P9-AFZ-164

FILM & VIDEO FINDER

Volume III

• *TITLE SECTION L-Z*
PAGE 3953-6434

Published for NICEM,
National Information Center for Educational Media,
a division of Access Innovations, Inc.,
by Plexus Publishing, Inc.

Fifth Edition, 1997. 3 volumes.

Film & Video Finder Vol. III

Published by Plexus Publishing, 143 Old Marlton Pike, Medford, New Jersey 08055.

ISBN: 0-937548-29-4
Fifth Edition. 1997. 3 volumes

L

L A Backwater - the Venice Canals 15 MIN
16mm
Color
LC 75-703265
Profiles the community of Venice, California, and its struggle to preserve its unique rural identity in the face of encroaching development and the spread of urban progress.
Geography - United States; Science - Natural; Sociology
Dist - USC **Prod** - USC 1975

L A Jazz 30 MIN
VHS / U-matic
$335.00 purchase
Fine Arts
Dist - ABCLR **Prod** - ABCLR

L A Jazz - a series 3 MIN
VHS
L A Jazz - a series
Color
Presents a series on the L A Jazz, containing one 60 minute videocassette and three 30 minute cassettes.
Fine Arts
Dist - ABCLR **Prod** - ABCLR

L A Jazz - a series
L A Jazz - a series 3 MIN
Dist - ABCLR

L A Justice 58 MIN
VHS / 16mm
Color (J)
$179.00 purchase, $75.00 rental _ #OD - 2208
Explores the Los Angeles County court system. Depicts a system overburdened by large numbers of criminal and civil cases. Portrays a judge, public defender, bounty hunter and prosecutor. Scrutinizes the obligations and the tactics of a defense attorney and looks at civil case settlements made outside the public court system.
Civics and Political Systems; History - United States
Dist - FOTH

L - Dopa and Parkinsonism 18 MIN
U-matic
Color (PRO)
LC 76-706052
Discusses indications for treating Parkinsonism with L - dopa. Describes dosage and possible side effects.
Health and Safety
Dist - USNAC **Prod** - WARMP 1970

L E a R - the League of Revolutionary Writers and Artists 31 MIN
U-matic / VHS
Color (H C A)
$250 purchase, $50 rental
Examines the history of the organization L E A R, founded in Mexico in 1934. Includes the views of L E A R members on the Mexican Revolution, the Spanish Civil War, and the occupation of Nicaragua by United Statres Marines. Includes archival footage, photos, murals, paintings, and poems by L E A R members. Produced by Yvette Nieves Cruz.
Fine Arts; Sociology
Dist - CNEMAG

L - 4 Earth Science Series
The Changing Earth 14 MIN
Dist - IITC

L I G H T 15 MIN
16mm
Color (I)
Offers a tribute to Thomas A Edison and a brief history of light which culminates with the invention of the incandescent light bulb and the machinery for its mass production.
Biography; History - United States; Science
Dist - DIRECT **Prod** - MIDMAR 1981

L I USA 31 MIN
16mm
Color
LC 72-702393
Pictures life in Long Island as a microcosm of America. Focuses on life in suburbia with its problems of pollution, planning, housing, health care, education and transportation.
Geography - United States; Social Science; Sociology
Dist - AVON **Prod** - AVON 1972

L is for the way you look 24 MIN
VHS
Color (G)
$60.00 rental, $250.00 purchase
Explores lesbian history and the women who have served as role models and objects of desire for young lesbians - from Martina Navratilova to Madonna, Simone de Beauvoir to Angela Davis. Reveals the director as she turns the camera on herself and friends to discuss how media images of lesbians affect the construction of identity. By Jean Carlomusto.
Fine Arts; History - World
Dist - WMEN

L L Bean 30 MIN
VHS / 16mm
Growing a Business Series
(H C)
$99.95 each, $1,295.00 series
Provides an example of a smooth running business in all respects, the L L Bean Company.
Business and Economics
Dist - AMBROS **Prod** - AMBROS 1988

L L Bean guide to outdoor photography 55 MIN
VHS
Color (H C A)
$29.95 purchase
Features outdoor photographer Lefty Kreh instructing in how to improve outdoor photography. Covers subjects including use of light, composing a picture, selection of equipment, and more.
Industrial and Technical Education
Dist - PBS **Prod** - WNETTV

L Model Microwave Ovens 25 MIN
VHS / 35mm strip / U-matic
Color (IND)
Teaches the experienced technician the new features and redesigned and reengineered components in the `L' model. Includes extensive 'hands on' exercises.
Home Economics; Industrial and Technical Education
Dist - WHIRL **Prod** - WHIRL

L S A T 240 MIN
VHS
Color (C A)
$59.95 purchase
Presents a review of appropriate skills for students planning to take the Law School Admission Test. Offers test - taking techniques, time - saving hints, multiple - choice strategies, and more. Includes study guide.
Education
Dist - PBS **Prod** - WNETTV

L Sound 14 MIN
U-matic / VHS
I - Land Treasure Series
Color (K)
English Language
Dist - AITECH **Prod** - UWISC 1980

LA 53 10 MIN
16mm / U-matic / VHS
Color (I J H)
Captures the sights, sounds, rhythms and feelings of railroading by following a freight train from Chicago to Los Angeles.
Social Science
Dist - JOU

La Abuela chicana 30 MIN
U-matic / VHS
La Esquina series
Color (H C A)
Depicts what happens when the grandmother of a Mexican - American family moves to Texas. Uses the story to try to reduce the minority isolation of Mexican - American students by showing the teenager as an individual, as a member of a unique cultural group and as a member of a larger complex society.
Sociology
Dist - GPN **Prod** - SWEDL 1976

La Acequia 10 MIN
16mm
Lifeways Series
Color (J)
LC 79-7018247
Depicts the cleaning of rural irrigation ditches in New Mexico, an annual tradition practiced since the arrival of the Spanish settlers in the 16th century.
Geography - United States; Sociology
Dist - BLUSKY **Prod** - BLUSKY 1980

La Acequia 14 MIN
U-matic / VHS / 16mm
Color
Portrays the traditional Hispanic agrarian practices and way of life of the people of the villages of northern New Mexico. Shows the gathering of the men of the village in early spring to clean the acequia, or water ditch so that the farmers can irrigate their crops.
Agriculture; Geography - United States; History - United States; Psychology; Science - Natural; Social Science; Sociology
Dist - ONEWST **Prod** - BLUSKY

La Alfombra Roja 9 MIN
16mm / U-matic / VHS
Color (SPANISH)
LC 73-702774
A Spanish version of 'THE RED CARPET.' Shows that when the doorman of a hotel rolls out the red carpet for the arrival of a Duke, the carpet keeps rolling through the streets and attracts a number of motorcycle policemen who pursue it to the dock where the titled visitor receives an impressive reception.
Foreign Language; Literature and Drama
Dist - WWS **Prod** - WWS 1960

La Bayadere 126 MIN
VHS
Color (G)
$39.95 purchase _ #1113
Presents the Kirov Corps de Ballet production of 'La Bayadere' filmed live at the Kirov Theatre. Stars Gabriella Komleva, Tatiana Terekhova and Rejen Abdyev.
Fine Arts; Foreign Language; Geography - World; Physical Education and Recreation
Dist - KULTUR

La Bayadere - The Royal Ballet 124 MIN
VHS
Color (G)
$19.95 purchase_#1326
Features dancers including Irek Moukhamedov and Darcey Bussell, performing the ballet La Bayadere. Presents the performance at Covent Garden, choreographed by Natalia Makarova for the Royal Ballet.
Fine Arts
Dist - KULTUR

La Belle Au Bois Dormant 3 MIN
16mm
Color
Presents Sleeping Beauty, one of the first commercials filmed in Gasparcolor, made with Jean Aurenche for Nicolas Wines, and contains Alexander Alexeieff's only example of puppet animation.
Business and Economics; Fine Arts; Literature and Drama
Dist - STARRC **Prod** - STARRC 1934

La Belle Epoque 60 MIN
VHS / U-matic
Color
$455.00 purchase
From an ABC TV program on the turn of the century.
History - United States; History - World
Dist - ABCLR **Prod** - ABCLR

La Belle Epoque 1890 - 1914 62 MIN
VHS
Color (S)
$39.95 purchase _ #833 - 9328
Explores the period 1890 - 1914 through the eyes of those who lived in it. Follows society's elite from London to Paris to New York, revealing how they lived, dressed and amused themselves in an age when the pursuit of beauty and romance was a way of life. Features Douglas Fairbanks as narrator and includes newsreel clips, paintings, photographs, period costumes and reenactments of the era.
History - United States; History - World; Home Economics; Social Science; Sociology
Dist - FI **Prod** - MMOA 1987

La Bellicosa 5 MIN
VHS / U-matic
Write on, Set 1 Series
Color (J H)
Consists of a lesson on adverbs.
English Language
Dist - CTI **Prod** - CTI

La Biblioteca - the Library 15 MIN
VHS / U-matic
Saludos
(P I G) (ENGLISH AND SPANISH)
$130 purchase, $25 rental, $75 self dub
Designed to introduce Spanish to the English speaking student at primary through intermediate levels. Seventeenth in a 25 part series.
Foreign Language
Dist - GPN

La Boheme 120 MIN
VHS
Color (S) (ITALIAN)
$39.95 purchase _ #623 - 9804
Stars Ileana Cotrubas and Neil Shicoff as Mimi and Rodolfo, the ill - fated lovers of 'La Boheme' by Puccini. Includes Thomas Allen and Marilyn Zschau as Marcello and Musetta. Lamberto Gardelli conducts the Royal Opera - Covent Garden production.
Fine Arts; Geography - World
Dist - FI **Prod** - NVIDC 1986

La Boheme 110 MIN
VHS / U-matic
Color (A)
Portrays a tale of love in the garretts of the Latin Quarter in Puccini's opera, La Boheme.

Fine Arts; Foreign Language
Dist - SRA **Prod** - SRA

La Boheme 142 MIN
VHS
Metropolitan opera series
Color (G) (ITALIAN WITH ENGLISH SUBTITLES)
$29.95 purchase
Stars Teresa Stratas, Renata Scotto, Jose Carreras, and Richard Stilwell in a performance of 'La Boheme' by Puccini. Conducted by James Levine. Produced and designed by Franco Zeffirelli. Includes a brochure with plot, historic notes, photographs, and production credits.
Fine Arts
Dist - PBS **Prod** - WNETTV 1982

La Boheme 141 MIN
VHS
Color (S) (ITALIAN)
$29.95 purchase _ #384 - 9365
Captures the Franco Zeffirelli production of 'La Boheme' by Puccini at the Metropolitan Opera House. Features Teresa Stratas as Mimi, Jose Carreras as Rudolfo, and Renata Scotto and Richard Stilwell. James Levine conducts.
Fine Arts; Foreign Language
Dist - FI **Prod** - PAR 1988

La Boheme - Luciano Pavarotti in 120 MIN
VHS
Color (G)
$39.95 purchase _ #1224
Presents the Genoa Opera Company production of 'La Boheme' performed during their historic tour of the People's Republic of China. Stars Luciano Pavarotti and Fiamma Izzo D'Amico filmed live at Beijing's Tianqiao Theatre.
Fine Arts; Foreign Language; Geography - World
Dist - KULTUR

La Bonne aventure 30 MIN
VHS
Paroles d'echanges 2 series
Color (J H) (FRENCH AND ENGLISH FRENCH)
#389002; LC 91-707692
Reveals that when two exchange students, Mike and Emily, and their hosts in Montreal renovate their club meeting area, an unusual adventure begins. Part of a series designed to build the confidence of new language learners.
Foreign Language; Geography - World; Sociology
Dist - TVOTAR **Prod** - TVOTAR 1990

La bonne aventure series

Aurevoir is not goodbye	15 MIN
The Bazaar	15 MIN
Christmas eve celebration	15 MIN
The Clock	15 MIN
The Commercial	15 MIN
The Deportation	15 MIN
The Explorers	15 MIN
The Good adventure	15 MIN
The Invention	15 MIN
Laughter	15 MIN
The Mistake	15 MIN
New Friends	15 MIN
Our Place	15 MIN
The Plans	15 MIN
The Prize	15 MIN
A Problem of feelings	15 MIN

Dist - GPN

La Caperucita Roja - 7 15 MIN
VHS
Amigos Series
Color (K) (SPANISH)
$125.00 purchase
Enables teachers with no knowledge of Spanish to introduce basic words to children in kindergarten through second grade. Uses simple concepts and music and features Perro Pepe, a six - foot orange dog, and Senorita Fernandez as instructors. Promotes awareness of and appreciation for Hispanic culture and sparks interest in the geography of Spanish - speaking countries. Part 7 is entitled 'La Caperucita Roja.'.
Foreign Language; Geography - World
Dist - AITECH

La Carrera 10 MIN
16mm
Color
LC 79-701313
Shows the 1978 Clasico del Caribe horserace, one of the most elegant horseraces in the world.
Physical Education and Recreation
Dist - PHILMO **Prod** - PHILMO 1979

La Carta - the Letter 15 MIN
U-matic / VHS
Saludos
(P I G) (ENGLISH AND SPANISH)
$130 purchase, $25 rental, $75 self dub
Designed to introduce Spanish to the English speaking student at primary through intermediate levels. Eleventh in a 25 part series.
Foreign Language
Dist - GPN

LA carwash 9 MIN
16mm
Color (G)
$40.00 rental
Experiments with dual screen projection in which the sound and picture exist as complete and separate entities. Captures the qualities of light and sound at a carwash in Los Angeles. Intentionally two - dimensional.
Fine Arts
Dist - CANCIN **Prod** - LIPZIN 1975

La Casa Y La Tierra De Loyola 20 MIN
U-matic / VHS / 16mm
Color (J H C) (SPANISH)
A Spanish language film. Shows the Basque countryside. Includes views of the ancestral house in the valley of Loyola and also the colorful St Ignatius day celebration in Azpeitia.
Foreign Language
Dist - IFB **Prod** - IFB 1955

La Cathedrale, La Ville, L'Ecole - Cathedral, City, School 52 MIN
16mm
Le Temp Des Cathedrales Series
Color
Explains the urban renaissance of the 13th century during which cathedral art and schools blossomed. Analyzes the concepts of cathedrals as homes of the people and cities as one big castle.
History - World; Religion and Philosophy
Dist - FACSEA **Prod** - FACSEA 1979

La Celula - Una Estructura En Funcionamiento, Pt 1 29 MIN
16mm / U-matic / VHS
Color (H C A) (SPANISH)
A Spanish language version of The Cell - A Functioning Structure, Pt 1. Describes the structure and functions of the living cell. Illustrates the processes by which cells nourish themselves and reproduce. Reveals the key functions of DNA and protein enzymes.
Foreign Language; Science - Natural
Dist - MGHT **Prod** - KATTNS 1978

La Celula - Una Estructura En Funcionamiento, Pt 2 30 MIN
U-matic / VHS / 16mm
Color (H C A) (SPANISH)
A Spanish language version of The Cell - A Functioning Structure, Pt 2. Explores the chemistry of the cell, showing how the cell manufactures proteins. Discusses how plant cells convert solar energy into chemical energy and how proteins are exported from the cell.
Foreign Language; Science - Natural
Dist - MGHT **Prod** - KATTNS 1978

La Cena 22 MIN
16mm
Color
LC 78-700194
Shows how 11 - year - old Pedrito works to buy medicine and a Christmas dinner for his sick mother, but loses his money to a gambler posing as a policeman. Explains how Pedrito then steals some food and is hit by a car as he flees from the police. Tells how the police promise to take Christmas dinner to Pedrito's mother while he is in the hospital.
Fine Arts
Dist - VALENJ **Prod** - VALENJ 1977

La Cenerentola - Cinderella 155 MIN
VHS
Color (S)
$39.95 purchase _ #623 - 9559
Presents the Glyndebourne production of 'La Cenerentola,' the Rossini adaptation of Cinderella. Stars American mezzo - soprano Kathleen Kuhlmann.
Fine Arts; Geography - World
Dist - FI **Prod** - NVIDC 1986

La Cenerentola - Cinderella 160 MIN
VHS
Color (G)
$39.95 purchase _ #CEN03
Presents the Salzburg Festival production of the opera La Cenerentola by Rossini. Stars bel canto singers Ann Murray and Francisco Araiza under the baton of Riccardo Chailly.
Fine Arts
Dist - HOMVIS **Prod** - RMART 1990

La Chambre 6 MIN
U-matic / VHS / 16mm
Color (J)
LC 72-702103
Uses animation, to show the frustration and confusion of a person trapped in a room. Shows how, as he tries to escape, the walls move and his tension increases. Reflects the feeling experienced when one is caught in a dilemma and there appears to be no way out. Without narration.
Fine Arts; Guidance and Counseling; Psychology; Sociology
Dist - IFB **Prod** - IFB 1971

La Champagne 23 MIN
16mm / U-matic / VHS
French Film Teaching Series
B&W (J H C) (FRENCH)
LC 70-707296
A French language film. Explores the life and activities in Champagne, including farming, grape harvesting, textile industries and markets. Shows glimpses of Troyes and Reims.
Foreign Language
Dist - IFB **Prod** - BRER 1947

La Chasse a Mort 15 MIN
U-matic / VHS / 16mm
La Maree Et Ses Secrets Series
Color (C A)
Foreign Language
Dist - FI **Prod** - FI

La Chinoise 95 MIN
16mm
Color (H C A) (FRENCH)
A French language film director by Jean - Luc Godard. Examines the militant New Left and the lives of five young Maoists plotting revolution from a Paris suburb.
Fine Arts; Foreign Language
Dist - NYFLMS **Prod** - PENBAK 1973

La Ciotat 31 MIN
16mm
Scenes de la vie Francaise series
Color (G)
$60.00 rental
Presents one in a series of French cities and scenes in which the material is woven together on an ordinary printer according to a certain pattern. Shows the port, the dry docks, workers leaving the shipyards, a tanker launched, fishermen and the beach.
Fine Arts; Geography - World
Dist - CANCIN **Prod** - LOWDER 1986

La Clase - the Classroom 15 MIN
U-matic / VHS
Saludos
(P I G) (ENGLISH AND SPANISH)
$130 purchase, $25 rental, $75 self dub
Designed to introduce Spanish to the English speaking student at primary through intermediate levels. Twentieth in a 25 part series.
Foreign Language
Dist - GPN

La Classification Animale 13 MIN
U-matic / VHS / 16mm
Color (I J H) (FRENCH)
A French - language version of the motion picture Putting Animals In Groups. Stresses that children can classify animals by observing their structure. Shows distinctive characteristics of mammals, birds, reptiles, amphibians, fishes and insects.
Foreign Language; Science - Natural
Dist - IFB **Prod** - IFB 1956

La Communaute Urbaine De Montreal 14 MIN
16mm
Color (G)
_ #106C 028 080
Shows various aspects of the territory and of the cultural and industrial life of greater Montreal. Is without spoken words.
Geography - World; History - World; Sociology
Dist - CFLMDC **Prod** - NFBC

La Conquista II 25 MIN
VHS
Hispanic culture video series
Color (J H)
$49.95 purchase _ #VK45876
Focuses on islands of the Caribbean and South America. Emphasizes how the conquistadors created a Hispanic culture. Part of a six - part series presenting the background and history of Spanish influences on the history, culture and society of different parts of the world.
History - World
Dist - KNOWUN

La Conquista (the Conquest) 25 MIN
VHS
Hispanic Culture Series
Color (I J H C A) (SPANISH)
Presents the importance and influence of Spain in the New World.
Foreign Language; Geography - World; History - World; Sociology
Dist - BENNUP **Prod** - VIDKNW 1986

La Conquista - the Spanish conquest of America 25 MIN
VHS
Hispanic culture video series
Color (J H)

$49.95 purchase _ #VK45043
Looks at the influence of Spain on the New World, emphasizing how the conquistadors created a Hispanic culture in the Western Hemisphere. Presents part of a six - part series that examines the background and history of Spanish influences on the history, culture and society of different parts of the world.
History - World
Dist - KNOWUN

La Couleur De La Forme 7 MIN
16mm
Color (H C)
Presents a collage film.
Fine Arts
Dist - CFS **Prod** - CFS 1969

La Divina 8 MIN
16mm
Color
LC 76-702332
Uses a juxtaposition of transcendental paintings and the activities in a car - washing establishment to satirize the preoccupation of the American people with cleanliness.
Fine Arts
Dist - USC **Prod** - USC 1968

La Dolce Festa - Little Italy, New York 31 MIN
16mm
Color (H C A)
LC 77-703179
Documents the 10 - day San Gennaro Festival, held each September in New York City's Little Italy to celebrate the liquification of the martyred saint's blood.
Geography - United States; History - United States; Religion and Philosophy; Social Science; Sociology
Dist - CECROP **Prod** - CECROP 1977

La Energia 27 MIN
U-matic / VHS / 16mm
Physical Science (Spanish Series
Color (H C A) (SPANISH)
A Spanish language version of Energy. Features three scientists discussing the nature of energy. Describes the equivalence of matter and energy and explains how energy changes into many forms and disperses itself into space. Suggests sources of energy which could replace those which deplete natural resources.
Foreign Language; Science - Physical; Social Science
Dist - MGHT **Prod** - SANDRS 1978

La Entrevista - the Interview, Film a 15 MIN
16mm
Spanish for You Series Unit 6
Color (I J)
Foreign Language
Dist - MLA **Prod** - LINGUA 1965

La Entrevista - the Interview, Film B 15 MIN
16mm
Spanish for You Series Unit 6
Color (I J)
Foreign Language
Dist - MLA **Prod** - LINGUA 1965

La Escuela De Perro Pepe - 10 15 MIN
VHS
Amigos Series
Color (K) (SPANISH)
$125.00 purchase
Enables teachers with no knowledge of Spanish to introduce basic words to children in kindergarten through second grade. Uses simple concepts and music and features Perro Pepe, a six - foot orange dog, and Senorita Fernandez as instructors. Promotes awareness of and appreciation for Hispanic culture and sparks interest in the geography of Spanish - speaking countries. Part 10 is entitled 'La Escuela De Perro Pepe.'.
Foreign Language; Geography - World
Dist - AITECH

La Esquina series

Cada quien hace su parte	30 MIN
Coconuts	30 MIN
El Chicano	30 MIN
La Abuela chicana	30 MIN
The Last hurrah	30 MIN
Rollos / roles	30 MIN
Roots / races	30 MIN
Superstar	30 MIN
The Walkout that never was	30 MIN

Dist - GPN

La Estrella Del Carnival (Cuba) 10 MIN
16mm
Color
Shows a nurse in Havana being chosen as the carnival queen. Presents one of the eclectic aspects of Cuba's revolutionary culture.
Geography - World; Social Science
Dist - CANWRL **Prod** - CANWRL 1965

La Estructura (Cuba) 12 MIN
16mm
Color
Gives a lyrical and impressionist treatment of the thermoelectric plant construction. Uses an unusual electric music track to complement the images.
Geography - World; Industrial and Technical Education; Science - Physical
Dist - CANWRL **Prod** - CANWRL

La Familia Silvestre Encuentra Hogar 11 MIN
U-matic / VHS / 16mm
Color (SPANISH)
LC 73-702771
A Spanish version of 'MAKE WAY FOR DUCKLINGS.' Follows Mrs Mallard as she leaves her home on an island in the Charles River and escorts her eight ducklings through hazardous Boston traffic to the public gardens where Mr Mallard is waiting for his family to join him.
Foreign Language; Literature and Drama
Dist - WWS **Prod** - WWS 1960

La Famille Martin 18 MIN
16mm / VHS / U-matic
French film reader series
B&W (J H C) (FRENCH)
Presents a French language film. Shows the activities of the Martin family when Madeline, the daughter who is in England, sends word that she will be home ahead of time. After many mishaps, they meet Madeline at the airport.
Foreign Language
Dist - IFB **Prod** - EFVA 1952

La Famille Senegalaise, Pt 1 - Trois Familles, Pt 2 - L'Education Et la Sante Publique 16 MIN
VHS / U-matic
Color (H C A) (FRENCH)
Explores family life in French speaking Africa, beginning with an overview of the culture and terrain of Senegal and showing aspects of traditional family life in two villages. The second part examines education, vocational training, community health, and the importance of the family.
Foreign Language; Sociology
Dist - IFB **Prod** - HAMPU 1986

La Fanciulla Del West 140 MIN
VHS
Color (S)
$39.95 purchase _ #623 - 9805
Presents the Royal Opera performance of 'La Fanciulla Del West' by Puccini. Stars Placido Domingo and Carol Neblett.
Fine Arts; Geography - World
Dist - FI **Prod** - NVIDC 1986

La Fantaisie De Melies 8 MIN
16mm
B&W (H C A)
LC FI68-7
Shows how special effects and camera tricks, such as stop photography and double exposures, were used in early films. Provides samples of phantasmagoria using three films - - extraordinary illusions, the enchanted well and the apparition - - copied from 35mm positives. A silent film.
Fine Arts
Dist - RMIBHF **Prod** - RMIBHF 1963

La Femme Infidele 102 MIN
16mm
Color (C A) (FRENCH (ENGLISH SUBTITLES))
A French language film. Presents a suspense drama. Includes English subtitles.
Fine Arts; Foreign Language
Dist - CINEWO **Prod** - CINEWO 1969

La Fiesta Mejicana - the Mexican Party 15 MIN
U-matic / VHS
Saludos
(P I G) (ENGLISH AND SPANISH)
$130 purchase, $25 rental, $75 self dub
Designed to introduce Spanish to the English speaking student at primary through intermediate levels. Twelfth in a 25 part series.
Foreign Language
Dist - GPN

La Fille Mal Gardee 100 MIN
VHS
Color (S)
$39.95 purchase _ #623 - 9563
Tells the story of country girl Lise who gets the man she loves in spite of her mother's plans. Features Lesley Collier and Michael Coleman in the leading roles. 'La Fille Mal Gardee,' composed by Herold, is choreographed by Frederick Ashton of the Royal Ballet.
Fine Arts; Geography - World; Physical Education and Recreation
Dist - FI **Prod** - NVIDC 1986

La Flor Y La Colmena 15 MIN
U-matic / VHS / 16mm
Color (J H) (SPANISH)
A Spanish - language version of the motion picture The Flower And The Hive. Shows the relationship between the activity of the bees and the fertility of field and orchard crops. Depicts the roles of the queen, drone and worker bees.
Science - Natural
Dist - IFB **Prod** - NFBC 1960

La Forza Del Destino 179 MIN
VHS
Color (S) (ITALIAN)
$39.95 purchase _ #384 - 9607
Features American soprano Leontyne Price in the lead role of 'La Forza Del Destino' by Verdi. Includes James Levine as conductor and Giuseppe Giacomini and Leo Nucci as other members of the cast in the production by the Metropolitan Opera.
Fine Arts; Foreign Language
Dist - FI **Prod** - PAR 1988

La France Contemporaine Series

Loin De Paris	10 MIN

Dist - EBEC

La France Telle Qu'Elle Est Series

Le Tourisme	19 MIN
Paris, Aujourd' Hui	19 MIN
Paris Hier	19 MIN
Un Hypermarche	19 MIN
Une Vile De Province	19 MIN

Dist - MEDIAG

La frontera 28 MIN
16mm
Color (SPANISH)
Views the border zone between the United States and Mexico. Portrays the meeting of two worlds with two standards of living through interviews with people living along the border zone.
Civics and Political Systems; Foreign Language; History - World; Sociology
Dist - HUDRIV **Prod** - HUDRIV

La Frustration - Est - Ce Que Je Finirai Par L'avoir 7 MIN
16mm
Emotions - French series
Color (FRENCH)
LC 75-704305
A French version of Frustration - How Can I Get It Right. Deals with a student's frustration caused by his inability to remember the lines of a play.
Foreign Language; Guidance and Counseling
Dist - MORLAT **Prod** - MORLAT 1974

La Gallinita Roja 16 MIN
U-matic / VHS / 16mm
Color (I J H) (SPANISH)
A Spanish version of The Little Red Hen.
Foreign Language
Dist - PHENIX **Prod** - FA 1961

La Gallinita Sabia 11 MIN
U-matic / VHS / 16mm
B&W (I J H) (SPANISH)
Spanish version of 'THE LITTLE RED HEN.' Combines art work and live action to depict the story. Narration is designed to provide frequent repetition.
Foreign Language
Dist - CORF **Prod** - CORF 1960

La Gare 18 MIN
16mm / U-matic / VHS
Comment Dit - On Series
Color (J H)
Features the rail station at Chateau - du - Loir, that serves both main and local lines. Shows how to buy a ticket, inquire about train times and for la consigne. Linguistically explains how changing the intonation of a question beginning 'Est - ce - que' can produce a statement.
Foreign Language
Dist - MEDIAG **Prod** - THAMES 1977

La Garonne 7 MIN
U-matic / VHS / 16mm
Chroniques De France Series
Color (H C A) (FRENCH)
LC 81-700764
A French language motion picture. Follows the course of the river Garonne.
Foreign Language; Geography - World
Dist - IFB **Prod** - ADPF 1980

La Gente Del Peru 11 MIN
U-matic / VHS / 16mm
Color (J H C) (SPANISH)
Spanish version of 'PEOPLE OF PERU.' Shows the people of the coastal desert, the people of the highland plains and the people of the Amazonic Jungle.
Foreign Language; Geography - World
Dist - IFB **Prod** - IFB 1961

La Gioconda 169 MIN
VHS
Color (S)
$39.95 purchase _ #833 - 9516
Offers the Vienna State Opera production of 'La Gioconda' by Ponchielli. Stars Placido Domingo, Eva Marton, Ludmilla Semtschuk, Kurt Rydl and Matteo Manuguerra. Adam Fischer conducts.
Fine Arts; Geography - World
Dist - FI **Prod** - RMART 1989

La gloire de mon pere - le chateau de ma mere 203 MIN
VHS
Color (G)
PdS25 purchase _ #ML-ART097
Dramatizes two connected stories by French author Marcel Pagnol. Provides English subtitles. Includes two videocassettes.
Fine Arts; Foreign Language
Dist - AVP

La Gloria De Espana (the Glory of Spain) 25 MIN
VHS
Hispanic Culture Series
Color (I J H C A) (SPANISH)
Explores the source of Spanish culture and presents a study of the heritage of Hispanic peoples.
Foreign Language; Geography - World; History - World; Sociology
Dist - BENNUP **Prod** - VIDKNW 1986

La Grande Breteche 24 MIN
VHS / U-matic
Orson Welles Great Mysteries Series
Color (I J C)
$89.00 purchase _ #3422
An English version of La Grande Breteche. Relates a tale of revenge, set in France during the Napoleonic wars. Presents a jealous husband who seals up a closet in which he suspects his wife's lover is hidden while his wife looks on in horror. Written by Honore de Balzac.
Literature and Drama
Dist - EBEC **Prod** - ANGLIA 1975

La grande illusion 50 MIN
VHS
Redemption song
Color; PAL (H C A)
PdS99 purchase
Features interviews with native Caribbeans who discuss the history of the islands. Focuses on the histories of Guadalupe and French Martinique. Fourth in a series of seven programs documenting the history of the Caribbean.
History - World
Dist - BBCENE

La grande notte a Verona - the festival of the greatest voices of opera 122 MIN
VHS
Color (G)
$24.95 purchase_#1376
Unites great opera performers in a concert to benefit the Jose Carreras International Leukemia Foundation. Features Jose Carreras, Ruggero Raimondi, Montserrat Caballe, Eva Marton, Samuel Ramey, Ileana Cotrubas and many others.
Fine Arts
Dist - KULTUR

La Grande Vitesse - the Work of Alexander Calder 16 MIN
16mm
Color
LC 72-702308
Shows American sculptor Alexander Calder as he completes work on stabiles, several large forty ton steel environmental sculptures.
Fine Arts
Dist - GVSC **Prod** - GVSC 1972

A La guerra 10 MIN
U-matic / VHS / 16mm
Color (A) (ENGLISH AND SPANISH BILINGUAL)
Discusses the struggle against poverty and racial discrimination by Puerto Ricans in New York since the 1950's. Portrays some of the art born of this struggle. Spanish/English bilingual version.
Fine Arts; History - United States; Sociology
Dist - CNEMAG **Prod** - CNEMAG 1979

La Guitarra Espanola 10 MIN
16mm / U-matic / VHS
Color (J) (SPANISH)
A Spanish - language beginning level version adapted from the motion picture I Am A Guitar. Shows how Ignacio Fleta and his sons lovingly shape and sand classical guitar frames, apply the inlaid rosette that is their trademark and polish the well - seasoned Cuban cedar, German spruce, Brazilian rosewood and hard African ebony that comprise the kind of instrument Andres Segovia or John Williams would wait a decade to play.
Fine Arts; Foreign Language
Dist - IFB **Prod** - IFB 1973

La Habanera 108 MIN
16mm / U-matic / VHS
Color; Captioned (A) (SPANISH (ENGLISH SUBTITLES))
Portrays modern Cuba through the story of the mid - life crisis of a female psychiatrist who is dedicated to her professional life as well as to her home and family. Spanish dialog with English subtitles.
Fine Arts; History - World
Dist - CNEMAG **Prod** - CNEMAG 1983

La Historia De Las Aztecas 19 MIN
U-matic / VHS / 16mm
Mexican Heritage (Spanish Series
Color (SPANISH)
LC 76-703909
A Spanish language version of The Story Of The Aztecs. Presents the accomplishments of the Aztecs, showing ruins of the Aztec empire. Points out their relationship to the Mexican people.
Foreign Language; Geography - World; History - World; Social Science; Sociology
Dist - FI **Prod** - STEXMF 1976

La Historia De Un Nino Esquimal 31 MIN
16mm / U-matic / VHS
Color (I) (SPANISH)
A Spanish - language version of the motion picture Angotee. Traces the life of an Eskimo from infancy to maturity. Shows him as an infant protected by his mother, as an adolescent accompanying his father on a hunt and as an adult setting up his own abode as a family man and hunter.
Foreign Language; Social Science; Sociology
Dist - IFB **Prod** - NFBC 1973

La Historia Romantica Del Tranporte Canadiense 11 MIN
16mm / U-matic / VHS
Color (SPANISH)
A Spanish language version of The Romance Of Transportation. Uses animation to show the growth of transportation in North America. Comments on the development of the canoe, oxcart, barge, steamboat, railroad, automobile, and airplane.
Foreign Language; Social Science
Dist - IFB **Prod** - NFBC 1954

La Idea De Los Numeros 14 MIN
U-matic / VHS / 16mm
Color (H C) (SPANISH)
A Spanish - language version of the motion picture The Idea Of Numbers - An Introduction To Number Systems. Discusses the development of number systems. Examines the earliest number concepts, the decimal system and the binary system which is now used in computers. Clarifies the concepts involved in the binary system.
Foreign Language; Mathematics
Dist - IFB **Prod** - IFB 1961

La Joconde - the Smile of the Mona Lisa 16 MIN
U-matic / VHS / 16mm
Color (J H C)
LC 77-701522
Presents the story of an obsession held since the creation of 'PORTRAIT OF MONA LISA' by Leonardo De Vinci.
Fine Arts
Dist - TEXFLM **Prod** - ARGOS 1970

LA, LA, Making it in Los Angeles 58 MIN
16mm
Color (H C A)
Focuses on the search for show business fame and fortune in the Los Angeles entertainment industry.
Fine Arts; Geography - United States; Sociology
Dist - DIRECT **Prod** - MOURIS 1979

LA Lakers 'just say no' anti - drug home video and song by winners, for winners 20 MIN
VHS
Color (P I J)
$14.98 purchase
Uses rap music and LA Lakers Magic Johnson, Kareem Abdul - Jabbar to bring an anti - drug message to youngsters. Teaches refusal skills. Includes a chronology of the filming of the message and clips of Laker games.
Fine Arts; Guidance and Counseling; Psychology; Sociology
Dist - BRODAT **Prod** - CBSFOX 1987

La Lengua 25 MIN
VHS
Hispanic Culture Series
Color (I J H C A) (ENGLISH, SPANISH)
Presents a background for the Spanish language - who speaks it, where and why.
Foreign Language; Geography - World; History - World; Sociology
Dist - BENNUP **Prod** - VIDKNW 1986

La Leyenda Del Alcalde De Zalamea 120 MIN
U-matic / VHS / 16mm
Color (SPANISH)
Offers a retelling of the story of the alcalde of Zalamea based on the plays of Lope and Calderon with its emphasis on the concepts of honor and loyalty.
Foreign Language; Literature and Drama
Dist - FOTH **Prod** - FOTH 1984

La linea 30 MIN
VHS
Crossroads of life series
Color (J H C G A R)
$24.95 purchase, $10.00 rental _ #35 - 8802 - 19; $24.95 purchase _ #87EE0802
Shows how 'the line' is drawn when Mike plans to marry his Mexican girlfriend Marina against his father's wishes. Reveals that in the end, Mike stands firm with his plans.
Religion and Philosophy; Sociology
Dist - APH **Prod** - CPH
CPH

La Llamada Telefonica - the Telephone Call, Film a 15 MIN
16mm
Spanish for You Series Unit 8
Color (I J)
Foreign Language
Dist - MLA **Prod** - LINGUA 1965

La Llamada Telefonica - the Telephone Call, Film B 15 MIN
16mm
Spanish for You Series Unit 8
Color (I J)
Foreign Language
Dist - MLA **Prod** - LINGUA 1965

La lucha 28 MIN
VHS
Color (J H C G A R)
$39.95 purchase, $10.00 rental _ #35 - 858344 - 93
Interviews El Salvador church leaders on the state of affairs in their war - torn country. Shows how the Salvadoran churches are responding to people's needs. Hosted by Mike Farrell.
Sociology
Dist - APH **Prod** - FRPR

La Lucha Contra Los Microbios 29 MIN
U-matic / VHS / 16mm
Color (H C) (SPANISH)
A Spanish - language version of the motion picture The Fight Against Microbes. Traces the development of methods to combat pathogenic bacteria. Shows the contributions of Jenner, Lister, Leeuwenhoek, Koch, Roux, Ehrlich, Domagh and Fleming.
Foreign Language; Health and Safety; Science - Natural
Dist - IFB **Prod** - OECD 1966

La Maggia 11 MIN
16mm / U-matic / VHS
B&W (I J H)
Creates an abstract composition by following a river's flow. Traces the river as it changes from a shallow yet swift - moving stream to deep quiet pools and as it passes and flows over rocks which have been whitened by the sun and shaped by the flow of the water through the ages. Explains that these rocks could be the basis for man's imitations found in expressionistic sculptures.
Fine Arts; Geography - World; Science - Physical
Dist - IFB **Prod** - AEKBRO 1973

La Maison 18 MIN
U-matic / VHS / 16mm
Comment Dit - On Series
Color (J H)
Presents a French family sunbathing, playing table tennis and tending flowers in the garden of a large house at Chateau - du - Loir. Linguistically shows that a question involving the inversion of verb and subject pronoun is answered by re - inversion of verb and pronoun.
Foreign Language
Dist - MEDIAG **Prod** - THAMES 1977

La Mandragola 97 MIN
16mm
B&W (C A) (ITALIAN (ENGLISH SUBTITLES))
An Italian language film with English subtitles about a husband who makes his wife take various fertility potions in order for her to provide him with an heir. Details how Gallimaco, a worldly blade and admirer of feminine beauty, conceives of a way by which he may possess the wife.
Foreign Language; Literature and Drama
Dist - TRANSW **Prod** - TRANSW 1967

La Maree Et Ses Secrets 75 MIN
VHS
Color (S) (FRENCH)
$450.00 purchase _ #825 - 9009
Combines an engaging story line with the language skills necessary for first and second year French students. Provides spoken French for listening comprehension, insights into some aspects of French life and motivation for learners at a variety of levels. Filmed on location in Cancale, features young people unwittingly involved in a dangerous mystery. Student Reader and Teacher's Notes accompany the series. Five 15 - minute programs on one cassette.
Foreign Language; Geography - World; History - World
Dist - FI **Prod** - BBCTV 1984

La Maree Et Ses Secrets Series
Chez Keravec 15 MIN
La Chasse a Mort 15 MIN
Les Choux - Fleurs De Saint - Brieuc 15 MIN
Les Surprises 15 MIN
Une Ombre Du Passe 15 MIN
Dist - FI

La meilleure occasion 13 MIN
16mm
Les Francais chez vous series
B&W (I J H)
Foreign Language
Dist - CHLTN **Prod** - PEREN 1967

La Mosca De La Fruta 21 MIN
16mm / U-matic / VHS
Color (H C A) (SPANISH)
A Spanish language version of The Fruit Fly - A Look At Behavior Biology. Examines the relationship of genes to behavior, using the fruit fly as a microcosm of life.
Foreign Language; Psychology; Science - Natural; Sociology
Dist - MGHT **Prod** - KATTNS 1978

La Moto 7 MIN
16mm / U-matic / VHS
Chroniques De France Series
Color (H C A) (FRENCH)
LC 81-700768
A French language motion picture. Shows the two - day motorcycle rally which begins at Val d'Isere in France.
Foreign Language; Geography - World
Dist - IFB **Prod** - ADPF 1980

La Mujer En Los Negocios 30 MIN
U-matic / VHS / 16mm
Behavior in Business (Spanish Series
Color (H C A) (SPANISH)
A Spanish language version of Women In Management - Threat Or Opportunity. Examines the effect of the women's liberation movement in several organizations and shows how leaders and managers are dealing with the situation.
Business and Economics; Foreign Language; Guidance and Counseling; Psychology; Sociology
Dist - MGHT **Prod** - MGHT 1976

La Musica De La Gente - the Music of the People 28 MIN
U-matic / VHS / 16mm
Color
Features the popular music of Hispanic people of the Southwest. Presents the music against the social and environmental background from which it developed.
Fine Arts; Geography - United States; History - United States; Sociology
Dist - ONEWST **Prod** - BLUSKY

La Musica De Los Viejos - Music of the Old Ones 28 MIN
16mm / U-matic / VHS
Color
Features the Hispanic folk music of the Southwest and the old musicians who preserve it.
Fine Arts; Geography - United States; History - United States; Sociology
Dist - ONEWST **Prod** - PMEDA

La Musique 13 MIN
16mm
En Francaise, Set 2 Series
Color (I J H C)
Foreign Language
Dist - CHLTN **Prod** - PEREN 1969

La Musique folklorique 48 MIN
VHS
Color (G) (FRENCH)
$39.95 purchase _ #W3488
Presents 11 well - known Franco - American songs recorded in picturesque settings including a French castle and a flower garden. Includes a short history of each song before it is performed. Provides insight into French culture. Provides written lesson plan with lyrics, vocabulary and ideas for related class projects.
Fine Arts; Foreign Language
Dist - GPC

La Naissance Du Kangourou Rouge 21 MIN
U-matic / VHS / 16mm
Color (H C A) (FRENCH)
A French - language version of the motion picture Birth Of The Red Kangaroo. Discusses all phases of marsupial reproduction. Explains oestrous cycle, gestation period and embryonic development. Shows the newly - born kangaroo climbing into the pouch where it develops for six months. Illustrates the basic structure and function of mammalian reproductive organs and describes mammalian embryonic development.
Foreign Language; Science - Natural
Dist - IFB **Prod** - CSIRFU 1966

La Naturaliez De La Materia 24 MIN
U-matic / VHS / 16mm
Physical Science (Spanish Series
Color (H C A) (SPANISH)
A Spanish language version of The Nature Of Matter. Probes the nature of atomic and subatomic particles. Discusses the concepts which led to the quantum theory. Emphasizes the particle - like and wave - like characteristics of the atomic constituents.
Foreign Language; Science - Physical
Dist - MGHT **Prod** - KATTNS 1978

La Navidad En Oaxaca 14 MIN
U-matic / VHS / 16mm
Mexican Heritage (Spanish Series
Color (SPANISH)
LC 76-703900
A Spanish language version of Christmas In Oaxaca. Shows Christmas celebrations in the Oaxaca region of Mexico, including folkloric dancers in vivid costumes, various customs of the region, students and a marimba band.
Foreign Language; Geography - World; History - World; Religion and Philosophy; Social Science
Dist - FI **Prod** - STEXMF 1975

La Noche d'amour 18 MIN
VHS
Color (G)
$40.00 purchase
Delves into Hollywood, where legends are born and souls die in the hell fire of licking tongues that aim to please where it hurts most.
Fine Arts
Dist - CANCIN **Prod** - KUCHAR 1986

La Notte Brava 96 MIN
16mm / U-matic / VHS
B&W (A) ((ENGLISH DUBBING))
Portrays contemporary life among aimless youth in Rome. English dubbed version.
Fine Arts; Sociology
Dist - CNEMAG **Prod** - CNEMAG 1961

La Ofrenda - The Days of the Dead 50 MIN
VHS / 16mm
Color (G) (ENGLISH & SPANISH W/ENGLISH SUBTITL ENGLISH & SPANISH W/SPANISH SUBTITLES)
Records the first days of November in Mexico when the souls of the dead visit the living and are welcomed in celebrations that combine ancient Indian traditions and Catholic ritual. Visits the ruins of Mitla, the Indians' gateway to the underworld, and follows this tradition to the Latino community in California where the holiday reinforces spiritual and cultural life in exile and children are encouraged to speak about death as a natural order of events, not to be feared. Includes satiric outdoor skits; processions; decoration of gravestones with special folk art; and colorful altars to the dead erected in homes with photos, candles, dolls and offerings of flowers and special foods. Produced by Lourdes Portillo and Susana Munoz.
Fine Arts; Religion and Philosophy; Social Science; Sociology
Dist - DIRECT

La Operacion 40 MIN
U-matic / VHS / 16mm
Color
Begins by noting that Puerto Rico has the world's highest incidence of female sterilization, with one - third of all Puerto Rican women of childbearing age having been sterilized. Documents the social, moral and religious issue as a means of population control with interviews of women, physicians, politicians and others.
Health and Safety; Science - Natural; Social Science; Sociology
Dist - CNEMAG **Prod** - CNEMAG 1982

La Peau De Chagrin 10 MIN
U-matic / VHS / 16mm
Color (H A)
LC 75-710557
Uses animation to tell the story of a poor and unhappy man who leaves his love to try his luck at gambling, loses his last penny, and then is given a magic skin which fulfills all wishes, but grows shorter as it is used.
Fine Arts; Foreign Language
Dist - IFB **Prod** - ZAGREB 1971

La Perichole 30 MIN
U-matic / VHS / 16mm
Who's Afraid of Opera Series
Color (J)
LC 73-703439
Features Joan Sutherland singing selected arias from the opera La Pericole.
Fine Arts
Dist - PHENIX **Prod** - PHENIX 1973

La Petite Ferme 12 MIN
16mm
Voix Et Images De France Series
Color (I) (FRENCH)
A French language film. Pictures the daily activities of a peasant family, living in the farm area of Etampes (Seine - et - Oise.).
Foreign Language
Dist - CHLTN **Prod** - PEREN 1962

La Petite Lilie 14 MIN
U-matic / VHS / 16mm
B&W (C A)
LC 78-701647
Presents a parody of the innocent, virtuous heroines of the early silent films. Shows Lilie, an orphan who hates her work as a seamstress and becomes a lady of the streets.
Fine Arts; Literature and Drama
Dist - PHENIX **Prod** - PHENIX 1975

La Petite Poule Rouge 16 MIN
U-matic / VHS / 16mm
Color (I) (FRENCH)
LC FIA67-2141
A French version of The Little Red Hen.
Foreign Language
Dist - PHENIX **Prod** - FA 1961

La Piazza San Marco, Venezia 7 MIN
16mm
B&W (G)
$10.00 rental
Relates the adventures of a young boy who discovers the greatest piazza in Italy. Uses film from 100 feet of Tri - X shot one overcast day in Venice with a mixture of stills and pencil drawings. For children of all ages. Produced by R Raffaello Dvorak.
Fine Arts; Geography - World
Dist - CANCIN

La Pinata 11 MIN
16mm
Color (H C) (SPANISH)
Uses animation to tell the story of Pepe, who works in a Mexican pinata factory. Designed for first - year Spanish classes.
Foreign Language
Dist - FILCOM **Prod** - SIGMA 1964

La piscine 13 MIN
16mm
En France avec Jean et Helene series
B&W (J H C)
LC 70-704512
Foreign Language
Dist - CHLTN **Prod** - PEREN 1967

La Place 18 MIN
U-matic / VHS / 16mm
Comment Dit - On Series
Color (J H)
Describes a visit to some of the businesses in the small town of Bauge on market day. Includes a boulangerie, a charcuterie, and a marchand de primeurs. Linguistically reviews how a change of intonation transforms a question into an affirmative answer.
Foreign Language
Dist - MEDIAG **Prod** - THAMES 1977

La Plage 18 MIN
U-matic / VHS / 16mm
Comment Dit - On Series
Color (J H)
Looks at the sandy beaches of les Sables - d'Olonne, which every summer attract thousands of children and adults to the seaside. Linguistically explains the principles governing the use of perfect and imperfect tense, matching the tense of an answer to a question to avoid confusion and error.
Foreign Language
Dist - MEDIAG **Prod** - THAMES 1977

La Plage 4 MIN
U-matic / VHS / 16mm
Color (H C A)
LC 81-701008
Presents an animated tale in which a man foresees the drowning of a woman who was sailing alone.
Fine Arts
Dist - PHENIX **Prod** - NFBC 1981

La Pomme 15 MIN
16mm
B&W (C A) (FRENCH (ENGLISH SUBTITLES))
A French language film. Presents an informal, impressionistic record of a contemporary artist's happy life with painting, love, people and the city. Includes English subtitles.
Fine Arts; Foreign Language
Dist - UWFKD **Prod** - UWFKD

La Poulette Grise 6 MIN
16mm / U-matic / VHS
Color (FRENCH)
A French language film. Features Norman Mc Laren's metamorphic images set to the lyrics of a French folksong about the little grey hen who nests in the church and the little brown hen who nests in the moon.
Fine Arts; Foreign Language
Dist - IFB **Prod** - NFBC 1947

La Premiere Soiree 8 MIN
16mm
Color (H C A)
Uses experimental techniques to create the moods and feelings of the poem La Premiere Soiree by Rimbaud.
Fine Arts; Literature and Drama
Dist - VIERAD **Prod** - VIERAD 1979

La Presencia Africana En Hispanoamerica 29 MIN
U-matic / VHS / 16mm
Color (H C A) (SPANISH)
A Spanish language program in three parts. Presents an overview of the history and culture of the peoples of African descent in Colombia, Ecuador and Venezuela.

Foreign Language; Sociology
Dist - IFB **Prod** - HAMPU 1987

La Primera Ciudad De Las Americas - Teotihuacan 18 MIN
U-matic / VHS / 16mm
Mexican Heritage
Color (SPANISH)
LC 76-703902
A Spanish version of America's First City - Teotihuacan. Visits the pyramids of Teotihuacan, 25 miles from Mexico City, pointing out the skills and artistry of the early Mexican people who built this city about 2,000 years ago. Notes that Teotihuacan was the first city built in the Americas.
Fine Arts; Foreign Language; Geography - World; History - World; Sociology
Dist - FI **Prod** - STEXMF 1975

La Princesse 5 MIN
16mm
Bonjour Line Series
Color (K P I)
A story about two farm children who meet a princess who changes their bread and leaves to cake and flowers.
Literature and Drama
Dist - CHLTN **Prod** - PEREN 1962

La Proprete - Si Vous Ne Pouvez Pas Vous Laver Les Mains, Mettez Un Pansement 9 MIN
16mm
Health
Color (FRENCH)
LC 76-700122
A French language version of the motion picture Cleanliness - If You Can't Wash Your Hands Wear A Band - Aid. Explores the world of germs, including where they live, what they do and how some of them get inside the human body and cause illness.
Foreign Language; Health and Safety
Dist - MORLAT **Prod** - MORLAT 1974

La publicite en France - volume I 26 MIN
VHS
Color (J H G) (FRENCH)
$45.00 purchase _ #W3437
Presents French television commercials about cosmetics, cars, clothing and similar products. Provides a glimpse of French culture and view of life. Includes script.
Foreign Language
Dist - GPC

La publicite en France - volume II 26 MIN
VHS
Color (J H G) (FRENCH)
$45.00 purchase _ #W4582
Presents French television commercials about cosmetics, cars, clothing and similar products. Provides a glimpse of French culture and view of life. Includes script.
Foreign Language
Dist - GPC

La publicite en France - volumes I and II 52 MIN
VHS
Color (J H G) (FRENCH)
$82.00 purchase _ #W5487
Contains a set of two videos that present French television commercials about cosmetics, cars, clothing and similar products. Provides a glimpse of French culture and view of life. Includes scripts.
Foreign Language
Dist - GPC

La Quebecoise 27 MIN
16mm
Color (G)
_ #106C 0172 114
Shows that the French Canadian women's image of today has changed. Senator Therese Casgrain, Judge Rejane Colas, a nun, a Playboy bunny and several feminists speak on the struggle to bring about change and the challenges still ahead.
History - World; Sociology
Dist - CFLMDC **Prod** - NFBC 1972

La Quete De Dieu - the Quest of God 52 MIN
16mm
Le Temp Des Cathedrales Series
Color
Analyzes the importance of monasteries among peasants and knights in the 11th century. Views Gerone's Apocalypse paintings of Saint - Vincent of Cardona and Tahull's frescoes.
History - World; Religion and Philosophy
Dist - FACSEA **Prod** - FACSEA 1979

La Raison avant la passion 80 MIN
16mm
Color (G)
$90.00 rental
Deals with the pain and joy of living in a large space - namely, Canada.
Fine Arts
Dist - CANCIN **Prod** - WIELNJ 1969

La Region Centrale 180 MIN
16mm
Color (FRENCH)
LC 74-701608
A French language film. Uses a specially designed camera mount in order to provide a new perspective on the scenery of the wilderness of northern Quebec.
Foreign Language; Geography - World; Industrial and Technical Education
Dist - CANFDC **Prod** - CFDEVC 1971

La Regione Centrale 190 MIN
16mm
Color (C)
$6000.00
Experimental film by Micihael Snow.
Fine Arts
Dist - AFA **Prod** - AFA 1971

La Reina 10 MIN
VHS / 16mm
Color (G)
$30.00 rental, $20.00 purchase
Contemplates on how individuals lose, as they grow up, their child's view of the world as a mystical universe continually reshaping itself. Looks at what happens when they split the real from the imaginary, yet if they listen to their waking dreams they can open ourselves to the mythical world once again. 1992 - 1993.
Fine Arts; Psychology; Sociology
Dist - CANCIN **Prod** - ALVARE

La Rentree - the Return to School 15 MIN
16mm
Toute la bande series
Color (J) (FRENCH)
LC 75-715482
A French language film. Tells the adventure of Caroline's and Victor's trip to a shop to buy their school supplies which brought Caroline's teacher's reprimands for wearing make - up.
Foreign Language
Dist - SBS **Prod** - SBS 1970

La Reproduccion De La Plantas 14 MIN
U-matic / VHS / 16mm
Color (SPANISH)
LC 72-702534
A Spanish language film. Shows the difference between sexual and asexual reproduction of plants and explains the processes involved in both methods. Describes self - pollination, cross - pollination and the improvement of plant strains by selective breeding.
Foreign Language; Science - Natural
Dist - CORF **Prod** - CORF 1958

La Reunion 11 MIN
16mm
Beginning Spanish Series
B&W (J) (SPANISH)
A Spanish language film. See series title for annotation.
Foreign Language
Dist - AVED **Prod** - CBF 1960

La Reunion - 29 15 MIN
VHS
Amigos Series
Color (K) (SPANISH)
$125.00 purchase
Enables teachers with no knowledge of Spanish to introduce basic words to children in kindergarten through second grade. Uses simple concepts and music and features Perro Pepe, a six - foot orange dog, and Senorita Fernandez as instructors. Promotes awareness of and appreciation for Hispanic culture and sparks interest in the geography of Spanish - speaking countries. Part 29 is entitled 'La Reunion.'.
Foreign Language; Geography - World
Dist - AITECH

La Robe De Chambre De Georges Bataille 70 MIN
U-matic / VHS
Color (FRENCH)
Features the 1983 Paris production by Foreman's Ontological/Hysterical Theatre.
Fine Arts; Foreign Language
Dist - KITCHN **Prod** - KITCHN

La Ronde 97 MIN
VHS
B&W (G)
$29.95 _ #RON010
Presents a view of the rituals of love and lovemaking in ten timeless sketches full of humor and tenderness. Adapts the play by Arthur Schnitzler set in turn - of - the - century Vienna. Directed by Max Ophuls.
Fine Arts; Literature and Drama; Psychology; Religion and Philosophy; Sociology
Dist - HOMVIS **Prod** - JANUS 1950

La Ropa De Ninas - Clothing for Girls 15 MIN
U-matic / VHS
Saludos
(P I G) (ENGLISH AND SPANISH)
$130 purchase, $25 rental, $75 self dub
Designed to introduce Spanish to the English speaking student at primary through intermediate levels. Sixth in a 25 part series.
Foreign Language
Dist - GPN

La Salamandre 125 MIN
16mm
B&W (FRENCH (ENGLISH SUBTITLES))
An English subtitle version of the French language, Swiss - made film. Follows incidents in the life of a young working - class Swiss girl, Rosemonde, who works at one job after another whenever the spirit and her sinking finances move her. Tells how she seeks out men who please her and sheds them when they start weighing her down.
Fine Arts; Foreign Language; Sociology
Dist - NYFLMS **Prod** - NYFLMS 1971

La Salud Mental Y La Communidad 31 MIN
U-matic / VHS / 16mm
B&W (H C)
LC 75-707257
A Spanish film. Dramatizes the process of developing and operating a community - - based mental health center whose function extends far beyond the diagnostic and treatment services of the traditional clinic. Traces the developments of the clinic and some of the problems that arise.
Foreign Language; Psychology
Dist - IFB **Prod** - MHFB 1931

La Sculpture Du Cuivre Au Chalumeau 14 MIN
16mm / U-matic / VHS
Color (H C A S) (FRENCH)
A French - language version of the motion picture Sculpturing Copper With A Torch. Shows the use of copper tube, wire, sheets and pipes in sculpturing. Explains the processes of forming, patching, enameling, brazing, cleaning and oxidation.
Fine Arts; Foreign Language
Dist - IFB **Prod** - MOTIVF 1965

La Senorita Y Su Perro - 12 15 MIN
VHS
Amigos Series
Color (K) (SPANISH)
$125.00 purchase
Enables teachers with no knowledge of Spanish to introduce basic words to children in kindergarten through second grade. Uses simple concepts and music and features Perro Pepe, a six - foot orange dog, and Senorita Fernandez as instructors. Promotes awareness of and appreciation for Hispanic culture and sparks interest in the geography of Spanish - speaking countries. Part 12 is entitled 'La Senorita Y Su Perro.'.
Foreign Language; Geography - World
Dist - AITECH

La Sopa De Piedras 11 MIN
U-matic / VHS / 16mm
Color (SPANISH)
LC 73-702775
A Spanish version of 'STONE SOUP.' Shows how three famished soldiers satisfy their hunger by tricking a group of gullible French peasants into supplying meat and vegetables for a pot of stone soup.
Foreign Language; Literature and Drama
Dist - WWS **Prod** - WWS 1960

La Soufriere 30 MIN
16mm
Color
Shows what happened when an earthquake was predicted on the island of Guadeloupe and all the residents, except for one, left. Directed by Werner Herzog.
History - World
Dist - NYFLMS **Prod** - UNKNWN 1977

La strada 107 MIN
VHS
Color (G) (ITALIAN (ENGLISH SUBTITLES) ITALIAN (ENGLISH DUBBING))
$29.95 purchase _ #S00917, #S00917A
Tells the story of a circus strongman who takes on a simple - minded waif as his assistant. Stars Anthony Quinn, Giulietta Masina, Richard Basehart, Aldo Silvana, and others. Music by Nino Rota. Directed by Federico Fellini.
Fine Arts; Physical Education and Recreation
Dist - UILL

La Sueno De Perro Pepe - 8 15 MIN
VHS
Amigos Series
Color (K) (SPANISH)
$125.00 purchase
Enables teachers with no knowledge of Spanish to introduce basic words to children in kindergarten through second grade. Uses simple concepts and music and features Perro Pepe, a six - foot orange dog, and Senorita Fernandez as instructors. Promotes awareness of and appreciation for Hispanic culture and sparks interest in the geography of Spanish - speaking countries. Part 8 is entitled 'La Sueno De Perro Pepe.'.
Foreign Language; Geography - World
Dist - AITECH

LA - suggested by the art of Edward Ruscha 28 MIN
VHS
Color (H C A)
$50.00
Presents the artist's view of Los Angeles as a basis for understanding the works of Edward Ruscha. Portrays the city through his work and includes interviews with him.
Fine Arts
Dist - ARTSAM **Prod** - MFV

La Superficie De La Tierra En Mapas 16 MIN
16mm / U-matic / VHS
Color (SPANISH)
LC 72-702531
A Spanish language film. Explains the process of mapmaking from the establishment of a network of control points, through the collection of detailed information, to final compilation and printing.
Foreign Language; Geography - World; Social Science
Dist - CORF **Prod** - CORF 1969

La Sylphide 81 MIN
VHS
Color (G)
$39.95 purchase _ #1126
Recreates the production of 'La Sylphide' by Taglioni performed in Paris on March 12, 1832. Includes the original costume and set designs completed by Pierre Lacotte in 1971. Stars Michael Denard, Ghislaine Thesmar and the Paris Opera Ballet Company.
Fine Arts; Foreign Language; Geography - World; Physical Education and Recreation
Dist - KULTUR

La Tapisserie De Bayeux 7 MIN
U-matic / VHS / 16mm
Chroniques De France Series
Color (H C A) (FRENCH)
LC 81-700762
A French language motion picture. Looks at the Bayeux Tapestry.
Foreign Language; Geography - World
Dist - IFB **Prod** - ADPF 1980

La Television - Linea Por Linea 11 MIN
16mm / U-matic / VHS
Color (H C) (SPANISH)
A Spanish - language version of the motion picture Television - Line By Line. Uses animation to explain the principles of television. Demonstrates how light energy is converted to electrical energy which is transmitted to a distant place by radio signal, and how the receiving picture - tube changes the radio signal to an image that is formed like the original, line by line.
Fine Arts; Foreign Language; Industrial and Technical Education; Science - Physical; Social Science
Dist - IFB **Prod** - IFB 1970

La Tercera Palabra 110 MIN
16mm
B&W (A) (SPANISH)
A Spanish language film. Tells the story of an aunt who hires a beautiful woman to teach her uneducated nephew.
Fine Arts; Foreign Language
Dist - TRANSW **Prod** - TRANSW

La Terre Est Une Femme 28 MIN
16mm
Color (FRENCH)
A French - language version of the motion picture The Land Is A Woman. Looks at the activities inherent in grape - growing and wine making in Virginia plus the romance they inspire in a vintner and his wife.
Agriculture; Foreign Language; Geography - United States
Dist - SCHDRC **Prod** - SCHDRC 1981

La Tete en fete 30 MIN
VHS
Paroles d'echanges 2 series
Color (J H) (FRENCH AND ENGLISH FRENCH)
#389004; LC 91-707718
Tells how the students plan a performance in their comfortably established club that will be a farewell to their exchange student friends who are returning to Ontario. Part of a series designed to build the confidence of new language learners.
Foreign Language; Geography - World; Sociology
Dist - TVOTAR **Prod** - TVOTAR 1990

La Tete Et Les Jambes 13 MIN
16mm
En Francais, set 1 series
Color (J A)
Foreign Language
Dist - CHLTN **Prod** - PEREN 1969

LA - the movie 14 MIN
VHS
Color (J H C)
$14.95 purchase _ #NA712
Geography - United States; History - World; Science - Physical
Dist - INSTRU **Prod** - NASA

La tragedie de Carmen 82 MIN
VHS
Color (G) (FRENCH)
$39.95 purchase _ #S01965
Presents British director Peter Brook's adaptation of the Bizet - Merimee opera 'Carmen.'
Fine Arts
Dist - UILL

La Tragedie De Carmen 82 MIN
VHS
Color (G) (FRENCH)
$44.95 purchase _ #V72154
Presents a production by Peter Brook featuring a re - ordered format for small orchestra and seven singers.
Fine Arts; Foreign Language
Dist - NORTNJ

La Traversee De L'Atlantique a La Rame - Crossing the Atlantic in a Small Boat 22 MIN
16mm
Color
Takes an improbable news item about a married couple's strange odyssey in a small boat and turns it into a narrative as the years pass and the journey continues.
Fine Arts
Dist - FILMWE **Prod** - FILMWE 1978

La Traviata 30 MIN
U-matic / VHS / 16mm
Who's Afraid of Opera Series
Color (J)
LC 73-703440
Features Joan Sutherland singing selected arias from the opera 'LA TRAVIATA.'.
Fine Arts
Dist - PHENIX **Prod** - PHENIX 1973

La Traviata 130 MIN
U-matic / VHS
Color
Presents the Augusta Opera's production of La Traviata at Columbus' Springer Opera House.
Fine Arts
Dist - MDCPB **Prod** - GPTV

La traviata 105 MIN
VHS
Color (G) (ITALIAN)
$29.95 purchase
Features Placido Domingo and Teresa Stratas in a film version of 'La Traviata' by Verdi. Directed and created by Franco Zeffirelli.
Fine Arts
Dist - PBS **Prod** - WNETTV

La Traviata 135 MIN
VHS
Color (S) (ITALIAN)
$39.95 purchase _ #395 - 9001
Presents the made - for - video Sir Peter Hall production of 'La Traviata' staged at Glyndebourne without an audience. Stars Marie McLaughlin, Walter MacNeil and Brent Ellis. Carefully replicates the original stage conception of Verdi.
Fine Arts; Geography - World
Dist - FI **Prod** - TVSOU 1988

La Traviata, and, Daughter of the Regiment - Vol 2 60 MIN
VHS
Who's Afraid of Opera Series
Color (K)
$29.95 purchase _ #1256
Presents Joan Sutherland and her puppet friends to make opera fun. Features excerpts from the operas 'La Traviata' and 'Daughter Of the Regiment' in Volume 2 of four volumes.
Fine Arts; Sociology
Dist - KULTUR

La Ultima Descarga 21 MIN
U-matic / VHS / 16mm
Color (IND) (SPANISH)
A Spanish - language version of the motion picture One Last Shock. Dramatizes the events leading to an electrical accident. Outlines the misuses of electrical equipment in the factory and office.
Foreign Language; Health and Safety
Dist - IFB **Prod** - MILLBK 1980

La Vallee De La Loire 24 MIN
U-matic / VHS / 16mm
Food and Wine from France
Color (H C A) (FRENCH)
A French language film tours the scenic and historic Loire River Valley region of France. Describes the area's major winemaking industry, highlighting vineyards, press houses, cellars and tasting rooms.
Geography - World; Home Economics
Dist - IFB **Prod** - POLNIS 1986

La Venta
VHS
Color (J H G) (SPANISH)
$44.95 purchase _ #MCV5011, #MCV5012
Presents a program on the history of Mexico.
History - World
Dist - MADERA **Prod** - MADERA

La Verbotene voyage 45 MIN
VHS
Color & B&W (G)
$50.00 purchase
Features an international cast of characters aboard an ocean liner. Mixes romantic intrique with labor revolts until the ship is torn apart - with the few tattered, yet still attractive, survivors confronting the dawn of a new and natural dominion. A collaboration between the filmmaker and his students.
Fine Arts; Literature and Drama
Dist - CANCIN **Prod** - KUCHAR 1989

La Vida Es Sueno 55 MIN
16mm / U-matic / VHS
Color (SPANISH)
Presents an example of the Spanish form of literature known as the auto written by Pedro Calderon De La Barca.
Foreign Language; Literature and Drama
Dist - FOTH **Prod** - FOTH 1984

La Vida Urbana 10 MIN
16mm / U-matic / VHS
Color (I J H) (SPANISH)
A Spanish language program. Shows a young Latin American boy visiting a coeducational school in Mexico City.
Foreign Language
Dist - IFB **Prod** - IFB 1963

La Vida Urbana - Boy's Voice 10 MIN
U-matic / VHS / 16mm
Elementary Spanish Series
Color (I J H)
LC FIA65-1544
Foreign Language
Dist - IFB **Prod** - IFB 1963

La Vida Urbana - Girl's Voice 10 MIN
U-matic / VHS / 16mm
Elementary Spanish Series
Color (I J H)
LC FIA65-5544
Foreign Language
Dist - IFB **Prod** - IFB 1963

La Vie Dans La Foret Feuillue 19 MIN
16mm / U-matic / VHS
Color (I J H) (FRENCH)
A French language version of the videocassette Life In The Deciduous Forest. Discusses life in the deciduous forest, tracing variations in temperature, moisture and light.
Foreign Language; Science - Natural
Dist - IFB **Prod** - IFB 1962

La vie de boheme 100 MIN
35mm / 16mm
B&W (G) (FRENCH WITH ENGLISH SUBTITLES)
Portrays a band of luckless Parisian bohemians - French poet Marcel, Albanian painter Rodolfo, Irish composer Schaunard and Mimi the cigarette girl, Rodolfo's lover. Draws from the 19th - century novel Scenes de la Vie de Boheme. Directed by Aki Kaurismaki, Finland.
Fine Arts; Geography - World
Dist - KINOIC

La Vie Tient a Plus D'Un Fil 12 MIN
U-matic / VHS / 16mm
Color (P I) (FRENCH)
A French - language version of the motion picture Puppet Magic. Gives a brief history of puppetry and details each step in the construction of marionettes. Shows the puppeteer at work making the marionettes come alive.
Fine Arts; Foreign Language
Dist - IFB **Prod** - INTNEW 1977

La Viejecita Del Zapato 11 MIN
16mm / U-matic / VHS
Color (I) (SPANISH)
LC FIA66-1743
A Spanish language film. Uses the nursery rhyme about the old woman and the shoe to develop beginning number vocabulary in Spanish.
Foreign Language
Dist - CORF **Prod** - CORF 1966

A La Ville 10 MIN
U-matic / VHS
Salut - French Language Lessons Series
Color
Focuses on the city. Includes the structures To (somewhere), In (a place), and At (a place). Covers addresses.
Foreign Language
Dist - BCNFL **Prod** - BCNFL 1984

La Vista De La Abuelita - Grandmother's Visit 15 MIN
VHS / U-matic
Saludos
(P I G) (ENGLISH AND SPANISH)

$130 purchase, $25 rental, $75 self dub
Designed to introduceSpanish to the English speaking student at primary through intermediate levels. Fourth in a 25 part series.
Foreign Language
Dist - GPN

La Vita (Life in a Tin) 7 MIN
16mm
Color (J)
Philosophizes about twentieth century man who is so caught up in the business of living that he forgets the meaning of life.
Guidance and Counseling; Religion and Philosophy
Dist - UWFKD **Prod** - UWFKD

Lab hood safety 13 MIN
U-matic / BETA / VHS
Color (IND G)
$495.00 purchase _ #600 - 20
Emphasizes the basic dos and don'ts for working safely in a laboratory hood. Shows how to select the correct hood and proper use.
Health and Safety; Industrial and Technical Education; Psychology
Dist - ITSC **Prod** - ITSC

Lab packing 13 MIN
VHS / U-matic / BETA
Handling hazardous waste series
Color; PAL (IND G) (SPANISH ITALIAN)
$175.00 rental _ #HWH - 500; $730.00 purchase, $175.00 rental _ #LAB001
Focuses on a waste packaging technique commonly used by hospitals, universities and other small quantity generators. Demonstrates simple time - saving and cost - effective methods of waste segregation and proper packing media and labeling. Includes leader's guide and 10 participant handouts. Part of a seven - part series which trains hazardous waste management workers.
Business and Economics; Health and Safety; Psychology; Sociology
Dist - BNA **Prod** - BNA
ITF

Lab safety 13 MIN
VHS
Chemistry master apprentice series
Color (H C)
$49.95 purchase _ #49 - 7201 - V
Highlights rules and procedures that help prevent serious accidents in the laboratory. Stages accidents to show the proper steps to take - eye wash, safety shower, fire extinguisher and the fire alarm system. Part of the Chemistry Master Apprentice series.
Health and Safety; Science; Science - Physical
Dist - INSTRU **Prod** - CORNRS

Lab Safety 12 MIN
U-matic / VHS / 16mm
Color (H C A)
LC 75-701425
Outlines safety procedures to follow when accidents occur in a chemistry laboratory. Demonstrates extinguishers for four different types of fires and shows procedures for using a fire blanket and for washing harmful chemicals out of the eyes and off the body.
Health and Safety; Science
Dist - IU **Prod** - NET 1975

Lab safety - the accident at Jefferson High
Videodisc
Color; CAV (J H)
$189.00 purchase _ #8L431
Uses light humor to present important lessons on lab safety. Shows how to use beakers, glass tubing, gas burners and other lab apparatus and equipment, how to handle all types of chemicals, how to react to emergencies and how to clean up. Barcoded for instant random access.
Science; Science - Physical
Dist - BARR **Prod** - BARR 1991

Lab Safety - the Accident at Jefferson High 18.5 MIN
VHS / 16mm / U-matic
Color (J H)
$435, $305, $335 purchase _ #A431
Uses light humor to present important lessons on lab safety. Shows proper storage of dangerous chemicals and the art of lab safety. Shows how to use beakers, glass tubing, gas burners, and other lab apparatus and equipment. Discusses how to handle all kinds of chemicals and how to react properly to emergencies plus how to clean up after using the lab. Provides information on what it means to be prepared for lab including wearing the right clothes and protective gear.
Health and Safety; Science
Dist - BARR **Prod** - BARR 1986

Label logic 18 MIN
U-matic / VHS / 16mm
Color (J) (SPANISH)
LC 79-713612
Informs buyer to read labels in order that he can make better judgments before making purchases. Discusses standards of quality and fill of container as checked scientifically by the food and drug administration.
Foreign Language; Home Economics
Dist - AIMS **Prod** - ASSOC 1968

Label the Behavior 30 MIN
U-matic / VHS
Stretch Concepts for Teaching Handicapped Children Series
Color (T)
Discusses physical, emotional and mental characteristics of exceptional children.
Education
Dist - HUBDSC **Prod** - HUBDSC

Label the behavior, not the child 30 MIN
16mm
Project STRETCH Series; Module 12
Color (T)
LC 80-700619
Depicts physical, emotional and mental characteristics of exceptional children and describes behavior patterns.
Education; Psychology
Dist - HUBDSC **Prod** - METCO 1980

Label to Table, Pt 1 29 MIN
U-matic / VHS / 16mm
Be a Better Shopper Series Program 5; Program 5
Color (H C A)
LC 81-701462
Looks at the information found on food labels, the coming of metric weight, open dating, drained weight labeling, universal product code and label graphics.
Home Economics
Dist - CORNRS **Prod** - CUETV 1978

Label to Table, Pt 2 29 MIN
16mm / U-matic / VHS
Be a Better Shopper Series Program 6; Program 6
Color (H C A)
LC 81-701463
Explores the legal aspects of food labeling, such as ingredient lists, federal standards and imitation and artificial products.
Home Economics
Dist - CORNRS **Prod** - CUETV 1978

Labeling 30 MIN
U-matic / VHS
Food for Life Series
Color
Home Economics; Social Science
Dist - MSU **Prod** - MSU

Labeling 14 MIN
BETA / VHS / U-matic
Hazard communication series
Color (IND G)
$395.00 purchase _ #820 - 06
Discusses the labels required on hazardous materials received from a manufacturer and the in - house labels used to identify containers of materials drawn from original containers. Covers DOT and NFPA labeling. Part of a series on hazard communication.
Health and Safety; Industrial and Technical Education; Psychology
Dist - ITSC **Prod** - ITSC

Labels 13 MIN
Videoreel / VT2
Living Better I Series
Color
Home Economics
Dist - PBS **Prod** - MAETEL

Labels and Distortion 30 MIN
VHS / U-matic
Language and Meaning Series
Color (C)
English Language; Psychology
Dist - GPN **Prod** - WUSFTV 1983

Labels - if You Label it this, it Can't be that 14 MIN
16mm / U-matic / VHS
Color (I)
LC 72-702952
Explains that although labels are convenient, they perpetuate misconceptions and sterotypes. Uses candid interviews with children to reveal the extent to which labels about people, particularly racial and ethnic groups, are erroneous. Illustrates the effect of words, names and labels on our attitudes and values.
Guidance and Counseling; Psychology; Sociology
Dist - ALTSUL **Prod** - NATBRG 1972

Labor and Delivery 19 MIN
16mm / U-matic / VHS
Pregnancy and Childbirth Series
Color (H C A)
LC 80-700671
Examines the stages of labor and shows the actual birth of a baby in the delivery room. Includes scenes of hospital care of the mother after delivery, care of the newborn and the first few days at home.
Health and Safety; Science - Natural
Dist - IFB **Prod** - DALHSU 1977

Labor and Delivery 29 MIN
U-matic / VHS
Tomorrow's Families Series
Color (H C A)
LC 81-706903
Describes the three main stages of childbirth and shows how these stages can be assisted by various techniques.
Health and Safety
Dist - AITECH **Prod** - MDDE 1980

Labor and delivery 14 MIN
U-matic / VHS
Color (SPANISH)
LC 77-73135
Defines stages of labor and discusses what the mother can expect physically and emotionally during these stages. Details cervical dilation and effacement, and explains medication before and during delivery, defines episiotomy and actual delivery of the baby followed by the placenta.
Foreign Language; Health and Safety; Sociology
Dist - MEDCOM **Prod** - MEDCOM

Labor and Management - How do they Come to Terms 30 MIN
U-matic / VHS
Economics USA Series
Color (C)
Business and Economics; Psychology
Dist - ANNCPB **Prod** - WEFA

Labor and Overhead Cost 60 MIN
BETA / VHS
Manufacturing Series
(IND)
Shows how direct labor and overhead data shoud be captured with computerized manufacturing and financial systems.
Business and Economics
Dist - COMSRV **Prod** - COMSRV 1986

Labor Day 15 MIN
U-matic
Celebrate Series
Color (P)
Social Science
Dist - GPN **Prod** - KUONTV 1978

Labor Day - East Chicago 25 MIN
16mm
Color (G)
$40.00 rental
Records a group of working - class Lions Club members and their families on a holiday outing. Views their contests and customs.
Civics and Political Systems; Fine Arts; History - United States; Sociology
Dist - CANCIN **Prod** - PALAZT 1979

Labor for Life 26 MIN
VHS
Color (H A)
Presents the history of childbirth in America from the turn of the century to the 1980s. Traces the changes in techniques of and attitudes toward childbirth.
Health and Safety
Dist - CEPRO **Prod** - CEPRO 1989

Labor in the Promised Land 52 MIN
VHS / U-matic
Color
Profiles union members who pride themselves on their skills, discipline and professionalism, while looking at the growth of nonunion construction in the sunbelt. Presents angry, poverty - level working people who are embracing unionism as a means of solving their economic problems.
Business and Economics
Dist - FI **Prod** - NBCNEW

Labor - its History 30 MIN
U-matic
It's Everybody's Business Series Unit 4, Managing a Business
Color
Business and Economics
Dist - DALCCD **Prod** - DALCCD

Labor - Management Relations 23 MIN
U-matic
Launching Civil Service Reform Series
Color
LC 79-706274
Gives an overview of the provisions of Title II and their implications for federal managers. Covers changes in administrative bodies, scope of negotiations, grievance arbitration procedures, and employee representational rights.
Business and Economics; Civics and Political Systems
Dist - USNAC **Prod** - USOPMA 1978

Labor - Management Relations in Japan 30 MIN
U-matic / VHS
Business Nippon Series
Color (A)
LC 85-702160
Business and Economics; History - World
Dist - EBEC **Prod** - JAPCTV

Labor - management relations in steel - conflict or cooperation 26 MIN
VHS
Color (G C)
$60.00 purchase, $18.50 rental _ #34267
Traces the roots and development of periods of conflict and cooperation between management and labor in the US steel industry. Ties the evolution to constantly changing industrial, national and international situations. Divides into three periods ranging from 1865 to the mid - 1980s.
Business and Economics; History - United States
Dist - PSU **Prod** - WPSXTV 1984

Labor more than Once 52 MIN
VHS / 16mm
Color (G)
$275.00 purchase, $65.00 rental
Chronicles the battle of Marianne MacQueen for custody and parental rights to her son. Looks at homophobia and objectively considers lesbianism and motherhood.
Civics and Political Systems; Sociology
Dist - WMEN **Prod** - LIZM 1983

Labor of love - childbirth without violence 27 MIN
8mm cartridge
Color (H C A)
Focuses on the technique of birth popularized by Dr Frederick Leboyer. Shows how this method tries to reduce the violence of birth.
Health and Safety; Science - Natural
Dist - PEREN **Prod** - MENTA

The Labor of Thy Hands 30 MIN
16mm
Eternal Light Series
B&W (H C A) (JEWISH)
LC 75-700970
Traces the development of contemporary labor legislation from its origins in Jewish teachings. (Kinescope).
Business and Economics; Religion and Philosophy
Dist - NAAJS **Prod** - JTS 1968

The Labor Reform Act of 1978 - Should Congress Provide more Protection for 59 MIN
U-matic
Advocates Series
Color
Presents Stephen I Schlossberg and Vincent J Atruzze debating Congress's role in providing protection for union organizing.
Business and Economics; Civics and Political Systems; Sociology
Dist - PBS **Prod** - WGBHTV

Labor Relations Management - Grievances 12 MIN
U-matic / VHS / 16mm
Labor Relations Management Series
(PRO A)
$395 Purchase, $95 Rental 5 days, $35 Preview 3 days
Focuses on the supervisor's role in an grievance discussion.
Business and Economics
Dist - ADVANM **Prod** - ADVANM

Labor Relations Management - Progressive Discipline 12 MIN
U-matic / VHS
Labor Relations Management Series
(PRO A)
$395 Purchase, $95 Rental 5 days, $35 Preview 3 days
Focuses on the supervisor's role in incorporating discipline in the corporate environment.
Business and Economics
Dist - ADVANM **Prod** - ADVANM

Labor Relations Management Series
Labor Relations Management - Grievances 12 MIN
Labor Relations Management - Progressive Discipline 12 MIN
Dist - ADVANM

Labor Songs 30 MIN
U-matic
Folklore - U S a Series
B&W
Features labor song writer Joe Glazer as he talks about how and why he writes labor songs.
Literature and Drama
Dist - UMITV **Prod** - UMITV 1967

Labor Symphony 20 MIN
VHS / 16mm
Ted Shawn and His Men Dancers Series
Color (C A)
$105.00 purchase, $20.00 rental _ #RB1249
Recreates the task - specific movements of workers in agriculture and industry through dance, with music by Jess Meeker.
Fine Arts
Dist - IU **Prod** - NENDOW 1986

Labor Unions 30 MIN
U-matic
It's Everybody's Business Series Unit 4, Managing a Business
Color
Business and Economics
Dist - DALCCD **Prod** - DALCCD

Labor Unions in Japan 30 MIN
VHS / U-matic
Business Nippon Series
Color (A)
LC 85-702161
Business and Economics; History - World
Dist - EBEC **Prod** - JAPCTV 1984

Labor unions - what you need to know 36 MIN
VHS
Color (H)
$159.00 purchase _ #06700 - 126
Presents a comprehensive overview of union operations. Shows how apprenticeships work, the differences between open and closed shops, the function of grievance channels, how and why arbitration is used, how strikes and boycotts can arise. Discusses union dues, shop stewards and other officers, various types of membership participation.
Business and Economics; Guidance and Counseling; Social Science; Sociology
Dist - GA **Prod** - GA

Labor Unions - what You Should Know
VHS
(G)
$139 purchase _ #PX06700V
Presents an overview of union operations, including how apprenticeships work, differences between open and closed shops, the functions of grievance channels, how and why arbitration is used, and how strikes and boycotts can arise. Discusses union dues and their purpose, and examines negotiations between labor and management, including collective bargaining techniques.
Business and Economics; Guidance and Counseling; Sociology
Dist - CAREER **Prod** - CAREER

The Laboratory Aspects of Diseases of the Testicle 35 MIN
16mm
Clinical Pathology Series
B&W (PRO)
LC 74-704997
Discusses testicular physiology and biochemistry. Points out factors in the assessment of testicular function, Leydig cell failure, sperm production, testicular biopsy evaluation, karyotyping analysis, and plasmatestosterone levels. Provides detailed information concerning pituitary involvement, LSH, FSH, use of radioactive isotopes in determination of malfunctions of testes, and Klinefelters syndrome. (Kinescope).
Science; Science - Natural
Dist - USNAC **Prod** - NMAC 1969

Laboratory conditions - using chemicals safely 13 MIN
8mm cartridge / VHS / BETA / U-matic
Color; PAL (IND G)
$395.00 purchase, $175.00 rental _ #LAB - 100
Informs on compliance with the OSHA Laboratory Chemical Standard. Illustrates proper laboratory procedures and what precautions workers should take. Shows how to detect the presence or release of hazardous chemicals in the work area, the physical and health hazards of chemicals, the various forms of chemicals and how they can enter the body. Explains the use of personal protective equipement and clothing and what to do in case of leaks or spills. Stresses the importance of checking the label and MSDS. Looks at environmental and medical monitoring, the use of engineering controls. Reviews procedures for taking emergency response action or calling for help and more. Includes a trainer's manual and ten participant manuals.
Health and Safety; Psychology; Science - Physical
Dist - BNA **Prod** - BNA

Laboratory Design for Microbiological Safety 34 MIN
16mm
Color
LC FIE67-511
Suggests the need for safety measures in the design of infectious disease laboratories. Describes and illustrates some of the principal building features and devices used to provide effective microbiological containment. Discusses the concept of primary and secondary barriers in preventing escape and spread of microorganisms.
Health and Safety; Science - Natural
Dist - USNAC **Prod** - USPHS 1966

Laboratory Design for Microbiological Safety 35 MIN
U-matic
Color
LC 80-736279
Points out problems concerning safety and functional use of microbiological laboratories. Describes some of the principal features and devices used to provide effective microbiological containment. Issued in 1966 as a motion picture.
Health and Safety; Science
Dist - USNAC **Prod** - USNCI 1980

Laboratory Design for Microbiological Safety, M - 1091 35 MIN
16mm
Color
Approaches safety problems in the design and construction of a microbiological laboratory from an engineering standpoint and describes the primary and secondary barrier concept for the containment of microorganisms.
Science; Science - Natural
Dist - NMAC **Prod** - DUART

Laboratory diagnosis of diphtheria series
Determination of types of C diphtheriae 11 MIN
Dist - USNAC

Laboratory Diagnosis of Rabies in Animals 30 MIN
U-matic
Color
LC 78-706275
Demonstrates laboratory techniques for examination of animals in the diagnosis of rabies. Shows the preparation of brain impressions, the inoculation of animals, the serum neutralization test and the fluorescent antibody test. Issued in 1961 as a motion picture.
Health and Safety; Science
Dist - USNAC **Prod** - USPHS 1978

Laboratory diagnosis of tuberculosis series
Preparation of a culture medium 14 MIN
Preparation of sputum specimens 67 FRS
Dist - USNAC

The Laboratory High Vacuum Technique, using Solder Glass 30 MIN
16mm
College Physics Film Program Series
B&W (C)
LC FIA68-1427
Demonstrates techniques for producing various electrode structures and mounting them onto regular glass headers.
Science; Science - Physical
Dist - MLA **Prod** - EDS 1968

Laboratory in the Desert 23 MIN
16mm
Color
LC 75-701180
Outlines living conditions in Las Vegas, Nevada. Shows a day in the life of technical personnel who commute daily from Las Vegas to Tonopah Test Range. Illustrates the capabilities of the range and the special techniques used to meet unique testing problems.
Civics and Political Systems; Education
Dist - USNAC **Prod** - USNRC 1969

Laboratory Methods for Airborne Infection , Pt 2, the Henderson Apparatus 34 MIN
16mm
Color
LC FIE65-87
Discusses aerosols and their use in studying diseases transmitted by air. Uses diagrams to explain the animal exposure chamber. Discusses the Henderson apparatus, which is especially useful in development of vaccine and drugs used in the treatment of respiratory diseases. Shows how laboratory workers are protected.
Health and Safety; Science
Dist - USNAC **Prod** - USACC 1959

Laboratory of Life 21 MIN
VHS / U-matic
Color (I J H A)
Leads a voyage of discovery into one of science's most educational areas of research. Linus Pauling explains in clear terms how DNA functions in the cell. Scientists demonstrate the manufacture of genetically engineered insulin.
Science - Natural
Dist - NGS **Prod** - NGS

Laboratory of the Body 30 MIN
U-matic / VHS
Color (PRO)
Describes the multi - discipline approach to modern dental research. Demonstrates a typical research problem, such as the effect of collagenase on collagen.
Health and Safety
Dist - WFP **Prod** - WFP

Laboratory Procedures for Complete Dentures, Pt 1 - Waxing and Flasking 12 MIN
U-matic / VHS / 16mm
Color (PRO)
Demonstrates the steps of waxing and flasking dentures. Shows the anatomical considerations of shaping the wax, and discusses investing procedures using artificial stone in sections. Illustrates removal of the wax, followed by sprinkling a characterizing veneer into the mold.
Health and Safety; Science
Dist - USNAC **Prod** - VADTC 1981

Laboratory Procedures for Complete Dentures, Pt 2 - Processing and Finishing 16 MIN
16mm / U-matic / VHS
Color (PRO)
Shows the handling and packing of flasked molds with methylmethacrylate resin, followed by recovery of the processed dentures. Illustrates finishing the dentures with polishing elements, and gives attention to preserving orientation indices to facilitate delivery of the dentures.
Health and Safety; Science
Dist - USNAC **Prod** - VADTC 1981

Laboratory safety 15 MIN
U-matic / VHS
Basic electricity and D C circuits - laboratory series
Color
Industrial and Technical Education; Science - Physical; Social Science
Dist - TXINLC **Prod** - TXINLC

Laboratory Safety Basics 55 MIN
VHS / U-matic
Color (H C A)
Includes basics of laboratory safety, and signs of life which examines the way symbols, color codes and number codes are employed to signal danger. Features also electrical and radiation hazards and biohazards which illustrate basic procedures and precautions related to dissection, live animals and microorganisms.
Health and Safety; Science
Dist - MOKIN **Prod** - CMLMS

Laboratory spills 11 MIN
BETA / VHS / U-matic
Color (IND G)
$495.00 purchase _ #601 - 20
Trains employees in procedures to be followed in the event of a small spill of acid, caustic or flammable liquid in a laboratory setting. Emphasizes awareness of potential hazards, location and proper use of safety equipment, clean - up material and appropriate first - aid procedures.
Health and Safety; Industrial and Technical Education; Psychology
Dist - ITSC **Prod** - ITSC

Laboratory Technique for Darkfield Microscopy 16 MIN
16mm
B&W
Explains the theory of darkfield microscopy, the preparation of slides and the use of a darkfield microscope.
Science
Dist - USNAC **Prod** - USN 1953

Laboratory Techniques 9 MIN
U-matic
Chemistry Videotapes Series
Color
Demonstrates laboratory techniques including bending glass to make a wash bottle. Introduces the pipette and the volumetric flask.
Science; Science - Physical
Dist - UMITV **Prod** - UMITV

Labor/Management EAP 17 MIN
U-matic / VHS
Color
Trains supervisors of union production workers in the techniques of employee assistance program (EAP) referral.
Business and Economics
Dist - WHITEG **Prod** - WHITEG

Labor's future with Gus Tyler 30 MIN
U-matic / VHS
World of ideas with Bill Moyers, session 2 series
Color; Captioned (A)
$39.95, $59.95 purchase _ #WIWM - 228
Features labor leader Gus Tyler, who began his career as an intellectual agitator on behalf of working men and women in the Depression, and who helped make the International Ladies' Garment Workers' Union one of the most progressive unions in organized labor. Shows that today Tyler works to preserve the union's influence at a time when garment industry jobs are dwindling and American manufacturing is on the decline. Discusses labor's place in the new global economy.
Business and Economics; Social Science; Sociology
Dist - PBS **Prod** - PBS

Labors of love 30 MIN
VHS
Color (G)
$450.00, $375.00 purchase, $45.00 rental
Presents four couples having four very different labors and deliveries. Discloses that no two childbirths are the same, that developing flexible expectations is important to preparing to have a baby. Shows how each couple comes to childbirth with expectations - some are met, some not. One couple opts for an epidural while another which had planned to use medication decides to go without. Reveals that for some a birthing room environment is important while for others the traditonal progression from labor room to delivery room is preferable or necessary. Witnesses an unscheduled cesarean, a vaginal delivery without medication, an induced labor, the birth of a second child and delivery of an 'elderly primip.' Produced and directed by Lis McElaney.
Health and Safety
Dist - POLYMR

Labor's political process 10 MIN
16mm / VHS
Color (G IND)
$5.00 rental
Overviews the AFL - CIO procedure followed in making an endorsement of a presidential candidate.
Business and Economics; Civics and Political Systems
Dist - AFLCIO **Prod** - LIPA 1987

Labor's struggle 30 MIN
VHS
America in perspective - US history since 1877 series
Color (H C G)
$99.00 purchase _ #AIP - 3
Describes the realities of working conditions in the late 19th - century United States. Analyzes the reactions of the working class during that period. Part of a 26 - part series.
Business and Economics; History - United States; Social Science
Dist - INSTRU **Prod** - DALCCD 1991

Labor's Turning Point 44 MIN
U-matic / VHS
Color
Conveys the upheaval created by a strike of Local 574, International Brotherhood of Teamsters. Gives a visual description of the socio - economic trauma of the Great Depression as it impacted on Minnesota's workers, businesses, banks and politics.
Business and Economics
Dist - NFPS UCV **Prod** - TCPT

Labour and delivery - 3 19 MIN
16mm / VHS / BETA / U-matic
Canadian hospitals Pregnancy - birth series
Color; PAL (PRO G)
PdS120, PdS128 purchase
Examines the stages of labor and shows the delivery in detail. Looks at the important 'transition phase.' Features a beautifully photographed birth in a delivery room. Part of a four - part series.
Health and Safety
Dist - EDPAT

Labour Law 15 MIN
VHS / 16mm
You and the Law Series
Color (S)
$150.00 purchase _ #275908
Employs a mixture of drama and narrative to introduce particular aspects of Canadian law. Presents some of the basic concepts and addresses some of the more commonly asked questions. Emphasis is on those elements of the law which are frequently misunderstood. 'Labour Law' discusses employer and employee relationships and the various laws and government agencies regulating the workplace. Topics include - the Employment Standards Act, Labour Relations Act, Labour Relations Board, Worker's Compensation Act, the Individual's Rights Protection Act, the Human Rights Commission and labor law exceptions.
Business and Economics; Civics and Political Systems; Geography - World; Guidance and Counseling; Social Science; Sociology
Dist - ACCESS **Prod** - ACCESS 1987

Labours of Eve series
Looks at issues relating to conception; childbirth and pregnancy through the eyes of six different women. Examines hysterectomy; multiple births; abortion; surrogate motherhood; artificial insemination; and egg donations to women unable to produce their own. Six programs constitute this series.

Helen's story	30 MIN
Jessie's story	30 MIN
Joan's story	30 MIN
Lori's story	30 MIN
Margaret's story	30 MIN
Mary's story	30 MIN

Dist - BBCENE

Labrador - Land Out of Time 30 MIN
VHS / U-matic
Color
Documents the problems in Labrador, where progress was long in coming and where the heritage of fishing and hunting has been replaced by forced government relocation and welfare.
Geography - World
Dist - JOU **Prod** - UPI

Labyrinths 28 MIN
16mm
Color
LC 80-700645
Depicts five astronauts, trapped in space, participating in a collective hallucination involving existential love, a planet and its dying sun, and a time traveler.
Fine Arts
Dist - MINEM **Prod** - MINEM 1979

The Lacemaker 108 MIN
16mm
Color (FRENCH (ENGLISH SUBTITLES))
Describes the ill - fated love affair between an awkward bourgeouis student and an inexperienced shop girl. Directed by Claude Goretta. With English subtitles.
Fine Arts; Foreign Language
Dist - NYFLMS **Prod** - UNKNWN 1977

The Lacemaker 107 MIN
VHS
Color (G)
$39.95 _ #LAC010
Presents a bittersweet twist on the Cinderella story in which a shy beautician falls in love with a handsome student. Depicts his inability to appreciate her inner beauty as the cause of her ultimate tragedy. Directed by Claude Goretta. Digitally remastered with new translation.
Fine Arts; Literature and Drama; Religion and Philosophy
Dist - HOMVIS **Prod** - JANUS 1977

Laceration - Principles and Techniques of Management 14 MIN
U-matic
Color (PRO)
Takes the student through the entire process of laceration management in the emergency room. Uses medical graphics, actual surgical film segments and discussion. Shows how to anesthesize and cleanse traumatic wounds, debride wounds prior to closure, suture wounds and manage the closed wound.
Health and Safety
Dist - UNM **Prod** - UNM

Lackluster 3 MIN
16mm
Color (G)
$15.00 rental
Plays with abstract animation of everyday objects in many colors.
Fine Arts
Dist - CANCIN **Prod** - PEARLY

Lacrosse 14 MIN
16mm
Color (G)
#2X70 I
Demonstrates how the ancient Indian game of Lacrosse is played, how Lacrosse sticks are made by Mohawk Indians, and how the Canadian Lacrosse Association helps to instruct teams.
Physical Education and Recreation; Social Science
Dist - CDIAND **Prod** - NFBC 1964

Lacrosse, Little Brother of War 14 MIN
16mm
Color
LC 75-704314
Traces the history of lacrosse from its origins as an Indian game of skill and bloodshed to its growing popularity today as an amateur sport and as a professional spectator sport.
Physical Education and Recreation; Social Science
Dist - CANFDC **Prod** - CANFDC 1974

Lacrosse series
VHS
N C A A instructional video series
Color (H C A)
$74.95 purchase _ #KAR1905V
Presents a four - part series on lacrosse. Focuses on basic skills, individual offensive and defensive skills, and goalkeeping.
Physical Education and Recreation
Dist - CAMV **Prod** - NCAAF

Lactation 41 MIN
VHS
Dairy Production And Management Series
Color (G)
$95.00 purchase _ #6 - 096 - 302P
Examines the external and internal anatomy of the udder in dairy cows, proper milking practices, abnormalities in mammary glands and milk composition and factors affecting milk production. Part of a five - part series on dairy management.
Agriculture; Business and Economics
Dist - VEP **Prod** - VEP

A Lad in the Lamp 16 MIN
16mm
Magnificent 6 and 1/2 Series
Color (K P I)
Presents the magnificent 'SIX AND 1/2' who find a lamp which they believe resembles a legendary one. When strange happenings take place, the small fry are convinced that it has magic powers.
Literature and Drama
Dist - LUF **Prod** - CHILDF 1970

Ladakh - in harmony with the spirit 86 MIN
VHS
Color (G)
$29.95 purchase _ #LAV
Portrays the kingdom of Ladakh, nestled high in the Himalayas. Compares life in Ladakh today with life in neighboring Tibet before the wholesale disruption of Tibetan culture and religious life by the Chinese government. Unfolds a landscape of sun and shadow, brilliant blue skies, towering mountains and deep, dark valleys, the play of deities and demons. Produced by Clemens Kuby.
Geography - World
Dist - SNOWLI

Ladakh - Little Tibet 30 MIN
U-matic / VHS
Journey into the Himalayas Series
Color (J S C A)
MV=$195.00
Looks at a remote area of Kashmir which has been closed to travel because of its location as India's northern border with China. Shows the Tibetan refugees who live there.
Geography - World; History - World
Dist - LANDMK **Prod** - LANDMK 1984

L'Adaptation a La Survie - Les Oiseaux 14 MIN
16mm / U-matic / VHS
Color (I J H) (FRENCH)
A French - language version of the motion picture Adaptations For Survival - Birds. Illustrates both structural and behavioral adaptations of birds to their environments and shows how these adaptations enable the birds to get sufficient food, to defend themselves and to reproduce enough offspring. Promotes discussion of evolution.
Foreign Language; Science - Natural
Dist - IFB **Prod** - IFB 1969

The Ladder 6 MIN
16mm / U-matic / VHS
Color (J)
LC 81-701612
Offers a symbolic tale about a man who climbs an actual ladder by going over and around those already on the ladder. Reveals him later at the bottom of the ladder writing his memoirs.
Fine Arts
Dist - PHENIX **Prod** - SFTB 1981

The Ladder of creation 52 MIN
16mm / VHS / U-matic
Ascent of man series
Color (H C A) (SPANISH)
LC 74-702262
Explores the controversy around the theory of evolution developed simultaneously by Alfred Wallace and Charles Darwin. Narrated by Dr Jacob Bronowski of the Salk Institute.
Science; Science - Natural
Dist - TIMLIF **Prod** - BBCTV 1973
BBCENE
AMBROS

The Ladder of creation - Pt 1 26 MIN
16mm / U-matic
Ascent of man series
Color (H C A)
LC 74-702262
Explores the controversy around the theory of evolution developed simultaneously by Alfred Wallace and Charles Darwin. Narrated by Dr Jacob Bronowski of the Salk Institute.
Religion and Philosophy; Science - Natural
Dist - TIMLIF **Prod** - BBCTV 1973

The Ladder of creation - Pt 2 26 MIN
16mm / U-matic
Ascent of man series
Color (H C A)
LC 74-702262
Explores the controversy around the theory of evolution developed simultaneously by Alfred Wallace and Charles Darwin. Narrated by Dr Jacob Bronowski of the Salk Institute.
Religion and Philosophy; Science - Natural
Dist - TIMLIF **Prod** - BBCTV 1973

Ladders 18 MIN
VHS / U-matic
Color (A IND)
Examines ladders used on construction sites. Features three grades of ladder and discusses the selection and handling, advantages and disadvantags of each. Provides safety tips.
Health and Safety
Dist - IFB **Prod** - CSAO 1986

Ladders 30 MIN
VHS
Firefighter I Video Series
Color (PRO G)
$125.00 purchase _ #35066
Shows crews using various types of ladders up to 35 feet to move both personnel and equipment. Stresses individual and team effort while demonstrating firefighting from ladders using hose and other equipment. Includes an instruction guide for review. Part of a video series on Firefighter I training codes to be used with complementing IFSTA manuals.
Health and Safety; Psychology; Social Science
Dist - OKSU **Prod** - OKSU

Ladders 29 MIN
16mm
B&W (H C A)
LC 76-701744
Demonstrates the standard procedures for carrying, footing, spotting, raising, securing and lowering straight and extension hand ladders from 14 feet to 50 feet in length.
Health and Safety
Dist - FILCOM **Prod** - LACFD 1954

Ladders 1 18 MIN
VHS
Firefighter I series
Color (IND)
$130.00 purchase _ #35632
Presents one part of a 19 - part series that is the teaching companion for IFSTA's Essentials of Fire Fighting manual. Defines basic types of ladders and explains how to use each type. Identifies parts and terms. Demonstrates basic ladder handling methods. Based on Chapter 8.
Health and Safety; Science - Physical; Social Science
Dist - OKSU **Prod** - ACCTRA

Ladders 2 17 MIN
VHS
Firefighter I series
Color (IND)
$130.00 purchase _ #35633
Presents one part of a 19 - part series that is the teaching companion for IFSTA's Essentials of Fire Fighting manual. Shows correct ladder placement. Demonstrates the procedures for raising and climbing ladders. Presents safety procedures when working with ladders. Based on Chapter 8.
Health and Safety; Science - Physical; Social Science
Dist - OKSU **Prod** - ACCTRA

Ladders and Aerial Apparatus 30 MIN
VHS
Firefighter II - III Video Series
Color (G PRO)
$145.00 purchase _ #35255
Demonstrates aerial ladders and apparatus during rescue and fire suppression operations. Identifies construction materials and load - safety features. Shows how to test ground and aerial ladders.
Agriculture; Health and Safety; Psychology; Social Science
Dist - OKSU **Prod** - OKSU

Ladders and Linemen 10 MIN
16mm / U-matic / VHS
Color (IND)
LC 76-701337
Points out how accidents can be avoided when using a ladder. Stresses the importance of selecting the right ladder for the job, especially when electricity is involved.
Guidance and Counseling; Health and Safety; Home Economics; Industrial and Technical Education
Dist - IFB **Prod** - EUSA 1974

Ladders and Lines - Number Line Concepts 20 MIN
U-matic
Let's Figure it Out Series
B&W (P)
Mathematics
Dist - NYSED **Prod** - WNYE 1968

Ladders and Scaffolds 60 MIN
U-matic / VHS
Mechanical Equipment Maintenance, Module 1 - Rigging and Lifting 'Series
Color (IND)
Industrial and Technical Education
Dist - LEIKID **Prod** - LEIKID

Ladies and Gentlemen of the Jury 28 MIN
16mm
Color (H A G)
Shows the problems of the drinking driver and the accidents that can be caused by such drivers.
Industrial and Technical Education; Psychology
Dist - FEDU **Prod** - USDT 1985

Ladies in Retirement 97 MIN
16mm
B&W
Describes a woman who will do anything to prevent her two sisters from being put into a mental institution, even if it means doing something grisly to her employer. Stars Ida Lupino and Elsa Lanchester.
Fine Arts
Dist - KITPAR **Prod** - CPC 1941

Ladies in Waiting 11 MIN
16mm
Family Life Education and Human Growth Series
Color (J)
LC FIA66-1177
Emphasizes the importance during pregnancy of balancing activity with rest and of practicing controlled relaxation and correct posture. Demonstrates breathing exercises to aid rest and ease labor.
Health and Safety; Physical Education and Recreation; Psychology; Sociology
Dist - SF **Prod** - MORLAT 1966

Ladies of Leisure 98 MIN
16mm
B&W
Tells how a wealthy young man falls in love with a street - smart girl. Depicts her attempted suicide after his parents refuse to let him marry her. Stars Barbara Stanwyck. Directed by Frank Capra.
Civics and Political Systems; Fine Arts
Dist - KITPAR **Prod** - CPC 1930

Ladies' tailor 92 MIN
VHS
Color (G)
$125.00 purchase
Spends a day in the life of a Jewish tailor's family in September 1941, Kiev, Russia, prior to the infamous execution of 96,000 Jews by the Nazis at Babi Yar. Portrays a Russian family, their home destroyed, sent by the Germans to lodge in the house of Isaac, the tailor. As the deportation of Kiev's Jews draws near, the two families meet and reveal their thoughts and feelings. Directed by Leonid Gorovets. Cinematography by A Ianovski.
Fine Arts; History - World; Literature and Drama; Religion and Philosophy; Sociology
Dist - NCJEWF

Ladies Wear the Blue 29 MIN
16mm
Color
LC 74-706481
Traces the history of Navy women from 1917 to the present. Stresses the importance of equal employment opportunity and highlights the changes the Navy has made to offer a more satisfying and rewarding career for women in naval service.
Civics and Political Systems; History - United States; Sociology
Dist - USNAC **Prod** - USN 1974

Ladies weight training 60 MIN
VHS
Weight training series
Color (G)
$39.99 purchase _ #MFV003V
Demonstrates a series of weight training exercises that are designed for beginning female lifters. Presents two different workouts to choose from.
Physical Education and Recreation; Science - Natural
Dist - CAMV **Prod** - CAMV 1988

The Lady and the Owl 28 MIN
16mm / U-matic / VHS
Color (H C A)
LC 76-702440
Features Key Mc Kiver of Vineland, Ontario, Canada, who, with the assistance of her husband, restores owls to their former health and vigor.
Science - Natural
Dist - WOMBAT **Prod** - NFBC 1975

Lady and the Tramp - a lesson in sharing attention 8 MIN
U-matic / VHS / 16mm
Disney's animated classics - lessons in living series
Color (P I)
LC 78-701725
Tells how a young boy fears the loss of attention that may accompany his parents having another child. Uses a scene from the animated film Lady And The Tramp to show that there is plenty of love to share when new people enter the scene.
Fine Arts; Guidance and Counseling
Dist - CORF **Prod** - DISNEY 1978

Lady Beware 17 MIN
16mm / U-matic / VHS
Color
Demonstrates techniques that women can use to protect themselves from the growing menace of personal assault. Includes details of security for home, car and phone, precautions for avoiding danger when out at night, the wisdom of flight, and what to do if escape isn't possible.
Sociology
Dist - PFP **Prod** - PFP

The Lady Bullfighter 21 MIN
U-matic / VHS
Color (C)
$249.00, $149.00 purchase _ #AD - 2135
Looks at Evelina Fabregas, Spain's only woman bullfighter.
Foreign Language; Geography - World; History - World; Physical Education and Recreation; Sociology
Dist - FOTH **Prod** - FOTH

A Lady Called Camille 29 MIN
U-matic
Color
LC 79-706663
Documents the devastation caused by Hurricane Camille. Tells how thousands of lives were saved because of emergency plans, trained rescue teams and help from thousands in volunteer groups and the military. Issued in 1971 as a motion picture.
Health and Safety; History - World; Sociology
Dist - USNAC **Prod** - USOCD 1979

A lady called camille 12 MIN
16mm 28 MIN
Color (P I J H) (SPANISH)
LC 75-700561; 74-704999; 74-705000
Tells the dramatic story of Hurricane Camille. Depicts the disaster, the advance warnings and evacuation efforts that saved thousands of lives before the storm and the relief and rescue operations which followed.
Health and Safety; History - World; Science - Physical; Sociology
Dist - USNAC **Prod** - USOCD 1971

Lady Constance Lytton 60 MIN
VHS
Shoulder to shoulder series
Color (G)
$59.95 purchase _ #SHOU - 103
Profiles Lady Constance Lytton, a member of the British aristocracy who joined the suffrage movement. Reveals that when she was imprisoned for her suffragist activities, she refused special treatment on account of her social status. Hosted by actress Jane Alexander.
Civics and Political Systems; History - World
Dist - PBS **Prod** - MKNZM 1988

Lady Day - the many faces of Billie Holiday 60 MIN
VHS
Masters of American music series
Color; B&W (G)
$29.95 purchase _ #1292
Documents the life of jazz singer Billie Holiday. Combines TV and movie footage, commentary from fellow musicians and singers, and narration from Holiday's autobiography, 'Lady Sings the Blue,' read by actress Ruby Dee. Includes Holiday's renditions of 'What a Little Moonlight Can Do,' 'Lover Man,' 'God Bless the Child.' Produced by Toby Byron - Multiprises.
Fine Arts
Dist - KULTUR

Lady Elaine Discovers Planet Purple 25 MIN
16mm
Purple Adventures of Lady Elaine Fairchilde Series Program 2
Color (K P S)
LC 80-700581
Presents Mr Rogers talking, singing and using puppets to tell a story about Lady Elaine's arrival home from Jupiter and her discovery of Planet Purple on the return trip. Discusses individual differences, handicaps, uniqueness and change.
Fine Arts; Guidance and Counseling; Literature and Drama
Dist - HUBDSC **Prod** - FAMCOM 1979

Lady Elaine Flies to Jupiter 29 MIN
16mm
Purple Adventures of Lady Elaine Fairchilde Series Program 1
Color (K P S)
LC 80-700581
Presents Mr Rogers talking, singing and using puppets to tell a story about Lady Elaine getting ready for her trip into space. Discusses individual differences, handicaps, uniqueness and change.
Fine Arts; Guidance and Counseling; Literature and Drama
Dist - HUBDSC **Prod** - FAMCOM 1979

Lady Elaine Wants Everything to be as it is on Planet Purple 24 MIN
16mm
Purple Adventures of Lady Elaine Fairchilde Series Program 3
Color (K P S)
LC 80-700581
Presents Mr Rogers talking, singing and using puppets to tell a story about Lady Elaine's attempts to make her neighborhood just like Planet Purple, where everything and everyone is the same. Discusses individual differences, including handicaps, uniqueness and change.
Fine Arts; Guidance and Counseling; Literature and Drama
Dist - HUBDSC **Prod** - FAMCOM 1979

Lady Fishbourne's Complete Guide to Better Table Manners 6 MIN
U-matic / VHS / 16mm
Color (J)
LC 78-700118
Uses animation in an illustration of proper eating etiquette.
Home Economics
Dist - CAROUF **Prod** - NFBC 1977

The Lady from Shanghai 87 MIN
16mm
B&W (C A)
Stars Orson Welles, Rita Hayworth and Everett Sloane in the story of murder on a leisurely pleasure cruise.
Fine Arts
Dist - TIMLIF **Prod** - CPC 1948

Lady in a Cage 93 MIN
U-matic / VHS / 16mm
B&W
Stars Olivia De Havilland as an invalid trapped in her home elevator.
Fine Arts
Dist - FI **Prod** - PAR 1964

Lady in Motion 28 MIN
16mm / VHS
Color (H)
$415.00, $205.00 purchase
Tells the story of Agnes Hammond, a 72 - year old rancher and breeder of champion Dachsunds. Highlights her home in the foothills of the Canadian Rockies.
Agriculture; Biography; Geography - World; Science - Natural; Sociology
Dist - FLMWST

The Lady in the Lincoln Memorial 18 MIN
16mm
Color (I)
LC 70-709231
Portrays the life of Marian Anderson as a struggling Negro singer in a prejudiced world through dramatized situations in her childhood and young adult years and through authentic photographs of her vocal and social triumphs. Includes photographs of her European tours and her historic concert at the Lincoln Memorial in 1939.
Biography; Civics and Political Systems; Fine Arts
Dist - SF **Prod** - NYT

The Lady is Willing 92 MIN
16mm
B&W
Stars Marlene Dietrich as an actress who finds an abandoned baby and insists on keeping it, hiring her own pediatrician (Fred MacMurray) and installing him in her hotel suite.
Fine Arts
Dist - KITPAR **Prod** - CPC 1942

Lady Lazarus - The Work of Sylvia Plath 25 MIN
VHS / 16mm
Color; B&W (G)
$75.00 rental, $250.00 purchase
Weaves a visual response to Sylvia Plath's own readings of her work, including 'Daddy,' 'Ariel' and selections from her novel The Bell Jar. Juxtaposes recordings of Plath's haunting voice, made during the final years before her death in 1963, with a figurative Lady Lazarus, a young woman acting as a spiritual medium for the writer during a seance. Celebrates this legendary writer, her macabre humor and the resonance and power of her words. By Sandra Levine.
Fine Arts; Literature and Drama
Dist - WMEN

Lady Marshall 21 MIN
16mm / VHS
Color (G)
$250.00 purchase, $60.00 rental
Visits Marshall Point, a small fishing village on the English speaking Atlantic coast of Nicaragua, where several Afro - Caribbean women run a flourishing boating operation. Reveals that the boat, donated by the Sandinista government and dubbed Lady Marshall, is the only boat in the area owned by women. Follows the activities of the women as they overturn fellow villagers' skepticism to gain economic independence, pride of achievement and a critical role in the functioning of their community. Produced by Maria Jose Alvarez and Marta Clarissa Hernandez.
Business and Economics; Geography - World; Sociology
Dist - WMEN

A Lady Named Baybie 58 MIN
16mm
Color
LC 81-700509
Shows the daily life of 64 - year - old Baybie Hoover, a blind gospel singer who earns her living performing on the street corners of New York City.
Fine Arts; Psychology
Dist - DIRECT **Prod** - STURTM 1980

The Lady of the Camellias 125 MIN
VHS
Color (G)
$39.95 purchase _ #1209
Presents the Hamburg Ballet production of 'The Lady Of The Camillias' choreographed and directed by John Neumeier to the music of Fredric Chopin in homage to world - famous prima ballerina Marcia Haydee. Stars Stuttgart's Haydee in the title role, along with Ivan Liska as Armand. The Symphony Orchestra of the NDR performs the score.
Fine Arts; Foreign Language; Geography - World; Physical Education and Recreation
Dist - KULTUR

Lady of the Rapids 11 MIN
16mm
Movietone Sports Series
Color
LC FI68-1545
Follows the adventures of Georgie White as she shoots the rapids of the Colorado river on its course through the Grand Canyon.
Geography - United States; Physical Education and Recreation
Dist - TWCF **Prod** - TWCF 1962

Lady of the Sea 20 MIN
U-matic / VHS / 16mm
Color (I J H C)
LC 78-701615
Presents the saga of a two - year journey around the world aboard a square - rigged sailing ship. Includes footage of the San Bias Islands, Pitcairn Island, Tahiti and Bali.
Geography - World
Dist - MGHT **Prod** - JONESF 1978

Lady on the Lower 13 MIN
16mm
Color (G)
LC 77-702402
Depicts the barge - lining activities of a towboat which hauls agricultural commodities on the Mississippi River.
Social Science
Dist - UMCSN **Prod** - UMCSN 1977

The Lady, or the Tiger by Frank Stockton 16 MIN
16mm / U-matic / VHS
Humanities - Short Story Showcase Series
Color (J H C)
Resets a story of the 1800's, The Lady, Or The Tiger, in the space age, adding helicopters, sportscars, penthouses and other touches.
Fine Arts; Literature and Drama
Dist - EBEC **Prod** - EBEC 1970
GA

Lady Sings the Blues 144 MIN
16mm / U-matic / VHS
Color
Features Diana Ross as the immortal blues singer Billie Holiday.
Fine Arts
Dist - FI **Prod** - PAR 1972

The Lady Vanishes 99 MIN
16mm
B&W
Tells how a middle - aged governess vanishes from a train and how the other passengers deny she was ever there. Directed by Alfred Hitchcock.
Fine Arts
Dist - REELIM **Prod** - UNKNWN 1938

The Lady Vanishes - Where are the Women in Film 29 MIN
U-matic
Woman Series
Color
Assesses the role of women in film. States that films have not reflected the struggle and changing status of American women, but have relegated them to secondary roles as victims of violence or on the brink of madness.
Fine Arts; Sociology
Dist - PBS **Prod** - WNEDTV

The Lady with the Dog 89 MIN
VHS
B&W (G) (RUSSIAN (ENGLISH SUBTITLES))
$29.95 purchase _ #1622
Presents a Soviet film, 1960, based on Anton Chekhov's 'The Lady With The Dog.' Tells the story of a bored banker, married, who meets a young woman, married, while on vacation in Yalta at the beginning of the century. They drift into an affair and into true love, but the conventions of society and their need to feel respectable force them to return to their old lives. They continue to meet clandestinely but cannot break from their pasts.
Fine Arts; Geography - World; Literature and Drama
Dist - KULTUR

The Lady with the ship on her head - 78
VHS
Reading rainbow series
Color; CC (K P)

$39.95 purchase
Joins LeVar as anchor of a wild and wacky news report, Headline News - all the news from the neck up, inspired by the book by Deborah Nourse Lattimore. Visits the largest barbershop in the world and offers a sneak preview of a hot new musical video. Part of a series offering a multicultural approach to generating reading enthusiasm with cross - curricular applications, hosted by LeVar Burton.
English Language; Literature and Drama
Dist - GPN **Prod** - LNMDP

The Lady Without Camelias - NY 10019 Stock NY 10019 106 MIN
U-matic / VHS / 16mm
B&W; Captioned (A) (ITALIAN (ENGLISH SUBTITLES))
Portrays the story of the discovery of a young salesgirl by a film producer, their collaboration and eventual marriage, their failure together in their careers, their separation and her inability to find a new lover or a renewed career.
Fine Arts
Dist - CNEMAG **Prod** - CNEMAG 1953

Lady Without Camelias, the 106 MIN
U-matic / VHS / 16mm
Captioned; B&W (A) (ITALIAN (ENGLISH SUBTITLES))
Portrays the story of the discovery of a young salesgirl by a film producer, their collaboration and eventual marriage, their failure together in their careers, their separation and her inability to find a new lover or a renewed career. Italian dialog with English subtitles.
Fine Arts
Dist - CNEMAG **Prod** - CNEMAG 1953

The Ladybird Beetle 11 MIN
VHS / 16mm / U-matic
Animal Families Series
Color (K P I)
$275, $195, $225 purchase _ #B424
Examines in detail the 'ladybug,' officially known as the ladybird beetle. Shows a ladybug laying her tiny eggs using close up photography. Follows the babies, or 'grubs,' leaving the eggs, the pupa stage and final metamorphosis into adulthood.
Science - Natural
Dist - BARR **Prod** - BARR 1986

Ladybird, Ladybird 25 MIN
VHS
Color (S)
$79.00 purchase _ #825 - 9548
Scrutinizes one of the world's best - loved insects, the ladybird. Uses incredibly close - up photography to trace the life cycles of the tiny carnivore, named for the Virgin Mary and one of nature's most effective predators. Narrated by David Attenborough.
Science - Natural
Dist - FI **Prod** - BBCTV 1988

Ladybug, ladybug 12 MIN
VHS
Natural history series
Color (I J H)
$60.00 purchase _ #A5VH 1102
Explores the world of a familiar and beneficial beetle, the ladybug. Shows how its ability to avoid predators and devour destructive insects makes it invaluable to human crops. Uses time - lapse photography to view the life cycle of the lady bug. Part of a series on natural history.
Science - Natural
Dist - CLRVUE **Prod** - CLRVUE

Ladybug, Ladybug 11 MIN
16mm / U-matic / VHS
Reading and Word Play Series
Color (P)
Presents a series of word - filled vignettes of ladybugs, flying squirrels and boys and girls to reinforce the words jump, fly, from, away, house, home and if.
English Language
Dist - AIMS **Prod** - PEDF 1976

Ladybug, Ladybug, Winter is Coming! 10 MIN
U-matic / VHS / 16mm
Color (P)
$265, $185 purchase _ #3708
Tells the story of a ladybug who is puzzled about the cold weather, asks other animals about it, and finds a safe place to stay until spring.
Science - Natural
Dist - CORF

The Ladykillers 90 MIN
16mm
Color
Features Alec Guinness as the head of a motley group of thieves planning the robbery of an armored truck. Shows how they plan to use an old lady's house as their base of operations, but how things go awry when she finds out about their plans. Directed by Alexander Mackendrick.
Fine Arts; Literature and Drama
Dist - LCOA **Prod** - CONPIC 1955

Lady's portion 30 MIN
VHS
Skirt through history
Color; PAL (H C A)
PdS65 purchase
Utilizes personal writings to document the lives of two early female journalists. Features Emile Peacocke and Bessie Parks, both of whom encountered sex discrimination and prejudice throughout their careers. Second in a series of six programs covering four centuries of women's history.
History - World; Sociology
Dist - BBCENE

Lafayette 99 MIN
16mm
Color (I)
Stars Orson Welles, Jack Hawkins and Michael Le Royer as Lafayette, the young French nobleman who spent his personal fortune and risked his life helping the United States win its independence.
Biography; History - United States
Dist - TWYMAN **Prod** - UNKNWN 1962

Lafcadio, the Lion who Shot Back 15 MIN
U-matic / VHS
Through the Pages Series no 10
Color (P)
LC 82-707378
Presents librarian Phyllis Syracuse reading from Shel Silverstein's story Lafcadio, The Lion Who Shot Back. Relates how a circus lion learns to become a trick shooter and becomes more and more like a person. Shows how a crisis forces him to decide whether he is a man or a lion.
English Language
Dist - GPN **Prod** - WVIZTV 1982

Lafcadio, the Lion who Shot Back 24 MIN
U-matic / VHS / 16mm
B&W (I)
LC 78-700115
Tells the story of a young lion, Lafcadio, who fails to make friends with hunters, then decides to become the world's greatest marksman, only to discover he has lost his own identity.
Guidance and Counseling; Literature and Drama
Dist - LCOA **Prod** - LCOA 1979

Laffin' Gas 7 MIN
16mm
B&W (K)
Presents a comedy about a dental assistant who takes over when the dentist steps out, thus causing a free - for - all. Features Charlie Chaplin.
Fine Arts
Dist - TWYMAN **Prod** - SENN 1914

L'Africaine 190 MIN
VHS
Color (S)
$49.95 purchase _ #833 - 9514
Stars Placido Domingo and Shirley Verrett in the San Francisco Opera production of 'L'Africaine' by Meyerbeer. Tells the story of explorer Vasco da Gama whose dangerous sea voyage takes him to the African coast. There he falls in love with the beautiful Selika. Produced by Lotfi Mansouri, designed by Wolfram Skalicki and directed by Maurizio Arena.
Fine Arts
Dist - FI **Prod** - RMART 1989

L'Afrique En Francais 37 MIN
U-matic
Color (H C A) (FRENCH)
Uses three French speaking Africans to introduce their homelands, Cameroun, Mali and Senegal. Describes aspects of life in those countries. Requires intermediate to advanced language skill in French.
Foreign Language; History - World
Dist - UILL **Prod** - UILL 1984

L'Afrique Noire Francophone series
Aspets divers - la terre et le climat - Pt 1 23 MIN
Aspets divers - le travail et les problems socio - economiques - Pt 4 23 MIN
Aspets divers - les activites du village - Pt 2 23 MIN
Aspets divers - les produits et les resources naturelles - Pt 3 23 MIN
Dist - IFB

L'Afrique Noire Francophone
Geographie Politique, Pt 4 - Le Zaire 48 MIN
Geographie Politique, Pt 1 - L'Afrique De L'Ouest - Le Senegal 48 MIN
Geographie Politique, Pt 3 - Le Cameroun Et Les Aspets De La Vie Camerounaise 48 MIN
Geographie Politique, Pt 2 - L'Afrique De L'Ouest - La Cote D'Ivoire 48 MIN
Dist - IFB

Lagoon of Lost Ships 52 MIN
U-matic / VHS / 16mm
Undersea World of Jacques Cousteau Series
Color (I)
History - World; Science - Natural; Science - Physical
Dist - CF **Prod** - METROM 1970

The Laguardia Story 25 MIN
16mm
Color (I J H C)
Laguardia sustained himself, through three terms as a Republican mayor in a Democratic city, by making zany public appearances and radio talks and by ballyhooing his accomplishments.
Biography; Civics and Political Systems; History - United States
Dist - SF **Prod** - SF 1965

Laguna Beach 30 MIN
VHS
John Stobart's WorldScape series
Color (A G)
$19.95 purchase _ #STO - 06
Features the vibrant southern California artist's community of Laguna Beach. Follows artist John Stobart as he travels the globe, painting directly from life, and demonstrates the simplicity of the method that has made him the foremost living maritime artist. Demonstrates Stobart's classical maritime style in numerous evocative settings around the world. Part of a series on painting outdoors.
Fine Arts
Dist - ARTSAM **Prod** - WORLDS

Laguna Beach Festival of Arts 10 MIN
16mm / U-matic / VHS
Color (J)
Presents the Laguna Beach Festival Of Arts, where living models replicate famous works of art.
Fine Arts; Geography - United States
Dist - MCFI **Prod** - IFADV 1980

Lahaina divers, Maui, Hawaii - fish show off 30 MIN
VHS
Scuba World series
Color (G)
$24.90 purchase _ #0442
Visits Maui Island in Hawaii. Investigates ancient underwater volcanic craters and showy fish.
Geography - World; Physical Education and Recreation
Dist - SEVVID

Lahaul and Spiti 20 MIN
16mm
Color (I)
Documents the scenic grandeur and life of the colorful people of lahaul and Spiti, up in the Himalayas. Explains that the area remains snowbound and cut off from the rest of the world for six months, but that in spring, life is stirred into activity.
Geography - World; History - World
Dist - NEDINF **Prod** - INDIA

Laila 12 MIN
16mm / U-matic / VHS
Color (I)
LC 82-700596
Shows the lifestyle and work of Laila Paatinen, a handicapped person who is the only female carpenter in Nova Scotia.
Education; Psychology
Dist - PHENIX **Prod** - NFBC 1981

Lake and River Kayaking 14 MIN
16mm
Outdoor Education White Water Paddling Series
Color
LC 74-703600
Demonstrates the handling of paddle and kayak in smooth water and white water.
Physical Education and Recreation
Dist - SF **Prod** - MORLAT 1973

Lake Bonneville - History's High - Water Mark 19 MIN
VHS / U-matic
Natural Science Specials Series Module Green
Color (I)
Creates an evolutionary picture of Lake Bonneville, a prehistoric lake, including the explorers and geologists who have studied its shoreline and fossils.
Geography - United States; History - World; Science - Physical
Dist - AITECH **Prod** - COPFC 1973

A Lake Community 15 MIN
U-matic / VHS
Why Series
Color (P I)
Discusses the living things found in a lake.
Science - Natural
Dist - AITECH **Prod** - WDCNTV 1976

Lake Erie 22 MIN
16mm
Color
Shows Roland Martin bass fishing in Lake Erie. Depicts how a dying lake was scientifically rehabilitated to restore one of the world's most productive freshwater fishing areas.
Geography - United States; Physical Education and Recreation
Dist - KAROL **Prod** - BRNSWK

Lake Michigan and the Illinois River - the Midwest Riviera 55 MIN
VHS
On the waterways series
Color (G H)
$29.95 purchase _ #OW11
Travels with the crew of the Driftwood from the straits of Mackinac through Lake Michigan to the Illinois River. Narrated by Jason Robards. Part of a 13 - part series on the history, geography, culture and ecology of North American waterways.
Social Science
Dist - SVIP

The Lake Michigan Coho - DDT Story 13 MIN
16mm
Environmental Science Series
Color
LC 72-700193
Shows why coho salmon were introduced into Lake Michigan, and how they were commercially marketed. Traces the discovery of DDT in the fish, the research that was done as a result, and the outcome of that research.
Agriculture; Geography - United States; Science - Natural
Dist - CIASP **Prod** - CIASP 1971

Lake Odyssey 26 MIN
16mm
Color (G)
_ #106C 0178 495
Shows the harvesting and recycling of lake weeds for animal fodder and compost.
Agriculture; Science - Natural
Dist - CFLMDC **Prod** - NFBC 1978

Lake Powell - jewel of the Colorado 30 MIN
VHS
Color (G)
$24.95 purchase _ #BOR - 6
Describes the historical background of the building of Glen Canyon Dam, Arizona. Examines the scenery and the recreational opportunities created by Lake Powell. Shows Glen Canyon Dam in operation.
Geography - United States
Dist - INSTRU **Prod** - USBR

Lake Superior - Hiawatha's Gitche Gumee 55 MIN
VHS
On the waterways series
Color (G H)
$29.95 purchase _ #OW06
Travels with the crew of the Driftwood through the sometimes violent and dangerous waters of the largest freshwater lake in North America. Narrated by Jason Robards. Part of a 13 - part series on the history, geography, culture and ecology of North American waterways.
Social Science
Dist - SVIP

Lake Superior - the Region Till Now 22 MIN
U-matic / VHS / 16mm
Color (I)
LC 73-703396
Provides general information on the people, economy, industry and geography of the Lake Superior region. Shows the people, industries and natural beauty in the watersheds of Michigan, Wisconsin, Minnesota and Ontario.
Business and Economics; Geography - United States; Geography - World
Dist - MCFI **Prod** - UWISC 1972

Lake Woebegone Loyalty Days 90 MIN
CD / VHS / Cassette
Color (G)
$19.95, $13.95, $9.95 purchase _ #16000, #15066, #15065
Joins the Minnesota Orchestra with Garrison Keillor. Includes pondering the experience of being Lutheran in 'The Young Lutheran's Guide To the Orchestra,' a parody of Benajamin Britten's 'The Young Person's Guide To The Orchestra.'.
Fine Arts; Literature and Drama; Religion and Philosophy
Dist - WCAT **Prod** - WCAT

Lakes 9 MIN
U-matic / VHS / 16mm
Color (P I)
LC 75-706844
Characterizes, defines and describes the physical features of lakes, how they are created and destroyed and their uses.
Science - Natural; Science - Physical
Dist - IU **Prod** - IU 1969

Lakes - Aging and Pollution 15 MIN
U-matic / VHS / 16mm
Color (P I J)
LC 70-710806
Features underwater photography and other techniques to explain the aging process of lakes. Examines plants, fish and animal life found in lake habitats. Investigates changing water quality and succession of organisms in lakes as they change from youth to middle age to old age and death. Emphasizes man's impact in speeding the aging process.
Science - Natural
Dist - CORF **Prod** - CENTEF 1971

Lakes and Streams 23 MIN
16mm / U-matic / VHS
Wilderness Ecology Series
Color (H C)
$540 purchase - 16 mm, $250 purchase - video _ #5752C
Talks about the importance of lakes and streams to the existence of different types of plants and animals. Explains how different seasons present different survival problems. Produced by Riverside Pix.
Science - Natural
Dist - CORF

Lakes as Earth features 15 MIN
VHS
Color (J H)
$45.00 purchase _ #A1VH 9429
Introduces lakes. Explains playa, pond, graben, slough, sink - hole, tam, lagoon, plunge - pool basin and other terms dealing with lakes.
Geography - World; Science - Physical
Dist - CLRVUE **Prod** - CLRVUE

Lakes, Rivers and Other Water Sources 17 MIN
U-matic / VHS / 16mm
Natural Phenomena Series
Color (J H)
Discusses the fresh water system consisting of lakes, rivers and underground water supplies. Deals with the origins of the water, the action of rivers, the ways a lake dies and forces that create the underground water supply. Introduces the concept of the continental divide and reviews the idea of the water cycle.
Geography - United States; Geography - World; Science - Natural; Science - Physical; Social Science
Dist - JOU **Prod** - JOU 1982

Lakeside Habitat 15 MIN
U-matic / VHS / 16mm
Animals and Plants of North America Series
Color (J)
LC 80-701735
Shows how the birds living at the lakeside return in spring.
Science - Natural
Dist - LCOA **Prod** - KARVF 1980

Lakha - A Tibetan lama 45 MIN
VHS / BETA
Color; PAL (G)
PdS3 purchase
Profiles one of Tibet's spiritual leaders living in Copenhagen with his Danish wife and children. Includes a return visit to Batang, Tibet, and a moving reunion with his people after 40 years in exile.
Fine Arts; Religion and Philosophy
Dist - MERIDT

The Lakota - One Nation on the Plains 30 MIN
U-matic / VHS / 16mm
Great Plains Experience Series
Color (H C)
History - United States; Social Science
Dist - GPN **Prod** - UMA 1976

Lamar Dodd - a Great Georgian 29 MIN
16mm
Great Georgians Series
Color
LC 75-703105
Presents a biographical study of artist and art educator Lamar Dodd, showing the relationship between his life - philosophy and his art.
Biography; Fine Arts; History - United States
Dist - UGA **Prod** - GCCED 1974

The Lamaze method 45 MIN
VHS
Color (G)
$19.95 purchase; $19.95 purchase _ #S00594
Presents a comprehensive guide to the LaMaze method of natural childbirth. Hosted by Patty Duke Astin. Developed by the American Society for Psychoprophylaxis.
Health and Safety
Dist - PBS **Prod** - WNETTV
UILL

Lamb and Pork 29 MIN
Videoreel / VT2
Cookin' Cajun Series
Color
Features gourmet - humorist Justin Wilson showing ways to cook lamb and pork with various ingredients.
Geography - United States; Home Economics
Dist - PBS **Prod** - MAETEL

Lamb chops 50 MIN
VHS
Cookbook videos series
Color (G)
$19.95 purchase _ #ALW144
Shows how to prepare lamb chops in short, easy - to - learn segments. Lists each ingredient as it is added in subtitles and visually reinforces spoken instructions. Gives recipe background and nutritional facts. Part of the Cookbook Videos series.
Home Economics; Social Science
Dist - CADESF **Prod** - CADESF

Lamb chops 50 MIN
VHS
Cookbook videos series; Vol 23
Color (G)
$19.95 purchase
Illustrates the four basic lamb chop cuts and demonstrates international recipes. Includes an abstract of recipes. Part of a series.
Home Economics; Social Science
Dist - ALWHIT **Prod** - ALWHIT

Lamb Retail Cuts Identification 17 MIN
VHS
Retail Cut Identification (Set C) Series
(C)
$79.95 _ CV113
Includes a live lamb, skeleton and carcass illustrating the major bones and retail cuts. Explains 23 retail cuts and other cuts with accepted industry names relating to location, major muscles and bones, shapes, exposed faces, and size. Recommended cooking techniques are also included.
Agriculture; Home Economics
Dist - AAVIM **Prod** - AAVIM 1989

Lamb Retail Cuts Identification 40 MIN
VHS
Color (G)
$79.95 purchase _ #6 - 040 - 114P
Uses a lamb carcass to relate major bones, muscles and wholesale cuts to retail cut identification. Identifies and explains 16 lamb retail cuts. Gives accepted industry names, size, color, shape, anatomical location and recommended cooking methods for each cut.
Agriculture; Business and Economics; Social Science
Dist - VEP **Prod** - VEP

Lamb Slaughter Technique 25 MIN
U-matic / VHS / 16mm
Color (C A)
LC FIA66-1425
Close - up photography shows step - by - step the modern methods used in the killing, skinning, evisceration and inspection of lambs.
Agriculture
Dist - CORNRS **Prod** - NYSCAG 1966

Lambada 60 MIN
VHS
Kathy Blake dance studios - let's learn how to dance series
Color (G A)
$39.95 purchase
Features dance instructors Kathy Blake and Gene Russo, who instruct viewers on the basics of the Lambada.
Fine Arts
Dist - PBS **Prod** - WNETTV

Lambchop and the Professor 24 MIN
VHS / U-matic
Color (K P I J)
Features Shari Lewis and Lambchop on a visit to a physics professor. Shows Lambchop helping the professor with several classroom experiments.
Fine Arts; Science - Physical; Sociology
Dist - SUTHRB **Prod** - SUTHRB

Lambda man 10 MIN
16mm
Color (G)
$25.00 rental
Features a filmpoem in which the voice of the narrator is that of a gay male, questioning the subjective myths in which he finds himself.
Fine Arts; Sociology
Dist - CANCIN **Prod** - TARTAG 1980

Lambert and Company 15 MIN
16mm
B&W
Presents Dave Lambert, of Lambert, Hendricks and Ross, with his newly formed quintet auditioning for RCA in 1964, shortly before his death. By D A Pennebaker.
Fine Arts
Dist - PENNAS **Prod** - PENNAS

Lambert, the Sheepish Lion 8 MIN
U-matic / VHS / 16mm
Color (K P I)
LC 72-700134
Presents a story about a lion cub that the stork delivered by mistake to a flock of lambs.
Literature and Drama
Dist - CORF **Prod** - DISNEY 1971

Lambeth Walk, Nazi Style 4 MIN
16mm

B&W
Offers a satiric view of Hitler and his elite guard marching and dancing to the popular World War II song The Lambeth Walk.
Fine Arts; Sociology
Dist - REELIM **Prod** - UNKNWN 1944

Lamellar Keratoprosthesis 7 MIN
16mm
Color
LC FIA66-877
Shows a research operation for replacing part of the opaque cornea by means of an optical prosthesis constructed of plastic and gold mesh.
Health and Safety
Dist - ACY **Prod** - ACYDGD 1962

Lameness of both Fore and Hindlimb 53 MIN
VHS / BETA
Color
Deals with the wobbler syndrome, compressed spinal cord, cut flexor tendons and other causes of lameness in horses. Covers the fundamentals of wound therapy.
Health and Safety; Physical Education and Recreation
Dist - EQVDL **Prod** - EQVDL

Lameness of the Forelimb, Pt 1 30 MIN
VHS / BETA
Color
Illustrates cases of forelimb lameness, including septic arthritis, hygroma and fractures.
Health and Safety; Physical Education and Recreation
Dist - EQVDL **Prod** - EQVDL

Lameness of the Forelimb, Pt 2 36 MIN
BETA / VHS
Color
Centers on the treatment of lameness occurring below the fetlock joint on the forelimb.
Health and Safety; Physical Education and Recreation
Dist - EQVDL **Prod** - EQVDL

Lameness of the Forelimb, Pt 3 46 MIN
BETA / VHS
Color
Deals with forelimb lameness between the shoulders of a horse in conjunction with prognosis and treatment of carpus.
Health and Safety; Physical Education and Recreation
Dist - EQVDL **Prod** - EQVDL

Lameness of the Forelimb, Pt 4 42 MIN
VHS / BETA
Color
Shows treatment techniques for the areas on a horse below the carpus down through fractures of the sesamoid bone.
Health and Safety; Physical Education and Recreation
Dist - EQVDL **Prod** - EQVDL

Lameness of the Forelimb, Pt 5 40 MIN
VHS / BETA
Color
Covers conditions and treatment of the forelimb of a horse. Discusses pastern joint subluxation, hoof wall loss, laminitis and more.
Health and Safety; Physical Education and Recreation
Dist - EQVDL **Prod** - EQVDL

Lameness of the Hindlimb, Pt 1 35 MIN
VHS / BETA
Color
Discusses hindlimb lameness in a horse. Includes diagnosis of wobbler syndrome and Achilles tendons.
Health and Safety; Physical Education and Recreation
Dist - EQVDL **Prod** - EQVDL

Lameness of the Hindlimb, Pt 2 23 MIN
BETA / VHS
Color
Covers signs of lameness in a horse's hock and below. Discusses bone spavin, weak flexor tendons and more.
Health and Safety; Physical Education and Recreation
Dist - EQVDL **Prod** - EQVDL

Lameness of the Hindlimb, Pt 3 42 MIN
BETA / VHS
Color
Reviews the causes of hindlimb lameness in a horse. Describes the joints and ligaments.
Health and Safety; Physical Education and Recreation
Dist - EQVDL **Prod** - EQVDL

Lament of the Reservation 24 MIN
16mm / U-matic / VHS
North American Indian Series Part 3
Color (H C)
Presents an uncompromising record of life on an Indian reservation - a life plagued by poverty, unemployment, hunger and infant mortality.
Social Science
Dist - MGHT **Prod** - MGHT 1971

Lamentations - Pt 3 20 MIN
VHS / 16mm
Unorganized Manager Series
Color (A PRO)
$790.00 purchase, $220.00 rental
Models effective communication skills for managers interacting with their staff. Shows how to set priorities and communicate them. Management training. Part of a series, 'The Unorganized Manager.'.
Guidance and Counseling; Psychology
Dist - VIDART **Prod** - VIDART 1990

L'Amico Fried's glamorous friends 12 MIN
16mm
Color (G)
$30.00 rental
Presents a pas de deux by Ondine and Sally Dixon. Features a traditional dramatic narrative and a formal approach.
Fine Arts
Dist - CANCIN **Prod** - JACBYR 1976

L'Amour a la quebecoise 30 MIN
VHS
Paroles d'echanges 2 series
Color (J H) (FRENCH AND ENGLISH FRENCH)
#389003; LC 91-707696
Reveals that the relationship of exhange students Mike and Emily takes an amorous turn, and their francophone friends complicate matters when the difficulties of communication become evident. Part of a series designed to build the confidence of new language learners.
Foreign Language; Geography - World; Sociology
Dist - TVOTAR **Prod** - TVOTAR 1990

L'Amour Fou 252 MIN
16mm
B&W (FRENCH)
A French language film. Portrays a young Paris theater director and his actress wife. Follows the couple's personal ups and downs and underscores the conflict between the theater and life.
Fine Arts; Foreign Language
Dist - NYFLMS **Prod** - NYFLMS 1968

L'Amour Live Series
Survival - from My Yondering Days 60 MIN
Dist - BANTAP

L'Amour Series
South of Deadwood - by Louis L'Amour 60 MIN
A Trail to the West - by Louis L'Amour 60 MIN
Where Buzzards Fly 60 MIN
Dist - BANTAP

Lamp at Midnight 76 MIN
VHS / U-matic
Color
Deals with three critical moments in the life of Galileo Galilei, the great astronomer whose physical observations of the universe by means of a telescope conflicted with the teachings of his church. Stars Melvyn Douglas and David Wayne.
Fine Arts; Literature and Drama
Dist - FOTH **Prod** - FOTH 1984

Lamps 15 MIN
Videoreel / VT2
Living Better II Series
Color
Shows how to make a lamp from a half - gallon bottle and a shade from heavy paper. Explains basic information for replacing cords, plugs and sockets.
Fine Arts; Home Economics
Dist - PBS **Prod** - MAETEL

Lamps and Electrical Outlets - Lamps and Chandeliers, Adding Electrical Outlets 30 MIN
BETA / VHS
Wally's Workshop Series
Color
Home Economics; Industrial and Technical Education
Dist - KARTES **Prod** - KARTES

Lampshade Crafting 45 MIN
VHS / BETA
Color
Explains techniques for the creation of lampshades and gives tips on placement within the home.
Fine Arts
Dist - HOMEAF **Prod** - HOMEAF

Lampshades 10 MIN
U-matic
Get it together series
Color (P I)
Teaches children two ways to make a lampshade.
Fine Arts
Dist - TVOTAR **Prod** - TVOTAR 1978

Lana Chimpanzee counts by 'numath' 15 MIN
VHS
Color (C G PRO)
$75.00 purchase, $13.00 rental _ #24178
Summarizes a software program developed to determine whether Lana, a chimpanzee, could learn to count through the use of a computer - monitored, video - formatted system. Shows Lana using a joystick - controlled cursor to touch a target number of boxes in order to obtain a reward. Illustrates her performance in various phases of the training program. Produced by Dr Duane Rumbaugh.
Psychology
Dist - PSU

Lana's story 26 MIN
VHS / U-matic
Color (PRO C)
$395.00 purchase, $80.00 rental _ #C860 - VI - 040
Documents the last six months in the life of Lana Beach, who died at age 43. Explores the impact of the dying process on the terminally ill patient and underscores hospice care. Includes comments by Beach, her husband, daughters and the physician. Interviews two other terminally ill patients.
Sociology
Dist - HSCIC

Lance 4 MIN
16mm
Color (P I J H C)
LC 72-700566
Presents a story about a young boy's fantasy involving an imaginary tiger and lion. Uses a technique in which the screen is split into three vertically parallel rectangles, with each section containing a different scene that unites with the others to form a full image.
Fine Arts
Dist - CFS **Prod** - PFIELO 1971

Lancelot of the Lake 83 MIN
16mm
Color (FRENCH)
Features the Knights of the Round Table returning from an unsuccessful quest for the Holy Grail. Shows how they have also failed individually in their personal vows of purity. as exemplified by Lancelot.
Fine Arts; Foreign Language
Dist - NYFLMS **Prod** - NYFLMS 1974

Lancez 10 MIN
U-matic / VHS
Salut - French Language Lessons Series
Color
Focuses on sports and command forms.
Foreign Language
Dist - BCNFL **Prod** - BCNFL 1984

The Land 30 MIN
16mm / U-matic / VHS
Great Plains Experience Series
Color (H C)
History - United States; Social Science
Dist - GPN **Prod** - UMA 1976

The Land 44 MIN
16mm
B&W
LC 75-700789
Portrays American agriculture during the Depression decade.
Agriculture; Business and Economics; History - United States
Dist - USNAC **Prod** - USAGA 1941

Land Above the Trees 20 MIN
16mm / U-matic / VHS
Color (J)
$415.00, $210.00 purchase, $40.00 rental
Explores the ecology of Alpine zones which exist between the treeline and summits of the major mountain chains in North America. Reveals that they are characterized by high snowfalls, extreme cold, and short, arid growing seasons.
Geography - World; Science - Natural; Science - Physical
Dist - BULFRG **Prod** - NFBC 1989

The Land Along the Water 10 MIN
U-matic / VHS / 16mm
Color; B&W (I J)
LC 76-702698
Characterizes the land that lies along oceans and large lakes in terms of its physical features and uses. Explains that differences in the physical appearance of land near shorelines may be caused by natural forces or by man building inland waterways and constructing recreational facilities.
Science - Natural; Science - Physical
Dist - IU **Prod** - NET 1969

Land and the People 57 MIN
16mm / U-matic / VHS
Age of Uncertainty Series
Color (H C A)
LC 77-701488
Focuses on the role of land in determining wealth and poverty and its effect on social and foreign policies. Based on the book The Age Of Uncertainty by John Kenneth Galbraith.
Business and Economics; Sociology
Dist - FI **Prod** - BBCL 1977

Land and the People, Pt 1 28 MIN
16mm / U-matic / VHS
Age of Uncertainty Series
Color (H C A)

LC 77-701488
Focuses on the role of land in determining wealth and poverty and its effect on social and foreign policies. Based on the book The Age Of Uncertainty by John Kenneth Galbraith.
Social Science; Sociology
Dist - FI **Prod** - BBCL 1977

Land and the People, Pt 2 29 MIN
U-matic / VHS / 16mm
Age of Uncertainty Series
Color (H C A)
LC 77-701488
Focuses on the role of land in determining wealth and poverty and its effect on social and foreign policies. Based on the book The Age Of Uncertainty by John Kenneth Galbraith.
Social Science; Sociology
Dist - FI **Prod** - BBCL 1977

Land and the People Series
The Desert 30 MIN
Mountains 30 MIN
The Plains 30 MIN
Dist - MDCPB

Land and the Pursuit of Happiness 32 MIN
16mm
Color
Discusses the use of land on a global scale, moving from an era of abundance to scarity. Focuses on the devastated forest land of the Olympic Peninsula in Washington State, the Rio Grande Valley, New Mexico, where water resources are scarce and the Waiahole - Waikane Valley in Hawaii, whose farmers fight against housing developments. Explains the reason for the downfall of the Anasazi Indians in Chaco Canyon, New Mexico.
Agriculture; Geography - United States; Geography - World
Dist - UCLA **Prod** - UCLA 1975

Land and Water 30 MIN
U-matic
Polka Dot Door Series
Color (K)
Presents a variety show for pre - school children. Includes songs, mime, stories, film sequences, talk, dance and fantasy figures. Each show emphasizes a particular theme such as numbers, feelings, exploring, music or time. Comes with parent teacher guide.
Fine Arts; Literature and Drama
Dist - TVOTAR **Prod** - TVOTAR 1985

Land and Water 25 MIN
16mm
Color (H C)
Shows the differences between peasant and plantation agriculture in a Mexican valley. Examines human ecology in relation to crops grown under conditions of drought, erosion and winter frost.
Agriculture; Geography - World; Science - Natural; Sociology
Dist - PSUPCR **Prod** - PSUPCR 1961

Land and Water in Iraq 14 MIN
16mm
Social Studies Program Series
Color (I J H)
LC FIA65-356
Provides a fragmentary view of some of the aspects of ecology of modern Iraq, dealing in particular with Mesopotamia and emphasizing those aspects of life between the Tigris and Euphrates that have probably remained unchanged since the time of the Sumerians. Dr Robert Adams explains with the aid of maps and diagrams the annual cycle of flooding and drought on the alluvial plains.
Geography - World; History - World
Dist - EDC **Prod** - EDS 1964

Land Beneath the Sea 24 MIN
16mm
Color
LC 70-702830
Demonstrates how marine geologists research the ocean bottom and learn about the ocean environment. Discusses the significance of marine geology and explains why a thorough knowledge of the ocean floor is essential in the use of the oceans for defense and economic purposes.
Science - Natural; Science - Physical
Dist - USNAC **Prod** - USNO 1968

Land Beneath the Sea 58 MIN
16mm
Color
LC 76-702833
Follows three dives by French and American deep - sea submersibles over the Rift Valley in the mid - Atlantic and uses the dives as a narrative device to explain plate tectonics theory.
Science; Science - Physical
Dist - MAETEL **Prod** - MAETEL 1976

Land Beneath the Sea, Pt 1 29 MIN
16mm
Color
LC 76-702833
Follows three dives by French and American deep - sea submersibles over the Rift Valley in the mid - Atlantic and uses the dives as a narrative device to explain plate tectonics theory.
Science - Physical
Dist - MAETEL **Prod** - MAETEL 1976

Land Beneath the Sea, Pt 2 29 MIN
16mm
Color
LC 76-702833
Follows three dives by French and American deep - sea submersibles over the Rift Valley in the mid - Atlantic and uses the dives as a narrative device to explain plate tectonics theory.
Science - Physical
Dist - MAETEL **Prod** - MAETEL 1976

The Land Burns 12 MIN
U-matic / VHS / 16mm
B&W (P I)
Discusses the northeastern 'DROUGHT REGION' in Brazil. Presents the story of Juan Amaro, a man who six years ago founded and settled on an abandoned ranch, with his wife and 11 children. Explains that today only four children survive, as a result of the sufferings in the droughts. Concludes with the realization that the family can no longer survive on the dried out ranch, so they decide to leave and go to the big city, where they hope things will be better.
Geography - World; Social Science; Sociology
Dist - CNEMAG **Prod** - PIC

Land Dayaks of Borneo 38 MIN
16mm
Color (C T)
LC FIA65-1667
Depicts life in Mentu Tapuh village, a border region between Indonesia and Malaysia. Pictures activities of Borneo's 50,000 land dayaks, including harvesting, dancing and canoe - making. Shows religious ceremonies, the harvest festival and games.
Geography - World; Social Science; Sociology
Dist - NYU **Prod** - GEDDES 1965

Land Des Schweigens Und Der Dunkelheit 87 MIN
16mm
Color (GERMAN (ENGLISH SUBTITLES))
A German language film with English subtitles. Documents society's lack of concern for the handicapped.
Foreign Language; Psychology; Sociology
Dist - WSTGLC **Prod** - WSTGLC 1971

Land Divers of Melanesia 30 MIN
U-matic / VHS / 16mm
Color (H C A)
LC 73-702697
Documents the salient features of the intact culture of Melanesia, including agriculture, play and ritual of bunlap on the Pentecost Island in the New Hebrides. Shows the relation between yam agriculture and ceremonies such as land - diving.
Agriculture; Geography - World; Sociology
Dist - PHENIX **Prod** - HUFSC

A Land Divided - India and Pakistan at War 15 MIN
16mm
Screen news digest series; Vol 14; Issue 5
B&W (J H)
LC 72-702748
Examines in depth the hatreds that triggered war between India and Pakistan and led to the creation of the Bangladesh Republic.
Geography - World; History - World
Dist - HEARST **Prod** - HEARST 1972

Land Drainage 25 MIN
16mm / U-matic / VHS
Color (J)
LC 81-700592
Explains that system drainage may be the solution to late planting and reduced crop yields. Discusses machines for laying plastic tile, the importance of adequate outlet systems, the treatment of fine - textured soils, and land smoothing.
Agriculture
Dist - CORNRS **Prod** - CUETV 1978

Land for Life 25 MIN
16mm
Color
LC 76-703065
Discusses the problem of population growth in the Lower Mainland of British Columbia in Canada. Explains what has been done to accommodate this growth without destroying the quality of life.
Geography - World; Science - Natural; Social Science; Sociology
Dist - BCDA **Prod** - BCDA 1974

Land for People, Land for Bears 15 MIN
16mm
Environmental Series - Landsat - Satellite for all Seasons Series
Color (J H A)
Looks at how the LANDSAT satellite supplies a new kind of data for land use mapping and wildlife habitat mapping, showing how the satellite's multispectral scanning instruments record the spectral signatures or reflectance values of the components of the Earth's surface.
Geography - World; Science - Natural; Science - Physical
Dist - USNAC **Prod** - NASA 1976

Land for Rose 83 MIN
VHS / 16mm
Color (G)
$350.00 purchase, $100.00 rental
Examines the popular movement in Brazil for land reform at an historic moment in the country's transition from dictatorship to democracy. Focuses on the comments and experiences of several women, including Rose, a young mother who gave birth to the first child born at a camp for landless peasants.
Agriculture; Geography - World; History - World; Sociology
Dist - CNEMAG **Prod** - CNEMAG 1987

Land from the North Sea 17 MIN
16mm / U-matic / VHS
Man and His World Series
Color (P I J H C)
LC 71-705479
Shows how man re - shapes his environment by use of sedimentation, dike construction and use of plant life. Teaches how man reclaims land from the sea.
Agriculture; Geography - World; Science - Natural
Dist - FI **Prod** - IFFB 1969

The Land is a Woman 28 MIN
16mm
Color
Looks at the activities inherent in grape - growing and wine making in Virginia plus the romance they inspire in a vintner and his wife.
Agriculture; Geography - United States
Dist - SCHDRC **Prod** - SCHDRC 1981

Land is Life 29 MIN
VHS / U-matic
Forest Spirits Series
Color (G)
Documents the history of the Oneidas' troubles over land. It begins with their trip from New York to Wisconsin and explores the allotment and subsequent loss of most of their land in Wisconsin. Now, little land for building remains on the reservation. Oneida who wish to return, cannot. The Oneida are trying to recover their lost land and improve the land they have.
Social Science; Sociology
Dist - NAMPBC **Prod** - NAMPBC 1975

Land is Life 30 MIN
VHS / U-matic
Forest Spirits Series
Color
Deals with the history of the land problems of the Oneida Indians of Wisconsin. Shows how the Oneidas are trying to recover land they lost and improve land which they control.
Geography - United States; History - United States; Social Science
Dist - GPN **Prod** - NEWIST

The Land is Rich 40 MIN
16mm
B&W
Traces the development of the Delano grape strike and documents the efforts of the workers to organize.
Agriculture; Business and Economics; Geography - United States
Dist - CANWRL **Prod** - RICHA 1967

Land, Labor and Capital 10 MIN
U-matic / VHS / 16mm
Economics for Elementary Series
Color (P I)
LC 72-703120
Introduces the student to the farmer to discover the importance of land, the mill foreman who emphasizes capital and a designer at a clothing factory who points out the merits of labor.
Business and Economics
Dist - AIMS **Prod** - EVANSA 1971

A Land Like no Other - Alaska 22 MIN
16mm
Color
LC 76-702834
Depicts the diversity of Alaska and the reactions of its visitiors. Includes views of 30 different localities.
Geography - United States; Geography - World
Dist - WESTRS **Prod** - WESTRS 1975

The Land Lives on 20 MIN
16mm
Color

LC 78-700391
Describes soil stewardship as the sense of responsibility for preserving the resources of air, land and water. Illustrates how soil stewards work effectively on farms, in urban areas and in industry.
Agriculture; Science - Natural
Dist - FINLYS **Prod** - NACD 1978

Land, location and culture - a geographical synthesis series
Attention - water at work - 5 60 MIN
Babylon to Bombay - the city through time 60 MIN
Capes, bays and the new geography - 1 60 MIN
The Changing face of the planet - human impact - 6 60 MIN
Conserve or consume - human use of resources - 8 60 MIN
The Internal city - 11 60 MIN
Our culture, our selves - 9 60 MIN
The Restless atmosphere - 4 60 MIN
Spatial interaction and location - 12 60 MIN
This Hazardous planet - 7 60 MIN
Too many people, too little space 60 MIN
Understanding the physical Earth - 3 60 MIN
Dist - INSTRU

Land - locked ark 30 MIN
VHS
Perspectives - natural science - series
Color; PAL; NTSC (G)
PdS90, PdS105 purchase
Looks at the technological spinoffs resulting from the study of the lifestyles, habits and breeding cycles of animals at the London Zoo.
Business and Economics; Science - Natural
Dist - CFLVIS **Prod** - LONTVS

Land of 10,000 Dumps 40 MIN
U-matic / VHS
Color
Takes a worrisome look at waste disposal in Minnesota.
Geography - United States; Science - Natural
Dist - WCCOTV **Prod** - WCCOTV 1981

The Land of Buddha 17 MIN
16mm
Color (I)
LC FIA65-1859
Uses 200 - year - old sculptures of the Ghuandara civilization, which are now lying in the northwestern part of Pakistan, to tell the story of the Gautama Buddha.
Fine Arts; Religion and Philosophy
Dist - FILMAS **Prod** - FILMAS 1965

The Land of cotton
16mm
March of time series
B&W (G)
$20.00 rental
Contains re - enactments. Presents part of a series formed by the founders of Time Magazine. Under 20 minutes in length.
Fine Arts; Literature and Drama
Dist - KITPAR **Prod** - MOT 1936

Land of Enlightenment 11 MIN
16mm
B&W (I)
Presents the route of a Chinese pilgrim through Bihar, 'THE LAND OF ENLIGHTENMENT.' Features all the places venerated by Buddhists.
Geography - World; Religion and Philosophy
Dist - NEDINF **Prod** - INDIA

Land of Fear, Land of Courage 60 MIN
VHS / U-matic
Color
$300 rental
Discusses the basic human rights of voting, owning property, deciding where and how to work, and protesting, which are denied to 83% of the people of South Africa. Includes a discussion with Anglican Bishop Desmond Tutu. Narrated by Edwin Newman.
History - World; Sociology
Dist - CCNCC **Prod** - CCNCC 1985

Land of Frost and Fire 15 MIN
U-matic / VHS
Other families, other friends series; Brown module; Iceland
Color (P)
Pictures the Icelandic countryside.
Geography - United States; Geography - World; Social Science
Dist - AITECH **Prod** - WVIZTV 1971

Land of Gold 13 MIN
16mm
Color
LC 79-701372
Chronicles the process of wheat farming and, through images of relics from years past, explores the relationship of humans to the land.
Agriculture; Sociology
Dist - ESSIA **Prod** - MARTSS 1979

The Land of Heart's Desire 29 MIN
16mm
Within America Series
Color (J)
Documents a time of decision in the lives of an Irish - American couple who after living 35 years in New York City consider retiring to the west coast of Ireland. Shows the couple torn between the power of their memories and the practical realities of the present.
Sociology
Dist - CEPRO **Prod** - CULLEN

Land of immigrants 16 MIN
16mm / VHS
Color (I J)
$310.00, $230.00 purchase, $60.00 rental
Discloses that people of different origins have immigrated at different periods for different reasons, that the United States has been molded by many cultures. Discusses the importance of tolerance in American growth.
History - United States; Psychology
Dist - CF

Land of immigrants; Rev. 16 MIN
U-matic / VHS / 16mm
Color (I J)
$49.95 purchase _ #P10089; LC 81-700985
Investigates the history United States immigration, focusing on how people of different origins have immigrated at different periods for different reasons. Considers the role of tolerance and how American culture has been molded by the many cultures of immigrants.
History - United States; Sociology
Dist - CF **Prod** - CF 1981

The Land of Israel 30 MIN
VHS
Shalom Sesame series
Color (K P)
$19.95 purchase _ #240
Stars Sesame Street Muppets and Mary Tyler Moore in an overview of Israel. Part of an eight - part series.
Geography - World; Sociology
Dist - ERGOM **Prod** - ERGOM

Land of Liberty, Pt 1 22 MIN
16mm
B&W (I J H C)
Early colonial history and the development of the republic to 1805. A pictorial history of the United States originally prepared for exhibition at the New York World's Fair.
History - United States
Dist - IU **Prod** - MPAA 1943

Land of Liberty, Pt 2 22 MIN
16mm
B&W (I J H C)
A pictorial history of the United States from 1805 to 1860.
History - United States
Dist - IU **Prod** - MPAA 1943

Land of Liberty, Pt 3 22 MIN
16mm
B&W (I J H C)
A pictorial history of the United States from 1860 to 1890.
History - United States
Dist - IU **Prod** - MPAA 1943

Land of Liberty, Pt 4 22 MIN
16mm
B&W (I J H C)
A pictorial history of the United States from 1890 to 1938.
History - United States
Dist - IU **Prod** - MPAA 1943

Land of Liberty, Pt 5 22 MIN
16mm
B&W (I J H C)
Depicts the developments in the U S during the years 1939 - 1958. Includes the significant events of World War II, of the Atomic Age and of the Cold War. Discusses domestic problems and describes the progress in scientific research, education and welfare.
History - United States
Dist - IU **Prod** - MPAA 1959

Land of look behind 88 MIN
VHS / 35mm / 16mm
Color (G)
$200.00, $250.00 rental
Presents a documentary on the funeral of reggae artist Bob Marley which becomes a dreamlike look at Jamaican culture. Directed by Alan Greenberg.
Fine Arts
Dist - KINOIC

Land of Lost Borders - the Chihuahuan Desert, Pt 1 27 MIN
16mm
Color
LC 82-700297
Studies the characteristics of the Chihuahuan Desert, with particular emphasis on the plants, animals and biomes.
Geography - United States; Geography - World; Science - Natural
Dist - ADAMSF **Prod** - GRDNH 1982

Land of milk and honey 19 MIN
VHS / U-matic / 16mm
Color (I J H)
$260.00, $310.00, $420.00 purchase, $45.00 rental
Looks at the lives of four contemporary diary farmers and their families. Presents a complex and varied lifestyle in the farmers' own words. Produced by the Pennsylvania Dairy Board.
Agriculture; Social Science
Dist - NDIM

Land of Muck and Money 25 MIN
16mm / VHS / BETA
Color
LC 77-702515
Presents correspondent Michael Maclear's examination of the phenomenon of mainstreeting in Canada. Notes that crime, fighting, alcoholism and related social problems can be seen on the streets of any urban center.
Geography - World; Social Science; Sociology
Dist - CTV **Prod** - CTV 1976

Land of Mystery 13 MIN
16mm
Travelbug Series
Color
An exciting jaunt through Yellowstone National Park, showing different views of canyon and falls.
Geography - United States
Dist - SFI **Prod** - SFI

Land of opportunity series
American rodeo 10 MIN
Sponge Divers 10 MIN
Dist - REP

Land of Our Fathers 60 MIN
VHS / U-matic
James Galway's Music in Time Series
Color (J)
Presents flutist James Galway discussing the renewed interest in the folk song and attempts to express in music the sense of homeland. Includes the song Londonderry Air and Dvorak's New World Symphony and Quartet in E - Flat.
Fine Arts
Dist - FOTH **Prod** - POLTEL 1982

Land of Our Fathers 30 MIN
16mm
B&W
States that the reasons for the biblical names of American towns and cities can be found in the Biblical roots of American civilization. (Kinescope).
Religion and Philosophy
Dist - NAAJS **Prod** - JTS 1954

Land of promise 57 MIN
VHS
B&W (G)
$39.95 purchase _ #206
Records the Yishuv - Jewish community of Palestine - in 1935. Features the halutzim - pioneers - recent refugees from Europe and the commerce, agriculture and industry of the period. Contrasts Palestinian cities, including 'old' and 'new' Jerusalem with kibbutzim, the new agricultural settlements. Includes original songs by Natan Alterman and commentary by Maurice Samuel.
History - World
Dist - ERGOM **Prod** - ERGOM 1993

The Land of promise - Ziemia obiecana 176 MIN
VHS
Color (G A) (POLISH WITH ENGLISH SUBTITLES)
$79.95 purchase _ #V273
Portrays three industrialists representing different ethnic groups in Poland - a Pole, a German and a Jew - who build a textile factory in Lodz at the turn of the century. Shows that they encounter problems with the overworked, underpaid workers. Based on a novel by Nobel Prize - winner Wladyslaw Reymont, depicting a society on the edge of change. Directed by Andrzej Wajda.
Fine Arts; History - World; Sociology
Dist - POLART

Land of Silence and Darkness 108 MIN
16mm
Color ((ENGLISH SUBTITLES))
Focuses on a woman who became blind and deaf in her youth, went into depression for 20 years, and emerged to become a tireless organizer of assistance to others in her situation. Directed by Werner Herzog. In English and German with English subtitles.
Biography; Fine Arts; Foreign Language; Guidance and Counseling
Dist - NYFLMS **Prod** - UNKNWN 1971

Land of Smiles 25 MIN
16mm
Eye of the Beholder Series
Color
LC 75-701891
Shows the beauty of Thailand, including her people and her temples.
Geography - World; Sociology
Dist - VIACOM **Prod** - RCPDF 1972

The land of sweet taps 57 MIN
VHS
Color (K P)
$19.95 purchase_#1387
Presents a beginner's tap class full of sweets and fun. Features an easy and enjoyable way for children to learn the fundamentals of tap dancing, including sounds, rhythms and steps. Especially appropriate for children ages 4 through 7.
Physical Education and Recreation
Dist - KULTUR

Land of the Bible Series
Dead Sea Scrolls 14 MIN
Exploring Ancient Cities 14 MIN
Jerusalem, the Sacred City 14 MIN
Life and Customs 14 MIN
A Pictorial Geography 14 MIN
Where Jesus Lived 15 MIN
Dist - FAMF

Land of the Big Ice 55 MIN
16mm
To the Wild Country Series
Color
LC 75-703400
Looks at the more than 8,000 square miles of Baffin Island's Cumberland Peninsula that have been set aside as the world's first arctic national park.
Geography - World; Science - Natural
Dist - KEGPL **Prod** - CANBC 1974

Land of the Bighorn 12 MIN
16mm
Color (A)
LC 77-703126
Discusses the attitudes of the Crow Indians towards land which is emerging as a recreational area behind the dam on the Bighorn River. Includes glimpses of water sports.
Physical Education and Recreation; Social Science
Dist - USNAC **Prod** - USNPS 1973

Land of the Book 28 MIN
16mm
Color (H C)
LC 78-701199
Brings alive the life and times of thousands of years ago in ancient Israel. Depicts the beauty of the land which gave birth to three great religions, the sites where heroic deeds took place and the towering splendor of the ancient works.
History - World; Literature and Drama
Dist - AVED **Prod** - GARNER 1967

The Land of the Book 30 MIN
16mm
B&W
Ralph Bellamy shows how the Bible can be viewed as a guide book to Israel - - it presents the past, present and future. Biblical sites shown include Solomon's mines, the plains of Armageddon, the River Jordan, Mt Tabor, Mt Zion, Galilee, Jerusalem, Carmel, Caesarea, Beersheba, the Negey and Acre. A companion film to 'THE PEOPLE OF THE BOOK.' (Kinescope).
Geography - World; Religion and Philosophy
Dist - NAAJS **Prod** - JTS 1959

Land of the Brahmaputra 12 MIN
16mm
B&W (I)
Follows the River Brahmaputra and its vagaries, which flow through Assam alternately ravaging and helping Assam to reap rich harvests. Includes view of the land and the people.
Geography - World; History - World
Dist - NEDINF **Prod** - INDIA

Land of the demons 60 MIN
VHS
Color (G)
$24.98 purchase _ #MH6380V-S
Examines the dangers and global implications of the war in the former Yugoslavia. Explores reasons for the hatred between the Serbians and the Muslims. Narrated by Peter Jennings.
Fine Arts; Religion and Philosophy; Sociology
Dist - CAMV

Land of the Dragon Series
Man of the Forest 25 MIN
Man of the People 25 MIN
Mountain of the Goddess 25 MIN
The Tiger's nest 25 MIN
Dist - LANDMK

Land of the drowned river 26 MIN
16mm
Audubon wildlife theatre series
Color (P A)
LC 76-710202
An ecological survey of the Del Mar Via Peninsula.
Science - Natural
Dist - AVEXP **Prod** - KEGPL 1968

Land of the elephants 70 MIN
VHS
Animals of Africa series
Color (I J H)
$25.00 purchase _ #A5VH 1500
Observes the African elephant battling, bathing and playing with its cohabitants in the jungle. Part of a nine - part series on African animals hosted by Joan Embery of the San Diego Zoo.
Geography - World; Science - Natural
Dist - CLRVUE

Land of the Friendly Animals 11 MIN
16mm / U-matic / VHS
Color (I J P)
$49.00 purchase _ #3100; LC 72-701973
Features the animals, people and the islands of the Galapagos. Emphasizes the many interesting animals including the giant tortoises, blue footed boobies, iguanas, great blue herons, sea lions, pelicans and flamingoes.
Science - Natural
Dist - EBEC **Prod** - EBEC 1972

Land of the Kapriska Purara 15 MIN
U-matic / VHS
Other families, other friends series; Brown module; Nicaragua
Color (P)
Pictures a park, a market and the Presidential Palace in Managua, Nicaragua.
Geography - World; Social Science; Sociology
Dist - AITECH **Prod** - WVIZTV 1971

The Land of the Lightening Brothers 26 MIN
VHS
Color (C)
$129.00 purchase _ #188 - 9022
Records a find of magnificent rock art depicting the Lightening Brothers, which the Wardman people see as part of their culture. Incorporates the traditional songs, ceremonies and stories associated with places where the art is located. The Lightening Brothers are legendary ancient beings who helped shape the traditional land of the northern aboriginal people of Australia.
Fine Arts; Geography - World; History - World; Religion and Philosophy; Sociology
Dist - FI **Prod** - FLMAUS 1987

Land of the Long Day 34 MIN
16mm
B&W (G)
#4X5N
Tells of a family of the Tununermuit tribe of Pond Inlet who must constantly search for food in the harsh climate of Canada's north. Shows how they move with the seasons and how they love the land and sea.
Social Science
Dist - CDIAND **Prod** - NFBC 1952

Land of the Long Day, Pt 1, Winter and Spring 19 MIN
U-matic / VHS / 16mm
Color (P I)
An Eskimo hunter tells of life in the North and describes the nature of the land.
Geography - World; Social Science
Dist - IFB **Prod** - NFBC 1952

Land of the Long Day, Pt 2, Summer and Autumn 19 MIN
U-matic / VHS / 16mm
Color (P I)
Describes a whale hunt and other techniques of living in the Arctic, especially in preparation of winter.
Geography - World; Social Science
Dist - IFB **Prod** - NFBC 1952

Land of the Loon 26 MIN
16mm
Color
LC 76-702023
Shows the wilderness of a Canadian wildlife sanctuary, Algonquin Park, its lakes and trails.
Geography - World; Science - Natural
Dist - KEGPL **Prod** - GIB 1975

Land of the loon 26 MIN
16mm
Audubon wildlife theatre series
Color (P A)
LC 70-710203
Examines the mood of a wilderness park through close - ups of many birds and animals in Algonquin Park in Ontario.
Science - Natural
Dist - AVEXP **Prod** - KEGPL 1969

The Land of the Peacock Throne 14 MIN
16mm
Screen news digest series; Vol 23; Issue 7
Color (I J H)
Describes 40 years of crises and unrest in Iran. Includes information on the rise of the Ayatollah Khomeini and the taking of American hostages.
Geography - World; History - World
Dist - HEARST **Prod** - HEARST 1981

Land of the Pharoahs 105 MIN
U-matic / VHS / 16mm
Color
Stars Jack Hawkins as an Egyptian Pharoah who orders a huge tomb for his burial and runs into problems with a conniving queen.
Fine Arts
Dist - FI **Prod** - WB 1955

Land of the Pineapple 15 MIN
U-matic / VHS
Other families, other friends series
Color (P)
Pictures a pineapple field, a sugar cane field and the Polynesian Cultural Village in Hawaii.
Geography - United States; Social Science
Dist - AITECH **Prod** - WVIZTV 1971

Land of the sea 26 MIN
16mm
Audubon wildlife theatre series
Color (P)
LC 70-709405
Explores the Canadian province of Nova Scotia and studies the famous tides of the Minas Basin with time - lapse photography. Describes the various underwater life and the Bay of Fundy tides.
Geography - World; Science - Natural
Dist - AVEXP **Prod** - KEGPL 1969

The Land of the Sleeping Mountains 60 MIN
U-matic / VHS / 16mm
Making of a Continent Series
Color (H C A)
Visits the Great Basin between the Wasatch Mountains of Utah and the Sierra Nevada of Nevada. Reveals that this was formed when the floor of the Pacific Ocean slid under the continent, pushing up the Sierra Nevada and cutting off moisture from the west.
Science - Physical
Dist - FI **Prod** - BBCTV 1983

Land of the tiger 60 MIN
U-matic / VHS
National Geographic video series
Color (J H A G)
$29.95 purchase
Presents an intimate portrait of the tiger, filmed in two national reserves in India throughout the seasons. Shows the predator stalking, capturing and devouring its prey, mating, caring for its cubs and marking territorial boundaries.
Geography - World; Science - Natural
Dist - PBS **Prod** - WNETTV
UILL

Land of the Tiger 25 MIN
16mm
Color (H C A)
Follows Fred Bear as he travels to India in search of Sher Kan, the great Bengal tiger. Portrays his experiences in the magnificent palace of his highness the Maharaja of Bundi and on the surrounding game trails. Shows him hunting the sambur, nilgai and axis deer.
Geography - World; Physical Education and Recreation
Dist - GFS **Prod** - GFS
HOMEAF

Land of the White Eagle - Part 1 - W Krainie orla bialego - Cz 1 95 MIN
VHS
Color (G A) (POLISH)
$24.95 purchase _ #V134, #V135
Offers a series of 10 - minute films highlighting Poland's history and traditions, her cultural heritage, architecture and landscape. Visits Gniezno, Zelazowa Wola, Poznan, Pszczyna, the Pieniny and Beskidy Mountains and the Eagle Nest trail between Cracow and Czestochowa. Also available with Polish narration. Part 1 of a 3 part series.
Geography - World
Dist - POLART

Land of the White Eagle - Part 3 - W Krainie orla bialego - Cz 3 90 MIN
VHS
Color (G A) (POLISH)
$24.95 purchase _ #V237, #V136
Offers a series of 10 - minute films highlighting Poland's history and traditions, her cultural heritage, architecture and landscape. Visits Czestochowa, Zamosc, Kalwaria, Zebrzydowska, Gdansk and Gdynia. Also available with Polish narration. Part 3 of a 3 part series.
Geography - World
Dist - POLART

Land of the White Eagle - Part 2 - W Krainie orla bialego - Cz 2 90 MIN
VHS
Color (G A) (POLISH)
$24.95 purchase _ #V165, #V227
Offers a series of 10 - minute films highlighting Poland's history and traditions, her cultural heritage, architecture and landscape. Visits Warsaw, Cracow, Wieliczka salt mine, Malbork, Torun, Wroclaw, Lodz and Szczecin. Also available with Polish narration. Part 2 of a 3 part series.
Geography - World
Dist - POLART

Land of their Own - the Face of Courage 30 MIN
VHS / U-matic
Color
Presents an 'original cast' western based on letters, diaries and photographs of the people who settled Nebraska. Includes photographs from the collection of the Nebraska Historical Society, many taken by Solomon D Butcher, Nebraska's pre - eminent pioneer photographer. Narrated by the late John G Neihardt, Nebraska's poet laureate.
History - United States
Dist - NETCHE **Prod** - NETCHE 1982

The Land of Third 15 MIN
VHS / U-matic
Magic Shop Series
Color (P)
LC 83-706146
Employs a magician named Amazing Alexander and his assistants to reinforce learning the letters of the alphabet.
English Language
Dist - GPN **Prod** - CVETVC 1982

Land - Part II
VHS
America the bountiful series
Color (G)
$89.95 purchase _ #6 - 402 - 002A
Examines the growth of early European settler population in America and the issues of control and use of land. Looks at the role of John Wallace in shaping the course of American agriculture. Observes the expansion of the American frontier at the close of the 18th century. Part of a six - part series on the history of American agriculture hosted by Ed Begley, Jr.
Agriculture; Biography; History - United States
Dist - VEP **Prod** - VEP 1993

Land Pollution - a First Film 8 MIN
U-matic / VHS / 16mm
Color
LC 74-701414
Tells how the American people can best use the land resources. Lists the many uses made of the land and explains that good land is not unlimited.
Geography - United States; Science - Natural; Social Science
Dist - PHENIX **Prod** - BEANMN 1974

The Land Speaks Out 12 MIN
16mm
Color
Points out that Israel is a modern country, rooted deeply in its historic past. Shows convenient vacation facilities at sea resorts and camping grounds combined with unique archaeological sites and beautiful scenery of the countryside.
Geography - World
Dist - ALDEN **Prod** - ALDEN

The Land that Came in from the Cold 13 MIN
U-matic / VHS / 16mm
Natural Phenomenon Series
Color (J)
LC 81-700681
Explores the glaciers of Glacier National Monument, showing how they have changed over the past 200 years. Points out that a glacier can be seen as a geological and zoological time line.
Geography - World; Science - Physical
Dist - JOU **Prod** - JOU 1980

Land that Time Forgot 90 MIN
16mm
Color (I A)
Based on the book by Edgar Rice Burroughs. Set in 1916, survivors from a torpedoed ship find themselves on a legendary island full of prehistoric monsters. Stars Doug McClure.
Fine Arts
Dist - TIMLIF **Prod** - AMICP 1974

Land that will not heal
U-matic / VHS / BETA
Search encounters in science series
Color; PAL (G H C)
PdS25, PdS33 purchase
Brings modern research efforts of the world's leading scientists into the classroom. Features one of a series of 24 mini - documentaries. Each film is 5 - 7 minutes in length.
Science; Science - Natural
Dist - EDPAT **Prod** - NSF

Land the Landing Force 29 MIN
16mm
Color
LC 74-706483
Shows operations of the naval amphibious forces.
Civics and Political Systems
Dist - USNAC **Prod** - USN 1967

Land the Landing Force - the History of Marine Amphibious Operations 28 MIN
16mm
Color
LC FIE62-30
Explains the development of the amphibious doctrine and its use in vertical assault.
Civics and Political Systems; History - United States
Dist - USNAC **Prod** - USMC 1960

The Land, the sea, the children there 24 MIN
U-matic / VHS
Young people's specials series
Color
Gives a lifestyle portrayal of two children, one from Maine and one from Nebraska.
Geography - United States; Sociology
Dist - MULTPP **Prod** - MULTPP

Land transport 15 MIN
VHS
Color; PAL (P I)
PdS25.00 purchase
Tells the history of overland travel, the development and routing of the rail and road networks and the use of land and conflicts raised by transport.
Geography - World; Social Science
Dist - EMFVL **Prod** - LOOLEA

Land transport through history 16 MIN
U-matic / VHS / BETA
Color; NTSC; PAL; SECAM (J H)
PdS58
Traces the development of land transportation, from the days when people walked or traveled by horse to the experimental cars of the future. Shows that road, canal and railroad networks were developed to serve growing industrial and urban communities. Follows the invention and evolution of motor cars to lead to discussion of the modern problems of road congestion and atmospheric congestion by exhaust fumes.
Industrial and Technical Education; Science - Natural; Social Science
Dist - VIEWTH

Land Use 29 MIN
VHS / 16mm
Washington Connection Series
Color (G)
$55.00 rental _ #WACO - 113
Civics and Political Systems; Social Science
Dist - PBS **Prod** - NPACT

Land Use and Misuse 13 MIN
U-matic / VHS / 16mm
Environmental Sciences Series
Color (J H)
LC 70-710056
Describes malpractice in the use of land surfaces without regard for erosion by wind and water, alteration of hydrologic cycle, contamination of ground water by irrigation and resulting changes in climate. Discusses phenomena, problems, effects, causes and possible solutions.
Agriculture; Science - Natural; Social Science; Sociology
Dist - LCOA **Prod** - DAVFMS 1975

Land Use in the City 30 MIN
VHS / U-matic
Living Environment Series
Color (C)
Discusses efficient use of land for the city and the countryside. Includes urban sprawl, zoning, subdivision regulation, environmental impact of population and industrial growth and the need for master planning.
Science - Natural
Dist - DALCCD **Prod** - DALCCD

Land Use on the Flood Plains 16 MIN
16mm / U-matic / VHS
Color (J H C)
LC 76-702976
Examines the relationship between flooding and land use. Explains that the proximity to transportation, energy and fertile soil has often outweighted the dangers of flood and offers dams, levies and flood - plan zoning as methods of controlling land use of flood plains.
Agriculture
Dist - IU **Prod** - IU 1976

Land Use Planning in the Town of Dunn 45 MIN
U-matic / VHS
B&W
Explores the negative and positive effects of land use planning in the town of Dunn.
Civics and Political Systems; Sociology
Dist - UWISC **Prod** - UWISC 1981

The Land was theirs 55 MIN
VHS
Color; B&W (G)
$50.00 purchase
Looks at Jewish farmers and their communities in New Jersey. Portrays immigrants in America adapting to new lifestyles and conventions while maintaining their cultural heritage. Produced and directed by Gertrude Dubrovsky.
Fine Arts; History - United States; Religion and Philosophy; Sociology
Dist - NCJEWF

Land where my fathers died 23 MIN
VHS / 16mm
Color (G)
$750.00, $250.00 purchase, $75.00 rental
Examines family dynamics and black masculinity. Portrays New Yorker Aziza Williams who visits her hometown with her boyfriend. Reveals that they visit her estranged father and irrepressible uncle, that their visit is disrupted by the damaging effects of alcoholism. Produced by Daresha Kyi.
Health and Safety; History - United States; Psychology; Sociology
Dist - WMEN

Land Where the Blues Began 59 MIN
U-matic / VHS / 16mm
Color
LC 82-700726
Presents a documentary about the culture of the Mississippi hill country.
Fine Arts; History - United States; Sociology
Dist - PHENIX **Prod** - MAETEL 1980

Land - with Love and Respect 26 MIN
16mm
Color (H C A)
LC 81-700594
Explores social and economic conflicts related to land - use decisions. Introduces information tools, such as topographic maps, air photos, soil studies, and resource inventories.
Agriculture
Dist - CORNRS **Prod** - CUETV 1979

Land Without Bread / Housing Problems 43 MIN
VHS / U-matic
B&W
Presents a documentary on the impoverished people living in the Las Hurdes region of Spain. Directed by Luis Bunuel. Explores the horrors and evils of the urban housing of the '30s through interviews with slum dwellers. Directed by Arthur Elton and Edgar Anstey.
Geography - World; History - World; Sociology
Dist - IHF **Prod** - IHF

Landbased Helicopter Operations - Functions 10 MIN
16mm
B&W
LC FIE59-237
Describes to helicopter pilots the many duties which they will be expected to perform in landbased helicopter operations and points out the versatility of the helicopter.
Guidance and Counseling; Industrial and Technical Education; Social Science
Dist - USNAC **Prod** - USN 1952

Landbased Helicopter Operations - Precautions 11 MIN
16mm
B&W
LC FIE59-236
Stresses the need for pilot alertness in helicopter operation and demonstrates night and rough - terrain operations.
Guidance and Counseling; Industrial and Technical Education; Social Science
Dist - USNAC **Prod** - USN 1952

Landet De Vandt (Conquered Land) 35 MIN
16mm
Color (DANISH)
A Danish language film. Presents interviews with old Moorland farmers who tell about their strenuous efforts to realize Enrico Dalgas' dream of fertilizing the moors of Jutland. Aims at proving that the history of the Danish health society reflects Denmark's development. Documents their work since 1866.
Agriculture; Foreign Language
Dist - STATNS **Prod** - STATNS 1966

Landfall 11 MIN
16mm
Color (G)
$35.00 rental
Encourages viewers to reject Newtonian notions of time and space by featuring the work of Quebec poet D G Jones, I Thought There Were Limits. Uses typography, graphics, timing and a method making of the words appear and disappear.
Fine Arts; Literature and Drama
Dist - CANCIN **Prod** - HANCXR 1983

Landfall no 1 6 MIN
16mm
Color
LC 76-701022
Presents a seascape film made on Prince Edward Island.
Geography - World; Industrial and Technical Education; Science - Natural
Dist - CANFDC **Prod** - CANFDC 1974

Landfill 12 MIN
16mm

Color
Proves that solid waste disposal need not be damaging to the environment. Depicts a regional transfer and landfill operation which serves a big city and several nearby suburban communities. Shows that it is designed to do a big job without the truck traffic, dust, noise and health problems which so often disturb citizens and arouse protest elsewhere.
Health and Safety; Science - Natural; Sociology
Dist - FINLYS **Prod** - FINLYS

Landforms and climates of the United States 20 MIN
U-matic / 16mm / VHS
Color (P I J)
$495.00, $375.00, $345.00 purchase _ #A613
Discusses the six major landforms of the United States - the Atlantic Coastal Plain, the Appalachian Highlands, the Interior Plains, the Rocky Mountains, the Intermountain Plateau and the Pacific Mountain Ranges. Looks at the characteristics of each of these landforms and their climate. Shows the effect that the shape of a landform and its distance from the equator have on climate.
Geography - United States
Dist - BARR **Prod** - CEPRO 1991

Landforms of the United States 30 MIN
VHS
Color (J H)
$39.95 purchase _ #IV115
Looks at the major physiographic provinces of the United States. Examines the geological forces which shapes each area and gives an overall view of the US as well as its specific regions.
Geography - United States; Science - Physical
Dist - INSTRU

The Landforms of Wyoming 30 MIN
VHS
Color (J H C)
$29.95 purchase _ #IVLWG
Reveals that the present landscape of Wyoming is the ever - changing product of a long series of events extending back in time to the beginning of Earth as a planet. Looks at the various landforms created by erosion, dendritic drainage patterns, landforms developed on flat - lying sedimentary rocks, tilted sedimentary rocks, folded and faulted rocks and landforms resulting from the action of glaciers and the wind. Looks at depositional landforms such as stream and playa lake deposits and volcano deposits.
Geography - United States; History - United States; Science - Physical
Dist - INSTRU

Landforms - what they are and How they are Shaped 66 MIN
U-matic / Slide
Color (J H C)
$259.00 purchase _ #01058 - 161
Provides an overview of the major types of landforms on the Earth with an account of the geological forces that produce them. In three parts.
Geography - World; Science; Science - Natural; Science - Physical
Dist - GA **Prod** - CRYSP

Landing Illusions - Short Landings 10 MIN
16mm
Color
LC 75-701304
Discusses optical illusions which can cause pilot error. Shows visibility restrictions on the glidepath caused by changing weather conditions.
Industrial and Technical Education; Psychology
Dist - USNAC **Prod** - USAF 1969

Landing on the Moon 28 MIN
16mm
Science Reporter Series
B&W (J H A)
LC 76-708127
Shows the inside of the lunar module, giving a simulated ride to the surface of the moon.
Industrial and Technical Education; Science - Physical
Dist - USNAC **Prod** - NASA 1966

The Landing Team 10 MIN
16mm
Logging Safety Series
Color (H C A)
Emphasizes the skill, safe working procedures and productive operations of the landing team. Shows professional landing teams at work in various conditions, terrains and locations.
Business and Economics; Health and Safety
Dist - RARIG **Prod** - RARIG 1968

Landing - Weather Minimums Investigation 21 MIN
16mm
Color
LC 75-700562
Examines problems faced by pilots making approaches under low visibility conditions. Depicts landings in deep, shallow and cloud base fog, in drizzle with and without windshield wipers and with misaligned instruments.
Industrial and Technical Education
Dist - USNAC **Prod** - USAF 1967

Landlord and Tenant 22 MIN
16mm
Color (J)
LC 76-700674
Takes a cinema - verite look at the opinions and attitudes held by landlords and tenants. Considers views from landlords, a welfare family with housing problems and a group of people responsible for organizing a tenant's union in a large housing project.
Sociology
Dist - OSUMPD **Prod** - OHHUM 1974

Landlord and Tenant Law 15 MIN
VHS / 16mm
You and the Law Series
Color (S)
$150.00 purchase _ #275903
Employs a mixture of drama and narrative to introduce particular aspects of Canadian law. Presents some of the basic concepts and addresses some of the more commonly asked questions. Emphasis is on those elements of the law which are frequently misunderstood. 'Landlord And Tenant Law' explains the rights, obligations and regulations governing both landlord and tenant. Leases and their stipulations for the right to privacy, sufficient notice, entry and exit inspections and damage deposits are discussed, as well as the Landlord and Tenant Act, and the Landlord and Tenant Advisory Board.
Civics and Political Systems; Geography - World
Dist - ACCESS **Prod** - ACCESS 1987

Landlord - Tenant Law 23 MIN
U-matic / VHS / 16mm
Law and the Citizen Series
Color (J)
LC 78-701830
Discusses the rights of tenants and landlords and raises questions concerning the landlords' obligation to maintain their apartments at legally imposed levels of habitability. Discusses the question of whether tenants should be allowed to deduct repair costs from the rent.
Civics and Political Systems; Home Economics; Sociology
Dist - BARR **Prod** - WILETS 1978

Landlords and Tenants 29 MIN
U-matic
You and the Law Series Lesson 16
Color (C A)
Discusses legal right and responsiblities that exist between landlords and tenants. Focuses on terms and basic clauses found in a typical lease.
Civics and Political Systems
Dist - CDTEL **Prod** - COAST

The Landman 16 MIN
16mm / VHS
(A PRO)
$325.00 purchase _ #30.0122, $300.00 purchase _ #50.0122
Explains common roles of a landman as a member of an exploration team.
Science - Physical; Social Science
Dist - UTEXPE **Prod** - UTEXPE 1977

Landmark 14 MIN
16mm
Color
LC 74-700711
Traces the development of nuclear power reactors in the United States and shows how their increased use in the future could ease the current energy crisis.
Industrial and Technical Education; Science - Natural; Science - Physical
Dist - USNAC **Prod** - ANL 1973

Landmark in Beta - Blocker Research - Findings of the Norwegian Multicenter Study Group 13 MIN
U-matic / VHS
Color (PRO)
Reports on the use of Timolol Maleate, a beta blocker, in a study population of nearly 2000 patients, which showed the effectiveness of the drug in reducing the risk of death and reinfarction in those who have survived the acute phase of a myocardial infarction.
Health and Safety
Dist - WFP **Prod** - WFP

Landmarks and Legends 30 MIN
VHS
Color (G)
$39.95 purchase _ #LALE - 000
Features landmarks in Washington, D.C., including Arlington National Cemetery, the Vietnam Veteran's Memorial and the house where Lincoln died. Tells the stories behind these landmarks. Hosted by Bryson Rash.
History - United States
Dist - PBS **Prod** - WETATV 1989

Landmarks in Psychology 53 MIN
VHS
Color (J H)
Highlights the principal contributions to modern psychology of Freud, Jung, Adler, Pavlov, Sullivan, Horney, Maslow, Watson, and Skinner. Through historical narrative and case study dramatization, your students learn the evolution of modern psychology.
Psychology
Dist - HRMC **Prod** - HRMC 1980

Landmarks of the Old Oregon Country 120 MIN
VHS / U-matic / BETA
Color (P I J H C G T A)
Shows pivotal themes and events in American and Pacific Northwest history shot at locations carefully chosen to correlate with historically significant places in Oregon, Washington, and Idaho. Include precontact Indians, exploration by sea and land, the inland fur trade, the work of missionaries to the Pacific Northwest, the Oregon Trail, early pioneer settlement, and Oregon statehood. Available is an extensive teacher's guide for upper elementary age group.
History - United States
Dist - OREGHS **Prod** - OREGHS 1986

Landmarks to Remember 20 MIN
U-matic
Exploring Our Nation Series
Color (I)
Highlights America's national monuments. Features the Washington Monument, the Jefferson Memorial, the Gettysburg battlefield, the Gateway Arch at St Louis, and Ft Laramie.
History - United States
Dist - GPN **Prod** - KRMATV 1975

Lands and Peoples of Oceania Series
The Island Continent - Australia 17 MIN
Dist - MCFI

Lands and Waters of Our Earth 11 MIN
U-matic / VHS / 16mm
Color (P)
Shows the many kinds of land and water forms on the earth's surface, such as hills, mountains, valleys and rivers.
Science - Natural; Science - Physical
Dist - CORF **Prod** - CORF 1956

Land's Edge 28 MIN
VHS / U-matic
Color
Shows human, animal and plant life along the ocean shore near Newport, Oregon. Features the natural beauty and the buildup of a storm.
Geography - United States; Science - Natural
Dist - MEDIPR **Prod** - MEDIPR 1974

The Lands of the Falling Waters 10 MIN
16mm
Color; B&W
Pictures scenes of South America including a flight to the world's highest waterfalls, Angle Falls, in Venezuela, Georgetown, capital of British Guiana and the Kaietur Falls.
Geography - World
Dist - PLP **Prod** - MILWOD 1958

LANDSAT - 15 years of learning 15 MIN
VHS
Color (J H C)
$14.95 purchase _ #NA202
Looks at the history and accomplishments of Landsat - the United States camera in space which was launched to photograph the surface of the Earth. Shows how space photography can be used to track changes on the Earth and to help in understanding ecosystems.
Industrial and Technical Education; Science - Natural; Science - Physical
Dist - INSTRU **Prod** - NASA

Landsat - Satellite for all Seasons Series
Remote Possibilities 15 MIN
Dist - USNAC

Landsbykirken (the Danish Village Church) 10 MIN
16mm
B&W ((DANISH SUBTITLES))
Presents the history of Danish country church architecture by showing how the church is used by the congregation, beginning with the celebration of Mass in a small and simple wooden church 800 years ago, and ending with the congregation singing in a village church of today. Shows the development and growth of the pattern of church architecture. Includes Danish subtitles.
Fine Arts; Geography - World
Dist - STATNS **Prod** - STATNS 1947

Landscape 18 MIN
16mm
B&W (G)
$35.00 rental
Studies the weather and landscape in the Hudson River valley.

Fine Arts; Geography - United States
Dist - CANCIN **Prod** - HUTTON 1987

The Landscape 30 MIN
U-matic / VHS
Designing the Environment Series
Color
Discusses the scope of architecture, which has expanded in recent years to include a consciousness of the entire ecological system of the planet and how this concern is now considered fundamental to good design.
Fine Arts; Science - Natural; Sociology
Dist - NETCHE **Prod** - NETCHE 1971

Landscape 37 MIN
16mm
Color (J)
Presents an adaptation of the Royal Shakespeare Company production of Harold Pinter's play, Landscape, staring Dame Peggy Ashcroft and David Waller.
Literature and Drama
Dist - CANTOR **Prod** - CANTOR

Landscape 8 MIN
16mm / U-matic / VHS
Color (H C A)
LC 75-703043
Uses animation to evoke memories of the past. Reflects images of reality into the world of fantasy.
Fine Arts
Dist - PHENIX **Prod** - HUFSC 1975

Landscape 30 MIN
VHS / 16mm
Chinese Brush Painting Series
Color (C A)
$85.00, $75.00 purchase _ 20 - 18
Explains the significance of Shan - Shui, depth, dimension and focus.
Fine Arts
Dist - CDTEL **Prod** - COAST 1987

Landscape - a Pattern of Change 19 MIN
16mm
Color (J)
LC 76-700566
Traces the changing patterns of land use as they affect a typical Australian town, using the example of Mudgee in New South Wales.
Geography - World; Sociology
Dist - AUIS **Prod** - FLMAUS 1975

Landscape After Battle 110 MIN
16mm
Color (POLISH (ENGLISH SUBTITLES))
Presents a love story set in a displaced persons camp in Poland after World War II. Directed by Andrzej Wajda. With English subtitles.
Fine Arts; Foreign Language
Dist - NYFLMS **Prod** - UNKNWN 1970

Landscape and cityscape 29 MIN
VHS
Photographic vision series
Color (G)
$49.95 purchase _ #RM115V-F
Considers the romantic movement in the evolution of photography. Presents the technical aspects of photography clearly and simply, including principles of the camera and techniques for controlling exposure, the use of various kinds of lighting, selection of appropriate lenses and film and basic darkroom techniques. Focuses on the world of photographers and photography - its history and evolution, its uses for personal development and expression, and the impact of photography on the world. Part of a 20-part series examining all aspects of the field of photography.
Industrial and Technical Education
Dist - CAMV
CDTEL

Landscape and Desire 58 MIN
16mm
Color; B&W (C)
$1600.00
Experimental film by Ken Kobland.
Fine Arts
Dist - AFA **Prod** - AFA 1981

Landscape and Light 30 MIN
VHS / U-matic
What a Picture - the Complete Photography Course by John Hedgecoe 'Series
Color (H C A)
Discusses the practicalities of landscape photography and how to capture mood and atmosphere through viewpoint, composition and the quality of light.
Industrial and Technical Education
Dist - FI

Landscape and Room 10 MIN
16mm
Color; Silent (C)
$200.00
Experimental film by David Haxton.
Fine Arts
Dist - AFA **Prod** - AFA 1978

The landscape architects 30 MIN
VHS
Up a gum tree with David Bellamy series
Color; PAL (H C A)
PdS65 purchase
Travels around Australia and looks at the flora and fauna of the continent. Traces the history of the aborigines and questions why they never became farmers. Employs David Bellamy as a tour guide. Part three of a five part series.
Geography - World; History - World
Dist - BBCENE

Landscape Artistry 30 MIN
VHS / BETA
Victory Garden Series
Color
Discusses planting on a deck. Pictures some landscape artistry in Boston and Lexington.
Agriculture; Physical Education and Recreation
Dist - CORF **Prod** - WGBHTV

Landscape Design 30 MIN
BETA / VHS
This Old House, Pt 1 - the Dorchester Series
Color
Considers gardening possibilities for a renovated house.
Industrial and Technical Education; Sociology
Dist - CORF **Prod** - WGBHTV

Landscape design presentation techniques 31 MIN
- Volume III
VHS
Landscape design series
Color (G)
$89.95 purchase _ #6 - 045 - 003A
Explores the scope of work and presentation techniques used by a garden designer, landscape contractor and landscape architect. Part of a series on landscape design.
Agriculture; Business and Economics
Dist - VEP **Prod** - VEP 1993

The Landscape design process - Vol II 26 MIN
VHS
Landscape design series
Color (G)
$89.95 purchase _ #6 - 045 - 002P
Looks in - depth at the landscape design process and the systematic procedure which helps to ensure the design of functional and attractive landscapes. Examines site analysis, development of the design program, schematic proposal, plan development and project installation. Part two of two parts.
Agriculture; Home Economics
Dist - VEP **Prod** - VEP

Landscape Design Series
Volume 1 - Introduction to Landscape Design 22 MIN
Dist - CSPC

Landscape design series
Presents a three - part series on landscape design. Includes the titles The Principle of Landscape Design, The Landscape Design Process, Landscape Design Presentation Techniques.
Landscape design presentation techniques - Volume III 31 MIN
The Landscape design process - Vol II 26 MIN
The Principles of landscape design - Vol I 22 MIN
Dist - VEP **Prod** - VEP

Landscape design series
Examines the principles of landscape design and design process in two parts.
Landscape design presentation techniques - Volume III 31 MIN
The Landscape design process - Vol II 26 MIN
The Principles of landscape design - Vol I 22 MIN
Dist - VEP **Prod** - VEP

Landscape equipment - loader - backhoe safety series 40 MIN
VHS
Backhoe safety series
Color (G)
$125.00 purchase _ #6 - 201 - 100A
Offers two videos which provide comprehensive safety education and easy - to - follow guidelines for loader - backhoe crews. Trains loader - backhoe operators on tape one. Discusses practical guidelines for other trades that work with loader - backhoes daily on tape two.
Agriculture; Health and Safety
Dist - VEP **Prod** - VEP

Landscape equipment maintenance series
Presents a five - part series on proper procedures for maintenance, safety and operation of power blowers, rotary edger - trimmers, 21 - inch rotary mowers, gas powered shears and string trimmers for landscaping.
Power Blower
Power Shears
Rotary Edger - Trimmer
String Trimmer
Twenty - One Inch Rotary Mower
Dist - VEP **Prod** - VEP

Landscape equipment safety for the 90s - power hand tools
VHS
Color (G)
$89.95 purchase _ #6 - 302 - 300S
Covers the latest features in line trimmers, hedge trimmers, power blowers, chain saws, and power pruners. Focuses on new OSHA safety requirements, how to select the right tool for the job, what protection should be used with each tool, and how to perform field maintenance checks.
Agriculture; Health and Safety
Dist - VEP **Prod** - VEP 1991

Landscape equipment safety for the 90s - push mowers 29 MIN
VHS
Color (G)
$89.95 purchase _ #6 - 302 - 311S
Covers new federal safety regulations for the 1990s and design features of push mowers. Shows equipment selection, personal safety and operating techniques from refueling to maintenance.
Agriculture; Health and Safety
Dist - VEP **Prod** - VEP 1991

Landscape equipment safety for the 90s - riding mowers 26 MIN
VHS
Color (G)
$89.95 purchase _ #6 - 302 - 303S
Covers new safety regulations for the 1990s, which mandated significant changes in the design and operation of riding mowers. Shows equipment selection, personal safety and operating techniques from refueling to maintenance.
Agriculture; Health and Safety
Dist - VEP **Prod** - VEP 1991

Landscape from a Dream - Paul Nash 30 MIN
16mm
Color (H A)
$660.00 purchase, $60.00 rental
Uses commentary from the autobiography of Paul Nash to trace his development from traditional English landscape artist to creating dreamlike vistas.
Fine Arts; Industrial and Technical Education
Dist - AFA **Prod** - ACGB 1978

Landscape in Painting 19 MIN
16mm / U-matic / VHS
Color
LC 74-700415
Surveys the history of landscape painting from the Roman period to the present day. Shows how the painting of landscapes in different historical periods differed in style, execution and intention.
Fine Arts
Dist - IFB **Prod** - SEABEN 1972

Landscape Irrigation Maintenance and Troubleshooting 26 MIN
VHS
Color (G)
$89.95 purchase _ #6 - 055 - 100P
Overviews the operation and maintenance of irrigation systems. Details sprinkler heads and drip emitters, pipes and fittings, field control wires and hydraulic tubing, valves, backflow prevention devices, mainlines and points of connection, and controllers. Utilizes a systematic approach to troubleshooting with the visual aid of a flowchart.
Agriculture
Dist - VEP **Prod** - VEP
CSPC

Landscape of Geometry Series
Cracking Up 15 MIN
It's Rude to Point 15 MIN
Lines that Cross 15 MIN
Lines that Don't Cross 15 MIN
The Range of Change 15 MIN
The Shape of Thing 15 MIN
Trussworthy 15 MIN
Up, Down and Sideways 15 MIN
Dist - TVOTAR

The Landscape of Pleasure 52 MIN
16mm / U-matic / VHS
Shock of the New Series
Color (C A)
LC 80-700986
Discusses the liberation of color which began in the late 19th century and which was amplified by Matisse and Derain. Points out the increasing personalization of art as seen in the work of Braque and Picasso.
Fine Arts
Dist - TIMLIF **Prod** - BBCTV 1980

Landscape painting 60 MIN
VHS
Color (G)
PdS19.95 purchase _ #A4-MC1
Presents a working conversation with the Salford artist Harold Riley while he paints a landscape in his own style and offers information about the basic rules of perspective, tone, and composition. Produced by Master Class.
Fine Arts
Dist - AVP

Landscape Painting with Harold Riley
VHS / U-matic
$24.95 purchase
Fine Arts
Dist - BEEKMN **Prod** - BEEKMN 1988

Landscape Suicide 95 MIN
16mm
Color (G)
Presents an independent production by James Benning. Offers strange murders by strange people.
Fine Arts; Literature and Drama
Dist - FIRS

Landscape Tools - Use and Safety 25 MIN
VHS
Color (G)
$89.95 purchase _ #6 - 091 - 100P
Teaches the importance of choosing the right tool for the job of landscaping and how the right selection adds to the job safety of the landscape worker. Examines safety precautions, proper clothing and back care. Emphasizes the value of tool care and storage. Shows several gardening tools in use, including the round and square point shovel, scoop shovel, rakes, forks, cultivators, hoe, picks and mattocks.
Agriculture; Health and Safety
Dist - VEP **Prod** - VEP

Landscape with Boots and Child 9 MIN
16mm
Color
LC 79-700233
Attempts to re - create the story behind a photograph that was found in Europe during World War II.
Fine Arts
Dist - POORI **Prod** - POORI 1978

Landscape with buildings 50 MIN
VHS
Spirit of the age series
Color (A)
PdS99 purchase
Examines the evolution of architecture in Britain since the Middle Ages. Part five of an eight-part series.
Fine Arts; Industrial and Technical Education
Dist - BBCENE

Landscapes 25 MIN
VHS
Exploring photography series
Color (A)
PdS65 purchase
Deals with a wide variety of approaches to landscape photography. Includes the work of Ernst Haas and John Blakemore. Explores the creative possibilities of still photography. Covers the major topics of interest to any photographer. Part of a six-part series hosted by Bryn Campbell.
Fine Arts; Industrial and Technical Education
Dist - BBCENE

Landscapes in pastel 30 MIN
VHS
Color (G)
PdS19.95 purchase _ #A4-ARG08
Demonstrates landscape painting in pastel from the first mark to the finished painting. Uses close focus camera to highlight details. Features Ken Jackson, who explains all materials as he uses them.
Fine Arts
Dist - AVP **Prod** - ARGUS

The Landscapes of Frederic Edwin Church 29 MIN
VHS
Color (G)
$29.95 purchase _ #CHU-01
Shows the grandeur of the American wilderness that inspired Frederic Edwin Church, leading artist of the Hudson River School. Displays the beauty of his romantic paintings.
Fine Arts
Dist - ARTSAM **Prod** - USNGA

Landscapes series
The Aspen parklands - the gentle wilderness 30 MIN
The Badlands and river valleys - echoes in stone 30 MIN
The Boreal forest - the strong woods 30 MIN
The Cypress Hills - Nunatak 30 MIN
The Grasslands - the great lone land 30 MIN
The Mountains - Headwaters 30 MIN
Precambrian Shield - the Bones of the Earth 30 MIN
Dist - ACCESS

Landscaping - Design 50 MIN
VHS
Art of Landscaping Series
(G)
$39.95 purchase _ #UH300V
Provides a step by step guide on designing, budgeting, constructing, and maintaining a landscaped garden.
Agriculture
Dist - CAMV **Prod** - CAMV

Landscaping Planting 50 MIN
VHS
Art of Landscaping Series
(G)
$29.95 purchase _ #UH200V
Discusses correct procedures for planting all sizes of trees, shrubs, ground covers, vines, flowers, grass, and hanging baskets.
Agriculture
Dist - CAMV **Prod** - CAMV

Landscaping - Shopping 50 MIN
VHS
Art of Landscaping Series
(G)
$29.95 purchase _ #UH100V
Offers many tips on shopping for the plants that will become part of the yard landscape. Discusses how to differentiate between good and bad plants, container sizes and soil ammendments.
Agriculture
Dist - CAMV **Prod** - CAMV

Landscaping with container plants
VHS
Color (G)
$89.95 purchase _ #6 - 110 - 100P
Presents detailed information for landscaping on how to choose different containers and select appropriate plants. Discusses planting techniques and maintenance.
Agriculture
Dist - VEP **Prod** - VEP

Landshapes 220 MIN
VHS
Color; PAL (J H)
PdS55 purchase
Presents a seven - program series - a 52 - minute program and six parts of 28 minutes each - on the landscape of the British Isles. Uses footage shot from the air to show the landscape going through a never - ending process of change. Contact distributor about availability outside the United Kingdom.
Geography - World; Science - Physical
Dist - ACADEM

Landslides - Descriptive 47 MIN
U-matic / VHS
Basic and Petroleum Geology for Non - Geologists - Landforms Series; Landforms
Color (IND)
Industrial and Technical Education; Science - Physical
Dist - GPCV **Prod** - PHILLP

L'ange 70 MIN
16mm
Color (G)
Presents an independent production by French filmmanker Patrick Bokanowski. Also available in 35mm film format.
Fine Arts
Dist - FIRS

Langevin Equation, Distribution Function and Boltzmann Equation
VHS / U-matic
Plasma Process Technology Fundamentals Series
Color (IND)
Describes the Langevin equation for electron motion which includes both the driving term from the electric field force and the opposing momentum - loss collisions between electrons and atoms, and their terminal velocities. Includes calculation of distribution function.
Industrial and Technical Education; Science - Physical
Dist - COLOSU **Prod** - COLOSU

Langston Hughes 60 MIN
VHS / 16mm
Voices and Visions Series
Color (H)
$8.00 rental _ #60731
Profiles Langston Hughes (1902 - 1967), who achieved distinction in poetry, drama, and fiction. Gwendolyn Brooks, James Baldwin, Amiri Baraka, and Arnold Rampersand explore Hughes' life and discuss such major influences on his work as jazz and blues music, the 1920's Harlem Renaissance, and his black heritage.
History - United States; Literature and Drama
Dist - PSU

Langston Hughes 24 MIN
35mm strip / VHS
Color (J H C A)
$93.00, $93.00 purchase _ #MB - 909729 - 4, #MB - 909709 - X
Portrays the life and work of African - American author Langston Hughes. Shows that Hughes' poetry, fiction, and autobiography all captured a unique 'insider' vision of black American life. Covers his beginnings in Joplin, Missouri, his college days at Columbia University, and his writing career on both sides of the Atlantic Ocean. Features selections from Hughes' works.
Literature and Drama
Dist - SRA **Prod** - SRA 1990

Langston Hughes 20 MIN
U-matic
Truly American Series
Color (I)
Biography; History - United States; Literature and Drama
Dist - GPN **Prod** - WVIZTV 1979

Langston Hughes 24 MIN
U-matic / VHS / 16mm
Color
LC 72-712703
Presents dramatized interpretive readings from Langston Hughes' best works. Includes a brief biography of the author's life.
Biography; History - United States; Literature and Drama
Dist - CAROUF **Prod** - WCAUTV 1971

Langston Hughes 30 MIN
VHS
Black Americans of achievement collection II series
Color (J H C G)
$49.95 purchase _ #LVCD6620V - S
Provides interesting and concise information on poet Langston Hughes. Part of a 10 - part series on African - Americans.
History - United States; Literature and Drama
Dist - CAMV

Langston Hughes - Part 6 60 MIN
VHS / U-matic
Voices and visions series
Color (G)
$45.00, $29.95 purchase
Uses interviews, music and dance performance to convey the work of poet Langston Hughes, who wrote of the beauty, dignity and heritage of blacks in America. Features James Baldwin and Hughes' biographer Arnold Rampersad. Part of a thirteen - part series on the lives and works of modern American poets.
Biography; History - United States; Literature and Drama
Dist - ANNCPB **Prod** - NYCVH 1988

Language 30 MIN
VHS / 16mm
Psychology - the Study of Human Behavior Series
Color (C A)
$99.95, $89.95 purchase _ 24 - 10
Describes how language is the product of learning, environmental influences and human genetic endowments.
Psychology
Dist - CDTEL **Prod** - COAST 1990

Language 30 MIN
VHS
Mind/Brain Classroom Series
Color (H G)
$59.95 purchase _ #MDBR - 109
Focuses on differing theories about the development of language. Intended for high school students.
Psychology
Dist - PBS **Prod** - WNETTV

Language 50 MIN
VHS
Human brain series
Color (H C A)
PdS99 purchase
Highlights recent advances in knowledge about the brain and its functions relative to speech. Uses case histories to illustrate individuals' triumphs over brain injury. Part of a seven-video set focusing on the self, memory, language, movement, sight, fear, and madness.
Psychology
Dist - BBCENE

Language 60 MIN
VHS
Mind Series
Color; Captioned (G)
$59.95 purchase _ #MIND - 107
Sets forth various theories on the origins of language. Shows that linguistic capacity is present even in people who cannot speak or hear. Considers the ways in which language shapes human perception.
Psychology
Dist - PBS **Prod** - WNETTV 1988

Language 30 MIN
U-matic / VHS / 16mm
Media Probes Series
Color (H C A)
Probes the impact of language on culture including a rehearsal and performance with the National Theatre of the Deaf, a look at the influence that the woman's movement has had on the newest Barnhart Dictionary, a seminar with the world's leading authority on abusive language and an animated Doonesbury strip extolling the virtues of California's Mellow - Speak. Hosted by Victor Borge.
English Language; Psychology; Sociology
Dist - TIMLIF **Prod** - LAYLEM 1982

Language - a Sign and Symbol System 30 MIN
U-matic / VHS
Language and Meaning Series
Color (C)
English Language; Psychology
Dist - GPN **Prod** - WUSFTV 1983

Language and Character 51 MIN
U-matic / VHS
Royal Shakespeare Company Series
Color
Discusses the Elizabethan relish of words - their resonances, onomatopeia, alliteration and antithesis. Deals with how Shakespeare uses language to define character and how his characters use heightened language to achieve their intentions. Includes examples from Love's Labour's Lost, Henry V, Julius Caesar and Hamlet.
Literature and Drama
Dist - FOTH **Prod** - FOTH 1984

Language and Communication 30 MIN
U-matic
Picking and Persuading a Jury Series
Color (PRO)
LC 81-706170
Suggests ways of ensuring clarity and comprehension in attorneys' communications with jurors.
Civics and Political Systems
Dist - ABACPE **Prod** - ABACPE 1980

Language and Communication 30 MIN
VHS / 16mm
Faces of Culture Series
Color (C A)
$85.00, $75.00 purchase _ 01 - 06
Describes the feelings and aspirations of expression in sounds and movements which constitute language.
Sociology
Dist - CDTEL **Prod** - COAST 1987

Language and gesture 60 MIN
VHS
Liturgy and the arts - Word, work and worship series
Color (R G)
$49.95 purchase _ #LAWW4
Includes examples of liturgical life and worship from across the United States. Examines current suppositions which prevail regarding liturgical life. Examines the rich drama of life unfolded in sign and symbols in the Roman Catholic Church. Traces the development of the liturgy in the history of the Church, the evolution of Church architecture and art, music and the 'appointments' used in worship, and discusses the language of the liturgy as well as the use of gesture and other modalities of expression in worship. Features Melanie Donohugh. Part of four parts on worship in the Roman Catholic Church.
Fine Arts; Religion and Philosophy
Dist - CTNA **Prod** - CTNA

Language and Hearing - Impaired Children 15 MIN
VHS / U-matic
Color (PRO)
Explains differences between normal language development and that of the hearing - impaired child. Delineates how to overcome the obstacles of teaching language skills.
Health and Safety; Psychology; Science - Natural
Dist - HSCIC **Prod** - HSCIC 1984

Language and Integration 28 MIN
16mm
Language - the Social Arbiter Series
Color
LC FIA67-463
A bi - racial panel of linguistic specialists discusses how language complicates and seems to interfere with the process of integration.
English Language; History - United States; Psychology; Sociology
Dist - FINLYS **Prod** - FINLYS 1966

Language and meaning series
Dominant metaphor and perception 30 MIN
The English Language - Racist and Sexist 30 MIN
Euphemism - Telling it Like it is 30 MIN
Euphemism and Social Change 30 MIN
The Function of Language - Perception 30 MIN
The Function of Language - the Social Dimensions 30 MIN
How meanings change 30 MIN
Kinesics - Motion and Meaning 30 MIN
Labels and Distortion 30 MIN
Language - a Sign and Symbol System 30 MIN
Language as Metaphor 30 MIN
Language Taboos - Cultural 30 MIN
Language Taboos - Grammatical 30 MIN
Levels of Abstraction and Meaning 30 MIN
The Manipulation of Language and Meaning 30 MIN
The Nature of Language - Brain and Mind 30 MIN
The Nature of Lanuage - the Linguistic Perspective 30 MIN
The Nature of Signs 30 MIN
The Nature of Symbols 30 MIN
The Past in Our Words 30 MIN
Proxemics - Distance 30 MIN
Some Misconceptions about Language - Pt 1 30 MIN
Some Misconceptions about Language - Pt 2 30 MIN
Standards, Styles and Keys 30 MIN
The Tunes of Language Intonation and Meaning 30 MIN
What do We Mean by Meaning 30 MIN
Why Meanings Change 30 MIN
Words - they Come and Go 30 MIN
Dist - GPN

Language arts holidays series
Christmas in pioneer times 15 MIN
Dist - MORLAT

Language Arts Series
The History of English 38 MIN
Dist - INCC

Language arts through imagination series
The Case of the missing space 16 MIN
What's an abra without a cadabra 15 MIN
Where does time fly 17 MIN
Dist - CORF

Language as Metaphor 30 MIN
U-matic / VHS
Language and Meaning Series
Color (C)
English Language; Psychology
Dist - GPN **Prod** - WUSFTV 1983

Language Assessment and Programming 29 MIN
U-matic / VHS
Mainstreaming the Exceptional Child Series
Color (T)
Discusses language assessment and programming in a mainstreaming situation.
Education; Psychology
Dist - FI **Prod** - MFFD

Language at Twelve 28 MIN
16mm
Color (C A)
LC 79-700525
Shows a group of twelve - year - olds as they participate in a language project. Points out differences in communication with parents, teachers and peers.
English Language; Psychology
Dist - AUIS **Prod** - FLMAUS 1976

Language - books and stories for young children 30 MIN
VHS
Calico pie series
Color (C A T)
$69.95 purchase
Presents part one of a 16 - part telecourse for teachers who work with children ages three to five. Discusses books and stories that can be used in the classroom. Hosted by Dr Carolyn Dorrell, an early childhood specialist.
Education; Psychology
Dist - SCETV **Prod** - SCETV 1983

Language construction company series
Adjectives and adverbs 18 MIN
Building a term paper - the master plan 18 MIN
Capitalization and punctuation 18 MIN
Clauses and phrases - parts make whole 18 MIN
Compound sentences - complex 18 MIN
More pronouns - more sub material 18 MIN
Nouns - Building blocks 18 MIN
Paragraph organization and style - the designer touch 18 MIN
Parts of speech - taking inventory 18 MIN
Personal pronouns - sub material 18 MIN
Simple sentence - basic construction 18 MIN
Underlining, italics, hyphenation, quotations - tricks of the trade 18 MIN
Verb mood and voice and problems verbs 18 MIN
Verb tenses - time matters 18 MIN
Verbs - being and doing 18 MIN
Dist - INSTRU

Language Development 7 MIN
U-matic
Take Time Series
(A)
Demonstrates the influence of parents and others caring for pre - schoolers on the physical and emotional development of the child.
Health and Safety; Psychology; Sociology
Dist - ACCESS **Prod** - ACCESS 1976

Language development 25 MIN
VHS / U-matic / BETA
Human development - first 2.5 years series
Color (C PRO)
$280.00 purchase _ #616.3
Discusses parent - child communication including turn - taking and 'motherese.' Describes the stages and sequences of language acquisition and development. Presents practical advice for improving a child's language ability. Part of a four - part series on the first 2.5 years of human development.
Health and Safety; Psychology; Social Science
Dist - CONMED **Prod** - CONMED

Language Experience Approach 20 MIN
U-matic / VHS / 16mm
Literacy Instructor Training Series
Color (T)
LC 78-700886
Focuses on literacy instruction techniques as well as the backgrounds and motivations of adult students.
Education; English Language
Dist - IU **Prod** - NEWPAR 1978

Language experience approach 30 MIN
16mm
Project STRETCH Series
Color (T)
LC 80-700618
Shows a kindergarten teacher demonstrating the principles of the language experience approach as the children in her class record events and create stories about those events.
Education; Psychology
Dist - HUBDSC **Prod** - METCO 1980

Language Experience Approach 28 MIN
VHS / U-matic
Helping Adults Learn Series
Color (C G T A)
Analyzes one method for teaching remedial reading that is designed to build on a student's prior knowledge and experience. Demonstrates the method in both a tutoring and a group learning environment, and it incorporates interviews with teachers and students.
Education; Psychology
Dist - PSU **Prod** - PSU 1987

The Language - Experience Approach to Teaching Reading - Grades 1 - 6 48 MIN
16mm
Color (C A)
LC 76-700039
Offers scenes from selected classroom sessions in which elements of the language - experience approach are being used in first, second and third grade classes. Helps teachers become acquainted with the language - experience system of reading instruction.
Education
Dist - UDEL **Prod** - UDEL 1975

Language Experience Story 13 MIN
VHS / 16mm
English as a Second Language Series
Color (A PRO)
$165.00 purchase _ #290310
Demonstrates key teaching methods for English as a Second Language - ESL teachers. Features a teacher - presenter who introduces and provides a brief commentary on the techniques, then demonstrates the application of the technique to the students. 'Language Experience Story' demonstrates the steps of developing and exploiting a language experience story with a low - level English class.
Education; English Language; Mathematics
Dist - ACCESS **Prod** - ACCESS 1989

Language Features, Pt 2 30 MIN
U-matic / VHS
Software Engineering - a First Course Series
Color (IND)
Discusses programming language features for scope control, exception handling, data encapsulation and structured central flow. Reviews and summarizes concepts of structured coding.
Industrial and Technical Education; Mathematics
Dist - COLOSU **Prod** - COLOSU

Language Features, Pt 3 30 MIN
VHS / U-matic
Software Engineering - a First Course Series
Color (IND)
Goes into structural programming concepts of single entry - single exit, 'structured' violations to single entry - single exit, the GOTO statement and uses of recursion.

Industrial and Technical Education; Mathematics
Dist - COLOSU **Prod** - COLOSU

A Language for Ben 52 MIN
U-matic / VHS
Color (C)
$249.00, $149.00 purchase _ #AD - 1713
Tells the story of Ben, the only deaf child in an English nursery school. Shows how he is helped by a signing teacher and others, both children and adults, pick up signing.
Guidance and Counseling; Health and Safety; Science - Natural
Dist - FOTH **Prod** - FOTH

Language in Action Series
Talking Ourselves into Trouble 29 MIN
Dist - IU

Language in Life
VHS / U-matic
Color
Science - Natural
Dist - MSTVIS **Prod** - MSTVIS

Language Instruction at the USAF Academy 25 MIN
16mm
Color
LC 74-706123
Illustrates progressive methods of teaching foreign languages at the Air Force Academy.
Civics and Political Systems; Education; Foreign Language
Dist - USNAC **Prod** - USAF 1962

Language (Interaction - Human Concerns in the Schools) 30 MIN
U-matic / VHS
Interaction - Human Concerns in the Schools Series
Color (T)
Analyzes the importance of language in an educational setting.
Education
Dist - MDCPB **Prod** - MDDE

Language, Learning and Children 30 MIN
U-matic / VHS
Language - Thinking, Writing, Communicating Series
Color
English Language
Dist - MDCPB **Prod** - MDCPB

Language of Algebra 16 MIN
U-matic / VHS / 16mm
Color (J H C)
Defines symbols, surveys their application in a modern world and illustrates their role in mathematics. Provides example problems and solutions.
Mathematics
Dist - IFB **Prod** - VEF 1956

The Language of being
VHS
Baby's world series
Color (G)
$29.95 purchase _ #DIS24160V-K
Instructs viewer on development of human babies as they learn verbal and physical skills. Shows infants grasping objects and using them as tools. Reveals the language babies use while learning adult language. Part of a three-part series that demonstrates the process of maturing from infancy into walking, talking, thinking human beings.
Health and Safety; Psychology
Dist - CAMV

The Language of Business 15 MIN
8mm cartridge / 16mm
Color
LC 75-701716; 74-705002
Dramatizes the need for being able to analyze facts and problem areas in a business so that decisions can be made. Shows the value of records in business management.
Business and Economics; Psychology
Dist - USNAC **Prod** - USSBA

The Language of Cells 145 MIN
U-matic
University of the Air Series
Color (J H C A)
$750.00 purchase, $250.00 rental
Relates the structure of the cell and how they work together to perform various functions for the body. Program contains a series of five cassettes 29 minutes each.
Science - Natural
Dist - CTV **Prod** - CTV 1978

The Language of Color
VHS / 35mm strip
$69.00 purchase _ #LS82 filmstrip, $79.00 purchase _ #LS82V VHS
Teaches how to use color in interior decorating, choose color in clothing, and how to understand one's own color preferences. Discusses the effect color has on one's emotions and actions.
Home Economics; Psychology
Dist - CAREER **Prod** - CAREER

The Language of Dance 29 MIN
16mm / U-matic / VHS
Time to Dance Series
B&W (C A)
Explains the basic element of emotion and shows how it can be transformed into a dance movement for one person, a group of dancers and an entire company. Presents the modern dance There Is A Time.
Fine Arts
Dist - IU **Prod** - NET 1960

The Language of editorial cartoons 15 MIN
VHS
Color (I J H)
$55.00 purchase _ #5480VD
Helps students to understand how editorial cartoons are created and why they are such an effective form of expressing opinion. Features many examples of cartoons and an insightful interview with a professional cartoonist. Includes a teacher's guide with a series of sequenced lessons teaching understanding of cartoons and how to draw them.
Civics and Political Systems; Fine Arts; Literature and Drama
Dist - KNOWUN **Prod** - KNOWUN 1992

The Language of Education 60 MIN
U-matic
Color
Lectures on language as the medium of education. Includes how language imposes a point of view and how culture is constantly created and negotiated.
Education
Dist - HRC **Prod** - OHC

Language of Faces 20 MIN
16mm
Color (J H A)
Presents the problems of survival in an age of materialism, arms races and fear of total annihilation. Suggests certain action of responsible citizenship.
Religion and Philosophy; Social Science; Sociology
Dist - YALEDV **Prod** - YALEDV

Language of Graphs, the 16 MIN
U-matic / VHS / 16mm
Color (J H)
LC 72-714992
Describes the bar, line, circle and equation graphs, and explains the special advantage of each. Points out some of the problems of interpreting these graphs.
Mathematics
Dist - CORF **Prod** - CORF 1972

The Language of life 20 MIN
VHS / U-matic
Catalyst series
Color (I J H)
$260.00, $310.00 purchase, $50.00 rental
Covers the subject of genetics. Includes selective breeding, genetic engineering, parthenogenesis, reproduction in the future and the importance of the gene pool.
Science - Natural
Dist - NDIM **Prod** - ABCTV 1991

The Language of life - understanding the genetic code 25 MIN
VHS
Color (H)
$99 purchase _ #10306VL
Introduces genetics and genetic code through animation and live - action footage of cells. Traces the flow of information from DNA to proteins through molecular language. The process of genetic mutation is also presented. Comes with interactive video quizzes; a teacher's guide; student activities; discussion questions; and 11 blackline masters.
Science - Natural
Dist - UNL

The Language of light 30 MIN
VHS
Color (G)
$24.95 purchase _ #S00935
Provides suggestions for the best uses of light in photography.
Industrial and Technical Education
Dist - UILL **Prod** - EKC

The Language of Maps 11 MIN
U-matic / 8mm cartridge
Color; B&W (I J H)
Uses aerial photography, topographic models and maps to show that the language of maps is composed of symbols representing natural and man - made features of the earth's surface.
Geography - World; Social Science
Dist - EBEC **Prod** - EBEC 1964

The Language of Maps 30 MIN
16mm
Starting Tomorrow Series
B&W (T)
LC 75-702435
Discusses the use of maps in the classroom.
Guidance and Counseling; Psychology; Social Science
Dist - WALKED **Prod** - EALING 1969

The Language of movement 24 MIN
VHS
Color (G)
$40.00 purchase
Shows a group of dance students from Central America, Europe and the United States demonstrating the power of creative dance in bridging international barriers through the universal language of movement. Features narration by Barbara Mettler at the Tucson Creative Dance Center.
Fine Arts; Physical Education and Recreation; Psychology; Social Science
Dist - METT **Prod** - METT 1985

The Language of Music 15 MIN
16mm / U-matic / VHS
Color (I J)
LC 77-702341
Introduces musical notation using both live action and animation. Traces the history of musical notation, demonstrates pitch and duration, explains notes and the musical scale and discusses the bass and treble clefs.
Fine Arts
Dist - MCFI **Prod** - NAF 1977

Language of Poetry 30 MIN
U-matic / VHS
Communicating through Literature Series
Color (C)
Literature and Drama
Dist - DALCCD **Prod** - DALCCD

Language of the Bee 15 MIN
VHS / 16mm
Color (J H)
LC FIA66-458
Dr Karl Von Frisch performs some experiments which led to his discovery of the language of the bees. The importance of an active, disciplined curiosity in scientific research is emphasized.
Science; Science - Natural
Dist - MIS **Prod** - MIS 1965

The Language of the Camera Eye 29 MIN
U-matic / VHS / 16mm
Photography - the Incisive Art Series
B&W (H C A)
LC FIA67-5069
Presents Ansel Adams and Beaumont Newhall as they analyze the photographs of Edward Weston, CartierBresson, Edward Steichen, Alfred Stieglitz and others.
Fine Arts; Industrial and Technical Education
Dist - IU **Prod** - NET 1962

Language of the Deaf 16 MIN
16mm / U-matic / VHS
Color (H C A S)
Explores the operation of Gallaudet College, the only liberal arts college in the world for the deaf.
Education; Guidance and Counseling
Dist - CAROUF **Prod** - CBSTV 1977

Language of the Mute Swan 14 MIN
U-matic / VHS / 16mm
Color; B&W (I J H)
LC FIA65-813
Tells the story of the swan from the ritual of courtship and nest building to the emergence of the first cygnet. Includes allusions to the works of Molnar, Hans Christian Anderson and Tchaikovsky.
Science - Natural
Dist - JOU **Prod** - JOU 1965

The Language of war 29 MIN
VHS
America's defense monitor series
Color (J H C G T A)
$25.00 purchase
Explores the impact of language on public debate and public policy, focusing on military - created terminology such as "pre - dawn vertical insertion," "violence processing," and "permanent pre - hostility." Questions whether such language is used to camouflage the reality of war. Interviews combat veterans, military historian Colonel Harry Summers, William Lutz, and others. Produced by Sandy Gottlieb.
Civics and Political Systems; Sociology
Dist - EFVP **Prod** - CDINFO 1990

Language Options 30 MIN
VHS / U-matic
Writing for a Reason Series
Color (C)
English Language
Dist - DALCCD **Prod** - DALCCD

Language Power for Peace 29 MIN
16mm
Big Picture Series
Color
LC 74-705003
Details the story of the Defense Language Institute.
Foreign Language
Dist - USNAC **Prod** - USA

Language Preschool 19 MIN
16mm
Regional Intervention Program Series
Color
LC 75-702410
Depicts preschool activities of the Regional Intervention Program, particularly those associated with language. Shows how the developmentally - delayed child is exposed to group activities and is forced to interact with other children in a variety of work and play situations.
Education; Psychology
Dist - USNAC **Prod** - USBEH 1973

Language Problems in the Schools 26 MIN
16mm
Language - the Social Arbiter Series
Color (H C T)
LC FIA67-5262
English and linguistic educators outline problems faced by teachers in helping children to communicate well in spoken and written standard English.
Education; English Language
Dist - FINLYS **Prod** - FINLYS 1966

Language - Program 7 60 MIN
VHS
Mind series
Color (G)
$69.95 purchase
Presents the seventh program of a nine - part series exploring the human mind. Examines the unique nature of human language, how it evolved, and its importance to thinking.
Psychology
Dist - PBS **Prod** - WNETTV

Language Programming 480 MIN
U-matic / VHS
(A PRO)
$650.00
Introduces all aspects of high and low level language for managers.
Computer Science
Dist - VIDEOT **Prod** - VIDEOT 1988

Language, Pt 7 60 MIN
VHS
Mind Series
Color (H)
$10.00 rental _ #60934
Examines the evolution of language and the particularly human ability for speech. Examines the individual's needs for communication and innate linguistic capacity.
Education; English Language; Social Science
Dist - PSU **Prod** - PBS

Language - puppets with young children 30 MIN
VHS
Calico pie series
Color (C A T)
$69.95 purchase
Presents part two of a 16 - part telecourse for teachers who work with children ages three to five. Discusses how puppets can be used in the classroom. Hosted by Dr Carolyn Dorrell, an early childhood specialist.
Education; Psychology
Dist - SCETV **Prod** - SCETV 1983

Language says it all - communicating with the hearing - impaired child 23 MIN
16mm / VHS
Color; Captioned (H C G)
$500.00, $250.00 purchase, $55.00 rental
Explores the difficulties of raising hearing - impaired children in hearing families. Shows four families understanding and fulfilling their deaf children's need for language and discussing first reactions on learning their child was deaf - one mother reveals how she stopped singing, smiling and talking to her new baby, activities done naturally with her other children. Explains how deafness interferes with normal parenting, causing children to withdraw in isolation and self doubt. In contrast, hearing children born into deaf families find parents who spontaneously know how to communicate. Shows the necessity for hearing family members to learn sign in order to accept the deaf child. Produced by Megan Williams and Rhyena Halpern for Tripod Films.
Education; Guidance and Counseling; Social Science; Sociology
Dist - FLMLIB

Language Taboos - Cultural 30 MIN
U-matic / VHS
Language and Meaning Series
Color (C)
English Language; Psychology
Dist - GPN **Prod** - WUSFTV 1983

Language Taboos - Grammatical 30 MIN
U-matic / VHS
Language and Meaning Series
Color (C)
English Language; Psychology
Dist - GPN **Prod** - WUSFTV 1983

Language Teaching in Context 25 MIN
16mm
Color (C T)
Demonstrates a new method of language teaching which associates objects, actions and events with the words. The context is a simulated foreign world of foreign people going about their affairs.
Education; English Language
Dist - WSUM **Prod** - WSUM 1959

Language techniques for the multi - handicapped learner 6 MIN
16mm
Color
LC 75-701306; 75-701305
Shows how deaf children learn to speak one syllable at a time until they have mastered a short phrase. Illustrates methods involving repetition and the association of pictures with words. Shows the use of tapes and films for individualized instruction.
Education; English Language; Guidance and Counseling
Dist - USNAC **Prod** - USBEH

Language - the social arbiter series

English teaching tomorrow	24 MIN
Language and Integration	28 MIN
Language Problems in the Schools	26 MIN
Linguistics and Education	22 MIN
The Nature of Language	28 MIN
Regional variations	28 MIN
Social Variations	27 MIN

Dist - FINLYS

Language - Thinking, Writing, Communicating Series

Apes and language	30 MIN
Communities of speech	30 MIN
Just Plain English	30 MIN
Language, Learning and Children	30 MIN
Men, Women, and Language	30 MIN
The Rhyme and Reason of Politics	30 MIN
The Shape of Language	30 MIN
The State of English	30 MIN
The Written Word	30 MIN

Dist - MDCPB

Language through Sight and Sound 18 MIN
U-matic / VHS / 16mm
Ways of Hearing Series
Color (C A)
Looks at the total communications (T.C.) philosophy of teaching hearing impaired children language, which advocates that hearing impaired children be encouraged to use all forms of communication in order to develop both receptive and expressive language. Includes sign language and fingerspelling along with auditory - oral training.
Education; Guidance and Counseling; Psychology
Dist - BCNFL **Prod** - BCNFL

Language Without Words 9 MIN
U-matic / VHS / 16mm
BSCS Behavior Film Series
Color
LC 74-701943
Examines a variety of nonverbal methods of communication used by animals, such as wolves, grouse, beavers and Siamese fighting fish.
Science - Natural
Dist - PHENIX **Prod** - BSCS 1974

Languages of the world
CD-ROM
(G) (MULTILINGUAL)
$889.00 purchase _ #2111
Features dictionaries of twelve of the world's most commonly used languages - Chinese, Danish, Dutch, English, Finnish, French, German, Italian, Japanese, Norwegian, Spanish, and Swedish. Enables users to search for translations, definitions, antonyms, synonyms and idioms of over seven million words. Japanese and Chinese terms can be displayed in either Kanji characters or Roman letters. In addition, this disc contains the Comprehensive Dictionary of American Idioms. For IBM PCs and compatibles, requires 640K RAM, DOS 3.1 or later, one floppy disk drive - hard disk recommended, one empty expansion slot, and an IBM compatible CD - ROM drive.
Foreign Language; Literature and Drama
Dist - BEP

Lani and the Sharkman 11 MIN
16mm
Color (J G)
Tells one of the legends of Hawaii from an ancient song that accompanied a hula. It is a tragic love story of a hula dancer and a sharkman.
Geography - United States; History - United States; Literature and Drama; Religion and Philosophy; Sociology
Dist - CINEPC **Prod** - TAHARA 1984

LANL Underground Testing 18 MIN
16mm
Color
LC 81-700290
Shows how data is collected from underground nuclear detonation tests.
Science
Dist - LASL **Prod** - LASL 1980

Lannan literary series

Allen Ginsberg - 2 - 25 - 89	87 MIN
Carlos Fuentes - 10 - 2 - 89	58 MIN
Carolyn Forche - 2 - 12 - 90	59 MIN
Ernesto Cardenal - 1 - 28 - 91	
Joy Harjo - 2 - 18 - 89	57 MIN
Kay Boyle - 9 - 11 - 89	58 MIN
Louise Gluck - 4 - 4 - 88	60 MIN
Lucille Clifton - 6 - 16 - 88	59 MIN
Robert Creeley - 4 - 13 - 90	58 MIN
Victor Hernandez Cruz - 4 - 17 - 89	58 MIN
Yehuda Amichai - 3 - 15 - 89	58 MIN

Dist - POETRY

Lantern Festival
VHS
Color (G) (MANDARIN CHINESE)
$25.00 purchase _ #9020
Presents a Mandarin Chinese language television program produced in the People's Republic of China.
Geography - World; Industrial and Technical Education; Literature and Drama
Dist - CHTSUI **Prod** - CHTSUI

Lanterns 10 MIN
U-matic
Get it together series
Color (P I)
Teaches children how to make a simple lantern from a tin can.
Fine Arts
Dist - TVOTAR **Prod** - TVOTAR 1978

Lanzarote - Land of Parched Earth 22 MIN
VHS / U-matic
Color (J S C G)
MV=$99.00
Exposes the beauty of the land and the lives of the people on one of the volcanic Canary Islands.
Geography - World; History - World
Dist - LANDMK **Prod** - INCAN 1986

Laos - Crossroads of Conflict 19 MIN
U-matic / VHS / 16mm
Color (H C A)
LC 72-703172
Discusses the geography, living habits, culture, history and present - day political conflicts of Laos and its people. Explains that the internationalism of Laos has been going for almost 100 years. Contrasts a legacy from the past with the anxieties of the present.
Civics and Political Systems; Geography - World; History - World; Sociology
Dist - FILCOM **Prod** - SIGMA 1970

Laos - Outpost in Peril 5 MIN
16mm
Screen news digest series
B&W
Explains in depth the free world's stake in the fate and future of Laos. Shows Laotian troops overlooking a bridge blown up by communist rebel guerillas.
Civics and Political Systems; Geography - World; History - World
Dist - HEARST **Prod** - HEARST 1961

Lap joint 4 MIN
BETA / VHS
Welding training - comprehensive - basic shielded metal arc welding series
Color (IND)
Industrial and Technical Education; Psychology
Dist - RMIBHF **Prod** - RMIBHF

Lap Joint V - Down 2 MIN
BETA / VHS
Welding Training (Comprehensive - Metal Inert Gas (M I G Welding 'Series
Color (IND)
Industrial and Technical Education; Psychology
Dist - RMIBHF **Prod** - RMIBHF

Lap Weld 7 MIN
VHS / BETA
Welding Training (Comprehensive - - - Oxy - Acetylene Welding 'Series
Color (IND)
Industrial and Technical Education; Psychology
Dist - RMIBHF **Prod** - RMIBHF

Lap Weld A1 3 MIN
VHS / BETA
Welding Training (Comprehensive - Tungsten Inert Gas (T I G Welding 'Series
Color (IND)
Industrial and Technical Education; Psychology
Dist - RMIBHF **Prod** - RMIBHF

Lap weld E7024 electrode 5 MIN
BETA / VHS
Arc welding and M I G welding series
Color (IND)
Industrial and Technical Education; Psychology
Dist - RMIBHF **Prod** - RMIBHF

Lap weld electrode 6 MIN
BETA / VHS
Arc welding and M I G welding series
Color (IND)
Industrial and Technical Education; Psychology
Dist - RMIBHF **Prod** - RMIBHF

Laparoscopic cholecystectomy 11 MIN
VHS
Color; CC (G C PRO)
$175.00 purchase _ #GS - 10
Explains gallbladder disease and notes that surgical removal of the gallbladder is the only permanent cure. Describes how laparoscopic cholecystectomy has replaced most traditional operations. Contact distributor for purchase price on multiple orders.
Health and Safety
Dist - MIFE **Prod** - MIFE 1995

Laparoscopic cholecystectomy - a patient education program 9 MIN
VHS
Color (G C PRO)
$200.00 purchase, $60.00 rental _ #4325S, #4325V
Educates thoroughly patient, family and nursing staff about the procedure of laparascopic choescystectomy. Uses actual views of the gallbladder through the laparoscope to describe the procedure. Answers common questions about gallstones: who gets them, what the stones are made of, how big they are, what symptoms they produce. Discusses the advantages of the procedure over other surgical methods, including hospital and recovery time, and examines post - operative guidelines. Produced by Dr John S Kennedy.
Health and Safety; Science - Natural
Dist - AJN

Laparoscopic gallbladder removal 45 MIN
VHS
Surgical procedures series
Color (C PRO G)
$149.00 purchase, $75.00 rental _ #UW4573
Shows how laparoscopic gall bladder surgery enables doctors to move around the patient's abdomen while shedding barely a drop of blood. Watches Dr James C Rosser, Jr - Akron General Medical Ctr, Akron, Ohio - use long, delicate instruments to remove a diseased gallbladder, leaving a scar small enough for a band - aid. Part of a 17 - part series recording surgical procedures in detail, with specialists who explain the ailment, the anatomical function of the part of the body being operated on, and how successful surgery might improve the patient's quality of life, hosted by Dr Donna Willis.
Health and Safety
Dist - FOTH

Laparoscopic hernia repair 45 MIN
VHS
Surgical procedures series
Color (C PRO G)
$149.00 purchase, $75.00 rental _ #UW4579
Focuses on laparoscopic surgeon Dr Carlos Gracia who closes a tear in the abdominal wall of a California policeman. Shows him inserting a piece of mesh into the abdomen, then stapling and suturing it, closing the opening of the inguinal hernia. The patient can return home in one day and expect to recover in one to two weeks, compared to open surgery recovery of six to eight weeks. Part of a 17 - part series recording surgical procedures in detail, with specialists who explain the ailment, the anatomical function of the part of the body being operated on, how successful surgery might improve the patient's quality of life. Hosted by Dr Donna Willis.
Health and Safety
Dist - FOTH

Laparoscopically assisted vaginal hysterectomy - LAVH 12 MIN
VHS
Color (G C PRO)
$175.00 purchase _ #OB - 121
Describes how this procedure can provide the benefits of vaginal hysterectomy to women who would otherwise require an abdominal procedure. Explains that all or part of the surgery may be performed through the laparoscope, while the uterus is removed through the vagina. Contact distributor for purchase price on multiple orders.
Health and Safety
Dist - MIFE **Prod** - MIFE

Laparoscopically assisted vaginal hysterectomy - LAVH 12 MIN
VHS
Color (G PRO C)
$250.00 purchase _ #OB - 121
Explains briefly both adominal and vaginal hysterectomies. Describes how laparoscopically assisted vaginal hysterectomy can avoid an abdominal procedure. Addresses common myths and concerns women have about hysterectomy such as sexual function, menopause, possible risks and symptoms to be aware of and when to notify their physicians.
Health and Safety
Dist - MIFE **Prod** - MIFE 1993

Laparoscopy 10 MIN
VHS
5 - part gynecological series
Color (G)
$100.00 purchase, $40.00 rental _ #5307S, #5307V
Demonstrates step - by - step the entire procedure of laparoscopy. Discusses the diagnostic use of laparoscopy and possible complications. Part of a five - part series on gynecology.
Health and Safety
Dist - AJN **Prod** - VMED

Laparoscopy - Refinements in Technique and Anesthesia 16 MIN
16mm
Color (PRO)
Depicts cold - light laparoscopy performed under local anesthesia plus neuroleptanalgesia, a state of psychic indifference.
Health and Safety; Science
Dist - SCITIF **Prod** - SCITIF 1970

Lapis 10 MIN
16mm
Color (J)
LC 75-701555
Presents an abstract art film composed of images produced by an analog computer. Explains the shifting kaleidoscopic patterns, mandalas and starbursts tracing a pattern of mystic meditation, accompanied by the sitar music of Ravi Shankar.
Fine Arts; Industrial and Technical Education
Dist - CFS **Prod** - WHITNY 1966
AFA

Laplace Transforms 38 MIN
U-matic / VHS
Calculus of Differential Equations Series
B&W
Mathematics
Dist - MIOT **Prod** - MIOT

Lapland Journey 13 MIN
16mm
Color
Portrays Sweden's unspoiled wilderness, showing the rich possibilities for relaxation which Norrland offers.
Geography - World; Sociology
Dist - SWNTO **Prod** - SWNTO

The Laplanders 18 MIN
16mm / U-matic / VHS
Color (P I)
Demonstrates how important reindeer are to the economy of the Lapps, providing food, shelter and income. Reveals how the animals still respond to ancient migratory instincts and cover great distances.
Geography - World; Science - Natural; Social Science
Dist - LUF **Prod** - LUF 1979

L'Appapartement 13 MIN
16mm
En France avec Jean et Helene series
B&W (J H C)
LC 73-700110
Foreign Language
Dist - CHLTN **Prod** - PEREN 1967

Lappedykker - Podiceps (Grebe) 5 MIN
16mm
Color
Presents a description of the grebe in its natural surroundings, accompanied by sound effects.
Science - Natural
Dist - STATNS **Prod** - STATNS 1965

Lapping 15 MIN
VHS
Color; PAL (J H IND)
PdS29.50 purchase
Describes the principles of fine lapping. Introduces the manufacturing of plane parallel pieces by using the example of a constant - speed lapping machine.
Industrial and Technical Education
Dist - EMFVL **Prod** - IFFB

Lapplandia 20 MIN
16mm
Color
Shows the rich possibilities of recreation offered to tourists by Lapland's mountains.
Geography - World; Sociology
Dist - SIS **Prod** - SWNTO 1964

The Large and Growly Bear 6 MIN
16mm / U-matic / VHS
Golden Book Storytime Series
Color (P)
Presents the story of a bear who can't scare anyone no matter how hard he tries until one day he scares himself.
Literature and Drama
Dist - CORF **Prod** - CORF 1977

Large Angles and Coordinate Axes 30 MIN
16mm
Trigonometry Series
B&W (H)
Describes trigonometric value of angles larger than 90 degrees. Discusses positive and negative angles, four quadrants of a circle and coordinates of a point. Explains methods of reducing large angles to equivalent smaller ones for use in trigonometric tables.
Mathematics
Dist - MLA **Prod** - CALVIN 1959

Large Animals of the Arctic 22 MIN
U-matic / VHS / 16mm
White Wildernes
Color (I J H) (PORTUGUESE NORWEGIAN DUTCH GERMAN SWEDISH)
Shows the relationship between the Arctic grass - eaters and the carnivores who prey on them.
Foreign Language; Science - Natural
Dist - CORF **Prod** - DISNEY 1963

Large Animals that Once Roamed the Plains 12 MIN
16mm / U-matic / VHS
Vanishing Prairie
Color (I J H) (SWEDISH GERMAN NORWEGIAN)
Glimpses the pronghorn antelope, bighorn sheep, cougar and other large animals that once roamed the American plains in large numbers but have now virtually disappeared.
Foreign Language; Science - Natural
Dist - CORF **Prod** - DISNEY 1963

Large Appliances 30 MIN
VHS / U-matic
Consumer Survival Series
Color
Presents tips on the purchase and care of large appliances.
Home Economics
Dist - MDCPB **Prod** - MDCPB

Large Bowel Obstruction 22 MIN
16mm
Color (PRO)
Discusses the problem of large bowel obstruction due primarily to carcinoma. Presents the indications for the various forms of treatment in relation to the site of obstruction, the competence or incompetence of the ileocecal valve and other pertinent factors.
Health and Safety; Science
Dist - ACY **Prod** - ACYDGD 1960

Large Business Film A 20 MIN
U-matic / VHS / 16mm
Job Interview - Whom would You Hire Series
Color (J H)
$430 purchase - 16 mm, $320 purchase - video
Shows job applicants from the point of view of the employer at a large business firm. A Dimension Film. Directed by Gary Goldsmith.
Business and Economics; Psychology
Dist - CF

Large Equipment
VHS
Color (G)
$89.95 purchase _ #6 - 300 - 302P
Emphasizes the danger of working around large landscaping equipment. Shows how to minimize risk. Uses the back hoe to demonstrate principles of familiarity with the equipment, the importance of operator training and the risks caused by modifying large equipment.
Agriculture; Health and Safety
Dist - VEP **Prod** - VEP

Large Group Instruction 28 MIN
16mm
Innovations in Education Series
Color
Dr Dwight Allen, professor of education at Stanford University, analyzes the effective use of large group instruction, discussing techniques, types and presentation modes.
Education
Dist - EDUC **Prod** - STNFRD 1966

Large metal power tools 45 MIN
VHS
Safety and operation series
Color (H A T)

$79.95 purchase _ #CV992
Discusses safety and proper operating procedures for the drill press, metal shear, abrasive cut - off machine, horizontal metal cutting band saw, grinder. Shows sharpening techniques for a twist drill, wood chisel, metal cold chisel, wood hatchet, grinding techniques for mushroom head on a metal punch and clawhammer and techniques for dressing a grinder wheel with a star type wheel dresser. Features Dr Bill Jowell of Sam Houston State University.
Health and Safety; Industrial and Technical Education
Dist - AAVIM **Prod** - AAVIM 1992

Large Numbers 15 MIN
U-matic / VHS
Math Matters Series
Color (I J)
Explains how to write and punctuate large numbers correctly.
Mathematics
Dist - AITECH **Prod** - STETVC 1975

Large Numbers 15 MIN
U-matic
Mathematical Relationship Series
Color (I)
Relates large number concepts to experience to help overcome the vagueness that surrounds them.
Education; Mathematics
Dist - TVOTAR **Prod** - TVOTAR 1982

The Large Passion 14 MIN
16mm
B&W
Features the final episodes of the life of Christ as it is captured by Albrecht Durer who grasped the importance of the medium of copperplate engraving, which was the artistic equivalent of printing.
Fine Arts; Religion and Philosophy
Dist - RADIM **Prod** - FILIM

Large scale asbestos removal operations 25 MIN
BETA / VHS / U-matic
Color (IND G)
$495.00 purchase _ #820 - 34
Explains procedures to be followed during large scale asbestos abatement projects. Describes how the area is prepared for asbestos removal, control measures used to minimize release of asbestos fibers, respiratory protection, personal protective equipment, asbestos removal, disposal and decontamination procedures.
Business and Economics; Health and Safety; Industrial and Technical Education; Psychology
Dist - ITSC **Prod** - ITCORP

Large scale visual arts workshop 25 MIN
VHS
Color (G C PRO)
$85.00 purchase, $45.00 rental
Demonstrates wall banners, murals and other decorative items that can be made by older residential - care patients using an overhead projector and simple art supplies. For residential - home activity directors. Package includes video and instruction booklet with reproducible ideas.
Health and Safety
Dist - TNF

Large Toys 25 MIN
VHS / U-matic
Blizzard's Wonderful Wooden Toys Series
Color (H C A)
Shows how to build a wagon and introduces a handbuilt rocking animal and a large toy crane.
Fine Arts
Dist - FI **Prod** - BBCTV

Large transformers - protective - devices and routine maintenance 60 MIN
U-matic / VHS
Electrical equipment maintenance series; Tape 1
Color (IND) (SPANISH)
Foreign Language; Industrial and Technical Education
Dist - ITCORP **Prod** - ITCORP

A Large Utility - Indiana Bell Telephone Company 20 MIN
VHS / U-matic
Clues to Career Opportunities for Liberal Arts Graduates Series
Color (C A)
LC 79-706054
Presents an interview with a representative from Indiana Bell Telephone Company. Enumerates the various jobs available to college graduates with liberal arts backgrounds in large, specialized companies.
Psychology
Dist - IU **Prod** - IU 1978

The Large White Butterfly 10 MIN
16mm
Color (P I J H)
Presents the life cycle of the large white butterfly from the pairing of the male and female to the emergence of the adult insect.
Science - Natural
Dist - VIEWTH **Prod** - GATEEF

Large wood power tools - I 35 MIN
VHS
Safety and operation series
Color (H A T)
$79.95 purchase _ #CV993
Discusses safety and proper operating procedures for the table saw, drill press, disc and belt sander. Shows how to make mitre cuts at different angles, ripping, crosscutting and making dado and rabbet cuts with the table saw. Features Charles Jedlicka.
Health and Safety; Industrial and Technical Education
Dist - AAVIM **Prod** - AAVIM 1992

Large wood power tools - II 35 MIN
VHS
Safety and operation series
Color (H A T)
$79.95 purchase _ #CV994
Discusses safety and proper operating procedures for the jointer, planer, radial arm saw and vertical band saw. Shows how to make mitre cuts at different angles, ripping and crosscutting with a radial arm saw. Features Charles Jedlicka.
Health and Safety; Industrial and Technical Education
Dist - AAVIM **Prod** - AAVIM 1992

Largemouth I 60 MIN
VHS
Color
Reveals the secrets of cattail bass, bull rushing the bass, coping with a cold front, and the underwater lures.
Physical Education and Recreation; Science - Natural
Dist - HOMEAF **Prod** - HOMEAF

Largemouth II 60 MIN
VHS
Color
Teaches the unique combination of rice and bass, flipping timber bass, boat deck bass, frog run bassing and jig and pig bass.
Physical Education and Recreation; Science - Natural
Dist - HOMEAF **Prod** - HOMEAF

Larks on a string 96 MIN
VHS / 35mm
Color (G) (CZECH WITH ENGLISH SUBTITLES)
$350.00 rental
Presents a wry comedy about a group of bourgeois dissidents who are inducted into the communist order as 'voluntary laborers' in a small town junk yard. Directed by Jiri Monzel.
Civics and Political Systems; Fine Arts
Dist - KINOIC **Prod** - IFEX 1990

Larnyx and Voice Series
Physiology of the Larynx Under Daily Stress 23 MIN
Dist - ILAVD

Laroussie the Saddlemaker 25 MIN
16mm / U-matic / VHS
World Cultures and Youth Series
Color (J)
Introduces a Moroccan boy named Laroussie who works as a brass and copper apprentice in his father's shop in the city of Fez. Reveals that the boy's true love is horses and that when an uncle provides him with the opportunity to make a saddle for an upcoming festival, Laroussie's father permits him to learn this new craft.
Geography - World; Sociology
Dist - CORF **Prod** - SUNRIS 1981

L'Arrivee a Paris 11 MIN
16mm / U-matic / VHS
B&W (H) (FRENCH)
A French language film. Follows the activities of two U S college students, who have come to Paris to study at the Sorbonne.
Foreign Language
Dist - IFB **Prod** - FFC 1951

Larry - an Amputee's Story 57 MIN
U-matic / VHS
Color (PRO)
Helps amputees, families and their health care providers cope with the special problems amputation brings.
Health and Safety; Psychology
Dist - HSCIC **Prod** - HSCIC 1984

Larry Eigner - 11 - 29 - 84
VHS / Cassette
Poetry Center reading series
Color (G)
$15.00, $45.00 purchase, $15.00 rental _ #608 - 515
Features the 1993 Poetry Center Book Award winner reading from his works at the Poetry Center, San Francisco State University.
Literature and Drama
Dist - POETRY

Larry Fagin 29 MIN
U-matic
Poets Talking Series
Color
Literature and Drama
Dist - UMITV **Prod** - UMITV 1975

Larry Fagin - 4 - 27 - 77 40 MIN
VHS / Cassette
Poetry Center reading series
B&W (G)
#256 - 209
Features the writer reading his works at the Poetry Center, San Francisco State University. Available only for listening purposes at the Center; not for sale or rent.
Literature and Drama
Dist - POETRY **Prod** - POETRY 1977

Larry Golsh 29 MIN
VHS / U-matic
American Indian artist series
Color (G)
Profiles Larry Golsh's artistry in gold and precious stones. Talks about himself as an artist and as an Indian in the art world. Discusses the ways his Indian heritage and his family have influenced his work.
Fine Arts; Social Science
Dist - NAMPBC **Prod** - NAMPBC 1982

Larry Goodell - 5 - 8 - 75 27 MIN
VHS / Cassette
Poetry Center reading series
Color (G)
$15.00, $45.00 purchase, $15.00 rental _ #126 - 97
Features the writer at the Poetry Center at San Francisco State University, reading selections from his books, The Staff Of Ometeotl; The Bowl of Ometeotl; The Book of Ometeotl; A Garden Of Ourselves; The Face Of Velma; and Dried Apricots. Includes an introduction by Kathleen Fraser.
Literature and Drama
Dist - POETRY **Prod** - POETRY 1975

Larry Gottheim series
Machete Gillette...Mama 45 MIN
Mnemosyne mother of muses 18 MIN
The Red thread 15 MIN
Dist - PARART

Larry Lebby and stone lithography 7 MIN
VHS / U-matic
Color (G A)
$35.00, $80.00 purchase _ #TCA13053, #TCA13052
Features Larry Lebby in an examination of the art of stone lithography. Discusses subjects including origins of the art, medium composition, choice of mediums, the process of creation, and more.
Fine Arts; Industrial and Technical Education
Dist - USNAC **Prod** - SMITHS 1983

Larry, Mr Jenkins and the Antique Car 15 MIN
16mm / U-matic / VHS
Creative Writing Series
Color (I J)
LC 73-700504
Presents three totally different stories about the same characters to provide a base for introducing story evaluation, as well as training in effective listening and speaking.
English Language
Dist - AIMS **Prod** - MORLAT 1972

The Larry P Case 30 MIN
U-matic / VHS
Law and Handicapped Children in School
Color (C A)
LC 79-706358
Reviews the background, content and progress of the Larry P versus Riles case, a class action suit brought by parents of Black children in the San Francisco school district to end the use of culturally biased IQ testing for placement.
Civics and Political Systems; Education; Psychology
Dist - IU **Prod** - IU 1979

Larry Rivers 28 MIN
16mm / VHS
Color (H C)
$600.00, $190.00 purchase, $75.00 rental; $600.00, $190.00 purchase, $75.00 rental
Portrays Larry Rivers, the artist, at work in his New York studio looking at some of his earlier works.
Fine Arts
Dist - BLACKW **Prod** - BLACKW 1973

Lars - Erik Magnusson - Larmag Investment Group, Amsterdam, Holland 47 MIN
VHS
Tycoons series
Color (J H G)
$225.00 purchase
Tells how cattle herdsman Lars - Erik Magnusson of Sweden became wealthy by investing in real estate, oil, and shopping centers among other activities.
Business and Economics
Dist - LANDMK

Larval Forms 20 MIN
U-matic / VHS
Color
Introduces roles that various larval forms play in the life cycle of both vertebrates and invertebrates. Includes such topics as planktonic larvae of erastaceans to the tadpoles of amphibians. Video version of 35mm filmstrip program, with live open and close.
Science - Natural
Dist - CBSC **Prod** - REXERC

Laryngectomy and Neck Dissection 22 MIN
16mm
Color (C)
LC FIA65-814
Demonstrates operative techniques of laryngectomy and radical neck dissection. Shows new closure and drainage procedures on dogs and humans. Closes with a dialogue between two laryngectomy patients using esophageal speech.
Health and Safety
Dist - OSUMPD **Prod** - OSUMPD 1964

Laryngectomy - Information for the Postoperative Patient 15 MIN
VHS / U-matic / BETA
(G PRO)
Portrays physical and emotional adjustments necessary after a laryngectomy.
Health and Safety
Dist - UTXAH **Prod** - UTXAH 1984

Laryngectomy - what it Means to You 34 MIN
U-matic / VHS
Color (A)
Discusses the implications of a total laryngectomy, including Medical and Surgical Aspects, Speech Without A Larynx, Physical Changes, Social And Emotional Adjustment and Marital and Family Adjustment.
English Language; Health and Safety; Science - Natural
Dist - USNAC **Prod** - VAMCNY 1984

The Larynx 17 MIN
VHS / U-matic
Anatomy of the head and neck series
Color (PRO C)
$395.00 purchase, $80.00 rental _ #C901 - VI - 070
Uses models to describe the skeletal framework of the larynx, with emphasis placed on the arytenoid cartilages. Uses prosected specimens and diagrams to demonstrate the main laryngeal muscles, the course and distribution of the recurrent and superior laryngeal nerves and the laryngeal vessels. Part of a series on head and neck anatomy produced by Shakti Chandra, Faculty of Medicine, University of Newfoundland.
Health and Safety; Science - Natural
Dist - HSCIC

The Larynx 86 MIN
U-matic
Head and Neck Anatomy Series
Color (PRO)
LC 78-706038
Explains the larynx and surrounding structures, including vocal cords, internal anatomy, arteries, veins and fascia. Discusses the function of deglutition and phonation in health and disease.
Science - Natural
Dist - USNAC **Prod** - NMAC 1976

The Larynx 13 MIN
U-matic / VHS / 16mm
Guides to Dissection Series
Color (C A)
Focuses on the head and neck. Demonstrates the dissection of the larynx.
Health and Safety; Science - Natural
Dist - TEF **Prod** - UCLA

Larynx, the, Pt 1 43 MIN
U-matic
Head and Neck Anatomy Series
Color (PRO)
LC 78-706038
Explains the larynx and surrounding structures, including vocal cords, internal anatomy, arteries, veins and fascia. Discusses the function of deglutition and phonation in health and disease.
Health and Safety; Science - Natural
Dist - USNAC **Prod** - NMAC 1976

Larynx, the, Pt 2 43 MIN
U-matic
Head and Neck Anatomy Series
Color (PRO)
LC 78-706038
Explains the larynx and surrounding structures, including vocal cords, internal anatomy, arteries, veins and fascia. Discusses the function of deglutition and phonation in health and disease.
Health and Safety; Science - Natural
Dist - USNAC **Prod** - NMAC 1976

Larynx - Unit 7 11 MIN
U-matic / VHS
Gross Anatomy Prosection Demonstration Series
Color (PRO)
Discusses the intrinsic muscles of the larynx including the arytemoideus, aryepiglotticus, cricoarytenoideus, thyroarytenoideus, cricothyroideus, thyroepiglotticus, as well as the folds in the mucosa of the larynx.
Health and Safety; Science - Natural
Dist - HSCIC **Prod** - HSCIC

Las Actividades - the Activities, Film A 15 MIN
16mm
Spanish for You Series Unit 5
Color (I J)
Foreign Language
Dist - MLA **Prod** - LINGUA 1965

Las Actividades - the Activities, Film B 15 MIN
16mm
Spanish for You Series Unit 5
Color (I J)
Foreign Language
Dist - MLA **Prod** - LINGUA 1965

Las Aventuras de Mafalda - Volume 1 60 MIN
VHS
Color (G) (SPANISH)
$39.95 purchase _ #W1754
Highlights linguistic characteristics of various regions through the cartoon adventures of a group of young people who view adults with a touch of humour. Video has 12 five - minute segments. Companion books are available separately.
Foreign Language
Dist - GPC

Las Aventuras de Mafalda - Volume 2 60 MIN
VHS
Color (G) (SPANISH)
$39.95 purchase _ #1755
Presents the adventures of cartoon character Mafalda and her friends, as they view the oddly humorous world of adults. Video has 12 five - minute segments based on various regional speech patterns. Companion books are available separately.
Foreign Language
Dist - GPC

Las Aventuras de Mafalda - Volumes 1 and 2 120 MIN
VHS
Color (G) (SPANISH)
$73.00 purchase _ #1756
Combines volumes 1 and 2 in a set. Shows the cartoon adventures of Mafalda and her friends as they view the adult world. Two videos contain a total of 24 five - minute lessons using various regional accents. Companion books are available separately.
Foreign Language
Dist - GPC

Las Flores - 14 15 MIN
VHS
Amigos Series
Color (K) (SPANISH)
$125.00 purchase
Enables teachers with no knowledge of Spanish to introduce basic words to children in kindergarten through second grade. Uses simple concepts and music and features Perro Pepe, a six - foot orange dog, and Senorita Fernandez as instructors. Promotes awareness of and appreciation for Hispanic culture and sparks interest in the geography of Spanish - speaking countries. Part 14 is entitled 'Las Flores.'.
Foreign Language; Geography - World
Dist - AITECH

Las Formas - 28 15 MIN
VHS
Amigos Series
Color (K) (SPANISH)
$125.00 purchase
Enables teachers with no knowledge of Spanish to introduce basic words to children in kindergarten through second grade. Uses simple concepts and music and features Perro Pepe, a six - foot orange dog, and Senorita Fernandez as instructors. Promotes awareness of and appreciation for Hispanic culture and sparks interest in the geography of Spanish - speaking countries. Part 28 is entitled 'Las Formas.'.
Foreign Language; Geography - World
Dist - AITECH

Las Madres - the mothers of Plaza de Mayo 64 MIN
16mm / VHS
Color (G)
$90.00, $125.00 rental, $295.00 purchase
Documents the Argentinian mothers' movement to demand to know the fate of 30,000 'disappeared' sons and daughters. Shows the empowerment of women in a society where women are expected to be silent and gives an understanding of Argentinian history in the 1970s and '80s.
Civics and Political Systems; Fine Arts; Sociology
Dist - WMEN **Prod** - MUNPOR 1985

Las Muchas Caras De Mexico 17 MIN
U-matic / VHS / 16mm
Mexican Heritage
Color (SPANISH)
LC 76-703913
A Spanish language version of The Many Faces of Mexico. Shows facets of the Mexican land and people.
Foreign Language; Geography - World; History - World
Dist - FI **Prod** - STEXMF 1976

Las Partes Del Cuerpo, Pt 1 - the Parts of the Body, Pt 1 15 MIN
VHS / U-matic
Saludos
(P I G) (ENGLISH AND SPANISH)
$130.00 purchase, $25.00 rental, $75.00 self dub
Designed to introduce Spanish to the English speaking student at primary through intermediate levels. Eighteenth in a 25 part series.
Foreign Language
Dist - GPN

Las Partes Del Cuerpo, Pt 2 - the Parts of the Body, PT 2 15 MIN
U-matic / VHS
Saludos
(P I G) (ENGLISH AND SPANISH)
$130.00 purchase, $25.00 rental, $75.00 self dub
Designed to introduce Spanish to the English speaking student at primary through intermediate levels. Nineteenth in a 25 part series.
Foreign Language
Dist - GPN

Las Primeras Ciudades De Los EEUU 52 MIN
U-matic / VHS
Espana Estuvo Alli Series
Color (C) (SPANISH)
$249.00, $149.00 purchase _ #AD - 1025
Focuses on St Augustine, Florida, and Sante Fe, New Mexico. Dramatizes Coronado's expedition. In Spanish.
Civics and Political Systems; Geography - World; History - United States; History - World
Dist - FOTH **Prod** - FOTH

Las Vegas, Your Best Bet 14 MIN
16mm
Color
LC 75-703106
Discusses the advantages of Las Vegas and of holding conventions there.
Business and Economics; Geography - United States
Dist - MCDO **Prod** - MCDO 1974

The LaSalle String Quartet, Pt I 30 MIN
Videoreel / VHS
LaSalle String Quartet Series
Color
Presents the LaSalle String Quartet using a set of instruments built by Nicolo Amati in the 1600s and performing Penderecki's 'Quartetto per archi', a composition which alters the normal sound of the instruments.
Fine Arts
Dist - NETCHE **Prod** - NETCHE 1970

The LaSalle String Quartet, Pt II 30 MIN
Videoreel / VHS
LaSalle String Quartet Series
Color
Uses Penderecki's 'Quartetto per archi', as a starting point for further exploration of modern composition.
Fine Arts
Dist - NETCHE **Prod** - NETCHE 1970

LaSalle String Quartet Series
The LaSalle String Quartet, Pt I 30 MIN
The LaSalle String Quartet, Pt II 30 MIN
Dist - NETCHE

Lascaux, Cradle of Man's Art 17 MIN
U-matic / VHS / 16mm
Color (H C A)
Photographs of the paintings by pre - historic man in the Lascaux Cave in southern France, first discovered in 1940. Also shows some of the important sites in the neighborhood and tells briefly something of prehistoric man.
Fine Arts; History - World; Science - Natural
Dist - IFB Prod - CHAP 1950

Lascaux - Cradle of Man's Art 17 MIN
16mm / U-matic / VHS
Color (I)
Explores the prehistoric wall paintings in the Lascaux cave of France.
Fine Arts; History - World; Sociology
Dist - IFB Prod - IFB 1952

Lascaux Treasures 15 MIN
U-matic / VHS
Color (H C A)
Uses documentary footage of the original prehistoric cave - paintings at Lascaux in southwest France to explain the importance of the site of an exact replica which is being built by international art experts.
Fine Arts; Geography - World
Dist - JOU Prod - JOU

The Laser 12 MIN
16mm
Color (I)
Explains the physics of light - the atom which emits it, radian energy, wave lengths and frequencies. Uses a solid - state ruby laser to demonstrate how it can generate an intense coherent beam of monochromatic light.
Science - Physical
Dist - SF Prod - SF 1967

Laser 11 MIN
16mm
Color
LC 79-701044
Enumerates the various ways in which lasers are used in communication, medicine and other fields.
Health and Safety; Industrial and Technical Education; Science; Science - Physical; Social Science
Dist - MGS Prod - ATAT 1979

The Laser - a Light Fantastic 30 MIN
Videoreel / VT1
Twenty - First Century Series
Color
Shows how the laser beam will some day be used as often and as easily as 20th century man now uses electricity.
Science; Science - Physical
Dist - MTP Prod - UCC

The Laser - a Light Fantastic 21 MIN
16mm / U-matic / VHS
Color (J)
LC FIA68-748
Shows the laser and explains how all the light waves travel simultaneously in exactly the same direction and at exactly the same frequency. Discusses the functions of the laser, such as making precise measurements, melting and welding metals, diamonds and other materials, communication, surgery and even to produce a new sort of three - dimensional image, called a hologram.
Business and Economics; Science - Physical
Dist - PHENIX Prod - CBSTV 1968

Laser and micro surgery 10 MIN
VHS
Infertility series
Color (G PRO C)
$150.00 purchase _ #SN - 337
Explores the use of laser and micro surgery in cases of female infertility. Part of a four - part series on infertility.
Health and Safety; Sociology
Dist - MIFE Prod - HOSSN

Laser Beam, the 20 MIN
16mm / U-matic / VHS
Color (H C A)
Uses animation to explain the laser process. Shows some of the applications of lasers in medicine, industry, communications, space exploration and holograms.
Industrial and Technical Education; Science - Physical
Dist - HANDEL Prod - HANDEL 1982

Laser capsulotomy 9 MIN
VHS
Color (G PRO C) (SPANISH)
$200.00 purchase _ #EY - 16
Describes the use of neodymium - YAG laser in the outpatient treatment of secondary cataracts. Helps patients to understand why the treatment has been recommended and explains the procedure, its benefits and operative and post - operative complications. Reviews patient compliance.
Health and Safety; Science - Natural
Dist - MIFE Prod - MIFE

Laser disc technology in the courtroom
VHS
Color (C PRO)
$99.95 purchase _ #FVZO70S
Outlines ways in which laser disc technology can be used in the courtroom. Suggests that the technology allows attorneys to quickly gain access to relevant materials, and makes transporting evidence easier. Deals with possible objections to its use.
Civics and Political Systems; Industrial and Technical Education
Dist - NITA Prod - NITA 1990

Laser Drilling 8 MIN
VHS / U-matic
Manufacturing Materials and Processes Series
Color
Shows how laser drilling works, the components, advantages and disadvantages.
Industrial and Technical Education
Dist - WFVTAE Prod - GE

Laser Fusion 18 MIN
16mm
Color
LC 78-700288
Explains the techniques and principles of the laser fusion program under development at the Los Alamos Scientific Laboratory. Discusses high - power lasers and describes future laser systems and conceptual laser fusion generating stations.
Industrial and Technical Education
Dist - LASL Prod - LASL 1977

A Laser Images Demonstration 10 MIN
16mm
Color (H C)
LC 77-714318
Uses argon, krypton and helium neon gas lasers to create multi - colored abstract patterns that flow to the accompaniment of electronic, rock and classical music.
Fine Arts; Industrial and Technical Education
Dist - CFS Prod - LASER 1971

Laser learning set 1 series
Presents Set 1 of a series of six theme - based interactive videodisc lessons. Requires a Pioneer LD - V2000 or 2200, with barcode reader and adapter, or a Pioneer LD - V4200 or higher. Includes the titles Jane Goodall and the Chimpanzees, The Gold Bug - Parts 1 and 2, First by Balloon, One Man Alone, and Woman With a Paintbrush. Includes user's guide, two readers for each lesson.
First by balloon
The Gold bug - Part 1
The Gold bug - Part 2
Jane Goodall and the chimpanzees
One man alone
Woman with a brush
Dist - BARR Prod - BARR 1971

Laser learning set 3 series
Presents Set 3 of a series of six theme - based interactive videodisc lessons. Requires a Pioneer LD - V2000 or 2200, with barcode reader and adapter, or a Pioneer LD - V4200 or higher. Includes the titles - The Winter of Despair, Magic Is..., Marvelous Mollusks, The Arctic's Timeless Challenge, The Magicians of Basketball, and Sizing up Sharks. Includes user's guide and two readers for each lesson.
The Arctic's timeless challenge
Magic is
The Magicians of basketball
Marvelous mollusks
Sizing up sharks
The Winter of despair
Dist - BARR Prod - BARR 1971

Laser learning set 2 series
Presents Set 2 of a series of six theme - based interactive videodisc lessons. Requires a Pioneer LD - V2000 or 2200, with barcode reader and adapter, or a Pioneer LD - V4200 or higher. Includes the titles Revolution - How It Began, Music That Won't Stand Still, To See the Summer Sky, From the Earth to the Moon, and Threatened. Includes user's guide and two readers for each lesson.
From the Earth to the Moon
Making things move
Music that won't stand still
Revolution - how it began
Threatened
To see the summer sky
Dist - BARR Prod - BARR 1971

Laser light therapy 11 MIN
16mm / VHS / U-matic
Color (A)
Describes how photocoagulation assists in treatment of diabetic and vascular retinopathies and macular diseases. Emphasizes general principles, benefits, limitations and complications.
Health and Safety; Industrial and Technical Education; Science - Natural
Dist - PRORE Prod - PRORE

Laser Physics 30 MIN
16mm
B&W (H C A)
LC 74-700173
Features Dr Marvin Hass, a research physicist at the U S Naval Research Laboratory in Washington, DC, who discusses the fundamentals of laser operation and simulated emission of radiation. Presents experiments using a high - power continuous argonion laser and a high resolution double grating spectrometer.
Science; Science - Physical
Dist - UNEBR Prod - UNL 1970

Laser Safety 11 MIN
16mm
Color
LC 75-703697
Describes hazards involved in the use of lasers. Shows how an eye injury can result either from direct or reflected exposure to laser beams and how fires result when flammable materials are pierced by laser beams. Explains safety precautions to be exercised by technicians using lasers.
Health and Safety; Science - Natural; Science - Physical
Dist - USNAC Prod - NASA 1973

Laser safety 18 MIN
VHS
Color (C G) (FRENCH)
$195.00 purchase, $40.00 rental _ #37239
Illustrates the hazards involved in using lasers. Shows safety techniques to prevent injuries to eyes and skin. Produced by Barry Pollack, Stanford University.
Health and Safety; Industrial and Technical Education
Dist - UCEMC

Laser Scanning of Active Semiconductor Devices 55 MIN
U-matic
Color
Presents new and powerful applications for laser scanning in semiconductor device design and reliability work.
Business and Economics; Industrial and Technical Education; Science - Physical
Dist - MTP Prod - USNBOS

Laser surgery 30 MIN
VHS
Perspectives - health and medicine - series
Color; PAL; NTSC (G)
PdS90, PdS105 purchase
Shows how a laser is used to cut a malignant tumor out of the brain.
Health and Safety; Industrial and Technical Education
Dist - CFLVIS Prod - LONTVS

Laser surgery for angle closure glaucoma 7 MIN
VHS
Color (G PRO C) (SPANISH)
$100.00 purchase _ #EY - 12
Educates and reassures patients scheduled to have laser surgery for angle closure glaucoma. Explains both the Argon and YAG lasers. Covers the advantages, risks and side effects of laser surgery.
Health and Safety; Science - Natural
Dist - MIFE Prod - MIFE

Laser surgery for open angle glaucoma 6 MIN
VHS
Color (G PRO C) (SPANISH)
$100.00 purchase _ #EY - 11
Reassures patients by explaining in detail how the physician will use the Argon laser to treat open angle glaucoma. Covers the procedure, advantages and risks along with post - operative side effects.
Health and Safety; Science - Natural
Dist - MIFE Prod - MIFE

Laser surgery of the cervix 10 MIN
VHS
Color (G PRO C) (SPANISH)
$250.00 purchase _ #OB - 89
Explains that laser surgery can be used to treat abnormal cells in the cervix, vagina and vulva. Shows how the colposcope is used in combination with the laser to destroy abnormal cells without damaging surrounding

health tissue. Discusses types of anesthesia that may be used, advantages and risks of the procedure and post surgery self - care. Recommends that the patient continue to see her physician regularly.
Health and Safety; Sociology
Dist - MIFE **Prod** - MIFE

Laser - the Light of the Future 30 MIN
16mm / U-matic / VHS
Experiment Series
Color; B&W (J)
Illustrates theoretical principles involved in laser light and documents how these principles were applied by scientists to produce the first laser. Demonstrates working lasers and their uses.
Science; Science - Physical
Dist - IU **Prod** - PRISM 1966

Laserblast 85 MIN
U-matic / VHS / 16mm
Color
Tells how a young man wears a pendant found from another world and soon finds that his will is being subjugated.
Fine Arts
Dist - FI **Prod** - UNKNWN 1978

Laserdisc learning series
The Adventures of Robin Hood
The Diary of Anne Frank
Excalibur
Good - bye my lady
The Grapes of wrath
The Great Gatsby
The Outsiders
Romeo and Juliet
Sounder
To kill a mockingbird
Twelve angry men
Dist - BARR

Laserimage 10 MIN
16mm
Color (P)
LC 77-701094
Introduces a new visual medium in which organic images generated from helium - neon and argon gas lasers convolute, evolve, burst and fuse into rhythms. Depicts cosmic flowers, electronic plasmas, cellular galaxies and primordial atoms.
Industrial and Technical Education; Science - Physical
Dist - CFS **Prod** - DRYER 1972

Lasers 29 MIN
VHS / 16mm
Discovery Digest Series
Color (S)
$300.00 purchase _ #707607
Explores a vast array of science - related discoveries, challenges and technological breakthroughs. Profiles and 'demystifies' research and development currently underway in many fields. Examines the use of lasers for cutting, communicating and fusing the atom.
Industrial and Technical Education; Psychology; Science; Science - Physical
Dist - ACCESS **Prod** - ACCESS 1989

Lasers 30 MIN
U-matic
Fast Forward Series
Color (H C)
Explains what lasers are and how they work and speculates on future refinements of the technology. Looks at some of the abilities of laser energy, a form of amplified light.
Computer Science; Industrial and Technical Education; Science
Dist - TVOTAR **Prod** - TVOTAR 1979

Lasers 22 MIN
VHS / U-matic
Color (I J H A)
Explores uses of lasers while surveying this widely applied technology. Uses dramatic animation to explain what lasers are and how they function.
Industrial and Technical Education
Dist - NGS **Prod** - NGS

Lasers - an Introduction 13 MIN
16mm / U-matic / VHS
Color (J)
$325.00, $235.00 purchase _ #3138
Explains laser operation, discrete spectra stimulation of atoms, and resonance.
Science - Physical
Dist - CORF

Lasers - an Introduction 13 MIN
U-matic / VHS / 16mm
Color (J)
Illustrates principles of laser operation, including concepts of coherent and incoherent light, continuous and discrete spectra, stimulation of atoms and resonance. Shows gaseous and crystalline lasers to be valuable tools in holography, communications, medicine and industry.
Science; Science - Physical
Dist - CORF **Prod** - CORF 1970

Lasers and Your Eyes 12 MIN
16mm
Color (IND)
LC 79-700052
Uses animation to explain lasers and their danger to the eyes. Describes the proper protective eye wear to be used in laser laboratories.
Health and Safety; Industrial and Technical Education
Dist - LASL **Prod** - LASL 1979

Lasers - Brighter than the sun 45 MIN
VHS / U-matic
Color (H G)
$280.00, $330.00 purchase, $60.00 rental
Looks at the special nature of laser light and its myriad uses in the areas of medicine, art, engineering and communications. Traces its invention in 1960, when it was little more than a curiosity, to the present, now an indispensable tool that has revolutionized all of life. Covers fiber optic and CD - ROM technology.
Industrial and Technical Education; Sociology
Dist - NDIM **Prod** - CANBC 1992

Lasers for eyes 26 MIN
VHS
Color (G)
$149.00 purchase, $75.00 rental _ #UW2356
Covers the five principal areas in which laser surgery is making important contributions - cataracts, macular degeneration, glaucoma, retinal tears, diabetic retinopathy. Explains what each area is and how it is repaired by laser surgery. Warns of potential dangers.
Health and Safety; Science - Natural
Dist - FOTH

Lasers from space 25 MIN
VHS
Sparky's animation series
Color (P I R)
$19.95 purchase, $10.00 rental _ #35 - 816 - 2020
Shows how Sparky and his friends make it through a solar energy accident. Suggests that they experience God's love and protection through the experience.
Literature and Drama; Religion and Philosophy
Dist - APH **Prod** - ANDERK

Lasers in manufacturing 35 MIN
VHS / 16mm
Manufacturing insights series
Color (A IND)
$200.00, $190.00 purchase _ #VT242, #VT242U
Shows how lasers can make welding, machining, gauging, and marking operations easier.
Business and Economics; Industrial and Technical Education
Dist - SME **Prod** - SME 1986

Lasers in manufacturing - a new look 26 MIN
VHS / 16mm
Manufacturing insights series
Color (A IND)
$200.00, $190.00 purchase _ #VT242, #VT242U
Shows how lasers are used for cutting, welding, drilling, heat treating, cladding, and scribing.
Business and Economics; Industrial and Technical Education
Dist - SME **Prod** - SME 1986

Lasers - the Light Fantastic 30 MIN
U-matic / VHS
Innovation Series
Color
Describes the variety of uses for lasers. Shows physicians using lasers to perform delicate eye surgery and discusses the scores of industrial uses.
Health and Safety; Industrial and Technical Education
Dist - PBS **Prod** - WNETTV 1985

Lasers - the Light Fantastic 26 MIN
U-matic / VHS
Color (C)
$249.00, $149.00 purchase _ #AD - 1979
Describes what lasers are and how they are used in industry and in medical applications.
Business and Economics; Health and Safety; Industrial and Technical Education; Psychology; Social Science
Dist - FOTH **Prod** - FOTH

Lassa Fever 57 MIN
16mm / VHS
Nova Series
(J H C)
$99.95 each
Focuses on the war against disease in Nigeria.
Health and Safety; Science; Sociology
Dist - AMBROS **Prod** - AMBROS 1985

Lassa Fever 57 MIN
U-matic / VHS
Nova Series
Color (H C A)
LC 83-707208
Tells about a medical missionary in Nigeria who died of an unknown fever which began to spread among the hospital staff and seemed immune to all treatment. Follows the efforts of a Yale research team as they discovered an effective treatment for the new tropical disease Lassa fever.
Health and Safety; History - World
Dist - TIMLIF **Prod** - WGBHTV 1982

Lassen Volcanic National Park 13 MIN
VHS / U-matic
Science in Our National Parks
Color (I J H C A)
Studies Mt Lassen's predecessor, the volcano Tehama. Highlights the process of succession after eruption, soil building, plants growing in Lassen volcanic, thermal areas, hot water algae, sulphur filled clays deposited along streams and animals found in the park.
Science - Natural
Dist - IFB **Prod** - CSPC 1986

Last Act for an Actor 20 MIN
16mm
Doctors at Work Series
B&W (H C A)
LC FIA65-1348
Shows the stages of rehabilitation that a troubled persons undergoes following a suicide attempt. Examines the effect of psychiatric interviews on the progress of the patient. Includes a discussion on the motives for suicide.
Health and Safety; Psychology
Dist - LAWREN **Prod** - CMA 1962

The Last Angry Man 100 MIN
16mm
B&W
Contrasts an elderly doctor who is primarily concerned in curing people with a doctor interested in money.
Fine Arts
Dist - TIMLIF **Prod** - CPC 1959

The Last Barrier - Crossing the Rhine 30 MIN
VHS / U-matic
World War II - GI Diary Series
Color (H C A)
History - United States
Dist - TIMLIF **Prod** - TIMLIF 1980

The Last Barrier - Crossing the Rhine 30 MIN
VHS / 16mm
World War II - G I Diary Series
(J H C)
$99.95 each, $995.00 series _ #18
Depicts the action and emotion that soldiers experienced during World War II, through their eyes and in their words. Narrated by Lloyd Bridges.
History - United States
Dist - AMBROS **Prod** - AMBROS 1980

The Last Boat Home 59 MIN
16mm
Color
LC 75-700451
Shows how citizens fought to preserve the Delta Queen, America's last riverboat, from Federal efforts intended to withdraw her from service.
Civics and Political Systems; History - United States; Social Science
Dist - LAGORC **Prod** - LAGORC 1975

The Last Bomb 35 MIN
U-matic / VHS / 16mm
Color
Describes the bombing of Japan by B - 29 airplanes and the dropping of the first atomic bomb on Japan.
Civics and Political Systems; Geography - World; History - United States
Dist - USNAC **Prod** - USAF

Last Call for Union Station 10 MIN
16mm
Color
LC 82-700331
Presents a documentary using the architecture of Union Station in Los Angeles to recall the heyday of the 1930's and 1940's using old stills and motion pictures.
Geography - United States; History - United States; Social Science
Dist - USC **Prod** - USC 1981

The Last Case 14 MIN
16mm
Color
LC 79-700234
Urges employees of small soft - drink bottling firms to oppose an FTC ruling through political activism.

Business and Economics; Civics and Political Systems
Dist - PEPSI Prod - PEPSI 1978

The Last Case of Polio 20 MIN
16mm
Color
Contains a number of episodes, including an animated one, showing how polio viruses are transmitted and their primary effect in humans. Traces recent trends in poliomyelitis incidence and demonstrates the care, precision and skill required to produce Orimune oral polio vaccine.
Health and Safety; Science
Dist - LEDR Prod - ACYLLD 1962

The Last Chance 29 MIN
16mm
To Live Again Series
Color
LC 74-705005
Discusses poverty as the theme of a Negro psychiatrist's interview with a white school drop - out.
Sociology
Dist - USNAC Prod - USSRS

The Last Chance 28 MIN
U-matic / VHS / 16mm
Color (J)
LC 80-700209
Tells how 3,000 acres of grasslands in Front Royal, Virginia, were dedicated in 1974 to the preservation of exotic animals threatened with extinction. Shows that human contact with the animals is minimal.
Science - Natural
Dist - BULFRG Prod - FNZOO 1979

Last chance detectives
VHS
Color (R P I J)
$19.99 purchase
Presents biblical values in stories about four 'ordinary' kids who make life more interesting by solving mysteries.
Guidance and Counseling; Literature and Drama; Religion and Philosophy
Dist - PROVID Prod - TYHP

Last Chance for the Navajo 27 MIN
16mm / U-matic / VHS
Color (J)
LC 78-700969
Examines the human rights issues in the struggle of the Navajo Indians to preserve their culture and land and at the same time cope with the realities of the economy.
Social Science; Sociology
Dist - MGHT Prod - ABCF 1978

Last chance garage 60 MIN
VHS
Color (G)
Presents step - by - step instruction in basic car repairs. Hosted by Brad Sears. Based on the long - running PBS television series.
Home Economics; Industrial and Technical Education
Dist - PBS Prod - WNETTV
UILL

Last Chance Garage Series

Air, water and fuel lines	30 MIN
Brake Installation	30 MIN
Car designs and the '40s	30 MIN
Cooling systems, thermostats, exhausts	30 MIN
Filters to Fiero	30 MIN
Fuel System - How it Works	30 MIN
Kit Car - Final Inspection	30 MIN
Motorcycles and Helmets	30 MIN
Reading Your Tires	30 MIN
Right Hose and Fuel Tanks	30 MIN
Suspension Test	30 MIN
Winter Wipers	30 MIN
Wiring, Batteries, Coolant and Upholstery	30 MIN

Dist - CORF

The Last Chance Stringband Live 52 MIN
VHS
Color (G)
$29.95 purchase
Presents 15 songs recorded live at the 1980 New Hampshire Folk Festival at Pat's Peak. Includes 'Chicken Reel,' 'Milwaukee Blues,' 'Leading The Right Life Now' and other traditional fiddle tunes, early country music and gospel on fiddle, banjo, mandolin and guitar. Features Ryan Thomson on fiddle.
Fine Arts
Dist - CAPFID Prod - CAPFID 1980

The Last chapter 85 MIN
16mm
B&W (G)
$100.00 rental
Depicts the richness of Jewish culture, both religious and secular, in Poland. Looks at the contributions of Jews to Polish life and the extreme economic and political vicissitudes to which Polish Jewry was subject over a thousand - year period. The last 'chapter' in the story is the Nazi onslaught. Includes some rare footage of Jewish life in early 20th - century Poland. Produced and directed by Benjamin and Lawrence Rothman. Narrated by Theodore Bikel.
Fine Arts; History - World; Sociology
Dist - NCJEWF

The Last Chapter 21 MIN
16mm
B&W (I)
Presents the last six months from the life of Jawaharlal Nehru, including his sudden illness, his recovery, his death and the funeral procession as well as the immersion of his ashes at the Holy Sangam. Provides intimate glimpses of the life of the late Prime Minister.
Biography
Dist - NEDINF Prod - INDIA

The Last Citizens - Pt 6 58 MIN
VHS
Struggle for Democracy Series
Color (S)
$49.00 purchase _ #039 - 9006
Explores the concept of democracy and how it works. Features Patrick Watson with Benjamin Barber of 'The Struggle For Democracy,' as host who travels to more than 30 countries around the world, examining issues such as rule of law, freedom of information, the tyranny of the majority and the relationship of economic prosperity to democracy. Part 6 considers the rights and responsibilities of citizens in a democratic state, and the value, meaning and power of democracy when a citizen has the opportunity to participate fully in the system.
Civics and Political Systems; History - World
Dist - FI Prod - DFL 1989

The Last cowboys 58 MIN
VHS
Color (G)
$24.95 purchase
Presents a historical perspective on cowboys. Tracks the lives of present day cowboys. Produced by John Howe.
History - United States; Literature and Drama
Dist - KUEDTV Prod - KUEDTV 1991

Last Crusade 50 MIN
VHS
Living Islam series
Color; PAL (H C A)
PdS99 purchase; Not available in the United States or Puerto Rico
Examines significant events in Islamic history and focuses specifically on the crusades. Provides information about the faith and many cultures of Islam with a particular emphasis on what it means to be a Muslim in today's world. Fifth in a series of five programs.
History - World; Religion and Philosophy
Dist - BBCENE

A Last Cry for Help 33 MIN
U-matic / VHS / 16mm
Color (H C)
LC 80-701289
Tells how a girl who appears to have everything going for her attempts suicide. Explains that her psychiatrist helps her realize that she must take control of her life.
Guidance and Counseling; Psychology; Sociology
Dist - LCOA Prod - ABCTV 1980

The Last dance 58 MIN
VHS
Color (H C G)
$445.00 purchase, $75.00 rental
Looks at the hopes, dreams and anxieties of American adolescents by focusing on a senior prom at a racially diverse high school. Shows the traditional problems of a prom, finding a date, finding the cash, as well as the problems of a generation that is slowly learning how to interact in a multi - racial environment. Questions how integrated American schools really are and to what extent the races are really mixing. Shatters stereotypes by showing white kids who struggle with broken homes and financial problems and minority kids who are articulate, accomplished and on the 'fast track.' Includes the voice of the counterculture - kids who mock senior proms and graduation itself. Produced for Green Room Productions.
History - United States; Sociology
Dist - FLMLIB Prod - ROSVUI 1991

The Last days of contrition 60 MIN
16mm
B&W (G)
$80.00 rental
Evokes a concern for light and shadow more typical of photographers. Travels from Venice, California through the Badlands to baseball stadiums in Buffalo and psychically from a mid - sixties anti - war perspective to a mid - eighties sense of urban despair. An auto trip stops for views of the US and the audience sees a postmodern landscape like a black version of Kerouac's On The Road. A Richard Kerr production.
Fine Arts; Geography - United States; Sociology
Dist - CANCIN

The Last days of Eddie Marsicano 30 MIN
VHS
Color (G)
$25.00 purchase
Documents writer, teacher and humorist Edward Marsicano, who offers his final comments, anecdotes, barbs and opinions about himself and the world he has known, after he was stricken with a rare and deadly type of cancer and told he didn't have long to live. Entertains with Ed's gallows humor as he holds forth on everything from microwaved bacon to literature to Nixon to Elvis and so on. Produced by Tyler Turkle.
Fine Arts; Literature and Drama; Sociology
Dist - CANCIN

Last Days of John Dillinger 52 MIN
U-matic / VHS / 16mm
Color
Recaptures the flavor of the early 1930's while detailing the events which led to the death of John Dillinger, the first person to be named Public Enemy Number One by the FBI.
Biography; History - United States; Sociology
Dist - FI Prod - WOLPER 1973

The Last Days of Living 58 MIN
U-matic / VHS
Color
Shares advanced and humanitarian methods of caring for the dying, including pain management and basic, creative techniques such as touching, music therapy and more.
Health and Safety; Psychology; Religion and Philosophy; Sociology
Dist - AJN Prod - NFBC
NFBC

Last Days of Living, Pt 1 29 MIN
16mm
Color (H C A)
LC 80-701514
Documents the efforts of the medical staff and volunteers at a special unit of Montreal's Royal Victoria Hospital as they tend to the special needs of the terminally ill. Explores the patients' evolving philosophies about their illnesses and impending deaths.
Health and Safety; Sociology
Dist - NFBC Prod - NFBC 1980

Last Days of Living, Pt 2 29 MIN
16mm
Color (H C A)
LC 80-701514
Documents the efforts of the medical staff and volunteers at a special unit of Montreal's Royal Victoria Hospital as they tend to the special needs of the terminally ill. Explores the patients' evolving philosophies about their illnesses and impending deaths.
Health and Safety; Sociology
Dist - NFBC Prod - NFBC 1980

The Last days of Maplewood 18 MIN
VHS / U-matic
Color (P I J)
$260.00, $310.00 purchase, $50.00 rental
Teaches the importance of recycling. Encourages children to become actively involved in recycling efforts at home and in their communities. Produced by the League of Women Voters of Maplewood.
Science - Natural
Dist - NDIM

The Last Days of Marilyn Monroe
VHS
Fine Arts
Dist - BERNGH Prod - BERNGH 1987

Last Days of Winter 90 MIN
VHS
Color (G) (MANDARIN CHINESE (ENGLISH SUBTITLES))
$45.00 purchase _ #6014A
Presents a Mandarin Chinese language movie produced in the People's Republic of China.
Fine Arts; Geography - World; Literature and Drama
Dist - CHTSUI Prod - CHTSUI

The Last Detail 105 MIN
16mm / U-matic / VHS

Color
Stars Jack Nicholson as a member of the Naval Shore patrol assigned to bring a prisoner back to the brig.
Fine Arts
Dist - FI **Prod** - CPC 1973

The Last diva 85 MIN
VHS / 16mm
Color; B&W (G) (ITALIAN WITH ENGLISH SUBTITLES)
$150.00 rental
Presents a documentary on the Italian silent screen actress Francesca Bertini. Directed by Gianfranco Mingozzi.
Fine Arts; History - World
Dist - KINOIC

Last Emperor
VHS
Color (G) (MANDARIN CHINESE (ENGLISH SUBTITLES))
$29.95 purchase _ #9016
Presents a Mandarin Chinese language television program produced in the People's Republic of China.
Geography - World; Industrial and Technical Education; Literature and Drama
Dist - CHTSUI **Prod** - CHTSUI

The Last emperor 164 MIN
VHS
Color (H C A)
$89.95 purchase _ #S02077
Tells the story of Pu Yi, China's last emperor who ascended to the throne at age three. Produced by Bernardo Bertolucci.
Civics and Political Systems; Fine Arts; History - World; Literature and Drama
Dist - UILL

Last Emperor of China Pu Yi 90 MIN
VHS
Color (G) (MANDARIN CHINESE (ENGLISH SUBTITLES))
$45.00 purchase _ #6004A
Presents a Mandarin Chinese language movie produced in the People's Republic of China.
Civics and Political Systems; Fine Arts; Geography - World; Literature and Drama
Dist - CHTSUI **Prod** - CHTSUI

The Last Empire, Intervention and Nuclear War 30 MIN
U-matic / VHS
Color (H C A)
Explores the connections between conventional and nuclear warfare and illustrates a mostly secret history of US foreign policy that included at least a dozen nuclear threats that had the potential to engage the US in a nuclear war.
Civics and Political Systems
Dist - CMBRD **Prod** - CMBRD 1987

Last Epidemic 21 MIN
U-matic / VHS
Color
A shortened version of the 1981 film and videotape The Last Epidemic. Documents a 1981 conference of the Physicians for Social Responsibility. Describes the effect of a nuclear attack on human life and on the environment. Argues for the necessity of ending the arms race.
Civics and Political Systems; Sociology
Dist - PSR **Prod** - PSR

The Last Epidemic 22 MIN
U-matic / 16mm
Color (J G)
$350.00 purchase, $50.00 rental
Conveys the consequences of one or more nuclear weapons on a civilian population. Describes environmental damage and the long range devastation to the planet.
Civics and Political Systems; Sociology
Dist - EFVP **Prod** - EFVP 1981

The Last Epidemic - Medical Consequences of Nuclear War 36 MIN
U-matic / VHS / 16mm
Color
Presents the speeches of Dr H Jack Geiger and others at the conference of Physicians for Social Responsibility which describe the probable medical consequences of nuclear attack on an American city.
Civics and Political Systems; Health and Safety
Dist - RCN **Prod** - RCN 1980

The Last Epidemic - the Medical Consequences of Nuclear Weapons and Nuclear War 47 MIN
U-matic / VHS
Color
Presents a series of excerpts from the conference on the medical consequences of nuclear weapons and nuclear war. Includes documentary footage, illustrations and demonstrations.
Civics and Political Systems; Health and Safety; Sociology
Dist - UWISC **Prod** - PSR 1980

Last exit to Brooklyn 102 MIN
35mm / 16mm
Color (A)
Adapts the novel by Hubert Selby, Jr. Tells the story of Harry Black, a strike secretary in a bitter labor dispute which erupts in a violent riot, and Tralala, a back alley Marilyn Monroe. Both are lost in a hopeless search to find love in a brutal world. Depicts prostitution, loveless sex, drug use and union corruption to chronicle the social breakdown of the 1950s, yet remains relevant in today's violent world. Contains all the violence, raw emotion and brutal humanity that made the book one of the most celebrated and most reviled of this century. Produced by Bernd Eichinger; directed by Uli Edel; screenplay by Desmond Nakano. Contact distributor for price.
Fine Arts; Psychology; Sociology
Dist - OCTOBF

The Last Fishermen 29 MIN
U-matic
Color
Profiles the commercial fishermen of the Great Lakes, focusing on their heritage of hard work and individualism and on the future of their industry.
Geography - United States; Industrial and Technical Education
Dist - PBS **Prod** - UWISCA

Last Flight 21 MIN
16mm
Doctors at Work Series
B&W (H C A)
LC FIA65-1349
A brain tumor is confirmed and located by skull films, EEG and arteriogram. Describes the symptoms and shows details of surgery for meningioma.
Health and Safety
Dist - LAWREN **Prod** - CMA 1963

The Last Flower 60 MIN
U-matic / VHS
Smithsonian World Series
Color (J)
Focuses on efforts to save plants, animals and precious objects. Includes efforts to restore Leonardo da Vinci's The Last Supper, a study of the herbal cures of tribal medicine in Kenya and the task of saving the golden lion tamarin monkey from extinction.
Fine Arts; Science - Natural
Dist - WETATV **Prod** - WETATV

The Last Freak in the World 25 MIN
16mm
Color
LC 75-704315
Presents a story about the relationship between a disenchanted young woman and an old - time carnival man she befriends.
Fine Arts; Guidance and Counseling
Dist - CANFDC **Prod** - CANFDC 1974

The Last Frontier 25 MIN
U-matic / 16mm / VHS
Color; Mono (G)
MV $185.00 _ MP $530.00 purchase, $50.00 rental
Features the growth in popularity of sport diving. Provides information regarding saftey equipment and diving hazards and highlights some of the most exotic scuba diving locations.
Physical Education and Recreation
Dist - CTV **Prod** - MAKOF 1981

Last Frontier Series
At peace with man 60 MIN
The Case for undersea sanctuaries 60 MIN
The Coral kingdom 60 MIN
Dive to the center of the Earth 60 MIN
Ghost Ship 60 MIN
King of the Artic 60 MIN
Maneater 60 MIN
Night Creatures 60 MIN
Of Artificial Reefs 60 MIN
Of Camouflage and Defence 60 MIN
The Predators 60 MIN
The Sea in miniature 60 MIN
The Sea of Cortez 60 MIN
Search for the Silver Fleet - Part One 60 MIN
Search for the Silver Fleet - Part Two 60 MIN
Shark reef 60 MIN
Shipwreck 60 MIN
The Silent Killers 60 MIN
Symphony beneath the sea 60 MIN
To Save a Whale 60 MIN
Whale Song 60 MIN
Dist - CTV

Last Frontier
Florida - a state of caring 60 MIN
The Last Mermaids 60 MIN
Dist - CTV

The Last Great Race on Earth 53 MIN
16mm / U-matic / VHS
Color (J)
LC 82-700853
Documents the 1979 Iditarod Trail Race from Anchorage to Nome, Alaska. Shows the 55 mushers as they participate in a 15 - day - long dogsled race of over 1,000 miles. Talks with leading contenders during the race.
Geography - United States; Physical Education and Recreation
Dist - FI **Prod** - BBCTV 1982

The Last hanging in Canada 29 MIN
VHS / 16mm
Moral question series
Color (C A G)
$90.00 purchase _ #BPN177911
Talks about the death penalty. Features the thoughts of two Florida prisoners on death row, a prison warden, an ethics professor, and a Salvation Army brigadier who witnessed Canada's last hanging in 1962.
History - World; Religion and Philosophy; Sociology
Dist - RMIBHF **Prod** - RMIBHF

The Last Hanging in Canada 30 MIN
U-matic
Color (A)
Provides a documentary examination of the death penalty and a discussion of it by prisoners, a warden, an ethics professor and a witness to Canada's last hanging in 1962.
Religion and Philosophy; Sociology
Dist - TVOTAR **Prod** - TVOTAR 1985

Last holiday 87 MIN
VHS
B&W (G)
$39.95 purchase _ #LAS080
Combines irony, humor and tenderness to portray shy George Bird who learns his days are numbered. Journeys with him for a last holiday, as he withdraws his life savings and dashes off to a fashionable seaside resort, where he is taken for a man of substance and becomes the favorite with his newfound aristocratic friends. Directed by Henry Cass. Remastered.
Fine Arts; Psychology; Sociology
Dist - HOMVIS **Prod** - JANUS 1950

Last Holiday 89 MIN
16mm
B&W
Presents a story of a little man struggling cleverly with ingenuity against the odds of modern life. Stars Alec Guinness.
Fine Arts; Sociology
Dist - LCOA **Prod** - STRAT

The Last Home 10 MIN
VHS / 16mm
Older Adults Series
(C)
$385.00 purchase _ #840VI043
Gives older adults' options and attitudes about the complex issue of institutionalization. Encourages health care professionals to deal with the elderly as individuals and to help them maintain a sense of independence in a dependent situation.
Health and Safety
Dist - HSCIC **Prod** - HSCIC 1984

The Last Horizon 60 MIN
VHS
Man on the rim - the peopling of the Pacific series
Color (H C)
$295.00 purchase
Explores the epic voyages of Polynesians using fast but frail outrigger canoes to settle island groups as far apart as Hawaii, Tahiti, New Zealand and Easter Island. Discloses that it took centuries for the Europeans to arrive in this part of the world and that world dominance is again shifting to the East and to the Pacific. Part of an 11 - part series on the people of the Pacific rim.
Geography - World; History - World; Sociology
Dist - LANDMK **Prod** - LANDMK 1989

The Last Hunger Strike 60 MIN
U-matic / VHS
Color
Relates how in the spring and summer of 1981 fifteen young men, prisoners in Northern Ireland, decided as a final form of protest to begin a hunger strike. Notes how over four months, ten of these men starved to death. Focuses on Michael James Devine, the last of the hunger strikers to die, and explores the day - to - day reality which compels a man to voluntarily surrender his life as a form of protest.
Geography - World; History - World
Dist - TAMERP **Prod** - TAMERP

The Last Hunger Strike - Ireland, 1981 56 MIN
VHS / U-matic
Color (A)
LC 83-707211
Highlights the political and social agony of Northern Ireland through a biographical sketch of Michael James Devine, an Irish Republican Army supporter who died in a hunger strike in 1981. Shows scenes of street violence and interviews with other IRA sympathizers.
History - World
Dist - ICARUS **Prod** - SEVDAY 1982

The Last Hunters - the Cod War 26 MIN
VHS / 16mm
Blue Revolution Series
Color (J)
$149.00 purchase, $75.00 rental _ #QD - 2285
Examines humanity's exploitation of the sea. The fifth of 16 installments of the Blue Revolution Series.
Industrial and Technical Education; Science - Natural
Dist - FOTH

The Last Hurrah 121 MIN
16mm
B&W
Examines the vanishing American tradition of the big city political 'Boss.' Stars Spencer Tracy and Pat O'Brien.
Civics and Political Systems; Fine Arts
Dist - TIMLIF **Prod** - CPC 1958

The Last hurrah 30 MIN
U-matic / VHS
La Esquina series
Color (H C A)
Presents a story centering on school politics. Uses the story to try to reduce the minority isolation of Mexican - American students by showing the teenager as an individual, as a member of a unique cultural group and as a member of a larger complex society.
Sociology
Dist - GPN **Prod** - SWEDL 1976

Last Jews of Radauti - song of Radauti 25 MIN
VHS
Jewish life around the world series
B&W (G)
$34.95 purchase _ #117
Studies Jews in a small Rumanian town. Meets the rabbi and shokhet. Shows preparation for the Sabbath, making challah and immersion in the mikveh. Directed by Laurence Salzmann.
History - World; Sociology
Dist - ERGOM **Prod** - ERGOM

The Last Journey 24 MIN
16mm
Color (C A)
Traces the dying traces of Jewish life in Russia through pictures taken by Nodar, a Jew about to leave the Soviet Union for the final time. Shows Russian Jews in synagogues, Jewish cemeteries and the scene of the Babi Yar massacre.
History - World; Religion and Philosophy
Dist - NJWB **Prod** - NJWB 1980

The Last journey 24 MIN
VHS
Color (G)
$34.95 purchase _ #119
Reveals that before Nodar Djindjihashvili, a Soviet Jew, left his homeland for the final time, he made a secret odyssey that took him into forty communities spanning 10,000 miles. Discloses that he recorded photographically Jewish life wherever he found Jews in the street, in the synagogues, even in cemeteries. Djindjihashvili looked for answers to the question of Jewish identity by stretching his vision from the Jews massacred at Babi Yar to those surviving day - to - day in remote parts of the Soviet Union.
Geography - World; History - World; Sociology
Dist - ERGOM

The Last journey of a genius 58 MIN
U-matic / VHS
Nova series
Color (H C A)
$250.00 purchase _ #HP - 5920C
Portrays Nobel Prize winning physicist Richard Feynman. Reveals his work on the atomic bomb during World War II, his tenure on the Challenger accident investigation board in 1986 and his whimsical quest to the obscure Central Asian country of Tannu Tuva in his final days. Part of the Nova series.
Biography; Science; Science - Physical
Dist - CORF **Prod** - WGBHTV 1989

Last Journey to Jerusalem 20 MIN
16mm
Living Bible Series
Color; B&W (J H T R)
Jesus tells the disciples of His coming death and Resurrection. James and John make their selfish ambitions known and Jesus rebukes them. In Jericho Jesus heals blind Bartinaeus. Jesus and his followers form the procession into Jerusalem.
Religion and Philosophy
Dist - FAMF **Prod** - FAMF

The last Khan of Khans 45 MIN
VHS
Storm from the east
Color; PAL (C H)
PdS99 purchase; Not available in the United States or Pacific Rim countries
Covers the end of the the Mongol empire's campaign of terror. Describes the life of Kublai Khan and the shift by the empire from physical conquest to trade conquest. Fourth in the four - part series Storm from the East, which presents the history of the Mongol empire.
Civics and Political Systems; History - World
Dist - BBCENE

The Last laugh 60 MIN
VHS / U-matic
Color (G)
$250.00 purchase, $100.00 rental
Documents a comedy workshop led by ten top - billed comedians for men with AIDS. Reveals that in three days, the fledgling comics and their mentors worked up original acts which they presented at a sold - out benefit at the Coconut Grove. Produced by Karen Babitt and Deborah Jones.
Health and Safety; Literature and Drama; Psychology; Sociology
Dist - FANPRO

The Last Laugh 70 MIN
VHS / U-matic
B&W (GERMAN)
Relates the story of an elderly man who as the doorman of a great hotel, has been demoted to washroom attendant due to his age. Directed by F W Murnau.
Fine Arts; Foreign Language
Dist - IHF **Prod** - IHF

The Last laugh (the drunk sequence) 14 MIN
U-matic / VHS / 16mm
Film study extracts series
B&W (J)
Presents an excerpt from the 1924 motion picture The Last Laugh. Tells how the doorman at a deluxe hotel is demoted to washroom attendant, gets drunk at his niece's wedding, and dreams he still holds his old job. Directed by Friedrich Murnau.
Fine Arts
Dist - FI **Prod** - UNKNWN

The Last leaf 21 MIN
VHS
Color (J H C)
$225.00 purchase
Tells the O Henry story of an artist who believes she will die of pneumonia when the last leaf falls from a tree outside her window. Reveals that her survival hinges on the willingness of one unlikely individual to risk everything in a secret, last - minute attempt to rid her of her morbid fixation. Produced by Chapman College.
Literature and Drama
Dist - PFP

Last lives - the manatee 15 MIN
VHS
Color (I J H)
$19.95 purchase _ #LL101
Visits Crystal River in Florida with two young boys and their father who snorkle with manatees and learn about their plight. Reveals that the mammals swim from the colder winter ocean water into the warmer spring - fed rivers of Florida where they encounter motorboats and other hazards which often kill or maim them. Filmed by Bill Lovin and produced by Marine Grafics.
Geography - United States; Science - Natural
Dist - ENVIMC

Last Love 11 MIN
16mm
Color (C)
$350.00 purchase, $30.00, $40.00 rental
Uses comic dream sequences and personal encounters to describe the tragic - comic aftermath of a love affair that has just ended. Offers comfort for one who has just ended a relationship. Produced by Cathy Zheutlin.
Fine Arts; Sociology
Dist - WMENIF

The Last lumberjacks 33 MIN
VHS
B&W (G)
$24.95 purchase _ #302 - 9
Includes historic photographs and documentary motion - picture footage taken of the last days of logging in Minnesota in a Carl H Henrikson, Jr. production.
History - United States; Industrial and Technical Education
Dist - MINHS

The last mammoth 50 MIN
VHS
Horizon series
Color; PAL (H C A)
PdS99 purchase; Not available in the United States
Investigates the disappearance of certain species at the end of the last ice age. Explains the new evidence surrounding the extinction of the woolly mammoth. Contrasts this evidence with the elephant, the last surviving relative of the mammoth.
Science - Natural; Science - Physical
Dist - BBCENE

Last Man on Earth 86 MIN
16mm
Color (H A)
Tells the story of the sole survivor of plague who is besieged by victims who arise at night thirsting for his blood. Stars Vincent Price.
Fine Arts
Dist - TIMLIF **Prod** - AIP 1964

The Last manatees 26 MIN
VHS
Challenge of the seas series
Color (I J H)
$225.00 purchase
Reveals that divers can approach manatees and stroke their stomachs. Discloses that because manatees are slow swimmers they are endangered by motor boats, and herbicides used in Florida that affect their reproduction. The prospects for the manatee are not good but the public has rallied to their defense. Part of a 26 - part series on the oceans.
Geography - United States; Science - Natural; Science - Physical
Dist - LANDMK **Prod** - LANDMK 1991

The Last march 11 MIN
16mm
Color (G)
$10.00 rental
Documents Memorial Day, 1969, where 50,000 people defied law and order to pay homage to People's Park. Presents footage originally shot for the BBC.
Fine Arts; Sociology
Dist - CANCIN **Prod** - LIPTNL 1970

The Last March 60 MIN
U-matic / VHS
Search for Alexander the Great Series
Color (C A)
LC 82-707383
Describes how Alexander the Great tries to further unify his kingdoms by having his Greek officers marry Persian women. Shows how he resumes his search for the ends of the world, which he continues until he dies in the year 323 BC.
Biography; History - World
Dist - TIMLIF **Prod** - TIMLIF 1981

The Last Marranos 65 MIN
VHS / 16mm
Sephardic Jewry series
Color (G) (PORTUGUESE WITH ENGLISH SUBTITLES)
$200.00 purchase
Features Portuguese Jews who were forced to accept conversion in 1497, five years after their expulsion from Spain. Discloses that the Jews, called 'marranos' by their Christian neighbors, tried to keep their Judaism alive. After 500 years of hiding their identities, some 100 Marranos remain in the village of Belmonte. Focuses primarily on interviews with surviving community members. Part two of program one of the Sephardic Jewry series which illuminates the histories of the Sephardic Diaspora communities and addresses the social and political issues confronting the Sephardim in the 20th century.
Fine Arts; History - World; Religion and Philosophy; Sociology
Dist - NCJEWF

The Last Mermaids 60 MIN
U-matic / 16mm / VHS
Last Frontier
Color; Mono (G)
MV $225.00 _ MP $550.00
Points out that with less than 1000 manatees now in existence, the need for public awareness and protection of these creatures is of prime importance.
Science - Natural
Dist - CTV **Prod** - MAKOF 1985

The Last Metro 133 MIN
16mm
Color (FRENCH)
A French language motion picture. Depicts life in the French theater during the Nazi occupation in World War II. Stars Catherine Deneuve and Gerard Depardieu. Directed by Francois Truffaut.
Fine Arts
Dist - UAE **Prod** - UAA 1980

The Last metro - Le Dernier metro 132 MIN
VHS
Color (G)
$39.95 _ #LAS070
Looks at the connections between personal relationships and political involvements. Follows a successful Jewish theatrical director forced to go underground in German - occupied Paris, 1942. Produced by Les Films du Carrosse.
Fine Arts; History - World; Psychology
Dist - HOMVIS

The Last mile - Mandela, Africa and democracy 30 MIN
VHS
Color (H C)
$250.00 purchase
Travels with Nelson Mandela through Ghana, Ivory Coast and Senegal. Discusses Africa's problems - the legacy of colonialism, one - party states, human rights, economic issues and the moves away from authoritarian rule to multi - party democracy.
Civics and Political Systems; Geography - World; History - World
Dist - LANDMK **Prod** - LANDMK 1993

Last Minute to Choose 23 MIN
16mm
Color (J H C A)
#3X118 ADMIN
Presents a number of interviews with young heroin addicts who describe how they got hooked and the extreme dangers they face as junkies. Includes very graphic scenes.
Guidance and Counseling; Health and Safety; Psychology; Sociology
Dist - CDIAND **Prod** - YOURF 1979

The Last Mooseskin Boat 28 MIN
16mm
Color (G)
_ #106C 0182 102
Records the passing of a tradition of the Shotah Dene who built mooseskin boats each spring to carry their families and cargo down the mountain rivers to trading settlements such as Fort Norman. Shows a man returning to the mountains to build one last mooseskin boat. Takes place in Northwest Territories.
Social Science
Dist - CFLMDC **Prod** - NFBC 1982
CDIAND

Last Movement of a New World Symphony 10 MIN
16mm
Color
LC 73-700487
Presents a cinematic joke in which a man is trying to put money into a parking meter before the time on it expires. Includes background music by Dvorak.
Fine Arts
Dist - TEMPLU **Prod** - TEMPLU 1972

The Last Nazi 72 MIN
16mm / U-matic / VHS
Color (J)
LC 77-700491
Features an interview between Canadian reporter Patrick Watson and Adolf Hitler's architect and Minister of War Armaments, Albert Speer, who responds calmly to questions about his 20 - year jail sentence for war crimes, his inclusion in Hitler's circle, his early years and his memoirs.
Biography; Civics and Political Systems; History - World; Psychology; Religion and Philosophy; Sociology
Dist - LCOA **Prod** - GLOBTV 1977

The Last Novelist 60 MIN
VHS / U-matic
World of F Scott Fitzgerald Series
Color (C)
Presents Fitzgerald kept alive by his dream of success in movies, while the romantic world of Hollywood kept a depressed nation's hopes alive in this dramatization of a Fitzgerald story.
Literature and Drama
Dist - DALCCD **Prod** - DALCCD

The Last of Life 28 MIN
16mm
Color (H C A)
LC 78-701800
Examines the physiological causes of aging and points out the problems that the elderly face in trying to function in a fast - paced, youth - oriented society.
Health and Safety; Psychology; Sociology
Dist - FLMLIB **Prod** - CANBC 1978

Last of the birds 60 MIN
VHS
Australian ark series
Color (G)
$19.95 purchase _ #S02054
Portrays bird life in Australia, focusing on endangered species.
Geography - World; Science - Natural
Dist - UILL

The Last of the Blue Devils 90 MIN
U-matic / VHS
Color
Tells the story of the music that came out of Kansas City during the 1920s and 1930s. Includes examples of the music of Count Basie, Lester Young, Buster Smith, Eddie Durham, Jimmy Rushing, Walter Page, Hot Lips Page, Ernie Williams, Bernie Moten, Big Joe Turner and Jay McShann.
Fine Arts; History - United States
Dist - DIRECT **Prod** - RICKRR 1980

The Last of the Caddoes 29 MIN
U-matic / VHS / 16mm
Color (J H C)
LC 83-706410
Presents a story about a young boy, living in rural Texas in the 1930's, who discovers that he is part Indian. Despite his parent's disapproval, he immerses himself in the folklore of the Caddo tribe and enters into a summer of self - discovery.
Literature and Drama; Social Science; Sociology
Dist - PHENIX **Prod** - HARK 1982

The Last of the Cuiva 65 MIN
VHS
Disappearing world series
Color (G C)
$99.00 purchase, $19.00 rental _ #51223
Reveals that the remaining members of the nearly extinct Cuiva tribe live in northeastern Colombia, surrounded by settlers' ranches. Discloses that only a few retain their traditional nomadic lifestyle and many work as day laborers for white ranchers. Shows how a once - proud people are being 'culturally killed.' Features anthropologist Bernard Arcand. Part of a series working closely with anthropologists who lived for a year or more in societies whose social structures, beliefs and practices are threatened by the expansion of technocratic civilization.
History - World; Sociology
Dist - PSU **Prod** - GRANDA 1971

Last of the Gladiators - Evel Knievel 105 MIN
VHS
Color; Stereo (G)
$39.98 purchase _ #TT8016
Features one of America's most exciting heros as he performs twenty - two jumps.
Industrial and Technical Education; Literature and Drama
Dist - TWINTO **Prod** - TWINTO 1990

Last of the Great Male Chauvinists 28 MIN
U-matic / VHS / 16mm
Color
Presents a story dealing with feminine fulfillment.
Religion and Philosophy; Sociology
Dist - PAULST **Prod** - PAULST

The Last of the Incas 28 MIN
U-matic / VHS / 16mm
Color (H C A)
LC 80-700250
Focuses on the High Andes of Peru, the region that spawned the Inca civilization. Discusses the social organization and art of the Incas and shows the lost city of Machu Picchu.
Social Science
Dist - JOU **Prod** - FRUCTN 1979

Last of the Jacks 15 MIN
16mm
Color
LC 78-700427
Uses archival photographs, old motion picture footage and filmed interviews with lumberjacks to describe logging operations in northern Minnesota after the turn of the century.
Agriculture; Geography - United States; History - United States; Social Science
Dist - MINHS **Prod** - MINHS 1977

Last of the jacks and The Last log drive 33 MIN
VHS
B&W (G)
$24.95 purchase _ #R - 30C
Uses photographs and documentary motion - picture footage to show the last days of logging in Minnesota. Produced by Carl H Henrikson, Jr.
History - United States
Dist - MINHS

Last of the Karaphuna 50 MIN
VHS / 16mm / U-matic
Color (G A)
$795.00, $595.00 purchase, $85.00 rental
Presents the plight of the Carib Indians who once dominated the West Indies and are now reduced in numbers to 2800. Discusses their efforts to preserve their ethnic and cultural identity.
Geography - World; History - World; Social Science
Dist - CNEMAG **Prod** - CNEMAG 1983

Last of the Log Drives 28 MIN
16mm
Color; B&W (P I J H C G T A)
Shows a river logging operation on the North Fork of the Clearwater River in Idaho. Sequences include forest, cutting, decking logs, hiring of men, building a floating bunk, etc.
Agriculture; Geography - United States
Dist - FO **Prod** - FO 1970

Last of the Mayas 27 MIN
16mm / U-matic / VHS
Color
Discusses the Mayan civilization which flourished in Central America from the 10th through the 14th centuries.
Social Science
Dist - HANDEL **Prod** - HANDEL 1981

The Last of the Mohicans 99 MIN
U-matic / VHS / 16mm
Color (J H)
Presents the story of the Indian scout Hawkeye and his Mohican companions, Chingachnook and his son Uncas. Based on the novel THE LAST OF THE MOHICANS by James Fenimore Cooper.
Literature and Drama
Dist - LUF **Prod** - LUF 1980

The Last of the Mohicans 91 MIN
16mm
B&W
Features Randolph Scott in an adaptation of James Fenimore Cooper's novel THE LAST OF THE MOHICANS.
Fine Arts; Literature and Drama
Dist - KITPAR **Prod** - UAA 1936

The Last of the Mohicans
Cassette / 16mm
Now Age Reading Programs, Set 3 Series
Color (I J)
$9.95 purchase _ #8F - PN68291x
Brings a classic tale to young readers. Filmstrip set includes filmstrip, cassette, corresponding book, classroom exercise materials and a poster. The read - along set includes student activity book, cassette and paperback.
English Language; Literature and Drama
Dist - MAFEX

The Last of the Mohicans 46 MIN
16mm / U-matic / VHS
Classic Stories Series
Color (J H)
Presents the story of the Indian scout Hawkeye and his Mohican companions, Chingachnook and his son Uncas. Based on the novel THE LAST OF THE MOHICANS by James Fenimore Cooper.
Literature and Drama
Dist - LUF **Prod** - LUF 1980

The Last of the Monsters 23 MIN
VHS / U-matic
Color
Focuses on the octopus and its survival skills. Shows it in its fascinating environment as it displays a variety of tricks to stay alive.
Science - Natural
Dist - NWLDPR **Prod** - NWLDPR

The Last of the New York cigar rollers 13 MIN
VHS / 16mm
Color (G)
$160.00, $265.00 purchase, $35.00 rental
Demonstrates and explains the nearly forgotten craft of making cigars by hand by New York City's last three cigar rollers. Explores the history behind their dying art, once an important industry in New York City, employing tens of thousands of workers of many nationalities.
Fine Arts
Dist - FIRS **Prod** - KRAMRK 1990

Last of the Persimmons 6 MIN
16mm
Color (C)
$194.00
Experimental film by Pat O'Neill.
Fine Arts
Dist - AFA **Prod** - AFA 1972

The Last of the Red Hot Dragons 27 MIN
16mm / U-matic / VHS
Color (P I)
Features King Lion and his followers who attempt to help the last dragon on earth who is trapped at the North Pole.
Literature and Drama
Dist - LUF **Prod** - LUF 1980

Last of the Wild Series
The Sea Lion 22 MIN
Dist - FI

Last one picked. . . first one picked on 68 MIN
VHS
Learning disabilities and social skills with Richard Lavoie series
Color (C H G)
$49.95, 49.95, 99.95; purchase _ #LAST-101-WC95, #LAST-102-WC95, #LAST-103-WC95
Employs Richard Lavoie as a host to describe the problems that children with learning disabilities face in social situations. Explains through examples how parents and teachers can help children affected by learning disabilities cope with scenarios outside the classroom.
Psychology
Dist - PBS **Prod** - WETATV 1994

The Last Outcasts 60 MIN
U-matic / VHS
Quest for the Killers Series
Color
Deals with the work of doctors and scientists in the remote hilltop villages of Nepal to overcome superstition and the longstanding stigmatization of leprosy, a disease many still believe to be a punishment from the gods.
Geography - World; Health and Safety; Religion and Philosophy; Sociology
Dist - PBS **Prod** - PBS

The Last parable 28 MIN
VHS / U-matic / 16mm
Color (J H G)
$275.00, $325.00, $545.00 purchase, $50.00 rental
Traces the importance and concept of wilderness in the history of humankind and its integration into world religions, myths and fairy tales. Justifies the vital need for wilderness and places where the mind and soul may think aloud. Produced by the Montana Department of Fish, Wildlife and Parks.
Science - Natural
Dist - NDIM

Last Paragraph 30 MIN
VHS / U-matic
Better Business Letters Series Lesson 4; Lesson 4
Color
Focuses on ending a business letter. Includes closing the sale, getting the check and avoiding trouble.
Business and Economics; English Language
Dist - TELSTR **Prod** - TELSTR
DELTAK

Last Patterns 29 MIN
Videoreel / VT2
Busy Knitter II Series
Color
Fine Arts; Home Economics
Dist - PBS **Prod** - WMVSTV

The Last Piano Sonata 28 MIN
U-matic / VHS
Beethoven by Barenboim Series
Color (C)
$249.00, $149.00 purchase _ #AD - 1232
Comments on Beethoven's Opus 111, his last sonata, which has only two movements, as though he had nothing further to say. Part of a thirteen - part series placing Beethoven, his music and his life within the context of his time and the history of music, Beethoven by Barenboim.
Fine Arts; History - World
Dist - FOTH **Prod** - FOTH

The Last picture show 50 MIN
VHS
Relative values series
Color (A)
PdS99 purchase
Explores fine art as big business. Today it is not unusual for art work to be bought as an investment rather than for aesthetic appreciation. Interviews distinguished critics, collectors, and artists to discover just how art is perceived in the modern world, how it is valued and promoted, and why artists are more important than the art they produce.
Fine Arts
Dist - BBCENE

The Last Picture Show 118 MIN
U-matic / VHS / 16mm
B&W
Depicts life in a dreary Texas town where an air of oppressive doom looms. Directed by Peter Bogdanovich.
Fine Arts
Dist - FI **Prod** - UNKNWN 1971

The Last Pony Mine 23 MIN
16mm
Color (J)
LC 72-702154
Examines the operation of the last pony coal mine in Iowa, and the feelings of its miners as the mine is threatened with closing.
Business and Economics; Geography - United States
Dist - IOWA **Prod** - IOWA 1972

The Last Prom 24 MIN
VHS / U-matic
Color (I A)
Tells the story of four teens on prom night and what occurs when drinking and driving are mixed.
Fine Arts; Health and Safety; Sociology
Dist - SUTHRB **Prod** - SUTHRB

The Last Prom 24 MIN
16mm / VHS
Color (C PRO)
$249.00, $349.00, $495.00 purchase _ #AD - 1121
Follows four drunk teenagers as they go for a spin in a car. Two are killed and the others scarred for life both pyhsically and emotionally. Teaches important lessons about peer pressure and the need to assert one's own idea of what is right.
Health and Safety; Psychology
Dist - FOTH **Prod** - FOTH 1990

The Last Rabbi 30 MIN
16mm
B&W
LC FIA64-1146
Portrays the heroism and courage of the victims of the Warsaw ghetto as evidenced in documents left by Jews in that ghetto. Relates how the last surviving rabbi refused to accept an opportunity to escape at the hands of the Nazis.
History - World; Religion and Philosophy
Dist - NAAJS **Prod** - JTS 1955

Last raid at Cabin Creek 90 MIN
VHS
Color (J H C G)
$49.95 purchase _ #SPD1V-S
Tells the true story of the final raid into what is now Northeastern Oklahoma. Reveals that the military operation was planned by Confederate Brigadier General Stand Watie and executed by Brigadier General Richard M Gano. The raid culminated in the capture of a Union wagon train with over 300 wagons valued at $1.5 million after a pitched battle on the banks of Cabin Creek. Meets a pioneer family named Martin who never recovered from the effects of the war in Indian Territory and visits the present - day Cabin Creek battlefield.
Civics and Political Systems; History - United States
Dist - CAMV

Last Reflections on a War 44 MIN
16mm
B&W (H C A)
LC FIA68-1938
Presents the critical comments and philosophies of Asian scholar and war correspondent, Bernard B Fall. Shows combat scenes in South Vietnam and illustrates the war's effect upon the people of Vietnam. Includes the comments which fall was recording when he was killed.
Geography - World; History - United States; History - World
Dist - IU **Prod** - NET 1968

The Last Refuge 29 MIN
16mm
Al Oeming - Man of the North Series
Color
LC 77-702868
Studies Al Oeming's game farm in Alberta, a 16 - hundred - acre outdoor laboratory for the breeding of threatened and endangered species. Focuses on the long vigil and treatment of a young wolf that is badly hurt.
Geography - World; Science - Natural
Dist - NIELSE **Prod** - NIELSE 1977

The Last resort 28 MIN
VHS / BETA
Color; PAL (G)
PdS20 purchase
Voices a cry of distress from Tibetan refugees who have been imprisoned and tortured. Addresses the consequences of China's invasion of Tibet.
Fine Arts; History - World
Dist - MERIDT

The Last Resort 60 MIN
U-matic / VHS
Color
Presents the human side of the confrontation at Seabrook, New Hampshire, where construction of a nuclear power project sparked opposition of local communities. Balances the arguments of the strongly pronuclear Governor Meldrim Thomson and nuclear utility officials against those of local citizens and project opponents.
Social Science; Sociology
Dist - GMPF **Prod** - GMPF

The Last Rhino 55 MIN
U-matic / VHS / 16mm
Color; B&W (K P I)
LC FIA67-1460
Tells the story of a young boy who tracks down a rhino who has been wounded and brings it back to his uncle's game preserve in East Africa.
Geography - World; Science - Natural
Dist - LUF **Prod** - CHILDF 1967

The Last right 29 MIN
VHS / U-matic / 16mm
Color (C)
$280.00, $330.00, $535.00 purchase, $65.00 rental
Depicts how one family confronts the illness and death experience of an elderly family member. Raises the ethical issues that surround family care - giving and the right of the elderly to choose how to live or die.
Health and Safety; Religion and Philosophy; Sociology
Dist - NDIM **Prod** - NFBC 1985

Last Rights 60 MIN
VHS
Color (G)
$125.00 purchase _ #LSTR - 000
Deals with the issue of euthanasia. Features the case of a New York physician who was involved in a 'mercy killing.' Presents the views of the Hemlock Society, an organization which defends euthanasia. Examines living wills and ways in which patients can control their own care.
Civics and Political Systems; Religion and Philosophy; Sociology
Dist - PBS **Prod** - WXXITV 1987

The Last Rite 15 MIN
16mm
B&W (C A)
Follows a young girl's gradual descent into schizophrenia.
Psychology
Dist - UWFKD **Prod** - UWFKD

Last Rites 30 MIN
16mm
Color
LC 79-700060
Presents the story of a young boy who is unable to accept his mother's death and tries to bring her back through magic rites. Shows how he finds solace from an unexpected source after his efforts to bring her back fail.
Fine Arts; Guidance and Counseling; Sociology
Dist - FLMLIB **Prod** - THOMAC 1979

The Last rodeo 30 MIN
VHS
Crossroads of life series
Color (G R)
Profiles Dusty Trail, an ex - rodeo star who dislikes being dependent on his daughter now that he is old. Shows how a rodeo cowboy teaches Dusty that there is a time for everything, including being dependent.
Guidance and Counseling; Literature and Drama; Religion and Philosophy
Dist - CPH **Prod** - CPH
APH

The Last Round 10 MIN
16mm / U-matic / VHS
Alcohol Abuse Series
Color
LC 77-700983
Follows a supervisor as he is confronted with evidence of one of his workers drinking on the job. Demonstrates how in - plant supervisors can recognize and deal with employees who have a drinking problem.
Business and Economics; Guidance and Counseling; Psychology; Sociology
Dist - JOU **Prod** - NSC 1976

The Last sailor
VHS
Color (G)
$39.80 purchase _ #0218
Documents the last days of working sail on the oceans, lakes and backwaters of the world. Sails in 12 countries on board Chinese junks, Nile River giassas, outrigger canoes.
History - World; Physical Education and Recreation
Dist - SEVVID

The Last Sailors
U-matic / VHS
Color
LC 84-706220
Captures some of the last sailing ships still in practical use during their final voyages. Ponders crafts and sailors with equal perception, focusing on the durable metal of both that allows them to survive the rugged life. Narrated by Orson Welles.
Social Science
Dist - ADFIPR **Prod** - ADFIPR 1984

Last Salmon Feast of the Celilo Indians 18 MIN
16mm
Color (I)
LC FIA63-68
Features scenes of Indians fishing for salmon, preparing the fish for the feast, partaking in the feast and dancing after the meal. Includes interviews with the participants.
Social Science
Dist - OREGHS **Prod** - OREGHS 1955

The Last scale 29 MIN
U-matic
Beginning piano - an adult approach series; Lesson 28
Color (H A)
Focuses on presentation of the scale and chords of F major. Reviews earlier scales and chords. Introduces Beethoven's 'Waltz In F,' the longest and most complex in the telecourse.
Fine Arts
Dist - CDTEL **Prod** - COAST

The Last sea 90 MIN
VHS
Haim Gouri series
B&W (G) (HEBREW AND YIDDISH WITH ENGLISH SUB)
$59.95 purchase _ #632
Shows how survivors of the Holocaust, realizing they had neither a home nor family, travelled by truck, by train, by foot over the Alps, across the sea in dangerously overcrowded ships to Israel. Written by Haim Gouri and produced by the Ghetto Fighters' House at Kibbutz Lohamei Hagetaot.
History - World; Sociology
Dist - ERGOM

The Last seduction 110 MIN
35mm / 16mm
Color (G)
$200.00 rental
Features a sardonic, fast - paced and diabolical film - noir thriller. Portrays Bridget, who knows what she wants, no matter who she walks over to get it. Hiding out in a small town with a million dollars she stole from her husband, she is bored and ready to spend it in New York City. She maneuvers to obtain her freedom by seducing an insurance valuer. Produced by Johanthan Shestack; directed by John Dahl; screenplay by Steven Barancik.
Fine Arts; Psychology; Sociology
Dist - OCTOBF

The Last seven months of Anne Frank 75 MIN
VHS
Willy Lindwer collection series
Color (G)
$49.95 purchase _ #651
Begins where the diary of Anne Frank leaves off. Brings together eight women who were with the Frank family in the concentration camps of Westerbork, Auschwitz - Birkenau and Bergen - Belsen. These eyewitnesses tell their harrowing story and reveal hitherto unknown details about the final months and days of Anne Frank's life. Graphic material. Part of eight documentaries on the Holocaust.
History - World
Dist - ERGOM **Prod** - LINDWE

The Last show on Earth 102 MIN
VHS
Color (J H C G)
$295.00, $395.00 purchase, $85.00, 95.00 rental
Tells the story of extinction on a global scale. Celebrates the efforts of people who are struggling to save Earth's endangered species. Loss of habitat, overpopulation, exploitation and greed are explored as the root causes of extinction. Designed to be entertaining as well as informative, a variety of musicians, including Elton John and Julian Lennon, contribute to the video. Viewpoints offered by Ben Kingsley, Sigourney Weaver, the Dalai Lama and many scientists. In four parts titled Endangered Species, Endangered Habitat, Endangered Cultures and Regaining Balance. Available only as a series on one cassette or on four separate cassettes for schools.
Fine Arts; Industrial and Technical Education; Science - Natural; Sociology
Dist - BULFRG **Prod** - CITV 1993

The Last stand - America's ancient forests 58 MIN
VHS / U-matic
Color (J H G)
$260.00, $310.00 purchase, $60.00 rental
Explores the natural history and the land use history of America's ancient forests. Looks at this vanishing ecosystem which is home to a beautiful array of plants and animals. Covers a wide variety of species and the heated battle that has erupted over the future of these ecosystems and the fate of the species within them. Produced by Ann J Prum. Available on two cassettes.
Agriculture; Fine Arts; Science - Natural
Dist - NDIM

Last stand at Little Big Horn 60 MIN
VHS
Color (I J H)
$19.95 purchase _ #PBS1046
Tells the story of what really happened at the Battle of Little Big Horn. Includes the views of the Lakota Sioux, Cheyenne and Crow. Uses journals, archives, oral histories and drawings to piece together the truth behind the mythic tale.
Social Science
Dist - KNOWUN **Prod** - PBS

Last Stand Farmer 25 MIN
16mm
Color (H C A)
LC 75-701414
Shows how an old Vermont farmer attempts to keep his farm operating in the face of rising taxes and lower farm output. Contrasts his philosophy with that of mass production on farms run by agribusiness enterprises.
Agriculture; Business and Economics; Geography - United States; Sociology
Dist - SILO **Prod** - SILO 1975
CANCIN

The Last Straw 20 MIN
U-matic / VHS / 16mm
B&W (H C A)
LC 74-700252
Tells about a bumbling, unhappy young man who seeks help from a doctor who turns out to be even more maladjusted than he is himself. Shows how, in spite of his incompetence, the doctor indirectly succeeds in helping the young man realize that while there are no simple solutions to his problems, he has a great deal to live for and should try to make the best of it.
Sociology
Dist - PHENIX **Prod** - PHENIX 1976

Last Stronghold of the Eagles 30 MIN
U-matic / VHS / 16mm
Color (J)
LC 81-701056
Explores the life cycle of the bald eagle, from courtship, through mating, to the raising and fledging of young eaglets. Culminates in the winter gathering of thousands of eagles in southeast Alaska, where human development now threatens their habitat.
Geography - United States; Science - Natural
Dist - LCOA **Prod** - NAS 1981

Last Summer 17 MIN
16mm / U-matic / VHS
Color (H C A)
LC 78-700931
Portrays three women as they make the transition from late pregnancy to early motherhood, emphasizing a primary life crisis.
Health and Safety; Psychology; Sociology
Dist - PEREN **Prod** - WEINSM 1978

Last Summer 97 MIN
16mm
Color (J)
Examines the lives of four young people during a single summer. Stars Richard Thomas and Barbara Hershey.
Fine Arts
Dist - CINEWO **Prod** - CINEWO 1969

Last Summer Won't Happen 60 MIN
U-matic / VHS / 16mm
Color
Traces the development of a group of individuals on the Lower East Side of New York from individual isolation and alienation to the beginnings of a sense of community and political activity.
Sociology
Dist - CNEMAG **Prod** - GESHUR 1968

The Last Supper and the resurrection - Tape 5 30 MIN
VHS
Jesus Christ series
Color (J H C G A)
$39.95 purchase, $10.00 rental _ #35 - 860577 - 1
Focuses on the events of the Last Supper and the resurrection of Jesus.
Literature and Drama; Religion and Philosophy
Dist - APH **Prod** - ABINGP

The Last Taboo 28 MIN
16mm / U-matic / VHS
Color (H C A)
LC 78-700195
Explores the feelings of six people who were sexually abused as children.
Guidance and Counseling; Psychology
Dist - CORF **Prod** - CAVPIC 1977

The last taboo - children who sexually abuse 40 MIN
VHS
Color (H C G)
$395.00 purchase, $65.00 rental
Shatters the Victorian notion of childhood innocence. Reveals that sexual abuse of children is committed by other children. New research shows that over one third of child abusers are under the age of 18 and one third of that group is under the age of 11. Shows how these abusers are part of a cycle of family abuse. Defines an abusive relationship as one where there is no informed consent, where there is an imbalance of power between the individuals concerned and where there is manipulation by the abuser. Discusses the reluctance of social workers to label a child as an abuser and the dearth of rehabilitation programs. Produced by Psychology News.
Sociology
Dist - FLMLIB **Prod** - CFTV 1993

The Last Tasmanian 101 MIN
16mm
Color
LC 80-700820
Follows the quest of two men to uncover the story of the Tasmanian aborigines. Offers an account of total genocide.
History - World; Sociology
Dist - TASCOR **Prod** - ARTIS 1977

The Last Tasmanian - Ancestors 17 MIN
U-matic / VHS / 16mm
Color (H C A)
LC 80-701158
Examines the geographical origin of Tasmania, describing how it became physically separated from Australia. Discusses how the resulting isolation affected the culture and lifestyle of the Tasmanian Aborigines through the years.
History - World; Sociology
Dist - CRMP **Prod** - ARTIS 1980

The Last Tasmanian - Extinction 63 MIN
U-matic / VHS / 16mm
Color (H C A)
LC 80-701159
Tells the story of a Tasmanian people, focusing on the British colonization of the island of Tasmania which began in 1803. Describes its use as a penal colony after which came the colonization which resulted in the extinction of the native inhabitants.
History - World; Sociology
Dist - CRMP **Prod** - ARTIS 1980

The Last temptation of Christ 163 MIN
35mm / 16mm / VHS
Color (G)
Presents a daring examination of the life of Christ by director Martin Scorsese. Stars Willem Dafoe who portrays Jesus as an insecure laborer torn betwen secular desires and service to God.
Fine Arts; Religion and Philosophy
Dist - KINOIC **Prod** - UPCI 1989

Last Thing on My Mind 39 MIN
Videoreel / VHS
B&W
Shows residents of two homes for the aging, one urban and one rural, telling what it means to spend one's last years in a home for the elderly.
Health and Safety; Sociology
Dist - CORNRS **Prod** - CUETV 1972

The Last Things 26 MIN
U-matic / VHS
Color (H C A)
$300.00
Shows the beauty and purpose of the stained glass windows in the churches built in the Middle Ages. Narrated by Malcolm Miller.
Fine Arts; History - World
Dist - LANDMK **Prod** - LANDMK 1986

Last Thursday Night 14 MIN
16mm
B&W
Tells the love story of young nonconformists who are part of a motorcycle crowd.

Fine Arts
Dist - NYU **Prod** - NYU

The Last to Know 45 MIN
16mm
Color
Discusses women's problems with alcohol and prescribed drugs.
Psychology; Sociology
Dist - NEWDAY **Prod** - FRIEDB

The Last Trail 58 MIN
16mm
B&W
Shows how Tom Dane rides to the rescue of an old friend's daughter and young son to help them save their stagecoach line from the bad guys. Stars Tom Mix and directed by Louis Seiler.
Fine Arts
Dist - KILLIS **Prod** - FOXFC 1927

The Last Tree 9 MIN
16mm / U-matic / VHS
Color
LC 75-703107
Traces the evolution of man from cell life and an intimate dependence on nature to his life in an artificial environment where he forgets his dependence on nature for survival.
Science - Natural; Sociology
Dist - PHENIX **Prod** - BRYSOB 1975

Last Tree 10 MIN
U-matic / VHS / 16mm
Color
Presents an ecological parable which traces the evolution of matter from the first amorphous blob right up to the emergence of man.
Science - Natural
Dist - PHENIX **Prod** - PHENIX 1975

Last Tuesday 14 MIN
VHS / 16mm
Color (PRO)
$445.00 purchase, $110.00 rental, $35.00 preview
Counsels the bank employee who has been robbed. Offers support and recognizes the fears and anxieties which accompany this experience. Enables employess to mentally cope with a robbery situation.
Business and Economics; Guidance and Counseling; Health and Safety; Psychology; Sociology
Dist - UTM **Prod** - UTM

Last Tuesday 14 MIN
VHS / U-matic
(PRO)
$445.00 purchase, $110.00 rental
Describes how to emotionally cope with a robbery. Stars Efrem Zimbalist Jr.
Sociology
Dist - CREMED **Prod** - CREMED 1987

The Last tycoon 124 MIN
VHS
Color (H C)
$89.00 purchase _ #04428 - 126
Stars Robert DeNiro, Robert Mitchum and Jack Nicholson in a film adaptation of the last, unfinished novel of F Scott Fitzgerald.
Fine Arts; Literature and Drama
Dist - GA **Prod** - GA

The Last Tycoon 122 MIN
U-matic / VHS / 16mm
Color
Offers an adaptation of F Scott Fitzgerald's novel THE LAST TYCOON, which details studio politics in early Hollywood. Stars Robert De Niro.
Fine Arts; Literature and Drama
Dist - FI **Prod** - PAR 1976

The Last Voyage of Henry Hudson 28 MIN
16mm
B&W (G)
_ #106B 0164 116
Shows Hudson who was looking for an open water route to the Orient but found, instead, an inland sea. Portrays the conflict between a man driven by his dream and the men who would not follow him.
Biography; History - World
Dist - CFLMDC **Prod** - NFBC 1964

The Last Wagon 29 MIN
16mm
Color (H A)
LC 70-715321
Traces the authentic music of the American cowboy to its actual source. Features the Western musicologist and folksigner, Katie Lee, who introduces a pair of original cowboy composers whose songs, philosophies, humor and anecdotes provide a glimpse into our vanished West.
Fine Arts; History - United States
Dist - UARIZ **Prod** - UARIZ 1971

The Last Waltz 117 MIN
16mm
Color
Records The Band's farewell concert, given in San Francisco in 1976. Directed by Martin Scorsese.
Fine Arts
Dist - UAE **Prod** - UNKNWN 1978

Last whalers - Portugal 20 MIN
U-matic / VHS / BETA
Color; PAL (G H C)
PdS40, PdS48 purchase
Travels to the Azores Islands, 900 miles off the coast of Portugal. Follows fishermen in pursuit of whales, a way of life which is vanishing.
Fine Arts
Dist - EDPAT

The Last Wild Virus 60 MIN
VHS / U-matic
Quest for the Killers Series
Color
Deals with the efforts of the World Health Organization to marshal its resources and manpower to eliminate smallpox from Bangladesh.
Geography - World; Health and Safety
Dist - PBS **Prod** - PBS

Last wilderness - Frazier Island 60 MIN
VHS
Australian ark series
Color (G)
$19.95 purchase _ #S02055
Portrays Australia's Frazier Island, a largely unspoiled and unexplored area.
Geography - World; Science - Natural
Dist - UILL

Last Word 48 MIN
VHS
Color
From the ABC TV program, 20 20. Presents a follow up to the Child Support program.
Sociology
Dist - ABCLR **Prod** - ABCLR 1983

The Last Word on Dinosaurs 26 MIN
U-matic / VHS
Color (C)
$249.00, $149.00 purchase _ #AD - 1824
Examines the fascination with dinosaurs - from dinosaur potholders and book ends to cartoon characters. Reveals that almost everything learned about them may be inaccurate. Shows that some dinosaurs were as small as chickens, speculates that some may have been extremely colorful, sleeker and more active than imagined.
Science - Natural; Science - Physical
Dist - FOTH **Prod** - FOTH

Last Words 12 MIN
16mm
B&W ((ENGLISH SUBTITLES))
Presents a Crete dialect motion picture with English subtitles. Focuses on a Cretan hermit forcibly brought back to society. Directed by Werner Herzog.
Fine Arts; Foreign Language
Dist - NYFLMS **Prod** - UNKNWN 1967

Last Year at Marienbad 93 MIN
16mm / U-matic / VHS
B&W
Relates how a man tries to convince a woman that they have met before and planned to run off together. Directed by Alain Resnais.
Fine Arts
Dist - FI **Prod** - UNKNWN 1961

Last year at Marienbad - the statues 12 MIN
16mm / U-matic / VHS
Film study extracts series
B&W (J)
Presents an excerpt from the 1961 motion picture Last Year At Marienbad. Shows a man reminding a woman of a conversation he claims they had last year at Marienbad. Directed by Alain Resnais.
Fine Arts
Dist - FI **Prod** - UNKNWN

Last Years of the Tsars 19 MIN
16mm / U-matic / VHS
Russian Revolution Series
B&W (H C)
Presents the story of tsarist Russia in the early years of the 20th century when the pleas of the millions of peasants and workers for mild reforms went unheard by the aristocracy but heard by others including a young revolutionary named Lenin.
Biography; Civics and Political Systems; History - World
Dist - FI **Prod** - GRANOV 1971

Lasting feelings - client and modeling tapes 173 MIN
VHS
Color; PAL; SECAM (G)
$170.00 purchase
Presents two tapes. Shows Leslie Cameron - Bandler guiding a client through NLP processes that change her feelings of jealousy in the client tape. Features Cameron - Bandler and Michael Lebeau who review the session recorded in the client tape, model the process and comment on the outcomes and interventions. Includes a 44 - page annotated transcript. All levels NLP, neuro - linguistic programming.
Guidance and Counseling; Psychology
Dist - NLPCOM **Prod** - NLPCOM

Lasting feelings - client tape 70 MIN
VHS
Color; PAL; SECAM (G)
$95.00 purchase
Features Leslie Cameron - Bandler who guides a client through NLP processes that change her feelings of jealousy and establish a sense of self - worth and confidence in her ability to sustain her relationship. Illustrates the Generative Chain Process. All levels NLP, neuro - linguistic programming.
Guidance and Counseling; Psychology
Dist - NLPCOM **Prod** - NLPCOM

Lasting feelings - modeling tape 103 MIN
VHS
Color; PAL; SECAM (G)
$95.00 purchase
Features Leslie Cameron - Bandler and Michael Lebeau who review the session recorded in the client tape, model the process and comment on the outcomes and interventions. Includes a 44 - page annotated transcript. All levels NLP, neuro - linguistic programming.
Guidance and Counseling; Psychology
Dist - NLPCOM **Prod** - NLPCOM

Latah - a Culture - Specific Elaboration of the Startle Reflex 39 MIN
16mm / VHS
Color (H C A)
$495.00, $160.00 purchase, $30.00 rental _ #CC3790
Examines the Malayasian culturally defined social role for individuals who startle strongly and easily, produced by Ronald Simons, MD, MA, under the auspices of the Institut Penyelidkan Perubatan in Malaysia.
Psychology; Sociology
Dist - IU **Prod** - GUG 1983

Latch, D - Type Flip - Flop and Registers
U-matic / VHS
Digital Techniques Series
Color
Industrial and Technical Education
Dist - HTHZEN **Prod** - HTHZEN

Latch - Key Families 23 MIN
U-matic / VHS
Color (G)
$249.00, $149.00 purchase _ #AD - 1597
Offers specific guidance to working parents with children who are left on their own after school. Explains how parents can provide for the physical safety and emotional needs of their children, how rules for conduct can best be set and chores assigned, so that the experience can help teach children maturity and independence.
Health and Safety; Sociology
Dist - FOTH **Prod** - FOTH

Latch/D - Type Flip - Flops and Registers
VHS / U-matic
Digital Techniques Video Training Course Series
Color
Industrial and Technical Education
Dist - VTRI **Prod** - VTRI

Late Autumn 127 MIN
16mm
Color (JAPANESE)
Relates the story of a young woman who announces that she is not ready for marriage. Shows the shocked reaction of her elders who are determined that she find a husband at once.
Fine Arts; Foreign Language; Guidance and Counseling; Sociology
Dist - NYFLMS **Prod** - NYFLMS 1960

Late chrysanthemums 101 MIN
VHS
B&W (G) (JAPANESE WITH ENGLISH SUBTITLES)
$79.95 purchase _ #VWA1080
Portrays four aging geishas who must grapple with lost youth and loneliness. Adapts three short stories by Fumiko Hayashi. Produced by Mikio Naruse.

Fine Arts
Dist - CHTSUI

Late Eye Report 6 MIN
16mm
B&W
LC 74-702997
Features an experimental film which presents a collage of realities which end up at zero.
Fine Arts; Industrial and Technical Education
Dist - CANFDC **Prod** - LICLIP 1973

Late for Supper 13 MIN
U-matic / VHS / 16mm
Safe at Home Series
Color (P I)
MV=$99.00
Explores the fact that many household accidents happen around suppertime. Reminds children that water and electricity don't mix, electrical appliances should always be unplugged when not in use and that stoves are for grownups.
Health and Safety
Dist - LANDMK **Prod** - LANDMK 1984

Late Gothic to early Renaissance 20 MIN
VHS
ARTV series
Color (J)
$44.95 purchase _ #E323; LC 90-708445
Offers two music videos which feature the art works of Giotto in 'I Am the Very Model of a Modern Major Painting Man' and of Masaccio in 'Cathedral Dreams.' Includes Botticelli and Jan Van Eyck. A third music video overviews all 40 artists discussed in the ten - part ARTV series which uses TV format, including 'commercials' which sell one aspect of an artist's style and a gossip columnist who gives little known facts about the artists.
Fine Arts
Dist - GPN **Prod** - HETV 1989

Late great Britons series
Questions the historical perception of six important figures in British history. Includes episodes about the lives of King Henry VIII, Queen Victoria, Winston Churchill, Charles Darwin, Robert Walpole and Oliver Cromwell.
Late great Britons series 180 MIN
Dist - BBCENE

Late Great Britons
Charles Darwin 30 MIN
Henry VIII 30 MIN
Oliver Cromwell 30 MIN
Queen Victoria - Pt 2 30 MIN
Robert Walpole 30 MIN
Winston Churchill 30 MIN
Dist - BBCENE

The Late Great God 30 MIN
U-matic / VHS / 16mm
Insight Series
Color; B&W (J) (SPANISH)
LC 71-702442
Follows a teenage girl, looking for meaning in life, who is drawn into a wild beach party where God is impeached.
Foreign Language; Psychology; Religion and Philosophy
Dist - PAULST **Prod** - PAULST 1968

The Late Great God 30 MIN
16mm / U-matic / VHS
Insight Series
Color; B&W (J)
LC 71-702442
Follows a teenage girl, looking for meaning in life, who is drawn into a wild beach party where God is impeached.
Psychology; Religion and Philosophy
Dist - PAULST **Prod** - PAULST 1968

The Late Great God 28 MIN
16mm / U-matic / VHS
Insight Series
Color; B&W (J) (SPANISH)
Describes a beach party at which God is put on trial.
Fine Arts; Foreign Language; Religion and Philosophy
Dist - PAULST **Prod** - PAULST

The Late Great Me - Story of a Teenage Alcoholic 71 MIN
16mm
Color (I)
LC 82-700563
Recounts how an emotionally troubled girl is led down the path to alcoholism by a boy who is equally emotionally disturbed. Shows how her life becomes one of deception, escape from reality and loss of responsibility. Reveals that she has a frightening accident which forces her to face her situation and, with the help of a teacher, attempt to overcome her illness.
Psychology; Sociology
Dist - WILSND **Prod** - WILSND 1982

The Late Great Planet Earth 46 MIN
16mm
Color (R)
Examines the prophecies of the ancient Hebrew seers as described in the book, THE LATE GREAT PLANET EARTH, by Hal Lindsey.
Guidance and Counseling; Religion and Philosophy
Dist - GF **Prod** - GF

The Late Middle Ages - the national monarchies - Parts 23 and 24 60 MIN
VHS / U-matic
Western tradition - part I series
Color (G)
$45.00, $29.95 purchase
Presents two thirty - minute programs tracing the history of ideas, events and institutions which have shaped modern societies hosted by Eugen Weber. Looks at the 200 years of war and plague which debiliated Europe during the latter part of the Middle Ages in part 23. Part 24 examines the emergence of a new, urban middle class while dynastic marriages established centralized monarchies. Parts 23 and 24 of a 52 - part series on the Western tradition.
Civics and Political Systems; Geography - World; Health and Safety; History - World; Sociology
Dist - ANNCPB **Prod** - WGBH 1989

The Late romantic age 19 MIN
VHS / U-matic
English literature series
Color (H C)
$250.00 purchase _ #HP - 6152C
Looks at the later part of the Romantic Age. Examines the lives, philosophies and works of major writers, including Byron, Shelley and Keats. Overviews Romantic literature's major themes and shows the connection between Classical and Romantic throught. Part of a two - part series on English literature.
Literature and Drama
Dist - CORF **Prod** - BBCTV 1990

Late Sequelae of Nonpenetrating Abdominal Trauma 27 MIN
16mm
Color (PRO)
Explains that visceral damage resulting from blunt trauma may initially escape detection because of minimal findings, diagnostic oversight and overshadowing injuries. Demonstrates the clinical radiologic and surgical aspects of the late sequelae of injuries to the liver, pancreas, spleen and intestine.
Health and Safety; Science
Dist - ACY **Prod** - ACYDGD 1963

Late Spring 107 MIN
16mm
B&W (JAPANESE)
Relates the story of an aging professor, a widower who lives outside Tokyo with his unmarried daughter, in perfect harmony and contentment that he knows cannot last. Shows how he arranges his daughter's marriage.
Fine Arts; Foreign Language; Sociology
Dist - NYFLMS **Prod** - NYFLMS 1949

Late summer blues 101 MIN
VHS
Color (G) (HEBREW WITH ENGLISH SUBTITLES)
$79.95 purchase _ #522
Tells of seven graduating high school students in 1970 Israel whose summer break is clouded by their impending induction into the army during the War of Attrition. Celebrates the innocence and idealism of Israeli youth while offering a grim reminder of the tragedy of war. Stars Dor Zweigenbom, Yoav Tsafir and Shahar Segal. Directed by Renen Schorr.
Fine Arts; History - World; Sociology
Dist - ERGOM **Prod** - ERGOM 1987

Late summer blues 101 MIN
16mm / VHS
Color (G) (HEBREW WITH ENGLISH SUBTITLES)
$300.00 rental
Portrays a group of seven 18 - year - olds who are on summer break just before their induction into the armed forces in Tel Aviv. Reveals that when the first of their comrades is killed in a training accident, the group must face decisions of far greater importance than most high school students. Directed by Renen Schorr.
Fine Arts; Geography - World; Sociology
Dist - KINOIC **Prod** - JANUS 1987

The Late Works 28 MIN
U-matic / VHS
Beethoven by Barenboim Series
Color (C)
$249.00, $149.00 purchase _ #AD - 1231
Reveals that Beethoven's late works are more compact, that he heightens the use of contrasts. Shows that he became a master of the small form. Part of a thirteen - part series placing Beethoven, his music and his life within the context of his time and the history of music, Beethoven by Barenboim.
Fine Arts; History - World
Dist - FOTH **Prod** - FOTH

The Later Campaigns of Francis Marion - Pt 8 30 MIN
VHS
And Then There were Thirteen Series
Color (H)
$69.95 purchase
Focuses on the battle campaigns of Francis Marion. Uses footage shot on battleground locations. Describes command personalities, weapons and uniforms. Part 8 of a twenty - part series on Southern theaters of war during the American Revolution.
Biography; Civics and Political Systems; Guidance and Counseling; History - United States
Dist - SCETV **Prod** - SCETV 1982

Later later Dutch master later 1 MIN
16mm
Color (G)
$5.00 rental
Presents a production conceived, performed and edited by Saul Levine with camera by Pelle Lowe.
Fine Arts
Dist - CANCIN **Prod** - LEVINE

Later that same Night 10 MIN
16mm
Color (C)
$224.00
Experimental film by Will Hindle.
Fine Arts
Dist - AFA **Prod** - AFA 1971

The Later Twentieth Century 28 MIN
U-matic / VHS
Survey of English Verse Series
Color (C)
$249.00, $149.00 purchase _ #AD - 1308
Considers the era from Dylan Thomas to Ted Hughes. Focuses on 'The Thought - Fox' by Hughes.
Fine Arts; Literature and Drama
Dist - FOTH **Prod** - FOTH

The Later Years 9 MIN
U-matic / VHS / 16mm
Color (H C A)
Deals with old age as the sum of all preceding stages, hopefully culminating in contentment and a healthy acceptance of death.
Psychology; Social Science; Sociology
Dist - PFP **Prod** - HUBLEY

The Later Years of the Woodleys 30 MIN
16mm
B&W
LC 74-705006
Illustrates the relationship between the aging process and ill health and shows how the social worker can be indispensable to appropriate medical care. Depicts the supervisory process and group supervision.
Business and Economics; Health and Safety; Sociology
Dist - USNAC **Prod** - USSRS

Lateral Cerebral Ventricle and the Fornix - a Self - Evaluation Exercise 18 MIN
VHS / U-matic
Neuroanatomy Series
Color (C A)
Health and Safety; Science - Natural
Dist - TEF **Prod** - UWO

Lateral Cerebral Ventricles and the Fornix 20 MIN
VHS / U-matic
Neuroanatomy Series
Color (C A)
Health and Safety; Science - Natural
Dist - TEF **Prod** - UWO

Lateral Corner Drop (Modified Sumi - Gaeshi) 3 MIN
16mm
Combative Measures - Judo Series Part 3K; Pt 3K
B&W
LC 75-700837
Demonstrates the lateral corner drop in judo and shows how to use this drop against attack.
Civics and Political Systems; Physical Education and Recreation
Dist - USNAC **Prod** - USAF 1955

Lateral Flap Cleft Lip Surgery Technique 18 MIN
16mm
Color (PRO)
Demonstrates an original method for closure of cleft lip through diagrams, actual technique and case results. Points out that the method can be adapted to use in both single and double cleft lip.
Health and Safety; Science
Dist - ACY **Prod** - ACYDGD 1962

Lateral Neck Superficial Structures 9 MIN
8mm cartridge
Anatomy of the Head and Neck Series
Color
LC 74-705007; 75-702012
Uses diagrams to present a dissection of superficial structures of the anterior and lateral neck. Shows the vessels and nerves transversing the external cervical fascia.
Science - Natural
Dist - USNAC **Prod** - USVA 1969

Lateral Sliding Flap 15 MIN
8mm cartridge
Color (PRO)
LC 75-700790; 75-701246
Demonstrates a periodontal technique involving a lateral sliding flap to cover the partially denuded root of a maxillary central incisor.
Health and Safety; Science
Dist - USNAC **Prod** - USVA 1971

Laterally Positioned Flap in Periodontics 15 MIN
16mm
Color
LC 75-702013; 74-705009
Shows how laterally positioned flaps are used to cover the denuded roots of a mandibular central incisor and maxillary molar. Shows how a partial or split thickness dissection is performed in order to leave periosteum at the donor sites.
Health and Safety; Science; Science - Natural
Dist - USNAC **Prod** - USVA 1968

Latex sky 8 MIN
16mm
B&W (G)
$10.00 rental
Employs the qualities of light and mass to create personal rhythms. Reacts to the depths experienced in dreaming.
Fine Arts; Psychology
Dist - CANCIN **Prod** - WOODBR 1974
CINEAS

Latex Test for Fibrin Degradation Products / Protamine Sulfate Paracoagulation 14 MIN
U-matic / VHS
Blood Coagulation Laboratory Techniques Series
Color
LC 79-707604
Demonstrates a convenient assay for fibrin degradation products and how to measure fibrin degradation products and monomers by dissociating the fibrin monomer complexes with protamine complexes.
Health and Safety; Science
Dist - UMICH **Prod** - UMICH 1977

Latex, the Market Builder 22 MIN
16mm
Color
Depicts the extent of production, technical service and new product development for Dow latexes. Depicts the Dow research commitment in latexes for the paper, textile, coatings and adhesives markets.
Business and Economics; Science
Dist - DCC **Prod** - DCC

The Lathe 15 MIN
16mm
Machine Shop Work Series
B&W (SPANISH)
LC 74-705010
Describes the characteristics and basic operations of the engine lathe.
Industrial and Technical Education
Dist - USNAC **Prod** - USOE 1942

The Lathe 15 MIN
16mm
Machine Shop Work Series Basic Machines
B&W
LC 74-705010
Describes the characteristics and basic operations of the engine lathe.
Industrial and Technical Education
Dist - USNAC **Prod** - USOE 1942

The Lathe 17 MIN
VHS / U-matic
Manufacturing Materials and Processes Series
Color
Covers major components of a lathe and its major functions.
Industrial and Technical Education
Dist - WFVTAE **Prod** - GE

Lathe - Chuck Work 13 MIN
16mm
Metalwork - Machine Operation Series
Color (I)
Parts of the lathe, mounting chucks and types, chucking work, taper turning and drilling, filing and polishing.
Industrial and Technical Education
Dist - SF **Prod** - MORLAT 1967

Lathe Cutting Tools Explained 40 MIN
VHS / 35mm strip
Color (H A IND)
#513XV7
Provides a hands on explanation of the various lathe cutting tools including how they are used, sharpened and cared for. Includes high speed steel tool bits, grinding high speed steel tool bits, and tool holders & carbide tools (3 tapes). Prerequisites required. Includes a Study Guide.
Education; Industrial and Technical Education
Dist - BERGL

The Lathe Explained 69 MIN
VHS / 35mm strip
Color (J H A IND)
#501XV7
Introduces the parts, accessories and operation of an engine lathe. Includes its basic parts, setting up work, its accessories, work operations on 3 and 4 jaw chucks, three ways to a taper, and cutting a thread (6 tapes). Prerequisites required. Includes a Study Guide.
Education; Industrial and Technical Education
Dist - BERGL

Lathe Safety
VHS / 35mm strip
Skills Related Safety Series
Color
$28.00 purchase _ #TX1E2 filmstrips, $58.00 purchase _ #TX1E2V VHS
Discusses the safe use and operation of a lathe.
Health and Safety
Dist - CAREER **Prod** - CAREER

Lathe Tools 11 MIN
VHS / U-matic
Introduction to Machine Technology, Module 2 Series; Module 2
Color (IND)
Focuses on types of lathe cutting tools and their uses. Includes high speed, insert type, parting tools, forming tools, boring tools and knurling tools.
Industrial and Technical Education
Dist - LEIKID **Prod** - LEIKID

Lathe - Work between Centers 13 MIN
16mm
Metalwork - Machine Operation Series
Color (I)
Setting up and turning work between centers, knurling, taper turning, filing and polishing.
Industrial and Technical Education
Dist - SF **Prod** - MORLAT 1967

Lathes for small - batch manufacture 9 MIN
VHS
Color; PAL (J H IND)
PdS29.50 purchase
Uses a fully automatic lathe to illustrate how the functions of the machine are guided and controlled by a system of cams and control discs. Shows lathes for copying turning, curve controlled automatic lathes and more.
Industrial and Technical Education
Dist - EMFVL **Prod** - IFFB

Latin America 30 MIN
35mm strip / VHS
Western man and the modern world series - Unit VIII
Color (J H C T A)
$72.00, $72.00 purchase _ #MB - 510458 - X, #MB - 510295 - 1
Examines the history of Latin America, focusing mostly on the modern era and its numerous political and social changes.
Civics and Political Systems; Geography - World; History - World
Dist - SRA

Latin America 30 MIN
U-matic / Kit / VHS
Western Man and the Modern World in Video
Color (J H)
$1378.12 the 25 part series _ #C676 - 27347 - 5, $69.95 the individual
Covers the history, geography and economy of Latin America. Explores the individual and societal impact of changing governments and ideologies in the Latin American countries.
Geography - World; History - World
Dist - RH

Latin America 20 MIN
16mm
B&W (LATIN)
LC 72-701049
Analyzes the political, social and economic factors affecting South American countries and their 200 million inhabitants. Pictures the development of South America and explains communist infiltration in Latin America.
Civics and Political Systems; Geography - World
Dist - USNAC **Prod** - USDD 1961

Latin America - Intervention in Our Own Backyard 26 MIN
U-matic / VHS / 16mm
Between the Wars Series
Color (H C)
Examines diplomatic relations between the United States and Latin America from the 19th century until 1933.
Civics and Political Systems; History - United States; History - World
Dist - FI **Prod** - LNDBRG 1978

Latin America - modern problems from ancient roots 61 MIN
VHS
Color (I J H)
$99.00 purchase _ #06133 - 026
Illustrates the political and eonomic challenges faced by the developing world. Explains colonialism, authoritarianism and revolution. Provides a historical overview of the Latin American region and portrays the everyday lives of families. Includes teachers' guide and library kit.
Geography - World; History - World; Social Science
Dist - INSTRU

Latin America - modern problems from ancient roots 61 MIN
VHS
Color (J H)
$99.00 _ #06133 - 026
Illustrates the political and economic challenges faced by the developing world. Explains colonialism, authoritarianism and revolution. Provides a historical overview of the region and portrays the everyday lives of various families. Includes teacher's guide and library kit.
Education; Geography - World; History - World; Social Science
Dist - GA

Latin American Cooking 22 MIN
16mm
Color (LATIN)
LC 70-706044
Introduces Latin American cooking using modern cooking equipment, and discusses the Indian and Spanish heritage in Latin American cooking. Shows the preparation of tortillas, tamales, enchiladas, Argentine beef roll stuffed with vegetables and eggs, anticuchos, mole poblano and other dishes popular in Latin American countries.
Home Economics
Dist - BUGAS **Prod** - BUGAS 1969

Latin American Cooking 22 MIN
16mm
Color (H C A) (SPANISH)
Presents the color of Latin American cooking. Explains how to make tortillas, tamales, enchiladas, mole poblano, and many others. Adapted from the cookbook, Latin Amaerican Cooking.
Home Economics
Dist - BUGAS **Prod** - BUGAS

Latin American Cooking and Louisiana Cajun Cooking 43 MIN
U-matic
Color (H C A)
Shows how to cook a variety of Latin American and Cajun foods using a gas range.
Geography - United States; Geography - World; Home Economics
Dist - BAILYB **Prod** - AGA 1986

Latin American Overview 25 MIN
U-matic / VHS / 16mm
Color (I J H)
LC 82-700645
Provides information about South America, Central America, Mexico and the Caribbean Islands. Covers a broad range of topics, including the people, culture, religion, geography and economics.
Geography - World; History - World
Dist - CRMP **Prod** - BIBICF 1982

Latin American Series - a Focus on People Series
Bolivia, Peru and Ecuador 19 MIN
The Caribbean 21 MIN
Central America 16 MIN
Chile and Argentina 19 MIN
Colombia and Venezuela 18 MIN
Mexico 17 MIN
North Brazil 18 MIN
South America - Overview 17 MIN
Dist - SF

Latin American Series - Focus on People Series
South Brazil 19 MIN
Dist - SF

Latin dances - Volume 3 50 MIN
VHS
Cal del Pozo's step this way - learn to dance series
Color (G A)
$19.95 purchase
Presents basic instruction in three Latin - based dances - the Tango, the Rumba, and the Cha Cha. Utilizes Cal del Pozo's method, which involves four simple foot movements, and provides computerized footprints to allow viewers to follow along more easily. Taught by del Pozo, who is a national ballroom dance champion and a Broadway dancer and choreographer.
Fine Arts
Dist - PBS **Prod** - WNETTV

Latin Exercises
Videodisc
(G) (LATIN)
$150.00 purchase
Offers a series of 60 individual Latin language computer drills for Allyn and Bacon's First Year Latin by Jenney et al. Reinforces classroom lessons. For Apple computer with 48K memory. Accompanied by a teacher's guide. Demo disk available.
Foreign Language
Dist - IFB

Latin Splendor - Spain and Portugal 20 MIN
U-matic / VHS
Color (J)
LC 82-706766
Gives an overview of Majorca and the Spanish cities of Madrid and Barcelona. Shows Portugal's beaches, port towns, Lisbon and the Catholic religious procession at Fatima.
Geography - World; History - World
Dist - AWSS **Prod** - AWSS 1980

Latino Profiles - Living in the U S Today 18 MIN
U-matic / VHS / 16mm
Color (J H C)
LC 76-701294
Takes a look at the lives and work of a variety of Latinos in the United States. Presents Latino people as they discuss their work their leisure, their goals and heritage and their pride in being Latinos.
Sociology
Dist - PHENIX **Prod** - PHENIX 1976

The Latissimus Dorsi Flap for Modified Radical Mastectomy 22 MIN
VHS / U-matic
Color (PRO)
Demonstrates a surgical technique for breast reconstruction which utilizes a latissimus dorsi musculocutaneous flap to give additional skin and cover for a breast implant.
Health and Safety
Dist - WFP **Prod** - WFP

Latitude 12 MIN
16mm / U-matic / VHS
Map Skills Series
Color (I J)
$350 purchase - 16 mm, $250 purchase - video _ #5193C
Discusses how points north and south of the equator are measured in degrees, and how they translate into miles. Produced by Christianson Productions, Inc.
Social Science
Dist - CORF

Latitude 10 MIN
U-matic
Geography Skills Series
Color (J H)
Shows how the Tropic of Cancer, Arctic Circle, Tropic of Capricorn and Antarctic Circles are measured using the equator as the starting point.
Computer Science; Education; Geography - World
Dist - TVOTAR **Prod** - TVOTAR 1985

Latitude 17 MIN
VHS / U-matic / 16mm
Map skills for beginners series
Color (I J)
$420.00, $250.00 purchase _ #HP - 5193C
Uses the animated exploits of wildlife photographer Natalie Haymaker to teach the concepts of measuring all points north and south of the equator by degrees. Shows why there is a worldwide relationship between latitude and climate, how degrees translate into miles, and how, in the northern hemisphere, latitude can be calculated in reference to the the North Star. Part of a series on map skills for beginners.
Geography - World; Science - Physical
Dist - CORF **Prod** - CHRISP 1989

Latitude and Longitude 9 MIN
16mm
Color (J H C G)
Explains how a ship can use latitude and longitude measurements to determine its position.
Geography - World; Social Science
Dist - VIEWTH **Prod** - GBI

Latitude and longitude 22 MIN
VHS
Color; CC (I J H) (ENGLISH AND SPANISH)
$110.00 purchase - #A51634
Uses animation to explain how early Greek astronomers developed a navigation system to locate any spot on Earth. Explains how latitude and longitude are used in modern location systems. Includes a teacher's guide.
Geography - World; Science - Natural
Dist - NGS **Prod** - NGS 1994

Latitude and Longitude 14 MIN
U-matic / VHS / 16mm
Color (I J) (SPANISH)
A Spanish language version of the film and videorecording Latitude And Longitude.
Social Science
Dist - EBEC **Prod** - EBEC 1981

Latitude and Longitude 9 MIN
U-matic / VHS / 16mm
Color (I J H)
Demonstrates that the location of a point on earth can be determined by using angular distances of measurement called latitude and longitude. Uses a globe to demonstrate the various relationships between latitude and longitude.
Geography - World
Dist - LUF **Prod** - LUF 1983

Latitude, longitude and time zones 13 MIN
VHS
Color; PAL (H)
Combines animation, live photography and representational models of the Earth to illustrate the development and use of the system of locating places on the surface of the Earth, using longitude and latitude. Considers the Earth's rotation in relationship to the sun and the prime meridian to show how world time zones were established.
Geography - World; Science - Physical; Social Science
Dist - VIEWTH **Prod** - VIEWTH

Latitude, Longitude and Time Zones 13 MIN
U-matic / VHS / 16mm
Color (I J)
Illustrates the development and use of the system of locating places on earth using latitude and longitude. Shows how world time zones are established.
Geography - United States; Geography - World
Dist - CORF **Prod** - CORF 1979

Latitude, Longitude and Time Zones 13 MIN
16mm / U-matic / VHS
Color (I J H)
$330, $240 purchase _ #4008
Shows are world time zones were established and how to locate places on the globe using latitude and longitude.
Social Science
Dist - CORF

Laton - a Handicapped Child in Need 15 MIN
16mm
Color
LC 76-702599
Shows the services provided for the handicapped by Head Start programs. Examines Head Start programs for physical and mental evaluation, dental care and hygiene.
Education; Health and Safety; Psychology
Dist - CFDC **Prod** - CFDC 1976

Laton Goes to School 15 MIN
16mm
Color (A)
LC 81-701205
Focuses on Laton, a symbolic handicapped child involved with the Head Start program. Shows the transition made by handicapped children from the Head Start program to the public school system.
Education; Psychology
Dist - CALVIN **Prod** - CALVIN 1978

Lattice multiplication
VHS
Lola May's fundamental math series
Color (I)
$45.00 purchase _ #10275VG
Presents an activity to practice the basic multiplication facts and multiplying numbers with many numbers before being taught compound multiplication. Comes with a teacher's guide and blackline masters. Part 25 of a 30 - part series.
Mathematics
Dist - UNL

Latvia 29 MIN
Videoreel / VT2
International Cookbook Series
Color
Features home economist Joan Hood presenting a culinary tour of specialty dishes from around the world. Shows the preparation of Latvian dishes ranging from peasant cookery to continental cuisine.
Geography - World; Home Economics
Dist - PBS **Prod** - WMVSTV

The Lau of Malaita 53 MIN
VHS
Disappearing world series
Color (G C)
$99.00 purchase, $14.00 rental _ #51156
Reveals that the extraordinary way of life of the Lau on their South Pacific islands kept them safe from enemies and disease for hundreds of years. Discloses that their 'life of custom' is threatened by Christianity and outside ideas. Features anthropologist Pierre Maranda. Part of a series working closely with anthropologists who lived for a year or more in societies whose social structures, beliefs and practices are threatened by the expansion of technocratic civilization.
History - World; Religion and Philosophy; Sociology
Dist - PSU **Prod** - GRANDA 1987

The Lau of Malaita - Pt 5 53 MIN
VHS
Disappearing World Series
Color (S)
$99.00 purchase _ #047 - 9005
Provides a precious record of the social structure, beliefs and practices of societies now threatened with imminent extinction by the pressures of our expanding technocratic civilization. Travels to the remote corners of three continents and features film crews who worked in close association with anthropologists who had spent a year or more living among the societies concerned. Part 5 looks at the Lau who have established an extraordinary way of life on their South Pacific Islands. For hundreds of years they have been safe from enemies and disease. Now their 'life of custom' is threatened by the spread of Christianity and ideas from the outside world.
Geography - World; History - World; Psychology; Religion and Philosophy; Social Science; Sociology
Dist - FI **Prod** - GRATV 1989

The Laubach way to English and reading video - based tutor workshops 330 MIN
VHS
Color (T G)
$399.00 purchase _ #692 - 4
Offers the Laubach way to English and reading video - based tutor workshops. Shows how to teach English and reading skills. Includes explanations, examples, complete leader's guides and handouts in photocopy master form.
Education; English Language
Dist - LAULIT **Prod** - LAULIT

The Laubach way to English video - based tutor workshop 180 MIN
VHS
Color (T G)
$299.00 purchase _ #693 - 2
Shows how to teach English reading skills. Includes explanations, examples, a complete leader's guide and handouts in photocopy master form.
Education; English Language
Dist - LAULIT **Prod** - LAULIT

The Laubach way to reading video - based 150 MIN
tutor workshop
VHS
Color (T G)
$299.00 purchase _ #691 - 6
Shows how to teach reading skills. Includes a leader guide and tutor handouts in photocopy format.
Education; English Language
Dist - LAULIT **Prod** - LAULIT

Laugh along with Lucy
VHS
Color (G)

$14.98 purchase _ #PD051
Presents footage of comedian Lucille Ball.
Fine Arts; Literature and Drama
Dist - SIV

Laugh and Cry 15 MIN
VHS / U-matic
Children in Action Series
Color
Psychology
Dist - LVN **Prod** - LVN

Laugh - it matters 30 MIN
VHS
Color (G)
$39.95 purchase
Looks at the benefits of laughter and gives practical suggestions on how to bring more laughter into your life through sight gags, jokes and funny stories. Two psychotherapists, Dr Annette Goodheart and Joyce Anisman - Saltman detail the many health benefits to be gained from laughter.
Health and Safety; Literature and Drama
Dist - HP

Laugh Lines - a Profile of Kaj Pindal 27 MIN
16mm
Color (J)
Offers a portrait of animator Kaj Pindal. Shows him at work creating zany cartoon characters, teaching students of animation and at home enjoying a full - size street car that tours his backyard.
Fine Arts; Industrial and Technical Education
Dist - NFBC **Prod** - NFBC 1979

The Laugh Track - 218 30 MIN
U-matic
Currents - 1985 - 86 Season Series
Color (A)
Explores the world of television comedy.
Fine Arts; Social Science
Dist - PBS **Prod** - WNETTV 1985

Laugh your way to health 60 MIN
VHS
Color (G)
$60.00 _ #VLY - H001
Features Annette Goodheart who explains her contention that laughter stimulates the cardiovascular system, massages internal organs, and exercises the human capacity to smile.
Health and Safety; Psychology
Dist - NOETIC

Laughing Alligator 21 MIN
U-matic / VHS
Color
Conveys the personal experiences of which the primitive landscape is composed. Juxtaposes sequences of body movements.
Fine Arts
Dist - KITCHN **Prod** - KITCHN

Laughing Gravy 19 MIN
16mm
B&W
Describes the havoc which ensues when Laurel and Hardy try to sneak an orphan puppy into their room.
Fine Arts
Dist - RMIBHF **Prod** - ROACH 1931

Laughing in the dark - from colored girl to woman of color - a journey from prison to power 30 MIN
VHS
Author's night at the Freedom Forum series
Color (G)
$15.00 purchase _ #V94 - 12
Focuses on Patricia Gaines, author of the book of the same title, in part of a series on freedom of the press, free speech and free spirit.
History - United States; Social Science; Sociology
Dist - FREEDM **Prod** - FREEDM 1994

Laughing, Learning and Driving
VHS
Color (P)
$12.95 purchase _ #V3139 - 10
Depicts comedian and traffic school instructor Steve Verret using humor to convey information about driving attitudes, laws and regulations, defensive driving and seat belts. Includes appearance by Joe Dolan, a Department of Motor Vehicles examiner who details the process of attaining a driver's license.
Education; Health and Safety; Industrial and Technical Education
Dist - SCHSCI

A Laughing matter 28 MIN
16mm / VHS / U-matic
Something special series
Color (I J H)
Portrays a young Caribbean boy who enters a contest to make a very depressed girl smile and 'accidentally' discovers his own talent is far more effective than imitating others. Features part of a series presenting contemporary interpretations of traditional folktales from around the world.
Literature and Drama; Sociology
Dist - OMFLTD **Prod** - TRIUNE 1990

Laughing matters 32 MIN
VHS
Color (G)
$250.00 purchase, $100.00 rental
Features the Project Return Players, an improvisational comedy group with a unique method for eliminating the social stigma of mental illness - humor. Reveals that a major goal of their performances is to demystify mental illness by encouraging open discussion and inviting members of the audience to ask questions. Emphasizes learning to cope with mental illness through a combination of therapy, medication and taking one day at a time. Produced by Rebecca Hantin.
Health and Safety; Literature and Drama; Psychology
Dist - BAXMED

The Laughing mirror, The Seven flames, Katalina and Katalin - Volume VI 34 MIN
VHS
European folktales series
Color (G)
$99.00 purchase, $50.00 rental _ #8262
Presents traditional East European stories brought to life by three of those countries' animators. Includes 'The Laughing Mirror' by Adrian Petringenaru of Romania, 'Katalina and Katalin' by Laurenti Sirbu of Romania and the Serbian fairy tale 'The Seven Flames' by Pavoa Stalter of Yugoslavia. Sixth volume of a six volume series of 18 European folktales produced by John Halas.
Fine Arts; Literature and Drama
Dist - AIMS **Prod** - EDPAT 1990

Laughs 8 MIN
16mm
Color (G)
$30.00 rental
Features cathode ray tubes conjuring the ghosts of favorite movie stars as they laugh at nothing. Captures their images traveling at the speed of light until they dissolve into silence.
Fine Arts
Dist - CANCIN **Prod** - WHITDL 1977

Laughter 15 MIN
U-matic / VHS
La Bonne Aventure Series
Color (K P)
Deals with French - American children. Shows that differences make the world interesting.
Foreign Language; Sociology
Dist - GPN **Prod** - MPBN

Laughter is Good Medicine 12 MIN
16mm / U-matic / VHS
Color
Presents an animated look at the role of laughter in relieving stress and aiding in better personal health. Shows how fellowship and a positive attitude toward life can help control anxiety and its effects and how a healthy lifestyle can prevent illness.
Guidance and Counseling; Health and Safety; Sociology
Dist - BBF **Prod** - BBF

Laughter is Holy 30 MIN
16mm
B&W
Portrays a chapter from Joe E. Brown's diary written during his personal appearances before American troops during World War II. Shows him battling a physical affliction as he performs, as well as the bombings and blackouts of many performances.
Biography; Fine Arts; History - World
Dist - WWPI **Prod** - GUIDAS 1959

Laughter through tears - Moti Peysi dem khazns - Skvoz slezy 92 MIN
35mm
Silent; B&W (G) (ENGLISH INTERTITLES SPANISH AND YIDDISH INTERTITLES)
Depicts the poverty and political repression of Jews in Czarist Russia in the late 1920s where official policy opposed the prevailing antisemitism of the populace. Constructs a skeptical portrait, both negative and positive, of prerevolutionary shtetl life. Based on Sholem Aleichem's stories 'Motl peysi, the Cantor's Son.' Contact distributor for rental fee.
History - World; Religion and Philosophy; Social Science; Sociology
Dist - NCJEWF

Launch control center 5 MIN
16mm
Apollo digest series
Color
LC 75-705011
Highlights the operations of launch control center at Cape Kennedy.
Industrial and Technical Education; Social Science
Dist - USNAC **Prod** - NASAMS 1969

Launch of the Saturn 5 4 MIN
U-matic
Apollo digest series
Color
LC 78-706980
Shows a typical launch of the Saturn 5, including assembly and transport to the launch pad preceding launching. Includes footage of separation of the first stage, taken from a mounted camera inside the second stage. Issued in 1969 as a motion picture.
Industrial and Technical Education; Science - Physical
Dist - USNAC **Prod** - NASA 1979

Launch of the Saturn V 4 MIN
16mm
Apollo digest series
Color
LC 74-705012
Depicts launch of Saturn V, Apollo, edited to music.
Industrial and Technical Education; Social Science; Sociology
Dist - USNAC **Prod** - NASAMS 1969

Launch Site to the Moon 3 MIN
16mm
Apollo digest series
Color
LC 74-705013
Tours Kennedy Space Center.
Industrial and Technical Education; Social Science
Dist - USNAC **Prod** - NASAMS 1969

Launch Windows for Lunar Landing 20 MIN
U-matic
Color
Describes the planning of a lunar mission with trajectories and physical capabilities which define these trajectories. Emphasizes the importance of the launch windows and earth reentry.
Industrial and Technical Education; Science - Physical
Dist - NASA **Prod** - NASA 1972

Launching a dream 14 MIN
VHS
Color (J H C)
$14.95 purchase _ #NA083
Examines the origins of the United States space program.
History - World; Science - Physical
Dist - INSTRU **Prod** - NASA

Launching Civil Service Reform Series WASHINGTON, DC 20409
The Senior Executive Service 30 MIN
Dist - USNAC

Launching Civil Service Reform Series
Labor - Management Relations 23 MIN
Merit Pay 18 MIN
A New Framework for Federal Personnel Management 30 MIN
Orientation to Civil Service Reform - a Discussion of the Highlights 31 MIN
Performance Appraisal and Workforce Discipline 22 MIN
Program Development Conference 29 MIN
Dist - USNAC

Launching the new government - 1789 - 1800 10 MIN
VHS
Color (I J H)
$59.00 purchase _ #MF - 4139
Examines the struggles of George Washington, Alexander Hamilton, Thomas Jefferson and John Adams to achieve stability for the new United States during the first 12 years of Constitutional government. Looks at how their work set the United States on a firm Contitutional course and portrays the critical events that shaped a working and lasting philosophy of government.
Civics and Political Systems; History - United States
Dist - INSTRU **Prod** - CORF

Launderette 10 MIN
VHS
Stop, look, listen series
Color; PAL (P I J)
Follows a teacher to a launderette where he finds two girls from school also doing their laundry. Watches them weigh their bundles, buy laundry detergent and put in coins to start the machines and all the phases of doing laundry.

Part of a series of films which start from some everyday observation and show more of what is happening, how and why. Builds vocabulary and encourages children to be more observant.
English Language; Home Economics; Social Science
Dist - VIEWTH

The Laundry Syndrome 23 MIN
16mm
Color (H)
LC 80-701231
Provides instruction in proper laundry techniques by telling a story about a woman who is a laundry junkie.
Home Economics
Dist - MTP **Prod** - USBCC 1980

Laundry Tips 13 MIN
Videoreel / VT2
Living Better I Series
Color
Home Economics
Dist - PBS **Prod** - MAETEL

Laura Chester - 3 - 29 - 87 35 MIN
VHS / Cassette
Poetry Center reading series
Color (G)
$15.00, $45.00 purchase, $15.00 rental _ #747 - 597
Features the experimental poet at the Poetry Center at San Francisco State University reading from her works, including selections from My Pleasure, performed with Summer Brenner, and In The Zone, with an introduction by Frances Phillips.
Literature and Drama
Dist - POETRY **Prod** - POETRY 1987

Laura Chester - 3 - 20 - 75 40 MIN
VHS / Cassette
Poetry Center reading series
Color (G)
$15.00, $45.00 purchase, $15.00 rental _ #109 - 83
Features the experimental poet at the Poetry Center of San Francisco State University, reading from her works, including selections from Night Latch and Primagravida.
Literature and Drama
Dist - POETRY **Prod** - POETRY 1975

Laura Clay - voice of change 56 MIN
VHS
Color (G)
$350.00 purchase, $95.00 rental
Profiles Laura Clay - 1849 - 1941 - a key figure in the woman's rights movement who devoted her life to the struggle for equal education opportunities, child custody rights, equal pay for equal work and the right to vote. Looks at her prominent roles in the National American Woman's Suffrage Association - today known as the League of Women Voters. Directed by Heather Lyons.
Fine Arts; History - World; Sociology
Dist - CNEMAG

Laura Reitman and Nancy Reynolds 30 MIN
U-matic / VHS
Eye on Dance - Second Time Around, Career Options for Dancers Series
Color
Fine Arts
Dist - ARCVID **Prod** - ARCVID

Laurel and Hardy Comedy Series
From Soup to Nuts 26 MIN
Leave 'Em Laughing 30 MIN
Men O War 24 MIN
Dist - RMIBHF

Laurel and Hardy Compendium 16 MIN
16mm
American Film Genre - the Comedy Film Series
B&W (H C A)
LC 77-701136
Presents excerpts from two Laurel and Hardy films, Air Raid Wardens, issued in 1943, and Hollywood Party, issued in 1934. Features a series of misadventures and mishaps as Laurel and Hardy try to contribute to the World War II war effort by volunteering as air raid wardens, and then attend a glamorous party in Hollywood. Exemplifies the comedy film genre.
Fine Arts
Dist - FI **Prod** - MGMA 1975

Laurel and Hardy festival series
Two tars 30 MIN
Dist - KITPAR
NCFP
RMIBHF

Laurel and Hardy festival series
Beau hunks 39 MIN
Dist - KITPAR
RMIBHF

Laurel and Hardy Festival Series
The Chimp 25 MIN
Swiss Miss 73 MIN
Dist - RMIBHF

Laurel and Hardy Go Visiting 3 MIN
16mm
Deals with the last footage of Oliver Hardy before his death.
Fine Arts
Dist - FCE **Prod** - FCE

The Laurel and Hardy Murder Case 28 MIN
16mm
B&W
Relates how Stan Laurel is mistaken for a missing heir. Shows how he and Oliver Hardy go to a creepy old house to claim his inheritance.
Fine Arts
Dist - RMIBHF **Prod** - ROACH 1930

The Laurel and Hardy Mystery Case 28 MIN
16mm
B&W
Tells how Ollie becomes convinced that Stan is the long - lost heir of the late tycoon Ebenezeer Laurel, which causes the pair to become involved with a strange butler, the police, heirs, black cats, a stormy night, murder and an assortment of suspects.
Fine Arts
Dist - RMIBHF **Prod** - ROACH 1930

Laurel with a moral 30 MIN
VHS
Color (K P R)
$11.99 purchase _ #35 - 82867 - 979
Presents Laurel, a storyteller whose subjects include self - esteem, obedience, generosity and God's love.
Literature and Drama; Religion and Philosophy
Dist - APH **Prod** - TYHP

Laurence Olivier - a life 159 MIN
VHS
Color (G)
$29.95 purchase _ #OLI010
Captures Olivier's genius and illustrates the legacy he left behind with film clips. Features Olivier recalling key partnerships, both on - and offstage, and reminiscences by many of his friends and colleagues, including Sir John Gielgud, Sir Ralph Richardson, Douglas Fairbanks, Jr, Dame Peggy Ashcroft and Olivier's wife, actress Joan Plowright. Edited and presented by Melvyn Bragg. Two tapes.
Fine Arts; Psychology
Dist - HOMVIS

Laurie and Pete - Birth 4
U-matic
Video birth library series
Color (J H G)
$100.00 purchase
Follows the childbirth experiences of Laurie and Pete, whose first child was born by emergency cesarean section at 32 weeks. Reveals that their next two babies were were successful vaginal deliveries, born at term with no complications. This time Laurie again goes into premature labor at 31 weeks. She spends the next four weeks on medication and bedrest. At 39 weeks when her membranes spontaneously break, she again delivers by VBAC - vaginal birth after cesarean. Part of a 15 - part series on childbirth education.
Health and Safety
Dist - POLYMR **Prod** - POLYMR

Laurie Duggan - 10 - 8 - 87
VHS / Cassette
Poetry Center reading series
Color (G)
$15.00, $45.00 purchase, $15.00 rental _ #772 - 613
Presents a reading by Australian poets. Features the writer reading from her books Under The Weather; The Great Divide; The Ash Range; and translations from The Epigrams of Martial, at the Poetry Center, San Francisco State University, with an introduction by Lyn Tranter.
Literature and Drama
Dist - POETRY

Laurie McDonald Series
Deux pieds 4 MIN
Duet for Tap and Galoshes 3 MIN
The Dying Swan 3 MIN
Minute Waltz 3 MIN
Dist - WMENIF

Laurie Simmons, a Teaser 5 MIN
U-matic / VHS
Cross - Overs - Photographers Series
Color
Fine Arts
Dist - ARTINC **Prod** - ARTINC

Laurie's operation 15 MIN
VHS
Zardips search for healthy wellness series
Color (P I)
LC 90-707997
Presents an episode in a series which help young children understand basic health issues and the value of taking good care of their bodies. Helps children overcome their fears about hospitals and surgery. Includes a teacher's guide.
Education; Health and Safety
Dist - TVOTAR **Prod** - TVOTAR 1989

L'Automne Est Une Aventure 11 MIN
U-matic / VHS / 16mm
Color (H) (FRENCH)
French version of 'AUTUMN IS AN ADVENTURE.' Depicts and narrates in simple French leaf raking, a marshmallow roast and a hike through the woods. Introduces a poem in French to encourage pupils to try their abilities in creative writing.
Foreign Language
Dist - CORF **Prod** - CORF 1960

Lautrec in Paris 29 MIN
Videoreel / VT2
Museum Open House Series
Color
Fine Arts; Geography - World
Dist - PBS **Prod** - WGBHTV

Lava and the River 20 MIN
16mm
Color (I J H C)
A story of the numerous lava flows which have made the Columbia Plateau, showing how they entombed plant and animal life. Points out the effects of the glacial melt - water action.
Geography - United States; Science - Natural; Science - Physical
Dist - MMP **Prod** - MMP 1959

Lava Beds National Monument 12 MIN
U-matic / VHS / 16mm
Color
Presents animation intercut with recent volcanic activity to trace the history of the Lava Beds National Monument in northern California. Describes shield volcanoes, lava tubes, pahoehoe lava and spatter cones, and traces the slow return of life to the area.
Geography - United States; Geography - World; History - United States; Science - Physical
Dist - USNAC **Prod** - USNPS 1981

Lavas of Etna 24 MIN
U-matic / VHS / 16mm
Color
Examines the form and structural complexity of Mount Etna, Europe's largest and most contemporary volcano, as well as the historic evolution of lava and ash types comprising the mountain's mantle. Demonstrates scientific analyses of the distribution of lava flows through chemical and X - ray analysis and mapping.
Geography - World; Science - Physical
Dist - MEDIAG **Prod** - OPENU 1982

Lavender 13 MIN
16mm / U-matic / VHS
Color (H C A)
LC 72-701946
Presents a film about two young lesbians whose past and present lives are examined through their own thoughts and feelings. Introduces a candid picture of lesbianism to help others understand and deal with its special life - style.
Psychology; Sociology
Dist - PEREN **Prod** - PEREN 1972

L'Aviateur 13 MIN
16mm
Les Francais chez vous series
B&W (I J H)
Foreign Language
Dist - CHLTN **Prod** - PEREN 1967

Lavinia Moyer and the Attic Theater 22 MIN
U-matic / VHS / 16mm
Working Artist Series
Color
Traces the Attic Theater's production of Wings, a play about stroke victims. Shows Lavinia Moyer, founder, involved in auditions, rehearsals, staging, comedy workshops and other activities.
Fine Arts; Health and Safety; Psychology
Dist - MARXS

L'Avventura 143 MIN
VHS
B&W (G)

$29.95 _ #AVV030
Tells the story of a young woman who disappears on a yachting trip. Portrays her lover and her best friend who lead a futile search then begin their own affair. Antonioni's tale of the idle rich, distinguished by his remarkable way of juxtaposing subjects in their environment, redefined our view of time and space in cinema.
Fine Arts; Psychology; Sociology
Dist - HOMVIS **Prod** - JANUS 1960
ANTONI

Law 30 MIN
VHS
How do you do - learning English series
Color (H A)
#317720
Shows that Frankie's undeserved parking ticket leads to a discussion with CHIPS about justice, law courts and simple legal terms. Describes how a trial works. Part of a series that helps newcomers learn English or improve their ability. Includes viewer's guide with grammar explanations and vocabulary drills, worksheets and two audio cassettes.
Civics and Political Systems; English Language
Dist - TVOTAR **Prod** - TVOTAR 1990

The Law 68 MIN
U-matic
Preventing Sexual Harassment in the Workplace Series
Color (A)
Explains the evolution of the federal law regarding sexual harrassment. Reviews the Civil Rights Act of 1964 and EEOC guidelines.
Business and Economics; Sociology
Dist - VENCMP **Prod** - VENCMP 1986

Law 20 TO 30 MIN
U-matic
Opportunity Profile Series
(H C A)
$99.95 _ #AI205
Illustrates the daily activities involved in a career in law. Working professionals in related jobs present the negative and positive aspects of such occupations.
Civics and Political Systems; Guidance and Counseling
Dist - CAMV **Prod** - CAMV

Law 20 MIN
VHS / 16mm
Citizens all Series
Color (H)
$150.00 purchase, $30.00 rental
Explores rule of law, the courts, and how the `best interests of the child' are determined in a child custody case.
Business and Economics; Civics and Political Systems
Dist - AITECH **Prod** - WHATV 1987

Law
U-matic / VHS
Opportunity Profile Series
$99.95 purchase _ #AJ104V
Provides advice on the skills and educational background desired by companies, the day to day activities of various careers, and the positive and negative aspects of various careers from corporate vice presidents, managers, and other working professionals.
Guidance and Counseling
Dist - CAREER **Prod** - CAREER

Law - a System of Order 18 MIN
U-matic / VHS / 16mm
Humanities Series
Color (J H)
LC 74-715412
Provides an introduction into the field of law.
Civics and Political Systems
Dist - MGHT **Prod** - MGHT 1972

The Law and Handicapped Children in School - Overview 30 MIN
VHS / U-matic
Law and Handicapped Children in School
Color (C A)
LC 79-706361
Reviews the provisions and background of the Education For All Handicapped Children Act of 1975 and the Rehabilitation Act of 1973.
Civics and Political Systems; Education; Psychology
Dist - IU **Prod** - IU 1979

Law and Handicapped Children in School
Annual review 30 MIN
The Due Process Hearing 30 MIN
The Due Process Panel 30 MIN
Educating the severely and profoundly handicapped 30 MIN
The Individualized Education Program 30 MIN
Individualized Education Program Case Conference 30 MIN
Integrating Handicapped Children in the Regular Classroom 30 MIN
The Larry P Case 30 MIN
The Law and Handicapped Children in School - Overview 30 MIN
Least Restrictive Environment - Resource Rooms and Special Classes 30 MIN
Least Restrictive Environment - Special Day and Residential Schools 30 MIN
Least Restrictive Environment Panel 30 MIN
Dist - IU

Law and Justice 30 MIN
U-matic
China After Mao Series
Color (CHINESE)
Discusses the many fluctuations within Chinese politics. Points to different bases of Chinese and western law and justice.
Civics and Political Systems; Geography - World
Dist - UMITV **Prod** - UMITV 1980

Law and Liability - a Security Perspective 15 MIN
U-matic / VHS
Health Care Security Training Series
Color
Defines legal powers and limitations of the security officer with emphasis on search, arrest and use of physical force.
Civics and Political Systems; Sociology
Dist - CORF **Prod** - GREESM 1984

Law and motion skills training 90 MIN
VHS
Color (PRO)
$149.00 purchase, $49.00 purchase _ #CP-69102
Uses case simulations to train lawyers in oral and written advocacy. Provides short segments of arguments covering nine motion topics. Includes a handbook.
Civics and Political Systems
Dist - CCEB

Law and Order 28 MIN
VHS / U-matic
Please Stand by - a History of Radio Series
(C A)
Fine Arts; History - United States; Psychology; Sociology
Dist - SCCON **Prod** - SCCON 1986

Law and Order 81 MIN
16mm / U-matic / VHS
B&W (J H C)
LC 72-708177
Presents a documentary of a layman's experience with the Kansas City police. Depicts the policeman's duties as disparate and difficult. Filmed during six weeks with the Kansas City Police Department.
Civics and Political Systems; Psychology; Social Science; Sociology
Dist - ZIPRAH **Prod** - WISEF

Law and Order 56 MIN
U-matic / VHS
We the People Series
Color (G)
$279.00, $179.00 purchase _ #AD - 1423
Considers that the power of police to search people and their homes is constitutionally limited - some say too limited. Looks at a case where police, who are often accused of violating the Fourth Amendment, are in court to oppose, on constitutional grounds, the police commissioner's drug - testing program. Part of a four - part series on the American Constitution.
Civics and Political Systems
Dist - FOTH **Prod** - FOTH

Law and persons with mental disability series
Presents a six - part series featuring Michael I Perlin, JD, on the law and persons with mental disability. Serves as a resource for attorneys practicing mental disability law, advocates working with mentally disabled individuals, mental health professionals, hospital administrators and other care providers subject to legal regulation. Includes The Involuntary Civil Commitment Process; The Right to Treatment; Institutional Rights, Community Rights and Homelessness; The Right to Refuse Treatment; Tort Law - The Legal Regulation of Mental Health Professionals; Power Imbalances; The Criminal Law Process.
The Criminal law process - Tape 6
The Involuntary civil commitment process - Tape 1
Power imbalances - Tape 5
The Right to refuse treatment - Tape 3
The Right to treatment, institutional rights, community rights and homelessnes - Tape 2
Tort law - the legal regulation of mental health professionals - Tape 4
Dist - BAXMED

Law and the Citizen Series
Contract law 23 MIN
Landlord - Tenant Law 23 MIN
Dist - BARR

The Law and the Family 145 MIN
U-matic
University of the Air Series
Color (J H C A)
$750.00 purchase, $250.00 rental
Shows that laws can help and also hinder the family and suggests specific changes in the laws. Program contains a series of five cassettes 29 minutes each.
Civics and Political Systems; Sociology
Dist - CTV **Prod** - CTV 1978

The Law and the Prophets 51 MIN
16mm / U-matic / VHS
Color (H A R)
LC FIA67-5966
Presents a biblical account of the Creation, the high points of the history of the Hebrew people and the developing of their faith through the time of the prophets. The prologue recounts the sin of Adam and Eve and closes with their banishment from the Garden of Eden.
Religion and Philosophy
Dist - MGHT **Prod** - NBCTV 1968

Law and the Prophets, the, Pt 1 27 MIN
U-matic / VHS / 16mm
Color (H C R)
LC FIA67-5966
Presents a biblical account of the creation, the high points of the history of the Hebrew people and the development of their faith through the time of the prophets. Recounts the sin of Adam and Eve and their banishment from the Garden of Eden. Depicts sacred themes by means of artwork.
Fine Arts; Religion and Philosophy
Dist - MGHT **Prod** - NBCTV 1968

Law and the Prophets, the, Pt 2 24 MIN
U-matic / VHS / 16mm
Color (H C R)
LC FIA67-5966
Presents a biblical account of the creation, the high points of the history of the Hebrew people and the development of their faith through the time of the prophets. Recounts the sin of Adam and Eve and their banishment from the Garden of Eden. Depicts sacred themes by means of artwork.
Fine Arts; Religion and Philosophy
Dist - MGHT **Prod** - NBCTV 1968

Law Enforcement 24 MIN
VHS / 16mm
Career Builders Video Series
Color
$85.00 purchase _ #V101
Examines a potential career choice by taking the viewer into the working environment and interviewing professionals on the demands, rewards and frustrations on the job.
Business and Economics; Civics and Political Systems; Sociology
Dist - EDUCDE **Prod** - EDUCDE 1987

Law Enforcement
U-matic / VHS
Work - a - Day America
$59.95 purchase _ #VV111V
Helps students achieve career vocational preparation. Stresses the four main points of career awareness and exploration, specific skills intended, employability skills needed, and real people sharing on the job experiences.
Guidance and Counseling
Dist - CAREER **Prod** - CAREER

Law Enforcement
VHS / U-matic
Career Builders Video Series
$95.00 purchase _ #ED101V
Uses actual professionals to talk about the job's demands, rewards, and frustrations. Shows the working environment of the career field.
Guidance and Counseling
Dist - CAREER **Prod** - CAREER

Law Enforcement - Civil Liability Series
The Negligent Use of Motor Vehicles 13 MIN
Dist - AIMS

Law Enforcement Education Series
What's a Cop 25 MIN
Dist - CORF

Law Enforcement Equipment Standards 7 MIN
16mm
Color (H C A)
LC 73-702596
Describes standards being developed for equipment used in the protection and safety of a policeman and patrol car,

and communications and standards for new equipment under the National Institute of Law Enforcement and Criminal Justice.
Civics and Political Systems; Sociology
Dist - USNBOS **Prod** - USNBOS 1972

Law Enforcement - Patrol Officers 19 MIN
VHS / U-matic
Ways of the Law Series
Color (H)
Dramatizes typical police officer problem situations. Presents discussions with former and present patrol officers.
Civics and Political Systems
Dist - GPN **Prod** - SCITV 1980

Law Enforcement - Patrol Procedures Series
Aggressive patrol 10 MIN
Driving under the influence 10 MIN
Felony vehicle stop 10 MIN
Observation and Perception 22 MIN
Probable cause - search and seizure 25 MIN
Dist - CORF

Law Enforcement - the Citizen's Role 19 MIN
VHS / U-matic
Ways of the Law Series
Color (H)
Discusses the citizen's role in law enforcement with county, state, city and national police.
Civics and Political Systems
Dist - GPN **Prod** - SCITV 1980

Law firm marketing and professional responsibility 50 MIN
VHS
Color (C PRO A)
$95.00 purchase _ #Y142
Examines methods of marketing law firm services and their ethical implications as determined by pertinent model rules, state statutes and court decisions.
Business and Economics; Civics and Political Systems
Dist - ALIABA **Prod** - CLETV 1991

Law firm marketing in the 90s 50 MIN
VHS
Color (A PRO C)
$95.00 purchase _ #Y701
Covers realistic ways for law practices of all sizes to obtain more business from new and existing clients.
Business and Economics; Civics and Political Systems
Dist - ALIABA **Prod** - CLETV 1992

Law firm policies on sexual harassment - Development and implementation 50 MIN
VHS
Color (C PRO A)
$95.00 purchase _ #Y151
Assists law firms in developing comprehensive and enforceable policies on sexual harassment applicable to both lawyers and support staff. Features a panel discussion with pre - recorded dramatizations of unlawful conduct sure to generate viewer discussion.
Civics and Political Systems; Sociology
Dist - ALIABA **Prod** - CLETV 1991

Law firms and ancillary business activities - Conflict between professionalism and the practice of law 50 MIN
VHS
Color (C PRO A)
$95.00 purchase _ #Y143
Examines the dangers of 'multiprofessional mixes' as put forth by critics who fear the erosion of the traditional attorney - client relationship as well as the conveniences and economic benefits claimed by proponents to be consistent with ethical and professional standards.
Business and Economics; Civics and Political Systems
Dist - ALIABA **Prod** - CLETV 1991

Law in the Schools 30 MIN
U-matic / VHS / 16mm
Legal Information for Law Enforcement Series
Color (PRO)
LC 76-701660
Examines law enforcement in relation to school campuses. Outlines the role of the police on school premises and suggests greater protection to curb violence and abate crime in schools.
Civics and Political Systems; Sociology
Dist - AIMS **Prod** - CAGO 1974

The Law machine 29 MIN
16mm
Government story series; No 9
Color
LC 70-707166
Discusses the steps through which a bill must pass before it becomes law. Points out the problems and strategies of leadership in steering a bill through Congress and the effect of individual personalities on passage of legislation.
Civics and Political Systems
Dist - WBCPRO **Prod** - WBCPRO 1968

The Law of Armed Conflict 21 MIN
U-matic / VHS / 16mm
Color
Presents an overview of laws of armed conflict in the air, on the sea and on the ground. Covers treaties and conventions and how they apply to members of the Air Force.
Civics and Political Systems; Sociology
Dist - USNAC **Prod** - USAF

Law of Cosines 30 MIN
VHS
Mathematics Series
Color (J)
LC 90713155
Explaines the law of cosines. The 107th of 157 installments in the Mathematics Series.
Mathematics
Dist - GPN

Law of cosines 30 MIN
VHS
Trigonometry series
Color (H)
$125.00 purchase _ #5014
Explains the law of cosines. Part of a 16 - part series on trigonometry.
Mathematics
Dist - LANDMK **Prod** - LANDMK

Law of Cosines 30 MIN
16mm
Trigonometry Series
B&W (H)
Derives the law of cosines and uses it to solve a problem in which either two sides and the included angle or three sides of a triangle are known.
Mathematics
Dist - MLA **Prod** - CALVIN 1959

The Law of Falling Bodies 13 MIN
U-matic / VHS
Mechanical Universe - High School Adaptation Series
Color (H)
Science - Physical
Dist - SCCON **Prod** - SCCON 1986

The Law of Falling Bodies 30 MIN
16mm / U-matic / VHS
Mechanical Universe Series
Color (C A)
Demostrates Galileo's experiments proving that all bodies fall with the same constant acceleration.
Science - Physical
Dist - FI **Prod** - ANNCPB

The Law of Gravitation - an Example of Physical Law 56 MIN
Videoreel / VHS
Feynman Lectures - the Character of Physical Law Series
B&W
Describes the history of the law of gravity, the method and its limitations.
Science - Physical
Dist - EDC **Prod** - EDC

The Law of magnets - Part 3 10 MIN
VHS
Magnets series
Color; PAL (P I J)
Examines the polar aspect of magnetism and how magnets attract each other. Part three of a five - part series on magnets.
Science - Physical
Dist - VIEWTH **Prod** - VIEWTH

Law of nature - East Africa - Part 13 8 MIN
VHS
Natures kingdom series
Color (P I J)
$125.00 purchase
Watches Masai warriors portray the movements of elephants in folklore and dance while other observers in a balloon view elephants, buffalo, gnus, a hyena and a giraffe. Part of a 26 - part series on animals showing the habitats and traits of various species.
Geography - World; Science - Natural
Dist - LANDMK **Prod** - LANDMK 1992

Law of Sines 30 MIN
16mm
Trigonometry Series
B&W (H)
Derives the law of sines and uses it to solve a problem in which two angles and the included side of a triangle are known. Describes a problem in which two sides and the angle opposite one of them are given and either of two solutions is possible.
Mathematics
Dist - MLA **Prod** - CALVIN 1959

Law of Sines 30 MIN
VHS
Mathematics Series
Color (J)
LC 90713155
Discusses the law of sines. The 106th of 157 installments in the Mathematics Series.
Mathematics
Dist - GPN

Law of sines 30 MIN
VHS
Trigonometry series
Color (H)
$125.00 purchase _ #5013
Explains the law of sines. Part of a 16 - part series on trigonometry.
Mathematics
Dist - LANDMK **Prod** - LANDMK

Law of Tangents 28 MIN
16mm
Trigonometry Series
B&W (H)
Derives the law of tangents and explains that it is significant because its ratio form is suitable to the use of logarithms for calculation. Shows a problem in which the law is utilized.
Mathematics
Dist - MLA **Prod** - CALVIN 1959

The Law of the Land 20 MIN
U-matic / VHS
Exploring Our Nation Series
Color (I)
Deals with the meaning and significance of the Constitution of the United States. Focuses on the Bill of Rights.
Civics and Political Systems
Dist - GPN **Prod** - KRMATV 1975

The Law of the Land 26 MIN
U-matic / VHS / 16mm
Color (J)
Looks at the use and misuse of land and what can be done to manage it more efficiently in the wake of urban sprawl, strip mining, leap - frog development, grotesque commercial districts and ruined scenery.
Social Science; Sociology
Dist - MCFI **Prod** - UFLA 1980

Law of the Sea 29 MIN
16mm
Color
LC 74-705014
Illustrates various legal problems that can arise at sea and their solutions.
Civics and Political Systems
Dist - USNAC **Prod** - USN 1970

Law of the Sea 28 MIN
U-matic / VHS / 16mm
Color (J)
LC 74-701912
Examines the state of maritime laws as related to Iceland, Ecuador, Alaska, England, the Netherlands, Denmark, Norway and the North Sea. Deals with off - shore fishing and mineral rights and discusses the concepts of freedom of the seas and the common heritage approach.
Civics and Political Systems; Social Science
Dist - JOU **Prod** - UN 1974

Law of the wild 26 MIN
VHS
Cliffhangers I series
B&W (G)
Features animal co - stars Rin - Tin - Tin, Jr and Rex. Hosted by cowboy hero Bob Custer. Includes six episodes.
Fine Arts
Dist - SCETV **Prod** - SCETV 1983

Law Office Management 160 MIN
VHS / U-matic
Color (PRO)
Discusses how to improve the efficiency and profitability of a law practice through recruiting, selecting and training personnel, jury and docket control and use of stored materials.
Business and Economics; Civics and Political Systems
Dist - ABACPE **Prod** - CCEB

Lawale 30 MIN
16mm
Color (G)
$50.00 rental
Portrays four women within the confines of the middle class and a world of endless afternoon teas, dinners and waiting. Gives the sense of a dream or a series of pauses like the arrest of time. Produced by Dore O.

Fine Arts; Sociology
Dist - CANCIN

Lawn and garden series

Annuals - hanging baskets 38 MIN
Basic gardening 59 MIN
Ground Covers 60 MIN
Grow Your Own Vegetables 55 MIN
Pruning 47 MIN
Success with Indoor Plants 57 MIN
Your Beautiful Lawn 48 MIN
Your beautiful roses 56 MIN
Dist - MOHOMV

Lawn and Gardening
VHS / U-matic
Work - a - Day America
$59.95 purchase _ #VV112V
Helps students achieve career vocational preparation. Stresses the four main points of career awareness and exploration, specific skills intended, employability skills needed, and real people sharing on the job experiences.
Guidance and Counseling
Dist - CAREER **Prod** - CAREER

The Lawn and Vacant Lot Community 15 MIN
U-matic / VHS
Why Series
Color (P I)
Discusses the living things found on lawns and vacant lots.
Science - Natural
Dist - AITECH **Prod** - WDCNTV 1976

Lawn Care 4.25 MIN
BETA / VHS / U-matic
School Housekeeping Series
(PRO A)
$225 _ #1016
Views basic information and methods of lawn care using various types of mowers.
Education; Guidance and Counseling
Dist - CTT **Prod** - CTT

Lawn Care 16.25 MIN
VHS / U-matic / BETA
Medical Housekeeping Series
(PRO A)
$225 _ #1016
Discusses the various methods that can be applied when using different kinds of mowers.
Education; Guidance and Counseling
Dist - CTT **Prod** - CTT

Lawn Care 48 MIN
BETA / VHS / 16mm
Color (G)
$39.95 purchase _ #VT1027
Teaches how to seed a lawn and maintain it. Covers liming and moss control, raking, thatching, mowing, and trimming. Taught by Ed Hume.
Agriculture
Dist - RMIBHF **Prod** - RMIBHF

Lawn Care 19.25 MIN
VHS / U-matic / BETA
Groundskeeping Series
(PRO A)
$225 _ #1017
Covers the basic methods used in lawn maintenance such as seeding, sodding, and fertilization.
Education; Guidance and Counseling
Dist - CTT **Prod** - CTT

Lawn Care 16.25 MIN
BETA / VHS / U-matic
Groundskeeping Series
(PRO A)
$225 _ #1016
Presents standard methods of mowing using various types of mowing machines.
Education; Guidance and Counseling
Dist - CTT **Prod** - CTT

Lawn Care 30 MIN
U-matic / VHS
Home Gardener with John Lenanton Series Lesson 19; Lesson 19
Color (C A)
Examines selection and use of mowers, mowing techniques and schedules and types of equipment for spreading fertilizer.
Agriculture
Dist - CDTEL **Prod** - COAST

Lawn Care 16.25 MIN
VHS / U-matic / BETA
Basic Housekeeping Series
(PRO A)
$225 _ #1016
Presents lawn care methods according to the use of various types of mowers.
Education; Guidance and Counseling
Dist - CTT **Prod** - CTT

Lawn care - Part 1 17 MIN
VHS
Color (H A G T)
$225.00 purchase _ #BM116
Covers basic lawn mowing techniques using small push mowers, several types of ride mowers and large tractor mowers. Places special emphasis on safety for both operator and bystander. Part one of a two - part series.
Agriculture; Health and Safety; Psychology
Dist - AAVIM **Prod** - AAVIM

Lawn Care (Part 2) 19.25 MIN
VHS / U-matic / BETA
Basic Housekeeping Series
(PRO A)
$225 _ #1017
Focuses on methods used in effective lawn care such as seeding, sodding, irrigation and others.
Education; Guidance and Counseling
Dist - CTT **Prod** - CTT

Lawn care - Part 2 20 MIN
VHS
Color (H A G T)
$225.00 purchase _ #BM117
Provides information on lawn care procedures such as seeding, sodding, fertilization, irrigation and weed control. Covers situations ranging from athletic field maintenance to spot seeding in established lawns. Part two of a two - part series.
Agriculture; Health and Safety; Psychology
Dist - AAVIM **Prod** - AAVIM

Lawn Care (Part 2) 19.3 MIN
VHS / U-matic / BETA
Medical Housekeeping Series
(PRO A)
$225 _ #1017
Gives important on data on lawn duties such as seeding, sodding, fertilization, and others.
Education; Guidance and Counseling
Dist - CTT **Prod** - CTT

Lawn Care (Pt 2) 19.25 MIN
VHS / U-matic / BETA
School Housekeeping Series
(PRO A)
$225 _ #1017
Covers information and methods that are useful in maintaining various types of lawns.
Education; Guidance and Counseling
Dist - CTT **Prod** - CTT

Lawn Equipment and Mowing Operations 29 MIN
U-matic
Grounds Maintenance Training Series
Color
Describes various types of mowers and lawn care equipment. Illustrates their use, maintenance care and safety precautions.
Agriculture
Dist - UMITV **Prod** - UMITV 1978

Lawn Installation 30 MIN
U-matic / VHS
Home Gardener with John Lenanton Series Lesson 11; Lesson 11
Color (C A)
Explains and demonstrates four methods of establishing a lawn. Suggests planting times and methods. Shows proper techniques of preparing the ground for planting.
Agriculture
Dist - CDTEL **Prod** - COAST

Lawns and Groundcovers 30 MIN
U-matic / VHS
Home Gardener with John Lenanton Series Lesson 10; Lesson 10
Color (C A)
Designed to help home gardener decide which type of grass or groundcover to use for a particular landscape purpose. Describes qualities and growing habits of most widely used grasses.
Agriculture
Dist - CDTEL **Prod** - COAST

Lawns - Planting and Care 60 MIN
U-matic / VHS
Ortho's Video Series
Color (A)
$24.95 _ #OR101
Gives the viewer tips on a complete process for planting and maintaining his lawn. Covers site preparation, installing a lawn, fertilizing, and more.
Agriculture; Science - Natural
Dist - AAVIM **Prod** - AAVIM

Lawrence Ferlinghetti - 3 - 5 - 76 30 MIN
VHS / Cassette
Poetry Center reading series
Color (G)
$15.00, $45.00 purchase, $15.00 rental _ #173 - 134A
Features the Beat poet reading his works at the Poetry Center, San Francisco State University, with an introduction by Lewis MacAdams.
Literature and Drama
Dist - POETRY **Prod** - POETRY 1976

Lawrence Ferlinghetti - 2 - 13 - 65 37 MIN
VHS / Cassette
NET Outtake series
B&W (G)
$15.00, $125.00 purchase, $15.00 rental _ #149 - 115
Features the Beat poet at City Lights Bookstore, which he founded, in San Francisco, and at his home reading The Situation in the West Followed by A Holy Proposal; The Jig is Up; and Dog. Part of a series of films composed of outtakes from the series USA - Poetry, which was produced in 1965 - 66 for National Educational Television, using all retrievable footage to provide rare glimpses of the poets in their own settings. Also features Net Outtake's program on Gary Snyder.
Literature and Drama
Dist - POETRY **Prod** - KQEDTV 1965

Lawrence Fixel - 10 - 4 - 87 120 MIN
VHS / Cassette
Poetry Center reading series
Color (G)
#932 - 629
Features the writer reading from his works at the Ruth Witt - Diamant Memorial Reading at the Poetry Center, San Francisco State University. Also includes readings by James Broughton, Robert Duncan, Rosalie Moore, Mark Linenthal, Shirley Taylor, Christy Taylor, Justine Fixel, Michael McClure, Gail Layton, and Stephen Witt - Diamant. Introduction by Frances Phillips. Slides of Ruth Witt - Diamant courtesy of Caryl Mezey. Available for listening purposes only at the Center; not for sale or rent.
Literature and Drama
Dist - POETRY **Prod** - POETRY 1987

Lawrence of Arabia 185 MIN
16mm
Color
Offers a biography of T E Lawrence, recounting his spectacular career and battles. Stars Peter O'Toole and Omar Sharif.
Biography; Fine Arts
Dist - TIMLIF **Prod** - CPC 1962

Lawrence of Arabia 221 MIN
U-matic / VHS / 16mm
Color
Relates the exploits of T E Lawrence, who helped forge the modern Arab nation.
Fine Arts
Dist - FI **Prod** - CPC 1962

Lawrence of Arabia 18 MIN
16mm
Color
An abridged version of the motion picture Lawrence Of Arabia. Tells the true story of T E Lawrence, the World War I British officer who united the Arabs against the Turks. Stars Peter O'Toole and Alec Guinness.
Biography; Fine Arts; History - United States
Dist - TIMLIF **Prod** - CPC 1982

Lawrence Raab 29 MIN
U-matic
Poets Talking Series
Color
Literature and Drama
Dist - UMITV **Prod** - UMITV 1975

Lawrence Weiner - Affected and or Effected 20 MIN
U-matic / VHS
Color
Presented by Lawrence Weiner.
Fine Arts
Dist - ARTINC **Prod** - ARTINC

Lawrence Weiner - Green as Well as Blue as Well as Red 20 MIN
U-matic / VHS
Color
Presented by Lawrence Weiner.
Fine Arts
Dist - ARTINC **Prod** - ARTINC

Lawrence Weiner - Shifted from Side to Side 1 MIN
U-matic / VHS
B&W

Offers illustrations of possibility.
Fine Arts
Dist - ARTINC **Prod** - ARTINC

Lawrence Weiner - There but for 20 MIN
U-matic / VHS
Color
Presented by Lawrence Weiner.
Fine Arts
Dist - ARTINC **Prod** - ARTINC

Lawrence Weiner - to and Fro and Fro and to and to and Fro and Fro and to 1 MIN
VHS / U-matic
B&W
Presents a comic introduction to the institution of conceptual art.
Fine Arts
Dist - ARTINC **Prod** - ARTINC

Lawrence Welk and His Champagne Music 10 MIN
16mm
Color
Presents Lawrence Welk and his orchestra playing his famous Champagne Music.
Fine Arts
Dist - RMIBHF **Prod** - UNKNWN

The Laws of Motion 29 MIN
Videoreel / VT2
Observing Eye Series
Color
Science - Physical; Sociology
Dist - PBS **Prod** - WGBHTV

The Laws of Motion, Pt 1 18 MIN
U-matic / VHS / 16mm
Physics in Action Series
Color (J H C)
Illustrates Newton's Laws of Motion as well as the principle of Conservation Of Momentum. Continued in the Laws of Motion, Pt 2.
Science - Physical
Dist - LUF **Prod** - LUF

The Laws of Motion, Pt 2 18 MIN
16mm / U-matic / VHS
Physics in Action Series
Color (J H C)
Illustrates Newton's Laws of Motion as well as the principle of Conservation of Momentum. Continued from the Laws of Motion, Pt 1.
Science - Physical
Dist - LUF **Prod** - LUF

Laws of Nature 5 MIN
16mm
Driver Education Series
Color (J)
LC FIA66-1004
Shows how the traffic engineer applies his knowledge of nature's laws and forces in determining safe speeds for vehicles to round curves.
Health and Safety
Dist - AMROIL **Prod** - AMROIL 1964

Laws of nature and driving 20 MIN
35mm strip / U-matic
Color (J H)
Shows how natural laws of gravity, friction, inertia and the force of impact affect us every time we get behind the wheel. Stresses the importance of knowing how these 'laws' affect vehicle performance and control in order to make driving safer and more enjoyable.
Health and Safety; Science - Physical
Dist - BUMPA **Prod** - BUMPA

The Lawyer 45 MIN
16mm
B&W; Color (G)
$100.00 rental
Discusses society and revolution. Transforms 'The Wretched of the Earth' into an American nightmare.
Fine Arts
Dist - CANCIN **Prod** - DEGRAS 1968

The Lawyer 29 MIN
U-matic
You and the Law Series Lesson 3
Color (C A)
Discusses several aspects of the lawyer. Includes training and qualifications necessary to be a lawyer, expected ethical principles and major forms of specialization.
Civics and Political Systems
Dist - CDTEL **Prod** - COAST

Lawyer from Boston 30 MIN
16mm
B&W (R)
Tells the story how Supreme Court Justice and Zionist Louis D Brandeis came to discover his Jewish heritage. (Kinescope).
Religion and Philosophy
Dist - NAAJS **Prod** - JTS 1956

The Lawyer, the farmer and the clerk 26 MIN
VHS
Ordinary people series
Color (G)
$190.00 purchase, $50.00 rental
Records June 25, 1993 when Ordinary People cameras, on hand to cover a constitutional negotiating process, captured footage of a tank smashing through the glass windows of Johannesburg's World Trade Center by the white right wing, to take over the negotiating chamber. Documents this day through the eyes of a clerk, a right wing extremist and a dispossessed black man. Exposes the precariousness of Africa's move toward democracy. Part of a series which chronicles an event in South Africa through the eyes of three or four 'ordinary' people, chosen to represent diverse backgrounds or dissimilar points of view. This current affairs series seeks to provide insight into the collective South African conscience.
Fine Arts; History - World
Dist - FIRS **Prod** - GAVSHO 1993

Lawyering skills series

Business planning	47 MIN
The Business transaction	30 MIN
Dispute Resolution	47 MIN

Dist - ABACPE

Lawyers 30 MIN
U-matic / VHS
Consumer survival series; Personal planning
Color
Presents tips on using lawyers.
Civics and Political Systems; Home Economics
Dist - MDCPB **Prod** - MDCPB

The Laxmi Bomb 15 MIN
U-matic / VHS / 16mm
Color (I J)
LC 82-706946
Presents an Indian fairy tale about a young boy who discovers a magical firecracker named after the goddess of good luck, Laxmi. Describes an adventure during which the boy overcomes the demon firecrackers with the help of Laxmi and saves other children who were captured by the demon.
Fine Arts; Geography - World; Literature and Drama
Dist - PHENIX **Prod** - KELTCS 1982

Lay it on the Line 22 MIN
16mm
Color
Discusses campaign fire management. Tells the story of a fire suppression organization set up for an all out campaign fire effort.
Social Science
Dist - FILCOM **Prod** - PUBSF

Lay Lady Lay 6 MIN
16mm / U-matic / VHS
Color
Shows how a hen is sent to the company psychiatrist after she loses pride in her work. Illustrates aspects of morale and production.
Business and Economics
Dist - PHENIX **Prod** - KRATKY 1978

Lay My Burden Down 60 MIN
U-matic / VHS / 16mm
B&W
Documents black tenant farmers in Alabama in 1966.
Social Science; Sociology
Dist - NEWTIM **Prod** - NEWTIM

Lay Therapy 30 MIN
U-matic / VHS
B&W
Uses excerpts from a regular meeting of lay therapists to help introduce the responsibilities of a lay therapist as a loving friend and link between the family and professional service agencies.
Psychology; Sociology
Dist - UWISC **Prod** - NCCAN

The Layered Silicone Mold Technique for Processing Dentures 30 MIN
16mm
Color
LC 74-705015
Presents a technique for processing mold in the upper half of the flask. Explains that this new method of processing produces extremely accurate dentures, free of adhering calcium sulphate film or particles and with the surfaces as smooth as the polished wax of the trial dentures.
Health and Safety
Dist - USVA **Prod** - USVA

Layering responses - 1 104 MIN
VHS
Creating therapeutic change series
Color; PAL; SECAM (G)
$95.00 purchase
Features Richard Bandler in the first part of a seven - part series on creating therapeutic change using advanced NLP, neuro - linguistic programming. Reveals that just solving problems often isn't enough and that time distinctions can be used to interlace beliefs, feeling states and 'chains' into complexes that generatively reorganize fundamental attitudes throughout a person's life. Recommended that tapes be viewed in order. Bandler sometimes uses profanity for emphasis, which may offend some people.
Health and Safety; Psychology
Dist - NLPCOM **Prod** - NLPCOM

Layering, Trimming, Clipping and Notching Seam Allowances 3 MIN
16mm
Clothing Construction Techniques Series
Color (J)
LC 77-701181
Illustrates techniques of layering, trimming, clipping and notching. Suggests where each technique would be used.
Home Economics
Dist - IOWASP **Prod** - IOWA 1976

Laying a foundation to introduce evidence 105 MIN
VHS
Color (PRO)
$149.00 purchase, $49.00 rental _ #CP-62901
Features 30 dramatized courtroom scenes with expert commentary covering each major type of foundation and alternative methods of using the evidence. Includes a handbook.
Civics and Political Systems
Dist - CCEB

Laying Concrete Block 15 MIN
16mm
Color (IND)
Stresses the importance of good mortar when used in masonry construction. Shows how the first course is laid in a full mortar bed and how vital the corner blocks and the first course are in laying the succeeding courses.
Industrial and Technical Education
Dist - MOKIN **Prod** - MOKIN

Laying Down Pipe 11 MIN
U-matic / VHS
Roughneck Training Series
Color (A PRO IND)
$175.00 purchase _ #40.0521
Shows how drill pipe and drill collars should be layed down, inspected and prepared for transport to the next location. Designed for entry - level rotary drill helpers.
Industrial and Technical Education; Social Science
Dist - UTEXPE **Prod** - UTEXPE 1983

Laying hardwood floors with Don Bollinger 60 MIN
VHS / BETA
Color (G A)
$29.95 _ #060055
Shows how to install a strip, plank or parquet hardwood floor. Features carpenter Don Bollinger. Also available in book format.
Fine Arts; Home Economics; Industrial and Technical Education
Dist - TANTON **Prod** - TANTON

Laying it on the line 28 MIN
16mm / VHS / BETA / U-matic
Color; PAL (IND)
PdS150, PdS158 purchase
Gives a general overview of planning excavation methods, laying and testing of two types of drainage materials - stoneware and PVC pipes. Shows modern procedures for correct installation methods. Produced by Film Victoria.
Industrial and Technical Education
Dist - EDPAT

Laying it on the Line 28 MIN
16mm
Color (IND)
LC 81-700709
Gives an overview of the planning, laying and testing of stoneware and PVC pipes.
Industrial and Technical Education
Dist - TASCOR **Prod** - VICCOR 1981

Laying Out and Forming Plywood 21 MIN
16mm
B&W

LC FIE52-313
Demonstrates how to lay out plywood using blueprint and templates, form plywood in a press, reinforce plywood and apply glue and varnish.
Industrial and Technical Education
Dist - USNAC **Prod** - USOE 1944

Laying Out and Installing Compartment Fixtures 12 MIN
16mm
B&W
LC FIE52-209
Explains how to locate installations on a planview blueprint, lay out ceiling fixtures and studs, lay out and burn a hole for the passage of cable and install ceiling fixtures.
Industrial and Technical Education
Dist - USNAC **Prod** - USOE 1945

Laying out and installing hangers 19 MIN
16mm
Shipbuilding skills series; Pipefitting; 5
B&W
LC FIE52-201
Explains how to measure and cut hanger legs to length, and how to install stool, angle iron bracket, strap, rod and saddle hangers.
Industrial and Technical Education
Dist - USNAC **Prod** - USOE 1944

Laying Out and Installing Kickpipes and Stuffing Tubes 16 MIN
16mm
B&W
LC FIE52-212
Shows how to locate the kickpipe or stuffing tube area, lay out the penetration area, cut or burn the penetration area and install the kickpipe or stuffing tube.
Industrial and Technical Education
Dist - USNAC **Prod** - USOE 1945

Laying Out and Installing Main Wireway 21 MIN
16mm
B&W
LC FIE52-211
Explains how to determine from the blueprint the route which cables are to follow and the size of the hangers to be used. Shows how to lay out the raceways, install flat bars and hangers and how to lay out penetration holes to but.
Industrial and Technical Education
Dist - USNAC **Prod** - USOE 1945

Laying Out, Drilling and Tapping Flanges on Sea Chest 19 MIN
16mm
B&W
LC FIE52-215
Points out the component parts of a sea chest. Explains how locations of flanges are checked, flanges leveled, stud hold centers laid out and stud holes drilled and tapped.
Industrial and Technical Education
Dist - USNAC **Prod** - USOE 1944

Laying Out Small Castings 16 MIN
16mm
Machine Shop Work Series Bench Work, no 6
B&W
LC FIE51-535
Explains how to lay out holes for drilling, locate a reference point and use hermaphrodite calipers, combination square and surface gage.
Industrial and Technical Education
Dist - USNAC **Prod** - USOE 1942

Laying, Pinning and Cutting a Pattern 4 MIN
16mm
Clothing Construction Techniques Series
Color (J)
LC 77-701169
Shows how to prepare the fabric for pattern layout. Demonstrates pinning the pattern on the correct grainline and cutting out the garment.
Home Economics
Dist - IOWASP **Prod** - IOWA 1976

Laying Pipe the Reel Way 24 MIN
16mm
Color
LC 80-701237
Describes the advantages of laying pipe on the ocean floor using the reel system operated from a ship.
Industrial and Technical Education
Dist - SFINTL **Prod** - SFINTL 1980

Laying the foundation for exhibits and witnesses at trial 57 MIN
VHS
Training the advocate series
Color (C PRO)
$115.00 purchase, $95.00 rental _ #TTA03
Uses a nuclear power plant accident case to teach basic trial advocacy skills. Gives guidelines for laying the foundation for exhibits and witnesses in a trial. Co - produced by the American Bar Association.
Civics and Political Systems
Dist - NITA **Prod** - NITA 1983

Laying the Foundation for Exhibits and Witnesses at Trial 49 MIN
VHS / U-matic
Training the Advocate Series
Color (PRO)
Establishes a basic checklist for the advocate to follow in laying foundations. Includes witness qualifications, relevance, the hearsay rule and 'magic words.'.
Civics and Political Systems
Dist - ABACPE **Prod** - AMBAR

Layout and Construction of a Straight - Run Stair 20 MIN
U-matic
Step by Step Series
(A)
Demonstrates the procedures of laying out and constructing a straight - run stair.
Industrial and Technical Education
Dist - ACCESS **Prod** - ACCESS 1984

Layout and Drilling Operations 60 MIN
VHS / U-matic
Mechanical Maintenance Basics, Module C - General Shop Practices 'Series
Color (IND)
Industrial and Technical Education
Dist - LEIKID **Prod** - LEIKID

Layout and imposition 25 MIN
VHS
Color (H C)
$79.95 purchase _ #SE - 4
Explains the necessary steps in setting up a job to be printed. Shows the most economical way to lay out a job taking press and bindery specifications into consideration. Includes common paper sizes, common folds, book layouts and shingling. The beginning of the job starts with information on how the job will be handled at the end in the bindery.
Industrial and Technical Education
Dist - INSTRU

Layout Cutting 29 MIN
Videoreel / VT2
Sewing Skills - Tailoring Series
Color
Features Mrs Ruth Hickman demonstrating layout cutting.
Home Economics
Dist - PBS **Prod** - KRMATV

Layout improvements for just-in-time 30 MIN
VHS / 16mm
Manufacturing insights series
Color (A IND)
$200.00, $190.00 purchase _ #VT393, #VT393U
Shows how changing machine layouts can result in inventory reduction, space reduction, and reduced work - in - process. Includes case studies.
Industrial and Technical Education; Psychology
Dist - SME **Prod** - SME 1990

Layout no 1 - Hole Location 19 MIN
VHS / 16mm
Machine Shop Series
(IND)
$80.00 purchase _ #KMS05
Shows how to accurately layout hole locations using basic layout tools such as the combination square, scriber, dividers, prick punch and center punch. Stresses the importance of working from proper reference points.
Industrial and Technical Education
Dist - RMIBHF **Prod** - RMIBHF

Layout no 1 - Hole Location 19 MIN
BETA / VHS
Machine Shop - Layout Series
Color (IND)
Explains how to layout hole locations using basic layout tools (combination square, scriber, dividers, prick punch and center punch). Stresses the importance of working from proper reference points.
Industrial and Technical Education
Dist - RMIBHF **Prod** - RMIBHF

Layout no 3 - Surface Plate 14 MIN
VHS / BETA
Machine Shop - Layout Series
Color (IND)
Demonstrates tools and procedures used when laying out work on the surface plate. Covers use of angle plate, surface gauge and vernier height gauge.
Industrial and Technical Education
Dist - RMIBHF **Prod** - RMIBHF

Layout no 3 - Surface Plate 14 MIN
VHS / 16mm
Machine Shop Series
(IND)
$71.00 purchase _ #KMS07
Demonstrates tools and procedures used in laying out work on the surface plate. Covers use of the angle plate, suface gauge, and the vernier height gauge.
Industrial and Technical Education
Dist - RMIBHF **Prod** - RMIBHF

Layout no 2 - Contours and Angles 19 MIN
VHS / BETA
Machine Shop - Layout Series
Color (IND)
Explains how to layout an irregular part from horizontal and vertical centerlines. Includes methods of laying out contours and angles.
Industrial and Technical Education
Dist - RMIBHF **Prod** - RMIBHF

Layout no 2 - Contours and Angles 19 MIN
VHS / 16mm
Machine Shop Series
(IND)
$83.50 purchase _ #KMS06
Continues procedures taught in 'Layout No 1'. Shows how to layout an irregular part from horizontal and vertical centerlines. Includes methods of laying out contours and angles.
Industrial and Technical Education
Dist - RMIBHF **Prod** - RMIBHF

Layout Tools for Metal Work 13 MIN
16mm
Metalwork - Hand Tools Series
Color (I)
Measuring and marking tools - try squares, dividers, calipers, scribers and punches, transferring design to metal and the use of layout fluids.
Industrial and Technical Education
Dist - SF **Prod** - MORLAT 1967

Lazy Days 29 MIN
16mm
B&W
Explains that for Farina a shady tree on a summer day is hard to resist, even though a 50 dollar prize is at stake. A Little Rascals film.
Fine Arts
Dist - RMIBHF **Prod** - ROACH 1929

Lazy Linda 15 MIN
VHS / 16mm
Managing Problem People Series
Color (A PRO)
$415.00 purchase, $195.00 rental
Portrays an employee who disrupts the department with incomplete assignments. Part of a series on managing 'problem' employees.
Business and Economics; Guidance and Counseling
Dist - VIDART **Prod** - VIDART 1990

Lazybones 79 MIN
16mm
B&W
Follows the circuitous love affair of Agnes and Lazybones, from the time he saves Agnes' sister from suicide, adopts the sister's daughter, returns from World War I and falls for his adopted daughter. Stars Buck Jones and Madge Bellamy. Directed by Frank Borzage.
Fine Arts
Dist - KILLIS **Prod** - FOXFC 1925

LBJ 240 MIN
VHS
Color & B&W (G)
$19.95 purchase _ #PBS365
Portrays the life of Lyndon Baines Johnson - LBJ, who rose from poor, rural Texas beginnings to become a political colossus who changed the American political landscape forever. Draws from a vast collection of photographs, film, family movies, news footage and the recollections of those closest to him.
Biography; Civics and Political Systems; History - United States
Dist - INSTRU **Prod** - PBS

LBJ - A Remembrance 29 MIN
VHS / U-matic
Color (J H G)
$280.00, $330.00 purchase, $50.00 rental
Covers the life of the former President through his friends, colleagues and adversaries.
Biography
Dist - NDIM **Prod** - GUG 1990

LBJ Goes to War, 1964 - 1965 60 MIN
U-matic / VHS / 16mm
Vietnam - a television history series; Episode 4
Color (H C A)
Reveals that after Kennedy's assassination in 1963, Lyndon Johnson inherited revolving door coups in South Vietnam as none of Diem's successor's was able to control the area. Shows that increasingly the NLF guerillas controlled the countryside as the national army disintegrated. States that secretly, Johnson approved open - ended deployment of U S troops.
History - United States; History - World
Dist - FI **Prod** - WGBHTV 1983

LBJ (Luther, Bobby, Jack) 15 MIN
16mm
Color
Presents a cultural assault on LBJ'S America, or, 'DR STRANGELOVE - FACT OR FICTION.'.
Civics and Political Systems
Dist - CANWRL **Prod** - CANWRL

LBJ - the Last Interview 43 MIN
16mm / U-matic / VHS
Color (H C A)
LC 73-703134
Presents an interview with Lyndon Baines Johnson. Discusses his strong commitment and many accomplishments regarding the Civil Rights Movement.
Biography; Civics and Political Systems
Dist - CAROUF **Prod** - CBSTV 1973

LCA short story library series

Antaeus	20 MIN
Butch minds the baby	30 MIN
The Chaparral Prince	20 MIN
The Cop and the anthem	23 MIN
The Invisible Boy	20 MIN
The Luck of Roaring Camp	27 MIN
The Monkey's Paw	27 MIN
Pardon Me for Living	30 MIN
Robbers, Rooftops and Witches	46 MIN
Split Cherry Tree	25 MIN

Dist - LCOA

LCA short story series
All summer in a day 25 MIN
Dist - LCOA

L'Chaim - To life 80 MIN
VHS
Color; B&W (G)
$90.00 purchase
Describes more than a century of Jewish life in Russia. Examines the historical and philosophical roots of the ORT movement, Organization for Rehabilitation through Training. Produced for Women's American ORT by Harold Mayer.
Fine Arts; History - World; Religion and Philosophy; Sociology
Dist - NCJEWF

Le Bain 18 MIN
VHS
Color (G)
$19.00 purchase
Expresses the pain of a young woman and her anger towards the man she loved who has abandoned her. Portrays her bathroom in amber hues where she plunges into her innermost thoughts, mortifying herself. When she forgives him she is set free from her anxieties. Reflects the eternal conflict between man and woman. Directed by Silas Shabelewska.
Fine Arts; Psychology; Religion and Philosophy
Dist - ALTFMW

Le Barbier De Seville 52 MIN
VHS
(G) (FRENCH)
$29.95 purchase _ #V72150
Presents a 1934 French language adaptation of the Italian opera by Rossini. Features Josette Day, Andre Bauge, Charpin and Jean Galland.
Fine Arts; Foreign Language
Dist - NORTNJ

Le Bonheur Et La Mort - Happiness and Death 52 MIN
16mm
Le Temp Des Cathedrales Series
Color
Demonstrates how the 14th century's secularization of art contrasts the anguish of death with the refined, festive life of hunting and princely pleasures.
History - World; Religion and Philosophy
Dist - FACSEA **Prod** - FACSEA 1979

Le Bourdon 11 MIN
16mm / U-matic / VHS
Color (H C) (FRENCH)
A French version of The Bumblebee. Illustrates all aspects of the life of the bumblebee.
Foreign Language
Dist - IFB **Prod** - IFB 1961

Le Bourgeois gentilhomme 97 MIN
VHS
Color (H C G) (FRENCH WITH SUBTITLES)
$99.00 purchase _ #DL45
Presents a Comedie Francaise production of Moliere's tale of a credulous and vain man who strives to be a gentleman. Features opulent sets and costumes.
Fine Arts; History - World; Literature and Drama
Dist - INSIM

Le Cafe 18 MIN
U-matic / VHS / 16mm
Comment Dit - On Series
Color (J H)
Shows drinks and a meal being ordered at the cafe Le Commerce, a typical cafe - restaurant at its busiest on market day. Linguistically looks at questions that require information in addition to that which is already present in the question itself.
Foreign Language
Dist - MEDIAG **Prod** - THAMES 1977

Le Chagrin Et La Pitie 260 MIN
16mm
Color (H C A)
LC 76-702631
Examines the occupation of France by the Germans during World War II using reminiscences of individuals and officials involved in the events at the time. Concentrates on the themes of collaboration and resistance.
Foreign Language; History - World
Dist - CINEMV **Prod** - NPSSRT 1972

Le chantier 13 MIN
16mm
En France avec Jean et Helene series; Set 1; Lesson 9
B&W (J H C)
LC 73-704505
Foreign Language
Dist - CHLTN **Prod** - PEREN 1967

Le chat va tomber 13 MIN
16mm
Les Francais chez vous series
B&W (I J H)
LC 72-704466
Foreign Language
Dist - CHLTN **Prod** - PEREN 1967

Le Choc Septique 21 MIN
U-matic / VHS
Color (PRO) (FRENCH)
A French language version of Septic Shock. Discusses the general pathophysiology of shock, the nine basic parts of evaluation (which include vital signs, cultures, CBC differential and a coagulation screen), chronologic treatment (which includes fluid therapy, pharmacologic agents and antibiotics) and differentiation of septic shock from hypovolemia.
Foreign Language; Health and Safety
Dist - UMICHM **Prod** - UMICHM 1976

Le Choix d'un ete 25 MIN
VHS
Paroles d'echanges 1 series
Color (J H) (FRENCH AND ENGLISH FRENCH)
#350103; LC 91-707588
Follows Helen, a wealthy girl from Toronto, who goes on an exchange trip to the Sherbrooke region of Quebec. Reveals that she has difficulty adjusting to her new surroundings and has trouble making friends. Part of a series that gives viewers a taste of authentic French - Canadian culture.
Foreign Language; Geography - World; Sociology
Dist - TVOTAR **Prod** - TVOTAR 1990

Le Cirque 8 MIN
U-matic / VHS / 16mm
Chroniques De France Series
Color (H C A) (FRENCH)
LC 81-700770
A French language motion picture. Looks at the lives of circus performers.
Foreign Language; Geography - World
Dist - IFB **Prod** - ADPF

Le coche d'eau 13 MIN
16mm
Les Francais chez vous series
B&W (I J H)
LC 76-704467
Foreign Language
Dist - CHLTN **Prod** - PEREN 1967

Le Cocktail 29 MIN
Videoreel / VT2
French Chef - French Series
Color (FRENCH)
A French language videotape. Features Julia Child of Haute Cuisine au Vin demonstrating how to make a cocktail. With captions.
Foreign Language; Home Economics
Dist - PBS **Prod** - WGBHTV

Le Conte Stewart, Landscape Painter 23 MIN
16mm
Color
LC 77-702268
Presents the historical and philosophical background of American painter Le Conte Stewart. Includes scenes of Stewart working outdoors and shows a large collection of his work in pastels, prints and oils as well as some of his drawings.
Fine Arts
Dist - SISEMF **Prod** - SISEMF 1977

Le Corbeau 92 MIN
16mm
B&W (FRENCH (ENGLISH SUBTITLES))
A French language motion picture with English subtitles. Tells how secretly circulated poison pen letters accuse a town doctor of incompetence and possibly murder.
Fine Arts; Foreign Language
Dist - KITPAR **Prod** - UNKNWN 1943

Le Corbusier 50 MIN
VHS
Museum Without Walls Series
Color (C)
LC 90713077
Documents the life and work of architect Le Corbusier. Depicts his major projects and studies his ideas about architecture and urban renewal. The third of eight installments of the Museum Without Walls Series.
Fine Arts
Dist - GPN

Le Cordon Bleu cooking series
Presents an eight - part series which details, with close - up footage, techniques and practical methods needed to prepare a fabulous assortment of dishes. Features the world - renowned chefs of Le Cordon Bleu's teaching staff. Includes vegetables, desserts, soups, salads, meats, fish, poultry and appetizers.

Appetizers	45 MIN
Desserts	45 MIN
Fish	45 MIN
Meats	45 MIN
Poultry	45 MIN
Salads	45 MIN
Soups	45 MIN
Vegetables	45 MIN

Dist - CAMV

Le Cycle De Reproduction De L'Ange De Mer 10 MIN
16mm / U-matic / VHS
Color (P I J H) (FRENCH)
A French - language version of the motion picture Reproduction Cycle Of Angel Fish. Explains the reproduction cycle of angel fish. Begins with the courtship and proceeds through the egg - laying, fertilization and incubation stages to the development of the newly - hatched fry.
Foreign Language; Science - Natural
Dist - IFB **Prod** - IFB 1971

Le Cycliste 5 MIN
16mm
Color (J)
LC 73-701225
Presents Le Cycliste, the great master of all cycles, in a mime.
Physical Education and Recreation
Dist - MARALF **Prod** - ALBM 1973

Le Dortoir 53 MIN
VHS
Color (H C G)
$225.00 purchase, $80.00 rental
Presents an adaptation of the stage production Le Dortoir, a bizarre dance drama. Tells an archetypal story of a man's journey back into memory and imagination to escape and, finally, overcome a personal crisis. Co - produced by CBC.
Fine Arts; Literature and Drama; Religion and Philosophy
Dist - CANCIN **Prod** - RHOMBS 1993

Le Facteur Qui S'Envole Et La Fleur 22 MIN
16mm
Bonjour Line Series

Color (K P I) (FRENCH)
A French language film. Two children decide to play a joke on the postman by hoisting him on a bicycle into the air with a hook and pulley from the barn and two little girls take a walk in the garden and pick a flower only to be chased by the watchman. Part 1 of a series.
Foreign Language
Dist - CHLTN **Prod** - PEREN 1962

Le Farfalle (the Butterflies) 5 MIN
16mm
Color
LC FIA65-1011
Uses live action, special effects and animation, intergrated with music, to give symbolic hints to the concept that women are like butterflies whose beauty is functional and that they can make butterflies with their sewing machines.
Home Economics
Dist - SVE **Prod** - SINGER 1965

Le Fauvisme 17 MIN
U-matic / VHS / 16mm
Color (H C) (FRENCH)
A French - language version of the motion picture Fauvism. Points out that the main contribution to modern painting of the Fauves was their use of color to express form, light and volume independent of subject matter or a given light. Includes examples from work by Vlaminck, Duchamp, Matisse and Dufy.
Fine Arts; Foreign Language
Dist - IFB **Prod** - LFLMDC 1972

Le Film est deja commence - Is the feature on yet 60 MIN
VHS
B&W (G)
$150.00 purchase
Presents the first attempt to break the tradition of normal filmic representation. Takes different filmic elements, such as sound, image, screen, theater, and disrupts them separately, then reintegrates them in a complex theatrical combination that includes 1 - image in an accelerated montage, out of sync with sound, drawn on with abstract motifs and symbols; 2 - Sound that is conceived as independent, an aesthetic and economical commentary on the art of films; a description of an imaginary film screening, etc. all mixed with a new music called lettrism; 3 - the elevation of the screen to the level of star; 4 - introduction in the theater of actors, who relate to themselves and to the film. Each video signed and dated by filmmaker, Maurice Lemaitre.
Fine Arts
Dist - CANCIN

Le Foyer International D'Accueil De Paris 7 MIN
U-matic / VHS / 16mm
Chroniques De France Series
Color (H C A) (FRENCH)
A French language film lists the facilities and activities available to foreign and provincial students in Paris, France. Includes lodging, cafeteria service, art exhibits, movies, music and theater.
Foreign Language; Geography - World
Dist - IFB **Prod** - ADPF 1980

Le Geant De La Prairie 21 MIN
U-matic / VHS / 16mm
Color (J A) (FRENCH)
A French - language version of the motion picture The Prairie Giant. Tells the story of the Canada goose and other birds. Shows geese in flight, nesting, raising their young and migrating south.
Foreign Language; Science - Natural
Dist - IFB **Prod** - COTTER 1968

Le Golem - the legend of Prague 96 MIN
VHS
Color (G) (FRENCH WITH ENGLISH SUBTITLES)
$79.95 purchase _ #418
Portrays the legend about Rabbi Judah Lowe of Prague who created the Golem in order to defend the Jews of Prague from a pogrom. Reveals that a generation later, the Jewish community is again threatened and the Golem is once again called upon to save their spiritual leader from execution. Stars Harry Baur with Roger Karl, Charles Dorat and Ferdinand Hart.
Literature and Drama; Religion and Philosophy; Sociology
Dist - ERGOM **Prod** - ERGOM 1935

Le Haut De Cagnes 10 MIN
16mm
Aspects De France Series
Color (H C) (FRENCH)
A French language film. Shows life in the old medieval town of Cagnes, situated on a hill above the Mediterranean. Points out that artists go there for inspiration from the quaint old homes.
Foreign Language
Dist - MLA **Prod** - WSUM 1952

Le journaliste 13 MIN
16mm
En France avec Jean et Helene series; Set 1; Lesson 8
B&W (J H C)
LC 78-704509
Foreign Language
Dist - CHLTN **Prod** - PEREN 1967

Le Magasin 5 MIN
16mm
Bonjour Line Series Part 2; Part 2
Color (K P I) (FRENCH)
A French language film. A merchant sells various objects to his patrons.
Foreign Language
Dist - CHLTN **Prod** - PEREN 1962

Le Mans - the Grand Prize 17 MIN
16mm
Color
Records the thrills, disappointments and rewards of the 24 - hour 1973 Grand Prix at Le Mans.
History - World; Physical Education and Recreation
Dist - MTP **Prod** - GC

Le Marais 13 MIN
16mm / U-matic / VHS
Sejour En France Series
Color (J H C) (FRENCH)
LC 72-702115
A French language film. Presents dramatic situations and dialog designed for comprehension by second - semester first year classes and second year classes. Features Jacques, an amateur of the Middle Ages, who takes Penny and Michele on a tour of the Place des Vosges where one of the last street vendors remains. Examines Jacques' collection of miniatures representing street merchants of a by - gone era.
Foreign Language; Geography - World
Dist - IFB **Prod** - IFB 1971

Le Marche 11 MIN
16mm
Voix Et Images De France Series
Color (I) (FRENCH)
A French language film. Depicts marketing on a Sunday morning in one of the workers' districts of Paris.
Foreign Language
Dist - CHLTN **Prod** - PEREN 1962

Le Merle 5 MIN
16mm / U-matic / VHS
Color (H C) (FRENCH)
LC FIA65-368
A French language film. Visualizes an old FrenchCanadian nonsense song. Simple white cut - outs on pastel backgrounds provide illustrations as the song relates how a blackbird loses parts of his body and then regains them two - and - three fold.
Foreign Language
Dist - IFB **Prod** - NFBC 1959
CFLMDC

Le Monde Sonore Des Sauterelles - the Musical World of Grasshoppers 38 MIN
16mm
Color (C) (FRENCH)
A French language film. Demonstrates certain experiments based on the presumption that locusts might be attracted by sound signals or ultra - sound signals. Uses this method for the destruction of migratory locusts.
Science - Natural
Dist - PSUPCR **Prod** - SFRS 1958

Le Mont Saint - Michel 12 MIN
16mm
Aspects De France Series
Color (H C) (FRENCH)
A French language film. Explores life in the islet community of Le Mont Saint - Michel with its gothic architecture that reflects the Middle Ages. Visitors come daily to see 'LA MERVEILLE DE L'OUEST.'.
Foreign Language
Dist - MLA **Prod** - WSUM 1955

Le Mouvement 14 MIN
16mm
Color (FRENCH)
LC FIA67-2356
Presents a French version of the 1967 motion picture 'MOTION.' Illustrates man in motion, showing such scenes as a small boy sliding down a bannister, an astronaut walking in space and free - falling parachutists.
Foreign Language
Dist - CRAF **Prod** - CNR 1967

Le Moyen Age 31 MIN
U-matic / VHS / 16mm
Color (H C A) (FRENCH)
LC 83-700670
A French - language version of the motion picture The Middle Ages. Traces the social, economic and cultural development of western Europe, emphasizing the life of the people during the middle ages.
Foreign Language; History - World
Dist - IFB **Prod** - IFB 1975

Le Musee Grevin 12 MIN
16mm / U-matic / VHS
Sejour En France Series
Color (J H C) (FRENCH)
LC 72-702102
A French language film. Presents a visit to a wax museum where Penny and Michele play a game trying to place the different figures of French history in their proper era. Shows how the director invites them to see how the models are made before placing them on display.
Foreign Language; Geography - World
Dist - IFB **Prod** - IFB 1970

Le Musee Rodin 13 MIN
16mm
En France avec Jean et Helene series; Set 1; Lesson 4
B&W (J H C)
LC 72-704510
Foreign Language
Dist - CHLTN **Prod** - PEREN 1967

Le Mystere Kuomiko - the Kuomiko Mystery 47 MIN
16mm
Color (H C A) (FRENCH (ENGLISH SUBTITLES))
LC 75-704370
A French language film with English subtitles. Features an interview with a young girl concerning her likes and dislikes and her feelings toward herself and the world. Reveals the mystery of individuality and the social mood of acceptance of estrangement characteristic of children of the atomic bomb era.
Foreign Language; Geography - World; Sociology
Dist - NYFLMS **Prod** - MARKC 1975

Le Nez 11 MIN
16mm
B&W
Presents Gogol's celebrated short story, The Nose, animated without words in fantastic moving pictures that capture the scene and spirit of 19th century Russia. Produced by Alexander Alexeieff and Claire Parker.
Fine Arts; History - World
Dist - STARRC **Prod** - STARRC 1963

Le Noel de Mickey 25 MIN
VHS
Color (G) (FRENCH)
$24.95 purchase _ #W5553
Adapts Charles Dickens' story about a tight - fisted boss who learns the true meaning of love at Christmas to an animated version starring the character Mickey Mouse.
Fine Arts; Foreign Language; Literature and Drama
Dist - GPC

Le Noir Et Le Blanc 13 MIN
16mm
En Francais, set 1 series
Color (J A)
Foreign Language
Dist - CHLTN **Prod** - PEREN 1969

Le pari 13 MIN
16mm
En France avec Jean et Helene series; Set 1; Lesson 1
B&W (J H C)
LC 76-704511
Foreign Language
Dist - CHLTN **Prod** - PEREN 1967

Le Parrain 30 MIN
U-matic / VHS
Franco File Series
Color (I)
Dramatizes family tradition in contemporary Franco - American life.
Sociology
Dist - GPN **Prod** - WENHTV

Le Partage Des Eaux 13 MIN
16mm
En Francais, set 2 series
Color (J A)
Foreign Language
Dist - CHLTN **Prod** - PEREN 1969

Le Pere 13 MIN
16mm
Family Relations - French Series
Color (K P) (FRENCH)
LC 76-700119
A French language version of the motion picture Call Me Dad. Provides an explanation of family relations.

Foreign Language; Sociology
Dist - MORLAT **Prod** - MORLAT 1974

Le Perroquet 11 MIN
16mm
Color (H C) (FRENCH)
A French language film. Uses animation to present the story of a parrot for beginning language students. Tells how Pedrito, a clever parrot, is kidnapped by a magician and then returned to his owners after a circus performance. Narration is by a native speaker.
Foreign Language
Dist - FILCOM **Prod** - SIGMA 1966

Le Petit Chaperon Rouge 14 MIN
U-matic / VHS / 16mm
Color (A) (FRENCH)
A French version of Little Red Riding Hood. Shows an object or action as it is being described. Uses repetition, recapitulation and visual aids to promote learning.
Foreign Language
Dist - PHENIX **Prod** - FA 1967

Le petit chaperon rouge - La belle et la bete 23 MIN
VHS
French fairy tales series
Color (I J) (FRENCH)
$39.95 purchase _ #W3457
Presents animated versions of the two fairy tales on video. For advanced level I students.
Foreign Language; Literature and Drama
Dist - GPC

Le Petit Coq Qui Reveille Le Soleil 11 MIN
U-matic / VHS / 16mm
B&W (I J H) (FRENCH)
French version of 'THE LITTLE ROOSTER WHO MADE THE SUN RISE.' Animated story of the rooster who discovers that his crowing does not make the sun rise, but who acquires pride in doing his job of waking his farmyard friends.
Foreign Language
Dist - CORF **Prod** - CORF 1962

Le Petit Theatre De Jean Renoir 100 MIN
16mm / U-matic / VHS
Color (H C A) (FRENCH)
LC 79-700669
A French language motion picture. Consists of three short comedies and a between - the - acts musical performance by Jeanne Moreau. Produced, directed and narrated by French film director Jean Renoir.
Fine Arts; Foreign Language; Literature and Drama
Dist - PHENIX **Prod** - RENOIR 1974

Le Petit Theatre De Jean Renoir, Pt 1 25 MIN
16mm / U-matic / VHS
Color (H C A) (FRENCH)
LC 79-700669
A French language motion picture. Consists of three short comedies and a between - the - acts musical performance by Jeanne Moreau. Produced, directed and narrated by French film director Jean Renoir.
Fine Arts
Dist - PHENIX **Prod** - RENOIR 1974

Le Petit Theatre De Jean Renoir, Pt 2 25 MIN
16mm / U-matic / VHS
Color (H C A) (FRENCH)
LC 79-700669
A French language motion picture. Consists of three short comedies and a between - the - acts musical performance by Jeanne Moreau. Produced, directed and narrated by French film director Jean Renoir.
Fine Arts
Dist - PHENIX **Prod** - RENOIR 1974

Le Petit Theatre De Jean Renoir, Pt 3 25 MIN
U-matic / VHS / 16mm
Color (H C A) (FRENCH)
LC 79-700669
A French language motion picture. Consists of three short comedies and a between - the - acts musical performance by Jeanne Moreau. Produced, directed and narrated by French film director Jean Renoir.
Fine Arts
Dist - PHENIX **Prod** - RENOIR 1974

Le Petit Theatre De Jean Renoir, Pt 4 25 MIN
U-matic / VHS / 16mm
Color (H C A) (FRENCH)
LC 79-700669
A French language motion picture. Consists of three short comedies and a between - the - acts musical performance by Jeanne Moreau. Produced, directed and narrated by French film director Jean Renoir.
Fine Arts
Dist - PHENIX **Prod** - RENOIR 1974

Le Pink Grapefruit 27 MIN
16mm / U-matic / VHS
Color (H C A)
LC 76-703954
Presents a portrait of the Spanish artist, Salvador Dali. Shows how his surrealism is carried over into his home and lifestyle. Includes a tour of the Salvador Dali Museum in Figueras, Spain, in which the artist discusses the building and collection.
Biography; Fine Arts
Dist - PHENIX **Prod** - YUNGLI 1976

Le Pique - Nique 15 MIN
U-matic / VHS / 16mm
Lettres D'un Ami Francais Series
Color (H C) (FRENCH)
A French language film. Pictures a French family on an outing in the Foret De Fontainebleau near Paris. Includes vocabulary dealing with food, table setting, games, traffic and weather.
Foreign Language
Dist - IFB **Prod** - IFB 1962

Le Plan Americain - the American Shot 16 MIN
16mm
Color
LC 80-701232
Tells how a young man who has stolen books from a bookstore in order to donate them to a public library meets and befriends a French - speaking young lady in a New York bookshop.
Fine Arts
Dist - WASSS **Prod** - WASSS 1979

Le Plus Petit Ange 14 MIN
16mm / U-matic / VHS
B&W (I J H C) (FRENCH)
French version of 'THE LITTLEST ANGEL.' Presents the story of a little angel who gave his most prized possessions to the baby Jesus and how God chose that gift to shine as an inspiration for all men.
Foreign Language
Dist - CORF **Prod** - CORF 1962

Le Pont 13 MIN
16mm
En Francais, set 1 series
Color (J A)
Foreign Language
Dist - CHLTN **Prod** - PEREN 1969

Le Printemps Est Une Aventure 11 MIN
U-matic / VHS / 16mm
B&W (I J H) (FRENCH)
French version of 'SPRING IS AN ADVENTURE.' Shows changes and activities which come with spring, such as flowers budding and blooming, eggs hatching and the planting of a garden.
Foreign Language
Dist - CORF **Prod** - CORF 1962

Le Quatorze Juillet 15 MIN
U-matic / VHS / 16mm
Lettres D'un Ami Francais Series
Color (H C) (FRENCH)
LC FIA65-1539
A French language film. Follows a brother and sister as they go by subway to the Champs - Elysees to watch the Bastile Day Parade, as they see an outdoor ball in front of the Invalides, as they observe carnival attractions and as they watch a fireworks display held over the Seine River.
Foreign Language
Dist - IFB **Prod** - IFB 1963

Le restaurant 13 MIN
16mm
En France avec Jean et Helene series; Set 1; Lesson 10
B&W (J H C)
LC 77-704514
Foreign Language
Dist - CHLTN **Prod** - PEREN 1967

Le Retour D'Afrique 109 MIN
16mm
B&W (FRENCH (ENGLISH SUBTITLES))
An English subtitle version of the French language, Swiss - made film. Presents a political parable about a young Swiss couple with radical leanings who find themselves on the brink of settling into a bourgeois life in Geneva. Includes screwball comedy elements as the couple decides to move to Algeria, but are stranded midway between the two continents.
Fine Arts; Foreign Language; Sociology
Dist - NYFLMS **Prod** - NYFLMS 1973

Le Rhin 7 MIN
U-matic / VHS / 16mm
Chroniques De France Series
Color (H C A) (FRENCH)
LC 81-700763
A French language motion picture. Presents the different faces of the Rhine river.
Foreign Language; Geography - World
Dist - IFB **Prod** - ADPF 1980

Le Socrate 90 MIN
16mm
Color (FRENCH)
A French language film. Deals with a poor wandering philosopher in a crisis who is being followed around the countryside by a police inspector.
Fine Arts; Foreign Language; Sociology
Dist - NYFLMS **Prod** - NYFLMS 1969

Le Tambou, the Drum of Haiti 19 MIN
16mm
Color
LC 74-700513
Shows the crafting of Haiti's unique tambou, a drum used in religious and cultural activities on the island, and points out its special place in the lives of the people.
Fine Arts; Religion and Philosophy; Social Science; Sociology
Dist - NLC **Prod** - NLC 1973

Le Tartuffe 110 MIN
VHS
Color (H C G)
$89.00 purchase _ #DL44
Stars Anthony Sher as Tartuffe, Moliere's evil character who worms his way into a wealthy Parisian household, in a Royal Shakespeare Company production.
Fine Arts; History - World; Literature and Drama
Dist - INSIM

Le Telephone 6 MIN
16mm
Voix Et Images De France Series
B&W (I) (FRENCH)
A French language film. Pictures Monsieur Brun waiting his turn at the telephone booth. Captures the changing intonations from mild irritation to despair.
Foreign Language
Dist - CHLTN **Prod** - PEREN 1962

Le Temp Des Cathedrales Series
Dieu est lumiere - god is light 52 MIN
La Cathedrale, La Ville, L'Ecole - Cathedral, City, School 52 MIN
La Quete De Dieu - the Quest of God 52 MIN
Le Bonheur Et La Mort - Happiness and Death 52 MIN
Le Tournant De 14e Siecle - the Turn of the 14th Century 52 MIN
Les Nations S'Affirment - Nations Assert Themselves 52 MIN
L'Europe De L'An Mil - Europe in the Year 1000 52 MIN
Roi, Chevalier Et Saint - King, Knight and Saint 52 MIN
Vers Des Temps Nouveaux - toward New Times 52 MIN
Dist - FACSEA

Le theatre des jeunes 13 MIN
16mm
En France avec Jean et Helene series; Set 1; Lesson 7
B&W (J H C)
LC 70-704515
Foreign Language
Dist - CHLTN **Prod** - PEREN 1967

Le Tourisme 19 MIN
U-matic / VHS / 16mm
La France Telle Qu'Elle Est Series
Color (H C)
Includes requesting a hotel room, ordering breakfast, asking for a campsite and visiting a Syndical d'Initiative. Shows tourist attractions around Saumer, interviews with a hotel proprietor and the director of a youth sports center.
Foreign Language; Geography - World
Dist - MEDIAG **Prod** - THAMES 1977

Le Tournant De 14e Siecle - the Turn of the 14th Century 52 MIN
16mm
Le Temp Des Cathedrales Series
Color
Shows that although Western Europe is ravaged by famine and black plague during the 14th century, spotty prosperity still occurs. Reveals that statesman patronize artists while the works of Dante and Giotto mingle the profane with the religious.
History - World; Religion and Philosophy
Dist - FACSEA **Prod** - FACSEA 1979

Le Vieux Paris 15 MIN
16mm
Toute la bande series; No 12

Color (J H C) (FRENCH)
LC 73-715479
A French language film. Presents the adventures of Caroline, Elisabeth and Jacques as they travel through the Ile de la Cite and the Palace des Vosges.
Foreign Language
Dist - SBS **Prod** - SBS 1970

Le Vilain Caneton 11 MIN
U-matic / VHS / 16mm
Color; B&W (I J H) (FRENCH)
French version of 'THE UGLY DUCKLING.' Follows the misfortunes of the unwanted Ugly Duckling who grows into a beautiful swan.
Foreign Language
Dist - CORF **Prod** - CORF 1960

Le Village, Un Village 22 MIN
16mm / U-matic / VHS
(France (from the Village Life Series
Color
Views life in Le Village, Sainte Alvere in the Dordogne region of France. Describes the annual village festival and shows the marriage of the town's motor mechanic to a girl from a smaller nearby town.
Geography - World; Sociology
Dist - JOU **Prod** - JOU 1979

Le Vin Rose 13 MIN
16mm
En Francais, set 1 series
Color (J A)
Foreign Language
Dist - CHLTN **Prod** - PEREN 1969

Le Violon De Gaston 25 MIN
16mm
Color (FRENCH)
_ #106C 0274 165
Geography - World
Dist - CFLMDC **Prod** - NFBC 1974

LEAA 29 MIN
VHS / 16mm
Washington Connection Series
Color (G)
$55.00 rental _ #WACO - 105
Civics and Political Systems; Social Science
Dist - PBS **Prod** - NPACT

Lead 10 MIN
BETA / VHS / U-matic
Hazard communication series
Color (IND G)
$295.00 purchase _ #830 - 04
Explains the potentially harmful effects of lead. Describes the symptoms associated with over - exposure. Explains the consequences of of untreated severe exposure. Discusses personal hygiene and administrative controls. Part of a series on hazard communication.
Health and Safety; Industrial and Technical Education; Psychology
Dist - ITSC **Prod** - ITSC

Lead - a four letter word
U-matic / VHS / BETA
Search encounters in science series
Color; PAL (G H C)
PdS25, PdS33 purchase
Brings modern research efforts of the world's leading scientists into the classroom. Features one of a series of 24 mini - documentaries. Each film is 5 - 7 minutes in length.
Science
Dist - EDPAT **Prod** - NSF

Lead, follow or get out of His way 30 MIN
VHS
Color (J H R)
$29.99 purchase, $10.00 rental _ #35 - 83543 - 533
Features Pat Hurley in a discussion on sharing one's Christian faith. Attempts to dispel common fears about evangelism.
Literature and Drama; Religion and Philosophy
Dist - APH **Prod** - WORD

Lead in Motion 20 MIN
16mm
Color
A revised version of The Lead Matrix. Documents the use of lead from Biblical times to the present, discussing the location of lead deposits, refining techniques, characteristics of lead and its use in industry.
Business and Economics; Geography - World; Industrial and Technical Education; Science - Physical; Social Science
Dist - USDIBM **Prod** - USDIBM

Lead in Motion 22 MIN
16mm
Color
Discusses lead in one of its most dense arrangements. Explains that lead, when refined, is one of the purest raw materials know to man. It resists vibrations and blocks radiation. Shows lead being mined and refined, with the careful extraction of such precious metals as copper, zinc and silver.
Geography - World; Science - Physical; Social Science
Dist - WSTGLC **Prod** - WSTGLC

Lead Paint Poisoning 5 MIN
16mm
Color (H C A)
LC 73-702597
Overviews the lead paint problem and some of the steps being taken by the Federal government, particularly the Department of Housing and Urban Development and the National Bureau of Standards, to overcome it.
Health and Safety; Social Science; Sociology
Dist - USNBOS **Prod** - USNBOS 1972

Lead Poisoning 26 MIN
U-matic / VHS
Color (C)
$249.00, $149.00 purchase _ #AD - 1915
Provides an in - depth look at the health hazards of lead. Explores what is being done to reduce and prevent lead contamination in air, water and soil. Examines advances made in the treatment of victims of lead poisoning.
Health and Safety; Science - Natural; Sociology
Dist - FOTH **Prod** - FOTH

Lead Poisoning 1 MIN
16mm
Color
LC 74-700347
Warns parents of children living in older homes and apartments of the dangers of lead poisoning. Uses cinema verite showing children playing in areas where cracked and peeling paint and plaster are obvious.
Health and Safety; Sociology
Dist - WSTGLC **Prod** - NPVLA 1973

Lead Poisoning Could Strike Your Child 22 MIN
U-matic / VHS / 16mm
Color (J)
Reveals the most common source of lead poisoning, the life - saving medical treatment applied to children who have eaten lead - contaminated paint, and the steps to decontaminate walls, ceilings and woodwork.
Health and Safety; Sociology
Dist - MCFI **Prod** - SPCTRI 1980

Lead poisoning - the effect on child health 28 MIN
VHS
Color (G)
$149.00 purchase, $75.00 rental _ #UW5115
Documents the disastrous effect of lead on child health. Features the mother of a child with severe lead poisoning who talks about her search for a lead - free house. A man recounts his early retirement because of lead poisoning from his job. An environmental and occupational health specialist discusses the range of environmental contaminants. Explains new research into the prevention of lead poisoning in children and a pioneering effort to stop lead poisoning.
Health and Safety
Dist - FOTH

Lead Poisoning - the Hidden Epidemic 10 MIN
16mm
Color (J)
LC 72-701738
Discusses the causes, testing for and preventative methods against childhood lead poisoning.
Guidance and Counseling; Health and Safety; Home Economics
Dist - LIFLMS **Prod** - LIFLMS 1972

The Lead Shoe 18 MIN
16mm
B&W (C)
$300.00
Experimental film by Sidney Peterson.
Fine Arts
Dist - AFA **Prod** - AFA 1949

The Lead Shoes 18 MIN
16mm
B&W (C A)
Features a film by Sidney Peterson dealing with paricide and the compulsive efforts to undo the deed.
Industrial and Technical Education; Sociology
Dist - GROVE **Prod** - GROVE

Lead your horse 61 MIN
VHS
Horse Care and Training Series
Color (H C A PRO)
$30.00 purchase _ #TA238
Shows the steps of training a horse to lead easily and safely at the side of the trainer. Includes the stages of training a horse, from the ten - day - old foal to the mature horse.
Agriculture; Physical Education and Recreation
Dist - AAVIM **Prod** - AAVIM 1990

Lead your horse 61 MIN
VHS / BETA
Horse care and training series
Color
Demonstrates the steps in training a horse to lead. Shows how to train horses from ten - day - old foals to mature adults.
Physical Education and Recreation
Dist - MOHOMV **Prod** - MOHOMV

Leadbelly 52 MIN
U-matic / VHS
Rainbow quest series
Color
Presents a solo performance by Pete Seeger in which he sings some of the songs composed by the famous black folksinger Hudie Ledbetter.
Fine Arts
Dist - NORROS **Prod** - SEEGER

The Leader - encouraging team creativity 23 MIN
VHS
Color (A PRO IND)
$549.00 purchase, $150.00 rental
Discusses the seven stages of team creativity - know the principles, pick a creative team, set the goal, generate ideas, sunthesize, verify, and accept and implement. Demonstrates each stage in a simulated exercise.
Business and Economics; Guidance and Counseling; Psychology
Dist - VLEARN **Prod** - EBEC

Leader of the Pack 30 MIN
VHS / 16mm
Marketing Series
Color (C A)
$130.00, $120.00 purchase _15 - 22
Features Yamaha Motorcycles' policy for setting prices.
Business and Economics
Dist - CDTEL **Prod** - COAST 1989

The Leader of the People 23 MIN
16mm / U-matic / VHS
Color (J)
LC 79-700486
Records the reactions of a little boy and his family as they listen to their grandfather's tales of his adventures as a wagon leader during the westward migrations on the American frontier. Based on the story The Leader Of The People by John Steinbeck.
Fine Arts; History - United States; Literature and Drama
Dist - BARR **Prod** - WILETS 1979

The Leader within 64 MIN
VHS / 16mm
Color (PRO)
$795.00 purchase, $225.00 rental
Features Dr Warren Bennis who interviews three successful leaders - General Dave Palmer of West Point, Frances Hesselbein of Girl Scouts of the USA and Max DePree from Herman Miller, a furniture manufacturer.
Business and Economics; Guidance and Counseling; Psychology
Dist - VICOM **Prod** - VICOM 1990

The Leader within 64 MIN
U-matic / VHS
Color (G PRO A)
$895.00, $795.00 purchase, $225.00 rental
Features Dr Warren Bennis who has spent over a decade interviewing and researching great leaders. Interviews three successful leaders from diverse organizations and shares their secrets of success.
Business and Economics; Guidance and Counseling; Psychology
Dist - MAGVID **Prod** - MAGVID 1989

The Leader within 64 MIN
VHS / U-matic
Color (G)
$895.00, $795.00 purchase, $225.00 rental
Features Dr Warren Bennis interviewing General Dave Palmer, Frances Hesselbein and Max DePree. Shows qualities fundamental to successful leadership.
Business and Economics; Guidance and Counseling; Psychology
Dist - VLEARN **Prod** - VPHI 1989

Leaders 11 MIN
16mm
Color (H C A)
LC 76-700567
Uses split - screen techniques in order to show the multi - disciplinary career opportunites available to officers in Australia's modern army.
Civics and Political Systems; Geography - World; Guidance and Counseling; Psychology
Dist - AUIS **Prod** - FLMAUS 1975

Leaders in American Medicine - a Mc Gehee Harvey, MD 60 MIN
U-matic
Color (PRO)
LC 78-706147
Presents an interview with Dr A Mc Gehee Harvey, who discusses the role of the physician in problem solving and explains his interest in the application of the scientific method to clinical problem solving.
Biography; Health and Safety
Dist - USNAC **Prod** - NMAC 1977

Leaders in American Medicine - a McGehee Harvey, MD 60 MIN
16mm
B&W
LC 79-700112
Presents Dr A McGehee Harvey discussing the role of the physician and the application of the scientific method in clinical problem solving. Examines the role of the United States in international medicine.
Health and Safety
Dist - USNAC **Prod** - NMAC 1978

Leaders in American Medicine - Abraham White, Ph D, D Sc 60 MIN
U-matic
Color (PRO)
LC 79-706863
Presents an interview with Dr Abraham White, consulting professor of biochemistry at Stanford University School of Medicine, who describes his research in the field of biochemistry and discusses changes in laboratories, equipment and grants during the 30 years of his career.
Biography; Health and Safety; Science - Natural
Dist - USNAC **Prod** - NMAC 1979

Leaders in American Medicine - Albert Baird Hastings, Ph D, Sc D 66 MIN
U-matic
B&W (PRO)
LC 76-706155
Discusses major research being done by Dr Albert Hastings while at Harvard University. Recounts his interest and research in electrolyte composition, tetany and parathyroid tetany, intermediary metabolism of lactic acid in the liver, the effect of chemicals on the mechanical work of the heart and other applications of biochemistry.
Biography; Health and Safety; Science - Natural
Dist - USNAC **Prod** - NMAC 1971

Leaders in American Medicine - Albert Baird Hastings, Ph D, Sc D 60 MIN
16mm
Color
LC 74-704527
Discusses some of the major research done by Dr Albert Hastings while at Harvard University, where he was Hamilton Kuhn Professor of Biological Chemistry. Recounts his interest and research in electrolyte composition, tetany and parathyroid tetany, intermediary metabolism of lactic acid in the liver, the effect of chemicals on the mechanical work of the heart and other applications of biochemistry.
Health and Safety; Psychology
Dist - USNAC **Prod** - NMAC 1971

Leaders in American Medicine - Alexander D Langmuir, MD 60 MIN
U-matic / VHS
Color
LC 80-706828
Presents Dr Alexander D Langmuir, former Chief Epidemiologist of the Center for Disease Control, discussing his career in epidemiology and his contributions at the Center for Disease Control.
Health and Safety
Dist - USNAC **Prod** - NMAC 1979

Leaders in American Medicine - Cecil J Watson, MD 58 MIN
16mm
B&W
LC 76-700094
Presents Dr Cecil J Watson discussing his career as a clinician, teacher and investigator. Stresses the need for a closer tie between medicine, research and teaching.
Health and Safety; Science
Dist - USNAC **Prod** - NMAC 1974

Leaders in American Medicine - Charles Huggins, MD 60 MIN
16mm
B&W
LC 74-704528
Recounts the life of Dr Charles Huggins and his research in endocrinology and prostatic cancer. Includes his work on bone marrow, his interest and work in the physiology and control of disease with the introduction of chemotherapy and his views on medical education and the future role of medicine.
Health and Safety; Psychology; Science - Natural
Dist - USNAC **Prod** - NMAC 1972

Leaders in American Medicine - David Seegal, MD 37 MIN
16mm
B&W (PRO)
LC 77-703506
Provides insight into the teaching methods used by Dr David Seegal at Columbia University. Examines the reasons for his effectiveness in motivating his students.
Health and Safety
Dist - USNAC **Prod** - NMAC

Leaders in American Medicine - Dorothy M Horstmann, MD 60 MIN
U-matic
Color (PRO)
LC 79-706864
Presents Dr Dorothy M Horstmann, professor of epidemiology and pediatrics at Yale University School of Medicine, discussing her interest in infectious diseases, her work in testing polio virus, her interest in rubella and future problems relating to infectious diseases.
Biography; Health and Safety
Dist - USNAC **Prod** - NMAC 1979

Leaders in American Medicine - Dwight L Wilbur, MD 59 MIN
16mm
B&W (PRO)
LC 77-703478
Presents an interview with Dr Dwight L Wilbur. Describes his family background and tells why he became a doctor. Examines his schooling at Stanford University and the University of Pennsylvania and his position at the Mayo Clinic. Explores his work with the American Medical Association.
Health and Safety
Dist - USNAC **Prod** - NMAC

Leaders in American Medicine - Emile Holman, MD 51 MIN
16mm
B&W
LC 76-700095
Presents Dr Emile Holman discussing his career in medicine at Stanford University, his experience as a Rhodes scholar and his research contributions in cardiovascular physiology and surgery with special emphasis on arteriovenous fistulae.
Health and Safety
Dist - USNAC **Prod** - NMAC 1974

Leaders in American Medicine - Franz J Ingelfinger, MD 59 MIN
39 MIN
16mm / U-matic
B&W; Color (PRO)
LC 77-703507; 77-706202
Describes the success of Dr Franz J Ingelfinger in two separate areas of medicine. Discusses his research accomplishments in gastroenterology and reviews the nine years he spent as editor of the New England Journal Of Medicine.
Health and Safety; Science
Dist - USNAC **Prod** - NMAC

Leaders in American Medicine - George L Engel, MD 61 MIN
16mm
B&W
LC 76-700096
Presents Dr George L Engel discussing the influence of his family and the strong need for self - identity which led to his dual specialization in internal medicine and psychiatry. Tells about his studies of the use of EEG tests on delirious patients, high altitude decompression sickness and psychosomatic factors of pain.
Health and Safety
Dist - USNAC **Prod** - NMAC 1974

Leaders in American Medicine - George W Corner, MD 57 MIN
16mm
B&W
LC 75-704432
Presents an interview with Dr George W Corner, who speaks of his early days at Johns Hopkins and the people who influenced his career in medicine. Includes comments on his studies of the menstrual cycle, its causes and effects and his discovery of the corpus luteum hormone later termed progesterone.
Guidance and Counseling; Health and Safety; Science
Dist - USNAC **Prod** - NMAC 1974

Leaders in American Medicine - Grace a Goldsmith, MD 58 MIN
16mm
Color
LC 75-704433
Presents an interview with Dr Grace A Goldsmith, who discusses her interest in nutritional and metabolic diseases. Recalls her research on drugs and diet and their effect on lipid metabolism and chronic cardiovascular diseases. Discusses her research on niacin, vitamin C and riboflavin, which led to the establishment of minimum daily requirements.
Health and Safety; Science; Social Science
Dist - USNAC **Prod** - NMAC 1974

Leaders in American Medicine - H W Magoun, MD 60 MIN
VHS / U-matic
Color
LC 80-706810
Presents H W Magoun, professor emeritus at the University of California at Los Angeles Brain Research Institute, discussing his career and his research in the field of poliomyelitis and electroencephalography.
Health and Safety
Dist - USNAC **Prod** - NMAC 1979

Leaders in American Medicine - Helen B Taussig, MD 50 MIN
16mm
B&W
LC 76-700097
Presents Dr Helen B Taussig describing her medical education at Johns Hopkins, where she later became the first woman to be appointed a full professor. Discusses her pediatric internship, her interest in congenital heart deformations and her reserach on pediatric malformations due to the use of thalidomide, which helped alert American officials to the dangers of the drug.
Health and Safety; Science
Dist - USNAC **Prod** - NMAC 1973

Leaders in American Medicine - Henry G Schwartz, MD 59 MIN
16mm
B&W (PRO)
LC 77-703508
Interviews Dr Henry G Schwartz, Professor of Neurological Surgery at Washington University School of Medicine. Describes his years in medical school and explains how a project on the regeneration of earthworms led him to specialize in anatomy and the physiology of the nervous system.
Health and Safety
Dist - USNAC **Prod** - NMAC

Leaders in American Medicine - Howard C Taylor, Jr, MD 57 MIN
16mm
B&W
LC 76-700098
Presents Dr Howard C Taylor describing the early days of internships in surgery and gynecology prior to the initiation of National Board exams. Tells about his career and its transition from gynecologic oncology to population studies. Discusses his papers in the areas of family planning, psychosomatic uterine congestion and endometrial hyperplasia.
Health and Safety
Dist - USNAC **Prod** - NMAC 1974

Leaders in American Medicine - Irvine H Page, MD 60 MIN
U-matic
Color (PRO)
LC 79-706865
Presents an interview with Dr Irvine H Page, director emeritus, Research Division, Cleveland Clinic, who discusses his life and work in the field of hypertension.
Biography; Health and Safety; Psychology
Dist - USNAC **Prod** - NMAC 1979

Leaders in American Medicine - Jacques Genest, MD, CC 51 MIN
16mm
B&W (PRO)
LC 77-700639
Presents an interview with Dr Jacques Genest. Discusses his medical education and numerous awards. Highlights the beginning of the Clinical Research Institute in Montreal.
Health and Safety
Dist - USNAC **Prod** - NMAC

Leaders in American Medicine - James V Warren, MD 60 MIN
U-matic / VHS
Color
LC 80-706811
Presents James V Warren, MD, discussing the circumstances that led him to a career in academic medicine at Ohio State University, Department of Medicine. Describes his use of the cardiac catheter and his thoughts on medical education and the future of internal medicine.
Health and Safety
Dist - USNAC **Prod** - NMAC 1979

Leaders in American Medicine - John F Enders, Ph D and Frederick C Robbins, MD 34 MIN
16mm
B&W
LC 75-704434
Presents Drs John F Enders and Frederick C Robbins discussing the discovery of the capacity of poliomyelitis virus to grow in vitro cultures of various tissues. Points out their contributions as part of a three - man team that won the 1954 Nobel Prize for medicine and physiology.
Health and Safety
Dist - USNAC **Prod** - NMAC 1974

Leaders in American Medicine - John P Hubbard, MD 58 MIN
16mm
B&W
LC 79-700107
Presents Dr John P Hubbard describing his career.
Health and Safety
Dist - USNAC **Prod** - NMAC 1979

Leaders in American Medicine - Jonathan E Rhoads, MD 57 MIN
16mm
B&W (PRO)
LC 77-703480
Highlights the significant achievements of Dr Jonathan E Rhoads' medical career at the University of Pennsylvania. Describes his early schooling and his college years. Examines his years in medical school and his decision to pursue a career in surgery.
Health and Safety
Dist - USNAC **Prod** - NMAC

Leaders in American Medicine - Joseph T Wearn, MD 48 MIN
16mm
B&W
LC 76-704033
Presents Dr Joseph T Wearn discussing his career, philosophy and experience as an educator with Dr Thomas Hale Ham, with whom he was associated in an experiment in medical education. Recalls how a young faculty was organized and a new curriculum adopted at Case Western Reserve University.
Education; Health and Safety
Dist - USNAC **Prod** - NMAC 1973

Leaders in American Medicine - Karl F Meyer, MD 59 MIN
16mm
B&W
LC 75-704435
Presents Dr Karl F Meyer describing his early education and discussing his work in the field of microbiology and immunology. Discusses his work in setting standards for quality control in the canning industry, his research efforts in the development of a vaccine against plague and his work in psittacosis, brucellosis, relapsing fever, valley fever and the toxic effects of shellfish poisoning.
Health and Safety; Science
Dist - USNAC **Prod** - NMAC 1974

Leaders in American Medicine - L T Coggeshall, MD 55 MIN
16mm
B&W (PRO)
LC 77-700640
Discusses the career of Dr L T Coggeshall as a teacher and researcher. Covers his studies and research in malaria immunology and chemotherapy as well as his role in helping to establish the University of Chicago School of Medicine.
Health and Safety
Dist - USNAC **Prod** - NMAC

Leaders in American Medicine - Leo G Rigler, MD 60 MIN
16mm
B&W
LC 76-704034
Presents Dr Leo G Rigler highlighting his lifetime experience and research in the science of radiology. Comments on the foundation of professional societies concerned with radiology and residency programs in Minnesota.
Health and Safety; Science
Dist - USNAC **Prod** - NMAC 1973

Leaders in American Medicine - Lester R Dragstedt, Ph D, MD 60 MIN
16mm
Color
LC 74-704526
Features Dr Lester Dragstedt and his first research on gastric ulcers and the cause of pain. Discusses his later research on physiology and peptic ulcers, which led to the introduction of vagotomy as a surgical technique for duodenal ulcers. Highlights Dragstedt's experiences in Europe, where he studied abdominal surgery.
Health and Safety; Science
Dist - USNAC **Prod** - NMAC 1972

Leaders in American Medicine - Martin M Cummings, MD 51 MIN
45 MIN
U-matic
B&W; Color (PRO)
LC 76-700099; 76-706146
Presents Dr Martin M Cummings, Director of the National Library of Medicine, giving a brief autobiographical profile and an historical review of the founding of the library. Emphasizes the role played by Dr John Shaw Billings in the development of the institution.
Health and Safety
Dist - USNAC **Prod** - NMAC 1973

Leaders in American Medicine - Matthew Walker, MD 56 MIN
16mm
B&W (PRO)
LC 77-700641
Discusses the medical career of Dr Matthew Walker. Tells about his efforts to train more surgeons, his responsibility for the success or failure of his students and his concern for the delivery of comprehensive health care to ghettos and rural areas.
Health and Safety
Dist - USNAC **Prod** - NMAC

Leaders in American Medicine - Maxwell Finland, M D 58 MIN
16mm
B&W (PRO)
LC 78-700758
Discusses the medical career of Dr Maxwell Finland from his years as a medical student to the 1970s. Comments on his interest in infectious diseases and his scientific insights in observations of patients and the use of clinical drugs.
Biography; Health and Safety
Dist - USNAC **Prod** - NMAC 1977

Leaders in American Medicine - Maxwell Finland, MD 58 MIN
U-matic
B&W (PRO)
LC 78-706085
Presents Dr Maxwell Finland discussing his medical career, his interest in infectious diseases, his scientific insights in observation of patients and the use of clinical drugs.
Biography; Health and Safety
Dist - USNAC **Prod** - NMAC 1977

Leaders in American Medicine - Maxwell M Wintrobe, MD 57 MIN
16mm
B&W
LC 76-700100
Presents Dr Maxwell M Wintrobe reviewing some of the major contributions in the area of hematology which bear his credits. Discusses his contributions in effecting a classification system for the anemias and his role in the development of more precise laboratory procedures and equipment.
Health and Safety; Science
Dist - USNAC **Prod** - NMAC 1974

Leaders in American Medicine - Medical Teaching Philosophies 30 MIN
16mm
B&W (PRO)
LC 76-703869
Expresses scientists' philosophies of medical education with excerpts from interviews with several leaders in the field.
Health and Safety
Dist - USNAC **Prod** - NMAC 1976

Leaders in American Medicine - Owen H Wangensteen, MD 60 MIN
U-matic
Color (PRO)
LC 76-706150
Describes the career of Dr Owen Wangensteen, including his work as a surgeon and his research experiments on the etiology of appendicitis and the etiology and surgical treatment of peptic ulcers and esophagitis. Emphasizes the importance of the history of medicine in medical education and the importance of encouraging and sharing opportunities with students.
Biography; Health and Safety
Dist - USNAC **Prod** - NMAC 1972

Leaders in American Medicine - Owen H Wangensteen, Md 60 MIN
16mm
B&W
LC 74-704530
Describes the career of Dr Owen Wangensteen, including his work as a surgeon and his research experiments on the etiology of appendicitis and the etiology and surgical treatment of peptic ulcers and esophagitis. Emphasizes the importance of the history of medicine in medical education and the importance of encouraging and sharing opportunities with students.
Health and Safety; Science
Dist - USNAC **Prod** - NMAC 1972

Leaders in American Medicine - Owsei Temkin, MD
VHS / U-matic
Color (PRO)
LC 81-707186
Presents an interview with Dr Owsei Temkin in which he recounts his arrival in the United States from Leipzig and his work at Johns Hopkins University with such personalities as Osler and Welch. Discusses the role of the sciences in the evolution of medicine as a profession.
Health and Safety
Dist - USNAC **Prod** - NMAC 1979

Leaders in American Medicine - Paul B Beeson, MD, and Eugene a Stead Jr, MD 60 MIN
16mm
B&W
LC 78-700953
Presents an interview with Paul B Beeson, MD, physician at the U S Veterans Administration, and Eugene A Stead Jr, MD, professor of medicine at Duke University Medical Center.
Health and Safety
Dist - USNAC **Prod** - NMAC 1977

Leaders in American Medicine - Paul B Besson, MD and Eugene a Stead, Jr, MD 60 MIN
U-matic
Color (PRO)
LC 78-706112
Presents an interview between Dr Paul B Besson, distinguished physician at the U S veterans Administration, and Dr Eugene A Stead, Jr, professor of medicine at Duke University Medical Center. Discusses their separate careers as well as their previous work together.
Biography; Health and Safety
Dist - USNAC **Prod** - NMAC 1977

Leaders in American Medicine - Robert H Williams, MD 60 MIN
16mm
B&W
LC 79-700113
Presents Dr Robert H Williams discussing his activities in the field of endocrinology.
Health and Safety
Dist - USNAC **Prod** - NMAC 1978

Leaders in American Medicine - Russell V Lee, MD 57 MIN
16mm
B&W (PRO)

LC 77-703479
Examines the medical career of Dr Russell V Lee. Describes his change from chemistry to medicine during his years at Stanford University. Examines his efforts to raise the standards of medical care in Palo Alto through the formation of a group medical clinic.
Health and Safety
Dist - USNAC **Prod** - NMAC

Leaders in American Medicine - Shields Warren, MD 61 MIN
16mm
B&W
LC 75-704419
Presents Dr Shields Warren discussing his academic career, his research in the pathology of diabetes, his association with the Atomic Energy Commission, his research in radiation pathology and the introduction of the use of isotopes in the biomedical field.
Health and Safety; Science
Dist - USNAC **Prod** - NMAC 1973

Leaders in American Medicine - T R Harrison, MD 55 MIN
16mm
B&W (PRO)
LC 77-700642
Discusses the career of Dr T R Harrison. Examines his years at Johns Hopkins, Vanderbilt and Peter Bent Brigham Hospital. Highlights his tenure as chairman of the Department of Medicine at the University of Alabama.
Health and Safety
Dist - USNAC **Prod** - NMAC

Leaders in American Medicine - W Montague Cobb, MD 58 MIN
16mm
B&W
LC 76-703870
Discusses the influence of parents and teachers on the goals and ideals of W Montague Cobb. Recounts his professional training, his work at Howard University and his role in helping to gain equal rights for Black physicians.
Guidance and Counseling; Health and Safety; Science
Dist - USNAC **Prod** - NMAC 1976

Leaders in American Medicine - Walsh Mc Dermott, MD 60 MIN
16mm
B&W
LC 74-704529
Presents the views of Dr Walsh Mc Dermott on the state of American medicine and on the future of medical education. Discusses Mc Dermott's early research on infectious diseases and his experimentation with laboratory animals in field testing of the antimicrobial drugs streptomycin and isoniazid. Recalls the development of a research program for prevention and control of tuberculosis in Navaho Indians and tells the problems that were solved.
Health and Safety; Psychology
Dist - USNAC **Prod** - NMAC 1971

Leaders in American Medicine - William Barry Wood, Jr, MD 60 MIN
16mm
B&W
LC 74-704531
Presents Dr William Barry Wood, Jr discussing his medical career as a student at Harvard and Johns Hopkins and as head of the Department of Medicine at Washington University in St Louis. Describes his work with mechanisms of disease, pneumococcal pneumonia and the pathogenesis of fever.
Education; Health and Safety
Dist - USNAC **Prod** - NMAC 1973

Leaders in American Medicine - William P Longmire, Jr, MD and Francis D Moore, MD 60 MIN
U-matic
Color (PRO)
LC 79-706866
Presents an interview between Dr William P Longmire, Jr, professor of surgery at the University of California at Los Angeles School of Medicine, and Dr Francis D Moore, professor of surgery at Harvard Medical School. Discusses their early careers in medicine and the discoveries in the field of surgery that became milestones during their careers.
Biography; Health and Safety
Dist - USNAC **Prod** - NMAC 1979

The Leaders - jazz in Paris 54 MIN
VHS
Color (G)
$29.95 purchase
Records a jazz concert in Paris.
Fine Arts
Dist - KINOIC **Prod** - RHPSDY

The Leaders of the Revolution, Pt 1 45 MIN
VHS / 16mm
Salisbury's Report on China - the Revolution and Beyond Series
Color (J)
$349.00 purchase, $175.00 rental _ #OD - 2227
Documents the major players and events over four decades of the Chinese revolution. Examines such figures as Mao Tse - Tung, Lin Chao - chi, Den Xiaoping, and the Gang Of Four. Focuses on the struggles, confrontations and scrambles for power. Features New York Times reporter Harrison Salisbury. The first of three installments of the series Salisbury's Report On China - The Revolution And Beyond.
Geography - World; History - World
Dist - FOTH

Leaders of the 20th century - portraits of power series

Adenauer - Germany reborn	24 MIN
Ben - Gurion - One place, one people	24 MIN
Churchill - voice of a lion	24 MIN
Churchill - voice of a prophet	24 MIN
De Gaulle - force of character	24 MIN
De Gaulle - republican monarch	24 MIN
Eisenhower - Years of Caution	24 MIN
Elizabeth II - winds of change	24 MIN
The End of the Old Order - 1900 - 1918	24 MIN
Franco - Caudillo of Spain	24 MIN
Hirohito - the Chrysanthemum Throne	24 MIN
Hitler - Revenge to Ruin	24 MIN
Kennedy - Years of Charisma	24 MIN
Khrushchev - the Bear's Embrace	24 MIN
Mahatma Gandhi - soul force	24 MIN
Mao - Long March to Power	24 MIN
Mao - Organized Chaos	24 MIN
Mohammed Reza Pahlavi - politics of oil	24 MIN
Nasser - People's Pharoah	24 MIN
Roosevelt - Hail to the Chief	24 MIN
Roosevelt - Manipulator - in - Chief	24 MIN
Tito - Power of Resistance	24 MIN
Truman - Years of Decision	24 MIN

Dist - LCOA

Leaders of Tomorrow 20 MIN
16mm
B&W (JAPANESE)
LC FIE52-1946
Portrays Japanese teen - age boys and girls learning the principles of democracy at the Youth Training Centers sponsored in Japan by the American Red Cross and the Allied Powers.
Civics and Political Systems; Education; Geography - World; Social Science; Sociology
Dist - USNAC **Prod** - USA 1949

The Leaders - Program 2 35 MIN
VHS
Ebony - Jet guide to black excellence series
Color (I J H)
$24.95 purchase _ #BLA130
Focuses on Douglas Wilder, Governor of Virginia; Marian Wright Edelman of the Children's Defense Fund; and James Comer, director Yale University's Child Study Center, who rose to leadership in the United States. Presents part of a three - part series by Ebony and Jet magazines to encourage young people to set goals and reach for their dreams.
Civics and Political Systems; Guidance and Counseling; History - United States; Psychology; Sociology
Dist - KNOWUN

Leadership 20 MIN
VHS / 16mm
Citizens all Series
Color (H)
$150.00 purchase, $30.00 rental
Considers why people run for office, concluding that political campaigns provide an opportunity for discussion and debate of important public issues.
Business and Economics; Civics and Political Systems
Dist - AITECH **Prod** - WHATV 1987

Leadership 18 MIN
U-matic / VHS / 16mm
Supervisory Development for Law Enforcement Series Part 1
Color
Uses dramatic re - creations of actual situations to illustrate the impact of various leadership styles and the effectiveness of the supervisor. Points out that leadership can be learned and that there is no absolutely right way to lead.
Business and Economics; Civics and Political Systems; Psychology; Social Science
Dist - CORF **Prod** - HAR

Leadership 20 MIN
VHS / U-matic
Effective Manager Series
Color
Business and Economics; Guidance and Counseling; Psychology
Dist - DELTAK **Prod** - DELTAK

Leadership 120 MIN
VHS
Color (G)
$2000.00 purchase
Presents a video seminar by Konosuke Matsushita Professor of Leadership at Harvard Business School, John Kotter. States that managers manage change, leaders create it - leadership can disrupt orderly planning systems and undermine management hierarchies, while management can discourage risk taking and enthusiasm needed for leadership. Both are necessary to prosperous organizations. Includes two videocassettes containing six 20 - minute modules, a facilitator's guide, viewer's guides, an audiocassette in which Fortune editor Geoffrey Colvin interviews Prof Kotter, and a summary card outlining seminar content.
Business and Economics; Guidance and Counseling; Psychology
Dist - NATTYL **Prod** - FOR 1990

Leadership 49 MIN
U-matic / 16mm / VHS
Human Journey Series
Color; Mono (J H C A)
MV #350.00 _ MP $450.00 purchase, $50.00 rental
Examines the qualities and personalities of some of our leaders. Includes interveiws with prominent figures in sports, education, business, politics, education and the millitary who discuss their veiws on leadership.
Guidance and Counseling; Sociology
Dist - CTV **Prod** - CTV

The Leadership Alliance 64 MIN
VHS / U-matic
Color (G PRO)
$995.00, $895.00 purchase, $250.00 rental
Features Tom Peters interviewing Pat Carrigan, Dennis Littky, Vaughn Beals and Ralph Stayer. Deals with management technique for economically unstable times.
Business and Economics; Guidance and Counseling; Sociology
Dist - VPHI **Prod** - VPHI 1989

Leadership alliance 60 MIN
VHS
Color (A PRO IND)
$895.00 purchase, $250.00 rental
Features Tom Peters in a look at leadership. Suggests that leadership must be present at all levels of an organization. Interviews several leaders in various settings.
Business and Economics; Guidance and Counseling; Psychology
Dist - VLEARN **Prod** - VPHI

The Leadership Alliance 60 MIN
VHS / 16mm
(C PRO)
$895.00 purchase, $225.00 rental
Gives successful examples of leadership in different areas of work from industry to education.
Education
Dist - VLEARN **Prod** - VPHI

The Leadership alliance 60 MIN
U-matic / VHS
Color (PRO G A)
$895.00, $995.00 purchase, $250.00 rental
Feaatures Tom Peters who introduces four successful managers exemplifying the principles of inspired leadership he feels are critical to achieving goals. Includes a viewer's guide.
Business and Economics; Guidance and Counseling; Psychology
Dist - EXTR **Prod** - VPHI

The Leadership alliance 64 MIN
U-matic / VHS
Color (G PRO A)
$995.00, $895.00 purchase, $250.00 rental
Presents Tom Peters on location with four outstanding leaders and before a live audience discussing the lessons of those leaders.
Business and Economics; Guidance and Counseling; Psychology
Dist - MAGVID **Prod** - MAGVID 1989

The Leadership alliance overview 30 MIN
U-matic / VHS
Color (PRO G A)
$495.00, $595.00 purchase, $175.00 rental
Presents an overview of the video The Leadership Alliance which features Tom Peters emphasizing the need for inspired leadership in businesses.
Business and Economics; Guidance and Counseling; Psychology
Dist - EXTR **Prod** - VPHI

The Leadership Alliance with Tom Peters 64 MIN
VHS / 16mm
Color (PRO)
$895.00 purchase, $185.00 rental, $50.00 preview
Features Tom Peters who investigates how outstanding leaders run their businesses. Discusses management innovations, empowering young people, creating work teams, delegating responsibility, and redefining management attitudes. Includes viewer's guide.
Business and Economics; Education; Guidance and Counseling; Psychology
Dist - UTM **Prod** - UTM

Leadership and Growth 30 MIN
U-matic / VHS
You - the Supervisor Series
Color
Business and Economics; Guidance and Counseling; Psychology
Dist - DELTAK **Prod** - PRODEV

Leadership and safety - your role in ensuring a safe workplace 17 MIN
VHS
Color (IND)
$495.00 purchase, $95.00 rental _ #BBP248
Train supervisors in safety issues including OSHA regulations and employees' rights and responsibilities. Includes a leader's guide, a participant workbook and reminder cards.
Guidance and Counseling; Health and Safety; Psychology
Dist - EXTR **Prod** - BBP

Leadership and Small Work Group Dynamics 27 MIN
16mm / U-matic / VHS
Management Development Series
Color
Presents Dr Verne J Kallejian who offers a chalkboard lecture in which he describes how to integrate the needs of people within an organization. Cites the family and the military as classic examples of need - oriented and task - oriented institutions and defines organizational efficiency as the optimization of the two factors.
Business and Economics; Psychology
Dist - UCEMC **Prod** - UCLA 1976

Leadership and technology management 14 MIN
VHS
Color (G C)
Describes the training program of the Center on Disabilities at Cal State U, Northridge. Overviews the five - day program to give the viewer a taste of the main themes of systems change and consumerism, the greater availability and utilization of technology among people with disabilities. Cosponsored with the California State Dept of Rehabilitation.
Health and Safety; Psychology
Dist - CSUN

Leadership and the One Minute Manager 80 MIN
U-matic / VHS / 16mm
Color (G)
Teaches managers how to build enthusiastic peak performers at all levels.
Business and Economics
Dist - VPHI **Prod** - VPHI 1985

Leadership and the one minute manager 80 MIN
VHS / U-matic / 16mm
One minute management system series
Color (G PRO A)
$1295.00, $1095.00, $995.00 purchase, $375.00, $325.00 rental
Presents Dr Ken Blanchard who shows how to use 'one minute manager' skills in leadership.
Business and Economics; Guidance and Counseling; Psychology
Dist - MAGVID **Prod** - MAGVID 1985

Leadership and the One Minute Manager
U-matic / VHS
Color
Discusses and teaches how managers can build enthusiastic peak performers at all levels of experience. Follows the One Minute Manager and Building the One Minute Manager Skills in the Dr Ken Blanchard - Dr Bob Lorber four - title management training courses.
Business and Economics; Psychology
Dist - CBSFOX **Prod** - CBSFOX

Leadership and the One Minute Manager 80 MIN
VHS / 16mm
(C PRO)
$1150.00 purchase, $310.00 rental
Shows four leadership styles, including directing, coaching, supporting and delegating. Teaches managers how to build enthusiastic peak performers at all levels of experience.
Education
Dist - VLEARN **Prod** - VPHI

The Leadership challenge 26 MIN
VHS
Color (A PRO IND)
$650.00 purchase, $125.00 rental
Suggests that leadership is a process, one which all managers can develop. Based on the book by James M Kouzes and Barry Z Posner.
Business and Economics; Guidance and Counseling; Psychology
Dist - VLEARN **Prod** - CRMF

The Leadership challenge 26 MIN
VHS
Color (PRO G A)
$725.00 purchase, $175.00 rental
Explores five principles of effective leadership that anyone can learn, giving examples of four successful managers who apply the principles to inspire others. Includes a leader's guide.
Business and Economics; Guidance and Counseling; Psychology
Dist - EXTR **Prod** - CRMP

The Leadership challenge - motivating a winning team 40 MIN
VHS
Women and leadership series
Color (A PRO)
$79.95 purchase _ #PB10V-B
Focuses on issues of interest to working women. Presents the 'Laws of Motivation' and examines the reasons why women are excellent natural motivators. Shows how women really can influence someone's motivational level. Part of a four-part series.
Business and Economics; Psychology; Sociology
Dist - CAMV

Leadership challenge series
The Leadership challenge - the two faces of power - Part I 45 MIN
The Leadership challenge - the two faces of power - Part II 45 MIN
Dist - EXTR

The Leadership challenge - the two faces of power - Part I 45 MIN
VHS
Leadership challenge series
Color (PRO IND A) (DUTCH FRENCH)
$695.00 purchase _ #VIMI15
Overviews problems associated to leadership roles. Discusses areas holding potential danger for those in positions of leadership - self assault, isolation from reality, transference, fear of success. Features Prof M Kets de Vries who also introduces to managers the idea of neurotic styles of organization, which he details in part II.
Business and Economics; Guidance and Counseling
Dist - EXTR

The Leadership challenge - the two faces of power - Part II 45 MIN
VHS
Leadership challenge series
Color (PRO IND A) (DUTCH FRENCH)
$695.00 purchase _ #VIM16
Details the five neurotic styles of organization introduced in part I - compulsive, depressive, detached, dramatic, suspicious. Identifies and teaches the implementation of positive leadership behaviors to those in management and supervisory positions. Features Prof M Kets de Vries.
Business and Economics; Guidance and Counseling
Dist - EXTR

Leadership - choosing the road less traveled 23 MIN
VHS
America's teenage video magazine series
Color (J H)
$95.00 purchase _ #2003VG
Delves into the structure of high school life and ways to bring out the leadership potential in students. Shows four different teenagers meeting to share feelings about leadership, social issues, high school spirit, success, and academics. Includes a discussion guide.
Guidance and Counseling; Psychology
Dist - UNL

Leadership - developing a talent for optimism
VHS
Color (C PRO G)
$30.00 purchase _ #930
Features Angela Barron McBride who presents the recent findings of current research on depression, relating its relevance to nursing as a field and to nurses as individuals. Concludes with individual and structural suggestions for developing a talent for optimism.
Guidance and Counseling; Health and Safety
Dist - SITHTA **Prod** - SITHTA 1987

Leadership Edge 18 MIN
VHS / 16mm
Color (C A)
$595.00 purchase, $150.00 rental _ #190
Shows three real - life leaders discussing and demonstrating their leadership strategies. Stresses that effective leadership is a skill that can be learned. Includes Leader's Guide.
Business and Economics; Guidance and Counseling; Psychology
Dist - SALENG **Prod** - SALENG 1987

Leadership Edge 18 MIN
VHS / 16mm
(C PRO)
$595.00 purchase, $135.00 rental
Shows three strategies that are common signatures of effective leaders, including communicating a clear sense of purpose, involving others, and demonstrating commitment.
Education
Dist - VLEARN

Leadership for a new era
VHS
Color (C PRO G)
$30.00 purchase, $15.00 rental _ #974 - P, #974 - R
Records the second in a series of keynote speeches from Sigma Theta Tau International's 1991 Biennial Convention held in Tampa, Florida. Features Sister Rosemary Donley who discusses traits of leaders and why leadership is needed.
Guidance and Counseling; Health and Safety
Dist - SITHTA **Prod** - SITHTA 1991

Leadership from within 90 MIN
BETA / VHS
Innerwork series
Color (G)
$49.95 purchase _ #W197
Looks at the difference between management and leadership. Defines leadership as that which moves forward to a new vision of the future while management maintains the status quo. Features James M Kouzes.
Guidance and Counseling; Psychology
Dist - THINKA **Prod** - THINKA

Leadership in action 17 MIN
VHS
Color (PRO A G)
$595.00 purchase, $175.00 rental
Presents comments on leadership principles by James Kouzes and Barry Posner. Uses DuPont Company's Bill Spencer as an example of extraordinary leadership achievement. Serves as a sequel to the videos The Leadership Challenge and The Credibility Factor.
Business and Economics; Guidance and Counseling; Psychology
Dist - EXTR **Prod** - CRMP

Leadership in QC Circles 22 MIN
VHS
(PRO)
Describes Quality Control activities in the context of the leader's participation and attitude. Presents the Plan, Do, Check, Action, or PDCA, cycle. Also shows how to motivate members, choose themes for the meeting, and how to collect and analyse data. Also details leaders' roles.
Business and Economics
Dist - TOYOVS **Prod** - JPC 1987

Leadership Issues - Theoretical and Pragmatic 30 MIN
16mm
Dimensions of Leadership in Nursing Series
Color (PRO)
LC 77-702472
Describes different approaches to leadership in nursing. Includes case studies which identify leadership behavior and skills. Defines leadership as a process rather than authority or power of position, emphasizing the interpersonal nature of leadership.
Health and Safety; Psychology
Dist - AJN **Prod** - AJN 1977

Leadership Link - Fundamentals of Effective Supervision Series
Managing Energy, Effort, Time, and Money 14 MIN
Peermanship 10 MIN
The Role of the Supervisor 17 MIN
Solid Performance Leadership 18 MIN
Straightforward Communication 19 MIN
Dist - DELTAK

Leadership - maximizing people potential 51 MIN
VHS
Color (A PRO)
$69.95 purchase _ #S01546
Features Sheila Bethel in a presentation of the most important leadership qualities, which include attention to detail, respect for the individual, willingness to risk, and others. Recommends that leaders avoid confusing leadership with command.
Business and Economics; Guidance and Counseling; Psychology
Dist - UILL

Leadership - maximizing people potential 55 MIN
VHS
Color (H C A)
$59.95 purchase
Features Sheila Murray Bethel, who shares her perspectives on successful leadership in the professional setting. Covers maximizing personal and professional potential, handling change more effectively, and other subjects.
Guidance and Counseling
Dist - PBS **Prod -** WNETTV

Leadership - Meeting the Challenge 9.3 MIN
BETA / VHS / U-matic
Supervisory Series
(PRO A)
$225 _ #1019
Presents the key responsibilities in supervisory incidents which can normally occur when managing a custodial team.
Education; Guidance and Counseling
Dist - CTT **Prod -** CTT

Leadership - meeting the challenge 10 MIN
VHS
Color (H A G T)
$225.00 purchase _ #BM119
Provides an overview of management and supervisory situations which are part of a supervisor's daily responsibilities.
Business and Economics; Guidance and Counseling; Psychology
Dist - AAVIM **Prod -** AAVIM

Leadership - people potential now 55 MIN
VHS
Speaking of success series
Color (H C G)
$39.95 purchase _ #PD12
Features Sheila Murray Bethel discussing how to become a successful role model, maximize professional potential, handle change more effectively, and build a winning professional environment. Part of a series.
Business and Economics
Dist - SVIP **Prod -** AUVICA 1993

Leadership Roles - First Line to Executive 45 MIN
U-matic / VHS
Nursing Career Development Series Pt 3
Color (PRO)
LC 81-707109
Describes the role of nurse as a leader and presents principles of effective management. Outlines the philosophical and detailed process of management practices for top leadership positions.
Health and Safety; Psychology
Dist - USNAC **Prod -** USVA 1981

Leadership Series Module 1
The Nature of Leadership 56 FRS
Dist - RESEM

Leadership series module 3
Applied leadership 18 MIN
Dist - RESEM

Leadership series
Presents three modules on leadership. Includes the titles The Nature of Leadership, Styles of Leadership, Applied Leadership.
Leadership series 52 MIN
Styles of leadership 72 FRS
Dist - RESEM **Prod -** RESEM 1981

Leadership skills by Aaron Alejandro 58 MIN
VHS
Color (H C G)
$79.00 purchase _ #CEV40321V
Uses humor and motivation to emphasize that individuals are not necessarily born with leadership abilities but must continuously work to develop them. Features Aaron Alejandro who conducts a fast - paced leadership workshop to develop and hone leadership skills. Encourages students to participate in their school and community and explains in detail how such participation affects their future.
Business and Economics; Guidance and Counseling; Psychology
Dist - CAMV

Leadership skills for women 26 MIN
VHS
Color (A PRO)
$495.00 purchase, $150.00 rental
Teaches ways women can develop their skills in working with others. Shows ways to effectively lead challenging people and situations.
Business and Economics; Guidance and Counseling; Sociology
Dist - DHB **Prod -** CRISP

Leadership style - balancing the needs of the leader, the people and the situation 33 MIN
VHS / BETA / U-matic
Color (G)
$495.00 purchase, $130.00 rental
Discusses leadership styles and shows how to choose appropriate leadership styles for accomplishment.
Business and Economics; Guidance and Counseling
Dist - AMEDIA **Prod -** WYVERN

Leadership - Style or Circumstance 30 MIN
U-matic / VHS / 16mm
Behavior in Business Film Series
Color (H C A)
LC 75-700170
Identifies and differentiates two diverse types of leaders, the relationship - oriented leader and the task - oriented leader. Shows how each type of leader can work effectively depending on the job situation.
Business and Economics; Psychology
Dist - CRMP **Prod -** CRMP 1975

Leadership - Style or Circumstance 28 MIN
16mm / VHS
#107583 - 6 3/4
Describes two broad categories of leaders, those who deal best with people and those who are oriented primarily towards tasks, and examines the importance of matching leadership style to a given situation.
Business and Economics
Dist - MGHT

Leadership Styles 20 MIN
VHS / U-matic
Color
Offers a dramatization showing how to work well with any type of boss, including the authoritarian boss, the humanitarian boss and the 'little bit of both' boss.
Psychology
Dist - AMA **Prod -** AMA

Leadership - the Critical Difference 60 MIN
Cassette / VHS
Effective Manager Series
Color (G)
$95.00 purchase _ #6429
Features Brian Tracy who offers step - by - step guidance on leadership. Includes a 60 - minute video, two audiocassettes and two workbooks. Part of a fourteen - part series.
Business and Economics; Civics and Political Systems; Guidance and Counseling; Psychology
Dist - SYBVIS

Leadership - the critical difference 60 MIN
VHS
Effective manager seminar series
Color (H C A)
$95.00 purchase _ #NGC745V
Presents a multimedia seminar on leadership. Consists of a videocassette, a 60 - minute audiocassette, and a study guide.
Business and Economics; Psychology
Dist - CAMV

Leadership video 3 MIN
VHS
Meeting opener motivation videos series
Color (G)
$89.00 purchase _ #MV4
Presents an inspiration video which incorporates breakthrough cinematography, stirring music and powerful lyrics to create a mood that enhances the impact of the desired message.
Business and Economics; Guidance and Counseling; Psychology
Dist - GPERFO

Leadership - Working with People
VHS / 16mm
(PRO)
$150.00 purchase _ #PS111
Shows the important role the manager has in assessing and developing of a philosophy of management as a basis for leadership. Identifies and analyzes various leadership styles.
Business and Economics
Dist - RMIBHF **Prod -** RMIBHF

Leadership - Working with People
U-matic / VHS
Principles of Management Series
Color
Stresses the importance of a manager in assessing and developing a philosophy of management as the basis for leadership. Identifies and analyzes the various leadership styles.
Business and Economics; Psychology
Dist - RMIBHF **Prod -** RMIBHF

Leadfoot 27 MIN
16mm / U-matic / VHS
Color (J H A)
Shows how Tom is so proud of his first car that he ignores the efforts of the police to get him to drive carefully. Explains that he eventually tumbles into a ravine while driving carelessly and kills his girlfriend. Stars Philip McKeon and Peter Barton.
Health and Safety
Dist - MEDIAG **Prod -** PAULST 1984

Leading a First Group Session 88 MIN
U-matic
Skills of Helping Series Program 2
Color (C A)
LC 80-707459
Explores some of the skills involved in leading a group session. Discusses clarifying purpose and role for group members, reaching for feedback, encouraging interaction, evaluating the first session, and other skills.
Guidance and Counseling; Psychology
Dist - SYRCU **Prod -** MCGILU 1980

Leading a First Group Session, Pt 1 44 MIN
U-matic
Skills of Helping Series Program 2
Color (C A)
LC 80-707459
Explores some of the skills involved in leading a group session. Discusses clarifying purpose and role for group members, reaching for feedback, encouraging interaction, evaluating the first session, and other skills.
Guidance and Counseling; Psychology
Dist - SYRCU **Prod -** MCGILU 1980

Leading a First Group Session, Pt 2 44 MIN
U-matic
Skills of Helping Series Program 2
Color (C A)
LC 80-707459
Explores some of the skills involved in leading a group session. Discusses clarifying purpose and role for group members, reaching for feedback, encouraging interaction, evaluating the first session, and other skills.
Guidance and Counseling; Psychology
Dist - SYRCU **Prod -** MCGILU 1980

Leading a service team 25 MIN
VHS
Color (PRO IND A)
Covers a day in the life of a high performance team at the IDS Financial Services division of American Express. Reveals that in the two years since Team 10 adopted the 'team - empowerment concept,' productivity has radically improved, up to 1000 percent in some areas.
Business and Economics; Psychology
Dist - VLEARN **Prod -** VLEARN 1990

Leading and following 27 MIN
VHS
Sunshine factory series
Color (P I R)
$14.99 purchase _ #35 - 83553 - 533
Features P J the repairman and kids in his neighborhood as they travel to the Sunshine Factory, a land populated by puppets, a computer and caring adults. Teaches a Biblically - based lesson on leading and following.
Religion and Philosophy
Dist - APH **Prod -** WORD

Leading and influencing I 44 MIN
VHS
Video guide to occupational exploration - the video GOE series

Color (J H C G)
$69.95 purchase _ #CCP1012V
Discusses occupations where people use mathematical information to make decisions or help others make decisions - Math and Statistics, Social Research, Business Administration, Finance, Business Management, and Contract and Claims. Interviews a statistician, urban planner, airport manager, accountant, contract administrator and a sociologist. Part of a 14 - part series exploring occupational clusters.
Business and Economics; Guidance and Counseling; Mathematics
Dist - CAMV **Prod** - CAMV 1991

Leading and influencing II 42 MIN
VHS
Video guide to occupational exploration - the video GOE series
Color (J H C G)
$69.95 purchase _ #CCP1013V
Discusses occupations where people use words and ideas to make decisions and influence others - Education and Library Services, Law, Administration Services, Communications, Promotions and Regulations Enforcement. Interviews a judge, prosecuting attorney, college president, environmental inspector, high school principal, television news producer, assignment editor and a fashion coordinator. Part of a 14 - part series exploring occupational clusters.
Business and Economics; Civics and Political Systems; Education; Guidance and Counseling; Social Science
Dist - CAMV **Prod** - CAMV 1991

Leading application 20 MIN
BETA / VHS / 16mm
Color (A PRO)
$86.00 purchase _ #KTI27
Covers cleaning, tinning, appplying, and paddle finishing lead fill.
Industrial and Technical Education
Dist - RMIBHF **Prod** - RMIBHF

Leading Discussions, Whole Class 49 MIN
U-matic / VHS
Strategies in College Teaching Series
Color (T)
LC 79-706291
Shows ways of stimulating different kinds of discussions and explains how to give directions and vary discussion format.
Education
Dist - IU **Prod** - IU 1977

Leading Group Discussions 27 MIN
16mm
Color (C T)
LC 77-703458
Demonstrates techniques for leading effective classroom discussions, including the abilities to respond to feelings, to clarify and summarize content, to pair feelings or content, to formulate stimulating questions and to provide feedback. Based on the book Facilitative Teaching - Theory And Practice by Joe Wittmer and Robert D Myrick.
Education; Psychology
Dist - EDMDC **Prod** - EDMDC 1977

Leading in a White Knuckle Decade 60 MIN
VHS / U-matic
Color (G PRO)
$895.00, $795.00 purchase, $225.00 rental
Features Dr. Warren Bennis who describes the four attributes shared by successful leaders. Answers two questions, how do people learn to lead, what do organizations do to promote or stifle leadership?
Business and Economics; Guidance and Counseling; Psychology
Dist - FI **Prod** - VPHI 1989

Leading in a White Knuckle Decade
VHS / 16mm
Color (PRO)
$795.00 purchase, $225.00 rental, $50.00 preview
Features Dr Warren Bennis who describes the qualities of successful leaders based on his research of leaders in many fields. Discusses applications to the world of business. Explains how one learns to lead and how organizations can encourage successful leadership.
Business and Economics; Education; Psychology
Dist - UTM **Prod** - UTM 1989

Leading questions 60 MIN
U-matic / VHS
Public mind series
Color; Captioned (A G)
$59.00, $79.00 purchase _ #MPUM - 102
Examines the power of professional pollsters to influence public opinion. Shows that techniques are designed to bring out the most emotional visuals with which to appeal to the increasingly indifferent society. Part of a series with Bill Moyers that examines the impact on democracy of a mass culture whose basic information comes from image - making, the media, public opinion polls, public relations and propaganda.
Business and Economics; Civics and Political Systems; Psychology; Sociology
Dist - PBS

Leading the change - Part 2 - manager version 21 MIN
VHS
New workplace series
Color (PRO IND A)
$525.00 purchase, $150.00 rental _ #QMR06B
Draws upon the expertise of several CEOs, managers, line workers and consultants as they discuss changes in the workplace and how they affect managers and employees. Promotes an understanding of the nature of change for managers of organizations undergoing transitions. By Quality Media Resources.
Business and Economics
Dist - EXTR

Leading the nation series
Customer - driven quality - Volume 1 30 MIN
Leading the nation - Total quality in the public sector 60 MIN
Team - based quality - Volume 1 30 MIN
Dist - EXTR

Leading the nation - Total quality in the public sector 60 MIN
VHS
Leading the nation series
Color (PRO IND A)
$1,090.00 purchase, $450.00 rental _ #ENT14A - B
Profiles in a two - part series two federal agencies - Sacramento Air Force Logistics Center and the IRS - that have changed by implementing quality. Includes helpful guidelines on understanding and implementing changes in the area of quality. Facilitator's Guide and Participant's Workbook are available.
Business and Economics; Civics and Political Systems
Dist - EXTR **Prod** - ENMED

Leading the Parade 13 MIN
16mm
Color
Features baton twirling performances by leading high school and college majorettes.
Physical Education and Recreation
Dist - FLADC **Prod** - FLADC

Leading the way 38 MIN
VHS
Color (A PRO IND)
$695.00 purchase, $150.00 rental
Teaches methods for dealing with change within an organization. Presents a flexible framework for dealing with change.
Business and Economics; Guidance and Counseling
Dist - VLEARN **Prod** - EFM

Leading the Way 40 MIN
VHS / 16mm
Color (PRO)
$695.00 purchase, $150.00 rental
Encourages managers to envision, plan and implement change in their own departments. Offers a flexible, realistic model for managing change.
Business and Economics; Psychology
Dist - VICOM **Prod** - VICOM 1990

Leading the way - Winning through change - Part 2 43 MIN
VHS
Color (PRO G A)
$695.00 purchase, $170.00 rental
Provides a four - step outline of the process of change as a basis for planning. Helps managers lead and avoid common mistakes during periods of change. Includes leader's guide.
Business and Economics; Guidance and Counseling; Psychology
Dist - EXTR **Prod** - AMA

Leading Your Horse 61 MIN
VHS / 16mm
(G)
$39.95 purchase _ #VT1068
Illustrates the steps in training a horse to lead easily and safely. Teaches the stages of training a horse, from the ten - day - old foal to the mature adult. Taught by Ron Palelek, top horse breeder.
Agriculture; Physical Education and Recreation
Dist - RMIBHF **Prod** - RMIBHF

Leadville 5 MIN
16mm
Color
Shows the dance - theatre of Alex Hay, in which man is portrayed as a machine.
Fine Arts
Dist - VANBKS **Prod** - VANBKS

Leadwork and plastic fillers - Vol 4 58 MIN
VHS
Collector car restoration home video libary series
Color (G)
$24.95 purchase
Shows how to select the right equipment, tools and supplies for leadwork and plastic fillers in collector cars. Demonstrates that many tools and equipment can be improvised at very little cost. Illustrates techniques. Part four of a six - part series on classic car restoration.
Industrial and Technical Education
Dist - COLLEC **Prod** - COLLEC 1993

Leaf 15 MIN
16mm
Color
LC 75-703516
Discusses the impact of leaf tobacco on the economic and social life of the United States.
Agriculture; Business and Economics; Health and Safety; Sociology
Dist - MTP **Prod** - TOBCCO 1974

The Leaf Eaters - Pt 22 30 MIN
16mm
Life on Earth series; Vol VI
Color (J)
$495.00 purchase _ #865 - 9043
Blends scientific data with wildlife photography to tell the story of the development of life. Features wildlife expert David Attenborough as host.
Science; Science - Natural; Science - Physical
Dist - FI **Prod** - BBCTV 1981

Leaf prints 11 MIN
U-matic / VHS / 16mm
Color (I)
LC 73-702683
Demonstrates a variety of print designs made with leaves.
Physical Education and Recreation; Science - Natural
Dist - LUF **Prod** - ACORN 1973

League of Arab States 28 MIN
Videoreel / VHS
International Byline Series
Color
Interviews Ambassador Clovis Maksoud, permanent observer of the League of Arab States to the United Nations. Focuses on the objectives of the League.
Business and Economics; Civics and Political Systems; Geography - World
Dist - PERRYM **Prod** - PERRYM

The League of gentlemen 115 MIN
VHS
B&W (G)
$39.95 purchase _ #LEA010
Joins a group of eight slightly shady, definitely desperate ex - army officers who plan to use their collective military talents to capture a bank. Presents a thriller full of comedy, suspense and a clever bank robbery. Directed by Basil Dearden. Digitally remastered.
Civics and Political Systems; Fine Arts; Sociology
Dist - HOMVIS **Prod** - JANUS 1960

The League of Nations - the Hope of Mankind 52 MIN
VHS / 16mm
Europe, the Mighty Continent Series no 7; No 7
Color
LC 77-701562
Discusses the aftermath of World War I, including the creation of the League of Nations, the problems of the Weimar Republic, the establishment of dictatorships in Poland, Yugoslavia and Hungary, and Mussolini's rise to power in Italy.
History - World
Dist - TIMLIF **Prod** - BBCTV 1976

The League of Nations - the Hope of Mankind, Pt 1 26 MIN
U-matic
Europe, the Mighty Continent Series no 7; No 7
Color
LC 79-707422
Discusses the aftermath of World War I, including the creation of the League of Nations, the problems of the Weimar Republic, the establishment of dictatorships in Poland, Yugoslavia and Hungary, and Mussolini's rise to power in Italy.
History - World
Dist - TIMLIF **Prod** - BBCTV 1976

The League of Nations - the Hope of Mankind, Pt 2 26 MIN
U-matic
Europe, the Mighty Continent Series no 7; No 7
Color
LC 79-707422
Discusses the aftermath of World War I, including the creation of the League of Nations, the problems of the Weimar Republic, the establishment of dictatorships in Poland, Yugoslavia and Hungary, and Mussolini's rise to power in Italy.
History - World
Dist - TIMLIF **Prod** - BBCTV 1976

A League of their own 27 MIN
VHS
Color (H C G)
$295.00 purchase, $55.00 rental
Recalls how a group of spirited women kept the sport of baseball alive during World War II when baseball players were drafted into the military. Interweaves archival footage and recollections of the players to portray the era when the women played a rough and tumble game but were expected to behave in a lady - like manner off the ball field. Produced by Kim Wilson and Kelly Candaele.
History - United States; History - World; Physical Education and Recreation
Dist - FLMLIB

League School for Seriously Disturbed Children Series
No Two of these Kids are Alike 28 MIN
One Hour a Week 18 MIN
Psycho - Educational Assessment 24 MIN
Teacher Support 15 MIN
Dist - USNAC

Leak detector operation and maintenance 360 MIN
U-matic 377 MIN
270 MIN
280 MIN
Color (IND)
Provides vacuum technology training for workers in the field. Set of 5 tapes, numbers 936 - 940.
Business and Economics; Psychology
Dist - VARIAN **Prod** - VARIAN 1986

Leak surveys - Parts I - III 66 MIN
Slide / VHS
Color (IND PRO)
$525.00, $500.00 purchase _ #55.2996, #15.2996
Presents a three - part series which trains employees about the types of leak surveys, tools and equipment used and methods employed in locating gas leaks. Includes three scripts and a workbook. Developed with the Southern Gas Association.
Health and Safety; Industrial and Technical Education; Psychology
Dist - UTEXPE

Leak Surveys, Pt 1 - Introduction 22 MIN
VHS / U-matic
Leak Surveys Series
Color (IND)
Describes what leak surveys are and their purpose. Explains components and properties of natural gas. Discusses the use of maps and recordkeeping and the three classes of gas leaks.
Social Science
Dist - UTEXPE **Prod** - UTEXPE 1983

Leak Surveys, Pt 3 - Field Operations 24 MIN
VHS / U-matic
Leak Surveys Series
Color (IND)
Covers the three methods of leak surveys, including vegetation, mobile and walking. Explains techniques unique to each method. Describes bar - hole tests and the use of probe bars in pinpointing a leak. Reviews the three classes of leaks and steps needed to classify a particular type of leak.
Industrial and Technical Education; Social Science
Dist - UTEXPE **Prod** - UTEXPE 1983

Leak Surveys, Pt 2 - Tools and Equipment 20 MIN
U-matic / VHS
Leak Surveys Series
Color (IND)
Discusses the combustible gas indicator, the flame pack, pipe locators and ethane detectors, all of which are used extensively in leak survey work.
Industrial and Technical Education; Social Science
Dist - UTEXPE **Prod** - UTEXPE 1983

Leak Surveys Series
Leak Surveys, Pt 1 - Introduction 22 MIN
Leak Surveys, Pt 3 - Field Operations 24 MIN
Leak Surveys, Pt 2 - Tools and Equipment 20 MIN
Dist - UTEXPE

Leak Test for Direct Reading Instruments 5 MIN
VHS / BETA
Color
Discusses manometers and water analysis experiments.
Health and Safety; Industrial and Technical Education; Science; Sociology
Dist - RMIBHF **Prod** - RMIBHF

Leakey 23 MIN
16mm / U-matic / VHS
Color (J)
Provides an intimate portait of Louis S B Leakey from his youth in Africa through his education at Cambridge to his seminal discoveries at Olduvai Gorge. Describes the work of his wife and son and the other scientists Leakey inspired, such as Jane Goodall, Dian Fossey and Birute Galdikas.
Biography; Science; Sociology
Dist - NGS **Prod** - NGS 1983

The Lean Body Workout 60 MIN
VHS
Color (G)
$29.95 purchase _ #1410
Shows how to increase lean muscle tissue which burns fat. Includes cardio - vascular conditioning.
Physical Education and Recreation; Science - Natural
Dist - SYBVIS **Prod** - SYBVIS

Lean legs and buns 45 MIN
VHS
Voigt fitness series
Color (G)
$19.95 purchase _ #GHM20002V
Uses a step bench and light weights to strengthen and sculpt the legs and buttocks. Features Karen Voigt as instructor. Part of a five - part series.
Physical Education and Recreation
Dist - CAMV

The Lean machine - a story about handling emotions 24 MIN
VHS
Human race club series
Color (P I)
$59.00 purchase _ #RB872
Uses animation to portray Maggie who mistakenly assumes that she will represent the club in the hometown go - cart derby. Reveals that her strong emotions cause trouble. Shows how to handle strong emotions. Part of a series teaching essential living skills.
Guidance and Counseling; Psychology
Dist - REVID **Prod** - REVID 1990

Leanne and Wayne 8 MIN
16mm
Color
LC 80-700907
Presents two examples of the care offered to socially disadvantaged children in Australia.
Geography - World; Home Economics; Sociology
Dist - TASCOR **Prod** - TASCOR 1977

The Leap 7 MIN
16mm
Color (J)
Presents an ordinary man who seems to interact physically with videographic apparitions, moving in and out of different space - time realities, fluctuating between the physical and the metaphysical with each stride of his leap toward freedom.
Fine Arts; Guidance and Counseling; Sociology
Dist - CANCIN **Prod** - UWFKD

The Leap 8 MIN
16mm / VHS
Color (G)
$20.00 rental
Theorizes on escaping from the confines of the past by a release of inner energy. Depicts an ordinary man interacting physically with video apparitions and moving in and out of different time - space realities. Produced by Tom DeWitt.
Fine Arts
Dist - CANCIN **Prod** - UWFKD 1968

Leaping silver and Atlantic salmon angling techniques 13 MIN
VHS
Color (G)
$29.90 purchase _ #0393
Watches casting champion Joan Salvato Wulff demonstrate the art of fly casting for Atlantic salmon on a river in Newfoundland, Canada.
Geography - World; Physical Education and Recreation; Science - Natural
Dist - SEVVID **Prod** - CTFL

Leaps and Bounds Series no 11
Rope Jumping 15 MIN
Dist - AITECH

Leaps and Bounds Series no 12
Underhand Throw and Catch 15 MIN
Dist - AITECH

Leaps and Bounds Series no 13
Overhand Throw and Ball Dodging 15 MIN
Dist - AITECH

Leaps and Bounds Series no 14
Projecting the Ball 15 MIN
Dist - AITECH

Leaps and Bounds Series no 15
Kicking 15 MIN
Dist - AITECH

Leaps and Bounds Series no 16
Striking 15 MIN
Dist - AITECH

Leaps and Bounds Series no 4
Locomotor Skills I 15 MIN
Dist - AITECH

Leaps and Bounds Series no 5
Locomotor Skills II 15 MIN
Dist - AITECH

Leaps and Bounds Series no 6
Locomotor Skills III 15 MIN
Dist - AITECH

Leaps and Bounds Series no 8
Tumbling I 15 MIN
Dist - AITECH

Leaps and Bounds Series no 9
Tumbling II 15 MIN
Dist - AITECH

Leaps and bounds series
Apparatus 15 MIN
Body awareness and control I 15 MIN
Body awareness and control II 15 MIN
Body awareness and control III 15 MIN
Creative movement 15 MIN
Dist - AITECH

Learn and earn series
Presents four series which present real - life training for aspiring professional and graphic arts students. Includes three programs in the Desktop Design series; three programs in the Paste - Up series; two programs in the Graphic Design series; and four programs in the Graphics Specialties series.
Learn and earn series 553 MIN
Dist - CAMV

Learn and earn with calligraphy 30 MIN
VHS
Color (H A T)
$39.95 purchase _ #DG119
Demonstrates eight different ways to learn and develop skills to produce calligraphic items for increased personal income. Considers invitations, certificates and awards, advertising, T - shirts, wine labels and framed quotations.
Fine Arts; Social Science
Dist - AAVIM **Prod** - AAVIM 1992

The Learn from Disappointments Game 11 MIN
16mm / U-matic / VHS
Learning Responsibility Series
Color (P)
LC 79-700563
Tells how a young girl learns that understanding disappointments often leads to something better.
Guidance and Counseling
Dist - HIGGIN **Prod** - HIGGIN 1979

Learn graphic design I
VHS / U-matic
Color (H C G)
$295.00, $295.00 purchase _ #02 - LGD
Shows how to create professional - looking documents and communicate messages clearly and effectively. Covers thinking through the design process, understanding the target audience, creating patterns and flow from page to page, designing for clarity and appeal, using type correctly and creatively. Features Jan V White and includes his book in course materials. Includes videotape, textbook and notebook. Published by VideoTutor.
Computer Science; Social Science
Dist - VIDEOT

Learn graphic design II
VHS / U-matic
Color (H C G)

$295.00, $295.00 purchase _ #02 - AGD
Presents part II of the Jan V White course on graphic design, including the book, Graphic Design for the Electronic Age. Covers using pictures to enhance communication, making pictures work with the type and other pictures, when to use charts or graphs to aid communication, selection of graph and chart format and designing a unique publication style. Includes videotape, textbook and notebook. Published by VideoTutor.
Computer Science; Social Science
Dist - VIDEOT

Learn graphic design series
Presents a two - part series on graphic design. Covers basic graphic design principles and their application to electronic production methods. Based on books by Jan White, who also hosts the series.
Editing by design
Graphic design for the electronic age
Dist - VLEARN

Learn how to save a life with first aid 30 MIN
VHS
Color (H A)
$19.95 purchase _ #DVC986V
Features an emergency physician and emergency medical technicians in a program covering first aid techniques. Covers CPR, the Heimlich Maneuver, and first aid techniques for a variety of situations.
Health and Safety
Dist - CAMV

Learn Japanese for business 70 MIN
VHS
Color (C A G PRO) (JAPANESE AND ENGLISH)
$79.95 purchase _ CPM1010
Introduces the basics of the Japanese language. Gives insights into the customs observed in the Japanese work day. Assumes no previous knowledge of Japanese. Produced by Shokai, Ltd, and Central Park Media. Includes text.
Business and Economics; Foreign Language; Sociology
Dist - CHTSUI

Learn not to burn 9 MIN
16mm
Color (I)
LC 76-701792
A revised edition of the 1975 film Learn Not To Burn. Shows some common fire hazards around the house, including smoking in bed, the kitchen stove and improper house wiring. Illustrates proper emergency escape procedures and shows what to do when one's clothing catches fire.
Guidance and Counseling; Health and Safety
Dist - NFPA **Prod** - NFPA 1976

Learn PageMaker 3.0 - basic to intermediate
VHS / U-matic
Color (H C G)
$295.00, $295.00 purchase _ #02 - PLS
Covers master pages, ruler guides, creating graphics with the toolbox, placing text manually and automatically, creating new text blocks, setting type and paragraph specifications, editing text, creating, applying and editing styles, placng graphics, text wrap, using tabs, working with layers, image control, templates and spot color. Teaches about Macintosh or PC. Includes videotape, guide and diskette. Published by VideoTutor.
Computer Science
Dist - VIDEOT

Learn PC Video Systems Introduction to Lotus 1 - 2 - 3
VHS / U-matic
Color (A)
Shows a complete training program for the Lotus 1 - 2 - 3 that is self paced. Explains which keys to press and what appears on the computer monitor.
Mathematics
Dist - DSIM **Prod** - DSIM

Learn programming today with Turbo Pascal 90 MIN
VHS
Visions video series
Color (A PRO)
$69.95 purchase
Enables the beginner to improve computer programming skills. Details how to program a computer and write programs. Provides easy-to-understand examples presented in clear, everyday language with high-tech production techniques and animation graphics. Hosted by Zack Urlocker. Includes workbook written by Keith Weiskamp. Part of a six-part series of training videos.
Computer Science
Dist - BORLND **Prod** - BORLND 1992

Learn snorkeling 30 MIN
VHS
Color (G)
$29.80 purchase _ #0283
Instructs on snorkeling. Uses easy to follow demonstrations which can be safely practiced in a pool, at the beach or in any calm shallow water.
Physical Education and Recreation
Dist - SEVVID

Learn Snorkeling 30 MIN
VHS
(H C A)
$39.95 purchase _ #BM340V
Teaches basic snorkeling skills, including clearing the mask, using swim fins, breathing from the snorkel, choosing equipment, as well as many safety techniques.
Physical Education and Recreation
Dist - CAMV

Learn Tai Chi - Chinese self - healing
VHS
Color (G)
$29.95 purchase _ #SV004
Presents Master Erle Montaigue teaching the graceful movements of 'yang' style Tai Chi.
Physical Education and Recreation; Psychology
Dist - SIV

Learn the ancient Chinese art of placement with feng shui 120 MIN
VHS
Color (G)
$29.95 purchase _ #V - FSV
Shows how to transform one's surroundings to a place of harmony and well - being. Teaches the secrets of an ancient philosophy for transforming the human environment.
Home Economics; Religion and Philosophy
Dist - WHOLEL

Learn the hammered dulcimer 60 MIN
VHS
Video music lesson series
Color (J H C G)
$29.95 purchase _ #TMV13V
Offers step - by - step hammered dulcimer instruction. Features studio musicians, composers, arrangers and educators who lend hands - on instruction about tuning the instrument, chord progressions, smooth and fluent style, timing and finger exercises, common note combinations, instrument set - up, special sound techniques. Includes examples of chord and scale theory, examples for technical improvement and songs to teach the principles of the instrument. Includes booklet. Part of a 16 - part series on musical instruction.
Fine Arts
Dist - CAMV

Learn the racing rules - Part 1
VHS
Color (G A)
$49.80 purchase _ #0076
Teaches the main rules of sailboat racing. Looks at limitations on the right - of - way boat, tacking situations, and before and after start luffing.
Physical Education and Recreation
Dist - SEVVID

Learn the racing rules - Part 2
VHS
Color (G A)
$49.80 purchase _ #0077
Teaches rules at marks and obstructions in sailboat racing. Describes exceptions to basic right - of - way rules.
Physical Education and Recreation
Dist - SEVVID

Learn the Typewriter Parts - Pt 1 10 MIN
VHS / 16mm
Type it Up Series
Color (S)
$500.00 series purchase _ #270304
Features detailed introductory typing instruction at the high school - adult level. Presents amusing interplay between the private detective - novice typist 'Bogie' and his perfectionist instructor 'Sam.' Explains what happens inside the typewriter whenever an activity is performed. Covers carriage, cylinder knob and line space regulator and explains how these parts are used when typing.
Business and Economics; Education
Dist - ACCESS **Prod** - ACCESS 1986

Learn the Typewriter Parts - Pt 2 11 MIN
VHS / 16mm
Type it Up Series
Color (S)
$500.00 series purchase _ #270305
Features detailed introductory typing instruction at the high school - adult level. Presents amusing interplay between the private detective - novice typist 'Bogie' and his perfectionist instructor 'Sam.' Further understanding is gained by an explanation of what happens inside the typewriter whenever an activity is performed. 'Learn The Typewriter Parts - Pt 2' explains the parts of a typewriter that make typing easier, such as the margin release, ribbon control, shift lock and tab. Also covers posture.
Business and Economics; Education; Physical Education and Recreation
Dist - ACCESS **Prod** - ACCESS 1986

Learn to boardsail 30 MIN
VHS
Color (G)
$100.00 rental _ #0136
Teaches beginning and intermediate boardsailing. Covers body position, wind awareness, steering, points of ail, tacking, jibing, rigging the board, getting under way, returning, knots, sail trim.
Physical Education and Recreation
Dist - SEVVID

Learn to dance - basic lesson - Vol 1 50 MIN
VHS
Learn to dance series
Color (G)
$29.95 purchase _ #PE709V
Teaches four basic foot movements which can be used in all traditional ballroom dances.
Fine Arts; Physical Education and Recreation
Dist - CAMV **Prod** - CAMV 1988

Learn to dance - Latin dances - Volume 3 50 MIN
VHS
Learn to dance series
Color (G)
$29.95 purchase _ #PE711V
Teaches four dances - the Tango, the Cha Cha, the Mambo, and the Rumba.
Fine Arts; Physical Education and Recreation
Dist - CAMV **Prod** - CAMV 1988

Learn to dance series
Presents a three - part series teaching the basics of ballroom dance. Instructs in techniques of the Waltz, Lindy or Jitterbug, Fox Trot, Tango, Cha Cha, Mambo, and the Rumba.
Learn to dance - basic lesson - Vol 1 50 MIN
Learn to dance - Latin dances - Volume 3 50 MIN
Learn to dance - swing era - Volume 2 50 MIN
Dist - CAMV **Prod** - CAMV 1988

Learn to dance series
Features Broadway choreographer and champion ballroom dancer Cal del Pozo who illustrates ballroom dancing. Teaches four simple foot movements and lets viewer follow the feet on the screen. Includes the basics, the Swing era, Latin dances and Texas style.
Learn to dance - Texas style
Dist - SIV

Learn to Dance Series
Learn to Dance Videos, Vol 1 50 MIN
Learn to Dance Videos, Vol 2 50 MIN
Learn to Dance Videos, Vol 3 50 MIN
Dist - WCAT

Learn to dance - swing era - Volume 2 50 MIN
VHS
Learn to dance series
Color (G)
$29.95 purchase _ #PE710V
Teaches three dances - the Waltz, the Lindy or Jitterbug, and the Fox Trot.
Fine Arts; Physical Education and Recreation
Dist - CAMV **Prod** - CAMV 1988

Learn to dance - 10 steps for the beginner
VHS
Color (G)
$44.95 purchase _ #GA000
Presents lessons in ballroom dancing.
Fine Arts; Physical Education and Recreation
Dist - SIV

Learn to dance - 10 steps for the beginner 80 MIN
VHS
Color (G A)
$44.95 purchase
Teaches the 10 basic steps of social dance for beginning dancers.
Fine Arts; Physical Education and Recreation
Dist - PBS **Prod** - WNETTV

Learn to dance - Texas style
VHS
Learn to dance series
Color (G)

$14.98 purchase _ #PD055
Features Broadway choreographer and champion ballroom dancer Cal del Pozo who shows how to dance Texas style. Teaches four simple foot movements and lets viewer follow the feet on the screen.
Fine Arts; Physical Education and Recreation; Sociology
Dist - SIV

Learn to Dance Videos, Vol 1 50 MIN
VHS
Learn to Dance Series
Color (G)
$19.95 purchase _ #16127
Introduces the four basic foot movements needed to learn any dance style. Features Broadway dancer and choreographer Cal del Pozo.
Fine Arts; Physical Education and Recreation
Dist - WCAT **Prod** - WCAT

Learn to Dance Videos, Vol 2 50 MIN
VHS
Learn to Dance Series
Color (G)
$19.95 purchase _ #16128
Presents dances of the Swing Era - foxtrot, waltz and jitterbug. Features Broadway dancer and choreographer Cal del Pozo.
Fine Arts; Physical Education and Recreation
Dist - WCAT **Prod** - WCAT

Learn to Dance Videos, Vol 3 50 MIN
VHS
Learn to Dance Series
Color (G)
$19.95 purchase _ #16129
Presents three popular Latin styles, cha - cha, rumba and tango. Features Broadway dancer and choreographer Cal del Pozo.
Fine Arts; Physical Education and Recreation
Dist - WCAT **Prod** - WCAT

Learn to follow Jesus - teaching children to put faith into action 50 MIN
VHS
Nanny and Isaiah adventure series
Color (K P I R)
$24.95 purchase _ #87EE0141
Presents an expanded version of the Nanny and Isaiah program 'The Winning Combination.' Tells how Nanny and Isaiah struggle to form a church softball team, learning along the way how to show love and concern for others. Features a guest appearance by St Louis Cardinals shortstop Ozzie Smith. Includes leader's guide.
Fine Arts; Guidance and Counseling; Literature and Drama; Religion and Philosophy
Dist - CPH **Prod** - CPH

Learn to Live with Stress - Programming the Body for Health 19 MIN
16mm / U-matic / VHS
Color
Presents interviews with Dr Hans Selye and Dr Herbert Benson, two authorities in the study of stress and its effects on the human brain and body. Describes stress as a force causing heart problems, hypertension and other threats to health, and discusses the possible use of meditation to treat people with high blood pressure. Uses an air traffic controller as an example to explain how man is affected by high - pressured and stressful jobs.
Health and Safety; Psychology
Dist - CNEMAG **Prod** - DOCUA

Learn to play autoharp 60 MIN
VHS
Color (G)
$34.95 purchase _ #VD - SEB - AU01
Features John Sebastian who provides a step - by - step learning guide to the autoharp. Shows how to hold the instrument, elementary chord theory, how to tune an autoharp and various ways to accompany favorite songs. Demonstrates fingerpicking techniques, how to find melody notes and scales to pick out melodies and play intrumentals in the styles of traditional players.
Fine Arts
Dist - HOMETA **Prod** - HOMETA

Learn to play bottleneck blues guitar 90 MIN
VHS
Color (G)
$49.95 purchase _ #VD - BOB - BN01
Features guitarist Bob Brozman who shows how to play the licks, runs, rhythms, harmonics and other techniques used by Robert Johnson, Charlie Patton, Bukka White and others. Demonstrates the basics of the Mississippi Delta blues form, open tunings and essential slide and right - hand picking techniques. Includes the songs Walking Blues, Can't Be Satisfied and Crossroads Blues and tablature.
Fine Arts
Dist - HOMETA **Prod** - HOMETA

Learn to play Cajun fiddle 90 MIN
VHS
Color (G)
$49.95 purchase _ #VD - DOC - FI01
Features Michael Doucet, the fiddler from Beausoleil. Breaks down the stylistic devices that give Cajun music its distinctive sounds - slurs, harmonies, ornaments and more. Teaches over a dozen waltzes, two - steps, blues and breakdowns, including Allons a Lafayette; Ma Chere Bebe Creole; Locassine Special; Jolie Blonde; J'ete Au Bal; Chere Toot Toot; Johnny Can't Dance; Tolan Waltz; Lake Arthur Stomp; Les Barres de la Prison; Les Veuves de la Coulee; The Reel de Nez Pique. Includes music.
Fine Arts
Dist - HOMETA **Prod** - HOMETA

Learn to play Irish fiddle series
Presents a two - part series featuring Kevin Burke. Covers rhythmic devices and other variations, including grace notes, ornaments, rolls and double - stops in Video One. Examines more complex rolls, triplets, grace notes, bowing techniques, rhythmic timing and phrasing in Video Two. Includes music.
Learn to play Irish fiddle series 195 MIN
Polkas, jigs and slides - Video One 90 MIN
Reels, jigs and gavottes - Video Two 105 MIN
Dist - HOMETA **Prod** - HOMETA

Learn to play traditional Hawaiian guitar 85 MIN
VHS
Color (G)
$49.95 purchase _ #VD - BOB - HW01
Features Bob Brozman who covers bar techniques, hand positions, scale patterns, Hawaiian tunings, vibrato, harmonic 'chimes' and more for guitar, Dobro, lap steel and pedal steel guitar players. Shows turnarounds, string pairs, slants with the bar and how to obtain the thirds and fifths of each scale. Illustrates Hawaiian classics - Mai Kai No Kauai, Maui Chimes, Moana Chimes and Uhe, Uhene. Includes tablature.
Fine Arts
Dist - HOMETA **Prod** - HOMETA

Learn to sail 106 MIN
VHS
Color (G A)
$39.80 purchase _ #0268
Presents a step - by - step basic to intermediate level course in sailing on board a 27 foot Soling. Features Steve Colgate.
Physical Education and Recreation
Dist - SEVVID

Learn to sail 106 MIN
VHS
Color (G)
$39.95 purchase
Presents an introductory, comprehensive sailing course. Covers all aspects of boat handling. Taught by Olympic sailor Steve Colgate.
Physical Education and Recreation
Dist - PBS **Prod** - WNETTV

Learn to Sail
VHS
Better Boating Series
(H C A)
$225.00 purchase series of 5 _ #BM300S
Discusses basic techniques for the beginning sailor. Explains parts of the boat, sailing terms, sailing knots, running and standing rigging, getting underway, setting the spinmaker, points of sail, emergency procedures and more.
Physical Education and Recreation
Dist - CAMV

The Learn to sail series - 1
VHS
Learn to sail series
Color (G A)
$49.90 purchase _ #0737
Presents part one of a two - part series on learning to sail. Covers sailing safety, the sailboat, lines and knots, what makes a boat sail, capsize recovery, man overboard, introduction to sails, using sails. Produced in cooperation with the United States Yacht Racing Union's Training Committee.
Health and Safety; Physical Education and Recreation
Dist - SEVVID

The Learn to sail series - 2
VHS
Learn to sail series
Color (G A)
$49.90 purchase _ #0738
Presents part two of a two - part series on learning to sail. Covers maneuvering upwind, maneuvering downwind, weather and currents, sailing well, leaving and returning, sailing drills. Uses slow motion, instant replay, stop action and animation. Produced in cooperation with the United States Yacht Racing Union's Training Committee.
Physical Education and Recreation
Dist - SEVVID

Learn to sail series
The Learn to sail series - 1
The Learn to sail series - 2
Dist - SEVVID

Learn to share Jesus - teaching children how to witness 40 MIN
VHS
Nanny and Isaiah adventure series
Color (K P I R)
$24.95 purchase _ #87EE0241
Presents an expanded version of the Nanny and Isaiah program Wonder Witness And Mighty Mouth. Tells how Nanny and Isaiah learn, through a series of adventures, that evangelism should involve everyday lives and relationships. Includes leader's guide.
Fine Arts; Guidance and Counseling; Literature and Drama; Religion and Philosophy
Dist - CPH **Prod** - CPH

Learn to sing Western harmony - sing the cowboy way 60 MIN
VHS
Color (G)
$29.95 purchase _ #VD - RID - VC01
Teaches Western harmony singing. Features Riders in the Sky who teach several well - known cowboy, folk and country songs in three and four - part harmony. Ranger Doug, Too Slim and Woody Paul break down their vocal arrangements, teaching melody and harmony lines both singly and in a group setting. Joey Miskulin is a special guest. Includes the songs Red River Valley, Tumbling Tumbleweed, Cool Water, Home on the Range, as well as music and lyrics.
Fine Arts
Dist - HOMETA **Prod** - HOMETA 1994

Learn to Ski Series
Ski Classic
Ski Esta
Ski Moderne
Skiing
Dist - SFI

Learn to speak French
CD-ROM
(G) (FRENCH)
$149.00 purchase _ #2641
Consists of 36 lessons with four native speakers reading in digitized sound. Includes grammar drills, listening exercises, and cultural notes on modern France. For Macintosh Classic, Plus, SE and II computers. Requires 1MB RAM, one floppy disk drive, and an Apple compatible CD - ROM drive.
Computer Science; Foreign Language
Dist - BEP

Learn to use money wisely...for children
VHS
Children's discovery series
Color (P I J)
$29.95 purchase _ #IV - 019
Discusses the pitfalls of poor money management and possible remedies.
Business and Economics; Home Economics
Dist - INCRSE **Prod** - INCRSE

Learn Xerox Ventura Publisher 2.0 professional extension
U-matic / VHS
Color (H C G)
$295.00, $295.00 purchase _ #02 - VPA
Covers all of the features of the Professional Extension including equations, tables, cross - references, variable insertion, vertical justification, the EDCO hyphenation dictionary, installation and EMS support. Includes videotape, guide and diskette. Published by VideoTutor.
Computer Science
Dist - VIDEOT

Learn yoga from a master 80 MIN
VHS
Color (G)
$29.95 purchase _ #V - YWS
Presents instruction in hatha yoga by Swami Satchidananda.
Physical Education and Recreation
Dist - PACSPI

Learner - Controlled Instruction 14 MIN
U-matic / 35mm strip
Dynamic Classroom Series
Color
Introduces the technique of learner - controlled instruction which allows the teacher and student to 'contract' on learning goals. Gives do's and don'ts, successes and failures.

Education; Psychology
Dist - RESEM **Prod** - RESEM

Learners with Problems 30 MIN
VHS / U-matic
Basic Education - Teaching the Adult Series
Color (T)
Shows how to cope with learners with problems when teaching adult basic education classes.
Education
Dist - MDCPB **Prod** - MDDE

Learning 30 MIN
VHS / 16mm
Psychology - the Study of Human Behavior Series
Color (C A)
$99.95, $89.95 purchase _ 24 - 07
Focuses on classical conditioning, operant conditioning and real - world applications to behavioral psychology.
Psychology
Dist - CDTEL **Prod** - COAST 1990

Learning 40 MIN
VHS / 16mm
Color (C)
$300.00 purchase _ #266301
Observes children learning. Demonstrates teaching strategies that accommodate the many ways in which children learn. Part 1 describes the variables that influence learning. Part 2 demonstrates one approach to accommodating learning styles. Part 3 illustrates how parents and teachers who understand learning styles can work together.
Education; Psychology; Sociology
Dist - ACCESS **Prod** - ACCESS 1986

Learning 10 MIN
16mm
Parent Education - Attitude Films Series
B&W
Education; Guidance and Counseling; Psychology; Sociology
Dist - TC **Prod** - TC

Learning 45 MIN
U-matic / VHS
Artificial intelligence series; Fundamental concepts, Pt 1
Color (PRO)
Discusses learning by being told and learning by examples and near misses. Features modeling, teaching, and an illustration.
Education; Psychology
Dist - MIOT **Prod** - MIOT

Learning 29 MIN
U-matic / VHS
One Strong Link Series
B&W
Psychology; Social Science
Dist - CORNRS **Prod** - CUETV 1971

Learning 5.1
VHS
WordPerfect 5.1 series
Color (G)
$49.95 purchase _ #VIA015
Teaches WordPerfect, version 5.1.
Computer Science
Dist - SIV

Learning - a happy experience 16 MIN
16mm / U-matic / VHS
Color (C A) (SPANISH LATIN)
LC 79-701587
Explains that elementary grade students with positive feelings toward school are happier and more receptive to learning. Demonstrates classroom techniques for creating a stimulating atmosphere.
Education; Psychology
Dist - ALTSUL **Prod** - BENSNS 1979

Learning - a Matter of Style 50 MIN
U-matic
Color (T)
Suggests ways teachers might accommodate various learning style elements in the classroom. Viewers develop diagnostic and prescriptive skills by participating in case studies of students with different learning styles.
Education; Psychology
Dist - AFSCD **Prod** - AFSCD 1986

Learning about Air 11 MIN
16mm / U-matic / VHS
Learning about Science Series
Color (P)
LC 76-700376
Presents a mime representing air appearing and disappearing as children experiment with soapbubbles, balloons, straws and a small windmill, demonstrating that air has weight, takes up space, exerts pressure and is a source of energy when in motion.
Science - Physical
Dist - AIMS **Prod** - ACI 1976

Learning about arthritis series
Ankylosing spondylitis 20 MIN
Coping with pain and emotions 15 MIN
The Many faces of arthritis 14 MIN
Osteoarthritis 20 MIN
Rheumatoid arthritis 17 MIN
Rheumatoid arthritis in children 19 MIN
Soft tissue syndrome and gout 12 MIN
Therapy and pain management 13 MIN
Dist - AIMS

Learning about cancer series
Presents a five - part series which takes an in - depth look at the detection and treatment of cancer and the emotional impact of the disease on patients and their families. Includes the titles Meeting the Challenge, The Time of Diagnosis, Surgery and Radiation, Chemotherapy, and Coping Emotionally.
Chemotherapy - 4 11 MIN
Coping emotionally - 5 13 MIN
Meeting the challenge - 1 15 MIN
Surgery and radiation - 3 14 MIN
The Time of diagnosis - 2 8 MIN
Dist - CF **Prod** - HOSSN 1976

Learning about Cells 16 MIN
U-matic / VHS / 16mm
Color (J)
LC 76-703645
Presents an introduction to the biological study of cell structure and function and examines the principles of cell growth and differentiation.
Science - Natural
Dist - EBEC **Prod** - EBEC 1976

Learning about Computers 11 MIN
16mm / U-matic / VHS
Color
Shows an elementary school student doing a report on computers as a homework assignment. Shows that a computer receives, stores and processes information very quickly.
Computer Science; Mathematics
Dist - NGS **Prod** - NGS 1984

Learning about courtesy 10 MIN
U-matic / BETA / 16mm / VHS
Beginning responsiblity series
Color (P)
$350,00, $250.00 purchase _ #JR - 5947C
Shows that courtesy means more than saying things like 'please' and 'thank you.' Uses animation and the story of Veronica, the mouse - child, to teach that courtesy requires both words and actions. Stresses the importance of courtesy because it helps people to get along better, resolve conflicts and feel better about themselves and others. Part of a series on beginning responsibilities.
Guidance and Counseling; Home Economics; Psychology; Social Science; Sociology
Dist - CORF **Prod** - CHRISP 1990

Learning about Diabetes Series
Control and complications 15 MIN
Diabetes and pregnancy 19 MIN
Diabetes and Young People 15 MIN
A New Way of Life 16 MIN
The Role of Insulin 19 MIN
Dist - AIMS

Learning about DOS computers
VHS
DOS series
Color (G)
$39.95 purchase _ #VIA031
Teaches about the DOS operating system in computers.
Computer Science
Dist - SIV

Learning about eating disorders series
Presents a five - part series which explores the problem of eating disorders. Includes the titles Starving and Binging, Anorexia Nervosa, Bulimia, Getting Help, and Changing Behavior.
Anorexia nervosa - 2 16 MIN
Bulimia - 3 15 MIN
Changing behavior - 5 16 MIN
Getting help - 4 15 MIN
Learning about eating disorders series 78 MIN
Starving and binging - 1 16 MIN
Dist - CF **Prod** - HOSSN

Learning about Electric Current 15 MIN
U-matic / VHS / 16mm
Introduction to Physical Science Series
Color (I J)
LC 74-703521
Examines the basic characteristics of electric current. Shows how electric current consists of a flow of electrons under the influence of an electric field and demonstrates the relationship between electric current and magnetism.
Science - Physical
Dist - EBEC **Prod** - EBEC 1974

Learning about Electricity 16 MIN
U-matic / VHS / 16mm
Color (P I)
$50 rental _ #9824
Describes concepts and vocabulary associated with uses of electricity.
Industrial and Technical Education; Science; Science - Physical
Dist - AIMS **Prod** - SAIF 1986

Learning about fairness 10 MIN
U-matic / BETA / 16mm / VHS
Beginning responsiblity series
Color (P)
$350.00, $250.00 purchase _ #JR - 5948C
Uses animation to tell the story of Martin, the mouse - child, who learns that before he can become king, he must learn to treat others fairly. Teaches that fairness involves considerations of equality, need and merit. Shows how to investigate a situation, listen to different viewpoints and draw conclusions that will be as fair as possible to everyone. Part of a series on beginning responsibilities.
Guidance and Counseling; Psychology; Sociology
Dist - CORF **Prod** - CHRISP 1990

Learning about Fire 12 MIN
16mm
Color (P I)
Reveals the mystery of fire and shows how to use it safely. Illustrates the difference between 'good fires' and 'bad fires', and between fireplace and campfire safety. Emphasizes that fire is a tool and not a toy.
Health and Safety
Dist - FILCOM **Prod** - FILCOM

Learning about Fruits We Eat 11 MIN
16mm / U-matic / VHS
Color (P I)
LC 70-706891
Discusses fruits from the tree, bush and vine to the market and table. Explains their remarkable variety in appearance and taste.
Agriculture; Health and Safety; Home Economics
Dist - CORF **Prod** - CORF 1970

Learning about Heart Attacks Series
Drugs and surgery 19 MIN
Meeting the emergency 13 MIN
Dist - AIMS

Learning about Heat 15 MIN
U-matic / VHS / 16mm
Color (I J) (SPANISH)
Teaches about heat.
Science - Physical
Dist - EBEC **Prod** - EBEC

Learning about Incentive Spirometry 11 MIN
U-matic / VHS
Color
LC 79-731359
Illustrates and explains the effects of deep breathing, then explains the role of incentive spirometry in respiratory care. Emphasizes the need for patient cooperation for best results.
Health and Safety; Science - Natural
Dist - MEDCOM **Prod** - MEDCOM

Learning about Jesus 20 MIN
BETA / VHS
Color (K P)
Tells the story of Jesus in animation for young children.
Literature and Drama; Religion and Philosophy
Dist - DSP **Prod** - DSP

Learning about Learning - Learning Research 29 MIN
16mm / U-matic / VHS
Focus on Behavior Series
B&W (H C A)
Explores the different strategies employed in developing new theoretical concepts about man's ability to learn. These studies conducted with human beings and animals have already led to changes in methods of instruction in schools and colleges.
Education; Psychology
Dist - IU **Prod** - NET 1963

Learning about Leaves 11 MIN
U-matic / VHS / 16mm

Color (I) (SPANISH)
Identifies pine needles, vegetable leaves, blades of grass and deciduous leaves. Demonstrates how leaves synthesize sugar and illustrates the life cycle of leaves.
Science - Natural
Dist - EBEC **Prod** - EBEC

Learning about letters 30 MIN
VHS
Sesame street home video series
Color (K P I)
$14.95 purchase; $19.95 purchase _ #S00818
Features Oscar, Big Bird, and the rest of the Sesame Street gang as they help children to learn the letters of the alphabet.
English Language; Literature and Drama
Dist - PBS **Prod** - WNETTV
UILL

Learning about Light 8 MIN
16mm / U-matic / VHS
Learning about Science Series
Color (P)
LC 76-700219
Explains some of the characteristics and properties of light. Shows how light rays may be reflected or refracted by transparent media and proves that light may be produced by the process of burning.
Science - Physical
Dist - AIMS **Prod** - ACI 1975

Learning about Light 15 MIN
U-matic / VHS / 16mm
Color (I J) (SPANISH)
Teaches about light and its properties.
Science - Physical
Dist - EBEC **Prod** - EBEC 1976

Learning about Liquids, Solids and Gases 11 MIN
16mm / U-matic / VHS
Learning about Science Series
Color (P)
LC 76-703648
Shows a group of children enjoying winter sports before moving indoors to pop corn, make taffy and perform some simple, easily - duplicated experiments which show the properties of and the differences among the three states of matter.
Science - Physical
Dist - AIMS **Prod** - ACI 1976

Learning about Magnetism 14 MIN
16mm / U-matic / VHS
Color (I J) (SPANISH)
Teaches about magnets and magnetism.
Science - Physical
Dist - EBEC **Prod** - EBEC 1975

Learning about Metric Measures 16 MIN
U-matic / VHS / 16mm
Color (P I J)
LC 79-711090
Introduces the basic concepts of the metric system. Identifies and defines the units of the metric stick. Uses the terms decimeter, centimeter, millimeter and meter. Shows the relationship of the metric and decimal systems.
Mathematics
Dist - PHENIX **Prod** - BOUNDY 1970

Learning about Nuclear Energy 15 MIN
16mm / U-matic / VHS
Color (I J) (SPANISH)
Teaches about the source and properties of nuclear energy.
Industrial and Technical Education; Science - Physical; Social Science
Dist - EBEC **Prod** - EBEC 1975

Learning about Nuclear Energy 15 MIN
U-matic / VHS / 16mm
Introduction to Physical Science Series
Color (I J)
LC 75-702353
Uses animation and practical demonstrations to explain the relationship between matter and nuclear energy. Presents the structure of the atom, the principles of nuclear fission and the difference between chemical energy and nuclear energy.
Science - Physical
Dist - EBEC **Prod** - EBEC 1975

Learning about numbers 30 MIN
VHS
Sesame Street home video series
Color (K P I)
$14.95 purchase
Features Oscar, Big Bird, and the rest of the Sesame Street gang as they help children to learn about numbers. Teaches children to count and recognize numbers from one to 20 and how to count objects.
Mathematics
Dist - PBS **Prod** - WNETTV

Learning about numbers 30 MIN
VHS
Color (K P I T)
$19.95 purchase _ #S00819
Features the Count and Big Bird, along with other members of the Sesame Street gang, as they teach children how to count from one to 20 and count objects as well.
Mathematics
Dist - UILL

Learning about Reptiles 12 MIN
U-matic / VHS / 16mm
Color (K P I)
LC 80-700149
Offers information on alligators, crocodiles, turtles, lizards and snakes, showing how they have adapted to their environments and how they take care of themselves.
Science - Natural
Dist - NGS **Prod** - NGS 1979

Learning about Science Series
Learning about Air 11 MIN
Learning about Light 8 MIN
Learning about Liquids, Solids and Gases 11 MIN
Learning about Solar Energy 12 MIN
Learning about Sound 8 MIN
Learning about Water 8 MIN
Dist - AIMS

Learning about science series
Learning about solar energy, Learning about liquids, solids and gases and Learning about air - Ccassette 1 30 MIN
Learning about water, Learning about light and Learning about sound - Cassette 2 30 MIN
Dist - EMFVL

Learning about sex series
How you are changing 15 MIN
Where do babies come from 10 MIN
Dist - APH

Learning about sex series
How you are changing 15 MIN
Dist - APH
CPH

Learning about sex series
Love, sex and God 10 MIN
Sex and the new you 15 MIN
Why boys and girls are different 6 MIN
Dist - CPH

Learning about Solar Energy 12 MIN
16mm / U-matic / VHS
Learning about Science Series
Color (P)
LC 76-700543
Shows a group of children as they experiment with energy from the Sun. Includes cooking on a solar cooker, playing with different colored paints to examine the relationship between color and heat and experimenting with solar panels and solar cells.
Science - Physical; Social Science
Dist - AIMS **Prod** - ACI 1975

Learning about solar energy, Learning about liquids, solids and gases and Learning about air - Ccassette 1 30 MIN
VHS
Learning about science series
Color; PAL (P I)
PdS35.00 purchase
Introduces children to the basic principles of science. Features part one of a two - part series.
Science; Science - Physical
Dist - EMFVL **Prod** - AIMS

Learning about Sound 17 MIN
U-matic / VHS / 16mm
Color (I J) (SPANISH)
Explains some of the characteristics and properties of sound.
Science - Physical
Dist - EBEC **Prod** - EBEC 1974

Learning about Sound 8 MIN
U-matic / VHS / 16mm
Learning about Science Series
Color (P)
LC 76-700220
Explains some of the characteristics and properties of sound. Shows the different ways in which sound travels through solid, liquid and gaseous media and describes other phenomena such as echoes and the character of sound vibrations.
Science - Physical
Dist - AIMS **Prod** - ACI 1975

Learning about Stroke 19 MIN
16mm / U-matic / VHS
Color (A)
Explains what happens when an individual suffers a stroke. Shows how the three types of cerebral vascular accidents affect blood supply to the brain. Discusses the major disabilities, both physical and emotional, that may result from stroke. Stresses the importance of beginning rehabilitation and retraining for the stroke patient immediately.
Health and Safety; Science - Natural
Dist - EBEC **Prod** - EBEC 1982

Learning about the heart series
Causes and risk factors 16 MIN
Dist - AIMS

Learning about the Human Body Series
Vision 16 MIN
Dist - UNL

Learning about the Reader 29 MIN
VHS / U-matic
Reading Comprehension Series
Color (T)
Education; English Language
Dist - HNEDBK **Prod** - IU

Learning about the world - Parents magazine - Volume 3 60 MIN
VHS
Color (A)
$19.95 purchase _ #S00986
Suggests that parents and toddlers can learn together through everyday activities. Covers activities such as chores, baths, sharing times, and the start of preschool.
Health and Safety; Home Economics; Psychology; Sociology
Dist - UILL

Learning about the zoo - planets
VHS
Growing up smarter series
Color (K P)
$14.95 purchase _ #MN010
Offers original stories that build beginning reading skills and teach about zoo animals and about the planets.
English Language; Literature and Drama; Science - Natural
Dist - SIV

Learning about Time in the Preschool Years 37 MIN
VHS / U-matic
B&W (PRO)
Helps children understand the concept of time. Illustrates strategies for encouraging children to recall the past, anticipate the future and observe and represent temporal sequences and intervals.
Education; Psychology
Dist - HSERF **Prod** - HSERF

Learning about Water 8 MIN
U-matic / VHS / 16mm
Learning about Science Series
Color (P)
LC 76-700221
Helps children understand the many ways in which water affects life on earth. Shows how water can be both a constructive force in helping man do work and a destructive force in destroying crops, land and livestock.
Science - Physical
Dist - AIMS **Prod** - ACI 1975

Learning about water, Learning about light and Learning about sound - Cassette 2 30 MIN
VHS
Learning about science series
Color; PAL (P I)
PdS35.00 purchase
Introduces children to the basic principles of science. Features part two of a two - part series.
Science; Science - Physical
Dist - EMFVL **Prod** - AIMS

Learning about Your Colostomy 16 MIN
U-matic / VHS
Color
LC 79-730905
Introduces the patient to the function of the digestive tract and colon. Shows events which take place in the hospital, and uses color graphics to explain the surgical procedure.
Health and Safety; Science - Natural
Dist - MEDCOM **Prod** - MEDCOM

Learning about Your Ileostomy 16 MIN
U-matic / VHS
Color
LC 78-730905
Introduces the function of the digestive tract and small intestine. Shows hospital events taking place before surgery, and uses color graphics to explain the procedure.
Health and Safety; Science - Natural
Dist - MEDCOM **Prod** - MEDCOM

Learning about Your Urostomy 13 MIN
U-matic / VHS
Color
LC 79-730905
Introduces the patient to the function of the urinary system. Discusses events which take place in the hospital before surgery, and uses color graphics to explain one type of surgical procedure, the ileal conduit.
Health and Safety; Science - Natural
Dist - MEDCOM **Prod** - MEDCOM

Learning addition - spelling
VHS
Growing up smarter series
Color (K P)
$14.95 purchase _ #MN011
Teaches basic math and spelling skills using sing - along.
English Language; Fine Arts; Mathematics
Dist - SIV

Learning all about cells and biology
CD-ROM
Color (J H)
$145.00 purchase _ #A3CD 4014M, #A3CD 4014B
Offers an interactive exploration of cells and biology. Examines basic theories and questions constituting the nucleus of biological science. Considers the conceptual evolution of the science and the history of biology from perspectives of pure classification, evolution, cell theory and organisms and societies as systems. Presents theories about life origins, biological characteristics and the fundamental structures of cells. Introduces the kingdoms of living things, one - celled and multicellular organisms and the fundamentals of cell activity, including respiration, metabolism and reproduction. Macintosh version requires 2MB RAM and color monitor. IBM version requires MCGA or VGA, Sound Blaster or compatible card for sound play.
Science - Natural
Dist - CLRVUE **Prod** - CLRVUE 1992

Learning all about dissection
CD-ROM
Color (J H)
$145.00 purchase _ #A3CD 4015M, #A3CD 4015B
Presents an interactive multimedia program which provides a thorough introduction and overview of dissection as a scientific tool. Defines and explains dissection as a carefully performed investigation of an organism's anatomy. Include in - depth studies of the earthworm, crayfish, perch, frog and fetal pigs, including the habitat, skeleton, sense organs, brain, appendages, means of locomotion, digestion, circulation and reproduction of each. Macintosh version requires 2MB RAM and color monitor. IBM version requires MCGA or VGA and SoundBlaster or compatible card for sound.
Science - Natural
Dist - CLRVUE **Prod** - CLRVUE 1992

Learning Alternatives through Instructional Media, Pt 1 30 MIN
16mm
Color (T PRO)
LC 74-700165
Features James G Buterbaugh, who establishes for educators of nursing a basic rationale for instructional development. Points out advantages of overhead projection, with a demonstration of a number of presentation models. Emphasizes elements which generally have been determined to improve instruction.
Education; Health and Safety; Psychology
Dist - UNEBR **Prod** - NTCN 1973

Learning Alternatives through Instructional Media, Pt 2 30 MIN
16mm
Color (T PRO)
LC 74-700167
Features James G Buterbaugh, who discusses for educators in nursing various instructional media, including videotape, recording systems, audio systems and others. Emphasizes the use of learning indexes for the selection of materials.
Education; Health and Safety; Psychology
Dist - UNEBR **Prod** - NTCN 1973

Learning and Behavior 27 MIN
16mm
Color
Shows how learning and conditioning are measured in the laboratory, uncovering important knowledge about the most fundamental processes in behavior.
Education; Psychology; Sociology
Dist - CCNY **Prod** - CBSTV

Learning and Behavior (the Teaching Machine) 26 MIN
U-matic / VHS / 16mm
B&W (H C A)
Shows how Drs B F Skinner and R J Herrnstein measure the learning process.
Psychology
Dist - CAROUF **Prod** - CBSTV

Learning and Behavior - the Teaching Machine 26 MIN
U-matic / VHS / 16mm
B&W (H C T)
LC FIA68-2417
Presents Drs B F Skinner and R J Herrnstein, who demonstrate how to measure the learning and conditioning process in the laboratory and show that all learning is dependent upon reward. The work of Dr Ivan Pavlov, 1904 Nobel Prize winner, is also discussed.
Education; Psychology
Dist - CAROUF **Prod** - CAROUF 1960

Learning and Development - Part 1 - Birth through Childhood 30 MIN
U-matic
Primer Series
Color (A)
Reveals that learning and development continue through life. Certain sequences of physical, linguistic, cognitive and social development are common to all including the retarded who can benefit from specialized, systematic training.
Education; Psychology
Dist - ACCESS **Prod** - ACCESS 1981

Learning and Development - Part 2 - Adolescence through Maturity 30 MIN
U-matic
Primer Series
Color (A)
Shows that school courses geared to the mentally handicapped, together with vocational programs, help such people to enter society independently and perhaps offer a marketable skill.
Education; Psychology
Dist - ACCESS **Prod** - ACCESS 1981

Learning and Liking it Series

Classical conditioning	45 MIN
Classroom environment	51 MIN
Extinction and differential reinforcement	42 MIN
Motivation	41 MIN
Positive Reinforcement	40 MIN
Punishment	44 MIN
Shaping and Scheduling	42 MIN
Use of Positive Reinforcement	49 MIN
Why Use Positive	33 MIN

Dist - MSU

Learning and Memory 30 MIN
VHS
Mind/Brain Classroom Series
Color (C A)
$59.95 purchase _ #MDBR - 103
Considers how memory and learning are related.
Psychology
Dist - FI **Prod** - WNETTV

Learning and Memory 60 MIN
VHS / U-matic
Brain, Mind and Behavior Series
Color (C A)
Discusses the mystery of memory.
Psychology
Dist - FI **Prod** - WNETTV

Learning and memory - Part 5 60 MIN
U-matic / VHS
Brain series
Color (G)
$45.00, $29.95 purchase
Investigates memory, forgetting, and learning. Uses the examples of a man with a most remarkable memory and a famous psychologist losing his memory. Part five of an eight - part series on the brain.
Psychology; Science - Natural
Dist - ANNCPB **Prod** - WNETTV 1984

Learning and Teaching 34 MIN
VHS / 16mm
Journeyworkers Series
Color (A PRO)
$250.00 series purchase _ #271201
Demonstrates effective approaches to developing reading and writing skills for tutors who require a clear, simple approach for instructing adult literacy. 'Learning And Teaching' shares the stories of four adult learners, the experience of seasoned tutors and introduces the stages of literacy development. The principle of learner - centered tutorials based on adult needs and interests is discussed, and an adult is followed through the process of enrolling in the program.
Education; English Language
Dist - ACCESS **Prod** - ACCESS 1987

Learning and Teaching of Concepts and Principles
U-matic / VHS
Learning System Design Series Unit 5
Color (T)
Discusses learning and teaching of concepts and principles, and learning and teaching of problem solving.
Education; Psychology
Dist - MSU **Prod** - MSU

Learning bluegrass dobro 90 MIN
VHS
Color (G)
$49.95 purchase _ #VD - CYN - DB01
Offers a hands - on dobro course with Cindy Cashdollar. Teaches essential right - hand techniques such as rolls, rhythm playing, crosspicking, tone control and damping, as well as valuable left - hand skills including bar techniques, chord building, hammer - ons and pull - offs, minor keys and more. Demonstrates four country tunes - Wildwood Flower, Fireball Mail, Sailor's Hornpipe and Wayfaring Stranger. Includes chords.
Fine Arts
Dist - HOMETA **Prod** - HOMETA

Learning bluegrass fiddle series
Presents a two - part series featuring Kenny Kosek. Teaches the basic melody for Jack of Diamonds then adds slides, open - string drones and bowing patterns for a bluegrass flavor in Video One. Moves on to slides, blues tones, rhythm patterns, slurs, fancy licks and endings, and other more advanced fiddle techniques and illustrates bluegrass classics in Video Two. Includes music.

Learning bluegrass fiddle - Video One	65 MIN
Learning bluegrass fiddle - Video Two	70 MIN

Dist - HOMETA **Prod** - HOMETA

Learning bluegrass fiddle - Video One 65 MIN
VHS
Learning bluegrass fiddle series
Color (G)
$39.95 purchase _ #VD - KOS - BF01
Features Kenny Kosek who teaches the basic melody for Jack of Diamonds, then adds slides, open - string drones and bowing patterns that give it bluegrass flavor. Continues on to classic country hoedowns - B'ile them Cabbage Down; Waterbound; Liberty - as Kosek introduces rhythm playing, melodic variations, double - stop harmonies and country - style bowing. Uses Bury Me Beneath the Willow to illustrate vibrato, slides, hammer - ons and legato - bowing. Includes music. Part one of a two - part series.
Fine Arts
Dist - HOMETA **Prod** - HOMETA

Learning bluegrass fiddle - Video Two 70 MIN
VHS
Learning bluegrass fiddle series
Color (G)
$39.95 purchase _ #VD - KOS - BF02
Features Kenny Kosek who teaches slides, blues tones, rhythm patterns, slurs, fancy licks and endings, and other more advanced fiddle techniques. Illustrates bluegrass classics such as Dixon County Blues; Pig in a Pen; Sally Goodin; Roll in My Sweet Baby's Arms; and Orange Blossom Special. Includes music. Part two of a two - part series.
Fine Arts
Dist - HOMETA **Prod** - HOMETA

Learning blues piano - Video Two 60 MIN
VHS
Blues piano series
Color (G)
$49.95 purchase _ #VD - COH - BR02
Features blues pianist David Cohen. Gives musical examples for those who have some background in blues piano. Teaches theory, blues scales and improvisation techniques, shuffle and straight - time rhythms, endings, intros and turnarounds and more. Part two of a three - part series.
Fine Arts
Dist - HOMETA **Prod** - HOMETA

Learning Booths 17 MIN
16mm
New Nursery School Series
Color (PRO)
LC 75-700791
Describes the use of learning booths in the responsive environment education program at the New Nursery School, Greeley, Colorado, operated by Colorado State University. Shows how the program aids disadvantaged children to improve language, learn problem - solving techniques, self - concepts, interpersonal relations and self - control.
Education; Psychology
Dist - USNAC **Prod** - USHHS 1969

Learning by Experience 10 MIN
U-matic / VHS
Making it Work Series
Color (H A)
Points out that finding the right job takes time and persistence. Shows Steve and his wife Ann reviewing his efforts and finding some things he could do better to improve his chances next time.
Guidance and Counseling; Psychology
Dist - AITECH **Prod** - ERF 1983

Learning centers 30 MIN
U-matic / VHS
Project STRETCH - Strategies to Train Regular Educators to Teach Children with Handicaps Series; Module 2
Color (PRO S T)
LC 80-706638
Demonstrates the concepts and skills necessary for designing and implementing learning centers.
Education; Psychology
Dist - HUBDSC **Prod** - METCO 1980

Learning Christian family communications
VHS
Color (G R)
$99.95 purchase _ #87EE0411
Presents a Bible - based study of communications within the family. Attempts to identify communication barriers, outline good communication skills, and show how to put those skills into practice. Includes leader's and participant's guides and copies of the 'Power of Praise' book and audiocassette.
Guidance and Counseling; Literature and Drama; Religion and Philosophy; Sociology
Dist - CPH **Prod** - CPH

Learning - Classical 19 MIN
Videoreel / VT2
Interpersonal Competence, Unit 05 - Learning Series; Unit 5 - Learning
Color (C A)
Features a humanistic psychologist who, by analysis and examples, discusses learning in the classical sense of the word.
Psychology
Dist - TELSTR **Prod** - MVNE 1973

Learning concept - introduction to personal computers 53 MIN
VHS
Color (H C A)
$175.00 purchase _ #GA05442V
Explains and demonstrates basic computer terms and applications. Includes a quick reference guide and library kit.
Computer Science
Dist - CAMV

Learning Concept - Introduction to Personal Computers 53 MIN
U-matic / VHS
Color
Demonstrates how easy personal computers are to use and introduces such common terms as RAM, DOS, run, load and save. Shows the variety of computer applications such as data bases, word processing, spreadsheets and graphics.
Computer Science; Industrial and Technical Education; Mathematics
Dist - GA **Prod** - GA 1984

Learning concept - the VisiCalc program 58 MIN
VHS
Color (J H)
$119.00 _ #05441 - 026
Uses the quick - teaching methods of video to put the program in operation right away for accounting, bookkeeping, statistics. Teaches what VisiCalc can do and how to apply its functions to students' needs.
Computer Science; Education; Mathematics
Dist - GA **Prod** - MICLRN

Learning country style piano 107 MIN
VHS
Color (G)
$49.95 purchase _ #VD - HOB - CP01
Features country and rock pianist Bob Hoban with special guest Vassar Clements. Teaches the country styles of Al Strickland, Moon Mullican, Webb Pierce, Floyd Cramer, 'Pig' Robbins and other greats. Shows how to use these styles with more modern innovations, chord constructions and tempos. Improves timing while the viewer learns about triads, shuffles, left and right - hand patterns, intros and endings, trills, solos, licks and variations, bass lines, hearing chord changes, accents, how to accompany a singer and more. Offers practice exercises, examples and points out common mistakes and problems. Includes a jam session with Clements and music.
Fine Arts
Dist - HOMETA **Prod** - HOMETA

Learning differences, problems and disabilities - an overview - Tape 1
VHS
Adults with learning disabilities teleconferences series
Color (PRO)
$35.00 purchase
Presents Dr Richard Cooper, president of the Center for Alternative Learning. Discusses learning differences, problems and disabilities. Part one of a four - part series on adults with learning disabilities.
Education; Psychology
Dist - KET **Prod** - KET 1991

Learning Disabilities 19 MIN
U-matic / VHS
Color (G)
$249.00, $149.00 purchase _ #AD - 1411
Examines the frequently misdiagnosed and misunderstood problem of learning disabilities. Emphasizes the importance of early diagnosis and treatment. Profiles a nine - year - old boy and his parents and teachers who detail the problems he faces in school and at home.
Education; Health and Safety; Psychology
Dist - FOTH **Prod** - FOTH

Learning disabilities 29 MIN
VHS
Helping adults learn series
Color (H G)
$140.00 purchase, $16.00 rental _ #36246
Looks at three Pennsylvania programs designed to meet the needs of learning disabled adults - the GED program at the State Regional Correctional Facility at Mercer; Project STRIDE; and the Reading Area Community College teacher education program. Outlines methods and strategies for helping students and discusses the definition of learning disability.
Education; Psychology
Dist - PSU **Prod** - WPSXTV 1991

Learning Disabilities 34 MIN
VHS / U-matic
Color
Shows teacher Beverly Doyle administering the Keywath Diagnosis Arithmetic Test.
Education; Mathematics; Psychology
Dist - UNEBO **Prod** - UNEBO

Learning disabilities and social skills with Richard Lavoie series
Last one picked. . . first one picked on 68 MIN
Dist - PBS

Learning Disabilities (Gates - McKillop Diagnostic Reading Test) 34 MIN
U-matic / VHS
Color
Shows teacher Beverly Doyle administering the Gates - McKillop Diagnostic Reading Test.
Education; Psychology
Dist - UNEBO **Prod** - UNEBO

Learning Disabled 20 MIN
U-matic
One Giant Step - the Integration of Children with Special Needs Series
Color (PRO)
Shows that most learning disabled children have a disorder in one or more of the basic psychological processes involved in understanding or using spoken or written language.
Education; Psychology
Dist - ACCESS **Prod** - ACCESS 1983

Learning DOS 2.0 - 3.3 Disk Operating Systems 42 MIN
VHS
Master Computer Software Easily Series
Color (G)
$29.95 purchase _ #60000
Shows how to use DOS 2.0 - 3.3 software for assembling a computer. Discusses using DOS commands, files, running programs, hints for successful computing, copying, deleting and formatting disks. Part of a nine - part series which breaks down into three sets of three units which discuss Lotus, DOS and Wordperfect. Any three units of the series can be purchased for $79.95.
Business and Economics; Computer Science; Education
Dist - CARTRP **Prod** - CARTRP

Learning DOS 2.0 - 3.3, Level I 42 MIN
VHS
Color; CC (G)
$29.95 purchase _ #LDLI
Concentrates on how to connect the components of an IBM PC. Discusses basic DOS commands. Gives an overview of the keyboard, basic DOS techniques, and how to avoid common errors.
Computer Science
Dist - APRESS

Learning DOS 5.0
VHS
DOS series
Color (G)
$49.95 purchase _ #VIA002
Teaches DOS 5.0.
Computer Science
Dist - SIV

Learning DOS - Level I 41 MIN
VHS
Learning DOS series
Color (G)
$29.95 purchase _ #6592
Uses slow, clear narration and graphics to go step - by - step through each operation in an introduction to MS - DOS.
Computer Science
Dist - ESPNTV **Prod** - ESPNTV

Learning DOS - Level II 35 MIN
VHS
Learning DOS series
Color (G)
$29.95 purchase _ #6593
Uses slow, clear narration and graphics to go step - by - step through each operation in part two of three parts on MS - DOS.
Computer Science
Dist - ESPNTV **Prod** - ESPNTV

Learning DOS - Level III 53 MIN
VHS
Learning DOS series
Color (G)
$29.95 purchase _ #6766
Uses slow, clear narration and graphics to go step - by - step through each operation in part three of three parts on MS - DOS.
Computer Science
Dist - ESPNTV **Prod** - ESPNTV

Learning DOS series
Presents a three - part series which uses slow, clear narration and graphics to go step - by - step through each operation in an introduction to MS - DOS. Teaches at levels I, II, and III.
Learning DOS - Level I 41 MIN
Learning DOS - Level II 35 MIN
Learning DOS - Level III 53 MIN
Learning DOS series 129 MIN
Dist - ESPNTV **Prod** - ESPNTV

Learning English - It's Harder than You Think 13 MIN
16mm
Color
LC 80-700821
Probes the reasons why some Australian migrants do not attempt to learn English.
English Language; Geography - World
Dist - TASCOR **Prod** - NSWF 1979

The Learning environment 30 MIN
Videoreel / VT2
Program development in the kindergarten series
B&W
Education
Dist - GPN **Prod** - GPN

Learning for a Lifetime - the Academic Club Method, Introduction 28 MIN
16mm
Learning for a Lifetime - the Academic Club Method Series Part 1
Color
Presents an overview of the Academic Club Method used at the Kingsbury Center Lab School. Shows how the traditional school day is transformed through the formation of clubs.

Education; Psychology
Dist - KINGS **Prod** - KINGS

Learning for a Lifetime - the Academic Club Method Series Part 1
Learning for a Lifetime - the Academic Club Method, Introduction 28 MIN
Dist - KINGS

Learning for a Lifetime - the Academic Club Method Series Part 4
Teaching History, Geography and Civics 27 MIN
Dist - KINGS

Learning for a Lifetime - the Academic Club Method Series Part 5
The Teacher as Club Leader 25 MIN
Dist - KINGS

Learning for a lifetime - the academic club method series
Developing reading readiness skills 28 MIN
The Setting up of a club 28 MIN
Dist - KINGS

Learning for Earning - a Montage 10 MIN
16mm
Color (J H)
LC 73-700528
Uses case history interviews to illustrate the major advantages of vocational education and describes 24 occupational courses with the accent on individualized learning.
Guidance and Counseling; Psychology
Dist - PART **Prod** - PART 1972

Learning for Living 80 HRS
VHS / U-matic
Color (G)
$4265.00, $2489.40 purchase
Offers 60 thirty - minute programs to teach functional reading, writing and mathematical skills for adults who cannot get or hold a job. Provides instruction in easy - to - understand and easy - to - use form for adults with below fourth - grade reading skills.
Business and Economics; Education; Guidance and Counseling; Psychology
Dist - SCETV **Prod** - SCETV 1989

Learning for the PC
VHS
PageMaker 4.0 series
Color (G)
$49.95 purchase _ #VIA038
Teaches PageMaker 4.0 desktop publishing for PCs.
Computer Science
Dist - SIV

Learning from Experience 20 MIN
16mm / U-matic / VHS
Color
Shows that the difference between a good salesman and a bad one is the ability to analyze and learn from experiences.
Business and Economics
Dist - DARTNL **Prod** - RANKAV

Learning from Experience 86 MIN
VHS / 16mm
Journeyworkers Series
Color (A PRO)
$250.00 series purchase _ #271202
Demonstrates effective approaches to developing reading and writing skills for tutors who require a clear, simple approach for instructing adult literacy. Illustrates several approaches for teaching adult literacy. Provides activities that help adults read and write. Covers the key points of using questions to teach and learn, assisted reading to focus on understanding content, assisted writing, using experience to read and write, learning the processes of writing, and selecting text for reading and lesson planning.
Education; English Language
Dist - ACCESS **Prod** - ACCESS 1987

Learning from Film and Television 27 MIN
VHS / U-matic
Instructional Technology Introduction Series
Color (C A)
Shows an opening film and TV research quiz that immediately involves the audience and demonstrates how each medium can be used effectively to expand learning experiences. Reviews disastrous ways to project a film. Depicts a teacher illustrating the importance of student involvement via media learning through preparation before viewing and planned follow - up activities.
Education; Industrial and Technical Education; Psychology
Dist - BCNFL **Prod** - MCGILU

Learning from others 20 MIN
VHS / U-matic
We are one series
Color (G)
Begins at the lodge of an uncle who is renowned as an arrow maker. Ni'bthaska and Teson learn to make arrows and listen to stories. Shows the scene switch to the field where Mother and oldest daughter are teaching the youngest daughter the secrets of planting the corn, as Grandmother taught them, so that 'it will remember to come back and feed them well.' Shows the boys called away from their arrow making by others who suggest a rabbit hunt to the meadow.
Social Science; Sociology
Dist - NAMPBC **Prod** - NAMPBC 1986

Learning from others - 37 9 MIN
VHS / U-matic
Life's little lessons - self - esteem 4 - 6 series
Color (I)
$129.00, $99.00 purchase _ #V666
Tells about unteachable Sydney Corporal. Shows that while roaming out in the swamp fighting by himself, he will not listen to his private who is trying to tell him that the war is over. He's still out there. Part of a 65 - part series on self - esteem.
English Language; Guidance and Counseling; Psychology; Social Science
Dist - BARR **Prod** - CEPRO 1992

Learning from Pets in the Classroom 15 MIN
U-matic / VHS / 16mm
Color; B&W (P I)
Shows how to organize the classroom for science and how to keep animals for observation. Views various classrooms where children are caring for pets, such as amphibians, insects and mammals.
Education; Science; Science - Natural
Dist - JOU **Prod** - ALTSUL 1961

Learning God's love - Tape 1 30 MIN
VHS
Little Marcy series
Color (K P R)
$11.99 purchase _ #35 - 887810 - 979
Features Little Marcy and her friends singing favorite Sunday school songs. Includes songs such as 'I'll be a Sunbeam,' 'This Little Light of Mine,' 'Oh How I Love Jesus,' and others.
Fine Arts; Religion and Philosophy
Dist - APH **Prod** - TYHP

Learning - How it Occurs 30 MIN
VHS / U-matic
Training the Trainer Series
Color (T)
Discusses the learning process. Tells how to identify and accommodate different learning styles.
Education; Psychology
Dist - ITCORP **Prod** - ITCORP

Learning How to Say no Series
How to Say no Without Losing Your Friends
Respect Yourself - Say no to Drugs
Dist - CAREER

Learning in a second language in the secondary curriculum - Cassette 1 52 MIN
VHS
Learning in a second language in the secondary curriculum series
Color; PAL (J H T)
PdS35.00 purchase
Focuses on bilingual pupils in mixed - ability groups talking, reading and writing. Features part one of a two - part series showing students acquiring English as their second language through participation in lessons across the secondary curriculum.
English Language; Foreign Language
Dist - EMFVL

Learning in a second language in the secondary curriculum - Cassette 2 57 MIN
VHS
Learning in a second language in the secondary curriculum series
Color; PAL (J H T)
PdS35.00 purchase
Focuses on changing schools to recognize bilingual students and reveals extracts from a teacher discussion regarding anti - racist approaches to language and bilingualism. Features part two of a two - part series showing students acquiring English as their second language through participation in lessons across the secondary curriculum.
English Language; Foreign Language; Sociology
Dist - EMFVL

Learning in a second language in the secondary curriculum series
Learning in a second language in the secondary curriculum - Cassette 1 52 MIN
Learning in a second language in the secondary curriculum - Cassette 2 57 MIN
Dist - EMFVL

Learning in America series
Examines the state of American education. Suggests that Americans are losing the education race with other nations such as Japan. Considers how rural and urban schools have difficulty providing good educations. Also examines questions such as textbook reform, teacher recruiting and how to improve education. Five - part series is hosted by Roger Mudd.
The Education race 60 MIN
Paying the freight 60 MIN
Teach your children 60 MIN
Upstairs downstairs 60 MIN
Wanted - a Million teachers 60 MIN
Dist - PBS **Prod** - WETATV

Learning independence - the teaching family model 24 MIN
VHS
Color (PRO G)
$15.00 purchase
Films a group home for children with special needs in Salina, Kansas, where the emphasis is on providing a family atmosphere for each person living there. Produced by the Media Support Services of the Bureau of Child Research.
Guidance and Counseling; Health and Safety
Dist - BEACH

The Learning Infant 30 MIN
U-matic
Growing Years Series
Color
Discusses the mental development of the child from birth to age three.
Psychology
Dist - CDTEL **Prod** - COAST

Learning is Searching - a Third Grade Studies Man's Early Tools 30 MIN
16mm
Studies of Normal Personality Development Series
B&W (C)
Shows a third grade studying tools and their origins. The process of search is stressed. Shows the relation of these studies to the group's other school activities.
Education; Psychology
Dist - NYU **Prod** - NYU 1955

Learning Laws - Respect for Yourself, Others and the Law Series
The High Road 13 MIN
That's My Bike 12 MIN
Too Much of a Good Thing 13 MIN
What's Wrong with Me 16 MIN
Who will be the Teacher 16 MIN
Dist - CORF

Learning Library Series
Caribbean Stories 50 MIN
Little Lou and His Strange Little Zoo 50 MIN
We Learn about the World 50 MIN
Dist - BENNUP

Learning machine 60 MIN
VHS
Nippon series
Color (A)
PdS99 purchase
Reveals that, since 1945, Japan has risen like a phoenix from the ashes to its position of industrial leadership in the world. Shows how an outstanding system of secondary education and the discipline of family life have led to a work ethos existing in no other country.
Business and Economics
Dist - BBCENE

Learning macros
VHS
Excel 4.0 series
Color (G)
$49.95 purchase _ #VIA045
Teaches about Excel 4.0 spreadsheet macros.
Computer Science
Dist - SIV

Learning Management 28 MIN
VHS / U-matic
Next Steps with Computers in the Classroom Series
Color (T)
Business and Economics; Computer Science; Industrial and Technical Education
Dist - PBS **Prod** - PBS

Learning Means Feeling as Well as Knowing 45 MIN
U-matic / VHS
B&W
Discusses affective learning, how attitudes about a subject influence the ability to comprehend it. Discusses the evaluatiion of affective objectives and methods for changing attitudes.
Psychology
Dist - BUSARG **Prod** - BUSARG

Learning mountain dulcimer 90 MIN
VHS
Color (G)
$39.95 purchase _ #VD - SHN - MD01
Features David Schnaufer on the mountain dulcimer. Starts with scales, fingerings and strumming and picking techniques. Teaches Wildwood Flower, then shows how to add chords and harmony notes and how to make use of guitar - style picking on the dulcimer. Includes arrangements of Tennessee Waltz and I'm So Lonesome I Could Cry.
Fine Arts
Dist - HOMETA **Prod** - HOMETA

Learning my 123s - money
VHS
Growing up smarter series
Color (K P)
$14.95 purchase _ #MN012
Teaches counting and about money to pre - schoolers.
Business and Economics; Mathematics
Dist - SIV

Learning my ABCs - shapes and colors
VHS
Growing up smarter series
Color (K P)
$14.95 purchase _ #MN013
Teaches the alphabet and about shapes and colors to pre - schoolers.
English Language; Psychology
Dist - SIV

Learning Objectives/Evaluating Learning Systems
VHS / U-matic
Learning System Design Series Unit 2
Color (T)
Education; Psychology
Dist - MSU **Prod** - MSU

The Learning of love 30 MIN
VHS / U-matic
Family portrait - a study of contemporary lifestyles series; Lesson 2
Color (C A)
Investigates the multitude of forms, developmental stages and feelings encompassed by the emotion of love. Charts love experiences from infancy to aging. Discusses love in a paired relationship.
Sociology
Dist - CDTEL **Prod** - SCCON

Learning - Operant 22 MIN
Videoreel / VT2
Interpersonal Competence, Unit 05 - Learning Series; Unit 5 - Learning
Color (C A)
Features a humanistic psychologist who, by analysis and examples, discusses learning by its operant definition.
Psychology
Dist - TELSTR **Prod** - MVNE 1973

Learning Our Language, Unit 2 - Dictionary Skills Series LINCOLN, NB 68501
They change their tune 20 MIN
Dist - GPN

The Learning Path 29 MIN
VHS / U-matic
Forest Spirits Series
Color (G)
Focuses on the confrontation between the Oneida and the Green Bay Curriculum Committee over the introduction of an Indian history and culture course in the city's high schools. Explores and evaluates ways of making the educational system aware of the needs of Native American students, by working within the system and from outside of it, using parental committees, supplemental education, alternative schools, and other methods.
Education; Social Science
Dist - NAMPBC **Prod** - NAMPBC 1975
GPN

The Learning path 59 MIN
VHS / 16mm
As long as the rivers flow series
Color (G)
$390.00 purchase, $75.00 rental
Explores the control of education as a means of Native American self - determination. Introduces three Edmonton elders who are educators working with younger natives. They recount harrowing experiences at reservation schools which fueled their resolution to preserve their language and identities. Blends documentary footage, dramatic re - enactments and archival film. Directed by Loretta Todd. Part of a five - part series dealing with the struggle of Native People in Canada to regain control over their destinies.
Education; Fine Arts; Social Science
Dist - FIRS **Prod** - CULRAY 1991

Learning Peachtree, accounting
VHS
Color (G)
$49.95 purchase _ #VIA032
Teaches Peachtree 5.0 accounting software.
Computer Science
Dist - SIV

Learning pedal steel guitar 90 MIN
VHS
Color (G)
$49.95 purchase _ #VD - BOU - ST01
Features Bruce Bouton who starts the viewer on the pedal steel guitar in the right way, teaching proper use of the bar, foot pedals, knee levers and volume pedals. Works in the E9 tuning to illustrate the 'natural' chords of the steel and how to play in all keys and the harmony scales that give the instrument its distinctive sound. Discusses picks and hand positioning, 'hand blocking,' 'pick blocking,' and other techniques to develop greater right - hand speed and flexibility. Offers classic licks, intros and endings of influential players and how they can be used in well - known country hits. Includes exercises, major to minor changes, chord inversions, string - lowering licks, unison licks, intros, endings and more.
Fine Arts
Dist - HOMETA **Prod** - HOMETA

Learning photography at home series
Applying the SLR 19 MIN
The Camera and automatic SLR 17 MIN
E - 6 processing in three steps 28 MIN
Filters 19 MIN
Dist - INSTRU

Learning plectrum banjo 90 MIN
VHS
Color (G)
$39.95 purchase _ #VD - WAC - PB01
Features Buddy Wachter on the plectrum banjo, which is better suited for solo playing than the shorter necked tenor banjo. Starts out with the essentials of pick techniques, holding the pick, proper wrist and hand positions, the tremolo, accents and dynamics, developing speed and control and detailed instruction on ten basic strums. Moves to the left hand to give proper fretting position, chord theory and structure, movable chords and left - hand exercises for strength and coordination. Teaches chord theory and 12 basic positions for major, minor, 7th, augmented and diminished chord formations. Includes chords and music.
Fine Arts
Dist - HOMETA **Prod** - HOMETA

The Learning Process 49 MIN
U-matic / 16mm / VHS
Human Journey Series
Color; Mono (J H C A)
MV $350.00 _ MP $450.00 purchase, $50.00 rental
Offers new insights into the processes of human learning. Discusses the biological processes that occur during learning, problems that hinder learning and methods that can be used to overcome learning disabilities.
Psychology; Science - Natural
Dist - CTV **Prod** - CTV

The Learning Process 25 MIN
U-matic
Biofeedback Strategies Series
Color (PRO)
Demonstrates general biofeedback learning strategies and discusses the external loop neurophysiological basis. Shows the frustrations and rewards of using biofeedback to elicit motor control that could not otherwise be used. Part 1 of a series.
Health and Safety; Psychology
Dist - AOTA **Prod** - AOTA 1981

Learning Professional Write 2.2
VHS
Professional Write 2.2 series
Color (G)
$39.95 purchase _ #VIA043
Teaches Professional Write 2.2.
Computer Science
Dist - SIV

Learning Responsibility Series
The Being on Time Game 11 MIN
The Common sense game 11 MIN
The Following instructions game 11 MIN
The Getting Organized Game 11 MIN
The Golden rule game 11 MIN
The Good manners game 13 MIN
The Good sport game 11 MIN
The Learn from Disappointments Game 11 MIN
The Respecting Others Game 11 MIN
The Sharing and not sharing game 11 MIN
Dist - HIGGIN

Learning rock 'n' roll piano 95 MIN
VHS
Color (G)
$49.95 purchase _ #VD - HOB - RP01
Features rock pianist Bob Hoban who takes catchy '50s and '60s rock 'n' roll piano styles - especially those made popular by Jerry Lee Lewis and Fats Domino - and brings them back in style. Shows how to do slides, rolls, melodic figures, rhythm patterns, shuffles, right - hand licks, slurs, solos, runs, single - note leads, 'pushed' notes and 'power beginnings.' Teaches the importance of proper finger - crossing techniques, exercises for smaller hands, how to develop muscle memory and the licks and techniques that enable the playing of hundreds of rock 'n' roll classics. Includes music.
Fine Arts
Dist - HOMETA **Prod** - HOMETA

Learning Strategies 11 MIN
16mm
One to Grow on Series
Color (T)
LC 73-701938
Shows a human relations program in action at a Cleveland, Ohio, school.
Guidance and Counseling; Psychology; Sociology
Dist - USNAC **Prod** - NIMH 1973

Learning strategies - acquisition and conviction - 2 66 MIN
VHS
Building and maintaining generalizations series
Color; PAL; SECAM (G)
$75.00 purchase
Features Richard Bandler in the second part of a six - part series on building and maintaining generalizations, using submodalities from advanced NLP, neuro - linguistic programming. Shows how people are motivated, learn, become convinced and generalize. Contains the first recorded descriptions of Bandler's time model. Recommended that tapes be viewed in order. Bandler sometimes uses profanity for emphasis, which may offend some people.
Health and Safety; Psychology
Dist - NLPCOM **Prod** - NLPCOM

Learning styles 30 MIN
16mm
Project STRETCH Series; Module 15
Color (T)
LC 80-700622
Shows how for a final examination, a group of college students must release a young girl from an enclosure, representing her environment, by determining what is her dominant learning style.
Education; Psychology
Dist - HUBDSC **Prod** - METCO 1980

Learning System Design Series Unit 1
Preview/Overview of Learning System Design
Dist - MSU

Learning System Design Series Unit 2
Learning Objectives/Evaluating Learning Systems
Dist - MSU

Learning System Design Series Unit 3
Task Descriptions - Task Analysis
Dist - MSU

Learning System Design Series Unit 4
General Principles of Learning and Motivation
Dist - MSU

Learning System Design Series Unit 5
Learning and Teaching of Concepts and Principles
Dist - MSU

Learning System Design Series Unit 6
Perceptual - Motor Skills - System Approach to Instruction
Dist - MSU

Learning tenor banjo 60 MIN
VHS
Color (G)
$39.95 purchase _ #VD - WAC - TB01
Features Buddy Wachter on the tenor banjo. Starts out with the essentials of pick techniques, holding the pick, proper wrist and hand positions, the tremolo, accents and dynamics, developing speed and control and detailed instruction on ten basic strums. Moves to the left hand to give proper fretting position, chord theory and structure, movable chords and left - hand exercises for strength and coordination. Teaches chord theory and 12 basic positions for major, minor, 7th, augmented and diminished chord formations. Includes chords and music.
Fine Arts
Dist - HOMETA **Prod** - HOMETA

Learning the Backstroke 11 MIN
16mm / U-matic / VHS
B&W (I J H C)
Illustrates techniques of the backstroke - position of body, timing, use of the flutterkick, starts, turns and practice. Uses slow motion underwater shots.
Physical Education and Recreation
Dist - IFB **Prod** - BHA 1965

Learning the Breast Stroke 11 MIN
16mm / U-matic / VHS
B&W (I J H C)
Shows the three basic steps of the breast stroke - the pull, kick and glide. Draws attention to arm and leg movements, position of body, proper breathing and practice methods.
Physical Education and Recreation
Dist - IFB **Prod** - BHA 1965

Learning the Butterfly Stroke 11 MIN
U-matic / VHS / 16mm
Color (J H)
LC FIA68-2863
Demonstrates body positions for leg kick, arm action, breathing and turning in the butterfly stroke. Uses underwater photography to illustrate specific movements. Shows proper starting position, the grab turn and the tumble.
Physical Education and Recreation
Dist - IFB **Prod** - BHA 1968

Learning the Crawl Stroke 16 MIN
U-matic / VHS / 16mm
B&W (I J H C)
Gives instruction in the techniques of the crawl, showing body position, leg and arm movement, proper breathing, timing, starts, turns and practice methods.
Physical Education and Recreation
Dist - IFB **Prod** - BHA 1965

Learning the Hard Way 15 MIN
VHS / 16mm
Color (H)
$225.00 purchase
Demonstrates that an educational program inside a prison improves a convict's chances upon release. Talks about convicts' efforts to learn and their reasons for trying.
Education; Sociology
Dist - FLMWST

Learning the Process 30 MIN
VHS / U-matic
Principles of Human Communication Series
Color (H C A)
Focuses on defining the basic principles of the nature of communication by presenting examples of the various components and explaining how they interrelate.
English Language; Psychology
Dist - GPN **Prod** - UMINN 1983

Learning the truth - the Bible as a story 30 MIN
VHS
Sharing the God story series
Color (G A R)
$39.95 purchase, $10.00 rental _ #35 - 822 - 2076
Features pastor Arndt Halvorson in an exposition of how people's lives are related to the story of the Gospel. Produced by Seraphim.
Religion and Philosophy
Dist - APH

Learning through Movement 32 MIN
16mm
B&W (C A S)
LC 70-711460
Explores learning concepts a child can experience in a creative dance class.
Physical Education and Recreation
Dist - SLFP **Prod** - BARLEN 1968

Learning through Play 28 MIN
U-matic
Color (J C)
Demonstrates the way handicapped and nonhandicapped preschool children in an integrated setting learn via their play. It is the story about the mainstreaming component at the Child Study Center at SDSU. It shows children freely manipulating their environment, exploring and discovering how things work. It was taped at the Child Study Center, which serves as a model demonstration program for University students, faculty and people from the community.
Education; Health and Safety; Psychology; Sociology
Dist - SDSC **Prod** - SDSC 1984

Learning through play 30 MIN
VHS
Parents' point of view series
Color (T A PRO)
$69.95 purchase
Presents advice on caring for children under five years old. Targeted to both parents and care givers. Considers how a child's play time can also be a learning experience. Hosted by Nancy Thurmond, ex - wife of Senator Strom Thurmond.
Education; Guidance and Counseling; Health and Safety
Dist - SCETV **Prod** - SCETV 1988

Learning through play - Module 7 Modules series
The Adult role in play 26 MIN
Dist - UTORMC

Learning through play - modules series module 5
Dramatic play 26 MIN
Dist - UTORMC

Learning through Play - Programs Series Program 2
The I and the Others 26 MIN
Dist - UTORMC

Learning through Play - Programs Series Program 3
Toying with Reality 27 MIN
Dist - UTORMC

Learning through play series
The I and the Others 27 MIN
Playspace 28 MIN
Rhyme and Reason 28.23 MIN
Toying with Reality 29 MIN
Dist - AITECH
UTORMC

Learning through play series
The Adult role in play 30 MIN
Children's playspace 30 MIN
Coping with problems 26 MIN
Dramatic Play 30 MIN
Pliable materials 30 MIN
Social Development 30 MIN
Waterplay 30 MIN
Dist - UTORMC

Learning through Problems - a Baby's Point of View 10 MIN
U-matic / VHS
B&W (PRO)
Observes events and problems from a baby's point of view. Shows how reaching, holding, moving and pulling can be complex for an infant. Suggests how baby's sensory - motor explorations can be turned into learning experiences.
Education; Psychology; Sociology
Dist - HSERF **Prod** - HSERF

Learning to add and subtract 30 MIN
VHS
Sesame street home video series
Color (K P I)
$14.95 purchase
Features Oscar, Big Bird, and the rest of the Sesame Street gang as they help children to learn how to add and subtract. Includes an activity book.
Literature and Drama; Mathematics
Dist - PBS **Prod** - WNETTV

Learning to be 20 MIN
U-matic / VHS
Folk Book Series
Color (P)
LC 80-706747
Presents folk stories that contain moral principles.
Literature and Drama; Religion and Philosophy
Dist - AITECH **Prod** - UWISC 1980

Learning to be a Good Sport 11 MIN
U-matic / VHS / 16mm
Beginning Responsibility Series
Color (P)
$320, $250 purchase _ #5078C
Shows the importance of being a good sport and how the fun in a game comes from participation. Produced by Christianson Productions.
Psychology
Dist - CORF

Learning to be Assertive - Advanced Skills 21 MIN
16mm / VHS
Color (J H C A PRO)
$395.00, $495.00 purchase, $75.00 rental _ #9956
Shows how to turn difficult situations into positive experiences. Deals with awkward social situations, shyness, and conflicts with families, teachers and friends. Teaches assertive skills.
Guidance and Counseling; Psychology
Dist - AIMS **Prod** - PANIM 1988

Learning to be Assertive - the Basic Skills 27 MIN
16mm / VHS
Color (J H C A PRO)
$395.00, $495.00 purchase, $75.00 rental _ #9941, #9941LD
Dramatizes a number of situations typical for adolescents and teenagers. Teaches young people that they can say `No'. Learning to be assertive skills.
Guidance and Counseling; Psychology
Dist - AIMS **Prod** - PANIM 1988

Learning to be Human Series
Snowbound 50 MIN
Dist - LCOA

Learning to be in East Africa 20 MIN
VHS / U-matic
Folk Book Series
Color (P)
Presents East African folk stories that contain moral principles.
Literature and Drama; Religion and Philosophy
Dist - AITECH **Prod** - UWISC 1980

Learning to be yourself - 1 21 MIN
VHS / U-matic / 16mm
Peer pressure series
Color (J H)
$470.00, $360.00, $330.00 _ #A974
Portrays 15 - year - old Jody Edwards who begins to understand how much she has let peer pressure affect her life. Reveals that she has been doing things just so others will like her. After a long talk with her older brother, Jody decides to pay more attention to her own feelings when she's making decisions and finds out that she has more fun when she does. Part of a two - part series on peer pressure.
Guidance and Counseling; Psychology; Sociology
Dist - BARR **Prod** - SAIF 1984

Learning to Breastfeed 22 MIN
16mm
Color (H C A)
LC 79-700568
Offers advice on breastfeeding by showing mothers as they nurse their babies for the first time.
Home Economics
Dist - POLYMR **Prod** - POLYMR 1979

Learning to care 20 MIN
VHS
Living with dying series
Color (H C G A R)
$29.95 purchase, $10.00 rental _ #4 - 85112
Interviews staff members of a nursing home. Teaches how to help alleviate a person's fear of death.
Religion and Philosophy; Sociology
Dist - APH **Prod** - APH

Learning to channel 59 MIN
VHS
Color (G)
$39.95 purchase
Features Meredith Lady Young, author of Agartha, a book telling of her experiences with channeling. Records a workshop and its participants as well as incidents in her personal life and a powerful meditation sequence.
Fine Arts; Literature and Drama; Religion and Philosophy
Dist - HP

Learning to Cope 25 MIN
U-matic / VHS / 16mm
Color
LC 78-701490
Depicts how seven people cope with the everyday problems of life.
Guidance and Counseling; Psychology
Dist - CORF **Prod** - MEHA 1978

Learning to dance in Bali 13 MIN
16mm / VHS
Character formation in different cultures series
B&W (G C)
$270.00, $105.00 purchase, $14.50 rental _ #24635
Traces the beginning of a Balinese infant's awareness of dance movement by visual and kinesthetic imitation in a session performed by I Mario, the most celebrated of Balinese dancers. Uses footage taken by Dr Bateson in the late 1930s and was completed in 1978 at the request of Dr Mead, whose extemporaneous narration is the last audio recording made by Mead before her death. Part of a series by Mead and Bateson.
Fine Arts; History - World; Sociology
Dist - PSU **Prod** - MEAD 1991

Learning to do God's work - Tape 2 30 MIN
VHS
Little Marcy series
Color (K P R)
$11.99 purchase _ #35 - 867829 - 979
Features Little Marcy and her friends singing favorite Sunday school songs. Includes songs such as 'The B - I - B - L - E,' 'Jesus Loves Me,' 'Do Lord,' and others.
Fine Arts; Religion and Philosophy
Dist - APH **Prod** - TYHP

Learning to do it right - 15 6 MIN
VHS / U-matic
Life's little lessons - self - esteem K - 3 - series
Color (K P)
$129.00, $99.00 _ #V614
Tells about Morgan Dodds who ran a 'no frills' dentist office even though he had never studied dentistry, and all his patients were afraid of dentists. Reveals that one of his patients, William, decided to become a dentist, learned all about teeth, came back, opened an office and practiced dentistry correctly, and people weren't afraid of the dentist anymore. Part of a 30 - part series on self - esteem.
Guidance and Counseling; Psychology
Dist - BARR **Prod** - CEPRO 1992

Learning to Enjoy 28 MIN
16mm
Prime Time Series
Color
LC 79-701485
Looks at some elderly people who have discovered that their later years can be satisfying if they make their own choices, take risks, and allow themselves to pursue the things that bring enjoyment.
Health and Safety; Psychology; Sociology
Dist - MTP **Prod** - SEARS 1979

Learning to fingerpick - beginning level 60 MIN
VHS
Learning to fingerpick series
Color (J H C G)
$49.95 purchase _ #HSPP01V
Requires only an elementary knowledge of guitar chords. Shows how to pick out a syncopated melody while maintaining a steady bass in the technique made popular by Chet Atkins, Merle Travis, Doc Watson and others.
Fine Arts
Dist - CAMV

Learning to fingerpick - intermediate level 60 MIN
VHS
Learning to fingerpick series
Color (J H C G)
$49.95 purchase _ #HSPP02V
Teaches a variety of left and right - hand guitar fingerpicking techniques, several traditional songs and instrumentals that give a more complete understanding of the guitar and its possibilities.
Fine Arts
Dist - CAMV

Learning to fingerpick series
Presents two programs on guitar fingerpicking at beginning and intermediate levels. Requires only an elementary knowledge of guitar chords for the beginning program. Teaches a variety of left and right - hand guitar fingerpicking techniques, several traditional songs and instrumentals that give a more complete understanding of the guitar and its possibilities in the intermediate program.
Learning to fingerpick - beginning level 60 MIN
Learning to fingerpick - intermediate level 60 MIN
Learning to fingerpick series 120 MIN
Dist - CAMV

Learning to flatpick series
Presents a three - part series on flatpicking featuring Steve Kaufmann and Happy Traum. Features Happy Traum in Video One teaching beginning country and bluegrass style. Steve Kaufmann teaches advanced bluegrass techniques in Video Two and how to develop speed and style in Video Three. Includes tablature and music.
Building bluegrass technique - video two 90 MIN
Developing speed and style - Video 3 90 MIN
Getting started - Video One 60 MIN
Dist - HOMETA **Prod** - HOMETA

Learning to Follow Instructions 12 MIN
16mm / U-matic / VHS
Beginning Responsibility Series
Color (P)
$295.00, $210.00 purchase _ #4295
Shows the importance of following instructions and shows how to follow them.
Guidance and Counseling; Psychology
Dist - CORF

Learning to Learn in Infancy 30 MIN
16mm
Head Start Training Series,
B&W (C T)
LC 74-701436
Stresses the essential role of curiosity and exploration in learning and points to the kinds of experience that cultivate and stimulate an eager approach to the world. Suggests ways in which adults can help infants make approaches, differentiate between objects and develop the earliest communication skills.
English Language; Psychology; Sociology
Dist - NYU **Prod** - VASSAR 1970

Learning to live in a world of plenty 21 MIN
VHS
Color (H C)
$59.00 purchase _ #513
Interviews Julian Simon. Presents good news about population, natural resources and pollution from the articulate economist.
Science - Natural; Social Science; Sociology
Dist - HAWHIL **Prod** - HAWHIL

Learning to live in a world of scarcity 27 MIN
VHS
Color (H C)
$59.00 purchase _ #515
Interviews Howard Odum, one of the founders of modern ecology, who explains his view that the world is seriously overpopulated and is running out of natural resources. States that humans have only two generations left to learn how to live in a world of scarcity.
Science - Natural; Social Science; Sociology
Dist - HAWHIL **Prod** - HAWHIL

Learning to Live on Your Own Series
Keeping Safe 28 MIN
The Most for Your Money 28 MIN
Where Your Money Goes 28 MIN
Dist - JOU

Learning to live series
Acquiring life scripts 30 MIN
Changing life scripts 30 MIN
Ego states 28 MIN
Feelings 30 MIN
Games 28 MIN
Strokes 28 MIN
Transactions 28 MIN
Dist - ECUFLM

Learning to live series
Time structures 30 MIN
Dist - ECUFLM
TRAFCO

Learning to Live Together 10 MIN
16mm
Parent Education - Attitude Films Series
B&W
Education; Guidance and Counseling; Sociology
Dist - TC **Prod** - TC

Learning to Live with Fear 5 MIN
16mm / U-matic / VHS
Communicating from the Lectern Series
Color (H C A)
Highlights the types of fears that are imaginary and those that are real and suggests how to deal with them.
English Language; Psychology
Dist - AIMS **Prod** - METAIV 1976

Learning to Look at Hands 8 MIN
16mm / U-matic / VHS
Learning to Look Series
Color (P)
LC 77-702729
Takes a close look at hands, showing that the way a hand is held may say something about what a person is thinking. Depicts fingers and thumbs in action.
Education; Psychology
Dist - MGHT **Prod** - MGHT 1969

Learning to look series
All kinds of buildings 8 MIN
Just Like in School 8 MIN
Learning to Look at Hands 8 MIN
Let's Find some Faces 9 MIN
On Your Way to School 8 MIN
What is a Family 7 MIN
Dist - MGHT

Learning to Manage Anger - the RETHINK Workout for Teens 32 MIN
VHS / BETA / U-matic
Color (I J H)
$200.00 purchase, $55.00 rental _ #3186VHS; LC 89716158
Teaches a seven - step method to manage feelings of anger successfully. Features Drs Karen Shanor and Cynthia White in discussions with a group of adolescents. Can be divided into segments for use in more than one session, or used in a single period.
Guidance and Counseling; Health and Safety; Psychology
Dist - RESPRC **Prod** - IMHIN 1988

Learning to massage 60 MIN
BETA
Color
Shows how to give an expert massage, focusing on intricate Swedish and Japanese accupressure massage.
Health and Safety
Dist - HOMET **Prod** - UNKNWN

Learning to obey your parents and seeing life from your parents' point of view - Tape 2 60 MIN
VHS
How to get along with your parents series
Color (J H R)
$10.00 rental _ #36 - 876002 - 533
Features Christian youth speaker Dawson McAllister discussing teenagers and their relationship with their parents. Consists of two 30 - minute segments which reveal the importance of parental discipline and encourage teenagers to try to see life from their parents' point of view.
Religion and Philosophy; Sociology
Dist - APH **Prod** - WORD

Learning to Observe 7 MIN
U-matic / VHS / 16mm
Color (I J)
LC 72-703176
Suggests ways in which we can improve our abilities to observe. Shows how viewers can strengthen skills in observing as they watch the antics of interesting animated characters.
English Language
Dist - PHENIX **Prod** - LEARN 1972

Learning to paint with Carolyn Berry series
Offers easy to follow, step - by - step methods for creating a finished painting or drawing from a blank canvas. Features an eight - part series covering everything from arranging or selecting your subjects to an explanation of the material needed and the specific techniques to be applied. Includes Portrait painting; Portrait drawing; Still life; Field flowers; Water color techniques; Perspective; and Basic Color, volume 1 and 2. Each episode is 30 - 70 minutes in length. Series is designed for students, hobbyists, amateur painters and professionals seeking new tips. Produced by Artists Video and directed by Christian Surette; 1991 - 1994. Video jackets available.
Basic color - Volume 1 70 MIN
Basic color - Volume 2 55 MIN
Field flowers 42 MIN
Perspective 30 MIN
Portrait drawing 60 MIN
Portrait painting 60 MIN
Still life 60 MIN
Water color techniques 30 MIN
Dist - CNEMAG

Learning to play blues guitar series
Presents a two - part series featuring Happy Traum. Covers 12 - bar blues form and progresses into right and left - hand techniques of traditional fingerstyle blues in Video One. Delves into the many possibilities and intricacies of blues in the key of A in Video Two and teaches new chord positions, bass runs, turnarounds, licks and solos.
Learning to play blues guitar - Video One 60 MIN
Learning to play blues guitar - Video Two 90 MIN
Dist - HOMETA **Prod** - HOMETA 1972

Learning to play blues guitar - Video One 60 MIN
VHS
Learning to play blues guitar series
Color (G)
$49.95 purchase _ #VD - HAP - BL01
Features Happy Traum who demonstrates the 12 - bar blues form. Progresses into the right and left - hand techniques of traditional fingerstyle blues. Requires only a working knowledge of basic guitar chords to learn blues chord

progressions, turnarounds, walking basses, picking techniques and blues riffs. Teaches several complete songs and instrumentals and the elements of blues improvisation. Part one of a two - part series.
Fine Arts
Dist - HOMETA **Prod** - HOMETA

Learning to play blues guitar - Video Two 90 MIN
VHS
Learning to play blues guitar series
Color (G)
$49.95 purchase _ #VD - HAP - BL02
Features Happy Traum who delves into the many possibilities and intricacies of blues in the key of A as played by Brownie McGhee, Big Bill Broonzy, John Hurt, Rev Gary Davis and other blues masters. Teaches new chord positions, bass runs, turnarounds, licks and solos. Includes several songs to work with, Betty and Dupree, Key to the Highway, Blood Red River, Come Back Baby, 12 Gates to the City. Part two of a two - part series.
Fine Arts
Dist - HOMETA **Prod** - HOMETA

Learning to Read Maps 12 MIN
16mm / U-matic / VHS
Color (P I)
LC 80-701806
Explains how maps are pictorial representations of real places, how physical features are represented as symbols on a map, how to find directions and how to calculate the distance to a destination.
Geography - World; Social Science
Dist - EBEC **Prod** - EBEC 1980

Learning to Read Music 29 MIN
Videoreel / VT2
Playing the Guitar I Series
Color
Fine Arts
Dist - PBS **Prod** - KCET

Learning to Relax 14 MIN
VHS / 16mm
Stress - Unwinding the Spring Series
Color (H C A PRO)
$195.00 purchase, $75.00 rental _ #8077
Teaches relaxation as a method of coping with stress.
Health and Safety; Psychology
Dist - AIMS **Prod** - HOSSN 1988

Learning to sail 72 MIN
VHS
Color (G A)
$39.90 rental _ #0828
Teaches sailing and sailing safety. Covers sailboat handling, sail trimming, safety and seamanship, right of way rules, docking, anchoring.
Physical Education and Recreation
Dist - SEVVID

Learning to Say no 60 MIN
VHS
Secret Intelligence Series
Color (G)
$59.95 purchase _ #SEIN - 103
Illustrates the disagreement within the CIA over the wisdom of being involved in covert operations. Reviews the attempts by Richard Nixon to use intelligence agencies to spy on his political foes. Shows that Congress began to investigate the intelligence community and its goals.
Civics and Political Systems; History - United States
Dist - PBS **Prod** - KCET 1989

Learning to Say no
VHS / U-matic
Color (I J)
Teaches assertiveness techniques. Emphasizes the sense of accomplishment, increased self - respect and admiration of others that result when young people are able to say 'No.'
Guidance and Counseling; Psychology; Sociology
Dist - SUNCOM **Prod** - SUNCOM

Learning to See 15 MIN
VHS / 16mm
Drawing with Paul Ringler Series
Color (I H)
$125.00 purchase, $25.00 rental
Outlines the principles of developing visual acuity for both perceptual and conceptual drawing.
Fine Arts; Industrial and Technical Education
Dist - AITECH **Prod** - OETVA 1988

Learning to See 15 MIN
16mm / U-matic / VHS
Human Senses Series
Color (P I)
Employs animation to show how light enters the eye and creates an upside - down image on the retina which the brain interprets. Presents optical illusions and lists the factors which affect what is seen.
Science - Natural
Dist - NGS **Prod** - NGS 1982

Learning to See - 2 15 MIN
VHS
Drawing with Paul Ringler Series
Color (I)
$125.00 purchase
Develops visual acuity for both perceptual and conceptual drawing. Focuses on the drawing process, for older students, rather than drawing specific objects. Part of a thirty - part series.
Fine Arts
Dist - AITECH **Prod** - OETVA 1988

Learning to see and understand - developing visual literacy
VHS
Color (J H C)
$197.00 purchase _ #00231 - 126
Explores the many modes of visual expression - the decorative arts, American Indian art, posters, cartoons, movie stills, advertising. Looks at the works of Leonardo, Goya, Lichtenstein, Rosenquist, Bierstadt, Picasso, Wyeth, Kelly, Albers and Matisse. Offers commentary from Marshall McLuhan, Stanley Kubrick, Ruth Benedict and Kurt Vonnegut. Includes teacher's guide and library kit. In two parts.
Fine Arts; Social Science
Dist - GA **Prod** - GA

Learning to Sew 57 MIN
BETA / VHS
Color
Discusses sewing equipment, fabrics, machine use, pattern choice and layout, darts, interfacing, gathering, piping, pockets and more.
Home Economics
Dist - HOMEAF **Prod** - HOMEAF

Learning to Speak - Pt 1 20 MIN
16mm
Color
LC 74-705018
Shows that the goal of instruction for the deaf child is to enable him to develop not normal, but intelligible communication. Concerns the characteristics of intonation, pitch articulation and vocal quality requisite to the attainment of intelligible speech within the phonological language system.
Education; English Language; Guidance and Counseling; Psychology
Dist - USNAC **Prod** - USHHS

Learning to Speak - Pt 2 20 MIN
VHS / U-matic
Color
LC 80-707416
Treats the perception of intonation patterns in the deaf child's attainment of intellectual speech within the phonological language system. Discusses how meaning is affected by stress, pitch, and phrasing, and by developing and improving speech rhythm.
Education; Psychology
Dist - USNAC **Prod** - USBEH 1980

Learning to Speak, Pt 2 25 MIN
16mm
Color
LC 74-705019
Concerns the perception on intonation patterns, how meaning is affected by stress, pitch and phrasing, and developing and improving speech rhythm.
Education; English Language; Guidance and Counseling; Psychology
Dist - USNAC **Prod** - USBEH

Learning to Swim Series
Survival Swimming 14 MIN
Dist - IFB

Learning to Swim with Artificial Aids 10 MIN
16mm / U-matic / VHS
B&W (I J H)
LC FIA68-2860
Presents the primary stages of beginner swimming - using artificial aids. Emphasizes free movement and confidence, then proceeds to basic strokes. Underwater photography clarifies movements and demonstrates buoyancy.
Physical Education and Recreation
Dist - IFB **Prod** - BHA 1968

Learning to teach Sunday school
VHS
Color (A T R)
$149.95 purchase _ #87EE0051
Trains both new and experienced Sunday school teachers. Deals with subjects including active learning, effective storytelling, preventive discipline, and others. Presents footage of actual Sunday school classes. Includes leader's and student guides.
Guidance and Counseling; Literature and Drama; Religion and Philosophy
Dist - CPH **Prod** - CPH
APH

Learning to tell the story 30 MIN
VHS
Sharing the God story series
Color (G A R)
$39.95 purchase, $10.00 rental _ #35 - 824 - 2076
Features pastor Arndt Halvorson in an exposition of how people's lives are related to the story of the Gospel. Produced by Seraphim.
Religion and Philosophy
Dist - APH

Learning to tell time - calendar
VHS
Growing up smarter series
Color (K P)
$14.95 purchase _ #MN014
Teaches pre - schoolers about time and the calendar.
Mathematics
Dist - SIV

Learning to Think Like a Manager 25 MIN
U-matic / VHS / 16mm
Color (H C A)
LC 83-700358
Chronicles the experiences of two new managers during their first three months on the job. Discusses the mistakes each makes, how to avoid these common pitfalls and suggests an active role for upper management in training new managers.
Business and Economics; Psychology
Dist - CRMP **Prod** - CRMP 1983
MGHT
VLEARN

Learning to Travel 22 MIN
16mm
Color (I J H)
Lays out the principles of trip - planning and trip - taking for handicapped passengers including how to choose the best transportation, how to find out trip information, what to take, how to find addresses and good travel behavior.
Education
Dist - PARPRO **Prod** - PARPRO

Learning to Type 30 MIN
U-matic / VHS / 16mm
Color (J H C A)
Introduces the student to the most recent typewriter equipment and to the basic skills used to override all typewriters from manual typewriter models to electronic typewriters and word processing machines.
Business and Economics; Mathematics
Dist - SF **Prod** - SF 1985

Learning to use ESP 30 MIN
BETA / VHS
Exploring parapsychology series
Color (G)
$29.95 purchase _ #S240
Focuses on the pioneering work of Czechoslovakian parapsychologist Dr Milan Ryzl. Shares his personal experiences as a hynpnotist and researcher. Describes his training methods and their practical application. Part of a four - part series on exploring parapsychology.
Psychology
Dist - THINKA **Prod** - THINKA

Learning to use the library 30 MIN
VHS
Color (H C G)
$69.95 purchase _ #RWR - 2
Reviews what libraries contain and how to access library material. Introduces the many information services available - print, nonprint and electronic materials, classification systems and the use of inter - library loans.
Education; Social Science
Dist - INSTRU **Prod** - FLCCJA 1991

Learning to use your senses 11 MIN
U-matic / VHS / 16mm
Color; B&W (K P)
LC FIA68-2526
Encourages children to verbalize sensory perceptions. Points out that people use their five senses automatically and explains how to learn about the environment by using the senses.
Science - Natural
Dist - EBEC **Prod** - EBEC 1968

Learning to Walk 8 MIN
16mm / U-matic / VHS
Color (H C A)
LC 80-700456
Tells the story of a lone figure who sets out on a purposeful stroll, only to be accosted by experts who demonstrate their ideas of the proper way he should walk.

Fine Arts
Dist - IFB **Prod** - ZAGREB 1980

Learning together or alone 30 MIN
VHS
Effective teacher telecourse series
Color (T)
$69.95 purchase, $50.00 rental
Covers the advantages and disadvantages of learning together or separately. Hosted by Dr Loren Anderson.
Education; Psychology
Dist - SCETV **Prod** - SCETV 1987

The Learning Tree 107 MIN
U-matic / VHS / 16mm
Color
Documents a year in the life of a black teenager in 1920's Kansas. Directed by Gordon Parks.
Fine Arts
Dist - FI **Prod** - WB 1969

Learning values with Fat Albert and the Cosby kids series
Uncle Monty's gone 14 MIN
Dist - MGHT

Learning Values with Fat Albert and the Cosby Kids, Set I Series
Check it out 13 MIN
Do your own thing 13 MIN
Dope is for dopes 14 MIN
The Hospital 12 MIN
Lying 13 MIN
The Runt 14 MIN
Summer Camp 13 MIN
What is a Friend 13 MIN
Dist - MGHT

Learning Values with Fat Albert and the Cosby Kids, Set II Series
Animal lover 14 MIN
Junk Food 14 MIN
An Ounce of Prevention 14 MIN
Smoke Gets in Your Hair 14 MIN
Take Two, They're Small 14 MIN
What's Say 14 MIN
You have something to offer 14 MIN
Dist - MGHT

Learning with film and video 15 MIN
VHS
Color (T A)
Shows how good teachers use film and video in the classroom and the benefits of using such media.
Education
Dist - VIEWTH **Prod** - VIEWTH

Learning with film and video 15 MIN
U-matic / VHS / 16mm
Color (A)
$55.00 purchase - 16 mm, $45.00 purchase - video
Shows how good teachers use film and video as an essential tool to provide learning experiences not otherwise available.
Education
Dist - CF **Prod** - CF

Learning with Film and Video 15 MIN
16mm / U-matic / VHS
Color (A)
$55 purchase - 16 mm, $45 purchase - video
Discusses how teachers use audio - visual materials to provide learning experiences. Made by the Los Angeles County Office of Education and Friends of Audio - visual Education.
Education
Dist - CF

Learning with Film and Video 15 MIN
16mm / VHS
Color
Discusses film and video as essential tools of learning and explains how film can bring the world into the classroom, motivate children to read, enhance basic skills development and enrich their learning experiences with exciting visual images. A live action film.
Education; Psychology
Dist - WWS **Prod** - FAC

Learning with Film and Video 15 MIN
U-matic / VHS / 16mm
Color (A C T)
Shows why film and video are indispensable teaching tools and how teachers use the media to provide learning experiences not otherwise available.
Education; Fine Arts; Guidance and Counseling
Dist - AIMS **Prod** - AIMS 1985

Learning WordPerfect for Windows
VHS
WordPerfect 5.1 series
Color (G)
$49.95 purchase _ #VIA028
Teaches WordPerfect, version 5.1, and its applications in Windows.
Computer Science
Dist - SIV

Lease Safety Tips for New Employees 23 MIN
VHS / U-matic
Color (IND)
Illustrates the more common potential hazards that a person may face on the lease and suggests ways to work safely and overcome these hazards.
Health and Safety; Social Science
Dist - UTEXPE **Prod** - UTEXPE 1978

Least Likely 20 MIN
16mm
Color
LC 82-700332
Presents a story about a man who was considered a loser in high school. Reveals that when he returns to the school for his class's tenth reunion as a rich and famous cartoonist, his calculated plan for revenge takes an unexpected turn and has unpredictable and humorous results.
Fine Arts
Dist - USC **Prod** - USC 1981

Least of My Brothers 27 MIN
U-matic / VHS / 16mm
Insight Series
B&W (H C A)
LC 76-705421
Tells of a college sophomore who faces an identity crisis, loses his faith and rediscovers life's purpose in the Peace Corps.
Guidance and Counseling; Psychology
Dist - PAULST **Prod** - PAULST 1966

The Least of these 15 MIN
VHS
Mission videos series
Color (G R)
$12.50 purchase _ #S12366
Portrays the life and work of Alice Brauer, a nurse who pursued a healing ministry to the people of India. Suggests that one person can indeed make a difference.
Guidance and Counseling; Literature and Drama; Religion and Philosophy
Dist - CPH **Prod** - LUMIS

Least Restrictive Environment Panel 30 MIN
U-matic / VHS
Law and Handicapped Children in School
Color (C A)
LC 79-706362
Presents a panel discussion on the requirements prescribed by PL94 - 142, the Education For All Handicapped Children Act of 1975, for providing the least restrictive educational environment for handicapped students.
Civics and Political Systems; Education; Psychology
Dist - IU **Prod** - IU 1979

Least Restrictive Environment - Resource Rooms and Special Classes 30 MIN
U-matic / VHS
Law and Handicapped Children in School
Color (C A)
LC 79-706363
Presents two teaching situations which illustrate the use of a multipurpose resource room for mildly retarded and/or learning disabled children, and special classes for hearing handicapped children.
Education; Psychology
Dist - IU **Prod** - IU 1979

Least Restrictive Environment - Special Day and Residential Schools 30 MIN
VHS / U-matic
Law and Handicapped Children in School
Color (C A)
LC 79-706365
Illustrates three educational alternatives for severely handicapped children, including a day school featuring specialized instruction, a residential school with personalized living environments and self - help facilities, and an innovative recreation camp.
Education; Psychology
Dist - IU **Prod** - IU 1979

Least restrictive environment - Tape 6 54 MIN
VHS
Legal challenges in special education series
Color (G)
$90.00 purchase
Details the leading cases on LRE, indicating what must precede a removal from regular education, when services must be provided in an integrated setting, what is the full continuum of services that must be available to insure that the least restrictive placement is chosen and how communicable diseases are to be taken into account. Features Reed Martin, JD. Includes resource materials. Part of a 12 - part series on Public Law 94 - 142.
Education
Dist - BAXMED

Leather 15 MIN
U-matic / VHS / 16mm
Rediscovery - Art Media Series
Color (I) (SPANISH)
LC 72-701127
Shows a leather craftsman using a variety of tools and several kinds of leather to make a simple pouch and belt and a more complicated shoulder bag and sandals. Includes basic instructions for making leather articles.
Fine Arts
Dist - AIMS **Prod** - ACI 1971

Leather I - Layout and Cutting 30 MIN
U-matic / VHS
Arts and Crafts Series
Color (H A)
LC 81-706989
Describes different types, grades, thicknesses, and uses of leather. Includes a demonstration of the fundamental techniques needed for developing a pattern, laying out the pattern on the leather stock and cutting out the item.
Fine Arts
Dist - GPN **Prod** - GPN 1981

Leather II - Assembly and Lacing 30 MIN
VHS / U-matic
Arts and Crafts Series
Color (H A)
LC 81-706992
Describes and demonstrates how to create leather articles using rivets, snaps, and sewing.
Fine Arts
Dist - GPN **Prod** - GPN 1981

Leather III - Carving and Finishing 30 MIN
U-matic / VHS
Arts and Crafts Series
Color (H A)
LC 81-706994
Describes abd demonstrates leather tooling, dying, finishing techniques and design transfer techniques.
Fine Arts
Dist - GPN **Prod** - GPN 1981

Leather in Your Life 23 MIN
16mm
Color
Tells the story of the processing and tanning of leather. Shows the many important uses of this material.
Business and Economics; Social Science
Dist - CCNY **Prod** - LIA

Leather Production 23 MIN
VHS
Video Field Trips
Color (J H)
$89.95 purchase _ #6 - 040 - 136P
Follows the step - by - step processes which transform a 'green' hide into leather at the IBP 'wet blue' hide tannery in Dakota City, Nebraska. Visits the Tony Lama boot factory in El Paso, Texas, and watches master craftsmen create a finished pair of boots. Part of a series of video field trips which follow raw materials from their natural environment through the processes which transform them into marketable products.
Agriculture; Business and Economics; Home Economics
Dist - VEP

Leather, Pt 3 - Leather Stamping 8 MIN
VHS / U-matic
Color
Explains and demonstrates different types of leather - stamping tools.
Fine Arts; Guidance and Counseling
Dist - HSCIC **Prod** - HSCIC

Leather, Pt 2 - Leather Carving 11 MIN
VHS / U-matic
Color
Introduces leather - carving techniques.
Fine Arts; Guidance and Counseling
Dist - HSCIC **Prod** - HSCIC

Leather series - leather finishing 6 MIN
VHS / U-matic
Leather series
Color
Shows how to apply four different leather finishes and explains when to use each one. Part five in a series of seven programs designed to acquaint occupational therapy students with leather activities.

Fine Arts; Guidance and Counseling
Dist - HSCIC **Prod** - HSCIC

Leather series - leather lacing 21 MIN
VHS / U-matic
Leather series
Color
Covers the four types of stitches used to lace leather pieces together. Last in a series of seven programs designed to acquaint occupational therapy students with leather activities.
Fine Arts; Guidance and Counseling
Dist - HSCIC **Prod** - HSCIC

Leather series - leather tooling 8 MIN
U-matic / VHS
Leather series
Color
Teaches techniques for decorating leather by tooling parts of the design. Part four in a series of seven programs designed to acquaint occupational therapy students with leather activities.
Fine Arts; Guidance and Counseling
Dist - HSCIC **Prod** - HSCIC

Leather series - setting an eyelet, a rivet, and a snap 9 MIN
U-matic / VHS
Leather series
Color
Demonstrates the setting of three types of leather fasteners, an eyelet, a rivet, and a snap. Part six in a series of seven programs designed to acquaint occupational therapy students with leather activities.
Fine Arts; Guidance and Counseling
Dist - HSCIC **Prod** - HSCIC

Leather series
Leather series - leather finishing 6 MIN
Leather series - leather lacing 21 MIN
Leather series - leather tooling 8 MIN
Leather series - setting an eyelet, a rivet, and a snap 9 MIN
Dist - HSCIC

Leather soul - working for a life in a factory town 43 MIN
VHS
Color (H C G)
$350.00 purchase, $65.00 rental
Follows the evolution of Peabody, Massachussetts and the lives of its working class inhabitants during the rise and fall of the leather tanning industry. Reveals that Peabody was once home to over 100 leather factories and developed a richly colorful social and political scene that flourished with the industrial boom. Today, Peabody's leather factories are silent, replaced by a high - tech computer industry that saved the town but not the jobs of the leather workers. Shows how sudden and unexpected technological progress has torn apart the fabric of communities. Features Studs Terkel as narrator. Produced by Picture Business and Bob Quinn.
Business and Economics; History - United States; Social Science
Dist - FLMLIB

Leather Stamping for Fun and Profit (#1889) 45 MIN
VHS
Color; Mono (J C)
George Hurst demonstrates how to easily make handsome and saleable leathercraft items using geometric stamping, 3 - D stamps and more.
Business and Economics; Fine Arts; Home Economics; Industrial and Technical Education
Dist - TANDY **Prod** - TANDY 1986

Leatherburning and Clock Making 86 MIN
BETA / VHS
Color
Presents a variety of leatherworking projects and then introduces basic instructions on clock making from kits.
Fine Arts
Dist - HOMEAF **Prod** - HOMEAF

Leathercraft, Pt 1 - Pattern Construction and Layout 27 MIN
U-matic / VHS
Color
Shows how to make a pattern for a leather item and how to cut out and prepare leather pieces for assembly.
Fine Arts; Guidance and Counseling
Dist - HSCIC **Prod** - HSCIC

Leatherman's training trilogy
VHS
Color (A PRO IND)
$3,500.00 purchase, $850.00 rental
Presents Dick Leatherman's three - part series on training corporate trainers.
Business and Economics; Guidance and Counseling; Psychology
Dist - VLEARN **Prod** - ITRC

Leatherneck Ambassadors 15 MIN
U-matic
Color
Features the performance of the Marine Corps in the International Festival of Music, Edinburgh, Scotland, 1958.
Civics and Political Systems; Fine Arts
Dist - USNAC **Prod** - USNAC 1972

Leathernick Ambassadors 14 MIN
16mm
Color
LC FIE67-122
Presents participation by Marines in the annual Edinburgh, Scotland, Military Tattoo.
Civics and Political Systems
Dist - USNAC **Prod** - USMC 1961

Leatherstocking tales 120 MIN
VHS
Color (J H C)
$179.00 purchase _ #05694 - 126
Presents a two - part adaptation of the wilderness sagas by James Fennimore Cooper. Includes tales from The Deerslayer, The Pathfinder, The Last Of The Mohicans, The Pioneers, and The Prairies.
History - United States; Literature and Drama
Dist - GA **Prod** - GA

The Leatherstocking Tales - New Perspectives 30 MIN
Videoreel / VHS
Color
Deals with James Fenimore Cooper's LEATHERSTOCKING TALES, in which he expresses the transcendence of the woodman.
Literature and Drama
Dist - NETCHE **Prod** - NETCHE 1970

Leave country sports alone 30 MIN
VHS
Open space series
Color; PAL (H C A)
PdS50 purchase; Available in the United Kingdom and Ireland only
Explores the reasons in favor of hunting. Describes 'country sports' as a humane method of controlling large numbers of predatory animals. Employs views of farmers, hunt members, veterinarians, and conservationists to challenge popular opinions on hunting.
Physical Education and Recreation; Sociology
Dist - BBCENE

Leave 'Em Laughing 30 MIN
16mm
Laurel and Hardy Comedy Series
B&W (P A)
LC 78-711883
Presents a Laurel and Hardy comedy in which Stan and Ollie muddle through the complications of a toothache, laughing gas and an eviction notice. Includes Edgar Kennedy as a police officer.
Fine Arts
Dist - RMIBHF **Prod** - ROACH 1927

Leave Herbert Alone 8 MIN
16mm / U-matic / VHS
Color (P I)
LC 75-702203
Presents a story about a young child who tries to play with her next door neighbor's cat. Shows how she disturbs the cat by constantly pursuing it, until she finds that if she is quiet and still the cat will come to her.
Science - Natural
Dist - AIMS **Prod** - MORLAT 1974

Leave Home Without it - 227 30 MIN
U-matic
Currents - 1985 - 86 Season Series
Color (A)
Reveals the personal debt that some people can amass with the unrestrained use of credit cards.
Business and Economics; Social Science
Dist - PBS **Prod** - WNETTV 1985

Leave it alone - dangerous substances around the home 10 MIN
VHS
Dr Cooper and his friends series
Color (T P) (FRENCH)
$50.00 purchase _ #PVK83, PVK41
Describes some commonly available substances with drug - like effects. Includes a teacher's guide and a poster.
Guidance and Counseling
Dist - ARFO **Prod** - ARFO

Leave it to You - OK
U-matic / 16mm
Color (A)
Explores the skills of delegation, what it is, how it is done, what can and cannot be delegated, the barriers and benefits.
Business and Economics; Psychology
Dist - BNA **Prod** - BNA 1983

Leave Me Alone, God 25 MIN
U-matic / VHS / 16mm
Insight Series
Color (H C A) (SPANISH)
Explains how a college professor who had denied the existence of God changes his mind after one of his students overdoses as a result of what he has taught her. Stars Richard Jordan.
Foreign Language; Guidance and Counseling; Psychology; Religion and Philosophy
Dist - PAULST **Prod** - PAULST
SUTHRB

The Leave - Taking 15 MIN
VHS / U-matic
Encounter in the Desert Series
Color (I)
Presents a Bedouin wedding ceremony. Ends a story of western visitors learning about the Bedouin way of life.
Geography - World; Social Science; Sociology
Dist - CTI **Prod** - CTI

Leave Yourself an Out 10 MIN
16mm
Expert Seeing Series
Color; B&W
Shows how to plan for emergencies and how to provide an 'ESCAPE ROUTE.'.
Health and Safety; Psychology
Dist - NSC **Prod** - NSC

Leaves 13 MIN
U-matic / VHS / 16mm
Color (P I)
LC 75-702443
Tells the story of a six year old boy's efforts to assist nature by replacing fallen leaves with his own creations made with construction paper, marking crayons and scissors. Portrays the mixture of reality and fantasy that is the child's world. With an original music score, but no narration.
Fine Arts; Psychology
Dist - AIMS **Prod** - PHILLR 1968

Leaves of absence 75 MIN
16mm
Color (G)
$200.00 rental
Contains images from the filmmaker's daily living and soul explorations. Uses color stocks with happy filmic accidents and shot and edited during the process of breaking away from her last family. Produced by Carmen Vigil.
Fine Arts
Dist - CANCIN

Leaves of Grass, Continued 10 MIN
16mm
B&W
Contrasts Walt Whitman's optimism for the future, in which he tried to foresee a great new life for the American city, with the congestion, squalor and filth produced by a city grown too big.
Science - Natural; Sociology
Dist - UPENN **Prod** - UPENN 1961

Leaves of green 11 MIN
VHS
Color; PAL (I J)
Presents a biological examination of the function of leaves. Shows how leaves absorb nitrogen and release oxygen, which is essential to all animal life, including humans.
Science - Natural
Dist - VIEWTH **Prod** - VIEWTH
STANF

Leaving 30 MIN
U-matic
Family and the Law Series
(H C A)
Explores a marriage breakdown and divorce proceedings.
Civics and Political Systems; History - World
Dist - ACCESS **Prod** - ACCESS 1980

Leaving and Coming Back 18 MIN
16mm
I Am, I Can, I will, Level II Series
Color (K P S)
LC 80-700569
Presents Mr Rogers exploring feelings people feel when separated from things and people they love.

Guidance and Counseling; Psychology
Dist - HUBDSC **Prod** - FAMCOM 1979

Leaving for School - Level 2 16 MIN
16mm
PANCOM Beginning Total Communication Program for Hearing Parents of Series
Color (K)
LC 77-700504
Education; Guidance and Counseling; Psychology; Sociology
Dist - JOYCE **Prod** - CSDE 1977

Leaving for the Sea 30 MIN
Videoreel / VHS
B&W
Portrays women's friendships in a dream - like fiction.
Sociology
Dist - WMENIF **Prod** - WMENIF

Leaving Home - a Family in Transition 28 MIN
16mm
Color (H C A)
LC 81-700472
Employs cinema verite techniques to show what happens when two young sisters decide to move away from home. Profiles the girls' desires for independence as well as for parental acceptance and approval.
Sociology
Dist - DIRECT **Prod** - PNTNGL 1980

Leaving school 15 MIN
VHS / U-matic
Work - the inside story series
Color (H C)
#389101; LC 91-706539
Looks at why young people leave school. Discusses finding a first job, dealing with rejection and adjusting to the world of work. Part of a series offering practical advice to teens entering the workforce.
Business and Economics; Guidance and Counseling; Psychology
Dist - TVOTAR **Prod** - TVOTAR 1991

Leaving the harbor 77 MIN
VHS
Color (G)
$85.00 purchase
Follows filmmaker Guido Gruczek as he travels from Long Island, through New England, and up to Montreal casting a film, although he only vaguely knows what it is about. Illustrates how art imitates life - how everyday occurrences and conversations become the scenes and dialogue for Gruczek's work. A film within a film.
Fine Arts; Geography - United States
Dist - CANCIN **Prod** - UNGRW 1991

Leaving the 20th Century Series
Arrival
Countdown
Departure
Dist - KITCHN

Lebanon 28 MIN
Videoreel / VHS
International Byline Series
Color
Interviews Ambassador Ghassan Tueni, permanent representative to the United Nations on Lebanon yesterday, today and tomorrow. Presents films on Lebanon. Hosted by Marilyn Perry.
Business and Economics; Civics and Political Systems; Geography - World
Dist - PERRYM **Prod** - PERRYM

Lebanon and the Crusades 12 MIN
U-matic / VHS / 16mm
Color (I)
Chronicles the three year campaign of the crusaders of Christian Europe to remove the Holy City of Jerusalem from the bonds of the Muslims. Looks at the fortresses the crusaders built along the Lebanese coast.
History - World
Dist - LUF **Prod** - LUF 1981

Lebanon, Israel and the PLO 28 MIN
VHS / U-matic
Color (H C A)
Examines the history that led to the confrontation between Israeli troops and the PLO in West Beirut.
History - World
Dist - JOU **Prod** - JOU

Lebanon - Land of Survivors 16 MIN
U-matic
Color
Illustrates Beirut during the summer of 1982, focusing on the devastation of the city and the nonpartisan aid given by Catholic Relief Services. Narrated by Joseph Curtin, Catholic Relief Services Program Director in Lebanon.
Geography - World; Sociology
Dist - MTP **Prod** - CATHRS

Lebanon - Modern Mosaic 29 MIN
VHS / 16mm
Countries and Peoples Series
Color (H C G)
$90.00 purchase _ #BPN128109
Takes the viewer from the traditional countryside of Lebanon to the ultramodern city of Beirut. Reveals some archaeological treasures of Baalbek and Byblos in contrast.
Geography - World; History - World
Dist - RMIBHF **Prod** - RMIBHF
TVOTAR

Lebanon Valley College - Guest Dan Smith, Program A 29 MIN
Videoreel / VT2
Sonia Malkine on Campus Series
Color
Features French folk singer Sonia Malkine and her special guest Dan Smith visiting Lebanon Valley College in Pennsylvania.
Fine Arts; Foreign Language; Geography - United States
Dist - PBS **Prod** - WITFTV

Lebanon Valley College - Guest Dan Smith, Program B 29 MIN
Videoreel / VT2
Sonia Malkine on Campus Series
Color
Features French folk singer Sonia Malkine and her special guest Dan Smith visiting Lebanon Valley College in Pennsylvania.
Fine Arts; Foreign Language; Geography - United States
Dist - PBS **Prod** - WITFTV

L'Ecluse 13 MIN
16mm
En France avec Jean et Helene series
B&W (J H C)
LC 73-704507
Foreign Language
Dist - CHLTN **Prod** - PEREN 1967

Lectra Nancy Side A, Side B 7 MIN
U-matic / VHS
Color
Produces dissonant images which are high gloss, confrontational and anti - authoritarian. Presented by Beth Berolzheimer, Wayne Fielding and Karl Hauser.
Fine Arts
Dist - ARTINC **Prod** - ARTINC

The Lecture and Role - Playing Strategy 30 MIN
16mm
Nursing - Where are You Going, How will You Get There Series
B&W (C A)
LC 74-700179
Dramatizes principles for presenting meaningful lectures and demonstrations.
Education; Health and Safety
Dist - NTCN **Prod** - NTCN 1971

Lecture Demonstrations in Electrochemistry 30 MIN
VHS
Chem 101 - Beginning Chemistry Series
Color (C)
$50.00 purchase, $21.00 rental _ #05129
Features sixteen un - narrated demonstrations including - conductivity of molten glass and tap water, migration of ions through gel, electrolysis of water, electrochemical energy, a variety of voltaic cells and others. Reactants are labeled by superimposed titles and a voltmeter scale is also superimposed over the demonstration where appropriate.
Science; Science - Physical
Dist - UILL **Prod** - UILL 1980

Lecture Demonstrations in Equilibrium 40 MIN
VHS
Chem 101 - Beginning Chemistry Series
Color (C)
$50.00 purchase, $21.00 rental _ #00146
Includes shifting and competing equilibria, free energy relationships, buffer action, hydrolysis of salts, solubility equilibria, "orange tornadoes," an oscillating reaction and others. Titrations are carried out in solutions with indicators, while the actual titration curve is being generated and superimposed on the screen.
Science - Physical
Dist - UILL **Prod** - UILL 1980

Lecture Eight, FORTRAN 30 MIN
VHS / U-matic
FORTRAN Series
Color
Talks about one dimensional arrays - array subscripts, a new statement DIMENSION, and Slash on Input FORMAT.
Industrial and Technical Education; Mathematics; Sociology
Dist - COLOSU **Prod** - COLOSU

Lecture Five, FORTRAN 30 MIN
U-matic / VHS
FORTRAN Series
Color
Discusses statement components logical variables and constants and logical format descriptor, plus header data.
Industrial and Technical Education; Mathematics; Sociology
Dist - COLOSU **Prod** - COLOSU

Lecture Four, FORTRAN 30 MIN
U-matic / VHS
FORTRAN Series
Color
Discusses real and integer types, statement components AND, OR and NOT, the order of operations, and using counter to terminate loop.
Industrial and Technical Education; Mathematics; Sociology
Dist - COLOSU **Prod** - COLOSU

Lecture Nine, FORTRAN 30 MIN
VHS / U-matic
FORTRAN Series
Color
Shows two - dimensional arrays, and searching for subscript pattern.
Industrial and Technical Education; Mathematics; Sociology
Dist - COLOSU **Prod** - COLOSU

Lecture Seven, FORTRAN 30 MIN
U-matic / VHS
FORTRAN Series
Color
Shows new statement DO and nested DO loops.
Industrial and Technical Education; Mathematics; Sociology
Dist - COLOSU **Prod** - COLOSU

Lecture Six, FORTRAN 30 MIN
U-matic / VHS
FORTRAN Series
Color
Shows new statement - Computed GO TO, predefined subprograms and labeled output.
Industrial and Technical Education; Mathematics; Sociology
Dist - COLOSU **Prod** - COLOSU

Lecture Ten, FORTRAN 30 MIN
VHS / U-matic
FORTRAN Series
Color
Discusses user - defined subprograms, new statements CALL and SUBROUTINE, and subprogram use.
Industrial and Technical Education; Mathematics; Sociology
Dist - COLOSU **Prod** - COLOSU

Lecture Three, FORTRAN 30 MIN
U-matic / VHS
FORTRAN Series
Color
Shows new statements GO TO and Logical IF. Lists statement components, relational operators and logical expression, attacking a problem, carriage control and debugging.
Industrial and Technical Education; Mathematics; Sociology
Dist - COLOSU **Prod** - COLOSU

Lee a Two Rivers 7 MIN
VHS
Color (C)
$250.00 purchase, $25.00, $35.00 rental
Presents a Canadian work of video art which celebrates women who live in harmony with the natural world. Features images of nature and music. Produced by Nicole Benoit.
Fine Arts; Geography - World; Sociology
Dist - WMENIF

Lee Baltimore - 99 years, what makes a poor man rich 17 MIN
U-matic / VHS / 16mm
American Character Series
Color (J H C)
LC 76-703008
Records the reminiscenses of Lee Baltimore, a 99-year-old ex - slave who is still a working farmer in Jasper County, Texas. Shows him plowing his fields with a horse and hand plow and demonstrates his interest in God and music.
History - United States; Sociology
Dist - EBEC **Prod** - ODYSSP 1976

Lee Iacocca 28 MIN
U-matic / VHS
Color (G)

$249.00, $149.00 purchase _ #AD - 2028
Presents a Phil Donahue program on Lee Iacocca, CEO of Chrysler Corporation. Chronicles the role of sales and marketing in the success and failure of a business.
Biography; Business and Economics; Industrial and Technical Education
Dist - FOTH **Prod** - FOTH

Lee Konitz - portrait of an artist as a saxophonist 83 MIN
VHS
Color (G)
$29.95 purchase
Focuses on jazz saxophonist Lee Konitz.
Fine Arts
Dist - KINOIC **Prod** - RHPSDY

Lee Krasner - the Long View 30 MIN
16mm
Color
LC 79-700392
Portrays abstract expressionist artist Lenore Krasner, focusing on her life, her studies and her marriage to Jackson Pollock. Shows the artist at work.
Fine Arts
Dist - AFA **Prod** - ROSEBA 1978

Lee Ritenour and Dave Grusin Live from the Record Plant 55 MIN
VHS
Color (S)
$29.95 purchase _ #726 - 9006
Presents internationally acclaimed guitarist Lee Ritenour and keyboardist Dave Grusin performing Rio Funk, Dolphin Dreams, St Elsewhere and five other pieces.
Fine Arts
Dist - FI **Prod** - VARJ 1989

Lee Suzuki - Home in Hawaii 19 MIN
U-matic / VHS / 16mm
Many Americans Series
Color (I J)
LC 73-702213
Presents a simple episode in the life of a 14 - year - old Hawaiian boy to provide a view of the island people whose multi - ethnic society makes them unique among our states. Provides glimpses of the human and social geography of Hawaii.
Geography - United States; Geography - World; Social Science; Sociology
Dist - LCOA **Prod** - LCOA 1973

Lee Theodore, Buzz Miller and Barbara Naomi Cohen - Stratyner 30 MIN
U-matic / VHS
Eye on Dance - Broadway Dance Series
Color
Focuses on the development of theatre dance.
Fine Arts
Dist - ARCVID **Prod** - ARCVID

Lee Theodore, Buzz Miller and Barbara Naomi Cohen - Stratyner 30 MIN
VHS / U-matic
Eye on Dance - Broadway Dance Series
Color
Focuses on the development of theatre dance.
Fine Arts
Dist - ARTRES **Prod** - ARTRES

Lee Trevino's golf tips for youngsters 40 MIN
VHS
Color (J H A)
$29.95 purchase _ #PM12677V
Features Lee Trevino with an introduction to the basics of golf. Covers subjects including grip, stance, putting, chipping, sand trap play, and more.
Physical Education and Recreation; Sociology
Dist - CAMV

Lee Trevino's priceless golf tips series
Presents a three - volume series on golf by Lee Trevino. Includes the titles Chipping and Putting, Getting out of Trouble and Swing Fundamentals Plus Distance and Control.
Chipping and putting 25 MIN
Getting out of trouble 25 MIN
Swing fundamentals plus distance and control 25 MIN
Dist - CAMV

Leeks - Trimming, Washing, Slicing, Dicing and Cutting for Julienne 8 MIN
U-matic / VHS
Color (PRO)
Home Economics; Industrial and Technical Education
Dist - CULINA **Prod** - CULINA

Leenya - Daughter of the Noble Blacks of Surinam 11 MIN
U-matic / VHS / 16mm
Captioned; Color (I J)
Looks at the life of Leenya, a young Bush Negro of Surinam.
Geography - World
Dist - IFB **Prod** - GORDAJ 1973

LEEP of the cervix 8 MIN
VHS
Color (PRO A)
$250.00 purchase _ #OB - 120
Aids health care professionals by providing viewers with information regarding the removal of cervical dysplasia through the procedure LEEP - loop electrosurgical excision procedure. Warns the viewer that cervical dysplasia left untreated may lead to cancer. Explains that LEEP offers an advantage over other treatment methods by providing a tissue specimen that can verify the degree of dysplasia, rule out cancer and verify that all abnormal tissue has been removed. Teaches patients what to expect during and after the procedure and covers the possible risks and normal recovery symptoms associated with LEEP.
Health and Safety
Dist - MIFE **Prod** - MIFE 1992

Lee's Parasol 25 MIN
16mm / U-matic / VHS
World Cultures and Youth Series
Color (I J A)
$520.00, $250.00 purchase _ #4112
Introduces Lee, a Thai girl who is making a beautiful parasol for her cousin, a Buddhist monk. Shows her in the process of constructing the parasol and then presenting it to her cousin as part of the ceremonies at the colorful Buddhist festival.
Fine Arts; Geography - World; Sociology
Dist - CORF **Prod** - CORF 1980

Leeward and windward video voyages series
Cruising the leeward islands - Volume 1
Cruising the windward islands - Volume 2
Dist - SEVVID

Left Atrial Myxoma Excision using the Superior Approach 9 MIN
U-matic / VHS
Color (PRO)
Shows the left atrial myxoma excision using the superior approach.
Health and Safety
Dist - WFP **Prod** - WFP

Left Brain, Right Brain 56 MIN
16mm
Nature of Things Series
Color (H C A)
LC 80-701983
Presents and demonstrates theories about the development of specialized roles within the human brain.
Psychology; Science - Natural
Dist - FLMLIB **Prod** - CANBC 1980

Left Brain - Right Brain - Part One 43.06 MIN
VHS
Using Your Creative Brain Series
Color (J H C)
LC 88-700272
Introduces students to the various powers, tasks and responses of each side of the brain.
Science - Natural
Dist - SRA **Prod** - SRA 1984

Left Colectomy for Carcinoma of the Rectosigmoid 15 MIN
U-matic / VHS
Color (PRO)
Describes left colectomy for carcinoma of the rectosigmoid.
Health and Safety
Dist - WFP **Prod** - WFP

The Left Handed Gun 102 MIN
U-matic / VHS / 16mm
B&W (C A)
Stars Paul Newman as Billy the Kid. Revolves around Billy's obsession with avenging the murder of his employer, a rancher shot during a new Mexico cattle drive.
Fine Arts
Dist - FI **Prod** - WB 1958

Left - handed memories 15 MIN
16mm
Color (G)
$20.00 rental
Pays homage to Will Hindle and his films. Introduces various images with words reflecting Hindle's film titles. Produced by Michele Fleming.
Fine Arts
Dist - CANCIN

The Left - Handed Woman 119 MIN
16mm
Color (GERMAN (ENGLISH SUBTITLES))
Focuses on a German housewife, living in Paris, who decides to become unmarried. Records her quiet 'war with the world' over three months of loneliness, near - breakdown, and adjustment. Directed by Peter Handke. With English subtitles.
Fine Arts; Foreign Language
Dist - NYFLMS **Prod** - UNKNWN 1978

Left Out 24 MIN
16mm / VHS
Family Issues - Learning about Life Series
Color (P I J H A)
$395.00, $495.00 purchase, $50.00 rental _ #9929
Deals with unemployment and its effect on family life. Amy, a 12 - year - old, feels left out because she can't afford to go on a field trip.
Guidance and Counseling; Sociology
Dist - AIMS **Prod** - NFBC 1987

The Left, Right Movie 7 MIN
16mm
Color (K P S)
LC 73-701041
Teaches and reinforces the concepts of left and right.
English Language; Guidance and Counseling
Dist - FILMSM **Prod** - FILMSM 1972

Left Ventricle Catheterization 14 MIN
16mm
B&W (PRO)
LC 77-701481
Presents the fundamental physiological relationship involved in left ventricle catheterization, using the retrograde technique. Shows the landmarks used for X - ray orientation, relevant cardiovascular structures visualized by opaque dye and the catheter - aortic valve - ventricular period relationship.
Health and Safety; Science; Science - Natural
Dist - USNAC **Prod** - NMAC 1973

Left Ventricular Hypertrophy 49 MIN
VHS / U-matic
Electrocardiogram Series
Color (PRO)
Teaches criteria for the diagnosis of left ventricular hypertrophy. Discusses increased magnitude of the mean QRS vector, ventricular repolarization abnormalities, and left axis deviation.
Health and Safety; Science; Science - Natural
Dist - HSCIC **Prod** - HSCIC 1982

The Left Wall of Cenotaph Corner 14 MIN
16mm
Color (J)
Traces the development of the chock or nut as an alternative to the hammered piton in rock climbing. Includes historical footage of two climbers ascending the left wall of Cenotaph corner in North Wales in 1964 using engineering nuts for direct aid.
Geography - World
Dist - CRYSP **Prod** - OAKCRK

Left wall of Centopath Corner 27 MIN
U-matic / VHS / BETA
Color; PAL (J H C G)
PdS45, PdS53 purchase
Traces the development of the chock as an alternative of the hammered piton. Includes unique footage of climbers ascending the Left Wall of Cenotaph Corner in North Wales.
Physical Education and Recreation
Dist - EDPAT

The Leg, Ankle and Foot 29 MIN
U-matic / VHS
Cyriax on Orthopaedic Medicine Series
Color
Examines the leg, ankle and foot for Achillis, tennis leg, sprained ankle, peroneal tendons, talocalcaean joint arthritis, loose body, dancer's heel, plantar fascitis and hallux.
Health and Safety; Science - Natural
Dist - VTRI **Prod** - VTRI

Leg Med Musik Og Sang - Music and Games 18 MIN
16mm
B&W (DANISH)
A Danish language film. Presents an on - the - spot report from various educational situations. Contributes to the debate about the teaching of music and singing in the kindergarten and the first school years.
Education; Fine Arts; Foreign Language
Dist - STATNS **Prod** - STATNS 1968

Leg - straightening procedure 45 MIN
VHS
Surgical procedures series
Color (G)
$149.00 purchase, $75.00 rental _ #UW4572
Watches as Dr Richard Davis - Asst Professor of Orthopedic Surgery, Univ of South Carolina - uses the Ilizarov technique to straighten the leg of 12 - year - old Richard. Involves threading wires through the bone and tying them to rings around the leg. The rings attach to adjustable rods which support the patient's weight when he stands. Lengthening is accomplished by separating the bones up to 1mm per day. Over months, bones can be lengthened as much as 8 inches. Part of a 17 - part series recording surgical procedures in detail, with specialists who explain the ailment, the anatomical function of the part of the body being operated on, and how successful surgery might improve the patient's quality of life, hosted by Dr Donna Willis.
Health and Safety; Science - Natural
Dist - FOTH

Legacies - episode 13 60 MIN
U-matic / VHS / 16mm
Vietnam - a television history series; Episode 13
Color (H C A)
Discusses the legacies of the Vietnamese war including delayed stress syndrome and the effects of Agent Orange. Shows that the volume of boat people demonstrated that a portion of the Vietnamese were so unable to relate to the victors that they risked their lives to escape.
History - United States; History - World
Dist - FI **Prod** - WGBHTV 1983

Legacies of the Depression on the Great Plains series
The Farm - Pt I 30 MIN
The Small town - Pt II 30 MIN
Dist - NETCHE

Legacies of the ice 12 MIN
U-matic / VHS / BETA
Color; NTSC; PAL; SECAM (I J)
PdS43
Describes glaciers, which form when more snow falls than melts, in terms of their movement and their effects upon the surface of the Earth. Shows how mountain glaciers widen and deepen valleys and, at high elevations, form cirques and horns. Reveals that continental glaciers can dig depressions, remove soil and smooth and fill uneven land. Glaciers melt water, erode the land, form lakes and help determine the level of ocean water. Humans gain from the effects of glaciation through farming the fertile soils of outwash, utilizing deposits of sand, gravel, clay and underground waters, and using glacial lakes for industrial and recreational purposes.
Geography - World; Science - Physical
Dist - VIEWTH

Legacies of the Ice Age 12 MIN
16mm / U-matic / VHS
Color (I J H)
LC 72-700500
Describes the formation and movement of different types of glaciers, and their effects on the land. Points out how glaciers benefit man.
Geography - World; Science - Physical
Dist - IU **Prod** - IU 1971

Legacies of the Ice Age 12 MIN
16mm
Color (J H C G)
Discusses glaciers and their movement and effects upon the earth's surface.
Geography - World; Science - Physical
Dist - VIEWTH **Prod** - GATEEF

Legacies of the Sixties 60 MIN
VHS / 16mm
Making Sense of the Sixties Series
Color (G)
$59.95 purchase _ #MSIX - N903
Reflects upon the Sixties from the perspective of 1990. Documents that America still faces many of the issues of that time. Part of a six - part series on the Sixties.
History - United States; Sociology
Dist - PBS **Prod** - WETATV 1990

Legacies - Volume 7 60 MIN
VHS
Vietnam - a television history series
Color (H C A)
$14.95 purchase
Presents 'Legacies,' the final episode of a 13 - part series covering the history of the Vietnam War.
History - United States
Dist - PBS **Prod** - WNETTV

Legacies - Volume 7 60 MIN
VHS
Vietnam - a television history series
Color (G)
$19.95 purchase _ #S01533
Presents the final episode of the 'Vietnam - A Television History' series. Considers the events that ended the Vietnam War.
History - United States
Dist - UILL **Prod** - PBS

Legacy 4 MIN
16mm
Color
LC 80-701233
Presents an overview of the development of the Earth's natural resources.
Social Science
Dist - BBF **Prod** - VINTN 1979

The Legacy 28 MIN
16mm
Color
LC 75-701181
Explains the total systems approach to fire safety and building protection. Focuses on the first GSA high - rise structure to include a total fire safety system, including a total sprinkler system, two - way voice communications, smoke detection equipment and other fire safety devices.
Health and Safety; Industrial and Technical Education
Dist - USNAC **Prod** - USGSA 1975

Legacy 22 MIN
VHS
Color (G)
$195.00 purchase, $50.00 rental
Examines the perpetuation of the romantic myths surrounding Christopher Columbus's 'discovery of the new world' in 1492. Introduces Native American Chief Roy Crazy Horse who visits the Dominican Republic, site of Columbus's first encounter with the Taino Indians. Contrasts European myths with the perspective of the indigineous Taino, who were subjected to a genocidal campaign of exploitation. Directed by Chief Roy Crazy Horse and Jeff Baker.
Fine Arts; History - World; Sociology
Dist - CNEMAG

Legacy - a Very Short History of Natural Resources 5 MIN
16mm
Color (J)
LC 80-701079
Uses claymation to recount the origins of the Earth's key energy resources.
Social Science
Dist - BBF **Prod** - BBF 1979

Legacy - a Very Short History of Natural Resources 5 MIN
16mm
Color
Presents a clay animation film on the history of natural resources. Shows a cosmic bang, gases turning to rain and the formation of oceans. Shows how vast resources from all previous life forms of matter are inside the earth, including oil, gas, coal, minerals and vast forests. Includes a brief look at the evolutionary process.
Fine Arts; Science - Natural; Science - Physical; Social Science
Dist - BBF **Prod** - VINTN

The Legacy - Children of Holocaust Survivors 23 MIN
VHS / 16mm
Color (S)
$400.00, $79.00 purchase _ #552 - 9021
Presents five children of concentration camp survivors discussing the painful effects their parents' horrifying experiences have had on their own lives. Shows them speaking of the 'conspiracy of silence' - their parents' attempts to shield their children from the hideous realities they have known.
Civics and Political Systems; History - United States; History - World; Sociology
Dist - FI

Legacy for a Loon 20 MIN
16mm
Color
Offers a scientifically accurate documentary on the behavior and life history of the common loon including scenes of courtship, nest building, incubation, territorial defense, egg hatching and other animals that are part of the loon's environment.
Science - Natural
Dist - BERLET **Prod** - BERLET 1982

Legacy in limbo 60 MIN
U-matic / VT1 / VHS
Color (G)
$59.95 purchase, $35.00 rental
Reveals that the Museum of the American Indian in New York City has the world's largest collection of Native American artifacts. Discloses, however, that only a small portion of the more than one million artifacts in the Museum collection are on public display; remaining artifacts are piled floor to ceiling in a Bronx warehouse. Museum officials want to move but New York City and New York State politicians are blocking the move, with threats, angry debate and lawsuits blocking every attempt to move to a better location. Meanwhile, the legacy of nearly every Indian culture in the Western Hemisphere is in limbo and at the mercy of the legal system.
Fine Arts; Social Science
Dist - NAMPBC **Prod** - WXXITV 1990

Legacy of a dream - Martin Luther King Jr 30 MIN
VHS
Color (J H C G)
$29.95 purchase _ #MH6067V
Examines the life and times of Martin Luther King, Jr. Features James Earl Jones as narrator.
Biography; Civics and Political Systems; History - United States
Dist - CAMV

Legacy of a genius - the story of Thomas Alva Edison 59 MIN
VHS
Color (A)
Documents the life and career of Thomas Edison. Shows that Edison invented, among other things, light bulbs, phonographs, and movie cameras. Interviews a variety of people on Edison's accomplishments. Hosted by Eric Sevareid.
History - United States; Science
Dist - SCETV **Prod** - SCETV 1986
PBS

Legacy of achievement 64 MIN
VHS
Legacy of achievement series
Color (PRO IND A)
$1095.00 purchase, $395.00 rental _ #JHP01
Combines Profiles of Achievement and Principles of Achievement - motivational programs designed to transcend differences of race, gender and culture. By Joan Holman productions.
Business and Economics; Psychology
Dist - EXTR

Legacy of achievement series
Legacy of achievement 64 MIN
Principles of achievement - Part 2 23 MIN
Profiles of achievement - Part I 41 MIN
Dist - EXTR

The Legacy of Anne Frank 29 MIN
U-matic / VHS / 16mm
Color (H A)
LC FIA68-106
Presents a portrayal of Anne Frank, using photographs of the house she lived in, her school and the Annex where she and her family were confined. Interviews her teacher and her father, emphasizing how their love and hope survived.
Civics and Political Systems; History - World; Religion and Philosophy
Dist - MGHT **Prod** - NBCTV 1967

The Legacy of Anne Sullivan 28 MIN
16mm
Color (K)
LC 79-702444
Demonstrates the work being done today to teach and rehabilitate deaf - blind children and adults. Describes the pioneering work of Anne Sullivan with Helen Keller.
Biography; Education; Health and Safety; Psychology
Dist - CMPBL **Prod** - PERKNS 1968

The Legacy of Currier and Ives 23 MIN
16mm
Color (I)
LC 76-701611
Surveys 19th century American life with Currier and Ives lithographs and period memorabilia. Includes such categories as general history, farming life, city life, sports and pastimes, riverlife, war scenes, life in the West, trains and patriotism.
Fine Arts; History - United States
Dist - ESMARK **Prod** - ESMARK

Legacy of Gemini 28 MIN
16mm
Color (H T)

LC FIE67-122
Summarizes the principal accomplishments of the Gemini two - man space flights - - includes astronaut training, rendezvous and docking of space vehicles, extravehicular activity and scientific experiments. Shows how these accomplishments will aid future manned space flights.
Industrial and Technical Education; Science; Science - Physical
Dist - NASA **Prod** - NASA 1967

Legacy of Gemini 30 MIN
U-matic / VHS
History of Space Travel Series
Color
Discusses the legacy of the Gemini space program.
Science - Physical
Dist - MDCPB **Prod** - NASAC

Legacy of Gemini WASHINGTON, DC 20409 18 MIN
U-matic / VHS
Color
LC 80-707381
Traces the major accomplishments of the Gemini manned spaceflight program and their relationships to the Apollo lunar landing program. Presents the 12 Gemini flights as a single composite flight. Issued in 1967 as a motion picture.
Industrial and Technical Education
Dist - USNAC **Prod** - NASA 1980

A Legacy of lifestyles 55 MIN
VHS
Africans series
Color (A)
PdS99 purchase _ Unavailable in USA or Canada
Features Ali Mazuri examining the history and peoples of Africa. Explores the role of the family in African society. Part of an eight-part series.
History - World; Sociology
Dist - BBCENE

A Legacy of lifestyles - Pt 2 60 MIN
VHS / U-matic
Africans series
Color (G)
$45.00, $29.95 purchase
Examines family structure in the varied countries of Africa. Includes matrilineal, patrilineal and polygamous traditions and the impact of modern cities on family ties. Part of a nine - part series hosted by Dr Ali Mazrui, Cornell University and University of Michigan.
History - United States; History - World; Sociology
Dist - ANNCPB **Prod** - WETATV 1988
BBCENE

The Legacy of Malthus 50 MIN
VHS
Developing stories II series
Color (G T)
$150.00 purchase, $75.00 rental
Challenges firmly held view that overpopulation is responsible for poverty. Intercuts scenes from the Napier Commission of enquiry into the Scottish Highland clearances, interviews contemporary Rajasthani Indian village women. Uses US news footage and modern propaganda films warning of the dire consequences of global population increase to argue that this is the same old debate dressed up with misleading statistics. Presents fourth video in second installment of the BBC series in which the BBC, with the guidance of Television Trust for the Environment, commissioned leading filmmakers from developing countries to create programs that deal with issues of people, population, and migration from the perspective of those directly affected by these crises.
Fine Arts; History - World; Social Science; Sociology
Dist - BULFRG **Prod** - BBCENE 1994

The Legacy of Rome 52 MIN
U-matic / VHS / 16mm
Saga of Western Man Series
Color (J)
LC FIA67-465
Describes the grandeur and imperial power of ancient Rome. Examines the influence on civilization of Roman achievements in the arts, the sciences, jurisprudence, and politics. Includes sequences filmed in Italy and in outposts of the Roman Empire from Libya to Scotland and from Jordan to the south of France.
History - United States; History - World
Dist - MGHT **Prod** - ABCTV 1966

Legacy of Rome, the, Pt 1 22 MIN
16mm / U-matic / VHS
Saga of Western Man Series
Color (J)
LC FIA67-465
Describes the grandeur and imperial power of ancient Rome. Examines the influence on civilization of Roman achievements in the arts, the sciences, jurisprudence, and politics. Includes sequences filmed in Italy and in outposts of the Roman Empire from Libya to Scotland and from Jordan to the south of France.
History - United States; History - World
Dist - MGHT **Prod** - ABCTV 1966

Legacy of Rome, the, Pt 2 30 MIN
U-matic / VHS / 16mm
Saga of Western Man Series
Color (J)
LC FIA67-465
Describes the grandeur and imperial power of ancient Rome. Examines the influence on civilization of Roman achievements in the arts, the sciences, jurisprudence, and politics. Includes sequences filmed in Italy and in outposts of the Roman Empire from Libya to Scotland and from Jordan to the south of France.
History - United States; History - World
Dist - MGHT **Prod** - ABCTV 1966

Legacy of the Crusaders 5 MIN
U-matic
See, Hear - the Middle East Series
Color (J)
Examines the history of the Crusaders and their goal of a Christian Jerusalem, their defeat and the fortresses that still stand.
Geography - World; History - World; Religion and Philosophy
Dist - TVOTAR **Prod** - TVOTAR 1980

Legacy of the Mamluks 28 MIN
16mm / VHS
Color (H A)
$250.00 purchase, $65.00 rental
Examines the culture of the Mamluks, a powerful Islamic sect that controlled trade routes between Europe, the Far East, and parts of Africa between 1250 and 1517. Shows how their culture exerted a marked influence on the West and reveals their contributions in painting, architecture, textiles, glassware, and ceramics.
Fine Arts; History - World
Dist - AFA **Prod** - NSAVIN 1987

Legacy of the Mountain Men 29 MIN
16mm
Color (J)
LC 80-701985
Shows modern day mountain men re - creating the spirit and activities of 19th century fur trappers at an annual gathering in the western United States. Depicts people using period tools and participating in hatchet - throwing and shooting contests while other members of the group explain why they enjoy re - enacting the harsh and often lonely life of the trapper.
History - United States; Physical Education and Recreation
Dist - BYU **Prod** - BYU 1980
EBEC

The Legacy of the Mountainmen 29 MIN
U-matic / VHS / 16mm
Color (J H A)
Tells the story of 19th century mountainmen who roamed the western wilderness in search of valuable, fur - bearing animals.
History - United States; Physical Education and Recreation
Dist - EBEC **Prod** - BYU 1980

The Legacy of the New Deal 30 MIN
U-matic / VHS
America - the second century series
Color (H C)
$34.95 purchase
Discusses the legacy of FDR and the New Deal, which created the expectation that the national government can respond to national concerns. Part of a 30-part series that examines social, political, and economic issues in the United States since 1875.
History - United States
Dist - DALCCD **Prod** - DALCCD
GPN

The Legacy of the Shoguns 56 MIN
VHS / U-matic
Japan Series
Color (H C A)
$125 purchase _ #5846C
Examines the 17th century traditions and hierarchy and shows how these traditions brought about a military power bent on world domination in World War II. A production of WTTW, Chicago.
History - World
Dist - CORF

Legacy of the spirits 52 MIN
16mm / VHS
Caribbean culture series
Color (G)
$500.00 purchase, $90.00, $60.00 rental
Shows Vodou as a valid and serious belief system. Interweaves Vodou ceremonies, scholarly information, music and images of ritual objects. Traces the religion from Africa to Haiti to New York City. Explains its theology, pantheon of spirits, possession, sacred drawings, Catholic influences, history of persecution. Filmed within the Caribbean communities of NYC. Part of a series on Caribbean culture by Karen Kramer.
Geography - United States; Geography - World; History - World; Religion and Philosophy; Sociology
Dist - DOCEDR **Prod** - DOCEDR 1985

Legacy of Wings 40 MIN
U-matic / VHS
Color
Recounts the pioneering work performed by Harold F Pitcairn. Shows how Pitcairn's work with autogyros led to the development of the modern helicopter. Chronicles the events that led to the establishment of Eastern Airlines.
Industrial and Technical Education; Social Science
Dist - MIRABC **Prod** - MIRABC 1983

A Legacy Restored 10 MIN
16mm / U-matic / VHS
Color
Recounts the history of the California State Capitol and its recent restoration.
Geography - United States; History - United States
Dist - UCEMC **Prod** - UCEMC

Legacy series

Bernini's Rome	29 MIN
The Crystal Year	30 MIN
The Stones of Amiens	29 MIN
The Sun king	29 MIN
Verdun	29 MIN
A Voice Cries Out	29 MIN

Dist - IU

Legal Affairs 30 MIN
VHS / U-matic
How People Age Fifty and Up Can Plan for a more Successful 'Retirement Series
Color
Contains information concerning contracts, buying, selling and renting. Includes estate planning and other obligations. Presented by David Ralston.
Civics and Political Systems; Sociology
Dist - SYLWAT **Prod** - RCOMTV

Legal aspects - laws you should know 59 MIN
VHS
How to start your own business series
Color (H A T)
$69.95 purchase _ #NC119
Looks at the legal aspects of businesses. Part of a ten - part series on starting a business.
Business and Economics
Dist - AAVIM **Prod** - AAVIM 1992

Legal aspects - Module II 14 MIN
VHS / U-matic
Supervision of self administration of medication series
Color (PRO C)
$395.00 purchase, $80.00 rental _ #C920 - VI - 018
Trains supervisory staff for developmentally disabled clients. Reveals that responsibility for the supervision of administering medications begins when a staff member first brings an individual to a doctor's office. Discloses that staff is responsible for overseeing the visit as well as for obtaining the correct medicines from a licensed pharmacy and seeing that the medications are properly taken and the interaction documented. Reviews the procedures for staff caring for individuals with special needs. Part of a five - part series presented by the Richmond State School Staff Development, Texas Dept of Mental Health and Mental Retardation.
Health and Safety; Psychology
Dist - HSCIC

Legal aspects of marriage 30 MIN
U-matic / VHS
Family portrait - a study of contemporary lifestyles; Lesson 10
Color (C A)
Describes basic legal requirements and some differences between state's laws. Presents common - law marriages and marriage contracts as variations of the traditional ceremony.
Civics and Political Systems; Sociology
Dist - CDTEL **Prod** - SCCON

The Legal Aspects of Negligence 20 MIN
VHS / 16mm
Color (PRO)
$295.00 purchase, $60.00 rental
Considers five legal aspects of negligence - understanding the difference between civil and criminal liability, understanding the difference between intentional tort and negligence, the five elements of negligence, vicarious liability, and four techniques to help prevent negligence.
Health and Safety
Dist - FAIRGH **Prod** - FAIRGH 1990

Legal Bibliography 52 MIN
U-matic / VHS
Legal Training for Children Welfare Workers Series
Color
Helps social workers feel more comfortable in the courtroom setting and helps develop their legal skills. Part 1 of a series.
Civics and Political Systems; Sociology
Dist - UWISC **Prod** - UWISC 1975

Legal challenges in special education series
Presents a 12 - part series on Public Law 94 - 142. Features Reed Martin, JD. Overviews Public Law 94 - 142 and Supreme Court cases on the law; shows how to develop a workable IEP and related services; discusses school health services; defines the least restrictive environment, the extended school year, discipline of handicapped students, what courts are requiring in the IEP, commonly made procedural mistakes by schools, preparing for a hearing and Section 504. Includes resource materials with each tape.

Americans With Disabilities Act - Tape 14	44 MIN
Attention deficit disorder - Tape 15	55 MIN
Discipline of handicapped students - Tape 8	38 MIN
Extended school year - Tape 7	33 MIN
How to develop an IEP that works - Tape 3	53 MIN
How to prepare for a hearing - Tape 11	68 MIN
Individuals With Disabilities Education Act - Tape 13	40 MIN
Least restrictive environment - Tape 6	54 MIN
Most common procedural mistakes which schools make - Tape 10	38 MIN
Overview of Public Law 94 - 142 - the wrongs Congress required schools to right - Tape 1	49 MIN
Related services	62 MIN
School health services - separating medicine from education - Tape 5	62 MIN
Section 1983 and public schools - Tape 17	40 MIN
Section 504 - expanding school's duties to handicapped students - Tape 12	60 MIN
The Supreme Court cases on Public Law 94 - 142	62 MIN
Traumatic brain injury - Tape 16	52 MIN
What courts are requiring in the IEP - Tape 9	78 MIN

Dist - BAXMED

Legal challenges in special education series
Features Reed Martin, attorney, in a 17 - part series on legal challenges in special education.

Americans With Disabilities Act - Tape 14	44 MIN
Attention deficit disorder - Tape 15	55 MIN
Discipline of handicapped students - Tape 8	38 MIN
Extended school year - Tape 7	33 MIN
How to develop an IEP that works - Tape 3	53 MIN
How to prepare for a hearing - Tape 11	68 MIN
Individuals With Disabilities Education Act - Tape 13	40 MIN
Least restrictive environment - Tape 6	54 MIN
Most common procedural mistakes which schools make - Tape 10	38 MIN
Overview of Public Law 94 - 142 - the wrongs Congress required schools to right - Tape 1	49 MIN
Related services	62 MIN
School health services - separating medicine from education - Tape 5	62 MIN
Section 1983 and public schools - Tape 17	40 MIN
Section 504 - expanding school's duties to handicapped students - Tape 12	60 MIN
The Supreme Court cases on Public Law 94 - 142	62 MIN
Traumatic brain injury - Tape 16	52 MIN
What courts are requiring in the IEP - Tape 9	78 MIN

Dist - BAXMED

The Legal considerations of broadcast news 23 MIN
VHS
Color (J H C)
$39.95 purchase _ #IVMC09
Takes a close look at many of the legal considerations that broadcast stations must follow when covering the news. Looks at libel, privacy, freedom of information, equal time provision for political candidates - section 315, the Fairness Doctrine and obscenity or nudity on television. Defines the legal terms and examines some important cases which defined the law as it stands.
Fine Arts; Literature and Drama
Dist - INSTRU

Legal environment of transportation 30 MIN
VHS
Business logistics series
Color (G C)
$200.00 purchase, $20.50 rental _ #34972
Examines the legal environment of transportation. Part of a 30 - part series on business logistics which deals with movement and storage of raw and finished products, and with managerial activities important for effective control of these operations. Interviews logistics managers of major US corporations and transportation companies. Uses on - site segments to demonstrate logistical carrier operations. Features program author Dr John Coyle.
Business and Economics; Social Science
Dist - PSU **Prod** - WPSXTV 1987

Legal Ethics - Applying the Model Rules Series IL 60611

Investigation	32 MIN

Dist - ABACPE

Legal Ethics - Applying the Model Rules Series

Advocacy	40 MIN
Counseling	34 MIN
Interviewing and the Lawyer - Client Relationship	43 MIN
Negotiation	35 MIN

Dist - ABACPE

Legal fees for handling estates - Current trends 60 MIN
VHS
Color (A PRO C)
$95.00 purchase _ #Y123
Features a wills and estates attorney, a probate judge and an Internal Revenue Service evaluator who outline the current controversy, trends and practices in the setting of legal fees for administering decedents' estates. Looks at this area in which abuse by attorneys allegedly has been rampant and has led the IRS to step up enforcement measures through fines, penalties and readjustments to rectify the situation.
Civics and Political Systems
Dist - ALIABA **Prod** - CLETV 1990

Legal forms of carriage 30 MIN
VHS
Business logistics series
Color (G C)
$200.00 purchase, $20.50 rental _ #34973
Examines the legal forms of carriage. Part of a 30 - part series on business logistics which deals with movement and storage of raw and finished products, and with managerial activities important for effective control of these operations. Interviews logistics managers of major US corporations and transportation companies. Uses on - site segments to demonstrate logistical carrier operations. Features program author Dr John Coyle.
Business and Economics; Social Science
Dist - PSU **Prod** - WPSXTV 1987

Legal information for law enforcement series

Civil liability of police officers	23 MIN
Forcible entry - Pt 2 - excuse and trickery	20 MIN
Law in the Schools	30 MIN
Parole, Probation and the Police	28 MIN
Traffic Violation Stops	23 MIN

Dist - AIMS

Legal issues confronting today's nurses series
Presents two videos providing information on the growing malpractice crisis. Shows how to reduce your risk of being sued by covering the basics of a nursing malpractice lawsuit and providing guidelines for reducing liability. Discusses appropriate documentation in medical records and an overview of legal terminology. The second part offers an inside perspective on a nursing malpractice lawsuit. Nurses see firsthand what to expect if they are named as a defendant or called as a witness. Includes advice to help them prepare for the legal interrogation.

Defending the nurse malpractice lawsuit - Part 2	25 MIN
How to reduce your risk of being sued - Part 1	26 MIN
Legal issues confronting today's nurses series	51 MIN

Dist - AJN **Prod** - WWC 1987

Legal issues in groundwater protection 210 MIN
VHS
Color (C PRO A)
$52.50, $150.00 purchase, #M701, #P207
Discusses topics such as basic elements of groundwater protection, the resource and the threat; federal regulatory framework to protect groundwater from industrial substances and hazardous wastes; emerging problems in aquifer protection, state responses, wellhead protection, FIFRA, and non - profit sources; and toxic torts involving groundwater contamination. This program was cosponsored by the Environmental Law Institute.
Civics and Political Systems; Science - Natural; Sociology
Dist - ALIABA **Prod** - ALIABA 1987

Legal Issues, Processes and Roles in Foster Care, Pt I 60 MIN
VHS / U-matic
B&W
Discusses various aspects of legal and judicial matters in foster care, including provisions of the Children's Code, juvenile court procedures, attorney and social worker roles, legal rights of children/parents/foster parents and issues arising from dealing with family matters.
Civics and Political Systems; Sociology
Dist - UWISC **Prod** - UWISC 1978

Legal Issues, Processes and Roles in Foster Care, Pt II 60 MIN
U-matic / VHS
B&W
Continues discussion of various aspects of legal and judicial matters in foster care.
Civics and Political Systems; Sociology
Dist - UWISC **Prod** - UWISC 1978

Legal Issues, Processes and Roles in Foster Care, Pt III 33 MIN
U-matic / VHS
B&W
Concludes discussion of various aspects of legal and judicial matters in foster care.
Civics and Political Systems; Sociology
Dist - UWISC **Prod** - UWISC 1978

Legal limits 35 MIN
VHS
Color (A PRO IND)
$895.00 purchase, $175.00 rental
Considers the legal implications of the supervisor's role within a corporation. Covers various potential legal situations and how they can be anticipated and dealt with successfully. Uses three video case studies to illustrate the principles discussed.
Business and Economics; Guidance and Counseling; Psychology
Dist - VLEARN

Legal limits - supervisory liability workshop 120 MIN
VHS
Color (A)
$895.00 purchase
Presents a four - part seminar to help supervisors realize the legal aspects of their decisions in such situations as giving negative employee reviews, terminating employees, and dealing with accusations of harassment. Emphasizes problem - solving using company policies. Includes two videos, a leader's guide and one participant's workbook. Available in two formats, Plant and Office. Additional materials available separately.
Business and Economics; Civics and Political Systems; Education
Dist - COMFLM **Prod** - COMFLM

Legal opinion letters in real estate transactions 90 MIN
VHS
Color (C PRO A)
$190.00 purchase _ #P245
Advises attorneys on the drafting techniques and substantive components of legal opinion letters prepared for buyers, sellers and lenders in anticipation of real estate sales and purchases.
Business and Economics; Civics and Political Systems
Dist - ALIABA **Prod** - CLETV 1988

Legal or Illegal 20 MIN
VHS / U-matic
Contract Series
Color (J H)
English Language
Dist - AITECH **Prod** - KYTV 1977

Legal Reference Materials 24 MIN
U-matic / VHS
Color
Discusses Maryland legal reference materials. Describes statutory and administrative law in terms of the library patron's reference questions.
Education; Literature and Drama; Social Science
Dist - LVN **Prod** - BCPL

Legal Requirements for Boatmen 18 MIN
16mm
Color
LC 74-705020
Discusses state and federal requirements for boatmen. Shows federal requirements for boat numbering and documenting, lifesaving devices, fire extinguishers, horns and whistles, lights and accident reports.
Health and Safety; Physical Education and Recreation; Social Science
Dist - USNAC **Prod** - USGEOS 1968

Legal research made easy - a roadmap through the law library maze 150 MIN
VHS
Color (G)
$89.95 purchase _ #LRME
Explains how to use all the basic legal research tools in the law library. Includes 40 page booklet.
Civics and Political Systems
Dist - NOLO **Prod** - NOLO
UNKNWN

Legal Rights 30 MIN
VHS / U-matic
Rights and Citizenship Series
Color
Civics and Political Systems; Social Science
Dist - CAMB **Prod** - MAETEL

The Legal side of evaluating performance 19 MIN
VHS
Color (G PRO)
$550.00 purchase, $130.00 rental
Trains managers and supervisors in the area of performance evaluation of employees. Stresses the importance of communicating expectations and standards, discussing problems an employee might have in meeting performance standards, documenting all importance facets of the appraisal process and avoiding bias.
Business and Economics; Psychology
Dist - AMEDIA **Prod** - AMEDIA 1991

The Legal side of performance appraisal - you be the judge 18 MIN
VHS
Color (A PRO IND)
$495.00 purchase, $95.00 rental
Discusses how to give a performance appraisal that will withstand legal challenges. Outlines four points that must be included in a successful appraisal. Includes a participation segment.
Business and Economics; Guidance and Counseling; Psychology
Dist - VLEARN **Prod** - BBP

The Legal system 30 MIN
VHS
Inside Britain 3 series
Color; PAL; NTSC (G) (BULGARIAN CZECH HUNGARIAN SPANISH POLISH ROMANIAN RUSSIAN SLOVAK UKRAINIAN ENGLISH WITH ARABIC SUBTITLES LITHUANIAN)
PdS65 purchase
Looks at the legal system of Great Britain, which conjures up for many a picture of bewigged barristers and stern - faced judges. Reveals that the British system is founded on principles and precedents shaped by centuries of experience and tradition. Shows how the legal system, from Commercial Law to Criminal Law, is the fundamental framework around which society has been built.
Civics and Political Systems
Dist - CFLVIS **Prod** - WATSHE 1993

The Legal System 30 MIN
U-matic / VHS
American Government 2 Series
Color (C)
Dramatizes vignettes to explain and illustrate many types of law. Clarifies many ways Americans settle their legal disputes through constitutional, administrative, statutory, criminal and civil laws.
Civics and Political Systems
Dist - DALCCD **Prod** - DALCCD

Legal Training for Children Welfare Workers Series Pt IV
Termination of Parental Rights 59 MIN
Dist - UWISC

Legal Training for Children Welfare Workers Series Pt V
General Court Strategy 55 MIN
Dist - UWISC

Legal Training for Children Welfare Workers Series
Children's code 58 MIN
Delinquency 58 MIN
Grantsmanship and funding 60 MIN
Innovative services for children and youth 58 MIN
Legal Bibliography 52 MIN
Protective Services 58 MIN
Dist - UWISC

Legal Typing - a Lawyer Defines a Good Legal Secretary 11 MIN
BETA / VHS
Typing - Legal Series
Color
Business and Economics; Civics and Political Systems
Dist - RMIBHF **Prod** - RMIBHF

Legal Typing - Course Introduction 17 MIN
BETA / VHS
Typing - Legal Series
Color
Business and Economics; Civics and Political Systems
Dist - RMIBHF **Prod** - RMIBHF

Legalization...how 29 MIN
VHS
America's drug forum series
Color (G)
$19.95 purchase _ #112
Looks at the issue of drug legalization. Asks what it means and how it would be implemented. Examines and critically analyzes a variety of models. Guests include David Boaz, vice president, CATO Institute, Joseph Galiber, New York State senator, Richard Cowan, Cowan Investments, Dr Ethan Nadelman, Princeton University, Richard Dennis, C&D Commodities.
Civics and Political Systems; Health and Safety; Psychology
Dist - DRUGPF **Prod** - DRUGPF 1991

The Legate 30 MIN
16mm
B&W
LC FIA65-1100
A drama of the Jewish struggle for religious freedom in Jerusalem in the middle of the second century B C. Describes the role of a Roman legate in making treaty arrangements with Simon Maccabeus, victorious leader of the Jewish movement. Features the celebration of the festival of Hanukkah.
History - World; Religion and Philosophy
Dist - NAAJS **Prod** - JTS 1965

Legault's Place 11 MIN
16mm
B&W
LC 79-711267
A story about an old man who wanted from life only to be left in peace to live with his memories in the familiar comfort of his aging cabin. Tells how the city began to build around him, how he evaded eviction and how he eventually became wealthy from the sale of his cabin.
Industrial and Technical Education; Physical Education and Recreation
Dist - UNKNWN **Prod** - FI 1965

Legend and Legacy - Pt 3 60 MIN
VHS
Raphael Series
Color (G)
$39.95 purchase _ #RAP-03
Looks at Raphael's influence on other artists and raises the complex issues of tradition, continuity and classical values. Reappraises the work of Raphael in light of the changes that are taking part in contemporary culture. Features David Thompson, former art critic of the London Times, as writer and narrator of the programs which were shot on location in Urbino, Perugia, Florence and Rome where the artist lived and worked. Part three of three parts.
Fine Arts
Dist - CRYSP **Prod** - RMART 1986
ARTSAM BBCL
FI

A Legend at Big Sur 15 MIN
16mm
Color (C A)
Presents a surrealistic cinepoem on Big Sur, California.
Fine Arts; Geography - United States
Dist - CFS **Prod** - CFS

Legend Days are Over 5 MIN
16mm / U-matic / VHS
Color
LC 73-702324
Presents in kinestasis animation various aspects of the life of the American Indian, conveying the human impact of the cultural change from the world of legend to modern life.
Psychology; Social Science; Sociology
Dist - PFP **Prod** - PFP 1973

The Legend of Arthur 26 MIN
U-matic / VHS
Color (C)
$249.00, $149.00 purchase _ #AD - 895
Examines the blend of history, myth, religion and dreams that contributed to the development of the Arthurian legend. Shows Glastonbury and other sites where the legend is set.
Literature and Drama; Religion and Philosophy
Dist - FOTH **Prod** - FOTH

The Legend of Corn 26 MIN
U-matic / VHS / 16mm
Color
Dramatizes an Ojibway Indian legend telling how the Great Manitou sent corn to keep the people from hunger.
Literature and Drama; Social Science
Dist - FOTH **Prod** - FOTH

The Legend of Duncan Falls 22 MIN
U-matic
Color
Dramatizes the story of David Duncan, one of the first white explorers of the Muskingum River in Ohio.
Biography; History - United States
Dist - HRC **Prod** - OHC

The Legend of El Dorado 25 MIN
16mm
Color (SPANISH)
Studies the myth and reality of gold as viewed through the pre - Columbian treasure of Bogota's Gold Museum.
Fine Arts; History - World
Dist - MOMALA **Prod** - OOAS 1983

The Legend of Harriet Tubman 15 MIN
VHS
Juba Series
Color (G)
$25.00 purchase _ #JUBA - 104
Focuses on the story of Harriet Tubman, the black woman who founded the Underground Railroad which helped slaves escape to Canada. Tells her story in the folklore tradition.
History - United States; Literature and Drama
Dist - PBS **Prod** - WETATV 1978
WETATV

The Legend of Hiawatha 60 MIN
VHS
Color (K P I J)
$29.95 purchase _ #S02078
Presents an animated version of the legend of Hiawatha, based on the epic poem by Longfellow.
Literature and Drama
Dist - UILL

The Legend of John Henry 11 MIN
U-matic / VHS / 16mm
Color (P I J)
LC 74-700614
Features Roberta Flack singing the scored narrative describing John Henry's stubborn refusal to allow a mechanized steam drill win the Chesapeake and Ohio railroad's drive through the big bend tunnel in West Virginia, in 1873. Explains that John Henry, fictionalized for his prowess and stamina as a steel driver, died beating the steam drill through the mountain.
Fine Arts; Literature and Drama
Dist - PFP **Prod** - BOSUST 1974

Legend of Johnny Appleseed 20 MIN
U-matic / VHS / 16mm
Color (I)
LC FIA59-727
Presents legend of John Chapman, Johnny Appleseed, in verse and in music sung by Dennis Day.
Literature and Drama
Dist - CORF **Prod** - DISNEY 1958

Legend of Lake Titicaca 22 MIN
U-matic / VHS / 16mm
Undersea world of Jacques Cousteau series
Color (G)
$49.95 purchase _ #Q10607
A shortened version of Legend Of Lake Titicaca. Features Jacques Cousteau and his divers in search of Inca treasure in Lake Titicaca, 12,000 feet above sea level. Shows how they discover a unique species of aquatic frog instead of the treasure.
Physical Education and Recreation
Dist - CF **Prod** - METROM 1971

The Legend of Lobo 68 MIN
16mm
Color
Presents the true story of Lobo the wolf, who leads his family and the wolf pack into lands uninvaded by man.
Fine Arts
Dist - TWYMAN **Prod** - DISNEY 1962

The Legend of Mark Twain 32 MIN
16mm
Color (I)
LC 77-706298
Traces Samuel Clemen's remarkable life and writing career concerning America and dramatizes selections from two of his well - known classics 'THE ADVENTURES OF HUCKLEBERRY FINN' and 'THE CELEBRATED JUMPING FROG OF CALAVERAS COUNTY.'.
Literature and Drama
Dist - BNCHMK **Prod** - ABCTV 1969

The Legend of Old Bill 9 MIN
16mm
Color (I) (AMERICAN SIGN)
LC 76-701688
Presents Willard Madsen relating, in American sign language for the deaf, his own story about a town hermit called Old Bill.
Education; Guidance and Counseling; Literature and Drama
Dist - JOYCE **Prod** - JOYCE 1975

The Legend of Paul Bunyan 13 MIN
16mm / U-matic / VHS
Color (I)
LC 74-703191
Depicts Paul Bunyan, who was no ordinary man. Points out that embodied in him are the qualities of the early pioneers who helped to fashion the character of America.
Literature and Drama
Dist - PFP **Prod** - BOSUST 1973

The Legend of Paul Bunyan 15 MIN
U-matic / VHS / 16mm
Magic Carpet Series
Color (P)
Presents an adaptation of the legend of Paul Bunyan.
Literature and Drama
Dist - GPN **Prod** - SDCSS 1977

The Legend of Paulie Green 30 MIN
U-matic / VHS
Dial A - L - C - O - H - O - L Series
Color (H)
Shows the progress of an advisor with a drinking problem. Introduces the daughter of an alcoholic mother to Alateen, an organization for children of alcoholics.
Sociology
Dist - GPN **Prod** - EFLMC

Legend of Rockmonotone 15 MIN
16mm
Color (H C A)
Recaptures the great days of the silent melodrama through the story of hero Rockmonotone, his sweetheart Lotta Passionata and the villian Dudley Dagger.
Fine Arts
Dist - UWFKD **Prod** - UWFKD

The Legend of Salt - a South East Asian Folk Tale 7 MIN
16mm
Folk Tales from Around the World Series
Color (P I)
LC 80-700573
Tells how the greed of an evil brother and a magic salt jar turned the ocean salty.
Literature and Drama
Dist - SF **Prod** - ADPF 1980

The Legend of Sleepy Hollow 46 MIN
U-matic / VHS / 16mm
Classic Stories Series
Color (I J H)
Portrays the story of the Headless Horseman which haunts the Hudson Valley near Tarrytown, New York. Based on the story The Legend Of Sleepy Hollow by Washington Irving.
Literature and Drama
Dist - LUF **Prod** - LUF 1979

The Legend of Sleepy Hollow 20 MIN
16mm / U-matic / VHS
Color (I J H)
LC 74-703801
Uses animation to tell Washington Irving's tale about a gangly schoolmaster and a headless ghost who haunts the Hudson River region.
Literature and Drama
Dist - CORF **Prod** - DISNEY 1974

The Legend of Sleepy Hollow 30 MIN
VHS
Rabbit ears collection series
Color (K P I J)
$12.95 purchase _ #247564
Tells the Washington Irving tale of Ichabod Crane and the headless horseman. Features actress Glenn Close as narrator.
Literature and Drama
Dist - KNOWUN **Prod** - RABBIT

The Legend of Sleepy Hollow 13 MIN
U-matic / VHS / 16mm
Color (P I J H C)
LC 71-715300
An animated film based on 'THE LEGEND OF SLEEPY HOLLOW,' by Washington Irving. Illustrates the spectral spirits and twilight superstitions that haunt the town of Sleepy Hollow.
Literature and Drama
Dist - PFP **Prod** - BOSUST 1972

The Legend of Sleepy Hollow 99 MIN
U-matic / VHS / 16mm
Color (I J H)
Portrays the story of the Headless Horseman which haunts the Hudson Valley near Tarrytown, New York. Based on the story The Legend Of Sleepy Hollow by Washington Irving.
Literature and Drama
Dist - LUF **Prod** - LUF 1979

The Legend of Sleepy Hollow 13 MIN
U-matic / VHS / 16mm
Color (I) (SPANISH)
A Spanish language version of the film, The Legend of Sleepy Hollow. Relates Washington Irving's classic American folk tale and the story of Ichabod Crane in an animated film which retains the richness of Irving's original language.
Fine Arts; Foreign Language; Literature and Drama
Dist - PFP **Prod** - PFP

Legend of Sunshine Mountain 25 MIN
VHS
Sparky's animation series
Color (P I R)
$19.95 purchase, $10.00 rental _ #35 - 814 - 2020
Portrays Sparky and his friends as they explore the Indian heritage in their area. Shows how they learn to trust God in the face of danger.
Literature and Drama; Religion and Philosophy
Dist - APH **Prod** - ANDERK

The Legend of Suram Fortress 89 MIN
VHS / 35mm / 16mm
Films of Sergei Paradjanov series
Color (G) (RUSSIAN WITH ENGLISH SUBTITLES)
$300.00, $400.00 rental
Presents the first film of director Sergei Paradjanov after more than a decade of persecution and imprisonment. Adapts an ancient Georgian legend about unrequited love and the vengeance of an abandoned woman. Reveals that the woman becomes a soothsayer and advises the prince who spurned her to bury his son in the walls of Suram Fortress to protect it during a siege.
Fine Arts; Religion and Philosophy
Dist - KINOIC **Prod** - IFEX 1985

Legend of the Birds 22 MIN
16mm
Color (H C A)
LC 72-706200
A narrator uses the natural rhythm of Longfellow's 'HIAWATHA' to describe the habits of New Zealand's birds and to tell the many Maori legends about birds.
Literature and Drama; Science - Natural
Dist - NZNFU **Prod** - NZNFU 1960

The Legend of the bluebonnet 20 MIN
VHS / U-matic / 16mm
Color (K P I)
$495.00, $375.00, $345.00 purchase _ #A615
Adapts an old Texas legend about the Commanche people. Reveals that the Commanches are suffering from drought and famine because of their selfishness. The Great Spirit refuses to send rain until they give up their most valued possession. A young orphan girl, She - Who - Is - Alone, sacrifices her beloved doll to save her people, and the bluebonnet, the Texas state flower, becomes a remembrance of her selflessness. Adapted by Tomie dePaola.
Literature and Drama; Social Science
Dist - BARR **Prod** - DF 1991

The Legend of the Boy and the Eagle 21 MIN
U-matic / VHS / 16mm
Color (P I J)
LC 76-701285
Presents an adaptation of the Legend of The Boy And The Eagle, a drama story about a young Hopi Indian boy who suffers grave consequences after he frees the sacred eagle of his tribe.
Literature and Drama; Social Science
Dist - CORF **Prod** - DISNEY 1976

Legend of the Cruel Giant 11 MIN
U-matic / VHS / 16mm
Color (K P)
LC 72-713873
Pictures an innocent fisherman releasing the genie and being rewarded with chests of jewels and gold. Shows how the genie grows into a cruel giant who brings plague and war into the world. Concludes with the fisherman tricking the genie back into the bottle.
Guidance and Counseling; Literature and Drama
Dist - CAROUF **Prod** - SYZMT 1971

Legend of the Ilima Blossoms 11 MIN
16mm
Color (I)
Presents the Hawaiian legend telling how the ilima blossoms appeared and why they could be worn only by those of royal lineage.
Geography - United States; Literature and Drama
Dist - CINEPC **Prod** - CINEPC

The Legend of the Indian paintbrush - 73
VHS
Reading rainbow series
Color; CC (K P)
$39.95 purchase
Journeys with a young Indian boy as he follows his vision quest to find the special gift he can give his people in a story retold and illustrated by Tomie dePaolo. Looks at the crucial role of Mother Earth in the art of the Pueblo Indians of New Mexico. Shows how they use natural materials in their pottery, buckskin painting and dance. Visits Taos Pueblo which provides a beautiful backdrop for LeVar and three Pueblo artists. Part of a series offering a multicultural approach to generating reading enthusiasm with cross - curricular applications, hosted by LeVar Burton.
English Language; Literature and Drama; Social Science
Dist - GPN **Prod** - LNMDP

Legend of the Indian Paintbrush - Lifecycle of the honeybees
VHS
Reading rainbow treasury series
Color (K P)
$12.95 purchase _ #516469
Presents two animated stories. Features Levar Burton as host. Part of a six - part series.
English Language; Fine Arts; Literature and Drama; Science - Natural
Dist - KNOWUN **Prod** - PBS

The Legend of the lightning bird 55 MIN
16mm / VHS
Life science - ecosystems series
Color (I J H C)
$795.00, $545.00 purchase, $80.00, $55.00 rental
Examines the Hammerkop, hammer - headed stork, which is viewed by African legend as the king of birds, having magical powers. Reveals that its virtually impregnable nest can weigh 200 pounds. Looks at the Egyptian stork and the kestrel - a small falcon. Covers the concepts of predator - prey population control, food webs, display - mating - bonding, nest building, rearing young, niches, communities, symbiosis and parasitism. Produced by Alan Root. Part of a series. Also available in 30 - minute version.
Geography - World; Science - Natural
Dist - BNCHMK

The Legend of the Lone Ranger 72 MIN
U-matic / VHS / 16mm
B&W
Tells how the Lone Ranger got his mask and became an intrepid crime fighter. Stars Clayton Moore and Jay Silverheels.
Fine Arts
Dist - FI **Prod** - UNKNWN 1957

Legend of the Magic Knives 11 MIN
16mm / U-matic / VHS
Color (I J H)
LC 72-711059
Portrays an ancient Indian legend in the setting of a totem village in the Pacific Northwest. Deals with an old chief who realizes that the carvings of an apprentice are superior to his and decides to knife him.
Literature and Drama; Social Science
Dist - EBEC **Prod** - EBEC 1971

Legend of the Niu 11 MIN
16mm
Color (G)
Tells one of the legends of Hawaii in which a boy shares his meager food with a hungry stranger. In return the islanders are given niu, the coconut, as a source of food, clothing and shelter.
Geography - United States; History - United States; Literature and Drama; Religion and Philosophy; Sociology
Dist - CINEPC **Prod** - TAHARA 1986

The Legend of the Paramo 22 MIN
U-matic / VHS / 16mm
Color (I) (SPANISH)
LC 78-700461
Portrays the cultural identity of South American people through the fantasy of a 12 - year - old boy in Colombia who recalls the legend of the Paramo, a desolate highland region near Caldas, Colombia, replete with stories of witchcraft and adventure.
Geography - World; Literature and Drama; Social Science; Sociology
Dist - PHENIX **Prod** - SAMPER 1967

Legend of the Red Maple Leaf 15 MIN
16mm / U-matic / VHS
Color (K P)
Presents a Chinese fairy tale about the impending marriage of Jade Blossom to Morning Star and the vow of the evil ruler Night Shadow to separate them. Relates the fantastic adventures which culminate in a happy ending.
Literature and Drama
Dist - TEXFLM **Prod** - AUDBRF

Legend of the Stick Game 30 MIN
U-matic
Real People Series
Color
Explores the functions of myth and legend in American Indian culture. Describes the role of the oral tradition.
Social Science; Sociology
Dist - GPN **Prod** - KSPSTV 1976

Legend of the Stick Game 29 MIN
VHS / U-matic
Real People Series
Color (G)
Recreates how the 'stick game' came to be. It illustrates some of the many functions of myth or legend in Native American culture and the role of the 'oral tradition.'.
Social Science
Dist - NAMPBC **Prod** - NAMPBC 1976

Legend of the White Snake 145 MIN
VHS
Color (G) (MANDARIN CHINESE)
$45.00 purchase _ #2004A
Presents a Mandarin Chinese language movie produced in the People's Republic of China.
Fine Arts; Geography - World; Literature and Drama
Dist - CHTSUI **Prod** - CHTSUI

Legend of Tianyun Mountain 127 MIN
VHS
Color (G) (CHINESE)
$45.00 purchase _ #1021C
Presents a film from the People's Republic of China.
Geography - World; Literature and Drama
Dist - CHTSUI

Legendary lineman
VHS
NFL series
Color (G)
$24.95 purchase _ #NFL2005V
Profiles several of the greatest linemen in National Football League history. Produced by NFL Films.
Literature and Drama; Physical Education and Recreation
Dist - CAMV

Legendary service 180 MIN
VHS
Color (A PRO IND)
$1,295.00 purchase, $250.00 rental
Features service experts Ken Blanchard, Gary Heil, and Richard Tate in an exploration of the ten fundamentals of 'legendary' customer service. Profiles service - oriented companies including Nordstrom, American Honda, and Domino's Pizza.
Business and Economics; Guidance and Counseling; Psychology; Sociology
Dist - VLEARN
FI
MAGVID
UTM
VICOM
VPHI

Legendary service overview 60 MIN
U-matic / VHS
Color (PRO A G)
$795.00, $895.00 purchase, $250.00 rental
Outlines ten basic principles in an overview of the video course Legendary Service. Shows visits to such customer service leaders as Nordstrom, American Honda, Domino's and Pacific Gas and Electric. Features Dr. Ken Blanchard, Gary Heil, and Richard Tate. Includes a worksheet.
Business and Economics; Guidance and Counseling; Psychology
Dist - EXTR **Prod** - VPHI

Legendary trails - everyman special series 200 MIN
VHS
Legendary trails - everyman special series
Color (A)
PdS200 purchase _ Unavailable in the USA
Explores four different expressions of the pilgrim's search - in the Himalayas, the mountains of Peru and the Pyrenees, and to Jerusalem.
Religion and Philosophy
Dist - BBCENE

Legendary voices - cantors of yesterday 55 MIN
VHS
B&W (G)
$49.95 purchase _ #765
Offers film recordings from the 1930s of outstanding cantors - David Roitman, Adolph Katchko, Samuel Malavsky, Josef Shlisky, Leibele Waldman, Moyshe Oysher and Yossele Rosenblatt. Includes an excerpt of Rosenblatt singing in a rowboat on the Jordan River.
Fine Arts; Religion and Philosophy; Sociology
Dist - ERGOM **Prod** - ERGOM

The Legendary West 53 MIN
16mm / U-matic / VHS
American Documents Series
Color (J H A)
Uses Hollywood motion pictures and archive material to trace the creation of the legend of the West. Compares the popular image of bandits, badmen, law officers and the American Indian with respect to the way it really was.
History - United States
Dist - LUF **Prod** - LUF 1976

Legendary Women in Dance - Syvilla Fort and Thelma Hill 30 MIN
U-matic / VHS
Third World Dance - Tracing Roots Series
Color
Fine Arts; Industrial and Technical Education; Sociology
Dist - ARCVID **Prod** - ARCVID

Legends of American skiing 80 MIN
VHS
Color; B&W (G)
$29.95 purchase
Documents the history of skiing in North America through photos, music and film, including footage from 1916.
Fine Arts; Physical Education and Recreation
Dist - NEFILM

Legends of bottleneck blues guitar 58 MIN
VHS
Color (G)
$24.95 purchase _ #VDZ - BG01
Presents rare, historical footage from 1965 - 1970 of some of the greatest slide blues guitarists. Features Son House, Fred McDowell, Mance Lipscomb, Johnny Shines, Furry Lewis and Jesse Fuller on a number of songs. Includes booklet.
Fine Arts
Dist - HOMETA **Prod** - HOMETA

Legends of country blues guitar - Volume 1 58 MIN
VHS
Color (G)
$24.95 purchase _ #VDZ - CG01
Presents rare footage from a myriad of sources depicting some of the greatest blues musicians. Features Mississippi John Hurt, Son House, Rev Gary Davis, Big Bill Broonzy, Robert Pete Williams, Mance Lipscomb, Henry Townsend, Brownie McGhee and Josh White. Includes the songs Silver City; Angel Child; Spike Driver; You're Going to Walk that Lonesome Valley Blues; Cairo Blues; Death Letter Blues; I Had a Woman in Hughes; Children of Zion; Worried Man Blues; How You Want it Done; John Henry; Blues in E; Mamie, Don't Kid Me; Jelly Jelly; Death Don't Have No Mercy; and a booklet.
Fine Arts
Dist - HOMETA **Prod** - HOMETA

Legends of country blues - Volume 2 60 MIN
VHS
Color (G)
$24.95 purchase _ #VDZ - CG02
Presents rare footage from a myriad of sources depicting some of the greatest blues musicians. Features Big Joe Williams - Sloppy Drunk Blues, Highway 49, Providence Help the Poor People; Bukka White - Aberdeen Mississippi Blues, Poor Boy; Rev Gary Davis - Buck Dance, Hard Walking Blues, Make - Believe Stunt, Keep Your Lamp Trimmed and Burning; Son House - Yonder Comes the Blues; Leadbelly - Goodnight Irene, The Grey Goose, Pick a Bale of Cotton, Take this Hammer; Houston Stackhouse - Cool Drink of Water; Sam Chatmon - Big Road Blues, That's All Right, Sam's Rag. Includes booklet.
Fine Arts
Dist - HOMETA **Prod** - HOMETA 1994

Legends of Easter Island 58 MIN
U-matic / VHS
Nova series
Color (H C A)
$250.00 purchase _ #HP - 5922C
Investigates the legends, artifacts and monoliths of Easter Island. Recalls that the original culture of peaceful statue builders and worshipers mysteriously disappeared 40 years after the discovery of Easter Island by Dutch admiral Jacob Rogeveen. Tries to explain where the present inhabitants came from, if they descended from the statue building culture, and why they abruptly stopped building colossal human figures. Part of a two - part series on Easter Island and part of the Nova series.
Fine Arts; History - World
Dist - CORF **Prod** - WGBHTV 1989

Legends of old time music
VHS
Color (G)
$22.50 purchase _ #VEST13026
Features Clarence Ashley, Doc Watson, Roscoe Holcomb, Sam McGee, Tommy Jarrell and others.
Fine Arts
Dist - ROUNDR **Prod** - VESTAP 1995

Legends of the Salmon People 26 MIN
16mm
Color (G)
#3X126
Presents three Indian legends which give insight into the Northwestern Coast Indian's way of life and the beliefs of the people. Discusses the subject clan system. Gives a short history of the possible backgrounds of the Salish, Haida, Bella Coola, Tlingt, and other groups.
Social Science
Dist - CDIAND **Prod** - DEVGCF 1977

Legends of traditional fingerstyle guitar 58 MIN
VHS
Color (G)
$24.95 purchase _ #VDZ - LF01
Presents archival footage of some of the greatest fingerstyle players when they were at their peak - Merle Travis - John Henry, Mus'rat, Lost John; Sam and Kirk McGee - Railroad Blues, Wheels, Victory Rag; Mance Lipscomb - Take Me Back, Run Sinner Run; Roscoe Holcomb - Poor Wayfaring Stranger; Elizabeth Cotten - Goin' Down the Road; Mama Your Papa Loves You; Freight Train, Vestapol; Doc Watson - Deep River Blues, Traveling Man; Doc and Merle Watson - When I Lay My Burden Down, Sitting on Top of the World, Got the Blues, Can't Be Satisfied; Josh White - John Henry; Brownie McGhee and Sonny Terry - Keys to the Highway; Rev Gary Davis - I Belong to the Band. Includes booklet.
Fine Arts
Dist - HOMETA **Prod** - HOMETA

The Legislative branch 58 MIN
U-matic / 16mm / VHS
Government as it is series
Color (J)
A shortened version of the motion picture The Legislative Branch. Analyzes how the United States Congress works by presenting interviews with several senators and congressmen. Narrated by Jack Anderson.
Civics and Political Systems
Dist - PFP **Prod** - EMLEN

The Legislative Game - Government Relations, Political Action 40 MIN
Videoreel / VHS
Color (A)
Provides instructions to allow AACD members to exercise political influence. Shows, in two parts, how to become involved in grassroots legislative action.
Civics and Political Systems
Dist - AACD **Prod** - AACD

The Legislative Process 30 MIN
VHS / 16mm
Government by Consent - a National Perspective Series
Color (I J H C A)
Focuses on the Japanese - American Reparation Bill (Civil Liberties Act) of1988 to illustrate the basic steps in lawmaking. Describes the points at which individuals can influence the outcome of legislation.
Civics and Political Systems
Dist - DALCCD **Prod** - DALCCD 1990

Legislative Report 29 MIN
U-matic
Woman Series
Color
Covers legislation that would benefit women, including child care, credit, national health insurance, displaced homemakers' legislation, and the Humphrey - Hawkins Bill.
Civics and Political Systems; Sociology
Dist - PBS **Prod** - WNEDTV

Legislative Report Update 29 MIN
U-matic
Woman Series
Color
Discusses attempts to lobby for women's issues.
Civics and Political Systems; Sociology
Dist - PBS **Prod** - WNEDTV

Legs and buttocks 60 MIN
VHS
Body sculpting series
Color (G)
$39.99 purchase _ #MFV019V
Presents a series of weight training exercises to shape the leg and buttock muscles.
Physical Education and Recreation; Science - Natural
Dist - CAMV **Prod** - CAMV 1988

Lehman Caves National Monument 12 MIN
16mm
Color (A)
LC 77-703222
Focuses on the formation of limestone caves featuring the singular effects in the Lehman Caves in Lehman Caves National Monument in Nevada.
Geography - United States; Science - Physical
Dist - USNAC **Prod** - USNPS 1971

Leiden Connection 20 MIN
16mm
Export Development Series
Color
LC 79-700108
Describes the trade opportunity program administered by the Industry And Trade Administration, including its computer matching service which brings together American sellers and foreign buyers.
Business and Economics
Dist - USNAC **Prod** - USIATA 1978

The Leidenfrost Effect 30 MIN
U-matic / VHS
Kinetic Karnival of Jearl Walker Pt 5
Color (H)
LC 83-706119
Presents physics professor Jearl Walker offering graphic and unusual demonstrations exemplifying the principles of the Leidenfrost effect, in which rapid evaporation prevents the immediate transfer of heat.
Science - Physical
Dist - GPN **Prod** - WVIZTV 1982

Leisure 10 MIN
16mm
B&W (G)
$10.00 rental
Dramatizes a social commentary with the interference of a three - hundred ton chunk of margarine.
Fine Arts
Dist - CANCIN **Prod** - KUCHAR 1966

Leisure 25 MIN
VHS
Dragon's tongue series
Color (J H G)
$195.00 purchase
Teaches basics of Putonghua, China's official language. Presents one video in a series of nineteen helping students develop comprehension skills by using only Chinese - no subtitles. Shows authentic scenes of Chinese homes, cities and the countryside. Features Colin Mackerras of Griffith University.
Foreign Language
Dist - LANDMK

Leisure 14 MIN
16mm / U-matic / VHS
Color (H C A)
LC 77-700625
Uses animation to bring to life period prints, paintings and archival photographs which illustrate the history of man's quest for leisure. Offers ideas on how leisure time will be spent in the future.
Physical Education and Recreation; Sociology
Dist - PFP **Prod** - FLMAUS 1977

Leisure 20 MIN
16mm
Color (H C A)
$365 purchase, $45 rental
Explores the possibility of a three day work week in the future and the problems created by too much leisure.
Sociology
Dist - CNEMAG **Prod** - DOCUA 1988

Leisure and Recreation 28 MIN
VHS / U-matic
Personal Finance and Money Management Series
Color (C A)
Business and Economics; Civics and Political Systems
Dist - SCCON **Prod** - SCCON 1987

Leisure and Recreation 30 MIN
VHS / U-matic
Personal Finance Series Lesson 7
Color (C A)
Presents travel and vacation options such as trip insurance, time - sharing arrangements, and home exchange programs. Discusses precautions to take before leaving on a vacation.
Sociology
Dist - CDTEL **Prod** - SCCON

Leisure and tourism 30 MIN
VHS
Inside Britain 3 series
Color; PAL; NTSC (G) (BULGARIAN CZECH HUNGARIAN SPANISH POLISH ROMANIAN RUSSIAN SLOVAK UKRAINIAN ENGLISH WITH ARABIC SUBTITLES LITHUANIAN)
PdS65 purchase
Shows how leisure and tourism have become major industries. Reveals that one of Britain's most popular cities - York - has managed to increase the number of visitors welcomed each year by concentrating on offering value for money services and attractions.
Geography - World; Sociology
Dist - CFLVIS **Prod** - CALYTV 1993

Leisure and Vacations 11 MIN
16mm / U-matic / VHS
Life in Modern France Series
Color (I J H)
Examines how the French spend their leisure time, including such activities as soccer, rugby, sailing, mountain climbing and touring.
Geography - World; Sociology
Dist - EBEC **Prod** - EBEC 1971

Leisure - attention all workaholics and churchaholics - Tape 3
VHS
Strengthening your grip series
Color (H C G A R)
$10.00 rental _ #36 - 892003 - 533
Features Chuck Swindoll in a discussion of leisure and its proper role for Christians.
Religion and Philosophy
Dist - APH **Prod** - WORD

Leisure Planning - a Gerontological Approach 22 MIN
VHS / U-matic
Color
Tells how to identify and manage problems in leisure planning for the elderly. Presents objective and subjective observations, and addresses twenty problems, psychological needs and goal statements.
Health and Safety; Psychology; Sociology
Dist - USNAC **Prod** - USVA

Leisure Time Photography 20 MIN
16mm / U-matic / VHS
Color (J)
Shows world class photographer Freeman Patterson conducting a course in 'making pictures,' the medium he considers to be the most accessible for leisure time pursuits and one offering unlimited opportunities for self - expression.
Fine Arts; Sociology
Dist - BCNFL **Prod** - HARDAP 1981

Leisure Time Photography 18 MIN
U-matic / VHS / 16mm
Color (H C A)
LC 80-701590
Describes photography as a hobby that provides people with a creative outlet and actually improves their ability to appreciate their surroundings. Shows professional photographer Freeman Patterson teaching students his beliefs and techniques.
Industrial and Technical Education
Dist - BCNFL **Prod** - BCNFL 1980

Leisure Time - USSR 12 MIN
16mm
Russia Today Series
Color (J H)
LC 73-701842
Examines how the Russian worker spends his increasing leisure time and how this affects the nature of Soviet society. Pictures common diversions such as concerts, the circus, amusement parks and sports.
Geography - World; Physical Education and Recreation
Dist - IFF **Prod** - IFF 1968

Leisureland Natal 14 MIN
16mm / VHS
Color (G)
Explores Durban and its surroundings. Includes an exploration of the Indian Ocean's shoreline north and south of Durban. Features area activities such as fishing, boating and sun bathing. Available for free loan from the distributor.
Geography - World
Dist - AUDPLN

L'Elisir D'Amore 132 MIN
VHS
Color (S) (ITALIAN)
$29.95 purchase _ #384 - 9608
Revives the elegant comedy by Donizetti, 'L'Elisir D'Amore' in a Metropolitan Opera production. Includes Nicola Rescigno as conductor and a cast of Luciano Pavarotti, Judith Blegen and Sesto Bruscatini.
Fine Arts; Foreign Language
Dist - FI **Prod** - PAR 1988

L'elisir d'amore 132 MIN
VHS
Metropolitan opera series
Color (G) (ITALIAN WITH ENGLISH SUBTITLES)
$29.95 purchase
Stars Luciano Pavarotti, Judith Blegen, Brent Ellis, and Sesto Bruscantini in a performance of 'L'Elisir D'Amore' by Donizetti. Conducted by Nicola Riscigno. Includes a brochure with plot, historic notes, photographs, and production credits.
Fine Arts
Dist - PBS **Prod** - WNETTV 1981

The Lemmings and Arctic Bird Life 21 MIN
16mm / U-matic / VHS
White Wilderness Series
Color (I) (DUTCH SWEDISH PORTUGUESE GERMAN NORWEGIAN)
Discusses the life of the Lemming. Illustrates how lakes and lagoons become havens for waterfowl and places for food for polar bears and ermine.
Geography - World; Science - Natural
Dist - CORF **Prod** - DISNEY 1964

The Lemon Drop Kid 91 MIN
16mm / U-matic / VHS
B&W (C A)
Stars Bob Hope as the Lemon Drop Kid who caused gangster Moose Moran to lose 10,000 dollars following a bad tip at the race - track.
Literature and Drama; Sociology
Dist - FI **Prod** - PAR 1951

The Lemon Grove Incident 58 MIN
U-matic / VHS / 16mm
Color (H C A)
$895 purchase - 16 mm, $595 purchase - video, $95 rental
Describes an attempted segregation of Hispanic and white children in the school district of Lemon Grove, California in the early 1930s. Recreates historic events and the racial climate in Depression era America. Dramatizes school board meetings and community meetings of Mexican American parents. Directed by Frank Christopher. Produced by Paul Espinosa.
Education; Social Science; Sociology
Dist - CNEMAG

Lemonade Suite 30 MIN
VHS / U-matic
Color (H C A)
LC 83-706042
Employs rhythmic instrumental compositions and fluid modern - dance movements to interpret selected poems by Gwendolyn Brooks. Relates the story of a girl who lusts for adventure, gets pregnant, suffers an abortion, then renews her vigor for life.
Literature and Drama
Dist - IU **Prod** - WINNER 1981

Lempad of Bali 55 MIN
VHS / U-matic
Color (J H C A)
$150.00
Describes the large body of art and architecture left by Lempad, a master artist of Bali who died at the age of 116 in 1978.
Fine Arts; History - World
Dist - LANDMK **Prod** - LANDMK 1986

Lemurs 27 MIN
U-matic / VHS / BETA
Stationary ark series
Color; PAL (G H C)
PdS50, PdS58 purchase
Discusses the recreation of humankind, nature and wildlife in part of a 12 - part series. Features Gerald Durrell. Filmed on location in Jersey, England.
Science - Natural
Dist - EDPAT

Len Chandler 52 MIN
VHS / U-matic
Rainbow quest series
Color
Features Pete Seeger and Len Chandler trading songs they have written including 'Keep On Keeping On,' and 'Beans in my Ears.'.
Fine Arts
Dist - NORROS **Prod** - SEEGER

Lena Kennedy 40 MIN
VHS
Color (H C G)
$79.00 purchase
Features the writer discussing her life in London's Cockney district and her use of childhood events and friendships for resource material. Talks about her works including Maggie; Autumn Alley; Nelly Kelly; and Lily, My Lovely.
Literature and Drama; Sociology
Dist - ROLAND **Prod** - INCART

Lena the Glassblower 25 MIN
U-matic / VHS / 16mm
World Cultures and Youth Series
Color (J)
Introduces Lena Sundberg who is glassblowing at the Orresfors Glassworks in Sweden. Follows her through her work at the factory as she learns the difficult breath control and dexterity needed to produce fine glasswork. Shows how she pursuades her parents to let her forego college for glassblowing.
Geography - World; Sociology
Dist - CORF **Prod** - SUNRIS 1981

Lena the Glassblower - Sweden 25 MIN
16mm / U-matic / VHS
World Cultures and Youth Series
Color (I J H A)
$520.00, $250.00 purchase _ #4261
Discusses the craft of glassblowing and a girl's decision to leave the university to become a glassblower.
Fine Arts
Dist - CORF

Lend a Paw 8 MIN
U-matic / VHS / 16mm
Color (P I)
LC 75-703560
Shows conflict between good and evil in the individual and poses typical dilemmas about self - worth and personal denial by presenting a story about Pluto's problem with a new kitten.
Fine Arts; Guidance and Counseling; Sociology
Dist - CORF **Prod** - DISNEY 1975

L'Enfant Et Les Sortileges 51 MIN
VHS
Color (K)
$39.95 purchase _ #833 - 9300
Involves a roomful of furnishings that come to life to seek revenge on a naughty young boy. Features choreography by Jiri Kylian who has adapted the opera 'L'Enfant Et Les Sortileges' by Ravel to dance. The Nederlands Dans Theater performs the piece and John McFarlane designed the stage.
Fine Arts; Physical Education and Recreation
Dist - FI **Prod** - RMART 1987

L'Enfant Et Les Sortileges 49 MIN
VHS
Color (K) (FRENCH)
$29.95 purchase _ #833 - 9320
Brings together children's book author Maurice Sendak as set designer, Cynthia Buchan singing the role of the naughty boy in 'L'Enfant Et Les Sortileges' by Ravel, and Simon Rattle conducting the London Philharmonic Orchestra. Offers a definitive production by Glyndebourne.
Fine Arts; Foreign Language
Dist - FI

Length 15 MIN
U-matic
Math Makers Two Series
Color (I)
Presents the math concepts of the origins of metric measurement, definitions of centimetres, millimetres and kilometres and problems involving measurement with body movements or activities.
Education; Mathematics
Dist - TVOTAR **Prod** - TVOTAR 1980

Length 25 MIN
VHS / U-matic
Metric Education Video Tapes for Pre and Inservice Teachers - K - 8 Series
Color
Discusses the most common metric units of length and presents guidelines for relating these lengths to everyday use.
Mathematics
Dist - PUAVC **Prod** - PUAVC

Length of a Plane Curve
U-matic
Calculus Series
Color
Mathematics
Dist - MDCPB **Prod** - MDDE

Lenin 39 MIN
U-matic / VHS / 16mm
B&W (J)
LC 78-700117
Documents the life and times of Lenin. Includes archival footage.
Biography; Business and Economics; History - World
Dist - LCOA **Prod** - GRANDA 1978

Lenin 40 MIN
VHS
Heroes and tyrants of the twentieth century series
Color (J H C G)
$29.95 purchase _ #MH6028V
Portrays Vladimir Ilyich Lenin, convict, prophet, exile, conspirator, and one of the greatest revolutionary thinkers in human history. Recreates the life of the leader of the Bolshevik Revolution and founder of the Russian Commmunist Party and the first head of the Soviet State. Reveals a ravaged and chaotic Russia and the fiery speeches of Lenin. Part of a six - part series on 20th - century leaders.
Civics and Political Systems; History - World
Dist - CAMV

Lenin and the Great Ungluing 57 MIN
U-matic / VHS / 16mm
Age of Uncertainty Series
Color (H C A)
LC 77-701489
Focuses on the breakup of the old political order in Soviet Russia under Lenin. Based on the book The Age Of Uncertainty by John Kenneth Galbraith.
Biography; Business and Economics; Civics and Political Systems
Dist - FI **Prod** - BBCL 1977

Lenin and the Great Ungluing, Pt 1 28 MIN
16mm / U-matic / VHS
Age of Uncertainty Series
Color (H C A)
LC 77-701489
Focuses on the breakup of the old political order in Soviet Russia under Lenin. Based on the book The Age Of Uncertainty by John Kenneth Galbraith.
History - World
Dist - FI **Prod** - BBCL 1977

Lenin and the Great Ungluing, Pt 2 29 MIN
U-matic / VHS / 16mm
Age of Uncertainty Series
Color (H C A)
LC 77-701489
Focuses on the breakup of the old political order in Soviet Russia under Lenin. Based on the book The Age Of Uncertainty by John Kenneth Galbraith.
History - World
Dist - FI **Prod** - BBCL 1977

Lenin Prepares for Revolution 22 MIN
U-matic / VHS / 16mm
Russian Revolution Series
B&W
LC 76-712763
Traces the role of Lenin as a revolutinary in his early life. Conveys the feeling of popularity he had with the masses and constant harassment from the government which was caused by his unswerving devotion to the overthrow of the Tsar. Portrays Lenin's leadership not as the cause of the revolution, but as an imprint on the revolution and modern Russia.
Biography; Civics and Political Systems; History - World
Dist - FI **Prod** - GRATV 1971

The Leningrad legend 71 MIN
VHS
Color; Hi-fi; Dolby stereo (G)
$29.95 purchase _ #1298
Features ballerina Natalia Makarova as host at a behind - the - scenes look at the Kirov Ballet. Recalls the company's past in clips and archival photos and focuses on the company's resolve to develop into a modern entity. Visits the Vaganova School where the tradition of classical ballet began 250 years ago.
Fine Arts; Geography - World
Dist - KULTUR **Prod** - KULTUR 1991

The Leningrad Mint 15 MIN
16mm / U-matic / VHS
Color (J H C)
LC 79-713872
Illustrates minting procedures at the Leningrad mint.
Business and Economics; Geography - World
Dist - CAROUF **Prod** - LENPSF 1971

The Leningrad Movie - Pt 12 58 MIN
VHS
Comrades Series
Color (S)
$79.00 purchase _ #351 - 9032
Follows twelve Soviet citizens from different backgrounds to reveal what Soviet life is like for a cross section of the 270 million inhabitants in the vast country of fifteen republics. Features Frontline anchor Judy Woodruff who also interviews prominent experts on Soviet affairs. Part 12 of the twelve - part series zooms in on controversial filmmaker Dinara Asnaova, who is also one of the USSR's few women directors. Goskino, the state cinema organization supplies the money for making films but also controls their production. Asanova bends the rules to create anomalistic films.
Civics and Political Systems; Fine Arts; Geography - World
Dist - FI **Prod** - WGBHTV 1988

Lennart Bruce - 2 - 13 - 75 30 MIN
VHS / Cassette
Poetry Center reading series
Color (G)
$15.00, $45.00 purchase, $15.00 rental _ #98 - 73
Features the writer reading from his works at the Poetry Center, San Francisco State University, with an introduction by Kathleen Fraser.
Literature and Drama
Dist - POETRY **Prod** - POETRY 1975

Lennart Bruce - 2 - 7 - 85 30 MIN
VHS / Cassette
Poetry Center reading series
Color (G)
$15.00, $45.00 purchase, $15.00 rental _ #612 - 518
Features the writer reading from his works at the Poetry Center, San Francisco State University, with an introduction by Jim Hartz.
Literature and Drama
Dist - POETRY **Prod** - POETRY 1985

Lenni Workman 25 MIN
VHS / U-matic
View from My Room is Great series
Color (H C)
Presents a video portrait of artist Lenni Workman.
Fine Arts
Dist - QUEENU **Prod** - KAA 1985

L'Ennui 18 MIN
16mm
B&W
LC 74-702740
Presents three short sequences with and without narration which create a synthesis of the real and the unreal.
Fine Arts
Dist - CANFDC **Prod** - ONCA 1973

Lenny 112 MIN
16mm
B&W (G)
$150.00 rental
Portrays the tortured self - destructive, brilliantly inventive comic Lenny Bruce, played by Dustin Hoffman. Uses material from Bruce's court trials which are 'performed' by Hoffman as part of his nightclub act. Bruce, who died in 1966, suffered from drug addiction and was harrassed by the police and courts for years. Starring Valerie Perrine and Jan Miner. Directed by Bob Fosse.
Fine Arts; Literature and Drama; Religion and Philosophy; Sociology
Dist - NCJEWF

Lenny Bruce on TV 35 MIN
16mm
B&W (H C A)
Presents the late comic Lenny Bruce as he appeared on two Steve Allen shows and in an unaired pilot for a show of his own. Asks if he was a sinner with a dirty mouth or a saint with a rusty halo.
Biography; Fine Arts
Dist - NYFLMS **Prod** - NYFLMS

Lenny Bruce - performance film 65 MIN
35mm / 16mm
B&W (G)
$150.00, $200.00 rental
Films an unexpurgated nightclub routine by Lenny Bruce in San Francisco just after his New York obscenity trial. Directed by John Magnuson.
Fine Arts; History - United States
Dist - KINOIC

Lenny Moore 20 MIN
16mm
Sports Legends Series
Color (I J)
Shows how Lenny Moore's speed and pass - receiving ability made him a football great. Follows his career from his days at Penn State University through all the years with the Baltimore Colts and Johnny Unitas. Features Lenny talking about film footage of some of his games.
Biography; Physical Education and Recreation
Dist - COUNFI **Prod** - COUNFI

Lenses 10 MIN
U-matic / VHS
Introductory Concepts in Physics - Light Series
Color (C)
$229.00, $129.00 purchase _ #AD - 1209
Shows the mechanism of the lens and of focusing.
Science - Physical
Dist - FOTH **Prod** - FOTH

Lenses 10 MIN
16mm
Light Series
B&W (J H)
Covers convex and concave lenses, object and image arrangements and the effect of increased curvature.
Science - Physical
Dist - VIEWTH **Prod** - GBI

Lenses and magnification 20 MIN
U-matic / 16mm / VHS
Color (P I J)
$530.00, $400.00, $370.00 purchase _ #A556
Uses a laser demonstration to demonstrate how important the lens is to magnification. Illustrates the bending and refracting of beams of light. Diagrams and photomicrography explain how the lenses in microscopes magnify images. Shows how the electron microscope, reflecting microscope and radio telescope magnify without lenses.
Industrial and Technical Education; Science - Physical
Dist - BARR **Prod** - MATVCH 1989

Lenses and perspective 9 MIN
VHS
Lessons in visual language series
Color (PRO G C)
$99.00 purchase, $39.00 rental _ #750
Shows that the position of the viewer - or of a camera - is the governing factor in the perception of spatial relationships in the third dimension. Discards the mistaken idea that lens focal length affects the appearance of depth. Features Peter Thompson as creator and narrator of a ten - part series on visual language. Produced by the Australian Film, Television and Radio School.
Industrial and Technical Education; Social Science
Dist - FIRLIT

Lenses - How they Work
Reviews the properties of light in order to better explain how the lenses in our eyes allow us to interpret light. Discusses the physics of man made lenses along with concave and convex lenses. Presents a wide variety of visuals of microscopes, telescopes and cameras highlighting this educational film about the different types of lenses.
Science - Physical
Dist - BARR **Prod** - BARR 1988

Lenses on Nature 27 MIN
U-matic / VHS
Color (K A)
Features nature photographers Len and Maria Zorn showing their techniques photographing birds, insects and flowers.
Industrial and Technical Education; Science - Natural
Dist - SUTHRB **Prod** - SUTHRB

Lent and Easter 20 MIN
VHS
Color (H C G A R)
$24.95 purchase, $10.00 rental _ #35 - 87356 - 460
Features ten dramatic vignettes of Lenten and Easter themes and devotions.
Literature and Drama; Religion and Philosophy
Dist - APH **Prod** - FRACOC

Lent and Holy Week
VHS / U-matic
Christian Year Series
Color (G)
Addresses themes of preparation of Holy Week.
Religion and Philosophy
Dist - CAFM **Prod** - CAFM

L'Entente Cordiale 10 MIN
U-matic / VHS / 16mm
Beginning French Conversation Series
B&W (J H) (FRENCH)
LC 71-702706
A French language film. Follows various customers through a Parisian grocery store, naming the items they purchase.
Foreign Language
Dist - IFB **Prod** - GATEP 1955

Lentil 9 MIN
U-matic / VHS / 16mm
B&W (K P)
An iconographic motion picture, using the original illustrations and story from the children's picture book by Robert Mc Closkey, about a boy who couldn't whistle and saved the day with his harmonica.
English Language
Dist - WWS **Prod** - WWS 1957

Leo - a Dream about a Lion 16 MIN
16mm / U-matic / VHS
Color (K P I)
LC 80-700264
Presents a story about a young girl who dreams that her stuffed toy lion comes to life and escapes to the wilderness. Tells how she runs in pursuit and encounters a wide variety of African animal life before finding her cub.
Fine Arts
Dist - ALTSUL **Prod** - CENRAM 1979

Leo at the Photgrapher 8 MIN
U-matic / VHS / 16mm
Color (P I)
Presents an animated tale about Leo the Lion and his adventures at a photographic studio.
Fine Arts
Dist - PHENIX **Prod** - KRATKY

Leo Beuerman 13 MIN
U-matic / VHS / 16mm
Color (I) (SPANISH FRENCH GERMAN)
LC 74-705599
Documents the life of Leo Beuerman, an unusual man physically handicapped since birth. Describes his ability to overcome diversity and his philosophy of life.
Biography; Education; Guidance and Counseling; Psychology
Dist - CORF **Prod** - CENTRO 1969

Leo Buscaglia 60 MIN
VHS / U-matic
John Callaway Interviews Series
Color
Education
Dist - PBS **Prod** - WTTWTV 1981

Leo Buscaglia - politics of love 50 MIN
VHS
Color (G)
$29.95 purchase _ #500817
Features Leo Buscaglia with his unique perspectives on love and life. Encourages viewers to free themselves from 'hang - ups' and build rewarding relationships.
Guidance and Counseling
Dist - PBS **Prod** - WNETTV
UILL

Leo Buscaglia Series

The Art of Being Fully Human	58 MIN
A Love Class	46 MIN
Speaking of Love	54 MIN
A Time to Live	50 MIN
Together	52 MIN

Dist - DELTAK

Leo Castelli - conversations on 30 years as a New York art dealer 29 MIN
VHS
Color (H C A)
$39.95 purchase _ #CAS-02
Portrays art dealer Leo Castelli and his impact on American art through his shows for various artists and his discussion about them and their work. Includes his view of the impact of the Minimalist and Conceptualist movements in the late 1960s.
Fine Arts
Dist - ARTSAM

Leo Claws 5 MIN
VHS / U-matic
Write on, Set 2 Series
Color (J H)
Deals with writing the business letter.
English Language
Dist - CTI **Prod** - CTI

Leo Lionni's Caldecotts
VHS
Color (K)
$66.00 purchase
Offers three titles - 'Alexander And The Wind - Up Mouse,' 'Frederick' and 'Swimmy.'.
Literature and Drama
Dist - PELLER

Leo on Vacation 11 MIN
16mm / U-matic / VHS
Color (K P I)
LC 75-702961
Depicts the misadventures of a circus lion whose plans for a quiet vacation in his African home backfire. Uses animation.
Fine Arts; Literature and Drama
Dist - PHENIX **Prod** - KRATKY 1975

Leo the Iconoclast 30 MIN
VHS
Saints and legions series
Color (H)
$69.95 purchase
Profiles Leo the Iconoclast. Part 20 of a twenty - six part series which introduces personalities, movements and events in ancient history responsible for the beginnings of Western Civilization.
History - World; Religion and Philosophy
Dist - SCETV **Prod** - SCETV 1982

Leo Tolstoy 172 MIN
35mm / VHS
Color (G) (RUSSIAN WITH ENGLISH SUBTITLES)
$300.00 rental
Depicts the struggles of author Leo Tolstoy. Directed by Sergei Gerasimov.
Fine Arts; Literature and Drama
Dist - KINOIC **Prod** - IFEX 1984

Leo Tolstoy 57 MIN
U-matic / VHS / 16mm
Third Testament Series
Color
Discusses the life and thought of Leo Tolstoy.
Biography; Literature and Drama; Religion and Philosophy
Dist - TIMLIF **Prod** - CANBC 1976

Leo Tolstoy's Epic War and Peace 380 MIN
VHS
Color (G)
$99.95 purchase _ #1180
Presents the uncut version of 'War And Peace' which was filmed entirely in Russia.
Fine Arts; Geography - World; Literature and Drama
Dist - KULTUR

Leon Garfield 8 MIN
16mm
Color (I J T)
LC 78-704568
Leon Garfield discusses how and why he writes and describes the research that goes into his books of high adventure.
English Language; Literature and Drama
Dist - CONNF **Prod** - PENGIN 1969

Leon Golub 12 MIN
U-matic
Color (H A)
$275.00 purchase, $50.00 rental
Features Leon Golub discussing his visual influences, his painting techniques and his keen interest in depicting the causes of violence. Produced by Bruce Beresford.
Fine Arts; Industrial and Technical Education
Dist - AFA

Leon Kass - Parts I and II 30 MIN
VHS
World of ideas with Bill Moyers - Season I - series
Color (G)
$59.95 purchase _ #BMWI - 119D
Interviews Dr Leon Kass, a physician and philosopher. Reveals that Kass believes science has raised questions which cannot be answered by scientific reasoning. Considers the moral implications of scientific questions such as euthanasia and reproductive technology. Hosted by Bill Moyers.
Religion and Philosophy
Dist - PBS

Leon 'Peck' Clark - Basketmaker 15 MIN
U-matic
Color (H C A)
LC 81-707514
Peck Clark, a Black Mississippi farmer, describes how he learned to make white oak baskets. Shows Mr. Clark gathering materials and creating a basket.
Fine Arts; Geography - United States; History - United States
Dist - SOFOLK **Prod** - SOFOLK 1981

Leona Tyler on Counseling, Pt 1 25 MIN
16mm
Color (C G)
Features Leona Tyler, former president of the American Psychological Association, discussing the role of the counselor in helping clients develop confusion and isolation as two problems facing young people, how to choose a counseling theory, and why she does not see changing human behavior as the whole objective of counseling.
Guidance and Counseling; Psychology; Sociology
Dist - AACD **Prod** - AACD 1973

Leona Tyler on Counseling, Pt 2 25 MIN
16mm
Color (C G)
Features Leona Tyler, former president of the American Psychological Association, treating the importance of client feelings in the counseling process, the growing need for counseling, reasons why school counselors could be more effective, and changes in the women's movement.
Guidance and Counseling; Psychology; Sociology
Dist - AACD **Prod** - AACD 1973

Leonard Bernstein - Candide
CD / Cassette / VHS
(G H A)
$25.95, $37.95, $34.95 purchase _ #20071, #20072, #20288
Presents a 1989 performance of 'Candide' by the London Symphony Orchestra and Chorus, conducted by Leonard Bernstein.
Fine Arts
Dist - WCAT **Prod** - WCAT

Leonard Bernstein - Serenade for violin and orchestra 43 MIN
VHS
Color (G)
$19.95 purchase_#1441
Presents Serenade for Violin and Orchestra based on Plato's Symposium, composed by Leonard Bernstein in 1954. Features Russian solo violinist, Dmitry Sitkovetsky, with the Ensemble Stuttgart performing this melodic and rhythmic work.
Fine Arts
Dist - KULTUR

Leonard Brooks 28 MIN
16mm
Color (G)
_ #106C 0176 011
Portrays the life and works of Canadian painter, Leonard Brooks.
Biography; Fine Arts
Dist - CFLMDC **Prod** - NFBC 1976

Leonard Easter, Rachal Harms and Nicholas Arcomano 30 MIN
U-matic / VHS
Eye on Dance - the Business and Law of Dance Series
Color
Discusses developing and protecting artistic assets.
Fine Arts
Dist - ARCVID **Prod** - ARCVID

Leonard Henny, How Nations Televise each Other, or Ronald Gone Dutch 28 MIN
U-matic / VHS
Color
Attacks the ideology and economics of mass media. Presented by Paper Tiger Television.
Fine Arts
Dist - ARTINC **Prod** - ARTINC

Leonard Unterberger, MA - Director, Family Workshop, Chicago 60 MIN
U-matic / VHS
Perceptions, Pt B - Dialogues with Family Therapists Series Vol II, 'Pt B4
Color (PRO)
Presents a young therapist who has trained probation officers and street workers based on an approach derived from the social awareness of the 1960's.
Guidance and Counseling; Psychology; Sociology
Dist - BOSFAM **Prod** - BOSFAM

Leonard Unterberger, MA - Just Making it - on Being White and Poor 60 MIN
U-matic / VHS
Perceptions, Pt B - Interventions in Family Therapists Series Vol II'Pt A4
Color (PRO)
Elicits from a young, low - income Chicago family its struggle to make their way in the world. Explores the family in its socio - economic context after a course of therapy.
Guidance and Counseling; Psychology; Sociology
Dist - BOSFAM **Prod** - BOSFAM

Leonard Z Lion Presents Learning about Your Heart Catheterization 16 MIN
U-matic / VHS
Color (K P I) (SPANISH)
Explains, in Spanish, the events of a cardiac catheterization. Prepares the child for the sights and sounds associated with this diagnostic procedures.
Foreign Language; Health and Safety; Science - Natural
Dist - UARIZ **Prod** - UARIZ

Leonard Z Lion Presents Learning about Your Heart Catheterization 16 MIN
VHS / U-matic
Color (K P I) (SPANISH)
Designed to be shown to parents and their children (ages 3 - 12) and features a lion. Explains the events that take place during cardiac catheterization. Prepares the child for the sights, sounds and sensations experienced.
Foreign Language; Health and Safety
Dist - UMICHM **Prod** - UMICHM 1981

Leonard Z Lion Presents Learning about Your Heart Operation 14 MIN
VHS / U-matic
Color (K P I) (SPANISH)
Designed to be shown to parents and their children (ages 3 - 12) and features a lion. Shows what occurs before and after a heart operation. Focuses on the sights, sounds and sensations experienced during hospitalization for heart surgery.
Foreign Language; Health and Safety
Dist - UMICHM **Prod** - UMICHM 1981

Leonard Z Lion Presents Learning about Your Heart Operation 14 MIN
VHS / U-matic
Color (K P I) (SPANISH)
Explains, in Spanish, what occurs before and after a heart operation. Uses animated characters to illustrate the events associated with hospitalization for heart surgery.
Foreign Language; Health and Safety; Science - Natural
Dist - UARIZ **Prod** - UARIZ

Leonard Z Lion Presents Learning about Your Operation 13 MIN
U-matic / VHS
Color (K)
Features Leonard Z Lion showing friend Peter what occurs before and after an operation. Focuses on the sights, sounds and sensations experienced during hospitalization.
Health and Safety; Psychology
Dist - UMICHM **Prod** - UMICHM 1983

Leonardo 28 MIN
U-matic / VHS
Once upon a Time - Man Series
Color (P I)
Follows the life of Leonardo da Vinci as Europe shifts from the Dark Ages to modern times. Animated.
Biography; History - World
Dist - LANDMK **Prod** - LANDMK 1981

Leonardo da Vinci 52 MIN
VHS / U-matic
Great masters series
Color (J H G)
$225.00, $275.00 purchase, $60.00 rental
Illuminates all facets of Leonardo's abiding genius from his paintings, anatomical studies, theories of light, military and mechanical engineering projects, sculpture and natural phenomena.
Fine Arts; History - World
Dist - NDIM **Prod** - GREMAS 1993

Leonardo Da Vinci and His Art 14 MIN
16mm / U-matic / VHS
Color (J H C)
$340, $240 purchase _ #1033
Describes the Renaissance art of Leonardo Da Vinci.
Fine Arts
Dist - CORF

Leonardo Da Vinci - Giant of the Renaissance 25 MIN
U-matic / VHS / 16mm
Color (J H C) (SPANISH)
Presents the life and work of Leonardo da Vinci. Shows examples of his art and scientific research.
Fine Arts
Dist - EBEC **Prod** - EBEC

Leonardo da Vinci - the visionary intellect 30 MIN
VHS
Color (G)
$29.95 purchase _ #ACE07V - F
Views the genius of da Vinci through his paintings, drawings, and inventive machine designs, with an overview of his life in Florence, Italy.
Fine Arts
Dist - CAMV

Leonardo da Vinci - virgin and child with Saint Anne 20 MIN
VHS
Color (G)
PdS10.50 purchase _ #A4-300415
Depicts the restoration of da Vinci's cartoon of c.1506 after it was attacked with a shotgun in 1987. Offers insight into the work of a conservator and into the methods and practices of da Vinci himself.
Fine Arts
Dist - AVP **Prod** - NATLGL

Leonardo - to Know How to See 55 MIN
16mm
Color (J)
LC 72-702400
A documentary on the life and works of Leonardo da Vinci, including both his artistic and scientific achievements.
Biography; Fine Arts
Dist - USNGA **Prod** - USNGA 1972

Leonid Kogan - Interpretations 60 MIN
VHS
Color (G)
$19.95 purchase _ #1131
Presents a colorful Soviet production of violinist Leonid Kogan playing Tchaikovsky, Glazunov, Brahms, Kreisler, Bizet and a set of Paganini variations accompanied on the piano by his daughter Nina. Reveals that Kogan died at the age of 58, barely 8 years after the death of David Oistrakh, leaving a vacuum in Soviet violin tradition from which it has never recovered.
Fine Arts; Geography - World
Dist - KULTUR

Leontyne Price 60 MIN
VHS / U-matic
John Callaway Interviews Series
Color
Fine Arts
Dist - PBS **Prod** - WTTWTV 1981

Leopard - Part 6 8 MIN
VHS
Safari TV series
Color (P I)
$125.00 purchase
Studies the daily life of the leopard. Part of a 13 - part series on African animals.
Geography - World; Science - Natural
Dist - LANDMK **Prod** - LANDMK 1993

Leopards, blankets and snow flakes - a 2 part documentary on the Apaloosa horse series
Joseph's trail 19 MIN
Top of the trail 19 MIN
Dist - FEDU

Leopold Allen, Brian Dube and Raymond Serrano 30 MIN
U-matic / VHS
Eye on Dance - Behind the Scenes Series
Color
Fine Arts
Dist - ARCVID **Prod** - ARCVID

Leopold Sedar Senghor 30 MIN
U-matic / VHS / 16mm
Creative Person Series
B&W (H C A)
LC FIA68-2199
Introduces Leopold Sedar Senghor, his poetry and the environment which his poems reflect. President Senghor also discusses his philosophy towards the blending of African and Western culture.
Fine Arts; Literature and Drama
Dist - IU **Prod** - NET 1967

Leopold, the See - through Crumbpicker 9 MIN
U-matic / VHS / 16mm
Color (K P)
LC 79-714120
Illustrates a story by James Flora about Leopold, the invisible crumbpicker and how he finally becomes visible.
Literature and Drama
Dist - WWS **Prod** - FIRE 1971

Leopold's maneuvers 15 MIN
VHS / U-matic
Color (PRO C)
$395.00 purchase, $80.00 rental _ #C881 - VI - 015
Trains obstetrical nurses and nursing students in Leopold's maneuvers for assessing and identifying the physical adaptation processes taking place between mother and fetus and for revealing the general location of the fetal heart and whether engagement has taken place. Reveals that the maneuvers also help identify stressors that may indicate high - risk situations for mother or baby during pregnancy, labor or delivery.
Health and Safety
Dist - HSCIC

Leper - Tredowata 100 MIN
VHS
Color (G A) (POLISH WITH ENGLISH SUBTITLES)
$39.95 purchase _ #V079
Presents a moving, melodramatic story of the forbidden love affair between a wealthy young nobleman and a beautiful teacher in a high society school. Shows that the town folk try to destroy the relationship between these two people of different social positions. Directed by Jerzy Hoffman.
Fine Arts; Religion and Philosophy
Dist - POLART

L'Epopee Canadienne De L'energie 25 MIN
16mm
Color (FRENCH)
LC 76-701328
A French language version of Great Canadian Energy Saga. Looks at the special importance of energy and energy resources.
Foreign Language; Geography - World; Social Science
Dist - IMO **Prod** - IMO

Leprosy 20 MIN
VHS / U-matic
Color
$335.00 purchase
Health and Safety
Dist - ABCLR **Prod** - ABCLR 1983

Leprosy Can be Cured 58 MIN
U-matic / VHS
Nova Series
Color (H C A)
$250 purchase _ #5129C
Shows scientists searching for a vaccine to control the spread of leprosy. Produced by WGBH Boston.
Health and Safety
Dist - CORF

Leptospirosis 16 MIN
16mm
Color
LC FIE61-27
Explains the different phases of leptospirosis. Discusses the possibility of human infection and points out the various aspects of the disease. For professional and laboratory personnel.
Agriculture; Health and Safety
Dist - USNAC **Prod** - USPHS 1960

Lerchenpark series - der held des tages 30 MIN
16mm
Lerchenpark series - der held des tages
B&W (GERMAN)
A German language motion picture. Focuses on a 55 - year - old bachelor whose temporary popularity disappears when he loses the final round of a TV quiz show.
Foreign Language; Psychology
Dist - WSTGLC **Prod** - WSTGLC 1971

Lerchenpark series - der held des tages
Lerchenpark series - der held des tages 30 MIN
Dist - WSTGLC

Lerchenpark series - die heiratsannonce 25 MIN
16mm
Lerchenpark series
B&W (GERMAN)
A German language motion picture. Gives an account of the confusion that results when a young attorney and her boyfriend place an advertisement in the newspaper to find a marriage candidate for her mother.
Foreign Language; Sociology
Dist - WSTGLC **Prod** - WSTGLC 1970

Lerchenpark series - Fraeulein Vogt 25 MIN
16mm
Lerchenpark series
B&W (GERMAN)
A German language motion picture. Explores the dilemma of a 30 - year - old woman whose widowed mother does everything she can to destroy her relationship with an admirer.
Foreign Language; Sociology
Dist - WSTGLC **Prod** - WSTGLC 1970

Lerchenpark series - Ordnung Muss Sein 30 MIN
16mm
Lerchenpark series
B&W (GERMAN)
A German language motion picture. Tells the story of a traveling salesman who refuses to accept his unfair dismissal from his company.
Foreign Language; Psychology; Sociology
Dist - WSTGLC **Prod** - WSTGLC 1971

Lerchenpark series
Lerchenpark series - die heiratsannonce 25 MIN
Lerchenpark series - Fraeulein Vogt 25 MIN
Lerchenpark series - Ordnung Muss Sein 30 MIN
Dist - WSTGLC

L'Ere Des Revolutions 26 MIN
U-matic / VHS / 16mm
Color (H C) (FRENCH)
LC 83-700669
A French - language version of the motion picture An Age Of Revolutions. Focuses on the French and Industrial Revolutions, ending with the Franco - Prussian War.
Foreign Language; History - World
Dist - IFB **Prod** - IFB 1976

Leroy 25 MIN
U-matic / VHS / 16mm
Insight series
Color (J)
LC 79-700645
Tells the story of a poor, illiterate couple who lose their home because of an unpaid medical bill. Relates that the man is jailed when he threatens the speculator who bought the house. Shows that when the man tells his story on television, he finds out that people do care.
Fine Arts; Sociology
Dist - PAULST **Prod** - PAULST 1977

Leroy Jenkens - Solo Violin 29 MIN
VHS / 16mm
Color
Presents solos by jazz violinist Leroy Jenkens.
Fine Arts
Dist - RHPSDY **Prod** - RHPSDY

LeRoy Walker Track and Field - Men Series
Fundamentals of running - men 17 MIN
The Jumping Events - Men 21 MIN
The Running Events - Men 21 MIN
The Throwing Events - Men 21 MIN
Dist - ATHI

LeRoy walker track and field - women series
Fundamentals of running - women 17 MIN
The Jumping Events - Women 15 MIN
The Running events - women 21 MIN
The Throwing Events - Women 20 MIN
Dist - ATHI

Les Amis - Friends 14 MIN
VHS / U-matic
Color (C A)
Documents the intimacy between an older man and a younger women. Emphasizes mutual responsibility for contraception.
Health and Safety; Psychology; Sociology
Dist - MMRC **Prod** - NATSF

Les Animaux 13 MIN
16mm
En Francais, set 2 series
Color (J A)
Foreign Language
Dist - CHLTN **Prod** - PEREN 1969

Les Antiquites 13 MIN
16mm
En Francais, set 2 series
Color (J A)
Foreign Language
Dist - CHLTN **Prod** - PEREN 1969

Les aventures de Monsieur Carre series
Dans le parc 8 MIN
En retard au bureau 8 MIN
Dist - IFB

Les Aventures de Tintin - le temple du soleil 92 MIN
VHS
Color (G) (FRENCH)
$39.95 purchase _ #5549
Tells an ancient Incan story with French comic character Tintin in the major role. Introduces beginning and intermediate - level French students to the cultural animated figure.
Fine Arts; Foreign Language; Literature and Drama
Dist - GPC

Les Baux De Provence 10 MIN
16mm
Aspects De France Series
Color (H C) (FRENCH)
A French language film. Depicts the remains of the castle of Les Baux.
Foreign Language
Dist - MLA **Prod** - WSUM 1956

Les Belles Couleurs 10 MIN
U-matic / VHS
Salut - French Language Lessons Series
Color
Focuses on colors, sizes, masculine and feminine adjectives, and demonstrative adjectives.
Foreign Language
Dist - BCNFL **Prod** - BCNFL 1984

Les Blues de Balfa 28 MIN
16mm / U-matic / VHS
Color (G)
$450.00, $250.00, $150.00 purchase
Traces the development of the musical Balfa family, renowned Cajun musicians of southwest Louisiana, and the first Cajun group to take their music outside of Louisiana. Reveals that Rodney and Will Balfa were killed in a car accident in 1979 but surviving member Dewey Balfa shares his memories. Includes the music of the Balfa Brothers, Rockin' Dopsie, Allie Young, Nathan Abshire, Tony Balfa and Raymond Francois and the Cajun Playboys. Produced and directed by Yasha Aginsky.
Fine Arts
Dist - FLOWER

Les Bons Debarras - Good Riddance 114 MIN
16mm
Color (FRENCH (ENGLISH SUBTITLES))
A French - language film with English subtitles. Tells the story of Manon, a precocious 13 - year - old girl who quietly and subtly rids her life of every deterrent to be the sole object of her mother's love.
Fine Arts; Foreign Language
Dist - IFEX **Prod** - PRISMA 1981

Les Brown series
Offers a series of motivational videos. Individual titles include You Deserve, Live Your Dreams - Get Past Your Fears, The Power to Change, Take Charge of Your Life and It's Possible.
It's possible 62 MIN
Les Brown series 242 MIN
Live your dreams - get past your fears 45 MIN
The Power to change 44 MIN
Take charge of your life 45 MIN
You deserve 48 MIN
Dist - JWAVID **Prod** - JWAVID 1981

Les cafes 13 MIN
16mm
En France avec Jean et Helene series; Set 1; Lesson 2
B&W (J H C)
LC 70-704504
Foreign Language
Dist - CHLTN **Prod** - PEREN 1967

Les Castors Au Travail 10 MIN
16mm / U-matic / VHS
Color (I J) (FRENCH)
A French language version of the videocassette Beavers At Work. Shows how beavers are suited to the environment and their work. Depicts baby beavers at play and adult beavers building homes.
Foreign Language; Science - Natural
Dist - IFB **Prod** - IFB 1964

Les Chansons De Bilitis 30 MIN
VHS / U-matic
Color
Presents a dance and reading set to music of the French poet Pierre Louys' series of poems which he claimed were inspired by ancient Greek verse. Uses the musical score of Claude Debussy which featured the delicate sounds of harp, flute and celeste woven into the narrative text of the poems. Shows a modern - day woman who studies her image in the waters of a pond and is transformed into the Grecian courtesan Bilitis.
Fine Arts; Literature and Drama
Dist - OHUTC **Prod** - OHUTC

Les Chateaux 16 MIN
16mm
Aspects De France Series
Color (H C) (FRENCH)
A French language film. Examines the architectural evolution of the chateaux, relating them to the life and times of their occupants.
Foreign Language
Dist - MLA **Prod** - WSUM 1966

Les chevaux 13 MIN
16mm
En France avec Jean et Helene series; Set 1; Lesson 12
B&W (J H C)
LC 77-704506
Foreign Language
Dist - CHLTN **Prod** - PEREN 1967

Les Choux - Fleurs De Saint - Brieuc 15 MIN
U-matic / VHS / 16mm
La Maree Et Ses Secrets Series
Color (C A)
Foreign Language
Dist - FI **Prod** - FI

Les Cles 14 MIN
16mm
Hand Operations - Woodworking - French Series
Color (FRENCH)
LC 75-704363
A French language version of Wrenches. Illustrates the versatilities and practicalities of a variety of wrenches.
Foreign Language; Industrial and Technical Education
Dist - MORLAT **Prod** - MORLAT 1974

Les Contes D'Hoffmann 149 MIN
VHS
(G) (FRENCH)
$44.95 purchase _ #V72151
Presents the opera by Offenbach as sung in French by Placido Domingo, Luciana Serra, Agnes Baltsa, and Ilena Cotrubas in a 1981 production. Libretto included.
Fine Arts; Foreign Language
Dist - NORTNJ

Les Crepes 5 MIN
16mm
Bonjour Line Series Part 1; Part 1
Color (K P I) (FRENCH)
A French language film. A little girl is making pancakes while her young brother secretly eats them one by one.
Foreign Language
Dist - CHLTN **Prod** - PEREN 1962

Les Dangers Du Travail En Espace Reduit 16 MIN
16mm / U-matic / VHS
Color (H A) (FRENCH)
A French - language version of the motion picture Confined Space Hazards. Stressses the correct procedure for working safely in confined spaces or areas. Shows a worker preparing to enter a tank as others take such safety precautions as blocking off intake and outlet pipes, locking and tagging all electrical switches, eliminating vapors from the space and testing the oxygen supply. Emphasizes the recognition of the hazardous space, planning for every eventuality and precision in remedial procedures.
Foreign Language; Health and Safety
Dist - IFB Prod - IAPA 1971

Les Dents - Les Gens Peuvent Vaincre Les Microbes 10 MIN
16mm
Health - French Series
Color (FRENCH)
LC 75-704341
A French language version of the motion picture Teeth - People Are Smarter Than Germs. Demonstrates how people who are taking care of their teeth are also looking after their health.
Foreign Language; Health and Safety
Dist - MORLAT Prod - MORLAT 1974

Les Femmes Connaissent La Mecanique 13 MIN
16mm
En Francais, set 1 series
Color (J A)
Foreign Language
Dist - CHLTN Prod - PEREN 1969

Les Francais chez vous series

Alice vient d'arriver	13 MIN
Aujourd'hui friture	13 MIN
Ce cavalier qui vient	13 MIN
Chasser est un plaisir	13 MIN
Dans deux heures	13 MIN
Dites - le avec des fleurs	13 MIN
Elle lui sourit	13 MIN
Est - ce que c'est ta veste	13 MIN
Fenetre sur jardin	13 MIN
Georges epousera	13 MIN
Il donne ses croissants aux oiseaux	13 MIN
Il faut tout lui enseigner	13 MIN
Il me regarde	13 MIN
Il n'en reste plus	13 MIN
Il y a beaucoup de place	13 MIN
Je n'ai rien a declarer	13 MIN
Je prends un tournevis	13 MIN
Je suis arrive avant vous	13 MIN
J'Y vais	13 MIN
La meilleure occasion	13 MIN
L'Aviateur	13 MIN
Le chat va tomber	13 MIN
Le coche d'eau	13 MIN
Mon ticket s'il vous plait	13 MIN
Nous avons faim	13 MIN
Nous irons peut - etre en Chine	13 MIN
A Nous les bijoux	13 MIN
Nous sommes seuls	13 MIN
Operation biberon	13 MIN
Pourquoi n'est - il pas la	13 MIN
Qu'est - ce que c'est	13 MIN
Qu'est - ce qu'il y a	13 MIN
Qui est - ce	13 MIN
Soudain le paradis	13 MIN
Symphonie realiste	13 MIN
Vendons ces meubles	13 MIN
Voila Gilbert, le voila	13 MIN
Vous, encore vous	13 MIN

Dist - CHLTN

Les Francaise Chez Vous Series

Ou Va - t - il, D'ou Vient - Il	13 MIN

Dist - CHLTN

Les Gardes De Caserne 4 MIN
16mm
Ceremonial Drill - French Series
Color (FRENCH)
LC 77-702844
A French language version of the motion picture The Quarters Guard. Demonstrates the military drill known as the Quarters Guard.
Civics and Political Systems; Foreign Language
Dist - CDND Prod - CDND 1976

Les Gens De Paris Au Temps Du Roi Soleil 60 MIN
U-matic / VHS
Color (C) (FRENCH)
$299.00, $199.00 purchase _ #AD - 1051
Pofiles the common people of Paris as well as the rich and famous whose lifestyle supported and exploited the commoners in the 17th century. Title translates as the people of Paris during the era of the Sun King, Louis XIV. A French language film.
Biography; Fine Arts; Foreign Language; Geography - World; History - World
Dist - FOTH Prod - FOTH

Les Grecs 29 MIN
U-matic / VHS / 16mm
Color (H C A) (FRENCH)
A French - language version of the motion picture The Greeks. Surveys Greek history and culture from the early Aegean civilizations to the conquests of Alexander.
Foreign Language; History - World
Dist - IFB Prod - IFB 1975

Les Insectes Sont Interessantes 11 MIN
16mm / U-matic / VHS
Color (I J) (FRENCH)
A French language version of the videocassette Insects Are Interesting. Examines the life histories, biologies and adaptations of insects. Stresses the importance of insects to man.
Foreign Language; Science - Natural
Dist - IFB Prod - DEU 1956

Les Insectes Sont Interessants 11 MIN
U-matic / VHS / 16mm
Color (C) (FRENCH)
A French version of 'INSECTS ARE INTERESTING.' Shows the biology, life cycle and adaptive abilities of insects.
Foreign Language
Dist - IFB Prod - IFB 1961

Les jeunes entrepreneurs series
Presents the three - video story of young teens, the robot they built, and the new - generation robot constructed. Develops intermediate - level language students' listening, comprehending, reading, writing and speaking skills through exercises and follow - up activities based on the story. Comes with three videos and teacher's guide with class activity material.

C'est un choix difficile	25 MIN
A quel prix la publicite	25 MIN
Un Premier prix	25 MIN

Dist - GPC

Les Jeux Sont Faits 105 MIN
16mm
B&W (H C A) (FRENCH)
A French language motion picture illustrating Jean - Paul Sartre's idea that man must exercise his free will and that to do so he must not depend on the past.
Foreign Language; Literature and Drama
Dist - TRANSW Prod - IFB 1947

Les Lunettes Astronomiques 13 MIN
16mm
En Francais, set 2 series
Color (J A)
Foreign Language
Dist - CHLTN Prod - PEREN 1969

Les McCann - Makin' it Real 29 MIN
U-matic
Interface Series
Color
Features musician - composer Les McCann singing, playing and talking about his music.
Fine Arts
Dist - PBS Prod - WETATV

Les McCann Trio 29 MIN
16mm / VHS
Jazz on Stage Series
Color
Fine Arts
Dist - RHPSDY Prod - RHPSDY

Les miserables 108 MIN
VHS
B&W (H C)
$79.00 purchase _ #03647 - 126
Stars Fredric March and Charles Laughton in the Victor Hugo drama about Jean Valjean, unjustly sentenced to years in the galleys, who emerges to build his life again. Produced in 1935.
Fine Arts; Literature and Drama
Dist - GA Prod - GA

Les Nations S'Affirment - Nations Assert Themselves 52 MIN
16mm
Le Temp Des Cathedrales Series
Color
Reveals how Gothic art meets with political and cultural resistance in Sicily and Spain while there is a renewal of Catholic spirituality in southern Italy. Shows examples of architectural rigidity including the cathedrals of Salisbury, Ely and Gloucester.
History - World; Religion and Philosophy
Dist - FACSEA Prod - FACSEA 1979

Les Oiseaux Qui Mangent De La Viande 6 MIN
16mm / U-matic / VHS
Color (C) (FRENCH)
French version of 'BIRDS THAT EAT FLESH.' Depicts and discusses the flesh - eaters' physical adaptations.
Foreign Language
Dist - IFB Prod - IFB 1952

Les Oiseaux Qui Mangent Des Graines 6 MIN
U-matic / VHS / 16mm
Color (ENGLISH, FRENCH)
Suggests that the physical structure of some birds adapts them for eating seeds. Shows that small size, agility and the shape of the bill are common characteristics of seed - eating birds.
Foreign Language; Science - Natural
Dist - IFB Prod - IFB 1963

Les Oiseaux Qui Mangent Des Insectes 6 MIN
16mm / U-matic / VHS
Color (ENGLISH, FRENCH)
A French language version of the English language film, Birds That Eat Insects. Shows how the physical structure of some birds is suitable for eating insects. Includes the swallow, nighthawk, kingbird, black billed cuckoo, woodpecker, flicker, robin and others.
Foreign Language; Science - Natural
Dist - IFB Prod - IFB 1963

Les Oiseaux Qui Mangent Des Poissons 6 MIN
U-matic / VHS / 16mm
Color (ENGLISH, FRENCH)
Describes how specialized structures enable some birds to catch and eat fish. Directs attention to the long toes and legs of wading birds such as the heron, the sharp pointed bill of the kingfisher and the talons of the osprey.
Foreign Language; Science - Natural
Dist - IFB Prod - IFB 1961

Les ondes 6 MIN
16mm
B&W (G)
$12.00 rental
Traces the paths of lunar, solar, and laser light to find common paths. By Wendy Blair.
Fine Arts
Dist - CANCIN

Les Ordres 107 MIN
16mm
Color (FRENCH (ENGLISH SUBTITLES))
A French language film with English subtitles. Describes the 1970 arrest and incarceration of 450 French Canadians without charges or explanation. Directed by Michel Brault.
Fine Arts; Foreign Language
Dist - NYFLMS Prod - UNKNWN 1974

Les Parfums 13 MIN
16mm
En Francais, set 2 series
Color (J A)
Foreign Language
Dist - CHLTN Prod - PEREN 1969

Les Passagers 90 MIN
16mm
B&W (FRENCH)
LC 74-702328
A French language motion picture. Presents the problems of Algerian emigrants working in France. Focuses on the problems of an Algerian youth from the time he leaves Algeria, through two years in Paris, to the time he decides to return to Algeria.
Foreign Language; Geography - World; Sociology
Dist - TRIFC Prod - CADI 1972

Les Petites Fugues 137 MIN
16mm
Color (FRENCH (ENGLISH SUBTITLES))
A French language film with English subtitles. Describes the adventures of a 66 - year - old farmhand who buys a motorbike. Directed by Yves Yersin.
Fine Arts; Foreign Language
Dist - NYFLMS Prod - UNKNWN 1979

Les Pinces 12 MIN
16mm
Hand Operations - Woodworking - French Series
Color (FRENCH)
LC 76-700147
A French language version of Pliers. Describes common types of pliers.
Foreign Language; Industrial and Technical Education
Dist - MORLAT Prod - MORLAT 1974

Les Precurseurs - Cezanne, Gauguin, Van Gogh 26 MIN
U-matic / VHS / 16mm
Color (H C) (FRENCH)
A French - language version of the motion picture The Precursors - Cezanne, Gauguin, Van Gogh. Portrays the influence of impressionism on artists Cezanne, Gauguin and Van Gogh, as exemplified in Cezanne's preoccupation with construction by volume, Gauguin's use

of descriptive backgrounds and bright color, and Van Gogh's attempt to evoke emotion rather than display craftsmanship.
Fine Arts; Foreign Language
Dist - IFB **Prod** - LFLMDC 1971

Les Prisonnieres 44 MIN
16mm
Color
LC 80-700306
Shows how a 15 - year - old American girl discovers her Huguenot heritage while attending school in France. Tells how she learns about Marie Durand, who was imprisoned for 38 years because of her beliefs.
History - United States; History - World; Religion and Philosophy
Dist - ADVENT **Prod** - ADVENT 1979

Les Prisonnieres, Pt 1 22 MIN
16mm
Color
LC 80-700306
Shows how a 15 - year - old American girl discovers her Huguenot heritage while attending school in France. Tells how she learns about Marie Durand, who was imprisoned for 38 years because of her beliefs.
Religion and Philosophy
Dist - ADVENT **Prod** - ADVENT 1979

Les Prisonnieres, Pt 2 22 MIN
16mm
Color
LC 80-700306
Shows how a 15 - year - old American girl discovers her Huguenot heritage while attending school in France. Tells how she learns about Marie Durand, who was imprisoned for 38 years because of her beliefs.
Religion and Philosophy
Dist - ADVENT **Prod** - ADVENT 1979

Les Pronoms Personnels Direct Et Indirect 15 MIN
U-matic / VHS
French from the French Language Videotapes - French Series
Color (FRENCH)
A French language videotape of The Direct And Indirect Personal Pronouns, Presents a lesson on various pronouns in French.
Foreign Language
Dist - UCEMC **Prod** - UCEMC

Les radio - taxis 13 MIN
16mm
En France avec Jean et Helene series; Set 1; Lesson 6
B&W (J H C)
LC 73-704513
Foreign Language
Dist - CHLTN **Prod** - PEREN 1967

Les Romains 23 MIN
U-matic / VHS / 16mm
Color (H C) (FRENCH)
LC 83-700671
A French - language version of the motion picture The Romans which surveys the political history of Rome from the Etruscans to Caesar, the unification of the peninsula and the growth of the empire.
Foreign Language; History - World
Dist - IFB **Prod** - DOOLYJ 1983

Les Saisons 14 MIN
16mm / U-matic / VHS
Color (J H C) (FRENCH)
LC 71-707280
A French language film. Provides a look at the changing seasons in France, particularly the winter sports season and the springtime with the Seine overflowing its banks.
Geography - World; Science - Natural
Dist - IFB **Prod** - IFB 1970

Les Silences de Manet 60 MIN
VHS
Color (H C A)
$39.95 purchase _ #MAN-02
Evokes 19th-century Paris through paintings by Edouard Manet. Reveals that, against his will, Manet was heralded as the leader of the avant-garde. Traces his refusal to be a part of the 'revolutionary' Impressionist movement, and his desperate longing for public approval. Coproduced with Didier Baussy.
Fine Arts
Dist - ARTSAM **Prod** - RMART

Les Surprises 15 MIN
U-matic / VHS / 16mm
La Maree Et Ses Secrets Series
Color (C A)
Foreign Language
Dist - FI **Prod** - FI

Les Tatouages de la memoire 34 MIN
VHS / 16mm
Color (C)
$500.00 purchase, $60.00, $80.00 rental
Presents a dream narrative sequence using symbols and dance to describe a woman's transmogrification into a raven who flies out of love and into death. Produced by Helen Doyle.
Fine Arts; Sociology
Dist - WMENIF

Les tournesols and Les tournesols colores 6 MIN
16mm
Color (G)
$20.00 rental
Features two films of fields of sunflowers. Adjusts the focus frame by frame in succession according to a series of patterns on particular plants in different parts of the field. Filmed at various focal lengths so the sunflowers combine during projection to form one image. The latter film is a capricious version of the former.
Fine Arts; Science - Natural
Dist - CANCIN **Prod** - LOWDER 1983

Les Trois Ours 15 MIN
U-matic / VHS / 16mm
Color; B&W (A) (FRENCH (FRENCH NARRATION))
A French version of The Three Bears with simple beginning French narration. Visualizes nouns, adjectives and verbs by the appropriate object or action on the screen.
Foreign Language
Dist - PHENIX **Prod** - FA 1960

Les troyens 253 MIN
VHS
Color (G) (FRENCH FRENCH WITH ENGLISH SUBTITLES)
$39.95 purchase _ #384 - 9509; $44.95 purchase _ #V72155; $39.95 purchase
Presents the Metropolitan Opera version of 'Les Troyens' by Berlioz. Features James Levine as conductor, Placido Domingo, Tatiana Troyanos and Jessye Norman in the cast.
Fine Arts; Foreign Language
Dist - FI **Prod** - PAR 1988
NORTNJ
PBS

Les Vedettes 26 MIN
16mm
Color (FRENCH)
LC FIA67-2235
French version of the 'THE ENTERTAINERS.' Presents a summary of the highlights of the 1966 Canadian Open Golf Championship, which was played in Vancouver from September 29th to October 3rd.
Foreign Language
Dist - MTP **Prod** - HSEGRM 1966

Les Verbes Pronominaux 10 MIN
U-matic / VHS
(French (from the French Language Videotapes (French Series
Color (FRENCH)
A French language videotape. Presents an intermediate French lesson. Illustrates the different uses of reflexive pronouns.
Foreign Language
Dist - UCEMC **Prod** - UCEMC

Les Voix Du Soleil 12 MIN
U-matic / VHS / 16mm
Color (H C) (FRENCH)
A French language film. Explains in animated form the benefits we derive directly and indirectly from the sun. Includes a brief history of the sun and the work of Galileo and Newton.
Foreign Language
Dist - IFB **Prod** - IFB

Les Voyageurs 30 MIN
U-matic / VHS
Franco File Series
Color (I)
Dramatizes cooperation in contemporary Franco - American life.
Sociology
Dist - GPN **Prod** - WENHTV

Lesbian erotica - volume I 45 MIN
VHS
Color (G A)
$60.00 purchase
Compiles three classic lesbian erotica films from 1974 - 1978. Includes Dyketactics; Double Strength; and Women I Love. See individual titles for description and availability for rental in 16mm format.
Fine Arts; Sociology
Dist - CANCIN **Prod** - BARHAM

A Lesbian in the pulpit 28 MIN
VHS
Color (H C G)
$295.00 purchase, $55.00 rental
Focuses on Sally Boyle, an ordained minister in the United Church of Canada, and Erin Shoomaker, executive director of an AIDS foundation, who have been living together as a lesbian couple for 4.5 years. Reveals that the membership of the United Church of Canada has been in great conflict over the issue of homosexuality - those subscribing to a strict reading of the Bible find it morally wrong and many question whether homosexuality is a choice or an inborn orientation.
Geography - World; Religion and Philosophy; Sociology
Dist - FLMLIB **Prod** - CANBC 1991

Lesbian Mothers 26 MIN
U-matic
B&W
Explores the social stigmas of being a lesbian mother in modern society through interviews with young people and their lesbian mothers.
Sociology
Dist - WMENIF **Prod** - WMENIF

Lesbian Mothers and Child Custody, Pt 1 29 MIN
U-matic
Woman Series
Color
Discusses lesbian mothers' struggle for custody of their children. Explains the controversy surrounding the question of parental fitness and its relationship to sexual preference.
Sociology
Dist - PBS **Prod** - WNEDTV

Lesbian Mothers and Child Custody, Pt 2 29 MIN
U-matic
Woman Series
Color
Presents Mary Jo Risher and Ann Foreman describing their efforts to reclaim custody of Mary Jo's 10 - year - old son, who was taken from the Risher - Foreman home and placed under his father's guardianship. Points out that Mary Jo's lesbianism was the central issue in the trial.
Sociology
Dist - PBS **Prod** - WNEDTV

Lesbians Against the Right 45 MIN
U-matic
Color
Discusses the attempts of the New Right to blame the ills of this society on the breakdown of the family, immigration and abortion. Discusses attempts which have been made to combat the New Right.
Sociology
Dist - WMENIF **Prod** - AMELIA

The Lesbos film 30 MIN
16mm
Color (G)
$60.00 rental
Documents the experiences of a group of American feminist students at the Aegean Women's Studies Institute on the island of Lesbos. Features classes in poetry, spirituality, writing and filmmaking.
Fine Arts; History - World; Sociology
Dist - CANCIN **Prod** - BARHAM 1981

Lesions of the Brain, Pt A - Stroke 41 MIN
16mm
B&W (PRO)
Presents Dr Michael E De Bakey of the Baylor University College of Medicine demonstrating his surgical treatment for cerebral vascular insufficiency caused by occlusive lesions in the arteries supplying the brain. Discusses the status of anticoagulants in the treatment of a stroke.
Health and Safety; Science; Science - Natural
Dist - UPJOHN **Prod** - UPJOHN 1961

Lesions of the Brain, Pt B - Head Injury 34 MIN
16mm
B&W (PRO)
Presents a panel of doctors discussing a skull fracture complicated by blood clots at successive stages of the case history. Examines the panelists' recommended course of therapy and emphasizes the cardinal signs of impending danger in the patient with a head injury.
Health and Safety; Science - Natural
Dist - UPJOHN **Prod** - UPJOHN 1961

Lesions of the Brain, Pt C - Parkinsonism 27 MIN
16mm
B&W (PRO)
Presents Dr Irving S Cooper of the New York University School of Medicine demonstrating his technique for relieving Parkinsonism by freezing the ventral lateral region of the thalamus by means of a cannula and liquid hydrogen. Includes Dr Mac Donald Critcheley of the National Hospital Queen Square, London, presenting two patients that illustrate the difference between Parkinsonian tremor and ideopathic or familial tremor.
Health and Safety; Science
Dist - UPJOHN **Prod** - UPJOHN 1961

Lesions of the Fallopian Tube 31 MIN
16mm
Color (PRO)
Shows various conditions which arise in the fallopian tubes including inflammatory diseases of acute, subacute and chronic stages. Illustrates diagnosis and treatment of tubal pregnancy.
Health and Safety; Science
Dist - ACY **Prod** - ACYDGD 1957

Leslie - a portrait of schizophrenia 57 MIN
VHS
Color (H C G)
$445.00 purchase, $75.00 rental
Portrays a remarkable young black man who suffers from paranoid schizophrenia. Tells of his hearing voices and experiencing hallucinations as a child. Recalls his experiences with drugs which may have triggered his illness. Produced by Chiz Schultz.
Health and Safety; Psychology
Dist - FLMLIB

Leslie Campbell - 5 - 9 - 80 60 MIN
VHS / Cassette
Poetry Center reading series
Color (G)
$15.00, $45.00 purchase, $15.00 rental _ #388 - 322
Features the writer talking about Gertrude Stein, discussing characters, entity writing, syntax and grammar at the Poetry Center, San Francisco State University. Includes readings from Stein's Melanctha, Tender Buttons, Lifting Belly and a selection from Patriarchal Poetry. Introduction by Tom Mandel.
Literature and Drama
Dist - POETRY **Prod** - POETRY 1980

Leslie Jane Pessemier, Mark Kloth and Rika Burnham 30 MIN
U-matic / VHS
Eye on Dance - Collaborations Series
Color
Features a performance of 'Esoterica' with Domy Reiter - Sofer, choreographer with the Bat - Dor Dance Company of Israel. Hosted By Celia Ipiotis.
Fine Arts
Dist - ARCVID **Prod** - ARCVID

Less Far than the Arrow 8 MIN
16mm / U-matic / VHS
Critical Moments in Teaching Series
Color (C A)
Presents an open - end film which examines the problems involved in motivating a high school class.
Education; Literature and Drama; Psychology
Dist - PHENIX **Prod** - CALVIN 1968

Less is more 14 MIN
U-matic / VHS / 16mm
Color (H C)
LC 75-703677
Examines the premise that a minimal use of natural resources can potentially produce large amounts of energy.
Science - Natural; Social Science
Dist - AIMS **Prod** - DURCEL 1975

Less is more - pollution prevention is good business 23 MIN
BETA / U-matic / VHS
Color (G)
$29.95, $130.00 purchase _ #LSTF11
Shows how industry is converting waste into salable products.
Science - Natural
Dist - FEDU **Prod** - USEPA 1986

Less Stress 14 MIN
U-matic / VHS / 16mm
Color (I J)
LC 79-700299
Introduces the concept of stress. Explains how stress affects the body and behavior. Includes vignettes that demonstrate ways of reducing stress.
Guidance and Counseling; Health and Safety; Psychology
Dist - CF **Prod** - KLINGL 1979

Less Stress in 5 Easy Steps
VHS
(A)
$295.00 purchase _ #82727
Demonstrates simple techniques for reducing stress and its negative effects. Discusses meditation, relaxation, self appreciation.
Psychology
Dist - CMPCAR

Less Stress in Five Easy Steps
BETA / VHS
Color
Presents a 'right brain' approach to stress managements, and provides techniques for recognizing stress, and integrating habitual and new stress reduction mechanisms, including breathing, exercise, imaging and music - video meditation. Emphasizes flexibility of response within a progressive framework of skills. Features Ed Asner.
Psychology
Dist - BRUMAZ **Prod** - BRUMAZ

Less stress in five easy steps 45 MIN
VHS
Color (H C A)
$89.95 purchase _ #MOP100V
Presents a series of exercises to help people overcome the effects of stress.
Physical Education and Recreation; Psychology
Dist - CAMV

Less than a Minute 6 MIN
16mm
Color
LC 80-700386
Examines the effect of noise on people and shows how earplugs can be used to help prevent hearing loss due to exposure to excessive noise.
Health and Safety; Science - Natural; Sociology
Dist - LEOARB **Prod** - LEOARB 1979

Less than nothing - a program about anorexia 7 MIN
VHS
Color (J H)
$49.95 purchase _ #WB493VG
Tells the story of Bonnie, a teenage girl who is suffering from anorexia. Shows the danger signs of eating disorders as Bonnie is eventually discovered binging. Discusses treatment, prevention and recognition of appetite disorders. Includes a teacher's guide and blackline masters.
Guidance and Counseling; Psychology
Dist - UNL

The Lesson 67 MIN
16mm
B&W (H C A)
LC 79-700913
Eugene Ionesco's play, 'THE LESSON,' which satirizes the interaction between pupil and professor.
Education; Industrial and Technical Education; Literature and Drama
Dist - GROVE **Prod** - GROVE 1966

Lesson and Analysis 29 MIN
U-matic / VHS
Working with the Beginning Teacher - Teaching Story Analysis Series
Color
Identifies skills needed by the beginning teacher.
Education
Dist - SPF **Prod** - SPF

A Lesson Doesn't End 30 MIN
16mm
Starting Tomorrow Series Unit 4 - New Ways in Elementary Science
B&W (T)
Describes classroom techniques dealing with science investigations using batteries, bulbs and wire.
Education; Science; Science - Physical
Dist - WALKED **Prod** - EALING

Lesson 8 - How Can Work be Done more Efficiently 24 MIN
VHS / 16mm
Man Management and Rig Management Series
(A PRO)
$250.00 purchase _ #40.0608
Shows how efficient use of equipment and manpower can reduce costs and increase job safety. Suggests methods for improving job efficiency and summarizes all nine lessons in the series.
Business and Economics; Industrial and Technical Education; Social Science
Dist - UTEXPE **Prod** - UTEXPE 1983

Lesson 5 - How do You Train Employees 21 MIN
VHS / 16mm
Man Management and Rig Management Series
(A PRO)
$250.00 purchase _ #40.0605
Tackles general problems and methods involved in teaching a new skill to an employee. Discusses the basic steps of teaching and points out that effective training can improve productivity.
Business and Economics; Industrial and Technical Education; Social Science
Dist - UTEXPE **Prod** - UTEXPE 1983

Lesson 4 - How do You Start Out a New Hand 20 MIN
VHS / 16mm
Man Management and Rig Management Series
(A PRO)
$250.00 purchase _ #40.0604
Defines morale and explains how it can affect a new worker's progress. Discusses special problems of new employees and advantages of proper training from the beginning of employment.
Guidance and Counseling; Industrial and Technical Education; Social Science
Dist - UTEXPE **Prod** - UTEXPE 1983

A Lesson in Learning 45 MIN
16mm
Color (T)
Presents spontaneous and unrehearsed classroom activity. Capsules a semester's curriculum.
Education; Religion and Philosophy
Dist - YALEDV **Prod** - YALEDV

A Lesson in love 29 MIN
VHS / 16mm
Watch your mouth series
Color (H)
$46.00 rental _ #WAYM - 113
Emphasizes language and communication skills for high school students. Notes the difference between formal and informal word usage.
Education; English Language; Social Science
Dist - PBS

A Lesson in Microcomputers - Hardware and Software
U-matic / VHS
Color
Gives a complete introduction to computer basics and helps review terms, functions and basic troubleshooting.
Industrial and Technical Education; Mathematics
Dist - GA **Prod** - GA

A Lesson on Change 12 MIN
16mm
Color (C A)
LC 72-702445
Presents a model of good teaching. Emphasizes the importance of taking advantage of teachable moments with children. Shows a teacher as she explains spontaneously to her second grade class the death of Dr Martin Luther King, Jr and the changes for which he gave his life.
Biography; Education
Dist - OSUMPD **Prod** - COLPS 1969

Lesson 1 - what is Management 23 MIN
VHS / 16mm
Man Management and Rig Management Series
(A PRO)
$250.00 purchase _ #40.0601
Demonstrates the value of basic management skills - planning, coordinating, and instructing. Examines who is responsible for developing these skills and the consequences of poorly developed skills.
Industrial and Technical Education; Social Science
Dist - UTEXPE **Prod** - UTEXPE 1983

Lesson Plans - Part I - Designing Effective Training - no 3 60 MIN
U-matic
Training the Trainer Series
Color (PRO)
Presents training sessions for professional training personnel. Includes goal selection, design and presentation of training material and evaluation and reports.
Industrial and Technical Education
Dist - VTRI **Prod** - VTRI 1986

Lesson Plans - Part II - Planning for Skills Training - no 4 60 MIN
U-matic
Training the Trainer Series
Color (PRO)
Presents training sessions for professional training personnel. Includes goal selection, design and presentation of training material and evaluation and reports.
Industrial and Technical Education
Dist - VTRI **Prod** - VTRI 1986

Lesson 7 - How do You Plan and Organize Work 21 MIN
VHS / 16mm
Man Management and Rig Management Series
(A PRO)
$250.00 purchase _ #40.0607
Explains how good planning is essential for effective management. Gives basic steps in planning and organizing work and demonstrates the effects of good and bad planning on company goals.
Business and Economics; Industrial and Technical Education; Social Science
Dist - UTEXPE **Prod** - UTEXPE 1983

Lesson 6 - where do you fit into the organization 20 MIN
VHS / 16mm
Man management and rig management series
(A PRO)
$250.00 purchase _ #40.0606
Shows how first - line supervisors function inside and outside the company. Emphasizes how good communication skills can benefit both the company and the employee.
Business and Economics; Industrial and Technical Education; Social Science
Dist - UTEXPE **Prod** - UTEXPE 1983

Lesson 3 - How do You Handle Personnel Problems 14 MIN
VHS / 16mm
Man Management and Rig Management Series
(A PRO)
$250.00 purchase _ #40.0603
Shows personnel problems that can occur, ho to handle them, and the the steps involved in solving them.
Guidance and Counseling; Industrial and Technical Education; Social Science
Dist - UTEXPE **Prod** - UTEXPE 1983

Lesson 2 - what is Leadership 14 MIN
VHS / 16mm
Man Management and Rig Management Series
(A PRO)
$250.00 purchase _ #40.0602
Defines leadership and describes its value in the workplace. Demonstrates improved productivity that can result from proper leadership.
Business and Economics; Industrial and Technical Education; Social Science
Dist - UTEXPE **Prod** - UTEXPE 1983

A Lesson with Steve Allen - an introduction to jazz piano 80 MIN
VHS
Color (G)
$29.95 purchase _ #VD - ALL - JP01
Overviews classic jazz piano ideas and techniques for the beginning player. Divulges the 'tricks of the trade' and 'gimmicks' that enhance keyboard style - trills, octave vibrato, 'fake runs,' blues riffs and more. Shows how any player, with a variety of simple techniques, can start to build arrangements and spice up jazz playing. Explores the basics of blues piano, including the use of boogie - woogie, stride and a variety of walking bass lines. Shows the use of moving 10ths in the bass as played by Teddy Wilson and and Art Tatum, how to add descending notes to vary a chord, play fast 4 - note riffs. Includes printed music.
Fine Arts
Dist - HOMETA **Prod** - HOMETA 1994

Lessons 14 MIN
16mm
Color (G)
$20.00 rental
Experiments with the influence of light on an object's appearance. Weaves scenes of everyday household rituals while a voice comments on the perceived implications. Produced by Rob Danielson.
Fine Arts
Dist - CANCIN

Lessons from a sheep dog 30 MIN
VHS
Color (H C G A R)
$49.99 purchase, $10.00 rental _ #35 - 82900 - 533
Tells the story of a castaway collie who comes to a sheep ranch and becomes an obedient and loving pet. Suggests that this is a parable of the sort of obedience and loving submission expected by God. Based on an account by author Phillip Keller.
Literature and Drama; Religion and Philosophy
Dist - APH **Prod** - WORD

Lessons from Gulam - Asian music in Bradford 49 MIN
VHS
Color (G)
$375.00 purchase, $50.00 rental
Visits Bradford, a small mill town in the north of England with a population of some 60,000 Muslims from South Asia. Studies Asian music within the community and contrasts music education in the schools with the very different kind of music performed within Islamic families. Focuses on Gulam Musa, originally from Gujerat, India, and of a Muslim subcaste whose members are traditionally barbers and musicians. Gulam specializes in singing qawwali, a genre of Muslim devotional music found in India and Pakistan.
Fine Arts; Geography - World; Religion and Philosophy
Dist - DOCEDR **Prod** - DOCEDR

Lessons from life sciences 145 MIN
U-matic
University of the air series
Color (J H C A)
$750.00 purchase, $250.00 rental
Looks at a variety of areas of biology and discusses how these areas affect each of us. Program contains a series of five cassettes of 29 minutes each.
Science - Natural
Dist - CTV **Prod** - CTV 1978

Lessons from the heart - taking charge of feelings series 50 MIN
VHS
Lessons from the heart - taking charge of feelings series
Color (I)
$269 purchase _ #10160VL
Guides children of upper elementary age toward an acceptance and understanding of their complex emotions and social situations. Features teen narrators who teach how to cope with feelings, self - esteem, mistakes, and expressing emotions. Includes interviews, dramatic vignettes, and graphics to illustrate the issues. Comes with four videos, four teacher's guides, discussion topics, and four sets of blackline masters.
Guidance and Counseling; Social Science
Dist - UNL

Lessons from the new workplace 20 MIN
VHS
Color (PRO)
$775.00 purchase, $195.00 rental
Reveals strategies for implementing a logical approach to organizational chaos and change by using nature's way of management and adaptation. Unlocks the doors to three workplace domains - information, relationships and vision. Shows how the US Army applied similar principles. Follows up Leadership and the New Science by Margaret Wheatley.
Business and Economics; Psychology
Dist - CRMF **Prod** - CRMF 1995

Lessons in cycling 60 MIN
VHS
Color (A G)
$39.95 purchase _ #NUV6099V-P
Combines basic and advanced techniques of cycling to teach ultra-bike-fitting, energy-efficient body positioning, fluid replacement and diet, and designing one's own optimum training program. Includes race footage from around the United States and training footage from Southern California.
Physical Education and Recreation
Dist - CAMV

Lessons in visual language series
Features Peter Thompson as creator and narrator of a ten - part series on visual language produced by the Australian Film, Television and Radio School. Includes the titles Framing, Shot Sizes and Framing Faults, The Third Dimension, Lenses and Perspective, Movement and Moving the Camera, Orientation of the Camera, Image and Screen, Editing, Rhythm, Music.

Editing	10 MIN
Framing	10 MIN
Image and screen	14 MIN
Lenses and perspective	9 MIN
Lessons in visual language series	107 MIN
Movement and moving the camera	11 MIN
Music	16 MIN
Orientation of the camera	11 MIN
Rhythm	10 MIN
Short sizes and framing faults	9 MIN
The Third dimension	7 MIN

Dist - FIRLIT

Lessons Learned from Aircraft Accidents - Know Your Aircraft 21 MIN
16mm
B&W
LC 74-705021
Discusses the problem of aircraft accidents resulting from aviators' lack of knowledge or disregard of aircraft limitations.
Health and Safety; Industrial and Technical Education; Social Science
Dist - USNAC **Prod** - USA 1967

Lessons of the Red Bead Experiment, Vol VIII
VHS
Deming Series
Color (G)
$595.00 purchase, $195.00 rental
Considers the lessons of the 'red bead' experiment. Part of a nine - part series produced by Dr W Edwards Deming, Prof Robert Reich and Ford CEO Donald Peterson. Illustrates the principles and implementation of the Deming philosophy.
Business and Economics; Guidance and Counseling; Psychology
Dist - VLEARN

Lessons of the red bead experiment - Volume VIII 25 MIN
VHS / U-matic
Deming library series
Color (G)
$595.00 purchase, $150.00 rental; $595.00 purchase, $150.00 rental _ #213 - 9013
Shows the strategies needed to ensure the future success of a business organization. Emphasizes removing the cause of failures. Part of a sixteen - part series on the business philosophy of Dr Deming.
Business and Economics; Guidance and Counseling; Psychology
Dist - VLEARN FI **Prod** - CCMPR 1989

Lessons of the red bead experiment - Volume VIII 25 MIN
VHS
Deming library series
Color (PRO A G)
$595.00 purchase, $150.00 rental
Points out procedures that can help strengthen a company through lower costs, higher profits, and better organization. Explains principles proposed by Dr. Edwards Deming. Part of a sixteen - volume series.
Business and Economics; Psychology
Dist - EXTR **Prod** - FI

Lessons on a Mannequin Series, Lesson III
High Elevation, Basic Layered Cut
Dist - MPCEDP

Lessons on a Mannequin Series, Lesson I
One Length Bob - Cut
Dist - MPCEDP

Lessons on a Mannequin Series, Lesson VI
Neckline Cut - with Curling Iron Technique
Dist - MPCEDP

Lessons on a mannequin series, lesson v
The Bi - level cut
Dist - MPCEDP

Lessons on a mannequin series
Includes six tapes which are generally used in sequence. Begins with starting the first lesson with a mannequin having fairly long hair. Shows through the sequence of haircuts the hair becoming shorter until it finally reaches a length which can no longer be cut. Shows various styling techniques and a permanent wave is given.
Wrapping a permanent wave - on a mannequin
Dist - MPCEDP **Prod** - MPCEDP

Lest we forget 5 MIN
VHS
Color (G)
$100.00 purchase _ #91F0880
Reminds audiences of the free enterprise spirit that gave America the highest standard of living in the world.
Civics and Political Systems; Psychology
Dist - DARTNL **Prod** - DARTNL

Lester Horton technique - the warm-up 45 MIN
VHS
Color (G)
$19.95 purchase_#1274
Exhibits the modern dance training method of Lester Horton. Demonstrates leg swings, fortifications and metatarsal presses - all aimed at increasing agility, strength and flexibility while avoiding injury. A good resource for non - dancers to do nonaerobic workout to relieve muscle stress.
Fine Arts; Physical Education and Recreation
Dist - KULTUR

Lester Wilson, Bernice Johnson 30 MIN
VHS / U-matic
Eye on Dance - Popular Culture and Dance Series
Color
Focuses on Black dancers and choreography in films. Features Roberto Gautier on Lower East Side clubs in New York. Hosted by Celia Ipiotis.
Fine Arts
Dist - ARCVID **Prod** - ARCVID

Let a Song be a Friend 15 MIN
U-matic / VHS
Strawberry Square Series
Color (P)
Fine Arts
Dist - AITECH **Prod** - NEITV 1982

Let a thousand parks bloom 27 MIN
16mm
Color (G)
$30.00 rental
Talks about the building of People's Park and its ultimate destruction which marked the end of an era.
Fine Arts; Sociology
Dist - CANCIN **Prod** - LIPTNL 1969

Let 'Er Buck 20 MIN
U-matic / VHS
Color
Documents the history of rodeos in Oregon, the transition from the range to the arena and the competition of the Pendleton Round - Up.
History - United States; Physical Education and Recreation
Dist - MEDIPR **Prod** - KOAPTV 1976

Let Everybody Help 10 MIN
16mm
Communications for Safety Series
B&W
Shows how to get employees talking about safety.
Business and Economics; Health and Safety
Dist - NSC **Prod** - NSC

Let Go 10 MIN
Videoreel / VT2
Janaki Series
Color
Physical Education and Recreation
Dist - PBS **Prod** - WGBHTV

Let Habit Help 10 MIN
16mm
Personal Side of Safety Series
B&W
Stresses developing safe habits and breaking unsafe habits.
Business and Economics; Health and Safety
Dist - NSC **Prod** - NSC

Let heaven and nature sing 30 MIN
VHS
Color (I J H C G A R)
$19.95 purchase _ #35 - 88141 - 87
Features wildlife and winter nature footage filmed in Yellowstone, Grand Teton National Park and Alaska's Glacier Bay. Utilizes Scripture readings and the Christmas music of Maranatha to complete the Christmas theme. Produced by Zondervan.
Industrial and Technical Education; Religion and Philosophy
Dist - APH

Let His Blood Fall on Our Heads
Videoreel / VT2
Jesus Trial Series Program 2
Color
LC 79-706738
Religion and Philosophy
Dist - TVBUS **Prod** - TVOTAR 1979

Let Katie do it 28 MIN
16mm
Movies - Our Modern Art Series
B&W
Presents a recently discovered film by D W Griffith, set in rural Maine in 1915.
Fine Arts
Dist - STRFLS **Prod** - SPCTRA 1973

Let Me Count the Ways, Baby 29 MIN
Videoreel / VT2
Our Street Series
Color
Sociology
Dist - PBS **Prod** - MDCPB

Let Me Count the Ways I Know Me 15 MIN
U-matic
Success in the Job Market Series
Color (H)
Describes the personal data sheet and the resume. Explores ways of gaining experience or specific skills in order to acquire desired jobs.
Guidance and Counseling; Psychology
Dist - GPN **Prod** - KUONTV 1980

Let Me Destroy My Own Life 21 MIN
U-matic
Color (H C)
LC 83-706243
Portrays Gary Gerbev, a rock and roll drummer, in striving for success in the music business. Explores his unique lifestyle on Long Island while he talks candidly and humorously about himself, his problems and his goals.
Business and Economics; Fine Arts; Sociology
Dist - ZUBLIL **Prod** - ZUBLIL 1981

Let me say this - Reflections on living in the nuclear age 30 MIN
U-matic / VHS / 16mm
Color
Examines the energy and enthusiasm with which many groups and individuals are working to avert nuclear disaster. Looks at four different groups, including children and teenagers, grassroots activists and politicians, academicians and professionals, and performing artists.
Civics and Political Systems; Science - Physical; Social Science
Dist - CNEMAG **Prod** - DISARM 1984

Let Me See 20 MIN
16mm
Color
LC FI54-131
Shows the nursery school for visually handicapped children in Los Angeles, California. Asks what can parents do to help a blind child, should he be treated like any normal - sighted child, and will he ever really become a useful member of society.
Education; Health and Safety; Psychology; Sociology
Dist - USC **Prod** - USC 1951

Let me see - No 8 series
Ants and worms 15 MIN
Dist - AITECH

Let Me See Series no 1
Pendulums 15 MIN
Dist - AITECH

Let Me See Series no 6
Water and Rain 15 MIN
Dist - AITECH

Let me see series
Air and wind 15 MIN
Forces 15 MIN
Sun 15 MIN
Dist - AITECH

Let Me Try - a Mentally Retarded Child 6 MIN
U-matic / VHS / 16mm
Like You, Like Me Series
Color (K P)
Tells the story of Wendy, a mentally retarded child whose grandmother wants to shield her from other children.
Education; Guidance and Counseling
Dist - EBEC **Prod** - EBEC 1977

Let My People Go 54 MIN
U-matic / VHS / 16mm
B&W (J)
LC FIA65-822
Describes the difficulties encountered by the Jews in their search for a homeland. Tells about the efforts of Theodore Herzl, the beginning of Zionism and the.
Geography - World; History - World; Religion and Philosophy
Dist - FI **Prod** - PMI 1965

Let My People Go, Pt 1 27 MIN
U-matic / VHS / 16mm
B&W (J)
LC FIA65-822
Describes the difficulties encountered by Jews in their search for a homeland. Discusses the efforts of Theodore Herzl and examines the beginnings of Zionism.
Religion and Philosophy
Dist - FI **Prod** - PMI 1965

Let My People Go, Pt 2 27 MIN
16mm / U-matic / VHS
B&W (J)
LC FIA65-822
Describes the difficulties encountered by Jews in their search for a homeland. Discusses the efforts of Theodore Herzl and examines the beginnings of Zionism.
Religion and Philosophy; Sociology
Dist - FI **Prod** - PMI 1965

Let Nature Work for You 12 MIN
16mm
Color
LC 74-705022
Illustrates how natural plant regeneration can be used to assist highway maintenance engineers in beautifying the right - of - way, after construction has been completed. Encourages maintenance crews to keep mowing operations to a minimum by not mowing the complete right - of - way, giving nature a chance to revegetate the areas with natural growth.
Industrial and Technical Education; Science - Natural; Sociology
Dist - USNAC **Prod** - USDTFH 1969

Let no Man Put Asunder 25 MIN
16mm
Perspective Series
Color
LC 73-702324
Shows how three divorced women have dealt with the problems of child rearing, loneliness, finances, employment and adjustment to the life of a single parent.
Guidance and Counseling; Sociology
Dist - WRCTV **Prod** - WRCTV 1973

Let no Man Regret 11 MIN
16mm / U-matic / VHS
Color (I)
LC 74-700100
Shows how the unspoiled beauty of nature is being endangered by man's pollution and uncontrolled development by illustrating the phrase, 'Let no man regret that I passed here.'.
Science - Natural; Sociology
Dist - HIGGIN **Prod** - HIGGIN 1973

Let none sell justice - a call to the healthcare ministry 27 MIN
U-matic / VHS
Color (R)
$100.00 purchase, $50.00 rental _ #395, #396, #397
Examines human relationships to reinforce imperatives of Catholic healthcare ministries.
Guidance and Counseling; Health and Safety; Religion and Philosophy
Dist - CATHHA

Let the church say amen 60 MIN
U-matic / VHS / 16mm
Color (A R)
LC 74-700101
Portrays the travels of a young Black student through the South as he prepares to become a minister. Shows the Black church from the inside and how it affects Black life in both urban and rural America. Explores a specific segment of the Black American experience while treating the larger theme of a young man seeking his role in life.
Guidance and Counseling; History - United States; Religion and Philosophy; Sociology
Dist - CHAMBA **Prod** - BRNSTC
ECUFLM UCBHM
UMCOM

Let the Current do the Work 20 MIN
VHS / U-matic
Color (J)
LC 82-706769
Considers rafts, canoes, and kayaks as alternatives to motor - powered excursions. Focuses on techniques, waterproof packing, loading, rigging 'for a flip' and 'after a flip' along with rescue techniques for boat and passenger.
Physical Education and Recreation
Dist - AWSS **Prod** - AWSS 1981

Let the doors be of iron 23 MIN
VHS
Color (H C G)
$195.00 purchase
Examines the history of Eastern State Penitentiary in Pennsylvania. Reveals that the institution, which opened in 1829, was built as an alternative to Philadelphia's Walnut Street Jail and conceived as a significant step toward more humane treatment and rehabilitation of criminals through separate confinement at hard labor. It served as a model for over 500 prisons worldwide and was finally closed in 1970. Narrated by Ed Asner.
History - United States; Sociology
Dist - LANDMK **Prod** - LANDMK 1992

Let the Fabric do the Work, Pt 1 29 MIN
Videoreel / VT2
Designing Women Series
Color
Home Economics
Dist - PBS **Prod** - WKYCTV

Let the Fabric do the Work, Pt 2 29 MIN
Videoreel / VT2
Designing Women Series
Color
Home Economics
Dist - PBS **Prod** - WKYCTV

Let the flour fly 60 MIN
VHS
Color (G A)
$39.95 purchase _ #MHG100V
Features accomplished bread baker Sue Holmes Hodder, who teaches viewers how to bake five different kinds of bread - Swedish Rye, Crunchy Oatmeal, Quick and Easy French, Grandma's Rolls, and traditional white.
Home Economics
Dist - CAMV

Let the Good Times Roll 99 MIN
16mm
Color (H C A)
Tells the story of rock and roll, the popular music of the 1950s, through a compilation of footage of performers of the day. Features Chuck Berry, Chubby Checker, Bo Diddley, Little Richard, The Five Satins, The Shirelles, The Coasters, and Bill Haley and The Comets.
Fine Arts; Sociology
Dist - TIMLIF **Prod** - CPC 1973

Let the needles do the talking - Evaluating the New Haven needle exchange
VHS
Color (C PRO G)
$150.00 purchase _ #92.01
Examines the legal needle exchange program implemented in November, 1990, in New Haven, Connecticut, to combat the spread of HIV - AIDS via needle sharing among New Haven's drug injectors. Reveals that a new data collection and analysis was developed which provided the needed parameters for mathematical models. Results suggest that the program has reduced HIV - AIDS incidence by 33 percent. New Haven Health Dept - AIDS Division. Edward H Kaplan, Elaine O'Keefe.

Business and Economics; Health and Safety; Psychology
Dist - INMASC

Let the student come first 7 MIN
U-matic / 35mm strip
Producing better learning series Module 1
Color
Points out that the teacher's goal is to see that students learn and therefore everything in the classroom should be directed toward the student's learning needs.
Business and Economics; Education; Psychology
Dist - RESEM **Prod** - RESEM

Let the Waters Run Free 22 MIN
16mm
Color
LC 73-702327
Explores one of the last natural stretches of the Missouri River and the free - flowing little White River of South Dakota. Shows the wildlife which flourishes there, the recreational use of the rivers and the effects of channelization and dam building on natural rivers.
Geography - United States; Industrial and Technical Education; Physical Education and Recreation; Science - Natural; Sociology
Dist - SDDGFP **Prod** - SDDGFP 1973

Let Them Come with Rain 20 MIN
16mm / U-matic / VHS
Color (J)
LC 75-704274
Discusses the problems of life and the potential for development in Botswana, a country in Southern Africa.
Geography - World; Social Science; Sociology
Dist - JOU **Prod** - UN 1975

Let Them Know 10 MIN
16mm
Safety Management Series
Color
Business and Economics; Health and Safety
Dist - NSC **Prod** - NSC

Let Them Learn 27 MIN
U-matic / VHS / 16mm
Project Discovery II Series
Color (A)
LC FIA68-562
Examines the characteristics of educational films which make them significant teaching materials. Illustrates the ways a film can be sued in a planned manner for a spontaneous teaching situation.
Education; Psychology
Dist - EBEC **Prod** - PORTA 1967

Let them live series
Bats 23 MIN
Desert big horn sheep 21 MIN
Grey Whale 22 MIN
Orangutan - the Man of the Forest 22 MIN
The Serengeti Lion 20 MIN
White Fin Dolphin 23 MIN
Dist - LUF

Let There be Light 58 MIN
16mm
B&W
LC 81-701576
Shows the treatment of combat neuropsychiatric patients in an Army hospital. Demonstrates narcosynthesis, hypnosis and psychiatric therapy for individuals and for groups.
Health and Safety
Dist - USNAC **Prod** - USASC 1981

Let There be Light 29 MIN
VHS / U-matic
Photo Show Series
Color
Shows that light does more than just expose film, its presence can be the reason you are taking the shot.
Industrial and Technical Education
Dist - PBS **Prod** - WGBHTV 1981

Let Us Teach Guessing 61 MIN
16mm
MAA Individual Lecturers Series
Color (H C)
LC FIA66-1276
Professor George Polya is shown guiding an undergraduate class to discover the number of parts into which 3 - space is divided by five arbitrary planes. He also identifies the steps in plausible reasoning and points out that they are relevant in attacking any mathematical problem.
Mathematics
Dist - MLA **Prod** - MAA 1966

Let Us Teach Guessing, Pt 1 30 MIN
16mm
Maa Individual Lecturers Series Basic
Color (H C)
LC FIA66-1276
Professor George Polya is shown guiding an undergraduate class to discover the number of parts into which 3 - space is divided by five arbitrary planes. He also identifies the steps in plausible reasoning and points out that they are relevant in attacking any mathematical problem.
Mathematics
Dist - MLA **Prod** - MAA 1966

Let Us Teach Guessing, Pt 2 30 MIN
16mm
Maa Individual Lecturers Series Basic
Color (H C)
LC FIA66-1276
Professor George Polya is shown guiding an undergraduate class to discover the number of parts into which 3 - space is divided by five arbitrary planes. He also identifies the steps in plausible reasoning and points out that they are relevant in attacking any mathematical problem.
Mathematics
Dist - MLA **Prod** - MAA 1966

Let Your Child Help You 11 MIN
16mm
Parent - Child Relations in the Early Years Series
B&W (C T)
Shows how young children may help at home and achieve a sense of accomplishment and responsibility as well as increased skill.
Guidance and Counseling; Psychology; Sociology
Dist - NYU **Prod** - NYU 1947

L'Etang 20 MIN
16mm / U-matic / VHS
Color (J H) (FRENCH)
A French - language version of the motion picture The Pond. Studies members of a pond community as they affect other members. Observes life forms above and below the surface of the water.
Foreign Language; Science - Natural
Dist - IFB **Prod** - IFB 1961

Lethal Arrhythmias 19 MIN
16mm
Intensive Coronary Care Multimedia Learning System (ICC/MMLS Series
Color (PRO)
LC 73-701774
Discusses lethal arrhythmias, including ventricular fibrillation, ventricular tachycardia and ventricular standstill. Describes pathophysiology, electrocardiographic pattern, clinical picture and treatment given.
Health and Safety
Dist - SUTHLA **Prod** - SUTHLA 1969

Lethal risk and AIDS speak 48 MIN
VHS
Color (J)
$638.00 purchase
Offers a two - part program on the AIDS and HIV crisis. Lethal Risk reveals that every year in America 12 million people are newly infected with a sexually transmitted disease, 65 percent of which are between 15 and 25 years of age. Looks at how HIV and AIDS are spreading rapidly through America's youth population. Explains HIV, how it is transmitted, how it affects the human immune system, and how it ultimately leads to AIDS and death. AIDS Speak interviews AIDS victims, students and others.
Health and Safety; Sociology
Dist - WRIED **Prod** - WRIED 1993

Let's all recycle 8 MIN
VHS
Color (P I) (SPANISH)
$160.00 purchase, $50.00 rental _ #8390
Features the official recycling mascot Woody Woodpecker who explains the three Rs - reducing what is thrown away, reusing whenever possible and recycling household items such as newspapers, aluminum cans, glass, plastics.
Science - Natural
Dist - AIMS **Prod** - LACDPW 1991

Let's be Flexible 15 MIN
VHS / U-matic
Strawberry Square Series
Color (P)
Fine Arts
Dist - AITECH **Prod** - NEITV 1982

Let's be frank about pork show 30 MIN
U-matic / VHS
Cookin' cheap series
Color
Presents cooks Larry Bly and Laban Johnson who offer recipes, cooking and shopping tips.
Home Economics
Dist - MDCPB **Prod** - WBRATV

Let's be Friends - an Emotionally Disturbed Child 6 MIN
U-matic / VHS / 16mm
Like You, Like Me Series
Color (K P)
Shows how a group of children decide to help one of their friends, a little girl with an emotional problem.
Education; Guidance and Counseling
Dist - EBEC **Prod** - EBEC 1977

Let's be pals 8 MIN
16mm
Talking films series
Color (G)
$16.00 rental
Presents the Talking Films series which employs non - camera animation, associative editing and text written or scratched into the emulsion. Joins words with images to tell the story or with the audience to promote direct interaction. This production engages the viewer in a dialogue about the nature of the film experience.
Fine Arts
Dist - CANCIN **Prod** - IRWINJ 1985

Let's be Rational about Fractions 30 MIN
U-matic / VHS
Adult Math Series
Color (A)
Shows adult math students what fractions are and how they are used.
Education; Mathematics
Dist - KYTV **Prod** - KYTV 1984

Let's begin - starting school 18 MIN
VHS
Color (K P)
$89.00 purchase _ #RB811
Looks at the activities of school.
Education
Dist - REVID **Prod** - REVID

Let's Bowl with Dick Weber 40 MIN
VHS
(H C A)
$29.95 purchase _ #CH700V
Examines the rules and stategies of bowling. Explains how to chose equipment, proper stance, ball delivery, release, aiming, and the mechanics of the game.
Physical Education and Recreation
Dist - CAMV

Let's Carve 10 MIN
16mm
B&W
LC 75-703194
Shows examples of sculpture and the kind of stone used for each. Also demonstrates how students can create their own material for carving.
Fine Arts
Dist - USC **Prod** - USC 1966

Let's Celebrate Holidays 49 MIN
U-matic / VHS
Let's Celebrate Holidays Series
Color (K P)
Containes 1 videocassette.
Guidance and Counseling; Psychology; Social Science
Dist - TROLA **Prod** - TROLA 1987

Let's Celebrate Holidays Series
Let's Celebrate Holidays 49 MIN
Dist - TROLA

Let's clear the air 16 MIN
VHS
Color (G A PRO IND)
$195.00 purchase _ #AH45273
Considers the issues and hazards of smoking in the workplace. Features former Surgeon General Dr C Everett Koop, business leaders and national experts.
Health and Safety; Psychology
Dist - HTHED **Prod** - HTHED

Lets Consider Our Future 23 MIN
16mm
Color (H C A)
#3X122I
Presents the lives of five Canadian Indian people, iincluding a nurse, a radio broadcaster, a translator, a marine biologist, and a manager. Discusses reasons for their career selections, their education and training, and more.
Social Science
Dist - CDIAND **Prod** - BOMI 1979

Let's Count 14 MIN
U-matic / VHS / 16mm
Color (P)
$340, $240 purchase _ #3409
Shows ordinal and cardinal numbers, tally marks, and numerals.
Mathematics
Dist - CORF

Let's Dance 29 MIN
U-matic
Challenge Series
Color (PRO)
Captures the charm, energy and talent of young dance students and shows the techniques that enhance the innovative approach of their teacher.
Fine Arts; Psychology
Dist - TVOTAR **Prod** - TVOTAR 1985

Let's Dance 30 MIN
U-matic
Magic Ring II Series
(K P)
Continues the aim of the first series to bring added freshness to the commonplace and assist children to discover more about the many things in their world. Each program starts with the familiar, goes to the less familiar, then the new, and ends by blending new and old information.
Education; Literature and Drama
Dist - ACCESS **Prod** - ACCESS 1986

Let's Dance with Arthur Murray 120 MIN
U-matic / VHS
Color (H C A)
Presents basic ballroom etiquette and shows how to perform the waltz, the cha cha, the foxtrot, the samba, the rumba and disco.
Fine Arts
Dist - TIMLIF **Prod** - TIMLIF 1982

Let's decorate 15 MIN
Videoreel / VT2
Art corner series
B&W (P)
Discusses decorations and gifts for the holiday season.
Fine Arts
Dist - GPN **Prod** - CVETVC

Let's draw elephants 15 MIN
U-matic / VHS
Let's draw series
Color (P)
Fine Arts
Dist - AITECH **Prod** - OCPS 1976

Let's draw series

Birds - let's draw	15 MIN
Boats - water	15 MIN
Cars - let's draw	15 MIN
Cartoon bodies	15 MIN
Cartoon faces - let's draw	15 MIN
Cats	15 MIN
Deer - let's draw	15 MIN
Dinosaurs - let's draw	15 MIN
Faces - Expressions	15 MIN
Halloween - Haunted House	15 MIN
Horses - let's draw	15 MIN
Let's draw elephants	15 MIN
Ovals	15 MIN
People	15 MIN
People - Figures in Action	15 MIN
Shapes, Pt 1	15 MIN
Shapes, Pt 2	15 MIN
Small Animals	15 MIN
Thanksgiving - let's draw	15 MIN
Underwater	15 MIN

Dist - AITECH

Let's Eat - a Comer 28 MIN
VHS / 16mm
Sonrisas Series
Color (T P) (SPANISH)
$46.00 rental _ #SRSS - 107
Shows the children using Carriage House to give a meal to the elderly. In Spanish and English.
Sociology
Dist - PBS

Let's Eat Food 35 MIN
16mm / U-matic / VHS
Color (H C A)
LC 76-701194
Examines the relationship between health and diet. Considers specific topics such as coronary heart disease, nutritional deprivation, iron deficiencies and the relationship of sugar to health.
Health and Safety; Home Economics; Social Science
Dist - MGHT **Prod** - CAPCC 1976

Let's experiment with water colors 15 MIN
Videoreel / VT2
Art corner series
B&W (P)
Shows how to manipulate paint and water to mix light and dark shades.
Fine Arts
Dist - GPN **Prod** - CVETVC

Let's explore a cave 21 MIN
VHS
Color (J H)
$29.95 purchase _ #IV112
Introduces caves and caverns and how they are formed. Explores the chemical and geological processes of cave formation. Visits Jewel Cave, Wind Cave, Lehman Cave and Timpanogos Cave National Monuments.
Geography - United States; Science - Physical
Dist - INSTRU

Let's explore a desert 17 MIN
VHS
Let's explore series
Color; CC (I)
$80.00 purchase _ #A51604
Joins a naturalist and his nephew in a walk in the Sonoran Desert of Arizona. Shows how animals and plants have adapted to the hot, dry conditions of the area, focusing on the unique saguaro cactus and its slow growth rate. Includes a teacher's guide.
Science - Natural
Dist - NGS **Prod** - NGS 1994

Let's explore a forest 17 MIN
VHS
Let's explore series
Color; CC (I)
$80.00 purchase _ #A51605
Follows Adrienne as her uncle shows her the living things found in the forests of the Great Smoky Mountains of Tennessee. Teaches about deciduous and evergreen trees, transpiration and photosynthesis, and insects and animals. Includes a teacher's guide.
Science - Natural
Dist - NGS **Prod** - NGS 1994

Let's explore a meadow 17 MIN
VHS
Let's explore series
Color; CC (I)
$80.00 purchase _ #A51608
Shows that a seemingly empty meadow in the Great Smoky Mountains of Tennessee is actually full of life, from grasshoppers to snakes. Includes an introduction to beekeeping. Includes a teacher's guide.
Science - Natural
Dist - NGS **Prod** - NGS 1994

Let's explore a seashore 16 MIN
VHS
Let's explore series
Color; CC (I)
$80.00 purchase _ #A51607
Follows a girl and her mother as they explore the seacoast of Maine. Shows the animals and plants that have adapted to marine conditions, focusing on those found in the inter - tidal zones. Includes a teacher's guide.
Science - Natural
Dist - NGS **Prod** - NGS 1994

Let's explore a wetland 17 MIN
VHS
Let's explore series
Color; CC (I)
$80.00 purchase _ #A51606
Introduces the plants and animals that live in a cypress swamp, part of a wildlife sanctuary in South Carolina. Includes a teacher's guide.
Science - Natural
Dist - NGS **Prod** - NGS 1994

Let's Explore Our World - Venture Read - Alongs 99 MIN
VHS / U-matic
Venture Read - Alongs Series
(P I)
Contains a read along cassette and 8 paperbacks.
Science; Science - Natural
Dist - TROLA **Prod** - TROLA 1986

Let's explore series

Let's explore a desert	17 MIN
Let's explore a forest	17 MIN
Let's explore a meadow	17 MIN
Let's explore a seashore	16 MIN
Let's explore a wetland	17 MIN

Dist - NGS

Let's Figure it Out Series

Changes and Exchange - Addition with Exchange	20 MIN
Constructing Houses - Facts about Threes	20 MIN
Doubles - multiples of two	20 MIN
Guess Again - Algebraic Concepts and the Distributive Property	20 MIN
Half 'N Half - Operations, Fractional Numbers	20 MIN
How many beans - averages in general	20 MIN
Hurry Up - Patterns in Multiplication	20 MIN
Ladders and Lines - Number Line Concepts	20 MIN
Mirror Images - Figures and Symmetry	20 MIN
Patterns - Aids in Generalization	20 MIN
Ready, get set, go - subtraction via time	20 MIN
Take a Guess - Estimation and Problem Solving	20 MIN
What's Missing - Missing Addends	20 MIN
What's the Rule - Concepts from Algebra	20 MIN
Wheels and Things - Linear Measurement	20 MIN

Dist - NYSED

Let's Find Life 8 MIN
U-matic / VHS / 16mm
Wonder Walks Series
Color (P I)
LC 75-712996
Describes the natural habitats of various animals that can be found in the urban environment.
Science - Natural; Social Science
Dist - EBEC **Prod** - EBEC 1971

Let's Find Out 15 MIN
16mm
African Primary Science Program Series
Color (P I T)
LC 70-713891
Shows how the local environment can be used to teach science in creative ways. Presents students of a primary class in Tanzania who are involved in using local insects to sharpen observation of questioning skills.
Education; Science
Dist - EDC **Prod** - EDC 1971

Let's Find some Faces 9 MIN
U-matic / VHS / 16mm
Learning to Look Series
Color (P)
Presents a look at faces and their many expressions and shapes.
English Language; Guidance and Counseling; Psychology
Dist - MGHT **Prod** - MGHT 1973

Let's Find Something Better to do 16 MIN
16mm / U-matic / VHS
Color (P I)
Examines vandalism at the grade shcool level by illustrating with puppets and live action. Stresses alternate behavior and responsibility for one's own actions.
Guidance and Counseling; Sociology
Dist - BCNFL **Prod** - BORTF 1983

Let's Finish the Job 11 MIN
16mm
Color (A)
LC 74-705025
Shows the many breeding areas of the Aedes aegypti mosquito in the modern city. Discusses the life cycle of the mosquito and describes steps necessary of eradicate it.
Health and Safety; Home Economics; Science - Natural
Dist - USNAC **Prod** - USPHS 1967

Let's get a move on 25 MIN
VHS
Color (P I J G)
$24.95 purchase _ #KVI103V - K
Helps children and parents survive the impact of changing places, saying goodbye, adjusting to new people, new situations and new spaces. Offers advice on making new friends, how kids can help with the move and ideas for keeping in touch with friends and loved ones left behind. Validates the emotions of children during a move and provides tools for dealing with them. Acknowledges children's fears, demystifies the moving process and offers advice through songs, narrative and real kids who tell about relocating. Includes activity guide.
Guidance and Counseling; Health and Safety
Dist - CAMV

Let's get along - conflict skills training 58 MIN
VHS
Color (P I)
$249 purchase _ #10385VG
Features Gary Wick, ventriloquist and comedian, teaching conflict skills. Presents programs on skills for solving differences; tone of voice; peace - making skills; and the importance of friends. Includes a reproducible teacher's guide.
Psychology; Social Science
Dist - UNL

Let's get along - conflict skills training series

How fights start and stop	14 MIN
Making and keeping friends	15 MIN
Nice things kids can do	16 MIN
What you say is what you get	13 MIN

Dist - UNL

Let's Get Away from it all 14 MIN
16mm
Color
Follows several visitors on their vacation in Pompano Beach, Florida.
Geography - United States; Physical Education and Recreation
Dist - FLADC **Prod** - FLADC

Let's Get it Back, America 29 MIN
16mm
Color
Presents George Washington, James Madison, Ben Franklin and Alexander Hamilton returning to Washington, DC and offering advice to an America whose government has grown far beyond what they envisioned.

Biography; Civics and Political Systems
Dist - USCHOC **Prod** - USCHOC 1980

Let's Get Organized 15 MIN
VHS / U-matic
Writer's Realm Series
Color (I)
$125.00 purchase
Provides some guidelines to organizing the subjects in a piece of writing.
English Language; Literature and Drama; Social Science
Dist - AITECH **Prod** - MDINTV 1987

Let's Get Together - Culture (Anthropology - Sociology) 15 MIN
VHS / U-matic
Two Cents' Worth Series
Color (P)
Shows Stuart, a Winnebago Indian, teaching his friend Chip about the colorful ceremonial dances his family does to make a living.
Social Science; Sociology
Dist - AITECH **Prod** - WHATV 1976

Let's Go for a Hike 15 MIN
VHS / U-matic
Mrs Cabobble's Caboose
(P)
Designed to teach primary grade students basic music concepts. Highlights melody, rhythm, harmony and the different families of musical instruments. Features Mrs. Fran Powell.
Fine Arts
Dist - GPN **Prod** - WDCNTV 1986

Let's Go Golfing
16mm
B&W
Bryon Nelson gives golf lesson in 13 segments.
Physical Education and Recreation
Dist - SFI **Prod** - SFI

Let's Go Out Together 13 MIN
U-matic / VHS / 16mm
Visit to Series
Color (P)
LC 77-703371
Presents children experiencing the diversity of city life through visits to an open market, a firehouse, a zoo and a construction site.
Guidance and Counseling; Social Science
Dist - JOU **Prod** - CCPEP 1977

Let's go power boating
VHS
Color (G)
$29.95 purchase _ #0189
Teaches about power boating. Covers terminology, safety gear, registration, Coast Guard exam, law, rules of the road, weather, loading, fueling, maintenance, trailering, boat hauling.
Physical Education and Recreation
Dist - SEVVID

Let's Go Sciencing, Unit III - Life Series
Mollusks 15 MIN
Dist - GPN

Let's go - success on the job 9 MIN
VHS
Employability skills videos series
Color (H G)
$48.00 purchase _ #JR104
Offers help for senior high students, people entering the job market, and adults in career transitions. Portrays newly hired employees who decipher a paycheck, identify benefits and examine civil rights regarding discrimination and harassment. They also explore positive work attitudes and habits, evaluate their own performances and learn about getting along with supervisors and co - workers.
Business and Economics; Guidance and Counseling
Dist - CENTER **Prod** - CENTER

Let's Go There Together 18 MIN
16mm
Color
LC 77-700296
Shows the ski areas of British Columbia.
Geography - World; Physical Education and Recreation
Dist - PCFCWA **Prod** - PETRIC 1976

Let's Help Recycle 11 MIN
U-matic / VHS / 16mm
Caring about Our Community Series
Color (P I)
LC 76-700544
Depicts a group of school children who come to a city council meeting to present a report on the need to stop waste and recycle materials. Shows that each child has conducted a study of one aspect of the problem and has a solution for it. Describes the recycling of paper, bottles and cans.
Science - Natural; Social Science
Dist - AIMS **Prod** - GORKER 1973

Let's Keep in Touch 28 MIN
16mm
Color
Describes how Medicare, with recommended supplementary insurance, can serve the needs of senior citizens.
Business and Economics; Health and Safety
Dist - MTP **Prod** - BALIN

Let's kill nanny 30 MIN
VHS
Open space series
Color; PAL (H C A)
PdS50 purchase; Available only in the United Kingdom
Describes the welfare state as debilitating to both the economy and the beneficiaries of the program. Uses information from a report published by the Adam Smith Institute and argues in favor of self - reliance.
Sociology
Dist - BBCENE

Let's learn about alcohol
VHS
Color (I J)
$79.50 purchase _ #AH46406
Uses an animated format to teach about alcohol. Reveals the dangers of alcohol use.
Health and Safety; Science - Natural
Dist - HTHED **Prod** - HTHED

Let's learn about bones and muscles
VHS
Color (K P I J)
$79.50 purchase _ #AH46354
Uses an animated format to teach about bones and muscles. Available in two editions, one for grades kindergarten through third grade and one for grades four through eight.
Science - Natural
Dist - HTHED **Prod** - HTHED

Let's learn about drugs
VHS
Color (I J)
$79.50 purchase _ #AH46405
Uses an animated format to teach about drugs and how to avoid them. Covers topics including peer pressure, the desire to be grown up, and the urge to show off.
Health and Safety; Science - Natural
Dist - HTHED **Prod** - HTHED

Let's learn about smoking
VHS
Color (I J)
$79.50 purchase _ #AH46407
Uses an animated format to teach about tobacco and its dangers. Presents strategies for dealing with peer pressure to smoke.
Health and Safety; Science - Natural
Dist - HTHED **Prod** - HTHED

Let's learn about the nervous system
VHS
Color (K P I J)
$79.50 purchase _ #AH46355
Uses an animated format to teach about the brain, spinal column, and nervous system. Available in two editions, one for grades kindergarten through third grade and one for grades four through eight.
Science - Natural
Dist - HTHED **Prod** - HTHED

Let's learn about your body
VHS
Color (K P I J)
$79.50 purchase _ #AH46350
Uses an animated format to teach about the major body systems, including the skeletal, muscular, cardiac, digestive, and others. Available in two editions, one for grades kindergarten through third grade and one for grades four through eight.
Science - Natural
Dist - HTHED **Prod** - HTHED

Let's learn about your digestive system
VHS
Color (K P I J)
$79.50 purchase _ #AH46356
Uses an animated format to teach about the digestive system, from the teeth to the endocrine system. Available in two editions, one for grades kindergarten through third grade and one for grades four through eight.
Science - Natural
Dist - HTHED **Prod** - HTHED

Let's learn about your heart
VHS
Color (K P I J)
$79.50 purchase _ #AH46351
Uses an animated format to teach about the heart, blood, and circulation. Available in two editions, one for grades kindergarten through third grade and one for grades four through eight.
Science - Natural
Dist - HTHED **Prod** - HTHED

Let's learn about your lungs
VHS
Color (K P I J)
$79.50 purchase _ #AH46352
Uses an animated format to teach about the respiratory system. Stresses the importance of caring for the lungs. Available in two editions, one for grades kindergarten through third grade and one for grades four through eight.
Science - Natural
Dist - HTHED **Prod** - HTHED

Let's learn about your teeth
VHS
Color (K P I J)
$79.50 purchase _ #AH46353
Uses an animated format to teach about dental hygiene and care. Stresses the importance of daily dental care. Available in two editions, one for grades kindergarten through third grade and one for grades four through eight.
Science - Natural
Dist - HTHED **Prod** - HTHED

Let's learn how to dance series
Features professional ballroom dancers Kathy Blake and Gene Russo in a 25 - part series teaching the various social dances, including the Tango, Fox Trot, Cha Cha, Samba, Jitterbug, and others.
Let's learn how to dance series 1500 MIN
Dist - CAMV **Prod** - CAMV

Let's Look at Castles 19 MIN
16mm / U-matic / VHS
Color (J H C)
LC 78-707247
Traces the development of the castle in England from the 11th century to the beginning of the 14th century. Explains early castle construction and various methods of castle attack and defense and includes the best examples of the period.
Fine Arts; History - World
Dist - IFB **Prod** - ATTICO 1968

Let's Look at Levers 10 MIN
16mm / U-matic / VHS
Color; B&W (P I)
Presents an introduction to levers. Shows how a lever works with examples of nail pulling and other common household uses.
Industrial and Technical Education; Science - Physical
Dist - JOU **Prod** - JOU 1961

Let's Look at New Zealand 15 MIN
16mm
Color (I J H)
LC FIA67-5305
Discusses the history, geography, culture, economic development and farm exports of New Zealand. Depicts the cities of Wellington and Auckland. Shows North Island's geysers and pools of hot mud and water.
Geography - World
Dist - SF **Prod** - TEXTBK 1966

Let's make a deal 11 MIN
VHS
Peacemakers series
CC; Color (I)
$89.95 purchase _ #10389VG
Gives simple strategies for conflicts where both parties come out winners. Demonstrates negotiation, compromise, problem solving, and apologizing. Includes a teacher's guide and blackline masters. Part two of a three - part series.
Psychology
Dist - UNL

Let's make a Deal - Cable Vs Dance 30 MIN
U-matic / VHS
Business and Law of Dance Series
Color
Business and Economics; Fine Arts; Industrial and Technical Education
Dist - ARCVID **Prod** - ARCVID

Let's make a Film 13 MIN
16mm
Color (P)
LC 79-714171
Explores the activities of the yellow ball workshop, Newton, Mass., Which involves young people from the ages of eight through eighteen who create their own films. Individual students demonstrate and discuss the steps involved in preparing their films and show the finished product.
Education; Fine Arts; Industrial and Technical Education
Dist - VANREN **Prod** - YELLOW 1971

Let's make a Map 11 MIN
U-matic / VHS / 16mm
Color; B&W (P I)
LC FIA65-35
Describes how the physical world is represented on a map. Illustrates comparative size and distance, and shows how a map can help us find our way from one place to another.

Social Science
Dist - PHENIX Prod - WILETS 1964

Let's make a Musical 29 MIN
U-matic
Music Shop Series
Color
Features Jerry Bilik as he composes a musical comedy on the spot to show how it's done.
Fine Arts
Dist - UMITV Prod - UMITV 1974

Let's make Music 30 MIN
VHS / 16mm
Favorite Music Stories Series
Color (P)
$39.95 purchase _ #CL6912
Presents music for children.
Fine Arts; Literature and Drama
Dist - EDUCRT

Let's make Music Volume 1 30 MIN
VHS / 16mm
Music Stories Series
Color (P)
$39.95 purchase _ #CL6905
Presents children's songs.
Fine Arts; Literature and Drama
Dist - EDUCRT

Let's make Up a Story 11 MIN
U-matic / VHS / 16mm
Color (P I)
LC 72-701934
Shows how you can use your imagination to make up your own stories with your own characters, settings and plots.
English Language; Literature and Drama
Dist - CORF Prod - CORF 1972

Let's Measure Series

Let's Measure - using Standard Units	14 MIN
Using Centimeters, Meters, and Kilometers	10 MIN
Using Grams and Kilograms	10 MIN
Using Milliliters and Liters	12 MIN
Using Standard Units	13 MIN

Dist - CORF

Let's Measure - using Standard Units 14 MIN
U-matic / VHS / 16mm
Let's Measure Series
Color (P)
LC 74-706797
Presents the story of Jimmy, who goes to measuring land and learns that to measure anything, units of the same size must be used and are called standard units.
Mathematics
Dist - CORF Prod - CORF 1970

Let's move it - Newton's laws of motion 15 MIN
VHS
Color (P I)
$89.00 purchase _ #RB806
Discusses Newton's three laws of motion. Observes that an object at rest remains at rest until a force makes it move. Once an object moves it moves forever unless a force stops it. Every action has an equal and opposite reaction. Considers the concepts of inertia, mass, acceleration, gravity and friction.
Science - Physical
Dist - REVID Prod - REVID

Let's obey 30 MIN
VHS
Quigley's village series
Color (K P I R)
$19.95 purchase, $10.00 rental _ #35 - 87 - 2504
Features Mr Quigley and his puppet friends. Shows how Mr Quigley tells the boys to pick only the ripe berries, and how the boys learn the importance of following directions. Produced by Jeremiah Films.
Literature and Drama; Religion and Philosophy
Dist - APH

Let's Party 30 MIN
VHS
Soapbox With Tom Cottle Series
Color (G)
$59.95 purchase _ #SBOX - 401
Investigates the use of drugs and alcohol by teenagers. Explores the reasons for using illicit substances. Hosted by psychologist Tom Cottle.
Guidance and Counseling; Health and Safety; Psychology; Sociology
Dist - PBS Prod - WGBYTV 1985

Let's party 30 MIN
VHS
Color (J H C G A)
$59.95 purchase _ #AH45186
Interviews seven teenagers on their experiences with substance abuse. Reveals that all of them agree that parents should accept the fact that teenagers will experiment with alcohol and drugs.
Guidance and Counseling; Health and Safety; Psychology; Sociology
Dist - HTHED Prod - PBS

Let's play baseball - with Ozzie Smith 50 MIN
VHS
Color (G T H J I)
$24.98 purchase _ #ABD1013V-P
Features shortstop Ozzie Smith teaching basic techniques and strategies to young baseball players. Includes warmups, stretching, mental preparation, communication between catcher and pitcher, pitching with runners on base, hitting stance, baserunning, and fielding. Emphasizes winning attitude in baseball and in life.
Physical Education and Recreation
Dist - CAMV

Let's Play Hospital 53 MIN
16mm
Color
LC 74-706373
Correlates a child's experiences in the hospital with what he feels about it. Shows how the hospital staff helps the children deal with their anxious feelings and describes a program of hospital - related play.
Health and Safety; Sociology
Dist - USNAC Prod - USOE

Let's Play Prisoners 24 MIN
U-matic / VHS
Julie Zando Series
Color (G)
$250.00, $200.00 purchase, $50.00 rental
Investigates female subjectivity. Uses several layers of first person narration to link power and love, dependency and differentiation. Asks whether all relationships between women are modeled after the early ambivalence of the mother - child relationship.
Fine Arts; Religion and Philosophy; Sociology
Dist - WMEN Prod - JUZAN 1988

Let's play safe 10 MIN
U-matic / VHS / 16mm
Color (I J)
LC 75-702575
Uses live photography and animation to show six playground accidents. Helps children understand the consequences of situations in which accidents occur.
Guidance and Counseling; Health and Safety
Dist - PEREN Prod - PORTA 1974
AIMS

Let's Play the Piano - and all those Keyboards 140 MIN
VHS
Color (G)
$39.95 purchase _ #1225
Prepares students of piano to play all forms of music including classical, country, jazz, pop and rock. Teaches how to read music and use chord accompaniment. Features Bud Conway as instructor.
Agriculture; Fine Arts
Dist - KULTUR

Let's pray - for every child - and grown - up - who needed help learning how to pray
VHS
Color (P I J H G)
$19.95 purchase _ #110 - 024
Teaches Muslims of all ages how to pray. Tells about the basics of Salat, Wudu, Adhan, Iqama, direction of prayer, number of rakats in each prayer, how to shorten prayer when traveling and more. Also available with book.
Religion and Philosophy
Dist - SOUVIS Prod - SOUVIS

Let's pretend 25 MIN
16mm / U-matic / VHS
Computer programme series; Episode 7
Color (J)
Explores the computers ability to be an accurate model or simulation of the real thing.
Business and Economics; Mathematics
Dist - FI Prod - BBCTV 1982

Let's Pretend 30 MIN
U-matic
Magic Ring I Series
(K P)
Introduces the series' main characters and the magical properties of the ring.
Education; Literature and Drama
Dist - ACCESS Prod - ACCESS 1984

Let's Pretend it 10 MIN
U-matic / VHS
Book, Look and Listen Series
Color (K P)
Deals with the skills to create stories from a variety of sources.
English Language; Literature and Drama
Dist - AITECH Prod - MDDE 1977

Let's Rejoice 10 MIN
U-matic / VHS / 16mm
Color (J H)
LC 73-702075
Offers glimpses of the lives of aged Jewish survivors of wartime Nazi concentration camps in Yugoslavia. Portrays their gradually - revealed resiliance after great hardships to stimulate an examination of life, the past and the future.
History - World; Sociology
Dist - WOMBAT Prod - WOMBAT 1973

Let's see 15 MIN
VHS
Art's place series
Color (K P)
$49.00 purchase, $15.00 rental _ #295810
Joins Jessie and Mrs Hooter as they go sightseeing. Shows Leo who plays some looking games with Doodles and Art, while Mirror tells the story of Little Tommy Tum. Features the art of Marc Chagall. Part of a series combining songs, stories, animation, puppets and live actors to convey the pleasure of artistic expression. Includes an illustrated teacher's guide.
Fine Arts
Dist - TVOTAR Prod - TVOTAR 1989

Let's Shape Up
VHS / U-matic
Color
Provides a base upon which dietitians can build a personal diet plan. Stresses exercise.
Physical Education and Recreation; Social Science
Dist - MEDFAC Prod - MEDFAC

Let's Split (Inner Thighs II) 29 MIN
Videoreel / VT2
Maggie and the Beautiful Machine - Feet and Legs Series
Color
Physical Education and Recreation
Dist - PBS Prod - WGBHTV

Let's Start at the Very Beginning 6 MIN
U-matic / VHS / 16mm
Communicating from the Lectern Series
Color (H C A)
Suggests that it is not necessary to recognize every person in the room before beginning the body of the speech. Shows effective and ineffective speech openings and notes how extensive background is not necessary when using quotes.
English Language
Dist - AIMS Prod - METAIV

Let's Take the Mystery Out of Power Brakes 22 MIN
16mm
Color (H C A)
LC 73-703375
Presents an analysis of power brake malfunctions and illustrates their correction by the installation of a replacement unit.
Industrial and Technical Education
Dist - BENDIX Prod - BENDIX 1971

Let's talk about AIDS 14 MIN
VHS
Color (P I)
$119.00 purchase _ #CG - 957 - VS
Presents information about AIDS in a style appropriate for students in grades 3 - 6. Conveys the information that AIDS cannot be contracted from casual contact and that elementary school children are unlikely to get it. Explains that it is contracted through an exchange of blood or other bodily fluids and reassures students.
Health and Safety
Dist - HRMC Prod - HRMC 1992

Let's talk about it series

Birthday	28 MIN
Male and female	22 MIN
The Parents	17 MIN
Puberty	18 MIN
The Teachers	19 MIN

Dist - EMFVL

Let's talk about it - Tape II 30 MIN
VHS
All about aging series
Color (A G)
$195.00 series purchase, $25.00 series rental
Describes relationships between older adults and adult chhildren. Covers the dynamics of communication and acceptance. Features the concerns of the aged. Part two of a four - part series not available separately. Includes workbook and provider's guide.
Psychology; Sociology
Dist - AGEVI Prod - AGEVI 1990

Let's Talk about Safety 10 MIN
16mm
Communication for Safety Series

B&W (C A)
Offers an approach to the universal problem of getting ideas across. Shows foremen how to use plain talk to put safety across, how to talk safety as easily as they talk bowling or baseball.
Health and Safety
Dist - NSC **Prod** - DUNN 1959

Let's talk about STD - testing for young men 12 MIN
VHS
Color (J H C)
$99.95 purchase _ #BO49 - V8
Presents street - wise role models for street - smart teens, speaking the language of urban audiences, motivating sexually active young women and men to get regular STD tests. Breaks through common myths, fears and social stigmas, personalize the risk, encourage condom use, and explain the screening procedure. Suggested to initiate discussion in one - on - one and group settings. Features 'Let's Talk About Sex,' the MTV rap hit by Salt 'n Pepa. See also companion volume for young women.
Guidance and Counseling; Health and Safety; Sociology
Dist - ETRASS **Prod** - ETRASS 1992

Let's talk about STD - testing for young women 12 MIN
VHS
Color (J H C)
$99.95 purchase _ #BO48 - V8
Presents street - wise role models for street - smart teens, speaking the language of urban audiences, motivating sexually active young women and men to get regular STD tests. Breaks through common myths, fears and social stigmas, personalize the risk, encourage condom use, and explain the screening procedure. Suggested to initiate discussion in one - on - one and group settings. Features 'Let's Talk About Sex,' the MTV rap hit by Salt 'n Pepa. See also companion volume for young men.
Guidance and Counseling; Health and Safety; Sociology
Dist - ETRASS **Prod** - ETRASS 1992

Let's Talk about Surgery 30 MIN
U-matic / VHS
Color
Considers medical versus surgical procedures. Looks at who really makes the decision to have surgery. Examines the idea of whether or not there is ever such a thing as 'minor surgery.'.
Health and Safety
Dist - AL **Prod** - UILCCC

Let's Talk about the Hospital Series
Going to the doctor 15 MIN
Going to the hospital 29 MIN
Having an Operation 17 MIN
A Visit to the Emergency Department 15 MIN
Wearing a Cast 17 MIN
Dist - FAMCOM

Let's talk about...responsibility 29 MIN
35mm strip / VHS
Color (I J)
$169.00, $129.00 purchase _ #2295 - SK, #2216 - SK
Examines questions of responsibility. Dramatizes situations ranging from the personal to the wider society. Helps students develop their personal senses of responsibility. Includes teacher's guide.
Education; Guidance and Counseling; Sociology
Dist - SUNCOM **Prod** - SUNCOM

Let's Talk Idioms 4.30 MIN
VHS
English Plus Series
(J H A)
Reveals proper usage of idioms in conversation as well as an introduction to colors.
English Language
Dist - AITECH **Prod** - LANGPL 1985

Let's Talk it Over - a Child with Epilepsy 6 MIN
U-matic / VHS / 16mm
Like You, Like Me Series
Color (K P)
Presents a story about Sandy, an epileptic child who is afraid of telling the other children about her condition.
Education; Guidance and Counseling
Dist - EBEC **Prod** - EBEC 1977

Lets Teach Signs 7 MIN
16mm
Color (H C A S)
LC 76-701689
Presents Herb Larson giving his views on teaching sign language to deaf students. Speaking as a deaf adult he advocates improving sign language skills as a means of acquiring a better understanding of English.
Guidance and Counseling; Psychology
Dist - JOYCE **Prod** - JOYCE 1975

Let's Think and be Safe 10 MIN
16mm / U-matic / VHS
Color (K P)
Dramatizes seven episodes around the major causes of accidents in schools. Shows what can happen and suggests ways to avoid these accidents. Combines animation and live action.
Health and Safety
Dist - AIMS **Prod** - PORTAP 1975

Let's Think Fat 15 MIN
Videoreel / VT2
Umbrella Series
Color
Health and Safety; Psychology; Social Science
Dist - PBS **Prod** - KETCTV

Let's try sharing 25 MIN
VHS
Big comfy couch series
Color (K P)
$14.99 purchase _ #0 - 7835 - 8305 - 2NK
Focuses on Loonette who learns that sharing isn't easy - even for clowns. Stimulates physical, mental and emotional growth. Shows youngsters how to deal with typical feelings and fears. Offers movement games and activities for developing coordination and motor skills. Builds positive attitudes toward books and reading. Part of a series.
English Language; Guidance and Counseling; Literature and Drama
Dist - TILIED **Prod** - PBS 1995

Let's Visit Series
Books - from start to finish 15 MIN
How to make a truck 9 MIN
Market Gardening 15 MIN
Sandwich stuff 15 MIN
Dist - BCNFL

Let's Walk Together 29 MIN
U-matic / VHS
Color (J H A)
LC 85-703548
Shows how abusive parents can develop more positive relationships with their children.
Sociology
Dist - EBEC **Prod** - BYU 1981

Let's Watch Plants Grow 10 MIN
16mm / U-matic / VHS
Color (P I)
A class watches plants grow. It learns that plants need water, minerals and sunlight.
Science - Natural
Dist - CORF **Prod** - CORF 1962

Let's Write a Story 11 MIN
U-matic / VHS / 16mm
Color (P I)
LC 78-701966
Presents three episodes as the basis for creative writing exercises.
English Language
Dist - CF **Prod** - CF 1978

Let's Write a Story 15 MIN
VHS / U-matic
Hidden Treasures Series no 5; No 5
Color (T)
LC 82-706529
Uses the adventures of a pirate and his three friends to explore the many facets of language arts. Focuses on punctuation and illustrates its use in reading and writing.
English Language
Dist - GPN **Prod** - WCVETV 1980

The Letter 15 MIN
U-matic / VHS / 16mm
Words and Pictures Series
Color (K P)
Tells of Toad's sadness that he has never received a letter. Reveals that Frog attempts to correct this by sending him a letter, but that Toad has a long wait when the letter is delivered by a snail.
English Language; Literature and Drama
Dist - FI **Prod** - FI

The Letter 17 MIN
VHS
Color (G)
$25.00 purchase
Depicts a symbolic rape by the Devil and a renewal of self - worth. Features actress Mary Lucas. Produced by Coni Beeson.
Fine Arts; Sociology
Dist - CANCIN

Letter carriers
VHS
Vocational visions career series
Color (H A)
$39.95 purchase _ #CDS502
Interviews people who are letter carriers. Answers questions about the educational requirements and necessary skills for the occupation, as well as its career opportunities, salary range and outlook for the future. Part of a series which examines the potential of various occupations.
Business and Economics; Guidance and Counseling; Psychology; Social Science
Dist - CADESF **Prod** - CADESF 1989

Letter from a Mother 10 MIN
16mm
B&W
LC FIE55-80
Shows an American mother's understanding of the role her son must play in defense of his country.
Civics and Political Systems; Guidance and Counseling; Social Science
Dist - USNAC **Prod** - USA 1955

Letter from an Airman 17 MIN
16mm
Color
LC 74-706124
Presents an airman's thoughts as he writes his brother about Air Force basic training.
Civics and Political Systems
Dist - USNAC **Prod** - USAF 1964

Letter from an Apache 11 MIN
VHS / U-matic
Color (I J)
Presents the story of an Apache who was kidnapped and lived with the Pimas and later the whites, where he studied medicine and became the first Native American physician.
History - United States; Social Science
Dist - CEPRO **Prod** - CEPRO 1986

Letter from an Unknown Woman 89 MIN
16mm
B&W
Stars Joan Fontaine as a woman who reveals her lifetime love for a concert pianist who fathered her child years ago and now can't even remember her. Tells how Fontaine's present husband challenges the pianist to a duel. Directed by Max Ophuls.
Fine Arts
Dist - KITPAR **Prod** - UPCI 1948

Letter from Siberia 60 MIN
16mm
Color (FRENCH)
Parodies the standard travelogue in its presentation of Siberia. Features an animated segment in which mammoths are described as a fashionable feature of Siberian life. Converts the Siberian gold rush into a full - blown Western, complete with Indians, cowboys rustlers, trappers and gunfights.
Foreign Language; Geography - World; Literature and Drama
Dist - NYFLMS **Prod** - NYFLMS 1957

The Letter of Application 30 MIN
VHS / U-matic
Writing for a Reason Series
Color (C)
English Language
Dist - DALCCD **Prod** - DALCCD

The Letter of Application and the Application Form 15 MIN
U-matic
Job Seeking Series
Color (H C A)
Tells how to use letters of application and application forms.
Guidance and Counseling; Psychology
Dist - GPN **Prod** - WCETTV 1979

The Letter on light blue stationery - a story about self - esteem 22 MIN
VHS
Human race club series
Color (P I)
$59.00 purchase _ #RB876
Uses animation to portray Pamela who is asked to write a sympathy letter to the family of a classmate who died. Part of a series teaching essential living skills.
Guidance and Counseling; Psychology; Sociology
Dist - REVID **Prod** - REVID 1990

Letter to a Friend 20 MIN
16mm
B&W
LC FIE52-1945
Explains how Japanese boys and girls correspond, as pen pals, with boys and girls of their own ages in the United States.

Guidance and Counseling; Sociology
Dist - USNAC **Prod** - USA 1951

Letter to a long lost friend 8 MIN
16mm
Color (G)
$20.00 rental
Stimulates the processes of memory bringing forth within the arc and shadow of time.
Fine Arts; Psychology
Dist - CANCIN **Prod** - RAYHER 1980

A Letter to Amy 7 MIN
16mm / U-matic / VHS
Color (K P)
LC 70-709266
Tells the story of Peter who is having a birthday party and although he has asked all his friends in person, he decides to write out one special invitation to a girl. Shows what happens before he reaches the mailbox, leaving him very mixed - up and worried about whether or not she will come to the party.
Literature and Drama
Dist - WWS **Prod** - WWS 1970

Letter to Brezhnev 94 MIN
16mm / 35mm
Color (G)
$250.00, $300.00 rental
Presents a pre - glasnost comedy about Teresa and Elaine, two working class women from Liverpool who search for some excitement in their dreary lives. Reveals that the women, on the town and on the prowl, spend the night with two Russian sailors on 24 - hour leave. Falling madly in love, Elaine writes to Brezhnev asking for permission to join her sailor in the Soviet Union. Brezhnev's reply causes a journalistic sensation, a family crisis and an unexpected response from the British government. Directed by Chris Bernard.
Civics and Political Systems; Fine Arts; Sociology
Dist - KINOIC

A Letter to Dad - a story of co - dependency 35 MIN
VHS
Color (G)
$295.00 purchase
Dramatizes the life of Megan Riley, a divorced mother of two teenagers who finally confronts the profoundly damaging effects of growing up in a dysfunctional family. Introduces Megan as she struggles with a life filled with despair and loneliness. Reveals that, returning to her childhood town she encounters the trauma of growing up with an unpredictable, violent alcoholic father and a co - dependent mother. Shows how Megan turns her life around with the help of an understanding therapist and begins building a healthy, fulfilling life.
Health and Safety; Sociology
Dist - FMSP

Letter to Jane 55 MIN
16mm
B&W ((ENGLISH NARRATION))
Studies the social issues raised by actress Jane Fonda and looks at her films and those of her father. Produced in France with English narration. Directed by Jean - Luc Godard and Jean - Pierre Gorin.
Fine Arts; History - World; Sociology
Dist - NYFLMS **Prod** - NYFLMS 1972

A Letter to Nancy 80 MIN
16mm
Color (H C A)
Deals with a romance between Carol Reed, daughter of a family of comfortable means, and the minister of a church serving mixed races in an underprivileged city area, which introduces young Nancy to the Reed family. Shows how through Nancy's plight, the family's selfcentered, complacent attitudes are jarred.
Religion and Philosophy
Dist - CPH **Prod** - CPH

Letter writing at work 19 MIN
16mm / VHS / U-matic
Color
LC 74-700687
Reviews letter writing skills for all employees who write letters as part of their job. Shows how the business letter can be made to fulfill its two main functions of messenger and ambassador.
Business and Economics; English Language
Dist - RTBL **Prod** - RANKAV 1972

Lettering
VHS
Drafting I series
(H C)
$59.00 _ CA139
Features various forms of lettering from vertical lettering to upper and lower case lettering.
Education; Industrial and Technical Education
Dist - AAVIM **Prod** - AAVIM 1989

Lettering Instructional Materials 22 MIN
U-matic / VHS / 16mm
Preparation of Audio - Visual Materials Series
Color; B&W (H C T)
Shows many types of letters and lettering devices, such as rubber stamps, stencil letters and mechanical scribers, which may be used to produce effective printing on display materials.
Education
Dist - IU **Prod** - IU 1955

Letters 9 MIN
16mm / U-matic / VHS
Color (J)
LC 74-701568
Shows how a new school in a rural village in Brazil brings opportunity and work for children and adults who cannot read.
Education; English Language; Geography - World
Dist - PHENIX **Prod** - SLUIZR 1974

Letters 30 MIN
U-matic
Today's Special Series
Color (K P)
Develops language arts skills in children. Programs are thematically designed around subjects of interest to youngsters. Action takes place in a department store where people, mannequins, puppets, comic characters and special guests present a light hearted approach to language arts.
Fine Arts; Literature and Drama; Psychology
Dist - TVOTAR **Prod** - TVOTAR 1985

Letters 11 MIN
16mm
Color (G)
$15.00 rental
Shares the filmmaker's realization that letters - written, mailed, read - are infused with so much love energy they become Valentines. Features four letters she and her son received over a number of years - a letter from Judy, a letter from worms, a letter from bugs and a letter from Ethan.
Fine Arts; Literature and Drama; Religion and Philosophy
Dist - CANCIN **Prod** - WILEYJ 1972

Letters C, D, E, F, G, H - Literki C, D , E, F, G, H 45 MIN
VHS
Color (K P) (POLISH)
$17.95 purchase _ #V155
Presents short, funny stories about the letters.
Education; Fine Arts; Literature and Drama
Dist - POLART

Letters from Morazan 55 MIN
U-matic / VHS / 16mm
Color
Tells the story of a guerilla offensive in the Morazan province of El Salvador. Shows preparation for battle and meetings of FMLN leaders and two remarkably filmed battles.
History - World
Dist - ICARUS **Prod** - RADIOV 1982

Letters from our lives 26 MIN
VHS
Color (J H C G)
$195.00 purchase, $45.00 rental
Pays homage to the United Nations' Decade of Disabled People in 1992. Features disabled women from around the globe who have written open letters to the world describing their individual struggles. Reveals that in certain parts of the world, being a woman demotes one to a second class citizen; being a disabled woman represents a double dose of discrimination. Looks at the sadness and hope of disabled women in Zimbabwe trying to survive on a daily basis and to create a better world for their children. Produced by Judy Jackson - Alma Productions.
Civics and Political Systems; Fine Arts; Geography - World; Health and Safety; Sociology
Dist - CANCIN

Letters from Viet Nam
16mm
Color
Views 60 helicopter combat missions flown by a young American pilot in Vietnam.
Civics and Political Systems; History - United States
Dist - DIRECT **Prod** - DREWAS 1965

Letters of John 60 MIN
VHS
Standard video Bible study series
Color (G A R)
$34.95 purchase, $10.00 rental _ #35 - 80135 - 2087
Examines the New Testament letters of John. Considers how the letters are related to John's Gospel and the book of Revelation, as well as examining the conflicts within the church at the time. Features several noted scholars. Includes leader's guide and study guide. Produced by Kerr Associates.
Literature and Drama; Religion and Philosophy
Dist - APH

Letters on ice 14 MIN
VHS
Postman Pat series
Color (P I)
$175.00 purchase
Reveals that the snow is frozen hard and Postman Pat gets stuck in a snowdrift. Shows that Ted Glenn gives Pat ice skates so he can deliver mail across a frozen lake. Part of a 13 - part animated puppet series which teaches values.
Guidance and Counseling; Literature and Drama
Dist - LANDMK **Prod** - LANDMK 1991

Letters to the World - Emily Dickinson and Walt Whitman 20 MIN
VHS / U-matic
American Literature Series
Color (H C A)
LC 83-706255
Offers a dramatization which presents interviews between a journalist and Emily Dickinson and Walt Whitman. Includes a conversation with students interested in their poems.
Literature and Drama
Dist - AITECH **Prod** - AUBU 1983

Letting go 29 MIN
VHS / U-matic
Color (C PRO A)
$285.00 purchase, $70.00 rental _ #4307S, 4307V
Shares the experiences of nurses and parents coping with the death of a child. Shows the child's point of view and illustrates how the child's feelings may be very different from those of the adults. Features two families who have recently lost a child.
Health and Safety; Sociology
Dist - AJN **Prod** - UFLA 1986

Letting go 10 MIN
VHS
Magnum eye series
Color (G)
$125.00 purchase, $30.00 rental
Spends time with people who have AIDS and with a doctor who works at the Wadell Clinic in San Francisco. Accompanies the doctor on her rounds as she visits patients, their families, friends and lovers in their homes and at hospices. Patients share their pain, disbelief, shame and hope and the doctor's view that strength and courage are needed to 'let go.' Directed by Paul Fusco. Part of a series by photographers from the Magnum Photo Agency.
Fine Arts; Health and Safety
Dist - FIRS **Prod** - MIYAKE 1993

Letting go 46 MIN
VHS / U-matic / Cassette
Florida through the decades as seen by High - Sheriff Jim Turner 'series
Color; PAL (G)
$79.95, $24.95, $9.95 purchase _ #1110
Portrays the life of a former High - Sheriff of Levy County, Florida, Jim Turner. Follows Turner in his old age. Portrays his death and reuniting with other characters in the series. Part eleven of an eleven - part historical docudrama.
Civics and Political Systems; Fine Arts; Health and Safety; History - United States; Sociology
Dist - NORDS **Prod** - NORDS 1991

Letting the Sun in 30 MIN
U-matic
Energy Efficient Housing Series
(A)
Discusses the option of passive solar energy supply.
Industrial and Technical Education; Social Science
Dist - ACCESS **Prod** - SASKM 1983

Lettre De Suisse, Une 10 MIN
16mm / U-matic / VHS
Color (H C)
Foreign Language
Dist - EBEC **Prod** - EBEC 1974

Lettres D'un Ami Francais Series
Chez Nous 12 MIN
Le Pique - Nique 15 MIN
Le Quatorze Juillet 15 MIN
Dist - IFB

Leucaena - a tree for all seasons 15 MIN
VHS
Fruits of the earth series
Color (G)
$175.00 purchase
Looks at a tree from Mexico that provides renewable fodder for cattle, firewood for fuel and wood for building materials. Considers what is necessary to improve cultivation of this agriculturally important pioneer plant.

Part of a series of 15 videos that describe everyday conditions in regions throughout the earth and look at plants available for environmentally sound, economically productive development.
Science - Natural
Dist - LANDMK

Leukemia 14 MIN
16mm
Doctors at Work Series
B&W (H C A)
LC FIA65-1350
Discusses three main forms of leukemia. Describes the incidence of leukemia in patients at various age levels.
Health and Safety
Dist - LAWREN **Prod** - CMA 1963

Leukemias 20 MIN
VHS / 16mm
(C)
$385.00 purchase _ #860VI069
Reviews blood films of cells from patients with the two main forms of acute leukemia as well as cells from patients with monocytic, granulocytic, limphoblastic leukemias and multiple myeloma. Demonstrates the histochemistry of white cells.
Health and Safety
Dist - HSCIC **Prod** - HSCIC 1986

L'Europe De L'An Mil - Europe in the Year 1000 52 MIN
16mm
Le Temp Des Cathedrales Series
Color
Looks at Western Europe during the year 1000 through views of the Abbey Of Tournus, the tapestries of Bayeaux and the bronze door of the church Saint - Michel.
History - World; Religion and Philosophy
Dist - FACSEA **Prod** - FACSEA 1979

Level 60 MIN
VHS / 16mm
Industrial Measurement Series
Color (PRO)
$695.00 purchase, $125.00 rental
Includes Introduction to Visual Level Sensors, Variable Displacement Devices, Pressure Measurement Sensors, Electrical Level Sensors, Ultrasonic and Sonic Sensors and Other Level Measurement Devices. Part of a five - part series on industrial measurement.
Industrial and Technical Education; Mathematics
Dist - ISA **Prod** - ISA

Level 5 - wooden staff skills
VHS
Mastering aikido series
Color (G)
$49.95 purchase _ #PNT000
Presents the fifth in a series of six videos explaining aikido, the least violent of Oriental martial arts, designed to defeat an attacker by harmonizing with the attacker's energy.
Physical Education and Recreation; Psychology
Dist - SIV

Level 4 - advanced defensive skills
VHS
Mastering aikido series
Color (G)
$49.95 purchase _ #PNT010
Presents the fourth in a series of six videos explaining aikido, the least violent of Oriental martial arts, designed to defeat an attacker by harmonizing with the attacker's energy.
Physical Education and Recreation; Psychology
Dist - SIV

Level 1 - fundamental skills
VHS
Mastering aikido series
Color (G)
$49.95 purchase _ #PNT001
Presents the first in a series of six videos explaining aikido, the least violent of Oriental martial arts, designed to defeat an attacker by harmonizing with the attacker's energy.
Physical Education and Recreation; Psychology
Dist - SIV

Level 6 - defense against multiple attackers
VHS
Mastering aikido series
Color (G)
$49.95 purchase _ #PNT011
Presents the sixth in a series of six videos explaining aikido, the least violent of Oriental martial arts, designed to defeat an attacker by harmonizing with the attacker's energy.
Physical Education and Recreation; Psychology
Dist - SIV

Level 3 - intermediate defensive skills
VHS
Mastering aikido series
Color (G)
$49.95 purchase _ #PNT003
Presents the third in a series of six videos explaining aikido, the least violent of Oriental martial arts, designed to defeat an attacker by harmonizing with the attacker's energy.
Physical Education and Recreation; Psychology
Dist - SIV

Level 2 - basic defensive skills
VHS
Mastering aikido series
Color (G)
$49.95 purchase _ #PNT002
Presents the second in a series of six videos explaining aikido, the least violent of Oriental martial arts, designed to defeat an attacker by harmonizing with the attacker's energy.
Physical Education and Recreation; Psychology
Dist - SIV

Level with me - honest communication 29 MIN
VHS
Color (J H)
$89.00 purchase _ #60412 - 026
Helps students learn more about themselves and their relationships within their families. Explores why families suffer from chronic communication breakdown and how people tend to manipulate instead of communicate. Uses lighthearted dramatic sketches to explain the five manipulative styles we all use.
Psychology; Social Science; Sociology
Dist - GA

Levels of Abstraction and Meaning 30 MIN
VHS / U-matic
Language and Meaning Series
Color (C)
English Language; Psychology
Dist - GPN **Prod** - WUSFTV 1983

Levels of Human Need 29 MIN
16mm
Supervisory Leadership Series
B&W (IND)
LC 72-703320
Business and Economics; Psychology
Dist - EDSD **Prod** - EDSD

The Lever 5 MIN
U-matic
Eureka Series
Color (J)
Demonstrates the principle of the lever in which the longer the arm of the lever to which force is applied, the less force needed.
Science; Science - Physical
Dist - TVOTAR **Prod** - TVOTAR 1980

The Lever 11 MIN
16mm
Color (P I J)
Defines and describes the basic parts of a lever. Develops the concepts of force, work and mechanical advantage.
Science - Physical
Dist - VIEWTH **Prod** - CENCO

Lever - a Simple Machine 15 MIN
U-matic / VHS
Why Series
Color (P I)
Discusses the characteristics of a lever.
Science - Physical
Dist - AITECH **Prod** - WDCNTV 1976

Lever, wheel and axle, pulley 11 MIN
VHS
Work, energy, and the simple machine series
Color (I J)
$55.00 purchase _ #1163VG
Demonstrates and explains three simple machines - the lever, wheel and axle, and the pulley. Shows everyday uses and explains their efficiency and advantages. Comes with a teacher's guide and 10 blackline masters. Part two of a four - part series.
Science - Physical
Dist - UNL

Lever, wheel and axle, pulley 9 MIN
VHS
Discovering simple machines series
CC; Color (P)
$55.00 purchase _ #1293VG
Introduces three simple machines - the lever, wheel and axle, and the pulley. Shows the relation between these machines and the principles behind their operation through demonstrations with common tools. Comes with a teacher's guide and seven blackline masters. Part two of a four - part series.
Science - Physical
Dist - UNL

Levers 12 MIN
16mm / U-matic / VHS
Simple Machines Series
Color (I J)
$315, $215 purchase _ #4481
Illustrates the workings of the lever and how it is used.
Industrial and Technical Education
Dist - CORF

Levi and Cohen - the Irish comedians 1 MIN
16mm
B&W (G)
$7.50 rental
Entertains with two grotesquely dressed and made - up comedians who begin hitting each other, while the audience becomes fed up and pelts them with rotten vegetables. Consists of a single brief shot, typical of many American productions during this period. Produced by American Mutoscope and Biograph Company.
Fine Arts
Dist - NCJEWF

Levi's for Feet 9 MIN
16mm
Color
LC 76-702658
Shows the joint development of Levi's for Feet by the Brown Shoe Company and Levi Strauss and Company. Explains their selling method.
Business and Economics
Dist - BRNSHO **Prod** - BRNSHO 1975

Levi's jeans 25 MIN
VHS
Design classics 1 series
Color (A)
PdS65 purchase _ Available in the United Kingdom and Ireland only
Uses archive film, period commercials, and interviews with key figures to examine the contribution to design made by some of the most successful products marketed in the 20th century. Part of a six-part series.
Business and Economics; Fine Arts
Dist - BBCENE

Levy and Goliath 100 MIN
35mm / 16mm / VHS
Color (G) (FRENCH WITH ENGLISH SUBTITLES)
$350.00 rental
Presents a comedy about two estranged brothers, one Hasidic, one married to a gentile, who cross paths for the first time in years because of a drug dealer named Goliath. Directed by Gerard Oury.
Fine Arts; Sociology
Dist - KINOIC

Lew Mathe 30 MIN
U-matic / VHS
Play Bridge with the Experts Series Pt 14
Color (A)
Presents bridge master Lew Mathe discussing bidding, dummy play and defensive problems.
Physical Education and Recreation
Dist - GPN **Prod** - KUHTTV 1980

Lewis and Clark 15 MIN
U-matic / VHS
Stories of America Series
Color (P)
Tells how Indian maiden Sacajawea helped Lewis and Clark cross the Rocky Mountains.
History - United States
Dist - AITECH **Prod** - OHSDE 1976

Lewis and Clark at the Great Divide 22 MIN
U-matic / VHS / 16mm
You are There Series
Color (I J)
LC 78-714893
Portrays the background, purposes and drama of the Lewis and Clark Expedition, concentrating on the events of 1805.
Geography - United States; History - United States
Dist - PHENIX **Prod** - CBSTV 1971

The Lewis and Clark expedition 20 MIN
VHS
Color (I J H)
$89.00 purchase _ #UL1923VA
Combines live reenactments, historic visuals and quotes from the journals of Lewis and Clark. Covers the purpose of the exploration, encounters with Native Americans, survival techniques and more. Includes teacher's guide and a set of duplicating masters.
Geography - United States; History - United States
Dist - KNOWUN

The Lewis and Clark journey 16 MIN
U-matic / VHS / 16mm
Color (I J)
LC FIA68-1799
Traces the expedition of Lewis and Clark using authentic records and pictures taken along the route.

Biography; History - United States; History - World
Dist - CORF **Prod** - CORF 1968

Lewis Hine and America 56 MIN
U-matic
Color (G A)
$10.00 rental
Profiles the life of social photographer Lewis Hine. Reveals that Hine was staff photographer for the National Child Labor Committee and his photographs were used in the crusade against child labor. Includes black and white photos of immigrants, child laborers, men and women at work in the mines, factories and mills during the first four decades of the 20th century.
Biography; History - United States; Industrial and Technical Education; Social Science; Sociology
Dist - AFLCIO **Prod** - ROSWHI 1984

Lewis Mumford on the city series Part 1
The City - heaven and hell 28 MIN
Dist - SF

Lewis Mumford on the city series Part 2
The City - cars or people 28 MIN
Dist - SF

Lewis Mumford on the city series Pt 3
The City and its region 28 MIN
Dist - SF

Lewis Mumford on the city series Pt 5
The City as man's home 28 MIN
Dist - SF

Lewis Mumford on the city series Pt 6
The City and the future 28 MIN
Dist - SF

Lewis Mumford on the City Series
The Heart of the City 28 MIN
Dist - SF

Lexington and Concord, April 19, 1775 15 MIN
U-matic / VHS / 16mm
Color (I J H)
Gives the background of Paul Revere's mission. Shows many sites connected with his ride.
History - United States
Dist - IFB **Prod** - BRDSHG 1965

Lexington, Concord, and independence 17 MIN
VHS
Color
$69.95 purchase _ #1804
Describes the events leading up to the Declaration of Independence, including the Continental Congress, battles at Lexington and Concord, and the appointment of George Washington as commander of the regular army.
History - United States
Dist - AIMS **Prod** - AIMS

Lexington, Concord and independence 17 MIN
16mm / U-matic / VHS
American history - birth of a nation series
Color (I J H)
LC FIA68-1118
Describes the battles at Lexington and at Concord. Discusses the heavy losses suffered by the British at Breed's Hill and Bunker Hill. Tells of the Continental Congress's appointment of George Washington as commander - in - chief of the regular army and its adoption of the Declaration of Independence. Number 4 of the series.
History - United States
Dist - AIMS **Prod** - CAHILL 1967

L'Halterophile Industriel 12 MIN
16mm / U-matic / VHS
Color (H A) (FRENCH)
A French - language version of the motion picture The Industrial Weightlifter. Presents a flexible model to illustrate how discs are pinched when weights are lifted when the backbone is curved. Demonstrates the correct method of lifting heavy objects and shows good posture, positioning and smooth application of lifting power. Emphasizes that extremely heavy items can be handled only with a special lifting device.
Business and Economics; Foreign Language; Guidance and Counseling; Health and Safety; Physical Education and Recreation
Dist - IFB **Prod** - IAPA 1965

L'Heure Espagnole 50 MIN
VHS
Color (G) (FRENCH (ENGLISH SUBTITLES))
$29.95 purchase _ #V72152
Presents a Glyndbourne Festival production of the tale of Torquemand by Ravel. Features sets and costumes designed by Maurice Sendak. Libretto included.
Fine Arts; Foreign Language
Dist - NORTNJ

L'Histoire D'Armagnac 19 MIN
U-matic / VHS / 16mm
Food and Wine from France Series
Color (H C A) (FRENCH)
A French language film visits the Gascogny region of France, introducing the people, the cuisine and the local brandy, Armagnac. Highlights the countryside, vineyards, distilleries, cellars, kitchens, restaurants, markets and local bullfights.
Geography - World; Home Economics
Dist - IFB **Prod** - POLNIS 1984

L'homme a la dague 26 MIN
VHS
Color (I J H) (FRENCH)
$39.95 purchase _ #W5474
Presents an episode from the French television series Les Enquetes de Sans Atout. Involves a teen - age detective in pursuit of a mysterious stranger. Uses colloquial French. For intermediate - level or higher language students.
Foreign Language
Dist - GPC

L'Hopital's rule 30 MIN
VHS
Calculus series
Color (C)
$125.00 purchase _ #6038
Explains L'Hopital's rule. Part of a 56 - part series on calculus.
Mathematics
Dist - LANDMK **Prod** - LANDMK

L'Hopital's Rule
U-matic
Calculus Series
Color
Mathematics
Dist - MDCPB **Prod** - MDDE

L'Hospital's Rule 20 MIN
VHS
Calculus Series
Color (H)
LC 90712920
Discusses L'Hospital's rule. The 48th of 57 installments of the Calculus Series.
Mathematics
Dist - GPN

Li Huiniang 95 MIN
VHS
Color (G) (MANDARIN CHINESE)
$45.00 purchase _ #2003B
Presents a Mandarin Chinese language movie produced in the People's Republic of China.
Fine Arts; Geography - World; Literature and Drama
Dist - CHTSUI **Prod** - CHTSUI

Li Shuang - Shuang 110 MIN
VHS
Color (G) (MANDARIN CHINESE)
$45.00 purchase _ #1068B
Presents a Mandarin Chinese language movie produced in the People's Republic of China.
Fine Arts; Geography - World; Literature and Drama
Dist - CHTSUI **Prod** - CHTSUI

Liability of accountants - Developments and trends 50 MIN
VHS
Color (C PRO A)
$95.00 purchase _ #Y141
Examines theories of liability, trouble areas that frequently spawn litigation and practical aspects of litigating accountant liability cases.
Business and Economics; Civics and Political Systems
Dist - ALIABA **Prod** - CLETV 1991

Liadov's The Enchanted lake
VHS
Music in motion series
Color (J H C G)
$75.00 purchase _ #MUS06V
Expresses visually what is heard in The Enchanted Lake by Liadov. Teaches classical music appreciation, develops interest and enhances listening enjoyment. Includes manual with suggestions for presenting the video, questions for discussion, research projects, correlations with other subject areas and listening and reading lists. Part of an eight - part series.
Fine Arts
Dist - CAMV **Prod** - MUSLOG

Liang and the Magic Paintbrush 30 MIN
U-matic / VHS
Reading Rainbow Series no 7
Color (P)
Presents an old Chinese legend about a boy who finds a paintbrush that magically brings brings pictures to life. Shows LeVar Burton participating in a lion dance in New York's Chinatown and exploring the world of computer art.
English Language; Social Science
Dist - GPN **Prod** - WNEDTV 1982

Liang Shanbo and Zhu Yingtai 120 MIN
VHS
Color (G) (MANDARIN CHINESE)
$45.00 purchase _ #2006B
Presents Mandarin Chinese language movies produced in the People's Republic of China.
Fine Arts; Geography - World; Literature and Drama
Dist - CHTSUI **Prod** - CHTSUI

Liberace live video 57 MIN
VHS
Color (G H A)
$19.95 purchase _ #20137
Features the late pianist Liberace in a 1985 performance with the London Philharmonic Orchestra. Performs a combination of classical and contemporary music, including 'I'll Be Seeing You,' 'You Made Me Love You,' 'Memories,' and others.
Fine Arts
Dist - WCAT **Prod** - WCAT

A Liberal Arts College for Men 18 MIN
16mm
College Selection Film Series
Color (J H A)
LC 74-713111
Students at Davidson College, an academically selective school located in a rural area in North Carolina, point out that selective admissions does not mean a constant struggle to remain in good standing if reasonable effort is exerted. Notes that students must travel to cities or to girls' schools in the area for an active social life.
Education; Guidance and Counseling
Dist - VISEDC **Prod** - VISEDC 1971

The Liberal tradition 60 MIN
VHS
Europe and America in the modern age - 1776 to the present series
Color (H C PRO)
$95.00 purchase
Presents a lecture by James Sheehan. Focuses on a critical period in European and American history and on leaders of the liberal movement. Part of a 20 - part series that looks at the last two centuries in Europe and America. Presents lectures by David M Kennedy and James Sheehan of Stanford University on such figures as Adam Smith, Marx, Lincoln, Washington, Jefferson, Freud, Margaret Sanger, Susan B Anthony and Jane Adams and their impact on the events of their day. For history resource material and continuing education courses.
Civics and Political Systems; History - United States; History - World
Dist - LANDMK

Liberalism and Conservatism
U-matic / VHS / 35mm strip
Political Idealogies of the Twentieth Century - Understanding the 'Isms Series
(J H C)
$159.00 purchase _ #06715 94
Traces the development of the conservative and liberal political philosophies from post Civil War to the present. Studies their positions on various issues. Features a dramatized debate on a proposed 'National Health Insurance Plan'. In 2 parts.
Business and Economics; Civics and Political Systems
Dist - ASPRSS **Prod** - GA

Liberalism and Conservatism
U-matic / VHS
Color (H)
Traces the formation of liberal and conservative alliances from the post - Civil War period through the present and studies the positions of each on a variety of issues.
Civics and Political Systems
Dist - GA **Prod** - GA

Liberalism Under Attack 30 MIN
U-matic
Realities
Color (A)
Delves into the political, social, economic and cultural trends of the 1980s. Probes a wide range of contemporary concerns. Each segment includes a guest speaker who is an expert in the field under discussion.
Business and Economics; Civics and Political Systems; Social Science; Sociology
Dist - TVOTAR **Prod** - TVOTAR 1985

Liberated Tops 15 MIN
Videoreel / VT2
Umbrella Series
Color
Home Economics
Dist - PBS **Prod** - KETCTV

Liberation 2 HRS
VHS
Master of Life Training Series
Color (G)

$29.95 purchase _ #VHS144
Contains two Video Hypnosis sessions which enhance clarity of focus, release of negative blocks and the experience of balance and harmony.
Health and Safety; Psychology; Religion and Philosophy
Dist - VSPU **Prod** - VSPU

Liberation 100 MIN
35mm / 16mm
Color; B&W (G)
$200.00 rental
Addresses the dramatic stories of the Allied campaign to liberate Europe during World War II and Adolf Hitler's genocidal war against the Jews. Begins in 1942 when Hitler was still at the height of his power and the Allies began envisioning a cross - channel invasion of Europe. Combines film footage, period music and radio broadcasts collected from archives around the world, to take the viewer behind the scenes where strategies and deceptions are revealed. Interwoven throughout are the stories of tragedy, courage and resistance of the Jews of Europe. Reaches its climax with the liberation of Paris, the Benelux countries, and the death camps, culminating with V - E Day. Produced by Arnold Schwartzman and Rabbi Marvin Hier; directed by Schwartzman.
Fine Arts; History - World
Dist - OCTOBF

The Liberation of Auschwitz 55 MIN
16mm / VHS
Color; B&W (G) (MULTILINGUAL)
$250.00 rental; $72.00 purchase
Contains previously unreleased footage filmed between January 27 and February 28, 1945. Features Alexander Woronsow, the only member of the Soviet camera crew of the film still alive in 1985. This footage, thought to have been lost until Woronsow's interview, augments the 18 - minute Soviet documentary used as evidence of Nazi war crimes at Nuremberg. Produced to mark the 40th anniversary of Auschwitz's liberation by the Soviet army. A post - war German film depicting Jewish life.
Civics and Political Systems; Fine Arts; History - World; Religion and Philosophy
Dist - NCJEWF

Liberation of Paris 34 MIN
16mm
B&W (C)
A documentary of the August, 1944, seige of Paris by the resistance movement. Begins in Nazi - controlled Paris one week before the arrival of allied troops. Shows the allies' arrival and the welcome given them.
History - World
Dist - RADIM **Prod** - LCFRCI 1944

Liberation of Rome 15 MIN
16mm
B&W
Industrial and Technical Education
Dist - FCE **Prod** - FCE

Liberation of Soviet Byelorussia 30 MIN
U-matic / VHS
Color
Presents a review of the defeat of Germany's Center Army Group and the liberation of Soviet Byelorussia during World War II.
Civics and Political Systems; History - World
Dist - IHF **Prod** - IHF

Liberation of Zoospores in the Alga Basicladia 4 MIN
16mm
Plant Science Series
Color (H C)
LC FIA65-823
Identifies the 'MOSS' on a 'MOSS - BACK' turtle as the Alga basicladia. An examination of filaments under a microscope shows darkening as zoospores mature, an exit pore forming and the escape of zoospores after the pore membrane bursts.
Agriculture; Science - Natural
Dist - MLA **Prod** - IOWA 1964

Liberation of Zoospores in the Alga Oedogonium 4 MIN
16mm
Plant Science Series
Color (H C)
LC FIA65-926
Shows asexual reproduction in the Alga oedogonium. Pictures cells in a filament which has modified to form zoospores, breaking of the filament, emergence of zoospores into a vesicle and the zoospores swimming after leaving the vesicle.
Agriculture; Science - Natural
Dist - MLA **Prod** - IOWA 1964

Liberation Series
Free for all 59 MIN
Good grief 60 MIN
She, he shall overcome 60 MIN
When will We Ever Learn 60 MIN
Dist - HRC

Liberation Theology - its Impact 25 MIN
U-matic / VHS / 16mm
Color (J H) (LATIN)
Talks about the problems of people in Latin America and the scriptural origins of liberation theology. Includes opponents of liberation theology. Produced by Mary Lou Reker and Dino Aranda.
Civics and Political Systems; Religion and Philosophy; Sociology
Dist - CWS

The Liberator 30 MIN
16mm
B&W (R)
Presents narration and choral and solo music to explain songs traditionally associated with Hanukkah and to explain other music influenced by the holiday theme. (Kinescope).
Religion and Philosophy
Dist - NAAJS **Prod** - JTS 1957

Liberator of the oppressed - Volume 4 30 MIN
VHS
Jesus of Nazareth series
Color (I J H C G A R)
$29.95 purchase, $10.00 rental _ #35 - 8317 - 1502
Presents excerpts from the Franco Zeffirelli film on the life and ministry of Jesus. Surveys the events of Jesus' early ministry, the arrest of John the Baptist, and presents some of the parables.
Literature and Drama; Religion and Philosophy
Dist - APH **Prod** - BOSCO

The Liberia tragedy 58 MIN
VHS
Color (G)
$350.00 purchase, $95.00 rental
Looks at the political history of Liberia, from the 1980 military coup led by Samual Doe to the 1989 rebellion which ousted him from power and led to civil war. Features extensive archival footage and interviews with Liberian journalists, former government officials and others. Directed by Hilton Fyle.
Fine Arts; History - World
Dist - CNEMAG

Libertarian Left 30 MIN
U-matic
Realities
Color (A)
Delves into the political, social, economic and cultural trends of the 1980s. Probes a wide range of contemporary concerns. Each segment includes a guest speaker who is an expert in the field under discussion.
Business and Economics; Civics and Political Systems; Social Science; Sociology
Dist - TVOTAR **Prod** - TVOTAR 1985

The Libertarians 29 MIN
U-matic / VHS / 16mm
B&W
Investigates the development of an urban working class in Brazil around the turn of the century. Shows how these immigrant laborers, confronted by brutal working conditions and poor wages, were instrumental in building a labor movement with a strong anarchist orientation.
History - World; Sociology
Dist - CNEMAG **Prod** - FIHOL

Liberty 60 MIN
U-matic / VHS
Six Great Ideas Series
Color (A)
Presents Dr Mortimer J Adler who declares that there is no such thing as liberty in itself. Points out that virtue and wisdom, circumstance and political forces each contain a singular aspect of freedom. Traces the thread that leads from one to the other.
Religion and Philosophy
Dist - FI **Prod** - WNETTV 1982

Liberty and justice - A Look at the American legal system 48 MIN
VHS / U-matic
Color (I J H)
$280.00, $330.00 purchase, $60.00 rental
Introduces students to the structure and function of the American legal system. Covers the history of the legal system, the Constitution, areas of law, pretrial and trial procedures, women and minorities. Produced by Cinegroup and San Diego County Bar Association.
Civics and Political Systems
Dist - NDIM

Liberty in a Featherbed - the Story of Thomas Kennedy 30 MIN
16mm
B&W
Tells the story of Thomas Kennedy, dramatizing the struggle in the legislature of Maryland to remove civil and political inequalities. (Kinescope).
Biography; Civics and Political Systems; History - United States
Dist - NAAJS **Prod** - JTS 1953

Liberty leading the people 30 MIN
VHS
Palette series
Color (G C)
$70.00 purchase, $12.50, rental _ #36401
Discloses that the use of color by Eugene Delacroix defines the allegorical Liberty Leading the People, a work that aroused passionate reactions when it was unveiled in 1831. Focuses on the female character of Liberty, fearless crossing a barricade while waving the French flag. Part of a 13 - part series which examines great paintings in a dynamic and dramatic way by moving into their creative spaces and spending time with the characters and their surroundings. Uses special video effects to investigate artistic enigmas and studies material, technique, style and significance. Narrated by Marcel Cuvelier, directed by Alain Jaubert.
Fine Arts
Dist - PSU **Prod** - LOUVRE 1992

Liberty mutual legends of golf 27 MIN
16mm
Color
Presents highlights of the Liberty Mutual Legends Of Golf tournament in Austin, Texas, won by Gary Brewer and Billy Caspar. Also features Sam Snead, Arnold Palmer, Julius Boros, Gene Sarazen, Don January and more.
Physical Education and Recreation
Dist - MTP **Prod** - LIBMIC

Liberty's Booty 50 MIN
VHS / U-matic
Color
Views middle - class, white prostitution. Concerns sexual demystification. Provides an ironic exposition of American 'permissivenss.'.
Fine Arts; Sociology
Dist - KITCHN **Prod** - KITCHN

Libra 39 MIN
16mm
Color
LC 79-700235
Depicts a futuristic, energy - abundant society which receives microwave energy from solar power satellites orbiting the Earth.
Social Science; Sociology
Dist - WORLDR **Prod** - WORLDR 1978

The Librarian 9 MIN
U-matic / VHS / 16mm
B&W (J H)
Emphasizes the background and training of a librarian. Illustrates the variety of ways in which a library provides service to the public.
Education; Guidance and Counseling; Psychology; Social Science
Dist - IFB **Prod** - CRAF 1958

The Librarian 15 MIN
VHS / 16mm
Harriet's Magic Hats IV Series
Color (P)
$175.00 purchase _ #207150
Presents thirteen new programs to familiarize children with more workers and their role in community life. Features Aunt Harriet's bottomless trunks of magic hats where Carrie has only to put on a particular hat to be whisked off to investigate the person and the role represented by the hat. 'The Librarian' shows Ralph looking for his favorite book. Carrie suggests that she might get a copy from Ella the librarian. Ella explains that books are labelled and placed on the shelf according to their own call numbers. Then she describes how different kinds of libraries help people.
Business and Economics; Education; Guidance and Counseling; Psychology; Social Science
Dist - ACCESS **Prod** - ACCESS 1986

Librarians Communicate 51 MIN
U-matic
Color
LC 78-706316
Discusses verbal and nonverbal communication used by library reference and public service staffs.
Education; Psychology
Dist - USNAC **Prod** - USHHS 1977

Libraries and the Pursuit of Happiness 29 MIN
U-matic / VHS / 16mm
Color
Describes the services provided by libraries and dispels some popular misconceptions as to what the library environment is really like. Discusses the role played by libraries and librarians in local communities.
Education; Social Science
Dist - EBEC **Prod** - EBEC 1981

Libraries are Kid Stuff 14 MIN
16mm / U-matic / VHS
Color (C A)
LC 78-712288
Services of the Myers Demonstration Library, Tucson, Arizona, are shown through the eyes of the children who use the elementary school library.
Education; Guidance and Counseling; Social Science
Dist - WWS **Prod** - UARIZ 1970

Libraries for Louisiana 20 MIN
16mm
Color (T)
LC FIA60-3458
Shows the value of Louisiana's library service. Presents librarians doing the job they love most, bringing books and other related materials to people wherever they are.
Education; Geography - United States
Dist - RAMSEY **Prod** - LASLIB

Libraries for the Kid in all of Us 1 MIN
U-matic
Color
Features children's comments about why they like the public library.
Education; Social Science
Dist - LVN **Prod** - MDPL

Libraries Without Bars 25 MIN
16mm
B&W (JAPANESE)
LC FIE52-1944
Shows modern improvements being made in Japanese libraries to stimulate interest in reading and to encourage appreciation of art, music and literature.
Civics and Political Systems; Education; Geography - World
Dist - USNAC **Prod** - USA 1951

Library 28 MIN
VHS
Elephant show series
Color (P I)
$95.00 purchase, $45.00 rental
Presents program 35 in the Sharon, Lois and Bram's Elephant Show series. Teaches reading readiness and social skills while engaging children in making music. Each program explores a new theme through adventure, fantasy, mystery and song with recording artists Sharon, Lois and Bram. Uses traditional materials which stress participation - action songs, sing - along songs, story songs, clapping songs, singing games, playground chants and folk songs from many different traditions. Includes teacher's guide co - authored by a music education specialist.
Fine Arts; Sociology
Dist - BULFRG **Prod** - CAMBFP 1991

The Library 14 MIN
BETA / VHS / U-matic / 16mm
Your town I series
Color (K P)
$245.00, $68.00 purchase _ #C50714, #C51473
Looks at the technology of a modern library - computers, community outreach programs, videocassettes and audiocassettes, records, storytime, special services for the disabled. Part of a five - part series on community services.
Social Science; Sociology
Dist - NGS **Prod** - NGS 1991

The Library - a Place for Discovery 17 MIN
U-matic / VHS / 16mm
Color (I) (SPANISH)
Highlights the services, materials and resources of public and school libraries. Explains how to use the card catalog, find books on the shelves and use the vertical files for pictures.
Education; Foreign Language; Social Science
Dist - EBEC **Prod** - EBEC

Library and Archival Disaster - Preparedness and Recovery 21 MIN
U-matic / VHS / 16mm
Color (G)
$98.00 purchase
Stresses the importance of having a carefully organized plan to deal with such occurrences as losing large portions of one's collections to disasters.
History - World; Psychology
Dist - BIBLIO **Prod** - BIBLIO 1987

Library and Archival Sciences 15 MIN
VHS / 16mm
(H C A)
$24.95 purchase _ #CS244
Describes the skills involved in working in the library and archival sciences.
Guidance and Counseling
Dist - RMIBHF **Prod** - RMIBHF

The Library game - fact and fantasy 14 MIN
VHS
Library game series
Color (H A G T)
$49.00 purchase _ #MC910
Teaches about the commonality of library organization, fiction and non - fiction, the Dewey Decimal System, and about the librarian as a special resource. Part one of a two - part series on libraries.
Education; Psychology; Social Science
Dist - AAVIM **Prod** - AAVIM

The Library game - research and reference
VHS
Library game series
Color (H A G T)
$49.00 purchase _ #MC915
Teaches about the card catalog system, locating library books and audiovisual materials, and other materials such as periodicals and the Reader's Guide. Part two of a two - part series on libraries.
Education; Psychology; Social Science
Dist - AAVIM **Prod** - AAVIM

Library game series
Fact and fantasy plus research and reference - the library game series
The Library game - fact and fantasy 14 MIN
The Library game - research and reference
Dist - AAVIM

Library Lens Sampler 10 MIN
U-matic / VHS
Color
Contains a sampler of the Baltimore County Public Library weekly five - minute news programs.
Education; Social Science; Sociology
Dist - LVN **Prod** - BCPL

Library Lobbying - a Primer for Trustees 15 MIN
U-matic / VHS
Color
Discusses the role of trustees in lobbying at the state level for library legislation.
Civics and Political Systems; Education; Social Science
Dist - LVN **Prod** - LVN

Library of Career Counseling Films Series
Is a Career in Mining, Petroleum or Gas Production for You 15 MIN
Dist - AITECH
COUNFI

Library of Career Counseling Films Series
How a Career Develops 15 MIN
Is a Career in Agri - Business for You 15 MIN
Is a Career in Atomic Energy for You 15 MIN
Is a Career in Banking for You 14 MIN
Is a Career in Bench Work for You 15 MIN
Is a Career in Business Administration for You 16 MIN
Is a Career in Electronics Manufacturing for You 16 MIN
Is a Career in Finance, Insurance or Real Estate for You 16 MIN
Is a Career in Fishing or Forestry for You 15 MIN
Is a Career in Food Preparation for You 15 MIN
Is a Career in Industrial Chemicals for You 15 MIN
Is a Career in Machining for You 16 MIN
Is a Career in Management for You 15 MIN
Is a Career in Motor Freight Transportation for You 15 MIN
Is a Career in Motor Vehicle or Equipment Manufacturing for You 16 MIN
Is a career in radio or television for you 15 MIN
Is a Career in Structural Work for You 15 MIN
Is a Career in the Aero - Space Industry for You 15 MIN
Is a Career in the Health Services for You 14 MIN
Is a Career in the Hotel or Motel Business for You 14 MIN
Is a Career in the Natural Sciences for You 15 MIN
Is a Career in the Professions for You 16 MIN
Is a Career in the Pulp and Paper Industry for You 20 MIN
Is a Career in the Restaurant Business for You 14 MIN
Is a Career in the Service Industries for You 15 MIN
Is a Career in the Social Sciences for You 14 MIN
Is a Career in the Telephone Business for You 15 MIN
Is a Career in the Textile or Apparel Industry for You 15 MIN
Is a railroad career for you 15 MIN
Is a Sales Career for You 15 MIN
The World of work 14 MIN
Dist - COUNFI

The Library of Congress 90 MIN
U-matic / VHS / 16mm
Color (H C A)
Looks at the collections and activities of the Library of Congress. Tells how the library serves Congress, scholars, other libraries, and copyright applicants.
Education; Social Science
Dist - FI **Prod** - WNETTV 1990

The Library of Congress - a Portrait of an American Institution 90 MIN
16mm / U-matic / VHS
Color (H C A)
LC 80-701169
Features an excursion through the vast collections and services of the Library of Congress. Includes an interview with Librarian of Congress Daniel J Boorstin.
Education; Geography - United States; Social Science
Dist - FI **Prod** - WNETTV 1980

The Library of Congress - a Portrait of an American Institution, Pt 1 30 MIN
16mm / U-matic / VHS
Color (H C A)
LC 80-701169
Features an excursion through the vast collections and services of the Library of Congress. Includes an interview with Librarian of Congress Daniel J Boorstin.
History - United States; Social Science
Dist - FI **Prod** - BBCTV 1980

Library of Management Skills 60 MIN
U-matic / VHS
(A PRO)
$450.00 purchase, $150.00 rental
Includes 8 courses to teach managers about strategic planning, marketing and new products, research and competitive analysis, information systems, time and cost estimates, interviewing, performance appraisals and report writing.
Computer Science
Dist - VIDEOT **Prod** - VIDEOT 1988

Library of the future series
Allows access to 450 of the world's most important literary works. Includes the full text of works by Aristotle, Chaucer, Marx, Melville, Shakespeare, Swift, Twain, and Voltaire, and many others, as well as historical documents, such as the Declaration of Independence and religious literature including the Bible and the Koran. Users can search by word, phrase, concept, name or date. For IBM PCs and compatibles, requires 640K RAM, DOS 3.1 or later, one floppy disk drive - hard disk recommended, one empty expansion slot, and an IBM compatible CD - ROM drive.
Library of the future series
Dist - BEP

Library of video backgrounds for post production series
Deep backgrounds - a library of video backgrounds for post production - Vol 1 60 MIN
Deep backgrounds - a library of video backgrounds for post production - Vol 2 60 MIN
Deep backgrounds - a library of video backgrounds for post production - Vol 3 60 MIN
Deep backgrounds - a library of video backgrounds for post production - Vol 4 60 MIN
Dist - SONYIN

Library Organization - Introduction 60 MIN
U-matic / VHS
Library Organization Series Pt 1
B&W
Education
Dist - UAZMIC **Prod** - UAZMIC 1977

Library Organization Series Pt 1
Library Organization - Introduction 60 MIN
Dist - UAZMIC

Library Reference Information - How to Locate and Use it 256 MIN
U-matic / VHS
Color (P I J H A)
LC 81-730306
Presents an introductory course on library usage. Includes locating information, using reference books, compiling a working bibliography, and using the card catalog.
Social Science
Dist - EDUACT **Prod** - EDUACT

Library Reference Section 15 MIN
16mm / U-matic / VHS
Color (I J)
LC 79-701652
Shows a school librarian demonstrating how to use basic reference tools to learn more about a subject.

Education; Social Science
Dist - PHENIX **Prod** - PERSPE 1979

Library report 25 MIN
U-matic / 16mm / VHS
Color (I J)
$550.00, $415.00, $385.00 purchase _ #C346
Uses humor to show students the steps for researching, organizing and writing a library report. Explores choosing and narrowing down a topic, organizing and outlining, finding information in the library, writing and revising a rough draft, taking notes. Produced by S S Wilson and Mark Chodzko.
Education; Psychology; Social Science
Dist - BARR **Prod** - UNDERR 1983

Library Sciences 15 MIN
BETA / U-matic / VHS
Career Success Series
Color (H C A)
$29.95 purchase _ #MX244 ; $29.95 _ #MX244
Portrays occupations in library sciences by reviewing required abilities and interviewing people employed in this field. Shows anxieties and rewards involved in pursuing a career as a librarian.
Education
Dist - CAMV **Prod** - CAMV

Library skills series
Presents a three - part series on library skills. Includes the titles 'Dictionary - the Adventure of Words,' 'Library World - 2nd Edition,' 'The Reference Section.'
Dictionary - the adventure of words - 1 16 MIN
Library skills series 58 MIN
Library world 20 MIN
The Reference section 22 MIN
Dist - BARR

Library Skills Series
Your Library and Media Center - How to Get the most from Them
Dist - CHUMAN

Library Skills Tapes Series
Almanacs, yearbooks and handbooks 4 MIN
Atlases and gazetteers 4 MIN
Biographical tools 4 MIN
Book index 7 MIN
The Card catalog 7 MIN
How to Use Dictionaries 8 MIN
How to Use Encyclopedias 6 MIN
The New York Times Index 6 MIN
Readers's Guide to Periodical Literature 7 MIN
Reviews and Criticisms 6 MIN
Special periodical index 6 MIN
Special Reference Materials 7 MIN
Writing a Research Paper 7 MIN
Dist - MDCC

Library world 20 MIN
VHS / U-matic / 16mm
Library skills series
Color (P I J)
$470.00, $360.00, $330.00 purchase _ #A547
Offers a fantasy tale to unlock the mysteries of library use. Explains the card catalog, the Reader's Guide, microfilm, audio materials, bilingual materials and computerized card catalogs and video libraries. Produced by Ron Becker. Part of a three - part series on library skills.
Education; Psychology; Social Science
Dist - BARR

The Library Zone - Where Every Patron is a VIP 9 MIN
U-matic / VHS
Color
Emphasizes the need for all library employees to give patrons courteous and good quality library service.
Education; Social Science
Dist - LVN **Prod** - PRATTE

Libre quiero ser - I want to be free 12 MIN
VHS
Color (I J H) (SPANISH)
$119.00 purchase _ #GW - 130 - VS
Uses a music video format that incorporates Latin and hip - hop music with interviews of teens to address six central themes - the powerful and deceptive advertising schemes used by tobacco companies to get young consumers hooked on their products; the social pressure to smoke as a way to be 'cool'; the social consequences of using tobacco in an increasingly smoke - free society; the heightened health risks for smokers; the highly addictive nature of tobacco and the drug nicotine; and the benefits of staying tobacco - free.
Guidance and Counseling; Health and Safety; Psychology
Dist - HRMC **Prod** - UCDEXT

Libya 28 MIN
Videoreel / VHS
Marilyn's Manhattan Series
Color
Features an interview with Mr Ibrahim Dharat, Counsellor for Economic Affairs, on the economic development of Libya. Includes a film clip on Libya's development. Hosted by Marilyn Perry.
Business and Economics; Civics and Political Systems; Geography - World
Dist - PERRYM **Prod** - PERRYM

Libya 28 MIN
Videoreel / VHS
International Byline Series
Color
Interviews Ambassador Mansur Rashid Kikhia on Libya's political position. Hosted by Marilyn Perry. Includes a film clip on Libya.
Business and Economics; Civics and Political Systems; Geography - World
Dist - PERRYM **Prod** - PERRYM

Libya (International Byline) 28 MIN
Videoreel / VHS
International Byline Series
Color
Interviews Mr Ahmed Shahati, Special Envoy of the Foreign Liaison Bureau in Tripoli, Libya, who was on a mission from the Socialist People's Libyan Arab Jamahiriya. Presents the Libyan view of relations between Libya and the United States.
Business and Economics; Civics and Political Systems; Geography - World
Dist - PERRYM **Prod** - PERRYM

Lice are not Nice 11 MIN
16mm / U-matic / VHS
Color (P I)
$25 rental _ #9781
Demonstrates all of the steps in the successful treatment of lice infestation.
Health and Safety
Dist - AIMS **Prod** - AIMS 1984

License 11 MIN
VHS / 16mm / U-matic
Color (J H C G)
$260, $180, $210 _ #B427
Explores the possible results of dangerous or careless driving.
Guidance and Counseling; Health and Safety; Industrial and Technical Education
Dist - BARR **Prod** - BARR 1986

License Plate Traffic Survey 12 MIN
16mm
Color
LC 74-705028
Demonstrates a method of conducting a traffic survey to obtain origination and destination information using motion picture photography and a computer.
Business and Economics; Social Science
Dist - USNAC **Prod** - USDTFH 1968

License to kill 45 MIN
VHS
Color; PAL (H C G)
PdS25 purchase
Examines traffic accidents in Great Britain, revealing that one in four road accidents involves a young driver and that male drivers under age 20 are six times more likely to have an accident than the population at large. Asks when the British government will tackle this 'license to kill.' Contact distributor about availability outside the United Kingdom.
Health and Safety; History - World
Dist - ACADEM

License to Kill 20 MIN
16mm / VHS
Color (G)
$425.00, $350.00 purchase, $55.00 rental
Examines both sides of the controversy surrounding the death penalty. Interviews those opposed and those in favor of capital punishment. Provides a cross - cultural survey, explains which countries use the death penalty, how often, for what reasons and the various methods used.
Civics and Political Systems; Sociology
Dist - CNEMAG **Prod** - FOXN 1984

License to Kill 28 MIN
16mm / U-matic / VHS
Color (A)
Examines the worldwide use of the death penalty, methods and reasons for its use, and arguments for and against it.
Civics and Political Systems; Sociology
Dist - CNEMAG **Prod** - CNEMAG 1984

License to kill 30 MIN
VHS
Open space series
Color; PAL (G)
PdS50
Looks at the problem of drinking and driving from the perspectives of four people who have lost family members in alcohol - related accidents. Explores their feelings about those responsible and the need for changes in the law. Contends that there is a need for greater government resourcing and more political will to tackle the problem.
Health and Safety; Industrial and Technical Education
Dist - BBCENE

Licensed practical nursing assistant refresher series
Cast techniques 20 MIN
Dressings 18 MIN
Early morning care - Pt 1 33 MIN
Early morning care - Pt 2 41 MIN
Early morning care - Pt 3 17 MIN
Infection Control 29 MIN
Intravenous Therapy 25 MIN
Post - operative care 15 MIN
Pre - Operative Admissions 11 MIN
Routine Admissions 11 MIN
Special Equipment 25 MIN
Traction 25 MIN
Dist - ACCESS

Licensing and Traffic Laws 29 MIN
VHS / U-matic
Right Way Series
Color
Discusses traffic laws, vehicle registration laws, vehicle inspection and equipment and maintenance laws.
Health and Safety
Dist - PBS **Prod** - SCETV 1982

Lickety - Split Licorice 8 MIN
16mm
Color
LC 74-702998
Tells a story about a boy and girl making licorice in their kitchen in order to stimulate the imagination of young people for writing, role playing and art work and to encourage recognition of differences between actuality and fantasy. Suggests that such common activities as making licorice can form the basis for engaging stories.
English Language; Literature and Drama
Dist - SF **Prod** - MORLAT 1972

Licorice Train 7 MIN
U-matic / VHS
Color
Delineates a ghetto youth's journey, via elevated train, into neighborhoods greatly different from his own, and indulges in various fantasies about what life is and might be like. Uses sweet background music to make an ironic contrast to the grim realities of the boy's existence.
Sociology
Dist - IFF **Prod** - IFF

Lid Reconstruction in Thermal Burns 11 MIN
16mm
Color
LC FIA66-880
Demonstrates the surgical correction of the cicatrical ectropion caused by a severe unilateral radiation burn.
Health and Safety
Dist - ACY **Prod** - ACYDGD 1962

Lidded Pots 28 MIN
Videoreel / VT2
Wheels, Kilns and Clay Series
Color
Features Mrs Peterson describing certain ceramic processes for her classroom at the University of Southern California. Illustrates lidded pots.
Fine Arts
Dist - PBS **Prod** - USC

L'Idee 27 MIN
16mm
B&W (GERMAN)
Presents a film by Berthold Bartosch, based on a book of 83 woodcuts by the Belgian artist, Frans Masereel, which was published in Germany in 1927, with a preface by Hermann Hesse. Makes a strong political statement about Europe just prior to the rise of Nazism, with the leading character, a slender, nude female figure, symbolizing the universal idealistic spirit in a world where good and evil constantly battle. Includes Arthur Honegger's score, thought to be the first to contain electronic instrumentation, which was created for the finished film in 1932.
Fine Arts; History - World
Dist - STARRC **Prod** - STARRC

Liderazgo 30 MIN
16mm / U-matic / VHS
Behavior in Business
Color (H C A) (SPANISH)
A Spanish version of Leadership - Style Or Circumstance. Shows that the effectiveness of different types of leadership depends upon the specific situation. Points out ways of developing leadership and insuring the effectiveness of such leaders once they are on the job.

Business and Economics
Dist - MGHT **Prod** - MGHT 1977

The Lie 29 MIN
U-matic / VHS / 16mm
Color (G) (SPANISH)
Presents a dramatic story of forgiveness.
Religion and Philosophy
Dist - CAFM **Prod** - CAFM 1973

Lie back and enjoy it 8 MIN
16mm
B&W (G)
$16.00 rental
Examines the politics of filmic representation of women under patriarchy. Consists of an image track of technologically manipulated images of women. Soundtrack is a dialogue between a man - filmmaker - and a woman of whom he's going to make a film. Produced by JoAnn Elam.
Fine Arts; Sociology
Dist - CANCIN

Liebe Mutter, Mir Geht Es Gut 91 MIN
16mm
Color (GERMAN (ENGLISH SUBTITLES))
Focuses on the lower - income and lower middle - class population. Documents the conflicts of the working class which commercial film productions generally ignore.
Foreign Language; Social Science
Dist - WSTGLC **Prod** - WSTGLC 1971

Liebesspiel (a Song Without Words) 2 MIN
16mm
B&W (I)
LC 72-703163
Uses animation to express the poetry of movement.
Fine Arts
Dist - GRAF **Prod** - FISCHF 1931

Lien on my soul and portrait not a dream - Parts 3 and 4 21 MIN
16mm
Breaking time
Color (G)
$60.00 rental
Offers a cityscape of New Haven which incorporates the 4th of July, a wedding, lovers, bikers and kids in a park Lien on My Soul. Witnesses Levine's mother's 'cry of rage' in Portrait Not a Dream. Part of a series, made between 1978 - 1983, that describes Levine's return to his hometown of New Haven in 1977 where he resumes working in his father's gas station. Confronts his past by looking back on the working people and places of his childhood and the automotive and petroleum base of that culture. Each film is a complete work and may be viewed separately.
Fine Arts; Geography - United States; Literature and Drama; Sociology
Dist - CANCIN **Prod** - LEVINE 1983

Lies 30 MIN
VHS / U-matic
Doris Chase concepts series
Color
Uses cost accounting to emphasize the spoken lie.
Business and Economics; Social Science; Sociology
Dist - WMEN **Prod** - CHASED

Lietuviskos Dainos Svente 20 MIN
VHS / U-matic
Color (LITHUANIAN)
Shows the first postwar traditional song and dance festival in Vilnius, Lithuania.
Fine Arts
Dist - IHF **Prod** - IHF

Lietuvos Dainu Svente 20 MIN
U-matic / VHS
Color (LITHUANIAN)
Features a song festival held in Vilnius, Lithuania, with dancing and singing groups from various parts of the country.
Fine Arts
Dist - IHF **Prod** - IHF

Life 135 MIN
VHS
Color (G) (MANDARIN)
$85.00 purchase _ #1077S
Presents a movie in two parts about life produced in the People's Republic of China.
Fine Arts
Dist - CHTSUI

Life 15 MIN
16mm
Color (H A)
LC 76-703697
Discusses general, known characteristics of life. Uses examples to show how life has adapted to Earth conditions and how certain life forms can withstand environmental shocks. Describes conditions on Mars, with the question raised as to the possibility of life existing there.
Science - Physical
Dist - USNAC **Prod** - NASA 1976

Life 101 - learning to say yes to life series 75 MIN
VHS
Life 101 - learning to say yes to life series
Color (J H R)
$99.95 purchase _ #35 - 84800 - 2042
Features Christian youth speaker Dawson McAllister discussing teenage depression and suicide. Includes interviews with teenagers at risk for suicide. Consists of two tapes. Produced by Shepherd Ministries.
Religion and Philosophy; Sociology
Dist - APH

Life 101 - Learning to say yes to life series
Life 101 - Learning to say yes to life - Tape 1 30 MIN
Life 101 - Learning to say yes to life - Tape 2 45 MIN
Life 101 - learning to say yes to life series 75 MIN
Dist - APH

Life 101 - Learning to say yes to life - Tape 1 30 MIN
VHS
Life 101 - Learning to say yes to life series
Color (J H R)
$10.00 rental _ #36 - 848001 - 2042
Features Christian youth speaker Dawson McAllister discussing teenage depression and suicide. Combines information in lecture form with interviews with teenagers at risk for suicide. Produced by Shepherd Ministries.
Religion and Philosophy; Sociology
Dist - APH

Life 101 - Learning to say yes to life - Tape 2 45 MIN
VHS
Life 101 - Learning to say yes to life series
Color (J H R)
$10.00 rental _ #36 - 848002 - 2042
Features Christian youth speaker Dawson McAllister discussing teenage depression and suicide. Combines information in lecture form with interviews with teenagers at risk for suicide. Produced by Shepherd Ministries.
Religion and Philosophy; Sociology
Dist - APH

Life After 60 - the Old Dream/New Dilemma 30 MIN
U-matic / VHS
Color
Looks into the lives of some Wisconsin elderly citizens, their needs and the care they receive. Talks about the necessity of community and government support ot help them continue to have choices and options concerning their care.
Health and Safety; Sociology
Dist - UWISC **Prod** - WMTVTV

Life After Breast Cancer 15 MIN
VHS / 16mm
Understanding Breast Cancer Series
Color (H C A PRO)
$195.00 purchase, $75.00 rental _ #8072
Deals with the emotions and coping after experiencing breast cancer.
Guidance and Counseling; Health and Safety
Dist - AIMS **Prod** - HOSSN 1988

Life After Death 35 MIN
16mm
Color
LC 79-700049
Presents Dr Lawrence Le Shan and Robert Monroe giving their views on the question of continuation after biological death. Interviews individuals who have experienced clinical death and have been revived.
Health and Safety; Psychology; Sociology
Dist - HP **Prod** - HP 1978

Life After Doomsday - Nuclear War 20 MIN
U-matic / VHS
Color
$335.00
Civics and Political Systems; Sociology
Dist - ABCLR **Prod** - ABCLR 1982

Life after downsizing - Part II 45 MIN
VHS
Change in the workplace series
Color (G C PRO)
$695.00 purchase, $35.00 preview
Presents part two of a three - part series guiding managers and employees through downsizing. Helps employees to overcome the fear, increased workload and hindered productivity that often accompany the loss of colleagues. Includes an 18 - minute managerial video and a 27 - minute employee video.
Business and Economics; Guidance and Counseling; Psychology
Dist - FI **Prod** - FLILN 1995

Life after life 57 MIN
VHS
Color (G)
$19.95 purchase _ #P32
Chronicles the stories of people with near - death experiences, including author Dannion Brinkly. Features Dr Raymond Moody.
Literature and Drama; Sociology
Dist - HP

Life after life 90 MIN
BETA / VHS
Innerwork series
Color (G)
$49.95 purchase _ #W417
Explores the significance of the near - death experience for understanding of the collective unconscious, emphasizing the value of wisdom and love as being primary in human life. Features Dr Raymond A Moody, Jr, psychiatrist.
Psychology; Religion and Philosophy; Sociology
Dist - THINKA **Prod** - THINKA

Life After the Curb - Recycling Processes
VHS / 16mm
Color (A)
Covers what is recyclable and where to recycle. Demonstrates processes and identifies end products.
Science - Natural; Sociology
Dist - CORNRS **Prod** - CORNRS 1990

Life after work 10 MIN
16mm / VHS / BETA / U-matic
Color; PAL (G)
PdS90, PdS98 purchase
Explores the importance of pre - retirement education and of planning ahead for a meaningful retirement.
Guidance and Counseling
Dist - EDPAT

Life Along a Malaysian River 17 MIN
U-matic / VHS / 16mm
Color (I J)
$195 video purchase, $295 film purchase or $30 rental
Studies the geography, daily life, people and transportation along the Rajang River in Malaysia.
Geography - World; Social Science
Dist - IFB

Life among the Test Tubes 30 MIN
U-matic / VHS
Zoolab Series
Color (J H)
$180.00 purchase
Introduces the careers available in the field of biology and Zoology.
Science - Natural
Dist - AITECH **Prod** - WCETTV 1985

The Life and Adventures of Nicholas Nickleby 479 MIN
U-matic / VHS
Color
Presents the Royal Shakespeare Company's production of Charles Dickens' novel THE LIFE AND ADVENTURES OF NICHOLAS NICKLEBY.
Literature and Drama
Dist - FOTH **Prod** - FOTH

The Life and art of William H Johnson 25 MIN
VHS
Color (J H C G)
$79.00 purchase _ #RO101V
Presents a portfolio of eight color reproductions which journey through the cotton patches of the South, the city streets of Harlem and the training camps of World War II as they explore the artistic development of artist William H Johnson. Reveals that Johnson was an expatriate during the 1930s but returned to New York in 1938, on the eve of World War II, prompted partly by the impending war and by the need to paint 'my own people.' Shows how he understood the importance of cultural roots in formulating an authentic, self - locating artistic expression. Includes teacher's guide.
Fine Arts; History - United States
Dist - CAMV

The Life and Assassination of the Kingfish
BETA / VHS
Color
Presents a portrayal by Ed Asner of the flamboyant and controversial Louisiana politician Huey Long.
Biography; Civics and Political Systems; History - United States
Dist - GA **Prod** - GA

The Life and Assassination of the Kingfish 97 MIN
16mm / U-matic / VHS
Color (H C A)
LC 80-700027
Examines the life and career of Louisiana Governor Huey Long, telling how he was idealized by some and despised by others. Explains how he changed the face of his State during his tempestuous political career and that he was preparing to run for the Presidency when he was assassinated in 1935.
Biography; Civics and Political Systems; Fine Arts; History - United States
Dist - LCOA **Prod** - TOMENT 1979

Life and Breath 15 MIN
16mm
Color
LC FIA68-2430
Describes the disease emphysema, and points out that it is the fastest growing lung ailment today.
Health and Safety; Science - Natural
Dist - AMLUNG **Prod** - CTRDA 1968

Life and Breath Series
Kids on Smoking 10 MIN
Smoking - a Report on the Nation's Habit 17 MIN
Smoking - How to Stop 23 MIN
Dist - JOU

Life and Customs 14 MIN
16mm
Land of the Bible Series
Color; B&W (I)
LC FIA67-1925
Shows many of the customs and practices of the people of the Bible lands. Emphasizes the relationship between the teachings of Jesus and the life and customs of the people.
Geography - World; Religion and Philosophy; Sociology
Dist - FAMF **Prod** - FAMF 1960

Life and Death 30 MIN
U-matic / VHS
Health, Safety and Well - Being Series
Color
Sociology
Dist - CAMB **Prod** - MAETEL

Life and death 30 MIN
VHS / U-matic
Forests of the world series
Color (I J H G)
$270.00, $320.00 purchase, $60.00 rental
Exposes insect infestations and air pollution, from pine bark beetles to acid rain, in New England, England, Sweden and Norway.
Science - Natural
Dist - NDIM **Prod** - NRKTV 1993

Life and Death - Dawson, Georgia 27 MIN
U-matic
Color
Documents the trial of five black men charged with the murder of a white man during a store robbery. Paints a picture of life and conflicting racial attitudes in a small Georgia town.
Civics and Political Systems; Sociology
Dist - PBS **Prod** - KANDIN

Life and Death in a Pond 15 MIN
16mm / U-matic / VHS
Color (H C)
Describes the struggle for survival which occurs in the waters of a pond from the fertilization of eggs through the quest for food to the eventual death of such creatures as frogs, newts, diving beetles and dragonfly nymphs.
Science - Natural
Dist - CORF **Prod** - CORF 1981

Life and Death in a Pond 15 MIN
16mm / U-matic / VHS
Color (J H C)
$370, $250 purchase _ #4136
Talks about the adaptation, development, and life cycles of the organisms in a pond.
Science - Natural
Dist - CORF

Life and death in ancient Egypt 50 MIN
VHS
Chronicle
Color; PAL (C H)
PdS99 purchase
Follows Dr Rosalie David as she uses non - destructive techniques to collect information from ancient Egyptian relics. Focuses on the scientific examination of mummies in the United Kingdom. Highlights an inter - disciplinary investigation into the cause of death of Egyptian mummies.
History - World; Sociology
Dist - BBCENE

Life and death in the Great Barrier Reef 60 MIN
VHS
Australian ark series
Color (G)
$19.95 purchase _ #S02056
Portrays the life cycle of Australia's Great Barrier Reef.
Geography - World; Science - Natural
Dist - UILL

Life and Death of a Cell 20 MIN
U-matic / VHS / 16mm
Color (H C A)
Uses an amoeba proteus to illustrate that the cell embodies all the functions and properties common to living things. Illustrates cell habitat, digestion and division, and explains the cause of cell death.
Science - Natural
Dist - UCEMC **Prod** - UCB 1959

Life and Death of a Tree 20 MIN
U-matic / VHS / 16mm
Color (H C A)
LC 80-700228
Explores the contributions of an oak tree to the ecology of other plants and animals.
Science - Natural
Dist - NGS **Prod** - NGS 1979

Life and Death of an African Pan 25 MIN
U-matic / VHS
Color (J H)
LC 84-706733
Tells the story of the creation, existence, and ultimate destruction of the shallow water - filled depressions called pans on the fringe of the Kalahari desert in Africa.
Science - Natural
Dist - CEPRO **Prod** - CEPRO 1982

The Life and death of Colonel Blimp 163 MIN
35mm
B&W (G)
Offers the restored version of a classically satirical look at the British military. Directed by Michael Powell and Emeric Pressburger.
Fine Arts; Literature and Drama
Dist - KINOIC

Life and Death of King John 155 MIN
VHS
Shakespeare series
Color (A)
PdS25 purchase
Stars Phyllida Law, Leonard Rossiter and John Thaw. Part of a series of plays by Shakespeare performed by leading stage and screen actors and interpreted by directors and producers such as Jonathan Miller, Elijah Mohinsky and Jack Gold.
Literature and Drama
Dist - BBCENE

Life and death on the Great Barrier Reef
VHS
Color (G)
$100.00 purchase _ #0913
Visits the Great Barrier Reef near Australia. Reveals that the reef is hundreds of miles long and that appearances are deceptive - what seem to be plants are really animals - and vice versa.
Science - Natural; Science - Physical
Dist - SEVVID

Life and debt - 2 50 MIN
VHS
Developing stories series
Color (H C G)
$150.00 purchase, $75.00 rental
Documents the effects of Brazil's $130 billion debt on its social and economic life, resulting from 500 years of domination and exploitation by Europeans, Americans and, now, Japanese. Links the assassination of 500 street children each year in Rio de Janeiro directly to Brazil's massive debt. A film by Octavio Bezerra for BBC Television. Part of a six - part series highlighting debates of the Earth Summit.
Business and Economics; Civics and Political Systems; Sociology
Dist - CANCIN **Prod** - BBCTV 1994

Life and Health Series
Alcoholism - a model of drug dependency 20 MIN
Dependence - a new definition 25 MIN
The Heart - Attack 27 MIN
The Heart - Counterattack 30 MIN
Dist - CRMP

Life and Liberty - for all who Believe 30 MIN
16mm / U-matic / VHS
Color (J)
Debates whether religious groups can use their freedom of religion to ban books and thus curtail other people's freedom of speech. Demonstrates how difficult it is to differentiate between parental discipline and child abuse.
Civics and Political Systems; Sociology
Dist - FI **Prod** - PAMWAY 1983

Life and Livelihood in the Bible 30 MIN
16mm
Eternal Light Series
B&W (H C A)
LC 72-700972
Features Maurice Samuel and Mark Van Doren, discussing and comparing practical day - to - day aspects of life in Bible times with their parallels in modern times. (Kinescope).
Religion and Philosophy
Dist - NAAJS **Prod** - JTS 1966

Life and Message of Swami Vivekananda 22 MIN
16mm
B&W (I)
Presents the biography of Swami Vivekananda, who, as the ardent disciple of Sri Ramakrishna Paramahamsa, made a deep impression at the Chicago Conference of World Religions. Portrays him as a humanist, patriot and exponent of Hindu philosophy.
Religion and Philosophy
Dist - NEDINF **Prod** - INDIA

The Life and Poetry of Julia De Burgos 28 MIN
16mm / U-matic / VHS
Captioned; Color (A) (SPANISH (ENGLISH SUBTITLES))
Portrays the life and work of the Puerto Rican poet Julia De Burgos.
Fine Arts; Literature and Drama
Dist - CNEMAG **Prod** - CNEMAG 1979

Life and soul 30 MIN
VHS
Lifesense series
Color; PAL (H C A)
PdS65 purchase; Not available in the United States
Examines the history of human development from the point of view of other species. Discusses the various religions of man as seen by the animals that are the focus of these religions. Part of the Lifesense series.
Science - Natural
Dist - BBCENE

The Life and Surprising Adventures of Robinson Crusoe 82 MIN
U-matic / VHS
Color (I J C A)
$99.00 purchase _ #4119
An English language version of the Soviet - made film. Relates the story of a man shipwrecked on a hostile uninhabited island who must survive alone. Shows how he acquires humility and a strange kind of contentment. Based on the novel The Adventures Of Robinson Crusoe by Daniel Defoe.
Literature and Drama
Dist - EBEC

Life and the Land Series
Chilcootin 18 MIN
Dist - CDIAND

Life and the Structure of Hemoglobin 28 MIN
U-matic / VHS / 16mm
Color (C A)
LC 76-700960
Describes the structure and mechanism of hemoglobin, as presented by Linus Pauling and other scientists, using computer animation.
Science - Natural
Dist - AIMS **Prod** - PAROX 1976

The Life and times of Allen Ginsberg 82 MIN
16mm / VHS
Color (G)
$1350.00, $490.00 purchase, $150.00 rental
Profiles one of the leading literary and cultural icons of the 20th century, the highly visible and controversial poet of the Beat and Hippie generations. Surveys the Beat Generation of the 1940s and 50s, the wild energy of the 60s, the disillusionment of the 70s and the cynicism and confusion of the 80s and 90s through Ginsberg's eyes. Uses a ten - year accumulation of more than 100 hours of film chronicling his life, including previously unseen material from Ginsberg's private archives. Features exclusive interviews with his contemporaries including Joan Baez, William Burroughs, Ken Kesey, Jack Kerouac, Abbie Hoffman, Timothy Leary, Norman Mailer and William F Buckley among others.
Fine Arts; Literature and Drama; Sociology
Dist - FIRS **Prod** - ARONJE 1993

The Life and times of Buffalo Bill Cody 20 MIN
VHS
Color (J H C G)
$34.95 purchase _ #OAP300V
Documents the eventful life of Colonel William F Cody to provide some of the most useful and historically accurate information available on the westward expansion of the United States and the Wild West. Reveals that Pony Express rider, buffalo hunter, calvary scout, entrepreneur and western legend Buffalo Bill's life spanned an important period of American history, that his experiences

exemplified the lifestyle of the Old West and the events in American history of that time. He knew almost the entire cast of characters of pioneer drama, including Sitting Bull, General Custer, Wild Bill Hickock and Annie Oakley.
Biography; History - United States
Dist - CAMV

The Life and times of John F Kennedy 60 MIN
VHS
Color (J H C G)
$29.95 purchase _ #WK227V
Examines the life of the 35th president, John F Kennedy, using live action and historic footage. Chronicles his attendance at prestigious schools, his role as secretary to his father when Joseph Kennedy served as ambassador to Great Britain, Kennedy as a naval officer during World War II, a reporter to the United Nations, his entrance into politics.
Biography; Civics and Political Systems; History - United States
Dist - CAMV

The Life and Times of Josiah Gardner, First Mate 55 MIN
VHS
Color (G)
$29.95 purchase _ #SS - 4
Tells the colorful story of the life at sea of Josiah Gardner, a fictional character. Reveals the career of a sailor in the 19th century. Features Glenn Gordinier, research associate and role player at Mystic Seaport, as Gardner.
Geography - World; History - World; Literature and Drama
Dist - MYSTIC **Prod** - MYSTIC

The Life and Times of Judge Roy Bean 124 MIN
16mm
Color
Stars Paul Newman as a slightly crazy judge who decides to restore law and order to his town, all for the love of Lily Langtry. Directed by John Huston.
Literature and Drama
Dist - TWYMAN **Prod** - UNKNWN 1972

Life and times of Peter Drucker 30 MIN
VHS
Business matters series
Color (A)
PdS65 purchase
Looks at the key ideas of Peter Drucker, grand old man of management. Asks, where did they start and how have they developed. Ends with a profile of the organization that he thinks is one of the best managed in the United States.
Business and Economics
Dist - BBCENE

The Life and Times of Rose Maddox
U-matic / VHS
(G)
$34.95 purchase, $25.00 rental
Documents Maddox's 50 year career in country music, which began at age 11 in California migrant camps to the Grand Ole Opry, major recording contracts and a place in the Country Music Hall of Fame's Walkway of the Stars.
Fine Arts
Dist - BAVC **Prod** - BAVC

The Life and Times of Rosie the Riveter 65 MIN
16mm
Color (J)
LC 81-700773
Presents five women reminiscing about their factory work during World War II. Points out that although the women were subjected to lower pay and discrimination, they had a positive response to the work. Includes archival and newsreel footage.
History - United States; Sociology
Dist - CLARTY **Prod** - CLARTY 1980

The life and times of Rosie the riveter 60 MIN
16mm
Color (G IND)
$10.00 rental
Records five women who talk about their experiences in the factories that built tanks, ships and bombers after the men went off to war in 1941 and 1942 and women were recruited for industrial jobs which had previously been closed to them. Tells what happened to these women when the war was over and the men came back to claim their jobs.
History - United States; Social Science; Sociology
Dist - AFLCIO **Prod** - FIELDC 1980

The Life and work of Paul
VHS
Color (I J H C G A R)
$19.95 purchase, $10.00 rental _ #35 - 81009 - 19
Consists of six short episodes which account for the life and ministry of the Apostle Paul. Covers Paul's background, character, conversion, ministry and trials.
Literature and Drama; Religion and Philosophy
Dist - APH **Prod** - FAMF

The Life and work of Paul
VHS
Color (I J H R G A)
$19.95 purchase _ #87EE1009
Gives an account of the life and ministry of the Apostle Paul. Profiles his background, character, conversion, ministry and trials.
Guidance and Counseling; Literature and Drama; Religion and Philosophy
Dist - CPH **Prod** - CPH

Life and Work of Sir James Hutton 28 MIN
U-matic / VHS
Earth Explored Series
Color
Focuses on the development of the theory of uniformitarianism, with field visits illustrating how geologists reconstruct the history of an area. Filmed in Scotland.
Science - Physical
Dist - PBS **Prod** - BBCTV

Life Another Way 55 MIN
U-matic
Color
Gives the story of a courageous woman who fought back from disabilities to become one of Canada's foremost crusaders for the rights of the disabled.
Psychology; Sociology
Dist - LAURON **Prod** - LAURON

Life Around Us Series
Animal communication 30 MIN
How Old is Old 30 MIN
More than Meets the Eye 30 MIN
Other Planets - no Place Like Earth 30 MIN
Small Wilderness 30 MIN
Dist - AMBROS

Life around us series
A Look at sound 30 MIN
Dist - AMBROS
TIMLIF

Life Around Us Series
After the whale 30 MIN
How Old is Old 30 MIN
Life in a Tropical Forest 30 MIN
The Lopsided wheel 30 MIN
The Losers 30 MIN
More than Meets the Eye 30 MIN
The Not - So - Solid Earth 30 MIN
Other Planets - no Place Like Earth 30 MIN
Rock - a - bye baby 30 MIN
Should Oceans Meet 30 MIN
Small wilderness 30 MIN
The Ultimate Machine 30 MIN
Dist - TIMLIF

Life Around Us (Spanish Series
Animal communication 30 MIN
The Losers 30 MIN
More than Meets the Eye 30 MIN
Should oceans meet 30 MIN
The Ultimate machine 30 MIN
Dist - TIMLIF

The Life around us - Video 4 47 MIN
VHS
Life science - secrets of science series
Color (I J H C)
$49.95 purchase
Presents two parts in two segments each, examining life forms from protozoa to mammals, the vast variety of insects inhabiting the Earth and looking at the behavior and importance of bees and the great diversity of plant life. Includes The Animal Kingdom and The World of Insects in Part I, The Busy Bees and A Planet of Plants in Part II. Hosted by Discover Magazine Editor in Chief Paul Hoffman. Fourth of four parts on life science.
Science - Natural
Dist - EFVP **Prod** - DSCOVM 1994

Life Around Us
Life in a Tropical Forest 30 MIN
Dist - TIMLIF

Life as an ethnic minority in Eastern Europe - 4 51 MIN
VHS
Eastern Europe - breaking with the past series
Color (H C G)
$50.00 purchase
Portrays the dramatic changes in the lives of ethnic Hungarians living in Romania in Let There Be Peace in this House, filmed during the last days of Ceausescu; Free Us From Evil, filmed after the revolution; Gravity, a Hungarian animation piece examining the challenges and dangers in breaking with the system. Part four of 13 parts.
Civics and Political Systems; History - World
Dist - GVIEW **Prod** - GVIEW 1990

Life at Salt Point (Salt Water Ecology) 15 MIN
U-matic / VHS / 16mm
Color (J H)
$370, $250 purchase _ #3874
Talks about how organisms adapt to open - sea, wave - swept, and tidal ecosystems.
Science - Natural
Dist - CORF

Life at Salt Point - Salt Water Ecology 15 MIN
U-matic / VHS / 16mm
Color (J)
LC 78-701753
Uses the natural laboratory of the California coast to study three salt water ecosystems. Examines habitat, adaption, food chains, filter feeding, and species interaction in each ecosystem through the use of underwater photography and photomicrography.
Science - Natural
Dist - CORF **Prod** - CORF 1978

Life at the End of the World 52 MIN
U-matic / VHS / 16mm
Undersea World of Jacques Cousteau Series
Color (I)
Science - Natural; Science - Physical
Dist - CF **Prod** - METROM 1970

Life at the Source - the Adventures of an Amazon Explorer 47 MIN
VHS / 16mm
Color (G)
$295.00 purchase, $75.00 rental
Recounts the story of Arno P Calderari, professional adventurer, jungle explorer, deep sea diver, treasure hunter and wildlife filmmaker, who has been dubbed 'Indiana Jones Arno' by the media. Reveals that he served as Technical Advisor for 'Raiders of the Lost Ark.' Interweaves his reminiscences with film footage of his many adventures and commentary on his role as an environmentalist and advocate for the preservation of rainforests.
History - World; Literature and Drama; Social Science; Sociology
Dist - CNEMAG **Prod** - CNEMAG 1989

Life at the Top 24 MIN
16mm
Color (J H C)
LC 77-701479
Examines population and national development patterns in industrialized France, Romania and the United Kingdom. Focuses on the question of family planning.
Guidance and Counseling; History - World; Sociology
Dist - SF **Prod** - UN 1975

Life at the water's edge 17 MIN
VHS
Color (I J H)
UK currency purchase
Looks at wetlands - ponds, lakes, rivers or marshes. Reveals that in some parts of the world they are prized as producers of food, or as a source of raw materials such as thatching grass and building poles - or as a haven for wildlife. Every year valuable wetland areas disappear and many others are threatened by dams, drainage schemes or pollution. Presented by World Wide Fund for Nature International.
Geography - World; Science - Natural; Social Science
Dist - VIEWTH

Life at Your Fingertips 13 MIN
U-matic / VHS / 16mm
Color (G)
MP=$260.00
Follows a sensational rock climber who shares with the viewer his feelings and emotions as he hangs onto the rock by his fingertips, using no safety equipment.
Physical Education and Recreation
Dist - LANDMK **Prod** - LANDMK 1986

Life before birth
VHS
Color (J H C G T A PRO)
$79.50 purchase _ #AH46306
Gives a visual presentation of the human reproductive process.
Health and Safety; Science - Natural
Dist - HTHED **Prod** - HTHED

Life between the Tides 20 MIN
U-matic / VHS / 16mm
Natural Phenomena Series
Color (I)
LC 77-703484
Portrays the diversity of animal life in the intertidal zone. Uses macro - and micro - cinematography to portray these animals in their natural environment.
Science - Natural
Dist - JOU **Prod** - CINEM 1977

Life Beyond Earth and the Mind of Man 25 MIN
16mm
Color (H A)
LC 76-700471
Features participants from a symposium held at Boston University in November 1972, exploring the implications of the possible existence of extraterrestrial life within the galaxy and the universe.
Science - Physical
Dist - USNAC **Prod** - NASA 1975

Life Cycle of a Fish 13 MIN
16mm / U-matic / VHS
Color (J H)
Focuses on the killifish, showing the process by which a fertilized egg develops into an approximate copy of its parents.
Science - Natural
Dist - FI **Prod** - MACMFL

The Life cycle of a flowering plant 11 MIN
VHS
Color; PAL (I J H)
PdS29
Examines the complete life cycle of a tomato plant, from germination of seed to dispersal of the plant's new seeds and fruits. Uses time - lapse photography to portray the main developmental changes as they occur. Demonstrates carefully and explains the emergence of the seedlings above the soil, the development of seed leaves and 'true' leaves, the appearance and pollination of flower buds, the development and growth of the fruit and the final dispersal of the seeds within the fruit. Makes a distinction between the 'cultivated' tomato illustrated in the program and the original wild tomato from which it came.
Science - Natural
Dist - BHA

Life Cycle of a Flowering Plant Series no 2
Mitosis 11 MIN
Dist - LUF

Life Cycle of a Flowering Plant Series no 3
Meiosis 7 MIN
Dist - LUF

Life cycle of a flowering plant series
Plant cell and male and female flower parts 11 MIN
Dist - LUF

Life Cycle of a Yeast Cell 17 MIN
16mm
B&W
Demonstrates the operation of the De Fonbrune pneumatic micro - manipulator and the making of microtools. Shows by diagram or microphotograph the sexual reproduction of yeast cells, asci and fusion of ascopores.
Science - Natural
Dist - SIUFP **Prod** - SILLU 1952

Life Cycle of Bass 22 MIN
16mm
Color
Introduces little - knowns facts about the life cycle of the largemouth bass, now considered the world's most popular freshwater game fish. Explains how these patterns of courtship, spawning, habit and habitat affect the angler.
Physical Education and Recreation; Science - Natural
Dist - KAROL **Prod** - BRNSWK

Life Cycle of Diphyllobothrium Latum 17 MIN
16mm
B&W
LC FIE52-2253
Explains and traces through animation and photomicrography the life cycle of the broad tapeworm of man.
Health and Safety; Science - Natural
Dist - USNAC **Prod** - USPHS 1950

Life Cycle of Endamoeba Histolytica in Dysenteric and Nondysenteric Amoebiasis 18 MIN
16mm
Color
LC FIE52-1124
Shows the parasites as cysts in an ulcerated colon. Demonstrates by animation how the amoeba divides into eight amoebulae which move about, and how the amoebae enter the blood. For medical personnel.
Health and Safety
Dist - USNAC **Prod** - USN 1948

Life Cycle of Endamoeba Histolytica in Dysenteric and Nondysenteric Amoebiasis 11 MIN
U-matic
Color (PRO)
LC 78-706102
Shows the parasites as cysts in an ulcerated colon and uses animation to demostrate how the amoeba divides into eight amoebulae which move and enter the blood. Issued in 1943 as a motion picture.
Health and Safety; Science - Natural
Dist - USNAC **Prod** - USN 1978

The Life Cycle of Insects - Complete Metamorphosis 20 MIN
U-matic / VHS / 16mm
Insect Series
Color
LC 80-700678
Examines the egg - larva - pupa - adult cycle of insect life, known as complete metamorphosis. Uses close - ups and time - lapse photography in viewing different stages of the life cycle of the butterfly, moth, mosquito and fly.
Science - Natural
Dist - IFB **Prod** - BHA 1977

The Life Cycle of Insects - Incomplete Metamorphosis 17 MIN
U-matic / VHS / 16mm
Insect Series
Color
LC 80-700679
Explains incomplete metamorphosis as extreme close - ups and speeded - up photography show how some insect eggs hatch into miniature versions of the adult and become adults through gradual stages. Illustrates the whole cycle of locust life and shows how cockroaches, walking sticks and aphids have a similar life cycle.
Science - Natural
Dist - IFB **Prod** - BHA 1977

The Life Cycle of Plants 28 MIN
U-matic / VHS
Life of Plants Series
Color (C)
$249.00, $149.00 purchase _ #AD - 1672
Examines the structural parts of plants. Looks at the life cycle of plants. Part of a series on plants.
Science - Natural
Dist - FOTH **Prod** - FOTH

Life cycle of the frog - KS 1 10 MIN
VHS
Color; PAL (P I)
PdS29.50 purchase
Introduces the amphibian group. Follows the reproduction of a frog - from tadpole and froglet to adult frogs.
Science; Science - Natural
Dist - EMFVL **Prod** - LOOLEA

Life Cycle of the Honey Bee 21 MIN
U-matic / VHS
Color (C)
$249.00, $149.00 purchase _ #AD - 1291
Examines the beehive in detail. Follows the complete life cycle of the bee.
Science - Natural
Dist - FOTH **Prod** - FOTH

Life Cycle of the Honeybee 13 MIN
16mm / U-matic / VHS
Bio - Science Series
Color
LC 80-706307
Shows the organization and specialization of the honeybee, including views of the new hive and the various activities of the workers, foragers, queen and young bees.
Science - Natural
Dist - NGS **Prod** - NGS 1976

The Life cycle of the honeybee - 36
VHS
Reading rainbow series
Color; CC (K P)
$39.95 purchase
Shows where honey comes from and how it is made in a book by Paula Z Hogan, illustrated by Geri K Stringenz. Visits a real - life beekeeper with LeVar and examines a beehive closely. Shows how honey is extracted from the combs and how important the queen bee is to the hive. Part of a series offering a multicultural approach to generating reading enthusiasm with cross - curricular applications, hosted by LeVar Burton.
English Language; Literature and Drama; Science; Science - Natural
Dist - GPN **Prod** - LNMDP

The Life Cycle of the Malaria Parasite 12 MIN
16mm / U-matic / VHS
Microbiology Teaching Series
Color (H C A)
Sexual and asexual cycles, including exorythrocytic stages, are depicted through the use of animation.
Health and Safety; Science - Natural
Dist - UCEMC **Prod** - UCEMC 1961

Life Cycle of the Silk Moth 11 MIN
16mm / U-matic / VHS
Bio - Science Series
Color (H C A)
Uses close - ups and slow motion to reveal in intricate detail the stages in the life of the silk moth. Examines mating, egg laying, egg hatching and the emergence of the caterpillar. Shows how a caterpillar uses its legs to hold on to various surfaces as it moves, how its jaws grind up the petiole of a leaf, and how it forms a cocoon. Shows the pupa slowly changing inside the cocoon and finally emerging as an adult moth.
Science - Natural
Dist - NGS **Prod** - NGS 1976

The Life cycle of the stars 26 MIN
16mm / U-matic / VHS
Cosmos series
Color (J H C)
Discusses the building blocks of matter, molecules, atoms, subatomic particles, leading to an explanation of the anatomy of stars. Shows how the different chemical elements are created and why there are atoms from distant galaxies in our own bodies.
Science - Physical
Dist - FI **Prod** - SAGANC 1980

The Life Cycle of Trichinella Spiralis 10 MIN
16mm
Color
Discusses the parasite which causes trichinosis.
Health and Safety; Science - Natural
Dist - UR **Prod** - UR

Life Cycles
Videodisc
Color (P)
Presents a remarkable visual record of how life begins in motion pictures, and still images on laser system video discs. Shows each segment of reproduction in animal and plant life, from cell division to courtship and birthing. Contains almost 4,000 color images, graphic illustrations and footage from 16 films.
Science - Natural
Dist - GPN **Prod** - GPN

The Life Cycles - Aging 30 MIN
U-matic / VHS
Focus on Society Series
Color (C)
Discusses the realities and stereotypes of aging.
Sociology
Dist - DALCCD **Prod** - DALCCD

Life Dances on 31.5 MIN
16mm
B&W (C)
Experimental film by Robert Frank.
Fine Arts
Dist - AFA **Prod** - AFA 1980

Life, death and denial - 2 43 MIN
VHS / U-matic
Glendon programs - a series
Color (C A)
$305.00, $275.00 purchase _ #V593
Integrates psychodynamic concepts and existential thought in regard to the knowledge of almost every human that death is inevitable. Shares the experiences of participants as children when they first learned about death, and reveals the methods they use as adults to deny their impending fate. Part of a 12 - part series featuring Dr Robert W Firestone, who is noted for his concept of the 'inner voice' and Voice Therapy.
Psychology; Sociology
Dist - BARR **Prod** - CEPRO 1991

The Life, Death and Recovery of an Alcoholic 26 MIN
16mm
Color (C A)
LC 77-701977
Traces the normal course of alcoholism from the first drink, through alcohol abuse and into alcohol addiction. Shows the psychological and chemical relationships which exist between an alcoholic and his employer, family and friends, the medical profession and the legal system.
Health and Safety; Psychology; Sociology
Dist - FMSP **Prod** - FMSP 1977

The Life, Death, and Recovery of an Alcoholic
16mm / U-matic / VHS
(H C A)
$395.00 purchase _ #81463 3/4 inch and #81455 VHS and #80747 film,
Discusses alcoholism prevention and treatment and counselor training. Demonstrates how an alcoholic's relationships, job performance, and life are affected by the disease of alcoholism.
Guidance and Counseling; Health and Safety; Psychology; Sociology
Dist - CMPCAR

Life, Death and Taxes Series

Chosen devices	29 MIN
An Exchangeable Value	29 MIN
First and great rule	29 MIN
The Fleeting estate	29 MIN
More than a Contract	29 MIN
Most Efficient Instrument	29 MIN
A Shifting of Risk	29 MIN
Specified Perils	29 MIN

Dist - UMITV

Life, Death and the American Woman 52 MIN
16mm
Color (J)
LC 78-701503
Covers causes, consequences and cures of common health problems experienced by American women.
Health and Safety; Science - Natural; Sociology
Dist - BESTF **Prod** - LNDBRG 1978

Life, Death and the American Woman, Pt 1 26 MIN
16mm
Color (J)
LC 78-701503
Covers causes, consequences and cures of common health problems experienced by American women.
Sociology
Dist - BESTF **Prod** - LNDBRG 1978

Life, Death and the American Woman, Pt 2 26 MIN
16mm
Color (J)
LC 78-701503
Covers causes, consequences and cures of common health problems experienced by American women.
Sociology
Dist - BESTF **Prod** - LNDBRG 1978

Life during the Mesozoic era 20 MIN
VHS
Color (J H C)
$39.95 purchase _ #IV145
Explores the life that developed from about 225 million years ago up through Cenozoic time. Reveals that while dinosaurs played a key role during this eera, there were many other forms of life, including insects and turtles, the bony fishes, flies, mosquitoes, lizards, birds and pterosaurs and snakes. Examines some mass extinction theories as to why life forms suddenly changed or died off.
Science - Physical
Dist - INSTRU

Life during the Paleozoic era 20 MIN
VHS
Color (J H C)
$39.95 purchase _ #IV144
Examines the Paleozoic era, a long period of time comprising seven periods from the Cambrian of over 600 million years ago through the Permian period. Examines fossil records and artists' drawings and dioramas of life in the Cambrian, Ordovician, Silurian, Devonian, Mississippian, Pennsylvanian and Permian periods. Looks at plant life, marine life and land life, including diatoms, algae, mosses, ferns, cycads, brachiopods, trilobites, crinoids, insects, reptiles, ammonites, sharks and fish. Discusses mass extinction theories and shows how the continents have moved.
Science - Physical
Dist - INSTRU

Life Endeath 7 MIN
16mm
Color (H C)
LC FIA67-5188
Presents an experimental film study of the abstract forms found in the flames of a fire to represent the cyclical nature of life from birth to death. Photographed by Erik Shiozaki.
Fine Arts
Dist - RADIM **Prod** - KAPR

Life flight 83 MIN
VHS
Color (H C G A R)
$39.95 purchase, $10.00 rental _ #35 - 844 - 8516
Explores the world of an emergency helicopter crew. Shows how the various crew members must deal with difficult choices all the time.
Health and Safety; Religion and Philosophy
Dist - APH **Prod** - VISVID

Life for life and moneymaking is inconsistent with life forces
VHS
Color (G R)
$29.95 purchase _ #C031
Features spiritual teacher Tara Singh who discusses the values of the Babylonian codes, 'A life for a life,' and moneymaking and the spiritual life.
Health and Safety; Psychology; Religion and Philosophy
Dist - LIFEAP **Prod** - LIFEAP

Life - Force 25 MIN
16mm
Color
LC 75-701893
Presents a documentary on Canadian painter Jack Chambers, exploring the creative energy which motivates the artist and his work.
Fine Arts
Dist - CANFDC **Prod** - MELFIL 1974

Life Force - a Salute to America's most Productive Industry - Agriculture 24 MIN
16mm
Color
LC 82-700738
Portrays the strength and closeness of farm families, their bond with the land and each other and how farmers combine business management, science, technology and plain hard work to make American agriculture the envy and wonder of the world.
Agriculture; Sociology
Dist - MTP **Prod** - FARMCB 1982

Life forms, animals and animal oddities 30 MIN
VHS
Tell me why series
Color (I J H)
$22.00 purchase _ #ABM019 - CV
Discusses animals, vertebrates, warm and cold - blooded animals, animal history, worms and animal oddities. Asks - what are protozoa, why do animals migrate, what animals live the longest, what is an echidna. Part of a series based on the book series by Arkady Leokum. Includes teacher's guide.
Science - Natural
Dist - CLRVUE **Prod** - CLRVUE

Life forms, animals, and animal oddities - Volume 7 30 MIN
VHS
Tell me why series
Color (K P I)
$19.95 purchase
Presents Volume 7 of the 'Tell Me Why' video encyclopedia series. Teaches children the facts about life forms, animals, and animal oddities.
Science - Physical
Dist - PBS **Prod** - WNETTV

Life from Life 10 MIN
16mm
Family Life and Sex Education Series
Color (K P)
Examines plants and trees producing the seeds for new life. Explains that all living things come from other living things of the same kind. Shows the mating, egg - laying, fertilization, hatching and early growth of angel fish and leopard frogs.
Science - Natural
Dist - SF **Prod** - SF 1968

Life from the Dead Sea 14 MIN
16mm
Color
Shows how the rich mineral resources from the Dead Sea, the lowest spot on earth, are extracted and processed.
Geography - World; Industrial and Technical Education
Dist - ALDEN **Prod** - ALDEN

Life from the sea 60 MIN
VHS
Miracle planet - the life story of Earth series
Color (I J H)
$100.00 purchase _ #A5VH 1322
Looks at the oceans that cover two - thirds of the Earth. Uses footage of an Australian tidal sea and limestone mountains in China to illustrate how living organisms created the atmospheric balance necessary for development of life on land. Part of a six - part series examining the intricate balance of systems known as planet Earth.
Geography - World; Science - Natural; Science - Physical
Dist - CLRVUE

Life from the Sea 26 MIN
16mm
Color
Demonstrates Japan's efforts to protect its fishery resources while endeavoring to develop inland and coastal supplies.
Geography - World; Industrial and Technical Education
Dist - MTP **Prod** - MTP

Life from the Sun 15 MIN
16mm / U-matic / VHS
Color (I J)
LC FIA65-343
Illustrates the sun's influence on earthly life and enumerates the physical and biological phenomena that are the direct results of the sun's energy.
Science - Natural; Science - Physical
Dist - IFB **Prod** - VEF 1963

Life Games 8 MIN
16mm
Color
LC 80-700874
Focuses on attitudes toward life.
Psychology
Dist - TASCOR **Prod** - VICCOR 1979

Life Goals - Setting Personal Priorities
VHS / 35mm strip
$132.00 purchase _ #HR619 filmstrip, $132.00 purchase _ #HR619V
Talks about determining what one wants from life and stresses that the skills of decision making are necessary to assist in setting personal priorities.
Guidance and Counseling; Psychology
Dist - CAREER **Prod** - CAREER

Life Goals - Setting Personal Priorities 35 MIN
VHS
Color (J H)
Guides your students through the steps necessary for making decisions about their goals in life. Emphasizes important decisionmaking skills, the need to clarify values, establish clear objectives, and develop strategies.
Education; Guidance and Counseling
Dist - HRMC **Prod** - HRMC 1976

Life Goes to the Movies Series Part 2

The War Years - Fabulous 1939, Then Global Conflict	35 MIN

Dist - TIMLIF

Life Goes to the Movies Series Pt 1

The Golden age of Hollywood - the Depression and a new optimism	35 MIN

Dist - TIMLIF

Life Goes to the Movies Series Pt 5

The Movies Today - a New Morality	37 MIN

Dist - TIMLIF

Life goes to the movies series

The Fifties - television and a new hollywood	27 MIN
The Post - war era - film noir and the Hollywood ten	20 MIN

Dist - TIMLIF

Life History of the Rocky Mountain Wood Tick 18 MIN
16mm
Color (H C)
Depicts the two - year life - cycle of the Rocky Mountain wood tick. Shows the biology of the various stages including adults, eggs, larvae and nymphs and shows such features as, adaptibility to environment, host requirements and natural controlling factors.
Agriculture; Science - Natural
Dist - USNAC **Prod** - USNAC 1969

Life in a Chinese commune 11 MIN
VHS
Color; PAL (P I J H)
Reveals that a commune is an economic, political and social unit collectively run by the people who live there. Shows the organization of a large agricultural commune to the north of Peking.
Civics and Political Systems; Geography - World; History - World; Sociology
Dist - VIEWTH **Prod** - VIEWTH

Life in a Drop of Water 10 MIN
16mm / U-matic / VHS
Color (I J)
$255.00, $180.00 purchase _ #3225; LC 73-701786
Uses photomicrography to reveal the amoeba, spirogyra, paramecium, volvox, hydra, rotifer and other living forms carrying on the basic life processes of moving, reacting, obtaining food and reproducing.
Science - Natural
Dist - CORF **Prod** - CORF 1973

Life in a Garden 13 MIN
16mm
Color
Shows insects, mammals and birds to be seen in a suburban or rural garden. Includes magnified photography.
Agriculture; Science - Natural
Dist - FENWCK **Prod** - FENWCK

Life in a lake 27 MIN
VHS / U-matic
Color (J H G)
$280.00, $330.00 purchase, $50.00
Shows how animals and plants can live together and flourish and maintain a balance of life. Includes the life cycles of dragonflies, salamanders, crayfish and other animal and plant species. Produced over a period of five years, by TV2 - Denmark.
Fine Arts; Geography - World; Science - Natural
Dist - NDIM

Life in a Pond 10 MIN
16mm / VHS / U-matic
Color (I J)
$265, $185 purchase _ #3171; LC 73-707610
On a field trip, high school boys and girls study life in a fresh water pond. They see a self - sustaining group of plants and animals sharing the problems of obtaining sunlight, food and water.
Science - Natural
Dist - CORF **Prod** - CORF 1970

Life in a Tropical Forest 30 MIN
16mm
Life Around Us
Color (SPANISH)
LC 78-700067
Surveys the jungles of Cambodia, the Amazon and the island of Barro Colorado to investigate various forms of animals and plant life found in tropical rain forests.
Geography - World; Science - Natural
Dist - TIMLIF **Prod** - TIMLIF 1971

Life in a Tropical Forest 30 MIN
U-matic / VHS / 16mm
Life Around Us Series
Color (I)
Aids in better understanding of life in the jungle, where man originated, and shows how some men study and protect its survival. Shows tropical rain forests in Cambodia, the Amazon and on the island of Barro Colorado near Panama.
Science - Natural; Sociology
Dist - TIMLIF **Prod** - TIMLIF 1971

Life in a tropical rainforest 14 MIN
U-matic / VHS / 16mm
Color (I J H) (DUTCH)
LC 77-707904
Documents life in a tropical rainforest, where warm weather and heavy rainfall encourage a wide variety of unique plant and animal life.
Geography - World; Science - Natural
Dist - PHENIX **Prod** - PHENIX 1977

Life in a Weaverbird Colony 20 MIN
16mm
Color (H C T)
Illustrates the breeding behavior of weaverbirds, including weaving of the nests by the male, territorial defense, courtship and pair formation, copulation, female behavior in lining the nest and feeding nestlings and the development of the young and their behavior.
Science - Natural
Dist - UCLA **Prod** - UCLA 1971

Life in ancient Egypt 36 MIN
VHS
Color (I J)
$60.00 purchase _ #CLV3310
Explores the social, cultural, political and religious aspects of daily life in ancient Egypt. Teaches about the Egyptians' way of life in both the city and country. Video transfer from filmstrip.
History - World
Dist - KNOWUN

Life in Ancient Egypt 30 MIN
U-matic / VHS / 16mm
Color (J H)
Reconstructs life in ancient Egypt through use of tomb art. Portrays farmers at work, scribes assessing taxes, wine makers and other work activities. Shows houses, family life, children's games and travel along the Nile.
History - World
Dist - VIEWTH **Prod** - GATEEF

Life in Ancient Rome 14 MIN
16mm / U-matic / VHS
Color (I J H) (SPANISH)
Re - creates scenes and activities in Rome during the reign of Emperor Trajan. Examines the characteristics and achievements of the Roman Empire. Considers how Roman ideas and culture influenced the development of Western civilization.
History - World
Dist - EBEC **Prod** - EBEC

Life in Ancient Rome 14 MIN
U-matic / VHS / 16mm
Captioned; Color (I J H)
Re - creates typical scenes in Rome during the reign of Emperor Trajan. Examines characteristics and achievements of the Roman Empire at the height of its power, points out some of the weaknesses in Roman society and considers the ways in which Roman ideas influenced the development of Western civilization.
History - World
Dist - EBEC **Prod** - EBEC 1964

Life in Britain in the forties series
English farmer 10 MIN
English foreman 10 MIN
Oxford student 10 MIN
Sadler Wells ballerina 18 MIN
Dist - EDPAT

Life in China - Agricultural Worker in the Commune 28 MIN
16mm
Color (J)
Relates to the common man in China and his place within the social structure of which he is a part. Portrays the communal structure of rural China today and reveals the place of the individual citizen within it.
Agriculture; Civics and Political Systems; Geography - World; Health and Safety; Sociology
Dist - UHAWAI **Prod** - UHAWAI 1972

Life in China - Industry 28 MIN
16mm
B&W (H)
LC 73-700264
Stresses the importance of industry in the development of mainland China, showing the operation of fertilizer and ceramics factories, a textile mill and a commune tea factory. Reviews the life of an industrial worker, including his living conditions, educational and health programs and the part which workers play in political and cultural demonstrations in the People's Republic of China.
Business and Economics; Geography - World; Social Science; Sociology
Dist - OSUMPD **Prod** - OSUPD 1972

Life in China - Mill Worker's Family 17 MIN
16mm
B&W
LC 72-713593
A view of life in the People's Republic of China, as revealed in the daily activities of the members of the family of a worker in a state - operated cotton mill.
Business and Economics; Geography - World; Social Science
Dist - OSUMPD **Prod** - OSUPD 1971

Life in Colombia series
Raguira 9 MIN
Dist - IFF

Life in Lost Creek - Fresh Water Ecology 15 MIN
U-matic / VHS / 16mm
Color (J)
$370.00, $250.00 purchase _ #3873; LC 78-701752
Uses the natural laboratory of a small mountain stream which flows into a peaceful pond to study three fresh water ecosystems. Examines habitat, adaptation, ecological niche, population and species interaction in each ecosystem through the use of underwater photography and photomicrography.
Science - Natural
Dist - CORF **Prod** - CORF 1978

Life in Mediterranean Lands 13 MIN
16mm / U-matic / VHS
Color (I J)
Focuses on the Mediterranean climate and explains how it affects the agricultural activities and lifestyles of people around the world.
Geography - World
Dist - CORF **Prod** - CORF 1978

Life in Mediterranean lands 13 MIN
VHS
Color (I J)
$59.00 purchase _ #MF - 3872
Examines the geography, crops and people in regions of Europe, North Africa, and even California, that share Mediterranean climate.
Geography - World
Dist - INSTRU **Prod** - CORF

Life in Modern France Series
A Better life tomorrow 10 MIN
Far from Paris 10 MIN
Leisure and Vacations 11 MIN
Dist - EBEC

Life in Parched Lands 30 MIN
U-matic / VHS / 16mm
World We Live in Series
Color (I J H)
LC 71-700239
Describes the techniques of conserving water used by plants and animals living in the Sonoran Desert of Mexico and the Southwestern United States.
Science - Natural
Dist - MGHT **Prod** - TIMELI 1968

Life in relation to death 120 MIN
VHS
Color (G)
$45.00 purchase _ #LIREDV
Features Lama Chagdud Tulku Rinpoche. Reveals that death is life's most overwhelming event. How the individual meets it - terrified and helpless, or with confidence and spiritual mastery - is within the power of the individual. Rinpoche's English is respoken by Tsering Everest.
Religion and Philosophy; Sociology
Dist - SNOWLI

Life in Samoa 11 MIN
16mm
Color (J H C)
Shows village life and a wedding ceremony in American Samoa.
Geography - World; History - World; Sociology
Dist - CINEPC **Prod** - TAHARA 1986

Life in Soviet Asia - 273 Days Below Zero 11 MIN
U-matic / VHS / 16mm
Man and His World Series
Color (I J H)
Looks at the transformation of wasteland to agricultural and industrial complexes in Soviet Asia.
Agriculture; Geography - World; History - World; Sociology
Dist - FI **Prod** - POLSKI 1974

Life in the balance 30 MIN
VHS
Lifesense series
Color; PAL (H C A)
PdS65 purchase; Not available in the United States
Examines the history of human development from the point of view of other species. Discusses the effects humans have on animals that are used for human gain or enjoyment.
Science - Natural
Dist - BBCENE

Life in the City 30 MIN
U-matic / VHS
Focus on Society Series
Color (C)
Talks of urban change, its cause and effects in St Louis.
Sociology
Dist - DALCCD **Prod** - DALCCD

Life in the colonies 30 MIN
U-matic / VHS
American story - the beginning to 1877 series
Color (C)
History - United States
Dist - DALCCD **Prod** - DALCCD

Life in the Deciduous Forest 19 MIN
16mm / U-matic / VHS
Living Science Series
Color (H C A)
LC FIA65-265
Describes the animals, plants and fungi found in a deciduous forest. Explains how they are affected by the seasonal changes. Traces the herbivore - carnivore food chains of the community.
Science - Natural
Dist - IFB **Prod** - CMPBL 1962

Life in the Desert 5 MIN
U-matic
See, Hear - the Middle East Series
Color (J)
Looks at the vanishing way of life of the desert people, the Bedouin, and how they survive in their arid, barren environment.
Geography - World; History - World; Religion and Philosophy
Dist - TVOTAR **Prod** - TVOTAR 1980

Life in the desert 60 MIN
VHS
Australian ark series
Color (G)
$19.95 purchase _ #S02057
Portrays the life cycle of Australia's deserts.
Geography - World; Science - Natural
Dist - UILL

Life in the desert system 20 MIN
VHS
Color (I J)
$89.95 purchase _ #10195VG
Observes the evolution and complexity of the desert ecosystem. Teaches the environmental interrelations of plants, animals, water, and the sun's energy in arid regions. Comes with an interactive video quiz; teacher's guide; discussion questions; and 11 blackline masters.
Geography - World; Science - Natural
Dist - UNL

Life in the Developing World Series Pt 2
Haiti - Education for the Future 30 MIN
Dist - GPN

Life in the Early Seas - Invertebrates and Fishes 11 MIN
16mm / U-matic / VHS
Evolution of Life Series
Color (I)
LC FIA67-5877
Discusses the formation of fossils and how evidence from fossils helped scientists learn more about life long ago.

Science - Natural
Dist - MGHT   Prod - MGHT   1968

Life in the Far East   16 MIN
16mm
Color (J H C G)
Presents a comprehensive picture of the way of life of the peoples of the Far East. Deals with village agriculture and life in the towns and cities.
Agriculture; Geography - World; Social Science; Sociology
Dist - VIEWTH   **Prod** - GATEEF

Life in the freezer   6 - 30 MIN. EPISODES
VHS
Color; PAL (H G)
PdS240 series purchase; not available in USA
Explores the wildlife of the continent of Antarctica in a six - part video series. Includes information on both aquatic and land varieties of plant and animal life. Hosted by David Attenborough. Episodes are also available individually.
Science - Natural
Dist - BBCENE

Life in the freezer series
The ice retreats   30 MINS.
Dist - BBCENE

Life in the freezer
The big freeze   30 MINS.
The bountiful sea   30 MINS.
The door closes   30 MINS.
Footsteps in the snow   30 MINS.
The race to breed   30 MINS.
Dist - BBCENE

Life in the Grasslands   11 MIN
U-matic / VHS / 16mm
Color (I J)
Gives an overview of life on the American prairie, examining plants, animals and weather.
Geography - United States; Science - Natural
Dist - EBEC   **Prod** - EBEC

Life in the herd   25 MIN
VHS
Color (H R)
$19.95 purchase _ #87EE0026
Features Christian humorist Pat Hurley in an exploration of whether it is possible to be popular and a Christian. Encourages teenagers to follow the example of Christ, not letting themselves be controlled by peer pressure. Stresses the need to create meaningful friendships. Includes Bible study.
Guidance and Counseling; Literature and Drama; Psychology; Religion and Philosophy
Dist - CPH   **Prod** - CPH

Life in the herd   30 MIN
VHS
Stop, look, and laugh series
Color (J H R)
$19.95 purchase, $10.00 rental _ #35 - 826 - 19
Teaches teenagers how to maintain their Christian faith in the face of peer pressure. Uses humor, comic vignettes and a question - and - answer session to present a Christian perspective. Hosted by Pat Hurley.
Literature and Drama; Religion and Philosophy
Dist - APH   **Prod** - CPH

Life in the Ocean   16 MIN
U-matic / VHS / 16mm
Color (I J H)
Illustrates many plants and animals of shore, shallow water and ocean depths relating them to each other, to their environment and to similar forms of life found on land.
Science - Natural
Dist - PHENIX   **Prod** - FA   1955

Life in the Past   15 MIN
U-matic / VHS / 16mm
Place to Live Series
Color (I J H)
Deals with the formation of the Grand Canyon. Shows different types of fossils from the Canyon's bands of rock.
Science - Physical
Dist - JOU   **Prod** - GRATV

Life in the Quick Lane   25 MIN
16mm
Color
Looks at the sport of drag racing which was once just a backyard hobby and is now a multi - million dollar business in which races are won and lost in the blink of an eye.
Physical Education and Recreation
Dist - MTP   **Prod** - SEARS

Life in the Sahara   15 MIN
16mm / U-matic / VHS
Color (I J H) (SPANISH)
Chronicles patterns of life in the desert. Emphasizes the importance of water, oasis vegetation and camels in the desert economy. Contrasts nomadic life - styles with Arab and Berber settlements.
Geography - World; Science - Natural; Sociology
Dist - EBEC   **Prod** - EBEC

Life in the salt marsh   30 MIN
VHS
Return to the sea series
Color (I J H G)
$24.95 purchase _ #RTS201
Reveals that the salt marsh is one of the most productive ecosystems on Earth. Discloses that in just a few inches of water the underwater camera can find some interesting marsh inhabitants. Includes a segment on Big Sweep, a nationwide effort to clean wetland areas. Part of a 13 - part series on marine life produced by Marine Grafics and University of North Carolina Public TV.
Science - Natural
Dist - ENVIMC

Life in the Sea   11 MIN
16mm / U-matic / VHS
Color; B&W (I J H)
Divides sea life into three groups - plankton, bottom dwellers and free swimmers. Shows how various animals capture food and protect themselves against natural enemies. Explains how sea life must depend upon a process of photosynthesis.
Science - Natural
Dist - EBEC   **Prod** - EBEC   1958

The Life in the sea   17 MIN
VHS
Junior oceanographer series
CC; Color (P I)
$69.95 purchase_#10368VG
Shows a variety of sea life from around the world through on - location footage. Includes topics such as types of plants in the oceans; types of animals; evolution; different types of ocean environments; and ocean adaptations. Comes with an interactive video quiz, a teacher's guide and six blackline masters. Part four of a four - part series.
Geography - World; Science - Natural; Science - Physical
Dist - UNL

Life in the Southern Seas   60 MIN
VHS
Australian ark series
Color (G)
$19.95 purchase _ #S02058
Portrays the life cycle of Australia's Southern Seas region.
Geography - World; Science - Natural
Dist - UILL

Life in the Thirties   52 MIN
16mm / U-matic / VHS
Project 20 Series
B&W (J)
Covers the Depression, FDR, Dust Bowl, 1936 election, 'RENDEZVOUS WITH DESTINY,' and the rise of Hitler, Mussolini and Hirohito. Alexander Scourby narrates.
History - United States
Dist - MGHT   **Prod** - NBCTV   1965

Life in the Thirties, Pt 1   26 MIN
16mm / U-matic / VHS
Project 20 Series
B&W (J)
Discusses the years 1930 to 1936 and such things as the Depression, the 1932 campaign, the FDR administration, demagogues of the era, and the 1936 campaign.
History - United States
Dist - MGHT   **Prod** - NBCTV   1965

Life in the Thirties, Pt 2   26 MIN
U-matic / VHS / 16mm
Project 20 Series
B&W (J)
Discusses the years 1936 to 1939 and such things as developments abroad leading to war, the rise of dictators in Europe and Japan, and the 1939 World's Fair.
History - United States
Dist - MGHT   **Prod** - NBCTV   1965

A Life in the Trees   58 MIN
U-matic / VHS
Life on Earth series; Program 12
Color (J)
LC 82-706503
Explores the evolution of primates in a wide range of geographic areas and explains the significance of binocular vision and grasping hands in successful adaptation to life in the trees.
Science - Natural
Dist - FI   **Prod** - BBCTV   1981

Life in the Trees - Pt 24   30 MIN
16mm
Life on Earth series; Vol VI
Color (J)
$495.00 purchase _ #865 - 9025
Blends scientific data with breathtaking wildlife photography to tell the story of the development of life. Features wildlife expert David Attenborough as host. Part 24 of 27 parts is entitled 'Life In The Trees.'.
Science; Science - Natural; Science - Physical
Dist - FI   **Prod** - BBCTV   1981

Life in the universe quartet   120 MIN
BETA / VHS
Color (G)
$69.95 purchase _ #Q364
Presents a four - part series on life in the universe. Includes 'The Implications of UFO Phenomena' with Dr Jacques Vallee, 'Aliens and Archetypes' with Terence McKenna, 'The Mystery of Creation' with Dr Richard Grossinger and 'Extra - Terrestrial Intelligence' with Dr James Harder.
History - World; Literature and Drama; Psychology; Religion and Philosophy; Science; Sociology
Dist - THINKA   **Prod** - THINKA

Life in the universe series
Aliens and archetypes   30 MIN
Extra - terrestrial intelligence   30 MIN
The Implications of UFO phenomena   30 MIN
The Mystery of creation   30 MIN
Dist - THINKA

Life in the Valley   15 MIN
16mm / U-matic / VHS
Place to Live Series
Color (I J H)
Describes the formation of valleys. Illustrates the plant and animal life and rock formations that are characteristic of valleys.
Science - Natural; Science - Physical
Dist - JOU   **Prod** - GRATV

Life in the Winter Forest   15 MIN
VHS / U-matic
Up Close and Natural Series
Color (P I)
$125.00 purchase
Reveals the adaptational skills of the animals in a forest region.
Agriculture; Science - Natural; Social Science
Dist - AITECH   **Prod** - NHPTV   1986

Life in the Womb - the First Stages of Human Development   40 MIN
VHS
Color (J)
LC 85-703930
Chronicles the course of human development from fertilization through the birth of a human being. Looks at both genetic and environmental influences on prenatal growth.
Health and Safety; Science - Natural; Sociology
Dist - HRMC   **Prod** - HRMC

Life in the Womb - the First Stages of Human Development
VHS / 35mm strip
$119.00 purchase _ #HR770 filmstrip, $139.00 purchase _ #HR770V HVS
Uses photographs of embryos and fetuses to document the course of human development from fertilization through birth.
Health and Safety; Psychology; Science - Natural; Sociology
Dist - CAREER   **Prod** - CAREER

Life in the Woodlot   17 MIN
16mm
Color (I J H C)
Reveals the complex pattern in which the seasons and the life cycles of man, animals and plants are interrelated.
Science - Natural
Dist - NFBC   **Prod** - NFBC   1960

A Life in Your Hands   15 MIN
16mm
Color
LC 75-703023
Dramatizes the effectiveness of cardiopulmonary resuscitation and how it can be used by laypersons to save thousands of lives each year. Concentrates on the use of cardiopulmonary resuscitation for heart attack victims.
Health and Safety
Dist - WSTGLC   **Prod** - ACTF   1975

Life Insurance   29 MIN
U-matic
You and the Law Series Lesson 14
Color (C A)
Studies life insurance policies and the effects of their legal elements. Describes some of the legal rights and obligations of the parties to a life insurance contract.
Business and Economics; Civics and Political Systems
Dist - CDTEL   **Prod** - COAST

Life Insurance   30 MIN
U-matic / VHS
Personal Finance Series Lesson 20
Color (C A)
Explores the basic elements of life insurance, including the kinds of companies that sell life insurance and the various plans and policies that are available. Provides guidelines to assist in determining how much individual life insurance is needed.

Business and Economics
Dist - CDTEL **Prod** - SCCON

Life Insurance 29 MIN
VHS / 16mm
You Owe it to Yourself Series
Color (G)
$55.00 rental _ #YOIY - 005
Business and Economics
Dist - PBS **Prod** - WITFTV

Life Insurance 14 MIN
Videoreel / VT2
Living Better II Series
Color
Discusses the different kinds of life insurance and explains some common insurance terms. Explains the qualifications and requirements of an insurance agent and then compares the rates of term and straight life policies.
Business and Economics; Home Economics
Dist - PBS **Prod** - MAETEL

Life Insurance 28 MIN
U-matic / VHS
Personal Finance and Money Management Series
Color (C A)
Business and Economics; Civics and Political Systems
Dist - SCCON **Prod** - SCCON 1987

Life is a serious business 7 MIN
16mm
Color; B&W (G)
$15.00 rental
Satirizes the self - help education film using the cliches of the genre.
Fine Arts; Literature and Drama
Dist - CANCIN **Prod** - MICHAL 1983

Life is Fragile 5 MIN
16mm
Color
LC 76-700185
Examines awareness of the value of human life and of the need for personal safety through an aesthetic theme without narration.
Guidance and Counseling; Health and Safety
Dist - SWBELL **Prod** - SWBELL 1976

Life is impossible 50 MIN
VHS
Horizon series
Color (A PRO C)
PdS99 purchase
Expresses frustration with our knowledge of how life works, but our inability to say how it began. Explains that molecular biology can make genes reproduce but cannot give them life. Asks whether something came before biology - perhaps beginning in the world below the ocean floor?
Dist - BBCENE

Life is Like a Domino 5 MIN
16mm
Color
LC 80-700360
Gives a demonstration of a domino design stunt and relates it to everyday life.
Fine Arts
Dist - CORPOR **Prod** - CORPOR 1980

Life is Precious - Buckle Them in 14 MIN
U-matic / VHS
Color (J)
LC 84-700432
Explains the need to use such restraining devices as seat belts and child car seats for children riding in automobiles. Shows the four development stages during which children need different kinds of protection.
Health and Safety; Sociology
Dist - FIESTF **Prod** - CMT 1983

Life is speed - get fast or go broke 65 MIN
VHS / U-matic
Color (G)
$995.00, $895.00 purchase, $250.00 rental
Visits four time - obsessed companies which are redefining entire industries while boosting profits and market share. Includes Titeflex, a flexible hose maker, Ingersoll - Rand, tool manufacturer, Cable News Network and Union Pacific Railroad. Reveals that teamwork, cutting new product development time, rapid decision - making and eliminating hierarchal layers of management were factors in these companies' success. Features Tom Peters as host. Includes extensive support material.
Business and Economics
Dist - VPHI **Prod** - VPHI 1990

Life is sweet 102 MIN
35mm / 16mm
Color (G)
Uses food as a means of expression in this painfully funny film. Centers on a working - class couple, their grown twin daughters, and a few bizarre neighbors. The whole family eats in front of the television, except for the anorexic twin who binges in private. Dad, a chef, dreams of the hitting the road in his mobile snack bar while Mum helps a neighbor open a new restaurant that serves delightful items such as pork cyst. Writer - producer Mike Leigh dissects a family coming apart, culminating in a poignant confrontation between mother and daughter. Produced by Simon Channing - Williams. Contact distributor for price.
Fine Arts; Home Economics; Sociology
Dist - OCTOBF

Life is Worth the Living 22 MIN
U-matic / VHS / 16mm
Color (H C)
LC 71-707248
Examines the high number of traffic accidents involving teenage drivers and insists on the need for driver training by professional instructors. Demonstrates many traffic violations and etiquette common among all drivers.
Health and Safety
Dist - IFB **Prod** - CHET 1968

Life, Liberty and the Pursuit of Happiness - a Celebration 21 MIN
16mm
Color
LC 75-702229
Presents examples of nonacademic art from the early days of America as seen in an exhibition staged by Marcel Breuer at the Whitney Museum Of American Art in New York.
Fine Arts
Dist - MTP **Prod** - PHILMO 1975

Life Lived in Celebration
16mm
Travel Tips from a Reluctant Traveler Series
Color; Stereo (H C G T A)
Religion and Philosophy
Dist - WHLION **Prod** - WHLION 1986

The Life - Long Rechargeable Pacemaker 9 MIN
VHS / U-matic
Color (PRO) (SPANISH)
Describes how a new type rechargeable, implanted pacemaker regulates the rhythm of the heart.
Health and Safety
Dist - WFP **Prod** - WFP

Life Lunches and Sensible Suppers
VHS
Cook for the Health of it Series
(C G)
$59.00_CA247
Gives food choices that are low in fat, salt, surgar.
Home Economics
Dist - AAVIM **Prod** - AAVIM 1989

Life matters series
Alzheimer's disease 29 MIN
Breast cancer 29 MIN
Dist - BAXMED

Life matters series
Arthritis 29 MIN
Glaucoma 29 MIN
Liver transplant 29 MIN
Rebuilding the body 29 MIN
Dist - BAXMED
PBS

Life matters series
Addiction 29 MIN
Dist - HTHED

Life matters series
Focuses on individuals who must deal with chronic or fatal illnesses. Deals with illnesses including addictions, AIDS, Alzheimer's, breast cancer, diabetes and liver diseases. Includes up - to - date information on relevant medical research. Series consists of 13 parts, and is hosted by Dr. Norman Kaplan.
AIDS 29 MIN
Alzheimer's disease 29 MIN
Depression 29 MIN
Diabetes 29 MIN
Epilepsy 29 MIN
Heart Attack 29 MIN
Obesity 29 MIN
Rebuilding the Body 29 MIN
Dist - PBS **Prod** - KERA 1989

Life minus three 10 MIN
16mm / VHS / BETA / U-matic
Color; PAL (G)
PdS115, PdS123 purchase
Teaches emergency procedures for heart attack, especially the vital three minutes needed to prolong life until experts arrive.
Health and Safety
Dist - EDPAT

The Life of a forest series
Introduces students to the birth and dynamics of growth in a forest. Explains forest flora and fauna; types of forests; and the aging process of old growth forests. Comes with two 15 - minute videos; a teacher's guide; interactive video quizzes; acitivities; discussion questions; and 17 blackline masters.
The Birth of a forest 15 MIN
A Forest grows old 15 MIN
Dist - UNL

Life of a Logo 23 MIN
16mm
Color
Follows the evolution of a live product logo using the stag which is a symbol of the Hartford Insurance group as an example.
Business and Economics; Psychology
Dist - MTP **Prod** - HFI

The Life of a Natural History Museum 14 MIN
U-matic
Color (I J)
Tours a museum of natural history showing the exhibits and research projects which explain what the term 'natural' means.
Science; Science - Natural
Dist - CEPRO **Prod** - CEPRO

Life of a Plant 11 MIN
16mm / U-matic / VHS
Color (I J H)
Portrays the growth of a flowering pea plant by means of time - lapse photography. Close - ups of the seed, germination and the growth of stem and roots are shown.
Science - Natural
Dist - EBEC **Prod** - EBEC 1950

The Life of a Red Blood Cell 10 MIN
16mm / VHS
Color (P I J)
$180.00, $225.00 purchase, $50.00 rental _ #8017
Introduces children to the circulatory system through the dramatization of a red blood cell manufactured in the bone marrow and following it as it joins others in the vein.
Science - Natural
Dist - AIMS **Prod** - AIMS 1989

The Life of a Red Cell 10 MIN
VHS / U-matic
Color (I J)
Uses animation and humor to introduce the blood circulatory system. Shows how a new red blood cell is made in the bone marrow and joins others in a blood vein. Follows its adventures through the entire system and back to the beginning of its path revealing the cyclic nature of the blood system.
Fine Arts; Science - Natural
Dist - EDMI **Prod** - EDMI 1983

The Life of Abraham Lincoln 16 MIN
16mm
B&W
LC 74-713154
Presents highlights from the life of Abraham Lincoln, beginning with his years in the Senate and ending with his death at Ford's Theater.
Biography; History - United States
Dist - RMIBHF **Prod** - EDISOT 1960

The Life of Anne Frank 30 MIN
VHS / U-matic
Color (H C G)
$199.00, $149.00 purchase _ #HVC - 643, #HHC - 643
Uses photos and excerpts from the diary of Anne Frank to portray the Frank family in Germany and Holland, shipment to the concentration camp, and final destiny.
Civics and Political Systems; History - World
Dist - ADL **Prod** - ADL 1991

The Life of Anne Frank 25 MIN
U-matic / VHS
Color (G)
$249.00, $149.00 purchase _ #AD - 1609
Tells the story of Anne Frank through quotations from her diary, pictures of her hiding place, photos from the Frank family album and documentary footage. Provides an understanding of the Holocaust, Fascism, anti - Semitism and racism.
Civics and Political Systems; History - United States; History - World; Sociology
Dist - FOTH **Prod** - FOTH

Life of Buffalo Bill 28 MIN
16mm
B&W
LC 70-713153
A biographical film about Buffalo Bill, featuring William F Cody in the prolog and epilog.
Biography; History - United States
Dist - RMIBHF **Prod** - BBPBFC

The Life of Christ
VHS
The Bible - American Sign Language translation series
Color (S R)
Presents an American Sign Language translation of the New Testament account of the life of Christ. Available on a free - loan basis from the Lutheran Church - Missouri Synod's Deaf Ministry.
Guidance and Counseling; Literature and Drama; Religion and Philosophy
Dist - CPH **Prod** - LUMIS

The Life of Christ as seen by a Puerto Rican woodcarver 47 MIN
16mm
Puerto Rican folkart expression - Las artesanias de Puerto Rico series
Color (SPANISH)
LC 79-701046
Focuses on the work of a little - known Puerto Rican woodcarver whose creations depict the life of Christ from birth to crucifixion and resurrection.
Fine Arts; Geography - United States
Dist - CASPRC **Prod** - CASPRC 1979

The Life of Christ as Seen by a Puerto Rican Woodcarver - Pt 1 24 MIN
16mm
Puerto Rican Folkart Expression - Las Artesanias De Puerto Rico 'Series
Color (SPANISH)
LC 79-701046
Focuses on the work of a little - known Puerto Rican woodcarver whose creations depict the life of Christ from birth to crucifixion and resurrection.
Fine Arts
Dist - CASPRC **Prod** - CASPRC 1979

The Life of Christ as Seen by a Puerto Rican Woodcarver - Pt 2 23 MIN
16mm
Puerto Rican Folkart Expression - Las Artesanias De Puerto Rico 'Series
Color (SPANISH)
LC 79-701046
Focuses on the work of a little - known Puerto Rican woodcarver whose creations depict the life of Christ from birth to crucifixion and resurrection.
Fine Arts
Dist - CASPRC **Prod** - CASPRC 1979

A Life of Dreams - Pt 1 60 MIN
VHS
The Wisdom of the dream - world of C G Jung series
Color (S)
$29.95 purchase _ #833 - 9546
Captures the essential spirit of C G Jung, a psychiatrist, a scholar, a painter and a traveler, but above all a healer and a dreamer. Part 1 of three parts follows Jung's life from his childhood, through his years as a hospital psychiatrist, to the initial influence of Freud and their disagreement and split.
Psychology; Religion and Philosophy
Dist - FI **Prod** - RMART 1989

Life of Elizabeth 10 MIN
16mm
News Magazine of the Screen Series
B&W
Presents a 1952 Screen News Digest excerpt showing the English royal couple's visit to Canada and the United States in 1952. Shows briefly Queen Elizabeth's early life. Shows colorful crown jewels in preparation for Queen Elizabeth's coronation in 1953. Covers the historic coronation and pagentry.
Biography; Geography - World; History - World
Dist - HEARST **Prod** - PATHE 1953

The Life of Emile Zola 32 MIN
16mm
B&W (H C)
An excerpt from the feature film of the same title. Depicts the trial of Emile Zola for slander and libel upon his exposure of the injustice of the French Army high command in condemning Dreyfus to Devil's Island.
Biography; Civics and Political Systems; Literature and Drama
Dist - IU **Prod** - WB 1946

The Life of Emile Zola 110 MIN
16mm
B&W
Traces the career of prolific French novelist Emile Zola, centering on his heroic defense of the unjustly persecuted Captain Dreyfus. Stars Paul Muni.
Biography; Fine Arts
Dist - UAE **Prod** - WB 1937

The Life of Leonardo da Vinci 270 MIN
VHS
Color (J H C G)
$99.95 purchase _ #QV001SV; $99.95 purchase _ #QV001SV - F
Chronicles in three parts the life of artist Leonardo da Vinci in 15th - century Italy. Looks at events and associations in his life that influenced his later work in part I. Parts II and III focus on his adult years and his work for Duke Ludonico Sforza in Milan. Parts IV and V tells of his later years and his rivalry with Michelangelo. Set of three videocassettes.
Fine Arts; History - World
Dist - CAMV

The Life of Leonardo da Vinci 270 MIN
VHS
Color (J H)
$129.00 purchase _ #60225 - 026
Describes the artist's life and delves into a serious study of his work. Looks at his investigations into almost every field of learning, from anatomy and history to physics and music. Part one chronicles his first 30 years, delineating the family and friends who influenced his later life. Parts two and three follow him from Florence to Milan to Venice then back to Florence, exploring his scientific and artistic achievements. Parts four and five discuss his rivalry with Raphael and his return to France. Deluxe leatherbound edition includes teacher's guide and library kit.
Education; Fine Arts; History - World
Dist - GA

Life of Mahatma Gandhi 28 MIN
16mm
Color (H C A)
LC 70-705737
A documentary account of the life of Gandhi, using newsreel footage.
Biography; Civics and Political Systems; History - World; Religion and Philosophy
Dist - FINDIA **Prod** - BAGAI 1963

Life of Mahatma Gandhi 80 MIN
16mm
Color (H C A)
LC 70-705737
A documentary account of the life of Gandhi, using newsreel footage.
Biography; Civics and Political Systems; History - World; Religion and Philosophy
Dist - FINDIA **Prod** - BAGAI 1950

The Life of Oharu 133 MIN
16mm
B&W (JAPANESE)
Covers several decades in the life of a Japanese courtesan, tracing her progress from innocent youth to an old woman begging through the streets. Examines the lifestyles to be found in feudal Japan.
History - World; Literature and Drama
Dist - NYFLMS **Prod** - NYFLMS 1952

Life of Oharu 133 MIN
VHS
B&W (G) (JAPANESE WITH ENGLISH SUBTITLES)
$55.95 purchase _ #VYR0976
Stars Kinuyo Tanaka. Portrays Oharu, daughter of a samurai in 17th century Japan. Oharu falls in love with a man of a lower class and after he is beheaded, she is forced to become the mistress of an important man to bear him an heir. After the child's birth she is forced into a marriage with a poor merchant who is later killed. Directed by Kenji Mizoguchi.
Literature and Drama; Sociology
Dist - CHTSUI

Life of Plants Series

Adaptation to site	28 MIN
The Ecology of the forest	28 MIN
The Life Cycle of Plants	28 MIN
Mushrooms and Fungi	28 MIN
Networks of Adaptation	28 MIN
Plant Defenses	28 MIN
Plants and Insects	28 MIN
Plants in the Scheme of Things	28 MIN
Playing with Fire	28 MIN
Survival Against the Odds	28 MIN
Vines and Other Parasites	28 MIN
Water and Plant Life	28 MIN
The World of green	28 MIN

Dist - FOTH

The Life of Riley - TV classics volume ten 52 MIN
VHS
B&W (G)
$29.95 purchase _ #MP1361
Presents a situation comedy from the 1950s with bite and social commentary. Stars Jackie Gleason as a blue collar riveter in two episodes. Includes an appearance by Lon Chaney, Jr.
Literature and Drama
Dist - INSTRU

The Life of Sojourner Truth - ain't I a woman 26 MIN
U-matic / BETA / 16mm / VHS
Color (J H)
$575.00, $250.00 purchase _ #JY - 6023L
Dramatizes the life of Sojourner Truth, famous orator who spoke out against slavery and for the rights of women. Portrays interviews with Frederick Douglas, Harriet Beecher Stowe, Abraham Lincoln and Sojourner Truth's diarist, Olive Gilbert.
History - United States; History - World; Sociology
Dist - CORF **Prod** - LCOA 1989

A Life of song - a portrait of Ruth Rubin 38 MIN
VHS
Color (G)
$34.95 purchase _ #920
Documents the life of octogenarian Dr Ruth Rubin who has spent her life collecting, preserving and transmitting the legacy of Yiddish folksongs. Follows her to various settings to observe her work. Features Cindy Marshall as host.
Fine Arts; Sociology
Dist - ERGOM **Prod** - ERGOM 1992

Life of Svankmajer - Death of Stalinism 27 MIN
16mm
Color (G)
Presents an independent production by Jan Svankmajer. Joins Czech animator Svankmajer at work on his latest creation, 'Death Of Stalinism.'.
Civics and Political Systems; Geography - World
Dist - FIRS

Life of the Bighorn Sheep 16 MIN
16mm
Color
Takes a look at the life history of the Rocky Mountain bighorn sheep beginning with the lambs born in spring on a protected rocky cliff. Relates the habitat, habits, predators and conservation story of the sheep.
Science - Natural
Dist - BERLET **Prod** - BERLET 1980

The Life of the forest 15 MIN
U-matic / 35mm strip
Color (J H C)
$43.95 purchase _ #52 3407B
Discusses the various habitats created by forest trees and the different types of organisms that live among them. Includes a teacher's guide.
Science - Natural
Dist - CBSC **Prod** - CBSC

Life of the Hermit Crab 24 MIN
16mm
Color
Explains that the hermit crab is grouped into the category of crustancea and describes its form and way of living.
Science - Natural
Dist - UNIJAP **Prod** - TOEI 1970

The Life of the mind - an introduction to psychology
VHS / Cassette
Color (C A)
$149.95, $89.95 purchase _ #RP - B639
Presents eight lectures which show how psychology governs the way we live and how mechanisms of the brain helped to shape that psychology. Features Associate Prof Richard Gerrig of Yale University as lecturer.
Psychology; Science - Natural
Dist - TTCO **Prod** - TTCO

Life of the Sockeye Salmon 25 MIN
U-matic / VHS / 16mm
Color (I)
LC 77-703483
Highlights spring in the Pacific Northwest, the season when the salmon eggs in river beds are beginning to hatch. Traces the development of the sockeye salmon as it completes a 6,000 - mile roundtrip journey.
Science - Natural
Dist - JOU **Prod** - WILFGP 1977

The Life of Thomas Jefferson 15 MIN
16mm
Color (P) (AMERICAN SIGN)
LC 76-701095
Presents, in American sign language, the life of Thomas Jefferson. Filmed at Independence Hall, Monticello, the University of Virginia and the Library of Congress. Signed by Louie J Fant, Jr.
Biography; Guidance and Counseling; Psychology
Dist - JOYCE **Prod** - JOYCE 1976

Life of Verdi 600 MIN
VHS
Color (G) (ITALIAN)
$124.95 purchase _ #1125
Presents the 10 hour unedited version of the mini series covering the life of Giuseppe Verdi. Features Ronald Pickup as Verdi and ballerina Carla Fracci as Giuseppina Strepponi, making her acting debut. Includes Renata Tebaldi, Maria Callas, Luciano Pavarotti and Birgit Nilsson singing from Verdi's works including 'Rigoletto,' 'Aida,' 'La Traviata,' in the original Italian.

Fine Arts
Dist - KULTUR

Life Offshore 16 MIN
U-matic / VHS
Color (IND)
Serves as a preview for the new employee about to work on an offshore production platform for the first time.
Business and Economics; Industrial and Technical Education; Social Science
Dist - UTEXPE **Prod** - UTEXPE

Life on a Dead Tree 11 MIN
16mm / U-matic / VHS
Color (P I)
Dave and Tommy have found an old dead tree in the woods. As they explore it, they find that it is the home of many different plants and animals such as lizards, beetles, crickets, slugs, fungus plants, tree salamanders, ants and gopher snakes.
Science - Natural
Dist - PHENIX **Prod** - FA 1957

Life on a Farm - Milking Time 13 MIN
VHS / 16mm
Color (P)
$280.00, $195.00 purchase
Visits a dairy farm with Brian and his grandfather. Follows the dairy cows from the pasture into the milking barn. The cows are milked, the milk transferred to holding tanks and then transported to the dairy by tanker truck.
Agriculture; Health and Safety; Science - Natural; Social Science; Sociology
Dist - LUF **Prod** - LUF

Life on a rotting log 15 MIN
U-matic / VHS
Animals and such series; Module blue - habitats
Color (I J)
Examines a rotting log as the habitat of countless creatures, each with its own means of survival.
Science - Natural
Dist - AITECH **Prod** - WHROTV 1972

Life on a Silken Thread 58 MIN
16mm
Nova Series
Color
Offers a close - up look at spiders and their functions, including molting.
Science - Natural
Dist - KINGFT **Prod** - WGBHTV

Life on a string 105 MIN
35mm / 16mm / VHS
Color (G) (CHINESE WITH ENGLISH SUBTITLES)
Portrays a blind boy on the harsh plains of central China who is promised sight if he devotes his life to music. Reveals that years later, the boy has grown into a blind old man who regards music as a path to higher truth. For his disciple, also blind, music is a sensual pleasure, a celebration of the here and now. Directed by Chen Kaige.
Fine Arts; Geography - World; Literature and Drama
Dist - KINOIC

Life on Earth 58 MIN
16mm
Color (G)
$60.00 rental
Records a year in the life of the filmmaker's family and friends. Centers on the birth and growth of his daughter Chloe.
Fine Arts; Literature and Drama; Psychology; Sociology
Dist - CANCIN **Prod** - LIPTNL 1972

Life on earth 240 MIN
VHS
Color (G)
$39.95 purchase
Presents a video encyclopedia of natural history. Discusses the marvels of nature, the secrets of evolution, and the wonder of life. Hosted by David Attenborough.
Science - Natural
Dist - PBS **Prod** - WNETTV

Life on Earth as I know it 8 MIN
U-matic / 16mm / VHS
Color (G)
$150.00 purchase, $40.00 rental
Tells the quirky love story of Lois and Kate. Produced by Penny McDonald of Australia.
Literature and Drama; Sociology
Dist - WMEN

Life on earth perhaps 29 MIN
VHS
Color (H C G T A)
$39.95 purchase, $25.00 rental
Uses a mixture of animation and documentary footage to show how the concept of warfare has evolved from glorified national sport to possible global suicide. Produced by Oliver Postgate.
Civics and Political Systems; History - World; Sociology
Dist - EFVP

Life on Earth Perhaps 29 MIN
U-matic / VT3
(G)
$95.00 purchase, $45.00 rental
Shows how war has evolved from a glorified national sport into possible global suicide. Uses the behavior of two warring neighbors to illustrate the absurdity of nuclear overkill.
Sociology
Dist - EFVP **Prod** - EFVP 1985

Life on Earth series - Vol II
The Segmented invertebrates - Pt 5 30 MIN
Dist - FI

Life on Earth series - Vol I
The Beginning of life - Pt 2 30 MIN
The Infinite variety - Pt 1 30 MIN
Dist - FI

Life on Earth series

The Amphibians - Pt 13	30 MIN
The Boney fishes - Pt 11	30 MIN
Building bodies	58 MIN
Building bodies - Pt 3	30 MIN
The Coming of insects - Pt 7	30 MIN
The Compulsive communicators	58 MIN
Compulsive Communicators - Pt 27	30 MIN
Conquest of the waters	58 MIN
Conquest of the waters - Pt 10	30 MIN
Dinosaurs and their descendants - Pt 15	30 MIN
The Early seas - Pt 4	30 MIN
The First forests - Part 3	58 MIN
The First forests - Part 6	30 MIN
Flowers and insects - Pt 8	30 MIN
From reptiles to birds - pt 16	30 MIN
The Hunters and the Hunted	58 MIN
The Hunters and the Hunted - Pt 23	30 MIN
The Infinite Variety	58 MIN
The Invasion of the Land	58 MIN
Invasion of the Land - Pt 12	30 MIN
The Leaf Eaters - Pt 22	30 MIN
A Life in the Trees	58 MIN
Life in the Trees - Pt 24	30 MIN
Life on Earth - Vol I	120 MIN
Life on Earth - Vol II	120 MIN
Life on Earth - Vol III	120 MIN
Life on Earth - Vol IV	120 MIN
Life on Earth - Vol V	120 MIN
Life on Earth - Vol VI	120 MIN
Life on Earth - Vol VII	90 MIN
Lord of the Air - Pt 17	30 MIN
Lords of the air	58 MIN
Mammals of the Sea - Pt 20	30 MIN
The Marsupials - Pt 19	30 MIN
The Primates - Pt 25	30 MIN
The Rise of mammals	58 MIN
The Swarming hordes	58 MIN
The Swarming Hordes - Pt 9	30 MIN
Theme and variation - pt 21	30 MIN
Theme and variations	58 MIN
Upright man - Pt 26	30 MIN
Victors of the dry land	58 MIN

Dist - FI

Life on Earth Video 240 MIN
VHS
Color (J)
$39.95 purchase _ #ESD 4212
Presents the most complete video produced on the development and evolution of life on earth, from the smallest, earliest forms to humans. Features David Attenborough as host.
Science; Science - Natural; Science - Physical
Dist - SCTRES **Prod** - SCTRES

Life on Earth - Vol I 120 MIN
VHS
Life on Earth series
Color (J)
$99.00 purchase
Blends scientific data with breathtaking wildlife photography to tell the story of the development of life. Features wildlife expert David Attenborough as host. Chronicles when, where and in what order the earth's more than four million species evolved. Volume I of seven volumes presents four 30 - minute programs entitled - 'The Infinite Variety,' 'The Beginning Of Life,' 'Building Bodies,' and 'The Early Seas.'.
Science; Science - Natural; Science - Physical
Dist - FI **Prod** - BBCTV 1981

Life on Earth - Vol II 120 MIN
VHS
Life on Earth series
Color (J)
$99.00 purchase
Blends scientific data with breathtaking wildlife photography to tell the story of the development of life. Features wildlife expert David Attenborough as host. Chronicles when, where and in what order the earth's more than four million species evolved. Volume II of seven volumes presents four 30 - minute programs entitled - 'The Segmented Invertebrates,' 'The First Forests,' 'The Coming Of Insects,' and 'Flowers And Insects.'.
Science; Science - Natural
Dist - FI **Prod** - BBCTV 1981

Life on Earth - Vol III 120 MIN
VHS
Life on Earth series
Color (J)
$99.00 purchase
Blends scientific data with breathtaking wildlife photography to tell the story of the development of life. Features wildlife expert David Attenborough as host. Chronicles when, where and in what order the earth's more than four million species evolved. Volume III of seven volumes presents four 30 - minute programs entitled - 'The Swarming Hordes,' 'Conquest Of The Waters,' 'The Boney Fishes,' and 'Invasion Of The Land.'.
Science; Science - Natural
Dist - FI **Prod** - BBCTV 1981

Life on Earth - Vol IV 120 MIN
VHS
Life on Earth series
Color (J)
$99.00 purchase
Blends scientific data with breathtaking wildlife photography to tell the story of the development of life. Features wildlife expert David Attenborough as host. Chronicles when, where and in what order the earth's more than four million species evolved. Volume IV of seven volumes presents four 30 - minute programs entitled - 'The Amphibians,' 'Victors Of The Dry Land,' 'Dinosaurs And Their Descendants,' and 'From Reptiles To Birds.'.
Science; Science - Natural
Dist - FI **Prod** - BBCTV 1981

Life on Earth - Vol V 120 MIN
VHS
Life on Earth series
Color (J)
$99.00 purchase
Blends scientific data with breathtaking wildlife photography to tell the story of the development of life. Features wildlife expert David Attenborough as host. Chronicles when, where and in what order the earth's more than four million species evolved. Volume V of seven volumes presents four 30 - minute programs entitled - 'Lord Of The Air,' 'The Rise Of Mammals,' 'The Marsupials,' and 'Mammals Of The Sea.'.
Science; Science - Natural
Dist - FI **Prod** - BBCTV 1981

Life on Earth - Vol VI 120 MIN
VHS
Life on Earth series
Color (J)
$99.00 purchase
Blends scientific data with breathtaking wildlife photography to tell the story of the development of life. Features wildlife expert David Attenborough as host. Chronicles when, where and in what order the earth's more than four million species evolved. Volume VI of seven volumes presents four 30 - minute programs entitled - 'Theme And Variation,' 'The Leaf Eaters,' 'The Hunters And The Hunted,' and 'Life In The Trees.'.
Science; Science - Natural
Dist - FI **Prod** - BBCTV 1981

Life on Earth - Vol VII 90 MIN
VHS
Life on Earth series
Color (J)
$99.00 purchase
Blends scientific data with breathtaking wildlife photography to tell the story of the development of life. Features wildlife expert David Attenborough as host. Chronicles when, where and in what order the earth's more than four million species evolved. Volume VII of seven volumes presents three 30 - minute programs entitled - 'The Primates,' 'Upright Man,' and 'Compulsive Communicators.'.
English Language; Psychology; Science; Science - Natural
Dist - FI **Prod** - BBCTV 1981

Life on ice 30 MIN
VHS / 16mm
Life science - ecosystems series
Color (I J H C)
$595.00, $535.00 purchase, $60.00, $55.00 rental
Uses underwater photography in Arctic Ocean waters under massive ice floes to observe the food chain of aquatic and terrestial organisms which evolved in extremely cold climates. Reveals the first link in the chain, a specially evolved algae which grows on the underside of ice flows in dim light and bitter cold. Crustaceans feed on the algae, and an increasingly complex food web of consumers leads to the top of the energy pyramid - small and large fish, seals, walruses, whales and polar bears. Covers the concepts of food chains, food webs, communities, adaptations for survival and ecological interactions between organizsms and environment.

Science - Natural
Dist - BNCHMK Prod - NFBC 1989

Life on Other Planets 18 MIN
16mm
Of Stars and Men
Color (J)
LC 76-701274
A revised version of the 1964 film Of Stars And Men. Tells the story of a man who gives up his hum - drum existence to seek truth through a philosophical quest. Based on the book Of Stars And Men by Dr Harlow Shapley.
Religion and Philosophy; Science - Physical
Dist - RADIM **Prod** - HUBLEY 1976

Life on Our Planet 12 MIN
U-matic
Color (G)
$350.00 purchase, $50.00, $40.00 rental
Contrasts the real life experiences of the characters with media portrayals of reality. Presented by Tess Payne.
Sociology
Dist - WMENIF **Prod** - WMENIF 1987

A life on prescription 60 MIN
VHS
Hypotheticals '94 series
PAL; Color; PAL (H C A)
PdS99
Examines moral and ethical dilemmas in the medical profession using fictionalized case studies. Focuses on the extent to which physicians will help patients to concieve the baby they want. Part one of a three part series.
Religion and Philosophy; Science - Natural
Dist - BBCENE

Life on the edge 26 MIN
VHS / U-matic
Survival in nature series
Color (J H)
$275.00, $325.00 purchase, $50.00 rental
Offers a study in wildlife ecology. Focuses on the mountain goat of North America. Looks at its survival in remote regions of high mountain ranges enduring the harshest of climates and exploiting food resources that no other animal is able to reach. Filmed against the backdrop of Alaskan landscape.
Geography - United States; Science - Natural
Dist - NDIM **Prod** - SURVAN 1990

Life on the edge of the Milky Way 30 MIN
VHS
Our solar system series
Color (G)
$195.00 purchase
Talks about characteristics of the sun, a star, and the planets. Looks at the history as well as the size and atmospheric conditions of the planets in the solar system. Part of a four - part series.
Science - Physical
Dist - LANDMK

Life on the forest floor - a first film 10 MIN
U-matic / VHS / 16mm
Color (I J) (FRENCH)
LC 72-703066
Explains that the forest floor is sheltered from strong sunlight and it is moist. Shows that the falling leaves and rotting stumps provide food and shelter for many kinds of animals and plants in this unique habitat.
Science - Natural
Dist - PHENIX **Prod** - NELLES 1972

Life on the Limit 26 MIN
16mm / U-matic / VHS
Botanic Man Series
Color (H C A)
Tells how the agricultural revolution enabled society to develop communities and cultures and also created the first man - made ecological disaster. Discusses how Hillong, in Assam, India, the wettest place on earth, became barren by such carelessness. New ecological disasters are created with concrete, asphalt, waste and poison.
Science - Natural
Dist - MEDIAG **Prod** - THAMES 1978

Life on the Macon Plateau 12 MIN
16mm / U-matic / VHS
Color
Features the Indian cultures of the Macon Plateau, particularly the Mississippian culture. Displays archeological evidence, pottery, tools, mound construction and grave goods at the Ocmulgee National Monument.
Geography - United States; History - United States; Social Science; Sociology
Dist - USNAC **Prod** - USNPS

Life on the Mississippi 115 MIN
U-matic / VHS / 16mm
Color
LC 81-700511
Presents an account of a young man's apprenticeship on the Mississippi River. Based on the book Life On The Mississippi by Mark Twain.
Geography - United States; Literature and Drama
Dist - FI **Prod** - GREAM 1980

Life on the Mississippi 120 MIN
VHS
Color (J H)
$39.00 purchase _ #05898 - 126
Tells of the experiences of Mark Twain as a riverboat captain before the Civil War.
History - United States; Literature and Drama
Dist - GA **Prod** - GA

Life on the Mississippi 120 MIN
U-matic / VHS
Color (H C A)
LC 81-707230
Dramatizes 18 months in the life of Mark Twain when, as a young man, he fulfilled his dream of becoming a river pilot.
History - United States; Literature and Drama
Dist - FI **Prod** - GREAM 1980

Life on the Mississippi
U-matic / VHS
Films - on - Video Series
Color (G C J)
$59.00 purchase _ #05898 - 85
Re - enacts Mark Twain's various experiences as a riverboat pilot before the Civil War.
Literature and Drama
Dist - CHUMAN

Life on the Mississippi 54 MIN
16mm / U-matic / VHS
Color (H C A)
An abridged version of the motion picture Life On The Mississippi. Presents an account of a young man's apprenticeship on the Mississippi River. Based on the book Life On The Mississippi by Mark Twain.
Biography; Geography - United States; History - United States
Dist - FI **Prod** - WNETTV 1980

Life on the Mississippi 47 MIN
VHS / U-matic
Color
Takes an expedition of the Mississippi River and the lives it touches through the narration of Mark Twain (Warren Frost). Reveals the story about today in terms of what survives of yesterday.
Geography - United States; Sociology
Dist - WCCOTV **Prod** - WCCOTV 1978

Life on the Mississippi, Pt 1 57 MIN
U-matic / VHS / 16mm
Color
LC 81-700511
Presents an account of a young man's apprenticeship on the Mississippi River. Based on the book Life On The Mississippi by Mark Twain.
Literature and Drama
Dist - FI **Prod** - GREAM 1980

Life on the Mississippi, Pt 2 58 MIN
U-matic / VHS / 16mm
Color
LC 81-700511
Presents an account of a young man's apprenticeship on the Mississippi River. Based on the book Life On The Mississippi by Mark Twain.
Literature and Drama
Dist - FI **Prod** - GREAM 1980

Life on the Streets 12 MIN
BETA / VHS / U-matic
(G)
$100.00 purchase
Explores the phenomenon of women who have dropped out of society and who live on the streets.
Sociology
Dist - CTV **Prod** - CTV 1985

Life on the Tundra 14 MIN
16mm / U-matic / VHS
Color (I)
LC FIA65-1392
Studies the tundra regions of the Canadian Arctic. Reveals the activities of various types of animal life such as nesting birds, musk - oxen and herds of caribou between the winter and spring seasons.
Science - Natural
Dist - EBEC **Prod** - NFBC 1965

Life or Breath 30 MIN
16mm / U-matic / VHS
Powerhouse Series
Color (I J)
Relates how relaxation exercises save a life when an ambassador's son is kidnapped.
Psychology
Dist - GA **Prod** - EFCVA 1982

Life or Death 25 MIN
16mm
Color
LC 77-700382
Contrasts the right and wrong ways of performing extrication, body survey, first aid and patient transport through the discussion of two ghosts concerning the emergency medical treatment they received at their fatal automobile accident.
Health and Safety
Dist - FILCOM **Prod** - FILCOM 1977

Life or Death in the Emergency Room 53 MIN
16mm / VHS
Color (J)
$795.00, $445.00 purchase
Features on - the - scene filming of actual events in the emergency room of St Mary's Medical Center in Long Beach, California.
Health and Safety
Dist - UNKNWN

Life or limb - the hemipelvectomy as a strike against cancer 20 MIN
VHS
Color (A PRO)
$175.00 purchase, $50.00 rental
Discusses the surgical and emotional effects of a hemipelvectomy operation, which is an amputation procedure used for some cancer cases. Interviews three cancer patients, two of whom have had the operation, who discuss the impact of cancer and amputation on their lives. Also offers comments from an osteopathic physician, an internist, and a clinical social worker. Includes instructional guide.
Health and Safety
Dist - UARIZ **Prod** - UARIZ

Life pact 23 MIN
16mm / VHS
Color (J H A C)
$395.00, $495.00 purchase, $75.00 rental _ #8154
Addresses the main reasons why teenagers attempt suicide - they feel alone and isolated.
Psychology; Sociology
Dist - AIMS **Prod** - MAGIC 1989

Life - Patent Pending 57 MIN
U-matic / VHS / 16mm
Nova Series
Color (H C A)
Presents breakthroughs in gene engineering and describes how scientists go about creating new forms of life. Tells how the impact of the gene bonanza affects industry, medicine and the scientific community.
Health and Safety; Science; Science - Natural
Dist - TIMLIF **Prod** - WGBHTV 1982

Life Planning 18 MIN
Videoreel / VT2
Interpersonal Competence, Unit 09 - Growth Series; Unit 9 - Growth
Color (C A)
Features a humanistic psychologist who, by analysis and examples, discusses life planning.
Psychology; Sociology
Dist - TELSTR **Prod** - MVNE 1973

Life positive - a drug abuse prevention curriculum 53 MIN
VHS
Color (I J)
$259.00 purchase _ #2202 - SK
Presents an instructional series on drug abuse prevention and education. Emphasizes providing accurate information about drugs and alcohol, enhancing coping skills, and strengthening students' self - esteem and self - image. Includes an instructional manual and a facilitator's videocassette.
Education; Psychology
Dist - SUNCOM

Life Safety in High Rise Fires 21 MIN
16mm
Color (A)
Describes a fire safety plan for high rise building occupants.
Health and Safety; Social Science
Dist - SF **Prod** - AREASX

Life Science 30 MIN
U-matic / VHS
New Voice Series
Color (H C A)
Dramatizes the experiences of the staff of a high school newspaper. Focuses on marriage.
Sociology
Dist - GPN **Prod** - WGBHTV

Life science - ecosystem series 390 MIN
VHS / 16mm
Life science - ecosystems series
Color (I J H C)
$7735.00, $6955.00 purchase
Presents thirteen thirty - minute programs on ecosystems in diverse parts of the world. Includes the titles Amate - the Great Fig Tree, Baobab - Portrait of a Tree, Birds of a Feather, Castles of Clay, Edge of Ice, Kopjes - Islands in a Sea of Grass, The Legend of the Lightning Bird, Life on Ice, Mzima - Portrait of a Spring, The Rains Came, A Season in the Sun, Together They Stand, The Year of the Wildebeest.
Geography - World; Science - Natural
Dist - BNCHMK

Life science - ecosystems series
Edge of ice 55 MIN
Kopjes - island in a sea of grass 55 MIN
The Legend of the lightning bird 55 MIN
Life on ice 30 MIN
Life science - ecosystem series 390 MIN
A Season in the sun 55 MIN
Dist - BNCHMK

Life Science for Elementary Series
Predators and Prey 9 MIN
Wild Animals Adapt 9 MIN
Wild Animals Catch Fish 9 MIN
Wildlife Families 9 MIN
Wildlife Mothers 9 MIN
Dist - AIMS

Life science - science in focus series 101 MIN
VHS
Life science - science in focus series
Color (J H)
$1975.00 purchase
Presents a five - part series on science. Includes the titles Energy, Heredity and Genetics, Enzymes, Control Mechanism, Waste and Global Pollution.
Science - Natural; Sociology
Dist - BNCHMK **Prod** - BNCHMK 1990

Life science - secrets of science series
Brain power - Video 3 47 MIN
From the beginning - Video 1 47 MIN
The Life around us - Video 4 47 MIN
Life's building blocks - Video 2 47 MIN
Dist - EFVP

Life Science Series
Explores the orderly and systematic classification of life within the animal and plant kingdoms. Provides an introduction to the characteristics whereby the simplest organisms through the most complex organisms are separated into groups within each kingdom.
All things animal 21 MIN
All things plant 19 MIN
Life Science Series
Dist - BARR **Prod** - BARR 1990

Life sciences
Kit / Videodisc
Newton's apple series
Color (I J H) (ENGLISH AND SPANISH)
$225.00 purchase _ #T81295; $325.00 purchase _ #T81290
Presents life sciences in a way that is interesting to children. Includes bees; plant growth; butterfly migration; hip replacement; aerobic exercise; HIV and AIDS; and Novocain (registered trademark). Higher - priced kit includes software for use on Macintosh computers only.
Health and Safety; Physical Education and Recreation; Science - Natural
Dist - NGS

Life sciences collection
CD-ROM
(G A)
$1895.00 purchase _ #1479
Includes abstracts and citations from more than 5,000 core journals, books, serial monographs, conference reports, international patents, and statistical publications covering English and foreign language publications. Current year plus two backfile years available. Updated quarterly. For IBM PCs and compatibles. Requires 640K RAM, DOS Version 3.1 or greater, one floppy disk drive - a hard disk drive is recommended, one empty expansion slot, and an IBM compatible CD - ROM drive.
Literature and Drama; Science - Natural
Dist - BEP

Life skills video series
Presents a two - part series on life skills. Includes the titles 'Building A Winning Attitude' and 'Understand And Be Understood.'
Build a winning attitude - success through motivation 30 MIN
Life skills video series 90 MIN
Understand and be understood - success through communication 60 MIN
Dist - CAMV

Life Span - How Long do We Live and Why 13 MIN
U-matic / VHS / 16mm
Captioned; Color (I J)
LC 72-703126
Compares the life span of an interest that may only live for a few days with that of other animals that may live for many years. Analyzes why there is such a difference in life span and how humans have increased their life span far beyond that of most animals.
Health and Safety; Science - Natural
Dist - JOU **Prod** - GLDWER 1972

Life Stances Genogram, Pt 7 41 MIN
U-matic / VHS
Relationship Growth Group Series
Color
Shows how to make life stance genograms of the family, enabling one to better understand behavior in personal encounters.
Guidance and Counseling; Psychology; Sociology
Dist - UWISC **Prod** - WRAMC 1979

Life Stances, Pt 6 45 MIN
VHS / U-matic
Relationship Growth Group Series
Color
Features lecture by Dr Donald R Bardill on life stances, the manner in which an individual approaches personal encounters. Discusses disfunctional, functional and and irrational life stances.
Guidance and Counseling; Psychology; Sociology
Dist - UWISC **Prod** - WRAMC 1979

Life Story of a Moth - the Silkworm 11 MIN
U-matic / VHS / 16mm
Captioned; Color (I)
Illustrates the structural and behavioral changes which occur during the process of metamorphosis in the silkworm moth. Includes close - ups of the molting process, the complex behavior of the larva, the emergence of the silkworm moth, its mating and the laying of eggs.
Science - Natural
Dist - EBEC **Prod** - EBEC 1964

Life Story of a Plant - about Flowers 7 MIN
16mm / U-matic / VHS
Color (P)
Follows the life cycle and processes of a plant. Shows how seeds develop and then are scattered to make new plants.
Science - Natural
Dist - EBEC **Prod** - NFBC 1965

Life Story of a Social Insect - the Ant 11 MIN
U-matic / VHS / 16mm
Basic Life Science Program Series
Color; B&W (I)
LC FIA68-408
Explains why ants are considered social insects. Shows how a new ant colony begins and the ways in which each ant works for the benefit of the colony. Identifies the three sections of an ant's body.
Science - Natural
Dist - EBEC **Prod** - EBEC 1968

Life story of an African Inyanga 27 MIN
VHS
Color (G)
$250.00 purchase, $50.00 rental
Portrays the selection and lifelong education of an Inyanga, an African healer who dispenses traditional herbal remedies. Examines the preparation and use of medicines, diagnoses and treatment of patients and the metaphysics and cosmology of Inyanga beliefs. Directed by Sith Yela.
Fine Arts; Health and Safety; History - World; Literature and Drama
Dist - CNEMAG

Life Story of the Earthworm 10 MIN
U-matic / VHS / 16mm
Color (I) (SPANISH)
Shows how the earthworm moves, feeds, reproduces and reacts to various stimuli. Demonstrates the relationship of the earthworm to the leech, sandworm and other annelids. Points out the worm's importance in improving the soil.
Science - Natural
Dist - EBEC **Prod** - EBEC

Life Story of the Hummingbird 16 MIN
16mm / U-matic / VHS
Color; B&W (I)
Shows physical characteristics and feeding, mating and nesting habits of hummingbirds. Depicts the care and growth of young birds. Uses high speed photography to reveal the hummingbird's unusual wing movement.
Science - Natural
Dist - EBEC **Prod** - EBEC 1963

Life Story of the Oyster 11 MIN
U-matic / VHS / 16mm
Color; B&W (I)
Demonstrates how the oyster develops into an adult and how the adult feeds, grows and reproduces. Shows the place of this mollusk in the marine food cycle.
Science - Natural
Dist - EBEC **Prod** - EBEC 1963

Life Story of the Paramecium 11 MIN
U-matic / VHS / 16mm
Color; B&W (I)
Depicts the life functions of the paramecium, showing how it feeds, grows, breathes, moves, reproduces, reacts to stimuli and gives off wastes. Explains that the basic unit of life is the individual cell.
Science - Natural
Dist - EBEC **Prod** - EBEC 1963

Life that lives on man 45 MIN
VHS
Horizon series
Color (A)
PdS99 purchase
Focuses on skin, one of the least studied organs of the body. Looks at the ecology of the bacteria, yeasts and animals that constitute the life that lives on humans, and demonstrates that the wee beasties have a profound influence on human life.
Science - Natural
Dist - BBCENE

The Life That's Left 29 MIN
U-matic / VHS / 16mm
(A)
$180.00, $450.00 purchase, $30.00, $40.00 rental
Explains the stages and psychological consequences of bereavement. Focuses on the process, what to expect and how to cope.
Sociology
Dist - GPN **Prod** - CHERIO 1979

Life through Fire 15 MIN
U-matic
Color (I)
Documents a new technique which uses fire productivity to improve wildlife habitat, water production and rangeland.
Science - Natural; Science - Physical; Social Science
Dist - CALDWR **Prod** - CSDWR

Life Times Nine 15 MIN
U-matic / VHS / 16mm
Color (I)
LC 74-701722
Presents Commercials for Life, a series of nine short films made by children ages 11 to 16.
Fine Arts
Dist - PFP **Prod** - INST 1974

Life Transitions 30 MIN
U-matic / VHS
Transitions Series Program 101
Color (A)
Features panels who relate moments of personal discovery and insight which evolved from their life transitions. Focuses on work, family and social changes which contributed to their learning. Includes such changes as employment and unemployment, aging, marriage and divorce.
Guidance and Counseling; Sociology
Dist - OHUTC **Prod** - OHUTC

Life Under Pressure 28 MIN
VHS / U-matic
Oceanus - the Marine Environment Series
Color (C A)
Science - Natural; Science - Physical
Dist - SCCON **Prod** - SCCON 1980

Life Under Pressure 30 MIN
VHS / U-matic
Oceanus - the Marine Environment Series Lesson 23
Color
Focuses on the three deep ocean zones and the basic physical water conditions within these zones. Discusses deep - water life forms.
Science - Natural; Science - Physical
Dist - CDTEL **Prod** - SCCON

Life under the pharaohs 21 MIN
VHS / U-matic
Egypt series
Color (J H C)
$250.00 purchase _ #HP - 6000C
Examines ancient paintings of everyday life from the tomb of an Egyptian nobleman, Sennufer. Looks at excavation work, artifacts and archaeology in Egypt. Studies the writing of hieroglyphics and the Rosetta Stone, and emphasizes the importance of scribes to ancient Egyptian civilization and its achievements. Part of a series on ancient Egypt.
Civics and Political Systems; English Language; History - World; Sociology
Dist - CORF **Prod** - BBCTV 1989

Life Under the Sea 17 MIN
VHS
Ocean Studies Series
Color
$69.95 purchase _ #4346
Reveal life amidst reefs in the shallow areas of the sea. Featured are the environment and ways of hermit crabs, starfish, sea urchins, lobsters, octopi, and moray eels.
Science - Natural; Science - Physical
Dist - AIMS **Prod** - AIMS

Life Under the Sea 16 MIN
16mm / U-matic / VHS
Color (I)
Reveals the colorful life on reefs in shallow areas of the sea. Shows pictures of hermit crabs, starfish, sea urchins, lobsters, octopus and eels.
Science - Natural; Science - Physical
Dist - AIMS **Prod** - PAR 1970

Life with Baby
16mm / U-matic / VHS
Color; Mono (H C T A)
Presents a program about and for beginning parents. Discusses parents and babies' needs, joys and frustrations, and the changes that parenthood causes.
Psychology; Sociology
Dist - TOGG **Prod** - TOGG 1984

Life with baby - how do the parents feel 27 MIN
VHS
Color (J H C G)
$295.00 purchase, $55.00 rental
Considers that every year children are abused and neglected by parents who feel overwhelmed by the task of raising a baby. Shows three families, one black and two white, adjusting to the emotional and physical demands of raising a baby. Meets a single teenage mother on welfare who lives at home with her family. One family talks of the isolation of being in a new community, away from family and friends, another expresses how their baby interferes with their personal relationship.
Psychology; Sociology
Dist - FLMLIB **Prod** - NECMHT 1988

Life with Diabetes Series
Diabetes mellitus - pregnancy counseling 15 MIN
A Team Approach to Patient Management 20 MIN
Twenty Seconds a Day - Coping with Diabetes 32 MIN
Dist - UMICH

Life with Father 118 MIN
16mm
B&W
Looks at life in the Day household in 1883 New York, emphasizing the bond of love which holds the children and parents together. Stars William Powell, Irene Dunne and Elizabeth Taylor. Directed by Michael Curitz. Based on the book Life With Father by Clarence Day.
Fine Arts
Dist - REELIM **Prod** - UNKNWN 1947

Life with Father 30 MIN
VHS / 16mm
Play Series
Color (H)
Presents Howard Lindsay and Russel Crouse's Life With Father, which tells the story of a father who attempts to run his home in a business - like manner. The first of eight installments of CTI's The Play Series, which attempts to give students an appreciation of the unique elements of the play through detailed examination of classic and trendsetting productions.
Fine Arts; Literature and Drama
Dist - GPN **Prod** - CTI 1990

Life with Father, Pt 1 40 MIN
16mm
Color
Presents a story of family life about author Clarence Day's youth in 1883 New York. Stars William Powell, Irene Dunne and Elizabeth Taylor. Directed by Michael Curtiz.
Fine Arts
Dist - TWYMAN **Prod** - WB 1947

Life with Father, Pt 2 39 MIN
16mm
Color
Presents a story of family life about author Clarence Day's youth in 1883 New York. Stars William Powell, Irene Dunne and Elizabeth Taylor. Directed by Michael Curtiz.
Fine Arts
Dist - TWYMAN **Prod** - WB 1947

Life with Father, Pt 3 39 MIN
16mm
Color
Presents a story of family life about author Clarence Day's youth in 1883 New York. Stars William Powell, Irene Dunne and Elizabeth Taylor. Directed by Michael Curtiz.
Fine Arts
Dist - TWYMAN **Prod** - WB 1947

Life with hypertension - practical approaches to therapy - focus on Prazosin 24 MIN
16mm
B&W (PRO)
LC 80-701234
Demonstrates practical approaches to therapy for hypertension patients.
Health and Safety
Dist - PFIZLB **Prod** - PFIZLB 1980

Life with St Helens 29 MIN
VHS / U-matic
Color
LC 82-706226
Presents a documentary on the eruption of Mount St Helens in 1980 from the viewpoint of the citizens in the vicinity of the volcano. Includes film footage of the eruption and the commentary of geologists, who offer the prospect of future eruptions.
Geography - United States; Geography - World; Sociology
Dist - PBS **Prod** - KSPSTV 1980

Life without a limb - amputees speak out 50 MIN
VHS
Color (G PRO)
$34.95 purchase
Shares the experiences of six adults facing the challenges of amputation. Features different levels of lower limb amputations. Addresses grief and loss, depression, motivation, phantom sensations - pain, and 'bouncing back' to become a whole person. Produced by Drs Steve Riggert and Roger Butterbaugh.
Health and Safety
Dist - FRAZRC

Life Without Cocaine 16 MIN
VHS / 16mm
Conquering Cocaine Series
Color (H A PRO)
$245.00 purchase, $75.00 rental _ #8100
Examines the social support systems which aid recovering addicts in enjoying a cocaine - free life.
Guidance and Counseling; Psychology
Dist - AIMS **Prod** - AIMS 1988

The Life you save 30 MIN
U-matic / VHS
Contemporary health issues series; Lesson 28
Color (C A)
Focuses on the cause and prevention of accidents. Offers first aid information.
Health and Safety
Dist - CDTEL **Prod** - SCCON

The Life You Save (First Aid) 17 MIN
U-matic / VHS / 16mm
Captioned; Color (J)
LC 73-702932
Presents four true cases where knowledge of basic first aid saved lives. Features Tim Donnelly of the 'EMERGENCY' TV series, describing the first aid method of each case.
Health and Safety
Dist - ALTSUL **Prod** - BURKSA 1973

Lifeboat 96 MIN
VHS
B&W (G)
$59.90 purchase _ #0335
Adapts the story 'Lifeboat' by John Steinbeck. Stars Tallulah Bankhead, William Bendix, Walter Slezak, Hume Cronyn and John Hodiak. Produced in 1944.
Literature and Drama
Dist - SEVVID

Lifeboats Under Gravity Davits - Launching Boats 25 MIN
16mm
B&W
LC FIE54-362
Shows the method of launching the merchant marine type of nested lifeboats using the 'WELIN GRAVITY DAVIT.' Demonstrates methods of launching at dockside and while underway at sea.
Civics and Political Systems; Health and Safety; Social Science
Dist - USNAC **Prod** - USN 1954

Lifeboats Under Gravity Davits - Recovering Boats 25 MIN
16mm
B&W
LC FIE54-363
Shows the single method of recovering the Merchant Marine type of nested lifeboats using the Welin Gravity Davit. Illustrates an actual recovery.
Civics and Political Systems; Health and Safety; Social Science
Dist - USNAC **Prod** - USN 1954

Lifecare - the Economics of Aging - 211 30 MIN
U-matic
Currents - 1985 - 86 Season Series
Color (A)
Shows the economic problems of the elderly in obtaining the proper medical and social care that they need.
Health and Safety; Social Science; Sociology
Dist - PBS **Prod** - WNETTV 1985

Lifeclimb 22 MIN
VHS / 16mm / U-matic
Color (C A)
LC 77-703265
Presents 64 - year - old Stan Zundell's description of the manner in which he has faced the difficulties and challenges of aging.
Health and Safety; Psychology; Sociology
Dist - PFP **Prod** - PFP 1977

Lifecycles
Videodisc
Color
Contains 4,000 color images, graphic illustrations and footage from 16 films gleaned from Oxford Scientific Firms, London, England. Portrays unique aspects of reproduction in animal and plant life from cell division to courtship and birthing, from pollination to budding.
Science - Natural
Dist - CBSC **Prod** - CBSC

Lifeline 12 MIN
VHS
Color (H)
Portrays South Africa's role as the protector of the Cape Sea Route, the Western World's major oil lifeline to the Middle East. Also portrays South Africa's role in World War II in an effort to explain its current importance as a strategic center between the Atlantic and the Indian oceans. Available for free loan from the distributor.
Geography - World; Social Science
Dist - AUDPLN

Lifeline - Dispatcher Communications 16 MIN
16mm / U-matic / VHS
Color
Presents the working dispatcher/communications environment in which a variety of complainant calls are received and proper dispatcher field responses are shown.
Civics and Political Systems; Social Science
Dist - CORF **Prod** - CORF

Lifeline express 60 MIN
VHS
QED series
Color; PAL (H C A)
PdS65 purchase
Features a unique train which has been converted into a mobile health clinic in India. Demonstrates how people in the most remote areas receive medical treatment for the first time.
Sociology
Dist - BBCENE

Lifeline in Space 14 MIN
16mm
Color (P I J H)
LC 70-712362
Presents a fictionalized account of the many roles man will be playing in space in the near future.
History - United States; Science - Physical
Dist - GRAF **Prod** - NOVLES 1971

Lifeline - preventing elder abuse 27 MIN
VHS
Color (G)
$24.95 purchase
Shows what elder abuse is and explains the obligation to report it. Discusses types of elder abuse; the abusers and the victims; the physical, behavioral, social, financial and caregiver indicators of abuse; how to report abuse; how to prevent abuse. Features Betty White as host.
Health and Safety
Dist - BAXMED

Lifeline to Learning 27 MIN
16mm
Color
LC 77-701440
Illustrates the special requirements of transporting handicapped school children and includes examples of how various school bus drivers encounter and respond to the needs of handicapped student passengers.
Health and Safety; Social Science
Dist - VISUCP **Prod** - VISUCP 1977

Lifelines 7 MIN
16mm
Color (G)
$10.00 rental
Combines animated line drawings with live photography of a nude model. Reflects a play on the title - living lines, life model, procreation and hand life line. Music by Teiji Ito.

Fine Arts
Dist - CANCIN **Prod** - EMSH 1960

Lifelines - a Career Profile Study 26 MIN
16mm / U-matic / VHS
Human Resources and Organizational Behavior Series
Color
Features Dr Edgar Schein, who discusses the insights of his research into career formation. Uses three case histories to explore Schein's concept of career anchors and looks at five categories of career anchors.
Guidance and Counseling; Psychology
Dist - CNEMAG **Prod** - DOCUA

Lifelines Series
Childbirth 30 MIN
Emergency medical care 30 MIN
Folk medicine 30 MIN
Forensic medicine 30 MIN
It's all in Your Mind 30 MIN
Medicine on the Tube 30 MIN
Nursing as a Profession 30 MIN
Sports medicine 30 MIN
The Treatment of Pain 30 MIN
Dist - MDCPB

Lifequest series
Immunology - the fighting edge 52 MIN
Dist - FOTH

Lifers 27 MIN
VHS
Color (S)
$79.00 purchase _ #386 - 9048
Examines the issue of life imprisonment. Goes inside maxiumum security prisons where 'lifers' candidly discuss their crimes and their frustrations over not being able to lead productive lives. Considers also the enormous cost to taxpayers of long incarcerations.
Civics and Political Systems; Sociology
Dist - FI **Prod** - CANBC 1988

Life's building blocks - Video 2 47 MIN
VHS
Life science - secrets of science series
Color (I J H C)
$49.95 purchase
Presents two parts in two segments each, examining blood, DNA, how cells function and form living organisms and how viruses work and prey on other organisms. Includes Blood and Our Bodies and DNA and Diversity in Part I, The Complex Cell and Understanding Viruses in Part II. Hosted by Discover Magazine Editor in Chief Paul Hoffman. Second of four parts on life science.
Science - Natural
Dist - EFVP **Prod** - DSCOVM 1994

Life's Clocks 27 MIN
16mm / VHS
Color (H A)
$395.00, $495.00 purchase, $75.00 rental _ #9990
Explains the science of chronobiology. Shows that different organisms have different internal rhythms which determine waking and sleeping as well as migration patterns and seasonal hibernation. Reveals also evidence of a connection between internal rhythms and mental illness and depression in humans.
Science - Natural
Dist - AIMS **Prod** - AIMS 1988

Life's Higher Goals 29 MIN
16mm
Color (H C)
Shows Bob Richards, two - time Olympic pole vault champion, giving one of his inspiring messages on living your life to the fullest. Illustrates persons who have overcome obstacles to become 'CHAMPIONS OF LIFE.'.
Guidance and Counseling; Physical Education and Recreation
Dist - NINEFC **Prod** - GEMILL

Life's lessons 60 MIN
VHS
Childhood series
Color (H C G)
$99.95 purchase _ #AMB105V - K
Reveals that between the ages of five and seven, children enter a new and distinctive stage of development. Shows the first day of school in several countries to illustrate how such universal milestones are recognized by different cultures. Looks at what recent research recommends for effective education. Part of a seven - part series on the journey from birth to adolescence.
Education; Health and Safety
Dist - CAMV

Life's little lessons - self - esteem 4 - 6 series
Accepting someone who is different - 1 8 MIN
Alcoholic parent - 2 12 MIN
Appreciating older people - 3 8 MIN
Arguing - 4 7 MIN
Being a shoplifter - 18 9 MIN
Being bossy - 5 10 MIN
Being conceited - 6 11 MIN
Being critical - 7 7 MIN
Being dependable - 8 10 MIN
Being greedy - 9 11 MIN
Being negative - 10 10 MIN
Being perfectionists - 11 10 MIN
Being picky - 12 11 MIN
Being possessive - 13 8 MIN
Being pushy - 14 11 MIN
Being self - centered - 15 14 MIN
Being self - conscious - 16 9 MIN
Being selfish - 17 7 MIN
Being trusted - 19 9 MIN
Being ungrateful - 20 12 MIN
Being yourself - 21 12 MIN
Child abuse - 22 12 MIN
CPR can save lives - 23 18 MIN
Criticizing others - 24 9 MIN
Doing your own work - 25 11 MIN
Doing your part - 26 15 MIN
Exaggerating - 27 7 MIN
Good example - 28 12 MIN
Gossiping - 29 7 MIN
Grieving - 30 11 MIN
Grumbling - 31 10 MIN
Hating - 32 9 MIN
Having the last word - 33 8 MIN
I can't...I won't - 34 7 MIN
Judging others - 35 8 MIN
Know - it alls - 36 12 MIN
Learning from others - 37 9 MIN
Listening - 38 12 MIN
Looking down on others - 39 10 MIN
Making excuses - 40 7 MIN
Manners - 41 13 MIN
Minding your own business - 42 13 MIN
New kid in town - 43 8 MIN
Overcoming handicaps - 44 16 MIN
Paying attention - 45 9 MIN
Peer pressure - 46 6 MIN
Relaxing time 11 MIN
Revenge - 48 10 MIN
Smiling - 51 8 MIN
Sticking to your word 8 MIN
Studying 7 MIN
Taking advantage of others - 54 12 MIN
Talking too much - 55 8 MIN
Telling secrets - 56 8 MIN
Tempers - 57 8 MIN
True love - 58 10 MIN
Trying too hard to please others - 59 8 MIN
Using people - 60 11 MIN
Using your head - 61 11 MIN
Vandalism - 62 9 MIN
Watching too much TV - 63 11 MIN
Water safety - 64 7 MIN
Working together - 65 9 MIN
Dist - BARR

Life's little lessons - self - esteem K - 3 - series
Anger - 1 12 MIN
Being a friend - 2 9 MIN
Being courteous - 3 13 MIN
Being deceitful - 4 5 MIN
Being insecure - 5 8 MIN
Being prejudiced - 6 7 MIN
Cheating - 7 6 MIN
First impressions - 8 6 MIN
Getting something for nothing - 9 7 MIN
Greed - 10 7 MIN
Having purpose - 11 10 MIN
Holding grudges - 12 7 MIN
Hurtful words - 13 12 MIN
Kind words - 14 6 MIN
Learning to do it right - 15 6 MIN
Loneliness - 16 6 MIN
Loyalty - 17 7 MIN
Lying - 18 9 MIN
Making decisions - 19 7 MIN
Overcoming fear - 20 13 MIN
Respecting elders - 21 9 MIN
Respecting privacy - 23 8 MIN
Respecting the law - 22 6 MIN
Sharing - 24 6 MIN
Showing off 6 MIN
Stealing - 26 8 MIN
Thankfulness - 27 8 MIN
Thoughtfulness - 28 8 MIN
Wasting time - 29 9 MIN
Work hard, play hard - 30 10 MIN
Dist - BARR

Life's little lessons series
Serving others 14 MIN
Setting goals 11 MIN
Dist - BARR

Life's work - four approaches to career counseling 160 MIN
VHS / 16mm / U-matic / BETA
Color (G)
$299.00 purchase, $150.00 rental
Explores career counseling as practiced in the field. Features four prominent career counselors as they each conduct a session with the same client. Offers an opportunity to examine and compare diverse methods and objects used in career counseling today. Counselors featured are Dr Howard Figler, Priscilla Claman, Acy Jackson and Barbara Sher.
Business and Economics; Guidance and Counseling; Psychology
Dist - CMBRD **Prod** - CMBRD 1993

Lifesavers - Fitness and Nutrition 20 MIN
U-matic / VHS / 16mm
Stress Management System Series
Color
Illustrates how sedentary lifestyles and improper eating habits take their toll on an individual's physical and emotional well - being. Shows how a properly balanced diet and regular fitness activity can help people work and play more effectively and enjoyably.
Physical Education and Recreation; Social Science
Dist - CORF **Prod** - MITCHG

Lifesaving and Water Safety Series
Boating safety and rescues 10 MIN
Defenses, releases and escapes 7 MIN
Nonswimming Rescues 7 MIN
Preventive Lifeguarding 9 MIN
Removal from the water 6 MIN
Snorkeling Skills and Rescue Techniques 13 MIN
Snorkelling Skills and Rescue Techniques 13 MIN
Special Equipment Rescues 9 MIN
Survival Swimming 7 MIN
Swimming Rescues 8 MIN
Dist - AMRC

Lifesense 180 MIN
VHS
Color; PAL (H C A)
PdS180 purchase; Not available in the United States
Traces the history of human development using the point of view of other species of animals. Includes six sections on Home Life; Seeds of Life; Partners for Life; Life & Soul; Human Life; and Life in the Balance.
Science - Natural
Dist - BBCENE

Lifesense series
Home life 30 MIN
Human life 30 MIN
Life and soul 30 MIN
Life in the balance 30 MIN
Partners for life 30 MIN
Seeds of life 30 MIN
Dist - BBCENE

Lifeskills 130 MIN
VHS
Color; PAL (G)
PdS55 purchase
Presents five 26 - minute programs discussing social situations which many people find difficult. Features Dr Robert Sharpe, behavioral psychologist, as presenter. Shows a panel dramatized versions of embarassing or awkward social situations. The panel comments on why the situation developed the way it did and are joined by an expert who makes a more detailed analysis. Portrays the correct way to handle the particular situation - settling arguments, negotiation, meeting people, intimacy and self - assertion. Contact distributor about availability outside the United Kingdom.
Home Economics; Psychology; Social Science; Sociology
Dist - ACADEM

Lifestories series
Includes six real life dramas of families confronted with different challenges. Covers topics of divorce in 'For Better, For Worse'; death of a spouse in 'In Loving Memory'; adoption in 'A Mother's Love'; Alzheimer's disease in 'Do You Remember?'; financial debt in 'Hard Times' and youth crime in 'Stephen's Going Straight.' Episodes are also available individually.
Lifestories series 180 MIN
Dist - BBCENE

Lifestories
Do you remember? 30 MINS.
For better, for worse 30 MINS.
Hard times 30 MINS.
In loving memory 30 MINS.
A mother's love 30 MINS.
Stephen's going straight 30 MINS.
Dist - BBCENE

Lifestory - a double helix 105 MIN
VHS
Horizon series
Color (A PRO C)
PdS99 purchase _ Unavailable in USA and Canada
Reflects the atmosphere of the early 1950s. Dramatizes the true story of a Briton, Francis Crick - played by Tim Pigott-Smith - and an American, Jim Watson - played by Jeff Goldblum - who built the first model of DNA structure.
Science - Natural
Dist - BBCENE

Lifestream - Collecion, Preparation and Administration of Blood and its Components 26 MIN
VHS / U-matic
Color (PRO)
Shows how modern techniques make it possible to greatly extend the collection and therapeutic use of blood and its components.
Health and Safety; Science - Natural
Dist - WFP **Prod** - WFP

Lifestudies - The Drug we drink - Talking Drink 40 MIN
VHS
Color; PAL (G)
PdS30 purchase
Presents two 20 - minute programs about alcohol and alcoholism. Examines the effect of alcohol on the body and looks at the safe limits, if there are any, of alcholic intake in The Drug We Drink. Talking Drink is a discussion program with a group of young people talking to Murial Gray, who examines their attitudes about drinking alcohol. Contact distributor about availability outside the United Kingdom.
Health and Safety; Psychology; Sociology
Dist - ACADEM

Lifestyle 30 MIN
U-matic
China After Mao Series
Color
Discusses experiences and observations of modern China.
Civics and Political Systems; Geography - World
Dist - UMITV **Prod** - UMITV

Lifestyle and Career Development 30 MIN
VHS
Infusing Gerontological Counseling into Counselor Preparation Series
Color (A PRO)
$65.00 purchase _ #77655
Identifies key concepts and activities important to career and lifestyle counseling with older persons.
Education; Guidance and Counseling; Health and Safety
Dist - AACD **Prod** - AACD 1988

Lifestyle Choices - Your Health, Baby's Health 29 MIN
VHS / 16mm
Your Health Series
Color (C)
$250.00 purchase _ #656301
Focuses on birthweight as the emerging new standard for gauging parental care from preconception to birth. Shows women that practicing positive lifestyle behaviors before and during pregnancy can greatly improve their changes of having healthy and normal birthweight babies. Examines critically the concept of birthweight and emphasizes lifestyle issues documented to have the greatest impact on birthweight such as nutrition, smoking, exercise - fitness, and drugs - alcohol.
Health and Safety; Psychology; Social Science; Sociology
Dist - ACCESS **Prod** - ACCESS 1987

Lifestyles 28 MIN
VHS
Elephant show series
Color (P I)
$95.00 purchase, $45.00 rental
Presents program 10 in the Sharon, Lois and Bram's Elephant Show series. Teaches reading readiness and social skills while engaging children in making music. Each program explores a new theme through adventure, fantasy, mystery and song with recording artists Sharon, Lois and Bram. Uses traditional materials which stress participation - action songs, sing - along songs, story songs, clapping songs, singing games, playground chants and folk songs from many different traditions. Includes teacher's guide co - authored by a music education specialist.
Fine Arts; Sociology
Dist - BULFRG **Prod** - CAMBFP 1988

Lifestyles and lifestages 30 MIN
VHS
Making a living work series
Color (G A)
$150.00 purchase _ #JW820V
Presents the theory of lifestages. Interviews career changers and others dealing with critical life decisions.
Business and Economics; Psychology
Dist - CAMV

Lifestyles for wellness - introduction 16 MIN
VHS / 16mm
Lifestyles for wellness series
Color (C A PRO)
Teaches the concept of wellness and motivates viewers to adopt healthy lifestyles. Uses first-hand accounts from people who have learned to live healthier lives. Features William Shatner. Part one of a five-part series.
Health and Safety; Physical Education and Recreation; Psychology
Dist - AIMS **Prod** - SANDE 1987
AJN

Lifestyles for wellness series
Fitness for wellness 11 MIN
Lifestyles for wellness - introduction 16 MIN
Nutrition for wellness 11 MIN
Dist - AIMS
AJN

Lifestyles in wellness series
Moderation in eating 11 MIN
Dist - AIMS
AJN

Lifestyles - leading killers of today
VHS
Color (J H C G A)
$79.50 purchase _ #AH46320
Surveys the 12 leading causes of death in the U S. Suggests that modern lifestyles are largely responsible for many of these deaths.
Health and Safety; Science - Natural
Dist - HTHED **Prod** - HTHED

Lifestyles - Lifestages 30 MIN
VHS / 16mm
Making a Living Work Series
Color (C)
$150.00 purchase _ #PAOT2V
Theorizes about different stages of life. Focuses on career changes and actions of those who have made important life decisions.
Guidance and Counseling; Psychology
Dist - JISTW

Lifestyles Lifestages 30 MIN
U-matic / VHS
Making a Living Work Series
(C A)
$225 _ #JWOT2V
Presents theory on lifestage and commentary from individuals attempting to change their careers.
Business and Economics
Dist - JISTW **Prod** - OHUTC

Lifestyles - Lifestages 30 MIN
VHS
Making a Living Work Series
$225.00 purchase _ #013 - 512
Discusses lifestage theory and changing careers.
Business and Economics; Guidance and Counseling
Dist - CAREER **Prod** - CAREER

Lifestyles/Lifestages 30 MIN
VHS / U-matic
Making a Living Work Series Program 102
Color (C A)
Focuses on lifestage theory and choosing lifestyles. Shows lifestyle and career changers talking about the momentum behind their decisions.
Guidance and Counseling; Psychology
Dist - OHUTC **Prod** - OHUTC

Lifetime Commitment - a Portrait of Karen Thompson 30 MIN
VHS / 16mm
Color (G)
$195.00 purchase, $60.00 rental
Tells the story of Sharon Kowalski who was critically injured and disabled in a car accident in 1983, and her lover, Karen Thompson, who has been fighting a legal battle against Sharon's family for the right to see Sharon and care for her. Documents Thompson's transformation from a closet lesbian to a leading activist for the rights of lesbian and gay couples and the disabled.
Civics and Political Systems; Fine Arts; Sociology
Dist - WMEN **Prod** - KIZEL 1988

Lifetime contract 55 MIN
VHS
Color (J H R)
$39.95 purchase, $10.00 rental _ #35 - 842 - 8936
Casts the classic struggle between good and evil in a modern - day light. Focuses on high school graduate Carl Trask, who must decide what he wants to do with his life. Produced by Bridgestone.
Psychology; Religion and Philosophy
Dist - APH

The Lifetime customer - a marriage of quality and customer satisfaction 60 MIN
VHS
Color; PAL (C G PRO)
$89.95, $69.95 purchase _ #90AST - V - M60
Discusses the competitive implications of linking quality and customer satisfaction through employee skill training. Shows a model for effective customer interaction and how to write a 'quality requirement.' Features Ron Galbraith, President, Management 21, Nashville TN; and Lynn Sellers, President, Transitions Unlimited, Houston TX.
Business and Economics; Education; Psychology
Dist - MOBILE **Prod** - ASTD 1990

The Lifetime customer - improved customer service 15 MIN
VHS
Color (PRO C)
$250.00 purchase, $70.00 rental _ #4391
Explains the cycle of how to create a lifetime customer - attraction; transaction; satisfaction; relationships; and commitment. Shows how to identify customer service problem areas and target specific areas of satisfaction.
Business and Economics; Health and Safety
Dist - AJN **Prod** - ENVINC

Lifetime Employment 28 MIN
U-matic / VHS / 16mm
Human Face of Japan Series
Color (H C A)
LC 82-700622
Shows how Japan must rely on imports for its economic survival and focuses on the Theory Z methods used to ensure a consistently high level of quality and productivity.
Business and Economics; Geography - World; History - World; Social Science
Dist - LCOA **Prod** - FLMAUS 1982

Lifetime Fitness 15 MIN
VHS / 16mm
All Fit with Slim Goodbody Series
Color (P I)
$125.00 purchase, $25.00 rental
Reviews the benefits of regular exercise even while doing chores and other daily activities.
Health and Safety; Physical Education and Recreation; Science - Natural
Dist - AITECH **Prod** - GDBODY 1987

A Lifetime in Photography 30 MIN
U-matic / VHS
Photographic Vision - all about Photography Series
Color
Industrial and Technical Education
Dist - CDTEL **Prod** - COAST

A Lifetime of Learning 28 MIN
VHS / U-matic
Color (PRO)
Depicts role of the University of Kansas Medical Center in the continuing education of the physician and surgeon in Kansas.
Health and Safety
Dist - WFP **Prod** - WFP

A Lifetime of photography 29 MIN
VHS
Photographic vision series
Color (G)
$49.95 purchase _ #RM120V-F
Presents a documentary on Max Yavno. Presents the technical aspects of photography clearly and simply, including principles of the camera and techniques for controlling exposure, the use of various kinds of lighting, selection of appropriate lenses and film and basic darkroom techniques. Focuses on the world of photographers and photography - its history and evolution, its uses for personal development and expression, and the impact of photography on the world. Part of a 20-part series examining all aspects of the field of photography.
Industrial and Technical Education
Dist - CAMV

Lifetime Protection 20 MIN
16mm
Color
Shows how styrofoam is finding wide use as a perimeter insulation and combination building insulation and plaster base for masonry residential construction. Explains the qualities of styrofoam and shows proper methods of installation.
Business and Economics; Industrial and Technical Education
Dist - DCC **Prod** - DCC 1956

Lifetime Weight Control - Diet Fact and Fiction
VHS
(G)
$69 purchase _ #LSWCV
Emphasizes that most diets don't work, and that going on and off diets is not only unhealthy, but likely to increase weight gain. Promotes moderate exercise as the key to losing weight. Introduces the Ten Calorie Plan as the safe, sane way to lose and maintain weight.
Guidance and Counseling; Health and Safety; Social Science
Dist - CAREER **Prod** - CAREER

Lifetimes of Change - Development and Growth 18 MIN
16mm / VHS

Color (I J H C A)
$245.00, $375.00 purchase, $30.00 rental _ #8012
Makes the point that as the years go by every living thing changes. Helps students perceive growth and developmental changes that are often slow and unnoticed by condensing events that normally take days, weeks, or years, into minutes.
Science - Natural
Dist - AIMS **Prod** - EDMI 1983

Lifetimes of Change - Development and Growth 18 MIN
U-matic / VHS
Color (I)
Illustrates how all living creatures, whether plants, animals or human beings, experience growth, development and change. Shows how man ages by a series of 15 portraits from infancy to old age. Cites three other examples for further exposition, including life - changes in toadstools, frog, and flowering plants.
Science - Natural
Dist - EDMI **Prod** - EDMI 1983

Lifewalks
U-matic / 16mm
Color (A)
Alerts people to the danger of being a pedestrian, gives safety tips and encourages people to walk safely.
Health and Safety
Dist - BNA **Prod** - BNA 1983

Lifeways Series
La Acequia 10 MIN
Dist - BLUSKY

Lifeways Series
Los Santeros 27 MIN
Dist - BLUSKY
ONEWST

Lifeways Series
Los Tejedores 28 MIN
Dist - ONEWST

Lifework
VHS / BETA
Adult Years - Continuity and Change Series
Color
Explores the role of work in adult lives, and discusses the new work ethic. Includes comments by a real estate agent, an executive, a factory worker, and the manager of a fast food restaurant.
Guidance and Counseling; Psychology
Dist - OHUTC **Prod** - OHUTC

The Lift 8 MIN
16mm
B&W
LC 72-702398
Explains how a man loses control of the machines in his mechanized world when an old elevator refuses to respond to his commands and eventually causes his death.
Fine Arts; Guidance and Counseling; Sociology
Dist - USC **Prod** - USC 1972

Lift 22 MIN
VHS
Color; PAL (J H G)
PdS15 purchase _ #1013
Portrays an energy conference to create an informal discussion of energy topics using characters drawn from life. Considers the facts, figures, as well as the emotions, surrounding the issues discussed, including the finite nature of fossil fuels and basic commodities such as plastic.
Social Science
Dist - UKAEA

Lift every voice - calling your pastor 17 MIN
VHS
Color (G A R)
$21.95 purchase, $10.00 rental _ #35 - 8115 - 2076
Encourages congregations to select ministers who come from traditionally underrepresented groups - women, minorities, people over 50 years old, and the disabled.
Religion and Philosophy
Dist - APH

Lift off 8 MIN
VHS / 16mm
Muppet meeting films series
Color (PRO)
$550.00 purchase, $300.00 rental, $30.00 preview
Presents Jim Henson's muppets who introduce and humorously comment on business meetings and breaks. Consists of three to four segments each approximately two and a half minutes.
Business and Economics; Psychology; Sociology
Dist - UTM

Lift the bandstand 50 MIN
VHS
Color; Stereo (G)
$29.95 purchase
Focuses on jazz artist Steve Lacy.
Fine Arts
Dist - KINOIC **Prod** - RHPSDY

Lift Truck Safety 12 MIN
U-matic / VHS
Steel Making Series
Color (IND)
Looks at the professional way to operate a lift truck. Stresses pre - shift inspection. Discusses proper driving techniques.
Business and Economics; Health and Safety; Industrial and Technical Education
Dist - LEIKID **Prod** - LEIKID

Lifting a curtain - conservation of Rubens' Crowning of St Catherine 30 MIN
BETA / U-matic / VHS
Color (G)
$59.95, $49.95 purchase
Documents the cleaning and restoration of the Peter Paul Rubens painting, The Crowning of St Catherine, in the collection of the Toledo Museum of Art. Features painting conservator Gabrielle Kopelman who explains and demonstrates the exacting technique required to clean and restore the 1633 painting to the original vibrancy it had as an altarpiece for a church in Malines, Belgium.
Fine Arts
Dist - ARTSAM **Prod** - TMART

Lifting - a Weight, a Way 10 MIN
16mm
Color
LC 74-705031
Illustrates proper methods of lifting parcels and sacks to reduce back injuries among postal employees. Features an olympic weightlifting champion applying proper techniques to actual postal operation.
Health and Safety; Social Science
Dist - USNAC **Prod** - USPOST 1970

Lifting and Analysis 17 MIN
U-matic / VHS
Color (A)
Discusses how to calculate parameters for safe lifting activity in specific situations. Intended for managers, supervisors, safety specialists and loss controllers.
Health and Safety; Psychology
Dist - USNAC **Prod** - USPHS 1981

Lifting Equipment 10 MIN
U-matic / VHS / 16mm
Safety in Construction Series
Color
Emphasizes safe operation of cranes and lifting equipment. Stresses the need to train operators in safe operations.
Health and Safety; Industrial and Technical Education
Dist - IFB **Prod** - NFBTE

Lifting injuries - analysis and solutions 17 MIN
VHS
Color (G IND)
$95.00 purchase _ #SHA10278
Shows how companies can reduce medical, accident and first aid reports and potential worker's compensation. Illustrates how to reduce risks to workers by calculating the acceptable load limit and the maximum permissable limits for each lifting activity. Demonstrates a relationship between exceeding these limits with injuries and lost work days. Examples are shown using these formula calculations, along with ways to make adjustments in order to reduce back injury.
Health and Safety
Dist - USNAC **Prod** - NIOSH 1981

Lifting - Man's Age Old Problem 14 MIN
16mm
Color (J)
Utilizes special photographic techniques to dramatize the functions of the back muscles and spine and to illustrate the efects of both correct and incorrect lifting methods. Suggests guidelines for use in establishing individual strength limits and offers advice on proper lifting techniques.
Health and Safety; Physical Education and Recreation; Science - Natural
Dist - AETNA **Prod** - AETNA 1964

Lifting properly 13 MIN
VHS / U-matic / BETA
Color; PAL (IND G)
$175.00 rental _ #AEB - 101
Shows the correct way to lift objects, push or pull them. Illustrates the use of carts and hand trucks, as well as the safe handling of drums and cylinders. Includes leader's guide and 10 workbooks.
Health and Safety; Physical Education and Recreation; Psychology; Science - Natural
Dist - BNA **Prod** - BNA

Lifting Safety 9 MIN
16mm
Color
Shows the proper technique for lifting heavy or bulky objects safely to avoid back and other injuries.
Health and Safety
Dist - RARIG **Prod** - RARIG

Lifting Techniques and Body Mechanics 20 MIN
VHS / U-matic
Color
Describes in non - technical terms what happens to the back when an object is lifted. Visualizes the spine with simple diagrams and a split - screen technique. Cites dangers to the back when an object is lifted incorrectly.
Health and Safety; Science - Natural
Dist - FAIRGH **Prod** - FAIRGH

Lifting Templates for a Foundation 23 MIN
16mm
B&W
LC FIE52-1210
Tells how to lift a template within the hull of a ship, and transfer the shape of the hull by use of measurements and cardboard.
Industrial and Technical Education
Dist - USNAC **Prod** - USN 1944

Lifting the Blackout - Images of North Korea 54 MIN
VHS / 16mm
Color (G)
$350.00 purchase, $90.00 rental
Examines the history, politics and culture of North Korea, including the daily life and aspects of many facets of North Korean society. Visits North Korean homes, schools, workplaces and recreation centers, as well as the demilitarized zone separating North and South Korea. Interviews North Koreans and Korea experts in the US.
Civics and Political Systems; Geography - World; History - United States; History - World
Dist - CNEMAG **Prod** - CNEMAG 1989

Lifting the Shadows 27 MIN
16mm
Color
Features four doctors discussing the effects of marijuana, alcohol and tobacco on sexual libido. Highlights the emotional impact on social and family relationships.
Psychology; Sociology
Dist - NARCED **Prod** - NARCED

Lifting Weight 10 MIN
16mm / U-matic / VHS
Inventive Child Series
Color (P I)
Views Grandpa and Boy hard at work lifting heavy sacks of grain and carrying them to the barn loft. Reveals that a dangling spider gives Boy the idea of pulling up the sacks with a rope and pulley. Demonstrates the concept of mechanical advantage.
History - World; Science - Physical
Dist - EBEC **Prod** - POLSKI 1983

Lifting Weight and Universal Vehicle 20 MIN
VHS / U-matic
Inventive Child Series
Color
$89.00 purchase _ #1582
Portrays the characters Boy and Grandpa who ease some of their problems after getting an idea from a spider (1st part). Presents Boy and Grandpa who construct a working vehicle from using observations (2nd part). Stresses childrens' creativity.
Psychology
Dist - EBEC

Ligado Technique 29 MIN
Videoreel / VT2
Playing the Guitar I Series
Color
Fine Arts
Dist - PBS **Prod** - KCET

Ligaments of the knee joint, the pathophysiology 20 MIN
U-matic / VHS
Color
Demonstrates the origins of knee instability preceded by explanation of the control functions of ligaments and semilunar cartilages.
Health and Safety
Dist - SPRVER **Prod** - SPRVER

Ligation and Stripping of Varicose Veins 23 MIN
16mm
Color (PRO)
Demonstrates a malleable stripper with detachable stripper heads. Illustrates the normal venous return and the disturbance found in varicose veins.
Health and Safety; Science
Dist - ACY **Prod** - ACYDGD 1961

The Ligation and Stripping Treatment of Varicose Veins 22 MIN
16mm
Color (PRO)
Shows the operative technique of the high sapheno femoral ligation together with the actual stripping technique.
Health and Safety; Science
Dist - ACY **Prod** - ACYDGD 1952

Light 25 MIN
VHS
Ask Oscar series
Color (P I)
$250.00 purchase
Asks where the sun goes at night, how mirrors work, what a rainbow is made of. Features Oscar the Mole who discusses elements of the solar system, photosynthesis, the rotation of the Earth and it's motion around the sun, refraction, the interdependency of light, energy, plants, animals and the speed of light. Part of a three - part series on basic science.
Science - Physical
Dist - LANDMK **Prod** - LANDMK 1990

Light 11.5 MIN
VHS / 16mm / U-matic
Color (K P I)
$275, $195, $225 purchase _ #A397
Introduces young children to basic properties and characteristics of light. Demonstrates how light bounces or reflects off smooth surfaces like calm water or mirrors. Introduces the concept of bending or refracting light to distort or enlarge images. Shows how water mist makes light break up into colors of the spectrum.
Science - Physical
Dist - BARR **Prod** - BARR 1986

Light 15 MIN
U-matic
Science Alliance Series
Color (I)
Examines the properties of light, refraction and reflection and tells of Edison's and Newton's experiments.
Science; Science - Physical
Dist - TVOTAR **Prod** - TVOTAR 1981

Light 15 MIN
VHS / U-matic
Arts Express Series
Color (K P I J)
Fine Arts
Dist - KYTV **Prod** - KYTV 1983

Light 4 MIN
16mm
From the Light Series
B&W (J H)
Reviews the physics of light. Progresses from elementary information to more advanced information.
Science - Physical
Dist - VIEWTH **Prod** - GBI

Light 15 MIN
VHS / 16mm
Challenge Series
Color (I)
$125.00 purchase, $25.00 rental
Illustrates the properties of light via laser demonstrations and following the production of a television program from the studio to the television set.
Science; Science - Physical
Dist - AITECH **Prod** - WDCNTV 1987

Light 10 MIN
VHS / U-matic / 16mm
Primary science series
Color (P I)
LC 91-705350
Illustrates the properties of light through simple observations. Explains how sunlight provides both light and heat. Includes two teacher's guides. Part of a series on primary science produced by Fred Ladd.
Science; Science - Physical
Dist - BARR

Light 14 MIN
U-matic / 16mm / VHS
Matter and energy for beginners series
Color (P)
$400.00, $250.00 purchase _ #HP - 5943C
Uses animation and live action to teach physical science. Stars Investigator Alligator and his friend Mr E, who investigate the mysteries of light. Part of a six - part series.
Science - Physical
Dist - CORF **Prod** - CORF 1990

Light 10 MIN
U-matic / VHS / 16mm
Art of Seeing Series
Color (I)
LC 70-704582
Explains that light is the phenomenon which makes visual experience possible. Shows how different kinds of light can change people's perceptions of the world. Discusses light as an important element in art. Illustrates ways in which artists have used light to achieve their expressive purposes.
Fine Arts; Science - Physical
Dist - FI **Prod** - AFA 1969

Light - 6 10 MIN
VHS / U-matic / 16mm
Primary science series
Color (K P I)
$265.00, $215.00, $185.00 purchase _ #B587
Illustrates the properties of light. Explains the reasons for shadows. Shows how reflected light can be a solar cooker. Considers the role of the sun in providing light and heat. Part of an 11 - part series on primary science.
Science - Physical
Dist - BARR **Prod** - GREATT 1990

Light - a First Film 13 MIN
16mm / U-matic / VHS
Color (P I)
Explores the pervasiveness of light as the basic form of energy, including its manifestations and transformations.
Science - Physical
Dist - PHENIX **Prod** - PHENIX 1982

The Light ahead - Fishke der krumer 95 MIN
VHS
Edgar G Ulmer's films series
B&W (G) (YIDDISH WITH ENGLISH SUBTITLES)
$69.95 purchase _ #738
Adapts a story by Mendele Mokher Seforim. Tells of a lame man, Fishke, who is the ward of the Jewish community and his love for the blind woman Hodi. Reveals that they are kept from marrying until a travelling bookseller turns the community's fear of the supernatural to the couple's advantage. Stars David Opatoshu, Helan Beverly and Isidore Cashier. Directed by Edgar G Ulmer and first released in 1937.
Fine Arts; Sociology
Dist - ERGOM **Prod** - ERGOM 1992

Light all about Us 10 MIN
U-matic / VHS / 16mm
Color (P I)
$265, $185 purchase _ #3280
Discusses the sources of light and energy.
Science - Physical
Dist - CORF

Light and Atmosphere 30 MIN
VHS / 16mm
Focus on Watercolor Series
Color (C A)
$85.00, $75.00 purchase _ 21 - 06
Demonstrates painting landscapes, atmospheric perspective, depth of field, historical development, and controlling color.
Fine Arts
Dist - CDTEL **Prod** - COAST 1987

Light and Color 14 MIN
16mm / U-matic / VHS
Color (I J) (SPANISH)
Explains what color is, how color is related to light, why a certain color looks the way it does, and the role color plays in the identification of chemical elements.
Foreign Language; Science - Physical
Dist - EBEC **Prod** - EBEC

Light and Color 15 MIN
VHS / U-matic
Why Series
Color (P I)
Discusses light and color.
Science - Physical
Dist - AITECH **Prod** - WDCNTV 1976

Light and color - 28 40 MIN
VHS
Conceptual physics alive series
Color (H C)
$45.00 purchase
Discusses the electromagnetic nature of light and its speed. Relates demonstrations of color addition to the colors of everyday things such as the blue sky, red sunsets, blue - green ocean and white clouds. Part 28 of a 35 - part series adapted from the college and high school textbook Conceptual Physics by Professor Paul Hewitt.
Science - Physical
Dist - MMENTE **Prod** - HEWITP 1992

Light and Easy, Pt 1 - a Measure of Responsibility 20 MIN
U-matic / VHS / 16mm
Color (J H A)
Presents Graham Kerr of 'Galloping Gourmet' fame, highlighting four factors he believes should be considered in planning menus. Includes aroma and emotion, nutrition, budget and effort.
Home Economics
Dist - CORNRS **Prod** - CUETV 1975

Light and Easy, Pt 2 - Elegant Low - Calorie Foods 30 MIN
16mm / U-matic / VHS
Color (J H A)
Presents Graham Kerr demonstrating techniques used to achieve specific nutrition and low - calorie dishes that have a gourmet touch.
Home Economics
Dist - CORNRS **Prod** - CUETV 1975

Light and Fresh Cooking 60 MIN
VHS
(H A)
$24.95 purchase _ #KA1000V
Illustrates the preparation of light, healthy meals selected by the staff of Bon Apetit magazine. Explains low fat cooking techniques, creative menu planning and artistic food presentation. Features chef Mark Peel making an Oriental meal.
Home Economics
Dist - CAMV **Prod** - CAMV

Light and Heat 15 MIN
VHS / U-matic
Why Series
Color (P I)
Discusses the characteristics of light and heat.
Science - Physical
Dist - AITECH **Prod** - WDCNTV 1976

Light and Images 10 MIN
U-matic / VHS / 16mm
Physical Science Series
Color (I J H)
$265, $185 purchase _ #4832C
Discusses how images are produced in cameras and the human eye.
Science - Physical
Dist - CORF

Light and Lenses 10 MIN
U-matic / VHS / 16mm
Color (J H C)
LC 74-701769
Uses diagrams and everyday examples from experience in order to show the basic properties of light and to describe how the application of various optical systems is used for photographic purposes.
Industrial and Technical Education; Science - Physical
Dist - JOU **Prod** - KVH 1973

Light and medicine of the future 110 MIN
VHS
Color (G)
$29.95 purchase _ #P17
Presents Dr Jacob Lieberman, OD, PhD explaining the concepts in his book. Deals with the effects of light and color on the human body, consciousness and human evolution.
Health and Safety; Literature and Drama; Science - Natural; Science - Physical
Dist - HP

Light and Shadow 7 MIN
16mm
Science Series
Color (K P I)
Experiments with shadows explain where the earth gets its light, what daytime and nighttime are, and the nature of a shadow.
Science - Physical
Dist - SF **Prod** - MORLAT 1967

Light and Shadow 11 MIN
U-matic / VHS
Introductory Concepts in Physics - Light Series
Color (C)
$229.00, $129.00 purchase _ #AD - 1220
Explains the relationship between light and shadow through a number of experiments - the casting of a simple shadow, casting the shadows of two objects on screen and other shades of light and shadow.
Science - Physical
Dist - FOTH **Prod** - FOTH

Light and shadow 19 MIN
16mm
Color (G)
$235.00 purchase, $30.00 rental _ #HPF - 685, #HRF - 685
Focuses on the lives and works of fifteen artists who came to Paris in the 1920s and 1930s, but died in the death camps of World War II.
Fine Arts; History - World
Dist - ADL **Prod** - ADL

Light and Shadow 30 MIN
VHS / 16mm
Focus on Watercolor Series
Color (C A)
$85.00, $75.00 purchase _ 21 - 08
Explains organizing light and shadow, daily rituals, hard and soft edges, and repetition of shapes and themes.
Fine Arts
Dist - CDTEL **Prod** - COAST 1987

Light and Shadow in the Holocaust 28 MIN
16mm
Color (H C A G)
Provides a look at art works of Jewish artists of the school of Paris before the Holocaust. Then it whows art created in the Theresienstadt concentration camp.
Fine Arts; Sociology
Dist - FEDU **Prod** - ISMUS 1985

Light and Shadow Techniques 15 MIN
Videoreel / VT2
Charlie's Pad Series
Color
Fine Arts
Dist - PBS **Prod** - WSIU

Light and Shadows 14 MIN
U-matic / VHS
Hands on, Grade 2 - Lollipops, Loops, Etc Series Unit 1 - Observing; Unit 1 - Observing
Color (P)
Gives experience in observing light and shadows.
Science
Dist - AITECH **Prod** - WHROTV 1975

Light and Sound Tools 29 MIN
VHS / 16mm
Villa Alegre Series
Color (P T)
$46.00 rental _ #VILA - 163
Presents educational material in both Spanish and English.
Education; Science - Physical
Dist - PBS

Light and the Electromagnetic Spectrum 14 MIN
U-matic / VHS / 16mm
Physical Science Series
Color (I J H)
$340, $230 purchase _ #4834C
Discusses the relationship between light and other forms of electromagnetic radiation.
Science - Physical
Dist - CORF

Light and what it Does 11 MIN
16mm / U-matic / VHS
Color (P) (SPANISH)
Demonstrates how light travels, how it is affected by different materials, what causes reflection and refraction and how light is used in many activities.
Foreign Language; Science - Physical
Dist - EBEC **Prod** - EBEC

Light as Information 30 MIN
U-matic / VHS
Perspective II Series
Color (J H C A)
$150.00
Explores a variety of science and technology subjects dealing with light and its use as a medium of communication. Shows how they work and discusses the implications of this new knowledge.
Computer Science; Science - Physical
Dist - LANDMK **Prod** - LANDMK 1981

Light at the end of the tunnel 10 MIN
16mm / VHS
Color (G)
$10.00 rental
Reenacts the metaphor of the emergence from the tunnel by interpreting literally the cliche after which it is named. Takes the viewer through a transformation from the dark and silent night into the light of day. Produced by Jerome Carolfi.
Fine Arts
Dist - CANCIN

A Light Beam Named Ray 20 MIN
16mm / U-matic / VHS
Color
LC 73-700265
Uses an animated light beam 'RAY' to explain the fundamentals of light, color and optics. Discusses the invisible neighbors of light and introduces the superlight and the laser beam. Covers sources of light, reflection, heliograph, refraction, shortsightedness and farsightedness, prisms, the color spectrum, the color wheel and white light.
Science - Physical
Dist - HANDEL **Prod** - HANDEL 1973

The Light Bulb 5 MIN
U-matic / VHS / 16mm
How It's made Series
Color (K)
Business and Economics
Dist - LUF **Prod** - HOLIA

Light Bulbs and the American Consumer 15 MIN
16mm
Color
Tells how to select the proper light bulbs for each residential application.
Home Economics
Dist - KLEINW **Prod** - KLEINW

Light, Color and the Visible Spectrum 13 MIN
U-matic / VHS / 16mm
Physical Science Series
Color (I J H)
$325, $230 purchase _ #4833C
Shows how the colors humans see depend on which of the wavelengths of white light reaches the eyes.
Science - Physical
Dist - CORF

Light, Dark and Daumier 29 MIN
Videoreel / VT2
Museum Open House Series
Color
Fine Arts; Geography - World
Dist - PBS **Prod** - WGBHTV

Light energy 14 MIN
Videodisc / VHS
Physical science series
Color (H J)
$99.95, $69.95 purchase _ #Q10347
Utilizes descriptions, illustrations and experiments to illustrate concepts of light energy. Explains how light sources occur through the transfer of energy and discusses the theory of photons. Features the wavelengths of light, the electromagnetic spectrum, and various examples of the particle - wave characteristics of light. Part of a series of six programs.
Science - Physical; Social Science
Dist - CF

The Light Fantastick 58 MIN
16mm
Color (J)
LC 76-702442
Discusses the use of animation and animation techniques.
Fine Arts; Industrial and Technical Education
Dist - NFBC **Prod** - NFBC 1974
CFLMDC

Light fixture 6 MIN
16mm
B&W (G)
$12.00 rental
Looks at a man who becomes the patient of a doctor - magician - orchestra conductor who appears to influence the forces of the unknown. Depicts visually the role of the conscious mind toward the unconscious. Produced by Steve Mobia.
Fine Arts; Psychology
Dist - CANCIN

Light following - part 1 6 MIN
16mm
B&W (G)
$12.00 rental
Explores a room using a flash to illuminate a space in fragments of light. Forces the viewer to reconstruct the space by connecting the image - events in time. Produced by Caroline Savage - Lee.
Fine Arts; Science - Physical
Dist - CANCIN

A Light for Debra 27 MIN
U-matic
Color
LC 79-706103
Presents an overview of the use of behavior modification through reinforcement as a tool to aid in concept, academic task and social development of the severely mentally retarded child.
Psychology
Dist - USNAC **Prod** - USBEH 1979

A Light for John 22 MIN
16mm
B&W
LC FIA59-308
Two days in the lives of a retarded man and his worrying mother are revealed. Shows the Depression and the hopelessness faced by both parties.
Guidance and Counseling; Health and Safety; Psychology
Dist - USC **Prod** - USC 1956

Light - form studies from Anaxagoras' stone 18 MIN
16mm
Color (G)
$24.00 rental
Relates the theory by Anaxagoras, first person to recognize the moon's luminance as reflected sunlight in 430 BC, in which he defines light as a separate entity and primary agent of vision. Employs camera variables to dramatize light reflection. Produced by Rob Danielson.
Fine Arts; Science - Physical
Dist - CANCIN

Light from Heaven 17 MIN
16mm
Book of Acts Series
Color; B&W (J H T R)
Presents the story of Saul of Tarsus and the stoning of Stephen. Reassures Christians on the firmness of their hope in Christ and shows sinners that everyone can be saved by Christ.
Religion and Philosophy
Dist - FAMF **Prod** - BROADM 1957

Light from within 30 MIN
U-matic / VHS
Developing Image Series
Color (J H)
Examines the trend toward graphic experimentation in photography.
Fine Arts; Industrial and Technical Education
Dist - CTI **Prod** - CTI

The Light Here Kindled 26 MIN
U-matic / VHS / 16mm
Color (I)
Re - creates the story of the pilgrims and their struggle for survival. Examines their living conditions, building of homes, food preparation, struggle with epidemic and starvation, practices of government and religion, and their ideas of education.
Civics and Political Systems; History - United States
Dist - IFB **Prod** - WGNDPA 1966

Light I - Refraction and Reflection 24 MIN
VHS / 16mm
Light Series
Color (I)
LC 90706234
Explains the principles of light refraction and reflection. Shows various optical illusions produced by light.
Science - Physical
Dist - BARR

Light II - waves, particles and photons 24 MIN
U-matic / VHS
Light series
Color (I J)
$325.00, $295.00 purchase _ #V193; LC 90-705972
Explores the particle and wave theories of light. Looks at scientific theory in the 17th century - Isaac Newton believed that light was composed of tiny, luminous particles, Christian Huygens believed light traveled in the form of waves. Reveals that in the 20th century Albert Einstein concluded that light was both wave and particle at the same time and called the particles photons. Studies refraction and reflection in relationship to lenses, binoculars, mirrors and telescopes. Part of a five - part series on light.
Fine Arts; Science; Science - Physical
Dist - BARR **Prod** - GLOBET 1989

Light III - the speed of light 24 MIN
VHS / U-matic
Light series
Color (I J)
$325.00, $295.00 purchase _ #V194; LC 90-705973
Traces the attempts of scientists over the centuries to describe the speed of light. Reveals that Galileo was the first to attempt to measure its speed. Part of a five - part series on light.
Fine Arts; Science; Science - Physical
Dist - BARR **Prod** - GLOBET 1989

A Light in the Darkness 33 MIN
16mm
B&W
Presents the story of Red Cross peacetime activities around the world.
Health and Safety
Dist - AMRC **Prod** - LRCSF 1964

The Light in the Forest 93 MIN
U-matic / VHS / 16mm
Color
Presents the story of a white youth raised by Delaware Indians who becomes involved in a series of conflicts as he reclaims his heritage in a village of Indian - hating men.
Fine Arts
Dist - FI **Prod** - DISNEY 1958

Light in the Sea 30 MIN
U-matic / VHS
Oceanus - the Marine Environment Series Lesson 21
Color
Discusses the importance of the light that penetrates the ocean to life on earth. Looks at the physical factors that influence the penetration of light in the sea.
Science - Natural; Science - Physical
Dist - CDTEL **Prod** - SCCON

Light Institute exercises with Chris Griscom - Tape 1 80 MIN
VHS
Windows to the sky series

Color (G)
$29.95 purchase
Presents the vision of Chris Griscom on the awarenesses required for the next century. Shows how to contact the Higher Self, radiate energy through the body and the electromagnetic benefits of spinning. Offers an 'Inner Child' exercise. Comments on the cosmic force of sexuality and moving from karmic relationship to soul recognition and advancement. Part one of a two - part series.
Health and Safety; Psychology; Religion and Philosophy
Dist - LIGHTI **Prod** - LIGHTI

Light is many Things 12 MIN
VHS / 16mm / U-matic
Color (K P I J)
$240, $170, $200 purchase _ #B234
Explores the nature of light as children experiment, observe, discover, and enjoy light in many different ways. Provides many visual experiences and teaches many facts about the nature of light. Explains that light is the source of heat, food, energy, light, and more.
Science - Physical
Dist - BARR **Prod** - BARR 1977

Light is right, cooking for health 60 MIN
VHS
Color (H C G)
$59.00 purchase _ #MC502
Demonstrates step - by - step a five - course, heart - healthy gourmet meal of less than 1,000 calories. Discusses the selection, preparation and presentation of the low - fat, low - calorie dishes in easy - to - understand format.
Health and Safety; Home Economics; Psychology; Social Science
Dist - AAVIM **Prod** - AAVIM 1992

Light IV - the laser and optical fibers 24 MIN
VHS / U-matic
Light series
Color (I J)
$325.00, $295.00 purchase _ #V195; LC 90-705975
Reveals that natural light is composed of different kinds of waves and photons. Considers that laser light cannot be found in nature, is produced artifically and is made up of identical photons which move in the same way and all at the same time. Part of a five - part series on light.
Fine Arts; Industrial and Technical Education; Science; Science - Physical
Dist - BARR **Prod** - GLOBET 1989

Light, Lenses and the Image 17 MIN
VHS / U-matic
Color (PRO)
Presents basic properties of lenses and their effects upon light in order to form an image on the retina. Explains the concepts of convergence and divergence. Discusses the effects of convex and concave lenses upon light rays and the ability of the lens to increase its power through the process of accommodation.
Health and Safety; Science - Natural
Dist - UMICHM **Prod** - UMICHM 1976

Light - Light and Shadows 15 MIN
U-matic / VHS
Featherby's Fables Series
Color (P)
Presents Mr Featherby who tells a story about a town that thought it was being terrorized by monsters. Shows how Captain Light finds that the culprits are shadows.
Science - Physical
Dist - GPN **Prod** - WVUTTV 1983

Light, lines and heavy fines 30 MIN
VHS
Metropolis series
Color; PAL (G)
PdS65 purchase
Presents the battle between city growth and automobile use. Traces the historical and technological evolution of modern cities. The program uses advanced graphics and dramatic recreation to reveal the hidden mechanisms that enable a metropolis to function. Part four of a six - part series.
Geography - World; Industrial and Technical Education
Dist - BBCENE

A Light Meal - 206 29 MIN
VHS
FROG series 2; Series 2; 206
Color (P I J)
$100.00 purchase
Offers the sixth program in series 2 by Friends of Research and Odd Gadgets. Lifts science off the textbook page into the real world to show how enjoyable and challenging science can be. In this episode, the Froggers wonder if it really can get so hot you could fry an egg on the sidewalk. With a little science and a little magic, lunch is served. Produced by Christopher Howard.
Home Economics; Science - Physical
Dist - BULFRG **Prod** - OWLTV 1993

Light Mechanics Series

Burnishing pivots	14 MIN
Truing Balance Wheels	14 MIN
Turning Brass with Hand Graver - Pt 1	14 MIN
Turning Brass with Hand Graver - Pt 2	11 MIN

Dist - USVA

Light Memories of Rio 33 MIN
VHS / 16mm
B&W (G)
$250.00 purchase, $55.00 rental
Examines the history of photography of in Brazil from 1839 and simultaneously traces the development of Rio de Janeiro as one of the world's major cities and a political and cultural center of Brazil. Blends computerized animation of photos by Brazil's major photographers with music by Brazilian composers of the same time to document Brazilian society, architecture, landscapes and political and social events.
Civics and Political Systems; Fine Arts; Geography - World; History - World; Industrial and Technical Education
Dist - CNEMAG **Prod** - CNEMAG 1987

The Light microscope - description, use and care 17 MIN
VHS / U-matic
Color (PRO C)
$395.00 purchase, $80.00 rental _ #C870 - VI - 040
Uses the Bausch and Lomb BB350 to demonstrate and explains each component of the compound binocular microscope and its function, and each step in its use and care. Details carefully the rationale behind each step. Presents by Dr Edith K MacRae.
Health and Safety; Science
Dist - HSCIC

Light Motif 4 MIN
16mm
Color
LC 76-703067
Shows light patterns which are variations of the sphere.
Fine Arts
Dist - CANFDC **Prod** - CANFDC 1975

The Light of Day 9 MIN
16mm
Color
LC 73-701040
Shows how color and daylight change in the environment from dawn through evening, in the city and the country.
Science - Physical; Social Science
Dist - FILMSM **Prod** - FILMSM 1972

The Light of Experience 52 MIN
U-matic / VHS / 16mm
Civilisation Series no 8; No 8
Color (J)
LC 75-708455
Surveys the development of Western civilization during the 17th century. Points out that the works of the Dutch painters - including Rembrandt, Frans Hals, Vermeer and Saenredam - show the revolutionary change in thought that replaced divine authority with experience, experiment and observation.
Fine Arts; History - World; Religion and Philosophy
Dist - FI **Prod** - BBCTV 1970

Light of Experience, the, Pt 1 24 MIN
16mm / U-matic / VHS
Civilisation Series no 8; No 8
Color (J H C)
LC 75-708455
Surveys the development of Western civilization during the 17th century. Points out that the works of the Dutch painters - including Rembrandt, Frans Hals, Vermeer and Saenredam - show the revolutionary change in thought that replaced divine authority with experience, experiment and observation.
History - World
Dist - FI **Prod** - BBCTV 1970

Light of Experience, the, Pt 2 28 MIN
16mm / U-matic / VHS
Civilisation Series no 8; No 8
Color (J H C)
LC 75-708455
Surveys the development of Western civilization during the 17th century. Points out that the works of the Dutch painters - including Rembrandt, Frans Hals, Vermeer and Saenredam - show the revolutionary change in thought that replaced divine authority with experience, experiment and observation.
History - World
Dist - FI **Prod** - BBCTV 1970

Light of Faith 33 MIN
U-matic / VHS / 16mm
Color (J)
Stars Lon Chaney and Hope Hampton in an updated variation of the Holy Grail legend.
Fine Arts
Dist - PHENIX **Prod** - HHP 1922

The Light of Faith 33 MIN
U-matic / VHS / 16mm
Color (H C A)
LC 76-703570
Previously entitled The Light In The Dark. Tells the story, without narration, of a softhearted thief, who steals a religious relic to cure a sick girl in a boardinghouse.
Fine Arts
Dist - PHENIX **Prod** - HHP 1976

Light of India 80 MIN
16mm
B&W
Presents the story of Gyandev, an outcast child who became one of India's great religious teachers. Features Indian spiritual music and religious songs.
Fine Arts; Geography - World; Religion and Philosophy; Sociology
Dist - FINDIA **Prod** - FINDIA

Light of the 21st Century 57 MIN
U-matic / VHS / 16mm
Nova Series
Color (H C A)
LC 79-701895
Investigates the use of lasers in the fields of medicine, dentistry, construction and communication. Explores possible developments in the use of lasers.
Industrial and Technical Education; Science; Science - Physical; Sociology
Dist - TIMLIF **Prod** - WGBHTV 1978

Light of the gods 28 MIN
VHS
Color (S) (ENGLISH AND GREEK)
$29.95 purchase _ #362 - 9003
Features Colleen Dewhurst who narrates the evolution of Greek art that spanned 500 years. Details the progression from the stylized stick figures of the Geometric period to the exquisitely carved and painted human images of the early - Classical era. Directed by Suzanne Bauman and shot on location, the release of this program coincided with the National Gallery of Art exhibit 'The Human Figure In Greek Art,' which toured museums across the country in 1989.
Fine Arts; History - World
Dist - FI **Prod** - NATLGL 1988

Light of the World 30 MIN
16mm
B&W (R)
Uses art and dramatized vignettes to illustrate Dr. Bob Jones' sermon; includes the story of Dr. Jones' mother's death.
Literature and Drama; Religion and Philosophy
Dist - UF **Prod** - UF

Light of Your Life 15 MIN
16mm / U-matic / VHS
Color (C A)
LC FIA68-2861
Discusses effects of glaucoma on vision and presents testing procedures which allow early discovery for remedial treatment.
Health and Safety; Science - Natural
Dist - IFB **Prod** - ISPB 1967

Light on Lasers 24 MIN
VHS / U-matic
Discovering Physics Series
Color (H C)
Defines the theory and construction of lasers in terms of the physical transitions or changes of the energy states of the atoms of lasing material and the optical geometry of the laser itself. Describes wide range of laser applications. Uses animated and computer graphics.
Industrial and Technical Education; Science - Physical
Dist - MEDIAG **Prod** - BBCTV 1983

Light on the Mountain 20 MIN
16mm
Color (J)
LC FIA66-357
Shows senior Girl Scouts from all over the United States at a roundup in Idaho. A cinema verite presentation of the behavior, the attitudes and the conversation of senior Girl Scouts from all over the United States. Without narration.
Guidance and Counseling; Physical Education and Recreation
Dist - GSUSA **Prod** - GSUSA 1965

Light Opera 3 MIN
16mm
Color (H C A)
LC 79-700121
Presents an experiment in the manipulation of light over a mylar surface in relation to a musical score.
Fine Arts
Dist - USC **Prod** - USC 1979

Light, Part 5 20 MIN
16mm
Color (H C A)
LC 78-701820
Presents a 1971 dance choreographed by Kei Takei in which a trio performs slow, liquid movements in an isolated pool of light.
Fine Arts
Dist - DANCE **Prod** - DANCE 1976

Light - play 7 MIN
16mm
Direct - on - film series
Color (G)
$15.00 rental
Demonstrates film techniques of hand - drawing, scratching and bleaching. Experiments with splicing including positive and negative images. First of three films in the Direct - on - Film series by Dirk De Bruyn.
Fine Arts
Dist - CANCIN

Light - Play Black, White, Gray 6 MIN
16mm
B&W
Illustrates the forms and relationships of the constructivist art of Moholy - nagy, leading exponent of modern design for architecture, painting, typography and theatre.
Fine Arts
Dist - RADIM **Prod** - MOHOLY

Light pressure for some heavy ideas 25 MIN
VHS
Lightly story series
Color (J H C)
$195.00 purchase
Studies the relationship of sound and light as shown in the Michaelson - Morley experiment, Planck's quantum theory, photons and Einstein's theory of relativity. Part of a four - part series on the physics and perception of light.
Science - Physical
Dist - LANDMK **Prod** - LANDMK 1992

Light Readings 20 MIN
16mm
B&W (G)
$700.00 purchase, $60.00 rental
Searches for women's voices in recorded history. Uses fragmented imagery to construct the experience of searching for what isn't there.
Fine Arts; History - World; Sociology
Dist - WMEN **Prod** - LIRHO 1978

Light Relections 15 MIN
16mm
Color
Studies the unusual effects obtained by moving, changing patterns of multi - colored lights and abstract mobiles.
Science - Physical
Dist - RADIM **Prod** - DAVISJ

Light Scattering 39 MIN
U-matic / VHS
Colloid and Surface Chemistry - Lyophilic Colloids Series
Color
Science; Science - Physical
Dist - KALMIA **Prod** - KALMIA

Light - Sensitive Materials 22 MIN
16mm
Fundamentals of Photography Series
Color
LC FIE52-1352
Discusses physics of light and color, and the classification and composition of light - sensitive materials.
Industrial and Technical Education; Science - Physical
Dist - USNAC **Prod** - USN 1948

Light series
Light I - Refraction and Reflection 24 MIN
Light II - waves, particles and photons 24 MIN
Light III - the speed of light 24 MIN
Light IV - the laser and optical fibers 24 MIN
Light V - infrared and ultraviolet radiation 24 MIN
Dist - BARR

Light Series
Lenses 10 MIN
Dist - VIEWTH

Light shaft 8 MIN
16mm
B&W (G)
$16.00 rental
Introduces filmmaker's obsession of cultivating visual ambiguities in the black theater where the ritualistic ray of light's main purpose is to reveal other places. Tampers with this process of recognition which results in ambiguities between notions of solidity and space among other things.
Fine Arts
Dist - CANCIN **Prod** - GRENIV 1975

A Light Shines in the Darkness 22 MIN
16mm
Color (I A)
Portrays the events from the Crucifixion through the Ascension climaxing the day of the Pentecost.
History - World; Religion and Philosophy
Dist - CAFM **Prod** - CAFM

Light - Site - Ings 13 MIN
VHS / 16mm
Color (G)
$150.00 purchase, $30.00 rental; LC 90712972
Documents the making of the public art piece, 'Holland Tunnel Drive - In Billboard,' a series of sequenced, painted images projected onto an 80' x 60' billboard at the entrance to Manhattan's Holland Tunnel. Raises questions about private and public spaces and the role of public art. Illustrates the preparation of the work, including the painting of glass slides by artist Leni Schwendinger.
Fine Arts; Geography - United States
Dist - CNEMAG **Prod** - CNEMAG 1990

Light Stage, Cinema, Radio, TV 30 MIN
VHS / U-matic
Afro - American Perspectives Series
Color (C)
Discusses black trends on the light stage, cinema, radio and television.
Fine Arts; History - United States
Dist - MDCPB **Prod** - MDDE

A Light still bright - the Ecumenical Patriarchate of Constantinople 57 MIN
VHS
Illuminations series
Color (G R)
#V - 1055
Documents the history of the Ecumenical Patriarchate of Constantinople, the church which serves as the spiritual headquarters of Eastern Orthodox Christianity. Tours the Patriarchate grounds. Explores the significance of the Patriarchate in Orthodox life. Available in both Greek and English - language versions, as well as in two separate half - hour parts.
Religion and Philosophy
Dist - GOTEL **Prod** - GOTEL 1990

The Light stuff 58 MIN
VHS / U-matic
Nova series
Color (H C A)
$250.00 purchase _ #HP - 5913C
Traces the evolution of the Daedalus, a 29 - foot, 68 pound gossamer plane with a wing span of 112 feet capable of cruising at only 15 miles per hour powered by the legs of a single human being. Records the flight of the Daedalus over the Aegean Sea. Part of the Nova series.
Industrial and Technical Education
Dist - CORF **Prod** - WGBHTV 1989

Light Style Gourmet Dinners - Part I
VHS
Cook for the Health of it Series
(C G)
$59.00_CA248
Shows how to prepare beef, pork, veal, and lamb in various creative ways.
Home Economics
Dist - AAVIM **Prod** - AAVIM 1989

Light Style Gourmet Dinners - Part II
VHS
Cook for the Health of it Series
(C G)
$59.00_CA249
Shows various methods for preparing beef, veal, lamb and pork.
Home Economics
Dist - AAVIM **Prod** - AAVIM 1989

A light that shines 21 MIN
VHS
Color (G R)
$12.50 purchase _ #S16065
Profiles four families whose faith brought them through crisis situations.
Guidance and Counseling; Literature and Drama; Religion and Philosophy
Dist - CPH **Prod** - LUMIS

Light - the Sun is the Source 15 MIN
VHS / U-matic
Featherby's Fables Series
Color (P)
Presents Captain Light who explains why plants need sunlight and comes to the rescue of campers and miners with his flashlight and candle.
Science - Physical
Dist - GPN **Prod** - WVUTTV 1983

A Light to Freedom 20 MIN
16mm
Color
LC FIA68-1374
Examines how the Canadian Salvation Army deals with juvenile delinquency, alcoholism, old age and prostitution.
Health and Safety; Sociology
Dist - SALVA **Prod** - SALVA

Light - Transparent, Translucent, Opaque 15 MIN
U-matic / VHS
Featherby's Fables Series
Color (P)
Tells how Captain Light is called upon to apprehend whoever has been stealing all man - made light sources in the Kingdom of Lightonia.
Science - Physical
Dist - GPN **Prod** - WVUTTV 1983

Light traps 10 MIN
16mm
Color (G)
$25.00 rental
Moves with a dance metered between the tempo of 60 cycles per second of electrified gas and camera shutter. Features manual harmonics. Produced by Louis Hock.
Fine Arts
Dist - CANCIN

Light V - infrared and ultraviolet radiation 24 MIN
VHS / U-matic
Light series
Color (I J)
$325.00, $295.00 purchase _ #V196; LC 90-705976
Examines the properties of infrared and ultraviolet light. Part of a five - part series on light.
Fine Arts; Science; Science - Physical
Dist - BARR **Prod** - GLOBET 1989

A Light Waltz 5 MIN
16mm
Color
LC 78-701491
Shows the manufacture of lights, accompanied by the music of Strauss.
Business and Economics
Dist - WEBC **Prod** - WEBC 1978

Light - Wave and Quantum Theories 13 MIN
U-matic / VHS / 16mm
Color (J H)
Introduces the accepted theory of light as consisting of both a wave motion and of discrete bundles or quanta of energy. Performs the Young's double - slit experiment to show the wave character of light. Discusses the photoelectric and Compton effects.
Science - Physical
Dist - CORF **Prod** - CORF 1961

Light waves - 30 30 MIN
VHS
Conceptual physics alive series
Color (H C)
$45.00 purchase
Explains and demonstrates wave interference and relates the phenomena to the colors seen in soap bubbles and gasoline on wet streets. Explains and demonstrates polarization. Part 30 of a 35 - part series adapted from the college and high school textbook Conceptual Physics by Professor Paul Hewitt.
Science - Physical
Dist - MMENTE **Prod** - HEWITP 1992

Light years 28 MIN
16mm
Color (G A)
$40.00 rental
Presents the work of filmmaker Gunvor Nelson. Evokes Nelson's displacement from her native Swedish culture. Uses wet ink on glass to create a constantly shifting image of a path leading to a house.
Fine Arts; Geography - World; History - United States; Industrial and Technical Education
Dist - PARART **Prod** - CANCIN 1987

Light years expanding 25 MIN
16mm
Field studies series
Color (G)
$55.00 rental
Traverses stellar distances in another of the 'Field Studies' series of collages combining live action and animation.
Fine Arts
Dist - CANCIN **Prod** - NELSOG 1987

Lighten up 37 MIN
VHS
Color (IND)
$495.00 purchase, $260.00 rental _ #AMI133
Shares tips on how employees can have fun in the workplace. Features humorist C W Metcalf with Humaerobics. Includes two videos and a hardbound copy of the book, Lighten up.
Business and Economics; Literature and Drama; Social Science
Dist - EXTR **Prod** - AMEDIA

Lighter cuisine 30 MIN
VHS
California style series
Color (H C G)
$19.95 purchase _ #IVN053V
Features expert chef instructors from the California Culinary Academy in San Francisco who share their secrets on light cuisine, California style. Part of a three - part series.
Home Economics
Dist - CAMV

Lighter - than - Air History - the Rigid Airship 45 MIN
VHS / U-matic
B&W
Examines the development of the airship between 1900 and 1947.
Industrial and Technical Education
Dist - IHF **Prod** - IHF

The Lighthouse that Never Fails 8 MIN
16mm
Color
Uses comedy to describe space flight.
Industrial and Technical Education; Science - Physical
Dist - THIOKL **Prod** - THIOKL 1961

Lighthouses of New England 30 MIN
VHS
Color (I J)
$19.95 purchase _ #ST - AT9385
Travels from Coney Island, New York, where the last civilian - operated lighthouse in the United States exists, to the rocky coast of Maine, for a nostalgic account of coastal beacons.
History - United States
Dist - INSTRU

Lighting 30 MIN
VHS / U-matic
You Can Fixit Series
Color
Demonstrates how to repair lighting.
Industrial and Technical Education
Dist - MDCPB **Prod** - WRJATV

Lighting 40 MIN
VHS
Color (G C H)
$99.00 purchase _ #DL491
Examines how lighting affects other aspects of stagecraft. Explains the use of instruments such as fresnels, ellipsoidals, and scoops. Demonstrates how lighting affects the appearance of faces and costumes.
Fine Arts
Dist - INSIM

Lighting and camera techniques series

Field production - lighting	24 MIN
Kodak master class - lighting Dances with Wolves	29 MIN
Kodak master class - lighting Dead Poets Society	28 MIN

Dist - INSTRU

Lighting and Composition 30 MIN
U-matic / VHS
What a Picture - the Complete Photography Course by John Hedgecoe 'Series Program 3
Color (H C A)
Explains the principles of composition in photographing still - life subjects in a controlled studio situation. Demonstrates the concept of depth of focus at a Normandy chateau and the challenge of photographing a wedding at an English village church.
Industrial and Technical Education
Dist - FI

Lighting and Staging Techniques for Television 100 MIN
U-matic / VHS
Color
Provides step - by - step instruction to visually exemplify the most current lighting and staging techniques essential for top quality television pictures.
Industrial and Technical Education
Dist - FIOREN **Prod** - FIOREN

Lighting Application for Video 30 MIN
U-matic / VHS
Video - a Practical Guide and more Series
Color
Provides the theory, rules and principles of video lighting. Demonstrates the creative use of backlighting, proper placement of lights and subjects on location and in the studios. Questions 'flat video lighting' precepts.
Fine Arts; Industrial and Technical Education
Dist - VIPUB **Prod** - VIPUB

Lighting in the executive offices 20 MIN
VHS
Color (H C)
$39.95 purchase _ #600210
Examines how to light a typical office situation. Shows how to mix daylight from the windows - and gelling windows - while using tungsten for fill light. Illustrates the use of patterns to create environments for a CEO. Discusses the concerns of a professional in taking equipment into the executive office and how to deal with them.
Business and Economics; Industrial and Technical Education
Dist - INSTRU

Lighting in the real world 65 MIN
VHS
Color (PRO G)
$119.00 purchase, $39.00 rental _ #624
Features cinematographer Dick Reisner who demonstrates how to use lighting gels and diffusion to solve common real - world lighting problems. Uses a series of carefully produced examples in typical studio, factory and office situations to show how to deal with combinations of daylight, incandescent and fluorescent color temperatures, how to elimiate glare, how to balance radically different levels in the same frame. Includes segments on location lighting, lighting in the studio office and studio lighting. Produced by Rosco Labs.
Industrial and Technical Education
Dist - FIRLIT

Lighting Techniques for New Sets 50 MIN
U-matic / VHS
Color
Demonstrates how to meet the special needs of TV sets specifically designed for news and weather programming.
Fine Arts; Industrial and Technical Education
Dist - FIOREN **Prod** - FIOREN

Lightly story series
Presents a four - part series on the physics and perception of light. Examines the evolving human understanding of light, light - refraction, electromagnetism, dispersion and the wave theory of light. Compares the human eye to the telescope, camera and television and looks at the relationship between light and sound.

A Glimmer of understanding	25 MIN
In a darkened room	25 MIN
Light pressure for some heavy ideas	25 MIN
Lightly story series	100 MIN
Rainbows and red skies	25 MIN

Dist - LANDMK **Prod** - LANDMK

Lightning and Precipitation Static - Causes and Effects on Aircraft - Damage and Protection 15 MIN
16mm
Color
LC 74-706484
Deals with the causes of lightning and precipitation static and tells their effect on aircraft. Focuses on damage and protection.
Industrial and Technical Education; Science - Physical
Dist - USNAC **Prod** - USN 1972

Lightning and Precipitation Static - Causes and Effects on Aircraft - Flash and Glow 19 MIN
16mm
Color
LC 74-706485
Deals with the causes of lightning and precipitation static and tells their effect on aircraft. Focuses on flash and glow.
Industrial and Technical Education; Science - Physical
Dist - USNAC **Prod** - USN 1972

Lightning and Precipitation Static - Causes and Effects on Aircraft - Future Aircraft 6 MIN
16mm
Color
LC 74-706486
Deals with the causes of lightning and precipitation static and tells their effect on aircraft. Focuses on aircraft design problems.
Industrial and Technical Education; Science - Physical
Dist - USNAC **Prod** - USN 1972

Lightning and Precipitation Static - Causes and Effects on Aircraft - Research 9 MIN
16mm
Color
LC 74-706487
Deals with the causes of lightning and precipitation static and tells their effect on aircraft. Focuses on research development and testing.
Industrial and Technical Education; Science - Physical
Dist - USNAC **Prod** - USN 1972

Lightning and Thunder 12 MIN
U-matic / VHS / 16mm
Color (I)
$295, $210 purchase _ #1668
Shows the causes of lightning and thunder and demonstrates safety practices to avoid being injured by lightning.
Health and Safety; Science - Physical
Dist - CORF

Lightning and Thunder 14 MIN
16mm / U-matic / VHS
Color (I)
LC FIA67-123
Demonstrates the time lapse between a lightning flash and the thunder that follows. Uses experiments with static electricity to show the cause of lightning. Shows safety practices against injury by lightning.
Health and Safety; Science; Science - Physical
Dist - CORF **Prod** - CORF 1967

The Lightning and Thunder Case 14 MIN
U-matic / VHS / 16mm
Simply Scientific Series
Color (P)
LC 81-700960
Demystifies the often - terrifying electrical storm and offers a set of safety rules for avoiding the dangers of lightning and thunder.
Geography - United States; Health and Safety; Science - Physical
Dist - LCOA **Prod** - LCOA 1981

Lightning Does Strike Twice 24 MIN
U-matic / VHS
Discovering Physics Series
Color (H C)
Describes some of the physical mechanisms responsible for the electrostatic charging of thunderclouds and the resulting precipitation and electrical lightning discharges. Uses animation to show conducting paths preceding lightning strikes and what to do about lightning.
Science - Physical
Dist - MEDIAG **Prod** - BBCTV 1983

The Lightning Rod Man 16 MIN
16mm / U-matic / VHS
Color (J)
Presents an adaptation of the short story by Herman Melville.
Literature and Drama
Dist - PFP **Prod** - DECHJ 1975

The Lightning Rod Thief 10 MIN
U-matic / VHS / 16mm
Color (K P)
Presents a humorous tale about a thief who steals only lightning rods and outwits two detectives who chase him from roof to roof. Ends with the thief getting a large charge.
Fine Arts; Literature and Drama
Dist - CAROUF **Prod** - GRIMP

Lightning tuning 25 MIN
VHS
Color (G A)
$39.95 purchase _ #0814
Shows how to tune the one design Lightning Class of sailboats. Provides information for other small sailboat racers. Produced by Shore Sail.
Physical Education and Recreation
Dist - SEVVID

Lightning War in the Middle East 14 MIN
16mm
Screen news digest series; Vol 10; Issue 1
B&W
LC FIA68-1654
Traces the roots of unrest that burst into conflict between Israel and Egypt in the lightning war of 1967.
History - World
Dist - HEARST **Prod** - HEARST 1967

Lightplay 28 MIN
16mm
B&W; Color (G)
$50.00 rental
Sketches a collection of ordinary activities such as biking, running, basketball, baseball, boating. Expresses a different visual temper of each particular activity. Filmed in New York's Central Park. Produced by Dave Gearey.
Fine Arts
Dist - CANCIN

Lights 24 MIN
VHS
Color (K P I)
$29.95 purchase _ #815
Uses animation to retell the Hanukah story - the struggle of a people to maintain their religious beliefs and observances in the face of adversity. Addresses the issue of religious freedom and 'the right to be different.' Voices by Paul Michael Glaser and Leonard Nimoy. Narrated by Judd Hirsch.
Fine Arts; Geography - World; Religion and Philosophy; Sociology
Dist - ERGOM **Prod** - ERGOM

Lights - a Hanukah fable 24 MIN
VHS
Color (K P I) (RUSSIAN)
$22.95 purchase _ #815
Presents an animated retelling of the Hanukah story. Addresses the struggle of a people to maintain its religious beliefs and observances in the face of adversity, as well as the issue of religious freedom and 'the right to be different.' Includes the voices of Paul Michael Glaser and Leonard Nimoy, narrated by Judd Hirsch.
Religion and Philosophy; Sociology
Dist - ERGOM

Lights, Action, Africa 55 MIN
16mm
Color
LC 83-700122
Portrays how photographers Joan and Alan Root photograph such unpredictable animals as cobras, wildebeests and hippos.
Geography - World; Industrial and Technical Education; Science - Natural
Dist - BNCHMK **Prod** - ROOTA 1983

Lights Breaking - Ethical Questions about Genetic Engineering 59 MIN
U-matic / VHS
Color (J H C A)
Features genetic engineering, where the manipulation of life forms at their most basic known level will be possible, where creation of new life forms will be a matter of will. Engaging in a series of conversations and images about the achievements and consequences of this biotechnology are three world class scientists, a poet, a theologian, and an ordinary citizen.
Religion and Philosophy; Science - Natural; Sociology
Dist - BULFRG **Prod** - CUSACK 1986

Lights, Camera, Lettuce 28 MIN
16mm
Color
LC 74-700546
Deals with the growing, harvesting, packing, care, preparation and varied uses of lettuce.
Agriculture; Home Economics; Social Science
Dist - MTP **Prod** - MTP 1973

Lights, Cameras, Accidents 20 MIN
VHS / U-matic
$335.00 purchase
Fine Arts
Dist - ABCLR **Prod** - ABCLR 1983

Lights have Limits 5 MIN
16mm
Driver Education Series
B&W (J)
LC FIA66-1005
Shows the blinding effect of high beam lights and the limitation of low beam lights. Tackles the problem of overdriving the headlights.
Health and Safety
Dist - AMROIL **Prod** - AMROIL 1964

Lights Running and Anchor 18 MIN
16mm
B&W
LC FIE52-933
Shows inland and international rules for color of lights, position and visibility for masthead, side, range and anchor lights and lights displayed by vessels being overtaken.
Civics and Political Systems; Health and Safety; Social Science
Dist - USNAC **Prod** - USN 1944

Lights, Vessels Being Towed 10 MIN
16mm
Color
LC FIE52-936
Gives inland light rules for barges and canal boats, scow barges, scows and nondescript vessels in New York harbor area and dump scows in new York harbor.
Civics and Political Systems; Health and Safety; Social Science
Dist - USNAC **Prod** - USN 1943

Lightweight lasagna 30 MIN
VHS
Richard Simmons slim cooking series
Color (H C G)
$19.95 purchase _ #FFO353V
Demonstrates step - by - step procedures for low - fat, high - flavor lasagna. Part of six - part series featuring Richard Simmons' health cuisine.
Home Economics
Dist - CAMV

Ligia Elena 7 MIN
16mm / VHS
Color (G)
$185.00, $160.00 purchase, $25.00 rental
Tells the tale of a young girl who disappoints her parents when she gets involved with a black trumpet player. Presents a put - down of consumerism, snobbery and racism. Produced by Francisco Lopez. Based on a song by Ruben Blades.
Psychology; Sociology
Dist - FIRS

Ligne D'Eau 8 MIN
16mm
Color (G)
$25.00 rental
Presents a first sketch of a new work staging the movements of objects and machines. By Yann Beauvais. Requires two projectors.
Fine Arts
Dist - CANCIN

Like a Beautiful Child 26 MIN
16mm
Color (A)
Reviews the struggle of hospital workers in New York to organize a union and improve wages that were less than welfare checks. Expresses what the union means to its members.
Business and Economics; Psychology
Dist - AFLCIO **Prod** - AFLCIO 1967

Like a prayer 30 MIN
U-matic / VHS
Color (G)
Offers seven perspectives on the ACTUP - WHAM demonstration in December, 1990, at St Patrick's Cathedral in New York City which protested the policies of Cardinal O'Connor on AIDS, birth control, reproductive rights and lesbian and gay rights.
Health and Safety; History - United States; Religion and Philosophy; Sociology
Dist - ACTUP **Prod** - DIVATV 1991

Like a roaring lion 46 MIN
VHS
Color (J H T PRO)
$149.00 purchase _ #AH45207
Tells the story of 16 - year - old Cathy Chambers, who wants to 'fit in' as the new kid in town. Shows that she faces a great deal of negative peer pressure to have sex, drink and try drugs. Provides guidance for saying no to peer pressure and in decision - making tactics.
Guidance and Counseling; Health and Safety; Psychology; Sociology
Dist - HTHED **Prod** - HTHED

Like a Rose 23 MIN
16mm
B&W
LC 75-703518
Focuses on the lonely and frustrating existence of two women currently serving 25 - year sentences in the Missouri State Penitentiary.
Geography - United States; Sociology
Dist - TOMATO **Prod** - TOMATO 1975

Like Any Child Only more So 29 MIN
U-matic / VHS / 16mm
Color (C A)
LC 78-701764
Profiles three families with children labeled as hyperactive. Presents the complex emotional, medical and environmental possibilities that may influence a child's behavior. Shows troublesome symptoms of hyperactivity as well as problems resulting from misunderstanding and mistreating the symptoms.
Psychology; Sociology
Dist - UCEMC **Prod** - ALLORN 1978

Like any other patient 26 MIN
VHS / U-matic
Color (A PRO)
$55.00, $110.00 purchase _ #TCA18034, #TCA18033
Interviews four patients with AIDS or HIV infection, and the wife of an AIDS patient. Discusses their reactions to their diagnoses, experiences with the health care system, and what they and their families want from health care providers. Designed for all employees at Veterans' Administration health care facilities. Includes a companion 44 - page book.
Health and Safety; Social Science
Dist - USNAC **Prod** - VAMCSL 1989

Like as the Lute 37 MIN
16mm
Color (H A)
$720.00 purchase, $60.00 rental
Follows Anthony Rooley, a new wave British lutenist who is reviving early music in Europe. Explores traditional lutecraft through visits and concerts with London lutemakers and Cairooud makers, scholars, concert performers and street musicians.
Fine Arts
Dist - AFA **Prod** - ACGB 1980

Like Cats and Dogs 23 MIN
U-matic / VHS
Color
Focuses on bobcats and coyotes and how different they are from domestic pets, but how much they are the same.
Science - Natural
Dist - NWLDPR **Prod** - NWLDPR

Like Coming to a New World 17 MIN
16mm
Color
LC 80-701570
Presents post - war migrants describing their lives in Australia.
Geography - World; Sociology
Dist - TASCOR **Prod** - NESWE 1979

Like Everybody Else 32 MIN
U-matic / VHS / 16mm
Color (H C A S)
LC 77-700735
Documents the life of the retarded adult in the community, showing a model program for achieving integration of retarded adults in society.
Health and Safety; Psychology; Sociology
Dist - STNFLD **Prod** - JLA 1976

Like Father, Like Son 15 MIN
16mm
Jackson Junior High Series
Color (J)
LC 76-704029
Shows how a son tries to approach the problem of alcoholism with his father, who is a problem drinker. Suggests methods of rehabilitation and sources of help.
Health and Safety; Psychology; Sociology
Dist - USNAC **Prod** - USOLLR 1976

Like it is Series

Assertive learning	29 MIN
Brown, Tony - Black Perspective on the News	30 MIN
Carmichael, Stokely	29 MIN
Cunningham, Reverend J F	29 MIN
Evans, Dr Thurman, M D	29 MIN
Gillespie, Marcia Ann	28 MIN
Green, Dr Robert	29 MIN
Hollis, Meldon	30 MIN
Johnson, Minnie	29 MIN
Jones, Dr Johnny	29 MIN
McGee, James - Dale Bertch	29 MIN
Mitchell, Parren	29 MIN
Moss, Reverend Otis	29 MIN
Page, Dr Joyce	29 MIN
Poussaint, Alvin	30 MIN
Robinson, Wilhelmena	29 MIN
Survival of the Black College	29 MIN
Wesley, Charles	29 MIN
Whitley, Joyce	29 MIN
Williams, Robert	29 MIN

Dist - HRC

Like it is - the Environment of Poverty, Pt 1 30 MIN
16mm
B&W (T)
Depicts the degenerating environment of poverty and how it warps and eventually destroys the human resources trapped in it. Reveals that a fouled environment not only impairs the physical fate of future generations, but also systematically infests and rots hearts, minds, values and hopes, dooming the poor even before they are born.
Psychology; Sociology
Dist - MLA **Prod** - MLA

Like it is - the Environment of Poverty, Pt 2 30 MIN
16mm
B&W (T)
Depicts the degenerating environment of poverty and how it warps and eventually destroys the human resources trapped in it. Reveals that a fouled environment not only impairs the physical fate of future generations, but also systematically infests and rots hearts, minds, values and hopes, dooming the poor even before they are born.
Psychology; Sociology
Dist - MLA **Prod** - MLA

Like it is - the Environment of Poverty, Pt 3 23 MIN
16mm
B&W (T)
Depicts the degenerating environment of poverty and how it warps and eventually destroys the human resources trapped in it. Reveals that a fouled environment not only impairs the physical fate of future generations, but also systematically infests and rots hearts, minds, values and hopes, dooming the poor even before they are born.
Psychology; Sociology
Dist - MLA **Prod** - MLA

Like Jake and me 15 MIN
U-matic / 16mm / VHS
Color (I)
$400.00, $280.00 purchase _ #JC - 67247
Adapts the book 'Like Jake and Me' by Mavis Jukes. Considers the issues of male roles in the story of a very sensitive and analytical ten - year - old boy who wants and needs the attention of his strong 'cowboy' stepfather. To complicate matters, Alex's mother is nine months pregnant with twins.
Literature and Drama; Sociology
Dist - CORF **Prod** - DISNEY 1981

Like Jake and Me
VHS / 35mm strip
Newbery Award - Winners Series
Color (I)
$35.00 purchase
English Language; Literature and Drama
Dist - PELLER

Like no Other Place Series

The Concrete Corridor	29 MIN
Fifty cents of every dollar	29 MIN
A Frontier, a Homeland	29 MIN
Grain - beyond the farmer's control	29 MIN
The Great black hope	29 MIN
Hook, line and limit	29 MIN
Newfoundland - You Can't Buy Freedom	29 MIN
P E I - the Million Acre Farm	29 MIN
Price of Power	29 MIN
Tuktoyaktuk - a Piece of the Action	29 MIN
Where have all the Cowboys Gone	29 MIN
Without an Industry, Without a Highway	29 MIN

Dist - TVOTAR

Like Ordinary Children 25 MIN
16mm / U-matic / VHS
Color (H C A)
Presents the viewpoint of a normal fourteen - year - old girl who visits handicapped children each week and contrasts it with those of a bright thirteen - year - old girl who has been handicapped since birth with a spinal deformity, Spina Bifida. Conveys the feelings and difficulties of the handicapped and of those who meet them.
Education; Psychology
Dist - MEDIAG **Prod** - THAMES 1973

Like Other People 37 MIN
U-matic / VHS / 16mm
Color (PRO)
LC 74-702340
Shows and discusses the feelings and attitudes of a group of physically handicapped people in an English institution for the handicapped. Emphasizes the fact that physically handicapped people have the same feelings and needs as normal people.
Education; Guidance and Counseling; Health and Safety; Psychology; Sociology
Dist - PEREN **Prod** - MHFC 1973

Like the Wind 59 MIN
U-matic
Color
Examines individual religious experience in America. Presents the stories of five people from different religious backgrounds who all share a deep spiritual commitment.
Religion and Philosophy; Sociology
Dist - PBS **Prod** - PPTN

Like two peas in a pod 55 MIN
VHS
Color (H C G)
$445.00 purchase, $75.00 rental
Focuses on three sets of identical twins in Quebec. Reveals that Luc and John feel an intense bond of affection and interests that to some degree excludes even their wives. Louis and Alphonse never married and continue to live together very harmoniously. Christiane and Christine, troubled by their interdependency, decided it was best to establish separate identities, and Christiane fell in love for the first time. Produced by Diane LeTourneau.
Sociology
Dist - FLMLIB **Prod** - NFBC 1991

Like water into sand 8 MIN
16mm
B&W; Color (G)
$24.00 rental
Illuminates a daughter's experience with her mother's suicide and her struggle with this final separation. Attempts to speak aloud poetically in the silence demanded by convention. Visual texture provided by underwater imagery, optical printing, 'bleached' color that fades and other techniques to enhance symbolic imagery. Produced by Susanne Fairfax.
Fine Arts; Sociology
Dist - CANCIN

Like who you are, be you - Volume 13 30 MIN
VHS
Our friends on Wooster Square series
Color (K P I R)
$34.95 purchase, $10.00 rental _ #35 - 87262 - 460
Presents religious concepts through storylines, songs and Scripture. Features puppet characters including Smedly, Troll and Sizzle.
Fine Arts; Literature and Drama; Religion and Philosophy
Dist - APH **Prod** - FRACOC

Like You, Dad - Wellness - 10 15 MIN
VHS
Your Choice - Our Chance Series
Color (I)
$180.00 purchase
Focuses on knowledge, attitudes and behaviors that influence drug free and drug use life styles. Emphasizes that effective drug abuse prevention education must begin before children are established users of tobacco, alcohol or other addictive drugs. Targets children in the vulnerable preteen years. Program 10 shows that Amy and Carol, worried about their father's smoking and sedentary habits, conspire with their mother to plan an active vacation, but Richard, their brother, demonstrates that Dad's habits are a model for him.
Guidance and Counseling; Health and Safety; Psychology; Sociology
Dist - AITECH **Prod** - AITECH 1990

Like You, Like Me Series

Doing things together - a child with a prosthetic hand	6 MIN
Everyone needs some help - a child with speech and hearing impairment	7 MIN
I Can do it - a Child with Double Braces	6 MIN
It's Up to Me - a Child with Asthma	7 MIN
Let Me Try - a Mentally Retarded Child	6 MIN
Let's be Friends - an Emotionally Disturbed Child	6 MIN
Let's Talk it Over - a Child with Epilepsy	6 MIN
See what I Feel - a Blind Child	6 MIN
When I Grow Up - Career Aspirations	6 MIN
Why Me - an Orthopedically Handicapped Child	7 MIN

Dist - EBEC

Liking Me - Building Self - Confidence
VHS / U-matic
Color (I J)
Examines the concept of self - esteem and its importance in school performance, in resisting peer pressure, and in coping with life. Includes teacher's guide.
Guidance and Counseling; Psychology; Sociology
Dist - SUNCOM **Prod** - SUNCOM

Liking yourself with no strings attached - self esteem 25 MIN
VHS
At - risk students video series
Color (I J H)
$98.00 purchase _ #AHV406
Looks at what makes people feel good and bad about themselves. Summarizes specific tips for building unconditional positive self esteem. Features students and teachers from The Tree of Learning School in Portland, Oregon. Includes a reproducible discussion guide with worksheets. Part of a five - part series on students at risk.
Health and Safety; Psychology; Sociology
Dist - CADESF **Prod** - CADESF 1990

Lil' Abner 78 MIN
16mm
B&W
Presents the comic strip Lil' Abner on the screen starring Buster Keaton, Granville Owen and Martha O'Driscoll.
Fine Arts
Dist - FCE **Prod** - FCE 1940

Lil Picard 30 MIN
VHS
Color (G)
$50.00 rental, $35.00 purchase
Presents Lil Picard, outrageous art world personality, telling her life story which reflects the history of the times. Records Picard's candid personal revelations as well as her career as a journalist and artist. Produced by Silvianna Goldsmith.
Fine Arts
Dist - CANCIN

Lil Picard, art is a party 10 MIN
VHS
Color (G)
$20.00 rental, $35.00 purchase
Records Lil Picard's 75th birthday party. Features attendance by all of the 'art world.' Produced by Silvianna Goldsmith.
Fine Arts
Dist - CANCIN

Lila 28 MIN
16mm
Color
$450 rental
Discusses the activities of 80 - year - old Lila Bonner - Miller as a psychiatrist, an artist, and a church leader. Discusses women's struggle for professional respect in their chosen work.
Health and Safety; Sociology
Dist - CCNCC IDIM **Prod** - CCNCC 1985

Lilac Time 27 MIN
16mm
History of the Motion Picture Series
B&W
Presents Colleen Moore and Gary Cooper in a melodrama of World War I pilots.
Fine Arts; History - World
Dist - KILLIS **Prod** - SF

L'Ile De La Cite 12 MIN
16mm / U-matic / VHS
Sejour En France Series
Color (J H C) (FRENCH)
LC 72-702104
A French language film. Dramatizes a situation in which an American girl and her French friend sightsee on the Ile St Louis.
Foreign Language
Dist - IFB **Prod** - IFB 1971

Lilias - alive with yoga 60 MIN
VHS
Color (G)
$39.95 purchase
Features Hatha Yoga expert Lilias Folan in two practice sessions teaching breathing exercises and yoga postures.
Physical Education and Recreation
Dist - PBS **Prod** - WNETTV

Lilias - alive with yoga - Volumes 1 and 2 120 MIN
VHS
Color (H C A)
$54.95 purchase
Features Lilias Folan in two courses in hatha yoga, one for beginners and one for more intermediate students. Each course also available separately, for $29.95 apiece.
Health and Safety; Physical Education and Recreation
Dist - YOGAJ **Prod** - YOGAJ

Lilies Grow Wild 16 MIN
16mm
Color
LC 80-700426
Presents a drama about the unsuccessful effort of a new teacher to impose discipline on an unruly student. Relates her discovery that love and personal attention are stronger than force.
Education
Dist - BYU **Prod** - BYU 1980

Lilies of Japan 28 MIN
16mm
Color
Explains that the Japanese have always felt a close affinity with nature and this is especially true with flowers. Points out that the lily is one flower which grows in abundance throughout Japan. Depicts the many different kinds of lilies which grow in Japan and the significance of this flower in the daily lives of the people.
Geography - World; Science - Natural; Social Science; Sociology
Dist - UNIJAP **Prod** - UNIJAP 1969

Lilies of the Field 94 MIN
U-matic / VHS / 16mm
B&W
Presents a story about ex - GI Homer Smith, who encounters five nuns attempting to farm some barren Arizona acreage. Stars Sidney Poitier and Lilia Skala.
Fine Arts
Dist - FI **Prod** - UAA 1963

Lilith 155 MIN
U-matic / VHS / 16mm
B&W (C A)
Stars Warren Beatty, Jean Seberg and Peter Fonda in the story of a girl who has created a world of her own.
Fine Arts
Dist - FI **Prod** - CPC 1964

The Lilith Summer 28 MIN
16mm / VHS
Color (I J H A)
Describes how an eleven - year - old girl and a 77 - year - old woman overcome their initial resentments and develop a sincere affection for each other. Based on the novel by Hadley Irwin. Available on laser disc.
Literature and Drama
Dist - AIMS APH **Prod** - WILETS 1985

Lillehei on Stagnant Shock 21 MIN
16mm
Upjohn Vanguard of Medicine Series
Color (PRO)
LC 73-702448
Presents visual evidence to support the concept of treating shock with vasodilators, rather than vasopressors, by utilizing cinemicrography of the mesentary microcirculation in living animals. Includes a demonstration of the step - by - step management of a patient in stagnant endotoxin shock secondary to abortion.
Health and Safety
Dist - UPJOHN **Prod** - UPJOHN 1968

Lillian Vernon - Making it in Mail Order 30 MIN
VHS / 16mm
(PRO G)
$89.95 purchase _ #DGP4
Tells the story of Lillian Vernon and her succes in mail order business. Gives tips for newcomers. Hosted by Dick Goldberg.
Business and Economics
Dist - RMIBHF **Prod** - RMIBHF

Lillies Grow Wild 16 MIN
16mm
Color (J H A)
LC 80-700426
Emphasizes that everyone is important. Shows how a rebellious boy is affected positively by the love and attention of a teacher.
Education; Guidance and Counseling; Psychology; Sociology
Dist - EBEC **Prod** - BYU 1981

Lilliput in Antarctica 48 MIN
VHS
Jacques Cousteau series
Color; CC (G)
$19.95 purchase _ #3043
Joins Jacques Cousteau and six children from around the world on a spectacular odyssey to Antarctica. Views huge glaciers, humpback whales, penguins and elephant seals. Part of a series by Cousteau featuring narration by actors and actresses who speak American English.
Geography - World; Science - Natural
Dist - APRESS

Lillith Summer
16mm / U-matic / VHS
Color (I J)
Tells the story of an unlikely friendship between a young girl and an old woman. Shows their developing understanding and acceptance of the many stages of life. Based on the novel by Irwin Hadley.
Literature and Drama; Sociology
Dist - AIMS **Prod** - PAR 1984

Lilly Dale - Messages from the spirit side of life 28 MIN
VHS
Color (G)
$250.00 purchase, $50.00 rental
Portrays Lily Dale, New York, one of America's oldest spiritualist communities, where just about everyone is a psychic or a medium who claims to communicate with the dead. Includes interviews and records their private readings, public healings and outdoor services. Directed by Andy Biskin.
Fine Arts; Religion and Philosophy; Sociology
Dist - CNEMAG

Lilly's World of Wax 28 MIN
VHS
Color (G)
$35.00 rental, $50.00 purchase
Presents Lilly who ran the 'World in Wax Musee' at Coney Island for 54 years until her retirement. Leads the viewer on a tour, narrated by Lilly, of the museum which is being dismantled to auction off its contents. Lilly insists on looking into the camera as she delivers her absurd and touching stories about the figures.
Fine Arts; History - United States
Dist - CANCIN **Prod** - PALAZT 1987

Lilting towards chaos 21 MIN
16mm
Color (G)
$40.00 rental
Chronicles a three - year period of the filmmaker's life. Attempts to capture his solipsism and self - centered introspection, emotions and dealings with the outside world. Invites the viewer to determine which musings are honest and useful and those which are circuitous and self - defeating.
Fine Arts; Literature and Drama; Psychology
Dist - CANCIN **Prod** - STREEM 1990

Lily - a Story about a Girl Like Me 14 MIN
16mm
Color
LC 78-700196
Documents the daily life of a ten - year - old girl with Down's Syndrome. Shows how a mentally retarded child can develop when raised in a normal home environment and taught in a regular classroom.
Education; Psychology
Dist - DAVFMS **Prod** - GRACEE 1977

Lily May Ledford 29 MIN
VHS / 16mm
Color (G)
$100.00 purchase _ #LEDFOVH
Utilizes interviews and performance footage to tell the story of Lily May Ledford, who led the first all - woman band on radio. Highlights Ledford's time in the early days of radio and her years growing up.
Fine Arts; Sociology
Dist - APPAL

Lily pad pond 10 MIN
U-matic / 16mm / VHS
Wild places series
Color (P)
$290.00, $250.00 purchase _ #HP - 6070C
Provides a close look at pond ecology. Surveys a pond from the surface to the bottom to discover a wealth of life. Shows the interaction of plants and animals which form an ecological balance. Part of a series teaching about different kinds of habitats which show how living things adapt to varying environments and how each creature depends upon others for existence. Produced by Partridge Film and Video, Ltd.
Science - Natural
Dist - CORF

Lima Family 19 MIN
16mm
B&W
LC FIE52-719
Depicts a day in the lives of the members of an upper class family of Lima, capital of Peru. Points out similarities to a family of the same class in the United States.
Geography - World; Social Science
Dist - USOIAA **Prod** - UWF 1944

The Limbic system - Part IV 27 MIN
VHS / U-matic
Gross anatomy of the human brain series
Color (PRO C)
$395.00 purchase, $80.00 rental _ #C901 - VI - 049
Focuses on the limbic system in part four of a four - part series on the gross anatomy of the brain. Presented by Dr Walter J Handelman, Department of Anatomy, Faculty of Medicine, University of Ottawa.
Health and Safety; Science - Natural
Dist - HSCIC

Limbic System, the, Pt I 60 MIN
U-matic
Nonbehavioral Sciences and Rehabilitation Series Part VIII
Color (PRO)
Presents terminology, major structures of the limbic lobe and associated structures composing the limbic system.
Psychology; Science - Natural
Dist - AOTA **Prod** - AOTA 1980

Limbic System, the, Pt II 60 MIN
U-matic
Nonbehavioral Sciences and Rehabilitation Series Part VIII
Color (PRO)
Shows limbic circuitry and function including behavioral substrates and major limbic system syndromes.
Psychology; Science - Natural
Dist - AOTA **Prod** - AOTA 1980

Limboid 25 MIN
16mm
Color (G)
$40.00 rental
Mixes lyrical, comical and disturbing symbolic imagery to illuminate this dreamlike narrative of a woman painter's transformation. Invites comparison between defensiveness and vulnerability. Produced by Steve Mobia.
Fine Arts
Dist - CANCIN

Limelight 144 MIN
VHS
B&W (G)
$29.98 purchase _ #S00251
Features Charlie Chaplin in a rare dramatic role as a failed comedian who helps a young dancer to stardom. Set before 1914 in the atmosphere of the London Music Hall. Co - stars Claire Bloom, Buster Keaton, and Nigel Bruce.
Fine Arts; Literature and Drama
Dist - UILL
RMIBHF

Limericks for Laughs 15 MIN
U-matic / VHS
Tyger, Tyger Burning Bright Series
Color (I)
Uses the limerick to demonstrate the uses of meter, rhyme, repetition and rhythm in poetry.
English Language; Literature and Drama
Dist - CTI **Prod** - CTI

Limestone 13 MIN
U-matic / VHS / 16mm
Color (I J)
LC 78-701137
Explains and simulates the formation of sedimentary rock, focusing on the importance of limestone as a natural resource. Shows how the rock is quarried and enumerates its major uses.
Science - Physical; Social Science
Dist - IU **Prod** - IU 1978

Limestone 16 MIN
VHS
Color; PAL (P I J)
PdS29
Compares and contrasts two major limestone areas, the oolitic limestone belt, especially the Bath and Corby areas, and the carboniferous limestone of the Pennine Hills. Introduces karst scenery. Shows other carboniferous limestone areas on a map.
Geography - World; Science - Physical
Dist - BHA

Limestone 20 MIN
U-matic / VHS
Chemistry in Action Series
Color (C)
$249.00, $149.00 purchase _ #AD - 1277
Looks at the industrial processing of limestone, calcium carbonate, into gravel for roadbuilding, sodium carbonate for glass - making, sand for quicklime and cement powder.
Industrial and Technical Education; Science - Physical
Dist - FOTH **Prod** - FOTH

Limestone - Iowa's Buried Treasure 26 MIN
16mm
Color
LC 74-700413
Explains the origin of limestone and shows mining and processing methods. Contrasts present rehabilitation methods with earlier practices, emphasizing the economic importance of limestone and suggesting the compatibility of mining and agriculture.
Geography - United States; Industrial and Technical Education
Dist - IOWA **Prod** - IOWALP 1974

The Limestone Legacy, Nature's Gift to Mankind 27 MIN
16mm
Color
LC 76-700378
Shows the many uses of limestone in construction, agriculture and industry, as well as in the home. Describes the geology and mining of limestone.
Industrial and Technical Education; Science - Physical; Social Science
Dist - UMO **Prod** - MOLPA 1975

Limestones 24 MIN
VHS / 16mm
Earth's Physical Resources Series
Color (S)
$200.00 purchase _ #236203
Presents a global view of the earth's resource potential. Features footage filmed in Britain, Europe and North America. 'Limestones' highlights the geological factors involved in the formation of the four major groups of limestone quarried in the United Kingdom. Demonstrates the chemical and physical properties of this raw material and its changing uses over time through maps and filmed segments of limestone ridges, quarries, buildings and manufacturing processes.
Business and Economics; Geography - World; Industrial and Technical Education; Science - Physical; Social Science
Dist - ACCESS **Prod** - BBCTV 1984

Limit 10 MIN
16mm
MAA Calculus Series
Color (H C)
LC 72-703521
Defines limit by the use of neighborhoods and illustrates use of the definition with examples of real valued functions of a single real variable in both continuous and discontinuous cases. An animated film narrated by Robert C Fisher.
Mathematics
Dist - MLA **Prod** - MAA 1967

Limit Curves and Curves of Infinite Length 14 MIN
U-matic / VHS / 16mm
Topology Short Films Series

Color (C A)
LC 81-700614
Describes the construction of limit curves from a sequence of approximation curves. Demonstrates that two of these curves have infinite length.
Mathematics
Dist - IFB **Prod** - IFB 1979

Limit curves and curves of infinite length 14 MIN
U-matic / VHS / BETA
Color; Silent; PAL (G H C)
PdS35, PdS43 purchase
Describes the construction of limit curves from a sequence of approximation curves by using computer - animated shorts. Includes Limit Curves I - The Circle; Limit Curves II - The Snowflake Curve; Limit Curves III - An Invalid Case; Limit Curves IV - Peano's Curve; Limit Curves V - Sierpinski's Curve; Curves of Infinite Length I - The Snowflake Curve; and Curves of Infinite Length II - Peano's Curve.
Industrial and Technical Education; Mathematics
Dist - EDPAT

Limit series
Explores limits of human achievement in engineering, focusing on international engineers facing their toughest career assignments. Asks how far physical limits can be pushed and what restraints exist in extending the scale of engineering projects.
Big plane 30 MIN
Deep tunnel 30 MIN
Fast ship 30 MIN
Long span 30 MIN
Space robot 30 MIN
Tall tower 30 MIN
Dist - BBCENE

Limit Surfaces and Space Filling Curves 11 MIN
U-matic / VHS / 16mm
Topology Short Films Series
Color (C A)
LC 81-700616
Gives four examples of infinite constructions in two and three dimensions.
Mathematics
Dist - IFB **Prod** - IFB 1979

Limit Switches, Torque Switches 60 MIN
U-matic / VHS
Electrtical Maintenance Training, Module 1 - Control Equipment 'Series
Color (IND)
Industrial and Technical Education
Dist - LEIKID **Prod** - LEIKID

The Limit Theorem 20 MIN
VHS
Calculus Series
Color (H)
LC 90712920
Discusses the limit theorem. The second of 57 installments in the Calculus Series.
Mathematics
Dist - GPN

Limit Theorems
U-matic
Calculus Series
Color
Mathematics
Dist - MDCPB **Prod** - MDDE

Limitations 30 MIN
VHS / U-matic
Pascal, Pt 2 - Intermediate Pascal Series
Color (H C A)
LC 81-706049
Reviews the primary problem areas that first - time Pascal users encounter. Goes over list of reasons for choosing Pascal along with major limitations in using Pascal in serious programming environments.
Industrial and Technical Education; Mathematics; Sociology
Dist - COLOSU **Prod** - COLOSU 1980

Limitations 30 MIN
VHS
Perspectives - natural science - series
Color; PAL; NTSC (G)
PdS90, PdS105 purchase
Looks at the ability of advanced microscopy to see deeper and deeper.
Science - Natural
Dist - CFLVIS **Prod** - LONTVS

Limitations of Heat Treatment 45 MIN
BETA / VHS / U-matic
Color
$400 purchase
Designs to minimize cracking and distortion. Shows types of cracking during heat treatment, including causes and prevention.
Science; Science - Physical
Dist - ASM **Prod** - ASM

Limited liability companies - Organization, taxation and development 210 MIN
VHS
Color (A PRO C)
$150.00, $200.00 purchase _ #M956, #P289
Explores many of the emerging issues in forming and using LLCs. Provides guidance on how to review the existing and new legislation in order to understand the comparative benefits of each act, and how to advise clients on the formation and operation of LLCs in a variety of situations. Study materials include a sample operating agreement, checklist and outlines.
Business and Economics; Civics and Political Systems
Dist - ALIABA **Prod** - ALIABA 1993

Limited Offer to Purchase 7 MIN
16mm
Color
LC 80-700909
Gives an explanation of the Australian Wool Corporation's 'Limited Offer to Purchase' scheme.
Business and Economics; Home Economics
Dist - TASCOR **Prod** - TASCOR 1977

The Limited Slip Differential - Pinion Operation and Service 10 MIN
VHS / 35mm strip
(H A IND)
#428XV7
Includes a Study Guide.
Education; Industrial and Technical Education
Dist - BERGL

Limits, a Formal Approach
U-matic
Calculus Series
Color
Mathematics
Dist - MDCPB **Prod** - MDDE

Limits, an Informal Approach
U-matic
Calculus Series
Color
Mathematics
Dist - MDCPB **Prod** - MDDE

Limits and continuity 30 MIN
VHS
Calculus series
Color (C)
$125.00 purchase _ #6005
Explains limits and continuity. Part of a 56 - part series on calculus.
Mathematics
Dist - LANDMK **Prod** - LANDMK

Limits and Continuity 30 MIN
VHS
Mathematics Series
Color (J)
LC 90713155
Discusses limits and continuity. The 114th of 157 installments in the Mathematics Series.
Mathematics
Dist - GPN

Limits and discipline techniques - Volume 5 60 MIN
VHS
Creative discipline series
Color (G A R)
$10.00 rental _ #36 - 85 - 1
Outlines limits for child discipline. Focuses on discipline techniques. Hosted by Dr Robert A Rausch.
Psychology; Sociology
Dist - APH **Prod** - ABINGP

Limits and Infinity
U-matic
Calculus Series
Color
Mathematics
Dist - MDCPB **Prod** - MDDE

Limits at Infinity 20 MIN
VHS
Calculus Series
Color (H)
LC 90712920
Discusses limits at infinity. The third of 57 installments of the Calculus Series.
Mathematics
Dist - GPN

Limits of Physical Force 19 MIN
16mm / U-matic / VHS
Police Civil Liability Series Part 3
Color
LC 79-701698
Explains how, when, and to what extent a police officer may use physical force. Covers topics such as the use and abuse of the police baton, flashlight and gunbelt.

Civics and Political Systems
Dist - CORF **Prod** - HAR 1979

The Limits of politics 30 MIN
VHS
America in perspective - US history since 1877 series
Color (H C G)
$99.00 purchase _ #AIP - 22
Describes the rise and fall of the 'imperial presidency.' Analyzes the significance of the Watergate scandal. Part of a 26 - part series.
Biography; Civics and Political Systems; History - United States
Dist - INSTRU **Prod** - DALCCD 1991

The Limits of power 30 MIN
VHS
America in perspective - US history since 1877 series
Color (H C G)
$99.00 purchase _ #AIP - 21
Examines the reasons why the United States engaged in the Vietnam War and why the nation eventually withdrew. Analyzes the effects of that conflict on the American people and policy makers. Part of a 26 - part series.
Civics and Political Systems; History - United States
Dist - INSTRU **Prod** - DALCCD 1991

Limits on the zeal of representation 25 MIN
VHS
Understanding modern ethical standards series
Color (C PRO)
#UEX03
Analyzes the American Bar Association's Model Rules of Professional Conduct. Emphasizes the limits on the zeal of representation, applying ABA standards to both attorneys and paralegals. Available only in series form for sale or rental.
Civics and Political Systems
Dist - NITA **Prod** - NITA 1985

Limits to Growth 30 MIN
U-matic / VHS / 16mm
Color (J)
Explores the fact that unless we control our world's population growth, its energy use, food in the Third World and pollution, a catastrophe will occur within this century. According to this study of world economic development, stability can be achieved only when economic growth is ended.
Business and Economics; Social Science; Sociology
Dist - MEDIAG **Prod** - THAMES 1972

Limits using continuity 30 MIN
VHS
Calculus series
Color (C)
$125.00 purchase _ #6036
Explains limits using continuity. Part of a 56 - part series on calculus.
Mathematics
Dist - LANDMK **Prod** - LANDMK

L'Immortelle 95 MIN
16mm
B&W (C A)
LC 75-707876
A mystery - drama in which a French professor goes in search of a woman with whom he once had a brief affair.
Fine Arts
Dist - GROVE **Prod** - COMOF 1969

LIMN I - III 17 MIN
16mm
Color (G)
$40.00 purchase
Features improvised edits where the subject is human gesture as the trace of sentiment and perception. Uses brief commonplace images. Produced by Konrad Steiner.
Fine Arts; Literature and Drama; Psychology
Dist - CANCIN

LIMN IV 13 MIN
16mm
Color (G A)
$35.00 rental
Presents the work of filmmaker Konrad Steiner. Refers the word 'limn' to the illumination of manuscripts with gold leaf. Offers tonal images of soft scarlet and yellow ochre and a sense of looking at a world which is up close.
Fine Arts; Industrial and Technical Education
Dist - PARART **Prod** - CANCIN 1988

L'Impressionnisme Et Le Neo - Impressionnisme 22 MIN
U-matic / VHS / 16mm
Color (H C) (FRENCH)
A French - language version of the motion picture Impressionism And Neo - Impressionism. Traces the history of modern painting through the works of Constable, Turner, Delacroix, Corot and Rousseau to Manet, the first impressionist. Compares Monet's 'Dejeuner Sur L'Herre' with Titan's 'Country Concert' to

show that Manet's space and plane concepts are concepts from classical painting. Examines the works of impressionist Monet, Degas, Cezanne, Pissaro and Renoir and new impressionists Seurat, Cross, Signac and Angrand.
Fine Arts; Foreign Language
Dist - IFB **Prod** - LFLMDC 1971

The Lin Family Shop 90 MIN
VHS
Color (G) (MANDARIN CHINESE (ENGLISH SUBTITLES))
$45.00 purchase _ #1003B
Presents a Mandarin Chinese language movie produced in the People's Republic of China.
Fine Arts; Geography - World; Literature and Drama
Dist - CHTSUI **Prod** - CHTSUI

Lin Tse - Hsu 107 MIN
VHS
Color (G) (MANDARIN CHINESE (ENGLISH SUBTITLES))
$45.00 purchase _ #1045B
Presents a Mandarin Chinese language movie produced in the People's Republic of China.
Fine Arts; Geography - World; Literature and Drama
Dist - CHTSUI **Prod** - CHTSUI

Lincoln 240 MIN
VHS
Color (J H C G)
$99.95 purchase _ #PAV1022V
Presents four parts on Abraham Lincoln. Examines Lincoln's roots in The Making of the President. The Pivotal Year examines Lincoln's presidency during the Civil War and the story behind the Gettysburg Address. I Want to Finish this Job - 1864 describes Lincoln's re - election campaign and his efforts to preserve the Union. Now He Belongs to the Ages - 1865 shows Lincoln's enemies plotting against him and the fanatical mania of assassin John Wilkes Booth who mirrored the collective rage of those who believed the President had dishonored their heritage and traditions.
Biography; History - United States
Dist - CAMV

Lincoln 15 MIN
U-matic
Celebrate Series
Color (P)
Civics and Political Systems; Social Science
Dist - GPN **Prod** - KUONTV 1978

Lincoln 200M I G Welding Machine Set - Up 20 MIN
VHS / BETA
Color (IND)
Explains the set - up for an Air Products M I G 150 wire feed machine.
Industrial and Technical Education; Psychology
Dist - RMIBHF **Prod** - RMIBHF

Lincoln - a Photobiography
VHS / 35mm strip
Newbery Award - Winners Series
Color (I)
$128.00 purchase
Biography; English Language; Literature and Drama
Dist - PELLER

Lincoln Center 12 MIN
16mm
B&W
Explains how 35,000 Puerto Rican families in New York City are driven from their homes to provide a cultural playground for the city's upper classes.
Social Science; Sociology
Dist - CANWRL **Prod** - CANWRL

The Lincoln Conspiracy 91 MIN
16mm / U-matic / VHS
Color (J H A)
Provides a step - by - step account of a conspiracy by high level government officials to forcefully remove President Lincoln from office and the successful cover - up of that conspiracy after the assassination. Stars Bradford Dillman and John Dehner.
Biography; Fine Arts; History - United States
Dist - LUF **Prod** - LUF 1979

The Lincoln Heritage Trail 28 MIN
16mm
Color (I)
Describes scenic highlights of the Lincoln heritage trail, a 993 mile trail through Illinois, Indiana and Kentucky. Shows where Lincoln lived, worked and traveled before he became President. Old photos, daguerrotypes, pen - and - ink sketches, water colors, drawings and modern photos show what life along the trail was like in Lincoln's time and today.
Biography; Geography - United States
Dist - AMROIL **Prod** - AMROIL 1964

The Lincoln - New Capital City 30 MIN
16mm
Great Plains Trilogy, 3 Series Explorer and Settler - the White Man 'Arrives; Explorer and settler - the white man arrives
B&W (J)
Portrays Nebraska's political and social history epitomized in the development of the city of Lincoln. Discusses the state's internal strife, its admission to the Union in 1867, and Lincoln's 'GOLDEN YEARS.' Shows Lincoln as the home of nationally prominent people.
Geography - United States; History - United States
Dist - UNEBR **Prod** - KUONTV 1954

Lincoln - Politician or Hero 24 MIN
U-matic / VHS / 16mm
American Challenge Series
B&W (J H)
Examines and interprets the political career of Abraham Lincoln against the backdrop of events which led to the Civil War. Shows him on the eve of assuming the Presidency as deeply disturbed by the campaign tactics he has just witnessed and in awe of the task before him. Uses excerpts from the motion picture Abe Lincoln In Illinois starring Raymond Massey and Gene Lockhart.
Biography; History - United States
Dist - FI **Prod** - RKOP 1975

Lincoln Speeches 58 MIN
Videoreel / VT2
Dialogue of the Western World Series
Color
Features Dean Robert A Goldwin of St John's College of Annapolis and three of his students discussing Lincoln Speeches with a special guest.
Biography; English Language; History - United States
Dist - PBS **Prod** - MDCPB

Lincoln - the Kentucky Years 18 MIN
16mm
Color (H)
LC 77-703223
Shows Lincoln's birthplace, providing insight into the humble beginnings and relationships which shaped the future President's character.
Biography; History - United States
Dist - USNAC **Prod** - USNPS 1972

Lincoln - Trial by Fire 52 MIN
16mm
Color (H C)
Examines the first two years of Abraham Lincoln's Civil War administration. Includes his disagreement with generals over military strategy, a hostile Congress and other problems.
Biography; History - United States
Dist - FI **Prod** - WOLPER 1974

Lincoln - Trial by Fire, Pt 1 - the Union Besieged (1861 - 1862) 26 MIN
16mm
Color (H C)
Examines the first two years of Lincoln's Civil War administration.
Biography; History - United States
Dist - FI **Prod** - WOLPER 1974

Lincoln - Trial by Fire, Pt 2 - Emancipation Proclamation (1862 - 1863) 26 MIN
16mm
Color (H C)
Examines the first two years of Lincoln's Civil War administration.
Biography; History - United States
Dist - FI **Prod** - WOLPER 1974

Lincoln's Gettysburg Address 15 MIN
U-matic / VHS / 16mm
Color (I J H C)
$25 rental _ #4348
Reviewed are the historical events of which Lincoln spoke at the famous battlefield.
Biography; Fine Arts; History - United States
Dist - AIMS **Prod** - AIMS 1973

Lincoln's Gettysburg Address 15 MIN
U-matic / VHS / 16mm
Great American Patriotic Speeches Series
Color (I J H C)
LC 73-701832
Features Charlton Heston.
Biography; English Language
Dist - AIMS **Prod** - EVANSA 1973

Lincoln's second inaugural address 25 MIN
U-matic / VHS
American documents series
Color (J H C)
$250.00 purchase _ #HH - 6266L
Gives a dramatic and insightful look at one of the most famous, influential and frequently quoted speeches of American history, the second inaugural address of Abraham Lincoln. Shows how Lincoln used the gravity of the times and his unique speaking ability to stir emotion and unite the nation. Part of a series on American documents.
Biography; English Language; History - United States
Dist - CORF **Prod** - LCA 1990

L'Incoronazione Di Poppea 155 MIN
VHS
Color (S) (ENGLISH SUBTITLES)
$39.95 purchase _ #623 - 9398
Presents the Glyndebourne production of 'L'Incoronazione Di Poppea' by Monteverdi. Stars Maria Ewing and Dennis Bailey.
Fine Arts; Geography - World
Dist - FI **Prod** - NVIDC 1986

Linda and Billy Ray from Appalachia 14 MIN
16mm / U-matic / VHS
Newcomers to the City Series
B&W (I J)
LC 74-710668
Presents the story of a family who moves from Appalachia to Cincinnati for better job opportunities. Shows how the family has a hard time adjusting to the ways of a big city.
Social Science
Dist - EBEC **Prod** - EBEC 1970

Linda and Richie's Choice 15 MIN
VHS / U-matic
Chemical People Educational Modules Series
Color (J)
Features interviews with kids recovering from drug and alcohol abuse. Stresses standing up to peer pressure.
Psychology; Sociology
Dist - CORF **Prod** - CORF

Linda Bechtold, Marlin MacKenzie, Howard Siegal 30 MIN
U-matic / VHS
Eye on Dance - Dancers' Bodies Series
Color
Focuses on the psychological aspects of dance performance and competition. Features Michael Vernon discussing Beryl Grey. Hosted By Irene Dowd.
Fine Arts
Dist - ARCVID **Prod** - ARCVID

Linda Darling - Hammond 29 MIN
VHS
Touching the future - dialogues on education series
Color (G)
$50.00 purchase, $11.50 rental _ #36271
Features Columbia University Education Prof Linda Darling - Hammond who also serves as codirector for the National Center on Restructuring. Cites teacher testing, changes in teacher education, an advisor system, realistic arrangements for parental involvement, and more community - like structure as ways of producing students capable of interdisciplinary problem - solving. Part of a series which interviews educational leaders on ways to improve American public school education. Features Dr Rodney Reed, dean of the College of Education at Penn State as host.
Education
Dist - PSU **Prod** - WPSXTV 1991

Linda - Encounters in the Hospital 29 MIN
16mm
Color (PRO)
LC 75-703048
Uses the case of a four - year - old girl as she prepares to have major surgery to illustrate how play therapy as instituted at the UCLA Center For The Health Sciences has strong, positive effects on children who suffer emotional stress when coming to the hospital.
Health and Safety; Psychology; Sociology
Dist - UCLA **Prod** - UCLA 1974

Linda Gregg - 3 - 11 - 82 30 MIN
VHS / Cassette
Poetry Center reading series
Color (G)
$15.00, $45.00 purchase, $15.00 rental _ #478 - 406
Features the writer reading her works at the Poetry Center, San Francisco State University.
Literature and Drama
Dist - POETRY **Prod** - POETRY 1982

Linda Laisure and HOME 30 MIN
VHS
Color (G C PRO)
$145.00 purchase, $45.00 rental
Highlights Linda Laisure's work with Alzheimer's patients in a look at her non - profit organization, Helping Our Mobile Elderly (HOME). Shows how the residential home's calm atmosphere helps the residents.
Health and Safety; Sociology
Dist - TNF

Linda Lavin 1 MIN
U-matic
ADL Celebrity Spot Series
Color
Uses television star Linda Lavin to pose questions about race, religion and ethnicity. Made in a television spot announcement format.

Sociology
Dist - ADL **Prod** - ADL

Linda Montano 26 MIN
U-matic / VHS
Color
Features an interview with Linda Montano. Presented by Kate Horsfield and Lyn Blumenthal.
Fine Arts
Dist - ARTINC **Prod** - ARTINC

Linda Roberts and Jessica Wolf 30 MIN
U-matic / VHS
Eye on Dance - Care and Feeding of Dancers Series
Color
Looks at the role of everyday movement habits in chronic injuries.
Fine Arts
Dist - ARCVID **Prod** - ARCVID

Linda Velzey is Dead 13 MIN
16mm / U-matic / VHS
Color (H C A)
LC 79-701106
Examines the dangers of hitchhiking by telling the story of one hitchhiker who was killed. Originally shown on the CBS television program 60 Minutes.
Sociology
Dist - CORF **Prod** - CBSTV 1979

Linda's Film on Menstruation 18 MIN
U-matic / VHS / 16mm
Color (J H)
LC 74-702871
Presents the story of a fifteen - year - old girl who experiences her menstrual period, describing the reaction of the girl and her sixteen - year - old boyfriend as they learn more about the subject of menstruation.
Guidance and Counseling; Health and Safety; Science - Natural
Dist - PHENIX **Prod** - PHENIX 1974

The Lindbergh Kidnapping Case
U-matic / VHS
(J H C A)
$97.00 purchase _ #04078 941
Details the controversial kidnapping of Charles Lindbergh's son.
Fine Arts; Sociology
Dist - ASPRSS

Line 15 MIN
U-matic / VHS
Arts Express Series
Color (K P I J)
Fine Arts
Dist - KYTV **Prod** - KYTV 1983

Line 15 MIN
VHS
Art's place series
Color (K P)
$49.00 purchase, $15.00 rental _ #295803
Shows how everyone experiments with lines in different ways - Art draws to music, Doodles shows how lines reveal feelings and others go sketching in the neighborhood. Features the artist Joan Miro. Part of a series combining songs, stories, animation, puppets and live actors to convey the pleasure of artistic expression. Includes an illustrated teacher's guide.
Fine Arts; Industrial and Technical Education
Dist - TVOTAR **Prod** - TVOTAR 1989

The Line 13 MIN
16mm
Color (H C A)
LC 78-709548
Views the first crossing of Australia by the New Standard Gauge Railway Line between Sydney and Perth. Natural sounds and folk music replace narration.
Geography - World; History - World; Industrial and Technical Education
Dist - AUIS **Prod** - ANAIB 1970

The Line 25 MIN
16mm
Screen Test Series
Color; Silent (J H C G T A)
Religion and Philosophy
Dist - WHLION **Prod** - WHLION

Line dances 60 MIN
VHS
Kathy Blake dance studios - let's learn how to dance series
Color (G A)
$39.95 purchase
Features dance instructors Kathy Blake and Gene Russo, who instruct viewers on the basics of line dances.
Fine Arts
Dist - PBS **Prod** - WNETTV

Line dancing is it 28 MIN
VHS
Color (G)
$22.95 purchase _ #PEP100V
Overviews basic line dance steps of five popular dances, including super freak, the freeze, slapping leather, the rise and Louisiana Saturday night.
Fine Arts; Physical Education and Recreation
Dist - CAMV

Line dancing with Christy Lane
VHS
Color (G)
$14.99 purchase _ #BHV030
Teaches five new line dances. Features Christy Lane.
Fine Arts; History - United States
Dist - SIV

Line describing a cone 30 MIN
16mm
B&W (G)
$40.00 rental
Deals with the projected light - beam itself, rather than treating it as a mere carrier of coded information, which is decoded when it strikes a flat surface like the screen. Exists only in the present or in the moment of projection. Every viewing position presents a different aspect for the viewer. Important conditions for projection will be sent with the film. An Anthony McCall production.
Fine Arts; Science - Physical
Dist - CANCIN

Line Driver and Receiver Applications, I Basic Systems 30 MIN
VHS / U-matic
Linear and Interface Circuits, Part II - Interface Integrated 'Circuits Series
Color (PRO)
Defines various data transmission systems and when and where used. Discusses single ended systems with available integrated circuits.
Industrial and Technical Education
Dist - TXINLC **Prod** - TXINLC

Line Drivers and Receivers Applications, II Advanced Systems 30 MIN
U-matic / VHS
Linear and Interface Circuits, Part II - Interface Integrated 'Circuits Series
Color (PRO)
Continues applications examples with differential and party - line systems, and advantages and disadvantages of using particular integrated circuits.
Industrial and Technical Education
Dist - TXINLC **Prod** - TXINLC

A Line in the sand 50 MIN
VHS
Color (G)
$19.98 purchase _ #UPC 30306 - 6124 - 3
Look at the events leading up to the Iraqi invasion of Kuwait. Features Peter Jennings who reports on the long standing relationship of Saddam Hussein's Iraq with the United States and other Western nations, and the impact of their support of Iraq's military build - up during the past decade.
History - World; Sociology
Dist - INSTRU **Prod** - ABCNEW

A Line in the sand - war or peace 50 MIN
VHS
Color (G)
$19.98 purchase _ #UPC 30306 - 6438 - 3
Presents a special aired on the eve of the United Nations deadline for Saddam Hussein to withdraw from Kuwait. Features Peter Jennings as host joining ABC News correspondents who report on what American forces will face in a military battle, the two men who brought about the conflict - George Bush and Saddam Hussein, and what many saw as the root of the crisis - oil.
Biography; Business and Economics; Civics and Political Systems; History - United States; History - World; Sociology
Dist - INSTRU **Prod** - ABCNEW

A Line in the sand - what did American win 50 MIN
VHS
Color (J H C G)
$29.98 purchase _ #MH6222V
Takes a special look at the war in Kuwait between Sadam Hussein of Iraq and George Bush of the United States, January 17, 1990, the '100 - hour war.' Features Peter Jennings.
History - United States; Sociology
Dist - CAMV

A Line is a line is a line 6 MIN
U-matic / VHS / 16mm
B&W (J)
LC 73-700998
Uses lines to create different images while J S Bach's Toccata and Fuge in D Minor is played on an organ. Outlines hundreds of everyday objects, set to grand music and merging into surprisingly dissimilar, yet seemingly logical shapes.
Fine Arts; Mathematics
Dist - IFB **Prod** - IFB 1972

Line of Apogee 46 MIN
16mm
Color
LC FIA68-149
This experimental film pictures the images that occur during a dream.
Fine Arts
Dist - FMCOOP **Prod** - WILMLM 1967

Line of Balance 14 MIN
16mm / U-matic / VHS
Color (IND)
Explains the principles and applications of the Line of Balance programming method for the planning and control of production. Shows how the method applies to any production process that involves repetitive or sequential operation.
Business and Economics
Dist - IFB **Prod** - WWP 1973

Line Prints 15 MIN
U-matic / VHS
Young at Art Series
Color (P I)
Fine Arts
Dist - AITECH **Prod** - WSKJTV

Line - Program 1 15 MIN
U-matic
Artscape Series
Color (I)
Shows children visiting an art gallery and entering a magic world of Artscape where they learn about lines in art.
Fine Arts
Dist - TVOTAR **Prod** - TVOTAR 1983

Line Segments 15 MIN
U-matic
Math Makers One Series
Color (I)
Presents the concepts of regions, lines, points, rays, line segments, regular polygon construction and nets.
Education; Mathematics
Dist - TVOTAR **Prod** - TVOTAR 1979

Line - Up Procedures for Tactical Telegraph Carrier Equipment 8 MIN
16mm
B&W
LC FIE53-604
Demonstrates the procedures for setting up tactical telegraph carrier equipment for two wire operations and emphasizes various tests to determine its operating efficiency.
Civics and Political Systems; Industrial and Technical Education; Social Science
Dist - USNAC **Prod** - USA 1953

Line Up Your Interview 11 MIN
16mm / U-matic / VHS
Get that Job Series
Color (H C A)
$280, $195 purchase _ #3546
Shows how to organize a resume and line up a interview to get a job.
Guidance and Counseling
Dist - CORF

Linea De Balance 14 MIN
16mm / U-matic / VHS
Color (IND) (SPANISH)
A Spanish - language version of the motion picture Line Of Balance. Explains the principles and applications of the Line of Balance programming method for the planning and control of production. Shows how the method applies to any production process that involves repetitive or sequential operation.
Business and Economics; Foreign Language
Dist - IFB **Prod** - WWP 1973

The Lineage 29 MIN
Videoreel / VT2
Our Street Series
Color
Sociology
Dist - PBS **Prod** - MDCPB

Lineage 29 MIN
16mm
Color (G)
$60.00 rental
Purports to reveal the processes and secrets of animation. Addresses basic issues of contemporary art such as illusionism, formalism, reflexivity, the narrrative, the time - space continuum and causality. Overcomes this didactic agenda with playful contradictions. Produced by George Griffin.
Fine Arts
Dist - CANCIN

Linear Accelerators in Radiation Therapy, Theory and Operation, Pts 1, 2 and 3 42 MIN
VHS / U-matic
Color
LC 82-706636
Introduces the basic components of the Linear Accelerator (LINAC), discusses their functions and describes the technical operation of the LINAC, including microwave cavities.
Health and Safety; Science; Science - Physical
Dist - USNAC **Prod** - USHHS 1982

Linear analog integrated circuits fundamentals and applications - a series
Linear analog integrated circuits fundamentals and applications'series
Color (IND)
Discusses in four modules, including 19 videotapes and 11 demonstrations, basics of complicated linear analog integrated circuits. Provides fundamental building blocks of circuit design as one useful circuit after another is analyzed and discussed. Module A - Bipolar Transistor Fundamentals - - ; Module B - Current Sources And Applications; Module C - The Differential Amplifier; Module D - Class A, B, and AB Output Stages - - .
Industrial and Technical Education
Dist - COLOSU **Prod** - COLOSU

Linear analog integrated circuits fundamentals and applications series
Linear analog integrated circuits fundamentals and applications - a series
Dist - COLOSU

Linear Analog Integrated Circuits Series
Module A - Bipolar Transistor Fundamentals and Basic Amplifier Circuits 45 MIN
Module B - Current Sources and Applications 45 MIN
Module C - the Differential Amplifier 45 MIN
Module D - Class A, B, and AB Output Stages and the MuA741 Operational Amplifier 45 MIN
Dist - COLOSU

Linear and Angular Measure 30 MIN
16mm
Mathematics for Elementary School Teachers Series no 16
Color (C)
Introduces fundamental concepts of geometry. Indicates that it is a deductive system. To be used following 'METRIC PROPERTIES OF FIGURES.'.
Mathematics
Dist - MLA **Prod** - SMSG 1963

Linear and Interface Circuits, Part II - Interface Integrated Circuits Series
DC Voltage Regulator Design 30 MIN
General Purpose Driver Circuits 30 MIN
Line Driver and Receiver Applications, I Basic Systems 30 MIN
Line Drivers and Receivers Applications, II Advanced Systems 30 MIN
Linear IC Technology - II 30 MIN
Semiconductor Memory Driver Applications 30 MIN
Sense Amplifiers 30 MIN
Translator Circuits 30 MIN
Voltage Regulator Applications 30 MIN
Dist - TXINLC

Linear and interface circuits - Pt II - Interface integrated circuits - series
Core memory driver applications 30 MIN
Dist - TXINLC

Linear and Interface Integrated Circuits, Part I - Linear Integrated Circuits Series
Comparator design 30 MIN
Linear I/C Technology 30 MIN
New Developments in Operational Amplifiers 30 MIN
Operational Amplifier Applications - I 30 MIN
Operational Amplifier Applications - II 30 MIN
Operational Amplifier Design - I 30 MIN
Operational Amplifier Design - II 30 MIN
Video and if Amplifiers 30 MIN
Dist - TXINLC

Linear and Interface Integrated Circuits, Part II - Interface Integrated Circuits Series
Linear IC Techology - I 30 MIN
Dist - TXINLC

Linear and interface integrated circuits, Pt I - linear integrated circuits series
Comparator applications 30 MIN
Dist - TXINLC

Linear Approximations 20 MIN
VHS
Calculus Series
Color (H)
LC 90712920
Examines linear approximations. The 56th of 57 installments of the Calculus Series.
Mathematics
Dist - GPN

Linear Continuous Time Dynamical Systems 42 MIN
U-matic / VHS
Modern Control Theory - Systems Analysis Series
Color
Industrial and Technical Education; Mathematics
Dist - MIOT **Prod** - MIOT

Linear Differential Equations 35 MIN
VHS / U-matic
Calculus of Differential Equations Series
B&W
Mathematics
Dist - MIOT **Prod** - MIOT

Linear Equations 30 MIN
U-matic
Introduction to Mathematics Series
Color (C)
Mathematics
Dist - MDCPB **Prod** - MDCPB

Linear Equations in One Unknown 30 MIN
16mm
Advanced Algebra Series
B&W (H)
Solves two word problems - - finding the point of no return in an airplane flight and computing the amount of alcohol needed to produce a certain percentage mixture in an automobile radiator.
Mathematics
Dist - MLA **Prod** - CALVIN 1960

Linear Estimation 44 MIN
VHS / U-matic
Probability and Random Processes - Statistical Averages Series
B&W (PRO)
Introduces linear estimation. Discusses mean - square estimators in this light.
Mathematics
Dist - MIOT **Prod** - MIOT

A Linear Fantasy 6 MIN
16mm
Color
LC 76-700134
Features a geometric scratch film with designs drawn directly on the surface film and color added.
Fine Arts; Industrial and Technical Education; Mathematics
Dist - ABOT **Prod** - ABOT 1974

Linear I/C Technology 30 MIN
VHS / U-matic
Linear and Interface Integrated Circuits, Part I - Linear Integrated'Circuits Series
Color (PRO)
Covers general overall technology considerations for all linear IC's including types of devices commonly used, their structures and characteristics.
Industrial and Technical Education
Dist - TXINLC **Prod** - TXINLC

Linear IC Technology - II 30 MIN
U-matic / VHS
Linear and Interface Circuits, Part II - Interface Integrated 'Circuits Series
Color (PRO)
Provides background for application of linear art and interface integrated circuits. Includes extension of first session for common devices, more exotic devices such as FET's, current source structures and dialectric isolation structures for complementary devices.
Industrial and Technical Education
Dist - TXINLC **Prod** - TXINLC

Linear IC Techology - I 30 MIN
U-matic / VHS
Linear and Interface Integrated Circuits, Part II - Interface 'Integrated Circuits Series
Color (PRO)
Includes this lesson as a repeat of Part I and should be used by engineers catering the Interface Circuits portion only.
Industrial and Technical Education
Dist - TXINLC **Prod** - TXINLC

Linear Inequalities 30 MIN
U-matic
Introduction to Mathematics Series
Color (C)
Mathematics
Dist - MDCPB **Prod** - MDCPB

Linear integrated circuits series
Power amplifier IC applications 30 MIN
Dist - TXINLC

Linear Measurement 10 MIN
16mm
Metric System Series
Color (P I)
Introduces the metric system of measurement. Discusses the shape of the earth, using the earth as a standard, why the metric system is a better system of measuring and the difficulties involved with people in changing to the metric system.
Mathematics
Dist - SF **Prod** - SF

Linear measurement
VHS
Lola May's fundamental math series
Color (P)
$45.00 purchase _ #10263VG
Introduces the concept of measuring the length and height of objects. Begins with nonstandard measures and proceeds to using inches in measurement. Comes with a teacher's guide and blackline masters. Part 13 of a 30 - part series.
Mathematics
Dist - UNL

Linear motion - 2 33 MIN
VHS
Conceptual physics alive series
Color (H C)
$45.00 purchase
Presents the concepts of speed, velocity and acceleration, introduced and supported with a variety of examples. Discusses free fall and the effects of air resistance on falling objects. Part 2 of a 35 - part series adapted from the college and high school textbook Conceptual Physics by Professor Paul Hewitt.
Science - Physical
Dist - MMENTE **Prod** - HEWITP 1992

Linear Programming 1 20 MIN
U-matic
Mathematical Concepts Series
B&W (J H)
Illustrates the usefulness of the linear programming model with a practical problem from the milk processing industry.
Mathematics
Dist - TVOTAR **Prod** - TVOTAR 1985

Linear Programming 2 20 MIN
U-matic
Mathematical Concepts Series
B&W (J H)
Shows how the linear programming model is altered by the imposition of new conditions on the real life situation.
Mathematics
Dist - TVOTAR **Prod** - TVOTAR 1985

Linear Programming, Pt 1 30 MIN
U-matic
Introduction to Mathematics Series
Color (C)
Mathematics
Dist - MDCPB **Prod** - MDCPB

Linear Programming, Pt 2 30 MIN
U-matic
Introduction to Mathematics Series
Color (C)
Mathematics
Dist - MDCPB **Prod** - MDCPB

Linear System Descriptions 40 MIN
U-matic / VHS
Probability and Random Processes - Linear Systems Series
B&W (PRO)
Discusses the characterization of a linear time - invariant (LTI) system in the time domain by its impulse response.
Mathematics
Dist - MIOT **Prod** - MIOT

Linear Time Invariant Dynamical Systems 52 MIN
U-matic / VHS
Modern Control Theory - Systems Analysis Series
Color
Industrial and Technical Education; Mathematics
Dist - MIOT **Prod** - MIOT

Linear Transformations 36 MIN
U-matic / VHS
Calculus of Linear Algebra Series
B&W
Mathematics
Dist - MIOT **Prod** - MIOT

Linearity Revisited 47 MIN
VHS / U-matic
Calculus of several Variables - Matrix - - Algebra Series; Matrix algebra

B&W
Mathematics
Dist - MIOT **Prod** - MIOT

Linebacker play
VHS
NCAA football videos - defensive series
Color (A G T)
$39.95 purchase _ #KAR1306V-P
Presents instruction on skills and drills given by NCAA coaches. Features Foge Fazio explaining linebacker techniques. One of a series of videos that provide coaching tips to offensive and defensive players and coaches. Series is available as individual cassettes, a set of offensive series, a set of defensive series, or both series combined.
Physical Education and Recreation
Dist - CAMV

Linebackers 60 MIN
VHS
One on One Coaching Series
(J H C)
$39.95 _ #CVN1050V
Presents football coach Goldsmith who demonstrates fundamentals and techniques for linebackers, including defensive strategy, reaction drills, pass drops, fumble recovery, hitting and more.
Physical Education and Recreation
Dist - CAMV **Prod** - CAMV

Linebreaking 11 MIN
VHS / U-matic / BETA
Color; PAL (IND G)
$175.00 rental _ #AEB - 113
Reveals that breaking a steamline or other types of pressurized or toxic pipes can be extremely dangerous. Presents a checklist of the safety procedures to use when breaking any line, using the easy - to - remember acronym CAUTION. Includes leader's guide and 10 workbooks.
Health and Safety; Industrial and Technical Education; Psychology
Dist - BNA **Prod** - BNA

The Lineman 14 MIN
U-matic / VHS / 16mm
Color (IND)
LC 76-701339
Explains why people become electrical linemen and what is involved in the job. Stresses that doing the job safely is the hallmark of the professional lineman.
Guidance and Counseling; Health and Safety; Industrial and Technical Education
Dist - IFB **Prod** - KROSTR 1975

Liner and Piston 20 MIN
16mm
B&W
LC FIE52-1365
Tells how to inspect liner, disassemble piston rod assembly, inspect slipper rod assembly, inspect piston assembly and piston, and replace rings.
Industrial and Technical Education
Dist - USNAC **Prod** - USN 1945

Liner Cementing 30 MIN
VHS / Slide / 16mm
Color (A PRO IND)
$160.00 purchase _ #11.1124, $170.00 purchase _ #51.1124
Defines liners, tells why they are used, and describes tools needed to set them. Discusses problems encountered and how to overcome or minimize them.
Industrial and Technical Education; Social Science
Dist - UTEXPE **Prod** - UTEXPE 1980

Lines 15 MIN
U-matic
Is the Sky Always Blue Series
Color (P)
Fine Arts
Dist - GPN **Prod** - WDCNTV 1979

Lines and Dots 7 MIN
16mm
Color (P I J H)
Shows blue dashes and red dots fighting each other whey they are brought in close contact with an unknown third power, which destroys the embattled signs and spreads over the screen like spilled paint.
Fine Arts; Industrial and Technical Education
Dist - SF **Prod** - SF 1970

Lines, Angles, Triangles, Quadrilaterals 13 MIN
U-matic / VHS / 16mm
Shape Hunting Series
Color (P I)
$315, $220 purchase _ #4023
Shows lines, angles, triangles, and quadrilaterals and how they relate to objects found in the physical world.
Mathematics
Dist - CORF

Lines in Relief - Woodcut and Block Printing 11 MIN
U-matic / VHS / 16mm
Color (I J H C)
Reviews the history of woodcuts and block printing from the Middle Ages to the present. Shows how a fine woodcut is made. Pictures the selection of tools and materials, transfer of design and techniques used in cutting the block.
Fine Arts
Dist - EBEC **Prod** - EBEC 1964

Lines in the sand 12 MIN
VHS / U-matic
Color; PAL (H C A)
$19.95 purchase
Provides a critical perspective on the management of the news media by the Pentagon during the Gulf war. Explores how information was controlled and news managed during the Gulf War to keep the disturbing realities of war from affecting the conscience of the US public. Contains an interview with a geology professor who lost his wife and four daughters in the American bomb shelter in Baghdad along with hundred of civilians. Raises questions concerning the way limited access to information shapes public opinion. Available also with a study guide at additional cost.
History - United States; Literature and Drama; Religion and Philosophy; Sociology
Dist - GRIWIR **Prod** - GRIWIR 1991

Lines of Fire 62 MIN
16mm
Color (G)
Presents an independent production by Brian Beker who served as writer and director. Looks at little known revolution in Burma against a military regime where 15,000 civilians were gunned down by government troops during a 1988 uprising. Explores the mercenary policies of the region where lumber is traded for captured student leaders and the US drug policy was determined by a former personal secretary of Nancy Reagan.
Civics and Political Systems; Geography - World; Sociology
Dist - FIRS

Lines of Force 10 MIN
U-matic
Color (H C A)
LC 81-706007
Presents an abstract montage of forms, colors and sounds. Utilizes split screen, live television and synthesized audio visual techniques.
Fine Arts
Dist - SYNAPS **Prod** - SYNAPS 1980

Lines of war - the drug war in Colombia 52 MIN
VHS
Color (H C G)
$445.00 purchase, $75.00 rental
Investigates the drug war in Columbia, cocaine capital of the world. Reveals that for almost a decade the United States has tried to smash drug cartels with small success. Coca growing has increased, spreading into new areas. For 5,000 years coca was used by Andean Indians to ease their harsh life but when Westerners manufactured coca into cocaine a bloody industry was unleashed. Criticizes rigid US policy pursuing foreign producers and traffickers and ignoring domestic social problems creating the demand. Reveals that extradition of drug traders to trial in the US has led to a blood bath against judges, politicians and law enforcement in Colombia and poor people in both countries have had their lives torn apart by drug wars.
Civics and Political Systems
Dist - FLMLIB **Prod** - CITV 1991

The Lines plan
VHS
Lines plan featuring Arno Day series
Color (G A)
$200.00 rental _ #0085
Features master boatbuilder Arno Day of Maine. Instructs on how to draw a complete line plan of any boat.
Fine Arts; Industrial and Technical Education; Physical Education and Recreation
Dist - SEVVID

Lines plan featuring Arno Day series
The Lines plan
The Lines plan no 1 - understanding lines 30 MIN
The Lines plan no 3 - drawing the lines 60 MIN
The Lines plan no 2 - taking lines 30 MIN
Dist - SEVVID

The Lines plan no 1 - understanding lines 30 MIN
VHS
Lines plan featuring Arno Day series
Color (G A)
$39.90 purchase _ #0482
Features master boatbuilder Arno Day of Maine. Covers the basics of boat lines - splines - and design, and teaches the meaning of hull lines.
Fine Arts; Industrial and Technical Education; Physical Education and Recreation
Dist - SEVVID

The Lines plan no 3 - drawing the lines 60 MIN
VHS
Lines plan featuring Arno Day series
Color (G A)
$49.90 purchase _ #0484
Features master boatbuilder Arno Day of Maine. Presents a full course in drawing line plans for any boat.
Fine Arts; Industrial and Technical Education; Physical Education and Recreation
Dist - SEVVID

The Lines plan no 2 - taking lines 30 MIN
VHS
Lines plan featuring Arno Day series
Color (G A)
$39.90 purchase _ #0483
Features master boatbuilder Arno Day of Maine. Shows how to take the lines from any boat.
Fine Arts; Industrial and Technical Education; Physical Education and Recreation
Dist - SEVVID

Lines that Cross 15 MIN
U-matic
Landscape of Geometry Series
Color (J)
Proves that when lines intersect the opposite angles created are equal. An archaeologist shows how a theodolite is used in triangulation.
Education; Mathematics
Dist - TVOTAR **Prod** - TVOTAR 1982

Lines that Don't Cross 15 MIN
U-matic
Landscape of Geometry Series
Color (J)
Illustrates the concept of parallel lines and instruments of navigation. Defines corresponding angles and how to use parallelograms.
Education; Mathematics
Dist - TVOTAR **Prod** - TVOTAR 1982

Lines - Vertical and Horizontal 13 MIN
U-matic / VHS / 16mm
Color (I J H C)
Presents pure non - objective art in which design and music are inseparable, as created by Norman McLaren and Evelyn Lambart.
Fine Arts
Dist - IFB **Prod** - NFBC 1963

Lingo 32 MIN
16mm
Color
LC 80-700300
Features a profile of T D Lingo and his unique theories about the mechanisms and potentials of the human brain.
Biography; Psychology; Science - Natural
Dist - TENST **Prod** - TENST 1979

Lingua - Alveloars 10 MIN
BETA / VHS
Speech Reading Materials Series
Color (A)
English Language
Dist - RMIBHF **Prod** - RMIBHF

Lingua - ROM
CD-ROM
(G A)
$489.00 purchase _ #2642
Includes 25 HyperGlot language tutors, with Chinese, French, German, Italian, Japanese, Russian and Spanish. For Macintosh Plus, SE and II computers. Requires 1MB RAM, floppy disk drive, Apple compatible CD - ROM drive.
Foreign Language
Dist - BEP

Lingual Delivery of Impacted Mandibular Third Molars 9 MIN
16mm
Color (PRO)
LC 77-703284
Shows a lingual delivery technique for removal of unerupted third molars.
Health and Safety; Science
Dist - USNAC **Prod** - VADTC 1977

Linguistics and Education 22 MIN
16mm
Language - the Social Arbiter Series
Color (H C T)
LC FIA67-5263
Three linguistics educators discuss the proposition that most laymen and some educators hold certain views about language which limit their effectiveness in teaching children standard English.
Education; English Language
Dist - FINLYS **Prod** - FINLYS 1966

Linguistics in Teaching of the Disadvantaged 30 MIN
VHS / U-matic
Color
Presents Dr. Beryl Loftman Bailey, Professor of English, Hunter College.
Education; English Language
Dist - NETCHE **Prod** - NETCHE 1969

Lining and Finishing the Details 29 MIN
Videoreel / VT2
Sewing Skills - Tailoring Series
Color
Features Mrs Ruth Hickman demonstrating how to line a coat and how to finish the details on it.
Home Economics
Dist - PBS **Prod** - KRMATV

Lining Techniques 4 MIN
16mm
Clothing Construction Techniques Series
Color (J)
LC 77-701175
Illustrates putting a separate lining in a skirt. Shows stitching lining, joining lining to fashion fabric at the waistline and zipper, completing the hem and anchoring the lining to the garment with crocheting.
Home Economics
Dist - IOWASP **Prod** - IOWA 1976

Lining the Coat 29 MIN
Videoreel / VT2
Sewing Skills - Tailoring Series
Color
Features Mrs Ruth Hickman demonstrating how to line a coat.
Home Economics
Dist - PBS **Prod** - KRMATV

Link analysis - a overview 30 MIN
VHS
Business logistics series
Color (G C)
$200.00 purchase, $20.50 rental _ #34968
Overviews link analysis. Part of a 30 - part series on business logistics which deals with movement and storage of raw and finished products, and with managerial activities important for effective control of these operations. Interviews logistics managers of major US corporations and transportation companies. Uses on - site segments to demonstrate logistical carrier operations. Features program author Dr John Coyle.
Business and Economics
Dist - PSU **Prod** - WPSXTV 1987

The Link and the Chain 28 MIN
16mm
Color
Sociology
Dist - WAORT **Prod** - WAORT 1980

Link between Us, the Electronics 28 MIN
VHS / U-matic
Color
Documents the daily influences of electronics products in people's lives. Features appearances by Eugene Fodor, Jim Henson, Lorin Maazel, Kenny Rogers, Eric Sevareid and Stevie Wonder.
Business and Economics; Industrial and Technical Education; Sociology
Dist - MTP **Prod** - ELECTR

Link Control Procedures 56 MIN
U-matic / VHS
Telecommunications and the Computer Series
Color
Discusses types of link control procedures.
Industrial and Technical Education; Mathematics
Dist - MIOT **Prod** - MIOT

The Link Sextant, Air 16 MIN
16mm
B&W
LC FIE52-984
Explains the operating principle of the sextant and the reading of the vernier scale. Shows two ways of making observations and how to grip the sextant when making observations.
Industrial and Technical Education; Mathematics; Science - Physical
Dist - USNAC **Prod** - USN 1943

Linking Arms 22 MIN
16mm
Color
LC 76-703240
Documents the work of Toronto sculptror Colette Whiten. Shows how she conceived the idea to link the arms of five men in one of her works.
Fine Arts
Dist - CANFDC **Prod** - CANFDC 1975

Linnaeus 18 MIN
16mm
Color
Presents the life of Sweden's great botanist, Carl Linnaeus, who devised the system of botanical classification and describes his contribution to science.
Geography - World; Science; Science - Natural
Dist - SIS **Prod** - SIS 1957

L'Innocenza Ed Il Placer - La Cinesi, and, Echo Et Narcisse 168 MIN
VHS
Color (S) (FRENCH)
$49.95 purchase _ #833 - 9316
Presents a double bill by Gluck recorded live at the rococo theater of the Schwetzingen Palace near Heidelberg. Includes a cast of Kurt Streit, Sophie Boulin, Christina Hoegman, Eva Maria Tersson, Deborah Massell and Peter Galliard. Rene Jacobs conducts the Concerto Cologne orchestra playing authentic Baroque instruments.
Fine Arts; Foreign Language; Geography - World
Dist - FI **Prod** - RMART 1987

Lino Manocchia, Ralph Marino and Federico Picciano 52 MIN
VHS / U-matic
Rainbow quest series
Color
Presents Italian folk music and a film of a group sing in an Italian village. Features Linco Manocchia, Ralph Marino and Federico Picciano.
Fine Arts
Dist - NORROS **Prod** - SEEGER

Linus Pauling - a century of science and life 28 MIN
VHS
Eminent scientist series
Color (J H)
$60.00 purchase _ #A2VH 4629
Features chemist Linus Pauling. Part of a series on scientists which discusses their childhood, educational backgrounds, decisions affecting their careers and illustrious achievements.
Science; Science - Physical
Dist - CLRVUE **Prod** - CLRVUE

Lion 22 MIN
16mm / U-matic / VHS
Animals, Animals, Animals Series
Color (P I)
Explores the lion and his dazzling role in art from the Alhambra to the Great Pyramid of Khufu to Rousseau's The Dream. Includes the story Androcles And The Lion. Hosted by Hal Linden.
Science - Natural
Dist - MEDIAG **Prod** - ABCNEW 1977

The Lion 18 MIN
U-matic / VHS / BETA
Color; PAL (G H C)
PdS40, PdS48 purchase
Views the relationships between members of a pride of lions and their interdependence on other animals.
Psychology; Science - Natural
Dist - EDPAT

The Lion 19 MIN
U-matic / VHS / 16mm
Color (P I J)
Features the relationship of a lion family, as well as its relationship to other animals. Highlights the ways in which the lioness cares for and caters to her cubs, the imperious nature of the father lion and the playfulness of the baby cubs.
Literature and Drama; Science - Natural
Dist - LUF **Prod** - CFD 1971

Lion - 4 10 MIN
U-matic / 16mm / VHS
Zoo animals series
Color (K P I)
$265.00, $215.00, $185.00 purchase _ #B605
Shows lions living in a wild animal park. Explains how lions behave in the wild and how they adjust to living in a park. Examines the role of the lioness in hunting for food and caring for the young cubs. Illustrates the physical characteristics of the lion. Part of a six - part series on zoo animals.
Science - Natural
Dist - BARR **Prod** - GREATT 1990

The Lion and the Eagle 60 MIN
16mm
Intertel Series
B&W (J)
Uses film clips to document from the point of view of the anglo - American alliance, the main events and personalities of the era from 1939 to the Vietnam War.
Civics and Political Systems; History - United States; History - World
Dist - IU **Prod** - NET 1966

Lion and the Eagle, the, Pt 1 30 MIN
16mm
Intertel Series
B&W (J)
LC FIA68-2201
Uses film clips to document from the point of view of the anglo - American alliance the main events and personalities of the era from 1939 to the Japanese surrender after World War II.
Fine Arts; History - World
Dist - IU **Prod** - NET 1967

Lion and the Eagle, the, Pt 2 30 MIN
16mm
Intertel Series
B&W (J)
LC FIA68-2202
Uses film clips to document the main events and personalities of the era from the end of World War II to the Vietnam War. Discusses the effect of the U N, SEATO, the Suez Crisis and the Vietnam War upon the anglo - American alliance.
Fine Arts; History - World
Dist - IU **Prod** - NET 1967

The Lion and the Horse 83 MIN
16mm
Color
Presents the story of Wildfire, a wild horse that is sold to a cruel rodeo owner and freed by a sympathetic cowpoke.
Fine Arts
Dist - TWYMAN **Prod** - WB 1952

The Lion and the Mouse 10 MIN
16mm / U-matic / VHS
Color (P)
$265, $185 purchase _ #1269
Shows how a mouse helps a lion with some dust in his eye. Animated.
Literature and Drama
Dist - CORF

The Lion and the Mouse 5 MIN
8mm cartridge / 16mm
Color (K P)
LC 77-701636
Presents an animated version of Aesop's fable about a mouse who saves a lion by chewing through the rope in which the lion is trapped.
Literature and Drama
Dist - BNCHMK **Prod** - NFBC 1977

Lion Dance 3 MIN
16mm
Color
Offers a graphic interpretation of the traditional Chinese lion dance utilizing traditional music. Employs visuals which are simple brush drawings and colors painted directly on the film.
Sociology
Dist - USC **Prod** - USC 1981

Lion game 4 MIN
VHS / 16mm
San - Ju - Wasi series
Color (G)
$120.00, $100.00 purchase, $20.00 rental
Watches Gunda, a young man, pretend to be a lion. Shows how he is 'hunted' and 'killed' by a group of boys. Part of a series by John Marshall about the Kung in Namibia and Botswana.
Geography - World; History - World; Physical Education and Recreation; Sociology
Dist - DOCEDR **Prod** - DOCEDR

Lion has seven heads 97 MIN
16mm
Color (ITALIAN PORTUGUESE (ENGLISH SUBTITLES) FRENCH SPANISH GERMAN)
Tells the story of revolution in Africa and Third World exploitation involving the CIA and the Portuguese.
Fine Arts; Foreign Language; History - World
Dist - NYFLMS **Prod** - NYFLMS 1970

Lion Head 29 MIN
Videoreel / VT2
Joyce Chen Cooks Series
Color
Features Joyce Chen showing how to adapt Chinese recipes so they can be prepared in the American kitchen and still retain the authentic flavor.
Geography - World; Home Economics
Dist - PBS **Prod** - WGBHTV

The Lion in Winter 134 MIN
U-matic / VHS / 16mm
Color
Stars Katherine Hepburn as Queen Eleanor and Peter O'Toole as King Henry II.
Biography; Fine Arts; History - World
Dist - FI **Prod** - UNKNWN 1968

The Lion in winter - 1946 and beyond - Part three 121 MIN
VHS
When the lion roars series
B&W/Color (G)
$19.98 purchase _ #6302453208
Follows the history of MGM through the collapse of the star and studio system, but not before the production of some of the greatest movie musicals ever made. Part of a three - part series on Metro Goldwyn Mayer - MGM which recalls the stars and the wealth of stories behind the movies they made.
Fine Arts; History - United States
Dist - INSTRU

Lion - Part 1 8 MIN
VHS
Safari TV series
Color (P I)
$125.00 purchase
Studies the daily life of the African lion. Part of a 13 - part series on African animals.
Geography - World; Science - Natural
Dist - LANDMK **Prod** - LANDMK 1993

The Lion reigns supreme - 1936 - 1945 - Part two 121 MIN
VHS
When the lion roars series
B&W/Color (G)
$19.98 purchase _ #6302453194
Covers MGM's brightest and busiest decade. Reveals that, after the tragic death of Irving Thalberg, Louis B Mayer became the sole head of MGM Studios and responsible for the glossy 'MGM' look. Looks at films such as Andy Hardy, The Thin Man series, The Wizard of Oz, Gone With the Wind and the films of World War II. Part of a three - part series on Metro Goldwyn Mayer - MGM which recalls the stars and the wealth of stories behind the movies they made.
Fine Arts; History - United States
Dist - INSTRU

The Lion Roars 10 MIN
Videoreel / VT2
Janaki Series
Color
Physical Education and Recreation
Dist - PBS **Prod** - WGBHTV

The Lion, the witch and the wardrobe 104 MIN
VHS
Color (K P I J)
$29.95 purchase _ #S02079
Presents an animated version of the C S Lewis children's story, 'The Lion, The Witch and The Wardrobe.' Produced in a collaborative effort by the Children's Television Workshop and Bill Melendez of 'Peanuts' fame.
Literature and Drama
Dist - UILL

The Lion, the witch and the wardrobe 95 MIN
VHS
Color (G R)
$29.95 purchase, $10.00 rental _ #35 - 8003 - 1518
Tells the story of two brothers and two sisters who are magically transported to Narnia, a land of talking animals and mythical creatures. Based on the book by C S Lewis.
Religion and Philosophy
Dist - APH **Prod** - SPAPRO

The Lion, the witch and the wardrobe 174 MIN
VHS
Chronicles of Narnia - Wonderworks collection series
Color (I J H)
$29.95 purchase _ #LIO02
Presents a segment from the C S Lewis fantasy in which animals speak, mythical creatures roam and children fight an epic battle against evil.
Guidance and Counseling; Literature and Drama
Dist - KNOWUN **Prod** - PBS

Lions 15 MIN
U-matic / VHS
Draw Man Series
Color (I J)
Gives a simple step - by - step approach for drawing a lion's head. Suggests ways of completing a wildlife picture.
Fine Arts
Dist - AITECH **Prod** - OCPS 1975

Lions 25 MIN
U-matic / 16mm
Untamed World Series
Color; Mono (J H C A)
$400.00 film, $250.00 video, $50.00 rental
Profiles the lion, the legendary king of beasts.
Science - Natural
Dist - CTV **Prod** - CTV 1971

Lions 14 MIN
VHS
Animal profile series
Color (P I)
$59.95 purchase _ #RB8112
Studies lions, who often sleep up to 22 hours a day. Part of a series on animals which looks at examples from the mammal, snake and bird classes, filmed in their natural habitat.
Science - Natural
Dist - REVID **Prod** - REVID 1990

Lions and Tigers 6 MIN
16mm / U-matic / VHS
Zoo Animals in the Wild Series
Color (P I)
$135, $95 purchase _ #4002
Talks about the habitations and behavior of lions and tigers.
Science - Natural
Dist - CORF

The Lion's cub 90 MIN
U-matic / VHS / 16mm
Elizabeth R series; No 1
Color
LC 79-707278
Portrays young Queen Elizabeth I during the brief reigns of her brother Edward and her sister Mary. Dramatizes her exile to the Tower because of her suspected relationship with courtier and political intriguer Thomas Seymour.
Biography; Civics and Political Systems; History - World
Dist - FI **Prod** - BBCTV 1976

The Lions Den 10 MIN
16mm
B&W
Presents a middle aged failure who looks at himself and his past. Explores the concept of frustration, and depicts a rather subtle form of self - delusion. Portrays the man talking about his parents, his past life as a Pimp, his clothes and his way of life.
Guidance and Counseling; Psychology; Sociology
Dist - UPENN **Prod** - UPENN 1967

The Lion's den 80 MIN
VHS
Color (G)
$490.00 purchase, $100.00 rental
Provides a document of the trials that confront Matthew Longden, a new teacher fresh out of college, in his classroom in London. Records his inability to maintain control over this mixed race, mixed gender and mixed ability class of 14 - year - olds. We watch as two more experienced teachers step in temporarily and demonstrate their techniques for dealing with unruly teenagers.He analyzes his own work with an educational consultant, who points out his flaws and helps him build a presence which will earn the teenagers respect. Offers insight into the psychological warfare which is a significant component of the educational process. Produced by Oliver Morse.
Education; Fine Arts
Dist - FIRS

Lion's den 40 MIN
VHS
Dovetails series
Color (K P I R)
$12.95 purchase _ #35 - 82 - 2064
Presents the Old Testament stories of the walls of Jericho, and of Gideon, Samson, Ruth, Hannah, King Solomon and others.
Literature and Drama; Religion and Philosophy
Dist - APH

Lions Love 110 MIN
16mm
Color
Offers a free - form look at the culture of the 1960's.
Fine Arts
Dist - TWYMAN **Prod** - UNKNWN

Lions of capitalism 55 MIN
VHS
Color; Captioned (G)
$19.95 purchase _ #S01051
Profiles leading U S capitalists, including J P Morgan, Andrew Carnegie, Henry Ford and Ray Kroc. Features archival kinescope footage and photographs of the men. Narrated by Orson Welles, Robert MacNeil and Lowell Thomas.
Biography; Business and Economics; History - United States
Dist - UILL

Lions of Dakar 50 MIN
VHS
Color (G) (FRENCH WITH ENGLISH SUBTITLES)
$49.95 purchase _ #W3492
Documents the life and music in Dakar, Senegal, in Africa. Presents performance by Afro Pop musicians Youssou n'Dour, Ismael Lo and Super Diamono and commentary by leading critics.
Fine Arts; Foreign Language; Geography - World
Dist - GPC

Lions of Etosha 60 MIN
VHS
Color (G)
$24.95 purchase _ #S01997
Portrays a pride of lions as they go through their day - to - day lives. Reveals that the pride is characterized by fierce loyalties, but by daily rivalries as well.
Science - Natural
Dist - UILL **Prod** - SIERRA

Lions of the African Night 59 MIN
VHS / U-matic
Color (G)
Focuses on a pride of 30 lions to capture the sights and sounds of Africa after dark. Follows the lions as they hunt and eventually succeed in bringing down a wildebeest.
Science - Natural
Dist - NGS **Prod** - NGS

The Lion's roar 50 MIN
VHS / 16mm / U-matic
Color (C A)
Presents the belief system of Tibetan Buddhism by following the living embodiment of human compassion and enlightenment, the Karmapas, on his journey from Sikkim in the Indian Himalayas to the U.S. and Europe.
Religion and Philosophy; Sociology
Dist - CEPRO **Prod** - CEPRO
SBHALA
SNOWLI

The Lion's roar - 1924 - 1936 - Part one 121 MIN
VHS
When the lion roars series
B&W/Color (G)
$19.98 purchase _ #6302453186
Chronicles the beginnings of Metro Goldwyn Mayer - MGM, beginning with He Who Gets Slapped in 1924. Reveals that MGM once boasted that it was home to 'more stars than the heavens.' Tells about Garbo, Tarzan and the Marx Brothers. Focuses on studio head Louis B Mayer and producer Irving Thalberg, who inspired the title characters in The Last Tycoon by F Scott Fitzgerald. Part of a three - part series on MGM which recalls the stars and the wealth of stories behind the movies they made.
Fine Arts
Dist - INSTRU

A Lion's tale 13 MIN
16mm
Color (G)
$25.00 rental
Portrays a daydreaming young man in pursuit of the elusive woman of his dreams and his continual setbacks due to the intrusion of the filmmaker's own tricks.
Literature and Drama; Sociology
Dist - CANCIN **Prod** - UNGRW 1968

Lipid Storage Disease - Past, Present and Future 60 MIN
VHS / U-matic
Color
Discusses the clinical and metabolic aspects of lipid storage diseases, emphasizing diagnosis and carrier detection as well as therapeutic approaches. Includes Gaucher's, Niemann - Pick, Fabry's and Tay - Sachs Diseases.
Health and Safety
Dist - USNAC **Prod** - USHHS

Lipids 45 MIN
VHS
Introductory principles of nutrition series
Color (C A PRO)
$70.00 purchase, $16.00 rental _ #50704
Discusses lipids. Part of a 20 - part series on nutrition. Emphasizes controversial nutritional issues and the principle instructional objectives.
Health and Safety; Social Science
Dist - PSU **Prod** - WPSXTV 1978

Lipswitch Mandibular Labial Vestibuloplasty 10 MIN
16mm
Color
LC 80-701861
Describes the lipswitch vestibuloplasty, a procedure to correct an inadequate mandibular labial sulcus. Explains that it is a relatively simple surgical procedure and can be done on an outpatient basis under local anesthesia.
Health and Safety
Dist - USNAC **Prod** - VADTC 1980

Liquid Crystals 29 MIN
Videoreel / VT2
Interface Series
Color
Business and Economics; Science - Physical
Dist - PBS **Prod** - KCET

The Liquid Fire 30 MIN
16mm

Eternal Light Series
B&W (H C A)
LC 79-700963
Portrays the adult life of Samuel Gompers, who served as President of the American Federation of Labor. (Kinescope).
Religion and Philosophy
Dist - NAAJS **Prod** - JTS 1967

Liquid hazardous waste 15 MIN
VHS / U-matic / BETA
Hazardous waste training series
Color (IND G A)
$730.00 purchase, $150.00 rental _ #LIQ001
Trains workers who collect, place in containers and store liquid hazardous waste. Demonstrates the use of approved containers, waste segregation techniques, personal protection equipment, approved transfer methods, labeling requirements, storage regulations and in - plant spill reporting. Part of a comprehensive seven - part series on hazardous waste training.
Health and Safety; Psychology
Dist - ITF **Prod** - BNA

Liquid hazardous waste 19 MIN
BETA / VHS / U-matic
Handling hazardous waste series
Color; PAL (IND G) (SPANISH ITALIAN FRENCH PORTUGUESE)
$175.00 rental _ #LWH - 100
Provides specialized training for personnel involved in collecting, placing in containers and storing liquid hazardous waste. Discusses the use of approved containers, waste segregation techniques, personal protective equipment, approved transfer methods, labeling requirements, storage regulations and in - plant spill reporting. Includes leader's guide and 10 participant handouts. Part of a seven - part series which trains hazardous waste management workers.
Business and Economics; Health and Safety; Psychology; Sociology
Dist - BNA **Prod** - BNA

Liquid Hazardous Waste 21 MIN
U-matic
Color (IND)
Provides specialized training for personnel involved in collection, containerization, and storage of hazardous waste in liquid form. Use of approved containers, personal protective equipment, approved transfer methods, labeling requirements, and storage regulations n are demonstrated and discussed.
Health and Safety; Industrial and Technical Education; Sociology
Dist - BNA **Prod** - BNA 1987

Liquid junction potentials - the ph and its measurement - buffer solutions - non - aqueous 56 MIN
U-matic / VHS
Electrochemistry - Pt III - thermodynamics of galvanic cells series
Color
Discusses liquid junction potentials, the pH and its measurement, buffer solutions and non - aqueous solvents.
Science; Science - Physical
Dist - MIOT **Prod** - MIOT

Liquid Junction Potentials, the Ph and its Measurement, Buffer Solutions, Non - Aqueous 56 MIN
U-matic / VHS
Electrochemistry Series
Color
Discusses liquid junction potentials, the pH and its measurement, buffer solutions and non - aqueous solvents.
Science; Science - Physical
Dist - KALMIA **Prod** - KALMIA

Liquid Level Measurement - 1 60 MIN
VHS
Fundamentals of Instrumentation and Control Series
Color (PRO)
$600.00 - $1500.00 purchase _ #ICLL1
Focuses on the operating principles of simple level measuring instruments, float - actuated instruments, displacers, magnetic float devices, conductance and capacitance probes, sonic and radiation instruments. Part of a nineteen - part series on the fundamentals of instrumentation and control, which is part of a 49 - unit set on instrumentation and control. Includes five workbooks and an instructor guide to support four hours of instruction.
Industrial and Technical Education; Mathematics; Psychology
Dist - NUSTC **Prod** - NUSTC

Liquid Level Measurement - 2 60 MIN
VHS
Fundamentals of Instrumentation and Control Series
Color (PRO)
$600.00 - $1500.00 purchase _ #ICLL2
Shows how to convert pressure measurements into equivalent liquid level measurements. Part of a nineteen - part series on the fundamentals of instrumentation and control, which is part of a 49 - unit set on instrumentation and control. Includes five workbooks and an instructor guide to support four hours of instruction.
Industrial and Technical Education; Mathematics; Psychology
Dist - NUSTC **Prod** - NUSTC

Liquid level measurement series
Differential pressure
Electrical, Sonic and Radiation Level Measurement
Float - actuated and magnetic - float devices
Introduction to Liquid Level Measurement
Pressure and level measurement concepts
Temperature Compensation and Maintenance
Dist - NUSTC

Liquid - Liquid Solvent Extraction 60 MIN
VHS
Systems Operations Series
Color (PRO)
$600.00 - $1500.00 purchase _ #RCSEG
Considers the principles of liquid - liquid solvent extraction involving the three stages of contacting, separation and solvent recovery. Covers equipment used and operator responsibilities. Part of a seventeen - part series on systems operations. Includes ten textbooks and an instructor guide to support four hours of instruction.
Education; Health and Safety; Industrial and Technical Education; Psychology
Dist - NUSTC **Prod** - NUSTC

Liquid Natural Gas 16 MIN
16mm
Color
LC 74-706048
Introduces and explains the science of cryogenics as applied to natural gas. Shows how liquid natural gas can be transported safely by truck and ship and how it may power a new generation of pollution free cars and buses.
Science - Physical; Social Science
Dist - BUGAS **Prod** - BUGAS 1969

Liquid Penetrant Testing 55 MIN
BETA / VHS / U-matic
Color
$400 purchase
Gives history and development of penetrants and basic principles.
Industrial and Technical Education; Science; Science - Physical
Dist - ASM **Prod** - ASM

Liquid Penetrant Testing 55 MIN
U-matic / VHS
Fundamentals of Nondestructive Testing Series ATLANTA, GA 30332
Color (PRO)
Reviews the basic principles, history and development of liquid penetrant testing. Shows how to interpret test results.
Industrial and Technical Education
Dist - AMCEE **Prod** - AMCEE

The Liquid Show 25 MIN
16mm
Start Here - Adventures into Science Series
Color
Features experiments that demonstrate the remarkable properties of ordinary liquids found in the home.
Science - Physical
Dist - LANDMK **Prod** - VIDART 1982

Liquid volume 15 MIN
U-matic
Studio M series
Color (P)
Focuses on the proper use of the one - half liter and the one - fourth liter.
Mathematics
Dist - GPN **Prod** - WCETTV 1979

Liquid waste and the kidney 5 MIN
VHS
Systems of the human body series
Color (I J)
$24.95 purchase _ #L9625
Uses animation to clarify the functions of the kidney. Part of a seven - part series on the human body, using the single - concept format.
Science - Natural
Dist - HUBDSC **Prod** - HUBDSC

Liquid waste and the kidney 9 MIN
16mm / VHS
Systems of the human body series
Color (J H C)
$80.00 purchase _ #194 W 0097, #193 W 2097
Introduces the relationship between liquid wastes and internal body processes. Uses animated sequences to trace the path of urine. Part of a series on the systems of the human body.
Science - Natural
Dist - WARDS **Prod** - WARDS

Liquids 20 MIN
U-matic
Chemistry 101 Series
Color (C)
Deals with characteristics of liquids with special attention to water. Defines and demonstrates density, viscosity, surface tension, cohesive and adhesive forces, calling attention to certain practical results in the behavior of various liquids.
Science; Science - Physical
Dist - UILL **Prod** - UILL 1975

Liquids Can Burn 13 MIN
U-matic / VHS / 16mm
Color (I)
LC 75-700079
Uses demonstrations and laboratory experiments to show the flammability of various liquids found in the home.
Guidance and Counseling; Health and Safety; Social Science
Dist - HIGGIN **Prod** - HIGGIN 1973

Liquids I - 19 39 MIN
VHS
Conceptual physics alive series
Color (H C)
$45.00 purchase
Develops the concepts of density, pressure and buoyancy. Uses a variety of demonstrations to illustrate these concepts. Introduces Archimedes' principle. Part 19 of a 35 - part series adapted from the college and high school textbook Conceptual Physics by Professor Paul Hewitt.
Science - Physical
Dist - MMENTE **Prod** - HEWITP 1992

Liquids II - 20 38 MIN
VHS
Conceptual physics alive series
Color (H C)
$45.00 purchase
Extends the discussion of Archimedes' principle with emphasis on the law of flotation. Illustrates concepts in fluids with a variety of demonstrations. Part 20 of a 35 - part series adapted from the college and high school textbook Conceptual Physics by Professor Paul Hewitt.
Science - Physical
Dist - MMENTE **Prod** - HEWITP 1992

Liquor liability litigation 210 MIN
VHS
Color (C PRO A)
$52.20, $150.00 purchase _ #M655, #P178
Assists lawyers whose practice includes liquor liability cases. Discusses 'dram shop' suits against bars and establishments that serve liquor and alcohol - related motor vehicle deaths. Among topics covered are how to conduct the investigation, evaluation, discovery, settlement, and trial.
Civics and Political Systems; Health and Safety
Dist - ALIABA **Prod** - ALIABA 1986

Liru 25 MIN
U-matic / VHS
Color (G)
$125.00 purchase, $50.00 rental
Dramatizes a Chinese American woman's search for ethnic and personal identity. Reveals that Liru grapples with the strained relations she has with her mother and her boyfriend. She must decide whether to stay in San Francisco to look after her mother or jet off to Yale to be with her Korean Japanese boyfriend. Produced and directed by Henry Chow.
History - United States; Psychology; Sociology
Dist - CROCUR

Lisa and Billy - Birth 8
VHS / U-matic
Video birth library series
Color (J H G)
$100.00 purchase
Follows the childbirth experiences of Lisa, 18, who had a miscarriage a year ago. Reveals that her boyfriend Billy is anxious about being there for the delivery and Lisa has a low tolerance for pain. Although the midwives encourage her to walk and labor with little medication, she has an epidural before she delivers. Includes no explicit views of the delivery. Part of a 15 - part series on childbirth education.
Health and Safety
Dist - POLYMR **Prod** - POLYMR

Lisa, Aus Dem Leben Einer Unentbehrlichen 94 MIN
16mm
Color (GERMAN (ENGLISH SUBTITLES))
A German language motion picture with English subtitles. Focuses on an editor's secretary whose recognition of her position and of her own needs, dreams, and problems lead to depressing visions and hysterical moods instead of to solutions.
Foreign Language; Psychology; Sociology
Dist - WSTGLC **Prod** - WSTGLC 1973

Lisa - Pay Attention 22 MIN
16mm
Color (C A)
LC 71-709400
Presents everyday situations in order to see how a child with a hearing impairment reacts to and may be hampered in the events that she and her teacher experience. Helps teachers become more aware of children's hearing problems.
Education; Psychology
Dist - AVEXP **Prod** - PLATTS 1970

Lisa Steele - some Call it Bad Luck 47 MIN
U-matic / VHS
Color
Examines the process of interrogation in the format of a cop show.
Fine Arts
Dist - ARTINC **Prod** - ARTINC

Lisa Steele - the Gloria Tapes 12 MIN
U-matic / VHS
Color
Depicts Gloria, who lacks the ability to speak on her own behalf. Uses the soap opera format.
Fine Arts
Dist - ARTINC **Prod** - ARTINC

Lisa - the Legacy of Sandra Blain 22 MIN
16mm / U-matic / VHS
Color (H C A)
LC 81-700728
Follows the recovery of a young woman from alcohol abuse and explains the problems confronting young women alcoholics. Stresses the need for mental, physical and spiritual recovery programs and mentions community agencies offering help for women alcoholics.
Health and Safety; Psychology; Sociology
Dist - AIMS **Prod** - CAHILL 1979

Lisa's World 30 MIN
U-matic
Color (J A)
Focuses on a family with a mildly - retarded seven - year - old child. Discusses the difficulties and rewards of raising the child in a normal home setting and the effects on other members of the family.
Psychology; Sociology
Dist - UMITV **Prod** - UMITV 1969

Lisbon 30 MIN
VHS
Color (G)
$29.95 purchase _ #S02024
Tours the Portuguese capital, Lisbon. Features visits to the Alfama, the Tower of Belem, the National Museum of Ancient Art, and more.
Geography - World
Dist - UILL

Lissajous Figures 27 MIN
16mm
B&W
LC 74-705037
Shows lissajous figures on an oscilloscope. Discusses them in terms of their general use of phase and frequency determinations, and demonstrates their use. (Kinescope).
Industrial and Technical Education; Science - Physical
Dist - USNAC **Prod** - USAF 1963

Lissy 90 MIN
16mm
B&W (G) (GERMAN WITH ENGLISH SUBTITLES)
$150.00 rental
Follows a young woman from her roots in the socialist working class to complicity with Nazi stormtroopers to, finally, rejection of both the Nazis and her husband who had joined the National Socialist Party. Interprets Franz Weiskopf's anti - fascist novel which sheds light on the parallel, differing and intersecting paths of Nazis and socialists between 1932 and 1934.
Civics and Political Systems; History - World; Religion and Philosophy
Dist - NCJEWF

Listen 19 MIN
VHS / 16mm
(C PRO)
$650.00 purchase, $135.00 rental
Helps people appreciate listening as a skill, appreciate its importance, and learn simple and practical techniques to make them good listeners.
Education
Dist - VLEARN **Prod** - MELROS

Listen 10 MIN
16mm / U-matic / VHS
Color (I J H K P) (SPANISH)
LC 72-701729
Uses visual images suggested by different kinds of music to stimulate a deeper appreciation of music.
English Language; Fine Arts; Foreign Language
Dist - ALTSUL **Prod** - BNJVD 1972

Listen 19 MIN
VHS / U-matic
Color
Demonstrates that listening is a valuable skill and shares a number of listening techniques. Suggests exercises to heighten skills.
English Language; Psychology; Social Science
Dist - VISUCP **Prod** - MELROS

Listen 19 MIN
VHS / 16mm
Color (PRO)
$650.00 purchase, $135.00 rental, $35.00 preview
Demonstrates how good listening skills lead to business success. Describes practical techniques which teach how to listen. Includes supporting text.
Business and Economics; Education; Psychology
Dist - UTM **Prod** - UTM

Listen
VHS
Management Development Series
Color (G)
$795.00 purchase, $185.00 rental
Changes the behavior of a manager who creates problems by failing. Part of a five - part series on management development.
Business and Economics; English Language; Guidance and Counseling; Psychology; Social Science
Dist - VLEARN **Prod** - MELROS

Listen 42 MIN
16mm
Color (J)
LC 76-701161
Shows the problems created for paper workers and their families by industrial noise pollution.
Business and Economics; Health and Safety; Psychology; Science - Natural; Sociology
Dist - UPIU **Prod** - UPIU 1974

Listen 30 MIN
16mm / U-matic / VHS
Western Maryland College Series
Captioned; Color
Presents a documentary on hearing loss, its causes, its psychological meaning and what can be done to cope with the problem.
Guidance and Counseling; Psychology; Science - Natural
Dist - USNAC **Prod** - WMARYC 1973

Listen and Learn 28 MIN
U-matic / VHS
Please Stand by - a History of Radio Series
(C A)
Fine Arts; History - United States; Psychology; Sociology
Dist - SCCON **Prod** - SCCON 1986

Listen and Say Series
A Sometimes Vowel 15 MIN
Dist - GPN

Listen, ask and answer - enhancing aural ability and oral facility - Tape 4 35 MIN
VHS
Teacher to teacher series
Color (T)
$100.00 purchase _ #887 - 0
Shows exerienced teachers in actual classroom settings presenting various instructional approaches to both new and veteran ABE and ESL teachers. Teaches creative techniques for instructing beginning ESL students - small - group work and tape recordings of real - life situations. Part four of a 12 - part series.
Education; English Language
Dist - LAULIT **Prod** - LAULIT

Listen Caracas 19 MIN
16mm / U-matic / VHS
Color (SPANISH)
Offers insights into the process of cultural genocide by presenting the last surviving Yecuana chief in the Amazon region who, with great dignity and urgency, describes the disrespectful attitude of colonizers and missionaries toward his people's beliefs and way of life.
Foreign Language; History - World; Social Science; Sociology
Dist - CNEMAG **Prod** - AZPURC

Listen Cindy 18 MIN
U-matic / VHS / 16mm
Color (I J)
LC 81-701562
Teaches the importance of developing good listening skills through the story of a girl who violates most of the rules of being a good listener in order to win a gold star for her paper on the subject.
English Language; Guidance and Counseling
Dist - CF **Prod** - CF 1981

Listen Hear 15 MIN
16mm / U-matic / VHS
Human Senses Series
Color (P I)
Deals with the causes of sound, how the brain receives and recognizes sounds and the effects of sound on people. Uses animation to identify the parts of the ear and shows what happens when sound waves enter human ears.
Science - Natural
Dist - NGS **Prod** - NGS 1982

Listen, Listen 18 MIN
U-matic / VHS / 16mm
Color
Presents an unusual and highly symbolic film, which shows real - life situations in which people are enjoying fulfilled lives. Motivates viewers to consider positive alternatives in their own lives.
Guidance and Counseling; Psychology
Dist - FORDFL **Prod** - FORDFL

Listen, Look and Learn 15 MIN
U-matic / VHS
All about You Series
Color (P)
Points out the different parts of the eye and describes the function of each. Illustrates how sound travels through the ear. Explains why some people must wear hearing aids and glasses.
Science - Natural
Dist - AITECH **Prod** - WGBHTV 1975

Listen, Please 12 MIN
16mm / U-matic
Modern Management Series
Color (IND)
Shows an audience of supervisors that they often think they're better listeners than they really are. Emphasizes the importance of listening in a supervisory job.
Business and Economics; Health and Safety; Psychology
Dist - BNA **Prod** - BNA 1960

Listen to Communicate 40 MIN
U-matic / VHS / 16mm
Color (C A)
LC 80-700601
Presents the basic concepts and skills of good listening.
English Language
Dist - CRMP **Prod** - MGHT 1980

Listen to Communicate, Pt 1 20 MIN
U-matic / VHS / 16mm
Color (C A)
LC 80-700601
Presents the basic concepts and skills of good listening.
Psychology
Dist - CRMP **Prod** - MGHT 1980

Listen to Communicate, Pt 2 20 MIN
16mm / U-matic / VHS
Color (C A)
LC 80-700601
Presents the basic concepts and skills of good listening.
Psychology
Dist - CRMP **Prod** - MGHT 1980

Listen to me - physical child abuse 17 MIN
VHS
Color (P I J H)
Portrays young Brian who comes to the aid of his little sister Lizbeth and his friend Jeffrey when he seeks outside help for physical child abuse. Reveals that Brian's mother beat him when he was the same age as Lizbeth, and Jeff's arm is broken and Brian fears worse will happen. A school counselor and an abuse agency helps Brian's family deal with their problem and shows all children that there is help that can make a change.
Sociology
Dist - VIEWTH **Prod** - VIEWTH

Listen to me - physical child abuse 17 MIN
U-matic / BETA / 16mm / VHS
Color (P I J)
$450.00, $350.00 purchase _ #JR - 5174M
Tells about young Brian who comes to the aid of his little sister Lizbeth and his friend Jeffrey, both of whom are battered children. Reveals that his mother blames and beats six - year - old Lizbeth when things go wrong - Brian received the same treatment when he was six. When Jeff's arm is broken, Brian is afraid worse things will happen. Through the help of a school counselor and an abuse agency, Brian's family learns to deal with their problem.

Sociology
Dist - CORF Prod - AZPRO 1988

Listen - to the butterfly
VHS
Video Biblical illustrator series
Color (H C G A R)
$24.99 purchase, $10.00 rental _ #35 - 83600 - 533
Likens the path of spiritual growth to the development of a Monarch butterfly. Emphasizes the importance of trust in the growth process.
Literature and Drama; Religion and Philosophy
Dist - APH Prod - WORD

Listen to the Kid - Adolescents Talk about Diabetes 15 MIN
U-matic / VHS
Color (PRO)
Designed to help health professionals and parents understand the special problems facing the adolescent with a chronic illness like diabetes. Includes interviews with teenagers about how diabetes affects their lives.
Health and Safety; Psychology
Dist - UMICHM Prod - UMICHM 1982

Listen to the mountains 22 MIN
8mm cartridge
Color (H C A)
LC 77-703266
Follows two couples on a three - week ski mountaineering expedition in California's Sierra Nevada mountains.
Geography - United States; Physical Education and Recreation
Dist - PFP Prod - JONESD 1977

Listen to the Music 15 MIN
U-matic
Music Box Series
Color (K P)
Explains mood music by matching music and pictures.
Fine Arts
Dist - TVOTAR Prod - TVOTAR 1971

Listen to what I'm drawing and Fight to be straight 13 MIN
VHS
Color (P I)
$189.00 purchase
Uses animation to present drug - use prevention concepts to youngsters. Portrays a musician named Plum who is lured into trying drugs and alcohol, even though his friends urge him not to in Listen to What I'm Drawing. Fight to Be Straight traces the development of a baby into a stong, healthy boxer who fights 'drugs' in the ring, and wins.
Guidance and Counseling; Health and Safety; Psychology
Dist - SELMED

Listen up 12 MIN
VHS
Color (J H)
$195.00 purchase, $75.00 rental _ #8416
Defines and clearly explains AIDS and HIV. Discusses the known ways of contracting the virus. Dispels myths and answers common questions.
Health and Safety
Dist - AIMS Prod - AJN 1992

Listen up - Part I 12 MIN
VHS
Listen - up series
Color (P I J)
$99.00 purchase, $40.00 rental _ #4318S, #4318V
Features the rap group Hard Corps and a host who present vital information on HIV and AIDS. Answers questions such as: What is AIDS? How is it spread? Can I get it at school? Gives answers in a reassuring manner and addresses misconceptions. Clearly spells out ways to avoid infection. Part one of a two - part series.
Health and Safety
Dist - AJN Prod - ENVINC

Listen up - Part II 17 MIN
VHS
Listen - up series
Color (T)
$99.00 purchase, $40.00 rental _ #4319S, #4319V
Helps teachers and health care workers to prepare to discuss HIV and AIDS with young people. Provides essential background information and explores what concepts can be taught to each age group. Shows how to convey information without lecturing. To be used with Part I of the two - part series.
Education; Health and Safety
Dist - AJN Prod - ENVINC

Listen - up series 29 MIN
VHS
Listen - up series
Color (P I J T)
$149.00 purchase _ #4320S
Presents two parts presenting information on HIV and AIDs. Focuses on youngsters in Part I and features a rap group and host who convey information on HIV and AIDS without lecturing. Part II helps teachers and health care workers to prepare to discuss HIV and AIDS with young people.
Education; Health and Safety
Dist - AJN Prod - ENVINC

Listen up - teacher's edition 17 MIN
VHS
Color (T PRO)
$195.00 purchase, $75.00 rental _ #8417
Instructs teachers on how to teach students at various grade levels about AIDS and HIV.
Education; Health and Safety
Dist - AIMS Prod - AJN 1992

Listen Well, Learn Well 11 MIN
U-matic / VHS / 16mm
Color (P I)
$280, $195 purchase _ #3370
Discusses the importance of effective listening.
English Language
Dist - CORF

Listen Well, Learn Well 11 MIN
U-matic / VHS / 16mm
Color (P I)
Shows listening problems and how to solve them.
Education
Dist - CORF Prod - CORF 1974

Listen while You Can 21 MIN
16mm / U-matic / VHS
Color (J)
Uses animation to define sound and to illustrate the construction of the ear. Explains types of ear damage and kinds of noise conditions that are dangerous.
Science - Natural; Science - Physical
Dist - IFB Prod - UKMD 1972

Listen, You'll See - what We Say Vs How We Say it 6 MIN
16mm / U-matic / VHS
(G)
Helps provide an understanding of the communication process and the many factors that influence it. Shows that how we say something is often more important than what we say. Animated.
Business and Economics; English Language; Psychology
Dist - SALENG Prod - NFBC 1983

Listening 20 MIN
16mm
All that I Am Series
B&W (C A)
Guidance and Counseling; Psychology
Dist - NWUFLM Prod - MPATI

Listening 29 MIN
16mm
Developing Communication Skills Series
B&W (IND)
LC 70-703322
Guidance and Counseling; Psychology; Social Science
Dist - EDSD Prod - EDSD

Listening - 38 12 MIN
VHS / U-matic
Life's little lessons - self - esteem 4 - 6 series
Color (I)
$129.00, $99.00 purchase _ #V667
Portrays Milly and Clarence Cooper, celebrating their 50th wedding anniversary. Reveals that the only thing 50 years together had done for those two was to make them good at 'not listening.' Shows how they learned to change. Part of a 65 - part series on self - esteem.
English Language; Guidance and Counseling; Psychology; Social Science
Dist - BARR Prod - CEPRO 1992

Listening - a Key to Problem - Solving 22 MIN
16mm / U-matic / VHS
Color (H C A)
Identifies causes of poor listening habits and ways to improve those habits. Shows how improved listening reduces problems, improves working relationships, and increases productivity. Discusses the need for sensitivity to both the facts and the feelings in oral messages and how to increase understanding of implied messages.
Business and Economics; English Language
Dist - AIMS Prod - AIMS

Listening and responding skills 15 MIN
VHS / U-matic
Color (PRO C)
$395.00 purchase, $80.00 rental _ #C850 - VI - 070
Teaches how to be aware of barriers to listening and responding effectively and how to observe effective communication techniques to use in problem solving. Presented by Kathleen M Tiernan.
English Language; Health and Safety; Social Science
Dist - HSCIC

Listening and Singing 15 MIN
U-matic / VHS
Pass it on Series
Color (K P)
Discusses musical instruments, clapping patterns and the differences between soft and loud.
Education; Fine Arts
Dist - GPN Prod - WKNOTV 1983

Listening and Speaking 30 MIN
VHS / U-matic
Basic Education - Teaching the Adult Series
Color (T)
Deals with listening and speaking when teaching adult basic education students.
Education
Dist - MDCPB Prod - MDDE

Listening and you 30 MIN
VHS / U-matic
Effective listening series; Tape 1
Color
Demonstrates skills to become a good listener. Focuses on becoming aware of listening styles. Shows how to make a personal profile.
English Language
Dist - DELTAK Prod - TELSTR
TELSTR

Listening assertively 28 MIN
U-matic / BETA / VHS
Communication skills 1 - basic series
Color (H C G)
$101.95, $89.95 purchase _ #CA - 48
Describes assertive listening as the process of tuning into what is being said, grasping the intended meaning of the message, reading nonverbal cues correctly and in context. avoiding preconceptions about the speaker or message, turning off personal biases, withholding judgment until necessary clarifications are made and responding with appropriate feedback and empathetic listening techniques. Part of a series on communication.
English Language; Social Science
Dist - INSTRU

Listening between the lines 16 MIN
VHS / 16mm / U-matic
Color (I J H)
LC 75-700990
Examines obstacles which interfere with listening, such as distractions and personal prejudices which color what a person hears. Explores the issues of interpretation and evaluation and shows how listening is an acquired ability.
English Language; Guidance and Counseling
Dist - HIGGIN Prod - HIGGIN 1975

Listening Beyond Words 21 MIN
16mm
Color
LC 74-700705
Revised edition of 'ARE YOU LISTENING.' Presents several brief sketches showing communication problems in a family, in a business and in school in order to analyze and correct failures in interpersonal relations.
Guidance and Counseling; Psychology; Sociology
Dist - BYU Prod - BYU 1973

Listening, Discrimination, Association, Memory, Description, Pt 1 14 MIN
U-matic / VHS
I - Land Treasure Series
Color (K)
English Language
Dist - AITECH Prod - NETCHE 1980

Listening, Discrimination, Association, Memory, Description, Pt 2 13 MIN
U-matic / VHS
I - Land Treasure Series
Color (K)
English Language
Dist - AITECH Prod - NETCHE 1980

Listening, Discrimination, Association, Memory, Description, Pt 3 15 MIN
VHS / U-matic
I - Land Treasure Series
Color (K)
English Language
Dist - AITECH Prod - NETCHE 1980

Listening emotions 30 MIN
U-matic / VHS
Effective listening series; Tape 7
Color
Explores emotional triggers and how they interfere with listening.
English Language
Dist - TELSTR Prod - TELSTR

Listening Eyes 19 MIN
16mm
Color

LC FIA52-324
Demonstrates how a deaf child and her classmates are taught by tutors of the deaf to listen with their eyes and speak almost as well as normal hearing children.
Education; Health and Safety; Psychology
Dist - USC **Prod** - USC 1947

Listening for Language 22 MIN
16mm / U-matic / VHS
Ways of Hearing Series
Color (C A)
Introduces two auditory methods of teaching hearing impaired children language, the auditory - oral and the auditory - verbal. Strives in both methods to teach the child listening skills which will enable him/her to communicate and function in a hearing world.
Education; English Language; Guidance and Counseling; Psychology
Dist - BCNFL **Prod** - BCNFL

Listening for more sales 10 MIN
U-matic / VHS / 16mm
Color (A) (SPANISH PORTUGUESE DUTCH)
Shows an unsuccessful sales effort and analyzes the various reasons why the effort broke down. Shows how to apply successful listening techniques to close a deal.
Business and Economics; English Language; Psychology
Dist - RTBL **Prod** - SANDYC

Listening for Results 10 MIN
U-matic / VHS / 16mm
Color (A)
Shows a salesman and manager attempting to plan a sales campaign and committing such listening errors as interrupting, failing to pay attention, making assumptions and jumping to conclusions. Reveals how these problems could have been avoided.
Business and Economics; English Language
Dist - RTBL **Prod** - SANDYC 1982

Listening for the Sale 19 MIN
U-matic / VHS / 16mm
Color
Presents humorous vignettes which are designed to show salespeople how to direct a customer simply by listening.
Business and Economics
Dist - MGHT **Prod** - CRMP 1981

Listening for the sale 20 MIN
16mm / U-matic / VHS
Color (H C A)
LC 81-700328
Demonstrates that listening is an acquired skill that salespeople must develop in order to be successful. Shows obstacles to listening and illustrates time - proven techniques for successful listening.
Business and Economics; English Language
Dist - CRMP **Prod** - CRMP 1982

Listening Leaders 30 MIN
VHS / 16mm
Color (A PRO)
$625.00 purchase, $235.00 rental
Observes General Electric, Polaroid, J C Penney and Riverside Methodist Hospital obtaining feedback from customers. Management training in customer service.
Business and Economics
Dist - VIDART **Prod** - NATTYL 1990

Listening leaders 30 MIN
VHS
Color (A PRO IND)
$625.00 purchase, $235.00 rental
Reveals that many top companies seek feedback from their customers. Shows how they use this information to improve or develop products and services. Targeted to managers.
Business and Economics; English Language; Guidance and Counseling; Psychology; Social Science
Dist - VLEARN **Prod** - VIDART

Listening makes a difference 7 MIN
U-matic / VHS / 16mm
Color (A)
Demonstrates the importance of active listening. Shows that by listening to prospective customers and asking questions, a salesman can discover a customer's needs and wants.
Business and Economics
Dist - SALENG **Prod** - SALENG

The Listening process 28 MIN
U-matic / BETA / VHS
Communication skills 1 - basic series
Color (H C G)
$101.95, $89.95 purchase _ #CA - 46
Overviews the listening process. Identifies the relationship of listening to effective communication skills. Part of a series on communication.
English Language; Social Science
Dist - INSTRU

Listening Skills 30 MIN
U-matic / VHS
Communication Skills for Managers Series
Color (A)
Emphasizes active listening - listening that entails specific skills to promote a desired outcome. Presents host Paula Prentiss stressing the need for a listener to be receptive, while Richard Benjamin talks about the two parts of active listening, taking it in and checking it out.
Business and Economics; English Language; Psychology
Dist - TIMLIF **Prod** - TIMLIF 1981

Listening Skills 10 MIN
VHS / 16mm
Color (A PRO)
$200.00 purchase
Demonstrates how people feel when other don't listen to them. Management training.
Business and Economics; English Language; Guidance and Counseling; Psychology
Dist - VIDART **Prod** - VIDART 1991

Listening Skills - How to be an Active Listener
U-matic / 35mm strip
Color (H C)
Demonstrates techniques for improving listening skills in interpersonal, school and job situations. Illustrates the physical and psychological factors that can influence one's ability to listen.
English Language
Dist - GA **Prod** - GA

Listening Skills - the Art of Active Listening 56 MIN
VHS
Color (J H C)
LC 85-703928
Tells how listening affects work, study and social relationships. Describes major listening faults and explains the techniques of good listening and how to improve comprehension.
English Language; Guidance and Counseling
Dist - HRMC **Prod** - HRMC

Listening, Speaking and Nonverbal Language Skills 15 MIN
16mm / U-matic / VHS
Communication Skills Series
Color (P I)
LC 77-700114
Identifies, through a series of humorous skits, abuses and misuses of listening, speaking and nonverbal language skills. Describes and demonstrates correct and appropriate ways of using these skills.
English Language
Dist - PHENIX **Prod** - MOCEP 1976

Listening - the art of understanding others video 16 MIN
VHS
Building better communication at work series
Color (G)
$395.00 purchase, $175.00 rental _ #BBCV1, #BBCV1R
Helps to develop the essential skills of attending, gather information and demonstrating understanding. Part of a series on enhancing communication in the workplace.
Business and Economics; English Language; Social Science
Dist - GPERFO

Listening - the Forgotten Skill Series
Techniques for Handling Difficult People and Listening to Yourself 16 MIN
Understanding the Listening Process 11 MIN
Dist - DELTAK

Listening - the key to productivity
VHS
Color (G)
$59.95 purchase _ #CO004
Demonstrates listening techniques for improving productivity.
Business and Economics; English Language; Social Science
Dist - SIV

Listening - the problem solver 20 MIN
VHS / U-matic / 16mm
Color (H C G)
$450.00, $345.00, $315.00 purchase _ #A313
Demonstrates the way to use listening skills to resolve problems in communication. Shows how to listen critically, creatively and sympathetically.
English Language; Social Science
Dist - BARR **Prod** - CALLFM 1981

Listening to Music 4 MIN
16mm
Listening to Music Series
Color (P I J)
Covers four types of instruments found in an orchestra - strings, brass, wind and percussion.
Fine Arts
Dist - VIEWTH **Prod** - GATEEF

Listening to Music Series
Flute, clarinet and bassoon 12 MIN
Listening to Music 4 MIN
Percussion Instruments 13 MIN
The String Trio 9 MIN
Trumpet, Horn and Trombone 11 MIN
Dist - VIEWTH

Listening to Others 14 MIN
VHS / 16mm
Color (PRO)
$295.00 purchase, $95.00 rental, $35.00 preview
Explains how open, direct relationships can be accomplished through good listening skills. Shows how caring listeners create an atmosphere of mutual trust in which problems can be solved, decisions can be made and good working relationships can be developed. Describes techniques for developing listeneing skills.
Business and Economics; Education; Psychology
Dist - UTM **Prod** - UTM

Listening to Others 14 MIN
U-matic / VHS
Hub of the Wheel Series
Color (G)
$249.00, $149.00 purchase _ #AD - 1562
Addresses the importance of listening. Presents some useful techniques for developing listening skills. Part of a ten - part series for office professionals.
Business and Economics; Computer Science; English Language
Dist - FOTH **Prod** - FOTH

Listening Under Pressure 15 MIN
16mm / U-matic / VHS
Courtesy Under Pressure Series
(PRO A)
$495, $150 Rental 5 days, $35 Preview 3 days
Explains the importance of using effective listening skills when answering the telephone for a business. Teaches fundamental skills such as minimizing distractions, and maintaining eye contact.
Business and Economics
Dist - ADVANM **Prod** - ADVANM

Listening Under Pressure
VHS
Telephone Courtesy Under Pressure Series
$199.00 purchase _ #012 - 800
Discusses how effective listening skills reduce pressure and improve efficiency.
Business and Economics; Social Science
Dist - CAREER **Prod** - CAREER

Listening with a Third Ear 30 MIN
U-matic
Color (PRO)
LC 80-706505
Highlights an interview between a psychiatric nurse and patient in order to create an awareness of unrecognized interactional dynamics operative in professional relationships.
Health and Safety
Dist - USNAC **Prod** - VAHSL 1978

Listening with the Third Ear 20 MIN
16mm
All that I Am Series
B&W (C A)
Fine Arts; Guidance and Counseling
Dist - NWUFLM **Prod** - MPATI

Lists 50 MIN
U-matic / VHS
Computer languages series; Pt 1
Color
Discusses programming techniques for list processing functions in computer languages.
Industrial and Technical Education; Mathematics; Sociology
Dist - MIOT **Prod** - MIOT

Liszt at Weimar 53 MIN
U-matic / VHS
Man and Music Series
Color (C)
$279.00, $179.00 purchase _ #AD - 1766
Considers the patronage of composers. Focuses on Liszt, brought to court by the Archduke of Weimar. Here Liszt composed the Sympnonic Poems and the Faust Symphony. Part of a 22 - part series that sets Western music into the historial and cultural context of its time.
Civics and Political Systems; Fine Arts; History - World
Dist - FOTH **Prod** - FOTH

Liszt, the Piano, and Craig Sheppard 26 MIN
U-matic / VHS / 16mm
Musical Triangles Series
Color (J)
Presents Hungarian pianist and composer Franz Liszt (1811 - 1886) who is regarded as the greatest pianist of his age. Features professional pianist Craig Sheppard performing some of Liszt's most famous compositions in a theater where Liszt himself once played concerts.

Fine Arts
Dist - MEDIAG **Prod** - THAMES 1975

Lisztomania 105 MIN
16mm
Color
Portrays Franz Liszt as a 19th century pop star who wavers between the pleasures of the flesh and an almost religious devotion to his music. Directed by Ken Russell.
Fine Arts
Dist - TWYMAN **Prod** - WB 1975

Litany of Breath 7 MIN
16mm
Color
Analyzes the question whether a person can remain silent during fascist - style repression.
Civics and Political Systems; Fine Arts
Dist - CANWRL **Prod** - CANWRL

Lite and easy workout 30 MIN
VHS
Esquire great body series
Color (H C A)
$19.99 purchase _ #EQGB06V
Presents the sixth of a nine - part exercise series oriented to women. Combines stretches and exercises. Developed by Deborah Crocker.
Physical Education and Recreation; Science - Natural
Dist - CAMV

The Litek Lamp 20 MIN
U-matic
Breakthrough Series
Color (H C)
Looks at the Litek lamp which emits more than 85 percent of its radiative energy in the visible band of the spectrum. The lamp is three times more efficient than the conventional light bulb and more convenient than the fluorescent tube.
Science; Science - Physical
Dist - TVOTAR **Prod** - TVOTAR 1985

Literacy
VHS
About the United Nations series
Color (J H C G)
$29.95 purchase _ #UNE91135V - S
Documents the work of the United Nations in promoting better living standards through education. Depicts the feelings of isolation and dependence shared by illiterates from both developed and developing countries. Gives students a better appreciation of their own education and they are encouraged to promote literacy in their own communities. Part of a seven - part series on the United Nations.
Civics and Political Systems; Education
Dist - CAMV **Prod** - UN

Literacy Instructor Training Series
Comprehension 20 MIN
Language Experience Approach 20 MIN
Patterns in Language 20 MIN
Talking it Over 20 MIN
Word Analysis Skills 20 MIN
Dist - IU

Literacy Lost 26 MIN
U-matic / VHS
Color (C)
$249.00, $149.00 purchase _ #AD - 1879
Estimates that there are 60 million functional illiterates in the United States currently, which puts the US 45th worldwide in literacy.
English Language; Psychology
Dist - FOTH **Prod** - FOTH

Literacy Lost - 215 30 MIN
U-matic
Currents - 1985 - 86 Season Series
Color (A)
Shows the concerns of the public and some educators over the slipping achievement scores of American students and the inability of many to read at even basic levels.
English Language; Social Science
Dist - PBS **Prod** - WNETTV 1985

Literary and Performing Arts 40 MIN
VHS / 16mm
Video Career Library Series
Color (H C A PRO)
$79.95 purchase _ #WW107
Shows occupations in the literary and performing arts such as writers, designers, musicians, actors and directors, painters, sculptors, photographers, editors, reporters, publicists, radio and television personalities, athletes, graphic artists and others. Contains current occupational outlook and salary information.
Business and Economics; Fine Arts; Guidance and Counseling
Dist - AAVIM **Prod** - AAVIM 1990

Literary Essay 1 30 MIN
VHS / U-matic
Communicating through Literature Series
Color (C)
Literature and Drama
Dist - DALCCD **Prod** - DALCCD

Literary Essay 2 30 MIN
VHS / U-matic
Communicating through Literature Series
Color (C)
Literature and Drama
Dist - DALCCD **Prod** - DALCCD

Literary - Performing Arts 40 MIN
U-matic / VHS
Video Career Library Series
(H C A)
$69.95
Covers duties, conditions, salaries and training connected with jobs in the performing arts field. Provides a view of employees in art related occupations on the job, and gives information concerning the current market for such skills. Revised every two years.
Fine Arts
Dist - CAMV **Prod** - CAMV

A Literate society - the computing machine I - Parts 1 and 2 60 MIN
U-matic / VHS
New literacy - an introduction to computers
Color (G)
$45.00, $29.95 purchase
Presents an introduction to computers and data processing. Discusses data versus information in Part 1. Explores the vast number of settings in which computers are used in the first part of two parts on computing machines and Part 2 of a 26 - part series on computers.
Computer Science; Industrial and Technical Education; Mathematics; Psychology
Dist - ANNCPB **Prod** - SCCON 1988

Literature 15 MIN
U-matic / VHS
Pass it on Series
Color (K P)
Identifies rhyming words and ways that poems and stories are different.
Education; Literature and Drama
Dist - GPN **Prod** - WKNOTV 1983

Literature 30 MIN
U-matic / VHS
Afro - American Perspectives Series
Color (C)
Discusses black trends in literature.
History - United States
Dist - MDCPB **Prod** - MDDE

Literature and psychology - characters in crisis 51 MIN
VHS
Color (J H)
$99.00 purchase _ #00279 - 026
Studies the effects of crisis and fantasy on the lives of a wide range of fictional characters. Shows how they deal with internal and external crises and the worlds of fantasy. Includes a dramatization of The Rocking - Horse Winner by D H Lawrence, along with a teacher's guide and library kit.
Education; Literature and Drama
Dist - GA

Literature - Behind the Words 30 MIN
U-matic
Humanities through the Arts with Maya Angelou Series
Lesson 17; Lesson 17
Color (C A)
Discusses some questions and topics basic to the critical, analytical approach to literature. Explores nature of creative process, writers' inspiration, role of rhythm in poetry and reasons for popularity of some modern fiction over others.
Literature and Drama
Dist - CDTEL **Prod** - COAST

Literature - fairy tales series 106 MIN
VHS / 16mm
Literature - fairy tales series
Color (P)
$2950.00, $2650.00 purchase
Presents ten fairy tales. Includes the titles 'The Brave Little Tailor', 'The Frog Prince', 'Little Red Riding Hood', 'Lucky Hans', 'Mother Holle', 'Puss in Boots', 'The Selfish Giant', 'The Steadfast Tin Soldier', 'The Table, the Donkey and the Stick', 'The Wolf and the Seven Goats'.
Literature and Drama
Dist - BNCHMK **Prod** - BNCHMK

Literature for Children 29 MIN
VHS / U-matic
Focus on Children Series
Color (C A)
LC 81-707451
Presents a noted children's librarian and educator exploring the place of books and literature in general in the live of young people from infancy to adolescence.
Education; Literature and Drama; Psychology
Dist - IU **Prod** - IU 1981

Literature - from Words, Truth 30 MIN
U-matic
Humanities through the Arts with Maya Angelou Series
Lesson 14; Lesson 14
Color (C A)
Traces evolution of the alphabet as the essential tool in written literature. Surveys characteristics of literature in each of the major periods of Western literature. Notes how various types of literature have portrayed humankind differently.
Literature and Drama
Dist - CDTEL **Prod** - COAST

Literature - Legacy for the Future 18 MIN
U-matic / VHS / 16mm
Humanities Series
Color (J H C)
LC 78-714101
An introduction to the study of literature.
Guidance and Counseling; Literature and Drama
Dist - MGHT **Prod** - MGHT 1971

The Literature of science fiction - an overview 37 MIN
VHS
Color (J H C A)
$93.00 purchase _ #MB - 540801 - 5
Presents a two - part examination of the genre of science fiction. 'What is Science Fiction' traces the roots of science fiction from Plato's Republic through Mary Shelley, Jules Verne, and H G Wells. 'The Study of Mankind' discusses science fiction's frequent focus on human problems and conflicts, and considers works by such authors as Isaac Asimov, Arthur Clarke, Ray Bradbury, and many others.
Literature and Drama
Dist - SRA **Prod** - SRA

Literature of Science Fiction Series
History of Science Fiction from 1938 to the Present 32 MIN
Lunch with John Campbell, Jr - an Editor at Work 28 MIN
New Directions in Science Fiction 25 MIN
Plot in Science Fiction 25 MIN
Science fiction films 30 MIN
Dist - UKANS

The Literature of Sports 29 MIN
Videoreel / VT2
One to One Series
Color
Literature and Drama; Physical Education and Recreation
Dist - PBS **Prod** - WETATV

Literature of the supernatural - worlds beyond reason 40 MIN
VHS
Color (J H)
$99.00 purchase _ #00265 - 026
Explores supernatural beings such as angels, demons, gods and spirits. Introduces the three witches of Shakespeare, Young Goodman Brown by Nathaniel Hawthorne, and The Strange Case of Dr Jekyll and Mr Hyde by Robert Louis Stevenson. Includes teacher's guide and library kit.
Education; Literature and Drama
Dist - GA

Literature, Pt 1 30 MIN
VHS / U-matic
Japan - the Living Tradition Series
Color (H C A)
Examines the literature in Japan.
History - World; Literature and Drama
Dist - GPN **Prod** - UMA 1976

Literature, Pt 2 30 MIN
U-matic / VHS
Japan - the Living Tradition Series
Color (H C A)
Examines the literature in Japan.
History - World; Literature and Drama
Dist - GPN **Prod** - UMA 1976

Literature - the Story Beyond 30 MIN
U-matic
Humanities through the Arts with Maya Angelou Series
Lesson 16; Lesson 16
Color (C A)
Defines good fiction and gives an overview of the history of fiction. Examines the basic elements of fiction through film and narrative of The Lottery read by Maya Angelou.
Literature and Drama
Dist - CDTEL **Prod** - COAST

Literature - the Synthesis of Poetry 30 MIN
U-matic
Humanities through the Arts with Maya Angelou Series Lesson 15; Lesson 15
Color (C A)
Centers on elements of poetry and on how those elements are fused to create a form that conveys the poet's meaning. Analyzes rhythm, imagery, repetition, meaning and rhyme.
Literature and Drama
Dist - CDTEL **Prod** - COAST

Literature with a message - protest and propaganda, satire and social comment
VHS
Color (J H C)
$197.00 purchase _ #00262 - 126
Analyzes literature written to rally support for causes, to satirize human folly, to protest injustice, to encourage idealism and spiritual rebirth. Examines literary propaganda in the Horatio Alger stories and the wartime speeches of Winston Churchill. Looks at examples of protest literature in the works of Alan Paton, Stephen Crane, e e cummings, Jonathan Swift, George Orwell, Arthur Miller. Includes teacher's guide and library kit. In two parts.
Literature and Drama; Religion and Philosophy; Sociology
Dist - GA **Prod** - GA

Lithography 25 MIN
VHS
Artists in print series
Color (A)
PdS65 purchase
Introduces the art of printmaking and illustrates basic printmaking techniques. Artists talk about their approach to the medium and are seen at all stages of making a print. Asks what a print is and explains the difference between an 'original' and a reproduction. Part of a five-part series.
Fine Arts; Industrial and Technical Education
Dist - BBCENE

Lithography 30 MIN
U-matic
Media and Methods of the Artist Series
Color (H C A)
Demonstrates drawing and printing on stone.
Fine Arts
Dist - TVOTAR **Prod** - TVOTAR 1971

Lithography 25 MIN
VHS / U-matic
Artist in print series
Color (H C A)
Shows a lithographer drawing directly onto lithographic zinc plates using a detailed drawing in colored pencils. Shows another lithographer spraying lithographic ink through masks onto his plates to build up the image in tones after which the plates are processed and proofed.
Industrial and Technical Education
Dist - FI **Prod** - BBCTV

The Lithuanian Ethnographic Ensemble 30 MIN
U-matic / VHS
Color
Shows actors, musicians and other artists of the renowned Lithuanian Ethnographic Ensemble combine their talents to perform Lithuanian polyphonic folks songs throughout scenic locations in their native land.
Fine Arts
Dist - IHF **Prod** - IHF

Litigating employment discrimination claims 210 MIN
VHS
Color (C PRO A)
$67.50, $160.00 purchase _ #M710, #P219
Provides lawyers with an understanding of the possibilities and techniques needed to successfully litigate and defend employment discrimination claims.
Civics and Political Systems; Social Science; Sociology
Dist - ALIABA **Prod** - ALIABA 1988

The Litter Monster 17 MIN
16mm / U-matic / VHS
Color (I J)
Presents an overview of the litter problem indicating the dollar costs per year to clean up littered areas. Points out that this money could be better used to support medical research or to fund better housing projects. Shows a variety of projects across the nation where young people have recognized the litter problem and are doing something about it.
Guidance and Counseling; Science - Natural; Sociology
Dist - HIGGIN **Prod** - HIGGIN 1972

Litterature francaise
CD-ROM
(G) (FRENCH)
$495.00 purchase _ #2272
Contains a collection of French literature from 380 authors, from the Chanson de Roland to 19th century novels and poetry. Produced by Act and Nathan Logiciels. Users can search by theme, form and technique, author, title, and historical event. Also includes an index of philosophic and literary terminology. For IBM PCs and compatibles, requires 640K RAM, DOS 3.1 or later, one floppy disk drive - hard disk recommended, one empty expansion slot, and an IBM compatible CD - ROM drive. A mouse is recommended.
Literature and Drama
Dist - BEP

The Litterbug 8 MIN
U-matic / VHS / 16mm
Color (P) (ITALIAN SPANISH SWEDISH)
Discourages littering. Hosted by Donald Duck.
Guidance and Counseling; Health and Safety; Science - Natural
Dist - CORF **Prod** - DISNEY 1962

Litterbug 5 MIN
16mm
Adventures in the High Grass Series
Color (K P I)
LC 74-702130
Depicts an insect community in puppet animation.
Guidance and Counseling; Literature and Drama; Science - Natural
Dist - MMA **Prod** - MMA 1972

Litters 9 MIN
16mm
Color
Tells what happens when a horde of rampaging letters lays waste to Coney Island by obstructing traffic, scattering litter, spray painting graffiti and harassing people. Shows how they are forced to rectify their damage and are imprisoned once again in trash barrels.
Fine Arts; Literature and Drama; Sociology
Dist - DIRECT **Prod** - MOURIS

Little 10 MIN
U-matic
Readalong Two Series
Color (P)
Provides young viewers with a flexible range of reading experiences through active involvement in reading and writing. Comes with teacher's guide and kit.
Education; English Language; Literature and Drama
Dist - TVOTAR **Prod** - TVOTAR 1976

The Little airplane that grew 9 MIN
U-matic / VHS / 16mm
Color (P I) (FRENCH)
LC 77-700602
Features an imaginative schoolboy who realizes his dream of flying his airplane.
Literature and Drama
Dist - LCOA **Prod** - LCOA 1969

Little Annie Rooney 97 MIN
16mm
B&W
Reveals that Little Annie Rooney, the daughter of a policeman, divides her time between getting into mischief and caring for her father and her brother, Tim. Reveals that when Annie's father is killed, Annie and Tim become intent on revenge. Stars Mary Pickford and William Haines. Directed by William Beaudine.
Fine Arts
Dist - KILLIS **Prod** - PICKFO 1925

Little Arliss 24 MIN
U-matic / VHS
American People and Places Series
Color (K)
$179.00, $79.00 purchase _ #AD - 1322
Presents a story of the American West in the late 1800s. Tells of Little Arliss, a twelve - year - old boy who tries to prove himself a man and succeeds, so that he isn't 'Little' Arliss any more. Part of a twelve - part series on American people and places.
Literature and Drama; Psychology; Sociology
Dist - FOTH **Prod** - FOTH

The Little Bear Keepers 51 MIN
16mm / U-matic / VHS
Featurettes for Children Series
Color (I J)
Presents the story of Pepiko, whose father is a zoo keeper. Tells how Pepiko learns that his favorite bear cub, Bruno, is about to be traded to another zoo and how Pepiko 'cub - naps' Bruno, embarking on a series of wild adventures.
Literature and Drama
Dist - FI **Prod** - AUDBRF

Little Bear - Sexual abuse prevention for children ages 4 - 9 30 MIN
VHS
Color (P I)
$149.00 purchase _ #3633 - V
Adapts a play written in 1981 which teaches children to recognize, prevent and report sexual abuse. Uses sights, sounds and language appropriate for young children. Animal characters show how to avoid sexual abuse and what to do if it occurs.
Health and Safety
Dist - KIDSRI **Prod** - NEWIST

Little Bear - Sexual abuse prevention for children ages 4 - 9 package 120
VHS
Color (P I T PRO C)
$199.00 purchase _ #3635 - V
Presents two programs on preventing sexual abuse of children. Includes a child's version featuring animal characters who show children how to prevent sexual abuse and what to do if it happens and an in - service program for teachers and other professionals who work with children to support the children's video. Teacher's manual and coloring book for children.
Health and Safety
Dist - KIDSRI **Prod** - NEWIST

Little Bear - Sexual abuse prevention for children ages 4 - 9 - Professional 30 MIN
VHS
Color (T PRO C)
$149.00 purchase _ #3634 - V
Supports the video of the same name teaching children to recognize, prevent and report sexual abuse as an in - service program for teachers and other professionals who work with children.
Health and Safety
Dist - KIDSRI **Prod** - NEWIST

Little Big Land 29 MIN
16mm
Earthkeeping Series
Color (H C A)
LC 73-703403
Describes how the tremendous growth of cities and highways has obliterated many of the Earth's natural systems. Explains the theories of urban experts who believe that total land - use planning and population control can help accommodate people and preserve the inherent values of the land.
Science - Natural; Sociology
Dist - IU **Prod** - WTTWTV 1973

Little Big Top 10 MIN
16mm
Color (I)
LC 78-700800
Takes a behind - the - scenes look at the everyday life of a small traveling circus troupe.
Physical Education and Recreation; Social Science; Sociology
Dist - NFBC **Prod** - NFBC 1978

Little big top 9 MIN
16mm
Amazing life game theater series
Color (K)
LC 72-701751
Uses a circus put on by life game players to teach mathematical concepts to pre - school children. Shows the children as they enjoy discovering geometric shapes in everything around them.
Mathematics
Dist - HMC **Prod** - HMC 1971

A Little Bit more Pregnant 29 MIN
Videoreel / VT2
Maggie and the Beautiful Machine - Pregnancy Series
Color
Health and Safety; Physical Education and Recreation
Dist - PBS **Prod** - WGBHTV

A Little Bit of Everything 15 MIN
U-matic / VHS
Soup to Nuts Series
Color (J H)
Shows Hansel and Gretel teaching the witch about empty calories and the need for a balanced diet. Presents private eye Max Lionel discussing the Case of the Neglected Nutrients.
Health and Safety; Social Science
Dist - AITECH **Prod** - GSDE 1980

A Little Bit of Paris 15 MIN
U-matic / VHS
Other families, other friends series; Red module; France
Color (P)
Pictures the Notre Dame Cathedral, Montmartre and the Eiffel Tower in Paris, France.

Geography - World; Social Science
Dist - AITECH Prod - WVIZTV 1971

A Little Bit Pregnant 29 MIN
Videoreel / VT2
Maggie and the Beautiful Machine - Pregnancy Series
Color
Health and Safety; Physical Education and Recreation
Dist - PBS Prod - WGBHTV

The Little Black Box 28 MIN
VHS / U-matic
Please Stand by - a History of Radio Series
(C A)
Fine Arts; History - United States; Psychology; Sociology
Dist - SCCON Prod - SCCON 1986

The Little Black Puppy 6 MIN
16mm / U-matic / VHS
Golden Book Storytime Series
Color (P)
Presents the story of a puppy who is disliked by a boy's family until it grows up.
Literature and Drama
Dist - CORF Prod - CORF 1977

Little Blocks 8 MIN
16mm
Exploring Childhood Series
Color (J)
LC 76-701888
Presents a situation in which a teenager has difficulty in working with a shy young boy. Shows the boy discussing the situation with his classmates.
Guidance and Counseling; Health and Safety; Psychology
Dist - EDC Prod - EDC 1976

Little Blue and Little Yellow 10 MIN
U-matic / VHS / 16mm
Color (P I)
An animated version of Leo Lionni's book in which Little Blue and Little Yellow turn green to the amazement of their friends and parents.
Literature and Drama
Dist - MGHT Prod - HILBER 1962

A Little boat 14 MIN
VHS / U-matic
En Francais series
Color (H C A)
Contrasts a pond on the Ile de - France and a school near Grenoble where the world's most unnavigable waterways are reconstructed in miniature.
Foreign Language; Geography - World
Dist - AITECH Prod - MOFAFR 1970

Little boxes 50 MIN
VHS
Horizon series
Color (A)
PdS99 purchase
Takes the position that real modern art exists in the home. Reveals that telephones and typewriters are more expressive of this age than many paintings and sculptures. Industrial designers have for years followed the rule that form follows function - but now all this is changing.
Fine Arts; Industrial and Technical Education
Dist - BBCENE

Little boy 54 MIN
16mm / VHS
Color (G)
$100.00 rental, $59.00 purchase
Views America through the lens of contemporary New Mexico, focusing on the harsh realities of Indian and Chicano life. Takes an anti - nuke stance and illuminates the dichotomy of a man - made environment vs. unforgiving landscape; high tech atomic power vs impoverished Native Americans and Chicanos; traditional cultural values vs new and alien ones; a law enforcement and penal system that upholds WASP standards of living vs a frontier lifestyle and mindset. Title is the name given by the Atomic bomb creators to that bomb built in New Mexico and dropped on Hiroshima. A Danny Lyon production.
Fine Arts; Geography - United States; Social Science; Sociology
Dist - CANCIN

Little boy of summer 30 MIN
VHS
Color (J H C G A R)
$24.95 purchase, $10.00 rental _ #35 - 8800 - 19
Tells the story of a little boy who learns about God's love from a major league baseball player.
Religion and Philosophy; Sociology
Dist - APH Prod - CPH

Little boy summer 30 MIN
VHS
Crossroads of life series
Color (G R)
$24.95 purchase _ #87EE0800
Tells how a major league baseball player leads a little boy to the understanding that God loves him.
Guidance and Counseling; Literature and Drama; Religion and Philosophy
Dist - CPH Prod - CPH

Little Brother Montgomery 30 MIN
U-matic
After Hours with Art Hodes Series
Color
Features blues piano player and singer Little Brother Montgomery. Includes the songs Mule Face Blues, Cow Cow Blues, Gonna Move On The Outskirts Of Town, and others.
Fine Arts
Dist - FAJAZZ Prod - FAJAZZ

The Little Brown Burro 23 MIN
U-matic / VHS / 16mm
Color (P I)
LC 79-700442
Presents the tale of a little donkey, belittled as useless, who comes to realize that by doing his best he can make his own special contributions.
Guidance and Counseling; Literature and Drama; Religion and Philosophy; Social Science
Dist - LCOA Prod - ATKINS 1979

The Little Brown Burro
VHS / BETA
Color
Tells the story of a little brown burro.
Literature and Drama; Physical Education and Recreation
Dist - EQVDL Prod - EQVDL

Little bug and Minderella - Volume 2 25 MIN
VHS
Filling station series
Color (K P I R)
$11.99 purchase _ #35 - 811319 - 979
Combines live action and animated sequences to teach the message that children are to obey their parents at all times.
Literature and Drama; Religion and Philosophy
Dist - APH Prod - TYHP

Little Businessman 28 MIN
16mm
Color (K P I)
Reveals that Luke's uncle wants to do away with Luke's pet dog. Describes an agreement which is reached wherein Luke pays his uncle to allow the old dog to live out his days in his uncle's house.
Literature and Drama
Dist - FI Prod - CANBC

Little by Little 14 MIN
U-matic / VHS
Strawberry Square Series
Color (P)
Fine Arts
Dist - AITECH Prod - NEITV 1982

Little by Little - a Portrait of Immigrant Women 30 MIN
U-matic
Challenge Series
Color (PRO)
Focuses on a group of immigrant women who take part in a job traiing program they hope will take them out of factory work.
Psychology; Sociology
Dist - TVOTAR Prod - TVOTAR 1985

The Little car 13 MIN
VHS
Color; PAL (K P I)
PdS29
Tells about a little car which dislikes its color - green - and wants to be red. Follows the car through its adventures, where it is treated as a magic car and not as part of real traffic.
Fine Arts; Religion and Philosophy
Dist - BHA

Little children - Part I 20 MIN
VHS
Joy of life series
Color (I J)
$175.00 purchase
Introduces parts of male and female bodies and the concepts of conception and genetic inheritance using an animated story format. Contains four five - minute segments. Segment 1 - Little Boys explains male genitalia. Segment 2 - Little Girls details female genitalia. Segment - Tiny Seeds explains the menstrual cycle and conception. Segment 4 - Chromosomes discusses genetics. Part of a series.
Health and Safety; Science - Natural
Dist - PFP Prod - EVENOP

Little Chimney Sweep 10 MIN
16mm
Lotte Reiniger's Animated Fairy Tales Series
B&W (K P I)
Shows the fairy tale 'LITTLE CHIMNEY SWEEP' in animated form based on the live shadow plays L Reiniger produced for BBC television.
Literature and Drama
Dist - MOMA Prod - PRIMP 1956

Little Christmas Elf 8 MIN
VHS / U-matic
Giant First Start Series
Color (K P)
$29.95 purchase _ #VL008
Tells the story of a Little Christmas Elf. Contains a 32 page hardcover book and a video.
English Language; Literature and Drama
Dist - TROLA

Little Church Around the Corner 60 MIN
16mm
B&W
LC 72-709612
A drama concerning an orphan who is reared to be a minister in a small mining town, but later becomes torn between his duty to the people of the town and his love for the mine owner's daughter, who wants him to preach in New York.
Fine Arts
Dist - WB Prod - WB 1923

Little City 31 MIN
16mm
Color (T)
LC 80-701362
Shows the learning activities and social interaction of retarded, emotionally handicapped and blind individuals living at Little City Foundation residential training community.
Education; Psychology
Dist - FLMLIB Prod - LICIFO 1980

Little computers - see how they run series

Character I/O Devices	18 MIN
CPU and memory	18 MIN
Data communication	18 MIN
Making Things Happen	18 MIN
Mass storage devices	18 MIN
Meet the Computer	18 MIN
Speech, Music and Graphics	18 MIN

Dist - GPN

Little computers...see how they run

Character I 0 Devices	18 MIN
Inside the Computer	18 MIN
Making things happen	18 MIN

Dist - GPN

Little David's adventure 52 MIN
VHS
Color (K P I R)
$19.99 purchase, $10.00 rental _ #35 - 83539 - 533
Uses animation, live action, special effects and music to present a time - travel account of the story of David and Goliath. Features contemporary Christian singer Sandi Patti.
Literature and Drama; Religion and Philosophy
Dist - APH Prod - WORD

A Little Death 30 MIN
U-matic / VHS / 16mm
Color (H C A)
Tells how a woman and a priest concoct a plan for teaching her husband a lesson. Based on Giovanni Boccaccio's Tales Of The Decameron.
Fine Arts; Literature and Drama
Dist - PHENIX Prod - PHENIX 1979

The Little Dog and the Bees 7 MIN
16mm / U-matic / VHS
Color (K P)
LC 83-700010
Presents an animated story in which a little dog and a kitten cross paths with a greedy alley cat when trying to keep him from taking some honeycomb from their friends the bees. Shows how the dog and the kitten come out ahead through ingenuity and teamwork.
Fine Arts
Dist - PHENIX Prod - ROMAF 1982

The Little Dog and the Chicks 8 MIN
16mm / U-matic / VHS
Little Dog Series
Color (I J)
LC 84-706793
Tells the story about Little Dog and his friend Kitten being mistakenly identified as their mother by a group of newborn chicks. They devise a clever plan to get the chicks back into their shells to be greeted by their real mother when they are 'born' a second time.
Fine Arts
Dist - PHENIX Prod - KRATKY

The Little Dog and the Goat 8 MIN
16mm / U-matic / VHS
Little Dog Series
Color (K P)
Presents the story of Little Dog and his friend Kitten helping a baby goat who has a bump on his head and thinks it was caused by Friend Squirrel carelessly throwing acorns. Explains that the real reason for the bump is that the goat is growing his first set of horns.
Fine Arts; Literature and Drama
Dist - PHENIX **Prod** - ROMAF

Little Dog Goes Fishing 8 MIN
U-matic / VHS / 16mm
Little Dog Series
Color (I)
LC 84-706794
Tells how several fish, too clever to allow themselves to be caught, come to the aid of their would - be captors when they fall into the river. The fishes' act of kindness makes the fishermen abandon fishing and they all part as friends.
Fine Arts
Dist - PHENIX **Prod** - KRATKY

The Little Dog Goes Skiing 8 MIN
U-matic / VHS / 16mm
Little Dog Series
Color (I)
LC 84-706795
Describes how Little Dog and Kitten make themselves comfortable in a warm, seemingly unoccupied cabin after a day of skiing until the irritable owner returns to evict them. Tells that when, as a result of his bad temper, the owner gets into trouble, Little Dog and Kitten rescue him and find themselves welcome in the cabin.
Fine Arts
Dist - PHENIX **Prod** - KRATKY

Little dog lost 48 MIN
16mm / U-matic / VHS
Animal featurettes series; Set 1
Color
LC 77-701893
Presents the story of Candy, a Welsh Cordy, who becomes lost from his master.
Literature and Drama
Dist - CORF **Prod** - DISNEY

Little Dog Lost 6 MIN
16mm / U-matic / VHS
Golden Book Storytime Series
Color (P)
Relates that while searching for their lost dog, Tim and Jody visit all kinds of neighborhood stores.
Literature and Drama
Dist - CORF **Prod** - CORF 1977

Little dog lost - Pt 1 24 MIN
16mm / U-matic / VHS
Animal featurettes series; Set 1
Color
LC 77-701893
Presents the story of Candy, a Welsh Corgy, who becomes lost from his master.
Fine Arts
Dist - CORF **Prod** - DISNEY

Little dog lost - Pt 2 24 MIN
U-matic / VHS / 16mm
Animal featurettes series; Set 1
Color
LC 77-701893
Presents the story of Candy, a Welsh Corgy, who becomes lost from his master.
Fine Arts
Dist - CORF **Prod** - DISNEY

Little Dog Series

The Little Dog and the Chicks	8 MIN
The Little Dog and the Goat	8 MIN
Little Dog Goes Fishing	8 MIN
The Little Dog Goes Skiing	8 MIN
The Little Pig	8 MIN
The Turtle	8 MIN
Who's the Cleanest	7 MIN

Dist - PHENIX

The Little Drummer Boy 25 MIN
U-matic / VHS / 16mm
Color (P I J H A)
$520 purchase _ #4445
Shows how a boy shares the gift of music with the baby Jesus. A Perspective film.
Literature and Drama; Social Science
Dist - CORF

The Little Drummer Boy 7 MIN
16mm / U-matic / VHS
Color
LC 78-708741
Shows the excitement felt by all who came to witness the birth in Bethlehem. Expresses the spirit of Christmas and inspires good will throughout the year.
Literature and Drama; Religion and Philosophy
Dist - WWS **Prod** - WWS 1968

The Little Drummer Boy - Book II 24 MIN
16mm / U-matic / VHS
Color
Presents Greer Garson narrating a puppet - animated story of how the Little Drummer Boy helped spread the word of the first Christmas.
Fine Arts; Religion and Philosophy
Dist - PERSPF **Prod** - PERSPF 1982

Little Dutch Boy 3 MIN
16mm
Color (P) (AMERICAN SIGN)
LC 76-701691
Tells in American sign language the story of the little Dutch boy who became a national hero when he saved his country from flooding by blocking a leak in a dyke with his hands. Signed for the deaf by Jack Burns.
Guidance and Counseling; Literature and Drama; Psychology
Dist - JOYCE **Prod** - JOYCE 1976

Little Dutch Island 15 MIN
U-matic / VHS
Other families, other friends series; Blue module; Aruba
Color (P)
Presents various features of the island of Aruba.
Geography - World; Social Science
Dist - AITECH **Prod** - WVIZTV 1971

The Little Engine that Could 10 MIN
16mm / U-matic / VHS
Color (P)
$265, $185 purchase _ #1510
Tells the story of a little engine that pulled a train full of toys to children on the other side of a mountain.
Literature and Drama
Dist - CORF

The Little Engine that Could 11 MIN
U-matic / VHS / 16mm
Color; B&W (P K)
Animated story of the little engine that pulled a trainload of toys to the children on the other side of the mountain.
Literature and Drama
Dist - CORF **Prod** - CORF 1963

A Little Extra Work 9 MIN
16mm
Color
LC 74-705038
Discusses the emotional conflicts involved in the working relationship between local and state health departments.
Health and Safety
Dist - USNAC **Prod** - USPHS

A Little fable 5 MIN
U-matic / VHS / BETA
Color; PAL (C G)
PdS20, PdS28 purchase
Asks are you part of the prejudice in your workplace.
Sociology
Dist - EDPAT

The Little Falls incident 7 MIN
16mm
Color (G)
$125.00 purchase, $30.00 rental _ #APF - 686, #ARF - 686
Visits a suburban New Jersey town which was the scene of an anti - Semitic incident. Interviews the people involved, the victim, her classmates, her mother, teacher and school principal.
History - United States; Sociology
Dist - ADL **Prod** - WCBSTV

A Little Fellow from Gambo 30 MIN
16mm
Color
_ #106C 0170 090N
Geography - World
Dist - CFLMDC **Prod** - NFBC 1970

A Little Flame 28 MIN
16mm
Color
LC 74-705039
Shows the dangers of fires carelessly caused by trash burning, smoking, brush and grass burning, campfires, and children playing with matches. Shows how John Weaver, a public spirited insurance man, helps to lick the fire problems in his community.
Health and Safety; Social Science
Dist - USNAC **Prod** - USDA 1965

Little Forest 8 MIN
16mm
Color (P I J H C)
LC 72-703328
Explores the nature of the essence of the forest. Examines the timelessness, the small and quiet phenomena and the equalness of all that occurs in the forest, from a deer being eaten away to a butterfly caught in a spider's web.
Agriculture; Science - Natural
Dist - MARALF **Prod** - ALBM 1972

The Little Foxes
BETA / VHS
B&W
Presents Lillian Hellman's drama of a Southern matriarch and the family she drives mercilessly. Starring Bette Davis.
Fine Arts; Geography - United States; Literature and Drama
Dist - GA **Prod** - GA

The Little Foxes 116 MIN
U-matic / VHS / 16mm
B&W (H)
Tells of a greedy, callous woman who deliberately sacrifices her family for her savage desire for wealth and social position.
Fine Arts; Literature and Drama
Dist - FI **Prod** - UNKNWN 1941

The Little Giants - the Inside Story of Your Glands 14 MIN
U-matic / VHS
Inside Story with Slim Goodbody Series
Color (P I)
Explores the electrical and chemical partnership between the brain and the endocrine system. Explains the functions and importance of the thyroid, pituitary, adrenal, the sex glands and the hypothalmus.
Science - Natural
Dist - AITECH **Prod** - GBCTP 1981

A Little Girl and a Gunny Wolf 6 MIN
U-matic / VHS / 16mm
Children's Storybook Theater Series
Color (P I)
Tells of a little girl who, in spite of her mother's warning, goes to pick flowers in the forest where she encounters a fabulous animal known as the Big, Bad Gunny Wolf.
Literature and Drama
Dist - AIMS **Prod** - ACI 1971

The Little Girl and the Tiny Doll 15 MIN
VHS / U-matic
Words and Pictures Series
Color (K P)
Tells the story of a little girl with her mother in a grocery store who discovers a tiny doll among the frozen food in the freezer. Reveals that over several days she brings the doll warm clothes, plays with it and finally is given permission by the clerk to take the doll home to live in a beautiful doll house. Emphasizes the letter d.
English Language; Literature and Drama
Dist - FI **Prod** - FI

Little girl lost - a troubled adolescent 28 MIN
VHS
Color (H C G)
$295.00 purchase, $55.00 rental
Portrays Joanne Shaver, a troubled teenager who met a violent death at the age of 17. Recalls her life as a happy little girl from a seemingly normal home, through her hostile preadolescence, to her becoming a runaway and a ward of the state. Reveals that she was turning away from a life of drugs and prostitution when she was locked out of her group home for an infraction of the curfew and reverted to the streets where she was murdered. Interviews her parents, her peers and counselors in an attempt to find out where society failed.
Sociology
Dist - FLMLIB **Prod** - CANBC 1993

A Little Help from Your Friends 15 MIN
VHS / U-matic
Writer's Realm Series
Color (I)
$125.00 purchase
Comments on the positive effect criticism can have on the writer's style.
English Language; Literature and Drama; Social Science
Dist - AITECH **Prod** - MDINTV 1987

Little house in the big woods 15 MIN
U-matic / VHS
Book bird series
Color (I)
Presents selections from Laura Ingalls Wilder's story of family life on the frontier.
English Language; Literature and Drama
Dist - CTI **Prod** - CTI

Little house under the moon 98 MIN
VHS
Color (G) (MANDARIN WITH ENGLISH SUBTITLES)
$45.00 purchase _ #5038B
Presents a movie produced in the People's Republic of China.
Fine Arts
Dist - CHTSUI

The Little Humpbacked Horse 85 MIN
VHS

Color (K)
$29.95 purchase _ #1204
Takes a magical tour through the land of flying horses, dancing fish and tumbling clowns in the Bolshoi Ballet production of 'The Little Humpbacked Horse.' Stars Maya Plisetskaya and Vladimir Vasiliev.
Fine Arts; Foreign Language; Geography - World; Physical Education and Recreation
Dist - KULTUR

Little Injustices - Laura Nader Looks at the Law 59 MIN
16mm
Odyssey Series
Color (H A)
Shows Laura Nader comparing treatment of 'little injustices' in a Mexican village to courtroom litigation over consumer complaints in the United States.
Civics and Political Systems; Home Economics; Sociology
Dist - DOCEDR **Prod** - DOCEDR 1981

Little Injustices - Laura Nader Looks at the Law 58 MIN
VHS / U-matic
Odyssey Series
Color
LC 82-706986
Presents anthropologist Laura Nader as she compares the Mexican and American legal systems and how they resolve consumer complaints.
Civics and Political Systems; Geography - World; Home Economics; Sociology
Dist - PBS **Prod** - PBA

Little Jesus - Hippy Hill 15 MIN
16mm
B&W (G)
$20.00 rental
Looks at the 'beautiful people' making vibrations with musical artifacts and smoking pot amongst herds of small children and pet dogs.
Fine Arts; Psychology
Dist - CANCIN **Prod** - PADULA 1969

Little Kids Don't do that - Troubled Children 29 MIN
U-matic
A Different Understanding Series
Color (PRO)
Gives case studies of two preschoolers with problems which reflect the importance of early diagnosis and intervention for children showing signs of emotional disturbance.
Psychology
Dist - TVOTAR **Prod** - TVOTAR 1985

Little Kids Don't do that - Troubled Children 29 MIN
VHS / 16mm
A Different Understanding Series
Color (G)
$90.00 purchase _ #BPN178010
Shows the importance of early diagnosis and intervention for children exhibiting signs of emotional disturbance. Presents case studies of 2 pre - schoolers. Features interviews with parents and professionals.
Psychology; Sociology
Dist - RMIBHF **Prod** - RMIBHF

Little League Baseball's Official Instruction Video
VHS / U-matic
Color
Physical Education and Recreation
Dist - MSTVIS **Prod** - MSTVIS

Little League Moochie 96 MIN
U-matic / VHS / 16mm
B&W
Tells the story of Moochie, a dedicated ten - year - old, who is determined to make the team. Explains that many of the lessons of life can be learned on the baseball diamond.
Fine Arts
Dist - FI **Prod** - DISNEY 1962

Little League's official how to play baseball 70 MIN
VHS
Color (K P I)
$19.95 purchase _ #S01349
Features Little League baseball players in an instructional film on baseball skills. Includes 19 segments, each covering a different topic, such as hitting, pitching, bunting, and others.
Physical Education and Recreation
Dist - UILL

Little League's Official How to Play Baseball by Video 70 MIN
VHS
(I J)
$49.95 _ #MST100V
Teaches the little leaguer the basics of baseball. Includes a discussion of how to handle the ball, the bases, when to run, catching and pitching, hitting the ball, and more.
Physical Education and Recreation
Dist - CAMV

Little Lie that Grew 30 MIN
16mm
B&W (P I)
LC 72-701647
Presents a nine - year - old boy who learns that telling the truth is always best when a little white lie grows until it is out of control.
Guidance and Counseling; Psychology
Dist - CPH **Prod** - CPH 1956

Little lieutenant 7 MIN
16mm
Color (H C A)
$30.00 rental
Looks at the late Weimar era with its struggles and celebrations leading up to world war. Accompanies John Zorn's arrangement of the Kurt Weill song, "Little Lieutenant of the Loving God". Includes labor footage, empty industrial landscapes, and battle newsreels. Produced by Henry Hills with Sally Silvers.
Civics and Political Systems; History - World
Dist - CANCIN

A Little Like Magic 24 MIN
16mm / VHS
Color (I)
$300.00, $225.00 purchase
Features the Famous People Players, a theater troupe of handicapped young adults under the direction of Diane Dupuy, who have played world wide.
Education; Fine Arts
Dist - UNKNWN

Little Lord Fauntleroy 102 MIN
16mm
B&W (P I)
Portrays a boy growing up in Brooklyn in the 1880's.
Fine Arts
Dist - FI **Prod** - FI

Little Lost Blue Rock 8 MIN
16mm
Color
LC 79-700236
Contrasts environmental conditions on Earth with those on the moon, emphasizing the difference made by the availability of water on Earth.
Science - Natural; Science - Physical
Dist - GROENG **Prod** - GROENG 1978

The Little Lost Burro 9 MIN
16mm
Color (K P I)
Tells how Blanco, the little white burro, sets out to find his mother who has been captured and taken away by men who sell wild burros to prospectors. Describes his adventures with a friendly rabbit, a ghost town and a hungry bobcat, and shows how he finds his mother after giving up all hope.
Literature and Drama
Dist - CORF **Prod** - CORF 1982

The Little Lost Burrow 9 MIN
U-matic / VHS / 16mm
Color (P I)
$245.00, $170.00 purchase _ #4062
Tells the story of a lost burro who goes to find his mother and has some adventures.
Literature and Drama; Science - Natural
Dist - CORF

The Little Lost Lamb, Saint Paul, a Good Friend of Jesus 26 MIN
VHS / BETA
Color (K P R)
Presents a puppet presentation of the Good Shepherd parable for children, and the story of Saint Paul in this computer animated program.
Literature and Drama; Religion and Philosophy
Dist - DSP **Prod** - DSP

Little Lou and His Strange Little Zoo 50 MIN
VHS
Learning Library Series
Color (K P I)
Portrays the adventures of a young black boy who lives in the city and becomes involved in learning activities in various subjects.
Literature and Drama
Dist - BENNUP **Prod** - VIDKNW

Little Lulu 24 MIN
16mm / U-matic / VHS
Color (I J)
LC 79-700085
Uses the comic strip character Little Lulu to illustrate the changing perceptions of male and female roles in society.
Guidance and Counseling; Sociology
Dist - CORF **Prod** - ABCTV 1979

Little Marcy series
Learning God's love - Tape 1 30 MIN
Learning to do God's work - Tape 2 30 MIN
Dist - APH

The Little Mariner - a True Fairy Tale 20 MIN
U-matic / VHS / 16mm
Color; B&W (P I)
LC FIA67-1770
Describes the port of Long Beach, California, from the point of view of a small boy who sails into the port an enchanted sailboat. Formerly titled 'LE PETIT MARINER.'.
English Language; Geography - United States; Literature and Drama; Science - Natural; Social Science
Dist - EBEC **Prod** - TIGERF 1966

The Little Marsupials 25 MIN
U-matic
Animal Wonder Down Under Series
Color (I J H)
Contains footage of the Honey Possum, an animal so small it can climb on flowers and feed on nectar and pollen. Includes the Nubat and the Red Tailed Wombenger.
Geography - World; Science - Natural
Dist - CEPRO **Prod** - CEPRO

Little Mary - America's Sweetheart 12 MIN
16mm
B&W (J A)
Tells about the career of Mary Pickford. In June of 1909, young Gladys Smith applied for work at the Biograph Studio. As Mary Pickford, the 16 - year - old girl had acquired an impressive list of credits in her 11 years on the stage. But stage roles for the young ingenue were scarce in the spring of 1909 when D W Griffith gave her her first bit role in films. Includes All On Account Of The Milk (1910) Ever Again (1910) The New York Hat (1912) and The Mender Of Nets (1912).
Biography; Fine Arts
Dist - RMIBHF **Prod** - RMIBHF

The Little match girl 24 MIN
U-matic / VHS
Young people's specials series
Color
Tells Hans Christian Andersen's classic story of a little girl's search for love at Christmas. Presented in a contemporary setting.
Fine Arts; Literature and Drama; Social Science; Sociology
Dist - MULTPP **Prod** - MULTPP

The Little Match Girl 17 MIN
U-matic / VHS / 16mm
Color (P I)
$405, $250 purchase _ #3967
Tells the tragic story of a little girl who sell matches on the streets on New Year's Eve. Puppet animated.
Literature and Drama
Dist - CORF

The Little Match Girl 15 MIN
VHS / 16mm
Stories and Poems from Long Ago Series
Color (I)
Uses the character of a retired sea captain to tell story of The Little Match Girl. The 12th of 16 installments of the Stories And Poems From Long Ago Series, which is intended to encourage young viewers to read and write.
Literature and Drama
Dist - GPN **Prod** - CTI 1990

The Little Match Girl 9 MIN
U-matic / VHS / 16mm
Classic Tales Retold Series
Color (P I)
LC 77-700095
Presents an adaptation of Hans Christian Andersen's tale about a little girl who is sent out on a bitterly cold Christmas Eve to sell her basket of matchsticks.
Fine Arts; Literature and Drama; Social Science
Dist - PHENIX **Prod** - PHENIX 1976

The Little Men of Chromagnon 8 MIN
U-matic / VHS / 16mm
Color (I)
LC 72-701356
An animated film which introduces the primary colors and their combinations.
Fine Arts; Science - Physical
Dist - IU **Prod** - NFBC 1971

The Little Mermaid 25 MIN
U-matic / VHS / 16mm
Color (P I) (FRENCH SPANISH)
A Spanish language version of the film, The Little Mermaid, an animated version of Hans Christian Anderson's story. Tells the story of a young mermaid who falls in love with a prince, sacrifices her voice to be with him in human form, and, when the prince marries another, nearly loses her soul, but instead is rewarded with everlasting happiness. Narrated by actor Richard Chamberlain.

Fine Arts; Foreign Language; Literature and Drama
Dist - PFP Prod - HUBLEY

The Little mermaid 60 MIN
VHS
Faerie tale theatre series
Color; CC (K P I J)
$19.95 purchase _ #CBS6802
Stars Pam Dawber and Treat Williams.
Literature and Drama
Dist - KNOWUN

The Little Mermaid 25 MIN
16mm / U-matic / VHS
Color
LC 74-700617
Presents Hans Christian Andersen's fairy story 'THE LITTLE MERMAID' about a little mermaid and her love for a prince.
Literature and Drama
Dist - PFP Prod - READER 1974

Little Miseries 27 MIN
U-matic / VHS / 16mm
Insight Series
Color (H C A)
Dissects the relationship between a young man and his overbearing aunt who raised him after his parents died. Shows that the aunt's behavior is really due to loneliness and the need for the young man's love. Stars John Ritter and Audra Lindley.
Guidance and Counseling; Psychology; Religion and Philosophy; Sociology
Dist - PAULST Prod - PAULST

Little monsters 30 MIN
VHS
QED series
Color; PAL (H C A)
PdS65 purchase
Explores food additives as a cause of hyperactivity in children. Reports specifically on the trials at Great Ormond Hospital and on youth offenders in the north of England. Promises controversial results.
Health and Safety; Sociology
Dist - BBCENE

Little Mouse's Big Valentine
VHS
Children's Literature on Video Series
Color (K)
$33.00 purchase
Literature and Drama
Dist - PELLER

Little Nino's pizzeria - 58
VHS
Reading rainbow series
Color; CC (K P)
$39.95 purchase
Reveals that Tony loves to help his dad make pizza at their family restaurant until his dad decides to open up a fancy new restaurant instead. Discloses that Tony always seems to be in the way until his father has a change of heart and decides he cannot stay away from his yummy pizza, from the story by Karen Barbour. LeVar decides to make his own pizza but what he doesn't realize is that his pizza has to feed an entire basketball team. Part of a series offering a multicultural approach to generating reading enthusiasm with cross - curricular applications, hosted by LeVar Burton.
English Language; Home Economics; Literature and Drama
Dist - GPN Prod - LNMDP

Little orphan Anna and a word to the wise - Volume 10 45 MIN
VHS
Flying house series
Color (K P I R)
$11.99 purchase _ #35 - 8959 - 979
Uses an animated format to present events from the New Testament era, as three children, a professor and a robot travel in the 'Flying House' back to that time. 'Little Orphan Anna' is based on the story of Harmon and his new wife, while 'A Word to the Wise' reflects the parables of the unjust judge and widow and the nobleman who spurns a wedding invitation.
Literature and Drama; Religion and Philosophy
Dist - APH Prod - TYHP

Little people 58 MIN
16mm / VHS
Color (H C G)
$850.00, $295.00 purchase, $85.00 rental
Offers a moving and sometimes funny documentary on the experience of being a dwarf among average - sized people. Shows how they encounter discrimination and have problems of access - reaching shelves in supermarkets. It is difficult for them to be taken seriously in the world of business. Yet, their struggles are all forgotten when they get together at their yearly national convention. Coproduced with Thomas Ott.
Sociology
Dist - FLMLIB Prod - KRAWZJ 1985

Little People Clothes 15 MIN
Videoreel / VT2
Umbrella Series
Color
Home Economics; Psychology; Social Science
Dist - PBS Prod - KETCTV

Little Peter's Tale 20 MIN
VHS
Gentle Giant Series
Color (H)
LC 90712920
Uses story to teach children universal truths. Fourteenth of 16 installments of the Gentle Giant Series, which takes stories from cultures throughout the world.
Health and Safety; Literature and Drama; Psychology
Dist - GPN

A Little Phantasy on a 19th Century Painting 4 MIN
16mm / U-matic / VHS
B&W (P)
Based on a nineteenth - century painting, 'ISLE OF THE DEAD,' by Arnold Boecklin. Animation artist Norman Mc Laren captures the mood of the original painting through light and movement. The island wakes to mysterious life and fades again into the dark.
Fine Arts
Dist - IFB Prod - NFBC 1947

The Little Pig 8 MIN
U-matic / VHS / 16mm
Little Dog Series
Color (K P)
Presents the story of Little Dog and Kitten trying to prevent a little pig from playing in a mud puddle and always getting dirty. Shows that their efforts are to no avail.
Fine Arts; Literature and Drama
Dist - PHENIX Prod - ROMAF

The Little Players 27 MIN
U-matic / VHS / 16mm
Color (J)
LC 83-700075
Introduces the Little Players, a puppet troupe whose repertoire is drawn from Shakespeare, Oscar Wilde and Noel Coward.
Fine Arts
Dist - WOMBAT Prod - LEHWIL 1982

The Little Players 59 MIN
16mm
Color
LC 81-700418
Focuses on the Little Players, a five - member theatrical troupe created by artists Frank Peschka and Bill Murdock.
Fine Arts
Dist - OPUS Prod - OPUS 1981

Little Plover (River) Project, a Study in Sand Plains Hydrology 35 MIN
16mm
Color
Shows how geologists and engineers collect and interpret data to determine the occurrence, movement and amount of water available in a particular area, how ground water and surface water are inter - related and how the effects of various water uses on stream flows and ground - water levels may be predicted.
Science - Natural; Science - Physical
Dist - USGEOS Prod - USGEOS 1963

The Little Prince 27 MIN
16mm
Color
Features an animated version of Saint Exupery's THE LITTLE PRINCE. Presents the fable of a prince who lived on a tiny planet watching over his three volcanoes and tending a single rose of great beauty. Shows how he goes to earth and makes friends with a fox who shares with him the secret of happiness.
Fine Arts; Guidance and Counseling; Literature and Drama; Sociology
Dist - BBF Prod - VINTN

The Little Prince 27 MIN
16mm
Color (P I J)
LC 79-701069
Uses the technique of clay animation to tell the story of a little prince who lives on a tiny planet and who travels to Earth to find the secret of happiness. Based on the book The Little Prince by Antoine de Saint - Exupery.
Fine Arts; Literature and Drama
Dist - BBF Prod - BBF 1979

The Little prince 88 MIN
VHS
Color (G)
$16.95 purchase _ #S02117
Presents a musical version of the Antoine de Saint - Exupery children's story 'The Little Prince,' in which a downed pilot and young space traveler become friends. Stars Richard Kiley, Steven Warner, Bob Fosse and Gene Wilder. Directed by Stanley Donen. Music by Lerner and Lowe.
Fine Arts; Literature and Drama
Dist - UILL

A Little Princess 160 MIN
VHS
WonderWorks Series
Color (P)
$79.95 purchase _ #766 - 9021
Tells the story of a wealthy and kind - hearted girl in Victorian England who is forced into a life of poverty. Stars Amelia Shankley, Nigel Havers. Based on the book by Frances Hodgson Burnett. Part of the WonderWorks Series which centers on themes involving rites of passage that occur during the growing - up years from seven to sixteen. Features young people as protagonists and portrays strong adult role models.
Fine Arts; History - World; Literature and Drama; Psychology; Social Science; Sociology
Dist - FI Prod - PBS 1990

A Little problem at home
VHS
Color (I J H G)
$195.00 purchase, $50.00 rental
Focuses on the unique problems of children in alcoholic familes where there is also family abuse - the double abuse of alcohol and of each other - physically, emotionally, sexually, by neglect or in combination. Features adult and adolescent children of alcoholics who speak candidly about growing up in a home with an alcoholic parent and how it affected their lives. Tells what steps they took to overcome the effects of being the child of an alcoholic.
Guidance and Counseling; Health and Safety; Sociology
Dist - NEWIST Prod - NEWIST

Little rabbit's loose tooth 11 MIN
VHS / U-matic
Color (P)
$250.00 purchase _ #HH - 6186L
Adapts 'Little Rabbit's Loose Tooth' by Lucy Bate. Tells a story about a little rabbit who wonders what she will be able to eat when she discovers she has a loose tooth. Demonstrates decision making and problem solving.
Literature and Drama; Psychology
Dist - CORF Prod - LCA 1990

The Little Rascals' Christmas Special 24 MIN
16mm
Color (K)
Uses animation to present a Christmas story featuring the Little Rascals. Shows how Spanky and Porky's mother buys them a train for Christmas with money she saved to buy a winter coat. Tells how her sacrifice and the boys' realization of it eventually involve a street - wise sidewalk Santa and the rest of the Little Rascals.
Literature and Drama; Religion and Philosophy; Social Science
Dist - CORF Prod - CORF 1982

A Little Rebellion Now and Then - Prologue to the Constitution 30 MIN
U-matic / VHS / 16mm
Color (H C A)
$540 purchase - 16 mm, $365 purchase - video
Dramatizes the years after the American Revolution, the framing of the Constitution, and the Constitutional Convention of 1787. Focusses on James Madison, Noah Webster, and Daniel Shays. A Calliope Production. Directed and produced by Randall Conrad and Christine Dall.
History - United States
Dist - CF

The Little Red Circle 8 MIN
16mm
Color (P)
Uses animation to introduce the principles of classification by physical attribute. Shows the basic attributes of objects, including color, shape and size.
Mathematics; Psychology; Science
Dist - SUTHRB Prod - RAMFLM 1977

The Little Red Hen 11 MIN
U-matic / VHS / 16mm
Color (P)
Uses both art and live action to retell the fable The Little Red Hen.
English Language; Literature and Drama
Dist - CORF Prod - CORF 1950

The Little Red Hen 10 MIN
U-matic / VHS / 16mm
Color (P)

$255, $180 purchase _ #312
Tells the story of a little red hen. Combines art and live animals.
Literature and Drama
Dist - CORF

Little Red Lighthouse 9 MIN
U-matic / VHS / 16mm
Color; B&W (K P)
An iconographic motion picture based on the children's book of the same title by Hildegarde Swift. Tells the story of a lighthouse who learns he is still useful even if a more powerful light has been installed on the great bridge.
English Language; Literature and Drama
Dist - WWS **Prod** - WWS 1956

Little Red Riding Hood 10 MIN
VHS / U-matic
Fairy Tale Series
Color (K P I)
Views the well - known story of Red Riding Hood's escape from the wolf. Comes with teacher's guide.
Literature and Drama
Dist - BNCHMK **Prod** - BNCHMK 1985

Little Red Riding Hood 13 MIN
16mm / U-matic / VHS
Color (P I)
LC 79-700958
Tells the story of Little Red Riding Hood and her adventures and dangers on the way to visit Grandmother.
Fine Arts; Literature and Drama
Dist - LCOA **Prod** - DEFA 1979

Little Red Riding Hood 9 MIN
16mm / U-matic / VHS
Color; B&W (P I A)
Re - creates the story book tale of Little Red Riding Hood.
English Language; Literature and Drama
Dist - PHENIX **Prod** - HARRY 1958

Little Red Riding Hood 17 MIN
16mm / U-matic / VHS
Color (P)
$405, $250 purchase _ #3947
Tells the traditional fairy tale of Red Riding Hood with background music and animation.
Literature and Drama
Dist - CORF

Little Red Riding Hood - a Balinese - Oregon Adaptation 17 MIN
16mm / VHS
Color (K)
$330.00, $49.00 purchase _ #975 - 9031
Retells the classic fairytale, 'Little Red Riding Hood,' through mime performed in a magnificent Oregon forest. Features Balinese masks which are carved before the camera. In the tradition of Prokofiev's 'Peter And The Wolf,' a different musical instrument personifies each character.
Fine Arts; Literature and Drama
Dist - FI **Prod** - SONNED 1983

Little Richard 30 MIN
16mm
B&W
LC FI67-114
Relates how Little Richard, a blue - tick hound, became trapped in a practically inaccessible hole while he was hunting raccoons and how he was rescued with the help of his owner, the neighbors and the phone and utility companies.
Literature and Drama
Dist - WB **Prod** - GE 1963

The Little riders 15 MIN
VHS
Books from cover to cover series
Color (P I G)
$25.00 purchase _ #BFCC - 105
Features Margaretha Shemin's book 'The Little Riders,' a tale about a girl, Johanna, who helps her grandparents remove little riders from the church steeple and hide them from the soldiers. Based on the German occupation of Holland during World War II.
English Language; Literature and Drama
Dist - PBS **Prod** - WETATV 1988

The Little Rivers 20 MIN
16mm
Color (J A)
LC 74-714056
Describes the difficulties which plague little urban streams such as the small creeks in the Buffalo metropolitan area. Explains the comprehensive planning program which proposes to provide a modern water resources system for this urban area.
Psychology; Science - Natural; Sociology
Dist - FINLYS **Prod** - FINLYS 1969

The Little Rooster who made the Sun Rise 11 MIN
U-matic / VHS / 16mm
Color (P)
Animated story of the rooster who discovers that his crowing does not make the sun rise, but who acquires pride in doing his job of waking his farmyard friends.
English Language; Social Science
Dist - CORF **Prod** - CORF 1961

Little School in the Desert 15 MIN
U-matic / VHS
Encounter in the Desert Series
Color (I)
Deals with the education of Bedouin children.
Geography - World; Social Science; Sociology
Dist - CTI **Prod** - CTI

The Little Shepherd and the First Christmas 19 MIN
U-matic / VHS / 16mm
Color (P I J H C A)
$435, $250 purchase _ #1766
Tells the story of a shepherd who brought a gift to the baby Jesus in Bethlehem.
Literature and Drama; Social Science
Dist - CORF

The Little Shop of Horrors 76 MIN
16mm
B&W (C A)
Tells of a simple - minded florist's helper who in an effort to impress his girlfriend, develops a hybrid plant which rejects ordinary plant foods and demands blood.
Fine Arts
Dist - KITPAR **Prod** - CORMAN 1960

Little Sinners 17 MIN
16mm
B&W
Explains how Spanky learns a morality lesson and gets a spiritual scare when he chooses fishing over Sunday school. A Little Rascals film.
Fine Arts
Dist - RMIBHF **Prod** - ROACH 1935

Little Sister 45 MIN
16mm
Color
LC 80-700068
Tells how a reunion of friends evolves into an emotional test for Ellen. Shows that the group's dynamic force threatens to clamp off her connection to an idealized past, impelling her to a painful confrontation with her oldest and most cherished friend.
Fine Arts
Dist - BRIMED **Prod** - BRIMED 1977

Little Sister, Pt 1 23 MIN
16mm
Color
LC 80-700068
Tells how a reunion of friends evolves into an emotional test for Ellen. Shows that the group's dynamic force threatens to clamp off her connection to an idealized past, impelling her to a painful confrontation with her oldest and most cherished friend.
Fine Arts
Dist - BRIMED **Prod** - BRIMED 1977

Little Sister, Pt 2 22 MIN
16mm
Color
LC 80-700068
Tells how a reunion of friends evolves into an emotional test for Ellen. Shows that the group's dynamic force threatens to clamp off her connection to an idealized past, impelling her to a painful confrontation with her oldest and most cherished friend.
Fine Arts
Dist - BRIMED **Prod** - BRIMED 1977

The Little Snowman
VHS
Children's Literature on Video Series
Color (K)
$33.00 purchase
Literature and Drama
Dist - PELLER

The Little Soot Slayer 10 MIN
16mm
Color (P I)
Presents a story of a little girl and her ingenious way of cleaning up the air.
Literature and Drama; Sociology
Dist - SF **Prod** - SF 1980

Little Stabs at Happiness 18 MIN
16mm
Color (C)
$560.00
Experimental film by Ken Jacobs.
Fine Arts
Dist - AFA **Prod** - AFA 1963

The Little Story, a Negligible Tale 7 MIN
16mm / U-matic / VHS
Color (J H C)
LC 77-701523
Presents an animated tale, based on a story by Ambrose Bierce, about a starving orphan girl who is showered with a whole assortment of delights on Christmas night. Shows how, as shopkeepers rush for the delights at dawn, they find the orphan dead.
Fine Arts; Literature and Drama; Social Science
Dist - TEXFLM **Prod** - LESFG 1977

The Little Sunshade (Umbrella) 32 MIN
16mm / U-matic / VHS
Color (K P I)
LC 73-702698
Presents a puppet film about a little old man who flies into a nursery on an umbrella, bringing all the toys to life and putting them in a circus show.
Literature and Drama
Dist - PHENIX **Prod** - PHENIX 1973

Little Swahili dancers 2 MIN
16mm
B&W (G)
$5.00 rental
Documents a troupe of young dancers performing African dance.
Fine Arts
Dist - CANCIN **Prod** - MERRIT 1972

A Little Swelling 56 MIN
VHS / U-matic
Color (H C A)
Shows a 16 - year old girl who becomes pregnant and how she deals with it.
Health and Safety; Psychology
Dist - MMRC **Prod** - MMRC

The Little Tadpole who Grew 10 MIN
U-matic / VHS / 16mm
Color (P)
$255 purchase - 16 mm, $180 purchase - video _ #3725
Shows the development of a tadpole into a frog.
Science - Natural
Dist - CORF

The Little Theatre of Jean Renoir 100 MIN
U-matic / VHS / 16mm
Color (H C A)
Presents a four - part film by French director Jean Renoir. Includes the stories The Last Christmas Dinner in which a beggar is rewarded for watching rich people eat by receiving the leftovers, The Electric Floor Waxer which is a musical about a woman in love with her parquet floor, Le Belle Epoque in which Jeanne Moreau sings badly and The King Of Yvetot which is a mid - life farce.
Fine Arts
Dist - TEXFLM **Prod** - JANUS 1969

Little Theatre of the Deaf 29 MIN
U-matic
Color
Features a children's play performed by the Little Theatre of the Deaf.
Education; Fine Arts
Dist - PBS **Prod** - NETCHE

A Little Thing Like Security 22 MIN
16mm
Color
LC 74-706374
Illustrates the time and effort spent to recover a document lost by a subcontractor. Shows how a single lapse in security consciousness can hurt a company.
Business and Economics
Dist - USNAC **Prod** - USDD 1972

Little Things 10 MIN
16mm
Color
LC 75-703598
Features an employee motivation film which presents a series of animated vignettes to show how good and bad habits can affect the employee.
Business and Economics; Fine Arts; Psychology
Dist - IBM **Prod** - IBMSGC 1975

Little Tim and the Brave Sea Captain 11 MIN
16mm / U-matic / VHS
Color
Tells the story of Tim, a stowaway on an ocean liner who braves a storm alongside the ship's captain. Uses illustrations to capture the rigors of shipboard life.
Literature and Drama; Social Science
Dist - WWS **Prod** - WWS

The Little time machine 15 MIN
VHS
Field trips series
Color (I J)

$34.95 purchase _ #E337; LC 90-708560
Portrays a class of scholars in the one - room Norlands School of the 1840s. Encourages the examination of the differences between the practices of the 19th and 20th century school. Part of a series which provides visual opportunities for children to 'visit' a variety of locations and activities as if they were on a field trip.
Education; Geography - United States; History - United States
Dist - GPN **Prod** - MPBN 1983

Little Tom Thumb 7 MIN
U-matic / VHS / BETA
Classic fairy tales series
Color; PAL (P I)
PdS30, PdS38 purchase
Tells the story of a boy who proves himself more clever than his brothers when he outwits the ogre and returns home with the treasure. Features part of a six - part series containing the essence of the Brothers Grimm, Charles Perrault and Hans Anderson.
Literature and Drama
Dist - EDPAT **Prod** - HALAS 1992

Little Toot 9 MIN
U-matic / VHS / 16mm
Color (P I)
LC 72-700133
A story about a mischievous tugboat whose antics get it banished beyond the 12 - mile limit until its heroic efforts during a storm bring it back to the harbor.
Geography - United States; Literature and Drama
Dist - CORF **Prod** - DISNEY 1971

The Little Train 14 MIN
16mm / U-matic / VHS
Color (P I)
LC 70-711645
Presents the story of a little train to show how easy it is to underrate the value of one's position. Tells how the little train, who shuttles coal continuously to the big long - distance trains, longs to see the world outside the train yards and finally jumps the tracks to have a merry time until his fuel runs out. Shows how he realizes the importance of his job when he is rescued and returns to see how the long distance trains were stranded because he was not there to bring them fuel.
Guidance and Counseling; Literature and Drama
Dist - PHENIX **Prod** - PHENIX 1969

The Little Train 11 MIN
16mm
Color (K P)
Describes how a small old - fashioned steam locomotive tries to prove its worth by racing a modern diesel engine.
Fine Arts
Dist - RADIM **Prod** - ZAGREB 1972

The Little Train of the Caipira 13 MIN
VHS
Music Experiences Series
Color
$69.95 purchase _ #1105
Introduced are Brazilian composer Heitor Villa Lobos and his work.
Fine Arts
Dist - AIMS **Prod** - AIMS

Little troll prince 45 MIN
VHS
Color (K P I R)
$12.95 purchase _ #35 - 830001 - 1518
Presents an animated Christmas parable in which the little troll prince's frozen heart is melted when he receives God's love. Features the voices of Vincent Price, Jonathan Winters, Cloris Leachman and Don Knotts. Animation done by Hanna - Barbera.
Literature and Drama; Religion and Philosophy
Dist - APH **Prod** - SPAPRO

The Little Tummy 15 MIN
U-matic / VHS / 16mm
Color
Portrays the tiny Paris restaurant called The Little Tummy, where kings and presidents pay 50 dollars for lunch. Documents Chef Bernard performing such masterpieces as baking three tiny quail in grape sauce, then throwing away all but the breasts.
Geography - World; Home Economics
Dist - KLEINW **Prod** - KLEINW

Little Twelvetoes 4 MIN
VHS / U-matic
Multiplication Rock Series
Color (P I)
Uses songs and cartoons to explore the mathematical possibilities of the number twelve.
Mathematics
Dist - GA **Prod** - ABCTV

Little Vera 110 MIN
VHS / 35mm / 16mm
Color (G) (RUSSIAN WITH ENGLISH SUBTITLES)
$300.00, $400.00 rental
Presents the first Russian film to show sex on screen and realistically depict life in the modern Soviet working class. Stars Natalia Negoda as Vera, a teenager solely interested in frequenting dance halls with her friends, but when one of her flings turns serious, she finds herself with live - in boyfriend and her life in shambles. Directed by Vasily Pichul.
Fine Arts; Psychology
Dist - KINOIC

Little visits with God - Volume 1 70 MIN
VHS
Color (P I R)
$15.95 purchase, $10.00 rental _ #35 - 8256 - 19
Uses puppets, animation and a storyteller to teach children how to live as a Christian. Considers topics including gossiping, being thankful, not looking down at others, and the strength God gives people. Includes a devotional guide.
Literature and Drama; Religion and Philosophy
Dist - APH **Prod** - CPH
CPH

Little visits with God - Volume 2 70 MIN
VHS
Color (P I R)
$15.95 purchase, $10.00 rental _ #35 - 8261 - 19
Uses puppets, animation and a storyteller to teach children how to live as a Christian. Considers topics including prayer, God's love, forgiveness, watching one's words, and self - esteem. Includes a devotional guide.
Literature and Drama; Religion and Philosophy
Dist - APH **Prod** - CPH

Little Wars 20 MIN
16mm
B&W
LC 79-701292
Takes a satirical look at a group of men who re - enact Civil War battles.
Fine Arts; Physical Education and Recreation
Dist - USC **Prod** - USC 1978

The Little white line that cried 5 MIN
16mm
Otto the auto - pedestrian safety - A series
Color (K P)
$30.00 purchase _ #150
Features Otto the Auto who emphasizes the need to cross at corners and intersections. Part of a series on pedestrian safety. Complete series available on 0.5 inch VHS.
Health and Safety
Dist - AAAFTS **Prod** - AAAFTS 1957

Little women 122 MIN
VHS
Color; CC (I J H)
$24.95 purchase _ #DB84
Stars June Allyson and Elizabeth Taylor in an adaptation of the story by Louisa May Alcott.
Literature and Drama
Dist - KNOWUN

Little Women 60 MIN
U-matic / VHS
Color (P I J)
Dramatizes Louisa May Alcott's classic LITTLE WOMEN in an animated video in the field of language arts.
Fine Arts; Literature and Drama
Dist - BRENTM **Prod** - BRENTM

Little Women
U-matic / VHS
Adolescent Literature Series
B&W (G C J)
$39 purchase _ #05693 - 85
Follows the lives of four sisters during the civil war. Stars Katherine Hepburn and Joan Bennett. Based on the story by Louisa May Alcott.
Fine Arts; Literature and Drama
Dist - CHUMAN
GA
KNOWUN

Little Yellow Fur 15 MIN
U-matic / VHS
Stories of America Series
Color (P)
Focuses on a young homesteader who makes friends with her Sioux neighbors.
History - United States
Dist - AITECH **Prod** - OHSDE 1976

Littleford Implant Film 8 MIN
16mm
Color (PRO)
Shows the use of the Subclavian Stick Sheath and the proper technique for implanting a pacer using this approach.
Health and Safety
Dist - CORDIS **Prod** - CORDIS

Littles - a series 13 MIN
VHS
Littles - a series
Color
Presents an animated series of the Littles. Contains 13 cassettes of 24 minutes each.
Literature and Drama
Dist - ABCLR **Prod** - ABCLR

Littles - a series
Littles - a series 13 MIN
Dist - ABCLR

The Littles, Pts 1 - 13 312 MIN
U-matic / VHS
(K P I)
$335.00 purchase
Fine Arts
Dist - ABCLR **Prod** - ABCLR

The Littlest angel 14 MIN
VHS
Color (K P I)
Tells the story of a bumbling little angel. Uses an animated format.
Literature and Drama; Religion and Philosophy
Dist - SCETV **Prod** - SCETV 1980

The Littlest Angel 14 MIN
16mm
Color (P I J H)
Presents the story of a little child who loses his way among the fluffy clouds. Explains that this little angel gives his dearest possession for love of the Christ child.
Literature and Drama; Religion and Philosophy
Dist - CORF **Prod** - CORF 1950

Littlest Hobo 77 MIN
16mm
B&W (I J)
Tells of a hobo German Shepherd dog and a wooly lamb rescued from the slaughterhouse who bring happiness to a broken - hearted boy and the will to walk to a little girl.
Fine Arts
Dist - CINEWO **Prod** - CINEWO 1958

The Littlest Outlaw 75 MIN
16mm
Color
Illustrates the fact that nothing can defeat a small boy armed with great personal courage and a deep devotion to a heroic horse.
Fine Arts
Dist - TWYMAN **Prod** - DISNEY 1956

The Littlest Pig 10 MIN
VHS / U-matic
Happy Time Adventure Series
Color (K P)
$29.95 purchase _ #VL006
Presents an adaptation of the book The Littlest Pig. Contains a 32 page hardcover book and a video.
English Language; Literature and Drama
Dist - TROLA

The Littlest Preppies 20 MIN
U-matic / VHS
Color
$335.00 purchase
Education
Dist - ABCLR **Prod** - ABCLR 1983

Liturgy and the arts - Word, work and worship series
Architecture - worship space 60 MIN
Art, vesture, vessels 60 MIN
Language and gesture 60 MIN
Music 60 MIN
Dist - CTNA

Liturgy, catechesis and the rite of acceptance 60 MIN
VHS
Introduction and overview of RCIA series
Color (R G)
$49.95 purchase _ #RCIA2
Assists Roman Catholic individuals and parish teams involved in the implementation of the Order of Christian Initiation of Adults in further understanding the periods and stages of the initiation process. Gives particular emphasis to the varieties of implementations and adaptation for various parish settings. Produced in collaboration with the North American Forum on the Catechumenate. Part of three parts on Roman Catholic initiation of adults.
Religion and Philosophy
Dist - CTNA **Prod** - CTNA

Liturgy of foundation 40 MIN
VHS
Advocacy lectures series
Color (C PRO)

$50.00 rental _ #EOX01
Presents lectures from various law school professors on principles of trial advocacy. Focuses on the liturgy of foundation.
Civics and Political Systems
Dist - NITA **Prod** - NITA

Liturgy of Foundation Laying and the Use of Exhibits 87 MIN
U-matic / VHS
Exhibit Series
Color (PRO)
Describes the major evidentiary considerations relevant to exhibits and steps in the proper procedure for introduction and use of exhibits in trials.
Civics and Political Systems
Dist - ABACPE **Prod** - ABACPE

Live a Little 30 MIN
16mm
Color; B&W (J H T R)
LC FIA67-5779
Rick, a young radio disc jockey, has a swinging glib patter that appeals to a large teenage following. He is not conscious of the real problems of the teenagers until one of his listeners is involved with a serious problem. He begins to examine his own goals for life.
Guidance and Counseling; Psychology; Sociology
Dist - FAMF **Prod** - FAMF 1967

Live and Learn 28 MIN
16mm
Color (C A)
LC 76-701599
Describes the process approach of the Kansas plan for educating special students. Explains how problem solving in daily living is incorporated into instruction and how students are taught to understand their own actions and the steps they must take to achieve their own goals.
Education; Psychology
Dist - UKANS **Prod** - UKANS 1974

Live and remember - Wo kiksuye 29 MIN
U-matic / VT1 / VHS
Color (G)
$49.95 purchase, $40.00 rental
Offers a documentary about the Lakota Sioux Nation's oral tradition, song and dance, medicine and the spirit world and perceptions of bicultural lifestyle discussed by Lakota elders, medicine men and traditional dancers, filmed on location at Rosebud Sioux Reservation. Opens with a look inside a Lakota Sweat Lodge ceremony - perhaps the most ancient rite of the Lakota Sioux people that continues today. Offers Lakota world views on the role of women in Indian society, alliances with animal nations, the Peace Pipe ceremony, the changing relationships both within the reservation community and with the non - Indian world. Produced by Henry Smith for the Solaris - Lakota Project.
Social Science
Dist - NAMPBC

Live at Preservation Hall 28 MIN
VHS / U-matic
Color
Features a performance of the Kid Thomas Band at the famous Preservation Hall jazz club in New Orleans' French Quarter.
Fine Arts
Dist - NOVID **Prod** - NOVID

Live Contortions 30 MIN
U-matic / VHS
B&W
Presents jazz - punk - noise artists James Chance and the Contortions live at Max's Kansas City.
Fine Arts
Dist - KITCHN **Prod** - KITCHN

Live from the battlefield - from Vietnam to Baghdad, 35 years in the world's war zones 30 MIN
VHS
Author's night at the Freedom Forum series
Color (G)
$15.00 purchase _ #V94 - 02
Focuses on Peter Arnett, CNN war correspondent and author of the book of the same title, in part of a series on freedom of the press, free speech and free spirit.
Social Science; Sociology
Dist - FREEDM **Prod** - FREEDM 1994

Live from the Met Highlights 70 MIN
VHS
(S) (ENGLISH, GERMAN, AND ITALIAN)
$29.95 purchase _ #384 - 9373
Highlights scenes from the following Metropolitan Opera productions - 'Don Carlo,' 'La Boheme,' 'Un Ballo In Maschera,' 'Tannhauser,' 'Lucia Di Lammermoor.' Features James Levine, Giuseppe Patane and Richard Bonynge as conductors, singers such as Placido Domingo, Mirella Freni, Teresa Stratas, Luciano Pavorotti, Eva Marton and Joan Sutherland.
Fine Arts; Foreign Language
Dist - FI **Prod** - PAR 1988

Live from the Met highlights - Volume 1 70 MIN
VHS
Metropolitan opera series
Color (G) (ITALIAN WITH ENGLISH SUBTITLES)
$29.95 purchase
Presents a collection of highlights from Metropolitan Opera performances. Includes scenes from 'The Bartered Bride,' 'Un Ballo In Maschera,' 'Don Carlo,' 'La Boheme,' 'Tannhauser,' and 'Lucia Di Lammermoor.' Includes a brochure with plot, historic notes, photographs, and production credits.
Fine Arts
Dist - PBS **Prod** - WNETTV 1986

Live Ghost 20 MIN
16mm
B&W (P A)
Features Laurel and Hardy as fish market employees who collaborate with the captain of a ghost ship in shanghaiing a crew. Shows how they are shanghaied themselves and suffer many ghostly experiences.
Fine Arts
Dist - RMIBHF **Prod** - ROACH 1934

Live Line Maintenance Series
Care and Maintenance of Tools and Protective Equipment
Cutting in disconnect switches - Pt 1
Cutting in disconnect switches - Pt 2
Deadend Insulator Replacement, Pt 1
Deadend Insulator Replacement, Pt 2
Insulator and Cross Arm Changeout, Pt 1
Insulator and Cross Arm Changeout, Pt 3
Insulator and Cross Arm Changeout, Pt 4
Pole replacement - pt 1
Pole replacement - pt 2
Reconductoring or Upgrading Voltage
Single Insulator Changeout
Temporary Grounding for De - Energized Maintenance
Dist - LEIKID

Live Lobster 24 MIN
16mm
Color
LC 77-700169
Traces an American lobster from a Midwest restaurant back to a trap off the coast of Maine. Includes an interview with the lobster fisherman and a sequence of a lobster in the process of moulting.
Business and Economics; Geography - United States; Industrial and Technical Education; Science - Natural
Dist - BODFIL **Prod** - DICEP 1977

Live or die 29 MIN
16mm / VHS
Color (J H C G)
$450.00, $335.00 purchase, $60.00 rental
Confronts the viewer with an essential choice - live in ways that keep the body healthy, or live in ways that make the body sick and, ultimately, results in premature death. Follows the lives of two likeable, successful people who both died at age 47.
Health and Safety; Psychology
Dist - CF **Prod** - WFP 1979
PEREN
WFP

Live poultry markets - the crossroads 11 MIN
U-matic / VHS
Biosecurity and the poultry industry series
Color (IND)
$40.00, $95.00 purchase _ #TCA18205, #TCA18204
Covers the importance of biosecurity in live poultry markets.
Agriculture; Health and Safety
Dist - USNAC **Prod** - USDA 1989

Live Show Special 30 MIN
U-matic
Today's Special Series
Color (K P)
Develops language arts skills in children. Programs are thematically designed around subjects of interest to youngsters. Action takes place in a department store where people, mannequins, puppets, comic characters and special guests present a light hearted approach to language arts.
Fine Arts; Literature and Drama; Psychology
Dist - TVOTAR **Prod** - TVOTAR 1985

Live Test of Westinghouse Washing Machines 7 MIN
VHS / U-matic
Color
Shows a classic television commercial in two segments, clothes being put into the washer and clothes being taken out.
Business and Economics; Psychology; Sociology
Dist - BROOKC **Prod** - BROOKC

Live the jazz - music revitalizes the elderly 28 MIN
VHS
Color (H C G)
$295.00 purchase, $55.00 rental
Captures the injection of live New Orleans jazz into nursing homes. Witnesses nursing home residents caught up in the rhythm, dancing together and twirling their parasols New Orleans style. Produced by Bobbie R Szyller, Evelyn Navarro and Donald R Perry. Longer, original version available.
Fine Arts; Health and Safety
Dist - FLMLIB

Live to Tell about it 40 MIN
U-matic / VHS
Color
Examines in detail the most common hazards causing lateral lift truck tipovers. Introduces the Clark safety seat and explains to lift truck operators how to protect themselves from serious injury in the event of a tipover.
Health and Safety
Dist - CLARKV **Prod** - CLARKV

Live Westinghouse Commercial for Refrigerators with Betty Furness 3 MIN
U-matic / VHS
Color
Shows a classic television commercial with Furness having problems opening the refrigerator door.
Business and Economics; Psychology; Sociology
Dist - BROOKC **Prod** - BROOKC

Live wires 12MIN
VHS
Color; PAL; NTSC (G IND)
PdS57, PdS67 purchase
Shows sensible measures for complying with the law concerning portable electric equipment. Focuses on a simple system of visual inspection which can detect 95 percent of damage to equipment or faults. Gives typical examples of what to look for and guidelines on the frequency of inspection.
Health and Safety; Psychology
Dist - CFLVIS

Live with it 25 MIN
U-matic
Color
Presents an informative commentary on what it's like to have diabetes. Focuses on the more subtle psychological aspects of the disease, on the mental outlook of those who've just learned they have it, rather than showing the diabetic how to take insulin or how to regulate his/her diet.
Health and Safety; Psychology
Dist - TEACHM **Prod** - WAHC

Live your dreams - get past your fears 45 MIN
VHS
Les Brown series
Color (G)
$69.95 purchase _ #TVL 1012
Develops the skills that will help overcome the fears that block life. Teaches ways to get past one's fears - by taking them head on.
Guidance and Counseling; Psychology
Dist - JWAVID **Prod** - JWAVID

Lived Time 12 MIN
16mm
Color; Silent (C)
$392.00
Experimental film by Martha Haslanger.
Fine Arts
Dist - AFA **Prod** - AFA 1978

The Liveliest Wire 59 MIN
Videoreel / VT2
Color
Features Ed Baumeister, supported by animation and filmed interviews, surveying the cable, its origins, current uses and forecasts for growth.
Fine Arts; Industrial and Technical Education; Social Science
Dist - PBS **Prod** - WGBHTV

Lively Art of Picture Books 57 MIN
16mm / U-matic / VHS
Color (C A)
Examines the qualities that lend vitality to good picture books through interviews with Barbara Cooney, Robert Mc Closkey and Maurice Sendak. Exhibits samples of the works of 36 illustrators plus the complete films 'TIME OF WONDER' and 'A SNOWY DAY.'.
English Language; Fine Arts; Literature and Drama
Dist - WWS **Prod** - WWS 1964

The Liver 15 MIN
U-matic / VHS / 16mm
Color
LC 80-700108
Discusses the structure and functions of the liver, including regulation of blood sugar level, metabolic activities involving amino acid linkage, excretion of poisons and storage of vitamins.
Science - Natural
Dist - IFB **Prod** - IFFB 1979

Liver 8 MIN
16mm
Color (H C A)
LC 79-700994
Uses animation to depict the various stages and symptoms of liver deterioration caused by alcohol abuse. Emphasizes the liver's regenerative powers, explaining that by ending alcohol abuse, an individual can regain much of his original liver capacity.
Health and Safety
Dist - FMSP **Prod** - HUBLEE 1979

Liver, Pancreas, and Spleen 14 MIN
U-matic / VHS / 16mm
Guides to Dissection Series
Color (C A)
Demonstrates the dissection of the liver, pancreas and spleen.
Health and Safety; Science - Natural
Dist - TEF **Prod** - UCLA

Liver Resection 18 MIN
16mm
Color (PRO)
Illustrates thoracoabdominal laparotomy with left hepatic lobectomy for a huge echinococcus cyst. Shows that the procedure involved partial evacuation and sterilization of the cyst with formaldehyde followed by mobilization of the cyst and the left lobe of the liver from multiple adherent adjacent organs and finally, resection through the left lobe of the liver.
Health and Safety; Science
Dist - ACY **Prod** - ACYDGD 1969

Liver Scan
VHS / U-matic
X - Ray Procedures in Layman's Terms Series
Color
Health and Safety; Science
Dist - FAIRGH **Prod** - FAIRGH

Liver transplant 29 MIN
VHS / U-matic
Life matters series
Color (G)
$175.00 purchase, $100.00 rental
Focuses on Kindra Poarch who was diagnosed at age 12 with Alagille's Syndrome, a rare and fatal liver condition. Shows Kindra and her parents talking about the ordeal of diagnosis, the difficulty of waiting for an organ after the decision was made to transplant and their feelings about the surgery - which they describe as both scary and exciting. Discusses the financial burden of the surgery and medication, but they never forgot that death was the alternative and they have never regretted the decision to transplant. Part of a 13 - part series that takes an in - depth look at the internal strength and convictions of people who live active and productive lives in spite of an illness that can be crippling or fatal.
Health and Safety
Dist - BAXMED **Prod** - KERA
PBS

Liverwort 5 MIN
U-matic / VHS
Color (C)
$229.00, $129.00 purchase _ #AD - 1286
Views the life cycle of ordinary liverwort or scale moss. Shows male and female thalluses and their reproductive cycles.
Science - Natural
Dist - FOTH **Prod** - FOTH

Liverwort - Alternation of Generations 16 MIN
16mm / U-matic / VHS
Color (H)
LC FIA65-1891
Shows alternation of generations in close - up and timelapse photography. Explains that liverworts need a damp environment and are dependent on water for their reproductive processes.
Science - Natural
Dist - CORF **Prod** - CORF 1965
VIEWTH

Lives 27 MIN
16mm
Color (ITALIAN NORWEGIAN GERMAN DANISH FRENCH)
LC 79-701234
Looks at the lives of five people who were affected by NATO. Stresses the resonance and textures of these lives in a free and democratic way of life.
Civics and Political Systems; Foreign Language
Dist - VISION **Prod** - NATO 1979

Lives and Lifestyles 12 MIN
16mm
Color
LC 79-700914
Presents representatives of four generations of people living in Maine, including a lobsterman, a great - grandmother, the young members of a commune and a dairy farming family who speak of change and how it is affecting their lives.
Geography - United States; Social Science; Sociology
Dist - POLYMR **Prod** - POLYMR

Lives of Performers 90 MIN
16mm
Color (G)
Presents an independent production by Yvonne Rainer. Offers fictional and real aspects of Rainer's dance company.
Fine Arts; Physical Education and Recreation
Dist - FIRS **Prod** - AFA 1972
AFA

The Lives of the Saints 26 MIN
VHS / U-matic
Every Window Tells a Story Series
Color (H C A)
$300.00
Shows the beauty and purpose of the stained glass windows in the churches built in the Middle Ages. Narrated by Malcom Miller.
Fine Arts; History - World
Dist - LANDMK **Prod** - LANDMK 1986

The Lives of the stars 60 MIN
U-matic / VHS / 16mm
Cosmos series; Program 9
Color (J)
LC 81-701154
Discusses molecules, atoms, and subatomic particles and explains the anatomy of stars and the forces acting on stellar interiors. Deals with stellar evolution, supernovae, and neutron stars. Uses an Alice In Wonderland sequence to explain gravitational effects. Based on the book Cosmos by Carl Sagan. Narrated by Carl Sagan.
Science - Physical
Dist - FI **Prod** - KCET 1980

Lives they Left Behind 116 MIN
VHS
Color (G) (MANDARIN CHINESE (ENGLISH SUBTITLES))
$45.00 purchase _ #6018A
Presents a Mandarin Chinese language movie produced in the People's Republic of China.
Fine Arts; Geography - World; Literature and Drama
Dist - CHTSUI **Prod** - CHTSUI

The Lives We Touch 30 MIN
16mm / U-matic / VHS
Color (H A)
Documents the Reform Jewish movement in America. Demonstrates unusual new community service programs.
Sociology
Dist - KLEINW **Prod** - KLEINW

The Livestock Farmer and the Four Flies 22 MIN
16mm
Color (J)
LC FIA67-469
Describes distinctive habits of the horn fly, the stable fly, the house fly and the face fly, showing the relationship of the life cycle and control methods for each.
Agriculture; Science - Natural
Dist - AMROIL **Prod** - AMROIL 1967

Livestock Feedstuffs Video Transfers Series
Offers a three - part series on lifestock feedstuffs. Considers the digestive systems of various species and focuses specifically on horses and swine.
Feeding horses
Introduction to Livestock Nutrition
Swine - Life - Cycle Feeding
Dist - VEP **Prod** - VEP 1967

Livestock fitting and showing - Set Q series
Fitting and showing of beef cattle
Fitting and showing of sheep 25 MIN
Fitting and showing of swine 19 MIN
Dist - AAVIM

Livestock handling 22 MIN
VHS
Color; PAL; NTSC (G)
PdS66, PdS77 purchase
Investigates the accidents and fatalities that occur every year to people working with animals. Shows how such accidents can be avoided through simple precautions and using common sense. Features Raymond Baxter who discusses with people in the agriculture industry problems which arise when dealing with bulls, cattle, hogs, sheep and horses. A veterinarian discusses some common zoonoses - animal diseases which can infect humans.
Agriculture; Health and Safety
Dist - CFLVIS

Livestock judging videos series
Beef judging practice
Judging beef breeding cattle
Judging beef cattle - meat quality grading
Judging dairy cattle 30 MIN
Judging market lambs
Judging market swine
Judging stockhorse performance classes
Judging swine practice class
Sheep judging practice
Dist - VEP

Living 10 MIN
16mm
Color
LC 80-701617
Offers an interpretation of the poem Living by Denise Levertov.
Fine Arts; Literature and Drama
Dist - LYTM **Prod** - LYTM 1980

Living 57 MIN
16mm / VHS
Heart of the Dragon Series
(J H C)
$99.95 each, $595.00 series
Follows a typical village family in China through an average day.
Geography - World; History - World
Dist - AMBROS **Prod** - AMBROS 1984

Living 20 MIN
VHS / 16mm
Trail Series
Color (I)
$150.00 purchase, $30.00 rental
Shows how every living thing needs food, water, shelter and living space.
Science - Natural
Dist - AITECH **Prod** - KAIDTV 1986

Living 57 MIN
16mm / U-matic / VHS
Heart of the Dragon Series Pt 7; Pt 7
Color (H C A)
Visits Maoping village in Zhejiang province in China, focusing on local peasants and their way of life. Follows the day - to - day life of one village family as they tend the land allocated to them by the state under the new 'responsibility' system and their own private plot.
Business and Economics; Civics and Political Systems; Geography - World; History - World
Dist - TIMLIF **Prod** - ASH 1984

The Living 3 MIN
16mm
B&W (I)
Issues an anti - war statement by blending scenes of statues coming alive, young girls dancing merrily to Pan's flute and the silent screams of bursting bullets.
Sociology
Dist - NJWB **Prod** - WOLMAN 1981

Living Africa - a Village Experience 34 MIN
U-matic / VHS / 16mm
Color (J)
Portrays the daily experinces and concerns of the people of Wassetake, a small village on the Senegal River in West Africa, emphasizing changes taking place within and outside the community.
Geography - World; History - World
Dist - IU **Prod** - IU 1984

Living American Theater Dance 11 MIN
16mm / U-matic / VHS
Color (I)
LC 82-700635
Shows how the American Dance Machine, under the direction of Leo Theodore, performs show - stopping numbers from musical plays. Presents interviews with Theodore and teacher Ann Reinking, as well as chats with troupe members about the company's purpose.
Fine Arts
Dist - PHENIX **Prod** - MAYQEN 1982

Living and dying with AIDS 77 MIN
VHS
Color (G)
$149.00 purchase, $75.00 _ #UW4591
Tells the story of a once flamboyant man and documents his final days dying of AIDS as he struggles for dignity in the presence of loving friends. Puts real faces on a deadly epidemic, examining gay life - styles and children with AIDS.
Health and Safety; Sociology
Dist - FOTH

Living and Income for Older Adults 14 MIN
Videoreel / VT2
Living Better II Series
Color
Explains the qualifications and procedure for applying for social security, Medicare, Medicaid and food stamps and tells how older adults use them for financial security when they retire. Suggests that an older adult may either live in a variety of facilities or at home with other family members.
Health and Safety; Psychology; Social Science; Sociology
Dist - PBS **Prod** - MAETEL

Living and non living things 12 MIN
16mm
B&W (I)
Shows the differences and similarities between living and non living things.
Science; Science - Natural
Dist - VIEWTH **Prod** - GBI

Living and non - living things 11 MIN
U-matic / VHS / 16mm
Captioned; Color (P)
$280.00 purchase - 16 mm, $195.00 purchase - video _ #3911
Surveys a variety of plants, animals and objects in order to clarify the differences between things that are alive and things that are not alive.
Science; Science - Natural; Science - Physical
Dist - CORF **Prod** - CORF 1978

Living and Working in Space 28 MIN
U-matic / VHS
Video Encyclopedia of Space Series
Color (C)
$249.00, $149.00 purchase _ #AD - 2112
Begins with the Skylab project which launched an unstaffed orbital workshop. Covers a host of experiments conducted in the US and by Spacelab, a European project, to study the effects of weightlessness on humans and the possibilities for working outside the laboratory in space. Part of an eleven - part series on space.
History - World; Industrial and Technical Education; Science - Physical
Dist - FOTH **Prod** - FOTH

Living and working in space - the countdown has begun 60 MIN
VHS
Color (J H C G)
$59.95 purchase _ #PBS01V - S
Offers dozens of interviews with today's space professionals, from a space doctor and the 'lunar lettuce man' to designers of space clothing and Mars vehicles. Interweaves a story of teacher Jaime Escalante and a former student with humorous, thought - provoking dramatizations of day - to - day activities in space. Stars Kathy Bates, Pat Morita, Jackee, Esai Morales, 'Weird Al' Yankovic and other personalities. Encourages students to study math and sicence in order to be prepared for the exciting, technology - based society that awaits them.
History - World; Industrial and Technical Education; Science; Science - Physical; Sociology
Dist - CAMV **Prod** - PBS 1993

Living Archeology 10 MIN
U-matic / VHS
Color (P I)
Demonstrates the value of archeology through the discovery of artifacts and views the lives of ancient people through the use of Indian hunting implements and stone tools.
History - World; Physical Education and Recreation; Sociology
Dist - ATLAP **Prod** - ATLAP

Living Arrangements and Services 15 MIN
U-matic
Aging in the Future Series
Color
Traces the historical development of specialized housing. Illustrates older people adapting to the rising costs of housing.
Health and Safety; Sociology
Dist - UMITV **Prod** - UMITV 1981

Living Arts of Japan 30 MIN
16mm
Color
Shows Japanese artisans at work, including an internationally known potter, a ceramic artist, Yuzen dyeing of kimono fabrics, a master of lacquer art, a bamboo weaver and an outstanding woodblock artist.
Fine Arts; Geography - World
Dist - MTP **Prod** - CONSUJ 1964

Living as a peaceful warrior 90 MIN
BETA / VHS
Innerwork series
Color (G)
$49.95 purchase _ #W355
Describes a way of life where the focused attention of the athlete is applied to all facets of daily life - from eating and walking to working and relating to others. Features Dan Millman, author of 'Way of the Peaceful Warrior.'
Guidance and Counseling; Physical Education and Recreation; Psychology
Dist - THINKA **Prod** - THINKA

Living Below the Line 60 MIN
U-matic / VHS
Frontline Series
Color
Presents an in - depth study of the U S welfare state, with fifteen and two - tenths percent of the American population trying to survive with some form of government assistance, and thirty - five million people trying to use various agencies and services, while trying to subsist during economic hard times.
Business and Economics; Civics and Political Systems; Guidance and Counseling; Sociology
Dist - PBS **Prod** - DOCCON

Living Better I Series

Breakfast	14 MIN
Building a sleeping area	12 MIN
Canisters	14 MIN
Choosing baby clothes	13 MIN
Cleaning house	14 MIN
Closet Space	13 MIN
Clothing for Preschool Children	14 MIN
Day care centers	13 MIN
Developing an infant's basic skills	13 MIN
Footstools	14 MIN
Free Form Papier Mache	13 MIN
Good grooming	14 MIN
Labels	13 MIN
Laundry Tips	13 MIN
Making a table	15 MIN
More Storage Space in the Kitchen	13 MIN
Nonfat Dry Milk	14 MIN
Patchwork Cover and Pillows	14 MIN
Selecting and Buying Clothes	13 MIN
Shoes for Children	13 MIN
Supermarket Dollar	14 MIN
Toys and Games for Five Years and Older	14 MIN
Using Gift Paper	15 MIN

Dist - PBS

Living better II series

Chicken I	15 MIN
Chickens II	15 MIN
Curtains I	12 MIN
Curtains II	13 MIN
Dashikis	13 MIN
Dental care	14 MIN
Draped Papier Mache	14 MIN
Envelope purses	14 MIN
Found things	13 MIN
Knitting	14 MIN
Lamps	15 MIN
Life Insurance	14 MIN
Living and Income for Older Adults	14 MIN
Molded Papier Mache	14 MIN
Rag Rugs	14 MIN
Scrambled Eggs and Canned Meat	14 MIN
Shopping for Insurance	14 MIN
Slip covering wooden chairs	13 MIN
A Spending Plan	14 MIN
Things of Value	14 MIN
Variety Meats	14 MIN
Ways with Pork	14 MIN
When Your Baby Needs a Doctor	14 MIN

Dist - PBS

Living Better Series

Toys and Games for Preschoolers	14 MIN

Dist - PBS

The Living Bible 25 MIN
16mm
Color (R)
Explains how the Bible was made available and understandable to the common man. Traces the development of the English Bible.
Guidance and Counseling; History - World; Religion and Philosophy
Dist - GF **Prod** - GF

Living Bible Series

Before Abraham was, I Am	20 MIN
Betrayal in gethsemane	15 MIN
Birth of John the Baptist	20 MIN
Birth of the Savior	15 MIN
Childhood of Jesus	15 MIN
The Crucifixion	20 MIN
First disciples	15 MIN
I Am the Resurrection	20 MIN
Jesus and the Fishermen	15 MIN
Jesus and the Lepers	15 MIN
Jesus at Nazareth and Capernaum	15 MIN
Jesus Before the High Priest	15 MIN
Jesus Heals the Man Born Blind	20 MIN
Jesus, Lord of the Sabbath	15 MIN
Jesus Teaches Forgiveness	15 MIN
Last Journey to Jerusalem	20 MIN
The Lord is Risen	15 MIN
The Lord's Ascension	15 MIN
Ministry of John the Baptist	20 MIN
Nicodemus	20 MIN
Thirty Pieces of Silver	15 MIN
Thy sins are forgiven	15 MIN
The Transfiguration	20 MIN
Trial Before Pilate	15 MIN
The Upper Room	15 MIN
Woman at the Well	15 MIN

Dist - FAMF

The Living Bird 14 MIN
U-matic / VHS / 16mm
Color (H C A)
Shows power of flight, types of food and nests of common birds. Includes a discussion of their senses of sight, smell and hearing.
Science - Natural
Dist - IFB **Prod** - DEU 1961

Living body - an introduction to human biology series

Aging	26 MIN
Cell duplication - growth and change	26 MIN
The Circulatory system - breath of life	26 MIN
The Circulatory system - hot and cold	26 MIN
The Circulatory system - life under pressure	26 MIN
The Circulatory system - two hearts that beat as one	26 MIN
Hormones - messengers	26 MIN
Introduction to Human Biology - Landscapes and Interiors	26 MIN
The Lower Digestive Tract - Breakdown	26 MIN
Mechanisms of Defense - Accident	26 MIN
Mechanisms of Defense - Internal Defenses	26 MIN
Muscles and Joints - Moving Parts	26 MIN
Muscles and Joints - Muscle Power	26 MIN
The Nervous System - Decision	26 MIN
The Nervous System - Nerves at Work	26 MIN
The Nervous System - Our Talented Brain	26 MIN
Reproduction - a New Life	26 MIN
Reproduction - Coming Together	29 MIN
Reproduction - into the World	26 MIN
Reproduction - Shares in the Future	26 MIN
Review of Human Biology - Design for Living	26 MIN
The Senses - Eyes and Ears	26 MIN
The Senses - Skin Deep	26 MIN
Sleep - Dream Voyage	26 MIN
The Upper Digestive Tract - Eating to Live	26 MIN
The Urinary Tract - Water	26 MIN

Dist - FOTH

Living body series
Presents a 26 - part series featuring diagrams, computer animation, medical photography, interior views of processes never seen before to introduce anatomy and physiology. Investigates sleep, digestion, the circulatory system, muscles and joints, the senses, the urinary tract, the nervous system, mechanisms of defense, reproduction, cell duplication, hormones, the aging process.

Living body series	713 MIN

Dist - FOTH

Living camera series

Adventures on the new frontier	54 MIN
Primary	54 MIN

Dist - DIRECT

The Living cell
VHS
Color (J H)
$59.95 purchase _ #193 W 0121
Introduces the characteristics of living organisms. Covers the basic structural and functional aspects of plant cells, along with a discussion of photosynthesis. Illustrates cell structure in one - celled and multicellular organisms. Emphasizes cellular specialization.
Science - Natural
Dist - WARDS **Prod** - WARDS

The Living Cell 15 MIN
16mm / U-matic / VHS
Cell Biology Series
Color (H C)
$420 purchase - 16 mm, $250 purchase - video _ #5221C ; $420, $250 purchase _ #5221C
Talks about cell specialization, the three regions of the cell, and the function of cells - plant, animal, and protist.
Science - Natural
Dist - CORF

The Living Cell - an Introduction 20 MIN
U-matic / VHS / 16mm
Color (H) (SPANISH)
A Spanish language version of the film and videorecording The Living Cell - An Introduction.
Foreign Language; Science - Natural
Dist - EBEC **Prod** - EBEC 1974

The Living Cell - DNA 20 MIN
16mm / U-matic / VHS
Color (H C) (SPANISH)
A Spanish language version of the film and videorecording The Living Cell - DNA.
Foreign Language; Science - Natural
Dist - EBEC **Prod** - EBEC 1976

Living Cell Series
Chemistry of the Cell 1 - the Structure of Proteins and Nucleic Acids 21 MIN
Chemistry of the Cell 2 - the Function of DNA and RNA in Protein Synthesis 16 MIN
Dist - MGHT

Living Cells 14 MIN
U-matic / VHS
Color (H C)
Shows there is much activity within a living cell. Illustrates modern film techniques which reveal that all parts of a living cell are in constant motion as compared to static nature shown in prepared microscopic slides.
Industrial and Technical Education; Science - Natural
Dist - EDMI **Prod** - EDMI 1983
AIMS

Living choices 16 MIN
U-matic / VHS
Color (G)
$250.00 purchase, $100.00 rental
Discusses the Patient Self - Determination Act which provides that all adults admitted to a health care facility receiving Medicare or Medicaid funding be informed of their rights to make decisions about their health care and that they be given written information about their right to complete advance directives.
Health and Safety
Dist - BAXMED **Prod** - TAKTEN 1993

The Living Christ 360 MIN
16mm / U-matic / VHS
Living Christ Series
Color (G)
Presents 12 episodes that depict the life of Christ.
Religion and Philosophy
Dist - CAFM **Prod** - CAFM 1958

Living Christ Series
Discipleship 30 MIN
Escape to Egypt 30 MIN
The Living Christ 360 MIN
Dist - CAFM

Living Christ series
Boyhood and baptism 30 MIN
Challenge of Faith 30 MIN
Conflict 30 MIN
Crucifixion and Resurrection 30 MIN
Fate of John the Baptist 30 MIN
Holy Night 30 MIN
Men of the Wilderness 30 MIN
Retreat and Decision 30 MIN
Return to Nazareth 30 MIN
Triumph and defeat 30 MIN
Dist - CAFM
ECUFLM

Living Christ series
Escape to Egypt 30 MIN
Dist - ECUFLM

The Living Constitution 30 MIN
VHS / 16mm
Government by Consent - a National Perspective Series
Color (I J H C A)
Illustrates that the U S Constitution is a "living document", which adapts to meet the needs of a dynamic nation.
Civics and Political Systems
Dist - DALCCD **Prod** - DALCCD 1990

The Living Constitution 30 MIN
VHS / U-matic
American Government Series; 1
Color (C)
Furnishes an in - depth look at the amendments, customs, usage and interpretation of the U S Constitution, with special attention to the 25th Amendment, the Child Labor Act and the Fair Labor Standards Act, to provide a better appreciation for a document that still works after 200 years.
Civics and Political Systems
Dist - DALCCD **Prod** - DALCCD

The Living Constitution 16 MIN
U-matic / VHS / 16mm
American history - birth of a nation series; No 7
Color (I) (SPANISH)
LC FIA68-1120
Describes the Constitutional Convention of 1787. Portrays how after months of argument and debate, a constitution presented by James Madison was signed by the delagates. Explains why this plan did not become law until the states were quaranteed a Bill Of Rights, which became the first ten amendments to the Constitution in 1791.
Civics and Political Systems; Foreign Language; History - United States
Dist - AIMS **Prod** - CAHILL 1967

A Living Constitution 24 MIN
16mm
Color (J A)
LC 70-714055
Shows how Pennsylvania modernized its archaic state constitution through a constitutional convention.
Civics and Political Systems
Dist - FINLYS **Prod** - FINLYS 1968

Living Creatures 15 MIN
U-matic / VHS
Arts Express Series
Color (K P I J)
Fine Arts
Dist - KYTV **Prod** - KYTV 1983

Living desert series
Animals at home in the desert 23 MIN
Predators of the Desert 22 MIN
Dist - CORF

Living Domiciliary Style 27 MIN
U-matic / VHS
Color
Illustrates domiciliary lifestyle, rehabilitative and therapeutic programs, recreational activities, rules and regulations in a VA domiciliary.
Civics and Political Systems; Guidance and Counseling; Health and Safety
Dist - USNAC **Prod** - VAMCSL

The Living Earth 25 MIN
VHS / U-matic / 16mm / BETA
Color (H G)
$390.00, $110.00 purchase _ #C50684, #C51457
Looks at planet Earth to discover how land, water, air and life are interdependent, working together as one global system. Examines new technologies which have expanded knowledge of Earth systems. Travels with scientists from the deepest oceans to outer space, from the deserts of Africa to Brazilian rain forest and Antarctica's ice cap. Shows how humans, who have inhabited Earth for a relatively brief time, have had such a profound effect on the planet.
Science - Natural; Science - Physical
Dist - NGS **Prod** - NGS 1991

The Living end 92 MIN
35mm / 16mm
Color (G)
Explores the consequences of gay male attraction in the 1990s with a postmodern black comedy. Focuses on the relationship between a pair of young, HIV - positive outcasts who become trapped in a strange, hostile Los Angeles. When a violent sexy drifter meets a bewildered writer, their casual affair turns into an odyssey escaping from the law up the West Coast, populated by lesbian serial killers, bizarre streetpeople, hysterical husband murderers and vicious gaybashers. Addresses the uncertainty, dislocation and seize - the - day urgency that have become an integral part of gay consciousness in America. Produced by Marcus Hu and Jon Gerrans. Written, directed, photographed and edited by Gregg Araki. Contact distributor for price.
Fine Arts; Health and Safety; Psychology; Sociology
Dist - OCTOBF

Living environment series
Air pollution 30 MIN
Antecedents of contemporary problems 30 MIN
Conservation of Vital Resources 30 MIN
Ecology concepts 1 30 MIN
Ecology concepts 2 30 MIN
Economic geology 30 MIN
Energy alternatives 30 MIN
Energy Problems 30 MIN
Environmental imperatives 30 MIN
Environmental perception 30 MIN
Food resources 30 MIN
Forest and man 30 MIN
Human Population Growth 30 MIN
Impact of Economic Systems 30 MIN
Impact of Political Systems 30 MIN
Individual Involvement 30 MIN
Land Use in the City 30 MIN
Myths of Technology 30 MIN
Population Growth 30 MIN
Solid Waste 30 MIN
Solutions and Projections 30 MIN
Water Pollution 30 MIN
Water Resources 30 MIN
Wildlife Management 30 MIN
Dist - DALCCD

Living Every Minute 12 MIN
16mm
Color (H C A)
Highlights the ways in which Carole Soucaze, a disabled woman, goes about her daily life and activities in her home in Nashville. Shows her working with the handicapped in her community while voicing her observations about the anger she experienced as she initially recuperated from her illness and the empathy she now feels toward her students and other students who are coping with physical disabilities.
Health and Safety; Psychology
Dist - LAWREN **Prod** - CBSTV 1982

Living forward, looking back 30 MIN
16mm / VHS
Color (G)
$250.00, $400.00 purchase, $50.00 rental
Interweaves the stories of six women who were profoundly affected by the choices available to them prior to the legalization of abortion. Explores the influence of family, friends and the prevailing sexual mores. Looks at the emotional consequences, illegal abortions, medical perspectives both pre - and post - Roe v Wade. Directed by Stephanie Hill.
Fine Arts; Health and Safety; Sociology
Dist - CNEMAG

Living Free 92 MIN
16mm
Color
Tells what happens when Elsa the Lioness goes back to the jungle and gives birth to three cubs.
Fine Arts; Science - Natural
Dist - TIMLIF **Prod** - CPC 1972

Living Glaciers 30 MIN
U-matic / VHS
Color (C)
$249.00, $149.00 purchase _ #AD - 2092
Focuses on Patagonia in southern Argentina, a desolate highland region where glaciers still flow from the Andes at daily speeds ranging from 50 centimeters to a whole meter. Examines life forms present, the glaciers themselves, and sites such as Lake Argentino which has some 150 different glaciers flowing into it.
Geography - World; Science - Physical
Dist - FOTH **Prod** - FOTH

The Living Goddess 30 MIN
16mm / U-matic / VHS
Color (J H C)
LC 79-700685
Explores the practice among the Newar people of Nepal of deifying selected female children as living representatives of ancient goddesses.
Religion and Philosophy; Sociology
Dist - WOMBAT **Prod** - CINETF 1979
CINETF

The Living Heart 28 MIN
U-matic / VHS
Color (C)
$249.00, $149.00 purchase _ #AD - 1479
Presents Dr Michael DeBakey, the pioneering heart surgeon. Describes coronary surgical procedures and their alternatives. Shows a coronary bypass procedure DeBakey developed, reviews risk factaors in atherosclerosis and discusses how to prevent heart disease.
Health and Safety; Science; Science - Natural
Dist - FOTH **Prod** - FOTH

Living in a nightmare 30 MIN
U-matic / VHS / 16mm
Color (H C A)
Studies Alzheimer's Disease using a nationwide survey of the illness, a look at two research projects in progress and candid interviews with patients of the disease and family members who care for them.
Health and Safety; Psychology
Dist - CORF **Prod** - WXYZTV 1983

Living in America - a hundred years of Ybor City 53 MIN
VHS
Color (H C G) (ENGLISH WITH SPANISH SUBTITLES)
$445.00 purchase, $75.00 rental
Portrays the long and rich tradition of Latin culture in Ybor City, Florida. Reveals that the community was founded in the 1880s when Cuban, Spanish and Italian immigrants arrived to work in the thriving cigar factors, and flourished until World War II when the effects of assimilation, urban renewal and the decline in the cigar industry led to its demise. Captures the colors, rhythms and texture of the close - knit ethnic enclave. Produced by Gayla Jamison.

Geography - United States; History - United States; Sociology
Dist - FLMLIB

Living in God's shadow
VHS
Greatest tales from the Old Testament series
Color (K P I R)
$29.95 purchase, $10.00 rental _ #35 - 832 - 528
Presents three stories from the Old Testament. Includes accounts of Job, Jonah, and the sacrifice of Isaac.
Literature and Drama; Religion and Philosophy
Dist - APH **Prod** - CAFM
CAFM

Living in South Africa 57 MIN
VHS
Color; PAL (G)
PdS100 purchase
Explores the environmental, social and moral legacies of post - Apartheid South Africa. Presents a Mark Newman, South Africa, production.
Fine Arts; Geography - World; Sociology
Dist - BALFOR

Living in space 23 MIN
VHS
Bright sparks series
Color (J H)
$280.00 purchase
Explores the theory that the sun may expand in the next 10 billion years, swallowing all the inner planets including the Earth. Looks at the technology of space colonization. Part of a 12 - part animated series on science and technology.
History - World; Industrial and Technical Education; Science - Physical
Dist - LANDMK **Prod** - LANDMK 1989

Living in space 8 MIN
16mm
Apollo digest series
Color
LC 74-705041
Deals with life support and routine activity in space.
History - World; Science - Physical; Social Science
Dist - USNAC **Prod** - NASAMS 1969

Living in space 35 MIN
VHS
Color (H C)
$129.00 purchase _ #111
Presents the history of space exploration and the prospects for the future where many people may be living in space. Includes a book of the same title from the Learning Power series.
History - World; Science; Science - Physical
Dist - HAWHIL **Prod** - HAWHIL 1991

Living in Space 28 MIN
U-matic / VHS
Video Encyclopedia of Space Series
Color (C)
$249.00, $149.00 purchase _ #AD - 2117
Reveals that the next step in space exploration will be the construction of an off - Earth habitat. Shows the design of the Space Shuttle as the first step. Considers the design of life, division of time, nature of food and the effect of zero - G on taste perception, clothing, and other aspects of human existence. Part of an eleven - part series on space.
History - World; Industrial and Technical Education; Science - Physical
Dist - FOTH **Prod** - FOTH

Living in space 38 MIN
U-matic / Kit / 35mm strip / VHS
Color (J H)
$79 two color sound filmstrips _ #C537 - 81125 - 7N, $129 one
Examines the prospects of living in space. Discusses the establishment of space stations and space colonies.
History - World; Science - Physical
Dist - RH

Living in space - Pt 1 - the case for regeneration 12 MIN
16mm
B&W
Introduces the concept of regenerative life support. Shows what is needed to provide people with clean fresh air, drinkable water, food, personal hygiene, waste disposal and temperature and humidity control.
History - World; Industrial and Technical Education; Science - Natural; Science - Physical
Dist - NASA **Prod** - NASA 1967

Living in space - Pt 3 - a technology for spacecraft design 12 MIN
16mm
Color
LC 74-705042
Shows the features that must be incorporated into a spacecraft intended for long duration manned space flight and the technology that is being developed to solve the numerous problems.
Industrial and Technical Education; Science - Physical; Sociology
Dist - NASA **Prod** - NASA 1966

Living in space - Pt 2 - regenerative processes 20 MIN
16mm
Color
LC FIE67-118
Shows the principles of physics, chemistry and mechanics employed in a regenerative life support system. Includes oxygen recovery, water purification, food and waste management, humidity and temperature control.
Home Economics; Science; Science - Natural; Science - Physical; Sociology
Dist - NASA **Prod** - NASA 1966

Living in space series - Part 1
A Case for regeneration 12 MIN
Dist - NASA

Living in Space Series Part 3
A Technology for Spacecraft Design 12 MIN
Dist - NASA

Living in the Age of Chaos 30 MIN
U-matic
Realities
Color (A)
Delves into the political, social, economic and cultural trends of the 1980s. Probes a wide range of contemporary concerns. Each segment includes a guest speaker who is an expert in the field under discussion.
Business and Economics; Civics and Political Systems; Social Science; Sociology
Dist - TVOTAR **Prod** - TVOTAR 1985

Living in the Future - Chips 15 MIN
16mm / U-matic / VHS
Living in the Future Series
Color (I J)
Describes a computer as a machine that processes information by performing a series of tasks according to a set of instructions. It works very fast, can make logical decisions, and is adaptable to a wide variety of processes and applications.
Industrial and Technical Education; Mathematics; Sociology
Dist - MEDIAG **Prod** - THAMES 1983

Living in the Future - Energy 15 MIN
U-matic / VHS / 16mm
Living in the Future Series
Color (I J)
Shows how modern society depends upon a great deal of energy, and such natural resources as coal, gas and oil are being used up at an ever - increasing rate and are becoming harder to find and more expensive to produce. Describes how electricity can be produced from the sun, wind or ocean tides or even in space.
Mathematics; Social Science; Sociology
Dist - MEDIAG **Prod** - THAMES 1983

Living in the Future - Evolution 15 MIN
U-matic / VHS / 16mm
Living in the Future Series
Color (I J)
States that the rapid changes the world has recently undergone were made possible by the use of the modern computer. Tells how it has evolved into an electronic tool that is more powerful, smaller, less expensive, more widely available and uses less energy than its predecessor, primarily because of the silicon chip.
Mathematics; Sociology
Dist - MEDIAG **Prod** - THAMES 1983

Living in the Future - Health 15 MIN
U-matic / VHS / 16mm
Living in the Future Series
Color (I J)
Describes how computers can be used to greatly increase human life expectancy. Patients interviews during routine checkups can be conducted by computer in order to save doctor's time. Tells how storage and retrieval of detailed and extensive medical records is enhanced by computers and artificial limbs are designed and controlled with microchips.
Health and Safety; Mathematics; Sociology
Dist - MEDIAG **Prod** - THAMES 1983

Living in the Future - Home 15 MIN
16mm / U-matic / VHS
Living in the Future Series
Color (I J)
Presents a tour of a specially equipped house in which a computer can control such activities as heating, lighting and cooking, while linking its residents with information sources and businesses outside to obtain services and merchandise.
Mathematics; Sociology
Dist - MEDIAG **Prod** - THAMES 1983

Living in the Future - Learning 15 MIN
16mm / U-matic / VHS
Living in the Future Series
Color (I J)
Shows how the computer is used as an educational tool to mediate or assist with training and instruction for learners of all ages and in all fields. Tells how schools will become activity and resource centers for individuals, families and work groups who learn from video and computer programs.
Education; Guidance and Counseling; Mathematics; Sociology
Dist - MEDIAG **Prod** - THAMES 1983

Living in the Future Series
Living in the Future - Chips 15 MIN
Living in the Future - Energy 15 MIN
Living in the Future - Evolution 15 MIN
Living in the Future - Health 15 MIN
Living in the Future - Home 15 MIN
Living in the Future - Learning 15 MIN
Living in the Future - Working 15 MIN
Living in the Future - World 15 MIN
Dist - MEDIAG

Living in the Future - Working 15 MIN
U-matic / VHS / 16mm
Living in the Future Series
Color (I J)
States that in a post - industrial society, computers will influence the working lives of most people. Describes robotics in industry, controls in manufacturing, information processing in offices and inventory and customer service in businesses will require a new knowledge of computers.
Business and Economics; Mathematics; Sociology
Dist - MEDIAG **Prod** - THAMES 1983

Living in the Future - World 15 MIN
U-matic / VHS / 16mm
Living in the Future Series
Color (I J)
Describes how computers make it possible to communicate around the world, translating information in many different languages and dialects at the touch of a button. Tells how this capability makes it possible to observe the need to effectively distribute resources to those in need.
Mathematics; Social Science; Sociology
Dist - MEDIAG **Prod** - THAMES 1983

Living in the Middle Atlantic States - Urban Complex 15 MIN
U-matic / VHS / 16mm
Color (I J H)
LC 74-701929
Surveys the geographic, economic and human activities in the Middle Atlantic states of New York, New Jersey, Pennsylvania, Delaware, Maryland and West Virginia.
Business and Economics; Geography - United States; Sociology
Dist - CORF **Prod** - CORF 1974

Living in the Rocky Mountain states - changing frontier lands 15 MIN
16mm / U-matic / VHS
Living in the United States series
Color (I J)
The second edition of Geography Of The Rocky Mountain States. Shows the land and the people of Montana, Idaho, Wyoming, Colorado, Utah and Nevada.
Geography - United States
Dist - CORF **Prod** - CORF

Living in the shadow of the test 30 MIN
VHS
Facing up to AIDS series
Color; PAL (H C A)
PdS65 purchase
Discusses the issues of living with AIDS with two infected men in London. Explores the quality of life that the two men have achieved as they receive the medical treatment necessary for them to live with the illness. Part one of a two - part series.
Health and Safety
Dist - BBCENE

Living in the soil 20 MIN
U-matic / VHS / 16mm
Exploring science series
Color (J H)
Discusses the creatures that live just above and below the earth's surface, showing that the great majority are less than one - fourth inch long.
Science - Natural
Dist - FI **Prod** - BBCTV 1982

Living in the United States series
Living in the Rocky Mountain states - changing frontier lands 15 MIN
Dist - CORF

Living in the USA 30 MIN
U-matic / BETA / 16mm / VHS

Color (G)
$600.00, $500.00 purchase, $100.00 rental
Prepares newcomers for the culture shock and practical realities of life in the United States. Overviews the cultural and regional diversity of the US and highlights challenges such as housing, banking, credit cards, schools, shopping, home appliances, driving, social customs and the importance of making friends. Also available in NSTC, PAL and SECAM formats.
Business and Economics; History - United States; Social Science; Sociology
Dist - COPGRG **Prod** - COPGRG

Living intuitively 30 MIN
VHS / BETA
Developing intuition series
Color (G)
$29.95 purchase _ #S235
States that learning to trust the intuition is a matter of practice and risk taking. Describes how to deal with the tensions associated with living as a spiritual being in a materialistic world. Features Shakti Gawain, author of 'Living in the Light' and 'Creative Visualization.' Part of a four - part series on developing intuition.
Psychology; Religion and Philosophy
Dist - THINKA **Prod** - THINKA

Living is Learning 30 MIN
U-matic
Action Options - Alcohol, Drugs and You Series
(H C A)
Summarizes insights into human behavior in learning how to meet challenges and make the most of them.
Psychology; Sociology
Dist - ACCESS **Prod** - ACCESS 1986

Living Islam series
Examines significant events in Islamic history and how they relate to modern Islam in a series of six programs. Provides information on the faith and many cultures of Islam with a particular emphasis on what it means to be a Muslim in today's world.
Among the non - believers 50 MIN
Foundations 50 MIN
Last Crusade 50 MIN
Dist - BBCENE

Living Islam
Challenges of the past 50 MIN
Paradise lies at the foot of the mother 50 MIN
Struggles with modernity 50 MIN
Dist - BBCENE

The Living jungle 26 MIN
16mm
Audubon wildlife theatre series
Color (P)
LC 73-709406
Shows unique jungle life in Panama. Explores the intricate relationships between the plants and animals in this tropical rainforest.
Geography - World; Science - Natural
Dist - AVEXP **Prod** - KEGPL 1969

The Living language 60 MIN
VHS
Moyers - The Power of the word series
Color; Captioned (G)
$59.95 purchase _ #MOPW - 102
Interviews James Autry and Quincy Troupe, two poets who make their livings in related fields. Presents Autry's poems, which are based both on the business world and Southern culture. Features Troupe, a literature and creative writing professor, reading his poems in a variety of settings including New York's Sing Sing prison. Hosted by Bill Moyers.
English Language; Literature and Drama
Dist - PBS

Living language French lessons 60 MIN
VHS
Color (G) (ENGLISH AND FRENCH)
$29.95 purchase
Presents a six - week course in the French language. Stresses gaining the ability to communicate in everyday situations, including the airport, hotel, streets, restaurants, and stores. Includes English subtitles.
Foreign Language
Dist - PBS **Prod** - WNETTV

Living language French video 50 MIN
VHS
Color (I J H) (FRENCH WITH ENGLISH SUBTITLES SPANISH WITH ENGLISH SUBTITLES)
$34.95 purchase _ #W5170, #W5171
Presents real - life situations involving practical conversations in French. Each conversation is spoken at a normal pace, with English subtitles, and then is repeated more slowly to help students develop fluency.
Foreign Language
Dist - GPC

Living Language French Video 60 MIN
BETA / VHS
Color
Provides instruction in conversational French.
Foreign Language
Dist - CROWNP **Prod** - CROWNP

Living language German lessons 60 MIN
VHS
Color (G) (ENGLISH AND GERMAN)
$29.95 purchase
Presents a six - week course in the German language. Stresses gaining the ability to communicate in everyday situations, including the airport, hotel, streets, restaurants, and stores. Includes English subtitles.
Foreign Language
Dist - PBS **Prod** - WNETTV

Living Language German Video 92 MIN
BETA / VHS
Color
Provides instruction in conversational German.
Foreign Language
Dist - CROWNP **Prod** - CROWNP

Living language Spanish lessons 60 MIN
VHS
Color (G) (ENGLISH AND SPANISH)
$29.95 purchase
Presents a six - week course in the Spanish language. Stresses gaining the ability to communicate in everyday situations, including the airport, hotel, streets, restaurants, and stores. Includes English subtitles.
Foreign Language
Dist - PBS **Prod** - WNETTV

Living Language Spanish Video 77 MIN
BETA / VHS
Color
Provides instruction in conversational Spanish.
Foreign Language
Dist - CROWNP **Prod** - CROWNP

Living Language Video - French 60 MIN
VHS / BETA
Color ((ENGLISH SUBTITLES))
Teaches the basics of French. Features real - life situations with English subtitles.
Foreign Language
Dist - NORTNJ **Prod** - NORTNJ

A Living legacy - the Woodrow Wilson House Museum 16 MIN
U-matic / VHS
Color (PRO)
$19.95, $12.98 purchase
Examines the problems and needs of historic house museums. Uses the Woodrow Wilson House Museum in Washington DC to address basic concerns of all museums and gives information on storage, environmental control, interpretation and preventive care of the house itself. Produced by the Center for Museum Studies at the Smithsonian for use in museum training.
Psychology
Dist - SMITHS

The Living leukocyte 12 MIN
U-matic
Microanatomy laboratory orientation series
Color (C PRO)
Demonstrates living examples of all five forms of normal leukocytes found in the peripheral blood.
Health and Safety; Science - Natural
Dist - UOKLAH **Prod** - UOKLAH 1986

Living life fully with Leo Buscaglia 58 MIN
U-matic / VHS
Color
Discusses Dr Buscaglia's message of accepting yourself using love as a force. Points out that the messaage was even more pertinent than usual because just a few months before this pryogram, Buscaglia had open heart surgery.
Psychology
Dist - PBS **Prod** - PBS 1982

Living life to the full 15 MIN
16mm / VHS / BETA / U-matic
Color; PAL (PRO)
PdS125, PdS133 purchase
Introduces the subject of hospice care for medical and non - medical personnel.
Health and Safety; Sociology
Dist - EDPAT

Living Lightning
U-matic / VHS
Color
Focuses on a season in the lives of a breeding pair of peregrine falcons. Follows them and their young into both triumph and tragedy.
Science - Natural
Dist - NWLDPR **Prod** - NWLDPR

The Living machine 13 MIN
VHS / U-matic / 16mm
This is you series
Color (P)
$400.00, $280.00 purchase _ #JC - 67282
Visits the 'World of Books,' a magical place where anything can happen. Stars Jiminy Cricket and the Mad Professor Peter Putterer who venture into the 'World of Machines' and explore the perfect living machine - the human body.
Fine Arts; Health and Safety; Science - Natural
Dist - CORF **Prod** - DISNEY 1990

The Living machine 60 MIN
U-matic / VHS / 16mm
Planet earth series
Color (C A)
Explores plate tectonics with scientists on location at Kilawea Volcano during an eruption, aboard a submersible craft as it dives to the bottom of the Atlantic. Discusses the causes of the worst earthquakes in American history.
Geography - World; Science - Physical
Dist - FI **Prod** - ANNCPB

Living machine 29 MIN
16mm
Color (G A)
$10.00 rental
Examines electronics technology from a 1960s perspective. Looks at machines which copy the human brain in calculating, remembering and prognosticating.
Computer Science; Sociology
Dist - AFLCIO **Prod** - NFBC 1963

The Living machine - Part 1 60 MIN
U-matic / VHS
Planet earth series
Color (G)
$45.00, $29.95 purchase
Looks at plate tectonics on location. Visits the erupting Kilauea volcano and the bottom of the Atlantic Ocean in the submersible craft Alvin. Part of a seven - part series on Planet Earth.
Geography - World; Science - Physical
Dist - ANNCPB **Prod** - WQED 1986

The Living machine - Pt 1 29 MIN
16mm
B&W (I)
Demonstrates the artificial intelligence of machines. Shows a chess game between an IBM computer and a champion player. Pictures simultaneous language translations in English and Russian done by computers.
Industrial and Technical Education; Mathematics; Sociology
Dist - SF **Prod** - NFBC 1963

The Living machine - Pt 2 30 MIN
16mm
B&W (I)
Explores the impact of computer technology on our society. Shows experiments in duplicating, electronically, our sensory perceptions. Provides the example of an artificial eye. Presents Dr Warren Mc Culloch and Dr Margaret Mead who give their views.
Mathematics; Sociology
Dist - SF **Prod** - NFBC 1963

Living Machines 57 MIN
U-matic / VHS / 16mm
Color
LC 80-700154
Focuses on the work of a group of biologists called natural engineers. Examines their methods of studying phenomena in nature, such as the aerodynamics of insects in flight or the feeding habits of marauding crabs.
Science; Science - Natural
Dist - FI **Prod** - WGBHTV 1980

The Living Maya - Program 1 58 MIN
U-matic / VHS
Living Maya series
Color
Introduces the Maya village of Chican. Witnesses the Maya's ability to resolve the many problems they face.
Geography - World; History - World; Social Science
Dist - UCEMC **Prod** - UCEMC

The Living Maya - Program 2 58 MIN
VHS / U-matic
Living Maya series
Color
Shows the strength and resourcefulness of a Maya family.
Geography - World; History - World; Social Science
Dist - UCEMC **Prod** - UCEMC

The Living Maya - Program 3 58 MIN
U-matic / VHS
Living Maya series
Color
Focuses on the relationships between Maya culture and religion and the cultivation of corn.
Geography - World; History - World; Social Science
Dist - UCEMC **Prod** - UCEMC

The Living Maya, Program 4 58 MIN
U-matic / VHS
Living Maya Series
Color
Explores assumptions, priorities and social values of the Mayas.
Geography - World; History - World; Social Science
Dist - UCEMC **Prod** - UCEMC

Living Maya Series
Presents a four - part series which documents life in a Yucatan village, focusing on one family over the course of a year. Introduces the village of Chican and the Colli Colli family in Program 1. Program 2 reveals that the family is hard pressed by an illness in the family and a drought which threatens their crucial corn crop. Program 3 focuses on the two youngest sons who plead to go to school in Merida - rejecting their family's traditional life. Program 4 shows the family resolving its difficulties even though the village harvests a mediocre corn crop. Produced by Hubert Smith.
The Living Maya - Program 1 58 MIN
The Living Maya - Program 2 58 MIN
The Living Maya - Program 3 58 MIN
The Living Maya, Program 4 58 MIN
Dist - UCEMC

Living metric 20 MIN
U-matic
Enter - metrics series
Color
Mathematics
Dist - MDCPB **Prod** - MDDE

Living Metrics - Count Me in 13 MIN
16mm / U-matic / VHS
Color (T)
LC 79-700307
Details ways in which metrics can be integrated into most school subjects.
Education; Mathematics
Dist - JOU **Prod** - CHIBED 1978

Living moments in Jewish Spain 21 MIN
VHS
In the footsteps of Marrano families series
Color (G)
$39.95 purchase _ #180
Introduces Jewish life in Medieval Spain as depicted in Jewish illuminated manuscripts of the period. Shows what everyday family life was like, how the Jewish holidays were celebrated, everyday activities and clothing styles. Includes accompanying Ladino music. Part of a series on the Marranos - Jews forced to convert and to live as Christians - from the Museum of the Jewish Diaspora - Beth Hatefutsoth.
History - World; Religion and Philosophy; Sociology
Dist - ERGOM

The Living Mosaic 27 MIN
16mm
Color (I J H C A)
Explores the great diversity of habitats and wildlife in the Tamaulipan biotic province of northeastern Mexico.
Geography - World; Science - Natural
Dist - ADAMSF **Prod** - TEXAIU 1985

Living music for Golden Mountains 27 MIN
U-matic / VHS / 16mm
Color
Documents the efforts of Leo Lew, a Chinese immigrant to America, to pass on the deep - rooted Cantonese folk music to new generations of Chinese - Americans. Traces Lew's life in America and shows some of the many problems facing the elderly in San Francisco's Chinatown. Presented in both English and Chinese with subtitles.
Fine Arts; Sociology
Dist - UCEMC **Prod** - DNGMEY 1982

Living - Non - living - once lived - evidence of past life 15 MIN
U-matic / VHS
Featherby's fables series
Color (P)
Tells how Mr Featherby's fossil center display at the library is being stolen, piece by piece. Shows how a newspaper reporter catches the thief.
History - World; Science; Science - Physical
Dist - GPN **Prod** - WVUTTV 1983

Living - non - living - once lived - grouping 15 MIN
U-matic / VHS
Featherby's fables series
Color (P)
Presents TV game show contestants who demonstrate how being able to group like objects develops skill in the area of organizing information.
Science; Science - Physical
Dist - GPN **Prod** - WVUTTV 1983

Living - non - living - once lived - identification 15 MIN
VHS / U-matic
Featherby's fables series
Color (P)
Shows a summer camp which provides the setting for a scavenger hunt during which living and non - living things are sought.
Science; Science - Physical
Dist - GPN **Prod** - WVUTTV 1983

Living - nonliving 15 MIN
U-matic / VHS
Hands on - Grade 2 - lollipops, loops, etc series
Color (P)
Gives experience in classifying living versus nonliving things. Unit three in the series.
Science
Dist - AITECH **Prod** - WHROTV 1975

The Living North 73 MIN
16mm
B&W
Fine Arts; Geography - World
Dist - FCE **Prod** - FCE

The Living ocean 25 MIN
U-matic / VHS
Color (J H C A G)
$235.00 purchase _ #51316
Shows how the oceans formed, how salinity is maintained, how the ocean floor provides evidence of tectonic activity, how the oceans figure in food webs, how the oceans affect both climate and weather and how mankind affects oceans.
Science; Science - Natural; Science - Physical
Dist - NGS

Living Ocean 26 MIN
VHS
Wonderstruck presents series
Color (I J)
$99.95 purchase _ #Q11174
Features marine biologist Stefani Hewlett who discusses dolphins, sea otters, baby seals, and the giant Pacific octopus. Illustrates the significance of the codfish worm and how a supposedly extinct prehistoric fish reappeared. Part of a series of 11 programs produced by the British Broadcasting Corporation and hosted by Bob McDonald.
Science; Science - Natural
Dist - CF

The Living Ocean - Pt 8 30 MIN
VHS
Wonderstruck Presents Series
Color (I)
$99.00 purchase _ #386 - 9062
Organizes science programs thematically for classroom use. Features Bob McDonald as host who makes learning fun with amazing science information and engaging activities. Part 8 of the eight part series travels below the waves to visit dolphins and beluga whales, coelacanths, sea otters, octopuses, baby seals and cod worms.
Geography - World; Science - Natural; Science - Physical
Dist - FI **Prod** - CANBC 1989

Living on our changing planet 23 MIN
U-matic / VHS / 16mm
Color (J)
Shows earthquake detectives, volcano watchers and disaster experts at work. Depicts an earthquake drill in Japan and scientists using lasers and computers to probe the earth.
Geography - World; Health and Safety; Science - Physical
Dist - NGS **Prod** - NGS 1984

Living on the edge - Shetland Islands and Channel Islands, UK 24 MIN
16mm / VHS
Amateur naturalist series
Color (I J H C G)
$495.00, $195.00 purchase
Shows how the inhabitants of rocky shored islands live in zones defined by the rise and fall of the tides - skate, dogfish, spider crab and sea urchin, flowers and lichens. Takes an underwater safari into a rockpool and observes a breeding area of seabirds in the cliffs. Part of a 13 - part series featuring a naturalist and a zoologist, Gerald and Lee Durrell, on field trips to different habitats.
Geography - World; Science - Natural
Dist - LANDMK **Prod** - LANDMK 1988

Living on the mud 23 MIN
16mm
Color (G)
$30.00 rental
Depicts the urbanization of the environment of 'flower children' in the 1970s. Pictures the shanty Bohemians of North Vancouver as a happy self - sustained community of independent people until bulldozers arrive.
Fine Arts; Geography - World; Sociology
Dist - CANCIN **Prod** - MALONS

Living on the River Agano 115 MIN
VHS
Color; PAL (G)
PdS100 purchase
Portrays the toll that industrialism has had on the River Agano in Japan, including the effects of dams and government regulations on the fishing industry. Looks at the mercury pollution from industrial dumping that has caused an increase of Minamata Disease among the people that live along the river. Produced by Sato Makoto of Japan.
Fine Arts; Geography - World; Industrial and Technical Education; Science - Natural; Social Science
Dist - BALFOR

Living on the Salmon Run
VHS / U-matic
Alaska Series
Color
Takes a look at commercial fishing in Alaska, the state's biggest industry. Shows a tough and bitter lifestyle through the eyes of a 17 - year - old boy.
Business and Economics; Geography - United States; History - United States; Industrial and Technical Education; Physical Education and Recreation
Dist - WCCOTV **Prod** - WCCOTV 1982

Living on your own video series
Presents a four - part video series dealing with the development of adult responsibilities. Covers subjects including money management, succeeding on one's first job, renting an apartment, and the nutrition of 'fast food.' Consists of four videocassettes and accompanying materials.
The Road to wise money management - planning, credit, and your paycheck 30 MIN
Dist - CAMV

The Living or Dead Test 29 MIN
16mm
Color (A)
Presents an experimental film by Diana Barrie in which parts of educational films are interspersed with pieces of colored leader and scratch animation.
Fine Arts
Dist - STARRC **Prod** - STARRC 1982

Living or Nonliving? 16 MIN
U-matic / VHS
Color (K P)
Uses sketches by an American Indian Artist and live action sequences of plants and animals to explore examples of how living things are nourished, how they grow and respond to the world, and how they produce other living things.
Science - Natural
Dist - NGS **Prod** - NGS

The Living past - Pt 1 15 MIN
16mm
B&W (I)
LC FIA56-886
Includes scenes of important events in American life between 1896 and 1905.
Fine Arts; History - United States
Dist - FCE **Prod** - FCE

The Living past - Pt 2 15 MIN
16mm
B&W (I)
LC FIA56-1249
Includes the early days of the horseless carriage, Columbus Circle 1900, Fifth Avenue in 1900, Spanish American War films, Duke of Windsor as a child, return of the Spanish War veterans, Dewey Flagship, Coney Island, death of President McKinley, Theodore Roosevelt takes oath of office, Justice Holmes.
Fine Arts; History - United States
Dist - FCE **Prod** - FCE

The Living past - Pt 3 15 MIN
16mm
B&W (I)
LC FIA56-1250
Includes President Theodore Roosevelt, the changing scene, New York's finest (police,) Rough Riders, Roosevelt's Conservation policies.
Fine Arts; History - United States
Dist - FCE **Prod** - FCE

The Living past - Pt 4 15 MIN
16mm
B&W (I)
LC FIA56-1251
Includes New York Giants (1905,) Bennett Cup Race (1905,) Roosevelt visits San Francisco, Gans - Nelson fight, nickelodeon movie from France, San Francisco earthquake, (unusual and complete coverage by cameramen from the Thomas A Edison studios.).
Fine Arts; History - United States
Dist - FCE **Prod** - FCE

Living philosophically quartet 120 MIN
BETA / VHS
Color (C A)
$69.95 purchase _ #Q374
Presents a four - part discussion on living philosophically. Includes Spirituality And The Intellect with Dr Jacob Needleman, Self And The Universe with Arthur M Young, The Primordial Tradition with Dr Huston Smith, and Self And Society with Dr Jane Rubin.
Psychology; Religion and Philosophy
Dist - THINKA **Prod** - THINKA

Living philosophically series
The Primordial tradition 30 MIN
Self and society 30 MIN
Self and universe 30 MIN
Spirituality and the intellect 30 MIN
Dist - THINKA

Living planet 31 MIN
16mm
Color
Goes on a spectacular aerial journey around the globe. Offers an opportunity to see the earth as a whole and to develop new visions and attitudes about a person's role in life.
Psychology; Science - Physical
Dist - MTP **Prod** - JOHNW

Living Planet Series Pt 11
Oceans 55 MIN
Dist - TIMLIF

Living Planet Series Pt 12
New Worlds 55 MIN
Dist - TIMLIF

Living Planet Series Pt 2
The Frozen World 55 MIN
Dist - TIMLIF

Living Planet Series Pt 5
Seas of Grass 55 MIN
Dist - TIMLIF

Living Planet Series Pt 9
The Margins of the Land 55 MIN
Dist - TIMLIF

Living Planet Series
The Baking deserts 55 MIN
The Building of the earth 55 MIN
The Community of the skies 55 MIN
The Frozen World 55 MIN
Jungle 55 MIN
The Margins of the Land 55 MIN
New Worlds 55 MIN
The Northern Forests 55 MIN
Oceans 55 MIN
Seas of Grass 55 MIN
Worlds Apart 55 MIN
Dist - AMBROS

Living Planet Series
Sweet Fresh Water 55 MIN
Dist - AMBROS
TIMLIF

Living planet series
The Baking deserts 55 MIN
The Building of the earth 55 MIN
The Community of the skies 55 MIN
Jungle 55 MIN
The Northern Forests 55 MIN
Worlds apart 55 MIN
Dist - TIMLIF

Living poetry 29 MIN
VHS / U-matic / 16mm
Color (H G)
$250.00, $300.00, $495.00 purchase, $60.00 rental
Focuses on the development of a poem over a one - year period by a major American poet. Uses archival footage and photographs to reflect the poems's influences while the camera probes the poet's thinking and feeling during the creative process.
Fine Arts; Literature and Drama
Dist - NDIM **Prod** - EDFLM 1988

Living poetry series
Casey at the bat 8 MIN
Dist - MGHT

Living proof 22 MIN
16mm / VHS / BETA / U-matic
Color; PAL (G)
PdS125, PdS133 purchase
Features the human side of heart surgery by people who have experienced it. Allays fears for anyone facing surgery and assists in recovery.
Health and Safety
Dist - EDPAT

Living prose series
Aesop's fables, Pt 1 12 MIN
Aesop's fables, Pt 2 10 MIN
Aesop's fables, Pt 3 12 MIN
Dist - MGHT

A Living queen 28 MIN
VHS
Color (H)
Depicts the life and role of Queen Margrethe II, Denmark's current sovereign. Product available for free loan from the distributor.
Geography - World; History - World
Dist - AUDPLN

Living rainforests 70 MIN
VHS
Color; PAL (J H G)
Explores the fate of the rainforests from an environmental perspective. Provides an educational resource for the study of rainforests in Environmental Studies across the National Curriculum. In four self - contained sections - Introducing the Amazon rainforest; Exploring rainforest ecology; Deforestation; The use of medicinal plants and conservation. Produced by Anna Culwick, United Kingdom. Price available on request.
Science; Science - Natural
Dist - EMFVL

The Living reef 22 MIN
VHS / U-matic
Color (I J A)
Reveals some of the teeming life on, under and behind Australia's Great Barrier Reef, one of the world's most remarkable collections of living things. Shows the reef's main structures, including gutters and caves along the sheltered edge, the shallow lagoon behind the crests of the reef, and an island formed from coral sand. Exhibits all kinds and shapes of coral, all kinds and shapes of fish, sponges, sea - squirts, tubeworms, stingrays, turtles and sharks.
Geography - World; Science - Natural; Science - Physical
Dist - EDMI **Prod** - EDMI 1976
AIMS

Living River 21 MIN
16mm
Color (I)
LC 74-702803
Presents an ecological story of a Pacific slope river and the life which it supports. Follows a river as it winds its way to the ocean, showing how the environment, both in and near the river, is shaped and influenced by its existence. Pictures the life cycle of the Pacific salmon from egg through alevin and fry to adult fish. Includes views of wildlife as well as underwater photography of salmon and trout. Filmed on Vancouver Island.
Geography - World; Industrial and Technical Education; Science - Natural
Dist - MMP **Prod** - MMP 1974

The Living rock 1 MIN
16mm
Caroline Avery series
Color (G A)
$10.00 rental
Presents the work of filmmaker Caroline Avery. Juxtaposes high and low images of children playing on the ground with cement pavement being laid.
Fine Arts; Industrial and Technical Education
Dist - PARART **Prod** - CANCIN 1989

Living Science Series
Around a big lake 17 MIN
The Boreal forest 19 MIN
Conservation and Balance in Nature 18 MIN
Life in the Deciduous Forest 19 MIN
The Pond 20 MIN
The Stream 15 MIN
Vacant Lot 21 MIN
Dist - IFB

Living Sculpture 22 MIN
16mm
Color (H C A)
LC 77-700731
Introduces sculptor Hart Tavel Goodman, who presents the intellectual and physical work involved in stone carving as exemplified by his own sculpture and that of other famous sculptors.
Fine Arts
Dist - WETFP **Prod** - WETFP 1976

The Living Smithsonian 60 MIN
VHS
Smithsonian world series
Color (G)
$49.95 purchase _ #SMIW - 401
Highlights the Smithsonian Institution and its people. Gives a behind - the - scenes look at the museums.
Fine Arts
Dist - PBS **Prod** - WETATV

Living Sober - the Class of '76 28 MIN
16mm
Color (C A)
Introduces recovered alcoholics of all ages who tell their stories of the pain of addiction and the freedom of recovery.
Health and Safety; Psychology
Dist - FMSP **Prod** - TRIAD 1976

The Living soil 9 MIN
16mm / Videodisc / VHS
Color (I J H A)
$160.00, $195.00, 395.00 purchase, $30.00 rental _ #8024
Illustrates by time - lapse photography the forces that create the soil and the many organisms that use and enrich it. Shows that rock - weathered by the action of water, wind, and the heat of the sun - is the 'parent,' producing soil that is then brought to life by rain.
Agriculture; Science - Natural; Science - Physical
Dist - AIMS **Prod** - EDMI 1983

The Living soil 9 MIN
16mm / VHS
Color (I J H)
Uses time - lapse photography to show how soil is created and used. Shows that weathered rock creates soil, and that rainfall sets the life process in motion.
Agriculture; Science - Natural; Science - Physical
Dist - AIMS **Prod** - CSIROA 1983
EDMI

Living spirit of '76 55 MIN
U-matic / VHS
Living spirit of '76 series
Color (I J)
Contains 1 videocassette.
Civics and Political Systems; Social Science
Dist - TROLA **Prod** - TROLA 1987

Living spirit of '76 series
Living spirit of '76 55 MIN
Dist - TROLA

The Living stone 33 MIN
16mm
Color (J A)
Pictures many aspects of Eskimo life and explains the Eskimo's belief in the legend that a spirit exists in every stick and stone, bird and beast. An elderly grandfather carves an image and relates its legend.
Literature and Drama; Social Science; Sociology
Dist - NFBC **Prod** - NFBC 1959

The Living Sun 30 MIN
16mm
Spectrum Series
B&W (H C A)
Depicts activities involved in outfitting and executing an expedition which uses aircraft in flight as platforms from which to observe a solar eclipse. Shows scientists at work before and during the expedition as they prepare and use equipment for recording the eclipse. Shows several views of the eclipse.
Science - Physical
Dist - IU **Prod** - NET 1967

Living systems 60 MIN
U-matic / VHS
Biology of cognition and language series
Color (A)
Presents biologist Humberto Maturana discussing living systems. Program four of the series.
Psychology; Science - Natural
Dist - UCEMC **Prod** - UCEMC

Living the Dream
VHS
Color (G)
$29.95 purchase _ #U891109011
Features Sonia Johnson, author of 'From Housewife To Heretic.'.
History - World; Religion and Philosophy; Sociology
Dist - BKPEOP **Prod** - SJOHN 1989

Living the Good Life with Helen and Scott Nearing 30 MIN
U-matic / VHS / 16mm
Color (J)
LC 77-703278
Shows that homesteading is not only viable in modern America, but beneficial to the individuals and society as well. Views Helen and Scott Nearing, who 45 years ago quit city life and went back to the land.
Agriculture; Guidance and Counseling; Social Science; Sociology
Dist - BULFRG **Prod** - BULFRG 1977

Living the life - child 25 MIN
VHS
Parenting and human development video series
Color (G)

$98.00 purchase _ #CDIL104V
Shows how children go about their daily business. Captures healthy interactions in the joy, affection and nurturing of others. Portrays unhealthy interactions in reactions to the anger, frustration and abuse of others. Developmental psychologists provide a conceptual framework for viewers. Includes discussion guide and reproducible worksheets. Part of a five - part series.
Guidance and Counseling; Health and Safety; Sociology
Dist - CAMV

Living the life - pre - schooler 25 MIN
VHS
Parenting and human development video series
Color (G)
$98.00 purchase _ #CDIL102V
Shows how preschoolers go about their daily business. Captures healthy interactions in the joy, affection and nurturing of others. Portrays unhealthy interactions in reactions to the anger, frustration and abuse of others. Developmental psychologists provide a conceptual framework for viewers. Includes discussion guide and reproducible worksheets. Part of a five - part series.
Guidance and Counseling; Health and Safety; Sociology
Dist - CAMV

Living the life - teen 25 MIN
VHS
Parenting and human development video series
Color (G)
$98.00 purchase _ #CDIL106V
Shows how teens go about their daily business. Captures healthy interactions in the joy, affection and nurturing of others. Portrays unhealthy interactions in reactions to the anger, frustration and abuse of others. Developmental psychologists provide a conceptual framework for viewers. Includes discussion guide and reproducible worksheets. Part of a five - part series.
Guidance and Counseling; Health and Safety; Sociology
Dist - CAMV

Living the life - teen parent 25 MIN
VHS
Parenting and human development video series
Color (G)
$98.00 purchase _ #CDIL108V
Shows how teen parents go about their daily business. Captures healthy interactions in the joy, affection and nurturing of others. Portrays unhealthy interactions in reactions to the anger, frustration and abuse of others. Developmental psychologists provide a conceptual framework for viewers. Includes discussion guide and reproducible worksheets. Part of a five - part series.
Guidance and Counseling; Health and Safety; Sociology
Dist - CAMV

Living the life - toddler 25 MIN
VHS
Parenting and human development video series
Color (G)
$98.00 purchase _ #CDIL100V
Shows how toddlers go about their daily business. Captures healthy interactions in the joy, affection and nurturing of others. Portrays unhealthy interactions in reactions to the anger, frustration and abuse of others. Developmental psychologists provide a conceptual framework for viewers. Includes discussion guide and reproducible worksheets. Part of a five - part series.
Guidance and Counseling; Health and Safety; Sociology
Dist - CAMV

Living the Second Time Around 25 MIN
U-matic / VHS / 16mm
Color (PRO)
Presents a story of the aging process and of Miriam Akins, depressed and lonely, who finds new values and goals for living. Shows the interaction between Miriam and her new employer.
Health and Safety; Psychology; Sociology
Dist - FEIL **Prod** - FEIL

Living the story 20 MIN
VHS
Color (G A R)
$19.95 purchase, $10.00 rental _ #4 - 85077
Stresses the need for good planning and motivational strategies in teaching church school classes.
Religion and Philosophy
Dist - APH **Prod** - APH

Living things and their environment 15 MIN
VHS / U-matic
Why Series
Color (P I)
Discusses living things and their environment.
Science; Science - Natural
Dist - AITECH **Prod** - WDCNTV 1976

Living Things are all Around Us 4 MIN
16mm / 8mm cartridge / VHS / U-matic
Most Important Person - Getting Along with Others Series
Color (K P I)
Follows as Johnny Running Bear learns to appreciate the living things of nature and finds it easier to make a friend at the day care center.
Guidance and Counseling; Psychology
Dist - EBEC **Prod** - EBEC 1972

Living Things are Everywhere 11 MIN
VHS / 16mm / U-matic
Color; B&W (P) (ARABIC)
Illustrates that living things may be found almost anywhere through the story of a young boy's discovery of various living things along a river bank.
Science - Natural
Dist - EBEC **Prod** - EBEC 1963

Living things can break too 8 MIN
16mm
Color (P)
LC 76-703635
Shows that the human body is a fragile machine and that the balance of what it takes to make the mechanism run smoothly is delicate. Portrays two children who discover how quickly living things can be killed by ordinary things found inside a house.
Guidance and Counseling; Health and Safety; Science - Natural
Dist - MALIBU **Prod** - MENKNS

Living things grow and change 15 MIN
U-matic / VHS
Animals and such series; Module red - life processes
Color (I J)
Shows how insects develop through a series of stages and how markings reveal age in trees and clam shells.
Science - Natural
Dist - AITECH **Prod** - WHROTV 1972

Living things in a drop of water 12 MIN
16mm / U-matic / VHS
Color (I)
Allows young science students to `look through the microscope' at a drop of pond water and see a variety of one - celled organisms called protists.
Science; Science - Natural
Dist - EBEC **Prod** - EBEC 1985

Living things reproduce 15 MIN
U-matic / VHS
Animals and such series
Color (I J)
Observes how living things reproduce and compares simple and complex methods of reproduction. Module Red of the series highlights life processes.
Science - Natural
Dist - AITECH **Prod** - WHROTV 1972

Living through it 27 MIN
16mm
Color (H C A)
LC 82-700428
Presents teacher and author Laura Knox interviewing Carole Soucaze, a young woman who suffered a catastrophic disability. Shows Miss Soucaze, a therapist herself, discussing her emotional reactions and growth through her illness and challenging those in the helping professions to consider how they behave toward disabled individuals.
Health and Safety; Psychology
Dist - LAWREN **Prod** - PRNTIP 1982

Living time - Sarah Jesup talks on dying 15 MIN
16mm
Color
Presents Sarah Jesup, a woman in her last two months of life, discussing the issues dying people face.
Psychology; Sociology
Dist - COFODY **Prod** - COFODY

Living together 30 MIN
U-matic / VHS
Oceanus - the marine environment series
Color
Defines symbiosis. Gives several examples of direct and indirect symbiosis. Discusses mutualism, commensalism and parasitism with the ocean world. Lesson 20 in the series.
Science - Natural; Science - Physical
Dist - CDTEL **Prod** - SCCON

Living together 60 MIN
U-matic / VHS
Discovery of animal behavior series
Color (J)
Portrays the work of Thorlief Schjelderup - Ebbe, Solly Zuckerman, Clarence Ray Carpenter, Frank Fraser Darling, William Hamilton and Amotz Zahavi who studied the communal living patterns of animals.
Science - Natural
Dist - FI **Prod** - WNETTV 1982

Living together 50 MINS.
VHS
The private life of plants
Color; PAL (H G)
PdS99 purchase; not available in USA, Canada
Reveals how certain plants can live in unlikely surroundings in order to promote their survival. Uses computer technology and time - lapse photography to highlight processes. Fifth in the six - part plant survival series, The Private Life of Plants. Hosted by David Attenborough.
Science - Natural
Dist - BBCENE

Living together 50 MIN
VHS
Trials of life series
Color (J H C G)
$29.98 purchase _ #TUR3089V - S
Looks at social behavior in animals. Part of a 12 - part series traveling with naturalist David Attenborough and his crew to exotic and dangerous places to observe the animal kingdom.
Science - Natural
Dist - CAMV **Prod** - TBSESI 1991

Living Together 28 MIN
16mm
B&W
LC 72-702205
Features three collective groups who discuss their experiences, and the rewards and drawbacks of communal living. Includes a statement by Margaret Mead on the value of these social experiments.
Psychology; Sociology
Dist - GSHDME **Prod** - GSHDME 1972

Living together 22 MIN
U-matic / VHS / 16mm
Neighbors series
Color (I J)
Examines the relationships within four European families and explores the future aspirations and ambitions of the parents and children for themselves. Compares these thoughts for the future against each family's current reality. Film four of the series.
Guidance and Counseling; Sociology
Dist - LUF **Prod** - LUF 1979

Living together 30 MIN
VHS / U-matic
Wild south series
Color (H C T G)
$295.00,$195.00 purchase, $30.00 rental
Shows human effects on the wetlands of New Zealand, including deforestation and swamp reclamation. Illustrates types of human - imposed problems facing ecosystems.
Geography - World; Science - Natural
Dist - ALTSUL **Prod** - ALTSUL 1987

Living Together 30 MIN
VHS / 16mm
Our Natural Heritage Series
Color (G)
$14.44 purchase _ #HSV4025
Explores relationships between growing things and their environment.
Psychology; Science - Natural
Dist - EDUCRT

The Living Tradition 120 FRS
VHS / U-matic
Color (H C)
Features 19th Century etchings and readings from Whitman's Leaves of Grass by Allen Ginsberg. Chronicles the poet's life.
Biography; Literature and Drama
Dist - CEPRO **Prod** - CEPRO

Living Traditions - Five Indian Women Artists 27 MIN
VHS / U-matic
Color (J)
Examines the relationship between traditional Indian values and the handiwork of five Indian women artists from Minnesota. Focuses on the role of culture handed down from generation to generation.
Social Science
Dist - UCV **Prod** - UCV

Living traditions quartet 120 MIN
VHS / BETA
Color (G)
$69.95 purchase _ #Q304
Presents a four - part series on living traditions. Includes The Way Of The Shaman with Dr Michael Harner, Francis Bacon And Western Mysticism with Peter Dawkins, Creation Spirituality with Dr Matthew Fox and Ancient Traditions In Modern Society with Dr Gay Gaer Luce.
Health and Safety; Religion and Philosophy
Dist - THINKA **Prod** - THINKA

Living traditions series
Ancient traditions in modern society 30 MIN
Creation spirituality 30 MIN
Francis Bacon and western mysticism 30 MIN
The Way of the shaman 30 MIN
Dist - THINKA

Living treasures of Japan 59 MIN
16mm / U-matic / VHS
Color (G)
Introduces nine Japanese artisans who are highly valued in Japan because of their particular skills. Looks at a potter, a dollmaker, a bellmaker, a swordmaker, a weaver - dyer, a papermaker, a Kabuki theatre actor, a musician and a puppeteer.
Fine Arts; Geography - World; History - World; Sociology
Dist - NGS **Prod** - NGS 1981
UILL

Living trees 16 MIN
16mm / Videodisc / VHS
Color (I J H A)
$295.00, $380.00, $395.00 purchase, $50.00 rental _ #9830
Defines and describes the parts and functions that all trees share. Shows how a trees carries water and minerals to the leaves, how the leaves make food for the tree by photosynthesis, and how that food is carried to the rest of the tree.
Science - Natural
Dist - AIMS **Prod** - WILETS 1986

Living under stress 30 MIN
VHS
Color (H C G)
$195.00 purchase
Investigates the cause of stress, how to live with it and how to avoid its worst consequences at every stage of life.
Guidance and Counseling; Health and Safety; Psychology
Dist - LANDMK **Prod** - LANDMK 1989

Living under the cloud - Chernobyl today 70 MIN
VHS
Color (G T)
$295.00 purchase, $85.00 rental
Exposes the effects of the 1986 Chernobyl nuclear plant disaster in which radioactive particles were carried across boundaries by wind and water, flora and fauna. Features Dr Vladimir Chernousenko, dying from exposure received as scientific director of the clean - up team, telling the truth about the accident. Reveals the former USSR's insufficient attempts to deal with the situation, includes videotaped recordings of the inhumane suicide missions of workers sent to rid the plant of radioactive debris, and tells how the sarcophagus built for containment is crumbling. The breakup of the USSR and its fragile economy cannot afford the expense of a massive cleanup. Produced by Teresa Metcalf.
Fine Arts; Health and Safety; History - World; Social Science; Sociology
Dist - BULFRG

Living under water 20 MIN
U-matic / VHS / 16mm
Exploring science series
Color (J H)
Shows that most of the ocean floor is covered by green plant life, floating pastures of microscopic single celled phytoplankton which are the feeding ground of the scarcely larger zooplankton.
Science - Natural
Dist - FI **Prod** - BBCTV 1982

Living Up North 24 MIN
16mm
Color
LC 76-702086
Discusses living in the Canadian North.
Geography - World; Sociology
Dist - PARA **Prod** - PARA 1974

Living up to death 90 MIN
VHS
Color (G)
$29.95 purchase _ #LIDEV
Records an evening talk by Sogyal Rinpoche in which he gives a comprehensive introduction to spiritual care for living and dying. Shows how the true meaning of life can be found through understanding death and impermanence. Explores the innermost essential nature of mind, pointing out how it is revealed through meditative practice. Gives practical advice on caring for the dying.
Religion and Philosophy; Sociology
Dist - SNOWLI

Living water 24 MIN
VHS
Color (G)
$29.95 purchase
Features photography by David Fortney. Includes Earth, a statement for world unity narrated by John Houseman.
Civics and Political Systems; Fine Arts; Geography - World
Dist - HP

Living Waters of the Big Cypress 14 MIN
16mm
Color
LC 80-701626
Presents a view of the Big Cypress National Preserve in Florida. Explains the role of water in the life cycle of this unique swamp and shows the wilderness habitats and plants and animals which inhabit them.
Geography - United States; Science - Natural
Dist - USNAC **Prod** - USNPS 1980

Living Waters of the Colorado 22 MIN
U-matic / VHS / 16mm
Color
Portrays life along the Colorado River and its tributaries. Examines the effects of man's activities in this area, concentrating on wildlife and recreational benefits of the Colorado River Storage Project. Includes scenes of Lake Powell and reservoirs at Flaming Gorge, Blue Mesa and Navajo.
Geography - United States; Industrial and Technical Education; Science - Natural; Social Science
Dist - USNAC **Prod** - USBR 1981

Living Way Out 25 MIN
16mm
Color (H A)
LC 78-701230
Depicts life in Shay Gap, a remote mining town in Western Australia. Presents residents and a social planner speaking on the problems of isolation and how they attempt to resolve them.
Geography - World; Sociology
Dist - AUIS **Prod** - FLMAUS 1976

Living well with arthritis series
Presents a five - part series on arthritis, discussing physical therapy, adaptive equipment, nursing issues, joint protection techniques, and coping with arthritis.
Adaptive equipment for arthritis - 2 9 MIN
Coping with arthritis - 5 12 MIN
Joint protection techniques for arthritis - 4 15 MIN
Nursing issues in arthritis - 3 11 MIN
Physical therapy for arthritis - 1 16 MIN
Dist - HSCIC **Prod** - BRMARH 1976

The Living wilderness 26 MIN
16mm
Audubon wildlife theatre series
Color (P A)
LC 73-710204
Studies the animals in the Rocky Mountains and how they adapt themselves to the changing environment of the mountains as winter turns to spring.
Geography - United States; Science - Natural
Dist - AVEXP **Prod** - KEGPL 1970

Living wills 30 MIN
VHS
Color (H C G)
$149.00 purchase, $75.00 rental _ #UW3111
Examines the concept of living wills and advance directives. Features Jamie Guth as host. Spends time with families in intensive care units, where they are forced to make decisions about lifesaving care. Shows how their experience may serve as a guide to viewers who may want to decide before the event whether they wish to be maintained on ventilators, fluids and drugs. Patients, their families and doctors also present their views of the situation.
Health and Safety; Sociology
Dist - FOTH

Living with a parent who takes drugs 21 MIN
VHS / U-matic
Color (I J H)
$250.00 purchase _ #HH - 6259L
Provides guidance for youngsters who are coping with a drug - abusing parent. Emphasizes that children are never responsible for these circumstances and encourages them to confide in an understanding adult.
Guidance and Counseling; Psychology; Sociology
Dist - LCA **Prod** - LCA 1990

Living with AIDS 28 MIN
VHS
Color (G)
$149.00 purchase, $75.00 _ #UW5333
Profiles several people with the HIV virus over the course of two years and examines the issues they face - medication, handling the emotional ups and downs, dealing with family members, paying for medical care, dealing with guilt. Profiles a 25 - year - old former drug abuser from New York City and her infected baby; a 29 - year - old female victim of sexual abuse; a musician; and a street wrestler. Examines alternative therapies and social support systems.
Health and Safety
Dist - FOTH

Living with AIDS 24 MIN
U-matic / VHS
Color (G)
$250.00 purchase, $100.00 rental
Chronicles the last six weeks in the life of 22 - year - old Todd Coleman who is afflicted with AIDS. Interviews Todd, his lover, his nurse, his social worker, his hospice. Focuses on the community support and the unconditional love given Todd as he grew weaker and less able to care for himself. Produced by Tina DiFeliciantonio.
Health and Safety; Sociology
Dist - BAXMED

Living with AIDS - 5 17 MIN
VHS
Coping with AIDS series
Color (H C G)
$250.00 purchase, $60.00 rental
Lists precautions persons with AIDS and those living with them must take to avoid bringing on opportunistic infections. Interviews long - term survivors of AIDS - ARC and their families who discuss the importance of attitude, determination and other nonmedical factors contributing to survival. Part of a five - part series for persons with AIDS and those involved with them, detailing medical and social aspects of living with AIDS. Resources are listed at the end of each program.
Health and Safety
Dist - CF **Prod** - HOSSN 1989

Living with an Alcoholic Parent
VHS / U-matic
Color (J H)
Presents young people revealing the fear, confusion, disappointment and anger they feel over their parents' drinking, and tell what crises prompted them to seek outside help. Encourages contacting Alateen and outlines their approach to dealing with alcoholism in the family.
Guidance and Counseling; Health and Safety; Sociology
Dist - GA **Prod** - AVNA

Living with angina 15 MIN
VHS
Color (G)
#FSR - 493
Presents a free - loan program which discusses the causes and types of treatment advances made in the last 15 years significant to angina management. Reviews drug therapy as well as certain procedures used to correct the angina such as coronary angioplasty and coronary artery bypass. Shows how to avoid situations that trigger angina pectoris attacks and explains how to take steps to improve cardiovascular fitness.
Health and Safety
Dist - WYAYLA **Prod** - WYAYLA

Living with Antabuse Therapy 18 MIN
VHS / U-matic
Color (A)
Discusses the effects, risks and problems of taking Antabuse and defines some restrictions for patients registered as veterans in the program.
Guidance and Counseling; Health and Safety; Sociology
Dist - USNAC **Prod** - VAMSLC 1984

Living with arthritis 60 MIN
VHS
Color (G)
$34.95 purchase _ CD45254
Features NFL All - Pro Quarterback Boomer Esiason, who had arthritis as a teenager, as host. Offers valuable tips on how to cope with arthritis.
Health and Safety; Physical Education and Recreation
Dist - HTHED **Prod** - ARTHF

Living with arthritis 14 MIN
VHS
Color (PRO A G) (SPANISH)
$250.00 purchase _ #AR - 05
Presents a complete look at the problems and available treatments for arthritis, from the careful depiction of how a joint works and interacts with muscles, tendons, ligaments and bursae to the development of the two major forms of arthritis. Stresses heat, exercise, rest and medication - HERM - as the best therapy. Includes occupational and physical therapies as well as a warning on 'miracle' cures.
Health and Safety
Dist - MIFE **Prod** - MIFE

Living with arthritis 50 MIN
U-matic / VHS
Bantam audio health series
Stereo (K P I J H C G T A S R PRO IND)
Gives facts about arthritis.
Health and Safety; Literature and Drama
Dist - BANTAP **Prod** - BANTAP

Living with asthma 16 MIN
VHS
Color; CC (G C PRO)
$175.00 purchase _ #PD - 06
Explains what asthma is and describes the elements of management, including medication, identifying and avoiding triggers, smoking cessation, exercise, peak flow

monitoring and immunotherapy. Contact distributor for purchase price on multiple orders.
Health and Safety
Dist - MIFE **Prod** - MIFE

Living with Baby 17 MIN
VHS / 16mm
New Mothers and Infant Care Series
Color (H C A PRO)
$195.00 purchase, $75.00 rental _ #8095
Emphasizes the necessity for new mothers to get the rest they need, to ask for help when they need it and to network with other new mothers.
Guidance and Counseling; Health and Safety; Home Economics; Sociology
Dist - AIMS **Prod** - HOSSN 1988

Living with Cancer 26 MIN
U-matic / VHS
Color (C)
$249.00, $149.00 purchase _ #AD - 1716
Reveals that every 30 seconds another person gets cancer, that every minute a cancer patient dies, but for each patient who dies there is one who lives to join the growing ranks of people living with cancer. Profiles three of these people.
Fine Arts; Health and Safety; Psychology
Dist - FOTH **Prod** - FOTH

Living with Cancer - a Conversation with Six Adolescent Cancer Patients 25 MIN
U-matic / VHS
Color (PRO)
Features six adolescent cancer patients describing their reactions to cancer. Includes the effect of illness on the family and friends, impact of chemotherapy and amputation, changes in personal relationships, self concept and dating.
Health and Safety; Sociology
Dist - UARIZ **Prod** - UARIZ

Living with cancer - the windstorms of life 28 MIN
VHS
Color (H C G)
$295.00 purchase, $55.00 rental
Profiles Dr Fred Lee, recognized by the National Institutes of Health as a leading researcher in prostate cancer. Explores Dr Lee's personal struggle with the cancer and the recognition of his own mortality. Shows the conflicts between his dedication to his work and his commitment to his family, his changed relationship to his patients when he becomes a patient, how he his sense of purpose has been transformed by the awareness of death. Produced by Ann Arbor Video, Inc.
Health and Safety; Sociology
Dist - FLMLIB

Living with Cancer - Three Perspectives
VHS
Color (J)
Examines the lives of several individuals stricken with cancer. These people explain how they face the common problems of managing pain, deciding on treatment, and facing prospect of death.
Health and Safety
Dist - HRMC **Prod** - HRMC 1986

Living with Cerebral Palsy 30 MIN
U-matic
(A)
Provides information and discusses the impact of the disorder on the entire family and provides an insight into the importance of available support service. A resource to parents of recently diagnosed CP children.
Health and Safety
Dist - ACCESS **Prod** - ACCESS 1978

Living with Chronic Illness 29 MIN
VHS / 16mm
Feelings Series
Color (G)
$55.00 rental _ #FEES - 107
Investigates how children with chronic illnesses deal with their friends and families. Features three 12 - year - olds.
Health and Safety; Sociology
Dist - PBS **Prod** - SCETV

Living with chronic illness - reaching for hope...learning to cope 33 MIN
VHS / U-matic
Color (PRO C G)
$395.00 purchase, $80.00 _ #C850 - VI - 107
Encourages group discussion about establishing and maintaining positive coping behavior in chronically ill children and their families. Presented by Carrie Goren Ingall and Dr Robert A Daughty.
Health and Safety; Sociology
Dist - HSCIC

Living with Computers 72 FRS
VHS / 16mm / U-matic
Skills for the New Technology - what a Kid Needs to Know Today 'Series
Color (P I)
LC 84-730288
Shows a magical young girl taking Elmer, a lovable, eccentric custodian, on a whirlwind tour to stress the importance of computer literacy by showing him how the computer is being used in homes, schools, and work places.
Guidance and Counseling; Psychology
Dist - CORF **Prod** - DISNEY

Living with Cystic Fibrosis 36 MIN
U-matic
Color (PRO)
Presents an overview of cystic fibrosis, the leading genetic killer of young people in the United States. Emphasizes its complications, diagnosis, personal and familiar impact, and the team approach for support.
Health and Safety; Science - Natural; Sociology
Dist - MTP **Prod** - CYSFIB

Living with Death 53 MIN
U-matic / VHS
Color
Reports on four months of research on the various aspects of death and how people deal with it.
Sociology
Dist - WCCOTV **Prod** - WCCOTV 1973

Living with Death - Unfinished Business 30 MIN
16mm / U-matic / VHS
Death and Dying Series
Color
LC 83-701006
From The Perspectives On Death And Dying Series. Presents Dr Elisabeth Kubler - Ross showing how dying patients can be assisted in accepting death. Includes scenes from Dr Kubler - Ross' workshops in which terminally ill people are counseled.
Sociology
Dist - CORF **Prod** - CBSTV 1983

Living with Diabetes 35 MIN
VHS
Color (G)
$24.95 purchase _ #6319
Discusses alternatives to insulin therapy and how to achieve healthy weight loss. Features experts from the Joslin Clinic of Boston.
Health and Safety; Physical Education and Recreation
Dist - SYBVIS **Prod** - SYBVIS

Living with Diabetes 19 MIN
U-matic / VHS
Color (C)
$249.00, $149.00 purchase _ #AD - 1971
Covers both childhood and adult - onset diabetes. Profiles various adult - onset diabetic patients to show the good effects of careful management of the disease and the dire effects of neglecting it. Shows how children with diabetes can be taught to accept their disease, learn to control it and lead complete and fulfilling lives.
Health and Safety; Psychology; Science - Natural; Sociology
Dist - FOTH **Prod** - FOTH

Living with Diabetes - Anything You Can Get, I Can Get Better 21 MIN
U-matic
Color
LC 80-706506
Explains the importance of personal hygiene and other preventive measures in living with diabetes.
Health and Safety
Dist - USNAC **Prod** - VAHSL 1979

Living with diabetes - by Biocom, Ltd 45 MIN
VHS / U-matic
Bantam audio health guides series
Stereo (K P I J H C G T A S R PRO IND)
Gives facts about diabetes.
Health and Safety
Dist - BANTAP **Prod** - BANTAP

Living with Diabetes - Meal Planning - Eat Right, Live Well 30 MIN
U-matic / VHS
Color (A)
Discusses the concept of meal planning in a diabetic diet for proper control of diabetes.
Health and Safety; Home Economics; Social Science
Dist - USNAC **Prod** - VAMCSL 1984

Living with Diabetes - the Exchange Lists, the Spice of Life 26 MIN
U-matic / VHS
Color (A)
Discusses food exchange lists and how to use them to maintain a proper diabetic diet.
Health and Safety; Social Science
Dist - USNAC **Prod** - VAMCSL 1984

Living with Diabetes - Your Future with a Difference 40 MIN
U-matic
Color
LC 80-706507
Features a doctor explaining treatments and probable lifestyle changes to a recently diagnosed diabetic and his family.
Health and Safety
Dist - USNAC **Prod** - VAHSL 1979

Living with disabilities 30 MIN
VHS
CC; Color (C H G A)
$59.95 purchase _ #CCNC-901-WC95
Describes how different people with disabilities live full and rich lives. Explains how a teenager who lives in a wheelchair spends his day in school. Hosted by Vidya Shaker. A high school athlete explains how to cope with an injury, and entertainer Queen Latifah discusses respect.
Health and Safety
Dist - PBS **Prod** - WTVSTV 1994

Living with Disaster 24 MIN
16mm
Color (J)
LC 79-700526
Emphasizes the need for long - term psychological and physical after - care of natural disaster victims.
Health and Safety; History - World; Psychology
Dist - AUIS **Prod** - FLMAUS 1975

Living with Dust 15 MIN
16mm
Color
LC 75-700356
Presents causes of dust in nature and industry and gives methods of controlling these conditions. Tells how different dusts affect the worker and what can be done to protect him.
Business and Economics; Health and Safety; Science - Natural; Social Science; Sociology
Dist - MMAMC **Prod** - MMAMC 1974

Living with Dying 19 MIN
U-matic / VHS / 16mm
Color
Presents four patients who discuss the emotional, social and medical problems which frequently accompany a life - threatening illness and how they have learned to cope with these problems.
Guidance and Counseling; Sociology
Dist - PRORE **Prod** - FILMA 1975

Living with dying 30 MIN
U-matic / VHS
Contemporary health issues series; Lesson 11
Color (C A)
Looks at attitudes toward death that have led to the rejection and isolation of the elderly and the institutionalization of the dying. Examines the ways in which people cope with impending death.
Sociology
Dist - CDTEL **Prod** - SCCON

Living with dying 50 MIN
VHS
Horizon series
Color; PAL (H C A)
PdS99 purchase
Follows the patients and staff in an NHS hospice and examines the hospice movement's philosophy of better care for the dying. Demonstrates the movement's emphasis on allowing terminal patients to maintain a normal life - style and to die without pain. Part of the Horizon series.
Health and Safety; Sociology
Dist - BBCENE

Living with dying series
Focuses on the issues surrounding death, grief and life after death. Interviews people who face death daily, primarily residents and employees of nursing homes. Consists of three videocassettes.
Exploring the mystery 20 MIN
Facing death 20 MIN
Learning to care 20 MIN
Dist - APH **Prod** - APH 1981

Living with electricity 15 MIN
VHS
Color; PAL (I J H)
PdS15 purchase _ #1012
Presents three short videos looking at the history of electicity. Uses archival footage to illustrate how the development and control of electricity has changed the ways in which humans lead their lives. Introduces the topics of electrical safety and control in terms of circuits and switches and logic gates. Encourages an interactive approach to learning. Includes booklets containing practical activities for the classroom and a teacher's handbook.
Health and Safety; Industrial and Technical Education; Science - Physical
Dist - UKAEA

Living with Glasnost and Perestroika - understanding the USSR today 70 MIN
VHS
Color (J H)
$129.00 _ #60125 - 026
Documents experts in Soviet affairs discussing these terms and explaining how they came about - from the abdication of the Czar through the birth of the USSR to the Soviet society of the 1980s. Gives their opinions about the implications of glasnost and perestroika and explains who they affected relations between the US and the Soviet Union. Includes teacher's guide and library kit.
Civics and Political Systems; Education; Fine Arts; History - World
Dist - GA

Living with good health series
AIDS 15 MIN
Drugs 15 MIN
Dist - AAVIM

Living with Grace, Alzheimer's Disease 28 MIN
U-matic / VHS
Color
Focuses on the life of one woman suffering from Alzheimer's disease, loss of memory, emotional swings, catastrophic reactions and confusion.
Health and Safety
Dist - UMDSM **Prod** - UMDSM

Living with high blood pressure 59 MIN
VHS
Color (G)
$34.95 purchase
Takes an in - depth look at hypertension. Explains the basic facts and dispels myths. Provides information on proper diet, exercise, weight control, medications, and more.
Health and Safety
Dist - PBS **Prod** - WNETTV

Living with high blood pressure 59 MIN
VHS
Color (G)
$39.95 purchase _ #KAR606
Explains what high blood pressure is, how heredity and lifestyle affect its levels. Shows how a patient can work with the medical profession to control high blood pressure. Features tennis champ and heart attack victim Arthur Ashe and medical experts.
Health and Safety
Dist - CADESF **Prod** - CADESF

Living with High Blood Pressure 60 MIN
VHS
(H C A)
$39.95 purchase _ #CST100V
Discusses high blood pressure and hypertension and how it kills without warning. Explains how risks can be controlled. Explores how heredity, lifestyle, and age can affect chances of contracting the disease. Describes the condition of high blood pressure and how it is examined as well as how it can be treated.
Health and Safety
Dist - CAMV **Prod** - CAMV

Living with Huntington's Disease 30 MIN
U-matic
(A)
Explores the physical and mental disabilities that characterize this hereditary illness and its effects on family members Co - produced by the Huntington Society of Canada.
Health and Safety
Dist - ACCESS **Prod** - ACCESS 1978

Living with IBD 21 MIN
VHS
Color (PRO A G)
$100.00 purchase _ #GI - 13
Helps young patients deal with the emotional effects of having an IBD and helps them understand how they can improve their lives. Explains what IBDs are, the effects of medications used in treatment and the possible need for bowel resection. Produced by the Patient Education Committee of the NFIC.
Health and Safety; Science - Natural
Dist - MIFE

Living with leukemia series
Emotional Concern 8 MIN
Good nutrition 7 MIN
Taking Care of Yourself 8 MIN
Understanding Leukemia 10 MIN
Dist - UTXAH

Living with loss - children with HIV
VHS
Hugs InVited - an educational and training series
Color (PRO C A)
$59.95 purchase _ #4824
Addresses the mortality of children infected with HIV, the virus that causes AIDS. Looks at the impact of HIV - infection on parents and siblings, confidentiality as it relates to family, friends, school and community.
Health and Safety
Dist - CWLOA **Prod** - CWLOA 1991

Living with love 15 MIN
U-matic / VHS
Inside-out series
Color
Stresses the benefits that love produces and shows how to cope with a lack of love in life. Explains the different ways in which love can be expressed.
Guidance and Counseling; Psychology
Dist - AITECH

Living with lung cancer 20 MIN
VHS / U-matic / BETA
(G)
Provides patients and families with information on how physicians diagnose lung cancer; patients with lung cancer relate through interviews how they learned to live with the disease.
Health and Safety; Science - Natural
Dist - UTXAH **Prod** - UTXAH 1985

Living with lung cancer 9 MIN
VHS / U-matic
Cancer education series
Color (G C PRO)
$195.00 purchase _ #C920 - VI - 046
Describes how physicians diagnose and treat lung cancer. Examines how patients learn to live with the disease. Features several people diagnosed with lung cancer who discuss their feelings about the disease and how they have managed to cope with the symptoms and treatment of the disease. Part of a four - part series presented by the University of Texas, MD Anderson Center.
Health and Safety; Science - Natural
Dist - HSCIC

Living with Nebraska's Water 27 MIN
16mm
Nebraska Water Resources Series
Color (H C A)
LC 74-700162
Illustrates natural water quality and pollution in Nebraska. Describes how nature creates the basic characteristics of the earth's surface and ground water and reviews the bacterial and chemical quality of both.
Geography - United States; Science - Natural; Science - Physical
Dist - UNEBR **Prod** - UNEBR 1971

Living with nuclear waste 12 MIN
16mm
Color (G)
$25.00 rental
Parodies 1950s educational films for elementary and high school students. Follows the Samsons, a modern family from the suburbs, up to their summer cabin where the local power company is building a nuclear waste disposal site. Uses flashbacks, animation and narration as the family evaluates the situation. Produced by Steve Westerlund.
Fine Arts; Literature and Drama; Social Science; Sociology
Dist - CANCIN

Living with parents - conflicts, comforts and insights 45 MIN
VHS
Color (J H)
$249.00 purchase _ #CG - 810 - VS
Explores conflicts between teenagers and parents. Discusses the dual pulls of wanting to be independent and wanting to be cared for. Looks at the ambivalence of parents who may find it hard to let go of their children. Gives students tactics for improving relationships with parents.
Guidance and Counseling; Psychology; Social Science; Sociology
Dist - HRMC **Prod** - HRMC

Living with parents who drink too much 18 MIN
VHS / 16mm
Color (I J)
$395.00, $345.00 purchase, $75.00 rental _ #8200
Helps children of alcoholics to understand alcolism, to know that they are not responsible for their parent's alcoholism and behavior. Emphasizes that such children need the support of someone with integrity with whom they can talk and from whom they can receive emotional support. Shows that joining a self - help group such as Children of Alcoholics is helpful.
Health and Safety; Sociology
Dist - AIMS **Prod** - AIMS 1990

Living with Peter 22 MIN
16mm
Color (J)
LC 74-702017
Explores the issue of living together without marriage.
Guidance and Counseling; Sociology
Dist - WEINSM **Prod** - WEINSM 1973

Living with spinal cord injury series
Presents a three - part series on spinal cord injuries. Includes Changes - coming to terms with spinal cord injury and beginning rehabilitation; Outside - the lifelong process by which some injured persons have created active and rewarding lives; and Survivors - explores the problems of growing old with a disability.
Changes 28 MIN
Outside 28 MIN
Survivors 28 MIN
Dist - FANPRO **Prod** - CORBTB 1973

Living with stress 16 MIN
16mm / U-matic / VHS
Color (A)
Describes what stress is. Shows how the body reacts to stressors - events that produce change.
Psychology
Dist - EBEC **Prod** - MIFE 1981

Living with stress 15 MIN
VHS
Color (PRO A) (SPANISH ARABIC)
$250.00 purchase _ #GN - 11
Helps the patient understand that even though drinking, smoking, or over - eating may give temporary relief from stress, the long term effects of these behaviors are damaging to health. Illustrates examples of good and bad stress and explains the basic 'fight or flight' response. Suggests that the most effective way to deal with stress is to find an enjoyable recreational activity, family interest, or hobby and participate in it on a regular basis. Helps patients identify with people in the program who explain how stress has affected them and how they have learned to cope with it.
Health and Safety; Psychology
Dist - MIFE **Prod** - MIFE 1991

Living with Stress 22 MIN
U-matic
Color (A)
Looks at typical daily stress - producing situations. Emphasizes that stress is a problem that each person must first understand and then deal with in an individual way.
Health and Safety; Psychology
Dist - GA **Prod** - XEROXF

Living with stress 25 MIN
16mm / VHS / BETA / U-matic
Color; PAL (G)
PdS140, PdS148 purchase
Gives details of stress - producing statistics.
Psychology
Dist - EDPAT

Living with stress
U-matic / VHS
(COR A)
$195.00 purchase _ #IE5222V
Investigates the impact of stress on many men and women who work for a major corporation at the middle management level.
Business and Economics; Psychology
Dist - CAREER **Prod** - CAREER

Living with technology 20 MIN
U-matic / VHS
You, me, and technology series
Color (J H)
; $150.00 purchase; LC 83-707177
Portrays the everyday, commonplace uses of technology through the familiar encounters of a fictitious suburban family with the clothing, communications, transportation and food industries. Uses dramatizations, archival artwork and stills to depict the development of technology. Emphasizes the trade - offs modern persons accept when they choose to use technology.
Sociology
Dist - AITECH **Prod** - TEMPLU 1983

Living with the City 24 MIN
16mm
Color (H C A)
LC 78-701231
Discusses developments in the preservation and rehabilitation of inner city areas of Sydney, Melbourne and Adelaide, Australia. Highlights the need for strong relationships between communities and government.
Geography - World; Sociology
Dist - AUIS **Prod** - FLMAUS 1975

Living with the dead 10 MIN
VHS
Magnum eye series
Color (G)
$125.00 purchase, $30.00 rental
Travels to the North Cemetery in Manila, the Philippines, where 5000 homeless people live among the gravestones. Looks at their poverty, which is so great they have moved their families into mausoleums, surreal homes where bones are swept out of crypts to make room

for furniture. A shantytown has arisen on top of the 15 foot high concrete wall that encloses the cemetery. Captures the strange stories of these dwellers. Directed by Misha Erwitt. Part of a series by photographers from the Magnum Photo Agency.
Fine Arts; Geography - World; Sociology
Dist - FIRS **Prod** - MIYAKE 1993

Living with the Landscape 14 MIN
16mm
Color (J H C G)
Discusses the relationship between man and the environment.
Science - Natural; Sociology
Dist - VIEWTH **Prod** - VIEWTH

Living with the spill 52 MIN
VHS
Color (G)
$390.00 purchase, $75.00 rental
Describes the effects of the Exxon Valdez oil spill on the community of Valdez, Alaska. Asks whether the disaster could have been prevented and whether the damage can ever be repaired.
Geography - United States; Science - Natural; Social Science
Dist - FIRS

Living with the Work Ethic 30 MIN
U-matic
Growing Old in Modern America Series
Color
Health and Safety; Sociology
Dist - UWASHP **Prod** - UWASHP

Living with tinnitus 9 MIN
VHS
Color (PRO A)
$250.00 purchase _ #OT - 15
Explains the problem of tinnitus for patients and their families. Explains symptoms, causes, evaluation, medical and surgical treatment options and risks. Uses state - of - the - art animation to depict the anatomy. For use in the practicing otolaryngologist's office and helpful to hospital patient educators or clinical staff.
Psychology; Science - Natural
Dist - MIFE **Prod** - MIFE 1992

Living with tomorrow 11 MIN
VHS
Color (G)
$14.95 purchase
Documents three ways of living with alternative energy sources. Visits a home wind - generator system, a community solar greenhouse and a double envelope house.
Social Science; Sociology
Dist - WMMI **Prod** - WMMI

Living with tradition 29 MIN
VHS / U-matic
Forest spirits series
Color (G)
Offers a glimpse at some of the Menominee people and the traditions they are trying to maintain. For a short period in their history, the Menominee of Wisconsin were not Indians. Under a federal process called 'termination,' the government ended the protected status of the Menominee as an Indian tribe. Their reservation became a country. Though they were forced to live like white people and outwardly lost some of their uniqueness, the Menominee kept a thread of their culture alive. Following a return to tribal status in 1973, the Menominee today are reaffirming their heritage.
Social Science; Sociology
Dist - NAMPBC **Prod** - NEWIST 1975
GPN

Living with trouble - crisis in the family
U-matic / VHS
Color (J H C)
Dramatizes the stories of three teenagers who cope with the task of carrying on their lives despite trouble in their families. Promotes understanding of family crises and how to take steps to make life personally rewarding. Includes teacher's guide.
Guidance and Counseling; Psychology; Sociology
Dist - SUNCOM **Prod** - SUNCOM
CAREER

Living with unresolved issues 30 MIN
VHS
Christian values in the business world series
Color (H C G A R)
$39.95 purchase, $10.00 rental _ #35 - 896 - 2076
Explores the creative tension that can exist between one's job and one's faith. Hosted by Bill Bockelman. Produced by Seraphim.
Business and Economics; Religion and Philosophy
Dist - APH

Living with wildlife 26 MIN
16mm
Color
Discusses man's impact on wildlife. Illustrates how best man can live and preserve his natural heritage of wildlife. Examines the economic, aesthetic, scientific, ecological and recreational roles of wildlife.
Science - Natural
Dist - STOUFP **Prod** - STOUFP 1982

Living with work 15 MIN
U-matic
Job skills series
(H C A)
Discusses how employment affects lifestyle. Encourages a healthy balance between work, family and leisure.
Business and Economics; Psychology
Dist - ACCESS **Prod** - ACCESS 1982

Living with your arrhythmia 15 MIN
VHS
Color (G)
#FSR - 494
Presents a free - loan program which teaches the causes of arrhythmia and what symptoms to look for. Discusses procedures to detect the abnormal heartbeat, including the stethoscope to listen to heart sounds and the EKG which measures the electrical impulses. Examines treatments in detail, medication therapy, pacemaker and electrical defibillators.
Health and Safety
Dist - WYAYLA **Prod** - WYAYLA

Living with your back 16 MIN
VHS / U-matic
Color (FRENCH)
LC 72-736646
Describes the intervertebral disks, their function and their relationship to the vertebrae. Includes demonstrations of good posture and proper body mechanics as they apply to helping the patient protect his/her back from further stress and strain. Demonstrates exercises designed to strengthen and tone the back - supporting muscles.
Health and Safety; Physical Education and Recreation; Science - Natural
Dist - MEDCOM **Prod** - MEDCOM

Living with your body series
Understanding the female body 15 MIN
Understanding the male body 15 MIN
Where babies come from 15 MIN
Dist - AAVIM

Living without kidneys 13 MIN
VHS
Color (G)
$125.00 purchase _ #CE - 119
Focuses on Patty who is an avid golfer, tennis player and cyclist. Reveals that she hikes and cross country skis and that, in the current year, she tried roller blades for the first time. But Patty has no kidneys. Since her kidneys failed when she was a young adult, she has experienced a variety of therapies, including an unsuccessful transplant, and she now depends on dialysis. Produced by Kathy Archibald.
Health and Safety; Science - Natural
Dist - FANPRO

Living wood - African masks and myths 12 MIN
16mm
Color (I)
LC 73-701042
Explains that to the African Black, the tree is a living thing and the masks he carves from the tree have a special power, a vital force. Attempts to reveal this vital force by showing the masks of Africa, as a tribesman relates the tales and myths of his people.
Geography - World; Social Science; Sociology
Dist - FILMSM **Prod** - GRADYM 1973

The Living word 28 MIN
VHS
Color (G A R)
$24.95 purchase, $10.00 rental _ #35 - 81 - 8936
Presents ten original songs based on passages from the Gospel of John.
Fine Arts; Literature and Drama; Religion and Philosophy
Dist - APH

Living world of the sea series
Egg into animal 12 MIN
Fish - master of movement, locomotion in the sea 12 MIN
The Survival Factor - Defense Mechanisms in the Sea 12 MIN
Dist - MIAMIS

Living Yoga 22 MIN
VHS / U-matic
Color
$39.95 purchase
Shows four classic pathways of 'union' (yoga) through the lives of disciples of Swami Satchidananda - hatha, the yoga of physical postures and breathing techniques; raja, the path of meditation and introspection; Karma, the way of selfless service; and bhakti, the yoga of love and devotion.
Health and Safety; Religion and Philosophy
Dist - HP **Prod** - HP

Living Yoga 20 MIN
VHS / U-matic
Color
Introduces the paths and practices that lead to the realization that living Yoga is living peacefully, healthfully and joyfully in all conditions.
Health and Safety; Religion and Philosophy
Dist - IYOGA **Prod** - IYOGA

Living Yoga - Four Yokes to God 20 MIN
16mm
Color (J)
LC 77-700747
Discusses the everyday practices of Hatha, Raja, Bhakti and Karma Yoga. Explains various Yoga postures, correct breathing, diet, meditation and the concepts of selfless service and true devotion.
Health and Safety; Religion and Philosophy
Dist - HP **Prod** - HP 1977

Livingstone - Clyde to Kalahari 23 MIN
U-matic / VHS / BETA
Color; NTSC; PAL; SECAM (I J)
PdS58
Follows the journey of David Livingstone across the African continent from west to east, when he discovered much of the Zambesi and the Victoria Falls. Shows parts of the Kalahari, the Kavango swamps, typical bush country, wild life and a bush fire. Reveals the problems facing an explorer more than a century ago in Africa.
Geography - World; History - World
Dist - VIEWTH

Liz 30 MIN
U-matic
Not one of the crowd series
Color (PRO)
Focuses on Liz who spent 18 months in a mental institution. Examines the lives of people with mental illnesses and the difficult transition from an institution to society.
Health and Safety; Psychology
Dist - TVOTAR **Prod** - TVOTAR 1981

Liz Fights Back 30 MIN
U-matic / VHS
K I D S - a Series
Color (H)
Continues Liz's story of coping after being sexually assaulted. Shows Liz and family attending a police line up but her attacker is not there. Though the police are discouraged, Liz and friends come up with a plan to trap her assailant.
Sociology
Dist - GPN **Prod** - CPOD

Liz Fights Back 30 MIN
VHS / U-matic
K - I - D - S
Captioned (H)
Continues the story of Liz from program 1. Investigates the aftermath of the rape. Second in a five part series.
Psychology; Sociology
Dist - GPN **Prod** - CPOSI 1981 - 1983

Liz Sits the Schlegels 26 MIN
16mm / U-matic / VHS
Color (I J)
Tells the story of Liz who gets a job sitting for three children. Describes Liz's difficulty in dealing with the oldest child who resents Liz's presence but comes to accept her when he almost endangers the lives of his younger brother and sister.
Guidance and Counseling; Literature and Drama; Psychology; Sociology
Dist - BCNFL **Prod** - PLAYTM 1985

Liza Bear - Earthglow 8 MIN
U-matic / VHS
Color
Visualizes phrases of a narrative poem. Involves indoor and outdoor sounds.
Fine Arts; Literature and Drama
Dist - ARTINC **Prod** - ARTINC

Liza Bear - Lost Oasis 10 MIN
U-matic / VHS
Color
Centers around the search for a lost oasis.
Fine Arts
Dist - ARTINC **Prod** - ARTINC

Liza Bear - Oned Nefifik, a Foreign Movie 28 MIN
U-matic / VHS
Color
Shows that the relation between the fact and experience of an event can be fluently and responsibly articulated.

Fine Arts
Dist - ARTINC **Prod** - ARTINC

Liza Bear - Polisario, Liberation of the Western Sahara 29 MIN
VHS / U-matic
Color
Deals with communications technology and production.
Fine Arts; Social Science
Dist - ARTINC **Prod** - ARTINC

Liza Bear - Title Advance, Les Conditions Du Travail 20 MIN
VHS / U-matic
Color
Deals with communications technology and production.
Fine Arts; Social Science
Dist - ARTINC **Prod** - ARTINC

Liza Bear - Towards a New World Information Order 60 MIN
VHS / U-matic
Color
Deals with communications technology and production.
Fine Arts; Social Science
Dist - ARTINC **Prod** - ARTINC

Lizard 11 MIN
U-matic / VHS / 16mm
See 'N Tell Series
Color (K P I)
LC 78-706310
Shows the lizard as it drinks dew from the grass and feeds on insects and spiders, sheds its skin and mates.
Science - Natural
Dist - FI **Prod** - PMI 1970

Lizard music 15 MIN
VHS
Storybound series
Color (I)
#E375; LC 90-713292
Presents a satire, 'Lizard Music' by D Manus Pinkwater, on modern culture and science fiction fantasy. Part of a 16 - part series designed to lead viewers to the library to find and finish the stories they encounter in the series.
English Language; Literature and Drama; Social Science
Dist - GPN **Prod** - CTI 1980

A Lizard tale 15 MIN
16mm / U-matic / VHS
Color (P I)
Reveals some facts about common lizards and how they adapt to their environment. Considers the importance of conservation from both a practical and aesthetic point of view.
Science - Natural
Dist - STANF **Prod** - STANF 1975

Lizards and Hermit crabs 10 MIN
VHS
Tiny tales series
Color (K P I)
$195.00 purchase
Presents two short animated stories narrated in rhyme by Ivor the spider. Tells a story about lizards in The Lizard's Tail and about hermit crabs in A Hermit Crab's Friend.
Literature and Drama
Dist - LANDMK **Prod** - LANDMK

Lizards of Oz 28 MIN
VHS
Color (P I J H)
$225.00 purchase
Views the world of lizards in their many varieties - skinks, dragons, monitors and goannas - and their many habitats. Shows close - ups of them and their interactions with dingos, scorpions, centipedes and snakes.
Science; Science - Natural
Dist - LANDMK

Lizzie - an Amazon Adventure 57 MIN
U-matic / VHS
River Journeys
Color (H C A)
$1225 purchase (entire series), $285 purchase (each)
Discusses the 1896 journey down the Amazon River of Lizzie Hessel.
Geography - World
Dist - CF

Lizzie and the baby - the childbirth for children video 19 MIN
VHS
Color (K P A)
$250.00 purchase _ #OB - 137
Shows three year old Lizzie, who is about to become a big sister, as she learns about pregnancy, birth, and the changes a baby can bring to the home. Provides parents with ideas to help prepare children aged 3 - 8 for the arrival of a new sister or brother. Produced by Injoy Productions. Contact distributor for purchase price on multiple orders.

Health and Safety; Sociology
Dist - MIFE

Llama Language 13 MIN
VHS / 16mm
Color (H C A)
Demonstrates how llamas and guanacos communicate with ear and tail movement and positions and illustrates the signals of warning when dealing with these cousins to the camel.
Psychology; Science - Natural
Dist - IOWA **Prod** - IOWA 1989

Llanito 51 MIN
VHS
B&W (G)
$59.00 purchase
Features those people who only operate on the fringes of society - Indians, Chicanos and a group of retarded Anglos. Portrays their collective martyrdom to American society by recording one of the retarded boys summarizing Christ's passion - a bizarre religious testament. Produced by Danny Lyon.
Fine Arts; Geography - United States; Psychology; Social Science; Sociology
Dist - CANCIN

LLETZ of the cervix 7 MIN
VHS
Color (PRO)
$250.00 purchase
Incorporates unique graphics and clear explanations to provide a reassuring presentation of the loop excision procedure.
Health and Safety; Sociology
Dist - LPRO **Prod** - LPRO

Lloyd J Reynolds - William M Geer 59 MIN
16mm
Men who Teach Series
B&W (C T)
LC FIA68-2615
Focuses on William Geer, lecturer in modern civilization and history at the University of North Carolina and Lloyd Reynolds, calligrapher and art historian, Reed College, Portland, Oregon. Samples their lectures, their counseling methods and their philosophies. Interviews present and former students.
Education
Dist - IU **Prod** - NET 1968

Lloyds of London 117 MIN
16mm
B&W
Tells the story of the founding of the world's most famous insurance company, and of two boyhood friends, Johnathan Blake and Horatio Nelson. Re - enacts the Battle of Trafalgar. Stars Freddie Bartholomew, Tyrone Power and Madeleine Carroll.
Business and Economics; Fine Arts
Dist - TWCF **Prod** - TWCF 1936

LLQ - Leatherman Leadership Questionaire
VHS / 16mm
(C PRO)
$600.00 purchase
Assesses leadership potential efficiently, quickly and inexpensively. Measures knowledge in 27 skill areas, providing data for managerial selection, career counseling, and needs assessment. Includes booklets for ten managers.
Education; Psychology
Dist - VLEARN **Prod** - INTRFL

LMNO 9.5 MIN
16mm
Color (C)
$325.00
Experimental film by Robert Breer.
Fine Arts
Dist - AFA **Prod** - AFA 1978

LNG, a special report 15 MIN
U-matic / VHS
Color (IND)
Demonstrates fire protection techniques for gaseous and liquified natural gas handlers. Overviews major fire testing with LNG from 1951 to 1972.
Health and Safety
Dist - ANSUL **Prod** - ANSUL 1974

Lo Espanol, Hoy, En Los EEUU 52 MIN
U-matic / VHS
Espana Estuvo Alli Series
Color (C) (SPANISH)
$249.00, $149.00 purchase _ #AD - 1031
Looks at the role of Hispanics in America today. Examines place names, festivals and dances, architecture and a large Spanish speaking population. In Spanish.
Foreign Language; History - United States; History - World; Sociology
Dist - FOTH **Prod** - FOTH

Load - Power Concept 30 MIN
VHS / U-matic
Color
Presents Dr. Howard V. McClusky, Professor of Adult Educational Psychology and Adult Education, University of Michigan, with the idea that life is a question of balancing our load of responsibilities against the power of our resources.
Psychology
Dist - NETCHE **Prod** - NETCHE 1971

Loaded Voltage Dividers 33 MIN
16mm
B&W
LC 74-705043
Defines and illustrates load. Shows how to determine the voltage at each tap and the current through the loads and voltage dividers. Leads the student through a problem of calculating the voltage and current through a loaded voltage divider. Shows how the direction of current flow and the polarity of the voltages across each resistor is determined. (Kinescope).
Industrial and Technical Education; Science - Physical
Dist - USNAC **Prod** - USAF 1964

The Loaded weapon 60 MIN
VHS / 16mm
Story of English series
Color (C)
PdS99 purchase
Shows how the Irish, in acquiring English as a second language, invested the tongue with unique characteristics and suggests that Ireland's current conflicts stem, in part, from cultural differences caused by language. Part 8 of the series.
English Language
Dist - BBCENE **Prod** - BBCTV 1986
FI
PSU

Loading and Firing a Bisque Kiln 28 MIN
Videoreel / VT2
Wheels, Kilns and Clay Series
Color
Features Mrs Peterson describing certain ceramic processes for her classroom at the University of Southern California. Demonstrates how to load and fire a bisque kiln.
Fine Arts
Dist - PBS **Prod** - USC

Loading and operating the autoclave in the dental office 8 MIN
BETA / VHS
Color (PRO)
Health and Safety; Science
Dist - RMIBHF **Prod** - RMIBHF

Loading and transporting the horse 13 MIN
BETA / VHS
Color
Demonstrates how to load and transport a horse.
Agriculture; Physical Education and Recreation
Dist - EQVDL **Prod** - EQVDL

Loading and Unloading Heavy Equipment on a Trailer 13 MIN
16mm / U-matic / VHS
Color (H C A)
LC 81-700593
Shows checks and safety precautions to follow when transporting heavy equipment on the highway. Demonstrates procedures for loading, unloading and transporting a backhoe and a bulldozer.
Health and Safety; Social Science
Dist - CORNRS **Prod** - CUETV 1979

Loading and unloading poles 21 MIN
16mm
B&W
LC 74-705044
Shows procedures for loading and unloading poles from a flatcar or trailer. Stresses safety precautions.
Health and Safety; Industrial and Technical Education
Dist - USNAC **Prod** - USA 1944

Loading dock safety and trailers 9 MIN
U-matic / BETA / VHS
Forklift operator training series
Color (IND G)
$395.00 purchase _ #817 - 24
Trains forklift operators. Identifies the areas to inspect on trailers, procedures to follow, loading and unloading procedures and general dock safety. Part of a series on skills in forklift operation.
Health and Safety; Industrial and Technical Education; Psychology
Dist - ITSC **Prod** - ITSC

Loads and Loading of General Transport Vehicles 18 MIN
16mm

B&W
LC 74-705045
Shows characteristics of the five types of military cargo transported via vehicle and the prescribed loading procedures for each. Emphasizes maximum authorized load, proper vehicle for given load and safety precautions.
Civics and Political Systems; Social Science
Dist - USNAC **Prod** - USA 1954

Loads of experience 15 MIN
VHS / U-matic / BETA
Color (IND G A)
$615.00 purchase, $125.00 rental _ #LOA007
Reveals that over fifty percent of all forklift accidents involve pedestrians. Incorporates accident prevention training for the lift truck driver and the co - worker in close proximity. Focuses on lifting, transporting and placing a load, and the responsibilities of those working around lift trucks.
Health and Safety; Psychology
Dist - ITF **Prod** - CREMED 1991

Loan fraud - internal and external
VHS
Color (A PRO IND)
$495.00 purchase, $149.00 rental
Presents a two - part program on loan fraud and its prevention. Interviews government and banking experts on how loan fraud can be detected and prevented. Narrated by Robert Stack and filmed on sites of several loan frauds.
Business and Economics; Civics and Political Systems; Sociology
Dist - VLEARN

The Loan officer as a super salesperson 40 MIN
VHS
Dream team series
Color (PRO)
$295.00 purchase, $150.00 rental _ #MAX03C
Shows how loan officers can sell with discretion and integrity. Includes a leader's guide. Part of an eight - part series. Produced by Marx Communications.
Business and Economics
Dist - EXTR

Loan path murder 50 MIN
VHS
Trial series
Color; PAL (H C A)
PdS99 purchase
Features the murder of a retired civil servant who is beaten to death on his way home. Presents the jury as they discuss a piece of evidence relating to the crime that has no apparent motive and no witnesses. First in a series of five programs filmed by the BBC in Scottish courts.
Civics and Political Systems; Sociology
Dist - BBCENE

Loans
VHS
Financial Planning and Management Series
(C G)
$59.00_CA275
Covers personal loans.
Business and Economics; Education
Dist - AAVIM **Prod** - AAVIM 1989

Loans and Credit 15 MIN
U-matic / VHS
Consumer Education Series
Color
Business and Economics; Home Economics
Dist - CAMB **Prod** - MAETEL

Loaves and fishes 26 MIN
VHS
How to save the Earth series
Color (J H C G)
$175.00 purchase, $45.00 rental
Travels to Africa and the North Sea. Asks how humans can prevent famines and protect the land and sea resources that provide their food. Melaku Worede, an Ethiopian and Jens Ole - Hojmann, from Denmark are the two featured green warriors.
Fine Arts; Health and Safety; Industrial and Technical Education; Science - Natural; Sociology
Dist - BULFRG **Prod** - CITV 1993

Lob and drop shot 29 MIN
U-matic / VHS
Vic Braden's tennis for the future series
Color
Physical Education and Recreation
Dist - PBS **Prod** - WGBHTV 1981

The Lob and the Smash 29 MIN
VHS / U-matic
Love Tennis Series
Color
Features Lew Gerrard and Don Candy giving tennis instructions, emphasizing the lob and the smash.
Physical Education and Recreation
Dist - MDCPB **Prod** - MDCPB

Lobbying 29 MIN
VHS / 16mm
Washington Connection Series
Color (G)
$55.00 rental _ #WACO - 114
Civics and Political Systems; Social Science
Dist - PBS **Prod** - NPACT

Lobbying 48 MIN
U-matic / BETA / VHS
Inquiry Series
Color; Mono (H C A)
$350.00 purchase, $50.00 rental
Reveals the often unrecognized activities of groups who are able to influence the governments' decisions.
Civics and Political Systems
Dist - CTV **Prod** - CTV

Lobbying - a case history 18 MIN
16mm / U-matic / VHS
Color (J H)
Presents a revised version of the 1952 motion picture Pressure Groups. Uses a case study to illustrate the legislative lobbying activities of various interest groups in conflict over a single issue.
Civics and Political Systems
Dist - EBEC **Prod** - EBEC 1977

Lobbying Congress - Influences and Interests - Pt 1 30 MIN
VHS / U-matic
Congress - We the People Series
Color
Illustrates different types of interest groups and their strategies and tactics, the mutual interdependence of Congress and interest groups, and congressional regulation of interest groups.
Civics and Political Systems
Dist - FI **Prod** - WETATV 1984

Lobbying for lives - lessons from the front 30 MIN
VHS / U-matic
Color (G)
$360.00, $325.00 purchase, $110.00 rental; $250.00 purchase, $50.00 rental _ #38107
Shows how Canadian health groups beat the powerful tobacco industry at its own political game and the lessons learned about influencing public opinion and Parliament. Interviews major figures on both sides of the issue. Includes documentary footage, television newsclips and a series of original drawings by political cartoonist Jerzy Kolacz.
Business and Economics; Civics and Political Systems; Geography - World; Health and Safety; History - World; Psychology; Sociology
Dist - MEDCIN UCEMC **Prod** - MEDCIN 1989

The Lobster 20 MIN
U-matic / VHS
Japanese Cuisine Series
Color (PRO)
Shows a live lobster dismembered, prepared, and served on a a small table resembling a sandy beach surrounded by cucumber waves and black pebbles.
Home Economics; Industrial and Technical Education
Dist - CULINA **Prod** - CULINA

Lobster 29 MIN
Videoreel / VT2
Joyce Chen cooks series
Color
Features Joyce Chen showing how to adapt Chinese recipes so they can be prepared in the American kitchen and still retain the authentic flavor. Demonstrates how to prepare lobster.
Home Economics; Industrial and Technical Education
Dist - PBS **Prod** - WGBHTV

Lobsterman 15 MIN
U-matic / VHS
Other families, other friends series
Color (P)
Describes how lobster is caught, cooked and sold in Maine. Module Blue of the series focuses on Maine.
Geography - United States; Geography - World; Home Economics; Social Science
Dist - AITECH **Prod** - WVIZTV 1971

Local anesthetics 30 MIN
16mm
Pharmacology series
B&W (C)
LC 73-703332
Health and Safety
Dist - TELSTR **Prod** - MVNE 1971

Local Area and Office Automation Series

Access and use	30 MIN
Components and organization	30 MIN
Designs and implementations	30 MIN
Impact and Issues	30 MIN

Dist - DELTAK

Local area networks 420 MIN
VHS / U-matic
(A PRO)
$2,520.00 ; $400.00, $450.00
Covers introductory issues for LANs. Provides practical guidelines.
Computer Science
Dist - VIDEOT **Prod** - VIDEOT 1988

Local Color
VHS / U-matic
Red Tapes Series
B&W
Pictures a deep, sculptural space taking America into past and future worlds. Uses essayistic language.
Fine Arts
Dist - KITCHN **Prod** - KITCHN

Local Color 116 MIN
16mm
Color (G)
Presents an independent production by Mark Rappaport. Offers a modernistic melodrama with four couples.
Fine Arts; History - United States; Literature and Drama
Dist - FIRS

Local Color - Bret Harte and Mary Wilkins Freeman 20 MIN
VHS / U-matic
American Literature Series
Color (H C A)
LC 83-706256
Offers dramatizations of two short stories, Bret Harte's Tennessee's Partner and Mary Wilkins Freeman's One Good Time.
Literature and Drama
Dist - AITECH **Prod** - AUBU 1983

Local exhaust ventilation systems 12 MIN
VHS
Color; PAL; NTSC (G IND)
PdS57, PdS67 purchase
Examines a typical local exhaust ventilation - LEV - system which consists of a hood or other type of inlet, ducting, fan and air cleaning device. Shows how each one of these parts needs to be properly designed, but the most important - the inlet - is often neglected. Considers a variety of types of LEVs to show the principles and the behavior of dust - laden air.
Health and Safety; Psychology
Dist - CFLVIS

Local government 30 MIN
VHS
Inside Britain 1 series
Color; PAL; NTSC (G) (BULGARIAN CZECH HUNGARIAN SPANISH POLISH ROMANIAN RUSSIAN SLOVAK UKRAINIAN ENGLISH WITH ARABIC SUBTITLES)
PdS65 purchase
Explains the functions of local government through meeting locally - elected officers, permanent officers, city employers and voluntary workers in Bradford, Yorkshire. Looks at the methods individual citizens can use to influence the management of services.
Civics and Political Systems
Dist - CFLVIS **Prod** - INFVIS 1991

Local Government 30 MIN
VHS / 16mm
Government by Consent - a National Perspective Series
Color (I J H C A)
Examines various types of local governments. Emphasizes that local government has a direct effect on individual lives and that individuals can affect government. Uses citizen activism in a suburb and in a large city as an example.
Civics and Political Systems
Dist - DALCCD **Prod** - DALCCD 1990

Local Government 30 MIN
VHS / U-matic
American Government Series; 1
Color (C)
Compares and contrasts many different forms of local government and ways people come into contact with them on a daily basis, often without realizing it. Examines the multiple layers of government - federal, state, county, city, special districts and specified authority.
Civics and Political Systems
Dist - DALCCD **Prod** - DALCCD

Local heroes - global change series

Against the odds - Pt 2	60 MIN
The Global connection - Pt 4	60 MIN
Power to Change - Pt 3	60 MIN
With Our Own Eyes - Pt 1	60 MIN

Dist - SCETV

Local Infiltration Anesthesia 9 MIN
U-matic / VHS
Medical Skills Films Series
Color (PRO)

Health and Safety
Dist - WFP **Prod** - WFP

Local Issue Series no 14
An Intellectual Caste System 30 MIN
Dist - IU

Localized Corrosion - Pitting and Crevice Corrosion 59 MIN
VHS / U-matic
Corrosion Engineering Series
Color (PRO)
Industrial and Technical Education; Science - Physical
Dist - GPCV **Prod** - GPCV

Locate yourself - are you spiritual or are you carnal 28 MIN
16mm
Christian home series
Color
LC 73-701552
Features personal and marriage counselor Henry Brandt who discusses the differences between those individuals who are guided by carnal drives and those who are spiritually directed in love, joy, peace, patience and the other gifts of the spirit. Presents a challenge for each person to find where they stand. Number one in the series.
Guidance and Counseling; Psychology; Religion and Philosophy
Dist - CCFC **Prod** - CCFC 1972

Locating and repairing leaks 17 MIN
16mm
Refrigeration service - domestic units series
B&W (IND)
LC FIE52-224
Shows how to test for sulphur dioxide and methyl chloride leaks, use the halide torch to locate freon leaks and repair several types of leaks. Number 3 in the Refrigeration service - domestic units series.
Industrial and Technical Education
Dist - USNAC **Prod** - USOE 1945

Locating Buttons and Buttonholes 4 MIN
16mm
Clothing Construction Techniques Series
Color (J)
LC 77-701198
Presents a step - by - step procedure for proper location of buttons and buttonholes. Includes an explanation of why certain button placements are made.
Home Economics
Dist - IOWASP **Prod** - IOWA 1976

Locating company information 15 MIN
VHS
Color (G C)
$100.00 purchase, $14.50 rental _ #23767
Offers an orientation to conducting business research in the library. Outlines the three basic steps involved in locating information for class assignments, job interviews, in - house business reports and for developing investment strategies - conducting preliminary background research, reviewing primary reference resources and locating reference resources.
Business and Economics; Education; Industrial and Technical Education
Dist - PSU **Prod** - WPSXTV 1986

Locating Holes, Drilling and Tapping in Cast Iron 18 MIN
16mm
Machine Shop Work Series Operations on the Drill Press, Vertical 'Drill, no 1
B&W
LC FIE52-552
Shows how to lay out a bolt circle having eight holes, to use the center punch as centers for drilling and to use a tapping chuck for set screws.
Industrial and Technical Education
Dist - USNAC **Prod** - USOE 1942

Locating Potential Employers 25 MIN
VHS / 16mm
Job Search - How to Find and Keep a Job Series
(H)
$69.00 _ #PA102V
Explains how to locate print sources that have information about job openings.
Guidance and Counseling
Dist - JISTW

Locating Potential Employers - Program 2 29 MIN
VHS / 16mm
Job Search - How to Find and Keep a Job
Color (H C A PRO)
$720.00 purchase _ #SD100
Explores the people and print resources for job possibilities as well as presenting ways to record information about employers. Available only as part of the complete series. Part 2 of 12 parts.

Business and Economics; Guidance and Counseling
Dist - AAVIM **Prod** - AAVIM 1990

Location analysis 30 MIN
VHS
Business logistics series
Color (G C)
$200.00 purchase, $20.50 rental _ #34979
Discusses location analysis. Part of a 30 - part series on business logistics which deals with movement and storage of raw and finished products, and with managerial activities important for effective control of these operations. Interviews logistics managers of major US corporations and transportation companies. Uses on - site segments to demonstrate logistical carrier operations. Features program author Dr John Coyle.
Business and Economics; Social Science
Dist - PSU **Prod** - WPSXTV 1987

Location lighting 22 MIN
VHS
Color (H C)
$39.95 purchase _ #600310
Takes a careful look at how to light for video or film in familiar locations such as fluorescent - lit factories or in unfamiliar locations such as under metal halide, sodium vapor or mercury vapor lighting. Offers instruction on how to achieve proper Kelvin and CC balance, how to determine which combination of light control filters is right and how to use the picture monitor, the waveform monitor and the Cinegel swatchbook to correct the lighting.
Industrial and Technical Education
Dist - INSTRU

Location of Decks and Compartments 17 MIN
16mm
B&W
Explains number and letter designations and deck and compartment arrangement aboard ship.
Civics and Political Systems; Social Science
Dist - USNAC **Prod** - USN 1948

Location sound recording 37 MIN
VHS
Color (PRO G)
$149.00 purchase, $49.00 rental _ #708
Features sound engineer Bill Linton who uses animation and demonstration to illustrate microphone types and pickup patterns. Discusses microphone selection and operating technique for dozens of location situations, from press conferences to strolling interviews, from parties to phone booths, from noisy streets to pastoral settings. Covers the special problems of lav mikes and radio mikes in separate sections. Produced by the Australian Film, Television and Radio School.
Fine Arts; Industrial and Technical Education
Dist - FIRLIT

Location techniques 30 MIN
VHS
Business logistics series
Color (G C)
$200.00 purchase, $20.50 rental _ #34980
Discusses location techniques. Part of a 30 - part series on business logistics which deals with movement and storage of raw and finished products, and with managerial activities important for effective control of these operations. Interviews logistics managers of major US corporations and transportation companies. Uses on - site segments to demonstrate logistical carrier operations. Features program author Dr John Coyle.
Business and Economics; Social Science
Dist - PSU **Prod** - WPSXTV 1987

The Loch 120 MIN
VHS
Sound (C G A)
PdS99 purchase
Depicts the scenery and wildlife of a Scottish loch, using one 30 minute program for each season. Employs the talents of musicians Eddie McGuire; Alasdair Nicholson; William Sweeney; and Sally Beamish. Directed by Mike Herd, a British natural history photographer.
Geography - World; Industrial and Technical Education; Science - Natural
Dist - BBCENE

Lock energy to zero 10 MIN
VHS / U-matic
Color (IND A)
LC 90-708695
Shows step - by - step the proper sequence and procedure to follow when shutting down, locking out and tagging equipment for maintenance and repair. Produced by Comprehensive Loss Management.
Health and Safety; Industrial and Technical Education; Psychology
Dist - IFB

Lock Former Machine Acme or Pipelock Seam 11 MIN
BETA / VHS
Metal Fabrication - Lock Former Machine Series
Color (IND)
Industrial and Technical Education; Psychology
Dist - RMIBHF **Prod** - RMIBHF

Lock Former Machine Pittsburgh Seam 14 MIN
VHS / BETA
Metal Fabrication - Lock Former Machine Series
Color (IND)
Industrial and Technical Education; Psychology
Dist - RMIBHF **Prod** - RMIBHF

Lock - Hold - Step
U-matic / VHS
Driving Safety Series
Color (IND)
Discusses proper method for getting in, on and around large trucks. Increases driver awareness on the importance of this method.
Health and Safety; Industrial and Technical Education
Dist - GPCV **Prod** - DCC

Lock - Out 8 MIN
VHS / U-matic
Take Ten for Safety Series
Color (IND)
Details the procedures to be followed when performing maintenance or repair on electrically - driven equipment.
Health and Safety; Industrial and Technical Education
Dist - CORF **Prod** - OLINC

Lock - out - tag - out 17 MIN
VHS
Color (IND G)
$395.00 purchase, $75.00 rental _ #8311
Explains what lockout - tagout is and how it protects employees from injury when servicing machinery. Provides examples of lock and tag devices used with electrical, pneumatic and hydraulic power systems. Illustrates common repair situations requiring lockout - tagout precautions. Complies with OSHA regulations.
Health and Safety
Dist - AIMS **Prod** - MARCOM 1991

Lock to zero 10 MIN
16mm / VHS / BETA / U-matic
Color; PAL (IND)
PdS150, PdS158 purchase
Shows step - by - step the proper sequence to follow when shutting down, locking out, and tagging equipment for maintenance and repair. Discusses electrical, hydraulic and pneumatic equipment. Includes manual and employee handbook.
Health and Safety
Dist - EDPAT **Prod** - CLMI 1988

Lock welt and self - lock window installation 12 MIN
VHS / BETA / 16mm
Color (A PRO)
$66.00 purchase _ #KTI29
Demonstrates the methodical installation of stationary glass using locking weatherstrips.
Industrial and Technical Education
Dist - RMIBHF **Prod** - RMIBHF

Locke and Berkeley 45 MIN
VHS
Great philosophers series
Color; PAL (H C A)
PdS99 purchase
Introduces the concepts of Western philosophy and two of its greatest thinkers. Features a contemporary philosopher who, in conversation with Bryan Magee, discusses Locke and Berkeley and their ideas. Part six of a fifteen part series.
Education; Religion and Philosophy
Dist - BBCENE

Locked inside 14 MIN
16mm
Color
LC 79-701373
Satirizes a man's obsession with the contents of a suitcase which his neighbor constantly carries.
Fine Arts; Literature and Drama
Dist - SIDCIN **Prod** - SIDCIN 1979

Locked Up and Left Out - Mothers in Prison 40 MIN
U-matic
Color (C H)
Reveals the emotional and physical trauma of imprisoned mothers and their children and discusses the solution attempted by the State of California.
Sociology
Dist - CSUS **Prod** - CSUS 1985

Locked up, locked out 30 MIN
U-matic / VHS / 16mm
Color
LC 73-702674
Shows what happens to 'problem' children from poor families and reveals the conditions in the children's treatment centers.
Home Economics; Sociology
Dist - CAROUF **Prod** - CBSTV 1973

Lockerbie - the local authority response 32 MIN
VHS
Color; PAL; NTSC (G PRO C)
PdS250 purchase
Presents a comprehensive overview of the many issues involved in the Local Authority response to the December 21, 1988 Pan American flight 103 explosion and crash over the Scottish market town of Lockerbie, which killed all 259 passengers and crew as well as 11 residents. Trains individuals involved with emergency planning. Produced by the Emergency Planning College.
Civics and Political Systems; Psychology; Science - Physical
Dist - CFLVIS

Lockheed L - 1011 Tristar 42 MIN
VHS / U-matic
Color
Traces the history of the development of the L - 1011 passenger plane from drawing board to actual test flights, including footage of assembly production techniques.
Industrial and Technical Education; Social Science
Dist - IHF **Prod** - IHF

Locking the door
VHS
Color (A) (DUTCH FRENCH GERMAN JAPANESE SPANISH)
$525.00 purchase
Emphasizes the importance of basic computer security measures, including limiting access to computers, protecting diskettes, removing physical hazards, logging off when leaving, and keeping passwords secure. Explains that computer data and hardware are assets for a business and should be protected as such.
Business and Economics; Computer Science; Education
Dist - COMFLM **Prod** - COMFLM

Lockout 22 MIN
VHS
Color (A)
$525.00 purchase
Uses a gameshow format to emphasize security procedures involving data and hardware. Checks viewer knowledge regarding accountability for data, classification of company information, proper disposal of secure information, and protection of data from unauthorized access or tampering.
Business and Economics; Computer Science; Education
Dist - COMFLM **Prod** - COMFLM

Lockout 11 MIN
BETA / VHS / U-matic
Color; PAL (IND G) (PORTUGUESE)
$175.00 rental _ #AEB - 107
Focuses on the reasons for lockout routines on both electrical and mechanical equipment and the logic behind them. Stresses the importance of following a company's lockout procedures. Details both the 'one - man, one - lock' and the 'supervised' lockout, illustrating the principles in action. Includes leader's guide and 10 workbooks.
Health and Safety; Industrial and Technical Education; Psychology
Dist - BNA **Prod** - BNA

Lockout for Safety 17 MIN
VHS / 16mm
Color (A IND)
LC 91705362
Trains workers in correct lockout procedures required by OSHA regulations. Demonstrates the six - step lockout procedure and the three - step restart procedure.
Education; Health and Safety; Psychology
Dist - IFB

Lockout - tagout 11 MIN
VHS / U-matic / BETA
Safety meetings series
Color (G IND)
$495.00 purchase, $95.00 rental _ #YHM7
Shows how to prevent on - the - job maintenance accidents through thorough lockout - tagout procedures.
Business and Economics; Health and Safety; Psychology
Dist - BBP **Prod** - BBP 1990

Lockout - tagout 12 MIN
VHS
Blueprints for safety series
Color (IND)
$249.00 purchase _ #CLM55
Presents guidelines for safety and compliance requirements, created by certified safety professionals. Includes an instructor's guide, training tips, a learning exercise, five employee handbooks, glossary of terms and template for transparencies.
Health and Safety
Dist - EXTR **Prod** - CLMI

Lockout - tagout 27 MIN
VHS
Color (G)
$495.00 purchase _ #4023 - HDLQ
Clarifies and defines safety procedures for preventing shock and injury. Also available as part of the complete Lockout - Tagout Program.
Health and Safety
Dist - KRAMES **Prod** - KRAMES

Lockout - tagout procedures 23 MIN
BETA / VHS / U-matic
Color (IND G A)
$610.00 purchase, $125.00 rental _ #LOC002
Identifies and illustrates proper lockout - tagout procedures for a variety of applications. Shows proper lockout - tagout and start - up sequences when working with four energy types - electrical, hydraulic - pneumatic, fluids and gases, and mechanical.
Health and Safety; Industrial and Technical Education; Psychology
Dist - ITF **Prod** - CREMED 1991

Locks and garage door openers - installing door locks, garage door opener 30 MIN
BETA / VHS
Wally's workshop series
Color
Industrial and Technical Education
Dist - KARTES **Prod** - KARTES

Locomotion 4 MIN
U-matic / VHS
Color (G)
$225.00 purchase, $75.00 rental
Tells the story of a spirited locomotive and caboose who are suddenly faced with a major obstacle while on the way to the station. By working together they overcome nearly impossible odds to solve their dilemma. Features computer animation and no narration.
Business and Economics; Guidance and Counseling
Dist - VLEARN **Prod** - ADVANM

Locomotion 30 MIN
VHS
Color (J H)
$120.00 purchase _ #A5VH 1195
Studies the locomotion of a broad spectrum of animals. Illustrates the principal types of locomotions found in protozoans, invertebrates, fish, amphibians, reptiles, birds and mammals. Includes teacher's guide with information on species shown and more detail on methods of locomotion.
Science - Natural
Dist - CLRVUE **Prod** - BBCTV

Locomotion 5 MIN
VHS
Color (COR)
$225.00 purchase, $75.00 five - day rental, $25.00 three - day preview _ #LOC
Stimulates discussion on a variety of managerial and problem solving issues. Serves as a session starter to focus on teamwork, goal setting, motivation, communication, and leadership. Includes a Leader's Guide. Available for three - day preview and five - day rental, as well as for lease or purchase.
Business and Economics; Guidance and Counseling; Psychology
Dist - ADVANM

Locomotion 16 MIN
U-matic / VHS / 16mm
Color
Celebrates the 15th anniversary of the world's first public passenger steam railway by showing scenes from railway history.
Social Science
Dist - LUF **Prod** - LUF 1979

Locomotion and feeding 17 MIN
VHS
Fresh water invertebrates series
Color (J H)
$99.95 purchase _#Q11167
Features fresh water invertebrates utilizing mircrophotography and focuses on locomotion, food gathering, and ingestion. Illustrates the differences between autotrophs and heterotrophs and features primitive predator and prey relationships. Presents a visual wrap - up which reiterates all technical names and major characteristics of each organism. Part of a series of three programs.
Science; Science - Natural
Dist - CF

Locomotion and Skeletons
VHS
Basic Biology And Biotechnology Series
Color (G)
$75.00 purchase _ #6 - 083 - 106P
Explores movements of animals and how those movements are made possible. Examines the endoskeleton of humans, the exoskeleton of crayfish and the earthworm hydroskeleton. Part of a series on basic biology.
Science - Natural
Dist - VEP **Prod** - VEP

Locomotion in the amoeba
VHS
BSCS Classic Inquiries Series
Color (H C)
$59.95 purchase _ #193 W 2214
Poses questions, raises problems and presents experimental data on locomotion in the amoeba. Part of a series on the life sciences.
Science - Natural
Dist - WARDS **Prod** - WARDS

Locomotion in the elderly - Tape 4 28 MIN
VHS
Increased mobility for the elderly series
Color (PRO)
$90.00 purchase _ #876
Teaches nurses and health professionals about wheelchair mobility skills and ambulation skills in the acute rehabilitation of elderly patients or for long term care settings. Presents the work of W Griggs and K S Black.
Health and Safety; Sociology
Dist - RICHGO **Prod** - RICHGO 1987

Locomotion of cancer cells in vivo compared with normal cells 21 MIN
16mm
Upjohn vanguard of medicine series
Color (PRO)
LC FIA68-150
Uses time - lapse cinemicrography to show how rapidly cancer cells move in respect to normal cells and pictures cancer cells engulfing and ingesting red and white blood cells.
Health and Safety; Science - Natural
Dist - UPJOHN **Prod** - UPJOHN 1967

Locomotion of Four - Footed Animals 15 MIN
U-matic / VHS / 16mm
Aspects of Animal Behavior Series
B&W
Shows all of the major animal gaits including walk, pace, single - foot, trot, bound, pronk, gallop, bipedal run and bipedal hop. Documents the type of locomotion with unique footage of a variety of mammals and reptiles.
Science - Natural
Dist - UCEMC **Prod** - UCLA 1980

Locomotion of the Horse 19 MIN
VHS / BETA
Color
Describes the Thoroughbred walk, trot, canter and gallop, as well as the Standardbred amble, pace and trot.
Physical Education and Recreation
Dist - EQVDL **Prod** - MSU

Locomotions and skeletons 29 MIN
U-matic
Introducing biology series; Program 12
Color (C A)
Describes varied movements of animals and how these movements are made possible. Details functions of the skeleton. Examines structure and function of the Haversian systems.
Science - Natural
Dist - CDTEL **Prod** - COAST

Locomotor skills
VHS
Children and movement video series
Color (H A T)
$29.95 purchase _ #MK803
Teaches about locomotor skills in children ages 3 to 6 years old. Part of a five - part series which guides in conducting physical education programs.
Physical Education and Recreation; Psychology
Dist - AAVIM **Prod** - AAVIM 1992

Locomotor Skills I 15 MIN
VHS / U-matic
Leaps and Bounds Series no 4
Color (T)
Demonstrates how to explain to primary students about walking, running, leaping, hopping, parts of the leg and foot, pushing, kinesthetic awareness, step size and cooperation in physical activities.
Physical Education and Recreation
Dist - AITECH

Locomotor Skills II 15 MIN
VHS / U-matic
Leaps and Bounds Series no 5
Color (T)
Explains how primary students can be taught about various types of jumping, developing force, pushing off and cooperating on the schoolyard.
Physical Education and Recreation
Dist - AITECH

Locomotor Skills III 15 MIN
U-matic / VHS
Leaps and Bounds Series no 6
Color (T)
Demonstrates how to explain to primary students about slides, gallops, skips, body part relationships and awareness, recognition of skills by their rhythmic pattern, dodging moving objects and people.
Physical Education and Recreation
Dist - AITECH

Locus 20 MIN
VHS / U-matic
Math Topics - Geometry Series
Color (J H C)
Mathematics
Dist - FI **Prod** - BBCTV

Locusts - the Now and Ancient Plague 9 MIN
16mm / U-matic / VHS
Real World of Insects Series
Color (I J)
LC 73-701799
Shows locusts mating and laying eggs. Views the developing nymphs which turn into swarming, destroying hordes. Gives examples of the coordinating efforts of the United Nations' Food and Agriculture Organization to control the locust population and prevent the damage they can cause.
Agriculture; Science - Natural
Dist - LCOA **Prod** - LCOA 1973

Locusts - the Now and Ancient Plague 10 MIN
U-matic / VHS / 16mm
Real World of Insects Series
Captioned; Color (P) (SPANISH)
Explores the behavior pattern of the locust, who has created critical food shortages over centuries. Discusses worldwide efforts to control this natural phenomenon.
Science - Natural
Dist - LCOA **Prod** - PEGASO 1973

Locusts - War Without End 57 MIN
16mm / U-matic / VHS
Nova Series
Color (H C A)
Shows how locusts can transform themselves from a group of harmless insects to a voracious swarm, capable of destroying all vegetation in their path. Depicts a frightening surge of a billion locusts, carpeting the ground and moving like a single, monstrous animal.
Agriculture; Science - Natural
Dist - TIMLIF **Prod** - WGBHTV 1982

Lodge Night 29 MIN
16mm
B&W
Tells how the black and white members of the Gang join the Cluck Cluck Klan. A Little Rascals film.
Fine Arts
Dist - RMIBHF **Prod** - ROACH 1923

The Lodger 66 MIN
16mm
B&W
Focuses on a boarding house tenant whose mysterious life causes him to be suspected as Jack the Ripper. Directed by Alfred Hitchcock.
Fine Arts
Dist - KITPAR **Prod** - UNKNWN 1926

Lodz symphony 20 MIN
16mm
B&W (G)
$50.00 rental
Portrays Lodz, Poland. Creates an empty world evoking the 19th - century industrial atmosphere populated with the ghosts of Poland's tragic past. Made between 1991 - 1993.
Fine Arts; Social Science
Dist - CANCIN **Prod** - HUTTON

Log 43 15 MIN
16mm
B&W
LC 75-703197
Presents a re - enactment based upon the Algier's Motel incident in which three people were killed during the Detroit riots in 1967.
Fine Arts
Dist - USC **Prod** - USC 1969

LOG - Apelco DXL 6000
VHS
Loran operation guide series
Color (G A)
$29.90 purchase _ #0754
Teaches Loran C programming for the Apelco DXL 6000 in nautical navigation. Shows how to enter the correct Loran chain for specific positions, how to program positions, determine the accuracy of a Loran C 'fix' and how to deal with the intricacies of specific machines.
Physical Education and Recreation; Social Science
Dist - SEVVID

Log Drive 30 MIN
16mm
B&W
_ #106B 0157 001N
Geography - World
Dist - CFLMDC **Prod** - NFBC 1957

Log Driver's Waltz
16mm
Color (I)
Presents an animated tale about a young girl who loves to dance and marries a log driver over his well - to - do landloving competition. Shows that driving logs down the river has made the young man the best dancing partner to be found.
Fine Arts
Dist - NFBC **Prod** - NFBC

LOG - Furuno LC 90
VHS
Loran operation guide series
Color (G A)
$29.90 purchase _ #0711
Teaches Loran C programming for the Furuno LC 90 in nautical navigation. Shows how to enter the correct Loran chain for specific positions, how to program positions, determine the accuracy of a Loran C 'fix' and how to deal with the intricacies of specific machines.
Physical Education and Recreation; Social Science
Dist - SEVVID

Log house - cabane de rondins 28 MIN
16mm / U-matic / VHS
Color (J) (FRENCH)
LC 79-701818
A French language motion picture. Observes a group of men as they build a log house. Follows the year - long process from the felling of pine trees to the installation of handmade kitchen counters.
Foreign Language; Industrial and Technical Education
Dist - BULFRG **Prod** - NFBC 1976

LOG - King 8001
VHS
Loran operation guide series
Color (G A)
$29.90 purchase _ #0729
Teaches Loran C programming for the King 8001 in nautical navigation. Shows how to enter the correct Loran chain for specific positions, how to program positions, determine the accuracy of a Loran C 'fix' and how to deal with the intricacies of specific machines.
Physical Education and Recreation; Social Science
Dist - SEVVID

Log of Mariner IV 27 MIN
16mm
Color (H A)
LC FIE67-96
A documentary account of the successful and rewarding Mariner 1964 - 65 fly - by mission to the planet Mars. Contains the first close - ups of Mars and planetary scientific conclusions resulting from the flight.
Science; Science - Physical
Dist - NASA **Prod** - NASA 1966

The Log Raft - a Norwegian Summer Story 25 MIN
U-matic / VHS / 16mm
Color (I J)
LC 72-700084
Shows the activities of three young children who spend the summer at an island cabin in the Norwegian fjords.
Geography - World; Literature and Drama
Dist - PHENIX **Prod** - PHENIX 1972

LOG - RayNav 550
VHS
Loran operation guide series
Color (G A)
$29.90 purchase _ #0427
Teaches Loran C programming for the RayNav 550 in nautical navigation. Shows how to enter the correct Loran chain for specific positions, how to program positions, determine the accuracy of a Loran C 'fix' and how to deal with the intricacies of specific machines.
Physical Education and Recreation; Social Science
Dist - SEVVID

LOG - RayNav 570
VHS
Loran operation guide series
Color (G A)
$29.90 purchase _ #0716
Teaches Loran C programming for the RayNav 570 in nautical navigation. Shows how to enter the correct Loran chain for specific positions, how to program positions, determine the accuracy of a Loran C 'fix' and how to deal with the intricacies of specific machines.
Physical Education and Recreation; Social Science
Dist - SEVVID

LOG - Si - Tex 787C
VHS
Loran operation guide series
Color (G A)
$29.90 purchase _ #0728
Teaches Loran C programming for the Si - Tex 787C in nautical navigation. Shows how to enter the correct Loran chain for specific positions, how to program positions, determine the accuracy of a Loran C 'fix' and how to deal with the intricacies of specific machines.
Physical Education and Recreation; Social Science
Dist - SEVVID

LOG - Si - Tex 797
VHS
Loran operation guide series
Color (G A)
$29.90 purchase _ #0710
Teaches Loran C programming for the Si - Tex 797 in nautical navigation. Shows how to enter the correct Loran chain for specific positions, how to program positions, determine the accuracy of a Loran C 'fix' and how to deal with the intricacies of specific machines.
Physical Education and Recreation; Social Science
Dist - SEVVID

LOG - Si - Tex EZ7
VHS
Loran operation guide series
Color (G A)
$29.90 purchase _ #0752
Teaches Loran C programming for the Si - Tex EZ7 in nautical navigation. Shows how to enter the correct Loran chain for specific positions, how to program positions, determine the accuracy of a Loran C 'fix' and how to deal with the intricacies of specific machines.
Physical Education and Recreation; Social Science
Dist - SEVVID

Logarithm - Exponential Functions 15 MIN
U-matic
Graphing Mathematical Concepts Series
(H C A)
Uses computer generated graphics to show the relationships between physical objects and mathematical concepts, equations and their graphs. Relates theoretical concepts to things in the real world.
Computer Science; Mathematics
Dist - ACCESS **Prod** - ACCESS 1986

The Logarithmic Decades 50 MIN
VHS / U-matic
Energy Issues and Alternatives Series
Color
Gives a brief historical overview of energy growth in the United States. Covers potential consequences if growth is continued.
Science - Natural; Social Science
Dist - UIDEEO **Prod** - UIDEEO

Logarithmic Differentiation 30 MIN
VHS
Mathematics Series
Color (J)
LC 90713155
Explains logarithmic differentiation. The 125th of 157 installments in the Mathematics Series.
Mathematics
Dist - GPN

Logarithmic differentiation 30 MIN
VHS
Calculus series
Color (C)
$125.00 purchase _ #6016
Explains logarthmic differentiation. Part of a 56 - part series on calculus.
Mathematics
Dist - LANDMK **Prod** - LANDMK

Logarithmic Functions 20 MIN
VHS
Calculus Series
Color (H)
LC 90712920
Discusses logarithmic functions. The 29th of 57 installments of the CalculusSeries.
Mathematics
Dist - GPN

Logarithmic Functions 30 MIN
U-matic
Introduction to Mathematics Series

Color (C)
Mathematics
Dist - MDCPB **Prod** - MDCPB

Logarithmic Functions and their Graphs 30 MIN
VHS
Mathematics Series
Color (J)
LC 90713155
Explains logarithmic functions and their graphs. The 90th of 157 installments in the Mathematics Series.
Mathematics
Dist - GPN

Logarithmic functions and their graphs 30 MIN
VHS
College algebra series
Color (C)
$125.00 purchase _ #4028
Explains logarithmic functions and their graphs. Part of a 31 - part series on college algebra.
Industrial and Technical Education; Mathematics
Dist - LANDMK **Prod** - LANDMK

Logarithms and the slide rule, lesson 1 30 MIN
16mm / U-matic / VHS
B&W (H C)
LC FIA67-5532
Traces the history of logarithms and the slide rule. Compares longhand multiplication and the exponential method. Defines logarithm and shows how to determine the characteristic of the logarithm of a number when the number is greater than or equal to unity.
Mathematics
Dist - IFB **Prod** - IFB 1960

Logarithms and the slide rule, lesson 2 30 MIN
U-matic / VHS / 16mm
B&W (H C)
LC FIA67-5533
Emphasizes the mantissa. Explains the use of the 'nine minus ten' convention when dealing with negative characteristics. Gives formal proof of the theorem 'the logarithm of a quotient is equal to the logarithm of the dividend minus the logarithm of the divisor.' Applies this to an example.
Mathematics
Dist - IFB **Prod** - IFB 1960

Logarithms and the Slide Rule, Lesson 3 30 MIN
U-matic / VHS / 16mm
B&W (H C)
LC FIA67-5534
Solves a problem requiring fourth power of the product of two numbers. Explains the method of computing mantissae. Explains and illustrates the technique of 'inserting a geometric mean between two numbers'.
Mathematics
Dist - IFB **Prod** - IFB 1960

Logarithms and the Slide Rule, Lesson 4 30 MIN
16mm / U-matic / VHS
B&W (H C)
LC FIA67-5535
Uses close - up photography to illustrate the use of a table of logarithms. Explains the method of looking up logarithms and antilogarithms.
Mathematics
Dist - IFB **Prod** - IFB 1960

Logarithms and the slide rule, lesson 5 30 MIN
16mm / U-matic / VHS
B&W (H C)
LC FIA67-5536
Explains the method of designing the slide rule. Illustrates logarithmic division of the scales and the basic use of the 'C' and 'D' scales for multiplication. Defines logarithm.
Mathematics
Dist - IFB **Prod** - IFB 1960

Logarithms and the slide rule, lesson 6 30 MIN
U-matic / VHS / 16mm
B&W (H C)
LC FIA67-5537
Describes division, using the 'C' and 'D' scales. Explains the principle of proportion in use of the slide rule. Demonstrates solving of 'combined multiplication and division' problems using the principle of proportion.
Mathematics
Dist - IFB **Prod** - IFB 1960

Logarithms and the Slide Rule, Lesson 7 30 MIN
U-matic / VHS / 16mm
B&W (H C)
LC FIA67-5538
Explains the 'C1' scale and shows its use for reciprocals, multiplication and division. Demonstrates the use of the 'A' and 'B' scales for squares and square roots. Shows how to determine which end of the 'A' scale to use in extracting square roots.
Mathematics
Dist - IFB **Prod** - IFB 1960

Logarithms and the Slide Rule, Lesson 8 30 MIN
U-matic / VHS / 16mm
B&W (H C)
LC FIA67-5539
Illustrates finding the area of a circle using the 'A' and 'B' scales. Explains cubes and cube roots, use of the 'S' scale for finding sines and cosines of angles, and use of 'T' scale for finding tangents of angles.
Mathematics
Dist - IFB **Prod** - IFB 1960

Logarithms and their properties 30 MIN
VHS
College algebra series
Color (C)
$125.00 purchase _ #4027
Explains logarithms and their properties. Part of a 31 - part series on college algebra.
Mathematics
Dist - LANDMK **Prod** - LANDMK

Logarithms and their Properties 30 MIN
VHS
Mathematics Series
Color (J)
LC 90713155
Explains logarithms and their properties. The 89th of 157 installments of the Mathematics Series.
Mathematics
Dist - GPN

Logdrivers 17 MIN
U-matic / VHS / 16mm
Color
Follows the spring log drive from timber stand to sawmill down the Coulouge River in Quebec, comparing the axes and horse - drawn sleds of the 1920s to modern equipment used today. A former logdriver recalls his days on the rivers and tells how this once common activity is rarer, though still carried on today.
Agriculture; Geography - World; History - World; Science - Natural
Dist - BCNFL **Prod** - BARNEM 1982

Logging 10 MIN
VHS
Skills - occupational programs series
Color (H A)
$49.00 purchase, $15.00 rental _ #316604; LC 91-708567
Outlines a typical logging operation and demonstrates the skills required by the crew. Part of a series featuring occupations in the skilled trades, in service industries and in business leading to careers in areas of demand and future growth. Includes teacher's guide with reproducible wooksheets.
Guidance and Counseling; Psychology
Dist - TVOTAR **Prod** - TVOTAR 1990

Logging Safety Series
The Landing Team 10 MIN
Dist - RARIG

Logging the Land 15 MIN
U-matic
North America - Growth of a Continent Series
Color (J H)
Stresses that forests are vital to North America's economic and ecological growth. Traces the history and growth of the continent's lumber industry.
Geography - United States; Geography - World
Dist - TVOTAR **Prod** - TVOTAR 1980

Logic 29 MIN
35mm strip / VHS
Color (J H C A)
$93.00, $93.00 purchase _ #MB - 481131 - 2, #MB - 512854 - 3
Seeks to develop students' logic. Covers the relationship between sound thinking and common sense, the search for truth, and ways of coming to conclusions. Examines concepts of logic.
Religion and Philosophy
Dist - SRA **Prod** - SRA

Logic Arrays 55 MIN
VHS / U-matic
Introduction to VLSI Design Series
Color (PRO)
Deals with the topics of logic minimization, AND and OR gates for Sum - of - Products implementation, the programmed logic array (PLA), and two - input decoding.
Industrial and Technical Education
Dist - MIOT **Prod** - MIOT

Logic Circuit Characteristics
U-matic / VHS
Digital Techniques Series
Color
Industrial and Technical Education
Dist - HTHZEN **Prod** - HTHZEN

Logic Circuit Operation 21 MIN
U-matic / VHS / 16mm
B&W (A)
Discusses the circuit operations of the various logic gates found in basic computers.
Industrial and Technical Education; Mathematics; Psychology
Dist - USNAC **Prod** - USAF 1970

Logic Concepts 48 MIN
U-matic / VHS
Digital Electronics Series
Color (PRO)
Industrial and Technical Education; Mathematics
Dist - MIOT **Prod** - MIOT

Logic for lawyers - a guide to clear legal thinking 218 MIN
VHS / Cassette
Color (PRO)
$295.00, $150.00 purchase, $150.00 rental _ #LOG1-000, #ALOG-000
Offers a practical guide on how logic applies in legal reasoning. Aids in avoiding errors in analyzing reported judicial opinions and in preparing and presenting a written or oral argument, in detecting error in the reasoning process of the adversary and in recognizing and avoiding logical fallacies. Includes a copy of the Judge Aldisert book, Logic for Lawyers.
Civics and Political Systems; Religion and Philosophy
Dist - AMBAR **Prod** - AMBAR 1992

Logic I
16mm
B&W
Tells how to define binary operations on the set (0.1).
Mathematics
Dist - OPENU **Prod** - OPENU

Logic II - Proof
16mm
B&W
Presents examples where proof is not an absolute quality. Investigates scientific and mathematical proof by looking at angles, triangles and axiomatics.
Mathematics
Dist - OPENU **Prod** - OPENU

Logic Modules - Task Description using an Algorithm 30 MIN
U-matic / VHS
Microprocessors for Monitoring and Control Series
Color (IND)
Introduces general block structure for digital systems, including block modules. Shows concept of using algorithms to design tasks and uses Euclid's algorithm as example.
Industrial and Technical Education; Mathematics; Sociology
Dist - COLOSU **Prod** - COLOSU

Logic Series
Avoiding Fallacies 28.34 MIN
Part One - using Logic in Everyday Life 28.34 MIN
Dist - SRA

Logical basis for equation transformation principles - Pt 1 32 MIN
16mm
Teaching high school mathematics - first course series; No 40
B&W (C T)
Mathematics
Dist - MLA **Prod** - UICSM 1967

Logical basis for equation transformation principles - Pt 2 33 MIN
16mm
Teaching high school mathematics - first course series; No 41
B&W (C T)
Mathematics
Dist - MLA **Prod** - UICSM 1967

Logical basis for equation transformation principles - Pt 3 35 MIN
16mm
Teaching high school mathematics - first course series; No 42
B&W (C)
Mathematics
Dist - MLA **Prod** - UICSM 1967

Logical Controls 30 MIN
U-matic / VHS
Computer Security Techniques Series
Color
Describes logical controls that can be designed into the computer system, including identification of system elements, authorization to perform transactions, surveillance of system activities and encryption of data.
Industrial and Technical Education
Dist - DELTAK **Prod** - DELTAK

Logical Data Base Design - the Key to Success 60 MIN
VHS / U-matic
Managing the Data Base Environment Series
Color
Examines the methods used to develop a logical data base model, the most important step in the development of the data base system.
Business and Economics; Industrial and Technical Education
Dist - DELTAK **Prod** - DELTAK

Logical level alignment 52 MIN
VHS
Color; PAL; SECAM (G)
$70.00 purchase
Features Robert Dilts. Demonstrates Dilts' way of eliciting and aligning all levels of experience - skills, abilities, beliefs and identity - to support change. Interviews Robin, seeking relief from severe arthritis. Intermediate level of NLP, neuro - linguistic programming.
Psychology
Dist - NLPCOM **Prod** - NLPCOM

Logical or Boolean Expressions - Table Representations, Map Representations 30 MIN
VHS / U-matic
Microprocessors for Monitoring and Control Series
Color (IND)
Gives sufficient introduction to Boolean Algebra for viewers to learn how to represent logical functions through algebraic equations and maps.
Industrial and Technical Education; Mathematics; Sociology
Dist - COLOSU **Prod** - COLOSU

Logical positivism and its legacy 45 MIN
VHS
Men of ideas series
Color; PAL (H C A)
PdS99 purchase; Not available in Canada.
Explains in simple terms the main developments in Western philosophy from the 19th century to the present day. Features a contemporary thinker discussing his ideas and beliefs on logical positivism with Bryan Magee. Part six of a fifteen part series.
Psychology; Religion and Philosophy
Dist - BBCENE

Logical power of computing schemes 50 MIN
U-matic / VHS
Computer languages series; Pt 1
Color
Lectures on the theoretical notions of computability and universality in computer languages.
Industrial and Technical Education; Mathematics; Sociology
Dist - MIOT **Prod** - MIOT

Logistic Support Management for Advanced Weapons 20 MIN
16mm
Color
LC FIE61-60
Defines the mission of a ballistic missile squadron and shows the component parts of weapon systems. Discusses the role of logistic support management in supplying prompt and accurate data, the role of an electronic data processing center and the procedures used in management by exception.
Civics and Political Systems
Dist - USNAC **Prod** - USDD 1960

Logistics for a Microteaching Clinic 28 MIN
16mm
Color (T)
Presents alternatives to the establishment of a pre - service or in - service microteaching clinic.
Education
Dist - EDUC **Prod** - EDUC

Logistics information systems 30 MIN
VHS
Business logistics series
Color (G C)
$200.00 purchase, $20.50 rental _ #34977
Examines logistics information systems. Part of a 30 - part series on business logistics which deals with movement and storage of raw and finished products, and with managerial activities important for effective control of these operations. Interviews logistics managers of major US corporations and transportation companies. Uses on - site segments to demonstrate logistical carrier operations. Features program author Dr John Coyle.
Business and Economics
Dist - PSU **Prod** - WPSXTV 1987

Logistics management system - LMS - Continuous flow manufacturing using knowledge based expert systems
VHS
Color (C PRO G)
$150.00 purchase _ #89.03
Visits IBM's Essex Junction, a Vermont facility, where the LMS is a real - time imbedded transaction - based integrated decision and knowledge based expert support system which serves as monitor and control for manufacturing flow or logistics. Reveals that its purpose is to improve tool utilization and serviceability and reduce cycle time, and is a critical component in major areas of the manufacturing facility. IBM. Gerald Sullivan, Kenneth Fordyce.
Business and Economics
Dist - INMASC

Logistics relationships in the firm 30 MIN
VHS
Business logistics series
Color (G C)
$200.00 purchase, $20.50 rental _ #34958
Examines logistics relationships in the firm. Part of a 30 - part series on business logistics which deals with movement and storage of raw and finished products, and with managerial activities important for effective control of these operations. Interviews logistics managers of major US corporations and transportation companies. Uses on - site segments to demonstrate logistical carrier operations. Features program author Dr John Coyle.
Business and Economics
Dist - PSU **Prod** - WPSXTV 1987

Logistics systems - a future perspective 30 MIN
VHS
Business logistics series
Color (G C)
$200.00 purchase, $20.50 rental _ #34983
Examines the future of logistics systems. Part of a 30 - part series on business logistics which deals with movement and storage of raw and finished products, and with managerial activities important for effective control of these operations. Interviews logistics managers of major US corporations and transportation companies. Uses on - site segments to demonstrate logistical carrier operations. Features program author Dr John Coyle.
Business and Economics; Sociology
Dist - PSU **Prod** - WPSXTV 1987

Logistics systems analysis 30 MIN
VHS
Business logistics series
Color (G C)
$200.00 purchase, $20.50 rental _ #34955
Discusses logistics systems analysis. Part of a 30 - part series on business logistics which deals with movement and storage of raw and finished products, and with managerial activities important for effective control of these operations. Interviews logistics managers of major US corporations and transportation companies. Uses on - site segments to demonstrate logistical carrier operations. Features program author Dr John Coyle.
Business and Economics
Dist - PSU **Prod** - WPSXTV 1987

Logo - the Computer as an Intellectual Tool 27 MIN
U-matic / VHS
New Technology in Education Series
Color (J)
LC 84-706536
Discusses computer literacy and the basis of LOGO, a computer educational language. Demonstrates the use of LOGO, including some student programming projects.
Education; Industrial and Technical Education
Dist - USNAC **Prod** - USDOE 1983

Logos 2 MIN
16mm
Color (H C)
Combines non - objective visuals and electronic music to produce optical illusions and a distortion of time perception.
Industrial and Technical Education
Dist - CFS **Prod** - CONGER

Lohengrin 220 MIN
VHS
(S) (GERMAN)
$39.95 purchase _ #384 - 9610
Presents the Metropolitan Opera production of 'Lohengrin' by Wagner. Features James Levine as conductor, a cast including Leonie Rysanek, Eva Marton and Peter Hofmann.
Fine Arts; Foreign Language
Dist - FI **Prod** - PAR 1988

Loin De Paris 10 MIN
U-matic / VHS / 16mm
La France Contemporaine Series
Color (H C) (FRENCH)
LC 77-714220
A French language film. Explores the lives of the four - fifths of the French population that live and work in the provinces. Shows the way environmental factors affect the various lifestyles. Examines the forces of change at work in the provinces of France.
Foreign Language; Geography - World; Sociology
Dist - EBEC **Prod** - EBEC 1971

The Loire Valley 24 MIN
16mm / U-matic / VHS
Food and Wine from France Series
Color (H C)
Tours the Loire River region of France, emphasizing the area's scenic and historic aspects. Describes the area's major winemaking industry and highlights the vineyards, press houses, cellars and tasting rooms.
Geography - World; Home Economics
Dist - IFB **Prod** - POLNIS 1986

Lois Jaffe, MSW - a Need to Know - a Family Faces Death 60 MIN
VHS / U-matic
Perceptions, Pt a - Interventions in Family Therapy Series Vol IV, 'Pt A8
Color (PRO)
Focuses on the effect of a terminal illness on the family. Features interviews with the family of a boy dying of acute myelogenous leukemia conducted by Lois Jaffe, who suffers from the same disease.
Guidance and Counseling; Psychology; Sociology
Dist - BOSFAM **Prod** - BOSFAM

Lois Jaffe, MSW - Associate Professor, University of Pittsburgh School of Social Work 60 MIN
VHS / U-matic
Perceptions, Pt B - Dialogues with Family Therapists Series Vol IV, 'Pt B8
Color (PRO)
Interviews Lois Jaffe, Who became a family therapist and social worker after raising a family. Reveals how contracting acute myelogenous leukemia focused her work on the seriously ill and dying.
Guidance and Counseling; Psychology; Sociology
Dist - BOSFAM **Prod** - BOSFAM

Lois' story 30 MIN
16mm
Color (G)
#AV - 1
Tells about the history of Alcoholics Anonymous. Available to Al - Anon membership only.
Guidance and Counseling; Health and Safety; Psychology
Dist - ALANON **Prod** - ALANON

L'Oiseau 4 MIN
16mm
Color
Transforms, enhances and interprets the force and beauty of a single bird in flight to present a unique visual experience.
Fine Arts
Dist - LILYAN **Prod** - LILYAN

Lokmanya Tilak 23 MIN
16mm
B&W (I)
Presents the life story of Lokmanya Tilak. Discusses the Indian struggle for independence.
History - World
Dist - NEDINF **Prod** - INDIA

Lola May's fundamental math series
Reinforces arithmetic skills and gives practice in mathematics. Features Dr Lola May as she teaches different approaches to numbers, addition, subtraction, time, multiplication, division, and fractions. Contains 30 videos with teacher's guides and blackline masters.
Addition facts to sums of 10
Addition facts to sums of 18
Addition of two - digit numbers
Beginning multiplication
Dividing by one digit
Equal, not equal, story problems
Equivalent fractions
Introduction to fractions
Lattice multiplication
Linear measurement
Multiplication facts
Multiplication of several digits
Number families
Numbers to 20
Numbers to 9
Numeration - ones and tens
Odd and even numbers
Order of fractions
Other number bases

Patterns
Place value through hundreds
Same and different
Shape, color, size
Subtraction facts to sums of 10
Subtraction of two and three - digit numbers
Time to 5 minutes
Time to 1 minute
Trading, check method, story problems
Using addition facts
Using subtraction facts
Dist - UNL

The Lollipop Opera 9 MIN
U-matic / VHS / 16mm
Color (K)
LC 74-713493
Don Freeman, cartoonist and illustrator, uses colored chalks to present an account of a young boy's visit to a barber shop.
Literature and Drama
Dist - PFP **Prod** - JOHNGL 1971

Lolly, Lolly, Lolly - Get Your Adverbs Here 3 MIN
VHS / U-matic
Grammar Rock Series
Color (P)
Uses a story about a special kind of store in order to demonstrate the function of adverbs as parts of speech.
English Language
Dist - GA **Prod** - ABCTV 1974

Lombardi
VHS
NFL series
Color (G)
$29.95 purchase _ #NFL62V
Profiles the late Vince Lombardi, who coached the Green Bay Packers to several National Football League championships. Produced by NFL Films.
Literature and Drama; Physical Education and Recreation
Dist - CAMV

Lombardi - commitment to excellence 26 MIN
16mm
Color (IND)
LC 76-701201
Presents a motivational film for sales and supervisory personnel based on Vince Lombardi's philosophy of pride in work, dedication to a job and will to succeed, presented through comments by his former players and associates and footage of football played under his direction.
Business and Economics; Physical Education and Recreation; Psychology
Dist - BBP **Prod** - COMMIT 1973

Lombardi - Commitment to Excellence 20 MIN
VHS / 16mm / U-matic
Color
Uses Vince Lombardi's gift for getting people to do better than they believed they could to leave a lasting impression on every employee.
Business and Economics; Psychology; Sociology
Dist - BBP **Prod** - BBP

Lomvie - uria aalge - guillemot 6 MIN
16mm
Color
Presents a description of the guillemot in its natural surroundings, accompanied by sound effects.
Science - Natural
Dist - STATNS **Prod** - STATNS 1965

London 30 MIN
VHS
Color (G)
$29.95 purchase _ #S02025
Tours London and nearby sites, including Bath, Windsor and Stonehenge. Gives a comprehensive view of London life, from the many historic sites to the most popular nightclubs.
Geography - World
Dist - UILL

London 40 MIN
16mm / U-matic / VHS
Touring Great Cities Series
Color
LC 78-700486
Shows the sights of London, including the London Zoo, Portobello Road and the Tower of London.
Geography - World
Dist - FI **Prod** - BBCTV 1977

London 3 MIN
16mm
Of all Things Series
Color (P I)
Discusses the city of London in England.
Geography - World
Dist - AVED **Prod** - BAILYL

London and the West - Pt 4 89 MIN
VHS
Great Houses of Britain Series
Color (S)
$29.95 purchase _ #057 - 9004
Joins art historian Viscount Norwich for a tour of twelve of Britain's great houses and castles. Teaches about British architecture, views the exquisite contents of the houses and surveys the magnificent grounds from a helicopter. Interviews the owners and caretakes - a fascinating cast of characters which includes a water - skiing marquis and an especially articulate kitchen maid. Part 4 tours Osterley Park House, a stunning example of neoclassical architecture, Claydon House, where Florence Nightingale was a frequent houseguest, and Lacock Abbey, with its fifteenth century cloisters and medieval frescoes.
Fine Arts; Geography - World; History - World; Sociology
Dist - FI

London bridge is falling down 9 MIN
16mm
Color (K P)
LC 71-703005
Uses illustrations by Peter Spier from the book 'London Bridge is Falling Down' to show the life and activity on the famous bridge as it appeared in the 18th century.
History - World; Social Science; Sociology
Dist - CONNF **Prod** - CONNF 1969

London - center of the world's art trade 27 MIN
16mm
Color
Takes a look behind the scenes of one of the major art centers, where masterpieces are traded daily.
Fine Arts
Dist - ROLAND **Prod** - ROLAND 1970

London clouds 4 MIN
16mm
Color (G)
$10.00 rental
Expounds on the idea that 'no matter where you arrive in legend, you find yourself at the point of departure.' Features soundtrack by Henri Pousseur. Also part of a package of four films by Wheeler Dixon.
Fine Arts
Dist - CANCIN **Prod** - WWDIXO 1986

London - Flower of Cities all 20 MIN
VHS
Color (S)
$19.95 purchase _ #423 - 9004
Tours historic London, St Paul's Cathedral, the Tower of London, Buckingham Palace and the Houses of Parliament, as well as theaters, concert halls, museums, shops and restaurants. Features breathtaking aerial photography of the Thames, the Royal Parks, Hampstead Heath and the Kew Gardens.
Fine Arts; Geography - World; History - World
Dist - FI

The London of William Hogarth 25 MIN
U-matic / VHS / 16mm
B&W (H C A)
LC 74-704374
Presents scenes from the satirical engravings of the 18th century artist William Hogarth which depict the everyday occurrences and some of the roudy activities of the citizenry. Pictures the story of marriage a la mode and scenes showing Hogarth's view of the human race.
Fine Arts; Geography - World; History - World
Dist - IFB **Prod** - BCF 1956

The London of William Hogarth 27 MIN
U-matic / VHS / 16mm
Color (H C A)
LC 80-706718
Uses the satirical engravings of William Hogarth to depict 18th century London life.
Fine Arts; History - World
Dist - IFB **Prod** - BCF 1977

The London Story 15 MIN
16mm
Color (G)
$50.00 rental
Presents a spy spoof about the unlikely alliance of three eccentric characters and their mission to uncover government foreign policy duplicity. Features famed London locales. Produced in assocation with the British Film Institute and Channel Four Television.
Civics and Political Systems; Fine Arts; Geography - World; Literature and Drama; Sociology
Dist - WMEN **Prod** - SALPOT 1987

London - the Musical Capital 53 MIN
U-matic / VHS
Man and Music Series
Color (C)
$279.00, $179.00 purchase _ #AD - 1772
Focuses on Georgian London toward the end of the 18th century. Reveals that Baroque music gave way to classical. Haydn made two extended visits to London. It would be 100 years before significant music was composed in London again. Part of a 22 - part series that sets Western music into the historial and cultural context of its time.
Fine Arts; Geography - World; History - World
Dist - FOTH **Prod** - FOTH

London Underground map 25 MIN
VHS
Design classics 1 series
Color (A)
PdS65 purchase _ Available world wide
Uses archive film, period commercials, and interviews with key figures to examine the contribution to design made by some of the most successful products marketed in the 20th century. Part of a six-part series.
Business and Economics; Fine Arts
Dist - BBCENE

Loneliness 11 MIN
VHS
Color (J H)
$79.95 purchase _ #10224VL
Explores loneliness in teenagers, social isolation, lack of compassion from others, abuse and other causes of social distance. Shows how counseling and positive ways of dealing with being lonely can help. Comes with a leader's guide, discussion topics and a blackline master.
Guidance and Counseling; Psychology; Social Science
Dist - UNL

Loneliness - 16 6 MIN
VHS / U-matic
Life's little lessons - self - esteem K - 3 - series
Color (K P)
$129.00, $99.00 _ #V615
Tells about Charlie McPhee, crabby old hermit, who had spent his life looking for treasure and scaring off his family and neighbors. Reveals that McPhee realized how lonely he was when some young boys befriended him and he found the treasure he'd been searching for - friends. Part of a 30 - part series on self - esteem.
Guidance and Counseling; Psychology
Dist - BARR **Prod** - CEPRO 1992

Loneliness - and Loving 17 MIN
U-matic / VHS / 16mm
Searching for Values - a Film Anthology Series
Color (J)
LC 72-703090
Tells how a young man, estranged from his family, his past, and himself, returns home to face emotions and conflicts he has chosen to keep suppressed.
Guidance and Counseling; Psychology; Sociology
Dist - LCOA **Prod** - LCOA 1972

Loneliness - the Empty Tree House 10 MIN
U-matic
Color (I J)
Tells how John's best friend moves away and leaves him reluctant to make friends with other children.
Fine Arts; Guidance and Counseling
Dist - GA **Prod** - GA

Lonely are the Brave 107 MIN
16mm
B&W
Pits a cowboy - outlaw against a sheriff in a flight for freedom. Stars Kirk Douglas and Walter Matthau.
Fine Arts
Dist - TWYMAN **Prod** - UPCI 1962

Lonely boy 27 MIN
16mm
B&W (H C A)
Uses the song I'm Just a Lonely Boy sung by Paul Anka, teenage idol of the fifties as the theme of a classic film in direct cinema about the 'pop' singer image. Emphasizes the creation of an 'image' that sells and the people who buy it.
Business and Economics; Fine Arts
Dist - NFBC **Prod** - NFBC 1962

The Lonely Crime 48 MIN
16mm
Perspective Series
Color
LC 73-700733
Probes the difficulties in applying legal and medical procedures to the crime of rape. Explains that rape is one of the hardest crimes to prove in court. Interviews women who have been raped, a convicted rapist and representatives of the police, prosecution and medical establishments.
Civics and Political Systems; Sociology
Dist - WRCTV **Prod** - WRCTV 1972

The Lonely Hunter 6 MIN
U-matic / VHS / 16mm
Inuit Legends Series
Color (K P)
Tells the story of an Inuit boy who lives alone, and befriends a baby seal. Relates how, although they enjoy each other's companionship, the seal senses the boy's need for human friends and calls on help from the Queen of the Sea, who finds a kayak with a young companion.

Geography - United States; Geography - World; Physical Education and Recreation; Science - Natural; Sociology
Dist - BCNFL **Prod** - ANIMET 1982

Lonely Island 7 MIN
16mm
Color (P I J)
Describes the animal and bird life of the Antarctic.
Geography - World; Science - Natural
Dist - AUIS **Prod** - ANAIB 1971

The Lonely Night 62 MIN
16mm / U-matic / VHS
B&W (A)
LC FIA54-757
Describes a woman's recovery from emotional disturbance, including the process of psychiatric treatment. Shows the kind of family life that can help build emotional strength.
Guidance and Counseling; Psychology; Sociology
Dist - IFB **Prod** - MHFB 1955

The Lonely office 29 MIN
16mm
Government story series; No 26
Color
LC 74-707167
Explains how and why the decision - making responsibility in every area of national life falls ultimately on the President, giving examples which illustrate the President's duties.
Biography; Civics and Political Systems
Dist - WBCPRO **Prod** - WBCPRO 1968

The Lonely passion of Brian Moore - creative process series 60 MIN
VHS
Creative process series
Color (G)
$89.95 purchase _ #S01984
Profiles Canadian author Brian Moore. Describes his birth in Ireland, his career as a journalist and how he came to write 15 novels in 30 years.
Literature and Drama
Dist - UILL **Prod** - NFBC

The Lonely scarecrow 11 MIN
U-matic / VHS / 16mm
Color (P)
$280, $195 purchase _ #1727; LC 74-706892
Tells a story about a talking scarecrow to present some basic concepts on cornfield ecology.
Literature and Drama; Science - Natural
Dist - CORF **Prod** - CORF 1970

The Lonely struggle - Marek Edelman, last hero of the Warsaw Ghetto Uprising 60 MIN
VHS
Willy Lindwer collection series
Color (G)
$39.95 purchase _ #657
Focuses on Marek Edelman, a cardiologist in Lodz, and sole surviving member of the leadership of the Warsaw Ghetto resistance. Gives an insider's account of the few hundred Jewish youngsters who encouraged the decimated ghetto population to rise up and fight against the Germans and fight to the last. Footage shot in Warsaw. Part of eight documentaries on the Holocaust.
History - World
Dist - ERGOM **Prod** - LINDWE

A Lonely woman - Kobieta samotna 94 MIN
VHS
Color (G A) (POLISH)
$29.95 purchase _ #V032
Portrays a woman raising her child in a small town. Shows that, deprived of help and friendship, she is left to her own resources.
Fine Arts; Psychology; Social Science; Sociology
Dist - POLART

Lonelyhearts 104 MIN
VHS
B&W (G)
$24.95 purchase _ #S01577
Tells the story of an idealistic journalist assigned to the 'Miss Lonelyhearts' column. Shows how the experience of dealing with other people's sordid tales affects his own life. Stars Montgomery Clift as the journalist. Based o the novel 'Lonelyhearts' by Nathanael West.
Literature and Drama
Dist - UILL

The Loner 32 MIN
VHS / U-matic
Color
Shows that we all have a little loner in us whom we both love and hate.
Fine Arts
Dist - KITCHN **Prod** - KITCHN

Lonesome cowboy 1 MIN
16mm
B&W (G)
$5.00 rental
Provides no description for this 27 second film.
Fine Arts
Dist - CANCIN **Prod** - MERRIT 1979

Lonesome cowboy 4 MIN
16mm
Color (G)
$5.00 rental
Creates a visual illustration of Elvis Presley's song by the same name in a Dirk Kortz production.
Fine Arts
Dist - CANCIN

Lonesome Ghosts 8 MIN
16mm / U-matic / VHS
Gang's all Here Series
Color
Shows what happens when the Ajax Ghost Exterminators consisting of Mickey Mouse, Donald Duck and Goofy encounter some lonesome ghosts.
Fine Arts
Dist - CORF **Prod** - DISNEY

The Lonesome Train 21 MIN
U-matic / VHS / 16mm
Color (J)
LC 74-700154
Uses anecdotes, historical accounts and legends, combined with contemporary drawings and photographs, to trace the progress of the funeral train of President Abraham Lincoln from Washington, DC, to Springfield, Illinois. Recounts stories about Lincoln's character and about the Lincoln legend.
Biography; History - United States
Dist - ALTSUL **Prod** - ROSBEG 1973

Long A sound 15 MIN
U-matic / Kit / VHS
Space station readstar series
(P)
$130.00 purchase, $25.00 rental, $75.00 self dub
Teaches phonics in a series designed to supplement second grade reading programs. Focuses on the long a sound. Sixth in a series of 25.
English Language
Dist - GPN

Long ago and far away series

As long as he can count the cows	29 MIN
Bill and Bunny	29 MIN
The Happy circus	28 MIN
The Silver cornet	29 MIN
What's a good story - Noah's ark	20 MIN

Dist - CORF

Long and High Jump 15 MIN
U-matic / VHS / 16mm
Women's Track and Field Series no 3
Color (J)
LC 79-700803
Focuses on long and high jump techniques in women's track and field.
Physical Education and Recreation
Dist - ATHI **Prod** - ATHI 1976

Long and High Jump, Pole Vaulting, Triple Jump 21 MIN
U-matic / VHS / 16mm
Men's Track and Field Series no 3
Color (I)
LC 79-700799
Focuses on techniques for the long and high jump, pole vaulting and triple jump.
Physical Education and Recreation
Dist - ATHI **Prod** - ATHI 1976

Long - and Short - Line Catheters - the Paths of Chemotherapy 12 MIN
U-matic
Color
Describes the indications for employing indwelling silicone central - venous catheters and then demonstrates the technique and locations for inserting both short - line and long - line catheters.
Health and Safety
Dist - UTEXSC **Prod** - UTEXSC

The long and short of it - how to take measurements 40 MIN
VHS
Color (H G)
$89.95 purchase _ #CCP0134-T
Explains standard and metric sytems of linear measuring. Helps vocational trade students to understand both systems of measurement. Includes tips for measuring accurately, rulers, and uses of measurement in different trades. Includes a videocassette, teacher's guide, and student worksheets.
Mathematics
Dist - CAMV

The Long and Short of Shadows 14 MIN
16mm
Fingermouse, Yoffy and Friends Series
Color (K P I)
LC 73-700440
Features Yoffy telling the story of villagers who exchange shadows for a day.
Guidance and Counseling; Literature and Drama
Dist - VEDO **Prod** - BBCTV 1972

Long and triple jump technique 27 MIN
VHS
Bill Dellinger's championship track and field series
Color (H C A)
$39.95 purchase _ #WES1701V
Features Bill Dellinger and the University of Oregon coaching staff, who teach the basic techniques of long and triple jumps. Presents drills to develop an athlete's potential and correct common errors in technique. Uses slow - motion film and on - screen graphics.
Physical Education and Recreation
Dist - CAMV

Long Beach Community Arts 53 MIN
U-matic / VHS
Shared Realities Series
Color (A)
Features a series of mini - documentaries involving community and art activities in Long Beach.
Fine Arts
Dist - LBMART **Prod** - LBMART 1983

Long Beach Museum of Art - Video 56 MIN
U-matic / VHS
Shared Realities Series
Color (A)
Presents an outline of the historical development of video at Long Beach, focusing on its origins and major activities.
Fine Arts
Dist - LBMART **Prod** - LBMART 1983

Long Beach olympiad 50 MIN
VHS / 16mm
Color
$49.80 purchase _ #0219
Covers the US Olympic sailing team.
Geography - World; Physical Education and Recreation
Dist - SEVVID **Prod** - OFFSHR
OFFSHR

Long Beach Operation Readiness 29 MIN
16mm
Color
LC 74-706488
Documents the largest training exercise in the history of Naval Reserve forces.
Civics and Political Systems
Dist - USNAC **Prod** - USN 1973

The Long Cast 30 MIN
16mm
B&W
Dramatizes the life of Adolph Ochs, who published the Chattanooga Times until he became affiliated with the New York Times, which he published from 1896 to 1935. (Kinescope).
History - United States; Industrial and Technical Education; Psychology; Social Science
Dist - NAAJS **Prod** - JTS 1963

The Long chain 52 MIN
16mm / U-matic / VHS
Connections series
Color (H C A)
LC 79-706746
Traces the connection between 17th century mercantile competition, the development of a coal - tar pitch to protect ship hulls, and the creation of waterproofed clothing, gaslight lamps, and nylon. Number 7 of the series.
History - World; Sociology
Dist - TIMLIF **Prod** - BBCTV 1979
AMBROS

The Long Chain 20 MIN
16mm
B&W
Examines the effects of multi - national corporations establishing branches in Third World countries. Interviews construction workers on buildings for U S companies in Bombay.
Business and Economics; Geography - World; Sociology
Dist - NEWTIM **Prod** - NEWTIM

The Long Childhood 52 MIN
16mm / VHS / U-matic
Ascent of Man Series
Color (H C A) (SPANISH)
LC 74-702267
Surveys the complex role of science in the cultural evolution of humanity. Narrated by Dr Jacob Bronowski of the Salk Institute.
Psychology; Religion and Philosophy; Science
Dist - TIMLIF **Prod** - BBCTV 1973
BBCENE
AMBROS

The Long Childhood - Pt 1 26 MIN
16mm / U-matic
Ascent of Man Series
Color (H C A)
LC 74-702267
Surveys the complex role of science in the cultural evolution of humanity. Narrated by Dr Jacob Bronowski of the Salk Institute.
Psychology; Sociology
Dist - TIMLIF **Prod** - BBCTV 1973

The Long Childhood - Pt 2 26 MIN
16mm / U-matic
Ascent of Man Series
Color (H C A)
LC 74-702267
Surveys the complex role of science in the cultural evolution of humanity. Narrated by Dr Jacob Bronowski of the Salk Institute.
Psychology; Sociology
Dist - TIMLIF **Prod** - BBCTV 1973

Long day's journey into night 170 MIN
VHS
B&W (G)
Portrays a troubled Connecticut family, including a drug - addicted mother and a son dying of tuberculosis. Based on the play by Eugene O'Neill. Stars Katherine Hepburn, Ralph Richardson, Jason Robards, Dean Stockwell, and others. Directed by Sidney Lumet.
Fine Arts; Literature and Drama
Dist - FI
GA
ABCLR
UILL

Long day's journey into night
U-matic / VHS
American literature series
B&W (G C J)
$89.00 purchase _ #05695 - 85
Re - enacts O'Neill's Broadway play. Stars Katherine Hepburn, Ralph Richardson, and Jason Robards.
Fine Arts
Dist - CHUMAN

Long distance commuting with the grey whale 24 MIN
VHS
Wild refuge series
Color (G)
$39.95 purchase
Follows a herd of gray whales as it moves from the Arctic down the Pacific coast, 7000 miles to breeding lagoons off the coast of Baja, Mexico. Stops at the uninhabited Channel Islands, to discover rookeries of California sea lions and the rare elephant seal. Part of a thirteen - part series on the North American wilderness. Each episode documents a different area and shows how animal species cope with their surroundings to survive.
Geography - World; Science - Natural
Dist - CNEMAG **Prod** - HOBELP 1976

Long E sound 15 MIN
U-matic / Kit / VHS
Space station readstar series
(P)
$130.00 purchase, $25.00 rental, $75.00 self dub
Teaches phonics in a series designed to supplement second grade reading programs. Explains the long e sound. Twenty first in a 25 part series.
English Language
Dist - GPN

Long eyes of earth 10 MIN
16mm
Films for music for film series
B&W/Color (G)
$50.00 rental
Investigates the link between sexual identity, spirituality and creativity. Focuses on the berdache, shaman or tribal priest of the Papago Indians, often a cross - dressing, homosexual male. Approaches ritual as a way of seeing. Includes music by Yvar Mikhashoff, Looking Through the Air, a poem, Shaman, by Paul Schmidt, Anthony deMare on piano, narration by Paul Schmidt.
Fine Arts; Sociology
Dist - CANCIN

The Long fist 24 MIN
U-matic
Color (J A)
Highlights episodes from a Hong Kong visit of Canadian kung fu devotees Gary Bush and Dennis Crawford. Shows viewers an open - air market, scenes of the city from a double - decker bus, visits to a restaurant and to Show Studios, the Hollywood of kung fu movies, and a demonstration of long fist techniques. Narrated by Bush and Crawford.
Geography - World; Physical Education and Recreation; Religion and Philosophy
Dist - MOBIUS **Prod** - MOBIUS 1982

The Long gray line 138 MIN
U-matic / VHS / 16mm
Color (I J H C)
Presents the story of Sergeant Marty Maher, the West Point athletic trainer who shaped the generations of cadets who have marched from West Point to influence our times.
Biography; Civics and Political Systems; Fine Arts
Dist - FI **Prod** - CPC 1955

A Long hard day on the ranch
CD-ROM
Discis Books on CD - ROM
(P I) (SPANISH)
$69.00 purchase _ #2559
Contains the original text and illustrations of A Long Hard Day on the Ranch by Audrey Nelson. Enhances understanding with real voices, music, and sound effects. Every word in the text has an in - context explanation, pronunciation and syllables, available through a click of the mouse. Spanish - English version available for an extra $5 per disc. For Macintosh Classics, Plus, II and SE computers, requires 1MB of RAM, one floppy disk drive, and an Apple compatible CD - ROM drive.
English Language; Literature and Drama
Dist - BEP

The Long Haul 30 MIN
U-matic / VHS / 16mm
Case Studies in Small Business Series
Color (C A)
Business and Economics
Dist - GPN **Prod** - UMA 1979

The Long Haul Men 17 MIN
16mm
Color (I J A)
LC FIA68-1245
Documents the experiences of a two - man driving team freighting produce from Mexico to the Canadian border. Shows glimpses of the changing terrain as the truck rolls on through day and night.
Business and Economics; Geography - United States; Social Science
Dist - NFBC **Prod** - NFBC 1966

A Long hours walk 29 MIN
U-matic / VHS / BETA
Color; PAL (G H C)
PdS60, PdS68 purchase
Shows how 85 percent of Columbia lives in barrios on the outskirts of Bogota and struggle against poverty, illness, hunger and premature death. Features Father Rene Garcia, a rebel Roman Catholic priest, as a guide.
Fine Arts; Geography - World; Social Science; Sociology
Dist - EDPAT **Prod** - IFF

Long I sound 15 MIN
U-matic / Kit / VHS
Space station readstar series
(P)
$130.00 purchase, $25.00 rental, $75.00 self dub
Teaches phonics in a series designed to supplement second grade reading programs. Discusses the long i sound. Thirteenth in a 25 part series.
English Language
Dist - GPN

Long irons 55 MIN
VHS
Name of the game is golf series
(H C A)
$49.95 purchase _ #SWC430V
Demonstrates basic golf skills, including correct swing for long shots, hooks and slices, tempo and proper alignment. Features slow motion photography.
Physical Education and Recreation
Dist - CAMV

Long Island transplant - a decade of progress, a century of hope 23 MIN
VHS / U-matic
Color (PRO C G)
$195.00 purchase _ #C911 - VI - 062
Reveals that more than 20,000 people suffer from end stage kidney disease. Discloses that for many of these patients a kidney transplant would either save their lives or greatly improve the quality of their lives. Features transplant recipients and those waiting for organs who discuss the issues they are facing. Presented by Transplantation Service, University Hospital, State University of New York at Stony Brook and Howard University Transplant Center, Washington, DC.
Health and Safety
Dist - HSCIC

The Long journey 26 MIN
VHS
Challenge of the seas series
Color (I J H)
$225.00 purchase
Examines salmon as a link between the deep sea and forest and mountains. Reveals that these fish provide food for the survival of whales and eagles and are the subject of international treaties protecting them from overfishing. Part of a 26 - part series on the oceans.
Science - Natural; Science - Physical
Dist - LANDMK **Prod** - LANDMK 1991

A Long journey
VHS
English as a second language - tutor training series
Color (G T PRO) (FRENCH)
$19.95 purchase _ #31044
Presents a human interest story to support the English as a Second Language - Tutor Training Kit.
English Language
Dist - LITERA

The Long journey home 27 MIN
U-matic / VHS
Color (G A)
$45.00, $110.00 purchase _ #TCA18236, #TCA18235
Covers the international effort to resettle and rebuild Afghanistan. Documents the unique collaborative effort, which involved United Nations agencies, donor countries, international volunteer organizations, and the Afghan people themselves. Produced by the US Information Agency.
Civics and Political Systems; Geography - World; Sociology
Dist - USNAC

Long Journey Home 58 MIN
16mm / VHS
Color (G)
$825.00, $100.00 purchase _ #LJHMVHS
Focuses on three Appalachian natives who still live in the area, have left or have returned. Describes the social and economic difficulties of Appalachian life.
Geography - United States; Guidance and Counseling; History - United States; Sociology
Dist - APPAL

Long Journey West 16 MIN
16mm
Color (P I J H)
Illustrates a family of pioneers on the trek from Massachusetts to the Midwest.
History - United States
Dist - VIEWTH **Prod** - GATEEF

Long Journey West - 1820 15 MIN
U-matic / VHS / 16mm
Pioneer Life Series
Color (I J)
Portrays highlights of a journey from Massachusetts to Illinois in the 1800's. Stresses hardships and shows the different types of transportation.
History - United States; Social Science
Dist - IU **Prod** - IU 1960

Long jump
VHS
Coaching men's field and track series
Color (H C G)
$59.95 purchase _ #TRS1253V
Features men's field and track coach Rick Sloan on the long jump. Offers a comprehensive series of teaching progressions beginning with the three starting variations, running mechanics, preparation for take off, take off and variations of in - flight and landing techniques. Part of a nine - part series.
Physical Education and Recreation
Dist - CAMV

Long jump 23 MIN
VHS
Track and field series
Color (J H C A)
$39.95 purchase _ #MXS450V
Features Dr Ken Foreman, former U S Olympic women's track coach, in a comprehensive program to teach skills of the long jump. Demonstrated by Olympian Martha Watson.
Physical Education and Recreation
Dist - CAMV

Long Jump APPROXIMATELY 33 MIN
U-matic / VHS
Women's Track & Field Videos Series
Color; B&W; Silent; Stereo; Mono (H C A)
Demonstrates techniques and drills by famous athletes for the long jump event. Prepared and narrated by coach Ken Foreman.
Physical Education and Recreation
Dist - TRACKN **Prod** - TRACKN 1986

Long jump
VHS
Coaching women's track and field series
Color (H C G)
$59.95 purchase _ #TRS1102V
Features women's field and track coaches Bob Meyers and Meg Ritchie on the long jump. Illustrates in detail the four phases of the long jump. Includes the teaching progressions of - Approach - mental keys and acceleration point; Take - off - how to coach correct techniques; In - flight - slow motion of proper position and body movements; Landing - critical mechanics and tips to achieve maximum projection. Part of a nine - part series.

Physical Education and Recreation
Dist - CAMV

Long jump 30 MIN
VHS
Track and field techniques series
Color (H C G)
$29.95 purchase _ #WK1100V
Features long jumper Lynn Davis who discusses the skill and improving performance. Part of a series.
Physical Education and Recreation
Dist - CAMV

The Long jump
VHS
NCAA instructional video series
Color (H C A)
$39.95 purchase _ #KAR2103V
Presents the first of a three - part series on field events. Focuses on the long jump.
Physical Education and Recreation
Dist - CAMV **Prod** - NCAAF

Long Jump 46 MIN
BETA / VHS
Women's Track and Field Series
Color
Physical Education and Recreation
Dist - MOHOMV **Prod** - MOHOMV

Long Jump APPROXIMATELY 60 MIN
VHS / U-matic
Frank Morris Instructional Videos Series
Color; B&W; Silent; Mono; Stereo (H C A)
Instructs athletes how to execute and improve performance of the Long Jump. Produced and Narrated by coach Frank Morris.
Physical Education and Recreation
Dist - TRACKN **Prod** - TRACKN 1986

The Long Jump 11 MIN
U-matic / VHS / 16mm
Athletics Series
Color (H C A)
LC 80-700340
Presents scenes of an international competition in the long jump, using slow - motion photography to demonstrate critical phases of the jump. Shows training exercises, and concludes with scenes of a long jump competition in the European Cup Semi - Finals.
Physical Education and Recreation
Dist - IU **Prod** - GSAVL 1980

Long Lance 55 MIN
VHS / 16mm
Color (S)
$790.00, $99.00 purchase _ #101 - 9104
Tells the true story of Sylvester Clark Long, a man marked by three racial identities. Discloses that Long dubbed himself Long Lance to escape the ghetto where he was born, and set out to exploit his Indian heritage. His deceptions carried him into the inner circles of celebrities and royalty - until they discovered the truth.
History - United States; Social Science
Dist - FI **Prod** - NFBC 1987

Long Lasting Blossoming Plants 29 MIN
Videoreel / VT2
Making Things Grow III Series
Color
Agriculture; Science - Natural
Dist - PBS **Prod** - WGBHTV

A Long Life 1 MIN
VHS / U-matic
Color
Uses TV spot format and panning technique to show a woman as she might look at 50, 40, 30, and 20 years of age. Encourages viewers to know which tests are necessary and when to take them for a long, healthy life.
Health and Safety
Dist - AMCS **Prod** - AMCS 1981

Long Live 29 MIN
Videoreel / VT2
Maggie and the Beautiful Machine - Easy Does it Series
Color
Physical Education and Recreation
Dist - PBS **Prod** - WGBHTV

Long Live the Heart 25 MIN
U-matic / VHS
Color
Shows how the heart works, the sophisticated diagnostic measures doctors have of looking at it, what happens when doctors have a heart attack and how heart attacks can be avoided. Features an actual cardio - catheterization procedure, in which one can see the patient's heart pumping through sophisticated X - ray techniques.
Health and Safety; Science; Science - Natural
Dist - MEDCOM **Prod** - MEDCOM

Long live the king 22 MIN
16mm
B&W (G)
$20.00 rental
Features an offbeat comedy about a princess who must find a husband in 24 hours or forfeit her throne. Uses a comic portrait of the clever Jew, a theme prevalent in silent films. Directed by Leo McCarey and produced by Roche Pathe. Stars Martha Sleeper, Oliver Hardy, Charles Chase and Max Davidson.
Dist - NCJEWF

Long live the lady 102 MIN
35mm
Color (G) (ITALIAN WITH ENGLISH SUBTITLES)
$300.00 rental
Presents a modern Italian farce which portrays a lavish dinner for wealthy businessmen which becomes a monstrous disaster as a group of lower - class teens are initiated into their professions as waiters. Directed by Ermanno Olmi.
Fine Arts; Sociology
Dist - KINOIC **Prod** - IFEX 1987

The Long March of the Suffragists 50 MIN
U-matic / VHS / 16mm
Yesterday's Witness in America Series
Color (H C A)
Recounts how women demonstrated to get the vote in 1916 by picketing the White House, being imprisoned, going on hunger strikes and being forcibly fed. Presents six suffragists who relate the final, dramatic years of their battle for the vote which culminated in victory in 1920.
History - United States; Social Science; Sociology
Dist - TIMLIF **Prod** - BBCTV 1982

The Long March South 29 MIN
VHS / U-matic
Journey into Thailand Series
Color (J S C A)
MV=$195.00
Reveals that the original Thais came from China, migrating slowly south through Burma and Thailand.
Geography - World; History - World
Dist - LANDMK **Prod** - LANDMK 1986

The Long Night 15 MIN
16mm
Color (J)
Presents the drama of a young man as he faces the reality of having tuberculosis. Provides information on the disease and explains how to prevent it.
Guidance and Counseling; Health and Safety
Dist - WSUM **Prod** - WSUM 1959

The Long Night 87 MIN
16mm
Color; B&W
Tells the story of a twelve - year - old boy in Harlem. Presents his search for money that was stolen from him, money which his mother desperately needs. Shows him finding his father on his search into the night. Based on the novel by Julian Mayfield.
Psychology; Sociology
Dist - BLKFMF **Prod** - BLKFMF

A Long Night with Lethal Guests 58 MIN
VHS
Color (S)
$129.00 purchase _ #188 - 9028
Follows medical researchers as they analyze malaria, work to develop a vaccine and slowly piece together the complex scientific and medical puzzle of one of the world's most deadly diseases. Reveals that malaria has reached epidemic proportions and that more than one half of the world's population is in danger of infection. Filmed largely in Papua New Guinea where malaria has traveled to even the remotest regions.
Business and Economics; Geography - World; Health and Safety; Science; Sociology
Dist - FI **Prod** - FLMAUS 1987

Long Nose 15 MIN
U-matic / VHS
Teletales Series
Color (P) (GERMAN)
$125.00 purchase
Introduces a children's tale that originates in Germany.
Education; Literature and Drama
Dist - AITECH **Prod** - POSIMP 1984

Long O sound 15 MIN
U-matic / Kit / VHS
Space station readstar series
(P)
$130.00 purchase, $25.00 rental, $75.00 self dub
Teaches phonics in a series designed to supplement second grade reading programs. Explains the long o sound. Sixteenth in a 25 part series.
English Language
Dist - GPN

Long Pants 60 MIN
16mm
B&W (J)
Stars Harry Langdon as a country boy pitted against city slickers in a series of adventures as he pursues a femme fatale.
Fine Arts
Dist - TWYMAN **Prod** - MGM 1927

Long rifle in revival 31 MIN
VHS / 35mm strip
Color (G)
$85.00, $20.00 purchase
Explores some of the history of the 'Kentucky' rifle and the contemporary phenomenon of revival of the manufacture and use of this historic weapon. Features gunsmiths and sharpshooters who demonstrate loading and firing operations.
Fine Arts; History - United States; Physical Education and Recreation
Dist - UWKY **Prod** - UWKY 1970

The Long road back 29 MIN
VHS
Color (J H C G)
$89.95 purchase, $45.00 rental _ #TTP143
Educates young people on the devastation of drug and alcohol abuse by letting them hear the stories of former addicts. Shows a group of high school students in an earnest and eye - opening encounter with recovering addicts, learning first - hand about both the costs of drug and alcohol abuse and the challenges of staying sober. Interviews residents of Marathon House, an intensive treatment program in Massachussetts. Recovering addicts talk candidly about losing family, friends, homes, livelihoods and their own self - esteem, and how they hope to change their lives as a result of living at Marathon House.
Fine Arts; Guidance and Counseling; Health and Safety
Dist - TURTID

The Long road back - Eastern Front 1943 - 45 52 MIN
VHS
Century of warfare series
Color (G)
$19.99 purchase _ #0 - 7835 - 8421 - 0NK
Follows the military campaigns of Adolf Hitler on the Eastern Front of the European theater in World War II, 1943 - 1945. Covers strategy, tactics, weapons, personalities, battles and campaigns, victories and defeats. Part of a 20 - part series on 20th - century warfare.
Civics and Political Systems; History - World; Sociology
Dist - TILIED

The Long Road Home 27 MIN
U-matic / VHS / 16mm
Insight Series
Color (H C A)
Depicts a man's encounter with God after he has run away from his fiancee on the eve of his wedding. Shows God teaching him that to love means to cope with disappointment and to overcome one's fears. Stars Martin Sheen and Harold Gould.
Guidance and Counseling; Psychology; Religion and Philosophy
Dist - PAULST **Prod** - PAULST

Long Road Home 27 MIN
U-matic / VHS
Color (J A)
Tells the story of a young man who panics the night before his wedding and learns about love and fidelity from God. Stars Harold Gould and Martin Sheen.
Fine Arts; Sociology
Dist - SUTHRB **Prod** - SUTHRB

Long Rope Jumping 17 MIN
16mm
Color (P I J H)
Promotes the physical education objectives of agility, rhythm, timing and alertness.
Physical Education and Recreation
Dist - MMP **Prod** - MMP 1967

Long Search Series no 11
Taoism - a Question of Balance 52 MIN
Dist - TIMLIF

Long Search Series no 2
Hinduism - 330 Million Gods 52 MIN
Dist - TIMLIF

Long Search Series no 6
Orthodox Christianity - the Rumanian Solution 52 MIN
Dist - TIMLIF

Long Search Series no 7
Judaism - the Chosen People 52 MIN
Dist - TIMLIF

Long search series
Alternative lifestyles in California - 52 MIN

West meets East
Buddhism - footprint of the Buddha - India 52 MIN
Buddhism - the land of the disappearing Buddha - Japan 52 MIN
Catholicism - Rome, Leeds, and the desert 52 MIN
Hinduism - 330 Million Gods 52 MIN
Judaism - the Chosen People 52 MIN
Orthodox Christianity - the Rumanian Solution 52 MIN
Reflections on the Long Search 52 MIN
Taoism - a Question of Balance - China 52 MIN
Dist - AMBROS

Long Search Series
African religions - Zulu Zion 52 MIN
Islam - There is no God but God 52 MIN
Protestant Spirit USA 52 MIN
Religion in Indonesia - the way of the ancestors 52 MIN
Dist - AMBROS
TIMLIF

Long search series
Alternative lifestyles in California - West meets East 52 MIN
Buddhism - footprint of the Buddha - India 52 MIN
Buddhism - the land of the disappearing Buddha - Japan 52 MIN
Catholicism - Rome, Leeds and the desert 52 MIN
Catholicism - Rome, Leeds and the desert - Pt 2 26 MIN
Reflections on the long search 52 MIN
Religion in Indonesia - the way of the ancestors - Pt 2 26 MIN
Dist - TIMLIF

The Long Shadow 32 MIN
16mm
Color
LC FIA68-216
Presents the early years of Abraham Lincoln's life showing the places of his birth, childhood, schooling, his work as a farmer, as a river boat pilot and as a surveyor, his study of law and politics and his early legislative years.
Biography; History - United States
Dist - USC **Prod** - USC 1968

Long shadows - the Civil War legacy 89 MIN
VHS / U-matic
Color (G)
$390.00 purchase
Portrays the ways the conflicts, issues, myths and effects of the Civil War, 1861 - 1865, continue to play a role in the national character and life of the United States. Interviews writers and historians John Hope Franklin, Studs Terkel, Robert Penn Warren, Tom Wicker, C Vann Woodward, Robert Coles, James Reston, Jr, former President Jimmy Carter and others. Considers a parallel between the Civil War and the Vietnam War. Produced by Ross Spears.
History - United States; Sociology
Dist - JAFP

The Long Ships 125 MIN
16mm / U-matic / VHS
B&W (C A)
Stars Richard Widmark and Sidney Poitier in an adventure - comedy of a robust band of Vikings on a desperate voyage in search of the legendary lost Golden Bell of St James.
Fine Arts
Dist - FI **Prod** - CPC 1964

Long span 30 MIN
VHS
Limit series
Color (A PRO IND)
PdS30 purchase _ Unavailable in USA and Canada
Describes Niels Gimsung's attempt to bring people together by building the world's first mile-long bridge. Part of a six-part series exploring limits of human achievement in engineering, focusing on international engineers facing their toughest career assignments. Asks how far physical limits can be pushed and what restraints exist in extending the scale of engineering projects.
Industrial and Technical Education
Dist - BBCENE

The Long Straight 60 MIN
U-matic / VHS / 16mm
Great Railway Journeys of the World Series
Color (J)
Travels the longest railroad line without a curve through Australia's Nullarbor Plain. Traces the Australian dream of a transcontinental railroad and rides on the antique Ghan train at a top speed of 17 miles per hour.
Geography - World; Social Science
Dist - FI **Prod** - BBCTV 1979

Long term AIDS 23 MIN
VHS
Color (A PRO)
$95.00 purchase _ #AH46226
Trains health professionals and others who care for people with AIDS. Focuses on nursing techniques and the psychosocial impact of caring for people with AIDS, particularly in a long - term care facility.
Health and Safety
Dist - HTHED **Prod** - HTHED

Long - term central venous catheters for pediatric patients 28 MIN
VHS
Color (PRO C)
$285.00 purchase, $70.00 rental _ #6516
Discusses the various types of pediatric long - term central venous access devices - partially implanted devices and totally implanted devices. Explains how to select the device, possible complications, nursing diagnosis, patient care and patient education.
Health and Safety
Dist - AJN **Prod** - HESCTV

The Long - Term Psychiatric Patient 40 MIN
16mm
Psychiatric - Mental Health Nursing Series
Color (PRO)
LC 76-701619
Presents a case study concerning a nurse's relationship with a long - term patient to demonstrate the principles, concepts and skills essential to therapeutic outcomes and rehabilitation. Shows opportunities for helping in patterns of social isolation, withdrawal and chronicity and methods for helping a patient move from very dependent to more independent modes of relating.
Health and Safety
Dist - AJN **Prod** - AJN 1976

Long - Term Stress Management 15 MIN
U-matic / VHS / 16mm
Stress Management System Series Film 3
Color (A)
Compares cause and effect with management of trauma stress cases.
Psychology
Dist - CORF **Prod** - CORF 1983

Long Tidal River 30 MIN
16mm
Color
Science - Natural
Dist - FENWCK **Prod** - FENWCK

A Long Time Ago 1 MIN
U-matic / VHS
Color
Shows Larry Hagman turning the anti - smoking message into a family affair by warning his daughter against smoking. Uses TV spot format.
Health and Safety; Sociology
Dist - AMCS **Prod** - AMCS 1983

Long time comin' 52 MIN
16mm / VHS
Color (G)
$90.00, $140.00 rental, $250.00 purchase
Profile two African - Canadian lesbian artists who bring political commitment and passion to their work and to their communities. Introduces Grace Channer, painter and Faith Nolan, singer and songwriter. Connects the creative process to political and sexual being.
Fine Arts; Sociology
Dist - WMEN **Prod** - BRAND 1993

Long Time Intervals 25 MIN
16mm
PSSC Physics Films Series
Color (H C)
Discusses the significance of long time intervals. Describes the radioactive dating process used in estimating the age of the earth.
Mathematics; Science - Physical
Dist - MLA **Prod** - PSSC 1959

Long time to grow, Pt 1 - two - and three - year - olds in nursery school 35 MIN
16mm
Studies of normal personality development series
Color
Follows the activities and learning behavior of nursery school children throughout the day and during different seasons of the year. Shows how teachers can offer help by setting limits. Discusses the necessary support, encouragement and the amount of supervision that pre - school children need.
Education; Psychology
Dist - NYU **Prod** - NYU 1951

Long Time to Grow, Pt 3 - Six - , Seven - and Eight - Year - Olds - Society of Children 30 MIN
16mm
Studies of Normal Personality Development Series
Color
Documents the entrance of children into a world of tradition, magic and customs that are resistant to change. Shows the growth of group cohesion leading toward cliques, peer groups and cleavages on the basis of interest and sex.
Psychology
Dist - NYU **Prod** - NYU 1957

Long Time to Grow, Pt 2 - Four and Five Year Olds in School 40 MIN
16mm
Studies of Normal Personality Development Series
B&W
Presents children ages four and five at work and play at the Vassar College Nursery School and the Poughkeepsie Day School.
Psychology
Dist - NYU **Prod** - NYU 1954

Long U sound 15 MIN
U-matic / Kit / VHS
Space station readstar series
(P)
$130 purchase, $25 rental, $75 self dub
Teaches phonics in a series designed to supplement second grade reading programs. Explains the long u sound. Twentieth in a 25 part series.
English Language
Dist - GPN

The Long valley - a study of bereavement 59 MIN
16mm / U-matic / VHS
Color (H C A)
LC 78-700525; 79-707823
Presents Dr Colin Murray Parkes, who lectures to a group of doctors, clergy, social workers and bereaved people about the process of grief. Describes the four stages of grief and explains how our reactions to grief have their origins in our evolution.
Guidance and Counseling; Psychology; Sociology
Dist - FI **Prod** - BBCTV 1978

Long View 28 MIN
16mm
Color (G)
_ #106C 0173 624
Shows that through the development of remote sensing technology in connection with satellites a view from space with a perspective and perception never before deemed feasible is now made possible. Details some of the practical applications and Canada's activity in this field, particularly where it concerns better management of natural resources and environment.
Geography - World; Science - Natural; Science - Physical
Dist - CFLMDC **Prod** - NFBC 1973

Long Vowel Sounds 15 MIN
VHS
Planet Pylon Series
Color (I)
Uses character Commander Wordstalker from Space Station Readstar to stress certain language arts skills or specific phonics. Studies long vowels. Intended to supplement third grade language curriculum. Includes a worksheet to be completed with the help of series characters.
Education; English Language
Dist - GPN

The Long Vowel Sounds 15 MIN
U-matic / VHS / 16mm
Reading Skills, Set 2 Series no 1
Color (P I)
LC 73-700980
Reviews the long and short vowel sounds. Shows through illustration and example three rules for long vowel sounds in long words.
English Language
Dist - JOU **Prod** - GLDWER 1972

The Long voyage home
VHS
Color (G)
$24.95 purchase _ #0721
Portrays the life of sailors in 1940 aboard a merchant ship in the North Atlantic. Shows the anxious crew searching the sky for German planes and hoping that they'll survive the journey home.
Fine Arts; History - World; Literature and Drama
Dist - SEVVID

The Long Voyage Home - Donne's Religious Poetry 45 MIN
VHS / U-matic
Survey of English Literature I Series
Color
Looks at John Donne's religious poetry.

Literature and Drama
Dist - MDCPB **Prod** - MDCPB

The Long Way Back 19 MIN
16mm / U-matic / VHS
B&W (A)
Shows lay persons how they can provide a link between the community and the patient in a mental hospital.
Psychology; Sociology
Dist - IFB **Prod** - CDNHW 1963

A Long Way from Home 15 MIN
VHS / U-matic
Other families, other friends series; Blue module; Mexico
Color (P)
Visits Acapulco and Teotihuacan in Mexico.
Geography - World; Social Science
Dist - AITECH **Prod** - WVIZTV 1971

A Long Way Home 22 MIN
U-matic / VHS / 16mm
Update Europe Series
Color (J H)
$495 purchase - 16 mm, $250 purchase - video _ #5179C
Discusses migration from countries in Southern to countries in Northern Europe. Produced by the BBC.
History - World
Dist - CORF

The Long Weekend - the Odds Get Shorter 23 MIN
16mm
Color
LC 74-706130
Dramatizes the risk of driving long distances on weekend trips. Depicts a professional gambler who relates the theories of gambling to a weekend fling of four Las Vegas - bound airmen.
Psychology; Social Science
Dist - USNAC **Prod** - USAF 1968

The Long years of experiment - 1844 - 1920 16 MIN
16mm
Twelve decades of concrete in American architecture series
Color
Industrial and Technical Education
Dist - PRTLND **Prod** - PRTLND 1965

The Longest Day
VHS / U-matic
Color (J H C A)
$97.00 purchase _ #05901 94
Tells the story of the D day landings at Normandy. Stars Richard Burton, Rod Steiger and John Wayne.
Fine Arts; History - United States
Dist - ASPRSS

The Longest hatred 156 MIN
VHS
Color; PAL (J H)
PdS55 purchase
Presents three 52 - minute programs looking at antisemitism, described as 'the longest and deepest hatred in human history.' Examines the history, present - day situation and possible ways of counteracting such an age - old problem. Contact distributor about availability outside the United Kingdom.
Sociology
Dist - ACADEM

The Longest River 29 MIN
VHS / U-matic
Color
Accompanies three young Americans as they raft down one of the world's most dangerous rivers, the Bio Bio in the Chilean Andes.
Geography - World
Dist - FLMLIB **Prod** - WINGS 1984

The Longest trail 58 MIN
16mm / VHS
Movement style and culture series
Color (H C G)
$950.00, $410.00 purchase, $60.00 rental _ #11291, #37263
Explores the dance traditions of American Indians. Shows more than 50 Native American dances and recounts one of the great human adventures - the settlement of the New World by people coming across the Bering Strait landbridge thousands of years ago. Part of a series on movement style and culture.
Fine Arts; Social Science; Sociology
Dist - UCEMC **Prod** - CHORP 1986

The Longest Wave 25 MIN
16mm
Color
Discusses the complexities of the absorption of the longest wave of Russian immigration to Israel.
Geography - World; Sociology
Dist - ALDEN **Prod** - UJA

Longevity - to Live to be 140 20 MIN
U-matic / VHS / 16mm
Color
Focuses on the Andean village of Vilcabamba, where there is a high percentage of people over 100 years old. Looks at the differences between this society and American society. Examines the factors leading to a long life and raises questions about American attitudes towards the old.
Health and Safety; Sociology
Dist - CNEMAG **Prod** - DOCUA

Longevity - to Live to be 140 24 MIN
U-matic / VHS / 16mm
Color (C A)
LC 79-700929
Discusses the phenomenon of longevity in the village of Vilcabambma, Ecuador, where 9 out of every 800 people are over 100 years old.
Health and Safety; Sociology
Dist - CNEMAG **Prod** - HOBLEI 1974

Longhorns 6 MIN
16mm
B&W
Shows the graceful rhythms of longhorns in motion.
Fine Arts
Dist - RADIM **Prod** - HARH

The Longhouse People 24 MIN
16mm
Color (J)
Pictures the life and religious ceremonies of the Longhouse People - - Iroquois Indians who adhere to the old religion. Shows their rain dances and healing ceremony performed by men of the false - face society.
Social Science; Sociology
Dist - NFBC **Prod** - NFBC 1950

Longine - Wittnauer Television Interviews - Senator Joseph R McCarthy and Dr Ralph E Lapp 26 MIN
U-matic / VHS
B&W
Presents two interviews from the Longine - Wittnauer Chronoscope broadcast on TV between 1951 and 1955. Features Senator Joseph R McCarthy and nuclear physicist Dr Ralph E Lapp discussing the term 'McCarthyism' and the rationale behind the development of the hydrogen bomb.
Biography; Civics and Political Systems; History - United States; Science - Physical
Dist - IHF
USNAC

Longines - Wittnauer Interviews - Adam Clayton Powell, Jr 11 MIN
VHS / U-matic
B&W (J A)
Portrays Congressman Adam Clayton Powell Jr in this interview first aired on CBS - TV on June 7, 1954. Powell, whose commentary in the 1950's following the 'Brown vs Board of Education' Supreme Court decision helped clarify the Negro community's hopes and goals. Discusses prejudice, integration in schools, churches, and the armed forces, interracial marriage and the Supreme Court decision.
History - United States
Dist - USNAC **Prod** - CBSTV 1954

Longitude 10 MIN
U-matic
Geography Skills Series
Color (J H)
Shows how the lines of longitude are related to local times, using the prime meridian and the sun.
Computer Science; Education; Geography - World
Dist - TVOTAR **Prod** - TVOTAR 1985

Longitude 16 MIN
U-matic / 16mm / VHS
Map skills for beginners series
Color (I J)
$350.00, $250.00 purchase _ #HP - 5194C
Uses the animated exploits of wildlife photographer Natalie Haymaker to demonstrate the location and role of the prime meridian. Shows how to measure longitude in degrees, time and miles, how longitude meridians are used to divide the world into time zones and how the distance between longitude lines get shorter away from the equator. Part of a series on map skills for beginners.
Geography - World; Science - Physical
Dist - CORF **Prod** - CHRISP 1989

Longitude 12 MIN
U-matic / VHS / 16mm
Map skills series
Color (I J)
$350.00 purchase - 16 mm, $250.00 purchase - video _ #5194C
Shows how longitude meridians are used to divide the world into time zones, and the location of the prime meridian. Produced by Christianson Productions, Inc.
Social Science
Dist - CORF

Longitude and latitude 11 MIN
VHS
Map reading series
Color (I J)
$24.95 purchase _ #S9047
Shows how to find grid locations on maps. Part of a five - part series teaching mapping skills in single - concept format.
Geography - World; Science - Physical; Social Science
Dist - HUBDSC **Prod** - HUBDSC

Longshoremen and automation - the changing face of the waterfront 30 MIN
VHS
Color (H C G)
$195.00 purchase, $40.00 rental _ #37480
Explores the impact of automation on the lives and work of longshoremen in San Francisco. Includes discussion guide. Features Ed Asner. Produced by Minott - Weihnacht.
History - United States; Social Science
Dist - UCEMC

Look Across the Channel 30 MIN
U-matic
Best Kept Secrets Series
Color (H C A)
Outlines the enduring lies that propagandists told their own people during World War II and the surprisingly tenacious hold they still have.
Civics and Political Systems; History - World
Dist - TVOTAR **Prod** - TVOTAR 1985

Look after your back 20 MIN
16mm / VHS / BETA / U-matic
Color; PAL (G T)
PdS150, PdS158 purchase
Indicates just how the back and spine works. Uses animation to show the workings of the spine in relation to the skull, ribs, pelvis, etc. Looks at the vertebrae in relation to the stress of moving.
Health and Safety
Dist - EDPAT

Look again 15 MIN
U-matic / VHS / BETA
Color; PAL (G H C)
PdS45, PdS53 purchase
Develops the idea that there are many aspects of our everyday world that have unsuspected mathematical implications. Investigates discreteness and continuity and problems connected with evaluating maxima and minima. Reveals the order in random doodling and concludes with the mathematics of a drunkard's walk.
Mathematics
Dist - EDPAT

Look Again at Garden Birds 22 MIN
U-matic / VHS / 16mm
Color (I J)
Introduces the common bird species found in gardens. Demonstrates how to achieve close views of these species as they nest, feed or bathe.
Science - Natural
Dist - VIEWTH **Prod** - GATEEF

Look Again at Gulls 25 MIN
16mm
Color (J H C G)
Shows how to recognize the different species of British gulls by their bills, leg colorings, tails and wings. Covers the six breeding species of Britain and details their life cycles.
Science - Natural
Dist - VIEWTH **Prod** - GATEEF

Look again series - Volume 1 29 MIN
VHS
Look again series
Color (P I J)
$250.00 purchase, $35.00 rental
Presents 3 programs from the Look Again series, without dialogue. Builds upon and develops children's natural interest in their surroundings. Includes Between the Walls, Connections and Snowballs and Sandcastles. See separate listings for content description.
Psychology; Science - Natural
Dist - BULFRG **Prod** - NFBC 1990

Look again series - Volume 2 28 MIN
VHS
Look again series
Color (P I J)
$250.00 purchase, $35.00 rental
Presents 3 programs from the Look Again series, without dialogue. Builds upon and develops children's natural interest in their surroundings. Includes Journey of the Blob, Topsy - Turvy and Night. See separate listings for content description.
Psychology; Science - Natural
Dist - BULFRG **Prod** - NFBC 1990

Look again series
Presents six films without dialogue to build upon and develop children's natural interest in their surroundings. Invites the viewer to share the wonder of two children as they investigate a variety of natural phenomena - the seasons, physical laws such as gravity, familiar living creatures, night, structures and their functions and ecological relationships. Encourages students to look more carefully and to appreciate the fascinating complexity of their environment. With teacher's guide.
Between the walls 10 MIN
Connections 10 MIN
Journey of the blob 10 MIN
Look again series - Volume 1 29 MIN
Look again series - Volume 2 28 MIN
Night 9 MIN
Snowballs and sandcastles 8 MIN
Topsy - Turvy 9 MIN
Dist - BULFRG **Prod** - NFBC 1990

A Look Ahead
16mm
B&W
Illustrates what to look for when analyzing fresh data. Discusses the need for so - called 'robust' statistics in the analysis of data from non - normal distributions.
Mathematics
Dist - OPENU **Prod** - OPENU

Look and do primary programs
Ancient Egypt - the world of art and architecture 28 MIN
Ancient Greece - the world of art and architecture 28 MIN
Ancient Rome - the world of art and architecture 28 MIN
Dist - ALARP

Look Around Us 29 MIN
Videoreel / VT2
Children's Fair Series
B&W (K P)
Science
Dist - PBS **Prod** - WMVSTV

Look around you in autumn 17 MIN
U-matic / VHS / 16mm
Look around you series
Captioned; Color (I)
LC 79-701775
Focuses on some of the taken - for - granted and unobserved events associated with the arrival of autumn.
Science - Natural
Dist - MCFI **Prod** - DEU 1978

Look around you in spring 17 MIN
U-matic / VHS / 16mm
Look around you series
Captioned; Color (I)
LC 79-701776
Focuses on some of the taken - for - granted and unobserved events associated with the arrival of spring.
Science - Natural
Dist - MCFI **Prod** - DEU 1978

Look around you in summer 17 MIN
16mm / U-matic / VHS
Look around you series
Captioned; Color (I)
LC 79-701777
Focuses on some of the taken - for - granted and unobserved events associated with the arrival of summer.
Science - Natural
Dist - MCFI **Prod** - DEU 1978

Look Around You in the Desert 18 MIN
U-matic / VHS / 16mm
Look Around You Series
Color (I J)
Shows what a desert is and how one is created. Introduces four distinctly different deserts that occupy the southwestern part of the United States and reveals how plants adapt to life in an arid land.
Geography - United States; Science - Natural
Dist - MCFI **Prod** - DEU

Look Around You in the Everglades 19 MIN
U-matic / VHS / 16mm
Color (I J)
Observes wildlife in the everglades in both the wet and dry seasons and explains how the mammals, birds and reptiles have adapted in remarkable ways to the harsh demands of survival.
Geography - United States; Science - Natural
Dist - MCFI **Prod** - DEU

Look Around You in the Zoo 17 MIN
16mm / U-matic / VHS
Look Around You Series
Color (P I J)
Introduces animals from North America, Africa, Asia and the Far East, South America, Australia and other parts of the world.
Science - Natural
Dist - MCFI **Prod** - DEU 1984

Look around you in winter 17 MIN
16mm / U-matic / VHS
Look around you series
Color (I J H)
LC 79-701779
Focuses on some of the taken - for - granted and unobserved events associated with the arrival of winter.
Science - Natural
Dist - MCFI **Prod** - DEU 1978

Look around you series
Look around you in autumn 17 MIN
Look around you in spring 17 MIN
Look around you in summer 17 MIN
Look Around You in the Desert 18 MIN
Look Around You in the Zoo 17 MIN
Look around you in winter 17 MIN
Dist - MCFI

A Look at a Community - the Dismal Swamp 15 MIN
U-matic / VHS
Hands on, Grade 5 - Our Environment Series
Color (I)
Looks at the community of life within a swamp.
Science - Natural
Dist - AITECH **Prod** - WHROTV 1975

A Look at cast therapy - 4 9 MIN
VHS
Orthopaedic nursing series
Color (PRO C G)
$395.00 purchase _ #R921 - VI - 005
Instructs nurses and nursing students on caring for patients after the application of the cast and splint. Part of a six - part series on orthopedic nursing.
Health and Safety
Dist - HSCIC **Prod** - UTXHSH 1993

A Look at Chemical Change 15 MIN
16mm / U-matic / VHS
Color (I J A)
LC 73-704749
Shows that different materials have different chemical reactions, using as an example a banana which has turned brown after having been left out on a table for several days.
Science - Physical
Dist - MGHT **Prod** - HANBAR 1970

Look at Greek - American Women Series
A Village in Baltimore 58 MIN
Village in Baltimore, a, Pt 1 29 MIN
Village in Baltimore, a, Pt 2 29 MIN
Dist - MOSESD

A Look at Growing Up - the Adolescent Years 30 MIN
U-matic / VHS
Here's to Your Health Series
Color (C T)
Points out that teenagers are caught in a biological 'squeeze play.' Shows they are neither child nor adult. Offers advice to parents and teenagers on ways to resolve their differences through negotiation. Talks to teen - agers about sex, peer acceptance and their attitudes towards adults.
Health and Safety; Psychology; Sociology
Dist - DALCCD **Prod** - DALCCD

A Look at Growing Up - the Early Years 30 MIN
VHS / U-matic
Here's to Your Health Series
Color (C T)
Shows a straightforward look at the common physical and emotional problems faced by children in the early years of life. Features a visit to a pediatric clinic. Discusses ways to help children cope with the divorce of their parents in this first of a two - part program on pediatrics.
Health and Safety; Psychology; Sociology
Dist - DALCCD **Prod** - DALCCD

A Look at Leaders 29 MIN
U-matic
Conversations with Allen Whiting Series
Color
Focuses on personalities, talents and foibles of world political leaders.
Civics and Political Systems
Dist - UMITV **Prod** - UMITV 1979

Look at Lines 15 MIN
U-matic / VHS
Young at Art Series
Color (P I)
Discusses lines in art.
Fine Arts
Dist - AITECH **Prod** - WSKJTV 1980

A Look at Liv 67 MIN
16mm / U-matic / VHS
Color (H C A)
Looks at the life of Norwegian actress Liv Ullmann, who discusses her work, her role as a woman in a shifting society, and her relationship with her daughter.
Biography; Fine Arts
Dist - TEXFLM **Prod** - MACMFL

A Look at Local Government 20 MIN
16mm
Government and Public Affairs Films Series
B&W (H C A)
Dr Charles Adrian, director, Institute for Community Development and Services, Michigan State University, describes conflicts between groups and between the central city and suburbs.
Civics and Political Systems; Sociology
Dist - MLA **Prod** - RSC 1960

A Look at Local Government - Dr Charles Adrian 20 MIN
16mm
Building Political Leadership Series
B&W (H C)
Civics and Political Systems
Dist - MLA **Prod** - RCS 1960

Look at Log Island 12 MIN
16mm
Color
Portrays the swinging Swedish capital at Stockholm, which originally was built on logs in the Stockholm archipelago.
Geography - World
Dist - SWNTO **Prod** - SWNTO 1965

A Look at Machine Knitting 28 MIN
U-matic / VHS
Color (J H C G T A)
Introduces machine knitting to the hobbyist and to those interested in starting a knitting business. Includes a machine demonstration and a discussion of the necessary skills, as well as profiles of knitters and suggestions about how to get started in a small knitting business.
Fine Arts
Dist - PSU **Prod** - PSU 1985

Look at Me Series no 2
The Working Mother 28 MIN
Dist - USNAC

Look at Me Series no 4
Fun with Dad 28 MIN
Dist - USNAC

Look at Me Series no 5
The Single Parent 28 MIN
Dist - USNAC

Look at Me Series
Building family relationships 30 MIN
Discipline 30 MIN
Exploring and Accepting Individual Traits 30 MIN
Exploring the World Together 30 MIN
Responsibilities and Rewards of Parenting 30 MIN
Separation 30 MIN
Understanding Sexuality 30 MIN
Dist - FI

Look at me series
Child/Parent relationships 28 MIN
Everyday parenting 28 MIN
Dist - PEREN

Look at me series
Everyday parenting 28 MIN
Grandmother and Leslie 28 MIN
Dist - USNAC

A Look at Percussion 29 MIN
Videoreel / VT2
American Band Goes Symphonic Series
B&W
Fine Arts
Dist - PBS **Prod** - WGTV

A Look at Rheumatoid Arthritis 30 MIN
Videoreel / VHS
Color
Explains the medical multidisciplinary approach for care of the Rheumatoid arthritis patient. Shows patients in physical therapy, occupational therapy and joint replacement surgery.
Health and Safety
Dist - UNDMC **Prod** - UNDMC

A Look at Science Fiction 30 MIN
VHS / U-matic
Communicating through Literature Series
Color (C)
Literature and Drama
Dist - DALCCD **Prod** - DALCCD

A Look at sound 30 MIN
16mm / U-matic / VHS
Life around us series
Color (I) (SPANISH)
Shows what causes sound, how it travels, how we hear it, and the effect is has on man and animals in an increasingly noisy world. Explains how the human ear receives sound - wave vibrations and reacts to them.
Science - Natural; Science - Physical
Dist - TIMLIF **Prod** - TIMLIF 1971
AMBROS

Look at sound 30 MIN
U-matic / VHS / BETA
Color; PAL (G H C)
PdS60, PdS68 purchase
Investigates the many aspects of hearing all over the world.
Psychology; Science - Physical
Dist - EDPAT

A Look at Southern China 20 MIN
U-matic / VHS
Color (J)
LC 82-706770
Visits Kunming and other cities and scenic landmarks in the southern part of China.
Geography - World; History - World
Dist - AWSS **Prod** - AWSS 1980

Look at that 11 MIN
U-matic / VHS / 16mm
Color (P I)
LC 70-700488
Defines and studies the basic art elements of line, form, pattern, texture and color. Emphasizes the discovery of these elements in a child's everyday life.
Fine Arts
Dist - PHENIX **Prod** - FILMSM 1968

A Look at the Castes 52 MIN
16mm
Phantom India series; Part 5
Color
Focuses on the castes in a village in Rajastan and shows how the social heirarchy established from birth acts as a rigid force in maintaining traditional Indian society.
Geography - World; Sociology
Dist - NYFLMS **Prod** - NYFLMS 1967

A Look at the Equipment 26 MIN
16mm
To Get from Here to There Series
Color (H)
Focuses on the motor vehicle with emphasis on good and bad automobile design.
Health and Safety; Psychology
Dist - PROART **Prod** - PROART

The Look at the Lives of Others 15 MIN
Videoreel / VT2
Images Series
Color (I)
Reviews GULLIVER'S TRAVELS by Jonathan Swift. Discusses literary forms and writing purposes.
English Language; Literature and Drama
Dist - GPN **Prod** - CVETVC

A Look at the sacraments - Part 1 30 MIN
VHS
Sacraments - Signs of faith and grace series
Color (R G)
$39.95 purchase _ #SACR1
Presents an overview of the sacraments of the Roman Catholic Church. Features Bruce Baumgarten. Introduces a series of eight parts on the sacraments.
Religion and Philosophy
Dist - CTNA **Prod** - CTNA

A Look at the Wild Side 22 MIN
16mm
Color
Shows two faces of Tasmania, the fertile land of the East and North and the wild mountainous land of the West and Central Plateau.
Fine Arts; Geography - World
Dist - TASCOR **Prod** - TASCOR 1968

A Look at traction therapy - 1 15 MIN
VHS
Orthopaedic nursing series
Color (PRO C G)
$395.00 purchase _ #R921 - VI - 007
Examines traction as a pulling force to a part of the body. Discusses how it is used for treatment of fractures, contractions of muscles and muscle spasms. Shows how effective traction prevents motion at the fracture site through skin, skeletal or manual traction methods. Reviews the purpose of each method and how it may be applied to the upper and lower extremities and the spine. Covers how to check for proper traction for potential problems. Part of a six - part series on orthopedic nursing.
Health and Safety
Dist - HSCIC **Prod** - UTXHSH 1993

Look at Us Now 21 MIN
VHS
Color (G)
$69.95 purchase
Profiles several individuals with disabilities to show how the use of assistive technology changed their lives. Highlights the practical use of assistive devices like reading machines, computers, special wheel chairs, vans and scooters.
Business and Economics; Health and Safety
Dist - SCETV **Prod** - SCETV 1989

Look at what I Can do 30 MIN
U-matic
Magic Ring I Series
(K P)
Shows children play games, run their own obstacle course, and magically join a disabled friend in swimming.
Education; Literature and Drama
Dist - ACCESS **Prod** - ACCESS 1984

A Look at You 13 MIN
16mm
Look at You Series
Color
Features two puppets, Orsen the dog and Webster the owl, who present concepts of the face and senses.
Science - Natural
Dist - ECI **Prod** - ECI

Look at You Now 15 MIN
VHS / U-matic
All about You Series
Color (P)
Shows the growth and development of babies, emphasizing their capabilities at various stages.
Science - Natural
Dist - AITECH **Prod** - WGBHTV 1975

A Look at You - on the Bus 9 MIN
16mm
Look at You Series
Color (P I)
Features two puppets, Orsen the dog and Webster the owl, who demonstrate correct ways to safely board, ride and exit a school bus.
Health and Safety; Social Science
Dist - ECI **Prod** - ECI

Look at You Series

A Look at You	13 MIN
A Look at You - on the Bus	9 MIN
A Look at You - the Body	8 MIN
A Look at You - the Muscles	8 MIN

Dist - ECI

A Look at You - the Body 8 MIN
16mm
Look at You Series
Color (P I)
Discusses physical components of the body. Includes discussion of all of the parts of the body individually and repeats them several times using different visuals each time, both abstract and real. Demonstrates the concepts of the whole versus parts, the self as an entity and the sense of touch.
Science - Natural
Dist - ECI **Prod** - ECI

A Look at You - the Muscles 8 MIN
16mm
Look at You Series
Color (P I)
Introduces concepts such as brain impulses to the muscles, admitting one's mistakes, group activities, colors, right and left and numbers.
Science - Natural
Dist - ECI **Prod** - ECI

Look at Zoos 12 MIN
16mm / U-matic / VHS
Color (P I)
Visits some of the world's major zoos, with special attention to unusual animals and the different manner in which animals are housed at each zoo.
Science - Natural
Dist - NGS **Prod** - NGS 1978

Look back in anger 114 MIN
VHS
Color; PAL (H)
PdS35 purchase
Presents the Renaissance Theatre Company's production of the post - war play by John Osborne. Portrays a self - destructive marriage propelled toward crisis point. Stars Emma Thompson and Kenneth Branagh. Contact distributor about availability outside the United Kingdom.
Literature and Drama; Sociology
Dist - ACADEM

Look back in anger 114 MIN
VHS
Color (G C H)
$69.00 purchase _ #DL290
Fine Arts
Dist - INSIM

Look Back in Anger
VHS / BETA
B&W
Presents John Osborne's play about an angry young man fighting the Establishment. Stars Richard Burton and Claire Bloom.
Literature and Drama
Dist - GA **Prod** - GA

Look back in anger 50 MIN
VHS
Doctors to be series
Color; PAL (C PRO)
PdS99 purchase
Highlights the change in outlook that many young doctors experience after completing medical school and beginning their work as qualified physicians. Last in the series Doctors To Be which follows a group of medical students from their initial screening through their work as newly qualified doctors.
Health and Safety
Dist - BBCENE

Look back in anger 30 MIN
VHS
Open space series
Color; PAL (H C A)
PdS50 purchase; United Kingdom and Ireland only
Features Sheila McKecknie of Shelter, the national campaign for the homeless, as she prepares to resign after ten years as director. Documents the successes and failures McKecknie witnessed during her tenure while also examining the political motivations behind her work and commitment to the homeless. Part of the Open Space series.
Sociology
Dist - BBCENE

Look Back in Sorrow 18 MIN
16mm / U-matic / VHS
Decades of Decision - the American Revolution Series
Color (H C A)
Presents a recreation of the dilemma faced by those who choose to leave their homeland after the colonies' resistance to England's oppressive taxation acts through the story of Samuel Carwen.
History - United States
Dist - NGS **Prod** - NGS 1975

Look Back to the Garden 28 MIN
U-matic / VHS / 16mm
Insight Series
Color; B&W (H C A)
LC 73-705423
A dramatization about the insecurity of an unwed young couple who are living together and are afraid of marriage and its responsibilities.
Guidance and Counseling; Psychology; Sociology
Dist - PAULST **Prod** - PAULST 1968

Look before you eat 22 MIN
U-matic / VHS / 16mm
Color (J H C A)
LC 78-700279
Looks at the relationship between eating habits and health by showing students who volunteer to reduce the amount of sugar, salt and fat in their diets and then report the results. Examines the roles of the food industry, fast food chains and vending machines in determining what foods are available.
Health and Safety; Home Economics
Dist - CF **Prod** - CF 1978

Look before you leap - the dropping - out crisis 30 MIN
VHS
Color (J H)
$89.00 purchase _ #CCP0052V
Features young people disussing their reasons for dropping out and the vast differences between the expectations and the reality of life after dropping out. Shows the abundance of choices available to high school graduates and the depleted job market available to drop - outs. Focuses upon the choices and alternatives available to all students contemplating dropping out - vocational schools, part - time work, counseling, financial aid, day care centers for teenage parents. Includes workbook.
Education; Guidance and Counseling
Dist - CAMV **Prod** - CAMV 1993

Look Beyond the Disability 29 MIN
16mm
Color (C A)
LC 78-701600
Highlights 16 services provided in Kansas for people who may be considered developmentally disabled.
Health and Safety; Psychology; Sociology
Dist - UKANS **Prod** - UKANS 1974

Look both Ways 19 MIN
16mm / U-matic / VHS
Color
Follows aircraft through normal and emergency air traffic activities. Emphasizes the importance of the air traffic controller viewing a situation both from his position and that of the pilot.
Industrial and Technical Education; Social Science
Dist - USNAC **Prod** - USAF

Look closely 15 MIN
Videoreel / VT2
Art corner series
B&W (P)
Creates awareness of pattern in nature through collecting nature objects and making crayon rubbings.
Fine Arts
Dist - GPN **Prod** - CVETVC

Look further than Tomorrow 34 MIN
16mm
B&W
LC 74-705047
Discusses the pros and cons of summer youth involvement programs in Washington, DC.
Civics and Political Systems; Guidance and Counseling; Psychology
Dist - USNAC **Prod** - USOJD 1967

Look Inside Russia 22 MIN
16mm
Color (H C A)
This is a film of pictures taken in Russia by an U S Agriculture delegation that visited there in 1955.
Geography - World; History - World
Dist - UNEBR **Prod** - UNL 1956

Look inside yourself 30 MIN
16mm
Mulligan stew series
Color (I)
Explains the reasons for eating breakfast and describes the digestive system.
Guidance and Counseling; Health and Safety; Science - Natural
Dist - GPN **Prod** - GPN

A Look into the Brain 18 MIN
16mm / U-matic / VHS
Color (J A)
Introduces the study of the brain and examines what researchers are discovering about its formation and function. Discusses the developmental stages of the brain, the traffic of electrical impulses and memory.
Science - Natural
Dist - IFB **Prod** - IFB

Look, Listen, and Lead 30 MIN
U-matic / VHS / 16mm
Color; Captioned
Discusses supervision, leadership, decision making, planning and performance appraisal. Suggests that managers should remain aware of and sensitive to the needs of their employees. Formerly titled The Goya Effect.
Business and Economics; Psychology
Dist - RTBL **Prod** - RANKAV

Look, listen and learn - Spanish club series
Fiesta - Volume 1 30 MIN
Los Animales - Volume 2 30 MIN
Dist - PEAPOD

Look Me in the Eye 30 MIN
Videoreel / VT2
Unconscious Cultural Clashes Series
Color
Psychology; Sociology
Dist - SCCOE **Prod** - SCCOE

Look mom, I'm fishing 40 MIN
VHS
Color (A G)
LC 90-712276
Provides information for parents who want to teach their children how to fish.
Health and Safety; Physical Education and Recreation
Dist - CPI
CREPRI
SEVVID

The Look of America, 1750 - 1800 26 MIN
U-matic / VHS / 16mm
Color (J)
LC 77-702099
Depicts the early years of the United States, describing the arts and crafts brought to the new world by British colonists. Reveals the lives of early Americans through historical artwork, maps, stills of homes, cities and tools of the era, and narration from colonists' writings.
Fine Arts; History - United States
Dist - PFP **Prod** - EAMES 1977

Look out 168 MIN
VHS
Color; PAL (P I)
PdS29.50 purchase
Encourages children to look at real things and to draw and paint them with confidence and pleasure. Includes three cassettes. Cassette 1, Making Marks, 58 minutes, introduces ideas for looking closely at familiar things and finding out about tools for drawing. Cassette 2, Making Color, 58 minutes, is concerned with looking at color, how light changes, mixing color and painting. Cassette 3, Working Away, 52 minutes, focuses on looking at the environment, drawing outdoors near the school, away on a day trip and drawing things that move.
Fine Arts
Dist - EMFVL

Look series
Presents a six-part series that strips away the glitz and glamor of the fashion business to look behind the scenes. Explores the mystique of the designer label and debates the meaning of style. Reveals the mysteries of material and unveils the interdependence between the fashion industry, the media, financiers, and the consumer.
Material world 50 MIN
Power of the press 50 MIN
Runway 50 MIN
Scenting the money 50 MIN
Uniform and function 50 MIN
Yves Saint Laurent 50 MIN
Dist - BBCENE

Look to the Children 10 MIN
16mm
Color
LC 79-700238
Surveys the various types of educational programs offered at the Rochester School for the Deaf. With captions.
Education; Guidance and Counseling; Psychology
Dist - ROCHDF **Prod** - ROCHDF 1978

A Look to the north - the Canadian health care system 36 MIN
VHS
Color (H C A G)
Explains the history and characteristics of the Canadian health system to United States audiences. Reveals that the Canadian Health Care System is a single payer, publicly funded health care system which provides health insurance to all legal residents of Canada.
Business and Economics; Geography - World
Dist - CANSCD **Prod** - CANSCD 1992

Look to the Sun 12 MIN
U-matic / VHS / 16mm
Color (PRO)
LC 77-702202
Explains principles of a sunlight collector and solar heat system. Shows various aspects of solar heat, including business, education, research and construction.
Industrial and Technical Education; Social Science
Dist - USNAC **Prod** - UDEN 1977

Look to Tomorrow 28 MIN
16mm
Color (PRO)
LC FIE68-71
Motivates the newly disabled serviceman to plan his vocational future by using the Veterans Administration vocational counselors.
Civics and Political Systems; Guidance and Counseling; Psychology
Dist - USVA **Prod** - VA 1968

Look Up at the Hawks 30 MIN
VHS / U-matic
(G)
Uses songs and readings to examine a Nebraska woman's thoughts and feelings about life in the Dust Bowl.
Fine Arts; History - United States; Literature and Drama
Dist - GPN **Prod** - NETV

Look - We have Come through 11 MIN
16mm / U-matic / VHS
B&W (H C A)
LC 81-700907
Presents an experimental film featuring hundreds of separate shots of a dancer in motion which have been edited to create the impression of seeing the dancer simultaneously from all perspectives.
Fine Arts; Industrial and Technical Education
Dist - PHENIX **Prod** - ELDERB 1977

Look what God made 30 MIN
VHS
Stories to remember series
Color (K P I R)
$14.98 purchase _ #35 - 85 - 2063
Uses animation and puppetry to present Biblical stories. Covers the stories of the earth's creation, Adam and Eve, Cain and Abel, Noah and the flood, and God's rainbow promise. Produced by Kids International.
Literature and Drama; Religion and Philosophy
Dist - APH

Look what I Can do / Can't do it Yet / Worrying 15 MIN
U-matic / VHS
Clyde Frog Show Series
Color (P)
Presents stories presented by Muppet - like Clyde Frog presenting stories emphasizing positive self - images, feelings of optimism and self - confidence.
Psychology
Dist - GPN **Prod** - MAETEL 1977

Look what We've Done to this Land 22 MIN
16mm
Color (I)
LC 74-701070
Shows the effects of strip mining and production of electricity on the people and land of the Four Corners area of the Southwest United States.
Geography - United States; Science - Natural; Social Science
Dist - BLUSKY **Prod** - CCHSE 1974

Look who's balking - the baby who wouldn't come out 15 MIN
VHS
Color (J H C A)
$195.00 purchase
Calls attention to conditions important to a baby's well - being through humor and drama about a baby who 'refuses' to be born. Talks about pre - and post - natal care, infant health and nutrition and discipline among the needs of infants. For educating young parents, especially teenagers. Uses idiomatic language. Created in association with USAA.
Health and Safety
Dist - PFP **Prod** - ASHAP

Look Who's Coming to Dinner 27 MIN
16mm
Color
Explains the environmental requirements in devastating a termite invasion. Discusses various insecticides.
Agriculture; Home Economics
Dist - MTP **Prod** - VELSIC

Look Who's Driving 8 MIN
16mm
Color (H C A)
Uses animation to show a normally careful driver who loses control of himself and his car when angered by another driver. Emphasizes the importance of good judgment and courtesy on the road.
Health and Safety
Dist - AETNA **Prod** - UPA 1953

Look Who's Living Next Door 30 MIN
16mm
Color (H C T)
Pictures Mike and Jerry, moving into an off - campus trailer court to explore their own ideas of morality. Portrays their neighbors who are a young doctoral candidate clergyman and his wife. Shows Mike living with a girl and Jerry finding no meaning in life. Presents Roy, a Black neighbor, unloading his feelings about racism. Challenges the young Christian couple to minister effectively to their various neighbors.
Guidance and Counseling
Dist - FAMF **Prod** - FAMF

Look who's talking 30 MIN
VHS
Nature series
Color (A)
PdS65 purchase _ Not available in the United States or Canada
Projects that the reason the world is in such a mess is that adults never learned to look after it. Reveals that environmental education is now compulsory in schools in the United Kingdom, while in Mexico City children are not learning about environmental problems, they're suffering from them. Follows young reporters who visit the World Summit for Children to discover whether the talk will lead to action.
Science - Natural
Dist - BBCENE

Look with Pride 5 MIN
16mm
Color (C A)
Reviews the scope of scientific investigation and credits the American Cancer Society volunteer for his vital role in helping to win the battle.
Health and Safety; Science; Sociology
Dist - AMCS **Prod** - AMCS

Lookback - a Musical Fantasy 54 MIN
16mm
Color
LC 74-703601
Presents a fantasy which reviews some of the common experiences of growing up, such as high school, friends, teachers and music.

Psychology
Dist - CFDEVC **Prod** - MLYNJ 1973

LookChangers 40 MIN
VHS
Color (G)
$39.95 purchase
Shows how to manage a wardrobe to produce more variety. Features Judith Rasband.
Home Economics
Dist - CONIMM **Prod** - CONIMM

Lookin' good 52 MIN
VHS / U-matic
K - 12 drug prevention video series
Color; Captioned (J)
$27.00, $52.00 purchase _ #TCA17517, #TCA17516
Features two programs on peer support groups that have helped teens overcome peer pressure to use drugs. Includes teacher's guide and information card.
Guidance and Counseling; Health and Safety; Psychology
Dist - USNAC **Prod** - USDED 1988

Looking 60 MIN
VHS
The Ring of truth series
Color (G)
$69.95 purchase _ #RNGO - 101
Using the example of Galileo and his telescope, explores how scientific tools have helped shape our perceptions of the world. Points out that many of these tools have been and are created in response to new scientific theories. Cites numerous examples of illusion to show that minds and vision interact to create illusions. Hosted by physics professor Philip Morrison.
Science - Physical
Dist - PBS **Prod** - PBA 1987

Looking after myself 36 MIN
VHS
Color; PAL (S)
PdS29.50 purchase
Features six programs designed specifically for youngsters with severe learning difficulties. Includes Cleaning my teeth; Washing my hands and face; Having a bath; Washing my hair; Shaving; and Dressing.
Guidance and Counseling; Psychology
Dist - EMFVL

Looking after young teeth 17 MIN
U-matic / VHS / BETA
Color; NTSC; PAL; SECAM (P I J H G)
PdS58
Reveals that one in three of the eight - year - olds in Great Britain has had an anesthetic to have badly decayed teeth removed. Asks why this occurs in spite of health education, fluoride toothpaste and the addition of fluoride in water supplies. Suggests a three - point plan to prevent the loss of children's teeth to decay - avoid sugar and sweet things; brush regularly; have regular checkups. Uses animation and real - life examples to show what causes tooth decay.
Health and Safety; Science - Natural
Dist - VIEWTH

Looking Ahead 30 MIN
VHS / U-matic
Stress Management - a Positive Strategy Series Pt 5
Color (A)
LC 82-706501
Examines physical fitness and nutritional awareness as they dovetail with effective stress management. Presents how the skills of day - to - day stress management transfer to the larger issues of life.
Psychology
Dist - TIMLIF **Prod** - TIMLIF 1982

Looking Ahead 8 MIN
U-matic
A Matter of Time Series
(A)
Offers a montage of vignetts which preview the retirement topics covered in succeeding programs.
Sociology
Dist - ACCESS **Prod** - ACCESS 1980

Looking ahead ... preparing to meet the future 60 MIN
VHS
Color (PRO H C)
$39.95 purchase _ #VII343V-J; $39.50 purchase _ #2948; #VOI01
Interviews Richard Bolles, author of What Color Is Your Parachute, Bill Morin, head of a large career-management company, and Anne Boe, author of Is Your 'Net' Working, to provide job hunters with tips. Targeted to all who are seeking jobs, and especially to professionals who have been laid off or otherwise outplaced.
Business and Economics; Guidance and Counseling; Psychology
Dist - CAMV
NEWCAR
EXTR

Looking at Animals Series
Bears 17 MIN
The Cat family 10 MIN
Cattle 16 MIN
The Dog family 10 MIN
Elephants 10 MIN
Insect Eaters 10 MIN
Pigs and Hippos 13 MIN
Rabbits and Hares 11 MIN
Rhinos 8 MIN
Sheep and Goats 12 MIN
Dist - IFB

Looking at art 29 MIN
VHS
Color (I J H)
$138.00 purchase _ #87 - 004827
Explores art and how it should be looked at with a group of students at an art museum. Uses numerous examples from the history of art to discuss different styles and techniques. Examines style through a montage tracing the many different schools of art. Introduces the basic elements of art - line, color, shape, value, pattern, mass, texture, repetition and variation. Develops art vocabulary.
Fine Arts
Dist - SRA **Prod** - SRA 1993

Looking at art - 11 24 MIN
VHS / U-matic
Think new series
Color (C G)
$129.00, $99.00 purchase _ #V586
Gives theoretical motivation and practical ideas about viewing art. Draws content from mathematics, science, history, human feelings, every human endeavor. Part of an 11 - part series that treats art as an essential mode of learning.
Fine Arts
Dist - BARR **Prod** - CEPRO 1991

Looking at Birds 10 MIN
U-matic / VHS / 16mm
Captioned; Color (P)
Illustrates the ways in which birds differ from other animals in appearance, body structure and behavior. Shows how they adapt to various places and conditions.
Science - Natural
Dist - EBEC **Prod** - EBEC 1964

Looking at Birds - an Introduction to Birdwatching 15 MIN
16mm
Color
Provides basic training in how to look at birds, to identify them and to begin to understand their behavior. Explains grouping of birds by habitat and family.
Physical Education and Recreation; Science - Natural
Dist - ACORN **Prod** - ACORN

Looking at Children 24 MIN
16mm
Color (T)
Portrays the early signs of health problems and conditions in children as seen frequently in the classroom by observant teachers. Depicts the important interactions of the teacher with parents and the school nurse to obtain appropriate remedial action.
Education; Sociology
Dist - MTP **Prod** - MLIC 1969

Looking at Gender Roles 60 MIN
U-matic
Perspectives on Women
Color (A)
Focuses on women in the economy, women and physical well being and how men and women are working to improve women's status in society.
Sociology
Dist - ACCESS **Prod** - ACCESS 1986

Looking at Mammals 11 MIN
16mm / U-matic / VHS
Captioned; Color (P)
Illustrates the importance of animal classification and shows the difference between birds, amphibians, reptiles and mammals.
Science - Natural
Dist - EBEC **Prod** - EBEC 1967

Looking at Ourselves 8 MIN
Videoreel / VT2
Interpersonal Competence, Unit 01 - the Self Series; Unit 1 - The self
Color (C A)
Features a humanistic psychologist who, by analysis and examples, discusses self - image.
Psychology; Sociology
Dist - TELSTR **Prod** - MVNE 1973

Looking at Plants Series
How Plants Climb 11 MIN
How Plants Move 11 MIN
How Seeds are made 15 MIN
How Seeds are Scattered 15 MIN
How Seeds Sprout 16 MIN
Dist - IFB

Looking at Processes
VHS / U-matic
Organizational Quality Improvement Series
Color
Shows how to determine the capabilities and characteristics of a manufacturing process. Explains how to identify and control production process variations.
Business and Economics; Psychology
Dist - BNA **Prod** - BNA

Looking at Reptiles 11 MIN
U-matic / VHS / 16mm
Color (P) (SPANISH)
Differentiates reptiles from other creatures by comparing body structure, respiratory system and manner of egg laying. Emphasizes the fact that reptiles were the first vertebrates to adopt a terrestrial life.
Foreign Language; Science - Natural
Dist - EBEC **Prod** - EBEC

Looking at size and shape series
At the junior level - Unit C 45 MIN
In the infants' school - Unit B 56 MIN
The Nursery school experience - Unit A 56 MIN
Secondary, first year - Unit D 36 MIN
Secondary, fourth year - Unit E 41 MIN
Strands of development - Unit F 32 MIN
Dist - EMFVL

Looking at Tomorrow - Thinking and Acting in the Real World 15 MIN
16mm
Color (J H)
Introduces the concepts of critical thought and action. Emphasizes the importance of critical thought to help people achieve the kind of future they want.
Guidance and Counseling
Dist - EPCOT **Prod** - EPCOT 1983

Looking Back 10 MIN
VHS / 16mm
Older Adults Series
(C)
$385.00 purchase _ #851VI023
Focuses on an elderly couple before the husband's death.
Health and Safety
Dist - HSCIC **Prod** - HSCIC 1986

Looking Back 30 MIN
U-matic / VHS
In Our Own Image Series
Color (C)
Fine Arts
Dist - DALCCD **Prod** - DALCCD

Looking back to the future - Raymond Loewy 60 MIN
VHS
Color (G)
$69.95 purchase _ #LBTF - 000
Profiles the life of industrial designer Raymond Loewy. Presents numerous examples of his work, including railroad locomotives, cars, boats, sewing machines and the interiors of the Concorde and Air Force One. Interviews Loewy, his wife, clients and fellow designers.
Fine Arts; Industrial and Technical Education
Dist - PBS

Looking backward, looking forward 30 MIN
VHS
America in perspective - US history since 1877 series
Color (H C G)
$99.00 purchase _ #AIP - 26
Discusses what Americans - as individuals, a society and a nation - have learned from their history and what they can expect to do with that knowledge as they approach the future. Part of a 26 - part series.
History - United States; Sociology
Dist - INSTRU **Prod** - DALCCD 1991

Looking Backward, Moving Forward 24 MIN
U-matic / VHS
Color
$335.00 purchase
Psychology
Dist - ABCLR **Prod** - ABCLR 1983

Looking backwards 28 MIN
VHS / U-matic
Color; B&W (G)
LC 77-700448
Presents footage from the Oregon Historical Society's collection documenting such phenomena from the past as an eastern Oregon wheat harvest with a 38 - horse team, President Harding dedicating the Oregon Trail Marker and salmon fishing with horse - drawn nets in the Columbia River. Utilizes early newsreels.
History - United States
Dist - MEDIPR **Prod** - OREGHS 1973
OREGHS

Looking down on others - 39 10 MIN
U-matic / VHS
Life's little lessons - self - esteem 4 - 6 series
Color (I)
$129.00, $99.00 purchase _ #V668
Portrays Stella Grundle who was a wonderful actress, but she thought she was better than anyone else. Shows how her pride brought her down and opened the way for her makeup person to get her role. Part of a 65 - part series on self - esteem.
Guidance and Counseling; Psychology
Dist - BARR **Prod** - CEPRO 1992

Looking for a Job? 30 MIN
U-matic
Color
Offers practical advice, including a 7 - step formula, to aid women in getting the job they want. Gives special advice to women seeking a job in an alternative, non - traditional, field.
Sociology
Dist - WMENIF **Prod** - WMENIF

Looking for a Job 15 MIN
U-matic
Job Skills Series
(H C A)
Deals with where and how to search for employment. Includes information on resumes and applications.
Business and Economics; Guidance and Counseling; Science - Physical
Dist - ACCESS **Prod** - ACCESS 1982

Looking for love - teenage parents
VHS / U-matic
Color (H)
Presents teenage mothers discussing their ambivalent feelings, from loving and worrying about their children to longing for lost adolescence and opportunities they might have had.
Psychology; Sociology
Dist - GA **Prod** - EDCC
CAREER
EDCC

Looking for love - teenage parents 30 MIN
U-matic / VHS
Vital link series
Color (J H C)
Presents the impact of teenage pregnancy on the young parents. Traces the choices and decisions caused by pregnancy.
Guidance and Counseling; Sociology
Dist - EDCC **Prod** - EDCC
GA
CAREER

Looking for Me 29 MIN
16mm
B&W
Investigates the therapeutic benefits of patterned movement in working with different types of students, including normal preschool children aged four and five, emotionally disturbed children, two autistic children and a group of adult teachers.
Psychology
Dist - NYU **Prod** - NYU

Looking for mushrooms 3 MIN
16mm
Color (G)
$8.00 rental
Searches for mushrooms in San Francisco and Mexico. Features music by John Lennon and special effects by Isauro Nava, Huatla De Jimenez, Mexico. Made between 1961 - 1967.
Fine Arts
Dist - CANCIN **Prod** - CONNER

Looking for Organic America 28 MIN
16mm / U-matic / VHS
Color (J)
LC 72-702204
Presents a picture of the organic farming movement in America today. Emphasizes the difference between conventional commercial farms and organic farms, and reveals the roles played by legislators, scientists, merchants and distributors in the development of organic farming.
Agriculture; Home Economics; Social Science; Sociology
Dist - BULFRG **Prod** - RPFD 1972

Looking for patterns in literature 30 MIN
VHS
Color (H C G)
$69.95 purchase _ #RWR - 24
Shows how to become skilled at perceiving patterns. Looks at the basic elements of setting, plot, theme, foreshadowing, figurative language and symbolism.
Literature and Drama
Dist - INSTRU **Prod** - FLCCJA 1991

Looking for perestroika 58 MIN
VHS / U-matic / BETA
Inside Gorbachev's USSR series
Color (H C A)
$125.00 purchase _ #JY - 6270C
Explores the promises and pitfalls of perestroika, where plans for economic reform are paralyzed by the fear of taking risks or losing power. Visits a coal mine, a state farm, a private business and the economic ministry in the Kremlin. Looks at problems of food supply and distribution and the effects of economic restructuring on the standard of living in the USSR. Part of a four - part series narrated by Hedrick Smith on the clash of modernization with Soviet tradition.
Agriculture; Business and Economics; Civics and Political Systems; Geography - World; History - World; Social Science; Sociology
Dist - CORF **Prod** - WGBHTV 1990

Looking for Santa Claus
VHS / 35mm strip
ALA Notable Children's Filmstrips Series
Color (K)
$33.00 purchase
Presents a children's story. Part of the American Library Association series.
English Language; Literature and Drama
Dist - PELLER

Looking for Series
Discovering Bridges 7 MIN
Travelling Together 7 MIN
Dist - FILMID

Looking for the Words - Teaching Functional Language Strategies 25 MIN
VHS / 16mm
Color (A)
$365.00 purchase, $55.00 rental _ #2841VHS
Shows how individuals with severe language deficiencies are able to learn functional verbal responses and language strategies.
Psychology
Dist - RESPRC **Prod** - RESPRC 1986

Looking for Yesterday 30 MIN
16mm / U-matic
Color
Illustrates why reality orientation doesn't help severely disoriented aged patients. Suggests an alternative therapy.
Health and Safety; Sociology
Dist - HRC **Prod** - OHC

The Looking Glass 28 MIN
U-matic
Color (C)
Experimental film by Juan Downey.
Fine Arts
Dist - AFA **Prod** - AFA 1981

Looking Good 19 MIN
16mm
Good Life Series
Color (S)
LC 81-700266
Uses a TV game show format to show appropriate grooming habits, including bathing, showering, brushing teeth and combing hair.
Education; Health and Safety
Dist - HUBDSC **Prod** - DUDLYN 1981

Looking Good - a Guide to Personal Grooming
VHS / 35mm strip
$119.00 purchase _ #IE6758 filmstrip, $159.00 purchase _ #IE6758V VHS
Discusses the care of the body, positive effects of body language, skin care and the treatment of acne, importance of good eating habits, sufficient sleep, regular exercise, and the maintenance of clothing.
Health and Safety
Dist - CAREER **Prod** - CAREER

Looking Good - a Guide to Personal Grooming
VHS / U-matic
Color (J H)
Discusses body language as a prelude to tips on selection and maintenance of clothing. Advises on skin care and cleanliness and stresses the importance of good eating habits, sufficient sleep and exercise, and the fact that a pleasing appearance helps develop a positive image.
Guidance and Counseling; Home Economics
Dist - GA **Prod** - GA

Looking Good on Paper
VHS / U-matic
Employability Skills Series
Color
Shows how to prepare thoroughly for and complete an employment application form which will make a favorable impression on a prospective employer.
Guidance and Counseling
Dist - CAMB **Prod** - ILCS

Looking in on Sunset 27 MIN
16mm
Color
Traces the history of Sunset Magazine from 1898 to modern times. Shows editors at work scouting and developing stories on travel, gardening, homes and food - the four subjects which set the West apart from the rest of the country.
Literature and Drama; Social Science; Sociology
Dist - MTP **Prod** - MTP

Looking Indoors 15 MIN
U-matic
Children and the Visual Arts Series
Color (PRO)
Encourages parents to interact with their children, stimulating their visual awareness and creative expression through activities indoors.
Education; Fine Arts
Dist - ACCESS **Prod** - ACCESS 1983

Looking into Things 13 MIN
U-matic / VHS / 16mm
Scientific Fact and Fun Series
Color (P I)
LC 80-700244
Tells how some common scientific instruments are used to extend the human senses. Shows how the length and mass of a fly is measured with various magnifiers and microscopes.
Mathematics; Science - Physical
Dist - JOU **Prod** - GLDWER 1979

Looking Out for Number One 52 MIN
U-matic / VHS
Color (G)
$249.00, $149.00 purchase _ #AD - 1926
Examines the ethics of our times. Looks at the increasingly unanswered plea for help of today's ever increasing poor. Interviews Jerry Rubin, Fran Lebowitz, Paul Gorman, Barbara Ehrenreich, Ramsey Clark, Ernest van den Haag and John Kenneth Galbraith.
Sociology
Dist - FOTH **Prod** - FOTH

Looking Out for Number One - the Ethics of the Eighties - 127 30 MIN
U-matic
Currents - 1984 - 85 Season Series
Color (A)
Reveals the attitudes and beliefs that are now prevelant.
Religion and Philosophy; Social Science
Dist - PBS **Prod** - WNETTV 1985

Looking Outdoors 15 MIN
U-matic
Children and the Visual Arts Series
Color (PRO)
Explores how nature provides a vast gallery of visual art.
Education; Fine Arts
Dist - ACCESS **Prod** - ACCESS 1983

Looking through 11 MIN
U-matic / VHS / BETA
Color; PAL (C G)
PdS30, PdS38 purchase
Discusses the breakdown of marriage.
Psychology; Sociology
Dist - EDPAT

Looking up 27 MIN
VHS / U-matic
Color (J H G)
$250.00, $300.00 purchase, $50.00 rental
Portrays a young man's recuperation from an automobile accident which left him paralyzed. Looks at his paraplegia and interviews him about his struggle and success in coming to terms with his condition and becoming productive after an initial period of despair. Produced by Fire Productions.
Fine Arts; Health and Safety
Dist - NDIM

Looking Up to Your Aviation Career 14 MIN
16mm
Color
LC 79-700821
Explores more than 60 career specialties in the field of aviation.
Guidance and Counseling; Industrial and Technical Education; Psychology
Dist - USNAC **Prod** - USFAA 1979

Looks - How they Affect Your Life 51 MIN
U-matic / VHS
Color (H C A)
Illustrates the social and psychological impact of fulfilling and not fulfilling the American standards of beauty.
Psychology
Dist - CORF **Prod** - GANNET

The Loom 50 MIN
16mm
Color (G)
$1461.00 purchase, $90.00 rental
Offers a multiple - superimposition hand - painted visual symphony of animal life of Earth.
Fine Arts
Dist - CANCIN **Prod** - BRAKS 1986

Loom in Essence 4 MIN
16mm
Color
LC 70-711309
A non - narrative study of a weaver at her loom.
Fine Arts
Dist - UMD **Prod** - UMD 1970

Loom Weaving 6 MIN
U-matic / VHS / 16mm
Creative Hands Series
Color (J H C)
Illustrates how to build a loom from a broom and a few pieces of wood. Shows how to thread the warp through the heddle, how to wind and use the bobbin, and the proper use of wool, cotton and other threads in making useful objects.
Fine Arts; Home Economics
Dist - IFB **Prod** - CRAF 1951

Looms of Time 45 MIN
16mm / U-matic / VHS
Color (H C A)
Reveals how a piece of silk was restored to an original piece of brocade which revealed several incidents from Chinese history.
History - World; Science - Physical
Dist - FI **Prod** - NHK 1973

The Loons 18 MIN
16mm / U-matic
Color (J H)
Tells a humorous story of six young teens who find success through the pursuit of health - conscious lifestyles. Emphasizes the importance of diet and exercise.
Health and Safety; Physical Education and Recreation; Social Science; Sociology
Dist - PEREN **Prod** - SCCL

The Loon's Necklace 11 MIN
16mm
Color (G) (FRENCH)
#4X7
Presents an Indian legend which explains the white band around the looon's neck.
Social Science
Dist - CDIAND **Prod** - IMO 1948

Loons of Amisk 15 MIN
16mm / U-matic / VHS
Animals and Plants of North America Series
Color (J)
LC 80-701736
Describes the habitats, nesting and feeding of the common loon.
Science - Natural
Dist - LCOA **Prod** - KARVF 1980

Loons, swans, geese, ducks, hawks - Volume 1 60 MIN
VHS
Audubon society videoguides to the birds of North America series
Color (G)
$29.95 purchase
Combines live footage and color photography in an Audubon Society bird watching program. Focuses on loons, swans, geese, ducks, hawks, and several other bird types. Uses bird sights and sounds, visual graphics, and maps to aid in the identification of bird types. Narrated by Michael Godfrey.
Science - Natural
Dist - PBS **Prod** - WNETTV

Loony Tom 11 MIN
16mm
B&W (G)
$15.00 rental
Presents the adventures of a slightly demented tramp cavorting through the world to make love to all the women he meets.
Fine Arts
Dist - CANCIN **Prod** - BROUGH 1951

The Loop 14 MIN
16mm
Intermediate Acrobatics Series Part 1
B&W
LC FIE52-1006
Instructs in the procedure of making the loop and the precautions to take before leaving the ground.
Industrial and Technical Education
Dist - USNAC **Prod** - USN 1943

Loopholes 30 MIN
VHS / U-matic
Money Puzzle - the World of Macroeconomics Series Module 4
Color
Takes a broad view of our taxation system. Illustrates to the viewer that though far from perfect the system contains mechanisms which serve as investment incentives.
Business and Economics; Sociology
Dist - MDCC **Prod** - MDCC

Loopings 16 MIN
U-matic / VHS
Numerical Control/Computerized Numerical Control - Advanced 'Programming Series Module 2
Color (IND)
Covers aspects of a loop statement and writing a program that contains a nested loop.
Business and Economics; Industrial and Technical Education
Dist - LEIKID **Prod** - LEIKID

Loops 3 MIN
16mm / U-matic / VHS
Color (C T)
An experimental film by Norman McLaren in which sound and visuals are created entirely by drawing upon film.
Fine Arts
Dist - IFB **Prod** - NFBC 1948

Loops
U-matic / VHS
PASCAL - a Modern Programming Language Series
Color
Describes loops and nested looping. Includes commands FORDO, WHILE, DO and REPEAT UNTIL.
Industrial and Technical Education; Mathematics
Dist - EDUACT **Prod** - EDUACT

Loose bolts 29 MIN
16mm / VHS / U-matic
Color
LC 74-700465
Deals with work on assembly lines. Interviews employees at a Ford automobile plant in order to show their reactions to this well - paid but potentially dehumanizing type of work.
Industrial and Technical Education; Sociology
Dist - ROLAND **Prod** - MRMKF 1973

Loose ends 25 MIN
VHS / 16mm
B&W (G)
$45.00 rental, $50.00 purchase
Looks at the process of internalizing the information that bombards the human race through a combination of personal experience and media in all forms and leads humanity to a state of psychological entropy and uniform inertness.
Fine Arts; Psychology
Dist - CANCIN **Prod** - STRANC 1979

Loose Ends 108 MIN
16mm
B&W
Focuses on two buddies with a terminal case of blue - collar blues.
Fine Arts
Dist - TWYMAN **Prod** - UNKNWN 1975

Loose ends - aging and losing control 100 MIN
VHS
Color (G)
$149.00 purchase, $75.00 rental _ #UW5361
Presents a view of the inside of an institution for the demented elderly. Films two months of living with a group of patients. Demands that the viewer confront personal fears of aging and losing control, accept the five main characters on their own terms, expand the sense of what is recognizably warm and human to encompass the often frightening world of these patients.
Health and Safety; Psychology
Dist - FOTH

Loose Forming 19 MIN
U-matic
Carpentry Apprenticeship Series
(H)
Identifies the main techniques and applications of loose forming which is the simplest type of formwork erected to fit special job requirements on site.
Industrial and Technical Education
Dist - ACCESS **Prod** - ACCESS 1983

A Loose Screw 29 MIN
Videoreel / VT2
Koltanowski on Chess Series
Color
Physical Education and Recreation
Dist - PBS **Prod** - KQEDTV

Loosening the Grip Series
Ain't goin' away 30 MIN
Alcohol and the body 30 MIN
Alcoholics anonymous 30 MIN
The End, the Beginning 30 MIN
The Experts on the causes 30 MIN
A Family matter 30 MIN
Louder than Words 30 MIN
An Ounce of Prevention 30 MIN
Picking Up the Tab 30 MIN
Special Treatment 30 MIN
Dist - GPN

Loot - the plundered heritage 29 MIN
U-matic / VHS
Color (H C)
$250.00 purchase _ #HP - 6316C
Documents the problems involved in preventing the destruction of the cultural history of Latin America. Surveys the battle of governments, museums, archaeologists and collectors over the artifacts of great pre - Columbian civilizations. Questions the competition between looters and archaeologists, the ways in which museums obtain historical objects and how art dealers and private collectors indirectly encourage looters and thieves.
Civics and Political Systems; Fine Arts; History - World; Sociology
Dist - CORF **Prod** - PFP 1990

Lope De Vega - Fuenteovejuna 142 MIN
U-matic / VHS
Color (SPANISH)
Offers an adaptation of Lope De Vega's play Fuenteovejuna.
Foreign Language; Literature and Drama
Dist - FOTH **Prod** - FOTH 1984

The Lopsided wheel 30 MIN
U-matic / VHS / 16mm
Life around us series
Color (J) (SPANISH)
Illustrates the development of the wheel, from its invention to its use in computer machinery. Highlights the problems created by wheels in the United States and other industrialized nations where there are too many, and in underdeveloped nations where there are not enough.
Social Science; Sociology
Dist - TIMLIF **Prod** - TIMLIF 1971

Lopsideland 5 MIN
U-matic / VHS / 16mm
Magic Moments, Unit 3 - Let's See Series
Color (K P I)
LC 70-705930
Shows children the way the world would look upside - down. Explains how to look at things from a different perspective.
English Language
Dist - EBEC **Prod** - EBEC 1969

L'Or Bleu Du Quebec 11 MIN
16mm
Color (FRENCH)
A French - language film which looks at the St Lawrence River and its many ports, each with its own personality. Shows that the river is one of the major reasons Quebec finds itself at the center of world commerce.
Foreign Language; Geography - World
Dist - MTP **Prod** - QDTFG

Loran C, a navigator's approach
VHS
Color (G A)
$39.80 purchase _ #0220
Discusses the role of Loran C. Explains its use and shows how, from antenna placement to waypoint programming.
Physical Education and Recreation; Social Science
Dist - SEVVID **Prod** - SEVVID

Loran operation guide series
Apelco 6100 - 6600
Apelco 6300
Apelco DXL 6500
II Morrow Tigershark
Impulse
Interphase
King 8008
LOG - Apelco DXL 6000
LOG - Furuno LC 90
LOG - King 8001
LOG - RayNav 550
LOG - RayNav 570
LOG - Si - Tex 787C
LOG - Si - Tex 797
LOG - Si - Tex EZ7
Lowrance LMS 200
Micrologic - Explorer
Micrologic - Voyager
Micrologic 7500 - 8000
North Star 800 and 800X
RayJeff L 100
RayNav 580
Searanger
Dist - SEVVID

Lorang's Way 69 MIN
U-matic / VHS / 16mm
Turkana Conversations Trilogy Series
Color (TURKANA (ENGLISH SUBTITLES))
Offers a multifaceted portrait of Lorang, the head of a Turkana tribal homestead. Shows that Lorang has seen the outside world and thinks his tribe's traditions will be affected by it. Presented in Turkana with English subtitles.
Foreign Language; History - World
Dist - UCEMC **Prod** - MCDGAL 1980

The Lorax 25 MIN
16mm / U-matic / VHS
Dr Seuss Series
Color (P I J)
LC 72-701659
Introduces the Dr Seuss character known as the Lorax in a fanciful tale with a serious theme - clean up the environment before it's too late.
Literature and Drama; Science - Natural
Dist - PHENIX **Prod** - CBSTV 1972

Lorca - a Murder in Granada 55 MIN
U-matic / VHS
Color (C) (SPANISH (ENGLISH NARRATION))
$299.00, $199.00 purchase _ #AD - 142
Presents a film autobiography of Garcia Lorca, containing family memorabilia, his drawings and paintings, and the only only remaining footage of the poet himself. Spanish with English narration.
Biography; Fine Arts; Foreign Language; Literature and Drama
Dist - FOTH **Prod** - FOTH

Lord and Father 45 MIN
16mm
Color (J)
LC 83-700635
Examines the intrafamily tension between a father who defends the cultivation of tobacco as a way of life and his son who questions both the justification of tobacco as a commercial good and the social system of share - crop tenancy used to cultivate it.
Agriculture; Sociology
Dist - APPAL **Prod** - APPAL 1983

Lord Durham 28 MIN
16mm
B&W (G)
_ #106B 0161 052
Explains when Durham opened the way for self government in Canada he closed the door on his own political success, but the policies he declared for Canada became the pattern for self rule in all the rest of the Commonwealth.
Biography; History - World
Dist - CFLMDC **Prod** - NFBC 1961

Lord Elgin and some Stones of no Value 58 MIN
VHS
Color (S)
$79.00 purchase _ #169 - 9001
Reconstructs the thievery of the British ambassador Lord Elgin who stripped the 'Elgin marbles' from the Parthenon in Greece and took them to Britain in the early 1800s. Reveals that today, despite a widespread call for their repatriation, the frieze and sculptures are still housed in the British Museum.
History - World; Sociology
Dist - FI **Prod** - CFTV 1987

Lord Hanson 32 MIN
VHS / 16mm
Take it from the Top Series
Color (A PRO)
$295.00 purchase
Features Lord Hanson, the founder of the Hanson Company, who discusses the success of his company and how he achieved that success. Part of a series featuring David Frost who interviews successful English businessmen.
Business and Economics; Geography - World; Guidance and Counseling; Psychology; Sociology
Dist - VIDART **Prod** - VIDART 1991

The Lord is My Shepherd 5 MIN
16mm
Song of the Ages Series
B&W (P I J)
LC 70-702124
Presents a modern interpretation of Psalm 22 using animated figures drawn on a blackboard.
Religion and Philosophy
Dist - FAMLYT **Prod** - FAMLYT 1964

The Lord is my shepherd - the 23rd Psalm for today 5 MIN
VHS
Color (J H G)
$89.00 purchase
Quotes the words of Psalm 23 of the Bible in a voiceover while picturing the misuse and destruction of natural resources across the world.
Religion and Philosophy
Dist - LANDMK

The Lord is Risen 15 MIN
16mm
Living Bible Series
Color; B&W (I)
Pictures the events of the resurrection, the placing of the special guard at the tomb, the rolling away of the stone, the discovery by the three women, Peter and John at the tomb, the two women and Jesus' appearance to Mary.
Religion and Philosophy
Dist - FAMF **Prod** - FAMF

Lord Jim
VHS
Color (G)
$59.90 purchase _ #0248
Adapts the novel 'Lord Jim' by Joseph Conrad. Stars Peter O'Toole, James Mason, Curt Jurgens, Eli Wallach, Jack Hawkins, Paul Lukas, Akim Tamiroff and Daliah Lavi.
Fine Arts; Literature and Drama
Dist - SEVVID

Lord Jim 154 MIN
16mm
Color
Based on the novel of the same name by Joseph Conrad. Tells the story of Jim, an officer in the 19th century British merchant marine, a man with such a powerful sense of guilt that he gives his life to atone for a single act of cowardice.
Fine Arts
Dist - TIMLIF **Prod** - CPC 1964

Lord of Asia 60 MIN
VHS / U-matic
Search for Alexander the Great Series Pt 3
Color (C A)
LC 82-707382
Shows Alexander the Great at the peak of his power as he becomes the ruler of Asia, subdues his longtime foe and overtakes Babylon and Persepolis. Reveals that although he marries, he soon returns to his first love - conquering the world.
Biography; History - World
Dist - TIMLIF **Prod** - TIMLIF 1981

Lord of the Air - Pt 17 30 MIN
16mm
Life on Earth series; Vol V
Color (J)
$495.00 purchase _ #865 - 9038
Blends scientific data with breathtaking wildlife photography to tell the story of the development of life. Features wildlife expert David Attenborough as host. Part 17 of 27 parts is entitled 'Lord Of The Air,' and chronicles the mastery of birds in the above ground realm.
Science; Science - Natural; Science - Physical
Dist - FI **Prod** - BBCTV 1981

Lord of the dance - destroyer of illusion 113 MIN
VHS
Color (G)
$59.00 purchase _ #FRLD
Focuses on Garwang Tojay Chenpo, a form of the deity Chenrezi, the Lord of the Dance. Visits Mani Rimdu, the major religious festival of the Everest regions where, during three weeks of ancient and secret ceremonies, the monks of Thubten Choling and Chiwong become Lord of the Dance - and with the compasion and power of gods, undertake heroic tasks. Produced by Richard Kohn.
Geography - World; Religion and Philosophy
Dist - SNOWLI FIRS **Prod** - SNOWLI 1985

Lord of the flies 90 MIN
VHS
B&W (G)
$29.95 purchase _ #LOR010; $69.00 purchase _ #05725 - 126; LC 71-707615
Brings the macabre novel by William Golding to the screen. Portrays a group of British schoolboys stranded on a remote and desolate island who try to organize themselves into a law - abiding society. Civilization is quickly forgotten as they descend into savagery and anarchy. Directed by Peter Brook. Digitally remastered.
Civics and Political Systems; Fine Arts; Guidance and Counseling; Psychology; Sociology
Dist - HOMVIS GA KITPAR **Prod** - JANUS HODGAP 1963

Lord of the Jungle 69 MIN
16mm
Bomba, the Jungle Boy Series
B&W (I)
Fine Arts; Literature and Drama
Dist - CINEWO **Prod** - CINEWO 1955

Lord of the North - Alexander Mackenzie 37 MIN
16mm
Color (G)
#3X931
Follows explorer Mackenzie in his search for the North passage where he encounters the Slave and Dogrib Indians, and ultimately travels to the Arctic Ocean.
Geography - World; History - World
Dist - CDIAND **Prod** - NFBC 1950

The Lord of the rings 133 MIN
VHS
Color (G)
$29.95 purchase _ #S00520
Presents an animated account of J R R Tolkien's fantasy trilogy, The Lord of the Rings. Features the voices of Christopher Guard, William Squire, John Hurt and more. Directed by Ralph Bakshi.
Literature and Drama
Dist - UILL

The Lord Passion - Misterium jeki Panskiej 40 MIN
VHS
Color (G A) (POLISH)
$24.95 purchase _ #V304, #V289
Shows the Passion of our Lord Jesus Christ achieved by the Franciscan Brothers. Depicts the last days of our Lord on Earth. Also available with Polish narration.
Fine Arts; History - World
Dist - POLART

Lord, why me 30 MIN
VHS
Color (H C G A R)
$29.95 purchase, $10.00 rental _ #35 - 845 - 8516
Interviews the Reverend Colonel Bill Rittenhouse on his faith and life adventures. Hosted by Peter White.
Literature and Drama; Religion and Philosophy
Dist - APH **Prod** - VISVID

The Lord's Ascension 15 MIN
16mm
Living Bible Series
Color; B&W (I)
Shows the appearances Jesus made on earth after His Crucifixion. Includes Jesus walking with the two on the road to Emmaus, appearing to the disciples, later again appearing before the disciples when Thomas was present, meeting the disciples at the Sea of Galilee, his appearance on the Mount of Olives and his Ascension to His Father.
Religion and Philosophy
Dist - FAMF **Prod** - FAMF

The Lords of Flatbush 85 MIN
16mm
Color
Presents a comedy about growing up in lower middle - class Brooklyn in the 1950's. Stars Sylvester Stallone and Henry Winkler.
Fine Arts
Dist - TWYMAN **Prod** - CPC 1974

Lords of the air 58 MIN
U-matic / VHS
Life on Earth series; Program 8
Color (J)
LC 82-706680
Describes the evolution of bird feathers as well as territorial behavior, courtship display, navigation and migration. Speculates on the extinction of the dinosaurs and why birds failed to inherit the earth.
Science - Natural
Dist - FI **Prod** - BBCTV 1981

Lords of the bush - Kenya - Part 18 8 MIN
VHS
Natures kingdom series
Color (P I J)
$125.00 purchase
Reveals that the Kenyan elephant, much reduced in numbers, consumes 300 pounds of food a day. Shows that they are matriarchal, that althogh elephants are very strong, they are very gentle. Part of a 26 - part series on animals showing the habitats and traits of various species.
Geography - World; Science - Natural
Dist - LANDMK **Prod** - LANDMK 1992

Lords of the Forest 29 MIN
VHS / U-matic
Journey into Thailand Series
Color (J S C A)
MV=$195.00
Shows Thailand's teak forests where elephants are still used commercially. Also shown is an Elephant Festival and a tug - of - war between one elephant and 150 soldiers.
Geography - World; History - World
Dist - LANDMK **Prod** - LANDMK 1986

Lords of the Forest
16mm
Color (J)
Shows animal life and ethnology of the Congo.
Science - Natural; Sociology
Dist - TWCF **Prod** - TWCF

The Lords of the Labyrinth 54 MIN
U-matic / VHS / 16mm
Color (H C A)
Visits the ruins of the city of Chan Chan in Peru which was once the greatest city in the Americas. Looks at the massive pyramids, huge courtyards, maze - like passages and thousands of cell - like buildings huddled inside walled compounds.
History - World
Dist - FI **Prod** - BBCTV 1976

Lords of the prairie - Venezuela - Part 24 8 MIN
VHS
Natures kingdom series
Color (P I J)
$125.00 purchase
Reveals that capybara are the largest rodents, reaching three feet in length and weighting more than 100 pounds. Shows how they cool themselves in water and guard against crocodiles by circling their young. Part of a 26 - part series on animals showing the habitats and traits of various species.
Geography - World; Science - Natural
Dist - LANDMK **Prod** - LANDMK 1992

Lords of the Sea 26 MIN
16mm / U-matic / VHS
Color (H C A)
Looks at the shark's nature and abilities.
Science - Natural
Dist - CORF **Prod** - CTV

The Lord's Prayer 27 MIN
16mm
Color (H C A)
Combines music and panoramic views of nature with the narration of Ralph W Sockman to interpret the Lord's Prayer. Filmed in Sequoia and King's Canyon National Parks.
Religion and Philosophy
Dist - CCNCC **Prod** - CCNCC

A Lorelie Called Sleep
U-matic / VHS
Driving Safety Series
Color (IND)
Looks at sleep while driving, how sleep - related accidents are a major cause of serious accidents, and what to do if you become drowsy while driving.
Health and Safety; Industrial and Technical Education
Dist - GPCV **Prod** - DCC

Loren Maciver, Pt 1 23 MIN
16mm
Color
Presents paintings by an American comtemporary painter, Loren Maciver. Reveals the transposition of objects, movement and color in city and country.
Fine Arts
Dist - RADIM **Prod** - FILIM

Loren Maciver, Pt 2 23 MIN
16mm
Color
Presents paintings by an American comtemporary painter, Loren Maciver. Reveals the transposition of objects, movement and color in city and country.
Fine Arts
Dist - RADIM **Prod** - FILIM

Lorenzo Ghiberti - the gates of paradise 30 MIN
VHS
Trecanni video library series
Color (G)
$29.95 purchase
Studies the cast bronze doors to the Florentine baptistery created by Lorenzo Ghiberti. Studies the building in relationship to other buildings in Florence. Part of a four - part series on Italian culture produced by Treccani Publishers and RAI, Italian broadcast network.
Fine Arts; History - World
Dist - CREPRI

Lorenzo Ghiberti - The Gates of Paradise 30 MIN
VHS
Treccani Italian Renaissance art series
Color (H C A)
$29.95 purchase
Presents the Florentine baptistry produced by Lorenzo Ghiberti. Examines the links between Gothic and Renaissance traditions exhibited in the work.
Fine Arts; History - World; Industrial and Technical Education
Dist - ARTSAM

Loretta Abbott and Al Perryman 30 MIN
U-matic / VHS
Eye on Dance - Partners in Dance Series
Color
Fine Arts
Dist - ARCVID **Prod** - ARCVID

Lori and Mike - Birth 2
VHS / U-matic
Video birth library series
Color (J H G)
$100.00 purchase
Follows the childbirth experiences of Lori and Mike in their first pregnancy. Reveals that they choose to have their baby in a hospital setting with a midwife and minimal medical intervention. During a difficult night of back labor, Mike rubs Lori's back while she showers for relaxation. Using a variety of laboring positions, she delivers a healthy baby the following morning. Part of a 15 - part series on childbirth education.
Health and Safety
Dist - POLYMR **Prod** - POLYMR

Lori - Art Therapy and Self Discovery 31 MIN
16mm
Color (PRO)
LC 78-700692
Demonstrates the use of art therapy in mental health rehabilitation based on a clinical case history by therapist Helen B Landgarten. Dramatizes the case of an emotionally disturbed 15 - year - old girl whose art therapy sessions help her emerge from depression and regain contact with herself and the world around her.
Health and Safety; Psychology
Dist - FILCOA **Prod** - FILCOA 1978

Lori Callies - 11 - 14 - 85 80 MIN
VHS / Cassette
Poetry Center reading series
Color (G)
$15.00 purchase, rental _ #673 - 555
Features the poet performing in a reading to benefit the San Francisco AIDS Foundation at the Poetry Center, San Francisco State University.
Health and Safety; Literature and Drama
Dist - POETRY **Prod** - POETRY 1985

Lori's story 30 MIN
VHS
Labours of Eve series
Color; PAL (A)
PdS50 purchase; Not available in the United States or Canada
Presents the story of Lori, a woman who agreed to act as a surrogate mother for her sister. Observes Lori as she talks about her feeling of isolation; her sister's lack of understanding; and the family pressures upon her to give up the child at birth. Nicky Singer narrates the series as it addresses issues of conception and pregnancy. Part four of a six - part series.
Health and Safety
Dist - BBCENE

Lorna Dee Cervantes - 4 - 24 - 85 34 MIN
VHS / Cassette
Poetry Center reading series
Color (G)
$15.00, $45.00 purchase, $15.00 rental _ #652 - 540
Features the Chicana writer at the Poetry Center at San Francisco State University, reciting her work Letter to David, a long poem consisting of letters to David Kennedy, son of John F Kennedy, with an introduction by Frances Mayes.
Literature and Drama
Dist - POETRY **Prod** - POETRY 1985

Lorna Dee Cervantes - 10 - 24 - 80 16 MIN
VHS / Cassette
Poetry Center reading series
Color (G)
#911 - 344
Features the Chicana writer reciting her works and five poems by Pancho Aguila during the Rebound Project reading at the Poetry Center, San Francisco State University. Available only for listening purposes at the Center; not for sale or rent.
Literature and Drama
Dist - POETRY **Prod** - POETRY 1980

Lorraine Hansberry - the Black Experience in the Creation of Drama 35 MIN
16mm / U-matic / VHS
Color (J)
LC 75-702526
Traces the artistic growth and vision of the black playwright Lorraine Hansberry, largely in her own words and in her own voice. Describes the author's childhood in Chicago, student days at the University of Wisconsin, work as a journalist in Harlem, life as a housewife in Greenwich Village and success on Broadway.
History - United States; Literature and Drama
Dist - FOTH **Prod** - MANTLH 1975

Lorraine, Pays Du Fer 11 MIN
16mm
Aspects De France Series
Color (H C) (FRENCH)
A French language film. Presents a close - up of a middle class Lorraine family.
Foreign Language
Dist - MLA **Prod** - WSUM 1966

Lorri 14 MIN
VHS / 16mm
Recovery Series
(G)
$50/3 Day VHS/3/4
Presents Lorri, a lesbian and recovering alcoholic, who has still not forgotten how out of control and sick she was before she sought help to overcome her addiction. Shows how after five years of sobriety, it still takes constant courage to live her life proudly.
Health and Safety; Sociology
Dist - BAXMED **Prod** - NFBC 1989

Lorry driver 10 MIN
VHS
Stop, look, listen series
Color; PAL (P I J)
Looks at a day in the life of a truck driver. Shows how he breakfasts before daylight, drives his truck to Newport Docks to deliver mine roof supports for export. On the way he stops for meals in roadside cafes. Watches the roof supports being loaded on the boat by a crane. Part of a series of films which start from some everyday observation and show more of what is happening, how and why. Builds vocabulary and encourages children to be more observant.
English Language; Social Science
Dist - VIEWTH

Los Alamos Computing Network 24 MIN
16mm
Color
LC 82-700062
Uses layman's terms to describe the Los Alamos Computing Network which deals with scientific calculations.
Business and Economics; Mathematics
Dist - LASL **Prod** - LASL 1982

Los Angeles 3 MIN
16mm
Of all Things Series
Color (P I)
Discusses the city of Los Angeles, California.
Geography - United States
Dist - AVED **Prod** - BAILYL

Los Angeles - the Making of a City 26 MIN
U-matic / VHS
Color (G)
$249.00, $149.00 purchase _ #AD - 1949
Traces the history and the diverse cultural and ethnic roots of the city of Los Angeles, California. Shows the elements that comprise both the myth and the reality of what will soon be America's most populous city, 'Angel City.'.
Geography - United States; Geography - World; History - United States; Sociology
Dist - FOTH **Prod** - FOTH

Los Angeles - the story of tent city 50 MIN
VHS
Color (H C G)
$195.00 purchase, $35.00 rental _ #37874
Looks at the lives and struggles of homeless people who been moved to an 'urban campground' in downtown Los Angeles. Focuses on a young street flower - seller, a likeable Vietnam veteran and his wife, a young mother of five who aspires to a singing career - while homeless leaders and city officials attempt to deal with the problem of homelessness before the campground must close. Directed by Tom Seidman.
Geography - United States; History - United States; Sociology
Dist - UCEMC

Los Animales - the Animals 15 MIN
U-matic / VHS
Saludos
(P I G) (ENGLISH AND SPANISH)
$130 purchase, $25 rental, $75 self dub
Designed to introduce Spanish to the English speaking student at primary through intermediate levels. Fourteenth in a 25 part series.
Foreign Language
Dist - GPN

Los Animales - Volume 2 30 MIN
VHS
Look, listen and learn - Spanish club series
Color (K P)
$19.95 purchase
Explores the world of animals in song, including a new version of The Three Little Pigs, and takes a trip to a farm and zoo. Features Jennifer Reyes and a diverse group of children who sing Latin American folk songs. Part of a series.
Foreign Language; Science - Natural
Dist - PEAPOD **Prod** - PEAPOD 1992

Los axiomas en el algebra 13 MIN
U-matic / VHS / 16mm
Color (J H) (SPANISH)
A Spanish - language version of the motion picture Axioms In Algebra. Defines an axiom as a statement accepted as true without proof. Shows how addition, subtraction,

multiplication and division axioms are applied to solving practical problems and how the root of each equation is used to check the solution.
Mathematics
Dist - IFB **Prod** - VEF 1960

Los Campesinos 60 MIN
VHS / U-matic
Bill Moyers' Journal Series
Color
Presents a look at Mexican farmers.
Agriculture; Geography - World; Sociology
Dist - PBS **Prod** - WNETTV 1975

Los Cinco Hermanos Chinos 10 MIN
16mm / U-matic / VHS
Color (SPANISH)
LC 73-702765
A Spanish version of the 'THE FIVE CHINESE BROTHERS.' Tells the story of five Chinese brothers who elude execution by virtue of their extraordinary individual qualities.
Foreign Language; Literature and Drama
Dist - WWS **Prod** - WWS 1960

Los Colones Ingles 52 MIN
U-matic / VHS
Espana Estuvo Alli Series
Color (C) (SPANISH)
$249.00, $149.00 purchase _ #AD - 1026
Looks at English expeditions to North America, the arrival of English, Dutch and French immigrants, Tierra de Ayllon and Tierra de Garay become Virginia, Maryland and Maine. In Spanish.
Geography - World; History - United States; History - World
Dist - FOTH **Prod** - FOTH

Los Colores De Miriam - 16 15 MIN
VHS
Amigos Series
Color (K) (SPANISH)
$125.00 purchase
Enables teachers with no knowledge of Spanish to introduce basic words to children in kindergarten through second grade. Uses simple concepts and music and features Perro Pepe, a six - foot orange dog, and Senorita Fernandez as instructors. Promotes awareness of and appreciation for Hispanic culture and sparks interest in the geography of Spanish - speaking countries. Part 16 is entitled 'Los Colores De Miriam.'.
Foreign Language; Geography - World
Dist - AITECH

Los Dias De La Semana - the Days of the Week 15 MIN
VHS / U-matic
Saludos
(P I G) (ENGLISH AND SPANISH)
$130 purchase, $25 rental, $75 self dub
Designed to introduce Spanish to the English speaking student at primary through intermediate levels. Thirteenth in a 25 part series.
Foreign Language
Dist - GPN

Los Espanoles En La Costa Atlantica Antes De 1607 54 MIN
U-matic / VHS
Espana Estuvo Alli Series
Color (C) (SPANISH)
$249.00, $149.00 purchase _ #AD - 1022
Covers the first black slaves in Bermuda, settlement of the Caribbean Islands, settlements in the Carolinas, Spaniards in America before Jamestown and Plymouth. In Spanish.
Geography - United States; Geography - World; History - World; Sociology
Dist - FOTH **Prod** - FOTH

Los Espanoles En La Costa Del Pacifico Antes De 1607 55 MIN
U-matic / VHS
Espana Estuvo Alli Series
Color (C) (SPANISH)
$249.00, $149.00 purchase _ #AD - 1024
Looks at the Spanish exploration of the US Pacific coast, the Spanish presence in California, the voyage of Juan de Fuca, the viceroy system. In Spanish.
Civics and Political Systems; Geography - World; History - United States; History - World
Dist - FOTH **Prod** - FOTH

Los Estados De La Materia 18 MIN
16mm / U-matic / VHS
Physical Science (Spanish Series
Color (H C A) (SPANISH)
A Spanish language version of The States Of Matter. Examines the characteristics of the states of matter and the atomic and molecular movements within solids, liquids and gases.
Foreign Language; Science - Physical
Dist - MGHT **Prod** - LOGANL 1978

Los Four 22 MIN
16mm
Color (J)
LC 79-700694
Presents the work of artists Frank Romero, Carlos Almaraz, Beto De La Rocha and Gilbert Sanchez Lujan and examines how the Mexican - American culture is embodied in their work. Follows their preparations for the first major exhibit of Chicano art in the United States.
Fine Arts; Sociology
Dist - IA **Prod** - LAC 1975

Los Fresnos Detention Center 17 MIN
U-matic
Color (J H A)
LC 82-707077
Shows the Immigration and Naturalization Service's detention facility at Los Fresnos, Texas, where illegal immigrants are held. Includes interviews with officials and detainees and tells what happens there. Discusses the increasing problem of illegal aliens from Latin America.
Civics and Political Systems; History - United States; Sociology
Dist - SWINS **Prod** - SWINS 1982

Los Gallos combativos 29 MIN
VHS / 16mm
Watch your mouth series
Color (H)
$46.00 rental _ #WAYM - 107
Emphasizes language and communication skills for high school students. Notes the difference between formal and informal word usage.
Education; English Language; Psychology; Social Science
Dist - PBS

Los Gamines - Colombia 28 MIN
16mm
Color
Tells the story of Father Xavier, a missionary working in with the street children of Bogota, Colombia. Shows how he converts them from thieving scavengers into hard - working, law - abiding citizens.
History - World; Religion and Philosophy; Sociology
Dist - MTP **Prod** - SCC

Los Habladores 17 MIN
U-matic / VHS / 16mm
El teatro classico
Color (H C) (SPANISH)
LC FIA68-1610
Dramatizes Cervantes' comedy about a talkative man who is invited to the home of another to break his wife of the same habit. Use in fourth year Spanish class or above.
Foreign Language
Dist - EBEC **Prod** - EBEC 1966

Los Indios 25 MIN
16mm
Eye of the Beholder Series
Color
LC 75-701472
Examines a group of South American Indians who are having difficulties in coping with modernization.
Social Science; Sociology
Dist - VIACOM **Prod** - RCPDF 1972

Los Mamiferos Vivientes 17 MIN
16mm / U-matic / VHS
Color (H C) (SPANISH)
Spanish version of The Living Mammal. Shows the characteristics held in common by all mammals and illustrates various ways in which they are adapted to live and struggle in different environments.
Foreign Language; Science - Natural
Dist - IFB **Prod** - IFB 1961

Los Mineros 60 MIN
VHS
Color; CC (G) (ENGLISH W/SPANISH VOICEOVER & ENG CC ENGLISH WITH CLOSED CAPTIONS)
Meshes archival footage, letters and personal testimony to retell the battle of the Mexican - American miners to form a union. Traces the history of copper mining in Arizona at the turn of the century where Latinos were delegated more dangerous tasks and earned less money than Anglo miners. Looks at the 1903 organized strike; 1931 deportation of the workers back to Mexico; recovery of the mines in the 1930s; and the formation of the Mexican Union during WWII. Produced by Hector Galan for PBS' American Experience.
Fine Arts; Social Science; Sociology
Dist - PBS **Prod** - PBS 1990

Los Nietos Kindergarten - a Camera Visit 25 MIN
16mm
B&W
Describes a Head Start - like program for disadvantaged children operated by a special public school kindergarten for Mexican - American children. Follows the children's unrehearsed activities while the director of the program is being interviewed.
Education; Psychology; Sociology
Dist - NYU **Prod** - VASSAR 1965

Los ninos abandonados - The Abandoned children 63 MIN
VHS
Color (G) (SPANISH WITH ENGLISH SUBTITLES)
$100.00 rental, $59.00 purchase
Looks at the harsh lives of street children in Colombia, South America, who form a class of untouchables becoming virtually invisible to the prosperous - even when they're asleep on city sidewalks. Documents the carefree and reasonably healthy boys and the girls who end up in brothels. A Danny Lyon production.
Fine Arts; Geography - World; Sociology
Dist - CANCIN

Los ninos cantan alabazas 25 MIN
VHS
Color (P I R) (SPANISH)
$12.88 purchase _ #35 - 85162 - 444
Features children at play while singing praise songs in Spanish. Includes such songs as 'Do Lord,' 'I've Got the Joy,' 'He's Got the Whole World in His Hands,' and others. Bilingual audiocassette and music book available at extra charge.
Fine Arts; Psychology; Religion and Philosophy
Dist - APH

Los Novios 29 MIN
VHS / 16mm
Que Pasa, U S A Series
Color (G)
$46.00 rental _ #QUEP - 118
Social Science; Sociology
Dist - PBS **Prod** - WPBTTV

Los Olmecs 56 MIN
U-matic / VHS
Color (C) (SPANISH)
$279.00, $179.00 purchase _ #AD - 2177
Focuses on the Olmecs, pre - Columbians who rose to power on the coast of the Gulf of Mexico. Looks at their highly developed culture and the architecture and sculpture which still stand.
Foreign Language; Geography - World; History - World; Social Science; Sociology
Dist - FOTH **Prod** - FOTH

Los Peregrinos modernos - give me your poor 20 MIN
VHS
We are one series
(I)
$45 purchase
Traces the Martinez family from its Latin American homeland to the United States. Focuses on problems with money and adjustment to using social programs. Sixth of an eight part series.
Sociology
Dist - GPN **Prod** - NCGE

Los Peregrinos modernos - give me your tired 20 MIN
VHS
We are one series
(I)
$45 purchase
Traces the Martinez family from its Latin American homeland to the United States. Focuses on problems when Mr. Martinez is injured at work. Seventh of an eight part series.
Sociology
Dist - GPN **Prod** - NCGE

Los Peregrinos modernos - I lift my lamp beside the golden door 20 MIN
VHS
We are one series
(I) (LATIN)
$45 purchase
Traces the Martinez family from its homeland in Latin America to the United States. Focuses on further cultural and personal adjustments the family makes. Eighth in an eight part series.
Sociology
Dist - GPN **Prod** - NCGE

Los Peregrinos modernos - send these to me 20 MIN
VHS
We are one series
(I)
$45
Traces the Martinez family from its Latin American homeland to the United States. Focuses on cultural differences highlighted by work and family issues. Fifth of an eight part series.
Sociology
Dist - GPN **Prod** - NCGE

Los Peregrinos modernos - the homeless 20 MIN
VHS
We are one series
(I)
$45 purchase
Traces the Martinez family from its native Latin America to the United States. Focuses on the death of a family member as a result of war, the political troubles and strengths of the homeland, and the family's flight. First of an eight part series.
Sociology
Dist - GPN **Prod** - NCGE

Los Peregrinos modernos - the huddled masses 20 MIN
VHS
We are one series
(I)
$45
Traces the Martinez family from its Latin American homeland to the United States. Focuses on their arrival in the strange new country. Third in an eight part series.
Sociology
Dist - GPN **Prod** - NCGE

Los Peregrinos Modernos - the Modern Pioneers Series

Give me your poor	15 MIN
Give me your tired	15 MIN
The Homeless	15 MIN
The Huddled Masses	15 MIN
I Lift My Lamp Beside the Golden Door	15 MIN
Send these to Me	15 MIN
The Wretched Refuse	15 MIN
Yearning to breathe free	15 MIN

Dist - GPN

Los Peregrinos modernos - the wretched refuse 20 MIN
VHS
We are one series
(I)
$45
Traces the Martinez family from its native Latin American homeland to the United States. Focuses on plans for the journey and church sponsorship. Second of an eight part series.
Sociology
Dist - GPN **Prod** - NCGE

Los Peregrinos modernos - yearning to breathe free 20 MIN
VHS
We are one series
(I)
$45 purchase
Traces the Martinez family from its Latin American homeland to the United States. Focuses on language and cultural issues brought out by new jobs. Fourth of an eight part series.
Sociology
Dist - GPN **Prod** - NCGE

Los Pinateros 16.5 MIN
U-matic / VHS / 16mm
Beginning Spanish Series
Color (J H) (SPANISH)
$390, $275, $305 _ #A531S
A Spanish language film which discusses the lifestyle and culture of a traditional Mexican family who have immigrated to the United States. Presents a look at the Mexican American experience.
Foreign Language; Geography - World; Guidance and Counseling; Psychology; Sociology
Dist - BARR **Prod** - BARR 1988

Los Que Dan Carino 23 MIN
U-matic / VHS / 16mm
B&W (C A) (SPANISH)
LC 75-707249
Depicts a typical family home as parents share work and play with the children and shows them at a family picnic where everyone has a chance to help, to be needed, to do something new and to be part of an exciting outing.
Foreign Language; Guidance and Counseling; Psychology
Dist - IFB **Prod** - MHFB 1963

Los Refugiados - The Refugees 27 MIN
VHS
Color (G) (ENGLISH & SPANISH W/ENG VOICEOVER)
Documents the reality of Salvadoran refugees living on Long Island. Describes the conditions that compelled them to leave their homeland. Fleeing the civil war in their country, 500,00 refugees escaped the death squads of El Salvador's military regime and made their way to the United States, where they are exploited by unscrupulous employers and live in constant fear of deportation. Videomakers Michael Ach and Mark Brady have worked closely with Salvadoran refugees and religious organizations that offer health, housing and educational support.
Business and Economics; Fine Arts; Sociology
Dist - ACH **Prod** - ACH 1986

Los Regalos - the Presents 15 MIN
VHS / U-matic
Saludos
(P I G) (ENGLISH AND SPANISH)
$130 purchase, $25 rental, $75 self dub
Introduces Spanish to the English speaking student at primary through intermediate levels. Seventh in a 25 part series.
Foreign Language
Dist - GPN

Los Salvajes 83 MIN
16mm
B&W (A) (SPANISH)
Reveals how a young girl is forced to marry a man of violent and brutal character and traces the problems that ensue.
Fine Arts; Foreign Language
Dist - TRANSW **Prod** - TRANSW

Los Santeros 27 MIN
16mm
Lifeways Series
Color (I)
LC 79-700660
Shows three New Mexican woodcarvers, or santeros, carving and painting their distinctive religious sculptures. Discusses their art and their heritage and shows historic examples of New Mexican carved, wooden saints.
Fine Arts; Geography - United States; Social Science; Sociology
Dist - BLUSKY **Prod** - BLUSKY 1979
ONEWST

Los Siete De La Raza 30 MIN
16mm
B&W
Presents seven Latino youths, recruiting street kids into a college Brown Studies program, who are charged with killing a plainclothesman. Explains that while they become victims of a press and police campaign to clean up the Latino community, their defense becomes the foundation of a revolutionary community organization.
Civics and Political Systems; Education; Social Science; Sociology
Dist - CANWRL **Prod** - CANWRL

Los Sures 58 MIN
U-matic / VHS / 16mm
Color (A)
Focuses upon the throbbing, thriving albeit poverty - ridden area in Brooklyn known as Los Sures. Examines the life of poor Hispanics, mostly Puerto Rican, struggling to successfully integrate themselves into mainstream America. Follows activities of auto - strippers, welfare permanents, advocates of strange cults and religions as well as street musicians, break dancers and card players.
Sociology
Dist - CNEMAG **Prod** - ECHDIX 1983

Los Tejedores 28 MIN
16mm / U-matic / VHS
Lifeways Series
Color (J)
LC 79-701826
Presents traditional weaving methods of Hispanic New Mexico and shows examples of Spanish weaving from the 18th and 19th centuries.
Fine Arts; Geography - United States; Sociology
Dist - ONEWST **Prod** - BLUSKY 1980

Los Tres Osos 15 MIN
U-matic / VHS / 16mm
Color (I J H) (SPANISH)
A Spanish language version of The Three Bears. Uses simple Spanish narration to relate the story as cartoons depict the scenes. Reviews basic sentences and asks the audience to repeat them.
Foreign Language
Dist - PHENIX **Prod** - FA 1960

Los Vendidos 30 MIN
16mm
Color (H C A)
Features El Teatro Campesino, discussing the evolution of the group, presenting a one - act play and performing a musical number which summarizes the group's aspirations and life work.
Fine Arts; Foreign Language
Dist - ETCO **Prod** - KNBCTV

Lose Weight Now
VHS
Color (G)
$19.95 purchase _ #VHS103
Uses two types of hypnosis and two types of subliminal suggestions.
Health and Safety; Physical Education and Recreation; Psychology
Dist - VSPU **Prod** - VSPU

Lose Weight with Alf Fowles 60 MIN
VHS / BETA
Color
Presents a program for weight loss based on deep relaxation and visual messages directed at the subconscious.
Health and Safety; Psychology
Dist - MOHOMV **Prod** - MOHOMV

The Loser 20 MIN
16mm
Patterns Series
Color (J H C)
LC 77-701383
Edited from the motion picture The Luck Of Ginger Coffey. Tells a story about a man's job difficulties which result when he lies about abilities he does not have and refuses to accept the kind of position for which he is qualified. Focuses on the conflict that arises when people are overly optimistic, while failing to grasp reality.
Fine Arts; Guidance and Counseling
Dist - SF **Prod** - SF 1977

Loser Take all 15 MIN
U-matic / VHS / 16mm
Bloomin' Human Series
Color
LC 78-701252
Presents the dilemma of a 14 - year - old Chicano boy who must decide whether to win a bicycle race or keep his challenger from being hurt in an accident.
Fine Arts; Guidance and Counseling
Dist - MEDIAG **Prod** - PAULST 1978

The Losers 30 MIN
U-matic / VHS / 16mm
Life Around Us Series
Color (I)
Studies the horse and its relationship to man. Portrays the horse in several roles - laying the foundation for the Western movie industry, participating in racing and acting as companions to the gauchos of Argentina. Questions the current usefulness of this animal.
Science - Natural
Dist - TIMLIF **Prod** - TIMLIF 1971

The Losers 30 MIN
16mm
Life Around Us (Spanish Series
Color (SPANISH)
LC 78-700080
Explores the historical relationship between horses and humans. Shows how the horse has served humans in work, war and play, but points out that the horse's usefulness is becoming limited.
Foreign Language; Physical Education and Recreation; Science - Natural
Dist - TIMLIF **Prod** - TIMLIF 1971

Losing a baby 25 MIN
VHS
Coping series
Color; PAL (G)
PdS25 purchase
Focuses on a young couple whose second child did not survive. Shares their story to help others who are in the same situation. Part of a series on coping with illness or tragedy. Contact distributor about availability outside the United Kingdom.
Guidance and Counseling; Sociology
Dist - ACADEM

Losing - a conversation with parents 20 MIN
U-matic / VHS
Color (J H C A)
Juxtaposes anorexia nervosa and forced starvation in third world countries where food is a weapon of political subjugation. Shows parents dealing with their daughter's death from anorexia. anorexia.
Psychology; Social Science
Dist - KITCHN **Prod** - KITCHN
WMENIF WMENIF

Losing control 58 MIN
VHS
Color (H C G T A)
$95.00 purchase, $45.00 rental
Presents a scenario where the two superpowers could be led into an unintended nuclear confrontation. Suggests that the danger of accidental nuclear war has escalated in the 1980s, as nuclear alerts have increased and the practice of "launch on warning" is being implemented. Considers possible solutions. Interviews experts including Senator Sam Nunn and former Defense officials Robert McNamara and Richard Perle. Produced by Gary Krane, Ideal Communication. Hosted by Bill Kurtis.
Civics and Political Systems; History - World; Sociology
Dist - EFVP

Losing Hearts and Minds 20 MIN
U-matic / VHS
Color

$335.00 purchase
Looks at the situation in Guatemala. From the ABC TV 20 - 20 program.
Geography - World; Sociology
Dist - ABCLR **Prod** - ABCLR 1982

Losing Hurts - but not Forever 10 MIN
VHS / 35mm strip
Coping with Loss Series
Color (I P)
$35.50 filmstrip, $45.50 video _ #1244; LC 88-713610
Teaches children the necessary attitudes and comforts for surviving a loss, whether from a move, divorce or death.
Psychology
Dist - MARSH **Prod** - MARSH 1988

Losing just the same 60 MIN
U-matic / VHS / 16mm
B&W (H C A)
LC FIA67-1088
Presents the story of a Black mother and her ten children who live on welfare but who dream of a world of Cadillac prestige and middle class status. A commentary on poverty in a Black urban ghetto.
History - United States; Psychology; Sociology
Dist - IU **Prod** - NET 1966

Losing the peace 30 MIN
VHS / 16mm
World of the 30s series
Color (J)
$149.00 purchase, $75.00 rental _ #OD - 2259
Examines difficulties faced by Versailles Treaty countries, the rise and fall of the Popular Front, the Leon Blum government, and the plebiscite in the Saar. Discusses the assassination of Alexander I of Yugoslavia. The second of 13 installments of The World of the 30s Series.
History - World
Dist - FOTH

Loss and Grieving - You and Your Patient 120 MIN
VHS / U-matic
Color (PRO)
LC 81-706293
Presents a study of death, dying and grief. Includes a discussion of the rights of the dying patient and guidelines for individuals working with the patient.
Health and Safety; Sociology
Dist - USNAC **Prod** - USVA 1980

Loss and Grieving - You and Your Patient, Pt 1 60 MIN
U-matic / VHS
Color (PRO)
LC 81-706293
Presents a study of death, dying and grief. Includes a discussion of the rights of the dying patient and guidelines for individuals working with the patient.
Sociology
Dist - USNAC **Prod** - USVA 1980

Loss and Grieving - You and Your Patient, Pt 2 60 MIN
U-matic / VHS
Color (PRO)
LC 81-706293
Presents a study of death, dying and grief. Includes a discussion of the rights of the dying patient and guidelines for individuals working with the patient.
Sociology
Dist - USNAC **Prod** - USVA 1980

The Loss of a Spouse 21 MIN
VHS / 16mm
Older Adults Series
(C)
$385.00 purchase _ #840VI042
Illustrates how a spouse's death affects each individual differently. Shows the importance of recognizing these differences and the symptoms of bereavement.
Health and Safety; Sociology
Dist - HSCIC **Prod** - HSCIC 1984

Loss of baby - death of a dream 45 MIN
VHS
Understanding maternal grief series
Color (C G)
$195.00 purchase, $50.00 rental _ #38179
Provides a general introduction to all the themes and issues covered in a five - part series on maternal grief. Includes discussions of the major psychological aspects of maternal grief with psychologist Margaret Nicol and neonatologist Dr Howard Chilton. Four women profiled in the series recount the experiences that helped them overcome their grief. Part of a series produced by Nicol, an Australian clinical psycologist specializing in the effects of reproductive loss on women's physical and mental health.
Guidance and Counseling; Health and Safety; Sociology
Dist - UCEMC

Loss of heat 20 MIN
16mm / VHS
Color (G)
$60.00 rental, $250.00 purchase
Weaves the stories of two lesbians in London and Spain who don't know each other but are connected by their common experiences of epilepsy, an 'invisible' illness. Looks at each woman's relationship with her lover. Reveals a sense of universality of epilepsy, its transgression across boundaries of culture and experience.
Health and Safety; Psychology; Sociology
Dist - WMEN **Prod** - DEVILL 1994

Loss of the will to live 15 MIN
U-matic / VHS
Color (PRO C)
$395.00 purchase, $80.00 rental _ #C901 - VI - 025
Helps caregivers develop positive psychosocial attitudes and behavior toward the aged. Discusses techniques which help patients to maintain the will to live. Presented by Dr Stephen Boy, Northern Essex College, Center for Nursing Education, Haverhill, Massachussetts.
Guidance and Counseling; Health and Safety; Psychology
Dist - HSCIC

Loss prevention
Videodisc
Financial FLASHFAX security series
(H A)
$1995.00
Instructs the employee in handling counterfeit currency, forged signatures and fraudulent checks and in basic internal control and auditing procedures. Can be customized for a particular financial institution. Includes practice material, quizzes and tests.
Business and Economics
Dist - CMSL **Prod** - CMSL

Loss Prevention for Business - Internal Crime 20 MIN
16mm / U-matic / VHS
Color
Discusses methods of preventing employee pilferage and theft, including persecution. Covers white collar crime including fraud, embezzlement, expense account cheating and computer data bank security breaches.
Business and Economics; Psychology; Sociology
Dist - CORF **Prod** - JACSTO

Loss Prevention for Business - Intrusion and Access Control 20 MIN
U-matic / VHS / 16mm
Color (A)
LC 77-700937
Shows methods for preventing a wide variety of externally perpetuated thefts. Stresses the need to identify and secure problem areas and demonstrates security training for key personnel.
Business and Economics; Sociology
Dist - CORF **Prod** - HAR 1978

Loss Prevention - Patient Property 18 MIN
VHS / 16mm
Color (PRO)
$295.00 purchase, $60.00 rental
Reminds caregivers of precautions necessary to prevent loss of patient property. Emphasizes the responsibility all healthcare givers have for protecting the patient from property loss.
Health and Safety
Dist - FAIRGH **Prod** - FAIRGH 1988

Loss prevention series
Job safety for clerical workers
Job safety for custodians
Job safety for food service workers
Job safety for maintenance workers
Job safety for teachers
Dist - AAVIM

Loss Prevention Series
Nine Dollars Plus One Dollar Equals 20 Dollars Shortchanged 27 MIN
Dist - BNA

Lost 93 MIN
VHS
Color (G)
$49.80 purchase _ #0258
Tells the true story of a 1973 voyage by a trimaran with three passengers from Vancouver, British Columbia to Costa Rica. Recounts that after traveling for two weeks, it capsized in a storm, leaving its crew adrift in the Pacific for 74 days.
Physical Education and Recreation
Dist - SEVVID

The Lost 600 18 MIN
16mm
Color
LC 80-700822
Emphasizes the dangers associated with foolish, unsafe and reckless behavior in and on the water. Covers still - water drownings, surfing, boating, yachting, water skiing, rock fishing, and swimming in home pools.
Health and Safety
Dist - TASCOR EDPAT **Prod** - NSWF 1978

Lost and found 30 MIN
U-matic
Today's Special Series
Color (K P)
Develops language arts skills in children. Programs are thematically designed around subjects of interest to youngsters. Action takes place in a department store where people, mannequins, puppets, comic characters and special guests present a light hearted approach to language arts.
Fine Arts; Literature and Drama; Psychology
Dist - TVOTAR **Prod** - TVOTAR 1985

Lost and found 27 MIN
16mm
Color (H)
Follows the progress of five young men who had little hope of finding a job before they entered Job Corps training programs.
Business and Economics; Guidance and Counseling; Psychology
Dist - AFLCIO **Prod** - USDL 1971

Lost and found 12 MIN
16mm / U-matic / VHS
Color (P I)
LC 78-708043
Discusses what one should do when one finds something that is lost and may be valuable to someone else. Gives children the opportunity to examine their own feelings both as finders and as losers.
Guidance and Counseling; Psychology; Social Science
Dist - PHENIX **Prod** - YEHU 1969

Lost and found in time and Voice in the wilderness - Vol 2 45 MIN
VHS
Flying house series
Color (K P I R)
$11.99 purchase _ #35 - 8951 - 979
Uses an animated format to present events from the New Testament era, as three children, a professor and a robot travel in the 'Flying House' back to that time. 'Lost and Found in Time' covers the boyhood of Jesus, while 'Voice in the Wilderness' tells the story of Jesus' baptism.
Literature and Drama; Religion and Philosophy
Dist - APH **Prod** - TYHP

Lost and found - Spatial Relationships (Geography) 14 MIN
VHS / U-matic
Two Cents' Worth Series
Color (P)
Shows that with help from a mime, Tracy and Ronnie learn to locate their favorite carnival rides using spatial directions.
Geography - United States
Dist - AITECH **Prod** - WHATV 1976

Lost and Lucky 60 MIN
U-matic / VHS
World of F Scott Fitzgerald Series
Color (C)
Examines the expatriate set that steamed to Europe in the 1920's in flight from 'Main Street' in this dramatization of a Fitzgerald story.
Literature and Drama
Dist - DALCCD **Prod** - DALCCD

The Lost army 58 MIN
16mm / VHS
Color (H C G)
$895.00, $445.00 purchase, $125.00, $75.00 rental
Traces the long cold trail - over two thousand years old - of the 'Lost Army of Cambyses' in Egypt. Records the expedition of American novelist Gary Chavetz who convinced people and agencies including National Geographic to back his exploration. Reports that state - of - the - art instruments and equipment balked, information from earlier travelers was wrong and Chavetz was forced to abandon his quest. Directed and edited by Ned Johnston and Susan Todd.
Geography - World; History - World
Dist - FLMLIB **Prod** - HUFSC 1989

Lost cat 27 MIN
VHS
B&W (G)
$25.00 purchase
Portrays Karen, a young black woman, who questions her marriage to Vince, a white man. Culminates when the cat runs away during a weekend visit by Karen's brother. The cat is played by a man in a cat suit. Explores issues of

personal identity and the nature of denial and sacrifice in relationships, while examining the current state of race relations in the US. Directed by Chris Brown.
Fine Arts; Psychology; Sociology
Dist - ALTFMW

Lost Cities of Copan and Tikal 14 MIN
16mm
Color
LC 74-703076
Explores the Mayan cities of Copan and Tikal and attempts to gain an insight into the characteristics of Mayan civilization through an examination of the ruins of their cities.
History - World; Sociology
Dist - CRTVLC **Prod** - CRTVLC 1974

Lost civilizations video series
Presents a ten - part series incorporating the newest research, evidence and discoveries; original cinematography in 25 countries on 5 continents; dramatized recreations of scenes from the past; three - dimensional computer graphics to reconstruct ancient cities and monumental feats of engineering; historic footage; and computer - animated maps. Covers the ancient history of Egypt, the Maya, Mesopotamia, the Aegean, Greece, China, Rome, Africa, the Incas and Tibet.

Aegean - legacy of Atlantis	50 MIN
Africa - a history denied	50 MIN
Ancient Egypt - quest for immortality	50 MIN
China - dynasties of power	50 MIN
Greece - a moment of excellence	50 MIN
Inca - secrets of the ancients	50 MIN
Maya - the blood of kings	50 MIN
Mesopotamia - return to Eden	50 MIN
Rome - the ultimate empire	50 MIN
Tibet - the end of time	50 MIN

Dist - TILIED **Prod** - TILIED 1974

Lost Command 129 MIN
U-matic / VHS / 16mm
Color (H C A)
Stars Anthony Quinn in an adventure story of a group of French paratroopers who have been defeated at Dien Bein Phu.
Fine Arts
Dist - FI **Prod** - CPC 1966

Lost Continent 92 MIN
16mm
B&W
Relates the experience of a group of scientist who land on a Pacific island searching for a stray missile and encounter prehistoric animals instead. Stars Cesar Romero and Hillary Brooke.
Fine Arts
Dist - REELIM **Prod** - LIPPRT 1951

Lost Control 45 MIN
U-matic / VHS / 16mm
B&W (J)
LC 76-701930
Shows men and women who acknowledge full responsibility for their addiction to drugs but who ask society to recognize their need for special help until they gain control of themselves.
Health and Safety; Sociology
Dist - PHENIX **Prod** - LYNCHE 1975

The Lost days of glory - Pt 1 29 MIN
Videoreel / VT2
Our Street Series
Color
Sociology
Dist - PBS **Prod** - MDCPB

The Lost days of glory - Pt 2 29 MIN
Videoreel / VT2
Our Street Series
Color
Sociology
Dist - PBS **Prod** - MDCPB

The Lost fringe benefit 25 MIN
VHS / U-matic / BETA / 16mm
Color (PRO)
$250.00 purchase, $75.00 rental
Portrays a city which discontinues the practice of supper money when a contract's language does not mention the practice. Shows that the union files a grievance, claiming that past practices cannot be discontinued without prior negotatiation. The arbitrator must decide whether an issue not covered by a contract may be arbitrated and whether the grievance should be sustained. Includes a discussion guide.
Business and Economics; Psychology; Sociology
Dist - AARA

The Lost fringe benefit, The Impasse 47 MIN
VHS / U-matic / BETA / 16mm
Color (PRO)
$400.00 purchase
Offers two films on dispute settlement in public employment. Portrays a dispute between a city and a union on the discontinuance of supper money in The Lost Fringe Benefit. Shows the negotiation between a city and a union on a new contract in which the city insists upon discontinuing the practice of supper money in The Impasse. Includes a discussion guide.
Business and Economics; Psychology; Sociology
Dist - AARA

The Lost Generations 20 MIN
16mm / U-matic / VHS
Color
Offers a verbal and visual diary of the bombing of Hiroshima and Nagasaki, revealing the effects on the populations of both cities.
Civics and Political Systems; History - World
Dist - FI **Prod** - FI

Lost gold mine 25 MIN
VHS
Sparky's animation series
Color (P I R)
$19.95 purchase, $10.00 rental _ #35 - 818 - 2020
Features Sparky and his friends as they search for a legendary treasure. Shows how they come to understand the perils of greed.
Literature and Drama; Religion and Philosophy
Dist - APH **Prod** - ANDERK

A Lost History 60 MIN
U-matic / VHS
Color
$300 rental
Narrates stories about famous Methodist women - Harriet Tubman; Francis Willard, who was denied the right to be a minister because she was a woman; Mary McLeod Bethune, one of the most influential Black women in American history, who founded a college and a hospital; and many others. An NBC documentary.
Religion and Philosophy; Sociology
Dist - CCNCC **Prod** - CCNCC 1985

Lost horizon 132 MIN
VHS
B&W (G)
$29.95 purchase _ #S01378
Tells the story of five airplane passengers who discover Shangri - La when their hijacked airplane crashes in the Himalayas. Stars Ronald Coleman, Jane Wyatt, Edward Everett Horton, and Sam Jaffe. Directed by Frank Capra.
Fine Arts; Literature and Drama
Dist - UILL

Lost Hunter 22 MIN
16mm
Basic Information Films Series
Color; B&W (J H C G T A)
Tells the story of a hunter who is lost in the wooded snow country, seeks shelter for the night in a cave, overcomes his panic and sends up smoke fires for searchers. First person narrations. Material derived from actual cases on file at the Idaho Department of Fish and Game.
Geography - United States; Health and Safety; Physical Education and Recreation
Dist - FO **Prod** - FO 1955

Lost in Death Valley 47 MIN
U-matic / VHS / 16mm
Teenage Years Series
Color (I J H)
Reveals what happens when five young members of a high school marching band are stranded in the desert when their single - engine plane crashes. Shows that traditional roles for male and females come into question as a shy girl who is the only one who knows how to deal with the dangers they face, shrinks from asserting herself, while an aggressive boy leads them on a trail headed for certain disaster.
Guidance and Counseling
Dist - TIMLIF **Prod** - ALAMAR 1984

Lost in Space 15 MIN
U-matic / VHS
It's all Up to You Series
Color (I J)
Shows how future societal alternatives may be predicted by a better understanding of the present society.
Sociology
Dist - AITECH **Prod** - COOPED 1978

Lost in the Barrens 15 MIN
VHS / U-matic
Book bird series
Color (I)
Tells of two boys lost in the subarctic forests of northern Canada. From the book by Farley Mowatt.
English Language; Literature and Drama
Dist - CTI **Prod** - CTI

Lost in the Crowd 43 MIN
16mm
Color
LC FIA67-474
Portray's God's search for the lost soul by showing how Easter vacation triggers the invasion of the beaches by thousands of high school and college young people in a frenzied search for sun, sand, surf, suds and sex. They soon lose their identity in a carnival of night clubs, go - go girls, bright lights and beer cans.
Psychology; Religion and Philosophy; Sociology
Dist - GF **Prod** - YOUTH 1966

Lost in the Fine Print 30 MIN
U-matic
Family and the Law Series
(H C A)
Deals with consumer law concerning purchase of motor vehicles.
Civics and Political Systems
Dist - ACCESS **Prod** - ACCESS 1980

Lost in the Mish - Mosh - Area Measure 13 MIN
U-matic
Color (P)
Tells how a famous detective selects the appropriate unit of measure in order to save a kidnapped professor.
Mathematics
Dist - GA **Prod** - DAVFMS

Lost in the Woods 30 MIN
U-matic / VHS
High Feather Series Pt 6; Pt 6
Color (I J)
LC 83-706052
Focuses on farming and the identification of edible foods in the wild.
Health and Safety; Social Science
Dist - GPN **Prod** - NYSED 1982

Lost in the Woods 23 MIN
U-matic / VHS / 16mm
Color (P I A)
Tells the story of a six - year - old boy who becomes lost in the woods while camping with his parents. Since he had previously learned about survival, he knows just what to do. Emphasizes simple survival techniques.
Health and Safety; Physical Education and Recreation
Dist - BCNFL **Prod** - CASSB 1984

Lost innocence 23 MIN
VHS
Color (J H)
$250.00 purchase
Portrays the horrors of street life faced every day by teenage runaways as seen by Sean, an innocent and naive 16 - year - old befriended by a street - wise kid who steers Sean into a self - destructive course of prostitution, drug abuse and eventual death.
Sociology
Dist - LANDMK **Prod** - LANDMK 1992

Lost is a feeling 15 MIN
VHS / 16mm / U-matic
Inside-out series
Color (I)
LC 73-702444
Helps children understand how persons can feel lost and threatened in new situations by introducing Amadore, a Puerto Rican who moves to Washington, DC, and attempts to make friends with a group of boys playing baseball. Shows how his efforts are marred by his inability to speak English.
Guidance and Counseling; Sociology
Dist - AITECH

The Lost jungle
VHS
Cliffhangers II series
B&W (G)
Features animal trainer Clyde Beatty and the Hagenbeck - Wallace animals in a jungle adventure. Tells how Beatty must recover a stolen treasure chest to protect the safety of Ruth Robinson and her ship - captain father. Includes six episodes.
Fine Arts
Dist - SCETV **Prod** - SCETV 1987

Lost Love - Another Senseless Tragedy 11 MIN
U-matic / VHS
Color (C A)
A light - hearted approach to the break - up of a love affair. Addresses romantic depression, rejection, loss, coping methods.
Health and Safety; Psychology
Dist - MMRC **Prod** - MMRC

Lost - Magician's Rabbit 15 MIN
U-matic / VHS
Magic Shop Series no 8
Color (P)
LC 83-706153
Employs a magician named Amazing Alexander and his assistants to explore the use of descriptive words.
English Language
Dist - GPN **Prod** - CVETVC 1982

The Lost Mission 19 MIN
VHS / U-matic
Color (I A)
Shows an archaeological discovery being made that establishes evidence of a culture that existed 3500 years ago.
Fine Arts; Sociology
Dist - SUTHRB **Prod** - SUTHRB

Lost Mixing Time of Dual - Drum Paver 30 MIN
16mm
Color
Highlights the importance of the simultaneous mixing interval in meeting mixing time specifications with dual - drum pavers. Shows some trouble spots and emphasizes the significance of proper adjustments to the batchmeter.
Industrial and Technical Education
Dist - USNAC **Prod** - USDTFH 1959

The Lost Pharaoh - the Search for Akhenaten 67 MIN
U-matic / VHS
Color (H C A)
Tells the story of an ancient pharaoh who was almost lost to history and the archeological sleuthing which went into piecing together information about him.
History - World; Science - Physical
Dist - NFBC **Prod** - NFBC

The Lost Phoebe 30 MIN
U-matic / VHS / 16mm
Color (H C A)
$575, $250 purchase _ #3946
Tells the story of a man who is drowned in the river when he believes that he sees his dead wife there and goes to join her. Produced by the American Film Institute. A Perspective film. Based on the story by Theodore Dreiser.
Literature and Drama
Dist - CORF

Lost Pigeon 15 MIN
VHS / 16mm / U-matic
Captioned; Color (I J) (SPANISH)
LC 74-700675
Deals with the concept of ownership and responsibility for one's actions by telling a story about a boy who lost one of his homing pigeons. Tells how the pigeon is injured by a group of boys and that one of the boys nurses it back to health. Raises the question of ownership of a bird.
Literature and Drama; Social Science
Dist - BARR **Prod** - BARR

The Lost Pilgrim 45 MIN
16mm
B&W
Describes the adventures of a lost pilgrim in a forest in 16th century France. Studies peasant life in a medieval village in a time of ignorance and religious obsession.
Geography - World; History - World
Dist - RADIM **Prod** - FILIM

Lost Production Highway Construction 30 MIN
16mm
Color
LC 74-705049
Examines minor delays that affect the production rates of key units of highway construction equipment, including power shovels, scrapers, hot - mix bituminous plants and concrete paver.
Industrial and Technical Education
Dist - USNAC **Prod** - USDTFH 1957

Lost Puppy 14 MIN
16mm / U-matic / VHS
Values for Grades K - 3 Series
Color (P)
LC 78-703954
An open - end film about a young girl's responsibility to obey her mother.
Guidance and Counseling; Sociology
Dist - CF **Prod** - CF 1969

The Lost republic 140 MIN
VHS / 35mm strip / U-matic
Color; B&W (H C A) (SPANISH (ENGLISH SUBTITLES))
$250 rental
Chronicles the years 1976 to 1983 in Argentina when the country was ruled by a military dictatorship. Describes political repression and human rights abuses. Directed by Miguel Perez.
Civics and Political Systems; History - World
Dist - CNEMAG

The Lost Secret 140 MIN
VHS
Color (G) (ENGLISH AND JAPANESE ENGLISH AND SPANISH ENGLISH AND GERMAN)
$295.00 purchase _ #SV7250
Presents an eleven - episode mystery in conversational English, emphasizing understanding of phrases rather than individual words. Teaches through cartoon strips, exercises and short readings that reinforce the video material. Created by Robert O'Neill and Martin Shovel. Includes two videocassettes, student book - available in German - English, Japanese - English or Spanish - English - and teacher's manual.
English Language
Dist - NORTNJ **Prod** - BBC

The Lost Sheep 13 MIN
U-matic / VHS / 16mm
Color (K P)
Uses cell and puppet animation to tell the story of a young shepherd who stumbles upon a mysterious underground kingdom while searching for his sheep. Shows how his kindness to his flock and loyalty to his job are rewarded.
Fine Arts; Literature and Drama
Dist - MOKIN **Prod** - CFET 1983

The Lost Sheep 15 MIN
16mm
Color (P I J H)
Uses puppets to tell the parable of the lost sheep.
Guidance and Counseling; Literature and Drama
Dist - YALEDV **Prod** - YALEDV

The Lost Sun 12 MIN
16mm
Animatoons Series
Color
LC FIA67-5512
The story of the barnyard trio - a rabbit, a pussy cat, and a dauntless duck - who search the skies for the sun which has disappeared. Relates how they find the sun and discover that those who want bright days must search for the sun.
Literature and Drama
Dist - RADTV **Prod** - ANTONS 1968

Lost Time - Occupational Back Injury 20 MIN
16mm
Color (A)
Examines the redesigning of work processes and lifting tasks to reduce the high incidence of back injuries.
Health and Safety
Dist - AFLCIO **Prod** - UORE 1981

Lost to the Revolution 28 MIN
U-matic / VHS / 16mm
Color
LC 81-700535
Looks at the final years of Imperial Russia through the legacy of Peter Carl Faberge, the renowned jeweler who created many fabulous designs for the Romanovs during the reigns of Czar Alexander III and Czar Nicholas II.
Fine Arts; History - World; Industrial and Technical Education
Dist - PHENIX **Prod** - FORBES 1981

Lost Twin Cities 60 MIN
VHS
Color (G)
$24.95 purchase _ #V - 003
Explores the architectural masterpieces and cultural icons that have disappeared from the Minneapolis - St Paul urban landscape over the last 50 years.
Fine Arts; History - United States
Dist - MINHS **Prod** - KTCATV

Lost Wax 9 MIN
U-matic / VHS / 16mm
Color (J)
LC 71-737623
Illustrates the lost wax process of casting metal images - - an ancient art still practiced today in India by itinerant craftsmen.
Fine Arts
Dist - AIMS **Prod** - KAP 1969

The Lost World of the Maya 36 MIN
U-matic / VHS / 16mm
Nova Series
Color (J)
LC 75-701996
Follows Eric Thompson, an authority on Mayan civilization, as he travels through Central America. Explains the theories that have been used to rationalize the decline of the Mayan culture.
History - World; Social Science
Dist - TIMLIF AMBROS **Prod** - BBCTV 1974

Lost World of the Medusa 50 MIN
U-matic / VHS
Color (H C A)
Explores the labyrinthine limestone islands of Palau in the Pacific, a lake filled with millions of medusa jellyfish, rain forests sprouting from coral rubble and vast caves haunted by whip scorpions, giant crickets and bats.
Geography - World; Science - Natural
Dist - FI **Prod** - WNETTV

The Lost World Revisited 28 MIN
16mm
Movies - Our Modern Art Series
B&W (J)
LC FIA68-3189
Discusses the 1925 motion picture The Lost World, based on a novel by Sir Arthur Conan Doyle, about the discovery of a river inhabited by gigantic pre - historic animals and which featured Lewis Stone, Wallace Beery, Bessie Love and Lloyd Hughes in the cast. Tells how Willis H O'brien used stop - motion photography in order to bring the pre - historic monsters to life.
Fine Arts; History - World
Dist - SF **Prod** - SPCTRA 1967

The Lost years of Jesus 92 MIN
VHS
Color (G)
$39.95 purchase _ #V - LY
Covers the 18 years in the life of Jesus not recorded in the Bible. Uses records found in an ancient Tibetan monastery along with information from the Akashic Records as a source. Discusses the Shroud of Turin and the Spear of Longinus. Includes footage shot in India, Europe and the United States.
Religion and Philosophy
Dist - PACSPI

Lot Acceptance Sampling 30 MIN
U-matic / VHS
Reliability Engineering Series
Color (IND)
Describes content and application of Military Standard 781C, 'Reliability Design Qualification and Product Acceptance Tests - Exponential Distribution.'.
Industrial and Technical Education
Dist - COLOSU **Prod** - COLOSU

Lot in Sodom 27 MIN
16mm
B&W (J)
A lyrical interpretation of the biblical story based on rhythmical arrangements of symbols rather than on chronological development of action.
Religion and Philosophy
Dist - TWYMAN **Prod** - WATWEB 1934

A Lot of Brass 15 MIN
U-matic / VHS
Mrs Cabobble's Caboose
(P)
Designed to teach primary grade students basic music concepts. Highlights melody, rhythm, harmony and the different families of musical instruments. Features Mrs. Fran Powell.
Fine Arts
Dist - GPN **Prod** - WDCNTV 1986

A Lot of living things 15 MIN
VHS / U-matic
Dragons, wagons and wax - Set 1 series
Color (K P)
Explains diversity in living things.
Science; Science - Natural
Dist - CTI **Prod** - CTI

LOTO - lockout tagout, your ticket to safety - Loteria - cierre y etiquette - su billete para la seguridad 15 MIN
U-matic / BETA / VHS
Safety - live action video series
Color (IND G) (SPANISH)
$495.00 purchase _ #800 - 18, #800 - 19
Instructs on the essential steps required to prevent injury from the unexpected release of electrical, mechanical, chemical, thermal, hydraulic, pneumatic and stored energy. Shows methods of identifying and neutralizing energy sources, lockout procedures, as well as testing and restarting equipment. Part of a series on safety.
Health and Safety; Industrial and Technical Education; Psychology
Dist - ITSC **Prod** - ITSC

Lots of Kids Like Us 28 MIN
VHS
Color (G)
$380.00 purchase _ #9510; $380.00 video purchase _ #82214, $425.00 film purchase _ #82206
Considers alcholism's effect on children. Shows children practical ways to take care of themselves, that their parents' addiction is not their fault, that they are not the only ones living in chemically dependent families.
Guidance and Counseling; Health and Safety; Sociology
Dist - HAZELB CMPCAR CORF **Prod** - ROGGTP

Lotte Eisner in Germany 34 MIN
16mm
Color (H C A)
LC 81-701028
Presents noted film critic Lotte Eisner, German born but long a resident of France, who offers her memoirs on film. Shows her reminiscing about meeting such greats as Eisenstein, Murnau and Pabst. Tells of her influence on various filmmakers.

Fine Arts
Dist - NYFLMS **Prod** - NYFLMS 1980

Lotte Goslar and Bertram Ross 30 MIN
U-matic / VHS
Eye on Dance - Great Performers Series
Color
Fine Arts
Dist - ARCVID **Prod** - ARCVID

Lotte Jacobi, a Film Portrait 24 MIN
16mm
Color
LC 79-701174
Examines the life of Lotte Jacobi, a noted portrait photographer.
Biography; Fine Arts; Industrial and Technical Education
Dist - UNH **Prod** - UNH 1979

Lotte Reiniger's animated fairy tales series

Caliph stork	10 MIN
Cinderella	10 MIN
The Frog prince	11 MIN
Gallant little tailor	10 MIN
The Grasshopper and the ant	10 MIN
Little Chimney Sweep	10 MIN
Puss in Boots	10 MIN
Sleeping Beauty	10 MIN
Snow White and Rose Red	13 MIN
Thumbelina	10 MIN

Dist - MOMA

Lotte Reininger's silhouette films series

Galathea	10 MIN

Dist - MOMA

Lottery and Information Prices - Risk Aversion 56 MIN
U-matic / VHS
Decision Analysis Series
Color
Industrial and Technical Education; Mathematics
Dist - MIOT **Prod** - MIOT

The Lottery by Shirley Jackson 18 MIN
16mm / U-matic / VHS
Humanities - Short Story Showcase Series
Color (J H C)
LC 77-707374
Presents Shirley Jackson's short story The Lottery.
Fine Arts; Literature and Drama
Dist - EBEC **Prod** - EBEC 1970

The Lottery video
VHS
Video chess mentor series
Color (G)
$24.95 purchase _ #JJ101
Presents professional gambler John Patrick explaining the strategies of lottery experts.
Physical Education and Recreation
Dist - SIV

Lotus 123 - Level II 74 MIN
VHS
Video professor's Lotus 123 series
Color (G)
$29.95 purchase _ #6595
Uses slow, clear narration and graphics to go step - by - step through each operation in an introduction to Lotus 123, part two in a three - part series.
Computer Science
Dist - ESPNTV **Prod** - ESPNTV

Lotus 123 - Level III 50 MIN
VHS
Video professor's Lotus 123 series
Color (G)
$29.95 purchase _ #6596
Uses slow, clear narration and graphics to go step - by - step through each operation in an introduction to Lotus 123, part three in a three - part series.
Computer Science
Dist - ESPNTV **Prod** - ESPNTV

Lotus 123 literacy
VHS
Computer software training series
Color (J H C G)
$49.95 purchase _ #AAT03V
Teaches Lotus 1 - 2 - 3 literacy in a comprehensive and easy - to - follow format. Illustrates actual commands and time saving techniques. Part of a 21 - part series on computer software.
Computer Science
Dist - CAMV

LOTUS 123 literacy - version 1 thru 2 .01
VHS
Excellence in computer literacy series
Color (G)
$49.95 purchase
Covers LOTUS 1 - 2 - 3, versions 1 through 2.01. Shows how to prepare and install the system and how to build simple and complex spreadsheets. Discusses the design of a basic workflow, editing, filing, printing and business graphics, special commands and shortcuts.
Computer Science
Dist - SMPUB **Prod** - SMPUB

Lotus 2.2 and 3.0 level II 65 MIN
VHS
Spreadsheet series
Color (J H C G)
$29.95 purchase _ #VP129V
Offers intermediate concepts in Lotus 2.2 and 3.0. Allows viewer to see keyboard and monitor simultaneously so that students can see the result of every keystroke. Part of a nine - part series on spreadsheets.
Business and Economics; Computer Science
Dist - CAMV

Lotus 2.2 and 3.0 level III 60 MIN
VHS
Spreadsheet series
Color (J H C G)
$29.95 purchase _ #VP137V
Offers advanced concepts in Lotus 2.2 and 3.0. Allows viewer to see keyboard and monitor simultaneously so that students can see the result of every keystroke. Part of a nine - part series on spreadsheets.
Business and Economics; Computer Science
Dist - CAMV

Lotus 3.1 multimedia training series
Presents three videos which train in the use of Lotus 3.1. Offers basic instruction, as well as instruction in editing and printing commands, creating spreadsheets and printing graphics. Includes three student workbooks and a data diskette.

Creating 3 - D spreadsheets with Lotus 3.1 - Part 2	75 MIN
Graphing features of Lotus 3.1 - Part 3	85 MIN
Introduction to Lotus 3.1 - Part 1	62 MIN

Dist - HALASI **Prod** - HALASI

LOTUS - a Project for World Peace 14 MIN
VHS
Color
Presents a videotaped slide shown by Paul Candylis on the subject 'LOTUS - A Project For World Peace.'
Education; Religion and Philosophy
Dist - IYOGA **Prod** - IYOGA

Lotus Agenda - Advanced Features 60 MIN
VHS / U-matic
(A PRO)
$275.00
Includes using category and view managers, tex, profile and data conditions.
Computer Science
Dist - VIDEOT **Prod** - VIDEOT 1988

Lotus Agenda - Complete Set 60 MIN
U-matic / VHS
(A PRO)
$495.00
Provides complete instruction on Lotus Agenda.
Computer Science
Dist - VIDEOT **Prod** - VIDEOT 1988

Lotus Agenda - Introduction to the Personal Information Manager 60 MIN
VHS / U-matic
(A PRO)
$275.00
Shows all skills necessary to utilize Agenda for business applications.
Computer Science
Dist - VIDEOT **Prod** - VIDEOT 1988

Lotus AmiPro 3.0 179 MIN
U-matic / VHS / BETA
Color; NTSC; PAL; SECAM (J H C G)
PdS99.95
Presents the popular word processor for use by a typical user. Features Karen Bottomley of Lotus Development - UK.
Computer Science
Dist - VIEWTH

Lotus Amipro 3.0 for Windows learning system 140 MIN
VHS
Color; CC (G H C IND PRO)
$595.00 purchase _ #MIC24
Teaches users the skills needed to master this word processing software program.
Computer Science
Dist - EXTR **Prod** - MICROV

Lotus Freelance Graphics 2.0 Windows 158 MIN
U-matic / VHS / BETA
Color; NTSC; PAL; SECAM (J H C G)
PdS99.95
Shows how to create high - quality presentations with the software. Trains both new and advanced users. Features Steve Dunbar of Lotus Development - UK.
Computer Science
Dist - VIEWTH

Lotus Improv for Windows 178 MIN
U-matic / VHS / BETA
Color; NTSC; PAL; SECAM (J H C G)
PdS99.95
Presents the successor to conventional spreadsheets. Shows users how to perform more advanced spreadsheet activities that usually create hassles in a conventional spreadsheet. Features Mark Benzies of Lotus Development - UK.
Computer Science
Dist - VIEWTH

Lotus in the West 28 MIN
16mm / U-matic / VHS
Color (J)
LC 80-701943
Explores the lives of two young Americans who have taken up residence in a Buddhist meditation center near downtown Los Angeles.
Religion and Philosophy
Dist - CAROUF **Prod** - BONTEJ 1980

Lotus Level II 74 MIN
VHS
Spreadsheet series
Color (J H C G)
$29.95 purchase _ #VP107V
Offers intermediate concepts on Lotus spreadsheets. Allows viewer to see keyboard and monitor simultaneously so that students can see the result of every keystroke. Part of a nine - part series on spreadsheets.
Business and Economics; Computer Science
Dist - CAMV

Lotus Level III 51 MIN
VHS
Spreadsheet series
Color (J H C G)
$29.95 purchase _ #VP115V
Offers advanced concepts on Lotus spreadsheets. Allows viewer to see keyboard and monitor simultaneously so that students can see the result of every keystroke. Part of a nine - part series on spreadsheets.
Business and Economics; Computer Science
Dist - CAMV

Lotus macros
VHS
Computer software training series
Color (J H C G)
$49.95 purchase _ #AAT08V
Teaches about Lotus macros in a comprehensive and easy - to - follow format. Illustrates actual commands and time saving techniques. Part of a 21 - part series on computer software.
Computer Science
Dist - CAMV

LOTUS macros - all versions
VHS
Excellence in computer literacy series
Color (G)
$49.95 purchase
Covers LOTUS macros. Shows how to plan and create macros for faster work and use data entry routines to speed up work. Discusses the creation of libraries and templates, documenting and 'de - bugging' macros.
Computer Science
Dist - SMPUB **Prod** - SMPUB

Lotus Notes 3.0 177 MIN
U-matic / VHS / BETA
Color; NTSC; PAL; SECAM (J H C G)
PdS99.95
Presents the most - used features of Lotus Notes and how to use it more effectively in group situations. Trains managers - users. Features Nigel Thomas of Lotus Development - UK.
Computer Science
Dist - VIEWTH

Lotus Notes 3.0 learning system 140 MIN
VHS
Color (G H C IND PRO)
$995.00 purchase _ #MIC20
Teaches users how to master this interoffice communications tool. Contains two videos.
Computer Science
Dist - EXTR **Prod** - MICROV

Lotus 1 - 2 - 3
U-matic / VHS
Micor Video Learning Systems Series
(A IND)
$495.00 purchase _ #MV200

Demonstrates the use of the Lotus 1 2 3.
Computer Science
Dist - CAMV

Lotus 1 - 2 - 3
Videodisc
(H A)
$2195.00
Teaches both the fundamentals and advanced features of Lotus 1 - 2 - 3 software for electronic spreadsheets. Explains use of formulas and range commands along with macros and templates. Six to ten hours.
Computer Science; Education
Dist - CMSL **Prod** - CMSL

Lotus 1 - 2 - 3
U-matic / VHS
Color
Shows how to use Lotus 1 - 2 - 3 - program efficiently and how to use the most frequently used commands.
Industrial and Technical Education; Mathematics
Dist - ANDRST **Prod** - LANSFD

Lotus 1 - 2 - 3, Level II 74 MIN
VHS
Master Computer Software Easily Series
Color (G)
$29.95 purchase _ #60010
Shows how to use Lotus software. Discusses range formatting, writing - copying formulas, absolute - relative cell addressing, changing cell appearance, database option, criterion on range headings, multiple criterion searches and printing. Part of a nine - part series which breaks down into three sets of three units which discuss Lotus, DOS and Wordperfect. Any three units of the series can be purchased for $79.95.
Business and Economics; Computer Science; Education
Dist - CARTRP **Prod** - CARTRP

Lotus 1 - 2 - 3, Level III 51 MIN
VHS
Master Computer Software Easily Series
Color (G)
$29.95 purchase _ #60011
Shows how to use Lotus software to create macros, numeric macros and command macros. Discusses creating, documenting, saving and printing graphics, key indicators and combining macros. Part of a nine - part series which breaks down into three sets of three units which discuss Lotus, DOS and Wordperfect. Any three units of the series can be purchased for $79.95.
Business and Economics; Computer Science; Education
Dist - CARTRP **Prod** - CARTRP

Lotus 1 - 2 - 3 2.2 and 3.0 introduction 47 MIN
VHS
Spreadsheet series
Color (J H C G)
$29.95 purchase _ #VP128V
Introduces concepts in Lotus 1 - 2 - 3 2.2 and 3.0. Allows viewer to see keyboard and monitor simultaneously so that students can see the result of every keystroke. Part of a nine - part series on spreadsheets.
Business and Economics; Computer Science
Dist - CAMV

Lotus 1 - 2 - 3 - Advanced Features - Spreadsheet Techniques, Graphics and Database Management 40 MIN
VHS / U-matic
(A PRO)
$275.00
Includes keyboard macros, typing alternatives, set up and use of macros for automating spreadsheet tasks.
Computer Science
Dist - VIDEOT **Prod** - VIDEOT 1988

Lotus 1 - 2 - 3 - advanced features - spreadsheet techniques, graphics and database managment - release 2.01
VHS
Color (H C G)
$325.00 purchase _ #07 - LOA
Discusses Lotus 1 - 2 - 3. Describes keyboard macros, the typing alternative, how to set - up and invoke useful macros for automating spreadsheet tasks, how to create bar and line charts and pie graphs, spreadsheet consolidation and how to use the database of Lotus. Includes a videocassette, a guide and a diskette.
Business and Economics; Computer Science
Dist - VIDEOT **Prod** - ANDRST

Lotus 1 - 2 - 3 - Advanced Macros 45 MIN
VHS / U-matic
(A PRO)
$275.00
Provides training in advanced macro features including creation of custom menus, macro concepts, debugging macros and making screens.
Computer Science
Dist - VIDEOT **Prod** - VIDEOT 1988

Lotus 1 - 2 - 3 - an Introduction to the Integrated Spreadsheet 40 MIN
VHS / U-matic
(A PRO)
$275.00
Introduces the use of the software and shows how to create a work sheet, enter data and format a worksheet.
Computer Science
Dist - VIDEOT **Prod** - VIDEOT 1988

Lotus 1 - 2 - 3 - an introduction to the integrated spreadsheet release 2.01
VHS
Color (H C G)
$325.00 purchase _ #07 - LOI
Introduces Lotus 1 - 2 - 3. Describes Lotus and its spreadsheets, how to create a worksheet, entering data, ranges, formulas, formatting the worksheet, editing data, macros, graphs, data management, printing and saving worksheets. Includes a videocassette, a guide and a diskette.
Business and Economics; Computer Science
Dist - VIDEOT **Prod** - ANDRST

LOTUS 1 - 2 - 3 - Beginning through Advanced Skills 250 MIN
Software / VHS / 16mm
Color (PRO)
$995.00 purchase, $40.00 preview
Teaches elementary and advanced features of the LOTUS 1 - 2 - 3 Computer system. Demonstrates step by step procedures. Includes five videotapes, five guidebooks, five demonstration disks, and Lotus 1 - 2 - 3 command chart.
Computer Science; Mathematics; Psychology
Dist - UTM **Prod** - UTM 1989

Lotus 1 - 2 - 3 - Complete Anderson Set
VHS / U-matic
(A PRO)
$495.00
Complete instruction on the use of Lotus 1 - 2 - 3 software,.
Computer Science
Dist - VIDEOT **Prod** - VIDEOT 1988

Lotus 1 - 2 - 3 - Creating and using Macros 43 MIN
VHS / U-matic
(A PRO)
$275.00
Shows how to build understanding and use of macros. Covers debugging macros and creating macro information screens.
Computer Science
Dist - VIDEOT **Prod** - VIDEOT 1988

Lotus 1 - 2 - 3 DOS version 2.4 & version 3.1 plus 177 MIN
U-matic / VHS / BETA
Color; NTSC; PAL; SECAM (J H G C)
PdS99.95
Covers the most - used features of the two widely - used versions of Lotus DOS. Highlights features specific to each version. Features Alan Baldwin of Lotus Development - UK.
Computer Science
Dist - VIEWTH

Lotus 1 - 2 - 3 - Executive Edition 120 MIN
U-matic / VHS
(A PRO)
$195.00, $250.00
Demonstrates all the basic of spreadsheets in addition to the integrated program functions of Lotus.
Computer Science
Dist - VIDEOT **Prod** - VIDEOT 1988

Lotus 1 - 2 - 3 introduction 43 MIN
VHS
Spreadsheet series
Color (J H C G)
$29.95 purchase _ #VP106V
Introduces concepts in Lotus 1 - 2 - 3. Allows viewer to see keyboard and monitor simultaneously so that students can see the result of every keystroke. Part of a nine - part series on spreadsheets.
Business and Economics; Computer Science
Dist - CAMV

Lotus 1 - 2 - 3 learning system 2.01
VHS / U-matic
Color (H C G)
$595.00, $495.00 purchase _ #07 - LMV
Trains first - time and advanced users of Lotus 1 - 2 - 3, release 2.01. Includes a videocassette, a guide and a diskette. Published by MicroVideo Learning Systems.
Business and Economics; Computer Science
Dist - VIDEOT

Lotus 1 - 2 - 3 Learning System Release 2 0 240 MIN
U-matic / VHS
(A PRO)
$495.00 $595.00
Provides all training required for first time users as well as advanced users. Shows how to create and format spreadsheets, data worksheets, graphics and databases.
Computer Science
Dist - VIDEOT **Prod** - VIDEOT 1988

Lotus 1 - 2 - 3 level II, version 2.2 and 3.0 65 MIN
VHS
Color (H C)
$29.95 purchase _ #VPS - 129
Shows how to create a basic spreadsheet. Discusses writing and copying formulas, absolute and relative cell addressing, creating named ranges, file combine command, using Lotus for database operations, sorting records, criterion range headings, multiple criterion searches, printing reports.
Computer Science
Dist - INSTRU

Lotus 1 - 2 - 3 level III, version 2.2 and 3.0 60 MIN
VHS
Color (H C)
$29.95 purchase _ #VPS - 137
Shows how to do file linkage. Teaches Avg, Min and Max functions, mixed relative and absolute address formulas, multiple ranges, calculating budget projections, worksheet windows, working with 'undo' for budget projections, data tables, range search, database tables, database functions.
Computer Science
Dist - INSTRU

Lotus 1 - 2 - 3 - Macros - Complete Anderson Set
U-matic / VHS
(A PRO)
$495.00
Provides complete training concerning macro function of Lotus.
Computer Science
Dist - VIDEOT **Prod** - VIDEOT 1988

Lotus 1 - 2 - 3 mentor series 480 - 720 MIN
Videodisc
Lotus 1 - 2 - 3 mentor series
(A PRO)
$1,990.00
Shows fundamentals and more complex concepts such as extended macros.
Computer Science
Dist - VIDEOT **Prod** - VIDEOT 1988

Lotus 1 - 2 - 3 mentor series
Lotus 1 - 2 - 3 mentor series 480 - 720 MIN
Dist - VIDEOT

Lotus 1 - 2 - 3 release 2.01 - beginning through advanced skills
U-matic / VHS
Color (H C G)
$1325.00, $1175.00 purchase _ #07 - LPC
Consists of five stand - alone modules on Lotus 1 - 2 - 3 Release 2.01. Allows users to master both the elementary and advanced features quickly and easily. Covers creating a spreadsheet, graphing, database management, macros, advanced functions and spreadsheet design. Includes 5 videocassettes, 5 guides and 5 diskettes. Published by Learn - PC.
Business and Economics; Computer Science
Dist - VIDEOT

Lotus 1 - 2 - 3 - release 2.01 - complete set
VHS
Color (H C G)
$595.00 purchase _ #07 - LOI - LOA
Presents two courses on Lotus 1 - 2 - 3, release 2.01. Describes Lotus and its spreadsheet, creating a worksheet, keyboard macros, how to set - up and invoke useful macros for automating spreadsheet tasks, how to create bar and line charts and pie graphs, spreadsheet consolidation and how to use the database of Lotus. Includes 2 videocassettes, 2 guides and 2 diskettes.
Business and Economics; Computer Science
Dist - VIDEOT **Prod** - ANDRST

Lotus 1 - 2 - 3 - release 2.2 and 3
VHS / U-matic
Color (H C G)
$595.00, $495.00 purchase _ #07 - M23
Covers the new features of Lotus 1 - 2 - 3, release 2.01 and 3. Looks at UNDO, database tables, annotating values, background printing, as well as the worksheet basics and the command menu. Includes a videocassette, a guide and a diskette. Published by MicroVideo Learning Systems.

Business and Economics; Computer Science
Dist - VIDEOT

Lotus 1 - 2 - 3 Release 2.2 and 3.0
VHS / BETA / U-matic
MS - DOS training video series
Color (G)
$1195.00 purchase, $275.00 rental
Offers introductory and advanced training in Lotus 1 - 2 - 3 Release 2.2 and 3.0. Shows how to name a range, perform an advanced calculation, use advanced macro commands.
Computer Science; Psychology
Dist - AMEDIA **Prod** - AMEDIA

Lotus 1 - 2 - 3 release 2.2 series
U-matic / VHS
Lotus 1 - 2 - 3 release 2.2 series
Color (H C G)
$1545.00, $1395.00 purchase _ #07 - NL2
Consists of six courses on Lotus 1 - 2 - 3 Release 2.2. Provides complete instructions on creating spreadsheets, using formuals, graphing, printing, advanced functions and more. Includes 6 videocassettes, 6 guides and a diskette. Published by Learn - PC.
Business and Economics; Computer Science
Dist - VIDEOT

Lotus 1 - 2 - 3 release 2.2 series
Lotus 1 - 2 - 3 release 2.2 series
Dist - VIDEOT

Lotus 1 - 2 - 3 - release 2.2 - three volume set
VHS
Color (H C G)
$895.00 purchase _ #07 - LVI - VII - III
Presents three courses on Lotus 1 - 2 - 3 - Release 2.2. Covers the new features, graphing, printing and managing large worksheets, and the advanced skills of Release 2.2. Includes 3 videocassettes, 3 guides and 3 diskettes.
Business and Economics; Computer Science
Dist - VIDEOT **Prod** - ANDRST

Lotus 1 - 2 - 3 release 2.2 transition
VHS / U-matic
Color (H C G)
$795.00, $695.00 purchase _ #07 - LL2
Offers two parts designed for previous Lotus users. Covers basic instructions on the 2.2 version in Moving Up With Lotus. Discusses comprehensively add - in programs such as Macro Library Manager Add - In Program and Allways. Includes 2 videocassettes, 2 guides and 2 diskettes. Published by Learn - PC.
Business and Economics; Computer Science
Dist - VIDEOT

Lotus 1 - 2 - 3 - release 2.2 - Volume I
VHS
Color (H C G)
$325.00 purchase _ #07 - LVI
Shows how to master the new features of Lotus 1 - 2 - 3 Release 2.2. Covers creating spreadsheets, working with formulas and functions, editing, formatting and printing the worksheet. Includes a videocassette, a guide and a diskette.
Business and Economics; Computer Science
Dist - VIDEOT **Prod** - ANDRST

Lotus 1 - 2 - 3 - release 2.2 - Volume II
VHS
Color (H C G)
$325.00 purchase _ #07 - VII
Covers graphing worksheet data, printing graphs, managing large worksheets and working with macros. Includes a videocassette, a guide and a diskette.
Business and Economics; Computer Science
Dist - VIDEOT **Prod** - ANDRST

Lotus 1 - 2 - 3 - release 2.2 - Volume III
VHS
Color (H C G)
$325.00 purchase _ #07 - III
Covers advanced skills of Release 2.2 - linking files, graphing linked data, using Allways and working with a database. Includes a videocassette, a guide and a diskette.
Business and Economics; Computer Science
Dist - VIDEOT **Prod** - ANDRST

Lotus 1 - 2 - 3 release 3
VHS / U-matic
Color (H C G)
$1545.00, $1395.00 purchase _ #07 - NL3
Trains new users of the Lotus 1 - 2 - 3 Release 3. Covers creating effective spreadsheets, customizing and printing spreadsheets, mastering linking and database management, harnessing the power of macros, utilizing advanced functions and creating and printing graphs. Includes 6 videocassettes, 6 guides and a diskette. Published by Learn - PC.
Business and Economics; Computer Science
Dist - VIDEOT

Lotus 1 - 2 - 3 - release 3 - complete set
VHS
Color (H C G)
$595.00 purchase _ #07 - LO3 - 3II
Presents two courses on Lotus 1 - 2 - 3 - Release 3. Covers new commands and the 3D environment, multiple files, linking files, creating a macro library and using record. Includes 2 videocassettes, 2 guides and 2 diskettes.
Business and Economics; Computer Science
Dist - VIDEOT **Prod** - ANDRST

Lotus 1 - 2 - 3 release 3 transition
VHS / U-matic
Color (H C G)
$795.00, $695.00 purchase _ #07 - LL3
Presents the most important new features of Release 3. Includes 2 videocassettes, 2 guides and 2 diskettes. Published by Learn - PC.
Business and Economics; Computer Science
Dist - VIDEOT

Lotus 1 - 2 - 3 - release 3 - Volume I
VHS
Color (H C G)
$325.00 purchase _ #07 - LO3
Covers Lotus 1 - 2 - 3 - Release 3. Teaches new worksheet commands, working in the 3D worksheet environment, consolidating data from multiple worksheets and working with graphs and data. Includes a videocassette, a guide and a diskette.
Business and Economics; Computer Science
Dist - VIDEOT **Prod** - ANDRST

Lotus 1 - 2 - 3 - release 3 - Volume II
VHS
Color (H C G)
$325.00 purchase _ #07 - 3II
Covers Lotus 1 - 2 - 3 - Release 3. Works with multiple files, linking files, graphing data, working with database tables, creating a macro library and using record. Includes a videocassette, a guide and a diskette.
Business and Economics; Computer Science
Dist - VIDEOT **Prod** - ANDRST

Lotus 1 - 2 - 3 - Windows level II 60 MIN
VHS
Windows applications series
Color (J H C G)
$29.95 purchase _ #VP157V
Offers intermediate concepts in Lotus 1 - 2 - 3 - Windows. Allows viewer to see keyboard and monitor simultaneously so that students can see the result of every keystroke. Part of an eight - part series on Windows.
Computer Science
Dist - CAMV

Lotus 1 - 2 - 3 Windows release 4.0 179 MIN
U-matic / VHS / BETA
Color; NTSC; PAL; SECAM (J H G C)
PdS99.95
Presents the most - used features of the software. Features John Ball of Lotus Development - UK.
Computer Science
Dist - VIEWTH

LOTUS Plans 1978 60 MIN
VHS / U-matic
Color
Explains the plans for the Light Of Truth Universal Shrine (LOTUS) by architect Vishwanath Watson.
Religion and Philosophy
Dist - IYOGA **Prod** - IYOGA

Lotus series
Getting started with 1 - 2 - 3 for Windows
Getting started with 1 - 2 - 3 release 2.3
Dist - SIV

Lotus - the latest and greatest
VHS
Computer software training series
Color (J H C G)
$49.95 purchase _ #AAT10V
Teaches Lotus concepts in a comprehensive and easy - to - follow format. Illustrates actual commands and time saving techniques. Part of a 21 - part series on computer software.
Computer Science
Dist - CAMV

Lotus video series
Offers a series designed to familiarize viewers with the ins and outs of Lotus 1-2-3. Provides information for both beginners and experts, using illustrations and analogies. Notes creators of series are sole authorized developers of video training for Lotus 1-2-3 software. Details commands and functions of software program. Includes eight videocassettes focusing on various aspects of the Lotus 1-2-3 program.
Getting started - AmiPro
Getting started - 1 - 2 - 3 Windows
Getting started with 1 - 2 - 3
Using power of 1-2-3 Windows
Using the power of Allways
Using the power of Ami Pro
Dist - CAMV

Lotus video series
Power of linking spreadsheets
Using the power of 1 - 2 - 3 Windows
Using the power of WYSIWYG
Dist - CAMV
SIV

Lotus wing 17 MIN
16mm
Color & B&W (G)
$30.00 rental
States that the world is recommitting sexual - political suicide. Comments on the military and Krazy. A Jerry Abrams production.
Fine Arts
Dist - CANCIN

LOTUS...the latest and greatest - version 1 thru 3.1
VHS
Excellence in computer literacy series
Color (G)
$49.95 purchase
Covers LOTUS 1 - 2 - 3, versions 1 through 3.1. Shows how to view multidimensional spreadsheets, use enhanced state - of - the - art graphics. Discusses 40 new features and improved printing abilities. Examines the built - in macro library and displays new linking features.
Computer Science
Dist - SMPUB **Prod** - SMPUB

Lou Gehrig - in a league all by himself 24 MIN
VHS
American lifestyle series; The Singular American
Color (I J H C A)
$70.00 purchase, $50.00 rental _ #9887; $69.95 purchase _ #S01322
Profiles New York Yankees baseball star Lou Gehrig. Follows Gehrig's brilliant baseball career, including his time playing with the likes of Babe Ruth. Covers Gehrig's struggles with the muscular disease that ultimately took his life. Includes footage of his memorable farewell speech at Yankee Stadium in 1939. Hosted and narrated by Hugh Downs.
Biography; Physical Education and Recreation
Dist - AIMS **Prod** - COMCO 1986
UILL

Lou Gehrig's Disease 20 MIN
U-matic / VHS
Color
$335.00 purchase
From the ABC TV program, 20 - 20.
Health and Safety; Sociology
Dist - ABCLR **Prod** - ABCLR 1984

Lou Rawls 28 MIN
Videoreel / VT2
People in Jazz Series
Color (G)
$55.00 rental _ #PEIJ - 107
Presents the jazz music of Lou Rawls. Features host Jim Rockwell interviewing the artist.
Fine Arts
Dist - PBS **Prod** - WTVSTV

Lou Stovall 14 MIN
U-matic / VHS
Color (G A)
$45.00, $95.00 purchase _ #TCA13049, #TCA13048
Features artist Lou Stovall on the art of silkscreening. Takes a step - by - step look at the silkscreening process.
Fine Arts; Industrial and Technical Education
Dist - USNAC **Prod** - SMITHS 1983

Loucheux Summer 28 MIN
16mm
Color (G)
#3X23
Documents activities at the summer fish camp of the Loucheux Indians in the Northwest Territory of Canada. Explains the Loucheux way of life.
Social Science
Dist - CDIAND **Prod** - CAMACT 1983

Loud Sounds, Soft Sounds 11 MIN
U-matic / VHS / 16mm
Color (P I)
LC 74-702709
Identifies certain common things by the sounds they make.
Science - Physical
Dist - STANF **Prod** - STANF 1969

Loud Talk - 8 15 MIN
VHS
Wordscape Series
Color; Captioned (I) (ENGLISH AND OLD ENGLISH)
$125.00 purchase
Uses the word 'cell' approach to teach vocabulary, opening each of sixteen 15 - minute programs with several word cells familiar to fourth graders and using these 'cells' to form compound words. Employs animated graphics to dramatize how compounds are 'built' of cells that form a seemingly endless series of new words and to teach that understanding cell words can help to understand the new words composed of them. Uses a series of vignettes to define and demonstrate a number of word cells related to loud talk. Reveals the classical, Old English and Native American origins of some familiar words.
English Language; Psychology
Dist - AITECH **Prod** - OETVA 1990

Loud visual noises 3 MIN
16mm
Color (G)
$138.00, $196.00 purchase, $12.00, $16.00 rental
Presents a hand - painted film by Stan Brakhage, dedicated to filmmaker Paul Lundahl who supplied the title. Includes collaborative soundtrack compiled by Joel Haertling with sound contributions by Die Totliche Doris - Germany; Zoviet France, Nurse with Wound - United Kingdom; The Hafler Trio; Joel Haertling; and IHTSO - Germany; on the sound version.
Fine Arts
Dist - CANCIN **Prod** - BRAKS 1986

Louder, please and The greatest 30 MIN
VHS
Davey and Goliath series
Color (P I R)
$19.95 purchase, $10.00 rental _ #4 - 8821
Presents two 15 - minute 'Davey and Goliath' episodes. 'Louder, Please' shows how Davey learns to be sensitive to others' needs through a deaf boy. 'The Greatest' deals with single - parent families. Produced by the Evangelical Lutheran Church in America.
Literature and Drama; Religion and Philosophy
Dist - APH

Louder than Our Words - Women and Civil Disobedience 36 MIN
VHS / U-matic
Color
Follows the experience of one women's affinity group, from their discussions through their arrests at the June 14, 1982, peace action during the United Nations Special Session on Disarmament. Addresses the historical use of civil disobedience by women to gain political rights.
Social Science; Sociology
Dist - GMPF **Prod** - GMPF
WMEN

Louder than words 60 MIN
VHS
Childhood series
Color (H C G)
$99.95 purchase _ #AMB102V - K
Shows why shyness and sociability have a distinct biological component. Explores how parents' expectations and actions come to shape a child's behavior and character. Part of a seven - part series on the journey from birth to adolescence.
Health and Safety; Psychology
Dist - CAMV

Louder than Words 30 MIN
VHS / U-matic
Loosening the Grip Series
Color (C A)
Health and Safety
Dist - GPN **Prod** - UMA 1980

A Louer 13 MIN
16mm
En Francais, set 1 series
Color (I J H C)
Foreign Language
Dist - CHLTN **Prod** - PEREN 1969

Louis Armstrong 12 MIN
16mm
Color
Portrays Louis Armstrong, whose musical innovations, influence and inspiration changed and enriched the course of American music.
Biography; Fine Arts; History - United States
Dist - COUNFI **Prod** - HEARST

Louis Armstrong 30 MIN
16mm
B&W
Presents a jazz concert in which Louis Armstrong is accompanied by other jazz greats.
Fine Arts
Dist - REELIM **Prod** - GOODYR 1962

Louis Armstrong 20 MIN
U-matic
Truly American Series
Color (I)
Biography; Fine Arts; History - United States
Dist - GPN **Prod** - WVIZTV 1979

Louis Armstrong
16mm
Color
Offers reflections on Louis Armstrong's personality as reflected through his music.
Biography; Fine Arts
Dist - DIRECT **Prod** - DREWAS 1968

Louis Armstrong 13 MIN
VHS / U-matic
Color
Records the career and life of jazz immortal Louis Armstrong. Includes Billy Taylor, Peggy Lee, Fred Robbins and Al Hibbler, who participate in this tribute.
Biography; Fine Arts; History - United States
Dist - KINGFT **Prod** - KINGFT

Louis Armstrong - the Gentle Giant of Jazz 29 MIN
16mm
American Life Style Series
Color
LC 79-700068
Examines the life of Louis Armstrong and his accomplishments as a jazz musician. Includes newsreel footage and archival photographs.
Biography; Fine Arts; History - United States
Dist - SHOWCO **Prod** - USFGC 1978

Louis Armstrong - the gentle giant of jazz 24 MIN
VHS
American lifestyle series; The Singular American
Color (I J H C A)
$70.00 purchase, $50.00 rental _ #9889
Profiles jazz trumpeter Louis 'Satchmo' Armstrong. Hosted and narrated by Hugh Downs.
Biography; Fine Arts
Dist - AIMS **Prod** - COMCO 1986

Louis Blue 60 MIN
16mm
Color (G)
$225.00 rental
Interviews country jazz artists of the 1920s who recall their glory days and play some of the music that made them legends. Directed by Terry Zwigoff.
Biography; Fine Arts; History - United States
Dist - KINOIC

Louis Comfort Tiffany - Artist in Glass 30 MIN
VHS / U-matic
Color
Looks at the glass sculpture of Louis Comfort Tiffany, most of which is housed at the Chrysler Museum in Norfolk, VA. Explores the cultural development of Art Nouveau and Art Deco.
Fine Arts
Dist - MDCPB **Prod** - WHROTV

Louis Farrakhan - April 5, 1984
VHS
Nightline news library series
Color (J H C)
$19.98 purchase _ #MH6143V - S
Focuses on Louis Farrakhan in a news story by the ABC News Team. Part of a series from the news program, Nightline.
History - United States; Sociology
Dist - CAMV **Prod** - ABCNEW 1984

Louis Ginsberg - 5 - 9 - 74 35 MIN
VHS / Cassette
Poetry Center reading series
Color (G)
$15.00, $45.00 purchase, $15.00 rental _ #48 - 35A
Features poet Louis Ginsberg reading from his works at the Poetry Center, San Francisco State University, with an introduction by Nanos Valaoritis.
Literature and Drama
Dist - POETRY **Prod** - POETRY 1974

Louis I Kahn - Architect 28 MIN
16mm
Color
Describes architect Louis I Kahn's early rebellion against the Bauhaus and the classical clarity of his later works. Shows his gradual mastery of interior light effects as he talks of the building's slice of the sun. Presents examples of his works, including the Yale University Art Gallery, the Salk Institute in San Diego, the Olivetti plant in Pennsylvania and the Kimball Art Museum in Texas.
Fine Arts
Dist - MUSLAR **Prod** - MUSLAR 1977

Louis James Hates School 12 MIN
U-matic / VHS / 16mm
Color (P I)
LC 80-700350
Tells how Louis James hates everything about school and decides he doesn't need to read or spell in order to find a job and make lots of money. Traces his misadventures and describes his realization of the real values of reading and spelling.
Guidance and Counseling; Literature and Drama
Dist - LCOA **Prod** - ARTASI 1980

Louis Joseph Papineau - the Demi God 27 MIN
16mm
B&W (G)
_ #106B 0161 053
Shows the life of Louis Joseph Papineau, a proud defiant man, skillful in parliamentary debate and Speaker of the Lower House. His sympathies were with the plain people pillaged by a mercantile ruling clique. When legislation became the instrument of private advantage, he brought government to a standstill.
Biography; History - World
Dist - CFLMDC **Prod** - NFBC 1961

Louis P Hammett 45 MIN
VHS / U-matic
Eminent Chemists - the Interviews Series
Color
Provides a tour of Dr Louis P Hammett's career and accomplishments as an industrial chemist and long - time professor at Columbia University. Reviews the evolution of physical organic chemistry.
Science; Science - Physical
Dist - AMCHEM **Prod** - AMCHEM 1982

Louis Pasteur 24 MIN
16mm / U-matic / VHS
Great Scientists Speak Again Series
Color (H A)
LC 76-702125
Presents Professor Richard Eakin of the department of Zoology, University of California giving a lecture in which he impersonates Louis Pasteur in the words, dress and manner of his time. Recounts Pasteur's study of right - handed and left - handed molecules of tartic acid, fermentation, spontaneous generation and different kinds of disease - producing bacteria.
Biography; Health and Safety; History - World; Science; Science - Natural
Dist - UCEMC **Prod** - QUICK 1975

Louis Pasteur 10 MIN
U-matic / VHS
Color (C)
$229.00, $129.00 purchase _ #AD - 1849
Presents a brief biography of scientist Louis Pasteur. Recollects his life and work as a model of science serving the public interest. He was the first to prove that microorganisms cause fermentation and disease and originated the first vaccines against rabies, anthrax and chicken cholera. He developed the process of pasteurization used to retard food spoilage.
Biography; Science; Science - Natural
Dist - FOTH **Prod** - FOTH

Louis Pasteur - Man of Science 30 MIN
16mm
B&W (I)
Presents a biography of Louis Pasteur from 1857, when he discovered that microbes caused fermentation, to his death in 1865. Describes his contribution to pasteurization and the development of the vaccine.
Biography; Health and Safety; Science
Dist - SF **Prod** - SF 1959

Louis Pasteur proves germs cause disease 20 MIN
VHS
Giant steps in science and society series
Color; CC (I J H)
$79.00 purchase _ #193
Shows that, if the importance of a scientist is judged by how much his or her work has benefited humanity, Louis Pasteur was, without question, the greatest scientist who ever lived. Illustrates why he was. Includes a teacher's guide. Part of a four - part series.
Health and Safety; Science; Science - Natural
Dist - HAWHIL **Prod** - HAWHIL 1994

Louis Pasteur - the Vaccine 24 MIN
VHS / 16mm
Color (I)
LC 90706255
Presents an account of the life and work of Louis Pasteur. Highlights Pasteur's key role in developing the principles of germ theory and vaccination.
Health and Safety; History - World; Psychology; Science; Science - Natural
Dist - BARR

Louis Simpson 29 MIN
U-matic
Poets Talking Series
Color
Literature and Drama
Dist - UMITV **Prod** - UMITV 1975

Louis the Fish 30 MIN
VHS / U-matic
Reading Rainbow Series no 5
Color (P)
Presents Vincent Gardenia narrating the story Louis The Fish about a man who turns into a fish and leading LeVar Burton on an exploration of exotic marine life, tide pools and dolphins.
English Language; Social Science
Dist - GPN **Prod** - WNEDTV 1982

Louis XIV's Great Century 28 MIN
VHS / U-matic
Once upon a Time - Man Series
Color (P I)
$99.00
Traces the evolution of French history from 1680 during the reign of Louis XIV, the Sun King. Animated.
Civics and Political Systems; History - World
Dist - LANDMK **Prod** - LANDMK 1981

Louis Zukofsky - 3 - 16 - 66 30 MIN
VHS / Cassette
NET Outtake series
B&W (G)
$15.00, $125.00 purchase, $15.00 rental _ #188 - 145
Features writer Louis Zukofsky at his New York City apartment reading part of A'9 and a long section from Catullus which he translated with his wife, Celia Zukofsky. Includes an extensive discussion of James Joyce, Walt Whitman, Ezra Pound and Basil Bunting, and footage of a walk through Manhattan. Part of a series of films composed of outtakes from the series USA - Poetry, which was produced in 1965 - 66 for National Educational Television, using all retrievable footage to provide rare glimpses of the poets in their own settings. Interviewed by Richard O Moore.
Guidance and Counseling; Literature and Drama
Dist - POETRY **Prod** - KQEDTV 1966

Louisa May Alcott
VHS / 35mm strip
Meet the Classic Authors Series
Color (I)
$39.95, $28.00 purchase
Portrays Louisa May Alcott. Part of a series on authors.
English Language; Literature and Drama
Dist - PELLER

Louisbourg 20 MIN
16mm
Color (G)
_ #106C 0172 553
Details what was involved in the restoration of the Fortress of Louisbourg, a fort originally built by King Louis XV during the French colonial era to protect French possessions in the new world. Located on the Atlantic shore of Cape Breton Island, considered to be the biggest archaeological dig in North America.
History - World; Sociology
Dist - CFLMDC **Prod** - NFBC 1972

Louise Bernikow - 11 - 20 - 80 60 MIN
VHS / Cassette
Poetry Center reading series
Color (G)
$15.00, $45.00 purchase _ #419 - 345
Features the writer reading from Among Women, a chapter on the friendship between Virginia Woolf and Katherine Mansfield, at the Poetry Center, San Francisco State University.
History - World; Literature and Drama; Sociology
Dist - POETRY **Prod** - POETRY 1980

Louise Burns, Kate Johnson and Jennifer Way 30 MIN
VHS / U-matic
Great Performers Series
Color
Fine Arts; Industrial and Technical Education
Dist - ARCVID **Prod** - ARCVID

Louise Erdich and Michael Dorris 27 MIN
VHS
Color (H C G)
$79.00 purchase
Features Native American writers Louise Erdich and Michael Dorris with Paul Bailey, discussing the cultural and political influence of American Indians in US society and literature. Talks about their works that include Beet Queen; Love Medicine and Yellow Raft in Blue Water.
Literature and Drama; Social Science; Sociology
Dist - ROLAND **Prod** - INCART

Louise Erdrich and Michael Dorris 30 MIN
VHS
World Of Ideas With Bill Moyers - Season I - series; Season I
Color (G)
$39.95 purchase _ #BMWI - 145
Interviews husband and wife writing team Louise Erdrich and Michael Dorris. Discusses their status as Native Americans and how this influences their writing. Hosted by Bill Moyers.
History - United States; Social Science
Dist - PBS

Louise Gluck - 5 - 10 - 90 29 MIN
VHS / Cassette
Poetry Center reading series
Color (G)
$15.00, $45.00 purchase, $15.00 rental _ #887
Features writer Louise Gluck reading from her book of poems, Ararat, at the Poetry Center, San Francisco State University, with an introduction by Robert Gluck.
Literature and Drama
Dist - POETRY **Prod** - POETRY 1990

Louise Gluck - 4 - 4 - 88 60 MIN
VHS / Cassette
Lannan Literary series
Color (G)
$15.00, $19.95 purchase, $15.00 rental _ #889
Features writer Louise Gluck reading from her four published books of poems, Firstborn; Descending Figure; The House On Marshland; and The Triumph Of Achilles, and from a collection of works in progress entitled Ararat, at the Los Angeles Theatre Center. Includes an interview by Lewis MacAdams. Part of a series of literary videotapes presenting major poets and writers from around the globe reading and talking about their work; readings were sponsored by The Lannan Foundation, a private contemporary arts organization.
Guidance and Counseling; Literature and Drama
Dist - POETRY **Prod** - METEZT 1988

Louise Gluck - 2 - 25 - 76 35 MIN
VHS / Cassette
Poetry Center reading series
Color (G)
$15.00, $45.00 purchase, $15.00 rental _ #169 - 132A
Features writer Louise Gluck reading from her works at the Poetry Center, San Francisco State University, with an introduction by Lewis MacAdams.
Literature and Drama
Dist - POETRY **Prod** - POETRY 1976

Louise Nevelson 25 MIN
16mm
Color (C A)
LC 73-701406
Features sculptor Louise Nevelson commenting on her art and telling of the development of the various periods in her work.
Fine Arts
Dist - CONNF **Prod** - CONNF 1971

Louise Nevelson in Process 29 MIN
VHS
Color (S)
$29.95 purchase _ #405 - 9166
Indicates that Louise Nevelson was in her 70s before American art critics recognized a woman's contribution to the sculpture of her country. Reveals that as an unrecognized woman sculptor she had little money for materials so she improvised with 'trash' found in the streets of New York to construct her special environmental art. Nevelson creates two new sculptures on camera, providing a rare opportunity for viewers to share in the unfolding of their unique sculptural process.
Fine Arts; Psychology; Sociology
Dist - FI **Prod** - WNETTV 1986

Louise Nevelson in Process 29 MIN
VHS
Color (I)
$29.95 purchase _ #HV - 667
Shows Louise Nevelson creating two new sculptures. Provides rare opportunity to share in the unfolding of her unique sculptural process.
Fine Arts
Dist - CRYSP **Prod** - CRYSP

Louise Nevelson in process 29 MIN
VHS
Color (H C A)
$29.95 purchase; $29.95 purchase _ #HV-667; $29.95 purchase _ #405-9166
Shows the creative process of Louise Nevelson as she creates two new sculptures while being filmed. Points out the lack of recognition in her early years that forced her to use found materials in her art.
Fine Arts
Dist - ARTSAM **Prod** - WNETTV
CRYSP
FI

Louise Torres 43 MIN
U-matic / VHS
Color (H C A)
Follows the Hispanic traditions of the mountain folk of northern New Mexico through the eyes of a 79 - year - old woman going about her simple tasks. Presents medicinal native plants and the casket she made for herself to spare her family the burden.
Sociology
Dist - CEPRO **Prod** - BLUSKY

Louisiana 60 MIN
VHS
Portrait of America series
Color (J H C G)
$99.95 purchase _ #AMB18V
Visits Louisiana and offers extensive research into the state's history. Films key locations and presents segments on history, government, education, folklore, science, journalism, sociology, industry, agriculture and business. Shows what is unique about Louisiana and distinctive about its regional culture and how it got to be that way. Includes study guide. Part of a 50 - part series.
Geography - United States; History - United States
Dist - CAMV

Louisiana Bass Champ 25 MIN
16mm
Color
LC 79-701048
Focuses on the Atchfalaya Basin in Louisiana, discussing its early settlement by French Canadians and showing the various types of wildlife found in the area.
Geography - United States
Dist - VICFIP **Prod** - VICFIP 1978

Louisiana Cajun Cooking 18 MIN
16mm
Color (H)
Shows the variety, styles and methods of cooking done by the Cajuns in Louisiana.
Home Economics
Dist - AGA **Prod** - AGA 1981

Louisiana films series
J'ai ete au bal - I went to the dance - the Cajun and Zydeco music of Louisiana 84 MIN
Yum, yum, yum 31 MIN
Dist - FLOWER

Louisiana Plantation 15 MIN
U-matic / VHS / 16mm
American Scrapbook Series
Color (I)
Depicts the early exploration of the southern United States. Discusses farming, slave labor and the eventual establishment of the large, self - sufficient plantations of the region.
Agriculture; History - United States
Dist - GPN **Prod** - WVIZTV 1977

The Louisiana Purchase 15 MIN
VHS
Color (J H C G)
$39.00 purchase _ #SOC130V
Describes the far - reaching effects on the US of the purchase of Louisiana Territory from the French in 1803. Shows how the Louisiana Purchase more than doubled the size of the United States without bloodshed, creating a new frontier and intensifying the struggle between slave and free states. Examines why Napoleon wanted Louisiana and why he sold it, how the Louisiana Purchase upset the balance of power in the American government, and how the acquisition of so much territory changed Americans' view of themselves and their future. Includes teacher's guide.
History - United States
Dist - CAMV

Louisiana Purchase - America's Best Buy 30 MIN
16mm
Great Plains Trilogy, 3 Series Explorer and Settler - the White Man 'Arrives; Explorer and settler - the white man arrives
B&W (H C A)
Describes the role of the Mississippi Valley in world diplomacy, pointing out the details and significance of the Louisiana Purchase. Traces the Lewis and Clarke expedition, their first camp in Nebraska, their council with the Indians and the significance of the expedition.
History - United States
Dist - UNEBR **Prod** - KUONTV 1954

Louisiana State
VHS
Campus clips series
Color (H C A)

$29.95 purchase _ #CC0031V
Takes a video visit to the campus of Louisiana State University. Shows many of the distinctive features of the campus, and interviews students about their experiences. Provides information on the composition of the student body, professors, academics, social life, housing, and other subjects.
Education
Dist - CAMV

Louisiana story 79 MIN
VHS
B&W (G)
$29.95 purchase _ #S01949
Documents the effects of oil industrialization on Louisiana, focusing on a boy's perspective. Directed by Robert Flaherty. Filmed in 1948.
Fine Arts; History - United States; Social Science
Dist - UILL

Louisiana Territory 15 MIN
U-matic / VHS / 16mm
United States Expansion Series
Color (J H)
$420 purchase - 16 mm, $250 purchase - video _ #5765C
Discusses the history of the Louisiana Territory and explains the influence of the French, Spanish, and English. A Donald Klugman communication production.
History - United States
Dist - CORF

Louisiana's Fabled Plantations 28 MIN
16mm
Tour Louisiana Travel Series
Color
LC 78-701559
Shows 22 Louisiana plantations which are open to the public.
Geography - United States
Dist - RAMSEY **Prod** - LATPA 1978

Louisville 13 MIN
16mm
Color
LC 75-703519
Tours the International Harvester Company's manufacturing plant at Louisville, including coverage of employee participation in its open house activities.
Business and Economics; Geography - United States; Guidance and Counseling
Dist - IH **Prod** - IH 1975

Loulou 110 MIN
16mm
Color (FRENCH (ENGLISH SUBTITLES))
A French language motion picture with English subtitles. Tells how a middle class woman leaves her husband for a leather - jacketed Romeo. Directed by Maurice Pialat.
Fine Arts; Foreign Language
Dist - NYFLMS **Prod** - UNKNWN 1980

The Louvre
BETA / VHS
Color
Tours the Louvre and explores both its collection of masterpieces and its dramatic history. Hosted by Charles Boyer.
Fine Arts; Geography - World
Dist - GA **Prod** - GA

The Louvre 53 MIN
VHS
Color (S)
$24.95 purchase _ #560 - 9001
Pays homage to the world's greatest collection of art, the Louvre. Reveals that every year more than two million visiters view its collection. Features Charles Boyer as host for a tour of the museum and the more than eight centuries of art it houses.
Fine Arts; Geography - World
Dist - FI **Prod** - FRIHOM 1988

The Louvre 44 MIN
16mm / VHS / U-matic
Humanities - the Fine Arts Series
Color (H C)
LC FIA67-1238
Traces the evolution of the Louvre in terms of the historical and cultural growth of France from the Renaissance. Provides close - ups of paintings and sculptures in this museum, which was once the residence of French kings. Narrated by Charles Boyer.
Fine Arts; History - World
Dist - EBEC **Prod** - NBCTV 1966

The Louvre - 1 105 MIN
BETA / VHS
Grand museum series
Color (G)
$29.95 purchase
Visits the Louvre. Offers close - up views of paintings with informative narrative rich in artistic and historic detail. Includes a chronological list of the works and artists shown. Part one of a three - parts series on famous art museums produced by Vistar.
Fine Arts
Dist - ARTSAM

Lovable Lyle 15 MIN
U-matic / VHS
Picture Book Park Series Red Module; Red module
Color (P)
Presents the children's story Lovable Lyle by Bernard Waber.
Literature and Drama
Dist - AITECH **Prod** - WVIZTV 1974

Love 30 MIN
VHS
How do you do - learning English series
Color (H A)
#317723
Shows how CHIPS learns about dating, romance and marriage. Part of a series that helps newcomers learn English or improve their ability. Includes viewer's guide with grammar explanations and vocabulary drills, worksheets and two audio cassettes.
English Language; Religion and Philosophy
Dist - TVOTAR **Prod** - TVOTAR 1990

Love 11 MIN
16mm
Family Life Education and Human Growth Series
Color (J H)
Presents the question of definition and responsibilities of love as opposed to the feelings of sex.
Guidance and Counseling; Psychology; Sociology
Dist - SF **Prod** - SF 1970

Love 2 MIN
16mm
Meditation Series
Color (I)
LC 80-700752
Creates a mood for discussion, thought, prayer or meditation on the subject of God is love.
Religion and Philosophy
Dist - IKONOG **Prod** - IKONOG 1975

Love 29 MIN
VHS / 16mm
Feelings Series
Color (G)
$55.00 rental _ #FEES-105; $69.95 purchase
Attempts to define love through the eyes and experiences of three fifth graders.
Sociology
Dist - PBS **Prod** - SCETV
SCETV

Love 27 MIN
VHS
Sunshine factory series
Color (P I R)
$14.99 purchase _ #35 - 83588 - 533
Features P J the repairman and kids in his neighborhood as they travel to the Sunshine Factory, a land populated by puppets, a computer and caring adults. Teaches a Biblically - based lesson on love.
Religion and Philosophy
Dist - APH **Prod** - WORD

Love and Adventure - Hamilton 45 MIN
Videoreel / VT2
Humanities Series Unit II - the World of Myth and Legend
Color
Literature and Drama; Religion and Philosophy
Dist - GPN **Prod** - WTTWTV

Love and Anarchy 108 MIN
16mm
Color (H C A)
LC 76-702145
Tells the story of shy country peasant who goes to the city with a plan to assassinate Benito Mussolini. Shows how his underground contact in the network of anarchists offers him a hideout in her brothel where he meets a young prostitute and falls in love.
Fine Arts
Dist - CINEMV **Prod** - CARDAR 1975

Love and Believe in Yourself
VHS
Color (G)
$19.95 purchase _ #VHS117
Uses two types of hypnosis and two types of subliminal suggestions.
Health and Safety; Psychology
Dist - VSPU **Prod** - VSPU

Love and Discipline, Self Esteem and Family Communications 60 MIN
BETA / VHS
Successful Parenting Series
Color
Guidance and Counseling; Religion and Philosophy; Sociology
Dist - DSP **Prod** - DSP

Love and Friendship at the Office 30 MIN
VHS / 16mm
(PRO G)
$89.95 purchase _ #DGP9
Talks about the difficulties and rewards of love and friendship in the office from the point of view of a president of an NBC TV affiliate who married her newscaster. Hosted by Dick Goldberg.
Business and Economics
Dist - RMIBHF **Prod** - RMIBHF

Love and Learn 10 MIN
U-matic
Color
LC 81-706222
Depicts the interaction between six preschoolers and six nursing home grandmothers who have been teamed for a weekly sharing of stories, games and affection.
Sociology
Dist - ADELPH **Prod** - ADELPH 1980

Love and Loneliness 29 MIN
U-matic / VHS
Young and Old - Reaching Out Series
Color (H C A)
LC 80-707180
Explores the satisfactions of love and the anguish of absence.
Guidance and Counseling; Psychology
Dist - PBS **Prod** - CRFI 1979

Love and Marriage
BETA / VHS
Adult Years - Continuity and Change Series
Color
Attempts to answer the question of love and marriage through a look at newlyweds, a Golden Wedding Anniversary couple, and a remarried couple.
Sociology
Dist - OHUTC **Prod** - OHUTC

Love and other sorrows 56 MIN
U-matic / 16mm / VHS
American short story series
Color (J H C A)
$750.00, $99.00 purchase _ #HP - 6216C
Adapts the short story 'First Love and Other Sorrows' by Harold Brodkey. Stars Stephen Mailer, Haviland Morris and Elizabeth Franz as the brother, older sister and widowed mother who try to impress each other, then finally try to relate to each other in a small American town in the 1950s. Produced by the American Playhouse.
Literature and Drama
Dist - CORF

Love and profit - the art of caring leadership 30 MIN
VHS
Color (PRO IND A)
$695.00 purchase, $195.00 rental _ #ETC20
Features James Autry, Fortune 500 executive and business consultant, presenting insight regarding humane management - including the elements of trust,honesty, special treatment and courage. Trains and inspires management teams. Includes leader's guide and participant's workbook. Other support materials available.
Business and Economics; Guidance and Counseling; Psychology
Dist - EXTR **Prod** - EXTR

Love and Sex 52 MIN
U-matic / VHS
Human Animal Series
Color (G)
$279.00, $179.00 purchase _ #AD - 1132
Provides an alternative look at sex as Phil Donahue shows women at a male strip club and a gay rights march. Considers also a teenage mother giving birth and a classroom where teachers and parents are trying to help teenagers come to grips with their sexual selves. Examines love, monogamy, heterosexuality and homosexuality in discussions with Dr William Masters and Dr June Reinisch. Part of a series by Phil Donahue on the Human Animal.
Health and Safety; Psychology; Religion and Philosophy; Sociology
Dist - FOTH **Prod** - FOTH

Love and the Goddess 58 MIN
Cassette / VHS
Power of Myth Series
Color (G)
$29.95, $9.95 purchase _ #XVLG, XALG; $39.95 purchase _ #TWOM - 105
Discusses romantic love. Examines the mythological image of women as goddess, virgin and Mother Earth. Part of the Power Of Myth series featuring Joseph Campbell.

Literature and Drama; Religion and Philosophy; Sociology
Dist - GAINST **Prod** - PBS
PBS
YELMON

Love and the Goddess
VHS / Cassette
Power of Myth Series
(G)
$29.95, $9.95 purchase
Features Joseph Campbell and Bill Moyers.
Literature and Drama; Religion and Philosophy
Dist - BKPEOP **Prod** - MFV

Love and the goddess
VHS
Power of myth series
Color (G)
$29.95 purchase
Presents 'Love And The Goddess,' the fifth part of the 'Power Of Myth' series with the late Joseph Campbell and Bill Moyers.
Religion and Philosophy
Dist - PBS **Prod** - WNETTV

Love at First Bite 96 MIN
16mm
Color (H C)
Presents the comedy about New York which has become so jaded, even Dracula doesn't scare its inhabitants. Stars Susan St James, George Hamilton and Richard Benjamin.
Fine Arts
Dist - TIMLIF **Prod** - AIP 1979

A Love Class 46 MIN
VHS / U-matic
Leo Buscaglia Series
Color
Psychology
Dist - DELTAK **Prod** - PBS

A Love Class with Leo Buscaglia 45 MIN
U-matic / VHS
Color
Presents Dr Leo Buscaglia in a question and answer session with a group of his students and friends in which he probes the dynamics of love and relationships.
Psychology
Dist - PBS **Prod** - KVIETV 1980

Love Conquers all - Love, Human, Divine Unlawful and Domesticated in the Canterbury Tales 45 MIN
VHS / U-matic
Survey of English Literature I Series
Color
Looks at the different types of love depicted in Chaucer's Canterbury Tales.
Literature and Drama
Dist - MDCPB **Prod** - MDCPB

Love games - Liebesspiel 2 MIN
16mm / VHS
B&W (G)
$16.50 rental
Creates in visual terms certain pure concepts best known otherwise through music. Exhibits a classical simplicity unique among filmmaker's works. The action sensuously expresses male - female duality.
Fine Arts
Dist - CANCIN **Prod** - FISCHF 1931

Love happens 12 MIN
16mm
Color (G)
$30.00 rental
Celebrates dance as an act of discovery and expression in the Haight - Ashbury ghetto. Features Michael McClure singing and Ken Kesey with his band of merrymakers. Produced by Bob Giorgio.
Fine Arts; History - United States; Religion and Philosophy
Dist - CANCIN

A love - hate affair 30 MIN
VHS
Cats series
Color; PAL (H C A)
PdS65 purchase
Describes the history of the domestic cat. Part two of a five part series.
Science - Natural
Dist - BBCENE

Love, Hatred, Friendship and God 120 MIN
U-matic / VHS
Color
Shows Sri Gurudev at Yogaville East where he answers questions on love, hatred, friendship and God.
Religion and Philosophy
Dist - IYOGA **Prod** - IYOGA

Love in Later Life 30 MIN
U-matic / VHS
Color (C A)
Affirms physical love as a life - long source of strength and pleasure. Shows a couple as they grew and changed through the years.
Health and Safety; Psychology
Dist - MMRC **Prod** - MMRC

The Love in my heart, it's okay to cry - Volume 8 60 MIN
VHS
Our friends on Wooster Square series
Color (K P I R)
$34.95 purchase, $10.00 rental _ #35 - 87174 - 460
Presents religious concepts through storylines, songs and Scripture. Features puppet characters including Smedly, Troll and Sizzle.
Fine Arts; Literature and Drama; Religion and Philosophy
Dist - APH **Prod** - FRACOC

Love in the Afternoon 126 MIN
16mm
B&W (J)
Presents Audrey Hepburn, Gary Cooper and Maurice Chevalier in the Billy Wilder story of the romance between a naive young music student and an aging millionaire swinger.
Fine Arts
Dist - CINEWO **Prod** - CINEWO 1957

Love in the Western World 145 MIN
U-matic
University of the Air Series
Color (J H C A)
$750.00 purchase, $250.00 rental
Shows five critical stages of the meaning of 'love' in the history of Western civilization and the 'solutions' that emerged in those stages which further our advance to the present. Program contains a series of five cassettes 29 minutes each.
History - World; Psychology; Sociology
Dist - CTV **Prod** - CTV 1977

Love is 1 MIN
16mm
Color
LC 72-702550
Presents an animated short - short, utilizing creative typography and colorful backgrounds to express the facetious concept that love may not always live up to its romantic reputation.
Fine Arts; Guidance and Counseling; Literature and Drama
Dist - USC **Prod** - USC 1972

Love is 15 MIN
U-matic
Can You Imagine Series
Color (P I)
Explains that a family is a close - knit group that will stick together.
Sociology
Dist - GPN **Prod** - WVIZTV

Love is a decision
VHS
Color (G R)
$129.95 purchase
Outlines a clear plan of Christian action for vital, healthy and growing relationships for engaged couples, newlyweds and veteran married people. Features Gary Smalley who stresses that love is a decision, not just a feeling, and that great marriages are achievements, not accidents. Demonstrates how honor is the the foundation for all healthy relationships, with honor there is hope that individuals can restore their relationship with God and loved ones. Includes six segments on two videos and a book and study guide.
Guidance and Counseling; Psychology; Religion and Philosophy; Sociology
Dist - GP

Love is Beautiful 15 MIN
16mm
Color (R)
Deals with the proper attitude toward sex, love and marriage in light of Christian scripture.
Guidance and Counseling; Religion and Philosophy
Dist - OUTRCH **Prod** - OUTRCH

Love is not enough 30 MIN
VHS
Color (H C G A R)
$39.95 purchase, $10.00 rental _ #35 - 83 - 2076
Features Lutheran theologian Joseph Sittler in a consideration of hunger issues. Emphasizes Sittler's point that Christians must do far more than 'throw crumbs' to the poor. Produced by Seraphim.
Religion and Philosophy; Sociology
Dist - APH

Love is the Answer 20 MIN
16mm
Color
LC 74-700351
Presents a story which compares the way a girl makes her husband's life better with the way silicones improve products.
Sociology
Dist - GE **Prod** - GE 1973

Love is to Grow on 24 MIN
16mm
Color
LC 77-701810
Shows the progress of Down's Syndrome children from birth through employment under a specialized and integrated educational system involving home, school and community environment.
Education; Psychology
Dist - MVI **Prod** - HCINST 1977

Love it - Leave it 15 MIN
16mm
Color (G)
$30.00 rental
Deals with patriotic color, football, nudity and parades set to a refrain of 'Love It' and coalescing into filmmaker's nightmare rendition of American the Awful.
Fine Arts; History - United States; Literature and Drama
Dist - CANCIN **Prod** - PALAZT 1973

Love it Like a Fool - a Film about Malvina Reynolds 28 MIN
16mm
Color (H C A)
LC 78-701586
Presents a biographical portrait of Malvina Reynolds, songwriter, performer, political activist and philosopher. Conveys her exuberance and enthusiasm for life through segments of her live performances, personal conversations and recordings of her songs.
Biography; Fine Arts
Dist - NEWDAY **Prod** - WNGRF 1977
AFA

Love Letter to Maryland 45 MIN
VHS / U-matic
Color
Tours the state of Maryland, visiting such locales as Deal Island, a quaint fishing village and Applegarth's boatyard in the beautiful town of Oxford.
History - United States
Dist - MDCPB **Prod** - MDCPB

Love letters 6 MIN
16mm
Color (A)
$10.00 rental
Satirizes everything everyone always wanted to see illustrated about sex but were afraid to ask. Gives the audience a light - hearted erotic abecedarian spoof.
Fine Arts; Literature and Drama
Dist - CANCIN **Prod** - COHENK 1972

Love, Liberty and the Pursuit of Conscience - John Adams and Massachusetts America 24 MIN
VHS
American Lifestyles II - Singular American Series
Color (I)
$70.00 purchase, $50.00 rental _ #9884
Narrates the story of John Adams, the second President and first Vice President of America and a tireless political leader with a passion for liberty. Hosted by E G Marshall.
Biography; History - United States
Dist - AIMS **Prod** - COMCO 1986

Love lorn giant, Enormous lies, Vixen & hare
U-matic / VHS / BETA
European folktale series
Color; PAL (P I)
PdS180, PdS188 purchase
Features folktales from Poland, Hungary and the USSR. Presents a series of 6 programs of 18 titles from 12 countries around the world. 3 animated programs per cassette.
Fine Arts; Literature and Drama
Dist - EDPAT **Prod** - HALAS

Love, Lynn 1 MIN
16mm
Color (G)
$10.00 rental
Expresses a poem from the filmmaker to her mother and grandmother.
Fine Arts; Literature and Drama; Sociology
Dist - CANCIN **Prod** - KIRBYL 1982

Love makes a family - gay parents in the '90s 16 MIN
VHS
Color (G)

$195.00 purchase, $100.00 rental _ #CJ - 116
Profiles a lesbian single mother who shares parenting with the gay father of her son; a lesbian couple, one of whom is deaf, who care for the children of a previous marriage, and a gay male couple with two adopted sons. Interviews a clinical psychologist and therapist who deal with gay families and their children. Produced by Remco Kobus, Marla Leech and Daniel Veltri.
Sociology
Dist - FANPRO

Love, marriage and family 60 MIN
VHS
Women of the world series
Color (G)
$59.95 purchase _ #WWRL - 102
Takes a look at marriage and family life throughout the world. Considers issues of monogamy, polygamy and differing styles of family life. Features actress Jane Seymour and Mila Mulroney, wife of the Canadian prime minister.
Sociology
Dist - PBS

Love Me and Leave Me 30 MIN
16mm
Footsteps Series
Color
LC 79-701549
Focuses on the relationship between parent and child, showing how this bond forms and how it affects the development of the child. Offers suggestions for making separations between parent and child easier.
Home Economics; Sociology
Dist - USNAC **Prod** - USOE 1978

Love - myth and mystery 30 MIN
VHS / U-matic
Art of being human series; Module 10
Color (C)
History - World; Literature and Drama; Religion and Philosophy
Dist - MDCC **Prod** - MDCC

Love note 60 MIN
VHS
Color (J H C G A R)
$49.95 purchase, $10.00 rental _ #35 - 824 - 2020
Tells how a young girl with cancer turned her back on her friends and family, until a new friend began to give her friendship, love and hope.
Guidance and Counseling; Health and Safety
Dist - APH **Prod** - ANDERK

The Love of Destiny 60 MIN
VHS
Color (G)
$19.95 purchase _ #1242
Showcases favorite operatic arias in a dramatic presentation. Features the works of Verdi, Puccini, Mascagni, Massinet and Donizetti.
Fine Arts
Dist - KULTUR

Love of Gardens, the, Pt 5 55 MIN
VHS
Hand and Eye Series - Vol III; Vol III; Pt 5
Color (S)
$99.00 purchase _ #386 - 9019
Melds together the past and the present in a celebration of handcrafted art. Traverses the globe to present the world's finest examples of sculpture, jewelry, glass, pottery, gardening, weaving and woodworking. Contemporary artisans demonstrate the ancient and innovative techniques they use to create their modern masterworks. Seven programs in four volumes. Part 5 takes viewers down the paths of some of the world's finest and most famous gardens.
Agriculture; Fine Arts
Dist - FI **Prod** - CANBC 1988

Love of God, feelings, sharing, joy - Volume 1 60 MIN
VHS
Our friends on Wooster Square series
Color (K P I R)
$34.95 purchase, $10.00 rental _ #35 - 87160 - 460
Presents religious concepts through storylines, songs and Scripture. Features puppet characters including Smedly, Troll and Sizzle. Explores concepts of the love of God, feelings, sharing and joy.
Fine Arts; Literature and Drama; Religion and Philosophy
Dist - APH **Prod** - FRACOC

Love of Life 91 MIN
16mm
Color (FRENCH (ENGLISH SUBTITLES))
Celebrates the life and work of pianist Arthur Rubenstein. Directed by Francois Reichenbach and S G Patris. With English subtitles.
Fine Arts; Foreign Language
Dist - NYFLMS **Prod** - UNKNWN 1968

Love of Life 30 MIN
U-matic / VHS / 16mm
Color (H C A)
LC 81-700002
Tells the story of a man's struggle for survival after he is deserted by his partner in the Canadian Klondike. Based on the story Love Of Life by Jack London. Narrated by Orson Welles.
Fine Arts; Literature and Drama; Sociology
Dist - LCOA **Prod** - NORCOM 1981

The Love of Three Oranges 118 MIN
VHS
Color (S)
$39.95 purchase _ #833 - 9272
Presents the Glyndebourne production of 'The Love Of Three Oranges' by Prokofiev. Stars Ryland Davies, Willard White and Nelly Morpurgo. Frank Cosaro directs, and Maurice Sendak, artist and author of children's books, creates a comic strip setting.
Fine Arts; Geography - World
Dist - FI **Prod** - NVIDC 1987

Love on Lushan Mountain 84 MIN
VHS
Color (G) (CHINESE WITH ENGLISH SUBTITLES)
$45.00 purchase _ #6052C
Presents a film from the People's Republic of China.
Geography - World; Literature and Drama
Dist - CHTSUI

Love on the run - L'Amour en fuite 95 MIN
VHS
Color (G)
$39.95 _ #LOV070
Features Truffaut's alter ego pursuing romance, his favorite pastime. Paints an affectionate portrait of Antione at 35, renewing old acquaintances, reliving bittersweet memories, and once again, taking a chance on love. Final film in the Antoine Doinel series. Produced by Les Films du Carrosse. Digitally remastered with new translation.
Fine Arts; Psychology; Religion and Philosophy; Sociology
Dist - HOMVIS

Love or money 25 MIN
VHS
Supervisors series
Color (A)
PdS50 purchase
Shows how supervisors can motivate their staff to get the best possible results, based on good relationships, delegation and incentives. Part of an eight-part series designed to help supervisors - particularly newly-appointed ones - to understand the demands of their individual roles through the experience of established supervisors who offer personal insights and strategies from within a framework of good practice.
Business and Economics; Psychology
Dist - BBCENE

Love potion number nine 6 MIN
16mm
B&W (G)
$10.00 rental
Features a humorous version of the classic legend in which a lovesick young man visits a gypsy fortune teller for relief. Presents a Fred Safran production.
Fine Arts; Literature and Drama; Religion and Philosophy
Dist - CANCIN

Love Seen 12 MIN
16mm
Color
LC 75-704319
Presents an analytic exercise in the ontology of the cinematic sex - scene.
Psychology; Sociology
Dist - CANFDC **Prod** - CANFDC 1974

Love, sex and God 10 MIN
VHS
Learning about sex series
Color (H R)
$12.95 purchase _ #87EE1026
Explains male and female sexual systems. Provides information on AIDS and venereal disease. Explores issues including sex in marriage, what to look for in a partner and the role of the family. Encourages teenagers to respect their bodies and maintain Christian standards for sex and dating.
Guidance and Counseling; Health and Safety; Literature and Drama; Religion and Philosophy; Sociology
Dist - CPH **Prod** - CPH

Love skills 56 MI
VHS
Color (C A)
$34.95 purchase
Offers chapters on sexual foreplay, positions, fantasies and obstacles to sexual fulfillment. Features five beautiful couples who demonstrate techniques. Contains sexually explicit material.
Fine Arts; Guidance and Counseling; Health and Safety; Physical Education and Recreation; Social Science
Dist - FCSINT

The Love Song of the Coocoo Birds 27 MIN
U-matic / VHS / 16mm
Insight Series
B&W (H C A)
LC 72-702005
Shows how an elderly couple, who are reduced to loneliness and poverty, manage to retain their dignity because their love for each other gives meaning to their lives.
Guidance and Counseling; Sociology
Dist - PAULST **Prod** - PAULST 1972

Love songs of the Miao in China 45 MIN
VHS
Color (H C G)
$350.00 purchase, $65.00 rental
Captures the lifestyle of the Miao who live deep in the mountains of southern China. Observes their courtship rituals which place a great deal of importance on love songs. Women and men woo each other with soulful songs and each year offers a regional festival, Pa - po - je, where the young go in search of marriage partners from another village. Focuses on a 17 - year - old girl who attends the festival and the everyday life of her family.
Geography - World; Guidance and Counseling; Sociology
Dist - FLMLIB **Prod** - NHK 1993

Love stories my grandmother tells - Part 1 30 MIN
16mm
B&W (G)
$60.00 rental
Portrays the filmmaker Dana Plays' 90 - year - old grandmother, Peggy Regler, reminiscing about her love affairs and significant relationships. Captures her memories of her failed first marriage, the true love she found with her second husband, writer Gustav Regler, and his tragic death in India. Juxtaposes the technological and political developments of the 20th century with the love affairs.
Fine Arts; Psychology; Sociology
Dist - CANCIN

Love Story 28 MIN
VHS
Color
$69.59 purchase _ #4077
Illuminated are the values and priorities needed to enjoy a meaningful life and fulfilling relationship.
Literature and Drama
Dist - AIMS **Prod** - AIMS

A Love Story 15 MIN
U-matic / VHS
Encounter in the Desert Series
Color (I)
Tells of marital customs among the Bedouins.
Geography - World; Social Science; Sociology
Dist - CTI **Prod** - CTI

Love Story 100 MIN
U-matic / VHS / 16mm
Color
Tells how a rich Harvard student and an ill - fated Radcliffe girl meet and fall in love. Stars Ryan O'Neal and Ali McGraw.
Fine Arts
Dist - FI **Prod** - PAR 1970

Love Story (and I Want Time) 28 MIN
U-matic / VHS / 16mm
Color (J A)
Edited from the motion picture Love Story. Traces the life of a young couple from their marriage to the untimely death of the young wife. Shows the needs of the dying and the grieving. Stars Ali McGraw and Ryan O'Neil.
Sociology
Dist - AIMS **Prod** - PAR 1977

Love Story - Donne's Love Poetry 45 MIN
VHS / U-matic
Survey of English Literature I Series
Color
Provides examples of John Donne's love poetry.
Literature and Drama
Dist - MDCPB **Prod** - MDCPB

A Love Story - the Canada Goose 23 MIN
U-matic / VHS
Color (K)
Visits the land of the Giant Canada Goose. Shows them raise their young in the face of constant danger from racoons, mink and man.
Science - Natural
Dist - NWLDPR **Prod** - NWLDPR

Love, Susan 15 MIN
U-matic / VHS / 16mm
Inside-out series
Color (I)
LC 73-702445
Helps children deal with the misunderstandings and conflicts that arise within even a loving family. Explains what happens when Susan's father arrives home from work, exhausted and troubled and rejects her pleas to look at the portrait that she has just painted. Depicts Susan's hurt and confusion.
Guidance and Counseling; Sociology
Dist - AITECH

Love Talks, Pt 1 30 MIN
U-matic / VHS
Color
Presents Dr Leo Buscaglia and a group of high school students who discuss the meaning of love and its risks. Emphasizes the idea that sharing love requires tolerance, compromise, respect and honesty.
Biography; Psychology
Dist - PBS **Prod** - PBS

Love Talks, Pt 2 30 MIN
VHS / U-matic
Color
Presents Dr Leo Buscaglia and a group of high school students who discuss the meaning of love and its risks. Emphasizes the idea that sharing love requires tolerance, compromise, respect and honesty.
Biography; Psychology
Dist - PBS **Prod** - PBS

Love Tapes - an Interactive Video Art Process 40 MIN
U-matic
B&W (A)
LC 81-706189
Presents eight individuals of various ages and lifestyles who are allowed three minutes each to express his or her perceptions and feelings about love.
Guidance and Counseling
Dist - FLMLIB **Prod** - CLARKW 1981

Love Tapes in New York 46 MIN
U-matic
B&W (A)
LC 80-707696
Shows eight people facing a video camera and expressing their perceptions of love.
Psychology
Dist - KINHOL **Prod** - CLARKW 1980

Love Tennis Series
Doubles Strategy 29 MIN
The Forehand 29 MIN
Interviews 29 MIN
Jargon, Scoring and Answers 29 MIN
The Lob and the Smash 29 MIN
The Return of the Serve 29 MIN
Singles Strategy 29 MIN
Dist - MDCPB

Love that Car 10 MIN
U-matic / VHS / 16mm
Color (H C A) (SPANISH)
LC FIA66-328
Presents a 'kidding - on - the - square' approach to the importance of car maintenance. Depicts the dilemmas in which several victims of carelessness find themselves.
Health and Safety; Industrial and Technical Education
Dist - AIMS **Prod** - PART 1967

Love that Pet 30 MIN
U-matic
Magic Ring II Series
(K P)
Continues the aim of the first series to bring added freshness to the commonplace and assist children to discover more about the many things in their world. Each program starts with the familiar, goes to the less familiar, then the new, and ends by blending new and old information.
Education; Literature and Drama
Dist - ACCESS **Prod** - ACCESS 1986

Love the Criminal, Hate the Crime 30 MIN
U-matic
Inside Japan Series
(H C A)
Gives an overview of the penal system of Japan and focuses on attitudes toward crime and punishment.
Geography - World; History - World
Dist - ACCESS **Prod** - ACCESS 1980

Love the first time around 15 MIN
VHS
Becoming independent series
Color (H G)
$79.00 purchase _ #CDHEC518V
Helps teens to understand the pitfalls inherent in the dating scene and introduces survival tips. Brings important developmental perspectives to the homronal urgency of teens. Part of a 13 - part series featuring practical life and consumer skills for teens venturing out into independence.
Guidance and Counseling; Health and Safety; Psychology; Social Science
Dist - CAMV

Love - the Ultimate Affirmation 58 MIN
VHS / U-matic
Color
Presents Dr Leo Buscaglia who offers a challenge to those who seek happiness and fulfillment in a relationship.
Psychology
Dist - PBS **Prod** - STSU 1979

Love those Trains 59 MIN
U-matic / VHS / 16mm
Color
Takes trips on famous trains such as Europe's Orient Express and the Salad Bowl Express which takes lettuce from California to New York. Interviews hoboes who use trains as their main method of transportation.
Social Science
Dist - NGS **Prod** - NGS 1984

Love Thy Customer 26 MIN
16mm
Color
LC FIA66-1283
Uses a kidding approach to show service writers how to better their relationship with the customers by doing things right the first time. Shows the customers as the service writers see them and the service writers and mechanics as the customers see them.
Business and Economics; Industrial and Technical Education
Dist - PART **Prod** - FMCMP 1966

Love to all, Lorraine 48 MIN
VHS
Color (G C H)
$139.00 purchase _ #DL490
Presents Elizabeth Van Dyke in a monologue that illuminates the moods, sufferings, goals and triumphs of playwright Lorraine Hansberry.
Fine Arts; History - United States
Dist - INSIM

Love to Kill 15 MIN
U-matic / VHS / 16mm
Searching for Values - a Film Anthology Series
Color (J)
LC 72-703094
Tells how six young boys, repulsed by their encounter with 'KILLING FOR SPORT' take action and become the victims themselves of society's violence. Explains that the boys free buffalo at a commercial buffalo preserve and that hunters, attempting to stop them, shoot and kill one of the boys.
Guidance and Counseling; Psychology; Science - Natural; Sociology
Dist - LCOA **Prod** - LCOA 1972

Love to write - creating an environment for writers - Tape 9 25 MIN
VHS
Teacher to teacher series
Color (T)
$100.00 purchase _ #888 - 9
Shows exerienced teachers in actual classroom settings presenting various instructional approaches to both new and veteran ABE and ESL teachers. Looks at a group of basic literacy students develop an understanding of themselves as writers as they learn the purpose of writing. Part nine of a 12 - part series.
Education; English Language
Dist - LAULIT **Prod** - LAULIT

Love, women and flowers - amor, mujeres y flores 58 MIN
VHS / U-matic / 16mm
Color (G) (SPANISH (ENGLISH SUBTITLES))
$295.00 purchase, $130.00, $100.00 rental
Looks at the production of flowers, which is Colombia's third largest export to the US and Europe. Reveals that the 60,000 women who work in the Colombian industry are routinely exposed to pesticides and fungicides, some of which are banned in the developed countries which export them to Colombia. Considers the dire health and environmental consequences of the unregulated use of agricultural chemicals. Produced by Marta Rodriguez and Jorge Silva.
Business and Economics; History - World; Social Science; Sociology
Dist - WMEN

Love your liver 45 MIN
VHS
Color (K P)
$60.00 purchase _ #CG - 977 - VS
Features rock musician and former drug abuser Jevon Thompson. Asks students and teachers to pretend to be livers, brains, lungs and a 'train' of positive and negative substances having their way with a kid's 'Best friend,' the human body.
Guidance and Counseling; Health and Safety; Psychology
Dist - HRMC **Prod** - HRMC 1992

Love your lungs 15 MIN
VHS
Color (P I J)
Portrays an older boy trying to persuade a younger friend to try a cigarette. Reveals that the boys are startled by the sudden appearance of a girl wearing a 'Love Your Lungs' T - shirt. Uses animation and dramatization to emphasize the importance of taking care of the respiratory system.
Health and Safety; Psychology; Science - Natural
Dist - VIEWTH **Prod** - VIEWTH

Loved, Honored and Bruised 25 MIN
16mm / U-matic / VHS
Color (H C A)
Documents the true story of Jeannie, beaten by her husband throughout the thirteen years of her marriage, who was too ashamed to ask for help. Tells how Jeannie and her five children were finally given shelter in a home for battered women and received counseling, financial aid, social support and legal aid to divorce her husband and start a new life.
Sociology
Dist - MEDIAG **Prod** - NFBC 1982

Lovejoy's Nuclear War 60 MIN
U-matic / VHS / 16mm
Color (J)
LC 75-704202
Describes how Sam Lovejoy burned a weather tower in Massachusetts which had been built prior to erecting a nuclear power plant. Explains that he took this action to protect other citizens from possible radioactive waste. Discusses the legal aspects of such a decision.
Civics and Political Systems; Science - Physical; Sociology
Dist - BULFRG **Prod** - GMPF 1975

Lovely, Lively Bavaria 23 MIN
16mm
Color
Records the changes that have turned parts of Bavaria into bustling centers of new industry and crafts. Describes Bavaria as taking its place in the mainstream of modern life while not seeming to change at all.
Geography - World; History - World
Dist - WSTGLC **Prod** - WSTGLC

Lovemaking 13 MIN
16mm
Color (A)
$25.00 rental
Presents an erotic rather than pornographic film.
Fine Arts
Dist - CANCIN **Prod** - BARTLS 1971

The Lovers 90 MIN
16mm
B&W (FRENCH (ENGLISH SUBTITLES))
Focuses on a provincial wife whose shallow life is changed by a night of love. Directed by Louis Malle. With English subtitles.
Fine Arts; Foreign Language
Dist - NYFLMS **Prod** - UNKNWN 1958

The Lovers 3 MIN
16mm
Color (G)
$10.00 rental
Contemplates the card from the Tarot, the Lovers, and examines the myths of romantic love in modern America. Produced by Beth Block.
Fine Arts; Religion and Philosophy
Dist - CANCIN

Lover's guide series
Advanced sex techniques 90 MIN
Better orgasms 60 MIN
Dist - FCSINT

The Lovers of Teruel 90 MIN
VHS
Color (G)
$39.95 purchase _ #1112
Combines the talents of Ludmila Tcherina, one of the greatest dance tragediennes of recent times, Raymond Rouleau, one of France's outstanding directors, cinematographer Claude Renoir and the music of Mikis Theodorakis ('Zorba The Greek'). Presents the conceptually revolutionary ballet, 'The Lovers Of Teruel.'.
Fine Arts; Foreign Language; Physical Education and Recreation
Dist - KULTUR

A Lover's Quarrel with the World 40 MIN
U-matic / VHS / 16mm
B&W (J)
LC 77-712364
Presents a portrait of the American poet Robert Frost, revealing his key philosophic and artistic views.
Biography; Fine Arts; Literature and Drama
Dist - PHENIX **Prod** - PFP 1970

Love's awakening 30 MIN
VHS
Color (G R)
$34.95 purchase, $10.00 rental _ #35 - 87395 - 460
Presents eight visual and musical meditations on love. Includes both secular and sacred songs, such as John Denver's 'Annie's Song,' Elton John's 'Love Song,' and 'Jesu, Joy of Man's Desiring.'
Fine Arts; Religion and Philosophy
Dist - APH **Prod** - FRACOC

Love's labors 60 MIN
VHS
Childhood series
Color (H C G)
$99.95 purchase _ #AMB103V - K
Explores the period between 6 months and 3 years. Reveals that every day brings startling evidence of rapid maturing of both the brain and the body - improved coordination, increased mobility, the first words, and an emerging sense of self. Part of a seven - part series on the journey from birth to adolescence.
Health and Safety; Psychology
Dist - CAMV

Love's labour's lost 120 MIN
VHS
BBC Shakespeare series
Color (G C H)
$109.00 purchase _ #DL454
Fine Arts
Dist - INSIM **Prod** - BBC

Love's Labour's Lost 120 MIN
VHS / 16mm
BBC's Shakespeare Series
(H A)
$249.95
Recounts the Shakespearean satire of the King of Navarre.
Literature and Drama
Dist - AMBROS **Prod** - AMBROS 1984

Love's Labour's Lost 29 MIN
Videoreel / VT2
Feast of Language Series
Color
Features Alan Levitan, associate professor of English at Brandeis University discussing Love's Labour's Lost by Shakespeare.
Literature and Drama
Dist - PBS **Prod** - WGBHTV

Love's Labour's Lost 120 MIN
U-matic / VHS
Shakespeare Plays Series
Color (H C A)
Offers a satire directed against intellectual pride and pedantry in which the king of Navarre and three of his lords vow to spend three years in study and not to see any women. Reveals that when the Princess of France arrives on a diplomatic mission with her three ladies, the men break their vow and fall in love with them.
Literature and Drama
Dist - TIMLIF **Prod** - BBCTV 1984

Loves of a blonde 89 MIN
VHS
B&W (G)
$39.95 purchase _ #LOV100
Studies with compassion the pathos of young love. Focuses on an idealistic factory worker who is seduced by a handsome musician and consequently falls in love with him, arriving at the Prague home of his parents full of hope. Produced by IFEX.
Fine Arts; Psychology; Religion and Philosophy
Dist - HOMVIS

Love's Sweet Song 29 MIN
Videoreel / VT2
Our Street Series
Color
Sociology
Dist - PBS **Prod** - MDCPB

Love's Tough Reach 30 MIN
VHS / U-matic
Color (J H A)
LC 85-703549
Tells the story of a father's love, understanding and respect for his wild daughter.
Sociology
Dist - EBEC **Prod** - BYU 1983

Lovesick 15 MIN
VHS
Color (I J H)
$75.00 purchase _ #433 - V8
Depicts boys and young men discussing their experiences with relationships, what they do 'for love,' and the sexual pressures they face from friends and society. Stimulates discussion about the nature of quality relationships for male and female audiences.
Guidance and Counseling; Health and Safety; Sociology
Dist - ETRASS **Prod** - ETRASS

Lovesick 28 MIN
16mm / U-matic / VHS
Color (H C A)
LC 76-702380
Shows a frustrated and lonely writer who tries to win the heart of a neighborhood prostitute. Results are funny, painfully sad and for a brief moment, successful in breaking through the harsh realities of life that often stifle the possibilities of love.
Fine Arts
Dist - PHENIX **Prod** - DNBAUM 1976

Lovey - a Circle of Children II 120 MIN
U-matic / VHS / 16mm
Color (H C A)
Tells the story of Mary McCracken, a special education teacher who must try to reach a little girl who has been diagnosed as schizophrenic or brain - damaged. Views Mary's personal life and shows how she must get over her divorce to venture forth with romance and a new life. Stars Jane Alexander.
Education; Fine Arts
Dist - TIMLIF **Prod** - TIMLIF 1982

Loving 6 MIN
16mm
Color (G)
$12.00 rental, $196.00 purchase
Says Cinema 16, 'The greens of the forest, the flesh tones of the lovers, the browns of earth, the sky and the sun evolve an expression of living in which the light consumes everything except the flesh of loving.'
Fine Arts
Dist - CANCIN **Prod** - BRAKS 1957

Loving and caring - Variations to lovemaking - Tape 3 52 MIN
VHS
Loving better series
Color (C A)
$34.95 purchase
Opens with a discussion of self - loving and explores masturbation. Uses humor to contrast the differing sexual behavior and priorities of two couples. Demonstrates three basic positions for intercourse, along with modifications and suggestions for greater pleasure. Illustrates a couple freely enjoying and demonstrating all the techniques and approaches introduced in earlier segments of the series. Contains explicit sexual material. Created by Dr Sheldon Kule, Clinical Assoc Prof and Chair, Dept of Psychiatry, New York College of Osteopathic Medicine.
Guidance and Counseling; Health and Safety; Physical Education and Recreation; Science - Natural; Social Science
Dist - FCSINT

Loving better series
The Basics - getting started - Tape 1 47 MIN
Discovery - Communicating through touch - Tape 2 53 MIN
Loving and caring - Variations to lovemaking - Tape 3 52 MIN
Sexual problems - Tape 5 40 MIN
Dist - FCSINT

Loving Couples 97 MIN
16mm / U-matic / VHS
Color (H C A)
Tells the stories of two couples, one married and one unmarried who regroup in rather unconventional ways. Stars Shirley MacLaine, James Coburn, Susan Sarandon and Stephen Collins.
Sociology
Dist - TIMLIF **Prod** - TIMLIF 1982

Loving Hands 23 MIN
16mm
Color
Shows how a mother can transmit love, energy, and well - being to her infant through massage. Directed by Frederick Leboyer.
Health and Safety; Home Economics
Dist - NYFLMS **Prod** - UNKNWN 1976

Loving Krishna 40 MIN
VHS / U-matic
Color (J H C A)
Looks at the worship of Krishna and examines the central concepts of Hindu sacred life.
Religion and Philosophy
Dist - CEPRO **Prod** - HUFSC 1986

Loving Me is Loving You 15 MIN
U-matic
Success in the Job Market Series
Color (H)
Shows a young man settling into his new job, explaining that he must learn to adapt to the change.
Guidance and Counseling; Psychology
Dist - GPN **Prod** - KUONTV 1980

Loving rebel 26 MIN
VHS / U-matic
Color (H C G)
$350.00, $325.00 purchase _ #V380
Profiles Helen Hunt Jackson, one of the 19th century's foremost advocates of Native American rights and one of its most celebrated writers. Features readings from her writings, photographs and drawings of Jackson's era.
Biography; Civics and Political Systems; History - United States; Literature and Drama; Social Science
Dist - BARR **Prod** - CEPRO 1987

Loving Relationships with Leo Buscaglia 50 MIN
U-matic / VHS
Color
Provides an affectionate trip through Leo Buscaglia's rich repertoire of warm family stories and personal experiences.
Biography; Psychology
Dist - PBS **Prod** - PBS

Loving Young Company 16 MIN
16mm
Color
Shows groups of American teenagers visiting Israel in the summer time. Follows their tour through the country, creating new friendships, acquainting themselves with the country and its people and having fun.
Geography - World
Dist - ALDEN **Prod** - ALDEN

Lovins on the Soft Path - an Energy Future with a Future 36 MIN
16mm / U-matic / VHS
Color (H C A)
LC 82-700651
Presents energy analysts Amory and Hunter Lovins who argue that the only long - term solution to the energy crisis lies in using energy efficiently and adopting appropriate renewable energy sources as opposed to nuclear power and coal.
Science - Natural; Social Science; Sociology
Dist - BULFRG **Prod** - ECECF 1982

Lovis James Hates School 11 MIN
U-matic / VHS / 16mm
Captioned; Color (P I)
Tells the story of young boy who decides to quit school for adventure, only to learn he needs to be back in school.
Fine Arts; Literature and Drama
Dist - LCOA **Prod** - ARTASI 1980

Low back extension exercises
U-matic / VHS
Physical therapy series
Color (PRO C G)
$195.00 purchase _ #C890 - VI - 008
Informs patient educators and patients about the benefits of low back extension exercises. Teaches effective techniques for minimizing pain and fatigue while enhancing the ability to perform daily activities. Part of a series by the physical therapy staff, St Luke's Hospital, Fargo, North Dakota.
Health and Safety; Physical Education and Recreation; Science - Natural
Dist - HSCIC

Low back flexion exercises
U-matic / VHS
Physical therapy series
Color (PRO C G)
$195.00 purchase _ #C890 - VI - 009
Informs patient educators and patients about the benefits of low back flexion exercises. Teaches effective techniques for minimizing pain and fatigue while enhancing the ability to perform daily activities. Part of a series by the physical therapy staff, St Luke's Hospital, Fargo, North Dakota.
Health and Safety; Physical Education and Recreation; Science - Natural
Dist - HSCIC

Low Back Pain 14 MIN
16mm / U-matic / VHS
Health Awareness Series
Color (H C A) (SPANISH)
LC 81-701105
Shows that low back pain is a common problem which can be caused by muscle strain, fatigue, certain chronic diseases and aging.
Health and Safety
Dist - JOU **Prod** - PRORE 1975

Low back pain
VHS
Color (PRO A G) (SPANISH ARABIC)
$250.00 purchase _ #OP - 07
Shows how to prevent low back pain. Provides guidelines for maintaining good posture while standing, walking, sitting and driving. Demonstrates proper body mechanics for lifting and reaching, and depicts recommended sleeping positions. Teaches the importance of regular exercise and weight control in developing a healthy back. Includes a discussion of the roles of the physician and physical therapist in managing back pain.
Science - Natural
Dist - MIFE **Prod** - MIFE 1991

Low back pain 30 MIN
VHS
At time of diagnosis series
Color (G)
$19.95 purchase _ #1 - 5757 - 7013 - XNK
Provides patients who are suffering from low back pain and their families with thorough, comprehensive and understandable information. Examines what is going on in the body and what might have caused the condition. Explains the type of medical professionals a patient may encounter and how the condition is monitored. Explores treatment options, including medication, surgery and lifestyle changes. Looks at practical issues surrounding the illness and answers the most common questions. Part of an ongoing series to provide the in - depth medical information patients and their families need to know.
Health and Safety; Science - Natural
Dist - TILIED **Prod** - TILIED 1996

Low Back Pain 17 MIN
VHS / U-matic
Color (PRO)
Identifies the symptoms of degenerative disc disease. Differentiates the cause of low back pain using a standard evaluation form (included with the program). Determines an appropriate treatment regimen for acute and chronic cases. Includes a discussion of several experimental treatment modalities.
Health and Safety
Dist - UMICHM **Prod** - UMICHM 1976

Low Back Pain 24 MIN
16mm / U-matic / VHS
Color
Examines low back pain as a major cause of lost production days, impaired work capacity, and pain - related distractions, errors and accidents. Presents Dr Hans Kraus, a noted orthopedic surgeon, who introduces five exercises to alleviate and prevent back pain.
Health and Safety; Psychology
Dist - CORF **Prod** - SPORP

Low Back Pain - Cause and Care 27 MIN
U-matic
Color (C)
Demonstrates patient education of three causes of back pain and its care.
Health and Safety; Science - Natural
Dist - UOKLAH **Prod** - UOKLAH 1980

Low Back Pain - Exercise and Lifestyle Management
U-matic / VHS
Color
Introduces the importance of proper muscle tone to minimize low back pain. Demonstrates an exercise program and techniques to limit the stresses and strains of physical activity on the lower back.
Physical Education and Recreation; Science - Natural
Dist - MIFE **Prod** - MIFE

Low birth weight infants
VHS
Mosby cameo series; Volume 1
Color (C PRO G)
$150.00 purchase
Features nurse researcher Dr Dorothy Brooten and her work. Part of a series featuring the work of outstanding nurse researchers.
Health and Safety
Dist - MOSBY **Prod** - SITHTA

Low Calorie 28 MIN
VHS / 16mm
What's Cooking Series
Color (G)
$55.00 rental _ #WHAC - 113
Home Economics
Dist - PBS **Prod** - WHYY

Low Choke Method 11 MIN
VHS / U-matic
Blowout Prevention and Well Control Series
Color (IND)
Shows conditions under which this variation of the Low Choke Method is used, the formation leak - off test and overview of Low Choke Method procedure.
Business and Economics; Industrial and Technical Education; Social Science
Dist - GPCV **Prod** - CAODC

Low energy houses to go 30 MIN
VHS
A House for all seasons series
Color (G)
$49.95 purchase _ #AHFS - 208
Shows that factory - built homes can be quite energy efficient in their own right. Documents the construction of an old fashioned post and beam house.
Business and Economics; Home Economics; Industrial and Technical Education; Science - Natural; Sociology
Dist - PBS **Prod** - KRMATV 1985

The Low - Fat Diet 10 MIN
VHS / U-matic
Color
LC 77-730426
Illustrates process of atherosclerosis and its development and emphasizes importance of low - fat diet, suggesting foods to be included and those to be avoided in well - balanced, low - fat diets.
Health and Safety; Home Economics; Science - Natural
Dist - MEDCOM **Prod** - MEDCOM

The Low - fat film 22 MIN
VHS
Color (H C G)
$480.00, $360.00 purchase, $60.00 rental
Follows four people with four different goals - losing weight, building muscle, achieving heart health and increasing personal energy. Shows how diet affects these goals. Explains cholesterol and examines fat in the diet - including a stunning sequence showing the results of a blood test before and after eating a fast food meal. Companion to Fast Food - What's In It For You.
Health and Safety; Physical Education and Recreation; Social Science
Dist - CF **Prod** - CF 1990

Low Fat Meat Preparation 13 MIN
16mm
Eat Right to Your Heart's Delight Series
Color (J H)
Presents a complete guide to the use of leaner cuts of beef with emphasis on selection of meat, proper trimming and deboning and preparation techniques that reduce saturated fats. Shows the proper use of marinades for tough, lean cuts like flank steak, examines extenders and their benefits with lean ground beef, gives stir - frying techniques and discusses the low - fat method of braising a pot roast and serving it with gravy.
Health and Safety; Home Economics; Social Science
Dist - IPS **Prod** - IPS 1976

Low Fire - Enamel on Copper 28 MIN
Videoreel / VT2
Wheels, Kilns and Clay Series
Color
Features Mrs Peterson describing certain ceramic processes for her classroom at the University of Southern California. Discusses appropriate temperatures for enamel on copper.
Fine Arts
Dist - PBS **Prod** - USC

Low Frequency Navigation 29 MIN
U-matic / VHS
Color (A)
Explains navigation by VLF or very low frequency signals. Includes nature of VLF waves, signal generation, waveguide theory, advantages of VLF signals and receiving antennas. Discusses omega VLF transmission system and uses for navigation including system problem areas.
Industrial and Technical Education
Dist - AVIMA **Prod** - FAAFL

Low impact aerobics 30 MIN
VHS
Esquire great body series
Color (H C A)
$19.99 purchase _ #EQGB04V
Presents the fourth of a nine - part exercise series oriented to women. Combines stretches and a low - impact aerobics workout. Developed by Deborah Crocker.
Physical Education and Recreation; Science - Natural
Dist - CAMV

Low level 22 MIN
VHS / U-matic
America at war series
Color (H C A)
$79.00 purchase _ #HP - 6287C
Looks at the role and evolution of low - flying bombers in warfare. Part of a war series produced by Lou Reda Productions, Inc.
Civics and Political Systems; History - United States; Industrial and Technical Education; Sociology
Dist - CORF

Low Level Air Navigation 22 MIN
16mm
Color
LC FIE61-88
Demonstrates flight planning and flight techniques to be used by carrier attack pilots in the navigation portion of the low level attack mission.
Civics and Political Systems; Industrial and Technical Education; Social Science
Dist - USNAC **Prod** - USN 1960

Low Level Radiation and Man 30 MIN
U-matic / VHS
Color
Presents Dr. Ernest J. Sternglass, University of Pittsburgh, discussing the threat of radiation to man, the effects of low level radiation on embryonic life stages and the correlation between radiation levels and mortality rates at test sites.
Science - Natural; Science - Physical
Dist - NETCHE **Prod** - NETCHE

Low - Level Wind Shear 16 MIN
U-matic / VHS
Color (A)
Defines wind shear as any change, gradual or abrupt, in wind speed and direction in a thin layer of the atmosphere. Notes danger potential of wind shear for aircraft takeoffs and landings. Describes research and detection techniques of Federal Government.
Industrial and Technical Education
Dist - AVIMA **Prod** - FAAFL

Low Level Wind Shear 16 MIN
16mm
Color
LC 78-701643
Describes research to refine airborne and ground - based wind shear detection techniques.
Industrial and Technical Education
Dist - USNAC **Prod** - USFAA 1978

Low Reynolds Number Flows 33 MIN
U-matic / VHS / 16mm
Fluid Mechanics Series
Color (H C)
LC 70-702987
Shows 'INERTIA - FREE' flows, in which every element of fluid is nearly in equilibrium under the influence of forces due to viscosity, pressure and gravity, the forces required to produce acceleration being comparatively very small.
Science - Physical
Dist - EBEC **Prod** - NCFMF 1967

Low Rider 22 MIN
U-matic / VHS
Color (J A) (SPANISH)
Discusses drinking, driving and youth. Depicts a typical situation in the Chicano community when two friends purchase a 'low rider.'.
Fine Arts; Foreign Language; Health and Safety; Psychology; Sociology
Dist - SUTHRB **Prod** - SUTHRB

Low Riders 23 MIN
VHS / U-matic
Images / Imagenes Series
Color
Describes low riders - the cars and drivers that flourish in Mexican - American communities.
Sociology
Dist - LVN **Prod** - TUCPL

Low Riders 22 MIN
16mm
Color (J)
LC 79-700695
Shows how two friends invest time, energy and money in customizing an old car only to have it wrecked because of drunken driving. Offers a solution to the problem of drinking and driving.
Health and Safety; Psychology; Sociology
Dist - IA **Prod** - USDTFH 1976

Low salt - low fat
VHS
Frugal gourmet - American classics series
Color (G)
$19.95 purchase _ #CCP828
Shows how to prepare low salt and low fat dishes in American cuisine. Features Jeff Smith, the Frugal Gourmet. Part of the nine - part series, American Classics.
Health and Safety; History - United States; Home Economics; Social Science
Dist - CADESF **Prod** - CADESF

Low Salt, Low Fat Cooking 30 MIN
BETA / VHS
Frugal Gourmet Series
Color
Demonstrates how to cook and dine avoiding salt and animal fat. Includes fish sauces, chicken thighs and herb and spice blends.

Health and Safety; Home Economics; Psychology
Dist - CORF Prod - WTTWTV

Low self esteem - why kids hurt themselves 25 MIN
VHS
At - risk students video series
Color (I J H)
$98.00 purchase _ #AHV404
Looks at the sensitive, fragile nature of the adolescent. Discusses failure and rejection and low self esteem as it relates to a wide variety of self destructive behavior. Features students and teachers from The Tree of Learning School in Portland, Oregon. Includes a reproducible discussion guide with worksheets. Part of a five - part series on students at risk.
Health and Safety; Psychology; Social Science; Sociology
Dist - CADESF Prod - CADESF 1990

Low Side - to - End Colorectal Anastomosis 28 MIN
16mm
Color (PRO)
Presents a technique for a low side - to - end colorectal anastomosis which offers greater technical ease, a more secure anastomosis and a larger anastomotic lumen than the conventional end - to - end anastomosis.
Health and Safety; Science
Dist - ACY Prod - ACYDGD 1968

Low Speed Car Crash Costs 22 MIN
16mm
Color (J)
LC 72-700543
Uses actual crash test scenes, charts, and chalkboard to demonstrate costs for 1969 standard automobiles.
Home Economics; Industrial and Technical Education
Dist - HF Prod - IIHS 1970

Low View from a Dark Shadow 29 MIN
Videoreel / VT2
Synergism - in Today's World Series
Color
Sociology
Dist - PBS Prod - WMVSTV

Low visibility 84 MIN
16mm
Color (G)
$175.00 rental
Tells the story of a survivor of a wilderness ordeal as seen through the eye of the news camera, hospital surveillance camera or the eyes of those around him. Portrays the survivor's insanity as a result of either some horrible trauma or a ruse to cover up a violent crime buried beneath the snow. Produced by Patricia Gruben and starring Larry Lillo.
Fine Arts
Dist - CANCIN

Low volume irrigation 7 MIN
VHS
Color (G)
$20.00 purchase _ #6 - 051 - 107A
Defines low volume or 'drip' irrigation and covers design, installation and maintenance considerations.
Agriculture
Dist - VEP Prod - TORO 1993

Lowdown on High Blood Pressure 10 MIN
U-matic / VHS
Color
Stresses the importance of controlling blood pressure. Useful as an aid in blood pressure screening, referral, follow - up and education.
Health and Safety; Science - Natural
Dist - AMRC Prod - AMRC

Lowdown series
Positive thinking 25 MIN
Sam 25 MIN
Dist - BBCENE

The lowdown
Gotta give up 25 MINS.
Dist - BBCENE

Lowell Fulson and Percy Mayfield - Mark Naftalin's Blue Monday Party 30 MIN
VHS
Color (G)
$24.95 purchase
Catches some of the blues of Lowell Fulson and Percy Mayfield.
Fine Arts
Dist - KINOIC Prod - RHPSDY

Lowell Herrero - the Graphic Process 28 MIN
16mm
Color
LC 73-701039
Presents Lowell Herrero, the creator of the calendar schedule of the San Francisco Giants baseball team for the 1972 season. Shows all phases of the work involved in graphics and printing.
Fine Arts; Industrial and Technical Education; Physical Education and Recreation
Dist - FILMSM Prod - FILMSM 1973

Lowell Thomas Remembers 1932 28 MIN
16mm
B&W (J H)
Looks at the major news events of the year 1932.
History - United States
Dist - RMIBHF Prod - RMIBHF 1976

Lowen and Bioenergetic Therapy 48 MIN
16mm
Color (H C A)
LC 75-701106
Features Dr Alexander Lowen describing his key ideas of bioenergetic therapy and demonstrating them in his work with a young female patient. Shows that Dr Lowen's theory is that the unconscious really exists in the muscle constrictions of the body and that therapy requires working with the body as opposed to the mind.
Psychology; Science - Natural
Dist - PSYCHF Prod - PSYCHF 1973

Lowen and Bioenergetic Therapy, Pt 1 24 MIN
16mm
Color
Features Dr Alexander Lowen, the foremost exponent of incorporating direct work with the body in the therapeutic process, who describes his key ideas of bioenergetic therapy and demonstrates them in his work with a young female patient. Describes Lowen's theory that the unconscious really exists in the muscle constrictions of the body and that therapy requires working with the body as opposed to the mind.
Health and Safety
Dist - PSYCHF Prod - PSYCHF

Lowen and Bioenergetic Therapy, Pt 2 24 MIN
16mm
Color
Features Dr Alexander Lowen, the foremost exponent of incorporating direct work with the body in the therapeutic process, who describes his key ideas of bioenergetic therapy and demonstrates them in his work with a young female patient. Describes Lowen's theory that the unconscious really exists in the muscle constrictions of the body and that therapy requires working with the body as opposed to the mind.
Health and Safety
Dist - PSYCHF Prod - PSYCHF

Lower Brainstem and Cerebellum Structures Related to the Fourth Ventricle 31 MIN
U-matic
Dissection of the Brain Series
Color (C)
Demonstrates the lobes of the cerebellum and the cerebellar peduncles. Surface landmarks of the medulla are identified as are some of the principle landmarks of the floor of the fourth ventricle.
Health and Safety; Science - Natural
Dist - UOKLAH Prod - UOKLAH 1978

Lower Depths, the 125 MIN
VHS
Japan Film Collection from SVS Series
B&W (G) (JAPANESE (ENGLISH SUBTITLES))
$59.95 purchase _ #K0649
Presents a movie produced in Japan. Features Akira Kurosawa as director. Stars Toshiro Mifune, Isuzu Yamada and Kyoko Kagawa.
Fine Arts; Geography - World
Dist - CHTSUI Prod - SONY 1957

The Lower Digestive Tract - Breakdown 26 MIN
U-matic / VHS / 16mm
Living Body - an Introduction to Human Biology Series
Color
Traces food as it enters the mouth and the process of breakdown and transformation occurs. Follows the food through the entire alimentary tract, showing how it is dissolved in acid, how the liver and gall bladder work, and how digestion and absorption work.
Science - Natural
Dist - FOTH Prod - FOTH 1985

Lower East Side - Seward Park 9 MIN
16mm
B&W (G)
$20.00 rental
Features a documentary of New York City's Lower East Side and Seward Park. Pictures Seward Park's Public Library and its neighborhood; pushcarts on various streets; a playground on the roof of Public School #31; boys diving in the East River; homeless men at the Salvation Army; games on a closed street; East Broadway; winter sports in Seward Park.
Fine Arts; Geography - United States; Religion and Philosophy; Sociology
Dist - NCJEWF

Lower Extremity, Pt 1
VHS / U-matic
Osteopathic Examination and Manipulation Series
Color (PRO)
Introduces manipulative procedures for the foot and ankle with identification of bony landmarks and an outline of the arch mechanism. Uses asymmetry of positional and tissue findings within the ankle and arch to direct the testing of mobility of local joints for dysfunction. Employs motion findings as a basis for treatment of foot and ankle dysfunction by manipulative procedures using the principles of direct technique.
Health and Safety; Science - Natural
Dist - MSU Prod - MSU

The Lower Mississippi - the working river 55 MIN
VHS
On the waterways series
Color (G H)
$29.95 purchase _ #OW12
Travels with the crew of the Driftwood on the Mississippi south of St Louis to explore the Old South and the problems of the new South. Narrated by Jason Robards. Part of a 13 - part series on the history, geography, culture and ecology of North American waterways.
Social Science
Dist - SVIP

The Lower plant forms 15 MIN
U-matic / VHS
Discovering series; Unit 7 - Plants
Color (I)
Science - Natural
Dist - AITECH Prod - WDCNTV 1978

The Lower South 25 MIN
U-matic / VHS / 16mm
United States Geography Series
Color (I J)
Surveys the diversity of the lower south, including Arkansas, Alabama, Mississippi, Louisiana, Georgia, Florida and South Carolina.
Geography - United States
Dist - NGS Prod - NGS 1983

Lower than the Angels 52 MIN
16mm / VHS / U-matic
Ascent of Man Series
Color (H C A) (SPANISH)
LC 74-702253
Explores the anatomical and intellectual changes which gave rise to human superiority among the animals. Narrated by Dr Jacob Bronowski of the Salk Institute.
Psychology; Science; Science - Natural
Dist - TIMLIF Prod - BBCTV 1973
BBCENE
AMBROS

Lower than the Angels - Pt 1 26 MIN
16mm / U-matic
Ascent of Man Series
Color (H C A)
LC 74-702253
Explores the anatomical and intellectual changes which gave rise to human superiority among the animals. Narrated by Dr Jacob Bronowski of the Salk Institute.
Science - Natural
Dist - TIMLIF Prod - BBCTV 1973

Lower than the Angels - Pt 2 26 MIN
16mm / U-matic
Ascent of Man Series
Color (H C A)
LC 74-702253
Explores the anatomical and intellectual changes which gave rise to human superiority among the animals. Narrated by Dr Jacob Bronowski of the Salk Institute.
Science - Natural
Dist - TIMLIF Prod - BBCTV 1973

Lower Urinary Tract Infections in Women
U-matic / VHS
Color (ARABIC SPANISH)
Explains the major causes of lower urinary tract infections in women along with a discussion of diagnosis and treatment. Emphasizes personal cleanliness as the best precaution against recurring or new infections.
Health and Safety
Dist - MIFE Prod - MIFE

Lower your cholesterol now 59 MIN
VHS
Color (J H C G)
$49.95 purchase _ #FA458V
Features a registered dietician who teaches viewers how to evaluate the amount of saturated fats, cholesterol and fiber in foods. Explains the differences in the multitudes of different kinds of oils and interviews a butcher who identifies the leanest cuts of meat, fish and poultry. Includes advice from a physician but not heavily oriented to science.
Health and Safety; Home Economics; Social Science
Dist - CAMV

The Lowfat living system 14 MIN
VHS
Color (H A)
$29.95 purchase _ #SF100V-H
Helps viewers learn the importance of eating, cooking, shopping, exercising and thinking the lowfat way in order to live a healthy lifestyle. Viewers learn how to make the right choices, even when dining out, without feeling deprived or like they're losing the willpower battle. Contains a 12-page guidebook, 128-page book and pocket slide-guide fat ruler.
Health and Safety; Home Economics
Dist - CAMV

Lowrance LMS 200
VHS
Loran operation guide series
Color (G A)
$29.90 purchase _ #0905
Teaches Loran C programming for the Lowrance LMS 200 in nautical navigation. Shows how to enter the correct Loran chain for specific positions, how to program positions, determine the accuracy of a Loran C 'fix' and how to deal with the intricacies of specific machines.
Physical Education and Recreation; Social Science
Dist - SEVVID

The Loyalists in the South - Pt 5 30 MIN
VHS
And Then There were Thirteen Series
Color (H)
$69.95 purchase
Considers the role of British Loyalists in the American South. Uses footage shot on location. Describes personalities. Part 5 of a twenty - part series on Southern theaters of war during the American Revolution.
Civics and Political Systems; Geography - United States; History - United States; Sociology
Dist - SCETV **Prod** - SCETV 1982

Loyalty - 17 7 MIN
VHS / U-matic
Life's little lessons - self - esteem K - 3 - series
Color (K P)
$129.00, $99.00 _ #V616
Reveals that nobody thought much of the Loser's Gang, but the gang knew what it meant to stick together. Shows the power of loyalty. Part of a 30 - part series on self - esteem.
Guidance and Counseling; Psychology
Dist - BARR **Prod** - CEPRO 1992

Loyola - Chicago
VHS
Campus clips series
Color (H C A)
$29.95 purchase _ #CC0027V
Takes a video visit to the campus of Loyola University in Chicago. Shows many of the distinctive features of the campus, and interviews students about their experiences. Provides information on the composition of the student body, professors, academics, social life, housing, and other subjects.
Education
Dist - CAMV

Loyola - New Orleans
VHS
Campus clips series
Color (H C A)
$29.95 purchase _ #CC0032V
Takes a video visit to the campus of Loyola University in New Orleans. Shows many of the distinctive features of the campus, and interviews students about their experiences. Provides information on the composition of the student body, professors, academics, social life, housing, and other subjects.
Education
Dist - CAMV

Lozanov Language Class 30 MIN
VHS / U-matic
B&W (T)
LC 84-707263
Includes remarks from Georgi Lozanov and clips from Evelina Gatora on teaching a beginning Italian class.
Education; Foreign Language; Psychology
Dist - LLI **Prod** - LLI 1984

LP 33 MIN
16mm
Color (G)
$35.00 rental
Collects twelve short silent films that deal with daily life and the mundane.
Fine Arts; Sociology
Dist - CANCIN **Prod** - LIPTNL 1969

L/R time constants 15 MIN
U-matic / VHS
Basic electricity and D C circuits - laboratory series
Color
Industrial and Technical Education; Science - Physical; Social Science
Dist - TXINLC **Prod** - TXINLC

LSAT review
VHS
Color (C)
$79.95 purchase _ #VAD002
Presents two videocassettes offering preparation review for the LSAT. Includes study guide.
Education
Dist - SIV

LSD 28 MIN
16mm
Color (H C A)
LC 74-705053
Features Walter Miner outlining how LSD was first discovered, discussing how it affects the brain and body, and stressing the extreme dangers of using LSD.
Health and Safety
Dist - USNAC **Prod** - USN 1967

LSD - 25 27 MIN
16mm
Color (J)
LC FIA68-148
Explains what LSD is and what it does. Begins with an LSD 'MOLECULE' saying, 'I AM A COMPLICATED THING, HERE IN COMPLICATED TIMES AND IN COMPLICATED PLACES. BUT NOW LET ME TELL YOU WHAT I REALLY AM AND WHAT I REALLY DO.'.
Health and Safety; Sociology
Dist - PROART **Prod** - PROART 1967

LSD - Insight or Insanity 28 MIN
16mm / U-matic / VHS
Color (J) (FRENCH PORTUGUESE SPANISH SWEDISH)
LC FIA68-964
Presents doctors, scientists and geneticists discussing the possible effects of LSD on the chromosomes. Examines the psychological and physiological effects of LSD use.
Foreign Language; Health and Safety; Sociology
Dist - PHENIX **Prod** - MILLRM 1968

LSD - the Other Side of Reality 21 MIN
16mm
Color (C A)
Examines the effects of LSD and its potential therapeutic uses in the field of mental health, featuring interviews with California researchers, clinicians and a rabbi.
Health and Safety; Sociology
Dist - KRONTV **Prod** - KRONTV 1964

LSD Trip - or Trap 20 MIN
16mm / U-matic / VHS
Color (J)
LC 76-702153
Presents facts about LSD, illustrating its use and tragic consequences when a teenage boy and a friend become involved in a car accident.
Health and Safety; Sociology
Dist - AIMS **Prod** - DAVP 1968

LTA History - Balloons 27 MIN
16mm
B&W
LC FIE52-1110
Traces the history of balloon experimentation covering problems discovered by outstanding men. Describes the modern uses of balloons.
History - World; Industrial and Technical Education
Dist - USNAC **Prod** - USN

Lubba Dubba - the Inside Story of Your Heart and Blood 15 MIN
VHS / U-matic
Inside Story with Slim Goodbody Series
Color (P I)
Presents Slim Goodbody introducing the circulatory system.
Science - Natural
Dist - AITECH **Prod** - UWISC 1981

Lube oil controls
VHS
Refrigeration training seminars by Bob Graham series
Color (G IND)
$55.00 purchase
Overs oil lube safety controls in detail. Part of a series of refrigeration training seminars by Bob Graham.
Industrial and Technical Education; Psychology; Science - Physical
Dist - AACREF **Prod** - AACREF 1990

Lubricating Ball Bearings 6 MIN
16mm
Color (IND)
Demonstrates a technique for ball bearing maintenance showing the proper procedure for removing deteriorated lubricant and replacing with fresh grease.
Industrial and Technical Education
Dist - MOKIN **Prod** - MOKIN

Lubrication 5 MIN
U-matic / VHS / 16mm
Basic Motorcycle Maintenance Series
Color (H C A)
LC 81-700699
Focuses on checking and changing oil in motorcycles. Discusses lubrication of cables.
Industrial and Technical Education
Dist - IFB **Prod** - PACEST 1980

Lubrication (1) 43 MIN
VHS / U-matic
Tribology 1 - Friction, Wear, and Lubrication Series
Color
Discusses fluid lubrication, boundary lubrication and the types of lubrication in between.
Industrial and Technical Education
Dist - MIOT **Prod** - MIOT

Lubrication (2) 45 MIN
U-matic / VHS
Tribology 1 - Friction, Wear, and Lubrication Series
Color
Discusses effect of reduction of surface energy on wear and types of lubricants which are effective in this regard.
Industrial and Technical Education
Dist - MIOT **Prod** - MIOT

Lubrication - a matter of care 20 MIN
U-matic / BETA / VHS
Color (IND G)
$295.00 purchase _ #800 - 01
Presents the basic principles of lubrication and why lubrication is important to plant operations and maintenance. Explains the basic procedures for changing oil or grease on a pump that can be taken out of service.
Health and Safety; Industrial and Technical Education; Psychology
Dist - ITSC **Prod** - ITSC

Lubrication Checks and Services 30 MIN
VHS / U-matic
Keep it Running Series
Color
Identifies the components of the engine's lubrication system and describes their functions. Explains the functions of lubricating oil, service requirements and how to change the oil.
Industrial and Technical Education
Dist - NETCHE **Prod** - NETCHE 1982

Lubrication in Healthy and Arthritic Joints 15 MIN
16mm
Color
Illustrates how joints are lubricated and explains the roles of articular cartilage and synovial fluid. Describes what happens when nature fails to lubricate joints, as in arthritis. Explains the difference between inflammatory and degenerative arthritis and explores various therapies.
Health and Safety; Science; Science - Natural
Dist - UPJOHN **Prod** - UPJOHN 1970

Lubrication of Electronic Equipment 9 MIN
16mm
Color
LC FIE56-58
Explains the importance of routine and methodical lubrication of electronic equipment according to recommended procedures.
Industrial and Technical Education
Dist - USNAC **Prod** - USN 1953

Lubrication system 35 MIN
VHS
Diesel engine maintenance video series
Color (G H)
$19.95 purchase _ #CEV00819V-T
Defines preventive maintenance for diesel engine owners and focuses on the lubrication system and the possible reasons for equipment failure. Discusses the importance of maintenence on the lubrication system, selecting oil, changing the oil and filter, and more.
Education; Industrial and Technical Education
Dist - CAMV

Lubrication Techniques 24 MIN
VHS / 16mm
Mechanical Maintenance Training Series
Color (H A)
$410.00 purchase, $110.00 rental
Describes different lubricants and additives and the proper lubrication techniques for chains, gears and all types of bearings.
Industrial and Technical Education
Dist - TAT **Prod** - TAT 1987

Lubrication - the Automobile 44 MIN
U-matic / VHS
Tribology 2 - Advances in Friction, Wear, and Lubrication Series

Color
Discusses the automobile and ways in which friction causes energy dissipation.
Industrial and Technical Education
Dist - MIOT **Prod** - MIOT

Lucha Corpi - 11 - 30 - 89 42 MIN
VHS / Cassette
Poetry Center reading series
Color (G)
$15.00, $45.00 purchase, $15.00 rental _ #866 - 675
Features the writer reading her works at the Poetry Center, San Francisco State University. Includes selections from City In The Mist, and some poems translated from Spanish by Catherine Rodriguez - Nieto. Introduction by Norma Alarcon.
Literature and Drama
Dist - POETRY **Prod** - POETRY 1989

Lucia 160 MIN
16mm
Color (SPANISH (ENGLISH SUBTITLES))
Dramatizes three separate periods in the Cuban struggle for liberation, showing the participation of Cuban women in that fight. Uses English subtitles.
Foreign Language; History - World; Sociology
Dist - TRIFC **Prod** - TRIFC 1969

Lucia - 3 89 MIN
VHS
Developing stories series
Color (H C G)
$150.00 purchase, $75.00 rental
Documents the effects of an oil - spill by a tanker during the night in the Philippines. Reveals that at dawn the fishing village of Bataan discovers the accident and soon the spill threatens not just marine life but the existence of the entire community. Chronicles the efforts of Lucia and her family to stay in the village, but the social forces are too strong and they are forced into the slums of Manila. A film by Mel Chionglo from a screenplay by Lino Brocka for Manila Inter - Film - BBC. Part of a six - part series highlighting debates of the Earth Summit.
Civics and Political Systems; Fine Arts; Science - Natural; Social Science; Sociology
Dist - CANCIN **Prod** - BBCTV 1994

Lucia Berlin - 2 - 24 - 84 18 MIN
VHS / Cassette
Poetry Center reading series
Color (G)
$15.00, $45.00 purchase _ #579 - 489
Features the poet reading her works at the Poetry Center, San Francisco State University, with an introduction by Jim Hartz.
Literature and Drama
Dist - POETRY **Prod** - POETRY 1984

Lucia Celebration 10 MIN
16mm
Color
Shows candle making, preparing for Christmas and Lucia Day celebration in Sweden.
Geography - World; Religion and Philosophy; Social Science
Dist - AUDPLN **Prod** - ASI

Lucia Di Lammermoor 128 MIN
VHS
(S) (ITALIAN)
$29.95 purchase _ #384 - 9508
Presents Dame Joan Sutherland in the lead of 'Lucia Di Lammermoor' by Donizetti. Features Richard Bonynge as conductor, Alfredo Kraus, Pablo Elvira and Paul Plishka in the cast of a lavish Metropolitan Opera production.
Fine Arts; Foreign Language
Dist - FI **Prod** - PAR 1988

Lucia Di Lammermoor
U-matic / VHS
Color (G)
Presents Anna Moffo as Lucia in this version set amidst highland castles.
Fine Arts
Dist - VAI **Prod** - VAI

Lucia di Lammermoor 128 MIN
VHS
Metropolitan opera series
Color (G) (ITALIAN WITH ENGLISH SUBTITLES)
$29.95 purchase
Stars Joan Sutherland, Alfredo Kraus, Pablo Elvira, and Paul Plishka in a performance of 'Lucia Di Lammermoor' by Donizetti. Conducted by Richard Bonynge. Includes a brochure with plot, historic notes, photographs, and production credits.
Fine Arts
Dist - PBS **Prod** - WNETTV 1982

Lucia Di Lammermoor 30 MIN
16mm / U-matic / VHS
Who's Afraid of Opera Series
Color (J)
LC 73-703432
Features Joan Sutherland singing the opera 'LUCIA DI LAMMERMOOR.' Features puppets in an opera box acting as a reviewing audience, conversing with the performers as they enter or leave front stage.
Fine Arts
Dist - PHENIX **Prod** - PHENIX 1973

Lucia Di Lammermoor 145 MIN
VHS
Color (G) (ITALIAN (ENGLISH SUBTITLES))
$39.95 purchase _ #1210
Presents Joan Sutherland in Lucia Di Lammermoor produced by the Australian Opera.
Fine Arts; Foreign Language
Dist - KULTUR

Lucia, Pt 1 54 MIN
16mm
Color (SPANISH (ENGLISH SUBTITLES))
Presents a woman embroiled in a tale of love and betrayal during Cuba's war for independence in 1865. Uses English subtitles.
Fine Arts
Dist - TRIFC **Prod** - TRIFC 1969

Lucia, Pt 2 53 MIN
16mm
Color (SPANISH (ENGLISH SUBTITLES))
Presents a woman involved in the overthrow of Cuban dictator Machado in 1933. Uses English subtitles.
Fine Arts
Dist - TRIFC **Prod** - TRIFC 1969

Lucia, Pt 3 53 MIN
16mm
Color (SPANISH (ENGLISH SUBTITLES))
Presents a woman confronting her husband's macho attitudes in the 1960's. Uses English subtitles.
Fine Arts
Dist - TRIFC **Prod** - TRIFC 1969

Luciano Pavarotti - Gala Concert 60 MIN
VHS
Color (G)
$19.95 purchase _ #1229
Presents the Luciano Pavarotti concert at the Olympia Hall in Munich, Germany. Contains 'Questa o quella' and 'La donna e mobile' from 'Rigoletto' and 'Amor ti vieta' from 'Fedora.'.
Fine Arts; Foreign Language; Geography - World
Dist - KULTUR

Lucie Rie 55 MIN
VHS
Omnibus series
Color (A)
PdS99 purchase
Features potter Lucie Rie in a discussion with host David Attenborough. Discusses her work on the eve of the opening of a major retrospective exhibition at the Victoria and Albert Museum in London in 1982.
Fine Arts
Dist - BBCENE

Lucifer, God's most beautiful angel 4 MIN
VHS
Color (G)
$10.00 rental, $15.00 purchase
Explores the Lucifer tale as manifested in man's realm in a film by Barry J Hershey.
Fine Arts
Dist - CANCIN

Lucifer rising 8 MIN
16mm
Color & B&W (G)
$10.00 rental
Depicts Lucifer as a bringer of light, God's beautiful but rebellious favorite, instead of the typical Christian personification of evil. Edits the original version, which was full of land and seascapes and performances by London's trendsetters and Marianne Faithfull, to add a haunting music track.
Fine Arts; Religion and Philosophy
Dist - CANCIN **Prod** - ANGERK 1989

Lucille Ball dies - Wednesday, April 26, 1989 30 MIN
VHS
Nightline series
Color (H C G)
$14.98 purchase _ #MP6172
Marks the death of comedienne and entertainer Lucille Ball, age 78.
Biography; Fine Arts
Dist - INSTRU **Prod** - ABCNEW 1989

Lucille Clifton - 6 - 16 - 88 59 MIN
VHS / Cassette
Lannan Literary series
Color (G)
$15.00, $19.95 purchase, $15.00 rental _ #892
Features the poet at the Los Angeles Theatre Center, reading from her books good woman - poems and a memoir and next - New Poems. Includes an interview conducted by Lewis MacAdams in the galleries of the Los Angeles Afro - American Museum. Part of a series of literary videotapes presenting major poets and writers from around the globe reading and talking about their work; readings were sponsored by The Lannan Foundation of Los Angeles, a private contemporary arts organization.
Guidance and Counseling; Literature and Drama
Dist - POETRY **Prod** - METEZT 1988

Luck in Loose Plaster 4 MIN
16mm
Color
Presents Sandy Moore's film entry selected from the 1985 Whitney Biennial Film and Video Exhibition.
Fine Arts
Dist - AFA **Prod** - AFA 1986

Luck is a Lady 29 MIN
Videoreel / VT2
Koltanowski on Chess Series
Color
Physical Education and Recreation
Dist - PBS **Prod** - KQEDTV

Luck of Laura Tedesco 27 MIN
Videoreel / VT2
Color
Explains that in April, 1972, Laura Tedesco, a waitress, won 50,000 dollars in Pennsylvania's lottery. Explores the fact that Laura and others who won big in 1970's lotteries have continued to win regularly in drawings and pools elsewhere.
Physical Education and Recreation; Sociology
Dist - PBS **Prod** - WQED

The Luck of Roaring Camp 27 MIN
U-matic / VHS / 16mm
LCA Short Story Library Series
Color (J)
LC 82-700411
Tells of the birth of a baby in a mining camp who is soon orphaned. Shows that the miners band together to raise the baby and he brings them luck in finding gold. Relates that their belief in him is so strong that they risk injury and death to save him from drowning. Based on the short story The Luck Of Roaring Camp by Bret Harte.
Literature and Drama
Dist - LCOA **Prod** - LCOA 1982

The Luck of the Stiffhams 30 MIN
VHS / U-matic
Wodehouse Playhouse Series
Color (C A)
Presents an adaptation of the short story The Luck Of The Stiffhams by P G Wodehouse.
Literature and Drama
Dist - TIMLIF **Prod** - BBCTV 1980

The Lucky Corner 17 MIN
16mm
B&W
Explains how a pretentious diner operator and his bratty son run Grandpa's lemonade stand off the block. Shows how Spanky and the Gang stage a parade which leads potential customers to the stand's new location. A Little Rascals film.
Fine Arts
Dist - RMIBHF **Prod** - ROACH 1936

The Lucky country - Australia - Part II 27 MIN
VHS
Children of two countries series
Color (P I J G)
$195.00 purchase
Follows eight Chinese children to Australia where they meet the Prime Minister, row a surf boat, visit an outback sheep ranch, take part in a lesson by radio in the famous 'School of the Air; and sample life in Sydney and Melbourne. Part two of a two - part series.
Geography - World; Sociology
Dist - LANDMK **Prod** - LANDMK 1987

Lucky Hans 11 MIN
VHS / U-matic
Fairy Tale Series
Color (K P I)
Shows the adventures of Hans as he journeys home trading gold for a series of less valuable items. Comes with teacher's guide.
Literature and Drama
Dist - BNCHMK **Prod** - BNCHMK 1985

Lucky Seven Sampson 4 MIN
U-matic / 35mm strip
Multiplication Rock Series
Color (P I)
LC 75-733963
Uses an original rock song illustrated by cartoon characters to demonstrate multiplication by seven.

Mathematics
Dist - GA **Prod** - ABCTV 1974

Lucky Strike (LSMFT) 1 MIN
VHS / U-matic
Color
Shows a classic television commercial with dancing cigarettes doing a square dance.
Business and Economics; Psychology; Sociology
Dist - BROOKC **Prod** - BROOKC

Lucky Thirteen 110 MIN
VHS
Color (G) (MANDARIN CHINESE (ENGLISH SUBTITLES))
$45.00 purchase _ #6026A
Presents a Mandarin Chinese language movie produced in the People's Republic of China.
Fine Arts; Geography - World; Literature and Drama
Dist - CHTSUI **Prod** - CHTSUI

Lucretia 5 MIN
U-matic / VHS
Write on, Set 1 Series
Color (J H)
Shows the correct use of the words 'Like' and 'As' in writing.
English Language
Dist - CTI **Prod** - CTI

Lucy - a Teenage Pregnancy 10 MIN
16mm / U-matic / VHS
Color (J H C)
Looks at the life of a 15 - year - old mother who is trying to make a life for herself and her baby in a crowded apartment in the projects with her nine siblings.
Sociology
Dist - PEREN **Prod** - PPSPRN

Lucy - aged 21 months, in foster care for 19 days 31 MIN
VHS
Young children in brief separation series
B&W (C G PRO)
$60.00 purchase, $12.00 rental _ #36105
Reveals that Lucy is too young to retain a clear memory of her absent mother, so she readily accepts the foster mother's care. Discloses that in spite of anxiety and resistive behavior, she manages well within the supportive relationship. However, Lucy's attachment to her foster mother causes conflict after her mother's return, and both women must cooperate in helping her through her anxiety. Part of a series on children in brief sepration.
Health and Safety; Psychology
Dist - PSU **Prod** - ROBJJ 1969

Lucy and Pete - Birth 12
U-matic
Video birth library series
Color (J H G)
$100.00 purchase
Follows the childbirth experiences of Lucy and Pete, who want to have their 8 - year - old son and 6 - year - old daughter present for the birth. Reveals that to strengthen the contractions, the midwife ruptures Lucy's membranes and encourages her to walk and use the Jacuzzi. Shows the two siblings present for the birth of the baby sister. Part of a 15 - part series on childbirth education.
Health and Safety
Dist - POLYMR **Prod** - POLYMR

Lucy Covington - Native American Indian 16 MIN
16mm / U-matic / VHS
Color (J H C)
LC 78-700932
Presents Lucy Covington, a grandchild of the last recognized chief of the Colville Indians. Tells how she led her people in a successful fight against the government's threat to close reservation.
Social Science
Dist - EBEC **Prod** - EBEC 1978

Lucy Swan
VHS
Color (G)
$350.00 purchase, $30.00 rental
Profiles Lucy Swan who was born on the Rosebud Reservation in South Dakota at the turn of the century. Shows how she accurately remembers the old ways, but does not entirely discount the new. 'This is the happiest time of my life,' she says without hesitation. She was chosen Outstanding Woman of the Year on the Cheyenne River Reservation.
Biography; History - United States; Social Science
Dist - ABBEY **Prod** - CALUME

Lucy's room 15 MIN
VHS
Color (G)
$195.00 purchase, $100.00 rental
Witnesses the struggle of a young couple trying to cope with the death of their first baby. Reveals that the wife responds to suggestions by therapists and is gradually coming to terms with the loss, but her husband is still filled with grief and has difficulty accepting the death and getting on with life. One day the wife helps an indigent and pregnant woman by paying part of her grocery bill and offering her the dead baby's crib. When the husband comes home and finds the two women in the baby's room, he reacts very badly. Later the needy woman comes back to ask for a job recommendation and the husband suddenly decides to give her the crib, beginning his healing. Produced by Brian Lindstrom.
Sociology
Dist - BAXMED

The Luddites 60 MIN
VHS
Color; PAL (J H)
PdS35 purchase
Examines industrialization and labor in the early 19th century when workers submitted to the impersonal discipline of mills, working 14 or 15 hour days in unsanitary and overheated conditions, living in crowded slums shut out from the beauty of nature. Reveals that young children were also employed, a new evil which mildly excited public concern, but the inhuman conditions under which families existed - tyranny and brutality under petty masters and overseers, disease and early death brought about by factory life - bred drunkenness, immorality and prostitution. The spontaneous reaction of workers to such evil was often to break the machines in the mills, the Luddite risings. Contact distributor about availability outside the United Kingdom.
History - World; Social Science
Dist - ACADEM

L'Udienza 111 MIN
16mm
Color (G) (ITALIAN (ENGLISH SUBTITLES))
Presents a provocative black comedy of passion and alienation, set against the intrigues of the modern - day Vatican. Stars Claudia Cardinale, Enzo Jannacci, Ugo Tognazzi, and Vittorio Gassman. Directed by Marco Ferreri.
Fine Arts
Dist - RIZACV **Prod** - RIZACV

Ludlow laughs - 59
VHS
Reading rainbow series
Color; CC (K P)
$39.95 purchase
Reveals that Ludlow is a big grump who never laughs or smiles, but one night he has the funniest dream ever and the whole world laughs with him. Features comedian Phyllis Diller as narrator of the story by Jon Agee. LeVar learns how to be funny from a 'comedy make - over specialist,' and viewers take a peek behind the scenes of a comedy club and meet a real - life stand - up comedian. Part of a series offering a multicultural approach to generating reading enthusiasm with cross - curricular applications, hosted by LeVar Burton.
English Language; Literature and Drama
Dist - GPN **Prod** - LNMDP

Ludlum on Ludlum - by Robert Ludlum 60 MIN
U-matic / VHS
Stereo (H C G T A S R PRO IND)
Shows Ludlum on background for stories, his role as writer, his life and personal interests.
Biography; History - United States; Literature and Drama
Dist - BANTAP **Prod** - BANTAP

Ludmila Semenyaka - Bolshoi Ballerina 60 MIN
VHS
Color (G)
$29.95 purchase _ #1260
Profiles the work of Bolshoi ballerina Ludmila Semenyaka. Includes excerpts from 'Swan Lake.'.
Fine Arts; Foreign Language; Geography - World; Physical Education and Recreation
Dist - KULTUR

Ludwig Van Beethoven 10 MIN
U-matic / VHS
Color (G)
$69.95 purchase _ #EX1864
Reveals that the story of the life of Ludwig van Beethoven is also the story of the music of love, war, majestic palaces and simple country roads.
Biography; Fine Arts
Dist - FOTH **Prod** - FOTH

Luigi Pirandello 58 MIN
VHS
Modern World - Ten Great Writers Series
Color (H)
$13.00 rental _ #60959
Portrays Luigi Pirandello, whose works 'Rules Of The Game,' 'Henry IV' and 'Six Characters In Searh Of An Author' analyzed relationships between outward appearance and inward reality to reveal the inner working of the human soul. Studies ten important European modernists writers through turn - of - the century settings, dramatizing their experiences and examining their principal works in a ten part series.
Literature and Drama
Dist - PSU **Prod** - FI
FI

Luigi Pirandello - 1867 - 1936 - Volume IX 58 MIN
VHS
Modern world - ten great writers series
Color (G)
$129.00 purchase _ #S01954
Profiles the Italian dramatist Luigi Pirandello, whose works explored the relationship between mask and reality. Uses drama, documentary, and literary criticism to portray Pirandello's experience, background and personal philosophy. Available for educational use only.
Literature and Drama
Dist - UILL

Luigi Pirandello - Pt 4 58 MIN
VHS
Modern World, the - 10 Great Writers Series
Color (S)
$129.00 purchase _ #833 - 9381
Profiles ten great Modernist writers whose work helped shape our world. Dramatizes the author's experiences and examines in - depth their various works. Part 4 presents Luigi Pirandello who analyzed the relationship between outward appearance and inward reality to reveal the inner workings of the human soul. Considers 'Rules Of The Game,' 'Henry IV' and 'Six Characters In Search Of An Author.'.
Fine Arts; Geography - World; Literature and Drama
Dist - FI **Prod** - LONWTV 1988

Luis Alfaro - 9 - 23 - 90 40 MIN
VHS / Cassette
Poetry Center reading series
Color (G)
$15.00, $45.00 purchase _ #946 - 713
Features Alfaro performing Downtown, which deals with racism, alcoholism, sexual and political diversity, and AIDS awareness, at the Poetry Center, San Francisco State University, with introductions by Robert Gluck and Margaret Crane.
Civics and Political Systems; Health and Safety; Literature and Drama; Sociology
Dist - POETRY **Prod** - POETRY 1990

Luisa Tenia Razon 11 MIN
16mm
Color (A) (SPANISH)
LC 72-700667
Tells how a young medical technician allays her mother - in - law's needless shame about the subject of uterine cancer. Makes it clear that cancer is nothing to be ashamed of, and that cancer of the uterus is a very curable cancer if detected early by a pap test and treated in time.
Foreign Language; Health and Safety
Dist - AMCS **Prod** - AMCS 1968

Luisa Torres 43 MIN
VHS / 16mm / U-matic
Color (H C A)
Follows the Hispanic traditions of the mountain folk of northern New Mexico through the eyes of a 79 - year - old woman going about her simple tasks. Presents medicinal native plants and the casket she made for herself to spare her family the burden.
Sociology
Dist - CEPRO **Prod** - BLUSKY

Luke 1 - 3
VHS
The Bible - American Sign Language translation series
Color (S R)
Presents an American Sign Language translation of the New Testament Gospel of Luke, chapters 1 through 3. Available on a free - loan basis from the Lutheran Church - Missouri Synod's Deaf Ministry.
Guidance and Counseling; Literature and Drama; Religion and Philosophy
Dist - CPH **Prod** - LUMIS

Luke, the Christian Deuteronomist 30 MIN
U-matic / VHS
Luke - the Theological Historian Series
Color (A)
Discusses Luke's keen interest in the book of Deuteronomy and how this earlier book helped him. Discusses the historical context in which Deuteronomy was written. Covers Luke's scriptural interpretation of Jesus' ministry.
Religion and Philosophy
Dist - UMCOM **Prod** - UMCOM 1981

Luke - the Theological Historian Series
The Birth of the Church, and the conversion of Saul of Tarsus 30 MIN
Eyewitnesses and servants of the Word 30 MIN
The Grumbling of the Faithful 30 MIN
Jesus' Way of Teaching and Preaching Scriptures 30 MIN
Luke, the Christian Deuteronomist 30 MIN
Luke's Account of Holy Week 30 MIN
Luke's Way of Reading His Scriptures, the Old Testament 30 MIN
Dist - UMCOM

Luke was There 32 MIN
16mm / VHS / U-matic
Color (P) (FRENCH SPANISH)
LC 76-702969; 80-701971
Tells the story of a boy whose disillusioning experiences with the adult world make him a runaway, until he learns the meaning of trust from a perceptive counselor at a children's shelter. An NBC Special Treat Program.
Guidance and Counseling; Sociology
Dist - LCOA **Prod** - LCOA 1976

Luke's Account of Holy Week 30 MIN
U-matic / VHS
Luke - the Theological Historian Series
Color (A)
Explains why the watching Pharisees felt that Jesus' entry into Jerusalem was blasphemous. Discusses the significance of the Last Supper. Explains the concepts of anamnesis and transubstantiation.
Religion and Philosophy
Dist - UMCOM **Prod** - UMCOM 1981

Luke's Way of Reading His Scriptures, the Old Testament 30 MIN
U-matic / VHS
Luke - the Theological Historian Series
Color (A)
Introduces the series and gives background information on Luke, the writer. Explains the 'septuagint' which Luke used for his scripture and how he used it. Concludes with a discussion of Luke's purposes for writing his scripture.
Religion and Philosophy
Dist - UMCOM **Prod** - UMCOM 1981

The Lull 15 MIN
VHS
Short story series
Color (J H)
#E373; LC 90-713140
Creates a mischievous character and deliberate misunderstandings in 'The Lull' by Suki. Part of a 16 - part series which introduces American short story writers and discusses the technical aspects of short story structure.
Literature and Drama
Dist - GPN **Prod** - CTI 1978

The Lull - by Saki 15 MIN
U-matic / VHS / 16mm
Short Story Series
Color (J H C A)
LC 83 - 706177
Tells about a politician who, seeking a respite from campaigning, ends up tending barnyard animals in his room due to a mischievously arranged misunderstanding. Based on the short stories The Lull and Louise by Saki.
Literature and Drama
Dist - IU **Prod** - IITC 1978

Lullaby 5 MIN
U-matic / VHS / 16mm
Color (K P I)
Uses intricate dough sculptures, folded paper and textured fabrics blended together to tell the animated story of a little dove.
Fine Arts
Dist - PHENIX **Prod** - GOTWAF

Lullaby 6 MIN
16mm
B&W (C A)
Presents a hilarious look at marriage several years after the vows have been taken.
Literature and Drama; Sociology
Dist - UWFKD **Prod** - UWFKD

Lullaby (Altato) 4 MIN
16mm / U-matic / VHS
Color (P I)
LC 80-700668
Offers an interpretation of a lullaby, showing pinwheels spinning, clocks, butterflies and balloons.
Fine Arts
Dist - IFB **Prod** - PANNOF 1977

Lulu in Berlin 52 MIN
VHS
Color; B&W (G)
$29.95 purchase
Takes a behind - the - scenes look at the film Lulu starring Louise Brooks. Interviews Hollywood exile Brooks. Directed by Richard Leacock and Susan Woll.
Fine Arts
Dist - KINOIC

Luma Nocturna 4 MIN
16mm
Color (C)
$129.00
Experimental film by Dennis Pies.
Fine Arts
Dist - AFA **Prod** - AFA 1974

Luma Nocturna 8 MIN
16mm
Color (A)
Presents an experimental film by Dennis Pies which suggests the subtle lights seen when dream and sleep state are penetrated.
Fine Arts
Dist - STARRC **Prod** - STARRC 1973

Lumaaq - an Eskimo Legend 8 MIN
16mm
Color (J)
Tells the story of a legend widely believed by the Povungnitik Inuit Eskimos.
Fine Arts; Literature and Drama; Social Science
Dist - NFBC **Prod** - NFBC 1975

Lumbar myelogram 14 MIN
VHS / U-matic
Color (PRO C G)
$195.00 purchase _ #C900 - VI - 014
Provides patients awaiting the lumbar myelogram procedure with a description and demonstration of the procedure that will help reduce anxiety. Interviews former myelogram patients who speak with candor about each stage of the process and physicians who discuss the many advantages of the procedure. Presented by Dr Harold Swanson.
Health and Safety
Dist - HSCIC

Lumbar Puncture 4 MIN
VHS / U-matic
Medical Skills Films Series
Color (PRO)
Health and Safety
Dist - WFP **Prod** - WFP

Lumbar Puncture 8 MIN
VHS / U-matic
Color (PRO)
Lists indications and contraindications for the procedure, contains graphics showing a step - by - step analysis and shows a 16mm film sequence of an actual lumbar puncture.
Health and Safety; Psychology; Science - Natural
Dist - UWASH **Prod** - UWASH

Lumbar Region, Pt 1 17 MIN
VHS / U-matic
Osteopathic Examination and Manipulation Series
Color (PRO)
Discusses the principle of introducing motion into the lumbar spine through the lower extremities in preparation for its use in the diagnosis of segmental dysfunction in the lumbar spine. Illustrates this principle further by the three direct manipulative techniques which are demonstrated.
Health and Safety; Science - Natural
Dist - MSU **Prod** - MSU

Lumbar Region, Pt 2 10 MIN
U-matic / VHS
Osteopathic Examination and Manipulation Series
Color (PRO)
Demonstrates palpatory examination and manipulative procedures for the lumbar spine with the patient in the seated position. Places emphasis on diagnostic information leading to improve localization of operator forces. Demonstrates both rotary and translatory types of motion testing.
Health and Safety; Science - Natural
Dist - MSU **Prod** - MSU

The Lumbar Spine I 25 MIN
U-matic / VHS
Cyriax on Orthopaedic Medicine Series
Color
Offers 11 manipulative techniques for the treatment of the lumbar spine.
Health and Safety; Science - Natural
Dist - VTRI **Prod** - VTRI

The Lumbar Spine II 22 MIN
VHS / U-matic
Cyriax on Orthopaedic Medicine Series
Color
Presents a non - manipulative treatment of disc lesions, including epidural local anaesthesia, traction and sclerosants.
Health and Safety; Science - Natural
Dist - VTRI **Prod** - VTRI

Lumber Grading
VHS / 35mm strip
$185.00 purchase _ #PX30699 filmstrips, $185.00 purchase _ #PX30699V
Discusses softwoods, hardwoods, plywood and veneer.
Industrial and Technical Education
Dist - CAREER **Prod** - CAREER

Lumber Production 35 MIN
VHS
Video Field Trips
Color (G)
$89.95 purchase _ #6 - 040 - 132P
Joins Spurlock Logging, Inc, in the forests of Woodville, Texas. Views the various steps in the logging process. Tours Champion International Corporation's plywood and stud mill in Camden, Texas. Demonstrates production of 2x4s, 4x4s and plywood. Interviews company executives. Part of a series of video field trips which follow raw materials from their natural environment through the processes which transform them into marketable products.
Agriculture; Industrial and Technical Education; Psychology; Social Science
Dist - VEP

The Lumiere Years 93 MIN
16mm
B&W (H C A)
Presents rare film footage of such historical events as the coronation of Czar Nicholas II, President McKinley preparing to invade Cuba and the Paris Exposition. Includes sequences from Europe, Africa, The Americas, Asia and India.
History - United States; History - World
Dist - FI **Prod** - FI 1974

Lumiere's train - Arriving at the station 9 MIN
16mm
B&W (G)
$20.00 rental
Deals with the subject of cinema itself as an apparatus of representation. Draws from two of cinema's pioneers, Louis Lumiere and Abel Gance. Using alternations between positive and negative, the film chronicles, in a highly kinetic manner, the coming to life and the birth of documentary and narrative fiction forms. Also part of the series Visual Essays on the origins of film.
Fine Arts
Dist - CANCIN **Prod** - RAZUTI 1979

Luminescence 9 MIN
16mm
Color (G)
$30.00 rental
Presents an abstract fantasy in collaboration with Ian Hugo.
Fine Arts
Dist - CANCIN **Prod** - EAGLE 1975

The Luminous Image 56 MIN
VHS / U-matic
Color
Documents an international exhibition of video installations held in the fall of 1984 in Amsterdam. Presented by the Stedelijk Museum.
Fine Arts
Dist - ARTINC **Prod** - ARTINC

Luminous Zone 30 MIN
16mm
Color; Silent (C)
$750.00
Experimental film by Barry Gerson.
Fine Arts
Dist - AFA **Prod** - AFA 1973

Lumpectomy 11 MIN
VHS / 16mm
Understanding Breast Cancer Series
Color (H C A PRO)
$195.00 purchase, $75.00 rental _ #8070
Discusses lumpectomy, removal of lumpy tissue from the breast.
Guidance and Counseling; Health and Safety
Dist - AIMS **Prod** - HOSSN 1988

Lumpy and Bumpy 14 MIN
16mm
Fingermouse, Yoffy and Friends Series
Color (K P I)
LC 73-700432
Follows Yoffy and his friends as they collect objects that are soft and objects that are hard.
Guidance and Counseling; Literature and Drama
Dist - VEDO **Prod** - BBCTV 1972

Lun 7 MIN
16mm
Color (G)
$15.00 rental
Utilizes puppet animation, found footage, optical printing and time - lapse photograhy. Narrates a poem; an ode to the moon. Produced by Steven Dye.
Fine Arts; Literature and Drama
Dist - CANCIN

Luna tune 2 MIN
16mm
Color (G)
$150.00 purchase, $25.00 rental
Uses sand animation lit from below, creating delicate silhouettes of sand figures as 84 - year - old lesbian poet Elsa Gidlow reads from her works. Produced by Carol Clement.
Fine Arts; Literature and Drama
Dist - WMEN

Lunacy 12 MIN
16mm / VHS
Color; B&W (G)
$15.00 rental
Dramatizes a certain craziness that occurs when the moon is full while exploring the root meaning of the word 'lunacy.' Interprets the surreal night when the moon intensifies life, causes strange behaviors and alters perceptual senses. Influenced by American experimental films of the 1940s and 1950s. Produced by Jerome Carolfi.
Fine Arts
Dist - CANCIN

Lunar Aspects 29 MIN
U-matic
Project Universe - Astronomy Series Lesson 3
Color (C A)
Explains the phases of the moon. Reviews basic data such as moon's size and distance from earth. Describes lunar and solar eclipses.
Science - Physical
Dist - CDTEL **Prod** - COAST

Lunar Geology 30 MIN
VHS / U-matic
Earth, Sea and Sky Series
Color (C)
Illustrates advances in lunar geology.
Science - Physical
Dist - DALCCD **Prod** - DALCCD

Lunar Geology 29 MIN
U-matic
Project Universe - Astronomy Series Lesson 7
Color (C A)
Contrasts data about the moon gathered by telescope and by space programs. Describes types of rock found on the moon.
Science - Physical
Dist - CDTEL **Prod** - COAST

Lunar Landing 1 - the Eagle has Landed 55 MIN
U-matic
NASA Tapes Series
Color (J)
LC 80-706111
Presents archival footage of Neil Armstrong's landing on and exploration of the moon's surface.
History - World; Industrial and Technical Education; Science - Physical
Dist - ASTROV **Prod** - NASA 1979

Lunar Landing - the Mission of Surveyor 1 16 MIN
16mm
Color
LC 75-701346
Presents a documentary account of the Surveyor I mission to land on the moon and send back close - up photographs of the lunar terrain. Shows the launching and the method by which the photographs were received.
Science - Physical
Dist - USNAC **Prod** - NASA 1967

The Lunar Module 5 MIN
16mm
Apollo digest series
Color
LC 74-705054
Gives a close - up look at the vehicle that made the actual touchdown on the lunar surface. Includes a view from the inside as well as an examination of the exterior.
History - World; Science; Science - Physical
Dist - USNAC **Prod** - NASA 1969

Lunar Orbit Rendezvous 21 MIN
16mm
Color
Discusses the groundwork conducted by the Mission Planning and Analysis Division in perfecting lunar rendezvous techniques.
Industrial and Technical Education; Science - Physical
Dist - NASA **Prod** - NASA

Lunar receiving lab 8 MIN
U-matic
Apollo digest series
Color
LC 79-706984
Shows the laboratory facilities of the Manned Spacecraft Center. Issued in 1969 as a motion picture.
Industrial and Technical Education; Science - Physical
Dist - USNAC **Prod** - NASA 1979

Lunar Samples of Apollo Eleven 8 MIN
U-matic
Color
Examines results of the preliminary investigation of the lunar samples. Includes biological and chemical studies and the distribution of the lunar material.
Science - Physical
Dist - NASA **Prod** - NASA 1972

Lunch is for wimps 30 MIN
VHS
Open space series
Color (A)
PdS50 purchase
Reveals that, across the United Kingdom, workers who were once dedicated, motivated and energetic are becoming exhausted, disillusioned and indifferent. Examines the economic climate of mass unemployment which forces employees, in an effort to avoid the axe, to do the work of two or even three people, to work extra hours and to take on extra responsibility, putting their friendships, family life and, ultimately, their health at risk.
Business and Economics; Sociology
Dist - BBCENE

The Lunch money 6 MIN
U-matic / 16mm / VHS
What should I do series
Color (P) (FRENCH)
$195.00, $120.00 purchase _ #JC - 67811
Uses animation to portray Susie whose lunch money has disappeared. Reveals that Hank knows that Red has it. Part of a series which dramatizes real life situations, gives possible options, alternatives and consequences, then leaves the final solution to students - for a learning situation which lasts.
Psychology; Sociology
Dist - CORF **Prod** - DISNEY 1970

Lunch Time with Babies 13 MIN
U-matic
Color (C A)
LC 81-706223
Observes children between the ages of three and 24 months of age as they eat lunch in a day care center. Discusses food preparation and nutritional information and describes how children play with food and utensils.
Home Economics
Dist - CORNRS **Prod** - CUETV 1981

Lunch with John Campbell, Jr - an Editor at Work 28 MIN
16mm
Literature of Science Fiction Series
Color (C A)
LC 72-700537
John W Campbell, Jr, late editor of Analog, discusses with Gordon Dickson and Harry Harrison the development of plot, theme and characters of a new story.
Literature and Drama
Dist - UKANS **Prod** - UKANS 1972

Lunches - Suppers
VHS / 35mm strip
Cook for the Health of it Series
(A)
$59.00 _ #RM6603
Uses standards set by the USDA and the HEW, to teach students the basic concepts of preparing lunches and suppers in a healthy manner. Includes cookbook.
Health and Safety; Home Economics
Dist - CAMV

Lunchroom Etiquette 10 MIN
U-matic / VHS / 16mm
Color (I)
Shows a variety of lunchroom situations and a variety of responses. Contrasts the positive and the not - so - positive responses to demonstrate the advantages of good manners. Deals with washing hands before eating, orderliness in line, carrying trays carefully, keeping the noise level low, and cleaning up after oneself.
Home Economics
Dist - AIMS **Prod** - AIMS 1982

A Lunchroom Goes Bananas 12 MIN
U-matic / VHS / 16mm
Beginning Responsibility Series
Color (P)
$305, $215 purchase _ #3917
Shows the importance of good manners in a school lunchroom.
Psychology; Social Science
Dist - CORF

Lundberg Family Farms 30 MIN
VHS / 16mm
Growing a Business Series
(H C)
$99.95 each, $1,295.00 series
Emphasizes the gains hard work can bring, through the story of the Lundberg Brothers and their rice farm.
Business and Economics
Dist - AMBROS **Prod** - AMBROS 1988

Lunes De Tormenta - 15 15 MIN
VHS
Amigos Series
Color (K) (SPANISH)
$125.00 purchase
Enables teachers with no knowledge of Spanish to introduce basic words to children in kindergarten through second grade. Uses simple concepts and music and features Perro Pepe, a six - foot orange dog, and Senorita Fernandez as instructors. Promotes awareness of and appreciation for Hispanic culture and sparks interest in the geography of Spanish - speaking countries. Part 15 is entitled 'Lunes De Tormenta.'.
Foreign Language; Geography - World
Dist - AITECH

Lung action and function 5 MIN
VHS
Systems of the human body series
Color (I J)
$24.95 purchase _ #L9624
Explains the function of the lungs. Details the interrelatedness of differing body systems. Part of a seven - part series on the human body, using the single - concept format.
Science - Natural
Dist - HUBDSC **Prod** - HUBDSC

Lung action and function 9 MIN
16mm / VHS
Systems of the human body series
Color (J H C)
$80.00 purchase _ #194 W 0096, #193 W 2096
Associates external evidences of breathing with internal body parts and the mechanics of breathing. Shows the expansion and collapse of the lungs. Part of a series on the systems of the human body.
Science - Natural
Dist - WARDS **Prod** - WARDS

Lung Cancer 60 MIN
VHS / 16mm
(C G)
$385.00 purchase _ #850VI025
Presents an overview of the causes, diagnosis, treatment and prevention of lung cancer.
Health and Safety
Dist - HSCIC **Prod** - HSCIC 1985

Lung Cancer - Early Diagnosis and Management 18 MIN
16mm
Color (PRO)
LC 72-700666
Shows physicians the preventive, diagnostic, and therapeutic measures by which they can help reduce the rising rates of morbidity and mortality from lung cancer.
Health and Safety
Dist - AMCS **Prod** - AMCS 1969

Lung Scanning in Pulmonary Disease 35 MIN
16mm
Color (PRO)
LC 77-707689
Demonstrates lung scanning as a valuable new diagnostic tool. Shows it aiding the radiologist in the interpretation of chest films and angiograms and serving as a screening procedure for routine or selective pulmonary angiography.
Health and Safety; Science; Science - Natural
Dist - SQUIBB **Prod** - SQUIBB 1967

Lung Scanning in Pulmonary Diseases 38 MIN
VHS / U-matic
Color (PRO)
Health and Safety; Science; Science - Natural
Dist - PRIMED **Prod** - PRIMED

Lung Ventilation Scan
U-matic / VHS
X - Ray Procedures in Layman's Terms Series
Color
Health and Safety; Science
Dist - FAIRGH **Prod** - FAIRGH

The Lungless Salamanders 16 MIN
U-matic / VHS / 16mm
Aspects of Animal Behavior Series
Color (J H C)
Examines the adaptive features of the lungless salamanders. Demonstrates the respiratory pattern of a typical lunged salamander and describes the probable events which led to the loss of lungs in plethodontids.
Science - Natural
Dist - UCEMC **Prod** - UCLA 1979

Lungs 10 MIN
16mm / Videodisc / VHS
Color (H C PRO)
$180.00, $225.00, $395.00 purchase, $30.00 rental _ #8018
Focuses on the lung and air passages of mammals. Demonstrates that the respiratory system of mammals has a structure that enables exchange of gases between the blood and external environment. Shows the lung's overall structure through dissection of a sheep's lung.
Science - Natural
Dist - AIMS **Prod** - EDMI 1982
EDMI

The Lungs - an Inside Story 11 MIN
U-matic / VHS / 16mm
Color (J)
LC 76-701943
Uses models and endoscopic photography within a human lung to reveal the structure of the lungs and how it affects their efficiency.
Science - Natural
Dist - CORF **Prod** - CORF 1976

Lungs and Removal of the Heart 10 MIN
16mm / U-matic / VHS
Guides to Dissection Series
Color (C A)
Focuses on the thoracic region. Demonstrates the dissection of the lungs and the removal of the heart.
Health and Safety; Science - Natural
Dist - TEF **Prod** - UCLA

The Lungs and Respiratory System 17 MIN
16mm / U-matic / VHS
Color (I J)
LC 75-702354
Describes the structure and functions of the human respiratory system and explains how the exchange of oxygen and carbon dioxide gases takes place in the lungs.
Science - Natural
Dist - EBEC **Prod** - EBEC 1975

The Lupinek Case 51 MIN
U-matic / VHS / 16mm
Featurettes for Children Series
Color (I J)
Tells how four talented children, guided by adults, operate a successful hand puppet theater. Shows how, when the puppets are stolen, the kids organize a search for the puppets, using techniques they remember from detective stories.
Guidance and Counseling; Literature and Drama
Dist - FI **Prod** - AUDBRF

Lupus 30 MIN
VHS
Color (G)
$149.00 purchase, $75.00 rental _ #UW3048
Reveals that lupus is an immune system disease that most often strikes young women. Shows that lupus affects more people than the more widely known multiple sclerosis, yet it remains a little - known disease. Looks at what may cause it and how it affects the people who suffer from it.
Health and Safety; Sociology
Dist - FOTH

Lupus - Wolf in Disguise 25 MIN
U-matic / VHS
Color
Explores ways to diagnose and treat the unusual disease of Lupus.
Health and Safety
Dist - MEDCOM **Prod** - MEDCOM

The Lure of Empire - America Debates Imperialism 27 MIN
U-matic / VHS / 16mm
Color (J H A) (SPANISH)
LC 73-702726
Gives an account of the annexation of the Philippines. Shows the debate on the floor of Congress over these islands, gained by chance during the United States' war with Spain to free Cuba.
Civics and Political Systems; Foreign Language; History - United States
Dist - LCOA **Prod** - LCOA 1974

Lure of the Everest 30 MIN
16mm
Color (I)
Records the attempts made by the Indian expedition of 1960 to conquer Everest. Highlights the elaborate preliminary arrangements and the camps set up at various heights.
Geography - World; Physical Education and Recreation
Dist - NEDINF **Prod** - INDIA

The Lure of the sea 15 MIN
VHS
Junior oceanographer series
CC; Color (P I)
$69.95 purchase_#10365VL
Addresses how the oceans have intrigued humans since the beginning of time in a format for elementary school age children. Poses questions such as what are oceans; who are oceanographers; why is it important to study oceans; and what is the difference between an ocean and a sea. Comes with an interactive video quiz, teacher's guide and six blackline masters. Part one of a four - part series.
Geography - World; Science - Natural; Science - Physical
Dist - UNL

The Lure of Water 11 MIN
U-matic
Color
Illustrates the dangers associated with recreation along the California State Water Project. Shows some of the more scenic places to enjoy while encouraging the safe use of the Project's many lakes and miles of aqueduct and bicycle trails.
Geography - United States; Health and Safety; Physical Education and Recreation
Dist - CALDWR **Prod** - CSDWR

The Lures of Death 15 MIN
U-matic / VHS / 16mm
Color (P)
Examines the deceptive lures child killers use to entice their victims into a trap of kidnapping, sexual abuse, torture or even death.
Sociology
Dist - CORF **Prod** - ABCTV

Luristan 14 MIN
16mm
Color (DANISH)
Presents an example of a half - nomadic civilization. Shows that the people live in a small village during the winter but during the summer the village is deserted, man and beast are on the plateau where they move from place to place to find pasture.
Foreign Language; Sociology
Dist - STATNS **Prod** - STATNS 1966

Lurk 38 MIN
16mm
B&W (G)
$45.00 rental
Sends up the mad scientist genre with a portrait of Prof Borealis and his luscious daughter Aurora, as the professor gets ready to try the first transplant of the new improved brain he has invented. Stars Edwin Denby and Red and Mimi Grooms.
Fine Arts; Literature and Drama
Dist - CANCIN **Prod** - BURCKR 1965

The Lusers 15 MIN
16mm
Color (J)
LC 80-701038
Presents Peter Hackes who reveals how to make a diet a real success by changing eating habits and increasing physical exercise. Discusses antistress foods, the memory diet, and creativity in dieting.
Health and Safety; Physical Education and Recreation
Dist - KLEINW **Prod** - KLEINW 1977

Lutes and delights 26 MIN
16mm / VHS
Morocco, body and soul series
Color (G)
$470.00, $260.00 purchase, $55.00 rental
Combines Arab and Moroccan poetry with accents from flamenco with Abdesadek Chekara and his orchestra, famous for their interpretations of Arab - Andalusian music. Features eleven 'noubas' or suites that came to North Africa when the Muslims and the Jews were expelled from Spain. Part of a series on Morocco's traditional music produced by Issa Genini.
Fine Arts; Literature and Drama
Dist - FIRS

Luther 108 MIN
VHS
Color (G A R)
$10.00 rental _ #36 - 81 - 2032
Profiles Martin Luther and his battles with the Roman Catholic Church. Emphasizes the political implications of Luther's dissent. Documents events such as the Diet of Worms, the Peasant's Revolt and the burning of the Papal Bull at Wittenberg. Stars Stacy Keach.
Literature and Drama; Religion and Philosophy
Dist - APH **Prod** - MAGNUM

Luther 112 MIN
U-matic / VHS / 16mm
Color
Chronicles 29 years in the life of Martin Luther. Stars Stacy Keach.
Biography; Fine Arts; Religion and Philosophy
Dist - FI **Prod** - UNKNWN

Luther and the Reformation 60 MIN
VHS / U-matic
James Galway's Music in Time Series
Color (J)
LC 83-706261
Presents flutist James Galway discussing the impact of the reformation on the history of music, focusing on the work of J S Bach and the importance of church organs and chorale singing.
Fine Arts
Dist - FOTH **Prod** - POLTEL 1982

Luther Metke at 94 60 MIN
VHS / U-matic
@Normal:Color (J)
LC 83-706261
@Normal:Presents flutist James Galway discussing the impact of the reformation on the history of music, focusing on the work of J S Bach and the importance of church organs and chorale singing.
Biography
Dist - UNKNWN **Prod** - UCLA 1982

Luther Metke at 94 27 MIN
VHS
Color (G C)
$195.00 purchase, $55.00 rental
Pictures the active later years of a poet, builder and community citizen who enjoys life and the world around him and is at peace. Presents his views on life, family and society through his comments and poetry.
Health and Safety
Dist - TNF **Prod** - NDIM 1979

Lutheran colleges and universities in the United States
VHS
Color (G R)
$12.50 purchase _ #S03044
Considers how a Lutheran higher education can be helpful. Profiles the colleges and seminaries of the Lutheran Church - Missouri Synod.
Guidance and Counseling; Literature and Drama; Religion and Philosophy
Dist - CPH **Prod** - LUMIS

Lutheran worship 20 MIN
VHS
Lutherans and their beliefs series
Color (J H C G A R)
$39.95 purchase, $10.00 rental _ #35 - 8110 - 2076
Features Dr Jerry L Schmalenberger in a consideration of Lutheran worship. Produced by Seraphim.
Religion and Philosophy
Dist - APH

Lutherans and their beliefs series

Baptism	20 MIN
Basic beliefs	20 MIN
The Creeds	20 MIN
Discipleship	20 MIN
Holy communion	20 MIN
Lutheran worship	20 MIN
The Reformation	20 MIN
Right or wrong for Lutherans	20 MIN
The Scriptures	20 MIN
Who are the Lutherans	20 MIN

Dist - APH

Luther's Choice 56 MIN
U-matic / VHS
Color (G)
$279.00, $179.00 purchase _ #AD - 2171
Tells the story of an inner - city youth who found the courage to break loose from the gang culture of his neighborhood. Shows him redirecting his life toward positive goals.
Fine Arts; Psychology; Sociology
Dist - FOTH **Prod** - FOTH

Luv 95 MIN
U-matic / VHS / 16mm
Color (C A)
Stars Jack Lemmon, Peter Falk and Elaine May in a comedy as it tells of a bright - eyed schemer who palms off his wife on an old college classmate in order to be free to marry another girl.
Fine Arts; Literature and Drama
Dist - FI **Prod** - CPC 1967

Luxembourg 30 MIN
VHS
Essential history of Europe
Color; PAL (H C A)
PdS65 purchase; Not available in Denmark
Presents the history and culture of Luxembourg from an insider's perspective. Eleventh in a series of 12 programs featuring the history of European Community member countries.
History - World
Dist - BBCENE

LVN Public Service Announcement Sampler
U-matic
Color
Presents a sampler for preview of the public service announcements produced for Maryland libraries. Updated regularly.
Education; Social Science
Dist - LVN **Prod** - LVN

Lycidas 18 MIN
U-matic / VHS / 16mm
Color
LC 77-702403
Presents an adaptation of the elegy Lycidas by John Milton. Combines paintings and music with a dramatic reading of the poem.

Fine Arts; Literature and Drama
Dist - UCEMC **Prod** - BIERJH 1977

Lydia Davis - 2 - 21 - 85 37 MIN
VHS / Cassette
Poetry Center reading series
Color (G)
$15.00, $45.00 purchase, $15.00 rental _ #617 - 522
Features the writer reading selections from Story and Other Stories and from The Thirteenth Woman, at the Poetry Center, San Francisco State University, with an introduction by Jim Hartz.
Literature and Drama
Dist - POETRY **Prod** - POETRY 1985

Lying 13 MIN
U-matic / VHS / 16mm
Learning Values with Fat Albert and the Cosby Kids, Set I Series
Color (K P I)
Tells how lies can get you in trouble. Explains that the gang's friend, Eddie, is back from Florida, where he says he wrestled alligators. Relates that the kids believe him and ask him to show them how to do it. Tells that everyone winds up covered with mud and wringing wet. Concludes with Eddie telling them that they should make up a story to tell their parents to avoid being reprimanded. At this point the kids realize that Eddie is a liar and has cried 'wolf' one too many times.
Guidance and Counseling
Dist - MGHT **Prod** - FLMTON 1975

Lying - 18 9 MIN
U-matic / VHS
Life's little lessons - self - esteem K - 3 - series
Color (K P)
$129.00, $99.00 _ #V617
Tells about Alvin's reputation for lying. Reveals that one day he saw a beautiful mermaid but nobody believed him because of his reputation, so Alvin decided telling the truth was better. Part of a 30 - part series on self - esteem.
Guidance and Counseling; Psychology
Dist - BARR **Prod** - CEPRO 1992

Lying and Cheating 29 MIN
VHS / 16mm
Feelings Series
Color (G)
$55.00 rental _ #FEES - 112
Presents sixth and seventh graders expressing their opinions on lying and its relation to self - respect. Features Dr Lee Salk.
Sociology
Dist - PBS **Prod** - SCETV
SCETV

Lyle, Lyle Crocodile - the musical house on East 88th St 25 MIN
VHS
Color (K P)
$12.95 purchase _ #095969
Tells the animated story of a family that moves into a new home and discovers that there's a crocodile in the bathtub.
Fine Arts; Literature and Drama
Dist - KNOWUN

Lyman H Howe's High Class Moving Pictures 28 MIN
U-matic / VHS / 16mm
Color (A)
Portrays the career of Lyman H Howe, a travelling exhibitor who brought motion pictures to America's towns and cities in the infancy of movies. Includes excerpts from some of Howe's own productions.
Biography; Fine Arts
Dist - CNEMAG **Prod** - CNEMAG 1983

Lyman - legend of the lakes
VHS
Color (G A)
$29.95 purchase _ #0911
Tells the story of a special boat designed for boating on the Great Lakes. Joins the Lyman Boat Owner's Association at their summer rendezvous. Views runabouts through cruisers.
Geography - United States; Physical Education and Recreation
Dist - SEVVID

Lyme disease 24 MIN
35mm strip / VHS
Color (J H C A)
$93.00, $93.00 purchase _ #MB - 909746 - 4, #MB - 909467 - 8
Examines the growing Lyme disease epidemic. Reveals that Lyme disease is caused by a microorganism, and usually transmitted from ticks to humans. Covers prevention and treatment, stressing the importance of catching the disease early on.
Health and Safety
Dist - SRA **Prod** - SRA 1990

Lyme Disease 26 MIN
U-matic / VHS
Color (C)
$249.00, $149.00 purchase _ #AD - 1714
Explains the symptoms of Lyme Disease and shows the culprit tick, its life and migratory cycles, the wildlife on which it feeds, and suggestions for avoiding its bite and removing it once attached. Warns that if Lyme Disease is unrecognized or incorrectly diagnosed, its complications can cause irreversible damage, death, and that neurological and physiological damage can occur to the fetus of an infected and untreated mother.
Health and Safety; Psychology; Science - Natural
Dist - FOTH **Prod** - FOTH

Lyme Disease - Danger in the Grass 13 MIN
VHS
Color (S)
$295.00 purchase, $75.00 rental _ #8164; LC 89716255
Explains how to spot Lyme Disease and what to do. Looks at high - risk areas and the tick that causes the disease.
Health and Safety; Sociology
Dist - AIMS **Prod** - ABCNEW 1989

Lyme Disease - Danger in the Grass 13 MIN
VHS / 16mm
Color (H C A)
$295.00 purchase, $75.00 rental _ #8164
Educates the public on Lyme Disease and how to avoid the suffering and permanent damage to the nervous system caused by the disease.
Health and Safety
Dist - AIMS **Prod** - ABCVID 1990

Lyme disease in our own backyard 56 MIN
VHS
Color (G)
$149.00 purchase, $75.00 rental _ #UW2865
Discloses that the tick - borne ailment, Lyme disease, may lie in wait in everyone's backyards. Features New Jersey health officials who trace the background of the disease, show its unpredictability and its devastating impact, and explain efforts to control it. Reveals that Lyme disease is a public health problem requiring community and individual vigilance. Teaches principles for controlling the disease for all who live in high - risk areas.
Health and Safety
Dist - FOTH

Lyme disease - what you need to know 19 MIN
VHS
Color (J H C A)
LC 90-700040
Presents sound current information on preventing, recognizing and treating Lyme disease. Helps in recognizing the symptoms at all stages and tells when and where to go for help and advice. Produced by Midnight Oil Productions.
Health and Safety; Sociology
Dist - HRMC
HSCIC

Lyme Regis 30 MIN
VHS
John Stobart's WorldScape series
Color (A G)
$19.95 purchase _ #STO - 04
Features one of the most ancient harbors in the world. The artist is joined by fellow artist Bert Wright. Follows artist John Stobart as he travels the globe, painting directly from life, and demonstrates the simplicity of the method that has made him the foremost living maritime artist. Demonstrates Stobart's classical maritime style in numerous evocative settings around the world. Part of a series on painting outdoors.
Fine Arts
Dist - ARTSAM **Prod** - WORLDS

The Lymphatic System 15 MIN
16mm / U-matic / VHS
Color (H C)
LC 80-700109
Discusses the relationship between the circulatory and the lymphatic systems. Explains the function of the lymphatic system and shows the flow of lymph through the lymphatic vessels.
Science - Natural
Dist - IFB **Prod** - IFFB 1979

Lymphography in Female Genital Cancer 25 MIN
16mm
Color
LC FIA66-52
Follows the diagnosis and treatment of genital malignancy in patients at the University of Miami School of Medicine. Demonstrates the application of direct lymphography in the treatment of carcinoma of the vulva and relates the results of the lymphatdenectomy operation.
Health and Safety
Dist - EATONL **Prod** - EATONL 1964

Lymphoid Organs 12 MIN
U-matic
Microanatomy Laboratory Orientation Series
Color (C)
Demonstrates the lymph node, the thymus gland and the spleen both in their general architecture and their individual diagnostic characteristics.
Health and Safety; Science - Natural
Dist - UOKLAH **Prod** - UOKLAH 1986

Lymphoproliferative Lesions of Salivary Glands and Upper Airways 55 MIN
U-matic
Color
Presents lymphoproliferative lesions, their systemic consequences and lymphomas of the head and neck.
Health and Safety
Dist - UTEXSC **Prod** - UTEXSC

Lyn Blumenthal - Social Studies, Pt 1, Horizontes 20 MIN
VHS / U-matic
Color
Presents a Cuban soap opera.
Fine Arts
Dist - ARTINC **Prod** - ARTINC

Lyn Blumenthal - Social Studies, Pt 2, the Academy 18 MIN
U-matic / VHS
Color
Suggests aggression, sexism and bigotry, Pictures an Academy Award stage.
Fine Arts
Dist - ARTINC **Prod** - ARTINC

Lyn Lifshin - not made of glass 55 MIN
U-matic / 16mm / VHS
Color (G)
$1000.00, $295.00 purchase, $125.00, $85.00 rental
Focuses on poet Lyn Lifshin. Interweaves thirty of her poems with a portrait of Lifshin and the history and continuing evolution of women writers. Produced by Mary Ann Lynch.
Literature and Drama; Sociology
Dist - WMEN

Lynda Benglis - Female Sensibility 14 MIN
U-matic / VHS
Color
Challenges patriarchal standards.
Fine Arts; Sociology
Dist - ARTINC **Prod** - ARTINC

Lynda Benglis - Mumble 20 MIN
U-matic / VHS
B&W
Presented by Lynda Benglis.
Fine Arts
Dist - ARTINC **Prod** - ARTINC

Lyndon B Johnson 17 MIN
U-matic / VHS
B&W
Traces the life of Lyndon Baines Johnson from his humble birth in 1908 to the beginning of his Presidency in 1963.
Biography
Dist - KINGFT **Prod** - KINGFT

Lyndon Johnson and the Tragedy of Vietnam 29 MIN
Videoreel / VT2
Course of Our Times II Series
Color
History - World
Dist - PBS **Prod** - WGBHTV

Lynn Rubright Video 30 MIN
VHS
Tell Me a Story Series
Color (K)
$19.95 purchase _ #W181 - 053
Features Lynn Rubright as storyteller. Includes 'How Woodpeckers Came To Be' and 'Six Wishes.' Part of an eight - unit series.
Literature and Drama
Dist - UPSTRT **Prod** - UPSTRT

Lynne Dreyer - 4 - 9 - 85
VHS / Cassette
Poetry Center reading series
Color (G)
$15.00, $45.00 purchase, $15.00 rental _ #630 - 530
Features the writer reading her works, Fade in the Morning Light and selections from Step Work, at the Poetry Center, San Francisco State University, with an introduction by Jim Hartz.
Literature and Drama
Dist - POETRY

Lyric anger 10 MIN
16mm
Color (G)

$20.00 purchase
Features a three - part film by Konrad Steiner which moves from terse storytelling to subjective brooding and to a dark psychological portrait of Orpheus.
Fine Arts
Dist - CANCIN

Lyrics - by Tim Rice 52 MIN
VHS
Color (G)
$14.95 purchase_#1377
Takes a musical journey through the career of Britain's lyricist, Tim Rice. Includes songs - Jesus Christ Superstar, I Don't Know How to Love Him, Don't Cry for Me Argentina, One Night in Bangkok and others.
Fine Arts
Dist - KULTUR

Lysistrata 97 MIN
VHS
Color (C A) (GREEK WITH ENGLISH SUBTITLES)
$99.00 purchase _ #DF213
Presents a contemporary adaptation of the comedy Lysistrata by Aristophanes shot on location at the Acropolis. Contains bawdy language.
Fine Arts; History - World; Literature and Drama
Dist - INSIM

M

M30 MIN
VHS
Cinematic eye series
Color (H)
$69.95 purchase, $40.00 rental
Considers the European movie 'M' within the context of its cultural, social and political milieu. Part 4 of a four - part series which reappraises classic European films as historic documents, aesthetic statements and as entertainment. Written and narrated by Benjamin Dunlap.
Fine Arts; History - World
Dist - SCETV **Prod** - SCETV 1977

M99 MIN
16mm / U-matic / VHS
B&W ((ENGLISH SUBTITLES))
Stars Peter Lorre and Ellen Widmann. Presents Fritz Lang's story of crime and pursuit. Tells the story of a child murderer who is sinister but also pitiable. Includes English subtitles.
Fine Arts; Foreign Language; Literature and Drama; Sociology
Dist - FI **Prod** - LANGF 1930

M95 MIN
VHS / U-matic
B&W (GERMAN)
Presents Peter Lorre as a notorious child killer hunted by the police and the underworld. Directed by Fritz Lang.
Fine Arts; Foreign Language
Dist - IHF **Prod** - IHF
UILL

M A R C 14 MIN
16mm
Color
LC 80-700766
Describes research being performed at the United States Meat Animal Research Center, whose goal is the development of new technology to increase the supply of high - quality red meats.
Agriculture; Industrial and Technical Education
Dist - USNAC **Prod** - USDA 1979

M C Higgins, the Great
35mm strip / VHS / Cassette
Newbery Award - Winners Series
Color (I)
$66.00, $24.00 purchase
English Language; Literature and Drama
Dist - PELLER

M F K Fisher - writer with a bite 28 MIN
VHS
Color (H G)
$250.00 purchase, $50.00 rental
Features intimate conversations with the American author and imaginatively visualized excerpts from her writings. Introduces her as not only a writer for the culinary arts, but also a novelist, essayist, short story writer and translator. Directed by Kathi Wheater.
Fine Arts; Literature and Drama
Dist - CNEMAG

M G M Studio Tour 57 MIN
16mm
B&W
Shows Norma Shearer, Zazu Pitts, Renee Adoree and Lew Cody in this nostalgic studio tour.
Fine Arts; Industrial and Technical Education
Dist - FCE **Prod** - FCE

M I G - fillet - vert - down fillet and butt welds 8 MIN
BETA / VHS
Arc welding and M I G welding series
Color (IND)
Industrial and Technical Education; Psychology
Dist - RMIBHF **Prod** - RMIBHF

M M in motion 45 MIN
VHS
Color; PAL (G)
PdS50 purchase
Portrays dancer and choreographer Mathilde Monnier in practice, production and performance.
Fine Arts
Dist - BALFOR **Prod** - OSTROV

M machine language 50 MIN
U-matic / VHS
Computer languages series; Pt 1
Color
Discusses addressing modes, instruction formats and types of instructions.
Industrial and Technical Education; Mathematics; Sociology
Dist - MIOT **Prod** - MIOT

M R - Mental Retardation 50 MIN
16mm
Color
Presents a survey of Wisconsin's mental retardation program, which demonstrates ways of coping with the condition of mental retardation and its many problems. Shows techniques of PKU testing and research in genetics, a multidisciplined approach to diagnosis and management, examples of severe retardation and recent advances in treatment. Depicts methods of handling the trainable and educable retarded, with emphasis on keeping the children at home.
Education; Psychology; Science; Sociology
Dist - NYU **Prod** - VASSAR

M - searching for a victim 12 MIN
16mm
Film study extracts series
B&W (J)
Presents an excerpt from the 1931 motion picture M. Depicts the child murderer, played by Peter Lorre, whistling obsessively as he stalks his new victim. Directed by Fritz Lang.
Fine Arts
Dist - FI **Prod** - UNKNWN

M Sound 14 MIN
VHS / U-matic
I - Land Treasure Series
Color (K)
English Language
Dist - AITECH **Prod** - NETCHE 1980

M25 - The Magic roundabout 52 MIN
VHS
First Tuesday series
Color; PAL (H C G)
PdS30 purchase
Describes six lanes of hell - the London orbital motorway - also known as M25. Examines the traffic jams and accidents of the M25 and how it presents motorway police with problem after problem, from drunk drivers to careless pedestrians and with police work ranging from issuing tickets to saving lives. Contact distributor about availability outside the United Kingdom.
History - World; Industrial and Technical Education
Dist - ACADEM **Prod** - YORKTV

MA - a Japanese concept 40 MIN
VHS
Color (G)
$90.00 purchase
Examines MA, a unique Japanese concept for time and space, in which the word MA was originally used to define the distance between two points or spaces, with importance attributed to the emptiness or silence of the space in between. Features two productions by Takahiko Iimura between 1975 - 1989. Includes MA - Space - time in the Garden of Ryoan - ji, a famous Zen garden, with text by Arata Isozaki and music by Takehisa Kosugi and MA - Intervals, an abstract consisting of black and clear spacings with a line between them.
Fine Arts; Religion and Philosophy
Dist - CANCIN

Ma Liang and the Magic Brush 15 MIN
U-matic / VHS
Sixteen Tales Series
Color (P I)
Tells The Chinese tale of how Ma Liang, rewarded for his hard work with a brush that makes everything he paints become real, outsmarts a greedy emperor and uses his magic brush for the good of his people.
Geography - World; Literature and Drama
Dist - AITECH **Prod** - KLCSTV

Maa Arithmetic Series
Ordered Pairs and the Cartesian Product 6 MIN
Dist - MLA

MAA Calculus Series
Area under a curve 15 MIN
Continuity of Mapping 10 MIN
The Definite integral 21 MIN
The Definite integral as a limit 10 MIN
A Function is a Mapping 10 MIN
Fundamental theorem of the calculus 10 MIN
I Maximize 10 MIN
Infinite Acres 10 MIN
Limit 10 MIN
Newton's Method 10 MIN
The Theorem of the Mean 10 MIN
Volume by shells 9 MIN
Volume of a solid of revolution 8 MIN
What is Area 20 MIN
Who Killed Determinants 57 MIN
Dist - MLA

MAA elementary arithmetic series
Addition and subtraction 7 MIN
Counting 9 MIN
Multiplication and Division 7 MIN
One to One Correspondence 10 MIN
Sets - union and intersection 6 MIN
What is a Set, Pt 1 14 MIN
What is a Set, Pt 2 7 MIN
Dist - MLA

Maa general mathematics series
Non - Standard Analysis, Pt 1 67 MIN
Non - Standard Analysis, Pt 2 67 MIN
Unsolved problems - three dimensions - Film 2 21 MIN
Unsolved problems - two dimensions - Film 1 22 MIN
Dist - MLA

MAA individual lecturers collegiate series
The Kakeya problem - Pt 1 30 MIN
The Kakeya problem - Pt 2 30 MIN
Dist - MLA

Maa Individual Lecturers Series Basic
Let Us Teach Guessing, Pt 1 30 MIN
Let Us Teach Guessing, Pt 2 30 MIN
Dist - MLA

Maa Individual Lecturers Series Collegiate
What is an Integral 61 MIN
Dist - MLA

MAA individual lecturers series
Applications of group theory in particle physics 60 MIN
Can You Hear the Shape of a Drum 65 MIN
Challenge in the Classroom - the Methods of R L Moore 54 MIN
Challenging Conjectures 40 MIN
The Classical groups as a source of algebraic problems 60 MIN
Differential topology - Lecture 1 60 MIN
Differential topology - Lecture 2 60 MIN
Differential topology - Lecture 3 60 MIN
Fixed points 60 MIN
Gottingen and New York - reflections on a life in mathematics 43 MIN
John Von Neumann 59 MIN
The Kakeya Problem 60 MIN
Let Us Teach Guessing 61 MIN
Mathematical Induction 60 MIN
Mathematical Induction, Pt 1 30 MIN
Mathematical Induction, Pt 2 30 MIN
Measure and Set Theory 47 MIN
Mr Simplex Saves the Aspidistra 32 MIN
Nim and Other Oriented Graph Games 63 MIN
Pits, peaks and passes - a lecture on critical point theory - Pt 1 48 MIN
Pits, peaks and passes - a lecture on critical point theory - Pt 2 26 MIN
Predicting at Random 43 MIN
The Search for Solid Ground 62 MIN
Topology 30 MIN
What is an Integral, Pt 1, Integrals are Averages 29 MIN
What is an Integral, Pt 2, Averages are Integrals 29 MIN
What is Mathematics and How do We Teach it 45 MIN
Dist - MLA

MAA mathematics series
Applications of the marriage theorem 47 MIN
Matching Theory - the Marriage Theorem 46 MIN
Singular Perturbation Theory and Geophysics 50 MIN
Dist - MLA

Mabel at the Wheel 25 MIN
16mm / U-matic / VHS
Charlie Chaplin Comedy Theater Series
B&W (I)
Presents one of the earliest Chaplin comedies in which he plays the role of a dastardly villain. Explains that aboard his motorcycle he tries to outsmart his rival at winning Mabel and the big race.
Fine Arts
Dist - FI **Prod** - MUFLM

Mabel Parker Hardison Smith 29 MIN
VHS / 16mm
Color (G)
$100.00 purchase _ #MPHSVHS
Traces the life of Mabel Parker Hardison Smith, a black Appalachian woman from the mining country of Kentucky. Features gospel music and archival and personal photographs.
Geography - United States; History - United States; Social Science; Sociology
Dist - APPAL

Ma'bugi' - Trance of the Toraja 21 MIN
16mm / U-matic / VHS
Color (H C)
LC 77-701038
Documents a religious trance ritual practiced in the Toraja highlands of Indonesia in order to restore health and prosperity to an afflicted village community.
Religion and Philosophy; Sociology
Dist - UCEMC **Prod** - CRYRHD 1974

Mac buyer's guide
CD-ROM
(G A)
$149.00 purchase _ #1611
Provides a source for thousands of Macintosh and Apple IIGS products. Includes all software, hardware, and accessories. Comes complete with description, system requirements, name, address, and telephone number of the supplier and prices. For Macintosh Plus, SE and II computers. Requires 1MB RAM, floppy disk drive, Apple compatible CD - ROM drive.
Computer Science; Home Economics
Dist - BEP

Mac Donald's Farm - Animals Go to School 11 MIN
U-matic / VHS / 16mm
Color (K P I)
LC 72-714069
Uses the format of a trip to a unique animal farm in order to observe animals performing unusual demonstrations of the stimulus - response - reward behavior concept in learning.
Psychology; Science - Natural; Social Science
Dist - AIMS **Prod** - CAHILL 1972

Mac in the USSR 40 MIN
VHS
Color (A)
PdS65 purchase
Reveals that, next to Coca-Cola, McDonald's is one of the great symbols of Western capitalism. Shows that in Moscow Big Mac represents hope, a direct emblem of perestroika - whereas in the West it stands for junk food. The largest McDonald's restaurant in the world opened in Moscow in 1990. Examines the events leading up the opening and talks with the Russian staff and the Canadian president of McDonald's.
Business and Economics
Dist - BBCENE

Mac Remembers Place Value - Place Value 15 MIN
U-matic / VHS
Figure Out Series
Color (I)
Tells the story of Alice's race to restore her computer friend's memory. Introduces the significance of place value and the meaning of the digit's location in a number.
Mathematics
Dist - AITECH **Prod** - MAETEL 1982

Mac Subtracts in Jail - Subtraction of Hundreds, Single Regrouping 15 MIN
U-matic / VHS
Figure Out Series
Color (I)
Demonstrates subtraction with only one regrouping, using the story of Mac's undercover venture to capture a computer embezzler.
Mathematics
Dist - AITECH **Prod** - MAETEL 1982

Mac Wilkins Gold Medal Discus Video 60 MIN
VHS / U-matic
Mac Wilkins Productions Videos Series
Color (J H C A)
Teaches the discus throw, explaining proper technique and training, drills. Narrated and demonstrated by Mac Wilkins, former discus world record holder.
Physical Education and Recreation
Dist - TRACKN **Prod** - TRACKN 1986

Mac Wilkins Productions Videos Series
Al Feurbach's basic 70' shot putting video 60 MIN
Mac Wilkins Gold Medal Discus Video 60 MIN
Dist - TRACKN

Macademic
CD-ROM
(G A)
$149.00 purchase _ #1826
Includes 7,500 programs and related files for education and instructional use with art, music, math, science, foreign languages, fun and games, teachers help and more. For Macintosh Plus, SE and II computers. Requires 1MB RAM, floppy disk drive, Apple compatible CD - ROM drive.
Computer Science
Dist - BEP

Macaroni, Nutrition and Numbers 13 MIN
16mm
Color (J)
Demonstrates the process of labeling the nutritional content of various foods.
Health and Safety; Home Economics; Social Science
Dist - MTP **Prod** - NMI

MacArthur
U-matic / VHS
Color (J C I)
Depicts the life of General Douglas MacArthur from World War II to the Korean conflict. Stars Gregory Peck.
Biography; Fine Arts; History - United States
Dist - GA **Prod** - GA

MacArthur and the war at sea - Volume 4
VHS
Crusade in the Pacific series
B&W (H C A)
$24.95 purchase
Covers the land and sea battles in the Pacific during World War II. Includes wartime footage and narration.
History - World
Dist - PBS **Prod** - WNETTV

The MacArthur report
16mm
B&W (G)
Features a biased 'report' which succeeds as a solid Truman putdown and is unintentionally amusing. Offers a short version, 9 minutes, $15.00 rental, or long, 13 minutes, $20.00 rental.
Biography; Fine Arts; History - United States; Literature and Drama
Dist - KITPAR **Prod** - UNEWSR 1952

Macbeth
U-matic / VHS
Classic Films - on - Video Series
B&W (G C J)
$79 purchase _ #05636 - 85
Screens the 1948 production of Shakespeare's tragedy. Stars Orson Wells.
Fine Arts
Dist - CHUMAN

Macbeth 148 MIN
VHS / 16mm
BBC's Shakespeare
(H A)
$249.95
Tells Shakespeare's tragedy of the warrior Macbeth who rises to the position of King of Scotland amidst terror and violence.
Literature and Drama
Dist - AMBROS **Prod** - AMBROS 1984

Macbeth 148 MIN
VHS / U-matic
Shakespeare Plays Series
Color (H C A)
Presents the play Macbeth by William Shakespeare about a warrior who is told by a trio of witches that he is fated to become King of Scotland and, therefore, with the aid of his wife, murders the king and assumes his throne. Reveals that the new king and his wife embark on a guilt - ridden reign of terror, murdering former friends and striking down the families of their adversaries.
Literature and Drama
Dist - TIMLIF **Prod** - BBCTV 1984

Macbeth 36 MIN
U-matic / VHS / 16mm
World of William Shakespeare Series
Color (H C A)
LC 78-700750
Presents a condensed version of William Shakespeare's play Macbeth.
Literature and Drama
Dist - NGS **Prod** - NGS 1978

Macbeth
VHS / U-matic
Color (J C I)
Presents Shakespeare's tragic play, Macbeth, in a restored, uncut version of the 1948 production starring Orson Wells.
Fine Arts; Literature and Drama
Dist - GA **Prod** - GA

Macbeth 148 MIN
VHS
BBC Shakespeare series
Color (G C H)
$109.00 purchase _ #DL455
Fine Arts
Dist - INSIM **Prod** - BBC

Macbeth 60 MIN
VHS / U-matic
Drama - play, performance, perception series; Dramatis personae
Color (H C A)
Explores methods of character development. Uses the play Macbeth as an example.
Literature and Drama
Dist - FI **Prod** - BBCTV 1978

Macbeth 30 MIN
U-matic / VHS
Shakespeare in Perspective Series
Color (J)
Presents an adaptation of Shakespeare's play Macbeth, the tragic story of an upright man, goaded by his ambition, and of the mental torment resulting from his crime. Includes the plays Julius Caesar, Romeo And Juliet and Hamlet on the same tape.
Literature and Drama
Dist - FI **Prod** - FI 1984

Macbeth 107 MIN
U-matic / VHS / 16mm
Color (I J H C)
Stars Maurice Evans and Judith Anderson as Lord and Lady Macbeth, in the Shakespeare play that deals with Scottish history.
Fine Arts; Literature and Drama
Dist - FI **Prod** - UNKNWN 1960

Macbeth 11 MIN
16mm / U-matic / VHS
Shakespeare Series
Color (H C A)
An excerpt from the play of the same title. Presents three scenes in which the three witches weave their spells and Act II, Scene 1 in which Macbeth contemplates the murder he is about to commit.
Fine Arts; Literature and Drama
Dist - IFB **Prod** - IFB 1974

Macbeth
U-matic / VHS
Color (G) (ITALIAN (ENGLISH SUBTITLES))
Presents Shakespeare's dark tragedy starring Kostas Paskalis and Josephine Barstow as the scheming Macbeths with MET star James Morris as Banquo. John Pritchard conducts.
Fine Arts
Dist - VAI **Prod** - VAI

Macbeth
VHS / U-matic
Shakespeare Series
B&W (G C J)
$79 purchase _ #05704 - 85
Re - enacts the 1948 version of Shakespeare's tragedy Stars Orson Welles.
Fine Arts; Literature and Drama
Dist - CHUMAN

Macbeth
VHS
Color (G)
$39.95 purchase _ #1115
Brings Shakespeare's mist - shrouded Scotti ction of
murder and intrigue to life in a Bolshoi Ba Theatre.
'Macbeth' taped live at Moscow's historic ia
Stars Alexei Fadeyechev in the title rol eographed
Timofeyeva as his unscrupulous cons orld; Physical
by Vasiliev to music by Molchanov.
Fine Arts; Foreign Language; Geogra
Education and Recreation
Dist - KULTUR 90 MIN

MacBeth
VHS ragedies series
Understanding Shakespeare -
Color; CC (I J H C)
$49.95 purchase _ #US03 ommentary by
Features key scenes, along s through the 16th - century
Shakespearean scholar s way for students to increase
language barrier to pro se classics. Includes a
their comprehension o
teacher's guide.
Literature and Drama
Dist - SVIP

Macbeth 149 MIN
VHS
Color (S) (ITALIAN)
$39.95 purchase _ #833 - 9318
Presents the Deutsche Opera Berlin production of 'Macbeth' by Verdi. Features a cast of Renato Bruson, Mara Zampieri, David Griffith, James Morris and Dennis O'Neill. Giuseppe Sinopoli conducts and the costume and set designs are by Luciano Damiani.
Fine Arts; Foreign Language; Geography - World
Dist - FI **Prod** - RMART 1988

Macbeth 89 MIN
VHS
B&W (G)
$59.95 purchase _ #S00521
Features Orson Welles as producer and star of Shakespeare's 'Macbeth.' Co - stars Jeanette Nolan, Dan O'Herlihy and Roddy McDowell.
Literature and Drama
Dist - UILL

Macbeth 148 MIN
U-matic / VHS
Color (C)
$399.00, $249.00 purchase _ #AD - 749 ; $399.00, $249.00 purchase _ #AD - 1251
Presents 'Macbeth' produced by Trevor Nunn with the Royal Shakespeare Company. Stars Ian McKellen and Judi Dench.
Literature and Drama
Dist - FOTH **Prod** - FOTH

Macbeth - Act I, Scene VII 8 MIN
U-matic / VHS / 16mm
Great Scenes from Shakespeare Series
Color (I)
LC 73-714376
Presents a lively form of entertainment which enables the viewer to focus on the atmosphere and theme of Shakespeare's Macbeth.
Literature and Drama
Dist - PHENIX **Prod** - SEABEN 1971

Macbeth - an Introduction 26 MIN
16mm / U-matic / VHS
Shakespeare Series
Color (J A)
LC 72-700980
Presents a version of Shakespeare's play 'MACBETH' Used narration to help bridge the transitions between the main sequences in the play.
Literature and Drama
Dist - PHENIX **Prod** - SEABEN 1968

Macbeth, Pt 1 - the Politics of Power 28 MIN
U-matic / VHS / 16mm
Humanities - the Drama Series
Color (H C)
Interprets and points out the relationships of the characters in the play Macbeth. Discusses the witches and the Monarch Duncan and considers how it is possible to portray Macbeth as a brutal murderer who remains a tragic hero. Narrated by Douglas Campbell.
Literature and Drama
Dist - EBEC **Prod** - EBEC 1964

Macbeth, Pt 3 - the Secret'st Man 33 MIN
U-matic / VHS / 16mm
Humanities - the Drama Series
Color (H C)
Emphasizes the capacity for good and evil within the same human heart. Macbeth reiterates that 'everyman is the secret'st man of blood.' Narrated by Douglas Campbell.
iterature and Drama
t - EBEC **Prod** - EBEC 1964

eth, Pt 2 - the Themes of Macbeth 28 MIN
n / U-matic / VHS
ities - the Drama Series
C)
w the entire play is built on the paradox, 'Nothing
t is not.' Explains that the world of Macbeth is
h appearances cannot be trusted. Narrated by
mpbell.
Literature and Drama
Dist - EB **Prod** - EBEC 1964

Macbeth re ns 130 MIN
VHS
Color; PAL (H)
PdS40 purchase
Presents a series 26 - minute parts relating some of the themes of Ma to the realities 20th - century life. Uses image assoc documentary and drama to encourage students k about the play and its background in relation eir own experiences. Contact distributor about availa outside the United Kingdom.
Literature and Drama; Soc
Dist - ACADEM

Macbeth RSC 146 MIN
VHS
Color; PAL (H)
PdS45 purchase
Presents the Trevor Nunn production of Macbeth on screen, using innovative production techniques. Stars Judi Dench and Ian McKellan. Contact distributor about availability outside the United Kingdom.
Literature and Drama; Sociology
Dist - ACADEM

Macbeth - the politics of power 28 MIN
VHS
Color (G C H)
$119.00 purchase _ #DL498
Examines how Shakespeare portrayed Macbeth as both a brutal murderer and a tragic hero. Features Douglas Campbell who interprets the role of characters in the play as they relate to the theme of power, and discusses problems he confronted when staging the play.
Fine Arts; Literature and Drama
Dist - INSIM

Macbeth - the secret'st man 28 MIN
VHS
Color (G C H)
$119.00 purchase _ #DL500
Examines Macbeth's tragic flaws to understand his capacity to hold both good and evil within one heart. Draws a parallel between Lady Macbeth's increasing madness and Macbeth's reaction to the murders.
Fine Arts; Literature and Drama
Dist - INSIM

Macedonia Baptist Choir 29 MIN
Videoreel / VT2
Changing rhythms series
Color
Presents the Macedonia Baptist Choir performing God Is, Blessed Be The Name, I'll Do His Will and We've Come A Long Way.
Fine Arts; History - United States
Dist - PBS **Prod** - KRMATV

MacGuide USA
CD-ROM
(G A)
$99.00 purchase _ #2211
Combines demonstration, shareware, freeware, product listing and review. Bulletin Board without the telephone lines or commercial information system expense. For Macintosh Plus, SE and II computers. Requires 1MB RAM, floppy disk drive, Apple compatible CD - ROM drive.
Computer Science
Dist - BEP

Mache Sculpture 13 MIN
16mm
Color (I)
LC 74-703049
Shows the techniques which can be used to create a variety of objects using papier - mache.
Fine Arts; Physical Education and Recreation
Dist - AVED **Prod** - AVED 1974

MacHenry 5 MIN
U-matic / VHS
Write on, Set 2 Series
Color (J H)
Presents a lesson in diction. Discusses the use of 'Awful' and 'Terrible' and 'Nice'.
English Language
Dist - CTI **Prod** - CTI

Machete Gillette...Mama 45 MIN
16mm
Larry Gottheim series
Color (G A)
$90.00 rental
Presents the work of filmmaker Larry Gottheim. Portrays the Dominican Republic using a pop song from the country as a backdrop. Uses the metaphor of the cutting edge of a machete as the wall between women and men, between natives of the republic and Haitians who come over to cut sugar cane, to a consideration of the divided self.
Fine Arts; Geography - World; History - World; Industrial and Technical Education; Sociology
Dist - PARART **Prod** - CANCIN 1989

Machiavelli's the Prince 90 MIN
VHS
Great Ideas Series
Color (H)
$14.00 rental _ #90439
Features Mortimer J. Adler in the second of five seminars of his Great Ideas Series, which exposes a group of high school students to the most important literary works of Western civilization. This installment examines Machiavelli's The Prince.
Civics and Political Systems; Education; Literature and Drama; Religion and Philosophy
Dist - PSU **Prod** - EBEC
EBEC

Machinability 56 MIN
BETA / VHS / U-matic
Color
$400 purchase
Presents machinability versus microstructure.
Industrial and Technical Education; Science
Dist - ASM **Prod** - ASM

Machine 10 MIN
16mm
Color (J A)
LC 70-712365
A deftly animated allegory on man and his inventions.
Fine Arts; Sociology
Dist - VIEWFI **Prod** - JANUS 1966

The Machine 12 MIN
U-matic / VHS
You and Your Personal Computer Series Part I
Color
Looks at the hardware which makes up the personal computer and shows what each part does and how it interrelates with each other part. Explains the logic, memory and control functions and what software is and how it's used.
Mathematics
Dist - VISUCP **Prod** - VISUCP

Machine - adding with fractions 10 MIN
16mm / VHS
Using fractions to add and subtract series
Color (I J H G)
$195.00, $125.00 purchase, $50.00 rental _ #8217
Portrays a boy who learns to use a 'number re - namer' machine that manufactures equivalent fractions. Part of a series teaching the use of fractions to add and subtract developed by the National Council of Teachers of Mathematics.
Mathematics
Dist - AIMS **Prod** - DAVFMS 1990

Machine Age 28 MIN
U-matic / VHS / 16mm
Color (J H)
LC 82-700151
Depicts a police officer whose first assignment is guarding a 17 - year - old runaway. Tells how the two become close and the policemen is torn between his responsibility and his attachment for the girl.
Fine Arts; Guidance and Counseling
Dist - FI **Prod** - NFBC 1980

Machine and Process Capability Studies 30 MIN
VHS / U-matic
Statistical Process Control Series
Color (PRO)
Provides an interactive video applications oriented training program that focuses on the role of the control chart as a powerful tool in monitoring quality. Lessons are designed to introduce shop floor operators, supervisors and technical personnel to the techniques of statistical process control.
Business and Economics; Mathematics
Dist - ITCORP **Prod** - ITCORP 1986

The Machine at Work 14 MIN
U-matic / VHS
You and Your Personal Computer Series Pt II
Color
Explains how the computer can handle the basic record - keeping functions of any business. Shows examples such as invoicing, inventory control, financial planning, graphics and word processing.
Mathematics
Dist - VISUCP **Prod** - VISUCP

Machine Brake Drum Ammco Brake Lathe 21 MIN
VHS / 16mm
Auto Mechanics Series
(G PRO)
$89.00 purchase _ #AM15
Discusses using the Ammco brake lathe on machine brake drums.
Industrial and Technical Education
Dist - RMIBHF **Prod** - RMIBHF

Machine Dreams 87 MIN
16mm
Color (G)
$490.00 purchase; $150.00 rental
Looks at the relationship between humankind and technology, exploring the ways machines embody our most fundamental hopes and fears.
Sociology
Dist - ICARUS
FIRS

Machine Embroidery 97 MIN
BETA / VHS
Color
Presents a series of projects that teach hoop improvements, outlining the variety of stitches, tapering, monogramming, applique and shading.

Home Economics
Dist - HOMEAF **Prod** - HOMEAF

Machine for Living 29 MIN
Videoreel / VT2
Design 2000 Series
B&W
Fine Arts; Industrial and Technical Education; Sociology
Dist - PBS **Prod** - WITFTV

Machine Hazard Awareness 17.5 MIN
U-matic / Kit / VHS
Color (IND A)
$475 purchase, $65 one week rental
Explains how to identify and recognize machine hazards, and how to understand guarding principles and recognize guarding qualities. Divided into four parts. The introduction lists possible hazards. The second part demonstrates and describes mechanical hazards. The third part discusses guarding techniques. The last part discusses guarding qualities.
Health and Safety
Dist - IFB

Machine Keyways on the Vertical Milling Machine (Straight and Woodruff)
VHS / U-matic
Milling and Tool Sharpening - Spanish Series
Color
Industrial and Technical Education
Dist - VTRI **Prod** - VTRI

Machine language 55 MIN
VHS / U-matic
Computer languages series; Pt 2
Color
Industrial and Technical Education; Mathematics; Sociology
Dist - MIOT **Prod** - MIOT

Machine - Master or Slave 14 MIN
16mm
B&W (H C T)
Uses a factory to illustrate problems management faces with the human and financial factors of technology. Asks such questions as, how can management coordinate its own self - interest with the needs of employees and consumers.
Business and Economics; Industrial and Technical Education; Psychology; Sociology
Dist - NYU **Prod** - NYU 1941

Machine - Metal Shop Safety
VHS / 35mm strip
Skills Related Safety Series
$36.00 purchase _ #TX1E1 filmstrips, $86.00 purchase _ #TX1E1V VHS
Teaches about machine and metal shop safety. Discusses shoes, goggles, hand tools, and machinery. oxyacetylene welding.
Health and Safety
Dist - CAREER **Prod** - CAREER

The machine of Eden 14 MIN
16mm
Color (G)
$28.00 rental, $454.00 purchase
Presents an experimental film by Stan Brakhage.
Fine Arts
Dist - CANCIN **Prod** - BRAKS 1970

Machine Operations - Sheet Metal 13 MIN
16mm
Metalwork - Machine Operation Series
Color (J H)
LC 72-700814
Sheet metal work - - the bar folder, slip - role former, standard brake and box, pan brake and hand forming.
Industrial and Technical Education
Dist - SF **Prod** - MORLAT 1967

Machine Quilting 1 60 MIN
VHS / BETA
Color
Introduces strip quilting, unique piecing, and the assembling of the quilt.
Home Economics
Dist - HOMEAF **Prod** - HOMEAF

Machine Quilting 2 87 MIN
VHS / BETA
Color
Demonstrates the time saving techniques of speed piecing. Covers quilt design, color selection, fabric prep, and quilting.
Home Economics
Dist - HOMEAF **Prod** - HOMEAF

Machine safeguarding 10 MIN
VHS
Supervisors' development program series
Color (IND)
$280.00 purchase _ #15490 - 2222
Explains the importance of safety practices around machinery. Features William Shatner as host. Part of a 13 - part series on employee safety which stresses the four - step SAFE model - Search for hazards, Assess risks, Find solutions, Enforce solutions.
Business and Economics; Health and Safety; Industrial and Technical Education; Psychology
Dist - NSC **Prod** - NSC

Machine Setup and Safety 14 MIN
VHS / U-matic
Numerical Control/Computerized Numerical Control, Module 1 - 'Fundamentals Series
Color (IND)
Covers cold start procedures, safety practices and features of the machine, establishing an origin point and determining tool length offsets.
Business and Economics; Industrial and Technical Education
Dist - LEIKID **Prod** - LEIKID

Machine Shop - Bandsaw Series
Safety and familiarization on the horizontal bandsaw 18 MIN
Safety and familiarization on the vertical bandsaw 25 MIN
Welding Bandsaw Blades 22 MIN
Dist - RMIBHF

Machine Shop - C N C Machine Operations Series
Bridgeport Series I, C N C Basic Set - Up and Machining 14 MIN
Bridgeport Series I, C N C Familiarization with Boss 6 Control 29 MIN
Bridgeport Series II Milling Machine 21 MIN
Numerical Control no 1 - Introduction to a Two Axis Vertical Mill 8 MIN
Numerical Control no 3 - Tape Controlled Drilling Operations 5 MIN
Numerical Control no 2 - Setup of Machine and Indexed Controls 19 MIN
Programming C N C - Absolute 14 MIN
Programming C N C - Incremental 23 MIN
Programming C N C, Circular Interpolation 20 MIN
Programming C N C, Drilling Cycles 19 MIN
Programming C N C, Special Milling Cycles 16 MIN
Repetitive Programming 15 MIN
Dist - RMIBHF

Machine Shop - Drill Press, Radial Drill, Drill Grinder Series
Drill Grinder no 1 - Block Diamond Model O 12 MIN
Hand Sharpening a Drill 16 MIN
Radial Drill no 1 - Familiarization and Basic Drill Operations 22 MIN
Radial Drill no 2 - Production, Drilling, Reaming and Tapping 22 MIN
Safety and Familiarization on Radial Arm Drill Press 26 MIN
Sharpening a Drill on the Drill Grinder 16 MIN
Dist - RMIBHF

Machine shop - engine lathe series
Aligning the tailstock 13 MIN
Cutting external threads on the engine lathe 39 MIN
Cutting internal threads 21 MIN
Cutting tapers using the compound rest 21 MIN
Cutting tapers using the tailstock offset method 23 MIN
Cutting tapers using the taper attachment 20 MIN
Cutting threads with a die 12 MIN
Drilling on the lathe 18 MIN
Facing and center drilling 17 MIN
Grinding a right - hand turning tool 26 MIN
Grinding lathe centers with the tool post grinder 21 MIN
Knurling 12 MIN
Measuring screw threads 10 MIN
Mounting cylindrical work in a four - jaw chuck 13 MIN
Mounting rectangular and irregular work in a four - jaw chuck 16 MIN
Principles of cutting - off 15 MIN
Safety and familiarization on the Clausing Colchester engine lathe 25 MIN
Safety and familiarization on the LeBlond engine lathe 22 MIN
Safety and familiarization on the South Bend engine lathe 30 MIN
Tapping threads on the engine lathe 22 MIN
Turning between centers 40 MIN
Using the four - jaw chuck 13 MIN
Using the three - jaw chuck 26 MIN
Dist - RMIBHF

Machine Shop - Jig Boring Operation Series
Jig Boring Operation no 5 - Boring Head Setup 19 MIN
Jig Boring Operation no 4 - Locating Holes on Rectangular Coordinates 22 MIN
Jig Boring Operation no 1 - Locating Lines and Edges 17 MIN
Jig Boring Operation no 6 - Precise Edge Location 14 MIN
Jig Boring Operation no 3 - Locating from a 'V' 22 MIN
Jig Boring Operation no 2 - Locating from Holes 29 MIN
Dist - RMIBHF

Machine shop - layout series
Basic layout procedures 12 MIN
Layout no 1 - Hole Location 19 MIN
Layout no 3 - Surface Plate 14 MIN
Layout no 2 - Contours and Angles 19 MIN
Dist - RMIBHF

Machine shop - milling machine series
Basic mill setup - casting and weldments, No 2 10 MIN
Basic mill setup - clamping procedures, No 1 10 MIN
Horizontal Mill no 5 - Milling a 90 Degree 'V' Groove 21 MIN
Horizontal Mill no 4 - Straddle Milling 20 MIN
Horizontal Mill no 2 - Milling Steps and Slots 21 MIN
Dist - CAMV
RMIBHF

Machine Shop - Milling Machine Series
Basic milling procedures 53 MIN
Cutting a keyway 26 MIN
Cutting a woodruff keyseat 30 MIN
Drilling on the Bridgeport Milling Machine 27 MIN
Finding the Center of a Shaft on the Vertical Milling Machine 16 MIN
Safety and Familiarization on the Bridgeport Series I Milling Machine 23 MIN
Safety and Familiarization on the Bridgeport Series II Milling Machine 21 MIN
Safety and Familiarization on the Horizontal Boring Mill 24 MIN
Safety and familiarization on the kearney and trecher milling machine - Pt 1 22 MIN
Safety and familiarization on the kearney and trecher milling machine - Pt 2 17 MIN
Squaring a Block 39 MIN
Using a Boring Head 22 MIN
Using the Index Head 29 MIN
Dist - RMIBHF

Machine Shop - Operations on the Horizontal Boring Mill Series
Setup for Rough Line - Boring
Dist - USNAC

Machine Shop Safety 17 MIN
U-matic / VHS
Safety Action for Employees Series
Color (IND)
Demonstrates safe operation of machine tools such as lathes, presses and grinds. Discusses housekeeping, personal safety and electrical lockouts.
Health and Safety; Industrial and Technical Education
Dist - GPCV **Prod** - GPCV

Machine Shop Safety 14 MIN
U-matic / VHS / 16mm
Color (J H)
Deals With protective procedures to prevent injury, respiratory protection, maintenance and correct handling of power and hand tools. Shows safety expert and accident victim stressing need to be safety conscious.
Health and Safety; Industrial and Technical Education
Dist - BCNFL **Prod** - BORTF 1983

Machine shop safety series
Cutting, bending and teamwork 18 MIN
Dist - NATMTB

Machine Shop Series Operation on the Internal Grinder, no 1
Grinding a Straight Hole 18 MIN
Dist - USNAC

Machine Shop Series
Basic layout procedures 12 MIN
Cylindrical grinder - No 1 - basic setup procedure and grinding methods 33 MIN
Cylindrical grinder - No 2 - shoulder grinding 14 MIN
Geometric Form and Positional Tolerancing 20 MIN
How to Read a Metric Micrometer 20 MIN
How to Read a Vernier Caliper 16 MIN
Layout no 1 - Hole Location 19 MIN
Layout no 3 - Surface Plate 14 MIN
Layout no 2 - Contours and Angles 19 MIN

Use and Care of the Micrometer 19 MIN
Dist - RMIBHF

Machine Shop - Shaper Series
Shaper no 3 - Machining Angles 11 MIN
Shaper no 2 - Squaring a Block 20 MIN
Dist - RMIBHF

Machine Shop - Surface Grinder Series
Inspecting 'V' Blocks 10 MIN
Safety and Familiarization on the Surface Grinder 33 MIN
Surface Grinder no 8 - Surface Grinding Problems 12 MIN
Surface Grinder no 5 - Grinding to Remove Warp 19 MIN
Surface Grinder no 4 - Squaring Up a Block 18 MIN
Surface Grinder no 1 - Mounting Work on a Magnetic Chuck 16 MIN
Surface Grinder no 7 - Grinding a 90 Degree 'V' 25 MIN
Surface Grinder no 6 - Grinding a Vertical Surface 16 MIN
Surface Grinder no 3 - Grinding Flat Surfaces 14 MIN
Surface Grinder no 2 - Mounting and Dressing the Wheel 10 MIN
Dist - RMIBHF

Machine Shop - Turret Lathe Series
Turret Lathe no 4 - Bar Turner Setup and Adjustment 18 MIN
Turret Lathe no 1 - Familiarization 17 MIN
Turret Lathe no 3 - Plunge Forming and Self - Opening Die Setups 12 MIN
Turret Lathe no 2 - Drilling, Tapping, Knurling, Forming 21 MIN
Dist - RMIBHF

Machine shop work - bench work - No 3
Fitting and scraping small bearings 24 MIN
Dist - USNAC

Machine Shop Work Bench Work Series
Reaming with Straight Hand Reamers 20 MIN
Dist - USNAC

Machine Shop Work - Fundamentals of Blueprint Reading Series
Principal Dimensions - Reference Surfaces, and Tolerances 12 MIN
Sectional Views and Projections - Finish Marks 15 MIN
Dist - USNAC

Machine Shop Work - Operation on the Shaper Series
Machining a Cast Iron Rectangular Block 25 MIN
Machining a Tool Steel V Block 21 MIN
Dist - USNAC

Machine shop work - operations of the drill press radial drill - a series
Machine shop work - operations of the drill press radial drill - a'series
Color
Countersinking, Counterboring And Spot Facing; Drilling And Tapping Cast Steel; Locating Holes, Drilling And Tapping In - - .
Industrial and Technical Education
Dist - USNAC Prod - USOE

Machine shop work - operations of the drill press radial drill - a series
Machine shop work - operations of the drill press radial drill - a series
Dist - USNAC

Machine shop work - operations on a broaching machine series
Double ram vertical surface broaching 28 MIN
Dist - USNAC

Machine Shop Work - Operations on the Centerless Grinding Machine Series no 3
Infeed Grinding Shouldered Work 23 MIN
Dist - USNAC

Machine Shop Work - Operations on the Centerless Grinding Machine Series no 4
Infeed Grinding a Shaft of Two Diameters 31 MIN
Dist - USNAC

Machine shop work - operations on the cutter grinder, no 5 - series
Sharpening a form relieved cutter 18 MIN
Dist - USNAC

Machine shop work - operations on the cutter grinder, no 1 - series
Sharpening a side milling cutter 23 MIN
Dist - USNAC

Machine shop work - operations on the cutter grinder, no 3 - series
Sharpening a shell end mill 17 MIN
Dist - USNAC

Machine shop work - operations on the drill press - radial drill - a series
Machine shop work series
B&W
Drilling And Tapping Cast Steel; Drilling To A Layout And Spotfacing Cast Iron.
Industrial and Technical Education
Dist - USNAC Prod - USOE

Machine Shop Work Operations on the Gear Hobbing Machine series
Hobbing a Spur Gear, Pt 2, Setting Up and Hobbing the Work 24 MIN
Dist - USNAC

Machine shop work - operations on the horizontal boring mill - a series
Machine shop work - operations on the horizontal boring mill - a'series
B&W; Color
Drilling, Tapping, Stub - Boring And Reaming; Setup For Face Milling With A Fixture.
Industrial and Technical Education
Dist - USNAC Prod - USOE

Machine shop work - operations on the horizontal boring mill - a series
Machine shop work - operations on the horizontal boring mill - a series
Dist - USNAC

Machine Shop Work - Operations on the Horizontal Boring Mill Series Number 6
Drilling, Tapping, Stub - Boring, and Reaming 22 MIN
Dist - USNAC

Machine shop work - operations on the horizontal boring mill series
Face milling with a fixture 16 MIN
Dist - USNAC

Machine Shop Work - Operations on the Internal Grinder Series no 2
Grinding a Deep Hole 18 MIN
Dist - USNAC

Machine Shop Work - Operations on the Internal Grinder Series no 3
Grinding and Facing a Blind Hole 17 MIN
Dist - USNAC

Machine shop work - operations on the metal cutting band saw - a series
Machine shop work - operations on the metal cutting band saw - a'series
B&W
Filing An Internal Irregular Shape; Sawing An Internal Irregular Shape.
Industrial and Technical Education
Dist - USNAC Prod - USOE

Machine shop work - operations on the metal cutting band saw - a series
Machine shop work - operations on the metal cutting band saw - a series
Dist - USNAC

Machine Shop Work - Operations on the Milling Machine Series no 3
Straddle Milling 17 MIN
Dist - USNAC

Machine Shop Work - Operations on the Milling Machine Series no 4
Plain Indexing and Cutting a Spur Gear 26 MIN
Dist - USNAC

Machine shop work - operations on the planer series
Planing a flat surface 22 MIN
Dist - USNAC

Machine Shop Work - Operations on the Surface Grinder Series no 1
Grinding a Parallel Bar - Setting Up the Machine 14 MIN
Dist - USNAC

Machine Shop Work - Operations on the Surface Grinder Series no 2
Grinding a Parallel Bar - Grinding Operations 15 MIN
Dist - USNAC

Machine Shop Work - Operations on the Surface Grinder Series no 5
Grinding Thin Discs 15 MIN
Dist - USNAC

Machine shop work - operations on the turret lathe series
Bar work, magnesium - necking and threading by use of attachment and by die head 23 MIN
Bar work, magnesium - setting up bar mechanism and roller turner 18 MIN
Bar work, magnesium - setting up multiple roller turner and turning a taper 17 MIN
Chuck work - setting up hexagon turret tools 22 MIN
Chuck work - setting up tools for combined cuts 16 MIN
Dist - USNAC

Machine Shop Work - Operations on the Vertical Boring Mill Series no 3
Facing, Turning, Boring, Grooving, and Chamfering 30 MIN
Dist - USNAC

Machine shop work - operations on the vertical milling machine - a series
Machine shop work series
B&W
Cutting A Dovetail Taper Slide; Cutting A Round End Keyway; Milling A Circular T - Slot; Milling A Helical Groove; Using A Shell End Mill.
Industrial and Technical Education
Dist - USNAC Prod - USOE

Machine shop work - precision measurement - a series
Machine shop work series
Color
Gage Blocks And Accessories; Precision Gage Blocks; Verniers.
Industrial and Technical Education
Dist - USNAC Prod - USOE

Machine shop work - precision measurement No 6 series
Precision gage blocks 18 MIN
Dist - USNAC

Machine Shop Work - Precision Measurement Series no 1
Steel Rule 14 MIN
Dist - USNAC

Machine Shop Work - Precision Measurement Series no 2
The Micrometer 15 MIN
Dist - USNAC

Machine shop work - precision measurement series
Height gages and test indicators 12 MIN
Dist - USNAC

Machine Shop Work Series Basic Machines
The Drill Press 10 MIN
The Lathe 15 MIN
The Milling Machine 15 MIN
The Shaper 15 MIN
Dist - USNAC

Machine Shop Work Series Bench Work, no 6
Laying Out Small Castings 16 MIN
Dist - USNAC

Machine Shop Work Series Bench Work - no 7
Centering Small Stock 12 MIN
Dist - USNAC

Machine Shop Work Series Bench Work
Reaming with Taper Hand Reamers 15 MIN
Dist - USNAC

Machine Shop Work Series Fundamentals of Blueprint Reading, no 3
Principal Dimensions, Reference Surfaces and Tolerances 12 MIN
Dist - USNAC

Machine Shop Work Series Fundamentals of Blueprint Reading series
Visualizing an Object 9 MIN
Dist - USNAC

Machine Shop Work Series Operations on a Broaching Machine, no 1
Broaching an Internal Keyway 23 MIN
Dist - USNAC

Machine Shop Work Series Operations on a Broaching Machine, no 2
Single Ram Vertical Surface Broaching 28 MIN
Dist - USNAC

Machine Shop Work Series Operations on the Center - Type Grinder, no 1
Grinding a Plain Pin, Pt 1, the 17 MIN

Grinding Wheel
Dist - USNAC

Machine Shop Work Series Operations on the Center - Type Grinder, no 2
Grinding a Plain Pin, Pt 2, Grinding Operations 17 MIN
Dist - USNAC

Machine Shop Work Series Operations on the Center - Type Grinder, no 3
Grinding a Slender Shaft with Back Rest 17 MIN
Dist - USNAC

Machine Shop Work Series Operations on the Centerless Grinding Machine, no 5
Endfeed Grinding a Tapered Pin 26 MIN
Dist - USNAC

Machine Shop Work Series Operations on the Drill Press, Radial Drill, no 1
Drilling and Tapping Cast Steel 19 MIN
Dist - USNAC

Machine Shop Work Series Operations on the Drill Press Sensitive Drill, no 1
Drilling a Hole in a Pin 10 MIN
Dist - USNAC

Machine Shop Work Series Operations on the Drill Press, Vertical Drill, no 1
Locating Holes, Drilling and Tapping in Cast Iron 18 MIN
Dist - USNAC

Machine Shop Work Series Operations on the Drill Press, Vertical Drill series
Countersinking, Counterboring and Spot Facing 20 MIN
Dist - USNAC

Machine Shop Work Series Operations on the Gear Hobbing Machine series
Hobbing a Spur Gear, Pt 1, Setting Up the Change Gears 15 MIN
Dist - USNAC

Machine Shop Work Series Operations on the Horizontal Boring Mill, no 6
Drilling, Tapping, Stub - Boring and Reaming 22 MIN
Dist - USNAC

Machine shop work series - operations on the horizontal boring mill
Face milling with a fixture 17 MIN
Dist - USNAC

Machine Shop Work Series Operations on the Internal Grinder, no 3
Grinding and Facing a Blind Hole 18 MIN
Dist - USNAC

Machine Shop Work Series Operations on the Metal Cutting Band Saw, no 1
Sawing an Internal Irregular Shape 32 MIN
Dist - USNAC

Machine Shop Work Series Operations on the Milling Machine, no 2
Straddle and Surface Milling to Close Tolerances 27 MIN
Dist - USNAC

Machine Shop Work Series Operations on the Milling Machine, no 5
Milling a Template 17 MIN
Dist - USNAC

Machine Shop Work Series Operations on the Milling Machine, no 8
Milling a Helical Cutter 18 MIN
Dist - USNAC

Machine Shop Work Series Operations on the Surface Grinder, no 1
Grinding a Parallel Bar, Pt 1, Setting Up the Machine 14 MIN
Dist - USNAC

Machine Shop Work Series Operations on the Surface Grinder, no 2
Grinding a Parallel Bar, Pt 2, Grinding Operations 15 MIN
Dist - USNAC

Machine Shop Work Series Operations on the Surface Grinder, no 4
Grinding a V Block 22 MIN
Dist - USNAC

Machine Shop Work Series Operations on the Vertical Boring Mill, no 1
Rough - Facing, Turning and Drilling 31 MIN
Dist - USNAC

Machine Shop Work Series Operations on the Vertical Milling Machine, no 1
Using a Shell End Mill 21 MIN
Dist - USNAC

Machine Shop Work Series Operations on the Vertical Milling Machine, no 4
Milling a Helical Groove 28 MIN
Dist - USNAC

Machine Shop Work Series Operations on the Vertical Milling Machine, no 5
Milling a Circular T - Slot 22 MIN
Dist - USNAC

Machine shop work series

Bar work - magnesium - Pt 3 - necking and threading by use of attachment and by die head	23 MIN
Boring holes with offset boring head	28 MIN
Boring to close tolerances	17 MIN
Cutting a taper with the compound rest and with a taper attachment	11 MIN
Cutting an external acme thread	16 MIN
Cutting an external national fine thread	12 MIN
Cutting an internal acme thread	22 MIN
Cutting teeth on a worm gear	17 MIN
Cutting threads with taps and dies	19 MIN
Drilling, boring and reaming work held in chuck	11 MIN
Filing an internal irregular shape	27 MIN
Filing and scraping small bearings	24 MIN
Fixed gages	17 MIN
Fundamentals of side cutting tools	11 MIN
Gage blocks and accessories	23 MIN
The Lathe	15 MIN
Machine shop work - operations on the drill press - radial drill - a series	
Machine shop work - operations on the vertical milling machine - a series	
Machine shop work - precision measurement - a series	
Machining work held in chuck - use of reference surfaces	24 MIN
The Micrometer	15 MIN
Operations on the horizontal boring mill - Setup for Face Milling with a Fixture - no 1	20 MIN
Plunge cut grinding	15 MIN
Reading a drawing of a valve bonnet	20 MIN
Reading a three - view drawing	10 MIN
Rough - Facing, Boring and Turning a Shoulder	22 MIN
Scraping flat surfaces	14 MIN
Setup for rough line - boring	15 MIN
Thrufeed grinding a straight pin	29 MIN
Turning a taper with the tailstock set over	17 MIN
Turning work held on a fixture	21 MIN
Turning work held on a mandrel	20 MIN
Turning Work of Two Diameters	14 MIN
Turning work on two diameters	14 MIN
The Turret Lathe - an Introduction	17 MIN
Using a boring bar between centers - work held on carriage	22 MIN
Using a follower rest	21 MIN
Using a steady rest	25 MIN
Using a steady rest when boring	21 MIN

Dist - USNAC

Machine shop work - single point cutting tools - spanish series
Fundamentals of end cutting tools 12 MIN
Dist - USNAC

Machine shopwork - operations of the turret lathe series
Chuck work - setting up hexagon turret tools, Pt 1 22 MIN
Chuck work - setting up tools for combined cuts, Pt 2 16 MIN
Dist - USNAC

Machine song 4 MIN
VHS / 16mm
B&W/Red (G)
$20.00 rental
Addresses the post - industrial human condition, which has grown increasingly dependent on machines and technology. Presents a stylized collage of photo - xerox animation. Produced by Chel White. Also available in video format in a group package entitled Five Films by Chel White.
Fine Arts; Social Science; Sociology
Dist - CANCIN

Machine Stitching Techniques 5 MIN
16mm
Clothing Construction Techniques Series
Color (J)
LC 77-701182
Describes four machine stitching techniques. Illustrates their correct location and possible uses. Shows the understitch, topstitch, stitch in the ditch and blind hemming stitch.
Home Economics
Dist - IOWASP **Prod** - IOWA 1976

Machine Story 4 MIN
U-matic / VHS / 16mm
Color
Offers an animated history of technology from the invention of the inclined plane, circa 8000 BC to the Saturn probe developed in 1980.
Fine Arts; Science; Sociology
Dist - PFP **Prod** - MILLRD

Machine Technology II - Engine Lathe Accessories Series
Vernier Scale and Vernier Caliper (Inside, Outside, and Dial Calipers) 15 MIN
Dist - CAMB

Machine Technology IV - Milling Series
Use of Plain and Side Milling Cutters on the Horizontal Milling Machine 15 MIN
Dist - CAMB

The Machine Tool - Principles and Operation 58 MIN
U-matic / BETA / VHS
Color
$400 purchase
Shows basic components in a machining process.
Industrial and Technical Education; Science
Dist - ASM **Prod** - ASM

Machine Tool Safety Series

Presses, Production and Protection	13 MIN
Safeguarding of Machine Tools	17 MIN
Safety Considerations in Die Design	14 MIN
Safety in Drilling, Milling and Boring Operations	17 MIN
Safety in Metal Turning Operations	17 MIN
The Turning Wheel - Safety in Grinding Operations	16 MIN

Dist - NATMTB

Machine Tools
VHS
Practical Woodworking Series
(C G)
$59.00 _ CA163
Shows safety practices for operation of machine tools used in woodwork such as the circular saw, band saw, jointed, shaper, and wood lathe.
Industrial and Technical Education
Dist - AAVIM **Prod** - AAVIM 1989

Machine Tools and Motions 22 MIN
16mm
B&W
LC FIA53-1132
Shows how the design of a machine's controls can improve the operator's efficiency and how operating levers can be extended and controls relocated so that the machine operator can load and unload the machine and manipulate the necessary controls with the least amount of effort and motion.
Industrial and Technical Education
Dist - GM **Prod** - GM 1951

Machine Trades 7 MIN
16mm / U-matic / VHS
Career Job Opportunity Film Series
Color
LC 74-706131
Describes job opportunities that are open to beginners, stressing good pay for entry workers and career ladder potential in the machine trades.
Guidance and Counseling; Industrial and Technical Education
Dist - USNAC **Prod** - USDLMA 1968

Machine Transcription - Transcription Technique 15 MIN
16mm
B&W
LC FIE52-73
Tells how to phrase dictation at various speeds, prepare for a day's work, compose a letter and correct errors in the transcriptions on the cylinder.
Business and Economics
Dist - USNAC **Prod** - USN 1943

Machine vision 50 MIN
VHS / 16mm
Manufacturing insights series
Color (A IND)
$200.00, $190.00 purchase _ #VT240, #VT240U
Gives an introduction to machine vision, binary, gray scale, and correlation.
Industrial and Technical Education; Psychology
Dist - SME **Prod** - SME 1985

Machine vision 45 MIN
U-matic / VHS
Artificial intelligence series; Computer vision, Pt 3
Color (PRO)
Features understanding constraints on observed intensity, history of machine vision, determinations, and manufacturing surface shading for synthetic images.
Mathematics; Psychology; Science - Physical
Dist - MIOT **Prod** - MIOT

Machine vision - a new look 20 MIN
VHS / 16mm
Manufacturing insights series
Color (A IND)
$200.00, $190.00 purchase _ #VT285, #VT285U
Shows the latest improvements in machine vision and how they are used for inspection and reverse engineering.
Industrial and Technical Education; Psychology
Dist - SME **Prod** - SME 1988

Machine Vision Technology 35 MIN
U-matic / VHS
Color
Explains the current types of machine vision systems in operation and how they can be used with welding, assembly and inspection applications. Demonstrates visual sensing, computer analysis and interpretation of critical factory data.
Industrial and Technical Education
Dist - SME **Prod** - SME

Machine Work Series Fundamentals of Blueprint Reading
Sectional Views and Projections, Finish Marks 15 MIN
Dist - USNAC

Machine Work Series Operations on the Engine Lathe
Rough Turning between Centers 15 MIN
Dist - USNAC

Machine workshop series
Cutting a short rack 18 MIN
Reduction of Radio Interference - Shipboard Installation 17 MIN
Dist - USNAC

Machines 15 MIN
U-matic
Science Alliance Series
Color (I)
Looks at simple machines such as the lever and the wheel and axle and explains how they work.
Science; Science - Physical
Dist - TVOTAR **Prod** - TVOTAR 1981

Machines, Engines and Motors 13 MIN
16mm / U-matic / VHS
Scientific Fact and Fun Series
Color; Captioned
LC 81-700633
Defines machines, engines and motors and relates them to everyday items. Discusses their interrelationships and describes the research process.
Industrial and Technical Education; Science - Physical
Dist - JOU **Prod** - GLDWER 1980

Machines that Move People 15 MIN
VHS / U-matic
Matter and Motion Series Module Green; Module green
Color (I)
Visits Transpo '72 to see past, present and future modes of transportation.
Science - Physical; Social Science
Dist - AITECH **Prod** - WHROTV 1973

Machines that Think 30 MIN
U-matic / VHS
Innovation Series
Color
Discusses the next generation of computers which will be the first to have true 'artificial intelligence.'.
Industrial and Technical Education; Mathematics
Dist - PBS **Prod** - WNETTV 1983

Machining a Cast Iron Rectangular Block 25 MIN
16mm
Machine Shop Work - Operation on the Shaper Series
B&W (SPANISH)
LC FIE51-523
Shows several processes, such as how to set the shaper ram stroke, adjust the shaper table, vise, vertical feed, head feed and crossfeed, and set up a rectangular cast iron block.
Industrial and Technical Education
Dist - USNAC **Prod** - USOE 1942

Machining a Rotor on the FMC Brake Lathe 5 MIN
VHS / 16mm
Auto Mechanics Series
(G PRO)
$48.00 purchase _ #AM19
Shows how to machine a rotor on the FMC brake lathe.
Industrial and Technical Education
Dist - RMIBHF **Prod** - RMIBHF

Machining a Tool Steel V Block 21 MIN
16mm
Machine Shop Work - Operation on the Shaper Series
B&W
LC FIE51-525
Shows how to lay out work for machining on a shaper, set up and position the ram stroke, and machine 'V' grooves and rectangular slots.
Industrial and Technical Education
Dist - USNAC **Prod** - USOE 1942

Machining and the Operation of Machine Tools, Module 4 - Milling and Tool Series
Gouging of 2 - and 4 - flute end mills 15 MIN
Identification of Parts and Operation of Horizontal Milling Machine 14 MIN
Identification of Parts and Operation of Vertical Milling Machine 15 MIN
Sharpening a Reamer between Centers 15 MIN
Sharpening Brazed Carbide Lathe Tools using a Universal Vise 15 MIN
Sharpening the Periphery of an End Mill 15 MIN
Sharpening the Periphery of Plain Milling Cutters and Side Mills 15 MIN
Use of the Face Milling Cutter on the Horizontal Mill 15 MIN
Dist - LEIKID

Machining and the Operation of Machine Tools, Module 1 - Basic Machine Technology Series
Contour band machine set - up and use of accessories 15 MIN
Contour hand machines - parts and accessories 15 MIN
Drill Presses - Sensitive and Radial 15 MIN
Handtools and their Use in Machine Technology 15 MIN
The Use of Layout Tools in Machine Technology 15 MIN
The Use of Measuring Tools in Machine Technology 15 MIN
Vernier Scale and Vernier Caliper 15 MIN
Dist - LEIKID

Machining and the Operation of Machine Tools, Module 3 - Intermediate Engine Lathe series
Cutting acme threads 15 MIN
Grinding forming tools and machine forms 15 MIN
Matching offset holes - face plate and 4 - jaw chuck 15 MIN
Matching shoulders and corners on the lathe 15 MIN
Roughing and finishing external threads on the lathe 15 MIN
Spring winding on the lathe 15 MIN
Using the steady rest and follower rest to machine on the lathe 15 MIN
Using the toolpost grinder on the lathe 15 MIN
Dist - LEIKID

Machining and the Operation of Machine Tools, Module 2 - Engine Lathe Series
Drilling, Boring and Reaming Work Held in a Lathe Chuck 15 MIN
Grinding a Round - Nose Finishing Tool 15 MIN
Mounting and Truing Work in the 4 - Jaw Independent Chuck 15 MIN
Dist - LEIKID

Machining and the operation of machine tools series
Cutting speeds and feeds for the engine lathe 15 MIN
Set - up for holding work to be milled 15 MIN
Dist - LEIKID

Machining Disk Brake Rotor Ammco Brake Lathe 22 MIN
VHS / 16mm
Auto Mechanics Series
(G PRO)
$91.00 purchase _ #AM16
Discusses using the Ammco brake lathe for machining disk brake rotors.
Industrial and Technical Education
Dist - RMIBHF **Prod** - RMIBHF

Machining Laminated Plastics 19 MIN
16mm
Plastics Series no 10
B&W
LC FIE51-302
Shows how to machine a typical laminated part, cut the tube stock to length on a circular saw, turn the outside diameters on a lathe, machine inside diameters by boring with a lathe and finish on a milling machine.
Industrial and Technical Education
Dist - USNAC **Prod** - USOE 1945

Machining Offset Holes - Face Plate and 4 - Jaw Chuck
U-matic / VHS
Intermediate Engine Lathe Operation Series
Color (SPANISH)
Industrial and Technical Education
Dist - VTRI **Prod** - VTRI

Machining Shoulders and Corners on the Lathe
U-matic / VHS
Intermediate Engine Lathe Operation Series
Color (SPANISH)
Industrial and Technical Education
Dist - VTRI **Prod** - VTRI

Machining work held in chuck - use of reference surfaces 24 MIN
16mm
Machine shop work series; Operations on the engine lathe; No 12
B&W (SPANISH)
LC FIE51-509
Explains how to select and machine surfaces to be used for reference, how to set up a workpiece accurately to the reference surfaces in a lathe chuck and how to use a boring bar to machine several internal surfaces.
Industrial and Technical Education
Dist - USNAC **Prod** - USOE 1944

Machinist
VHS / U-matic
Work - a - Day America
$59.95 purchase _ #VV113V
Helps students achieve career vocational preparation. Stresses the four main points of career awareness and exploration, specific skills intended, employability skills needed, and real people sharing on the job experiences.
Guidance and Counseling
Dist - CAREER **Prod** - CAREER

Machinist's Vice 15 MIN
U-matic / VHS
Blueprint Reading for Machinists Series
Color (IND)
Shows how to read an assembly line drawing and a bill of material. Demonstrates how to interpret cross - sectioned views.
Industrial and Technical Education
Dist - LEIKID **Prod** - LEIKID

Machismo 16 MIN
U-matic / VHS
Color (G)
$249.00, $149.00 purchase _ #AD - 1633
Shows machismo flourishing in Brazil where a man can kill his wife because he thinks or imagines she may have glanced at another man. Reveals that there is an inconvenient law which requires the killer's disappearance for a few days, but when those days have elapsed, he cannot be punished for 'defending his honor.' From a '60 Minutes' program.
Civics and Political Systems; Geography - World; Sociology
Dist - FOTH **Prod** - FOTH

Machito - a Latin Jazz Legacy 58 MIN
16mm
Color (H A)
$1000.00 purchase, $125.00 rental
Follows the birth and development of Latin jazz music in America. Focuses on Cuban - born musician Machito. Includes interviews with Dizzie Gillespie, Tito Puente and Dexter Gordon.
Fine Arts
Dist - AFA
ICARUS

Machorka - Muff 18 MIN
16mm
B&W
Attacks West Germany's rearmament and revival of its militaristic tradition in the Adenauer era. Spotlights a former Nazi officer working his way back to society and official good standing. Based on a story by Heinrich Boll.
Civics and Political Systems; Geography - World; History - United States; Literature and Drama
Dist - NYFLMS **Prod** - NYFLMS

Mach's Gut 75 MIN
VHS
Color (S) (GERMAN)

$450.00 purchase _ #825 - 9441
Teaches basic skills in German. Uses three different techniques to illustrate the workings of the German language - role playing sketches to demonstrate conversational German, documentary sequences to show Austrian people using the language in everyday situations, and signpost sequences which extract key words and phrases and reinforce them through graphics. Five 15 - minute programs on one cassette. Notes accompany the series.
Foreign Language; Geography - World; History - World
Dist - FI **Prod** - BBCTV 1987

Machu Picchu 15 MIN
16mm
Color (G)
$30.00 rental
Traces the layers of rocks, patterns and structure of the ancient Incan city and temple in the Peruvian Andes.
Geography - World
Dist - CANCIN **Prod** - BARHAM 1981

Macintosh and TJ 96 MIN
16mm
Color (P I)
Fine Arts
Dist - FI **Prod** - FI

Macintosh series
Getting to know your Macintosh, Mac SE, Plus 50 MIN
Introduction to PageMaker 2.0a 69 MIN
PageMaker 2.0a level II 58 MIN
Dist - CARTRP

Mackenna's Gold 128 MIN
U-matic / VHS / 16mm
Color (J)
Stars Gregory Peck and Omar Sharif in a Western drama of 17 men and four women in pursuit of gold, through deserts, canyons and mountains.
Fine Arts
Dist - FI **Prod** - CPC 1969

Mackenzie Valley Pipeline 28 MIN
16mm
Color (H)
#3X51 I
Describes the opinions of Indians concerning the Mackenzie Valley Pipeline in the aftermath of the Berger Report. Explains how the Indians feel that all developments should be controlled by native people.
Social Science; Sociology
Dist - CDIAND **Prod** - NCG 1975

Mackinac Bridge Diary 27 MIN
16mm
Color (H C A)
Describes the story of the conversion of steel, wire and concrete into the world's longest suspension bridge, spanning the Straits of Mackinac.
Business and Economics; Social Science
Dist - USSC **Prod** - USSC

Maclarification 4 MIN
16mm
Color
LC 75-703199
Presents fluid lines, patterns, colors and lively music in a style similar to the experimental films of Canadian film artist Norman Mc Laren.
Fine Arts
Dist - USC **Prod** - USC 1966

Maclear series
All the Messiah's men 25 MIN
The Axis - thirty years after 25 MIN
The British Connection 25 MIN
Chayita and the 500 million 25 MIN
Children of main street 25 MIN
The Elliot Lake Example 25 MIN
The Gods in the tower 25 MIN
The Greatest gamble of all 25 MIN
Guns Across the Border 25 MIN
Homicide, Zone One 25 MIN
Into the Madding Crowd 25 MIN
The Merchants of Peace 25 MIN
The Miracle Seekers 25 MIN
The Most Thankless Job on Earth 25 MIN
Rum Paradise 25 MIN
Running dogs and other fables 25 MIN
The Wired - in World of Zen 25 MIN
Dist - CTV

The MacMillan Video Almanac for Kids 60 MIN
BETA / VHS
Color
Presents a visual almanac for children that teaches general worldly information in an entertaining format.
Fine Arts; Literature and Drama
Dist - HOMEAF **Prod** - HOMEAF

The Macmillan Video Almanac for Kids 60 MIN
BETA / VHS
Color (K P I)
Presents eight subjects - soap bubble magic, a journey into space, a secret language, body talk, kite flying, volcanoes, drawing faces and string figures. Based on The Macmillan Illustrated Almanac For Kids.
Physical Education and Recreation; Science - Physical
Dist - CARAVT **Prod** - MACLS
UILL

MacNeil - Lehrer Newshour Series
Team Spirit 10 MIN
Dist - PBS

MacNeil/Lehrer Newshour 60 MIN
VHS
Color (G)
$24.95 purchase _ #MLNH - 000
Presents an in - depth look at major news stories of the day. Hosted by Robert MacNeil and Jim Lehrer.
Civics and Political Systems; Fine Arts; Literature and Drama
Dist - PBS **Prod** - PBS

Macrame 15 MIN
U-matic / VHS / 16mm
Rediscovery - Art Media Series
Color (I) (SPANISH)
LC 72-702161
Points out that the ancient art of knotting known as macrame has had a great revival in recent years and shows how to make the few basic knots, how to combine them to form simple and useful objects and how to create various effects.
Fine Arts
Dist - AIMS **Prod** - ACI 1972

Macrame 30 MIN
U-matic / VHS
Arts and Crafts Series
Color (H A)
LC 81-706190
Demonstrates and explains the basics of macrame construction, from cutting the cord to whipping and knotting techniques. Shows artistic macrame creations such as wall hangings, necklaces, and plant hangings.
Fine Arts
Dist - GPN **Prod** - GPN 1981

Macro 7.03 MIN
U-matic / VHS
Photo Tips Series
Color (J H A)
Introduces the equipment and technique involved in macrophotography.
Fine Arts; Industrial and Technical Education
Dist - AITECH **Prod** - TURR 1986

Macro and micro perspectives of logistics systems 30 MIN
VHS
Business logistics series
Color (G C)
$200.00 purchase, $20.50 rental _ #34956
Examines macro and micro perspectives of logistics systems. Part of a 30 - part series on business logistics which deals with movement and storage of raw and finished products, and with managerial activities important for effective control of these operations. Interviews logistics managers of major US corporations and transportation companies. Uses on - site segments to demonstrate logistical carrier operations. Features program author Dr John Coyle.
Business and Economics
Dist - PSU **Prod** - WPSXTV 1987

Macro and real time photography 14 MIN
VHS
Color (PRO G)
$99.00 purchase, $39.00 rental _ #763
Features Peter Parks of Oxford Scientific Films. Demonstrates how the close - up photography techniques developed by Oxford for nature films can be applied to 'real time' special effects work for commercials and features. Shows how the impression of huge events can be created on a miniature scale. Produced by the Australian Film, Television and Radio School.
Industrial and Technical Education
Dist - FIRLIT

Macro models 14 MIN
VHS / U-matic
Real world economic series
Color (J H)
$240.00, $290.00 purchase, $60.00 rental
Shows a variety of models, what variables constitute different models, how they are constructed and how they give us insight into the economy. Explains how an economy works and how these models can indicate ways to cure possible problems in the economy. Discusses supply, consumption, gross national product and other terms.
Business and Economics
Dist - NDIM **Prod** - REALWO 1993

Macroeconomic basics 60 MIN
VHS
Macroeconomics series
Color (H C G)
$89.00 purchase _ #GSU - 312
Presents basic macroeconomic theory. Discusses aggregate demand, aggregate supply and macroeconomic equilibrium. Examines the effects of changes in investment and government spending. Interviews Dr Sidney Jones, Asst Secretary of the Economic Policy Department of the Treasury. Part of a 24 - part series instructed by Dr Edward F Stuart, Northwestern University, which focuses on a description of the major economic policy - making bodies in the United States and their interrelationships.
Business and Economics
Dist - INSTRU

Macroeconomic concepts - GNF 60 MIN
VHS
Macroeconomics series
Color (H C G)
$89.00 purchase _ #GSU - 309
Discusses macroeconomic concepts. Defines the gross national product - GNP. Part of a 24 - part series instructed by Dr Edward F Stuart, Northwestern University, which focuses on a description of the major economic policy - making bodies in the United States and their interrelationships.
Business and Economics
Dist - INSTRU

Macroeconomic Performance 45 MIN
VHS / U-matic
Economic Perspectives Series
Color
Discusses various aspects of macroeconomic performance.
Business and Economics
Dist - MDCPB **Prod** - MDCPB

Macroeconomic policy - the political dimension 60 MIN
VHS
Macroeconomics series
Color (H C G)
$89.00 purchase _ #GSU - 324
Discusses the political dimensions of making macroeconomic decisions. Interviews Dr John Taylor, member of the Council of Economic Advisors. Part of a 24 - part series instructed by Dr Edward F Stuart, Northwestern University, which focuses on a description of the major economic policy - making bodies in the United States and their interrelationships.
Business and Economics
Dist - INSTRU

Macroeconomic theories - classical and Keynesian 60 MIN
VHS
Macroeconomics series
Color (H C G)
$89.00 purchase _ #GSU - 313
Presents classical and Keynesian macroeconomic theories. Discusses the income - expenditure approach, the consumption and saving functions and investment demand and its determinants. Part of a 24 - part series instructed by Dr Edward F Stuart, Northwestern University, which focuses on a description of the major economic policy - making bodies in the United States and their interrelationships.
Business and Economics
Dist - INSTRU

Macroeconomics 45 MIN
U-matic / VHS
Economic Perspectives Series
Color
Discusses various aspects of macroeconomics.
Business and Economics
Dist - MDCPB **Prod** - MDCPB

Macroeconomics series
Banking and the federal reserve system 60 MIN
Budgets, deficits and the public debt 60 MIN
The Circular flow of goods and money 60 MIN
Economic fluctuations 60 MIN
The Economic problem - scarcity and choice 60 MIN
Economic reasoning and economic theory 60 MIN
Fiscal policy 60 MIN
Fiscal policy and monetary policy 60 MIN
The Inflation - unemployment trade off 60 MIN
Introduction to macroeconomics 60 MIN
Keynesian equilibrium 60 MIN
Macroeconomic basics 60 MIN
Macroeconomic concepts - GNF 60 MIN
Macroeconomic policy - the political dimension 60 MIN
Macroeconomic theories - classical and Keynesian 60 MIN
Market analysis - demand and supply 60 MIN

Market equilibrium 60 MIN
Monetary policy - differing views 60 MIN
Money and the economy 60 MIN
National income and its components 60 MIN
The Nature of money 60 MIN
The Production possibilities frontier 60 MIN
Public debt - international effects 60 MIN
The Role of markets and money 60 MIN
Dist - INSTRU

Macromolecules - Polymerization Thermoplastics 60 MIN
U-matic / VHS
Chemistry Training Series
Color (IND)
Discusses fibers formed from macromolecules, polymerization of ethylene at high pressure, polystyrene, macromolecules of different shapes, modification with acrylonnitrile and the extrusion of thermoplastics.
Science; Science - Physical
Dist - ITCORP **Prod** - ITCORP

Macros and Other Advanced Features of Lotus 1 - 2 - 3 100 MIN
U-matic / VHS
(A PRO)
$495.00, $595.00
Shows how to use macros and how to build and use auto exec. Also discusses advanced functions, database functions and spreadsheet design.
Computer Science
Dist - VIDEOT **Prod** - VIDEOT 1988

Macros and Other Advanced Features of Lotus 1 - 2 - 3 - Learn - PC Video Systems
VHS / U-matic
Color
Covers spreadsheet consolidation and macros in a self - paced training program.
Business and Economics; Industrial and Technical Education
Dist - DSIM **Prod** - DSIM

Mac's factory, or shortcuts in multiplying with fractions 10 MIN
VHS
Children's encyclopedia of mathematics - multiplication and division of fractions series
Color (I)
$49.95 purchase _ #8356
Illustrates multiplication with fractions shortcuts. Part of a seven - part series on multiplication and division with fractions.
Mathematics
Dist - AIMS **Prod** - DAVFMS 1991

Mac's Fame is Multiplied - Multiplication , Two Digits Times Three Digits 15 MIN
U-matic / VHS
Figure Out Series
Color (I)
Uses the story of Mac's campaign for mayor to introduce the hand - held calculator and explain how to estimate the answer before using a calculator.
Mathematics
Dist - AITECH **Prod** - MAETEL 1982

Mac's Mill 12 MIN
U-matic / VHS / 16mm
Color (J)
LC 83-700184
Focuses on a New Brunswick resident who runs a waterpowered mill built in 1909. Discusses balanced ecology, intelligent use of natural resources, and the possibility of earning a living without the aid of 20th century technology.
Science - Natural; Social Science
Dist - BULFRG **Prod** - NFBC 1976

Macular degeneration 4 MIN
VHS
5 - part retina series
Color (G)
$75.00 purchase, $40.00 rental _ #5314S, #5314V
Discusses symptoms, diagnosis, the importance of early detection. Describes fluorescein angiography, laser photocoagulation and low - vision aids in treatment and rehabilitation. Part a five - part series on the retina.
Health and Safety; Science - Natural
Dist - AJN **Prod** - VMED

Macular Degeneration 4 MIN
VHS / U-matic
Color
Discusses one of the conditions of aging which seriously impairs vision. Explains the human eye, and how macular degeneration occurs when cells in the macula begin to die. Reassures patient that macula degeneration while serious, will not cause total blindness.
Health and Safety; Science - Natural
Dist - MEDCOM **Prod** - MEDCOM

Macular Degeneration
VHS / U-matic
Color
Helps the patient understand how central vision is lost as macular degeneration progresses. Includes a review of the eye's anatomy, process of sight, and the areas affected. Explains follow - up monitoring using the Amsler Grid.
Science - Natural
Dist - MIFE **Prod** - MIFE

Macumba, trance and spirit healing 43 MIN
VHS / 16mm
Color (H C G)
$650.00, $395.00 purchase, $65.00 rental
Observes that in today's stressful world, millions of people turn to spiritism for help. Shows the roots and beliefs of African spirit religions in Rio de Janeiro and the United States. Spiritism believes in communication with the supernatural world through mediums and trance, as in macumba and voodoo. Reveals that trance healing techniques are being used by the medical profession to treat schizophrenics, epilectics and drug addicts and to achieve personal and social equilibrium. Produced by Madeleine Richeport.
Geography - World; Health and Safety; History - United States
Dist - FLMLIB

The Mad Bomber 5 MIN
VHS / U-matic
Write on, Set 1 Series
Color (J H)
Deals with the use of the phrases 'Is where' and 'Is when' in writing.
English Language
Dist - CTI **Prod** - CTI

The Mad Chemist 10 MIN
16mm
Color (P I)
Shows how a 'mad chemist' creates a green - skinned Frankenstein monster which he hooks up to a 'happiness machine.' Demonstrates the futility of finding happiness through chemical means.
Health and Safety
Dist - PROART **Prod** - PROART 1969

Mad Dog 5 MIN
16mm
Color
LC 79-701374
Tells how a doll comes to life to seek retribution against a playful dog who tore apart her fellow stuffed animals.
Fine Arts
Dist - ADELPH **Prod** - ADELPH 1978

Mad Morrie 12 MIN
16mm / VHS / BETA / U-matic
Color; PAL (IND)
PdS115, PdS123 purchase
Highlights hazards in an automotive repair workshop by following a train of catastrophes which beset Morris, who has much to learn about safe workshop practices. Contains some comical overtones to strengthen the safety message.
Health and Safety; Industrial and Technical Education
Dist - EDPAT **Prod** - TASCOR 1982

Mad River 58 MIN
16mm
Color
Presents a portrait of a rural community caught in a crossfire between demands for increased protection of the environment and concern for jobs and economic development. Focuses on a coalition of displaced workers, their unions, and community groups, which joined together to reopen a closed plywood mill as a community - owned cooperative.
Business and Economics; Social Science
Dist - CANCIN **Prod** - FINLIN 1981

Mad River - Plant Closures in the Redwoods 55 MIN
U-matic / VHS
Color (H A)
LC 81-707596
Uses the example of a timber community near California's Mad River to examine the use of natural resources and the conflict between those who desire increased protection of the environment and those who are concerned with jobs and economic development.
Agriculture; Business and Economics; Science - Natural; Social Science
Dist - FINLIN **Prod** - FINLIN 1982

The Mad Whirl 71 MIN
Videoreel / VT2
Toys that Grew Up II Series
Color
Fine Arts
Dist - PBS **Prod** - WTTWTV

Madagascar I 25 MIN
16mm / U-matic
Untamed World Series
Color; Mono (J H C A)
$400.00 film, $250.00 video, $50.00 rental
Explores the changing landscape and unusual wildlife of the island of Madagascar. wildlife.
Geography - World; Science - Natural
Dist - CTV **Prod** - CTV 1973

Madagascar II 25 MIN
16mm / U-matic
Untamed World Series
Color; Mono (J H C A)
$400.00 film, $250.00 video, $50.00 rental
Explores the plant and animal life found on the island of Madagascar, including the Lemur, the Aye - Aye, and a variety of natural vegetation.
Geography - World; Science - Natural
Dist - CTV **Prod** - CTV 1973

Madagascar, or, Caroline Kennedy's sinful life in London 2 MIN
16mm
Color (G)
$250.00 purchase, $10.00 rental
Features Caroline Kennedy dancing at a gala ball in London. Portrays the morning after as she attempts to make frozen orange juice in the kitchen with mixed results. Intercut with footage of an Africn tribe who advise the viewer to 'dance now, for tomorrow we go.' Soundtrack courtesy of Alan Lomax.
Fine Arts
Dist - CANCIN **Prod** - WWDIXO 1976

Madam 28 MIN
U-matic / VHS / 16mm
Insight Series
B&W (H C A)
LC 70-705425
A dramatization about a woman who publishes a pornographic magazine catering to insecure males, is challenged by an assistant, and ultimately breaks down, revealing her own hatred of sex, life and herself.
Guidance and Counseling; Psychology
Dist - PAULST **Prod** - PAULST 1967

Madame Bovary
BETA / VHS
B&W
Presents Flaubert's story about a young woman trapped in an unhappy marriage. Stars Jennifer Jones, Van Heflin, James Mason and Louis Jourdan.
Fine Arts; Literature and Drama
Dist - GA **Prod** - GA

Madame Butterfly 143 MIN
VHS
Color (S) (ITALIAN)
$39.95 purchase _ #833 - 9302; $39.95 purchase _ #S01689
Offers the La Scala production of 'Madame Butterfly' by Puccini starring Yasuko Hayashi in the title role. Includes a cast of Peter Dvorsky, Hak - Nam Kim and Giorgio Zancanaro. Lorin Maazel conducts.
Fine Arts; Foreign Language; Geography - World
Dist - FI **Prod** - RMART 1987
UILL

Madame Butterfly 140 MIN
VHS
Color (S) (ITALIAN)
$39.95 purchase _ #623 - 9806
Presents Puccini's 'Madame Butterfly' staged in the Arena di Verona. Stars Raina Kabaivanska.
Fine Arts; Foreign Language; Geography - World
Dist - FI **Prod** - NVIDC 1986

Madame Butterfly 140 MIN
U-matic / VHS
Color (A) (ITALIAN)
Presents Puccini's tragedy, Madame Butterfly, in a production which tranforms the Arena di Verona into a magical setting of Japanese gardens and cherry trees.
Fine Arts; Foreign Language
Dist - SRA **Prod** - SRA

Madame C J Walker 30 MIN
VHS
Black Americans of achievement video collection series
Color (J H C G)
$39.98 purchase _ #LVC6610V
Portrays entrepreneur Madame C J Walker through interviews with leading authorities, rare footage and archival photographs. Part of 12 - part series on noted black Americans.
History - United States
Dist - CAMV

Madame C J Walker 17 MIN
35mm strip / VHS
Notable black Americans series

Color (J H C T A)
$45.00 purchase _ #MB - 909836 - 3, #MB - 539719 - 6
Presents a biographical sketch of Madame C J Walker, a black businesswoman who fought racist and sexist barriers to become America's first self - made millionairess. Includes archival photographs and original illustrations.
Biography; History - United States; History - World; Social Science; Sociology
Dist - SRA

Madame Chiang Kai - shek 26 MIN
16mm
History Makers of the 20th Century Series
B&W (J H A)
Uses rare actuality footage to portray the personal life and history - making deeds of Madame Chiang Kai - Shek.
Biography; History - World
Dist - SF **Prod** - WOLPER 1965

Madame Dubarry 85 MIN
16mm
B&W ((GERMAN SUBTITLES))
A silent motion picture with German subtitles. Tells the story of Madame Dubarry, who advanced from seamstress to become the mistress of Louis XV. Hated by the people for her lavishness, after the king's death is brought before the revolutionary court, sentenced and executed. Influenced by Max Reinhardt's monumental stage productions.
Fine Arts; Foreign Language
Dist - WSTGLC **Prod** - WSTGLC 1919

Made and bottled in Kentucky 59 MIN
VHS
Color (G I J H)
$19.95 purchase _ #MW16
Shows the technology of distilling, along with interviews with families whose ancestors began today's distilleries.
History - United States
Dist - SVIP

Made for Art 15 MIN
VHS
Art's place series
Color (K P)
$49.00 purchase, $15.00 rental _ #295807
Celebrates Art's birthday, as his friends use a variety of media to create art for him. Part of a series combining songs, stories, animation, puppets and live actors to convey the pleasure of artistic expression. Includes an illustrated teacher's guide.
Fine Arts
Dist - TVOTAR **Prod** - TVOTAR 1989

Made for television 5 MIN
16mm
Color (G)
$20.00 rental
Juxtaposes excerpts from television to a sound track of extraordinary facts about humans and their environment. Exposes the exploitative nature of television advertising.
Business and Economics; Fine Arts; Literature and Drama
Dist - CANCIN **Prod** - FARWIL 1981

Made in America 60 MIN
VHS
Entrepreneurs - an American adventure series
Color (H C A)
$59.95 purchase
Highlights the issues currently faced by the manufacturing industry while looking at its past and future. Examines the role of the assembly line in the development of American industry. Suggests that mass production helped the US become dominant in industries such as steelmaking, automobile production and textile manufacturing. Narrated by Robert Mitchum. Part of a six-part series.
Business and Economics; Education; Social Science
Dist - PBS **Prod** - CUNLIM 1986
CAMV

Made in Barbados 20 MIN
U-matic / VHS / 16mm
One World Series
Color (J H)
Shows how some Caribbean islands must choose to use available labor to manufacture goods from imported raw materials.
Business and Economics; Geography - World; History - World
Dist - FI **Prod** - BBCTV 1982

Made in Britain 52 MIN
16mm / U-matic / VHS
Destination America Series
Color (J)
Describes how the British, highly skilled and seeking prosperity, were model immigrants. Interviews and historic pictures portray what life in America was like for the English and Welsh who were able to reap the material rewards of America's expanding economy.
History - United States; History - World; Sociology
Dist - MEDIAG **Prod** - THAMES 1976

Made in China - a search for roots 30 MIN
16mm / VHS
Color (H C G)
$550.00, $295.00 purchase, $55.00 rental
Follows Lisa Hsia, born and raised in Illinois, who grew up typically American in an assimilated home where Chinese food was her only tie to her heritage. Reveals that Hsia travels to China and established residence with her aunt and uncle who are unaccustomed to independent young women. Hsia gets into a few scrapes when she ventures around China because she doesn't know the rules, but she gradually settles in, learning about her rich and interesting background and discovers some truths about herself. Produced by Lisa Hsia.
Geography - World; History - World; Sociology
Dist - FLMLIB

Made in Japan 30 MIN
U-matic / VHS
Japan - the Changing Tradition Series LINCOLN, NB 68501
Color (H C A)
History - World
Dist - GPN **Prod** - UMA 1978

Made in Japan, Pt 1 - Cultural Influences on Industry 16 MIN
U-matic / VHS / 16mm
Color (H C A)
Delineates the integral link between Japan's cultural tradition and its modern corporate structure. Discusses family and educational values that shape Japanese attitudes toward work. Explains why the intense loyalty between employer and employee has done so much to promote industrial productivity in Japan.
Business and Economics; History - World
Dist - CORF **Prod** - WABCTV 1982

Made in Japan, Pt 2 - Business Practices and Changing Lifestyles 22 MIN
U-matic / VHS / 16mm
Color (H C A)
Examines the business practices responsible for Japan's booming economy. Looks at the way Japan views management, research, long - range planning, re - investment, profit - making and training. Interviews corporate heads, the head of the Japanese Productivity Center, government leaders and workers.
Business and Economics; History - World
Dist - CORF **Prod** - WABCTV 1982

Made in Japan - Ukiyo - E Prints 29 MIN
Videoreel / VT2
Museum Open House Series
Color
Geography - World; Industrial and Technical Education
Dist - PBS **Prod** - WGBHTV

Made in Maine 8 MIN
16mm
Color (G)
$20.00 rental
Takes a closeup look at the visual riches around a lake in Maine.
Fine Arts; Geography - United States
Dist - CANCIN **Prod** - BURCKR 1970

Made in Mississippi - Black Folk Art and Crafts 20 MIN
16mm
Color (J A)
LC 76-700025
Features folk art, crafts and architecture in rural Mississippi. Presents people discussing their work and telling how they learned each tradition.
Fine Arts; History - United States; Literature and Drama; Sociology
Dist - SOFOLK **Prod** - YUMDS 1975

Made in Sweden 26 MIN
16mm
Color
LC FIA66-1389
Shows how the natural resources of Sweden are used, pointing out that modern industrialism helps to give Sweden a high standard of living.
Geography - World
Dist - SWNTO **Prod** - SWEDIN 1957

Made in the Bronx
16mm
Color
Shows a diverse range of people from a shattered Bronx neighborhood determined to rebuild their community. Addresses the value and necessity for all people to experience their creativity.
Psychology; Social Science; Sociology
Dist - SULANI **Prod** - SULANI

Made manifest 12 MIN
16mm
Color (G)
$472.00 purchase, $20.00 rental
Comments on I Corinthians 1 - 13.
Fine Arts
Dist - CANCIN **Prod** - BRAKS 1980

Made on Rails - a History of the Mexican Railroad Workers 40 MIN
VHS / 16mm
Color (G) (SPANISH (ENGLISH SUBTITLES))
$250.00 purchase, $50.00 rental; LC 89715647
Examines the history of one of Mexico's most combative unions, the railroad workers, from the 1920s through the present day. Includes archival footage and interviews with suriving participants. Focuses on key periods such as the 1923 rejection of the offical government union, the 1938 nationalization of the railroads and the great strike of 1958 - 1959. Spanish dialogue with English subtitles.
Business and Economics; History - World; Social Science
Dist - CNEMAG **Prod** - CNEMAG 1988

Made to Wear - Wool's a Natural 15 MIN
16mm
Color
Describes, in chronological order, how the fashion trends set by couturiers are translated into clothing. Discusses the interaction of the fashion designer and fabric designer, and includes the charting of sample fabrics. Shows the mechanical process of cutting and manufacturing garments. Conveys wool's quality and versatility while emphasizing the importance of 'investment' dressing in today's economy. Narrated by Orson Welles.
Home Economics
Dist - WSTGLC **Prod** - WSTGLC

Madeira 15 MIN
16mm
Color
LC FIA65-1871
Describes the Portuguese island of Madeira, whose inhabitants remain almost untouched by western technology. Pictures the age - old methods and practices which are still maintained in farming, in growing and processing grapes for wine, in fishing and in embroidery. Includes views of the mountainous island and of the relaxed amusements available to the tourist. Filmed in Madeira.
Geography - World
Dist - RADIM **Prod** - MACKIN 1965

Madeira - Atlantic Paradise 15 MIN
VHS / U-matic
Color (I)
Familiarizes third through fifth grade pupils with other nations' cultures. Builds understanding by studying differences that might divide or cause confusion between various ethnic groups.
Home Economics; Psychology
Dist - GPN

Madeleine Kamman Cooks 90 MIN
U-matic / VHS
Video Cooking Series
Color
$49.95 purchase; $39.95 purchase
Begins with a simple Caribbean salad of whole sauteed shrimp with cantaloupe, avocados and an imaginative dressing combining lime juice, rum, mustard and cream.
Home Economics
Dist - BAFBRG **Prod** - BAFBRG 1986

Madeleine L'Engle - Star - gazer 30 MIN
VHS / U-matic
Color (G P I J H C)
$69.00, $99.00 purchase, $55.00 rental
Portrays the author of A Wrinkle In Time speaking candidly of her early years, her work as a writer and her personal philosophy. Features L'Engle fielding classroom questions from her young fans. Narrated by Julie Harris. Produced by Martha Wheelock.
Literature and Drama
Dist - ISHTAR

Madeleines 29 MIN
Videoreel / VT2
French Chef - French Series
Color (FRENCH)
A French language videotape. Features Julia Child of Haute Cuisine au Vin demonstrating how to prepare madeleines. With captions.
Foreign Language; Home Economics
Dist - PBS **Prod** - WGBHTV

Madeline 7 MIN
U-matic / VHS / 16mm
Color
Uses animation to describe the adventures of an irrepressible French school girl and her life in boarding school. Based on the book Madeline by Ludwig Bemelman.
Fine Arts; Literature and Drama
Dist - CF **Prod** - BOSUST 1969
LCOA

Madeline 7 MIN
16mm / U-matic / VHS
Color (P I)
$165 purchase - 16 mm, $115 purchase - video
Discusses what happens when Madeline has her appendix out. Produced by Stephen Bosustow. Based on the book by Ludwig Bemelman.
Health and Safety; Literature and Drama
Dist - CF

Madeline
VHS / 16mm
Color (K)
$18.88 purchase _ #HTV22194
Presents Christopher Plummer narrating Ludwig Bemelman's story; from an HBO production.
Literature and Drama
Dist - EDUCRT

Madeline 7 MIN
U-matic / VHS / 16mm
Color (P I) (SPANISH)
Tells the story of a young french girl in Paris who goes to the hospital to have her appendix removed.
Fine Arts; Foreign Language; Literature and Drama
Dist - LCOA **Prod** - RANK 1969

Madeline Gleason - 5 - 15 - 74 120 MIN
VHS / Cassette
Poetry Center reading series
Color (G)
$15.00 purchase, rental _ #54 - 36A
Presents the poet reading from her works at the Poetry Center, San Francisco State University. Features Poets of the Forties, nine writers in one event, distributed as one tape. Includes co - readers James Broughton, Robert Duncan, William Everson, Robert Horan, Janet Lewis, Richard Moore, Rosalie Moore and Tom Parkinson.
Literature and Drama
Dist - POETRY **Prod** - POETRY 1974

Madeline's Dream 20 MIN
U-matic / VHS / 16mm
Gestalt Series
Color (H C)
LC 74-706490
Using the Gestalt method, a young girl re - lives a repetitive dream and discovers some basic truths about herself.
Education; Psychology
Dist - FI **Prod** - PMI 1969

Madeline's rescue 35 MIN
VHS
Children's circle collection series
Color (K P I)
$14.95 purchase _ #WK1170
Offers a collection of Madeline stories by Ludwig Bemelman. Includes title story along with Madeline and the Bad Hat and Madeline and the Gypsies.
Fine Arts; Literature and Drama
Dist - KNOWUN

Madera - Plastico - Una Nueva Dimension 12 MIN
U-matic / VHS / 16mm
Color (H C) (SPANISH)
A Spanish - language version of the motion picture Wood Plastic - A New Dimension. Demonstrates the use of the catalyst heat system in making wood plastic. Shows how the usual disadvantages of wood are minimized by this process and presents a commercial use for the new material.
Business and Economics; Foreign Language; Science - Physical
Dist - IFB **Prod** - HOLTMB 1969

Madhur Jaffrey's Far Eastern Cookery 61 MIN
VHS
Color (S)
$29.95 purchase _ #781 - 9039
Evokes the atmosphere of exotic countries such as Thailand and Sumatra. Features master chef Madhur Jaffrey who teaches how to make Spicy Beef Salad, Mange - Tout Stir Fried With Prawns, Smoky Aubergines In Lime Sauce and other recipes.
Fine Arts; Health and Safety; Home Economics; Sociology
Dist - FI **Prod** - BBCTV 1989

Madhur Jaffrey's Indian Cookery 61 MIN
VHS
Color (S)
$29.95 purchase _ #781 - 9038
Shows how to prepare eight appetizing and authentic Indian dishes using ingredients that are readily available. Features Madhur Jaffrey who provides recipes icluding Tandoori - Style Chicken, Lemony Chicken With Fresh Coriander, Red Lamb Or Beef Stew, Spiced Basmati Rice and Deep - Fried Puffy Bread.
Fine Arts; Geography - World; Health and Safety; Home Economics; Industrial and Technical Education; Sociology
Dist - FI **Prod** - BBCTV 1989

Madi 26 MIN
16mm / VHS
Color (I)
LC 89715687
Dramatizes the difficulties of adolescence. Considers the questions of revenge and forgiveness. Explores similarities and differences in cultures.
Education; Guidance and Counseling; History - World; Psychology
Dist - BARR

Madigan's Million 95 MIN
16mm / U-matic / VHS
Color (J)
Stars Dustin Hoffman as the mild - mannered undercover agent who is sent on a round - the - world chase.
Literature and Drama
Dist - FI **Prod** - IDEAL 1966

Madina Boe 40 MIN
16mm
B&W
Explains how the people of Guinea Bissau have liberated two - thirds of their country. Describes a people's war fought by a people's army, where poets, peasants and doctors fight side - by - side.
Civics and Political Systems; Sociology
Dist - CANWRL **Prod** - CANWRL

The Madison School Plan 18 MIN
16mm / U-matic / VHS
Color (C A) (SPANISH)
LC 73-714325
Presents a plan for intergrating exceptional children into the regular school program. Explains that children are allowed to take part in regular classes as well as being instructed by the specialized faculty of a learning center.
Education
Dist - AIMS **Prod** - SMUSD 1971

Madmax 93 MIN
16mm
Color (H A)
Tells the story of a desolate, lawless future where leather suited cops protect highways from suicidally daring drivers and roving motorcycle gangs. Stars Mel Gibson.
Fine Arts
Dist - TIMLIF **Prod** - AIP 1980

Madness 50 MIN
VHS
Human brain series
Color (H C A)
PdS99 purchase
Highlights recent advances in knowledge about the brain and its functions relative to mental health. Uses case histories to illustrate individuals' triumphs over brain injury. Part of a seven-video set focusing on the self, memory, language, movement, sight, fear, and madness.
Psychology
Dist - BBCENE

Madness 60 MIN
U-matic / VHS
Brain, Mind and Behavior Series
Color (C A)
Discusses schizophrenia.
Psychology
Dist - FI **Prod** - WNETTV

Madness 30 MIN
VHS
Mind/Brain Classroom Series
Color (H G)
$59.95 purchase _ #MDBR - 101
Deals with mental illnesses. Intended for high school students.
Psychology
Dist - PBS **Prod** - WNETTV

Madness and Medicine 49 MIN
U-matic / VHS / 16mm
Color (J)
Explores the quality of mental institutions. Examines the relatively radical therapies of drugs, electroshock therapy, and psychosurgery.
Psychology
Dist - CRMP **Prod** - ABCTV 1977

Madness and Medicine 48 MIN
U-matic / VHS / 16mm
Color (H C A)
LC 77-701413
Takes a critical look at mental health institutions and their diverse treatment programs, which help some patients but prove damaging to others.
Health and Safety; Psychology
Dist - MGHT **Prod** - ABCTV 1977

Madness and Medicine, Pt 1 25 MIN
U-matic / VHS / 16mm
Color (H C A)
LC 77-701413
Takes a critical look at mental institutions and their diverse treatment programs, which help some patients but prove damaging to others.
Psychology
Dist - MGHT **Prod** - ABCTV 1977

Madness and Medicine, Pt 2 24 MIN
16mm / U-matic / VHS
Color (H C A)
LC 77-701413
Takes a critical look at mental institutions and their diverse treatment programs, which help some patients but prove damaging to others.
Psychology
Dist - MGHT **Prod** - ABCTV 1977

Madness and Method - the Play within the Play - Hamlet as Playwright 45 MIN
U-matic / VHS
Survey of English Literature I Series
Color
Looks at the play within a play in Shakespeare's work Hamlet.
Literature and Drama
Dist - MDCPB **Prod** - MDCPB

Madness on trial 50 MIN
VHS
Horizon series
Color (H C A)
PdS99 purchase
Calls attention to conflicts that arise when a mentally ill person becomes involved in a crime. Talks about punishment versus treatment.
Civics and Political Systems; Health and Safety; Psychology
Dist - BBCENE

Madness - Part 7 60 MIN
VHS / U-matic
Brain series
Color (G)
$45.00, $29.95 purchase
Illustrates the effects of a split between the thinking and feeling parts of the brain, schizophrenia. Chronicles scientific efforts to pinpoint the brain's anatomical changes. Part six of an eight - part series on the brain.
Psychology; Science - Natural
Dist - ANNCPB **Prod** - WNETTV 1984

Madness series
Outlines the history of mental illness since the medieval period. Includes methods of treatment and public perception of mental illness. Comprises five episodes which are also available individually. Based on Jonathan Miller's history of mental illness.
Madness series 300 MIN
Dist - BBCENE

Madness
Brainwaves 60 MIN
In two minds 60 MIN
Out of sight 60 MIN
The talking cure 60 MIN
To define true madness 60 MIN
Dist - BBCENE

Madonna, child and Saint Anne 30 MIN
VHS
Palette series
Color (G C)
$70.00 purchase, $12.50, rental _ #36403
Portrays in a desolate landscape, the Virgin Mary who tries to restrain the Christ child who plays with a lamb as Saint Anne watches over them. Reveals that the meaning of the painting by Leonardo da Vinci has evoked questions since its creation in 1510, but its message still remains a mystery. Part of a 13 - part series which examines great paintings in a dynamic and dramatic way by moving into their creative spaces and spending time with the characters and their surroundings. Uses special video effects to investigate artistic enigmas and studies material, technique, style and significance. Narrated by Marcel Cuvelier, directed by Alain Jaubert.
Fine Arts
Dist - PSU **Prod** - LOUVRE 1992

Madonna with Chancellor Rolin 30 MIN
VHS
Palette series
Color (G C)
$70.00 purchase, $12.50, rental _ #36402
Reveals that Flemish master Jan Van Eyck is said to have invented the art of oil painting and perfected it by applying paint to the canvas in transparent layers, a technique which allowed him to create works such as the Madonna in 1436. Offers a landscape and gallery with figures of unusual depth, detail and complexity. Part of a 13 - part series which examines great paintings in a dynamic and dramatic way by moving into their creative spaces and spending time with the characters and their surroundings. Uses special video effects to investigate artistic enigmas and studies material, technique, style and significance. Narrated by Marcel Cuvelier, directed by Alain Jaubert.

Fine Arts
Dist - PSU **Prod** - LOUVRE 1992

Madrid 57 MIN
VHS
Color (G) (SPANISH)
$39.95 purchase _ #W1404, #W1405
Views sites in Madrid, Spain that highlight its history, including the Prado Museum, Plaza Mayor, the Royal Palace and other locations from Medieval times to the 20th century. Focuses on aspects of culture expressed through art, dancing and bullfighting.
Foreign Language; Geography - World; Sociology
Dist - GPC

Madrid 30 MIN
VHS
Color (G)
$29.95 purchase _ #S02026
Tours Madrid, the capital of Spain. Features the Prado, shops, palaces, gardens, and side trips to Toledo and Segovia.
Geography - World
Dist - UILL

Madrid - Capital De Espana 18 MIN
U-matic / VHS / 16mm
Spanish Language Series
Color (J H C) (SPANISH)
LC 73-707306
A Spanish language film for first year Spanish students. Views Madrid, Spain - - the principle streets, the airport, Spain's tallest building, monuments and statues, the bull ring and a bull fight. Visits the Prado Museum featuring the paintings of El Greco, Goya and Velasquez.
Foreign Language
Dist - IFB **Prod** - IFB 1969

Madrid, N M 9 MIN
16mm
Color (I)
LC 79-700760
Uses poetry, music and scenes of empty houses and sunrises to present a portrait of a ghost town in New Mexico.
Fine Arts
Dist - BLUSKY **Prod** - BLUSKY 1978

Madura, Madura 26 MIN
VHS
Color (C)
$165.00 purchase, $30.00 rental _ #CC4135
Examines a health clinic in rural Indonesia which offers both basic medical care and health and nutrition education. Explains the Indonesian government's program in adult literacy and creation of art cooperatives.
Civics and Political Systems; Geography - World; History - World; Sociology
Dist - IU **Prod** - NFBC 1990

Maedchen in uniform 90 MIN
VHS
B&W (G)
$24.95 _ #MAE030
Tells the story of a lonely girl's crush on a female teacher in a strict boarding school. Features an early feminist classic, originally banned in Germany and censored in the US, a decision later reversed with Eleanor Roosevelt's help. The all - female production, directed by Leontine Sagan, stands out for its sensitive acting and tender portrayal of female love.
Fine Arts; Psychology; Sociology
Dist - HOMVIS **Prod** - JANUS 1931

Maedchenkrieg 148 MIN
16mm
Color (GERMAN (ENGLISH SUBTITLES))
A German language motion picture with English subtitles. Deals with a German family in Prague between 1936 and 1946 that eventually must choose between monetarty and emotional ruin and return to a defeated and destroyed Germany. A television production of Martin Bieler's novel MAEDCHENKRIEG.
Foreign Language; History - World; Literature and Drama; Sociology
Dist - WSTGLC **Prod** - WSTGLC 1977

Maelstrom 1 MIN
16mm
Color
LC 72-702401
Presents an old woman who takes a ride on the carousel of life and is flooded with memories of her past.
Education; Fine Arts; Sociology
Dist - USC **Prod** - USC 1972

Maestro instructional series
Presents a ten - part series which supplements class lessons and reinforces private lessons on ten musical instruments. Offers clear - cut examples and demonstrations on how to unpack and assemble the instruments, proper hand position and instrumental nomenclature. Discusses notes, breathing, posture, reading music and care and maintenance of the instruments. Includes booklets. Instruments covered are the flute, clarinet, saxophone, trombone, trumpet, tuba, snare drum, violin, viola and cello.

Cello for beginners	50 MIN
Clarinet for beginners	50 MIN
Flute for beginners	50 MIN
Saxophone for beginners	50 MIN
Snare drum for beginners	50 MIN
Trombone for beginners	50 MIN
Trumpet for beginners	50 MIN
Tuba for beginners	50 MIN
Viola for beginners	50 MIN
Violin for beginners	50 MIN

Dist - CAMV

Magazine I 30 MIN
VHS
Perspectives - science in action - series
Color; PAL; NTSC (G)
PdS90, PdS105 purchase
Demonstrates a miscellany of new products.
Business and Economics; Science
Dist - CFLVIS **Prod** - LONTVS

Magazine I - Birds, Beasts, and Breathing Fish 25 MIN
16mm / U-matic / VHS
Untamed World Series
Color; Mono (J H C A)
$400.00 film, $250.00 video, $50.00 rental
Profiles seven unusual animals, including the zebroids, the eland, the lungfigh, the mole rat, the scorpion, chameleon, and a pair of mating storks.
Science - Natural
Dist - CTV **Prod** - CTV 1970

Magazine II 30 MIN
VHS
Perspectives - science in action - series
Color; PAL; NTSC (G)
PdS90, PdS105 purchase
Shows how new ideas spring to the minds of many different people - not all of them trained scientists.
Business and Economics; Fine Arts; Science
Dist - CFLVIS **Prod** - LONTVS

Magazine II - Bats, Birds, and Bigger Beasts 25 MIN
16mm / U-matic / VHS
Untamed World Series
Color; Mono (J H C A)
$400.00 film, $250.00 video, $50.00 rental
Reveals the immense value of nature's scavengers to the balance of the environment. Looks specifically at the vulture and its contributions as well as other beasts.
Science - Natural
Dist - CTV **Prod** - CTV 1970

Magazine rack
CD-ROM
(G A)
$99.00 purchase _ #2871
Features more than 300 of 1990's most popular magazines. Divides into four categories - business and industry, general interest, health and fitness, and computers. For IBM PC and compatibles. Requires 640K RAM, DOS Version 3.1 or greater, floppy disk drive - a hard disk drive is recommended, one empty expansion slot, and an IBM compatible CD - ROM drive.
Computer Science; Literature and Drama
Dist - BEP

Magazines to Transparencies 12 MIN
16mm / U-matic / VHS
Color (H C A)
Demonstrates the making of transparencies from magazine photographs with common materials - - scissors, rubber cement and sheets of frosted acetate.
Education
Dist - IFB **Prod** - FLORSU 1958

Magellan and Cortes - Pizarro and other conquistadors 33 MIN
VHS
Age of exploration series
Color (I J)
$60.00 purchase _ #CLV402 - 2
Presents two programs on Magellan and Cortes, Pizzarro and other conquistadors. Shows how explorers and their discoveries led to new concepts on the size, shape and varied peoples of the world. Covers the period from 1450 to 1600. Combines period artifacts, works of art and narrated personal accounts of the explorers themselves. Part of two parts. Enhanced video from filmstrip.
History - World
Dist - KNOWUN

Magenta Geryon series

Adagio - part I	8 MIN
In a summer garden - part 2	15 MIN
Winter light - part 3	9 MIN

Dist - CANCIN

Maggi Hambling 30 MIN
VHS
Making their mark series
Color (A)
PdS65 purchase _ Unavailable in South Africa
Profiles Maggi Hambling, who has a unique drawing style and way of working. Introduces the viewer to practical and aesthetic aspects of the skill of drawing. Part of a six-part series.
Fine Arts
Dist - BBCENE

Maggie 20 MIN
VHS
Color (G)
$89.00 purchase, $40.00 rental
Features an interview with Maggie Kuhn, founder of the Gray Panthers, who speaks out on the need for an intergenerational movement, what old and young have in common, the 'four M's' for older adults, the importance of spiritual dimension, caregivers and care receivers and the Gray Panther Growl. Presents a production by Dr James V Gambone, Points of View.
Fine Arts; Guidance and Counseling; Health and Safety; Sociology
Dist - TNF

Maggie, a Girl of the Streets - a Novel by Stephen Crane 15 MIN
U-matic / VHS / 16mm
Novel Series
Color (J H C A)
LC 83-700040; 83 - 706269
Presents the story of an impoverished young woman living a life of violence, cruelty and despair in New York City's Lower East Side in the 1890's. Based on the novel MAGGIE, A GIRL OF THE STREETS by Stephen Crane.
Literature and Drama
Dist - IU **Prod** - IITC 1982

Maggie and the Beautiful Machine - Backs Series

The Back - Pt 1	29 MIN
The Back, Pt 2	29 MIN
Maintenance	29 MIN
Posture	29 MIN
The Upper Back	29 MIN

Dist - PBS

Maggie and the beautiful machine - bellies series

Abdominals	29 MIN
Basics - abdominals	29 MIN
Breathe	29 MIN
Pot Bellies	29 MIN
Side Abdominals	29 MIN

Dist - PBS

Maggie and the Beautiful Machine - Easy Does it Series

Chairs - Pt 1	29 MIN
Chairs - Pt 2	29 MIN
Flexibility	29 MIN
Long Live	29 MIN
Slow and Easy	29 MIN

Dist - PBS

Maggie and the Beautiful Machine - Eating Series

Dieting	29 MIN
Goodies	29 MIN
I Never See Maggie Alone	29 MIN
Ten Ugly Pounds	29 MIN
Thoroughbreds	29 MIN

Dist - PBS

Maggie and the beautiful machine - feet and legs series

Basics - thighs	29 MIN
The Feet	29 MIN
The Inner Thighs	29 MIN
Knees	29 MIN
Let's Split (Inner Thighs II)	29 MIN

Dist - PBS

Maggie and the beautiful machine - general shape - up series

The Best ones	29 MIN
Combinations	29 MIN
Test - Pt 1	29 MIN
Test - Pt 2	29 MIN

Dist - PBS

Maggie and the Beautiful Machine - Hips and the Bottom Series

Four Walls	29 MIN
Hips and Bottom, Pt 2	29 MIN

Dist - PBS

Maggie and the Beautiful Machine - Maggie and Her Willing Accomplices Series

The Chest	29 MIN
Chin and neck	29 MIN
Hips and Bottom, Pt 1	29 MIN
When in Rome	29 MIN

Dist - PBS

Maggie and the beautiful machine - Maggie and her willing accomplices series
The Face 29 MIN
Dist - PBS

Maggie and the Beautiful Machine - Pregnancy Series
Babies and bellies 29 MIN
Delivery 29 MIN
A Little Bit more Pregnant 29 MIN
A Little Bit Pregnant 29 MIN
A Round Seven Months 29 MIN
Dist - PBS

Maggie and the Beautiful Machine - Shape - Up Now for Kids Series
Kids' Stuff 29 MIN
When You and I were Young Maggie 29 MIN
Dist - PBS

Maggie Gee 45 MIN
VHS
Color (H C G)
$79.00 purchase
Features the writer discussing with Sheila McCleod how to write about world problems and experimenting with styles and formats. Talks about her works that include The Burning Book and Light Years.
Literature and Drama; Sociology
Dist - ROLAND **Prod** - INCART

Maggie Kuhn - Wrinkled Radical 27 MIN
U-matic / VHS / 16mm
Color (G)
LC 77-700770
Profiles Gray Panthers leader Maggie Kuhn and her efforts to protect the rights of the elderly. Interviews her in her home, working in the Panthers' Philadelphia offices and speaking with groups about discrimination against the aged.
Civics and Political Systems; Health and Safety; History - World
Dist - IU **Prod** - WNETTV 1977

Magic - 205 29 MIN
VHS
FROG series 2; Series 2; 205
Color (P I J)
$100.00 purchase
Offers the fifth program in series 2 by Friends of Research and Odd Gadgets. Lifts science off the textbook page into the real world to show how enjoyable and challenging science can be. In this episode, the Froggers blend chemistry, physics and a magician's flair, sleight of hand and optical illusions to produce great results. Produced by Christopher Howard.
Science - Physical
Dist - BULFRG **Prod** - OWLTV 1993

Magic and Catholicism 34 MIN
16mm
Color
Shows how the people of the Bolivian highlands blend in thought and practice the religion of their ancestors and their conquerors. Demonstrates how a fatal automobile accident provides occasion for expressions of both faiths in an effort to influence events.
Geography - World; Religion and Philosophy
Dist - WHEELK **Prod** - AUFS

Magic and Music 17 MIN
16mm / U-matic / VHS
Color (P)
LC 74-703802
Uses animation to depict modern and classical music. Enacts Rimsky - Korsakoff's Flight of the Bumblebee and excerpts from Beethoven's Sixth Symphony.
Fine Arts
Dist - CORF **Prod** - DISNEY 1974

The Magic balloons 16 MIN
U-matic / VHS / 16mm
Color (P I)
LC 70-700603
Presents an art film without narration about a little boy on the beach who sells balloons which become real people to him.
Fine Arts; Literature and Drama
Dist - LCOA **Prod** - LCOA 1969

Magic Bill 7 MIN
U-matic / VHS / 16mm
Color (I)
Presents Magic Bill, a sweet - talking drug dealer and Bruce Weitz from Hill Street Blues. Discusses how not to be fooled into thinking drugs are harmless.
Psychology; Sociology
Dist - CORF **Prod** - WQED

The Magic boy's Easter
VHS
Color (G R)
$19.95 purchase
Describes how a lame youth who works for a first - century Jerusalem magician comes to believe that Christ is the Savior.
Guidance and Counseling; Literature and Drama; Religion and Philosophy
Dist - CPH **Prod** - LUMIS

The Magic braid 112 MIN
VHS
Color (G) (CHINESE WITH ENGLISH SUBTITLES)
$45.00 purchase _ #6043C
Presents a film from the People's Republic of China by Feng Yicai.
Geography - World; Literature and Drama
Dist - CHTSUI

Magic Broom 13 MIN
U-matic / VHS
Happy Time Adventure Series
Color (K P)
$29.95 purchase _ #VM115
Presents an adaptation of the book Magic Broom. Contains a 32 page hardcover book and a video.
English Language; Literature and Drama
Dist - TROLA

The Magic Bullet 27 MIN
U-matic / VHS / 16mm
Perspective Series
Color (J)
Discusses the medical uses of isolated individual antibodies.
Health and Safety; Science; Science - Natural
Dist - STNFLD **Prod** - LONTVS

Magic carpet series
Aesop and his fables 15 MIN
Aladdin and his magic lamp 15 MIN
The Butterfly tray 15 MIN
The Legend of Paul Bunyan 15 MIN
The Monkey and the Crocodile 15 MIN
Paul Revere's Ride 15 MIN
The Princess of the Full Moon 15 MIN
Rip Van Winkle 15 MIN
The Story of John Henry 15 MIN
The Story of Molly Pitcher 15 MIN
Why Rabbits have Long Ears 15 MIN
Why Spiders Hide in Dark Corners 15 MIN
Dist - GPN

Magic Carpets - an Introduction to Oriental Rugs 75 MIN
VHS
Color (G)
$35.00 purchase
Shows how Oriental rugs are made and evaluated. Considers kilims and knotted rugs, patterns and symbols, and care. Features Kitty Davenport as host.
Home Economics
Dist - WGTETV **Prod** - WGTETV

Magic Circle Series
Bleacher feature 12 MIN
Kids in conflict 12 MIN
The Pinch 12 MIN
Dist - ECUFLM

Magic Circle Series
Kids and Conflicts 12 MIN
Dist - MMA

Magic Circle Series
The Bleacher Feature 12 MIN
Kids and Conflict 12 MIN
Dist - UMCOM

The Magic coach - exercise and nutrition for fitness 18 MIN
VHS
Color (I J H)
$295.00 purchase, $75.00 rental _ #8386
Features champion bodybuilder Ellen Morrow who portrays a coach with magical powers and gives teenagers lessons in fitness, including aerobics, muscle strength and flexibility, and advice on nutrition.
Physical Education and Recreation; Social Science
Dist - AIMS **Prod** - MAGICC 1991

Magic Day 22 MIN
16mm
Color (H C A)
Shows how such public agencies as transportation, police, fire and public health departments work to protect a teen - age girl during one day. Also explains the protective services of volunteer agencies.
Health and Safety; Social Science; Sociology
Dist - WSUM **Prod** - WSUM 1954

Magic E 15 MIN
U-matic / Kit / VHS
Space Station Readstar series
(P)
$130.00 purchase, $25.00 rental, $75.00 self dub
Teaches phonics in a series designed to supplement second grade reading programs. Focuses on the letter e. Third in a 25 part series.
English Language
Dist - GPN

Magic Explained 4 MIN
16mm
Color (A)
Presents a hand colored silent experimental film by Diana Barrie which shows her as a female magician with magic wands, fires and lightning makes herself disappear.
Fine Arts
Dist - STARRC **Prod** - STARRC 1980

The Magic fiddle 8 MIN
VHS / U-matic
Timeless tales series
Color (P I)
$110.00, $160.00 purchase, $60.00 rental
Tells the tale of a simple old servent who is given a magical fiddle that makes people dance.
Literature and Drama
Dist - NDIM **Prod** - TIMTAL 1993

The Magic Fishbone 11 MIN
U-matic / VHS / 16mm
Color (I J)
LC 83-700374
Relates what happens when a good fairy aids an impoverished family with a magic fishbone that may only be used once. Based on a story by Charles Dickens.
Literature and Drama
Dist - PHENIX **Prod** - KRATKY 1982

The Magic Flute 160 MIN
VHS
Color (G)
$39.95 purchase _ #1212
Offers the Australian Opera production of 'The Magic Flute' by Mozart in English. Features Yvonne Kenny as Pamina, Richard Bonynge conducting.
Fine Arts
Dist - KULTUR

The magic flute
CD-ROM
Audio notes series
(G) (ENGLISH AND GERMAN)
$66.00 purchase _ #2621
Contains The Magic Flute by Mozart - 143 minutes of digital audio, with commentary and annotation. Includes the entire German libretto, a complete English translation, spoken summaries - in English or German - of the dialogue, long - form analysis of the music, the story of the opera, sound glossary, and musical and character indices. HyperCard 1.2 included. Requires a Macintosh with at least 1 MB of RAM, a hard disk drive with at least 6.5 MB of free space, an Apple compatible CD - ROM drive, and headphones or external speakers.
Fine Arts
Dist - BEP

The Magic Flute 21 MIN
U-matic / VHS / 16mm
Color (K P)
Tells the story of a minstrel and a lord of a castle who does not like music. Reveals that when the king breaks the minstrel's lute, a nightingale helps him to escape the lord's range.
Fine Arts; Literature and Drama
Dist - CAROUF **Prod** - GRIMP

The Magic Flute
U-matic / VHS
Color (G) (ITALIAN (ENGLISH SUBTITLES))
Presents the David Hockney production conducted by Bernard Haitink and featuring Benjamin Luxon and Felicity Lott.
Fine Arts; Foreign Language
Dist - VAI **Prod** - VAI

The Magic Flute 10 MIN
16mm / U-matic / VHS
Color (K P)
Uses animation to tell how a minstrel inspires the wrath of a lord who hates music.
Fine Arts; Literature and Drama
Dist - CAROUF **Prod** - CAROUF

Magic flute 134 MIN
VHS
Color (G)
$59.95 purchase _ #S00834
Presents Ingmar Bergman's adaptation of the Mozart opera 'The Magic Flute.' Stars Ulric Cold, Josef Kostlinger, Erik Saeden, Birgit Nordin and Irma Urrila.
Fine Arts
Dist - UILL

The Magic Flute 134 MIN
VHS

Color (S) (GERMAN)
$29.95 purchase _ #384 - 9351
Interprets 'The Magic Flute' by Mozart in a production by cinematic master Ingmar Bergman. Offers Eric Ericson as conductor and a cast of young Swedish singers.
Fine Arts; Foreign Language
Dist - FI **Prod** - PAR 1973

The Magic Flute 164 MIN
VHS
Color (S) (GERMAN)
$59.95 purchase _ #055 - 9009
Presents the Glyndebourne production of 'The Magic Flute' by Mozart. Offers David Hockney as set designer, singing by Felicity Lott and Benjamin Luxon, and Bernard Haitink as conductor of the London Philharmonic.
Fine Arts; Foreign Language
Dist - FI **Prod** - VAI 1988

The Magic Flute 8 MIN
16mm
Color
Offers a Fox and Crow satire on the foibles of mankind.
Fine Arts; Literature and Drama
Dist - TIMLIF **Prod** - TIMLIF 1982

A Magic Garden Christmas 60 MIN
VHS
Color (K)
$12.98 purchase _ #TT8122
Features Carole and Paula along with their furry friend Sherlock singing Christmas songs for the whole family.
Literature and Drama; Religion and Philosophy
Dist - TWINTO **Prod** - TWINTO 1990

Magic Garden Playalong Music Rhymes and Happy Times
VHS / 16mm
Color (K)
$9.88 purchase _ #PPI616
Presents actresses from the TV show with songs for children.
Fine Arts; Literature and Drama; Psychology
Dist - EDUCRT **Prod** - PIONR

Magic Gift of Rongo 11 MIN
16mm
Color; B&W (J H)
A story of an inept young fisherman who becomes skillful after he learns net making from a demigod, which he captured by chance.
Literature and Drama
Dist - CINEPC **Prod** - CINEPC

Magic Grandpa 8 MIN
U-matic / VHS / 16mm
Color (I J)
Uses puppet animation to tell a story about a lazy brother who is tricked into learning industrious habits.
Fine Arts; Religion and Philosophy
Dist - PHENIX **Prod** - KRATKY 1980

Magic Hands 7 MIN
16mm / U-matic / VHS
Magic Moments, Unit 2 - Let's do Series
Color (K P I)
LC 70-702912
Shows four make - believe sequences in which children use their hands to make wishes come true.
Education; English Language; Psychology
Dist - EBEC **Prod** - EBEC 1969

The Magic Harp 26 MIN
U-matic / VHS / 16mm
Color
Dramatizes a story from the Llanos country of southern Venezuela about a boy who saved his family from destitution through the power and beauty of his music.
Geography - World; Literature and Drama
Dist - FOTH **Prod** - FOTH

The Magic Hat 23 MIN
U-matic / VHS / 16mm
Unicorn Tales Series
Color (P I)
LC 80-700547
Presents a contemporary story, based on the fairy tale The Emperor's New Clothes, about a young boy who is having difficulties making friends in a new city and receives a magic hat guaranteed to make everyone like him. Shows how he learns some truths about friendships and the powers of the special hat.
Fine Arts; Literature and Drama
Dist - MGHT **Prod** - MGHT 1980

The Magic Horse 57 MIN
16mm
Color (P I)
Presents the first full - length Russian color cartoon in an English language version.
Fine Arts
Dist - FI **Prod** - FI

The Magic Horse 56 MIN
VHS / U-matic
Color
Features a Russian cartoon based on one of the most popular children's folk tales about a boy who befriends a magical horse.
Fine Arts; Foreign Language
Dist - IHF **Prod** - IHF

The Magic House 17 MIN
16mm / U-matic / VHS
Color (P I)
LC 70-712539
Presents a modern fantasy about children who are unhappy with household chores and the family pecking order. Reveals what happens when their wishes come true and they discover a difference between getting what they wished for and getting what they wanted. Provides insight into the idea of mutual responsibility in society.
Psychology; Sociology
Dist - PHENIX **Prod** - KINGSP 1970

Magic in the Fingers 16 MIN
16mm
B&W (I)
Presents child maestros who perform on different musical instruments with considerable talent.
Fine Arts
Dist - NEDINF **Prod** - INDIA

Magic in the Sky 57 MIN
16mm
Color
Presents a documentary that investigates the impact of U S and Canadian television on Eskimos in the Arctic and their struggle to establish their own network. Provides examples of the effects television can have on any culture.
Fine Arts; Social Science; Sociology
Dist - NFBC **Prod** - NFBC 1981

Magic in the Wind 5 MIN
VHS / U-matic / 16mm
Color; Mono (G)
MV $85.00 _ MP $75.00 purchase, $50.00 rental
Traces the steps required to prepare for a ocean sailing race.
Physical Education and Recreation
Dist - CTV **Prod** - MAKOF 1982

Magic is
Videodisc
Laser learning set 3 series; Set 3
Color; CAV (P I)
$375.00 purchase _ #8L5414
Looks at the art of illusion in the performance of magic. Discusses famous magicians such as Houdin, Blackstone and Houdini. Illustrates a conjuring trick with a toy rabbit. Part of a series of six theme - based interactive videodisc lessons. Includes user's guide, two readers. Requires a Pioneer LD - V2000 or 2200, with a barcode reader and adapter, or a Pioneer LD - V4200 or higher.
Fine Arts
Dist - BARR **Prod** - BARR 1992

Magic Johnson - always showtime
VHS
Color (G)
$19.95 purchase _ #FOX000
Combines an interview with footage of impossible shooting and ball handling.
Physical Education and Recreation
Dist - SIV

The Magic Lantern Movie 9 MIN
16mm
Color
Traces the Magic Lantern's history and shows slides depicting travel scenes, familiar stories, jokes and tricks. Illustrates the basic principles of all future projection of slides, as well as movies. Includes scenes from George Melies' 1903 film, The Magic Lantern, with music selected from works played on antique music boxes which were used with slide presentations of the 19th century. Produced by Maxine Haleff, with narration written by Cecile Starr and animation by Bob Fontana.
Fine Arts
Dist - STARRC **Prod** - STARRC

The Magic Lantern Show - and How it Grew - a History of Movies 14 MIN
16mm
Screen news digest series
B&W (I)
LC 76-701236
Focuses on the birth and growth of the art of cinema. Includes film clips from early classics, both silent and sound. Explains the development of color film, high speed photography and sophisticated cameras.
Fine Arts; History - United States; Industrial and Technical Education
Dist - HEARST **Prod** - HEARST 1975

Magic Letters 16 MIN
16mm
Color (K P I)
Demonstrates the teaching formation of letters and the relationship of the capital and small letter. Includes the letters A, B, C, D, E, F and G.
English Language
Dist - SF **Prod** - SF 1968

Magic library series
Baseball hero 15 MIN
A Fairy's tale 15 MIN
From back to front 15 MIN
Goblin mischief 15 MIN
Golden wishes 15 MIN
A Hero seeks adventure 15 MIN
An Indian Cinderella 15 MIN
Meeting in space 15 MIN
Poetry please 15 MIN
The Real princess 15 MIN
Timid dinosaurs 15 MIN
The Trickster 15 MIN
Witches and mice 15 MIN
Dist - TVOTAR

The Magic Machines 14 MIN
U-matic / VHS / 16mm
Color (J H)
Documents the lifestyle and art of Robert Gilbert, a sculptor who transforms society's junk into magic machines that bring fantasy to life.
Fine Arts
Dist - PFP **Prod** - PFP 1970

Magic Man 24 MIN
U-matic / VHS / 16mm
World According to Nicholas Series
Color (P I J)
Shows Nicholas preferring to perform magic with his uncle rather than studying for school. Reveals that he soon discovers that both learning magic and school require study and imagination.
Guidance and Counseling
Dist - LUF **Prod** - LUF 1980

Magic Moments Series
Holding on 5 MIN
Dist - EBEC

Magic Moments, Unit 5 - Let's Play Series
Choosing up 6 MIN
Guessing Game 7 MIN
Join Hands, Let Go 8 MIN
Matching Up 4 MIN
Dist - EBEC

Magic Moments, Unit 4 - Let's Pretend Series
Getting Even 3 MIN
Magic Sneakers 8 MIN
Dist - EBEC

Magic Moments, Unit 1 - Let's Talk Series
Me Too 3 MIN
What if 3 MIN
Whose Shoes 3 MIN
Dist - EBEC

Magic Moments, Unit 3 - Let's See Series
Hands Grow Up 6 MIN
Lopsideland 5 MIN
Toes Tell 6 MIN
Dist - EBEC

Magic Moments, Unit 2 - Let's do Series
Magic Hands 7 MIN
Dist - EBEC

The Magic Moth 22 MIN
U-matic / VHS / 16mm
Color (P)
LC 76-700379
Presents a film version of the book THE MAGIC MOTH. Depicts the death of a child, the reactions of the other family members and the process which the family goes through during this crisis. Deals realistically with death from the point of view of a young boy.
Sociology
Dist - CORF **Prod** - CENTRO 1976

The Magic Movies of Georges Malies 56 MIN
Videoreel / VT2
Toys that Grew Up II Series
Color
Fine Arts
Dist - PBS **Prod** - WTTWTV

Magic Numbers 20 MIN
16mm
Color (K P I)
Demonstrates the teaching formation of numbers. Shows the relationship between a numeral, its name and its meaning. Includes the numbers 1, 2, 3, 4, 5, 6, 7, 8, 9 and 10.
Mathematics
Dist - SF **Prod** - SF 1968

The Magic of a Counter 14 MIN
U-matic / VHS / 16mm
Color (P I J)
LC 77-704530
Introduces the basic concepts of decimal numeration through the use of blocks and a large counter.
Mathematics
Dist - PHENIX **Prod** - BOUNDY 1969

Magic of Color 15 MIN
U-matic / VHS
Young at Art Series
Color (P I)
Discusses color in art.
Fine Arts
Dist - AITECH **Prod** - WSKJTV 1980

Magic of Dance Series
The Ebb and flow 52 MIN
The Magnificent Beginning 52 MIN
Out of the Limelight, Home in the Rain 52 MIN
The Romantic Ballet 52 MIN
The Scene changes 52 MIN
What is New 52 MIN
Dist - TIMLIF

Magic of Disneyland 21 MIN
U-matic / VHS / 16mm
Color (I J H)
LC 72-701375
Shows the revised version of 'GALA DAY AT DISNEYLAND - A VISIT TO THE HAPPIEST PLACE ON EARTH.'.
Geography - United States; Physical Education and Recreation; Sociology
Dist - CORF **Prod** - DISNEY 1970

The Magic of Fire 23 MIN
16mm / U-matic / VHS
Color
LC 74-705058
Illustrates how fires and explosions occur and describes the safe use and control of commonly used gases and flammable liquids by tabletop displays and laboratory demonstrations. Points out the various industrial fires and fire hazards in the home with instruction on their prevention.
Health and Safety; Science - Physical
Dist - USNAC **Prod** - USBM 1965

The Magic of Herself the elf 24 MIN
VHS
Color (P)
Presents an animated version of 'The Magic of Herself the Elf.' Tells about Herself who leads a madcap band of tiny elves whose magical powers protect the workings of nature. When Herself's power is stolen by the villains Thorn and his daughter Poison Ivy, she is imprisoned in a secret garden, but eventually she returns to her rightful place as guardian of nature's precarious balance.
Fine Arts; Literature and Drama; Science - Natural
Dist - VIEWTH **Prod** - VIEWTH

The Magic of Ireland 12 MIN
16mm / U-matic / VHS
Color (J H)
LC 80-707500
Offers an introduction to the history, literature, countryside and people of Ireland.
Geography - World; History - World
Dist - CORF **Prod** - SPECTR 1978

Magic of Ireland 12 MIN
U-matic / VHS / 16mm
Color (H C A)
LC 80-701758
Looks at historical sites, cathedrals and literary landmarks in Ireland.
Geography - World; History - World
Dist - CORF **Prod** - SPEF 1979

The Magic of Lassie 100 MIN
U-matic / VHS / 16mm
Color
Stars James Stewart, Mickey Rooney and Alice Faye in the story of a kidnapped collie.
Fine Arts; Science - Natural
Dist - FI **Prod** - UNKNWN 1978

The Magic of magnets 12 MIN
VHS
Electricity and magnetism series
Color (I)
$55.00 purchase _ #1213VG
Explores magnetism and its special relationship to electricity. Explains how magnetism can produce electricity and electricity can produce magnetism. Comes with a teacher's guide and 10 blackline masters. Part three of a five - part series.
Science - Physical
Dist - UNL

Magic of Manatee 15 MIN
16mm
Color
Presents a scenic tour of Manatee County, Florida.
Geography - United States; Physical Education and Recreation
Dist - FLADC **Prod** - FLADC

The Magic of Model Railroading 15 MIN
16mm
Color
Discusses the joys of model railroading.
Physical Education and Recreation; Social Science
Dist - MORAIL **Prod** - MORAIL

The Magic of numbers 40 MIN
VHS
Color (H C PRO)
$225.00 purchase
Traces the history and development of numbers and mathematics from ancient times to the age of computers. Makes use of demonstrations and animation to emphasize concepts. For upper - level high school and college levels, and for professional teachers of mathematics.
Mathematics
Dist - LANDMK

Magic of Oil Painting Series
Floral 29 MIN
Morning Scene 29 MIN
Seascape 29 MIN
Still Life 29 MIN
Summer Landscape 29 MIN
Sunset 29 MIN
Dist - PBS

Magic of the Atom Series no 1
Atom Smashers 18 MIN
Dist - HANDEL

Magic of the atom series No 28
The Atomic fingerprint 13 MIN
Dist - HANDEL

Magic of the atom series No 29
Atomic power production 14 MIN
Dist - HANDEL

Magic of the Atom Series no 30
Radioisotope Scanning in Medicine 16 MIN
Dist - HANDEL

Magic of the atom series No 31
Atomic energy for space 17 MIN
Dist - HANDEL

Magic of the atom series No 32
The Atom - underground 20 MIN
Dist - HANDEL

Magic of the atom series No 33
The Atom and the environment 22 MIN
Dist - HANDEL

Magic of the atom series
The Atom and archaeology 25 MIN
The Atom in the hospital 21 MIN
Atom in the Hospital, the 21 MIN
The Riddle of Photosynthesis 15 MIN
Dist - HANDEL

The Magic of the Atom - the Riddle of Photosynthesis 15 MIN
16mm
Color (J)
Explains the role of photosynthesis in the production of food in nature. Details the complex sequence of chemical processes that occur and identifies some of the intermediary compounds formed by plants in the process of producing food stuffs.
Science - Physical
Dist - USERD **Prod** - ATOMEC

The Magic of the Bolshoi ballet 60 MIN
VHS
Color (G)
$29.95 purchase _ #1222
Presents a collection of historic performances by leading dancers of the Bolshoi Ballet Company. Features Maya Plisetskaya, Galina Ulanova, Vladimir Vasiliev, Natalia Bessmertnova, Ekaterina Maximova. Includes scenes from 'The Sleeping Beauty,' 'Romeo And Juliet,' 'Don Quixote,' 'Giselle' and 'Swan Lake.'.
Fine Arts; Foreign Language; Geography - World; Physical Education and Recreation
Dist - KULTUR

Magic of the Mind 29 MIN
U-matic
Everybody's Children Series
Color (PRO)
Compares creativity, wit, intuition and fantasy with the mental skills that the educational system has traditionally stressed.
Home Economics; Psychology; Sociology
Dist - TVOTAR **Prod** - TVOTAR 1985

Magic of the Mind 29 MIN
VHS / 16mm
Everybody's Children Series
(G)
$90.00 purchase _ #BPN16115
Compares creativity, wit, intuition, and fantasy with reason and logic. Discusses their place in the traditional educational system. Comprises part of a series which examines child raising in modern society.
Psychology; Sociology
Dist - RMIBHF **Prod** - RMIBHF

Magic of the Mountains 11 MIN
16mm
Color (I)
Studies the color and splendor investing the beautiful valley of Kashmir as spring gives place to summer and again as autumn lights up the valley in gorgeous tints of fascinating beauty which slowly fade out with the advent of winter.
Geography - World; History - World
Dist - NEDINF **Prod** - INDIA

The Magic of TV 12 MIN
VHS / U-matic
Getting the most out of TV series
Color (P I J)
$195.00, $245.00 purchase, $50.00 rental
Shows how technicians create special effects, dissolves and slow motion. Looks at distinguishing fantasy from reality. Part of a seven - part series.
Fine Arts; Industrial and Technical Education
Dist - NDIM **Prod** - YALEU 1981

The Magic of TV 12 MIN
16mm / U-matic / VHS
Getting the most Out of TV Series
Color (I J)
LC 81-700100
Shows how special effects and slow - motion photography are used to enhance television programming and explains the techniques behind various special effects. Helps children distinguish between fantasy and reality.
Fine Arts; Sociology
Dist - CORF **Prod** - TAPPRO 1981

The Magic of Venice
VHS
International travel films from Doug Jones series
Color (G H)
$19.95 purchase _ #IT12
Explores Venice.
Geography - World
Dist - SVIP

The Magic of Virginia 14 MIN
16mm
Color
LC FIA67-2146
Tells the importance of proper public relations training, particularly when attracting out - of - state visitors.
Geography - United States
Dist - VADE **Prod** - VADE 1966

The Magic of Walt Disney World 30 MIN
U-matic / VHS / 16mm
Color
LC 74-700278
Provides a tour of the unique vacation destination area of Disneyland. Shows the aesthetics which are achievable with careful and innovative community planning.
Geography - United States; Physical Education and Recreation; Social Science
Dist - CORF **Prod** - DISNEY 1973

The Magic of Walt Disney World 25 MIN
16mm
Color
Features a tour of Walt Disney World, a vacation kingdom of entertainment for the whole family.
Geography - United States; Physical Education and Recreation
Dist - FLADC **Prod** - FLADC

The Magic of Water 25 MIN
16mm
Color
LC 76-701466
Shows the techniques of irrigation.
Agriculture
Dist - CENTWO **Prod** - CENTWO 1975

The Magic orange 8 MIN
16mm
B&W (P I G)
$20.00 rental
Tells the story of a boy who steals an orange and explores London while under its magical influence. Stimulates discussion on values, morality, time, reality, imagination and dreams. Positive and negative imagery with some animation. Produced by R Raffaello Dvorak.
Fine Arts; Guidance and Counseling
Dist - CANCIN

Magic pages series

The Adventures of Egbert the Easter egg	15 MIN
The Aminal	14 MIN
Bears on Hemlock Mountain	15 MIN
Billy goat in the chili patch	15 MIN
The Book of giant stories	15 MIN
The Case of the hungry stranger	12 MIN
The Dragon in the clock box	15 MIN
The Duchess Bakes a Cake	15 MIN
The Eggs and three gold pieces	15 MIN
The Fish from Japan	14 MIN
The Five Chinese brothers	15 MIN
The Green Machine by Polly Cameron	15 MIN
Hansel and Gretel	
How Six found Christmas	15 MIN
Ira Sleeps Over	13 MIN
Jim and the Beanstalk	15 MIN
Messy Sally	13 MIN
My Father's Dragon and the Hundred Dresses	15 MIN
A Pair of Red Clogs	15 MIN
The Seamstress of Salzburg	15 MIN
A Selection of Fables	15 MIN
The Singing Trilogy	15 MIN
Sometimes It's Turkey, Sometimes It's Feathers	14 MIN
Sphero, the Reluctant Snowball	15 MIN
The Stone Soup	12 MIN
The Troll Music	15 MIN
You Look Ridiculous Said the Rhinocerus to the Hippopotamus	15 MIN

Dist - AITECH

The Magic Pipes 15 MIN
16mm
Color (P I) (GERMAN SPANISH)
LC 77-701813
Shows that the town of Kufstein, Austria, runs by the knowledge that every day its famous organ will play beautiful music. Tells that one day, however, something very mysterious and funny happens to the organ and the town.
Fine Arts; Foreign Language; Literature and Drama
Dist - SF **Prod** - DOKUMP 1977

The Magic Pony 80 MIN
16mm
Color (P I)
Fine Arts; Science - Natural
Dist - FI **Prod** - FI

The Magic Pony 11 MIN
16mm / U-matic / VHS
Favorite Fairy Tales and Fables Series
Color (P)
$280, $195 purchase _ #4148
Tells the story of a pony who helps a boy find magical objects and become king.
Literature and Drama
Dist - CORF

The Magic Pony - a Russian Fairy Tale 11 MIN
16mm / U-matic / VHS
Favorite Fairy Tales and Fables Series
Color (K P)
Presents the Russian fairy tale The Magic Pony. Shows how a strange looking pony uses his magic to help his young master, Ivan, find a marvelous sun bird and an enchanted ring for a cruel czar. Tells how the pony uses his magic again when the wicked ruler demands to be made young again and Ivan becomes ruler.
Literature and Drama
Dist - CORF **Prod** - CORF 1980

The Magic Pony Ride 23 MIN
U-matic / VHS / 16mm
Unicorn Tales Series
Color (P I)
LC 80-700549
Presents a contemporary story, based on the fairy tale The Ugly Duckling, about a lonely little girl and a weary pony who meet a magic man. Tells how he transforms the street into a technicolor playground and the pony into a unicorn which the little girl rides with joy.
Fine Arts; Literature and Drama
Dist - MGHT **Prod** - MGHT 1980

The Magic Powder Called Portland Cement 27 MIN
16mm
Color (IND)
LC 82-700032
A revised version of the motion picture From Mountains To Microns. Describes the cement hydration process and the production of Portland cement from raw materials to the finished product. Includes scenes from various cement plants which show the use of new technology to conserve fuel and control pollution and describes the work of the Portland Cement Association.
Industrial and Technical Education; Sociology
Dist - PRTLND **Prod** - PRTLND 1979

Magic Prison - a Dialogue Set to Music 36 MIN
U-matic / 16mm / VHS
Humanities - Poetry Series
Color (H C)
LC 74-702913
Presents a dramatized dialogue of letters between Emily Dickinson and a stranger, Colonel T W Higginson, revealing the unique qualities of mind and character of this American poet. Dramatizes some of the most moving moments in the poet's life.
Literature and Drama
Dist - EBEC **Prod** - EBEC 1969

Magic Ring I Series

Big, small, near and far	30 MIN
Color my rainbow	30 MIN
Everyone lives someplace special	30 MIN
Let's Pretend	30 MIN
Look at what I Can do	30 MIN
Mud, Sand, Clay and Cake	30 MIN
A New Baby	30 MIN
Our Hospital Friends	30 MIN
The Recipe Maker	30 MIN
A Sound Idea	30 MIN
A Visit with Winter	30 MIN
The Whatsit and the Zoo	30 MIN

Dist - ACCESS

Magic Ring II Series

Day camp	30 MIN
Everyone has a Body	30 MIN
Glimmer and glow	30 MIN
Imagine that	30 MIN
Let's Dance	30 MIN
Love that Pet	30 MIN
Nightlife	30 MIN
Sounds of Music	30 MIN
This Means that	30 MIN
Watchamacallit - the Mystery Machine	30 MIN
Wheels, Wings and Other Things	30 MIN
Who's in Our Family	30 MIN
The Wonderful World of Wet	30 MIN

Dist - ACCESS

Magic rites - Divination by animal tracks - Dogon 7 MIN
16mm
African village life - Mali series
Color (C)
Geography - World; Social Science; Sociology
Dist - IFF **Prod** - BRYAN 1967

Magic rites - Divination by chicken sacrifice - Dogon 7 MIN
16mm
African village life - Mali series
Color (C)
Geography - World; Social Science; Sociology
Dist - IFF **Prod** - BRYAN 1967

The Magic Rolling Board 15 MIN
16mm / U-matic / VHS
Color
LC 76-702844
Takes a look at the joys and pleasures of skateboarding.
Physical Education and Recreation
Dist - PFP **Prod** - MCGIF 1976

The Magic Scarab - Superstition 12 MIN
U-matic / VHS / 16mm
Forest Town Fables Series
Color (K P)
LC 74-700398
Uses a puppet story to explore the fallacy of belief in superstition, emphasizing self - reliance. Shows how Oni and the other puppets find out whether or not a good luck charm really works when Oni reluctantly enters the spelling contest without it.
Guidance and Counseling; Literature and Drama
Dist - CORF **Prod** - CORF 1974

The Magic school bus inside the Earth - 66
VHS
Reading rainbow series
Color; CC (K P)
$39.95 purchase
Follows a quirky teacher and her students on a field trip that they'll never forget in a story by Joanna Cole, illustrated by Bruce Degen. Follows LeVar on his own adventure when he visits California Caverns. Views stalgmites, stalactites and other crystal formations while LeVar experiences 'spelunking' with a real - life cave expert. Part of a series offering a multicultural approach to generating reading enthusiasm with cross - curricular applications, hosted by LeVar Burton.
English Language; Literature and Drama; Physical Education and Recreation; Science; Science - Physical
Dist - GPN **Prod** - LNMDP

The Magic Sense
U-matic / VHS
Body Human Series
Color
Explores the mystery and beauty of the body's living camera, the eye, showing how an image is formed and work of an eye surgeon including that of a cataract that must be shattered and clouded fluid removed to restore vision to a 30 - year - old, blind from diabetes, of spastic eye muscles that keep a thirteen - month - old boy with a giant retinal tear. Illustrates how a man, tragically blinded, overcame his blindness using remembered images to interpret information from his other senses.
Health and Safety; Industrial and Technical Education
Dist - MEDCOM **Prod** - MEDCOM

Magic Shapes 10 MIN
16mm
Color (K P I)
Reinforces the learning of basic shapes as readiness for reading, writing and mathematics. Includes the circle, square, triangle, rectangle, diamond and cross.
Mathematics
Dist - SF **Prod** - SF 1968

The Magic Shop 12 MIN
16mm / U-matic / VHS
Humanities - Short Story Classics Series
Color (J H)
LC 80-701812
Presents a story about a father who takes his son to the Genuine Magic Shop, where they encounter surprises and some unusual disappearances. Based on the short story The Magic Shop by H G Wells.
Fine Arts; Literature and Drama
Dist - EBEC **Prod** - EBEC 1980

The Magic Shop - in - Service 15 MIN
VHS / U-matic
Magic Shop Series
Color (T)
LC 83-706145
Presents an overview designed to acquaint teachers with the use of the 14 Magic Shop programs, which teach language arts concepts.
Education; English Language
Dist - GPN **Prod** - CVETVC 1982

Magic Shop Series no 10
Capital Idea 15 MIN
Dist - GPN

Magic Shop Series no 11
End it Right 15 MIN
Dist - GPN

Magic Shop Series no 12
Yours Truly 15 MIN
Dist - GPN

Magic Shop Series no 13
Quote, Unquote 15 MIN
Dist - GPN

Magic Shop Series no 2
Rhyming Words 15 MIN
Dist - GPN

Magic Shop Series no 4
One Plus One Equals New 15 MIN
Dist - GPN

Magic Shop Series no 6
Name it 15 MIN
Dist - GPN

Magic shop series no 7
Action words 15 MIN
Dist - GPN

Magic Shop Series no 8
Lost - Magician's Rabbit 15 MIN
Dist - GPN

Magic Shop Series no 9
The Opposite - same Machine 15 MIN
Dist - GPN

Magic Shop Series

The Land of Third	15 MIN
The Magic Shop - in - Service	15 MIN
Who, what, When, Where and Why	15 MIN

Dist - GPN

A Magic Show 30 MIN
16mm
Color (J H C G)
$450 purchase, $45 rental
Expresses the concerns of teachers, students, and administrators about communities trying to cut school expenses by cutting appropriations for the arts.
Education; Fine Arts
Dist - DHF **Prod** - DHF 1980

Magic Sneakers 8 MIN
U-matic / VHS / 16mm
Magic Moments, Unit 4 - Let's Pretend Series
Color (K P I)
LC 78-702914
Tells the story of a boy who finds a pair of magic sneakers and outwits an evil monster who wants to take the shoes away from him.
English Language
Dist - EBEC **Prod** - EBEC 1969

The Magic square 7 MIN
VHS
Children's encyclopedia of mathematics - meeting numbers series
Color (K P I)
$49.95 purchase _ #8348
Shows how to use addition and subtraction. Part of a six - part series on numbers.
Mathematics
Dist - AIMS **Prod** - DAVFMS 1991

The Magic Square 8 MIN
16mm
Mathematics for Elementary School Students - Whole Numbers Series
Color (P)
LC 73-701844
Mathematics
Dist - DAVFMS **Prod** - DAVFMS 1974

The Magic Stick 12 MIN
16mm
Color (K P I)
LC 71-700760
Dramatizes a story about a hedgehog who finds a stick, and a rabbit who believes it has magical powers.
Fine Arts; Literature and Drama
Dist - RADTV **Prod** - RADTV 1969

Magic tales 35 MIN
VHS
Storytellers collection series
Color (K P I)
$14.95 purchase _ #ATL423
Offers four tales of magic. Features four of the United States' most accomplished storytellers. Part of a four - part series.
Literature and Drama
Dist - KNOWUN

Magic - the Sleeveless way
VHS
Children's discovery series
Color (P I J)
$29.95 purchase _ #IV - 039
Features Sleeveless, the Magician, who shows how to turn simple household items such as cups, soda bottles, pencils, thread and crumpled paper into magic tricks.
Physical Education and Recreation
Dist - INCRSE **Prod** - INCRSE

The Magic thinking cap 30 MIN
VHS
Color (G P I)
$29.95 purchase _ #TJT100V-K
Presents a program designed to spark conversation between parents and children. Uses a storyline that parallels the tale of The Boy Who Cried Wolf to help parents consider angry feelings and children deal with peer pressure. Integrates video and real personal situations. Recommended for children of ages 7 to 12 and their parents.
Psychology; Sociology
Dist - CAMV

The Magic Touch 12 MIN
16mm
B&W (I)
Shows some of the exquisite arts and crafts India's artisans produce all over the country.
Fine Arts
Dist - NEDINF **Prod** - INDIA

The Magic Vine 15 MIN
U-matic / VHS
Stepping into Rhythm Series
Color (P)
Encourages children to respond to the parts of a song - words, rhythm and melody through body movement.
Fine Arts; Physical Education and Recreation
Dist - AITECH **Prod** - WVIZTV

The Magic Walking Stick 15 MIN
VHS
Gentle Giant Series
Color (K)
LC 90712405
Uses story to teach children universal truths. Second of 16 installments of The Gentle Giant Series featuring stories from cultures throughout the world.
Health and Safety; Literature and Drama; Psychology
Dist - GPN **Prod** - CTI 1988

The Magic Water 7 MIN
16mm / U-matic / VHS
Inuit Legends Series
Color (K P)
Tells how an Eskimo boy has learned to hunt and fish although blind. Cites how he catches fish to feed hungry baby seals leaving the mother seal to help him. Highlights how she visits the Queen of the Sea who rewards the youngster by restoring his sight.
Geography - United States; Geography - World; Physical Education and Recreation; Science - Natural; Sociology
Dist - BCNFL **Prod** - ANIMET 1982

A Magic Way of Going - the Thoroughbred 10562 50 MIN
16mm / U-matic / VHS
Color (I)
LC 84-706166
Analyzes the thoroughbred racehorse's ability to run using the comments of expert researchers, reproductions of art masterpieces and examinations of museum specimens.
Agriculture; Physical Education and Recreation
Dist - WOMBAT **Prod** - CANBC 1983

Magic Weapons for Healthy Teeth 15 MIN
U-matic / VHS / 16mm
Color (P I)
LC 79-700878
Presents a dentist who uses magic to teach facts about dental hygiene to a young boy. Explains how plaque builds up on teeth and the values and techniques of proper brushing and flossing.
Health and Safety; Home Economics
Dist - AIMS **Prod** - AIMS 1978

The Magic Well 14 MIN
16mm / U-matic / VHS
Color (P I)
LC 76-702366
Presents an adaptation of the Grimm brothers' fairytale entitled Frau Holle, in which two sisters journey to an enchanted land where kindness is rewarded by Mother Holle. Shows how the girls' journeys have very different results.
Guidance and Counseling; Literature and Drama
Dist - CORF **Prod** - CORF 1976

Magic Wheel 6 MIN
16mm
Color
Tells the story of Henry Joliff and the business machines he helped to make. Shows how these machines are made and used. Presents a trip to the famous school of business developed by the National Cash Register Company for the purpose of training its representatives.
Business and Economics; Psychology
Dist - CCNY **Prod** - NCR

Magic Words 10 MIN
U-matic / VHS / 16mm
Color (P I)
LC 71-713507
Humorously portrays the joys and sorrows of languages, the function of written words, and the quirks of rhyme, synonyms, and alliteration.
English Language; Literature and Drama
Dist - PHENIX **Prod** - KINGSP 1971

Magic Work - Shop of Reveron 23 MIN
VHS / U-matic
Color (SPANISH)
Shows the fantastic life of the Venezuelan painter Armando Reveron through his objects and dolls at his studio.
Fine Arts
Dist - MOMALA **Prod** - MOMALA

The Magic Workshop of Reveron 23 MIN
16mm
Color (J) (SPANISH)
LC 82-700847
Details the fantastic life of the Venezuelan painter Reveron through the objects and dolls at his studio.
Fine Arts; Foreign Language; History - World
Dist - MOMALA **Prod** - OOAS 1982

Magic World of Art, Part I 26 MIN
U-matic
Magic World of Art Series
Color (K P I)
Shows how to draw a basic face.
Fine Arts
Dist - CEPRO **Prod** - CEPRO

Magic World of Art, Part II 26 MIN
U-matic
Magic World of Art Series
Color (K P I)
Shows how to draw an angry, smiling and surprised face.
Fine Arts
Dist - CEPRO **Prod** - CEPRO

Magic World of Art, Part III 18 MIN
U-matic
Magic World of Art Series
Color (K P I)
Shows how to draw an old face, an infant's face and a cartoon face.
Fine Arts
Dist - CEPRO **Prod** - CEPRO

Magic World of Art Series
Magic World of Art, Part I 26 MIN
Magic World of Art, Part II 26 MIN
Magic World of Art, Part III 18 MIN
Dist - CEPRO

Magical Death 28 MIN
16mm
Yanomamo Series
Color (C)
LC 74-702978
Relates the religious activities of a political leader and shaman from a village in Venezuela to the political and social organization in a Yanomamo Indian group.
Geography - World; Religion and Philosophy; Sociology
Dist - DOCEDR **Prod** - PSU 1973

Magical Disappearing Money 11 MIN
U-matic / VHS / 16mm
Consumer Education Series
Color (J) (SPANISH)
LC 72-703429
Portrays a cheerful, slightly scatterbrained 'food expert witch' appearing in a supermarket and working her magic to draw the customers around her. Shows her explaining with accompanying magic why certain purchases of the customers are unwise. Pictures the wiser customers returning to their shopping.
Foreign Language; Home Economics
Dist - ALTSUL **Prod** - LEARN 1972

A Magical Field Trip to the Denver Mint 14 MIN
16mm / VHS
Color (P I)
$280.00, $335.00 purchase, $50.00 rental _ #8131
Teaches about the Denver mint and the money making process through a fantasy tale.
Business and Economics
Dist - AIMS **Prod** - FIETF 1989

A Magical Field Trip to the Dinosaur Museum 15 MIN
16mm / VHS
Color (P)
$295.00, $375.00 purchase, $50.00 rental _ #8176
Teaches about fossils and dinosaurs through a fantasy tale.
Fine Arts; Science - Natural; Science - Physical
Dist - AIMS **Prod** - FIETF 1990

A Magical field trip to the mapmaker 17 MIN
16mm / VHS
Color (P I)
$425.00, $295.00 purchase, $75.00 rental _ #8414
Uses the magic of Rosie O'Flanigan to take two children on a magical field trip to see how maps are made, what a surveyor does and the symbols and terms that are used on most maps.
Geography - World; Social Science
Dist - AIMS **Prod** - FIETF 1991

A Magical Field Trip to the Post Office 15 MIN
16mm / VHS
Color (P)
$295.00, $375.00 purchase, $50.00 rental _ #8175
Explains the necessity for stamps through a fantasy tale.
Business and Economics; Physical Education and Recreation
Dist - AIMS **Prod** - FIETF 1990

A Magical journey 90 MIN
BETA / VHS
Innerwork series
Color (G)
$49.95 purchase _ #W061
Contains three complete programs by Terence McKenna, founder of Botanical Dimensions. Includes 'Hallucinogens and Culture,' 'Time and the I Ching' and 'The Human Future,' which proposes four key elements of a responsible future - feminism, space exploration, cybernetics and hallucinogens.
Fine Arts; History - World; Psychology; Religion and Philosophy; Sociology
Dist - THINKA **Prod** - THINKA

Magical Malaysia 25 MIN
16mm / U-matic / VHS
Color (H C A)
Visits the verdant jungles, exotic creature and striking religious shrines of Malaysia together with the cities of Kuala Lampur and Penang. Shows traditional dances, shadow puppets, cottage industries and small - scale farms.
Geography - World
Dist - IFB **Prod** - POLNIS 1984

Magical Mother Nature - the four seasons 20 MIN
VHS
Color (P)
$89.00 purchase _ #RB845
Looks at the importance of changing seasons to the world. Considers the weather changes that occur with each season and how these changes affect animal, plant and human communities.
Science - Natural; Science - Physical
Dist - REVID **Prod** - REVID 1990

Magical Mystery Coat 13 MIN
16mm
B&W
LC 79-701177
Tells how a budding young composer is unable to write a song for the high school variety show because he lacks confidence in himself. Shows how the gift of Paul Mc Cartney's overcoat inspires him.
Fine Arts
Dist - KINGCH **Prod** - KINGCH 1979

Magical mystery tour 60 MIN
VHS
Color (G)
$29.95 purchase _ #S02008
Stars the Beatles in their third feature film, a bus tour that spoofs bus tours. Features several Beatles hits, including 'Magical Mystery Tour,' 'I Am The Walrus,' 'Fool On The Hill.'
Fine Arts
Dist - UILL

The Magician 13 MIN
U-matic / VHS / 16mm
B&W (I J H)
Presents an anti - war film in the form of allegory about a magician who attracts a group of children at the beach. Shows how he begins by amusing them with innocent tricks, then leads them in playing with toy guns and finally, has them playing with real guns.
Literature and Drama; Sociology
Dist - LUF **Prod** - LUF

The Magician 20 MIN
16mm
Magnificent 6 and 1/2 Series
Color (P I)
Tells the story of a magician who was invited to a surprise party by some children who experiment with the star performer's equipment.
Fine Arts; Literature and Drama
Dist - LUF **Prod** - CHILDF 1970

Magician 29 MIN
VHS / 16mm
Sonrisas Series
Color (T P) (ENGLISH AND SPANISH)
$46.00 rental _ #SRSS - 104
Teaches children to accept the handicapped. In Spanish and English.
Health and Safety; Sociology
Dist - PBS

The Magicians of basketball
Videodisc
Laser learning set 3 series; Set 3
Color; CAV (P I)
$375.00 purchase _ #8L5417
Tells the story of the Harlem Globetrotters and their sensational contribution to basketball. Part of a series of six theme - based interactive videodisc lessons. Requires a Pioneer LD - V2000 or 2200, with barcode reader and adapter, or a Pioneer LD - V4200 or higher. Includes user's guide, two readers.
Fine Arts; History - United States; Physical Education and Recreation
Dist - BARR **Prod** - BARR 1992

Magick lantern cycle 180 MIN
16mm
Color (G)
$300.00 rental
Features a collection of productions made between 1947 - 1980. Includes Fireworks; Puce Moment; Eaux D'Artifice; Inauguration of the Pleasure Dome; Scorpio Rising; Kustom Kar Kommandos; Invocation of my Demon Brother; Rabbit's Moon; and Lucifer Rising. Titles also available separately.
Fine Arts; Literature and Drama; Psychology; Religion and Philosophy
Dist - CANCIN **Prod** - ANGERK

Magna Carta, Pt 1, Rise of the English Monarchy 16 MIN
U-matic / VHS / 16mm
Color (J H C)
Traces the history of England from the Norman invasion in 1066 to the crowning of King John in 1199. Discusses the concept of feudalism and the conflict between the English kings and barons.
History - United States; History - World
Dist - EBEC **Prod** - EBEC 1959

Magna Carta, Pt 2, Revolt of the Nobles and the Signing of the Charter 16 MIN
U-matic / VHS / 16mm
Color (J H C)
Dramatizes the events after the crowning of King John which brought the conflict between kings and barons to a climax, leading to the drafting of the Magna Carta.
History - United States; History - World
Dist - EBEC **Prod** - EBEC 1959

The Magnasync Story 8 MIN
16mm
Color (J)
Discusses magnasync motion picture sound recording equipment which is available to film producers.
Fine Arts
Dist - RVIERA **Prod** - MAGSYN 1959

Magnesium Oxide - Sulfur Dioxide Recovery Process 12 MIN
16mm
Color
LC 78-701895
Describes the magnesium oxide - sulfur dioxide recovery process used in two power stations. Provides an overview of the sulfur dioxide control problem, discusses possible solutions and examines the chemistry and equipment involved in the process.
Business and Economics; Science - Natural; Sociology
Dist - USNAC **Prod** - USEPA 1978

The Magnet as a Compass Needle 12 MIN
U-matic / VHS
Introductory Concepts in Physics - Magnets Series
Color (C)
$229.00, $129.00 purchase _ #AD - 1174
Shows how to make and use a compass needle and demonstrates a ship's compass.
Science - Physical
Dist - FOTH **Prod** - FOTH

Magnet Earth 50 MIN
16mm / U-matic / VHS
Color (H C A)
Explores current research into the earth's magnetic field and examines the effects it has on living organisms.
Science; Science - Physical
Dist - FI **Prod** - BBCTV 1982

A Magnet Laboratory 20 MIN
16mm
PSSC Physics Films Series
B&W (H C)
Shows equipment used in producing strong magnetic fields. Demonstrates magnetic effects of currents and the magnetism of iron.
Science - Physical
Dist - MLA **Prod** - PSSC 1960

Magnetic Amplifiers 39 MIN
16mm
Color
LC 76-701535
Discusses the use and advantages of magnetic amplifiers in controlling electric power. Uses schematics and graphs of the ideal hysteresis loop to illustrate the theory behind the operation and construction of saturable reactors and self - saturating reactors.
Industrial and Technical Education
Dist - USNAC **Prod** - USAF 1963

Magnetic Bubble Memories - MBM 30 MIN
VHS / U-matic
Microcomputer Memory Design Series
Color (IND)
Shows magnetic bubble memory (MBM) features, MBM technology and device organization, operation of an MBM system, inter - facing MBM with microprocessors and design examples.
Industrial and Technical Education; Mathematics; Sociology
Dist - COLOSU **Prod** - COLOSU

Magnetic Confinement 24 MIN
U-matic / VHS
Discovering Physics Series
Color (H C)
Explores plasma which can be contained and controlled by magnetic force fields at very hot temperatures. Shows how collisions of plasma molecules cause fusion. Uses models, demonstrations, and animation to illustrate behavior of charge particles in various magnetic field geometrics.
Science; Science - Physical
Dist - MEDIA **Prod** - BBCTV 1983

Magnetic Cores, Pt 1 - Properties 29 MIN
16mm
B&W
LC 74-705060
Depicts properties of magnetic cores and their application in data processing systems. Shows how information is stored and transferred from one core to another.
Industrial and Technical Education; Mathematics; Science - Physical
Dist - USNAC **Prod** - USA 1962

Magnetic Cores, Pt 2 - Basic Circuits 30 MIN
16mm
B&W
LC 74-705061
Describes the features and functions of single - diode, split - winding and inhibit transfer loops. Shows the application of these loops singly or in combination.
Industrial and Technical Education
Dist - USNAC **Prod** - USA 1962

Magnetic Disc Interfacing, Pt 1 48 MIN
U-matic / VHS
Microprocessor Interfacing Series
Color
Industrial and Technical Education; Mathematics
Dist - MIOT **Prod** - MIOT

Magnetic Disk Interfacing, Pt 2 44 MIN
U-matic / VHS
Microprocessor Interfacing Series
Color
Industrial and Technical Education; Mathematics
Dist - MIOT **Prod** - MIOT

Magnetic Effects in Space 14 MIN
16mm
Skylab Science Demonstrations Series
Color
LC 76-703698
Illustrates basic principles of science by utilizing film footage from Skylab in - flight science demonstrations. Discusses experiments in which magnetic effects in space are shown from Skylab television transmission and demonstration equipment.
Industrial and Technical Education; Science; Science - Physical
Dist - USNAC **Prod** - NASA 1975

Magnetic, Electric and Gravitational Fields 11 MIN
U-matic / VHS / 16mm
B&W (I J) (SPANISH)
Through demonstrations and drawings, shows characteristics of magnetic, electric and gravitational fields. Defines field as an area in which a force can be felt. Shows how the earth's gravitational field affects objects on the earth.
Science - Physical
Dist - EBEC **Prod** - EBEC 1962

The Magnetic field - Part 4 18 MIN
VHS
Magnets series
Color; PAL (P I J)
Illustrates the magnetic field through observation of the attraction of iron filings by a magnet. Demonstrates that the field exists in three - dimensional space. Part four of a five - part series on magnets.
Science - Physical
Dist - VIEWTH **Prod** - VIEWTH

The Magnetic field - vector fields and hydrodynamics - Parts 35 and 36 60 MIN
U-matic / VHS
Mechanical universe and beyond - Part II series
Color (G)
$45.00, $29.95 purchase
Looks at the law of Biot and Sarvart, the force between electric currents and Ampere's law in Part 35. Reveals that force fields have definite properties of their own suitable for scientific study in Part 36. Parts of a 52 - part series on the mechanics of the universe.
Science; Science - Physical
Dist - ANNCPB **Prod** - SCCON 1985

Magnetic Fields 15 MIN
U-matic / VHS
Experiment - Physics Level 1 Series
Color (C)
$249.00, $149.00 purchase _ #AD - 1965
Demonstrates some of the phenomena associated with magnetic fields. Includes induction, the Hall effect and eddy currents. Part of a series of videos demonstrating physics experiments which are too impractical to perform in a classroom laboratory.
Education; Psychology; Science - Physical
Dist - FOTH **Prod** - FOTH

Magnetic Fields 18 MIN
U-matic / VHS
Introductory Concepts in Physics - Magnets Series
Color (C)
$229.00, $129.00 purchase _ #AD - 1173
Demonstrates the magnetic force field space around magnets through the collection of iron filings with a magnet.
Science - Physical
Dist - FOTH **Prod** - FOTH

Magnetic Fields and Electric Currents, Pt 1 14 MIN
U-matic / VHS / 16mm
Color (I J H)
LC 73-700193
Explores the magnetic properties associated with a wire carrying a direct electric current. Uses models to demonstrate the existence of a magnetic field in the vicinity of a current - carrying conductor. Establishes properties of the magnetic field, such as direction and strength by experimentation.
Science; Science - Physical
Dist - PHENIX **Prod** - PHENIX 1972

Magnetic Fields and Electric Currents, Pt 2 13 MIN
U-matic / VHS / 16mm
Color
LC 74-700074
Investigates what happens when magnetic fields interact. Studies the effect by observing the magnetic fields of permanent magnets which are attracting and repelling other magnets. Shows that similar effects occur when the interacting fields are produced by electric currents. Uses the principles demonstrated to explain the operation of a simple electric motor.
Science - Physical
Dist - PHENIX **Prod** - PHENIX 1973

Magnetic Force 9 MIN
U-matic / VHS
Introductory Concepts in Physics - Magnets Series
Color (C)
$229.00, $129.00 purchase _ #AD - 1171
Demonstrates that magnets have different shapes and exert different levels of magnetic force.
Science - Physical
Dist - FOTH **Prod** - FOTH

Magnetic Highway 28 MIN
16mm
Color
Demonstrates the sophistication reached by modern motor carrier operations, looks at career opportunities available in the trucking industry, and provides a view of electronic communications and motor freight management.
Guidance and Counseling; Social Science
Dist - MTP **Prod** - ATA

Magnetic Levitation 20 MIN
U-matic
Breakthrough Series
Color (H C)
Looks at a possible new high speed transportation system using linear induction and linear synchronous motors which would produce, in effect, a flying train.
Science; Social Science
Dist - TVOTAR **Prod** - TVOTAR 1985

Magnetic Memory 25 MIN
16mm
Color
Explains how magnetic tape has added a new dimension to the memory of man. Outlines many uses of magnetic tape, describes the manufacturing process and discusses the controls exercised to produce tape.
Business and Economics; Education
Dist - MMAMC **Prod** - MMAMC 1961

Magnetic North 27 MIN
U-matic / VHS / 16mm
Victory at Sea Series
B&W (J H)
Documents World War II battles in the Polar region from Murmansk to Alaska.
Civics and Political Systems; History - United States; History - World
Dist - LUF **Prod** - NBCTV

Magnetic Particle and Radiographic Inspection 65 MIN
BETA / VHS / U-matic
Color
$400.00 purchase
Contains two tapes.
Guidance and Counseling; Industrial and Technical Education; Psychology
Dist - ASM **Prod** - ASM

Magnetic Particle Testing 55 MIN
BETA / VHS / U-matic
Color
$400.00 purchase
Gives history and development of magnetic particle testing.
Science; Science - Physical
Dist - ASM **Prod** - ASM

Magnetic Tape Interfacing, Pt 1 45 MIN
VHS / U-matic
Microprocessor Interfacing Series
Color
Industrial and Technical Education; Mathematics
Dist - MIOT **Prod** - MIOT

Magnetic Tape Interfacing, Pt 2 45 MIN
U-matic / VHS
Microprocessor Interfacing Series
Color
Industrial and Technical Education; Mathematics
Dist - MIOT **Prod** - MIOT

Magnetism 68 MIN
16mm / U-matic / VHS
B&W
Discusses aspects of magnetism.
Science - Physical
Dist - USNAC **Prod** - USAF

Magnetism 7 MIN
U-matic / VHS / 16mm
Basic Electricity Series
Color (H C A)
Describes the uses of magnetism; the kinds of magnets; the magnetic field; lines of force; polarity; the concentration of lines of force at the poles; induced magnetism; temporary and permanent magnets; polar attraction and repulsion.
Science - Physical
Dist - IFB **Prod** - STFD 1979

Magnetism 21 MIN
U-matic / VHS / 16mm
B&W
LC 79-707509
Discusses aspects of magnetism.
Science - Physical
Dist - USNAC **Prod** - USAF 1979

Magnetism 13 MIN
16mm
Electricity Series
Color (J H A)
Magnetism - - North and South poles, magnetic fields and lines of force, the compass, electrons and magnetic field, electromagents and solenoids.
Science - Physical
Dist - SF **Prod** - MORLAT 1967

Magnetism 10 MIN
VHS
Junior electrician series
CC; Color (P I)
$55.00 purchase _ #1333VG
Explains magnets and the relationship between magnetism and electricity. Demonstrates the workings of magnets. Comes with a teacher's guide and blackline masters. Part two of a four - part series.
Science - Physical
Dist - UNL

Magnetism and beyonds - Quad VI 60 MIN
VHS
Mechanical universe - high school adaptation series
Color (H)
$75.00 purchase _ #MU - Q6
Presents four programs on physics. Includes - Magnetic Fields - examines the contributions of Gibert, Oersted and Ampere to explain the interaction between magnetic field and a moving charge; Electromagnetic Induction - explains Faraday's law which related induced electric fields and changing magnetic flux; Alternating Current - introduces alternating current and the development of the rationale of using it for electric power transmission, including the history of the transformer and the contributions of Thomas Edison and Nikola Tesla; The Michelson - Morley Experiment - describes how two American scientists, Michelson and Morley, performed their experiment to detect ether and the implication of their results.
Science - Physical
Dist - INSTRU

Magnetism and electricity 60 MIN
VHS / U-matic
Electrical maintenance training series; Module A - AC and DC theory
Color (IND)
Industrial and Technical Education
Dist - LEIKID **Prod** - LEIKID

Magnetism and Electricity 15 MIN
U-matic / VHS
Matter and Motion Series
Color (I)
Considers the relationship between magnets and electricity.
Science - Physical
Dist - AITECH **Prod** - WHROTV 1973

Magnetism and electromagnetic and magnetic induction - 33 41 MIN
VHS
Conceptual physics alive series
Color (H C)
$45.00 purchase
Examines electromagnets, motors, generators, and magnetic levitation, using many examples and demonstrations. Part 33 of a 35 - part series adapted from the college and high school textbook Conceptual Physics by Professor Paul Hewitt.
Science - Physical
Dist - MMENTE **Prod** - HEWITP 1992

Magnetism and Fields of Force 13.5 MIN
16mm / VHS / U-matic
Physical Science Learning Lab Series
Color (I J P)
$305.00, $215.00, $245.00 purchase _ #A300; LC 81-700084
Investigates a variety of substances, including the Earth itself, to find which ones may have magnetic properties.
Science - Physical
Dist - BARR **Prod** - BARR 1981

Magnetism at Work 12 MIN
16mm
Color (J H C)
LC 75-707624
Provides a brief history of magnetism, from discovery through compasses, magnetic fields, and electromagnetics. Demonstrates important points by actual laboratory experiments. Explains what magnetism is, covering diamagnetism, paramagnetism, ferromagnetism and domains. Presents a series of modern applications, including a simplified demonstration of one of magnetism's roles in medicine.
Science - Physical
Dist - GE **Prod** - GE 1970

Magnetism in Space 19 MIN
16mm
Skylab Science Demonstrations Series
Color (H A)
LC 76-703699
Describes basics of magnetism through demonstrations on Earth and in space on board Skylab. Reviews familiar magnetic effects and applications of magnets on Earth and shows how these effects are observable in space in new and different ways.
Science - Physical
Dist - USNAC **Prod** - NASA 1975

Magnetism - Magnetic Field, Pt 1 3 MIN
16mm
B&W ((DANISH SUBTITLES))
Shows that in a magnet the molecules lie in a certain order, whereas in a piece of iron they lie in a disorderly way, but will become ordered if a magnet is brought near to the iron. Includes Danish subtitles.
Foreign Language; Science - Physical
Dist - STATNS **Prod** - STATNS 1950

Magnetism - Magnetic Field, Pt 2 3 MIN
16mm
B&W ((DANISH SUBTITLES))
Shows the movements of free electrons in a magnetic field. Includes Danish subtitles.
Foreign Language; Science - Physical
Dist - STATNS **Prod** - STATNS 1950

Magnetism - no 5 60 MIN
U-matic
AC/DC Electronics Series
Color (PRO)
One of a series of electronic and electrical training sessions for electronics workers on direct and alternating current and how to work with each.
Industrial and Technical Education; Science - Physical
Dist - VTRI **Prod** - VTRI 1986

Magnetism of Place 30 MIN
U-matic
Visions - Artists and the Creative Process Series
Color (H C A)
Shows how Newfoundland artists are inspired by the sea.
Fine Arts; History - World
Dist - TVOTAR **Prod** - TVOTAR 1983

Magnetism, Pt 1 34 MIN
U-matic
B&W
LC 79-707509
Defines magnets, discusses their characteristics, and explains the theory of molecular arrangement in a magnet.
Science - Physical
Dist - USNAC **Prod** - USAF 1979

Magnetism - Pt 1; 2nd ed. 15 MIN
U-matic
Search for science series; Unit V - Electricity
Color (I)
Presents an explanation of the nature of magnetism.
Science - Physical
Dist - GPN **Prod** - WVIZTV

Magnetism, Pt 2 34 MIN
U-matic
B&W
LC 79-707509
Discusses terms such as permeability and flux. Explains the characteristics of temporary and permanent magnets. Concludes with a presentation of the basic shapes in which magnets are found.

Science - Physical
Dist - USNAC **Prod** - USAF 1979

Magnetism - Pt 2; 2nd ed. 15 MIN
U-matic
Search for science series; Unit V - Electricity
Color (I)
Shows how man's knowledge of magnetism allowed him to produce an electric motor.
Science - Physical
Dist - GPN **Prod** - WVIZTV

Magnetism, Pt a 34 MIN
16mm
B&W
LC 74-705062
Defines magnets and explains the difference between natural and artificial magnets. Discusses the characteristics of magnetic lines of force about a magnet and the laws of repulsion and attraction. Explains the theory of molecular arrangement in a magnet. (Kinescope).
Science - Physical
Dist - USNAC **Prod** - USAF

Magnetism, Pt B 34 MIN
16mm
B&W
LC 74-705063
Discusses magnetic terms - permeability, retentivity, flux, reluctance, residual magnetism and magnetic shielding. Explains the characteristics of temporary and permanent magnets, concluding with a presentation of the basic shapes in which magnets are generally found. (Kinescope).
Science - Physical
Dist - USNAC **Prod** - USAF

Magneto Ignition 6 MIN
U-matic / VHS / 16mm
Power Mechanics Series
Color (J)
LC 73-703244
Presents basic information about the theory, maintenance, and tune - up of a magneto ignition.
Industrial and Technical Education
Dist - CAROUF **Prod** - THIOKL 1969

Magnetochemistry 20 MIN
U-matic / VHS
Experiment - Chemistry Series
Color (C)
$249.00, $149.00 purchase _ #AD - 1071
Examines the electron configuration and oxidation state of the metal ion in a compound by measuring the change in weight of a sample of the compound in a magnetic field gradient. Part of a series on experiments in chemistry.
Education; Psychology; Science; Science - Physical
Dist - FOTH **Prod** - FOTH

Magnetron 40 MIN
16mm
B&W
LC 74-705064
Explains basically, how the traveling wave magnetron operates. Discusses the filters that exist in the magnetron and their effects on electron motion. Reviews the basic requirements of an oscillator and shows how the magnatron meets these requirements. Points out factors that determine power and frequency and emphasizes the effects of varying magnetic fields.
Industrial and Technical Education; Science - Physical
Dist - USNAC **Prod** - USAF

Magnetron Sputtering 35 MIN
U-matic / VHS
Plasma Sputtering, Deposition and Growth of Microelectronic Films 'for VLSI Series
Color (IND)
Compares normal discharge and magnetron - enhanced sputtering in terms of deposition rate, film adhesion, stress and step coverage.
Industrial and Technical Education; Science - Physical
Dist - COLOSU **Prod** - COLOSU

Magnets 15 MIN
U-matic
Science Alliance Series
Color (I)
Shows how to make a magnet and an electromagnet and demonstrates the laws of magnetism.
Science; Science - Physical
Dist - TVOTAR **Prod** - TVOTAR 1981

Magnets 10 MIN
VHS
Take a look 2 series
Color (P)
$49.00 purchase, $15.00 rental _ #353808; LC 91-708020
Explores basic principles of magnetism by testing a variety of materials to discover whether or not they are magnetic. Part of a series that takes a hands - on approach to the principles of science.
Psychology; Science; Science - Physical
Dist - TVOTAR **Prod** - TVOTAR 1990

Magnets 12 MIN
U-matic / 16mm / VHS
Matter and energy for beginners series
Color (P)
$400.00, $250.00 purchase _ #HP - 5949C
Uses animation and live action to teach physical science. Stars Investigator Alligator and his friend Mr E, who investigate the properties of magnets. Part of a six - part series.
Science - Physical
Dist - CORF **Prod** - CORF 1990

Magnets and their Uses 10 MIN
U-matic / VHS / 16mm
Color; B&W (P I)
LC 76-703366
Uses animation to illustrate the characteristics and properties of magnets. Demonstrates that a magnet has two poles and shows every - day use of magnets.
Science - Physical
Dist - PHENIX **Prod** - KAHANA 1964

Magnets for Beginners 11 MIN
U-matic / VHS / 16mm
Color (P)
$265.00, $195.00 purchase _ #1660; LC FIA65-1906
Shows what materials magnets attract, what a magnetic field is, what poles are and how magnetic force can pass through objects. Uses iron filings suspended in glycerin to show magnetic field in three dimensions.
Science - Physical
Dist - CORF **Prod** - CORF 1965

Magnets, Magnetism and Electricity 9 MIN
16mm / U-matic / VHS
Color (P I J)
LC 71-705148
Describes the major characteristics of magnets and shows how compasses and magnets are used to detect a magnetic field. Includes an animated sequence to show the relation of the electron spin in atoms in a magnet to the electron flow in a current of electricity.
Science - Physical
Dist - MGHT **Prod** - MGHT 1970

Magnets, Magnets 13 MIN
VHS / 16mm / U-matic
Color (K P)
$295.00, $205.00, $235.00 purchase _ #A446
Gives youngsters a basic introduction to magnets, explaining many facts about them. Demonstrates what magnets do - lift metal objects, pull bits of iron out of sand, magically float in a tube, or even lift huge chunks of iron.
Science - Physical
Dist - BARR **Prod** - BARR 1986

Magnets - magnets 13 MIN
U-matic / 16mm / VHS
Color; Captioned (K P)
$295.00, $235.00, $205.00 purchase _ #A446
Gives youngsters a basic introduction to magnets.
Science - Physical
Dist - BARR **Prod** - GREATT 1986

Magnets series
The Compass - Part 5 13 MIN
The Law of magnets - Part 3 10 MIN
The Magnetic field - Part 4 18 MIN
The Power of a magnet - Pt 2 9 MIN
What a magnet does - Part 1 10 MIN
Dist - VIEWTH

Magnets - the Dragon's Secret 15 MIN
16mm / U-matic / VHS
Color (K P)
LC 82-700082
Uses the story of a knight in clanking armor to demonstrate what magnets are, how they work and their many uses.
Literature and Drama; Science - Physical
Dist - EBEC **Prod** - EBEC 1981

Magnificat 50 MIN
16mm / VHS
(J A)
$75.00 rental
Presents a tradional version of Bach's Magnificat in D, crosscut with a jazz version. Available on two reels for schools.
Fine Arts
Dist - BULFRG

Magnificat 50 MIN
16mm / U-matic / VHS
Color; Stereo (J)
$750.00, $275.00 purchase, $75.00 rental
Documents a perfomance of Bach's Magnificat by Tafelmusik and the Tudor Singers juxtaposed with a jazz version by Bobby McFerrin, Ann Mortifee and the New Swingle Singers.
Fine Arts
Dist - BULFRG **Prod** - RHOMBS 1989

Magnificat for Solo, Chorus and Orchestra , BWV 243 34 MIN
U-matic / VHS
Color (C)
$229.00, $129.00 purchase _ #AD - 995
Presents the Magnificat for Solo, Chorus and Orchestra, BWV 243, by Johann Sebastian Bach, performed at the 800 - year - old church of St Nicholas in Leipzig. Features Heidi Riess, Peter Schreier, Gothart Stier and the New Bach Collegium Maximum in performance.
Fine Arts; History - World
Dist - FOTH **Prod** - FOTH

Magnificence in Trust 28 MIN
U-matic / VHS / 16mm
Color
Shows Glacier Bay National Monument, Katmai National Monument and Mount McKinley in Alaska.
Geography - United States; History - United States
Dist - USNAC **Prod** - USNPS

The Magnificent Adventure 80 MIN
16mm
B&W (J)
Witnesses an adventure from the book of Acts and the life of St Paul. Includes the stoning of Stephen, the vision of St Paul on the Damascus Road, his missionary journeys and other significant events.
Religion and Philosophy
Dist - CAFM **Prod** - CAFM

The Magnificent Adventure - the Life of the Apostle Paul 80 MIN
VHS / BETA
B&W
Covers the life of the Apostle Paul.
Religion and Philosophy
Dist - DSP **Prod** - DSP

The Magnificent Ambersons
VHS / BETA
B&W
Presents a story about Victorian America based on Booth Tarkington's novel THE MAGNIFICENT AMBERSONS, directed by Orson Welles.
History - United States; Literature and Drama
Dist - GA **Prod** - GA

The Magnificent Beginning 52 MIN
U-matic / VHS / 16mm
Magic of Dance Series
Color (J)
Describes the first real ballet school, founded by King Louis XIV of France. Tells how the courtly dances of 17th century France eventually led to the worldwide phenomenon of ballet.
Fine Arts
Dist - TIMLIF **Prod** - BBCTV 1980

Magnificent Canada Goose 11 MIN
16mm / U-matic / VHS
Color (I)
Follows the Canada goose from its migration north through the breeding season to the gathering of the flocks for the migration south. Shows wild life refuges and the work of the U S Fish and Wild Life Service and state conservation departments.
Geography - World; Science - Natural
Dist - IFB **Prod** - IFB 1954

A Magnificent Century 29 MIN
16mm
Industrial Revolution Series
Color
Deals with the consequences of the industrial revolution for the people who went through it.
History - United States; History - World
Dist - MTP **Prod** - LIBFUN

The Magnificent Ditch 28 MIN
16mm
Color
LC FIA66-742
Dramatizes an old muleskinner describing life on the Chesapeake and Ohio Canal at the turn of the twentieth century. Includes scenes of the Potomac Valley, Harper's Ferry, Salty Dog Tavern, Paw Paw Tunnel and the Canal Museum at Great Falls.
History - United States
Dist - WMALTV **Prod** - WMALTV 1966

Magnificent Gift 64 MIN
16mm
Color (G)
#3X48 I
Gives an overview of the fur trade industry and its role in openning western Canada for settlement.
History - World; Physical Education and Recreation
Dist - CDIAND **Prod** - CANBC 1978

Magnificent Heritage 55 MIN
16mm
Color (J)

LC FIA65-831
Dramatizes John Leland's role in the struggle for religious liberty in America.
History - United States; Religion and Philosophy
Dist - BROADM **Prod** - BROADM 1964

The Magnificent Major 23 MIN
U-matic / VHS / 16mm
Unicorn Tales Series
Color (P I)
LC 80-700545
Presents a contemporary story, based on the children's book The Wizard Of Oz, about a little girl who hates to read, is transported to a society of non - readers and suddenly finds herself on trial for having a book. Shows how when she is forced to defend herself she reads aloud, enchanting both the court and herself, and returns with a different outlook on reading.
Fine Arts; Literature and Drama
Dist - MGHT **Prod** - MGHT 1980

The Magnificent Matador 94 MIN
16mm / U-matic / VHS
Color (C A)
Stars Anthony Quinn and Maureen O'Hara in a portrayal of the beauty, grace and daring of the dangerous sport of bullfighting.
Geography - World; Physical Education and Recreation
Dist - FI **Prod** - TWCF 1955

Magnificent Micronesia
VHS
Color (G)
$14.90 purchase _ #0607
Visits Micronesia. Explores Palau, Truk, Lagoon and Ponape. Includes underwater photography.
Geography - World; Industrial and Technical Education
Dist - SEVVID

The Magnificent Moose 16 MIN
16mm / U-matic / VHS
North American Species Series
Color (P I J)
Follows the events of a moose year, from the birth of calves, the attack of a predatory wolf pack, the training of young to feed and swim, the growing of antlers, to the climactic autumn encounters between male bulls.
Science - Natural
Dist - BCNFL **Prod** - KARVF 1984

Magnificent obsession - the life of Edward Teller 28 MIN
VHS
Eminent scientist series
Color (J H)
$60.00 purchase _ #A2VH 1012
Features nuclear physicist Edward Teller. Part of a series on scientists which discusses their childhood, educational backgrounds, decisions affecting their careers and illustrious achievements.
Science; Science - Physical; Sociology
Dist - CLRVUE **Prod** - CLRVUE

Magnificent recipes for brunch
VHS
Video cooking library series
Color (J H G)
$19.95 purchase _ #KVC923V
Illustrates the preparation of brunch through step - by - step demonstrations. Covers everything needed from ingredients to equipment, with clear explanations of cooking techniques. Includes recipes. Part of a 22 - part series.
Home Economics
Dist - CAMV

Magnificent 6 and 1/2 Series

The Astronoughts	21 MIN
Billy the Kid	18 MIN
Bob a job	16 MIN
Five survive	15 MIN
Ghosts and Ghoulies	21 MIN
A Good deed in time	18 MIN
It's not Cricket	16 MIN
Kontiki Kids	17 MIN
A Lad in the Lamp	16 MIN
The Magician	20 MIN
Peewee Had a Little Ape	20 MIN
Peewee's Pianola	16 MIN
The Ski Wheelers	14 MIN
That's all We Need	16 MIN
Up for the cup	15 MIN
Up the creek	14 MIN
When Knights were Bold	17 MIN

Dist - LUF

Magnifying glass 10 MIN
VHS / U-matic / 16mm
Primary science series
Color (P I)
LC 91-705335
Explains the magnifying glass, a basic tool of science. Describes microscopes and other lenses. Includes two teacher's guides. Part of a series on primary science produced by Fred Ladd.
Science; Science - Natural; Science - Physical
Dist - BARR

Magnifying glass - 7 10 MIN
U-matic / 16mm / VHS
Primary science series
Color (K P I)
$265.00, $215.00, $185.00 purchase _ #B588
Explains what a magnifying glass does and how it works. Shows how a microscope uses magnifying lenses to help see things that are too small for the unaided eye to see. Part of an 11 - part series on primary science.
Business and Economics; Science - Physical
Dist - BARR **Prod** - GREATT 1990

Magnolia Gardens - Charleston 30 MIN
BETA / VHS
Victory Garden Series
Color
Presents the Magnolia Gardens in Charleston.
Agriculture; Physical Education and Recreation
Dist - CORF **Prod** - WGBHTV

Magnum eye series
Features a series of 10 minute films by photographers from the Magnum Photo Agency. Exemplifies the goals of Magnum, founded in 1947 by Robert Capa and Henri Cartier - Bresson, which aim to give the world images capturing the poignancy of the human experience, from John Kennedy to the student who defied a tank at Tiananmen Square. Includes 17 titles - Croatia in Crisis; Getting Out; Jab Jab; Cocaine True, Cocaine Blue; El Otro Lado - The Other Side; Gospel and Blues, A Spell in the Mississippi Delta; Joey Goes to Wigstock; Letting Go; On the US Nuclear Highway; The People Next Door; The Russian Prison, A Separate Life; Living with the Dead; Opening Hearts; A Peruvian Equation; Scared Again - Jews in Berlin; Sidewalk Santas; and Waiting for Madonna.

Cocaine true, cocaine blue	10 MIN
Croatia in crisis	10 MIN
Getting out	10 MIN
Gospel and blues - a spell in the Mississippi Delta	10 MIN
Jab jab	10 MIN
Joey goes to Wigstock	10 MIN
Letting go	10 MIN
Living with the dead	10 MIN
The Magnum eye series	170 MIN
On the US nuclear highway	10 MIN
Opening hearts	10 MIN
The People next door	10 MIN
A Peruvian equation	10 MIN
The Russian prison - A separate life	10 MIN
Sacred again - Jews in Berlin	10 MIN
Sidewalk Santas	10 MIN
Waiting for Madonna	10 MIN

Dist - FIRS **Prod** - MIYAKE

Magoo's Puddle Jumper 7 MIN
U-matic / VHS / 16mm
Mister Magoo Series
Color (K P I J)
LC 79-700042
A reissue of the 1956 motion picture Magoo's Puddle Jumper. Shows how Mr Magoo accidentally drives his new automobile under water. Shows that Mr Magoo fails to realize that he is surrounded by marine life.
Fine Arts; Literature and Drama
Dist - CF **Prod** - BOSUST 1978

Magpie Lays an Egg 17 MIN
16mm
Color (P I)
Relates what happens when the circus comes to town and the star penguin disappears. Tells what occurs when the Chiffy kids and one goose egg enter the picture.
Literature and Drama; Science - Natural
Dist - LUF **Prod** - LUF 1979

Magpie's Talking Duck 17 MIN
16mm
Color (P I)
Covers what happens when the Chiffy Kids enter a duck in a pet show and convince the judges that it can really talk.
Literature and Drama; Science - Natural
Dist - LUF **Prod** - LUF 1979

Magritte 14 MIN
16mm
Color
Presents an interview with painter Rene Magritte as he discusses his rarely seen modern works and the values of modern art.
Fine Arts
Dist - GROVE **Prod** - GROVE

Magritte - the False Mirror 22 MIN
U-matic / VHS / 16mm
Color (J A)
LC 71-712010
Discusses the Belgian painter, Rene Magritte, using an assemblage of the painter's images. The spoken commentary is confined to a few of Magritte's own statements about his intentions and an occasional pertinent anecdote from his close friends, Mesens and Scutenaire.
Fine Arts
Dist - FI **Prod** - FI 1971

Maguindanao Kulintang Ensembles from Mindanao, the Philippines 16 MIN
16mm
Ethnic Music and Dance Series
Color (J)
LC 72-700256
Explains that the Maguindanao people of Mindanao, the Philippines, have a complex and highly developed style of gong music. Describes the main instrument, the kulintang, and shows other types of large hanging gongs and drums.
Fine Arts; Geography - World
Dist - UWASHP **Prod** - UWASH 1971

The Mahabharata 318 MIN
VHS
Color (G C H)
$149.00 purchase _ #DL273
Stages the saga of the war between two feuding clans in ancient India. Directed by Peter Brook.
Fine Arts; History - World
Dist - INSIM

Mahalia Jackson 34 MIN
U-matic / VHS / 16mm
Color (J)
LC 81-700919
Documents the life of American gospel singer Mahalia Jackson. Includes footage of Miss Jackson singing such songs as Down By The Riverside, A Closer Walk With Thee and Move On Up A Little Higher.
Fine Arts; Religion and Philosophy
Dist - PHENIX **Prod** - SCHWEJ 1980

Mahalia Jackson Sings Spirituals
VHS / U-matic
Color
History - United States
Dist - MSTVIS **Prod** - MSTVIS

The Maharajas - Imperialism by Conspiracy 25 MIN
16mm / U-matic / VHS
Color (H C A)
LC 77-700646
Presents, through historical narration and the commentary of the former maharaja of Patiala in the Punjab, the story of the English East India Company and the alliance that developed between the maharajas and the British. Shows the wealth and lifestyles of the maharajas and their eventual loss of power.
Civics and Political Systems; History - World; Sociology
Dist - CORF **Prod** - CFDLD 1977

Maharishi Mahesh 28 MIN
U-matic / VHS / BETA
Faces of India series
Color; NTSC; PAL; SECAM (J H C G)
PdS58
Visits the 'Show - biz' Swami. Follows the camera into his home where it becomes a part of his environment. Part of a series of portraits on film presenting a cross section of characters from real life.
Fine Arts; History - World
Dist - VIEWTH

Mahatma Gandhi 10 MIN
U-matic / VHS
Color (G)
$229.00, $129.00 purchase _ #AD - 1855
Reveals that after studying law in England, Mahatma Gandhi sought his fortune in South Africa. Discloses that what he found brought him to the spiritual road of non - violent resistance which he would follow for the rest of his life. He remained true to his ideals through wars, famine, civil strife and India's political difficulties.
Biography; History - World; Religion and Philosophy
Dist - FOTH **Prod** - FOTH

Mahatma Gandhi - silent revolution 38 MIN
VHS / U-matic / 16mm
Color (H C)
LC 75-707273
Documents the record of Gandhi's plan for basic education and shows the plan operating three areas in agricuture, education and industrial training.
Education; Religion and Philosophy; Social Science
Dist - IFB **Prod** - PILGRM 1969

Mahatma Gandhi - soul force 24 MIN
16mm / U-matic / VHS
Leaders of the 20th century - portraits of power series
Color (H C A)

LC 80-701089
Explores Mahatma Gandhi's philosophy of non - violence. Narrated by Henry Fonda.
Biography; History - World; Religion and Philosophy
Dist - LCOA **Prod** - NIELSE 1980

The Mahogany connections 29 MIN
U-matic / VHS
Survivors series
Color (H C)
$250.00 purchase _ #HP - 6106C
Reveals that the odds against a tiny mahogany tree seedling reaching adulthood are enormous - if it withstands a host of natural dangers it may then be imperiled by man. Shows how human activities both protect and jeopardize the mahogany. Part of a series on the issue of wildlife conservation and the enormity of the task of protecting wildlife and wilderness.
Science - Natural; Social Science
Dist - CORF **Prod** - BBCTV 1990

Mai Zetterling's Stockholm 25 MIN
U-matic / VHS / 16mm
Cities Series
Color (H C A) (SPANISH)
LC 80-701297
A shortened version of the motion picture Mai Zetterling's Stockholm. Presents actress - writer - director Mai Zetterling on a tour of Stockholm, Sweden.
Geography - World; Sociology
Dist - LCOA **Prod** - NIELSE 1980

Mai Zetterling's Stockholm 50 MIN
U-matic / VHS / 16mm
Cities Series
Color (I) (SPANISH)
LC 78-701707
Presents Swedish actress Mai Zetterling as she takes Stockholm.
Geography - World; Sociology
Dist - LCOA **Prod** - NIELSE 1978

The Maids 28 MIN
VHS / 16mm
Color (G)
$225.00 purchase, $60.00 rental
Looks at history of domestic labor since slavery and ambivalence felt by black women towards the work. Offers sophisticated analysis of racial and sexual division of labor, indicates that as black women moved from domestic labor into other job sectors, white - owned entrepreneurial maid services primarily employing white women have been created. Domestic service is considered demeaning because of long hours, menial toil and low pay. Historically, it was one of the few occupations open to black women in America. Produced by Muriel Jackson.
History - United States; Social Science; Sociology
Dist - WMEN **Prod** - MUJAC 1985

Maids and madams 52 MIN
VHS
Color (H C G)
$195.00 purchase, $75.00 rental
Examines Apartheid through the complex relationship between black household worker nd white employer. Offers the domestic situation as a microcosm of the racial issues dividing the country. Over a million black women live in a state of domestic bondage, underpaid, working long hours, at the mercy of draconian laws which separate them from their own families. Written and directed by Mira Hamermesh.
Geography - World; History - World; Sociology
Dist - FLMLIB

Maids of Wilko - Panny z Wilka 111 MIN
VHS
Color (G A) (POLISH WITH ENGLISH SUBTITLES)
$49.95 purchase _ #V256
Shows that after a long absence, Wiktor returns to a place where he once spent happy holidays. Attempts to recapture at least a trace of the moods of his youth, but there is no return to the past. Directed by Andrzej Wajda.
Fine Arts; Literature and Drama; Psychology
Dist - POLART

Mail and Female 11 MIN
16mm
B&W
Explains that when Alfalfa is made president of the He - Man Woman Haters' Club, he must rush after Darla to retrieve a love letter he has sent her. A Little Rascals film.
Fine Arts; Literature and Drama
Dist - RMIBHF **Prod** - ROACH 1937

The Mail Distribution Clerk 15 MIN
16mm
Color
LC 74-705065
Tells what the duties of a mail distribution clerk are and demonstrates the inside work at a post office.
Social Science
Dist - USNAC **Prod** - USPOST

The Mail Handler 12 MIN
16mm
Color
LC 74-705066
Demonstrates the responsibilities of the mail handler at a large post office.
Social Science
Dist - USNAC **Prod** - USPOST

Mail it Right 12 MIN
16mm
Color (H A)
LC 76-701591
Shows secretarial practices which save time and money for businesses and get the best service at the post office. Gives the recommended methods for preparing first - class mail and introduces the correct address format for mechanized sorting in post offices.
Social Science; Sociology
Dist - USNAC **Prod** - USPS 1975

Mail Order Beauty Racket 20 MIN
VHS / U-matic
Color
$335.00 purchase
From the ABC TV 20 20 program.
Sociology
Dist - ABCLR **Prod** - ABCLR 1983

Mail order sales 30 MIN
U-matic / VHS
Consumer survival series; Shopping
Color
Presents tips on purchasing something by mail order.
Home Economics; Social Science
Dist - MDCPB **Prod** - MDCPB

The Mailbox 24 MIN
16mm
Color (J H A)
LC 77-702102
Tells the story of an elderly widow who waits and waits for a letter from her children. Relates that when the letter finally arrives, the woman dies before she can read it.
Guidance and Counseling; Health and Safety; Psychology; Sociology
Dist - EBEC **Prod** - BYU 1977

Main Dish Delights
VHS
Microwave Cooking Series
(C G)
$59.00_CA259
Illustrates a variety of main dishes.
Home Economics
Dist - AAVIM **Prod** - AAVIM 1989

Main event
VHS
Color (G)
$39.80 purchase _ #0275
Documents the 1981 World Offshore Powerboat Championship.
Physical Education and Recreation
Dist - SEVVID

Main Idea 30 MIN
VHS / U-matic
Teaching Reading Comprehension Series
Color (T PRO)
$180.00 purchase,$50.00 rental
Covers the techniques involved in identifying the main idea of the story and methods of teaching the student these techniques.
Education; English Language
Dist - AITECH **Prod** - WETN 1986

Main idea road 20 MIN
U-matic / VHS
Efficient reading - instructional tapes series
Color
Shows how to learn the ways to find key words and ideas and how to read for the main idea.
English Language
Dist - TELSTR **Prod** - TELSTR

The Main motion 28.37 MIN
U-matic / VHS
Meeting will come to order series
(G)
Combines narration and dramatization to illustrate the basic rules of parliamentary procedure. Written by the Members of the National Association of Parliamentarians following the revised Robert's Rules of Order.
Civics and Political Systems; English Language
Dist - GPN **Prod** - NETV 1983

Main Street 29 MIN
16mm
Color (A)
LC 79-701275
Focuses on the economic and esthetic plight of Main Street, America. Describes how concerned merchants and consulting preservationists have joined forces in many cities and towns to revitalize the commercial and architectural advantages of downtown business areas.
Geography - World; Sociology
Dist - NTHP **Prod** - NTHP 1979

Main street 18 MIN
BETA / VHS / U-matic
Color (IND G A)
$777.00 purchase, $150.00 rental _ #MAI021
Instructs employees about working with chemicals, precautions to take to avoid injury and what to do if accidents occur. Discusses chemicals likely to be used in the workplace - solvents, poisons, gases, explosives and carcinogens. Trains those who work with hazardous chemicals in non - manufacturing organizations.
Health and Safety; Psychology
Dist - ITF **Prod** - BNA 1991

Main Street - a Charge of Rape 15 MIN
VHS
Color (S)
$79.00 purchase _ #322 - 9284
Reveals that one in five college women becomes a victim of forced sex, often on a first date. Considers that ninety percent of these rapes go unreported. Features NBC News' Maria Shriver who examines societal attitudes about 'date rape.'.
Guidance and Counseling; Health and Safety; Psychology; Sociology
Dist - FI **Prod** - NBCNEW 1987

Main Street - Bitter Harvest 9 MIN
VHS
Color (S)
$79.00 purchase _ #322 - 9295
Discloses that the US is home to about 50,000 teenage migrant workers. Reveals that their plight is often ignored by society at large. Most migrant workers live and die in poverty. The dream of leaving the fields requires education but nine out of ten migrant children never graduate from school. From dawn until suppertime they must work in the fields leaving no time to attend classes.
Agriculture; Health and Safety; History - World; Psychology; Social Science; Sociology
Dist - FI **Prod** - NBCNEW 1987

Main Street - Growing Up Gay 10 MIN
VHS
Color (S)
$79.00 purchase _ #322 - 9294
Takes a hard look at the lives of teenage homosexuals through interviews with a gay teenage man and a young lesbian. Features NBC News correspondent Bill Schechner. Both youngsters share the stories of how they confronted their sexual identities and the resulting problems.
Health and Safety; Psychology; Sociology
Dist - FI **Prod** - NBCNEW 1987

Main Street Gym 6 MIN
16mm
B&W
A study of an old boxing gym in the Los Angeles area.
Fine Arts; Physical Education and Recreation
Dist - USC **Prod** - USC 1968

Main Street - He's My Brother 9 MIN
VHS
Color (J)
$79.00 purchase _ #322 - 9296
Focuses on 16 - year - old Kay whose 12 - year - old brother Bobbie is autistic. Reflects the challenges and rewards of having a handicapped sibling.
Health and Safety; Psychology; Sociology
Dist - FI **Prod** - NBCNEW 1987

Main Street - no Smoking 7 MIN
VHS
Color (J)
$79.00 purchase _ #322 - 9290
Reveals how teenagers perceive cigarette smoking. Looks at what various communities around the country are doing to help prevent kids from starting. Teens themselves discuss their attitudes and experiences, providing influential anti - smoking role models.
Guidance and Counseling; Health and Safety; Psychology; Sociology
Dist - FI **Prod** - NBCNEW 1987

Main Street - Sex and the American Teenager 45 MIN
VHS
Color (J)
$79.00 purchase _ #322 - 9276
Asks if today's adolescents are as free and open in their sexual attitudes as they'd like us to think. Features Bryan Gumbel and sex therapist Dr Ruth Westheimer as hosts, joined by 12 teenagers who openly reveal their personal feelings on this sensitive subject.
Guidance and Counseling; Health and Safety; Psychology; Sociology
Dist - FI **Prod** - NBCNEW 1986

Main street - your right to know 17 MIN
VHS / U-matic / BETA
Color; PAL (IND G) (SPANISH)
$175.00 rental _ #MSF - 100
Illustrates the hazards and precautions for solvents, poisons, corrosives, gases, explosives and carcinogens for employees who work with chemicals. Shows why chemical safety is also important off the job and show how to use Material Safety Data Sheets - MSDS. Includes leader's guide and 10 workbooks.
Business and Economics; Health and Safety; Psychology; Science - Physical
Dist - BNA **Prod** - BNA

Main video series
Presents a series of seven programs on telephone skills and customer service. Leader's guides and additional support material provided.
Five forbidden phrases 18 MIN
Hall of shame 20 MIN
Main video series 138 MIN
On follow - up 17 MIN
On incoming calls 17 MIN
Dist - TELDOC **Prod** - TELDOC

Maine 60 MIN
VHS
Portrait of America series
Color (J H C G)
$99.95 purchase _ #AMB19V
Visits Maine. Offers extensive research into the state's history. Films key locations and presents segments on history, government, education, folklore, science, journalism, sociology, industry, agriculture and business. Shows what is unique about Maine and distinctive about its regional culture and how it got to be that way. Includes study guide. Part of a 50 - part series.
Geography - United States; History - United States
Dist - CAMV

The Maine bear 15 MIN
VHS
Field trips series
Color (I J)
$34.95 purchase _ #E337; LC 90-708570
Visits the Northern Maine woods where the Black Bear is found. Observes the activities conducted in research about and management of this animal, both in summer and winter. Part of a series which provides visual opportunities for children to 'visit' a variety of locations and activities as if they were on a field trip.
Education; Science - Natural
Dist - GPN **Prod** - MPBN 1983

Mainly for pupils - a very good place to start - melody making - Cassette 5 58 MIN
VHS
Sounds like mine series
Color; PAL (P I)
PdS29.50 purchase
Features a series devised to explore musical creativity and composing in the classroom, provoke thought and stimulate discussion.
Fine Arts
Dist - EMFVL

Mainly for pupils - one plus one - gemini - Cassette 6 57 MIN
VHS
Sounds like mine series
Color; PAL (P I)
PdS29.50 purchase
Features a series devised to explore musical creativity and composing in the classroom, provoke thought and stimulate discussion.
Fine Arts
Dist - EMFVL

Mainly for pupils - pulse, pulse, pulse - Cassette 4 66 MIN
VHS
Sounds like mine series
Color; PAL (P I)
PdS29.50 purchase
Features a series devised to explore musical creativity and composing in the classroom, provoke thought and stimulate discussion.
Fine Arts
Dist - EMFVL

Mainly for teachers - a normal activity - Cassette 1 39 MIN
VHS
Sounds like mine series
Color; PAL (T)
PdS29.50 purchase
Features a series devised to explore musical creativity and composing in the classroom, provoke thought and stimulate discussion.
Fine Arts
Dist - EMFVL

Mainly for teachers - many voices - talking stick - Cassette 3 58 MIN
VHS
Sounds like mine series
Color; PAL (T)
PdS29.50 purchase
Features a series devised to explore musical creativity and composing in the classroom, provoke thought and stimulate discussion.
Fine Arts
Dist - EMFVL

Mainly for teachers - sinfonietta education - Cassette 2 58 MIN
VHS
Sounds like mine series
Color; PAL (T)
PdS29.50 purchase
Features a series devised to explore musical creativity and composing in the classroom, provoke thought and stimulate discussion.
Fine Arts
Dist - EMFVL

Mainly Math Series
Common fractions 20 MIN
Decimal fractions 20 MIN
Directed Numbers, Pt 1 20 MIN
Directed Numbers, Pt 2 20 MIN
Motion Geometry 20 MIN
Number Patterns 20 MIN
Percentages 20 MIN
Plane Geometry 20 MIN
Probabilities, Pt 1 20 MIN
Probabilities, Pt 2 20 MIN
Ratios and Proportions 20 MIN
Scientific notation 20 MIN
Statistics and Graphs, Pt 1 20 MIN
Statistics and Graphs, Pt 2 20 MIN
Dist - GPN

A Mainly Musical Decision 15 MIN
U-matic
It's Mainly Music Series
Color (I)
Shows children visiting a school where music, art, dance and drama are taught in addition to the regular school curriculum.
Fine Arts
Dist - TVOTAR **Prod** - TVOTAR 1983

The Mainstay of the Mails 13 MIN
16mm
Color
LC 74-705068
Shows the complexity and importance of maintaining the equipment and buildings of today's postal system. Illustrates the latest mechanization equipment and stresses the need for highly skilled maintenance employees.
Business and Economics; Industrial and Technical Education; Social Science
Dist - USNAC **Prod** - USPOST

Mainstream 30 MIN
U-matic
Real People Series
Color
Focuses on the resurgence of pride in tribal values among the Indians of the Northwestern United States.
Social Science; Sociology
Dist - GPN **Prod** - KSPSTV

Mainstream 25 MIN
VHS / U-matic
Real People Series
Color (G)
Shows a journey in which a young Coeur d'Alene Indian women recalls her father, her childhood, and her tribe's history. She becomes aware that the reservation and her past remain a secure haven, a source of energy and inspiration, the root place of her being. It is a story common to many young Indians in today's mainstream who are seeking and finding new pride in their own tribal values and identities.
Social Science
Dist - NAMPBC **Prod** - NAMPBC 1976

Mainstream 7 MIN
16mm
Color (G)
$20.00 rental
Dips into oblivion. Transforms the infinite span of thought into spatial - temporal micromoments. A Jerry Abrams production.
Fine Arts
Dist - CANCIN

Mainstreaming 26 MIN
U-matic
Color (H)
Provides information concerning the real - life integration of a number of disabled children into public schools.
Psychology; Sociology
Dist - ESST **Prod** - ESST 1980

Mainstreaming 30 MIN
16mm
Project STRETCH Series
Color (T)
LC 80-700614
Features three special educators who discuss the reasons for the movement toward mainstreaming handicapped children and the major models of service to these children and their teachers.
Education; Psychology
Dist - HUBDSC **Prod** - METCO 1980

Mainstreaming secondary special vocational needs student series
Amplification in education 98 MIN
Analysis of reading materials 30 MIN
Assessing learner needs 30 MIN
Behavior management 30 MIN
Cognitive base for language acquisition and remediation 80 MIN
Diagnostic Procedures with the Language Disordered Child 111 MIN
Evaluation 30 MIN
Foundations of behavior modification 100 MIN
Individual Education Programs 30 MIN
Instructional Planning 30 MIN
Instructional Resources 30 MIN
Job Placement and Follow - Up 30 MIN
Sequencing Instruction 30 MIN
Special Needs Learner Characteristics 30 MIN
Dist - PUAVC

Mainstreaming Techniques - Life Science and Art 12 MIN
U-matic / VHS / 16mm
Special Education Curriculum Design - a Multisensory Approach Series
Color (T)
LC 80-706558
Illustrates the involvement activities, interactions and responses of handicapped children in a mainstreamed life science and art program. Features classroom experiments with live organisms, including suggestions for adaptation in teaching strategy and equipment modification to provide for individual modes of learning. Based on the book Laboratory Science And Art For Blind, Deaf, And Emotionally Handicapped Children by Doris Hadary.
Education; Psychology
Dist - MGHT **Prod** - MGHT 1979

Mainstreaming the Exceptional Child Series
Behavior - Assessment and Programming 29 MIN
Delivery systems 29 MIN
Human Relations in the Classroom 29 MIN
Introduction to Exceptionality, Pt 1 29 MIN
Introduction to Exceptionality, Pt 2 29 MIN
Language Assessment and Programming 29 MIN
Mathematics - Assessment and Programming 29 MIN
Overview of Mainstreaming 29 MIN
Parent Involvement 29 MIN
Reading - assessment and programming 29 MIN
School and Classrooms 29 MIN
Whither the Mainstream 29 MIN
Dist - FI

Mainstreams and Cross Currents 29 MIN
U-matic
Visions - the Critical Eye Series
Color (H C)
Explores modernist art and related subjects such as methods of marketing, drawbacks involved in adopting theories of mainstream art, the role of the critic and the ways in which art can express religious experience.
Fine Arts
Dist - TVOTAR **Prod** - TVOTAR 1985

Mainstreet Soldier 36 MIN
16mm
Color
LC 77-702955
Documents the life of a 48 - year - old alcoholic who has spent the last 28 years on and around Winnipeg's Main Street Skid Row district. Follows him to his favorite haunts and listens to what he has to say about himself and his life.
Health and Safety; Psychology; Sociology
Dist - CANFDC **Prod** - YAKIR 1972

Maintainability Engineering 28 MIN
U-matic / VHS
Color
Covers Maintainability Engineering principles, corrective and preventive maintenance practices, equipment operating and downtime categories, maintenance personnel factors and safety factors.
Industrial and Technical Education
Dist - UAZMIC **Prod** - UAZMIC

Maintainability Operational Availability, and Preventive Maintenance of Series Pt 1
Course Objectives, Downtimes and their Distributions 60 MIN
Dist - UAZMIC

Maintainability, Operational Availability and Preventive Maintenance of Series Pt 5
Steady State Availability Applications, Availability Improvement Considerations, 60 MIN
Dist - UAZMIC

Maintainability, operational availability and preventive maintenance of series
Design practices for better maintainability, and preventive maintenance theory 60 MIN
Dist - UAZMIC

Maintaing and troubleshooting electric motors series
VHS / 16mm
Maintaining and troubleshooting electric motors series
Color (H A)
Presents a series of training films demonstrating the maintenance and troubleshooting of various types of electric motors.
Industrial and Technical Education
Dist - TAT Prod - TAT 1989

Maintaining a Lawn 29 MIN
Videoreel / VT2
Dig it Series
Color
Features Tom Lied offering tips for keeping a lawn healthy and problem - free and suggesting ways to get rid of problems that may occur.
Agriculture; Science - Natural
Dist - PBS Prod - WMVSTV

Maintaining a Winning Team 30 MIN
U-matic / VHS
Managerial Game Plan - Team Building through MBO Series
Color
Emphasizes on pulling back at agreed - to intervals to review how plans are working. Stresses the role of leadership. Shows how to maintain a winning team by keeping their attention directed to operating problems rather than problem personalities.
Business and Economics; Psychology
Dist - PRODEV Prod - PRODEV

Maintaining and Troubleshooting Electric Motors Series
AC motors 21 MIN
DC Motors 23 MIN
Maintaing and troubleshooting electric motors series
Maintaining Motors 17 MIN
Motor Nameplates 19 MIN
Troubleshooting Motors 21 MIN
Dist - TAT

Maintaining Centrifugal Pumps 24 MIN
VHS / 16mm
Mechanical Maintenance Training Series
Color (H A)
$410.00 purchase, $110.00 rental
Describes maintenance and operation of centrifugal pumps.
Industrial and Technical Education
Dist - TAT Prod - TAT 1987

Maintaining Fruit Quality 43 MIN
16mm
Color
LC 77-702856
Discusses methods of keeping fruit healthy until it reaches the consumer.
Health and Safety; Home Economics; Social Science
Dist - BCDA Prod - BCDA 1977

Maintaining Good Working Conditions 9 MIN
16mm
Problems in Supervision Series
B&W (SPANISH)
LC FIE62-55
Shows two supervisors describing specific ways they improved working conditions.
Business and Economics; Foreign Language; Guidance and Counseling; Psychology
Dist - USNAC Prod - USOE 1944

Maintaining Ideal Weight, Avoiding Excess Fat, Saturated Fat and Cholesterol 28 MIN
VHS / U-matic
Eat Well, be Well Series
Color (H C A)
Introduces guidelines Nos. 2 and 3 - Maintain Ideal Weight And Avoid Too Much Fat, Saturated Fat and Cholesterol. Explores the effects of fat types on the body and alerts us to the dangers of obesity.
Health and Safety; Social Science
Dist - JOU Prod - JOU 1983

Maintaining moral purity - Tape 4 25 MIN
VHS
Church leaders under fire series
Color (A R PRO)
$10.00 rental _ #36 - 84 - 222
Deals with the issue of sex scandals between church leaders and laity. Offers guidelines for maintaining moral purity while working closely with others. Produced by Priority Publishing.
Religion and Philosophy
Dist - APH

Maintaining Motors 17 MIN
VHS / 16mm
Maintaining and Troubleshooting Electric Motors Series
Color (H A)
$465.00 purchase, $110.00 rental
Demostrates motor maintenance, lubrication, cleaning, inspection and servicing.
Industrial and Technical Education
Dist - TAT Prod - TAT 1989

Maintaining Quality Standards 10 MIN
16mm
Problems in Supervision Series
B&W
LC FIE52-78
A supervisor learns that quality as well as quantity is necessary and how quality standards can be achieved and maintained.
Business and Economics
Dist - USNAC Prod - USOE 1944

Maintaining Quality Standards 10 MIN
16mm
Problems in Supervision Series
B&W (SPANISH)
LC 74-705069
Tells how a supervisor learns that quality as well as quantity production is necessary and how such quality standards can be achieved and maintained.
Business and Economics; Foreign Language; Guidance and Counseling
Dist - USNAC Prod - USOE 1944

Maintaining the Deep Fat Fryer 20 MIN
VHS / BETA
Color (G PRO)
$59.00 purchase _ #QF31
Details steps used to clean, filter and fill the deep fat fryer.
Home Economics
Dist - RMIBHF Prod - RMIBHF

Maintaining the elderly in community 48 MIN
VHS
Color (G C)
$39.95 purchase
Looks at practical ways congregations have developed to maintain contact with older members who can no longer attend services and programs these congregations' leaders have developed to assist the elderly to remain in the community. Considers work through Columbus Hospital, The Ark, a Jewish organization, and the Lutheran Social Services group.
Health and Safety; Religion and Philosophy
Dist - TNF Prod - TNF

Maintaining the Hub Service Type Helicopter - Rotor Systems and Related Controls 16 MIN
16mm
B&W
LC FIE60-30
Illustrates basic steps in the removal of rotor blades and hub, snubbers, flap restrainers and dampers. Shows procedures for setting blade angle of incidence and checking control cable tensions.
Industrial and Technical Education; Social Science
Dist - USNAC Prod - USN 1952

Maintaining Workers' Interest 13 MIN
16mm
Problems in Supervision Series
B&W (C A) (SPANISH)
LC FIE52-79; FIE62-58
Dramatizes instances of employees doing poor work because their jobs do not interest them and shows what the supervisor should do to detect and remedy such situations.
Business and Economics
Dist - USNAC Prod - USOE 1944

Maintaining your PC
VHS
Computer software training series
Color (J H C G)
$49.95 purchase _ #AAT13V
Shows how to maintain a PC in a comprehensive and easy - to - follow format. Illustrates actual commands and time saving techniques. Part of a 21 - part series on computer software.
Computer Science
Dist - CAMV

Maintenance 26 MIN
VHS / U-matic
Right Way Series
Color
Describes basic car care and maintenance.
Health and Safety; Industrial and Technical Education
Dist - PBS Prod - SCETV 1982

Maintenance 29 MIN
Videoreel / VT2
Maggie and the Beautiful Machine - Backs Series
Color
Physical Education and Recreation
Dist - PBS Prod - WGBHTV

Maintenance and Exterior Repairs - Household Maintenance, Exterior Repairs 30 MIN
BETA / VHS
Wally's Workshop Series
Color
Home Economics; Industrial and Technical Education
Dist - KARTES Prod - KARTES

Maintenance and Inspection of the Float and Pressure Type Carburetors 28 MIN
16mm / U-matic / VHS
B&W (IND)
Shows visual inspection, adjustment, removal and replacement of carburetors installed in Army aircraft.
Education; Industrial and Technical Education
Dist - USNAC Prod - USA

Maintenance and Property 30 MIN
U-matic
Family and the Law Series
(H C A)
Deals with a divorced couple who must negotiate a settlement in the courts.
Civics and Political Systems; History - World
Dist - ACCESS Prod - ACCESS 1980

Maintenance and Repair of Steam Condensers - Circulating Water Side 17 MIN
16mm
B&W
LC FIE52-2128
Explains the principle and operation of the steam condenser and shows the procedures of preparing, cleaning, inspecting, repairing and testing a condenser.
Civics and Political Systems; Social Science
Dist - USNAC Prod - USN 1952

Maintenance and Show Grooming 72 MIN
VHS / BETA
Color
Covers horse grooming techniques. Includes body clipping, mane and tail care and hoof preparation.
Health and Safety; Physical Education and Recreation
Dist - EQVDL Prod - CSPC

Maintenance, Lubrication and Troubleshooting 29 MIN
U-matic
Radiographic Processing Series
Color (C)
LC 77-706135
Presents guidelines for the maintenance and lubrication of automatic radiographic processors.
Health and Safety; Industrial and Technical Education; Science
Dist - USNAC Prod - USVA 1975

Maintenance Management Series
Computerized Maintenance Systems 30 MIN
Evaluating the maintenance program 30 MIN
The Maintenance Organization 30 MIN
Maintenance Safety and Efficiency 30 MIN
Maintenance Systems and Documentation 30 MIN
Parts and Materials 30 MIN
Preventive and Predictive Maintenance 30 MIN
Scheduling 30 MIN
Work Execution 30 MIN
Dist - ITCORP

Maintenance of Energized Circuits - Use of Hot Line Tools on Circuits of Over 5,000 Volts 20 MIN
U-matic / VHS / 16mm

Color (IND)
Outlines specific tasks in maintenance of energized circuits carrying over 5,000 volts. Emphasizes personal safety in use of high voltage equipment and ground and pole - top work.
Industrial and Technical Education
Dist - USNAC **Prod** - USAF

Maintenance of Energized Circuits - Use of Rubber Protective Equipment 19 MIN
16mm / U-matic / VHS
Color (IND)
Outlines work tasks in maintenance of energized high voltage circuits. Covers hazards and countermeasures, protective equipment, work crew safety, use of high voltage maintenance equipment and pole - top safety procedures.
Industrial and Technical Education
Dist - USNAC **Prod** - USAF

Maintenance of High - Voltage Circuit Breakers and Switchgear - 4 kV and Over 60 MIN
VHS
Transformers, Switchgear and Batteries Series
Color (PRO)
$600.00, $1500.00 purchase _ #EMMHV
Describes the operating principles of high - voltage circuit breakers and switchgear. Shows how circuit breakers extinguish an arc and how protective systems work in conjunction with the breakers. Part of a four - part series on transformers, switchgear and batteries, which is part of a 29 unit set on electrical maintenance. Includes 10 textbooks and an instructor guide which provide four hours of instruction.
Education; Health and Safety; Industrial and Technical Education; Psychology
Dist - NUSTC **Prod** - NUSTC

Maintenance of Low - Voltage Circuit Breakers and Switchgear - Under 4 kV 60 MIN
VHS
Transformers, Switchgear and Batteries Series
Color (PRO)
$600.00, $1500.00 purchase _ #EMMLV
Explains switch functions, protective functions and how a breaker interrupts a circuit. Part of a four - part series on transformers, switchgear and batteries, which is part of a 29 unit set on electrical maintenance. Includes 10 textbooks and an instructor guide which provide four hours of instruction.
Education; Health and Safety; Industrial and Technical Education; Psychology
Dist - NUSTC **Prod** - NUSTC

Maintenance of Microwave Power Tubes 34 MIN
16mm / U-matic / VHS
Color (A)
Outlines procedures for the care and handling of the magnetron and kleptron power tubes used in radar and tropospheric communications equipment.
Industrial and Technical Education
Dist - USNAC **Prod** - USAF 1959

Maintenance of Precision Roller Chain Drives 17 MIN
VHS
Power Transmission Series II - Selection, Application and 'Maintenance Series
Color (A)
$265.00 purchase, $50.00 rental _ #57974
Explains that since a chain has no side - flex capacity, shaft alignment, both horizontal and vertical, is critical. Shows how to check alignment, sag, tension and lubrication. Describes types of chains, including slip fit, tap fit, press fit, offset link. Lists types of lubrication, explaining the role of drive speed in selection. Discusses the effect of air temperature on viscosity. Explains ANSI dimensions, and components of precision chains.
Industrial and Technical Education
Dist - UILL **Prod** - MAJEC 1986

The Maintenance Organization 30 MIN
VHS / U-matic
Maintenance Management Series
Color
Discusses maintenance management goals and process. Describes leadership and time management techniques. Deals with centralized and decentralized shops.
Business and Economics; Psychology
Dist - ITCORP **Prod** - ITCORP

Maintenance Painting 26 MIN
16mm
Color
Shows pictorially what all parties concerned, from the designer to the man with the paint brush, should know about maintenance painting.
Home Economics; Industrial and Technical Education
Dist - HERC **Prod** - HERC

Maintenance Practices 60 MIN
VHS
Maintenance Practices Series
Color (PRO)
$600.00, $1500.00 purchase _ #GMMPR
Introduces the steps for completing a typical maintenance job. Teaches safety and tagging procedures, preventive maintenance programs and some general maintenance techniques. Part of a two - part series on maintenance practices, part of a set on general and mechanical maintenance. Includes 10 textbooks and an instructor guide which provide four hours of instruction.
Education; Health and Safety; Industrial and Technical Education; Psychology
Dist - NUSTC **Prod** - NUSTC

Maintenance Practices Series
Maintenance Practices 60 MIN
Print Reading and Use 60 MIN
Dist - NUSTC

Maintenance Procedures - Ansul Dry Chemical Hand Portable Extinguishers 17 MIN
VHS
Color (IND)
Details how an examination of fire extinguishers will reveal the need for any repair, recharge, replacement or testing necessary to assure effective, safe operation.
Health and Safety
Dist - ANSUL **Prod** - ANSUL

Maintenance Procedures - Ansul Dry Chemical Wheeled Extinguishers 11 MIN
VHS
Color (IND)
Demonstrates examination of a dry chemical wheeled fire extinguisher which will reveal the need for any repair, recharge, replacement or testing necessary to help assure effective, safe use. Stresses good maintenance procedures.
Health and Safety
Dist - ANSUL **Prod** - ANSUL

Maintenance Procedures - Ansul Large Dry Chemical Hand Hose Line Systems 13 MIN
VHS
Color (IND)
Demonstrates how a thorough examination of a large dry chemical hand hose line fire extinguishing system will reveal the need for any repair, recharge, replacement or testing necessary to help assure safe, effective use. Stresses good maintenance procedures.
Health and Safety
Dist - ANSUL **Prod** - ANSUL

Maintenance Safety and Efficiency 30 MIN
VHS / U-matic
Maintenance Management Series
Color
Examines plant, shop and field safety. Pursues shop and field efficiency.
Business and Economics; Psychology
Dist - ITCORP **Prod** - ITCORP

Maintenance Safety in Aviation - Murphy's Law 17 MIN
16mm
B&W
LC 74-705070
Tells how improper installation of aircraft equipment can cause accidents.
Health and Safety; Industrial and Technical Education
Dist - USNAC **Prod** - USN

Maintenance Systems and Documentation 30 MIN
U-matic / VHS
Maintenance Management Series
Color
Defines the functions of documentation. Describes work request systems and maintenance history files. Discusses evaluating contractor performance.
Business and Economics; Psychology
Dist - ITCORP **Prod** - ITCORP

Maintenance Tank Cleaning - Butterworth Method 31 MIN
16mm
B&W
LC FIE52-1264
Explains how purposes govern procedures to be followed and shows basic techniques in applying the Butterworth method.
Industrial and Technical Education; Social Science
Dist - USNAC **Prod** - USN 1950

The Maitland & Morpeth string quartet 29 MIN
VHS
Color; PAL (G)
PdS50 purchase
Tells a story based on Nick Enright's poem about a violin - playing couple whose hobby grows. Features The Carl Pini Quartet. Produced by Anne Joliffe for Jollification Ltd.
Fine Arts; Literature and Drama
Dist - BALFOR

Maitre 11 MIN
16mm
Color (I)
LC 78-701050
Uses animation, without narration, to present an abstract expression of the dilemma of an artist in search of success and recognition.
Fine Arts
Dist - SIM **Prod** - CITE 1967

Maitre De L'Ungava 28 MIN
16mm
Color (FRENCH)
A French - language film which shows the caribou in his courageous struggle for life in Quebec.
Foreign Language; Geography - World; Science - Natural
Dist - MTP **Prod** - QDTFG

Maize in Metal 15 MIN
U-matic / VHS
Explorers Unlimited Series
Color (P I)
Visits a food canning company to show the complexity of the food industry.
Business and Economics; Social Science
Dist - AITECH **Prod** - WVIZTV 1971

Majdanek 1944 65 MIN
VHS
Color; B&W (G) (MULTILINGUAL)
$72.00 purchase
Contains testimony from survivors and witnesses to the atrocities in the concentration and extermination camp Majdanek, erected near Lublin in 1941 and liberated on July 23, 1944. Provides a record of the Majdanek Nazi war crimes trial. Produced by Irmgard and Bengt von zur Muhlen. English and German with English subtitles.
Fine Arts; History - World; Religion and Philosophy
Dist - NCJEWF

Majestic Brass, Pt 1 15 MIN
U-matic / VHS
Musical Instruments Series
Color
Fine Arts
Dist - GPN **Prod** - WWVUTV

Majestic Brass, Pt 2 16 MIN
VHS / U-matic
Musical Instruments Series
Color
Fine Arts
Dist - GPN **Prod** - WWVUTV

The Majestic Canadian Rockies 20 MIN
VHS / U-matic
Color (J)
LC 82-706771
Shows the Canadian Rockies and discusses the mountains in reference to the park areas in Jasper, Banff, Alberta, and Calgary.
Geography - World
Dist - AWSS **Prod** - AWSS 1980

The Majestic Clockwork - Pt 1 26 MIN
16mm / U-matic
Ascent of Man Series
Color (H C A)
LC 74-702260
Focuses on the contributions of Newton and Einstein to the evolution of physics. Explores the revolution that ensued when Einstein's theory of relativity upset Newton's description of the universe. Narrated by Dr Jacob Bronowski of the Salk Institute.
History - World; Science - Physical
Dist - TIMLIF **Prod** - BBCTV 1973

The Majestic Clockwork - Pt 2 26 MIN
16mm / U-matic
Ascent of Man Series
Color (H C A)
LC 74-702260
Focuses on the contributions of Newton and Einstein to the evolution of physics. Explores the revolution that ensued when Einstein's theory of relativity upset Newton's description of the universe. Narrated by Dr Jacob Bronowski of the Salk Institute.
History - World
Dist - TIMLIF **Prod** - BBCTV 1973

The Majestic Eagles of North America 12 MIN
16mm
Color (P I)
LC 85-703606
Presents the story of the American eagle.
History - United States; Science - Natural
Dist - EBEC **Prod** - EBEC 1985

The Majestic Wapiti 16 MIN
16mm / U-matic / VHS
North American Species Series
Color (P I J)
Depicts the successful adaptation of the Wapiti (elk or red deer) to the open western woods.
Science - Natural
Dist - BCNFL **Prod** - KARVF 1984

Major Amputations for Arteriosclerosis - Technic and Rehabilitation 13 MIN
16mm
Color (PRO)
Shows the importance of simple techniques of amputation and early provision of temporary limbs in patients receiving amputations for above - knee and below knee amputation. Illustrates the methods for measuring the artificial limbs and constructing them.
Health and Safety; Science
Dist - ACY **Prod** - ACYDGD 1959

Major Barbara 131 MIN
VHS
B&W (G)
$39.95 purchase _ #MAJ010
Adapts the play by George Bernard Shaw which tells the story of Barbara Undershaft, daughter of a wealthy munitions manufacturer and an ardent member of the Salvation Army. Uses ironic humor and social satire in war - torn England. Unabridged and fully restored; remastered.
Fine Arts; Literature and Drama; Sociology
Dist - HOMVIS **Prod** - JANUS 1941

Major Barbara 121 MIN
16mm
B&W
Features Wendy Hiller as an idealistic Salvation Army soldier dedicated to saving the poor from the abuses of the rich. Shows her conflict with her father, a wealthy munitions manufacturer who believes that the poor can be saved through intelligent manipulation of money. Features Rex Harrison as a lovestruck intellectual caught in the middle of the conflict. Directed by Gabriel Pascal. Based on the play Major Barbara by George Bernard Shaw.
Fine Arts; Literature and Drama
Dist - LCOA **Prod** - UAA 1941

Major Burns
U-matic / VHS
Burns - Emergency Management Series
Color
Focuses on the appropriate care for major burn patients in the field and in the emergency department. Explains illustrates and simulates each step. Discusses various physical and medical ramifications to further aid in determining proper emergency care.
Health and Safety
Dist - VTRI **Prod** - VTRI

Major Burns 20 MIN
VHS / U-matic
Medical Crisis Intervention Series
Color (PRO)
Teaches how to recognize and initiate treatment for patients suffering with major burns. Discusses how to direct the activity of paramedics at the scene, how to stabilize patients, anticipation of post - burn complications and provision of initial therapy.
Health and Safety
Dist - LEIKID **Prod** - LEIKID

Major Divisions and Areas of Function 19 MIN
U-matic / VHS
Neurobiology Series
Color (PRO)
Identifies by means of brain specimens and diagrams the anatomical landmarks of the cerebral hemispheres, the lobes of the brain and their subdivisions, and the functional areas related to the cerebrocortical structure.
Health and Safety; Science - Natural
Dist - HSCIC **Prod** - HSCIC

Major Dundee 134 MIN
U-matic / VHS / 16mm
Color (J)
Stars Charlton Heston as Union Army Major Dundee leading a troop of misfits and killers against a marauding Apache chieftain who has massacred a company of U S Cavalry and escaped back to his sanctuary in Mexico.
Civics and Political Systems; Fine Arts
Dist - FI **Prod** - CPC 1965

Major Illness in the Family 30 MIN
U-matic
Health Care Today Series
Color (H A)
Dramatizes how a major, confining illness of one member affects the daily life of a family.
Health and Safety
Dist - TVOTAR **Prod** - TVOTAR 1985

Major Illnesses and the Family 29 MIN
VHS / 16mm
Health Care Today series
Color (H C G)
$90.00 purchase _ #BPN109808
Shows, through dramatization, how a major, confining illness of a family member affects the daily life of the whole family.
Health and Safety; Sociology
Dist - RMIBHF **Prod** - RMIBHF

Major League Hitting Secrets 30 MIN
VHS
(J H C)
$34.95 _ #MXS8207V
Baseball coach Vada Pinson teaches the secrets of bat acceleration, shifting the body to handle curve balls, low pitches, and fast balls. Offers tips on bunting.
Physical Education and Recreation
Dist - CAMV

Major Medical Syndromes Series

Acute myocardial infarction	20 MIN
Cirrhosis	20 MIN
Congestive Heart Failure	20 MIN
Dissecting Aortic Aneurysm	20 MIN
Meningitis	20 MIN

Dist - USNAC

Major or Minor 14 MIN
VHS / U-matic
Stepping into Rhythm Series
Color (P)
Encourages children to distinguish between major and minor modes through ear training.
Fine Arts
Dist - AITECH **Prod** - WVIZTV

Major Overhaul
VHS / 35mm strip
Small Engine Know - How Series
$85.00 purchase _ #DXSEK040 filmstrip, $85.00 purchase _ #DXSE040V VHS
Teaches disassembly and cleaning, inspection and servicing, and reassembly and starting of small engines.
Education; Industrial and Technical Education
Dist - CAREER **Prod** - CAREER

Major Phyla Series

Anthropods - insects and their relatives	11 MIN
Arthropods - Insects and their Relatives	11 MIN
Classifying plants and animals	11 MIN
Echinoderms and mollusks	16 MIN
Fungi - the One Hundred Thousand	7 MIN
The Invertebrates	13 MIN
Mosses, Liverworts and Ferns	14 MIN
Protozoa - Structures and Life Functions	17 MIN
Simple Organisms - Algae and Fungi	14 MIN
Simple Organisms - Bacteria	15 MIN
Sponges and Coelenterates - Porous and Sac - Like Animals	11 MIN
Worms - flat, round and segmented	16 MIN

Dist - CORF

Major religions series
Travels from the great cathedrals of Europe to a street in Shanghai. Looks at the traditions and practices of the great religions with experts like John Blofeld and Huston Smith. Contains five films entitled Christian Mysticism; Buddhism - The Path to Enlightenment; Taoism; Hinduism and the Song of God; and The Sufi Way. See individual titles for descriptions.

Major religions series	160 MIN

Dist - HP

Major Structural Repairs of Plastic Boats 20 MIN
16mm
Color
LC 74-706489
Shows the methods and materials used for repairing major structural damage to fiberglass reinforced plastic boats.
Physical Education and Recreation; Social Science
Dist - USNAC **Prod** - USN 1972

Major Venereal Disease 24 MIN
VHS / U-matic
Emergency Management - the First 30 Minutes, Vol III Series
Color
Illustrates the symptoms, diagnosis and treatment of gonorrhea and syphilis.
Health and Safety
Dist - VTRI **Prod** - VTRI

A Majority of One 153 MIN
U-matic / VHS / 16mm
Color (I J H C)
Stars Rosalind Russell and Alec Guiness in the story of a Brooklyn matron who suddenly finds herself enroute to Japan with her daughter and diplomat son - in - law.
Fine Arts; Geography - World
Dist - FI **Prod** - WB 1961

Majority Rule and Minority Rights 20 MIN
VHS / 16mm
Citizens all Series
Color (H)
$150.00 purchase, $30.00 rental
Probes the conflict between majority rule and minority rights as reflected in a school's no - smoking policy, which a majority favors but which also angers smokers.
Business and Economics; Civics and Political Systems
Dist - AITECH **Prod** - WHATV 1987

Makai - the Documentary of an Open Ocean Dive 28 MIN
16mm
Color
LC 74-706491
Shows the preparation and employment of a mobile saturation dive off the coast of Ohau, Hawaii. Combines underwater photography with descriptions of diving research sponsored by the Bureau of Medicine Surgery, the Office of Naval Research and the Navy supervisor of diving.
Civics and Political Systems; Science - Physical
Dist - USNAC **Prod** - USN 1973

Makarova returns 60 MIN
VHS
Color; Hi-fi; Dolby stereo (G)
$29.95 purchase _ #1297
Records the return of ballerina Natalia Makarova to the Kirov Ballet nearly 20 years after her defection from the USSR. Includes excerpts from Makarova's performance in Eugene Onegin on the Kirov stage and personal reflections on her career.
Fine Arts; Geography - World
Dist - KULTUR **Prod** - KULTUR 1991

Make a family video album
VHS
Color (H G A)
$19.95 purchase _ #ED100
Shows the novice how to use a home video camera, with no scripting necessary, to produce a family video album from old photographs, slides, films, news clippings and other family memorabilia.
Fine Arts; Industrial and Technical Education; Sociology
Dist - AAVIM **Prod** - AAVIM

Make a joyful and beautiful noise 100 MIN
VHS
Color (G)
$49.95 purchase _ #S01828
Gives guidelines for improving one's singing ability. Covers topics including posture, breathing, vocal tone, range and register, resonance, diction and more. Suggests exercises for improving tone and breaking bad singing habits. Hosted by Jeffrey Sandborg.
Fine Arts
Dist - UILL

Make a Joyful Sound 54 MIN
16mm
B&W
LC FIA66-841
Shows how teachers affect the musical interests of 450 youngsters chosen for the New Jersey All - State High School Chorus and Orchestra. Includes sequences of their concert at Symphony Hall, Newark, New Jersey.
Fine Arts
Dist - CBSTV **Prod** - WCBSTV 1965

Make a Noise 25 MIN
16mm
Start Here - Adventures and Science Series
Color
Explains what sound is, why some sounds are musical and how to experiment with vibrations.
Science - Physical
Dist - LANDMK **Prod** - VIDART 1983

Make a print 15 MIN
Videoreel / VT2
Art corner series
B&W (P)
Describes manipulating objects such as fingers or salvage shapes to make a print.
Fine Arts
Dist - GPN **Prod** - CVETVC

Make a Print - with a Potato or Tomato 60 MIN
BETA / VHS
Children's Crafts Series
Color (K P)
Demonstrates making prints with fruits and vegetables and objects such as kitchen tools and old toys.
Fine Arts
Dist - MOHOMV **Prod** - MOHOMV

Make a Puppet - make a Friend 56 MIN
BETA / VHS
Children's Crafts Series

Color (K P)
Demonstrates how to make a puppet out of a paper bag, how to make clothes for paper dolls and how to make snowflakes by cutting and folding paper.
Fine Arts
Dist - MOHOMV **Prod** - MOHOMV

Make a splash - volunteer 30 MIN
VHS
Color (G)
$29.95 purchase _ #S01435
Encourages viewers to do volunteer community work. Interviews volunteers who tell of their experiences. Produced by the Junior Leagues of Chicago and Evanston, IL.
Social Science; Sociology
Dist - UILL

Make a Wish 15 MIN
VHS / U-matic
Mrs Cabobble's Caboose
(P)
Designed to teach primary grade students basic music concepts. Highlights melody, rhythm, harmony and the different families of musical instruments. Features Mrs. Fran Powell.
Fine Arts
Dist - GPN **Prod** - WDCNTV 1986

Make a Wish 5 MIN
U-matic / 16mm / VHS
Color (H C G T A)
LC 76-703728
Health and Safety; Sociology
Dist - PSU **Prod** - PSU 1973

Make Believe 26 MIN
VHS
Ordinary people series
Color (G)
$190.00 purchase, $50.00 rental
Visits the town of Schweizer - Reineke and its neighboring township, Ipelegeng. Observes two simultaneous ceremonies - one for the African National Congress, the other for the Afrikaner Resistance Movement. Three children witness these diametrically opposed events, demonstrating their innocence as they grapple with long standing prejudices not fully understood. Reveals the future of a country where children grow up entrenched in hatred. Part of a series which chronicles an event in South Africa through the eyes of three or four 'ordinary' people, chosen to represent diverse backgrounds or dissimilar points of view. This current affairs series seeks to provide insight into the collective South African conscience.
Fine Arts; History - World; Sociology
Dist - FIRS **Prod** - GAVSHO 1993

Make - Believe Marriage 33 MIN
16mm / U-matic / VHS 33 MIN
Color; Captioned (J H A) (SPANISH)
LC 79-700322; 79-700323
A shortened version of the motion picture Make - Believe Marriage. Presents a classroom experiment in marriage. Shows how the teenagers in Mr Webster's high school marriage class are paired off, take vows, draw up a budget, have make - believe babies, learn to deal with unemployment and eventually decide whether to continue the marriage or get a divorce. An ABC After School Special.
Foreign Language; Guidance and Counseling; Sociology
Dist - LCOA **Prod** - LCOA 1979

Make 'em laugh 270 MIN
VHS
Color (G PRO)
$199.95 purchase _ #4242EG
Presents a three - video humor seminar covering how, when, where and why to use humor in programs. Shows how to use humor effectively to maintain attention in a presentation and to leave an impact upon the audience. Features Tom Antion.
Business and Economics; English Language; Literature and Drama
Dist - EXEGAL

Make 'Em Laugh 28 MIN
U-matic / VHS
Please Stand by - a History of Radio Series
(C A)
Fine Arts; History - United States; Psychology; Sociology
Dist - SCCON **Prod** - SCCON 1986

Make Fewer Motions - Motion Economy 18 MIN
16mm
Color
LC 75-701274
Shows principles of motion economy which enables workers to perform tasks with less fatigue and increased output. Shows how to select a job for analysis and how to use a motion economy chart.
Business and Economics; Psychology
Dist - USNAC **Prod** - USA 1973

Make Germany Pay 20 MIN
16mm / U-matic / VHS
Twentieth Century History Series
Color (H C A) (GERMAN)
Presents a portrait of life in Germany after its defeat in World War I. Shows the serious financial inflation and the problems caused by French and Belgian occupation of the Ruhr. Ends with Germany joining the League Of Nations in 1926.
History - World
Dist - FI **Prod** - BBCTV 1981

Make Germany Pay - Pt 1 20 MIN
16mm
Twentieth Century History Series - Vol I
Color (S)
$380.00 purchase _ #548 - 9230
Illuminates the events and issues which shaped our modern world. Uses archival footage, maps, drawings, feature film segments, paintings and posters to illustrate historic events. The first thirteen programs are available separately on 16mm. Part 1 of Volume I of thirteen programs, 'Make Germany Pay,' takes an in - depth look at the critical problems Germany faced from its defeat in World War I to its acceptance by the League of Nations in 1926.
Civics and Political Systems; Geography - World; History - United States; History - World; Sociology
Dist - FI **Prod** - BBCTV 1981

Make it count 260 MIN
VHS
Color; PAL (H C G)
PdS55 purchase
Presents ten 26 - minute programs teaching survival skills to people who have problems with numbers, such as those who can neither understand nor use the basic principles of arithmetic or who find it difficult to recognize numbers at all. Uses supermarket checkouts and factory wage offices to put addition and subtraction within the context of daily life, as well as to avoid any hint of 'classroom.' Contact distributor about availability outside the United Kingdom.
Education; Mathematics; Psychology
Dist - ACADEM

Make it Easy on Yourself 30 MIN
U-matic / VHS
Adult Math Series
Color (A)
Explains cancellation and some of the rules about how fractions fit together.
Education; Mathematics
Dist - KYTV **Prod** - KYTV 1984

Make it Fit 29 MIN
Videoreel / VT2
Designing Women Series
Color
Home Economics
Dist - PBS **Prod** - WKYCTV

Make it Happen 30 MIN
U-matic / VHS / 16mm
Color (PRO)
No descriptive information available.
Business and Economics
Dist - DARTNL **Prod** - DARTNL 1969

Make it Happen 22 MIN
16mm
Color (J H)
LC 83-701003
Suggests that women need to strive for respect rather than approval in their work and personal lives. Presents the comments of women on the planning, retraining and rethinking they went through to obtain such jobs as carpenter and stockbroker.
Sociology
Dist - MOBIUS **Prod** - MOBIUS 1982

Make it Lamb, 1,2,3 32 MIN
U-matic / VHS
Color (PRO)
Presents facts about lamb and its desirability as a restaurant menu item. Demonstrates cooking methods, including roasting, sauteing and pan broiling, and making an aromatic stew from the shank.
Home Economics; Industrial and Technical Education
Dist - CULINA **Prod** - CULINA

Make it Move 32 MIN
16mm
Color
LC 75-703202
Presents an original 'documentary' musical comedy. Satirizes student life in the Department of Cinema of the University of Southern California. Contains such original songs as Make It Move, A Splice Is Nice, Kodachrome Blues, Patio Patter, My Star and Love Laughed. (A USC Cinema Graduate Workshop production.).
Fine Arts
Dist - USC **Prod** - USC 1965

Make Light of Lifting 17 MIN
U-matic / VHS / 16mm
Color
Presents various manual lifting techniques designed to prevent back injury.
Health and Safety
Dist - IFB **Prod** - MILLBK

Make Mine Metric 13 MIN
U-matic / VHS / 16mm
Color
LC 75-703599
Presents a light - hearted introduction to the metric system and the situations it will cause in our daily habits when driving speeds, supermarket purchases, dress sizes and other every - day items are recast into metric figures.
Home Economics; Mathematics
Dist - PFP **Prod** - BRAVC 1975

Make Mine Music 75 MIN
16mm / U-matic / VHS
Color
Presents an all - animated musical fantasy, including a cast of famous musicians and singers.
Fine Arts
Dist - FI **Prod** - DISNEY 1946

Make music fun
VHS
Color; PAL (K P)
PdS20 purchase
Presents a fun look at music, musical instruments old and new and rhythm song. Features Lucie Skeaping in a 30 - part series of programs from 7 - 10 minutes each. Contact distributor about availability outside the United Kingdom and individual titles in the series.
Fine Arts
Dist - ACADEM

Make My People Live 57 MIN
16mm / VHS
Nova Series
(J H C)
$99.95 each
Explores the plight of American Indians, who suffer disease in greater numbers than other Americans, and yet have inadequate facilities on their reservations.
Science; Social Science; Sociology
Dist - AMBROS **Prod** - AMBROS 1983

Make nursing your business 55 MIN
U-matic / VHS
Color (C PRO)
$275.00 purchase, $75.00 rental _ #42 - 2299, #42 - 2300, #42 - 2299R, #42 - 2300R
Covers everything from how to obtain start - up capital to personal self - assessment and skill - building techniques. Reveals exactly what it takes to be a successful entrepreneur. Profiles one of the most successful nursing centers in the nation and takes a close look at a hospital's case management program run by nurse entrepreneurs.
Business and Economics; Health and Safety
Dist - NLFN **Prod** - NLFN

Make or break 104 MIN
VHS
Color; PAL (G)
PdS40 purchase
Presents four 26 - minute programs. Follows the arduous and often amusing training of volunteer recruits to the marriage guidance profession. Contact distributor about availability outside the United Kingdom.
Sociology
Dist - ACADEM

Make Room for Dad 15 MIN
U-matic / 35mm strip
Color
LC 79-`730076;
Helps parents expecting to face cesarean section know what to expect by following an expectant couple from their classes and into the delivery room. Shows actual delivery of their little girl.
Sociology
Dist - MEDCOM **Prod** - MEDCOM

Make Room for Daddy 23 MIN
U-matic / VHS
Color
Presents a four - part series on the changing role of fatherhood.
Sociology
Dist - WCCOTV **Prod** - WCCOTV 1982

Make Sure they See You 10 MIN
16mm
Expert Seeing Series
Color; B&W
Shows how to communicate with other drivers and pedestrians.
Health and Safety; Psychology
Dist - NSC **Prod** - NSC

Make the phone work for you 12 MIN
VHS
Color (J H C G)
$59.00 purchase _ #CBR1077V
Shows telephone techniques that will help to get more done, serve customers better and sell more products and services. Teaches the valuable skills of what to ask before putting customers on hold; how to soothe irate callers; how to end a call diplomatically; how to win at the telephone - tag game; why individuals should make an 'interruption list' and more.
Business and Economics; Psychology; Social Science
Dist - CAMV

Make the Right Move
VHS
Color (G)
$49.00 purchase _ #CCP0005V
Looks at lease agreements, security deposits, house rules and waivers, renting terminology and what to ask about an apartment before renting. Comes with manual and is available in Beta and 3/4 inch U - matic.
Home Economics; Social Science
Dist - CADESF **Prod** - CADESF 1988

Make the Right Move - the Apartment Rental Game
U-matic / VHS
(C A)
$49.00 _ #CCP0005V
Focuses on the issues young adults face when choosing an apartment for the first time. Using graphics and humorous scenarios, the video covers such points as how to use classified advertisements, choosing a leasing agreement, understanding rent terminology and others.
Social Science; Sociology
Dist - CAMV **Prod** - CAMV

Make today count 19 MIN
VHS / U-matic / 16mm
Color (H G)
$250.00, $300.00, $425.00 purchase, $50.00 rental
Addresses the subject of terminal illness. Presents frank interviews with persons facing their own terminal illness or the death of a family member. Proivides encouragement for group discussions and support group involvement. Produced by the Partners Against Substance Abuse.
Guidance and Counseling; Sociology
Dist - NDIM

Make top scores every time 30 MIN
VHS
Go to the head of the class collection
Color (H C A)
$29.95 purchase _ #LF704V
Presents strategies for test preparation. Helps students determine their best learning styles. Includes a booklet.
Education; Psychology
Dist - CAMV

Make training worth every penny 18 MIN
VHS
Color (G)
$550.00 purchase, $170.00 rental _ #V1064 - 06
Instructs managers in methods of training and evaluation to ensure that employee training is effective. Features Dr Jane Holcomb presenting her three - step process for obtaining good results. Includes video, leader's guide and Holcomb's book Make Training Worth Every Penny. Additional copies of the book are available separately.
Psychology
Dist - BARR

Make - Up and Juggling 30 MIN
VHS / U-matic
Behind the Scenes Series
Color
Fine Arts
Dist - ARCVID **Prod** - ARCVID

Make - up Artist 15 MIN
U-matic
Harriet's Magic Hats II Series
(P I J)
Teaches the ways actors and actresses are prepared for movies and television by means of make up.
Guidance and Counseling
Dist - ACCESS **Prod** - ACCESS 1983

Make - Up for the Theater 20 MIN
U-matic / VHS / 16mm
Color
Demonstrates the application of stage make - up. Shows how to account for differences in sexes and stage lighting.
Fine Arts
Dist - UCEMC **Prod** - UCEMC

Make - Up for Women 60 MIN
VHS / 16mm
(G)
$39.95 purchase _ #VT1078
Shows proper make - up application techniques. Discusses how to prepare the skin before applying make - up and the various soaps, astringents, and facial creams that can be used. Shows which foundation to use and how to do shading and highlighting. Teaches about correct color matching and how to apply powder, rouge, eye shadow, eyeliner, mascara, and lipstick. Taught by Barry Koper, Hollywood make - up artist.
Home Economics
Dist - RMIBHF **Prod** - RMIBHF

Make - Up for Women 60 MIN
VHS / BETA
Color
Shows how to apply make - up properly and effectively.
Home Economics
Dist - MOHOMV **Prod** - MOHOMV

Make - up for Women 60 MIN
BETA
Color
Explains how women can enhance their natural beauty through make - up.
Home Economics
Dist - HOMET **Prod** - CINAS

Make - up techniques with David Nicholas series 300 MIN
VHS
Make - up techniques with David Nicholas series
Color (H C G)
$199.95 purchase _ #BY200SV
Presents a five - part series featuring makeup artist David Nicholas. Discusses ethnic makeup, basic makeup techniques and cosmetics, makeup for heavyset women, reconstructive and corrective makeup, men's skin care and makeup techniques.
Home Economics; Sociology
Dist - CAMV

The Make - up workshop 90 MIN
VHS
Technical theatre series
Color (J H C G)
$95.00 purchase _ #DSV004V
Follows several students through an actual make - up workshop. Consults each student individually with their specific character's design and application. Covers supplies and tools, facial anatomy, preparing the face, middle age make - up, old age make - up, special effects and more. Includes teacher's guide. Part of a five - part series on theater techniques.
Fine Arts
Dist - CAMV

Make Up Your Mind 29 MIN
Videoreel / VT2
That's Life Series
Color
Psychology
Dist - PBS **Prod** - KOAPTV

Make Up Your Mind about Alcohol 9 MIN
VHS
Color (H C A)
$60.00 purchase, $20.00 rental
Shows how teenagers can teach fifth and sixth graders about alcohol use and abuse. Part of a three session program.
Guidance and Counseling; Psychology
Dist - CORNRS **Prod** - CORNRS 1985

Make up your mind - skillful decisions 30 MIN
VHS
Color (J H C G)
$99.00 purchase _ #LS148V
Teaches a six - step system to improve decision making skills.
Guidance and Counseling; Psychology
Dist - CAMV

Make Way for Ducklings 11 MIN
U-matic / VHS / 16mm
B&W (K P)
The picture book classic by Robert McCloskey. Iconographic filming with original score by Arthur Kleiner.
English Language; Literature and Drama
Dist - WWS **Prod** - WWS 1955

Make Way for the Past 28 MIN
16mm
Color
LC 77-700384
Tells the stories of five people who have restored almost forgotten 18th - century houses.
Guidance and Counseling; Industrial and Technical Education
Dist - WSTGLC **Prod** - RIC 1976

Make winter driving safer 13 MIN
16mm / VHS
Color (H G)
$65.00, $30.00 purchase _ #305, #500
Outlines the adjustments in skills necessary for winter driving and the precautions motorists should take to prepare a car for cold weather. Emphasizes the proper techniques to anticipate and avoid potential accidents due to skidding on ice and snow, how to recover from a skid and the proper use of 'jumper cables'.
Health and Safety; Industrial and Technical Education
Dist - AAAFTS **Prod** - AAAFTS 1982

Make Your Blood do Double Duty 14 MIN
16mm
Color
LC 75-702473
Stresses the need for a continuous supply of volunteer blood donors within the U S Navy.
Health and Safety; Science; Science - Natural; Sociology
Dist - USNAC **Prod** - USN 1973

Make Your Investigation Count 11 MIN
U-matic
Color (IND)
Shows the steps of an effective accident investigation, including interviewing witnesses, and deciding the difference between immediate and basic causes of accidents. Supervisors learn that investigations are not complete until permanent actions are taken to prevent recurrence.
Health and Safety; Industrial and Technical Education; Sociology
Dist - BNA **Prod** - ERESI 1984

Make your own arrangement 30 MIN
Videoreel / VT2
Designing home interiors series; Unit 13
Color (C A)
Discusses selecting adaptable furnishings for smaller environments such as apartments and condominiums.
Home Economics
Dist - CDTEL **Prod** - COAST

Make Your Own Wine 60 MIN
VHS / BETA
Color
Provides step - by - step instruction in the techniques of wine making.
Home Economics
Dist - MOHOMV **Prod** - MOHOMV

Make your way - Cassette 4 54 MIN
VHS
Exploring your neighbourhood series
Color; PAL (P I)
PdS29.50 purchase
Provides a framework within which children can investigate their neighborhood. Helps them develop skills and techniques which enable them to satisfy their curiosity. Part four of a four - part series.
Social Science; Sociology
Dist - EMFVL

Make Yourself House Rich 60 MIN
U-matic / VHS
Sylvia Porter Series
Stereo (H C G T A S R PRO IND)
Shows strategies for mining the untapped dollars in your home.
Business and Economics; Literature and Drama; Social Science
Dist - BANTAP **Prod** - BANTAP 1986

Makeover madness - Volume 11 25 MIN
VHS
Filling station series
Color (K P I R)
$11.99 purchase _ #35 - 811416 - 979
Combines live action and animated sequences to teach the message that people are beautiful because they are created in God's image.
Literature and Drama; Religion and Philosophy
Dist - APH **Prod** - TYHP

Makes me wanna holler - a young black man in America 30 MIN
VHS
Author's night at the Freedom Forum series
Color (G)
$15.00 purchase _ #V94 - 05
Focuses on Nathan McCall, author of the book of the same title, in part of a series on freedom of the press, free speech and free spirit.
History - United States; Social Science; Sociology
Dist - FREEDM **Prod** - FREEDM 1994

Makeshift Solutions 18 MIN
16mm / U-matic / VHS
History Book Series
Color
Uses paintings, graphics and animation to describe the organization of the workers of Europe in response to the unemployment created by the industrial crisis. Discusses the expeditions of Stanley in Africa and its colonizations.
Business and Economics; History - World; Social Science; Sociology
Dist - CNEMAG **Prod** - TRIFC 1974

Makeup for the theater - Part I 60 MIN
VHS
Color (G C H)
$99.00 purchase _ #DL260
Looks at the underlying principles of makeup design - how light and shadow work on the facial structure. Uses split - screen inserts to show the makeup chart as the paint is applied. Illustrates how to create male and female characters, how to create a period appearance, and how to construct a hairpiece. Part one of two parts.
Fine Arts
Dist - INSIM

Makeup for the theater - Part II 60 MIN
VHS
Color (G C H)
$99.00 purchase _ #DL319
Looks at the underlying principles of makeup design - how light and shadow work on the facial structure. Uses split - screen inserts show the makeup chart as the paint is applied. Demonstrates two complete make - ups, plus how to create old and fantasy faces. Part two of two parts.
Fine Arts
Dist - INSIM

Makhalipile - the Dauntless One 54 MIN
VHS / 16mm
Color (G)
$350.00 purchase, $90.00 rental
Profiles Archbishop Trevor Huddleston who became known as 'Makhappile,' the dauntless one, after he became a champion of the black people of Johannesburg, South Africa, in the fifties. Interweaves interviews and archival footage to chronicle Archbishop Huddleston's life and work and his continuing commitment to the destruction of apartheid. Includes interviews with Oliver Tambo, Desmond Tutu, Helen Joseph and Sir Shridath Ramphal.
Civics and Political Systems; Geography - World; History - World; Sociology
Dist - CNEMAG **Prod** - IDAFSA 1989

Makimono 38 MIN
16mm
Color (G)
$50.00 rental
Features an independent film from Hamburg by Werner Nekes, who founded the Hamburg Cooperative in 1967 and has run the Hamburger Filmschau since then. Unfolds a continuously varying impression of a representation of a landscape.
Fine Arts
Dist - CANCIN

Makin' Hole in the Eighties 31 MIN
U-matic / VHS / 16mm
Color (A PRO)
$160.00 purchase _ #30.0120, $375.00 purchase _ #50.0120
Introduces today's drilling industry from seismic exploration to action on the rig floor. Designed for nontechnical audiences.
Industrial and Technical Education; Social Science
Dist - UTEXPE **Prod** - UTEXPE 1981

Makin' sweet harmony 14 MIN
VHS / U-matic
Music and me series
Color (I)
LC 80-706748
Introduces the concept of harmony through participation, listening and learning a song about harmony.
Fine Arts
Dist - AITECH **Prod** - WDCNTV 1979

Making a Book 15 MIN
U-matic / VHS
Word Shop Series
Color (P)
Literature and Drama
Dist - WETATV **Prod** - WETATV

Making a Call - Getting through 8 MIN
VHS
Spanish Plus Series
(J H A) (SPANISH)
Teaches how to talk about time and then details phone conversation in Spanish.
Foreign Language
Dist - AITECH **Prod** - LANGPL 1985

Making a Call - Leaving a Message 7 MIN
VHS
Spanish Plus Series
(J H A)
Features the Spanish instruction for answering the telephone and asking for someone on the phone.
Foreign Language
Dist - AITECH **Prod** - LANGPL 1985

Making a Cello 40 MIN
16mm
Color (H A)
$700.00 purchase, $60.00 rental
Documents the felling of a 225 - year - old spruce in a Swiss forest and its shipment to Berkshire, England, where musical instrument maker Alec McCurdy begins to work it into a cello. Features other woods also.
Fine Arts
Dist - AFA **Prod** - CCGB 1977

Making a Choice 10 MIN
16mm
Parent Education - Information Films Series
B&W (S)
Describes the procedure for selecting and teaching the second lip - reading word.
Guidance and Counseling; Psychology
Dist - TC **Prod** - TC

Making a cold bend on a hand powered machine 13 MIN
16mm
Shipbuilding skills series; Pipefitting; 4
B&W
LC FIE52-202
Discusses the importance of bends in marine pipe installation. Shows how to measure pipe for bends and how to operate a hand - bending machine.
Industrial and Technical Education
Dist - USNAC **Prod** - USOE 1944

Making a Connection
U-matic / VHS
Working Offshore Series
Color (IND)
Covers procedures for making up a joint of pipe including getting the joint ready, placing it in the mousehole, cleaning and doping threads, unlatching the kelly on the new joint, stabbing and making up the new joint and other roughneck duties in making a connection.
Business and Economics; Industrial and Technical Education; Social Science
Dist - GPCV **Prod** - GPCV

Making a Connection 12 MIN
U-matic / VHS
Roughneck Training Series
Color (IND)
Identifies points that the drilling crew should be aware of when adding a mousehole joint to the drill string. Includes inspection, preparation and procedures.
Business and Economics; Industrial and Technical Education; Social Science
Dist - UTEXPE **Prod** - UTEXPE 1983

Making a Continuous Lapped Placket 5 MIN
16mm
Clothing Construction Techniques Series
Color (J)
LC 77-701206
Illustrates how to prepare the placket area by marking and reinforcing stitching. Presents the option of using a bias or straight grain placket strip, and shows how to reinforce the placket at the point of strain.
Home Economics
Dist - IOWASP **Prod** - IOWA 1976

Making a Core Box for a Flanged Pipe Elbow 21 MIN
16mm
B&W
LC FIE52-126
Explains how to use a pattern layout in making a core box, design a core box, lay out a curved core piece, turn the core cavity in a curved piece, assemble a core box having a curved core piece and finish the core box.
Industrial and Technical Education
Dist - USNAC **Prod** - USOE 1945

Making a Core Box for a Machine Base 12 MIN
16mm
B&W
LC FIE52-130
Shows how a patternmaker, working from a casting, goes about the job of designing a core box, examines the casting, visualizes the problem, makes the layout and constructs the pattern and core boxes.
Industrial and Technical Education
Dist - USNAC **Prod** - USOE 1945

Making a Core Box for a Tail Print 18 MIN
16mm
B&W
LC FIE52-135
Explains how to use dry sand cores in molding holes in castings, use a pattern layout to make a core box, distinguish between core and core print, add the core and determine the parting line of a core box.
Industrial and Technical Education
Dist - USNAC **Prod** - USOE 1945

Making a Core Box for a Vertical Core 19 MIN
16mm
B&W
LC FIE52-125
Explains the function of the sand core. Depicts how to make a half box, use parted boxes, use a layout pattern in making a core box, prepare core box pieces and assemble a core box.
Industrial and Technical Education
Dist - USNAC **Prod** - USOE 1945

Making a Difference 27 MIN
16mm
Color (PRO)
Documents the role of the OTR in the 70's. Shows patients from all age groups receiving occupational therapy services for physical and psychosocial dysfunctions.
Health and Safety
Dist - AOTA **Prod** - AOTA 1972

Making a difference - a mother's guide to prenatal care - Haga la diferencia 20 MIN
VHS
Having a baby series
Color (H G PRO) (SPANISH)
$195.00 purchase _ #E910 - VI - 032, #E910 - VI - 048
Identifies unhealthy behaviors expectant mothers should avoid and beneficial habits that should become part of their daily lives. Part of a six - part series on all aspects of birth, from prenatal to postnatal care of the mother and care of the newborn infant.
Health and Safety; Sociology
Dist - HSCIC **Prod** - UTXHSH 1991

Making a difference on patrol 12 MIN
VHS
In crime's wake victim assistance training series
Color (C PRO G)
$50.00 purchase
Explores the initial reactions to be expected from crime victims. Part of a five - part series of in - training videos for victim advocates - social workers, domestic intervention specialists, police officers and other victim services personnel. Includes a discussion guide developed by the Police Executive Research Forum.
Guidance and Counseling; Sociology
Dist - SELMED

Making a difference - Restoring the Earth around us 28 MIN
VHS
Color (J H C G)
$195.00 purchase, $45.00 rental
Begins with a brief history of environmental destruction during ancient times then leads into three portraits of present - day efforts to reverse environmental damage. Includes volunteers replanting sequoia trees; operating a fish hatchery to return salmon to rivers; and planting thousands of trees in downtown Los Angeles. Produced by George Spies.
Fine Arts; Science - Natural; Social Science
Dist - BULFRG

Making a Fabric Covered Belt 5 MIN
16mm
Clothing Construction Techniques Series
Color (J)
LC 77-701217
Shows making a professional - looking, fabric - covered belt using commercial belting. Describes a method for achieving the desired length and shows using the belting as a guide for achieving the correct size fabric tube.
Home Economics
Dist - IOWASP **Prod** - IOWA 1976

Making a Faced Opening for a Pleated Sleeve Closure 4 MIN
16mm
Clothing Construction Techniques Series
Color (J)
LC 77-701210
Shows how to make a faced opening and how to attach the cuff to a sleeve that has this type of opening.
Home Economics
Dist - IOWASP **Prod** - IOWA 1976

Making a Five Tuck Splice 26 MIN
16mm
B&W
LC FIE52-24
Pictures the preparation of a cable for splicing. Shows how to make the first tuck and the four succeeding tucks.
Industrial and Technical Education
Dist - USNAC **Prod** - USOE 1944

Making a flat position open butt weld/ making a flat position closed butt 22 MIN
U-matic / VHS / 16mm
Arc welding series
Color (H C A)
Describes how to make a flat position open butt weld, a flat position closed butt weld and butt welding steel rods end to end.
Industrial and Technical Education
Dist - CORNRS **Prod** - CUETV 1981

Making a Good Impression 15 MIN
U-matic / VHS
Color (PRO)
LC 80-706812
Presents the steps involved in making a custom ear mold for an air - conduction hearing aid.
Health and Safety
Dist - USNAC **Prod** - BRENTW 1976

Making a Good Thing Better 11 MIN
16mm
Color (PRO)
LC 74-703662
Shows how use of a tamper - resistant package of Tubex narcotics and barbiturates helps strengthen drug security programs in hospitals and clinics.
Health and Safety
Dist - WYLAB **Prod** - WYLAB 1970

Making a Half - Slip 13 MIN
16mm
Home Economics - Clothing Series
Color (J H A)
LC 79-709993
Shows the procedure of making a half - slip, analyzing the marking and measuring, sewing the pieces together and adding the waistband and the lace.
Home Economics
Dist - SF **Prod** - MORLAT 1968

Making a horizontal tee weld 10 MIN
16mm / U-matic / VHS
Arc welding series
Color (H C A)
Industrial and Technical Education
Dist - CORNRS **Prod** - CUETV 1981

Making a Living 8 MIN
16mm
B&W
Tells the story of man who tries to get a job on a newspaper by stealing a rival's camera and racing to the newspaper's office with pictures of an auto accident. Stars Charlie Chaplin.
Fine Arts
Dist - TWYMAN **Prod** - MSENP 1914

Making a Living Work Series Program 101
Change 30 MIN
Dist - OHUTC

Making a Living Work Series Program 102
Lifestyles/Lifestages 30 MIN
Dist - OHUTC

Making a Living Work Series Program 104
Skills 30 MIN
Dist - OHUTC

Making a Living Work Series Program 107
Occupational Research 30 MIN
Dist - OHUTC

Making a living work series
Presents an eight - part series covering different aspects of making a career in the business world. Considers subjects including change, lifestage theory, values, skill transfer, decision making, and more.
Lifestyles and lifestages 30 MIN
Skills 30 MIN
Dist - CAMV

Making a Living Work Series
Change 30 MIN
Dist - CAMV
CAREER

Making a living work series
Occupational Research - the Job Search 30 MIN
Values 30 MIN
World of work 30 MIN
Dist - CAMV
CAREER
JISTW

Making a living work series
Decision making 30 MIN
Dist - CAMV
JISTW

Making a Living Work Series
Making Change 30 MIN
Dist - CAMV
JISTW
OHUTC

Making a Living Work Series
Provides a series of eight titles on eight VHS tapes which discuss various aspects of establishing a career.
Lifestyles - Lifestages 30 MIN
Making a Living Work Series 30 MIN
Making Change 30 MIN
Skills 30 MIN
Dist - CAREER **Prod** - CAREER 1914

Making a living work series
Decision making 30 MIN
Dist - CAREER
JISTW

Making a Living Work Series
Change 30 MIN
Lifestyles - Lifestages 30 MIN
Lifestyles Lifestages 30 MIN
Skills 30 MIN
Dist - JISTW

Making a living work series
Decision making 30 MIN
World of work 30 MIN
Dist - OHUTC

Making a Mask 6 MIN
16mm / U-matic / VHS
Creative Hands Series
Color (I J H C)
Shows how to make two kinds of masks - - tie - on and slipover - - out of wet paper and paste.
Fine Arts
Dist - IFB **Prod** - CRAF 1951

Making a Master Developed Layout, Pt 1 20 MIN
16mm
B&W
LC FIE52-13
Demonstrates how to make the complete pattern or master developed layout for a bulkhead in an airplane fin, using a master contour template.
Industrial and Technical Education
Dist - USNAC **Prod** - USOE 1944

Making a Master Developed Layout, Pt 2 - and Making the Form Block 16 MIN
16mm
B&W
LC FIE52-11
Explains how to complete the master developed layout by calculating and scribing the form block lines. Shows how to make the form block.
Industrial and Technical Education
Dist - USNAC **Prod** - USOE 1944

Making a Matchboard Pattern 21 MIN
16mm
Precision Wood Machining Series Fundamentals of Patternmaking, no 8
B&W
LC FIE52-124
Shows how to sketch a matchboard, make patterns, prepare gates to connect patterns, prepare the runner for the cope side, assemble the matchboard, turn a draft taper on a hole and attach flask fixtures.
Industrial and Technical Education
Dist - USNAC **Prod** - USOE 1945

Making a Melody 29 MIN
U-matic
Song Writer Series
Color
Shows composer Jerry Bilik as he examines five sets of lyrics, chooses one, and, at the end of 29 minutes, has written a tune.
Fine Arts
Dist - UMITV **Prod** - UMITV 1977

Making a Mosaic 10 MIN
16mm
Color; B&W (I)
Demonstrates the making of a mosaic by ADA Korsakaite from sketch to completion by the use of ceramic tile and commercial tessary. Shows examples of work done by Juan O' Gorman, Millard Sheets and Chavez Morado.
Fine Arts
Dist - AVED **Prod** - ALLMOR 1955

Making a Neckband Collar 5 MIN
16mm
Clothing Construction Techniques Series
Color (J)
LC 77-701193
Demonstrates making a shirt - type collar that has the neckband cut in one with the collar. Illustrates stitching the front edges of the collar and band accurately, clipping and notching where appropriate.
Home Economics
Dist - IOWASP **Prod** - IOWA 1976

Making a Newspaper 13 MIN
U-matic / VHS
Under the Yellow Balloon Series
Color (P)
Shows Ruth's grandfather, a newspaper editor, showing her the steps in putting out a newspaper for the Animal Lover's Club.
Literature and Drama; Social Science
Dist - AITECH **Prod** - SCETV 1980

Making a One - Piece Flat Pattern 22 MIN
16mm
Precision Wood Machining Series Fundamentals of Pattern Making, no 1
B&W
LC FIE52-118
Shows how to identify the parts of the molding flask, to use shrinkage rules, to prepare the pieces, to make identical castings and to finish the patterns.
Industrial and Technical Education
Dist - USNAC **Prod** - USOE 1945

Making a Paid Political Announcement 7 MIN
16mm
Color (C)
$400.00
Experimental film by Howard Fried.
Fine Arts
Dist - AFA **Prod** - AFA 1988

Making a Pattern for a Flanged Pipe Elbow 18 MIN
16mm
B&W
LC FIE52-123
Illustrates how to make a right - angle layout, turn out separate core prints, make split flanges, set flanges into core prints, assemble half the pattern on the layout, dowel an elbow pattern and apply leather fillets.
Industrial and Technical Education
Dist - USNAC **Prod** - USOE 1945

Making a Pattern for a Machine Molded Steel Globe and Angle Valve 14 MIN
16mm
Precision Wood Machining Series Problems in Patternmaking
B&W
LC FIE52-134
Explains how machine molding affects pattern design and how a patternmaker designs and constructs a pattern for a valve body, including the gating system.
Industrial and Technical Education
Dist - USNAC **Prod** - USOE 1945

Making a Pattern for a Three - Part Mold 20 MIN
16mm
B&W
LC FIE52-122
Discusses the reasons for the three - part pattern. Shows how to make the layout, segment the body or center section, eliminate the end grain on large flanges and turn large work on the end of the lathe.
Industrial and Technical Education
Dist - USNAC **Prod** - USOE 1945

Making a Pattern Requiring a Cover Core 14 MIN
16mm
B&W
LC FIE52-128
Explains how molding and coring problems lead to the choice of a cover core, and shows how a pattern - maker designs patterns and core boxes requiring a cover core.
Industrial and Technical Education
Dist - USNAC **Prod** - USOE 1945

Making a Pattern Requiring Box Construction 17 MIN
16mm
B&W
Explains how the patternmaker approaches the task of making a pattern for a duplicate of a casting, examines and measures the casting, visualizes the problem and constructs the pattern.
Industrial and Technical Education
Dist - USNAC **Prod** - USOE

Making a Pattern Requiring Segmental Construction 13 MIN
16mm
Precision Wood Machining Series Problems in Patternmaking
B&W
LC FIE52-89
Explains why segmental construction is a preferred method for some patterns and shows how a patternmaker designs and constructs a pattern for a gear blank which requires segmental construction.
Industrial and Technical Education
Dist - USNAC **Prod** - USOE 1945

Making a Pattern using a Green and a Dry Sand Core 14 MIN
16mm
B&W
LC FIE52-127
Illustrates how a green sand core is molded. Tells how a patternmaker determines when to allow for a green sand core, how he designs a pattern allowing for a green sand core and how he visualizes and constructs a particular pattern.

Industrial and Technical Education
Dist - USNAC **Prod** - USOE 1945

Making a Pattern with a Horizontal Core 14 MIN
16mm
B&W
LC FIE52-121
Explains when a horizontal core is used and how to allow for shrinkage in bronze. Shows how to lay out fillets, make horizontal core prints, true up a parting plane, dowel a pattern with a horizontal core and turn.
Industrial and Technical Education
Dist - USNAC **Prod** - USOE 1945

Making a Pattern with a Tail Print 19 MIN
16mm
B&W
LC FIE52-120
Shows how to mold castings with holes, make a rough sketch for visualizing the actual casting, use a dry sand core, form core cavities by using tail prints and make a layout including tail prints.
Industrial and Technical Education
Dist - USNAC **Prod** - USOE 1945

Making a Picture 30 MIN
U-matic / VHS
What a Picture - the Complete Photography Course by John Hedgecoe'Series Program 1
Color (H C A)
Introduces the working principles of a camera and encourages an understanding of the basic elements of light, shape, form and pattern within the setting of a small family circus.
Industrial and Technical Education
Dist - FI

Making a Pinata 11 MIN
16mm
Color (P I)
LC 73-702456
Shows how a pinata is made of paper mache formed around a balloon and decorated with tissue paper ruffles. Presents ideas for pinatas for most of the major holidays of the year.
Fine Arts
Dist - ATLAP **Prod** - ATLAP 1969

Making a Pointed Collar (with Seam on Outer Three Sides) 5 MIN
16mm
Clothing Construction Techniques Series
Color (J)
LC 77-701192
Illustrates a technique in which the upper and under collars are stitched from the same pattern piece. Shows how the outer seam is stitched and understitched before the end seams, thus keeping the under collar from showing.
Home Economics
Dist - IOWASP **Prod** - IOWA 1976

Making a Purchase - Ikura Desu Ka 28 MIN
U-matic / VHS
Japanese for Beginners Series
Color (C) (JAPANESE)
$249.00, $149.00 purchase _ #AD - 2101
Shows how to ask 'How much.' Looks at the denominations of Japanese currency. Shows how to say 'No' or 'I don't understand.' Teaches Japanese numbers and etiquette. Part of the Japanese for Beginners Series.
Foreign Language; Geography - World; History - World; Mathematics; Psychology; Social Science; Sociology
Dist - FOTH **Prod** - FOTH

Making a Recovery Bed 10 MIN
16mm
B&W
LC FIE59-133
Demonstrates the procedure to be followed and the equipment and supplies needed to arrange a bed unit in the hospital ward or room to ensure a safe, warm, comfortable bed for the patient returning from surgery.
Health and Safety
Dist - USNAC **Prod** - USN 1957

Making a Revolution 52 MIN
16mm / VHS
America Series
(J H C)
$99.95 each, $595.00 series
Describes the events, people, and atmosphere leading up to the American Revolution.
Geography - United States; History - United States
Dist - AMBROS **Prod** - AMBROS 1973

Making a revolution 52 MIN
VHS / 16mm / U-matic
America - a personal history of the United States series; No 3
Color (J) (SPANISH)
LC 74-701572
Describes how the diverse colonies grew together in common complaints against the mother country. Presents Alistair Cooke who traces the American tradition of turning to arms in the face of trouble.
History - United States
Dist - TIMLIF **Prod** - BBCTV 1972

Making a revolution - Pt 1 26 MIN
16mm / U-matic
America - a personal history of the United States series; No 3
Color (J)
LC 74-701572
Describes how the diverse colonies drew together in common complaints against the mother country. Presents Alistair Cooke who traces the American tradition of turning to arms in the face of trouble.
History - United States
Dist - TIMLIF **Prod** - BBCTV 1972

Making a revolution - Pt 2 26 MIN
U-matic / 16mm
America - a personal history of the United States series; No 3
Color (J)
LC 74-701572
Describes how the diverse colonies drew together in common complaints against the mother country. Presents Alistair Cooke who traces the American tradition of turning to arms in the face of trouble.
History - United States
Dist - TIMLIF **Prod** - BBCTV 1972

Making a Round Collar 4 MIN
16mm
Clothing Construction Techniques Series
Color (J)
LC 77-701191
Illustrates a technique in which the upper and under collars are from the same pattern piece. Shows how the under collar is extended one - eighth inch beyond the upper collar, thus preventing it from showing.
Home Economics
Dist - IOWASP **Prod** - IOWA 1976

Making a Segmented Pattern 22 MIN
16mm
B&W
LC FIE52-119
Explains how to plan segmentation of the pattern, lay out the segments and web, assemble the pattern, prepare a recessed hub and finish the pattern.
Industrial and Technical Education
Dist - USNAC **Prod** - USOE 1945

Making a serving hatch using hand and power tools - Part one of Unit D - Carpentry and joinery - Cassette 7 51 MIN
VHS
Building crafts - the teaching and learning process series
Color; PAL (J H IND)
PdS29.50 purchase
Features part of an 18 - part series which observes teaching and learning in a variety of workshop situations. Includes such skills as plumbing, brickwork, carpentry, painting and decorating.
Industrial and Technical Education
Dist - EMFVL

Making a serving hatch using hand and power tools - students' attempts - Part two of Unit D - Carpentry and joinery -Cassette 8 24 MIN
VHS
Building crafts - the teaching and learning process series
Color; PAL (J H IND)
PdS29.50 purchase
Features part of an 18 - part series which observes teaching and learning in a variety of workshop situations. Includes such skills as plumbing, brickwork, carpentry, painting and decorating.
Industrial and Technical Education
Dist - EMFVL

Making a Simple Core 15 MIN
16mm
Foundry Practice Series Bench Molding, no 2; Bench molding; No 2
B&W
LC FIE52-107
Demonstrates how to prepare sand for coremaking, make a small cylindrical core in either one or two pieces, assemble a two - piece core and locate a vertical core in a mold to provide necessary venting. Shows how core gases escape when a mold is poured.
Industrial and Technical Education
Dist - USNAC **Prod** - USOE 1944

Making a sound decision 28 MIN
16mm
Color
LC FIA66-484
Shows the craftsmanship needed to design, manufacture and install a Reuter pipe organ.
Computer Science; Fine Arts
Dist - REUTER **Prod** - REUTER 1965

Making a Sound Film 13 MIN
U-matic / VHS / 16mm
Films about Filmmaking Series
Color (J)
LC 73-701923
Demonstrates the recording, editing and mixing of various types of sound with the visual images of a film. Describes the equipment used, the techniques involved, the procedures for synchronized dialog, voice over, music and sound effects.
Fine Arts; Industrial and Technical Education
Dist - IFB **Prod** - IFB 1973

Making a summary judgment motion 105 MIN
VHS
Color (PRO)
$65.00, $149.00 purchase, $49.00 rental _ #CP-53284, #CP-63284
Uses vignettes to illustrate important concepts in moving for summary judgment, including discovery, drafting, burden of proof, supporting, timing, challenge to sufficiency, and appeal. Includes tape program materials.
Civics and Political Systems
Dist - CCEB

Making a table 15 MIN
Videoreel / VT2
Living better I series
Color
Fine Arts; Industrial and Technical Education
Dist - PBS **Prod** - MAETEL

Making a thread pouch 13 MIN
16mm
Home economics - clothing series
Color (J H A)
LC 71-709991
Reviews threading of the bobbin and straightening the material. Shows pinning the thread pouch, sewing the seams and finishing the seams.
Home Economics
Dist - SF **Prod** - MORLAT 1968

Making a Trip 18 MIN
U-matic / VHS
Roughneck Training Series
Color (IND)
Points out factors rotary helpers should consider in order to make a round trip in a proper and safe manner.
Business and Economics; Industrial and Technical Education; Social Science
Dist - UTEXPE **Prod** - UTEXPE 1983

Making a video program 49 MIN
VHS
Color (PRO G)
$149.00 purchase, $49.00 rental _ #703
Overviews the video production process from scriptwriting and preproduction planning to editing, sweetening, titling and preview screening. Illustrates every step in the planning and production of a dramatic scene. Discusses script breakdown and storyboarding, planning for adequate coverage, setup on location, portable recorder operation basics, power requirements and batteries, camera white - balance procedure, exposure control, basic three - point lighting, mic types, patterns and placement, shot sizes and framing, eyelines, headroom and screen direction, actor - director communications. Produced by the Australian Film, Television and Radio School.
Industrial and Technical Education
Dist - FIRLIT

Making a Vinyl Repair Grain Matrix 9 MIN
VHS / BETA
Color (A PRO)
$58.50 purchase _ #KTI41
Deals with auto body repair. Shows the fabrication of a graining matrix, using Uticolor and a heat gun to cure.
Industrial and Technical Education
Dist - RMIBHF **Prod** - RMIBHF

Making a Wire Template 19 MIN
16mm
B&W
LC FIE52-1190
Shows how to draw lay - out measurements with blueprints, transfer blueprints, find the radius with a beam compass and bend a template.
Industrial and Technical Education; Mathematics
Dist - USNAC **Prod** - USN 1944

Making a work sampling study 23 MIN
U-matic / VHS / 16mm
Color (H C A)
Shows the steps used in making the work sampling study, including defining the problem, taking the preparatory steps, designing the study, making the observations, analyzing and summarizing the data, and reporting the results.
Business and Economics; Guidance and Counseling; Psychology
Dist - UCEMC **Prod** - UCB 1957

Making a wrapped and soldered splice 15 MIN
16mm
Aircraft work series; Control cables; No 1
B&W
LC FIE52-35
Demonstrates how to make a ball soldered terminal, prevent the wires from unlaying when cut, fit a cable to a thimble and make the wire wrap.
Industrial and Technical Education
Dist - USNAC **Prod** - USOE 1944

Making Advances - what Organizations must do about Sexual Harassment 30 MIN
VHS / 16mm
(G A PRO)
$600.00 purchase _ #AG - 5140M
Shows how to establish and maintain a harassment free work environment.
Psychology; Sociology
Dist - CORF **Prod** - CORF 1982

Making an occupied bed 25 MIN
VHS / U-matic / BETA
Basic patient care - comfort and hygiene series
Color (C PRO)
$150.00 purchase _ #127.3
Presents a video transfer from slide program which stresses bedmaking as one of the most important nursing actions for providing patient comfort. Demonstrates procedural steps for bedmaking while focusing on the purpose of each. Presents variations of steps for meeting specific patient needs. Part of a series on basic patient care.
Health and Safety
Dist - CONMED **Prod** - CONMED

Making an occupied bed 15 MIN
VHS
Color (C PRO G)
$395.00 purchase _ #R940 - VI - 004
Shows healthcare professionals how to make a bed while the bed is occupied. Demonstrates how to move a patient safely in the bed to allow for a linen change, how to remove soiled linen from the bed and how to make the bed. Discusses making mitred corners, making toe pleats, using a flat sheet as a bottom sheet and making an open bed.
Health and Safety
Dist - HSCIC **Prod** - BALLSU 1994

Making an Occupied Bed 19 MIN
U-matic / VHS
Basic Nursing Skills Series
Color (PRO)
Health and Safety
Dist - BRA **Prod** - BRA

Making an occupied bed 28 MIN
16mm
Directions for education in nursing via technology series; Lesson 5
B&W (PRO)
LC 74-701778
Discusses the source and collection of clean linen and demonstrates a method of making an occupied bed.
Health and Safety
Dist - WSUM **Prod** - DENT 1974

Making an Operational Analysis 29 MIN
16mm
Job Instructor Training Series
B&W (IND)
LC 77-703324
Business and Economics; Psychology
Dist - EDSD **Prod** - EDSD

Making an unoccupied bed 22 MIN
16mm
Directions for education in nursing via technology series; Lesson 3
B&W (PRO)
LC 74-701776
Discusses the source and collection of clean linen and demonstrates a method for making an unoccupied bed. Shows the use of a contour sheet and draw sheet.
Health and Safety
Dist - WSUM **Prod** - DENT 1974

Making an Unoccupied Bed 14 MIN
16mm
B&W
LC FIE59-134
Demonstrates the procedures to be followed and the equipment and supplies needed to arrange a unit in a hospital ward or room.
Health and Safety
Dist - USNAC **Prod** - USN 1957

Making and Cutting the Lining 29 MIN
Videoreel / VT2
Sewing Skills - Tailoring Series
Color
Features Mrs Ruth Hickman demonstrating how to make and cut lining.
Home Economics
Dist - PBS **Prod** - KRMATV

Making and keeping friends 15 MIN
VHS
Let's get along - conflict skills training series
Color (P I)
$69.95 purchase _ #10384VG
Explains the importance of making and keeping friends. Features Gary Wick, ventriloquist and comedian, as he shows kids conflict skills and the importance of communication. Includes a reproducible teacher's guide. Part of a four - part series.
Guidance and Counseling; Psychology
Dist - UNL

Making and meaning - the Wilton diptych 25 MIN
VHS
Color (G)
PdS15.50 purchase _ #A4-300451
Reveals the newly cleaned Wilton diptych, a small altarpiece commissioned by Richard II and painted around 1395 to 1399. Notes the diptych's complex religious and secular symbolism and the light it sheds on Richard himself and the medieval culture which he exemplified.
Fine Arts
Dist - AVP **Prod** - NATLGL

Making and playing homemade instruments 60 MIN
VHS
Color (K P I J)
$19.95 purchase _ #VD - MAX - HM01
Shows kids how to make a banjo out of a bleach bottle, or a conga drum from an oatmeal box, or maracas from frozen orange juice cans. Features Cathy Fink and Marcy Marxer who invite three youngsters to help them make and play these and other homemade instruments. Includes a yardstick mouthbow, bottle cap castanets and a washtub bass. Needs only simple tools and inexpensive, easy - to - find materials.
Fine Arts
Dist - HOMETA **Prod** - HOMETA

Making and Repairing Tubing Connections 18 MIN
16mm
Refrigeration Service Series Commercial Systems, no 5
B&W
LC FIE52-263
Shows how to straighten copper tubing, how to work, cut and dress copper tubing, how to make a flare for various sizes of tubing and how to sweat in a connector to cover a break.
Industrial and Technical Education
Dist - USNAC **Prod** - USOE 1944

The Making and sterilization of an innoculating loop/development of aseptic 32 MIN
U-matic / VHS
Color
Includes three presentations titled The Making And Sterlization Of An Innoculating Loop, The Development Of Aseptic Technique and Pure Culture Techniques. Covers characteristics of a well - made innoculating loop and techniques for making the loops, the use and development of an oaseptic technique to maintain purity during the transfer of stock cultures and isolated colonies and the concept of a pure culture as well as a demonstration of two isolation techniques typically employed in the microbiology laboratory.
Science; Science - Natural
Dist - AVMM **Prod** - AMSM

Making and using Bias Strips 6 MIN
16mm
Clothing Construction Techniques Series
Color (J)
LC 77-701229
Demonstrates how to cut, shape and join bias strips and shows where and how to use bias. Includes piping and bias facings.
Home Economics
Dist - IOWASP **Prod** - IOWA 1976

Making Appraisals Effective 30 MIN
U-matic / VHS
Management for Engineers Series
Color
Business and Economics; Industrial and Technical Education; Psychology
Dist - SME **Prod** - UKY

Making Arrangements 29 MIN
U-matic
Song Writer Series
Color
Shows how songs can be improved by a group working together.
Fine Arts
Dist - UMITV **Prod** - UMITV 1977

Making babies series
Presents two 26 - minute programs about embryo research. Includes the titles For the Childless and For Parents at Risk. A companion booklet accompanies each program. Contact distributor about availability outside the United Kingdom.
For parents at risk 26 MIN
For the childless 26 MIN
Making babies series 52 MIN
Dist - ACADEM

Making Basic Plumbing Repairs 60 MIN
VHS / BETA / 16mm
Color (G)
$39.95 purchase _ #VT1033
Shows how to make basic plumbing repairs such as fixing a leaky faucet or unclogging a drain. Taught by Jerry Jones.
Industrial and Technical Education
Dist - RMIBHF **Prod** - RMIBHF

Making Behavioral Objectives Meaningful Series
Behavioral Objectives and Accountability 30 MIN
Objectives in the Affective Domain 30 MIN
Objectives in the Cognitive Domain 30 MIN
Dist - SPF

Making Bound Buttonholes 6 MIN
16mm
Clothing Construction Techniques Series
Color (J)
LC 77-701199
Demonstrates a method of making bound buttonholes which is suitable for a wide variety of fabrics. Shows how the buttonhole location is marked and illustrates how a fabric piece is attached to form the lips of the buttonhole.
Home Economics
Dist - IOWASP **Prod** - IOWA 1976

Making Bound Buttonholes 29 MIN
Videoreel / VT2
Sewing Skills - Tailoring Series
Color
Features Mrs Ruth Hickman demonstrating how to make bound buttonholes.
Home Economics
Dist - PBS **Prod** - KRMATV

Making Bread 6 MIN
U-matic / VHS
Color
Shows the machinery and the machinations of a bread making factory. Uses wit in its presentation.
Business and Economics; Home Economics; Industrial and Technical Education
Dist - MEDIPR **Prod** - MEDIPR 1979

Making Button Loops 5 MIN
16mm
Clothing Construction Techniques Series
Color (J)
LC 77-701201
Shows preparing button loops from bias fabric strips and using lined or graph paper as an aid for getting the loops evenly spaced and the same size.
Home Economics
Dist - IOWASP **Prod** - IOWA 1976

Making career decisions
VHS
Employability skills videos series
Color (H G)
$48.00 purchase _ #JR108
Offers help for senior high students, people entering the job market, and adults in career transitions. Focuses on how to make effective career decisions by using career and labor market information and well as information about personal interest, values and financial needs and also how to find this information.
Business and Economics; Guidance and Counseling
Dist - CENTER **Prod** - CENTER 1993

Making Change 30 MIN
VHS
Making a Living Work Series
$225.00 purchase _ #013 - 579
Portrays two case studies showing people reacting to and planning for change in their career and lifestyles.
Business and Economics; Guidance and Counseling
Dist - CAREER **Prod** - CAREER

Making Change 30 MIN
VHS / U-matic
Making a Living Work Series
(C A)
$225.00 purchase _ #JWOT8V
Relates case studies which exemplify reactions to changes in work and life styles.
Business and Economics; Education
Dist - JISTW **Prod** - OHUTC
OHUTC
CAMV

Making Change 9 MIN
U-matic / VHS / 16mm
Color (P)
Teaches the names, values and relationships of coins, how to make change and the use of decimals in money notation.
Mathematics; Social Science
Dist - PHENIX **Prod** - PHENIX 1977

Making Change for a Dollar 13 MIN
16mm / U-matic / VHS
Color (P)
$325, $235 purchase _ #3408
Shows how to tell the value of different coins and how to add them together to make change.
Mathematics
Dist - CORF

Making Change Work 9 MIN
U-matic / 35mm strip
Introduction of Change Series
Color
Offers five simple steps to avoid the major pitfalls of introducing change. Covers timing, preparation and the actual implementation.
Business and Economics; Psychology
Dist - RESEM **Prod** - RESEM

Making children's picture books - Shirley Hughes, Babette Cole and Pat Hutchins 42 MIN
VHS
Color (H C G)
$79.00 purchase
Features the writers and illustrators discussing with Heather Neill how children's books are conceived, written and put together with drawings for a completed work. Talks about the importance of imaginative characters as well as realism in children's works, and the resources each artist uses for inspiration in her writing and drawing.
Literature and Drama
Dist - ROLAND **Prod** - INCART

Making Choices 29 MIN
VHS / 16mm
Villa Alegre Series
Color (P T)
$46.00 rental _ #VILA - 151
Presents educational material in both Spanish and English.
Education; Psychology
Dist - PBS

Making choices - an interactive sexual decision making videodisc program
Videodisc
Color (J H C)
$495.00 purchase
Presents an interactive videodisc program which lets students see the potential consequences of their decisions without having to suffer from them. Uses a common 'home alone' situation to ask students to make one decision which leads them to another and then another. Each decision is a discussion point for students to explore various degrees of risk and safety. Requires a simple videodisc player and a remote.
Health and Safety; Psychology; Social Science; Sociology
Dist - SELMED

Making choices for quality health care 20 MIN
VHS
Color (G)
$149.00 purchase _ #4042 - HDLQ
Looks at effective health care consumer skills in action. Teaches viewers how to obtain quality care at lower cost. Includes a 16 - page leader's guide. Also available as part of the complete Quality Health Care Program.
Home Economics
Dist - KRAMES **Prod** - KRAMES

Making cold calls easy and profitable
VHS
Color (G PRO)
$49.95 purchase _ #585 - 67
Improves mental and emotional preparation for making cold calls. Covers creating an effective script, recognizing customer needs, using soft sell techniques and rehearsing presentations. Discusses rejection and how to deal with it.
Business and Economics
Dist - MEMIND

Making Composite Color Slides with a Rear Projection System 8 MIN
U-matic
Color
LC 77-706052
Discusses equipment, materials and procedures used for making composite slides.
Education; Industrial and Technical Education
Dist - USNAC **Prod** - NMAC 1976

Making connections through geometry - the search beneath the sea 24 MMIN
VHS
Color (I J H)
$189.00 purchase _ #FG - 114 - VS
Follows two teens on a scuba diving adventure who discover some strange tiles on the ocean floor. Reveals that their discovery leads them into a search for a long - lost treasure ship. In the process they investigate a wide range of geometric skills and concepts - the relationship between angles and polygons, tessellations, methods of estimating the height of a distant lighthouse, maps, properties of similar figures. Includes hands - on material - tiles, navigational charts and worksheets, student booklets and a teacher's resource guide.
Geography - World; Mathematics
Dist - HRMC **Prod** - HRMC 1994

Making Contact 20 MIN
U-matic
Neighbours - a Training Program for Community Volunteers Series
Color (A)
Gives a description of what should lead up to and take place in the first meeting between an ESL tutor and student and a discussion by several tutors of their experiences in this situation.
Social Science
Dist - ACCESS **Prod** - ACCESS 1985

Making Contact - a Beginning in Speech and Language Therapy 9 MIN
16mm
Color
LC 74-705072
Provides an introduction to the field of speech pathology. Concentrates on the role of the clinician in relation to children who do not communicate or relate.
Education; English Language; Psychology
Dist - USNAC **Prod** - USHHS 1971

Making Contacts 29 MIN
U-matic / VHS
Photo Show Series
Color
Features an introduction to the darkroom, including photograms and how to take processed film and make a contact sheet, and prepare it for printing.
Industrial and Technical Education
Dist - PBS **Prod** - WGBHTV 1981

Making Cuffs 6 MIN
16mm
Clothing Construction Techniques Series
Color (J)
LC 77-701207
Illustrates attaching a cuff to the lower edge of a gathered sleeve. Discusses both one - piece and two - piece cuffs and shows the different techniques for applying interfacing for the two cuff constructions.
Home Economics
Dist - IOWASP **Prod** - IOWA 1976

Making customer service happen 30 MIN
VHS
Color (A PRO IND)
$875.00 purchase, $185.00 rental
Emphasizes the concept that customer service must be a priority at all levels of a company, not merely those which deal directly with the public. Focuses on how the manager can improve service in his or her department.
Business and Economics; Guidance and Counseling; Psychology
Dist - VLEARN **Prod** - MELROS

Making dance films 30 MIN
VHS / U-matic
Dance on television and film series
Color
Fine Arts
Dist - ARCVID **Prod** - ARCVID

Making Dances 90 MIN
16mm
Color
LC 81-700433
Includes interviews, rehearsal and performance sequences with choreographers Trisha Brown, Lucinda Childs, David Gordon, Douglas Dunn, Kenneth King, Meredith Monk and Sara Rudner.
Fine Arts
Dist - BLACKW **Prod** - BLACKW 1980

Making Dances, Pt 1 30 MIN
16mm
Color
LC 81-700433
Includes interviews, rehearsal and performance sequences with choreographers Trisha Brown, Lucinda Childs, David Gordon, Douglas Dunn, Kenneth King, Meredith Monk and Sara Rudner.
Fine Arts
Dist - BLACKW **Prod** - BLACKW 1980

Making Dances, Pt 2 30 MIN
16mm
Color
LC 81-700433
Includes interviews, rehearsal and performance sequences with choreographers Trisha Brown, Lucinda Childs, David Gordon, Douglas Dunn, Kenneth King, Meredith Monk and Sara Rudner.
Fine Arts
Dist - BLACKW **Prod** - BLACKW 1980

Making Dances, Pt 3 30 MIN
16mm
Color
LC 81-700433
Includes interviews, rehearsal and performance sequences with choreographers Trisha Brown, Lucinda Childs, David Gordon, Douglas Dunn, Kenneth King, Meredith Monk and Sara Rudner.
Fine Arts
Dist - BLACKW **Prod** - BLACKW 1980

Making Dances - 7 Post - Modern Choreographers 90 MIN
U-matic / VHS
Color
Reflects the diversity of contemporary dance. Documents the work and ideas of Trisha Brown, Lucinda Childs, David Gordon, Douglas Dunn, Kenneth King, Meredith Monk and Sara Rudner.
Fine Arts
Dist - BLACKW **Prod** - BLACKW

Making Darts, Tucks and Pleats 5 MIN
16mm
Clothing Construction Techniques Series
Color (J)
LC 77-701177
Shows stitching darts and securing threads with a tailor's knot. Illustrates making regular tucks, narrow pin tucks and pleats.
Home Economics
Dist - IOWASP **Prod** - IOWA 1976

Making Decisions 15 MIN
U-matic / VHS
By the People Series
Color (H)
Presents a model for thoughtful decision - making in the political process.
Civics and Political Systems; Social Science
Dist - CTI **Prod** - CTI

Making decisions - 19 7 MIN
VHS / U-matic
Life's little lessons - self - esteem K - 3 - series
Color (K P)
$129.00, $99.00 _ #V618
Tells about Vincent I Peabody, Jr, who had inherited his father's company. Reveals that he was a VIP - Very Incompetent Person - because he was afraid of making decisions. Shows how he decided to ask for help, start making his own decisions and become a VIP - Very Intelligent Person. Part of a 30 - part series on self - esteem.
Guidance and Counseling; Psychology
Dist - BARR **Prod** - CEPRO 1992

Making Decisions about Sex 25 MIN
16mm / U-matic / VHS
Color (J H)
LC 81-701564; 81 - 707577
Presents a group of teenagers who candidly assess their decisions and the circumstances that influenced them to either have or refrain from sex.
Guidance and Counseling; Health and Safety; Psychology
Dist - CF **Prod** - CF 1981

Making Decisions / Doing what You Think is Right / Why Am I Punished 15 MIN
U-matic / VHS
Clyde Frog Show Series
Color (P)
Presents stories presented by Muppet - like Clyde Frog presenting stories emphasizing positive self - images, feelings of optimism and self - confidence.
Psychology
Dist - GPN **Prod** - MAETEL 1977

Making Delegation Work for You
U-matic / VHS
Color
Sharpens the manager's ability to make appropriate delegation decisions through group sessions, activities and self - assessment exercises.
Business and Economics; Psychology
Dist - AMA **Prod** - AMA

Making diversity work 23 MIN
VHS
FYI career and personal performance series
Color (G)
$99.00 purchase _ #FYI14
Shows how to develop the awareness and skills necessary to recognize and tolerate differences and to form productive work groups. Teaches the practical process that unites employees and focuses their energy to serve the mission and goals of the organization.
Business and Economics; Psychology
Dist - GPERFO

Making do 50 MIN
VHS
Color (G)
$295.00 purchase, $95.00 rental
Looks at the 'informal economy' of countries in Asia, Africa and Latin America including handicrafts, light manufacturing, salvage operations, construction, street vendors, and laundries. Provides a detailed overview of this parallel lifestyle which operates on the margins of society's formal economy and legal system, and provides people in some 100 nations of the Third World with a means of survival. Directed by German Gutierrez.
Business and Economics; Fine Arts; Social Science
Dist - CNEMAG

Making 'do the Right Thing' 58 MIN
16mm / VHS
Color (G)
$895.00, $390.00 purchase, $125.00 rental
Records the creation of the film by Spike Lee, 'Do The Right Thing,' for ten weeks during the summer of 1988 in Brooklyn's Beford - Stuyvesant. Reveals the motivations for many artistic decisions made by Lee. Considers the explosive cultural and political issues raised in the film. By St Clair Bourne.
Fine Arts; History - United States
Dist - FIRS **Prod** - FIRS 1989
ICARUS

Making effective presentations 32 MIN
VHS
Color (C PRO)
$285.00 purchase, $70.00 rental _ #4317S, #4317V
Offers vignettes in an interactive format which demonstrate the right and wrong way for health care teachers to deliver stronger, more compelling presentations. Shows how to prepare, present and wrap up effectively. Presented by the Center for Instructional Support.
English Language; Health and Safety
Dist - AJN

Making effective sales calls - Part 2 47 MIN
VHS
Real selling series
Color (A PRO)
$395.00 purchase, $150.00 rental
Presents the second of a five - part series on sales. Portrays real sales persons on sales calls. Covers subjects including determining sales strategies, gaining credibility, personalizing sales presentations, and more.
Business and Economics; Psychology
Dist - VLEARN

Making effective teller referrals 20 MIN
VHS
Color (A PRO IND)
$595.00 purchase
Demonstrates that bank tellers, through even the most routine customer transactions, have many opportunities to promote sales. Presents vignettes for role play practice of sales opportunities.
Business and Economics; Psychology; Social Science
Dist - VLEARN

Making Ends Meet 11 MIN
16mm
Color
LC 74-705997
Shows, via film - a - graph technique, the successful operation of a day - care center in Perry, Georgia, where limited funds are available.
Business and Economics; Industrial and Technical Education; Sociology
Dist - USNAC **Prod** - USSRS 1969

Making Ends Meet - the Family Spending Plan 12 MIN
U-matic
Color; Mono (H C)
Outlines the process of developing a family budget. Featuring a young family, illustrates the importance of communication in developing and using a spending and savings plan.
Business and Economics; Home Economics
Dist - UWISCA **Prod** - UWISCA 1985

Making everyday events special 30 MIN
VHS
Parents' point of view series
Color (T A PRO)
$69.95 purchase
Presents advice on caring for children under five years old. Targeted to both parents and care providers. Considers how everyday family events can be made into special occasions. Hosted by Nancy Thurmond, ex - wife of Senator Strom Thurmond.
Education; Guidance and Counseling; Health and Safety
Dist - SCETV **Prod** - SCETV 1988

Making excuses - 40 7 MIN
U-matic / VHS
Life's little lessons - self - esteem 4 - 6 series
Color (I)
$129.00, $99.00 purchase _ #V669
Portrays Lyle Tucker who lived in a little Western town and had learned that excuses could get him out of a lot of work and avoid trouble. Reveals that he also had a reputation for being undependable and he almost lost Betsy because of it. Part of a 65 - part series on self - esteem.
Guidance and Counseling; Psychology
Dist - BARR **Prod** - CEPRO 1992

Making Eye Glass Lenses 5 MIN
U-matic / VHS / 16mm
European Studies - Germany Series
Color (H C A)
LC 76-700747
Describes the modern German eye glass manufacturing industry as well as the historical development of the process.
Business and Economics; Geography - World
Dist - IFB **Prod** - MFAFRG 1973

Making felt rugs 9 MIN
U-matic / VHS / BETA
Pushtu tribe series
Color; PAL (G H C)
PdS30, PdS38 purchase
Provides insights into how the Pushtu mountain nomads live, focusing upon their reliance on crafts for both function and beauty. Shows women making felt mats for beds and decoration and men shearing the tribal sheep. Without narration. Part of a four - part series.
Fine Arts; Geography - World; Sociology
Dist - EDPAT **Prod** - IFF

Making Felt Rugs - Pushtu 9 MIN
16mm
Mountain Peoples of Central Asia Series
Color (K P I J H C)
Provides insights into how the Pushtu mountain nomads live, focusing upon their reliance on crafts to supply both function and beauty. Shows how women of the Pushtu tribe make felt mats for their families' comfort and for decorating the hard floor of their black camel hair tents, while Pushtu men shear the tribal sheep. Describes their Moslem wives who pound and separate the wool fibers, deftly flicking their hands over the flattened, outstretched wool and pressing in the vivid colors.
Fine Arts; Geography - World; Sociology
Dist - IFF **Prod** - IFF

Making Folded and Fake Cuffs 6 MIN
16mm
Clothing Construction Techniques Series
Color (J)
LC 77-701212
Shows how to make a fake cuff which achieves the effect of a regular cuff cut, but eliminates bulk. Includes the more conventional folded cuff, with a formula for achieving the desired width and length.
Home Economics
Dist - IOWASP **Prod** - IOWA 1976

Making French and Flat Fell Seams 5 MIN
16mm
Clothing Construction Techniques Series
Color (J)
LC 77-701183
Defines French and flat fell seams and identifies where they might be used. Illustrates steps in making both types of seams.
Home Economics
Dist - IOWASP **Prod** - IOWA 1976

Making Friends 29 MIN
Videoreel / VT2
Our Street Series
Color
Sociology
Dist - PBS **Prod** - MDCPB

Making Friends 15 MIN
VHS / 16mm
Color (P)
$180.00 purchase
Models skills for meeting people and developing friendships for the benefit of young children. Includes leader's guide.
Guidance and Counseling; Health and Safety; Psychology; Sociology
Dist - CHEF **Prod** - CHEF

Making Friends 15 MIN
VHS / U-matic
Out and about Series
Color (P)
Depicts Molly's difficulties in making new friends at school after her best friend moves away. Explains that at first she meets rejection, but that a fable about a rhinoceros and a tickbird encourages her to keep trying.
Guidance and Counseling
Dist - AITECH **Prod** - STSU 1984

Making friends 8 MIN
U-matic / VHS
Songs for us series
Color (P)
$250.00 purchase _ #JC - 67701
Presents a live - action music video which teaches children the value of friendship and the importance of working things out when there are differences of opinion. Underscores the idea that friends can be found anywhere. Part of the Songs for Us series.
Fine Arts; Psychology
Dist - CORF **Prod** - DISNEY 1989

Making fun of others isn't fun at all, love is a special gift - Volume 6 60 MIN
VHS
Our friends on Wooster Square series
Color (K P I R)
$34.95 purchase, $10.00 rental _ #35 - 87172 - 460
Presents religious concepts through storylines, songs and Scripture. Features puppet characters including Smedly, Troll and Sizzle.
Fine Arts; Literature and Drama; Religion and Philosophy
Dist - APH **Prod** - FRACOC

Making futures real - requisite change for weight loss and maintenance - client and modeling tapes 170 MIN
VHS
Color; PAL; SECAM (G)
$170.00 purchase
Presents two tapes. Illustrates Leslie Cameron - Bandler in a demonstration of the positive effects of building a compelling future life possibility, offering subtle interventions of effective weight loss and maintenance. Features Cameron - Bandler and Michael Lebeau who review the session recorded in the client tape, model the process and comment on the outcomes and interventions. Includes a 63 - page annotated transcript. All levels NLP, neuro - linguistic programming.
Physical Education and Recreation; Psychology
Dist - NLPCOM **Prod** - NLPCOM

Making futures real - requisite change for weight loss and maintenance - client session 80 MIN
VHS
Color; PAL; SECAM (G)
$95.00 purchase
Features Leslie Cameron - Bandler who demonstrates the positive effects of building a compelling future life possibility. Focuses on subtle interventions of effective weight loss and maintenance. All levels NLP, neuro - linguistic programming.
Physical Education and Recreation; Psychology
Dist - NLPCOM **Prod** - NLPCOM

Making futures real - requisite change for weight loss and maintenance - modeling tape 80 MIN
VHS
Color; PAL; SECAM (G)
$95.00 purchase
Features Leslie Cameron - Bandler and Michael Lebeau who review the session recorded in the client tape, model the process and comment on the outcomes and interventions. Includes a 63 - page annotated transcript. All levels NLP, neuro - linguistic programming.
Physical Education and Recreation; Psychology
Dist - NLPCOM **Prod** - NLPCOM

Making Gathers 3 MIN
16mm
Clothing Construction Techniques Series
Color (J)
LC 77-701178
Illustrates the use of gathering threads and suggests stitch length. Shows pinning and stitching the gathered layer to the ungathered layer, finishing with two rows of stitching and trimming to reduce bulk in the finished hem.
Home Economics
Dist - IOWASP **Prod** - IOWA 1976

Making Government Work series
County Government 30 MIN
Dist - GPN

Making government work
Administrative agencies 30 MIN
The Future of government 30 MIN
Good citizenship 30 MIN
The Governor 30 MIN
How a Bill Becomes a Law 30 MIN
Municipal Government 30 MIN
Political Action Kit 30 MIN
Political parties 30 MIN
Power 30 MIN
Taxation 30 MIN
You and the Courts 30 MIN
Dist - GPN

Making Gunpowder - Tajik 10 MIN
16mm
Mountain Peoples of Central Asia Series
B&W (K P I J H C)
Shows how the Tajik people of Badakstan, in northeastern Afghanistan, follow their ancient custom of making gun powder.
Civics and Political Systems; Geography - World; Sociology
Dist - IFF **Prod** - IFF

Making Haiku 8 MIN
U-matic / VHS / 16mm
Color (P I J)
LC 72-700983
Introduces and explains the form of haiku and presents scenes from nature which inspire haiku. Emphasizes the simplicity and beauty of this form of poetry and encourages students' creativity in composing their own.
English Language; Fine Arts; Literature and Drama
Dist - EBEC **Prod** - EBEC 1972

Making healthy choices series
Addresses the key wellness issues facing people today. Looks at how people make daily choices about what to eat, who to spend time with, how to react to changes and challenges, and more. Contains six programs that examine five key areas of wellness including eating, myths our culture has built up around eating and weight, how exercise can be part of a normal lifestyle and that it doesn't have to hurt to be effective, how stress can be healthy and how physical and emotional reactions can be used to examine our lives, how good relationships are essential for good health, and how to begin a new lifestyle in the pursuit of better health. Includes leader's guide and participant workbooks.
Healthy change 20 MIN
Healthy eating 20 MIN
Healthy exercise 20 MIN
Healthy lifestyle 20 MIN
Healthy relationships 20 MIN
Healthy stress 20 MIN
Dist - WHLPSN

Making humor work 20 MIN
VHS
Color (A PRO)
$495.00 purchase, $150.00 rental
Shows how to use humor to reduce stress and increase productivity on the job and in daily living.
Business and Economics; Literature and Drama; Psychology
Dist - DHB **Prod** - CRISP

Making Ideas Happen 22 MIN
16mm
Color
LC 81-700560
Provides a look at aluminum production facilities in many parts of the United States as well as in France and Australia, showing how it is made and the markets it serves.
Business and Economics; Industrial and Technical Education
Dist - MTP **Prod** - MTP 1981

Making is choosing - a fragmented life - a broken line - a series of observations 104 MIN
VHS / 8mm cartridge
Color (G)
$150.00 rental, $80.00 purchase
Portrays six years of the filmmaker's life made up of impressionistic observations organized in a way that testifies to the 'fragmented life' of the film's full title. Includes some concrete happenings such as the birth of a daughter and moving his home from San Francisco to El Paso.
Fine Arts; Literature and Drama; Sociology
Dist - CANCIN **Prod** - VARELA 1989

Making it 29 MIN
U-matic
A Different Understanding Series
Color (PRO)
Explores the feelings of three teenagers on aspects of life that deeply concern them, school, close friendships, competition, family relations and sex.
Psychology; Sociology
Dist - TVOTAR **Prod** - TVOTAR 1985

Making it 18 MIN
16mm
Color
LC 76-703324
Discusses the role of sex in personal relationships.
Guidance and Counseling; Health and Safety; Psychology; Sociology
Dist - MORLAT **Prod** - MORLAT 1975

Making it 29 MIN
VHS / 16mm
A Different understanding series
Color (G)
$90.00 purchase _ #BPN178004
Gives the views of 3 teenagers on aspects of life they are concerned with. Discusses school, close friendships, competition, family relations, and sex. Features footage of these teens in daily life contrasted with footage of teens in the fifties. Co - produced with the Mental Health Division, Health and Welfare, Canada.
Sociology
Dist - RMIBHF **Prod** - RMIBHF

Making it Better - How Everyone Can Create a Safer Workplace
U-matic / 16mm
Color (A)
Shows how to motivate workers to make their workplace safer for themselves and others.
Health and Safety
Dist - BNA **Prod** - BNA 1983

Making it Count 12 MIN
U-matic
A Matter of Time Series
(A)
Tells the story of a retired couple who spend their time in solitary ways. As a result, each resents the other and a compromise has to be found to save the marriage.
Sociology
Dist - ACCESS **Prod** - ACCESS 1980

Making it count, 24346 SEATTLE, WA 98124 series
Additional programming capabilities 30 MIN
Dist - BCSC

Making it count series
Acquiring computer systems 30 MIN
Batch processing 30 MIN
Computer Aids to Management 30 MIN
Computer Operation Centers 30 MIN
Computers and Society 30 MIN
Evaluating Computer Resources 30 MIN
History of Computing 30 MIN
Information Representation 30 MIN
Introduction and preview - making it count series 30 MIN
An Introduction to Programming 30 MIN
Microcomputers 30 MIN
Multiprogramming and Multiprocessing 30 MIN
Networks and Distributed Data Processing 30 MIN
Online Processing 30 MIN
Review and Preview 30 MIN
System Analysis - Design 30 MIN
System Analysis - Development and Implementation 30 MIN
System Analysis - Problem Definition 30 MIN
Word Processing in Office Systems 30 MIN
Dist - BCSC

Making it Cozy 30 MIN
U-matic
Energy Efficient Housing Series
(A)
Discusses insulation and R value. Explains why different insulation is needed in different places.
Industrial and Technical Education; Social Science
Dist - ACCESS **Prod** - SASKM 1983

Making it Happen 17 MIN
Videoreel / VHS
Color
Focuses on whether or not winning is a 'feminine' attribute. Explores the lives of three sportswomen. Highlights women's major contributions to sports history.
Physical Education and Recreation; Sociology
Dist - EDC **Prod** - EDC

Making it happen 30 MIN
VHS
How do you manage series
Color (A)
PdS65 purchase
Shows how to have influence at work and how to negotiate at every level. Looks at negotiation as something that humans do all the time; at how to find ways around obstacles and the win-win approach; and managing conflict and crisis. Part of a six-part series featuring Dr John Nicholson, a business psychologist who specializes in helping people to develop new attitudes and ways of thinking to improve both job performance and satisfaction.
Business and Economics; Psychology
Dist - BBCENE

Making it in the Organization 18 MIN
U-matic / VHS / 16mm
Color (H C A)
LC 80-700116
A revised version of the Canadian motion picture Living In The Company. Shows how an employee's attitudes toward his work, his supervisor, his responsibility, and his organization affect job performance and satisfaction.
Guidance and Counseling; Psychology
Dist - SALENG **Prod** - WILCOD 1980

Making it in the USA - the secret of america's winners 30 MIN
U-matic
Adam Smith's money world 1985 - 1986 season series; 209
Color (A)
Attempts to demystify the world of money and break it down so that small as well as large businesses and it's people understand and adjust to new social and economic trends. Reports on the major economic stories and discoveries of 1985 and 1986.
Business and Economics
Dist - PBS **Prod** - WNETTV 1986

Making it in the World of Work 26 MIN
U-matic / VHS / 16mm
Color (J H C)
LC 72-701770
Discusses importance of life - style goals in choosing a compatible career. Includes discussion with young workers in nine different occupations.
Guidance and Counseling; Psychology
Dist - ALTSUL **Prod** - NORMBP 1972

Making it Live 60 FRS
VHS / U-matic
Basic Sales Series
Color
Demonstrates that knowing the product or service being sold and being able to tell about it with enthusiasm and conviction is a key to sale success.
Business and Economics; Psychology
Dist - RESEM **Prod** - RESEM

Making it Move 10 MIN
16mm / U-matic / VHS
Color (H C)
LC 80-700118
Illustrates the various stages in the process of cell animation.
Fine Arts; Industrial and Technical Education
Dist - PHENIX **Prod** - HALAS 1979

Making it official 12 MIN
16mm
Color (G IND)
$5.00 rental
Reveals that elections are often lost because large numbers of union members don't vote and many aren't even registered to vote. Looks at the role of union volunteers in checking membership lists provided by the state federation and helping to register other union members through person to person contact. Produced by the Labor Institute of Public Affairs for COPE.
Business and Economics; Civics and Political Systems
Dist - AFLCIO **Prod** - LIPA

Making it on Your Own - Building a Private Law Practice 50 MIN
VHS / U-matic
Color (PRO)
Designed for the lawyer considering going into solo practice or already in independent practice. Focuses on problems of law office management, financing, time management, counseling and client relations.
Business and Economics; Civics and Political Systems
Dist - ABACPE **Prod** - ABACPE

Making it on Your Own - Consumer Education
U-matic / VHS
Color (J H)
Help young people aquire the skills needed to move successfully into the adult world.
Home Economics
Dist - CAREER **Prod** - CAREER 1979

Making it on your own - managing your money 22 MIN
VHS
Color (H)
$49.00 purchase _ #60351 - 025
Portrays Carol, a teenager, who learns the necessity of budgeting. Reveals that it does not take long before she finds herself deeply in debt, having spent way beyond her means. Worse yet, her car breaks down and she can't afford to fix or replace it. Part of a series.
Business and Economics; Home Economics; Sociology
Dist - GA **Prod** - GA

Making it on your own - your own place 21 MIN
VHS
Color (H)
$49.00 purchase _ #60350 - 025
Follows two young men as they find an apartment and then find out about the realities of independence - apartment leases, moving expenses, cooking, shopping, budgeting. Reveals that through trial and error they figure out how to solve their problems and discover a new life - style. Part of a series.
Home Economics; Sociology
Dist - GA **Prod** - GA

Making it ... safe 60 MIN
VHS
Color (G)
$29.95 purchase
Examines and analyzes the problems confronting sexually active people as a result of the AIDS epidemic. Features Dr Marian E Dunne as host. Looks at what is safe - safer - safest. Offers practical insights and approaches and safe and sensible solutions.
Health and Safety
Dist - FCSINT

Making it Stick - no 7 60 MIN
U-matic
Training the Trainer Series
Color (PRO)
Presents training sessions for professional training personnel. Includes goal selection, design and presentation of training material and evaluation and reports.
Industrial and Technical Education
Dist - VTRI **Prod** - VTRI 1986

Making it work 30 MIN
VHS
Color (G C)
$199.00 purchase, $45.00 rental
Focuses on the first nursing - care facility in Minnesota to accept AIDS patients. Dramatizes how the staff dealt with their fear and lack of knowledge about the disease.
Health and Safety; Sociology
Dist - TNF

Making it Work 20 MIN
16mm
B&W (I)
LC FIA59-812
Illustrates the techniques in the work of the church press secretary.
Religion and Philosophy
Dist - ADVENT **Prod** - ADVENT 1960

Making it Work Series

The Application	11 MIN
How Am I Doing	15 MIN
How do I find a job	13 MIN
I'm Here to Work - Now what	12 MIN
The Interview	11 MIN
Learning by Experience	10 MIN
Making the most of Yourself	14 MIN
Opening Doors	13 MIN
Practical Planning	15 MIN
Say that One more Time	14 MIN
Tests and Stress	12 MIN
You have a Job Offer - Now what	13 MIN

Dist - AITECH

Making it Young 28 MIN
U-matic / VHS / 16mm
Developing Your Potential Series
Color (I J H)
Stresses that involvement and effort are the keys to developing one's potential and being successful.
Psychology
Dist - JOU **Prod** - SCCL

Making Judgments 15 MIN
U-matic / VHS
By the People Series
Color (H)
Provides criteria which can be used in making judgments about political issues.
Civics and Political Systems; Social Science
Dist - CTI **Prod** - CTI

Making kitchen cabinets by Paul Levine 60 MIN
BETA / VHS
Color (G A)
$29.95 _ #060033
Shows how to make high - quality, Euro - style kitchen cabinets with common workshop tools and standard hardware. Features carpenter Paul Levine. Also available in book format.
Fine Arts; Home Economics; Industrial and Technical Education
Dist - TANTON **Prod** - TANTON

Making Learning its Own Reward 18 MIN
VHS / U-matic
Color
Depicts motivational problems of a student who lacks the intrinsic motivation to pass spelling. Shows how together he and his teacher decide on an appropriate motivational reward.
Education; Psychology
Dist - UNEBO **Prod** - UNEBO

Making Legislators Accountable 27 MIN
U-matic
Color (A)
Demonstrates how the lobbying process works and its success in improving the voting records of Representatives who regularly hear from their constituents.
Civics and Political Systems
Dist - AFLCIO **Prod** - LIPA 1984

Making Line Graphs 14 MIN
U-matic / VHS
Hands on, Grade 4 - Cars, Cartoons, Etc Series Unit 2 - Measuring
Color (I)
Gives experience in making line graphs.
Mathematics
Dist - AITECH **Prod** - WHROTV 1975

Making love - Part III 20 MIN
VHS
Joy of life series
Color (I J)
$175.00 purchase
Uses an animated story format to discuss being in and making love. Contains four five - minute segments. Segment 9 - Making Love discusses being in love as a unique experience, then talks about intercourse and orgasms. Segment 10 - Protecting Yourself talks of the risks involved in lovemaking such as sexually transmitted diseases, including AIDS, and how to minimize risk by limiting partners and using condoms. Segment 11 - Conception presents the topic in detail. Segment 12 - The Baby's Coming shows an egg's development from fertilization to childbirth. Part of a series.
Guidance and Counseling; Health and Safety
Dist - PFP **Prod** - EVENOP

Making Maps 14 MIN
U-matic / VHS
Hands on, Grade 4 - Cars, Cartoons, Etc Series Unit 2 - Measuring; Unit 2 - Measuring
Color (I)
Gives experience in making maps.
Mathematics; Social Science
Dist - AITECH **Prod** - WHROTV 1975

Making marriage work - Part 1
VHS
Help - our family is unraveling series
Color (G A R)
$29.95 purchase, $10.00 rental _ #35 - 861328 - 527
Features Howard and Jeanne Hendricks with insights on marriage and parenting. Outlines the communication process within a marriage that cultivates intimacy.
Sociology
Dist - APH **Prod** - MIS

Making meaning - integrated language arts - Across the curriculum - Tape 4 22 MIN
VHS
Making meaning - integrated language arts series
Color (T C PRO)
$295.00 purchase, $125.00 rental _ #614 - 232X01
Shows how to teach reading, writing, listening and speaking across the curriculum by using a whole language approach. Watches as teachers use the natural elements of language learning to help children learn subjects through reading and writing about them rather than by learning facts in isolation; encourage students to use personal experiences as the reference point for learning subject material; let responses to student work guide lessons and still meet strict district curriculum requirements. Includes a comprehensive facilitator's guide and When Writers Read by Jane Hansen. Part four of five parts on whole language education.
Education
Dist - AFSCD **Prod** - AFSCD 1992

Making meaning - integrated language arts - Assessment - Tape 5 22 MIN
VHS
Making meaning - integrated language arts series
Color (T C PRO)
$295.00 purchase, $125.00 rental _ #614 - 233X01
Shows how assessment in a whole language approach differs from traditional approaches. Visits classrooms to show how evaluation starts by observing what students know and can do. Demonstrates the use of anecdotal records, conferences, teacher observations, student records and portfolios to evaluate students. Includes a comprehensive facilitator's guide and When Writers Read by Jane Hansen. Part four of five parts on whole language education.
Education
Dist - AFSCD **Prod** - AFSCD 1992

Making meaning - integrated language arts - Introduction - Tape 1 22 MIN
VHS
Making meaning - integrated language arts series
Color (T C PRO)
$295.00 purchase, $125.00 rental _ #614 - 229X01
Shows the necessity of new literacies such as thinking skills, writing for multiple purposes and reading for greater depth. Illustrates how a whole language approach teaches reading and writing in the same natural way that speech is learned. Motivates students by using literature as a vehicle for exploring language arts. Teaches the fundamental skills of grammar, phonics and spelling in the context of student work rather than in isolation. Explains how to group students for increasing learning rather than on the basis of ability and how to use assessment strategies that guide instruction and involve the learner. Includes a comprehensive facilitator's guide and When Writers Read by Jane Hansen. Part one of five parts on whole language education.
Education
Dist - AFSCD **Prod** - AFSCD 1992

Making meaning - integrated language arts - Primary grades - Tape 2
VHS
Making meaning - integrated language arts series
Color (T C PRO)
$295.00 purchase, $125.00 rental _ #614 - 230X01
Visits three classrooms using a whole language approach to teaching reading, writing, listening and speaking to K - 3 students. Explains the importance of time, choice, response, structure and community to instructional decisions. Shows how allowing students to choose their own reading materials and writing topics increases their motivation to learn. Demonstrates the use of shared book experiences, collaborative writing projects, reading conferences, writing conferences and modeling of the writing process. Includes a comprehensive facilitator's guide and When Writers Read by Jane Hansen. Part two of five parts on whole language education.
Education
Dist - AFSCD **Prod** - AFSCD 1992

Making meaning - integrated language arts series
VHS
Making meaning - integrated language arts series
Color (T C PRO)
$1165.00 purchase, $395.00 rental _ #614 - 228X01
Shows how to implement a whole language approach in schools. Includes five videos, a facilitator's guide and the book, When Writers Read, by Jane Hansen. Provides a comprehensive staff development resource for informing staff, parents and other audiences of how a whole language approach adapts natural elements of language learning to the teaching of reading, writing, listening and speaking in school; persuading school board members and community groups that a whole language approach helps students develop the skills they need for future success; showing teachers how a whole language approach empower them to make better instructional decisions for their students.
Education
Dist - AFSCD **Prod** - AFSCD 1992

Making meaning - integrated language arts - Upper elementary grades - Tape 3 23 MIN
VHS
Making meaning - integrated language arts series
Color (T C PRO)
$295.00 purchase, $125.00 rental _ #614 - 231X01
Visits two fifth - grade classrooms to show teachers using the natural elements of language learning in upper elementary grades. Illustrates examples of guided reading, read - aloud dialog journals, observations of the writing process, oral presentations and mini - lessons that teachers use when groups within the class need specific instruction in spelling, grammar or other skills.

Demonstrates how teachers provide time for students to explore literature and connect real life to what they learn in school. Includes a comprehensive facilitator's guide and When Writers Read by Jane Hansen. Part three of five parts on whole language education.
Education
Dist - AFSCD **Prod** - AFSCD 1992

Making Meetings Count
16mm / U-matic
Color (C A)
Dramatizes ways that business meetings can go wrong and shows how to prepare and run an effective meeting.
Business and Economics; Psychology
Dist - PHENIX **Prod** - PHENIX

Making Meetings Count 15 MIN
U-matic / VHS / 16mm
Color (H C A)
Shows a young business woman presenting a new idea and failing to convince her boss of its worthiness. Provides relevant business instruction while pointing out what went wrong with her presentation and what steps to take to run an effective presentation.
Business and Economics; Psychology
Dist - PHENIX **Prod** - MATVCH 1983

Making Meetings Work 18 MIN
VHS / 16mm
(C PRO)
$395.00 purchase, $100.00 rental
Presents time saving tips to make meetings more efficient.
Education
Dist - VLEARN

Making Memories 25 MIN
VHS / U-matic
Color
Probes the many mystifying aspects of memory with aid of leading experts and a quiz testing viewers on their recall. Includes a segment with two amnesia patients, one who has regained his memory and one who is still trying. Features memory feats by mathematical genius 'Willie the Wizard' and former basketball star Jerry Lucas.
Health and Safety; Psychology
Dist - MEDCOM **Prod** - MEDCOM

Making money with Major Munchy - explorations in probability 28 MIN
VHS
Color (I J H)
$175.00 purchase _ #FG - 117 - VS
Shows how four teens are challenged to win a cereal box contest after watching a whacky TV commercial for Major Munchy cereal. Reveals that to win the prize, they need to collect a set of letters in specially marked boxes of cereal. To do this they need to model the problem in probability and statistics. A variety of methods are used for modeling, including selecting letters at random with replacement, simulating purchases using number cubes, using computer - generated tables of random letters and even using a computer program in BASIC to run hundreds or thousands of trials. Includes a teacher's resource book.
Mathematics
Dist - HRMC **Prod** - HRMC 1994

Making Mortise and Tenon Joints
VHS
Video Workshops Series
$29.95 purchase _ #FW800
Shows a master craftsman demonstrating his techniques for making mortise - and - tenon joints.
Education; Industrial and Technical Education
Dist - CAREER **Prod** - CAREER

Making Mortise and Tenon Joints with Frank Klausz 60 MIN
VHS / BETA
Color (H C A)
Teaches how to make joints that are fundamental to good furniture making. Comes with booklet.
Industrial and Technical Education
Dist - TANTON **Prod** - TANTON

Making Movie Music 29 MIN
U-matic
Music Shop Series
Color
Discusses how Jerry Bilik makes music for movies.
Fine Arts
Dist - UMITV **Prod** - UMITV 1974

Making music 26 MIN
VHS
Wonderstruck presents series
Color (I J)
$99.95 purchase _#Q11169
Presents music from a scientific perspective in five separate segments explaining sound waves, conduction, acoustics, and resonance. Provides information on how to construct a gutbucket and includes on - location visits to a guitar maker, a steel drum band, and a glass orchestra. Part of a series of 11 programs produced by the Canadian Broadcasting Corporation and hosted by Bob McDonald.
Fine Arts
Dist - CF

Making Music 12 MIN
VHS / U-matic
Color (P I)
Presents Michael Small who guides the viewer through the fun and hard work of writing and playing music for a living.
Fine Arts
Dist - SF **Prod** - SF 1972

Making Music - Pt 1 30 MIN
VHS
Wonderstruck Presents Series
Color (I)
$99.00 purchase _ #386 - 9055
Organizes science programs thematically for classroom use. Features Bob McDonald as host who makes learning fun with amazing science information and engaging activities. Part 1 of the eight part series explores the sciences of sound and music through demonstrations and activities with a glass orchestra, a gutbucket, acoustic and electric guitars, steel drums and a study of resonance.
Fine Arts; Science - Physical
Dist - FI **Prod** - CANBC 1989

Making Music - the Emerson String Quartet 28 MIN
U-matic / VHS
Color
Provides a close look at the personal and musical qualities that must combine to make an ensemble of excellence.
Fine Arts
Dist - VINEVI **Prod** - VINEVI

Making music - the symphony orchestra 25 MIN
VHS
Color (J H C G)
$100.00 purchase _ #CLE673V
Goes behind the scenes with the Denver Young Artist Orchestra as it prepares for performance. Intersperses interviews with the conductor and orchestra members with footage of the orchestra's early rehearsals, seating auditions, dress rehearsal and final performance. Discusses the structure and organization of the symphony orchestra, the different sections, the instruments in each section and the responsibilities of the musicians and conductor. Includes a teacher's guide with program summary, list of learning objectives and notes about the orchestra, conductor and music.
Fine Arts
Dist - CAMV

Making New Friends 15 MIN
U-matic / VHS
Mrs Cabobble's Caboose
(P)
Designed to teach primary grade students basic music concepts. Highlights melody, rhythm, harmony and the different families of instruments. Features Mrs. Fran Powell.
Fine Arts
Dist - GPN **Prod** - WDCNTV 1986

Making Numbers Work 24 MIN
16mm
Color (A)
Shows how to use numbers more effectively, how to mentally work with numbers quickly and how to present or read data in such a way as to highlight significant trends.
Business and Economics; Mathematics
Dist - VISUCP **Prod** - MELROS 1983

The Making of a Ballet 38 MIN
VHS / U-matic
Color (I A)
Focuses on choreographer Rudi van Dantzig who spends most of his life in theaters and at rehearsals where he creates most of his ballets.
Fine Arts
Dist - SUTHRB **Prod** - SUTHRB

Making of a champion
VHS
Color (G A)
$39.80 purchase _ #0221
Features young sailing champions who give tips on how to win races. Includes Tom Blackaller, Dave Ullman, Dave Perry and Russ Silvestri.
Physical Education and Recreation
Dist - SEVVID

Making of a Clinician, Pts 1 and 2 86 MIN
16mm
B&W (PRO)
LC 77-703505
Presents a discussion between Dr David Seegal and four medical students about teaching methods. Includes his decalogue of nonprofessional virtues and describes the self - evaluation recommended for students.
Education; Health and Safety; Psychology
Dist - USNAC **Prod** - NMAC 1977

Making of a Clinician - Teaching the Medical Student to Teach 86 MIN
U-matic / VHS
Color (PRO)
LC 77-706200
Presents a discussion between Dr David Seegal and four medical students about teaching methods.
Health and Safety
Dist - USNAC **Prod** - NMAC 1977

The Making of a College Athlete 26 MIN
U-matic / VHS
Color (C)
$249.00, $149.00 purchase _ #AD - 1719
Reveals that thirty percent of high school football and basketball players are functionally illiterate. Stresses that these athletes bring fame and fortune to their schools but seventy percent of them do not graduate. As a result, their inferior educations limit them economically and in career choices. Examines both the efforts of the NCAA to establish minimum academic requirements and the costly exploitation of young male athletes.
Education; Physical Education and Recreation; Sociology
Dist - FOTH **Prod** - FOTH

Making of a continent II series
Collision course - Pt 1 58 MIN
The Great river - Pt 3 58 MIN
The Rich, High Desert - Pt 2 57 MIN
Dist - FI

The Making of a continent - Part 1 110 MIN
VHS
Making of a continent series
Color (I J H)
$190.00 purchase _ #A5VH 1293
Explores the river running through the Colorado Plateau as it leaves a record of the Earth's earliest environment in The Corridors of Time. Looks at the Great Basin which was formed when the floor of the Pacific slid under North America and pushed up the Sierra Nevada Mountains in The Land of the Sleeping Mountains. Part one of a three - part series on the geological events that shaped the North American continent.
Geography - United States; Geography - World
Dist - CLRVUE

The Making of a continent - Part 2 110 MIN
VHS
Making of a continent series
Color (I J H)
$190.00 purchase _ #A5VH 1295
Reveals that the birth of the Sierra Nevada created California's central valley which made history with its wealth of gold and rich soil in The Price of Gold. Journeys to the wasteland of Canada's Great Slave Lake, littered with the remains of continental collisions and fossilized remains from the earliest days of the planet in Collision Course. Part two of a three - part series on the geological events that shaped the North American continent.
Geography - United States; Geography - World; History - United States; Science - Physical
Dist - CLRVUE

The Making of a continent - Part 3 110 MIN
VHS
Making of a continent series
Color (I J H)
$190.00 purchase _ #A5VH 1296
Views the breadbasket of the world, the Great Plains which rest on miles of ancient sediment, and the Great Lakes, created in the last ice age, in The Rich, High Desert. Travels down the Mississippi River and reveals that it was created by the tilting of the Rocky Mountains and the diversion of rivers during the ice ages, in The Great River. Part three of a three - part series on the geological events that shaped the North American continent.
Geography - United States; Geography - World
Dist - CLRVUE

Making of a continent series
Presents a three - part series of six programs on the geological events which shaped the North American continent. Studies the Colorado Plateau, the Great Basin, the Sierra Nevada Mountains, Great Slave Lake, the Great Plains, the Great Lakes and the Mississippi.
The Making of a continent - Part 1 110 MIN
The Making of a continent - Part 2 110 MIN
The Making of a continent - Part 3 110 MIN
Making of a continent series 330 MIN
Dist - CLRVUE

Making of a Continent Series
Eighteen corridors of time 60 MIN
The Land of the Sleeping Mountains 60 MIN
The Price of Gold 60 MIN
Dist - FI

The Making of a crew
VHS
Color (G PRO)
$24.95 purchase _ #0013
Looks at a lifeboat station. Examines the methods and high standards for putting together a crew and how crew members work together.
Health and Safety; Physical Education and Recreation; Psychology
Dist - SEVVID **Prod** - SEVVID

The Making of a Documentary 21 MIN
16mm / U-matic / VHS
Color (H C A)
LC 73-703128
Takes the viewer through all the pre - planning and research stages into actual shooting and final editing, to the end result - the documentary.
Fine Arts; Industrial and Technical Education
Dist - CAROUF **Prod** - CBSTV

The Making of a Film 30 MIN
VHS / U-matic
Communicating through Literature Series
Color (C)
Fine Arts
Dist - DALCCD **Prod** - DALCCD

The Making of a Live Television Show 26 MIN
U-matic / VHS / 16mm
Color (J)
LC 79-713375
Describes the production of a live television show, from the first meeting of the writers, to the dance rehearsal and to the final performance. Shows the pressure on the director and points out that a good television presentation requires much preplanning and work. Includes views of Johnny Carson, Jimmy Durante, the Golddiggers, Bob Finkel and Bill Foster.
Fine Arts; Social Science; Sociology
Dist - PFP **Prod** - BRAVER 1971

The Making of a live television show 22 MIN
VHS
Exploring mass communication series
Color (J H C)
$39.95 purchase _ #IVMC02
Goes behind the scenes of a live, local television show. Follows the host from dressing room to the set. Shows the many people it takes to produce a live program, including producer, director, video technicians and talent.
Fine Arts; Guidance and Counseling
Dist - INSTRU

The Making of a Live TV Show 24 MIN
U-matic / VHS / 16mm
Color
Looks at the preparation and televising of the annual Emmy Awards show. Moves from rehearsal halls and production meetings to the actual events. Uses split screen effects to emphasize the parts played by all members of the production company.
Fine Arts; Industrial and Technical Education
Dist - PFP **Prod** - BRAVC

The Making of a magazine 35 MIN
VHS
Color (H C)
$39.95 purchase _ #IVMC20
Explores the history of the magazine in the United States. Goes behind the scenes in two American magazines, a city magazine and a regional magazine. Meets the publisher, editor, art director, photographer and layout director. Examines the business aspects of a magazine, including promotions, targeted advertising and subscriptions.
Literature and Drama
Dist - INSTRU

The Making of a nation 85 MIN
VHS
Color (J H C G)
$89.95 purchase _ #CLE004CV
Traces the earliest years of the United States as a nation, a period of unparalleled growth and expansion. Begins with the new Constitution and George Washington's inauguration to detail the events - the commanding personalities, purchases, declared and undeclared prizes war - that helped the thirteen new states grow into a land that would stretch from coast to coast. Concludes with the formation of a new antislavery party and the nomination of Abraham Lincoln.
Biography; Civics and Political Systems; History - United States
Dist - CAMV

The Making of a Natural History Film 52 MIN
U-matic / 16mm
Nova Series
Color (J) (SPANISH)
LC 75-702717
Follows naturalists and biologists as they use modern film techniques and technology to film a variety of biological phenomena.
Fine Arts; Industrial and Technical Education; Science
Dist - TIMLIF **Prod** - BBCTV 1974

Making of a Natural History Film 52 MIN
16mm / VHS
Nova Series
(J H C)
$99.95 each
Shows Oxford graduates attempting to film rare sights.
Science; Sociology
Dist - AMBROS **Prod** - AMBROS

The Making of a Package Deal 30 MIN
16mm / U-matic / VHS
Enterprise Series
Color (C A)
Shows how various entertainment industries join forces to create properties which have huge potential for profits in various media.
Business and Economics; Fine Arts; Literature and Drama; Sociology
Dist - LCOA **Prod** - WGBHTV 1981

The Making of a Plague 13 MIN
16mm
Color
Documents the damage created by the gypsy moth caterpillar, a voracious pest that is a threat to all living trees. Records this severe plague and shows control efforts to stop its rapid spread across the United States and Canada.
Agriculture; Science - Natural
Dist - CHEVRN **Prod** - CHEVRN 1971

The Making of a Quarterback (with Roger Staubach) 30 MIN
U-matic / VHS / 16mm
Color
LC 81-701057
Presents the former Dallas Cowboys quarterback, Roger Staubach, and the Cowboys assistant coach, Dan Reeves, employing close - up demonstrations, scrimmage plays and NFL game footage to illustrate the fundamental skills of quarterbacking and training. Includes scenes of Staubach executing specific conditioning exercises, ball handling and passing techniques, and huddle leadership, and shows the importance of a winning philosophy of leadership.
Physical Education and Recreation; Psychology
Dist - LCOA **Prod** - INVISN 1981

Making of a Salesman Series Session 1, Pt 2
Closings - Techniques and Characteristics of Effective Closers
Dist - PRODEV

Making of a Salesman Series Session 4
Dual Channel Communication - Psychology of Selling
Dist - PRODEV

Making of a Salesman Series Session 5
Problem Solving Selling
Dist - PRODEV

Making of a Salesman Series Session 6, Parts 1 and 2
Motivational Selling - What Motivates You
Dist - PRODEV

Making of a Salesman Series Session 7
Selling Strategies - Steps to Sale
Dist - PRODEV

Making of a Salesman Series Session 8
Time and Territory Management
Dist - PRODEV

Making of a salesman series
Communication and listening skills - logical selling
Developing effective presentation skills - who sells most
The Real World of Selling
Dist - PRODEV

The Making of a Song 30 MIN
VHS / U-matic
Color
$335.00 purchase
Fine Arts
Dist - ABCLR **Prod** - ABCLR

The Making of a television programme 25 MIN
VHS
Color; PAL (I J H)
PdS40 purchase
Goes behind the scenes at Emmerdale to show what a scriptwriter does, what happens on outside location, who is involved in studio work. Explores the world of television and encourages students to think about the television programming they watch. Includes booklet and TV Studio Poster. Contact distributor about availability outside the United Kingdom.
Fine Arts; Literature and Drama
Dist - ACADEM

The Making of an Alcoholic 28 MIN
VHS / U-matic
Color (J A)
Shows a chart on the making of an alcoholic that looks at how one person might become an alcoholic.
Health and Safety; Psychology; Sociology
Dist - SUTHRB **Prod** - SUTHRB

The Making of ancient iron 38 MIN
VHS
Color (C G)
$195.00 purchase, $50.00 rental _ #38177
Records the construction and operation of the largest model ever built of a late Iron Age iron smelting furnace. Shows how the field of experimental archaeology helps to understand the past. The goal of 'Smelt 1991' was to take the results of field excavations in Germany and use them to explore the social and technical issues associated with early large - scale iron production. Follows the project from beginning to end, providing historical context on the late Iron Age and documenting the final results of the experiment. Produced by Evan L Johnson.
Sociology
Dist - UCEMC

Making of Bronco Billy 11 MIN
16mm
B&W (H C A)
Features G M Anderson in the role he made famous, Bronco Billy. A silent film.
Fine Arts
Dist - RMIBHF **Prod** - SPOOR 1913

The Making of Comrades 28 MIN
VHS
Color (S)
$79.00 purchase _ #351 - 9020
Documents the making of the documentary 'Comrades.' Features series producer Richard Denton and producers Alan Bookbinder and Olivia Lichtenstein discussing their unique experiences in this special documentary.
Fine Arts; Geography - World; History - World
Dist - FI **Prod** - BBCTV 1987

The Making of Fanny and Alexander 110 MIN
VHS
Color (G)
$29.95 purchase
Presents a film on the making of the motion picture Fanny and Alexander, both directed by Ingmar Bergman.
Fine Arts
Dist - KINOIC

The Making of Flaws 5 MIN
U-matic / VHS
Write on, Set 1 Series
Color (J H)
Teaches the active and passive voice.
English Language
Dist - CTI **Prod** - CTI

The Making of Gandhi - Mr Attenborough and Mr Gandhi 51 MIN
16mm / U-matic / VHS
Color (J A G)
Details the struggles of Attenborough and actor Ben Kingsley to bring Gandhi's life and philosophy to the screen. Features historic footage, scenes from the film, and on location interviews which are combined to show the courageous commitment that went into making the Academy Award winning film.
Fine Arts; Industrial and Technical Education
Dist - DIRECT **Prod** - CPC 1983

The Making of Hatupatu 15 MIN
VHS
Color; PAL (P I J H)
Presents a Maori myth acted by puppets. Introduces the concepts of mythology and religion as way in which humans ask questions about the meaning of life.
Literature and Drama; Religion and Philosophy
Dist - VIEWTH

The Making of JSA - Job Safety Analysis 21 MIN
U-matic / BETA / VHS
Color (IND G)
$495.00 purchase _ #827 - 10
Uses the humorous interaction between a 'wild' video producer and conservative safety director to illustrate the components of JSA such as criteria for job selection, breaking the job into steps, identifying the hazards at each step and developing procedures to eliminate hazards. Covers the use of the JSA, including self - reference guides, training for new workers, equipment safety maintenance checklists and accident analysis.
Business and Economics; Health and Safety; Industrial and Technical Education; Psychology
Dist - ITSC **Prod** - ITSC

Making of Kabuki Medea 24 MIN
VHS
Color (H C A)
$99.00 purchase, $26.00 rental _ #57986
Reviews unique characteristics of kabuki theater, explains compound word which includes music, dance and acting. Shows costume design and props. Features Shozo Sato conducting a class on intonation techniques, creating a wig and demonstrating make - up.
Fine Arts; Geography - World
Dist - UILL **Prod** - UILL 1985

The Making of Letters 30 MIN
VHS / U-matic
Alphabet - the Story of Writing Series
Color
Deals with the making of the first paper in Egypt, the creation of the reed pen, how letters emerged from symbols, and the Roman letter.
English Language; History - World
Dist - WSTGLC **Prod** - WSTGLC

The Making of Letters 28 MIN
16mm
Alphabet - the Story of Writing Series
Color
Shows how early records were kept on clay and wax tablets and discusses heiroglyphics, the making of papyrus, the cutting of a reed pen, the development of the alphabet and Roman lettering.
English Language; History - World
Dist - FILAUD **Prod** - CFDLD 1982

Making of Mankind Series
Beyond Africa 55 MIN
A Human Way of Life 55 MIN
In the Beginning 55 MIN
Settling Down 55 MIN
The Survival of the Species 55 MIN
Dist - AMBROS
BBCENE
TIMLIF

The Making of Mind and Power - the Naval War College 19 MIN
16mm
Color
LC 74-706492
Looks at the Naval War College as an educational institution, developing new concepts and original free - world maritime strategic thought.
Civics and Political Systems; Education
Dist - USNAC **Prod** - USN 1970

The Making of Miss Saigon 75 MIN
VHS
Color (H C G)
$79.00 purchase _ #DL289
Goes behind the scenes to follow the making of a broadway hit, from conception through rehearsals to an all - star opening night. Features performance footage from the original London production.
Fine Arts
Dist - INSIM

The Making of Ohio 35 MIN
VHS
Color (J H C)
$29.95 purchase _ #IV04
Explores the geological forces at work to shape what is now the state of Ohio. Features Dr Jane Forsythe of the Geophysical Dept at Bowling Green State University and looks at the fossil record and shows other geological processes which formed the land, including running water and glaciers. Shows some of the plants and animals which once covered most of the area. Investigates how sedimentary rock - limestone, dolomite and sandstone - were formed and how glaciers shaped Ohio.
Geography - United States; History - United States; Science - Physical
Dist - INSTRU

The Making of Raiders of the Lost Ark 58 MIN
16mm
Color (I)
LC 82-700617
Shows how colorful stunts from the motion picture 'Raiders Of The Lost Ark' were created for the screen. Includes interviews with the stars, Harrison Ford and Karen Allen, director Steven Spielberg, the producers, the cinematographer, the stunt director and others.
Fine Arts
Dist - DIRECT **Prod** - LUCAS 1982

The Making of Rocky - the American Dream Continues 24 MIN
U-matic / VHS / 16mm
Color (P A G)
Presents the real life story of Sylvester Stallone and the screen story of his character, Rocky Balboa. Features clips from the Rocky films.
Fine Arts; Industrial and Technical Education; Sociology
Dist - DIRECT **Prod** - NIERNG 1982

The Making of Russia - 1480 - 1860 26 MIN
VHS / 16mm / U-matic
World - a Television History Series
Color (J H C)
MP=$475.00
Pictures the birth of the first Russian dynasty, the Ruriks, following the Viking expansion in the Ukrainian river system. Shows the rise of Muscovy and the later conquests of Siberia. Under Catherine the Great and her successors Russia developed into a power in the west. Peasant unrest led to the disintegration of the Tsarist regime.
History - World
Dist - LANDMK **Prod** - NETGOL 1985

The Making of Russia - 1480 - 1860 30 MIN
VHS
World - A Television history series
Color (C A T)
$55.00 rental
Covers developments in Russia in the period from 1480 to 1860. Based on 'The Times Atlas of World History.' Serves as part 21 of a 26 - part telecourse. Available only to institutions of higher education.
History - World; Sociology
Dist - SCETV **Prod** - SCETV 1986

The Making of Star Wars 52 MIN
16mm / U-matic / VHS
Color (I)
Shows the making of the motion picture Star Wars, including explanations of some of the special effects and visits to location sets in Tunisia.
Fine Arts
Dist - FI **Prod** - KURTZG 1979

Making of Star Wars, the, Pt 1 26 MIN
U-matic / VHS / 16mm
Color (I)
Shows the making of the motion picture Star Wars, including explanations of some of the special effects and visits to location sets in Tunisia.
Fine Arts
Dist - FI **Prod** - KURTZG 1979

Making of Star Wars, the, Pt 2 26 MIN
U-matic / VHS / 16mm
Color (I)
Shows the making of the motion picture Star Wars, including explanations of some of the special effects and visits to location sets in Tunisia.
Fine Arts
Dist - FI **Prod** - KURTZG 1979

The Making of television news 60 MIN
VHS
Color (H C)
$39.95 purchase _ #IVMC01
Presents two parts on television newscasting. Looks at the process of producing television news in part one, visiting a typical market newsroom to show the process of news gathering, reporting, editing and final on - air presentation. Part two shows the process that a reporter uses in editing a story for a 6 PM newscast. Uses television graphics to explain the videotape editing process, including control track, and insert and assembly modes. Shows how the show is ordered for the newscast, the interaction of reporter, producer and the news director.
Fine Arts; Guidance and Counseling; Literature and Drama
Dist - INSTRU

The Making of the Arabs 50 MIN
U-matic / VHS
Arabs - a living history series
Color (H C A)
MV=$495.00
Introduces the viewer to the rich variety of life, opinion and history that exists in the Arab world.
Geography - World; History - World
Dist - LANDMK **Prod** - LANDMK 1986

The Making of the Frog King 12 MIN
U-matic / VHS / 16mm
Brothers Grimm Folktales Series
Color (P I J H)
LC 81-700810
Shows how the motion picture version of the fairy tale The Frog King was made.
Fine Arts; Literature and Drama
Dist - DAVT **Prod** - DAVT 1982

Making of 'the Frog King,' the 9 MIN
U-matic / VHS
Children's Folktales Series
Color
Tells how the Frog King was brought to life with real people and live frogs.
Literature and Drama
Dist - FILMID **Prod** - FILMID

The Making of the Garden - Pt 1 56 MIN
VHS
First Eden Series
Color (S)
$129.00 purchase _ #825 - 9502
Presents a spectacular portrait of the Mediterranean Sea and the variety of plants and animals that call the region home. Features David Attenborough as narrator. Part 1 of four parts witnesses the birth and growth of the great sea - a story that begins 6.5 million years ago. Illustrates the geographical richness of the region, the ecological diversity of its wildlife, and the social complexity of its ancient peoples.
Geography - World; History - World; Science - Physical; Sociology
Dist - FI **Prod** - BBCTV 1988

Making of the President, 1964 79 MIN
16mm
B&W
LC FIA66-462
Describes the 1964 political conventions and the presidental campaigns, beginning with John F Kennedy's death and ending with Lyndon B Johnson's election. Based on the book of the same title by Theordore H White.
Biography; Civics and Political Systems
Dist - WOLPER **Prod** - XEROX 1965

Making of the President, 1964, Pt 1 42 MIN
16mm
B&W
Describes the 1964 political conventions and the presidential campaigns, beginning with John F Kennedy's death and ending with Lyndon B Johnson's election. Based on the book of the same title by Theodore H White.
Civics and Political Systems
Dist - WOLPER **Prod** - XEROX 1965

Making of the President, 1964, Pt 2 38 MIN
16mm
B&W
Describes the 1964 political conventions and the presidential campaigns, beginning with John F Kennedy's death and ending with Lyndon B Johnson's election. Based on the book of the same title by Theodore H White.
Civics and Political Systems
Dist - WOLPER **Prod** - XEROX 1965

The Making of the President - 1972 90 MIN
16mm / U-matic / VHS
Color (H C A)
LC 79-707820
Tells the story of Richard Nixon and his men, including the campaign, the convention, the Eagleton Affair, the Committee to Re - Elect the President, the Plumbers, Colson, E Howard Hunt, G Gordon Liddy, M Cord, John Erlichman and Bob Haldeman. Traces Nixon's political career from his early political days to his Communist witchhunt. Based on the book 'The Making Of The President - 1972' by Theodore White.
Biography; Civics and Political Systems; History - United States
Dist - TIMLIF **Prod** - TIMLIF 1973

Making of the President, the, 1960 80 MIN
U-matic / VHS / 16mm
B&W (I J)
Analyzes the campaign for President in 1960 as cameras follow John F Kennedy and Richard Nixon. Based on the book by Theodore H White.
Biography; Civics and Political Systems
Dist - FI **Prod** - METROM 1964

Making of the President, the, 1960, Pt 1 40 MIN
U-matic / VHS / 16mm
B&W
Analyzes the presidential campaign of 1960.
Civics and Political Systems
Dist - FI **Prod** - METROM 1964

Making of the President, the, 1960, Pt 2 40 MIN
U-matic / VHS / 16mm
B&W
Analyzes the presidential campaign of 1960.
Civics and Political Systems
Dist - FI **Prod** - METROM 1964

Making of the President, the, 1964 80 MIN
U-matic / VHS / 16mm
B&W
LC 70-711270
Outlines events in the presidential campaign of 1964, beginning with the early efforts of Barry Goldwater and ending with Lyndon Johnson's victory.
Biography; Civics and Political Systems; History - United States
Dist - FI **Prod** - METROM

Making of the President, the, 1964, Pt 1 40 MIN
16mm / U-matic / VHS
B&W
LC 70-711270
Outlines events in the presidential campaign of 1964, beginning with the early efforts of Barry Goldwater and ending with Lyndon Johnson's victory.
Civics and Political Systems
Dist - FI **Prod** - METROM 1963

Making of the President, the, 1964, Pt 2 40 MIN
16mm / U-matic / VHS
B&W
LC 70-711270
Outlines events in the presidential campaign of 1964, beginning with the early efforts of Barry Goldwater and ending with Lyndon Johnson's victory.
Civics and Political Systems
Dist - FI **Prod** - METROM 1963

Making of the President, the, 1972 90 MIN
VHS / 16mm / U-matic
Color (SPANISH)
LC 78-700038; 78-700036
Documents the 1972 Presidential campaign which resulted in the landslide reelection of Richard Nixon.
Biography; Civics and Political Systems; Foreign Language; History - United States
Dist - TIMLIF **Prod** - TIMLIF 1972

The Making of the Television News 40 MIN
U-matic / VHS
BBC TV Production Training Course Series
Color (C)
$279.00, $179.00 purchase _ #AD - 2083
Offers a behind - the - scenes view of how television news is produced. Shows how newscasters and the production team decide which stories to use, how they should be presented and how long each story should run. Part of a twelve - part series on TV production by the BBC.
Fine Arts; Geography - World; Industrial and Technical Education
Dist - FOTH **Prod** - FOTH

The Making of the U S a - 1776 - 1890 30 MIN
VHS
World - a television history series
Color (C A T)
$55.00 rental
Covers developments in the United States in the period from 1776 to 1890. Based on 'The Times Atlas of World History.' Serves as part 22 of a 26 - part telecourse. Available only to institutions of higher education.
History - World; Sociology
Dist - SCETV **Prod** - SCETV 1986

The Making of the United States of America 1776 - 1890 26 MIN
U-matic / VHS / 16mm
World - a television history series
Color (J H C)
MP=$475.00 purchase
Follows the development of the country from the signing of the Declaration of Independence through the expansion westward, to the development of industry, which made America one of the most powerful countries in the world.
History - United States; History - World
Dist - LANDMK **Prod** - NETGOL 1985

The Making of them 40 MIN
VHS
40 minutes series
Color (A)
PdS65 purchase
Reveals that every September, a number of eight-year-old boys leave home to start their first term at boarding school. States that, for the next ten years, these boys will spend most of their time living away from their families. It will be 'the making of them,' says one mother, but some who have gone through the process feel that the experience has severely damaged their lives.
Health and Safety; Sociology
Dist - BBCENE

Making Offon 18 MIN
16mm
Color (G)
$25.00 rental
Recreates the making of the short film classic Offon. Shows video production techniques using a studio switcher.
Fine Arts; Industrial and Technical Education
Dist - CANCIN **Prod** - BARTLS 1981

Making opera 88 MIN
VHS
Color (G)
$29.98 purchase _ #VU458V - F
Shows all aspects of staging an opera, from music and stage action practices through set design and building, costume planning, fittings, and dress rehearsal to the final production. Features Verdi's La Forza del Destino as produced by the Canadian Opera Company.
Fine Arts
Dist - CAMV

Making Overtures - the Story of a Community Orchestra 28 MIN
U-matic / VHS / 16mm
Color (J H A)
Shows Northumberland Community Orchestra whose members range from students in their teens to seniors in their eighties, and from business executives to hog farmers. Depicts the musicians' endless enthusiasm for music making, their creative methods of fundraising and their collective will to survive.
Fine Arts; Social Science; Sociology
Dist - BULFRG **Prod** - RHOMBS 1985

Making paper 15 MIN
VHS
Field trips series
Color (I J)
$34.95 purchase _ #E337; LC 90-708562
Explores a paper mill which produces the thin, shiny paper used to print magazines. Begins with the stockpile of logs and gives special emphasis to quality control measures at the plant. Part of a series which provides visual opportunities for children to 'visit' a variety of locations and activities as if they were on a field trip.
Business and Economics; Education; Social Science
Dist - GPN **Prod** - MPBN 1983

Making Pattern, Core Boxes and Assembling Core for a Water - Cooled Motor Block 15 MIN
16mm
B&W
LC FIE52-133
Explains how a patternmaker constructs the pattern and master core boxes, checks the working core boxes, and pastes up and assembles test cores.
Industrial and Technical Education
Dist - USNAC **Prod** - USOE 1945

Making Picture Frames
VHS
Construction Technology Series
$99.00 purchase _ #BX28V
Industrial and Technical Education
Dist - CAREER **Prod** - CAREER

Making Picture Frames 17 MIN
VHS
(G A IND)
$99.00 purchase _ #W28V7
Describes two ways to make a picture frame. Study Guide included.
Industrial and Technical Education; Physical Education and Recreation
Dist - BERGL

Making Points 11 MIN
16mm
Color (J)
Shows adolescent boys being interviewed by a television reporter about their plans for the future, but giving answers actually offered by girls. Examines differences in the behavior of men and women.
Psychology; Sociology
Dist - DIRECT **Prod** - MIDMAR 1980

Making Product Recommendations and Closing the Call 15 MIN
U-matic / VHS
Telemarketing for Better Business Results Series
Color
Business and Economics; Psychology
Dist - DELTAK **Prod** - COMTEL

Making Quilt Designs - Vol 3 60 MIN
VHS
Quilting with Joe Cunningham and Gwen Marston Series
(H A)
$39.95 purchase _ #BIQ003V
Explains how to draft straight line patterns, clamshells, cables, fans, and other quilting designs.
Fine Arts; Home Economics
Dist - CAMV **Prod** - CAMV

Making responsible decisions 30 MIN
VHS
Color (I J H)
$40.00 purchase _ #B025 - V8
Covers all aspects of sexual decision making, encouraging teens to abstain. Features Connie and Michael who lead an all African - American cast as they discuss sexual intercourse, visit a family planning clinic, share their differing opinions, and finally negotiate a mutual solution. Offers insights into the pressures that influence sexual decision making. Shows where to get reliable information and resources. Increases the ability to say 'no' through the use of assertiveness skills. Recognizes the risks of teen pregnancy and STDs and teaches about effective means of birth control. Includes 51 - page leader's guide, a script, and instructions for producing the play.
Guidance and Counseling; Health and Safety; Psychology; Social Science
Dist - ETRASS **Prod** - ETRASS

Making sausages 10 MIN
VHS
Stop, look, listen series
Color; PAL (P I J)
Watches the teacher who goes to buy sausages and has to wait while the butcher makes some. Shows how the meat is taken from cold storage, chopped, made into sausage meat and stuffed into a casing. Part of a series of films which start from some everyday observation and show more of what is happening, how and why. Builds vocabulary and encourages children to be more observant.
English Language; Industrial and Technical Education; Social Science
Dist - VIEWTH

Making Seaweeds Worth Eating 22 MIN
U-matic / VHS
Color
Presents current information on seaweed cultivation and food products. Looks at cultivation, processing and preparation of seaweed types and algae for food products. Video version of 35mm filmstrip program with live open and close.
Science - Natural
Dist - CBSC **Prod** - BMEDIA

Making Sense 26 MIN
16mm / U-matic / VHS
Children Growing Up Series
Color (C A)
Illustrates how a baby first has to distinguish between self and non - self. Shows deliberately constructed situations and experiments that provide systematic knowledge of how a child sees and makes sense of the world.
Home Economics; Psychology; Sociology
Dist - FI **Prod** - BBCTV 1971

Making Sense 25 MIN
U-matic / VHS / 16mm
Children Growing Up Series
Color (H C A)
Demonstrates how a child sees and makes sense of the world.
Psychology
Dist - FI **Prod** - BBCTV 1981

Making sense 30 MIN
U-matic / VHS
Supersense series
Color (H C)
$250.00 purchase _ #HP - 5806C
Examines the question of whether animals think in some human sense of the word or if they are totally instinctive creatures. Speculates that animals seem to combine learning with instinct. Part of a series which deals with different facets of animal awareness.
Psychology; Science - Natural
Dist - CORF **Prod** - BBCTV 1989

Making sense of a big number 14 MIN
VHS / U-matic
It figures series
Color (I)
Shows that Zeke plans to collect a hundred thousand bottle caps until he learns to picture how many that would be. Includes an animated segment in which the Duke of York's baker needs help thinking about 10,000 muffins. Number 21 of the It Figures Series.
Mathematics
Dist - AITECH **Prod** - AITECH 1982

Making sense of content 98 MIN
VHS / 16mm
Journeyworkers series
Color (A PRO)
$250.00 series purchase _ #271204
Demonstrates effective approaches to developing reading and writing skills for tutors who require a clear, simple approach for instructing adult literacy. Demonstrates strategies for helping adults understand the content of what they read and to write about their own ideas so that others can understand them. Discusses several key points - drawing inferences, anticipating audiences' knowledge and responses, main idea - detail relationships, recognizing and recalling text information and responding to content.
Education; English Language
Dist - ACCESS **Prod** - ACCESS 1987

Making Sense of it 13 MIN
16mm / U-matic / VHS
Scientific Fact and Fun Series
Color (P I)
LC 80-700715
Illustrates the human senses by means of a trip through a wooded area. Explains how a scientist identifies and classifies living things.
Science - Natural
Dist - JOU **Prod** - GLDWER 1979

Making sense of our senses 13 MIN
VHS
Space education series
Color (J H G T A)

$49.00 purchase, $15.00 rental _ #335704; LC 91-706536
Explains in detail the three types of senses used by the human body to detect motion and what happens when the brain receives conflicting messages from these sensors. Part of a series that provides teachers and students with information regarding the latest experimentation with weightlessness. Includes teacher's guide.
Industrial and Technical Education; Science; Science - Natural
Dist - TVOTAR **Prod** - TVOTAR 1989

Making sense of the real world 25 MIN
VHS / U-matic
Computers in control series
Color (H C A)
Examines the range of sensors available for entering information into the computer and discusses the difference between the analog and digital world.
Industrial and Technical Education; Mathematics
Dist - FI **Prod** - BBCTV 1984

Making sense of the sixties series
Breaking Boundaries, Testing Limits 60 MIN
In a dark time 60 MIN
Legacies of the Sixties 60 MIN
Picking Up the Pieces 60 MIN
Seeds of the Sixties 60 MIN
We Can Change the World 60 MIN
Dist - PBS

Making sense of words 48 MIN
VHS / 16mm
Journeyworkers series
Color (A PRO)
$250.00 series purchase _ #271203
Demonstrates effective approaches to developing reading and writing skills for tutors who require a clear, simple approach for instructing adult literacy. Illustrates strategies for helping adults in recognize and spell words. Includes predicting words through language, meaning, and print cues, developing a sight strategy - the ability to recognize words by sight, associating letter and sounds, and analyzing word parts to identify and spell words.
Education; English Language
Dist - ACCESS **Prod** - ACCESS 1987

Making sense out of nonsense 29 MIN
U-matic / VHS
Coping with kids series
Color (T)
Education; Psychology
Dist - FI **Prod** - MFFD

Making Sense Out of Nonsense 30 MIN
U-matic / VHS
Coping with Kids Series
Color
Identifies basic assumptions underlying Adler's approach and how a child's position in the family affects behavior.
Guidance and Counseling; Sociology
Dist - OHUTC **Prod** - OHUTC

Making Sense with Outlines 10 MIN
16mm / U-matic / VHS
Color (I J)
LC 77-700493
Presents the basic structure and benefits of using outlines to organize ideas with an example of how a student uses an outline in writing about glass recycling.
English Language; Guidance and Counseling
Dist - CORF **Prod** - CORF 1977

Making sense with outlines 10 MIN
U-matic / VHS / 16mm
Color (I J)
$255, $180 purchase _ #3428
Explains the structure, mechanics, style, and form of outlines.
English Language
Dist - CORF

Making Sense with Sentences 16 MIN
U-matic / VHS / 16mm
Color (I)
LC 75-700093
Shows how to state ideas in complete sentences.
English Language
Dist - CORF **Prod** - CORF 1975

Making Serpent 32 MIN
16mm
Color (G)
$50.00 rental
Describes the process behind the making of the short film Serpent, including how to structure a nonverbal narrative, how to shoot film for editing, how to find archetypal images in daily life.
Fine Arts; Industrial and Technical Education
Dist - CANCIN **Prod** - BARTLS 1980

Making sex fun - Volume 3 90 MIN
VHS
Better sex video series
Color (C A)
$29.95 purchase
Shows how maintaining an exciting sex life takes creativity and the willingness to explore. Introduces new types of activities which can bring novelty and variety to a relationship, including sexual aids, role - playing, costumes and the thrill of adventurous locations. Contains explicit sexual material. Created by three of America's top sex educators - Dr Judy Seifer, Fellow of the Masters & Johnson Institute; Dr Michael Kollar, sex therapist; and Dr Roger Libby, USA Today columnist.
Guidance and Counseling; Health and Safety; Physical Education and Recreation; Science - Natural; Social Science
Dist - FCSINT

Making, Shaping and Treating Steel Series
The Blast Furnace 8 MIN
The Electric Arc Furnace 7 MIN
Hot rolling of steel sheets 7 MIN
The Open Hearth Furnace 7 MIN
Semi - Finished Steel 8 MIN
Dist - USSC

Making, Shaping and Treatment of Steel Series
Chemistry of Iron and Steel 14 MIN
Dist - USSC

Making Sheet Metal Repairs 19 MIN
16mm
B&W
LC FIE52-277
Explains how to remove the damaged area around a hole, lay out trim lines, prepare the hole to receive the patch, 'bump' out plug and doubler, mark and drill plug and doubler, and rivet completed patch to the part.
Industrial and Technical Education
Dist - USNAC **Prod** - USOE 1945

Making Soft Dolls 60 MIN
VHS / 16mm
(G)
$39.95 purchase _ #VT1083
Gives detailed instruction on body construction of five different dolls. Shows how to contour dolls.
Fine Arts
Dist - RMIBHF **Prod** - RMIBHF

Making soft dolls 60 MIN
BETA / VHS
Crafts and decorating series
Color
Demonstrates body construction of five different soft dolls.
Fine Arts
Dist - MOHOMV **Prod** - MOHOMV

Making Soft Dolls 55 TO 60 MIN
VHS
Morris Craft Series
(A)
$29.95 _ #MX406V
Features Lee Maher, renowned craft designer, as he demonstrates various soft doll craft ideas.
Fine Arts
Dist - CAMV **Prod** - CAMV

Making space 15 MIN
VHS
Art's place series
Color (K P)
$49.00 purchase, $15.00 rental _ #295805
Shows how Art is making space in the gallery for some new pictures, and doesn't know what to do with the old ones. Demonstrates how to recognize and draw space and distance. Features the paintings of Paul Klee and Tom Thomson. Part of a series combining songs, stories, animation, puppets and live actors to convey the pleasure of artistic expression. Includes an illustrated teacher's guide.
Fine Arts
Dist - TVOTAR **Prod** - TVOTAR 1989

Making special friends 27 MIN
U-matic
Color (J C)
Documentary dealing with social acceptance of handicapped children mainstreamed into public schools. Shot on location at Lindbergh Elementary School in San Diego, California. Shows children with various types of handicaps in the classroom. Dr. C. Lynn Fox, SDSU Education professor, demonstrates ways the teacher can improve the social climate in the classroom and encourage friendship among handicapped and non - handicapped children.
Education; Health and Safety; Psychology; Sociology
Dist - SDSC **Prod** - SDSC 1982

Making Square or V - Shaped Corners 5 MIN
16mm
Clothing Construction Techniques Series
Color (J)
LC 77-701184
Demonstrates reinforcing the inside corner, clipping to stitching, pinning and stitching two layers together and finishing to reduce bulk. Includes reinforcement of the corner with fusible interfacing.
Home Economics
Dist - IOWASP **Prod** - IOWA 1976

Making stress work for you 20 MIN
VHS
Color (H C G A R)
$39.95 purchase, $10.00 rental _ #35 - 872 - 2076
Presents pastor Erling Wold in a discussion of stress. Offers Biblical and personal insights into coping with stress. Produced by Seraphim.
Health and Safety; Religion and Philosophy
Dist - APH

Making subjects and verbs agree 14 MIN
U-matic / VHS
Grammar mechanic
(I J)
Designed to help intermediate students apply the rules of grammar. Focuses on agreement of subjects and verbs. Seventh in a series of 16.
English Language
Dist - GPN **Prod** - WDCNTV

Making T - Joint, Lap Joint and Outside Corner Welds all Positions with Aluminum, Steel 15 MIN
VHS / U-matic
Welding III - TIG and MIG (Industry Welding Series
Color
Health and Safety; Industrial and Technical Education
Dist - CAMB **Prod** - CAMB

Making telephone appointments 18 MIN
VHS
Color (A PRO IND)
$495.00 purchase, $150.00 rental
Presents tips for making telephone appointments. Covers subjects including how to ask questions, how to make sure not to be put on hold or to leave a message to call back, and ending each call on a positive note.
Business and Economics; Home Economics; Social Science
Dist - VLEARN **Prod** - TELDOC

Making telephone appointments 21 MIN
BETA / VHS / U-matic
International series
Color (A G)
$495.00 purchase, $150.00 rental
Enables the sales force to recognize the importance of the telephone as a sales tool. Covers understanding the fear of rejection, getting past the secretary, and the seven 'key rules' that should be followed when making appointments by phone. Includes leader's guide and additional support material.
Business and Economics; Psychology
Dist - TELDOC **Prod** - GOWER

Making the ADA work for you 23 MIN
VHS
Color (G PRO)
$595.00 purchase, $140.00 rental _ #V259D - 06, #V259V - 06
Emphasizes attitudes and laws that affect hiring disabled workers, pointing out ways to overcome obstacles. Focuses on the disabled individual's needs and assets that a company must keep in mind. Uses six skits to illustrate possible solutions to problems. Video is available either open or closed captioned.
Health and Safety
Dist - BARR

Making the American dream work for our children 30 MIN
VHS
Color (A)
Explores the state of affairs for at - risk children in the schools. Reveals that many school counselors are overwhelmed with the tasks of helping students with family and personal problems while also attempting to help others with college entrance. Focuses on examples of at - risk programs which stress hope and second chances. Suggests that social and economic conditions may be part of the problem.
Psychology; Sociology
Dist - SCETV **Prod** - SCETV 1990

Making the American Scrape Oboe Reed 27 MIN
16mm
Color (H)
LC 73-711315
A musician demonstrates the detailed steps that are necessary for making a good oboe reed.
Fine Arts
Dist - UILL **Prod** - UILL 1971

Making the Boss Look Good 10 MIN
U-matic / 35mm strip
Effective Office Worker Series
Color
Stresses the importance of assisting the manager or supervisor in many different ways. Offers tips on handling mail, visitors, appointments, phone calls and travel.
Psychology
Dist - RESEM **Prod** - RESEM

Making the change - Part 1 - employee version 21 MIN
VHS
New workplace series
Color (PRO IND A)
$525.00 purchase, $150.00 rental _ #QMR06A
Draws upon the expertise of several CEOs, managers, line workers and consultants as they discuss changes in the workplace and their affect upon managers and employees. Promotes an understanding of the nature of change for employees in organizations undergoing transitions. By Quality Media Resources.
Business and Economics
Dist - EXTR

Making the closing argument 59 MIN
VHS
Winning at trial series
Color (C PRO)
$115.00 purchase, $95.00 rental _ #WAT08
Uses a wrongful death case to teach the skills of trial advocacy. Focuses on the skills involved in making closing arguments. Includes excerpts from the trial, comments from the lawyers involved, and critiques.
Civics and Political Systems; Education
Dist - NITA **Prod** - NITA 1986

Making the connection 30 MIN
VHS
Perspective - computers and electronics - series
Color; PAL; NTSC (G)
PdS90, PdS105 purchase
Takes a look at mimicking the connections formed in the human brain to produce 'clever' computers.
Computer Science
Dist - CFLVIS **Prod** - LONTVS

Making the Difference 14 MIN
16mm
Color
LC 77-700170
Uses six short segments to show how General Aviation airplanes serve the public every day in both critical and common situations.
Industrial and Technical Education; Social Science
Dist - MTP **Prod** - GEAVMA 1976

Making the Difference 5 MIN
16mm
Color (H C A)
LC 80-701039
Instructs police officers in proper conduct on the witness stand. Shows how to prepare and review notes, have a pretrial conference with the prosecutor, present a professional appearance, speak clearly and conversationally, and avoid distractions.
Civics and Political Systems
Dist - KLEINW **Prod** - KLEINW 1978

Making the Dream Come True 38 MIN
U-matic
A Different Understanding Series
Color (PRO)
Shows mothers attempting to teach their children how to communicate successfully. Interviews a speech and language pathologist.
Psychology
Dist - TVOTAR **Prod** - TVOTAR 1985

Making the Dream Come True, Pt 1 16.5 MIN
VHS / 16mm
A Different Understanding Series
Color (G)
$90.00 purchase _ #BPN178006
Stresses that parents should encourage their language delayed child to develop to full potential. Shows mothers attempting to teach their children how to communicate successfully. Features Speech Language Pathologist Ayala Manolson. Part 1 of a 2 part tape.
Education; Psychology
Dist - RMIBHF **Prod** - RMIBHF

Making the Dream Come True, Pt 2 16.5 MIN
VHS / 16mm
A Different Understanding Series
Color (G)
$90.00 purchase _ #BPN178007
Emphasizes parents' responsibility to encourage their language - delayed child to develop to full potential. Show mothers trying to teach their children successful communication skills. Features Speech Language Pathologist Ayala Manolson. Part 2 of a 2 part tape.
Education; Psychology
Dist - RMIBHF **Prod** - RMIBHF

Making the Future Work 22 MIN
U-matic / VHS
Color (C A)
Focuses upon the need for creative leadership and forward thinking as the means to shape America's social, economic and political future.
Civics and Political Systems
Dist - CORF **Prod** - CORF

Making the Interview Work - Five Ways to Improve Interviewing 25 MIN
U-matic / VHS
Videosearch Employment Interview Series
Color
Business and Economics; Fine Arts; Guidance and Counseling; Psychology
Dist - DELTAK **Prod** - DELTAK

Making the most of a Guest Speaker 10 MIN
VHS / 16mm
English as a Second Language Series
Color (A PRO)
$165.00 purchase _ #290304
Demonstrates key teaching methods for English as a Second Language - ESL teachers. Features a teacher - presenter who introduces and provides a brief commentary on the techniques, then demonstrates the application of the technique to the students. 'Making The Most Of A Guest Spaker' demonstrates the important steps in planning and implementing lessons which have been built around a guest speaker.
Education; English Language; Mathematics
Dist - ACCESS **Prod** - ACCESS 1989

Making the most of making mistakes - a lesson on learning from mistakes 14 MIN
VHS
Lessons from the heart - taking charge of feelings series
Color (I)
$89.95 purchase _ #10166VG
Shows children how to learn from mistakes rather than letting them undermine self - confidence. Uses dramatic vignettes, interviews, and graphics to teach acceptance of feelings and apologizing if mistakes hurt others. Comes with a teacher's guide, discussion questions, and two blackline masters. Part three of a four - part series.
Guidance and Counseling
Dist - UNL

Making the most of MIDI
VHS
Color (G)
$29.95 purchase _ #BC013
Explains the use of MIDI in digital musical instruments. Features MIDI expert Marc Mann. Includes reference chart, trouble shooting tipsheet, and implementation chart.
Fine Arts
Dist - SIV

Making the most of on - the - Job Changes
U-matic / VHS
Team Building for Administrative Support Staff Series
Color
Explores the nature of organizational change and the employee's role in adapting to and suggesting changes. Shows how chance can play a positive role in the work environment.
Business and Economics; Psychology
Dist - AMA **Prod** - AMA

Making the most of the micro series

At the end of the line	25 MIN
Everything is under control	25 MIN
Getting down to BASIC	25 MIN
Getting down to business	25 MIN
Introducing graphics	25 MIN
Keeping a record	25 MIN
Moving pictures	25 MIN
Sounds interesting	25 MIN
Strings and things	25 MIN
The Versatile machine	25 MIN

Dist - FI

Making the most of your campus visit 15 MIN
VHS
College bound series
Color (H)
$69.00 purchase _ #05521 - 126
Tours the University of Pennsylvania, meets the dean of admissions and watches a college interview. Shows how to prepare for a visit and what to look for while on campus. Part of a five - part series on choosing the right college.
Education; Guidance and Counseling; Psychology
Dist - GA **Prod** - GA

Making the most of Your Campus Visit
VHS
College Bound Series
$69.00 purchase _ #IE05527V
Discusses the purpose of a campus visit and to gain from it.
Education
Dist - CAREER **Prod** - CAREER

Making the most of Your Money
U-matic / VHS
Color (J H)
Teaches young consumers the skills of using and spending money wisely, and how to avoid the common problems that beset the economically unwary. Includes saving, buying a car, understanding contracts, and budget dating.
Home Economics; Mathematics
Dist - EDUACT **Prod** - EDUACT

Making the most of Yourself 14 MIN
U-matic / VHS
Making it Work Series
Color (H A)
Explains that Bill is willing to take additional training, adjust his schedule as needed and fulfill his commitment when tired, while Bobby isn't. Dramatizes how body language, choice of words and tone of voice are important to effective communication.
Guidance and Counseling
Dist - AITECH **Prod** - ERF 1983

Making the News Fit 28 MIN
VHS / U-matic
Color (H C A)
$250 purchase, $50 rental
Examines press coverage of the war in El Salvador and analyzes media treatment of major issues. Also examines the role of the U.S. Government in defining the news and political pressures that journalists encounter when their reports conflict with United States Government accounts. Direted by Beth Sanders.
Civics and Political Systems; Literature and Drama
Dist - CNEMAG

Making the Occupied Bed 15 MIN
16mm
B&W
LC FIE59-135
Demonstrates the procedure to be followed and the supplies and equipment needed to arrange a bed unit in the hospital room or ward while the bed is occupied by a patient.
Health and Safety
Dist - USNAC **Prod** - USN 1957

Making the right connection - buying home entertainment components
VHS
Consumer skills series
Color (J H G)
$79.95 purchase _ #CCV706
Uses a problem solving approach to show how to make an informed decision about buying home entertainment components. Shows how to shop for a television set, video cassette recorder - VCR, and a stereo system. Discusses warranties and the pros and cons of service contracts. Part of a series on consumer skills.
Home Economics; Industrial and Technical Education
Dist - CADESF **Prod** - CADESF

Making the right moves 30 MIN
VHS
Color (A PRO IND)
$375.00 purchase
Interviews five African - American corporate managers on their experiences. Suggests that hard work and the willingness to learn can take a person far in business.
Business and Economics; Guidance and Counseling; History - United States; Psychology; Sociology
Dist - VLEARN **Prod** - SWBELL

Making the Sale 5.35 MIN
VHS
Spanish Plus Series
(J H A) (SPANISH)
Discusses the pronunciation of numbers 1 through 10 as well as verb endings and comparing adjectives in Spanish.
Foreign Language
Dist - AITECH **Prod** - LANGPL 1985

Making the Surgical (Postoperative) Bed 19 MIN
16mm
Nurse's Aid, Orderly and Attendant Series
Color
LC 70-704827
Demonstrates the proper procedures to be followed in making a safe surgical/postoperative bed.
Guidance and Counseling; Health and Safety
Dist - COPI **Prod** - COPI 1969

Making the transition to training 46 MIN
VHS / 16mm
(C PRO)
$450.00 purchase
Teaches trainers how to motivate, use visual aids, ask and answer questions, and promote interaction. Demonstrates how evaluation can be used to both the trainer's and the trainee's advantage.
Education
Dist - VLEARN **Prod** - GPCV

Making the Transition to Training
U-matic / VHS
Color (IND)
Shows how the former field hand must become acquainted with the tools of training to be an effective trainer. Teaches how to motivate, how to use visual instructional aids, how to ask and answer questions, how to promote interaction and how evaluation can be used to both trainer and trainee advantage.
Education; Industrial and Technical Education
Dist - GPCV **Prod** - GPCV

Making the Unoccupied (Closed) Bed 19 MIN
16mm
Nurse's Aid, Orderly and Attendant Series
Color
LC 76-704826
Demonstrates the proper way to make an unoccupied bed, emphasizing quick, easy safe and sanitary procedures.
Guidance and Counseling; Health and Safety
Dist - COPI **Prod** - COPI 1969

Making the unoccupied - closed - bed 13 MIN
U-matic
Nurse's aide, orderly and attendant series
Color (H C A)
Demonstrates how to make an unoccupied bed, emphasizing quick, easy, safe and sanitary procedures.
Health and Safety; Science
Dist - COPI **Prod** - COPI 1969

Making their mark series
Profiles six artists who have different drawing styles, personalities, and ways of working. Introduces the viewer to practical and aesthetic aspects of the skill of drawing. Features Sir Hugh Casson, Maggi Hambling, David Gentleman, Charlotte Fawley, Roy Marsden, and Mike Wilks.

Charlotte Fawley 30 MIN
David Gentleman 30 MIN
Maggi Hambling 30 MIN
Mike Wilks 30 MIN
Roy Marsden 30 MIN
Sir Hugh Casson 30 MIN
Dist - BBCENE

Making Things Grow I Series

Dutch Bulbs 30 MIN
Gesneriads 30 MIN
Horticultural Presents 30 MIN
The Pot problem 30 MIN
Potting 30 MIN
Questions and Answers - Making Things Grow I 30 MIN
Soils 30 MIN
The Succulents 30 MIN
Dist - PBS

Making Things Grow II Series

Accent plants 30 MIN
Artificial Lighting 30 MIN
The Cool window 30 MIN
Dividing 30 MIN
Ferns 30 MIN
Forcing bulbs 30 MIN
Indoor Topiary 30 MIN
Massing a Window 30 MIN
Questions and Answers - Making Things Grow II 30 MIN
Short Day Problems 30 MIN
Dist - PBS

Making Things Grow III Series

Arranging 29 MIN
A Children's show 29 MIN
Dormancy 29 MIN
Fall Duties 29 MIN
Gifts that Grow 29 MIN
Have You Ever been to Kew 29 MIN
High Summer 29 MIN
Long Lasting Blossoming Plants 29 MIN
Mea Culpa 29 MIN
More Cuttings 29 MIN
Moving on 29 MIN
The Portable Garden 29 MIN
Questions and answers III - making things grow III 29 MIN
Questions and Answers IV - Making Things Grow III 29 MIN
Seeds 29 MIN
Short Cuts 29 MIN
Softwood Cuttings 28 MIN
Starting from Scratch 29 MIN
Summer Hanging Plants 29 MIN
Summering House Plants 29 MIN
Supermarket - Ten Cent Store 29 MIN
Variety 29 MIN
Window Boxes 29 MIN
Dist - PBS

Making Things Happen 18 MIN
VHS / U-matic
Little Computers - See How they Run Series
Color (J)
LC 81-706846
Goes step - by - step through the process of developing a program that will make a toy mouse move on command. Reviews the application of similar systems to control mechanisms such as sensors that keep track of time, count and respond to pressure and temperature changes.
Computer Science; Mathematics
Dist - GPN **Prod** - ELDATA 1980

Making things happen 18 MIN
U-matic / VHS
Little computers...see how they run
(G)
Explains how small computers receive, process, store and transmit information. Uses dialogue, graphics and demonstrations. Focuses on making a toy mouse run and turn on command and reviews similar systems. Sixth in a series of eight.
Computer Science
Dist - GPN

Making things move 11 MIN
U-matic / VHS / 16mm
Color (P) (SPANISH)
Shows examples of forces that make things move, forces that keep things from moving and forces that make things more difficult to move.
Science - Physical
Dist - EBEC **Prod** - EBEC

Making things move
Videodisc
Laser learning set 2 series; Set 2
Color; CAV (P I)
$375.00 purchase _ #8L5411
Explains the art of animation. Shows an animator at work. Illustrates different animation techniques. Shows how animated and live - action films differ and how to make flip - book animation. Part of a series of six theme - based interactive videodisc lessons. Requires a Pioneer LD - V2000 or 2200, with a barcode reader and adapter, or a Pioneer LD - V4200 or higher. Includes a user's guide, two readers.
Fine Arts; Industrial and Technical Education
Dist - BARR **Prod** - BARR 1992

Making Things Move 25 MIN
U-matic / VHS
Computers in Control Series
Color (H C A)
Discusses the application of computer technology to electric motors. Features a new growth industry called animatronics, which uses computers and small motors to make lifelike statues that talk and move.
Industrial and Technical Education; Mathematics
Dist - FI **Prod** - BBCTV 1984

Making Things to Learn 11 MIN
16mm
Early Childhood Educational Study Series
B&W (T)
LC 73-705608
Shows people working to build educational materials and children using the materials in their classrooms. Filmed at several public and private schools and head start classrooms in the Boston area.
Education; Guidance and Counseling; Psychology
Dist - EDC **Prod** - EDS 1970

Making things work series

Battered pictures 15 MIN
Care of birds 15 MIN
Chair Problems 15 MIN
Cut Christmas trees 15 MIN
Furniture stains 15 MIN
Household smells 15 MIN
Mending Books 15 MIN
Mending China and Glass 15 MIN
Pewter 15 MIN
Rug Spots 15 MIN
Small Electrical Repairs 15 MIN
Waste not 15 MIN
Window Problems 15 MIN
Wrappings 15 MIN
Dist - PBS

Making tomorrow's polymers 240 MIN
VHS
Color (C PRO)
$400.00 purchase _ #V - 4200 - 17106
Teaches about five new block copolymers. Explores free radical induced polymerization and how it can be used in research, as well as linear step - growth polymerizations. Covers carbocationic polymerization, free radical induced polymerization, linear step - growth polymerization and anionic and transition metal catalyzed polymerization. Joseph P Kennedy, H James Harwood, Frank Harris and Roderic P Quirk instruct. Includes four videos and a course study guide.
Industrial and Technical Education; Science - Physical
Dist - AMCHEM **Prod** - AMCHEM 1989

Making up the room 9 MIN
16mm / U-matic / VHS
Professional hotel and tourism programs series
Color (J)
LC 74-700222
Shows proper responsibilities of a maid making up a check - out room with special emphasis given to thoroughness in cleaning.
Health and Safety; Home Economics
Dist - NEM **Prod** - NEM 1970

Making womb for baby 140 MIN
VHS
Color (G)
$29.95 purchase
Takes a comprehensive look at pregnancy and childbirth. Covers the do's and don'ts of pregnancy, including a prenatal exercise program. Hosted by obstetrician Dr Dave David.
Health and Safety
Dist - PBS **Prod** - WNETTV

Making work easier 15 MIN
U-matic / VHS
Why series
Color (P I)
Discusses the characteristics of work.
Psychology; Science - Physical
Dist - AITECH **Prod** - WDCNTV 1976

Making Your Case 27 MIN
U-matic / VHS
Color (A)
Illustrates the principles of effective presentation through the use of a dream technique. Shows Alice, pension plan presenter, dreaming she is presenting pensions to the Queen of Hearts and her court and doing a poor job of it. Presents the Mad Hatter and the March Hare rescuing her and teaching her how to be more effective.
Business and Economics; Psychology
Dist - XICOM **Prod** - XICOM

Making Your Case 24 MIN
U-matic / VHS
Color
Stresses the importance of preliminary research, making proper notes and rehearsing before making a presentation.
Business and Economics; English Language
Dist - VISUCP **Prod** - VIDART

Making Your Kitchen Store more 23 MIN
VHS
Color (G)
$19.95 purchase _ #6116
Shows how to create more storage space in the kitchen.
Home Economics; Industrial and Technical Education; Sociology
Dist - SYBVIS **Prod** - HOMES

Making your kitchen store more 23 MIN
VHS
Better homes and gardens video library series
Color (G)
$19.95 purchase
Presents more than 60 ideas to help improve use of kitchen space. Shows how to revamp wall cabinets, window areas, base cabinets, and more.
Home Economics
Dist - PBS **Prod** - WNETTV

Making your life a masterpiece - lessons from terminal illness 30 MIN
VHS
Insights - topics in contemporary psychology series
Color (H C G)
$89.95 purchase _ #ARG - 104
Features three people diagnosed as terminally ill from cancer who discuss how that news forced them to reevaluate their lives, change their values and how they made their lives into masterpieces. Shares important lessons. Part of a four - part series on contemporary psychology.
Guidance and Counseling; Health and Safety; Psychology; Sociology
Dist - INSTRU

Making your money count 53 MIN
VHS
Color (G)
$19.95 purchase _ #1788
Offers advice on managing cash, savings, investments, long term planning, and educational financing.
Business and Economics; Education; Mathematics
Dist - ESPNTV **Prod** - ESPNTV

Making Your Money Grow 28 MIN
U-matic / VHS
Personal Finance and Money Management Series
Color (C A)
Business and Economics; Civics and Political Systems
Dist - SCCON **Prod** - SCCON 1987

Making your money grow 30 MIN
U-matic / VHS
Personal finance series
Color (C A)
Offers an introduction to investments, including federal and state laws governing investments. Describes some sources for investment information. Lesson 15 in the Personal Finance Series.
Business and Economics
Dist - CDTEL **Prod** - SCCON

Making your point 30 MIN
VHS
FYI video series
Color (H C G)
$79.95 purchase _ #AMA84009V
Shows how to increase the impact of what one says and how it is said with practical tips and techniques. Part of a seven - part series on professional and personal skills for the workplace.
Business and Economics; English Language; Guidance and Counseling; Psychology; Social Science
Dist - CAMV **Prod** - AMA 1991

Making your point
VHS
FYI video series
Color (J H C G)
$79.95 purchase _ #AMA84009V
Shows how to increase the impact of power of what one says and how it is said with reliable and practical tips and techniques. Part of a 12 - part series on professional and personal skills for the work place.
Business and Economics; Guidance and Counseling; Social Science
Dist - CAMV **Prod** - AMA

Making your point without saying a word 30 MIN
VHS
Color (G PRO)
$79.95 purchase _ #738 - 67
Gives expert advice on how to use gestures, posture, eye contact, tone of voice and facial expression to get ideas across and get wanted results. Shows how to increase impact and power of presentations, incease self - awareness and identify and control nonverbal messages being sent.
Psychology; Social Science
Dist - MEMIND **Prod** - AMA

Making Your Voice Heard 10 MIN
U-matic / VHS
Hub of the Wheel Series
Color (G)
$249.00, $149.00 purchase _ #AD - 1568
Reveals that a business's public image begins with the telephone. Shows telephone techniques designed to enhance a company's telephone image. Part of a ten - part series for office professionals.
Business and Economics; English Language; Industrial and Technical Education
Dist - FOTH **Prod** - FOTH

The Makioka Sisters 140 MIN
VHS
Color (G) (JAPANESE WITH ENGLISH SUBTITLES)
$59.95 purchase _ #R5MSR
Portrays the four daughter of a merchant family who face the end of a gentle way of life. Adapts the novel by Junichiro Tanizaki. Directed by Kon Ichikawa.
Fine Arts; Sociology
Dist - CHTSUI

Mako 30 MIN
U-matic
Pearls Series
Color (H C A)
Presents a Hollywood actor discussing the world of Asian movie stereotypes.
Fine Arts; Sociology
Dist - GPN **Prod** - EDFCEN 1979

Malabrigo 84 MIN
VHS / 35mm strip / U-matic
Color (H C A) (SPANISH (ENGLISH SUBTITLES))
$250 rental
Portrays a young Peruvian woman in her search for her missing husband. Examines the lack of help she is able to obtain from police, villagers, and employees of the hotel where she is staying. Talks about the danger she and those helping her also find themselves in. Directed by Alberto Durant.
History - World; Industrial and Technical Education; Sociology
Dist - CNEMAG

Malagan art of New Ireland 18 MIN
VHS / U-matic
Color (G)
$100.00, $39.95 purchase
Documents a contemporary Malagan in New Ireland, Papua, New Guinea. Reveals that this elaborate ceremony honors clan ancestors through days of dancing, feasting, singing and speechmaking which culminate in the dramatic unveiling of large wooden sculptures hidden in secret enclosures near clan burial grounds.
History - World; Religion and Philosophy; Sociology
Dist - ARTSAM **Prod** - MIA

Malagan Labadama - a tribute to Buk - Buk 58 MIN
VHS / 16mm
Institute of Papua New Guinea Studies series
Color (G)
$400.00 purchase, $120.00, $60.00 rental
Portrays a malagan labadama for the deceased Buk - Buk organized by three Kaparau brothers from Pantagin village of New Ireland. Reveals that Buk - Buk had been the top chief of the Mandak region and served under the German colonial administration and witnessed Japanese and Australian occupations. A malagan is a carved, painted representation given ceremonially in honor of a deceased person as a final morturary offering, as well as the spirit represented by the carving and the festivities accompanying its presentation. Part of a series by Chris Owen.
History - World; Sociology
Dist - DOCEDR **Prod** - IPANGS 1982

Malakapalakadoo Skip Two 10 MIN
VHS / U-matic
Color (P I)
$49.00 purchase _ #3525
Presents imaginative problem - solving through clay animation and invites youngsters to practice their own creative abilities.
Fine Arts; Psychology
Dist - EBEC

Malakapalakadoo, Skip Two 10 MIN
U-matic / VHS / 16mm
Color (J)
LC 78-700673
Introduces imaginative approaches to problem solving. Presents two children disguised as beanbags entering into the magical land of Malakapalakadoo and meeting a kindly but helpless king.
Guidance and Counseling; Psychology
Dist - EBEC **Prod** - EBEC 1977

Malanga 3 MIN
16mm
B&W (G)
$5.00 rental
Presents Gerard Malanga, poet and dancer, performing his works. Progresses from 24 frame sections to smaller ones with the sound synchronized to its corresponding scene. Produced by Keewatin Dewdney.
Fine Arts
Dist - CANCIN

Malaria Control Series
Rearing and Handling of Anopheles Mosquitoes 16 MIN
Dist - USNAC

Malaria control series
Preparation and staining of blood films 17 MIN
Dist - USPHS

Malaria - Images of a Reality 13 MIN
16mm
Color
LC 78-701126
Examines the worldwide resurgence of malaria, discussing the disease, its cause, how it affects victims, and what can be done about it.
Health and Safety; Sociology
Dist - DYP **Prod** - UNEP 1978

Malas Companias 29 MIN
VHS / 16mm
Que Pasa, U S a Series
Color (G)
$46.00 rental _ #QUEP - 114
Social Science; Sociology
Dist - PBS **Prod** - WPBTTV

Malatesta 80 MIN
16mm
Color (GERMAN)
Documents a group of Latvian refugees who attempted to put the law of universal equality among men into practice in London in 1910. Shows how their siege of Sidney Street was doomed to failure but still has significance.
Civics and Political Systems; Foreign Language; History - World
Dist - WSTGLC **Prod** - WSTGLC 1970

Malay Fisherman of Sabak 11 MIN
16mm
Human Family, Pt 1 - South and Southeast Asia Series
Color (I)
Depicts the fishing village of Sabak, located along the shores of the China Sea in Malaysia. Explains that the Sabak fishermen form into small groups or associations. Tells the story of Ismail Bin Awang, the leader of one of these associations, and his family.
Geography - World; Social Science; Sociology
Dist - AVED **Prod** - AVED 1972

Malaysia 10 MIN
16mm
Color
Describes Malaysia, with emphasis on the east coast.
Geography - World
Dist - PMFMUN **Prod** - FILEM 1975

Malaysia 51 MIN
VHS
Asian insight series; Part 4
Color (S)
$79.00 purchase _ #118 - 9016
Introduces the people and the cultures of the Asian Pacific. Presents a balanced, objective interpretation of the region's history. Illuminates past and present social structure, mores, beliefs, art and architecture to give a well - rounded look at this newly influential area. Part 4 of six parts considers Malaysia, a Moslem state in a Chinese - dominated market. Examines the problems of a multiracial society and an irony common to Southeast Asia - Chinese economic strength in a country where the Chinese are a minority.
Foreign Language; Geography - World; History - World; Religion and Philosophy
Dist - FI **Prod** - FLMAUS 1987

Malaysia 25 MIN
16mm / U-matic / VHS
Untamed World Series
Color; Mono (J H C A)
$400.00 film, $250.00 video, $50.00 rental
Discusses the animals and vegetation of the Malaysian peninsula.
Geography - World; Science - Natural
Dist - CTV **Prod** - CTV 1973

Malaysia in Brief 26 MIN
16mm
Color
Describes the main industries of Malaysia.
Geography - World
Dist - PMFMUN **Prod** - FILEM 1973

Malaysian Parliament 9 MIN
16mm
B&W
Shows the formal opening of the new Parliament building in Malaysia and the first ceremonial meetings of the House of Representatives and the Senate.
Civics and Political Systems; Geography - World
Dist - PMFMUN **Prod** - FILEM 1964

Malaysian river boy 15 MIN
U-matic / VHS / BETA
Color; NTSC; PAL; SECAM (I J)
PdS58
Offers a detailed social study of two families living in Sarawak whose lives are dominated by a river which provides the only means of communication. Reveals that one family group is Sea Dayaks who live in an upriver longhouse, the other is Chinese who live in a small town. Introduces the principal crops of the area and vividly illustrates journeys on both the upper and lower river.
Geography - World; History - World
Dist - VIEWTH

Malaysian take - away 30 MIN
VHS
Nature series
Color; PAL (G)
PdS65 purchase; Not available in the United States, Canada or Japan
Probes the timber boom in the Malaysian district of Sarawak. Contends that the boom will be over by 1997 and those who profit are mostly Malaysian politicians and Chinese and Japanese businessmen. The program looks at the communities that benefit from logging money, and the danger of the destroying such resources.

Agriculture; Geography - World
Dist - BBCENE

Malaysian Village 18 MIN
U-matic / VHS
Color (I J)
Visits a Malaysian village family of husband, wife and six children. Reveals that the father, a former fisherman, now drives a school bus. Shows food preparation, school, traditional wedding, games, sports and church.
Geography - World; History - World
Dist - EDMI Prod - EDMI 1974

Malbangka country 30 MIN
16mm / U-matic / VHS
Australian institute of aboriginal studies series
Color
Portrays an Aboriginal family that has moved back to its original homestead following unsuccessful government attempts at resettlement in small towns with missionary schools.
History - World; Social Science
Dist - UCEMC Prod - AUSIAS 1979

Malcolm Bradbury 35 MIN
VHS
Color (H C G)
$79.00 purchase
Features the British writer with A S Byatt discussing writing using comic forms and the modern literary movement. Talks about his works including Eating People is Wrong; The History Man; and Cuts - A Very Short Novel.
Literature and Drama
Dist - ROLAND Prod - INCART

Malcolm Brewer - Boat Builder 18 MIN
U-matic / VHS / 16mm
American Character Series
Color (J H C)
LC 76-703010
Focuses on Malcolm Brewer, a 77 - year - old resident of Camden, Maine, who still builds boats by hand with the tools he has used for years. Tells of his life built on self - reliance and joy in hard work.
History - United States; Sociology
Dist - EBEC Prod - ODYSSP 1976

Malcolm Campbell - Man Against Time 15 MIN
BETA / VHS
B&W
Portrays Malcolm Campbell, who drove 302 mph in 1935.
Physical Education and Recreation
Dist - STAR Prod - STAR

Malcolm Forbes - Forbes Magazine, USA 47 MIN
VHS
Tycoons series
Color (J H G)
$225.00 purchase
Shows how Malcolm Forbes became a millionaire through ownering and publishing Forbes Magazine. Shows how he invested his money in art and crafts and his interests in cycling and ballooning.
Business and Economics
Dist - LANDMK

Malcolm X 23 MIN
16mm / U-matic / VHS
Color (I A)
LC 79-712702
Dramatizes the life of Malcolm X from his early childhood up to the time of his death with excerpts from his writings.
History - United States
Dist - CAROUF Prod - WCAUTV 1971

Malcolm X 30 MIN
VHS
Black Americans of achievement video collection series
Color (J H C G)
$39.98 purchase _ #LVC6612V
Portrays civil rights leader Malcolm X through interviews with leading authorities, rare footage and archival photographs. Part of 12 - part series on noted black Americans.
History - United States
Dist - CAMV

Malcolm X 15 MIN
U-matic / VHS
Color (G)
$229.00, $129.00 purchase _ #AD - 1751
Profiles Malcolm X. Describes his struggle for black equality.
Biography; Civics and Political Systems; History - United States
Dist - FOTH Prod - FOTH

Malcolm X - El Haji Malik El Shabazz 60 MIN
VHS
B&W (H)
$49.00 purchase _ #60419 - 025
Tells the story of Malcolm X and the Black Muslim movement.
Biography; History - United States; Religion and Philosophy
Dist - GA Prod - GA 1992

Malcolm X - make it plain 150 MIN
VHS
CC; Color (H C A)
$99.95 purchase _ AMEX-666-WC95; $125.00 purchase _ AMEI-633-WC95
Provides 'the definitive biography' of Malcolm X. Describes his change from 'Detroit Red' when he entered prison to 'Malcolm X' when he was released. Includes interviews, archival footage, photographs and an original film score.
History - United States
Dist - PBS Prod - BSIDE 1993

Malcolm X Speaks 44 MIN
16mm
B&W (I)
LC 73-701013
Documents the life and thought of Malcolm X. Includes his most important speeches, seminar interviews and dialogues with those who knew him best (including his wife and children.).
Biography; History - United States; Religion and Philosophy
Dist - GROVE Prod - ABCM 1970

Malcolm X - Struggle for Freedom 22 MIN
16mm
B&W (J)
LC 73-700845
Portrays Malcolm X at a time when his views were changing to include the world situation with regard to the race problem. Includes interviews filmed during Malcolm X's trip to Europe and Africa shortly before his assassination in the United States, interspersed with scenes of African rebellion.
Biography; Civics and Political Systems; History - United States; Psychology; Sociology
Dist - GROVE Prod - GROVE 1966

Malcom X - El Hajj Malik El Shabazz 60 MIN
VHS
Black history series
Color (J H C G)
$29.95 purchase _ #XE1504V
Details the life of Malcolm X, considered to be one of the 20th century's most controversial and charismatic civil rights leaders. Shows how he influenced the way American society perceived black people during his short life. Part of a six - part series on Afro - American history.
Biography; Civics and Political Systems; History - United States
Dist - CAMV

Maldives and Fiji Islands 28 MIN
Videoreel / VHS
International Byline Series
Color
Interviews the ambassadors from the Maldives and Fiji Islands. Includes slides and a short film clip on both countries. Presents a special program on island nations.
Business and Economics; Civics and Political Systems; Geography - World
Dist - PERRYM Prod - PERRYM

The Male 28 MIN
VHS
Human body - reproduction - series
Color (J H G)
$89.95 purchase _ #UW4183
Covers physiological information about the sexual functions of the male human body. Examines the events at the moment of insemination that determine that a child will be a boy, the hormones responsible for developing male sex characteristics and sexual behavior, and how semen is produced. Covers the events of puberty and possible causes of male sterility. Part of a 39 - part series featuring computer animation, medical photography, electron micrography, full - color drawings and diagrams and three - dimensional working models to cover the workings of the human body.
Health and Safety; Science - Natural; Sociology
Dist - FOTH

The Male 29 MIN
U-matic
Introducing biology series; Program 28
Color (C A)
Discusses the role of the male in human reproduction. Provides a basic overview of the anatomy of the male reproductive system. Covers birth control and venereal disease.
Health and Safety; Science - Natural
Dist - CDTEL Prod - COAST

Male anatomy and physiology
VHS
Understanding yourself and your body series
Color (I J)
$69.00 purchase _ #MC313
Examines the anatomy and physiology of the human male. Discusses sperm production - spermatogenesis, ejaculation and fertilization in a teacher - student dialogue. Explains female and male chromosomes briefly.
Health and Safety; Psychology; Sociology
Dist - AAVIM Prod - AAVIM 1992

Male and female 22 MIN
VHS
Let's talk about it series
Color; PAL (I J)
PdS29.50 purchase
Explores children's concepts of the sexes with their teachers, learning about anatomical differences, the process of fertilization and conception. Part of a five - part series on sex education.
Health and Safety; Sociology
Dist - EMFVL

Male and Female Homosexuality and Bisexuality
U-matic / VHS
Independent Study in Human Sexuality Series
Color (PRO)
Health and Safety; Psychology; Sociology
Dist - MMRC Prod - MMRC

The Male body 20 MIN
U-matic / Kit / VHS
Growing up
(J)
Describes the male body and the changes it undergoes in adolescence. Focuses on the reproductive system. Third in a six part series.
Science - Natural; Sociology
Dist - GPN

Male Cartoon Figure 15 MIN
Videoreel / VT2
Charlie's Pad Series
Color
Fine Arts
Dist - PBS Prod - WSIU

Male Catheterization, Pt 1 9 MIN
16mm
Urological Nursing Series
Color
LC 76-712980
Explains the purpose of catheterization and shows the techniques involved in preparing a male patient for the procedure. Describes the essential functions of the organs of the urinary system and the two basic types of catheterization.
Health and Safety; Science
Dist - TRNAID Prod - TRNAID 1969

Male Catheterization, Pt 2 11 MIN
16mm
Urological Nursing Series
Color
LC 70-712981
Describes the techniques involved in using a simple catheter and a foley retention catheter for male patients. Emphasizes the importance of minimizing patient discomfort and trauma.
Health and Safety; Science
Dist - TRNAID Prod - TRNAID 1969

Male citizens 99 MIN
VHS
Color (G) (MANDARIN)
$45.00 purchase _ #5031B
Presents a movie produced in the People's Republic of China.
Fine Arts; Sociology
Dist - CHTSUI

The Male factor in infertility 26 MIN
VHS / 16mm
Color (G)
$149.00, $249.00, purchase _ #AD - 1908
Reveals that research shows that male infertility, believed to be on the increase, is an important factor in at least half the couples who are unable to conceive. Explores the newly found causes, corrective techniques, and the psychological implications through interviews with patients, researchers, and medical experts.
Science - Natural
Dist - FOTH Prod - FOTH 1990

Male - female communication skills - Module II 20 MIN
8mm cartridge / VHS / BETA / U-matic
Smarter together series
Color; CC; PAL (PRO G)
$795.00 purchase
Presents three units taking an in - depth look at how women and men interact - Mutual Respect; Conflict Resolution; Power, Position, Purpose. Challenges participants to identify areas where communications can be improved by using the S - M - A - R - T assessment tool. Facilitates dialog between women and men and improves their communication skills. Includes a trainer's manual and 20 participant manuals. Part of a two - module series.
Business and Economics; Psychology; Social Science; Sociology
Dist - BNA Prod - BNA 1994

The Male - female crisis 50 MIN
VHS
Creating family series
Color (H C G A R)
$10.00 rental _ #36 - 871503 - 460
Features marriage counselor and therapist Clayton Barbeau in an exploration of conflicts between males and females.
Guidance and Counseling; Psychology; Religion and Philosophy; Sociology
Dist - APH **Prod** - FRACOC

Male Genital - Rectal Examination 12 MIN
U-matic / VHS
Color (PRO)
Outlines systematic approach to the male genital - rectal examination.
Health and Safety; Science - Natural
Dist - HSCIC **Prod** - HSCIC 1984

Male genitalia 12 MIN
VHS / U-matic / BETA
Techniques of physical diagnosis - a visual approach series
Color (PRO)
$350.00 purchase
Reviews the techniques for genital examination, hernia and lymph node assessment and rectal and prostate examination. Concludes with a test for occult blood. Part of series by Dr Donald W Novey teaching the basic skills of physical examination as seen through the eyes of the examiner.
Health and Safety
Dist - MEDMDS

Male Genitalia, Anus and Hernias 12 MIN
16mm
Visual Guide to Physical Examination (2nd Ed Series
Color (PRO)
LC 81-701521
Demonstrates the physical examination of the male genitalia, anus and hernias, showing necessary procedures, manipulations, pacing, positions and patient - examiner interaction.
Health and Safety
Dist - LIP **Prod** - LIP 1981

Male Genitourinary Examination 24 MIN
VHS / U-matic
Color (PRO)
Demonstrates techniques used in examining the male genitourinary system and how to differentiate normal from abnormal findings.
Health and Safety; Science - Natural
Dist - HSCIC **Prod** - HSCIC 1982

The Male Health Profile 30 MIN
U-matic / VHS
Here's to Your Health Series
Color (C T)
Traces male development from the fetus through old age. Examines biological and cultural factors that influence male behavior.
Health and Safety; Psychology
Dist - DALCCD **Prod** - DALCCD

Male involvement project trigger film 3 MIN
U-matic / VHS / 16mm
Color
Attempts to give young men the realization that they should examine the potential effects that sexual activity can have on their lives and encourages them to seek information or advice from their local family or health clinic.
Health and Safety; Sociology
Dist - PEREN **Prod** - PEREN 1983

Male Makeover
VHS / U-matic
Color
Demonstrates the intricacies of pointing and other methods of hair shaping and beard trimming.
Education; Home Economics
Dist - MPCEDP **Prod** - MPCEDP 1984

Male masturbation 6 MIN
VHS / 16mm
Color (C A)
$125.00, $79.00 purchase, $50.00 rental
Portrays masturbation in terms of realistic gratification and tension release. Demonstrates nipple stimulation, penile erection, testicle movement, ejaculation and muscle spasm. Explicit. By Dr David McWhirter.
Health and Safety; Sociology
Dist - FCSINT **Prod** - FCSINT 1976

Male Masturbation 6 MIN
U-matic / VHS
Color (C A)
Portrays male masturbation in terms of realistic gratification and tension release.
Health and Safety; Psychology
Dist - MMRC **Prod** - MMRC

Male Menopause 29 MIN
U-matic
Color
Focuses on the real and imagined sexual problems of the middle - aged American male as seen by a physician and a sociologist.
Psychology; Science - Natural
Dist - UMITV **Prod** - UMITV 1974

The Male orgasm 53 MIN
VHS
Sex - A Lifelong pleasure
Color (C A)
$29.95 purchase
Reveals the causes of premature ejaculation and gives proven techniques for delaying orgasm. Leads step - by - step through topics including childhood conditioning, the orgasm reflex and type of stimulation. Covers sensual massage, genital massage, masturbation, ways to delay orgasm and advanced lovemaking positions to maximize pleasure. Contains explicit sexual material. Produced by psychologist Goedele Liekens and Dr Michael Perry. From Holland.
Guidance and Counseling; Health and Safety; Physical Education and Recreation; Sociology
Dist - FCSINT

The Male Pelvis 15 MIN
16mm / U-matic / VHS
Guides to Dissection Series
Color (C A)
Focuses on the pelvis and perineum. Demonstrates the dissection of the male pelvis.
Health and Safety; Science - Natural
Dist - TEF **Prod** - UCLA

Male Pelvis - Unit 20 24 MIN
VHS / U-matic
Gross Anatomy Prosection Demonstration Series
Color (PRO)
Describes the arteries, muscles, and nerves of the pelvic wall. Discusses structures which pass from the posterior abdominal wall into the pelvis, the major structures of the pelvis and structures related to them, the blood vessels of the pelvis, and structures related to the prostate.
Health and Safety; Science - Natural
Dist - HSCIC **Prod** - HSCIC

Male Perineum 19 MIN
U-matic / VHS / 16mm
Cine - Prosector Series
Color (PRO)
Examines the parts and planes of the bony pelvis.
Science - Natural
Dist - TEF **Prod** - AVCORP

The Male Perineum 16 MIN
U-matic / VHS / 16mm
Guides to Dissection Series
Color (C A)
Focuses on the pelvis and perineum. Demonstrates the dissection of the male perineum.
Health and Safety; Science - Natural
Dist - TEF **Prod** - UCLA

Male Perineum - Unit 22 15 MIN
U-matic / VHS
Gross Anatomy Prosection Demonstration Series
Color (PRO)
Discusses the male penis, the layers of the perineum and its vessels and nerves, and the deeper aspect of the perineum, which is divided into two regions, the aval triangle and the U G triangle.
Health and Safety; Science - Natural
Dist - HSCIC **Prod** - HSCIC

The Male Physician and the Female Patient 15 MIN
VHS / U-matic
Color (PRO)
Dramatizes encounters between female patients and male physicians, and accuses some doctors of sexism.
Health and Safety; Sociology
Dist - HSCIC **Prod** - HSCIC 1977

Male Radical Mastectomy 20 MIN
U-matic / VHS
Breast Series
Color
Health and Safety; Science - Natural
Dist - SVL **Prod** - SVL

Male rape 25 MIN
VHS
Open space series
Color; PAL (H C A)
PdS50 purchase
Investigates male rape and the unwillingness of society to acknowledge its existence. Reports that male rape victims are often hesitant to seek help through fear of not being believed or of being labeled homosexual. Challenges the typical belief that men who rape other men are homosexual. Features male rape victims who talk about their victimization.
Sociology
Dist - BBCENE

Male Reproductive System I 14 MIN
U-matic
Microanatomy Laboratory Orientation Series
Color (C)
Demonstrates the convoluted tubules with emphasis on the developing sex cells and the sustentacular Sertoli cells.
Health and Safety; Science - Natural
Dist - UOKLAH **Prod** - UOKLAH 1986

Male Reproductive System II 12 MIN
U-matic
Microanatomy Laboratory Orientation Series
Color (C)
Covers the accessory sex glands in the male, the prostate gland, seminal vesicle and Cowpers glands.
Health and Safety; Science - Natural
Dist - UOKLAH **Prod** - UOKLAH 1986

Male Reproductive System - Pt 1 - Testis, Epididymis, Vas Deferens, Ampulla 39 MIN
U-matic / VHS
Histology review series
Color (PRO)
Covers anatomy, functions, and histological organizations of the testis, epididymis, vas deferens, and ampulla.
Health and Safety; Science - Natural
Dist - HSCIC **Prod** - HSCIC

Male Reproductive System - Pt 2 - Accessory Organs - Prostate, Seminal Vesicle, Cowper's 36 MIN
U-matic / VHS
Histology review series
Color (PRO)
Presents information about organs of the male reproductive system including the seminal vesicle, prostate gland, Cowper's gland, and penis.
Health and Safety; Science - Natural
Dist - HSCIC **Prod** - HSCIC

Male Sexuality - Infancy to Old Age
VHS / U-matic
Continuing Medical Education - Basic Sexology Series
Color (PRO)
Health and Safety; Psychology
Dist - MMRC **Prod** - TIASHS

Male Stress Syndrome 28 MIN
U-matic / VHS
Color (G)
$249.00, $149.00 purchase _ #AD - 1247
Considers male stress, its causes and cures, its effect on women and the differences between male and female stress. Features Phil Donahue, Dr Georgia Witkin - Laniol, author of 'The Male Stress Syndrome,' and tennis pro Arthur Ashe.
Psychology; Sociology
Dist - FOTH **Prod** - FOTH

Malecite Fancy Basket - Vanniere Fantasie Malecite 12 MIN
16mm
Color (G) (FRENCH)
#2X83I
Illustrates the Malecite Indian art of basket making. Demonstrates how two Malecite Indians from the Kingsclear Reserve make baskets out of black ash and sweet grass.
Fine Arts; Social Science
Dist - CDIAND **Prod** - BAILEY 1977

Malevich Suprematism 9 MIN
16mm
Color (H A)
$270.00 purchase, $45.00 rental
Features Soviet pioneer of modern painting, Malevich, 1878 - 1935, who worked to establish what he called 'the supremacy of pure sensibility' by combining and juxtaposing flat, nonobjective, geometrical elements.
Fine Arts; Industrial and Technical Education
Dist - AFA **Prod** - ACGB 1970

Mali 60 MIN
VHS
Under African skies series
Color (A)
PdS99 purchase
Reviews the music of Mali. Explores how African music reflects its culture, religion, and politics. Seeks out the diverse music of Africa to find out where it comes from, what it means, and where it's going. Part of a five-part series.
Fine Arts; Geography - World
Dist - BBCENE

Malice in Bigotland (Industry Version) 21 MIN
16mm
Color (A)
LC 78-700999
Deals with the destructive force of prejudice through the story of an executive who, having revealed his prejudices

while interviewing potential employees, goes home and dreams about a sinister carnival called Bigotland where prejudice and hatred are sold. Introduced by Charlton Heston.
Psychology; Sociology
Dist - ESMRDA **Prod** - ESMRDA 1978

Malice in Bigotland - school version 21 MIN
16mm
Color (J)
LC 78-700991
Deals with the destructive force of prejudice through the use of a fantasy in which a class of students are transported to a carnival playground where the main attraction is the House of Racial Stereotypes. Introduced by Charlton Heston.
Psychology; Sociology
Dist - ESMRDA **Prod** - ESMRDA 1978

Malice in wonderland 30 MIN
VHS
Wildlife on one series
Color; PAL (H C A)
PdS65 purchase
Examines the coral reefs of the Red Sea. Describes the predators of the coral reef and explains how they are in turn prey. Employs the use of underwater photography to view the activity of a coral reef.
Geography - World
Dist - BBCENE

The Mallee Fowl 25 MIN
U-matic
Animal Wonder Down Under Series
Color (I J H)
Shows the Mallee Fowl building a huge conical mound which acts as an incubator.
Geography - World; Science - Natural
Dist - CEPRO **Prod** - CEPRO

The Mallet 11 MIN
16mm / U-matic / VHS
Color (J)
LC 80-700597
Presents a story about a futuristic, antiseptic food factory where workers select healthy chicks, while rejects are carried along a conveyor belt until they are crushed by a mallet and dropped into a garbage bin. Tells how a single black chick rebels against his fate before the mallet strikes.
Industrial and Technical Education; Social Science
Dist - IFB **Prod** - DUNAV 1978

A Mallet of Luck 55 MIN
U-matic / VHS
Japanese Cuisine Series
Color (PRO)
Demonstrates the preparation of a Mallet of Luck - broiled sea bream between cedar chips, shaped rice, a ribbon box of pressed egg white, yolk, and seaweed, and other garde - manger work.
Home Economics; Industrial and Technical Education
Dist - CULINA **Prod** - CULINA

Mallorca - an Island Paradise 15 MIN
16mm
Color (C A)
Explains that Mallorca lies in the blue Mediterranean just off the coast of Spain, and has a deeply penetrating history. Points out that some of its cities were founded before the time of Christ and this sun - splashed island was known to the Phoenicians, Greeks and Carthaginians, and yet today, the island offers elegant hotels, villas and beaches that lure vacationers from all over the world.
Geography - World
Dist - MCDO **Prod** - MCDO 1965

Malmaison and Josephine 26 MIN
U-matic / VHS
Castles of France Series
Color (C) (FRENCH (ENGLISH SUBTITLES))
$249.00, $149.00 purchase _ #AD - 1504
Focuses on Malmaison, of the era of Napoleon. Reveals that it was purchased by Josephine who brought Napoleon there for a brief happy period followed by divorce, illness and Josephine's death. Part of a six - part series on castles of France. In French with English subtitles.
Fine Arts; Foreign Language; Geography - World; History - World
Dist - FOTH **Prod** - FOTH

Malmo - Gateway to the North 13 MIN
16mm
Color
Explains that because of its location on the southern coast of Sweden, the city of Malmo has become one of the most important industrial centers in the country and is presently in the midst of a tremendous Industrial expansion.
Business and Economics; Geography - World; Social Science; Sociology
Dist - AUDPLN **Prod** - ASI

Malnala 103 MIN
U-matic / VHS / 16mm
Captioned; Color (A) (SPANISH (ENGLISH SUBTITLES))
Portrays the runaway African slaves in Cuba in the 19th century who were political rebels in the war of independence against the Spanish. Third part of a trilogy including 'The Other Francisco' and 'The Bounty Hunter.' Spanish dialog with English subtitles.
Civics and Political Systems; Fine Arts; History - World; Sociology
Dist - CNEMAG **Prod** - CNEMAG 1979

Malnutrition - Diagnosis and Therapeutic Alternatives 40 MIN
VHS / U-matic / 16mm
Nutrition and Health Series
Color (PRO C)
$577.50 purchase _ #840VI029A - B
Defines and discusses the major causes of malnutrition in the world population at large and in hospitalized patients. Includes the various clinical techniques available to diagnose malnutrition and to correct imbalances. Consists of two videocassettes.
Psychology; Social Science
Dist - HSCIC **Prod** - HSCIC 1983

Malnutrition in a Third World Community 23 MIN
16mm
Color (C)
LC 80-701545
Studies malnutrition in the Philippines. Covers infant feeding practices, breast feeding and supplements, and the problems of poverty.
Geography - World; Health and Safety
Dist - PSUPCR **Prod** - PSUPCR 1980

Malocclusion 15 MIN
VHS / 16mm / U-matic
Color
Defines the problem and examines causes and effects. Includes bruxism and TMJ syndrome. Explains diagnosis and treatment, including splints and equilibration.
Health and Safety; Science - Natural
Dist - PRORE **Prod** - PRORE

Malocclusion - Causes and Effects 9 MIN
U-matic / VHS / 16mm
Color (A)
Defines malocclusion and examines the causes and effects. Presents information on bruxism, results of not replacing missing teeth, high spots and TMJ syndrome.
Health and Safety; Science - Natural
Dist - PRORE **Prod** - PRORE

Malocclusion - Diagnosis and Treatment 7 MIN
U-matic / VHS / 16mm
Color (PRO)
Discusses the need for early diagnosis and treatment of malocclusion. Stresses the role the patient can play in correction of the disorder.
Health and Safety; Science - Natural
Dist - PRORE **Prod** - PRORE

Malpractice 19 MIN
U-matic / VHS
Color (C)
$249.00, $149.00 purchase _ #AD - 1458
Profiles an obstetrician who describes the measures he is taking to safeguard himself against malpractice suits. Interviews an obstetrician - gynecologist who is being sued seven years after a normal delivery and an attorney who sees malpractice suits as a necessary means for policing the medical profession.
Civics and Political Systems; Health and Safety; Psychology
Dist - FOTH **Prod** - FOTH

Malpractice 44 MIN
16mm
Nursing and the Law Series
B&W
LC 78-703193
Defines negligence and the meaning of proximate cause.
Civics and Political Systems; Health and Safety
Dist - AJN **Prod** - VDONUR 1968

Malpractice - Pt 1 8 MIN
U-matic
Medical - Legal Issues - Observations Series
(A)
Deals with pertinent medical and legal issues in today's complex world of medicine. Co - produced by the Alberta Law Foundation.
Civics and Political Systems; Health and Safety
Dist - ACCESS **Prod** - ACCESS 1984

Malpractice - Pt 5 - Compensation 11 MIN
U-matic
Medical - Legal Issues - Observations Series
(A)
Deals with pertinent medical and legal issues in today's complex world of medicine. Co - produced by the Alberta Law Foundation.
Civics and Political Systems; Health and Safety
Dist - ACCESS **Prod** - ACCESS 1984

Malpractice - Pt 4 - the American Influence 8 MIN
U-matic
Medical - Legal Issues - Observations Series
(A)
Deals with pertinent medical and legal issues in today's complex world of medicine. Co - produced by the Alberta Law Foundation.
Civics and Political Systems; Health and Safety
Dist - ACCESS **Prod** - ACCESS 1984

Malpractice - Pt 6 - Hospital Responsibilities 7 MIN
U-matic
Medical - Legal Issues - Observations Series
(A)
Addresses hospital responsibilities in malpractice situations.
Health and Safety
Dist - ACCESS **Prod** - ACCESS 1984

Malpractice - Pt 3 - the Canadian Medical Protective Association 12 MIN
U-matic
Medical - Legal Issues - Observations Series
(A)
Deals with pertinent medical and legal issues in today's complex world of medicine. Co - produced by the Alberta Law Foundation.
Health and Safety
Dist - ACCESS **Prod** - ACCESS 1984

Malpractice - Pt 2 - Standard of Care 12 MIN
U-matic
Medical - Legal Issues - Observations Series
(A)
Deals with pertinent medical and legal issues in today's complex world of medicine. Co - produced by the Alberta Law Foundation.
Health and Safety
Dist - ACCESS **Prod** - ACCESS 1984

Malta 28 MIN
Videoreel / VHS
International Byline Series
Color
Interviews Ambassador Victor Gauci, permanent representative of Malta to the United Nations. Discusses the conference on the Law of the Sea. Describes the attractions of his country. Includes film clips.
Business and Economics; Civics and Political Systems; Geography - World
Dist - PERRYM **Prod** - PERRYM

The Maltese cross movement 7 MIN
16mm
Color (G)
$10.00 rental
Draws together threads of the producer's life such as a childhood myth, drug trips, mathematics and language. Uses a slowed - down version of hypermontage to explore many themes at once. Title is also the name of a book of collages. Produced by Keewatin Dewdney.
Fine Arts
Dist - CANCIN

The Maltese Falcon 100 MIN
16mm
B&W
Presents a crime film with Sam Spade as the private detective.
Fine Arts
Dist - UAE **Prod** - UNKNWN

The Maltese Unicorn 23 MIN
U-matic / VHS / 16mm
Unicorn Tales Series
Color (P I)
LC 80-700543
Presents a contemporary story, based on the fairy tale 'The Boy Who Cried Wolf', about a mischievous boy who tries to prove he didn't break the Maltese Unicorn. Shows how with the help of a famous detective, he discovers the guilty party and the learns the value of being a man of his word.
Fine Arts; Literature and Drama
Dist - MGHT **Prod** - MGHT 1980

Malvina Reynolds and Jack Elliot 52 MIN
VHS / U-matic
Rainbow quest series
Color
Presents Malvina Reynolds singing her famous 'Little Boxes.' Presents Jack Elliott singing some of Woody Guthrie's songs.
Fine Arts
Dist - NORROS **Prod** - SEEGER

Mama Awethu 53 MIN
VHS / 16mm
Color (G)

$390.00, $995.00 purchase, $75.00, $125.00 rental
Follows the daily lives of five black South African women in the townships around Cape Town. Reveals the inhuman legacy of the apartheid system and how township life has necessitated their involvement in the struggle for better living conditions and equal rights. Records the grinding poverty in the midst of one of the richest countries on the planet; the near - total lack of social services and utilities; the occasional riots; and drive - by shootings by white supremists. Produced by Bethany Yarrow.
Fine Arts; History - World; Sociology
Dist - FIRS

Mama Don't Allow
VHS / 35mm strip
ALA Notable Children's Filmstrips Series
Color (K)
$33.00 purchase
Presents a children's story. Part of the American Library Association series.
English Language; Literature and Drama
Dist - PELLER

Mama don't allow - 30
VHS
Reading rainbow series
Color; CC (K P)
$39.95 purchase
Reveals that when Miles gets a saxophone for his birthday, neither his parents nor his neighbors can stand the racket. Discloses that when Miles and his Swamp Band are invited to the Alligator Ball, no one guesses what's in store for them. Visits an alligator farm in Louisiana with LeVar, journeys down the Mississippi in a riverboat and meets one of New Orlean's hottest jazz saxophonists. Part of a series offering a multicultural approach to generating reading enthusiasm with cross - curricular applications, hosted by LeVar Burton.
English Language; Fine Arts; Geography - United States; Literature and Drama
Dist - GPN **Prod** - LNMDP

Mama goes to war 18 MIN
16mm
Cuba - a view from inside series
Color (G)
$300.00 purchase, $40.00 rental
Follows a group of women through their military training for the territorial militia. Features part of a 17 - part series of shorts by and about Cuban women. Directed by Guillermo Centeno. Illustrated catalog available. Contact distributor for programming advice and discount package rental fees.
Fine Arts; History - World; Literature and Drama; Sociology
Dist - CNEMAG

Mama's going to buy you a mockingbird 15 MIN
VHS
More books from cover to cover series
Color (I G)
$25.00 purchase _ #MBCC - 106
Tells the story of Jeremy, a boy who, with the help of his friend Tess, learns to accept the fact that his father is dying of cancer. Based on the book 'Mama's Going to Buy You a Mockingbird' by Jean Little. Hosted by John Robbins.
Education; English Language; Literature and Drama
Dist - PBS **Prod** - WETATV 1987

Mama's Little Pirate 19 MIN
16mm
B&W
Tells how dreams of a pirate's treasure lead the Little Rascals into a huge underground room with a giant footprint on the muddy floor.
Fine Arts
Dist - RMIBHF **Prod** - ROACH 1934

Mama's Pushcart - Ellen Stewart and 25 Years of La MaMa, ETC 54 MIN
VHS / 16mm
Color (G)
$295.00 purchase, $75.00 rental
Portrays Ellen Stewart, founder of New York's LaMaMa Experimental Theater Company. Interviews LaMaMa artists Peter Brook, Harvey Fierstein and Elizabeth Swados and presents archival and performance footage and an original soundtrack by Swados.
Fine Arts; Geography - United States; History - United States
Dist - WMEN **Prod** - RODI 1988

Mambo 60 MIN
VHS
Kathy Blake dance studios - let's learn how to dance series
Color (G A)
$39.95 purchase
Features dance instructors Kathy Blake and Gene Russo, who instruct viewers on the basics of the Mambo. First of two parts.
Fine Arts
Dist - PBS **Prod** - WNETTV

Mambo
VHS
Arthur Murray dance lessons series
Color (G)
$19.95 purchase _ #MC046
Offers lessons in classic ballroom dancing from instructors in Arthur Murray studios, focusing on the mambo. Part of a 12 - part series on various ballroom dancing styles.
Fine Arts; Physical Education and Recreation; Sociology
Dist - SIV

Mambo II 60 MIN
VHS
Kathy Blake dance studios - let's learn how to dance series
Color (G A)
$39.95 purchase
Features dance instructors Kathy Blake and Gene Russo, who instruct viewers on the basics of the Mambo. Second of two parts.
Fine Arts
Dist - PBS **Prod** - WNETTV

Mambo mouth 56 MIN
VHS
Color; CC (G)
Eviscerates Latino stereotypes in a series of stand - up routines by comedian John Leguizamo. Records the comedian adopting various characters such as an obnoxious and sexist talk - show host who dispenses machismo advice to callers; a Cuban cabana boy romancing an aging Floridian in hopes of obtaining a green card; a homeboy with a boombox who giddily details his loss of virginity to a prostitute; and more. Humor tinged with pathos is seen in Pepe, an incarcerated illegal alien whose ethnic dissembling culminates in a poignant plea for understanding. Reinventing himself as a corporate Japanese success story, John discovers that his intrinsic Latino personality refuses to be suppressed for long. Produced by Jeff Ross for Martin Bregman Productions.
Fine Arts; Literature and Drama; Sociology
Dist - AMBROS

Mame 131 MIN
16mm
Color
Tells the story of a youngster who comes to live with his Bohemian aunt.
Fine Arts
Dist - TWYMAN **Prod** - WB 1974

Mamele - Little Mother 95 MIN
VHS
Joseph Green Yiddish film classics series
B&W (G) (YIDDISH WITH ENGLISH SUBTITLES)
$79.95 purchase _ #720
Stars Molly Picon who portrays Khavtshe, the youngest daughter of a widower left with the responsibility of tending house for a helpless and indifferent family of seven. Costars Edmund Zayenda and Max Bozyk. Directed by Joseph Green.
Fine Arts; Sociology
Dist - ERGOM **Prod** - ERGOM 1938

The Mammal palace 31 MIN
16mm
B&W (G)
$30.00 rental
Depicts the turbulent relationships of disturbed individuals who live in an apartment house. Stars Donna Kerness and husband Hopeton Morris, Frank Meyer and Zelda Keiser. Shot in reversal film.
Fine Arts; Psychology
Dist - CANCIN **Prod** - KUCHAR 1969

The Mammalian heart 15 MIN
16mm / VHS
Color (H C PRO)
$320.00, $250.00 purchase, $50.00 rental _ #8019
Explains the structure and functioning of the mammalian heart using the heart of the sheep and the dog as examples. Using radiocinematography, shows the passage of blood through the heart, lungs, and major vessels.
Science; Science - Natural
Dist - AIMS **Prod** - AIMS 1982

Mammals 30 MIN
VHS
Tell me why series
Color (I J H)
$22.00 purchase _ #ABM020 - CV
Discusses mammals, whales, pinnipeds, manatees, elephants, bats, primates. Asks why whales are considered mammals, if polar bears hibernate, and is the chimpanzee a monkey. Part of a series based on the book series by Arkady Leokum. Includes teacher's guide.
Science - Natural
Dist - CLRVUE **Prod** - CLRVUE

Mammals 14 MIN
VHS
Vertebrate series
Color; PAL (I J H)
Determines that the structure of their bodies and the size of their brains makes mammals the most highly developed animals on Earth. Examines three mammal groups - egg - laying, marsupial and placental - to introduce their common characteristics, how they have adapted to different environments, and the differences in the development and parental care of their young. Part of a series on vertebrate animals.
Science - Natural
Dist - VIEWTH

Mammals 10 MIN
U-matic / VHS / 16mm
All about Animals Series
Color (P)
Illustrates the characteristics of familiar and exotic mammals.
Science - Natural
Dist - AIMS **Prod** - BURGHS 1978

Mammals 14 MIN
U-matic / VHS / 16mm
Vertebrates series
Color (I J H)
$365.00, $250.00 purchase _ #4459
Talks about the differences in development, care of offspring, and physical characteristics among different types of mammals.
Science - Natural
Dist - CORF

Mammals 12 MIN
16mm / U-matic / VHS
Color (K P I)
LC 80-700148
Identifies the characteristics of mammals. Shows that household pets may be relatives of large, wild animals.
Science - Natural
Dist - NGS **Prod** - NGS 1979

Mammals 13 MIN
VHS
Jr zoologist series
Color (P I)
$49.50 purchase _ #UL2071VB; $59.95 purchase _ #2071VG
Focuses on the mammal class in the animal kingdom. Includes a teacher's booklet with lesson plans and activities. Part of a four - part series.
Science - Natural
Dist - KNOWUN
UNL

Mammals 3 MIN
16mm
Of all Things Series
Color (P)
LC FIA65-1431
Presents a vignette picturing classes of mammals.
Science - Natural
Dist - AVED **Prod** - BAILYL 1961

Mammals 15 MIN
VHS / U-matic
Up Close and Natural Series
Color (P I)
$125.00 purchase
Examines the characteristics and various types of mammals.
Science - Natural
Dist - AITECH **Prod** - NHPTV 1986

Mammals - a first film 11 MIN
U-matic / VHS / 16mm
Color (P I)
Describes the similarities that mammals have in common and also shows the many different places in the world where mammals live. Includes discussion of the beautiful, unusual and sometimes comic shapes that mammals have.
Science - Natural
Dist - PHENIX **Prod** - PHENIX 1982

Mammals - a multimedia encyclopedia
CD-ROM
Color (P I J H G)
$99.00 purchase _ #80922, #80926
Offers entries on more than 200 mammals, 700 photos, 155 animal vocalizations, movie clips, fact boxes and essays, a classification game, glossary, 150 range maps. For Macintosh or DOS. Includes teacher's edition. Contact distributor for hardware requirements.
Science - Natural
Dist - NGS

Mammals - a multimedia encyclopedia
CD-ROM
(G)

$149.00 purchase _ #1531
Brings the animal kingdom to life on the computer screen. Provides interactive access to information on more than 200 mammals, with essays on each animal, vital statistics, range maps, graphic images - some in full motion video, and authentic vocalizations. Produced by National Geographic Society in conjunction with IBM. For IBM PCs and compatibles, requires 640K RAM, DOS 3.1 or later, one floppy disk drive - hard disk recommended, one empty expansion slot, an IBM compatible CD - ROM drive, and a color EGA or VGA monitor. Mouse recommended.
Literature and Drama; Science - Natural
Dist - BEP **Prod** - NGS

Mammals and milk 11 MIN
16mm / U-matic / VHS
Color (K P I)
LC 72-712328
Shows that animals are all alike in the respect that they produce milk to feed their young. Also useful in early sex education and to stimulate language arts discussion.
Science - Natural
Dist - AIMS **Prod** - ASSOCF 1971

Mammals and milk 14 MIN
U-matic / VHS / 16mm
Color (P I)
Shows that, although animals are different, they are all alike in one respect - they have mammary glands and they all produce milk to feed their young.
Science - Natural
Dist - AIMS **Prod** - AIMS 1971

Mammals and their Young 15 MIN
U-matic / VHS
Animal World Series
Color (K P)
$79.95 purchase _ #51321
Presents a variety of mammals in their natural habitats.
Education; Science; Science - Natural
Dist - NGS

Mammals are interesting 12 MIN
U-matic / VHS / 16mm
Color (I J)
Views of many different animals are included to illustrate the distingushing characteristics of mammals.
Science - Natural
Dist - EBEC **Prod** - EBEC 1953

Mammals of Africa and India 11 MIN
16mm / U-matic / VHS
Color
LC FIA67-1455
Depicts elephants, rhinoceroses and hippos, emphasizing physical appearance, eating habits and behavior in a zoo as contrasted with life in the wilds.
Science - Natural
Dist - MCFI **Prod** - HOE 1967

Mammals of the Sea 29 MIN
VHS / U-matic
Color
Examines the biological role and importance of Pacific marine mammals and the controversies that surround them.
Science - Natural; Science - Physical
Dist - PBS **Prod** - OSU 1980

Mammals of the Sea - Pt 20 30 MIN
16mm
Life on Earth series; Vol V
Color (J)
$495.00 purchase _ #865 - 9041
Blends scientific data with breathtaking wildlife photography to tell the story of the development of life. Features wildlife expert David Attenborough as host. Part 20 of 27 parts is entitled 'Mammals Of The Sea.'.
Science; Science - Natural; Science - Physical
Dist - FI **Prod** - BBCTV 1981

The Mammals of Victoria 30 MIN
16mm
Silent; Color (H C A)
$90.00 rental
Features a series of ocean tide waves, sometimes with mountains in the background, hand-painted patterns, and abstractions composed of distorted shapes in shades of blue. Reveals increasingly recognizable shapes of birds, humans, boats and water interspersed with bursts of fire and other shapes and images. Produced by Stan Brakhage as a companion piece to "A Child's Garden" and "The Serious Sea".
Fine Arts
Dist - CANCIN

Mammals - Seals and Otters 28 MIN
VHS / U-matic
Oceanus - the Marine Environment Series
Color (C A)
Science - Natural; Science - Physical
Dist - SCCON **Prod** - SCCON 1980

Mammals - Seals and Otters 30 MIN
VHS / U-matic
Oceanus - the Marine Environment Series Lesson 18
Color
Discusses the ancestry of marine mammals. Looks at the three main groups of marine mammals and compares their basic characteristics. Differentiates between seals and sea lions.
Science - Natural; Science - Physical
Dist - CDTEL **Prod** - SCCON

Mammals - Volume 9 30 MIN
VHS
Tell me why series
Color (K P I)
$19.95 purchase
Presents Volume 9 of the 'Tell Me Why' video encyclopedia series. Teaches children the facts about mammals.
Science - Physical
Dist - PBS **Prod** - WNETTV

Mammals - Whales 30 MIN
VHS / U-matic
Oceanus - the Marine Environment Series Lesson 19
Color
Focuses on a typical marine mammal, the whale. Distinquishes between cetaceans. Explains functions of odontoceti sonar. Discusses current states of whaling and its effect on existing whale populations.
Science - Natural; Science - Physical
Dist - CDTEL **Prod** - SCCON

Mammals - Whales 28 MIN
VHS / U-matic
Oceanus - the Marine Environment Series
Color (C A)
Science - Natural; Science - Physical
Dist - SCCON **Prod** - SCCON 1980

Mammals with hoofs 11 MIN
VHS
Color; PAL (I J H)
Reveals that hoofed mammals are among the most common domesticated animals and exist in great variety in the wild. Shows that these mammals can be divided into two classes - the even - toed - pigs, deer, hippo, and the odd - toed - horses, rhino, and shows their activities, diets and special adaptations.
Science - Natural
Dist - VIEWTH

Mammary Augmentation and Construction with Omentum 19 MIN
16mm
Cine Clinic Series
Color (PRO)
Shows the technique for one - stage subcutaneous mastectomy and reconstruction, mammary augmentation and delayed mammary construction with re - located omentum. Discusses the indications, feasibility and limitations.
Health and Safety; Science
Dist - NMAC **Prod** - ACYDGD 1970

Mammography
VHS / U-matic
X - Ray Procedures in Layman's Terms Series
Color
Health and Safety; Science
Dist - FAIRGH **Prod** - FAIRGH

Mammography 12 MIN
VHS
Color (G PRO C) (SPANISH)
$200.00 purchase _ #OB - 69
Reveals that routine mammography can reduce deaths from breast cancer by as much as 40 percent because mammography is the only way to detect breast cancer in its early stages. Emphasizes the necessity of early detections, shows exactly what is involved in the mammographic procedure, and why. Uses detailed animation to show the difference in the size of lumps discovered through self - examination and mammography.
Health and Safety; Sociology
Dist - MIFE **Prod** - MIFE

Mammography of the augmented breast 8 MIN
VHS
Color (C PRO)
$250.00 purchase
Demonstrates proper implant manipulation for optimal visualization of the entire breast. Approved for 1 hour of CME credits.
Health and Safety
Dist - LPRO **Prod** - LPRO

Mammography Technique 27 MIN
16mm
B&W
LC 74-733992
Details the radiographic procedure for detection of breast cancer. Emphasizes positioning of the patient, coning procedures and film exposure and development. Restricted to radiologists. (Kinescope).
Health and Safety
Dist - USNAC **Prod** - USPHS 1965

Mammography - the life saving image 7 MIN
VHS / U-matic
Color (PRO)
$200.00 purchase, $60.00 rental _ #5284S, #5284V
Demonstrates mammography and explains that it takes little time, is rarely uncomfortable and generates a minimal amount of radiation. Emphasizes that early detection of breast cancer requires monthly breast self - examination, annual examinations by a professional and mammography on a regular basis.
Health and Safety; Sociology
Dist - AJN **Prod** - LPRO 1989

Mammoth and Mastodon - Elephants on the Plains 30 MIN
16mm
Great Plains Trilogy, 1 Series in the Beginning - the Primitive Man; In the beginning - the primitive man
B&W (H C A)
Traces the development and migration of the enormous old world mammoths and mastodons of the Ice Age. Describes the hunting of them by early man on the great plains and their extinction during the Ice Age.
Science - Natural
Dist - UNEBR **Prod** - KUONTV 1954

Mammoth Cave national park, Kentucky 30 MIN
VHS
Color (G)
$29.95 purchase _ #S01851
Explores Kentucky's Mammoth Cave, which is the longest cave on earth. Reviews related history.
Geography - United States; Physical Education and Recreation
Dist - UILL

Mammy Water - in search of the water spirits in Nigeria 59 MIN
16mm / VHS
Color (C G A)
$350.00, $995.00 purchase, $60.00 rental _ #38097, #11410
Explains that Mammy Water is a pidgin English name for a local water goddess worshipped by the Ibibio, Ijaw, and Igbo speaking peoples of southeastern Nigeria. Her various cults are led predominantly by priestesses. Shows numerous rituals and ceremonies associated with Mammy Water, while devotees provide commentary. Produced by Dr. Sabine Jell - Bahlsen.
Geography - World; Religion and Philosophy; Sociology
Dist - UCEMC

A Man, a Plan, a Canal, Panama 58 MIN
U-matic / VHS
Nova Series
Color (H C A)
$250 purchase _ #5264C
Examines the history of the Panama Canal and shows how vessels are raised and lowered. Produced by WGBH Boston.
Geography - World
Dist - CORF

Man Abuses Man - Lifestyle Abuses 30 MIN
U-matic / VHS
Color
Reveals facts about how the American lifestyle has incorporated health abuses without much regard for the grave consequences. Discusses importance of restructuring lives and relates how the pregnant woman should care for herself, thus giving a better health start to her unborn child.
Health and Safety; Physical Education and Recreation; Sociology
Dist - FAIRGH **Prod** - FAIRGH

Man after God's own heart 30 MIN
VHS
Our dwelling place series
Color (K P I R)
$14.95 purchase _ #35 - 8820 - 7756
Presents an animated account of children in an orphanage as they explore the rooms of an old mansion, finding Biblical stories coming to life. Includes the Old Testament accounts of David and Goliath, David and Jonathan, David's rise to become king of Israel, and Elijah and the ravens.
Literature and Drama; Religion and Philosophy
Dist - APH

Man Against Fire 28 MIN
16mm / U-matic / VHS
Color (I) (SPANISH)
LC 74-705077
Shows the latest in firefighting methods and fire prevention.
Health and Safety; Science - Natural; Social Science
Dist - USNAC **Prod** - USDA 1969

Man Alive 12 MIN
16mm
Color (C A)
Illustrates the importance of seeking competent medical advice when cancer is suspected. Uses animation to humorously draw a parallelism between the problems of physical symptoms and the symptoms of an automobile.
Health and Safety
Dist - AMCS **Prod** - AMCS 1952

Man Alive Series
David 28 MIN
Jocelyn 28 MIN
May's Miracle 28 MIN
Dist - FLMLIB

Man alone and loneliness - the dilemma of the modern society
VHS
Color (J H C)
$197.00 purchase _ #00235 - 126
Explores the many faces of loneliness. Shows how the visions of artists, innovators and explorers can often set these individuals apart from the rest of society. Discusses the change in American attitudes about loneliness, from the chosen solitude of the early settlers to the compelling group - mindedness of modern times. Includes teacher's guide and library kit. Two parts.
History - United States; Psychology; Sociology
Dist - GA **Prod** - GA

Man Amplifiers 29 MIN
Videoreel / VT2
Interface Series
Color
Business and Economics; Science - Physical
Dist - PBS **Prod** - KCET

A Man and a River 15 MIN
16mm
Color
LC 74-705078
Tells the story of Thomas Hart Benton, famous painter, author, conservationist and raconteur, and his great love for the Buffalo River, a clear - running waterway that winds through the Ozark Hills of northwestern Arkansas.
Biography; Geography - United States
Dist - USNAC **Prod** - EPA 1973

Man and Environment 25 MIN
U-matic / VHS / 16mm
Untamed World Series Series
Color; Mono (J H C A)
$400.00 film, $250.00 video, $50.00 rental
Studies men of varying cultures and societies who are coping with the elements of their respective environments.
Geography - World; Social Science
Dist - CTV **Prod** - CTV 1969

A Man and His Dog Out for Air 2 MIN
16mm
B&W (C)
$129.00
Experimental film by Robert Breer.
Fine Arts
Dist - AFA **Prod** - AFA 1957

Man and His Environment I - Rainforest Family 17 MIN
U-matic / VHS / 16mm
Man and His Environment Series
Color (I J H)
LC 70-712251
Shows the Choco Indians of Central and South America who are typical of the hunting and gathering societies explains that because of their extreme isolation, each child is taught by his parents the many skills necessary to live in the forest. Shows how they adapt to the forest environment by using available forest materials to make their houses, clothing, tools and utensils.
Geography - World; Psychology; Social Science
Dist - PHENIX **Prod** - MITC 1971

Man and His Environment II - Food from the Rainforest 17 MIN
U-matic / VHS / 16mm
Man and His Environment Series
Color (I J H)
LC 74-712252
Shows how the Choco Indians of Central and South America supply most of their own food by hunting, fishing, gathering and simple agriculture. Tells how boys hunt and fish with their fathers while girls learn to gather and prepare food with their mothers. Shows how surplus products are taken away by canoe to to the trading post which is several days journey away.
Geography - World; Psychology; Social Science
Dist - PHENIX **Prod** - MITC 1971

Man and his environment - in harmony and in conflict
VHS
Color (J H C)
$197.00 purchase _ #00206 - 126
Stresses the need for making a conscious choice to live in harmony with the environment. Proposes that planning, studies of the growth of cities and their problems as well as the suggestions of architects can aid in the creation of a harmonious environment. Includes teacher's guide and library kit. In two parts.
Science - Natural; Sociology
Dist - GA **Prod** - GA

Man and His Environment Series
Man and His Environment I - Rainforest Family 17 MIN
Man and His Environment II - Food from the Rainforest 17 MIN
Dist - PHENIX

Man and His Gold 28 MIN
16mm
Color
LC 79-701375
Shows the many and varied roles that gold has played and continues to play for man. Demonstrates gold's unique properties which make it both desirable and useful.
Business and Economics; Science - Physical
Dist - MTP **Prod** - GOLDIC 1979

Man and His Habits 13 MIN
16mm
Foremanship Training Series
Color
LC 74-705079
Shows how man's habits endanger his safety by becoming routine when carried over to his work. Shows the worker how to acquire safe work habits by practicing safety at home and on the job.
Health and Safety
Dist - USNAC **Prod** - USBM 1969

A Man and His Men 30 MIN
16mm
Color (R)
Takes a look at the life of a professional football player. Spotlights Tom Landry, coach of the Dallas Cowboys and how his Christian faith affects his work.
Guidance and Counseling; Physical Education and Recreation
Dist - GF **Prod** - YOUTH

Man and His Sport Series
The Athletes 27 MIN
Sports Medicine 28 MIN
Swimmer 26 MIN
Dist - AUIS

A Man and his wife weave a hammock 12 MIN
16mm / VHS
Yanomamo series
Color (G)
$250.00, $150.00 purchase, $25.00 rental
Observes a village headman, Moawa, who weaves a cotton hammock while his wife swings in her own hammock, occasionally touching his leg in a loving manner. Shows the wife watching and teasing as she plays with their baby. Part of a series on the Yanomamo Indians of Venezuela by Timothy Asch and Napoleon Chagnon.
Geography - World; Social Science; Sociology
Dist - DOCEDR PSUPCR **Prod** - DOCEDR 1975

Man and His World 22 MIN
U-matic / VHS / 16mm
Color (I J)
LC 74-701737
Creates a metaphorical portrait of the inhabitants of the earth. Shows a group of Negro teen - agers playing with a soccer ball as titles appear on the screen which tell of the vulnerable suspension of the planet in time and space. The admonishment to people is Do Not Blow its chances for survival.
Guidance and Counseling; Science - Physical; Sociology
Dist - AIMS **Prod** - GROENG 1969

Man and His World Series
Bangkok 18 MIN
Bargemen on the Rhine 13 MIN
Coffee planters near Kilimanjaro 14 MIN
Cooperative farming in East Germany 15 MIN
Cork from Portugal 14 MIN
Dairy Farming in the Alps 16 MIN
Deep sea trawler 18 MIN
Diamond Mining in East Africa 9 MIN
Egyptian villagers 14 MIN
Favela - diary of a slum 17 MIN
Highland Indians of Peru 18 MIN
Indian Villagers in Mexico 12 MIN
Industrial Beginnings in West Pakistan 17 MIN
Industrial Region in Sweden 18 MIN
Industrial Worker in Kenya 13 MIN
Israeli Kibbutz 19 MIN
Japanese Farmers 17 MIN
Land from the North Sea 17 MIN
Life in Soviet Asia - 273 Days Below Zero 11 MIN
Man Changes the Nile 13 MIN
Masai in Tanzania 14 MIN
Miners of Bolivia 15 MIN
New Life for a Spanish Farmer 18 MIN
North Sea Islanders 19 MIN
A Norwegian Fjord 13 MIN
Oasis in the Sahara 16 MIN
Oil in Libya 15 MIN
Over the Andes in Ecuador 18 MIN
Plateau Farmers in France 15 MIN
Rainy Season in West Africa 14 MIN
Ranchero and gauchos in Argentina 17 MIN
Rice Farmers in Thailand 19 MIN
River Journey on the Upper Nile 18 MIN
River People of Chad 20 MIN
Romania 18 MIN
Sugar in Egypt 13 MIN
Three Brothers in Haiti 17 MIN
Timber in Finland 15 MIN
Tokyo Industrial Worker 17 MIN
Two Brothers in Greece 15 MIN
Venezuela 14 MIN
Winemakers in France 15 MIN
Wool in Australia 19 MIN
Yugoslavian Coastline 14 MIN
Dist - FI

Man and Music Series
The Age of Reason 53 MIN
Beethoven - the Age of Revolution 53 MIN
Beethoven - the Composer as Hero 53 MIN
The Golden age 53 MIN
Haydn and the Esterhazys 53 MIN
The Italian connection 53 MIN
Liszt at Weimar 53 MIN
London - the Musical Capital 53 MIN
Monteverdi in Mantua 53 MIN
Mozart - a Genius in His Time 53 MIN
Mozart - Dropping the Patron 53 MIN
Music at the Court of Louis XIV 53 MIN
Music for a Nation 53 MIN
Music for the World 53 MIN
Music of an Empire 53 MIN
The New Music 53 MIN
Out of the Darkness 53 MIN
Schubert - the Young Romantic 53 MIN
The Search for a Voice 53 MIN
Turn of the Century 53 MIN
The Voice of Britannia 53 MIN
The Waltz City 53 MIN
Dist - FOTH

Man and Radiation 29 MIN
16mm
Color
LC FIE64-193
Discusses the discovery of radiation, the different types, and its beneficial applications in medicine, industry, agriculture, power and research.
Agriculture; Business and Economics; Health and Safety; Science - Physical
Dist - USERD **Prod** - USNRC 1963

Man and Resources 145 MIN
U-matic
University of the Air Series
Color (J H C A)
$750.00 purchase, $250.00 rental
Explains various instances of man's confrontation with a limit to his growth and man's solution to each problem posed by the apparent limitations. Program contains a series of five cassettes 29 minutes each.
Social Science
Dist - CTV **Prod** - CTV 1976

Man and Safety - Communications 30 MIN
U-matic / VHS / 16mm
Color
Discusses the need for better communication and its importance in preventing accidents. Reenacts several accidents to show the consequences of too much or too little information, unclear messages and emotional difficulties.
Health and Safety; Psychology
Dist - USNAC **Prod** - USAF 1983

Man and Safety - Physical Limitations 23 MIN
VHS / U-matic
Color
LC 73-702416; 82-706286
Describes man's physical limitations and relates them to human error accidents. Reconstructs several accidents to show the consequences of exceeding one's physical capabilities.
Health and Safety; Science - Natural
Dist - USNAC **Prod** - USAF 1963

Man and Safety - Physiological Limitations 26 MIN
16mm
Color (J H)
LC 77-701151
Discusses the boundaries beyond which human efficiency breaks down and accidents occur. Considers the added complexity of equipping man to survive environments of outer space.
Health and Safety; Industrial and Technical Education; Science - Natural; Science - Physical
Dist - USNAC **Prod** - USAF 1963

Man and Safety - Supervision 26 MIN
U-matic / VHS / 16mm
Color
Discusses supervision and its role in human failure accidents. Dramatizes several accidents to show the consequences of poor supervision and illustrates the role of positive supervision in preventing a major catastrophe.
Business and Economics; Health and Safety
Dist - USNAC **Prod** - USAF 1983

Man and Safety - Tools 28 MIN
16mm
Color
LC 81-700788
Enacts accidents on the ground, in the air and in the mountains to show how misuse of tools can lead to disaster. Points out the importance of selecting and correctly using proper tools for specific purposes.
Health and Safety; Industrial and Technical Education
Dist - USNAC **Prod** - USAF 1981

The Man and the Atom - Challenge of Our Times 17 MIN
16mm
B&W
LC FIA68-1655
Uses historic films to illustrate the crises and challenges of the Atomic Age.
History - United States; Science - Physical
Dist - HEARST **Prod** - HEARST 1967

Man and the Atom, Pt 1 30 MIN
U-matic
B&W
Surveys the role of the Atomic Energy Commission in the nation's atomic energy program. Reviews the atom's place in national defense and the peaceful use of nuclear explosives. Surveys radioisotopes and their many applications.
Civics and Political Systems; Health and Safety; Science - Physical
Dist - USNAC **Prod** - USNAC 1972

Man and the Atom, Pt 2 30 MIN
U-matic
B&W
Surveys the role of the Atomic Energy Commission and their guidance of research for both defense and research purposes.
Civics and Political Systems; Health and Safety; Science - Physical
Dist - USNAC **Prod** - USNAC 1972

Man and the Changing Earth - Science, Social Studies
VHS / U-matic
Color
Provides the necessary background for understanding current problems. Discusses forces that change our environment, the balance of the ecosystem, effects, the beginning of the industrial revolution, and the rise and problems of cities.
Science - Natural; Social Science
Dist - EDUACT **Prod** - EDUACT

Man and the FBM 28 MIN
16mm
Color
LC FIE61-90
Shows the U S Navy's fleet ballistic missile submarine and discusses the recruitment and training of the personnel who will operate the nuclear weapons system.
Civics and Political Systems
Dist - USNAC **Prod** - USN 1960

Man and the forest - part 5 series
Decorative woods and fuel 20 MIN
Dist - MMP

Man and the Forest Series Part 4
Native Transplants and Crude Drugs 18 MIN
Dist - MMP

Man and the Forest Series
The Cedar tree 11 MIN
Decorative foliage 20 MIN
Red Man and the Red Cedar 12 MIN
Seed cones and reforestation 23 MIN
Dist - MMP

The Man and the Giant 8 MIN
U-matic / VHS / 16mm
Color (H C A)
Shows Inuit Indians acting out a legend about a captured hunter.
Social Science
Dist - PHENIX **Prod** - NFBC 1978

The Man and the Giant - an Eskimo Legend 8 MIN
U-matic / VHS / 16mm
Color (J)
LC 79-700670
Dramatizes an Inuit legend about a hunter who is taken captive by a giant.
Literature and Drama; Social Science
Dist - PHENIX **Prod** - NFBC 1978

Man and the Industrial Revolution 20 MIN
16mm / U-matic / VHS
History of Man Series
Color (J)
LC 79-708551
Describes the beginnings of the first industrial revolution in Europe, its spread and its social, political and technological implications.
Business and Economics; History - World; Psychology; Sociology
Dist - MGHT **Prod** - MGHT 1970

The Man and the Land 28 MIN
16mm
Color
LC 74-701771
Shows how American farmers, using up - to - date agricultural techniques, feed the people of the United States and provide food for millions of people overseas.
Agriculture; Health and Safety; Industrial and Technical Education
Dist - INDFB **Prod** - INDFB 1974

Man and the Rise of Civilization 19 MIN
U-matic / VHS / 16mm
History of Man Series
Color (J)
LC 70-708549
Deals with the general process of becoming civilized. Shows how urbanization and specialization of functions occurred within civilizations. Emphasizes that great civilizations grew at various times in all parts of the world, among all men.
History - World; Psychology; Sociology
Dist - MGHT **Prod** - MGHT 1970

The Man and the Rocket
16mm
Screen news digest series
B&W (H)
Presents a report on the Grissom flight and the earlier launchings of the Discoverer XXVI, Tiros III, and Midas III. Volume four, issue one of the Screen News Digest series.
Industrial and Technical Education; Science - Physical
Dist - HEARST **Prod** - HEARST 1961

Man and the 'Second' Industrial Revolution 19 MIN
U-matic / VHS / 16mm
History of Man Series
Color (J)
LC 72-708552
Shows how man is using new technological knowledge to change the world and to reach out to new worlds. Poses the problems that have come with this knowledge, overpopulation, pollution and the ability to destroy the environment. Provides a point of departure for discussion on how the future history of man will be written.
History - World; Psychology; Sociology
Dist - MGHT **Prod** - MGHT 1970

The Man and the Snake 26 MIN
U-matic / VHS / 16mm
Color
LC 75-704203
Features the short story by Ambrose Bierce about a young man's visit to the home of a zoologist who keeps and studies snakes with the locale changed from post - Civil War America to Victorian England.
Literature and Drama
Dist - PFP **Prod** - JOCF 1975

Man and the State - Burke and Paine on Revolution 28 MIN
U-matic / VHS / 16mm
Man and the State Series
Color
LC 74-700157
Features Thomas Paine who was a leading radical and revolutionary in 1792. Presents Edmund Burke who is a most articulate conservative. Shows Burke and Paine debating their conflicting views of man, political change and liberty while elements of the French Revolution are acted out in microcosm before them. Explains the government of the United States as related to the ideas under discussion.
Biography; Civics and Political Systems; History - United States
Dist - BARR **Prod** - WILETS 1974

Man and the State - Hamilton and Jefferson on Democracy 26 MIN
16mm / U-matic / VHS
Man and the State Series
Color (J)
LC 75-702538
Discusses Alexander Hamilton's and Thomas Jefferson's differing views of democracy.
Biography; Civics and Political Systems; History - United States
Dist - BARR **Prod** - WILETS 1975

Man and the State - Machiavelli on Political Power 28 MIN
16mm / U-matic / VHS
Man and the State Series
Color (J)
Presents the political ideas of Niccolo Machiavelli, which havo had a tremendous impact on society. Machiavelli is forced to debate his ideas. Questions if his politics is a politics of realism, and does he show the world as it is today. An open ended film.
Biography; Civics and Political Systems; History - World; Literature and Drama
Dist - BARR **Prod** - WILETS 1972

Man and the State - Marx and Rockefeller on Capitalism 26 MIN
16mm / U-matic / VHS
Man and the State Series
Color (J H)
Features Karl Marx and John D Rockefeller, who are temporarily brought back to life by a future society in order to debate the basic ideas of communism and capitalism as they evolved up to the last quarter of the 20th century. Shows how the conflict between these ideas is reflected in the main social and economic tensions in the world today.
Biography; Business and Economics; Civics and Political Systems; History - World
Dist - BARR **Prod** - WILETS 1977

Man and the State - Roosevelt and Hoover on the Economy 25 MIN
U-matic / VHS / 16mm
Man and the State Series
Color (J)
LC 76-701292
Explores what would happen if Herbert Hoover and Franklin Roosevelt were forced to confront one another and debate their reasons for acting or failing to act during the Great Depression. Evaluates the conflicting views of both men on deficit financing bureaucracy and the role the federal government plays in people's lives.
Biography; Business and Economics; Civics and Political Systems; History - United States
Dist - BARR **Prod** - WILETS 1976

Man and the State Series
Man and the State - Burke and Paine on Revolution 28 MIN
Man and the State - Hamilton and Jefferson on Democracy 26 MIN
Man and the State - Machiavelli on Political Power 28 MIN
Man and the State - Marx and Rockefeller on Capitalism 26 MIN
Man and the State - Roosevelt and Hoover on the Economy 25 MIN
Man and the State - the Trial of Socrates 29 MIN
Dist - BARR

Man and the State - the Trial of Socrates 29 MIN
U-matic / VHS / 16mm
Man and the State Series
Color (J)
LC 75-714083
Explains the significance of the trial and death of Socrates in the history of Western civilization as reflected in the works of Plato, Xenophon and Aristophanes, as well as in other Greek sources.
History - World; Literature and Drama; Religion and Philosophy; Sociology
Dist - BARR **Prod** - WILETS 1971

Man and the Universe Series
Time - Measurement and Meaning 26 MIN
Dist - EBEC

Man and Water 28 MIN
16mm
Color
LC 78-701697
Offers a look at a river system and concludes that the farmer, rancher and environmentalist must work together to prevent degradation of the river.
Science - Natural; Sociology
Dist - CONICO **Prod** - CONICO 1978

Man and Woman 33 MIN
16mm / U-matic / VHS
Great Themes of Literature Series
Color (J)
LC 73-702547
Presents an edited version of Franco Zeffirelli's film The Taming Of The Shrew, which is based on Shakespeare's play. Features Richard Burton as the clever and boisterous Petruchio, who woos and weds the flamboyant and resistant Katherine, played by Elizabeth Taylor.
Literature and Drama; Sociology
Dist - LCOA **Prod** - LCOA 1973

Man and woman and animal 10 MIN
16mm
Color (H C A)
$35.00 rental
Explores men and women as united by the history of nature in contrast with the traditional trinities. Produced by Valie Export.
Science - Natural
Dist - CANCIN

Man and woman - myths and stereotypes 36 MIN
VHS
Color (J H)
$99.00 purchase _ #00267 - 026
Examines how literature, art, movies, media and music perpetuate artificial male and female sex roles. Traces the history of sexual stereotypes through the writings of Sylvia Plath and Simone de Beauvoir and looks at how writers such as Shakespeare, Wordsworth and Byron idealized woman as beautiful and unobtainable. Includes teacher's guide and library kit.
Education; Literature and Drama; Sociology
Dist - GA

A Man and Woman's Guide to Breast Examination 5 MIN
U-matic / VHS / 16mm
Color
LC 76-700380
Uses live action and animation in presenting a guide to breast examination. Shows how a husband learns to examine his wife for the early detection of breast cancer.
Health and Safety; Sociology
Dist - UCEMC **Prod** - RTOMP 1976

Man, Animal, Climate and Earth 30 MIN
16mm
Great Plains Trilogy, 2 Series Nomad and Indians - Early Man on the 'Plains; Nomad and Indians - early man on the plains
B&W (J)
Discusses discovery of early human camp sites in southwestern Nebraska. Describes what is known about the climate, the behavior of streams and the animals and men.
Science - Physical; Social Science
Dist - UNEBR **Prod** - UNEBR 1954

Man as He Behaves 30 MIN
16mm
Science Reporter Series
B&W
LC FIA65-1665
Outlines lab research concerning human behavior and explains the need for methods to gauge human behavior indirectly and objectively. Demonstrates how cooperation and competition are tested by observing subjects operating machines. Suggests that research leads to an understanding of mental health.
Psychology
Dist - IU **Prod** - MIOT 1967

Man as hero - tragic and comic
VHS
Color (J H C)
$197.00 purchase _ #00215 - 126
Defines heroes as those who have had a profound effect on the lives of people or have influenced the course of history. Studies six individuals - David, Michelangelo, Joan of Arc, Beethoven, Napoleon and Einstein, as well as contemporary heroes Martin Luther King, Jr, Pete Seeger, Malcolm X and Ralph Nader. Includes teacher's guide and library kit. In two parts.
History - United States; History - World; Sociology
Dist - GA **Prod** - GA

Man as Hunter and Food Gatherer 19 MIN
16mm / U-matic / VHS
History of Man Series
Color (J)
LC 77-708548
Shows representatives of the last remaining hunting and food - gathering tribes, who exist today much as men did thousands of years ago.
History - World; Sociology
Dist - MGHT **Prod** - MGHT 1970

Man as symbol maker - creating new meanings
VHS
Color (J H C)
$197.00 purchase _ #00249 - 126
Analyzes how women and men have used symbols since earliest times to express basic ideas about themselves and the world in which they live. Examines the impact of symbols and images used in art and literature. Includes teacher's guide and library kit. In two parts.
Fine Arts; Literature and Drama; Social Science
Dist - GA **Prod** - GA

The Man behind the gavel 29 MIN
16mm
Government story series; No 6
Color
LC 70-707171
Discusses the role of the speaker of the House of Representatives, pointing out that he is the second most powerful elected official in the United States. Shows how individual speakers from Henry Clay to Sam Rayburn have interpreted and wielded that power.
Civics and Political Systems
Dist - WBCPRO **Prod** - WBCPRO 1968

The Man Behind the Mask 50 MIN
U-matic / VHS
Color (J)
LC 84-706202
Reviews the life of Heinrich Schiemann, the man who was long recognized as the Father of Archeology until it was discovered that virtually all his achievements were fakery.
Biography; Science; Science - Physical
Dist - FI **Prod** - BBCTV 1982

Man Belongs to the Earth 22 MIN
16mm
Color
LC 75-703833
Deals with the natural environment of cities, the desert, the oceans and the mountains. Shows the dread waste and destruction threatening the environment and points out natural wonders that should be preserved. Presents the problems and some solutions. Includes scenes photographed throughout the 50 states.
Science - Natural; Science - Physical
Dist - USNAC **Prod** - USBIC 1974

The Man between 104 MIN
16mm
B&W
Features James Mason as a shadowy figure who becomes caught between West and East Berlin when he falls in love with a woman. Directed by Sir Carol Reed.
Fine Arts
Dist - KITPAR **Prod** - UNKNWN 1953

Man Blong Custom 52 MIN
U-matic / VHS / 16mm
Tribal Eye Series
Color (H C A)
Demonstrates the importance of tribal sculpture to the culture of the Western Pacific islands. Shows how Christianity has both succeeded and failed in some instances to replace the tribal sculpture tradition.
Fine Arts; History - World; Sociology
Dist - TIMLIF **Prod** - BBCTV 1976

Man builds - man destroys series
A City with a future 30 MIN
The Seamless web 30 MIN
Dist - GPN

A Man Called Bee - Studying the Yanomamo 40 MIN
16mm
Yanomamo Series
Color
LC 75-702654
Follows anthropologist Napoleon Chagnon as he collects anthropological field data among the Yanoama Indians of southern Venezuela.
Geography - World; Sociology
Dist - DOCEDR **Prod** - DOCEDR 1974

The Man Called Bogart 26 MIN
16mm
B&W
LC FI68-174
Follows the career of Humphrey Bogart, from his unsuccessful early films and his gangster films, to his greatest films, including Treasure of the Sierra Madre, The African Queen and The Caine Mutiny.
Biography; Fine Arts
Dist - WOLPER **Prod** - WOLPER 1963

Man Called 'Duce,' a - Benito Mussolini in Perspective 15 MIN
16mm
Screen news digest series; Vol 14; Issue 7
B&W (J H)
Documents the rise and fall of Benito Mussolini.
Biography; History - World
Dist - HEARST **Prod** - HEARST 1972

A Man Called Edison 28 MIN
16mm
B&W (I A)
Presents the contributions of Thomas A Edison to the motion picture through his early kinetoscope films. Provides a vivid panorama of early moviemaking.
Biography; Fine Arts
Dist - SF **Prod** - SPCTRA 1970

A Man Called Flintstone 87 MIN
16mm
Color (J H C)
Presents an animated feature, starring Fred Flintstone and the whole Flintstone gang as Fred impersonates a well known secret agent and pursues his mission of tracking down the enemy operative.
Fine Arts
Dist - TIMLIF **Prod** - HANBAR 1966

A Man called Luther 40 MIN
VHS
Color (J H C G A R)
$29.50 purchase, $10.00 rental _ #35 - 80 - 254
Documents the life of Martin Luther. Hosted by Dr Lee Roy Brandes. Produced by Encounter, Inc.
Religion and Philosophy
Dist - APH

A man called Norman 50 MIN
VHS
Color (I J H C G A R)
$69.00 rental _ #36 - 81 - 2025
Profiles Mike Adkins, who credits a man called Norman with changing his life. Shows that Norman was rejected by church - going people. Produced by Focus on the Family.
Religion and Philosophy
Dist - APH

Man Changes the Nile 13 MIN
U-matic / VHS / 16mm
Man and His World Series
Color (P I J H C)
LC 76-705480
Explains how man uses his ingenuity to take advantage of the Nile River for both power and irrigation.
Agriculture; Geography - World; Science - Natural
Dist - FI **Prod** - FI 1969

A Man dies 45 MIN
16mm
Color (H)
Features the teenagers of the Bristol Church Youth Club in England who present a contemporary form of the medieval mystery play, using drama, Rock and Roll music and dancing, and modern dress to tell the story of the Passion of Christ and its meaning for today.
Fine Arts; Guidance and Counseling; Literature and Drama
Dist - YALEDV **Prod** - YALEDV

Man - eaters of India 60 MIN
VHS
National Geographic video series
Color (G)
$29.95 purchase
Portrays the deadly cats of Kumaon, India, and Jim Corbett, the man who saved them from extinction.
Science - Natural
Dist - PBS **Prod** - WNETTV

Man Enough for the Job 25 MIN
U-matic / VHS / 16mm
Color (I)
Uses a teenager and his family to show the purpose and work of 4 - H clubs, and their contributions to America.
Agriculture; Guidance and Counseling; Psychology; Sociology
Dist - IFB **Prod** - OFP 1961

A Man Escaped 100 MIN
16mm
B&W (FRENCH)
Tells how French resistance leader Andre Devigny escaped from a Nazi prison in Lyon just hours before he was to be executed.
Fine Arts; Foreign Language; History - World
Dist - NYFLMS **Prod** - NYFLMS 1956

Man - Flying - Mountain - Kite 11 MIN
16mm
Color
LC 76-700381
Presents a visual essay of mountain hang gliders in Montana and Idaho, filmed from a balloon, helicopter and glider.
Physical Education and Recreation
Dist - BITROT **Prod** - BITROT 1975

A Man for all seasons 120 MIN
VHS
Color (G A)
$79.95 purchase _ #TNO102AE
Takes viewers back to the era of Reformation England, focusing on the religious and ethical conflicts between Sir Thomas More and King Henry VIII. Stars Charlton Heston, Vanessa Redgrave, and Sir John Gielgud. Originally broadcast on the TNT cable network.

Fine Arts; History - World; Literature and Drama
Dist - TMM **Prod** - TMM

A Man for all seasons 120 MIN
VHS
Color (J H C)
$89.00 purchase _ #05733 - 126
Portrays the rift between Sir Thomas More and King Henry VIII. Stars Paul Scofield and Robert Shaw.
Civics and Political Systems; History - World
Dist - GA **Prod** - GA

Man from Deer Creek, the, the Story of Ishi
VHS / U-matic
Color
Tells the story of Ishi, a Yahi Indian who was the last Indian in America to grow up without contact with 'American civilization.'.
Social Science; Sociology
Dist - MMPRO **Prod** - MMPRO

The Man from Inner Space 27 MIN
U-matic / VHS / 16mm
Insight Series
Color (H C A)
Analyzes the problems of having faith through the story of a space man who promises to solve all the earth's problems if the population will let go of 'all else,' including nuclear weapons, so that he can take over within them. Stars James Franciscus and Louis Gossett.
Psychology; Religion and Philosophy
Dist - PAULST **Prod** - PAULST

The Man from Laramie 104 MIN
16mm
Color
Tells how Will Lockhart travels to New Mexico to find and kill the man who sold guns to the Apaches who killed his brother. Stars James Stewart.
Fine Arts
Dist - TIMLIF **Prod** - CPC

The Man from Maisinicu 117 MIN
U-matic / VHS / 16mm
Captioned; B&W (A) (SPANISH (ENGLISH SUBTITLES))
Presents espionage and counter intelligence activity during the early years of the Cuban revolution.
Civics and Political Systems; Fine Arts; History - World
Dist - CNEMAG **Prod** - CNEMAG 1973

The Man from NECA 20 MIN
16mm
Color (J H C)
LC 71-704743
Narration and a series of episodes document the variety of services provided to members of NECA, and emphasizes the chapter manager's role and status in chapter activities.
Business and Economics; Industrial and Technical Education
Dist - FINLYS **Prod** - NECA 1967

Man from Nowhere 58 MIN
16mm
Color (I J)
Tells how Alice's life with her great - uncle is disrupted when a sinister man appears to tell her that her life is in danger. Describes how four local urchins befriend her by setting a trap for the stranger.
Fine Arts
Dist - LUF **Prod** - LUF 1978

Man - his growth and development, birth through adolescence - a series
Man - his growth and development, birth through adolescence - a'series
B&W
Adolescence - A Cultural Phenomenon; Adolescent Idealism And Realism ; Adolescent Sexuality; Cognitive Functioning - Ages 6 - 13; Consolidation And Growth; Coping With The Toddler; Emerging Consciousness; Emotional Development Of The Infant; Heredity And Behavior; Infant And Society, The; Intellectual Development - Ages 6 - 13; Language Development; Man - His Growth And Development, Birth - - ; Path To Adulthood; Peer Groups - Ages 3 - 13; Play Activities - Ages 6 - 13; Preschooler - Concept Development; Preschooler - Psycho - Sexual Development; Rudiments Of Self Concept; School And The Child; Sex Roles - Ages 3 - 13; Toddler, The - Origins Of Independence.
Psychology
Dist - AJN **Prod** - VDONUR 1967

Man - his growth and development, birth through adolescence - a series
Man - his growth and development, birth through adolescence - a series
Dist - AJN

Man hunt 31 MIN
BETA / VHS / U-matic
Color (C A G)
$870.00 purchase, $240.00 rental
Stars John Cleese who shows how to use the interviewing process for recognizing talent. Hones interviewing skills by showcasing three typical problems and their solutions. Demonstrates the proper way to prepare to meet candidates, listen to what is said and probe into sensitive areas.
Business and Economics; Guidance and Counseling; Psychology
Dist - VIDART **Prod** - VIDART

Man Hunt 31 MIN
U-matic / VHS
Color (A)
Employs humorous examples to demonstrate effective and ineffective techniques for drawing out a candidate during a job interview. Emphasizes preparation and good questions.
Business and Economics; Psychology
Dist - XICOM **Prod** - XICOM

The Man Hunters 52 MIN
U-matic / VHS / 16mm
Color (I A)
LC 77-711316
Explores the time and the place where man first walked on the earth.
History - World; Science - Natural
Dist - FI **Prod** - FI 1971

Man Hunters, Pt 1 26 MIN
16mm / U-matic / VHS
Color (I A)
LC 77-711316
Explores the time and the place where man first walked on the earth.
History - World
Dist - FI **Prod** - FI 1971

Man Hunters, Pt 2 26 MIN
U-matic / VHS / 16mm
Color (I A)
LC 77-711316
Explores the time and the place where man first walked on the earth.
History - World
Dist - FI **Prod** - FI 1971

Man in a bubble 15 MIN
16mm
B&W (G)
$45.00 rental
Introduces Sidney Peterson, one of the originators of the American avant - garde cinema, and his classic films made in San Francisco between 1947 and 1950. Features a short documentary about personal acoustical space in an age of intolerable noise. Fragmented views of New York and Chicago are seen in his street photography.
Fine Arts; Sociology
Dist - CANCIN

The Man in Charge 18 MIN
16mm
Color
LC 74-706493
Discusses the problems of leadership on the small unit level in the Marine Corps. Emphasizes the importance of identifying the overall concepts of leadership by the individual Marine.
Civics and Political Systems; Psychology
Dist - USNAC **Prod** - USN 1973

Man in Command 29 MIN
16mm
Color
LC 75-700792
Shows training career opportunities offered to line officers in the U S Navy.
Civics and Political Systems; Psychology
Dist - USNAC **Prod** - USN 1968

Man in Flight 19 MIN
16mm
Color
LC FIE61-91
Depicts the research being carried on at the School Of Aviation Medicine, Brooks Air Force Base, Texas, to insure man's comfort and safety in flight.
Industrial and Technical Education
Dist - USNAC **Prod** - USAF 1945

The Man in Green 19 MIN
16mm
Color
LC 74-705080
Tells the story of the state forestry organizations. Shows the different kinds of foresters and where they function.
Agriculture; Civics and Political Systems; Social Science; Sociology
Dist - USNAC **Prod** - USDA 1970

Man in His Environment 29 MIN
U-matic / VHS / 16mm
Color (I)
LC 76-702946
Presents a film essay on the checks and balances of the natural cycle, showing how the processes that regulate other forms of life ultimately regulate humans as well. Explores ramifications of human overpopulation, wastefulness of modern industrial society and disruption caused by many agricultural methods.
Guidance and Counseling; Science - Natural; Sociology
Dist - UCEMC **Prod** - FMNH 1976

Man in Society 36 MIN
U-matic / VHS
Color
Includes 36 half - hour videotapes.
Sociology
Dist - TELSTR **Prod** - TELSTR

Man in Space, the Second Decade 28 MIN
U-matic
Space in the 70's Series
Color
LC 79-706964
Reviews achievements of manned space flight during the 1960's and shows programs for manned flight during the 1970's. Describes programs that are technically feasible and desirable beyond 1980. Issued in 1971 as a motion picture.
History - World; Industrial and Technical Education; Science - Physical; Sociology
Dist - USNAC **Prod** - NASA 1979

A Man in the box 8 MIN
16mm
Color (G)
$10.00 rental
Features the film camera looking inward and defining itself by how it sees the world yet it never sees anything but itself. Presents a camera's photographic memory, trying to focus in upon its own image.
Fine Arts; Industrial and Technical Education
Dist - CANCIN **Prod** - RAYHER 1978

The Man in the Cast Iron Suit 25 MIN
U-matic / VHS / 16mm
Insight Series
Color (J)
LC 79-700756
Depicts three generations of the Hayes family struggling to fulfill themselves and learning from their grandfather that neither physical prowess or economic success will fulfill the human being.
Fine Arts; Guidance and Counseling; Sociology
Dist - PAULST **Prod** - PAULST 1976

Man in the dark sedan 5 MIN
16mm
Color (G)
$10.00 rental
Combines nature photography with rural landscapes. Features Snakefinger performing title song while rolling down a deserted road in an old sedan pulled by minions. Directed by Graeme Whifler.
Fine Arts
Dist - CANCIN

Man in the Desert 19 MIN
16mm
Color (J)
LC 72-702257
Examines the human and environmental effects of man's use of the Australian desert.
Geography - World; Science - Natural
Dist - AUIS **Prod** - ANAIB 1970

Man in the Fifth Dimension 33 MIN
16mm
Color
Features Billy Graham who guides the viewer through space and time into the realm of the fifth dimension, the spirit.
Biography; Guidance and Counseling; Religion and Philosophy
Dist - NINEFC **Prod** - WWP

The Man in the iron lung 51 MIN
VHS / U-matic
Color (C PRO)
$395.00 purchase, $80.00 rental _ #C920 - VI - 050
Describes to the physician the iron lung as an alternative to modern respirators. Teaches nurses and physical therapists practical methods of care to patients in the iron lung. Confirms to patients and their families that a patient with respiratory failure can lead a happy and productive life. Presented by Louisiana State University School of Medicine.
Health and Safety; Science - Natural
Dist - HSCIC

The Man in the Iron Mask 113 MIN
16mm
B&W
Tells what happens when twin Dauphins are born to Louis XIII of France and one of them is spirited away to be raised by the Three Musketeers. Stars Louis Hayward and Joan Bennett. Based on the novel The Man in the Iron Mask by Alexandre Dumas.
Fine Arts; Literature and Drama
Dist - KITPAR **Prod** - UAA 1939

The Man in the Ironic Mask - Jonathan Swift - the Modest Proposal and the Second 45 MIN
VHS / U-matic
Survey of English Literature I Series
Color
Analyzes Jonathan Swift's Modest Proposal and the Second Voyage Of Gulliver.
Literature and Drama
Dist - MDCPB **Prod** - MDCPB

The Man in the Middle 25 MIN
U-matic / VHS / 16mm
Color (J)
Records the daily efforts to seek an elusive peace in Lebanon as seen through the eyes of members of the multinational peacekeeping body stationed in the country. Shows that since 1978, the force has had to cope not only with the problem of maintaining a stable buffer zone between Lebanese guerillas and Christian militia, but also with separating Israeli soldiers and PLO members.
History - World
Dist - LUF **Prod** - LUF 1982

Man in the Middle 22 MIN
U-matic / VHS / 16mm
Color
Discusses the role of the supervisor who is sandwiched between the need for full production and the health and safety needs of his employees. Discusses attitudes toward safety.
Business and Economics; Health and Safety
Dist - IFB **Prod** - MILLBK

The Man in the Moon Remembers 5 MIN
U-matic / VHS / 16mm
Color
Uses animation and film footage from the Apollo moon landings to depict the history of the moon.
History - World; Science - Physical
Dist - USNAC **Prod** - NASM

Man in the Sea - the New Frontier 14 MIN
16mm
B&W (J H)
LC 70-703536
Presents a study of man's attempts to push back the frontiers of the sea.
Science - Natural; Science - Physical
Dist - HEARST **Prod** - HEARST 1969

Man in the Sea - the Story of Sea Lab II 28 MIN
U-matic
Color
LC 79-708130
Describes the U S Navy's Sea Lab II experiment. Includes underwater photography inside in the vehicle and of the sea around it. Issued in 1966 as a motion picture.
Science; Science - Physical
Dist - USNAC **Prod** - USN 1979

The Man in the silk hat 96 MIN
35mm / 16mm / VHS
Color tint (G) (FRENCH WITH ENGLISH SUBTITLES)
$150.00, $250.00 rental
Uses clips from his funniest films to recall the career of French silent screen comedian, Max Linder. Directed by Maud Linder.
Fine Arts; Literature and Drama
Dist - KINOIC

The Man in the White Suit 85 MIN
16mm
B&W
Presents a comedy about a young man whose discovery of a miracle fabric leads him to discover some contradictions upon which society is based. Features Alec Guinness.
Fine Arts; Literature and Drama
Dist - LCOA **Prod** - EALPRO 1952

Man in the Wilderness 105 MIN
16mm
Color
Presents the story of a trapper who is mauled by a grizzly bear and left for dead by his companions. Tells how he sets out to recover his furs and to wreak revenge.
Fine Arts
Dist - TWYMAN **Prod** - WB 1968

Man into space - the story of rockets and space science series
Early rockets and dreams of space 24 MIN
Pioneers and Modern Rockets 24 MIN
Satellites and Men in Orbit 24 MIN
Target Moon 24 MIN
Dist - AIMS

Man into Space - the Story of Rockets and Space Sciences Series
Exploring the Planets 24 MIN
Dist - AIMS

Man is His Own Worst Enemy 12 MIN
16mm / U-matic / VHS
Color (I) (ARABIC SPANISH FRENCH)
Features cartoon character Professor Von Drake discussing the struggle between reason and emotion in man. Emphasizes the need to seek a balance between the two.
Foreign Language; Guidance and Counseling; Psychology
Dist - CORF **Prod** - DISNEY 1975

Man is Responsible to the Earth 15 MIN
16mm
Color
LC 75-702891
Explains that pesticides have been an invaluable aid for improving quantity and quality in crops, but that they have been used incorrectly and unnecessarily in some instances. Presents insect scouting as a tool for determining the need for insecticide use, including an example of the control and savings realized with pea growing.
Agriculture
Dist - USNAC **Prod** - USEPA 1975

Man Isn't Dying of Thirst 22 MIN
16mm
Color
Explains the effects of LSD on the body, based on scientific research done in Czechoslovakia.
Health and Safety; Psychology
Dist - DANPRO **Prod** - DANPRO

A Man like Eva 92 MIN
35mm / 16mm / VHS
Color (G) (GERMAN WITH ENGLISH SUBTITLES)
$250.00, $300.00 rental
Presents a bizarre, fictionalized account of the life of film director Rainer Warner Fassbinder starring one of his leading actresses, Eva Mattes. Directed by Radu Gabrea.
Fine Arts
Dist - KINOIC

Man - Loading and Budgeting in Project Planning 30 MIN
VHS / 16mm
Project Management Series
Color (PRO)
$400.00 purchase, $100.00 rental
Includes Manload Charts, Resource Allocation, Costing, Budget Formats, Computers in Project Management and 'Kick - off' Presentation. Part of a six - part series on project management.
Business and Economics; Industrial and Technical Education; Psychology
Dist - ISA **Prod** - ISA

Man Looks at the Moon 15 MIN
16mm / U-matic / VHS
Color (I J H)
Presents line drawings, rare photographs taken through telescopes, and dramatic films taken both in mission control rooms and by astronauts to show what is currently known about the moon's geology.
Science - Physical
Dist - EBEC **Prod** - EBEC 1970

Man Machine Charts 22 MIN
U-matic / 16mm / VHS
B&W; Mono (C A)
Describes the construction and use of a man with a machine chart.
Science - Natural
Dist - UIOWA **Prod** - UIOWA 1953

Man - made Diamond 12 MIN
16mm
Color
Demonstrates the process of producing industrial diamonds. Shows how to accelerate nature's process of changing carbon into diamonds.
Industrial and Technical Education
Dist - GE **Prod** - GE

Man - made Famine 50 MIN
U-matic / VHS
Color (J H C A)
Talks about the lack of technical assistance given to Africa's women farmers and how this is a major reason for the food shortages there. Narrated by Glenda Jackson. A production of New Internationalist Publications Limited.
Social Science; Sociology
Dist - CWS

Man - made Land - Mizushima Coastal Industrial Area 27 MIN
16mm
Color
Explains that Mizushima is a typical country town near the sea in Japan. Shows what happens when next to an old market town a whole new industrial complex rises. Points out that here we have things Japanese, things Western, the traditional and the new all fused into a new kind of place to live, modernized by industrial transformation.
Geography - World; Social Science
Dist - UNIJAP **Prod** - KAJIMA 1965

Man - made Man 15 MIN
U-matic / VHS / 16mm
Twenty - first Century Series
Color (J)
LC 75-702567
A shortened version of the 1967 motion picture Man - Made Man. Discusses modern developments that have been made in the area of vital organ transplants and artificial organs. Illustrates the progress that has been made and presents several problems yet to be solved.
Health and Safety; Sociology
Dist - MGHT **Prod** - CBSTV 1975

The Man made World 15 MIN
U-matic
North America - Growth of a Continent Series
Color (J H)
Examines North America's manufacturing process. Describes the interdependence of primary, secondary and tertiary industries and looks at factors that influence their location.
Geography - United States; Geography - World
Dist - TVOTAR **Prod** - TVOTAR 1980

Man Makes a Desert 11 MIN
U-matic / VHS / 16mm
Color; B&W (I) (SPANISH)
Illustrates the changes that can occur when man upsets the delicate balance between the plants and animals that inhabit an area. Explains that through scientific study man is attempting to reclaim the land by reversing the changes he made.
Agriculture; Geography - United States; Science - Natural; Science - Physical
Dist - PHENIX **Prod** - FA 1964

Man makes a desert 10 MIN
U-matic / VHS / BETA
Color; NTSC; PAL; SECAM (J H)
PdS32
Reveals that a desert was accidentally formed in the southwestern part of the United States when poor farming and ranching practices disturbed the natural environment and the delicate balance between plant and animal life that inhabited the area. Discloses that grassland was destroyed, land was plowed and overgrazed and that grass gave way to desert plant life. Shows how attempts are being made to reverse desertification and to reclaim the land. Illustrates how a grassland ecosystem works, how humans disrupt such ecosystems and what has been learned. Includes shots of deserts in the United States and around the world.
Geography - United States; Geography - World; Science - Natural
Dist - VIEWTH

Man Management and Rig Management Series Lesson 1
What is Managment? 23 MIN
Dist - UTEXPE

Man Management and Rig Management Series Lesson 2
What is Leadership? 14 MIN
Dist - UTEXPE

Man Management and Rig Management Series Lesson 8
How Can Work be Done more Efficiently 24 MIN
Dist - UTEXPE

Man management and rig management series
How do you handle personnel problems? 14 MIN
How do you plan and organize work 21 MIN
How do you start out a new hand? 20 MIN
How do you train employees? 21 MIN
Introduction 25 MIN
Lesson 8 - How Can Work be Done more Efficiently 24 MIN
Lesson 5 - How do You Train Employees 21 MIN
Lesson 4 - How do You Start Out a New Hand 20 MIN
Lesson 1 - what is Management 23 MIN
Lesson 7 - How do You Plan and Organize Work 21 MIN
Lesson 6 - where do you fit into the organization 20 MIN
Lesson 3 - How do You Handle 14 MIN

Personnel Problems
Lesson 2 - what is Leadership 14 MIN
Where do You Fit into the Organization 20 MIN
Dist - UTEXPE

Man, Monsters and Mysteries 25 MIN
U-matic / VHS / 16mm
Color (I J H)
LC 74-700279
Tells the story of famous 'monster' Nessie of Loch Ness from 1933 to the present. Reveals the existence of ancient legends and writings concerning the Scottish monster.
Geography - World; History - World; Literature and Drama; Religion and Philosophy
Dist - CORF **Prod** - DISNEY 1973

Man must Work 15 MIN
16mm
Color
Describes the work therapy program called 'CHIRP' (Community Hospital Industrial Rehabilitation Program) being conducted at the Veterans' Administration Hospital in Brockton, Massachusetts. Shows how patients are assigned to jobs which enable them to participate in one of society's basic economic functions - productive work.
Geography - United States; Guidance and Counseling; Health and Safety; Social Science; Sociology
Dist - AMEDA **Prod** - HOFLAR

A Man Named Lombardi 55 MIN
U-matic / VHS / 16mm
Color (J)
Reveals the total commitment of Vince Lombardi both as a player and as a coach. Narrated by George C Scott.
Biography; Physical Education and Recreation
Dist - LUF **Prod** - LUF 1972

Man of Aran 74 MIN
VHS
B&W (H C G)
$29.95 purchase _ #MAN100
Portrays life on the Aran Islands, a desolate waste of rocks off the coast of Ireland and home to a small fishing village engaged in a daily battle against its magnificent opponent, the sea. Captures in dramatic detail the tragedy and beauty of the life of an Aranite family.
Fine Arts; Literature and Drama
Dist - INSTRU HOMVIS **Prod** - FLAH 1934

Man of Aran 77 MIN
16mm
B&W (J)
$845.00 purchase _ #398 - 0001
Presents the poetic tribute of Robert Flaherty to the hardy people of Aran Island, a rocky crag off the coast of Ireland. Shows that every day the inhabitants of Aran must fight for survival against gale - force winds and thunderous waves sweeping in from 3000 miles of the storm - tossed Atlantic Ocean.
Geography - World; History - World
Dist - FI

Man of Faith 22 MIN
16mm
B&W (J)
Dramatizes Mark's account of Christ healing the man who is paralyzed. Shows how many came to follow Jesus and depicts Jesus' great influence through His teachings and ministry.
Religion and Philosophy
Dist - CAFM **Prod** - CAFM

Man of Kintail 30 MIN
16mm / U-matic / VHS
B&W (J)
LC FIA68-1662
Presents events in the life of Robert Tait McKenzie, Canadian physician, physical education professor and sculptor. Describes the physical education programs and rehabilitation centers he established and includes displays of his sculpture.
Biography; Fine Arts; Physical Education and Recreation
Dist - IFB **Prod** - CHET 1968

Man of La Mancha 121 MIN
16mm
Color
Stars Peter O'Toole in a musical version of Don Quixote.
Fine Arts
Dist - UAE **Prod** - UAA 1972

Man of Leather 20 MIN
U-matic / VHS / 16mm
Captioned; Color (A) (PORTUGUESE (ENGLISH SUBTITLES))
Portrays the life of the 'vaquero', the cowboy of the Brazilian Northeast.
Fine Arts
Dist - CNEMAG **Prod** - CNEMAG

Man of letters series
D H Lawrence 60 MIN
George Orwell 60 MIN
Graham Greene 60 MIN
W Somerset Maugham 60 MIN
Dist - MDCPB

Man of Lightning 29 MIN
U-matic
Color
Presents a drama of the long - vanished world of the Cherokee in the years before European contact. Explores the demanding morality and complex spirit world of the earliest Americans. Also available in two - inch quad and one - inch videotape.
Social Science
Dist - NAMPBC **Prod** - GASU

Man of marble - Czlowiek z marmuru 160 MIN
VHS
Color (G A) (POLISH WITH ENGLISH SUBTITLES)
$79.95 purchase _ #V276
Tells the story of a young filmmaker trying to reconstruct a truthful picture of a Stalinist past, a past obscured by 20 years of changing propaganda in an Andrzej Wajda production.
Fine Arts; Sociology
Dist - POLART

A Man of peace 40 MIN
VHS / BETA
Color; PAL (G)
PdS18, $36.00 purchase
Travels with His Holiness the Dalai Lama to Norway to receive the Nobel Peace Prize in Oslo, December 1989. Follows his visits to Trondheim and Bergen and the Arctic region of Samiland. Captures His warmth, wisdom, compassion and humor. Co - produced by the Office of Information and International Relations.
Fine Arts; History - World; Religion and Philosophy
Dist - MERIDT **Prod** - MERIDT 1989

A Man of principle 90 MIN
35mm
Color; PAL (G)
Follows a simple man's rise to power who is known as El Condor, the head of a group of assassins. Fashions a subdued thriller, part expose and part psychological drama, based on the bitter political struggles between conservative and liberal parties in 1948 Columbia. A Procinor Ltd production, Columbia. Contact distributor about price availability outside the United Kingdom. This film is not available in West Germany, Spain, Greece, France, Eastern Europe and Latin America.
Civics and Political Systems; History - World; Literature and Drama
Dist - BALFOR

The Man of the beatitudes - Volume 8 30 MIN
VHS
Jesus of Nazareth series
Color (I J H C G A R)
$29.95 purchase, $10.00 rental _ #35 - 8321 - 1502
Presents excerpts from the Franco Zeffirelli film on the life and ministry of Jesus. Surveys the events of Jesus' raising of Lazarus, Peter's profession of faith, the Sermon on the Mount, and Mary and Martha at Bethany.
Literature and Drama; Religion and Philosophy
Dist - APH **Prod** - BOSCO

Man of the Forest 25 MIN
16mm
Land of the Dragon Series
Color (H C A)
Describes the Manas Game Sanctuary on the Manas River in south - eastern Bhutan. Features Suraj Kumar Pradhan, a forest ranger, and shows some of his activities in preserving the wildlife of the area.
Geography - World; Science - Natural
Dist - LANDMK **Prod** - NOMDFI 1983

The Man of the House 29 MIN
Videoreel / VT2
Our Street Series
Color
Sociology
Dist - PBS **Prod** - MDCPB

The Man of the House 8 MIN
U-matic / VHS
Color
Concerns the problems of four - year - old David, who tries to take on the role of grown - up protector of the house while his father is on a business trip. Depicts David promising to protect his mother against all sorts of monsters. Portrays his reconciliation with reality as resolving the problems of wrestling with impossible goals while maintaining self - respect.
Psychology
Dist - PRIMED **Prod** - PRIMED

Man of the People 25 MIN
16mm
Land of the Dragon Series
Color (H C A)
Presents a description of life in the village of Punakha, in Bhutan's central valley. Features Samthen Dorji, a moderately wealthy farmer who is also a village headman, and his family.
Geography - World
Dist - LANDMK **Prod** - NOMDFI 1983

Man of the Trees 25 MIN
U-matic / VHS / 16mm
Color
Recounts Richard St Barbe - Baker's efforts to bring world attention to the alarming rate at which trees are being felled and the dangers of overgrazing. Shows Baker's 1952 Sahara crossing and ecological survey. Sketches his early life in the forests of Canada, colonial Kenya and Nigeria. Reveals his support of the Chipko people of India and explores his involvement in New Zealand.
Science - Natural
Dist - JOU **Prod** - JOU 1982

Man of vision 30 MIN
VHS
Our dwelling place series
Color (K P I R)
$14.95 purchase _ #35 - 8835 - 7756
Presents an animated account of children in an orphanage as they explore the rooms of an old mansion, finding Biblical stories coming to life. Includes the Old Testament accounts of Daniel in Babylon, the fiery furnace, the lion's den, and the handwriting on the wall.
Literature and Drama; Religion and Philosophy
Dist - APH

Man of Wheat - the Saga of Glen Miller 28 MIN
U-matic / VHS / 16mm
Color
LC 81-701129
Introduces Glen Miller, a wheat farmer in eastern Washington state who started a small farm in 1943 that has now expanded to include thousands of acres of wheat. Recounts Miller's life and shows how his farm has grown into a business which includes sons and grandsons, who man more than a dozen great harvesting tractors.
Agriculture; Sociology
Dist - PFP **Prod** - MARTSS 1981

Man Oh Man 18 MIN
16mm / VHS
Color (G)
$380.00, $230.00 purchase, $45.00 rental
Looks at the forces which mold young boys into men. Features men from all walks of life who speak with sadness and humor about what is expected of them and how they often feel they fail.
Psychology; Sociology
Dist - NEWDAY **Prod** - COMEPA

Man oh man - growing up male in America 18 MIN
16mm / VHS
Color (H C PRO T R)
LC 87-706979
Documents the societal pressures of being an American man. Uses interviews with young men, as well as perspectives from a young woman. Created by J Clements for High Tide Productions.
History - United States; Sociology
Dist - NEWDAY

Man on a horse 10 MIN
16mm
B&W (G)
$20.00 rental
Offers the original film adaptation of Malcolm Lowry's Under The Volcano. Features music by Jack Bruce and Pete Brown.
Fine Arts
Dist - CANCIN **Prod** - FERGCO 1980

Man on a Skateboard 20 MIN
16mm
Color (J H T R)
LC 70-702458
A study of the attitudes of a church and a community toward a severely handicapped man, a multiple amputee. Shows him with his family, driving a car, operating a newsstand and being ignored by modern church people in his own community.
Guidance and Counseling; Health and Safety; Psychology; Social Science; Sociology
Dist - FAMF **Prod** - JONY 1969

The Man on Cloud Mountain 55 MIN
VHS
Color (G)
$39.95 purchase
Features a Buddhist retreat center in Castle Rock, Washington. Translates a talk given there by Shodo Harada Roshi, abbot of Sogenji, a Zen teaching monastery.

Fine Arts; Health and Safety; Religion and Philosophy
Dist - HP

The Man on the Flying Trapeze 8 MIN
16mm
Color
Presents an animated version of the song The Man On The Flying Trapeze.
Fine Arts
Dist - TIMLIF **Prod** - TIMLIF 1982

Man on the Hot Seat - Explosives Safety, Egress Systems 29 MIN
16mm
Color
LC 80-701138
Explains the egress team concept and shows how to maintain and inspect aircraft explosive egress systems. Simulates two fatal accidents caused by careless repair of the egress systems. Stresses the importance of effective and safe maintenance procedures and delineates appropriate guidelines.
Civics and Political Systems; Industrial and Technical Education
Dist - USNAC **Prod** - USAF 1963

Man on the Moon
VHS / U-matic
Color (J C I)
Presents Walter Cronkite narrating a CBS documentary tracing the birth and development of the United States Space Program.
Fine Arts; History - World; Science - Physical
Dist - GA **Prod** - GA

Man on the rim - the peopling of the Pacific series 660
VHS
Man on the rim - the peopling of the Pacific series
Color (H C)
$2895.00 purchase
Presents an 11 - part series on the people of the Pacific rim. Chronicles the spread of Asians to Australia, New Guinea, North America, South America, Indonesia, the 'Bronze Age' in Southeast Asia, the technical superiority of ancient China, the struggle of Japan to create an identity separate from that of China, South American and Mexican cultures and Polynesian adventurers.
Geography - World; History - World; Social Science; Sociology
Dist - LANDMK **Prod** - LANDMK 1989

The Man or Woman for the Job 15 MIN
16mm
Color
LC 74-705084
Points out the importance of effective employee recruitment and selection procedures through the experiences of a small print shop owner who learns the hard way that such procedures are necessary. Shows various sources of employees.
Business and Economics; Education; Guidance and Counseling; Psychology
Dist - USNAC **Prod** - USSBA

Man Overboard 30 MIN
BETA / VHS
Under Sail Series
Color
Tells what to do when someone falls overboard, when a line gets caught in the propeller and when a boat capsizes. Introduces sailboat racing.
Physical Education and Recreation
Dist - CORF **Prod** - WGBHTV

Man Shapes His World 145 MIN
U-matic
University of the Air Series
Color (J H C A)
$750.00 purchase, $250.00 rental
Discusses man's role in changing the face of the earth and talks on problems of ownership, use and control of strategic world areas. Program contains five cassettes 29 minutes each.
Geography - World
Dist - CTV **Prod** - CTV 1978

Man - Sized Job 28 MIN
16mm
Color
LC 72-702405
Deals with the recruitment of newspaper carrier boys. Shows how newspaper carrier boys form a vital link between the newspaper and its readers, and tells the importance of providing youngsters with a challenging job that rewards them for their personal effort, and gives them a sense of responsibility and accomplishment.
Guidance and Counseling; Social Science
Dist - AVON **Prod** - NYT 1972

The Man that Corrupted Hadleyburg 40 MIN
U-matic / VHS / 16mm
American Short Story Series
Color (J H C) (SPANISH)
Presents an adaptation of Mark Twain's short story The Man That Corrupted Hadleyburg. Tells about a small town that is visited by a stranger who concocts a scheme to test the honesty of the town's leading citizens.
Fine Arts; Literature and Drama
Dist - CORF **Prod** - LEARIF 1980
CDTEL
GA

The Man that Gravity Forgot 9 MIN
16mm / U-matic / VHS
Color (P I)
Uses animation to present the extraordinary life of Bram, the only man in the world who is not affected by the force of gravity. Illustrates the zany things that happen when you weigh nothing at all and reveals the important role that gravity plays in our lives.
Literature and Drama; Science - Physical
Dist - CORF **Prod** - CORF 1979

Man the Creator 13 MIN
16mm
B&W (I)
Depicts the art and craft of pottery since ancient times. Reveals the many changes effected in recent times in regard to the wheel and firing methods.
Fine Arts
Dist - NEDINF **Prod** - INDIA

Man, the esthetic being 60 MIN
U-matic / VHS
Art of being human series
Color (H C A)
Discusses the esthetic aspects of man.
Fine Arts
Dist - FI **Prod** - FI 1978

Man - the Incredible Machine 28 MIN
U-matic / VHS / 16mm
Color (J)
LC 76-703411
Uses photographs and recording techniques in examining the human body, including the heart, lungs, blood vessels, skeleton and joints, muscles, ears, skin, eyes and brain.
Science - Natural
Dist - NGS **Prod** - NGS 1975

Man - the Measure of all Things 52 MIN
16mm / U-matic / VHS
Civilisation Series
Color (J)
LC 74-708452
Surveys the development of Western civilization during the 15th century as evidenced especially in the work of Botticelli, Masaccio, Bellini, Giorgione, Van Eyck and Alberti. Number four of the Civilization series.
Fine Arts; History - World
Dist - FI **Prod** - BBCTV 1970

Man - the Measure of all Things, Pt 2 28 MIN
U-matic / VHS / 16mm
Civilisation Series
Color (J H C)
LC 74-708452
Surveys the development of Western civilization during the 15th century as evidenced especially in the work of Botticelli, Masaccio, Bellini, Giorgione, Van Eyck and Alberti. Number four of the Civilization series.
History - World
Dist - FI **Prod** - BBCTV 1970

The Man, the Music and the Marine - John Philip Sousa Marches to Greatness 24 MIN
VHS
American Lifestyles II - Singular American Series
Color (I)
$70.00 purchase, $50.00 rental _ #9885
Looks into the life of the 'March King,' John Philip Sousa, who composed world - famous marches in the America of the early 1900s. Hosted by E G Marshall.
Biography; Fine Arts
Dist - AIMS **Prod** - COMCO 1986

The Man, the Snake and the Fox 14 MIN
16mm
Color (G)
#2X103 I
Dramatizes an Ojibway Indian legend using puppets who teach a moral lesson about keeping promises. Told by anthropologist Basil Johnson.
Social Science
Dist - CDIAND **Prod** - NFBC 1979
MOKIN

Man, the Symbol Maker 25 MIN
16mm
Science of Life Series
Color (J)
LC 81-700848
Discusses nonverbal human communication and examines the difference between animal signals and symbols. Shows how a chimpanzee was taught to symbolize and looks at the possible dangers of the symbolic process.
Psychology
Dist - WARDS **Prod** - CRIPSE 1981

Man to Man 30 MIN
U-matic / VHS / 16mm
B&W (C A)
Shows the importance of dependable personal relationships to mental health.
Guidance and Counseling; Psychology
Dist - IFB **Prod** - MHFB 1954

A Man to Ride the River with 15 MIN
U-matic / VHS / 16mm
American Scrapbook Series
Color (I)
Traces the life and explorations of Juan Bautiste de Anza, who led an expedition in 1774 through the desert to San Francisco.
History - United States
Dist - GPN **Prod** - WVIZTV 1977

The Man Upstairs 6 MIN
16mm
B&W
LC 76-703783
Shows a meeting between skid row alcoholics and Bible - thumping evangelists.
Guidance and Counseling; Religion and Philosophy; Sociology
Dist - YORKU **Prod** - YORKU 1975

The Man we call Juan Carlos 27 MIN
VHS / 16mm
Color (G)
Portrays a Guatemalan campesino turned guerilla. Looks at unrest in Guatemala. Features music by Bruce Cockburn.
Geography - World; History - World
Dist - ASTRSK **Prod** - ASTRSK 1990

Man, what a Party - 12 20 TO 25 MIN
VHS
If You Paint, You See more Series
Color (I)
Asks children to draw human figures in action using patches of color or sketchy lines.
Education; Fine Arts
Dist - AITECH

A Man, When He is a Man 66 MIN
16mm / VHS
Color (G) (SPANISH (ENGLISH SUBTITLES))
$350.00 purchase, $130.00, $90.00 rental
Illustrates the social climate and cultural traditions which feed 'machismo' and allow the domination of women in Latin America. Reveals the comic element of male posturing and its serious consequences. Set in Costa Rica.
Geography - World; Psychology; Sociology
Dist - WMEN **Prod** - VASAR 1982

The Man who Brought Happiness 5 MIN
16mm
Color (I)
LC 80-700859
Provides a modern restatement of the parable of the talents. Tells the story of a stranger who shares his happiness with villagers who see it only as bread and how a little child leads them to see that only when they use their happiness will they know it.
Fine Arts; Guidance and Counseling
Dist - ALBA **Prod** - ALBA 1977

The Man who could not see far enough 33 MIN
16mm
Color (G)
$60.00 rental
Uses literary, structural, autobiographical and performance metaphors to construct a series of tableaux that evoke the act of vision, the limits of perception and the rapture of space. Ranges in subject from a solar eclipse to an ascent of the Golden Gate Bridge. A Peter Rose production.
Fine Arts; Psychology
Dist - CANCIN

Man who Dances - Edward Villella 54 MIN
16mm
Bell Telephone Hour Series
Color
LC FIA68-1003
Depicts the dancer's exhausting world of classes, rehearsals and performances as revealed through the experiences of one of America's bravura dancers, Edward Villella. Includes scenes from performances of George Balanchine's Tarantella, Glinkiana and the Rubies section of The Jewels.
Fine Arts
Dist - DIRECT **Prod** - ATAT 1968

The Man who Didn't Belong 7 MIN
16mm
Human Side of Supervision Series
Color (IND)
LC 73-701930
Presents an incident illustrating results of a communications breakdown with a new employee. Answers questions of how much orientation is enough, how much initial break - in and training is enough and where to find the explanations of a high rate of turnover of employees.
Business and Economics; Psychology
Dist - VOAERO **Prod** - VOAERO 1972

The Man who Digs for Fish 13 MIN
16mm
Color (J)
Reveals the conservation methods of Frank Jenkinson, who digs up newly - hatched salmon in the Jarvis Inlet to protect them from dying before reaching maturity. Shows how his methods have increased the salmon population from 500 to 25,000.
Science - Natural
Dist - NFBC **Prod** - NFBC 1979

The Man who Envied Women 125 MIN
16mm
Color (G)
Presents an independent production by Yvonne Rainer. Tells the story of a self - satisfied womanizer, Jack Deller, the man 'who knows almost too much about women.'.
Fine Arts; Guidance and Counseling; Literature and Drama; Psychology; Sociology
Dist - FIRS

The Man who Had no Dream 7 MIN
U-matic / VHS / 16mm
Color (K P I)
LC 81-701567
Tells an animated story about wealthy Mr Oliver who couldn't sleep or dream until he found an injured bird and repaired its wing. Emphasizes the need to work for others and the importance of being needed. Illustrates that money alone cannot buy happiness and that satisfaction comes from setting goals and working to achieve them. Based on the book The Man Who Had No Dream by Adelaide Holl.
Fine Arts; Guidance and Counseling; Literature and Drama
Dist - CF **Prod** - BOSUST 1981

The Man who Had to Sing 10 MIN
16mm
Color (J)
LC 72-700418
A story about the life of a man who was pushed, shoved, kicked and bounced around because, during all of his life, he expressed himself in a fashion that did not harmonize with those around him.
Psychology
Dist - MMA **Prod** - ZAGREB 1971

The Man who Knew How to Fly 10 MIN
16mm / U-matic / VHS
Color (I)
LC 83-700011
Tells of a man who discovers that he has the power to fly and shows how earthbound scholars demand that he make so many changes in his takeoff and landing procedures that he finds that he no longer can fly.
Fine Arts
Dist - PHENIX **Prod** - KRATKY 1982

The Man who knew too much 120 MIN
VHS
Color (G)
$59.95 purchase _ #S01122
Presents a remake of the 1934 Hitchcock thriller of the same name. Stars James Stewart and Doris Day.
Fine Arts
Dist - UILL

The Man who knew too much 84 MIN
VHS
B&W (G)
Presents the 1934 Alfred Hitchcock film 'The Man Who Knew Too Much,' which many believe led to his US film directing career. Tells the story of a young girl who is kidnapped in hopes of keeping her parents silent about an assasination plot. Stars Leslie Banks, Edna Best, Peter Lorre, and others.
Fine Arts
Dist - UILL
KITPAR

The Man who Left His will on Film 93 MIN
16mm
B&W (JAPANESE)
Traces the life of a filmmaker who commits suicide by studying the meaning of the last footage he shot. Presents numerous scenes of Japanese cities and countryside in an effort to find out more about the young man.
Fine Arts; Foreign Language; Geography - World
Dist - NYFLMS **Prod** - NYFLMS 1970

The Man who Loved Bears 50 MIN
16mm
Color
LC 78-700291
Tells the story of a man who discovers the tracks of a Grizzly bear in Colorado, where they are thought to be extinct. Follows his efforts to raise a cub to the point where she can survive on her own in the wild.
Science - Natural
Dist - STOUFP **Prod** - STOUFP 1977

The Man who Loved Machines 9 MIN
VHS / 16mm
Color (I J H)
$225 film, $60 video, $25 rental
Provides an introduction to energy forms and energy conservation. Tells the story of a man who learns that machines powered by fossil fuel are not always the appropriate answer.
Science - Natural; Social Science
Dist - BULFRG **Prod** - BULFRG 1984

The Man who Loved Numbers 58 MIN
U-matic / VHS
Nova Series
Color (H C A)
$250 purchase _ #5277C
Examines the life of mathematician Srinivasa Ramanujan, and looks at contemporary mathematicians who study formulas in his notebooks. Produced by WGBH Boston.
Mathematics
Dist - CORF

The Man who made up his mind 50 MIN
VHS
Horizon series
Color; PAL (G)
PdS99 purchase
Presents the work of Gerald Edelman, a scientist who challenges the existing view of the brain as an information processing machine. Explains Edelman's theory of the brain as an evolving ecosystem which works in a similar fashion to natural selection. Looks at the supporters who hail him as the new Darwin and those who are skeptical of his work.
Industrial and Technical Education; Science - Natural
Dist - BBCENE

The Man who Mistook His Wife for a Hat 75 MIN
U-matic / VHS
Color (C)
$299.00, $199.00 purchase _ #AD - 1557
Collects the case studies neurologist Oliver Sacks encountered in his work. Focuses on the title story about Dr P who is diagnosed with visual agnosia, in which he can see but cannot make sense of what he sees. Reveals that Dr P has Alzheimer's Disease and uses music to give coherence to his visual life.
Health and Safety; Psychology; Science - Natural
Dist - FOTH **Prod** - FOTH

Man who moved mountains 50 MIN
VHS
Horizon series
Color; PAL (H C J)
PdS99 purchase; Not available in the United States or Canada
Describes the geologic discovery in the 1930's by Harold Wellman that the Earth's crust is fluid. Indicates that while his ideas were originally rejected, they have led to a theory about how mountains are built. Part of the Horizon series.
Science; Science - Physical
Dist - BBCENE

The Man who Mugged God 28 MIN
16mm / U-matic / VHS
Insight Series
Color (H C A)
Depicts what happens when a man mugs someone who turns out to be God. Details God's explanation that He loves all creatures, especially the poor. Stars Warren Oates and Harold Gould.
Guidance and Counseling; Psychology; Religion and Philosophy
Dist - PAULST **Prod** - PAULST

The Man who named the world 52 MIN
VHS
Visionaries series
Color (C G)
$195.00 purchase
Profiles Prof James Lovelock, British atmospheric scientist and research scientist for NASA who is responsible for the Gaia hypothesis, which states that the world is a single organism that has been alive for 3.5 billion years. Reveals that Lovelock was the first to seek out chlorofluorocarbons - CFCs - in the atmosphere and invented the instrument for their detection. Part of a four - part series about innovative ideas on intelligence, genetics, evolution, agriculture and economics.
Science; Science - Physical
Dist - LANDMK **Prod** - LANDMK 1990

The Man who Needed Nobody 30 MIN
U-matic / VHS
Money Puzzle - the World of Macroeconomics Series
Color
Illustrates the meaning of comparative advantage as a crucial element in trading. Looks at international trade. Module 14 of the Money Puzzle - the world of macroeconomics series.
Business and Economics; Sociology
Dist - MDCC **Prod** - MDCC

A Man who Needs no Introduction 5 MIN
U-matic / VHS / 16mm
Communicating from the Lectern Series
Color (H C A)
Shows proper forms of guest introduction and describes how to give a speech of thanks.
English Language
Dist - AIMS **Prod** - METAIV 1976

The Man who Read Books 17 MIN
16mm
Color
LC 79-701293
Presents a speculative fantasy about a meek librarian who loves and understands books and is fighting a new process that will eliminate all printed matter.
Fine Arts
Dist - USC **Prod** - USC 1979

The Man who Shot the Pope 52 MIN
VHS / U-matic
Color (H C A)
LC 83-706305
Discusses the findings of a nine - month investigation of the shooting of Pope John Paul II by terrorist Mehmet Ali Agca. Traces Agca's life from his boyhood in Turkey to the present, building a case for the theory that he was employed by the Soviet Union to slay the pope.
Religion and Philosophy; Sociology
Dist - FI **Prod** - NBCNEW 1982

The Man who Talks to Water 29 MIN
16mm
Color
LC 78-701560
Discusses the importance of long - range water planning. Surveys man's efforts to put water to his uses and shows major water - moving projects in the Western United States.
Science - Natural; Social Science
Dist - MTP **Prod** - AMERON 1978

The Man who Thought with His Hat 14 MIN
16mm / VHS
Color (G)
$245.00, $295.00 purchase, $50.00 rental _ #8004
Tells the story of Alec Noll, the President of Agonia in the Pacillic Islands. He thinks with his hat but when he loses it his government goes into panic. Akala, a little girl, finds the hat and despite her seeming unimportance teaches Alec enormously so that he never needs his hat again. Swedish satire.
Fine Arts; Foreign Language; Literature and Drama
Dist - AIMS **Prod** - EDMI 1985

The Man who Tried to Kill the Pope 16 MIN
U-matic / VHS
Color (H C A)
Examines the life Of Mehmet Ali Agca, the man who attempted to assasinate Pope John Paul II in St Peter's Square in Rome on May 13, 1981. Looks at the political atmosphere in Turkey, which it is believed gives rise to terrorists and their activities.
Geography - World; History - World; Sociology
Dist - JOU **Prod** - JOU

The Man who Wanted to Fly - a Japanese Tale 11 MIN
U-matic / VHS / 16mm
Color (P)
LC 76-701177
Presents a story about a man who seemed to learn how to fly, but who had good reason to keep the secret to himself.
Literature and Drama
Dist - CORF **Prod** - CORF 1969

The Man who Went Blue Sky 27 MIN
U-matic / VHS / 16mm
Insight Series
Color; B&W (J)
LC 75-700940
Presents a story about an inventor of impractical creations. Shows how he goes to work for a large company to invent useful things and how he learns that playful inspiration and creativity can be more important than practicality or money.
Guidance and Counseling; Sociology
Dist - PAULST **Prod** - PAULST 1974

The Man who would be King 129 MIN
16mm
Color (H C)
Presents the adventures of two men in British - controlled India in the 19th century. Stars Sean Connery and Michael Caine. Based on the work by Rudyard Kipling.
Fine Arts; Literature and Drama
Dist - CINEWO **Prod** - CPC 1975

A Man with a Movie Camera 69 MIN
U-matic / VHS
B&W
Offers a classic experimental Russian film directed by Dziga Vertov.
Fine Arts
Dist - IHF **Prod** - IHF

Man with a Problem 17 MIN
16mm
B&W (C T)
LC 72-700825
Shows the admission of an alcoholic to a clinic. Describes the etiology, follows the diagnosis and treatment of the case and discusses the team approach by psychiatrists and psychologists. Demonstrates the treatment of alcoholism by aversion and relaxation techniques and illustrates the learning of new habit patterns based on a system of operant conditioning.
Health and Safety; Psychology
Dist - PSUPCR **Prod** - UADEL 1967

Man with a Suitcase 30 MIN
16mm
B&W
LC FI67-113
Accounts the experiences of a West German citizen who smuggled his fiancee out of East Germany by carrying her through the border check - station in a suitcase. Includes commercials from the original telecast.
Civics and Political Systems; Geography - World
Dist - WB **Prod** - GE 1962

Man with Gun Calls - an Analysis of Officers Killed 14 MIN
VHS / 16mm
Color (PRO)
$295.00 purchase, $75.00 rental _ #8179
Illustrates survival tactics on a man - with - gun call. Informs through reenactments of true risks and review of new vital statistics on such calls.
Civics and Political Systems; Psychology
Dist - AIMS **Prod** - AIMS 1990

Man with not time for beauty 30 MIN
VHS / U-matic
Art of being human series
Color (C)
History - World; Literature and Drama; Religion and Philosophy
Dist - MDCC **Prod** - MDCC

The Man with the Torque Wrench 10 MIN
16mm
B&W
Demonstrates proper use of torquing equipment and emphasizes the importance of torquing and the serious consequences that may result from improper torquing. Shows different types of torque wrenches used by the air force.
Civics and Political Systems; Industrial and Technical Education
Dist - USNAC **Prod** - USAF 1958

The Man Without a Country 25 MIN
U-matic / VHS / 16mm
B&W (I J H)
LC FIA55-324
Based on the book The Man Without A Country by Edward Everett Hale. Portrays a judge, swearing in new American citizens, as he relates the story of an American naval officer who rejected and damned his country in a burst of anger.
Civics and Political Systems; Literature and Drama
Dist - MGHT **Prod** - CROSBY 1953

Man without pigs 60 MIN
16mm / VHS
Institute of Papua New Guinea Studies series
Color (G)
$400.00 purchase, $120.00, $60.00 rental
Reveals that John Waiko is the first Papua New Guinean to become a professor. Discloses that when he returned to his home village of Tabara to celebrate his achievement with his own people of the Benandere clan, his people were not impressed because he had not accumulated the desirable wealth of pigs valued by their culture. Part of a series by Chris Owen.
History - World; Sociology
Dist - DOCEDR **Prod** - IPANGS 1990

A Man Writes to a Part of Himself 58 MIN
U-matic / VHS
Color (J)
Portrays poet Robert Bly. Shows him at his northern Minnesota farm. Recounts his early struggles in New York City.
Literature and Drama
Dist - UCV **Prod** - UCV

A Man Writes to a Part of Himself 58 MIN
VHS / U-matic
Documentaries on Art Series
Color (G)
$120.00, $80.00 purchase, $45.00, $30.00 rental
Portrays poet Robert Bly. Shows his sense of humor and love of life. Produced by Center for International Education, Michael Hazard, Greg Pratt and Intermedia Arts.
Biography; Literature and Drama
Dist - IAFC

The Man you loved to hate 90 MIN
VHS / 16mm
Color; B&W (G)
$150.00 rental
Portrays the bizarre career of film director Erich von Stroheim through interviews with those who worked with him and knew him and clips from his films. Offers a detailed study of a man whose perverse aberrations regarding women, art and finances made him a Hollywood outcast. Directed by Patrick Montgomery.
Fine Arts
Dist - KINOIC

Mana the Magic Spear 11 MIN
16mm
Color (G)
Tells of one of the legends of Hawaii in which the boy Kio steals a magic spear which eventually kills him, teaching the Hawaiians that ill use of power ends tragically.
Geography - United States; History - United States; Literature and Drama; Religion and Philosophy; Sociology
Dist - CINEPC **Prod** - TAHARA 1986

Manabu Mabe Paints a Picture 13 MIN
16mm
Color (J H C)
LC 75-700285
Presents Japanese - Brazilian artist Mabe creating an abstract painting.
Fine Arts
Dist - MOMALA **Prod** - OOAS 1964

Manage it series
Emphasizes the 'management' in stress management by teaching powerful skills for handling stress at home and on the job. Demonstrates different relaxation techniques to use to manage stress. Contains six programs that teach how to identify personal stressors; help identify stress overload and explore three important types of stress management strategies; define relationships and develop communication skills; identify stress-related addictive behaviors; assess job stress by identifying drainers and energizers in the workplace; and reevaluate current coping patterns and personal values to set goals and make real changes. Each program includes leader's guide and participant workbooks.

Addictive patterns - Pt 4	20 MIN
Interpersonal conflict	20 MIN
Job stress	20 MIN
Stress overload	20 MIN
Stress traps	20 MIN
Survival skills	20 MIN

Dist - WHLPSN

Manage meetings that get results 60 MIN
VHS
Effective manager seminar series
Color (H C A)
$95.00 purchase _ #NGC750V
Presents a multimedia seminar on how to manage meetings effectively. Consists of a videocassette, a 60 - minute audiocassette, and a study guide.
Business and Economics; Psychology
Dist - CAMV

Manage Your Career - the U S Army Civilian Career Management Program 30 MIN
16mm
B&W
Explains the objectives, principles and benefits of the U S Army Civilian Career Management Program, which is designed to provide formalized education or training, self - development activities and appropriate experience.
Civics and Political Systems; Guidance and Counseling; Psychology
Dist - USNAC **Prod** - USA

Manage Your Stress 52 MIN
U-matic / VHS / 16mm
Color (C A)
LC 80-700600
Describes how to manage stress in the work environment.
Psychology
Dist - CRMP **Prod** - MGHT 1980

Manage Your Stress, Pt 1 26 MIN
16mm / U-matic / VHS
Color (C A)
LC 80-700600
Describes how to manage stress in the work environment.
Psychology
Dist - CRMP **Prod** - MGHT 1980

Manage Your Stress, Pt 2 26 MIN
16mm / U-matic / VHS
Color (C A)
LC 80-700600
Describes how to manage stress in the work environment.
Psychology
Dist - CRMP **Prod** - MGHT 1980

Manage your time to build your territory 30 MIN
VHS
Color (G)
$565.00 purchase, $150.00 rental _ #91F0867
Features sales trainer Joe Batten who shows how to plan and organize sales territory.
Business and Economics; Psychology
Dist - DARTNL **Prod** - DARTNL 1991

Managed care is here - are you ready 34 MIN
U-matic / VHS
Color (C PRO)
%i $275.00 purchase, $75.00 rental _ #42 - 2307, #42 - 2306, #42 - 2307R, #42 - 2306R
Gives a complete overview of what managed care is and how it is used in a variety of settings. Interviews Joseph A Califano, Jr, former Secretary of Health, Education and Welfare, who recounts how managed care and its reliance on nursing is destined to become the mainstay of health care delivery in the United States.
Health and Safety
Dist - NLFN **Prod** - NLFN

The Managed Forest 26 MIN
16mm
Color
LC 77-702956
Presents the problems of multiple land use and vanishing wildlife habitat.
Science - Natural
Dist - MEPHTS **Prod** - MEPHTS 1976

Managed Milking 8 MIN
U-matic
Color; Mono (H C)
Demonstrates proper milking techniques for dairy farmers. Shows what happens when the cow isn't stimulated at the proper time, and suggests systems for milking in stanchion barns and milking parlors.
Agriculture
Dist - UWISCA **Prod** - UWISCA 1977

Management 23 MIN
U-matic / VHS
How to be more Successful in Your Own Business Series
Color (G)
$279.00, $179.00 purchase _ #AD - 2002
Provides insights into the many aspects of management which the small business owner must address in order to survive and prosper. Features Jim Sanders of the US Small Business Administration. Part of an eight - part series on successful business management moderated by David Susskind.
Business and Economics; Guidance and Counseling; Psychology
Dist - FOTH **Prod** - FOTH

Management 15 MIN
VHS / U-matic / BETA
Career Success Series
(H C A)
$29.95 _ MX201
Portrays occupations in management by reviewing required abilities and interviewing people employed in this field. Shows anxieties and rewards involved in pursuing a career in management.
Business and Economics; Education; Guidance and Counseling
Dist - CAMV **Prod** - CAMV

Management 15 MIN
VHS
Career success series
Color (H C A)
$29.95 purchase _ #MX201
Presents an introduction to management careers. Covers the necessary skills, and interviews people in these careers on the rewards and stresses involved.
Business and Economics; Education; Psychology
Dist - CAMV

Management 30 MIN
U-matic
It's Everybody's Business Series Unit 4, Managing a Business
Color

Business and Economics
Dist - DALCCD **Prod** - DALCCD

Management
VHS
Dynamics of business series
Color (H C A)
$139.00 purchase _ #MAS02V
Explores basic management concepts. Considers subjects including management functions, planning and control, human resources, and leadership styles.
Business and Economics; Psychology
Dist - CAMV

Management 45 MIN
VHS / U-matic
Corporate Network Strategy Series
Color
Explores the reasons that executives and managers must get involved in decisions concerning the communications networks that are springing up in corporations.
Industrial and Technical Education; Psychology; Social Science
Dist - DELTAK **Prod** - DELTAK

Management - a Joint Venture 8 MIN
VHS / U-matic
Color
Contains eight half - hour videotapes on business management.
Business and Economics; Psychology
Dist - TELSTR **Prod** - TELSTR

Management Action Program Series
Customer service 22 MIN
Innovation 27 MIN
Productivity through People 29 MIN
Dist - VIDART

Management - acute staphylococcal endocarditis
VHS
Color (PRO)
#MR - 189
Presents a free - loan program which trains medical professionals. Contact distributor for details.
Health and Safety; Science - Natural
Dist - WYAYLA **Prod** - WYAYLA

Management and Business Games 12 MIN
U-matic / 35mm strip
Dynamic Classroom Series
Color
Shows how to use complex and simple management games, group and individual games. Points out the purpose, definition and uses of games and cautions of dangers in overusing.
Education; Psychology
Dist - RESEM **Prod** - RESEM

Management and Commerce - Accounting
VHS
Video Career Series
$29.95 purchase _ #MD190V
Shows students going on the job to learn the variety of skills required for this occupation and the special training or educational requirements. Discusses various hiring procedures and what is involved in joining a professional association or union.
Education; Guidance and Counseling
Dist - CAREER **Prod** - CAREER

Management and Commerce - Business and Data Processing Machine Operations
VHS
Video Career Series
$29.95 purchase _ #MD192V
Shows students going on the job to learn the variety of skills required for this occupation and the special training or educational requirements. Discusses various hiring procedures and what is involved in joining a professional association or union.
Education; Guidance and Counseling
Dist - CAREER **Prod** - CAREER

Management and Commerce - Clerk - Bank, Insurance and Commerce
VHS
Video Career Series
$29.95 purchase _ #MD193V
Shows students going on the job to learn the variety of skills required for this occupation and the special training or educational requirements. Discusses various hiring procedures and what is involved in joining a professional association or union.
Education; Guidance and Counseling
Dist - CAREER **Prod** - CAREER

Management and Commerce - Financial Business Services
VHS
Video Career Series
$29.95 purchase _ #MD197V
Shows students going on the job to learn the variety of skills required for this occupation and the special training or educational requirements. Discusses various hiring procedures and what is involved in joining a professional association or union.
Education; Guidance and Counseling
Dist - CAREER **Prod** - CAREER

Management and Commerce - Management and Private Enterprise
VHS
Video Career Series
$29.95 purchase _ #MD201
Shows students going on the job to learn the variety of skills required for this occupation and the special training or educational requirements. Discusses various hiring procedures and what is involved in joining a professional association or union.
Education; Guidance and Counseling
Dist - CAREER **Prod** - CAREER

Management and Commerce - Sales and Commodities
VHS
Video Career Series
$29.95 purchase _ #MD203
Shows students going on the job to learn the variety of skills required for this occupation and the special training or educational requirements. Discusses various hiring procedures and what is involved in joining a professional association or union.
Education; Guidance and Counseling
Dist - CAREER **Prod** - CAREER

Management and Commerce - Secretarial Services
VHS
Video Career Series
$29.95 purchase _ #MD204V
Shows students going on the job to learn the variety of skills required for this occupation and the special training or educational requirements. Discusses various hiring procedures and what is involved in joining a professional association or union.
Education; Guidance and Counseling
Dist - CAREER **Prod** - CAREER

Management and leadership skills for women series
Presents a three - part series on women in management. Describes good and bad leadership traits and offers a quiz on leadership skills in Volume 1. Volume 2 shows how to motivate people to accept unpopular but necessary policies, handle new recruits and delegate. Volume 3 offers tips on turning a work group into a work team and moving people through the stages of change.
Management and leadership skills for women - Volume 1 90 MIN
Management and leadership skills for women - Volume 2 90 MIN
Management and leadership skills for women - Volume 3 90 MIN
Dist - CAMV **Prod** - CARTRP

Management and leadership skills for women - Volume 1 90 MIN
VHS
Management and leadership skills for women series
Color (J H C G)
$99.95 purchase _ #CTK072V
Describes the five best and worst leadership traits and presents a quiz to determine one's skill for motivating others. Shows how to identify and manage different working styles. Part one of a three - part series on women in management.
Business and Economics; Guidance and Counseling; Psychology; Social Science
Dist - CAMV **Prod** - CARTRP 1991

Management and leadership skills for women - Volume 2 90 MIN
VHS
Management and leadership skills for women series
Color (J H C G)
$99.95 purchase _ #CTK073V
Describes how to get people to accept an unpopular but necessary policy, ways to avoid a new recruit disaster, how to delegate and why one must appraise one's own performance regularly. Part two of a three - part series on women in management.
Business and Economics; Guidance and Counseling; Psychology; Social Science
Dist - CAMV **Prod** - CARTRP 1991

Management and leadership skills for women - Volume 3 90 MIN
VHS
Management and leadership skills for women series
Color (J H C G)
$99.95 purchase _ #CTK074V
Presents a 10 - point program for turning a work group into a team, how to move people through the stages of change - oblivion, rebellion, adaptation and motivation. Part three of a three - part series on women in management.
Business and Economics; Guidance and Counseling; Psychology; Social Science
Dist - CAMV **Prod** - CARTRP 1991

Management and Motivation - Version I - Management and Motivation - Pt 1
U-matic / VHS
Color
Offers a basic framework for organizing thoughts and perceptions about people and how to develop one's self - perception in management.
Business and Economics; Psychology
Dist - AMA **Prod** - AMA

Management and Motivation, Version II - Personality Styles
U-matic / VHS
Color
Offers a five - part series on improving sales performance with effective management of different personality styles.
Business and Economics; Psychology
Dist - AMA **Prod** - AMA

Management and Motivaton - Version I - Management and Motivation - Pt 3
VHS / U-matic
Color
Presents a presentation on understanding what it is that different types of personalities want in a job and what they need in a job if they are to be successful.
Psychology
Dist - AMA **Prod** - AMA

Management and Organization 10 MIN
VHS / 16mm
Secondary Physical Education Series
Color (C)
$95.00 purchase _ #264004
Familiarizes teachers with Secondary School Physical Education, an expanded curriculum that emphasizes the lifestyle implications of regular physical activity. 'Management And Organization' emphasizes the importance of increasing the amount of activity time during class.
Education; Mathematics; Physical Education and Recreation
Dist - ACCESS **Prod** - ACCESS 1986

Management and ownerships options for independent hospitals - a series
Management and ownerships options for independent hospitals - a series
Color
Explores the alternative management options available to independent hospitals and the advantages and disadvantages of each arrangement in two video tapes.
Business and Economics; Health and Safety; Psychology
Dist - AHOA **Prod** - AHOA

Management and ownerships options for independent hospitals - a series
Management and ownerships options for independent hospitals - a series
Dist - AHOA

Management and Treatment of the Violent Patient Series
The Assaultive patient 30 MIN
Calming and medicating violent patients in the emergency room 30 MIN
Differentiating personality, psychodynamic, toxic and organic causes of violence 30 MIN
Overview of Management and Treatment Issues in Acute Intervention in Emergency Room 30 MIN
Psychotherapy and Medication 30 MIN
Restraints, Seclusion and a Demonstration of Applying Restraints 30 MIN
Victims - their Circumstances, Management and Legal Issues 30 MIN
Dist - HEMUL

Management by Motivation 12 MIN
U-matic / 35mm strip
Improving Managerial Skills Series
Color
Offers a comprehensive list of ways to motivate workers on almost any job and an introduction to job enrichment.
Business and Economics; Psychology
Dist - RESEM **Prod** - RESEM

Management by Objectives 8 MIN
16mm
Color (J)

LC 76-704019
Examines, through the use of animation, the process of management by objectives. Defines four basic stages that can be used as guidelines in achieving better management and personal fulfillment.
Business and Economics; Psychology
Dist - BESTF **Prod** - NILCOM 1973

Management by Objectives 30 MIN
U-matic / VHS
Color
Presents Dr. Bruce A. Kirchoff, University of Nebraska - Omaha, discussing management by objectives. Uses dramatic vignettes to illustrate the key points - setting of objectives by the manager, use of objectives as guidelines for day - to - day action and involvement of all organization members in setting and using objectives.
Business and Economics; Guidance and Counseling
Dist - NETCHE **Prod** - NETCHE 1973

Management by Objectives - an Overview 57 FRS
U-matic / VHS
Management by Objectives Series Module 1
Color
Introduces management by objectives (MBO) by identifying its component parts and by briefly describing the process of the MBO system. Discusses the relationship of MBO to the overall management process and its dependency upon participative management.
Business and Economics; Psychology
Dist - RESEM **Prod** - RESEM

Management by Objectives Series Module 1
Management by Objectives - an Overview 57 FRS
Dist - RESEM

Management by Objectives Series Module 2
Goal Setting 10 MIN
Dist - RESEM

Management by Objectives Series Module 3
Installing Management by Objectives 58 FRS
Dist - RESEM

Management by Objectives Series
MBO I - what is MBO 13 MIN
MBO II - Developing Objectives 14 MIN
MBO III - Performance Appraisal 14 MIN
Dist - CRMP

Management by Objectives Series
Applying management by objectives 29 MIN
Establishing Performance Criteria 29 MIN
Innovation by Objectives 29 MIN
Job Responsibilities and Measurement 29 MIN
Organizational Goal - Planning 29 MIN
Problem solving by objectives 29 MIN
Dist - EDSD

Management by objectives series
Presents three modules on management by objectives. Includes the titles Management by Objectives - An Overview, Goal Setting and Installing Management by Objectives.
Management by objectives series 29 MIN
Dist - RESEM **Prod** - RESEM

Management by responsibility
VHS / U-matic / Cassette
Color (G)
$6000.00, $80.00 purchase
Trains in management of employees. Illustrates the levels of human development, from marginal to super achiever and shows how to motivate and stimulate growth in all levels. Features Dr G Michael Durst. Available in video or audio format. Video format includes 11 videocassettes.
Business and Economics; Guidance and Counseling; Psychology
Dist - TRASYS **Prod** - TRASYS 1982

Management by Responsibility Series
The Achievement level 60 MIN
The Conformist Level (Section a) 48 MIN
The Conformist Level (Section B) 20 MIN
Implementation of MBR process - feedback and recognition - section a 28 MIN
Implementation of MBR process - feedback and recognition - section B 30 MIN
Implementation of MBR Process - Goal Setting 38 MIN
Implementation of MBR Process - Phase I - Motivation (Section a) 35 MIN
Implementation of MBR Process - Phase I - Motivation (Section B) 25 MIN
Implementation of MBR Process - Phase II - Delegation 54 MIN
Introduction to Responsible Management (Section a) 40 MIN
Introduction to Responsible Management (Section B) 28 MIN
The Process of growth - Section A 48 MIN
The Process of Growth (Section B) 28 MIN
The Responsible Level 40 MIN
The Self - Protective Level (Section a) 28 MIN
The Self - Protective Level (Section B) 40 MIN
The Unconscious level - Section A 25 MIN
The Unconscious level - Section B 33 MIN
Dist - DELTAK

Management by time series
Presents four modules on management by time. Includes the titles The Time of Our Lives, Analyzing Our Time Usage, Using Others to Save Time, Our Time is Our Time.
Management by time series 45 MIN
Dist - RESEM **Prod** - RESEM 1982

Management Challenges 20 MIN
U-matic / VHS
Effective Manager Series
Color
Business and Economics; Guidance and Counseling; Psychology
Dist - DELTAK **Prod** - DELTAK

Management Change - the People Issues 45 MIN
VHS / U-matic
Management Strategies for Office Automation Series
Color
Discusses the organizational impacts of office automation, the importance of preparing the organization for change and strategies for doing that.
Business and Economics; Industrial and Technical Education; Psychology
Dist - DELTAK **Prod** - DELTAK

Management - Conducting Effective Meetings
16mm / U-matic / VHS
Color (C)
Techniques for holding productive meetings are described and enacted.
Business and Economics; Psychology
Dist - AIMS **Prod** - AIMS 1986

Management Control of System Schedule and Cost 55 MIN
U-matic / VHS
Systems Engineering and Systems Management Series
Color
Presents program management techniques. Illustrates the application of PERT for controlling schedule.
Industrial and Technical Education
Dist - MIOT **Prod** - MIOT

Management Controls 11 MIN
16mm
Running Your Own Business Series
Color
Outlines how to get the most useful help out of accountancy. Summarizes the essential ingredients of the proper uses of accounting.
Business and Economics
Dist - EFD **Prod** - EFD

Management Development Series
Effective leadership 32 MIN
Emotional Styles in Human Behavior 24 MIN
Group Leadership - the History of the Group Process Movement 28 MIN
Human Considerations in Management 29 MIN
Importance of Relationships in Organizational Life - Why People Need People 16 MIN
Leadership and Small Work Group Dynamics 27 MIN
The Managerial Grid 35 MIN
Organizational Development 30 MIN
Problem solving in groups 25 MIN
Some Personal Learnings about Interpersonal Relationships 33 MIN
Ways of Dealing with Conflict in Organizations 27 MIN
Dist - UCEMC

Management Development Series
The Appraisal interview
Listen
Say what You Want
Teams and Leaders
Thirty Ways to make more Time
Dist - VLEARN

Management Development System Design 90 MIN
VHS / U-matic
(A PRO)
$180.00 purchase members, $200 purchase non - members, $50.00 rental
Features Patricia A McLagan, President of McLagan and Associates as she discusses development of management talent in the Information Age.
Business and Economics; Education
Dist - ASTD **Prod** - ASTD

Management Diagnostic Series
Evaluating Organizational Effectiveness
Dist - DELTAK

Management emergency medical priorities 14 MIN
U-matic / VHS
Emergency medical training series; Lesson 22
Color (IND)
Teaches importance and procedures for setting priorities of treatment of an individual who has suffered multiple injuries.
Health and Safety; Industrial and Technical Education
Dist - LEIKID **Prod** - LEIKID

Management - Emphasize Your Strengths 22 MIN
U-matic / VHS / 16mm
Color (H C G)
$520, $365, $395 _ #A988
Shows that good managers are able to recognize what they do very well, what they do well enough, and where they need to concentrate their development efforts. Discusses time management, assignment of personnel, personnel counseling, delegation, and involving employees in planning, problem solving and decision making.
Business and Economics; Psychology; Social Science; Sociology
Dist - BARR **Prod** - BARR 1985

Management Faces the Waves of Change 30 MIN
U-matic / VHS
Third Wave Series
Color
Business and Economics; Sociology
Dist - DELTAK **Prod** - TRIWVE

Management for Engineers Series
Control techniques for the engineer manager 30 MIN
Creating an Effective Team 30 MIN
Decision making techniques 30 MIN
Effective communication 30 MIN
Making Appraisals Effective 30 MIN
Motivational Techniques for Engineers 30 MIN
Organizing Technical Activities 30 MIN
Participative Management 30 MIN
Planning Technical Activities 30 MIN
Role of the Engineer Manager 30 MIN
Selecting and Managing Projects 30 MIN
Time Management 30 MIN
Dist - SME

Management for the '90s - Quality Circles Series
How do you start 30 MIN
Should We 30 MIN
What are they 30 MIN
Dist - DELTAK

Management, Gear and Maintenance, Pt 1 44 MIN
VHS
Woodlot Harvesting Kit Series
Color (G)
$95.00 purchase _ #6 - 096 - 401P
Presents three segments on woodlot management concepts, woodlot harvesting gear and chain saw maintenance. Part one of two parts on on woodlot harvesting.
Agriculture; Industrial and Technical Education; Social Science
Dist - VEP **Prod** - VEP

Management Implications of SQL/DS 30 MIN
VHS / U-matic
SQL/DS and Relational Data Base Systems Series
Color
Addresses some of the basic concerns about relational data base and SQL/DS. Focuses on such topics as conversion, implementation and performance associated with SQL/DS.
Business and Economics; Industrial and Technical Education
Dist - DELTAK **Prod** - DELTAK

Management Improvement - It's Your Business 16 MIN
16mm
Color
LC FIE61-93
Shows through the use of animation that good management means effective use of men, money, materials and facilities.
Business and Economics; Psychology
Dist - USNAC **Prod** - USN 1959

Management in Action Series
Conducting a Performance Appraisal 13 MIN
Conducting a Salary Discussion 10 MIN
Conducting a Termination 8 MIN
Defining the job 9 MIN
Discussing Career Goals 11 MIN
Giving positive feedback 7 MIN
Handling Personal Problems 11 MIN
Improving Employee Performance 11 MIN

Taking Disciplinary Action 10 MIN
Dist - CORF

Management in Private Enterprise 15 MIN
VHS / 16mm
(H C A)
$24.95 purchase _ #CS201
Describes the skills involved in management of private enterprise. Features interviews with professionals in the field.
Guidance and Counseling
Dist - RMIBHF Prod - RMIBHF

Management in the service economy 59 MIN
VHS
Color (PRO IND A) (DUTCH FRENCH)
$695.00 purchase _ #VIM06
Features Prof R Van Dierdonck discussing how interaction takes place between managing and marketing an operation. Emphasizes to the service - related business manager the necessity of organization procedural and interpersonal skills and expertise. Strategies for success are also discussed.
Business and Economics
Dist - EXTR

Management information and risk management
VHS
Dynamics of business series
Color (H C A)
$139.00 purchase _ #MAS07V
Examines basic concepts of management information and risk management. Covers subjects including business information systems, data processing systems, risk management, and careers in business.
Business and Economics
Dist - CAMV

Management issues 28 MIN
U-matic
Psychotropic drugs and the health care professional series
Color
Presents various issues and topics which should be considered by health care professionals when working with clients.
Health and Safety; Psychology
Dist - UWASHP Prod - UWASHP

Management Issues 11 MIN
U-matic / VHS / 16mm
It Can't be Home Series
Color
Contrasts indifferent and concerned attitudes displayed by a nursing home admissions officer toward a prospective patient. Shows why nursing home menus should be varied and nutritious. Examines the dubious use of sedatives to maintain a quiet atmosphere.
Health and Safety; Psychology; Sociology
Dist - USHHS Prod - USHHS

Management meeting breaks 10 MIN
VHS / U-matic / BETA
Humatoons meeting breaks series
Color (C A G)
$525.00 purchase, $260.00 rental
Presents a series of short, comic vignettes for management meeting breaks featuring a repertory cast of actors as real business people in cartoon - like situations. Includes The Huddle, Relay Race, Break Huddle, The Champ, The Gymnast.
Business and Economics; Literature and Drama
Dist - VIDART Prod - VIDART

Management of a hydrothermal generating system
VHS
Color (C PRO G)
$150.00 purchase _ #89.07
Looks at new algorithms for larger scale nonlinear programming and network flow optimization with side constraints which were developed to enable rapid solution of problems while allowing optimal analysis in short turnaround time. Shows that this series of models for managing reservoirs and generating facilities has had a profound effect on planning and operation and provided direct savings of millions of dollars annually.
Business and Economics; Social Science
Dist - INMASC

Management of Abnormal Tone in Head Trauma Patients - Strategies for Occupational Therapists 25 MIN
U-matic
Color (PRO)
Demonstrates three major reflex patterns in the lower level head trauma patient and techniques used to facilitate more normal positions for functions. Identifies high level balance and postural problems which inhibit function in the ambulatory patient with head trauma. Describes improved postural adaptations.
Health and Safety
Dist - RICHGO Prod - RICHGO

The Management of Acute Renal Failure 12 MIN
U-matic / VHS
Color (PRO)
Provides a succinct analysis of management of fluid and electrolyte problems in acute renal failure.
Health and Safety
Dist - UMICHM Prod - UMICHM 1978

Management of Acute Upper Gastrointestinal Bleeding 30 MIN
U-matic / VHS
Color
Describes dignostic and therapeutic approach for management of patients bleeding from the upper gastrointestinal tract.
Health and Safety
Dist - ROWLAB Prod - ROWLAB

Management of Advanced and Neglected Surgical Lesions 25 MIN
16mm
Color (PRO)
Portrays the treatment of numerous advanced surgical lesions from patients in Eastern Kentucky (Appalachia.) Emphasizes technical operative features.
Health and Safety; Science
Dist - ACY Prod - ACYDGD 1964

Management of Airway Obstruction 11 MIN
U-matic / VHS
Cardiopulmonary Resuscitation Series
Color (PRO)
Shows how to successfully manage airway obstruction whether victim is conscious, becomes unconscious, or is found unconscious and whether the blockage is caused by an anatomical structure or a foreign body, such as food.
Health and Safety
Dist - HSCIC Prod - HSCIC 1984

Management of Alcohol Dependency in the Medical Patient 27 MIN
U-matic
Color (PRO)
Discusses the disease concept of alcoholism. Demonstrates specific techniques for drawing up an alcoholic patient profile.
Health and Safety
Dist - AYERST Prod - AYERST

Management of Angina Pectoris by Coronary Angioplasty 32 MIN
U-matic / VHS
Color (PRO)
Describes coronary angioplasty - a recent approach in the management of angina pectoris. Discusses criteria used for the selection of patients, preparations prior to the procedure and management following the procedure. Uses a cineradiograph to illustrate balloon dilatation of arterial blockage.
Health and Safety
Dist - UMICHM Prod - UMICHM 1982

Management of breast cancer series
Presents three - parts on managing breast cancer. Includes two programs on managing early stage breast cancer, Asymptomatic Mass - A Team Approach and Palpable Symptomatic Mass - From Risk Management to Adjuvant Therapy; and Management Strategies for Advanced Cancer.
Management of breast cancer series 97 MIN
Management of early stage breast cancer - asymptomatic mass - a team approach - 1 31 MIN
Management of early stage breast cancer - palpable symptomatic mass - from risk management to adjuvant therapy - 2 33 MIN
Management strategies for advanced breast cancer - 3 33 MIN
Dist - HSCIC Prod - MCVA 1982

Management of Breast Feeding 15 MIN
16mm
B&W
Provides answers to an expectant mother's questions about breast feeding. Uses diagrams to explain engorgement, the anatomy of the breast and the nursing procedure. Demonstrates the technique of manual expression of breast milk.
Health and Safety; Home Economics; Sociology
Dist - UWASHP Prod - JENSGD 1959

Management of Bronchial Asthma 20 MIN
U-matic / VHS
Color (PRO)
Presents the physiologic processes which influence the patency of the airway. Divides the management of asthma into three treatment phases including treatment of an acute attack, treatment of chronic asthma and treatment of ventilatory failure.
Health and Safety
Dist - UMICHM Prod - UMICHM 1974

Management of Burn Trauma Wounds 29 MIN
U-matic / 35mm strip
Burn Trauma Series
Color (PRO)
Details management of burn trauma wounds in terms of three major objects - adequate nutrition for tissue regeneration, prevention of invesive wound infection, and removal of necrotic tissue. Leads to successful wound closure when each objective is achieved.
Health and Safety; Psychology
Dist - BRA Prod - BRA

Management of Burns, Pt 1 - Supportive Care 18 MIN
16mm
B&W
Explains the diagnosis, care and treatment of patients suffering from burn injuries.
Civics and Political Systems; Health and Safety
Dist - USNAC Prod - USA 1958

Management of Burns, Pt 2 - Local Care 15 MIN
16mm
B&W
Describes procedures followed in the dressing and operating rooms, including cleansing the wound, debridement of the skin, occlusive dressing treatment, air treatment and skin grafting.
Civics and Political Systems; Health and Safety
Dist - USNAC Prod - USA 1958

Management of Child Behavior in the Dental Office 38 MIN
16mm / U-matic / VHS
B&W
Shows how to guide a child's behavior in ways that will help him accept dental care in his early years and allow the dentist to treat him efficiently and safely.
Health and Safety; Home Economics
Dist - USNAC Prod - IU

Management of Classroom Environment 30 MIN
U-matic / VHS
Teaching Students with Special Needs Series
Color
Revues student behavior and gives suggestions for creating a positive teaching - learning environment in the classroom.
Psychology
Dist - PBS Prod - MSITV 1981

Management of Cleft Lip and Cleft Palate Deformities 11 MIN
16mm
Color (PRO)
LC 76-703700
Shows when a primary care physician should refer patients to specialists of the ongoing care team. Focuses on the management of cleft lip and cleft palate deformities.
Health and Safety
Dist - USNAC Prod - NMAC 1976

Management of complex wounds 28 MIN
VHS
Wound care series
Color (PRO C)
$285.00 purchase, $70.00 _ #4402
Reveals that healing a complex wound requires excellent assessment and intervention skills, as well as aggressive management of complications and familiarity with the wide variety of wound care products available. Reviews the basics of wound assessment. Discusses in detail, wound cleansing, disinfection, debridement, dressing and packing. Explains how to choose appropriate product for each step, based upon the patient's wound, with an emphasis on infection, the most common complication. Stresses the importance of documentation and guidelines for proper documentation. Emphasizes aggressive wound management and proper documentation and communication. Part two of two parts on complex wounds or three parts on wound care.
Health and Safety
Dist - AJN Prod - AJN 1995

The Management of Compound Fractures 17 MIN
16mm
Color (PRO)
Demonstrates the first aid, resuscitation and definitive treatment of compound tibial fractures. Illustrates wound excision with primary closure and wound excision with delayed primary closure.
Health and Safety; Science
Dist - ACY Prod - ACYDGD 1961

Management of coppice woodland-episode 4 25 MIN
VHS
Spirit of trees series

Color (G)
$195.00 purchase, $50.00 rental
Examines the art of coppicing, an ancient method of managing trees. Shows how this has important contemporary applications in the sustainable management of woodland trees. Part of an eight - part series on trees and their relationship with the world around them. Hosted by environmentalist Dick Warner, who meets with conservationists, scientists, folklorists, woodsmen, seed collectors, forest rangers, wood turners and more.
Agriculture; Science - Natural; Social Science
Dist - CNEMAG

Management of Data Communications 42 MIN
U-matic / VHS
Telecommunications and the Computer Series
Color
Discusses planning functions and implementation and operations in data communications.
Industrial and Technical Education; Mathematics
Dist - MIOT **Prod** - MIOT

Management of Domestic Violence 17 MIN
VHS / U-matic
Crisis Intervention Series
Color (PRO)
Illustrates on - the - scene management of a spouse - beating situation by both emergency medical technicians and police.
Health and Safety; Sociology
Dist - GPN **Prod** - SBG 1983

Management of Drug Overdose 10 MIN
VHS / U-matic
Color (PRO)
Discusses the five basic principles in the management of drug overdose, recognition of respiratory depression, support of respiration and circulation, identification of the causative agent, elimination of the causative agent and psychiatric support of the patient.
Health and Safety; Psychology
Dist - UMICHM **Prod** - UMICHM 1973

Management of ear protection 20 MIN
VHS
Color; PAL; NTSC (IND G)
PdS60, PdS70 purchase
Shows managers and industrial trainers the importance of protecting the hearing of workers from damage due to excessive noise. Demonstrates the importance of using the correct type of ear protectors suited to the work being performed and adapted to fit the individual worker correctly. Reveals that a noise measurement survey can determine suitable ear protection depending on noise level and frequency.
Guidance and Counseling; Health and Safety; Psychology
Dist - CFLVIS

Management of early stage breast cancer - asymptomatic mass - a team approach - 1 31 MIN
VHS
Management of breast cancer series
Color (PRO C G)
$395.00 purchase _ #R931 - VI - 002
Allows viewers to explain the importance of early detection and diagnosis of asymptomatic lesions; select mammographic screening to identify suspicious hallmarks of malignancy; describe the role of needle localization in diagnosis; outline an appropriate surgical approach to the asymptomatic lesion; discuss the rationale for breast conservation; and illustrate how a woman choose therapy for an asymptomatic mass. Addresses the emotions and questions of patients faced with decisionmaking in the management of breast cancer, including psychological issues, second opinions, family information and genetic counseling. Part of a three - part series on managing breast cancer.
Health and Safety; Sociology
Dist - HSCIC **Prod** - MCVA 1993

Management of early stage breast cancer - palpable symptomatic mass - from risk management to adjuvant therapy - 2 33 MIN
VHS
Management of breast cancer series
Color (PRO C G)
$395.00 purchase _ #R931 - VI - 003
Focuses on the management of patients with a symptomatic mass in the breast. Addresses questions ranging from the selection procedures to the specific details of treatment of the primary lesion. Includes a discussion on the appropriateness of adjuvant therapies. Opens by reviewing the legal responsibilities of physicians in the documentation and diagnosis of breast cancer. Presents guidelines for keeping physicians 'out of the courtroom.' Part of a three - part series on managing breast cancer.
Health and Safety; Sociology
Dist - HSCIC **Prod** - MCVA 1993

Management of Esophageal Carcinoma 36 MIN
16mm
Color (PRO)
Outlines one method of managing carcinoma of the esophagus. Includes staging of the operation, preliminary bypass of esophagus with colon to relieve obstruction, irradiation before resection and total thoracic esophagectomy.
Health and Safety; Science
Dist - ACY **Prod** - ACYDGD 1969

Management of Fresh Water Near Drowning 13 MIN
VHS / U-matic
Color (PRO)
Discusses the phenomenon of the near drowning victim with emphasis on the initial and delayed effects of immersion. Shows the importance of obtaining an appropriate history and x - ray and of observing the near drowning victim for cardiac dysrhythmias, hyperbolemia and pulmonary edema. Includes ten necessary elements to be used in the manage - ment of near drowning patients and difficulties which may arise during management.
Health and Safety
Dist - UMICHM **Prod** - UMICHM 1973

Management of Gallstones Outside the Gallbladder 30 MIN
VHS / U-matic
Color
Discusses the management of retained or newly formed calculi in the bileducts of patients who had undergone cholecystectomy.
Health and Safety
Dist - ROWLAB **Prod** - ROWLAB

Management of Gastrointestinal Tubes 21 MIN
16mm
Color (PRO)
Demonstrates the insertion, care and types of gastro - intestinal tubes as well as indications for use.
Health and Safety; Science
Dist - ACY **Prod** - ACYDGD 1970

Management of Heparin Therapy 20 MIN
U-matic / VHS
Color (PRO)
Considers the questions of how heparin should be administered, by what route, for how long and how it should be monitored. Compares heparin with oral anticoagulants and gives reasons why one is more appropriate than the other in certain situations. Discusses common laboratory assays for heparin measurement including the Thrombin Clotting Time.
Health and Safety; Science
Dist - UMICHM **Prod** - UMICHM 1977

Management of herpes simplex in pregnant women and neonates 58 MIN
VHS / U-matic
Color (PRO C)
$395.00 purchase, $80.00 rental _ #C850 - VI - 050
Focuses on increasing problems associated with herpes simplex - HSV - as it relates to the pregnant woman and the neonate. Outlines appropriate diagnostic methodology for the physician and presents a detailed decision making approach to case management during pregnancy. Discusses specific approaches to managing the neonate following delivery. Presented by Drs Sergio Stagno and Richard O Davis.
Health and Safety
Dist - HSCIC

Management of Hydrocephalus with the Denver Shunt 19 MIN
U-matic / VHS
Color (PRO)
Demonstrates how to surgically implant a Denver Shunt in an infant in order to drain excess fluid from the brain.
Health and Safety
Dist - WFP **Prod** - WFP

Management of Interfering and Annoying Behavior - Normalization 129 MIN
U-matic / VHS
Meeting the Communications Needs of the Severely/Profoundly 'Handicapped 1980 Series
Color
Discusses the humane and ethical techniques available for reducing or eliminating the interfering and annoying behaviors of severely and profoundly handicapped persons.
Psychology; Social Science
Dist - PUAVC **Prod** - PUAVC

Management of Interfering and Annoying Behavior - Normalization 154 MIN
U-matic / VHS
Meeting the Communication Needs of the Severely/Profoundly 'Handicapped 1981 Series
Color
Addresses four areas included in elimination of inappropriate behaviors which interfere with language acquisition.
Psychology; Social Science
Dist - PUAVC **Prod** - PUAVC

The Management of malignant cardiac arrhythmias - Volume 9
VHS / 8mm cartridge
Cardiology video journal series
Color (PRO)
#FSR - 511
Presents a free - loan program, part of a series on cardiology, which trains medical professionals. Contact distributor for details.
Health and Safety
Dist - WYAYLA **Prod** - WYAYLA

Management of Malignant Melanoma of the Trunk 37 MIN
16mm
Color (PRO)
Presents rationale of regional node dissection for melanoma of the trunk. Demonstrates anatomic choice of appropriate lymph node basic and techniques of dissection.
Health and Safety; Science
Dist - ACY **Prod** - ACYDGD 1970

Management of mass casualties - Pt 6 - sorting 13 MIN
16mm
Color
LC FIE59-205
Discusses problems concerning the identification of various types of casualties likely to be encountered in nuclear weapon warfare, where the medical personnel and facilities available are inadequate to meet the medical requirements.
Health and Safety
Dist - USNAC **Prod** - USA 1959

Management of Massive Hemorrhage from the Lower Gastrointestinal Tract 21 MIN
16mm
Color (PRO)
Points out that massive bleeding from the lower gastrointestinal tract presents both internist and surgeon with an exceedingly difficult problem in diagnosis and treatment. Discusses diagnostic and therapeutic measures.
Health and Safety; Science
Dist - ACY **Prod** - ACYDGD 1966

The Management of Maturity Onset Diabetes Mellitus 117 MIN
VHS / U-matic
Color (PRO)
LC 81-706294
Discusses managing patients with maturity onset diabetes.
Health and Safety
Dist - USNAC **Prod** - USVA 1980

The Management of maturity onset diabetes mellitus - Pt 1 58 MIN
U-matic / VHS
Color (PRO)
LC 81-706294
Discusses managing patients with maturity onset diabetes.
Health and Safety
Dist - USNAC **Prod** - USVA 1980

The Management of maturity onset diabetes mellitus - Pt 2 59 MIN
U-matic / VHS
Color (PRO)
LC 81-706294
Discusses managing patients with maturity onset diabetes.
Health and Safety
Dist - USNAC **Prod** - USVA 1980

Management of Menopause Related Problems 45 MIN
VHS
Health and Hygiene Series
(A)
$39.95 purchase _ #KV230V
Describes symptoms and treatments of menopause related problems.
Health and Safety
Dist - CAMV

Management of microprocessor technology series

Advanced software	53 MIN
Basic software for product development	48 MIN
Future trends	56 MIN
Introduction	57 MIN
Microprocessor - Based Product Opportunities	56 MIN
Microprocessor Architecture I	50 MIN
Microprocessor Architecture II	49 MIN

Product development 58 MIN
Real Time Systems 57 MIN
Strategic Impact of Technology 44 MIN
Dist - MIOT

The Management of Open Traumatic Dislocation 11 MIN
16mm
Color (PRO)
Shows that open wounds of joints must be treated promptly and the positioning and draping of the extremity must be such so that manipulation can be carried out as necessary.
Health and Safety; Science
Dist - ACY **Prod** - ACYDGD 1962

Management of Organic Headache 23 MIN
U-matic
Color (PRO)
LC 76-706054
Describes how headaches can be signals which alert physicians to the possibility of organic disease. Discusses various tests which verify the physician's diagnosis.
Health and Safety
Dist - USNAC **Prod** - WARMP 1970

Management of Pain Series Module 1
Neurophysiology of Pain 24 MIN
Dist - BRA

Management of pain series module 3
Assessment of pain 21 MIN
Dist - BRA

Management of Pain Series Module 4
Physiologic Modulation of Pain 28 MIN
Dist - BRA

Management of Pain Series Module 5
Pain Control through Behavior Modification 23 MIN
Dist - BRA

Management of Pain Series
Psychodynamics of Pain 19 MIN
Dist - BRA

Management of Peptic Ulcer Disease 30 MIN
VHS / U-matic
Color
Discusses the pathophysiology of duodenal ulcer, the basis for selecting specific treatments for short term and long term healing of duodenal ulcer and the result of these treatments.
Health and Safety
Dist - ROWLAB **Prod** - ROWLAB

Management of Postdate Pregnancy
U-matic / VHS
Color (PRO)
Discusses management of pregnancies which remain undelivered for two weeks or more beyond the estimated date of confinement. Presents guidelines for precise pregnancy dating, screening for complications, fetal assessment tests, use of real - time ultrasonography and delivery of the postmature infant. Outlines fetal and neonatal risks associated with postdate delivery. Emphasizes careful monitoring and conservative management.
Health and Safety
Dist - UMICHM **Prod** - UMICHM 1983

Management of Premature Labor 9 MIN
VHS / U-matic
Color (PRO)
Includes considerations for consultation, proper techniques of monitoring during delivery, means of minimizing trauma and the organization of personnel and equipment for the preterm infant.
Health and Safety
Dist - UMICHM **Prod** - UMICHM 1983

The Management of Severe Burns in Children 20 MIN
16mm
Color (PRO)
LC FIA66-53
Discusses and illustrates the care given severely burned children at Children's Hospital, Columbus, Ohio. Focuses on the coordinated efforts of physicians, nurses, physiotherapists, social workers, dietitians and ancillary personnel.
Health and Safety
Dist - EATONL **Prod** - EATONL 1965

Management of Technological Innovation Series
Communication in science and technology 48 MIN
Corporate - R and D Interface Management 34 MIN
Innovation in Industrial Organizations 49 MIN
Motivating Scientists and Engineers 45 MIN
Technical Venture Strategies 49 MIN
User Needs and Industrial Innovation 42 MIN
Dist - MIOT

Management of the Above Knee Amputee 24 MIN
U-matic / VHS
B&W
Shows a 60 - year - old man demonstate the bandaging of his unshaped stump, measuring and applying a shrinker sock, applying an above knee prosthesis and ambulating with a prosthesis and crutches.
Health and Safety
Dist - BUSARG **Prod** - BUSARG

Management of the Adult Respiratory Distress Syndrome 30 MIN
VHS / U-matic
Color (PRO)
Discusses the adult pathophysiological abnormalities underlying the adult respiratory distress syndrome. Presents variables involved in the treatment of this disease and in maximizing the oxygen delivery to the tissues.
Health and Safety
Dist - UMICHM **Prod** - UMICHM 1982

Management of the Alcohol Dependency in the Medical Patient 25 MIN
16mm
Color
LC 75-700147
Discusses medical practices in the management of alcoholism, including diagnosis, confrontation of the patient, recruitment into the treatment network and pharmacotherapy. Use live action and animation.
Health and Safety; Psychology; Sociology
Dist - AYERST **Prod** - AYERST 1974

Management of the Below Knee Amputee 17 MIN
U-matic / VHS
B&W
Demonstrates bandaging a mature below knee stump and measuring and applying a shrinker sock. Shows the components of a PTS prothesis with a medical wedge while the subject is attaching the prosthesis and then walking with a walker.
Health and Safety
Dist - BUSARG **Prod** - BUSARG

Management of the Crushed Chest 13 MIN
U-matic / VHS
Color (PRO)
Reviews pathological changes occurring in crushing injuries of the chest and illustrates the principles of management.
Health and Safety; Science - Natural
Dist - PRIMED **Prod** - PRIMED

Management of the drug dependent person - heroin 30 MIN
16mm
Directions for education in nursing via technology series; Lesson 91
B&W (PRO)
LC 74-701870
Discusses a program established at a methadone clinic in an outpatient department of a private hospital. Describes the program of a nonsubstitute protected environment approach to treatment of heroin addiction.
Health and Safety
Dist - WSUM **Prod** - DENT 1974

Management of the heat shield of the space shuttle orbiter - priorities and recommendations based on risk analysis
VHS
Color (C PRO G)
$150.00 purchase _ #93.04
Reveals that tiles of the space shuttle orbiter are critical to safety at re - entry - 80 percent of the risk can be attributed to 15 percent of the tiles. Examines the importance of systems couplings and the need for additional tile testing in the risk - critical areas. Recommendations were estimated to be a 7 percent reduction in overall accident probability, equaling about $5 billion and the lives of the astronauts.
Business and Economics; Science - Physical
Dist - INMASC

Management of the Leprosy Patient 19 MIN
16mm
Color
LC FIE61-49
Discusses the work done with leprosy patients at the Public Health Service Hospital at Carville, Louisiana. Shows the effectiveness of sulfone drugs in treatment. Explains the importance of rehabilitation, which includes restoring muscular function, teaching vocational skills and building self - confidence.
Health and Safety; Psychology
Dist - USNAC **Prod** - USPHS 1960

Management of the Postdate Pregnancy 10 MIN
VHS / 16mm
Problems in High Risk Pregnancy, Pt II
(C)
$385.00 purchase _ #850VI063
Covers the problem of diminished placental function, postdate placenta, the consequences of placental insufficiency, fetal hemodynamics, assessment of fetal condition in postdate pregnancy, and management of labor and meconium aspiration in the newborn.
Health and Safety
Dist - HSCIC **Prod** - HSCIC 1985

Management of Third Degree Burns in a Newborn 16 MIN
16mm
Color
LC 74-706133
Provides a clinical demonstration of the management of third degree burns of the genitalia and lower extremities suffered by a male infant within an hour after birth.
Health and Safety
Dist - USNAC **Prod** - USA 1969

Management of Thoracic Injuries 29 MIN
16mm
Color (PRO)
Demonstrates the basic principles underlying the treatment of thoracic injuries by model and animal demonstrations and shows application of these principles in the care of patients. Emphasizes practical measures for maintenance of uninterrupted respiratory function in the presence of severe trauma.
Health and Safety; Science
Dist - ACY **Prod** - ACYDGD 1962

Management of Thoracic Trauma 26 MIN
VHS / U-matic
Color (PRO)
Discusses the more common surgical thoracic emergencies in the categories of penetrating and non - penetrating trauma. Presents the pathophysiology of thoracic trauma, the evaluation of patients with chest trauma, the initiation of appropriate therapy and some of the life - threatening injuries which may occur with little, or no, external evidence.
Health and Safety; Psychology
Dist - UMICHM **Prod** - UMICHM 1977

The Management of Time 10 MIN
16mm
Color
LC 74-700545
Shows how a successful businessman organizes his time to his best advantage in order to educate middle management executives on methods of utilizing time.
Business and Economics; Psychology
Dist - NILCOM **Prod** - NILCOM 1974

Management of Time Series Module 1
The Time of Our Lives 63 FRS
Dist - RESEM

Management of time series module 2
Analyzing our time usage 10 MIN
Dist - RESEM

Management of Time Series Module 3
Using Others to Save Time 10 MIN
Dist - RESEM

Management of Time Series Module 4
Our Time is Our Time 13 MIN
Dist - RESEM

Management of total parenteral nutrition - Part 1 25 MIN
BETA / VHS / U-matic
Tubes, tubes, tubes series
Color (C PRO)
$280.00 purchase _ #610.4
Delineates the specific indications for total parenteral nutrition - TPN. Discusses selections of access routes, including advantages and disadvantages of various venous access devices. Examines TPN solutions in terms of individual patient needs and responses. Reveals that handling and storage of solutions include both measures to maintain the integrity of the solutions and identification of problems. Focuses on the nurse's use of equipment and supplies with special emphasis on the use of volumetric pump in administration of solutions. Produced by the School of Nursing, State University of New York at Stony Brook. Part of a five - part series on feeding tubes and intravenous therapy.
Health and Safety
Dist - CONMED

Management of total parenteral nutrition - Part 2 24 MIN
VHS / U-matic / BETA
Tubes, tubes, tubes series
Color (C PRO)

$280.00 purchase _ #610.5
Guides the nurse in the use of comprehensive baseline studies in the ongoing monitoring of the patient's status. Discusses the prevention, detection and treatment of complications such as electrolyte - acid - base imbalances and hyperglycemia. Explores common causes of catheter - related problems including infection, blockage, emboli, breaks or tears and dislodgement with emphasis on how the nurse can provide safeguards to minimize their occurence. Produced by the School of Nursing, State University of New York at Stony Brook. Part of a five - part series on feeding tubes and intravenous therapy.
Health and Safety
Dist - CONMED

Management of Upper Airway Obstruction 12 MIN
VHS / U-matic
Color (PRO)
Outlines the indications and the steps in management of upper airway obstruction from various causes. Points out error in improper techniques and demonstrates proper approaches for oral airways, bronchoscopy, naso and oro - tracheal intubation and tracheostomy.
Health and Safety; Science - Natural
Dist - PRIMED **Prod** - PRIMED

Management of upper and lower airways 17 MIN
VHS / U-matic
Color (PRO C)
$395.00 purchase, $80.00 rental _ #C870 - VI - 020
Introduces nursing and medical students to the most commonly used artificial airways. Discusses the need to establish and maintain an artificial airway in patients with life - threatening injury or illness who cannot sustain normal respiratory function. Describes the oropharyngeal, nasopharyngeal, esophageal and endotracheal airways and outlines insertion of each airway, first on an anatomical model, then on a patient. Looks at contraindications for each method.
Health and Safety; Science - Natural
Dist - HSCIC

Management of Upper and Lower Gastrointestinal Bleeding 30 MIN
U-matic / VHS
Color
Discusses the management of upper and lower gastrointestinal bleeding. Considers the resuscitation and examination of the bleeding patient, diagnosis of the cause of bleeding and therapy.
Health and Safety
Dist - ROWLAB **Prod** - ROWLAB

Management of Vesicant Extravasation 53 MIN
U-matic
Color
Shows how to care for the relatively rare phenomenon of vesicant extravasation resulting from drug injection and infiltration into surrounding skin.
Health and Safety
Dist - UTEXSC **Prod** - UTEXSC

Management of Viral Hepatitis 19 MIN
VHS / U-matic
Color (PRO)
Describes the overlap of hepatitis A and hepatitis B and the differential diagnosis of acute viral hepatitis in the pre - icteric and icteric phases of viral hepatitis. Covers the specific points in the management of viral hepatitis, the approach in evaluating and managing patients with hepatitis B antigen and the indications for gamma globulin prophylaxis.
Health and Safety
Dist - UMICHM **Prod** - UMICHM 1974

Management of Work Series Module 2
Planning 9 MIN
Dist - RESEM

Management of Work Series Module 3
Organizing 12 MIN
Dist - RESEM

Management of Work Series Module 4
Directing 14 MIN
Dist - RESEM

Management of work series Module 5
Controlling 53 FRS
Dist - RESEM

Management of work series
Presents five modules on supervising others. Includes the titles The Successful Manager, Planning, Organizing, Directing, Controlling.
Management of work series 58 MIN
The Successful manager 62 FRS
Dist - RESEM **Prod** - RESEM 1974

Management Organization and Critical Job Elements 120 MIN
U-matic / VHS
AMA's Program for Performance Appraisal Series
Color
Describes the principles on which successful organizations are based, and the contribution of accurate statements of critical job elements to the smooth functioning of a management unit and to the clarification of management goals.
Business and Economics; Psychology
Dist - AMA **Prod** - AMA

Management Organization and Position Description 28 MIN
Videoreel / VT2
How to Improve Managerial Performance - the AMA Performance 'Standards Program Series
Color (A)
LC 75-704233
Features James L Hayes, president of the American Management Associations, exploring nine principles on which successful organizations are based. Shows the contribution made by accurate position descriptions to the smooth functioning of a management unit.
Business and Economics; Psychology
Dist - AMA **Prod** - AMA 1974

Management organization and position descriptions 29 MIN
VHS / U-matic
Color
Shows how to bypass 'organizational layering,' avoid corporate relationships and bring the basics of responsibility and accountability into sharp focus.
Business and Economics; Psychology
Dist - AMA **Prod** - AMA

Management Perspective of Office Automation 45 MIN
VHS / U-matic
Management Strategies for Office Automation Series
Color
Provides an overview of the justifications, benefits, tools and organizational issues associated with the introduction of office automation.
Business and Economics; Industrial and Technical Education; Psychology
Dist - DELTAK **Prod** - DELTAK

Management practices for beef cattle - I 25 MIN
VHS
Cattle production - set I series; Set L
(C)
$79.95 _ CV147
Provides instruction in basic management practices for beef cattle including - handling, retraint and facilities, identification, vaccination, growth stimulant implantation, dehorning, plus a summary and quizzes.
Agriculture; Health and Safety
Dist - AAVIM **Prod** - AAVIM 1989

Management Practices for Beef Cattle -II 46 MIN
VHS
Cattle Production (Set L) Series; Set L
(C)
$79.95 _ CV148
Outlines management practices for beef cattle including surgical and bloodless castration, external parasites and treatment, internal parasites and treatment, and palpation.
Agriculture
Dist - AAVIM **Prod** - AAVIM 1989

Management Presentation
U-matic / VHS
Implementing Quality Circles Series
Color
Examines the ways to present a solution to management. Covers assembling data and using visual aids. Lists pitfalls.
Business and Economics; Psychology
Dist - BNA **Prod** - BNA

Management - Pt 1 - Listening for Understanding 30 MIN
U-matic / VHS / 16mm
Color (C)
Dramatizes the importance of effective communication for managers.
Business and Economics
Dist - GPN **Prod** - UMA 1981

Management - Pt 2 - Work Redesign 30 MIN
U-matic / VHS / 16mm
Color (C)
Introduces the recent and highly respected Hackman/Oldham model of work design.
Business and Economics
Dist - GPN **Prod** - UMA 1981

The Management revolution - I
VHS
Power of change series
Color (G PRO)
$795.00 purchase, $200.00 rental
Features Dr Gerald Ross and Michael Kay who provide an overview of the changes transforming American business. Reveals that these changes include the emergence of mass customization and the fragmentation of markets into specialized niches. Introduces 'The Molecular Management Structure.' Part one of two parts.
Business and Economics; Psychology; Sociology
Dist - AMEDIA **Prod** - AMEDIA 1993

Management science - I 150 MIN
U-matic / VHS
For all practical purposes - introduction to contemporary 'mathematics series
Color (G)
$130.00, $85.00 purchase
Presents a five - part module on management science. Includes an overview and the titles 'Street Smarts,' 'Trains, Planes and Critical Paths,' 'Juggling Machines' and 'Juicy Problems.' Demonstrates how the mathematical concepts of management science enable society to run more efficiently. Part of a series on contemporary mathematics produced by the Consortium for Mathematics and Its Applications - COMAP. On three videocassettes. Hosted by Professor Solomon Garfunkel.
Mathematics
Dist - ANNCPB

Management science module - juicy problems - Part 5 and statistics module - overview - Part 6 60 MIN
VHS / U-matic
For all practical purposes - introduction to contemporary 'mathematics series
Color (G)
$45.00, $29.95 purchase
Concludes the Management Science module. Uses linear programming, the corner principle, the simplex method and the Karmarkar algorithm to help business and government make the best use of available resources in Part 5. Overviews the Statistics module. Shows how data is collected, organized and analyzed so that statistical conclusions can be valid and unbiased in Part 6. Parts of a 26 - part series on contemporary mathematics produced by the Consortium for Mathematics and Its Applications - COMAP. Hosted by Professor Solomon Garfunkel.
Mathematics
Dist - ANNCPB

Management science module - overview - street smarts - Parts 1 and 2 60 MIN
U-matic / VHS
For all practical purposes - introduction to contemporary 'mathematics series
Color (G)
$45.00, $29.95 purchase
Overviews the Management Science module. Shows how society can run more efficiently through using mathematical techniques to find the best schedules and routes in Part 1. Cities and towns with routing problems such as mail delivery graph an 'Euler circuit' to find the most efficient routes in Part 2. Parts of a five - part Management Science module and a 26 - part series on contemporary mathematics. Produced by the Consortium for Mathematics and Its Applications - COMAP. Hosted by Professor Solomon Garfunkel.
Mathematics
Dist - ANNCPB

Management science module - trains, planes and critical paths - juggling machines - Parts 3 and 4 60 MIN
U-matic / VHS
For all practical purposes - introduction to contemporary 'mathematics series
Color (G)
$45.00, $29.95 purchase
Introduces algorithms - 'nearest neighbor,' 'greedy' - which aid in solving complex routing problems in Part 3. Shows different kinds of list processing algorithms to solve scheduling problems. Discusses bin - packing, how to use the least space to accommodate the most objects in Part 4. Parts of a five - part Management Science module and a 26 - part series on contemporary mathematics. Produced by the Consortium for Mathematics and Its Applications - COMAP. Hosted by Professor Solomon Garfunkel.
Mathematics
Dist - ANNCPB

Management series
Presents a five-part series that focuses on the strategies and tactics businesses should take to succeed. Includes tips on creating a successful business plan, finding new customers, how to start and operate a business, dealing with sexual harassment, and hiring and firing. Includes ten videocassettes and written support material for each volume in the series.
Building a successful business plan for your company 36 MIN
Finding new customers for your new business
Hiring and firing - things you need to know
Dist - CAMV

A Management sexual harassment prevention program - Part I 41 MIN
U-matic / VHS / BETA
Intent vs impact series
Color; CC; PAL (PRO G IND)
$895.00 purchase
Shows managers the nuts and bolts of recognizing subtle sexual harassment and how to deal with sexual harassment situations. Covers quid pro quo harassment, hostile work environment, receiving a sexual harassment complaint, talking with the alleged harasser, questions and answers. Includes a trainer's manual and 20 participant manuals. Part one of two parts on preventing sexual harassment.
Business and Economics; Psychology; Social Science; Sociology
Dist - BNA **Prod** - BNA

Management Skill Development Series
Assertiveness and salesmanship for managers
Building teamwork
Motivating People
Solving Communication Problems
Welcome to Management
Dist - RMIBHF

Management skills for church leaders series
Covers management skills necessary for successful church leaders. Includes topics such as organization, goal setting, motivation, volunteers, and managing time and money. Consists of six 60 - minute tapes.
Additional management skills - Tape 6 60 MIN
Building the team with member talents - Tape 4 60 MIN
Motivating volunteers and staff - Tape 3 60 MIN
Our mission, our goals - goal setting for individuals, committees, and the institution - Tape 2 60 MIN
Preparing for success - the organization of your church - Tape 1 60 MIN
Time and money - making the most of scarce resources - Tape 5 60 MIN
Dist - APH

Management Skills for Nurses Series
Moving Up - Making the Transition to Head Nurse 31 MIN
Organizing - Making it all Happen 28 MIN
Planning - Preparing for Action 26 MIN
Dist - AJN

Management Skills for Supervisors Series
A Manager's Role and Function Unit
Motivation Unit
Problem - Solving Unit
Dist - TIMLIF

Management skills series
Presents a five - part series on management skills produced by Health and Sciences Network. Includes the titles How to Develop a Departmental Budget; Time Management Skills; Effective Supervisor Skills; Problem Solving and Conflict Resolution; Communication Skill.
Communication skills 28 MIN
Effective supervisor skills 28 MIN
How to develop a departmental budget 28 MIN
Management skills series 140 MIN
Problem solving and conflict resolution 28 MIN
Time management skills 28 MIN
Dist - AJN

Management Skills Series
Clear writing - Pt 1 and Pt 2 - Anne H Carlisle
Communication skills, Joseph A Robinson
Competitive analysis, Victor H Prushan
Conducting a Performance Appraisal, James F Carey
Conducting Effective Meetings, David B Norris
Effective management style - Arnold Ruskin
Engineer as business person, David B Norris
Estimating Time and Cost, Ward V Speaker
Interviewing Techniques, Richard J Pinsker
Marketing New Products, Victor H Prushan
Motivation and Team Building, Susan Pistone
Negotiating Techniques, Arnold Ruskin
Recruiting Talented People, J Kenneth Lund
Strategic Planning, William S Birnbaum
Time Management, E Byron Chew
Your Career, J Kenneth Lund
Dist - AMCEE

Management skills video series - Coaching and motivation 20 MIN
VHS
Management skills video series
Color (PRO IND A)
$495.00 purchase, $99.00 rental _ #BLR01A
Uses a humorous approach to teach motivational skills. Helps managers and team leaders learn simple techniques in developing and implementing an individual motivation plan. By BLR.
Business and Economics; Psychology
Dist - EXTR

Management skills video series
Management skills video series - Coaching and motivation 20 MIN
Dist - EXTR

Management strategies for advanced breast cancer - 3 33 MIN
VHS
Management of breast cancer series
Color (PRO C G)
$395.00 purchase _ #R931 - VI - 004
Focuses on the goals and options of therapy for patients who either initially present an advanced cancer problem or experience failure of their initial treatment approach. Discusses appropriate follow - up plans and the available treatment therapies including radiotherapy, endocrine therapy and chemotherapy. Discusses pain management strategies and counseling with respect to genetic risk factors. Part of a three - part series on managing breast cancer.
Health and Safety; Sociology
Dist - HSCIC **Prod** - MCVA 1993

Management Strategies for Office Automation Series
Management Change - the People Issues 45 MIN
Management Perspective of Office Automation 45 MIN
Office Automation Game Plan 45 MIN
Survey of Office Automation Applications 45 MIN
Dist - DELTAK

Management System for School Disruption and Violence 26 MIN
U-matic / VHS / 16mm
Color (T)
Presents a profile of basic management skills at work in four schools that have been turned around from a pattern of disruption and violence.
Education; Sociology
Dist - PHENIX **Prod** - PHENIX 1984

Management Technique 30 MIN
U-matic / VHS
Bees and Honey Series
Color
Discusses the agricultural calendar and management problems in beekeeping.
Agriculture; Science - Natural
Dist - MDCPB **Prod** - WGTV

Management Theories X and Y 10 MIN
16mm
Color (PRO)
Features Dr Warren Schmidt who presents a distillation of Douglas Mc Gregor's key concepts on managerial assumptions.
Business and Economics
Dist - UCLA **Prod** - UCLA 1970

Management Training Series
Managing by Exception
Managing Stress
Motivating to Achieve Results
Performance Appraisal
Dist - DELTAK

Management turned upside down - Volume I 30 MIN
VHS
What America does right series
Color (G C PRO)
$795.00 purchase, $225.00 rental
Presents the first of two parts drawing from the book What America Does Right by Bob Waterman. Shows how three companies are building work forces for tomorrow with strategies such as horizontal management, cross - functional teams and reengineering.
Business and Economics; Industrial and Technical Education; Psychology
Dist - FI **Prod** - ENMED 1995

A Management View of Structured Techniques 30 MIN
VHS / U-matic
Structured Techniques - an Overview Series
Color
Discusses structured techniques from a management viewpoint, focusing on how structured techniques can be used to combat many serious software problems, such as poor program quality and low productivity.
Industrial and Technical Education; Psychology
Dist - DELTAK **Prod** - DELTAK

Management's Five Deadly Diseases - a Conversation with Dr W Edwards Deming 16 MIN
U-matic / VHS / 16mm
Color (C A)
Describes aspects of American management style that adversely affect productivity and diminish American capacity for competitiveness.
Business and Economics
Dist - EBEC **Prod** - EBEC 1984

Management's new responsibilities - Pt 2 28 MIN
VHS
Subtle sexual harassment series
Color (PRO IND COR A)
$425.00 purchase, $150.00 rental
Examines legal responsibilities and liabilities on sexual harassment issues facing management. Nationally-recognized experts look at elements of a sound policy and how to handle complaints. Dramatizes the question of indirect victims, organizational liability in client-employee harassment, compliments and acts of 'kindness,' and rumors. Part two of two-part series.
Sociology
Dist - VIDART

Management's Role in Health and Safety 15 MIN
16mm
Color
LC 74-705089
Defines management's responsibility for the health and safety of the men working in our nation's mines. Points out various environmental health problems, safety hazards, and offers possible solutions, with emphasis on effective safety training.
Guidance and Counseling; Health and Safety; Industrial and Technical Education; Psychology; Science - Natural
Dist - USNAC **Prod** - USDA 1972

The Manager and the Law 19 MIN
U-matic / VHS / 16mm
Professional Management Program Series
Color (J) (SPANISH)
LC 76-700187
Uses a series of short dramatizations to present six guidelines based on general principles of law to assist managers in reducing legal risks to themselves and their organizations.
Business and Economics; Civics and Political Systems; Guidance and Counseling; Psychology
Dist - NEM **Prod** - NEM 1975

The Manager as coach
VHS
Color (G PRO)
$199.95 purchase _ #20536EG
Presents a three - volume video set which reveals that the principles of coaching - practiced and perfected by winning athletic coaches for decades - have been proved as techniques for motivating people and bringing about behavioral change. Presents coaching principles in a business context. Shows how to create team bonding, loyalty and commitment, as well as how a manager can be both supportive and demanding. Features Marion Howell.
Business and Economics; Physical Education and Recreation; Psychology
Dist - EXEGAL

The Manager in the Automated Office 30 MIN
U-matic / VHS
Impact of Office Automation on People Series
Color
Examines the impact of office automation on the manager and the adaptations the manager will have to make in this new office environment.
Business and Economics; Industrial and Technical Education; Psychology
Dist - DELTAK **Prod** - DELTAK

Manager of the Year 11 MIN
VHS / 16mm
(C PRO)
$595.00 purchase, $135.00 rental
Focuses on effective listening techniques. Describes what to do before, during and after listening.
Education
Dist - VLEARN

Manager of the Year - Effective Listening 20 MIN
16mm / VHS
Color (C A)
$595.00 purchase, $150.00 rental _ #191
Introduces listening skills - what to do before, during and after listening. Breaks messages into two parts and teaches how to listen for feelings as well as for facts. Includes Leader's Guide.
Business and Economics; English Language; Guidance and Counseling; Psychology
Dist - SALENG **Prod** - SALENG 1987

Manager - to - Manager Series
Module 5 - Getting Approval from Authorized Departments 12 MIN
Module 4 - Helping Colleagues Handle Problems 13 MIN
Module 1 - Overcoming Resistance to Change 12 MIN
Module 3 - Dealing with Difficult People 11 MIN
Module 2 - Gaining Cooperation from Peers 11 MIN
Dist - UTM

Manager Under Pressure 15 MIN
16mm
Color (J)
LC 76-703973
Uses animation and live action to tell the story of a manager confronted with intense personal and professional conflicts. Shows how he must analyze the alternatives and solutions available to him and how the experience of a pressure situation can be a time for gaining perspective and learning about oneself.
Business and Economics; Guidance and Counseling; Psychology
Dist - XICOM **Prod** - BOSUST 1977

Manager Under Pressure 17 MIN
U-matic / VHS
Color (A)
Demonstrates in a humorous manner five basic patterns for coping with pressure in a business setting. Emphasizes the fifth pattern, seeking perspectives and alternatives.
Business and Economics; Psychology
Dist - XICOM **Prod** - XICOM

Manager Wanted 28 MIN
U-matic / 8mm cartridge / VHS / 16mm
Color; B&W (H C) (JAPANESE NORWEGIAN GERMAN PORTUGUESE SWEDISH DANISH FRENCH DUTCH)
Stresses the importance of training subordinates to handle a supervisor's work so that the supervisor may be elevated when the opportunity arises.
Business and Economics; Foreign Language
Dist - RTBL **Prod** - RTBL 1964

Managerial Control 20 MIN
U-matic / VHS / 16mm
Color (A) (SPANISH)
Reveals how simple control procedures help supervisors and managers keep their operations within budget and on schedule without losing sight of their goals. Deals with standards, measurement and corrective action.
Business and Economics; Foreign Language
Dist - NEM **Prod** - NEM

Managerial Decision Making
VHS / U-matic
Principles of Management Series
Color
Defines decision making, and explores the parameters of the decision - making environment.
Business and Economics; Psychology
Dist - RMIBHF **Prod** - RMIBHF

Managerial Decision Making
VHS / 16mm
(PRO)
$150.00 purchase _ #PS104
Defines decision making, and explores the limits of the decision making environment.
Business and Economics
Dist - RMIBHF **Prod** - RMIBHF

Managerial finance in action
VHS
Color (A PRO IND)
Presents an overview of finance principles for executives with little or no prior training in the subject. Covers subjects including budgeting of costs, projecting sales, and cash flow. Intended for use in a three - day workshop format.
Business and Economics
Dist - VLEARN

Managerial game plan - team building through MBO series
Developing the plan - Pt 1 30 MIN
Developing the plan - Pt 2 30 MIN
Gaining commitment 30 MIN
Maintaining a Winning Team 30 MIN
The Name of the Game 30 MIN
Dist - PRODEV

The Managerial Grid 35 MIN
U-matic / VHS / 16mm
Management Development Series
B&W (C A)
LC 78-701806
Explains a useful system for evaluating management methods. Shows the system applied to various situations in order to determine the attitudes, values, degree of commitment, creativity and conflict that can be expected under different management methods.
Business and Economics; Psychology
Dist - UCEMC **Prod** - UCLA 1963

Managerial Stress 30 MIN
VHS / U-matic
Business of Management Series Lesson 23; Lesson 23
Color (C A)
Interviews managers as they discuss personal sources of stress and the steps they take to alleviate it. Looks at the direct action large corporations have taken to reduce employee stress.
Business and Economics; Psychology
Dist - SCCON **Prod** - SCCON

The Managerial World 30 MIN
U-matic / VHS
Business of Management Series Lesson 1; Lesson 1
Color (C A)
Features working managers and professors of management as they explore the five inter - dependent functions that represent the heart of management.
Business and Economics; Education; Psychology
Dist - SCCON **Prod** - SCCON

Managers Can Avoid Wasting Time 30 MIN
VHS / 16mm
Harvard Business Review Video Series
(A PRO)
$650.00 purchase _ #AG - 4879M
Defines critical organizational needs and demonstrates techniques for handling them with solid practical management strategies.
Business and Economics; Psychology
Dist - CORF **Prod** - WGBH 1987

The Manager's Environment
VHS / 16mm
(PRO)
$150.00 purchase _ #PS103
Discusses how internal and external influences can determine which managerial decisions are or are not acceptable.
Business and Economics
Dist - RMIBHF **Prod** - RMIBHF

A Manager's Introduction to Workers' Compensation 17 MIN
U-matic
Color (IND)
Exposes middle managers and supervisors to the high costs of accidents, presents the history and rationale for workers' compensation, explains the extent of coverage, types of disabilities, available benefits, types of insurance, and how the program is administered.
Business and Economics
Dist - BNA **Prod** - ALLIED 1986

Manager's job - folklore and fact 30 MIN
VHS / 16mm
Harvard business review video series
(A PRO)
$650.00 purchase _ #AG - 5114M
Defines critical organizational needs and demonstrates techniques for handling them with solid practical management strategies.
Business and Economics; Psychology
Dist - CORF **Prod** - WGBH 1987

Manager's Job Responsibilities 3 MIN
Videoreel / VT2
SUCCESS, the AMA Course for Office Employees Series
Color
LC 75-704219
Shows office employees that they share some of the same overall organizational responsibilities with their supervisors. Suggests that employees should recognize the many different roles they have in meeting these responsibilities.
Business and Economics; Psychology
Dist - AMA **Prod** - AMA 1972

Manager's Operating Realities 10 MIN
Videoreel / VT2
SUCCESS, the AMA Course for Office Employees Series
Color
LC 75-704209
Presents an instructional course for office employees. Provides insights into the problems and pressures with which today's managers must deal. Offers a definition of management, identifies three major managerial activities and uses dramatized examples in order to show the five basic operating realities faced by managers.
Business and Economics; Psychology
Dist - AMA **Prod** - AMA 1972

A Manager's Role and Function Unit
VHS / U-matic
Management Skills for Supervisors Series
Color (A)
Covers the basic responsibilities, roles and skills expected of those in the beginning ranks of management. Shows how managers function within the organization, their relationship to upper management, peers and employees, and their effects on productivity and the organization at large.
Business and Economics; Psychology
Dist - TIMLIF **Prod** - TIMLIF 1984

The Manager's Role in the Productivity Movement 13 MIN
VHS / 16mm
(PRO)
Describes the manager's role in the productivity movement.
Business and Economics
Dist - TOYOVS **Prod** - JPC 1987

A Manager's Roles in QC Circle Activities 20 MIN
VHS
(PRO)
Outlines the role of Quality Control promoters clearly. Shows how Quality Control circles, or QC circles, were started as a part of Total Quality Control, and investigates the effects of QC circles upon company operations. Describes five installation stages and their purpose, effects and taboos.
Business and Economics
Dist - TOYOVS **Prod** - JPC 1987

Managers with impact - versatile and inconsistent 30 MIN
VHS / 16mm
Harvard business review video series
(A PRO)
$650.00 purchase _ #AG - 4904M
Defines critical organizational needs and demonstrates techniques for handling them with solid practical management strategies.
Business and Economics; Psychology
Dist - CORF **Prod** - WGBH 1987

Managing 27 MIN
VHS
Minding my own business series
Color (H C G)
$225.00 purchase
Features women entrepreneurs who have developed businesses. Discusses management and operation of their new business. Part of a six - video series that highlights the personal experiences of business owners in getting started.
Business and Economics
Dist - LANDMK

Managing a drug free environment 13 MIN
VHS
Color (A PRO IND)
$495.00 purchase, $125.00 rental
Focuses on the role and responsibility of managers in dealing with drug abuse in the workplace. Uses case studies to help managers recognize and deal with situations.
Business and Economics; Guidance and Counseling; Psychology
Dist - VLEARN **Prod** - EBEC

Managing a flock series
Applying health care practices 22 MIN
Feed and water delivery systems 27 MIN
Feeding the farm flock 26 MIN
Fencing 21 MIN
Sheep handling, using equipment and sheep psychology 18 MIN
Dist - HOBAR

Managing a Play 11 MIN
16mm / U-matic / VHS
B&W (H)
Describes the responsibilities of the publicity director and manager.
Business and Economics; Fine Arts
Dist - IFB **Prod** - IFB 1951

Managing a Structured Programming Project 15 MIN
16mm
Structured Program Design Series
Color
LC 81-700499
Explains how data processing managers can develop and evaluate programs using the structured approach.
Business and Economics
Dist - EDTRCS **Prod** - EDTRCS 1981

Managing a successful compliance examination 47 MIN
VHS
Dream team series
Color (IND PRO)
$295.00 purchase, $150.00 rental _ #MAX03G
Introduces Lucy Griffin and Phillips Gay with advice for bankers on meeting compliance examiners. Includes a leader's guide. Part of an eight - part series. Produced by Marx Communications.
Business and Economics
Dist - EXTR

Managing adversity - 10 30 MIN
VHS
Venturing...the entrepreneurial challenge series
Color (G)
$14.95 purchase
Shows how entrepreneurs have responded to adversities faced in venturing. Part ten of a 13 - part series on the steps involved in starting and developing an entrepreneurial company. Viewers' guide available separately. Sponsored under a grant from the Farmers Home Administration to help small and rural businesses.
Business and Economics; Psychology
Dist - VTETV **Prod** - VTETV 1992

Managing and implementing 30 MIN
U-matic / VHS / 16mm
Advertising the small business series
(A)
$180 VC purchase, $450 film purchase, $350 reduced film purchase, $30
Discusses how to advertise for a small business. Focuses on writing and designing ads. Second in a two part series.
Business and Economics
Dist - GPN **Prod** - NETCHE 1981

Managing and understanding behavior problems in Alzheimer's disease and related disorders 170 MIN
VHS
Color (G C PRO)
$295.00 purchase
Presents a series of ten videos that form a complete training program for caregivers who work with Alzheimer's patients. Helps in identifying and developing ways to cope with common problems, including agitation, paranoia and depression. Package includes ten videos and manual.
Health and Safety; Sociology
Dist - TNF

Managing and using PC memory 150 MIN
VHS
Self - teaching video learning package series
Color (G PRO)
$295.00 purchase _ #7MM60
Features Mark Minasi, author, editor and PC veteran who explores all types of PC memory, memory upgrades, and memory managers. Teaches how to differentiate among the types of memory, and what each can and cannot do; maximize the performance of existing applications with a memory management strategy; evaluate programs that utilize PC memory above 640K; create and use upper memory blocks - UMBs; reallocate 'newly found' memory; and take advantage of DOS 5.0's memory manager to recover memory for your programs. Includes a comprehensive course workbook. Part of a series.
Computer Science
Dist - TECHIN

Managing and using the Data Resource 20 MIN
VHS / U-matic
User - Directed Information Systems Series
Color
Presents the concepts of data management and user application development. Discusses data base concepts and explores the structures and techniques which must support it for data base to be an effective tool for the user.
Business and Economics; Industrial and Technical Education; Psychology
Dist - DELTAK **Prod** - DELTAK

Managing anxiety and depression in the elderly
VHS
Color (PRO)
#ATV - 366
Presents a free - loan program which trains medical professionals. Contact distributor for details.
Health and Safety; Psychology
Dist - WYAYLA **Prod** - WYAYLA

Managing application development 30 MIN
VHS / U-matic
Application development without programmers series
Color
Suggests goals for DP management and new methodologies for achieving those goals to capitalize on new techniques for application development.
Industrial and Technical Education; Psychology
Dist - DELTAK **Prod** - DELTAK

Managing assaultive patients series
Self - protection and recovery 18 MIN
Team strategies and containment 16 MIN
Dist - CONMED

Managing at the speed of change 27 MIN
VHS
Color (PRO IND A)
$795.00 purchase, $195.00 rental _ #MEN02
Analyzes reaction to change through a message from Daryl Conner. Offers hope and help for managers facing the pressures of change. Includes facilitator's manual. By Mentor Media. Includes facilitator's manual.
Business and Economics; Psychology
Dist - EXTR

Managing Behavior in School 30 MIN
VHS / U-matic
Developing Discipline Series
Color (T)
Presents the principal, a classroom teacher, the counselor, a librarian and a student from the Vandenberg Middle School who speak to the value and impact of the discipline program described in the Developing Discipline series.
Education; Guidance and Counseling; Psychology; Sociology
Dist - GPN **Prod** - SDPT 1983

Managing Business Organization 29 MIN
U-matic / VHS
Business File Series
Color
Business and Economics
Dist - PBS **Prod** - PBS

Managing by Decision - Making 11 MIN
U-matic / 35mm strip
Improving Managerial Skills Series
Color
Offers an easy - to - follow set of rules for increasing a supervisor's decision - making skills.
Business and Economics; Psychology
Dist - RESEM **Prod** - RESEM

Managing by Exception
U-matic / VHS
Management Training Series
Color
Business and Economics; Psychology
Dist - DELTAK **Prod** - THGHT

Managing by wandering around 24 MIN
VHS
Color (A PRO IND)
$795.00 purchase, $185.00 rental
Portrays several managers who 'wander around' the workplace on a regular basis. Shows the reactions and comments of their staffs. Suggests that there are several different management styles that can be used with this practice.
Business and Economics; Guidance and Counseling; Psychology
Dist - VLEARN **Prod** - MELROS

Managing Change 30 MIN
U-matic / VHS / 16mm
Color (C A PRO)
$995.00 purchase, $165.00 rental
Presents a supervisory package to motivate employees to cope with change. Includes two videotapes, leader's guide, participant's manual, overhead transparencies, cards and wall chart.
Business and Economics; Psychology
Dist - VICOM **Prod** - VICOM 1990

Managing Change 23 MIN
16mm / U-matic / VHS
Color (A)
LC 81-701618
Illustrates and suggests solutions to some of the special problems that confront managers when it is their responsibility to manage change. Shows how, when a new assembly line is installed and new products are introduced in an English laminating factory, unexpected problems arise.
Business and Economics; Psychology
Dist - IFB **Prod** - MILLBK 1981

Managing Change 21 MIN
VHS / 16mm
ITC Supervisory Methods, Module 16, Series
(C PRO)
$995.00 purchase, $165.00 rental
Shows positive and negative reactions to change, along with behavior modeling. Participants apply the managing change model to an actual change experience. Includes materials for an eight hour training session.
Education
Dist - VLEARN **Prod** - INTRFL

Managing change 20 MIN
VHS
Color (A PRO)
$495.00 purchase, $150.00 rental
Presents ways managers can help employees through a four - step process to deal with change. Uses examples from industry to explain the process.
Guidance and Counseling
Dist - DHB **Prod** - CRISP

Managing Change - the Human Dimension 33 MIN
VHS / 16mm
Color (C PRO)
$645.00 purchase, $150.00 rental
Gives ten reasons people resist change, along with management strategies to help people see change as an opportunity, and guidelines for managing major changes.
Education
Dist - VLEARN **Prod** - GOODMI
GOODMI

Managing Changing Priorities 60 MIN
VHS / BETA
Manufacturing Series
(IND)
Evaluates the interdependencies of production schedules and the importance of managing change. Teaches techniques for keeping schedules up to date and for responding to the customer and factory needs that cause schedule changes.
Business and Economics
Dist - COMSRV **Prod** - COMSRV 1986

Managing chemotherapy side effects - taking good care of yourself 33 MIN
VHS
Color (PRO C G)
$250.00 purchase, $70.00 rental _ #4388
Gives patients an overview of the side effects that result from chemotherapy treatment and methods for managing them. Features individuals of varying ages, backgrounds and cancer diagnoses describing their experiences and demonstrating coping methods they found effective. Includes graphic and animated representations of how chemotherapy works and why side effects occur. Emphasizes the importance of a partnership among the patient, significant others and healthcare team. Facilitates a sense of patient control over treatment through a positive representation of a fearful situation.
Health and Safety
Dist - AJN **Prod** - UIHC

Managing childhood asthma - a parent's guide 30 MIN
VHS
Color (G)
$39.95 purchase _ #MTI001V-K
Presents information about childhood asthma, including how to become active partners with your healthcare professionals, asthma medicine and its use, and recognizing your child's asthma triggers. Asserts that the child's activities will not have to be limited with proper management of the condition.
Health and Safety
Dist - CAMV

Managing conflict 13 MIN
VHS / U-matic
Applied management series
Color
Business and Economics
Dist - DELTAK **Prod** - ORGDYN

Managing Conflict - How to make Conflict Work for You 15 MIN
U-matic / VHS / 16mm
Color (H C A)
LC 78-701792
Illustrates several strategies for dealing with conflict, discussing both advantages and disadvantages of each strategy.
Business and Economics; Guidance and Counseling; Sociology
Dist - SALENG **Prod** - SALENG 1978

Managing conflict - Part 3 21 MIN
VHS
Straight talk on teams series
Color (PRO IND A)
$450.00 purchase, $95.00 rental _ #BBP132C
Presents part three of a four - part series. Uses the expertise of Allan Cox to enable managers to take an in - depth look at team building. Includes a leader's guide and workbook.
Business and Economics; Psychology
Dist - EXTR **Prod** - BBP

Managing Conflict Productively 120 MIN
U-matic / Cassette
Color; Stereo (A)
Presents techniques for turning conflict into a positive force, contributing to efficiency and stimulating creative problem solving and innovation.

Business and Economics; Psychology
Dist - UNIVAS **Prod** - UNIVAS

Managing consumer credit delinquency in the US economy
VHS
Color (C PRO G)
$150.00 purchase _ #91.06
Focuses on optimal allocation of collection efforts to correctly classify delinquent accounts which has reduced harassment of good customers and allowed effective concentration on those accounts most likely to respond. Reveals that validity and effectiveness of the optimization modeling used has demonstrated its effectiveness for GE Capital and for use in any other collection environment. General Electric Capital. William M Makuch, Jeffrey L Dodge, Joseph G Ecker, Donna C Granfors, Gerald J Hahn.
Business and Economics
Dist - INMASC

Managing Creatively 21 MIN
16mm / U-matic / VHS
Color
LC 83-700597
Encourages managers to take an imaginative approach and recognize barriers to creativity. Tells the story of a manager who has fallen into a stagnant routine and copes with crises in a piecemeal manner while exhibiting dynamic leadership and resourcefulness in his private life. Shows how he changes his approach to management.
Business and Economics
Dist - IFB **Prod** - MILLBK 1982

Managing creativity 70 MIN
VHS
Color (PRO IND A G) (DUTCH FRENCH)
$695.00 purchase _ #VIM13
Highlights the relationship between creativity and change - emphasizing development of creative process within an organization. Includes procedures helpful to managers and others - removing barriers, developing a creative process for planning, forming idea sources, initiating motivational stimuli and setting up communication and evaluation methods. Discussion presented by Prof Simon Majaro.
Business and Economics; Fine Arts; Psychology
Dist - EXTR

Managing cultural differences series
The Cosmopolitan Manager
Family delocation coping skills
Improving the Productivity of International Managers
Transnational Manager as Cultural Change Agents
Transnational Managers as Intercultural Communicators
Understanding Cultural Differences
Dist - GPCV

Managing Dancers 30 MIN
VHS / U-matic
Business and Law of Dance Series
Color
Business and Economics; Fine Arts; Industrial and Technical Education
Dist - ARCVID **Prod** - ARCVID

Managing differences - valuing diversity - Part I 30 MIN
VHS
Valuing diversity series
Color (A PRO IND)
$695.00 purchase, $100.00 rental
Presents the first of a seven - part series on diversity in the workplace. Argues that diversity can be a strength if properly handled. Dramatizes situations leading to conflict and poor performance, showing how they can be better handled. Covers evaluation, development, and motivation of diverse employees.
Business and Economics; Guidance and Counseling; Psychology; Sociology
Dist - VLEARN

Managing Difficult Customers 20 MIN
VHS / 16mm
Color (H C A)
$495.00 purchase, $150.00 rental _ #197
Provides specific techniques for managing three types of difficult customers over the phone. Vignettes show how to handle angry, talkative and demanding customers. Includes Leader's Guide.
Business and Economics; Psychology
Dist - SALENG **Prod** - ALCONG 1990

Managing diversity 22 MIN
VHS
Color (PRO G A)
$725.00 purchase, $175.00 rental
Illustrates potential problems through scenes involving gender, racial, and ethnic differences among employees. Encourages viewing diversity as a positive, not negative, characteristic that can be used to advantage. Presents cultural consultants Kanu Kogod and Selma Myers.
Business and Economics; Guidance and Counseling; Psychology
Dist - EXTR **Prod** - CRMP

Managing diversity 25 MIN
VHS
Color (PRO IND A)
Shows how to operate on the job with co - workers of different ethnic backgrounds.
Business and Economics
Dist - CRMF **Prod** - CRMF 1990

Managing earaches in children 15 MIN
VHS
Color (G C PRO)
$100.00 purchase _ #CC - 12
Shows why children are more likely to get ear infections than adults. Gives tips to temporarily relieve discomfort until the child can be treated by a physician. Shows parents the structure of the middle ear and demonstrates how blockage of the Eustachian tubes can cause buildup of fluid and resulting pain. Discusses medications the doctor may prescribe including antibiotics, antihistamines and decongestants. Mentions the need for possible corrective surgery. Stresses that parents should always contact a physician when ear infections occur.
Health and Safety; Science - Natural
Dist - MIFE **Prod** - MIFE

Managing effective programs series
Safety, health, and loss control - managing effective programs - a series
Dist - AMCEE

Managing emergency medical priorities 14 MIN
VHS / U-matic
Emergency medical training series
Color
Defines priority injuries and shows how to determine and establish priorities and how to treat brain, chest and abdominal emergencies as priorities.
Health and Safety
Dist - VTRI **Prod** - VTRI

Managing Employee Morale 25 MIN
U-matic / VHS
Motivation and Productivity Series
Color
Discusses methods for improving employee morale including fact - finding, letting people participate in decisions and using channels of upward communication.
Psychology
Dist - BNA **Prod** - BNA

Managing Energy, Effort, Time, and Money 14 MIN
U-matic / VHS
Leadership Link - Fundamentals of Effective Supervision Series
Color
Business and Economics; Health and Safety; Psychology
Dist - DELTAK **Prod** - CHSH

Managing Financial Resources - Long Term Funds 29 MIN
VHS / U-matic
Business File Series
Color
Business and Economics
Dist - PBS **Prod** - PBS

Managing Financial Resources - Short Term Funds 29 MIN
VHS / U-matic
Business File Series
Color
Business and Economics
Dist - PBS **Prod** - PBS

Managing for commitment 25 MIN
VHS
Color (A PRO)
$495.00 purchase, $150.00 rental
Teaches how to increase the loyalty of employees through building mutual trust between the company and the worker. Based on the book by Carol Kinsey Goman.
Business and Economics; Psychology
Dist - DHB **Prod** - CRISP

Managing for customer care 27 MIN
BETA / VHS / U-matic
Color (A G)
$595.00 purchase, $195.00 rental
Introduces a management development program designed to assist supervisors in managing their people to a superior level of service. Evaluates the concepts of empowering people, under - promising and over - delivering, and leading by example.
Business and Economics
Dist - TELDOC **Prod** - WYVERN 1991

Managing for Productivity 30 MIN
VHS / U-matic
Business of Management Series Lesson 26; Lesson 26
Color (C A)
Examines the various aspects of the Japanese approach to management. Looks at whether or not the techniques that work in Japan would have the same result in the United States. Looks at ways a manager can coordinate productivity efforts.
Business and Economics; Geography - World; Psychology
Dist - SCCON **Prod** - SCCON

Managing for Results 10 MIN
U-matic / 35mm strip
Human Side of Management Series
Color
Shows how to create a goal - setting environment and how to manage it. Develops techniques for helping supervisors bring employee goals and organization goals closer together.
Business and Economics; Psychology
Dist - RESEM **Prod** - RESEM

Managing frontline service 28 MIN
VHS
Color (A PRO IND)
$730.00 purchase, $235.00 rental
Trains frontline staff in customer service. Combines dramatic vignettes and demonstrations of customer service techniques.
Business and Economics; Guidance and Counseling; Psychology
Dist - VLEARN **Prod** - VIDART

Managing Frontline Service 28 MIN
VHS / 16mm
Color (A PRO)
$730.00 purchase, $235.00 rental
Encourages supervisors to treat frontline staff as their most valued customers. Shows how to select, train, coach and celebrate the staff which deals with the public and customers.
Business and Economics
Dist - VIDART **Prod** - NATTYL 1990

Managing growth - 8 30 MIN
VHS
Venturing...the entrepreneurial challenge series
Color (G)
$14.95 purchase
Describes ways of effectively managing the chaos inherent in growth. Part eight of a 13 - part series on the steps involved in starting and developing an entrepreneurial company. Viewers' guide available separately. Sponsored under a grant from the Farmers Home Administration to help small and rural businesses.
Business and Economics; Psychology
Dist - VTETV **Prod** - VTETV 1992

Managing harmony
VHS
The Respectful workplace - redefining workplace violence series
Color (IND)
$425.00 purchase, $150.00 rental _ #QMR08C
Helps businesses end hostility, intimidation, harassment and other damaging behavior in the workplace. Includes a facilitator guide, handouts and overhead transparencies. Part of a three - part series. Produced by Quality Media Resources.
Business and Economics; Guidance and Counseling; Health and Safety; Social Science; Sociology
Dist - EXTR

Managing harmony - Pt 3 26 MIN
VHS
The respectful workplace - Redefining workplace violence series
Color (PRO IND COR A)
$425.00 purchase, $150.00 rental, $50.00 preview
Examines the cost of workplace violence, including personal and organizational liability, and how management must work to preclude it. It redefines workplace violence and helps organizations put an end to the destructive conflicts that occur on a daily basis.
Sociology
Dist - VIDART

Managing Hemorrhoids
U-matic / VHS
Color (ARABIC)
Explains how over - strained blood vessels can result in hemorrhoids (both internal and external) and how proper diet and bowel habits can alleviate the discomfort. Discusses surgery as a possible but unlikely option.
Health and Safety
Dist - MIFE **Prod** - MIFE

Managing Human Resources 29 MIN
VHS / U-matic
Business File Series
Color
Business and Economics
Dist - PBS **Prod** - PBS

Managing Information 29 MIN
U-matic / VHS
Business File Series
Color
Business and Economics; Industrial and Technical Education
Dist - PBS **Prod** - PBS

Managing Information Technology 30 MIN
VHS / U-matic
Strategic Impact of Information Technology Series
Color
Discusses the problems and implications of information technology from a top management viewpoint. Outlines considerations for planning and implementing information technology.
Industrial and Technical Education; Social Science
Dist - DELTAK **Prod** - DELTAK

Managing institutionalization of strategic decision support for the Egyptian cabinet
VHS
Color (C PRO G)
$150.00 purchase _ #89.06
Reveals that macro strategic issues and - or management and technological development needs of 28 large projects in Egypt involved strategic decision making at a cabinet level. Shows that the introduction, development and use of DSS in different ministries, sectors and governorates suggested that managing institutionalization is as important as model building - an explicit, complimentary and integrated process. Government of Egypt. Hisham El Sherif.
Business and Economics; Civics and Political Systems; Psychology
Dist - INMASC

Managing Interruptions 30 MIN
U-matic / VHS
Time Management for Management Series Pt 5
Color (A)
Explains that one key to managing interruptions effectively is to anticipate them whenever possible. Shows how to block out time on daily calendars for anticipated or routine matters and how to establish policies with secretaries or assistants for handling unexpected interruptions.
Business and Economics; Psychology
Dist - TIMLIF **Prod** - TIMLIF 1981

Managing Job Related Stress 30 MIN
16mm
Dimensions of Leadership in Nursing Series
Color (PRO)
LC 81-700111
Emphasizes the importance of helping employees who are undergoing stress. Presents vignettes of four stressful situations.
Health and Safety; Psychology
Dist - AJN **Prod** - CATTN 1979

Managing job stress series
Presents information to help employees conquer on - the - job stress through a six - session video course. Covers the topics of workplace pressure, employee roles and expectations, employee workload, interpersonal conflict and pressures, coping with change in the workplace, and managing work and homelife.

Balancing work and home	15 MIN
Clarifying roles and expectations	15 MIN
Controlling the workload	15 MIN
Handling workplace pressure	15 MIN
Managing job stress series	90 MIN
Managing people pressures	15 MIN
Surviving the changing workplace	15 MIN

Dist - ADVANM

Managing job stress series
Takes aim at the universal problem of work-related stress. Helps the viewer address a variety of work-environment issues with audiences of blue-collar workers, white-coller workers, students, managers, executives, professionals and volunteers. Contains six programs which deal with the sources and potential damage of on-the-job stress and five quick skills to manage it; the stated and unspoken expectations causing stress; how workloads create stress and four skills for controlling the workload; handling conflict with co-workers; coping with changes in the workplace; and four skills to help balance life in and outside of work. Each program includes leader's guide and participant workbook.

Balancing work and home	20 MIN
Clarifying roles and expectations	20 MIN
Controlling the workload	20 MIN
Handling workplace pressure	20 MIN
Managing people pressures	20 MIN
Surviving the changing workplace	20 MIN

Dist - WHLPSN

Managing large scale asbestos removal operations 13 MIN
U-matic / BETA / VHS
Color (IND G)
$495.00 purchase _ #820 - 33
Trains managers on large scale asbestos removal operations. Explains what should be done before removal starts, what is required during the removal and disposal process. Covers proper notification procedures, how to assess a job and important facts to gather prior to awarding an asbestos removal contract.
Business and Economics; Health and Safety; Industrial and Technical Education; Psychology
Dist - ITSC **Prod** - ITSC

Managing large scale asbestos removal operations - Large scale asbestos removal operations 38 MIN
BETA / VHS / U-matic
Color (IND G)
$795.00 purchase _ #820 - 33, #820 - 34
Presents two videos on large scale asbestos removal operations. Discusses the management of such a project, what should be done before removal, requirements during removal and disposal, notification procedures and the process of awarding a contract. Explains the procedures to be followed during asbestos abatement projects in the second video.
Business and Economics; Health and Safety; Industrial and Technical Education; Psychology
Dist - ITSC

Managing Learning - Developing Skills 24 MIN
VHS / 16mm
Color (A PRO)
$605.00 purchase, $185.00 rental
Shows how to develop and manage training in the workplace rather than in the classroom.
Business and Economics; Guidance and Counseling; Psychology
Dist - VIDART **Prod** - VIDART 1990

Managing Learning, Part 2 30 MIN
VHS / 16mm
(C PRO)
$135.00 purchase, $135.00 rental
Emphasizes that every manager should be a training manager. Shows managers how to identify training needs based on performance, mobilize resources, then implement, monitor and evaluate training.
Education
Dist - VLEARN **Prod** - VIDART

Managing Learning - the Concept 24 MIN
VHS / 16mm
(C PRO)
$575.00 purchase, $135.00 rental
Shows arguments for using training to meet the challenges of technical, organizational and financial change.
Education
Dist - VLEARN **Prod** - VIDART

Managing Meetings 30 MIN
U-matic / VHS
Communication Skills for Managers Series
Color (A)
Presents hosts Richard Benjamin and Paula Prentiss giving guidelines on when to call a meeting, how to prepare for it, how to establish leadership and how to stick to the agenda.
Business and Economics; English Language; Psychology
Dist - TIMLIF **Prod** - TIMLIF 1981

Managing Meetings that Get Results 60 MIN
Cassette / VHS
Effective Manager Series
Color (G)
$95.00 purchase _ #6420
Features Brian Tracy who shows how to keep meetings short and to the point and productive. Includes a 60 - minute video, two audiocassettes and two workbooks. Part of a fourteen - part series.
Business and Economics; Civics and Political Systems; Guidance and Counseling; Psychology; Social Science
Dist - SYBVIS

Managing Microcomputers - the Microcomputer Game 30 MIN
VHS / U-matic
Ready or not Series
Color
Stresses the idea of determining what needs and groups of students will be served by microcomputers.
Education; Industrial and Technical Education
Dist - PCATEL **Prod** - NCSDPI

Managing momentum - Part 7 16 MIN
VHS
Total quality management - Ten elements for implementation series
Color (PRO IND A)
$300.00 purchase _ #GO02G
Presents part seven of a ten - part series which outlines a course of continuous improvement. Helps organizations, such as educational institutions, manufacturing operations, hospitals and service industries. Includes extensive workshop materials. By Goal - QPC.
Business and Economics; Psychology
Dist - EXTR

Managing Motivation 11 MIN
16mm / U-matic / VHS
Color (A)
LC 81-700295
Illustrates how to increase employee motivation.
Business and Economics; Psychology
Dist - SALENG **Prod** - SALENG 1981

Managing our countryside - I 30 MIN
VHS
Inside Britain 3 series
Color; PAL; NTSC (G) (BULGARIAN CZECH HUNGARIAN SPANISH POLISH ROMANIAN RUSSIAN SLOVAK UKRAINIAN ENGLISH WITH ARABIC SUBTITLES LITHUANIAN)
PdS65 purchase
Reveals that the British landscape, prized for its scenic beauty, is threatened with irreversible change. Looks at the impact of human activity upon the countryside. Shows that new agricultural practices, growing tourism and pollution are putting at risk those qualities that Britons prize about their land. Part one of two parts.
Geography - World; Science - Natural
Dist - CFLVIS **Prod** - OPTIC 1993

Managing our countryside - II 30 MIN
VHS
Inside Britain 3 series
Color; PAL; NTSC (G) (BULGARIAN CZECH HUNGARIAN SPANISH POLISH ROMANIAN RUSSIAN SLOVAK UKRAINIAN ENGLISH WITH ARABIC SUBTITLES LITHUANIAN)
PdS65 purchase
Looks at conservation and land management. Shows how, in an age of multi - purpose land use, immediate and coordinated action is needed, involving national and local legislation, environmental groups, farmers, landowners and the public. Part two of two parts.
Geography - World; Science - Natural
Dist - CFLVIS **Prod** - OPTIC 1993

Managing our resources 30 MIN
VHS / U-matic
Forests of the world series
Color (J H G)
$270.00, $320.00 purchase, $60.00 rental
Covers a range of issues from tree farms to ecosystem management in the United States, New Zealand and parts of Africa. Touches on the vital chemical resources for medicine extracted from trees and private forest lands and the risks of monoculture tree farms.
Science - Natural
Dist - NDIM **Prod** - NRKTV 1993

Managing pain 18 MIN
VHS
Color (G)
$149.00 purchase, $75.00 rental _ #UW5255
Looks at what can be done about pain besides taking aspirin. Shows how some doctors brush off patients with pain, while others are staffing Pain Centers. Examines some of the latest research on the nature of pain and its treatment and points out old standby treatments such as massage.
Health and Safety
Dist - FOTH

Managing People 52 MIN
Cassette / U-matic / VHS
Wharton Executive Development Video Series
Color (G)
$249.00, $189.00 purchase
Features Dr Charles Dwyer, University of Pennsylvania. Explains why managers lapse into self - limiting styles of management. Teaches substitute behaviors which expand human influence and maximize organizational power. Includes the video, a 48 - minute audiocassette and a study guide. Part of a series.
Business and Economics; Guidance and Counseling; Psychology
Dist - KANSKE

Managing people 68 MIN
VHS
Color (PRO IND A) (DUTCH FRENCH)
$695.00 purchase _ #VIM09
Describes styles of management - characteristics, behavior features, advantages and disadvantages, outcomes of each. Assists managers in understanding the value of forming appropriate matches between themselves and employees. Presenter Prof Paul Evans uses the viewpoint of the line managers.
Business and Economics
Dist - EXTR

Managing People for Project Success 30 MIN
U-matic / VHS
Project Management Series
Color
Tells how to motivate a project team. Demonstrates leadership styles. Deals with conflict resolution.
Business and Economics; Psychology
Dist - ITCORP **Prod** - ITCORP

Managing People for Project Success 30 MIN
VHS / 16mm
Project Management Series
Color (PRO)
$400.00 purchase, $100.00 rental
Includes Motivating Your Project Team, Leadership Styles, Manager Authority and Interpersonal Influences and Conflict Resolution. Part of a six - part series on project management.
Business and Economics; Industrial and Technical Education; Psychology
Dist - ISA **Prod** - ISA

Managing people pressures 20 MIN
VHS
Managing job stress series
Color (A PRO IND COR)
$95.00 purchase _ #VJSV4
Takes aim at a problem faced by almost everyone - work-related stress. Addresses various work-environment issues that affect everyone from blue-collar workers to executives to volunteers. Outlines how workers can best manage conflict to reduce workplace stress. Describes six skills that help workers better manage people pressures. Includes leader guide and five participant guides. Part four of a six-part series.
Psychology
Dist - WHLPSN

Managing people pressures 15 MIN
VHS
Managing job stress series
Color (COR)
$89.00 purchase _ #WMP/WPA
Provides information to help employees assess the extent and cause of 'people pressures' at work. Presents various methods of handling interpersonal conflict, demonstrating how to apply each example to a situation an employee may have experienced. Offers six skills for managing people pressures on the job. Part of a six - part series.
Guidance and Counseling; Psychology
Dist - ADVANM

Managing people problems - are you really listening 15 MIN
VHS
Color (C)
$31.50 rental _ #24169; $31.50 rental _ #24169
Presents advice on how to listen to employees and determine their underlying fellings and attitudes.
Business and Economics; Guidance and Counseling; Social Science
Dist - PSU **Prod** - EBEC
EBEC

Managing people problems series
Are you really listening 15 MIN
Dealing with Different Personalities 14 MIN
Motivating employees trapped on a plateau 18 MIN
Dist - VLEARN

Managing people through change 19 MIN
VHS / U-matic / 16mm
Color (H C A)
$495.00, $375.00, $345.00 purchase _ #A563; $55.00 purchase, $130.00 rental; LC 90-705191
Demonstrates the four phases people typically go through in response to corporate changes. Examines the manager's role in each phase. Includes teacher's guide.
Business and Economics; Guidance and Counseling; Psychology
Dist - BARR **Prod** - BARR 1989
VLEARN

Managing performance - 3
U-matic / VHS / BETA
Synergy - EEO, diversity and management series
Color; CC; PAL (IND PRO G)
$895.00 purchase
Reveals that EEO liabilities as well as low morale and productivity can be avoided when managers take a proactive response to problems. Discloses that problems don't go away when they are ignored - they frequently get worse. Uses case studies to illustrate problems related to - co - worker issues and hostile environments; sexual harassment; workforce reductions and EEO issues. Includes 20 participant manuals. Part of a series showing managers how to apply EEO guidelines in managing a diverse workforce.
Business and Economics; Guidance and Counseling
Dist - BNA **Prod** - BNA

Managing performance problems 26 MIN
VHS / 16mm / U-matic
Color (C A G PRO)
$525.00, $375.00, $400.00 _ #C515; $595.00 purchase, $140.00 rental
Gives insights into dealing with the employee who is performing poorly despite supervisory efforts to motivate and develop the employee. Dramatizes some of the most common job performance problems such as a disorganized employee, a person whose personal problems are affecting job performance, two employees with conflicting work styles or one with a poor job fit. Stresses the importance of dealing with performance deficiencies by following an organized process.
Business and Economics; Social Science
Dist - BARR **Prod** - BARR 1987
VLEARN

Managing PMS - A Delicate balance 20 MIN
VHS / U-matic
Color (J H G)
$240.00, $290.00 purchase, $50.00 rental
Features leading authorities who explain Premenstrual Syndrome. Looks at its characteristics, its possible causes and current treatment options. Produced by Madison Pharmacy Associates.
Health and Safety
Dist - NDIM

Managing PMS - a delicate balance 38 MIN
VHS
Color (G I J H)
$49.95 purchase _ #SD03
Studies what PMS is and isn't, the origins, causes, and symptoms of PMS, self help techniques, prescription therapy, the pros and cons of treatment options, and how others can understand and help the PMS patient. Includes a second part, an audio cassette featuring a 10 - minute exercise - relaxation segment.
Health and Safety; Sociology
Dist - SVIP

Managing possessions 35 MIN
VHS
Color (R G)
$19.95 purchase _ #9322 - X
Features Christian financial expert Larry Burkett who discusses the management of possessions, including major purchases and insurance plans.
Business and Economics; Religion and Philosophy
Dist - MOODY **Prod** - MOODY 1994

Managing problem people series - case studies in leadership 85 MIN
VHS
Managing problem people series
Color (A PRO IND)
$2,115.00 purchase, $590.00 rental
Presents six dramatic vignettes exploring how apathy and resentment develop in employees. Suggests that managerial behavior can often be a causal factor in such cases.
Business and Economics; Guidance and Counseling; Psychology
Dist - VLEARN **Prod** - VIDART

Managing Problem People Series
Big Mouth Billy 17 MIN
Lazy Linda 15 MIN
Moaning Minnie 19 MIN
Rulebound Reggie 12 MIN
Silent Sam 16 MIN
Wimpy Wendy 18 MIN
Dist - VIDART

Managing problem people series
Managing problem people series - case studies in leadership 85 MIN
Dist - VLEARN

Managing process safety - a view from the top 16 MIN
VHS
Color (IND)
$495.00 purchase, $95.00 rental _ #800 - 80
Provides an overview of process safety for top and middle management. Reviews the primary elements of a chemical safety program from a management perspective.
Business and Economics; Health and Safety
Dist - ITSC **Prod** - ITSC

Managing Production and Inventory using Forecasts 60 MIN
VHS / BETA
Manufacturing Series
(IND)
Shows the integration of forecasting with production and inventory functions.
Business and Economics
Dist - COMSRV **Prod** - COMSRV 1986

Managing quality dynamics 78 MIN
VHS
Color (PRO IND A) (DUTCH FRENCH)
$695.00 purchase _ #VIM18
Addresses the origination of a 'quality culture' within an organization. Assists managers in implementing quality standards by the process of repetition, understanding ISO 9000 quality standards and developing market - driven quality. Features Prof James Teboul. Introduces the video Implementing Quality Dynamics.
Business and Economics
Dist - EXTR

Managing riparian areas on forest lands 28 MIN
VHS / U-matic / Slide
Watershed management series
Color (H C A)
$130.00 purchase, $25.00 rental _ #987
Examines the nature, functions and benefits of riparian areas on forest lands. Discusses the effects of forest practices on lakes, ponds and streams, including the observed effects of increased sunlight on stream temperature and fish populations, the role of large and small woody debris in the quality and quantity of animal habitat and issues of mass soil movement.
Agriculture; Industrial and Technical Education; Science - Natural; Social Science
Dist - OSUSF **Prod** - OSUSF 1991

Managing Risk 29 MIN
U-matic / VHS
Business File Series
Color
Business and Economics
Dist - PBS **Prod** - PBS

Managing Safety Yourself 15 MIN
U-matic / VHS
Foreman's Accident Prevention Series
Color (IND)
Reviews nine 'how to' principles of good supervision for promoting safe workmanship. Contains an exercise of seven observation examples in which the foreman must detect an unsafe act or condition.
Health and Safety
Dist - GPCV **Prod** - GPCV

Managing sales stress 39 MIN
VHS
Color (PRO IND A)
$495.00 purchase, $95.00 rental _ #BBP121
Shows how stress is a built - in hazard in a sales career where personal profit hinges on individual performance. Helps salespeople learn how to turn stress into profit. Includes Companion Leader's Guide.
Business and Economics; Health and Safety; Psychology
Dist - EXTR **Prod** - BBP

Managing Secretions in Chronic Lung Disease - Emphysema
U-matic / VHS
Color (ARABIC SPANISH)
Shows how failure of ciliary action and the cough mechanisms in chronic lung disease, such as asthma, chronic bronchitis or emphysema, can be managed by means of bronchodilators, expectorants and postural drainage.
Health and Safety; Science - Natural
Dist - MIFE **Prod** - MIFE

Managing space and time for safe driving
U-matic / VHS
Color (H G)
$60.00, $40.00 purchase _ #569, #449
Shows how good drivers continually adjust their driving to maintain a safe space cushion in traffic. Stresses the need for maintaining safe following distances and the active use of the eyes in knowing what is going on ahead, to the sides and behind the driver.
Health and Safety
Dist - AAAFTS **Prod** - AAAFTS 1991

Managing spinal injury in sport series
Football - a case study 15 MIN
Hockey - a Case Study 15 MIN
Overview 15 MIN
Swimming - a Case Study 15 MIN
Dist - ACCESS

Managing Stress
U-matic / VHS
Management Training Series
Color
Business and Economics; Psychology
Dist - DELTAK **Prod** - THGHT

Managing Stress 33 MIN
U-matic / VHS / 16mm
Color (H C A)
LC 78-701934
Examines the productivity of various levels of stress. Shows how to recognize undue stress and how to handle stress.
Psychology
Dist - MGHT **Prod** - MGHT 1978

Managing Stress 30 MIN
VHS
Who's in Charge Series
Color (G)
$19.95 purchase
Examines the management of stress. Features Dr Scott Sheperd. Part of a four - part series.
Health and Safety; Psychology
Dist - WGTETV **Prod** - WGTETV

Managing stress 15 MIN
VHS / 16mm
Your health series
Color (S)
$150.00 purchase _ #276001
Provides useful information about general health issues. Outlines briefly three basic steps individuals can take towards reducing and controlling stress in their lives.
Health and Safety; Psychology; Sociology
Dist - ACCESS **Prod** - ACCESS 1987

Managing Stress 19 MIN
U-matic / VHS
Color (G)
$249.00, $149.00 purchase _ #AD - 1379
Distinguishes between positive stress, which can strengthen the immune system, and negative stress, which can increase the likelihood of heart disease, high blood pressure and cancer. Shows the effects of different types of stress and how an individual can reduce stress.
Health and Safety; Psychology; Science - Natural; Sociology
Dist - FOTH **Prod** - FOTH

Managing Stress and Anger
VHS / U-matic
Administrative Woman Series
Color (A)
Shows experts telling how to make stress a positive influence if one recognizes and manages it. Looks at causes of stress, importance of self - talk to reduce it and steps involved in conflict resolution.
Business and Economics; Psychology
Dist - GPCV **Prod** - GPCV

Managing Stress, Anxiety and Frustration 55 MIN
VHS
Color (H C)
LC 85-703931
Defines stress, analyzes its causes and effects, and provides stress managing techniques including biofeedback, meditation, progressive relaxation and guided imagery.
Psychology
Dist - HRMC **Prod** - HRMC

Managing Stress, Anxiety, and Frustration 50 MIN
VHS
Color (H)
Defines stress and analyzes its causes and effects. Provides specific techniques for managing stress, including meditation, and progressive relaxation.
Psychology
Dist - IBIS **Prod** - IBIS 1980

Managing stress for mental fitness 20 MIN
VHS
Color (A PRO)
$495.00 purchase, $150.00 rental
Looks at stress management techniques that can be used at work and at home for mental health. Uses interviews and role - plays to emphasize ways to recognize the effects of stress on individuals.
Business and Economics; Health and Safety; Psychology
Dist - DHB **Prod** - CRISP 1993

Managing stress - Part 1 21 MIN
VHS / U-matic / BETA
Stress series
Color (C PRO)
$150.00 purchase _ #131.7
Presents a video transfer from slide program which describes the relaxation response as a means of preventing and alleviating undue stress. Surveys several techniqes for eliciting the response, including yoga, meditation, autogenic training and progressive relaxation. Discusses biofeedback as an avenue for learning control of the autonomic nervous system. Part of a series on stress.
Health and Safety; Psychology; Religion and Philosophy
Dist - CONMED **Prod** - CONMED

Managing stress - Part 2 28 MIN
VHS / U-matic / BETA
Stress series
Color (C PRO)
$150.00 purchase _ #131.8
Presents a video transfer from slide program which emphasizes the assessment of past stressful experiences and the realistic anticipation of future stressors as important aspects of planning for and controlling stress. Describes characteristics of the 'effective coper' and presents the 'stress innoculation program' as one means of improving coping techniques. Suggests several ways to slow down a busy life and examines the pros and cons of leaving a stressful environment. Part of a series on stress.
Health and Safety; Psychology
Dist - CONMED **Prod** - CONMED

Managing stress series
The Time bomb within 14 MIN
What the World Dishes Out 15 MIN
What You Bring on Yourself 15 MIN
Dist - CENTEF
CORF

Managing the aggressive patient 30 MIN
VHS
Color (PRO C)
$285.00 purchase, $70.00 rental _ #6529
Points out factors that may increase agitation in an aggressive patient. Identifies the clients at risk for aggressive behavior and analyzes nursing interventions that minimize aggression. Covers verbal and non - verbal cues to watch for and what to do and not to do in a heated situation. The importance of understanding how to minimize the risks associated with aggressive patients cannot be overly - stressed. Reveals that it is easier to identify and minimize behaviors that indicate agitation than to manage an out - of - control client. Uses scenarios to illustrate key concepts.
Health and Safety
Dist - AJN **Prod** - HESCTV

Managing the data base environment series
Concerns of End Users 60 MIN
Data administration 60 MIN
Data base is a change in management 60 MIN
Logical Data Base Design - the Key to Success 60 MIN
The View from the Top 60 MIN
Dist - DELTAK

Managing the Decision 60 MIN
VHS / U-matic
Missiles of October - a Case Study in Decision Making Series
Color
Business and Economics; Civics and Political Systems; History - World
Dist - DELTAK **Prod** - LCOA

Managing the Executive Branch 60 MIN
U-matic / VHS
Every Four Years Series
Color (I)
LC 81-706957
Explores how a president gets things done. Examines the growth in presidential staff and the ways modern presidents have worked with their staff members.
Civics and Political Systems
Dist - AITECH **Prod** - WHYY 1980

Managing the experience of labor and delivery
Videodisc
(PRO C)
$1300.00 purchase _ #C891 - IV - 024
Presents a Level III interactive program to train third and fourth year nursing students and nurses. Simulates normal labor and delivery beginning with the introduciton of the laboring patient and husband as she is admitted to the hospital. Requires student selection of patient assessment information and active participation in collecting data. Offers four distinct sections - Beginning of Administration, Beginning of Labor, Beginning of Delivery and Other Entry Options. Ask distributor about specific technical requirements. Presented by Barbara R Gilman, Elizabeth Weiner and Jeffry Gordon, University of Cincinnati Medical Center.
Computer Science; Health and Safety
Dist - HSCIC

Managing the Information Resource 45 MIN
VHS / U-matic
Information Resource Management - Challenge for the 1980s Series
Color
Defines and explains information management and its implications for organizations of today and tomorrow.
Industrial and Technical Education; Psychology
Dist - DELTAK **Prod** - DELTAK

Managing the Job 66 FRS
VHS / U-matic
Effective Office Worker Series
Color
Looks at the five 'w's' of organization and offers 13 ways to better organization.
Psychology
Dist - RESEM **Prod** - RESEM

Managing the Journey 60 MIN
VHS / U-matic
Color (G PRO)
$795.00, $695.00 purchase, $250.00 rental
Discusses the four levels of change and the four successive leadership styles which enhance the process of change. Features Dr Ken Blanchard, author of the 'One Minute Manager.'
Business and Economics; Guidance and Counseling; Psychology
Dist - VPHI **Prod** - VPHI 1989

Managing the journey 75 MIN
U-matic / VHS
Color (G PRO A)
$995.00, $895.00 purchase, $250.00 rental
Examines organizational behavior. Shows managers and leaders how to bring about change. Features Dr Ken Blanchard.
Business and Economics; Guidance and Counseling; Psychology; Sociology
Dist - MAGVID **Prod** - MAGVID 1989

Managing the Journey
VHS / 16mm
Color (PRO)
$895.00 purchase, $250.00 rental
Features Dr Ken Blanchard. Teaches managers and leaders how to bring about change. Discusses the four levels of change and the leadership styles each level requires.
Business and Economics; Guidance and Counseling; Psychology
Dist - VICOM **Prod** - VICOM 1990

Managing the Journey 75 MIN
VHS / 16mm
Color (PRO)
$695.00 purchase, $255.00 rental, $50.00 preview
Features Dr Ken Blanchard who shows how to affect change in businesses. Discusses different leadership styles and how to gradually empower employees with more responsibility. Includes support materials.
Business and Economics; Education; Psychology; Sociology
Dist - UTM **Prod** - UTM

Managing the knowledge specialists 10 MIN
U-matic / VHS
Meeting the challenge with Dr Warren Bennis series
Color (C A G)
$250.00 purchase _ #V215
Presents Drs Warren Bennis and Peter Drucker who conduct a seminar on managing knowledge specialists. Gives examples of what has worked in real companies. Focuses on the responsibility of management for providing solutions in a rapidly changing global economy. Part of a five - part series.
Business and Economics; Computer Science; Industrial and Technical Education
Dist - BARR **Prod** - HILSU 1992

Managing the old growth forest 21 MIN
VHS / U-matic
Color (H C G)
$310.00, $285.00 purchase _ #V390
Interviews people who represent both sides of the debate over 'old growth' forests. Includes representatives of the forest products industry and scientists.
Agriculture; Business and Economics; Science - Natural; Social Science
Dist - BARR **Prod** - CEPRO 1987

Managing the Overseas Assignment 29 MIN
VHS / U-matic
Going International Series
Color (A)
LC 84-706118
Explains cultural and business practices in various foreign countries, such as Japan,. Saudi Arabia, Venezuela, India, England and Mexico in order to help American families adjust to living abroad.
Geography - World; Social Science
Dist - COPGRG **Prod** - COPGRG 1983

Managing the quality of your clinical practice 31 MIN
VHS
Color (C PRO)
$250.00 purchase, $100.00 rental _ #42 - 2575, #42 - 2575R
Shows nurses how they can achieve quality care on a professional and personal level. Orients staff nurses and students to quality initiatives in any health care setting. Features staff nurses who share their feelings about improving the quality of their practice - from communication to careful documentation to juggling the demands of a high - pressure job. Quality experts from leading hospitals give practical ideas to make continuous quality improvement work for nurses and their patients. Includes facilitator's guide and CEs - certification education units.
Business and Economics; Health and Safety
Dist - NLFN **Prod** - NLFN

Managing the relationship - 6 45 MIN
VHS
Working with Japan series
Color (C PRO G)
$395.00 purchase, $175.00 rental _ #825
Examines a number of difficult management issues often arising in trans - Pacific alliances. Presents practical solutions from veteran Japanese and Western business people. Discusses selecting and training personnel for working with the Japanese, the roles of suppliers and and qualitiy expectations. Examines the differences in ethical standards, problem - solving styles and government regulations. Looks at building business relationships with Japan into global strategies for success in corporate development, marketing, human resources and technology. Part six of a six - part series on business relations with Japan. Produced by Intercultural Training Resources, Inc.
Business and Economics; Civics and Political Systems; Geography - World; Home Economics; Psychology
Dist - INCUL

Managing the Transition 30 MIN
U-matic / VHS
Third Wave Series
Color
Business and Economics; Sociology
Dist - DELTAK **Prod** - TRIWVE

Managing the Transition to IRM 45 MIN
U-matic / VHS
Information Resource Management - Challenge for the 1980s Series
Color
Examines the critical issues of information management and discusses what organizations can do today to implement it.
Industrial and Technical Education; Psychology
Dist - DELTAK **Prod** - DELTAK

Managing the troubled employee 24 MIN
U-matic / VHS
Color (A)
$275.00 purchase, $50.00 rental
Provides managers with an approach to the detection and confrontation of the troubled employee.
Business and Economics; Psychology
Dist - SUTHRB **Prod** - SUTHRB
VLEARN

Managing the troubled employee 30 MIN
VHS / U-matic / BETA
Color; CC (G IND PRO C)
Demonstrates a practical, five - step recognition - intervention process that enables managers and supervisors to deal effectively and legally with troubled employees. Emphasizes that managers should focus on performance issues rather than becoming involved in employees' personal lives or infringing on their rights. Includes a trainer's manual and 20 participant manuals.
Business and Economics; Guidance and Counseling; Psychology
Dist - BNA **Prod** - BNA

Managing the turmoil creating by implementing TQM - the transition phase 70 MIN
VHS
Color; PAL (C G PRO)
$89.95, $69.95, $16.00 purchase _ #92AST - V - M49, #92AST - M49
Shows how to assess a company on the continuum of total - quality management. Focuses on phase II - transition - of a three - part, quality - implementation model. Describes how turmoil is a sign of success and a necessary stage. Participants share their experiences with TQM implementation and shows techniques to manage the change, including ways to handle constructive dissent. Uses real life case strategies and audience participation to enliven the presentation. Features Elaine Biech and Dan Greene, partners, ebb associates, Portage WI.
Business and Economics; Psychology
Dist - MOBILE **Prod** - ASTD 1992

Managing time 11 MIN
VHS / U-matic
Applied management series
Color
Business and Economics
Dist - DELTAK **Prod** - ORGDYN

Managing Time - Professional and Personal 30 MIN
U-matic / VHS
Time Management for Management Series Pt 6
Color (A)
Shows managers how they can make use of all their time, personal as well as professional, and balance demands in both spheres. Details how to define and accomplish their free time activities, relating each to long - term goals.
Business and Economics; Psychology
Dist - TIMLIF **Prod** - TIMLIF 1981

Managing to be green 30 MIN
VHS
Business matters series
Color (A)
PdS65 purchase
Visits three firms that have decided that good environmental practices are vital for success in the 1990s with Richard North. Talks to directors, managers and staff about changing attitudes and practices, environmental audits, selling 'greenness' and the role of environmental consultants.
Business and Economics; Science - Natural
Dist - BBCENE

Managing to keep the customer 30 MIN
VHS
Color (G A)
$195.00 purchase _ #VMKEEP - 721
Presents a video version of the book 'Managing To Keep The Customer' by Robert L Desatnick, former human resources vice - president for both McDonald's and Chase Manhattan Bank. Covers strategies for developing superior customer service performance at all levels. Includes a copy of the book.
Business and Economics; Guidance and Counseling; Psychology
Dist - PRODUC **Prod** - PRODUC

Managing to Survive 28 MIN
U-matic / VHS / 16mm
Finance for Managers Series
Color (A)
LC 81-701630
Dramatizes the events which lead to the bankruptcy of an English furniture - manufacturing firm. Designed to promote discussion of general financial principles and specific problems related to roles of managers and the development of supporting skills and attitudes.
Business and Economics
Dist - IFB **Prod** - LOYDSB 1980

Managing to Win 23 MIN
VHS / U-matic
Color (A)
Shows former University of Arkansas football coach Lou Holtz explaining how he motivates and manages his teams to win, just as a businessmen must motivate and manage his employees. Treats related issues that bear on both sports and business success. Narrated by Pat Summerall.
Business and Economics; Physical Education and Recreation; Psychology
Dist - SFTI **Prod** - SFTI

Managing underground storage tanks 18 MIN
U-matic / VHS / BETA
Color (G PRO)
$29.95, $130.00 purchase _ #LSTF42
Explains installation, corrosion protection, leak detection and tank inventory. Shows how leaks from USTs contaminate soil and shows methods for dealing with leaks.
Industrial and Technical Education
Dist - FEDU **Prod** - USEPA 1987

Managing Up 17 MIN
VHS / 16mm
Color (PRO)
$450.00 purchase, $85.00 rental, $50.00 preview
Illustrates and reinforces practical techniques for partnership between employees and employer. Shows employees behavior management and cooperation with the supervisor. Based on book by Michael LeBoeuf. Includes support materials.
Business and Economics; Psychology
Dist - UTM **Prod** - UTM

Managing urinary incontinence in older adults 120 MIN
VHS
Virginia Geriatric Education Center Video Conference series
Color (G C PRO)
$149.00 purchase, $55.00 rental
Deals with diagnosing, treating and managing incontinence of patients in the home, in the nursing home and in residential care settings.
Health and Safety
Dist - TNF **Prod** - VGEREC

Managing with Alzheimer's Disease 30 MIN
VHS / U-matic
Color
Focuses on solutions to the problems encountered by anyone caring for a person with Alzheimer's disease. Includes information on when and how to choose a nursing facility.
Health and Safety; Psychology
Dist - GSHDME **Prod** - GSHDME

Managing with Alzheimer's disease 29 MIN
VHS
Color (G PRO C)
$200.00 purchase _ #NR - 01
Teaches skills for caregivers within the home of the Alzheimer's patient. Emphasizes the need to create a calm, consistent routine environment. Helps family and friends to understand the medical and psychiatric evaluations required to rule out other conditions. Recommends that the impaired person be included in decision making as much as possible.
Health and Safety
Dist - MIFE **Prod** - MIFE

Managing with Daceasy 4.3
VHS
Daceasy 4.3 series
Color (G)
$29.95 purchase _ #VIA051
Shows how to manage Daceasy 4.3 in accounting.
Computer Science
Dist - SIV

Managing Your Boss 30 MIN
VHS / 16mm
Harvard Business Review Video Series
(A PRO)
$650.00 purchase _ #AG - 4979M
Demonstrates how to communicate needs and goals to superiors in order to create more effective, productive relationships.
Business and Economics; Psychology
Dist - CORF **Prod** - WGBH 1987

Managing Your Emotions 11 MIN
16mm / U-matic / VHS
Color (J H C)
$270, $190 purchase _ #3119
Shows how children can deal with strong emotions and respond constructively to them.
Psychology
Dist - CORF

Managing your high blood pressure with drugs 4 MIN
VHS / U-matic
Color
Explains necessity for controlling high blood pressure, or hypertension, which if untreated can damage the blood circulatory system and lead to kidney failure, stroke, heart disease or other complications. Describes benefits and possible side effects of physician - prescribed drugs and cites importance of developing habit of taking medication regularly and keeping a record of it.
Health and Safety; Science - Natural
Dist - MEDCOM **Prod** - MEDCOM

Managing your law firm series
Basic financial management 40 MIN
How to Avoid Self - Malpractice 40 MIN
Winning Isn't Everything - Improving Client Relations 35 MIN
Dist - ABACPE

Managing Your Molecule 15 MIN
VHS / U-matic
Time Management for Managers and Professionals Series
Color
Business and Economics; Psychology
Dist - DELTAK **Prod** - DELTAK

Managing Your Personal Finances
VHS
Color (H C A PRO)
$89.00 purchase _ #MC900
Demonstrates how to handle personal income and expenses, develop credit worthiness and avoid financial pitfalls.
Business and Economics
Dist - AAVIM **Prod** - AAVIM 1990

Managing Your Time 63 FRS
U-matic / VHS
Effective Office Worker Series
Color
Shows office workers more than 20 ways to manage their time more effectively. Offers tips for saving time in typing, filing and dictation.
Psychology
Dist - RESEM **Prod** - RESEM

Managing Your Time 18 MIN
U-matic / VHS
Hub of the Wheel Series
Color (G)
$249.00, $149.00 purchase _ #AD - 1565
Highlights the importance of time planning. Provides details for developing a pro - active time plan. Describes techniques for protecting the plan once it is established. Part of a ten - part series for office professionals.
Business and Economics
Dist - FOTH **Prod** - FOTH

Managing Your Time 18 MIN
VHS / 16mm

Color (PRO)
$295.00 purchase, $95.00 rental, $35.00 preview
Explains the importance of time management in the business world. Describes techniques for establishing and maintaining a time management plan.
Business and Economics; Education; Psychology
Dist - UTM **Prod** - UTM

Managing your time - Just another Monday 14 MIN
VHS
The Employee development series
Color (PRO IND A)
$495.00 purchase, $150.00 rental _ #ITC29
Presents part four of a ten - part series designed to prepare employees for coping with workplace demands in a skillful and confident manner. Enables supervisors and managers to improve their skills and abilities as they work with their peers. Includes a leader's guide, instructions for self - study and a participant's booklet.
Business and Economics; Guidance and Counseling
Dist - EXTR **Prod** - ITRC

Managing your weight without dieting 25 MIN
VHS
Color (I J H C)
$169.00 purchase _ #FG - 111 - VS
Offers an easy - to - understand approach to weight management using proper nutrition and appropriate exercise. Explores why young people are so prone to high - fat diets and why they shun regular exercise. Focuses on teens becoming obsessed with thinness - especially young women - and how this can lead to dangerous eating disorders. Addresses healthy eating and exercise habits that students can use throughout their lifetime. Exposes popular weight - reduction frauds such as wrapping the body in plastic, fad diets and reducing creams. Consultant - Lori Wiersema.
Health and Safety; Physical Education and Recreation; Social Science
Dist - HRMC **Prod** - HRMC 1994

Managing Yourself 30 MIN
U-matic / VHS
Stress Management - a Positive Strategy Series Pt 3
Color (A)
LC 82-706501
Studies how to manage anxiety through the management of thoughts, feelings and reactions to stress by using relaxation skills and behavioral techniques.
Psychology
Dist - TIMLIF **Prod** - TIMLIF 1982

Manassas 15 MIN
U-matic / VHS
Color (J A)
Portrays the first (Bull Run) and second battles of Manassas. Illustrates the consequences paid by both North and South in the Civil War.
History - United States
Dist - USNAC **Prod** - USNPS 1983

Mance Lipscomb in concert 60 MIN
VHS
Color (G)
$24.95 purchase _ #VDZ - LP01
Focuses on guitarist Mance Lipscomb, son of a former slave and a tenant farmer who played guitar and sang songs for his neighbors. Reveals that he was 'discovered' in 1960 and within a short while was recording albums and performing at festivals and clubs nation wide. Presents a 1969 television concert which includes the songs So Different Blues; Take Me Back; Going Down Slow; Keep on Trucking; Alcohol Blues; Angel Child; Silver City; Night Time is the Right Time; Key to the Highway; You Got to See Your Mama Every Night; Mama Don't Allow; Long Way to Tipperary; Baby, You Don't Have to Go; When the Saints Go Marching in; Motherless Children; I Want to Do Something for You.
Fine Arts
Dist - HOMETA **Prod** - HOMETA 1994

Manchild Revisited - a Commentary by Claude Brown 60 MIN
VHS
Color (G)
$100.00 purchase _ #MANC - 000
Features author Claude Brown as he gives an inside view of urban black life. Focuses on the lives of young black men, suggesting that crime, disillusionment and fear are destroying their future. Offers suggestions for solving these problems.
Sociology
Dist - PBS **Prod** - WXXITV 1987

Mandabi 90 MIN
16mm
Color (I)
LC 76-707580
A story about a man who receives a money order that threatens to destroy the traditional fabric of his life is used to point out the problems of modern Africa as a civilization struggling to recapture its own rich heritage after colonial corruption.
Geography - World; History - World; Psychology; Sociology
Dist - GROVE **Prod** - DOMIR 1969

The Mandala 60 MIN
VHS
The Buddhist path with Detong Cho Yin series
Color (G)
$34.95 purchase _ #P13f
Explains the complete Buddhist path to enlightenment. Features Buddhist nun Detong Cho Yin, who gives insights and meditations for the beginner or advanced practitioner. Demonstrates visualizations to place the mind within tantric practice. Part of a series of six easy - to - follow videos.
Religion and Philosophy
Dist - HP

Mandala - world of the mystic circle 50 MIN
VHS
Color (G)
$29.95 purchase _ #MAWOMY
Documents the creation and ritual dismantling of the sacred Kalachakra sand mandala by four Tibetan monks during August, 1991, in the Buffalo Museum of Art. Explores the universal motif and archetype of the mandala on a myriad of levels through revealing interviews with the monks and with others. Depicts numerous examples of mandalas from nature and other cultures. Produced by Martin McGee.
Religion and Philosophy
Dist - SNOWLI

Mandalas - vision of heaven and earth 17 MIN
VHS
Color (G)
$29.95 purchase
Features a flowing sequence of images that evoke our sense of the sacred in all life. Presents a production by Mirtala Bentov, artist and wife of scientist Itzhak Bentov.
Fine Arts
Dist - HP

Mandarin Pancakes 29 MIN
Videoreel / VT2
Joyce Chen Cooks Series
Color
Features Joyce Chen showing how to adapt Chinese recipes so they can be prepared in the American kitchen and still retain the authentic flavor. Demonstrates how to prepare mandarin pancakes.
Geography - World; Home Economics
Dist - PBS **Prod** - WGBHTV

The Mandarin Revolution 57 MIN
16mm / U-matic / VHS
Age of Uncertainty Series
Color (H C A)
LC 77-701490
Focuses on the worldwide slump that threatened economic disaster after World War I and the role of economist John Maynard Keynes' ideas on saving the West. Based on the book The Age Of Uncertainty by John Kenneth Galbraith.
Business and Economics
Dist - FI **Prod** - BBCL 1977

Mandarin Revolution, the, Pt 1 28 MIN
16mm / U-matic / VHS
Age of Uncertainty Series
Color (H C A)
LC 77-701490
Focuses on the worldwide slump that threatened economic disaster after World War I and the role of economist John Maynard Keynes' ideas on saving the West. Based on the book The Age Of Uncertainty by John Kenneth Galbraith.
Business and Economics
Dist - FI **Prod** - BBCL 1977

Mandarin Revolution, the, Pt 2 29 MIN
16mm / U-matic / VHS
Age of Uncertainty Series
Color (H C A)
LC 77-701490
Focuses on the worldwide slump that threatened economic disaster after World War I and the role of economist John Maynard Keynes' ideas on saving the West. Based on the book The Age Of Uncertainty by John Kenneth Galbraith.
Business and Economics
Dist - FI **Prod** - BBCL 1977

Mandela 135 MIN
VHS
Color (G)
$79.95 purchase _ #S02118
Presents a dramatic biography of black South African leader Nelson Mandela. Traces Mandela's shift in philosophy from passive resistance to armed struggle. Stars Danny Glover and Alfre Woodard. Written by Ronald Harwood. Filmed in Zimbabwe.
Geography - World; Sociology
Dist - UILL

Mandela 52 MIN
U-matic / VHS / 16mm
Color (J H C A)
Account of the extraordinary public and private relationship between the imprisoned leader of black resistance to apartheid, the George Washington of black South Africa, and his wife who took up the burden of leadership.
Geography - World; History - United States; History - World; Sociology
Dist - CANWRL **Prod** - CANWRL 1986

Mandela - the man and his country 50 MIN
VHS
Color (G)
$19.98 purchase _ #UPC 30306 - 6023 - 3; $19.98 purchase _ #UPC 30306 - 6023 -3
Chronicles the life of Nelson Mandela against the backdrop of South African politics. Includes rare footage and exclusive interviews.
Civics and Political Systems; History - World
Dist - INSTRU **Prod** - ABCNEW
CAMV

Mandibular Block Anesthesia - Gow - Gates Technique 9 MIN
16mm
Color
LC 79-700986
Describes the Gow - Gates method of mandibular block anesthesia, as well as extra - and intra - oral landmarks.
Health and Safety
Dist - USNAC **Prod** - VADTC 1978

Mandibular movements 12 MIN
VHS / U-matic
Color (C PRO)
$395.00 purchase, $80.00 rental _ #C881 - VI - 011
Introduces medical students to procedures for examination and assessment of mandibular and condylar movements. Shows that a kinesiograph and headgear fitted with transducers offers the means for accurate examination of mandibular movements. Presented by Dr Max O Hutchins.
Health and Safety; Science - Natural
Dist - HSCIC

Mandibular Prognathism 43 MIN
16mm
Color
LC FIE56-30
Demonstrates the two - stage operation for the correction of a mandibular prognathism. Shows in considerable detail preoperative and postoperative studies as well as the two stages of the operation. Includes inserts of X - ray studies and medical sketches demonstrating various stages in the surgical procedure.
Health and Safety; Science - Natural
Dist - USNAC **Prod** - USVA 1956

Mandibular Reconstruction - Cancellous Bone from the Iliac Crest in an Alloplastic Mesh 21 MIN
VHS / U-matic
Color (PRO)
Shows an implantable material, 'alloplastic mesh,' which can be easily molded and cut, used to reconstruct osseous contour defects. Demonstrates the technique to reconstruct a large section of a patient's mandible which had been resected to remove a tumor.
Health and Safety
Dist - WFP **Prod** - WFP

Mandibular Vestibuloplasty with Skin Graft 18 MIN
16mm
Color (PRO)
LC 77-701470
Demonstrates the surgical procedure for increasing the quantity of the mandibular denture bearing area by lowering the buccal, labial and lingual muscular attachments and introducing a skin graft.
Health and Safety; Science - Natural
Dist - USNAC **Prod** - VADTC 1977

Mandolin of Bill Monroe series
Presents a two - part series featuring Bill Monroe, 'Father of Bluegrass.' Demontrates the mandolin techniques and repertoire of Monroe on over 25 tunes in Video One. Includes bluegrass musician Sam Bush who dissects 16 pieces played by Monroe, taking them apart in note - by - note detail. Uses split - screens and close - ups, as well as replays of Monroe's demonstrations on Video Two.
A Detailed analysis by Sam Bush - video two 90 MIN
Mandolin of Bill Monroe series 180 MIN
One - on - one with the master - Video One 90 MIN
Dist - HOMETA **Prod** - HOMETA 1977

The Mandolin of Norman Blake 90 MIN
VHS
Color (G)

$49.95 purchase _ #VD - BLA - MN01
Features Norman Blake with Nancy Blake on guitar and second mandolin. Teaches old - time instrumentals in the Celtic and Southern mountain tradition. Shares Norman Blake's personal tips and advice on tuning, phrasing, ornaments, double - stops, tremolos, drones, split - strings and more. Featues the songs John Brown's March; Campbell's Farewell to Red Gap; The Hollow Poplar; Father's Hall; The Little Fair Child; Jack Danielson's Reel; Green Castle Hornpipe; Mandolin Fanfare; and Blake's March. Includes tablature.
Fine Arts
Dist - HOMETA **Prod** - HOMETA

Mandrills 12 MIN
VHS
Animal profile series
Color (P I)
$59.95 purchase _ #RB8126
Studies mandrills, the largest baboons and also the largest members of the monkey family. Examines the colorful faces and the limb adaptation of baboons which allows them to walk long distances. Part of a series on animals which looks at examples from the mammal, snake and bird classes, filmed in their natural habitat.
Science - Natural
Dist - REVID **Prod** - REVID 1990

Mandy's Checkup 15 MIN
16mm
Color (K)
LC 81-701639
Uses clowns to show what a physical checkup is like. Points out that it is not painful or unpleasant, and that just because a person feels fine does not mean that he or she is healthy.
Health and Safety; Home Economics
Dist - USNAC **Prod** - USDHHS 1981

Mandy's Grandmother 30 MIN
U-matic / VHS / 16mm
Color (I J)
$89.00 purchase _ #SO1107; LC 79-700655
Presents a story about a young tomboy and her prim grandmother who quickly forget the disappointment of their first meeting and become friends. Based on the book Mandy's Grandmother by Liesel Skorpen. Features Maureen O'Sullivan and Amy Levitan.
Fine Arts; Literature and Drama
Dist - PHENIX **Prod** - SUGERA 1978
UILL

Maneater 60 MIN
VHS / U-matic / 16mm
Last Frontier Series
Color; Mono
MV $225.00 _ MP $550.00
Gives account of the most unwelcome visitor to the Florida Coast - the shark. John Stoneman and members of the Foundation for Ocean Research investigate.
Science - Natural
Dist - CTV **Prod** - MAKOF 1985

Manejando El Cambio 23 MIN
U-matic / VHS / 16mm
Color (A) (SPANISH)
A Spanish - language version of the motion picture Managing Change. Illustrates and suggests solutions to some of the special problems that confront managers when it is their responsibility to manage change. Shows how, when a new assembly line is installed and new products are introduced in an English laminating factory, unexpected problems arise.
Business and Economics; Foreign Language; Psychology
Dist - IFB **Prod** - MILLBK 1981

Manet 30 MIN
VHS
Tom Keating on painters series
Color (J H C G)
$195.00 purchase
Focuses on the painter Manet. Features Tom Keating who recreates the painting of Manet exactly as the artist did the original work and gives biographical information. Part of a six - part series on painters.
Fine Arts
Dist - LANDMK **Prod** - LANDMK 1987

Manet, an innovator in spite of himself 15 MIN
16mm
Color
Reveals that Manet's paintings were the harbingers of modern art even though they were ridiculed by critics of his time. Shows that his Olympia was called the first truly modern painting and his works inspired such impressionists as Renoir and Monet.
Fine Arts
Dist - FACSEA **Prod** - LEEN 1980

Manet - the heroism of modern life 25 MIN
VHS
Color (G)
PdS15.50 purchase _ #A4-300432
Celebrates the complexity and richness of Manet's paintings and their blend of tradition and modernity. Examines the artist's commitment to painting the history of his own era, tracing the development of his painting during the 1860s and exploring the way he used art to comment on his own time. Assesses the debt owed by Manet to the Spanish artists, especially Velasquez and Goya. Documents Manet's 1865 visit to Spain.
Fine Arts
Dist - AVP **Prod** - NATLGL

Mangement's new responsibilities - Program 2 28 MIN
VHS
Subtle sexual harassment series
Color (G C PRO)
$425.00 purchase, $150.00 rental
Examines the liabilities and responsibilities managers and supervisors bear in setting standards for interpersonal and professional behavior in the work place. Pays close attention to the critical role managers must play in identifying cases of sexual harassment - blatant or subtle, addressing complaints and enforcing organization policies designed to eliminate harassment from the work environment. Part two of a two - part series on sexual harassment. Includes leader's guide and handouts.
Business and Economics; Psychology
Dist - VTCENS

Mangrove Swamps 25 MIN
U-matic / VHS / 16mm
Untamed World Series
Color; Mono (J H C A)
$400.00 film, $250.00 video, $50.00 rental
Looks at the mangrove tree and the swampland environment that is its home. Shows other vegetation and some animals found in the swamps also.
Science - Natural
Dist - CTV **Prod** - CTV 1972

Manhatta 10 MIN
16mm
B&W (G)
$20.00 rental
Presents a visual document and love poem of the New York bustle in the early 1920s by Strand and Sheller.
Fine Arts; Geography - United States
Dist - KITPAR

Manhattan 96 MIN
16mm
B&W
Stars Woody Allen as a television writer whose quest for the perfect woman leads him through a variety of relationships. Features Meryl Streep, Diane Keaton, Mariel Hemingway and Michael Murphy.
Fine Arts
Dist - UAE **Prod** - UNKNWN 1979

Manhattan Street Band 24 MIN
U-matic / VHS / 16mm
Color (I)
Presents young men from the streets of the Lower East Side of New York. Illustrates their unerring sense of musical style, steel drums, bongos and vibraphone which comprise the Manhattan Street Band.
Fine Arts; Geography - United States; Social Science
Dist - CAROUF **Prod** - GESEA

Manhole - mac
CD-ROM
(G A)
$59.00 purchase _ #1971m
Provides a journey to fantasy and wonder for kids of all ages. Uses Hypercard. For Macintosh Plus, SE and II computers. Requires 1MB RAM, floppy disk drive, Apple compatible CD - ROM drive.
Computer Science
Dist - BEP

Manhole - pc
CD-ROM
(G A)
$79.00 purchase _ #1971p
Provides a journey to fantasy and wonder for kids of all ages. For IBM PC and compatibles. Requires 640K RAM, DOS Version 3.1 or greater, floppy disk drive - hard disk drive recommended, one empty expansion slot, and an IBM compatible CD - ROM drive.
Computer Science
Dist - BEP

Manic depression I 40 MIN
VHS
Color (J H C G A)
$125.00 purchase _ #AH45645
Describes the nature and origin of manic depression, also known as bipolar disorder. Reveals that many famous people suffered from manic depression. Hosted by Brock Morris, MD.
Health and Safety; Psychology
Dist - HTHED **Prod** - HTHED

Manic depression II 20 MIN
VHS
Color (J H C G A)
$125.00 purchase _ #AH45646
Describes the nature and origin of manic depression, also known as bipolar disorder. Covers treatment options and reviews the biological causes of depression. Hosted by Brock Morris, MD.
Health and Safety; Psychology
Dist - HTHED **Prod** - HTHED

Manic depression series
Describes the nature and origin of manic depression, also known as bipolar disorder. Stresses the biological cause of depression, and covers treatment options. Reveals that many famous people suffered from manic depression. Hosted by Brock Morris, MD.
Manic depression series 60 MIN
Dist - HTHED **Prod** - HTHED

Manic depression - the agony and the ecstasy - Part I - the illness 33 MIN
VHS / U-matic
Color (PRO C)
$395.00 purchase, $80.00 rental _ #C901 - VI - 002
Examines the nature and characteristics of bi - polar disorder. Presents a general description of the disease along with the diagnostic criteria of each stage. Features Dr Brock A Morris who presents his theory regarding the possible historical origins of the conditon. Describes scientific studies of manic depressives and medical tests to determine treatment plans. Part one of a two - part series.
Health and Safety
Dist - HSCIC

Manic depression - the agony and the ecstasy - Part II - the treatment 33 MIN
U-matic / VHS
Color (PRO C)
$395.00 purchase, $80.00 rental _ #C901 - VI - 003
Examines the nature and characteristics of bi - polar disorder. Discusses the biochemical traits of the condition with a focus on the two principal neural transmitters implicated in the breakdown. Features Dr Brock A Morris. Presents an in - depth look at treatment programs past and present. Part two of a two - part series.
Health and Safety
Dist - HSCIC

Manic depression - the agony and the ecstasy series 66 MIN
VHS
Manic depression - the agony and the ecstasy series
Color (PRO C G)
$312.00 purchase _ #R901 - VI - 002S
Presents a two - part series on manic depression - bipolar disorder. Discusses the illness and the treatment. Produced by Dr Brock A Morris, Brazos Psychiatric Hospital, Waco, Texas, in association with Mending the Mind and Dub - L Tape Productions.
Health and Safety; Psychology
Dist - HSCIC

Manic depression - the agony and the ecstasy series
Manic depression - the agony and the ecstasy series 66 MIN
Dist - HSCIC

Manic Depressive Illness 17 MIN
VHS / U-matic
Color (PRO)
LC 77-730522
Discusses disturbances in mood which may reach from mania to severe depression. Discusses the classification of manic - depression and explains the types, manic, depressed and circular. Reviews lithium carbonate, a drug frequently considered in the care of patients with manic - depressive illness.
Health and Safety; Psychology
Dist - MEDCOM **Prod** - MEDCOM

Manifest destiny 30 MIN
VHS
American adventure series
Color (G)
$150.00 purchase _ #TAMA - 119
Emphasizes the Mexican - American War and its impact on U S expansion. Features the settlers who migrated to California, Oregon, Texas and other areas acquired in the war. Investigates the reasons for the conflict.
History - United States
Dist - PBS

Manifold II 10 MIN
U-matic / VHS
Color (PRO)
Shows how to assemble and use a new manifold which helps simplify multiple pressure lines used in hemodynamic monitoring.
Health and Safety
Dist - WFP **Prod** - WFP

Manila 11 MIN
16mm / U-matic / VHS
Color (J)
Explores the city of Manila, from Rizal Park to Port Santiago in the old Spanish City. Views the Chinese district, the churches, shopping centers, modern office buildings and traffic.
Geography - World; Sociology
Dist - LUF **Prod** - LUF 1979

Manimals 29 MIN
16mm / U-matic / VHS
Color
LC 78-700198
Explores the world of exotic pets and the emotions surrounding them, ranging from love and ego to comedy and tragedy.
Science - Natural
Dist - PHENIX **Prod** - OPUS 1978

Manioc Bread 11 MIN
16mm
Indians of the Orinoco - the Makiritare tribe series
Color (J H C)
Shows Makiritare women making bread from manioc roots, after removing a poison by squeezing the scraped and shredded remains in mammoth hand - woven basket - tubes. Explains that from the flour they make yuca or cassava bread, a staple of the Makiritare diet. Part of an eight - part series on the Makiritare Indians of Venezuela.
Geography - World; Home Economics; Social Science; Sociology
Dist - IFF **Prod** - IFF 1972
EDPAT

Manipulation and Actualization 30 MIN
U-matic
Color
Illustrates eight different manipulative techniques which are predominately used by people today. Discusses recent developments in the 'Manipulation and Actualization' theory.
Psychology
Dist - PSYCHF **Prod** - PSYCHF

Manipulation of dental bases and cements 15 MIN
U-matic / VHS
Color (C PRO)
$395.00 purchase, $80.00 rental _ #D840 - VI - 039
Teaches dental students, hygienists and assistants the proper techniques and procedures for using the three most widely used dental cements - zinc phosphate, zinc polycarboxylate and reinforced zinc oxide. Presented by Drs W Franklin Caughman and James W O'Hara.
Health and Safety
Dist - HSCIC

The Manipulation of Language and Meaning 30 MIN
U-matic / VHS
Language and Meaning Series
Color (C)
English Language; Psychology
Dist - GPN **Prod** - WUSFTV 1983

The Manipulative Client 30 MIN
16mm
Psychiatric - Mental Health Nursing Series
Color (PRO)
LC 77-700135
Presents course instructors Grayce Sills and Doreen James Wise and guest Mary R Bock reviewing the psychodynamics underlying manipulative behavior. Discusses nursing intervention with emphasis on consistence and communication. Shows everyday situations demonstrating manipulative behavior.
Health and Safety; Psychology
Dist - AJN **Prod** - AJN 1977

Manipulative Techniques to Assist Fluid Flow 14 MIN
VHS / U-matic
Osteopathic Examination and Manipulation Series
Color (PRO)
Applies principles of manipulation to treatment of somatic findings common in patients with upper respiratory infections. Directs palpatory examination for disturbances in tissue fluid flow to related areas of tissue tension and congestion. Demonstrates soft tissue and articulatory techniques in the cervical and thoracic spinal regions, the anterior cervical compartment and the thoracic cage.
Health and Safety; Science - Natural
Dist - MSU **Prod** - MSU

Manitoba Fish Tale 30 MIN
16mm
Color
Shows three fishermen traveling to the remote lakes of Manitoba to catch the fighting smallmouth bass, northern pike, Winnipeg perch and walleye pike.
Geography - World; Physical Education and Recreation
Dist - KAROL **Prod** - BRNSWK

Mankiller - a chief and her people 30 MIN
VHS
Author's night at the Freedom Forum series
Color (G)
$15.00 purchase _ #V94 - 04
Focuses on Wilma Mankiller, former head of the Cherokee Nation and author of the book of the same title, in part of a series on freedom of the press, free speech and free spirit.
Civics and Political Systems; Social Science; Sociology
Dist - FREEDM **Prod** - FREEDM 1994

Mankind and the Atom 20 MIN
16mm
Screen news digest series
B&W
Illustrates the birth and history, crises and challenges of the Atomic Age. Volume 10, issue two of the Screen News Digest series.
History - World; Psychology; Science - Physical; Sociology
Dist - HEARST **Prod** - HEARST 1967

Mankinda 10 MIN
16mm
B&W (G)
$15.00 rental
Experiments with the combination of verse and hand - painted images creating graphic as well as verbal excitement.
Fine Arts; Literature and Drama
Dist - CANCIN **Prod** - VANBKS 1959

Manlio Argueta - 11 - 13 - 86 67 MIN
VHS / Cassette
Poetry Center reading series
Color (G)
$15.00, $45.00 purchase _ #725 - 583
Features Argueta reading from his works, including an excerpt from a novel, at the Poetry Center, San Francisco State University. Includes an interview with question and answer session with Carlos Peron as translator.
Literature and Drama
Dist - POETRY **Prod** - POETRY 1986

Manloading and Budgeting in Project Planning 30 MIN
VHS / U-matic
Project Management Series
Color
Describes manload charts. Covers resource allocation and budget formats. Explores the use of computers in project management.
Business and Economics; Psychology
Dist - ITCORP **Prod** - ITCORP

Manly Bacon, Unholey and Two - Minute Mousse 15 MIN
Videoreel / VT2
Umbrella Series
Color
Home Economics; Psychology; Social Science
Dist - PBS **Prod** - KETCTV

Manmade Extinction 15 MIN
16mm
Science in Action Series
Color (C)
Deals with the efforts of ecologists and research scientists to stave off and control the extermination of the many species imperiled by modern civilization.
Science; Science - Natural
Dist - COUNFI **Prod** - ALLFP

Manna of the South Seas 20 MIN
16mm
Color (I J H)
Shows the many uses of the coconut in the Fiji Islands - for food, to make baskets and for trade in the form of copra.
Geography - World
Dist - MMP **Prod** - MMP 1954

Manne and Jazz 21 MIN
16mm
B&W
LC 75-703204
Presents a documentary depicting the professional and private life of Shelly Manne, a jazz musician.
Fine Arts
Dist - USC **Prod** - USC 1965

Manned Space Flight 1964 14 MIN
16mm
Color
Reports NASA'S manned flight programs. Includes the two - man Gemini earth - orbital and the three - man Apollo lunar landing missions.
Science; Science - Physical
Dist - THIOKL **Prod** - NASA 1964

Manned Space Flight - New Goals, New Challenges 19 MIN
16mm
Color
Shows where we stand today in manned space flight and where we will be in the future if present capability is applied to such imminent developments as Skylab, space stations and space shuttles.
Industrial and Technical Education; Science - Physical
Dist - NASA **Prod** - NASA

The Manned Spacecraft Center - Where Tomorrow Begins 30 MIN
16mm
Color
Depicts the role of the NASA Manned Spacecraft Center in the nation's space flight programs from Mercury, Gemini and Apollo through Skylab and programs of the future.
History - United States; History - World; Industrial and Technical Education; Science - Physical
Dist - NASA **Prod** - NASA

Mannerism - Italy - 10 15 MIN
VHS
Art history II - survey of the Western World series
Color (I)
$125.00 purchase
Discusses painters of the Italian school of mannerism, Parmigianino, Pontormo, Bronzino, Tintoretto and Michelangelo. Presents chatecteristic works of the artists, connects their works to the literature, religion and history of their times.
Fine Arts; Geography - World; History - World
Dist - AITECH **Prod** - WDCNTV 1989

Manners - 41 13 MIN
VHS / U-matic
Life's little lessons - self - esteem 4 - 6 series
Color (I)
$129.00, $99.00 purchase _ #V670
Shows that when Cousin Clem visits his wealthy relatives in the city, they turn up their noses at his poor taste in clothes and awkward manners. Reveals that there's more to having good manners than knowing which fork to use. Part of a 65 - part series on self - esteem.
Guidance and Counseling; Home Economics; Psychology; Social Science; Sociology
Dist - BARR **Prod** - CEPRO 1992

The Manners and Morals of High Capitalism 60 MIN
U-matic / VHS / 16mm
Age of Uncertainty Series
Color (H C A)
LC 77-700662
Looks at the robber baron industrial capitalists of the late 19th century. Based on the book The Age Of Uncertainty by John Kenneth Galbraith.
Biography; Business and Economics
Dist - FI **Prod** - BBCL 1977

Manners and Morals of High Capitalism, the, Pt 2 30 MIN
U-matic / VHS / 16mm
Age of Uncertainty Series
Color (H C A)
LC 77-700662
Looks at the robber baron industrial capitalists of the late 19th century. Based on the book The Age Of Uncertainty by John Kenneth Galbraith.
Business and Economics
Dist - FI **Prod** - BBCL 1977

Manners are Lots of Fun 19 MIN
U-matic / VHS
Manners are Lots of Fun Series
Color (K P)
Contains 1 videocassette.
Guidance and Counseling; Home Economics; Psychology
Dist - TROLA **Prod** - TROLA 1987

Manners are Lots of Fun Series
Manners are Lots of Fun 19 MIN
Dist - TROLA

Manners at work 18 MIN
VHS
Color (PRO)
$89.00 purchase _ #60407 - 025
Shows etiquette as a social invention with the power to smooth rough edges in human interaction. Demonstrates that good manners are a career asset as well as a way to build confidence.
Guidance and Counseling; Home Economics; Psychology; Sociology
Dist - GA **Prod** - GA 1992
VLEARN

Manners in Public 11 MIN
U-matic / VHS / 16mm
Color (P)
$270, $190 purchase _ #3255
Shows the importance of good manners in public and what is appropriate behavior in a particular situation.
Psychology; Social Science
Dist - CORF

Manners - the Magic Words 16 MIN
VHS / 16mm / U-matic
Color (K P I)
$375, $265, $295 _ #A403
Discusses the importance of being polite and courteous. Depicts how good manners make life easier.
Literature and Drama; Psychology
Dist - BARR **Prod** - BARR 1986

Manners...yes, even in a part - time job 25 MIN
35mm strip / VHS
Color (J H C A)
$93.00, $93.00 purchase _ #MB - 512993 - 0, #MB - 512981 - 7
Utilizes cartoons and humor to illustrate the importance of manners in the workplace. Focuses on service - oriented jobs such as restaurants, supermarkets, and department stores. Encourages viewers to consider how they would have handled the situations presented. Covers first impressions and getting hired.
Education; Guidance and Counseling; Psychology; Sociology
Dist - SRA **Prod** - SRA 1988

The Mannikin 28 MIN
16mm / U-matic / VHS
Classics, Dark and Dangerous Series
Color (SPANISH)
LC 76-703938
Presents a supernatural story by Robert Bloch about a young singer who is possessed by a demon. Features Ronee Blakley and Keir Dullea.
Literature and Drama
Dist - LCOA **Prod** - LCOA 1977

Manoeuvre 115 MIN
U-matic / VHS / 16mm
B&W (H C A)
LC 80-700498
Documents NATO war games where NATO conducts maneuvers to test how fast reinforcements from the United States can come to the aid of NATO forces already stationed in Western Europe. Follows an infantry tank company from Fort Polk, Louisiana, through various stages of the training exercises to a simulated war near the East German border.
Civics and Political Systems; Fine Arts
Dist - ZIPRAH **Prod** - WISEF 1980

Manon 152 MIN
VHS
Color (S) (FRENCH)
$29.95 purchase _ #384 - 9701
Presents the New York City Opera production of 'Manon' by Massenet. Features Beverly Sills as lead in an elegant rococo production of an early 18th - century French story.
Fine Arts; Foreign Language
Dist - FI **Prod** - PAR 1989

Manon 115 MIN
VHS
Color (S)
$39.95 purchase _ #623 - 9405
Stars Jennifer Penney as Manon and Anthony Dowell as Des Grieux in the Royal Ballet production of 'Manon' by Massenet. Features Kenneth MacMillan as choreographer.
Fine Arts; Geography - World; Physical Education and Recreation
Dist - FI **Prod** - NVIDC 1986

Manon des sources 114 MIN
VHS
Color (H C A)
PdS19.95 purchase _ #ML-6306523
Dramatizes Marcel Pagnol's novel. Stars Yves Montand. Includes English subtitles.
Fine Arts; Foreign Language
Dist - AVP

Manon Lescaut 126 MIN
VHS / U-matic
Color (A)
Presents the story of an obsessive love that begins in pre - revolutionary France in the always popular Puccini opera, Manon Lescaut.
Fine Arts; Foreign Language
Dist - SRA **Prod** - SRA

Manon lescaut 135 MIN
VHS
Metropolitan opera series
Color (G) (ITALIAN WITH ENGLISH SUBTITLES)
$29.95 purchase
Stars Placido Domingo, Renata Scotto, and Pablo Elvira in a performance of 'Manon Lescaut' by Puccini. Conducted by James Levine. Includes a brochure with plot, historic notes, photographs, and production credits.
Fine Arts
Dist - PBS **Prod** - WNETTV 1980

Manon Lescaut 135 MIN
VHS
Color (S) (ITALIAN)
$29.95 purchase _ #384 - 9554
Presents the Metropolitan Opera production of 'Manon Lescaut' by Puccini. Includes Gian Carlo Menotti as director, Placido Domingo and Renata Scotto in the cast.
Fine Arts; Foreign Language
Dist - FI **Prod** - PAR 1988

Manon Lescaut 130 MIN
VHS
Color (S)
$39.95 purchase _ #623 - 9807
Features Kiri te Kanawa in her first portrayal of the title role of 'Manon Lescaut' by Puccini. Includes Placido Domingo and Thomas Allen in the cast of the Royal Opera production. Giuseppe Sinopoli conducts.
Fine Arts; Geography - World
Dist - FI **Prod** - NVIDC 1986

The Manor house mystery - problem - solving in geometry 27 MIN
VHS
Detective stories for math problem solving series
Color (I J H)
$175.00 purchase _ #CG - 914 - VS
Reveals that Billy and Jodie have been hired by a shady - looking detective to help solve a mystery about a haunted house and a treasure. Shows that the clues begin to unfold when they find the handbook of the Sigma Delta club, a secret society. The handbook lays out a series of tasks leading to the treasure - and a secret passage. Includes clue kit with blueprints, copies of the secret handbook, diagrams, triangles, empty grids and photos of the peculiar bookcase in the treasure room. Requires students to pool problem - solving skills and geometry skills. Part of a series.
Literature and Drama; Mathematics; Psychology
Dist - HRMC **Prod** - HRMC

Manos a La Obra - the Story of Operation Bootstrap 59 MIN
16mm / U-matic / VHS
Color (H C A)
Looks at Puerto Rico's Operation Bootstrap, the highly vaunted economic development plan undertaken in the Fifties that was to provide a role model for economic development throughout the Americas. Surveys Puerto Rican history from the 1930s through the 1980s when Fortune Magazine has labeled Puerto Rico's economy as Operation Welfare.
Geography - United States; History - United States
Dist - CNEMAG **Prod** - CPRS

Manos a La Obra - the Story of Operation Bootstrap - Pt I 28 MIN
U-matic / 16mm
Presente Series
Captioned; Color (SPANISH (ENGLISH SUBTITLES))
Chronicles Puerto Rico's history from the peaceful revolution and U S invasion in 1898 when its peaceful and natural state was changed forever. Reveals how the contradictory historical forces led to the industrialization and transformation of Puerto Rican society.
Civics and Political Systems; History - United States; History - World; Social Science; Sociology
Dist - KCET **Prod** - KCET

Manos a La Obra - the Story of Operation Bootstrap - Pt II 29 MIN
U-matic / 16mm
Presente Series
Captioned; Color (SPANISH (ENGLISH SUBTITLES))
Chronicles the history of U S involvement in the underdeveloped country of Puerto Rico. Uses filmclips, archival newspapers, government propaganda films and candid interviews with key figures in recent Puerto Rican history to emphasize the purpose of Operation Bootstrap to attract U S capital to Puerto Rico by offering tax - free earnings and calling the island the 'showcase of the Americas.' Reveals the industrialization experience in a land that was free.
Business and Economics; Civics and Political Systems; History - United States; Social Science; Sociology
Dist - KCET **Prod** - KCET

Manouane River Lumberjacks 28 MIN
16mm
B&W
_ #106B 0162 059N
Geography - World
Dist - CFLMDC **Prod** - NFBC 1962

Manowan - Forest Adventure - Manowan Aux Bois 52 MIN
16mm
Color (G) (FRENCH)
3X46 I
Describes the hunting and field trip of a group of Manowan Indian boys and girls in the legendary Quebec forest. Illustrates procedures for making a camp site, skills required to become self sufficient in the forest, how to hunt and trap beaver, and how to ice fish with a net, all with an understanding of the need to maintain the ecological balance. In 2 parts.
Physical Education and Recreation; Science - Natural; Social Science
Dist - CDIAND **Prod** - GRATTO 1976

Manpower Management 30 MIN
U-matic / VHS
Color
Presents Dr. James W. Walker, US International University, discussing employee motivation, compensation, manpower training and organizational planning. Treats human resources as assets to the business.
Business and Economics; Psychology
Dist - NETCHE **Prod** - NETCHE 1969

Manrique 26 MIN
U-matic / VHS
Color (H C A)
$99.00
Shows the extraordinary creations of Cesar Manrique, an internationally acclaimed artist, sculptor and designer.
Fine Arts
Dist - LANDMK **Prod** - LANDMK 1986

A Man's a Man for all that 14 MIN
16mm
Color
Tells a story set in a small diner during World War II in which a recently discharged soldier brings unexpected rivalry between four women.
Fine Arts
Dist - USC **Prod** - USC

Man's Best Friend 15 MIN
U-matic / VHS
Pass it on Series
Color (K P)
Discusses pets and caring for pets.
Science - Natural
Dist - GPN **Prod** - WKNOTV 1983

Man's Best Friend 60 MIN
U-matic
Color (G)
Explores the special symbiotic relationship existing between man and dog.
Science - Natural
Dist - PBS **Prod** - WNETTV 1987

Man's Best Friends 60 MIN
U-matic / VHS / 16mm
Color (A)
Examines the needs of animals used in research in relation to the needs of science. Discusses the views of animal lovers, who maintain that far too many animals are consumed in medical research, and such research is not only cruel but mostly unnecessary. Notes that the issue has not been realistically addressed by all parties but does require considered study, and soon.
Health and Safety; Science; Science - Natural
Dist - CNEMAG **Prod** - PACSFM 1985

Man's Effect on the Environment 14 MIN
U-matic / VHS / 16mm
Color (J H)
LC 74-711141
Shows some of the effects of man's exploitation of natural resources from the time of the earliest colonists. Raises questions as to the quality of life such environmental changes might produce.
Science - Natural
Dist - PHENIX **Prod** - PHENIX 1970

A Man's Hand 21 MIN
16mm
Doctors at Work Series
B&W (H C A)
LC FIA65-1351
Shows how a finger crippled in an accident is examined and treated in an operation. Discusses the anatomy and functioning of the hand.
Health and Safety; Science - Natural
Dist - LAWREN **Prod** - CMA 1962

A Man's Hands 5 MIN
16mm
Color (I A)
LC 72-711722
Dramatizes man's favorite appendage squeezing, poking, playing, fixing and touching.
Fine Arts; Science - Natural
Dist - VIEWFI **Prod** - PROKP 1970

Man's Impact on the Environment 15 MIN
VHS / 16mm
Ecosystems of the Great Land Series
Color (I H)
$125.00 purchase, $25.00 rental
Summarizes concepts introduced in the preceding programs as part of a discussion of how humans interact with the environment.

Geography - United States; Science - Natural
Dist - AITECH **Prod** - ALASDE 1985

Man's Impact on the Environment 23 MIN
16mm
Color (H C)
Reveals how man has caused dangerous changes in his environment. Shows that man is the single most important factor affecting the 'Balance of Nature.' Explains the tragic consequences of man's almost complete encroachment upon his environment.
Science - Natural
Dist - MLA **Prod** - MLA

Man's Impact on the Environment 20 MIN
16mm
Science of Life Series
Color (J)
LC 81-700849
Discusses ecological and social consequences of a fuel - intensive economy for agriculture, population, urbanization, production and marketing, and resources.
Home Economics; Science - Natural
Dist - WARDS **Prod** - CRIPSE 1981

Man's interdependence with other organisms 14 MIN
U-matic / VHS
Discovering series; Unit 8 - Ecology
Color (I)
Science; Science - Natural
Dist - AITECH **Prod** - WDCNTV 1978

Man's nature 30 MIN
16mm
Color (G)
$40.00 rental
Presents a William T Wiley production. No description provided.
Fine Arts
Dist - CANCIN

A Man's Place 25 MIN
16mm
Color (J)
LC 81-701335
Presents four men who are pursuing nontraditional male roles, and their families, who tell how the men enjoy roles as homemaker, worker in a traditionally female job, parenting, and sharing family responsibilities.
Sociology
Dist - CUNY **Prod** - CUNY 1979

Man's Place in the Universe 30 MIN
VHS / U-matic
Ethics in America Series
Color (H C A)
Presents George Abell, author and astronomy professor, tracing the origin of the solar system through photographic slides. Focuses on the need for continuing space exploration, the prospects for life in outer space and the ethical issue involved in possible encounters with other human beings.
Religion and Philosophy; Science - Physical
Dist - AMHUMA **Prod** - AMHUMA

A Man's Reach 33 MIN
16mm
B&W (J H C)
LC FIA65-835
Describes the functions and responsibilities of a school superintendent and points up his relationship to the school system. Reveals the demanding nature of the position.
Education
Dist - OSUMPD **Prod** - OSUMPD 1964

A Man's Reach Should Exceed His Grasp 24 MIN
U-matic / VHS / 16mm
Color (I)
Presents the history of flight and man's reach for a new freedom through aviation and the exploration of space, recounting developments from the Wright Brothers' flight to the landing on the Moon and plans for future missions to other planets. Emphasizes the creative role of research and cites statements by scientists, writers, poets and philosophers which document man's search for knowledge. Narrated by Burgess Meredith.
Industrial and Technical Education; Physical Education and Recreation; Science; Social Science
Dist - USNAC **Prod** - NASA 1972

Man's Search for Identity
U-matic / VHS
Color
Explains that the struggle for identity is life - long and that it may be shaped publicly or privately. Describes the awakening of self using passages from The Catcher In The Rye, The Red Badge Of Courage, The Lord Of The Flies, The Diary Of Anne Frank, Black Boy and The Invisible Man.
Fine Arts; Guidance and Counseling; Literature and Drama; Psychology
Dist - GA **Prod** - CHUMAN

Man's Shortcomings 13 MIN
16mm
Foremanship Training Series
Color
LC 74-705085
Shows how man's personality quirks may endanger his and other workers' safety. Gives suggestions to avoid or change this mental attitude and prevent these nonsensical actions.
Guidance and Counseling; Health and Safety; Psychology; Sociology
Dist - USNAC **Prod** - USBM 1969

Man's Thumb on Nature's Balance 51 MIN
16mm
Color (J)
Explains that animals live in nature in a relationship of predator and prey keeping their numbers in balance until man gets involved in the equation. Shows that man brings about profound changes in the total environment that often lead the other animals to the danger of extinction. Examines the weeding out of deer herds, the regulation of bird species and the selective 'Harvesting' of the seal crop.
Science - Natural
Dist - NBCTV **Prod** - NBCTV 1971

Man's Thumb on Nature's Balance, Pt 1 23 MIN
16mm
Color (J)
Explains that animals live in nature in a relationship of predator and prey keeping their numbers in balance until man gets involved in the equation. Shows that man brings about profound changes in the total environment that often lead the other animals to the danger of extinction. Examines the weeding out of deer herds, the regulation of bird species and the selective 'Harvesting' of the seal crop.
Science - Natural
Dist - NBCTV **Prod** - NBCTV 1971

Man's Thumb on Nature's Balance, Pt 2 28 MIN
16mm
Color (J)
Explains that animals live in nature in a relationship of predator and prey keeping their numbers in balance until man gets involved in the equation. Shows that man brings about profound changes in the total environment that often lead the other animals to the danger of extinction. Examines the weeding out of deer herds, the regulation of bird species and the selective 'Harvesting' of the seal crop.
Science - Natural
Dist - NBCTV **Prod** - NBCTV 1971

A Man's Woman 52 MIN
VHS / 16mm
Color (G)
$295.00 purchase, $90.00 rental; LC 89715751
Dramatizes an intriguing analysis of the ideological and social implications of the anti - women women's movement. Follows the assassination of the fictional Clovis Kingsley, a powerful 'pro - family' anti - feminist right wing ideologue. Investigates Kingsley's life and ideological mission to reveal a complex and contradictory account of the anti - feminist movement.
Literature and Drama; Psychology; Sociology
Dist - CNEMAG **Prod** - CNEMAG 1988

Mansion of the Doomed 93 MIN
16mm
Color
Focuses on a scientist who will do anything to restore his daughter's sight, including using the eyeballs from her fiancee and other unlucky victims.
Fine Arts
Dist - TWYMAN **Prod** - UNKNWN 1975

Manson's Blood Fluke 16 MIN
16mm
B&W
LC FIE53-290
Uses primarily animation photomicography to demonstrate stages in the life cycle of schistosoma mansoni in secondary and primary hosts, to depict the biologic relationships between the blood fluke and its hosts, man and snail, and to explain the pathology of Manson's schistosomiasis in man. For professional use.
Health and Safety; Science - Natural
Dist - USNAC **Prod** - USPHS 1948

Mansube Machlidar 11 MIN
16mm
B&W (I)
Illustrates the development of fisheries in village ponds which have enabled the village panchayats to earn revenue.
Agriculture; Business and Economics
Dist - NEDINF **Prod** - INDIA

Mantegna - the Triumph of Caesar 24 MIN
16mm
Color (H A)
$475.00 purchase, $50.00 rental
Explores a series of paintings, 'The Triumph Of Caesar', by Florentine artist Andrea Mantegna, 1431 - 1506.
Fine Arts; Industrial and Technical Education
Dist - AFA **Prod** - ACGB 1973

Mantis and wasp 25 MIN
VHS
Nature watch series
Color (P I J H C)
$49.00 purchase _ #320215; LC 89-715858
Explores the physical traits, bunting skills, nest - building, and life cycles of the mantis and the wasp. Part of a series that explores the curious and uncommon characteristics of a variety of mammals, insects, birds and sea creatures.
Science - Natural
Dist - TVOTAR **Prod** - TVOTAR 1988

The Manton Plan 13 MIN
16mm
Color
LC 80-700910
Shows how a local municipality in Australia goes about establishing a Disaster Plan.
Health and Safety; History - World; Social Science
Dist - TASCOR **Prod** - TASCOR 1977

Manual Alphabet 16 MIN
16mm
PANCOM Beginning Total Communication Program for Hearing Parents of 'Series Level 2
Color (K)
LC 77-700504
Education; Guidance and Counseling; Psychology; Sociology
Dist - JOYCE **Prod** - CSDE 1977

Manual Cutting a Bevel - Freehand 13 MIN
16mm
Welding Procedures Series Oxygen Cutting
B&W
LC FIE52-290
Shows how to select a tip for bevel cutting, clean a tip, adjust oxygen and acetylene pressure for bevel cutting and cut a bevel with minimum drag. Number two - Oxygen cutting of the Welding procedures series.
Industrial and Technical Education
Dist - USNAC **Prod** - USOE 1944

Manual Cutting a Shape - Freehand Guided 16 MIN
16mm
Welding Procedures Series Oxygen Cutting
B&W
LC FIE52-291
Shows how to make plywood template for cutting, make a tip guide device, position a template for cutting, use the guide device and use a circle cutting device. Number three of the Welding procedures series.
Industrial and Technical Education
Dist - USNAC **Prod** - USOE 1944

Manual Cutting to a Line - Freehand 21 MIN
16mm
Welding Procedures Series Oxygen Cutting, no 1
B&W
LC FIE52-289
Shows how to assemble an oxyacetylene cutting outfit, select proper cutting tip, adjust oxygen and acetylene delivery pressures, adjust the preheating cutting flames, make a 90 degree free - hand cut and disassemble the cutting outfit.
Industrial and Technical Education
Dist - USNAC **Prod** - USOE 1944

Manual Data Input 17 MIN
U-matic / VHS
Numerical Control/Computerized Numerical Control, Module 1 - 'Fundamentals Series
Color (IND)
Examines the parts of the manual data input keyboard. Discusses entering and storing programs and entering tool length offsets.
Business and Economics; Industrial and Technical Education
Dist - LEIKID **Prod** - LEIKID

Manual English Vocabularies 100 MIN
VHS / U-matic
Color (S)
Demonstrates Signing Exact English (SEE) vocabulary words. Presents fingerspelling, signing, and usage of words in a sentence.
Education; Guidance and Counseling; Psychology
Dist - GALCO **Prod** - GALCO 1975

Manual handling series
Watch their backs 18 MIN
Watch your back 14 MIN
Dist - CFLVIS

Manual Lifting 19 MIN
VHS / U-matic
Safety Action for Employees Series
Color (IND)
Describes and demonstrates correct manual lifting techniques and how unsafe lifting can lead to serious injury.
Health and Safety
Dist - GPCV **Prod** - GPCV

Manual Load Handling in the Warehouse 12 MIN
16mm / VHS
Safety on the Job Series
Color (C A PRO)
$245.00, $295.00 purchase, $75.00 rental _ #8178
Emphasizes the do's and don't's of warehouse activities and shows workers how to handle products safely and efficiently.
Health and Safety; Psychology
Dist - AIMS **Prod** - AIMS 1990

Manual load handling in the warehouse 12 MIN
VHS
Safety on the job series
Color (G IND)
$99.95 purchase _ #6 - 203 - 017A
Presents the do's and don'ts of warehouse procedure. Shows workers how to handle products safely, inspect loads for hazards, how to lift properly and how to use special warehouse tools. Part of a series on job safety.
Health and Safety; Science - Natural
Dist - VEP **Prod** - VEP 1993

Manual Positive Pressure Ventilation 9 MIN
U-matic / VHS
Medical Skills Films Series
Color (PRO)
Health and Safety
Dist - WFP **Prod** - WFP

Manual Sampling of Petroleum and Petroleum Products 25 MIN
Slide / VHS / 16mm
Color (A IND)
$240.00, $250.00 purchase _ #13.2987, #53.2987
Surveys various procedures and equipment used in manual sampling. Covers the various containers used, including lines and tanks.
Industrial and Technical Education; Mathematics; Social Science
Dist - UTEXPE

Manuel Jimenez - Woodcarver 29 MIN
U-matic / 16mm
Presente Series
Color (SPANISH)
Profiles the life of Manuel Jimenez, the woodcarver whose dream came true. Shows how he became interested in the art after years of herding animals and plowing the fields. Follows the woodcarver's process from selecting a tree to adding the finishing touches. In Spanish with English voice - over. Filmed in Arrazola, Oaxaca, Mexico.
Biography; Fine Arts; Geography - World; Industrial and Technical Education
Dist - KCET **Prod** - KCET

Manuel's Box - a Videotape for Special Education 58 MIN
VHS
B&W (C A)
$110.00 purchase, $18.00 rental
Shows one child's cognitive and emotional development over a two - year period during which he received intensive individual intervention at the Bloomingdale Head Start Programs.
Psychology
Dist - CORNRS **Prod** - BLOOF 1980

Manufacture of Planet Pinions 14 MIN
16mm
Color
Examines the machining and inspection processes of planet pinions.
Business and Economics
Dist - GM **Prod** - GM

The Manufactured epidemic 30 MIN
VHS / U-matic
Contemporary health issues series
Color (C A)
Identifies smoking as a contributing factor in a number of disease processes. Examines the characteristics of smokers and describes the nature of the drug nicotine. Discusses the difficulty of breaking the smoking habit in light of national economic interests. Lesson 20 of the Contemporary Health Issues series.
Health and Safety; Psychology
Dist - CDTEL **Prod** - SCCON

Manufacturing 30 MIN
U-matic / VHS
Videosearch Performance Appraisal - Case Studies Series
Color
Fine Arts; Psychology
Dist - DELTAK **Prod** - DELTAK

Manufacturing 6 MIN
16mm / U-matic / VHS
Kingdom of Could be You Series
Color (K P I)
Guidance and Counseling
Dist - EBEC **Prod** - EBEC 1974

Manufacturing 10 MIN
U-matic
Color (P)
Takes a tour of the Hershey chocolate factory to show how a candy bar is produced. Examines the entire manufacturing process, from raw materials to finished product.
Business and Economics; Guidance and Counseling
Dist - GA **Prod** - MINIP

Manufacturing and Construction Series - 12 Titles on 12 VHS Tapes -
Career Profiles - Manufacturing and Construction Service Series
Dist - CAREER

Manufacturing and Construction Series
Career profiles - analytical laboratory technician
Career profiles - auto body repairer
Career Profiles - Automobile Mechanic
Career Profiles - Communications Electronics Technicians
Career Profiles - Construction Technology
Career Profiles - Electrical Equipment
Career Profiles - Electronics Engineering Technician
Career Profiles - Machinist
Career Profiles - Marine and Small Engine Repair
Career Profiles - Mechanican Design
Career Profiles - Service Technician
Career Profiles - Welding
Dist - CAREER

Manufacturing automation - a key to productivity series
CAD / CAM - the computer in manufacturing 30 MIN
Implementation, impact and change 30 MIN
Implications for MIS 30 MIN
The New manufacturing environment 30 MIN
Using industrial robots 30 MIN
Dist - DELTAK

Manufacturing Control 180 MIN
U-matic
Electronics Testing, Quality - Reliability and Manufacturing Control'Series
Color (IND)
Discusses material control, production control, and material requirements planning for the manufacture of electronic printed circuit boards and components. Includes scheduling, inventory, procurement and floor control.
Business and Economics; Industrial and Technical Education
Dist - INTECS **Prod** - INTECS

Manufacturing costs 52 MIN
BETA / VHS / U-matic
Color (A PRO)
$200.00 purchase
Offers a seminar developing the principles of simplified cost accounting through three easy - to - understand examples. Uses lectures and chart work presentations, as well as a visit to a corporate controller's office for a round table discussion.
Business and Economics; Psychology
Dist - TAMMFG **Prod** - TAMMFG 1991

Manufacturing - IBM 20 MIN
VHS / U-matic
Clues to Career Opportunities for Liberal Arts Graduates Series
Color
LC 79-706055
Interviews a representative of IBM and enumerates the jobs available in large corporations for college graduates with liberal arts backgrounds.
Business and Economics; Guidance and Counseling
Dist - IU **Prod** - IU 1978

Manufacturing insights series
Adaptive control 38 MIN
Advances in computer numerical control 27 MIN
Automated assembly 34 MIN
Automated inspection - non - destructive testing 30 MIN
Automated material handling 29 MIN
CAD - CAM 25 MIN
CAD - CAM networking 36 MIN
CAD - CAM workstations 30 MIN
Composites in manufacturing 31 MIN
Cutting tools 28 MIN
DFM - design for manufacturability 30 MIN
Factory data collection 30 MIN
Flexible automated circuit board assembly 30 MIN
Flexible manufacturing cells 28 MIN
Flexible manufacturing systems 50 MIN
Hazardous waste minimization 30 MIN
Implementing just-in-time 27 MIN
Implementing total quality management 30 MIN
Lasers in manufacturing 35 MIN
Lasers in manufacturing - a new look 26 MIN
Layout improvements for just-in-time 30 MIN
Machine vision 50 MIN
Machine vision - a new look 20 MIN
Personal computers in manufacturing 28 MIN
Programmable controllers 27 MIN
Robots in assembly and packaging 45 MIN
Robots in surface preparation 26 MIN
Robots in welding and painting 35 MIN
Sensors 30 MIN
Setup reduction for just-in-time 30 MIN
Simulation 28 MIN
Simultaneous engineering 45 MIN
Superabrasives and precision grinding 30 MIN
Tooling for composites 24 MIN
Dist - SME

Manufacturing Materials and Processes Series
Abrasive flow machine 11 MIN
Abrasive machining 11 MIN
Broaching and Shaping 16 MIN
Casting 28 MIN
Chemical Milling 11 MIN
Cleaning 15 MIN
Computer Applications in Industry 17 MIN
Drilling and Boring 25 MIN
Electrical Discharge Machining 17 MIN
Electrochemical Grinding 14 MIN
Electrochemical Machining 13 MIN
Electroplating 17 MIN
Finishing and Deburring 16 MIN
Forging 19 MIN
Gages and measurements 15 MIN
Heat Treating 15 MIN
Interactive Graphics 10 MIN
Introduction to coatings and painting 15 MIN
Introduction to Joining 9 MIN
Introduction to Metallurgy 11 MIN
Introduction to Sheet Metal 9 MIN
Laser Drilling 8 MIN
The Lathe 17 MIN
Materials Testing 10 MIN
Milling 9 MIN
Non - Destructive Testing 16 MIN
Powder metallurgy 14 MIN
Rolling 11 MIN
Sheet Metal Processing 19 MIN
Soldering and Brazing 17 MIN
Welding 15 MIN
Dist - WFVTAE

Manufacturing Materials Series
Presents a four - part series on manufacturing materials. Includes the titles 'Ceramics,' 'Plastics,' 'Metals' and 'Textiles.'
Ceramics 21 MIN
Metals 22 MIN
Plastics 21 MIN
Textiles 21 MIN
Dist - BARR **Prod** - GLOBET 1978

The Manufacturing Midwest 15 MIN
U-matic / VHS / 16mm
U S Geography Series
Color (J)
LC 76-701771
Examines the manufacturing resources of the Midwest region of the United States.
Business and Economics; Geography - United States; Geography - World; Social Science
Dist - MGHT **Prod** - MGHT 1976

The Manufacturing plan 180 MIN
U-matic
Electronics testing, quality - reliability and manufacturing control'series
Color (IND)
Discusses facility planning for the manufacture of electronic components and boards. Includes facility requirements, site selection, plant layouts, material handling, production, and guidelines for successful operation.
Business and Economics; Industrial and Technical Education
Dist - INTECS **Prod** - INTECS

Manufacturing process - 4 13 MIN
VHS
Exploring technology education - manufacturing - series
Color (I)
$180.00 purchase
Introduces six manufacturing processes - separating, cutting, forming, casting, conditioning, assembling and finishing. Demonstrates many of these processes in a foundry. Builds the technological literacy vital for current and future careers. Part of the Exploring Technology Series.
Business and Economics; Education; Industrial and Technical Education; Social Science
Dist - AITECH **Prod** - AITECH 1990

Manufacturing process planning 15 MIN
VHS / 16mm
Exploring technology series
Color (I J)
$180.00 purchase, $25.00 rental
Introduces common and innovative processes. Production in a steel foundy and the handcrafting of a violin illustrate separating, forming, molding, conditioning, assembling and finishing.
Business and Economics
Dist - AITECH **Prod** - AITECH 1990

Manufacturing process planning - 5 15 MIN
VHS
Exploring technology education - manufacturing - series
Color (I)
$180.00 purchase
Emphasizes that to be competitive, manufacturers must plan for quality control, productivity and for new products. Builds the technological literacy vital for current and future careers. Part of the Exploring Technology Series.
Business and Economics; Education; Industrial and Technical Education; Social Science
Dist - AITECH **Prod** - AITECH 1990

Manufacturing Series
Achieving inventory and stores record accuracy 60 MIN
Analyzing variances and projecting costs 60 MIN
Bill of material applications for master production scheduling 60 MIN
Budget performance measurement 60 MIN
The Business planning process 60 MIN
Buyer and the law 60 MIN
The Buyers job 60 MIN
Capacity and Resource Planning 60 MIN
Capacity Control and Production Reporting 60 MIN
Capacity Planning 60 MIN
Communicating schedules 60 MIN
Computer aided purchasing 60 MIN
Controlling components, supplies, tooling, documentation and production reporting 60 MIN
Controlling engineering documentation 60 MIN
Controlling workloads and capacity utilization 60 MIN
Customer relations 60 MIN
Defining the role of physical materials management 60 MIN
Demand management 60 MIN
Developing a standard cost roll up 60 MIN
Developing cost standards 60 MIN
Developing the budget 60 MIN
Disbursement 60 MIN
Dispatching Overview 60 MIN
Estimating and Delivering Quotations 60 MIN
Executing the schedule 60 MIN
Factors that Determine and Affect Master Production Scheduling Features 60 MIN
Final Assembly Scheduling 60 MIN
Forecast requirements in a manufacturing environment 60 MIN
How MRP Helps Production Scheduling 60 MIN
How MRP Works in Manufacturing 60 MIN
Identifying and Reporting Variances 60 MIN
Improving Stores Operations through Performance Measurement 60 MIN
International Purchasing 60 MIN
Inventory Count Reconciliation and Adjustment 60 MIN
Inventory Management 60 MIN
Labor and Overhead Cost 60 MIN
Managing Changing Priorities 60 MIN
Managing Production and Inventory using Forecasts 60 MIN
Master Production Scheduling Features and Methods 60 MIN
Master Schedule Planning Reports 60 MIN
Material Movement and Inventory Cost 60 MIN
Meeting Customer Needs and Expectations 60 MIN
The Nature and Source of Demand 60 MIN
Negotiation 60 MIN
Operations Planning 60 MIN
Order Alterations, Reschedules and Returns 60 MIN
Order Entry and Delivery Promising 60 MIN
An Overview of Master Production Scheduling 60 MIN
Performance Measurements 60 MIN
Planning Manufacturing Capacity 60 MIN
Planning Manufacturing Lot Sizes 60 MIN
Policies and Procedures 60 MIN
Procurement performance measurement 60 MIN
Procurement Planning and Contracting 60 MIN
Product Definition 60 MIN
Product Development 60 MIN
Product Producibility 60 MIN
Product Release 60 MIN
Productivity measurement 60 MIN
Purchasing Material and Service Cost 60 MIN
Receipt Administration 60 MIN
Receiving 60 MIN
Recognizing and Solving Capacity Problems 60 MIN
Replanning Solutions to Production Problems 60 MIN
Responsibilities of Configuration Managment 60 MIN
Role of Production Scheduling 60 MIN
Scheduling Operation Sequence 60 MIN
Selecting Forecasting Techinques 60 MIN
Solving Budget Problems 60 MIN
Stocking and Location Control 60 MIN
Subcontract manufacturing, scheduling and control 60 MIN
Supplier Performance Measurement 60 MIN
Supply Management 60 MIN
What is Configuration Managment 60 MIN
Work Center Supervisor's Job 60 MIN
Working with Intrinsic Forecasting Techniques 60 MIN
Dist - COMSRV

Manufacturing systems 15 MIN
VHS / 16mm
Exploring technology series
Color (I J)
$180.00 purchase, $25.00 rental
Introduces intermittent, continuous and customs systems and their essential elements.
Business and Economics
Dist - AITECH **Prod** - AITECH 1990

Manufacturing systems - 2 14 MIN
VHS
Exploring technology education - manufacturing - series
Color (I)
$180.00 purchase
Introduces intermittent, continuous and custom manufacturing systems and their essential elements. Builds the technological literacy vital for current and future careers. Part of the Exploring Technology Series.
Business and Economics; Education; Industrial and Technical Education; Social Science
Dist - AITECH **Prod** - AITECH 1990

Manufacturing systems explained
VHS / 35mm strip
$239.00 purchase _ #017 - 732 filmstrips, $239.00 purchase _ #017 -
Discusses the Universal Systems Model and stresses the value of people and information as resources. Talks about the use of resources such as materials, tools, machines, capital, and time. Provides an introduction to forming, separating, combining, and conditioning processes, and talks in depth about each. Explores reasons for and methods of control, and talks about products and their impacts.
Social Science
Dist - CAREER BERGL **Prod** - CAREER

Manufacturing Systems Technology 60 MIN
VHS / 16mm
Color (H A)
$299.00 purchase _ T11
Identifies five components of the Universal System Model, defines resources and explores four types of processes.
Business and Economics; Industrial and Technical Education
Dist - BERGL **Prod** - BERGL 1990

Manufacturing technology 30 MIN
VHS
Success by the numbers - the applied vocational math video series
Color (G H)
$149.00 purchase _ #CDAMV118V-T
Interviews professionals in different careers as they explain the uses of mathematics in their jobs. Demonstrates the importance of mathematics in measuring and calculating part sizes and discusses calipers, tape measures and geometric calculations required in the industrial sector.
Business and Economics; Education
Dist - CAMV

Manufacturing the Ducor Catheter 10 MIN
16mm
Color (PRO)
Illustrates the manufacturing and quality control of the Ducor catheter.
Business and Economics; Health and Safety
Dist - CORDIS **Prod** - CORDIS

Manufacturing with Plastics 25 MIN
VHS / U-matic
Technical Studies Series
Color (H C A)
Discusses manufacturing with plastics.
Industrial and Technical Education
Dist - FI **Prod** - BBCTV 1981

Manure Storage 16 MIN
VHS / U-matic
Agricultural Accidents and Rescue Series
Color
Focuses on gases as often being the major concern in rescues from manure storage facilities. Stresses the importance of restraint and personal protection.
Agriculture; Health and Safety
Dist - PSU **Prod** - PSU

The Manxmen 25 MIN
16mm
Eye of the Beholder Series
Color
LC 75-701896
Surveys the Isle of Man, a little known island set in the midst of the Irish Sea. Points out that it is all that remains of an ancient Norse Kingdom and contains a wealth of stories.
Geography - World
Dist - VIACOM **Prod** - RCPDF 1974

Many Adventures of Winnie the Pooh Series
Winnie the Pooh and the Blustery Day 25 MIN
Winnie the Pooh and the Honey Tree 26 MIN
Winnie the Pooh and Tigger Too 26 MIN
Dist - CORF

Many Americans Series
Felipa - north of the border 17 MIN
Geronimo Jones 21 MIN
Lee Suzuki - Home in Hawaii 19 MIN
Matthew Aliuk - Eskimo in Two Worlds 18 MIN
Miguel - Up from Puerto Rico 15 MIN
Siu Mei Wong - who Shall I be 18 MIN
Todd - Growing Up in Appalachia 14 MIN
Dist - LCOA

The Many Cities of Boston 17 MIN
16mm
Color (J)
LC 75-709034
Features Daniel P Moynihan and Charles V Hamilton who discuss the new period in our national history when, for many, confrontation is replacing the democratic process, when established institutions are being questioned and found wanting. Studies Boston as representative of any city in the United States, its black ghetto, Roxbury, which is raging with violence and Dover, white and prosperous, which is helping Roxbury to help itself. Concludes with the statement that the cities are our civilization, they are in trouble now, but these troubles must be worked out in order to survive.
Geography - United States; Guidance and Counseling; History - United States; Psychology; Social Science; Sociology
Dist - NBCTV **Prod** - NBCTV 1969

Many Different Gifts 50 MIN
16mm
Color
LC 74-703215
Focuses on the planning and preparation by the Nova Community for a liturgy for the second Sunday in Advent and shows how each element is incorporated in the finished liturgy.
Religion and Philosophy
Dist - MMM **Prod** - NOVAC 1974

Many Different Stories 15 MIN
U-matic
Color (I)
Teaches writing skills while telling the story of Chris who returns from the library with a book of story poems.
Education; English Language; Literature and Drama
Dist - TVOTAR **Prod** - TVOTAR 1982

Many Faces of Argonne 60 MIN
16mm
Color
LC FIE64-167
Depicts the Argonne National Laboratory in Argonne, Illinois, showing objectives, methods and hardware of the broad range of nuclear research conducted by a national laboratory of the U S Atomic Energy Commission.

Civics and Political Systems; Geography - United States; Science; Science - Physical
Dist - USERD **Prod** - ANL 1963

The Many faces of arthritis 14 MIN
VHS / 16mm
Learning about arthritis series
Color (H C A PRO)
$195.00 purchase, $75.00 rental _ #8083
Considers the many ways in which arthritis manifests.
Health and Safety; Science - Natural
Dist - AIMS **Prod** - HOSSN 1988

The Many Faces of Mexico 17 MIN
16mm / U-matic / VHS
Mexican Heritage Series
Color
LC 76-703912
Shows facets of the Mexican land and people.
Geography - World; History - World
Dist - FI **Prod** - STEXMF 1976

The Many Faces of Mexico 30 MIN
16mm
Color (C A)
LC FIA65-836
Illustrates attractions and activities of Mexico, ranging from ancient ruins to modern industrial facilities. Includes views of Guaymas, Mazatlan, Guadalajara, Acapulco, Taxco and Mexico City.
Geography - World
Dist - MCDO **Prod** - DAC 1964

The Many Faces of Renaissance Man 145 MIN
U-matic
University of the Air Series
Color (J H C A)
$750.00 purchase, $250.00 rental
Explains the ideals and downfall of the Renaissance thought and society. Program contains a series of five cassettes 29 minutes in length.
Geography - World; Religion and Philosophy
Dist - CTV **Prod** - CTV 1977

The Many faces of Sherlock Holmes 58 MIN
VHS
Color (H C T A)
$79.95 purchase _ #S01324
Presents a sort of biographical sketch of the literary sleuth Sherlock Holmes. Interviews Sir Arthur Conan Doyle, creator of Holmes. Features footage from theatrical Holmes films.
Literature and Drama
Dist - UILL

The Many faces of television
U-matic
Visual learning series
Color (T)
Presents television professionals discussing why television has been so successful. Session two of the Visual learning series.
Education; Fine Arts; Industrial and Technical Education
Dist - NYSED **Prod** - NYSED

Many Happy Returns 10 MIN
16mm
Color (I J)
LC 76-703109
Presents an animated film outlining basic principles of reincarnation through the adventures of a child.
Fine Arts; Religion and Philosophy
Dist - ASSRE **Prod** - JDDS 1972

Many happy returns 15 MIN
VHS / U-matic
Dragons, wagons and wax - Set 2 series
Color (K P)
Shows how people change physically as they grow older.
Science; Science - Natural
Dist - CTI **Prod** - CTI

Many Happy Returns 26 MIN
16mm / VHS
Color (I)
$495.00, $295.00 purchase
Tells the story of Barney, 23 years old, a clown for children's birthday parties, and Beth, 13 years old, who was smitten with Barney five years earlier when he performed at her birthday party. Reveals that Beth brings out all her feminine wiles and a great deal of makeup to waylay Barney upon his exit from entertaining Beth's little brother's party. This comedy of unrequited puppy love was written by Willie Reale.
Guidance and Counseling; Health and Safety; Literature and Drama; Psychology
Dist - LUF **Prod** - LUF

Many hear - some listen 12 MIN
16mm / U-matic / VHS
Art of communication series
Color (J H C A)
$295, $210 purchase _ #74541
Shows three types of listening styles, and discusses the importance of effective listening.
English Language
Dist - CORF

Many hear - some listen 12 MIN
U-matic / VHS / 16mm
Art of communication series
Color (H C A)
Examines several listening styles and points out that effective listening involves the listener as well as the speaker.
Business and Economics; English Language
Dist - CORF **Prod** - CENTRO

Many luscious lollipops 11 MIN
VHS
Ruth Heller language stories series
Color (P I)
$44.95 purchase _ #SAV9041
Provides enrichment and understanding about adjectives in a program. Teaches English grammar. Part of a four - part series adapting picture books that teach grammar by Ruth Heller.
English Language
Dist - KNOWUN

The Many masks we wear
VHS
Color (J H C)
$197.00 purchase _ #00241 - 126
Explores the idea of the mask for concealment and expression. Gives a chronology of the use of masks in religion, ritual, theater, art and society. Studies the ritualistic and functional aspects of the mask in societal and psychological contexts, using works such as Games People Play by Eric Berne. Includes teacher's guide and library kit. Two parts.
Psychology; Social Science; Sociology
Dist - GA **Prod** - GA

Many Men Say 5 MIN
16mm
Song of the Ages Series
B&W (H C A)
LC 77-702118
Presents a modern interpretation of Psalm 4 using the dramatization about a scrubwoman who, while cleaning a newsroom, hears the sounds of the happenings of the world and sweeps these absurdities away.
Religion and Philosophy
Dist - FAMLYT **Prod** - FAMLYT 1964

The Many modes of media 28 MIN
U-matic / BETA / VHS
Communication skills 2 - advanced series
Color (H C G)
101.95, $89.95 purchase _ #CA - 20
Covers the identification of four literary genre. Discusses literature as a medium of communication. Overviews the origins of mass media. Discusses the effect of mass media on history and society. Part of a 26 - part series.
Literature and Drama; Social Science; Sociology
Dist - INSTRU

Many Moons 13 MIN
16mm / U-matic / VHS
Color (P I)
LC 74-703644
Presents an adaptation of the story about the princess who desired the moon and the jester who devised a way to fulfill her wish.
Literature and Drama
Dist - MGHT **Prod** - MGHT 1975

Many Moons 10 MIN
16mm
Color (P)
$210.00 purchase _ #215 - 0007
Recreates the children's story by James Thurber about Princess Lenore who desires the moon. Reveals that when none of the king's wise counselors can obtain it for her, it is the court jester who finds a way to fulfill her wish.
Fine Arts; Literature and Drama
Dist - FI **Prod** - TEXFLM 1983

Many Races Hopemobile 58 MIN
16mm
Color (P I J H C)
Presents the story of the many races hopemobile, a motorized library distributing literature on black heritage and culture.
History - United States
Dist - GCCED **Prod** - GCCED 1971

The Many Styles of Music 15 MIN
U-matic
It's Mainly Music Series
Color (I)
Teaches children about the many styles of music and the versatility of different musical instruments.
Fine Arts
Dist - TVOTAR **Prod** - TVOTAR 1983

Many though one 30 MIN
VHS
Maryknoll video magazine presents series
Color (G)
$14.95 purchase
Examines seven ancient rites used in Cairo, Egypt Catholic Church worship that evoke traditional Church history and art.
Religion and Philosophy
Dist - MARYFA

Many Voices 10 MIN
16mm
Color
LC 76-703434
Shows ethnic and racial participation in the Bicentennial. Discusses cultural pluralism and intergroup cooperation in American society, showing the wide variety of people who have contributed to the building of the nation. Offers a sampling of ethnic and multicultural Bicentennial projects across the country.
History - United States
Dist - USNAC **Prod** - USARBA 1976

Many Voices - a Vous D'Agir 18 MIN
16mm
Color (H C A) (FRENCH)
#2X27 I
Explains the responsibilities of the chief and the band council on Indian reserves.
Social Science
Dist - CDIAND **Prod** - ANCS 1977

Many wonder 40 MIN
VHS
Short stories - video anthology series
Color (H G)
$59.95 purchase
Spins a tale about an overly generous New York woman pursued by three bachelors with different agendas. Directed by Craig Lowry. Part of a sixteen - part anthology of short dramas by young American filmmakers.
Fine Arts; Literature and Drama; Sociology
Dist - CNEMAG

The Many Worlds of Carlos Fuentes-Pt 1 60 MIN
VHS / U-matic
Bill Moyers' Journal Series
Color
Presents an interview with Carlos Fuentes, the Mexican author and authority on Third World countries.
Civics and Political Systems; Geography - World; Literature and Drama; Social Science
Dist - PBS **Prod** - WNETTV 1980

The Many Worlds of Carlos Fuentes-Pt 2 60 MIN
U-matic / VHS
Bill Moyers' Journal Series
Color
Presents an interview with Carlos Fuentes, the Mexican author and authority on Third World countries.
Civics and Political Systems; Geography - World; Literature and Drama; Social Science
Dist - PBS **Prod** - WNETTV 1980

Many Worlds of Nature Series

Adaptation	11 MIN
The Birds' nest	12 MIN
The Bird's year - variety and change	12 MIN
Environment manipulation	12 MIN
Evergreens	14 MIN
Flowers	13 MIN
The Marsh	12 MIN
The Monarch and the Milkweed	11 MIN
The Oak	12 MIN
Of Birds, Beaks and Behavior	11 MIN
Partners	13 MIN
Patterns	12 MIN
Pollination Mechanisms	12 MIN
Protective Coloration	13 MIN
Seed Dispersal	12 MIN
Surviving the Cold	12 MIN
Tree Blossoms	12 MIN

Dist - CORF

Manzana Por Manzana 35 MIN
VHS / U-matic
Color (SPANISH)
Introduces the vast process of reconstruction in Northern Nicaragua. Explains the Nicaraguan revolution through songs, statements and views of local Nicaraguan activities.
History - World
Dist - ICARUS **Prod** - YASHGR

Manzanar 16 MIN
VHS / U-matic
Japanese American experience in World War II series
Color (G)
$99.00 purchase, $30.00 rental
Captures the emotions of filmmaker Robert A Nakamura as he revisits Manzanar, where he was interned as a child. Recalls his childhood experiences there.

Biography; History - United States; Sociology
Dist - CROCUR **Prod** - VISCOM 1971

Mao by Mao 20 MIN
U-matic / VHS
Color
Offers an autobiography of Chinese leader Mao Tse - Tung drawn from his writings, diaries, speeches and personal notes. Includes the first photos in which Mao appeared as well as a look at the 1949 Shanghai victory parade, filmed by Henri Cartier - Bresson.
Biography; History - World
Dist - FOTH **Prod** - FOTH 1984

Mao - Long March to Power 24 MIN
16mm / U-matic / VHS
Leaders of the 20th century - portraits of power series
Color (H C A) (SPANISH DANISH)
Portrays Mao Tse - Tung's rise to power as he competed against nationalist rival Chiang Kai - Shek.
Biography; Civics and Political Systems; History - World
Dist - LCOA **Prod** - NIELSE 1979

Mao - Organized Chaos 24 MIN
U-matic / VHS / 16mm
Leaders of the 20th century - portraits of power series
Color (H C A) (SPANISH DANISH)
Shows the philosophy of Mao's Little Red Book, and how the chaos of the cultural revolution produced the greatest order China had ever known.
Biography; Civics and Political Systems; History - World
Dist - LCOA **Prod** - NIELSE 1979

Mao to Mozart - Isaac Stern in China
VHS / BETA
Color
Provides insights into east and west through Isaac Stern's tour of China and the resulting cultural exchange.
Geography - World
Dist - GA **Prod** - GA

Mao Tse - tung 26 MIN
16mm / U-matic / VHS
Biography Series
B&W (J)
LC FIA67-1385
Presents a biography of Mao tse - tung, the head of the Chinese Communist Party. Shows how he was influenced by the democratic revolution of Sun - Yat - sen in the 1920's and how he engineered a Communist takeover in China.
Biography; Civics and Political Systems; Geography - World; History - World
Dist - MGHT **Prod** - WOLPER 1964

Mao Tse - Tung 13 MIN
U-matic / VHS
Color (G)
$229.00, $129.00 purchase _ #AD - 1862
Looks briefly at the life of Mao Tse - Tung. Considers also the transformation of China from a dynastic empire to a government run by and for the peasants, from a feudal agrarian society to an organized, highly - centralized Communist country.
Biography; Civics and Political Systems; Geography - World; History - World
Dist - FOTH **Prod** - FOTH

Mao Tse Tung Profile 17 MIN
VHS / U-matic
Color (H C A)
Documents the life of Mao Tse - tung, from his role in the overthrow of the Man Chu dynasty to the opening of China to the Western nations.
Biography; History - World
Dist - JOU **Prod** - UPI
UILL

Mao Tse - Tung Remakes China 29 MIN
Videoreel / VT2
Folk Guitar Plus Series
Color
History - World
Dist - PBS **Prod** - WGBHTV

Mao Tse - Tung, the greatest revolutionary of our time 17 MIN
16mm
Color (G)
$20.00 rental
Reflects upon the contributions of Mao Tse-Tung. Gives a sweeping view of the proletariat's ascendancy to power, from the Paris Commune and the Russian Revolution to the Cultural Revolution. Represents revolutionary filmmakers in the 1960s whose work provides a window to that period.
Civics and Political Systems; Fine Arts; History - World; Social Science
Dist - CANCIN **Prod** - SINGLE 1978

Mao Zedong and his son 108 MIN
VHS
Color (G) (MANDARIN)
$45.00 purchase _ #0295C
Presents a documentary about Mao Zedong and his son produced in the People's Republic of China.
Fine Arts
Dist - CHTSUI

Maori 22 MIN
16mm / U-matic / VHS
Color (J A)
Presents a comprehensive look at the past, present and future of the Maori people, descendants of the original inhabitants of New Zealand. Portrays the stresses and pulls of this rural, traditional people as they move to the cities for jobs and urban lifestyles.
Geography - World; Sociology
Dist - UNKNWN **Prod** - NFUNZ

Maori Arts and Culture 29 MIN
16mm
Color (J A)
Shows the magnificent carving of the early Maori and explains the reasons for the decline and renaissance of Maori art. Points out that in the decoration of some new meeting houses, Maori artists and craftsmen are again producing fine work.
Fine Arts; Geography - World; History - World; Social Science
Dist - UNKNWN **Prod** - NFUNZ

Map and Globe Skills - Introduction 20 MIN
VHS / U-matic
Map and Globe Skills Series
Color (I J)
Provides information on maps and globes by showing visits to the Library of Congress map division and to the American Automobile Association's cartographic department.
Social Science
Dist - GPN **Prod** - WCVETV 1978

Map and Globe Skills Series

Earth, direction and time	20 MIN
Geographical Forms	20 MIN
Map and Globe Skills - Introduction	20 MIN
Map Reading	20 MIN
Map Usage	20 MIN
Types of maps	20 MIN

Dist - GPN

Map and globe terms 18 MIN
VHS
Geography tutor series
Color (J H C G)
$49.95 purchase _ #BM101V-S
Defines and explains standard map terms. Illustrates topics which are easily referenced through an on-screen digital timer. Includes teacher's guide and glossary. Part of a six-part series on geography.
Geography - World; Social Science
Dist - CAMV
GA

Map and globe terms 18 MIN
VHS
Geography tutor series
Color (J H)
$49.00 _ #60456 - 026
Features part of an six - part series on geography packed with illustrated terms, concepts and site studies to reinforce specific content. Includes teacher's guide.
Education; Geography - World
Dist - GA

The Map Collectors 30 MIN
U-matic
Maps - Horizons to Knowledge Series
Color
Gives an historical review of map societies of cartographers and collectors. Looks at examples of rare maps.
Geography - United States; Geography - World; Social Science
Dist - UMITV **Prod** - UMITV 1980

A Map for Mr Meep 17 MIN
16mm / VHS
Color (P)
$370.00, $355.00 purchase, $60.00 rental
Teaches about reading maps through a story with Margaret, Marsha and the unusual Mr Meep. Introduces map basics, including how to read legends and directions. The principles of reading a neighborhood map are then extended to understanding maps of towns, states, nations, and the world.
Geography - World; Social Science
Dist - HIGGIN **Prod** - HIGGIN 1986

Map Grids 10 MIN
U-matic
Geography Skills Series
Color (J H)
Teaches the simple scientific method of determining location by means of a map grid and its advantages and disadvantages.
Computer Science; Education; Geography - World
Dist - TVOTAR **Prod** - TVOTAR 1985

Map of California - Highlands and their Uses 18 MIN
16mm
Color (I J H)
LC FIA67-8
Shows how the highlands, ranging from 1,000 to 14,000 feet above sea level, are used to grow apricots and peaches, to raise sheep and cattle, to mine ore, to provide lumbering and military bases and to serve as recreation sites for national and state parks.
Agriculture; Geography - United States; Social Science
Dist - ACA **Prod** - ACA 1966

Map of life - science, society and the human genome project 46 MIN
VHS
Color (J H)
$60.00 purchase _ #A5VH 1264
Takes a look at the quest to map and sequence the entire human genome. Features Dr James D Watson, former head of the Natl Center for Human Genome Research, who explains the goals of the massive 15 - year project. Dr Walter Gilbert explains some of the science behind mapping and sequencing genes and how scientists are using this information to understand how genes control the functions of the human body. Drs Louis Sullivan and Bernadine Healy discuss how the results of the project will revolutionize biomedicine and how society must deal with the many ethical issues surrounding the research.
Health and Safety; Science - Natural
Dist - CLRVUE **Prod** - CLRVUE 1992

Map projection 11 MIN
VHS
Map reading series
Color (I J)
$24.95 purchase _ #S9048
Presents three major map projections. Part of a five - part series teaching mapping skills in single - concept format.
Geography - World; Science - Physical; Social Science
Dist - HUBDSC **Prod** - HUBDSC

Map projections in the computer age 11 MIN
VHS
Color (I J H)
$59.00 purchase _ #MF-3076; $270.00, $190.00 purchase _ #3076
Reveals that a recent development in mapmaking, the use of computers, has allowed cartographers to produce accurate and specialized versions of maps more quickly than ever before. Shows cylindrical, conic, azimuthal and equal - space projections, revealing the functions and distortions of each. Points out that computers produce maps mathematically instead of by projection and that they can generate a map which is a combination of several different projections.
Geography - World
Dist - INSTRU **Prod** - CORF
CORF

Map Reading 16 MIN
U-matic / VHS / 16mm
Color
Presents a boy trying to find a present hidden in a park. Tells how he learns from his father about directions, the use of a compass, scales for distances and map symbols.
Social Science
Dist - HANDEL **Prod** - HANDEL 1981

Map Reading 20 MIN
U-matic
Map and Globe Skills Series
Color (I J)
Imparts basic map reading information. Explains distance determination and scales and symbols interpretation.
Social Science
Dist - GPN **Prod** - WCVETV 1979

Map reading - 1 12 MIN
VHS
Color; PAL (P I)
PdS25.00 purchase
Explains the advantages of using maps for accurate direction in the absence of signposts. Looks at symbols on the map and their meaning. A continuation from Following Directions.
Social Science
Dist - EMFVL **Prod** - LOOLEA

Map Reading and Trip Planning 30 MIN
Videoreel / VT2
Sportsmanlike Driving Series
B&W (C A)
Health and Safety; Physical Education and Recreation; Social Science; Sociology
Dist - GPN **Prod** - AAAFTS

Map reading II 17 MIN
16mm / VHS

Color (J H)
$370.00, $340.00 purchase
Portrays two students who are taking a trip from Los Angeles to San Diego. Looks at maps of the two cities as well as of the State of California. Shows how to convert map distances in ground distances, the use of checkpoints to verify progress, map symbols. Stresses safe driving.
Geography - United States; Health and Safety; Social Science
Dist - HANDEL **Prod** - HANDEL 1990

Map reading series
Presents a five - part series teaching mapping skills in single - concept format. Includes Earth and Scale, Longitude and Latitude, Map Projection, Contour Mapping, Profile Mapping.
Contour mapping 10 MIN
Earth and scale 11 MIN
Longitude and latitude 11 MIN
Map projection 11 MIN
Profile mapping 8 MIN
Dist - HUBDSC **Prod** - HUBDSC 1990

Map skills 18 MIN
VHS
Geography tutor series
Color (J H C G)
$49.95 purchase _ #BM103V-S
Introduces students to actual use of map skills. Illustrates covered topics which are easily referenced through an on-screen digital timer. Includes teacher's guide and glossary. Part of a six-part series on geography.
Geography - World; Social Science
Dist - CAMV
GA

Map skills for beginners - directions 10 MIN
VHS
Map skills for beginners series
Color; PAL (P I J H)
Teaches about directions such as left and right based on body orientation, and north, south, east and west based on the North Star and the rising and setting sun. Looks at the use of a map and compass. Part of a series on map skills.
Geography - World; Science - Physical; Social Science
Dist - VIEWTH **Prod** - VIEWTH

Map skills for beginners - globes 10 MIN
VHS
Map skills for beginners series
Color; PAL (P I J H)
Teaches about the use of globes in representing the bodies of water and land masses of Earth. Considers the poles, equator, labeling the oceans, continents and countries. Part of a series on map skills.
Geography - World; Science - Physical; Social Science
Dist - VIEWTH **Prod** - VIEWTH

Map skills for beginners - maps 10 MIN
VHS
Map skills for beginners series
Color; PAL (P I J H)
Teaches about maps. Looks at the use of scale and symbols, reading a legend, directions, using a grid to find certain locations with ease. Part of a series on map skills.
Geography - World; Science - Physical; Social Science
Dist - VIEWTH **Prod** - VIEWTH

Map skills for beginners series
Latitude 17 MIN
Longitude 16 MIN
Dist - CORF

Map skills for beginners series
Map skills for beginners - directions 10 MIN
Map skills for beginners - globes 10 MIN
Map skills for beginners - maps 10 MIN
Dist - VIEWTH

Map skills - latitude 12 MIN
VHS
Map skills series
Color; PAL (H)
Features animated wildlife photographer Natalie Haymaker who teaches how all points north or south of the equator are measured in degrees, why there is a definite worldwide relationship between latitude and climate. Shows how degrees translate into miles and how, in the northern hemisphere, latitude can be calculated in reference to the North Star. Part of a series on map skills.
Geography - World; Science - Physical; Social Science
Dist - VIEWTH **Prod** - VIEWTH

Map skills - longitude 12 MIN
VHS
Map skills series
Color; PAL (H)
Features animated wildlife photographer Natalie Haymaker who demonstrates the location and role of the prime meridian, measurement of longitude in degrees, time and miles, how longitude meridians are used to divide the globe into time zones. Demonstrates that the distance between longitude lines diminishes as they range in distance from the equator. Part of a series on map skills.
Geography - World; Science - Physical; Social Science
Dist - VIEWTH **Prod** - VIEWTH

Map skills - physical features 12 MIN
VHS
Map skills series
Color; PAL (H)
Features animated outdoorsman Lance Bolder who attempts to climb the highest mountain on the island and shows how he learns some important lessons about how a map indicates physical features. Looks at map indicators for various bodies of water, including the difference between a gulf, a bay, a lake and an ocean. Shows that elevation is determined in relationship to sea level and how land contours are treated on maps. Part of a series on map skills.
Geography - World; Science - Physical; Social Science
Dist - VIEWTH **Prod** - VIEWTH

Map Skills - Recognizing Physical Features 11 MIN
U-matic / VHS / 16mm
Map Skills Series
Color (I J)
LC 79-704816
Compares map symbols with physical features, shows how colors represent elevation and defines physical features, such as gulf, peninsula, island, strait, channel, tributary, plain and plateau.
Geography - United States; History - United States; Social Science
Dist - CORF **Prod** - CORF 1969

Map skills - scale 12 MIN
VHS
Map skills series
Color; PAL (H)
Features animated outdoorsman Lance Bolder as he attempts to escape an erupting volcano. Shows that Bolder discovers how important it is to understand scale in map reading. Compares the concept of scale to actual objects. Illustrates scale through ratio, unit comparison and bar scales. Part of a series on map skills.
Geography - World; Science - Physical; Social Science
Dist - VIEWTH **Prod** - VIEWTH

Map skills series
Latitude 12 MIN
Longitude 12 MIN
Map Skills - Recognizing Physical Features 11 MIN
Map Skills - Understanding Latitude 11 MIN
Map Skills - Understanding Longitude 11 MIN
Map Skills - using Different Maps Together 11 MIN
Map Skills - using Scale 11 MIN
Physical Features 12 MIN
Scale 12 MIN
Using Maps Together 12 MIN
Dist - CORF

Map skills series
Map skills - latitude 12 MIN
Map skills - longitude 12 MIN
Map skills - physical features 12 MIN
Map skills - scale 12 MIN
Map skills - using maps together 12 MIN
Dist - VIEWTH

Map Skills - Understanding Latitude 11 MIN
U-matic / VHS / 16mm
Map Skills Series
Color
LC 76-713535
Traces the development of latitude in exploration and map - making. Introduces tropic, temperate and frigid climate zones; and shows the relationship between latitude and climate.
Geography - World; Science - Physical; Social Science
Dist - CORF **Prod** - CORF 1971

Map Skills - Understanding Longitude 11 MIN
16mm / U-matic / VHS
Map Skills Series
Color
LC 70-713536
Shows how meridians are drawn, how longitude and time are related, and how to use longitude with latitude to pinpoint the exact locations of places.
Geography - World; Social Science
Dist - CORF **Prod** - CORF 1971

Map Skills - using Different Maps Together 11 MIN
U-matic / VHS / 16mm
Map Skills Series
Color (I J)
LC FIA66-34
Maps of the same scale and projection are combined to reveal relationships between natural features of the earth, human use and social and political features. Animation is used.
Social Science
Dist - CORF **Prod** - CORF 1966

Map skills - using maps together 12 MIN
VHS
Map skills series
Color; PAL (H)
Features animated outdoorsman Lance Bolder who shows how to use information from several maps of the same scale to reveal information on a single area. Emphasizes the value of combining information from elevation maps, transportation maps, physical feature maps, rainfall maps and natural resource maps. Underscores the meaning and significance of colors, lines and symbols on maps. Part of a series on map skills.
Geography - World; Science - Physical; Social Science
Dist - VIEWTH **Prod** - VIEWTH

Map Skills - using Scale 11 MIN
U-matic / VHS / 16mm
Map Skills Series
Color (I J)
LC 72-713534
Compares scale models with actual objects to define scale. Introduces the main types of scales and shows how to use them to estimate distances.
Geography - World; Mathematics; Social Science
Dist - CORF **Prod** - CORF 1971

Map Symbols 10 MIN
U-matic
Geography Skills Series
Color (J H)
Teaches an understanding of map legends and the techniques of identifying and locating information thorugh different sizes and shapes of symbols.
Computer Science; Education; Geography - World
Dist - TVOTAR **Prod** - TVOTAR 1985

Map Usage 20 MIN
U-matic
Map and Globe Skills Series
Color (I J)
Explains important map elements, including grid, index systems and legends. Features a taxi driver discussing the importance of maps in his work.
Social Science
Dist - GPN **Prod** - WCVETV 1979

Map your way to better grades 30 MIN
VHS
Go to the head of the class series
Color (H C A)
$29.95 purchase _ #LF703V
Teaches the notetaking strategy known as 'mindmapping,' which is a visual way of recording data. Includes a booklet.
Education; Psychology
Dist - CAMV

Mapandangare, the Great Baboon 10 MIN
U-matic / VHS / 16mm
Color (P I J)
LC 78-702009
Provides a basic introduction to African musical instruments and shows how they are made. Features musicologist Andrew Tracy, who illustrates the role of music in African storytelling by having children chant responses as he relates a tale of a brave baboon.
Fine Arts; Geography - World
Dist - ALTSUL **Prod** - TEGNID 1978

MAPC - medical aseptic protective care 18 MIN
U-matic / VHS
Color (PRO C)
$395.00 purchase, $80.00 rental _ #C850 - VI - 106
Explains Medical Aseptic Protective Care - MAPR - a system for limiting the spread of microorganisms. Shows how, by following MAPR procedures, medical professionals and hospital personnel can help prevent the spread of communicable disorders to other patients and among themselves. Presented by Mary Beth O'Holleran, RN.
Health and Safety
Dist - HSCIC

Maple 4 MIN
16mm
Color (K P)
LC 80-700759
Presents a story about a sad child who is offered a variety of material things, but only becomes happy when she receives the gift of friendship.
Guidance and Counseling; Literature and Drama
Dist - IKONOG **Prod** - IKONOG 1976

The Maple and the Crown - the Royal Family in Canada 88 MIN
VHS
Color (S)
$79.00 purchase _ #386 - 9044
Presents rare film footage that captures history though the experiences of the British Royal Family. Features the full panoply of splendid state events from the 1939 Canadian Peace Tour of King George VI to Elizabeth II's magnificent coronation in Westminster Abbey and the fairy - tale wedding of Charles and Diana, as well as intimate family moments.
Civics and Political Systems; Geography - World; History - World
Dist - FI **Prod** - CANBC 1988

The Maple Leaf Forever 10 MIN
16mm / U-matic / VHS
Color (I J H)
LC 77-703187
Uses authentic costumes, buildings and language to re - create the life of a small Canadian town in the middle of the 19th century, the time of the celebration of that country's nationhood.
Geography - World; History - World; Social Science
Dist - JOU **Prod** - TFW 1977

Maple Spring 14 MIN
16mm / U-matic / VHS
Color (P I J)
Illustrates how a family works together, when the spring thaw begins in the north, to harvest the sap from the sugar maple trees on their farm. Shows many uses they make from the syrup, on fresh bread, butter - raisin tarts, and finally, a 'sugaring off' party to celebrate the end of harvest.
Agriculture; Science - Natural; Social Science; Sociology
Dist - BCNFL **Prod** - NELVNA 1979

The Maple Sugar Farmer 29 MIN
U-matic / VHS / 16mm
Yesterday and Today Series
Color (I)
LC 73-701667
Portrays Sherman Graff, a 72 - year - old maple sugar farmer who lives in Southern Illinois. Features Graff explaining how to make both maple syrup and maple sugar the way his ancestors did six generations ago.
Agriculture
Dist - AIMS **Prod** - HINDAV 1973

Maple Syrup 13 MIN
16mm / U-matic / VHS
Color (I)
LC 79-701797
Shows how maple syrup is produced, from the sapping of trees to the treatment and storage of sap.
Agriculture; Science - Natural
Dist - MCFI **Prod** - UWISC 1978

Maple syrup making 15 MIN
VHS
Field trips series
Color (I J)
$34.95 purchase _ #E337; LC 90-708575
Visits a maple syrup making operation and discusses the history of syrup making, the processes of tapping trees, gathering sap and the making and selling of syrup. Part of a series which provides visual opportunities for children to 'visit' a variety of locations and activities as if they were on a field trip.
Agriculture; Education; Social Science
Dist - GPN **Prod** - MPBN 1983

Mapping 60 MIN
VHS
The Ring of truth series
Color (G)
$69.95 purchase _ #RNGO - 103
Traces the history of mapping from the ancient Greeks to the satellite mapmakers of modern times. Shows how simple methods of the past could create accurate maps. Hosted by physics professor Philip Morrison.
Science - Physical
Dist - PBS **Prod** - PBA 1987

Mapping Australia 21 MIN
16mm
Color
LC FIA68-1741
Describes the mapping of Australia, from the initial aerial and ground surveys to the final printing of the completed sheet. Illustrates the importance of cartography in the nation's development.
Geography - World; Social Science
Dist - AUIS **Prod** - ANAIB 1968

Mapping feminism 40 MIN
VHS
Color (G)
$149.00 purchase
Takes the camera of Lisa Robinson onto the campus sidewalks of Univ of California, Berkeley, to ask the question of both males and females, 'Are you a feminist, and what does that mean.' Reveals that, with less than 16 percent of college women identifying themselves as feminists, the answers offered are anything but clearcut. Shows how the word 'feminism' has become extemely fuzzy in usage.
Sociology
Dist - MILMED **Prod** - MILMED 1993

Mapping for Defense 14 MIN
16mm
Color
LC 79-707416
Explains the method by which maps are developed from initial survey information.
Social Science
Dist - CDND **Prod** - CDND 1968

Mapping it out 30 MIN
Videoreel / VT2
Designing home interiors series; Unit 6
Color (C A)
Shows the drawing of a floor plan to enable students to better understand the concept of scale, placement of windows and doors, and architectural symbols.
Fine Arts; Home Economics
Dist - CDTEL **Prod** - COAST

Mapping of History - the History of Mapping 30 MIN
U-matic
Maps - Horizons to Knowledge Series
Color
Describes the earliest maps, showing cultural and political influences of the time. Explores modern map making techniques.
Geography - United States; Geography - World; Social Science
Dist - UMITV **Prod** - UMITV 1980

Mapping Our World 26 MIN
U-matic / VHS
Color (C)
$249.00, $149.00 purchase _ #AD - 1901
Traces the development of mapmaking from an art to a science. Starts with maps concocted from the tales of travelers and embellished by the mapmakers imagination. Shows the elements of modern mapmaking, computers, remote sensing technology, computer - generated imagery from satellites and radar emanations from space vehicles.
Geography - World; History - World; Science - Physical; Social Science
Dist - FOTH **Prod** - FOTH

Mapping the Land 15 MIN
U-matic
North America - Growth of a Continent Series
Color (J H)
Traces the patterns of immigration to North America from the late fifteenth century to the present. Also includes map making, latitude, longitude and time zones.
Geography - United States; Geography - World
Dist - TVOTAR **Prod** - TVOTAR 1980

Mapping the Products of the Human Genome 59 MIN
U-matic
Color
Discusses the anatomy of the cell and its molecular constituents.
Health and Safety; Science - Natural
Dist - UTEXSC **Prod** - UTEXSC

Mapping the Weather 26 MIN
VHS / 16mm
Blue Revolution Series
Color (J)
$149.00 purchase, $75.00 rental _ #QD - 2288
Examines the economic and human effects of the weather and efforts to measure it and forecast it. The eighth of 16 installments of the Blue Revolution Series.
Geography - World; Science - Natural; Science - Physical
Dist - FOTH

Mapping your world 17 MIN
BETA / VHS / U-matic / 16mm
Color (I J)
$280.00, $79.00 purchase _ #C50657, #C51448
Studies maps. Shows how information is coded through names, colors, lines, numbers and direction. Looks at how latitude and longitude are used to locate places on a map, how scale determines distances and a compass rose determines direction. Discusses theme maps which may focus on railroads, waterways, bedrock geology or natural resources.
Geography - World; Social Science
Dist - NGS **Prod** - NGS 1990

Mappings and Functions
16mm
B&W
Shows how a graph can be used to represent a particular situation. Defines abstract mappings and functions.
Mathematics
Dist - OPENU **Prod** - OPENU

Maps and Globes - an Introduction 17 MIN
16mm / U-matic / VHS
Color (P I J)
LC 80-701954
Introduces basic map reading skills and indicates the diversity of information available from maps.
Geography - World; Social Science
Dist - ALTSUL **Prod** - ALTSUL 1980

Maps and Landmarks 11 MIN
16mm / U-matic / VHS
Color (P I)
LC 78-711142
Tells how children use objects in their environment as landmarks to help them find their way. Traces a family's trip to grandmother's house and back, first showing the real objects used as landmarks, then a model of the area and a simple pictorial map. Provides an opportunity to apply the basic understandings to major landmarks on a physical map of the United States.
Social Science
Dist - PHENIX **Prod** - PHENIX 1971

Maps and Weather Vanes 6 MIN
16mm
Basic Facts about the Earth, Sun, Moon and Stars Series
Color (P I)
LC 70-709361
Describes the making of maps and weather vanes.
Science - Physical; Social Science
Dist - SF **Prod** - MORLAT 1967

Maps and what they tell us
VHS
Using maps, globes, graphs, tables, charts and diagrams series
Color (I J H)
$49.50 purchase _ #UL1033VJ
Shows how to interpret data in maps. Presents part of a five - part series on basic globe skills and understanding data from pictorial and other graphic representations.
Geography - World
Dist - KNOWUN

Maps are Fun 11 MIN
16mm / U-matic / VHS
Color (P I)
Shows a cartographer as he helps a young boy prepare a map of his paper route. Defines legend, scale and grid. Discusses the use of color in maps and exhibits some different types of maps.
Geography - World; Social Science
Dist - CORF **Prod** - CORF 1963

Maps for a Changing World 18 MIN
U-matic / VHS / 16mm
Color (I J)
LC 81-700057
Discusses the history of mapmaking. Explores the problems of depicting accurate representations of a round earth. Offers information on symbols, legends and scales, and takes a look at aerial photography.
Geography - World; Social Science
Dist - EBEC **Prod** - EBEC 1980

Maps - From quill to computer 26 MIN
VHS / U-matic / 16mm
Color (J H G)
$280.00, $330.00, $515.00 purchase, $55.00 rental
Introduces the history of maps from ancient times to the present. Shows how in earlier times maps were often superb works of art and vehicles for the cartographer's imagination. Now maps are produced automatically from the computerized data of surveillance satellites and aircraft.
Geography - World
Dist - NDIM **Prod** - CANBC 1985

Maps - Horizons to Knowledge Series

The Map Collectors	30 MIN
Mapping of History - the History of Mapping	30 MIN
The New Horizons	29 MIN
Production and Printing	30 MIN
To Measure the Earth	30 MIN

Dist - UMITV

Maps - How to Read Them 14 MIN
U-matic / VHS / 16mm
Color (I J)
Uses the legend of the map along with its scale and compass rose to show how maps help locate important places, trace routes from place to place and calculate distance.

Geography - United States; Geography - World; Social Science
Dist - PHENIX Prod - PHENIX 1982

Maps - know where you're going 16 MIN
U-matic / 16mm / VHS
Color (K P I)
$345.00, $270.00, $240.00 purchase _ #A979
Teaches the fundamentals of reading maps. Shows how maps are pictures or drawings of land and what's on it, how a map is drawn to scale and how distances can be measured using the scale and a ruler. Looks at the key to maps and symbols, how to read the index and use grids to locate streets and addresses, the points of the compass.
Geography - United States; Geography - World; Social Science
Dist - BARR Prod - SAIF 1984

Maps Show Our Earth 10 MIN
U-matic / VHS / 16mm
Color (P)
LC 73-701638
Explains how colors and key symbols are used on maps, how maps can be used together and how they relate to a globe.
Geography - World; Mathematics; Social Science
Dist - CORF Prod - CORF 1973

Maps - Symbols and Terms 15 MIN
U-matic / VHS / 16mm
Color (I)
LC 83-700115
Discusses map symbols, common and practical uses of maps, and the concepts and related language of direction, scale and projection.
Geography - United States; Social Science
Dist - AIMS Prod - AIMS 1983

Maps - where am I 12 MIN
U-matic / VHS / 16mm
Color (P) (SPANISH)
LC 83-700196
Takes a helicopter ride over a neighborhood and translates the vertical view into a flat map. Discusses the use of colors, symbols, map scale, distance scale, and direction.
Geography - United States; Social Science
Dist - AIMS Prod - AIMS 1982
INSTRU

Maps - where am I 11 MIN
VHS
Color (P) (SPANISH)
$49.95 purchase _ #9711D3
Helps kids to relate the three - dimensional world in which they live to the two - dimensional world of maps by taking some children on a helicopter ride over a neighborhood and translating that view into a flat map.
Geography - World
Dist - INSTRU

Mara - Mara - Marathon 3 MIN
U-matic / VHS
Metric Marvels Series
Color (P I)
Shows how Meter Man uses a track meet to explain kilometers and other metric distances.
Fine Arts; Mathematics
Dist - GA Prod - NBCTV 1978

Marasmus 24 MIN
16mm
Color (G)
$50.00 rental
Offers 'A woman's response to technology - the jet lag of birth.' Coproduced by Betzy Bromberg and Laura Ewig.
Fine Arts; Sociology
Dist - CANCIN

Marat Sade 115 MIN
VHS
Color (G C H)
$109.00 purchase _ #DL209
Presents Peter Brook's version of the Peter Weiss play, in which the Marquis de Sade, confined to an asylum, directs the other patients in a reenactment of the assassination of French revolutionary Jean - Paul Marat.
Fine Arts
Dist - INSIM

Marathon 10 MIN
16mm
Color
LC 73-700735
Documents the progress of a 52 - hour dance marathon which was held by students at the University of Maryland to raise money for the Muscular Dystrophy Association of America.
Physical Education and Recreation; Sociology
Dist - UMD Prod - UMD 1972

Marathon 8 MIN
16mm
Color
LC 78-700429
Shows the running of the New York Marathon.
Physical Education and Recreation
Dist - COMCOR Prod - MHT 1977

The Marathon 50 MIN
U-matic / 16mm
Olympiad Series
Color; Mono (J H C A)
$650.00 film, $350.00 video, $50.00 rental
Examines the marathon through Olympic history, focusing on Abebe Bikila and his historic 1960 race.
Physical Education and Recreation
Dist - CTV Prod - CTV 1976

The Marathon 50 MIN
BETA / 16mm / VHS
Color
LC 77-702541
Presents a television special from the CTV program Olympiad which highlights dramatic moments in the history of the Olympic marathon competitions. Includes newsreel footage from 1908 to 1976.
Physical Education and Recreation
Dist - CTV Prod - CTV 1976

Marathon 28 MIN
VHS
Elephant show series
Color (P I)
$95.00 purchase, $45.00 rental
Presents program 17 in the Sharon, Lois and Bram's Elephant Show series. Teaches reading readiness and social skills while engaging children in making music. Each program explores a new theme through adventure, fantasy, mystery and song with recording artists Sharon, Lois and Bram. Uses traditional materials which stress participation - action songs, sing - along songs, story songs, clapping songs, singing games, playground chants and folk songs from many different traditions. Includes teacher's guide co - authored by a music education specialist.
Fine Arts; Sociology
Dist - BULFRG Prod - CAMBFP 1989

Marathon challenge 60 MIN
VHS
Track and field series
Color (J H C A)
$39.95 purchase _ #MXS460V
Features Dr Ken Foreman, former U S Olympic women's track coach, in a comprehensive program to teach skills of Marathon running. Follows eight runners as they set out to meet the Marathon challenge. Covers subjects including buying the right shoes, proper training, diet advice, hill running, exercises, and more.
Physical Education and Recreation
Dist - CAMV

The Marathon Challenge 60 MIN
BETA / VHS
Color
Presents instruction and advice for the runner training for a marathon.
Physical Education and Recreation
Dist - MOHOMV Prod - MOHOMV

Marathon Fever 24 MIN
16mm
Color
LC 81-700396
Follows a marathon race from start to finish.
Physical Education and Recreation
Dist - CANTOR Prod - ALPERT 1979

Marathon fever - dare to excel 24 MIN
U-matic / VHS
Guidance, health, and drug prevention series
Color (G A)
$129 purchase _ #06861 - 851
Documents the experiences of four ordinary people who tackle the challenge of running a 26 mile marathon. Focuses on the rigors of achieving unusually high goals. Presents running as an alternative to drug use.
Physical Education and Recreation; Psychology
Dist - CHUMAN Prod - GA
GA

Marathon Man 125 MIN
16mm / U-matic / VHS
Color
Tells how a graduate student is caught up in intrigue involving a vicious Nazi criminal. Stars Dustin Hoffman, Roy Scheider and Laurence Olivier.
Fine Arts
Dist - FI Prod - PAR 1976

The Marathon - Pt 1 25 MIN
BETA / 16mm / VHS
Color
LC 77-702541
Presents a television special from the CTV program Olympiad which highlights dramatic moments in the history of the Olympic marathon competitions. Includes newsreel footage from 1908 to 1976.
Physical Education and Recreation
Dist - CTV Prod - CTV 1976

The Marathon - Pt 2 25 MIN
16mm / VHS / BETA
Color
LC 77-702541
Presents a television special from the CTV program Olympiad which highlights dramatic moments in the history of the Olympic marathon competitions. Includes newsreel footage from 1908 to 1976.
Physical Education and Recreation
Dist - CTV Prod - CTV 1976

Marathon - the Ultimate Challenge 15 MIN
16mm / VHS
Color (J H A)
$265.00, $330.00 purchase, $50.00 rental _ #8013
Views the experiences of a runner during the Vancouver International Marathon, a run of 26 miles.
Physical Education and Recreation; Psychology
Dist - AIMS Prod - EDMI 1983

Marathon Woman - Miki Gorman 28 MIN
16mm
Color (H C A)
LC 81-700389
Presents Miki Gorman, twice winner of both the New York and Boston marathons, who describes her metamorphosis from sports observer to dedicated runner.
Physical Education and Recreation
Dist - FLMLIB Prod - FLMLIB 1982

Marble Game 12 MIN
16mm
Vignette Series
B&W (T)
LC 73-707933
Focuses on a group of pre - school children at Cambridge Neighborhood House playing an impromptu game of marbles.
Education; Guidance and Counseling; Psychology; Sociology
Dist - EDC Prod - EDS 1969

Marbleized paper, crayons with paint, and other resists 56 MIN
VHS / 16mm
Children's crafts series
(K P)
$39.99 purchase _ #VT1065
Shows how to make marbleized paper. Demonstrates different kinds of art projects of materials that resist and defines 'resist.' Discusses primary and secondary colors. Suggests gift ideas, such as cards and booklets. Taught by Julie Abowitt, Multi - Arts Coordinator for the Seattle Public Schools.
Fine Arts
Dist - RMIBHF Prod - RMIBHF
MOHOMV MOHOMV

Marbury V Madison 36 MIN
16mm
Equal Justice Under Law Series
Color (H C)
LC 78-700000
Presents a dramatization of the landmark U S Supreme Court decision in Marbury v Madison which established the Supreme court's responsibility to review the constitutionality of acts of Congress.
Civics and Political Systems; History - United States
Dist - USNAC Prod - USJUDC 1977

Marbury Vs Madison
U-matic / VHS / 35mm strip
Supreme Court Decisions that Changed the Nation Series
(J H C)
$59.00 purchase=FS _ #06803 94, $69.00 purchase=MV _ #06803 94
Explores the lasting impact of the Marbury versus Madison supreme court case, which clarified the power of the judiciary. Features historical photography.
Civics and Political Systems
Dist - ASPRSS Prod - GA
GA

Marc and Ann 27 MIN
16mm / U-matic / VHS
Color (G)
$500.00, $350.00, $250.00 purchase
Portrays Marc and Ann Savoy, a young Cajun musical couple. Reveals Marc as a musician and master accordion - builder, irreverent storyteller and outspoken promoter of his culture, and Ann, mother of four and author of Cajun Music - A Reflection of a People.
Fine Arts; Geography - United States
Dist - FLOWER Prod - BLNKL 1991

Marc Brown video series - Set I
VHS
Marc Brown video series
Color (K)
$63.00 purchase
Presents 'Arthur's Tooth' and 'Arthur's Eyes.'.
Literature and Drama
Dist - PELLER

Marc Brown video series - Set II
VHS
Marc Brown video series
Color (K)
$63.00 purchase
Presents 'Arthur's Teacher Trouble' and 'Arthur Goes To Camp.'.
Literature and Drama
Dist - PELLER

Marc Brown video series - set III
VHS
Marc Brown video series
Color (K)
$63.00 purchase
Presents 'Dinosaurs Divorce' and 'Dinosaurs Beware.'.
Literature and Drama
Dist - PELLER

Marc Brown video series
Marc Brown video series - Set I
Marc Brown video series - Set II
Marc Brown video series - set III
Dist - PELLER

Marc Chagall 26 MIN
U-matic / VHS / 16mm
Color (J)
LC FIA66-1478
Examines the style and content of Marc Chagall's paintings and discusses his contribution to 20th - century art.
Biography; Fine Arts
Dist - MGHT **Prod** - AUERBH 1965

Marc Chagall 52 MIN
VHS
Color (S)
$39.95 purchase _ #833 - 9004
Explores the life and work of Marc Chagall. Documents the history of a poor Russian Jew who became the grand old man of French art.
Fine Arts; History - World; Sociology
Dist - FI **Prod** - RMART 1986

Marc Chagall 25 MIN
U-matic / VHS / 16mm
Color (H C A)
LC 81-706534
Explores the life and work of Marc Chagall, depicting his works on canvas, in sculpture and in stained glass. Discusses Chagall's contribution to 20th-century art.
Fine Arts
Dist - CRMP **Prod** - AUERBH 1965
MGHT

Marc Chagall - the Colours of Passion 24 MIN
16mm / U-matic / VHS
Color (J)
LC 79-701245
Focuses on the diverse artistic achievements of Marc Chagall. Explains Chagall's often perplexing subject matter and passion for color in terms of his stated desire to create a world where anything is possible. Includes examples of his work, along with a discussion of his background and the influences of impressionism, cubism and Russia on his work.
Biography; Fine Arts
Dist - IFB **Prod** - IFB 1979

Marc goes to hospital 25 MIN
16mm / VHS / BETA / U-matic
Color; PAL (K P I)
PdS125, PdS133 purchase
Explains what happens when a child has to go into the hospital. Takes the fear out of operations. Narrated by a doctor who explains why the medical procedures have to be done, followed by a Ward Sister who escorts the viewer through the domestic routine. Upbeat, positive production for children.
Health and Safety; Psychology; Sociology
Dist - EDPAT

Marceau on Mime 22 MIN
U-matic / VHS / 16mm
Color (I)
LC 74-701701
Presents mime artist Marcel Marceau discussing the history of mime and his personal credo as a mime artist.
Fine Arts
Dist - AIMS **Prod** - GOULDP 1973

Marcel a Paris 24 MIN
16mm / U-matic / VHS
Color (FRENCH)
Follows the adventures of nine - year - old Marcel as he tries to earn money in Paris.
Foreign Language
Dist - IFB **Prod** - IFB 1969

Marcel a Paris 23 MIN
U-matic / VHS / 16mm
Color (J H C) (FRENCH)
LC 79-709670
Provides experience with simple sentences and vocabulary spoken at a conversational tempo.
Foreign Language
Dist - IFB **Prod** - IFB 1970

Marcel in Paris 10 MIN
U-matic / VHS / 16mm
Color (P I J H)
LC 70-712917
Follows a small boy as he explores the streets of Paris and witnesses the wonders of the city. Portrays the Eiffel Tower, Champs d'Elysee and the Tuileries.
Geography - World
Dist - FI **Prod** - FI 1972

Marcel Proust 58 MIN
VHS
Modern world - ten great writers series
Color (H)
$13.00 rental _ #60960
Examines Marcel Proust's 'Remembrance Of Things Past,' both a novel about time and memory and a social satire. Part of a ten-part series that studies ten important modernist European writers by placing them against turn - of - the - century settings, dramatizing their own experiences and looking at their principal works.
Literature and Drama
Dist - PSU **Prod** - FI
FI

Marcel Proust 15 MIN
U-matic / VHS / 16mm
Color (H C A)
$365, $235 purchase _ #4053
Examines the life of artist Marcel Proust, focussing on his book, Remembrance Of Things Past. Narrated by Israel Berman. A Perspective film.
Fine Arts; Literature and Drama
Dist - CORF

Marcel Proust - 1871 - 1922 - Volume IV 58 MIN
VHS
Modern world - ten great writers series
Color (G)
$129.00 purchase _ #S01955
Profiles French author Marcel Proust. Uses drama, documentary, and literary criticism to portray Proust's experience, background and personal philosophy. Available for educational use only.
Literature and Drama
Dist - UILL

Marcel Proust - Pt 5 58 MIN
VHS
Modern World, the - 10 Great Writers Series
Color (S)
$129.00 purchase _ #833 - 9382
Profiles ten great Modernist writers whose work helped shape our world. Dramatizes the author's experiences and examines in - depth their various works. Part 5 presents Marcel Proust and his 'Remembrance Of Things Past.'.
Fine Arts; Geography - World; Literature and Drama
Dist - FI **Prod** - LONWTV 1988

Marcello, I'm So Bored 8 MIN
16mm
Color
LC 75-703205
Combines modern music and pop - art style to mirror the contemporary American social landscape with its growing lack of sincere human feeling and emotional involvement.
Guidance and Counseling; Psychology; Social Science; Sociology
Dist - USC **Prod** - USC 1967

March 10 MIN
VHS / U-matic
Emma and Grandpa series
(K P)
$180 VC purchase, $30 VC five day rental, $110 self dub
Uses simple rhyming couplets to help kindergartners and first graders understand nature and seasonal changes. Highlights the importance of conservation. Focuses on pond life. Third in a 12 part series.
Science - Natural
Dist - GPN **Prod** - GRIFN 1983

March 25 - Greek Independence Day 28 MIN
VHS
Illuminations series
Color (G R)
#V - 1017
Reviews the history of Greek independence. Documents the War of Independence and its supporters, including Lord Byron. Interviews scholars on the 400 years of Ottoman rule of Greece, the similarities between Greek and American struggles for independence, and other subjects. Emphasizes the significance of Greek Independence Day from ethnic and religious perspectives.
Fine Arts; History - World
Dist - GOTEL **Prod** - GOTEL 1988

March - a portrait of Eleanor Anderson 24 MIN
VHS
Color (G)
$125.00 purchase, $15.50 rental _ #36250
Interviews nursing home resident Eleanor Anderson, age 92, who keeps a sense of well - being by sustaining a high level of activity, interaction and personal interests, and by exercising body and mind. Shows how personal photographs lend a sense of immediacy and nostalgia as she looks back at her life. Challenges the notion of the elderly as anonymous and lacking in purpose by referring to her fellow residents as strong individuals with histories, preferences, skills and personalities. Produced by Robert Steele.
Guidance and Counseling; Health and Safety; Psychology; Social Science
Dist - PSU

The March for disarmament 27 MIN
VHS
Color (G)
$39.95 purchase
Chronicles the June 12, 1982 march and rally for peace and disarmament in New York City. Reveals that nearly one million people joined the protest. Interviews Dick Gregory, Joan Baez, Theodore Bikel, Holly Near, Randall Forseberg.
History - United States; Religion and Philosophy; Sociology
Dist - WMMI **Prod** - WMMI 1982

March for Life 20 MIN
VHS / BETA
Color
Expounds the position against abortion and covers the 1986 March for Life.
Religion and Philosophy; Sociology
Dist - DSP **Prod** - DSP

March in April 60 MIN
VHS
Color (G)
$390.00 purchase, $75.00 rental
Features a personal record of the historic 1993 Gay Civil Rights March on Washington, DC by documenting Mark and several of his friends from around the country who have come to stay with him for that week. Delves into the personal lives of these gay men, their worries, relationships with families, etc. Features encounters with political figures. Produced by Stephen Kinsella.
Civics and Political Systems; Fine Arts; Sociology
Dist - FIRS

March of the Wooden Soldiers 70 MIN
16mm
B&W
Stars Laurel and Hardy in an adaptation of Victor Herbert's operetta Babes In Toyland. Shows how Laurel and Hardy try to help Bo Peep save her home from the evil Barnaby.
Fine Arts
Dist - FI **Prod** - ROACH 1934

March of time - America at war series 678 MIN
VHS
B&W (G)
$149.95 purchase _ #S02121
Presents a six - part series of newsreel excerpts covering the American effort in World War II.
History - United States
Dist - UILL

March of time - America at war series
American defense - Pt 1 122 MIN
American defense - Pt 2 126 MIN
Friend and foe - Pt 1 116 MIN
Friend and foe - Pt 2 87 MIN
Friend and foe - Pt 3 87 MIN
On the homefront 114 MIN
Dist - UILL

March of time - American fashion and leisure 1945 - 1950 105 MIN
VHS
March of time series
B&W (G)
$24.95 purchase _ #S01517
Uses newsreel footage from 1945 to 1950 to present a view of American fashion and leisure trends. Originally produced by Time magazine.
History - United States; Home Economics
Dist - UILL **Prod** - TIMLIF

March of time - American lifestyles 1939 - 1950 series 540 MIN
VHS
B&W (G)
$149.70 purchase _ #S01514
Uses newsreel footage from 1939 to 1950 to present a view of American culture during that period. Consists of six 90 - minute tapes. Originally produced by Time magazine.
History - United States
Dist - UILL **Prod** - TIMLIF

March of time - Americans prepare 1939 - 1940 118 MIN
VHS
March of time series
B&W (G)
$24.95 purchase _ #S01521
Uses newsreel footage from 1939 to 1940 to present a view of Americans as they prepared for possible involvement in World War II. Originally produced by Time magazine.
History - United States
Dist - UILL **Prod** - TIMLIF

March of time - Americans prepare 1940 - 1941 113 MIN
VHS
March of time series
B&W (G)
$24.95 purchase _ #S01522
Uses newsreel footage from 1940 to 1941 to present a view of Americans as they prepared for possible involvement in World War II. Originally produced by Time magazine.
History - United States
Dist - UILL **Prod** - TIMLIF

March of time - America's youth 1940 - 1950 90 MIN
VHS
March of time series
B&W (G)
$24.95 purchase _ #S01518
Uses newsreel footage from 1940 to 1950 to present a view of American young people and the challenges they faced. Originally produced by Time magazine.
History - United States; Sociology
Dist - UILL **Prod** - TIMLIF

March of time - post - war problems and solutions series 125 MIN
VHS
B&W (G)
$124.90 purchase _ #S02128
Presents a five - part series of newsreel excerpts covering the post - World War II era in the US and abroad.
History - United States; History - World
Dist - UILL

March of time - post - war problems and solutions series

America's post - war problems - Part 1	125 MIN
America's post - war problems - Part 2	119 MIN
Modern main street, USA	120 MIN
Post - war problems beyond - Pt 3	107 MIN
Post - war problems beyond - Pt 4	125 MIN

Dist - UILL

March of time - praying for peace 1940 - 1941 71 MIN
VHS
March of time series
B&W (G)
$24.95 purchase _ #S01526
Uses newsreel footage from 1940 to 1941 to present a view of the Vatican and its response to World War II. Originally produced by Time magazine.
History - World; Religion and Philosophy
Dist - UILL **Prod** - TIMLIF

March of time series
The Land of cotton
Dist - KITPAR

March of Time Series

Demagogues and do - gooders	20 MIN
Exits and Entrances	20 MIN
Is Everybody Listening	20 MIN
The Movies March on	20 MIN
Under the Clouds of War	20 MIN

Dist - TIMLIF

March of time series

March of time - American fashion and leisure 1945 - 1950	105 MIN
March of time - Americans prepare 1939 - 1940	118 MIN
March of time - Americans prepare 1940 - 1941	113 MIN
March of time - America's youth 1940 - 1950	90 MIN
March of time - praying for peace 1940 - 1941	71 MIN
March of time - show business - the postwar years 1946 - 1950	92 MIN
March of time - show business - the war years 1939 - 1945	73 MIN
March of time - the American family - the postwar years 1946 - 1948	89 MIN
March of time - the American family - the war years 1941 - 1945	89 MIN
March of time - the battle beyond 1939 - 1940	107 MIN
March of time - the battle beyond 1940 - 1941	117 MIN
March of time - the military prepares 1930 - 1941	124 MIN

Dist - UILL

March of Time Series

Frontiers of the Mind	52 MIN
Frontiers of the Mind, Pt 1	26 MIN
Frontiers of the Mind, Pt 2	26 MIN
Seven days in the life of the president	60 MIN

Dist - WOLPER

March of time - show business - the postwar years 1946 - 1950 92 MIN
VHS
March of time series
B&W (G)
$24.95 purchase _ #S01519
Uses newsreel footage from 1946 to 1950 to present a view of American show business and its changes after World War II. Originally produced by Time magazine.
Fine Arts; History - United States
Dist - UILL **Prod** - TIMLIF

March of time - show business - the war years 1939 - 1945 73 MIN
VHS
March of time series
B&W (G)
$24.95 purchase _ #S01520
Uses newsreel footage from 1939 to 1945 to present a view of American show business and its role in maintaining morale during World War II. Originally produced by Time magazine.
Fine Arts; History - United States
Dist - UILL **Prod** - TIMLIF

March of time - the American family - the postwar years 1946 - 1948 89 MIN
VHS
March of time series
B&W (G)
$24.95 purchase _ #S01515
Uses 1940s newsreel footage to present a view of the American family at that time. Originally produced by Time magazine.
History - United States; Sociology
Dist - UILL **Prod** - TIMLIF

March of time - the American family - the war years 1941 - 1945 89 MIN
VHS
March of time series
B&W (G)
$24.95 purchase _ #S01516
Uses newsreel footage from 1941 to 1945 to present a view of American families and how they responded to World War II. Originally produced by Time magazine.
History - United States; Sociology
Dist - UILL **Prod** - TIMLIF

March of time - the battle beyond 1939 - 1940 107 MIN
VHS
March of time series
B&W (G)
$24.95 purchase _ #S01523
Uses newsreel footage from 1939 to 1940 to present a view of Americans as they prepared for possible involvement in World War II. Originally produced by Time magazine.
History - United States
Dist - UILL **Prod** - TIMLIF

March of time - the battle beyond 1940 - 1941 117 MIN
VHS
March of time series
B&W (G)
$24.95 purchase _ #S01524
Uses newsreel footage from 1940 to 1941 to present a view of Americans as they prepared for possible involvement in World War II. Originally produced by Time magazine.
History - United States
Dist - UILL **Prod** - TIMLIF

March of time - the great depression series 544 MIN
VHS
B&W (G)
$149.95 purchase _ #S02134
Presents a six - part series on the events of the Great Depression, covering the years 1935 through 1937. Uses newsreel footage to portray the events.
History - United States
Dist - UILL

March of time - the Great Depression series

Economy blues	81 MIN
Prosperity ahead	103 MIN
Reality and America's dreams	98 MIN
Time marches in	85 MIN
Trouble beyond our shores	80 MIN
War and labor woes	107 MIN

Dist - UILL

March of time - the military prepares 1930 - 1941 124 MIN
VHS
March of time series
B&W (G)
$24.95 purchase _ #S01525
Uses newsreel footage from 1930 to 1941 to present a view of the American armed forces as they prepared for possible war. Originally produced by Time magazine.
History - United States
Dist - UILL **Prod** - TIMLIF

March of time - trouble abroad series 480 MIN
VHS
B&W (G)
$149.95 purchase _ #S02173
Presents a six - part series of newsreel excerpts covering events in the US and worldwide from June 1937 to August 1939.
History - United States; History - World
Dist - UILL

March of time - trouble abroad series

Germany and other problems	76 MIN
Spotlight on war	91 MIN
Tensions increase	76 MIN
Uncle Sam, the observer	75 MIN
War abroad, depression at home	71 MIN
War, peace and America	91 MIN

Dist - UILL

March on Paris 1914 of Generaloberst Alexander Von Kluck and His Memory of Jessie 75 MIN
16mm
Color
LC 77-701814
Dramatizes the reminiscences of German General Alexander von Kluck concerning the campaign of his army from the Belgian border to the Battle of the Marne and his romance with Jessie Holladay.
Biography; History - United States
Dist - FMCOOP **Prod** - HAWKSP 1977

March on Paris 1914 of Generaloberst Alexander Von Kluck and His Memory of Jessie - Pt 1 38 MIN
16mm
Color
LC 77-701814
Dramatizes the reminiscences of German General Alexander von Kluck concerning the campaign of his army from the Belgian border to the Battle of the Marne and his romance with Jessie Holladay.
History - World
Dist - FMCOOP **Prod** - HAWKSP 1977

March on Paris 1914 of Generaloberst Alexander Von Kluck and His Memory of Jessie - Pt 2 37 MIN
16mm
Color
LC 77-701814
Dramatizes the reminiscences of German General Alexander von Kluck concerning the campaign of his army from the Belgian border to the Battle of the Marne and his romance with Jessie Holladay.
History - World
Dist - FMCOOP **Prod** - HAWKSP 1977

March on the Pentagon 21 MIN
16mm
B&W (G)
$20.00 rental
Portrays over 100,000 people who came to Washington, DC in October of 1967, to oppose the war in Vietnam. Looks at the rally assembled in front of the Washington Monument and records their march to the Pentagon, where they were met by US troops, marshalls, tear gas, etc. A David Ringo production.
Fine Arts; Sociology
Dist - CANCIN

March on Washington - the Bonus Marches 15 MIN
16mm
Color
Examines tactics of rebellion groups, pointing out that today's rebels against the establishment don't deserve credit for inventing protest, but are merely refining a process that has been characteristic of the means by which much progress has been achieved in the United States.

Civics and Political Systems; Sociology
Dist - REAF **Prod** - INTEXT

March or Die 106 MIN
16mm
Color
Presents an adventure story about the French Foreign Legion.
Fine Arts
Dist - SWANK **Prod** - CPC

Marching Mizzou 11 MIN
16mm
Color
LC 76-702845
Portrays the color, pageantry and precision of the University of Missouri's marching band. Includes behind - the - scenes preparation and a halftime show.
Fine Arts; Physical Education and Recreation
Dist - UMO **Prod** - UMO 1976

Marching out - Wymarsz 108 MIN
VHS
Color; B&W (G A) (POLISH)
$24.95 purchase _ #V088
Presents a documentary about Pilsudski's Legions and other Polish military formations fighting for Poland's independence in the years 1914 - 1921.
Fine Arts; History - World
Dist - POLART

Marching Percussion 11 MIN
16mm
How to Series
Color (J H)
Covers the elements involved in building a championship marching percussion section, including the precision method, tonality in percussion, selecting instruments, mallets, carrying devices, timptoms and how to write for them, scoring music, field positioning and visual presentation.
Fine Arts; Physical Education and Recreation
Dist - MCCRMK **Prod** - MCCRMK 1974

Marching - Rifles Section 12 MIN
16mm
Color
Offers information on rifle handling, spinning and tossing for the marching band show.
Physical Education and Recreation
Dist - MCCRMK **Prod** - MCCRMK 1978

Marching Show Design 12 MIN
16mm
Color
Shows the Bridgemen approach to planning and designing a field marching show.
Physical Education and Recreation
Dist - MCCRMK **Prod** - MCCRMK 1978

Marching the Colours 3 MIN
U-matic / VHS / 16mm
Color (P I J H C)
An experiment in film animation, made by Guy Glover without a camera, visualizing a military march in geometric, abstract patterns of color.
Fine Arts
Dist - IFB **Prod** - NFBC 1942

Marching to a different drummer - the life and career of Jonas Salk 28 MIN
VHS
Eminent scientist series
Color (J H)
$60.00 purchase _ #A2VH 1051
Features physician Jonas Salk, who developed the polio vaccine. Part of a series on scientists which discusses their childhood, educational backgrounds, decisions affecting their careers and illustrious achievements.
Health and Safety; Science
Dist - CLRVUE **Prod** - CLRVUE

Marci 15 MIN
VHS
Straight from the shoulder series
Color (J H)
$85.00 purchase _ #ESGV1502V
Explores the issue of teenage suicide and its relationship to substance abuse through the true story of Marci. Reveals that Marci's parents introduced her to alcohol at age ten and by the time she was 16 she had attempted suicide twice. Describes the escalation of her feelings of loneliness, her last and almost successful suicide attempt, her visit to the hospital and her slow treatment. Part of a three - part series.
Guidance and Counseling; Health and Safety; Psychology
Dist - CAMV

Marciano - Charles 30 MIN
16mm
IBC Championship Fights, Series 1 Series
B&W
Physical Education and Recreation
Dist - SFI **Prod** - SFI

Marciano - Louis 30 MIN
16mm
IBC Championship Fights, Series 1 Series
B&W
Physical Education and Recreation
Dist - SFI **Prod** - SFI

Marciano - Moore 29 MIN
16mm
IBC Championship Fights, Series 1 Series
B&W
Physical Education and Recreation
Dist - SFI **Prod** - SFI

Marciano - Moore 30 MIN
16mm
IBC Championship Fights, Series 2 Series
B&W
Physical Education and Recreation
Dist - SFI **Prod** - SFI

Marco Polo 22 MIN
U-matic / VHS / 16mm
Color (I J)
Presents an animated version of the adventures of Marco Polo who traveled across Europe and Asia to secure the overland route to Cathay.
Fine Arts; History - World
Dist - LUF **Prod** - LUF 1979

Marco Polo's Travels 19 MIN
U-matic / 16mm / VHS
B&W; Captioned (I J H) (SPANISH)
Re - creates the adventures that Marco Polo described in his book. Dramatizes the differences between Eastern and Western cultures by showing scenes in Kubla Khan's court. Indicates the impact upon medieval Europe of Polo's account.
History - World
Dist - EBEC **Prod** - EBEC 1955

Marco Polo's Travels 28 MIN
VHS / U-matic
Once upon a Time - Man Series
Color (P I)
$99.00
Shows Marco Polo leaving Venice for the Mongol Empire where he spent 20 years as advisor to the Khan. Animated.
History - World
Dist - LANDMK **Prod** - LANDMK 1981

Marcos - Aquino - February 5, 1986
VHS
Nightline news library series
Color (J H C)
$19.98 purchase _ #MH6154V - S
Overviews the political confrontation between Ferdinand Marcos and Corazon Aquino in a news story by the ABC News Team. Part of a series from the news program, Nightline.
History - World
Dist - CAMV **Prod** - ABCNEW 1986

Marcus Garvey 30 MIN
VHS
Black Americans of achievement collection II series
Color (J H C G)
$49.95 purchase _ #LVCD6618V - S
Provides interesting and concise information on Black nationalist leader Marcus Garvey. Part of a 10 - part series on African - Americans.
Guidance and Counseling; History - United States
Dist - CAMV

Marcus Garvey and the UNIA Papers 28 MIN
U-matic / VHS
Color
History - United States
Dist - SYLWAT **Prod** - RCOMTV 1984

Marcus Garvey - toward Black Nationhood 42 MIN
VHS / U-matic
Color (J)
LC 84-706039
Combines archival material and live interviews with Marcus Garvey, Jr and others to introduce the life and work of the pioneer Black nationalist leader Marcus Garvey.
History - United States
Dist - FOTH **Prod** - WGRMTV 1983

Marcuse and the Frankfurt School 45 MIN
VHS
Men of ideas series
Color; PAL (H C A)
PdS99 purchase; Not available in Canada.
Explains in simple terms the main developments in Western philosophy from the 19th century to the present day. Features a contemporary thinker discussing his ideas and beliefs with Bryan Magee. Part three of a fifteen part series.
Psychology; Religion and Philosophy
Dist - BBCENE

MARCY personalized training video - how to use your home - gym 105 MIN
VHS
Color (H C A)
$49.99 purchase _ #MFV001V
Presents a comprehensive look at home gym workouts. Explains and demonstrates more than 50 different exercises, all of which can be done with either free weights or weight machines. Includes a personal workout checklist. Part of the MARCY - muscular strengthening, aerobic conditioning, regularity in training, concern for safety, and youthful appearance - series.
Physical Education and Recreation; Science - Natural
Dist - CAMV

Mardi gras 17 MIN
VHS / 16mm
Color (I J H G)
$295.00, $29.95 purchase
Explores the origin and history of Mardi Gras in American and the extent of Mardi Gras festivities today. Focuses on customs, traditions, masquerade balls, street costumes and parades in New Orleans and Mobile, Alabama.
History - United States; Religion and Philosophy; Social Science
Dist - KAWVAL **Prod** - KAWVAL

Mare Island flexible manufacturing workstation 14 MIN
U-matic / VHS
Color (A PRO)
$50.00, $95.00 purchase _ #TCA17892, #TCA17891
Presents a technical interim report on the Mare Island Flexible Manufacturing Workstation Research Facility. Describes the automated machining process for a typical flangepart. Produced by the US Department of Commerce's National Institute of Standards and Technology.
Business and Economics; Industrial and Technical Education; Sociology
Dist - USNAC

Mare Nostrum 27 MIN
U-matic / VHS / 16mm
Victory at Sea Series
B&W (J H)
Describes the military command of the Mediterranean from 1940 to 1942.
Civics and Political Systems; History - United States; History - World
Dist - LUF **Prod** - NBCTV

Mare Tranquillitatis - Flagstaff, Arizona 12 MIN
16mm
Color
LC 74-706375
Documents the construction of an area simulating a lunar crater field. Shows how the site near Sunset Crater in Arizona was prepared by using explosives and compares the aerial photographs of the completed construction to those of the lunar surface.
Geography - United States; Industrial and Technical Education; Science; Science - Physical
Dist - USNAC **Prod** - USGEOS 1969

Margaret 13 MIN
16mm
B&W (J)
LC 76-701866
Tells about a mildly retarded girl who, apart from a short period in an institution, has lived happily at home with her family. Shows how, now that she is 14 years old, she appears to be unaware that she is different although her parents worry about the future.
Health and Safety; Psychology; Sociology
Dist - AUIS **Prod** - AUSDSS 1975

Margaret Atwood 52 MIN
VHS
Color (H C G)
$79.00 purchase
Features the writer discussing her works about women and the theme of 'breaking out.' Includes her works The Handmaid's Tale; The Edible Woman; Life Before Man; Surfacing; Bodily Harm, among others. Reviews her poetry and short stories. Interview by Hermoine Lee.
Literature and Drama; Religion and Philosophy
Dist - ROLAND **Prod** - INCART

Margaret Atwood - an Interview 28 MIN
U-matic
Color
Presents Margaret Atwood discussing the writing process, poetry poetry and the special problems of women writers, such as learning to be persistent in order to get published. Explains some of the reasons behind Canadian Nationalism.
History - World; Literature and Drama; Sociology
Dist - WMENIF **Prod** - WMENIF

Margaret Atwood - 5 - 3 - 78 60 MIN
VHS / Cassette
Poetry Center reading series
Color (G)
$15.00, $45.00 purchase _ #284 - 238
Features the Canadian writer reading her works at the Poetry Center, San Francisco State University. Includes a question and answer session.
Literature and Drama
Dist - POETRY **Prod** - POETRY 1978

Margaret Atwood - once in August - creative process series 60 MIN
VHS
Margaret Atwood - once in August - creative process series
Color (G)
$89.95 purchase _ #S01985
Interviews Canadian author Margaret Atwood and her family. Shares Atwood's writing philosophy of presenting clear - cut, dramatic choices for her characters.
Literature and Drama
Dist - UILL **Prod** - NFBC

Margaret Atwood - once in August - creative process series
Margaret Atwood - once in August - creative process series 60 MIN
Dist - UILL

Margaret Beals and Dr Jay Adlersberg 30 MIN
U-matic / VHS
Dancers' Health Alert Series
Color
Fine Arts; Health and Safety
Dist - ARCVID **Prod** - ARCVID

Margaret Becker 60 MIN
VHS
Front row concert video series
Color (G R)
$14.95 purchase _ #VCV3109
Features the music of contemporary Christian artist Margaret Becker. Presented in an acoustic format.
Fine Arts; Guidance and Counseling; Literature and Drama; Religion and Philosophy
Dist - GF

Margaret Cesa - 9 - 11 - 80 30 MIN
VHS / Cassette
Poetry Center reading series
Color (G)
$15.00, $45.00 purchase, $15.00 rental _ #409 - 335
Features the writer reading her works from Slide Show Book at the Poetry Center, San Francisco State University.
Literature and Drama
Dist - POETRY **Prod** - POETRY 1980

Margaret Crane - 9 - 28 - 89 15 MIN
VHS / Cassette
Poetry Center reading series
Color (G)
$15.00, $45.00 purchase, $15.00 rental _ #870 - 669
Features the writer performing Roadkill with Scott MacLeod at the Poetry Center, San Francisco State University, with an introduction by Robert Gluck.
Literature and Drama
Dist - POETRY **Prod** - POETRY 1989

Margaret Laurence, First Lady of Manawaka 53 MIN
16mm
Color (G)
_ #106C 0178 390
Traces the life of Margaret Laurence, one of Canada's most celebrated authors, from her birth in a small prairie town in Manitoba. Includes readings from her work by Canadian actress Jane Eastwood.
Biography; Literature and Drama
Dist - CFLMDC **Prod** - NFBC 1978

Margaret Mead 30 MIN
16mm
B&W (H C A)
LC FIA67-5107
Anthropologist Margaret Mead appraises human values with relation to man's potential for complete selfannihilation. She explains that an understanding of human traditions, philosophy and action is necessary to give the future a meaningful value. (Kinescope).
Biography; Religion and Philosophy; Sociology
Dist - MLA **Prod** - USC 1964

Margaret Mead 12 MIN
U-matic / VHS
Color (G)
$229.00, $129.00 purchase _ #AD - 1844
Documents the life of Margaret Mead, a pioneer in the science of anthropology.
Biography; Science; Sociology
Dist - FOTH **Prod** - FOTH

Margaret Mead - an Interview 20 MIN
U-matic
Color
Features anthropologist and author Margaret Mead talking about the influence of women in her life, her own work and experiences.
Sociology
Dist - WMENIF **Prod** - WMENIF

Margaret Mead - Cultural Factors in Population Control
U-matic / VHS
B&W
Discusses the cultural factors in population control in a talk by Dr Margaret Mead.
Sociology
Dist - UWISC **Prod** - VRL 1970

Margaret Mead - Taking Note 59 MIN
16mm
Odyssey Series
Captioned; Color (J A)
$125.00 purchase _ #ODYS-212
Profiles Margaret Mead's personal history and intellectual contributions, based on interviews held shortly before her death, old family and field photographs, and on converstions with a variety of her friends, family and former students.
Biography; Sociology
Dist - DOCEDR **Prod** - DOCEDR 1981
PBS

Margaret Price sings Ruckert Lieder 30 MIN
VHS
Color (G)
$19.95 purchase_#1434
Features the artistry of soprano Margaret Price as she performs Mahler's orchestral songs, written in 1905. Presents the Ludwigsburg Palace Festival Orchestra accompanying her.
Fine Arts
Dist - KULTUR

Margaret Sanger - A Public nuisance 28 MIN
VHS
Color (G)
$60.00 rental, $250.00 purchase
Highlights Sanger's pioneering strategies of using media and popular culture to advance the cause of birth control. Tells the story of her arrest and trial, using actuality films, vaudeville, courtroom sketches and re - enactments, video effects and Sanger's own words. Looks at how she effectively changed public discussion of birth control from issues of mortality to issues of women's health and economic well - being. Directed by Terese Svoboda and Steve Bull.
Fine Arts; Sociology
Dist - WMEN

Margaret Sloan on Black Sisterhood 29 MIN
U-matic
Woman Series
Color
Presents Margaret Sloan discussing sexism and feminism and how they relate to black women in the movement.
Sociology
Dist - PBS **Prod** - WNEDTV

Margaret Tait 41 MIN
16mm
Color (H A)
$900.00 purchase, $75.00 rental
Explores the films of Scottish artist Margaret Tait.
Fine Arts
Dist - AFA **Prod** - ACGB 1984

The Margaret Thatcher years 60 MIN
VHS
Color (J H C G)
$29.95 purchase _ #SVC5005V
Portrays the reign of Margaret Thatcher as Prime Minister in Great Britain. Interviews colleagues and opponents, uses footage from the Falklands War, the miners' strike, Thatcher's close brush with death in Brighton to examine Thatcher and the British political system and process.
History - World
Dist - CAMV

Margaret's story 30 MIN
VHS
Labours of Eve series
Color; PAL (A)
PdS50 purchase; Not available in the United States or Canada
Examines the story of Margaret, a woman who became pregnant despite having a total hysterectomy. Observes Margaret as she tackles with the fact that in every other similar case the baby has died and the mother is at risk. Nicky Singer presents the series. Part one of a six - part series.
Health and Safety; Sociology
Dist - BBCENE

Marge Piercy 46 MIN
VHS
Color (H C G)
$79.00 purchase
Features the writer talking with Nikki Gerrard about using novels to express one's view of women's experience. Discusses her work including Fly Away Home; Braided Lives; Woman on the Edge of Time; and Small Changes.
Literature and Drama
Dist - ROLAND **Prod** - INCART

Margia Kramer - Freedom of Information Tape - 1, Jean Seberg 18 MIN
VHS / U-matic
Color
Documents the FBI's surveillance and harassment of Jean Seberg. Conveys contradictions between her public and private personas.
Fine Arts
Dist - ARTINC **Prod** - ARTINC

Margia Kramer - Freedom of Information Tape 3, the CIA Guerrilla Manual 4 MIN
VHS / U-matic
Color
Deals with First Amendment rights.
Fine Arts
Dist - ARTINC **Prod** - ARTINC

Margia Kramer - Freedom of Information Tape 2 - Progress and Access 36 MIN
U-matic / VHS
Color
Tells how computerization contributes to the isolating tendencies of capitalist culture.
Fine Arts; Social Science
Dist - ARTINC **Prod** - ARTINC

Margia Kramer - no more Witchhunts, a Street Festival 17 MIN
VHS / U-matic
Color
Focuses on a New York City street festival protesting the rise of neo - McCarthyism.
Fine Arts
Dist - ARTINC **Prod** - ARTINC

Margia Kramer - Progress, Memory 5 MIN
U-matic / VHS
Color
Deals with First Amendment rights.
Civics and Political Systems; Fine Arts
Dist - ARTINC **Prod** - ARTINC

Margin of Acceptability
VHS / 35mm strip
Electronic Soldering Series
$42.00 purchase _ #LXES2 filmstrip, $62.00 purchase _ #LXES2V VHS
Demonstrates how the margin of acceptability is narrowed and delineated.
Education; Industrial and Technical Education
Dist - CAREER **Prod** - CAREER

Margin of Safety 4 MIN
16mm
Driver Education Series
Color (H C)
LC FIA66-1006
Discusses the distance that should be maintained between vehicles going in the same direction. Stresses the importance of looking well ahead of one's own car.
Health and Safety
Dist - AMROIL **Prod** - AMROIL 1964

Margin of Safety - Psychological Distance Under Danger 16 MIN
16mm
B&W (H C)
Reports on an experiment showing that subjects (college students) allow greater margins of safety under dangerous conditions and that they change to a slower pace than is characteristic under conditions of no danger. Provides an illustration of how an experment of this kind is conducted.
Psychology
Dist - PSUPCR **Prod** - PSUPCR 1955

Margin seal procedure for esthetic silicone facial prostheses 13 MIN
VHS / U-matic
Color (C PRO)
$395.00 purchase, $80.00 rental _ #D871 - VI - 035
Outlines the development of a silicone facial prosthesis and presents the margin seal technique. Shows the procedures for accurately matching skin color and texture. Presented by Dr Ariyadasa Udagama.
Health and Safety
Dist - HSCIC

Marginal People 28 MIN
U-matic / VHS / 16mm
Color (J)
Depicts the plight of the newly independent country of Bangladesh in terms of the need to establish a new international order.
Geography - World; History - World
Dist - LUF **Prod** - LUF 1979

The Margins of the Land 55 MIN
16mm / U-matic / VHS
Living Planet Series Pt 9
Color (H C A)
Looks at life along the coastlines and shows how mangroves with their roots help to expand the coastline.
Science - Natural
Dist - TIMLIF **Prod** - BBCTV 1984

The Margins of the Land 55 MIN
16mm / VHS
Living Planet Series
(J H C)
$99.95 each, $595.00 series
Examines the lives of creatures who live in mud and sand.
Science; Science - Natural; Science - Physical
Dist - AMBROS **Prod** - AMBROS 1984

Margo 11 MIN
16mm
Color
Presents a discussion on masturbation and techniques. Includes bathing, use of body oils, using a mirror to examine genitals and manual clitoral and breast stimulation to orgasm. Shows the stages of the sexual response cycle.
Guidance and Counseling; Psychology; Sociology
Dist - MMRC **Prod** - MMRC

The Margot Fonteyn Story 90 MIN
VHS
Color (S)
$39.95 purchase _ #833 - 9522
Captures Dame Margot Fonteyn on the eve of her 70th birthday telling her life story. Includes archival film and interviews with mentors, partners and proteges such as Ninette de Valois, Frederick Ashton, Robert Helpmann and Rudolf Nureyev.
Fine Arts; Geography - World; Physical Education and Recreation
Dist - FI **Prod** - RMART 1989

Marguerite 30 MIN
VHS / U-matic
New Voice Series
Color (H C A)
Dramatizes the investigations of the staff of a high school newspaper. Focuses on prostitution.
Sociology
Dist - GPN **Prod** - WGBHTV

Marguerite a La Ferme 15 MIN
U-matic / VHS / 16mm
Color (J H) (FRENCH)
A French language film. Follows a girl as she visits, works and plays on her cousins' farm.
Foreign Language
Dist - IFB **Prod** - IFB 1962

Maria 40 MIN
16mm
Color (A)
Portrays a unionizing attempt at a Canadian plant led by a woman named Maria. Recognizes that besides management, she also faces obstacles from her family and fiance who do not understand her new role as a union organizer.
Business and Economics; Sociology
Dist - AFLCIO **Prod** - CANBC 1979

Maria and Julian's Black Pottery 11 MIN
16mm
Color (H A)
$190.00 purchase, $30.00 rental
Presents a classic 1938 documentary which features Maria Martinez and her husband Julian at home in New Mexico's Ildefonso Pueblo creating their famous black - on - black pottery.
Fine Arts
Dist - AFA **Prod** - SIFP 1978

Maria and many others 22 MIN
VHS
Color (G)
$175.00 purchase, $45.00 rental
Visits the spectacular region of Ecuador's Andes mountains which is among the nation's poorest areas. Follows 14 - year - old Maria as she helps her mother with domestic chores and tend their small farm. Makes the observation that, since 70 percent of men leave to earn livings in other areas, girls are often married by age 15 and know how to run the household, but have never known the leisure time to play as a child.
Fine Arts; Social Science; Sociology
Dist - FIRS **Prod** - JENKIN 1993

Maria and the Coconuts 15 MIN
VHS / U-matic
Other families, other friends series; Blue module; Mexico
Color (P)
Visits Mexico City, Tula and Taxco.
Geography - World; Social Science
Dist - AITECH **Prod** - WVIZTV 1971

Maria Callas 92 MIN
VHS
Color (G)
$19.95 purchase_#1437
Offers a glimpse into the rise and fall of controversial opera singer Maria Callas. Contains extensive archival film footage.
Biography; Fine Arts
Dist - KULTUR

Maria Callas 1959 Hamburg concert 68 MIN
VHS
B&W (G) (ITALIAN)
$39.95 purchase _ #1155
Features opera diva Maria Callas in a 1959 concert performance in Hamburg, Germany.. Includes selections from 'La Vestale,' 'Macbeth,' 'Don Carlo,' and other operas.
Fine Arts
Dist - PBS **Prod** - WNETTV 1959
KULTUR

Maria Callas 1962 Hamburg Concert 66 MIN
VHS
B&W (G) (ITALIAN AND FRENCH)
$39.95 purchase _ #1156
Presents diva Maria Callas in concert at Hamburg, Germany in 1962. Offers from 'Carnaval Romain' - the Overture, 'Le Cid' - Pleurez, mes yeux, 'Carmen' - Habanera and Seguidilla, 'Ernani' - Ernani, involami, 'Cenerentola' - Nacqui' all'affanno, and 'Don Carlo' - O Don fatale. Conducted by Georges Pretre.
Fine Arts; Geography - World
Dist - KULTUR

Maria Callas - Life and Art 80 MIN
VHS
Color; B&W (G)
$29.95 purchase _ #1168
Presents a performance biography of Maria Callas which gives new insight into the private character of one of the century's greatest divas. Celebrates her singing and dramatic skills, explores the woman behind the public persona and the conflict between her personal aims and ambitions. Includes rare footage from private collections and film archives combined with performance excerpts from 'Tosca,' 'Norma,' 'Carmen.' Touching personal reminiscences by Zeffirelli, Guilini and Gorlinsky.
Fine Arts; Foreign Language; History - World
Dist - KULTUR

Maria Callas - life and art 78 MIN
VHS
Color (G) (ENGLISH AND ITALIAN)
$29.95 purchase
Presents a comprehensive video account of the life, music and passions of Maria Callas. Shows Callas in several performance excerpts, including 'Tosca,' 'La Traviata,' and more. Includes interviews with famous friends.
Fine Arts
Dist - PBS **Prod** - WNETTV

Maria - Indian pottery of San Ildefonso 27 MIN
VHS
Color (G)
$29.95 purchase
Features Indian potter Maria Martinez who demonstrates the traditional Indian ways of pottery making. Begins with the spreading of sacred corn, and moves to gathering and mixing clay, construction and decorating of pottery and building the fire mound.
Fine Arts; Social Science
Dist - ARTSAM **Prod** - HOLDAY

Maria Magdalena 70 MIN
16mm
Color (GERMAN)
A German language motion picture. Projects Friedrich Hebbel's classical drama, 'Maria Magdalena,' into the present.
Fine Arts
Dist - WSTGLC **Prod** - WSTGLC 1973

Maria Montessori, Follow the Child 49 MIN
16mm
Color
LC 79-700393
Documents the life of Maria Montessori, physician and educator in the field of early childhood development. Includes accounts by individuals who worked with her and scenes from Montessori classrooms.
Biography; Education; Psychology
Dist - DCASS **Prod** - DCASS 1978

Maria Montessori, Follow the Child, Pt 1 24 MIN
16mm
Color
LC 79-700393
Documents the life of Maria Montessori, physician and educator in the field of early childhood development. Includes accounts by individuals who worked with her and scenes from Montessori classrooms.
Education
Dist - DCASS **Prod** - DCASS 1978

Maria Montessori, Follow the Child, Pt 2 25 MIN
16mm
Color
LC 79-700393
Documents the life of Maria Montessori, physician and educator in the field of early childhood development. Includes accounts by individuals who worked with her and scenes from Montessori classrooms.
Education
Dist - DCASS **Prod** - DCASS 1978

Maria Morzeck 101 MIN
16mm
Color (GERMAN (ENGLISH SUBTITLES))
A German language film with English subtitles. Tells the story of Maria Morzeck, a coy and progressive girl in East Berlin whose brother is involved in broadcasting a taped Adenauer speech on a factory announcement system and is subsequently arrested and imprisoned. Continues as Maria meets Paul Dreister, the judge who sentenced her brother, who admires her, and with whom she plays along even though she despises him in hopes of obtaining a reduced prison term for her brother.
Fine Arts; Foreign Language
Dist - WSTGLC **Prod** - WSTGLC 1976

Maria - 3 - Amina - 4 - Unit 2 45 MIN
VHS
Play it out series
Color; PAL (I J T)
PdS29.50 purchase
Features Maria, who learns about peer group pressure and rejection and Amina, who deals with intimidation by someone with greater power. Part of a series of six programs in three units in which youngsters face a set of dilemmas typical in everyday life and explore the consequences of their decisions through discussion and role play. Provides guidance for teachers in using role play in the classroom.
Guidance and Counseling; Psychology; Sociology
Dist - EMFVL

Mariachi - the Music, the Spirit 28 MIN
U-matic / 16mm
Color (SPANISH, ENGLISH)
Gives an account of the first Tucson International Mariachi Conference, a five - day celebration of Mexican music and culture where people compete and learn. Features discussions by participants explaining the difficulty in learning the techniques and the years of training required to master mariachi music. Includes appearances by Don Silvestre Vargas giving the history of the music and Lola Beltran, one of Mexico's mariachi singers. In Spanish and English with English voice - over.
Fine Arts; Sociology
Dist - KCET **Prod** - KUATTV

Marian Anderson 20 MIN
U-matic
Truly American Series
Color (I)
Biography; Fine Arts; History - United States
Dist - GPN **Prod** - WVIZTV 1979

Marian Anderson 60 MIN
VHS
Color (H C A)
$69.95 purchase _ MRAN-000-WC95
Examines Ms Anderson's reflections about the people, events and influences that contributed to shaping her development as an artist.
Civics and Political Systems; Fine Arts; History - United States
Dist - PBS **Prod** - WETATV 1991

Marian Vectors - Vector Studies 12 MIN
VHS
Color (G)
$29.95 purchase, $16.00 rental _ #S03321
Uses mathematical formulas to bridge the gap between sonic and visual art, enabling the viewer to hear and see a mathematical process. Demonstrates each movement expressing a single process mapped directly into color and pitch, produced with the help of a computer.
Computer Science; Fine Arts; Mathematics; Psychology
Dist - UILL **Prod** - BEVANS 1989

Marianne Moore 60 MIN
VHS / 16mm
Voices and Visions Series
Color (H)

$8.00 rental _ #60732
Compares the life and poetry of Marianne Moore (1887 - 1972), both of which were colorful and eccentric. Full of paradox and 'wild decorum', her poems are modern, natural, and earthy on the one hand, and old - fashioned, artful and moralistic on the other. Grace Schulman and others offer insights into and read from her poems.
Literature and Drama
Dist - PSU

Marianne Moore - Part 8 60 MIN
U-matic / VHS
Voices and visions series
Color (G)
$45.00, $29.95 purchase
Analyzes the paradoxes of the poetry of Marianne Moore. Features critics and friends of Moore such as Monroe Wheeler, Grace Shulman and Patricia Willis. Part of a thirteen - part series on the lives and works of modern American poets.
Biography; History - United States; Literature and Drama
Dist - ANNCPB **Prod** - NYCVH 1988

Maria's story - a portrait of love and survival in El Salvador's civil war 53 MIN
16mm / VHS
Color (H C G) (SPANISH)
$850.00, $445.00 purchase, $125.00, $85.00 rental
Portrays a 39 - year - old mother of three who is a leader in the guerilla movement in El Salvador. Reveals that Maria Serrano is a down - to - earth woman whose passion for social justice dominates her life. Produced by Pamela Cohen and Catherine M Ryan.
History - World
Dist - FLMLIB

Maricela 62 MIN
VHS
Wonderworks collection series
Color (I J H)
$29.95 purchase _ #MAR200
Tells about a young girl who struggles to find her place in the United States when her mother, who was a teacher in El Salvador, must now work as a housekeeper.
Guidance and Counseling; Literature and Drama; Sociology
Dist - KNOWUN **Prod** - PBS 1986

Mariculture of Porphyra 21 MIN
U-matic / VHS
Color (JAPANESE)
Discusses commercial culture of Porphyra as a food crop and its role in Japanese culture and cuisine. Includes the cultivation, processing, marketing and use of Porphyra. Video version of 35mm filmstrip program, with live open and close.
Science - Natural
Dist - CBSC **Prod** - BMEDIA

Marie 95 MIN
16mm
Color
Tells the story of a teenage girl who suspects that her father has been murdered, possibly by her mother, from whom he had been separated. Stars Maria Schell.
Literature and Drama; Sociology
Dist - WSTGLC **Prod** - WSTGLC

The Marie Celeste - Unit E 49 MIN
VHS
Drama forum series
Color; PAL (T)
PdS35.00 purchase
Shows part of an hour - long drama session and story development with Andy Mathieson and his class of third - and fourth - year juniors - nine to eleven year - olds - in unit five of a ten - unit series of observational material on the work of drama teachers.
Education; Fine Arts
Dist - EMFVL

Marie - Claire Blais - an Interview 30 MIN
U-matic
Color
Presents Marie - Claire Blais talking about herself and her writing. Tells of the barriers that confronted women writers as evidenced by the long historical tradition of women's adopting male pseudonyms in order to get published and gain acceptance as authors.
Literature and Drama; Sociology
Dist - WMENIF **Prod** - WMENIF

Marie Curie - a Love Story 32 MIN
U-matic / VHS / 16mm
Biographies Series
Color (J H C A)
$640, $250 purchase _ #77529
Examines the life of scientist Marie Curie, including the discovery of Polonium and Radium.
Biography; Science
Dist - CORF

Marie Curie - a Love Story 32 MIN
U-matic / VHS / 16mm
Advance of Science Series
Color (J H C A)
$640, $250 purchase _ #77529
Shows the life of Dr. Curie and Marie Cuire who discovered Radium.
Science
Dist - CORF

Marie Curie finds radium and radioactivity 20 MIN
VHS
Giant steps in science and society series
Color; CC (I J H)
$79.00 purchase _ #191
Visits the office and laboratory of Marie Curie in Paris. Reveals how Curie and her husband Pierre worked long hours in a nearby shed to discover the new element radium and how Marie Curie coined the word 'radioactivity' to describe the strange behavior of the newly discovered atoms of radium. Includes a teacher's guide. Part of a four - part series.
Science; Science - Physical
Dist - HAWHIL **Prod** - HAWHIL 1994

Marie Et Le Cure 30 MIN
16mm
B&W (C A) (FRENCH)
A French language film. Tells the story of a country girl whose arrival leads to tragedy.
Foreign Language
Dist - UWFKD **Prod** - UWFKD

Marie Louise collects bric-a-brac 50 MIN
VHS
Signs of the times series
Color (A)
PdS99 purchase
Takes viewers 'through the keyhole' into ordinary late 20th-century homes in Britain to see what people's perceptions of good and bad taste really are. Examines how younger men are undermining women's traditional sovereignty in the home. Part one of a five-part series.
Fine Arts; Home Economics; Industrial and Technical Education
Dist - BBCENE

Marie Sets 15 MIN
VHS
Color (G)
$29.95 purchase, $16.00 rental
Presents colored motion fractals in kaleidoscopic variety coupled with music derived from the same mathematical formulas in an early work by Brian Evans which he produced on a CRAY XMP supercomputer.
Computer Science; Fine Arts; Mathematics; Psychology
Dist - UILL **Prod** - BEVANS 1988

Marijuana 30 MIN
VHS
Video encyclopedia of psychoactive drugs series
Color (J H G)
$44.95 purchase _ #LVP6617V
Presents the most up - to - date research in clinical and laboratory studies on marijuana. Discusses the effects of marijuana on the mind and body, addiction and abuse, recovery and rehabilitation, medical uses, importation and distribution facts, user methodology and current trends. Part of a series.
Guidance and Counseling; Psychology
Dist - CAMV

Marijuana 15 MIN
VHS
Color (J H C G)
$85.00 purchase _ #ESGV2502V
Presents experts in the field of drug abuse discussing the physical and psychological effects of marijuana use. Shows how THC, the psychoactive ingredient in pot, travels through the human body to the brain and explains the short and long - term symptoms of smoking pot.
Guidance and Counseling; Psychology
Dist - CAMV

Marijuana 34 MIN
16mm / U-matic / VHS
Color (J H A) (FRENCH SPANISH)
LC FIA68-2661
Discusses the physical dangers, emotional dependency and legalities of using marijuana. Interviews users and non - users. Narrated by singer Sonny Bono.
Guidance and Counseling; Health and Safety; Sociology
Dist - PHENIX **Prod** - AVANTI 1968

Marijuana 10 MIN
U-matic / VHS / 16mm
Drug Information Series
Color
Discusses the characteristics of marijuana. Identifies the signs of use and abuse, the pharmacological and behavioral effects, and the short - and long - term dangers.
Health and Safety
Dist - CORF **Prod** - MITCHG 1982

Marijuana
VHS
Substance abuse video library series
Color (T A PRO)
$125.00 purchase _ #AH45141
Presents information on the abuse of marijuana. Details the history of marijuana, how it is abused, short - term physical and psychological effects, dependency and overdose risks, and treatment. Developed by Brock Morris and Kevin Scheel.
Guidance and Counseling; Health and Safety; Psychology; Sociology
Dist - HTHED **Prod** - HTHED

Marijuana Alert 20 MIN
U-matic / VHS / 16mm
Color (J H)
LC 83-700384
Looks at the effects of marijuana on the human body, including the reproductive organs, lungs, heart and brain.
Health and Safety
Dist - PHENIX **Prod** - GREENF 1982

Marijuana and Human Physiology 22 MIN
U-matic / VHS
Color (H C G T A)
$50 rental _ #9823
Describes physiological aspects of marijuana use.
Guidance and Counseling; Psychology; Science - Natural; Sociology
Dist - AIMS **Prod** - AIMS 1986

Marijuana and the mind - addiction 19 MIN
VHS
Marijuana and the mind series
Color (I J H G PRO)
$295.00 purchase, $75.00 rental _ #8268
Looks at the addictive qualities of marijuana. Explains the symptoms of addiction. Part of a series on marijuana.
Guidance and Counseling; Psychology
Dist - AIMS **Prod** - AIMS 1990

Marijuana and the mind - addiction and intoxication 22 MIN
VHS / Videodisc / 16mm
Marijuana and the mind series
Color (I J H G PRO)
$495.00, $395.00 purchase, $75.00 rental _ #8210, #9832 - LD
Looks at current research on the effects of marijuana on the brain which reveals that the drug concentrates in the two areas of the brain which control memory, learning, movement and thought. Part of a series on marijuana.
Guidance and Counseling; Psychology
Dist - AIMS **Prod** - AIMS 1990

Marijuana and the mind - intoxication 16 MIN
VHS
Marijuana and the mind series
Color (I J H G PRO)
$295.00 purchase, $75.00 rental _ #8267
Shows how the action of marijuana on the brain creates intoxication. Contrasts the difference in brain efficiency between sober and intoxicated individuals. Part of a series on marijuana.
Guidance and Counseling; Psychology
Dist - AIMS **Prod** - AIMS 1990

Marijuana and the mind series
Marijuana and the mind - addiction 19 MIN
Marijuana and the mind - addiction and intoxication 22 MIN
Marijuana and the mind - intoxication 16 MIN
Dist - AIMS

Marijuana as medicine 29 MIN
VHS
America's drug forum series
Color (G)
$19.95 purchase _ #113
Reveals that many argue that marijuana is uniquely effective as a medicine for glaucoma and cancer patients. Discloses that the United States government owns and operates a marijuana farm in Mississippi expressly to provide marijuana to sick people. Asks if the US should be in the pot growing business and what role, if any, marijuana has in medicine and how widely available it should be. Guests include Lester Grinspoon of Harvard Med School, Mahmoud ElSouhy of the University of Mississippi Research Institute of Pharmaceutical Sciences, Robert Randall of the Alliance for Cannabis Therapeutics, Steve Rodgers, detective with the Nutley, New Jersey Police Dept.
Health and Safety; Psychology
Dist - DRUGPF **Prod** - DRUGPF 1991

Marijuana, Driving, and You 13 MIN
16mm / U-matic / VHS
Color (J)
LC 81-700749
Investigates the psychological and motor - response effects of marijuana. Tells how marijuana use affects driving.

Health and Safety
Dist - AIMS **Prod** - PORTA 1980

Marijuana - Facts, Myths and Decisions
VHS / U-matic
(J H C)
$189.00 purchase _ #06780 941
Presents basic facts about marijuana use. Explains the plant's chemical properties and how they effect the body. Concentrates on the social aspects of using marijuana, the possibility of psychological addiction and how young people can avoid pressure form their peers to experiment.
Guidance and Counseling
Dist - ASPRSS **Prod** - ASPRSS

Marijuana - Facts, Myths, and Decisions 45 MIN
U-matic / VHS
Color (I J H)
LC 81-706152
Describes the chemical properties of marijuana and explains the way it affects the human body. Presents arguments for and against its use and legalization, and points to the possibility of psychological addiction. Encourages students to base their decisions on facts about the drug and not on peer pressure.
Health and Safety
Dist - GA **Prod** - GA 1981

Marijuana in Medicine 32 MIN
U-matic
Color
Explains the program at the University of Texas M D Anderson Hospital for using marijuana in medicine.
Health and Safety
Dist - UTEXSC **Prod** - UTEXSC

Marijuana in the 90s 35 MIN
VHS
Color (H G C PRO)
$500.00 purchase
Features Dr David Ohlms who re - examines older studies on the effects of marijuana and introduces new research. Reveals that marijuana definitely is not a 'safe' drug. Looks at how the quality and 'strength' of marijuana have changed over the years. Educates professionals in chemical dependency treatment programs, patients in treatment and serves as a part of prevention programs.
Guidance and Counseling; Psychology
Dist - FMSP

Marijuana - Playing for High Stakes
VHS / 35mm strip
$37.50 purchase _ #015 - 653 filmstrip, $47.50 purchase _ #015 - 658
Discusses the dangers of experimenting with drugs. Examines common misconceptions about marijuana and encourages students to avoid all types of drugs.
Health and Safety; Psychology; Sociology
Dist - CAREER **Prod** - CAREER

Marijuana - the Great Escape 20 MIN
16mm / U-matic / VHS
Color (I J H)
LC 71-708044
Presents the story of George Willis, a young drag racer, who uses marijuana. Shows that not everyone will die as a result of using marijuana but every user sacrifices control of his own will, judgement and perception. Demonstrates the established effects of marijuana and emphasizes the possibility of psychological dependence.
Guidance and Counseling; Health and Safety; Sociology
Dist - PHENIX **Prod** - PHENIX 1970

Marijuana - the Hidden Danger 30 MIN
VHS / U-matic
Color (J H C)
LC 80-707446
Explains what marijuana does to the mind, body and behavior of those who smoke it.
Health and Safety; Psychology; Sociology
Dist - CORF **Prod** - WABCTV 1979

Marijuana - Up Close 30 MIN
U-matic / VHS
Color (I)
LC 82-706436
Dispels common myths about the use of marijuana. Discusses its wide use and details its physical effects.
Health and Safety
Dist - GPN **Prod** - WVIZTV 1981

Marijuana update 22 MIN
U-matic / VHS
Color (G)
$249.00 purchase _ #7459
Interviews five people who discuss how they were introduced to marijuana and how they initially believed it was harmless. Reveals that the drug of choice of the sixties is now more powerful because of chemicals used in the growing process. Looks at the common indicators of marijuana use and the physical hazards associated with its use.
Guidance and Counseling; Health and Safety; Psychology; Sociology
Dist - VISIVI **Prod** - VISIVI 1991

Marijuana use and its effects
VHS
Color (J H C G A PRO)
$79.50 purchase _ #AH46338
Uses medical photography and art to demonstrate the medical damage caused by marijuana use. Focuses on marijuana's damage to nervous, respiratory and reproductive systems.
Guidance and Counseling; Health and Safety; Psychology; Science - Natural
Dist - HTHED **Prod** - HTHED

Marilyn and Orrin
VHS / 16mm / U-matic
Portraits of goodbye series
Color (A)
Looks at a couple who divorce after 13 years of marriage. Looks at the wife's feelings of guilt, anger and helplessness and the husband's struggle to overcome his own guilt and adjust to his life as a bachelor.
Sociology
Dist - ECUFLM **Prod** - UMCOM 1980

Marilyn Chin - 10 - 26 - 89 40 MIN
VHS / Cassette
Poetry Center reading series
Color (G)
$15.00, $45.00 purchase, $15.00 rental _ #860 - 671
Features the poet reading from her works at the Poetry Center, San Francisco State University, with an introduction by Robert Gluck.
Literature and Drama
Dist - POETRY **Prod** - POETRY 1989

Marilyn French 48 MIN
VHS
Color (H C G)
$79.00 purchase
Features the writer with Sarah Dunant, discussing sexuality, motherhood, and childrearing and their influence on writing. Talks about her works that include The Women's Room; The Bleeding Heart; and Her Mother's Daughter.
Literature and Drama; Sociology
Dist - ROLAND **Prod** - INCART

Marilyn Hacker - 5 - 4 - 77 50 MIN
VHS / Cassette
Poetry Center reading series
Color (G)
$15.00, $45.00 purchase, $15.00 rental _ #258 - 211
Features the writer reading her works at the Poetry Center, San Francisco State University.
Literature and Drama
Dist - POETRY **Prod** - POETRY 1977

Marilyn Monroe - behind the legend 60 MIN
VHS
Color (H C T A)
$39.95 purchase _ #S01325
Profiles the life of actress Narilyn Monroe. Interviews co - stars and professional associates. Features home movie footage of Monroe, as well as clips from many of her professional films.
Biography; Fine Arts; History - United States
Dist - UILL

Marilyn Schorin and Wendy Banker 30 MIN
VHS / U-matic
Eye on Dance - Dancers' Health Series
Color
Focuses on two differing perspectives of dancers' nutrition. Includes 'Esoterica' with Harvy Lichtenstein. Hosted by Irene Dowd.
Fine Arts
Dist - ARCVID **Prod** - ARCVID

Marilyn times five 13 MIN
16mm
B&W (G)
$600.00 purchase
Views a young woman, allegedly Marilyn Monroe, with harsh scrutiny in an old girlie film. Uses a repetitive five cycles to view her body and play her song, 'I'm through with Love.' to examine the power of images in United States culture. Features Arline Hunter. Made between 1968 - 1973.
Fine Arts; Sociology
Dist - CANCIN **Prod** - CONNER

Marilyn's Manhattan series
Arab League 28 MIN
Austria 28 MIN
Bhutan 28 MIN
Ecuador 28 MIN
German Democratic Republic - Tape 2 28 MIN
German Democratic Republic - Tape 1 - Leipzig 28 MIN
Jordan 28 MIN
Libya 28 MIN
Philippines 28 MIN
Saudi Arabia 28 MIN
Special - Cyprus 28 MIN
Under - Secretary General of U N for the Office of Press Information 28 MIN
United Nations Chief of Protocol 28 MIN
Zambia 28 MIN
Dist - PERRYM

Marilyn's window 4 MIN
16mm
Color (G)
$322.00 purchase, $12.00 rental
Offers stream - of - visual - consciousness images of Marilyn's window remembered from inside out.
Fine Arts
Dist - CANCIN **Prod** - BRAKS 1988

Marimba Music of Mexico 8 MIN
16mm
Ethnic Music and Dance Series
B&W (J)
LC 72-700255
Presents a performance of marimba music of southern Mexico. Explains that the pieces played are examples of the traditional songs from the regions of Tabasco and Tehuantepec.
Fine Arts; Geography - World
Dist - UWASHP **Prod** - UWASH 1971

Marina Popovich 20 MIN
U-matic / VHS
Color
Features Lieutenant Colonel Marina Popovich, the Soviet test pilot and engineer who set 13 world records. Begins with the romantic aspects of flying which had been primarily a man's profession and follows with a biography of Marina illustrated by interviews and off - screen commentary.
Biography; History - World; Industrial and Technical Education
Dist - IHF **Prod** - IHF

Marina Warner 40 MIN
VHS
Color (H C G)
$79.00 purchase
Features the writer talking with Lisa Appignanesi about the place of women in fiction and mythology and the influence of gender and religion on literature. Discusses her writings including Joan of Arc - The Image of Female Heroism and The Skating Party.
Literature and Drama; Religion and Philosophy
Dist - ROLAND **Prod** - INCART

Marine Animals of the Open Coast - a Story of Adaptation 22 MIN
16mm
Color (I)
Shows the interrelationships between sea anemone, sea urchin, barnacle, other marine animals and their surroundings. Describes the five general types of food on which they depend.
Science - Natural
Dist - MMP **Prod** - MMP 1963

Marine Biologist 15 MIN
U-matic / 16mm / VHS
Career Awareness
(I)
$130 VC purchase, $240 film purchase, $25 VC rental, $30 film rental
Presents an empathetic approach to career planning, showing the personal as well as professional attributes of marine biologists. Highlights the importance of career education.
Guidance and Counseling; Science - Physical
Dist - GPN

Marine Biology - Life in the Tropical Sea 11 MIN
U-matic / VHS / 16mm
Color (I J H)
LC 76-700053
Presents a documentary by Jacques Cousteau about the many marine animal groups living in tropical waters, largely within coral reefs. Emphasizes the need to preserve the delicate balance of this environment.
Science - Physical
Dist - PHENIX **Prod** - LIVDC 1975

Marine command post operations - Who's in charge 15 MIN
VHS
Color (IND PRO)
$189.00 purchase, $65.00 rental
Presents a team approach from Marine Command Post Operations. Advises that ship's crews, marine agencies, port authorities and fire departments can benefit from understanding the interest, responsibilities and contributions to be made by the many groups and agencies involved in a major marine fire emergency.
Health and Safety
Dist - JEWELR

Marine Corps Junior ROTC 20 MIN
16mm
Color

LC 74-705093
Shows how the students, in uniforms, participate in drill team and drum and bugle corps activities, sanctioned rifle matches and other appropriate activities.
Civics and Political Systems; Education
Dist - USNAC **Prod** - USN 1972

Marine Delicacies 9 MIN
16mm
B&W (I)
Shows how the abundant quantity of fish along the Indian coastline is caught with modern equipment and how it is processed and scientifically canned.
Business and Economics
Dist - NEDINF **Prod** - INDIA

Marine diesel engine maintenance 75 MIN
VHS
Color (G A)
$39.95 purchase _ #0854
Covers the maintenance of marine diesel engines. Looks at electrical, exhaust and cooling systems. Explains troubleshooting, maintenance, diagnostics, bleeding the diesel, batteries, turbo chargers, blowers, filters.
Industrial and Technical Education; Physical Education and Recreation
Dist - SEVVID

Marine Diesel Engines for Power Boats 16 MIN
16mm
B&W
LC FIE52-1070
Shows the BUDA marine diesel engines DA, DB and DD. Explains the mechanical operation of the DB and its points of difference from the Dd.
Industrial and Technical Education
Dist - USNAC **Prod** - USN 1942

Marine engine mechanic 4.5 MIN
VHS / 16mm
Good works 5 series
(A PRO)
$40.00 purchase _ #BPN238010
Presents the occupation of a marine engine mechanic. Gives a profile of a young person who is either undergoing an apprenticeship or has recently completed training in this field. Takes the viewer on a tour of this person's workplace and explains the practical skills and training offered by employers and schools. Gives a better understanding of the demand for skilled workers today and the potential for personal growth.
Guidance and Counseling
Dist - RMIBHF **Prod** - RMIBHF

Marine engineer officer 5 MIN
U-matic
Good work series
Color (H)
Provides useful, up to date information on various occupations to aid high school students in career selection. Available in five series of ten jobs each.
Education; Guidance and Counseling; Social Science
Dist - TVOTAR **Prod** - TVOTAR 1981

Marine firefighting series
Exploring fire's chemistry
Interior firefighting
Portable extinguisers
Portable extinguishers
Use of foam
Water and fire
Dist - GPCV

Marine Flowers 31 MIN
U-matic / VHS / 16mm
Color (H C)
Describes the structures, behaviors and life cycles of coelenterates, multicelled animals that have inhabited the seas for at least a billion years. Shows how they live in a relationship of mutual exploitation and examines the two - stage life cycle of polyp and medusa.
Science - Natural
Dist - IFB **Prod** - TOKYO 1976

Marine gas engine maintenance 75 MIN
VHS
Color (G A)
$39.95 purchase _ #0819
Covers the maintenance of marine gas engines. Looks at electrical, fuel, exhaust, cooling and ignition systems. Explains troubleshooting, maintenance, diagnostics, lay - up, batteries.
Industrial and Technical Education; Physical Education and Recreation
Dist - SEVVID

Marine Gas - Turbine Engine - Trouble Shooting 16 MIN
16mm
Color
LC FIE58-16
Describes the general procedure for locating the cause of trouble when a gas - turbine engine fails to start, to attain power, to keep oil pressure or to maintain performance.
Industrial and Technical Education
Dist - USNAC **Prod** - USN 1954

Marine Gas Turbine Engines - Principles of Operation 19 MIN
16mm
Color
LC FIE53-153
Explains the basic principles of the gas turbine engine, some variations in the design of turbines currently in use and the applications of the gas turbine in the operation of pumps, boats, trucks and helicopters.
Industrial and Technical Education
Dist - USNAC **Prod** - USN 1953

Marine Gas Turbine Engines - the Boeing 502 - 10c Engine 22 MIN
16mm
Color
Demonstrates the construction, operation and maintenance of the 502 - 10c engine.
Industrial and Technical Education
Dist - USNAC **Prod** - USN 1960

Marine Gas Turbine Engines - the Solar T - 45 Engine 23 MIN
16mm
Color
LC FIE61-94
Discusses the basic concept behind the gas turbine engine, its assembly and operation, unit accessories and their functions and how to operate the unit.
Industrial and Technical Education
Dist - USNAC **Prod** - USN 1960

Marine hurricane preparedness
VHS
Tell me why series
Color (G)
$29.90 purchase _ #0724
Shows how to prepare for a hurricane. Instructs yachtsmen, marinas, yacht clubs and boatyards.
Physical Education and Recreation; Science - Physical
Dist - SEVVID

Marine Invertebrates of the Chesapeake Bay 9 MIN
16mm
Color (I J H)
Shows shallow water invertebrates from the low order hydroid to high order crab in their natural habitat.
Science - Natural
Dist - VADE **Prod** - VADE 1963

Marine mammals of the Gulf of Maine 24 MIN
VHS
Color (G)
$19.95 purchase
Presents footage of whales and seals taken over 20 years by researchers from Allied Whale laboratory. Brings out the laboratory's history and its contributions to knowledge of marine mammals.
Fine Arts; History - United States; Science - Natural
Dist - NEFILM

Marine Marvels 11 MIN
16mm
B&W (I)
Shows the large variety of fish that exists in the Indian marine world and covers the two aquariums at Bombay and Trivandrum.
Science - Natural
Dist - NEDINF **Prod** - INDIA

Marine Meteorology 30 MIN
VHS / U-matic
Oceanus - the Marine Environment Series Lesson 11
Color (C A)
Traces the fundamental change in the composition of the earth's atmosphere since its formation. Discusses weather and the cause of the seasons.
Science - Natural; Science - Physical
Dist - CDTEL **Prod** - SCCON 1980
SCCON

Marine Pollution 30 MIN
U-matic / VHS
Oceanus - the Marine Environment Series Lesson 28
Color (C A)
Focuses on pollution of oceans. Explains problems that exist in determining pollution levels in the ocean. Discusses some of the effects of specific pollutants.
Science - Natural; Science - Physical
Dist - CDTEL **Prod** - SCCON 1980
SCCON

Marine Science 10 MIN
U-matic
Color (P)
Focuses on the role played by marine scientists in safeguarding the resources of the sea.
Guidance and Counseling; Science - Natural
Dist - GA **Prod** - MINIP

Marine Science 6 MIN
U-matic / VHS / 16mm
Kingdom of Could be You Series
Color (K P I)
Guidance and Counseling
Dist - EBEC **Prod** - EBEC 1974

Mariner - Mars 1969 21 MIN
16mm
Color (J)
LC 75-710695
Reviews the principal facts known, and theories held, about Mars prior to 1969. Presents the scientific information obtained from the two Mariner spacecraft that passed close by it in 1969. Incorporates numerous photographs of the Martian surface.
Science; Science - Physical
Dist - NASA **Prod** - NASA 1971

Mariner Mars Space Probe - President Kennedy Remembered - Focus on the Aswan Dam 20 MIN
16mm
Screen news digest series; Vol 7; Issue 5
B&W (H C)
Focuses on the events of 1964. Shows the preparation and launching of the Mariner spacecraft for a journey to Mars. Recalls the death of President Kennedy. Shows the Aswan Dam in Egypt, pointing out its value.
History - United States; Science; Science - Physical
Dist - HEARST **Prod** - HEARST 1965

Marines, 1965 15 MIN
16mm
Color
LC 74-705094
Highlights Marine Corps activities during 1965, including battle operations and civic action in the Dominican Republic and Vietnam.
Civics and Political Systems; History - United States
Dist - USNAC **Prod** - USMC 1966

Marines - 65 25 MIN
VHS / U-matic
Color
Highlights the activities under President Johnson of the U S Marine Corps, who fought in two hemispheres - the Dominican Republic and Vietnam.
Civics and Political Systems; History - United States; History - World
Dist - IHF **Prod** - IHF

Marines in Perspective 8 MIN
16mm
Color
LC 76-702711
Shows prospective Marine recruits the types of duties available to them while serving in the Marine Corps.
Civics and Political Systems; Guidance and Counseling
Dist - USNAC **Prod** - USMC 1975

Marinetek Waypointer
VHS
Color (G A)
$29.90 purchase _ #0908
Shows how to install, set up and use the Loran C, Marintek Waypointer model.
Physical Education and Recreation; Social Science
Dist - SEVVID

Maring in Motion 16 MIN
16mm / U-matic / VHS
Color (C G T A)
Shows a visual study of the movement style used by the Maring, swidden horticulturalists living on the slopes of the Bismarck Mountains in New Guinea. Horeometric analysis of body movement shows how Maring dance utilizes and emphasizes the movement patterns which occur in work and play.
Fine Arts; Sociology
Dist - PSU **Prod** - PSU 1968

The Marinos 9 MIN
U-matic / VHS / 16mm
American Family - an Endangered Species Series
Color (H C A)
Discusses the divorce and bitter custody fight of the parents of three children.
Sociology
Dist - FI **Prod** - NBCNEW 1979

Mario and the Marvelous Gift 20 MIN
16mm
Animatoons Series
Color (K P I)
LC FIA68-1535
Relates the story of a marvelous gem which spread happiness until it was broken by the henchmen of a wicked witch.
Literature and Drama
Dist - RADTV **Prod** - ANTONS 1968

Mario and the Marvelous Gift - Pt 1 11 MIN
16mm
Animatoons Series
Color
LC FIA67-5502
The story of the marvelous gem which spread happiness, and Mario, the little boy who struggled against evil forces to bring a broken gem to the good fairy of the blue star to repair it.
Fine Arts
Dist - RADTV **Prod** - ANTONS 1967

Mario and the Marvelous Gift - Pt 2 11 MIN
16mm
Animatoons Series
Color
LC FIA67-5503
Describes how Mario was captured by a witch and how the good fairy of the blue star removed the spell from a marvelous gem, saying that happiness and joy belong to those who remain honest and true.
Fine Arts
Dist - RADTV **Prod** - ANTONS 1968

Mario Lanza - the American Caruso 68 MIN
VHS
Color (G)
$19.95 purchase_#1295
Contains clips from the movies and records of American tenor Mario Lanza, known for his films - The Great Caruso and The Toast of New Orleans - and his records - Be My Love and others. Gives a frank presentation of his turbulent life. Hosted by Placido Domingo.
Biography; Fine Arts
Dist - KULTUR

Mario Lanza - the American Caruso 68 MIN
VHS
Color; B&W (G)
$29.95 purchase _ #1295
Documents the life of classical American tenor, Mario Lanza. Includes clips from his popular films and recordings, and interviews with co - workers Zsa Zsa Gabor, Anna Moffo, Kathryn Grayson and Joe Pasternak to portray Lanza's turbulent life. Features tenor Placido Domingo as host.
Biography; Fine Arts
Dist - KULTUR **Prod** - KULTUR 1991

Mario Sanchez - Painter of Memories 17 MIN
16mm
American Folk Artists Series
Color (J)
LC 78-700604
Presents a study of the life and work of Cuban - American wood painter Mario Sanchez. Includes the artist's reminiscences about his family and old neighborhood, as well as his commentary on the techniques and subject matter typifying his work.
Fine Arts
Dist - BOWGRN **Prod** - BOWGRN 1978

Mario Vargas Llosa 48 MIN
VHS
Color (H C G)
$79.00 purchase
Features the writer talking with John King about looking at society through satire, and the role of mass culture and intellectualism in a writer's development. Discusses his writings including La Casa Verde; Aunt Julia and the Scriptwriter; The War Of The End Of The World; and The True Story of Alejandro Mayta.
Literature and Drama
Dist - ROLAND **Prod** - INCART

Marion Weinstein - stand - up witch
VHS / Cassette
Color (G)
$20.00, $9.95 purchase
Presents Marion Weinstein, witch and stand - up comic, performing a comedic act at the Top of New York's Village Gate.
Fine Arts; Literature and Drama; Religion and Philosophy
Dist - EMAGIC **Prod** - EMAGIC

Marionette Theatre 29 MIN
U-matic
Off Stage Series
Color
Focuses on adaptations of Greek plays by a puppeteer who uses as many as 18 figures at once.
Fine Arts
Dist - UMITV **Prod** - UMITV 1975

Mariposa 60 MIN
U-matic / VHS
Rainbow Movie of the Week Series
Color (J A)
Shows how the son of a Mexican tenant farmer rescues his own dreams and those of his neighbors when he devises a plan to raise enough money to save their land and secure their financial future.
Sociology
Dist - GPN **Prod** - RAINTV 1981

Marisa and the Mermaid - Florida's War on Water Weeds 14 MIN
16mm
Color (I J H C)
LC FIA66-744
Employs underwater photography to demonstrate the central and southern Florida Flood Control District's war on aquatic weeds. Explains the importance of placing sea cows and marisa snails in weed - infested areas to eat the weeds.
Geography - United States; Health and Safety; Science - Natural
Dist - FDC **Prod** - CSFFCD 1965

Marital Adjustment
VHS
Marriage, Family Living and Counseling Series
(C G)
$59.00_CA231
Discusses marriage and the family relationship.
Guidance and Counseling
Dist - AAVIM **Prod** - AAVIM 1989

The Marital Dance - a Study of Movement in Therapy, Pt 1 52 MIN
U-matic / VHS
Color (PRO)
Uses the movements of dance to illustrate the predictable patterns of a marital relationship. Presents a series of edited interview sequences with a married couple. Shows how the therapist demonstrates the recurrent dysfunctional patterns and how the couple comes to recognize the roles they play.
Psychology; Sociology
Dist - PSU **Prod** - PSU

The Marital Dance - a Study of Movement In Therapy, Pt 2 32 MIN
U-matic / VHS
Color (PRO)
Uses the movements of dance to illustrate the predictable patterns of a marital relationship. Presents a series of edited interview sequences with a married couple. Shows how the therapist demonstrates the recurrent dysfunctional patterns and how the couple comes to recognize the roles they play. Comprises the second of two parts.
Psychology; Sociology
Dist - PSU **Prod** - PSU

Marital deduction trusts 50 MIN
VHS
Color (A PRO C)
$95.00 purchase _ #Y506
Features an expert panel with a number of practical articles, checklists and forms in the accompanying study guide. Addresses the complex issues surrounding marital deduction trusts.
Business and Economics; Civics and Political Systems; Sociology
Dist - ALIABA **Prod** - CLETV 1993

A Marital Therapy Consultation 60 MIN
VHS
Color (PRO)
$69.95 Videotape _ #3777
Shows how calling in a guest consultant can help a marital counseling session by, among other things, providing a new style of intervention or breaking an impasse in the therapy.
Psychology
Dist - BRUMAZ **Prod** - DUKEDP 1984

Marivaux - La Double Inconstance 135 MIN
U-matic / VHS
Color (C) (FRENCH)
$399.00, $249.00 purchase _ #AD - 1492
Presents 'La Double Inconstance' by Marivaux in French.
Foreign Language; History - World; Literature and Drama; Sociology
Dist - FOTH **Prod** - FOTH

Mark 11 MIN
16mm
B&W (J)
LC 76-701868
Tells about a young quadriplegic who is confined to a wheelchair after an accident. Shows how he is concerned about his studies and prospects for employment while his family worries about the future when they will not be around to care for him.
Health and Safety; Psychology; Sociology
Dist - AUIS **Prod** - AUSDSS 1975

Mark 10 MIN
U-matic / VHS / 16mm
People You'd Like to Know Series
Color (I J H)
LC 78-701951
Tells the story of 14 - year - old Mark, who has a reading problem but who is working to overcome it.
Education; English Language; Psychology
Dist - EBEC **Prod** - WGBHTV 1978

The Mark Cresse school of baseball 120 MIN
VHS
Color (J H C G)
$49.00 purchase _ #CH4000SV
Presents two volumes offering helpful hints, strategies and different techniques for baseball players at every level. Uses language and visual demonstation techniques that any novice baseball player can understand and put into practical use on the playing field. Volume 1 covers offense - hitting, bunting, and baserunning, with a special section on pitching. Volume 2 covers defense - cathing, infielding and outfielding. Features Los Angeles Dodgers' coach Mark Cresse.
Physical Education and Recreation
Dist - CAMV

Mark Harris - Something about a Writer 23 MIN
U-matic
Color (H C A)
Explores the attitudes and techniques of writing of Mark Harris, university professor and author of BANG THE DRUM SLOWLY.
Biography; Literature and Drama
Dist - CEPRO **Prod** - CEPRO

Mark II Articulator Procedure 60 MIN
U-matic
Color (C)
Demonstrates the procedure for obtaining a facebow registration, retruded position registration and lateral excursion registration of the mandible and the utilization of these records to accurately mount study models in articulator and set the condular controls to stimulate the relationships of the patient's teeth.
Health and Safety; Science - Natural
Dist - UOKLAH **Prod** - UOKLAH 1986

Mark Linenthal - 10 - 4 - 87 120 MIN
VHS / Cassette
Poetry Center reading series
Color (G)
#928 - 629
Features the writer reading from his works at the Ruth Witt - Diamant Memorial Reading at the Poetry Center, San Francisco State University. Also includes readings by James Broughton, Robert Duncan, Rosalie Moore, Shirley Taylor, Christy Taylor, Justine Fixel, Lawrence Fixel, Michael McClure, Gail Layton, and Stephen Witt - Diamant. Introduction by Frances Phillips. Slides of Ruth Witt - Diamant courtesy of Caryl Mezey. Available for listening purposes only at the Center; not for sale or rent.
Literature and Drama
Dist - POETRY **Prod** - POETRY 1987

Mark of a Man 17 MIN
16mm
Color
Presents an anti - recruiting film. Shows how the Army trains its men to fight against the people of Vietnam. Presents recent veterans of the Vietnamese war who describe their experiences.
Civics and Political Systems
Dist - CANWRL **Prod** - CANWRL

The Mark of Excellence 11 MIN
16mm
Color
Compares the oilfield firefighter, Red Adair, to Astronaut Neil Armstrong.
Biography; Industrial and Technical Education; Science; Science - Physical
Dist - NASA **Prod** - NASA

The Mark of Lilith 32 MIN
16mm / VHS
Color (G)
$350.00 purchase, $75.00 rental
Weaves together the story of Zena, a black lesbian researching why the goddesses of one culture become the demons of another, and Lillia, a white vampire who wants to get away from her bloodsucking companion Luke. Reveals that Zena and Lillia meet at a horror movie where the woman always dies in the last reel. Their relationship enables Lillia to stop being a predator or victim and provides answers for Zena. Produced by Bruna Fionda, Polly Gladwin, Isiling Mack - Nataf.
Fine Arts; Literature and Drama; Psychology; Sociology
Dist - WMEN **Prod** - FGMN 1986

A Mark of Quality 14 MIN
U-matic
Color
A tour for the housewife from feedlot to pack plant to supermarket and back into her own kitchen. Tells how the Federal Meat Grading Service helps the shopper by providing a guide to buying quality meat.

Guidance and Counseling; Home Economics; Social Science
Dist - USDA **Prod** - USDA 1972

The Mark of Quality - Case 13 MIN
16mm
Color
LC 80-700359
Offers a look behind the scenes in research and manufacturing at J I Case Company, one of the world's largest makers of agricultural and construction equipment.
Business and Economics
Dist - CORPOR **Prod** - CASE 1980

Mark of the clown 15 MIN
VHS
Color (I J H C G A R)
$10.00 rental _ #36 - 82 - 1521
Introduces clown ministry as an option for churches. Suggests that it can be used in a wide variety of settings, including retreats, workshops and worship services.
Religion and Philosophy
Dist - APH **Prod** - MMM

The Mark of the D P Professional 30 MIN
VHS / U-matic
Recruiting and Developing the D P Professional Series
Color
Business and Economics; Guidance and Counseling; Psychology
Dist - DELTAK **Prod** - DELTAK

The Mark of Zorro 77 MIN
16mm
B&W
Presents the first of the swashbuckler costume films Douglas Fairbanks Sr made.
Fine Arts
Dist - KITPAR **Prod** - UAA 1920

The Mark of Zorro 91 MIN
BETA
B&W
Stars Douglas Fairbanks as Zorro, the crusader for the rights of the Mexican people.
Fine Arts
Dist - RMIBHF **Prod** - UNKNWN 1920

The Mark of Zorro 90 MIN
16mm
B&W
Introduces Zorro, the famous Mexican Robin Hood who carves his initial wherever he goes in his efforts to preserve the rights of oppressed Mexicans. Stars Douglas Fairbanks, Sr and Marguerite de la Motte. Directed by Fred Niblo.
Fine Arts
Dist - KILLIS **Prod** - UNKNWN 1920

Mark of Zorro, the 121 MIN
VHS / BETA
Silent; B&W
Stars Douglas Fairbanks as the heroic Zorro.
Fine Arts
Dist - VIDIM **Prod** - UNKNWN 1920

Mark 1 - 6
VHS
The Bible - American Sign Language translation series
Color (S R)
Presents an American Sign Language translation of the New Testament Gospel of Mark, chapters 1 through 6. Available on a free - loan basis from the Lutheran Church - Missouri Synod's Deaf Ministry.
Guidance and Counseling; Literature and Drama; Religion and Philosophy
Dist - CPH **Prod** - LUMIS

Mark Russell Specials 90 MIN
VHS
Color (G)
$79.95 purchase _ #MRCS - 000
Features highlights from satirist and political commentator Mark Russell's live performances. Includes a special collection of his songs.
Civics and Political Systems; Literature and Drama
Dist - PBS **Prod** - WNEDTV

Mark 7 - 11
VHS
The Bible - American Sign Language translation series
Color (S R)
Presents an American Sign Language translation of the New Testament Gospel of Mark, chapters 7 through 11. Available on a free - loan basis from the Lutheran Church - Missouri Synod's Deaf Ministry.
Guidance and Counseling; Literature and Drama; Religion and Philosophy
Dist - CPH **Prod** - LUMIS

Mark Tobey Abroad 30 MIN
U-matic / VHS / 16mm
Color (A)
LC 73-702699
Presents a tribute to the artist, Mark Tobey, as an old man. Tobey talks about himself, his art and other artists and demonstrates his always creative ability in drawing, music, poetry and observations on life in general.
Fine Arts; Guidance and Counseling; Religion and Philosophy
Dist - PHENIX **Prod** - HUFSC 1973

Mark Twain 30 MIN
VHS
Famous authors series
Color (J H G)
$225.00 purchase
Looks at the life and career of the American writer through selections from his works. Uses the music and events of his time, including his stints as a reporter, prospector, riverboat pilot, speaker and humorist. Part of a series of videos about 24 major American and British authors. Videos are also available in a set.
History - United States; Literature and Drama
Dist - LANDMK

Mark Twain 26 MIN
16mm / U-matic / VHS
Biography Series
B&W (I)
Presents a biography of Mark Twain showing his experiences and varied environments which furnished material for his stories, essays and novels.
Biography; Literature and Drama
Dist - MGHT **Prod** - WOLPER 1963

Mark Twain
VHS / 35mm strip
Meet the Classic Authors Series
Color (I)
$39.95, $28.00 purchase
Portrays Mark Twain. Part of a series on authors.
English Language; Literature and Drama
Dist - PELLER

Mark Twain - a musical biography 88 MIN
VHS
Color; CC (I J H)
$24.95 purchase _ #32990
Portrays the life of Samuel Clemens in a musical program.
Biography; Literature and Drama
Dist - KNOWUN

Mark Twain and the Automated Office 12 MIN
16mm
Color
LC 79-700728
Uses the personage of Mark Twain to underscore Commercial Union Leasing Corporation's human approach to computers. Emphasizes the flexibility and importance of time, time - saving and time - stretching.
Business and Economics; Mathematics
Dist - CULC **Prod** - CULC 1978

Mark Twain - Background for His Works 14 MIN
16mm / U-matic / VHS
Color (J)
$340.00; $240.00 purchase _ #3898; LC 78-700511
Uses rare motion picture footage to introduce Mark Twain and show scenes from his boyhood home in Hannibal, Missouri, and from locations in the East where he wrote the recollections of his life. Dramatizes excerpts from many of his works.
Biography; Literature and Drama
Dist - CORF **Prod** - CORF 1978

Mark Twain - Beneath the Laughter 58 MIN
16mm / U-matic / VHS
Color
LC 80-700170
Presents dramatic re - creations showing Mark Twain as a somber old man of 74, mourning his daughter's death.
Biography; Literature and Drama
Dist - PFP **Prod** - FALM 1979

Mark Twain Gives an Interview 14 MIN
16mm
Color (I J H C)
$350.00 purchase _ #1235
Re - creates an interview with Mark Twain, portrayed by Hal Holbrook.
Biography; Literature and Drama
Dist - CORF **Prod** - CORF 1961

Mark Twain - How I Came into the Literary Profession 25 MIN
U-matic / VHS / 16mm
Color (I J H C A)
$560, $250 purchase _ #5103C
Talks about Mark Twain's life as a satirist, realist, essayist, lecturer, reporter, and novelist. Filmed in his house in Hartford, Connecticut.
Literature and Drama
Dist - CORF

Mark Twain - HUCKLEBERRY FINN 29 MIN
Videoreel / VT2
One to One Series
Color
Presents readings from HUCKLEBERRY FINN by Mark Twain.
Literature and Drama
Dist - PBS **Prod** - WETATV

Mark Twain, Huckleberry Finn and the Mississippi - a video commentary 25 MIN
VHS
Color (J H)
$89.00 purchase _ #05529 - 126
Covers background information about Mark Twain and his work. Focuses on the deeper implications of Huckleberry Finn. Features Richard Brodhead of Yale University.
Literature and Drama
Dist - GA **Prod** - GA

Mark Twain, Huckleberry Finn and the Mississippi River - a Video Commentary
U-matic / VHS
American Literature Series
(G C J)
$89 purchase _ #05529 - 85
Explains why Huckleberry Finn is considered to be one of the best pieces of American Fiction. Interviews Richard Brodhead of Yale University. Shows the deeper implications of Twain's work.
Literature and Drama
Dist - CHUMAN

Mark Twain, Louisa may Alcott, Herman Melville 55 MIN
35mm strip / VHS / 16mm
Meet the Classic Authors Series
Color (I)
$89.95 purchase
Features the lives and work of American authors Louisa May Alcott, Mark Twain,and Herman Melville, focusing on motivations behind the writing. Set 2 of a 4 part series.
Education; Literature and Drama
Dist - JANUP **Prod** - JANUP

Mark Twain - When I was a Boy 25 MIN
U-matic / VHS / 16mm
Color (H C A)
Portrays Mark Twain's life along the Mississippi River, as a boy growing up, later as a young cub and pilot on the glamorous stern - wheeled steamboats and finally as a world - renowned writer reflecting back on those days.
Biography; Literature and Drama
Dist - NGS **Prod** - NGS 1977

Mark Twain's a Connecticut Yankee in King Arthur's court 60 MIN
VHS
Color (G)
$64.95 purchase _ #S02039
Presents a dramatization of Mark Twain's story 'A Connecticut Yankee in King Arthur's Court.' Stars Richard Basehart, Roscoe Lee Browne, and Paul Rudd.
Literature and Drama
Dist - UILL **Prod** - WQED 1978

Mark Twain's America 54 MIN
U-matic / VHS / 16mm
Project 20 Series
B&W (J)
Re - creates the life of Mark Twain and the age in which he lived. Shows historical highlights, including the frontier towns, Manhattan in the gay 90's and Twain's stagecoach journey through the West.
Biography; History - United States; Literature and Drama
Dist - MGHT **Prod** - NBCTV 1960

Mark Twain's America, Pt 1 27 MIN
U-matic / VHS / 16mm
Project 20 Series
B&W (J)
Re - creates the life of Mark Twain and the age in which he lived. Shows historical highlights, including the frontier towns, Manhattan in the gay 90's and Twain's stagecoach journey through the West.
Literature and Drama
Dist - MGHT **Prod** - NBCTV 1960

Mark Twain's America, Pt 2 27 MIN
16mm / U-matic / VHS
Project 20 Series
B&W (J)
Re - creates the life of Mark Twain and the age in which he lived. Shows historical highlights, including the frontier towns, Manhattan in the gay 90's and Twain's stagecoach journey through the West.
Literature and Drama
Dist - MGHT **Prod** - NBCTV 1960

Mark Twain's 'Connecticut Yankee'
VHS / U-matic
Color
Literature and Drama
Dist - MSTVIS **Prod** - MSTVIS

Mark Twain's Hartford home 24 MIN
VHS
Color (H C T A)
$69.95 purchase _ #S01323
Tours Mark Twain's Victorian home in Hartford, Connecticut. Includes samples of Twain's wit, photographs, and anecdotes from his life.
Biography; Fine Arts; Literature and Drama
Dist - UILL

Mark Twain's Hartford Home 24 MIN
16mm / U-matic / VHS
American lifestyle series; Cultural leaders
Color (I J H)
Features E G Marshall touring the home of Mark Twain.
Geography - United States
Dist - AIMS **Prod** - COMCO 1978

Mark - Up 90 MIN
U-matic / VHS / 16mm
Energy War Series
Color
Covers the frantic lobbying through the final test vote of the congressional struggle over President Carter's energy proposal.
Civics and Political Systems; History - United States; Social Science
Dist - PENNAS **Prod** - PBS

Mark Va a La Escuela - 11 15 MIN
VHS
Amigos Series
Color (K) (SPANISH)
$125.00 purchase
Enables teachers with no knowledge of Spanish to introduce basic words to children in kindergarten through second grade. Uses simple concepts and music and features Perro Pepe, a six - foot orange dog, and Senorita Fernandez as instructors. Promotes awareness of and appreciation for Hispanic culture and sparks interest in the geography of Spanish - speaking countries. Part 11 is entitled 'Mark Va A La Escuela.'.
Foreign Language; Geography - World
Dist - AITECH

Mark Van Doren - Poems and Criticism 29 MIN
Videoreel / VT2
One to One Series
Color
Presents the poetry of Mark Van Doren.
Literature and Drama
Dist - PBS **Prod** - WETATV

Marked for failure 60 MIN
16mm
America's crises series
B&W (C A)
LC FIA66-824
Examines the situation in New York City's Harlem section, revealing the profound handicaps to learning and efforts being made to overcome these disadvantages.
Education; History - United States; Psychology; Sociology
Dist - IU **Prod** - NET 1965

Marken (the Field) 18 MIN
16mm
Color
Depicts animal life in the open field, accompanied by sound effects.
Science - Natural
Dist - STATNS **Prod** - STATNS 1962

The Market 29 MIN
16mm
Corporation Series
B&W (H C A)
LC 74-702397
Presents supermarket chain owner Sam Steinberg, who discusses the three main forces in the battle of the marketplace, including suppliers, competitors and consumers.
Business and Economics; Geography - World
Dist - NFBC **Prod** - NFBC 1973

The Market - Allocating a Surplus 10 MIN
16mm / U-matic / VHS
Foundations of Wealth Series
Color
Shows the possible solutions to the problem of allocating the surplus created by the division of labor and mechanization.
Business and Economics
Dist - FOTH **Prod** - FOTH

Market analysis - demand and supply 60 MIN
VHS
Macroeconomics series
Color (H C G)
$89.00 purchase _ #GSU - 307
Discusses demand and supply analysis. Features part of a 24 - part series instructed by Dr Edward F Stuart, Northwestern University, which focuses on a description of the major economic policy - making bodies in the United States and their interrelationships.
Business and Economics
Dist - INSTRU

Market and product expansion - 6 30 MIN
VHS
Venturing...the entrepreneurial challenge series
Color (G)
$14.95 purchase
Highlights entrepreneurs who have been very successful at expanding their products and markets, both domestically and internationally. Part six of a 13 - part series on the steps involved in starting and developing an entrepreneurial company. Viewers' guide available separately. Sponsored under a grant from the Farmers Home Administration to help small and rural businesses.
Business and Economics; Psychology
Dist - VTETV **Prod** - VTETV 1992

Market Cattle Grading 23 MIN
VHS
Meat Animal Grading (Set I) Series
(C)
$79.95 _ CV136
Displays the fundamentals of slaughter cattle evaluation and grading including an evaluation of slaughter cattle based on predicted U S Quality Grade and U S Yeild Grade.
Agriculture
Dist - AAVIM **Prod** - AAVIM 1989

Market Clearing Price 23 MIN
U-matic / VHS / 16mm
People on Market Street Series
Color (H A)
LC 77-702405
Explains how the price of a good equates the amount of that good demanded with the amount supplied. Explains how inventories help to provide reliable supply at more predictable prices.
Business and Economics
Dist - CORF **Prod** - FNDREE 1977

Market Economy of the United States 15 MIN
U-matic / VHS / 16mm
Color (J H)
LC 80-700947
Defines the concept of limited resources and outlines the features of traditional, market, and command economies. Shows freedom of choice, competition, and the profit motive to be the major components of a market economy and illustrates how these principles work in real life.
Business and Economics
Dist - PHENIX **Prod** - GREENF 1980

Market equilibrium 60 MIN
VHS
Macroeconomics series
Color (H C G)
$89.00 purchase _ #GSU - 308
Discusses market equilibrium. Looks at market changes. Part of a 24 - part series instructed by Dr Edward F Stuart, Northwestern University, which focuses on a description of the major economic policy - making bodies in the United States and their interrelationships.
Business and Economics
Dist - INSTRU

Market failure - monopoly 30 MIN
VHS
Introductory economics series
Color; PAL (J H C G)
PdS29.50 purchase
Looks at the efficiencies of monopoly and how government - created monopoly can be eliminated. Explains that removing an inefficient natural monopoly is more difficult. Features Ellen Roseman and Professor John Palmer describing three methods. Part of a four - part series.
Business and Economics
Dist - EMFVL **Prod** - TVOTAR

Market Gardener 15 MIN
U-matic
Harriet's Magic Hats II Series
(P I J)
Shows how vegetables are grown in fields or greenhouses and how they are weeded, sprayed, harvested, washed, sorted and packaged for sale.
Guidance and Counseling
Dist - ACCESS **Prod** - ACCESS 1983

Market Gardening 15 MIN
U-matic / VHS / 16mm
Let's Visit Series
Color (P I)
Shows how Wing Lee and his family supply fresh produce for the city's supermarkets and greengrocers from their six - acre market garden. Describes traditional methods of Chinese cultivation. Explains the steps in raising vegetables and how Lee works to keep labor and profit within the family unit.
Agriculture; Social Science
Dist - BCNFL **Prod** - BCNFL 1984

Market in Berlin 15 MIN
16mm
B&W
Shows the routine activities at the weekly farmers' market on Wittenberg Square, the idyllic small - town life amidst the Berlin metropolis.
Fine Arts
Dist - WSTGLC **Prod** - WSTGLC 1929

Market Place in Mexico 13 MIN
U-matic / VHS / 16mm
Captioned; Color (P I J)
LC 75-701083
Examines socioeconomic conditions in a rural Mexican marketplace. Shows how people, such as a serape maker, a potter and a rope maker, are dependent on one another's skills. Points out the similarities and differences between the contemporary market and its ancestor, the Aztec market of 500 years ago.
Geography - World; Social Science
Dist - ALTSUL **Prod** - ALTSUL 1974

Market planning - segmentation and positioning for higher growth and profits 60 MIN
VHS
Color (PRO IND A) (DUTCH FRENCH)
$695.00 purchase _ #VIM21
Defines necessary steps in defining a effective marketing plan. Encourages marketing managers to maintain the necessary balance between market shares initiatives which are long term and profits which are short term. Prof Peter Doyle takes a practical approach to the subject.
Business and Economics
Dist - EXTR

Market Research 30 MIN
U-matic / VHS
Marketing Perspectives Series
Color
Gives marketing information systms and their components, primary and secondary data, traditional methods of information gathering and test marketing as an information method.
Business and Economics; Education
Dist - WFVTAE **Prod** - MATC

Market research - an ingredient for success 54 MIN
VHS
How to start your own business series
Color (H A T)
$69.95 purchase _ #NC116
Looks at the role of market research. Part of a ten - part series on starting a business.
Business and Economics
Dist - AAVIM **Prod** - AAVIM 1992

Market stall holder 10 MIN
VHS
Stop, look, listen series
Color; PAL (P I J)
Shows a typical day at a market. Looks at the erection of stalls and their loading with goods before the customers arrive. Examines the variety of goods, from vegetables to wigs. At the end of the selling day, the sellers pack up their unsold wares, the stalls are dismantled and the litter is swept up for collection. Part of a series of films which start from some everyday observation and show more of what is happening, how and why. Builds vocabulary and encourages children to be more observant.
Business and Economics; English Language; Social Science
Dist - VIEWTH

Market structure 13 MIN
VHS / U-matic
Real world economics series
Color (J H)
$240.00, $290.00 purchase, $60.00 rental
Includes materials on what is meant by the term 'market,' competition, how an auction market sets price, monopoly, oligopoly, price wars and cartels, and government intervention.
Business and Economics
Dist - NDIM **Prod** - REALWO 1993

Market Swine Grading 32 MIN
VHS
Meat Animal Grading (Set I) Series
(C)
$79.95 _ CV137
Gives the fundamentals of evaluating market barrows and gilts based on the degree of muscling, back fat and last rib as well as U S D A Grade.
Agriculture
Dist - AAVIM **Prod** - AAVIM 1989

A Market town 14 MIN
VHS
Color; PAL (P I J)
PdS29
Shows the development of a rural market center - Sudbury, Suffolk - at a bridging point, as well as the changing function of the market, the town's sphere of influence, recent development and population as a result of overflow from London.
Geography - World
Dist - BHA

The Marketeers - Careers in Marketing 13 MIN
16mm
Working Worlds Series
Color (I J H)
LC 75-701545
Explores the variety of careers available in marketing and distribution.
Guidance and Counseling; Psychology
Dist - FFORIN **Prod** - OLYMPS 1974

Marketing 30 MIN
U-matic
It's Everybody's Business Series Unit 5, Operating a Business
Color
Business and Economics
Dist - DALCCD **Prod** - DALCCD

Marketing
U-matic
Matter of taste series; Lesson 1
Color (H A)
Shows that the modern cook has virtually unlimited choices of fresh, nutritious foods all year round. Discusses how to have a successful marketing trip, from weekly menu plans to buying according to season.
Home Economics
Dist - CDTEL **Prod** - COAST

Marketing 30 MIN
VHS / 16mm
Growing a Business Series
(H C)
$99.95 each, $1,295.00 series
Examines the importance of good marketing to a successful business.
Business and Economics
Dist - AMBROS **Prod** - AMBROS 1988

Marketing 27 MIN
VHS
Minding my own business series
Color (H C G)
$225.00 purchase
Features women entrepreneurs who have developed businesses. Discusses how they marketed their skill or service in beginning their new business. Part of a six - video series that highlights the personal experiences of business owners in getting started.
Business and Economics
Dist - LANDMK

Marketing 27 MIN
U-matic / VHS
How to be more Successful in Your Own Business Series
Color (G)
$279.00, $179.00 purchase _ #AD - 2004
Looks at marketing strategies. Considers planning, setting goals, pricing in relation to competition, costs and demand, forecasting sales and budget, using and measuring the effectiveness of advertising. Part of an eight - part series on successful business management moderated by David Susskind.
Business and Economics
Dist - FOTH **Prod** - FOTH

Marketing
VHS
Dynamics of business series
Color (H C A)
$139.00 purchase _ #MAS03V
Explores basic marketing concepts. Considers subjects including marketing functions, marketing mix, channels of distribution, promotion, and selling.
Business and Economics
Dist - CAMV

Marketing a Product Range 25 MIN
VHS
Color (S)
$149.00 purchase _ #825 - 9654
Reveals how successful companies constantly update and improve their product range to keep their percentage of the market. Provides viewers with a thorough understanding of marketing processes. A discussion guide comes with the program.
Business and Economics; Psychology
Dist - FI **Prod** - BBCTV 1989

Marketing and customer service
VHS
School to work - communications connections for the real world 'series
Color (J H C G)
$149.00 purchase _ #CDCOM106V
Discusses why communications skills are a vital part of careers in marketing and customer service. Meets the requirements for integrating academic communication skills with the vocational work world of the Carl Perkins Applied Technology Act. Part of a ten - part series.
Business and Economics; Guidance and Counseling; Social Science
Dist - CAMV

Marketing and Distribution 10 MIN
U-matic
Color (P)
Shows the many careers involved in designing, researching, testing, marketing, advertising and distributing a product.
Business and Economics; Guidance and Counseling
Dist - GA **Prod** - MINIP

Marketing and Distribution 6 MIN
16mm / U-matic / VHS
Kingdom of Could be You Series
Color (K P I)
Guidance and Counseling
Dist - EBEC **Prod** - EBEC 1974

Marketing and Distributive Education 24 MIN
U-matic / VHS
Color (J H)
Discusses career options and trends in marketing. Focuses on careers in sales, advertising, physical distribution and management.
Guidance and Counseling
Dist - IFB

The Marketing and manufacturing edge - Volume III 25 MIN
VHS
Color (PRO IND A)
Presents the case history of the introduction and marketing of Gillette's new Sensor Razor.
Business and Economics; Psychology
Dist - ENMED **Prod** - ENMED 1990

Marketing and Sales 21 MIN
VHS / 16mm
Video Career Library Series
Color (H C A PRO)
$79.95 purchase _ #WW109
Shows occupations in marketing and sales such as insurance sales, real estate agents, sales representatives, retail salespersons, transportation ticket clerks, travel agents, stockbrokers and others. Contains current occupational outlook and salary information.
Business and Economics; Guidance and Counseling
Dist - AAVIM **Prod** - AAVIM 1990

Marketing and Sales 21 MIN
VHS
Video Career Library Series
(G)
$69.95 _ #CJ119V
Covers duties, conditions, salaries and training connected with jobs in the marketing and sales fields. Provides a view of employees in sales related occupations on the job, and gives information on the current market for such skills. Revised every two years.
Business and Economics; Guidance and Counseling
Dist - CAMV **Prod** - CAMV

Marketing and sales - 5 30 MIN
VHS
Venturing...the entrepreneurial challenge series
Color (G)
$14.95 purchase
Features entrepreneurs who are extremely creative in their marketing techniques, particularly in their 'guerilla' - or low cost - marketing. Part five of a 13 - part series on the steps involved in starting and developing an entrepreneurial company. Viewers' guide available separately. Sponsored under a grant from the Farmers Home Administration to help small and rural businesses.
Business and Economics; Psychology
Dist - VTETV **Prod** - VTETV 1992

Marketing and statistics 10 MIN
VHS
Commercial chicken production series
Color (G)
$39.95 purchase _ #6 - 050 - 106A
Discusses marketing and statistics in poultry farming. Part of a six - part series on commercial chicken production.
Agriculture; Social Science
Dist - VEP **Prod** - UDEL

Marketing and the law - an introduction 35 MIN
VHS / U-matic
Antitrust counseling and the marketing process series
Color (PRO)
Outlines the legal counsel's role in marketing decision - making and discusses the nature of marketing, the marketing concept and the product life cycle.
Business and Economics; Civics and Political Systems
Dist - ABACPE **Prod** - ABACPE

Marketing Communications 30 MIN
U-matic / VHS
Marketing Perspectives Series
Color
Shows basic processes of communication in sales skills, steps in the sales process, importance of personal motivation to a salesperson, factors to be assessed in establishing sales territories and methods of organizing a sales force.
Business and Economics; Education
Dist - WFVTAE **Prod** - MATC

Marketing Communications
VHS
Marketing Video Series
$89.95 purchase _ #RPMP17V
Discusses how the basic process of communications relates to sales.
Business and Economics
Dist - CAREER **Prod** - CAREER

Marketing Concepts 29 MIN
U-matic / VHS
Business File Series
Color
Business and Economics
Dist - PBS **Prod** - PBS

Marketing Distribution 29 MIN
VHS / U-matic
Business File Series
Color
Business and Economics
Dist - PBS **Prod** - PBS

Marketing electronic information series
Presents an eight - part series on marketing electronic information. Includes the titles What Is Marketing Electronic Information - and Hot Trends; Distribution and Direct Mail; Budgeting for Your Marketing Plan; The New Media - What You Must Know; INTERNET - The New Marketing Opportunity; Training and Customer Service; Exhibitions and Trade Shows; Field Sales and Telemarketing. Eight videos.
Budgeting for your marketing plan
Distribution and direct mail
Exhibitions and trade shows
Field sales and telemarketing
INTERNET - The New marketing opportunity
The New media - what you must know
Training and customer service
What is marketing electronic information - and hot trends
Dist - DEJAVI **Prod** - DEJAVI

Marketing for Black Physicians 25 MIN
VHS / 16mm
(C PRO)
$385.00 purchase _ #870VI023
Stresses to residents that they must have a marketing plan that will help them establish the most successful practice.
Health and Safety
Dist - HSCIC **Prod** - HSCIC 1987

Marketing integrity - ethics issues for government contractors 26 MIN
VHS
Color (A)
$500.00 purchase, $150.00 rental _ #V1069 - 06
Promotes awareness of ethical problems in manufacturing, bidding, and supplying for government - related contracts. Encourages establishment of company standards for conduct of business. Includes video and leader's guide.
Business and Economics
Dist - BARR **Prod** - ETHICS

Marketing Management 30 MIN
VHS / U-matic
Marketing Perspectives Series
Color
Covers the efforts of the marketing concept of goal - setting by corporations, role of market information in the decision making process and other aspects of marketing management.
Business and Economics; Education
Dist - WFVTAE **Prod** - MATC

Marketing mystique - Pt 5 30 MIN
U-matic / VHS
Profiles in progress series
Color (H C)
$325.00, $295.00 purchase _ #V550
Reveals that in India tourism has become the biggest foreign - exchange earner. Examines India's position as the world's largest democracy and one of its oldest cultures. Asia's biggest hotel chain, the Taj, has had a

strong role in dispelling the myths and misconceptions about India while providing a strong base of employment and training in the service industry. Part of a 13 - part series on people who are moving their tradition - bound countries into modern times.
Business and Economics; Geography - World
Dist - BARR **Prod** - CEPRO 1991

Marketing New Products, Victor H Prushan
VHS / U-matic
Management Skills Series
Color (PRO)
Business and Economics; Psychology
Dist - AMCEE **Prod** - AMCEE

Marketing perspectives series
Advertising - broadcast 30 MIN
Advertising - print 30 MIN
Agents and brokers 30 MIN
Channels of Distribution 30 MIN
Communications management 30 MIN
Consumer buying behavior 30 MIN
Consumerism 30 MIN
Direct Marketing 30 MIN
Future trends 30 MIN
Government and its influences 30 MIN
Industrial Markets 30 MIN
International Marketing 30 MIN
Market Research 30 MIN
Marketing Communications 30 MIN
Marketing Management 30 MIN
Marketing Strategies 30 MIN
Marketing Today 30 MIN
Marketing Variables 30 MIN
Packaging and Labeling 30 MIN
Physical Distribution 30 MIN
Pricing Strategies 30 MIN
Pricing Theories 30 MIN
Product development 30 MIN
Product Management 30 MIN
Retail Location 30 MIN
Retailing 30 MIN
Service Marketing 30 MIN
Target Markets 30 MIN
Wholesalers and Distributors 30 MIN
Dist - WFVTAE

Marketing Practices 19 MIN
U-matic / VHS
Financing, Starting and Marketing a Flock Series
Color
Discusses a variety of factors that affect the value of market lambs.
Agriculture
Dist - HOBAR **Prod** - HOBAR

Marketing Pricing Strategy 29 MIN
U-matic / VHS
Business File Series
Color
Business and Economics
Dist - PBS **Prod** - PBS

Marketing Product Strategy 29 MIN
U-matic / VHS
Business File Series
Color
Business and Economics
Dist - PBS **Prod** - PBS

Marketing Promotional Strategy 29 MIN
U-matic / VHS
Business File Series
Color
Business and Economics
Dist - PBS **Prod** - PBS

Marketing quality 15 MIN
16mm / VHS / BETA / U-matic
Quality series
Color; PAL (PRO IND)
PdS135, PdS143 purchase
Describes the dual role that marketing and quality plays in the operations of the viewer's company. Features a production by the Institute of Quality Assurance. Part of a three - part series.
Business and Economics; Psychology
Dist - EDPAT

Marketing Research Pays Off 13 MIN
16mm
Color
LC FIE59-192
Tells the story of agricultural marketing research, showing USDA scientists at work improving marketing methods, reducing processing and handling costs and expanding the market for farm products.
Agriculture
Dist - USNAC **Prod** - USDA 1959

Marketing research series
The Basics, Pt 1 30 MIN
Creative approaches, Pt 2 30 MIN
Dist - GPN

Marketing Series
Presents a series that offers a thorough introduction to marketing as it relates to contemporary living and society's changing needs.
All the right moves 30 MIN
Because It's There 30 MIN
Breaking through the Clutter 30 MIN
Coming of age 30 MIN
Deliverance 30 MIN
Driving Passion 30 MIN
The Fastest game in town 30 MIN
The Fresh Connection 30 MIN
Gold in the hills 30 MIN
Great expectations 30 MIN
The Green Machine 30 MIN
Jeans, Jewels, and Jogging Shoes 30 MIN
Just Another Oil Company 30 MIN
Leader of the Pack 30 MIN
Movers and Shakers 30 MIN
Off and Running 30 MIN
Polishing the Apple 30 MIN
Prophesy 30 MIN
The Road to Success 30 MIN
Sky Fox 30 MIN
Testing the Waters 30 MIN
'Tis the Seasoning 30 MIN
What Makes Amos Famous 30 MIN
What the Market will Bear 30 MIN
Dist - CDTEL **Prod** - COAST 1959

Marketing Strategies 30 MIN
U-matic / VHS
Marketing Perspectives Series
Color
Shows how to develop marketing strategies, the importance of technological changes on product lines management and how the shortage of products affects marketing management.
Business and Economics; Education
Dist - WFVTAE **Prod** - MATC

Marketing strategies and tactics for the aging product 60 MIN
VHS / U-matic
Antitrust counseling and the marketing process series
Color (PRO)
Discusses alternatives available to a company manager charged with the responsibility of reducing a product's cost by recasting the distribution system. Evaluates the risks.
Business and Economics; Civics and Political Systems
Dist - ABACPE **Prod** - ABACPE

Marketing strategies and tactics for the dominant product 39 MIN
VHS / U-matic
Antitrust counseling and the marketing process series
Color (PRO)
Raises questions concerning permissable strategies and tactics for marketing a dominant product, especially with reference to pricing, meeting competition, advertising intensity and the introduction of flanking or blocking brands.
Business and Economics; Civics and Political Systems
Dist - ABACPE **Prod** - ABACPE

Marketing Strategy 51 MIN
Cassette / U-matic / VHS
Wharton Executive Development Video Series
Color (G)
$249.00, $189.00 purchase
Features Drs Thomas S Robertson and David J Reibstein. Illustrates the essential concepts of modern marketing. Presents a Market Strategy Audit procedure and a step - by - step process for incorporating good marketing fundamentals into a cohesive marketing plan. Includes the video, a 71 - minute audiocassette and a study guide. Part of a series.
Business and Economics
Dist - KANSKE

Marketing Strategy 51 MIN
Cassette / VHS
Wharton School of Business Executive Development Video Series
Color (G)
$189.00 purchase _ #6237
Shows how to assess customer needs and position products, how to price products and identify objectives. Includes a 51 - minute video, one audiocassette and a guidebook.
Business and Economics
Dist - SYBVIS

Marketing strategy for fast growth 60 MIN
VHS
Effective manager seminar series
Color (H C A)
$95.00 purchase _ #NGC753V
Presents a multimedia seminar on marketing strategy. Consists of a videocassette, a 60 - minute audiocassette, and a study guide.
Business and Economics; Psychology
Dist - CAMV

Marketing Strategy for Fast Growth 60 MIN
Cassette / VHS
Effective Manager Series
Color (G)
$95.00 purchase _ #6423
Features Brian Tracy who shows how to define where a business is, where the busines should go and how to get there. Includes a 60 - minute video, two audiocassettes and two workbooks. Part of a fourteen - part series.
Business and Economics; Civics and Political Systems; Guidance and Counseling; Psychology
Dist - SYBVIS

Marketing Successes for Coca Cola - Why they Work
VHS
$97 purchase _ #PX4747
Provides an inside look at the master plan for selling Coca Cola. Reveals the thoughts behind the successful marketing strategy of Coca Cola. Includes a look at some of the company's best TV commercials and an analysis of why they have worked so well.
Business and Economics
Dist - CAREER **Prod** - CAREER

Marketing Successes of Coca - Cola - Why they Work 30 MIN
VHS / 16mm
(PRO)
$89.95 purchase _ #DGP36
Reveals the thoughts behind the marketing strategy of Coca - Cola USA and analyzes why it works. Hosted by Dick Goldberg.
Business and Economics
Dist - RMIBHF **Prod** - RMIBHF

Marketing Techniques 20 MIN
VHS / U-matic
Consumer Squad Series
Color
Illustrates marketing techniques and the steps consumers can take to counteract them.
Business and Economics; Home Economics
Dist - PBS **Prod** - MSITV 1982

Marketing the Myths 25 MIN
U-matic / VHS / 16mm
Color; PAL (H C A) (FRENCH JAPANESE)
PdS50, PdS58 purchase; LC 77-701009
Presents a collection of 24 television commercials from around the world. Aims to assist in the study of television advertising and its influence on modern society and culture. Includes several commercials in Japanese and a few in French.
Business and Economics; Fine Arts; Social Science
Dist - PHENIX **Prod** - PHENIX 1977
EDPAT

Marketing to Minorities 30 MIN
VHS / 16mm
(PRO G)
$89.95 purchase _ #DGP35
Explains the strategies and techniques of Tom Burrell, the most successful ad man in marketing to blacks. Also features Pete Sealey, vice president of Coca Cola, and William Youngclaus, the vice president of McDonald's. Hosted by Dick Goldberg.
Business and Economics
Dist - RMIBHF **Prod** - RMIBHF

Marketing Today 30 MIN
U-matic / VHS
Marketing Perspectives Series
Color
Points out the benefits of marketing in the U S economic system and to the individual firm. Shows marketing functions, differentiating between marketing and selling.
Business and Economics; Education
Dist - WFVTAE **Prod** - MATC

Marketing Today
VHS
Marketing Video Series
$89.95 purchase _ #RPMP01V
Teaches how to tell the difference between marketing and selling. Discusses the benefits of marketing in the United States economic system.
Business and Economics
Dist - CAREER **Prod** - CAREER

Marketing Variables 30 MIN
VHS / U-matic
Marketing Perspectives Series
Color
Shows how to control variables in the marketing mix and addresses the external factors which affect the marketing mix.
Business and Economics; Education
Dist - WFVTAE **Prod** - MATC

Marketing Variables
VHS
Marketing Video Series
$89.95 purchase _ #RPMP02V
Explains a 'marketing mix' and defines its controlling variables. Discusses how marketing mixes are adjusted to reflect changes in the marketplace.
Business and Economics
Dist - CAREER **Prod** - CAREER

Marketing Video Series
Channels of Distribution
Marketing Communications
Marketing Today
Marketing Variables
Dist - CAREER

Marketing where your competition is NOT 45 MIN
VHS
Color (G)
$59.95 purchase
Helps business owners to analyze and enhance their markets, marketing positions and strategies. Discusses finding a marketing niche; the difference between competitor and competition; SWAD comparison charts; making the competition 'play your game.'
Business and Economics
Dist - TOMKAT **Prod** - TOMKAT 1994

Marketing - winning customers with a workable plan
VHS
Small business video library series
Color (PRO J H C G)
$39.95 purchase _ #VPR001V
Presents marketing strategies for the small business person, with special emphasis on free or low - cost sources of critical information and assistance. Combines instruction, case studies, personal insights and informal panel discussions. Includes a comprehensive workbook to stimulate thinking and provide step - by - step instructions for writing, analyzing, planning and implementing constructive change for any business. Part of a four - part series for budding entrepreneurs.
Business and Economics
Dist - CAMV

Marketing - winning customers with a workable plan - Volume 1 45 MIN
VHS
Small business video library series
Color (G)
$29.95 purchase _ #BC01
Shows how to develop a marketing plan. Includes workbook. Part of a series for small businesses, sole proprietors and students. Developed by the Small Business Administration and Bell Atlantic.
Business and Economics
Dist - SVIP

Marketing Your Records Management Programs
U-matic / VHS
Color
Presents a records management program, and explains how to show the high - cost impact of current records handling practices, set up a short and long - term plan, develop cost and savings projections, develop a productivity measurement scenario, and present plans to management. Features Dennis F Morgan, a nationally recognized leader in the records management field.
Business and Economics
Dist - CAPVID **Prod** - CAPVID

Marketing your voice 46 MIN
VHS
Elaine Clark voice - over series
Color (J H C G)
$39.95 purchase _ #DES03V
Presents the final step to getting voice - over work. Shows how to make a demo tape, mailings to agents or advertising agencies, promotional ideas and etiquette on the job or audition. Part of a three - part series by Elaine Clark on the field of voice - overs.
English Language; Fine Arts
Dist - CAMV

Marketing yourself in the hidden job market - Tape 2
VHS
Find the job you want and get it series
Color (H A T)
$99.00 purchase _ #ES135
Considers employment in lesser known job markets. Part of a four - part series on employment.
Business and Economics; Guidance and Counseling; Psychology
Dist - AAVIM

The Marketplace 30 MIN
U-matic / VHS
Photographic Vision - all about Photography Series
Color
Industrial and Technical Education
Dist - CDTEL **Prod** - COAST

The Marketplace 15 MIN
16mm
Color
LC 79-700433
Explains how local weights and measures officials ensure accuracy in the marketplace. Follows an inspector through a typical workday, observing as he tests scales in a produce market, checks the accuracy of gasoline pumps, and verifies the weights of prepackaged foods.
Mathematics
Dist - USNAC **Prod** - USNBS 1978

The Marketplace 29 MIN
VHS
Photographic vision series
Color (G)
$49.95 purchase _ #RM119V-F
Shows how the field of photography can function as a career. Presents the technical aspects of photography clearly and simply, including principles of the camera and techniques for controlling exposure, the use of various kinds of lighting, selection of appropriate lenses and film and basic darkroom techniques. Focuses on the world of photographers and photography - its history and evolution, its uses for personal development and expression, and the impact of photography on the world. Part of a 20-part series examining all aspects of the field of photography.
Industrial and Technical Education
Dist - CAMV

Marketplace 2000 90 MIN
VHS / U-matic
Color (G PRO A)
$1050.00, $950.00 purchase, $225.00 rental
Features Dr Ken Dychtwald who predicts that the focus of the American marketplace will shift from youth to middle aged and older consumers.
Business and Economics
Dist - MAGVID **Prod** - MAGVID 1990

Marketplace 2000 90 MIN
VHS / 16mm
Color (PRO)
$950.00 purchase, $225.00 rental
Features Dr Ken Dychtwald, expert on middle aged and mature consumers. Predicts changes in demography and redistribution of wealth which will alter the consumer marketplace.
Business and Economics
Dist - VICOM **Prod** - VICOM 1990

Marketplace 2000 90 MIN
VHS / U-matic
Color (G PRO)
$1090.00, $950.00 purchase, $225.00 rental
Discusses change, innovation in American marketplace. Outlines changes in demography and redistribution of wealth which will cause some market segments to decline and others to rise. Describes ten most important characteristics of tomorrow's consumer. Predicts product design, advertising and marketing techniques that may be successful in the future. Two 45 - minute videos featuring Dr Ken Dychtwald, author of 'Age Waves.'.
Business and Economics; Fine Arts; Industrial and Technical Education; Psychology; Social Science; Sociology
Dist - VPHI **Prod** - VPHI 1990

Marketplace ethics - issues in sales and marketing 29 MIN
VHS
Color (A)
$500.00 purchase, $150.00 rental _ #V1070 - 06
Promotes awareness of ethical problems in sales and marketing of products. Encourages establishment of company standards for conduct of business in relation to product representation, non - acceptance of gifts, whistleblowing, competitor relationships and customer dealings. Includes video and leader's guide.
Business and Economics
Dist - BARR **Prod** - ETHICS

Marketplace - explaining the stock market 20 MIN
VHS
Color (I J H)
$55.00 purchase _ #5484VD; $59.95 purchase _ #KUN5484V
Takes a close look at the inner workings of the 'financial nerve center' of the United Staes. Explains how the stock market works and its importance in the US economic system. Examines some of the issues likely to dominate news about the stock market in the 1990s.
Business and Economics; Sociology
Dist - KNOWUN **Prod** - KNOWUN 1992
CAMV

A Marketplace for the Nation 5.5 MIN
U-matic / VHS / 16mm
Color (H C A)
$145 purchase - 16 mm, $110 purchase - video
Depicts the stock market. Shows competition between buyers and sellers on the New York Stock Exchange and explains how the stock market stimulates economic growth and provides investment opportunity. Produced by the New York Stock Exchange Foundation, Inc.
Business and Economics
Dist - CF

The Marketplace in the Port of Barcelona 15 MIN
16mm
Rudolf Nureyev's Film of Don Quixote Series
Color
LC 78-701878
Fine Arts
Dist - SF **Prod** - WRO 1978

Marketplace prophets 60 MIN
VHS
Color (R)
$29.95 purchase _ #479 - 9
Portrays 100 years of Catholic social justice teaching, from the 1891 encyclical Rerum Novarum to the groups and individuals working for social justice today. Includes discussion guide.
Religion and Philosophy; Sociology
Dist - USCC **Prod** - USCC 1991

Marketplace Series
Money in the Marketplace 15 MIN
Dist - EBEC

Marketplace, the 55 MIN
U-matic / VHS
Your Money Series
(H C A)
$29.95 _ #MX1211V
Instructs viewers on the basic concepts of investing. Covers the New York Stock Exchange, the American Stock Exchange, penny markets and others.
Business and Economics
Dist - CAMV **Prod** - CAMV

The Marketplaces 55 MIN
BETA / VHS
Investing Series
Color
Discusses the investment opportunities in a range of markets, from the American Stock Exchange and the Commodities Market to the Penny Market.
Business and Economics
Dist - MOHOMV **Prod** - MOHOMV

The Marketplaces 55 MIN
VHS / 16mm
(G)
$39.95 purchase _ #VT1073
Teaches about the opportunities to invest. Covers the arenas for invesment from the most conservative to the riskiest - the New York Stock Exchange, American Stock Exchange, Over - the - counter market, Penny Market and Commodities market. Introduces financial vocabulary, and explains the broker - dealer's role. Discusses some of the rules and protections of each market and gives the knowledge necessary for making beneficial financial decisions.
Business and Economics
Dist - RMIBHF **Prod** - RMIBHF

Markets and Prices - do they Meet Our Needs 30 MIN
VHS / U-matic
Economics USA Series
Color (C)
Business and Economics
Dist - ANNCPB **Prod** - WEFA

Markets, Prices and Equilibrium I 45 MIN
U-matic / VHS
Economic Perspectives Series
Color
Discusses the economic concepts of markets, prices and equilibrium.
Business and Economics
Dist - MDCPB **Prod** - MDCPB

Markets, Prices and Equilibrium II 45 MIN
VHS / U-matic
Economic Perspectives Series
Color
Discusses the economic concepts of markets, prices and equilibrium.
Business and Economics
Dist - MDCPB **Prod** - MDCPB

Marking 17 MIN
VHS / 16mm / U-matic
Information Security Briefing Series

Color (A)
Discusses how National Security Information should be marked in regard to classification. Presents how derivative classification must be marked. Discusses use of acronyms, abbreviations and special markings.
Civics and Political Systems
Dist - USNAC **Prod** - USISOO 1982

Marking Symbols and Applications 16 MIN
BETA / VHS
Color (IND)
Explains the marking symbols used in various sheet metal shops, which help to eliminate the possibility of making mistakes in layout assembly and fabrication of various fittings and metal fabrications.
Industrial and Technical Education; Psychology
Dist - RMIBHF **Prod** - RMIBHF

Marking Time 28 MIN
16mm / U-matic / VHS
Understanding Space and Time Series
Color
Explains Einstein's theory of relativity as meaning that space and time are relative, depending on the motion of the observer. Uses an imaginary space voyage to demonstrate how 50 years and a vast distance to one person may be a few weeks and a much shorter distance to another.
Science - Physical
Dist - UCEMC **Prod** - BBCTV 1980

Marks of a disciple 44 MIN
VHS
Building the family of God series
Color (R G)
$29.95 purchase _ #6111 - 5
Shows how ordinary Christians can change their world and practice discipleship. Features Dr John MacArthur.
Literature and Drama; Religion and Philosophy
Dist - MOODY **Prod** - MOODY

Marks of reference 12 MIN
16mm
Color (G)
$35.00 rental
Works through and resolves the filmmaker's 'inner rectangles.'
Fine Arts
Dist - CANCIN **Prod** - DOBERG 1980

Marks of the ancestors - ancient Indian rock art of Arizona 43 MIN
VHS / U-matic
Color (G)
$59.95 purchase
Explores rock art in Arizona. Travels to six different regions - Cerro Prieto, north of Tucson - Hohokam culture; South Mountain Park, Phoenix area - Hohokam culture; Verde Valley, Sedona area - Archaic, Sinaguan and Yavapai culture; Wupatiki National Monument, Crack - in - Rock site - Hopi and Pueblo cultures; Black Mountains, near Kingman - Archaic or Hualapai culture; and Canyon de Chelly National Monument - Basketmaker, Pueblo and Navajo cultures. Features Native Americans and archaeologists at the sites discussing current knowledge of rock art, such as hunting magic, shamanism and migration symbols. Also addresses the problem of vandalism. By Echo Productions.
Geography - United States; Social Science; Sociology
Dist - NAMPBC **Prod** - ECHOPR 1993

Marlboro - the Type of Man who Smokes Marlboro 1 MIN
U-matic / VHS
Color
Shows a classic television commercial relating smoking and working.
Business and Economics; Psychology; Sociology
Dist - BROOKC **Prod** - BROOKC

Marlene 96 MIN
VHS
Color; B&W (G)
$39.95 purchase _ #S02170
Presents a biographical sketch of Marlene Dietrich. Includes excerpts from her films.
Fine Arts
Dist - UILL

Marlene 27 MIN
16mm
B&W
Features Marlene, an adopted 15 year old from a broken home, who is committed to a youth services institution for being a stubborn child. Follows her through placements, interviews with social workers, arguments with friends, discussions with her mother and confrontations with probation officers after being accused of stealing a car.
Sociology
Dist - IMAGER **Prod** - HALLM

Marlin to the Fly 23 MIN
Videoreel / VT2
Color
Tells the story of the late Dr Webster Robinson's history - making achievement of catching a striped marlin with a fly rod, caught off Baja California, Mexico.
Physical Education and Recreation
Dist - PBS **Prod** - WPBTTV

Marloo - the Red Kangaroo 22 MIN
16mm
Australian Wildlife Series
Color (I)
Presents the life history of Marloo, the red kangaroo. Explains that this marsupial is in danger of extinction due to droughts and man's progress. Follows the daily activities of the female, the male and their young.
Geography - World; Science - Natural
Dist - AVEXP **Prod** - AVEXP

Marloo, the red kangaroo 12 MIN
VHS
Color; PAL (I J H)
Studies the life pattern of the Australian red kangaroo, called marloo by the aborigines. Describes habitat feeding, mating and birth. Shows in detail the physical characteristics of the marsupial kangaroos - body structure, adaptability of the tail as a useful appendage, nursing and raising the young 'joeys.'
Geography - World; Science - Natural
Dist - VIEWTH **Prod** - VIEWTH

The Marmes Archaeological Dig 18 MIN
16mm
Color (I)
LC 72-701378
Describes the oldest fully documented discovery of early man in the Western hemisphere, the remains of the marmes man found in southeast Washington. Emphasizes the techniques which anthropologists, archeologists, geologists, and other scientists use in the field and laboratory to reconstruct man's past.
History - World; Science - Physical; Sociology
Dist - UWASHP **Prod** - KIRL 1972

Marmosets 27 MIN
U-matic / VHS / BETA
Stationary ark series
Color; PAL (G H C)
PdS50, PdS58 purchase
Discusses the recreation of humankind, nature and wildlife in part of a 12 - part series. Features Gerald Durrell. Filmed on location in Jersey, England.
Science - Natural
Dist - EDPAT

Marmosets and tamarins 12 MIN
VHS
Animal profile series
Color (P I)
$59.95 purchase _ #RB8113
Studies marmosets and tamarins, the world's smallest monkeys. Includes action - packed footage of these creatures scurrying about, wrestling, chasing, and helping to carry newborn twins on their backs. Part of a series on animals which looks at examples from the mammal, snake and bird classes, filmed in their natural habitat.
Science - Natural
Dist - REVID **Prod** - REVID 1990

Marmot mountain - Yellowstone below zero 48 MIN
VHS
BBC wildlife specials series
Color (G)
$24.95 purchase _ #MAR08
Visits the Tyrol Mountains of Austria to view marmots who struggle for four months to gain enough nourishment to last them for eight months under the snow in Marmot Mountain. Examines the beauty and dramatic change in lifestyle which takes place in Yellowstone Park during the first few weeks of winter in Yellowstone Below Zero.
Literature and Drama; Science - Natural
Dist - HOMVIS **Prod** - BBCTV 1990

Marmots 25 MIN
U-matic / VHS / 16mm
Untamed Frontier Series
Color; Mono (J H C A)
$400.00 film, $250.00 video, $50.00 rental
Introduces the habits and behaviour of the Marmot, featuring footage of the meadows in the Swiss Alps where they live.
Geography - World; Science - Natural
Dist - CTV **Prod** - CTV 1975

Marmots of the Pacific Northwest 18 MIN
16mm
Color (I)
LC 72-701379
Examines the hibernation, reproduction, feeding and social interaction of the Olympic marmot in his natural environment.
Geography - United States; Science - Natural
Dist - UWASHP **Prod** - KIRL 1972

Marnie 130 MIN
VHS
Color (G)
$24.95 purchase _ #S00903
Presents Alfred Hitchcock's tale of a beautiful kleptomaniac cured by the love of a rich man, who makes her his wife. Stars Tippi Hedren, Sean Connery, and Martin Gabel.
Fine Arts
Dist - UILL

Maronites between Flower and Gun 27 MIN
U-matic / VHS
In the Footsteps of Abraham Series
Color (J H C A)
MV=$375.00
Fighting against Byzantium and Islam, Christian populations in Syria took shelter on Mount Lebanon. There they have stayed and forged an identity which is one of the major factors of the ongoing Lebanese conflict.
Religion and Philosophy
Dist - LANDMK **Prod** - LANDMK 1984

Maronites between flower and gun - 6 30 MIN
U-matic / VHS / BETA
Abraham's posterity series
Color; PAL (G H C)
PdS50, PdS58 purchase
Follows the journeys which Abraham made some 4000 years ago. Offers a dramatic interpretation at the events which are today tearing the region apart. Part of a thirteen - part series. A Cine & Tele Production, Brussels, Belgium.
Fine Arts; Religion and Philosophy
Dist - EDPAT

Marooned 134 MIN
16mm
Color
Describes the plight of American astronauts who are trapped in an orbiting spacecraft. Stars Gregory Peck, Richard Crenna, and David Janssen.
Fine Arts
Dist - TWYMAN **Prod** - CPC 1969

The Marquee Mystery - using Structural Analysis 9 MIN
U-matic
Alexander Hawkshaw's Language Arts Skills Series
Color
Tells how a movie house employee almost loses his job when the letters on the marquee tumble down. Shows how Alexander and his friends save the day by using structural analysis.
English Language
Dist - GA **Prod** - LUMIN

Marquette
VHS
Campus clips series
Color (H C A)
$29.95 purchase _ #CC0103V
Takes a video visit to the campus of Marquette University in Wisconsin. Shows many of the distinctive features of the campus, and interviews students about their experiences. Provides information on the composition of the student body, professors, academics, social life, housing, and other subjects.
Education
Dist - CAMV

Marquette and Joliet - voyage of discovery 14 MIN
VHS
Color (I J)
$59.00 purchase _ #MF - 3619; $350.00, $245.00 purchase _ #3619
Documents and recreates the journey recorded in the journal of Jesuit missionary and explorer Jacques Marquette. Traces the journey across Lake Michigan, along the rivers of Wisconsin, down the Mississippi and their return to Lake Michigan.
History - United States; History - World
Dist - INSTRU **Prod** - CORF 1975
CORF

Marquette Park 25 MIN
16mm
Color (G)
$30.00 rental
Records the unsettling reactions of white residents to a black march into their own neighborhood. Looks at the role played in generating hostility by local Nazi organizations. Note - Marquette Park and Marquette Park II may be rented together a lower price. Contact distributor for details.
Civics and Political Systems; Fine Arts; History - United States; Sociology
Dist - CANCIN **Prod** - PALAZT 1976

Marquette Park 62 MIN
U-matic / VHS
Color
Presents the issues and emotions involved in the American Nazi Party's radical confrontations against integrationists, communists and police in Chicago's Marquette Park in the 1970s. Shows a march into a Black neighborhood halted by police in October 1975, Nazi efforts to inflame angry whites opposed to a black civil rights march in June 1976 and a Nazi rally at the peak of the organization's visibility in June 1978. Not recommended for young or impressionable audiences.
Civics and Political Systems; History - United States; Sociology
Dist - IHF **Prod** - IHF

Marquette Park II 35 MIN
16mm
Color (G)
$55.00 rental
Looks at the media who is covering the event of a march by the Chicago - based Nazi Party. Gives viewer a flag - waving antifascist crazy, followed by Nazi clubhouse antics, displayed in turn by an emblematic TV screen in the center of the frame, which is a sly comment on the media identity of the event. The intercutting of the media's presence, the Nazi's activities and the media reporting points out how seriously the press treats an eminently ludicrous display. Note - Marquette Park and Marquette Park II may be rented together for a lower price. Contract distributor for details.
Civics and Political Systems; Fine Arts; History - United States; Social Science; Sociology
Dist - CANCIN **Prod** - PALAZT 1980

Marquiritare 25 MIN
U-matic / VHS / 16mm
Untamed World Series Series
Color; Mono (J H C A)
$400.00 film, $250.00 video, $50.00 rental
Features the Marquiritare peoples of Venezuala whose ancient culture survives unchanged in a changing world.
Geography - World; Social Science; Sociology
Dist - CTV **Prod** - CTV 1973

Marquis 88 MIN
16mm / VHS
Color (A)
$1250.00, $490.00 purchase, $150.00 rental
Adapts the Marquis de Sade's obscene romance novel Justine with an offbeat twist. Tells the bizarre story of the Marquis, an aristocratic canine imprisoned for blasphemy, who engages Colin, his animated erect penis, in philosophic debates about art, politics and sexual freedom. Also features a masochistic rooster as the prison governor; a camel as a Jesuit priest; and a cow as Justine, the innocent victim of a royal rape. Conceived and written with art direction by Roland Topor. Produced by Henri Xhonneux.
Fine Arts; Literature and Drama
Dist - FIRS

Marriage 17 MIN
U-matic / VHS / 16mm
Color
Looks at various aspects of marriage from the wedding to the golden anniversary.
Sociology
Dist - PEREN **Prod** - PEREN

Marriage 20 MIN
U-matic / VHS
Contract Series
Color (J H)
English Language
Dist - AITECH **Prod** - KYTV 1977

Marriage 48 MIN
VHS / U-matic / 16mm
Human Journey Series
Color; Mono (J H C A)
MV $350.00 _ MP $450.00 purchase $50.00 rental
Reveiws the changing moods of marriage. Through the eyes of couples living together, just married or ppreparing for marriage, this program studies the potentials and problems of marriage. Program includes interveiws with several marriage counselors and well known.
Science - Natural; Sociology
Dist - CTV **Prod** - CTV

Marriage 25 MIN
16mm / U-matic / VHS
Gestalt Series
Color (H C)
LC 78-706491
Using two married couples, Dr Frederick Perls demonstrates the Gestalt method of achieving achieving a more honest communication in marriage.
Psychology; Sociology
Dist - FI **Prod** - PMI 1969

Marriage
Videoreel / VHS
Home Series Pt 3; Pt 3
Color
Focuses on a young couple who feel, despite the woman's earlier failed marriage and an increasing trend toward informal relationships, that their commitment to each other can best be expressed by a traditional wedding.
Sociology
Dist - EDC **Prod** - EDC

Marriage 14 MIN
16mm
Family Life Education and Human Growth Series
Color (J H A)
Contrasts the lives of two couples, one marrying right out of high school and the other couple who waited.
Guidance and Counseling; Psychology; Sociology
Dist - SF **Prod** - SF 1970

Marriage 30 MIN
U-matic
Transitions - Caught at Midlife Series
Color
Examines some of the marital problems that may hit hard at mid - life.
Psychology; Sociology
Dist - UMITV **Prod** - UMITV 1980

Marriage 30 MIN
VHS
Skirt through history
Color; PAL (H C A)
PdS65 purchase
Documents the life of Anne Lister, born in 1791 and the owner of an estate in Halifax. Utilizes her journal writings to narrate her secret life as a lesbian. First in a series of six programs featuring women in history.
History - World; Sociology
Dist - BBCENE

Marriage and After 14 MIN
16mm
B&W (J)
Explains that the happiness of the married couple is quite often marred when the family grows into unmanageable proportions. Emphasizes the plea for family planning.
Guidance and Counseling; Sociology
Dist - NEDINF **Prod** - INDIA

Marriage and Common - Law 15 MIN
VHS / 16mm
You and the Law Series
Color (S)
$150.00 purchase _ #275901
Employs a mixture of drama and narrative to introduce particular aspects of Canadian law. Presents some of the basic concepts and addresses some of the more commonly asked questions. Emphasis is on those elements of the law which are frequently misunderstood. 'Marriage And Common - Law' reveals that many of the legal privileges and protections assured by marriage do not extend to common - law relationships. Identifies the differences between marriage and living common - law. The rights of children from a common - law relationship and the legal ramifications of a common - law partner's death are examined.
Civics and Political Systems; Geography - World; Sociology
Dist - ACCESS **Prod** - ACCESS 1987

Marriage and the Family 30 MIN
U-matic
Faces of Culture - Studies in Cultural Anthropology Series Lesson 9; Lesson 9
Color (C A)
Reviews various forms of marriage and family structure. Introduces some of the terms used to distinguish marriage and family patterns and demonstrates these concepts in their specific cultural contexts.
Sociology
Dist - CDTEL **Prod** - COAST

The Marriage Circle 86 MIN
16mm
B&W
Tells the story of a five - way love affair in Vienna. Directed by Ernst Lubitsch.
Fine Arts
Dist - KITPAR **Prod** - UNKNWN 1923

Marriage, Family Living and Counseling
VHS / U-matic
Color (J H)
Describes and interprets the basic problems of marriage and family life. This program explores major concerns as expressed by teenagers and secondary college instructors.
Guidance and Counseling; Home Economics; Sociology
Dist - CAREER **Prod** - CAREER 1974

Marriage, Family Living and Counseling Series
The Engagement
Marital Adjustment
Marriage - Sometimes it Doesn't Work
Marriage - Sometimes it Works
Money Management
The Nature of Marriage
The New Generation
The Wedding
Dist - AAVIM

Marriage - Family - Self 30 MIN
VHS / U-matic
Health, Safety and Well - Being Series
Color
Sociology
Dist - CAMB **Prod** - MAETEL

The Marriage game 90 MIN
U-matic / VHS / 16mm
Elizabeth R series; No 2
Color
LC 77-701549
Dramatizes Queen Elizabeth I's romance with the Earl of Leicester, who became her constant companion but who never succeeded in becoming her husband.
Biography; Civics and Political Systems; History - World
Dist - FI **Prod** - BBCTV 1976

Marriage - God's style 50 MIN
VHS
God's blueprint for the Christian family series
Color (R G)
$29.95 purchase _ #6138 - 7
Features Dr Tony Evans. Offers insights into marriage from a conservative Christian viewpoint. Part of six parts on marriage, parenting and families.
Guidance and Counseling; Literature and Drama; Religion and Philosophy; Sociology
Dist - MOODY **Prod** - MOODY

Marriage in the middle years 30 MIN
U-matic / VHS
Family portrait - a study of contemporary lifestyles series; Lesson 28
Color (C A)
Deals with recognition of physiological and psychological changes in the years when children leave home. Evaluates resources that aid in adjustment.
Sociology
Dist - CDTEL **Prod** - SCCON

Marriage in the shadows 96 MIN
16mm
B&W (G) (GERMAN WITH ENGLISH SUBTITLES)
$150.00 rental
Presents post - war Germany's first attempt to address antisemitism and the Holocaust. Focuses on the years, 1933, 1938 and 1945. Examines how events in Nazi Germany affected the lives of an intermarried couple, Hans Weiland and Elizabeth Maurer, a famous Jewish actress whom the Nazis barred from the stage. Based on a true story by Hans Scheikart.
Fine Arts; History - World; Religion and Philosophy; Sociology
Dist - NCJEWF

Marriage is for Keeps 30 MIN
16mm
Color; B&W (J H T R)
LC FIA67-5777
A young married couple becomes increasingly aware that communication is breaking down between them. Arguments and misunderstandings are frequent. With the help of their pastor - counselor, each learns to see himself through the other's eyes, and they begin to find answers to their problems.
Guidance and Counseling; Psychology; Sociology
Dist - FAMF **Prod** - FAMF 1966

Marriage - is it a Health Hazard 30 MIN
U-matic / VHS / 16mm
Women Series
Color (H C A)
Points out that married women make up the largest percentage of first admissions to psychiatric hospitals suffering from depression. Reveals that they also consume the greatest quantity of tranquilizers and sleeping pills. Shows how this can result from a seemingly happy marriage as many women come to feel devoured by their dependents.
Psychology; Sociology
Dist - LUF **Prod** - LUF 1979

Marriage of Figaro 168 MIN
VHS
Color (G) (ITALIAN WITH ENGLISH SUBTITLES)
$59.95 purchase
Features Kiri Te Kanawa in a performance of 'The Marriage Of Figaro' by Mozart, along with John Pritchard conducting the London Philharmonic.
Fine Arts
Dist - PBS **Prod** - WNETTV

The Marriage of Figaro 168 MIN
VHS
Color (S) (ITALIAN (ENGLISH SUBTITLES))
$59.95 purchase _ #055 - 9010
Offers the Glyndebourne production of 'The Marriage Of Figaro' by Mozart. Features Iliana Cotrubas, Frederica von Stade, Kiri te Kanawa and Benjamin Luxon in the cast and John Pritchard conducting.
Fine Arts; Foreign Language
Dist - FI **Prod** - VAI 1988
VAI

Marriage of Figaro 25 MIN
16mm
B&W (J) ((ENGLISH NARRATION))
Presents a condensed version of Mozart's comic opera The Marriage Of Figaro as performed by the Metropolitan Opera Company. Uses English narration.
Fine Arts
Dist - SELECT **Prod** - OFF

The Marriage of Maria Braun 120 MIN
16mm
Color (GERMAN (ENGLISH SUBTITLES))
Tells the story of a German woman whose husband is missing in the Second World War and who mobilizes herself upward while waiting for him to return. Directed by Rainer Werner Fassbinder. With English subtitles.
Fine Arts; Foreign Language
Dist - NYFLMS **Prod** - UNKNWN 1978

The Marriage of Siva and Parvathi 40 MIN
U-matic / VHS
Color
Presents a contemporary play portraying the Yogic approach to training the mind.
Religion and Philosophy
Dist - IYOGA **Prod** - IYOGA

Marriage on the Rocks 109 MIN
U-matic / VHS / 16mm
Color (C A)
Stars Frank Sinatra, Dean Martin and Deborah Kerr in a marital comedy about an advertising agency executive who is bored with marriage after 19 years.
Literature and Drama; Sociology
Dist - FI **Prod** - WB 1965

Marriage - Part 3 30 MIN
VHS
Sacraments - Signs of faith and grace series
Color (R G)
$39.95 purchase _ #SACR3
Explores the sacrament of marriage to bring about a better understanding of the meaning of the rite through examination of the actions, symbols and words. Features Bruce Baumgarten. Part three of an eight - part series on the sacraments.
Religion and Philosophy; Sociology
Dist - CTNA **Prod** - CTNA

Marriage renewal video from H Norman Wright series
Communication - key to your marriage
Holding on to romance
How to speak your spouse's language
Dist - GOSPEL

The Marriage Savers 29 MIN
U-matic
Woman Series
Color
Offers advice on choosing a marriage counselor.
Psychology; Sociology
Dist - PBS **Prod** - WNEDTV

Marriage Series
We do, We do 11 MIN
The Weekend 16 MIN
You Haven't Changed a Bit 15 MIN
Dist - FRACOC

Marriage - Sometimes it Doesn't Work
VHS
Marriage, Family Living and Counseling Series
(C G)
$59.00_CA230
Discusses marriages that do not work.
Guidance and Counseling; Sociology
Dist - AAVIM **Prod** - AAVIM 1989

Marriage - Sometimes it Works
VHS
Marriage, Family Living and Counseling Series
(C G)
$59.00_CA229
Covers notions about marriages that work.
Guidance and Counseling; Sociology
Dist - AAVIM **Prod** - AAVIM 1989

Married couples 28 MIN
VHS / U-matic
Issues of cystic fibrosis series
Color (PRO C)
$395.00 purchase, $80.00 rental _ #C891 - VI - 044
Offers excerpts from a two - hour interview session involving married couples of whom one partner has cystic fibrosis. Discusses physical deterioration, abandonment, anger, fear of desertion and having children. Part of a 13 - part series on cystic fibrosis presented by Drs Ivan Harwood and Cyril Worby.
Health and Safety; Science - Natural; Sociology
Dist - HSCIC

Married Lives Today 19 MIN
U-matic / VHS / 16mm
Color (I J H C)
LC 75-704005
Shows glimpses of three couples which survey the range of interpersonal experiences and reactions in various contemporary marriage relationships.
Sociology
Dist - PHENIX **Prod** - SILSHA 1975

Married with a star 33 MIN
VHS
Willy Lindwer collection series
Color (G)
$39.95 purchase _ #653
Offers the film recording of the marriage of Max Werkendam and Clara de Vries on May 25, 1942, in the heart of Amsterdam's Old Jewish Quarter, in Nazi - occupied Holland. Reveals that for almost 50 years the film of the wedding lay untouched. Now uncovered, it focuses on the story of the ill - fated couple and their weddings guests, most of whom did not survive the war. Part of eight documentaries on the Holocaust.
History - World; Sociology
Dist - ERGOM **Prod** - LINDWE

Marriott at Kennedy 13 MIN
VHS / U-matic
Color (PRO)
Gives a view of the operation of the Marriott flight kitchen at Kennedy Airport in New York. Shows the management, control systems, kitchens, storerooms and offices, and details food preparation and presentation.
Home Economics; Industrial and Technical Education
Dist - CULINA **Prod** - CULINA

Marry Me, Marry Me 87 MIN
16mm
Color (C A) (FRENCH (ENGLISH SUBTITLES))
Presents a comedy about a man who turned everything he touched to marriage. Includes English subtitles.
Foreign Language; Literature and Drama
Dist - CINEWO **Prod** - AA 1969

Marrying 57 MIN
16mm / VHS
Heart of the Dragon Series
(J H C)
$99.95 each, $595.00 series
Exaines the traditions of the Japanese marriage and the influences modern women's beliefs are having on them.
Geography - World; History - World
Dist - AMBROS **Prod** - AMBROS 1984

Marrying 57 MIN
16mm / U-matic / VHS
Heart of the Dragon Series Pt 8; Pt 8
Color (H C A) (CHINESE)
Examines the central role of the family in Chinese society, the changing status of women and the reactions of a rural community to the government policy of birth control, which seeks to limit children to one per family.
Geography - World; History - World; Sociology
Dist - TIMLIF **Prod** - ASH 1984

The Marrying Kind 96 MIN
16mm / U-matic / VHS
B&W (J)
Stars Judy Holliday, Aldo Ray and Madge Kennedy in the story of a marriage of two people who face the varying problems of money and moppets with heartfelt honesty.
Sociology
Dist - FI **Prod** - CPC 1952

Mars 29 MIN
U-matic
Project Universe - Astronomy Series Lesson 9
Color (C A)
Reviews overall characteristics of Mars. Presents historical perspective on the interest which Mars has generated during the past century. Shows some of the findings of Mariner explorations.
Science - Physical
Dist - CDTEL **Prod** - COAST

Mars alive 50 MIN
VHS
Horizon series
Color; PAL (H C A)
PdS99 purchase; Not available in Sweden
Explores the plans of different nations to change the environment of the planet Mars to sustain human life.
History - World; Science - Natural; Science - Physical
Dist - BBCENE

Mars and Beyond 15 MIN
16mm
Color
LC 76-703871
Traces the Viking Mission to Mars to explore the biochemical components of life. Demonstrates the chemical conditions involved in the experiment and discusses the potential significance of the biochemical findings in relation to past, present and future Martian life.
Industrial and Technical Education; Science - Natural; Science - Physical
Dist - USNAC **Prod** - NASA 1976

Mars - Chemistry Looks for Life 26 MIN
16mm / U-matic / VHS
Color
LC 78-701384
Shows how the Viking Mission facilitated the study of life on Mars.
Industrial and Technical Education; Science - Natural; Science - Physical
Dist - WARDS **Prod** - CHEMED 1978

Mars in 3 - D - Images from the Viking Mission 32 MIN
16mm
Color
LC 79-701441
Presents images of the Martian surface photographed from various angles by the Viking orbiter and its two test landers.
Science - Physical
Dist - NASA **Prod** - NASA 1979

Mars - is There Life 15 MIN
16mm
Color (H A)
LC 76-703701
Discusses possible past history of Mars and its present surface topography of volcanoes, ice caps, steam beds, impact craters, canyons and wind - eroded surfaces. Examines the Viking lander and its biology experiments in relation to the search for life on Mars. Encourages discussion of life forms that might be able to survive on Mars and the potential significance of their discovery.
History - World; Science - Physical
Dist - USNAC **Prod** - NASA 1976

Mars Minus Myth 22 MIN
U-matic / VHS / 16mm
Color (J H C)
Presents pictures and data from the Mariner Nine and Viking missions to Mars. Discusses origins of land forms, the discovery of water ice in the polar caps and the improbability of life.
Science - Physical
Dist - CF **Prod** - CF 1977

Mars minus myth; Rev. 22 MIN
VHS
Color (J H C A)
$49.95 purchase _ #Q10921
Features a scientist who explains the major findings and the photographs of the Mariner 9 and Viking missions to Mars. Discusses the origins of land form, discovery of water in the past, the improbability of life and other matters. Directed by Ben Shedd.
Guidance and Counseling; Science - Physical
Dist - CF

Mars - the Red Planet 30 MIN
VHS / BETA
Color
Reveals, through the eyes of Mariner and Viking robot satellites, the red planet, its mysterious past, and its enormous mountains and canyons which dwarf anything found on Earth. Includes color photos from Mars' surface.
Science - Physical
Dist - CBSC **Prod** - CBSC

Mars, the Red Planet 30 MIN
VHS
Color (J)
$29.95 purchase _ #ES 8320
Discovers Mars, a planet whose mountains, plains and canyons dwarf anything found on earth. Traces highly imaginative theories of Mars from its discovery in 1669 to the historic landing of the Viking space vehicle on its surface.
History - World; Industrial and Technical Education; Science - Physical
Dist - SCTRES **Prod** - SCTRES

Mars - the Search Begins 29 MIN
16mm
Color
LC 74-706376
Examines the planet Mars, using pictures taken by the Mariner IX spacecraft.
Science - Physical
Dist - USNAC **Prod** - NASA 1974

Mars - the Search for Life Begins 15 MIN
16mm
Science in Action Series
Color (C)
Investigates some of the attempts of scientists to determine whether or not there is life beyond the earth. Includes one of the space probes sent to Mars in the 1970's, Mariner 9, which photographed the entire Martian surface in nearly a year of operation and provided material for much experimentation and speculation.
Science; Science - Natural; Science - Physical
Dist - COUNFI **Prod** - ALLFP

The Marsh 12 MIN
U-matic / VHS / 16mm
Many Worlds of Nature Series
Color (I)
Explores the habitat and food chains of the marsh.
Science - Natural
Dist - CORF **Prod** - SCRESC

Marsh and Swamp 15 MIN
U-matic / VHS
Up Close and Natural Series
Color (P I)
$125.00 purchase
Explores the swampland environment and surveys various aspects of the food chain.
Agriculture; Science - Natural; Social Science
Dist - AITECH **Prod** - NHPTV 1986

Marsh Treasures 13 MIN
16mm
Color (I J)
Points out the vast treasures of oil, salt and sulfur found along the gulf coast marsh lands. Shows special machines and mining processes used to overcome the hazards of mining in water and swamp land.
Geography - United States; Science - Natural
Dist - MLA **Prod** - DAGP 1961

Marsha 24 MIN
U-matic / VHS
Color (J)
Presents a story of a mentally retarded teenage girl, exploring her conflict at home and her relationship with the community. Provides a personal glimpse of her problems as well as her achievements.
Health and Safety; Psychology
Dist - ATLAP **Prod** - ATLAP

Marsha and Harry 10 MIN
VHS / U-matic
Color (H C A)
Presents a humorous look at the trials, tribulations and joys of first time sexual intercourse. Introduces topics essential to all sexuality discussion groups.
Health and Safety; Psychology; Sociology
Dist - MMRC **Prod** - SFTCEN

Marsha M Linehan on borderline personality disorder series
Treating borderline personality disorder - the dialectical approach 35 MIN
Understanding borderline personality disorder - the dialectical approach 35 MIN
Understanding borderline personality disorder - the dialectical approach and Treating borderline personality - the dialectical approach 70 MIN
Dist - GFORD

Marshal Blucher - a portrait against the background of an epoch 70 MIN
VHS
Glasnost film festival series
B&W (H C G T A) (RUSSIAN (ENGLISH SUBTITLES))
$59.95 purchase, $35.00 rental
Presents a Soviet film shown at the Glasnost Film Festival. "Marshal Blucher - A Portrait Against The Background Of An Epoch" examines the state of affiars in the Soviet Union in the 1930s through the example of Red Army commander Marshal Blucher. Reveals that although the Marshal was much admired, he was arrested in 1938 and died in Stalin's torture chambers.
Business and Economics; Civics and Political Systems; History - World; Sociology
Dist - EFVP

Marshall High Fights Back 58 MIN
U-matic / VHS / 16mm
Color (J A G)
Presents the story of how a Chicago high school, a community, and its children find the power within themselves to make changes for the better under a new principal and his successor. Examines the growing concern for quality education that affects all American communities.
Education; Social Science; Sociology
Dist - DIRECT **Prod** - DREWAS 1985

Marshall Holman's maximum bowling 45 MIN
VHS
Color (H C A)
$29.95 purchase _ #SUM210V
Features professional bowler Marshall Holman with a five - point program to improve a bowler's performance. Covers the five points of rhythm, slide, hand position, release point, and follow - through. Uses slow and stop - motion photography to analyze and demonstrate each point.
Physical Education and Recreation
Dist - CAMV

Marshall Ho'o Tai chi 90 MIN
VHS
Color (G)
$39.95 purchase _ #1117
Presents 9 simple temple exercises, a 27 - movement short form based on the Yang style, and some push hands and self defense techniques. Instructions come in a daily repeatable format. For beginners and those who want to compare styles.
Physical Education and Recreation
Dist - WAYF

Marshall Islands - Living with the Bomb - Pt 2 28 MIN
VHS
Human Face of the Pacific Series, the
Color (S)
$79.00 purchase _ #118 - 9002
Looks behind the romance and mystery of the islands of the South Seas to reveal the islands as they really are - a heterogeneous group of countries and colonies struggling to meet the challenges of the modern world while trying to preserve their cultural identities. Part 2 of six parts scrutinizes the Marshall Islands, United States Trust Territory, whose native people were relocated and their culture vanquished because of the American testing of nuclear bombs in their territory.
Geography - World; History - United States; History - World; Science - Physical; Sociology
Dist - FI **Prod** - FLMAUS 1987

Marshall maintenance programs series
Boiler operation - fireside 16 MIN
Coupling alignment 23 MIN
Electrical safety - low voltage situations 12 MIN
Mechanical seal installation 20 MIN
Rigging equipment over the floor 16 MIN
Rigging wire rope slings 18 MIN
Dist - ITSC

Marshall maintenance training programs series
Pipefitting - cutting - reaming - threading 18 MIN
Reading piping drawings 17 MIN
Rigging equipment over the floor 16 MIN
Rotary gear pumps - Pt 1 14 MIN
Rotary gear pumps - Pt 2 14 MIN
Rotary joints - installation and maintenance 13 MIN
Soldering and brazing copper tubing 13 MIN
Taper key, installation and removal 14 MIN
The Theodolite 13 MIN
V - belts proper care 15 MIN
Dist - LEIKID

The Marshall - Marchetti Cysto - Urethropexy for the Correction of Stress Incontinence 20 MIN
16mm
Color (PRO)
LC FIA66-54
Illustrates Dr Spellman's adaptation of the MarshallMarchetti cysto - urethropexy procedure and defines his recommendations for incontinence tests and procedural application.
Health and Safety
Dist - EATONL **Prod** - EATONL 1963

Marshall - Marchetti - Krantz Procedure 9 MIN
U-matic / VHS
Gynecologic Series
Color
Health and Safety
Dist - SVL **Prod** - SVL

The Marshall plan and postwar Europe 35 MIN
35mm strip / VHS
Turning points series
Color (J H C T A)
$84.00, $84.00 purchase _ #MB - 540372 - 2, #MB - 510016 - 9
Examines the Marshall Plan, which helped the nations of Western Europe recover economically from World War II. Documents the beginning of the Cold War and the formation of both NATO and the Warsaw Pact. Features excerpts from the speeches of General Marshall, President Harry Truman, and Winston Churchill.
Civics and Political Systems; History - United States; History - World
Dist - SRA **Prod** - SRA 1989

Marshall, Texas - Marshall, Texas 90 MIN
U-matic / VHS
Walk through the 20th Century with Bill Moyers Series
Color
Describes the small town of Marshall, Texas, which in the past has been resistant to change but now is moving forward at a faster pace.
Civics and Political Systems; History - United States; History - World
Dist - PBS **Prod** - CORPEL 1982

Marshes of the Mississippi 13 MIN
16mm
Color (I J)
Shows the land building work of the Mississippi River along the Gulf of Mexico, the daily spreading and development of some three million tons of sediment into spongy land. Points out the dependence of animal life on specific plants of the area.
Geography - United States; Science - Natural
Dist - MLA **Prod** - DAGP 1960

The Marshes of 'Two' Street 29 MIN
Videoreel / VT2
Synergism - in Today's World Series
Color
Sociology
Dist - PBS **Prod** - KVIETV

Marshland is not Wasteland 14 MIN
16mm
Color (P I J H)
LC FIA63-1055
Explains that marshlands are among the most productive lands on earth, pointing out that marsh grasses provide food for the growth of organisms, that algae become food for tiny water animals, which are then eaten by the larger animals and fish. Discusses the wide spread annihilation of coastal marshes, pointing out that their destruction also means the destruction of spawning and nursery grounds of many species of Commercial and sports fishes.
Science - Natural
Dist - FENWCK **Prod** - WILCOX 1962

Marshlands - Where the Action is 20 MIN
VHS / U-matic
Natural Science Specials Series Module Green
Color (I)
Examines the interrelationships and interdependencies of plants and animals within the marsh community. Suggests improving marshland management.
Science - Natural
Dist - AITECH **Prod** - COPFC 1973

Marsupialization of a Hydatid Cyst of Echinococcus Granulosus in the Liver 14 MIN
16mm
Color (PRO)
LC FIE64-109
Demonstrates the serologic and radiologic findings confirming the diagnosis of hydatid cyst in a 21 - yearold white male. Shows the surgical treatment of the patient leading to complete recovery.
Health and Safety
Dist - USNAC **Prod** - USPHS 1963

Marsupialization of an Anterior Maxillary Residual Cyst 7 MIN
U-matic
Color (PRO)
LC 76-706220
Illustrates a surgical technique for the marsupialization of a maxillary cyst. Explains the advantages and indications for this procedure.
Health and Safety
Dist - USNAC **Prod** - USVA 1968

Marsupials 25 MIN
U-matic / VHS / 16mm
Untamed World Series
Color; Mono (J H C A)
$400.00 film, $250.00 video, $50.00 rental
Explains that with the exception of the American opossums, marsupials are found only in Australia and then goes on to profile several species in great detail.
Geography - World; Science - Natural
Dist - CTV **Prod** - CTV 1973

The Marsupials - Pt 19 30 MIN
16mm
Life on Earth series; Vol V
Color (J)
$495.00 purchase _ #865 - 9020
Blends scientific data with breathtaking wildlife photography to tell the story of the development of life. Features wildlife expert David Attenborough as host. Part 19 of 27 parts is entitled 'The Marsupials.'.
Science; Science - Natural; Science - Physical
Dist - FI **Prod** - BBCTV 1981

Marta Meszaros series
Adoption 89 MIN
The Girl 86 MIN
Riddance 84 MIN
Dist - KINOIC

Martell Cognac - One of the World's more Civilized Pleasures 15 MIN
16mm
Color
Highlights Martell cognac, favorite of all France, and the dedication of eight generations of the Martell family.
History - World; Sociology
Dist - MTP Prod - MARTLJ

Martha 9 MIN
U-matic / VHS / 16mm
Zoom Series
Color (P I)
Introduces Martha Ann Rudolph who has suffered from epilepsy since birth. Shows her ice skating with friends, sledding, volunteering at a hospital and sharing her feelings with her peers who also have epilepsy.
Health and Safety; Psychology
Dist - FI Prod - WGBHTV 1978

Martha Ann and the Mother Store 7 MIN
16mm / U-matic / VHS
Wrong Way Kid Series
Color (J H)
LC 83-700944
Uses animation to tell the story of Martha Ann who does not want to pick up her toys, go to bed early, or clean her shoes as her mother requires. Shows how she goes to the Mother Store for a trade - in, but after trying out several new mothers, she discovers that her own is the best of all. Based on the book Martha Ann And The Mother Store by Nathaniel and Betty Jo Charnley.
Guidance and Counseling; Literature and Drama
Dist - CF Prod - BOSUST 1983

Martha Bowers, Myrna Renaud 30 MIN
VHS / U-matic
Eye on Dance - Politics and Comment In - Dance Series
Color
Discusses contemporary dancers' social and political concerns. Features 'Esoterica' with William Starrett. Looks at a humorous escapade in Dublin.
Fine Arts
Dist - ARCVID Prod - ARCVID

Martha C Nussbaum 30 MIN
VHS
World of ideas with Bill Moyers - Season I - series
Color (G)
$39.95 purchase _ #BMWI - 147
Interviews philosophy and classics professor Martha C Nussbaum. Shares her convictions that the insights of the ancient Greeks are still quite valid today. Hosted by Bill Moyers.
Religion and Philosophy
Dist - PBS

Martha Clarke 54 MIN
U-matic / VHS / 16mm
Color
LC 81-700345
Portrays artist Martha Clarke as she creates an evening of original theatrical dance.
Fine Arts
Dist - PHENIX Prod - CHOPRA 1980

Martha Clarke and Senta Driver 30 MIN
U-matic / VHS
Eye on Dance - Comdey and Outrage in Dance Series
Color
Fine Arts
Dist - ARCVID Prod - ARCVID

Martha Clarke, Pt 1 27 MIN
16mm / U-matic / VHS
Color
LC 81-700345
Portrays artist Martha Clarke as she creates an evening of original theatrical dance.
Fine Arts
Dist - PHENIX Prod - CHOPRA 1980

Martha Clarke, Pt 2 27 MIN
16mm / U-matic / VHS
Color
LC 81-700345
Portrays artist Martha Clarke as she creates an evening of original theatrical dance.
Fine Arts
Dist - PHENIX Prod - CHOPRA 1980

Martha Graham - an American Original in Performance 93 MIN
VHS
B&W (G)
$39.95 purchase _ #1177
Contains three historic performances by Martha Graham. Presents 'A Dancer's World,' 'Night Journey' and 'Appalachian Spring' with music by Aaron Copland.
Fine Arts; Physical Education and Recreation
Dist - KULTUR

The Martha Graham Dance Company 90 MIN
16mm / U-matic / VHS
Dance in America Series
Color (H C A)
LC 77-702339
Focuses on Martha Graham and her influence on modern dance.
Fine Arts
Dist - IU Prod - WNETTV 1976

Martha Graham - the dancer revealed 60 MIN
VHS
Color (G)
$24.95 purchase_#1388
Documents the life and work of modern dancer Martha Graham. Shows extracts of her work including Acts of Light, Errand into the Maze, Frontier, Appalachian Spring, American Document, Primitive Mysteries and Night Journey.
Fine Arts
Dist - KULTUR

Martha Mitchell 29 MIN
Videoreel / VT2
Changing rhythms series
Color
Presents vocalist Martha Mitchell, backed by the Billy Wallace Trio. Interviews songwriter Rudy Jackson talking about the problems of publishing a song.
Fine Arts; History - United States
Dist - PBS Prod - KRMATV

Martha Rosler 56 MIN
U-matic / VHS
Color
Features an interview with Martha Rosler. Presented by Kate Horsfield and Lyn Blumenthal.
Fine Arts
Dist - ARTINC Prod - ARTINC

Martha Rosler - a Simple Case for Torture, or How to Sleep at Night 62 MIN
VHS / U-matic
Color
Makes explicit references to historical and political events.
Fine Arts
Dist - ARTINC Prod - ARTINC

Martha Rosler - Domination and the Everyday 32 MIN
VHS / U-matic
Color
Includes both images and texts. Contains a social framework.
Fine Arts
Dist - ARTINC Prod - ARTINC

Martha Rosler - if It's Too Bad to be True, it Could be Disinformation 17 MIN
U-matic / VHS
Color
Combines facts, figures, newspaper reports, anecdotes, autobiographical material, mass media images and questions in a social framework.
Fine Arts; Sociology
Dist - ARTINC Prod - ARTINC

Martha Schlamme 52 MIN
U-matic / VHS
Rainbow quest series
Color (GERMAN)
Features German - born Martha Schlamme singing several songs in German while accompanied by Abraham Stockman on piano.
Fine Arts
Dist - NORROS Prod - SEEGER

Marthain 40 MIN
16mm
Color (G)
$75.00 rental
Concerns the political, spiritual and poetic aspects of survival in Ireland. Weaves together found footage, interviews and wildly unpredictable monologlues into a portrait of the Irish psyche. The title is the Irish word for the act of surviving. Featuring the Abbey Theatre actor John Molloy.
Geography - World
Dist - CANCIN Prod - FARWIL 1979

Martha's Vineyard 30 MIN
VHS
John Stobart's WorldScape series
Color (A G)
$19.95 purchase _ #STO - 10
Features the artist's summer home. Follows artist John Stobart as he travels the globe, painting directly from life, and demonstrates the simplicity of the method that has made him the foremost living maritime artist. Demonstrates Stobart's classical maritime style in numerous evocative settings around the world. Part of a series on painting outdoors.
Fine Arts
Dist - ARTSAM Prod - WORLDS

Martial Arts - Fun, Protection and Self - Improvement 25 MIN
U-matic / VHS
Color (J H C A)
Features a visit with two of the most respected martial arts instructors and practitioners in the world, Master Yoshimitsu Yamada and Professor Ronald Duncan.
Physical Education and Recreation; Psychology; Sociology
Dist - GERBER Prod - SIRS

Martial arts series
Presents a five - part series on the martial arts. Covers the basics of karate and judo, concepts of self - defense, and self - defense strategies for women.
Basic judo 60 MIN
Karate - Part 2 60 MIN
Self - defense 60 MIN
Self - defense for women 60 MIN
Dist - CAMV

Martial arts series
Karate - Part 1 60 MIN
Dist - CAMV
MOHOMV

Martial qigong 150 MIN
VHS
Color (G)
$49.95 purchase _ #1145
Teaches the Circling Horses qigong form with martial arts applications. Includes movements from a wide variety of classical martial arts including T'ai chi, and is intended for martial artists of any style. Demonstrates the 44 movements, fundamental principles, step by step instructions with repetition, closeups, different angles, and slow motion. By Eo Omwake.
Physical Education and Recreation
Dist - WAYF

The Martian chronicles - the expeditions 100 MIN
VHS
Color (J H)
$29.00 purchase _ #05726 - 126
Stars Rock Hudson in a story about the colonization of a distant world by Ray Bradbury.
Literature and Drama
Dist - GA Prod - GA

Martian in Moscow, Film 1 9 MIN
U-matic / VHS / 16mm
Martian in Moscow Series
Color (H C A) (RUSSIAN)
A Russian - language motion picture which deals with shopping for clothes and toys in Moscow.
Foreign Language; Geography - World
Dist - IFB Prod - HALAS 1977

Martian in Moscow, Film 2 10 MIN
U-matic / VHS / 16mm
Martian in Moscow Series
Color (H C A) (RUSSIAN)
A Russian - language motion picture which deals with visiting the cafeteria, the river and the health centern Moscow.
Foreign Language; Geography - World
Dist - IFB Prod - HALAS 1977

Martian in Moscow, Film 3 10 MIN
U-matic / VHS / 16mm
Martian in Moscow Series
Color (H C A) (RUSSIAN)
A Russian - language motion picture dealing with such topics as a balloon chase over Moscow and a visit to the Kremlin and the Bolshoi Ballet School.
Foreign Language; Geography - World
Dist - IFB Prod - HALAS 1977

Martian in Moscow, Film 4 11 MIN
16mm / U-matic / VHS
Martian in Moscow Series
Color (H C A) (RUSSIAN)
A Russian - language motion picture dealing with a ride on the Moscow underground and an outing in Gorki Park.
Foreign Language; Geography - World
Dist - IFB Prod - HALAS 1977

Martian in Moscow Series
Martian in Moscow, Film 1 9 MIN
Martian in Moscow, Film 2 10 MIN
Martian in Moscow, Film 3 10 MIN
Martian in Moscow, Film 4 11 MIN
Dist - IFB

The Martian Investigators 28 MIN
16mm
Color (I)
LC 70-705153
Presents the team of scientists who built and controlled the experiments of Mariners 6 and 7 that passed close to Mars in July and August 1969, and sent back photographs of the Martian surface and scientific data that expanded our knowledge of the planet. Gives the preliminary results of the missions.
Science - Physical
Dist - NASA **Prod** - NASA 1969

Martin Amis 35 MIN
VHS
Color (H C G)
$79.00 purchase
Features the American writer discussing literary heroes and their characterization with Ian McEwan. Talks about his novels The Rachel Papers, Dead Babies and his essay collection The Moronic Inferno.
Literature and Drama
Dist - ROLAND **Prod** - INCART

Martin and Abraham Lincoln 15 MIN
U-matic / VHS
Stories of America Series
Color (P)
Recounts a Civil War incident involving Abraham Lincoln and the son of an Andersonville prisoner.
Biography; History - United States
Dist - AITECH **Prod** - OHSDE 1976

Martin Chambi and the Heirs of the Incas 50 MIN
U-matic / VHS / 16mm
Color (H C A) (SPANISH (ENGLISH SUBTITLES))
$795 purchase - 16 mm, $495 purchase - video, $85 rental
Examines the work of Peruvian photographer Martin Chambi. Discusses the reasons for Chambi's documentary photographs of Peruvian Indians and includes photographs of Macchu Pichu. Directed by Paul Yule and Andy Harries.
Fine Arts; History - World
Dist - CNEMAG

Martin Chuzzlewit 300 MIN
VHS
Color (G)
PdS99 purchase _ Unavailable in USA and Canada
Tells about old Martin Chuzzlewit, estranged from his grandson but concerned about who will inherit his riches when he dies. Reveals that his relatives, a criminal and, perhaps murderous lot, bring forth all their cunning and greed in the hope of securing the inheritance. David Lodge adapts the Charles Dickens comedy, Paul Schofield leads the cast in the title role, supported by John Mills, Tom Wilkinson, Philip Franks and Elizabeth Spriggs.
Literature and Drama
Dist - BBCENE

Martin Chuzzlewit 29 MIN
U-matic
Dickens World Series
Color
Examines Dickens' problems of learning to deal with rascals and with the world around him.
Literature and Drama
Dist - UMITV **Prod** - UMITV 1973

Martin Chuzzlewit 330 MIN
VHS
CC; Color (G)
$150.00 purchase _ #MAST-400-WC95
Describes the adventures of Martin Chuzzlewit in this adaptation of the Charles Dickens novel. Includes the actions of various characters of Victorian England as they struggle to gain `fame, fourtune, position and power.' Features Paul Scofield, Emma Chambers, and Sir John Mills.
Literature and Drama
Dist - PBS **Prod** - WGBH BBCENE 1994

Martin Kahan, Rodney Nugent and Louis Falco 30 MIN
VHS / U-matic
Eye on Dance - Dance on TV and Film Series
Color
Looks at dance and new music videos. Hosted by Celia Ipiotis.
Fine Arts
Dist - ARCVID **Prod** - ARCVID

Martin Luther 120 MIN
VHS
B&W (G A R)
$49.95 purchase, $10.00 rental _ #35 - 834 - 8516
Depicts the Protestant reformer Martin Luther. Examines the social conditions which may have influenced Luther's ideas. Also available in abridged 30 - minute edition at lower price.
Literature and Drama; Religion and Philosophy
Dist - APH **Prod** - VISVID

Martin Luther 100 MIN
16mm
B&W (H C)
Depicts the life of Martin Luther, including his acceptance into the Augustinian Order. Part 1 discusses his questioning of accepted teaching and the posting of the 95 theses. Part 2 tells about Luther's trial where he refused to recant his writings. Part 3 describes his life at Wartburg Castle and his marriage.
Biography; Religion and Philosophy
Dist - CPH **Prod** - LUTHER 1953

Martin Luther and Catholicism 30 MIN
U-matic
Realities
Color (A)
Delves into the political, social, economic and cultural trends of the 1980s. Probes a wide range of contemporary concerns. Each segment includes a guest speaker who is an expert in the field under discussion.
Business and Economics; Civics and Political Systems; Social Science; Sociology
Dist - TVOTAR **Prod** - TVOTAR 1985

Martin Luther and John Calvin - Tape 4 40 MIN
VHS
Cloud of witnesses series
Color (J H C G A R)
$39.95 purchase, $10.00 rental _ #35 - 860046 - 1
Profiles Reformation leaders Martin Luther and John Calvin. Filmed on location.
Religion and Philosophy
Dist - APH **Prod** - ABINGP

Martin Luther - Excerpt 29 MIN
16mm
B&W (C)
Presents the life work of Luther from the time of his views as Augustinian monk, through his ordination as a priest, his self doubts, opposition to sales of indulgences, posting of the 95 theses, debate with eck, excommunication, burning of papal decree and refusal to recant before a diet of worms.
Biography; History - World; Religion and Philosophy
Dist - IU **Prod** - TFC 1971

Martin Luther - heretic 70 MIN
VHS
Color (C J H G A)
$49.95 purchase _ #87EE0111; $49.95 purchase, $10.00 rental _ #35-871-19
Profiles the life of Martin Luther. Documents the events leading up to Luther's withdrawal from the Roman Catholic Church, an event which prompted the Protestant Reformation. Available in both segmented and uninterrupted versions.
Biography; Guidance and Counseling; Literature and Drama; Religion and Philosophy
Dist - CPH **Prod** - CPH
APH

Martin Luther, His Life and Time 101 MIN
BETA / VHS
Silent; B&W
Traces the life and work of Martin Luther, focusing on his early years.
Biography; Religion and Philosophy
Dist - VIDIM **Prod** - UNKNWN 1924

Martin Luther King 103 MIN
U-matic / VHS
Color
Examines Martin Luther King's life.
History - United States
Dist - NORTNJ **Prod** - NORTNJ

Martin Luther King 28 MIN
16mm
Meet the Press Series
B&W
LC 72-701448
Dr Martin Luther King explains the Negro non - violent resistance movement being practiced in the South. A discussion with Ned Brooks, moderator, Mae Craig, Anthony Lewis, Lawrence Spivak and Frank Van Der Linden.
Biography; Civics and Political Systems; History - United States; Psychology; Sociology
Dist - NBCTV **Prod** - NBCTV 1960

Martin Luther King 15 MIN
U-matic
Celebrate Series
Color (P)
Biography; Civics and Political Systems; History - United States; Social Science
Dist - GPN **Prod** - KUONTV 1978

Martin Luther King commemorative collection 120 MIN
VHS
Color (H C A)
$29.95 purchase
Presents a commemoration of the life and work of Dr Martin Luther King Jr. Features the recollections of the people who knew King best - including Andrew Young, Jimmy Carter, Ted Kennedy, Bill Cosby, and others. Concludes with an anthology of King's speeches.
History - United States
Dist - PBS **Prod** - WNETTV

Martin Luther King commemorative collection 115 MIN
VHS
Color; B&W (G)
$29.95 purchase _ #S02162
Consists of two programs which pay tribute to Martin Luther King and his ideals. 'In Remembrance of Martin' interviews Bill Cosby, Jimmy Carter, and other King admirers on their memories of the man, and includes footage of the civil rights struggle. 'The Speeches of Martin Luther King' includes all the major speeches King gave.
Biography; Civics and Political Systems; English Language; History - United States
Dist - UILL

Martin Luther King commemorative collection 115 MIN
VHS
Color (J H C G)
$39.95 purchase _ #MH1502V
Celebrates the life Martin Luther King, Jr, - 1929 - 1968 - in two volumes. Features anecdotes and insights from Coretta Scott King, Archbishop Desmond Tutu, Bill Cosby, Senator Edward Kennedy, Andrew Young, Dick Gregory, Ralph Abernathy, Joan Baez and John Lewis in the first part - In Remembrance of Martin. Presents King's speeches in part two - The Speeches of Martin Luther King.
Biography; Civics and Political Systems; English Language; History - United States
Dist - CAMV

Martin Luther King day 10 MIN
VHS
Color (K P I)
$69.95 purchase _ #10014VG
Highlights the career of America's foremost civil rights leader, Dr Martin Luther King Jr. Explains Dr King's contribution, history, and belief in nonviolence. Shows the congressional passage of Dr King's birthday as a national holiday. Includes a guide.
Civics and Political Systems; History - United States
Dist - UNL

Martin Luther King - from Montgomery to Memphis 27 MIN
16mm
B&W (G)
$40.00 rental _ #ERF - 773
Documents milestones in the life of Martin Luther King, Jr, from 1954 when he spearheaded the Montgomery, Alabama bus boycott until his assassination in Memphis, Tennessee in 1968.
Biography; Civics and Political Systems; History - United States
Dist - ADL **Prod** - ADL

Martin Luther King - I have a dream 25 MIN
VHS
Color (H C A)
$14.95 purchase
Features Dr Martin Luther King Jr giving his famous 'I Have A Dream' speech in Washington, D C. Also includes historic footage of the activities of the civil rights movement.
History - United States
Dist - PBS **Prod** - WNETTV

Martin Luther King, Jr 24 MIN
U-matic / VHS / 16mm
Great Americans Series
Color (J H G)
Examines Martin Luther King, Jr's career, his belief in the non - violent protest and the impact of his leadership on the civil rights movement using documentary footage and the voices of people in the most prominent issues of his life. Demonstrates how King helped establish the Public Accommodations Act, the Voting Rights Act and the Open Housing Act.
Biography; History - United States
Dist - EBEC **Prod** - EBEC 1981

Martin Luther King, Jr 30 MIN
VHS
Black Americans of achievement video collection series
Color (J H C G)

$39.98 purchase _ #LVC6604V
Portrays civil rights leader, the Reverend Martin Luther King, Jr, through interviews with leading authorities, rare footage and archival photographs. Part of 12 - part series on noted black Americans.
History - United States
Dist - CAMV

Martin Luther King, Jr
VHS
Speeches collection series
Color (J H C G)
$29.95 purchase _ #MH1410V
Offers a collection of speeches by Martin Luther King, Jr. Part of a ten - part series on the addresses of the 20th - century's most powerful speakers. Witnesses the signing of peace treaties, the inciting of world wars, the making of history with words.
Biography; Civics and Political Systems; English Language; History - United States
Dist - CAMV

Martin Luther King, Jr 27 MIN
U-matic / VHS
Color (G)
$229.00, $129.00 purchase _ #AD - 1745
Looks at Martin Luther King, Jr, an ordained minister who used the principles of non - violence promulgated by Gandhi in the struggle for freedom, justice and equality for American blacks. Examines his role in the Southern Christian Leadership Conference.
Biography; Civics and Political Systems; History - United States
Dist - FOTH **Prod** - FOTH

Martin Luther King, Jr - a Man of Peace 30 MIN
16mm / U-matic / VHS
B&W (J)
LC FIA68-3150
Dr Martin Luther King discusses contemporary questions - - the role of organized religion as an instrument to bring social change, the future of the civil rights movement and the possibility of his own violent death.
Biography; Civics and Political Systems; History - United States; Psychology; Religion and Philosophy; Sociology
Dist - JOU **Prod** - JOU 1968

Martin Luther King, Jr - a New Dawn - a New Day 29 MIN
VHS / U-matic
Color
Depicts events in the life of Martin Luther King, Jr. Presented in a montage by artist Melusena Carl Whitlock.
History - United States; Sociology
Dist - SYLWAT **Prod** - RCOMTV 1985

Martin Luther King, Jr. - Black History month 15 MIN
VHS
America's special days series
Color (K P) (SPANISH)
$23.95 purchase
Tells about Martin Luther King, Jr and his efforts to promote civil rights. Shows school children celebrating his life and visits his birthplace. Looks at exhibits in the Civil Rights museum, including the Rosa Parks bus. Challenges children to explore friendship with others.
Civics and Political Systems; Social Science
Dist - GPN **Prod** - GPN 1993

Martin Luther King, Jr - commemorative collection 115 MIN
VHS
Color (J H C)
$39.00 purchase _ #03880 - 126
Presents two documentaries on Dr Martin Luther King, Jr - In Remembrance of Martin and The Speeches of Martin Luther King, Jr.
Biography; Civics and Political Systems; English Language; History - United States; Religion and Philosophy
Dist - GA **Prod** - GA

Martin Luther King, Jr Day - the Making of a Holiday 28 MIN
U-matic / VHS
Color (G)
$249.00, $149.00 purchase _ #AD - 1691
Tells the story of how celebrating Martin Luther King, Jr's birthday became law. Relates how his widow, Coretta Scott King, carries on his work. Includes Stevie Wonder, Bill Cosby, Harry Belafonte, Diana Ross and host LeVar Burton.
Biography; Civics and Political Systems; History - United States
Dist - FOTH **Prod** - FOTH

Martin Luther King, Jr - from Montgomery to Memphis 27 MIN
U-matic / VHS / 16mm
B&W (J)
LC 72-704537
Traces the life of Martin Luther King when he first rose to national prominence as a result of his leadership in a struggle against bus segregation in Montgromery, Alabama - - his civil rights campaigns in Albany, Georgia and Birmingham, Alabama, and the massive march in Washington, helped bring about meaningful civil rights legislation - - he was awarded the Nobel Peace Prize in 1964 and he was assassinated In Memphis, on April 4, 1968.
History - United States
Dist - PHENIX **Prod** - FA 1969

Martin Luther King, Jr - His Message Today 28 MIN
U-matic / VHS
Color (G)
$249.00, $149.00 purchase _ #AD - 1692
Looks at the legacy of Martin Luther King, Jr. Interviews his widow, Coretta Scott King, his son, Martin Luther King, III, Rev Dr Joseph Lowery and Walter E Fauntroy. From a Phil Donahue program.
Biography; Civics and Political Systems; History - United States
Dist - FOTH **Prod** - FOTH

Martin Luther King, Jr - I have a Dream
VHS / U-matic
(J H C A)
$19.00 purchase - #03794 941
Presents Reverend Martin Luther King's monumental 'I have a Dream' speech, recorded on August 28, 1963, in its entirety along with scenes of the Civil Rights Struggle.
History - United States
Dist - ASPRSS

Martin Luther King Jr - I have a dream 28 MIN
VHS
B&W (G)
$14.95 purchase _ #S02009
Presents Martin Luther King Jr's famous 'I Have A Dream' speech, given in August 1963 in Washington DC. Includes film clips of the civil rights movement.
Biography; Civics and Political Systems; English Language; History - United States
Dist - UILL

Martin Luther King, Jr Memorial Special 30 MIN
U-matic
Color (J C)
Takes KPBS Director of Black Ethnic Affairs, Anasa Briggs, to her hometown, San Bernardino, where she interviews the Honorable Mayor Holcomb, Assembly Speaker Willie Brown, and other public figures. They discuss the multiethnic community's involvement with the Martin Luther King, Jr. Memorial and the scholarship Fund Committee which secured donations of $45,000 to commission Mexican sculptor, Julio Martinez Soto, to build the 11 - foot Bronze Memorial Statue in San Bernardino's City Hall.
Fine Arts; History - United States
Dist - SDSC **Prod** - SDSC

Martin Luther King, Jr - Portrait of an American 28 MIN
U-matic / VHS
Color (G)
$249.00, $149.00 purchase _ #AD - 1690
Shows the background and education, the practical and spiritual sources of the dream of Martin Luther King, Jr. Explains his achievements as an American who shouldered the task of unifying America and recalling the pluralistic history of and moral consciousness of the country.
Biography; Civics and Political Systems; History - United States
Dist - FOTH **Prod** - FOTH

Martin Luther King Jr - the Assassin Years 26 MIN
U-matic / VHS / 16mm
Nobel Prizewinners Series
Color (J)
LC 78-700558
Blends sequences photographed in Montgomery, Alabama, with newsreel footage to recapture the crusade of Nobel Prize winner Martin Luther King Jr and his leadership in the Civil Rights Movement.
Biography; History - United States
Dist - CORF **Prod** - CFDLD 1978

Martin Luther King Jr - the Assassin Years 26 MIN
16mm / U-matic / VHS
Biographies Series
Color (J H C A)
$575, $250 purchase _ #77530
Examines the leadership of Martin Luther King Jr during the civil rights movement.
Civics and Political Systems; History - United States; Sociology
Dist - CORF

Martin Luther King, Jr - the search for black identity 32 MIN
VHS
Color (J H)
$99.00 _ #06038 - 026
Features speeches to illustrate Dr King's eloquence and conviction for the civil rights movement and philosophy of nonviolent action. Traces the history of black leadership and the impact of King's methods. Includes teacher's guide and library kit.
Education; Fine Arts; History - United States
Dist - GA

Martin Luther King - the legacy 79 MIN
VHS
Color; PAL (J H)
PdS40 purchase
Reveals the character of one of the greatest orators of the 20th century, and the embodiment of the Civil Rights movement in the United States. Assesses the extent to which Martin Luther King's dream has been realized for the black people of America. Contact distributor about availability outside the United Kingdom.
Biography; Civics and Political Systems; History - United States
Dist - ACADEM

Martin Luther King - the Man and the March 83 MIN
16mm
B&W (C A)
LC FIA68-1939
Records the history of the late Dr Martin Luther King's 'POOR PEOPLE'S MARCH,' shows Dr King conferring with aides, speaking at rallies and visiting schools.
Biography; Civics and Political Systems; History - United States
Dist - IU **Prod** - NET 1968

Martin Luther - Protestant reformer 26 MIN
VHS / U-matic
Stamp of greatness series
Color (J H)
$280.00, $330.00 purchase, $50.00 rental
Documents the life of Martin Luther, whose reformation of the Church he loved led to the founding of a new one, which changed the course of world history.
Religion and Philosophy
Dist - NDIM **Prod** - TYNT 1990

Martin Luther, Pt 1 - the Ninety - Five Thesis 40 MIN
16mm
B&W (H C A)
Portrays Luther's acceptance into the Augustinian order, his inner spiritual turmoil, journey to Rome, apoointment as Professor of Theology at Wittenberg University, questioning of the accepted teaching and interpretations of scripture, preaching against indulgences and posting of the ninety - five thesis on the eve of All Saints Day, October 31, 1517.
Religion and Philosophy
Dist - CPH **Prod** - CPH

Martin Luther, Pt 3 - Champions of the Faith 30 MIN
16mm
B&W (H C A)
Shows Luther taken by friends to Wartburg Castle, after he is condemend by both Pope and Emperor and under sentence of death, where he completes translation of the New Testament. Closing scene is back at the castle church in Wittenberg with Luther standing before his congregation. Closes to the rousing strains of 'A MIGHTY FORTRESS IS OUR GOD.'.
Religion and Philosophy
Dist - CPH **Prod** - CPH

Martin Luther, Pt 2 - by Faith Alone 30 MIN
16mm
B&W (H C A)
Portrays the early attempts by the church to link Luther with John Hus, the Leipzig debates with John Eck, Luther's release from the vows of the Augustinian order, his condemenation by Pope Leo X, and burning of the Papal Bull on December 10, 1520. Shows Luther's trial.
Religion and Philosophy
Dist - CPH **Prod** - CPH

Martin Meets the Pirates 26 MIN
U-matic / VHS / 16mm
Color (I J)
Presents the story of Martin who is tempted to join a street gang until he learns the gang has demanded 'protection money' from his younger sister and her friend. Shows brother and sister rallying the neighborhood to scare off the gang.
Literature and Drama; Psychology; Sociology
Dist - BCNFL **Prod** - PLAYTM 1985

Martin the cobbler 27 MIN
VHS
Color (G R)
$10.00 rental _ #36 - 82 - 1439
Tells the story of Martin, a poor cobbler who receives an unexpected visit from the Lord.
Literature and Drama; Religion and Philosophy
Dist - APH **Prod** - BBF

Martin the emancipator 46 MIN
VHS
Color (G)
$59.95 purchase _ #S02168; $59.99 purchase, $10.00 rental _ #35-80-8975
Profiles the life and work of Dr Martin Luther King Jr. Features footage from Dr King's leadership of the black civil rights movement. Interviews friends and admirers of Dr King, including Coretta Scott King, Jesse Jackson, Rosa Parks, Andrew Young, Charlton Heston, and many others.
Biography; Civics and Political Systems; History - United States; Sociology
Dist - UILL
APH

Martine Van Hamel, Hector Mercado 30 MIN
U-matic / VHS
Eye on Dance - Dancers' Bodies Series
Color
Discusses physical and emotional changes as the dance artist matures. Features 'Esoterica' with costume designer Willa Kim. Hosted by Irene Dowd.
Fine Arts
Dist - ARCVID **Prod** - ARCVID

Martita Goshen - Dance 15 MIN
U-matic / VHS
Pass it Along Series
Color (I)
$130.00 purchase, $25.00 rental, $75.00 self dub
Focuses upon Martita Goshen leading an entire elementary school in an improvisational dance as she weaves a story about the endangered species of the Earth. Tells interesting information about whales, then leads students in animal inspired dance moves on the beach. Notes grace in animal movement inspires dance.
Fine Arts; Science - Natural
Dist - GPN **Prod** - SCITV

Marty Hogan's Power Racquetball 30 MIN
VHS
(J H C A)
$39.95 _ #PAV598V
Explains how to develop a stronger racquetball game. Discusses all serving techniques, arm extension drills, playing angles, the ceiling shot, lob, and hitting the ball on the fly.
Physical Education and Recreation
Dist - CAMV

Marty Liquori's runner's workout 60 MIN
VHS
Color (H C A)
$29.95 purchase _ #BV825V
Features runner Marty Liquori with an introduction to running. Covers running techniques, training schedules, equipment, avoiding injuries, and more.
Physical Education and Recreation; Science - Natural
Dist - CAMV

Marty's moonride 40 MIN
VHS
Color (P I R)
$19.95 purchase, $10.00 rental _ #35 - 89 - 2020
Portrays a child who claims to have ridden on a spaceship. Uses this story to teach the concept that God cares about children.
Literature and Drama; Religion and Philosophy
Dist - APH **Prod** - ANDERK

Marusska and the Wolf 15 MIN
U-matic / VHS / 16mm
Color (I J H C)
LC 83-700375
Presents an animated version of the Moravian tale of Marusska, a poor mountain girl, and the consequences that befall her later in her life as a result of trying to free a duchess imprisoned in a castle she happens upon as a girl.
Literature and Drama
Dist - PHENIX **Prod** - KUBRIC 1982

Marusska and the Wolf Castle 15 MIN
U-matic / VHS / 16mm
Color (I J H C)
Presents an animated version of the Moravian tale of Marusska, a poor mountain girl, and the consequences that befall her later in her life as a result of trying to free a duchess imprisoned in a castle she happens upon as a girl.
Literature and Drama
Dist - PHENIX **Prod** - KUBRIC 1982

Marva 17 MIN
16mm / U-matic / VHS
Color (C T)
LC 80-700097
Relates the story of Marva Collins, who resigned from the Chicago school system after 14 years and used her retirement to start a school for the impoverished students in Chicago's all - black west side. Shows how she emphasizes basic subjects, especially reading, by using the classics. Originally shown on on the CBS television program 60 Minutes.
Education
Dist - CAROUF **Prod** - CBSTV 1980

Marvel - a Jakarta Boy 17 MIN
16mm
Asian Neighbors - Indonesia Series
Color (H C A)
LC 75-703583
Examines the life of a young migrant boy in Jakarta, Indonesia. Shows how he works hard so that he can fulfill his life's goal of getting an education.
Geography - World; Social Science
Dist - AVIS **Prod** - FLMAUS 1975

The Marvella Bayh Story 10 MIN
16mm
Color (H C A)
LC 77-701312
Presents Marvella Bayh, who encourages women to have medical checkups and breast examinations by telling how she faced having breast cancer and how she returned to a full, active life.
Guidance and Counseling; Health and Safety; Sociology
Dist - AMCS **Prod** - AMCS 1973

Marvelous Machines - Expendable People 48 MIN
U-matic / VHS
Color (H C A)
LC 84-706264
Visits the Monongahela Valley to study the depressed steel industry that once was the region's lifeblood. Probes the causes and senses the multi - faceted effects of steel's decline in the U S.
Business and Economics; Industrial and Technical Education
Dist - FI **Prod** - NBCNEW 1983

The Marvelous March of Jean Francois 18 MIN
16mm
Color (P I)
Presents the adventures of Jean Francois, a small drummer boy in Napolean's Grande Armee.
Fine Arts
Dist - SF **Prod** - SF 1970

The Marvelous Math Caper 11 MIN
U-matic / VHS / 16mm
Color (P I)
LC 77-703399
Uses a story about a superhuman little girl in order to explore problem solving, logical thinking and mathematical solutions.
Mathematics
Dist - BARR **Prod** - BARR 1977

Marvelous mollusks
Videodisc
Laser learning set 3 series; Set 3
Color; CAV (P I)
$375.00 purchase _ #8L5415
Defines, describes and illustrates mollusks. Discusses their habits and the beauty and variety of their shells. Part of a series of six theme - based interactive videodisc lessons. Requires a Pioneer LD - V2000 or 2200, with barcode reader and adapter, or a Pioneer LD - V4200 or higher. Includes user's guide, two readers.
Science - Natural
Dist - BARR **Prod** - BARR 1992

Marvels in Miniature 15 MIN
16mm
Color (J)
Shows underwater life of the barrier reef under the magnifying glass, depicting the thousands of small particles that go to make up the plankton upon which the smallest of fishes feed. Features sea creatures, from the smallest of diatoms to the ghost shrimp and the sea worm.
Science - Natural
Dist - AUIS **Prod** - ANAIB 1950

The Marvels of Industrial Robots 36 MIN
U-matic / VHS
Color (H C A)
Shows the newest of the industrial robots - precision work - robots that locate, lift, sort, weld, assemble and package in light or darkness, cold or heat. Recognizes the inevitability and potentialities of industrial robots.
Sociology
Dist - CORF **Prod** - CENTRO 1983

Marvels of the Mind 23 MIN
U-matic / VHS / 16mm
Color (H C A)
LC 80-700227
Explores the complex structures and processes of the human brain using photographic sequences, pictures of extremely thin sections of brain tissues, and computer simulation.
Science - Natural
Dist - NGS **Prod** - NGS 1980

Marvin Bell 29 MIN
U-matic
Poets Talking Series
Color
Literature and Drama
Dist - UMITV **Prod** - UMITV 1975

Marx Brothers Mosaic 27 MIN
16mm
B&W
Presents the Marx Brothers' one - reel shorts 'The Incredible Jewel Robbery,' 'Pigskin Capers' and 'This Is War' mounted onto a single reel.
Fine Arts; Literature and Drama
Dist - CFS **Prod** - CFS

Marx for Beginners 7 MIN
16mm / U-matic / VHS
Color
Presents an animated motion picture which highlights the major philosophical and economic theories of Karl Marx.
Civics and Political Systems
Dist - ICARUS **Prod** - CUCMBR 1983

Marx, Pt 4 - Ethics, Marxism as Ideology , Leninism 30 MIN
U-matic
From Socrates to Sartre Series
Color
Discusses the Marxist theory of ethics and focuses on Marxism as ideology. Offers a look at Leninism.
Religion and Philosophy
Dist - MDCPB **Prod** - MDCPB

Marx, Pt 1 - His Life, His Work as Official Doctrine 30 MIN
U-matic
From Socrates to Sartre Series
Color
Traces the life of Karl Marx and examines his work as official doctrine.
Religion and Philosophy
Dist - MDCPB **Prod** - MDCPB

Marx, Pt 3 - Class Conflict, Withering Away of the State 30 MIN
U-matic
From Socrates to Sartre Series
Color
Examines Marx's ideas on class conflict and the withering away of the state.
Religion and Philosophy
Dist - MDCPB **Prod** - MDCPB

Marx, Pt 2 - Metaphysics, Dialectical Materialism 30 MIN
U-matic
From Socrates to Sartre Series
Color
Discusses metaphysics and dialectical materialism in the work of Marx.
Religion and Philosophy
Dist - MDCPB **Prod** - MDCPB

Marxism - the Theory that Split a World 25 MIN
16mm / VHS / U-matic
Color (H C A) (SPANISH)
LC 76-708186
Outlines the history and significance of Marxism by interviews witpeople who knew Karl Marx or were influenced by his ideas.
Biography; Business and Economics; Civics and Political Systems; History - World
Dist - LCOA **Prod** - INCC 1970

Marxist philosophy 45 MIN
VHS
Men of ideas series
Color; PAL (H C A)
PdS99 purchase; Not available in Canada.
Explains in simple terms the main developments in Western philosophy from the 19th century to the present day. Features a contemporary thinker discussing his ideas on Marxist philosophy with Bryan Magee. Part two of a fifteen part series.
Psychology; Religion and Philosophy
Dist - BBCENE

The Marxist tradition and America 60 MIN
VHS
Europe and America in the modern age - 1776 to the present series

Color (H C PRO)
$95.00 purchase
Presents a lecture by David M Kennedy. Focuses on a critical period in European and American history and on leaders of the time. Part of a 20 - part series that looks at the last two centuries in Europe and America. Series presents lectures by David M Kennedy and James Sheehan of Stanford University on such figures as Adam Smith, Marx, Lincoln, Washington, Jefferson, Freud, Margaret Sanger, Susan B Anthony and Jane Adams and their impact on the events of their day. For history resource material and continuing education courses.
Civics and Political Systems; History - United States; History - World
Dist - LANDMK

Mary and Joseph 25 MIN
VHS
Greatest stories ever told series
Color (K P I R)
$19.95 purchase, $10.00 rental _ #35 - 80 - 2020
Uses an animated format to present the New Testament account of Jesus' birth, childhood and development.
Literature and Drama; Religion and Philosophy
Dist - APH **Prod** - ANDERK

Mary and Melvin 29 MIN
VHS / 16mm
Watch your mouth series
Color (H)
$46.00 rental _ #WAYM - 102
Emphasizes language and communication skills for high school students. Notes the difference between formal and informal word usage.
Education; English Language; Psychology; Social Science
Dist - PBS

Mary Ann Glendon 30 MIN
U-matic / VHS
World of ideas with Bill Moyers, season 1 series
Color (A G)
$39.95, $59.95 purchase _ #BMWI - 144
Features Mary Ann Glendon, professor of comparative law at Harvard University. Talks about abortion in the US and Europe and how Glendon believes Roe v Wade gave rise to misinterpretation of the abortion issues in the US. Part of a series in which Bill Moyers interviews outstanding individuals whose ideas and work have enhanced our society.
Psychology; Sociology
Dist - PBS **Prod** - PATV 1989

Mary Anthony and Bettie DeJong 30 MIN
U-matic / VHS
Eye on Dance - Dance on TV Series
Color
Looks at the roots of dance on television and in film. Presents an excerpt from 'Nine Variations on a Dance Theme,' a film by Hillary Harris. Features Birgit Cullberg in 'Esoterica.'.
Fine Arts
Dist - ARCVID **Prod** - ARCVID

Mary Carter Smith Video 30 MIN
VHS
Tell Me a Story Series
Color (K)
$19.95 purchase _ #W181 - 052
Features Mary Carter Smith as storyteller. Includes 'John Henry,' 'Moseoatunya,' 'The Cowtail Switch,' 'The Talking Skull,' 'Zunn Gali Gali' and 'Can Of Corn Colors.' Part of an eight - unit series.
Literature and Drama
Dist - UPSTRT **Prod** - UPSTRT

Mary Cassatt - Impressionist from Philadelphia 30 MIN
VHS
Originals - women in art series
Color (G)
$39.95 purchase _ #CAS-01; LC 78-701104
Portrays the life of Mary Cassatt, an early American Impressionist from Philadelphia. Reveals her personal story, her years in Paris, her relationship with Degas, the influence of her prominent Philadelphia family and the places where she painted and lived. Discloses that she hated conventional art and only began to paint seriously when Degas invited her to show her works with other Impressionists. Illustrates a selection of her work.
Fine Arts
Dist - ARTSAM **Prod** - WNETTV 1978
CAMV
FI

Mary Catherine Bateson 30 MIN
VHS
World of ideas with Bill Moyers - Season I - series
Color (G)
$39.95 purchase _ #BMWI - 127
Interviews anthropologist and author Mary Catherine Bateson on changing roles for women. Discusses traditional gender roles and questions why women are forced to choose between conflicting commitments. Hosted by Bill Moyers.
Sociology
Dist - PBS

Mary Daly Presents Gyn - Ecology 80 MIN
U-matic
B&W
Features Mary Daly discussing the liberation of women. Focuses on the global dimension of atrocities against women. Celebrates the becoming of the radical feminist.
Sociology
Dist - WMENIF **Prod** - WMENIF

Mary Gordon and Margaret Drabble 45 MIN
VHS
Color (H C G)
$79.00 purchase
Features the writers discussing writing about mother - child relationships and how they have been described in literature. Talks about their works that include The Millstone; The Needle's Eye; Final Payments; and Men and Angels.
Literature and Drama; Sociology
Dist - ROLAND **Prod** - INCART

Mary Had a Little Lamb 3 MIN
U-matic / VHS
Color; Mono (K P)
Points out that more than 150 years after its creation, Hale's five verse poem has found new life. De Paola's serene images of rural life in the 1830's blend with poignant narration and original chamber music to create a treatment of Americana. Mary is a red haired, pig tailed schoolgirl with a cuddly, fleecy lamb constantly at her side. The rich colors and authentic period details produce a romantic consistency that carries the tale through its final tableau, where students in Mary's class learn why the lamb is so faithful.
English Language; Fine Arts; Literature and Drama
Dist - WWS **Prod** - WWS 1985

Mary Hinkson and Zachary Solov 30 MIN
VHS / U-matic
Eye on Dance - Update, Topics of Current Concern Series
Color
Discusses dancers' changing attitudes. Looks at 'Esoterica' with Frederick Franklin. Hosted by Celia Ipiotis.
Fine Arts
Dist - ARCVID **Prod** - ARCVID

Mary Kate's War 25 MIN
U-matic / VHS / 16mm
Decades of Decision - the American Revolution Series
Color (H C A)
Presents a recreation of the story of Mary Katherine Goddard, postmistress of Baltimore and publisher of the Maryland Journal. Demonstrates her courage in upholding the freedom of the press and her struggle for a place in society equal to that of a man.
Biography; History - United States; History - World
Dist - NGS **Prod** - NGS 1975

The Mary Kay Story 30 MIN
VHS / 16mm
(PRO G)
$89.95 purchase _ #DGP1
Tells the story of Mary Kay Ash, founder of Mary Kay Cosmetics. Hosted by Dick Goldberg.
Business and Economics
Dist - RMIBHF **Prod** - RMIBHF

Mary Kingsley 52 MIN
U-matic / VHS / 16mm
Ten who Dared Series
Color
LC 77-701579
Dramatizes Mary Kingsley's 1893 journey along the Ogowe and Rembwe Rivers of Africa's West Coast, where she studied the native cultures of the cannibalistic tribes.
Biography; History - World; Sociology
Dist - TIMLIF **Prod** - BBCTV 1976

Mary Kingsley - West Africa, 1893, Pt 1 26 MIN
16mm
Ten who Dared Series
Color (I A)
Special classroom version of the film and videorecording Mary Kingsley - West Africa, 1893.
History - World
Dist - TIMLIF **Prod** - BBCTV 1977

Mary Kingsley - West Africa, 1893, Pt 2 26 MIN
16mm
Ten who Dared Series
Color (I A)
Special classroom version of the film and videorecording Mary Kingsley - West Africa, 1893.
History - World
Dist - TIMLIF **Prod** - BBCTV 1977

Mary Lou at Saratoga 29 MIN
U-matic / VHS
Color
Follows Mary Lou Vanderbilt Whitney through the social whirl of Saratoga's racing season.
Fine Arts
Dist - KITCHN **Prod** - KITCHN

Mary Lou Williams - music on my mind 60 MIN
U-matic / 16mm / VHS
Color (G)
$750.00, $250.00 purchase, $130.00, $90.00 rental
Pays tribute to American composer - arranger - pianist Mary Lou Williams. Traces her mastery of swing, bebop and modern jazz piano. Interviews Dizzy Gillespie, Buddy Tate and Williams. Reveals that at the height of her career she dropped out of music to work with drug addicted musicians in Harlem. Fifteen years later she picked up her career and composed the first jazz mass to be performed at St Patrick's Cathedral in New York. Produced by Joanne Burle and narrated by Roberta Flack.
Fine Arts; Sociology
Dist - WMEN

Mary Lyon - Precious Time 30 MIN
U-matic / VHS / 16mm
Color (G)
$425 video purchase, $525 film purchase or $45 rental
Studies the life of educator Mary Lyon from her girlhood to her founding of Mount Holyoke in 1837. Focuses on the educational emancipation and cultural democratization of women and on Lyons' spiritual orientation.
Biography; Sociology
Dist - IFB

Mary McLeod Bethune 30 MIN
VHS / U-matic
Color
Discusses why Mary McLeod Bethune was memorialized with a commemorative postage stamp, a memorial statue, the Bethune Museum - Archives National Historic Site, and the Bethune - Cookman College.
History - United States
Dist - SYLWAT **Prod** - RCOMTV 1985

Mary McLeod Bethune 30 MIN
VHS
Black Americans of achievement collection II series
Color (J H C G)
$49.95 purchase _ #LVCD6616V - S
Provides interesting and concise information on educator Mary McLeod Bethune. Part of a 10 - part series on African - Americans.
History - United States
Dist - CAMV

Mary of Mile 18 12 MIN
16mm
Color (I J)
Describes the life of a young girl growing up on a farm in a remote Mennonite community. Includes full animation of visuals.
Fine Arts; Religion and Philosophy
Dist - NFBC **Prod** - NFBC 1982

Mary of Scotland
VHS / U-matic
B&W (J H C A)
$19.00 purchase _ #05819 941
Dramatizes the life of Mary, Queen of Scotland, cousin and rival of Queen Elizabeth. Stars Katherine Hepburn.
Biography; Fine Arts
Dist - ASPRSS

Mary of Scotland 123 MIN
VHS
B&W (H C)
$49.00 purchase _ #05819 - 126
Stars Katharine Hepburn as Mary, Queen of Scots, cousin and rival to Elizabeth I of England.
Civics and Political Systems; History - World
Dist - GA **Prod** - GA

Mary Poppins
VHS
Disney classics on video series
Color; CC (K P I)
$29.95 purchase _ #017307
Presents the Disney verion of Mary Poppins on video.
Fine Arts; Literature and Drama
Dist - KNOWUN **Prod** - DISNEY

Mary, Queen of Scots - Pt 5 20 MIN
VHS
Tudors Series
Color (I)
$79.00 purchase _ #825 - 9425
Paints a detailed and historically accurate picture of the Tudor period, 1485 - 1603, in British history. Examines historical trends over a broad time period or concentrates on one aspect of the era. The dramatizations are based on source material and the locations are authentic. Part 5 of seven parts recreates through dramatizations and documentary film the tragic life of Mary, Queen of Scots, and her relationship with Queen Elizabeth I.

Civics and Political Systems; History - World; Religion and Philosophy
Dist - FI **Prod** - BBCTV 1987

Mary Rawlyk 25 MIN
VHS / U-matic
View from My Window is Great series
(H C)
Presents a video portrait of feminist printmaker Mary Rawlyk.
Fine Arts; Industrial and Technical Education
Dist - QUEENU **Prod** - KAA 1985

Mary S Mc Dowell 50 MIN
16mm
Profiles in Courage Series
B&W (I J H)
LC FIA65-1422
Documents the pacifist convictions of Mary Mc Dowell, a Quaker teacher, who was dismissed from her position in Brooklyn and brought to trial because she refused to take a loyalty pledge, engage in Red Cross work and help sell liberty bonds at the close of World War I.
Biography; History - World
Dist - SSSSV **Prod** - SAUDEK 1964

Mary S Mc Dowell, Pt 1 25 MIN
16mm
Profiles in Courage Series
B&W (J)
Presents the story of a teacher who stood by her religious beliefs and was forced out of her job.
Religion and Philosophy
Dist - SSSSV **Prod** - SAUDEK 1966

Mary S Mc Dowell, Pt 2 25 MIN
16mm
Profiles in Courage Series
B&W (J)
Presents the story of a teacher who stood by her religious beliefs and was forced out of her job.
Religion and Philosophy
Dist - SSSSV **Prod** - SAUDEK 1966

Mary Stuart 140 MIN
VHS
Color (S)
$39.95 purchase _ #623 - 9396
Reveals that Dame Janet Baker chose the title role in this English National Opera production of 'Mary Stuart' by Donizetti for her farewell to the London stage. Includes Rosalind Plowright in the role of Elizabeth I as her costar.
Fine Arts; Geography - World
Dist - FI **Prod** - NVIDC 1986

Mary White 102 MIN
VHS
Color (J H C)
$39.00 purchase _ #04441 - 126
Portrays the real life of the daughter of a newspaper editor who rejected her life of wealth and set off to find her own identity. Stars Kathleen Beller and Ed Flanders.
Biography; History - United States; History - World
Dist - GA **Prod** - GA

Mary Wigman - When the Fire Dances between the Two Poles 43 MIN
U-matic / VHS / 16mm
B&W
Reveals the work and philosophy of choreographer Mary Wigman. Shows highlights of Wigman's performances from 1923 through her final solo in 1942. Describes her work with students following her retirement from the stage.
Fine Arts
Dist - UCEMC **Prod** - MACSNY 1982

Maryknoll video magazine presents series

Beyond the killing fields	30 MIN
Buddhism and black belts	30 MIN
Call and response	30 MIN
China church - old roots, new shoots	30 MIN
Folks like us	30 MIN
Karibu - Welcome	30 MIN
Many though one	30 MIN
Mosque	30 MIN
No longer colonies - Hong Kong 1997 , Macau 1999	30 MIN
Once upon a time	30 MIN
A Place to call home - Posadas	30 MIN
Something new out of Africa	30 MIN
Walking with the Buddha	30 MIN

Dist - MARYFA

Maryland 60 MIN
VHS
Portrait of America series
Color (J H C G)
$99.95 purchase _ #AMB20V
Visits Maryland. Offers extensive research into the state's history. Films key locations and presents segments on history, government, education, folklore, science, journalism, sociology, industry, agriculture and business. Shows what is unique about Maryland and distinctive about its regional culture and how it got to be that way. Includes study guide. Part of a 50 - part series.
Geography - United States; History - United States
Dist - CAMV

Maryon Kantaroff 18 MIN
16mm
B&W
LC 77-702960
Visits Canadian sculptor Maryon Kantaroff in her studio and observes as she creates a sculpture. Shows a wide variety of her works.
Fine Arts
Dist - CANFDC **Prod** - RYALLS 1974

Mary's story 30 MIN
VHS
Labours of Eve series
Color; PAL (A)
PdS50 purchase; Not available in the United States or Canada
Presents the story of Mary, a woman who contracted AIDS from a sperm donor after an unsuccessful program of artificial insemination. Examines the effect on Mary as she copes with an AIDS infection nine years after her attempt at insemination. Nicky Singer narrates the series as it looks at issues of pregnancy and conception. Part five of a six - part series.
Health and Safety
Dist - BBCENE

The Marzipan pig 30 MIN
VHS
Rabbit ears collection series
Color; CC (K P I J)
$12.95 purchase _ #328800
Tells about a sweet pig who charms a lonely mouse, a lovesick owl, a curious bee and a weary flower.
Literature and Drama
Dist - KNOWUN **Prod** - RABBIT

Ma's Motors 28 MIN
16mm
Color
Portrays a disabled boy's struggle in Taiwan for a chance to learn auto mechanics at Ma's Motors.
Education; Geography - World; Psychology
Dist - MTP **Prod** - MARYFA 1982

Mas Numeros - more Numbers 15 MIN
VHS / U-matic
Saludos
(P I G) (ENGLISH AND SPANISH)
$130 purchase, $25 rental, $75 self dub
Designed to introduce Spanish to the English speaking student at primary through intermediate levels. Ninth in a 25 part series.
Foreign Language
Dist - GPN

Masaccio 40 MIN
VHS
Three painters 2 series
Color (A)
PdS65 purchase _ Available only in the UK
Explores the work of the painter Masaccio, hosted by painter and critic Sir Lawrence Gowing. Based on the concept that Masaccio's work represents a distinct stage in the development of European painting between the Renaissance and the present day. Discusses the historical and social backgrounds against which the artist worked, but concentrates on examining a small number of canvases. Includes views of the places which particularly inspired the artist.
Fine Arts
Dist - BBCENE

Masada 12 MIN
16mm
Color
Depicts Professor Yigael Hadin leading the excavations at Masada, the last Jewish stronghold against the Roman legions in the first millennium. Shows the hundreds of volunteers from all over the world who participate.
Geography - World; History - World
Dist - ALDEN **Prod** - ALDEN

Masada 30 MIN
16mm
Eternal Light Series
B&W (H C A)
LC 72-700964
Presents a documentary filmed in Israel, showing the excavations on the site of the ancient rock - fortress of Masada. Includes an interview of Dr Yigael Yadin, Israeli archeologist in charge of these excavations. Discusses the significance of the discoveries at Masada, indicating that it was valiantly defended as the last outpost of resistance to Roman tyranny, in 73 C E. (Kinescope).
History - World; Religion and Philosophy; Science - Physical
Dist - NAAJS **Prod** - JTS 1967

Masada - a story of heroism 28 MIN
VHS
Archaeology series
Color (G)
$29.95 purchase _ #221
Recalls the 2000 - year - old story of the Jewish community which chose self - destruction rather than surrender to the Roman legion below the mountain of Masada. Features Walter Zanger as host.
History - World; Religion and Philosophy; Sociology
Dist - ERGOM **Prod** - ERGOM

Masai in Tanzania 14 MIN
U-matic / VHS / 16mm
Man and His World Series
Color
LC 70-705481
Shows the life styles and dress of the African tribe, the Masai. Emphasizes the economy and social attitudes of this tribe and its relationship with neighboring tribes.
Geography - World; History - United States; Sociology
Dist - FI **Prod** - PMI 1969

Masai manhood 53 MIN
VHS
Disappearing world series
Color (G C)
$99.00 purchase, $19.00 rental _ #51215
Reveals that Masai warriors of East Africa live on the fringes of society and are not permitted to marry and are excluded from tribal decision making. Focuses on the lives of these young men until the time of the eunoto, a dramatic four - day ceremony that marks their transition from warrior to elder. Features anthropologist Melissa Llewelyn - Davies. Part of a series working closely with anthropologists who lived for a year or more in societies whose social structures, beliefs and practices are threatened by the expansion of technocratic civilization.
Religion and Philosophy; Sociology
Dist - PSU **Prod** - GRANDA 1987

Masai Manhood 53 MIN
16mm
Disappearing World Series
Color (A)
LC 80-701658
Looks at the seven - year period in the life of Masai men during which they serve as warriors.
Geography - World; Sociology
Dist - INSHI **Prod** - GRATV 1980

Masai women 52 MIN
VHS
Disappearing world series
Color (G C)
$99.00 purchase, $14.00 rental _ #51152
Look at the women of the Masai - from childhood through marriage to old age - and their role in a completely male - dominated society. Features anthropologist Melissa Llewelyn - Davies. Part of a series working closely with anthropologists who lived for a year or more in societies whose social structures, beliefs and practices are threatened by the expansion of technocratic civilization.
Sociology
Dist - PSU **Prod** - GRANDA 1974

Masai Women 52 MIN
16mm
Disappearing World Series
Color (A)
LC 80-701666
Looks at the women of the Masai tribe, tracing their passage into womanhood and examining their daily lives.
Geography - World; Sociology
Dist - INSHI **Prod** - GRATV 1980

Masai Women - Pt 10 52 MIN
VHS
Disappearing World Series
Color (S)
$99.00 purchase _ #047 - 9010
Provides a precious record of the social structure, beliefs and practices of societies now threatened with imminent extinction by the pressures of our expanding technocratic civilization. Travels to the remote corners of three continents and features film crews who worked in close association with anthropologists who had spent a year or more living among the societies concerned. Part 10 looks at the women of the Masai who are animal herders in the East African Rift Valley. The women are considered in their roles from childhood through marriage and old age - in a completely male - dominated society.
Geography - World; History - World; Psychology; Social Science; Sociology
Dist - FI **Prod** - GRATV 1989

Masajes cardiacos 11 MIN
U-matic / VHS / 16mm
Emergency resuscitation - Spanish series
Color (C A) (SPANISH)
A Spanish - language version of the motion picture Closed Chest Cardiac Massage. Introduces the technique of closed chest cardiac massage.

Foreign Language; Health and Safety
Dist - IFB **Prod** - UKMD

Masculin Et Feminin 13 MIN
16mm
En Francais, set 2 series
Color (J A)
Foreign Language
Dist - CHLTN **Prod** - PEREN 1969

Masculine and feminine 14 MIN
VHS / U-matic
En Francais series
Color (H C A)
Presents two humorous sketches involving the opposite sexes.
Foreign Language; Geography - World
Dist - AITECH **Prod** - MOFAFR 1970

Masculine or Feminine - Your Role in Society 19 MIN
16mm / U-matic / VHS
Color (J A)
LC 78-710851
Shows that society defines the roles of male and female and considers the effect of these stereotypes on individual development.
Guidance and Counseling; Psychology; Social Science
Dist - CORF **Prod** - CORF 1971

Mashi Warak and Mashi Kussa 26 MIN
U-matic / VHS
Color (PRO)
Demonstrates stuffing and how it is used in Middle Eastern cuisine. Grape leaves are stuffed with a lamb and rice filling and steamed, and squash is stuffed with a similar filling and cooked with a Marinara sauce.
Home Economics; Industrial and Technical Education
Dist - CULINA **Prod** - CULINA

Mashiko Village Pottery, 1937 22 MIN
U-matic / VHS / 16mm
B&W
Presents the creation of a number of pieces in the workshop of Totaro Sakuma in Mashiko, Japan, illustrating the preparation of the clay and the throwing, glazing, decorating, and firing of the pottery. Also highlighted are the designs of the great teapot painter Minagawa Masu. Restored by Marty Gross.
Fine Arts
Dist - PSU **Prod** - PSU 1984

The Mashpee Wampanoags - Tribal Identity 29 MIN
VHS / U-matic
People of the First Light Series
Color (G)
Shows how the members of the Mashpee Wampanoag Tribe live, work, and maintain the long standing culture of their ancestors on the same lands the tribe has inhabited thousands of years. Developers have recently reshaped the ancestral lands into new communities for urban living. Shows how the Native American community now devotes its energies to preserving the knowledge and understanding of what it means to be a Mashpee Wampanoag Indian. Both young and old share in the responsibility for preserving their unique heritage.
Sociology
Dist - NAMPBC **Prod** - NAMPBC 1979

The Mashpee Wamponogs 30 MIN
U-matic
People of the First Light Series
Color
Social Science; Sociology
Dist - GPN **Prod** - WGBYTV 1977

The Mask 35 MIN
16mm
Color (PRO)
LC 80-700856
Explains that alcohol may mask symptoms of both physical and mental disorders and suggests how police can use a system of observation that begins when a person is first seen.
Civics and Political Systems
Dist - USNAC **Prod** - USPHS 1980

The Mask 34 MIN
16mm
B&W
LC FIA65-3427
Explains that alcohol may mask symptoms of both physical and mental disorders and suggests a system of observation for police. Emphasizes the significance of alcoholism as a problem confronted most frequently by policemen and stresses the increasingly humanitarian role of the police.
Health and Safety; Sociology
Dist - USPHS **Prod** - LAAMH 1964

Mask 30 MIN
VHS / U-matic
Doris Chase concepts series
Color
Charts the subsconcious journey of a black woman, unravelling history, and discovering her true source of strength.
Sociology
Dist - WMEN **Prod** - CHASED

The Mask 4 MIN
16mm
Color (P)
LC 77-702961
Presents a story about two African boys, various comical animals and a mask.
Geography - World; Literature and Drama; Science - Natural
Dist - CANFDC **Prod** - CANFDC 1976

The Mask 5 MIN
16mm
Song of the Ages Series
B&W (J)
LC 72-702130
Presents a modern interpretation of Psalm 61, using scenes of a circus clown applying his make - up.
Religion and Philosophy
Dist - FAMLYT **Prod** - FAMLYT 1964

Mask and face covering 20 MIN
VHS
Color (I J H)
$39.95 purchase _ #CP724
Portrays the many ways humans have sought to alter, disguise, protect, adorn and immortalize the human face. Shows symbolic, ritualistic, primitive, historic and contemporary masks. Includes an Eskimo Seal mask, Peruvian mummy mask, an Apache mask and more.
Fine Arts
Dist - KNOWUN

Mask Layout 55 MIN
VHS / U-matic
Introduction to VLSI Design Series
Color (PRO)
Deals with transformation of a circuit design to a geometrical layout, using the design rules. Gives detailed example and shows influence of design rules on the order of design.
Industrial and Technical Education
Dist - MIOT **Prod** - MIOT

Mask Patterns and their Constraints 55 MIN
VHS / U-matic
Introduction to VLSI Design Series
Color (PRO)
Covers shapes for mask patterns, formal languages, student design examples, design rules, and classes of design.
Industrial and Technical Education
Dist - MIOT **Prod** - MIOT

Masked Dance (Dogon People) 6 MIN
VHS / U-matic
African Village Life (Mali Series
Color
Fine Arts; Geography - World; History - World; Sociology
Dist - IFF **Prod** - IFF

Masked incident 6 MIN
16mm
B&W (G)
$15.00 rental
Provides no description.
Fine Arts
Dist - CANCIN **Prod** - MERRIT 1979

Masked madness in Switzerland 30 MIN
VHS
World of festivals series
Color (J H C G)
$195.00 purchase
Travels to Basel, Switzerland at 4:00 am, to hear the sound of drums and fife, and see outlandishly costumed figures with grotesque masks and huge lanterns atop their heads. Reveals that every day comic floats, brass bands and noisy crowds throng the streets, at night spectacular balls are held. Part of a 12 - part series on European festivals.
Geography - World; Social Science
Dist - LANDMK **Prod** - LANDMK 1988

Maskerade 10 MIN
16mm
B&W (J)
Shows African masks photographed to the rhythm of native music.
Fine Arts; Geography - World; Social Science; Sociology
Dist - REMBRT **Prod** - REMBRT

Maskerade 99 MIN
16mm
B&W (GERMAN)
A German language motion picture. Portrays the wife of a surgeon who follows a famous painter into his studio and posses for a picture, dressed only in a mask and a muff, the grand prize she has won in the tombola that night. Unveils the happenings of the next day, when this picture appears in the newspaper and all Vienna recognizes the muff.
Foreign Language; Literature and Drama
Dist - WSTGLC **Prod** - WSTGLC 1934

Masking 13 MIN
BETA / VHS
Color (A PRO)
$68.50 purchase _ #KTI40
Deals with auto body repair.
Industrial and Technical Education
Dist - RMIBHF **Prod** - RMIBHF

The Maskmaker 9 MIN
U-matic / VHS / 16mm
Art of silence, pantomimes with Marcel Marceau series
Color (J H C)
LC 75-703450
Explains that for Marcel Marceau, the Maskmaker is one who represents humanity, with all the faces humanity can possess. Includes the classic symbols for comedy and tragedy.
Fine Arts
Dist - EBEC **Prod** - EBEC 1975

MaskMaker 130 MIN
VHS
Color (P I J H G)
$39.95 purchase _ #MAS - 11
Offers a complete course in the fabrication and painting of papier mache masks, giving the viewer all of the basic skills necessary to enjoy papier mache mask - making for a lifetime. Gives people of all ages the opportunity to enjoy a very special means of personal exploration and expression, as Jackie Miller's clear, content - rich teaching style guides them through her complete 10 - hour course in fabricating, dry finishing, and painting wearable papier mache masks.
Fine Arts
Dist - ARTSAM **Prod** - JOHNST

Maskmaking introduction 35 MIN
VHS
Color (I J H)
$39.95 purchase _ #CP792
Presents an easy - to - follow, hands - on approach to making a variety of masks with basic materials, including paper plates, paper bags, aluminum pie tins, cardboard, balloons and more.
Fine Arts
Dist - KNOWUN

Maskmaking introduction 35 MIN
VHS
Maskmaking series
Color (J H C G)
$49.95 purchase _ #CPC792V
Looks at making a variety of masks with basic materials, including paper plates, paper bags, aluminum pie tins, corrugated cardboard, balloons, paper headbands and clay. Includes an easy - to - follow introduction to maskmaking with examples of masks from different cultures and masks made by students. Part one of two parts.
Fine Arts
Dist - CAMV

Maskmaking series
Presents two parts on maskmaking. Shows how to make a variety of masks with basic materials in Maskmaking Introduction. Illustrates methods used to construct masks, expanding on techniques in Maskmaking Introduction, in Maskmaking Workshop.
Maskmaking introduction 35 MIN
Maskmaking workshop 50 MIN
Dist - CAMV

Maskmaking workshop 50 MIN
VHS
Maskmaking series
Color (J H C G)
$49.95 purchase _ #CPC793V
Shows methods used to construct masks expanding on techniques in Maskmaking Introduction. Demonstrates how to use plaster gauze on a person's face and then use that mask as a press - mold for paper and clay. Illustrates the use of wire and crumpled paper as armatures for maskmaking. Looks at historic masks as a background for ideas and inspiration. Second of two parts.
Fine Arts
Dist - CAMV

Maskmaking workshop 50 MIN
VHS
Color (I J H)
$39.95 purchase _ #CP793
Shows how to make masks using plaster gauze on a model and a press - mold for paper, clay and plaster gauze. Covers wire and crumpled paper as armatures for maskmaking.
Fine Arts
Dist - KNOWUN

Masks 12 MIN
16mm / U-matic / VHS
Color (J)
Displays a collection of primitive and modern masks. Discusses the role of masks in the cultural and artistic life of various peoples. Explains how masks are used in rituals and in dramatizing myths and legends.
Fine Arts; Sociology
Dist - PHENIX **Prod** - PEGF 1962

Masks 10 MIN
U-matic
Get it Together Series
Color (P I)
Teaches children how to make a mask from papier - mache and a balloon.
Fine Arts
Dist - TVOTAR **Prod** - TVOTAR 1978

Masks and face coverings 20 MIN
VHS
Color (J H C G)
$49.95 purchase _ #CPC744V
Portrays the many ways humans have sought to alter, disguise, protect, adorn and immortalize the human face. Shows symbolic, ritualistic, primitive, historic and contemporary masks. Illustrates 80 examples, including an Eskimo Seal Mask, a Peruvian mummy mask, an African helmet mask, a Mixtec mosaic work, an Apache devil mask.
Fine Arts; Sociology
Dist - CAMV

Masks and mask making - masks from many cultures 21 MIN
VHS
Color (G)
$39.95 purchase _ #MAS - 10
Presents masks from different regions of the world and from diverse cultures. Includes images of over 100 masks combined with sequences of dances and festivals where masks are worn. Shows masks worn at the Mardi Gras and examples from the Dominican Republic, New Guinea, Bali, China, Tibet, Japan, Korea, Africa, Mexico, Guatemala, Bolivia, and a variety made by North American Indians.
Fine Arts; Social Science
Dist - ARTSAM **Prod** - CRYSP

Masks from many cultures 21 MIN
VHS
Color (J H C G)
$49.95 purchase _ #CPC745V; $39.95 purchase _ #CP745
Overviews images of over 100 masks combined with sequences of dances and festivals where masks are worn in traditional ceremonies. Shows masks worn at the Mardi Gras in New Orleans and an artist from the Dominican Republic making a mask for a festival who uses papier mache over a clay mold. Shows him wearing the finished mask. Presents examples from New Guinea, Bali, China, Tibet, Japan, Korea, Africa, Mexico, Guatemala, Bolivia, as well as a variety of masks by North American Indians.
Fine Arts; Sociology
Dist - CAMV
KNOWUN

Masks - How We Hide Our Emotions 30 MIN
VHS
Color (J H)
Challenges your students to examine the psychological masks we all wear, and explore the problems that arise when the masks fail to reflect our true feelings.
Guidance and Counseling; Health and Safety
Dist - HRMC **Prod** - HRMC

The Masks of culture 25 MIN
VHS / U-matic
Color (J H G)
$250.00, $300.00 purchase, $50.00 rental
Explains the importance in tribal ceremonies of ritual wooden masks of Native American cultural traditions. Gives weight to the role of masks in all cultures as symbolic representations of the inner self and the world around.
Fine Arts; Social Science
Dist - NDIM **Prod** - GRY 1992

Masks of eternity 60 MIN
VHS
Moyers - Joseph Campbell and the power of myth series
Color (G)
$39.95 purchase _ #TWOM - 106
Interviews the late mythological scholar Joseph Campbell. Presents Campbell's observations on concepts of God, religion and eternity. Reveals that Campbell views myth as a 'mask of God,' or a metaphor for all outside the visible world. Hosted by Bill Moyers.
Religion and Philosophy; Social Science; Sociology
Dist - PBS

Masks of Eternity 58 MIN
VHS
Power of Myth Series
Color (G)
$29.95, $9.95 purchase _ #XVME, XAME
Examines the mythological image of god, religion and eternity as revealed in Christianity, Buddhism, the beliefs of Navajos, Jung and others. Part of the Power Of Myth series featuring Joseph Campbell.
Literature and Drama; Religion and Philosophy; Social Science
Dist - GAINST **Prod** - PBS

Masks of Eternity
VHS / Cassette
Power of Myth Series
(G)
$29.95, $9.95 purchase
Features Joseph Campbell and Bill Moyers.
Literature and Drama; Religion and Philosophy
Dist - BKPEOP **Prod** - MFV

Masks of eternity
VHS
Power of myth series
Color (G)
$29.95 purchase
Presents 'Masks Of Eternity,' the sixth and final part of the 'Power Of Myth' series with the late Joseph Campbell and Bill Moyers.
Religion and Philosophy
Dist - PBS **Prod** - WNETTV

Masks of eternity, vol 6 60 MIN
VHS
Power of Myth series
Color (G)
$29.95 purchase _ #687
Features storyteller Joseph Campbell who provides challenging insights into the concepts of God, religion and eternity as revealed in Christian teachings, Navajo tradition, writings by Jung and others. Part of a six - part series on Joseph Campbell with introductions by Bill Moyers.
Literature and Drama; Religion and Philosophy
Dist - YELMON **Prod** - PBS

Masks of illusion 8 MIN
16mm / VHS
Color (G)
$20.00 rental, $200.00, $50.00 purchase
Presents the masks of sculptor Horace Washington. Envisions his creative process through a variety of film effects.
Fine Arts
Dist - CANCIN **Prod** - KNWLDB 1986

Maslow and Self - Actualization, no 1 30 MIN
16mm
Color (C T)
LC FIA68-1961
Dr Abraham Maslow discusses the dimensions of selfactualization and elaborates on recent research and theory related to honesty, awareness, freedom and trust.
Psychology
Dist - PSYCHF **Prod** - PSYCHF 1968

Maslow and Self - Actualization, no 2 30 MIN
16mm
Color (C)
LC FIA68-1961
Dr Abraham Maslow discusses the dimensions of selfactualization and elaborates on recent research and theory related to honesty, awareness, freedom and trust.
Psychology
Dist - PSYCHF **Prod** - PSYCHF 1968

Maslow's Hierarchy of Needs 15 MIN
U-matic / VHS / 16mm
Color (A)
Presents Abraham Maslow's analysis of the role of needs in human motivation and indicates its relevance to supervisors, managers and students.
Guidance and Counseling; Psychology
Dist - SALENG **Prod** - SALENG 1975

Maslow's Hierarchy of Needs 15 MIN
VHS / 16mm
(C PRO)
$550.00 purchase, $135.00 rental
Shows the relevance of Maslow's theory to superiors, managers, and sales personnel. Helps viewers understand what motivation is. Helps improve interpersonal relationships and organizational effectiveness.
Education
Dist - VLEARN

Masonry
VHS / 35mm strip
Masonry Series
$295.00 purchase _ #DXMAS5 filmstrips, $295.00 purchase _ #DXMAS5V VHS
Provides instruction in the elements of masonry with an emphasis on safety.
Industrial and Technical Education
Dist - CAREER **Prod** - CAREER

Masonry Block Explained 60 MIN
VHS / 16mm
Color (H A)
$289.00 purchase _ M41
Demonstrates the manufacture of masonry blocks. Details the safe operaton of a power mixer and shows the viewer how to properly lay out and construct a masonry block wall using 8 inch blocks.
Industrial and Technical Education
Dist - BERGL **Prod** - BERGL 1989

Masonry, Second Series
VHS
Masonry Series
$295.00 purchase _ #DXMSS000 filmstrips, $295.00 purchase _
Discusses mortar mixer, masonry, and hydraulic saws, nomenclature, brick, block, pattern bonds, joints, brick veneer, composite, cavity, and intersecting walls, pilasters, chases, and a single flue chimney.
Industrial and Technical Education
Dist - CAREER **Prod** - CAREER

Masonry Series
Masonry
Masonry, Second Series
Dist - CAREER

Masque 25 MIN
16mm
B&W
LC 78-711327
Tells how a girl has a profound effect on the relationship of two guys who live together.
Fine Arts
Dist - USC **Prod** - USC 1970

Masque of the Red Death 10 MIN
U-matic / VHS / 16mm
Color (H C)
LC 70-708570
An adaptation of the story Masque Of The Red Death by Edgar Allan Poe, about a count who locks himself and his court inside his castle in order to avoid the plague only to be destroyed by the plague masquerading as a seductive woman.
Literature and Drama
Dist - MGHT **Prod** - ZAGREB 1970

Masque of the Red Death 88 MIN
16mm
Color (H A)
Describes a medieval Italian prince who practices devil worship while the plague rages outside. When he holds a ball, death is an uninvited guest. Directed by Roger Corman. Stars Vincent Price.
Fine Arts
Dist - TIMLIF **Prod** - AIP 1964
TWYMAN

The Masque of the Red Death 89 MIN
U-matic / VHS / 16mm
Color (H C)
Based on the short story The Masque Of The Red Death by Edgar Allan Poe. Dramatizes the macabre tale of a Renaissance prince who holds a masque ball during the time of the Red Death plague. Stars Vincent Price.
Fine Arts; Literature and Drama
Dist - FI **Prod** - CORMAN 1964

Masquerade 28 MIN
VHS
Elephant show series
Color (P I)
$95.00 purchase, $45.00 rental
Presents program 15 in the Sharon, Lois and Bram's Elephant Show series. Teaches reading readiness and social skills while engaging children in making music. Each program explores a new theme through adventure, fantasy, mystery and song with recording artists Sharon, Lois and Bram. Uses traditional materials which stress participation - action songs, sing - along songs, story songs, clapping songs, singing games, playground chants and folk songs from many different traditions. Includes teacher's guide co - authored by a music education specialist.
Fine Arts; Sociology
Dist - BULFRG **Prod** - CAMBFP 1989

Masquerade 27 MIN
16mm / U-matic / VHS
Color
Presents the inhabitants of an imaginary planet as they prepare for a masquerade. Focuses on the importance of creativity. From the studio of Co Hoedeman, creator of the Claymation technique.
Fine Arts; Literature and Drama
Dist - MEDIAG **Prod** - NFBC 1985

Masquerade 100 MIN
VHS
Color (G) (MANDARIN CHINESE)
$45.00 purchase _ #6008A
Presents a Mandarin Chinese language movie produced in the People's Republic of China.
Fine Arts; Geography - World; Literature and Drama
Dist - CHTSUI **Prod** - CHTSUI

Masquerade 5 MIN
16mm
Color (G)
$15.00 rental
Uses animation with hand - painted engraved cut - outs on a full - color background. Portrays scenes of a duel in a snowy forest, Harlequin dying, Red Indian with wings of victory and a cat - masked woman.
Fine Arts
Dist - CANCIN **Prod** - JORDAL 1981

The Masquerader 10 MIN
16mm
B&W
Features Charlie Chaplin posing as a woman.
Fine Arts
Dist - FCE **Prod** - FCE 1914

The Masqueraders 10 MIN
16mm
B&W (J)
Charlie Chaplin, Charlie Chase and Minta Durfee star in the comic story of a male actor who, after being fired, returns to the movie studio disguised as a woman. A silent film.
Fine Arts
Dist - RMIBHF **Prod** - SENN 1914

Mass 15 MIN
U-matic
Math Makers One Series
Color (I)
Presents the math concepts of mass, relationships beween grams, kilograms and tons and mass and cost problems.
Education; Mathematics
Dist - TVOTAR **Prod** - TVOTAR 1979

Mass 5 MIN
U-matic
Eureka Series
Color (J)
Tells how mass is measured and shows how it differs from size.
Science; Science - Physical
Dist - TVOTAR **Prod** - TVOTAR 1980

Mass and Density - Investigating Matter 20 MIN
U-matic / VHS / 16mm
Color (I J)
$60 rental _ #9812
Experiments are conducted that demonstrate Law of Conservation of Mass, how changes in volume affect density and how buoyancy works.
Science; Science - Physical
Dist - AIMS **Prod** - SAIF 1986

Mass and volume 15 MIN
U-matic / VHS
First films on science series
Color (P I)
Introduces concepts of mass and volume. Demonstrates that objects can have the same volume but different masses and the same mass but different volumes.
Mathematics; Science - Physical
Dist - AITECH **Prod** - MAETEL 1975

Mass and Weight 24 MIN
VHS / U-matic
Metric Education Video Tapes for Pre and Inservice Teachers (K - 8 'Series
Color
Presents the most common units of mass and relates this to everyday objects. Includes activities such as finding the mass of an object, matching containers of equal mass and distinguishing between mass and weight.
Mathematics
Dist - PUAVC **Prod** - PUAVC

Mass and Weight in Orbit
U-matic / VHS
Experiments in Space Series
Color
Distinguishes weight from mass. Depicts astronauts lifting weights in space.
Science - Physical
Dist - EDMEC **Prod** - EDMEC

Mass for the Dakota Sioux 20 MIN
16mm
B&W (C)
$392.00
Experimental Film by Bruce Baillie.
Fine Arts
Dist - AFA **Prod** - AFA 1964

Mass for the Dakota Sioux 20 MIN
VHS / 16mm
B&W (G)
$45.00 rental
Reveals the contradiction between the form of the Mass and the theme of Death. Uses a collage of images. 1963 - 1964.
Fine Arts; Religion and Philosophy; Sociology
Dist - CANCIN **Prod** - BAILB

Mass media 30 MIN
VHS
Color (H C)
$89.95 purchase _ #TSI - 122
Demonstrates the influence of mass media on individuals, on society and on culture. Shows how mass media makes the world smaller through instantaneous communication and how it helps set the national agenda.
Social Science; Sociology
Dist - INSTRU

Mass of Atoms 47 MIN
16mm
Physics Films Series
B&W (J H C)
LC FIA67-5928
Depicts an experiment to determine the masses of a helium atom and a polonium atom. Shows the various laboratory techniques involved and necessary precautions to take during the experiment.
Science - Physical
Dist - MLA **Prod** - PSSC 1967

The Mass of atoms - Pt 1 20 MIN
16mm
PSSC physics films series
B&W (J H C)
LC FIA67-5928
Depicts the first part of an experiment to determine the masses of a helium atom and a polonium atom. Shows the various laboratory techniques involved and necessary precautions to take during the experiment.
Science; Science - Physical
Dist - MLA **Prod** - PSSC 1967

The Mass of atoms - Pt 2 27 MIN
16mm
PSSC physics films series
B&W (J H C)
LC FIA67-2929
Depicts the last part of an experiment to determine the masses of a helium atom and a polonium atom. Shows the various laboratory techniques involved and necessary precautions to take during the experiment.
Science; Science - Physical
Dist - MLA **Prod** - PSSC 1967

Mass Preschool Testing 30 MIN
U-matic / VHS
Hearing Screening Series
Color
Discusses mass preschool testing, the most promising method to detect hearing difficulties while they can still be treated with reasonable success. Presents a scenario for the organization and implementation of such a program.
Guidance and Counseling; Health and Safety; Science - Natural
Dist - NETCHE **Prod** - NETCHE 1971

Mass production procedures in apparel manufacturing series
Eagleknit makes basics right 25 MIN
Eiseman Tradition 21 MIN
JH Collectibles Story 23 MIN
Overview of Apparel Manufacturing 14 MIN
Dist - IOWA

The Mass Spectrometer 22 MIN
16mm / U-matic / VHS
Color (H C)
Shows the application of mass spectrometry in both industry and research and describes in detail the principle of operation of the direction focusing type. Describes briefly the double focusing type.
Science - Physical
Dist - VIEWTH **Prod** - MULLRD

Mass Spectrometry 30 MIN
U-matic / VHS
Color
Presents Dr. Larry Keefer, head of the Chemistry Unit, National Cancer Institute and Dr. James Loo, former mass and nuclear spectrometrist, University of Nebraska Medical Center, introducing theory and methods of mass spectrometry and fragmentation factors.
Science - Physical
Dist - NETCHE **Prod** - NETCHE 1970

Mass Spectrometry 33 MIN
U-matic / VHS / 16mm
Color (C)
LC 70-713031
Introduces the techniques of mass spectrometry, shows how the spectrometer operates and describes the kinds information that the instrument yields.
Mathematics; Science; Science - Physical
Dist - MEDIAG **Prod** - WILEYJ 1971

Mass Spectrometry 20 MIN
U-matic / VHS
Experiment - Chemistry Series
Color (C)
$249.00, $149.00 purchase _ #AD - 1064
Uses a mass spectrometer to investigate two aspects of electron bombardment of gas phase atoms and molecules. Part of a series on experiments in chemistry.
Education; Psychology; Science; Science - Physical
Dist - FOTH **Prod** - FOTH

Mass storage devices 18 MIN
U-matic / VHS
Little computers - see how they run series
Color (J)
LC 81-706844
Takes a practical look at problems and solutions in the area of information storage and retreival. Covers the relative cost of various options and describes the advantages and disadvantages of a number of storage methods.
Computer Science; Mathematics
Dist - GPN **Prod** - ELDATA 1980

Mass transit - up, up and away 22 MIN
U-matic / VHS / 16mm
Color (J)
Discusses the shape of travel in the future, as affected by over - population, pollution, and technology. Presents possibilities for capsule cars, jet belts and high-speed monorails.
Social Science
Dist - CNEMAG **Prod** - DOCUA

Mass Wasting - Dry 7 MIN
VHS
Color (C)
$34.95 purchase _ #193 E 2071
Depicts rock slide and temporary damming, rockfall by weathering, dry slumping and talus formation. Teacher's guide provided.
Science - Physical
Dist - WARDS

Mass wasting - dry 8 MIN
VHS
Geology stream table series
Color (H C)
$24.95 purchase _ #S9004
Treats dry erosion in a single - concept format, using models and NASA footage. Part of a 12 - part series on stream tables.
Agriculture; Geography - World; Science - Physical
Dist - HUBDSC **Prod** - HUBDSC

Mass Wasting - Moist 8 MIN
VHS
Color (C)
$34.95 purchase _ #193 E 2072
Demonstrates shoreline slumping, mudflows and earthflows. Teacher's guide provided.
Science - Physical
Dist - WARDS

Mass wasting - moist 8 MIN
VHS
Geology stream table series
Color (H C)
$24.95 purchase _ #S9005
Treats wet erosion in a single - concept format, using models and NASA footage. Part of a 12 - part series on stream tables.
Agriculture; Geography - World; Science - Physical
Dist - HUBDSC **Prod** - HUBDSC

The Massachusetts 54th Colored Infantry 60 MIN
VHS
CC; Color (C H G A)
$69.95 purchase _ #AMEI-403-WC95
Describes the history of the Massachusetts 54th Colored Infantry, a unit made up of African American free men and former slaves that fought for the Union Army during the Civil War. Explains that this was the first all black regiment in the United States Army. Includes a lesson plan for teachers.
History - United States
Dist - PBS **Prod** - JASH 1991

Massachusetts College of Art
VHS
Campus clips series
Color (H C A)
$29.95 purchase _ #CC0108V
Takes a video visit to the campus of the Massachusetts College of Art. Shows many of the distinctive features of the campus, and interviews students about their experiences. Provides information on the composition of the student body, professors, academics, social life, housing, and other subjects.

Education
Dist - CAMV

Massachusetts Institute of Technology
VHS
Campus clips series
Color (H C A)
$29.95 purchase _ #CC0054V
Takes a video visit to the campus of M I T - the Massachusetts Institute of Technology. Shows many of the distinctive features of the campus, and interviews students about their experiences. Provides information on the composition of the student body, professors, academics, social life, housing, and other subjects.
Education
Dist - CAMV

Massachusetts Story 58 MIN
16mm
Color (H C A)
LC 78-701435
Examines the issues relating to off - shore oil drilling in Massachusetts, using the comments of local businesspeople, regional political figures, ecological experts and oil industry spokespersons.
Business and Economics; Geography - United States; Science - Natural; Social Science; Sociology
Dist - MASHAM **Prod** - MASHAM 1977

Massachusetts Story
U-matic / VHS
Color
Examines the way people live, work and play on Cape Cod, the Islands and New Bedford and the challenge to that way of life by the plans to exploit energy resources on the Georges Bank.
Geography - United States; Science - Natural; Social Science; Sociology
Dist - LAWDET **Prod** - LAWDET

Massachussetts 60 MIN
VHS
Portrait of America series
Color (J H C G)
$99.95 purchase _ #AMB21V
Visits Massachussetts. Offers extensive research into the state's history. Films key locations and presents segments on history, government, education, folklore, science, journalism, sociology, industry, agriculture and business. Shows what is unique about Massachussetts and distinctive about its regional culture and how it got to be that way. Includes study guide. Part of a 50 - part series.
Geography - United States; History - United States
Dist - CAMV

Massacre 50 MIN
VHS
Watergate series
Color; PAL (H C A)
PdS99 purchase; Not available in the United States or Canada
Investigates the events of the Watergate Affair that led to Richard Nixon's resignation in 1974. Features Nixon's attempt to bypass existing laws and avoid public exposure of the Watergate Affair. Presents the Watergate investigators and those convicted of Watergate crimes. Fourth in a five - part series.
Civics and Political Systems; History - United States
Dist - BBCENE

Massacre in Nanjing 104 MIN
VHS
Color (G) (MANDARIN)
$45.00 purchase _ #0326C
Presents a movie produced in the People's Republic of China.
Fine Arts
Dist - CHTSUI

Massacre of marines in Beirut - Monday, October 24, 1983 30 MIN
VHS
Nightline series
Color (H C G)
$14.98 purchase _ #MP6140
Documents the massacre of 242 marines by Islamic extremist bombs, after the marines had been dispatched to Beirut, Lebanon, by Ronald Reagan against the advice of military advisors.
Biography; Fine Arts; History - United States
Dist - INSTRU **Prod** - ABCNEW 1983

Massage 48 MIN
VHS / U-matic
Color (C A)
Combines a complete instruction unit on the art of giving relief and pleasure through touch with analysis of cultural taboos concerning touch.
Psychology
Dist - MMRC **Prod** - MMRC

Massage and meditation 54 MIN
VHS
Color (A PRO)
$29.95 purchase
Demonstrates a variety of massage and meditation techniques for both professionals and students. Presents a visual tour of the lymphatic system, showing reflexology points and chakras. Soundtrack also available separately on audiocassette.
Health and Safety; Religion and Philosophy; Science - Natural
Dist - SCANPS **Prod** - HARMNY 1987

Massage for beginners - a Cayce - Reilly massage workshop 60 MIN
VHS
Color (G)
$39.95 purchase _ #P59
Shows how to give a relaxing, therapeutic massage at home and teaches how to develop your own powers of healing touch with the unique rhythmic movement of the Cayce - Reilly massage technique.
Health and Safety
Dist - HP

Massage for everyone
VHS
To your health series
Color (G)
$29.95 purchase _ #IV - 048
Discusses massage therapy, its techniques, benefits and history as taught and endorsed by the Swedish Institute.
Health and Safety; Physical Education and Recreation
Dist - INCRSE **Prod** - INCRSE

Massage for health 70 MIN
VHS
Color (G)
$29.95 purchase _ #6027
Teaches easy - to - follow Western style massage techniques for the whole body. Features Shari Belafonte - Harper. Includes 42 - page Handbook and massage oil.
Health and Safety; Physical Education and Recreation
Dist - SYBVIS **Prod** - SYBVIS

Massage for health 70 MIN
VHS
Color (G)
$29.95 purchase
Presents a comprehensive introduction to Swedish massage techniques for the entire body. Also teaches self - massages and stretches. Hosted by Shari Belafonte - Harper and several massage professionals.
Physical Education and Recreation
Dist - PBS **Prod** - WNETTV

Massage for relaxation
VHS
Color (G)
$19.95 purchase _ #NU006
Shows simple techniques for use on oneself or others.
Health and Safety; Psychology
Dist - SIV

Massage - introduction for beginners 91 MIN
VHS
Color (G)
$39.95 purchase
Presents a comprehensive introduction to the art of massage. Hosted by massage therapist Stephen Abraham.
Physical Education and Recreation
Dist - PBS **Prod** - WNETTV

Massage of the lower extremity 34 MIN
VHS / U-matic
B&W
Demonstrates massage of the lower extremity, review of the anatomy of leg muscles and lists the equipment needed.
Health and Safety
Dist - BUSARG **Prod** - BUSARG

Massage of the upper extremity 40 MIN
U-matic / VHS
Color
Demonstrates massage of the upper extremity, including a list of equipment needed and a review of the anatomy.
Health and Safety
Dist - BUSARG **Prod** - BUSARG

Massage - simple 50 MIN
VHS
Color (G)
$19.95 purchase
Presents a comprehensive massage program, focusing on nine body areas commonly susceptible to tensions and aches. Includes Swedish, Shiatsu, and sports medicine techniques.
Physical Education and Recreation
Dist - PBS **Prod** - WNETTV

The Massasauga rattler 16 MIN
U-matic / VHS / BETA
Color (I J H)
$29.95, $130.00 purchase _ #LSTF81
Explains how reptiles can be the animals most adversely affected by habitat disruption because they have relatively little mobility. Shows how a colony of rattlers was monitored in a shrinking New York wetland. Includes teacher's guide. Produced by Nature Episodes assisted by the New York State Dept of Environmental Conservation and the Toronto Zoo.
Science - Natural
Dist - FEDU

The Masses and the Millionaires - the Homestead Strike 26 MIN
16mm / U-matic / VHS
Color (J) (SPANISH)
LC 73-702727;
Recreates the bloody strike at the Carnegie Steel Company in 1892.
Business and Economics; History - United States; Social Science; Sociology
Dist - LCOA **Prod** - LCOA 1974

Masseter and Temporal Muscles 14 MIN
8mm cartridge / 16mm
Anatomy of the Head and Neck Series
Color (PRO)
LC 75-701248
Uses a cadaver to follow the anatomical dissection of the head, neck, temporomandibular joints, masticatory muscles, deep spaces of the face and the third division of the trigeminal nerve.
Science - Natural
Dist - USNAC **Prod** - USVA 1969

Massey series
What you are is 150 MIN
What you are is where you see 75 MIN
Dist - VPHI

Massey Tapes Series
What You are is , Pt 1 30 MIN
What You are is , Pt 2 60 MIN
What You are is , Pt 3 30 MIN
What You are Is'nt Necessarily what You will be 60 MIN
Dist - CBSFOX

Massey Tapes Series
What You are is Where You See 75 MIN
Dist - CBSFOX
MAGVID
VPHI

Massey Tapes Series
What You are is Where You were When 90 MIN
Dist - CBSFOX
VPHI

Massey Triad 180 MIN
VHS / 16mm
(C PRO)
$1495.00 purchase, $375.00 rental
Shows how attitudes, prejudices, and ways of reacting to change are programmed into each generation. Stresses the need to move from a fixed viewpoint to a flexible point of view. Includes three one - hour programs, The Past, The Present, and The Future.
Education
Dist - VLEARN **Prod** - VPHI

Massey triad series
Presents a three - part series which explores the development of value systems. Stresses the need for self - understanding in order to work with others more efficiently. Looks at intergenerational conflict. Features Morris Massey.
What you are is not what you have to be - Part B 69 MIN
What you are is what you were when - Part A 64 MIN
Dist - MAGVID **Prod** - MAGVID

Massing a Window 30 MIN
Videoreel / VT2
Making Things Grow II Series
Color
Agriculture; Fine Arts; Science - Natural
Dist - PBS **Prod** - WGBHTV

The Massive Mirror 29 MIN
U-matic
Visions - the Critical Eye Series
Color (H C)
Explores modernist art and related subjects such as methods of marketing, drawbacks involved in adopting theories of mainstream art, the role of the critic and the ways in which art can express religious experience.
Fine Arts
Dist - TVOTAR **Prod** - TVOTAR 1985

Massive Pulmonary Embolism - Surgical Treatment 14 MIN
16mm
Color
LC FIA68-760
Portrays the emergency surgical management treatment of otherwise lethal massive pulmonary emboli. Demonstrates pulmonary embolectomy using cardio pulmonary bypass. Shows methods of temporary circulatory support with a portable heart - lung machine.
Health and Safety; Science - Natural
Dist - GENT **Prod** - UMIAMI 1967

Massive Transfusion 22 MIN
VHS / 16mm
(C)
$385.00 purchase _ #870VI063
Offers a thorough overview of massive transfusion. Describes the types of patients likely to require it, its goals, common and rare complications associated with the procedure, and treatements for these complications.
Health and Safety
Dist - HSCIC **Prod** - HSCIC 1987

Mast Bumping - Causes and Prevention 20 MIN
U-matic / VHS / 16mm
Color (A)
Offers instruction to helicopter pilots on excessive rotor flopping, explains in - flight conditions which precede mast bumping and shows actions pilots must take to avoid accidents.
Civics and Political Systems; Industrial and Technical Education
Dist - USNAC **Prod** - USA 1982

Mast - Making for the King 17 MIN
16mm
Color (J H A)
Presents the history of mast - making in New England which goes back to 1634, when a shipment of pines was sent to England to be hewn into masts for the ships of the king's navy. Shows the process of selecting a mast tree, preparing the bed, building a platform for choppers, felling the tree and hauling the 80 - foot log with many yokes of oxen.
History - United States; Industrial and Technical Education
Dist - UNH **Prod** - UNH 1977

MAST - Military Assistance to Safety and Traffic 19 MIN
16mm
Color
LC 75-702411
Introduces MAST, a program dedicated to providing military medical assistance to civilians in need by utilizing helicopters and medical corpsmen during emergencies. Outlines the capabilities of aeromedical evacuation helicopters and crews.
Health and Safety; History - World; Sociology
Dist - USNAC **Prod** - USA 1974

Mastectomy 14 MIN
VHS / 16mm
Understanding Breast Cancer Series
Color (H C A PRO)
$195.00 purchase, $75.00 rental _ #8071
Considers various sorts of surgery used in treating breast cancer.
Guidance and Counseling; Health and Safety
Dist - AIMS **Prod** - HOSSN 1988

Mastectomy education series
Presents a five - part series on mastectomy education presented by physical therapist Jan Anthes, Zaira Becker, RN, Linda Waldren, RN, Pilar Gonzalez, RN and Leatha Ross, RN. Includes the titles Pre and Post - Operative Education, Feelings and Coping, Feelings of the Husband and Post - Mastectomy Exercises, Parts 1 and 2.
Feelings and coping 20 MIN
Feelings of the husband 21 MIN
Post - mastectomy exercises - Pt 1 10 MIN
Post - mastectomy exercises - Pt 2 30 MIN
Pre and post - operative education 25 MIN
Dist - HSCIC

Master and Slave 11 MIN
16mm
Color (G)
Tells one of the legends of Hawaii in which a pampered young chief abuses a slave who later saves his life when a volcano erupts. In gratitude, slavery is abolished in the land by the chief.
Geography - United States; History - United States; Literature and Drama; Religion and Philosophy; Sociology
Dist - CINEPC **Prod** - TAHARA 1986

Master Bathroom 30 MIN
BETA / VHS
This Old House, Pt 2 - Suburban '50s Series
Color
Features remodeling a master bathroom. Shows how to build kitchen cabinets.
Industrial and Technical Education; Sociology
Dist - CORF **Prod** - WGBHTV

Master Class I 30 MIN
U-matic / VHS
Grant Johannesen - Pianist Series
Color
Presents Grant Johannesen with his master class of students at the University of Nebraska - Lincoln.
Fine Arts
Dist - NETCHE **Prod** - NETCHE 1973

Master Class II 30 MIN
VHS / U-matic
Grant Johannesen - Pianist Series
Color
Continues Grant Johannesen's work with his class, stressing concentration before an audience and the need to explore a piece.
Fine Arts
Dist - NETCHE **Prod** - NETCHE 1973

Master class in directing with Joanne Akalaitis 40 MIN
VHS
Color (G C H)
$179.00 purchase _ #DL340
Leads three actors through Jane Akalaitis' method of approaching a text through physicality. Shows a first rehearsal of Jean Genet's The Screens and teaches how the complex physicality of the play can be realized. Demonstrates how to convey an idea by creating a mask of facial muscles. Following the rehearsal, the actors give their reactions to Akaitis' method of approaching the text.
Fine Arts
Dist - INSIM

Master Class with Menuhin 56 MIN
16mm / U-matic / VHS
Color; Stereo (H)
$850.00, $310.00 purchase, $45.00 rental
Documents a masterclass for Canadian violin students given by Sir Yehudi Menuhin.
Fine Arts
Dist - BULFRG **Prod** - RHOMBS 1989

Master computer software easily series
DOS 2.0 - 3.3 Level II 36 MIN
DOS 2.0 - 3.3 Level III 52 MIN
Introduction to Lotus 1 - 2 - 3 43 MIN
Introduction to Wordperfect 5.0 58 MIN
Learning DOS 2.0 - 3.3 Disk Operating Systems 42 MIN
Lotus 1 - 2 - 3, Level II 74 MIN
Lotus 1 - 2 - 3, Level III 51 MIN
Wordperfect 5.0, Level II 60 MIN
Wordperfect 5.0, Level III 60 MIN
Dist - CARTRP

Master Cooking Course 60 MIN
VHS / U-matic
(H C A)
$39.95 _ #OP100V
Features Craig Claiborne and Pierre Franey, authorities on cooking, as they cover the finer points of cooking by demonstrating the methods for preparing four complete meals.
Home Economics
Dist - CAMV **Prod** - CAMV

Master in the Colonies 30 MIN
VHS / 16mm
World of the 30s Series
Color (J)
$149.00 purchase, $75.00 rental _ #OD - 2266
Describes efforts by European colonial rulers to convince native peoples to imitate European appearance and behavior. Examines exceptions such as Gandhi and notes how the Salt March signaled the end of Colonialism throughout the world. The ninth of 13 installments of The World Of the 30s Series.
History - United States; History - World
Dist - FOTH

The Master Key to Success 180 MIN
Cassette / VHS
Color (G)
$189.00 purchase _ #XVMKS
Presents the Napoleon Hill formula for success and prosperity. Includes two 90 - minute videos, four audiocassettes, transcript, summary cards and action book.
Psychology; Social Science; Sociology
Dist - GAINST

Master Misery 40 MIN
16mm / VHS
Color (G)
$495.00, $295.00 purchase, $60.00 rental
Presents a film based on a short story by Truman Capote. Offers an allegory on the spiritual battle to regain lost innocence and overcome alienation. Features Sylvia, looking for meaning in a mundane world, who meets Mr Revercomb who buys dreams. By Elizabeth Dimon.
Fine Arts; Literature and Drama
Dist - CNEMAG **Prod** - CNEMAG 1989

The Master Musicians of Jahjouka 58 MIN
VHS / U-matic
Color (GERMAN DUTCH)
Documents the rich musical history of a remote Moroccan village that has been unusually affected by westernization. Shows people who believe their music to possess healing powers. Shows the musicians performing as ancient ceremonies are described.
Fine Arts; Foreign Language; Social Science
Dist - MENASS **Prod** - MENASS 1983

The Master of Ballantrae 89 MIN
16mm
Color
Offers an adaptation of Robert Louis Stevenson's novel THE MASTER OF BALLANTRAE. Stars Errol Flynn.
Fine Arts; Literature and Drama
Dist - TWYMAN **Prod** - WB 1953

Master of Life
VHS
Color (G)
$19.95 purchase _ #VHS105
Uses hypnosis and subliminal suggestions.
Health and Safety; Psychology
Dist - VSPU **Prod** - VSPU

Master of Life Training Series
Dharmic destiny and soul goals 2 HRS
Liberation 2 HRS
Self - Creation 2 HRS
Success on Every Level 2 HRS
Dist - VSPU

The Master of Light - a Biography of Albert A Michelson 25 MIN
16mm / U-matic / VHS
Color (H A)
Depicts the life of Albert A Michelson, with the aid of computer graphics, archival stills and historic film footage. Describes him as America's first Nobel Prize winner in physics, and artist and musician as well as a scientist who pioneered in light research.
Biography; History - World; Science - Physical
Dist - CNEMAG **Prod** - ONEPAS 1984

The Master of Samarkand - Pt 10 58 MIN
VHS
Comrades Series
Color (S)
$79.00 purchase _ #351 - 9030
Follows twelve Soviet citizens from different backgrounds to reveal what Soviet life is like for a cross section of the 270 million inhabitants in the vast country of fifteen republics. Features Frontline anchor Judy Woodruff who also interviews prominent experts on Soviet affairs. Part 10 of the twelve - part series examines Abdugaffar Khakkulov, an Uzbek descendant of the Mongol armies which invaded the region close to the Afghan border during the Middle Ages, and his daily life as a member of the Moslem community.
Civics and Political Systems; Geography - World; History - World; Religion and Philosophy
Dist - FI **Prod** - WGBHTV 1988

Master of the Art 30 MIN
16mm / U-matic / VHS
Powerhouse Series
Color (I J)
Shows how some kids use self - discipline to restore a security director's job.
Psychology
Dist - GA **Prod** - EFCVA 1982

Master of the Performing Arts - Maureen Forrester 28 MIN
16mm
Color (G)
_ #106C 0178 390
Goes behind the curtain to see one of Canada's musical stars with a group of students teaching, discussing her art and performing.
Biography; Fine Arts
Dist - CFLMDC **Prod** - NFBC 1981

Master of the Shadows - Pt 5 26 MIN
VHS
Human Face of Indonesia Series, the
Color (S)
$99.00 purchase _ #118 - 9040
Focuses on the lives of five very different Indonesians. Presents an enthralling and informative picture of the life and culture of Indonesia by putting their personal stories into the broader context of the modern country. Part 5 of five parts views Bali, the most famous place in Indonesia. Asks if its traditional culture can survive the pressures of tourism. Tells the story of a man whose life is dedicated to nurturing his ancient culture, illustrating the conflict between the old and the new.
Geography - World; History - World
Dist - FI **Prod** - FLMAUS 1987

Master of the wind 11 MIN
VHS / U-matic
Color (G)
$335.00 purchase, $95.00 rental
Stresses principles of effective decision - making and competitive excellence. Tells the story of three top glider pilots competing for the National Soaring Championship.
Business and Economics; Guidance and Counseling; Industrial and Technical Education; Psychology
Dist - VLEARN **Prod** - VANTCO

Master photographers series
Looks at professional photographers from Europe and North America who started their careers early in the 20th century and who are considered pioneers in their specific fields. A six-part series.
Alfred Eisenstaedt 35 MIN
Andre Kertesz 35 MIN
Andreas Feininger 35 MIN
Ansel Adams 35 MIN
Bill Brandt 35 MIN
Jacques - Henri Lartigue 35 MIN
Dist - BBCENE

Master Production Scheduling Features and Methods 60 MIN
VHS / BETA
Manufacturing Series
(IND)
Identifys the features and methods of master production scheduling and their applications.
Business and Economics
Dist - COMSRV **Prod** - COMSRV 1986

The Master Race 20 MIN
VHS / U-matic
History in Action Series
Color
Discusses the Nazi concept of racial superiority and their attempts to achieve it. Deals with the secret police and the German concentration camps.
History - World
Dist - FOTH **Prod** - FOTH 1984

Master Raster 9 MIN
VHS
Color (C)
$300.00 purchase, $25.00, $35.00 rental
Incorporates computer animation, fluorescently colored images, television commercials, muzak, and absurd news items to suggest that television reduces society to an indiscriminate amalgamation of palatable bits. Produced by Mary Ellen Lower and Video Vision.
Industrial and Technical Education; Psychology; Sociology
Dist - WMENIF

Master Salt and the Sailor's Son - Pt 7 16 MIN
VHS
Words and Pictures Series
Color (P)
$49.00 purchase _ #548 - 9871
Uses animated stories to improve reading and vocabulary skills. Discusses the story content of each program and suggests several activities that relate to the story and the lessons learned. Part 7 of the seven part series tells the exciting adventure of little Sammy Salt who stows away aboard the Jolly Jack and sails to the Coconut Island.
English Language; Fine Arts; Literature and Drama
Dist - FI **Prod** - BBCTV 1984

Master Schedule Planning Reports 60 MIN
BETA / VHS
Manufacturing Series
(IND)
Defines the data and information that are required to make effective decisions, which reports are used in the decision making process and how those reports are used.
Business and Economics
Dist - COMSRV **Prod** - COMSRV 1986

Master search Bible
CD-ROM
(G A)
$795.00 purchase _ #2341
Provides a comprehensive biblical reference library of classic and contemporary works. Links three Bible versions to studies in language, history, geography, archaeology and ancient cultures. Contains 13 Bibles and references. For Macintosh Plus, SE and II computers. Requires 1MB RAM, floppy disk drive, Apple compatible CD - ROM drive.
Literature and Drama; Religion and Philosophy
Dist - BEP

The Master Singers of Nuremberg 20 MIN
16mm
Musical Masterpieces Series
B&W
Presents Franco Farrara directing the Radio Philharmonic Orchestra of Italy playing 'PRELUDE, THIRD ACT OVERTURE' from Wagner's 'THE MASTER SINGERS OF NUREMBERG.'.
Fine Arts
Dist - SG **Prod** - SG

Master Smart Woman 28 MIN
16mm / VHS
Color (G)
$500.00, $250.00 purchase, $65.00 rental
Re - evaluates the contribution of Sarah Orne Jewett to American literature. Describes Jewett as critically acclaimed in the 19th century and an important role model for a generation of women writers. Features stills from turn of the century photographers Chansonetta Emmons and Emma Coleman, critiques of Jewett's work, and excerpts from her fiction and autobiography.
Biography; History - United States; Literature and Drama
Dist - WMEN **Prod** - MORRJ 1984

The Master Teacher 10 MIN
16mm
Dr Bob Jones Says Series
Color (R)
Dr. Bob Jones, Sr. speaks about basic life truths.
Religion and Philosophy
Dist - UF **Prod** - UF

Master teacher - a portrait of Walter Robert 28 MIN
VHS / U-matic
Color (H C G)
$150.00 purchase, $25.00 rental _ #RC1273VU, #RC1273VH
Profiles Walter Robert, pianist, scholar and teacher of renown at Indiana University. Presents Robert conducting master classes and critiques and candidly discussing his teaching philosophy. Interviews fellow faculty members master violinist Joseph Gingold and Charles Webb. Produced by Susanne Schwibs and Indiana University Radio and TV Service.
Fine Arts
Dist - IU

The Master Thief 15 MIN
U-matic / VHS / 16mm
Color (P I)
LC 73-701728
Presents an animated puppet film based upon a fairy tale by the Grimm brothers. Shows a count who tells a master thief that he will remain free if he can steal the count's favorite horse while it is being guarded. Follows the thief as he is given another challenge by the count after he is successful with the horse.
Fine Arts; Literature and Drama
Dist - IU **Prod** - NET 1970

The Master Touch 18 MIN
16mm
Color
Combines live action and animation and stars Captain Silversides, who not only drives cars and sailboats but owns and operates a Gleaner Combine on his farm. Explains the different efficiency features on his Gleaner.
Agriculture
Dist - IDEALF **Prod** - ALLISC

Master Weavers of the Andes 15 MIN
U-matic / VHS / 16mm
Color (J)
LC 78-701920
Examines the craft of weaving as practiced by the Quechua Indians near Cuzco, Peru. Points out that, except for the use of chemical dyes, the processes of spinning and weaving are practiced as they have been for centuries.
Fine Arts; Geography - World; Social Science
Dist - EBEC **Prod** - CINECO 1978

The Masterbuilders 15 MIN
U-matic / VHS / 16mm
RSPB Collection Series
Color (I J H)
LC 84-707100
Exhibits what is considered the most intelligent of all birds, the weaverbird of Africa. Shows its nest - building techniques that involve actual tying of the first knot in its woven nest. Discloses male birds, after nest building, in the display ritual to attract female birds.
Science - Natural
Dist - BCNFL **Prod** - RSFPB 1983

Mastering aikido series
Presents a series of six videos explaining aikido, the least violent of Oriental martial arts, designed to defeat an attacker by harmonizing with the attacker's energy. Titles collected here include Fundamental Skills, Basic Defensive Skills, Intermediate Defensive Skills, Advanced Defensive Skills, Wooden Staff Skills and Defense Against Multiple Attackers.
Level 5 - wooden staff skills
Level 4 - advanced defensive skills
Level 1 - fundamental skills
Level 6 - defense against multiple attackers
Level 3 - intermediate defensive skills
Level 2 - basic defensive skills
Dist - SIV

Mastering goal setting 25 MIN
BETA / U-matic / VHS
Color (G PRO)
$595.00, $495.00 purchase, $225.00 rental _ #PM0021
Features Dr Kenneth Blanchard who introduces the SMART model of goal - setting. Focuses on two very different companies and how they handle goal - setting. Shows why employees become more self - assured and self - reliant when the goals they are working on are clear.
Business and Economics; Guidance and Counseling; Psychology; Social Science
Dist - BLNCTD **Prod** - BLNCTD

Mastering Grammar 30 MIN
VHS / U-matic
Business of Better Writing Series
Color
Deals with the mastering of grammar as part of improving business writing skills.
Business and Economics
Dist - KYTV **Prod** - KYTV 1983

Mastering iaido
VHS
Sword series
Color (G)
$49.95 purchase _ #PNT005
Presents 10th Dan Master Katsuo Yamaguchi teaching the art of the samurai sword.
Physical Education and Recreation; Psychology
Dist - SIV

Mastering Job Safety Analysis 15 MIN
VHS / U-matic
Foreman's Accident Prevention Series
Color (IND)
Teaches first - line supervisors how to develop a step - by - step procedure for breaking down the elements of a job so it can be performed with maximum safety.
Health and Safety
Dist - GPCV **Prod** - GPCV

Mastering jujutsu series
Collects all three volumes of a jujutsu series taught by 8th Dan Master Shizuya Sato.
Volume 1
Volume 2
Volume 3
Dist - SIV

Mastering kendo
VHS
Sword series
Color (G)
$49.95 purchase _ #PNT006
Presents 10th Dan Master H. Takano teaching Japan's most practical martial art.
Physical Education and Recreation; Psychology
Dist - SIV

Mastering kobujutsu
VHS
Sword series
Color (G)
$49.95 purchase _ #PNT004
Presents 10th Dan Master Yoshio Sugino demonstrating the Boken, Naginata and Bojutsu.
Physical Education and Recreation; Psychology
Dist - SIV

Mastering Math Skills 29 MIN
U-matic / VHS
Integration of Children with Special Needs in a Regular Classroom 'Series
Color
Presents a program for elementary school children with learning disabilities and behavioral problems. Emphasizes long - term memory, progression from concrete to abstract ideas and visual - spatial problems. Provides lessons in mathematics.
Education; Mathematics; Psychology
Dist - AITECH **Prod** - LPS 1975

Mastering Mechanics 30 MIN
U-matic / VHS
Business of Better Writing Series
Color
Deals with the mastering of mechanics as part of improving business writing skills.
Business and Economics
Dist - KYTV **Prod** - KYTV 1983

Mastering memos 15 MIN
VHS
Color (J H C G PRO)
$59.00 purchase _ #CBR1074V
Helps viewers improve their memo-writing abilities. Details how to write concise, informative memos. Focuses on teaching viewers how to reduce rambling; avoid wasting space; answer three important questions in every memo; become an audience-minded writer; write in a conversational style; and more.
Business and Economics; English Language; Social Science
Dist - CAMV

Mastering Microsoft Windows
VHS
Computer software training series
Color (J H C G)
$49.95 purchase _ #AAT15V
Teaches Microsoft Windows mastery in a comprehensive and easy - to - follow format. Illustrates actual commands and time saving techniques. Part of a 21 - part series on computer software.
Computer Science
Dist - CAMV

Mastering money - Pt 6 30 MIN
U-matic / VHS
Profiles in progress series
Color (H C)
$325.00, $295.00 purchase _ #V551
Focuses on Singapore, a city - state which is attractive to multinational companies. Looks at the success of Singapore and the globalization of capital, finance and markets in an increasingly interdependent world. Part of a 13 - part series on people who are moving their tradition - bound countries into modern times.
Business and Economics; Civics and Political Systems; Geography - World; History - World
Dist - BARR **Prod** - CEPRO 1991

Mastering performance appraisals 26 MIN
VHS
Color (A)
$525.00 purchase
Illustrates correct and incorrect procedures for employee evaluations through dramatizations. Helps supervisors organize their methods to avoid legal complications. Package includes a leader's guide with exercise material. Additional copies available separately.
Business and Economics; Civics and Political Systems; Education
Dist - COMFLM **Prod** - COMFLM

Mastering performance management 90 MIN
VHS / BETA / U-matic
Color (G PRO)
$1095.00, $995.00 purchase, $225.00 rental _ #PM0006
Uses an investigative journalism format to present the three phases of the performance management process - Performance Planning, Day - to - Day Coaching and Performance Evaluation. Presents four vignettes to illustrate how the process works.
Business and Economics; Psychology
Dist - BLNCTD **Prod** - BLNCTD

Mastering performance management 61 MIN
VHS / BETA / U-matic
Color (G)
$795.00 purchase, $225.00 rental
Offers four parts on performance management. Shows how to set SMART goals - Specific, Measurable, Attainable, Relevant, Trackable. Trains in giving feedback, identifying KRAs - Key Result Areas, listening and working together to achieve team and organizational goals.
Business and Economics; Psychology; Social Science
Dist - AMEDIA **Prod** - AMEDIA

Mastering Punctuation 30 MIN
U-matic / VHS
Business of Better Writing Series
Color
Deals with the mastering of punctuation as part of improving business writing skills.
Business and Economics
Dist - KYTV **Prod** - KYTV 1983

Mastering Spelling 30 MIN
VHS / U-matic
Business of Better Writing Series
Color
Deals with the mastering of spelling as part of improving business writing skills.
Business and Economics
Dist - KYTV **Prod** - KYTV 1983

Mastering the art of cross examination
VHS
Color (PRO C)
$1995.00 purchase _ #FVMACOS
Features Irving Younger as moderator. Teaches cross examination skills using a combination of information, demonstrations and analysis, including Younger's 'Ten Commandments of Cross Examination.' Includes six books, one program planner's guide and 11 videocassettes.
Civics and Political Systems
Dist - NITA **Prod** - NITA 1987

Mastering the art of cross examination series
Features the late law professor Irving Younger in an examination of various types of witnesses and how to cross examine each type. Uses lecture and demonstration for each witness type. Co - produced by the American Bar Association. Eleven - part series includes problem - solving exercise books, a teacher's manual and a planner's guide.

Cross examining the biased witness 31 MIN
Cross examining the child witness 39 MIN
Cross examining the expert accountant witness 52 MIN
Cross examining the expert attorney witness 55 MIN
Cross examining the expert medical witness 35 MIN
Cross examining the eyewitness 52 MIN
Cross examining the hostile witness 52 MIN
Cross examining the law enforcement witness 41 MIN
Cross examining the sympathetic witness 48 MIN
Cross examining the well - prepared witness 59 MIN
Cross examining the witness of the opposite sex 46 MIN
Dist - NITA **Prod** - NITA 1987

Mastering the art of cross examination with Irving Younger series
Cross examining the eyewitness 52 MIN
Dist - AMBAR

Mastering the basics - a guide for the woman golfer 40 MIN
VHS
Color (J H A)
$29.95 purchase _ #KOD412V
Presents LPGA professional instructor and former college coach Annette Thompson with an introduction to the basics of golf for women. Focuses on developing the fundamentals of a good golf swing. Examines the problems most commonly faced by golfers of all ability levels.
Physical Education and Recreation
Dist - CAMV

Mastering the bow and arrow sports 10 MIN
U-matic / VHS / 16mm
Archery series
Color (I)
LC 79-700778
Focuses on mastering the sport of archery.
Physical Education and Recreation
Dist - ATHI **Prod** - ATHI 1978

Mastering the midfield advantage - Part 1
VHS
Winning at soccer with Bobby Charlton series
Color (J H A)
$29.95 purchase _ #SLS017V
Features English soccer coach Bobby Charlton in an introduction to the midfielder position in soccer. Shows that the midfielder must have good all - around skills, including shooting, passing, tackling, and ball control.
Physical Education and Recreation
Dist - CAMV

Mastering the midfield advantage - Part 2
VHS
Winning at soccer with Bobby Charlton series
Color (J H A)
$29.95 purchase _ #SLS012V
Features English soccer coach Bobby Charlton in an introduction to the midfielder position in soccer. Shows that the midfielder must have good all - around skills, including running off the ball, decoy running, creating space, and winning the ball.
Physical Education and Recreation
Dist - CAMV

Mastering the new global economy 10 MIN
VHS / U-matic
Meeting the challenge with Dr Warren Bennis series
Color (C A G)
$250.00 purchase _ #V216
Presents the Drs Warren Bennis and Peter Drucker who conduct a seminar on mastering the new global economy. Gives examples of what has worked in real companies. Focuses on the responsibility of management for providing solutions in a rapidly changing global economy. Part of a series of five - parts.
Business and Economics; Computer Science; Industrial and Technical Education
Dist - BARR **Prod** - HILSU 1992

Mastering traumatic memories I - introduction, interview, abreaction 92 MIN
VHS
Mastering traumatic memories series
Color (PRO)
$150.00 purchase, $50.00 rental _ #D - 228
Presents a comprehensive introduction to techniques for dealing with traumatic experiences of clients. Emphasizes dissociative responses. Illustrates a model preparatory interview and a sample abreactive session. Includes identifying indicators for not doing abreactive work, controlling intense affect, hypnotic induction, ideomotor signals, time distortion, safety for vulnerable alter personalities. Part of a three - part series featuring Dr Judith Peterson, Dr Roberta Sachs and Kathy Steele, RN.
Psychology
Dist - CAVLCD **Prod** - CAVLCD

Mastering traumatic memories II - special issues 73 MIN
VHS
Mastering traumatic memories series
Color (PRO)
$125.00 purchase, $40.00 rental _ #D - 229
Presents a series of role playing vignettes for exploring difficult clinical situations in dealing with clients who have had traumatic experiences. Discusses alter personalities who block therapy, character pathology, spontaneous abreactions, homicidal alter personalities, self multilation, out - of - control behavior. Part of a three - part series featuring Dr Judith Peterson, Dr Roberta Sachs and Kathy Steele, RN.
Psychology
Dist - CAVLCD **Prod** - CAVLCD

Mastering traumatic memories III - advanced techniques 36 MIN
VHS
Mastering traumatic memories series
Color (PRO)
$95.00 purchase, $35.00 rental _ #D - 299A
Demonstrates specific therapeutic techniques for clients who have had traumatic experiences. Includes age regression, hypnotic fractionation, time distortion, managing touch, using the BASK model, cognitive restructuring. Part of a three - part series featuring Dr Judith Peterson, Dr Roberta Sachs and Kathy Steele, RN.
Psychology
Dist - CAVLCD **Prod** - CAVLCD

Mastering traumatic memories series
Presents a three - part series with therapeutic techniques for clients who have had traumatic experiences. Includes the titles 'Introduction, Interview, Abreaction', 'Special Issues', 'Advanced Techniques'. Features Dr Judith Peterson, Dr Roberta Sachs and Kathy Steele, RN.

Mastering traumatic memories I - introduction, interview, abreaction 92 MIN
Mastering traumatic memories II - special issues 73 MIN
Mastering traumatic memories III - advanced techniques 36 MIN
Dist - CAVLCD **Prod** - CAVLCD

Masterpiece 26 MIN
16mm
Color
LC 76-702448
Presents an imaginative look at the future.
Sociology
Dist - CANFDC **Prod** - ATFICO 1975

A Masterpiece of Spanish Painting 25 MIN
16mm
Color (C T)
Shows 26 large panels of a Spanish masterpiece - The Retablo of Ciudad Rodrigo by Fernando Gallego. Gives a stylistic and iconographic explanation of this Hispano - Flemish masterpiece which was presented to the University of Arizona by the Kress Foundation in 1960.
Fine Arts
Dist - UARIZ **Prod** - ATWOOD 1962

Masterpieces at the Met 61 MIN
VHS
Color (S)
$29.95 purchase _ #412 - 9060
Features Philippe de Montebello, Director of the Metropolitan Museum of Art, who leads a tour of masterpieces from the Met's permanent collection. Covers more than five thousand years of world civilization and features paintings such as 'Cypresses' by van Gogh and 'Young Woman With A Water Jug' by Vermeer, artifacts from Egyptian tombs, African wood sculptures, medieval tapestries, and other art objects from around the world.
Fine Arts; Geography - World; History - World
Dist - FI **Prod** - MMOA 1988

Masterpieces of Chinese Art 28 MIN
16mm / U-matic / VHS
Color (H C A)
Exhibits some 50 pieces of Chinese art including ancient bronzes from the Shang dynasty, jade articles spanning some 3,000 years of artistic development and porcelain wares including Ju ware. Covers carved lacquer and calligraphy.
Fine Arts; History - World
Dist - LUF **Prod** - LUF 1974

Masterpieces of the Met 61 MIN
VHS
Color (J)
$29.95 purchase _ #HV - 904
Features the director of the Metropolitan Museum of Art as host. Leads a tour of masterpieces from the Met's permanent collection spanning more than five thousand years of world civiliztion.
Fine Arts
Dist - CRYSP **Prod** - CRYSP

Masterpieces of the Met 61 MIN
Videodisc / VHS
Color (G)
$29.95, $39.95 purchase _ #MAS01, #MAS01LD
Overviews more than 5,000 years of civilization through a tour of masterpieces from the permanent collection of the Metropolitan Museum of Art. Features Philippe de Montebello, Director.
Fine Arts; History - World; Sociology
Dist - HOMVIS **Prod** - MMOA 1990

Master's Figure Drawing Class - Composition - Anatomy, Male and Female 20 MIN
U-matic
Color (H C)
LC 79-706395
Shows the composition and anatomy of male and female figures.
Fine Arts
Dist - SRA **Prod** - SRA 1979

Master's Figure Drawing Class - Female Gesture 20 MIN
U-matic
Color (J H)
LC 79-706389
Shows how to draw the female gesture.
Fine Arts
Dist - SRA **Prod** - SRA 1979

Master's Figure Drawing Class - Female Proportions 20 MIN
U-matic
Color (J H C)
LC 79-706390
Shows how to draw female proportions.
Fine Arts
Dist - SRA **Prod** - SRA 1979

Master's Figure Drawing Class - Female Quick Sketch 20 MIN
U-matic
Color (H C)
LC 79-706393
Shows how to draw a quick sketch of the female figure.
Fine Arts
Dist - SRA **Prod** - SRA 1979

Master's Figure Drawing Class - Male Gesture 20 MIN
U-matic
Color (J H C)
LC 79-706391
Shows how to draw the male gesture.
Fine Arts
Dist - SRA **Prod** - SRA 1979

Master's Figure Drawing Class - Male Proportions 20 MIN
U-matic
Color (H C)
LC 79-706392
Shows how to draw male proportions.
Fine Arts
Dist - SRA **Prod** - SRA 1979

Master's Figure Drawing Class - Male Quick Sketch 20 MIN
U-matic
Color (H C)
LC 79-706394
Shows how to draw a quick sketch of the male figure.
Fine Arts
Dist - SRA **Prod** - SRA 1979

Master's Figure Drawing Class - Review Female, Seated 20 MIN
U-matic
Color (H C)
LC 79-706396
Offers a review of drawing the seated female figure.
Fine Arts
Dist - SRA **Prod** - SRA 1979

Masters in our own house - French and English relations in Canada 30 MIN
VHS
Remaking of Canada - Canadian government and politics in the 1990s 'series
Color (H C G)
$89.95 purchase _ #WLU - 511
Discusses the need of Quebec for political recognition of its distinctness, reasons for the rise of separatism in Quebec, the problems bilingualism and multiculturalism pose for Quebec and the continuing challenge of Quebec nationalism to Canadian unity. Part of a 12 - part series incorporating interviews with Canadian politicians and hosted by Dr John Redekop.
Civics and Political Systems; History - World
Dist - INSTRU **Prod** - TELCOL 1992

Masters of American music series
Lady Day - the many faces of Billie Holiday 60 MIN
Dist - KULTUR

Masters of Animation - North America 85 MIN
VHS
Color (J)
$29.95 purchase _ #HV - 914
Showcases the best in animation from the US and Canada. Interviews Norman McLaren. Presents works by thirteen animators including Lamb, the Hubleys, Disney, Patel and Back.
Fine Arts; Geography - World; Industrial and Technical Education
Dist - CRYSP **Prod** - CRYSP

Masters of animation series
Presents a four - part series representing the achievements of 7000 animation artists from 13 countries. Surveys United States' animation in Volume 1. Volume 2 discusses European animation. Volume 3 looks at the works of Ivanov - Vano, Atamanov, Norstein and others and Volume 4 looks at children's animation in Japan.
Masters of animation - Volume 1 85 MIN
Masters of animation - Volume 2 87 MIN
Masters of animation - Volume 3 113 MIN
Masters of animation - Volume 4 86 MIN
Dist - CAMV

Masters of animation series
Eastern Europe - Vol III 113 MIN
Great Britain and Western Europe - Vol II 87 MIN
Japan and Computer Animation - Vol IV 56 MIN
North America - Vol I 85 MIN
Dist - FI

Masters of animation - Volume 1 85 MIN
VHS
Masters of animation series
Color (J H C G)
$39.95 purchase _ #HVS60V
Discusses American animators - Chuck Jones, Barrie Nelson and Leo Salkin. Examines excerpts of animation from Walt Disney productions. Part of a four - part series representing the achievements of 7000 animation artists from 13 countries.
Fine Arts; Industrial and Technical Education
Dist - CAMV

Masters of animation - Volume 2 87 MIN
VHS
Masters of animation series
Color (J H C G)
$39.95 purchase _ #HVS61V
Discusses the role of European animators in establishing animation as a sophisticated form of entertainment. Part of a four - part series representing the achievements of 7000 animation artists from 13 countries.
Fine Arts; Industrial and Technical Education
Dist - CAMV

Masters of animation - Volume 3 113 MIN
VHS
Masters of animation series
Color (J H C G)
$39.95 purchase _ #HVS62V
Covers the works of animation greats Invanov - Vano, Atamatov, Norstein and others. Part of a four - part series representing the achievements of 7000 animation artists from 13 countries.
Fine Arts; Industrial and Technical Education
Dist - CAMV

Masters of animation - Volume 4 86 MIN
VHS
Masters of animation series
Color (J H C G)
$39.95 purchase _ #HVS63V
Discusses Japanese animation and noted animation programs for children. Part of a four - part series representing the achievements of 7000 animation artists from 13 countries.
Fine Arts; Industrial and Technical Education
Dist - CAMV

The Masters of Disaster 30 MIN
U-matic / VHS / 16mm
Color (I)
Shows how a caring, creative teacher motivates black elementary school kids to organize a championship chess team.
Education; Sociology
Dist - IU **Prod** - IU 1985

Masters of Hang Gliding 28 MIN
16mm
Color
LC 79-700394
Shows hang gliding as it is practiced in various parts of the United States and at the Master of Hang Gliding Championship at Grandfather Mountain, North Carolina.
Physical Education and Recreation
Dist - MORTON **Prod** - MORTON 1978

Masters of inner space 26 MIN
VHS / U-matic
Color (J H G)
$280.00, $330.00 purchase, $60.00 rental
Explores the design features of fishes. Gives an intimate view of the way fishes are equipped for life in the ocean, with their special kind of physical make - up, use of color and sensory equipment.
Science - Natural; Science - Physical
Dist - NDIM **Prod** - TVNZ 1992

Masters of Modern Sculpture, Pt 1 - the Pioneers 58 MIN
VHS / U-matic
Color
Introduces the major sculptors of the 20th century and looks closely at their works. Includes Rodin, Degas, Rosso, Bourdelle, Maillol, Lehmbruck, Matisse, Picasso, Lipchitz, Laurens, Epstein, Boccioni, Duchamp - Villon, Gonzales and Brancusi.
Fine Arts
Dist - BLACKW **Prod** - BLACKW

Masters of Modern Sculpture, Pt 3 - the New World 58 MIN
U-matic / VHS
Color
Introduces the major sculptors of the 20th century and looks closely at their works. Includes David Smith, Louise Nevelson, David Hare, Ibram Lassaw, Theodore Roszak, Herbert Ferber, Louise Baurgeois, John Chamberlain, Mark Di Suvero, Isamu Noguchi, George Rickey, Barnett Newman, Tony Smith, George Segal, Donald Judd, Claes Oldenburg, Robert Morris, Richard Serra, Carl Andre, Edward Kienholz, Christo, Michael Heizer and Robert Smithson.
Fine Arts
Dist - BLACKW **Prod** - BLACKW

Masters of Modern Sculpture, Pt 2 - Beyond Cubism 58 MIN
U-matic / VHS
Color
Introduces the major sculptors of the 20th century and looks closely at their works. Includes Vladimir Tatlin, Naum Gabo, Antoine Pevsner, Marcel Duchamp, the Dada Artists, Man Ray, Joan Miro, Jean Arp, Max Ernst, Alexander Calder, Alberto Giacometti, Henry Moore, Barbara Hepworth, Germaine Richier, Cesar, Gunther Uecker, Heinz Mack, Otto Piene, Joseph Beuys, Arman, Yves Klein, Daniel Spoerri, Jean Tinguely, Anthony Caro and Gilbert & George.
Fine Arts
Dist - BLACKW **Prod** - BLACKW

Masters of Modern Sculpture Series no 1
The Pioneers 59 MIN
The Pioneers - Pt 1 30 MIN
The Pioneers - Pt 2 29 MIN
Dist - BLACKW

Masters of Modern Sculpture Series no 3
The New World 59 MIN
New World, the, Pt 1 30 MIN
New World, the, Pt 2 29 MIN
Dist - BLACKW

Masters of Modern Sculpture Series Pt 2
Beyond Cubism, Pt 2 29 MIN
Dist - BLACKW

Masters of modern sculpture series
Beyond Cubism 59 MIN
Beyond Cubism , Pt 1 30 MIN
Dist - BLACKW

Masters of Our Musical Heritage 8 MIN
U-matic / VHS
Color
Contains eight half - hour videotapes on the history of music.
Fine Arts
Dist - TELSTR **Prod** - TELSTR

Masters of Tap 61 MIN
VHS
Color (S)
$39.95 purchase _ #086 - 9006
Brings together three of the world's greatest tap dancers for a sentimental journey through the history of the art form. Features Charles 'Honi' Coles, Chuck Green and Will Gaines demonstrating their mastery and historical footage of other tap greats.
Fine Arts; Physical Education and Recreation
Dist - FI **Prod** - IFPAL 1988

Masters of the Congo Jungle 88 MIN
U-matic / VHS / 16mm
Color (J)
Looks at African flora, fauna and native life.

Geography - World
Dist - PHENIX **Prod** - STORCH 1975

Masters of the Wok 29 MIN
16mm / U-matic / VHS
Taste of China Series
Color (J)
History - World; Home Economics
Dist - UCEMC **Prod** - UCEMC 1984

Masterworks of Painting 51 MIN
U-matic / VHS
Color (A)
Introduces the principles of great painting through the art of European and American masters. Views the great movements up to the recent past.
Fine Arts
Dist - SRA **Prod** - SRA

Mastery at Sea 30 MIN
16mm
B&W
LC FIE65-103
Traces the development of modern seapower, using historical footage showing great batteships from World War I, aircraft carriers, submarines and missile - bearing vessels, including Polaris submarines.
Civics and Political Systems
Dist - USDS **Prod** - NATO

The Mastery of Space 58 MIN
16mm
Color (P)
LC FIE64-73
Traces the development of Project Mercury and the manin - space program. Documents the flight of Freedom 7 and the earth orbital flight of Friendship 7 on February 20, 1962. Reports briefly on Project Gemini, Apollo and Saturn booster.
Science; Science - Physical
Dist - NASA **Prod** - NASA 1962

Mastic asphalt - Part one of Unit F - Cassette 11 58 MIN
VHS
Building crafts - the teaching and learning process series
Color; PAL (J H IND)
PdS29.50 purchase
Features part of an 18 - part series which observes teaching and learning in a variety of workshop situations. Includes such skills as plumbing, brickwork, carpentry, painting and decorating.
Industrial and Technical Education
Dist - EMFVL

Mastic asphalt - the students' attempts - Part two of Unit F - Cassette 12 41 MIN
VHS
Building crafts - the teaching and learning process series
Color; PAL (J H IND)
PdS29.50 purchase
Features part of an 18 - part series which observes teaching and learning in a variety of workshop situations. Includes such skills as plumbing, brickwork, carpentry, painting and decorating.
Industrial and Technical Education
Dist - EMFVL

Mastoidectomy and Tympanoplasty
VHS / U-matic
Color
Shows how the normal ear works, how chronic middle ear infections can lead to ruptured ear drum or begin to invade and destroy bone.
Science - Natural
Dist - MIFE **Prod** - MIFE

Mastri - a Balinese Woman 18 MIN
16mm
Asian Neighbors - Indonesia Series
Color (H C A)
LC 75-703583
Explores the lives of a Balinese couple in their village. Contrasts their day - to - day activities and religious beliefs with the Bali known to tourists.
Geography - World; Social Science; Sociology
Dist - AVIS **Prod** - FLMAUS 1975

Masturbation - Men 18 MIN
U-matic / VHS
Color (C A)
Men between the ages of 20 and 50 share their patterns of masturbation. Provides insight and reassurance about a topic rarely discussed openly by men.
Health and Safety; Psychology
Dist - MMRC **Prod** - MMRC

A Masturbatory story 15 MIN
U-matic / VHS / 16mm
Color (J H)
Appraises and explains the needs and desires involved with male masturbation. Destroys the fallacies that have surrounded masturbation for centuries.
Guidance and Counseling; Health and Safety; Psychology
Dist - PEREN **Prod** - DOOMOR

Masuo Ikeda - Printmaker 14 MIN
U-matic / VHS / 16mm
Color (J H)
LC 73-702193
Features Masuo Ikeda, a modern Japanese artist who lives in New York. Observes as he creates a color print from copper plates and explains how he finds ideas and how he creates his prints. Shows his procedure and tools in close - up detail as he makes the plates, pulls proofs, checks and corrects the proofs, makes corrections on the plates and pulls the finished prints.
Fine Arts
Dist - AIMS **Prod** - ACI 1973

Matador 50 MIN
U-matic / VHS
Color (C) (SPANISH)
$299.00, $199.00 purchase _ #AD - 964
Looks at bullfighting in Spain. Examines the breeding and training of bulls, the societal implications of the pursuit, and an actual bullfight in Seville.
Foreign Language; Geography - World; History - World; Physical Education and Recreation; Sociology
Dist - FOTH **Prod** - FOTH

The Match factory girl 70 MIN
16mm / 35mm
Color (G) (FINNISH WITH ENGLISH SUBTITLES)
Portrays the bleak existence of Iris, a young factory worker in modern day Finland. Reveals that Iris is cruelly ignored at home, at work and in the dreary nightclubs she frequents. A new red dress complicates her situation when it leads to a one - night stand with a business man who leaves her pregnant. Scorned by her family and one time lover, Iris mixes rat poison with water and... Directed by Aki Kaurismaki.
Fine Arts; Sociology
Dist - KINOIC

Match girl 25 MIN
16mm
Color (G)
$32.00 rental
Dramatizes the fantasy experiences of an aspiring young actress. Features Andy Warhol and Vivian Kurz. Adapted from the story by Hans Christian Anderson. Music by the Rolling Stones. Produced by Andrew Meyer.
Fine Arts; Literature and Drama
Dist - CANCIN

The Match that started my fire 19 MIN
VHS / 16mm
Color (G)
$60.00 rental, $295.00 purchase
Presents an experimental comedy in which the joy of sexual pleasure is discovered and experienced by women in their childhood and early teens. Features women telling their hilarious anecdotes of climbing a rope, descending a slide, being stung by insects and so forth - all of which were 'the match that started their fire.' Celebrates the physical world and female orgasm through a visual montage of images evoking a world of 1960s kitsch and nostalgia, with occasional darker hints of taboo and transgression. By Cathy Cook.
Fine Arts; Sociology
Dist - WMEN

Matchbox menagerie - Corfu, Greece 24 MIN
VHS / 16mm
Amateur naturalist series
Color (I J H C G)
$495.00, $195.00 purchase
Discovers a cache of stagnant water in an overgrown garden in Corfu, Greece. Reveals a world of microscopic life. Lizards are caught and a mealworm colony is established to feed them. A cage is built to house caterpillars. Part of a 13 - part series featuring a naturalist and a zoologist, Gerald and Lee Durrell, on field trips to different habitats.
Geography - World; Science - Natural
Dist - LANDMK **Prod** - LANDMK 1988

Matches 9 MIN
16mm / U-matic / VHS
Color (P I)
LC 70-713213
Uses the story about two children who find a book of matches near their club house to demonstrate the need for safety rules and the exercise of individual responsibility.
Guidance and Counseling; Health and Safety
Dist - ALTSUL **Prod** - BELLDA 1971

Matching - Greater than, Less than 15 MIN
U-matic
Measure Up Series
Color (P)
Explains how to match numerals to given sets of objects with up to nine elements. Shows the order of the numbers one to nine.
Mathematics
Dist - GPN **Prod** - WCETTV 1977

Matching leadership style to the situation 60 MIN
VHS
Color (A PRO IND)
$750.00 purchase, $250.00 rental
Uses an interactive video format to apply leadership skills to a variety of situations. Demonstrates both appropriate and inappropriate leadership styles.
Business and Economics; Guidance and Counseling; Psychology
Dist - VLEARN

Matching Offset Holes - Face Plate and 4 - Jaw Chuck 15 MIN
VHS / U-matic
Machining and the Operation of Machine Tools, Module 3 - 'Intermediate Engine Lathe Series
Color (IND)
Industrial and Technical Education
Dist - LEIKID **Prod** - LEIKID

Matching People and Positions 10 MIN
U-matic / 35mm strip
Assessing Employee Potential Series
Color
Shows how employee evaluation can be made easier and more effective through careful analysis of job requirement and the qualifications of the person being considered.
Business and Economics; Psychology
Dist - RESEM **Prod** - RESEM

Matching Plaids in Darts and Seams by Slip Stitching 29 MIN
Videoreel / VT2
Sewing Skills - Tailoring Series
Color
Features Mrs Ruth Hickman demonstrating how to match plaids in darts and seams by slip stitching.
Home Economics
Dist - PBS **Prod** - KRMATV

Matching Seams and Pleats in Plaid 29 MIN
Videoreel / VT2
Sewing Skills - Tailoring Series
Color
Features Mrs Ruth Hickman showing how to match seams and pleats in plaid.
Home Economics
Dist - PBS **Prod** - KRMATV

Matching Shoulders and Corners on the Lathe 15 MIN
VHS / U-matic
Machining and the Operation of Machine Tools, Module 3 - 'Intermediate Engine Lathe Series
Color (IND)
Industrial and Technical Education
Dist - LEIKID **Prod** - LEIKID

Matching the Computer to Your Curriculum
VHS / Software / Kit / U-matic
New Horizons Series
(PRO)
$1595 series purchase
Provides teachers with strategies and steps for gradually introducing the computer into classrooms.
Computer Science
Dist - AITECH **Prod** - ALASDE 1986

Matching Theory - the Marriage Theorem 46 MIN
16mm
MAA Mathematics Series
B&W (C A)
LC 74-702787
Contains an extended introduction to the marriage theorem and some of its elementary consequences, shifting to a proof of the theorem and a separate result, Sperner's Theorem.
Mathematics
Dist - MLA **Prod** - MAA 1974

Matching Up 4 MIN
U-matic / VHS / 16mm
Magic Moments, Unit 5 - Let's Play Series
Color (K P I)
LC 73-705939
Uses a split - screen technique to match pairs of feet with the rest of the body.
English Language
Dist - EBEC **Prod** - EBEC 1969

Matching your needs with funding source interests - organizing staff and developing materials 55 MIN
VHS
Winning grants series
Color (G A)
$1,795 member purchase, $1,995 non member purchase
Presents seminars on succesful grant writing. Focuses on organizing staff and materials to tailor funding source information to applicant needs. First of ten segments.

Business and Economics; Education
Dist - GPN **Prod** - UNEBR

The Matchlock Gun
35mm strip / VHS / Cassette
Newbery Award - Winners Series
Color (I)
$66.00, $14.00 purchase
English Language; Literature and Drama
Dist - PELLER

The Matchseller 13 MIN
16mm
Color (G)
$20.00 rental
Conjures up a fairytale made in England. Assembles a 1950s carnival rock 'n' roll background in which a young bride uses a socerer's charm to procure a husband. A Laurie Lewis production.
Fine Arts; Literature and Drama
Dist - CANCIN

Mate Location by a Moth 5 MIN
U-matic / VHS
Color (J H C)
Shows how a male moth can locate a female moth in complete darkness by scent and touch. Provides a useful case study of scientific method, and illustrates how a special camera was used that amplified dim light to avoid disturbing the moths.
Industrial and Technical Education; Science - Natural
Dist - EDMI **Prod** - EDMI 1977

Mate selection and marriage readiness 30 MIN
U-matic / VHS
Family portrait - a study of contemporary lifestyles series; Lesson 9
Color (C A)
Discusses the selection of a mate and the factors governing that decision. Covers exogamy and endogamy and the process of mate selection as a multi - stage development. Includes values that figure in marriage readiness such as age, education, religion and personality.
Sociology
Dist - CDTEL **Prod** - SCCON

Mateo 17 MIN
16mm / U-matic / VHS
Color (I J H)
LC 81-701032
Relates the story of a young farm boy who runs away from home and goes to a large city where he learns some valuable, but painful, lessons before he is reunited with his parents.
Fine Arts; Foreign Language; Guidance and Counseling; Sociology
Dist - PHENIX **Prod** - PHENIX 1980

Material Handling 15 MIN
VHS / 16mm
(H C A)
$24.95 purchase _ #CS174
Describes the skills involved in material handling and presents interviews with people involved in the field.
Guidance and Counseling
Dist - RMIBHF **Prod** - RMIBHF

Material Handling 15 MIN
VHS / U-matic / BETA
Career Success Series
(H C A)
$29.95 _ #MX174
Portrays occupations in materials handling by reviewing required abilities and interviewing people employed in this field. Shows anxieties and rewards involved in pursuing a career in material handling.
Education; Guidance and Counseling; Industrial and Technical Education
Dist - CAMV **Prod** - CAMV

Material handling equipment for bulk solids 60 MIN
VHS
Equipment operations series
Color (PRO)
$600.00 - $1500.00 purchase _ #OTMHE
Introduces material handling concepts, types of major equipment, associated equipment and measuring systems. Covers safety precautions, physical characteristics of material to be handled and proper selection of equipment. Part of a twenty - part series on equipment operation. Includes ten textbooks and an instructor guide to support four hours of instruction.
Business and Economics; Civics and Political Systems; Health and Safety; Industrial and Technical Education; Mathematics; Psychology; Sociology
Dist - NUSTC **Prod** - NUSTC

Material handling of bulk liquids 60 MIN
VHS
Equipment operations series
Color (PRO)
$600.00 - $1500.00 purchase _ #OTMHL
Covers moving bulk liquids from the plant or refinery into rail and tank cars and barges. Emphasizes the safe handling of hazardous materials and following the safety regulations established by governmental regulatory agencies. Part of a twenty - part series on equipment operation. Includes ten textbooks and an instructor guide to support four hours of instruction.
Business and Economics; Civics and Political Systems; Health and Safety; Industrial and Technical Education; Mathematics; Psychology; Sociology
Dist - NUSTC **Prod** - NUSTC

Material handling of bulk solids 60 MIN
VHS
Equipment operations series
Color (PRO)
$600.00 - $1500.00 purchase _ #OTMHS
Covers moving bulk solids from the plant into rail and tank cars and barges and vice versa. Considers the equipment used for loading, unloading, conveying, weighing and measuring bulk solids. Emphasizes the safe handling of hazardous materials and following safety regulations established by governmental agencies. Part of a twenty - part series on equipment operation. Includes ten textbooks and an instructor guide to support four hours of instruction.
Business and Economics; Civics and Political Systems; Health and Safety; Industrial and Technical Education; Mathematics; Psychology; Sociology
Dist - NUSTC **Prod** - NUSTC

Material Handling Principles in Transportation 20 MIN
16mm
B&W
Shows the deplorable waste of money, time and manhours when material handling and loading prqctices are faulty. Emphasizes the importance of using the right equipment to transport items. Demonstrates right and wrong methods of handling cargo.
Social Science
Dist - USNAC **Prod** - USDD 1960

Material Movement and Inventory Cost 60 MIN
VHS / BETA
Manufacturing Series
(IND)
Teaches how to translate costs associated with material movement and inventory into their financial equivalent.
Business and Economics
Dist - COMSRV **Prod** - COMSRV 1986

Material Removal 30 MIN
U-matic / VHS
Color
Discusses the elctrochemical discharge machining methods as they are applied to exotic metals. Explains the advantages and disadvantages of electrochemical grinding and machining.
Business and Economics; Industrial and Technical Education
Dist - SME **Prod** - CONNTV

Material Removal - Principles 20 MIN
U-matic / VHS
Engineering Crafts Series
Color (H C A)
Industrial and Technical Education
Dist - FI **Prod** - BBCTV 1981

Material safety data sheets 12 MIN
VHS / U-matic / BETA
Color (IND G A)
$455.00 purchase, $125.00 rental _ #MAT002
Educates employees on the use of Material Safety Data Sheets - MSDS. Teaches line - level employees where to look on an MSDS for specific information. Explains the terminology and shows how to use MSDS information for safety purposes.
Health and Safety; Psychology
Dist - ITF **Prod** - CREMED 1991

Material safety data sheets - IX ; Rev. 14 MIN
8mm cartridge / VHS / BETA / U-matic
Chemsafe 2000 series
Color; CC; PAL (IND G)
$395.00 purchase, $175.00 rental _ #CS2 - 900
Offers a user's guide to the MSDS. Includes explanations of common scientific terms to assist employees in understandingthe health and physical hazards of chemicals. Explains graphically each part of the MSDS in an easy - to - remember, step - by - step format. Includes a glossary of important terms. Part of a nine - part series providing comprehensive training in chemical safety. Includes a trainer's manual and ten participant handouts.
Health and Safety; Psychology; Science - Physical
Dist - BNA **Prod** - BNA 1994

Material Selection
VHS
Advanced Woodworking Series
(C G)
$59.00 _ CA171
Shows how to select the proper materials appropriate to the project.
Industrial and Technical Education
Dist - AAVIM **Prod** - AAVIM 1989

The Material that can do almost anything, 1950 - 1964 21 MIN
16mm
Twelve decades of concrete in American architecture series
Color
Industrial and Technical Education
Dist - PRTLND **Prod** - PRTLND 1965

Material world 50 MIN
VHS
Look series
Color (A)
PdS99 purchase _ Unavailable in the USA
Describes how Miyake, Versace, and Lacroix cut their cloth. Strips away the glitz and glamor of the fashion business to look behind the scenes. Explores the mystique of the designer label and debates the meaning of style. Reveals the mysteries of material and unveils the interdependence between the fashion industry, the media, financiers, and the consumer. Part of a six-part series.
Home Economics
Dist - BBCENE

Materials 15 MIN
16mm / U-matic / VHS
Craft, Design and Technology Series
Color (I J)
Points out that of all the materials suitable for workshops, plastic is more versatile than wood, metal or clay, even though a large quantitiy of energy is required to extract each. Plastic can be produced by chemists from petroleum so that it possesses properties designed to suit specific applications.
Business and Economics; Sociology
Dist - MEDIAG **Prod** - THAMES 1983

Materials - and all that stuff 30 MIN
VHS
Calico pie series
Color (C A T)
$69.95 purchase
Presents part 12 of a 16 - part telecourse for teachers who work with children ages three to five. Discusses materials that can be used in the classroom. Hosted by Dr Carolyn Dorrell, an early childhood specialist.
Education; Psychology
Dist - SCETV **Prod** - SCETV 1983

Materials Handling
VHS / U-matic
Pulp and Paper Training - Thermo - Mechanical Pulping Series
Color (IND)
Covers transport and handling of chips in a typical system from the chip receiving end through to the chip bin. Demonstrates different methods of conveying, such as belt, screw, chip washing, safety arrangements and operating variables.
Industrial and Technical Education
Dist - LEIKID **Prod** - LEIKID

Materials Handling 12 MIN
VHS / U-matic
Color
Shows how to forklift, dolly and hand - truck materials from place to place and how to move materials without getting hurt.
Health and Safety
Dist - FILCOM **Prod** - FILCOM

Materials handling 16 MIN
VHS / U-matic
Industrial safety series
Color (IND)
Discusses how to load pallets and trucks, safe use of two - wheel hand trucks and forklift trucks, safe use of gravity conveyors and power conveyors and working on a hook - on team. Includes working with different types of ladders and mobile scaffolding.
Health and Safety; Industrial and Technical Education
Dist - LEIKID **Prod** - LEIKID

Materials handling and low back pain 29 MIN
U-matic / VHS
Color (IND C G)
$395.00 purchase, $80.00 rental _ #C901 - VI - 058
Explores new approaches to improving safety in the workplace and recognizes worker input as a key element in creating optimal work environments. Instructs on how to exercise, methods of preventing and coping with the physiological and psychological manifestations of pain. Produced by William Fletcher, Callisto Productions, Cleveland.
Health and Safety; Psychology
Dist - HSCIC

Materials handling and packaging in logistics 30 MIN
VHS
Business logistics series
Color (G C)
$200.00 purchase, $20.50 rental _ #34967
Examines materials handling and packaging in logistics. Part of a 30 - part series on business logistics which deals with movement and storage of raw and finished products, and with managerial activities important for effective control of these operations. Interviews logistics managers of major US corporations and transportation companies. Uses on - site segments to demonstrate logistical carrier operations. Features program author Dr John Coyle.
Business and Economics
Dist - PSU **Prod** - WPSXTV 1987

Materials handling and storage 10 MIN
VHS
Supervisors' development program series
Color (IND)
$280.00 purchase _ #15492 - 2222
Explains the importance of safety practices in materials handling and storage. Features William Shatner as host. Part of a 13 - part series on employee safety which stresses the four - step SAFE model - Search for hazards, Assess risks, Find solutions, Enforce solutions.
Business and Economics; Health and Safety; Industrial and Technical Education; Psychology
Dist - NSC **Prod** - NSC

Materials Handling Equipment Operation - Gantry Truck and Warehouse Cranes 21 MIN
16mm
B&W
LC FIE55-206
Shows the uses and operations of gantry truck and warehouse cranes and discusses safety precautions.
Health and Safety; Industrial and Technical Education
Dist - USNAC **Prod** - USN 1953

Materials - Key to Progress 17 MIN
16mm
Color
LC FIE59-226
Portrays the over - all technical mission of the USAF materials research and development program and emphasizes the important contributions of industry and science to its progress.
Civics and Political Systems
Dist - USNAC **Prod** - USDD 1958

Materials management 30 MIN
VHS
Business logistics series
Color (G C)
$200.00 purchase, $20.50 rental _ #34960
Examines materials management. Part of a 30 - part series on business logistics which deals with movement and storage of raw and finished products, and with managerial activities important for effective control of these operations. Interviews logistics managers of major US corporations and transportation companies. Uses on - site segments to demonstrate logistical carrier operations. Features program author Dr John Coyle.
Business and Economics
Dist - PSU **Prod** - WPSXTV 1987

Materials revolution 30 MIN
VHS
Perspectives - industrial design - series
Color; PAL; NTSC (G)
PdS90, PdS105 purchase
Reveals that, over 50 years ago, a team of British scientists invented terylene, the precursor of now ubiquitous human - made materials. Shows that current research is engaged in the development of processes and products that do not harm the environment.
Fine Arts; Science - Natural
Dist - CFLVIS **Prod** - LONTVS

Materials - Session 5
VHS
English as a second language - tutor training series
Color (G T PRO)
$70.00 purchase _ #31050
Demonstrates common materials used as props in language teaching. Concentrates on the specifics of using experience approach with non - literates - telling time, counting money, job - related and other everyday needs using the tutoring approaches presented. Shows how to use the ESLOA assessment. Fifth of seven videos that support the English as a Second Language - Tutor Training Kit.
Education; English Language
Dist - LITERA

Materials Testing 10 MIN
U-matic / VHS
Manufacturing Materials and Processes Series
Color
Covers types of metal testing.
Industrial and Technical Education
Dist - WFVTAE **Prod** - GE

Maternal Behavior in the Female Rat and its Modification by Cortical Injury 10 MIN
16mm
B&W
Presents studies of animal behavior from the American Museum of Natural History in New York.
Science - Natural
Dist - PSUPCR **Prod** - PSUPCR

Maternal Deprivation in Young Children 30 MIN
16mm
B&W (C T)
The first part shows some of the disorders caused by prolonged maternal deprivation. The second part shows the progress of children under psychotherapy.
Psychology; Sociology
Dist - NYU **Prod** - ASSM 1953

Maternal filigree 23 MIN
16mm
Color (G)
$45.00 rental
Explores development of psychic partners in cycles of sexuality, birth and death. Weaves symbolism with archaic imagery into a kind of fluid dance. Second in a loose trilogy by Sandra Davis.
Fine Arts
Dist - CANCIN

Maternity Hospital Routine 15 MIN
16mm
Family Life Education and Human Growth Series
Color (J)
Shows the hospital maternity ward and labor room including pre - delivery tests, the work of doctors and nurses during delivery, methods of baby identification and the care given in the recovery room.
Health and Safety; Sociology
Dist - SF **Prod** - MORLAT 1967

Mates, Martyrs and Masters 27 MIN
U-matic / VHS / 16mm
Color (A)
Dramatizes methods of improving performance by not letting emotional needs conflict with supervisory responsibilities. Includes establishing priorities, delegating tasks, taking risks and initiating change.
Guidance and Counseling; Sociology
Dist - SEVDIM **Prod** - SEVDIM

Matewan 130 MIN
35mm / 16mm
Color (G)
Portrays a real - life incident that occurred during the savage union industry struggles in the early 1920s. Delves deeply into the moral and social issues that helped forge the American labor movement of the early twentieth century. Based on a tragic showdown between West Virginia miners and management known as the Matewan Massacre. Produced by Peggy Rajski and Maggie Renzi; written and directed by John Sayles. Contact distributor for price.
Business and Economics; Civics and Political Systems; Fine Arts; History - United States; Social Science
Dist - OCTOBF

Math 29 MIN
VHS / 16mm
Breaking the Unseen Barrier Series
Color (C)
$180.00, $240.00 purchase _ #269704
Demonstrates through dramatic vignettes effective teaching strategies to help students with learning disabilities reach their full potential. Offers insight into integrating learning disabled students into the classroom. 'Math' focuses on Wayne, grade one and bright, who has only a vague notion of counting and difficulty determining the size of objects. Without assistance, this math learning disability will create problems for Wayne as he grows older. Nick is a high school student who has grasped many of the basic concepts of math but when questions are framed in word or story format, Nick struggles to find the answers. Explores strategies for helping students like Wayne and Nick.
Education; Mathematics; Psychology
Dist - AITECH **Prod** - ACCESS 1988

Math - a moving experience
VHS
Color (P)
$39.95 purchase _ #245 - 25632
Allows young children to explore counting, shapes, and vocabulary through classroom experiences integrating mathematics, movement, and imagination. Enhances creativity, spontaniety, and individuality, and develops a wholistic learning environment for both teachers and children.
Mathematics; Physical Education and Recreation
Dist - AAHPER **Prod** - AAHPER

Math - all Skill Areas and Problem Types 120 MIN
U-matic / VHS
SAT Exam Preparation Series
Color
Education; Mathematics
Dist - KRLSOF **Prod** - KRLSOF 1985

Math and spell well flash cards
VHS
Color (P I)
$94.90 purchase _ #CZ300
Presents two programs which teach basic math and spelling skills. Includes eight videocassettes.
English Language; Mathematics
Dist - SIV

Math and young children - Part I 30 MIN
VHS
Calico pie series
Color (C A T)
$69.95 purchase
Presents part seven of a 16 - part telecourse for teachers who work with children ages three to five. Discusses how math can be taught in the classroom. Hosted by Dr Carolyn Dorrell, an early childhood specialist.
Education; Psychology
Dist - SCETV **Prod** - SCETV 1983

Math and young children - Part II 30 MIN
VHS
Calico pie series
Color (C A T)
$69.95 purchase
Presents part eight of a 16 - part telecourse for teachers who work with children ages three to five. Discusses how math can be taught in the classroom. Hosted by Dr Carolyn Dorrell, an early childhood specialist.
Education; Psychology
Dist - SCETV **Prod** - SCETV 1983

Math Anxiety 29 MIN
16mm
Color
LC 81-700538
Highlights a course for math - anxious adults.
Education; Mathematics
Dist - EDC **Prod** - JASON 1980

Math Anxiety - We Beat it, So Can You 29 MIN
U-matic / VHS
Color
Focus on math anxiety experienced by students of all ages. Discusses the nature and pervasive effects of math anxiety. Demonstrates one method to control the anxiety through a supportive, non - threatening teaching style. Shows scenes from a math anxiety classroom.
Education; Mathematics
Dist - EDC **Prod** - EDC

Math country series
Hot and heavy - temperature and weight 14 MIN
Dist - AITECH

Math Cycle Series
Addition facts 16 MIN
Area 15 MIN
Checking addition and subtraction 16 MIN
Computers 16 MIN
Distance, weight and volume 15 MIN
Division 16 MIN
Division extended 15 MIN
Division facts 15 MIN
Division with remainders 15 MIN
Equality and inequality 16 MIN
Estimation - Rounding to Tens 15 MIN
Fractions 16 MIN
Graphs 16 MIN
Introduction to Decimals 15 MIN
Measurement - introduction to distance mass and volume 16 MIN
Measurement - Time and Temperature 16 MIN
Money 16 MIN
Multiplication 16 MIN
Multiplication Facts 15 MIN
Multiplication Without Renaming 15 MIN
Parts and Wholes 16 MIN
Perimeter 15 MIN
Place Value 15 MIN
Place Value Extended 15 MIN
Renaming in Addition 16 MIN
Renaming in Addition Extended 15 MIN
Renaming in Multiplication 15 MIN
Renaming in Subtraction 16 MIN
Renaming in Subtraction Extended 15 MIN
Review and Summary 15 MIN
Subtraction Facts 16 MIN
Dist - GPN

Math factory - geometry series
Points and line segments 15 MIN
Dist - GPN

Math factory, module 5 - fractions series
Fooling with fractions 15 MIN
Dist - GPN

Math Factory, Module I - Sets Series
Introducing Sets 15 MIN
Joining Sets - Addition 15 MIN
Nonequivalent Sets - Inequalities 15 MIN
Separating Sets 15 MIN
Dist - GPN

Math factory, Module II - geometry series
Angles and other figures 15 MIN
Circles 15 MIN
Curves 15 MIN
The Great game contest 15 MIN
Dist - GPN

Math factory, module iii - number patterns series
Addition with Zero and One 15 MIN
Attention to tens 15 MIN
Beginning Concepts in Multiplication 15 MIN
Building number patterns 15 MIN
Place Value, Face Value 15 MIN
Dist - GPN

Math Factory - Module IV - Problem Solving Series
Addition of Tens and Ones 15 MIN
Renaming in Addition 15 MIN
Writing Number Sentences 15 MIN
Dist - GPN

Math Factory, Module V - Fractions Series
Fraction Action 15 MIN
Fraction Magic 15 MIN
Presenting One - Third 15 MIN
What's Half, What's a Fourth 15 MIN
Dist - GPN

Math Factory, Module VI - Money Series
Dollar scholar 15 MIN
Money Business 15 MIN
Solving Money Problems 15 MIN
What Buys more 15 MIN
Dist - GPN

Math factory - problem solving series
Relating multiplication and division 15 MIN
Dist - GPN

Math factory series
Set numeration 15 MIN
Sets of coins 15 MIN
Subtraction of tens and ones 15 MIN
Dist - GPN

Math flash cards
VHS
Color (P I)
$49.95 purchase _ #CZ100
Teaches basic skills in mathematics - addition, subtraction, multiplication and division. Includes four videocassettes.
Mathematics
Dist - SIV

Math for Beginners Series
Addition 12 MIN
Division 12 MIN
Multiplication 12 MIN
Subtraction 12 MIN
Dist - CORF

Math for life series
Presents a four - part series which reviews basic mathematics skills. Focuses on the daily application of these skills. Covers fractions, decimals, percents, and consumer math. Includes a study guide for each part.
Consumer math 120 MIN
Decimals 120 MIN
Fractions 240 MIN
Math for life series 600 MIN
Percents 120 MIN
Dist - CAMV

Math for Medications 7 MIN
U-matic / VHS
Color
Focuses on the mathematics necessary for pharmacists and physicians.
Health and Safety; Mathematics
Dist - TELSTR **Prod** - TELSTR

Math for the Construction Trades
VHS / 35mm strip
Color
$185.00 purchase _ #PX30700 filmstrips, $185.00 purchase _ #PX30700V
Describes how to estimate concrete foundations, subfloors and stair treads, and sheathing.
Education; Industrial and Technical Education; Mathematics
Dist - CAREER **Prod** - CAREER

Math Makers One Series
Capacity 15 MIN
Decimals 15 MIN
Division 15 MIN
Graphing 15 MIN
Line Segments 15 MIN
Mass 15 MIN
Money 15 MIN
Multiplication 15 MIN
Problem Solving 15 MIN
Temperature 15 MIN
Transformations 15 MIN
Dist - TVOTAR

Math Makers Two Series
Angles 15 MIN
Area 15 MIN
Length 15 MIN
Math Review 1 15 MIN
Math Review 2 15 MIN
Number Properties 15 MIN
Patterns 15 MIN
Perimeter 15 MIN
Symmetry 15 MIN
Tessellations 15 MIN
Three - D Shapes 15 MIN
Two - D Shapes 15 MIN
Volume 15 MIN
Dist - TVOTAR

Math Matters Series Blue Module
Fractions I 15 MIN
Fractions II 15 MIN
Metric System - Linear Measure 15 MIN
Metric System - Weight and Capacity 15 MIN
Quadrilaterals 15 MIN
Triangles 15 MIN
Dist - AITECH

Math Matters Series Green Module
Percent 14 MIN
Probability I 14 MIN
Probability II 14 MIN
Unit Pricing 15 MIN
Dist - AITECH

Math matters series
Area I 14 MIN
Area II 14 MIN
Data graphs 15 MIN
Large Numbers 15 MIN
Properties of zero and one 15 MIN
Volume I 15 MIN
Volume II 15 MIN
Dist - AITECH

Math Minus Mystery 6 MIN
U-matic / VHS / 16mm
Color (T)
LC 75-702729
Explains a teacher education program to train undergraduate college students to teach elementary school mathematics.
Education; Mathematics
Dist - AMEDFL **Prod** - NSF 1975

Math minus mystery
U-matic / VHS / BETA
Search encounters in science series
Color; PAL (G H C)
PdS25, PdS33 purchase
Brings modern research efforts of the world's leading scientists into the classroom. Features one of a series of 24 mini - documentaries. Each film is 5 - 7 minutes in length.
Mathematics; Science
Dist - EDPAT **Prod** - NSF

Math Mission 2 - Overview 15 MIN
U-matic / VHS
Math Mission 2 Series
Color (T)
LC 82-706319
Shows selected segments from programs in the Math Mission 2 series. Demonstrates the format used, explains the philosophy of the program, and gives a preview of the content.
Mathematics
Dist - GPN **Prod** - WCVETV 1981

Math Mission 2 Series
Characteristic Characters 15 MIN
Everything in its place 15 MIN
It's Time 15 MIN
Math Mission 2 - Overview 15 MIN
The Missing Addends 15 MIN
Money Matters 15 MIN
Part of Something 15 MIN
Pints, Quarts and Pottles 15 MIN
A Place for Everything 15 MIN
Plus and Minus 15 MIN
Predictions and reflections 15 MIN
Puzzling Problems 15 MIN
The Shape of Things 15 MIN
Shapes and more Shapes 15 MIN
Dist - GPN

Math - no mystery series
Division - round two 15 MIN
Dist - GPN

Math patrol three series
Addition four 15 MIN
Addition three 15 MIN
Division one 15 MIN
Division two 15 MIN
Multiplication One 15 MIN
Multiplication Two 15 MIN
Subtraction Four 15 MIN
Subtraction Three 15 MIN
Dist - TVOTAR

Math Patrol Two Series
Adding One 15 MIN
Adding Two 15 MIN
Math, who Needs it 15 MIN
Shapes 15 MIN
Solids 15 MIN
Subtraction One 15 MIN
Subtraction Two 15 MIN
Dist - TVOTAR

Math - Quantitative Comparison 120 MIN
VHS / U-matic
SAT Exam Preparation Series
Color
Education; Mathematics
Dist - KRLSOF **Prod** - KRLSOF 1985

Math readiness series
This one with that one 10 MIN
Up, down, all around - directional relationships 10 MIN
Which Go Together - Set Building 10 MIN
Dist - CORF

Math Review 1 15 MIN
U-matic
Math Makers Two Series
Color (I)
Presents the math concepts of multiplication of multiples, questions involving bar graphs, division, ratio and addition.
Education; Mathematics
Dist - TVOTAR **Prod** - TVOTAR 1980

Math Review 2 15 MIN
U-matic
Math Makers Two Series
Color (I)
Presents the math concepts of subtraction of time, multiplication of a whole number by a fraction, concepts of time and addition and subtraction of money.
Education; Mathematics
Dist - TVOTAR **Prod** - TVOTAR 1980

Math Review and Math Shortcuts
U-matic / VHS
Drafting - Blueprint Reading Basics Series
Color (IND)
Industrial and Technical Education
Dist - GPCV **Prod** - GPCV

Math review for the A C T
U-matic / VHS
Standardized video exam review series
Color (H C A)
$39.95 _ #VA210V
Shows effective strategies to use when taking the ACT for math. Includes study guide.
Education
Dist - CAMV **Prod** - CAMV 1989

Math review for the A C T 120 MIN
VHS
Test preparation video series
Color (H G A)
$39.95 purchase _ #VAI110
Features experienced teachers who guide students through math review courses for the ACT. Includes tips, 'insider' test taking strategies and confidence building hints. Stresses problem solving.
Education; Mathematics; Psychology
Dist - CADESF **Prod** - CADESF

Math Review for the G R E
U-matic / VHS
Standardized Video Exam Review Series
Color (H T)
$39.95 _ #VA610V
Features instructors with experience who council viewers on effective strategies to use in taking the G R E. Includes study guide.
Education
Dist - CAMV **Prod** - CAMV 1986

Math Review for the GED 120 MINUTES
VHS / 16mm
Test Preparation Video Series
Color (H)

$39.95 _ VAI 100
Reviews mathematics for GED test takers. Testing strategies and problem solving techniques are given.
Education; Psychology
Dist - CADESF **Prod** - CADESF

Math review for the GMAT
VHS / U-matic
Standardized video exam review series
Color (H T)
$39.95 _ #VA710V
Shows effective strategies to use in taking the math portion of the GMAT. Includes study guide.
Education
Dist - CAMV **Prod** - CAMV 1987

Math Review for the SAT - PSAT 120 MINUTES
VHS / 16mm
Test Preparation Video Series
Color (H)
$39.95 _ VAI 104
Reviews mathematics for SAT and PSAT test takers. Testing strategies and problem solving techniques are given.
Education; Psychology
Dist - CADESF **Prod** - CADESF

Math Review for the S A T - P S A T
U-matic / VHS
Standardized video exam review series
Color (H C)
$39.95 _ #VA110V
Shows effective strategies to use in taking SAT and PSAT exams. Includes study guide.
Education
Dist - CAMV **Prod** - CAMV 1989

Math Review, Pt 1
U-matic / VHS
Industrial Training, Module 1 - Plant Principles Series; Module 1 - Plant principles
Color (IND)
Focuses on basic mathematics for the shop operator. Includes numbers, addition, subtraction, multiplication and division.
Industrial and Technical Education; Mathematics
Dist - LEIKID **Prod** - LEIKID

Math Review, Pt 2
U-matic / VHS
Industrial Training, Module 1 - Plant Principles Series; Module 1 - Plant principles
Color (IND)
Studies averages, fractions, decimals and percentages.
Industrial and Technical Education; Mathematics
Dist - LEIKID **Prod** - LEIKID

Math Review, Pt 3
VHS / U-matic
Industrial Training, Module 1 - Plant Principles Series; Module 1 - Plant principles
Color (IND)
Includes algebra, the equation and symbols.
Industrial and Technical Education; Mathematics
Dist - LEIKID **Prod** - LEIKID

The Math - science encounter 25 MIN
U-matic / 16mm / VHS
Color (P I J)
$550.00, $415.00, $385.00 purchase _ #C358
Shows how mathematics and science are an important part of everyday life. Follows Todd who gets an 'F' in math and is taken off the soccer team. The only way to get back on the team is through special tutoring. His tutor is a strange girl who makes rockets propelled by vinegar and baking soda, uses algebra to measure the height of trees and looks at the stars through a telescope.
Education; Mathematics; Science
Dist - BARR **Prod** - CHODZK 1984

Math that Counts Series
The Caretaker's Dilemma 10 MIN
King Vat - Introduction to Decimals 13 MIN
Dist - EBEC

Math Topics - Geometry Series
Circles - Pt 4 20 MIN
Exterior angles 20 MIN
Grids 20 MIN
Locus 20 MIN
Points and line 20 MIN
Dist - FI

Math topics - statistics series
Data collection 20 MIN
Data reduction 20 MIN
Data representation 20 MIN
Probability I 20 MIN
Probability II 20 MIN
Dist - FI

Math Topics - Trigonometry Series
Scale Factor 20 MIN
Similar Shapes 20 MIN
Sine Graph 20 MIN
Sine of Obtuse Angles 20 MIN
Turning 20 MIN
Dist - FI

Math tutor series
Algebraic terms and operations - Part 1 47 MIN
Factoring and solving quadratic equations - Part 3 23 MIN
Solving algebraic equations of the first degree and inequalities - Part 2 57 MIN
Solving simultaneous equations and inequalities algebraically and geometrically - Part 4 29 MIN
Verbal problems and introduction to trigonometry - Part 5 43 MIN
Dist - PBS

Math vantage videos series
Presents a five - part series using interactive learning, interdisciplinary approaches, mathematical connections, student involvement and exploration to enable students to use patterns to explain, create and predict situations. Includes Discovering Patterns; Patterns with Ten; Sequences and Ratios; Tessellations; Networks, Paths and Knots.
Discovering patterns
Networks, paths and knots
Patterns with ten
Sequences and ratios
Tessellations
Dist - SUNCOM **Prod** - NEBMSI 1984

Math ... who needs it 58 MIN
VHS
Color (H J)
$39.95 purchase _ FASE001V-G
Features celebrities such as Bill Cosby, Terri Garr, and Dizzy Gillespie to convince students that math is necessary in real life. Visits the classroom of Jaime Escalante, well-known math teacher who inspired the movie Stand and Deliver. Presents uses of math in fashion, skateboard design, sports, music and more.
Education; Mathematics
Dist - CAMV

Math, who Needs it 15 MIN
U-matic
Math Patrol Two Series
Color (P)
Presents a review of the concepts presented in the series.
Education; Mathematics
Dist - TVOTAR **Prod** - TVOTAR 1977

Math Works Series
Estimating - Estimating by Rounding 15 MIN
Estimating - Other Estimation Strategies 15 MIN
Measurement - Dividing Regions into Subregions for Finding Area 15 MIN
Measurement - Finding Areas of Rectangles 15 MIN
Measurement - the Difference between Perimeter and Area 15 MIN
Mental Computation - using Mental Computation for Addition 15 MIN
Probability - possible outcomes 15 MIN
Problem Solving - Identifying the Problem 15 MIN
Problem solving - looking for a pattern 15 MIN
Problem solving - simplifying the problem 15 MIN
Problem solving - using diagrams and models 15 MIN
Problem Solving - using Graphs 15 MIN
Problem solving - using maps 15 MIN
Problem Solving - using Tables 15 MIN
Ratio - Forming Ratios 15 MIN
Statistics - Analyzing Data 15 MIN
Statistics - Collecting Data 15 MIN
Statistics - Sampling 15 MIN
Dist - AITECH

Mathemagic, Unit III - Geometry Series
Rectangles and Right Angle 20 MIN
Dist - GPN

Mathematical Calculations of Glaze Formulas 28 MIN
Videoreel / VT2
Wheels, Kilns and Clay Series
Color
Features Mrs Peterson describing certain ceramic processes for her classroom at the University of Southern California. Shows how to use mathematical calculations of glaze formulas.
Fine Arts
Dist - PBS **Prod** - USC

Mathematical concepts series
Applications of transformations 20 MIN
Conceptual Models 20 MIN
Descriptive and causal models 20 MIN
Dilatations and similarity 20 MIN
Distance preserving transformations 20 MIN
From reality to models 20 MIN
Introduction to Transformations 20 MIN
Linear Programming 1 20 MIN
Linear Programming 2 20 MIN
Dist - TVOTAR

Mathematical Curves 10 MIN
16mm / U-matic / VHS
Color (J H)
$49.95 purchase _ Q10756; LC 77-703300
Presents an animated montage of the names and shapes of 14 mathematical curves from ellipse to spiral, helix to hyperbola. Shows the prevalence of mathematics in our daily lives.
Mathematics
Dist - CF **Prod** - WATSOC 1977

Mathematical eye - Series 1 260 MIN
VHS
Mathematical eye series
Color; PAL (I J)
PdS45 purchase
Presents ten programs of 26 minutes each that stimulate interest and enthusiasm in mathematics. Includes the topics - circles; decimals; lines and networks; maps and co - ordinates; measurement; near enough; Fibonacci and prime numbers; triangle and square numbers; statistics; working things out. Part of a three part series on mathematics using documentary film, cartoons and high - tech graphics to introduce projects and open - ended investigations, with questioning commentary to provoke active viewing. Each series includes an experiment pack for pupils and detailed teacher notes. Contact distributor about availability outside the United Kingdom.
Mathematics
Dist - ACADEM

Mathematical eye - Series 2 260 MIN
VHS
Mathematical eye series
Color; PAL (I J)
PdS45 purchase
Presents ten programs of 26 minutes each that stimulate interest and enthusiasm in mathematics. Includes the topics - area and volume; equations and formulae; fractions and percentages; graphs; logic and problem solving; numbers; probability; ratio and scale; shapes and angles; symmetry. Part of a three part series on mathematics using documentary film, cartoons and high - tech graphics to introduce projects and open - ended investigations, with questioning commentary to provoke active viewing. Each series includes an experiment pack for pupils and detailed teacher notes. Contact distributor about availability outside the United Kingdom.
Mathematics
Dist - ACADEM

Mathematical eye - Series 3 80 MIN
VHS
Mathematical eye series
Color; PAL (I J)
PdS30 purchase
Presents four programs of 20 minutes each that stimulate interest and enthusiasm in mathematics. Includes the topics - patterns in numbers; primes, squares and cubes; triangles and Fibonacci numbers; design and construction. Part of a three part series on mathematics using documentary film, cartoons and high - tech graphics to introduce projects and open - ended investigations, with questioning commentary to provoke active viewing. Each series includes an experiment pack for pupils and detailed teacher notes. Contact distributor about availability outside the United Kingdom.
Mathematics
Dist - ACADEM

Mathematical eye series
Mathematical eye - Series 1 260 MIN
Mathematical eye - Series 2 260 MIN
Mathematical eye - Series 3 80 MIN
Dist - ACADEM

Mathematical Induction 60 MIN
16mm
Maa Individual Lecturers Series
Color (J H)
Professor Leon Henkin develops the principle of mathematical induction through a number of simple examples.
Mathematics
Dist - MLA **Prod** - MAA 1960

Mathematical Induction, Pt 1 30 MIN
16mm
MAA Individual Lecturers Series
Color (H C)
LC FIA63-464
Professor Leon Henkin develops the principle of mathematical induction through a number of simple examples.

Mathematics
Dist - MLA **Prod** - MAA 1960

Mathematical Induction, Pt 2 30 MIN
16mm
MAA Individual Lecturers Series
Color (H C)
LC FIA63-464
Professor Leon Henkin develops the principle of mathematical induction through a number of simple examples and proves the principle using the axiom that states that the positive integers are well - ordered.
Mathematics
Dist - MLA **Prod** - MAA 1960

Mathematical Investigations Series
Mathematical Investigations - Vol I 40 MIN
Mathematical Investigations - Vol II 40 MIN
Mathematical Investigations - Vol III 40 MIN
Mathematical Investigations - Vol IV 40 MIN
Mathematical Investigations - Vol V 40 MIN
Dist - FI

Mathematical Investigations - Vol I 40 MIN
VHS
Mathematical Investigations Series
Color (I)
$79.00 purchase
Challenges students to ask probing questions and motivates them to explore answers. Does not suggest that there is a single correct answer to a problem. Develops independent investigative thinking. Volume I of five volumes presents four 10 - minute programs - 'Pascal's Triangle I,' 'Gears,' 'Arithmetic Progressions,' and 'Shuffles.'.
Education; Mathematics
Dist - FI **Prod** - BBCTV 1988

Mathematical Investigations - Vol II 40 MIN
VHS
Mathematical Investigations Series
Color (I)
$79.00 purchase
Challenges students to ask probing questions and motivates them to explore answers. Does not suggest that there is a single correct answer to a problem. Develops independent investigative thinking. Volume II of five volumes presents four 10 - minute programs - 'Pascal's Triangle II,' 'Mazes,' 'Geometric Progressions,' and 'Numbers As Codes.'.
Education; Mathematics
Dist - FI **Prod** - BBCTV 1988

Mathematical Investigations - Vol III 40 MIN
VHS
Mathematical Investigations Series
Color (I)
$79.00 purchase
Challenges students to ask probing questions and motivates them to explore answers. Does not suggest that there is a single correct answer to a problem. Develops independent investigative thinking. Volume III of five volumes presents four 10 - minute programs - 'Fly On The Wall,' 'Projections,' 'In Proportion,' and 'Scale Up.'.
Education; Mathematics
Dist - FI **Prod** - BBCTV 1988

Mathematical Investigations - Vol IV 40 MIN
VHS
Mathematical Investigations Series
Color (I)
$79.00 purchase
Challenges students to ask probing questions and motivates them to explore answers. Does not suggest that there is a single correct answer to a problem. Develops independent investigative thinking. Volume IV of five volumes presents four 10 - minute programs - 'Folds,' 'The Right Shape,' 'Decimals Forever,' and 'How Likely.'.
Education; Mathematics
Dist - FI **Prod** - BBCTV 1988

Mathematical Investigations - Vol V 40 MIN
VHS
Mathematical Investigations Series
Color (I)
$79.00 purchase
Challenges students to ask probing questions and motivates them to explore answers. Does not suggest that there is a single correct answer to a problem. Develops independent investigative thinking. Volume V of five volumes presents four 10 - minute programs - 'Get The Facts,' 'Rolling,' 'Patterns,' and 'Time Graph.'.
Education; Mathematics
Dist - FI **Prod** - BBCTV 1988

Mathematical Mystery Tour 57 MIN
16mm / VHS
Nova Series
(J H C)
$99.95 each
Discusses the solidity of ancient math as well as the vastness of new mathematical advances.
Mathematics; Science; Sociology
Dist - AMBROS **Prod** - AMBROS 1985

Mathematical Problems I 30 MIN
U-matic / VHS
Teaching Children with Special Needs Series
Color (T)
Discusses the teaching of mathematical problem - solving skills to children with special needs.
Education
Dist - MDCPB **Prod** - MDDE

Mathematical Problems II 30 MIN
VHS / U-matic
Teaching Children with Special Needs Series
Color (T)
Discusses the teaching of mathematical problem - solving skills to children with special needs.
Education
Dist - MDCPB **Prod** - MDDE

Mathematical reasoning - problem solving and grid - ins
VHS
Test taking - SAT I series
Color (H A)
$49.95 purchase _ #VA863V-G
Helps students study for the SAT scholastic aptitude test. Uses a test-taking instructor to guide viewer. Outlines what to expect on the test, how to prepare, and tips to getting a higher score. Each program 120-160 minutes in length. Part of a five-part series.
Education; Mathematics
Dist - CAMV

Mathematical reasoning - quantitative comparisons
VHS
Test taking - SAT I series
Color (H A)
$49.95 purchase _ #VA847V-G
Helps students study for the SAT scholastic aptitude test. Uses a test-taking instructor to guide viewer. Outlines what to expect on the test, how to prepare, and tips to getting a higher score. Each program 120-160 minutes in length. Part of a five-part series.
Education; Mathematics
Dist - CAMV

Mathematical Relationship Series
Approximating and estimating 15 MIN
Fractions 15 MIN
Games, Puzzles and Logic 15 MIN
Geometric Shapes 15 MIN
Large Numbers 15 MIN
The Metric System 15 MIN
Number Patterns 15 MIN
Probability 15 MIN
Ratio 15 MIN
Time 15 MIN
What are Numbers 15 MIN
Dist - TVOTAR

Mathematical Relationships Series
The Metric System 13 MIN
Dist - NBCTV

Mathematical relationships series
Statistics 15 MIN
Dist - TVOTAR

Mathematical treasure hunting - the search for the SS Central America
VHS
Color (C PRO G)
$150.00 purchase _ #91.02
Shows how a combination of historical, statistical, analytic and subjective methods was used to generate a probability distribution for the location of the wreck SS Central America, lost 130 years ago off the coast of South Carolina. Reveals that the Columbus - America Discovery Group successfully completed this unusual treasure hunt for an estimated $1 billion in gold bars and coins, as well as valuable historical information. Columbus - America Discovery Group. Lawrence D Stone.
Business and Economics; Science - Physical
Dist - INMASC

Mathematics - an Animated Approach to Fractions Series Part 1
Familiarity with Fractions and Multiplication of Fractions 12 MIN
Dist - FI

Mathematics - an Animated Approach to Fractions Series Part 2
Renaming Fractions and Addition of Fractions 12 MIN
Dist - FI

Mathematics - an animated approach to fractions series
Subtraction, division and mixed numbers 12 MIN
Dist - FI

Mathematics and physics series
Bernoulli's Principle - why an airplane flies 15 MIN
Energy, work, power and force 31 MIN
Measurement of area and volume 23 MIN
Newton's Law of Motion 31 MIN
Sound and its Effects 22 MIN
Temperature, pressure and fluids - Pt 1 gases 30 MIN
Temperature, pressure and fluids - Pt 2 liquids 16 MIN
Dist - AVIMA

Mathematics and the special child 29 MIN
16mm
Project STRETCH Series; Module 20
Color (T)
LC 80-700627
Demonstrates how to use concrete, manipulative materials to teach abstract concepts.
Education; Mathematics; Psychology
Dist - HUBDSC **Prod** - METCO 1980

Mathematics and the special student 30 MIN
U-matic / VHS
Project STRETCH - Strategies to Train Regular Educators to Teach Children with Handicaps Series; Module 20
Color (T S)
LC 80-706656
Demonstrates how to use concrete, manipulative materials to teach abstract concepts.
Education; Psychology
Dist - HUBDSC **Prod** - METCO 1980

Mathematics - Assessment and Programming 29 MIN
VHS / U-matic
Mainstreaming the Exceptional Child Series
Color (T)
Discusses mathematics assessment and programming in a mainstreaming situation.
Education; Mathematics; Psychology
Dist - FI **Prod** - MFFD

Mathematics for Elementary School Students - Whole Numbers Series
Array Back When 8 MIN
The Beast of Ragoo Lagoon 8 MIN
The Big story 8 MIN
Double Trouble 8 MIN
How Big is a Million 8 MIN
It's a Small World 8 MIN
The Magic Square 8 MIN
Nuts to You 8 MIN
Shape Up 8 MIN
Something's Missing 8 MIN
A Thousand and One Naughts 8 MIN
Dist - DAVFMS

Mathematics for elementary school teachers - a series
Mathematics for elementary school teachers - a series
Color
A sequentially arranged series for teacher training. Pre - Number Ideas; Whole Numbers; Names For Numbers; Numeration Systems; Place Value And Addition; Addition And Subtraction; Addition And Subtraction Techniques; Multiplication; Division; Multiplication Techniques; Division Techniques; Sentences, Number Line; Points, Lines, Planes; Polygons And Angles; Metric Properties Of Figures; Linear And Angular Measure; Factors And Primes; Introducing Rational Numbers; Equivalent Fractions; Addition And Subtraction Of Rational Numbers; Multiplication Of Rational Numbers; Division Of Rational Numbers; Decimals; Ratio, Rate, Percent;.
Education; Mathematics
Dist - MLA **Prod** - SMSG

Mathematics for elementary school teachers - a series
Mathematics for elementary school teachers - a series
Dist - MLA

Mathematics for Elementary School Teachers Series no 3
Names for Numbers 30 MIN
Dist - MLA

Mathematics for Elementary School Teachers Series no 5
Place Value and Addition 30 MIN
Dist - MLA

Mathematics for elementary school teachers No 6 series
Addition and subtraction 30 MIN
Dist - MLA

Mathematics for elementary school teachers - No 7 series
Addition and subtraction techniques 30 MIN
Dist - MLA

Mathematics for Elementary School Teachers Series no 8
Multiplication 30 MIN
Dist - MLA

Mathematics for Elementary School Teachers Series no 10
Multiplication Techniques 30 MIN
Dist - MLA

Mathematics for Elementary School Teachers Series no 12
Sentences, Number Line 30 MIN
Dist - MLA

Mathematics for Elementary School Teachers Series no 15
Metric Properties of Figures 30 MIN
Dist - MLA

Mathematics for Elementary School Teachers Series no 16
Linear and Angular Measure 30 MIN
Dist - MLA

Mathematics for Elementary School Teachers Series no 17
Factors and Primes 30 MIN
Dist - MLA

Mathematics for Elementary School Teachers Series no 18
Introducing Rational Numbers 30 MIN
Dist - MLA

Mathematics for elementary school teachers series no 19
Equivalent fractions 30 MIN
Dist - MLA

Mathematics for elementary school teachers -No 20 series
Addition and subtraction of rational numbers 30 MIN
Dist - MLA

Mathematics for elementary school teachers series - No 23
Decimals 30 MIN
Dist - MLA

Mathematics for Elementary School Teachers Series no 25
Congruence and Similarity 30 MIN
Dist - MLA

Mathematics for Elementary School Teachers Series no 26
Solid Figures 30 MIN
Dist - MLA

Mathematics for Elementary School Teachers Series no 28
Measurement of Solids 30 MIN
Dist - MLA

Mathematics for Elementary School Teachers Series no 29
Negative Rational Numbers 30 MIN
Dist - MLA

Mathematics for elementary school teachers series
Division techniques 30 MIN
Points, lines, planes 30 MIN
Polygons and angles 30 MIN
Pre - number ideas 30 MIN
Ratio, rate, percent 30 MIN
The Real Numbers 30 MIN
Whole Numbers 30 MIN
Dist - MLA

Mathematics for primary - addition 9 MIN
U-matic / VHS / 16mm
Mathematics for primary series
Color (P I) (SPANISH)
Uses bunnies, boats, helicopters and roller skates to illustrate the operation of addition.
Mathematics
Dist - AIMS **Prod** - PAR 1977

Mathematics for primary - division 8 MIN
U-matic / VHS / 16mm
Mathematics for primary series
Color (P I) (SPANISH)
Illustrates the concept of division by depicting animated shoes, balls, cards and chairs.
Mathematics
Dist - AIMS **Prod** - PAR 1977

Mathematics for primary - multiplication 7 MIN
16mm / U-matic / VHS
Mathematics for primary series
Color (P I) (SPANISH)
Discusses the operation of multiplication by showing bottles in rows, socks in pairs, cars in columns, and pencils in jars.
Mathematics
Dist - AIMS **Prod** - PAR 1977

Mathematics for primary series
Mathematics for primary - addition 9 MIN
Mathematics for primary - division 8 MIN
Mathematics for primary - multiplication 7 MIN
Mathematics for primary - subtraction 8 MIN
Dist - AIMS

Mathematics for primary - subtraction 8 MIN
U-matic / VHS / 16mm
Mathematics for primary series
Color (P I) (SPANISH)
Uses animated objects to illustrate the concept of subtraction.
Mathematics
Dist - AIMS **Prod** - PAR 1977

Mathematics for the '80s Grade Six Series
Decimals - ordering decimals 15 MIN
Estimation - Estimation Strategies for Division 15 MIN
Estimation - Estimation Strategies for Multiplication 15 MIN
Estimation - Reasonableness of Answers 15 MIN
Fractions - Multiplication with Fractions and Mixed Numbers 15 MIN
Fractions - Subtracting Mixed Numbers 15 MIN
Geometry and Measurement - Measuring Angles 15 MIN
Geometry and Measurement - Measuring Volume 15 MIN
Measurement - Precision and Estimation 15 MIN
Mental Computation - using Mental Computation for Multiplication 15 MIN
Problem solving - drawing and interpreting tables and diagrams 15 MIN
Problem solving - guess - check - revise 15 MIN
Problem solving - solving a simpler problem 15 MIN
Problem solving - using logical reasoning 15 MIN
Ratio, Proportion, Percent 15 MIN
Statistics - Sampling 15 MIN
Statistics - Understanding Mean, Median, and Mode 15 MIN
Dist - AITECH

Mathematics for Tomorrow's World, Part I - Thinking, Learning, Living
VHS / U-matic
Color
Points out the changing role of mathematics in the classroom. Presents the challenging implications for today's mathematics teacher.
Mathematics
Dist - FILMID **Prod** - FILMID 1983

Mathematics for Tomorrow's World, Part II - the Shape of Things to Come
U-matic / VHS
Color
Offers an opportunity to explore and utilize geometry at the elementary level.
Mathematics
Dist - FILMID **Prod** - FILMID 1983

Mathematics - Fundamental Operations Series
Bases and exponents 5 MIN
Factoring Numbers 5 MIN
Dist - PHM

Mathematics (GMAT), Lesson 3
U-matic / VHS
GMAT/Graduate Management Admission Test Series
Color (C A)
Education; Mathematics
Dist - COMEX **Prod** - COMEX

Mathematics - Graphing Series
Four Quadrants 13 MIN
Graphing an equation 14 MIN
Point coordinates - quadrant one 13 MIN
Dist - PHM

Mathematics (GRE), Lesson 3
U-matic / VHS
GRE/Graduate Record Examination Series
Color (H A)
Education; Mathematics
Dist - COMEX **Prod** - COMEX

Mathematics in Music 30 MIN
U-matic
Changing Music Series
Color
Fine Arts
Dist - PBS **Prod** - WGBHTV

Mathematics learning activities series
Multiplication, division and fractions - Part 2 36 MIN
Numeration, addition and subtraction - Part 1 52 MIN
Dist - UCALG

Mathematics - life's number game 20 MIN
U-matic / VHS / 16mm
Color (I J H)
$465.00, $250.000 purchase _ #3764
Presents a series of vignettes showing people solving job - related and everyday problems with mathematics. Illustrates the occupations and daily situations that require a thorough knowledge of basic math.
Mathematics
Dist - CORF **Prod** - CORF 1979

Mathematics of Choice and Chance, Program 5 - Confident Conclusions 30 MIN
VHS / U-matic
For all Practical Purposes - Fundamentals of Mathematics Series
Color (C A)
Focuses on the concept of a confidence interval and describes what opinion polls do and do not reveal. Explains formula for computing confidence intervals, how confidence in statistical conclusion is related to sample size and how to analyze a sampling distribution.
Mathematics
Dist - FI **Prod** - ANNCPB

Mathematics of choice and chance, Program 4 - odds - on favorite 30 MIN
VHS / U-matic
For all practical purposes - fundamentals of mathematics series
Color (C A)
Analyzes how long - term patterns of chance events can be predicted by observing the operation of a casino. Introduces elementary probability concepts and analyzes normal curves, standard deviation and expected value. Demonstrates use of the Central Limit Theorem.
Mathematics
Dist - FI **Prod** - ANNCPB

Mathematics of choice and chance, Program 1 - overview 30 MIN
U-matic / VHS
For all practical purposes - fundamentals of mathematics series
Color (C A)
Introduces the major themes of statistics - collecting, organizing and picturing data and drawing conclusions from data. Explains bias and randomness by looking at formal and informal public opinion polls and examining a major medical experiment. Presents inference as a tour through a telephone factory and games of chance in a visit to a casino.
Mathematics
Dist - FI **Prod** - ANNCPB

Mathematics of choice and chance, Program 2 - behind the headlines 30 MIN
U-matic / VHS
For all practical purposes - fundamentals of mathematics series
Color (C A)
Explores how surveys and public opinion polls work. Examines how the unemployment rate is determined and what statistical evidence means. Explains the difference between a survey and an experiment and how chance is used in random sampling.
Mathematics
Dist - FI **Prod** - ANNCPB

Mathematics of choice and chance, Program 3 - picture this 30 MIN
U-matic / VHS
For all practical purposes - fundamentals of mathematics series
Color (C A)
Focuses on exploratory data analysis, emphasizing the human eye and brain as the best devices for seeing and recognizing patterns. Introduces histograms, medians, quartiles and the concept of an outlier with one variable and moves to situations with two variables to introduce scatterplots and box plots.
Mathematics
Dist - FI **Prod** - ANNCPB

Mathematics of Personal Finance 30 MIN
U-matic
Introduction to Mathematics Series
Color (C)

Mathematics
Dist - MDCPB **Prod** - MDCPB

Mathematics of the Honeycomb 13 MIN
16mm / VHS
Color
States that the elegance of the honeycomb, admired by the Greek mathematician Pappus, was not fully appreciated until modern mathematical methods were applied. Shows a historical and analytical approach to the honeycomb problem leading to an appreciation of the importance of mathematics in science and engineering.
Mathematics; Science; Science - Natural
Dist - MIS **Prod** - MIS 1977

Mathematics Review, Tape 1 45 MIN
VHS / U-matic
S A T / A C T Examination Video Review Series
Color (H A)
Reviews basic math skills to prepare the SAT/ACT examination.
Education; Mathematics
Dist - COMEX **Prod** - COMEX

Mathematics Review, Tape 2 45 MIN
U-matic / VHS
S A T / A C T Examination Video Review Series
Color (H A)
Includes percentage problems, tax, interest formula and percent increase and decrease problems similar to the ones on the SAT/ACT examination.
Education; Mathematics
Dist - COMEX **Prod** - COMEX

Mathematics Review, Tape 3 45 MIN
U-matic / VHS
S A T / A C T Examination Video Review Series
Color (H A)
Includes basic algebra skills as tested on the SAT/ACT examination.
Education; Mathematics
Dist - COMEX **Prod** - COMEX

Mathematics Review, Tape 4 45 MIN
VHS / U-matic
S A T / A C T Examination Video Review Series
Color (H A)
Includes problems involving prime numbers, and simple and weighted averages as tested on the SAT/ACT examination.
Education; Mathematics
Dist - COMEX **Prod** - COMEX

Mathematics Review, Tape 5 45 MIN
VHS / U-matic
S A T / A C T Examination Video Review Series
Color (H A)
Includes problems involving radicals, properties and symbolic algebra as tested on the SAT/ACT examination.
Education; Mathematics
Dist - COMEX **Prod** - COMEX

Mathematics Review, Tape 6 45 MIN
VHS / U-matic
S A T / A C T Examination Video Review Series
Color (H A)
Includes word problems, consecutive integer problems and age problems as tested on the SAT/ACT examination.
Education; Mathematics
Dist - COMEX **Prod** - COMEX

Mathematics Review, Tape 7 45 MIN
U-matic / VHS
S A T / A C T Examination Video Review Series
Color (H A)
Includes basic geometry problems and problems involving different relationships between figures as tested on the SAT/ACT examination.
Education; Mathematics
Dist - COMEX **Prod** - COMEX

Mathematics Review, Tape 8 45 MIN
VHS / U-matic
S A T / A C T Examination Video Review Series
Color (H A)
Includes solid geometry problems, analytical geometry problems and chart and graph problems as tested on the SAT/ACT examination.
Education; Mathematics
Dist - COMEX **Prod** - COMEX

Mathematics Series
Absolute value equations and inequalities 30 MIN
Addition and subtraction of radical expressions 30 MIN
Addition and subtraction of rational expressions 30 MIN
Addition, subtraction and multiplication of polynomials 30 MIN
Advanced area problems 30 MIN
Advanced volume problems 30 MIN
Algebra of functions 30 MIN
Angles, degrees and radians 30 MIN
Applications that lead to equations involving rational expressions 30 MIN
Applications that Lead to Linear Equations 30 MIN
Applications that lead to quadratic equations 30 MIN
Applications to business 30 MIN
Applications to growth and decay 30 MIN
Applications to physics 30 MIN
Area 30 MIN
Areas, antidifferentiation and the fundamental theorem of calculus 30 MIN
Average rate of change and slope of lines 30 MIN
Binomial theorum 30 MIN
Circles, Pt 1 30 MIN
Circles, Pt 2 30 MIN
Circles, the midpoint formula and the distance formula 30 MIN
Complex fractions 30 MIN
Complex numbers 30 MIN
Composite functions and the chain rule 30 MIN
Compound inequalities 30 MIN
Constructions, Part 1 30 MIN
Constructions, Pt 2 30 MIN
Coordinate geometry 30 MIN
Decimals - addition, subtraction and rounding 30 MIN
Decimals - division, conversion to fractions 30 MIN
Definite integrals and areas 30 MIN
Definite integrals, substitution and integration by parts 30 MIN
The Delta - process and instantaneous rates of change 30 MIN
Differentiation and approximation 30 MIN
Differentiation rules - power and sums 30 MIN
Division of polynomials, the remainder theorem and the factor theorem 30 MIN
Division of rational expressions 30 MIN
Equations involving rational expressions 30 MIN
Equations of straight lines 30 MIN
Equations with rational expressions 30 MIN
Evaluating Trigometric Functions 30 MIN
Exponential Functions and their Graphs 30 MIN
EYP, log and differentiation 30 MIN
Factoring 30 MIN
Factoring Binomials 30 MIN
Factoring, Pt 1 30 MIN
Factoring, Pt 2 30 MIN
Factors and Multiples 30 MIN
Formulas for lines 30 MIN
Fractions - Least Common Denominator, Addition and Subtraction 30 MIN
Fractions - Multiplication and Division 30 MIN
Functions 30 MIN
Functions and their Graphs 30 MIN
General Factoring 30 MIN
Graph sketching 30 MIN
Graphing linear equations 30 MIN
Graphing rational functions 30 MIN
Graphing trigometric functions - Pt 1 30 MIN
Graphing trigometric functions - Pt 2 30 MIN
Graphs of linear inequalities 30 MIN
Greatest common factor and factoring trinomials 30 MIN
Implicit Differentiation 30 MIN
Inequalities 30 MIN
Integration by Parts 30 MIN
Integration Formulas 30 MIN
Intercepts, Distance and Slope 30 MIN
Introduction to Non - Euclidean Geometries 30 MIN
Introduction to Proofs 30 MIN
Introduction to Trigometric Functions 30 MIN
Inverse Functions 30 MIN
Inverse Functions and their Derivatives 30 MIN
Inverse Trigometric Functions 30 MIN
Law of Cosines 30 MIN
Law of Sines 30 MIN
Limits and Continuity 30 MIN
Logarithmic Differentiation 30 MIN
Logarithmic Functions and their Graphs 30 MIN
Logarithms and their Properties 30 MIN
Miscellaneous Equations 30 MIN
Miscellaneous Quadratic Equations Solved by Factoring 30 MIN
More Exponents and Introduction to Radicals 30 MIN
Multiplication and Division of Radical Expressions 30 MIN
Multiplication and Division of Rational Expressions 30 MIN
Operations on Polynomials 30 MIN
Operations on Rational Expressions 30 MIN
Operations on Real Numbers 30 MIN
Operations on Signed Numbers 30 MIN
Optimization using Differentiation - Critical Points 30 MIN
Parallel Lines 30 MIN
Percent and Applications 30 MIN
Percent and Applications, Pt 2 30 MIN
Perimeter and Area 30 MIN
Polar coordinates 30 MIN
Polynomial and rational inequalities 30 MIN
Polynomial Functions 30 MIN
Postulates and basic terms 30 MIN
The Product and Quotient Rules 30 MIN
Quadratic Functions 30 MIN
Quadrilaterals 30 MIN
Radical Equations 30 MIN
Radical Expressions 30 MIN
Rational exponents 30 MIN
Rational expressions - Pt 1 30 MIN
Rational Expressions, Pt 2 30 MIN
Rational root theorem 30 MIN
Rectangular Coordinates and Graphing 30 MIN
Related Rates 30 MIN
Right triangle applications 30 MIN
Second derivative, inflection points and concavity 30 MIN
Shifting and Reflecting Graphs 30 MIN
Similarity 30 MIN
Simplifying Radicals 30 MIN
Simultaneous Equations 30 MIN
Slope and Graphing Inequalities 30 MIN
Solids 30 MIN
Solving Absolute Value Equations 30 MIN
Solving Absolute Value Inequalities 30 MIN
Solving Equations 30 MIN
Solving Linear Equations 30 MIN
Solving Linear Inequalities 30 MIN
Solving Quadratic Equations 30 MIN
Solving Quadratic Equations by Completing the Square 30 MIN
Solving Quadratic Equations by Factoring 30 MIN
Solving Quadratic Equations by the Quadratic Formula 30 MIN
Substitution 30 MIN
Systems of equations 30 MIN
Systems of Nonlinear Equations 30 MIN
Tangent Lines 30 MIN
Taylor's Formula 30 MIN
Triangles, Pt 1 30 MIN
Triangles, Pt 2 30 MIN
Trigometric Equations 30 MIN
Trigometric Form, Demoivre's Theorum and Nth Roots of Complex Numbers 30 MIN
Trigometric Functions of General Angles 30 MIN
Trigometric Identities, Pt 1 30 MIN
Trigometric Identities, Pt 2 30 MIN
Trigometric Identities, Pt 3 30 MIN
Trigonometry Functions 30 MIN
Vertical and Horizontal Asymptotes 30 MIN
Volume Problems 30 MIN
Whole Numbers - Division 30 MIN
Whole Numbers - Multiplictions, Order of Operations 30 MIN
Word Problems 30 MIN
Dist - GPN

Mathematics, Tape 1
U-matic / VHS
New GED Examinations Series
Color (H A)
Reviews material for the high school equivalency examination (GED). Explains the GED mathematics examination. Covers fractions.
Education; Mathematics
Dist - COMEX **Prod** - COMEX

Mathematics, Tape 1 45 MIN
U-matic / VHS
CLEP General Examinations Series
Color (H A)
Prepares students for the College Level Examination Program (CLEP) tests in Mathematics. Gives an introduction to CLEP mathematics and basic arithmetic.
Education; Mathematics
Dist - COMEX **Prod** - COMEX

Mathematics, Tape 2
VHS / U-matic
New GED Examination Series
Color (H A) (SPANISH)
Reviews material for the high school equivalency examination (GED). Discusses fractions, ratios and proportions.
Education; Foreign Language; Mathematics
Dist - COMEX **Prod** - COMEX

Mathematics, Tape 3 45 MIN
U-matic / VHS

CLEP General Examinations Series
Color (H A)
Prepares students for the College Level Examination Program tests in Mathematics. Focuses on modern mathematics, probability and statistics.
Education; Mathematics
Dist - COMEX **Prod** - COMEX

Mathematics, tape 4 45 MIN
VHS / U-matic
CLEP general examinations series
Color (H A) (SPANISH)
Prepares students for the College Level Examination Program tests in Mathematics. Focuses on geometry.
Education; Mathematics
Dist - COMEX **Prod** - COMEX

Mathematics, Tape 4
VHS / U-matic
New GED Examination Series
Color (H A) (SPANISH)
Reviews material for the high school equivalency examination (GED). Covers percentages.
Education; Foreign Language; Mathematics
Dist - COMEX **Prod** - COMEX

Mathematics, tape 5
U-matic / VHS
New GED examination series
Color (H A) (SPANISH)
Reviews material for the high school equivalency examination (GED). Focuses on several aspects of geometry.
Education; Mathematics
Dist - COMEX **Prod** - COMEX

Mathematics, Tape 5 45 MIN
U-matic / VHS
CLEP General Examinations Series
Color (H A)
Prepares students for the College Level Examination Program tests in Mathematics. Covers number systems, functions, symbolic algebra and radicals.
Education; Mathematics
Dist - COMEX **Prod** - COMEX

Mathematics through Discovery 25 MIN
16mm
B&W (T)
LC FIE63-346
Shows how skilled instructors use a learner discovery method to teach new concepts in mathematics at elementary and secondary school levels.
Education
Dist - USNAC **Prod** - USOE 1963

Mathematics Today Series
Challenge in the Classroom - the Methods of R L Moore - Pt 1 27 MIN
Challenge in the Classroom - the Methods of R L Moore - Pt 2 27 MIN
Measures and Set Theory 50 MIN
The Search for Solid Ground 45 MIN
Theory of limits - Pt 3 13 MIN
Theory of limits - Pt 1 - limits of sequences 34 MIN
Theory of limits - Pt 2 - limits of functions and limit processes 38 MIN
Topology with Raoul Bott and Marston Morse 30 MIN
What is Mathematics and How do We Teach it, Pt 1 22 MIN
What is Mathematics and How do We Teach it, Pt 2 23 MIN
Dist - MLA

Mathematics - Unending Search for Excellence 25 MIN
16mm
B&W (T)
LC FIE63-347
Reports on the current audio - visual aids used in teaching new mathematics.
Education; Mathematics
Dist - USNAC **Prod** - USHHS 1962

Mathias Kneisel 96 MIN
16mm
Color (GERMAN)
Tells the story of a Bavarian who dreams of making his fortune in America, but whose poverty leads to his stealing, shooting a policeman, and finally being executed.
Foreign Language; Sociology
Dist - WSTGLC **Prod** - WSTGLC 1971

Mathilde mohring 40 MIN
16mm
Color (GERMAN (ENGLISH SUBTITLES))
Tells the story of Mathilde, who manipulates the student Hugo Grassman into marrying her and procures a mayor's position for him. Continues as Hugo, unable to fulfill all of Mathilde's expectations, falls sick and dies. Ends with Mathilde realizing her selfishness and becoming a better person as a result of it.
Fine Arts; Foreign Language
Dist - WSTGLC **Prod** - WSTGLC 1977

Math's Alive
16mm
Color
Explains the ways in which a teacher can make the study of mathematics more real and alive for the student.
Education; Mathematics
Dist - SUTHLA **Prod** - SUTHP

Maths for beginners - addition 12 MIN
VHS
Maths for beginners series
Color; PAL (P)
Features animated character Calculating Kangaroo who induces youngsters to think about numbers and their relationships in addition. Part of a series introducing the four basic arithmetic operations and the relationships between them. Shows how to recognize and use number patterns to simplify the process of memorizing number facts and solving problems.
Mathematics
Dist - VIEWTH **Prod** - VIEWTH

Maths for beginners - division 12 MIN
VHS
Maths for beginners series
Color; PAL (P)
Features animated character Calculating Kangaroo who shows that division answers how many equal groups of how many in each equal group. Part of a series introducing the four basic arithmetic operations and the relationships between them. Shows how to recognize and use number patterns to simplify the process of memorizing number facts and solving problems.
Mathematics
Dist - VIEWTH **Prod** - VIEWTH

Maths for beginners - multiplication 12 MIN
VHS
Maths for beginners series
Color; PAL (P)
Features animated character Calculating Kangaroo who visits an animated underwater world and shows that multiplication is finding out how many when joined in equal groups. Part of a series introducing the four basic arithmetic operations and the relationships between them. Shows how to recognize and use number patterns to simplify the process of memorizing number facts and solving problems.
Mathematics
Dist - VIEWTH **Prod** - VIEWTH

Maths for beginners series
Maths for beginners - addition 12 MIN
Maths for beginners - division 12 MIN
Maths for beginners - multiplication 12 MIN
Maths for beginners - subtraction 12 MIN
Dist - VIEWTH

Maths for beginners - subtraction 12 MIN
VHS
Maths for beginners series
Color; PAL (P)
Features animated character Calculating Kangaroo who asks youngsters how many are left or how many more. Part of a series introducing the four basic arithmetic operations and the relationships between them. Shows how to recognize and use number patterns to simplify the process of memorizing number facts and solving problems.
Mathematics
Dist - VIEWTH **Prod** - VIEWTH

Mathscore One Series
Angles - a good turn 20 MIN
Axes and grids - get co - ordinated 20 MIN
Capacity, volume and mass - fill it up 20 MIN
Decimals - get the point 20 MIN
Fractions - Bits and Pieces 20 MIN
Graphs - graphic description 20 MIN
Place Value - Know Your Place 20 MIN
Sequences - what next 20 MIN
Symmetry and Shapes - Mirror Image 20 MIN
Tesselations and Area - a Cover Up 20 MIN
Dist - FI

Mathscore two series
Angles - a matter of degree 20 MIN
Axes and grids - graphs rule, ok 20 MIN
Capacity, volume and mass - massive ending 20 MIN
Decimals - fine adjustment 20 MIN
Fractions - Half and Half 20 MIN
Graphs - Picture Story 20 MIN
Place Value - Take it Away 20 MIN
Sequences - Numbers Growing 20 MIN
Symmetry and Shapes - S for Shapes 20 MIN
Tesselations and Area - Space Count 20 MIN
Dist - FI

Mathways series
Areas of circles and cylinders 15 MIN
The Decimal point 15 MIN
Volume 15 MIN
Dist - AITECH

Matina Horner - Portrait of a Person 16 MIN
U-matic / VHS / 16mm
Color (H C A)
LC 75-700656
Discusses Matina Horner's concerns as sixth president of Radcliffe College. Presents, in humorous cartoon form with her own narration, her famous research on the expectations of women and their apparent fear of success.
Biography; Education; Sociology
Dist - PHENIX **Prod** - PHENIX 1975

Matinee at the Bijou, no 01 90 MIN
U-matic
Color
Includes a cartoon, a short subject, a segment of a serial, a coming attraction, and the 1935 feature film The Lost City.
Fine Arts
Dist - PBS **Prod** - BIJOU

Matinee at the Bijou, no 02 90 MIN
U-matic
Color
Includes a cartoon, a short subject, a segment of a serial, a coming attraction, and the 1937 feature film Movie Struck.
Fine Arts
Dist - PBS **Prod** - BIJOU

Matinee at the Bijou, no 03 90 MIN
U-matic
Color
Includes a cartoon, a short subject, a segment of a serial, a coming attraction, and the feature film West Of The Divide.
Fine Arts
Dist - PBS **Prod** - BIJOU

Matinee at the Bijou, no 04 90 MIN
U-matic
Color
Includes a cartoon, a short subject, a segment of a serial, a coming attraction, and the 1934 feature film The Lost Jungle.
Fine Arts
Dist - PBS **Prod** - BIJOU

Matinee at the Bijou, no 05 90 MIN
U-matic
Color
Includes a cartoon, a short subject, a segment of a serial, a coming attraction, and the 1932 feature film Winds Of The Wasteland.
Fine Arts
Dist - PBS **Prod** - BIJOU

Matinee at the Bijou, no 06 90 MIN
U-matic
Color
Includes a cartoon, a short subject, a segment of a serial, a coming attraction, and the 1934 feature film Polooka.
Fine Arts
Dist - PBS **Prod** - BIJOU

Matinee at the Bijou, no 07 90 MIN
U-matic
Color
Includes a cartoon, a short subject, a segment of a serial, a coming attraction, and the 1938 feature film The Man From Music Mountain.
Fine Arts
Dist - PBS **Prod** - BIJOU

Matinee at the Bijou, no 08 90 MIN
U-matic
Color
Includes a cartoon, a short subject, a segment of a serial, a coming attraction, and the 1939 feature film Flying Deuces.
Fine Arts
Dist - PBS **Prod** - BIJOU

Matinee at the Bijou, no 09 90 MIN
U-matic
Color
Includes a cartoon, a short subject, a segment of a serial, a coming attraction, and the 1934 feature film Submarine Alert.
Fine Arts
Dist - PBS **Prod** - BIJOU

Matinee at the Bijou, no 10 90 MIN
U-matic
Color
Includes a cartoon, a short subject, a segment of a serial, a coming attraction, and the 1943 feature film Million Dollar Kid.
Fine Arts
Dist - PBS **Prod** - BIJOU

Matinee at the Bijou, no 11 90 MIN
U-matic
Color
Includes a cartoon, a short subject, a segment of a serial, a coming attraction, and the 1942 feature film Wildcat.
Fine Arts
Dist - PBS **Prod** - BIJOU

Matinee at the Bijou, no 12 90 MIN
U-matic
Color
Includes a cartoon, a short subject, a segment of a serial, a coming attraction, and the feature films Yellow Rose Of Texas and Song Of Texas.
Fine Arts
Dist - PBS **Prod** - BIJOU

Matinee at the Bijou, no 13 90 MIN
U-matic
Color
Includes a cartoon, a short subject, a segment of a serial, a coming attraction, and the 1943 feature film Gung Ho.
Fine Arts
Dist - PBS **Prod** - BIJOU

Matinee at the Bijou, no 14 90 MIN
U-matic
Color
Includes a cartoon, a short subject, a segment of a serial, a coming attraction, and the 1947 feature film It's A Joke, Son.
Fine Arts
Dist - PBS **Prod** - BIJOU

Matinee at the Bijou, no 15 90 MIN
U-matic
Color
Includes a cartoon, a short subject, a segment of a serial, a coming attraction, and the 1944 feature film Cowboy Commandos.
Fine Arts
Dist - PBS **Prod** - BIJOU

Matinee at the Bijou, no 16 90 MIN
U-matic
Color
Includes a cartoon, a short subject, a segment of a serial, a coming attraction, and the 1947 feature film Philo Vance Returns.
Fine Arts
Dist - PBS **Prod** - BIJOU

Mating behavior in the cockroach
VHS
BSCS Classic Inquiries Series
Color (H C)
$59.95 purchase _ #193 W 2212
Poses questions, raises problems and presents experimental data on social behavior in chickens. Part of a series on the life sciences.
Science - Natural
Dist - WARDS **Prod** - WARDS

Mating Behavior of the Honey Bee 13 MIN
16mm
Color (C A)
LC 74-713860
Documents research methods for studying mating behavior of the honey bee. Shows reactions of drones to the tethered queen, to the queen confined in a small cage, to the odor of the queen, to the queen bee suspended at various altitudes, and to artificial models of queen bees with various characteristics.
Science - Natural
Dist - PSUPCR **Prod** - NSF 1971

Mating Dances 25 MIN
16mm / U-matic / VHS
Untamed World Series
Color; Mono (J H C A)
$400.00 film, $250.00 video, $50.00 rental
Describes the courtship dances and ritual displays of a variety of animals and then looks at their function and purpose.
Science - Natural
Dist - CTV **Prod** - CTV 1970

The Mating Season 96 MIN
BETA / VHS
Color (P)
Features a romantic comedy about a high - strung lawyer and a laid - back laundromat owner. Stars Lucie Arnaz and Laurence Lockinbill.
Fine Arts; Sociology
Dist - LCOA **Prod** - LCOA

Matins 3 MIN
16mm
Color (G)
$121.00 purchase, $12.00 rental
Offers a film made on the occasion of and inspired by the marriage of Jim and Lauren Tenney.
Fine Arts; Sociology
Dist - CANCIN **Prod** - BRAKS 1988

Matisse 40 MIN
VHS
Three painters 1 series
Color (A)
PdS65 purchase
Explores the work of the painter Matisse, hosted by painter and critic Sir Lawrence Gowing. Based on the concept that Matisse's work represents a distinct stage in the development of European painting between the Renaissance and the present day. Discusses the historical and social backgrounds against which the artist worked, but concentrates on examining a small number of canvases. Includes views of the places which particularly inspired the artist.
Fine Arts
Dist - BBCENE

Matisse - a Sort of Paradise 30 MIN
16mm / U-matic / VHS
Color (I A)
LC 79-712012
Takes the viewer on a lyrical trip through the world of Matisse as seen in his painting. Reveals the idyllic quality of his works.
Fine Arts
Dist - FI **Prod** - BCACGB 1969

Matisse - a Sort of Paradise 30 MIN
16mm
Color (H A)
$525.00 purchase, $60.00 rental
Documents the gathering of pictures from all over the world for a massive 1968 London retrospective of the works of Henri Matisse, 1869 - 1954.
Fine Arts; Industrial and Technical Education
Dist - AFA **Prod** - ACGB 1969

Matisse and the Fauves 20 MIN
16mm / U-matic / VHS
Color (H C)
LC 79-707247
Documents the search of Henri Matisse and other painters from a greater intensity of color, based upon their belief that the impact of painting comes from its colored surface. Shows Matisse's developing use of bold, simplified brushwork and brilliant, unnatural color.
Fine Arts
Dist - IFB **Prod** - IFB 1970

Matisse in Nice 28 MIN
VHS
Color (G)
$29.95 purchase _ #MAT03
Documents the history of Henry Matisse who left Paris in 1917 to live in Nice on the French Riviera. Shows how he was influenced by the Mediterranean Sea and its light over the next 13 years.
Fine Arts; Geography - World; History - World
Dist - HOMVIS **Prod** - USNGA 1990

Matisse - Voyages 58 MIN
VHS
Color (J)
$39.95 purchase _ #HV - 902
Traces the brilliantly colored work of Matisse from his early canvases and images of dance and music to his cut - out pieces. Incorporates archival footage and a wealth of paintings.
Fine Arts; History - World
Dist - CRYSP **Prod** - CRYSP

Matisse - Voyages 58 MIN
VHS
Color (H C A)
$39.95
Presents the great variety of works by Matisse, from paintings to cutout pieces and decorations for the Chapel of the Rosary in Vence, France. Includes discussion of his involvement in the Fauvist movement. Makes use of archival footage, photographs, and excerpts from his 'Notes of a Painter.'
Fine Arts
Dist - ARTSAM **Prod** - RMART

Matisse - Voyages 58 MIN
VHS
Color (S)
$39.95 purchase _ #833 - 9530
Traces the development of Matisse's brilliantly colored work from his early canvases, images of dance and music, and odalisques to his cut - out pieces and decorations for the Chapel of the Rosary at Vence. Draws on a wealth of paintings, archival footage, photographs and extracts from 'Notes Of A Painter' by Matisse to capture the richness of his legacy. Didier Baussy directs.
Fine Arts; History - World
Dist - FI **Prod** - RMART 1989

Matrices 30 MIN
U-matic
Introduction to Mathematics Series
Color (C)
Mathematics
Dist - MDCPB **Prod** - MDCPB

Matrices I have met by Paul Halmos 60 MIN
VHS
AMS - MAA joint lecture series
Color (PRO G)
$59.00 purchase _ #VIDHALMOS - VB2
Describes selected matrices, their properties and the problems connected with them. Discusses questions of matrix approximation, unitary dilation of matrices, subnormal matrices and square roots of matrices. Recorded in New Orleans.
Mathematics
Dist - AMSOC **Prod** - AMSOC 1986

Matrioska 5 MIN
16mm / U-matic / VHS
Color (K P A)
LC 70-710379
An animated film which shows enamelled wooden Russian dolls performing a Russian folk dance.
Fine Arts
Dist - MGHT **Prod** - NFBC 1970

Matrix 6 MIN
U-matic / VHS / 16mm
Color (I A)
LC 70-711330
Presents horizontal and vertical lines, squares and cubes where all motion is a long closed invisible pathway.
Fine Arts
Dist - PFP **Prod** - WHIT 1970

Matrix 6 MIN
16mm
Color (C)
$196.00
Experimental film by John Whitney.
Fine Arts
Dist - AFA **Prod** - AFA 1971

The Matrix diagram - Part 6 19 MIN
VHS
Memory jogger plus series
Color (PRO IND A)
$495.00 purchase _ #GO01F
Presents part six of a seven - part series featuring Michael Brassard. Uses an interactive format giving viewers hands - on experience with topic. By Goal - QPC. Includes extensive workshop materials.
Business and Economics; Psychology
Dist - EXTR

Matrix materials 51 MIN
BETA / VHS / U-matic
Composites I the basics series
Color
$400 purchase
Thermosetting organic resins such as polyesters, epoxies, and polyimides.
Industrial and Technical Education; Science
Dist - ASM **Prod** - ASM

Matt and the Missing Parts 8 MIN
16mm
Human Side of Supervision Series
Color (IND)
LC 73-701931
Studies human motives, how they can be misunderstood, how they affect all layers of supervision, how they are symptoms of even deeper personal and company problems and how significant they can be to the welfare of any company.
Business and Economics; Psychology
Dist - VOAERO **Prod** - VOAERO 1972

Mattehw Geller - Everglades City 98 MIN
VHS / U-matic
Color
Features a fairy tale. Gives equal weight to characters, plot and environment.
Fine Arts; Literature and Drama
Dist - ARTINC **Prod** - ARTINC

Matteo and Alan Lynes 30 MIN
U-matic / VHS
Eye on Dance - Dance in Religion and Ritual Series
Color
Focuses on the cultural experience reflected in dance. Looks at a performance of 'Esoterica' with Robert Cohan. Hosted by Julinda Lewis.
Fine Arts
Dist - ARCVID **Prod** - ARCVID

Matter 22 MIN
VHS
Understanding science video series
Color (I J H)
$39.95 purchase _ #KUS202
Explores the general and physical properties of matter, as well as phase changes. Discusses weight and mass, Boyle's law and more. Part of a six - part series on science.
Science - Physical
Dist - KNOWUN

Matter 10 MIN
VHS
Take a look 2 series
Color (P)
$49.00 purchase, $15.00 rental _ #353803; LC 91-707960
Defines matter and shows how it can take the form of a solid, liquid or gas. Part of a series that takes a hands - on approach to the principles of science.
Psychology; Science; Science - Physical
Dist - TVOTAR **Prod** - TVOTAR 1990

Matter 15 MIN
U-matic
Science Alliance Series
Color (I)
Introduces the states of matter, solid, liquid and gas and demonstrates how matter can change from one state to another.
Science; Science - Physical
Dist - TVOTAR **Prod** - TVOTAR 1981

Matter 15 MIN
VHS
Understanding science series
Color (J H)
$39.00 purchase _ #60487 - 026
Part of a series that presents difficult scientific concepts in an easy - to - understand format designed with natural stopping points so the instructor can choose when to stop for classroom discussion.
Science - Physical
Dist - GA **Prod** - GA 1993

Matter and Energy 14 MIN
U-matic / VHS / 16mm
Color (J H)
LC 72-700862
Presents properties and states of matter, potential and kinetic energy and the rule of energy in chemical changes.
Science - Physical
Dist - CORF **Prod** - CORF 1972

Matter and energy
VHS
Color; PAL (H)
Begins with the universe as an enormous system of matter and energy to show examples of properties and states of matter, the relationship between kinetic and potential energy and the role of energy in chemical changes. Uses the law of conservation of matter and energy as related to nuclear fission and fusion to lead to the modern concept of the equivalence of matter and energy.
Science - Physical
Dist - VIEWTH **Prod** - VIEWTH

Matter and Energy 13 MIN
16mm / U-matic / VHS
Color (J H)
$315, $220 purchase _ #1710
Discusses energy and its relation to chemical changes. Talks about nuclear fission and nuclear fusion.
Science - Physical
Dist - CORF

Matter and Energy 11 MIN
16mm
Of Stars and Men (2nd Ed Series
Color (J)
LC 76-701274
A revised version of the 1964 film Of Stars And Men Tells the story of a man who gives up his hum - drum existence to seek truth through a philosophical quest. Discusses man's place in the universe through an examination of time, one of life's basic elements. Based on the book OF STARS AND MEN by Dr Harlow Shapley.
Religion and Philosophy; Science - Physical
Dist - RADIM **Prod** - HUBLEY 1976

Matter and energy for beginners series
Electricity 15 MIN
How materials change 12 MIN
Light 14 MIN
Magnets 12 MIN
Solid, liquid, gas 12 MIN
Sound
Dist - CORF

Matter and energy series
Presents a four - part series presenting the latest theories and understandings of atomic structure and the relationships of matter and energy. Includes the titles Energy - What Is It; Matter - What Is It; Matter - How Is It Put Together; Energy from the Atom - Nuclear Power; and 25 blackline masters.
Energy - what is it 10 MIN
Energy from the atom - nuclear power 10 MIN
Matter - how is it put together 10 MIN
Matter - what is it 10 MIN
Dist - HRMC **Prod** - UNL 1976
UNL

Matter and its Properties 15 MIN
VHS / 16mm
Challenge Series
Color (I)
$125.00 purchase, $25.00 rental
Introduces the world of physics through various demonstrations and experiments.
Science; Science - Physical
Dist - AITECH **Prod** - WDCNTV 1987

Matter and Minerals 30 MIN
VHS / U-matic
Earth, Sea and Sky Series
Color (C)
Explores the history and make - up of matter. Concentrates on minerals, the basic building blocks of the earth and of many astronomical bodies.
Science - Physical; Social Science
Dist - DALCCD **Prod** - DALCCD

Matter and motion - module red - series
Earth resources 15 MIN
The Earth's past 15 MIN
Dist - AITECH

Matter and Motion Series Module Blue
Our polluted waters 15 MIN
Radioactivity and the environment 15 MIN
Sounds around us 15 MIN
Dist - AITECH

Matter and Motion Series Module Brown
It's about time 15 MIN
Weather 15 MIN
Dist - AITECH

Matter and Motion Series Module Green
Machines that move people 15 MIN
Simple machines 15 MIN
Dist - AITECH

Matter and Motion Series Module Red
The States of matter 15 MIN
Thinking about rocks 15 MIN
Dist - AITECH

Matter and Motion Series
About Christmas trees 15 MIN
About energy 15 MIN
Days and seasons 15 MIN
Magnetism and electricity 15 MIN
Something in the air 15 MIN
Dist - AITECH

Matter and the molecular theory 13 MIN
16mm / U-matic / VHS
Color (J)
$325.00, $235.00 purchase _ #3177
Presents inductive demonstrations and experiments to show evidences for the existence of atoms and molecules. Shows how crystal lattices, individual crystallites, diffusion in solids, liquids and gases, Brownian movement and electron micrographs add support to the molecular theory.
Science - Physical
Dist - CORF **Prod** - CORF 1970

Matter - building blocks of the universe 15 MIN
VHS
Color (P I)
$89.00 purchase _ #RB803
Studies matter and its presently known components - protons, electrons and neutrons. Examines atomic structure, elements, compounds, physical states - solids, liquids and gases, and the action of heat in changing the physical states of substances.
Science - Physical
Dist - REVID **Prod** - REVID

Matter Changes 13.5 MIN
16mm / VHS / U-matic
Physical Science Learning Lab Series
Color (I J P)
$305, $215, $245 purchase _ #A298; LC 81-700085
Shows how electrons govern chemical change and illustrates molecular motion in solids, liquids and gases.
Science - Physical
Dist - BARR **Prod** - BARR 1981

Matter - how is it put together 10 MIN
VHS
Matter and energy series
Color (I J H)
$55.00 purchase _ #GW - 5108 - VS; $59.95 purchase _ #1263VG
Concentrates on the states of matter and how matter can change from one state to another. Describes the three states of matter common to human experience. Present also the fourth state of matter, plasma. Part three of a four - part series presenting the latest theories and understandings of atomic structure and the relationships of matter and energy. Includes blackline masters.
Science - Physical
Dist - HRMC **Prod** - UNL 1992
UNL

Matter in Balance 30 MIN
U-matic
Dimensions in Science - Chemistry Series
Color (H C)
Contrasts equilibrium as a balance between opposing forces with dynamic equalibrium in which molecular processes are balanced.
Science; Science - Physical
Dist - TVOTAR **Prod** - TVOTAR 1979

Matter into Energy 10 MIN
16mm / U-matic / VHS
Color (I J)
$265, $185 purchase _ #77537
Shows how matter converts into energy and discusses nuclear reactions.
Science - Physical
Dist - CORF

Matter is Everything 12 MIN
16mm / VHS / U-matic
Physical Science Learning Lab Series
Color (I J P)
$275, $195, $225 purchase _ #A297; LC 81-700086
Shows the relationships among matter, mass, properties, elements, compounds, molecules, atoms, protons, neutrons and electrons.
Science - Physical
Dist - BARR **Prod** - BARR 1981

Matter is made of 15 MIN
VHS / U-matic
First Films on Science Series
Color (P I)
Discusses the properties of molecules. Shows how, with different arrangement of molecules, matter takes different forms. Includes experiments that show how to detect very large molecules and that demonstrate molecular motion.
Science; Science - Physical
Dist - AITECH **Prod** - MAETEL 1975

Matter, Matter Everywhere - How Materials Change 11 MIN
U-matic / VHS / 16mm
Matter, Matter Everywhere Series
Color (P)
LC 72-706716
Shows that some changes in materials result in new materials with different characteristics.
Science - Physical
Dist - CORF **Prod** - CORF 1970

Matter, Matter Everywhere - its Smallest Parts 14 MIN
16mm / U-matic / VHS
Matter, Matter Everywhere Series
Color (P)
LC 75-706714
Shows how the concept of atoms and molecules accounts for the three forms of matter. Children discover what molecules might be like and how they are believed to behave.
Science - Physical
Dist - CORF **Prod** - CORF 1970

Matter, Matter Everywhere - Mixing and Dissolving 11 MIN
16mm / U-matic / VHS
Matter, Matter Everywhere Series
Color (P)
LC 79-706715
Introduces the characteristics of mixtures and solutions. Shows children combining familiar materials and then try to separate them in order to learn about mixtures and solution.
Science - Physical
Dist - CORF **Prod** - CORF 1970

Matter, Matter Everywhere Series
How materials change 11 MIN
Matter, Matter Everywhere - How Materials Change 11 MIN
Matter, Matter Everywhere - its Smallest Parts 14 MIN
Matter, Matter Everywhere - Mixing and Dissolving 11 MIN
Matter, Matter Everywhere - Solids, Liquids and Gas 11 MIN
Solid, Liquid, Gas 11 MIN
Dist - CORF

Matter, Matter Everywhere - Solids, Liquids and Gas 11 MIN
U-matic / VHS / 16mm
Matter, Matter Everywhere Series
Color (P)
LC 77-706713
Explores ways of describing matter and explains how the three states of matter differ.
Science - Physical
Dist - CORF **Prod** - CORF 1970

The Matter of Air 30 MIN
16mm
Starting Tomorrow Series Unit 4 - New Ways in Elementary Science
B&W (T)
Shows how elementary science lessons that are activity oriented can be undertaken using the simplest materials, even in a highly formal classroom.
Education; Science
Dist - WALKED **Prod** - EALING

A Matter of balance 23 MIN
16mm / U-matic
Color (J H C)
$375.00, $300.00 purchase, $100.00 rental
Discusses the internal balancing mechanisms of the body and how they are affected by drugs. Discusses three different classes of drugs - uppers - stimulants, downers - barbituates and all - arounders - psychedelics.
Health and Safety; Psychology
Dist - CNMD **Prod** - CNMD 1987

A Matter of balance 20 MIN
VHS
Color (J H G)
$325.00 purchase
Examines the effects of psychoactive drugs. Teaches physiology and brain chemistry in an easy - to - understand manner. Helps to disarm the lure of drug and alcohol use. Shows users how drugs manipulate their brain chemistry and negatively impact behavior.
Guidance and Counseling; Psychology; Sociology
Dist - FMSP

A Matter of balance 20 MIN
VHS / U-matic / BETA
Color; PAL (IND G)
$175.00 rental _ #ASF - 112
Reveals that falls account for about 20 percent of all industrial accidents, that some are caused by unsafe working conditions. Considers that most result from victims taking chances, acting unsafely or not being alert to danger. Examines situations and actions that cause falls. Includes leader's guide and 10 workbooks.
Health and Safety; Psychology
Dist - BNA **Prod** - BNA

Matter of Chance 28 MIN
U-matic
Color (A)
LC 77-703362
Features a hospital - based sickle - cell anemia counseling program. Differentiates sickle cell disease from sickle cell trait and discusses the chances of hereditary transmission.
Health and Safety; Science - Natural
Dist - USNAC **Prod** - VADTC 1977

A Matter of Choice 28 MIN
16mm
Color
LC 76-703246
Looks at far - reaching prospects of nuclear development and its benefits and consequences.
Industrial and Technical Education; Science - Physical; Social Science
Dist - CANFDC **Prod** - TETRA 1975

A Matter of choice 60 MIN
VHS / U-matic
Winds of change series
Color (G)
$59.95 purchase
Travels to the Hopi Nation in an effort to understand their struggle to find their place in the modern world. Interviews tribal members offering rare insights into the personal side of acculturation and assimilation. Looks at the remarkable importance of women and uncles in Hopi social structure, and how the exodus of their youth to the cities threatens their very survival.
Social Science
Dist - NAMPBC

A Matter of choice - a program confronting teenage sexual abuse 20 MIN
VHS
Color (J H)
$95.00 purchase _ #1373VG
Addresses the topic of date and acquaintance rape for teenagers. Discusses refusal, definitions of sexual assault, and the myths about rape. Features interviews with victims, perpetrators and professionals as they tell stories and give advice. Includes a leader's guide and blackline masters.
Sociology
Dist - UNL

Matter of Choice - Question De Choix 14 MIN
16mm
Color (H C A) (FRENCH)
#2X30I
Explains the process of electing a new band chief for an Indian reservation. Focuses on both election procedures and the responsibilities of the office.
Social Science
Dist - CDIAND **Prod** - ALBCOM 1975

Matter of clarity 30 MIN
16mm
Color (G)
$55.00 rental
Completes the loose trilogy of a cycle of discovery. Brings to resolution the themes of Blakean revelation of the sensuality of perception through rich imagery of the natural world. Produced by Sandra Davis.
Fine Arts
Dist - CANCIN

A Matter of Concern - Organizing Emergency Field Care of Athletes 12 MIN
16mm / U-matic / VHS
Football Injury Prevention Series
Color (I J H)
Explains emergency treatment of the injured football player, with instructions for the person assigned first aid responsibility, including how to recognize and handle serious injuries.
Physical Education and Recreation
Dist - ATHI **Prod** - ATHI

A Matter of Conscience - Henry VIII and Thomas more 30 MIN
U-matic / VHS / 16mm
Western Civilization - Majesty and Madness Series
Color (H C A)
LC 72-702775
Accentuates the historic clash between Henry VIII and Sir Thomas More as a prototypical confrontation between state policy and an individual who is living in opposition to it.
Civics and Political Systems; History - World; Sociology
Dist - LCOA **Prod** - CPC 1972

A Matter of Contamination Sense 10 MIN
16mm
B&W (PRO)
Discusses the hazards present when handling radioactive substance and the principles and practice of contamination drills.
Health and Safety; Science - Physical
Dist - UKAEA **Prod** - UKAEA 1958

The Matter of David J 16 MIN
U-matic / VHS / 16mm
Under the Law, Pt 2 Series
Color (I J H C)
LC 75-703574
Tells a story about a boy who agrees to drive a getaway truck in a robbery to raise money to pay for a motorcycle. Shows how he must accept responsibility for the consequences of the robbery when it results in a shooting.
Civics and Political Systems; Sociology
Dist - CORF **Prod** - USNEI 1975

A Matter of degree 30 MIN
U-matic / VHS
Contemporary health issues series; Lesson 4
Color (C A)
Examines the stress that is characteristic of life in twentieth - century America. Focuses on three sources of stress and looks at specific means by which individuals can combat the effects of stress.
Psychology
Dist - CDTEL **Prod** - SCCON

A Matter of degrees 27 MIN
VHS
Always a river video collection series
Color (G)
Contact distributor about rental cost _ #N92 - 032
Takes an unusual tour through a museum, giving a history of surveying and a demonstration of present surveying methods.
Geography - United States; Industrial and Technical Education
Dist - INDI

A matter of degrees - applying intermediate - temperature thermal pipe insulation 20 MIN
VHS
Color (IND)
$395.00 purchase, $95.00 rental _ #800 - 60
Explains safe and correct techniques for installing calcium silicate and fiberglass insulation on pipes, valves, flanges, elbows and tees. Discusses personal protective equipment and procedures to follow if asbestos is discovered.
Health and Safety; Psychology
Dist - ITSC **Prod** - ITSC

A Matter of Doing Something to Live 20 MIN
U-matic
B&W
Documents the life and work experiences of women in the Thompson/Nicola region of British Columbia, a northern farming area, from the 19th to the mid - 20th centuries. Looks at the work options available to women during this period, links these choices to the economic system and Canadian society's expectations of women and examines the effects of the work options upon women's lives.
History - World; Sociology
Dist - WMENIF **Prod** - WMENIF

A Matter of expectations - 1 30 MIN
16mm / VHS / BETA / U-matic
Parenting the child who is handicapped series
Color; PAL (G PRO)
PdS150, PdS158 purchase
Deals with the practical issues of raising the handicapped child within the family and community setting. Presents part of a three - part series.
Health and Safety; Social Science; Sociology
Dist - EDPAT

A Matter of Fat 26 MIN
U-matic / VHS
Color (C)
$249.00, $149.00 purchase _ #AD - 1907
Examines biochemical and genetic explanations for obesity. Considers the see - saw effect of dieting and the 'set point' theory. Shows ongoing research into the biochemistry of weight gain.
Health and Safety; Psychology; Social Science
Dist - FOTH **Prod** - FOTH

A Matter of Fat 99 MIN
16mm
Color (H C A)
LC 77-714184
Examines several aspects of the problem of over - weight in a documentary about the ordeal of a fat man and his struggle to lose weight.
Guidance and Counseling; Health and Safety; Physical Education and Recreation
Dist - NFBC **Prod** - NFBC 1969

Matter of Fiction Series no 10
The Outsiders 20 MIN
Dist - AITECH

Matter of fiction series no 2
A Slave's tale 20 MIN
Dist - AITECH

Matter of Fiction Series

Ash road	20 MIN
Donbas and the Endless steppe	20 MIN
Undertow and Count Me Gone	20 MIN
White Mountains and the City of Gold and Lead	20 MIN
The Year of the jeep	20 MIN

Dist - AITECH

Matter of heart 107 MIN
35mm / 16mm / VHS
Color; B&W (G)
$150.00, $200.00 rental
Portrays Carl Gustav Jung. Directed by Mark Whitney.
Fine Arts; Psychology
Dist - KINOIC

A Matter of Inconvenience 10 MIN
U-matic / VHS / 16mm
Color (A)
LC 74-703164
Depicts a group of young skiers on the slopes of Lake Tahoe, Nevada. Explains that they are either blind or amputees, showing that a disability does not have to be a handicap, but only a matter of inconvenience.
Guidance and Counseling; Health and Safety; Physical Education and Recreation
Dist - STNFLD **Prod** - STNFLD 1974

A Matter of Independence 16 MIN
16mm
Color
LC 77-703225
Discusses the experiences of handicapped students at St Andrew's Presbyterian College. Shows their lives in mobile home units adapted to accommodate individuals in wheelchairs.
Education; Psychology
Dist - USNAC **Prod** - STANPC 1976

A Matter of Indifference 48 MIN
U-matic / VHS / 16mm
B&W (H C A)
LC 74-703304
Presents a critique of society's ambivalence toward the aged. Includes an interview with Maggie Kuhn, founder of the Gray Panther movement.
Health and Safety; Sociology
Dist - PHENIX **Prod** - PHENIX 1974

A Matter of Insurance 52 MIN
16mm / U-matic / VHS
Fight Against Slavery Series no 3; No 3
Color
LC 78-700502
Recounts an incident involving a slave captain who murdered 130 Africans by throwing them overboard and was then brought to trial, not on a murder charge but for an insurance claim. Shows how this dramatically changed public opinion on slavery.
History - United States; Sociology
Dist - TIMLIF **Prod** - BBCTV 1977

Matter of Job Protection 12 MIN
16mm
Color
LC 74-700823
Presents an animated story of the last day in the career of a letter carrier.
Guidance and Counseling; Social Science
Dist - CRAF **Prod** - CRAF 1972

A Matter of judgment - conflicts of interest in the workplace 30 MIN
VHS
Color (A)
$500.00 purchase, $150.00 rental _ #V1065 - 06
Points out areas of business that may lead to conflicts of interest, such as vendor relationships, hiring practices, consulting abuses and family involvment. Uses short skits to present legally questionable activities as thought - provoking material. Includes a group leader's guide with the video.
Business and Economics; Psychology
Dist - BARR **Prod** - ETHICS

A Matter of Life and Death 30 MIN
U-matic / VHS / 16mm
Moving Right Along Series
Color (J H A)
Demonstrates how students face the possibility of losing a teacher they idolize when he suffers a stroke. Shows that as they learn to come to terms with the inevitability of death, they help the teacher begin his recovery.
Sociology
Dist - CORF **Prod** - WQED 1983

A Matter of life or death - withdrawing life support 20 MIN
VHS
Color (H C G)
$295.00 purchase, $55.00 rental
Asks whether a terminally ill patient has the right to say, 'I'd rather die now.' Extracts from the video Who Lives, Who Dies. Interviews Dr David Finley, Director of Critical Care, Roosevelt Hospital, New York, who believes the patient's wishes should be respected. Addresses bioethical issues relating to individual patients and to society as a whole. Questions whether money spent to prolong the process of dying should be redirected to patients who are currently denied basic care. Produced for Public Policy Productions.
Civics and Political Systems; Sociology
Dist - FLMLIB **Prod** - RWEIS 1988

Matter of minutes - pulp and paper - hydrogen sulfide 22 MIN
BETA / VHS / U-matic
Color (IND G)
$395.00 purchase _ #601 - 05
Discusses the dangers of hydrogen sulfide, H2S, to workers in the pulp and paper industry. Emphasizes the extremely poor warning qualities of H2S and the fact that it is heavier than air.
Health and Safety; Industrial and Technical Education; Psychology
Dist - ITSC **Prod** - ITSC

Matter of minutes - wastewater - hydrogen sulfide 21 MIN
BETA / VHS / U-matic
Color (IND G)
$395.00 purchase _ #601 - 06
Discusses the dangers of hydrogen sulfide, H2S, to workers in the wastewater treatment industry.
Health and Safety; Industrial and Technical Education; Psychology
Dist - ITSC **Prod** - ITSC

A Matter of Opportunity 27 MIN
16mm
Color (J H)
Focuses on the many opportunities available to students who decide on a career in medicine.
Health and Safety
Dist - AMEDA **Prod** - AMEDA

A Matter of people - Pt 7 30 MIN
VHS / U-matic
Profiles in progress series
Color (H C)
$325.00, $295.00 purchase _ #V552
Addresses specific individuals and institutions who are making a difference in their societies around the world. Examines the role of three specific elements in helping Third World nations compete while keeping up with the rising expectations of their growing populations - the media, the business community and political leadership. Part of a 13 - part series on people who are moving their tradition - bound countries into modern times.
Business and Economics; Geography - World; Sociology
Dist - BARR **Prod** - CEPRO 1991

A Matter of Perspective 8 MIN
16mm
Color
LC 74-705099
Shows a problematical situation intended as a stimulus to guide group discussion. Describes a young mother's difficulty in having her children vaccinated at a county clinic.
Health and Safety; Home Economics; Sociology
Dist - USNAC **Prod** - NMAC

Matter of principle - polygamy in the mountain west 58 MIN
VHS
Color (G)
$19.95 purchase
Takes an unprecedented look at the history, controversy and contemporary practice of polygamy in the American West. Produced by Ken Verdoia.
History - United States; Religion and Philosophy; Sociology
Dist - KUEDTV **Prod** - KUEDTV 1990

A Matter of promises 60 MIN
VHS / U-matic
Winds of change series
Color (G)
$59.95 purchase
Introduces members of the Onondaga, Navajo and Lummi leadership, including Audrey Shenandoah, clan mother, who states that she has lived within the geopolitical boundaries of the US but has never considered herself 'American.' Interviews tribal members and documents external and internal forces that threaten their national sovereignty. Gives a brief history of political activism with archival footage.
Social Science
Dist - NAMPBC

A Matter of Protection 28 MIN
16mm
Color (A)
LC FIE64-115
Shows how the public health service helped to combat the Asian flu epidemic of 1957, how it seeks causes and cures of many diseases and how it helps to safeguard the nation's health. Explains how the nation's resources are mobilized.
Health and Safety
Dist - USNAC **Prod** - USPHS 1963

A Matter of protection - barrier techniques for healthcare workers 16 MIN
VHS
Color (C PRO G)
$395.00 purchase _ #R930 - VI - 016
Trains healthcare workers exposed to microorganisms who need to protect themselves and their patients. Demonstrates some barrier techniques healthcare workers can use to reduce the spread of microorganisms to themselves and their patients and to reduce the risk of infection in the healthcare facility. Produced at Norwalk Hospital, Norwalk, Connecticut.
Health and Safety
Dist - HSCIC

A Matter of Respect 18 MIN
U-matic / VHS / 16mm
Color (H)
Uses the dramatization of a teen love affair to emphasize male sexual responsibility.
Guidance and Counseling; Health and Safety; Psychology; Sociology
Dist - USNAC **Prod** - USHHS

A Matter of respect 18 MIN
U-matic / 16mm / VHS
Color (J H C)
$190.00, $95.00 purchase _ #TCA03812, #TCA03813, #TCA05102
Dramatizes a teenage love affair. Focuses on the male's need to exercise sexual responsibility. Includes teacher's guide.
Health and Safety; Science - Natural
Dist - USNAC **Prod** - CFDISC 1980

A Matter of Seconds 30 MIN
16mm
Color; B&W (C T)
Concerns three elderly people who had accidents in the home as a result of a lack of safety measures.
Health and Safety; Sociology
Dist - CFDC **Prod** - CFDC

A Matter of Size 29 MIN
U-matic
Color
Examines the effects of bigness and smallness on American life. Surveys the growing frustration felt by many as the result of big business and big government.
Sociology
Dist - PBS **Prod** - WMHTTV

A Matter of Size - Power and People 29 MIN
VHS / U-matic
Color
Considers questions of size, power, politics, economics and culture. Presents divergent views. Originally aired on PBS.
Fine Arts
Dist - KITCHN **Prod** - KITCHN

A Matter of state - the atom - Parts 5 and 6 60 MIN
VHS / U-matic
World of chemistry series
Color (C)
$45.00, $29.95 purchase
Presents parts 5 and 6 of the 26 - part World of Chemistry series. Examines matter in its three principal states - gases, liquids and solids - relating the visible world to the submicroscopic. Explains changes in matter at the molecular level. Reviews models of the atom from the ancient to the modern view. Two thirty - minute programs hosted by Nobel laureate Roald Hoffmann.
Science - Physical
Dist - ANNCPB **Prod** - UMD 1990

A Matter of survival 17 MIN
VHS
Color (C PRO)
$195.00 purchase, $75.00 rental _ #42 - 2433, #42 - 2433R
Targets the safe handling, containment and disposal of sharps. Includes a hands - on video and three copies of an instructor's manual, including a post - test. Uses real - life dramatizations to demonstrate the correct way to handle sharps to minimize risk and enhance protection. Features first - hand stories from health care workers who were infected by or exposed to accidental needlesticks.
Health and Safety
Dist - NLFN **Prod** - NLFN

A Matter of Taste 14 MIN
U-matic / VHS / 16mm
Human Senses Series
Color (P I)
Employs animation to show how taste information is sent from cells in taste buds on the tongue along nerve pathways to the brain. Describes the four common tastes and shows that what people eat depends on where they live and their personal experiences.
Science - Natural
Dist - NGS **Prod** - NGS 1982

Matter of taste series
Beverages
Bread
Cheese and milk
Eggs
Fish
Fruit
Grains and legumes
Herbs, spices, and oils
Kitchen equipment
Marketing
Meat
Pasta
Pastry
Poultry
Presentation
Salads
Soups
Sugar
Varietal Meats
Vegetables 30 MIN
Dist - CDTEL

A Matter of the mind 60 MIN
VHS
Frontline Series
Color; Captioned (G)
$150.00 purchase, $95.00 rental _ #FRON - 415K
Examines mental illness from the perspective of those who deal with it. Focuses on patients at Central Manor, a Minnesota halfway house for people with mental illnesses.
Health and Safety
Dist - PBS **Prod** - DOCCON 1989

A Matter of Time 20 MIN
VHS / U-matic
Once upon a Time Series
Color (P I)
Presents literary selections that deal with adventures in time and space and looks at the world of tomorrow.

English Language; Literature and Drama
Dist - AITECH **Prod** - MDDE 1977

A Matter of Time 97 MIN
16mm
Color (H A)
Tells the story of a chambermaid in pre - WWI Europe who is taught to love life by an eccentric contessa. Stars Liza Minnelli, Ingrid Bergman, Charles Boyer. Directed by Vincent Minneli.
Fine Arts
Dist - TIMLIF **Prod** - FWTVP 1976

A Matter of Time 30 MIN
U-matic / VHS / 16mm
Color (J H A)
LC 81-700958
Chronicles the painful period of growth which occurs for Lisa when she discovers that her mother has a malignant tumor and only a few months to live. Shows the girl emerging from her mother's shadow and discovering her own special talent.
Guidance and Counseling; Sociology
Dist - LCOA **Prod** - TAHSEM

A Matter of Time 22 MIN
16mm
Color
LC 77-701815
Deals with the safe operation of large construction machines. Shows a series of accident vignettes, some described by the actual operators involved and others by witnesses.
Health and Safety; Industrial and Technical Education
Dist - PILOT **Prod** - CLARK 1976

A Matter of time series

Farley's folly	13 MIN
The Hours are good	13 MIN
It all adds up	11 MIN
Looking Ahead	8 MIN
Making it Count	12 MIN
No Place to Go	14 MIN
Staying in Tune	9 MIN
Two for the road	12 MIN

Dist - ACCESS

A Matter of Understanding - the Coyote, His Story 27 MIN
16mm
Color (C A)
LC 77-703226
Examines the life and habits of coyotes and explains why they are misunderstood by man.
Science - Natural
Dist - USNAC **Prod** - USEPA 1977

Matter - Volume 2 18 MIN
VHS
Understanding science series
Color (I J)
$39.95 purchase _ #SC02
Presents experiments and demonstrations that can be easily repeated in the classroom. Includes a teacher's guide. Part of a six - part series explaining difficult scientific ideas in an informal way.
Science; Science - Physical
Dist - SVIP

Matter Waves 28 MIN
16mm
B&W (H C)
Presents a modern version of the original experiment which showed the wave behavior of the electron. Shows electron diffraction patterns on a flourescent screen and discusses the electron diffraction experiments of G p Thomson.
Science; Science - Physical
Dist - MLA **Prod** - PSSC 1962

Matter Waves 10 MIN
U-matic
Wave Particle Duality Series
Color (H C)
Looks at Broglie's prediction that light sometimes behaves like wave and sometimes like particles.
Science; Science - Physical
Dist - TVOTAR **Prod** - TVOTAR 1984

Matter - what is it 10 MIN
VHS
Matter and energy series
Color (I J H)
$55.00 purchase _ #GW - 5107 - VS; $59.95 purchase _ #1243VG
Introduces students to the structure of matter. Uses descriptions of particle accelerators and how they are used to explore atoms to clarify some of the latest information about the building blocks of matters. Part two of a four - part series presenting the latest theories and understandings of atomic structure and the relationships of matter and energy. Includes blackline masters.
Science - Physical
Dist - HRMC **Prod** - UNL 1992
UNL

The Matter with Me 15 MIN
U-matic / VHS / 16mm
Color (H C A)
LC 72-702406
Follows the movements of a twelve - year - old Black boy through two worlds - one White, one Black. Shows the boy in various places in these two worlds and presents both worlds through the boy's eyes.
Guidance and Counseling; Sociology
Dist - AIMS **Prod** - MONWIL 1972

Matters of life and death 50 MIN
VHS
Doctors to be series
Color; PAL (C PRO)
PdS99 purchase
Covers some of the difficult situations doctors - in - training encounter in their work with patients. Focuses on the emotional strain that medical students bear. Fourth in the series Doctors To Be which follows a group of medical students from their initial screening through their work as newly qualified doctors.
Health and Safety
Dist - BBCENE

Matters of the Heart 30 MIN
U-matic / VHS
Innovation Series
Color
Looks at the research effort underway to combat heart disease. Discusses new diagnostic techniques as well as experimental methods of treatment.
Health and Safety; Science - Natural
Dist - PBS **Prod** - WNETTV 1983

Matthew 6 MIN
16mm
Color
LC 77-700385
Follows a three - year - old child's exploration of a meadow.
Psychology
Dist - ASPTEF **Prod** - ASPTEF 1976

Matthew 15 MIN
VHS / U-matic
Changing Series
Color (J H)
Looks at Matthew, a wild brawler whose violent behavior culminates in attempted suicide after he is arrested for robbing a gas station.
Sociology
Dist - AITECH **Prod** - WGTETV 1980

Matthew 13 - 16
VHS
The Bible - American Sign Language translation series
Color (S R)
Presents an American Sign Language translation of the New Testament Gospel of Matthew, chapters 13 through 16. Available on a free - loan basis from the Lutheran Church - Missouri Synod's Deaf Ministry.
Guidance and Counseling; Literature and Drama; Religion and Philosophy
Dist - CPH **Prod** - LUMIS

Matthew 17 - 21
VHS
The Bible - American Sign Language translation series
Color (S R)
Presents an American Sign Language translation of the New Testament Gospel of Matthew, chapters 17 through 21. Available on a free - loan basis from the Lutheran Church - Missouri Synod's Deaf Ministry.
Guidance and Counseling; Literature and Drama; Religion and Philosophy
Dist - CPH **Prod** - LUMIS

Matthew 26 - 28
VHS
The Bible - American Sign Language translation series
Color (S R)
Presents an American Sign Language translation of the New Testament Gospel of Matthew, chapters 26 through 28. Available on a free - loan basis from the Lutheran Church - Missouri Synod's Deaf Ministry.
Guidance and Counseling; Literature and Drama; Religion and Philosophy
Dist - CPH **Prod** - LUMIS

Matthew Aliuk - Eskimo in Two Worlds 18 MIN
U-matic / VHS / 16mm
Many Americans Series
Color (I J)
LC 73-701259
Tells the story of Matthew, an Eskimo boy assimilated into the city life of Anchorage and his Uncle Isak, from a hunting village in the north, who represents a different tradition.
Geography - United States; Psychology; Social Science
Dist - LCOA **Prod** - LCOA 1973

Matthew 5 5 5 MIN
16mm
Color (H C R)
LC 73-702538
Discusses chapter five, verse five of the gospel of Matthew, in the New Testament. Juxtaposes views of argumentative, 'INVOLVED' humanity with the poor, the derelict and the oppressed. Poses the question, 'WHO IS THE MEEK.' Views a grave, its preparation and closing as one suggestion of 'INHERITING THE EARTH.'.
Literature and Drama; Religion and Philosophy
Dist - FRACOC **Prod** - FRACOC 1973

Matthew 5 - 9
VHS
The Bible - American Sign Language translation series
Color (S R)
Presents an American Sign Language translation of the New Testament Gospel of Matthew, chapters 5 through 9. Available on a free - loan basis from the Lutheran Church - Missouri Synod's Deaf Ministry.
Guidance and Counseling; Literature and Drama; Religion and Philosophy
Dist - CPH **Prod** - LUMIS

Matthew Henson 30 MIN
VHS
Black Americans of achievement collection II series
Color (J H C G)
$49.95 purchase _ #LVCD6619V - S
Provides interesting and concise information on explorer Matthew Henson. Part of a 10 - part series on African - Americans.
History - United States
Dist - CAMV

Matthew Manning - a Study of a Psychic 27 MIN
16mm
Color
LC 75-704205
Describes the experiences of Matthew Manning, a young British psychic.
Psychology; Religion and Philosophy
Dist - USCAN **Prod** - RAYMDB 1975

Matthew Manning - Study of a Psychic 30 MIN
VHS / U-matic
Color
Shows the life of English psychic Matthew Manning including his work with scientists trying to discover what produces his talent.
Psychology; Religion and Philosophy
Dist - HP **Prod** - HP

Matthew Merian - European Engraver and Historian (1593 - 1650) 14 MIN
16mm
B&W
Presents the photo - journalism of the troubled age during the 17th century, showing the engraving of large and crowded scenes of city and country life in war and peace by Merian.
Fine Arts
Dist - ROLAND **Prod** - ROLAND

Matthew 1 - 4 and Psalms 19 and 23
VHS
The Bible - American Sign Language translation series
Color (S R)
Presents an American Sign Language translation of the New Testament Gospel of Matthew, chapters 1 through 4, as well as Psalms 19 and 23. Available on a free - loan basis from the Lutheran Church - Missouri Synod's Deaf Ministry.
Guidance and Counseling; Literature and Drama; Religion and Philosophy
Dist - CPH **Prod** - LUMIS

Matthew - portrait of a one - year old 25 MIN
VHS
Citizen 2000 child development series
Color (H C G)
$295.00 purchase, $55.00 rental
Features pediatrician Dr Aidan Macfarlane who demonstrates the accomplishments of a one - year - old child in his examination of Matthew. Shows that Matthew exhibits a variety of motor and communication skills and is of special interest because of his multicultural upbringing, of Chinese ancestry growing up in England. He will learn no English until he goes to school. Part of a series on child development which is following a group of children over a period of 18 years - from their birth in 1982 until they become adults in the year 2000. Produced by Dove Productions for Channel 4.
Health and Safety; Psychology
Dist - FLMLIB **Prod** - CFTV 1993

Matthew 10 - 12 and Psalm 1
VHS
The Bible - American Sign Language translation series
Color (S R)
Presents an American Sign Language translation of the New Testament Gospel of Matthew, chapters 10 through 12, and Psalm 1. Available on a free - loan basis from the Lutheran Church - Missouri Synod's Deaf Ministry.

Guidance and Counseling; Literature and Drama; Religion and Philosophy
Dist - CPH **Prod** - LUMIS

Maturational lag and specific language disabilities 30 MIN
16mm
Slingerland screening tests for identifying children with specific language series Part A
B&W
Discusses maturational lag and Specific Language Disability as well as those borderline children who might be regarded as 'high risk' for failure. Explains the purpose of the Slingerland screening tests.
Education; English Language; Psychology
Dist - EDPS **Prod** - EDPS

Mature Faith 45 MIN
VHS / BETA
Psychological Growth and Spiritual Development Series
Color (G)
Psychology; Religion and Philosophy
Dist - DSP **Prod** - DSP

The Mature Woman 30 MIN
16mm
Color (C A)
LC 79-700916
Explains how myths, stereotypes and the media influence society's attitudes toward aging, especially aging women.
Business and Economics; Fine Arts; Psychology; Sociology
Dist - AACD **Prod** - AMERGA 1976

The Maturing Female 14 MIN
16mm
Family Life Education and Human Growth Series
Color (J H)
Shows through a story that the teenager is rarely experienced enough to know her friends or herself as well as she think she does.
Guidance and Counseling; Psychology
Dist - SF **Prod** - SF 1970

The Maturing Market 30 MIN
VHS / U-matic
Information Industry - Strategic Planning Considerations Series
Color
Explores the maturing of the marketplace and the resulting restructuring among information services, two of the top change issues facing information industry strategists.
Industrial and Technical Education
Dist - DELTAK **Prod** - DELTAK

Maturing Patterns in a Dancer's Life 30 MIN
VHS / U-matic
Dancers' Health Alert Series
Color
Fine Arts; Health and Safety
Dist - ARCVID **Prod** - ARCVID

The Maturing Shakespeare 28 MIN
U-matic / VHS
Survey of English Verse Series
Color (C)
$249.00, $149.00 purchase _ #AD - 1297
Follows the development of Shakespeare as a dramatist. Features locations and excerpts from his plays.
Fine Arts; Literature and Drama
Dist - FOTH **Prod** - FOTH

Maturity matrix linear programming comes of age
VHS
Color (C PRO G)
$150.00 purchase _ #86.02
Shows how the Darling model is a financial planning simulator which changes dynamically through time, allows analysis and projection of changes in income of financial institutions, and supports establishment of precise market hedges. Reveals that this microcomputer model has been installed in over 400 banks since 1982, and has increased their collective earnings by $500 million in one year alone. George Darling and Associates. John Lastavica.
Business and Economics; Computer Science
Dist - INMASC

Mau Mau 51 MIN
16mm / VHS / U-matic
Color (H C)
An edited version of the motion picture Mau Mau. Analyzes the history of post World War II political events in Kenya. Documents how British over - reaction to a movement for native representation in the Kenyan colonial government led to repression and persecution. Presents a narrative account of how white settlers in Kenya responded to the nationalistic aspirations expressed through the Mau Mau movement.
History - United States; History - World
Dist - FI **Prod** - FI 1973

Maud Hart Lovelace 1892 - 1980 - a Minnesota Childhood 14 MIN
VHS / U-matic
Color (P I J)
LC 84-730300
Portrays Lovelace's childhood in relation to her well - known Betsy - tacy books. Includes historical photographs and illustrations from the books. Explains the concept of historical fiction.
Biography; Literature and Drama
Dist - HERPRO **Prod** - HERPRO 1984

Maud Lewis - a World Without Shadows 10 MIN
U-matic / VHS / 16mm
Color (J)
LC 79-700007
Presents a posthumous tribute to Maud Lewis, an untutored Nova Scotia painter.
Fine Arts
Dist - PHENIX **Prod** - NFBC 1978

Maui 30 MIN
VHS
John Stobart's WorldScape series
Color (A G)
$19.95 purchase _ #STO - 03
Features Charles Lindbergh's grave and other interesting and beautiful sites. Follows artist John Stobart as he travels the globe, painting directly from life, and demonstrates the simplicity of the method that has made him the foremost living maritime artist. Demonstrates Stobart's classical maritime style in numerous evocative settings around the world. Part of a series on painting outdoors.
Fine Arts
Dist - ARTSAM **Prod** - WORLDS

Maui and His Kite 11 MIN
16mm
Color (I)
Tells the story of Maui, demi - god hero of Polynesia, who assembles a kite of bamboo and tapa cloth and with a magic wind Calabash given to him by wind boy makes a flying machine.
Literature and Drama; Social Science
Dist - CINEPC **Prod** - CINEPC

Mauna Kea - on the verge of other worlds 60 MIN
VHS
Color (G)
$125.00 purchase _ #MKOW - 000
Tells how the extinct Hawaiian volcano Mauna Kea is being used as an observatory. Reveals that four major telescopes are operated on the mountain, with more to come. Uses animated special effects to simulate recent discoveries.
Science - Physical
Dist - PBS **Prod** - HAWAPT 1989

Maureen Duffy 45 MIN
VHS
Color (H C G)
$79.00 purchase
Features the British writer and poet with Elaine Feinstein discussing writing as a career and noting how to find inspiration to write various forms like narratives and poems. Talks about her work that includes Gor Saga; Londoners; and Capital and Changes.
Literature and Drama
Dist - ROLAND **Prod** - INCART

Maurice 135 MIN
35mm / 16mm
Color (G)
Traces the sexual awakening of a young man torn between his own longings and the confines of Edwardian England. Adapts the novel by E M Forster and gives voice to his own inner conflicts. Tells the story of Maurice who enters Cambridge, falls in love with Clive and has an intense but platonic love affair. When Clive marries, the rejected lover consults a doctor and a hypnotist in hopes of curing his homosexuality. Eventually, Maurice becomes a respectable businessman and finds a happy and honest relationship with a man from a class far beneath him. Produced by Ismail Merchant; screenplay by Kit Hesketh - Harvey and James Ivory; stars Hugh Grant, James Wilby, Rupert Graves, Dehholm Elliott, Simon Callow and Ben Kingsley. Contact distributor for price.
Fine Arts; Psychology; Sociology
Dist - OCTOBF

Maurice 27 MIN
16mm / U-matic / VHS
Color (A)
Examines the events of Oct 19, 1983 when members of Grenada's Provisional Revolutionary Government were assassinated. Portrays the following US invasion.
Civics and Political Systems; History - World
Dist - CNEMAG **Prod** - CNEMAG 1984

Maurice Bejart - the Love of Dance 60 MIN
VHS / U-matic
Color
Fine Arts
Dist - ABCLR **Prod** - ABCLR

Maurice Chevalier 58 MIN
U-matic / VHS
B&W (C)
$249.00, $149.00 purchase _ #AD - 1349
Portrays a most beloved song - and - dance man, Maurice Chevalier. Traces his career with archival footage from Montmartre to Hollywood.
Biography; Fine Arts; Foreign Language; History - World
Dist - FOTH **Prod** - FOTH

Maurice Hines, Mercedes Ellington, Dean Badolato and Valarie Pettiford 30 MIN
VHS / U-matic
Eye on Dance - Broadway Dance Series
Color
Looks at today's 'Broadway gypsies.'.
Fine Arts
Dist - ARTRES ARCVID **Prod** - ARTRES ARCVID

Maurice Schwartz film series
Maurice Schwartz films series 193 MIN
Dist - ERGOM

Maurice Schwartz films series 193 MIN
VHS
Maurice Schwartz film series
B&W (G) (YIDDISH WITH ENGLISH SUBTITLES)
$130.00 purchase _ #711
Presents actor Maurice Schwartz in two sound films. Includes Tevye and Uncle Moses.
Literature and Drama; Sociology
Dist - ERGOM **Prod** - ERGOM 1939

Maurice Schwartz films series
Tevye - Tevye der Milkhiker 96 MIN
Uncle Moses 87 MIN
Dist - ERGOM

Maurice Sendak 14 MIN
U-matic / VHS / 16mm
Color (C A)
LC FIA66-971
Maurice Sendak, in his studio apartment, speaks of his favorite composers and expresses his admiration for painters and illustrators of the past. He discusses ways these artists have influenced his own work and traces the development of the book 'WHERE THE WILD THINGS ARE.'.
Literature and Drama
Dist - WWS **Prod** - WWS 1966

Maurice Sendak 45 MIN
VHS
Color (H C G)
$79.00 purchase
Features the writer and illustrator talking with Paul Vaughan about his books for children, what makes a successful children's book and adapting books for opera. Discusses his works including Where the Wild Things Are; Outside Over There; and Higgledy Piggledy Pop.
Fine Arts; Literature and Drama
Dist - ROLAND **Prod** - INCART

The Maurice Sendak Library 35 MIN
VHS / 16mm
Children's Circle Video Series
Color (K)
$18.88 purchase _ #CCV021
Presents Maurice Sendak stories for children.
Literature and Drama
Dist - EDUCRT

Maurice Sendak's Really Rosie 35 MIN
VHS
Children's circle collection series
Color (K P I)
$14.95 purchase _ #WK1179
Presents a collection of stories by Maurice Sendak. Includes Alligator's All Around; Chicken Soup with Rice; One Was Johnny, Pierre.
Fine Arts; Literature and Drama
Dist - KNOWUN

Mauritius 28 MIN
Videoreel / VHS
International Byline Series
Color
Interviews Sir Harold Walter, Minister of External Affairs of Mauritius. Shows the beauty of Mauritius and the lifestyles of its people. Hosted by Marilyn Perry.
Business and Economics; Civics and Political Systems; Geography - World
Dist - PERRYM **Prod** - PERRYM

Maurits Escher - Painter of Fantasies 27 MIN
16mm / U-matic / VHS
Color (H C A)
$400 purchase - 16 mm, $295 purchase - video, $50 rental
Portrays the life of M.C. Escher, the graphic artist whose work combines fact, fantasy, mirror images, and symmetrical shapes. Includes interviews with M. C. Escher.
Biography; Fine Arts
Dist - CNEMAG **Prod** - DOCUA 1988

Mauro the Gypsy 43 MIN
16mm
Color (P I)
Tells about Mauro and his gypsy family having to move on.
Literature and Drama
Dist - LUF **Prod** - LUF

Maury Wills on Baserunning 60 MIN
VHS / BETA
Color
Demonstrates baserunning techniques, from the time the batter - runner leaves home plate until he scores or the inning ends. Features Maury Wills, the man who broke Ty Cobb's base - stealing record.
Physical Education and Recreation
Dist - MOHOMV **Prod** - MOHOMV

Mavericks and misfits
VHS
NFL series
Color (G)
$24.95 purchase _ #NFL2006V
Profiles several of the National Football League's most colorful players, 'mavericks and misfits' alike. Produced by NFL Films.
Literature and Drama; Physical Education and Recreation
Dist - CAMV

Max 20 MIN
16mm / U-matic / VHS
Color (J)
LC 79-700679
Presents a story about an aspiring actress who stays late one night to work on her performance in a Broadway show. Tells how she meets the night watchman, an ex - vaudevillian, who, after hearing her emote, says that she would be better off marrying a doctor. Concludes with her insisting on pursuing her acting career.
Fine Arts
Dist - CAROUF **Prod** - GILLAX 1979

Max Adrian as George Bernard Shaw 90 MIN
16mm
Color (J)
Features British actor Max Adrian in a one - man show as the playwright, George Bernard Shaw. Presents lines from Shaw's own writing to evoke the spirit of the playwright from age 38 to just before his death at 93.
Biography; Fine Arts; Literature and Drama
Dist - CANTOR **Prod** - CANTOR

Max Almy - Deadline 4 MIN
U-matic / VHS
Color
Considers corporate demand and personal drive.
Fine Arts
Dist - ARTINC **Prod** - ARTINC

Max Almy - Leaving the 20th Century 11 MIN
VHS / U-matic
Color
Compares social retardation and technical progress.
Fine Arts
Dist - ARTINC **Prod** - ARTINC

Max Almy - Modern Times 30 MIN
VHS / U-matic
B&W
Explores personal relationships and women's roles.
Fine Arts
Dist - ARTINC **Prod** - ARTINC

Max Almy - Perfect Leader 4 MIN
U-matic / VHS
Color
Addresses the coding of a politician for an effective television image.
Fine Arts
Dist - ARTINC **Prod** - ARTINC

Max Bill 16 MIN
16mm
Color
LC 77-700386
Introduces painter Max Bill, including views of his exhibits and of the painter at work.
Fine Arts; Sociology
Dist - COMSKY **Prod** - COMSKY 1976

Max Ernst - Journey into the Subconscious (1891 - 1976) 12 MIN
16mm
Color
Follows Max Ernst into the undersea world of the subconscious where people are confused with birds and forests melt.
Fine Arts
Dist - ROLAND **Prod** - ROLAND

Max Havelaar 170 MIN
35mm
Color; PAL (G)
Travels to the poverty - stricken province of Lebek in 19th century Java. Portrays Max Havelaar, a flamboyant young Dutch official who is sent there to take over the role of Assistant - Resident when his predecessor dies under mysterious circumstances and the province is left in turmoil. Directed by Fons Rademakers for PT Mondial Motion Pictures and Fons Rademakers Produktie, Netherlands. Contact distributor for price and availability outside the United Kingdom.
Civics and Political Systems; Fine Arts; Literature and Drama; Sociology
Dist - BALFOR

Max made mischief 30 MIN
16mm / VHS
Color (C T G)
$430.00, $70.00 purchase, $38.00, $18.00 rental _ #35650
Uses the Maurice Sendak story, Where the Wild Things Are, to demonstrate a literary curriculum developed by Sonia Landes. Shows how third graders explore plot structure, the nature of poetry and the use of illustrations. Includes print material.
English Language; Literature and Drama
Dist - PSU **Prod** - MASON 1978

Max made Mischief - an Approach to Literature 30 MIN
16mm
Color (C T)
LC 78-700675
Shows a third grade class as two teachers try out a new curriculum which uses Maurice Sendak's children's book Where The Wild Things Are to introduce the children to the study and appreciation of literature. Shows the teachers in a discussion with Sendak.
Literature and Drama
Dist - DOCUFL **Prod** - MASON 1977

Max Planck and the World of Atoms 24 MIN
U-matic / VHS
Color (C)
$249.00, $149.00 purchase _ #AD - 2196
Introduces Max Planck and the world he created through his quantum theory. Shows how the theory was developed and its current applications in photo - electro - chemical experiments and atomic spectroscopy.
Science; Science - Physical
Dist - FOTH **Prod** - FOTH

Max Tishler 30 MIN
VHS
Eminent chemists videotapes series
Color (H C G)
$60.00 purchase _ #VT - 025
Meets chemist Max Tishler. Part of a series glimpsing into the history of chemistry and offering insights into the successes, trials and tribulations of some of the most distinguished names in the world of chemistry.
Science
Dist - AMCHEM

Max Und Moritz 80 MIN
16mm
Color (GERMAN)
A German language motion picture. Presents the story of two boys who aggravate the townspeople by constantly thinking up new pranks until the furious miller takes justice into his own hands. A musical production of a picture book by Wilhelm Busch.
Foreign Language; Literature and Drama
Dist - WSTGLC **Prod** - WSTGLC 1956

The Maxillary Lateral Incisor, Information Phases 11 MIN
BETA / VHS
Color (PRO)
Describes the cosmetic changes occurring after this restoration.
Health and Safety
Dist - RMIBHF **Prod** - RMIBHF

Maxillary Sinus 4 MIN
U-matic
Microanatomy Laboratory Orientation Series
Color (C)
Reviews the relationship of the maxillary sinus to the upper molar teeth.
Health and Safety; Science - Natural
Dist - UOKLAH **Prod** - UOKLAH 1986

Maxillofacial Prosthetics - Fabrication of a Nasal Prosthesis 19 MIN
VHS / U-matic
Color (PRO)
Demonstrates techniques used in fabricating a nasal prosthesis from the material PDM siloxane. Shows preparation of the stone mold, casting, pressing and heating.
Health and Safety; Science
Dist - USNAC **Prod** - VAMCNY

Maxima and Minima in several Variables 34 MIN
U-matic / VHS
Calculus of several Variables - Matrix - - Algebra Series; Matrix algebra
B&W
Mathematics
Dist - MIOT **Prod** - MIOT

Maximizing Input with Aphasic Patients 102 MIN
VHS / U-matic
Color
Emphasizes maximizing activation of the brain. Gives attention to the role of cues, syntactic and semantic complexity.
Education; Psychology
Dist - PUAVC **Prod** - PUAVC 1981

Maximizing memory in the elderly 25 MIN
VHS / U-matic
Color (PRO C)
$395.00 purchase, $80.00 rental _ #C920 - VI - 049
Reviews ways to maintain or improve memory in the elderly. Looks at the effects of memory loss on health and self - concept. Presented by Dr Robin West, University of Florida, Geriatric Education Center.
Health and Safety; Psychology
Dist - HSCIC

Maximizing revenues through optimum control of the amount of product offered at various prices - yield management of American Airlines
VHS
Color (C PRO G)
$150.00 purchase _ #91.01
Shows how American Airlines Decision Technologies is actively involved in maximizing revenue from airline flights, railroad runs, hotel rooms, rental car fleets and cruise ships. Reveals that yield management controls reservation availability through overbooking, class code control and traffic management and that system revenue is maximized by considering traffic flow through centrally located hub airports. Revenue has increased by 5 percent, an estimated $1.4 billion over three years. American Airlines Decision Technologies. Barry C Smith, John F Leimkubler, Ross M Darrow.
Business and Economics
Dist - INMASC

Maximizing Witness Cooperation 22 MIN
16mm / U-matic / VHS
Color (PRO)
LC 76-703654
Dramatizes the problem of the uncooperative witness and gives police officers guidelines on how to deal with witnesses and overcome problems.
Civics and Political Systems; Psychology; Sociology
Dist - CORF **Prod** - HAR 1977

Maximizing Your Conferences Resources 18 MIN
U-matic / 35mm strip
Conference Leading Skills Series
Color
Outlines some ways for getting a conference off to a positive start. Shows ways to get the group participating and the different 'roles' of conferees.
Business and Economics; English Language; Psychology
Dist - RESEM **Prod** - RESEM

Maximum 14 MIN
16mm
Color (H C A)
LC FIA66-481
Presents a montage featuring Swedish ballet dancers. Illustrates good work habits and physical conditioning for female office workers and homemakers.
Fine Arts; Physical Education and Recreation
Dist - AETNA **Prod** - AETNA 1965

Maximum Effort 28 MIN
U-matic / VHS / 16mm
Color
Looks at the racing prowess of the Kialoa, an 80 - foot modern maxi - boat.
Physical Education and Recreation
Dist - OFFSHR **Prod** - OFFSHR 1981

Maximum marriage series
Features Tim Timmons in a presentation of his concepts for 'Maximum Marriage.' Covers topics such as living together versus marriage, marriage types, differences between men and women, and more. Four - part series includes study guides.
The Eleven battlegrounds of marriage - Part 2 50 MIN
How do you spell relief - Part 4 50 MIN
Why are women so weird and men so strange - Part 3 50 MIN
Why marriage when you can live together - Part 1 50 MIN
Dist - APH **Prod** - WORD 1981

Maximum - Minimum Problems 20 MIN
VHS
Calculus Series
Color (H)
LC 90712920
Discusses maximum - minimum problems. The 14th of 57 installments of the Calculus Series.
Mathematics
Dist - GPN

Maximum security 15 MIN
VHS
Color (A)
$525.00 purchase
Follows a data security "offender" from one violation to the next, showing how breaches of computer security compromise a company's information assets. Emphasizes important do's and don'ts of data protection.
Business and Economics; Computer Science; Education
Dist - COMFLM **Prod** - COMFLM

Maxine Hong Kingston - talking story 60 MIN
U-matic / VHS
Color (G)
$250.00 purchase, $50.00 rental
Takes a personal look at the life and work of Maxine Hong Kingston. Explores the principal themes and concerns in her books, her views on Chinese and American culture, feminism and pacifism, the importance of ghosts, mythology and dreams. Follows Kingston to her childhood home in Stockton, California, and to Hawaii, where she wrote The Woman Warrior. Features B D Wong as narrator.
Biography; Literature and Drama; Religion and Philosophy; Sociology
Dist - CROCUR **Prod** - KQEDTV 1990

Maxine Singer 30 MIN
VHS
World Of Ideas With Bill Moyers - Season I - series
Color (G)
$39.95 purchase _ #BMWI - 138
Interviews David Puttnam, a filmmaker whose works include 'Chariots of Fire' and 'The Killing Fields.' Theorizes that the film industry is partially to blame for societal problems including violence and greed. Suggests that the film industry must accept responsibility for its influence on society.
Business and Economics; Guidance and Counseling; Religion and Philosophy; Science - Physical; Sociology
Dist - PBS

Maxine Sullivan - love to be in love 48 MIN
VHS
Color & B&W (G)
$295.00 purchase, $70.00 rental
Presents a film portrait of Maxine Sullivan - 1911 - 1987 - the jazz vocalist who rose from a Pennsylvania steeltown domestic and singer with no formal training to become one of the foremost black female vocalists in America. Includes clips from vintage Hollywood films, TV appearances and her last recording session. Produced and directed by Greta Schiller.
Biography; Fine Arts; History - United States
Dist - CNEMAG

Max's chocolate chicken 35 MIN
VHS
Children's circle collection series
Color (K P I)
$14.95 purchase _ #WK1196
Offers a collection of children's stories which includes the title story along with Each Peach Pear Plum; Picnic; and The Circus Baby.
Fine Arts; Literature and Drama
Dist - KNOWUN

Maxwell - Boltzmann Distribution 4 MIN
16mm
Kinetic Theory by Computer Animation Series
Color (H C A)
LC 73-703249
Presents particles in a box which are started off with the same speed in random directions. Shows that as they collide, their speeds change. Develops histograms at different temperatures to illustrate the steady - state distribution of speeds. Includes two - dimensional Maxwell - Boltzmann curves which are superimposed over the histograms.
Science; Science - Physical
Dist - KALMIA **Prod** - KALMIA 1973

Maxwell Mouse 8 MIN
VHS / U-matic
Giant First Start Series
Color (K P)
$29.95 purchase _ #VM019
Tells the story of Maxwell Mouse. Contains a 32 page hardcover book and a video.
English Language; Literature and Drama
Dist - TROLA

Maxwell Mouse - Great Bunny Race
VHS / 16mm
Video Read - Alongs Series
Color (K)
$8.88 purchase _ ISBN #5109 - 18601 - 3
Features animated stories and songs as lessons in children learning word skills. Available in a series of six similar videos.
Fine Arts; Literature and Drama
Dist - EDUCRT

Maxwell Street blues - Chicago blues and gospel 56 MIN
VHS
Color (G)
$29.95 purchase
Offers some Chicago blues and gospel music from the Maxwell Street Blues.
Fine Arts
Dist - KINOIC **Prod** - RHPSDY

Maxwellian and Druyvesteyn Distributions
U-matic / VHS
Plasma Process Technology Fundamentals Series
Color (IND)
Cites Maxwellian and Druyvesteyn distributions as derived from the Boltzmann equation and compares them. Gives their respective dependence on electron energy. Outlines evaluation of the collision integral and Boltzmann equation for these cases. Discusses the importance of 'tail electrons' and how they 'wag.'.
Industrial and Technical Education; Mathematics; Science - Physical
Dist - COLOSU **Prod** - COLOSU

Maxwell's equations - optics - Parts 39 and 40 60 MIN
U-matic / VHS
Mechanical universe...and beyond - Part II series
Color (G)
$45.00, $29.95 purchase
Portrays James Clerk Maxwell who discovered that displacement current produces electromagnetic waves, or light, in Part 39. Reveals that many properties of light are properties of waves, including reflection, refraction and diffraction in Part 40. Parts of a 52 - part series on the mechanics of the universe.
Science; Science - Physical
Dist - ANNCPB **Prod** - SCCON 1985

May 10 MIN
U-matic / VHS
Emma and Grandpa series
Color (K P)
$180 VC purchase, $30 VC five day rental, $110 self dub
Uses simple rhyming couplets to help kindergartners and first graders understand nature and seasonal changes. Highlights the importance of conservation. Focuses on the importance of grass as a native crop. Fifth in a 12 part series.
Science - Natural
Dist - GPN **Prod** - GRIFN 1983

May 1968 10 MIN
16mm
Color
Presents a brief account of the organizing work of the French students in Paris during April and May of 1968. Shows the brutal repression of the state to try and crush the newly formed worker student alliance.
Geography - World; Sociology
Dist - CANWRL **Prod** - CANWRL

May 30, 1431 14 MIN
VHS / 16mm
Newscast from the Past Series
Color (I J H)
$58.00 purchase _ #ZF224V
Uses TV news format to portray May 30, 1431 - a retrospective of Joan of Arc who has just died, a lawsuit against Johann Gutenberg the inventor of the printing press, human sacrifice by the Aztecs, the beginning of the Renaissance in Florence, and other events. Six different historical dates in series.
History - World; Social Science
Dist - SSSSV **Prod** - ZENGER 1984

May Day - May Day 30 MIN
VHS
Color (G A)
$20.00 purchase
Presents footage filmed in seven countries on International Labour Day 1987. Looks at the abuse of trade unionists' human rights and their struggle to make their voices heard and achieve official recognition. Focuses on Guatemala.
Business and Economics; Civics and Political Systems; Social Science; Sociology
Dist - AMNSTY **Prod** - AMNSTY 1987

May I help you - commendable customer service 30 MIN
VHS
Clerical skills series
Color (H C G)
$79.95 purchase _ #CCP0054V
Trains entry level employees on contact with the public as cashiers, food service workers, sales clerks and customer service representatives. Shows beginning workers how to provide good customer service - and a good company image - through maintaining a good attitude, projective positive body language, using the correct tone of voice and developing rapport with the customer. Explains and demonstrates proven techniqes to placate angry customers who populate the nightmares and daily life of front line personnel. Includes workbook with reproducible worksheets. Part of a series on clerical skills.
Business and Economics; Guidance and Counseling; Psychology; Social Science
Dist - CAMV **Prod** - CAMV 1992

May I help you - commendable customer service 30 MIN
VHS
Office skills series
Color (PRO)
$79.95 purchase _ #CCP0054V
Helps employees improve their customer service skills. Stresses that good customer service skills are crucial to help businesses retain customers. Offers advice on maintaining a good attitude; projecting positive body language; using the correct tone of voice; developing rapport with the customer; how to placate angry customers; and more. Presents viewers with examples of good and bad customer service. Includes workbook with reproducible worksheets.
Business and Economics; Psychology
Dist - CAMV

May I Speak to Mr Page 25 MIN
16mm
Color (C A)
Presents firsthand reports of Christian literature work in 19 countries. Shows the travels of Mr Page commitments from the Wheaton office to all parts of the world.
Literature and Drama; Religion and Philosophy
Dist - CBFMS **Prod** - CBFMS

May I Speak to the Women of the House? 28 MIN
U-matic
Color
Examines life conditions for single mothers and government inaction regarding these women. Follows a single mother through daily activities as she tries to provide food, clothing and care for her six children on monthly government benefits of $663.
Sociology
Dist - WMENIF **Prod** - OTCME

May I suggest 10 MIN
U-matic / VHS / BETA
Color (A)
#FC42
Presents a training film that entertains while it teaches suggestive selling. Focuses on eight specific tips for increasing sales. Explores selling areas such as using descriptive phrases, helping customers make a choice and looking for signs of celebration.
Industrial and Technical Education
Dist - CONPRO **Prod** - CONPRO

May it be 29 MIN
16mm
Color
LC 76-700384
Shows Israel after the Yom Kippur War and just before the tragedy at Ma'alot and continues to New York to see Jews in need and the people who help them. Hosted by Herschel Bernardi.
History - United States; History - World; Sociology
Dist - ALDEN **Prod** - UJA 1975

May O'Donnell, Ray Green, Kenneth Rinker and Tim DeBaets 30 MIN
U-matic / VHS
Eye on Dance - the Business and Law of Dance Series
Color
Fine Arts
Dist - ARCVID **Prod** - ARCVID

May Peace Begin with Me 29 MIN
16mm
Color
LC 73-700737
Shows four young men, including a Pole, an Iraqui and two Israeli - born Jews, as they leave their frontier kibbutz for family holidays in the city. Follows their journey and family experiences to reveal the diversity of their backgrounds and the meaning of the land as it affects new and older generations in Israel.
History - World; Sociology
Dist - GUG **Prod** - GUG 1972

may sailing
VHS
Under sail with Robbie Doyle series
Color (G A)
$19.90 purchase _ #0401
Demonstrates a short sail in a harbor. Reviews the balance of forces involved in sailing and some of the necessary tools. Covers points of sail and wind direction and care and maintenance of equipment. Features Robbie Doyle.
Physical Education and Recreation
Dist - SEVVID

May Sarton live
16mm / Cassette
Color (G H C)
$49.00, $10.00 purchase
Features May Sarton's poetry reading in Los Angeles, 1987.
Literature and Drama
Dist - ISHTAR

May Sarton - writing in the upward years 30 MIN
VHS
Writing in the upward years series
Color (G C)
$195.00 purchase, $55.00 rental
Focuses on the effect of aging on the creative process as demonstrated in the writings of poet May Sarton. Features readings by and interviews with the poet, along with photographs of her life journey.
Fine Arts; Health and Safety; Literature and Drama
Dist - TNF

May We Help You? 1 MIN
U-matic / VHS
Color (SPANISH)
Illustrates message of answering public questions about cancer with stylized photography of inner workings of telephone. Uses TV spot format.
Foreign Language; Health and Safety
Dist - AMCS **Prod** - AMCS 1982

The Maya 30 MIN
VHS
Indians of North America video series
Color; B&W; CC (P I J)
$39.95 purchase _ #D6657
Overviews the history of the Maya. Combines interviews with leading authorities on Native American history with live footage and historic stills. Part of a ten - part series.
Social Science
Dist - KNOWUN

The Maya 30 MIN
VHS
Indians of North America series
Color (J H C G)
$49.95 purchase _ #LVCD6657V - S
Interviews Mayan leaders who discuss their nation's history. Includes location footage at Mayan communities where children and elders discuss what it means to be Native American today. Part of a 10 - part series on Indian culture.
History - World; Social Science
Dist - CAMV

Maya Angelou 35 MIN
VHS
Color (H C G)
$79.00 purchase
Features the multi - talented American writer, dancer and activist discussing her works and the influence of her experiences on her writing. Talks about her autobiographical works I Know Why the Caged Bird Sings; Gather Together in My Name; Singin' and Swingin' and Gettin' Merry like Christmas; and The Heart of a Woman.
Literature and Drama
Dist - ROLAND **Prod** - INCART

Maya Angelou 29 MIN
U-matic / VHS
Creativity with Bill Moyers Series
Color (H C A)
LC 83-706228
Tells how thirty years after she left it, Maya Angelou, poet, musician and actress returns to Stamps, Arkansas, the rural southern town where she grew up.
Fine Arts; Literature and Drama; Psychology
Dist - PBS **Prod** - CORPEL 1982

Maya Angelou on creativity 30 MIN
VHS
Color (G)
$19.95 purchase _ #X008
Interviews poet Maya Angelou who revisits her hometown with Bill Moyers.
Biography; Literature and Drama
Dist - STRUE **Prod** - PAV 1993

Maya Angelou - rainbow in the clouds 60 MIN
VHS
CC; Color (C H G A)
$69.95 purchase _ #MANG-000-WC95
Describes the life of poet Maya Angelou. Explains the meaning of 'faith' in everyday lives of people. Angelou, an activist and teacher presents her philosphy.
History - United States; Literature and Drama
Dist - PBS **Prod** - WTVSTV 1994

Maya Angelou Series
Maya Angelou - the Writer 30 MIN
Dist - NETCHE

Maya Angelou - the Writer 30 MIN
U-matic / VHS
Maya Angelou Series
Color
Presents Maya Angelou, discussing her relationship with her mentor, James Baldwin, her work regimen and performing two of her favorite compositions - 'No Loser, No Weeper' and 'And Still I Rise.'.
Literature and Drama
Dist - NETCHE **Prod** - NETCHE 1982

The Maya - Crocodile City 30 MIN
U-matic / VHS
Color (H C A)
Chronicles a dig in Belize, where archeologists and local workers uncovered an ancient Mayan civilization centered at Lamanai. Discusses the culture of the Mayans and the reasons for their demise.
Geography - World; History - World; Social Science; Sociology
Dist - JOU **Prod** - CANBC

Maya Lords of the Jungle 58 MIN
U-matic / VHS
Odyssey Series
Color
LC 82-706433
Visits ancient sites on the Yucatan Peninsula where new findings are forcing a reappraisal of the past of the Mayans.
History - World; Science - Physical; Social Science; Sociology
Dist - PBS **Prod** - PBA

Maya Lords of the Jungle 59 MIN
16mm
Odyssey Series
Color (J H A)
Shows the Maya civilization of Central America. Suggests an interpretation of Mayan society that shows the use of agriculture and salt as trade items.
Agriculture; History - World; Sociology
Dist - DOCEDR **Prod** - DOCEDR 1981

Maya series
Brujo - Shaman 55 MIN
Tajimoltik - five days without name 30 MIN
Via Dolorosa - The Sorrowful way 10 MIN
Dist - DOCEDR

Maya - the blood of kings 50 MIN
VHS
Lost civilizations video series
Color (G)
$19.99 purchase _ #0 - 7835 - 8270 - 6NK
Reveals the dark rituals of human mutilation as Maya rulers draw their own blood to offer to their gods. Observes Mayan culture at its peak - its towering pyramids, life - and - death ball games, extensive glyphs - then probes its mysterious decline. Part of a ten - part series incorporating the newest research, evidence and discoveries; orginal cinematography in 25 countries on 5 continents; dramatized recreations of scenes from the past; three - dimensional computer graphics to reconstruct ancient cities and monumental feats of engineering; historic footage; and computer - animated maps.
History - World
Dist - TILIED **Prod** - TILIED 1995

Mayakovsky - the Poetry of Action 22 MIN
16mm / U-matic / VHS
Color (H C A)
LC 72-702964
Presents a portrait, in his own words and tells through his own paintings and drawings of the poetic genius, Vladimir Mayakovsky, who cast a hypnotic spell over the artistic and literary life of Russia in the twenties.
Biography; Fine Arts; Geography - World; Literature and Drama
Dist - FOTH **Prod** - MANTLH 1972

Mayaland 40 MIN
16mm / U-matic / VHS
Color
Discusses the Maya civilization, focusing on sites in Mexico, Guatemala and Honduras.
Social Science
Dist - FI **Prod** - MACM

Mayaland Safari 33 MIN
16mm
Color (J)
LC 70-701923
Relates the story of the Mayans, showing five ancient Mayan cities. Describes the advanced Mayan Stone - Age civilization. Presents illustrations of Mayan architecture, sculpture, pottery and textile products.
Fine Arts; History - World; Science - Physical; Sociology
Dist - AVED **Prod** - HENSON 1964

The Mayan Mystery 17 MIN
U-matic / VHS / 16mm
Color (I A)
LC 70-706793
Shows the ruins of the major Mayan cities in Mexico, Guatemala and the Honduras. Lists possible explanations for the decline of the Mayas.
Geography - World; Science - Physical
Dist - AIMS **Prod** - HP 1970

Mayan Rainforest Farming 29 MIN
VHS
Ecology Workshop Series
Color (J H C G)
$195 purchase, $50 rental
Points that Mayan farmers continue a sustainable form of rainforest agriculture despite the decimation of tropical rainforests. Points that these farmers grow a variety of vegetables and non - food crops beneath their fruit - trees.
Science - Natural; Science - Physical
Dist - BULFRG **Prod** - BULFRG 1987

Mayan voices - American lives 56 MIN
16mm / VHS
Color (G)
$895.00, $390.00 purchase, $125.00 rental
Visits a community of Maya who have fled Guatemala's political violence to settle in a wholly new environment - Indiantown, Florida. Contrasts the experiences of families who have been in this small agricultural town since the outbreak of violence in Guatemala in the early 1980s with the struggle of those who continue to arrive in search of better lives. Demonstrates the impact the influx of 5,000 people with a foreign language and culture has on the predominantly white community. Explores issues of identity, cultural intergration, migration and social change.
Fine Arts; Social Science; Sociology
Dist - FIRS

The Mayans - apocalypse then 27 MIN
VHS / U-matic
Color (J H C G)
$395.00, $365.00 purchase _ #V446
Presents detailed footage of several well - preserved Mayan cities. Examines the complex Mayan civilization. Addresses the sudden demise of the culture through a review of various hypotheses which explain the abandonment of Mayan cities in 900 AD.
Geography - World; History - World; Social Science; Sociology
Dist - BARR **Prod** - CEPRO 1988

The Mayas 11 MIN
U-matic / VHS / 16mm
Color (I J H C)
Surveys the Mayan civilization, pointing out the history, culture and achievements of the Indians. Pictures the ruins of the ancient city of Tikal in Guatemala, Uxmal and Chichen Itza.
History - World; Sociology
Dist - CORF **Prod** - CORF 1957

Maybe I Am - the Story of a Teenage Alcoholic 30 MIN
VHS
Color (I H)
Examines the symptoms of alcoholism and the effects on those close to the alcoholic, through telling a story of a 'typical' teenage alcoholic.
Guidance and Counseling; Health and Safety; Psychology; Sociology
Dist - HRMC **Prod** - HRMC 1985

Maybe Next Week Sometime 30 MIN
16mm
Color (I)
LC 75-701088
Examines black roots music as it exists in the rural South. Includes music ranging from folk and rock to spirituals and the ceremonial music of the Yoruba people of South Carolina.
Fine Arts; Sociology
Dist - RADIM **Prod** - BOWRTD 1975

Maybe Tomorrow 20 MIN
Videoreel / VT2
Color
Emphasizes the implications of interracial romance within the Black community and the influence the community has on them.
Sociology
Dist - PBS **Prod** - SPRHIL

Mayday 15 MIN
16mm
Black Liberation Series
B&W
Presents the events of the MayDay rally at San Francisco's federal building in honor of Huey P Newton, minister of defense of the Black Panther party and political prisoner.
History - United States
Dist - CANWRL **Prod** - CANWRL 1969

Mayday 15 MIN
16mm
B&W (G)
$15.00 rental
Records a rally held on May 1st by the revolutionary Black Panther Party to free their leader, Huey P Newton. Represents revolutionary filmmakers in the 1960s whose work provides a window to that period.
Civics and Political Systems; Fine Arts; History - United States; Sociology
Dist - CANCIN **Prod** - SINGLE 1969

Mayday 16 MIN
U-matic / VHS / BETA
Color; NTSC; PAL; SECAM (H C G)
PdS95
Moves step - by - step through a resuscitation code. Highlights the medical team members and their responsibilities. Stresses the importance of teamwork and coping strategies.
Health and Safety; Psychology
Dist - VIEWTH

Mayday, Mayday 50 MIN
16mm / U-matic / VHS
Color (I)
Portrays what happens when a plane crashes and young Mark and Allison set out in the wilderness to seek help for their injured parents. Shows them learning to rely on each other and courageously keeping going despite being threatened by a pack of wild dogs, an angry rattlesnake and the ever - increasing threat of nightfall. Produced for the ABC Weekend Specials.
Literature and Drama
Dist - CORF **Prod** - ABCLR 1983

Mayday - Mayday 30 MIN
VHS
Perspectives - transport and communication - series
Color; PAL; NTSC (G)
PdS90, PdS105 purchase
Examines the rigorous safety training of workers upon North Sea oil rigs.
Health and Safety; Industrial and Technical Education; Psychology
Dist - CFLVIS **Prod** - LONTVS

The Mayflower Story 25 MIN
16mm
Color
Shows the building of the Mayflower II, an exact duplicate of the pilgrim ship. Describes its voyage across the Atlantic and pictures the arrival of the ship at Plymouth.
History - United States; History - World; Industrial and Technical Education
Dist - MTP **Prod** - AERO 1957

The Mayfly - Ecology of an Aquatic Insect 15 MIN
U-matic / VHS / 16mm
Biology Series Unit 1 - Ecology; Unit 1 - Ecology
Color (J H)
LC 73-701886
Shows a small, delicate mayfly and species called hexagenia bilineata along parts of the Mississippi River. Includes laboratory shots where the natural environment of the mayfly was duplicated to permit a more controlled study of its habits. Shows the lifespan of all mayfly species.
Science - Natural
Dist - EBEC **Prod** - EBEC 1973

Mayhem 20 MIN
16mm
Color; B&W (G A)
$60.00 rental
Presents the work of filmmaker Abigail Child. Engages in multi - layered analysis of gender roles and cinematic conventions. Juxtaposes image and sound, shapes and gestures, documentary and narrative. Creates a dark and gloomy underworld of crime and corruption and a psychological drama of sexual poetics and the erotic.
Fine Arts; History - United States; Industrial and Technical Education; Psychology; Sociology
Dist - PARART **Prod** - FMCOOP 1987

Mayhem - part 6 20 MIN
16mm / VHS
Is this what you were born for series
B&W (G)
$60.00 rental
Depicts a film noir setting, where soap opera thrillers and Mexican comic books generate the action. Creates a film in which Sound is the Character. Focuses on sexuality and the erotic.
Fine Arts
Dist - CANCIN **Prod** - CHILDA 1987

Mayor Ed Koch 60 MIN
U-matic / VHS
John Callaway Interviews Series
Color
Civics and Political Systems; Geography - United States
Dist - PBS **Prod** - WTTWTV 1981

Maypo Animated Commercial 1 MIN
VHS / U-matic
Color
Shows a classic animated television commercial with the line, 'I Want My Maypo.'.
Business and Economics; Psychology; Sociology
Dist - BROOKC **Prod** - BROOKC

May's Miracle 28 MIN
16mm
Man Alive Series
Color (H C A)
LC 82-701184
Presents a documentary about May Lemke who adopted a blind severely retarded and cerebral palsied baby. Tells how the boy at age 16 suddenly began to play the piano. Shows how he performs on the piano with vigorous emotion and imitates singers from the past. Points out that May believes that what happened was a miracle, but certainly her steadfast mothering contributed to the development of his unusual potential.
Psychology; Sociology
Dist - FLMLIB **Prod** - CANBC 1982

Mazda Mood 3 MIN
16mm
Color
LC 78-701313
Presents a 'teaser' shown to Mazda automobile dealers to introduce the Mazda RZ - 7 car.
Business and Economics; Industrial and Technical Education
Dist - DEULAU **Prod** - DEULAU 1978

The Maze 81 MIN
16mm
B&W
Presents a horror story with frightstricken women, strange monsters and a corridor of hideous winged bats. Stars Richard Carlson and Veronica Hunt. Available In 3 - D.
Fine Arts
Dist - KITPAR **Prod** - UNKNWN 1953

The Maze 30 MIN
16mm
Films at the Frontier of Psychological Inquiry Series
Color (H C A)
LC 72-702199
Studies t8e case of William Kurelek, a professional artist who was once a patient in a mental hospital, in order to investigate the cause, nature, and cure of a common mental disorder. Tells how his illness was evident in his paintings, and includes interviews with his psychiatrist, priest and family.
Health and Safety; Psychology
Dist - HMC **Prod** - HMC 1971

Mazurek Dabrowskiego 57 MIN
VHS
Color (G A) (POLISH)
$29.95 purchase _ #V120
Reveals the history and tradition of the Polish anthem.
Fine Arts; History - World
Dist - POLART

Mazurka 95 MIN
16mm
B&W (GERMAN)
Reviews the case of the famous pianist Michailow, who is shot by the singer Vera in a nighclub because he had ruined her marriage 15 years earlier and is attempting to seduce her daughter. Based on actual documents of a murder trial.
Foreign Language; Literature and Drama; Sociology
Dist - WSTGLC **Prod** - WSTGLC 1935

Mbambim, a Lineage Head in Aytkkpere, North to Go 23 MIN
U-matic / VHS
B&W (C G T A)
Portrait of a headman of patrilineage, comprising about eighty people, in a small Anufo village in North Togo. Mbambim's difficulty in exercising authority over the members of his family does not fit the role of lineage head, forced upon him because he is the eldest man of the lineage. Shows an analysis of the situation by a diviner and the ensuing ceremony, performed by the lineage as a whole, to reestablish Mbambim's position and to stress the unity of his lineage.
Social Science; Sociology
Dist - PSU **Prod** - PSU 1973

Mbira Dza Vadzimu - Dambatsoko, an Old Cult Center with Muchatera and Ephat Mujuru 51 MIN
VHS / U-matic
Mbira Series
Color
Focuses on the life of the late Muchatera Mujuru, leader of one of the few remaining traditional cult centers in Shona country in Zimbabwe. Looks at various aspects of his life and the life of his adherents at Dambatsoko. Shows several kinds of ceremonies.
Fine Arts; Geography - World
Dist - PSU **Prod** - PSU

Mbira Dza Vadzimu - Dambatsoko, an Old Cult Centre with Muchatera and Ephat Mujuri 51 MIN
16mm
Mbira Series
Color (H C A)
LC 78-700698
Shows traditional South African cult ceremonies performed by Muchatera and Ephat Mujuru, including a spirit possession ceremony, prayers and a blood sacrifice.
Geography - World; Religion and Philosophy; Sociology
Dist - PSUPCR **Prod** - ZANTZA 1978

Mbira Dza Vadzimu - Dambatsoko, an Old Cult Centre with Muchatera and Ephat Mujuri, Pt 1 25 MIN
16mm
Mbira Series
Color (H C A)
LC 78-700698
Shows traditional South African cult ceremonies performed by Muchatera and Ephat Mujuru, including a spirit possession ceremony, prayers and a blood sacrifice.
Religion and Philosophy
Dist - PSUPCR **Prod** - ZANTZA 1978

Mbira Dza Vadzimu - Dambatsoko, an Old Cult Centre with Muchatera and Ephat Mujuri, Pt 2 26 MIN
16mm
Mbira Series
Color (H C A)
LC 78-700698
Shows traditional South African cult ceremonies performed by Muchatera and Ephat Mujuru, including a spirit possession ceremony, prayers and a blood sacrifice.
Religion and Philosophy
Dist - PSUPCR **Prod** - ZANTZA 1978

Mbira Dza Vadzimu - Religion at the Family Level with Gwanzura Gwenzi 66 MIN
16mm
Mbira Series
Color (H C A)
LC 78-700702
Presents the daily activities of South African Gwanzura Gwenzi from his weekdays in the city to his weekends at home in the Tribal Trust Lands. Shows a bira - spirit seance.
Geography - World; Religion and Philosophy; Sociology
Dist - PSUPCR **Prod** - ZANTZA 1978

Mbira dza vadzimu - religion at the family level with Gwanzura Gwenzi 66 MIN
VHS / 16mm
Color (G C)
$735.00, $170.00 purchase, $32.00 rental _ #60286
Establishes the essential religious background for a series on the use of the traditional mbira in the cultural life of the Mashona people of Rhodesia by examining the life of a man in his early 40s. Shows him at work in a western urban town and at home in the tribal lands on the weekend, where he hosts an all - night mbira, or spirit seance, the main expression of Shona religious ritual. His sister is the family medium, his grandfather the spirit who possesses her and the guests are members of his family, past and present, and neighbors. Part of a series co - produced with Andrew Tracey.
Religion and Philosophy; Sociology
Dist - PSU **Prod** - ZANTZA 1978

Mbira Dza Vadzimu - Religion at the Family Level with Gwanzura Gwenzi, Pt 1 33 MIN
16mm
Mbira Series
Color (H C A)

LC 78-700702
Presents the daily activities of South African Gwanzura Gwenzi from his weekdays in the city to his weekends at home in the Tribal Trust Lands. Shows a bira - spirit seance.
History - World
Dist - PSUPCR **Prod** - ZANTZA 1978

Mbira Dza Vadzimu - Urban and Rural Ceremonies with Hakurotwi made, Pt 1 22 MIN
16mm
Mbira Series
Color (H C A)
LC 78-700701
Presents Hakurotwi Mude, a South African singer and leader of a professional group of mbira players, as he performs at an informal urban bira, at a sacrifice and at a funeral.
Religion and Philosophy
Dist - PSUPCR **Prod** - ZANTZA 1978

Mbira Dza Vadzimu - Urban and Rural Ceremonies with Hakurotwi Mude 45 MIN
16mm
Mbira Series
Color (H C A)
LC 78-700701
Presents Hakurotwi Mude, a South African singer and leader of a professional group of mbira players, as he performs at an informal urban bira, at a sacrifice and at a funeral.
Fine Arts; Geography - World; Religion and Philosophy; Sociology
Dist - PSUPCR **Prod** - ZANTZA 1978

Mbira Dza Vadzimu - Urban and Rural Ceremonies with Hakurotwi Mude, Pt 2 23 MIN
16mm
Mbira Series
Color (H C A)
LC 78-700701
Presents Hakurotwi Mude, a South African singer and leader of a professional group of mbira players, as he performs at an informal urban bira, at a sacrifice and at a funeral.
Religion and Philosophy
Dist - PSUPCR **Prod** - ZANTZA 1978

Mbira Dza Vadzimu - Urban and Rural Ceremonies with Hakurotwi Mudhe 45 MIN
U-matic / VHS
Mbira Series
Color
Presents a portrait of Hakurotwi Mudhe, singer and leader of a professional group of mbira players. Shows him in various kinds of performances. Includes an informal urban Friday night bira, a sacrifice and a funeral.
Fine Arts; Geography - World
Dist - PSU **Prod** - PSU

Mbira - Matepe Dza Mhondoro, a Healing Party 21 MIN
VHS / U-matic
Mbira Series
Color
Presents a re - enactment of a healing ceremony in order to show the performance of two complete songs on one type of mbira. Features the famous matepe player Saini Murira as he leads a group of four players. Includes traditional healing dances.
Fine Arts; Geography - World
Dist - PSU **Prod** - PSU

Mbira - Matepe Dza Mhondoro - a Healing Party 20 MIN
16mm
Color (H C A)
LC 78-700695
Features a reenactment of the healing ceremony of a South African tribe.
Fine Arts; Geography - World; Religion and Philosophy; Sociology
Dist - PSUPCR **Prod** - ZANTZA 1978

Mbira music - the spirit of Zimbabwe 52 MIN
VHS
Color (G)
$149.00 purchase _ #EX3083
Features the music and traditions of Zimbabwe.
Fine Arts
Dist - FOTH

Mbira - Njari, Karanga Songs in Christian Ceremonies with Simon Mashoko 24 MIN
16mm
Mbira Series
Color (H C A)
LC 78-700696
Shows Simon Mashoko, a South African rural Catholic catechist, as he performs on the mbira at beer and dance parties, in catechism classes and at a church service in his home.
Fine Arts; Geography - World; Religion and Philosophy; Sociology
Dist - PSUPCR **Prod** - ZANTZA 1978

Mbira - Njari - Karanga songs in Christian ceremonies with Simon Mashoko 24 MIN
VHS / 16mm
Color (G C)
$335.00, $115.00 purchase, $18.00 rental _ #33042
Focuses on Magwenyambira Simon Mashoko, rural Catholic catechist and njari mbira player famous in Shona country. Reveals that Mashoko has mastered the traditional spirit repertoire and has adapted the mbira successfully for use in the Catholic Church. Shows him moving and performing in the traditional sphere, at a beer party and a dance party, and at a catechism class and a Sunday church service held in his home. Part of a series co - produced with Andrew Tracey.
Fine Arts; Religion and Philosophy; Sociology
Dist - PSU **Prod** - ZANTZA 1977

Mbira Series

Mbira - Matepe Dza Mhondoro, a Healing Party	21 MIN
Mbira - the Technique of the Mbira Dza Vadzimu	19 MIN
Mbira Dza Vadzimu - Dambatsoko, an Old Cult Center with Muchatera and Ephat Mujuru	51 MIN
Mbira Dza Vadzimu - Urban and Rural Ceremonies with Hakurotwi Mudhe	45 MIN

Dist - PSU

Mbira Series

Mbira - Njari, Karanga Songs in Christian Ceremonies with Simon Mashoko	24 MIN
Mbira - the Technique of Mbira Dza Vadzimu	19 MIN
Mbira Dza Vadzimu - Dambatsoko, an Old Cult Centre with Muchatera and Ephat Mujuri	51 MIN
Mbira Dza Vadzimu - Dambatsoko, an Old Cult Centre with Muchatera and Ephat Mujuri, Pt 1	25 MIN
Mbira Dza Vadzimu - Dambatsoko, an Old Cult Centre with Muchatera and Ephat Mujuri, Pt 2	26 MIN
Mbira Dza Vadzimu - Religion at the Family Level with Gwanzura Gwenzi	66 MIN
Mbira Dza Vadzimu - Religion at the Family Level with Gwanzura Gwenzi , Pt 1	33 MIN
Mbira Dza Vadzimu - Urban and Rural Ceremonies with Hakurotwi made, Pt 1	22 MIN
Mbira Dza Vadzimu - Urban and Rural Ceremonies with Hakurotwi Mude	45 MIN
Mbira Dza Vadzimu - Urban and Rural Ceremonies with Hakurotwi Mude, Pt 2	23 MIN

Dist - PSUPCR

Mbira - the Technique of Mbira Dza Vadzimu 19 MIN
16mm
Mbira Series
Color
LC 78-700697
Introduces the musical technique and sound of mbira dza vadzimu as played by Ephat Mujuru, a leading mbira player. Demonstrates some of the rhythmic and harmonic elements of the music, using animation and freeze - frame techniques. Features the use of improvisation, different styles of playing and the combination of two mbiras in duet.
Fine Arts; Geography - World; Sociology
Dist - PSUPCR **Prod** - ZANTZA 1978

Mbira - the Technique of the Mbira Dza Vadzimu 19 MIN
U-matic / VHS
Mbira Series
Color
Provides an introduction to the musical technique and sound of the Mbira dza Vadzium as played by Ephat Mujuru. Demonstrates some of the rhythmic and harmonic elements of the music through animation and freeze - frame techniques. Presents various traditional songs to illustrate the use of improvisation, different styles of playing and the combination of two mbiras in duet.
Fine Arts; Geography - World
Dist - PSU **Prod** - PSU

MBO I - what is MBO 13 MIN
16mm / U-matic / VHS
Management by Objectives Series
Color (A)
Presents skeptical Charlie at a management by objectives training session where he asks pertinent questions about the philosophy and implementation of management by objectives.
Business and Economics; Psychology
Dist - CRMP **Prod** - BOSUST 1981

MBO II - Developing Objectives 14 MIN
16mm / U-matic / VHS
Management by Objectives Series
Color (A)
Presents precise guidelines for well - written objectives.
Business and Economics; Psychology
Dist - CRMP **Prod** - BOSUST 1981

MBO III - Performance Appraisal 14 MIN
U-matic / VHS / 16mm
Management by Objectives Series
Color (A)
Illustrates the process of management by objectives in action through the techniques of a good performance appraisal.
Business and Economics; Psychology
Dist - CRMP **Prod** - BOSUST 1981

Mc Carthy Vs Welch 25 MIN
U-matic / VHS / 16mm
Men in Crisis Series
B&W (J H C)
LC 76-706741
Features televised hearings of the Senate commitee investigating charges ranging from black mail to treason brought by Sen Mc Carthy against the Army.
Civics and Political Systems; History - United States
Dist - FI **Prod** - WOLPER

Mc Culloch V Maryland 36 MIN
16mm
Equal Justice Under Law Series
Color (H C)
LC 78-700001
Presents a dramatization of the landmark U S Supreme Court case of Mc Culloch v Maryland in which the Court struck down Maryland's attempt to tax a federally chartered bank.
Civics and Political Systems; History - United States
Dist - USNAC **Prod** - USJUDC 1977

Mc Laren Films Series

Opening Speech - Mc Laren	7 MIN

Dist - IFB

MC Squared - the Prometheus Factor 10 MIN
16mm
Color
LC 80-701246
Traces man's use of non - renewable fuel resources from the invention of the steam engine to mass production and excessive consumption. Explores ways of meeting energy needs through the use of wastes, renewable resources and the forces of nature.
Social Science
Dist - MTP **Prod** - GAPAC 1980

MC68000 Microprocess Series

Program Manipulation Instructions	30 MIN

Dist - COLOSU

MC68000 microprocessor series

Advanced instructions	30 MIN
Arithmetic, data and control instructions	30 MIN
Asynchronous bus and function control pins	30 MIN
Indirect Addressing Modes	30 MIN
Introduction to the Programming Model	30 MIN
Modern Programming Practices	30 MIN
Processing States and Exception	30 MIN
Program Exercises	30 MIN
Simple Addressing Modes	30 MIN

Dist - COLOSU

McAllister's Dream 30 MIN
U-matic / VHS
Color
Centers on 43 - year - old Fred McAllister, an actor for almost 25 years, who is still waiting for artistic success between the commercials he does to make ends meet. Reveals that he is torn between the desires of his girlfriend and his agent, but that he finally gets his chance when a friend asks him to audition for a major film.
Fine Arts
Dist - MDCPB **Prod** - MDCPB

McBroom's Zoo - the Finches' Fabulous Furnace 15 MIN
U-matic / VHS
Best of Cover to Cover 1 Series
Color (P)
Literature and Drama
Dist - WETATV **Prod** - WETATV

McCarthy - death of a witch hunter 50 MIN
VHS
Color (H C T A)
$29.95 purchase _ #S01326
Presents a highly personal documentary about Senator Joseph McCarthy, known for his anti - Communist 'witch hunts' of the early 1950s. Reveals that McCarthy abused his power and played on American fears of Communism. Includes footage from the 1954 Army - McCarthy hearings. Produced by Emile de Antonio.

Biography; Civics and Political Systems; History - United States
Dist - UILL

McCulloch Vs Maryland
U-matic / VHS / 35mm strip
Supreme Court Decisions that Changed the Nation Series
Color (J H C)
$69.00 purchase=MV _ #06808 94, $59.00 purchase=FS _ #06808 94
Exlpores the lasting impact of the national bank case, McCulloch versus Maryland, which established the 'imperial powers' of the federal government.
Civics and Political Systems
Dist - ASPRSS GA Prod - GA

McGee and me series
Back to the drawing board - Episode 6
The Big lie - Episode 1
Do the bright thing - Episode 7
The Not - so - great escape
Skate expectations - Episode 4
A Star in the breaking - Episode 2
Twister and shout
Dist - APH

McGee and me - Take me out of the ball game 30 MIN
VHS
Color (K P I J G R)
$19.95 purchase _ #404VSV
Features Nicholas and McGee, who learn that it is important to keep things in the right perspective and to put their faith in God rather than people. Includes a special appearance by Los Angeles Dodger pitcher Orel Hershiser. Produced by Focus on the Family.
Guidance and Counseling; Literature and Drama; Religion and Philosophy
Dist - GF

McGee and me - 'Twas the fight before Christmas 30 MIN
VHS
Color (K P I J G R)
$19.95 purchase _ #416VSV
Features Nicholas and McGee as they go through a series of misadventures near Christmas. Shows that they learn what the true meaning of Christmas can and should be.
Guidance and Counseling; Literature and Drama; Religion and Philosophy
Dist - GF

McGee, James - Dale Bertch 29 MIN
U-matic
Like it is Series
Color
Discusses urban planning, including planning for the poor and the problem of urban sprawl.
Sociology
Dist - HRC Prod - OHC

McGraw - Hill science and technical reference set
CD-ROM
(H C A)
$264.00 purchase _ #1241
Contains two authoritative reference works on one disc - the McGraw - Hill Concise Encyclopedia and the McGraw - Hill Dictionary of Scientific and Technical Terms. Covers the physical, earth and life sciences, and engineering. The Concise Encyclopedia contains over 7300 signed articles, and the Dictionary of Scientific and Technical Terms includes 98,500 terms. Articles may be browsed, read, printed, or copied to a file. For IBM PCs and compatibles, requires at least 640K RAM, DOS 3.1 or later, one floppy disk drive - hard disk recommended, one empty expansion slot, and an IBM compatible CD - ROM drive.
Business and Economics; Industrial and Technical Education; Literature and Drama; Science - Natural; Science - Physical
Dist - BEP

McGruff on Halloween 14 MIN
VHS / 16mm
Color (P I)
$345.00, $275.00 purchase, $75.00 rental _ #8212
Stresses safety, giving tips to make Halloween both safe and fun. Emphasizes that costumes should be fire retardant, light in color. Recommends makeup rather than masks. Outlines dos and don'ts regarding trick or treating. Recommends attending club or neighborhood party.
Health and Safety; Social Science; Sociology
Dist - AIMS Prod - AIMS 1990

McGruff on Vandalism 16 MIN
16mm / VHS
McGruff the Crime Dog Series
Color (P I)
$325.00, $395.00 purchase, $75.00 rental _ #8136
Explains how vandalism hurts everyone. Features McGruff the Crime Dog.
Guidance and Counseling; Sociology
Dist - AIMS Prod - AIMS 1990

McGruff the Crime Dog Series
McGruff on Vandalism 16 MIN
McGruff's Gang Alert 16 MIN
McGruff's Guide to Personal Safety 9 MIN
Dist - AIMS

McGruff's Gang Alert 16 MIN
16mm / VHS
McGruff the Crime Dog Series
Color (P I)
$325.00, $395.00 purchase, $75.00 rental _ #8135
Explains how street gangs hurt the community and disrupt the lives of residents. Features McGruff the Crime Dog.
Guidance and Counseling; Health and Safety; Sociology
Dist - AIMS Prod - AIMS 1990

McGruff's Guide to Personal Safety 9 MIN
16mm / VHS
McGruff the Crime Dog Series
Color (K P I)
$195.00, $230.00 purchase, $50.00 rental _ #9915; LC 89-710717; 89-710718
Helps children to understand that they have personal space and the right to protect it. Helps them to understand the difference between friends and strangers. Features McGruff the Crime Dog.
Health and Safety
Dist - AIMS Prod - AIMS 1987

McGruff's self - care alert 17 MIN
16mm / VHS
Color (P I)
$395.00, $295.00 purchase, $75.00 rental _ #8211
Shows youngsters how to protect themselves when they're home alone. Looks at how to safely carry and use housekeys, check houses before entering, and to make sure that doors and windows are locked once inside. Considers answering the phone and door, who to allow in the house when adults are not present, what to do in case of an emergency.
Health and Safety; Sociology
Dist - AIMS Prod - AIMS 1990

McKonkey's Ferry - Christmas 1776 28 MIN
U-matic
Color
Re - creates George Washington's victories at the Battle of Trenton.
History - United States
Dist - PBS Prod - NJPBA

MCRI Medicine Training Tape 51 MIN
VHS / U-matic
Color
Shows step - by - step procedure which each child and family goes through during evaluations at Meyer Children's Rehabilitation Institute of the University of Nebraska Medical Center. Shows the home visit by a nurse, a family social work interview, a psychological testing session, a medical evaluation, a staffing, and the resulting interpretation.
Health and Safety; Psychology
Dist - UNEBO Prod - UNEBO

MDTA Building Towards a Job Future 5 MIN
U-matic / VHS / 16mm
Career Job Opportunity Film Series
Color
LC 74-706137
Shows how this major program under the Manpower Development and Training Act makes use of experienced instructors and realistic work settings to train people in occupations in which there are known labor shortages.
Education; Social Science
Dist - USNAC Prod - USDLMA 1967

Me 85 MIN
16mm
Color
LC 75-704321
Presents the story of a young man whose cluttered personal life prevents him from becoming a writer.
Guidance and Counseling; Literature and Drama
Dist - CFDEVC Prod - CFDEVC 1974

Me 17 MIN
U-matic / VHS / 16mm
Color (P I)
$395.00, $250.00 purchase _ #72021; LC 72-702507
Deals with self image, identity and personal worth. Shows that each person is unique and each individual's identity is worth preserving and nurturing. Concludes with the statement that damage can be caused by trying to change your image to someone or something you are not.
Guidance and Counseling; Psychology
Dist - CORF Prod - PHENIX 1972

Me 10 MIN
16mm
Color
LC 72-700046
Draws a parallel between the integrity of the guitar craftsman and the pride of workmanship in all the people who are involved in the manufacture of intricate computers.
Fine Arts; Industrial and Technical Education; Mathematics; Sociology
Dist - RCAM Prod - RCAM 1971

ME 1 6 MIN
U-matic / VHS
Professional Engineering Review Series
Color (PRO)
Covers energy systems, thermal and fluid processes on six 60 - minute videotaped lectures.
Industrial and Technical Education
Dist - AMCEE Prod - NCSU

ME 2 7 MIN
VHS / U-matic
Professional Engineering Review Series
Color (PRO)
Covers mechanical analysis and design on seven 60 - minute videotaped lectures.
Industrial and Technical Education
Dist - AMCEE Prod - NCSU

Me - a Cop 29 MIN
16mm
Color (J)
LC 74-703252
Shows some of the incidents which happen to a policeman on his daily duties. Helps encourage young people of high school and college age to consider a career in law enforcement.
Civics and Political Systems; Guidance and Counseling; Social Science; Sociology
Dist - WGTV Prod - WGTV 1974

Me - a Self - Awareness Film 10 MIN
U-matic / VHS / 16mm
Color (P I)
LC 74-703481
Creates an awareness of personal identity, the five senses, feelings and the Golden rule. Uses a combination of live action, music, animation and mime.
Guidance and Counseling; Science - Natural
Dist - CORF Prod - MCDOCR 1974

Me, a Teen Father? 13 MIN
U-matic / VHS / 16mm
Color (J H C A)
$325, $235 purchase _ #80510
Tells about the problems of a teenage boy who discovers his girl friend is pregnant.
Psychology; Sociology
Dist - CORF

Me, a Teen Father 13 MIN
U-matic / VHS / 16mm
Color (J)
LC 80-701594
Explores the pressures, guilt, ambivalence, anguish, anger and moments of nostalgic tenderness of a teenage boy who has just learned that his girlfriend is pregnant.
Health and Safety; Sociology
Dist - CORF Prod - GORKER 1980

Me Alone, on My Own 20 MIN
VHS / U-matic
Once upon a Town Series
Color (P I)
Explores literary selections that deal with personal problems and the need to face them.
English Language; Literature and Drama
Dist - AITECH Prod - MDDE 1977

Me, an Alcoholic 24 MIN
U-matic / VHS / 16mm
Color (J)
Presents a dramatization about a male teenage alcoholic who refuses to admit he has a problem. Follows him from a drunk - driving apprehension to court and then to sessions with a local Alcoholic Rehabilitation Program worker.
Health and Safety; Psychology; Sociology
Dist - CORF Prod - SRSPRD

Me and Dad's New Wife 33 MIN
U-matic / VHS / 16mm
Teenage Years Series
Color
LC 77-702485
Tells the story of a seventh grade girl who, on her first day back in school, discovers her father's new wife is to be her math teacher. Provides insight into the feelings of guilt, anger and insecurity which divorce may arouse in a teenager. Based on the book A Smart Kid Like You by Stella Pevsner.
Guidance and Counseling; Sociology
Dist - TIMLIF Prod - WILSND 1976

Me and Mom - an Autobiography 23 MIN
U-matic / VHS
Color
Presents a one - woman show about a family of four who represent a composite self. Deals with inter - generational conflict and affection.
Fine Arts; Sociology
Dist - KITCHN **Prod** - KITCHN

Me and my back - back safety 22 MIN
BETA / VHS / U-matic
Safety - live action video series
Color (IND G)
$495.00 purchase _ #827 - 25
Shows how to reduce back stress on and off the job. Explains the function of the spinal column, the effect of lifting, stress and force. Demonstrates proper techniques for back care and maintenance through exercise, good posture and safe work practices. Part of a series on safety.
Health and Safety; Industrial and Technical Education; Psychology
Dist - ITSC **Prod** - ITSC 1990

Me and My Brother 91 MIN
16mm
B&W
Studies the alienation of a man who lives and travels with his brother and the poet Allen Ginsberg. Shows that his alientation is severe enough to be labeled schizophrenia.
Fine Arts; Psychology
Dist - NYFLMS **Prod** - NYFLMS 1968

Me and My Robot
U-matic / VHS
CNN Special Reports
(J H C)
$129.00 purchase _ #31380 941; $129.00 purchase _ #31380 - 851
Investigates the function and application of robots in society.
Industrial and Technical Education; Sociology
Dist - ASPRSS **Prod** - TURNED
CHUMAN

Me and My Senses 10 MIN
16mm / U-matic / VHS
Color (P I)
LC 74-712540
Helps children discover the world around them by taking them on a sensory trip to the zoo, emphasizing their senses of sight, sound, touch, taste and smell.
Psychology
Dist - PHENIX **Prod** - KINGSP 1970

Me and Rubyfruit program 18 MIN
VHS
Works of Sadie Benning series
Color (A)
$225.00 purchase, $75.00 rental
Presents four autobiographical shorts by Sadie Benning. Examines the space of Benning's bedroom in If Every Girl Had a Diary. Me and Rubyfruit has Benning asking, 'Why don't you marry me.' Living Inside portrays hating school, living in a small town and feeling queer. New Year considers teen angst in a world that's too sick to care. Produced by Benning.
History - United States; Literature and Drama; Sociology
Dist - WMEN

Me and Stella 25 MIN
16mm / VHS / U-matic
Color (J H C A)
LC 77-701016
Interviews Elizabeth Cotton, whose success in song - writing proves that age and race need not be impediments to life.
Fine Arts
Dist - PHENIX **Prod** - ASHUR 1977

Me and the Colonel 110 MIN
16mm / U-matic / VHS
B&W (H C A)
Stars Danny Kaye as a refugee of the Nazi hordes nearing Paris. Shows how he acquires an ancient Rolls Royce and joins forces with a reluctant, resentful Polish colonel to begin a rollicking, racing chase across France to freedom.
Fine Arts
Dist - FI **Prod** - CPC 1958

Me and the Monsters 10 MIN
16mm
Color (P)
Presents a light sing along approach to the problems of small children, including a discussion of drugs.
Psychology; Sociology
Dist - BBF **Prod** - BBF

Me and We 17 MIN
VHS / 16mm
(C PRO)
$500.00 purchase, $135.00 rental
Shows, in an animated fable, a new supervisor establishing a communication pipeline by observing and listening to each member of the group. Shows how he develops a four - point plan to bring them together in a cooperative, productive team.
Education
Dist - VLEARN

Me and We 17 MIN
U-matic / VHS / 16mm
Quality, Production and Me Series
Color (A) (DUTCH SPANISH PORTUGUESE SWEDISH)
Tells the story of a new supervisor who is responsible for keeping the organization's communication pipeline open. Shows how the supervisor develops a four - point plan to bring employees together in a cooperative, productive team.
Business and Economics; Foreign Language; Psychology
Dist - RTBL **Prod** - PORTA 1982

Me and You 12 MIN
U-matic / VHS / 16mm
Quality, Production and Me Series
Color (A) (SPANISH NORWEGIAN PORTUGUESE DUTCH)
Explains how supervisors can make sure employees develop to their maximum potential.
Business and Economics; Foreign Language; Psychology
Dist - RTBL **Prod** - PORTA 1982

Me and You 17 MIN
16mm
Color
LC 79-701178
Uses animation to show new supervisors the importance of dealing with new employees on an individual, rather than impersonal, level.
Business and Economics; Psychology
Dist - UPJOHN **Prod** - UPJOHN 1979

Me and You Kangaroo 19 MIN
16mm / U-matic / VHS
Captioned; Color (P I)
LC 74-701705
Presents a story about the love of a young Australian boy for the baby kangaroo which he raises after its mother has been accidentally killed by a car.
Geography - World; Literature and Drama; Science - Natural
Dist - LCOA **Prod** - LCOA 1974

Me muero por fumar - I'm dying for a smoke 30 MIN
VHS
Color (I J H) (SPANISH)
$39.95 purchase _ #B050 - V8
Offers the first culturally specific smoking cessation video created for the Hispanic community. Combines dramatic and documentary segments to give teens and adults the motivation and techniques to kick the smoking habit. Stresses that everyone around a smoker is also smoking involuntarily.
Guidance and Counseling; Psychology
Dist - ETRASS **Prod** - ETRASS

Me - my best friend - a lesson on self - esteem 12 MIN
VHS
Lessons from the heart - taking charge of feelings series
Color (I)
$89.95 purchase _ #10167VG
Presents a teen narrator teaching about self - esteem and finding the good in one's self. Uses vignettes, graphics, and interviews to illustrate respect and accepting feelings. Comes with a teacher's guide, discussion questions and two blackline masters. Part two of a four - part series.
Guidance and Counseling; Psychology
Dist - UNL

Me, Myself 12 MIN
U-matic / VHS / 16mm
Vignettes Series
Color (J)
LC 73-701775
Presents four vignettes leading to discussions on self image and the meaning of maturity.
Guidance and Counseling; Sociology
Dist - MEDIAG **Prod** - PAULST 1973

Me, myself ... and drinking 23 MIN
VHS
Me, myself ... series
Color (I J H)
$139.00 purchase _ #B006 - V8
Gives middle school students accurate, objective information about the mental, physical, and social effects of alcohol. Offers four vignettes in which teens are confronted with tough alcohol - related situations and model effective problem - solving skills. A counselor explains the advertising strategies used to lure young consumers. Includes program guide and catalog cards.
Health and Safety
Dist - ETRASS **Prod** - ETRASS

Me, myself ... and drugs 35 MIN
VHS
Me, myself ... series
Color (I J H)
$159.00 purchase _ #B007 - V8
Gives grades 5 - 9 an understanding of the cultural pressures and consequences of drug use. Defines a drug as any substance, legal or illegal, that affects the way the mind or body works. Students examine the message they get to use drugs from adults, commercials, and peers; the major groups of drugs; how drugs work within the body; and constructive ways to deal with peer pressure. Includes program guide and catalog cards.
Guidance and Counseling; Health and Safety; Psychology
Dist - ETRASS **Prod** - ETRASS

Me, Myself and I 15 MIN
U-matic / VHS
Pass it on Series
Color (K P)
Demonstrates happy and sad feelings and stresses treating others in a nice way.
Education; Guidance and Counseling
Dist - GPN **Prod** - WKNOTV 1983

Me, myself ... and smoking 22 MIN
VHS
Me, myself ... series
Color (I J H)
$139.00 purchase _ #B005 - V8
Uses a devil's advocate approach to teach grades 5 - 9 about the hazards of cigarettes. Features a wise - cracking PR man for the tobacco industry who tries to convince Denise and Tom that smoking is great, but the teens finds flaws in each of his absurd arguments. Includes program guide and catalog cards.
Health and Safety
Dist - ETRASS **Prod** - ETRASS

Me, myself ... series
Me, myself ... and drinking 23 MIN
Me, myself ... and drugs 35 MIN
Me, myself ... and smoking 22 MIN
Dist - ETRASS

The Me of the Moment 20 MIN
U-matic / VHS
Readers' Cube Series
Color (I)
Presents dramatizations of literary works that deal with the search for self - knowledge and self - understanding.
English Language; Literature and Drama
Dist - AITECH **Prod** - MDDE 1977

Me power - building self - confidence 20 MIN
VHS
Color (H)
$159.00 purchase _ #08386 - 126
Outlines a program for building self - esteem. Shows how to develop constructive behavior patterns and follow easily applied techniques for setting goals, recognizing personal accomplishments and overcoming insecurity in new situations.
Health and Safety; Psychology; Sociology
Dist - GA **Prod** - AVNA

Me Too 3 MIN
16mm / U-matic / VHS
Magic Moments, Unit 1 - Let's Talk Series
Color (K P I)
LC 74-705923
Tells of a young boy who destroys a sand castle built by a group of children who excluded him from their play. Discusses feelings of rejection.
English Language
Dist - EBEC **Prod** - EBEC 1969

Mea Culpa 29 MIN
Videoreel / VT2
Making Things Grow III Series
Color
Agriculture
Dist - PBS **Prod** - WGBHTV

The Meaders family - North Georgia potters 31 MIN
VHS / 16mm
Color (G C)
$340.00, $70.00 purchase, $20.50, $13.00 rental _ #33090
Depicts Meaders family members as they work at the family kiln in Cleveland, Georgia, using styles and techniques that remain largely unchanged since 1893. Interviews family members who discuss and demonstrate each step in the complex process, from digging the clay and grinding it in a mule - powered mill, to throwing, glazing and firing large crocks and pitchers.
Fine Arts; History - United States
Dist - PSU **Prod** - SIFP 1978
SFA

The Meadow - an Ecosystem 13 MIN
16mm / U-matic / VHS
Color (I J H)
LC 76-700245
Considers the relationship of plant and animal organisms in the ecological community of a meadow.
Science - Natural
Dist - BARR **Prod** - BARR 1976

Meadowcroft Rockshelter 30 MIN
16mm
B&W
LC 77-701816
Explores the on - site and laboratory investigations into the archeological dig at the Meadowcraft Rockshelter in Pennsylvania.
Science - Physical; Sociology
Dist - UPITTS **Prod** - UPITTS 1976

Meadowlark Lemon Presents the World 17 MIN
16mm / U-matic / VHS
Color
LC 79-700058
Features basketball star Meadowlark Lemon introducing basic map - reading skills. Provides comic definitions of sphere, equator, axis and hemisphere. Explains how to use longitude and latitude lines.
Geography - World; Social Science
Dist - PFP **Prod** - PFP 1979

The Meadow's Green 25 MIN
U-matic / VHS
Color
Presents the Bread and Puppet Theatre's two day 'Domestic Fair and Resurrection Circus,' with 118 puppeteers, more than 50 different shows, and exhibits on the meadows that serve as a stage.
Fine Arts
Dist - GMPF **Prod** - GMPF

Meal Planning 30 MIN
VHS / U-matic
Food for Life Series
Color
Home Economics; Social Science
Dist - MSU **Prod** - MSU

Meal Planning and Preparation 16 MIN
16mm / U-matic / VHS
Color (J H C A)
$410.00, $250.00 purchase _ #80502; LC 81-701384
Demonstrates basic procedures in meal planning and preparation, including menu planning, grocery shopping, and precise scheduling for the preparation of each dish.
Home Economics
Dist - CORF **Prod** - CENTRO 1981

Meal presentation and etiquette video basics series
Focuses on step-by-step, graphically presented techniques in a working kitchen. Viewers learn many ideas for preparing meals for groups and how to feel comfortable and confident when entertaining.
Entertaining - meal styles - when to serve what
Etiquette - how not to impress royalty
Meal timing - juggling ten balls at once
Presentation of the meal - are you being stared at
Dist - CAMV

Meal timing - juggling ten balls at once
VHS
Meal presentation and etiquette video basics series
Color (G)
$39.95 purchase _ #CDKIT144V-H
Offers many ideas for preparing meals for groups and how to feel comfortable and confident when entertaining. Demonstrates food cooking and managing tips to properly coordinate all of the dishes to be ready at the same time.
Home Economics
Dist - CAMV

Meals for Two
BETA / VHS
Video Cooking Library Series
Color
Demonstrates the preparation of recipes such as London Broil with Mushroom Sauce, Rice Salad and Ice Cream Crepes.
Home Economics
Dist - KARTES **Prod** - KARTES

Meals in a Half Hour 12 MIN
16mm
Eat Right to Your Heart's Delight Series
Color (J H)
Gives many time - saving hints on the selection of foods, meal planning and advance preparation, providing four quick - meal demonstrations, all low in fat and cholesterol. Features linguini and clam sauce, broiled dinner, salisbury steak, turkey - noodle soup, home - made frozen dinners that can be thawed fast and lunchtime suggestions.
Health and Safety; Home Economics; Psychology
Dist - IPS **Prod** - IPS 1976

Mealtime 29 MIN
VHS / 16mm
Villa Alegre Series
Color (P T)
$46.00 rental _ #VILA - 139
Presents educational material in both Spanish and English.
Education; Home Economics
Dist - PBS

Mean
VHS
Probability and statistics series
Color (H C)
$125.00 purchase _ #8004
Provides resource material about the meaning of mean for help in the study of probability and statistics. Presents a 60 - video series, each part 25 to 30 minutes long, that explains and reinforces concepts using definitions, theorems, examples and step - by - step solutions to tutor the student. Videos are also available in a set.
Mathematics
Dist - LANDMK

Mean, nasty, ugly Cinderella 15 MIN
VHS
Creative writing series
Color (I)
$315.00, $235.00 purchase, $60.00 rental
Shows how characters influence stories. Part of a four - part series set in a classroom with a small demonstration group of students and a teacher of creative writing. Projector stops are provided to encourage viewer participation in creative thinking and writing paralleling that done by the group onscreen. Directed by Bud Freeman.
English Language; Fine Arts; Literature and Drama
Dist - CF

Mean Streets 112 MIN
16mm
Color
Dramatizes the struggle of a man climbing the hierarchy of a Mafia family in New York City. Directed by Martin Scorcese.
Fine Arts
Dist - SWANK **Prod** - WB

Meaning 60 MIN
VHS / U-matic
Computer Dialogue - the Key to Successful Systems Series
Color
Discusses the growth of technology and the need for better managment tools, the development of dialogues to aid management, the power of graphics dialogues in portraying complex data relationships and new dialogue capabilities supported by distributed processing and intelligence.
Industrial and Technical Education
Dist - DELTAK **Prod** - DELTAK

Meaning in Child Art 11 MIN
16mm
Color (C T)
Shows how art classes can help develop the child's sensitivity to himself and his environment. Illustrates the philosophy that in teaching art to children, the process is more important than the final product. Uses average work, such as all children can produce, to show how much the child can become involved in his own expression.
Education; Fine Arts; Psychology
Dist - PSUPCR **Prod** - PSU 1955

Meaning in Communication 19 MIN
Videoreel / VHS
Interpersonal Competence, Unit 02 - Communication Series; Unit 2 - Communication
Color (C A)
Features a humanistic psychologist who, by analysis and examples, discusses communication and its meaning in interacting with others.
Psychology; Sociology
Dist - TELSTR **Prod** - MVNE 1973

Meaning in Modern Painting, Pt 1 23 MIN
U-matic / VHS / 16mm
Humanities - the Fine Arts Series
Color (H C)
LC FIA67-1958
Portrays works by Picasso, Klee, Mondrian, Cezanne and other modern artists to illustrate their belief that painting and sculpture need not mirror visible reality. Discusses these artists theories of reality in art.
Fine Arts
Dist - EBEC **Prod** - EBEC 1967

Meaning in Modern Painting, Pt 2 17 MIN
U-matic / VHS / 16mm
Humanities - the Fine Arts Series
Color (H C)
LC FIA67-1958
Includes works by Picasso, Klee, Mondrian, Cezanne and other modern artists to illustrate their belief that painting and sculpture need not mirror visible reality. Discusses these artists theories of reality in art.
Fine Arts
Dist - EBEC **Prod** - EBEC 1967

Meaning is more than Words 14 MIN
VHS / U-matic
Thinkabout Series Giving and Getting Meaning
Color (I)
LC 81-706108
Shows Tina, Jody, Adam And Dave having a series of adventures originating from the meaning - giving signals that surround the words people use, including emphasis, intonation, context, pauses and nonverbal behaviors.
Psychology
Dist - AITECH **Prod** - SCETV

Meaning of Addition and Subtraction, Dr W G Quast 20 MIN
16mm
Teaching Modern School Mathematics - Struc - Ture and Use Series
Color; B&W (K P I)
Mathematics
Dist - HMC **Prod** - HMC 1971

Meaning of AEs 50 MIN
U-matic / VHS
Computer languages series; Pt 1
Color
Discusses funtionality, development of the normal value algorithm from intuitive notions of meaning and the substitution rule in computer languages.
Industrial and Technical Education; Mathematics; Sociology
Dist - MIOT **Prod** - MIOT

The Meaning of Communication 30 MIN
16mm
Nursing - R Plus M Equals C, Relationship Plus Meaning Equals 'Communication Series
B&W (C A)
LC 74-700205
Presents a working definition of communication and describes typical communication gaps.
Health and Safety; Psychology
Dist - NTCN **Prod** - NTCN 1971

The Meaning of Democracy 20 MIN
16mm
Government and Public Affairs Films Series
B&W (H C)
Dr E E Schattschneider, Professor of Governement, Wesleyan University, develops the basic premise of democracy, its respect for the individual and for his personal freedoms.
Civics and Political Systems
Dist - MLA **Prod** - RSC 1960

The Meaning of Democracy - Dr E E Schattschneider 20 MIN
16mm
Building Political Leadership Series
B&W (H C)
Civics and Political Systems
Dist - MLA **Prod** - RSC 1960

Meaning of madness series
The Institution of insanity 23 MIN
The Medicine man 25 MIN
Psychiatry comes of age 24 MIN
Rights and rituals 23 MIN
Dist - PSU

The Meaning of Multiplication, Dr Marilyn J Zweng 19 MIN
16mm
Teaching Modern School Mathematics - Struc - Ture and Use Series
Color; B&W (K P I)
Mathematics
Dist - HMC **Prod** - HMC 1971

The Meaning of nutrition 75 MIN
VHS
Color (J H C A)
$186.00 purchase _ #MB - 513006 - 8
Seeks to dispel common myths and misinformation about nutrition. Features photos of appealing foods from all four food groups, showing that good nutrition can be tasty, too. Consists of two volumes.
Health and Safety; Social Science
Dist - SRA **Prod** - SRA 1988

The Meaning of Our Experience 38 MIN
16mm / U-matic / VHS
Color (C A)
Presents a group of middle class people who share important and intimate aspects of their lives, not only to learn from each other but in the realization that sharing oneself is a key to self - development.

Guidance and Counseling; Psychology
Dist - FI Prod - ROBERJ 1974

Meaning of Our Experience 37 MIN
16mm
Color (C A)
Focuses on adults participating in a life experience workshop based on the conviction that people can learn from each other and that sharing oneself is a key to self development.
Psychology
Dist - NYU Prod - NYU

The Meaning of the Pledge 10 MIN
U-matic / VHS / 16mm
American Values for Elementary Series
Color (P I)
LC 72-703122
Features Ben Murphy who visits a typical grade class to find out what the students think the pledge means. Provides a springboard for classroom discussion and inquiry.
Civics and Political Systems; Social Science
Dist - AIMS Prod - EVANSA 1972

The Meaning of the whole 65 MIN
Cassette
Beyond fragmentation - memory of the whole series
Color; PAL (G C PRO)
$150.00, $25.00 purchase _ #V9333, #T9333
Features Fred Kofman who pushed the boundaries of current thinking about the nature of reality. Speculates on what it means to perceive, act, communicate and learn - what it means to be human. Part three of three parts on breaking down the myth that human relationships can be separated into their constituent parts and showing how this myth is slowly being replaced by an appreciation for interconnectedness and the integrity of the whole.
Business and Economics; Psychology; Sociology
Dist - PEGASU

The Meaning of Tibetan Buddhist chanting 27 MIN
VHS
Color (G)
$21.95 purchase _ #THMC
Features Thubten Pende, American, who became a Buddhist monk in the Tibetan tradition and studied under the Dalai Lama in Dharamsala, India. Discusses the chanting and disciplines of Tibetan Buddhism and illustrates Tibetan art which symbolizes the ideas and techniques of Buddhism.
Religion and Philosophy
Dist - SNOWLI Prod - SNOWLI

Meaningful Use of Time 29 MIN
U-matic / VHS
How People Age 50 and Up Can Plan for a more Successful Retirement 'Series
Color
Focuses on making the best use of time. Presented By Bill Oriol, Associate Director, International Center for Social Gerontology.
Health and Safety; Sociology
Dist - SYLWAT Prod - RCOMTV

Means, medians, and modes of grouped data
VHS
Probability and statistics series
Color (H C)
$125.00 purchase _ #8006
Provides resource material about the meaning of mean, median and mode of group data for help in the study of probability and statistics. Presents a 60 - video series, each part 25 to 30 minutes long, that explains and reinforces concepts using definitions, theorems, examples and step - by - step solutions to tutor the student. Videos are also available in a set.
Mathematics
Dist - LANDMK

A Means of assistance to ambulation - crutch walking 31 MIN
16mm
Directions for education in nursing via technology series; Lesson 68
B&W (PRO)
LC 74-701844
Identifies various types of crutches. Demonstrates preparation of patient and four types of gaits, ascending and desending stairs, and sitting in and rising from a chair.
Health and Safety
Dist - WSUM Prod - DENT 1974

Meanwhile 3 MIN
16mm
B&W (G)
$15.00 rental
Surveys filmmaker's room in stop motion, very speedy. Looks at an encounter between a girl, a cat and a plant in the garden next door. Breathing on the soundtrack enhances both sections.

Agriculture; Fine Arts; Home Economics
Dist - CANCIN Prod - PEARLY

Meanwhile back at the ranch - 44
VHS
Reading rainbow series
Color; CC (K P)
$39.95 purchase
Follows Rancher Hicks to Sleepy Gulch in the story by Trinka Hakes Noble, illustrated by Tony Ross, and reveals that he misses a very eventful, surprise - filled day back home. Experiences the Old West with LeVar as he rides a stagecoach across the Arizona desert and visits Old Tuscon, an authentic Western town. LeVar also gets a taste of the life of a cowboy when he dons true western garb - spurs, chaps and an official ten - gallon hat. Meets a talented stunt woman who demonstrates rope tricks and horseback stunts. Part of a series offering a multicultural approach to generating reading enthusiasm with cross - curricular applications, hosted by LeVar Burton.
English Language; History - United States; Literature and Drama; Physical Education and Recreation
Dist - GPN Prod - LNMDP

Measles (Rubeola) in Children 2 MIN
U-matic / VHS / 16mm
Color (C)
LC FIA68-260
Shows measles patients 5 to 9 days after exposure displaying the preliminary symptoms of conjunctivitis, upper respiratory tract infection, catarrh, and Koplick spots, and 12 to 19 days after exposure when the rash appears on the face and spreads to the neck and trunk.
Health and Safety
Dist - UCEMC Prod - UCEMC 1961

Measurable Functions
16mm
B&W
Presents the measurable functions as an extension of the Lebesgue integrable functions.
Mathematics
Dist - OPENU Prod - OPENU

Measure and Set Theory 47 MIN
16mm
MAA Individual Lecturers Series
B&W (H C T)
Professor Stanislaw Ulam defines measure and lectures on the existence of measures and the uniqueness where they exist. He discusses the Banach - Tarski paradox and the work of Godel and Paul Cohen.
Mathematics
Dist - MLA Prod - MAA 1966

Measure for Measure 145 MIN
VHS / 16mm
BBC's Shakespeare Series
(H A)
$249.95
PResents the Shakesepearean comedy of crime and premarital sex.
Literature and Drama
Dist - AMBROS Prod - AMBROS 1979

Measure for Measure 145 MIN
VHS / U-matic
Shakespeare Plays Series
Color (H C A)
LC 79-706934
Presents Shakespeare's comedy about life in Vienna where sexual relationships between unmarried people are punishable by death. Centers on Isabella, who is torn between her attempts to save her brother's condemned life and her vows to God. Stars Kate Nelligan, Tom Piggott - Smith and Christopher Strauli.
Literature and Drama
Dist - TIMLIF Prod - BBCTV 1979

Measure for measure 145 MIN
VHS
BBC Shakespeare series
Color (G C H)
$109.00 purchase _ #DL456
Fine Arts
Dist - INSIM Prod - BBC

Measure for Measure 29 MIN
Videoreel / VT2
Feast of Language Series
Color
Features Alan Levitan, associate professor of English at Brandeis University discussing Measure For Measure by Shakespeare.
Literature and Drama
Dist - PBS Prod - WGBHTV

Measure Length - Think Metric 9 MIN
16mm / U-matic / VHS
Think Metric Series
Color
LC 74-701237
Explains the importance of measuring length. Defines the standard metric units of length, the meter, centimeter, millimeter and kilometer through the story of two boys who explore their neighborhood with a meter stick and centimeter rule and discover the comparative size of things around them.
Mathematics
Dist - BARR Prod - BARR 1974

Measure Length - Think Metric 9 MIN
U-matic / 16mm
Color (K P I) (SPANISH)
Defines the standard metric units of length.
Foreign Language; Mathematics
Dist - BARR Prod - BARR

Measure of a Moment 55 MIN
16mm
Color
Portrays the stirring pageant presented at the Congregational General Council in Omaha in 1956, with Raymond Massey as narrator.
Religion and Philosophy
Dist - YALEDV Prod - YALEDV

Measure of Air Flow with a Thermal Anemometer 11 MIN
VHS / BETA
Color
Discusses ventilation, air flow and anemometers.
Health and Safety
Dist - RMIBHF Prod - RMIBHF

The Measure of America 26 MIN
U-matic / VHS / 16mm
Color (J H C G T A)
$50 rental _ #9786; $69.95 purchase _ #501498
Provides an articulation of many of the most traditional and fundamental concepts of American social, economic, and political life. Shows scenes of Americans at work and play and familiar symbols of national pride.
History - United States; Sociology
Dist - AIMS Prod - AIMS 1984
UILL

The Measure of Man 9 MIN
16mm
Color (P I)
LC 77-703378
Uses animation to present a brief history of measurement and common metric units.
Mathematics
Dist - BESTF Prod - EFCR 1977

A Measure of understanding 29 MIN
U-matic / VHS
Captioned; Color (A) (DUTCH)
Discusses effective communication, techniques for clearing up conflicting meanings, how to recognize the 'double level' of a verbal message, and the causes and prevention of communication breakdown. Available captioned for the deaf. Also available in Dutch and Spanish.
Psychology
Dist - RTBL Prod - RTBL

A Measure of Understanding 29 MIN
16mm / U-matic / 8mm cartridge / VHS
Color; B&W (C A) (DUTCH SPANISH)
LC 79-714888
Demonstrates how to clear up conflicting, double messages and determine the real intent of incongruent communication.
Foreign Language; Guidance and Counseling; Psychology
Dist - RTBL Prod - RTBL 1970

Measure of worth 15 MIN
VHS / U-matic / 16mm
Color (G)
$300.00, $175.00 purchase, $45.00 rental
Makes the connection between eating disorders and advertising images. Presents the stories of three young women suffering from Anorexia Nervosa. Produced by Kristin Porter.
Psychology; Sociology
Dist - WMEN

Measure, Take, Pepper 10 MIN
U-matic
Readalong Two Series
Color (P)
Provides young viewers with a flexible range of reading experiences through active involvement in reading and writing. Comes with teacher's guide and kit.
Education; English Language; Literature and Drama
Dist - TVOTAR Prod - TVOTAR 1976

Measure Up Series
Addition - sums to Ten 15 MIN
Addition and subtraction of Two - digit numbers 15 MIN
Awareness of numbers 15 MIN
Conservation of Discrete Objects 15 MIN
Conservation of Liquids and Solids 15 MIN

Counting in Order 13 MIN
Equal and not equal 15 MIN
Equalizing 15 MIN
Fractions, Pt 2 15 MIN
Fun and games 15 MIN
Geometry 15 MIN
Graphing 15 MIN
Grouping and Partitioning to Twenty 15 MIN
Matching - Greater than, Less than 15 MIN
Measurement, Pt 1 15 MIN
Measurement, Pt 2 15 MIN
Mixed Operation - Sums to Six 15 MIN
Mixed Operations to Sums of Ten 15 MIN
Place Value - Pt 1 15 MIN
Place Value - Pt 2 15 MIN
Place Value - Pt 3 15 MIN
Place Value - the Teens 15 MIN
Readiness for Addition and Subtraction 15 MIN
Subtraction - Sums to Six 15 MIN
Subtraction - Sums to Ten, Pt 1 15 MIN
Subtraction - Sums to Ten, Pt 2 15 MIN
Sums Up to Six 15 MIN
Time, Pt 1 15 MIN
Time, Pt 2 15 MIN
Dist - GPN

Measure volume - think metric 9 MIN
U-matic / VHS / 16mm
Think metric series
Color
LC 74-701239
Introduces the concept of measuring volume in metric units. Shows young people as they measure the volumes of things in their home.
Mathematics
Dist - BARR **Prod** - BARR 1974

Measure Weight - Think Metric 9 MIN
16mm / U-matic / VHS
Think Metric Series
Color (SPANISH)
LC 74-701238
Introduces the concept of measuring weight in metric units. Shows two girls as they visit a chemist to learn about the standard units of weight. Tells how they use their new knowledge to compare the weight of common things in their home and to bake a metric cake.
Mathematics
Dist - BARR **Prod** - BARR 1974

The Measured loaf 15 MIN
VHS / U-matic
Dragons, wagons and wax - Set 1 series
Color (K P)
Explains the methods of measuring matter.
Mathematics; Science; Science - Physical
Dist - CTI **Prod** - CTI

Measurement 30 MIN
VHS
Perspectives - science in action - series
Color; PAL; NTSC (G)
PdS90, PdS105 purchase
Discusses the fact that the very fabric of society is based on the standards of time, length and weight. Shows how measurements are achieved with accuracy using units of measurement from the National Physical Laboratory in London.
Mathematics
Dist - CFLVIS **Prod** - LONTVS

Measurement 21 MIN
16mm
PSSC Physics Films Series
B&W (H C)
Discusses the art of measurement, using the speed of a rifle bullet as an example. Discusses such problems as noise, bias, use of black boxes and the element of decision.
Mathematics; Science - Physical
Dist - MLA **Prod** - PSSC 1959

Measurement 26 MIN
VHS
Color (G)
$195.00 purchase
States that without the ability to measure weight, length and time society would have remained static and progress would have been impossible.
Mathematics
Dist - LANDMK **Prod** - LANDMK 1992

Measurement 15 MIN
U-matic / VHS
First Films on Science Series
Color (P I)
Presents measurement as an important process used constantly in everyday life. Focuses on the different things that need to be measured, the practical reasons for measuring them and the instrument used to measure them.
Mathematics
Dist - AITECH **Prod** - MAETEL 1975

Measurement and Man 16 MIN
U-matic / VHS / 16mm
Color; B&W (P I)
LC FIA66-463
Demonstrates the importance of mathematics in measurement, observation, communication and data recording.
Mathematics; Science
Dist - IU **Prod** - IU 1965

Measurement and Statistics 16 MIN
16mm
Basic Psychology Series
Color (H C A)
LC 76-702921
Examines basic concepts in measurement and statistics in psychology, including scales of measurement, measures of central tendency and dispersion and the normal curve.
Psychology
Dist - EDMDC **Prod** - EDMDC 1973

Measurement - Dividing Regions into Subregions for Finding Area 15 MIN
VHS / U-matic
Math Works Series
Color (I)
Shows how to divide irregular region into subregions to determine total area.
Mathematics
Dist - AITECH **Prod** - AITECH

Measurement - Finding Areas of Rectangles 15 MIN
U-matic / VHS
Math Works Series
Color (I)
Demonstrates the formula for finding the area of a rectangle.
Mathematics
Dist - AITECH **Prod** - AITECH

Measurement for Valve String Installed Height 5 MIN
VHS / 16mm
Auto Mechanics Series
(G PRO)
$48.00 purchase _ #AM24
Shows how to measure for valve string installed height.
Industrial and Technical Education
Dist - RMIBHF **Prod** - RMIBHF

Measurement - introduction to distance, mass and volume 16 MIN
U-matic / VHS
Math cycle series
Color (P)
Shows how to measure distance, mass and volume.
Mathematics
Dist - GPN **Prod** - WDCNTV 1983

Measurement of a patient's blood pressure 30 MIN
VHS / U-matic
Color (PRO C)
$395.00 purchase, $80.00 rental _ #C861 - VI - 062
Uses a logical and uncomplicated approach to teach the beginning student how to measure blood pressure. Shows how to select the proper cuff size, apply it, palpate the brachial artery, determine the pressure and record it in thepatient's medical record. Describes the structure and use of two types of cuffs - the pocket aneroid and the hand aneroid. Presented by Dr John W Sponaugle.
Health and Safety; Science - Natural
Dist - HSCIC

Measurement of area and volume 23 MIN
VHS / U-matic
Mathematics and physics series
Color (IND)
Defines and describes plane surfaces and three dimensional solids. Develops formulas for calculating and how they work. Includes discussion of circular measurement and spherical volume.
Mathematics; Science - Physical
Dist - AVIMA **Prod** - AVIMA 1980

The Measurement of Blood Pressure 23 MIN
VHS / U-matic
Blood Pressure Series
Color (PRO)
LC 79-706006
Presents examples of blood pressure readings on a standard mercury manometer in order to provide a test on the hearing and recording of blood pressure measurements.
Health and Safety
Dist - IU **Prod** - IU 1978

Measurement of Blood Pressure in Dental Practice 8 MIN
U-matic
Color (PRO)
LC 79-706751
Defines blood pressure and related terms and demonstrates a technique for measuring blood pressure in dental practice.
Health and Safety
Dist - USNAC **Prod** - MUSC 1978

Measurement of Cerebral Blood Flow in Health and Disease 50 MIN
U-matic
Color
Discusses the technique of measuring cerebral blood with external probes. Discusses the measurement of blood flow with CT scan.
Health and Safety; Science - Natural
Dist - UTEXSC **Prod** - UTEXSC

Measurement of Electrical Impedence in Single Cell Suspensions as a Rapid Assay 32 MIN
U-matic
Color
Discusses cellular metabolism before and after the induction of electrical current.
Health and Safety
Dist - UTEXSC **Prod** - UTEXSC

Measurement of Impulse Response 11 MIN
VHS / U-matic
Probability and Random Processes - Linear Systems Series
B&W (PRO)
Demonstrates the relative invariance of linear time - invariant system responses to the detailed shape of a pulse input of short duration but fixed area.
Mathematics
Dist - MIOT **Prod** - MIOT

Measurement of Length 10 MIN
16mm
Measurement Series
Color (J)
LC 76-703207
Introduces various aspects of linear measurement and the use of such tools as a decimal inch and metric rule, inside and outside calipers and a metric micrometer.
Mathematics
Dist - PSU **Prod** - PSU 1972

Measurement of Petroleum and Petroleum Product Cargoes Aboard Marine Vessels 40 MIN
Slide / VHS / 16mm
Color (A IND)
$285.00, $295.00 purchase _ #13.2983, #53.2983
Identifies procedures and equipment for measuring petroleum aboard marine vessels. Covers basic petroleum characteristics and measurement techniques. Describes marine tankers and outlines principles of basic construction. Reviews marine terminology.
Industrial and Technical Education; Mathematics; Social Science
Dist - UTEXPE

Measurement of Solids 30 MIN
16mm
Mathematics for Elementary School Teachers Series no 28
Color (T)
Presents the standard formulas for determining the volume of various solids. Employs physical models to introduce the concept of volume. To be used following 'AREA.'.
Mathematics
Dist - MLA **Prod** - SMSG 1963

Measurement of Surface and Interfacial Tensions of Liquids 1 25 MIN
VHS / U-matic
Colloid and Surface Chemistry - Surface Chemistry Series
B&W (PRO)
Science - Physical
Dist - MIOT **Prod** - MIOT

Measurement of Surface and Interfacial Tensions of Liquids 2 37 MIN
VHS / U-matic
Colloid and Surface Chemistry - Surface Chemistry Series
B&W (PRO)
Science - Physical
Dist - MIOT **Prod** - MIOT

Measurement of Surface and Interfacial Tensions of Liquids, Pt 1 25 MIN
U-matic / VHS
Colloid and Surface Chemistry - Surface Chemistry Series
Color
Science; Science - Physical
Dist - KALMIA **Prod** - KALMIA

Measurement of Surface and Interfacial Tensions of Liquids, Pt 2 37 MIN
U-matic / VHS
Colloid and Surface Chemistry - Surface Chemistry Series
Color
Science; Science - Physical
Dist - KALMIA **Prod** - KALMIA

A Measurement of the Acceleration of Gravity - Falling Body 8 MIN
16mm
Color; B&W (C)
Presents a physics experiment in which two photoelectric cells are arranged for use in measuring the time of transit through a known vertical distance.
Science; Science - Physical
Dist - PUAVC **Prod** - PUAVC 1961

A Measurement of the Acceleration of Gravity with Kater's Pendulum 21 MIN
16mm
B&W (C)
Uses Kater's pendulum in a gravity experiment.
Science; Science - Physical
Dist - PUAVC **Prod** - PUAVC 1961

Measurement of the Corrosion Potential and Corrosion Current 46 MIN
U-matic / VHS
Corrosion Engineering Series
Color (PRO)
Industrial and Technical Education; Science - Physical
Dist - GPCV **Prod** - GPCV

A Measurement of the Universal Gravitational Constant with the Cavendish Balance 27 MIN
16mm
Color; B&W (C)
Quantitive determination of the universal gravitational constant is achieved with a sensitive torsion balance with a long vibration time. Time lapse photography is used to reduce observation time.
Science - Physical
Dist - PUAVC **Prod** - PUAVC 1961

Measurement of Vapor Pressure 12 MIN
16mm
Experimental General Chemistry Series
B&W
Offers the procedure for determining the heat of vaporization of a liquid by studying its vapor pressure at various temperatures.
Science; Science - Physical
Dist - MLA **Prod** - MLA

Measurement of Weight 12 MIN
16mm
Measurement Series
Color (J)
LC 76-703208
Shows how scales work, demonstrating both spring scales and balances. Explains why balance - type scales are used for laboratory work and shows the procedure for weighting with both the triple beam balance and analytical balance.
Mathematics
Dist - PSU **Prod** - PSU 1972

Measurement - Precision and Estimation 15 MIN
U-matic / VHS
Mathematics for the '80s Grade Six Series
(I)
$125.00 purchase
Analyzes the use of increasingly precise intruments to provide increasingly precise measurements.
Mathematics
Dist - AITECH **Prod** - AITECH 1987

Measurement, Pt 1 15 MIN
U-matic
Measure Up Series
Color (P)
Discusses how to measure length, area and volume with non - standard units.
Mathematics
Dist - GPN **Prod** - WCETTV 1977

Measurement, Pt 2 15 MIN
U-matic
Measure Up Series
Color (P)
Shows how to measure length in meters.
Mathematics
Dist - GPN **Prod** - WCETTV 1977

Measurement readiness series
Big and small 10 MIN
Fast and slow 11 MIN
Heavy and Light 13 MIN
Hot and Cold 10 MIN
Dist - CORF

Measurement Series
Measurement of Length 10 MIN
Measurement of Weight 12 MIN
Understanding the Metric System 8 MIN
Why Measure 6 MIN
Dist - PSU

Measurement Techniques 9 MIN
VHS / 16mm
Food Preparation Techniques Series
Color (H C A)
Demonstrates measurement techniques for the American kitchen and the food preparation laboratory of liquids, dry ingredients, shredded ingredients, shortening and other items.
Home Economics; Psychology
Dist - IOWA **Prod** - IOWA 1989

Measurement - the Difference between Perimeter and Area 15 MIN
VHS / U-matic
Math Works Series
Color (I)
Illustrates the difference between perimeter and area by showing that the perimeter can surround very different areas.
Mathematics
Dist - AITECH **Prod** - AITECH

Measurement - the foundation of chemistry - modeling the unseen - Parts 3 and 4 60 MIN
VHS / U-matic
World of chemistry series
Color (C)
$45.00, $29.95 purchase
Presents parts 3 and 4 of the 26 - part World of Chemistry series. Looks at the importance of accuracy and precision in measurement to modern chemistry. Examines the use of models to explain phenomena which are beyond the realm of ordinary perception. Emphasizes a classic model which explains the behavior of gases. Two thirty - minute programs hosted by Nobel laureate Roald Hoffmann.
Mathematics; Science; Science - Physical
Dist - ANNCPB **Prod** - UMD 1990

Measurement - Time and Temperature 16 MIN
U-matic / VHS
Math Cycle Series
Color (P)
Tells how to read a clock and a thermometer.
Mathematics
Dist - GPN **Prod** - WDCNTV 1983

Measurement Tools - 1 60 MIN
VHS
Handtools and Hardware Series
Color (PRO)
$600.00, $1500.00 purchase _ #GMMT1
Introduces units of measurements, along with the different types of measurement tools. Describes rules, tapes, calipers and torque wrenches, their use and appropriate care. Part of a seven - part series on handtools and hardware, part of a larger set on general and mechanical maintenance. Includes 10 textbooks and an instructor guide which provide four hours of instruction.
Education; Industrial and Technical Education; Psychology
Dist - NUSTC **Prod** - NUSTC

Measurement Tools - 2 60 MIN
VHS
Handtools and Hardware Series
Color (PRO)
$600.00, $1500.00 purchase _ #GMMT2
Describes measurement tools and concepts not covered in Part 1. Examines vernier calipers, micrometers, inside micrometers, depth gauges, telescoping gauges, dial indicators, their care and calibration. Part of a seven - part series on handtools and hardware, part of a larger set on general and mechanical maintenance. Includes 10 textbooks and an instructor guide which provide four hours of instruction.
Education; Industrial and Technical Education; Psychology
Dist - NUSTC **Prod** - NUSTC

Measurement - Use of the Analytical Balance 24 MIN
16mm
Experimental General Chemistry Series
Color
Introduces the student to the nature and measurement of mass. Shows how to operate automatic analytical balances and the degree of accuracy that can be expected from the different types. Shows proper techniques for weighing different kinds of materials.
Mathematics; Science; Science - Physical
Dist - MLA **Prod** - MLA

Measurement with Light Waves 15 MIN
16mm
Engineering Series
B&W
LC FIE52-264
Discusses the principles of measurement with light waves, nature of light waves, cause of interference bands and use of these bands in ultra - precision measurement. Shows gage block inspection procedures.
Science - Physical
Dist - USNAC **Prod** - USOE 1944

Measurements for Custom Orthopedic Shoes, VA Form 10 - 2908 17 MIN
U-matic / VHS
Color
LC 80-707595
Demonstrates the correct technique for measuring feet, as required to complete VA form 10 - 2908.
Health and Safety
Dist - USNAC **Prod** - USVA 1980

Measures and Set Theory 50 MIN
16mm
Mathematics Today Series
B&W (H)
LC FIA66-1280
Outlines the background and principal of measure theory, including both finitely and countably additive measures. Explores the relationship of these measures to set theory, concentrating on recent developments of the continuum hypothesis.
Mathematics
Dist - MLA **Prod** - COEMM 1966

Measures for Air Quality 4 MIN
16mm
Color (H C A)
LC 73-702598
Describes new air quality measurement techniques and calibration standards being developed by the National Bureau of Standards to help improve the accuracy of measuring air pollution. Includes the use of a laser to measure air pollution levels, the sulphur dioxide fluorescence detector and the permeation tube.
Science - Natural
Dist - USNBOS **Prod** - USNBOS 1972

Measures of Distance 15 MIN
U-matic / VHS
Color (G)
$250.00, $200.00 purchase, $50.00 rental
Explores the renewal of friendship between mother and daughter during a brief family reunion in war - torn Lebanon in 1981. Experiences the silence and isolation imposed by war.
History - World; Religion and Philosophy; Sociology
Dist - WMEN **Prod** - MONHA 1988

Measuring 13 MIN
U-matic / VHS / 16mm
Science Processes Series
Color (P)
LC 70-703314
Shows that measuring is an indispensable part of daily life. Illustrates that measurements can be qualitative, larger than or smaller than, but that standard limits are necessary for communicating among people. Presents a brief description and comparison of the English and metric systems of measurement.
Mathematics
Dist - MGHT **Prod** - MGHT 1970

Measuring 20 MIN
VHS / 16mm
Trail Series
Color (I)
$150.00 purchase, $30.00 rental
Considers carrying capacity and limiting factors as they apply to wildlife populations. Shows human intervention.
Science - Natural
Dist - AITECH **Prod** - KAIDTV 1986

Measuring - a Way of Comparing 10 MIN
U-matic / VHS / 16mm
Color (P I)
LC FIA68-387
Shows that measuring is a way of comparing. Begins with a boy comparing the length of two trains and a girl comparing the height of two dolls. Explains that we often want to know more about two objects than which is longer or taller. Demonstrates the measuring of length, width and volume.
Mathematics
Dist - PHENIX **Prod** - BOUNDY 1967

Measuring and Calibration 60 MIN
U-matic / VHS
Quality Assurance Series
Color (IND)
Deals with tolerances, measuring, calibration program and metrication.
Business and Economics; Industrial and Technical Education; Mathematics
Dist - LEIKID **Prod** - LEIKID

Measuring and Layout Tools 30 MIN
U-matic / VHS
Aircraft Hardware, Hand Tools and Measuring Devices Series
Color (IND)
Contains information on precision measuring instruments and tools used for transferring dimensions on paper to the materials of fabrication.
Industrial and Technical Education; Mathematics
Dist - AVIMA **Prod** - AVIMA

Measuring and Layout Tools 13 MIN
16mm
Hand Tools for Wood Working Series no 6; No 6
Color (J H A)
LC FIA67-964
Demonstrates the use of measuring tools and layout tools.
Industrial and Technical Education
Dist - SF **Prod** - MORLAT 1967

Measuring and using electricity 12 MIN
VHS
Electricity and magnetism series
Color (I)
$55.00 purchase _ #1223VG
Introduces measurement of electric power and terms such as wattage, amperage and voltage. Presents the basic requirements for and the two types of circuits. Comes with a teacher's guide and six blackline masters. Part four of a five - part series.
Industrial and Technical Education; Science - Physical
Dist - UNL

Measuring Blood Pressure 25 MIN
U-matic / VHS
Basic Nursing Skills Series Tape 8; Tape 8
Color (PRO)
Includes measuring body temperature. Covers measuring pulse and respiratory rates. Discusses nurse - patient relations.
Health and Safety
Dist - MDCC **Prod** - MDCC

Measuring Blood Pressure 20 MIN
U-matic / VHS
Blood Pressure Series
Color (PRO)
Presents proper blood pressure measurement techniques with emphasis on selection and care of equipment, selection of the appropriate size cuff and explanation of the ausculatory gap.
Health and Safety
Dist - IU **Prod** - NICEPR 1980

Measuring Blood Pressure 10 MIN
16mm
Color
Stresses the importance of having blood pressure measured, while pointing out that 60 million Americans have high blood pressure but only about half of them know it.
Health and Safety
Dist - MTP **Prod** - MTP

Measuring Blood Pressure 10 MIN
16mm
Color (PRO)
LC 76-700288
Reviews basic steps involved in measuring blood pressure and offers advice on techniques that may help assure more accurate reading. Includes a brief overview of the problem of high blood pressure in the United States.
Health and Safety; Science
Dist - MESHDO **Prod** - MESHDO 1976

Measuring - Blood Pressure, Body Temperatures, Pulse and Respiratory Rates 25 MIN
U-matic / VHS
Basic Nursing Skills Series
Color (PRO)
Health and Safety
Dist - BRA **Prod** - BRA

Measuring brain gain - 1
U-matic / VHS / BETA
Search encounters in science series
Color; PAL (G H C)
PdS25, PdS33 purchase
Brings modern research efforts of the world's leading scientists into the classroom. Features one in a series of 24 mini - documentaries. Each film is 5 - 7 minutes in length.
Science; Science - Natural
Dist - EDPAT **Prod** - NSF

Measuring common kitchen ingredients
VHS
Kitchen video series
$59.00 purchase _ #FY100V
Teaches the importance of kitchen safety and following directions. Uses kitchen video transfers and graphic photography.
Home Economics; Industrial and Technical Education
Dist - CAREER **Prod** - CAREER

Measuring customer satsifaction 25 MIN
VHS
Color; CC (IND)
$495.00 purchase, $150.00 rental _ #CRI49
Shows how to mount an effective program to surpass customer expectations. Includes a leader's guide and workbooks.
Business and Economics; Social Science
Dist - EXTR **Prod** - CRISP

Measuring Distance 15 MIN
VHS / U-matic
Why Series
Color (P I)
Discusses measuring distance.
Mathematics
Dist - AITECH **Prod** - WDCNTV 1976

Measuring External and Internal Threads
VHS / U-matic
Intermediate Engine Lathe Operation Series
Color (SPANISH)
Industrial and Technical Education
Dist - VTRI **Prod** - VTRI

Measuring Hearing 11 MIN
VHS / U-matic
Color
LC 80-707423
Explains that procedures employed in measuring the learning - impaired child's auditory capacity may vary according to the age of the child, the stimulus presented, and the response anticipated. Presents several evaluation techniques.
Health and Safety; Psychology
Dist - USNAC **Prod** - USBEH 1980

Measuring in Astronomy - How Big, How Far 12 MIN
U-matic / VHS / 16mm
Color (I J)
LC 71-700649
Discusses how surveyors use their knowlege of geometry and properties common to triangles to measure the large distances on the curved surface of the earth.
Mathematics
Dist - PHENIX **Prod** - DSFI 1969

Measuring in Science 14 MIN
U-matic / VHS
Whatabout Series
Color (J)
Demonstrates how an archaeologist uses measuring to reconstruct and understand the fossil remains of a mammoth.
Science
Dist - AITECH **Prod** - AITECH 1983

Measuring Ingredients and Following Recipes
VHS
$79 purchase _ #PX30755V
Demonstrates weighing foods on different scales, measuring wet and dry ingredients, and cooking the meat sauce. Uses a professional kitchen staff, chef and his assistants to provide demonstrations.
Home Economics
Dist - CAREER **Prod** - CAREER

Measuring Instructional Effectiveness 30 MIN
U-matic / VHS
Training the Trainer Series
Color (T)
Shows how to measure instructional effectiveness. Covers preparing written and performance tests, scoring tests and using reaction sheets.
Education; Psychology
Dist - ITCORP **Prod** - ITCORP

Measuring instruments 60 MIN
U-matic / VHS
Mechanical maintenance basics series
Color (IND) (SPANISH)
Focuses on use and care of measuring instruments including steel rule, vernier calipers, thickness gauge, micrometers.
Industrial and Technical Education
Dist - ITCORP **Prod** - ITCORP

Measuring is Important 17 MIN
U-matic / 16mm
Color (I)
Shows a sixth grade class learning the fundamentals of measuring. Shows how the measurement of length, weight, volume, time and temperature apply in daily life. Introduces the metric system.
Mathematics
Dist - BARR **Prod** - SAIF

Measuring Large Distances 29 MIN
16mm
PSSC Physics Films Series
B&W (H C)
Describes the place of triangulation, parallax and the inverse square law for light in geophysics and astronomy. Uses models of the earth, moon and stars.
Mathematics; Science - Physical
Dist - MLA **Prod** - PSSC 1959

Measuring, Marking and Sawing Wood 14 MIN
U-matic / VHS / 16mm
Vocational Skillfilms - Woodworking Skills Series
Color (IND)
Demonstrates the correct methods for measuring wood using the rule and tri - square. Deals with the selection of saws and the techniques of sawing. Shows correct tool care procedures.
Industrial and Technical Education
Dist - RTBL **Prod** - RTBL 1982

Measuring Molecules 20 MIN
16mm
Science Twenty Series
Color (P A)
LC 72-710540
Shows students being taken through tunnels to appreciate the size of molecules.
Science; Science - Physical
Dist - SF **Prod** - PRISM 1970

Measuring Motion
Software / BETA
Force, Weight and Motion Measurement Series
Color (PRO)
$600.00 - $1500.00 purchase _ #IDMEM
Describes how a typical valve position detector measures and indicates linear displacement. Checks and calibrates a valve position detector. Part of a three - part series on force, weight and motion measurement. Interactive training system includes course administrator guide, videodisc and computer software.
Industrial and Technical Education; Mathematics; Psychology
Dist - NUSTC **Prod** - NUSTC

Measuring My Success 30 MIN
U-matic / VHS
Money Puzzle - the World of Macroeconomics Series Module 6
Color
Shows how the performance of the economy is measured in terms of gross national product, net national product, national income and the consumer price index.
Business and Economics; Sociology
Dist - MDCC **Prod** - MDCC

Measuring pipe, tubing, and fittings 15 MIN
U-matic
Shipbuilding skills series; Pipefitting
B&W
LC 80-707268
Identifies types of pipes, tubing, and fittings and shows how to use basic measuring tools. Explains how to measure pipe for offsets and how to make allowances for fittings and offsets when measuring pipes. Issued in 1944 as a motion picture.
Industrial and Technical Education
Dist - USNAC **Prod** - USOE 1980

Measuring Process Variables 60 MIN
U-matic / VHS
Instrumentation Basics - Process Concepts Series Tape 2; Process concepts; Tape 2
Color (IND)
Industrial and Technical Education; Mathematics
Dist - ISA **Prod** - ISA

Measuring screw threads 10 MIN
VHS / BETA
Machine shop - engine lathe series; No 21
Color (IND)
Explains two common methods of measuring screw threads, thread triangles and a thread micrometer. Discusses the tables used in each method and proper technique for measuring.
Industrial and Technical Education; Psychology
Dist - RMIBHF **Prod** - RMIBHF

Measuring Shadows - the Universe Today 28 MIN
16mm / U-matic / VHS
Understanding Space and Time Series
Color
Discusses the structure of the universe and the research that led to man's present understanding of it.
Science - Physical
Dist - UCEMC **Prod** - BBCTV 1980

Measuring Short Distances 20 MIN
16mm
PSSC Physics Films Series
B&W (H)
Discusses the ways to measure short distances, including the centimeter scale, microscopic dimensions and atom dimensions. Explains the calibration of instruments.

Mathematics; Science - Physical
Dist - MLA **Prod** - PSSC 1959

Measuring Speed 14 MIN
U-matic / VHS
Hands on, Grade 4 - Cars, Cartoons, Etc Series Unit 2 - Measuring; Unit 2 - Measuring
Color (I)
Gives experience in measuring speed.
Mathematics
Dist - AITECH **Prod** - WHROTV 1975

Measuring success - Part 5 13 MIN
VHS
Breakthrough improvement in quality series; Pt 5
Color (PRO IND A)
$495.00 purchase, $175.00 rental _ #GP133E
Presents part five of a five - part series developed by Florida Power and Light's - Qualtec Quality Service. Pictures the principles that make up policy management and gives organizations a resource to help achieve and keep a competitive advantage.
Business and Economics
Dist - EXTR **Prod** - GPERFO

Measuring Techniques 15 MIN
16mm / U-matic / VHS
Biological Techniques Series
Color (H C)
Demonstrates the basic techniques and equipment used to measure length and volume and to determine concentrations.
Science; Science - Natural
Dist - IFB **Prod** - THORNE 1961

Measuring techniques - linear, volume, temperature 17 MIN
VHS
Color (J H)
$145.00 purchase _ #A5VH 1006
Uses clear demonstrations and wording to present methods for selecting the appropriate measurement instrument, reading the measurement accurately and recording the proper - significant - measurement. Illustrates specific measuring techniques relating to the properties of length, volume and temperature.
Mathematics; Science
Dist - CLRVUE **Prod** - CLRVUE

Measuring Temperature 15 MIN
U-matic / VHS
Why Series
Color (P I)
Discusses measuring temperature.
Mathematics
Dist - AITECH **Prod** - WDCNTV 1976

Measuring Temperature 5 MIN
U-matic
Eureka Series
Color (J)
Explains how Anders Celsius invented the Celsius thermometer using the expansion of mercury as a gauge to measure temperature.
Science; Science - Physical
Dist - TVOTAR **Prod** - TVOTAR 1980

Measuring the Blood Sugar - Chemstrip BG 24 MIN
VHS / U-matic
Color (PRO)
Demonstrates Bio - Dynamics products. Provides a basic understanding of how strip products work.
Health and Safety; Science - Natural
Dist - MEDFAC **Prod** - MEDFAC 1983

Measuring the Blood Sugar - Dextrostix and Visidex 18 MIN
U-matic / VHS
Color (PRO)
Demonstrates Ames products and how strip products react to glucose. Describes the Glucometer and its use.
Health and Safety; Science - Natural
Dist - MEDFAC **Prod** - MEDFAC 1982

Measuring the Performance of Textiles - Textile Testing Series no 2
Textile Testing using the Instron 22 MIN
Dist - CORNRS

Measuring the Performance of Textiles - Textile Testing Series no 5
Frazier Air Permeability Instrument 15 MIN
Dist - CORNRS

Measuring the Performance of Textiles - Textile Testing Series no 6
Frazier Compressometer 7 MIN
Dist - CORNRS

Measuring the performance of textiles - textile testing series No 14
Atlas fadeometer 16 MIN
Dist - CORNRS

Measuring the performance of textiles - textile testing series

Abrasion - accelerator - Pt 2	11 MIN
Abrasion - CSI stoll tester - Pt 4	13 MIN
Abrasion - introduction, wyco tester - Pt 1	10 MIN
Abrasion - taber abraser - Pt 3	9 MIN
Atlas fadeometer	17.75 MIN
Color difference meter	16 MIN
Flammability - Pt 2	9.25 MIN
Flammability - Pt 3	8.9 MIN
Flammability - Pt I	16.75 MIN
Frazier Air Permeability Instrument	15 MIN
Frazier Compressometer	8 MIN
Guarded hot plate	13 MIN
Introduction to the Instron	38 MIN
Textile Testing using the Instron	16 MIN

Dist - CORNRS

Measuring the Temperature of Petroleum and Petroleum Products 23 MIN
U-matic / VHS
Color (IND)
Discusses temperature measurement and considers proper procedures, equipment care and safety. Conforms to current API Manual of Petroleum Measurement Standards.
Business and Economics; Industrial and Technical Education; Mathematics; Social Science
Dist - UTEXPE **Prod** - UTEXPE

Measuring the Universe 10 MIN
16mm / U-matic / VHS
Color (I J H) (SPANISH)
LC 72-702461
Explains how astronomers have used geometry, the spectrum and apparent brightness to measure the distance between earth and stars in the universe. Demonstrates how powerful telescopes enable man to determine distances of stars outside the galaxy.
Foreign Language
Dist - PHENIX **Prod** - DSFI 1969

Measuring Things 3 MIN
U-matic / VHS / 16mm
Color; Captioned
Mathematics
Dist - HANDEL **Prod** - HANDEL

Measuring Things 1 - Distance, Time Temperature 17 MIN
U-matic / VHS / 16mm
Color (P I)
Introduces methods for simple determination of length, time and temperature. Stresses American ways of measurement, but brief comparisons with the metric system are made. Features simple experiments.
Mathematics
Dist - HANDEL **Prod** - HANDEL 1984

Measuring Time 15 MIN
VHS / U-matic
Why Series
Color (P I)
Discusses measuring time.
Mathematics
Dist - AITECH **Prod** - WDCNTV 1976

Measuring time - calendars and clocks 14 MIN
U-matic / VHS / 16mm
Color (I J H)
$49.95 purchase _ #Q10907
Traces people as timekeepers from the earliest observation of celestial phenomena to atomic timekeeping devices. Utilizes animation to demonstrate the need for leap days and to explain the basis of solar and lunar calendars. Describes a variety of clocks.
Mathematics
Dist - CF **Prod** - IFFB 1984

Measuring Tools 13 MIN
U-matic / VHS
Introduction to Machine Technology, Module 1 Series; Module 1
Color (IND)
Discusses the need for measuring tools. Tells how to identify and use such tools as rules, calipers, micrometers and gauge blocks.
Industrial and Technical Education
Dist - LEIKID **Prod** - LEIKID

Measuring Tools Explained 60 MIN
VHS / 35mm strip
(J H IND)
#503XV7
Introduces and explains how to use and take measurements with a variety of commonly used measuring tools. Includes the Vernier caliper, the outside micrometer, inside micrometers, depth gages, dial indicators, and protractors and 'JO' blocks (6 tapes). Prerequisite required. Includes a Study Guide.
Education; Industrial and Technical Education; Sociology
Dist - BERGL

Measuring Units - an Introduction 14 MIN
U-matic / VHS / 16mm
Color (P I)
LC FIA68-388
Explains all of the basic units of measurement - - width, length, height, square and cubic. Begins with the simple method of measurement of a string with a stick then moves to area measurement and finally to cubic space measurement.
Mathematics
Dist - PHENIX **Prod** - BOUNDY 1967

Measuring Up 13 MIN
16mm / U-matic / VHS
Fitness for Living Series
Color (J H)
LC 82-700733
Explains the necessity and importance of physical fitness testing. Gives students instruction on how to monitor their own fitness.
Physical Education and Recreation
Dist - CORF **Prod** - DISNEY 1982

Measuring Up 30 MIN
U-matic / VHS
Villa Alegre Series
Color (K P)
Psychology; Social Science; Sociology
Dist - MDCPB **Prod** - BCTV

Measuring Up 15 - 30 MIN
U-matic / Kit / VHS
Business Computing...Cut Down to Size
(G A)
Introduces undergraduate and graduate business students to the applications of computer capabilities to business. Focuses on small computers, hardware and software. First in a five part series.
Computer Science
Dist - GPN

Measuring using urns, cups and spoons 20 MIN
VHS / 16mm
(G PRO)
$59.00 purchase _ #QF14
Demonstrates measuring techniques for both liquid and dry ingredients. Discusses the correct methods of weighing dry and liquid ingredients by using various measuring containers.
Home Economics
Dist - RMIBHF **Prod** - RMIBHF

Measuring Valve Guides 6 MIN
VHS / 16mm
Auto Mechanics Series
(G PRO)
$51.00 purchase _ #AM33
Shows how to measure valve guides.
Industrial and Technical Education
Dist - RMIBHF **Prod** - RMIBHF

Measuring Valve Stem Height 00 MIN
VHS / 16mm
Auto Mechanics Series
(G PRO)
$53.00 purchase _ #AM25
Shows how to measure valve stem height.
Industrial and Technical Education
Dist - RMIBHF **Prod** - RMIBHF

Measuring Volumes of Liquids 11 MIN
16mm / U-matic / VHS
Basic Laboratory Techniques in Chemistry Series
Color (H C)
LC 73-703056
Shows the correct use of graduated cylinders and pipets (volumetric and graduated.) Emphasizes accurate reading of the meniscus and proper handling of the equipment.
Science
Dist - LUF **Prod** - SCHLAT 1972

Measuring Weight
Software / BETA
Force, Weight and Motion Measurement Series
Color (PRO)
$600.00 - $1500.00 purchase _ #IDMEW
Shows how to determine the weight of objects using equal and unequal arm balances. Verifies balance beam accuracy. Describes how strain gauge and piezoelectric load cells are used to measure weight. Part of a three - part series on force, weight and motion measurement. Interactive training system includes course administrator guide, videodisc and computer software.
Industrial and Technical Education; Mathematics; Psychology
Dist - NUSTC **Prod** - NUSTC

Measuring Weight 15 MIN
U-matic / VHS
Why Series
Color (P I)
Discusses measuring weight.
Mathematics
Dist - AITECH **Prod** - WDCNTV 1976

Measuring Your Blood Pressure using a Wrap - Around Cuff 9 MIN
U-matic / VHS
Color
Describes the benefits of taking accurate blood pressure readings, the equipment used and the procedure for taking and recording blood pressure readings to the person interested in taking his own blood pressure.
Health and Safety
Dist - UMICHM **Prod** - UMICHM 1980

Measuring Your Clarity 13 MIN
U-matic / VHS
Put it in Writing Series
Color
English Language
Dist - DELTAK **Prod** - DELTAK

Meat 113 MIN
VHS / 16mm
(G H)
$350.00 purchase, $150.00 rental
Documents the process by which cattle and sheep are turned into consumer products at a large feed lot and packing plant. Directed by Frederick Wiseman.
Fine Arts; Social Science
Dist - ZIPRAH **Prod** - WISEF

Meat
U-matic
Matter of taste series; Lesson 12
Color (H A)
Discusses various ways to prepare meat. Demonstrates two main dishes. Shows how to carve one's own steaks and chops from whole cuts of meat.
Home Economics
Dist - CDTEL **Prod** - COAST

Meat 60 MIN
U-matic / VHS
Way to Cook with Julia Child
(C A)
$34.95 _ #KN200V
Features popular cooking teacher, Julia Child, as she demonstrates various recipes for cooking meat.
Home Economics; Industrial and Technical Education
Dist - CAMV **Prod** - CAMV

Meat
VHS
Way to Cook - Julia Child Series
$29.95 purchase _ #5 INCH 45 RPM RECORD733V
Features Julia Child demonstrating how to prepare a variety of dishes using meat.
Home Economics; Industrial and Technical Education
Dist - CAREER **Prod** - CAREER

Meat and Meat Packing 14 MIN
16mm / U-matic / VHS
Color (I J H)
Describes how the workers of a meat - packing plant clean, cut and inspect carcasses. Shows how meat is smoked and how sausages are prepared.
Agriculture; Psychology; Social Science
Dist - IFB **Prod** - KRUSE 1957

Meat and Poultry - How to Select Them 19 MIN
U-matic / VHS / 16mm
Color (J H C)
LC 76-703545
Uses a young reporter's interview with a butcher to show consumers how to select the best quality meat and poultry for their needs. Shows how to recognize desirable characteristics of chicken and such meats as veal, lamb, beef, pork and hamburger. Provides a variety of tips, along with hints on cooking cheaper cuts.
Home Economics
Dist - ALTSUL **Prod** - ALTSUL 1976

Meat Animal Grading (Set I) Series
Feeder cattle grading 20 MIN
Market Cattle Grading 23 MIN
Market Swine Grading 32 MIN
Dist - AAVIM

Meat Buying - a Time of Decision 25 MIN
16mm
Color (H C A)
LC 79-705158
Traces the history of beef procuction and retailing in the United States from its inception to the present day. Covers USDA inspection and grading, nutrition of meat and information on buying, indicating the best beef buys and modern methods of preparation and cooking.
Health and Safety; Home Economics; Industrial and Technical Education; Social Science
Dist - ADOL **Prod** - ADOL 1970

Meat cookery 18 MIN
16mm / U-matic / VHS
Color (J)
$460.00, $250.00 purchase _ #80503; LC 81-701115
Demonstrates different methods of cooking various cuts of beef depending upon the tenderness and fat content. Includes instructions on the use of a meat thermometer and proper carving techniques.
Home Economics
Dist - CORF **Prod** - CENTRO 1981

A Meat - Cooperative 10 MIN
16mm
B&W (H C A)
Tells the story of how a meat - cooperative was formed on the Lower East Side of New York to side step high prices, poor quality and weight cheating by local supermarkets.
Business and Economics; History - United States; Home Economics; Psychology; Sociology
Dist - CANWRL **Prod** - CANWRL 1968

Meat cutting 56 MIN
VHS
Meat cutting and handling series
Color (H G)
$99.00 purchase _ #31314 - 027
Covers techniques for beef rib, loin cuts, beef round, chuck cuts, pork cuts, lamb cuts and veal cuts. Presents part of a two - part series.
Education; Industrial and Technical Education
Dist - GA

Meat cutting and handling series
Teaches students the professional way to work with meat and poultry. Includes two videos, Meat Cutting and Meat Handling.
Meat cutting 56 MIN
Meat handling 28 MIN
Dist - GA

Meat Cutting - Beef I 55 MIN
VHS
Meat Videos From The University Of Nebraska Series
Color (G)
$79.95 purchase _ #6 - 010 - 101P
Illustrates separating the forequarter from the hindquarter on beef carcassess and dividing the forequarter into wholesale and retail cuts. Part one of two - parts on beef and part of a larger meat cutting series.
Agriculture; Business and Economics; Social Science
Dist - VEP **Prod** - UNEBR

Meat Cutting - Beef II 55 MIN
VHS
Meat Videos From The University Of Nebraska Series
Color (G)
$79.95 purchase _ #6 - 010 - 102P
Illustrates dividing the hindquarter into wholesale and retail cuts. Part one of two - parts on beef and part of a larger meat cutting series.
Agriculture; Business and Economics; Social Science
Dist - VEP **Prod** - UNEBR

Meat Cutting - Lamb 60 MIN
VHS
Meat Videos From The University Of Nebraska Series
Color (G)
$79.95 purchase _ #6 - 010 - 103P
Shows how to cut lamb carcasses into proper wholesale cuts and divide them into retail cuts. Part of a series on meat cutting.
Agriculture; Business and Economics; Social Science
Dist - VEP **Prod** - UNEBR

Meat Cutting - Pork 55 MIN
VHS
Meat Videos From The University Of Nebraska Series
Color (G)
$79.95 purchase _ #6 - 010 - 104P
Shows standard wholesale and retail cuts of pork. Studies the fine points of cutting and trimming for quality and profit. Part of a series on meat cutting.
Agriculture; Business and Economics; Social Science
Dist - VEP **Prod** - UNEBR

Meat Cutting Procedures - Beef I 55.26 MIN
U-matic / VHS
Animal Slaughtering - Meat Cutting
(PRO)
Shows accepted meat cutting techniques for beef. First of three parts.
Agriculture; Industrial and Technical Education
Dist - GPN **Prod** - NETV

Meat Cutting Procedures - Beef II 55.54 MIN
U-matic / VHS
Animal Slaughtering - Meat Cutting
(PRO)
Shows accepted meat cutting techniques for beef. Second of three parts.
Agriculture; Industrial and Technical Education
Dist - GPN **Prod** - NETV

Meat Cutting Procedures - Beef III 8.25 MIN
VHS / U-matic
Animal Slaughtering - Meat Cutting
(PRO)
Shows accepted meat cutting techniques for beef. Third of three parts.
Agriculture; Industrial and Technical Education
Dist - GPN **Prod** - NETV

Meat Cutting Procedures - Lamb 1.00.23 MIN
VHS / U-matic
Animal Slaughtering - Meat Cutting
(PRO)
Shows accepted meat cutting techniques for lamb.
Agriculture; Industrial and Technical Education
Dist - GPN **Prod** - NETV

Meat Cutting Procedures - Pork 54.36
VHS / U-matic
Animal Slaughtering - Meat Cutting
(PRO)
Shows accepted meat cutting techniques for pork.
Agriculture; Industrial and Technical Education
Dist - GPN **Prod** - NETV

Meat Cutting Procedures - Turkey 10.16 MIN
U-matic / VHS
Animal Slaughtering - Meat Cutting
(PRO)
Shows the accepted meat cutting techniques for turkey.
Agriculture; Industrial and Technical Education
Dist - GPN **Prod** - NETV

Meat Cutting - Turkey
VHS
Meat Videos From The University Of Nebraska Series
Color (G)
$79.95 purchase _ #6 - 010 - 106P
Shows the standard wholesale and retail cutting of turkey. Part of a series on meat cutting.
Agriculture; Business and Economics; Social Science
Dist - VEP **Prod** - UNEBR

The Meat fight 14 MIN
VHS / 16mm
San - Ju - Wasi series
Color (G)
$270.00, $140.00 purchase, $30.00 rental
Reveals how leadership among the Kung derives from talent and experience. Shows how a conflict over an antelope, which was killed by a hunter from one band but found and distributed by a hunter from another, is resolved without violence and without a formal political organization. Part of a series by John Marshall about the Kung in Namibia and Botswana.
Geography - World; History - World; Physical Education and Recreation; Sociology
Dist - DOCEDR **Prod** - DOCEDR

Meat handling 28 MIN
VHS
Meat cutting and handling series
Color (H G)
$99.00 purchase _ #30828 - 027
Includes portion products, portion control and how to handle meat safely and properly. Presents part of a two - part series.
Education; Industrial and Technical Education
Dist - GA

Meat Inspection and Grading 15 MIN
U-matic
Meats in Canada Series
(A)
Explains the differences between inspection and grading by Canadian standards and the differences between Canadian and American standards.
Agriculture; History - World; Home Economics
Dist - ACCESS **Prod** - ACCESS 1983

Meat - It's not what it used to be 26 MIN
U-matic / VHS
Color (C)
$249.00, $149.00 purchase _ #AD - 1895
Looks at changes in meat as a food supply. Considers changing tastes, consumer demand for leaner meats and new methods to produce more protein from fewer animals. Examines how the most nutrition can be gotten from meat.
Health and Safety; Psychology; Social Science; Sociology
Dist - FOTH **Prod** - FOTH

Meat Judging Practice - I 30 MIN
VHS
Meat Judging Practice (Set D) Series
(C)
$69.95 _ CV115
Shows beginning meat judging including 30 retail cuts as well as nine quality carcasses, four judging classes, two sets of questions, and official placings. Recommended for FFA or 4 H meat judging teams.
Agriculture
Dist - AAVIM **Prod** - AAVIM 1989

Meat Judging Practice - II 30 MIN
VHS
Meat Judging Practice (Set D) Series
(C)
$69.95 _ CV116
Give students a chance to practice judging meats by showing thirty retail cuts as well as nine carcasses. Includes four judging classes, two sets of questions, and official placings at the end of each class so students can check their own self scoring.

Agriculture
Dist - AAVIM **Prod** - AAVIM 1989

Meat Judging Practice (Set D) Series
Meat Judging Practice - I 30 MIN
Meat Judging Practice - II 30 MIN
Meats Judging Practice - III 29 MIN
Meats Judging Practice - IV 32 MIN
Dist - AAVIM

The Meat of the matter - pt 1 29 MIN
U-matic / VHS / 16mm
Be a better shopper series program 7; Program 7
Color (H C A)
LC 81-701464
Explains meat grading, meat tenderizing and meat labeling. Discusses the relationshop of cut to tenderness in beef, pork and lamb along with the variety of ground meat products.
Home Economics
Dist - CORNRS **Prod** - CUETV 1978

The Meat of the matter - pt 2 29 MIN
U-matic / VHS / 16mm
Be a better shopper series program 8; Program 8
Color (H C A)
LC 81-701465
Deals with how to get the best buy on meat. Discusses meat merchandizing, butcher - performed services and buying from bulk - meat dealers.
Home Economics
Dist - CORNRS **Prod** - CUETV 1978

The Meat of the matter - pt 3 29 MIN
U-matic / VHS / 16mm
Be a better shopper series program 9; Program 9
Color (H C A)
LC 81-701466
Looks at sources of protein in other than meat, including grains, seeds, nuts and dairy products. Discusses hams and other cured meats and poultry products and fish.
Home Economics
Dist - CORNRS **Prod** - CUETV 1978

Meat Retailing 15 MIN
U-matic
Meats in Canada Series
(A)
Describes butchering and the best cuts of meat, product prices and their marketability as well as the roles of the packing plant and the bulk wholesaler.
Agriculture; History - World; Home Economics
Dist - ACCESS **Prod** - ACCESS 1983

Meat Videos From The University Of Nebraska Series
Animal slaughter - pork 28 MIN
Animal slaughter - turkey
Meat Cutting - Beef I 55 MIN
Meat Cutting - Beef II 55 MIN
Meat Cutting - Lamb 60 MIN
Meat Cutting - Pork 55 MIN
Meat Cutting - Turkey
Retail Cut ID - Beef
Dist - VEP

Meatless Menus 11 MIN
16mm
Eat Right to Your Heart's Delight Series
Color (J H)
Provides four complete meals nutritionally balanced, recognizing the need for less meat in our diets. Emphasizes complementary proteins, with descriptive art work to show the eight essential amino acids and how they are completed by proper combinations of proteins in each meal. Shows artistic displays of grains, legumes, nuts and vegetables to add to the appeal of meals without meat. Includes lunchbox suggestions.
Health and Safety; Home Economics; Psychology
Dist - IPS **Prod** - IPS 1976

Meats 45 MIN
VHS
Le Cordon Bleu cooking series
Color (H C G)
$24.95 purchase _ #LCB005V
Details, with close - up footage, techniques and practical methods needed to prepare a fabulous assortment of meats. Features the world - renowned chefs of Le Cordon Bleu's teaching staff. Part of an eight - part series.
Home Economics
Dist - CAMV

Meats Coming West 29 MIN
Videoreel / VT2
Frying Pans West Series
Color
Presents host Sam Arnold, presenting western recipes on cooking meats.
Home Economics
Dist - PBS **Prod** - KRMATV

Meats in Canada series
Animals for food 15 MIN
Consumer Concerns about Meat 15 MIN
Conversion of meat to muscle 15 MIN
Handling and Cooking Meat in the Home 15 MIN
Meat Inspection and Grading 15 MIN
Meat Retailing 15 MIN
Processed meats 15 MIN
Safety of meats 15 MIN
Dist - ACCESS

Meats Judging Practice I 30 MIN
VHS
Meats Judging Practice Series
Color (G)
$69.95 purchase _ #6 - 040 - 115P
Includes a 570 - point practice contest with 30 retail meat cuts, nine carcasses to quality grade, four carcass - wholesale cut - retail cut classes, two sets of questions and official placings. Shows cuts at the end of each videotape for self - scoring. Part one of four - parts on meat judging practice.
Agriculture; Business and Economics; Social Science
Dist - VEP **Prod** - VEP

Meats Judging Practice II 30 MIN
VHS
Meats Judging Practice Series
Color (G)
$69.95 purchase _ #6 - 040 - 116P
Includes a 570 - point practice contest with 30 retail meat cuts, nine carcasses to quality grade, four carcass - wholesale cut - retail cut classes, two sets of questions and official placings. Shows cuts at the end of each videotape for self - scoring. Part two of four - parts on meat judging practice.
Agriculture; Business and Economics; Social Science
Dist - VEP **Prod** - VEP

Meats Judging Practice III 30 MIN
VHS
Meats Judging Practice Series
Color (G)
$69.95 purchase _ #6 - 040 - 117P
Includes a 570 - point practice contest with 30 retail meat cuts, nine carcasses to quality grade, four carcass - wholesale cut - retail cut classes, two sets of questions and official placings. Shows cuts at the end of each videotape for self - scoring. Part three of four - parts on meat judging practice.
Agriculture; Business and Economics; Social Science
Dist - VEP **Prod** - VEP

Meats Judging Practice - III 29 MIN
VHS
Meat Judging Practice (Set D) Series
(C)
$69.95 _ CV117
Exhibits advanced meats judging employing thirty retail cuts, nine carcasses to qaulity grade, four judging classes, two sets of questions, and official placings at the end of the tape so students can check their self scores.
Agriculture
Dist - AAVIM **Prod** - AAVIM 1989

Meats Judging Practice - IV 32 MIN
VHS
Meat Judging Practice (Set D) Series
(C)
$69.95 _ CV118
Give students opportunity to judge meat using thirty retail cuts, nine carcasses to quality grade, four judging classes, two sets of questions, and official placings at the end of the tape so students can check their self scores.
Agriculture
Dist - AAVIM **Prod** - AAVIM 1989

Meats Judging Practice IV 30 MIN
VHS
Meats Judging Practice Series
Color (G)
$69.95 purchase _ #6 - 040 - 118P
Includes a 570 - point practice contest with 30 retail meat cuts, nine carcasses to quality grade, four carcass - wholesale cut - retail cut classes, two sets of questions and official placings. Shows cuts at the end of each videotape for self - scoring. Part four of four - parts on meat judging practice.
Agriculture; Business and Economics; Social Science
Dist - VEP **Prod** - VEP

Meats Judging Practice Series
Meats Judging Practice I 30 MIN
Meats Judging Practice II 30 MIN
Meats Judging Practice III 30 MIN
Meats Judging Practice IV 30 MIN
Dist - VEP

Meats, Seafood and Poultry
VHS
Food Preparation
$185.00 purchase _ #PX1141V; $185.00 purchase _ #PX1141V filmstrip
Provides fundamental information about the three principal types of entrees. Describes how these foods appear in the market and how to store them before cooking. Demonstrates suitable cooking methods.
Health and Safety; Home Economics; Social Science
Dist - CAREER **Prod** - CAREER

Mecate - A New song 50 MIN
16mm / VHS
Color (G)
$895.00, $480.00 purchase, $100.00 rental
Illustrates the peasants' cultural movement in Nicaragua. Shows how music, theater and poetry are part of their everyday life and their efforts to improve their lives. Produced by Felix Zurita de Higes.
Fine Arts; History - World; Literature and Drama; Social Science; Sociology
Dist - FIRS

The Mechanic 15 MIN
U-matic
Harriet's Magic Hats III Series
(P I J)
Teaches children that an auto mechanic fixes or replaces parts that break or wear out.
Guidance and Counseling
Dist - ACCESS **Prod** - ACCESS 1985

Mechanical Advantage and Friction 5 MIN
U-matic
Eureka Series
Color (J)
Compares the mechanical advantage of an inclined plane with a lever.
Science; Science - Physical
Dist - TVOTAR **Prod** - TVOTAR 1980

Mechanical Aids 10 MIN
U-matic / VHS / 16mm
Safety in Construction Series
Color
Shows common mistakes associated with using the saw bench, skill saw, concrete mixer, dumper and electrical hand tools. Defines procedures which should become routine for safe work habits.
Health and Safety; Industrial and Technical Education
Dist - IFB **Prod** - NFBTE

Mechanical Capers for Fun and Fitness 12 MIN
16mm
Color (P I)
Depicts physical activities in which children imitate the motions of earth moving and highway building machinery and equipment.
Physical Education and Recreation
Dist - MMP **Prod** - MMP 1967

Mechanical component reliability prediction, probabilistic design for reliability series
Component reliability and its confidence limit - designing a specified reliability 60 MIN
Dist - UAZMIC

Mechanical Compounds 8 MIN
VHS / 16mm / U-matic
You Need to Know Series
Color (A PRO IND)
$175.00 purchase _ #30.0114, $150.00 purchase _ #50.0114
Industrial and Technical Education; Social Science
Dist - UTEXPE **Prod** - UTEXPE 1981

Mechanical Crabs 10 MIN
U-matic / VHS / 16mm
Color (J)
LC 79-700671
Uses animation to tell a science fiction story about a military scientist who develops the ultimate weapon, automatic machines shaped like crabs and strong enough to devour metal and crush anything in their path.
Fine Arts; Literature and Drama; Social Science
Dist - PHENIX **Prod** - SFSP 1977

Mechanical Disorders of the Lumbar Spine 35 MIN
U-matic
Evaluation of Low Back Pain Series
Color (C)
Discusses segmetal instability, the facet syndrome, spinal stenosis and disc disorders.
Health and Safety; Science - Natural
Dist - UOKLAH **Prod** - UOKLAH 1978

Mechanical drives, couplings and alignment 120 MIN
VHS / U-matic
Mechanical equipment maintenance series
Color (IND) (SPANISH)
Deals with couplings, alignment, belts, chains, speed reducers and vibration.
Industrial and Technical Education
Dist - ITCORP **Prod** - ITCORP

Mechanical electricity; 2nd ed. 15 MIN
U-matic
Search for science series; Unit V - Electricity
Color (I)
Surveys two ways of creating electricity and discovers the things which make possible mechanical electricity.
Science - Physical
Dist - GPN **Prod** - WVIZTV

Mechanical energy 15 MIN
Videodisc / VHS
Physical science series
Color (I J)
$99.95, $69.95 purchase _ #Q10334
Utilizes descriptions, illustrations and experiments to illustrate concepts of mechanical energy. Explains how mechanical energy exerts a force in solid, liquid and gas states and how we use these forces to work. Describes potential and kinetic energy and how machines provide mechanical advantage. Part of a series of six programs.
Science - Physical
Dist - CF

Mechanical Energy and Thermal Energy 22 MIN
16mm
PSSC Physics Films Series
B&W (H C)
Shows several models to illustrate both the bulk motion and random motion of molecules. Shows their interconnection as the energy of bulk motion. Discusses thermal conduction and absolute temperature scale.
Science - Physical
Dist - MLA **Prod** - PSSC 1959

Mechanical engineering 25 MIN
VHS
Career encounters series
Color (J H C A)
$95.00 purchase _ #MG3412V-J
Presents a documentary-style program that explores a career in mechanical engineering. Features professionals at work, explaining what they do and how they got where they are. Emphasizes diversity of occupational opportunities and of men and women in the field. Offers information about new developments and technologies and about educational and certification requirements for entering the profession. One of a series of videos about professions available individually or as a set.
Business and Economics; Guidance and Counseling; Industrial and Technical Education
Dist - CAMV

Mechanical engineering career encounters 28 MIN
VHS
Career encounters video series
Color (J H)
$89.00 purchase _ #4258
Offers a documentary on careers in the field of mechanical engineering. Visits workplaces and hears professionals explain what they do, how they got where they are and why they find the work so rewarding. Emphasizes human diversity in the professions. Dispels myths, misconceptions and stereotypes and offers practical information about the requirements for entering the field. Part of a 13 - part series.
Business and Economics; Guidance and Counseling; Industrial and Technical Education
Dist - NEWCAR

Mechanical engineering - No 6 28 MIN
VHS / U-matic
Career encounters series
Color (H C)
$110.00, $95.00 purchase
Looks at the role of the mechanical engineer and how this profession affects and controls everyday life. Outlines the educational requirements for the field. Sponsored by the American Society of Mechanical Engineers.
Business and Economics; Guidance and Counseling; Industrial and Technical Education; Psychology
Dist - PLEXPU **Prod** - PLEXPU 1990

Mechanical engineering technician 5 MIN
U-matic
Good work series
Color (H)
Provides useful, up to date information on various occupations to aid high school students in career selection. Available in five series of ten jobs each.
Education; Guidance and Counseling; Industrial and Technical Education
Dist - TVOTAR **Prod** - TVOTAR 1981

Mechanical engineering technician 5 MIN
VHS / 16mm
Good works 4 series
Color (A PRO)
$40.00 purchase _ #BPN225806
Presents the occupation of a mechanical engineering technician. Gives a profile of a young person who is either undergoing an apprenticeship or has recently completed training in this field. Takes the viewer on a tour of this person's workplace and explains the practical skills and training offered by employers and schools. Gives a better understanding of the demand for skilled workers today and the potential for personal growth.
Guidance and Counseling
Dist - RMIBHF **Prod** - RMIBHF

Mechanical Equipment Maintenance, Module 1 Rigging and Lifting Series
Hand Operated Hoists 60 MIN
Ladders and Scaffolds 60 MIN
Power Operated Hoists and Cranes 60 MIN
Dist - LEIKID

Mechanical equipment maintenance - Module 1 - rigging and lifting series
Forklifts and mobile cranes 60 MIN
Dist - LEIKID

Mechanical equipment maintenance, Module 1 rigging and lifting - a series
Mechanical equipment maintenance series
Color (IND)
Focuses on several aspects of rigging and lifting. Forms one of twenty - one modules in mechanical maintenance training. Forklifts And Mobile Cranes; Hand Operated Hoists; Ladders And Scaffolds; Power Operated Hoists And Cranes.
Industrial and Technical Education
Dist - LEIKID **Prod** - LEIKID

Mechanical Equipment Maintenance, Module 2 - Mechanical Drives, Couplings Series
Couplings, Alignment and Belts 60 MIN
Dist - LEIKID

Mechanical Equipment Maintenance - Module 2 - Mechanical Drives, Couplings Series
Chains, Speed Reducers, Vibration 60 MIN
Dist - LEIKID

Mechanical equipment maintenance, Module 3 - packing and seals - a series
Mechanical equipment maintenance series
Color (IND)
Covers maintenance aspects of bearings and lubrication. Comprises one of twenty - one modules in mechanical maintenance training. Mechanical Seals; Pump And Valve Packing.
Industrial and Technical Education
Dist - LEIKID **Prod** - LEIKID

Mechanical Equipment Maintenance, Module 3 - Packing and Seals Series
Mechanical Seals 60 MIN
Pump and Valve Packing 60 MIN
Dist - LEIKID

Mechanical Equipment Maintenance, Module 4 - Bearings and Lubrication Series
Anti - friction bearings 60 MIN
Plain Journal Bearings 60 MIN
Dist - LEIKID

Mechanical equipment maintenance, Module 5 - centrifugal pumps - a series
Mechanical equipment maintenance series
Color (IND)
Focuses on disassembly, repair and assembly of pumps and rotors. Comprises one of twenty - one modules in mechanical maintenance training. Pump Assembly; Pump Disassembly; Rotor Assembly; Rotor Repair.
Industrial and Technical Education
Dist - LEIKID **Prod** - LEIKID

Mechanical Equipment Maintenance, Module 5 - Centrifugal Pumps Series
Pump Assembly 60 MIN
Pump Disassembly 60 MIN
Rotor Assembly 60 MIN
Rotor Repair 60 MIN
Dist - LEIKID

Mechanical Equipment Maintenance, Module 6 - Special Centrifugal Pumps 60 MIN
VHS / U-matic
Color (IND)
Covers standardized end suction and vertical pumps. Comprises one of twenty - one modules in mechanical maintenance.
Industrial and Technical Education
Dist - LEIKID **Prod** - LEIKID

Mechanical Equipment Maintenance, Module 7 - Piping Series
General Maintenance 60 MIN
Heat Exchangers 60 MIN
Strainers, Filters, and Traps 60 MIN
Tubing and Piping 60 MIN
Dist - LEIKID

Mechanical equipment maintenance, Module 8 - valves series
Diaphragm and Butterfly Vavles 60 MIN
Gate Valves 60 MIN
Glove valves 60 MIN
Dist - LEIKID

Mechanical Equipment Maintenance, Module 9 - Air Compressors Series
Cylinder maintenace - reciprocating compressors 60 MIN
Rotary Compressors 60 MIN
Valve Amintenance - Reciprocating Compressors 60 MIN
Dist - LEIKID

Mechanical equipment maintenance, module 9 - boiler and boiler equipment series
Boiler equipment 60 MIN
Dist - LEIKID

Mechanical Equipment Maintenance, Module 10 - Boiler and Boiler Equipment Series
Tube Repair 60 MIN
Dist - LEIKID

Mechanical Equipment Maintenance, Module 11 - Coal and Ash Handling Equipment Series
Ash handling equipment 60 MIN
Coal Handling Equipment 60 MIN
Dist - LEIKID

Mechanical equipment maintenance, Module 12 - diesel engines - a series
Mechanical equipment maintenance series
Color (IND)
Focuses on maintenance of diesel engines. Forms one module of a twenty - one module section on mechanical maintenance training. Diesel Systems; Preventive Maintenance, Pt 1; Preventive Maintenance, Pt 2.
Industrial and Technical Education
Dist - LEIKID **Prod** - LEIKID

Mechanical equipment maintenance, module 12 - diesel engines series
Diesel systems 60 MIN
Preventive maintenance - Pt 1 60 MIN
Preventive maintenance - Pt 2 60 MIN
Dist - LEIKID

Mechanical Equipment Maintenance, Module 13 - Vibration Analysis 60 MIN
U-matic / VHS
Color (IND)
Covers measurements, evaluation and correction. Comprises one of twenty - one mechanical maintenance training modules.
Industrial and Technical Education
Dist - LEIKID **Prod** - LEIKID

Mechanical equipment maintenance, Module 14 - relief valves - a series
Mechanical equipment maintenance series
Color (IND)
Covers operation and maintenance of safety and relief valves. Forms one of twenty - one mechanical maintenance training modules. Electrically Operated Relief Valves; Steam And Gas Safety Valves.
Industrial and Technical Education
Dist - LEIKID **Prod** - LEIKID

Mechanical Equipment Maintenance, Module 14 - Relief Valves Series
Electrically Operated Relief Valves 60 MIN
Steam and Gas Safety Valves 60 MIN
Dist - LEIKID

Mechanical Equipment Maintenance, Module 15 - Advanced Alignment 60 MIN
VHS / U-matic
Color (IND)
Examines double dial indicator techniques. Comprises one of twenty - one mechanical maintenance training modules.
Industrial and Technical Education
Dist - LEIKID **Prod** - LEIKID

Mechanical equipment maintenance, Module 16 - hydraulic equipment - a series
Mechanical equipment maintenance series
Color (IND)
Covers maintenance of hydraulic equipment. Forms one of twenty - one modules in mechanical maintenance training. Basic Hydraulics, Cylinder Overhaul; Gear Pumps, Vane Pumps.
Industrial and Technical Education
Dist - LEIKID **Prod** - LEIKID

Mechanical Equipment Maintenance, Module 16 - Hydraulic Equipment Series
Basic hydraulics, cylinder overhaul 60 MIN
Gear Pumps, Vane Pumps 60 MIN
Dist - LEIKID

Mechanical equipment maintenance, Module 17 advanced pipefitting - a series
Mechanical equipment maintenance series
Color (IND)
Covers instruction and mainteance of piping. Comprises one of twenty - one modules in mechanical maintenance training. Blueprints, Piping Layout; Joint Lubrication; Piping Prepartion And Installation; Plastic Piping.
Industrial and Technical Education
Dist - LEIKID **Prod** - LEIKID

Mechanical Equipment Maintenance, Module 17 - Advanced Pipefitting Series
Blueprints, piping layout 60 MIN
Joint Lubrication 60 MIN
Piping Preparation and Installation 60 MIN
Dist - LEIKID

Mechanical Equipment Maintenance Series
Advanced alignment 60 MIN
Advanced pipefitting 240 MIN
Air compressors 180 MIN
Bearings and lubrication 180 MIN
Boilers and boiler equipment 120 MIN
Centrifugal Pumps 240 MIN
Coal and ash handling equipment, conveyors 120 MIN
Diesel engines 180 MIN
Hydraulic Equipment 120 MIN
Mechanical drives, couplings and alignment 120 MIN
Packing and Seals 120 MIN
Piping 240 MIN
Relief Valves 120 MIN
Rigging and Lifting 240 MIN
Specialized Centrifugal Pumps 60 MIN
Valves 240 MIN
Vibration Analysis 60 MIN
Dist - ITCORP

Mechanical equipment maintenance series
Mechanical equipment maintenance, Module 12 - diesel engines - a series
Mechanical equipment maintenance, Module 14 - relief valves - a series
Mechanical equipment maintenance, Module 16 - hydrauic equipment - a series
Mechanical equipment maintenance, Module 17 advanced pipefitting - a series
Mechanical equipment maintenance, Module 5 - centrifugal pumps - a series
Mechanical equipment maintenance, Module 1 rigging and lifting - a series
Mechanical equipment maintenance, Module 3 - packing and seals - a series
Plastic piping 60 MIN
Tilting pad, oil film, trust bearings 60 MIN
Dist - LEIKID

Mechanical equipment maintenance - Spanish series
Diesel engines 180 MIN
Piping 240 MIN
Relief valves 120 MIN
Rigging and lifting 240 MIN
Vibration Analysis 60 MIN
Dist - ITCORP

Mechanical equipment maintenance - valves series, Module 8
Control valves 60 MIN
Dist - LEIKID

Mechanical Fields 22 MIN
VHS / U-matic
Video Career Library Series
(H C A)
$69.95 _ #CJ122V
Covers duties, conditions, salaries, and training connected with jobs in the mechanical field. Provides a view of employees in mechanical related occupations and gives information concerning the current market for such skills. Revised every two years.
Guidance and Counseling; Industrial and Technical Education
Dist - CAMV **Prod** - CAMV

Mechanical Fields 22 MIN
VHS / 16mm
Video Career Library Series
Color (H C A PRO)
$79.95 purchase _ #WW112
Shows occupations in mechanical fields such as automobile and diesel engine mechanics, auto body repairers, heavy equipment mechanics, heating, air conditioning and refrigeration mechanics, and others. Contains current occupational outlook and salary information.
Agriculture; Business and Economics; Guidance and Counseling
Dist - AAVIM **Prod** - AAVIM 1990

Mechanical I 42 MIN
VHS
Video guide to occupational exploration - the video GOE series
Color (J H C G)
$69.95 purchase _ #CCP1005V
Breaks down into Engineering, Managerial, Operations and Engineering Technology. Interviews a drafter who uses CAD, computer programmer, landscape architect, chemical engineer, construction and statistical superintendent, pilot instructor, boat captain and a surveyor. Part of a 14 - part series exploring occupational clusters.
Agriculture; Business and Economics; Computer Science; Guidance and Counseling; Industrial and Technical Education
Dist - CAMV **Prod** - CAMV 1991

Mechanical II 45 MIN
VHS
Video guide to occupational exploration - the video GOE series
Color (J H C G)
$69.95 purchase _ #CCP1006V
Breaks down into Craft and Craft Technology, Material and Quality Control, and Vehicle and Operations. Interviews a pipefitter - plumber, brick layer, chef, heavy equipment inspector, meter reader, auto repair estimators, water treatment plant operator and an EMT. Part of a 14 - part series exploring occupational clusters.
Business and Economics; Guidance and Counseling; Industrial and Technical Education
Dist - CAMV **Prod** - CAMV 1991

Mechanical Interest and Ability in a Home - Raised Chimpanzee, Pt 1 17 MIN
16mm
B&W (C T)
Briefly demonstrates the structure and function of a chimpanzee's hands, following the development of manual dexterity from age eight months to six years in such activities as playing with blocks and toys, fastening snap - and - ring sets, attempting to tie knots, filing nails and using carpenter's tools.
Psychology; Science - Natural
Dist - PSUPCR **Prod** - PSUPCR 1954

Mechanical Interest and Ability in a Home - Raised Chimpanzee, Pt 2 18 MIN
16mm
B&W (C T)
Shows a female chimpanzee's behavior in response to water from ages nine months to six years and behavior in response to fire from ages three to five years. Demonstrates cigarette smoking, sand play, scribbling, use of knife, stringing of beads and use of needle and thread at various ages.
Psychology; Science - Natural
Dist - PSUPCR **Prod** - PSUPCR 1954

Mechanical Interest and Ability in a Home - Raised Chimpanzee, Pt 3 16 MIN
16mm
B&W (C T)
Shows a female chimpanzee's responses to and usage of such objects as lights and light switches, electric fan, telephone, phonograph, music - box, mirror, iodine applicator, toys and blocks. Covers ages two to five years.
Psychology; Science - Natural
Dist - PSUPCR **Prod** - PSUPCR 1954

Mechanical Interest and Ability in a Home - Raised Chimpanzee, Pt 4 18 MIN
16mm
B&W (C T)
Presents instances of formal training, including putting on clothes, using a toilet chair, eating with a spoon, opening bottles, cans and jars, pouring coffee, using faucets and solving classical problems.
Psychology; Science - Natural
Dist - PSUPCR **Prod** - PSUPCR 1954

Mechanical maintenance basics, module a - hand tools series
Chisels, hacksaws, files, reamers, power drills 60 MIN
Vises, Clamps, Pliers, Screwdrivers, Wrenches 60 MIN
Dist - LEIKID

Mechanical Maintenance Basics, Module B - Measuring Instruments 60 MIN
U-matic / VHS
Color (IND)
Covers steel rule, Vernier calipers, thickness gauges and micrometers. Comprise one of twenty - one modules on modules on mechanical maintenance training.
Industrial and Technical Education
Dist - LEIKID **Prod** - LEIKID

Mechanical maintenance basics, module C - general shop practices - a series
Mechanical maintenance basics series
Color (IND)
Focuses on drilling, grinding and cutting practices. Forms one of twenty - one modules on mechanical maintenance basics. Cutting; Grinding; Layout And Drilling Operations.
Industrial and Technical Education
Dist - LEIKID **Prod** - LEIKID

Mechanical Maintenance Basics, Module C - General Shop Practices Series
Cutting 60 MIN
Grinding 60 MIN
Layout and Drilling Operations 60 MIN
Dist - LEIKID

Mechanical Maintenance Basics, Module D - Mechanical Print Reading 60 MIN
VHS / U-matic
Color (IND)
Covers symbols, layout drawings, print reading and interpretation. Comprises one of twenty - one modules.
Industrial and Technical Education
Dist - LEIKID **Prod** - LEIKID

Mechanical maintenance basics series
General Shop Practices 180 MIN
Hand tools 120 MIN
Measuring instruments 60 MIN
Mechanical print reading 60 MIN
Dist - ITCORP

Mechanical maintenance basics series
Mechanical maintenance basics, module C - general shop practices - a series
Dist - LEIKID

Mechanical Maintenance Training Series
Presents a series on the maintenance and operation of mechanical equipment.
Lubrication Techniques 24 MIN
Maintaining Centrifugal Pumps 24 MIN
Dist - TAT **Prod** - TAT

The Mechanical man and the wild goat 30 MIN
VHS
Davey and Goliath series
Color (P I R)
$19.95 purchase, $10.00 rental _ #4 - 8822
Presents two 15 - minute 'Davey and Goliath' episodes. 'The Mechanical Man' compares Goliath with Davey's robot, teaching that Goliath can love Davey because he has the gift of life from God. 'The Wild Goat' illustrates sacrifice for the love of another, as Davey returns a wild goat to his mountain habiat. Produced by the Evangelical Lutheran Church in America.
Literature and Drama; Religion and Philosophy
Dist - APH

Mechanical Melodies 5 MIN
16mm
Color (I)
LC 73-700488
Shows the beautifully shaped parts inside the mechanical pianorchestra as they move, beat, tap and turn fantastic patterns while creating gay music.
Fine Arts
Dist - CONNF **Prod** - STONEB 1973

The Mechanical Monsters 8 MIN
16mm
B&W
Illustrates the Superman cartoon from the famed Fleischer studios.
Fine Arts
Dist - FCE **Prod** - FCE

Mechanical Needle 9 MIN
U-matic / VHS / 16mm
Inventive Child Series
Color (P I)
Shows how a woodpecker who uses his beak to help Boy mend a torn sail gives Boy the idea for inventing a sewing machine using a needle with an eye in the point attached to a wheel driven by a foot pedal.
History - World; Science - Physical
Dist - EBEC **Prod** - POLSKI 1983

Mechanical Operation of the Model 28 Teletypewriter - Automatic Typer Selecting 11 MIN
16mm
B&W
LC FIE58-29
Shows the chain of action in the automatic typer of the Model 28 teletypewriter from the signal generator to and through the selecting mechanism that operates the code bars.

Business and Economics
Dist - USNAC **Prod** - USN 1954

Mechanical Operation of the Model 28 Teletypewriter - Function Mechanism 11 MIN
16mm
B&W
LC FIE58-31
Shows the mechanical chain of action in the function mechanism of the Model 28 teletypewriter. Emphasizes the operation of the function clutch as opposed to the main shaft clutch.
Business and Economics
Dist - USNAC **Prod** - USN 1954

Mechanical Operation of the Model 28 Teletypewriter - Keyboard Transmitting 13 MIN
16mm
B&W
LC FIE58-28
Shows the mechanical operation of the keyboard transmitting mechanism of the Model 28 teletypewriter. Traces the action from the key punched to the signal generator and explains each part in the chain between keyboard and generator.
Business and Economics
Dist - USNAC **Prod** - USN 1954

Mechanical Operation of the Model 28 Teletypewriter - Type Box Positioning Mechanism 20 MIN
16mm
B&W
LC FIE58-30
Shows the chain of action of the mechanical levers that position the type box of the Model 28 teletypewriter in the proper position so that the letter or figure key that is punched may be printed.
Business and Economics
Dist - USNAC **Prod** - USN 1954

Mechanical Packing Aboard Ship 30 MIN
16mm
B&W
LC FIE52-1081
Demonstrates how to pack a spiral wound gasket and a steam reciprocating pump rod, repack a centrifugal part, and replace packing around a condenser tube.
Civics and Political Systems; Industrial and Technical Education
Dist - USNAC **Prod** - USN 1948

The Mechanical Paradise 52 MIN
16mm / U-matic / VHS
Shock of the New Series
Color (C A)
LC 80-700984
Takes a look at Western art between 1870 and 1914. Shows how art adapted to a fragmented world by depicting its subjects in a fragmented manner, specifically through cubism. Describes the work of Delaunay, Duchamp, and Picabia.
Fine Arts
Dist - TIMLIF **Prod** - BBCTV 1980

Mechanical Power Transmission 42 MIN
VHS / 35mm strip
(H A IND)
#820XV7
Introduces the basics of mechanical power transmission, focusing on bearings, pulleys and gears. Includes fundamental principles, bearings - types and maintenance, and gear drives (3 tapes). Includes a Study Guide.
Education; Industrial and Technical Education
Dist - BERGL

Mechanical Power Transmission Series
Bearings 19 MIN
Chain and Chain Drives 17 MIN
From muscle to machine 16 MIN
Gears and Gear Drives 18 MIN
Shafting, Couplings and Joining Devices 18 MIN
V - Belts and V - Belt Drives 19 MIN
Dist - LUF

Mechanical print reading 60 MIN
U-matic / VHS
Mechanical maintenance basics series
Color (IND) (SPANISH)
Focuses on symbols, layout drawings, print reading and interpretation.
Industrial and Technical Education
Dist - ITCORP **Prod** - ITCORP

Mechanical Refrigeration - How it Works 22 MIN
16mm
B&W (H A)
LC FIE52-77
Explains the function, theory and operation of a refrigeration system.
Industrial and Technical Education
Dist - USNAC **Prod** - USN 1947

Mechanical Seal Installation 20 MIN
16mm
Color (IND)
Demonstrates the function and installation of single inside, double inside and single outside mechanical seals. Deals with ways of preventing seal wear to keep maintenance expense at a minimum.
Industrial and Technical Education
Dist - MOKIN **Prod** - MOKIN

Mechanical seal installation 20 MIN
U-matic / BETA / VHS
Marshall maintenance programs series
Color (IND G)
$395.00 purchase _ #800 - 55
Explains the function and installation of a single inside, double inside and single outside mechanical seals. Discusses in detail prevention of seal wear, seal lubrication and the importance of keeping maintenance expenses to a minimum.
Health and Safety; Industrial and Technical Education; Psychology
Dist - ITSC **Prod** - ITSC

Mechanical Seals 60 MIN
VHS
Pumps Series
Color (PRO)
$600.00, $1500.00 purchase _ #GMMES
Identifies the different types of mechanical seals. Describes how they work. Shows how to disasseble a pump properly and prepare it for a mechanical seal. Teaches how to install various types of mechanical seals. Part of a seven - part series on pumps, which is part of a set on general and mechanical maintenance. Includes 10 textbooks and an instructor guide which provide four hours of instruction.
Education; Health and Safety; Industrial and Technical Education; Psychology
Dist - NUSTC **Prod** - NUSTC

Mechanical Seals 60 MIN
U-matic / VHS
Mechanical Equipment Maintenance, Module 3 - Packing and Seals 'Series
Color (IND)
Industrial and Technical Education
Dist - LEIKID **Prod** - LEIKID

Mechanical - Semichemical Pulping Basics 60 MIN
VHS
Systems Operations Series
Color (PRO)
$600.00 - $1500.00 purchase _ #PMMSB
Describes the function and operation of equipment found in typical mechanical and semichemical pulping systems. Covers basic woodyard equipment. Includes ten textbooks and an instructor guide to support four hours of instruction.
Education; Industrial and Technical Education; Psychology
Dist - NUSTC **Prod** - NUSTC

Mechanical - Semichemical Pulping Operations 60 MIN
VHS
Systems Operations Series
Color (PRO)
$600.00 - $1500.00 purchase _ #PMMSO
Builds on the concepts presented in pulping basics. Starts with the operation of chip receiving and storing systems and devices such as chip bins, conveyors, vibrators and elevators. Addresses grinder and refiner operations, and washer and thickener operations. Includes ten textbooks and an instructor guide to support four hours of instruction.
Education; Health and Safety; Industrial and Technical Education; Psychology
Dist - NUSTC **Prod** - NUSTC

The Mechanical switch 15 MIN
U-matic / VHS
Basic electricity and D C circuits - laboratory series
Color
Industrial and Technical Education; Science - Physical; Social Science
Dist - TXINLC **Prod** - TXINLC

Mechanical Testing of Metals 45 MIN
U-matic / BETA / VHS
Color
$300 purchase
Shows elastic and plastic deformation.
Industrial and Technical Education; Psychology; Science - Physical
Dist - ASM **Prod** - ASM

Mechanical Troubleshooting 60 MIN
U-matic / VHS
Air Conditioning and Refrigeration - - Training Series
Color (IND)
Explores general procedures for troubleshooting, short cycling, high discharge pressure and low suction pressure.
Education; Industrial and Technical Education
Dist - ITCORP **Prod** - ITCORP

The Mechanical universe - and beyond - part I series 780 MIN
U-matic / Videodisc / VHS
The Mechanical universe - and beyond series
Color (G)
$1000.00, $500.00, $350.00 purchase
Presents the first half of the 52 - part 'The Mechanical Universe...And Beyond' series. Combines computer graphics and dramatic reenactments of great moments in the history of science. Traces the interaction of ideas from the time of Aristotle to Einstein.
Science; Science - Physical
Dist - ANNCPB **Prod** - SCCON 1985

Mechanical universe - and beyond - Part I series
Resonance - waves - Parts 17 and 18 60 MIN
Dist - ANNCPB

The Mechanical universe and beyond - Part II series 780 MIN
U-matic / Videodisc / VHS
The Mechanical universe and beyond series
Color (G)
$1000.00, $500.00, $350.00 purchase
Presents the second half of the 52 - part 'The Mechanical Universe...And Beyond' series. Combines computer graphics and dramatic reenactments of great moments in the history of science. Traces the interaction of ideas from the time of Aristotle to Einstein to quantum mechanics and beyond.
Science; Science - Physical
Dist - ANNCPB **Prod** - SCCON 1985

Mechanical universe - and beyond - Part II series
Beyond the mechanical universe - static electricity - Parts 27 and 28 60 MIN
The Magnetic field - vector fields and hydrodynamics - Parts 35 and 36 60 MIN
Dist - ANNCPB

Mechanical universe - and beyond - Pt II series
From atoms to quarks - the quantum mechanical universe - Pts 51 and 52 60 MIN
Dist - ANNCPB

Mechanical universe . . . and beyond - Pt 1 series
Energy and eccentricity - navigating in space - Pts 23 and 24 60 MIN
Dist - ANNCPB

The Mechanical universe - and beyond series 1560 MIN
U-matic / Videodisc / VHS
The Mechanical universe - and beyond series
Color (G)
$1750.00, $950.00, $650.00 purchase
Presents the complete 52 - part 'The Mechanical Universe...And Beyond' series. Combines computer graphics and dramatic reenactments of great moments in the history of science. Traces the interaction of ideas from the time of Aristotle to Einstein to quantum mechanics and beyond.
Science; Science - Physical
Dist - ANNCPB **Prod** - SCCON 1985

Mechanical Universe and Beyond Series
The Mechanical Universe and Beyond - Vol I 60 MIN
The Mechanical Universe and Beyond - Vol II 60 MIN
The Mechanical Universe and Beyond - Vol III 60 MIN
The Mechanical Universe and Beyond - Vol IV 60 MIN
The Mechanical Universe and Beyond - Vol IX 60 MIN
The Mechanical Universe and Beyond - Vol V 60 MIN
The Mechanical Universe and Beyond - Vol VI 60 MIN
The Mechanical Universe and Beyond - Vol VII 60 MIN
The Mechanical Universe and Beyond - Vol VIII 60 MIN
The Mechanical Universe and Beyond - Vol X 60 MIN
The Mechanical Universe and Beyond - Vol XI 60 MIN
The Mechanical Universe and Beyond - Vol XII 60 MIN
The Mechanical Universe and Beyond - Vol XIII 60 MIN
Dist - SCCON

The Mechanical Universe and Beyond - Vol I 60 MIN
VHS
Mechanical Universe and Beyond Series
Color (S)
$29.95 purchase _ #118 - 9088
Combines state - of - the - art visuals with solid information to present the fundamentals of physics. Makes abstract concepts and mathematical processes understandable and offers an intellectual and philosophical base for physics comprehension. Features Professor David Goodstein of the California Institute of Technology as host. Volume I of thirteen volumes presents the titles 'Beyond The Mechanical Universe' and 'Static Electricity.'.
Science - Physical
Dist - SCCON **Prod** - CIT 1986

The Mechanical Universe and Beyond - Vol II 60 MIN
VHS
Mechanical Universe and Beyond Series
Color (S)
$29.95 purchase _ #118 - 9089
Combines state - of - the - art visuals with solid information to present the fundamentals of physics. Makes abstract concepts and mathematical processes understandable and offers an intellectual and philosophical base for physics comprehension. Features Professor David Goodstein of the California Institute of Technology as host. Volume II of thirteen volumes presents the titles 'The Electric Field' and 'Potential And Capacitance.'.
Science - Physical
Dist - SCCON **Prod** - CIT 1986

The Mechanical Universe and Beyond - Vol III 60 MIN
VHS
Mechanical Universe and Beyond Series
Color (S)
$29.95 purchase _ #118 - 9090
Combines state - of - the - art visuals with solid information to present the fundamentals of physics. Makes abstract concepts and mathematical processes understandable and offers an intellectual and philosophical base for physics comprehension. Features Professor David Goodstein of the California Institute of Technology as host. Volume III of thirteen volumes presents the titles 'Voltage, Energy And Force' and 'The Electric Battery.'.
Science - Physical
Dist - SCCON **Prod** - CIT 1986

The Mechanical Universe and Beyond - Vol IV 60 MIN
VHS
Mechanical Universe and Beyond Series
Color (S)
$29.95 purchase _ #118 - 9091
Combines state - of - the - art visuals with solid information to present the fundamentals of physics. Makes abstract concepts and mathematical processes understandable and offers an intellectual and philosophical base for physics comprehension. Features Professor David Goodstein of the California Institute of Technology as host. Volume IV of thirteen volumes presents the titles 'Electic Circuits' and 'Magnets.'.
Science - Physical
Dist - SCCON **Prod** - CIT 1986

The Mechanical Universe and Beyond - Vol IX 60 MIN
VHS
Mechanical Universe and Beyond Series
Color (S)
$29.95 purchase _ #118 - 9096
Combines state - of - the - art visuals with solid information to present the fundamentals of physics. Makes abstract concepts and mathematical processes understandable and offers an intellectual and philosophical base for physics comprehension. Features Professor David Goodstein of the California Institute of Technology as host. Volume IX of thirteen volumes presents the titles 'Velocity And Time' and 'Mass, Momentum, Energy.'.
Science - Physical
Dist - SCCON **Prod** - CIT 1986

The Mechanical Universe and Beyond - Vol V 60 MIN
VHS
Mechanical Universe and Beyond Series
Color (S)
$29.95 purchase _ #118 - 9092
Combines state - of - the - art visuals with solid information to present the fundamentals of physics. Makes abstract concepts and mathematical processes understandable and offers an intellectual and philosophical base for physics comprehension. Features Professor David Goodstein of the California Institute of Technology as host. Volume V of thirteen volumes presents the titles 'Magnetic Fields' and 'Vector Fields And Hydrodynamics.'.
Science - Physical
Dist - SCCON **Prod** - CIT 1986

The Mechanical Universe and Beyond - Vol VI 60 MIN
VHS
Mechanical Universe and Beyond Series
Color (S)
$29.95 purchase _ #118 - 9093
Combines state - of - the - art visuals with solid information to present the fundamentals of physics. Makes abstract concepts and mathematical processes understandable and offers an intellectual and philosophical base for physics comprehension. Features Professor David Goodstein of the California Institute of Technology as host. Volume VI of thirteen volumes presents the titles 'Electromagnetic Induction' and 'Alternating Current.'.
Science - Physical
Dist - SCCON **Prod** - CIT 1986

The Mechanical Universe and Beyond - Vol VII 60 MIN
VHS
Mechanical Universe and Beyond Series
Color (S)
$29.95 purchase _ #118 - 9094
Combines state - of - the - art visuals with solid information to present the fundamentals of physics. Makes abstract concepts and mathematical processes understandable and offers an intellectual and philosophical base for physics comprehension. Features Professor David Goodstein of the California Institute of Technology as host. Volume VII of thirteen volumes presents the titles 'Maxwell's Equations' and 'Optics.'.
Science - Physical
Dist - SCCON **Prod** - CIT 1986

The Mechanical Universe and Beyond - Vol VIII 60 MIN
VHS
Mechanical Universe and Beyond Series
Color (S)
$29.95 purchase _ #118 - 9095
Combines state - of - the - art visuals with solid information to present the fundamentals of physics. Makes abstract concepts and mathematical processes understandable and offers an intellectual and philosophical base for physics comprehension. Features Professor David Goodstein of the California Institute of Technology as host. Volume VIII of thirteen volumes presents the titles 'The Michelson - Morley Experiment' and 'The Lorentz Transformation.'.
Science - Physical
Dist - SCCON **Prod** - CIT 1986

The Mechanical Universe and Beyond - Vol X 60 MIN
VHS
Mechanical Universe and Beyond Series
Color (S)
$29.95 purchase _ #118 - 9097
Combines state - of - the - art visuals with solid information to present the fundamentals of physics. Makes abstract concepts and mathematical processes understandable and offers an intellectual and philosophical base for physics comprehension. Features Professor David Goodstein of the California Institute of Technology as host. Volume X of thirteen volumes presents the titles 'Temperature And Gas Law' and 'Engine Of Nature.'.
Science - Physical
Dist - SCCON **Prod** - CIT 1986

The Mechanical Universe and Beyond - Vol XI 60 MIN
VHS
Mechanical Universe and Beyond Series
Color (S)
$29.95 purchase _ #118 - 9098
Combines state - of - the - art visuals with solid information to present the fundamentals of physics. Makes abstract concepts and mathematical processes understandable and offers an intellectual and philosophical base for physics comprehension. Features Professor David Goodstein of the California Institute of Technology as host. Volume XI of thirteen volumes presents the titles 'Entropy' and 'Low Temperatures.'.
Science - Physical
Dist - SCCON **Prod** - CIT 1986

The Mechanical Universe and Beyond - Vol XII 60 MIN
VHS
Mechanical Universe and Beyond Series
Color (S)
$29.95 purchase _ #118 - 9099
Combines state - of - the - art visuals with solid information to present the fundamentals of physics. Makes abstract concepts and mathematical processes understandable and offers an intellectual and philosophical base for physics comprehension. Features Professor David Goodstein of the California Institute of Technology as host. Volume XII of thirteen volumes presents the titles 'The Atom' and 'Particles And Waves.'.
Science - Physical
Dist - SCCON **Prod** - CIT 1986

The Mechanical Universe and Beyond - Vol XIII 60 MIN
VHS
Mechanical Universe and Beyond Series
Color (S)
$29.95 purchase _ #118 - 9100
Combines state - of - the - art visuals with solid information to present the fundamentals of physics. Makes abstract concepts and mathematical processes understandable and offers an intellectual and philosophical base for physics comprehension. Features Professor David Goodstein of the California Institute of Technology as host. Volume XIII of thirteen volumes presents the titles 'From Atoms To Quarks' and 'The Quantum Mechanical Universe.'.
Science - Physical
Dist - SCCON **Prod** - CIT 1986

The Mechanical Universe - High School Adaptation 360 MIN
VHS / U-matic
Color (H)
Provides an exciting array of audiovisual resources for classroom instruction that include closeups of complicated and expensive experiments, animation sequences, and historical reenactments of the beginnings of physics.
Science - Physical
Dist - SCCON **Prod** - SCCON 1986

Mechanical universe - high school adaptation series

Conservation laws and fundamental forces - Quad II	60 MIN
Electricity - Quad V	60 MIN
From Kepler to Einstein - Quad IV	60 MIN
Kinematics and scientific methods - Quad III	60 MIN
Magnetism and beyonds - Quad VI	60 MIN
Modern physics - Quad VII	60 MIN
Physics on Earth and in the heavens - Quad I	60 MIN

Dist - INSTRU

Mechanical Universe - High School Adaptation Series

Angular momentum	15 MIN
The Apple and the moon	12 MIN
Conservation of Energy	15 MIN
Conservation of Momentum	8 MIN
Curved space and black holes	12 MIN
The Fundamental sources	16 MIN
Harmonic Motion	12 MIN
Inertia	18 MIN
Introduction to Waves	10 MIN
Kepler's Laws	14 MIN
The Law of Falling Bodies	13 MIN
The Millikan Experiment	15 MIN
Moving in Circles	7 MIN
Navigating the Space	18 MIN
Newton's Laws	240 MIN
Temperature and the Gas Laws	16 MIN

Dist - SCCON

Mechanical universe series
Covers 28 different concepts in physics from Newton's Laws to Special Relativity. Uses 3 - D graphics created at the Jet Propulsion Laboratory in California, historic reenactments and close - ups of complicated and expensive experiments in combination to make abstract concepts and mathematical processes interesting and understandable. Includes topics such as navigation in space, magnetic fields, the law of inertia and curved space and black holes. Accompanies each video with printed guides for students and teachers. Contact distributor about availability outside the United Kingdom.
The Mechanical universe series
Dist - ACADEM

Mechanical Universe Series

Angular momentum	30 MIN
The Apple and the moon	30 MIN
Conservation of Energy	30 MIN
Conservation of Momentum	30 MIN
Derivatives	30 MIN
Energy and Eccentricity	30 MIN
From Kepler to Einstein	30 MIN
The Fundamental Forces	30 MIN
Gravity, electricity, magnetism	30 MIN
Harmonic Motion	30 MIN
Harmony of the spheres	30 MIN
Inertia	30 MIN
Integration	30 MIN
Introduction to the Mechanical Universe	30 MIN
The Kepler Problem	30 MIN
The Law of Falling Bodies	30 MIN
The Millikan Experiment	30 MIN
Moving in Circles	30 MIN
Navigating in Space	30 MIN

Newton's Laws 30 MIN
Potential energy 30 MIN
Resonance 30 MIN
Torques and Gyroscopes 30 MIN
Vectors 30 MIN
Waves 30 MIN
Dist - FI

Mechanical universe...and beyond - Part I series
Angular momentum - torques and gyroscopes - Parts 19 and 20 60 MIN
Conservation of energy - potential energy - Parts 13 and 14 60 MIN
Conservation of momentum - harmonic motion - Parts 15 and 16 60 MIN
Derivatives - inertia - Parts 3 and 4 60 MIN
Gravity, electricity, magnetism - the Millikan experiment - Parts 11 and 12 60 MIN
Integration - the apple and the moon - Parts 7 and 8 60 MIN
Introduction to the mechanical universe - the law of falling bodies - Parts 1 and 2 60 MIN
Kepler to Einstein - harmony of the spheres - Parts 25 and 26 60 MIN
Kepler's three laws - the Kepler problem - Parts 21 and 22 60 MIN
Moving in circles - fundamental forces - Parts 9 and 10 60 MIN
Vectors - Newton's laws - Parts 5 and 6 60 MIN
Dist - ANNCPB

Mechanical universe...and beyond - Part II series
The Atom - particles and waves - Parts 49 and 50 60 MIN
Electric circuits - magnetism - Parts 33 and 34 60 MIN
The Electric field - potential and capacitance - Parts 29 and 30 60 MIN
Electromagnetic induction - alternating current - Parts 37 and 38 60 MIN
Entropy - low temperature - Parts 47 and 48 60 MIN
Maxwell's equations - optics - Parts 39 and 40 60 MIN
The Michelson - Morley experiment - the Lorentz transformation - Parts 41 and 42 60 MIN
Temperature and gas laws - engine of nature - Parts 45 and 46 60 MIN
Velocity and time - mass, momentum, energy - Parts 43 and 44 60 MIN
Voltage, energy and force - the electric battery - Parts 31 and 32 60 MIN
Dist - ANNCPB

Mechanical ventilation series
Presents a two - part series on mechanical ventilation. Includes the titles Essentials for Nursing Care and Complications and Weaning.
Complications and weaning - Part 2 28 MIN
Essentials for nursing care - Part 1 28 MIN
Dist - AJN **Prod** - HOSSN 1986

Mechanical waves 20 MIN
VHS / U-matic / 16mm
Energy and waves series
Color (H C)
$450, $315, $345 purchase _ #A353; LC 83-700640
Uses real - life examples and laboratory experiments to explain the properties of mechanical waves. Explores wave amplitude, frequency, wavelength, velocity, pulse, bore, periodic waves, standing waves, the law of reflection, diffraction, the Doppler effect and interference.
Science - Physical
Dist - BARR **Prod** - BARR 1983

Mechanics 15 MIN
VHS / 16mm
(H C A)
$24.95 purchase _ #CS158
Describes the skills necessary to be a mechanic. Features interviews with mechanics about their jobs.
Guidance and Counseling
Dist - RMIBHF **Prod** - RMIBHF

Mechanics 15 MIN
BETA / VHS / U-matic
Career success series
Color (H C A)
$29.95 purchase _ #MX158
Portrays occupations in mechanics by reviewing required abilities and interviewing people employed in this field. Shows anxieties and rewards involved in pursuing a career as a mechanic.
Education; Guidance and Counseling; Industrial and Technical Education
Dist - CAMV **Prod** - CAMV

Mechanics - college physics series
Fixed system of orbiting bodies 7 MIN
Dist - MLA

Mechanics' Liens and Related Remedies 120 MIN
U-matic / VHS / Cassette
Color; Mono (PRO)
Looks at the procedureal demands of mechanics' lien law. Explains alternative remedies such as stop notices and bond claims. Includes topics such as priorities, enforcement of lien and effects of bankruptcy on remedies.
Civics and Political Systems
Dist - CCEB **Prod** - CCEB

Mechanics of Flight in Flying Foxes 8 MIN
U-matic / VHS / 16mm
Aspects of Animal Behavior Series
Color (H C A)
LC 75-702962
Uses ultra - slow - motion photography inside an experimental wind tunnel to analyze the flight of large bats.
Science; Science - Natural
Dist - UCEMC **Prod** - UCLA 1974

Mechanics of fluids series
Characteristics of Laminar and Turbulent Flow 25 MIN
Effects of fluid compressibility 17 MIN
Fluid motion in a gravitational field 23 MIN
Form, drag, lift and propulsion 23 MIN
Fundamental principles of flow 23 MIN
Introduction to the Study of Fluid Motion 24 MIN
Dist - UIOWA

Mechanics of Life - Blood and Circulation 8 MIN
U-matic / VHS / 16mm
Mechanics of Life Series
Color (I)
LC 72-711091
Uses X - ray photography and animation to describe how the human blood system is designed. Shows the composition of blood through microphotography and discusses the role of each blood component.
Science - Natural
Dist - PHENIX **Prod** - EOTHEN 1971

Mechanics of Life - Bones and Joints 8 MIN
U-matic / VHS / 16mm
Mechanics of Life Series
Color (I)
LC 77-711095
Describes the skeletal construction of the human body. Notes that although a unity of pattern exists in the skeletal structures of vertebrates, each organism has developed a skeleton that provides support and allows movements needed for its particular lifestyle.
Science - Natural
Dist - PHENIX **Prod** - EOTHEN 1971

Mechanics of Life - Breathing and Respiration 9 MIN
U-matic / VHS / 16mm
Mechanics of Life Series
Color (I)
LC 76-711092
Points out that organisms with very small volumes, such as amoebae, can get the oxygen they need through the membranes that define their bodies. Shows that larger organisms have developed systems that increase the surface area that can be used for oxygen - carbon dioxide transfer. Notes that the lung system in the human provides a very large surface for gas exchange, but is very delicate.
Science - Natural
Dist - PHENIX **Prod** - EOTHEN 1971

Mechanics of Life - Digestion and the Food We Eat 9 MIN
16mm / U-matic / VHS
Mechanics of Life Series
Color
LC 70-711093
Points out that the body needs a well - balanced diet in order to remain healthy. Explains that a good diet provides the right amounts of proteins, fats, carbohydrates, vitamins and minerals. Describes the process of preparing foods rich in these basic materials for use within the body.
Science - Natural
Dist - PHENIX **Prod** - EOTHEN 1971

Mechanics of Life - Muscles and Movement 10 MIN
16mm / U-matic / VHS
Mechanics of Life Series
Color
LC 73-711094
Explains what muscles are and how they work. Describes the difference between voluntary and involuntary muscles, and stresses that good posture and proper exercise help muscles work efficiently.
Science - Natural
Dist - PHENIX **Prod** - EOTHEN 1971

Mechanics of Life Series
Mechanics of Life - Blood and Circulation 8 MIN
Mechanics of Life - Bones and Joints 8 MIN
Mechanics of Life - Breathing and Respiration 9 MIN
Mechanics of Life - Digestion and the Food We Eat 9 MIN
Mechanics of Life - Muscles and Movement 10 MIN
Dist - PHENIX

Mechanics of Love 7 MIN
16mm
B&W (C)
$280.00
Experimental film by Willard Maas.
Fine Arts
Dist - AFA **Prod** - AFA 1955

The Mechanics of movement - Part 1 23 MIN
VHS
Cutting edge series
Color (G)
$150.00 purchase _ #8023
Examines research conducted by seven researchers at the Human Performance Laboratory, Faculty of Physical Education, University of Calgary. Part of a five - part series on the latest research and technology developments in Western Canada.
Geography - World; Physical Education and Recreation; Science
Dist - UCALG **Prod** - UCALG 1989

The Mechanics of Television
U-matic
Visual Learning Series Session 4
Color (T)
Explains the physical principles behind the television picture. Demonstrates the operation of a color television set and videocassette player.
Education; Fine Arts; Industrial and Technical Education
Dist - NYSED **Prod** - NYSED

The Mechanics of toys 12 MIN
VHS
Color; PAL (P I)
PdS25.00 purchase
Takes a first look at wheels, levers, cogs, energy storage and power transmissions. Evaluates familiar toys.
Science - Physical
Dist - EMFVL **Prod** - LOOLEA

The Mechanic's Tool Box 30 MIN
U-matic / VHS
Aircraft Hardware, Hand Tools and Measuring Devices Series
Color (IND)
Describes tools to be included in every mechanic's tool box plus use of special tools for particular jobs.
Industrial and Technical Education
Dist - AVIMA **Prod** - AVIMA

Mechanism of Alkene Bromination 20 MIN
U-matic / VHS
Experiment - Chemistry Series
Color (C)
$249.00, $149.00 purchase _ #AD - 1065
Carries out the bromination of propene in the absence and presence of chloride ions so that students may infer likely reaction mechanisms based on product distributions measured in a gas - liquid chromatograph. Part of a series on experiments in chemistry.
Education; Psychology; Science; Science - Physical
Dist - FOTH **Prod** - FOTH

Mechanism of an Organic Reaction 20 MIN
16mm
CHEM Study Films Series
Color (H)
A study of the hydrolysis of the ester methyl benzoate shows that the discovery of a reaction mechanism includes a determination of the chemical equation, the structures of the reactants and products, the fate of each atom of the reactants and the structures of the intermediate molecules. Discusses bond polarity.
Science - Physical
Dist - MLA **Prod** - CHEMS 1962

Mechanism of an organic reaction 20MIN
VHS / 16mm
Chem study video - film series
Color (H C)
$320.00, $99.00 purchase, $29.00 rental _ #192 W 0890, #193 W 2036, #140 W 4166
Uses hydrolysis of an organic ester to show that discovery of a reaction mechanism - the actual steps by which a reaction proceeds - includes a determination of the chemical equation, the structures of the reactants and the structures of the intermediate molecules. Gives the concepts of bond polarity. Part of a series for teaching chemistry to high school and college students.

Science - Physical
Dist - WARDS **Prod** - WARDS 1990

Mechanism of Impairment in Spinal Cord Injury, Part 1 — 15 MIN
Slide / VHS / 16mm
Nursing Management in Neurogenic Bladder Series
Color (PRO)
$50.00, $80.00, $100.00 purchase, $30.00, $35.00 rental _ #8016
Presents information on neurogenic bladder conditions. Focuses on the mechanism of impairment resulting from spinal cord injury. Presents the work of Y C Wu, MD, R King, MS, RN, and W Griggs, MSN, RN. Slide program includes 54 slides and audiocassette accompanied by study guide package.
Health and Safety; Science - Natural
Dist - RICHGO **Prod** - RICHGO 1980

Mechanisms for Voice Frequency Change — 10 MIN
16mm
Color
Surveys available information on vocal fold lengthening and thinning, cricoid cartilage rocking and the upward position of the larynx in the neck as voice frequency is increased. Analyzes the interaactions of these factors and explains the mechanics responsible for laryngeal alternations.
Science - Natural
Dist - UCEMC **Prod** - UCSF 1977

Mechanisms of air ventilation in labyrinth fishes — 12 MIN
VHS
Color (G C)
$70.00 purchase, $14.00 rental _ #23948
Features three species of the Anabantoid family - African bush fish, gourami and climbing perch, labyrinth fish which possess accessory breathing organs that allow them to survive in low - oxygen and oxygen - free water. Employs live - action and slow - motion photography, graphics models, dissection and X - ray cinematography to demonstrate the process.
Science - Natural
Dist - PSU **Prod** - IWIF 1987

Mechanisms of Bacterial Transformation — 56 MIN
U-matic
Color
Discusses advances in the research about bacterial transformation and gives attention to DNA cycling.
Health and Safety
Dist - UTEXSC **Prod** - UTEXSC

Mechanisms of Chip Formation — 22 MIN
U-matic
Color
Shows the physical characteristics of various metals during machining, turning, shaping or drilling. Explains behavior of several types of metal under stress of a sharper blade.
Science - Physical
Dist - UMITV **Prod** - UMITV 1967

Mechanisms of Defense - Accident — 26 MIN
16mm / U-matic / VHS
Living Body - an Introduction to Human Biology Series
Color
Points out that the body is like a self - supporting hospital, able to deal on its own with wounds, bacterial invasions, fractures and obstructions to its various passages. Follows the sequence of events over seconds or weeks when skin or bone are damaged, and shows the defensive reactions of blood clotting, fever and mending bone fracture.
Science - Natural
Dist - FOTH **Prod** - FOTH 1985

Mechanisms of Defense - Internal Defenses — 26 MIN
16mm / U-matic / VHS
Living Body - an Introduction to Human Biology Series
Color
Discusses the mechanisms of defense used by the body when bacteria or viruses invade the whole system. Shows the roles of the spleen, the lymphatic system and the white blood cells, and explains the body's production of antibodies. Uses the common cold as an example to follow the sequence from viral attack to recovery.
Science - Natural
Dist - FOTH **Prod** - FOTH 1985

Mechanisms of Disease - Host Defenses Series
Dynamics of Immunocompetence 19 MIN
Hypersensitivity and Autoimmunity 16 MIN
Immunodeficiency Diseases 16 MIN
Nonspecific Defense Mechanisms 15 MIN
Dist - BRA

Mechanisms of Neurosurgical Football Injuries — 14 MIN
U-matic
Color
Consists of actual high school, college and professional football plays which have caused serious and fatal head and spinal injuries.
Health and Safety; Physical Education and Recreation
Dist - UMITV **Prod** - UMITV 1967

Mechanisms of Respiratory Clearance — 15 MIN
U-matic / VHS / 16mm
Color
Shows the mechanisms of cilia beating, the influence of mucus load and the measurement and significance of the viscoelasticity of mucus. Describes how variations on these factors determine the clearance of mucus.
Science - Natural
Dist - USNAC **Prod** - VAMBNY 1982

Mechanization — 10 MIN
U-matic / VHS / 16mm
Foundations of Wealth Series
Color
Shows how mechanization contributes to the creation of wealth.
Business and Economics; Social Science
Dist - FOTH **Prod** - FOTH

Meconium Ilues and the Meconium Plug Syndrome — 18 MIN
16mm
Color (PRO)
Explains that among the strange catastrophes that befall the intestinal tract of the newborn infant, meconium ileus and obstruction due to meconium plug are among the rarest and the most difficult to treat. Illustrates four distinct types of obstruction due to meconium.
Health and Safety; Science
Dist - ACY **Prod** - ACYDGD 1958

Medal of Honor — 30 MIN
VHS / U-matic
World War II - GI Diary Series
Color (H C A)
History - United States; History - World
Dist - TIMLIF **Prod** - TIMLIF 1980

Medal of Honor — 30 MIN
VHS / 16mm
World War II - G I Diary Series
(J H C)
$99.95 each, $995.00 series _ #23
Depicts the action and emotion that soldiers experienced during World War II, through their eyes and in their words. Narrated by Lloyd Bridges.
History - United States; History - World
Dist - AMBROS **Prod** - AMBROS 1980

Medal of Honor - a Team Man — 5 MIN
16mm
B&W
LC 74-705105
Cites Forrest Vosler for bravery and self - sacrifice while serving as a radio operator - air gunner on a mission over Bremen, Germany, in 1943.
Civics and Political Systems; History - United States
Dist - USNAC **Prod** - USAF 1967

Medal of Honor - Ace of Aces — 5 MIN
16mm
B&W
LC 74-705106
Cites Captain Eddy Rickenbacker for his heroism as a World War I fighter pilot.
Biography; Civics and Political Systems; History - United States
Dist - USNAC **Prod** - USAF 1967

Medal of Honor - America Strikes Back — 7 MIN
16mm
B&W
LC 74-706138
Cites General James Doolittle for leadership in the first air raid over Tokyo.
Biography; History - United States
Dist - USNAC **Prod** - USAF 1967

Medal of Honor - Burning Ploesti Oil — 7 MIN
16mm
B&W
LC 74-705107
Cites Col Leon Johnson and Col John Krane for bravery in Ploesti oil raids.
Biography; Civics and Political Systems
Dist - USNAC **Prod** - USAF 1967

Medal of Honor - by Act of Congress — 5 MIN
16mm
B&W
LC 75-703725
Cites Charles A Lindbergh for navigational skill and courage in his historic flight from New York to Paris.
Biography; Industrial and Technical Education; Science
Dist - USNAC **Prod** - USAF 1967

Medal of Honor - Capt Hilliard A Wilbanks — 10 MIN
16mm
Color
LC 75-703749
Cites the late Capt Hilliard A Wilbanks, a forward air control pilot, for saving the lives of many Americans by using his small plane to divert enemy fire in Vietnam combat.
Biography; Civics and Political Systems; Industrial and Technical Education
Dist - USNAC **Prod** - USAF 1968

Medal of Honor - Capt Jay Zeamer — 5 MIN
16mm
B&W
LC 74-706139
Cites Captain Jay Zeamer, bomber pilot for heroism during World War II reconnaissance mission.
Biography; History - United States
Dist - USNAC **Prod** - USAF 1967

Medal of honor collection — 288 MIN
VHS
Color (J H)
$69.95 purchase _ #CFE9606V-S
Draws intimate and dramatic portraits of ordinary men who discovered extraordinary courage in themselves and, thereby, won America's Medal of Honor. Offers six videocassettes which tell stories of soldiers in World War II, both in Europe and the Pacific, Korea, and Vietnam. Features stories of brothers Walter and Roland Ehlers at Omaha Beach, Richard Bong in the Pacific, Don Ross and John Finn at Pearl Harbor, William Barber in Korea, and Sammy Davis and Jimmie Howard in Vietnam.
History - United States; History - World
Dist - CAMV

Medal of Honor - Heading Home — 5 MIN
16mm
B&W
LC 74-705108
Cites Captain William R Lawley for heroism and exceptional flying skill on a heavy bombardmanet mission over enemy occupied Europe.
Biography; Civics and Political Systems
Dist - USNAC **Prod** - USAF 1967

Medal of Honor - One for One — 5 MIN
16mm
B&W
LC 74-706140
Pays tribute to Major Bernard Fisher, the first Vietnam hero to receive the Medal of Honor for saving a fellow pilot's life in the Battle of Ashau.
Biography; History - United States
Dist - USNAC **Prod** - USAF 1967

Medal of Honor - One Man Air Force — 7 MIN
16mm
B&W
LC 74-705109
Cites Col James H Howard for his valor as a World War II fighter pilot.
Biography; Civics and Political Systems; History - United States
Dist - USNAC **Prod** - USAF 1967

Medal of Honor - Only a Few Returned — 5 MIN
16mm
B&W
LC 74-705110
Cites Sgt Maynard Smith for his fearlessness as World War II B - 17 gunner.
Biography; Civics and Political Systems; History - United States
Dist - USNAC **Prod** - USAF 1967

Medal of Honor - Pacific Age — 5 MIN
16mm
B&W
LC 74-705112
Cites Major Richard Bong for bringing down over 40 enemy aircraft.
Biography; Civics and Political Systems; History - United States
Dist - USNAC **Prod** - USAF 1969

Medal of Honor Rag — 54 MIN
U-matic / VHS
Color (H C A)
Presents the story of a black Vietnam veteran who won the Congressional Medal of Honor and was later shot and killed while holding up a supermarket in Detroit. Offers an imaginary dialogue between the soldier and a psychiatrist in which they come to the conclusion that the medal had a terrible effect on the soldier's life.
Civics and Political Systems; Guidance and Counseling; History - United States
Dist - FI **Prod** - CHOPRA 1983

Medal of honor series
Presents six parts featuring intimate and dramatic portraits of ordinary men who discovered extraordinary courage within themselves and earned America's highest tribute. Includes three parts on World War II - brothers Walter and Roland Ehlers in the European theater, Richard Bong and Howard Gilmore in the Pacific theater, and Don Ross and John Finn at Pearl Harbor and in the Pacific; one part on Korea - Captain William Barber; two parts on Vietnam - Sgt Sammy Davis in Part I, Sgt Jimmie Howard and his 17 Marines in Part II.
Medal of honor series 288 MIN
Dist - CAMV

Medal of Honor - Seven Down 5 MIN
16mm
B&W
LC 74-705113
Cites Major Willaim Shomg for downing seven World War II enemy aircraft.
Biography; Civics and Political Systems; History - United States
Dist - USNAC Prod - USAF 1969

Medal of Honor - Trial by Fire 4 MIN
16mm
B&W
LC 74-705114
Pays tribute to Sgt Edward Erwin, who ditched an ignited phosphorous bomb from his aircraft during a World War II raid over enemy territory.
Biography; Civics and Political Systems; History - United States
Dist - USNAC Prod - USAF 1969

Medal of Honor - with One Hand 4 MIN
16mm
B&W
LC 74-705115
Cites Lt John Morgan who single - handedly guided his plane to a target during a World War II raid over Europe.
Civics and Political Systems; History - World
Dist - USNAC Prod - USAF 1967

Medea 107 MIN
VHS
B&W (G C H)
$99.00 purchase _ #DL421
Features Judith Anderson in the title role.
Fine Arts; Literature and Drama
Dist - INSIM

Medea
VHS / U-matic
Color (G) (ITALIAN (ENGLISH SUBTITLES))
Presents Maria Callas as Medea in her only non - operatic film.
Fine Arts; Literature and Drama
Dist - VAI Prod - VAI

Medea 70 MIN
VHS
Color (G)
$39.95 purchase _ #1114
Interprets freely the classic drama 'Medea' by Euripides in one act. Features Georgiy Aleksidze and Elgudja Zhgenti as writers and directors. Stars Marina Goderdzishvili and Vladimir Julukhadze. Musical score by Revaz Gabichvadze.
Fine Arts; Foreign Language; Geography - World; Physical Education and Recreation
Dist - KULTUR

Medea 90 MIN
U-matic / VHS
Color
Presents an adaptation of Euripedes' classic play Medea, starring Zoe Caldwell and Judith Anderson.
History - World; Literature and Drama
Dist - FOTH Prod - WQED 1983

Medea 110 MIN
VHS
Color (G C H) (GREEK WITH ENGLISH SUBTITLES)
$139.00 purchase _ #DL392
Stages Euripides' play as it would have been perfomred in 5th - century Greece, BC, with lines delivered in the authentic pitched sing - song fashion - in accordance with recent linguistic discoveries.
Fine Arts
Dist - INSIM

Medex - the Person 25 MIN
U-matic
Color
LC 76-706055
Reviews the Medex program to extend the physician's capacity to provide care through the utilization of paraphysicians.
Health and Safety
Dist - USNAC Prod - WARMP 1972

Medex - the Program 28 MIN
U-matic
Color
LC 76-706056
Reviews the Medex program to extend the physician's capacity to provide care through the utilization of paraphysicians.
Health and Safety
Dist - USNAC Prod - WARMP 1972

The Media 75 MIN
VHS
Color; PAL (J H)
PdS40 purchase
Presents five programs of 15 minutes each exploring the media and its effects. Encompasses advertising, the theater, publishing, special effects and the program makers of television. Contact distributor about availability outside the United Kingdom.
Fine Arts; Sociology
Dist - ACADEM

Media and Campaigning 30 MIN
U-matic / VHS
American Government Series; 1
Color (C)
Reveals the importance of using the mass media effectively in political campaigns.
Civics and Political Systems
Dist - DALCCD Prod - DALCCD

The Media and Human Rights 60 MIN
VHS
Color (H)
$10.50 rental _ #60658
Features Ted Koppel and a panel of human - rights specialists, politicians, and print and broadcast journalists discussing the coverage of human rights issues in South Africa, Poland and the Philippines. Emphasizes human rights in the media and discusses how to make it a foreign policy concern.
Civics and Political Systems; Literature and Drama; Sociology
Dist - PSU Prod - PBS
PBS

Media and message 60 MIN
VHS / U-matic
Art of being human series
Color (H C A)
Discusses the role of media in society.
Sociology
Dist - FI Prod - FI 1978

Media and methods of the artist series

Acrylic 1	30 MIN
Acrylic 2	30 MIN
Assemblage	30 MIN
Collage	30 MIN
Egg tempera	30 MIN
Gouache	30 MIN
Intaglio	30 MIN
Lithography	30 MIN
Monoprints	30 MIN
Mural Techniques 1	30 MIN
Mural Techniques 2	30 MIN
Oil Equipment	30 MIN
Oil Pigments	30 MIN
Oil Techniques 1	30 MIN
Oil Techniques 2	30 MIN
Oil Techniques 3	30 MIN
Pastel	30 MIN
Pencils and Paper	30 MIN
Pens and Inks	30 MIN
Printing Techniques	30 MIN
Relief	30 MIN
Sculpture 1	30 MIN
Sculpture 2	30 MIN
Serigraphs	30 MIN
Sticks	30 MIN
Watercolor	30 MIN

Dist - TVOTAR

Media clip art
CD-ROM
(G A)
$350.00 purchase _ #2291
Provides 650 M of Desktop Publishing Images. Uses Postscript and TIFF formats, in both black and white and in color. For Macintosh Plus, SE and II computers. Requires 1MB RAM, floppy disk drive, Apple compatible CD - ROM drive.
Computer Science; Industrial and Technical Education
Dist - BEP

Media darling 8 MIN
16mm
B&W (G)
$25.00 rental
Portrays the American Media Machine as vampires in search of a bloody soundbite in a Thad Povey production.
Fine Arts; Sociology
Dist - CANCIN

Media Dreams 10 MIN
16mm
B&W
Portrays a man who returns from a business trip with a 'BARBIE' doll which he has purchased as a gift for his three - year - old daughter. Explains that his wife and daughter won't be home until the next day and during that evening the 'BARBIE' doll comes to life and seduces him.
Fine Arts; Psychology; Sociology
Dist - UPENN Prod - UPENN 1964

Media for managers 40 MIN
VHS
Color (PRO IND A)
$695.00 purchase, $195.00 rental _ #CFM04
Confronts the need for managers to be able to communicate with the media. Teaches managers to understand the media, do media interviews, avoid traps, get news coverage and communicate in a crisis. Includes a pocket guide. By Communications for Management Inc Intl.
Business and Economics; Psychology; Social Science
Dist - EXTR

Media for Presentations 20 MIN
16mm / U-matic / VHS
Color (J)
LC 79-700586
Discusses the advantages of audiovisual communication. Describes the characteristics of various media, including charts, graphs, photographs, presentation boards, overhead and opaque projectors, slides, filmstrips, 16mm and 8mm film, videotape and audio media.
Education; Fine Arts; Industrial and Technical Education; Social Science
Dist - IU Prod - IU 1978

Media in Politics 90 MIN
U-matic / VHS
Media Studies Series
Color (C)
$399.00, $249.00 purchase _ #AD - 2059
Features Tony Schwartz who illustrates the media concepts he has employed successfully on behalf of countless political candidates before and after they took office. Offers practical examples of media use to advance candidates and political causes.
Civics and Political Systems; Computer Science; English Language; Fine Arts; Psychology; Sociology
Dist - FOTH Prod - FOTH

Media in the Classroom 48 MIN
VHS / U-matic
Strategies in College Teaching Series
Color (T)
LC 79-706190
Shows how to use various media in the classroom to increase student involvement and to improve the quality of instruction.
Education
Dist - IU Prod - IU 1977

Media kit
VHS / 35mm strip
Color (H A)
$79.00, $69.00 purchase _ #LS30V, #LS30F
Examines the impact of mass media on family life. Suggests that mass media influence behaviors, and conflict with 'traditional values.' Includes support materials.
Psychology; Sociology
Dist - CAMV

Media man 60 MIN
VHS
Color; B&W (G)
Begins in the filmmakers' garden where Danny Lyon is growing blemish free tomatoes in expectation of Jesse Helms, or someone from the NEA coming to dinner. Views Lyon smashing a large rotten pumpkin as he announces that he is making a film about America. Then things get crazy. Bleak Beauty's answer to CNN, NBC and all things false and electronic, in which the filmmakers age five years in the production. By Danny Lyon and Nancy Lyon. Contact distributor for price.
Fine Arts; Literature and Drama; Sociology
Dist - CANCIN

Media - Massaging the Mind 19 MIN
U-matic / VHS / 16mm
Color
Depicts future techniques for delivering the media's message, including satellites, lasers and holograms. Shows how newspapers and magazines will be radically altered by the continual speed - up of electronic journalism. Explores the role television has in shaping politicians.
Civics and Political Systems; Literature and Drama; Social Science; Sociology
Dist - CNEMAG Prod - DOCUA

Media only 47 MIN
VHS
Color (H G)
$295.00 purchase, $65.00 rental
Takes a behind - the - scenes look at media coverage of the 1992 Republican National Convention where, for one hectic week, 15,000 members of the working press crowded into Houston's Astrodome complex. Features interviews with the journalists themselves and shows the operations of newsgathering. Produced by Margaret O'Brien - Molina and Rick Christie.
Civics and Political Systems; Fine Arts; Literature and Drama; Sociology
Dist - CNEMAG

Media probes series
Design 30 MIN
The Future 30 MIN
Language 30 MIN
Photography 30 MIN
Political spots 30 MIN
Soap Operas 30 MIN
Soundaround 30 MIN
TV News 30 MIN
Dist - TIMLIF

Media skills for Haitian activists 50 MIN
VHS
Color (G)
$16.95 purchase
Features a workshop with Gwen McKinney, whose public relations firm represents President Aristide and journalist Alfredo Lopez. Sponsored by Americans for Aristide. Includes training manual.
Business and Economics; Social Science
Dist - GREVAL

Media Studies Series
Guerilla Media 120 MIN
Media in Politics 90 MIN
Secrets of Effective Radio Advertising 75 MIN
Dist - FOTH

Media Utilization 29 MIN
VHS / U-matic
Instructional Technology Introduction Series
Color (C A)
Illustrates the problems a teacher may encounter when not pre - viewing a film before using. Shows several media consultants being interviewed as to the many media resources available. Concludes with look at opaque projector.
Education
Dist - BCNFL **Prod** - MCGILU

Media war in El Salvador 22 MIN
VHS / 16mm
Color (G)
$190.00 purchase, $50.00 rental; $45.00 rental
Shows how the three major political parties in El Salvador are trying to use the media for their own purposes during that country's civil war. Discloses that two parties, the Christian Democrats and ARENA, imported advertising consultants from the US and mounted media campaigns copying the successful Reagan - Bush 'Tuesday Team' of 1984. The third party, FMLN - FDR, has broadcast regularly over Radio Venceremos since the beginning of the war.
Civics and Political Systems; Geography - World; History - United States; Literature and Drama; Sociology
Dist - FIRS **Prod** - FIRS 1989
ICARUS

Median Sternotomy and Elective Cardiac Arrest in Open Heart Surgery 36 MIN
16mm
Color (PRO)
Shows the operative techniques used in heart - lung surgery at Stanford University hospitals. Demonstrates the repair of intracardiac defects through the median sternotomy incision.
Health and Safety; Science
Dist - ACY **Prod** - ACYDGD 1958

Mediastinoscopy using Bivalve Speculum 16 MIN
16mm
Color
LC 74-715463
Uses operative scenes, anatomic drawings, and cadaver views to demonstrate the technique of mediastinoscopy using a bivalve speculum. Presents case reports to show the application of mediastinoscopy in evaluating pulmonary disease.
Health and Safety; Science
Dist - SQUIBB **Prod** - KAISRF 1971

Mediating 57 MIN
16mm / U-matic / VHS
Heart of the Dragon Series Pt 10; Pt 10
Color (H C A)
Analyzes the breakdown of a Chinese marriage and the pressures that are brought on the couple to reconcile their differences.
Geography - World; History - World; Sociology
Dist - TIMLIF **Prod** - ASH 1984

Mediating 57 MIN
16mm / VHS
Heart of the Dragon Series
(J H C)
$99.95 each, $595.00 series
Focuses on the method of handling divorce and reconciliation in China.
Geography - World; History - World
Dist - AMBROS **Prod** - AMBROS 1984

Mediation - 107 30 MIN
U-matic
Currents - 1984 - 85 Season Series
Color (A)
Reveals the means and methods available for mediation of disputes.
Business and Economics; Social Science
Dist - PBS **Prod** - WNETTV 1985

Mediation - Catalyst to Collective Bargaining Series
Stalemate 29 MIN
Dist - IU

Mediation - negotiating settlements 33 MIN
BETA / VHS / U-matic
Color (PRO)
$90.00 purchase
Portrays a guest who comes for dinner, falls down the stairs and threatens to sue. Shows the mediation process and demonstrates how mediation can be a viable alternative for settling such claims. Shows how to guide opposing parties in open discussions and private 'caucuses' to a satisfactory conclusion. Includes a discussion guide.
Civics and Political Systems; Psychology
Dist - AARA **Prod** - AARA

Mediation of a commercial dispute - a construction case study 45 MIN
VHS / U-matic / BETA
Color (PRO)
$125.00 purchase
Introduces the mediation process within the context of a substantial commercial dispute. Examines the difficulties presented to the mediator by adversarial disputants and their lawyers. Focuses on the role, technique and ethics of the mediator. Includes a discussion guide.
Industrial and Technical Education; Psychology
Dist - AARA **Prod** - AARA

Mediation of a contruction dispute 35 MIN
VHS / U-matic / BETA
Color (PRO)
$90.00 purchase
Portrays an architect, a contractor, an owner and a tenant who argue their differing points of view of a complex contruction dispute. Shows a mediator steering the parties to a resolution. Introduces industrial mediation. Includes a discussion guide.
Industrial and Technical Education; Psychology
Dist - AARA **Prod** - AARA

Mediation - the Win - Win Solution 15 MIN
VHS / Slide
Color (A)
$20.00 purchase
Presents some of the innovative techniques available for settling certain disputes out of court. Conciliation, mediation, arbitration, and other types of problem resolution at the neighborhood level, are assisting in the nationwide effort to relieve the over burdened court system.
Civics and Political Systems
Dist - AARP **Prod** - AARP 1986

Medic 4 24 MIN
U-matic / VHS
Color
Presents a dramatic story about a typical 24 - hour day for a para - medic team of the St Paul Fire Department.
Health and Safety; Science
Dist - WCCOTV **Prod** - WCCOTV 1974

Medical 30 MIN
U-matic
Fast Forward Series
Color (H C)
Examines genetic engineering, microsurgery, diagnostic medicine and the new machines for these and other medical uses.
Computer Science; Health and Safety; Science
Dist - TVOTAR **Prod** - TVOTAR 1979

Medical and Health Workers 13 MIN
U-matic / VHS / 16mm
Community Helpers Series
Color (P I)
$315, $220 purchase _ #79524
Shows the many different types of medical personnel and how they work with other community helpers to help people in the community.
Social Science; Sociology
Dist - CORF

Medical and Institutional Aspects 40 MIN
U-matic
Sexuality and Physical Disability Series
Color
Presents the issue of sexuality of the physically disabled through the perspectives of the past and current institutional practices. Presents a sampling of devices used to deal with altered sexual performance.
Health and Safety; Psychology
Dist - UMITV **Prod** - UMITV 1976

The Medical and Surgical Management of Angina Pectoris 58 MIN
U-matic / VHS
Color (PRO)
LC 81-706295
Discusses the diagnosis of significant coronary disease and the management of stable angina pectoris by medical and surgical therapy.
Health and Safety
Dist - USNAC **Prod** - USVA 1980

Medical and Surgical Treatment of Dizziness 50 MIN
VHS / U-matic
Dizziness and Related Balance Disorders Series
Color
Health and Safety
Dist - GSHDME **Prod** - GSHDME

The Medical and Surgical Treatment of Valvular Heart Disease 92 MIN
16mm
Boston Medical Reports Series
B&W (PRO)
LC 74-705116
Discusses various types of acquired valvular cardiac defects including clinical and hemodynamic assessment, indications for and results of surgery.
Health and Safety; Science - Natural
Dist - NMAC **Prod** - NMAC 1968

Medical applications of electromagnetism 56 MIN
VHS
Color (G)
$149.00 purchase, $75.00 rental _ #UW5117
Reveals that the first recorded case of a broken bone being mended by electricity was in 1812, but the greater part of the medical profession still regards the use of electricity in this fashion with suspicion. Shows how some doctors in England are using electromagnetism to accelerate healing, mend bones and help heroin addicts overcome the agonies of withdrawal. Looks at the pioneering work of a Swedish radiologist who is treating breast and lung cancer victims with direct current electricity.
Health and Safety
Dist - FOTH

Medical asepsis 30 MIN
16mm
Directions for education in nursing via technology series; Lesson 1
B&W (PRO)
LC 74-701773
Discusses means of transmission of microorganisms and prevention of transmission. Demonstrates hand washing and applies the concepts of medical asepsis to nursing activities in the hospital.
Health and Safety
Dist - WSUM **Prod** - DENT 1974

Medical Aspects 28 MIN
U-matic / VHS
Color (J A)
Features Dr Max A Schneider as he discusses the various parts of the body affected by excessive drinking.
Health and Safety; Psychology; Sociology
Dist - SUTHRB **Prod** - SUTHRB

Medical aspects of alcohol - An Encyclopedia on alcohol and human physiology - Part I 27 MIN
VHS
Medical aspects of alcohol series
Color; CC (J H G) (SPANISH)
$425.00 purchase
Illustrates the effects of alcohol on the liver, heart, pancreas, kidneys and other organs of the body. Features Dr Max A Schneider. Updates the older version, using computer

animated graphics, the fashion and styles of the 1990s. Discusses alcohol as a toxic drug and the diseases that are a result of alcohol use. Part one of two parts.
Guidance and Counseling; Health and Safety; Psychology; Sociology
Dist - FMSP **Prod** - FMSP 1994

Medical aspects of alcohol - an encyclopedia on alcohol and human physiology - Part II 24 MIN
VHS
Medical aspects of alcohol series
Color; CC (J H G) (SPANISH)
$425.00 purchase
Discusses the effects of alcohol upon the brain and nerve tissue. Features Dr Max A Schneider. Updates the older version, using computer animated graphics, the fashion and styles of the 1990s. Discusses alcohol as a toxic drug and the diseases that are a result of alcohol use. Part two of two parts.
Guidance and Counseling; Health and Safety; Psychology; Sociology
Dist - FMSP **Prod** - FMSP 1994

Medical Aspects of Alcohol, Pt 1 30 MIN
U-matic / VHS
Color (J A)
Presents a detailed overview of the signs and symptoms of disease resulting from the use of alcohol and other drugs. Constitutes the first of a two - part series.
Health and Safety; Psychology; Sociology
Dist - SUTHRB **Prod** - SUTHRB

Medical Aspects of Alcohol, Pt 2 30 MIN
U-matic / VHS
Color (J A)
Presents the second of a two - part overview of the signs and symptoms of disease resulting from the use of alcohol and other drugs.
Health and Safety; Psychology; Sociology
Dist - SUTHRB **Prod** - SUTHRB

Medical aspects of alcohol series
Presents two parts which discuss the effects of alcohol upon the liver, heart, pancreas, kidneys and other organs, as well as the brain and nerve tissue. Features Dr Max A Schneider. Updates the older version, using computer animated graphics, the fashion and styles of the 1990s. Discusses alcohol as a toxic drug and the diseases that are a result of alcohol use.
Medical aspects of alcohol - An Encyclopedia on alcohol and human physiology - Part I 27 MIN
Medical aspects of alcohol - an encyclopedia on alcohol and human physiology - Part II 24 MIN
Dist - FMSP **Prod** - FMSP

Medical aspects of co - dependency 28 MIN
VHS
Color (J H G)
$379.00 purchase
Uses computer - generated medical diagrams and interviews with family members to thoroughly describe the nature and scope of co - dependency. Features Dr Max A Schneider who explains the physical and emotional strains that a drug or alcohol abuser places on family, friends and co - workers.
Guidance and Counseling; Health and Safety; Psychology
Dist - FMSP **Prod** - FREDER

Medical Aspects of Disability - Course Lecture Series
The Emergence of Our Largest Minority - the Disabled on Independent Living 53 MIN
Psychological Issues in the Rehabilitation Process 56 MIN
Psychology of Disability - Working with and Motivating the Difficult Client 57 MIN
Stroke - Recent Trends and Treatments 80 MIN
Substance Abuse and Physical Disability 41 MIN
The Traumatically Brain Injured Patient - Acute Rehabilitative Aspects 36 MIN
Vocational Rehabilitation and the Individual with Head Trauma 51 MIN
Dist - RICHGO

Medical Aspects of Diving, Pt 1 - Mechanical Effects of Pressure 28 MIN
U-matic
Color
LC 80-706862
Provides information on the safety and efficiency of persons concerned with diving and underwater swimming. Describes physiological pressure stresses. Issued in 1962 as a motion picture.
Health and Safety
Dist - USNAC **Prod** - USN 1980

Medical Aspects of Diving, Pt 1 - the Mechanical Effects of Pressure 30 MIN
16mm
Color
LC FIE63-32
Explains how underwater swimmers and divers can prevent harm to themselves by avoiding the application of unequal pressures from the air and the water.
Health and Safety; Science - Natural
Dist - USNAC **Prod** - USN 1962

Medical Aspects of Diving, Pt 2 - Effects of Elevated Partial Pressures of Gases 28 MIN
16mm
Color
LC FIE63-31
Explains how the body is affected by what you breathe and the pressure at which you breathe it.
Health and Safety; Science - Natural
Dist - USNAC **Prod** - USN 1962

Medical Aspects of High Intensity Noise - Ear Defense 21 MIN
16mm
B&W
Points out the hazards associated with high noise levels produced by jet aircraft and other noisy equipment found ashore and aboard ship.
Health and Safety; Science - Natural
Dist - USNAC **Prod** - USN 1955

Medical Aspects of High Intensity Noise - General Effects 21 MIN
16mm
B&W
Explains the increasingly serious hazards of high intensity noise. Describes the nature of noise and some of its physiological and psychological effects.
Civics and Political Systems; Health and Safety; Science - Natural
Dist - USNAC **Prod** - USN 1955

Medical aspects of mind altering drugs 30 MIN
VHS
Color (J H G)
$399.00 purchase
Illustrates the mental and physical effects of drugs on human physiology. Combines dramatic vignettes, computer graphics and charts with a discussion of the most important information about the most commonly abused drugs. Groups mind - altering drugs into six major categories - marijuana; sedative hypnotics; narcotics; inhalants; hallucinogens; and stimulants. Covers substances such as alcohol, tranquilizers, heroin, demerol, nitrates, PCP, LSD, cocaine and crack.
Guidance and Counseling; Health and Safety; Psychology
Dist - FMSP **Prod** - FREDER

Medical Aspects of Nuclear Radiation 20 MIN
16mm
Color (H A)
LC FIE52-2069
Explains effects of radiation upon the human body, internal and external radiation hazards, and the relative gravity of the hazards of nuclear radiation, blast and heat.
Health and Safety
Dist - USNAC **Prod** - USA 1952

Medical aspects of tobacco 27 MIN
VHS
Color; CC (J H G) (SPANISH)
$395.00 purchase
Combines a dramatic story, animated graphics and interviews with information about the effects of tobacco. Pays particular attention to pregnant women, youth, minorities, recovering addicts and recovering alcoholics. Features Dr Max A Schneider.
Guidance and Counseling; Health and Safety; Psychology
Dist - FMSP **Prod** - FMSP

Medical Assistant
U-matic / VHS
Work - a - Day America
$59.95 purchase _ #VV114V
Helps students achieve career vocational preparation. Stresses the four main points of career awareness and exploration, specific skills intended, employability skills needed, and real people sharing on the job experiences.
Guidance and Counseling
Dist - CAREER **Prod** - CAREER

Medical Assistant's Transcribing 6 MIN
BETA / VHS
Typing - Medical Series
Color
Business and Economics; Health and Safety
Dist - RMIBHF **Prod** - RMIBHF

Medical Audit Process 14 MIN
U-matic / VHS
Color (PRO)
Presents a way of evaluating the patterns and quality of medical practice.
Health and Safety
Dist - UMICHM **Prod** - UMICHM 1975

Medical benefits from exercise
VHS
Color (J H C G A PRO)
$79.50 purchase _ #AH46315
Describes the medical benefits of exercise. Shows how exercise benefits each of the body's organs.
Physical Education and Recreation; Science - Natural
Dist - HTHED **Prod** - HTHED

Medical Care during Pregnancy 29 MIN
U-matic / VHS
Tomorrow's Families Series
Color (H C A)
LC 81-706898
Explains that medical care and advice during pregnancy are most important to the health of the mother and baby.
Health and Safety
Dist - AITECH **Prod** - MDDE 1980

Medical Care for the McDaniel Family - a Compact Course in Family Medicine 60 MIN
VHS / U-matic
Color (PRO)
Introduces family medicine in six two - hour workshop sessions. Presents an encounter between members of a family practice group and the McDaniel family.
Health and Safety
Dist - HSCIC **Prod** - HSCIC 1980

Medical Careers 26 MIN
16mm
Color (H C A)
$425 purchase, $55 rental
Surveys the variety of medical careers open today, exploring the motives, requirements, and rewards of different medical jobs.
Health and Safety; Science
Dist - CNEMAG **Prod** - DOCUA 1988

Medical Careers - It's not all Dr Kildare 26 MIN
U-matic / VHS / 16mm
Color (J)
LC 76-701184
Presents some of the medical careers open to young people today and surveys professionals explaining their reasons for entering the medical field. Suggests factors young people should think about when considering a medical career.
Guidance and Counseling; Health and Safety; Psychology; Science
Dist - CNEMAG **Prod** - DOCUA 1976

Medical Cisis Intervention Series
Minor Burns 20 MIN
Dist - LEIKID

Medical Committee for Human Rights 15 MIN
16mm
Color
Shows the medical committee's role during the long strike at San Francisco State College and the need for a tactical knowledge of first aid as the struggles of student demonstrations intensify.
Geography - United States; Health and Safety; Sociology
Dist - CANWRL **Prod** - CANWRL

Medical Crisis Intervention Series
Major Burns 20 MIN
The Psychotic Assaultive Patient 20 MIN
The Suicidal Patient 20 MIN
Dist - LEIKID

Medical Effects of Alcohol 13 MIN
U-matic / VHS / 16mm
Color (A)
Shows the effects of alcohol on the human body over a period of years.
Health and Safety; Psychology; Sociology
Dist - EBEC **Prod** - MIFE 1984

Medical effects of alcohol use 12 MIN
VHS
Color (PRO A) (SPANISH)
$150.00 purchase _ #GN - 09
Explains the damaging effects of alcohol use in an objective and non - judgmental way. Explains how alcohol affects every area of the body including outward effects as well as the internal effects on organs such as fatty liver, esophageal tears, stomach ulcers and Central Nervous System disturbances. Describes typical withdrawal symptoms and explains how patients may not be aware that these symptoms relate to alcohol use. Cautions patients about the interaction of drugs like cold medicines with alcohol.
Guidance and Counseling; Health and Safety; Psychology
Dist - MIFE **Prod** - MIFE

Medical Effects of the Atomic Bomb, Pt 1 - Physics, Physical Destruction, Casualty 32 MIN
16mm
Color
LC FIE52-1730
Explains nuclear physics, fission and general reaction, thermal energy and mechanical force, nuclear radiation and ionizing effects. Portrays the physical destruction and casualty effects of atomic bombing.
Health and Safety; Science - Physical
Dist - USNAC **Prod** - USA 1950

Medical Emergencies in the Dental Office 25 MIN
16mm
Color (PRO)
LC 79-701697
Presents a series of simulated medical emergencies occurring in a dentist's office and explains the recommended management of these emergencies.
Health and Safety
Dist - USNAC **Prod** - NMAC 1979

The Medical Ethic 30 MIN
VHS / U-matic
Ethics in America Series
Color (H C A)
Presents Louis Lasagna, professor of medicine, and Robert M Veatch, senior associate at the Institute of Society, Ethics and the Life Sciences, outlining changing attitudes in medical ethics and decisions confronting the profession. Focuses on rights of patients, sustaining life in seemingly hopeless cases, use of placebos and doctor - patient relationships.
Health and Safety; Religion and Philosophy; Sociology
Dist - AMHUMA **Prod** - AMHUMA

Medical Ethics and Aging - Medicine as an Instrument of Social Control 30 MIN
VHS / U-matic
Color (PRO)
Shows four physicians in a conversation about medicine as an institution of social control. Raises moral, religious and ethical questions.
Health and Safety; Sociology
Dist - HSCIC **Prod** - HSCIC 1982

The Medical Examination of Your Eyes 13 MIN
U-matic / VHS / 16mm
Color (H C A) (SPANISH)
Discusses the benefits and techniques of regular ophthalmological examinations, explaining diagnostic procedures and possible treatments for several conditions.
Foreign Language; Health and Safety
Dist - JOU **Prod** - PRORE 1974

The Medical Examination of Your Eyes 13 MIN
U-matic / VHS / 16mm
Color (H C A)
Discusses the benefits and techniques of regular ophthalmological examinations, explaining diagnostic procedures and possible treatments for several conditions.
Health and Safety
Dist - JOU **Prod** - JOU 1974

Medical Experimentation - Informed Consent - Part 1 10 MIN
U-matic
Medical - Legal Issues - Observations Series
(A)
Deals with pertinent medical and legal issues in today's complex world of medicine. Co - produced by the Alberta Law Foundation.
Health and Safety; Sociology
Dist - ACCESS **Prod** - ACCESS 1984

Medical Experimentation - Informed Consent - Part 2 10 MIN
U-matic
Medical - Legal Issues - Observations Series
(A)
Deals with pertinent medical and legal issues in today's complex world of medicine. Co - produced by the Alberta Law Foundation.
Health and Safety; Sociology
Dist - ACCESS **Prod** - ACCESS 1984

Medical Experimentation - Informed Consent - Part 3 10 MIN
U-matic
Medical - Legal Issues - Observations Series
Deals with pertinent medical and legal issues in today's complex world of medicine. Co - produced by the Alberta Law Foundation.
Health and Safety; Sociology
Dist - ACCESS **Prod** - ACCESS 1984

Medical Facts for Pilots 25 MIN
16mm
Color
LC 74-705117
Provides a look at some of the fundamental physical, physiological and psychological limitations in flight. Alerts pilots to such aeromedical factors as disorientation, the effect of alcohol, oxygen requirements and pilot vision.
Health and Safety; Industrial and Technical Education; Psychology; Social Science
Dist - USFAA **Prod** - FAAFL 1970

Medical health aide
VHS
Day in a career series
Color (J H T G)
$89.00 purchase _ #VOC09V-J
Presents information about the occupation of medical health aide, of the careers that the United States Department of Labor projects as potentially successful by the year 2000. Profiles in detail the work day of a real person, with candid interviews and work situations and information about the educational requirements, credentials, job outlook, salaries, important associations, and contacts in the field. One of a series of ten videos, lasting 15 to 22 minutes, available individually or as a set.
Business and Economics; Guidance and Counseling; Science
Dist - CAMV

The Medical History 20 MIN
VHS / 16mm
(C)
$385.00 purchase _ #850VI129
Exposes the viewer to types of patients who impede the progress of the medical history interview. Includes nonverbal, hostile, seductive and overly verbal patients. Shows how to build a good relationship with both problem and non - problem patients in order to gather the fullest amount of information possible.
Health and Safety
Dist - HSCIC **Prod** - HSCIC 1985

The Medical History
VHS / U-matic
Color
Health and Safety; Psychology
Dist - MEDMDS **Prod** - MEDMDS

Medical home health aide 18 MIN
VHS
Get a life - a day in the career guidance series
Color (H C A)
$89.00 purchase _ #886696-11-X
Takes viewers through a day in the life of a medical home health aide, who explains why she entered the field, what it takes to be effective and what her plans for the future are. Show in-service classes, on-site nursing supervision and a typical day with the HHA and one of her patients. Notes that the training does not require a degree and the pay is moderate, yet this is a very important job with major responsibilities. Part of a ten-part series.
Business and Economics; Guidance and Counseling; Health and Safety
Dist - VOCAVD **Prod** - VOCAVD 1995

Medical home health aide
VHS
Day in a career series
Color (C H A)
$89.00 purchase _ #VOC09V-G
Presents one of a ten-part series of videocassettes featuring various careers with the highest potential for success in the years before 2000. Profiles the detailed workday of a real person, with interviews and work situations. Includes information about educational requirements, credentials, job outlook, salaries, and important associations and contacts. Each program 15 to 22 minutes in length.
Business and Economics; Guidance and Counseling; Science
Dist - CAMV

Medical housekeeping series
Basics of carpet care 22 MIN
Basics of floor care - Part one 17 MIN
Basics of Floor Care (Part 2) 17.25 MIN
Custodial safety 15 MIN
Institutional Restroom Cleaning 20.5 MIN
Introduction to housekeeping 14 MIN
Isolation Room Cleaning 13.25 MIN
Kitchen Sanitation 16 MIN
Lawn Care 16.25 MIN
Lawn Care (Part 2) 19.3 MIN
Operating room cleaning 14 MIN
Patient Room Cleaning 13.5
Shower and locker room 14 MIN
Dist - CTT

The Medical Interview 13 MIN
U-matic
Patient Interview - Science or Art Series
Color (PRO)
Presents a complete medical interview of a new patient by the chief medical resident of the Larue Carter Hospital in Indianapolis.
Health and Safety; Psychology
Dist - PRIMED **Prod** - PRIMED

Medical joinery 30 MIN
VHS
Perspective 10 series
Color; PAL; NTSC (G)
PdS90, PdS105 purchase
Shows how a baby born with a disfigured face defect is restored to normality within days of birth. Looks at how a man's face, deformed by cancer, is reconstructed to allow him to face the world again. Rebuilding faces damaged by accident or disease combines the skills of surgeons and computer scientists.
Health and Safety
Dist - CFLVIS **Prod** - LONTVS 1993

Medical Lab Technician 15 MIN
VHS / 16mm
(H C A)
$24.95 purchase _ #CS159
Describes the skills involved in being a medical lab technician. Features interviews with people working in the field.
Guidance and Counseling
Dist - RMIBHF **Prod** - RMIBHF

Medical Laboratory Technician 17 MIN
16mm
Color
LC 77-703726
Describes the U S Navy's training program for medical laboratory technicians. Discusses classroom and on - the - job training in various branches, admission requirements, length of the course and career opportunities.
Civics and Political Systems; Guidance and Counseling; Psychology; Science
Dist - USNAC **Prod** - USN 1974

Medical Laboratory Technician 15 MIN
BETA / VHS / U-matic
Career Success Series
(H C A)
$29.95 _ #MX159
Portrays occupations in medical laboratory technics by reviewing required abilities and interviewing people employed in this field. Shows anxieties and rewards involved in pursuing a career as a medical lab technician.
Education; Guidance and Counseling; Health and Safety; Science
Dist - CAMV **Prod** - CAMV

Medical Laboratory Techniques Series
Serological Technique - Venipuncture 7 MIN
Dist - USNAC

Medical Laboratory Technology
VHS / U-matic
$24.95 purchase
Science
Dist - BEEKMN **Prod** - BEEKMN 1988

Medical Legal Aspects of Amniocentesis for Prenatal Diagnosis 13 MIN
U-matic / VHS / 16mm
Color
Discusses the legal aspects of amniocentesis that physicians need to be aware of.
Civics and Political Systems; Health and Safety
Dist - USNAC **Prod** - USHHS

Medical - Legal Aspects of Amniocentesis for Prenatal Diagnosis 13 MIN
16mm
Color (PRO)
LC 79-700987
Discusses some of the legal aspects of amniocentesis.
Civics and Political Systems; Health and Safety
Dist - USNAC **Prod** - NMAC 1979

Medical Legal Implications in the Management of Benign and Malignant Breast Disease 37 MIN
VHS / 16mm
(C)
$385.00 purchase _ #850VI051
Presents the medical ethical, and legal implications of managing breast cancer. Emphasizes careful discussion of available alternatives with the patient and recordkeeping that documents that thoughtful process leading to clinical decisions.
Health and Safety
Dist - HSCIC **Prod** - HSCIC 1985

Medical - Legal Issues - Observations Series
Abortion 10 MIN
Contraception 7 MIN
The Definition of death 9 MIN
The Deformed neonate 10 MIN
The Dying Patient 14 MIN
Experimentation on the Voiceless - 10 MIN

the Child
Experimentation on the Voiceless - the Mentally Incompetent 11 MIN
Informed Consent - the Full Disclosure of Risks 11 MIN
Informed Consent - the Physician's Point of View 10 MIN
Malpractice - Pt 1 8 MIN
Malpractice - Pt 5 - Compensation 11 MIN
Malpractice - Pt 4 - the American Influence 8 MIN
Malpractice - Pt 6 - Hospital Responsibilities 7 MIN
Malpractice - Pt 3 - the Canadian Medical Protective Association 12 MIN
Malpractice - Pt 2 - Standard of Care 12 MIN
Medical Experimentation - Informed Consent - Part 1 10 MIN
Medical Experimentation - Informed Consent - Part 2 10 MIN
Medical Experimentation - Informed Consent - Part 3 10 MIN
Medical Research - Means and Criteria 15 MIN
Medical Research - Regulation 15 MIN
The No Code 10 MIN
The Right to Refuse Treatment 14 MIN
Sterlization 10 MIN
Sterlization - the Mentally Handicapped 10 MIN
Dist - ACCESS

Medical - Legal Issues Series
Death and dying 30 MIN
Experimentation 30 MIN
Informed Consent 30 MIN
Negligence and Error 30 MIN
Reproduction 30 MIN
Resource Allocation 30 MIN
Rights and Responsibilities 30 MIN
The Voiceless 30 MIN
Dist - ACCESS

Medical malpractice - home repairs - car rental
U-matic / VHS
Consumer survival series
Color
Discusses various aspects of medical malpractice, home repair and car rentals.
Civics and Political Systems; Health and Safety; Home Economics
Dist - MDCPB **Prod** - MDCPB

Medical malpractice litigation - new strategies for a new era series 361 MIN
Cassette
Medical malpractice litigation - new strategies for a new era series
Color (PRO)
$595.00, $150.00 purchase, $300.00 rental _ #MED2-000, #AME2-000
Offers a seven - part series that discusses and demonstrates innovative litigation strategies and techniques developed in response to the rapidly changing climate in which medical malpractice cases are litigated. Covers case evaluation, pretrial and trial strategies, jury selection, opening statements and expert witnesses. Includes demonstrations by skilled trial lawyers, interviews of those conducting the demonstrations and panel discussions. Includes study guides.
Civics and Political Systems
Dist - AMBAR **Prod** - AMBAR 1987

Medical malpractice - the physician as witness 35 MIN
U-matic / VHS
Color (PRO)
$385.00 purchase _ #840VI079
Portrays a physician in two roles - the first involving professional negligence, the second involves physician as a witness in a malpractice case.
Business and Economics; Civics and Political Systems; Health and Safety
Dist - HSCIC **Prod** - HSCIC 1984

Medical management of kidney stones 10 MIN
VHS
Color (PRO A G)
$250.00 purchase _ #UR - 03
Explains the basic methods of medical management - hydration, alkalinization, diet modification and medication. Discusses stone development and reviews the common symptoms. Emphasizes that compliance with diet, fluid intake and medication is essential for life - long management. Developed in cooperation with and endorsed by the American Urological Association.
Science - Natural
Dist - MIFE **Prod** - MIFE

Medical Management of Spinal Spasticity 22 MIN
16mm
Color (PRO)
Shows examinations, case histories, treatment and a discussion on the pathophysiology of spasticity caused by spinal cord lesions.
Health and Safety
Dist - GEIGY **Prod** - GEIGY

Medical Management of the Hypertensive Patient 16 MIN
U-matic / VHS
Color (PRO)
Presents two methods of patient management which may be used when antihypertensive therapy is indicated. Covers the elements of both techniques and methods to ensure patient compliance with prescribed therapies.
Health and Safety; Science - Natural
Dist - UMICHM **Prod** - UMICHM 1981

Medical Management of the Sexually Abused Child 24 MIN
VHS / U-matic
Color (PRO)
Provides medical information to professionals who may be called on to deal with sexually abused children.
Health and Safety; Psychology; Sociology
Dist - HSCIC **Prod** - HSCIC 1984

Medical Management - Role of the Nurse in Establishing a Diagnosis 40 MIN
U-matic
Critical Care Nursing - Acutely Ill Patients with Coronary Artery 'Disease Series
Color (PRO)
LC 79-706224
Illustrates the risk factors associated with coronary artery disease. Demonstrates complete cardiac assessment, including ausculation of heart sounds and evaluation of pulses, EKG'S and chest X - rays. Discusses indication for Swan - Ganz catheter, use of medications and interprofessional relationships between nursing and medical staff.
Health and Safety
Dist - USNAC **Prod** - AJN 1978

Medical - Moral - Legal Issues 44 MIN
16mm
Nursing and the Law Series
B&W
LC 79-703370
A physician, a priest and a layer discuss organ transplants, abortion, sterilization and the maintenance of life in terminal illness.
Civics and Political Systems; Health and Safety; Religion and Philosophy; Sociology
Dist - AJN **Prod** - VDONUR 1968

Medical Office Instruments 26 MIN
BETA / VHS
Color
Discusses instruments used in a physician's office.
Health and Safety
Dist - RMIBHF **Prod** - RMIBHF

Medical personnel 14 MIN
U-matic / VHS
Tax tips on tape series
Color; Captioned (A PRO IND)
$20.00, $40.00 purchase _ #TCA17628, #TCA17627
Covers tax law for medical personnel. Focuses on the deductibility of using part of a home as an office, as well as of travel expenses for trips to professional meetings.
Business and Economics; Civics and Political Systems; Social Science
Dist - USNAC **Prod** - USIRS 1988

Medical Potential of Lasers 21 MIN
16mm
Upjohn Vanguard of Medicine Series
Color (PRO)
LC 76-713212
Explains and demonstrates the potential of lasers in experimental medicine and surgery, in microbiology, and in analytic and diagnostic procedures.
Health and Safety; Science
Dist - UPJOHN **Prod** - UPJOHN 1971

Medical Problems 30 MIN
VHS / U-matic
Teaching Students with Special Needs Series
Color
Features a discussion of the impact of medical problems on the educational performance of special - needs students and chronic problems teachers should be aware of it.
Health and Safety
Dist - PBS **Prod** - MSITV 1981

Medical problems associated with alcoholism
VHS
Color (J H C G A PRO)
$79.50 purchase _ #AH46302
Uses medical photography and art to demonstrate the medical damage caused by alcoholism. Explains causes, treatments and prevention strategies.
Guidance and Counseling; Health and Safety; Psychology; Science - Natural; Sociology
Dist - HTHED **Prod** - HTHED

Medical Problems of the Addict 35 MIN
16mm
Films and Tapes for Drug Abuse Treatment Personnel Series
Color (PRO)
LC 73-702454
Covers a range of medical problems presented by addicts and drug abusers. Discusses the medical techniques for withdrawing an individual from opiates and barbiturates. Includes the drug abuser as a patient, serum hepatitis and other infections, respiratory problems, anemia, abscesses, skin lesions, tetanus and endocarditis.
Education; Health and Safety; Psychology; Sociology
Dist - NIMH **Prod** - NIMH 1973

The Medical record profession - No 9 28 MIN
VHS / U-matic
Career encounters series
Color (H C)
$110.00, $95.00 purchase
Addresses the potential for growth within the medical records profession. Shows how medical record professionals process, manage and disseminate the information critical to patient care and enable physicians, nurses, technicians and other health care workers to communicate in an accurate and expedient way. Defines the educational requirements for the field.
Business and Economics; Computer Science; Guidance and Counseling; Psychology; Science
Dist - PLEXPU **Prod** - PLEXPU 1990

Medical Records
VHS / U-matic
Work - a - Day America
$59.95 purchase _ #VV115V
Helps students achieve career vocational preparation. Stresses the four main points of career awareness and exploration, specific skills intended, employability skills needed, and real people sharing on the job experiences.
Guidance and Counseling
Dist - CAREER **Prod** - CAREER

Medical Records - Written Link to Patient Care 11 MIN
U-matic
Color
Describes the functions of the University of Texas MD Anderson's Dept of Medical Records.
Health and Safety
Dist - UTEXSC **Prod** - UTEXSC

Medical Research - Means and Criteria 15 MIN
U-matic
Medical - Legal Issues - Observations Series
(A)
Deals with pertinent medical and legal issues in today's complex world of medicine. Co - produced by the Alberta Law Foundation.
Health and Safety; Sociology
Dist - ACCESS **Prod** - ACCESS 1984

Medical Research - Regulation 15 MIN
U-matic
Medical - Legal Issues - Observations Series
(A)
Deals with pertinent medical and legal issues in today's complex world of medicine. Co - produced by the Alberta Law Foundation.
Health and Safety; Sociology
Dist - ACCESS **Prod** - ACCESS 1984

Medical Residency Training at Wilford Hall USAF Hospital 21 MIN
16mm
Color
LC 74-706141
Cites the USAF Hospital, Wilford Hall, for the quality of its professional care, contributions to clinical medicine and support of orbital space flights. Describes 11 residence programs, fellowships and other educational opportunities for physicians and surgeons.
Health and Safety
Dist - USNAC **Prod** - USAF 1965

Medical Risk Management - Plan for Action 31 MIN
U-matic / VHS
Color
Stresses that hospitals that do not learn from their mistakes are destined to repeat them. Describes how a liability control system works and shows a typical system in action.
Civics and Political Systems; Health and Safety
Dist - TEACHM **Prod** - TEACHM

Medical robots 30 MIN
VHS
Perspective 10 series
Color; PAL; NTSC (G)
PdS90, PdS105 purchase
Looks at a machine that can set the path of probes into the brain. Reveals that it is one of a series of robots helping surgeons in the operating theater. Designers are also working on a robot to guide the surgeons's drill in operations to repair broken thigh bones, and another to perform prostate removals. Examines the implications for doctor and patient alike.
Computer Science; Health and Safety
Dist - CFLVIS **Prod** - LONTVS 1993

The Medical School and the Community - How are they Related 29 MIN
16mm
Concepts and Controversies in Modern Medicine Series
B&W (PRO)
LC 74-705118
Emphasizes that the function of medicine involves community health at all levels and that good medical care depends upon further development of excellence at the medical schools.
Health and Safety
Dist - NMAC **Prod** - NMAC 1969

Medical Sciences - Dentistry
VHS
Video Career Series
$29.95 purchase _ #MD210V
Shows students going on the job to learn the variety of skills required for this occupation and the special training or educational requirements. Discusses various hiring procedures and what is involved in joining a professional association or union.
Education; Guidance and Counseling
Dist - CAREER **Prod** - CAREER

Medical Sciences - Medicine
VHS
Video Career Series
$29.95 purchase _ #MD211V
Shows students going on the job to learn the variety of skills required for this occupation and the special training or educational requirements. Discusses various hiring procedures and what is involved in joining a professional association or union.
Education; Guidance and Counseling
Dist - CAREER **Prod** - CAREER

Medical Sciences - Optometry
VHS
Video Career Series
$29.95 purchase _ #MD212V
Shows students going on the job to learn the variety of skills required for this occupation and the special training or educational requirements. Discusses various hiring procedures and what is involved in joining a professional association or union.
Education; Guidance and Counseling
Dist - CAREER **Prod** - CAREER

Medical Sciences - Pharmacy
VHS
Video Career Series
$29.95 purchase _ #MD213V
Shows students going 'on the job' to learn the variety of skills required for this occupation and the special training or educational requirements. Discusses various hiring procedures and what is involved in joining a professional association or union.
Education; Guidance and Counseling
Dist - CAREER **Prod** - CAREER

Medical self - help series
Artificial Respiration 16 MIN
Bleeding and Bandaging 28 MIN
Burns 14 MIN
Emergency childbirth 28 MIN
Fractures and Splinting 28 MIN
Healthful Living in Emergencies 28 MIN
Infant and Child Care 14 MIN
Nursing Care of the Sick and Injured 28 MIN
Radioactive fallout and shelter 28 MIN
Shock 14 MIN
Transportation of the injured 14 MIN
Dist - USNAC

Medical Skills Films Series
Arterial Puncture 9 MIN
Cardiac arrest and defibillation 9 MIN
Central Venous Pressure Measurement 9 MIN
Emergency Nasal Packing 9 MIN
External cardiac compression 9 MIN
Gastric Lavage 9 MIN
Intermittent Pressure Breathing 9 MIN
Intravenous Techniques - Infusion 9 MIN
Local Infiltration Anesthesia 9 MIN
Lumbar Puncture 4 MIN
Manual Positive Pressure Ventilation 9 MIN
Nasogastric Intubation 9 MIN
Paracentesis (Abdominal) 9 MIN
Proctosigmoidoscopy 9 MIN
Removal of a Superficial Foreign Body from the Eye 9 MIN
Thoracentesis 9 MIN
Tracheostomy 9 MIN
Urethral Catheterization 9 MIN
Veni - Puncture 9 MIN
Ventricular Defibrillation 9 MIN
Dist - WFP

Medical Skills Library Series
Endotracheal Intubation 9 MIN
Gastric Lavage 14 MIN
Tonometry 9 MIN
Venous Cutdown 9 MIN
Dist - SUTHLA

Medical Supply System, U S Army, Pt 1 - Organization and Administration 24 MIN
16mm
B&W
LC 74-705120
Describes the mission and operational relationship of the major organizations within the Medical Supply System.
Civics and Political Systems; Health and Safety
Dist - USNAC **Prod** - USA 1967

Medical Supply System, U S Army, Pt 2 - Operations at Conus and Overseas Installations 22 MIN
16mm
B&W
LC 74-705119
Demonstrates Medical Supply operations at a typical depot in CONUS (Ft Knox.).
Civics and Political Systems; Health and Safety
Dist - USNAC **Prod** - USA 1967

Medical Technology 26 MIN
U-matic / VHS
Color (I J H A)
Introduces the Aboriginals, the first people to inhabit the island continent of Australia, and recreates the coming of Europeans, convicts and their guards from England.
Geography - World
Dist - NGS **Prod** - NGS

Medical Terminology - Adjectival Endings 16 MIN
BETA / VHS
Color (PRO)
$76.00 purchase _ #KHO107
Health and Safety
Dist - RMIBHF **Prod** - RMIBHF

Medical Terminology - Five Basic Rules 21 MIN
BETA / VHS
Color (PRO)
$88.50 purchase _ #KHO104
Reviews the five rules for forming and identifying medical terms.
Health and Safety
Dist - RMIBHF **Prod** - RMIBHF

Medical Terminology - Prefixes 19 MIN
BETA / VHS / 16mm
Color (PRO)
$83.50 purchase _ #KHO106
Discusses prefixes used in medical terminology.
Health and Safety
Dist - RMIBHF **Prod** - RMIBHF

Medical Terminology Series
Introduction to Medical Terminology 20 MIN
Pronunciation of Medical Terminology 15 MIN
Spelling Medical Terminology 18 MIN
Dist - HSCIC

Medical Terminology - Suffixes 7 MIN
BETA / VHS / 16mm
Color (PRO)
$53.50 purchase _ #KHO105
Discusses suffixes used in medical terminology.
Health and Safety
Dist - RMIBHF **Prod** - RMIBHF

Medical Terminology - Verbal Derivatives 15 MIN
VHS / BETA / 16mm
Color (PRO)
$73.50 purchase _ #KHO108
Discusses verbal derivatives used in medical terminology.
Health and Safety
Dist - RMIBHF **Prod** - RMIBHF

Medical Terminology - Word Roots 17 MIN
BETA / VHS
Color (PRO)
$78.50 purchase _ #KHO109
Health and Safety
Dist - RMIBHF **Prod** - RMIBHF

Medical Terminology - Word Roots II 21 MIN
BETA / VHS
Color (PRO)
$88.50 purchase _ #KHO110
Health and Safety
Dist - RMIBHF **Prod** - RMIBHF

Medical Tests 30 MIN
U-matic / VHS
Here's to Your Health Series
Color (C T)
Reviews medical testing. Takes away some of the mystique surrounding medical testing. Encourages people to recognize their right to be an active participant during medical testing.
Health and Safety; Science
Dist - DALCCD **Prod** - DALCCD

Medical Transcribing 8 MIN
VHS / BETA
Typing - Medical Series
Color
Business and Economics; Health and Safety
Dist - RMIBHF **Prod** - RMIBHF

Medical Treatment of Headache 45 MIN
VHS / 16mm
(C)
$385.00 purchase _ $850VI064
Covers the diagnosis and treatment of functional headache, and the management of headache symptoms in the presence of a number of possible etiologies such as brain tumor, neck muscle spasm, and sinusitis.
Health and Safety
Dist - HSCIC **Prod** - HSCIC 1985

Medical Typing - Consultation Report 4 MIN
BETA / VHS
Typing - Medical Series
Color
Business and Economics; Health and Safety
Dist - RMIBHF **Prod** - RMIBHF

Medical Typing - Discharge Summary or Clinical Resume 6 MIN
BETA / VHS
Typing - Medical Series
Color
Business and Economics; Health and Safety
Dist - RMIBHF **Prod** - RMIBHF

Medical Typing - Electroencephalogram 6 MIN
VHS / BETA
Typing - Medical Series
Color
Business and Economics; Health and Safety
Dist - RMIBHF **Prod** - RMIBHF

Medical Typing - Filing Rules 10 MIN
VHS / BETA
Typing - Medical Series
Color
Business and Economics; Health and Safety
Dist - RMIBHF **Prod** - RMIBHF

Medical Typing - History and Physical 12 MIN
BETA / VHS
Typing - Medical Series
Color
Business and Economics; Health and Safety
Dist - RMIBHF **Prod** - RMIBHF

Medical Typing - Introduction 6 MIN
BETA / VHS
Typing - Medical Series
Color
Business and Economics; Health and Safety
Dist - RMIBHF **Prod** - RMIBHF

Medical Typing - Laboratory 17 MIN
BETA / VHS
Typing - Medical Series
Color
Business and Economics; Health and Safety
Dist - RMIBHF **Prod** - RMIBHF

Medical Typing - Medical Records 12 MIN
BETA / VHS
Typing - Medical Series
Color
Business and Economics; Health and Safety
Dist - RMIBHF **Prod** - RMIBHF

Medical Typing - Operative Report 4 MIN
VHS / BETA
Typing - Medical Series
Color
Business and Economics; Health and Safety
Dist - RMIBHF **Prod** - RMIBHF

Medical Typing - Radiology 16 MIN
VHS / BETA
Typing - Medical Series
Color

Business and Economics; Health and Safety
Dist - RMIBHF Prod - RMIBHF

A Medical view 30 MIN
VHS
Color (PRO)
$195.00 purchase _ #2929
Features a training program for medical professionals by Astrid Heger. Teaches accurate diagnosing of child sexual abuse, how to conduct sensitive, nontraumatic interviews and how to successfully deal with the legal system. Produced by Children's Institute International. Includes a syllabus.
Health and Safety; Psychology
Dist - GFORD

The Medical Witness 35 MIN
16mm
We Can Help Series
Color (PRO)
LC 77-703246
Dramatizes a physician's experience in preparing for and testifying in court on a child abuse case. Enumerates important do's and don'ts in testifying.
Home Economics; Sociology
Dist - USNAC Prod - NCCAN 1977

The Medical Witness and Juvenile Court 35 MIN
U-matic / VHS
Color (PRO)
Focuses on a mock contested child - dependency hearing to familiarize expert medical witnesses with courtroom formalities.
Civics and Political Systems; Health and Safety
Dist - UARIZ Prod - UARIZ

Medicare Patient Classification - Assigning DRGs 32 MIN
U-matic / VHS
Color
Stresses the need of a basic understanding of the new Medicare payment system. Features in - depth interviews with staff members of a New Jersey hospital where a cost - based reimbursement plan has been instituted. Helps staff understand the structure of DRG's, the importance of the patient's principal diagnosis and recording of secondary diagnoses in assuring proper payment to the hospital as well as the effects of case - mix load on financial viability.
Business and Economics; Health and Safety
Dist - AHOA Prod - AHOA

The Medicated generation 28 MIN
VHS
Color (G C PRO)
$400.00 purchase, $100.00 rental
Documents questions aged patients have about the medicines that are prescribed for them.
Health and Safety
Dist - TNF

The Medicated Generation - Medication 56 MIN
VHS / U-matic
Color
Addresses the special concerns of the elderly in medication management and the responsibilities of health professionals to support the elderly by communicating information and caring.
Health and Safety
Dist - UMDSM Prod - UMDSM

Medicated Society Series no 1
Drugs through the Ages 60 MIN
Dist - NMAC

Medicated Society Series no 6
The Drug Approach to Mental Illness 60 MIN
Dist - NMAC

Medicated Society Series no 7
Experimental Design of Anti - Cancer Agents 60 MIN
Dist - NMAC

Medicated Society Series no 8
Drugs in Prevention of Heart Attacks 60 MIN
Dist - NMAC

Medicated Society Series no 9
Diseases Due to Drug Treatment 60 MIN
Dist - NMAC

Medicated society series
The Effects of drugs on the unborn child 60 MIN
Dist - NMAC

Medicating Children 23 MIN
VHS / U-matic
Color
Presents important information for nursing students and nurses about administering medications to children of various ages. Presents general considerations and details related to all routes of medication administration, safety factors in calculation and administration, and comfort measures.
Health and Safety
Dist - AJN Prod - UNCN

Medicating the elderly 28 MIN
VHS / U-matic
Color (PRO)
$275.00 purchase, $60.00 rental _ #7508S, #7508V
Stresses the need for a careful drug history and using the fewest drugs and smallest doses possible for elderly patients. Reveals that elderly confusion may be drug induced. Discusses patient education on safety and drug purposes. Considers the special problems of the elderly - greater use of medication, physiological changes and decreased ability to deal with stress. Looks at balancing a drug's therapeutic effects with its risks.
Health and Safety
Dist - AJN Prod - HOSSN 1985

Medicating the Geratric Patient 24 MIN
VHS / 16mm
Color (PRO)
$295.00 purchase, $60.00 rental
Discusses how drug metabolism is affected in the presence of liver disease, decreased cardiac output, urinary retention and or constipation. Covers symptoms which suggest an adverse reaction to medication, plus content related to various drug groups.
Health and Safety
Dist - FAIRGH Prod - FAIRGH 1986

Medication administration - Module I
Videodisc
Color (C PRO)
$995.00 purchase _ #J22205, #J22203
Covers oral, topical and parenteral medication administration. Uses audio, full motion video and graphics to tutor on site selection and injection techniques for intradermal, subcutaneous, intramuscular and Z - track injections. Shows the types of needles and syringes. Informs on factors to consider when making a selection. Overviews aseptic technique, proper handling of vials and ampules. Demonstrates mixing medications in a syringe. Provides guidelines for administering oral medications, eye and ear drops, pastes, ointments and creams and positioning, considerations for pediatric and geriatric patients. Level III interactive, 5.25 or 3.5 diskettes, part of a series. Produced by Thomas Jefferson University. Ask AJN about hardware requirements.
Health and Safety
Dist - AJN

Medication and safety 13 MIN
VHS
Color (IND)
$250.00 purchase, $95.00 rental _ #BBP201
Addresses the issue of over - the - counter and prescription drug use on the job. Includes a leader's guide.
Health and Safety
Dist - EXTR Prod - BBP

Medication Errors 28 MIN
VHS / U-matic
Color
Examines the types of medication errors that occur most often in hospitals today - vignettes focus on these errors (wrong drug, patient, dosage, time, or route). Recommends procedures for avoiding medication errors and stresses the importance of patient feedback.
Health and Safety
Dist - PSU Prod - PSU 1984

The Medication history interview 122 MIN
U-matic / VHS
Color (PRO)
Teaches students how to take accurate medication history. Treats drug use, reactions, compliance, open - ended and closed questions, non verbals, anxiety, and reassurance. Includes 15 min audiocassette and 125 page paperback.
Health and Safety
Dist - HSCIC Prod - HSCIC 1981

Medication use by the elderly - implications for nurses 30 MIN
VHS
Color (C PRO)
$285.00 purchase, $70.00 rental _ #4329S, #4329V
Shows a variety of elderly clients in various community settings and a nurse practitioner who elicits a drug history from an elderly client. Illustrates proper procedures in taking the history, how physiological aging affects drug absorption, distribution, metabolism and excretion, and covers principles of prescribing for the elderly. Addresses drug interactions and food - drug interaction as well as certain problematic drugs for the elderly.
Health and Safety
Dist - AJN Prod - BELHAN

Medications administration and absorption series
Presents five video programs and a software simulation program on medications administration and absorption. Includes the video titles Oral Medications Administration; Administration and Absorption of Parenteral Medications; Administration and Absorption of Topical Medications; Administration of Intravenous Medications; Venipuncture Technique; and Medications Mediadisks, IBM - compatible software.
Administration and absorption of parenteral medications 28 MIN
Administration and absorption of topical medications 24 MIN
Administration of intravenous medications 22 MIN
Oral medication administration 23 MIN
Venipuncture technique 22 MIN
Dist - CONMED

Medications and elders - a delicate balance 33 MIN
VHS
Color (G PRO)
$165.00 purchase, $55.00 rental
Explains that older patients' bodies handle medications differently so that prescribing drugs must be done with care. Emphasizes drug choices that work best for elderly patients for various conditions. For professional education.
Health and Safety
Dist - TNF

Medications and You - a Special Report 13 MIN
VHS / U-matic
Color
Encourages patients to ask questions and accept responsibility for caring for themselves. Answers typical questions regarding prescription medications.
Health and Safety
Dist - UARIZ Prod - UARIZ

Medications - Avoiding Errors
U-matic / VHS
Color
Illustrates the types of medication errors, the steps in medication administration which reduce opportunity for error and other measures designed to prevent medication error.
Health and Safety
Dist - FAIRGH Prod - FAIRGH

Medications - to Feel Your Best 9 MIN
U-matic
Diabetes Care at Home Series
(A)
Outlines techniques used at home in the preparation, administration and storage of different types of insulin and oral medications.
Health and Safety
Dist - ACCESS Prod - ACCESS 1983

The Medici and Palazzo Vecchio - the Florentine Republic and ducal Florence 50 MIN
VHS
Trecanni video library series
Color (G)
$39.95 purchase
Tours the Palazzo Vecchio built during the 1300s and transformed later into a royal fortress by Cosimo I de'Medici. Part of a four - part series on Italian culture produced by Treccani Publishers and RAI, Italian broadcast network.
Fine Arts; History - World
Dist - CREPRI

The Medici and Palazzo Vecchio - The Florentine republic and ducal Florence 60 MIN
VHS
Treccani Italian Renaissance art series
Color (H C A)
$39.95 purchase
Chronicles the history of the palazzo Vecchio and diagrams its building plan. Shows its rooms and displays their decoration over two centuries of occupation.
Fine Arts; History - World
Dist - ARTSAM

The Medici and the library - manuscripts and printed books in Renaissance Florence 50 MIN
VHS
Trecanni video library series
Color (G)
$29.95 purchase
Tours the Laurentian Library in Florence, Italy. Tells stories of the great bibliophiles Cosimo the Elder and Lorenzo the Magnificent and the expert scribes they employed. Shows the beautiful books and manuscripts created by these masters. Part of a four - part series on Italian culture produced by Treccani Publishers and RAI, Italian broadcast network.
History - World; Literature and Drama; Social Science
Dist - CREPRI

The Medici and the library - Manuscripts and printed books in Renaissance Florence 30 MIN
VHS
Treccani Italian Renaissance art series
Color (H C A)
$29.95 purchase
Tours the Laurentian Library in Florence. Tells of the bibliophiles Cosimo the Elder and Lorenzo the Magnificent and the scribes they employed and shows the books and manuscripts they produced.
Fine Arts; History - World; Industrial and Technical Education; Social Science
Dist - ARTSAM

Medicinal Drug Development at the Walter Reed Army Institute of Research 19 MIN
16mm
Color (PRO)
LC 79-710663
Describes the search for new drugs for the prevention and treatment of drug - resistant Plasmodium falciparum malaria. Outlines the drug development program at Walter Reed Army Institute of Research which uses a computerized chemical information system to track over 350,000 medicinal chemicals through selection, testing, approval by the Federal Drug Administration, and clinical trials around the world.
Health and Safety
Dist - USNAC **Prod** - WRAIR 1979

Medicine 15 MIN
BETA / VHS / U-matic
Career Success Series
(H C A)
#MX211
Portrays occupations in medicine by reviewing required abilities and interviewing people employed in this field. Shows anxieties and rewards involved in pursuing a career as a doctor.
Education; Guidance and Counseling; Health and Safety; Science
Dist - CAMV **Prod** - CAMV

Medicine 15 MIN
VHS / U-matic
Watch Your Language Series
Color (J H)
$125.00 purchase
Highlights the use of medical terms and the language structure involved.
English Language; Social Science
Dist - AITECH **Prod** - KYTV 1984

Medicine 23 MIN
VHS
Bright sparks series
Color (P I)
$280.00 purchase
Explores modern medical advances. Part of a 12 - part animated series on science and technology.
Health and Safety
Dist - LANDMK **Prod** - LANDMK 1989

Medicine
VHS / U-matic
Career Builders Video Series
$95.00 purchase _ #ED107V
Uses actual professionals to talk about the job's demands, rewards, and frustrations. Shows the working environment of the career field.
Guidance and Counseling
Dist - CAREER **Prod** - CAREER

Medicine 29 MIN
VHS / 16mm
Discovery Digest Series
Color (S)
$300.00 purchase _ #707618
Explores a vast array of science - related discoveries, challenges and technological breakthroughs. Profiles and 'demystifies' research and development currently underway in many fields. 'Medicine' scrutinizes artificial knees, a TENS unit which blocks pain, biofeedback to reduce aches and pains and a profile of geneticist Dr Bob Church.
Health and Safety; Psychology; Science
Dist - ACCESS **Prod** - ACCESS 1989

Medicine 15 MIN
VHS / 16mm
(H C A)
$24.95 purchase _ #CS211
Describes the skills necessary to go into the field of medicine. Features interviews with people working in the field.
Guidance and Counseling
Dist - RMIBHF **Prod** - RMIBHF

Medicine 24 MIN
VHS / 16mm
Career Builders Video Series
Color
$85.00 purchase _ #V107
Examines a potential career choice by taking the viewer into the working environment and interviewing professionals on the demands, rewards and frustrations on the job.
Business and Economics; Health and Safety; Sociology
Dist - EDUCDE **Prod** - EDUCDE 1987

Medicine and Mercy 26 MIN
U-matic / VHS
Color (C)
$249.00, $149.00 purchase _ #AD - 1924
Considers the interplay between technology, ethics and the quality of human life, the definition of life and death and the thesis that humans have a right to die. Looks at two important court decisions pertaining to the cessation of artificial life - support systems. Examines the legal and ethical arguments on both sides of the issue.
Civics and Political Systems; Health and Safety; Religion and Philosophy; Sociology
Dist - FOTH **Prod** - FOTH

Medicine and Mercy - 120 30 MIN
U-matic
Currents - 1984 - 85 Season Series
Color (A)
Focuses on mercy care and mercy death by today's medical profession.
Health and Safety; Social Science; Sociology
Dist - PBS **Prod** - WNETTV 1985

Medicine and Money 48 MIN
16mm / U-matic / VHS
Color (H C A)
LC 77-701514
Investigates the factors which have turned the practice of medicine into an industry. Discusses problems connected with federally funded programs such as Medicare and Medicaid and focuses on the lack of accountability for both quality and cost of health care.
Social Science
Dist - MGHT **Prod** - ABCF 1976

Medicine and Money, Pt 1 24 MIN
U-matic / VHS / 16mm
Color (H C A)
LC 77-701514
Investigates the factors which have turned the practice of medicine into an industry. Discusses problems connected with federally funded programs such as Medicare and Medicaid and focuses on the lack of accountability for both the quality and cost of health care.
Business and Economics; Health and Safety; Social Science
Dist - MGHT **Prod** - ABCF 1976

Medicine and Money, Pt 2 24 MIN
U-matic / VHS / 16mm
Color (H C A)
LC 77-701514
Investigates the factors which have turned the practice of medicine into an industry. Discusses problems connected with federally funded programs such as Medicare and Medicaid and focuses on the lack of accountability for both the quality and cost of health care.
Business and Economics; Health and Safety; Social Science
Dist - MGHT **Prod** - ABCF 1976

Medicine and Related Fields 30 MIN
VHS / 16mm
Video Career Library Series
Color (H C A PRO)
$79.95 purchase _ #WW105
Shows occupations in medicine and related fields such as physicians, dentists, veterinarians, optometrists, registered nurses, pharmacists, chiropractors, physician's assistants and others. Contains current occupational outlook and salary information.
Business and Economics; Guidance and Counseling; Health and Safety
Dist - AAVIM **Prod** - AAVIM 1990

Medicine and Related Fields 30 MIN
VHS / U-matic
Video Career Library Series
(H C A)
$69.95 _ #CJ115V
Covers duties, conditions, salaries and training connected with jobs in the medicine field. Provides a view of employees in various medicine related occupations, and gives information concerning the current market for such skills. Revised every two years.
Guidance and Counseling; Health and Safety
Dist - CAMV **Prod** - CAMV

Medicine and the Physician in Western Civilization - the Seventeenth and 23 MIN
16mm
Color
Details the changing role and image of the physician and other health practitioners in the 17th and 18th centuries. Discusses medical education, approaches to disease, the care of the insane and the poor, and major figures and discoveries of this period.
Health and Safety; Science
Dist - USC **Prod** - USC 1980

Medicine Behind Bars 29 MIN
U-matic
Color
Examines the quality of health care behind bars. Features interviews with inmates at Jackson State Prison.
Health and Safety; Sociology
Dist - UMITV **Prod** - UMITV 1977

Medicine, Drugs and You - a First Film 12 MIN
U-matic / VHS / 16mm
Color (P I J)
Discusses safe, intelligent use of substances which may help or harm us depending on our attitudes. Tells how drugs are found, how pharmacists do their work, proper usage and the differences between drugs.
Health and Safety
Dist - PHENIX **Prod** - BRUNOS 1983

Medicine fiddle 81 MIN
VHS
Color (H C G)
$295.00 purchase, $60.00 rental _ #37154
Celebrates the fiddling and dancing traditions of Native and Metis families on both sides of the United States and Canadian border. Reveals that although European in origin, the fiddling and step - dancing tradition of both Indian and mixed - blood descendants now reflects a strong Native American influence and is sustained largely by Native spiritual ideals. Weaves music, dance and storytelling featuring Ojibwa, Menominee, Metis and Ottawa fiddlers and dancers. Produced by Michael Loukinen for Up North Films.
Social Science
Dist - UCEMC

Medicine Flower and Lone Wolf and R C Gorman 60 MIN
VHS / U-matic
American Indian artists - part 1 series
Color (G)
$69.95 purchase
Profiles artists Grace Medicine Flower and her brother Joseph Lonewolf, potters from Santa Clara Pueblo in New Mexico. Looks at how they have revived and extended the traditional forms and techniques of their pre - Columbian ancestors in their work. Introduces R C Gorman, Navajo painter and printmaker, who works in his Taos, New Mexico studio, completing one of a suite of paintings dedicated to the Navajo woman, his primary subject.
Fine Arts; Social Science
Dist - NAMPBC **Prod** - PBS

Medicine Flower and Lonewolf 29 MIN
U-matic / VHS
American Indian Artists Series
Color
Focuses on American Indian artists Grace Medicine Flower and her brother Joseph Lonewolf, both potters from Santa Clara Pueblo in New Mexico.
Fine Arts; Social Science
Dist - PBS **Prod** - KAETTV

Medicine Flower and Lonewolf 29 MIN
VHS / U-matic
American Indian artist series; Pt 1
Color (G)
Join their teacher and father, Camilio Sunflower Tafaya, in search of clay, they mold their pottery from the recovered clay, polish and incise it, and finally fire it. Discuss technical and aesthetic considerations. The two potters have revived and expanded the techniques of graffito and polychrome.
Fine Arts; Social Science
Dist - NAMPBC **Prod** - NAMPBC 1979

Medicine for the Layman Series WASHINGTON, DC 20409
Cancer - what is it 60 MIN
Dist - USNAC

Medicine for the layman series
Genetics and recombinant DNA 60 MIN
Dist - MTP
USNAC

Medicine for the layman series
Arthritis 60 MIN
Biofeedback - therapeutic self - control 60 MIN
Blood transfusions - benefits, risks 60 MIN
Breast cancer 60 MIN
Cancer and the environment 60 MIN
Cancer Treatment 60 MIN
Cholesterol, diet, and heart disease 60 MIN
Control and therapy of genetic disease 45 MIN
Heart Attacks 60 MIN
Immunity 60 MIN
Interferon 60 MIN
Obesity and Energy Metabolism 60 MIN
Peptic Ulcer 60 MIN
Stroke 60 MIN
Dist - USNAC

Medicine in Action Series no 3
Breakbone Fever, 'DENGUE' 8 MIN
Dist - USNAC

Medicine in Sport 30 MIN
U-matic / VHS
Perspective II Series
Color (J H C A)
$150.00
Explores a variety of science and technology subjects dealing with light and its use as a medium of communication. Shows how they work and discusses the implications of this new knowledge.
Science - Physical
Dist - LANDMK **Prod** - LANDMK

Medicine - Living to be 100 22 MIN
16mm / VHS / U-matic
Color (J)
Looks at areas of medical research aimed at prolonging life. Discusses radiation therapy, preventive medicine, heart transplants, and other topics.
Health and Safety; Social Science
Dist - CNEMAG **Prod** - DOCUA

The Medicine man 25 MIN
VHS
Meaning of madness series
Color (C G PRO)
$175.00 purchase, $19.00 rental _ #35077
Looks at the history of medical ideas concerning insanity and shows how traditional psychiatry justified its practices. Uses archival footage and illustrative graphics to document historical treatments, including 'causing considerable commotion' - swinging or rotating the body to cause vertigo and sickness, inducing an insulin coma and administering electroconvulsive therapy. Highlights research on recording and interpreting the electrical energy of the brain to aid in the diagnosis and treatment of mental illness. Part of a four - part series which traces the history of psychiatry in a societal context from the mid - 1800s to modern - day England.
History - United States; Psychology
Dist - PSU **Prod** - BBC 1982

Medicine man I 120 MIN
VHS
Color (G)
$120.00 purchase _ #1014
Features Dr Steven Langer who interviews Moshe Feldenkrais and his work in Awareness Through Movement. Offers four programs entitled The Beginning, On Teaching and Learning, What Is Awareness Through Movement, On Exercise. Part one of two parts.
Health and Safety; Physical Education and Recreation; Science - Natural
Dist - FKRAIS **Prod** - FKRAIS 1981

Medicine man I and II 240 MIN
VHS
Color (G)
$200.00 purchase
Features Dr Steven Langer who interviews Moshe Feldenkrais and his work in Awareness Through Movement. Offers eight programs entitled The Beginning, On Teaching and Learning, What Is Awareness Through Movement, On Exercise, On Posture, On Breathing, The Basis of the Feldenkrais Method, On Working With Cerebral Palsy. In two parts.
Health and Safety; Physical Education and Recreation; Science - Natural
Dist - FKRAIS **Prod** - FKRAIS

Medicine man II 120 MIN
VHS
Color (G)
$120.00 purchase _ #1015
Features Dr Steven Langer who interviews Moshe Feldenkrais and his work in Awareness Through Movement. Offers four programs entitled On Posture, On Breathing, The Basis of the Feldenkrais Method, On Working With Cerebral Palsy. Part two of two parts.
Health and Safety; Physical Education and Recreation; Science - Natural
Dist - FKRAIS **Prod** - FKRAIS 1981

Medicine on the Tube 30 MIN
VHS / U-matic
Lifelines Series
Color
Discusses medicine on television.
Health and Safety; Sociology
Dist - MDCPB **Prod** - UGATV

The Medicine Show 28 MIN
16mm
Color
LC 76-700920
Presents conservationist H H Gilman, who lectures on the value of soil and water conservation.
Science - Natural; Social Science
Dist - UNEBR **Prod** - UNEBR 1974

Medicine - Volume 15 30 MIN
VHS
Color (K P I)
$19.95 purchase
Presents Volume 15 of the 'Tell Me Why' video encyclopedia series. Tells children the basic facts about medicine.
Science - Physical
Dist - PBS **Prod** - WNETTV

Medicines, Drugs and Poisons 10 MIN
U-matic / VHS / 16mm
Our Wonderful Body Series
Color (P)
$255, $180 purchase _ #3434
Shows the importance of following a doctor's instructions and reading labels on containers.
Health and Safety
Dist - CORF

Medicines used during Pregnancy 5 MIN
U-matic / VHS
Color (H C A)
LC 84-706397
Emphasizes the dangers of using any medicines during pregnancy without a doctor's permission. Covers drugs known to cause serious fetal abnormalities, drugs suspected of causing problems, and those for which there is no conclusive evidence.
Health and Safety
Dist - USNAC **Prod** - USFDA 1983

The Medieval Castle 18 MIN
16mm / U-matic / VHS
B&W (I J H C G)
Looks at the development of the medieval castle beginning with the early Norseman wooden motte and baily form which was susceptible to attack by fire. Shows the advent of stone castles and the life that went on in them, the development of the keep, the siege operations and how the defenses gradually improved to withstand them.
Fine Arts; History - World; Sociology
Dist - VIEWTH **Prod** - GBI

Medieval conflict - faith and reason - Program 2 52 MIN
16mm / VHS
Day the universe changed series
Color (H C G)
$695.00, $300.00 purchase, $75.00 rental
Reveals that after the Roman Empire, the questioning attitude derived from the Greeks gave way for centuries to the teachings of St Augustine who cared only about 'life' after death. Discloses that 11th - century crusaders invading Spain captured a treasure trove from the Arabs - Greek, Roman and Arab scientific knowledge - leading to the creation of universities and causing bitter conflicts between scientific inquiry and Christianity. Part of a ten - part series on Western thought hosted by James Burke.
History - World; Religion and Philosophy; Sociology
Dist - CF **Prod** - BBCTV 1986

The Medieval Crusades 27 MIN
16mm / U-matic / VHS
Color (J H) (SPANISH)
Follows the fate of one family and their manor through the First Crusade. Reviews the most important later Crusades and the influence of the crusaders on life in Europe.
Foreign Language; History - World
Dist - EBEC **Prod** - EBEC

Medieval England - the Peasants' Revolt 31 MIN
16mm / U-matic / VHS
Western Civilization - Majesty and Madness Series
Color (J H C) (FRENCH SPANISH)
LC 70-708187
Portrays the men and women of the Middle Ages and discusses the Peasants' Revolt of 1381 which reveals the condition of slavery and the weaknesses of the feudal system such as its oppressive tax structure, its cruelty and its social inequity.
History - World; Sociology
Dist - LCOA **Prod** - KING 1969

The Medieval Guilds 21 MIN
16mm / U-matic / VHS
Color (I J H C) (SPANISH)
Traces the development of a medieval town from a feudal manor to a commercial center in the late middle ages. Tells of the emergence and significance of gilds. Photographed in old gild towns of Western Europe.
History - World
Dist - EBEC **Prod** - EBEC 1956

The Medieval Kings 60 MIN
U-matic / VHS / 16mm
Royal Heritage Series
Color (H C A)
Explains that the medieval kings of England left their mark on great castles and abbeys. Visits Westminster, Caernarvon Castle and some early royal tombs in France. Presents Queen Elizabeth who comments on the jewel - studded State Crown.
Civics and Political Systems; History - World
Dist - FI **Prod** - BBCTV 1977

Medieval Life - the Monastery 15 MIN
U-matic / VHS / 16mm
Color (I J H C) (AFRIKAANS)
Depicts the pattern of life in the Spanish monastery during the 15th century.
History - World; Religion and Philosophy
Dist - AIMS **Prod** - ACI 1970

The Medieval Manor 22 MIN
U-matic / VHS / 16mm
Color (I J H C)
Describes the way of life in the feudal community of Montbref. Includes a look at peasant life, local justice, a noble marriage and the position of the Church.
History - World
Dist - EBEC **Prod** - EBEC 1956

Medieval manuscripts 30 MIN
VHS / U-matic
Color (C)
$89.95 purchase _ #EX1617
Explores the origins of medieval manuscripts, the process of illumination, the materials used, the function of scriptoria and how the works were selected.
Fine Arts; Literature and Drama
Dist - FOTH **Prod** - FOTH

The Medieval Mind 26 MIN
U-matic / VHS / 16mm
Humanities - Philosophy and Political Thought Series
Color (H C)
LC 73-704170
Points out the tensions and conflicts of the middle ages, and shows how the architecture of the cathedrals reflects the uneasy balance of opposing forces with their soaring columns, arches and flying buttresses. Explains how this left a permanent mark on Western civilization.
Fine Arts; History - World
Dist - EBEC **Prod** - EBEC 1969

The Medieval Monastery 17 MIN
16mm
B&W (I J H C G)
Features monastic life at the medieval Buckfast Abbey. Shows the monks illuminating manuscripts, gardening, meeting in the chapter house and dining in the refectory. Stresses the importance of the medieval monastery as a center of scholarship and culture.
History - World; Religion and Philosophy
Dist - VIEWTH **Prod** - GBI

The Medieval Monument 30 MIN
U-matic / Kit / VHS
Western Man and the Modern World in Video
Color (J H)
$1378.12 the 25 part series _ #C676 - 27347 - 5, $69.95 the individual
Examines the pervasive influence of the church on medieval life. Traces the changes from Romanesque to Gothic. Focuses on cathedrals.
Fine Arts; History - World
Dist - RH

The Medieval movement 30 MIN
35mm strip / VHS
Western man and the modern world series - Unit II
Color (J H C T A)
$72.00, $72.00 purchase _ #MB - 510422 - 9, #MB - 510223 - 4
Tours many of Europe's most spectacular cathedrals, all built in medieval times. Suggests that the church held a powerful influence in medieval Europe. Discusses the changes in architecture from Romanesque to Gothic.
Fine Arts; History - World
Dist - SRA

Medieval philosophy 45 MIN
VHS
Great philosophers series
Color; PAL (H C A)
PdS99 purchase
Introduces the concepts of Western philosophy and its greatest thinkers. Features a contemporary philosopher who, in conversation with Bryan Magee, discusses most influential thinkers of the medieval period and their ideas. Part three of a fifteen part series.
History - World; Religion and Philosophy
Dist - BBCENE

Medieval realms 40 MIN
VHS / CD-ROM
Color; PAL (I J)
PdS150 purchase ; PdS55 purchase
Presents two 40 - minute programs on all aspects of medieval life in the Great Britain. Examines issues ranging from the development of the monarchy to the health of the poor in films based around the Magna Carta and the Luttrell Psalter, both housed in the British Library. Shows these very important manuscripts, which are never shown to the public in close - up or in their entirety.

Covers almost all the major features of Britain's medieval past and the legacy of the Middle Ages to the modern world. Includes a comprehensive resource pack with illustrative material. A supporting CD - ROM is available separately. Contact distributor about availability outside the United Kingdom.
History - World
Dist - ACADEM

Medieval Series
Medieval Society - the Nobility 13 MIN
Medieval Society - the Villagers 11 MIN
Medieval Times - Guilds and Trade 14 MIN
Medieval Times - Role of the Church 14 MIN
Medieval Times - the Crusades 14 MIN
Dist - CORF

Medieval Society 30 MIN
U-matic / VHS / 16mm
Color (J H)
Establishes the closely integrated structure of society by showing different aspects of late medieval life. Focuses on the function of the monarch, barons, the church and the towns. Details the organization of a small manor and its various classes of occupants. Ends with a great banquet at the Baron's castle.
History - World; Sociology
Dist - VIEWTH **Prod** - GATEEF

Medieval Society - the Nobility 13 MIN
16mm / U-matic / VHS
Medieval Series
Color (H)
LC 76-701924
Simulates daily life in the thirteenth century, showing the roles performed by nobles and clergy.
History - World; Sociology
Dist - CORF **Prod** - CORF 1976

Medieval Society - the Villagers 11 MIN
U-matic / VHS / 16mm
Medieval Series
Color
LC 76-701923
Depicts life in the Middle Ages, showing medieval villagers, including a reeve and a serf, explaining something of their life and work.
History - World; Sociology
Dist - CORF **Prod** - CORF 1976

Medieval theater - Mary of Mijmeghen 20 MIN
VHS
Color (C A)
$119.00 purchase _ #DF329
Examines the York Mystery Cycle and Everyman to trace the evolution of the theater of the Middle Ages. Includes footage of director Johann de Meester of Holland directing the Dutch medieval drama Mary of Mijmeghen to show how a morality play might actually have been staged.
Literature and Drama
Dist - INSIM

Medieval theater - the play of 'Abraham and Isaac' 26 MIN
VHS
Color (G C H)
$129.00 purchase _ #DL430
Dramatizes the production of a play at an English estate in 1482 by a family of traveling players. Shows the relationship of medieval drama to the attitudes of the aristocracy and the doctrines of the church.
Fine Arts
Dist - INSIM

Medieval Times - Guilds and Trade 14 MIN
U-matic / VHS / 16mm
Medieval Series
Color (I J H C)
LC FIA65-410
Discusses the rise of the Venetian and Genoese merchant princes and the formation and spread of the guilds or hanses. Illustrates the economic role of craft guilds in medieval society and relates the guilds to today's European Common Market. Scenes in Europe visualize medieval trade.
History - World
Dist - CORF **Prod** - CORF 1965

Medieval Times - Role of the Church 14 MIN
16mm / U-matic / VHS
Medieval Series
Color (H C)
Illustrates the influences of the Church on medieval society, and describes the role of the church in shaping European history. Captures the spirit of the times through re - enactments and by studying the cathedrals, churches and art works of the Middle Ages.
History - World; Religion and Philosophy
Dist - CORF **Prod** - CORF 1961

Medieval Times - the Crusades 14 MIN
U-matic / VHS / 16mm
Medieval Series
Color (I J H C)
LC FIA65-1040
Re - evaluates the effects of the crusades, the religious wars which wracked Europe and the Near East for almost two centuries. Pictures some historical sites and examines original sources of information. Characterizes the crusades as a divisive force in history.
History - World
Dist - CORF **Prod** - CORF 1965

Medieval to Elizabethan Poetry 28 MIN
U-matic / VHS
Survey of English Verse Series
Color (C)
$249.00, $149.00 purchase _ #AD - 1296
Illustrates the period of development of modern English with songs from anonymous poets and the poetry of John Skelton. Samples the poetry of Tomas Wyatt, Tichbourne, Nashe, Walter Raleigh, Marlowe, Drayton and Shakespeare.
Fine Arts; Literature and Drama
Dist - FOTH **Prod** - FOTH

The Medieval Village 19 MIN
16mm
B&W (I J H C G)
Traces the social history of Laxton, England, a village which still uses the medieval open field system. Begins with monuments and documents including the first map of Laxton's three open fields divided into strips. Compares these with today's continued use of the three open fields.
Agriculture; History - World
Dist - VIEWTH **Prod** - GBI

Medieval weaponry 90 MIN
VHS
Combat for the stage and screen series
Color (PRO C G)
$275.00 purchase, $90.00 rental _ #621
Discusses the military technology and combat technique of the medieval period. Shows moves and safe techniques for broadsword, sword and shield and quarterstaff combat. Features David Boushey as instructor and producer. Part of a three - part series on stage and screen combat.
Fine Arts; History - World
Dist - FIRLIT

Medieval women 24 MIN
VHS / U-matic
Color (J H C G)
$245.00 purchase, $50.00 rental
Looks at how women were portrayed in the illuminated manuscripts of the thirteenth through sixteenth centuries. Reveals that the Church was uncomfortable about women, but viewed them as saints if they were pure, pious and chaste - St Catherine of Alexandria. Other women were regarded as a risk to men's souls and, therefore, sinners - Salome and Queen Herodias. Depicts women going about their daily lives, running households, farm chores, blacksmithing, managing dairies, mining, involved in cottage industries such as silkworm breeding and silk spinning, writing, producing art and music. Features Prof Joyce Salisbury.
Business and Economics; Guidance and Counseling; History - World; Religion and Philosophy; Sociology
Dist - IFB **Prod** - GBCTP 1989

The Medieval world 14 MIN
VHS
Color; PAL (H)
Considers the walled city of York, England, the Flemish guildhalls of Ghent and the cathedral in Chartres, France. Portrays knights, feudalism, Chaucer's pilgrims, castles and crusades for an understanding of Medieval times.
History - World; Religion and Philosophy
Dist - VIEWTH

Medieval world 50 MIN
VHS
Spirit of the age series
Color (A)
PdS99 purchase
Examines the evolution of architecture in Britain since the Middle Ages. Part one of an eight-part series.
Fine Arts; Industrial and Technical Education
Dist - BBCENE

Medieval World, the 14 MIN
U-matic / VHS / 16mm
Color (I J H C)
Portrays medieval times, discussing knights and feudalism, Chaucer's pilgrims, castles and crusades. Uses the English - walled city of York, the Flemish guildhalls of Ghent and the French cathedral of Chartres to supply the background.
History - World
Dist - CORF **Prod** - CORF 1980

Mediggo 30 MIN
16mm
Color
Presents a scriptural detective story of the city of Solomon buried beneath ruins.
Religion and Philosophy
Dist - CAFM **Prod** - CAFM

Medina 15 MIN
16mm
Color (G)
$25.00 rental
Documents the old cities of Morocco.
Fine Arts
Dist - CANCIN **Prod** - BARTLS 1972

Medisense 20 MIN
16mm
Color (A)
Looks at the magnitude and complexity of health cost inflation. Shows how sky - rocketing health costs directly and indirectly affects employees. Demonstrates that both positive and direct action is both necessary and possible to change the health systems for the benefit of all.
Health and Safety
Dist - JONEST **Prod** - DRUKRR

Meditation
VHS
Color (G)
$29.95 purchase _ #MED000
Introduces the philosophy, benefits and practical uses of meditation, especially for stress reduction.
Health and Safety; Psychology; Religion and Philosophy
Dist - SIV

Meditation 29 MIN
16mm
Real Revolution - Talks by Krishnamurti Series
B&W
LC 73-703034
Features Indian spiritual leader Krishnamurti who explains the process of meditation, which he defines not as concentration of self - stimulation but as the acute awareness of a quiet mind. Gives as the philosophy that man can free himself from his troubled image of of himself by finding life beyond daily existence through meditation.
Guidance and Counseling; Religion and Philosophy
Dist - IU **Prod** - KQEDTV 1968

Meditation 60 MIN
VHS
The Buddhist path with Detong Cho Yin series
Color (G)
$34.95 purchase _ #P13b
Explains the complete Buddhist path to enlightenment. Features Buddhist nun Detong Cho Yin, who gives insights and meditations for the beginner or advanced practitioner. Includes discussion, exercises, chakras and visualizations. Part of a series of six easy - to - follow videos.
Religion and Philosophy
Dist - HP

Meditation Crystallized - Lama Govinda on Tibetan Art 14 MIN
16mm
Color
LC 73-700376
Presents Lama Govinda, artist, author and one of the world's foremost interpreters of Tibetan Buddhism, discussing Tibetan art as an expression of the deepest and most meaningful levels of the human psyche and a crystallization of centuries of meditation.
Fine Arts; Geography - World
Dist - HP **Prod** - HP 1973

Meditation IV 5 MIN
16mm
Color (G)
$15.00 rental
Travels through inner landscapes and different levels of consciousness. Investigates the media artist caught between nature and technology by utilizing 3 - D computer animation and other techniques. Produced by Kevin Deal.
Fine Arts
Dist - CANCIN

Meditation on Violence 12 MIN
16mm
B&W (H C A)
Presents a choreography of the movements and rhythms of Wu - Tang and Saolin schools of Chinese boxing filmed by Mayan Deren.
Fine Arts
Dist - GROVE **Prod** - GROVE

Meditation series
Teaches the viewer how to relax, calm mind and body and feel peace and well - being. Contains five films entitled The Art of Meditation; Meditation - The Inward Journey; Meditation Crystallized; Going with the Flow; and Zen and Now. See individual titles for descriptions.
Meditation series 87 MIN
Dist - HP

Meditation series
Amen 2 MIN
Faith 2 MIN
Glory be 2 MIN
Hope 2 MIN
Joy 2 MIN
Love 2 MIN
Peace 2 MIN
Prayer 2 MIN
Self 2 MIN
Trust 2 MIN
Wonder 2 MIN
Dist - IKONOG

Meditation - the Inward Journey 20 MIN
16mm
Color (H C A)
LC 77-701611
Defines meditation as an inward power, as a journey which, when successful, enables the traveler to see himself as if he were someone else and to see others as if they were he.
Guidance and Counseling; Religion and Philosophy
Dist - HP **Prod** - HP 1977

Meditation - Yoga, T'ai Chi and Other Spiritual Trips 18 MIN
16mm / U-matic / VHS
Color
Points out that two and a half million people are trying zen, yoga and other old Asian meditational techniques on this continent today. Visits teacher Marie Paulyn at a school of hatha - yoga, interviews author and philosopher Alan Watts at home on his ferry boat in San Francisco Bay and looks at theatre students working on traditional T'ai Chi forms.
Religion and Philosophy
Dist - CNEMAG **Prod** - DOCUA

Meditative experience quartet 120 MIN
VHS / BETA
Color (G)
$69.95 purchase _ #Q314
Presents a four - part series on the meditative experience. Includes 'Tibetan Buddhist Meditation' with Dr Ole Nydahl, 'What Is Kundalini' with Dr Lee Sannella, 'Benefits of Long Term Meditation' with Shinzen Young and 'Cultivating Mindfulness' with Dr Charles T Tart.
Psychology; Religion and Philosophy; Science - Natural
Dist - THINKA **Prod** - THINKA

Meditative experience series
Benefits of long - term meditation 30 MIN
Cultivating mindfulness 30 MIN
Tibetan Buddhist meditation 30 MIN
What is Kundalini 30 MIN
Dist - THINKA

Mediterranan and African collection series
Israel - the holy land 60 MIN
Dist - CAMV

Mediterranean and African collection series
Presents a five-part series on the Mediterranean and Africa. Teaches about the people, culture and history of Greece, Israel, Kenya, Jordan, and more. Visits historic buildings, monuments and landmarks. Examines the physical topography of locations. Also part of a larger series entitled Video Visits that travels to six continents.
Greece - playground of the gods 60 MIN
Jordan - the desert kingdom 60 MIN
Kenya safari - essence of Africa 60 MIN
Mediterranean and African collection series 300 MIN
Pearls of the Mediterranean 60 MIN
Dist - CAMV **Prod** - WNETTV

Mediterranean Cookery - Egypt, Turkey, Morocco and Greece 88 MIN
VHS
Color (S)
$29.95 purchase _ #781 - 9024
Celebrates the exotic cuisine of Egypt, Turkey, Morocco and Greece. Demonstrates 23 Mediterranean specialties including Kibbeh, Couscous and Sltifatho. Features cooking writer Claudia Roden as host.
Fine Arts; Geography - World; Health and Safety; Home Economics; Industrial and Technical Education; Sociology
Dist - FI **Prod** - BBCTV 1989

Mediterranean Cookery - France, Italy, and Spain 88 MIN
VHS
Color (S)
$29.95 purchase _ #781 - 9023
Introduces the cuisine of France, Italy and Spain. Features Claudia Roden as host. Teaches how to make 27 different recipes, including Ratatouille, Gazpacho Andaluz and Involtini.
Fine Arts; Geography - World; Health and Safety; Home Economics; Industrial and Technical Education; Sociology
Dist - FI **Prod** - BBCTV 1989

Mediterranean - cradle or coffin 58 MIN
VHS
Cousteau series
Color (G)
$29.90 purchase _ #0771
Joins Jacques Cousteau and the crew of the Calypso on the Mediterranean Sea. Reveals that it is a return for Costeau from 30 years before when he found the sea teeming with marine life. He returns to a marine desert and tells what happened, and how to make the Mediterranean capable of supporting marine life again. Part of a series featuring Cousteau.
Geography - World; Science - Natural; Sociology
Dist - SEVVID **Prod** - COUSTS

The Mediterranean Front 26 MIN
U-matic / VHS
B&W (G)
$249.00, $149.00 purchase _ #AD - 1610
Shows the efforts of the 'free' French to gather and train in North Africa and take part in the British and American campaign to liberate Italy. Documentss the campaign that followed the Mediterranean landings as it fought its way across Europe as far as the Danube, and ends with Marshal Keitel's final surrender.
Geography - World; History - United States; History - World; Sociology
Dist - FOTH **Prod** - FOTH

Mediterranean Mosaic 27 MIN
16mm / U-matic / VHS
Victory at Sea Series
B&W (J H)
Looks at the importance of Gibraltar and Malta during World War II and the enemy fleets in the Mediterranean.
Civics and Political Systems; History - United States; History - World
Dist - LUF **Prod** - NBCTV

Mediterranean mosaic, Guadalcanal, rings around Rabaul and mare nostrum 108 MIN
VHS
Victory at sea series
B&W (G)
$24.95 purchase _ #S01155
Contains four episodes from the Victory at Sea series, documenting the US Navy battles of World War II. 'Mediterranean Mosaic' covers Allied and enemy fleet operations around Gibraltar and Malta, while 'Guadalcanal' gives a total perspective on that battle. 'Rings Around Rabaul' focuses on the Japanese effort to control the Solomon Islands, and 'Mare Nostrum' deals with the struggle for control of the Mediterranean and North Africa.
Civics and Political Systems; History - United States
Dist - UILL

A Mediterranean Prospect 58 MIN
U-matic
Nova Series
Color
LC 80-707475
Discusses the pollution of the Mediterranean Ocean. Tells how the pollution problems facing the 18 countries along the Mediterranean have gotten the nations working together with the exception of Albania. Tells how the number of marine research laboratories contributing to the battle against pollution emergencies has risen from less than a dozen in four countries to 83 in 16 countries.
Geography - World; Sociology
Dist - PBS **Prod** - BBCTV 1980

The Mediterranean World 23 MIN
U-matic / VHS / 16mm
Color; B&W (I J H) (SPANISH)
Explains the significance of the Mediterranean region in the development of Western civilization. Depicts life today in Greece, Italy and the Arab countries, stressing the importance of the region as a focal point of world tension.
Geography - World
Dist - EBEC **Prod** - EBEC 1961

Medium 60 MIN
U-matic / VHS
Computer Dialogue - the Key to Successful Systems Series
Color
Examines the explosive growth of interactive technology and introduces the modes and devices of human - computer conversation.
Industrial and Technical Education
Dist - DELTAK **Prod** - DELTAK

The Medium
U-matic / VHS
(G)
Presents Marie Powers and Leo Coleman in their Broadway roles as Madam Flora and Tobe in Menotti's melodrama. Conducted by Thomas Schippers.
Fine Arts
Dist - VAI **Prod** - VAI

Medium Cool
VHS / BETA
Color
Presents a documentary - style drama about the events inside and outside the Chicago Democratic National Convention of 1968.
Civics and Political Systems
Dist - GA **Prod** - GA

The Medium is the masseuse - a Balinese massage 30 MIN
VHS / 16mm
Color (G)
$650.00, $250.00 purchase, $55.00, $50.00 rental
Interviews Jero Tapakan, a Balinese spirit medium, who also practices as a masseuse when possession is not auspicious. Focuses on Jero's treatment of Ida Bagus, a member of nobility from a neighboring town. Treatment includes a thorough massage, administration of eye drops, an infusion and a special paste for the chest. Includes a detailed discussion about the nature and treatment of illness, as well as informal banter between Jero, her other patients and people in her household. By Linda Connor, Patsy Asch and Timothy Asch.
Geography - World; Health and Safety; Religion and Philosophy
Dist - DOCEDR **Prod** - DOCEDR

Medium rare...hold the cottage 10 MIN
VHS / 16mm
Color (G)
Takes a whimsical and slightly twisted look at the Ontario, Canada ritual of going to the cottage with a stop at Weber's Charcoal Broiled en route.
Geography - World; Literature and Drama; Physical Education and Recreation
Dist - ASTRSK **Prod** - ASTRSK 1990

Medlars on Line - Medline 23 MIN
U-matic / VHS
Color (PRO)
Explains the concept of on - line retrieval of bibliographic citations to medical literature by use of communications terminals in medical libraries throughout the United States.
Education; Health and Safety; Industrial and Technical Education; Mathematics; Sociology
Dist - USNAC **Prod** - USHHS

Medley of Danish, Pt 1
U-matic / VHS
Medley of Danish Series
Color
Home Economics; Industrial and Technical Education
Dist - CULINA **Prod** - CULINA

Medley of Danish, Pt 2
VHS / U-matic
Medley of Danish Series
Color
Home Economics; Industrial and Technical Education
Dist - CULINA **Prod** - CULINA

Medley of Danish Series
Medley of Danish, Pt 1
Medley of Danish, Pt 2
Dist - CULINA

Medline - current plus backfiles to 1966
CD-ROM
(G PRO C)
$2795.00 purchase _ #1459d
Corresponds to three printed indexes - Index Medicus, Index to Dental Literature and International Nursing Index. Accesses abstracts and citations from 3,200 journals. Monthly updates. IBM PCs and compatibles require at least 640k RAM, DOS 3.1 or later, one floppy disk drive - hard disk recommended, one empty expansion slot, and an IBM compatible CD - ROM drive.
Health and Safety; Literature and Drama
Dist - BEP **Prod** - NLM

Medline - current plus 4 backfile yrs
CD-ROM
(G PRO C)
$1695.00 purchase _ #1459b
Corresponds to three printed indexes - Index Medicus, Index to Dental Literature and International Nursing Index. Accesses abstracts and citations from 3200 journals. Monthly updates. IBM PCs and compatibles require at least 640k RAM, DOS 3.1 or later, one floppy disk drive - hard disk recommended, one empty expansion slot, and an IBM compatible CD - ROM drive.
Health and Safety; Literature and Drama
Dist - BEP **Prod** - NLM

Medline - current plus 9 backfile yrs
CD-ROM
(G PRO C)
$1495.00 purchase _ #1459a
Correponds to three printed indexes - Index Medicus, Index to Dental Literature and International Nursing Index. Accesses abstracts and citations from 3200 journals. Quarterly updates. IBM PCs and compatibles require at

least 640k RAM, DOS 3.1 or later, one floppy disk drive - hard disk recommended, one empty expansion slot, and an IBM compatible CD - ROM drive.
Health and Safety; Literature and Drama
Dist - BEP **Prod** - NLM

Medline - current year
CD-ROM
(G PRO C)
$1,250.00 purchase _ #1459c
Corresponds to three printed indexes - Index Medicus, Index to Dental Literature and International Nursing Index. Accesses abstracts and citations from 3200 journals. Monthly updates. IBM PCs and compatibles require at least 640k RAM, DOS 3.1 or later, one floppy disk drive - hard disk recommended, one empty expansion slot, and an IBM compatible CD - ROM drive.
Health and Safety; Literature and Drama
Dist - BEP **Prod** - NLM

Medoonak the Stormmaker 13 MIN
U-matic / VHS / 16mm
Color
LC 76-702031
Interprets a Micmac Indian legend about Medoonak the stormmaker, enacted by members of the Mermaid Theater of Wolfville, Nova Scotia, using mime, dance and narration.
Literature and Drama; Social Science
Dist - IFB **Prod** - NFBC 1975

The Medulla Oblongata 15 MIN
U-matic / VHS
Neurobiology Series
Color (PRO)
Identifies the macroscopic structures of the medulla oblongata using brain specimens and diagrams. Discusses briefly physiology and pathology of the medulla oblongata where applicable.
Health and Safety; Science - Natural
Dist - HSCIC **Prod** - HSCIC

Medullary Nailing 17 MIN
U-matic / VHS
Color
Illustrates the indication, principles and performance of both closed and open medullary nailing.
Health and Safety
Dist - SPRVER **Prod** - SPRVER

Medusa Challenger 25 MIN
16mm / U-matic / VHS
Color (I)
LC 79-700138
Tells the story of what happens when a flower vendor and his nephew are separated when a drawbridge is raised to allow the Medusa Challenger, the largest freighter on the Great Lakes, to pass.
Fine Arts
Dist - PHENIX **Prod** - KOCHP 1978

Meecology 26 MIN
16mm
Color (P I)
LC 75-700123
Portrays children from rural, suburban, urban and inner - city surrounding and shows how each relates to their environment in an ecologically productive way.
Science - Natural; Sociology
Dist - CHRSTP **Prod** - MCDONS 1974

Meerkats Unlimited, and, the Impossible Bird 57 MIN
VHS
Color (S)
$24.95 purchase _ #781 - 9021
Follows the adventures of a band of curious 12 - inch - tall mongoose - like creatures whose 'philosophy' is all for one, one for all, in 'Meerkats United.' Explores the remarkable world of the ostrich which is nine feet tall and weighs 300 pounds in 'The Impossible Bird.' The ostrich cannot fly but runs 40 miles per hour. Filmed in Kenya. Narrated by David Attenborough.
Geography - World; Science - Natural
Dist - FI **Prod** - BBCTV 1988

Meet a working painter - Neil Welliver 18 MIN
VHS
Color (I J H)
$138.00 purchase _ #87 - 004812
Travels to the coast of Maine to meet painter Neil Welliver. Joins Welliver in the wilderness as he works on a small canvas portraying a stream rushing through a snow - covered wood. Returns to Welliver's studio where he talks about his work and demonstrates his techniques of working in oil, watercolor and print. Tours Welliver's most recent exhibition at the Marlborough Gallery in New York City.
Fine Arts
Dist - SRA **Prod** - SRA 1992

Meet a working sculptor - Martine Vaugel 22 MIN
VHS
Color (I J H)
$138.00 purchase _ #87 - 004817
Travels to the studio of Martine Vaugel to watch as she creates a full figure bronze sculpture of Mahatma Gandhi. Shows how she begins by crafting a small maquette figure to be used as a guide thorughout the sculpting process. When Vaugel is satisfied that the intricate details are just right, an artisan makes a huge negative - mold of the piece. Visits a foundry to observe the lost - wax bronze casting process.
Fine Arts
Dist - SRA **Prod** - SRA 1992

Meet an Orchestra Musician Series
At the rehearsal 15 MIN
Before the Concert 30 MIN
In the Music Store 15 MIN
Dist - AITECH

Meet and Greet 15 MIN
VHS / U-matic
Children in Action Series
Color
Psychology
Dist - LVN **Prod** - LVN

Meet Ashley Bryan - storyteller, artist, writer
VHS
Color (I J H)
$85.00 purchase _ #87 - 005010
Visits storyteller, writer and illustrator Ashley Bryan at his home on an island off the coast of Maine. Explains how his work with folktales and American spirituals is a way to share his African ancestry with others. Bryan retells a traditional Nigerian tale and adapts a West Indian folktale in Turtle Knows Your Name. Shows how he rehearses with neighbors to develop his stories and watches his work on illustrations for his new book.
Fine Arts; History - United States; Literature and Drama
Dist - SRA **Prod** - SRA 1993

Meet ... Bradley Harrison Pickelsimer 35 MIN
16mm
Color (G)
$60.00 rental
Features an experimental documentary about a Kentucky drag queen, Bradley Harrison Pickelsimer, who ran his own bar on Main Street in Lexington. Records his colorful personality whom the filmmaker, Heather McAdams, found to be both entertaining and deep. Bradley's observations were similar to McAdams' views on life even though their backgrounds were miles apart. McAdams witnessed firsthand people laughing at him or dismissing him altogether just because he was a cross - dresser - the film makes a social statement that the United States hasn't really progressed very far as a society.
Fine Arts; Sociology
Dist - CANCIN

Meet D W
VHS
Color (K)
$33.00 purchase
Presents two stories by Marc Brown - 'D W Flips' and 'D W All Wet.'.
Literature and Drama
Dist - PELLER

Meet George Washington, Pt 1 26 MIN
16mm
Project 20 Series
Color (I)
LC 70-706055
Presents a factual look at the life of George Washington as portrayed in his own words, as well as in letters and diaries of his contemporaries and in newspapers of the time.
Biography
Dist - NBCTV **Prod** - NBCTV 1969

Meet George Washington, Pt 2 26 MIN
16mm
Project 20 Series
Color (I)
LC 70-706055
Presents a factual look at the life of George Washington as portrayed in his own words, in letters and diaries of his contemporaries and in newspapers of the time.
Biography
Dist - NBCTV **Prod** - NBCTV 1969

Meet Jerry Leavy 43 MIN
16mm
Color
LC 74-706377
Shows that a bilateral upper extremity amputee can be completely independent in the activities of his daily life. Shows Jerry Leavy driving a car and flying a plane.
Health and Safety; Psychology
Dist - USNAC **Prod** - USOE

Meet John Doe 135 MIN
16mm
B&W
Features Gary Cooper as an unemployed man picked as the 'typical American' by a newspaper publisher. Tells how he discovers that he is being exploited to further the publisher's political ambitions. Stars Barbara Stanwyck, Edward Arnold and Walter Brennen. Directed by Frank Capra.
Fine Arts
Dist - REELIM **Prod** - WB 1941

Meet Lisa 5 MIN
16mm / U-matic / VHS
Color (P) (SPANISH)
LC 74-714064
Presents a statement of the world as seen by a brain damaged child. Involves her parents, friends and attitudes towards her in general.
Psychology
Dist - AIMS **Prod** - LEARN 1971

Meet Margie 10 MIN
U-matic / VHS / 16mm
Color (J)
LC 76-700290
Tells the story of Margie, who, like many young people throughout the nation, is getting her education on her own, and on a shoestring. Shows that although living at a dollar - figure poverty level, she uses energy, imagination and creativity to gain a rich life. Explains that she travels by bike, belongs to a food co - op, trades chores with her neighbors and barters her skills for someone else's thereby reducing her cash need.
Business and Economics; Guidance and Counseling; Home Economics; Social Science
Dist - ALTSUL **Prod** - ALTSUL 1976

Meet Marlon Brando 28 MIN
16mm
B&W
Presents improvisational conversations between Marlon Brando and interviewers of the TV world providing a personal portrait of the major film star.
Biography; Fine Arts
Dist - MAYSLS **Prod** - MAYSLS 1965

Meet me in Miami Beach 18 MIN
VHS
Color (G)
$50.00 purchase
Features three elderly Jews in their nineties, who have retired to Miami Beach. Shares their search for a fountain of youth, the Jewish community that thrived in this unlikely setting, and the inevitability of growing old and losing friends. Reveals the contrasts between the remaining shtetl community with the new youth culture that has infused the beach communities. Directed by Bonnie C Cohen.
Fine Arts; Health and Safety; Religion and Philosophy; Social Science
Dist - NCJEWF

Meet Me in St Louis 2 MIN
U-matic / VHS / 16mm
B&W
Offers a sequence done for a 1962 television special.
Fine Arts
Dist - PFP **Prod** - EAMES 1962

Meet me, Jesus 15 MIN
16mm
Color (G)
$30.00 rental
Deals with the birth and regrowth, ultimate destruction and rebirth of civilization with underlying theme of loss of innocence, dignity and hope. Uses found footage as well as original material and hand painting on film.
Industrial and Technical Education; Psychology; Sociology
Dist - CANCIN **Prod** - UNGRW 1966

Meet me tonight in dreamland 7 MIN
16mm
Color (G)
$30.00 rental
Travels through the underworld of the inner mind and out of darkness with the carnival neon of American pop heaven, including lust, bountiful breasts and military invasion.
Fine Arts
Dist - CANCIN **Prod** - WHITDL 1975

Meet Meter Man 3 MIN
U-matic / VHS
Metric Marvels Series
Color (P I)
Introduces the animated superhero Meter Man, who specializes in converting distances to metric terms by using his magic Metric Measuring Stick.
Fine Arts; Mathematics
Dist - GA **Prod** - NBCTV 1978

Meet Mr Lincoln 27 MIN
16mm / U-matic / VHS
B&W (I J H C)
Old photographs, pictures, newspapers and posters review the life of Lincoln. Portraits of Civil War soldiers, their camps and battles, and scenes of cities and backwoods reconstruct the America Lincoln knew in the 1860's.
Biography; History - United States
Dist - EBEC **Prod** - NBCTV 1960

Meet Mr Noise 26 MIN
16mm
Color
LC 74-705121
Points out hazards of working in an area of vibration and noise. Shows how noise of heightened intensity can impair hearing and general health. Demonstrates how properly fitted protective devices worn by personnel reduces adverse effects of noise.
Health and Safety; Science - Natural
Dist - USNAC **Prod** - USAF 1962

Meet Mr Stork 17 MIN
16mm / U-matic / VHS
Color
Introduces Artie Elgart, an auto parts distributor who also runs the Golden Cradle adoption agency and spends most of his time finding babies for childless couples. Explains that unlike most adoption agencies, the Golden Cradle provides the birth - mother with the best possible care, paid for by the adopting couple. Originally shown on the CBS program 60 Minutes.
Sociology
Dist - CAROUF **Prod** - CBSTV

Meet NIC - the nursing interventions classification system
VHS
Practice of nursing series
Color (C PRO)
$275.00 purchase, $100.00 rental _ #42 - 2658, #42 - 2658R
Examines a new standardized classification system that describes the treatments nurses perform. Recalls how researchers at the University of Iowa developed the NIC system which labels, defines and categorizes 336 nursing interventions. Shows how to use the system and how it compares to other taxonomies. Visits hospitals, schools and other practice settings where NIC is being pioneered. Experts discuss NIC's applications in research, computerization and the public policy arena where NIC is likely to streamline and standardize documentation, and help nurses to prove their worth in a competitive, cost - based health care system. Produced with the Iowa Intervention project.
Health and Safety
Dist - NLFN **Prod** - NLFN

Meet Professor Balthazar Series
Arts and Flowers 9 MIN
Bim, Bam, Bum 10 MIN
Doctor don't little 9 MIN
Hat - on - flier 10 MIN
Of Mouse and Ben 10 MIN
Stumble Bumps 10 MIN
Dist - IFB

Meet Professor Balthazar Series
Victor's Egg - O - Mat 10 MIN
Dist - ZAGREB

Meet Professor Balthazar
Snow Time for Comedy 10 MIN
Dist - IFB

Meet the Actors 11 MIN
16mm
Color (I)
Shows that wild animals, born to kill, can be taught to go through their hair - raising routines without so much as missing a cue. Stars Tamba, the humorous chimpanzee, and Humpy, the talking camel.
Fine Arts; Literature and Drama; Science - Natural
Dist - AVED **Prod** - AVED 1961

Meet the Caldecott illustrator - Jerry Pinkney 21 MIN
VHS
Color (J H C T A)
$129.00 purchase _ #MB - 002845 - 1
Profiles artist Jerry Pinkney, whose artwork in children's books has won him the Caldecott Award. Shows Pinkney at work. Interviews Pinkney on his artistic outlook.
Fine Arts
Dist - SRA **Prod** - SRA 1991

Meet the Classic Authors Series
Charles Dickens, Jules Verne, Robert Louis Stevenson 55 MIN
Edgar Allan Poe, James Fenimore Cooper, Washington Irving 55 MIN
Jack London, Rudyard Kipling, H G Wells 55 MIN
Mark Twain, Louisa may Alcott, Herman Melville 55 MIN
Dist - JANUP

Meet the classic authors series
Charles Dickens
Edgar Allan Poe
H G Wells
Herman Melville
Jack London
James Fennimore Cooper
Jules Verne
Louisa May Alcott
Mark Twain
Robert Louis Stevenson
Rudyard Kipling
Washington Irving
Dist - PELLER

Meet the Classic Authors Videos - Set I
VHS
Color (I)
$89.95 purchase
Features portraits of authors whose works have weathered the test of time. Includes Edgar Allan Poe, James Fennimore Cooper and Washington Irving. Also available as single titles.
Literature and Drama
Dist - PELLER

Meet the Classic Authors Videos - Set II
VHS
Color (I)
$89.95 purchase
Features portraits of authors whose works have weathered the test of time. Includes Mark Twain, Louisa May Alcott and Herman Melville. Also available as single titles.
Literature and Drama
Dist - PELLER

Meet the Classic Authors Videos - Set III
VHS
Color (I)
$89.95 purchase
Features portraits of authors whose works have weathered the test of time. Includes Charles Dickens, Jules Verne and Robert Louis Stevenson. Also available as single titles.
Literature and Drama
Dist - PELLER

Meet the Classic Authors Videos - Set IV
VHS
Color (I)
$89.95 purchase
Features portraits of authors whose works have weathered the test of time. Includes Jack London, Rudyard Kipling and H G Wells. Also available as single titles.
Literature and Drama
Dist - PELLER

Meet the Computer 18 MIN
U-matic / VHS
Little Computers - See How they Run Series
Color (J)
LC 81-706563
Describes basic computer functions and presents information about some of the most familiar small computers such as Apple II, Atari 400 and Texas Instruments' 99/4.
Mathematics
Dist - GPN **Prod** - ELDATA 1980

Meet the DC - 9 10 MIN
16mm
Color (C A)
Serves as an introduction to the DC - 9. It literally 'TAKES APART' its most important features and compoments.
Industrial and Technical Education; Social Science
Dist - MCDO **Prod** - DAC 1966

Meet the Masters Series
El Greco 29 MIN
Michelangelo 29 MIN
Mondrian 29 MIN
Paul Cezanne 29 MIN
Paul Klee 29 MIN
Rembrandt 29 MIN
Seurat 29 MIN
Tintoretto 29 MIN
Toulouse - Lautrec 29 MIN
Dist - UMITV

Meet the Neighborhood 15 MIN
U-matic
We Live Next Door Series
Color (K)
Shows children the value of old things as the residents of Nutdale protest the replacement of the old neighborhood store with a supermarket.
Psychology; Social Science
Dist - TVOTAR **Prod** - TVOTAR 1981

Meet the Press series
Martin Luther King 28 MIN
Robert Taft - January 7, 1951 28 MIN
Dist - NBCTV

Meet the Sioux Indian 11 MIN
U-matic / VHS / 16mm
Color; B&W (I J)
Portrays the varied daily activities of the men and women of the Sioux as they preserve their food, decorate their clothes and build their tepees. Made on Pine Ridge reservation of North Dakota.
Social Science; Sociology
Dist - IFB **Prod** - DEU 1949

Meet what You Eat 18 MIN
16mm
Color (I J H)
Offers a lesson in basic nutrition. Includes an introduction to the basic food groups and nutrient interspersed with historical food anecdotes.
Health and Safety; Social Science
Dist - FILAUD **Prod** - SWIFT 1979

Meet Your Animal Friends 52 MIN
VHS / 16mm
Color (K)
$195.00 purchase; $29.95 purchase _ #S00598
Introduces animals to children in 23 short segments. Lynn Redgrave narrates.
Science - Natural
Dist - FLMWST
UILL

Meet Your Parent, Adult, Child 9 MIN
U-matic / VHS / 16mm
Transactional Analysis Series
Color (J) (DUTCH SWEDISH)
LC 75-702804
Uses animation to explain why people have difficulty communicating on the same level. Explains the transactional analysis theory that each person develops a parent, child and adult ego state early in childhood upon which later relationships depend. Stresses the importance of effective interpersonal relationships.
Psychology
Dist - PHENIX **Prod** - CBSTV 1975

Meeting Artists 15 MIN
U-matic / VHS
Primary Art Series
Color (P)
Considers the artist at work through visits to the studios of sculptor Edgar Britton, weaver Kathryn Wertenberger, potter Henry Mead and painter Mina Conant.
Fine Arts; Social Science
Dist - AITECH **Prod** - WETATV

Meeting at Night 20 MIN
16mm
Color
LC FIE52-943
Shows five basic meeting situations and the proper night whistle signals on the ocean, in inland waters and in narrow channels. Explains the causes of head - on collisions and shows emergency action signals.
Health and Safety; Social Science
Dist - USNAC **Prod** - USN 1943

Meeting Breakers - Customizers
VHS / 16mm
(PRO)
$80.00 purchase _ #MDSV
Presents thirty amusing vignettes for use in meetings or conventions, or to use in in - house video productions. Covers topics such as teamwork, office romance, meeting and conventión foibles, sexism, the sales force, the office, and the production plant.
Business and Economics
Dist - RMIBHF **Prod** - RMIBHF

Meeting breaks series
Are you really listening 4 MIN
Closing time 4 MIN
The Customer is king 3 MIN
Hound dog blues with Lenny Henry 4 MIN
Insurance mania - Part 1 7 MIN
Insurance mania - Part 2 11 MIN
Mel and Griff - Part 1 7 MIN
Mel and Griff - Part 2 7 MIN
Nobody's perfect 4 MIN
Quality - why bother 8 MIN
When a group is a team 4 MIN
Dist - VIDART

Meeting change creatively - Part 10 14 MIN
VHS
Employment development series
Color (PRO IND A)

$495.00 purchase, $150.00 rental _ #ITC36
Presents part ten of a ten - part series designed to prepare employees to cope with workplace demands in a skillful and confident manner. Enables supervisors and managers to improve their skills and abilities as they work with their peers. Includes a leader's guide, instructions for self - study and participant's booklet.
Business and Economics; Guidance and Counseling
Dist - EXTR **Prod** - ITRC

Meeting Customer Needs and Expectations 60 MIN
BETA / VHS
Manufacturing Series
(IND)
Defines the responsibilities and functions of the customer service representative.
Business and Economics
Dist - COMSRV **Prod** - COMSRV 1986

The Meeting - Eddie finds a home 30 MIN
VHS
Color (K P I G R)
$14.95 purchase _ #412VSV
Features a New York City youth center director, Ben Davidson, who takes Eddie, an orphan pup, into his home. Shows how they read the Bible together and discuss the idea that Jesus can be their friend.
Literature and Drama; Religion and Philosophy
Dist - GF

Meeting Emotional Needs in Childhood - Groundwork of Democracy 33 MIN
16mm
Studies of Normal Personality Development Series
B&W (C T)
Suggests ways parents and teachers contribute to the kinds of attitudes toward people and the sense of community responsibility the seven - to ten - year - old child is developing as he grows to adulthood.
Education; Psychology; Sociology
Dist - NYU **Prod** - NYU 1947

Meeting fractions series
Presents a four - part series introducing fractions developed by the National Council of Teachers of Mathematics. Includes the titles 'Cavemen - an Introduction to Fractions,' 'Watermelons - Equivalent Fractions,' 'Genie and Clam - Comparing Fractions' and 'Knights - What Comes After One - Third.'

Cavemen - an introduction to fractions	12 MIN
Genie and clam - comparing fractions	8 MIN
Knights - what comes after one - third	11 MIN
Watermelons - equivalent fractions	10 MIN

Dist - AIMS **Prod** - DAVFMS 1947

The Meeting Ground 15 MIN
16mm
Color
LC 74-705122
Tells of the recruitment of prior - service Marines for enlistment in the U S Marine Corps Reserve.
Civics and Political Systems; Guidance and Counseling
Dist - USNAC **Prod** - USMC 1969

Meeting Gulf People who are Meeting the Challenge 25 MIN
16mm
Color
LC 77-702486
Introduces the Gulf Oil Corporation advertising campaign. Features Gulf employees who explain the challenge of their particular jobs and how they contribute to Gulf's overall effort.
Business and Economics
Dist - COMCRP **Prod** - GULF 1976

Meeting in Progress 43 MIN
U-matic / 8mm cartridge / VHS / 16mm
Color; Captioned; B&W (H C A) (DUTCH SWEDISH SPANISH DANISH FRENCH GERMAN JAPANESE PORTUGUESE NORWEGIAN)
LC 73-700186
Offers a means of teaching conference leadership through group participation. Asks trainees to decide at 12 critical points in a typical problem - solving conference which group relations or task function they would use if they were the leader.
Business and Economics; Foreign Language; Psychology; Sociology
Dist - RTBL **Prod** - RTBL 1969

Meeting in space 15 MIN
VHS
Magic library series
Color (P)
LC 90-707946
Tells a space and science fiction story. Raises children's awareness of a sense of story in order to enrich and motivate language, reading and writing skills. Includes teacher's guide. Part of a series.
Education; English Language; Literature and Drama
Dist - TVOTAR **Prod** - TVOTAR 1990

Meeting in the Desert 15 MIN
U-matic / VHS
Encounter in the Desert Series
Color (I)
Introduces a Western family to Bedouin nomads.
Geography - World; Social Science; Sociology
Dist - CTI **Prod** - CTI

Meeting Individual Needs 30 MIN
U-matic / VHS
Reading is Power Series no 2
Color (T)
LC 81-707517
Uses interviews and candid classroom scenes to show how innovative teachers are developing strategies to help the student learn to read at a pace suited to his or her individual needs.
English Language
Dist - GPN **Prod** - NYCBED 1981

Meeting ISO 9000 standards - a briefing for chemical laboratories 180 MIN
VHS
Color (C PRO)
$2200.00 purchase _ #V - 6100 - 26881
Examines ISO 9000 certification and whether or not the standards can be implemented at viewers' facilities. Shows how to assess whether implementation of the standards is worth the time, energy and cost of certification and how to avoid pitfalls in the implementation process. Demonstrates how to ascertain the real costs of implementing ISO 9000 standards in a laboratory. Owen B Mathre, of E I du Pont de Nemours & Co, and Steven B Oblath, of Research Associates, speak. Suzan L Jackson, Johannes Schmid and Barbara N Sutter serve as panelists. Includes two videos and a course study guide.
Industrial and Technical Education; Science
Dist - AMCHEM **Prod** - AMCHEM 1993

Meeting Leading Series
Planning for Impact 40 MIN
Dist - DELTAK

Meeting Leading Series
Conducting and Managing the Meeting 30 MIN
Dist - DELTAK
PRODEV

Meeting Leading Series

Planning for Impact and Control	30 MIN
Preview Program	30 MIN

Dist - PRODEV

Meeting Nature's Challenge 19 MIN
16mm
Color
LC 80-700302
Tells the story of Ohio Medical Products' role in the development of medical life - support technology, showing how interaction between medical practitioners and design engineers contributes to the solution of critical - care and life - support problems.
Business and Economics; Health and Safety
Dist - OHMED **Prod** - OHMED 1980

Meeting Near Mafeking 23 MIN
16mm
Color
Presents the story of six Scouts out on a hiking trip who find themselves going through time and space ending up in the midst of Scouting's origins.
Sociology
Dist - BSA **Prod** - BSA 1982

Meeting Objections
U-matic / VHS
Telephone Selling Series
Color (IND)
Lists basic objection types like need more information, as to price, doubts value and can't afford, stalls and miscellaneous. Shows how to handle negative reactions, such as is objection clear, probing or paraphrasing until clear, getting prospect's reaction and, if favorable, close, and if negative, offer more information or continue probe but avoid argument. Includes six sales demonstrations and two sets of role plays.
Business and Economics; Psychology; Social Science
Dist - COLOSU **Prod** - COLOSU

The Meeting of Minds 15 MIN
U-matic / VHS
Color (A)
Presents techniques for breaking down barriers that prevent sales. Shows how to establish rapport with customers and ease their doubts.
Business and Economics
Dist - XICOM **Prod** - XICOM

A Meeting of Minds 22 MIN
16mm
Color
LC 78-701438
Discusses the need for open communication and objectivity in conducting employment rating interviews.
Business and Economics; Psychology
Dist - CONED **Prod** - CONED 1978

The Meeting of Minds 14 MIN
VHS / U-matic
Sales Communications Series
Color
Illustrates the way to identify and remove barriers to create a meeting of the minds and make the sale.
Business and Economics
Dist - VISUCP **Prod** - VISUCP

Meeting of the Minds 3 MIN
16mm / VHS
Caffeine Capers - Reel 1 - Series
Color (PRO)
$175.00 purchase, $99.00 rental
Presents a humorous vignette about a business meeting between high level policy makers.
Psychology
Dist - UTM

Meeting of two queens - Encuentros enre dos reinas 14 MIN
VHS
Color (A)
$200.00 purchase, $50.00 rental
Casts Greta Garbo and Marlene Dietrich as lovers - Queen Christina meets the Scarlet Empress. Links the queens through the motifs of the cigarette and meaningful gazes and gestures. Edited and produced by Cecilia Barriga.
Fine Arts
Dist - WMEN

Meeting opener motivation videos series
Presents a series of five inspirational videos which incorporate breakthrough cinematography, stirring music and powerful lyrics to create a mood that enhances the impact of the desired message. Includes the concepts of Quality, Service, Teamwork, Leadership and Wellness.

Leadership video	3 MIN
Quality video	3 MIN
Service video	3 MIN
Teamwork video	3 MIN
Wellness video	3 MIN

Dist - GPERFO

Meeting Place 9 MIN
16mm
Color
LC 72-700599
A recuiting film which takes the prospective student on a tour of Temple University. Emphasizes the broad spectrum of educational, intellectual, and recreational facilities that are available at this Philadelphia University.
Education; Guidance and Counseling
Dist - TEMPLU **Prod** - TEMPLU 1971

Meeting Residents' Needs 12 MIN
16mm / U-matic / VHS
It Can't be Home Series
Color
Shows the importance of meaningful work, social relationship and recreation for nursing home residents.
Health and Safety; Psychology; Sociology
Dist - USNAC **Prod** - USHHS 1976

Meeting Robbers 35 MIN
16mm / VHS
#109067 - 3 3/4
Demonstrates how managers can plan and conduct a meeting properly, keeping it on track and avoiding frustration and wasted time.
Business and Economics
Dist - MGHT

The Meeting Robbers 20 MIN
16mm
Color (C)
$27.50 rental _ #23811
Describes seven types of personalities who rob meetings of time, creativity and productivity. Provides strategies for diplomatically dealing with these personalities and having a meeting that meets common goals.
Business and Economics
Dist - PSU **Prod** - CRMP
VLEARN

Meeting Steam Vessels 18 MIN
16mm
B&W
LC 74-705123
Gives examples of steam vessels meeting on the ocean and in inland waters. Demonstrates whistle signals for various situations and shows how to figure the degree of a vessel's turn at various distances.
Civics and Political Systems; Social Science
Dist - USNAC **Prod** - USN 1943

Meeting Strangers - Red Light, Green Light 20 MIN
U-matic / VHS / 16mm
Color (P I) (SPANISH)

LC 76-702462
Helps the child to understand when the meeting of strangers might be potentially dangerous and provides him with specific suggestions for behavior at such times.
Guidance and Counseling; Health and Safety; Psychology
Dist - PHENIX **Prod** - PHENIX 1969

Meeting the challenge - 1 15 MIN
VHS
Learning about cancer series
Color (G)
$250.00 purchase, $60.00 rental
Takes an in - depth look at the detection and treatment of cancer and the emotional impact of the disease on patients and their families. Part 1 of a five - part series.
Health and Safety
Dist - CF **Prod** - HOSSN 1989

Meeting the challenge of hazardous waste 29 MIN
BETA / U-matic / VHS
Color (G)
$29.95, $130.00 purchase _ #LSTF10
Examines the roles of government, industry and communities in reducing environmental threats. Looks at new treatment technologies.
Sociology
Dist - FEDU **Prod** - USEPA 1988

Meeting the Challenge of Prospective Reimbursement for Employees 18 MIN
VHS / U-matic
Color
Focuses on Employees at Memorial Hospital. Shows them realizing the importance of their contribution to this medical facility.
Health and Safety; Industrial and Technical Education
Dist - CREMED **Prod** - CREMED

Meeting the Challenge of Prospective Reimbursement for Managers 27 MIN
U-matic / VHS
Color
Focuses on an official at Memorial Hospital who, after becoming a patient at his own hospital, automatically changes his opinions.
Health and Safety; Industrial and Technical Education
Dist - CREMED **Prod** - CREMED

Meeting the challenge with Dr Warren Bennis series
Presents a five - part series with Drs Warren Bennis and Peter Drucker who conduct a seminars on doing business and managing employees. Gives examples of what has worked in real companies. Focuses on the responsibility of management for providing solutions in a rapidly changing global economy.
The Challenge of change 10 MIN
Information - based organizations and the knowledge worker 10 MIN
Managing the knowledge specialists 10 MIN
Mastering the new global economy 10 MIN
The special demands of service workers and women employees 10 MIN
Dist - BARR **Prod** - HILSU

Meeting the communication needs of the severely - profoundly handicapped 1981 series
Assessment of visual acuity 76 MIN
Dist - PUAVC

Meeting the communication needs of the severely - profoundly handicapped 1980 series
Cognitive development 145 MIN
Dist - PUAVC

Meeting the communication needs of the severely - profoundly handicapped 1981 series
Cognitive development 175 MIN
Communication assessment 160 MIN
Communication intervention 159 MIN
Motor Development - Assessment and Intervention 159 MIN
Pragmatic development 146 MIN
Dist - PUAVC

Meeting the Communication Needs of the Severely/Profoundly Handicapped 1981 Series
Behavioral Assessment of Hearing 89 MIN
Management of Interfering and Annoying Behavior - Normalization 154 MIN
Nonspeech Communication - Augmentative Systems 330 MIN
Semantics and Syntax 168 MIN
Dist - PUAVC

Meeting the communications needs of the severely - profoundly handicapped 1980 series
Cognitive assessment 121 MIN
Communication assessment 138 MIN
Communication intervention 107 MIN
Focusing on next environments for communication training 108 MIN
Oral Motor Problems 45 MIN
Pragmatic development 112 MIN
Dist - PUAVC

Meeting the communications needs of the severely - profoundly handicapped series
Phonological development 130 MIN
Dist - PUAVC

Meeting the Communications Needs of the Severely/Profoundly Handicapped 1980 Series
Behavioral Analysis and Operant Techniques 144 MIN
Hearing 60 MIN
Management of Interfering and Annoying Behavior - Normalization 129 MIN
Nonspeech Communication - Augmentative Systems 314 MIN
Parent Training 150 MIN
Preparing the Sensory and Visual Perceptual Motor Prerequisites for Communication 50 MIN
Syntactic and Semantic Development 136 MIN
Dist - PUAVC

Meeting the Emergency 13 MIN
VHS / 16mm
Learning about Heart Attacks Series
Color (H C A PRO)
$195.00 purchase, $75.00 rental _ #8078
Examines emergency procedures for coping with a heart attack.
Guidance and Counseling; Health and Safety
Dist - AIMS **Prod** - HOSSN 1988

Meeting the Man - James Baldwin in Paris 27 MIN
16mm
Color (H C A)
LC 72-702628
Presents a documentary on James Baldwin as a Black man, a writer and a political figure.
Biography; History - United States; Literature and Drama
Dist - IMPACT **Prod** - IMPACT 1972

Meeting the meeting challenge 35 MIN
VHS
Color (A PRO IND)
$660.00 purchase, $155.00 rental
Discusses how to conduct meetings more successfully. Covers topics including getting the meeting started, encouraging participation, handling conflict, and getting commitment to group decisions. Pauses at 12 different points to allow for audience discussion.
Business and Economics; Guidance and Counseling; Psychology
Dist - VLEARN **Prod** - RTBL

Meeting the Meeting Challenge 35 MIN
VHS / 16mm
(C PRO)
$630.00 purchase, $150.00 rental
Shows a meeting in progress. Stops for audience discussion at 12 critical points, including getting started, encouraging participation, handling conflict, and getting commitment to group decisions. Updated version of the classic, Meeting In Progress.
Psychology
Dist - VLEARN

Meeting the Needs of the Physically Handicapped 10 MIN
16mm
Exceptional Learners Series
Color (T S)
LC 79-700713
Shows handicapped children in a regular classroom situation and in a classroom where handicapped students use special facilities and equipment.
Education; Psychology
Dist - MERILC **Prod** - MERILC 1978

Meeting the Union Challenge Series
Unions - Awareness and Organizing Tactics
Unions - Strategies for Prevention
Dist - GPCV

Meeting the world - Parents video magazine - Volume 2 45 MIN
VHS
Color (A)
$19.95 purchase _ #S01204
Describes how parents can discover and help to develop their children's capabilities. Discusses topics including motor development, childproofing the home, discipline, day care and more.
Psychology; Sociology
Dist - UILL

Meeting will come to order series
Amending a motion 28.03 MIN
By - laws, voting and elections 29.33 MIN
Incidental and other motions 28 MIN
The Main motion 28.37 MIN
Order of precedence 24.11 MIN
Organizing a new society 28.40
Dist - GPN

A Meeting with the enemy 22 MIN
16mm
B&W (G)
$25.00 rental
Describes events following a national referendum on nuclear disarmament which is successful but is countered with an attempt by the American military to stage a mock nuclear war in order to retain their power. Depicts a popular uprising that blocks the military but is aborted by 'other' forces. Set in the year 1992. Produced by Niccolo Caldararo. Music by Tom Wells, Ali Pimera and Brain Damage.
Civics and Political Systems; Fine Arts
Dist - CANCIN

Meeting Your Micro and the World of Computing
Software / VHS / Kit / U-matic
New Horizons Series
(PRO)
$1595 series purchase
Introduces the many uses of computers in contemporary work and education environments.
Computer Science
Dist - AITECH **Prod** - ALASDE 1986

Meetings, bloody meetings 30 MIN
VHS / U-matic / BETA
Color; CC (C A G)
$870.00 purchase, $240.00 rental
Stars John Cleese who portrays a thoroughly inefficient chairperson who dreams he is hauled up before a court for negligent conduct of meetings. Gives an in - depth demonstration of the disciplines, techniques and attitudes required to make meetings shorter and more productive.
Business and Economics; Psychology
Dist - VIDART **Prod** - VIDART 1993
VISUCP
VLEARN

Meetings, Health Care, and Safety - How to Hold a Meeting 30 MIN
U-matic / VHS
Color
Provides practical information on conducting an effective meeting. Illustrates how to develop a productive meeting atmosphere.
Business and Economics; Psychology
Dist - CREMED **Prod** - CREMED

Meetings - Isn't There a Better Way? 32 MIN
VHS / U-matic
Color
Places emphasis on teaching leaders and participants collaborative problem - solving techniques in achieving consensus. Identifies four types of meetings - presentation, feedback, problem - solving and decision - making, and explains how to run each.
Business and Economics; Guidance and Counseling; Social Science
Dist - VISUCP **Prod** - VISUCP

Meetings that work! 21 MIN
VHS
Color (COR)
$495.00 purchase, $150.00 five - day rental, $35.00 three - day preview _ #UMW/UTM
Guides management in developing methods of preparing for and holding more productive and efficient staff meetings. Teaches how to plan a creative agenda, prepare your staff, take advantage of chance meetings, become more organized, and evaluate past meetings. Includes a leader's guide.
Business and Economics
Dist - ADVANM

Meetings with remarkable men 108 MIN
35mm / 16mm / VHS
Color (G)
$250.00, $300.00 rental
Draws on the works of G I Gurdjieff to follow one man's search for an ancient brotherhood of knowledge which has passed its wisdom through thousands of years. Directed by Peter Brooks.
Fine Arts; Religion and Philosophy
Dist - KINOIC **Prod** - CORINT 1979

Meg Green's financial workout
VHS
Color (A)
Features financial planner Meg Green who shows how to organize finances using simple exercises and workout tips. Covers taxes, investments, insurance, retirement planning and estate planning. Includes a hands-on financial organizer.
Business and Economics
Dist - SIV
CAMV

Mega - Building - Giants Cast Long Shadows 17 MIN
16mm / U-matic / VHS
Color
Explains that some people see skyscrapers as heralds of the life style of the urban future while others see them as unthinking giantism. Depicts various "mega - buildings" around the world and anlyzes their effects.
Fine Arts; Science - Natural; Sociology
Dist - CNEMAG **Prod** - DOCUA

MegaCode 28 MIN
VHS
Color (C PRO)
$285.00 purchase, $70.00 rental _ #4293S, #4293V
Underscores the belief that nurses must be prepared to function in a code and demonstrates that clearly, precisely and in sequential order. Dramatizes in a hospital setting the correct order of actions that must be taken in a life - threatening situation, such as a cardiac and - or respiratory arrest. Offers a team approach for running mock or practice codes as well as for actual cardiopulmonary resuscitation. Demonstrates the assigning of roles, CPR, defibrillation, IV lines, equipment setup and medication administration. Includes a guide with drug information, code protocols, cardiac arrest worksheet. Produced by Rogue Valley Medical Center.
Health and Safety
Dist - AJN

Megan at 2 30 MIN
U-matic / VHS
Say it with sign series; Pt 33
Color (H C A) (AMERICAN SIGN)
Presents Lawrence Solow and Sharon Neumann Solow introducing American Sign Language used by the hearing - impaired. Emphasizes signs having to do with a two - year - old named Megan.
Education
Dist - FI **Prod** - KNBCTV 1982

Megapolis 29 MIN
16mm
Earthkeeping Series
Color (H C A)
LC 73-703404
Explains that even though there exists the technology to build socially responsible cities which provide for varying lifestyles, American cities are growing so big that one city is growing into another forming one huge sprawling man - made environment of megapolis. Ascribes this condition to apathy.
Science - Natural; Sociology
Dist - IU **Prod** - WTTWTV 1973

Megatrends 57 MIN
Cassette / U-matic
Mono; Color (G)
Deals with the nature of the new tech society. Based on John Naisbitt's nonfiction work, Megatrends. Includes Six cassettes.
Business and Economics
Dist - VPHI **Prod** - VPHI 1985

Megatrends - Short Cut Version 25 MIN
VHS / 16mm
(C PRO)
$495.00 purchase, $175.00 rental
Presents a short cut version of Megatrends.
Education
Dist - VLEARN **Prod** - VPHI

Meggido - City of Destruction 29 MIN
U-matic / VHS / 16mm
Color (H C R)
LC 80-700652
Provides a guided view of excavations at Meggido, Israel, conducted by archaeologist Yigael Yadin of Hebrew University. Relates the interpretation of the Old Testament of the architectural and cultural clues which tie together the excavated cities of Meggido, Hazor and Gezer as parts of Solomon's kingdom.
History - World; Science - Physical; Sociology
Dist - IU **Prod** - CAFM 1980

Megohmmeters, voltage testers, clamp - on ammeters 60 MIN
U-matic / VHS
Electrical maintenance training series; Module B - Test instruments
Color (IND)
Industrial and Technical Education
Dist - LEIKID **Prod** - LEIKID

The Mehinacu 52 MIN
VHS
Disappearing world series
Color (G C)
$99.00 purchase, $19.00 rental _ #51224
Focuses on the month - long fruit harvest celebration of the Mehinacu who live near the river Xingu in the central Brazilian rain forest. Reveals that the peaceful Mehinacu way of life is threatened by road builders who plan to cut through the forest. Features anthropologist Thomas Gregor. Part of a series working closely with anthropologists who lived for a year or more in societies whose social structures, beliefs and practices are threatened by the expansion of technocratic civilization.
Sociology
Dist - PSU **Prod** - GRANDA 1974

Mei - Mei Berssenbrugge - 4 - 21 - 76 41 MIN
VHS / Cassette
Poetry Center reading series
Color (G)
$15.00, $45.00 purchase _ #197 - 154
Features the writer reading her works at the Poetry Center, San Francisco State University.
Literature and Drama
Dist - POETRY **Prod** - POETRY 1976

Mei - Mei Berssenbrugge - 9 - 28 - 82 30 MIN
VHS / Cassette
Poetry Center reading series
Color (G)
$15.00, $45.00 purchase _ #498 - 421
Features the writer reading her works at the Poetry Center, San Francisco State University.
Literature and Drama
Dist - POETRY **Prod** - POETRY 1982

Mei - Mei Berssenbrugge - 2 - 22 - 90 40 MIN
VHS / Cassette
Poetry Center reading series
Color (G)
$15.00, $45.00 purchase _ #874 - 679
Features the writer reading from her books Empathy and Hiddenness at the Poetry Center, San Francisco State University, with an introduction by Laura Moriarty.
Literature and Drama
Dist - POETRY **Prod** - POETRY 1990

The Meier chronicles
VHS
Edward Meier series
Color (G)
$59.95 purchase _ #GB001
Visits the contact sites of Edward Meier's over 100 claimed encounters with aliens.
Science - Physical; Sociology
Dist - SIV

The Meiji Adventure 30 MIN
VHS / U-matic
Journey into Japan Series
Color (J S C G)
MV=$195.00
Reveals the history of the Meiji period when the iron rule of the Shoguns waned and aggressive industrialization and military preparations were begun.
Geography - World; History - World
Dist - LANDMK **Prod** - LANDMK 1986

The Meiji Period - 1868 - 1912 58 MIN
U-matic / VHS
Japan Past and Present Series
Color (G)
$279.00, $179.00 purchase _ #AD - 2154
Reveals that the arrival of Commodore Perry in 1854 set the stage for Japan's dramatic leap from the Middle Ages into modernity. Discloses that Japan's ports were forced open - the English, French, Russians and Dutch demanded and got the same privileges. In 1868 the last shogun gave way to a 15 - year - old Emperor who dressed in Western - style clothes. Part of a five - part series on Japan past and present.
Civics and Political Systems; Geography - World; History - World; Sociology
Dist - FOTH **Prod** - FOTH

The Meiji Transformation 28 MIN
VHS / U-matic
Japan - the Changing Tradition Series
Color (A)
LC 80-706224
Uses drawings, period films and sound effects to chronicle the reign of Meiji, Emperor of Japan.
Civics and Political Systems; History - World
Dist - GPN **Prod** - UMA 1979

Mein kampf - Hitler's rise and fall 117 MIN
VHS
Color (J H C G)
$39.95 purchase _ #CPM13V
Illustrates Hitler's attempt to conquer the world. Contains footage from the archives of the Nazi SS Elite Guard and is filled with actual scenes of the horrors of the time. Witnesses Hitler's rise to power, the extermination campaign waged by the German government, its failure and the fall of Hitler and his comrades.
Civics and Political Systems; History - World
Dist - CAMV

Meiosis 15 MIN
VHS
Color (J H) (SPANISH)
$99.00 purchase _ #3669 - 026
Takes the viewer up close to illustrate the complex process of meiosis. Highlights the role of meiosis in sexual reproduction in both plants and animals. Includes teacher's guide.
Education; Science - Natural
Dist - GA **Prod** - EBEC
EBEC

Meiosis
VHS
Basic science series
Color (J H) (ENGLISH AND SPANISH)
$39.95 purchase _ #MCV5020
Focuses on meiosis, presenting only basic concepts. Includes teacher's guide and review questions. Combines computer animation and the use of 'sheltered language' to help students acquire content vocabulary, become comfortable with scientific language and achieve success in science curriculum. Part of a series on basic science concepts.
Science; Science - Natural
Dist - MADERA **Prod** - MADERA

Meiosis 26 MIN
U-matic / 35mm strip
Color (H C)
$43.95 purchase _ #52 1644
Introduces the basic mechanisms of meiosis, sources of genetic variability, cytology. Compares meiosis and mitosis. Includes a teacher's guide.
Science - Natural
Dist - CBSC **Prod** - BMEDIA

Meiosis 7 MIN
U-matic / VHS / 16mm
Life Cycle of a Flowering Plant Series no 3
Color
LC 73-703050
Uses the apple tree as a model, as well as time - lapse microphotography and animation, to explain and reinforce the concept of meiosis.
Science - Natural
Dist - LUF **Prod** - SCHLAT 1971

Meiosis 12 MIN
U-matic / VHS / 16mm
Color (C)
Shows how the number of chromosomes in germ cells is halved. An introductory flow chart shows the fertilization meiosis cycle.
Science - Natural
Dist - IFB **Prod** - CSIROA 1956

Meiosis in lilium anthers 26 MIN
VHS
Color (J H)
$49.95 purchase _ #193 W 0130
Illustrates first and second division in lily anthers. Covers meiosis - first division, meiosis - second division, and includes two timed review quizzes of 15 questions each which cover mixed meiotic stages and cell structures. Illustrates proper microsearch techniques. Produced by the University of New Brunswick.
Science - Natural
Dist - WARDS

Meiosis - the key to genetic diversity 26 MIN
VHS
Color (J H C)
$169.00 purchase _ #CG - 875 - VS
Helps to clarify the process of meiosis for students by first developing an uderstanding of the problems that meiosis solves for the organism. Uses clear animation and photo - micrography to demonstrate how each step of meiosis contributes to the solution of those problems. Presents some fundamental concepts of genetics to illustrate how meiosis, including crossing - over, contributes to genetic diversity.
Science - Natural
Dist - HRMC **Prod** - HRMC

Meiosis - the key to genetic diversity 26 MIN
VHS
Color (J H)
$170.00 purchase _ #A5VH 1269
Presents two parts which shows why meiosis is important to sexually reproducing organisms. Shows how an organism's sex cells are formed through the process of meiosis, focuses on how meiosis reduces by half the normal diploid number of chromosomes and illustrates each step of meiosis from prophase I through telophase II in the first part. The second part explains why genetic diversity is important and how it strengthens a species, describing random segregation of chromosomes during meiosis and detailing how the crossing over of genes between homologous chromosomes results in still more variation.
Science - Natural
Dist - CLRVUE **Prod** - CLRVUE 1992

The Meiotic Mix 10 MIN
U-matic
Organic Evolution Series
Color (H C) (FRENCH)
Traces the development of various theories of evolution beginning with the Biblical account of creation and going on to discuss Darwin, Mendel and others. Ties together the microscopic and macroscopic, genetics and heredity, cell reproduction and breeding populations. Available in French. Comes with teacher's guide.
Science
Dist - TVOTAR **Prod** - TVOTAR 1986

Meji 4 MIN
16mm
B&W (G)
$5.00 rental
Records a children's festival day in Tokyo. Features lots of Nikons with mothers and children in traditional dress. A Rob Savage production.
Fine Arts; Geography - World; Religion and Philosophy; Sociology
Dist - CANCIN

The Mekong 57 MIN
U-matic / VHS
River Journeys
Color (H C A)
$1225 purchase (entire series), $285 purchase (each)
Discusses the journeys of William Shawcross across the Mekong River in southeast Asia. Relates his journeys in Vietnam, Kampuchea, and Laos. Produced by BBC - TV and RKO Pictures for public television.
Geography - World
Dist - CF

Mekong 26 MIN
U-matic / VHS / 16mm
Color (J H)
Geography - World; History - United States; History - World
Dist - EBEC **Prod** - SIPC 1967

Mekong Farmer of Thailand 14 MIN
16mm
Human Family, Pt 1 - South and Southeast Asia Series
Color (I)
Tells the story of Soi and his family who live in Huei Suem, a village in the northeast of Thailand, far down the Mekong River.
Geography - World; Social Science; Sociology
Dist - AVED **Prod** - AVED 1972

Mel and Griff - Part 1 7 MIN
U-matic / VHS
Meeting breaks series
Color (C A PRO)
$295.00 purchase
Offers a funny look at virtually every aspect of a business meeting. Includes 'Start of Day,' 'Pre - Coffee,' 'Speaker Intro' and 'Big Build Up.' Features Mel Smith and Griff Rhys Jones. Produced by Playback.
Business and Economics; Literature and Drama; Psychology
Dist - VIDART

Mel and Griff - Part 2 7 MIN
U-matic / VHS
Meeting breaks series
Color (C A PRO)
$295.00 purchase
Offers a funny look at virtually every aspect of a business meeting. Includes 'Questions and Answers,' 'Post Critical Speaker,' 'Mental Attitude' and 'Statistics.' Features Mel Smith and Griff Rhys Jones. Produced by Playback.
Business and Economics; Literature and Drama; Psychology
Dist - VIDART

Mel Lewis
VHS
Color (G)
$29.95 purchase _ #1273
Presents late drummer Mel Lewis fronting the big band which has performed every Monday night for more than a decade at New York's Village Vanguard. Features a young seventeen - piece ensemble performing three pieces by Herbie Hancock and one by Bob Brookmeyer.
Fine Arts
Dist - KULTUR

Mel on Wheels 19 MIN
U-matic / VHS / 16mm
Color (J)
LC 82-700156
Tells about Melvin Manger, who was born with severe cerebral palsy and led a sheltered life until, with the help of friends and an electric wheelchair, he learned to become more independent. Shows how now, in his sixties, he is able to participate in the community.
Education; Psychology
Dist - CF **Prod** - WRMFZY 1982

Melancholy Maybe 23 MIN
16mm
Color
LC 77-702965
Features excerpts from the screenplay Last Card by John Kuti, depicting a tragic relationship between two lovers.
Fine Arts; Guidance and Counseling; Literature and Drama
Dist - ONCA **Prod** - ONCA 1976

Melanesian Nightmare 27 MIN
16mm / U-matic / VHS
Victory at Sea Series
B&W (J H)
Highlights the New Guinea campaign during World War II.
Civics and Political Systems; History - United States; History - World
Dist - LUF **Prod** - NBCTV

Melanesian nightmare, D - day, Roman renaissance and killers and the killed 108 MIN
VHS
Victory at sea series
B&W (G)
$24.95 purchase _ #S01157
Contains four episodes from the Victory at Sea series, documenting the US Navy battles of World War II. 'Melanesian Nightmare' documents the Japanese attempt to occupy Port Moresby, and 'D - Day' covers the planning of the D - Day operation. 'Roman Renaissance' highlights the Allied convoy of 160,000 soldiers to Sicily, while 'Killers and the Killed' deals with the Allied struggle against German U - boats in the Atlantic.
Civics and Political Systems; History - United States
Dist - UILL

Melanomas - Diagnosis and Treatment 21 MIN
16mm
Color (PRO)
Shows a large variety of malignant melanomas. Traces their natural history and outlines the differential diagnosis of moles with special attention to junctional nevi. Depicts the diagnosis and treatment of a patient with melanoma. Demonstrates wide surgical excision of localized lesions.
Health and Safety; Science
Dist - AMCS **Prod** - AMCS 1973

Melbourne, Florida at its Best 15 MIN
16mm
Color
Explores the community of Melbourne, Florida.
Geography - United States
Dist - FLADC **Prod** - FLADC

Melbourne Olympic Games 22 MIN
16mm
Color (H C)
LC FIA59-558
Records action shots of numerous track and field events of the 16th Olympiad held at Melbourne, Australia. Depicts the colorful pageantry and spirit of the age - old Olympic games for the general public as well as sports fans.
Geography - World; Physical Education and Recreation
Dist - COCA **Prod** - HANDY 1958

Meli 21 MIN
U-matic / VHS / 16mm
Color
LC 80-701330
Examines the struggles and joys of Meli Davis Kaye, who has managed to raise a family while at the same time continuing her work as a dancer and mime artist.
Fine Arts; Sociology
Dist - IDIM **Prod** - IDIM 1980

Melies - Catalogue 9 MIN
16mm
Color
LC 70-704322
Presents a homage to Georges Melies, 1862 - 1938, a founder of the cinema.
Biography; Fine Arts
Dist - CANFDC **Prod** - CANFDC 1973

Melina Mercouri's Athens 25 MIN
U-matic / VHS / 16mm
Cities Series
Color (H C A)
LC 80-701091
Presents actress Melina Mercouri as she tours her native Athens and explains the music, poetry and legends of Greece. Includes views of the Acropolis, the Port of Pireaus and the Monasteraki.
Geography - World; Sociology
Dist - LCOA **Prod** - NIELSE 1980

Melinda's blind 24 MIN
16mm
Young people's specials series
Color
LC 80-700283
Tells the story of a young girl who encounters difficulty in learning to live in a world of darkness. Shows her eventual triumph over the problems of depression, fear, bitterness and lack of confidence.
Fine Arts; Guidance and Counseling; Psychology
Dist - MULTPP **Prod** - MULTPP 1979

Mellah 30 MIN
16mm
B&W (I)
LC 72-700014
Tells the story of a young boy from the Mellah, the slum quarter of Casablanca, and how his life was changed by going to a vocational school sponsored by the organization for rehabilitation through training.
Guidance and Counseling; Psychology; Sociology
Dist - WAORT **Prod** - WAORT 1955

Mellem to Kultutrer (between Two Cultures) 54 MIN
16mm
B&W (DANISH)
Examines and documents the conditions and effects of developmental work in SouthEastern Mexico.
Foreign Language; Geography - World
Dist - STATNS **Prod** - STATNS 1967

Mellow Moods 29 MIN
Videoreel / VT2
Changing rhythms series
Color
Presents the free - form electronic rock sound of the Mellow Moods in Ain't No Sunshine, What's Going On, Who Was He and Slipping Into Darkness.
Fine Arts; History - United States
Dist - PBS **Prod** - KRMATV

Melodic Inversion 9 MIN
16mm
Color
Reflects the inner world of man in quest of the ideal, beautiful, desirable and unattainable through a visual melodic study of transposal in which colors with fluid movements reveal the moods embedded in the theme.
Fine Arts; Religion and Philosophy
Dist - RADIM **Prod** - HUGOI

Melodies 14 MIN
U-matic / VHS
Music and Me Series
Color (P I)
Discusses musical melodies.
Fine Arts
Dist - AITECH **Prod** - WDCNTV 1979

Melody 15 MIN
U-matic
Music Box Series
Color (K P)
Demonstrates melody and the possible range of high and low sounds.
Fine Arts
Dist - TVOTAR **Prod** - TVOTAR 1971

Melody 28 MIN
VHS / U-matic
Old Friends - New Friends Series
Color
Presents portraits of Lesley Frost Ballantine, daughter of poet Robert Frost and herself a poet and author, and of famous black blues singer John Jackson.
Fine Arts; History - United States; Literature and Drama
Dist - PBS **Prod** - FAMCOM 1981

Melody 8 MIN
U-matic / VHS / 16mm
Color (K P I) (SPANISH)
LC 73-701493
Tells the story of Melody, a bird who meets, sings and plays with instruments of the brass, woodwind, string and rhythm families.
Fine Arts
Dist - AIMS **Prod** - SAIF 1972

Melody and Pitch 21.5 MIN
U-matic / VHS
You Can make Music Series
Color (K P I)
$360, $390 purchase _ #V124
Demonstrates that a melody is a group of tones with definite pitches. Shows viewers how to distinguish between low and high pitches. Introduces the concept of scale to children.
Fine Arts
Dist - BARR **Prod** - BARR 1987

Melody and Scale 25 MIN
VHS / U-matic
You Can make Music Series
Color (K P I)
$360, $390 purchase _ #V125
Explores the concept of melody, emphasizing the subtle pitch changes which occur within a typical melody. Teaches the five tone scale of do, re, mi, fa, so.
Fine Arts
Dist - BARR **Prod** - BARR 1987

Melody and Timbre 25 MIN
VHS / U-matic
Arts Express Series
Color (K P I J)
Fine Arts
Dist - KYTV **Prod** - KYTV 1983

Melody - Bi - Lingual 15 MIN
U-matic / VHS / 16mm
Color (K P I)
LC 74-702703
Presents the story of Melody, a bird who sings rather than chirps. Explains how she discovers all the instruments of the orchestra in the process of looking for a friend.
Fine Arts
Dist - AIMS **Prod** - SAIF 1973

The Melody Lingers on 28 MIN
U-matic / VHS
Please Stand by - a History of Radio Series
(C A)
Fine Arts; History - United States; Psychology; Sociology
Dist - SCCON **Prod** - SCCON 1986

A Melody of Birds and Flowers 20 MIN
VHS / U-matic
Color (J)
LC 82-706772
Shows the egret, laughing gull, golden eagle and other birds, along with views of flowers in various regions of America.
Science - Natural
Dist - AWSS **Prod** - AWSS 1980

Melody Time 75 MIN
U-matic / VHS / 16mm
Color
Presents a musical fantasy based on American tall tales and ballads.
Fine Arts
Dist - FI **Prod** - DISNEY 1948

The Melon tossing game 15 MIN
VHS / 16mm
San - Ju - Wasi series
Color (G)
$270.00, $140.00 purchase, $30.00 rental
Observes women from three Kung bands who have gathered at a mangetti grove to play an intense game involving dance and tossing a melon. Reveals that men intrude and dance spectacularly and an old woman, N - aoka, goes into a trance - like state, but the dance disintegrates when N - ai, the wife of the male dancer Gunda, teases and taunts N - aoka. Part of a series by John Marshall about the Kung in Namibia and Botswana.
Fine Arts; Geography - World; History - World; Physical Education and Recreation; Psychology; Sociology
Dist - DOCEDR **Prod** - DOCEDR

Meltdown - Volume 3 45 MIN
VHS
Bubblegum crash series
Color (A) (JAPANESE WITH ENGLISH SUBTITLES)
$34.95 purchase _ #CPM92003
Presents a Japanese animated film. Viewer discretion is advised as some films contain strong language or violence.
Fine Arts
Dist - CHTSUI

Melting Point Determination 17 MIN
U-matic / VHS
Organic Chemistry Laboratory Techniques Series
Color
Shows procedures for determining a melting point. Demonstrates various types of apparatus. Illustrates the principles behind phase changes.
Science; Science - Physical
Dist - UCEMC **Prod** - UCLA

The Melting Pot 24 MIN
16mm
B&W (I J)
Pictures California's growth in terms of its varied peoples, from the days of the Indian through the immigration of national groups. Shows the contributions of the various nationalities to modern civilization.
Geography - United States; History - United States
Dist - MLA **Prod** - ABCTV 1963

The Melting pot 30 MIN
U-matic / VHS
Art America series
Color (H C A)
$43.00 purchase
Shows the urban environment in the work of American artists. Provides background on the social and cultural context of the works. Part of a 20-part series.
Fine Arts
Dist - CTI **Prod** - CTI
GPN

Melting Statues/Jazz Dance 30 MIN
U-matic / VHS
Doris Chase Dance Series
Color
Features performances by Kei Takei, Mel Pate and John Parton, and animation with Gay Delanghe.
Fine Arts; Physical Education and Recreation
Dist - CHASED **Prod** - CHASED

Melvin Arbuckle, Famous Canadian 5 MIN
16mm
Color (I)
Presents an animated look at a childhood prank perpetrated on the Canadian prairies.
Fine Arts; Literature and Drama
Dist - NFBC **Prod** - NFBC 1980

Melvin Calvin 45 MIN
VHS / U-matic
Eminent Chemists - the Interviews Series
Color
Discusses and demonstrates the work of Dr Melvin Calvin on porphyrins and his work on photosynthesis.
Science; Science - Natural; Science - Physical
Dist - AMCHEM **Prod** - AMCHEM 1982

Melvyn Bragg 45 MIN
VHS
Color (H C G)
$79.00 purchase
Features the British writer with Frank Delaney discussing his writing and championing of the arts. Talks about his works including The Hired Man; Without a City Wall; and the non - fiction titles Speak for England and Laurence Olivier.
Literature and Drama
Dist - ROLAND **Prod** - INCART

A Member of Society 10 MIN
16mm / U-matic / VHS
BSCS Behavior Film Series
Color
LC 74-702354
Discusses animals as members of their ecological society and the importance of each type to the ecological balance of the environment.
Science - Natural
Dist - PHENIX **Prod** - BSCS 1974

Member of the Wedding 91 MIN
U-matic / VHS / 16mm
B&W (J)
Stars Julie Harris, Ethel Waters and Brandon De Wilde. Portrays a young girl who teeters on the thin edge of heartbreak and minor tragedy because of her enormous sense of loneliness.
Fine Arts; Literature and Drama
Dist - FI **Prod** - CPC 1952

Members of the Original Chorus Line Talk about Where they have Gone Since Then 30 MIN
VHS / U-matic
Broadway Series
Color
Fine Arts; Industrial and Technical Education
Dist - ARCVID **Prod** - ARCVID

Membrane Filtration Procedure - Fecal Determination in Wastewater and Wastewater 22 MIN
BETA / VHS
Color
Complete title is Membrane Filtration Procedure - Fecal Determination In Wastewater And Wastewater Effluent - Membrane Filtration Technique. Discusses water reuse, sewage purification, water and the membrane filtration technique in wastewater technology.
Health and Safety; Industrial and Technical Education; Science; Social Science
Dist - RMIBHF **Prod** - RMIBHF

Membrane Oxygenation in Extracorporeal Life Support 6 MIN
16mm
Color
LC 73-700890
Demonstrates the use of the general electric membrane oxygenator in open heart surgery. Shows how the unit is connected to the human body to provide oxygenated blood.
Health and Safety; Science - Natural
Dist - GE **Prod** - GE 1972

Membrane Potential 10 MIN
VHS / 16mm
Color (I)
$95.00
Defines membrane potential and uses computer animation to show how a cell maintains a constant membrane potential.
Science - Natural
Dist - FLMWST

Membrane Potentials - Incomplete Selectivity, Bi - Ionic Potentials, Filtration through 40 MIN
U-matic / VHS
Colloids and Surface Chemistry Electrokinetics and Membrane - - 'Series
B&W
Teaches membrane potentials. Shows incomplete selectivity, hi - ionic potentials and filtration through membrane.
Science - Physical
Dist - MIOT **Prod** - MIOT

Membrane Potentials, Incomplete Selectivity, Bio - Ionic Potentials, Filtration through 40 MIN
U-matic / VHS
Colloid and Surface Chemistry - Electrokinetics and Membrane Series
Color
Discusses membrane potentials, incomplete selectivity, bio - ionic potentials and filtration through membrane.
Science; Science - Physical
Dist - KALMIA **Prod** - KALMIA

Membranes 41 MIN
U-matic / 35mm strip
Color (H C)
$43.95 purchase _ #52 1616
Discusses how lipid and protein molecules come together to form cellular membranes. Illustrates the fluid mosaic and pathways of transportation within the membrane. Includes a teacher's guide.
Science - Natural
Dist - CBSC **Prod** - BMEDIA

Membranes and transport 24 MIN
VHS
Color (J H)
$99.00 purchase _ #4785 - 026
Looks at the cell's ability to transport substances selectively into, out of and around itself. Concentrates on how membrane systems work. Includes teacher's guide.
Education; Science - Natural
Dist - GA **Prod** - EBEC

Memling - Painter of Bruges 27 MIN
U-matic / VHS / 16mm
Color (H C A)
Evokes the civilization of Bruges, Belgium, near the end of the Middle Ages through the paintings of Flemish artist, Memling. Shows how Memling depicts the customs, rich costumes, religious beliefs and economics of his time.
Biography; Fine Arts
Dist - IFB **Prod** - IFB 1974

The Memo book - Aus der ferne 28 MIN
16mm
Color (A)
$60.00 rental
Seeks to remake the male body in a celebratory flow of communion and despair, mythos and logos. Invites the viewer into an erotic dream labyrinth. Produced by Matthias Meuller. This film is S8mm blown up to 16mm.
Fine Arts; Science - Natural
Dist - CANCIN

Memo from a Grateful Spy 10 MIN
16mm / U-matic / VHS
Color
LC 81-701171
Uses vignettes in illustrating that information disclosure in an organization is due to employee negligence and careless security practices. Asks employees to consider how they may be contributing unintentionally to a security problem and urges them to take action to prevent information loss.
Business and Economics; Psychology; Sociology
Dist - CORF **Prod** - XEROXF 1981

Memo from a Grateful Spy 10 MIN
U-matic / VHS / 16mm
Color (SPANISH)
Discusses action to be taken to prevent information loss.
Foreign Language; History - World
Dist - CORF **Prod** - XEROXF

Memo from Machiavelli 50 MIN
VHS
Timewatch series
Color; PAL (G)
PdS99 purchase
Presents the works of Niccolo Machiavelli and their relevance in politics today. Examines recent discussion that Machiavelli may have been a pragmatic patriot rather than a master of sinister and unscrupulous intrigue as traditionally believed. British politicians put forward their views on Machiavelli's legacy. Ian Richardson reads extracts from The Prince.
Civics and Political Systems
Dist - BBCENE

Memo to the President 48.30 MIN
U-matic / 16mm / VHS
Inquiry Series
Color; Mono (H C A)
MV $350.00 _ MP $600.00 purchase, $50.00 rental
Examines the close economic relationship between Canada and the United States but, also underlines the growing differences between the two countries. This program reflects the concerns Canadians have about limiting energy related wastes and conservation of energy resources for their own growth and prosperity.
Civics and Political Systems; Science - Natural; Social Science
Dist - CTV **Prod** - CTV

Memoirs of a Movie Palace 45 MIN
16mm
Color
LC 80-700326
Explores the aura and significance of a grand, pre - Depression movie palace through the recollections of a vaudevillian, patrons, the theater's decorator, and its former manager, projectionist and organist.
Fine Arts
Dist - BLACKW **Prod** - BLACKW 1980

Memoirs of a Movie Palace, Pt 1 23 MIN
16mm
Color
LC 80-700326
Explores the aura and significance of a grand, pre - Depression movie palace through the recollections of a vaudevillian, patrons, the theater's decorator, and its former manager, projectionist and organist.
Fine Arts
Dist - BLACKW **Prod** - BLACKW 1980

Memoirs of a Movie Palace, Pt 2 22 MIN
16mm
Color
LC 80-700326
Explores the aura and significance of a grand, pre - Depression movie palace through the recollections of a vaudevillian, patrons, the theater's decorator, and its former manager, projectionist and organist.
Fine Arts
Dist - BLACKW **Prod** - BLACKW 1980

Memoirs of an everyday war 29 MIN
16mm / VHS
Color (G)
$515.00, $280.00 purchase, $55.00 rental
Tells the personal stories of four people who took extraordinary risks in Pinochet's Chile to become catalysts in the pro - democracy movement. Addresses issues which continue to be crucial to Chileans as they struggle to establish a firm democracy. Produced by the Cinemateca Chilena.
Civics and Political Systems; Fine Arts; Social Science
Dist - FIRS

Memorabilia 49 MIN
16mm / VHS
B&W (G)
$75.00 rental, $75.00 purchase
Delves into filmmaker Edward Jones' family filmed over a period of six years. Includes scenes of his grandmother's family, his sister's family and the painting and sculpture of friends. Mainly about the passage of time, growing older and dying, babies being born, etc. 'Consolation and transcendence are sought through celebration and art.'
Fine Arts; Sociology
Dist - CANCIN **Prod** - JONESE 1981

Memorable Moments 28 MIN
16mm
Color (H C)
LC FIA64-740
Uses a story about a little lost girl to show various floats that participated in the Tournament of Roses Parade at Pasadena, California, in 1963.
Geography - United States; Social Science
Dist - TRA **Prod** - TRA 1963

Memorandum 58 MIN
16mm
B&W (H C)
LC FIA67-5695
Deals with Goering's memorandum of July, 1941, which set in motion Nazi concentration camps and other methods of exterminating the Jews of Germany. Depicts a group of Bergen - Belsen survivors on a visit to the camp. Uses German and British footage to show alternating scenes of the past and of today's Germany.
Civics and Political Systems; Geography - World; History - World; Psychology; Sociology
Dist - NFBC **Prod** - NFBC 1966

Memorandum on Security 9 MIN
16mm
Color
LC FIE59-209
Shows research activity being carried on in various universities, research centers and industrial laboratories for the department of defense and explains the purpose of security regulations and procedures required to enforce them.
Civics and Political Systems; Education
Dist - USNAC **Prod** - USA 1959

Memorandum, Pt 1 27 MIN
16mm
B&W (H C)
Based on the memorandum dated July 21, 1941 from Herman Goering to SS Chief Reinhardt which set in motion the machinery that Hitler said would be the 'FINAL SOLUTION' to the Jewish question.
History - World
Dist - NFBC **Prod** - NFBC

Memorandum, Pt 2 27 MIN
16mm
B&W (H C)
Based on the memorandum dated July 21, 1941 from Herman Goering to SS Chief Reinhardt which set in motion the machinery that Hitler said would be the 'FINAL SOLUTION' to the Jewish question.
History - World
Dist - NFBC **Prod** - NFBC

Memorandum to Industry 31 MIN
16mm
Color
LC 74-705125
Shows not only what industry should do, but what industry is doing in planning its civil defense preparations. Tells what various industries have accomplished to provide fallout shelter for employees and the public, to assure continuity of company management in the event of an attack on the United States.
Business and Economics; Civics and Political Systems; Sociology
Dist - USNAC **Prod** - USOCD 1966

Memorial
16mm
Color (H C A)
LC 73-702554
Re - enacts the battle of the Somme. Marches over battlegrounds now covered with grain. Conveys the futility and valor of war.
Geography - World; History - World; Sociology
Dist - MMA **Prod** - MMA 1972

Memorial Day 21 MIN
16mm
B&W
Tells the story of a small New England town's observance of Memorial Day with special emphasis on the part played in it by a young sailor who has just returned from active duty in Korea.
Civics and Political Systems; Geography - United States; History - United States
Dist - USNAC **Prod** - USN 1952

Memorial Day 14 MIN
VHS / U-matic
Color (I)
LC 83-706967
Conveys the meaning of Memorial Day by viewing a traditional parade in East Hampton, New York.
Social Science
Dist - DIRECT **Prod** - DIRECT 1984

Memorial Day 15 MIN
U-matic
Celebrate Series
Color (P)
Civics and Political Systems; Social Science
Dist - GPN **Prod** - KUONTV 1978

Memorial Day
VHS
Why We Celebrate - Video Series
Color (P)
$39.95 purchase
English Language; Literature and Drama; Social Science
Dist - PELLER

Memorial Day portrayed 8 MIN
16mm
Color (G)
$15.00 rental
Portrays a reunion of friends and comrades. Struggles with the past to be present.
Fine Arts; Psychology
Dist - CANCIN **Prod** - LEVINE 1975

Memorial Day - Veterans' Day 15 MIN
VHS
America's special days series
Color (K P) (SPANISH)
$23.95 purchase
Looks at two days to honor those who serve the country, Memorial Day and Veterans' Day. Shows ceremonies being held at the Tomb of the Unknowns at Arlington National Cemetery and visits other monuments. Talks about our nation's respect for those who died in our country's service.
Civics and Political Systems; Social Science
Dist - GPN **Prod** - GPN 1993

Memories 26 MIN
U-matic / VHS
Color (PRO)
Deals with anyone who comes in contact with parents after they have experienced a stillbirth, miscarriage, or infant death.
Health and Safety; Sociology
Dist - HSCIC **Prod** - HSCIC 1982

Memories 30 MIN
VHS
How do you do - learning English series
Color (H A)
#317712
Shows that Frankie throws a party for CHIPS and herself and together they look back on all that he has learned in his short life. Part of a series that helps newcomers learn English or improve their ability. Includes viewer's guide with grammar explanations and vocabulary drills, worksheets and two audio cassettes.
English Language; Psychology
Dist - TVOTAR **Prod** - TVOTAR 1990

Memories Along the Patapsco 30 MIN
U-matic / VHS
Color
Looks at the history and development of the Howard County community of Elkridge, Maryland, once a busy seaport.
Geography - United States; History - United States
Dist - LVN **Prod** - HCPL

Memories from Eden 57 MIN
16mm / U-matic / VHS
Nova Series
Color (H C A)
LC 79-701897
Explains how zoos are involved in breeding and public education programs that will affect the future of both animal and human life. Discusses the idea that with the world losing 15 million acres of wilderness every year zoos may become the last refuge of wildlife.
Science - Natural; Sociology
Dist - TIMLIF **Prod** - WGBHTV 1978

Memories from the department of amnesia 13 MIN
VHS
Color (G)
$200.00 purchase, $50.00 rental
Presents an experimental video about the process of grieving - the way in which memory operates and the emotions it arouses. Enunciates the painful phases of grieving - dealing with the inevitability of death, the transitional void between one's world and nothing, and a new sense of clarity. Offers an elegy to the mother of director Janice Tanaka, whose attempts to maintain balance and security were constantly disrupted by social, cultural, political and personal forces beyond her control.
Guidance and Counseling; Psychology; Sociology
Dist - CROCUR

Memories I - Basic Concepts 30 MIN
U-matic / VHS
Digital Sub - Systems Series
Color
Discusses types of memory cells available and develops fundamentals of storage configurations. Develops basic configurations of shift register, random access (RAM's) and read only memories (ROM's).
Industrial and Technical Education; Mathematics; Sociology
Dist - TXINLC **Prod** - TXINLC

Memories II - Applications 30 MIN
U-matic / VHS
Digital Sub - Systems Series
Color
Takes basic theory developed in previous session and shows how to design with RAM's and ROM's through five examples.
Industrial and Technical Education; Mathematics; Sociology
Dist - TXINLC **Prod** - TXINLC

Memories, motivations - phases of social work 8 MIN
VHS
Color (C PRO)
$150.00 purchase _ #6840
Looks at the stages of development within the career of a social worker. Offers studies in 'heroism' - idealism, 'depression' - memories of failure, and 'optimism' - the emergence of competent and mature social workers.
Business and Economics; Psychology; Sociology
Dist - UCALG **Prod** - UCALG 1981

Memories of an Old Cowboy 9 MIN
16mm
Color (P I)
LC 80-700238
Uses animation to tell a story about an aging cowboy who recalls the exciting old days of the wild, wild West when he was a sheriff of a small town, defending it against all malefactors. Questions whether his memory of these events is real or if he has just seen too many westerns.
Fine Arts
Dist - SF **Prod** - POLSKI 1980

Memories of an unborn baby 4 MIN
16mm
Color (G)
$5.00 rental
Describes itself as 'warm multiple imagery.'
Fine Arts
Dist - CANCIN **Prod** - LIPTNL 1966

Memories of childhood and war - 6 51 MIN
VHS
Eastern Europe - breaking with the past series
Color (H C G)
$50.00 purchase
Presents three segments on the tragedy of World War II - Gaudiopolis, excerpts from a Hungarian documentary on children orphaned by the war; The Man Who Saved the Lives of Children, which portrays Hungarian Gabor Stzelho; and When Were You Born, an exploration of the experience of war by Hungarian filmmaker Gyorgy Szilagy. Part six of 13 parts.
Civics and Political Systems; History - World; Sociology
Dist - GVIEW **Prod** - GVIEW 1990

Memories of Family 24 MIN
16mm
Color (H C A)
LC 77-701850
Deals with the effect of the family on the individual.
Guidance and Counseling; Sociology
Dist - POLYMR **Prod** - FIE 1977

Memories of Gustav Holst 27 MIN
VHS
Color (G)
$129.00 purchase _ #EX3865
Examines the life of English composer Gustav Holst. Features Imogen Holst, who shows where and how Holst lived and from where he drew some of his themes.
Dist - FOTH

Memories of hell 57 MIN
U-matic / VHS
Color (H C A)
$420.00, $395.00 purchase _ #V430
Traces the history of 1,800 young men from New Mexico who, in 1941, were sent to the Philippines just months before World War II began. Reveals that what started as a yearlong tour of duty turned into years of virtual hell as these young men survived one of the war's most brutal battles and subsequent prisoner of war experiences. Examines the special bonds of friendship which has been maintained among these men.
History - United States; History - World; Sociology
Dist - BARR **Prod** - CEPRO 1987

Memories of Mewar 10 MIN
16mm
B&W (I)
Explains that Mewar, the cradle of Rajput chivalry, still echoes with the tales of its rulers and the songs of Meerabai, the princess turned saint. Shows the ancient palaces of Udaipur built with granite and marble and embellished with sculpture.
Fine Arts; History - World
Dist - NEDINF **Prod** - INDIA

Memories of Prince Albert Hunt 30 MIN
U-matic
Color
Uses experimental techniques to tell the story of Prince Albert Hunt, a fiddler from East Texas who performed during the 1920's.
Biography; Fine Arts
Dist - PBS **Prod** - KERA

Memories of Tata 52 MIN
VHS
Color (G)
$295.00 purchase, $95.00 rental
Offers an intimate and revealing portrait of the immigrant Central American family of filmmaker Sheldon Schiffer woven from his own childhood memories and reminiscences of his grandparents, mother and aunt. Interviews the family patriarch, nicknamed Tata, who discusses his notions of what it was to be a man, including the need to command respect, macho views of sexuality, emotional outbursts, threat of physical violence and sexist notions of childrearing - all at the expense of losing the love of his entire family. Directed by Sheldon Schiffer.
Fine Arts; Sociology
Dist - CNEMAG

Memories of the Cangaco 26 MIN
16mm
B&W (J) (LATIN)
Explains that banditry has long been an important social phenomenon in Latin America, at times serving the peasantry as a vehicle for social protest. Portrays the Brazilian bandit of the 1930's, his motivations and activities.
Geography - World; Sociology
Dist - NYFLMS **Prod** - NYFLMS

Memory 50 MIN
VHS
Human brain series
Color (H C A)
PdS99 purchase
Highlights recent advances in knowledge about the brain and its functions relative to memory. Uses case histories to illustrate individuals' triumphs over brain injury. Part of a seven-video set focusing on the self, memory, language, movement, sight, fear, and madness.
Psychology
Dist - BBCENE

Memory 30 MIN
U-matic / VHS / 16mm
Color (C)
LC 80-700849
Shows how to improve long - term memory, which is used most often for intellectual and organizational tasks. Provides proven methods of categorizing and referencing memories in order to facilitate fast, efficient recall.
Business and Economics; Psychology
Dist - CRMP **Prod** - CRMP 1980
MGHT

Memory 30 MIN
VHS / 16mm
Psychology - the Study of Human Behavior Series
Color (C A)
$99.95, $89.95 purchase _ 24 - 08
Explains research in the nature and workings of memory; defines amnesia and Alzheimer's disease.
Psychology
Dist - CDTEL **Prod** - COAST 1990

Memory - all echo 27 MON
VHS
Color (G)
$275.00 purchase, $75.00 rental
Uses the work of late Korean American writer Theresa Hak Kyung Cha, Dictee, to explore cultural identity and displacement. Interweaves passages by Cha with archival footage, recent scenes of turmoil in Korea and re - enactments portraying Cha's childhood.
Biography; Geography - World; History - United States; History - World; Sociology
Dist - WMEN **Prod** - TRIMIN 1990

Memory and Intelligence 45 MIN
16mm
Piaget's Developmental Theory Series
Color (FRENCH (ENGLISH SUBTITLES))
LC 75-712350
Features the Swiss psychologist, Jean Piaget, presenting his new work on memory and intelligence at the International Congress of Preschool Educational Specialists in Kyoto, Japan. Includes English subtitles to supplement Piaget's presentation in French.
Psychology
Dist - DAVFMS **Prod** - DAVFMS 1971

Memory and Pride 24 MIN
U-matic / VHS / 16mm
Gestalt Series
Color (H C)
LC 71-706492
Outlines the Gestalt approach to anxiety as Dr Frederick Perls works with a young woman who is self - conscious about her height.
Psychology
Dist - FI **Prod** - PMI 1969

Memory and Storage 30 MIN
U-matic
Fast Forward Series
Color (H C)
Traces the development of electronic memory from relays and tubes to transistors and integrated circuits and on to new technologies involving Josephson junctions and magnetic bubble memory.
Computer Science; Science
Dist - TVOTAR **Prod** - TVOTAR 1979

Memory and the elderly 20 MIN
VHS / U-matic
Mind and body series
Color (PRO C)
$395.00 purchase, $80.00 rental _ #C850 - VI - 121
Presents an analysis of diseases and conditions known to cause dementia. Includes Alzheimer's disease and multiple infarct dementia. Looks at personal and family problems caused by dementia. Presented by Dr Raymond Vickers, Michael O'Callahan and Dr Jonathan A Freedman. Part of a series.
Health and Safety; Psychology
Dist - HSCIC

Memory Array, the and the Decoding Logic of a Memory System 30 MIN
U-matic / VHS
Microcomputer Memory Design Series
Color (IND)
Shows organization of RAM and ROM devices in an array, and sets out techniques and implementations of address decoding logic - linear selection, fully decoding and decoding using bipolar PROM.
Industrial and Technical Education; Mathematics; Sociology
Dist - COLOSU **Prod** - COLOSU

Memory circus 35 MIN
VHS
Color (G)
$29.00 purchase
Presents an allegorical story of a woman's search through her past and present for the love and faith she must find within herself. Weaves a convoluted tale of magic, carnival tricks and fantasy to the point where the audience has trouble distinguishing past from present. Directed by Mary Kuryla.
Fine Arts; Literature and Drama; Psychology
Dist - ALTFMW

Memory eye 6 MIN
16mm
Color (G)
$17.50 rental
Examines the process of remembering. Explores the places where memory is held and the importance of its flickering images.
Fine Arts; Psychology
Dist - CANCIN **Prod** - ALVARE 1989

Memory - Fabric of the Mind 28 MIN
U-matic / VHS
Color (G)
$249.00, $149.00 purchase _ #AD - 1738
Considers how brain chemistry might explain memory. Asks if long term memory is a kind of permanent pattern on the structure of the brain and what kind of structural changes occur. Looks at where changes might occur and examines forgetting. Visits several internationally - renowned memory research labs.
Psychology; Science - Natural; Sociology
Dist - FOTH **Prod** - FOTH

Memory Fixing 67 MIN
U-matic / VHS / 16mm
Color (C A)
Presents business training consultant Dr Ken Cooper introducing techniques that will help business executives develop alertness, save time and improve productivity.
Psychology
Dist - FI **Prod** - PROSOR 1983
PROSOR

Memory Functions and Economics 60 MIN
Videoreel / VT1
Semiconductor Memories Course Series no 1
Color (IND)
Chracterizes the memory functions of sequentially accessed, random accessed and fixed program memories.
Industrial and Technical Education
Dist - TXINLC **Prod** - TXINLC

Memory Game 15 MIN
U-matic
Know Your World Series
(I J)
Shows students playing a memory training game.
Science
Dist - ACCESS **Prod** - ACCESS 1981

Memory Interface Timing 30 MIN
U-matic / VHS
Interface Programming (6809 Series
Color (IND)
Shows how buffered and buffer - free address and data buses are designed. Identifies desirable bus - extender properties and timing constraints for memory devices and uses them in actual examples.
Industrial and Technical Education; Mathematics; Sociology
Dist - COLOSU **Prod** - COLOSU

Memory is made of this 30 MIN
16mm / U-matic / VHS
Mr Microchip Series
Color (I J H)
Explains the various types of memory, RAM, ROM and floppy disk, and how information is put into the computer memory. Clarifies the differences between human memory (associative) and the computer's perfect memory.
Mathematics
Dist - JOU **Prod** - JOU

Memory jogger plus series
Includes seven videos, featuring Michael Brassard, which use an interactive, hands - on approach. Educates employees in the use of the Seven Management and Planning Tools. By Goal - QPC. Includes extensive workshop materials.
The Affinity diagram - Part 2 34 MIN
The Interrelationship diagraph - Part 3 26 MIN
Introductory - memory jogger plus series - Part 1
The Matrix diagram - Part 6 19 MIN
The Prioritization matrices - Part 5 34 MIN
The Process decision program chart - Part 7 23 MIN
The Tree diagram - Part 4 29 MIN
Dist - EXTR

Memory of a moment 10 MIN
VHS / U-matic
Color (G)
$39.95, $29.95 purchase _ #HVC - 789, #HHC - 789
Reunites Robert Waisman who had been imprisoned in Buchenwald, a German concentration camp, and Leon Bass, a black American who participated in the liberation of the camp, on the 40th anniversary of the liberation of the camp. Reveals that Bass, now a history teacher, was a soldier in a segregated army, and that he was the first black man Waisman had ever seen.
Civics and Political Systems; Guidance and Counseling; History - United States; History - World; Religion and Philosophy; Sociology
Dist - ADL **Prod** - PBS

Memory of Christmas 12 MIN
U-matic / VHS / 16mm
Simple Gifts Series
Color (I)
Presents a series of dramatic photographs which illustrates playwrights Moss Hart's achingly impoverished childhood reminiscence from his autobiography Act One. Describes two Christmases a generation apart that illustrate the gap that existed between himself and his father and how the gap was finally bridged.
Literature and Drama; Religion and Philosophy; Social Science
Dist - TIMLIF **Prod** - WNETTV

Memory of the Camps 58 MIN
VHS
Frontline Series
Color; Captioned (G)
$59.95 purchase _ #FRON - 318K
Provides evidence on film of the Nazi Holocaust. Shows numerous scenes from the camps at Dachau, Auschwitz and Buchenwald, including gas chambers, crematoria, medical experimentation labs and surviving prisoners. Filmed by British and American film crews who accompanied Allied forces as they liberated the camps.
History - World
Dist - PBS **Prod** - DOCCON 1985

Memory of the Park 9 MIN
16mm
Color
LC 72-700190
Presents an impression of the movements, color, sound and people in Washington Square Park in New York City.
Geography - United States; Social Science
Dist - CRAR **Prod** - CRAR 1972

Memory Pictures 24 MIN
U-matic / VHS
Pratibha Parmar Series
Color (G)
$250.00, $200.00 purchase, $50.00 rental
Profiles gay East Indian photographer Sunil Gupta and his work. Examines his portrayal of sexual and racial identity in relation to personal and familial identity. Includes a storyteller portrayed by Asian actress Meer Syal to provide poetic reflection and a visual construct of the historical context of migration.
Fine Arts; Industrial and Technical Education; Religion and Philosophy; Social Science; Sociology
Dist - WMEN **Prod** - PARMAR 1989

Memory, Pt 1 15 MIN
VHS / U-matic
I - Land Treasures Series
Color (K)
English Language
Dist - AITECH **Prod** - UWISC 1980

Memory, Pt 2 13 MIN
VHS / U-matic
I - Land Treasure Series
Color (K)
English Language
Dist - AITECH **Prod** - NETCHE 1980

Memory skills 25 MIN
VHS
Color (H C A)
$89.00 purchase _ #60408 - 027
Teaches visualization methods that are fun to use and eliminate much of the nervousness and fear of failure from later recall tests.
Psychology
Dist - GA **Prod** - GA

Memory Technologies, Microcomputer Organization and Operation 30 MIN
U-matic / VHS
Microcomputer Memory Design Series
Color (IND)
Covers introduction, memory technologies, semiconductor memories, block diagram of a microcomputer and its operation, and general organization of a memory unit.
Industrial and Technical Education; Mathematics; Sociology
Dist - COLOSU **Prod** - COLOSU

Memory - what's in it for me 60 MIN
VHS
Color (A PRO)
$69.95 purchase _ #S01547
Stresses the concept of associativity as a key to memory improvement. Hosted by memory expert David Markoff.
Psychology
Dist - UILL

Memotion Examples 20 MIN
16mm
Color
Explains that memotion photography is one method of analyzing motion and time study work. Features examples of memotion including a street operation performed by a crew from a gas company, operation of a railroad yard with humping operations and a crew operation in a steel foundry.
Business and Economics; Industrial and Technical Education
Dist - CCNY **Prod** - MUNDEL

Memphis Belle 42 MIN
16mm
B&W
LC FIE54-318
Tells the story of the B - 17, the flying fortress.
Civics and Political Systems; Industrial and Technical Education
Dist - USNAC **Prod** - USDD 1944

The Memphis Belle 43 MIN
VHS / U-matic
B&W
Documents the final mission of the Flying Fortress 'Memphis Belle' as it led a squadron of bombers in a daring daylight attack on the submarine pens at Wilhelmshaven during World War II.
Civics and Political Systems; History - United States
Dist - IHF **Prod** - IHF

Memphis - the new design 23 MIN
VHS
Color (J H C T A)
$93.00 purchase _ #MB - 481065 - 0
Introduces the Memphis design style of furniture. Notes that Memphis styles often mock Bauhaus and Scandinavian design.
Fine Arts; Industrial and Technical Education
Dist - SRA **Prod** - SRA

Memphis - the New Design Series
And Then There was Memphis 11.15 MIN
Part One - Redesigning Our Modern World 11.17 MIN
Dist - SRA

Men Against Tanks/Engineers to the Front 48 MIN
VHS / U-matic
Color (GERMAN)
Presents training drama of an entrenched German infantry platoon, unsupported by aircraft, heavy weapons or reinforcements which must repel an overwhelming attack of Soviet T - 34 tanks.
Civics and Political Systems; Foreign Language
Dist - IHF **Prod** - IHF

Men and self - care video
VHS
Health care consumerism system series
Color (G)
$179.00 purchase _ #WMV08
Focuses on the three most critical areas of men's health. Shares over 20 steps men can take to immediately reduce the greatest threats to good health. Part of a ten - part series.
Home Economics; Sociology
Dist - GPERFO **Prod** - GPERFO

Men and the Sea 9 MIN
16mm
Color
LC 75-701593
Shows the operations of Exxon Corporation as it searches for oil beneath the North Atlantic.
Business and Economics; Industrial and Technical Education; Science - Natural; Social Science
Dist - EXXON **Prod** - EXXON 1975

Men and Women in Management 29 MIN
16mm
Color
Interviews male executives who discuss their growing personal and professional awareness of women in management positions.
Business and Economics; Sociology
Dist - IMPACT **Prod** - STURTM

Men and women - partners at work 18 MIN
VHS
Color (A PRO)
$495.00 purchase, $150.00 rental
Models steps leading to effective teamwork between men and women on the job. Examines the styles each brings to the work ethic. Notes ways sexual harassment can be reduced or prevented as well as ways to deal with it in the workplace.
Business and Economics
Dist - DHB **Prod** - CRISP

Men are just desserts 30 MIN
VHS
Going the distance - women taking charge in the 90s series
Color (J H C G)
$29.95 purchase _ #JJ1548V
Discloses to women viewers that men are not the 'complete meal' in their lives, not even the 'main course,' but just desserts. Watches Diane as she discovers that a postponed marriage is her unexpected ticket to a new and surprisingly life - with or without a man. Discovers how 'nutritional' men can be when women are the ones in control of their feelings, relationships and lives. Part of a three - part series on women in the 90s.
Psychology; Sociology
Dist - CAMV

Men at Bay 26 MIN
16mm / U-matic / VHS
Color (J H C)
LC 70-712558
Presents a case history of the imminent destruction of San Francisco Bay, an example of the overwhelming environmental problems facing every major American city. Uses graphic photography and interviews of the angry and confused San Francisco residents.
Geography - United States; Science - Natural
Dist - PHENIX **Prod** - KINGSP 1970

Men bathing 14 MIN
16mm / VHS
San - Ju - Wasi series
Color (G)
$270.00, $140.00 purchase, $30.00 rental
Observes the visit of five Kung men to Nama pan, a small lake. Reveals that Ti - kay has come to wash clothes acquired while rescuing his band's wives from Boers, the others came to bathe. Sexual jokes are exchanged with pleasure and hilarity. Part of a series by John Marshall about the Kung in Namibia and Botswana.
Geography - World; History - World; Literature and Drama; Sociology
Dist - DOCEDR **Prod** - DOCEDR

Men, Depression and Desperation 28 MIN
U-matic / VHS
Color (G)
$249.00, $149.00 purchase _ #AD - 1259
Reveals that members of the 'stronger sex' can be overwhelmed by crisis - death, divorce, job loss - and often seek escape through isolation, drugs or even suicide. Features Dr Herbert Freudenberger and Phil Donahue who seek to help men find ways to acknowledge, express and come to grips with crisis.
Guidance and Counseling; Health and Safety; Psychology; Sociology
Dist - FOTH **Prod** - FOTH

The Men from Boeing 24 MIN
16mm
Color
LC 80-700212
Shows the effort and skill required of Boeing's 747 aircraft on - ground crew as they are brought in to fix an airplane which crashed off the runway in Frankfurt, Germany.
Industrial and Technical Education
Dist - WELBIT **Prod** - BOEING 1980

The Men from the Boys 28 MIN
16mm
Big Picture Series
Color
LC 82-700089
Shows how new recruits are transformed into trained soldiers during the first eight weeks of basic training, focusing on the role of the assigned drill sergeant and the reactions of the young inductees.
Civics and Political Systems
Dist - USNAC **Prod** - USA 1982

Men in Cages 56 MIN
16mm / U-matic / VHS
B&W (H C)
LC 74-701924
Investigates the criminal, from first offender to the hardened repeater, and his life behind bars. Shows some of the worst penal institutions.
History - United States; Psychology; Sociology
Dist - CAROUF **Prod** - CBSTV 1966

Men in Cages, Pt 1 26 MIN
U-matic / VHS / 16mm
B&W (H C)
LC FIA67-1453
Investigates the criminal, from first offender to the hardened repeater, and his life behind bars. Shows some of the worst penal institutions.
Sociology
Dist - CAROUF **Prod** - CBSTV 1966

Men in Cages, Pt 2 26 MIN
U-matic / VHS / 16mm
B&W (H C)
LC FIA67-1453
Investigates the criminal, from first offender to the hardened repeater, and his life behind bars. Shows some of the worst penal institutions.
Sociology
Dist - CAROUF **Prod** - CBSTV 1966

Men in crisis series
Presents a five - part series on men in crisis. Includes the titles Fathers, Sons and Trust; Feelings, Alcohol and Manhood; Self - Esteem and Empowerment; Heroes and Identity; A Way Back - Redefining Masculinity.

Fathers, sons and trust 37 MIN
Feelings, alcohol and manhood 25 MIN
Heroes and identity 25 MIN
Self - esteem and empowerment 28 MIN
A Way back - redefining masculinity 21 MIN
Dist - CONMED

Men in Crisis Series
Mc Carthy Vs Welch 25 MIN
Mitchell Vs Military Tradition 25 MIN
Roosevelt Vs Isolation 25 MIN
Dist - FI

Men in Early Childhood Education 24 MIN
16mm
Color
Depicts men sharing their interests and feelings in early childhood settings. Documents the reactions of parents, children and colleagues. Shows the men's expressions of joys and frustrations at working in an intellectually stimulating, though underpaid, profession.
Education; Psychology; Sociology
Dist - DAVFMS **Prod** - DAVFMS

The Men in the Cockpit 25 MIN
BETA / 16mm / VHS
Color
LC 77-702516
Examines the problems and dangers of pilot fatigue and jet lag during long, nonstop domestic flights and on international runs with multiple time zone changes.
Health and Safety; Industrial and Technical Education; Social Science
Dist - CTV **Prod** - CTV 1976

Men in War 104 MIN
16mm
B&W
Focuses on a platoon during the Korean War, showing how it must reach a specified destination regardless of the odds.
Fine Arts
Dist - KITPAR **Prod** - UAA 1957

Men, Machines and the Secretary 24 MIN
U-matic / VHS / 16mm
Color
Documents how a company reorganized its use of secretaries because of the introduction of a word processor. Studies the replacement of the conventional system of personal secretaries with administrative support centers in the headquarters office of a large multi - national oil company.
Business and Economics
Dist - MEDIAG **Prod** - OPENU 1981

Men O War 24 MIN
16mm
Laurel and Hardy Comedy Series
B&W
LC 71-711884
Presents a Laurel and Hardy comedy in which Ollie tries to stretch the 15 cents they have between them to cover refreshments for four, Stan gets stuck with the check, plays a one - armed bandit and hits the jackpot.
Fine Arts
Dist - RMIBHF **Prod** - ROACH 1929

Men of Action 30 MIN
U-matic / VHS
Japan - the Changing Tradition Series
Color (H C A)
History - World
Dist - GPN **Prod** - UMA 1978

Men of Bronze 58 MIN
U-matic / VHS / 16mm
Color (H C A)
Focuses on the 369th Combat Regiment, an all - black unit which spent more time under fire during World War I than any other regiment.
History - United States
Dist - FI **Prod** - KILLIS 1977
UILL

Men of Bronze, Pt 1 30 MIN
U-matic / VHS / 16mm
Color (H C A)
LC 78-701108
Tells the story of the U S Army's 359th regiment. Uses rare photographs, film from the National Archives of the United States and France and interviews of veterans to show how the regiment brought American jazz to Europe.
Civics and Political Systems
Dist - FI **Prod** - KILLIS 1978

Men of Bronze, Pt 2 29 MIN
16mm / U-matic / VHS
Color (H C A)
LC 78-701108
Tells the story of the U S Army's 359th regiment. Uses rare photographs, film from the National Archives of the United States and France and interviews of veterans to show how the regiment brought American jazz to Europe.
Civics and Political Systems
Dist - FI **Prod** - KILLIS 1978

The Men of Company 208 28 MIN
U-matic
Color (H C A)
Follows a group of young men going through basic training at the Great Lakes Naval Base.
Civics and Political Systems; History - United States
Dist - CEPRO **Prod** - CEPRO

Men of Courage 15 MIN
U-matic / VHS / 16mm
Odyssey Series
Color
Focuses on the many explorers whose lives are linked with the discovery and exploration of Antarctica. Profiles Captain James Cook, Dumont D'Urville, Charles Wilkes, james Ross and others.
Geography - World; History - World
Dist - GPN **Prod** - KRMATV

The Men of Dark Tears 40 MIN
16mm
Color
LC 72-702408
Presents the story of a young Crete revolutionary and his relationship with a middle aged Greek wanderer during one of the many revolts against the Turkish Empire in 1889. Explains that through their relationship and experiences, the young man learns that humanity transcends national boundaries and ethnic hatreds.
Fine Arts; History - World; Sociology
Dist - USC **Prod** - USC 1972

Men of Destiny Volume I - World Political Figures
VHS / U-matic
B&W (J H C A)
$59.00 purchase _ #04451 94
Records the lives and achievements of over 30 leaders in twentieth century history including Winston Churchill, Herbert Hoover, and Mahatma Gandhi. Features period newsreels.
Biography; Fine Arts; History - World
Dist - ASPRSS

Men of Destiny Volume II - Artists and Innovators
U-matic / VHS
B&W (J H C A)
$59.00 purchase _ #04450 94
Presents the achievements of over thirty world reknowned artists and innovators of the twentieth century, including Marie Curie, Thomas Edison, Albert Einstein, and Charles Lindbergh.
Biography; Fine Arts; History - World
Dist - ASPRSS

Men of ideas series
Explains in simple terms the main developments in Western philosophy from the 19th century to the present day. Features fifteen distinguished thinkers who discuss their ideas with Bryan Magee.

Heidegger and modern existentialism 45 MIN
The Idea of Chomsky 45 MIN
The Ideas of Quine 45 MIN
An Introduction to philosophy 45 MIN
Logical positivism and its legacy 45 MIN
Marcuse and the Frankfurt School 45 MIN
Marxist philosophy 45 MIN
Moral philosophy 45 MIN
Philosophy - the social context 45 MIN
Philosophy and literature 45 MIN
Philosophy and politics 45 MIN
The Philosophy of language 45 MIN
The Philosophy of science 45 MIN
The Spell of linguistic philosophy 45 MIN
The Two philosophies of Wittgenstein 45 MIN
Dist - BBCENE

Men of Iron 20 MIN
U-matic / VHS / 16mm
Color (IND)
Tells how working with iron and steel high in the sky requires training, experience and a concern for safety. Gives safety precautions for workers and also shows the manufacture and installation of laminated wooden beams.
Health and Safety; Industrial and Technical Education; Psychology
Dist - IFB **Prod** - CSAO

Men of justice 29 MIN
16mm
Government story series; No 39
Color
LC 73-707172
Discusses the human aspects of the Supreme Court, showing how the personalities and prejudices of the justices affect their interpretations of the law.
Civics and Political Systems
Dist - WBCPRO **Prod** - WBCPRO 1968

Men of little faith 55 MIN
VHS
Microbes and men
Color; PAL (C PRO H)
PdS99 purchase; Not available in the United States
Explains Pasteur's discovery of vaccines. Describes the rivalry between Pasteur and Koch as they search for the germ that causes cholera. Third in the six - part series Microbes and Men, which covers the history and development of modern medicine.
Health and Safety; Science
Dist - BBCENE

Men of Maintenance - Southeast Asia 15 MIN
16mm
Color
LC 74-706142
Highlights aircraft maintenance operations in Southeast Asia. Depicts specialized personnel using sophisticated electronic equipment to check out complex aircraft systems.
Geography - World; Industrial and Technical Education
Dist - USNAC **Prod** - USAF 1968

Men of Pontiac 11 MIN
16mm
Destination - Dotted Line Series no 1
B&W
LC 70-707695
A typical salesman discusses techniques of good salesmanship and the advantages of running a Pontiac dealership.
Business and Economics
Dist - GM **Prod** - GM 1952

Men of the Canefields 20 MIN
16mm
B&W (H C)
Explains that time is the crucial factor in getting sugar cane to the sugar mill. Shows how a Cuban volunteer work crew spends long hours in the fields and still attends classes. Views recreational activities enjoyed by the crew.
Agriculture; Civics and Political Systems; Education; Geography - World
Dist - CANWRL **Prod** - ICAIC 1967

Men of the Sea 28 MIN
16mm
Color
LC 74-705127
Portrays the story of Navy combat art.
Civics and Political Systems
Dist - USNAC **Prod** - USN 1970

Men of the Tall Ships 60 MIN
16mm
Color
LC 78-701498
Presents a story about the men who sailed across the Atlantic to New York City for the Operation Sail '76 competition.
Geography - World; Physical Education and Recreation
Dist - DIRECT **Prod** - DREWAS 1978

Men of the Wilderness 30 MIN
16mm / U-matic / VHS
Living Christ Series

Color
Depicts John the Baptist imprisoned as Jesus' ministry begins.
Religion and Philosophy
Dist - CAFM **Prod** - CAFM
ECUFLM

Men on women, women on men 60 MIN
VHS
Women of the world series
Color (G)
$59.95 purchase _ #WWRL - 103
Focuses on changing roles for both men and women. Interviews psychologist Dr Toni Grant, Claire Rayner and Barbara Cartland. Features women such as German steel magnate Viola Hallman who have made lives for themselves.
Business and Economics; Sociology
Dist - PBS

Men Under Siege - Life with the Modern Woman 33 MIN
16mm / U-matic / VHS
Color (A)
LC 80-701690
Offers a portrait of American men in the late 1970's, showing how they have reacted to changes in women's roles.
Sociology
Dist - CORF **Prod** - ABCNEW 1979

Men who are working with women in management 28 MIN
16mm
Are you listening series
Color (J)
LC 80-701124
Tells how some male executives have coped with training, advancing, advising and criticizing their women colleagues. Shows how they have changed their personal and corporate awareness due to the new status of women.
Guidance and Counseling; Psychology; Sociology
Dist - STURTM **Prod** - STURTM 1973

The Men who danced - the story of Ted Shawn's male dancers 1933 - 1940 30 MIN
VHS
Color; B&W (J H C G)
LC 90-708813
Presents the story of the first all - male dance company in the United States, Ted Shawn's Male Dancers. Includes historical footage of the company performing in the 1930s and illustrates the choreography of Ted Shawn.
Fine Arts; History - United States; Sociology
Dist - DANCOR **Prod** - DANCOR 1989

Men who dared series
Burke and Wills - Australia, 1860 - Pt 1 26 MIN
Dist - TIMLIF

Men who Feed the World 14 MIN
16mm
Color
Presents the story of Jimmy and his prize winning Swiss calf, Heida.
Agriculture; Sociology
Dist - FLADC **Prod** - FLADC

Men who Hate Women and the Women who Love Them 28 MIN
U-matic / VHS
Color (G)
$249.00, $149.00 purchase _ #AD - 1156
Addresses the issues of heterosexual relationships between men who hate women and the unfortunate women who love men who hate women. Features Phil Donahue and Dr Susan Forward, author of 'Men Who Hate Women And The Women Who Love Them.'.
Guidance and Counseling; Psychology; Religion and Philosophy; Sociology
Dist - FOTH **Prod** - FOTH

Men who molest - children who survive 52 MIN
VHS / 16mm
Color (H C G)
$850.00, $450.00 purchase, $80.00 rental
Explores the lives of four child molesters. Reveals that three of them are in treatment at the nation's largest community - based facility, Northwest Treatment Associates of Seattle. Witnesses dramatic group therapy sessions in which they struggle to control their deviancy. Shows how devastating this crime is to children. Lucy Berliner works with a little girl who confronts her molesting uncle in prison so that she can see that what happened was not her fault. Produced by Racbel Lyon.
Sociology
Dist - FLMLIB

Men who teach series
Abraham Kaplan 59 MIN
Abraham Kaplan, Pt 1 30 MIN
Abraham Kaplan, Pt 2 29 MIN
Gerald Holton 59 MIN
Howard E Mitchell 59 MIN
Lloyd J Reynolds - William M Geer 59 MIN
Norman Jacobson 59 MIN
Dist - IU

The Men who Tread on the Tiger's Tail 60 MIN
VHS / U-matic
B&W (JAPANESE (ENGLISH SUBTITLES))
Tells a story set in 12th Century Japan of a clan lord hunted by his brother, the reigning shogun. Describes his flight with six followers and their disguise as monks and how the border magistrate allows them to pass. Based on the Kabuki drama Kanjincho. Directed by Akira Kurosawa. With English subtitles.
History - World; Literature and Drama; Sociology
Dist - IHF **Prod** - IHF

Men with Green Faces 29 MIN
16mm
Color
LC 74-705129
Shows functions and a cross section of life of the Navy's frogmen commandos, the Seals. Covers the excitement of parachute jump training and the quiet of jungle patrols.
Civics and Political Systems
Dist - USNAC **Prod** - USN 1969

Men with Wings 14 MIN
16mm
B&W
LC 74-706144
Describes the courage and the achievements of pilots whose efforts over the last half century have given aviation a rich heritage. Includes the Korean conflict, which marked the beginning of the jet age.
Civics and Political Systems; Industrial and Technical Education
Dist - USNAC **Prod** - USDD 1963

Men - Women - After the Revolution 58 MIN
VHS / 16mm
(G)
$275.00 purchase, $150.00, $75.00 rental
Interviews twelve people about the uncertainty of sexuality in the 1980s.
Sociology
Dist - FANPRO **Prod** - FANPRO 1989

Men, Women and Children 20 MIN
U-matic / VHS
Color
Tells about fire in the home, their real causes and the resulting injury and destruction.
Health and Safety; Home Economics
Dist - FPF **Prod** - FPF

Men, Women, and Language 30 MIN
U-matic / VHS
Language - Thinking, Writing, Communicating Series
Color
English Language
Dist - MDCPB **Prod** - MDCPB

Men, women, angels and harps 29 MIN
VHS
Color (H G)
$250.00 purchase, $50.00 rental
Explores the harp and its social functions throughout its 5000 year history. Features performances by Carrol McLaughlin and her partner, pianist - composer Bill Marx, son of Harpo, who reminisces about his famous father, a pretty mean harpist himself when he wasn't cutting up with his brothers. Directed by Laura Paglin.
Fine Arts
Dist - CNEMAG

Men, Women, Sex and AIDS 49 MIN
VHS
Color (S)
$79.00 purchase _ #322 - 9283
Considers the various issues surrounding AIDS. Features correspondent Tom Brokaw who interviews experts, victims and young people to delineate what constitutes responsible and safe sexual behavior and how early and how explicitly young people should be informed about AIDS. Brokaw asks if enough money is being endowed to AIDS research and what effect the rapidly multiplying number of victims is having on healthcare facilities, insurance programs and social security benefits.
Health and Safety; Sociology
Dist - FI **Prod** - NBCNEW 1987

Menagerie 22 MIN
16mm
Color (K P I J H)
LC FIA67-5629
A collection of eight short animated films created by children, ages 8 - 16, students at the pilot film workshop of the Lexington School of Modern Dance, 1967. Includes techniques of black and white clay animation, color, cut - outs, tear - outs, collage and flip cards.
Fine Arts; Literature and Drama
Dist - CELLAR **Prod** - LSMD 1967

The Mende 51 MIN
VHS
Disappearing world series
Color (G C)
$99.00 purchase, $19.00 rental _ #51225
Portrays 260 Mende people living in the forest of Sierra Leone to show the successful and the unlucky, the clowns and gossips, happy households and divided ones. Reveals that the Mendes recognize a supernatural world that affects all aspects of their daily routine. Features anthropologist Mariane Ferme. Part of a series working closely with anthropologists who lived for a year or more in societies whose social structures, beliefs and practices are threatened by the expansion of technocratic civilization.
Sociology
Dist - PSU **Prod** - GRANDA 1990

Mendelian genetics 27 MIN
VHS
Color (J H)
$100.00 purchase _ #A5VH 1258
Explains Mendel's basic principles of genetics - dominance, segregation and independent assortment. Invites students to make hypotheses about Mendel's experiments and compares their predictions with Mendel's outcomes. Shows how Punnett Squares are used to determine the possible outcomes of specified matings - genetic crosses, to combine the symbols for traits, and to predict the appearance of offspring - Phenotype - and the actual genetic make - up of offspring - Genotype.
Science - Natural
Dist - CLRVUE **Prod** - CLRVUE 1992

Mendel's Laws 14 MIN
16mm / U-matic / VHS
Genetics Series
Color (J H C)
$350, $245 purchase _ #1312
Discusses the work of scientist Gregor Mendel, and how it relates to genetics.
Science; Science - Natural
Dist - CORF

Mendelssohn and Bach - Israel Philharmonic Orchestra conducted by Zubin Mehta 48 MIN
VHS
Huberman Festival series
Color (G)
$19.95 purchase_#1359
Presents Schlomo Mintz performing Mendelssohn's Concerto in E Minor. Combines the violin expertise of Mintz and Isaac Stern in a performance of Bach's Concerto in D Minor for Two Violins and String Orchestra.
Fine Arts
Dist - KULTUR

The Mendelssohn Concerto 22 MIN
16mm
Color (P)
Shows children and teenagers dancing classical ballet to the music of Mendelssohn.
Education; Fine Arts; Psychology
Dist - WSUM **Prod** - WSUM 1956

Mendelssohn's Midsummer Night's Dream 20 MIN
16mm
Musical Masterpieces Series
B&W
Franco Ferrara directs the Radio Philharmonic Orchestra of Italy playing 'NOCTURNE,' 'SCHERZO' and 'WEDDING MARCH' from Mendelssohn's 'MIDSUMMER NIGHT'S DREAM.'.
Fine Arts
Dist - SG **Prod** - SG

Mending Bodies and Souls 30 MIN
U-matic
North of Sixty Degrees - Destiny Uncertain Series
Color (H C)
Examines the effects of the stress caused by rapid change and the problems of acculturation in northern people.
Geography - United States; Geography - World; History - World
Dist - TVOTAR **Prod** - TVOTAR 1985

Mending Books 15 MIN
Videoreel / VT2
Making Things Work Series
Color
Home Economics
Dist - PBS **Prod** - WGBHTV

Mending China and Glass 15 MIN
Videoreel / VT2
Making Things Work Series
Color
Fine Arts
Dist - PBS **Prod** - WGBHTV

Mending hearts 59 MIN
VHS / U-matic
Color (G)
$295.00 purchase, $100.00 rental
Documents two years in the lives of four individuals who have contracted HIV in different ways while they struggle to come to terms with reality and change their lives to accommodate their diagnosis. Interviews two physicians, Drs. Richard Dubois and Jim Braude, whose practice is largely AIDS patients.
Health and Safety
Dist - BAXMED **Prod** - BAXMED 1992

Mending Wall 10 MIN
U-matic / VHS / 16mm
Reading Poetry Series
Color (J H)
LC 72-700189
Presents Leonard Nimoy reading the poem Mending Wall by Robert Frost, as scenes evocative of the poem are pictured. Shows the words of the poem as it is reread to appropriate scenes.
Literature and Drama
Dist - AIMS **Prod** - EVANSA 1972

Mendocino 14 MIN
16mm
Color (G)
$20.00 rental
Documents a summer the filmmaker spent in Mendocino, California. Features portraits of a painter and a unicyclist.
Fine Arts
Dist - CANCIN **Prod** - WALLIN 1968

Meninges - Hemisection of the Brain Principle Features of the Brainstem 32 MIN
U-matic
Dissection of the Brain Series
Color (C)
Demonstrates the relationship of the meninges to the brain. Principle features of the brainstem following longitudinal sectioning of the brain along its sagittal axis are reviewed.
Health and Safety; Science - Natural
Dist - UOKLAH **Prod** - UOKLAH 1978

Meningitis 20 MIN
U-matic / VHS
Major Medical Syndromes Series
Color (PRO)
LC 80-706595
Focuses on meningitis by covering the basic pathophysiology of the condition, clinical signs and symptoms, and laboratory tests. Includes animated segments.
Health and Safety
Dist - USNAC **Prod** - NMAC 1979

Meningitis - the urgent diagnosis 52 MIN
VHS
Color (G)
$149.00 purchase, $75.00 rental _ #UW4658
Gives an account of three families as they wait for hours in intensive care when their three small children fight for their lives against meningitis. Illustrates the horror of the disease as well as the irrefutable argument for early diagnosis and treatment.
Health and Safety
Dist - FOTH

Meniskus of Japan 25 MIN
16mm
Diaries no 1 - no 8 - 1979 - 1983
Color (G)
$35.00 rental
Features part eight of an eight - part series by Andras Szirtes.
Fine Arts; Literature and Drama
Dist - CANCIN

Menneskets Natur (Man's Nature) 15 MIN
16mm
Color (DANISH)
Portrays pollution of nature by modern man.
Foreign Language; Science - Natural
Dist - STATNS **Prod** - STATNS 1970

Mennonites of Ontario 16 MIN
U-matic
Color (J)
Traces the influx of several waves of Mennonites into Ontario, Canada. Describes the community which has resulted from the mixture of traditional Mennonites with more liberal members of that sect. Examines their common values.
Religion and Philosophy; Sociology
Dist - BULLER **Prod** - BULLER

Menopause 10 MIN
VHS
Color (G PRO C)
$200.00 purchase _ #OB - 79
Provides an overview of what to expect physically and emotionally during menopause. Explains how the drop in estrogen level causes changes throughout the whole body, in the circulatory and bone system as well as the reproductive system. Shows patients ways to minimize adverse effects and lead a more healthy life.
Health and Safety; Sociology
Dist - MIFE **Prod** - MIFE

Menopause 7 MIN
VHS / U-matic
Color
Defines menopause. Explains physiologic changes responsible for menopause and basic principles of treatment.
Science - Natural; Sociology
Dist - MEDFAC **Prod** - MEDFAC 1981

Menopause 10 MIN
VHS / 16mm / U-matic
Color (A PRO) (SPANISH)
Discusses menopause and the benefits and limitations of the various treatments for it.
Foreign Language; Health and Safety; Psychology
Dist - PRORE **Prod** - PRORE

Menopause 19 MIN
U-matic / VHS / 16mm
Woman Talk Series
Color (H C A)
States that there is no way of determining, in advance, how a particular woman will react to this stage of her life. Explains that the only preparation is to try to thoroughly understand what menopause is and why it can cause certain physical symptoms. Gives a detailed, animated explanation of the menopause process.
Health and Safety; Sociology
Dist - CORF **Prod** - CORF 1983

Menopause 15 MIN
VHS / U-matic
Color (G C PRO)
$175.00 purchase _ #OB - 119
Details the menopausal experience of an individual woman. Features eight older women discussing their menopause interspersed with the main story line. Discusses mild estrogen therapy.
Health and Safety; Sociology
Dist - MIFE **Prod** - MIFE

Menopause and beyond 60 MIN
VHS
Sexuality and aging series
Color (G)
$29.95 purchase
Discusses sexual health issues that affect all women during menopause and the years that follow. Includes the specific topics of the pros and cons of hormone therapy, osteoporosis, urinary incontinence and the value of Kegel exercises. Interviews menopausal women and their partners who share their feelings about menopause and how aging has affected their sexuality and health in general.
Health and Safety
Dist - FCSINT

Menopause and the time before menopause 30 MIN
VHS
At time of diagnosis series
Color (G)
$19.95 purchase _ #1 - 5757 - 7006 - 7NK
Provides patients who are encountering menopause and their families with thorough, comprehensive and understandable information. Examines what is going on in the body and what might have caused the condition. Explains the type of medical professionals a patient may encounter and how the condition is monitored. Explores treatment options, including medication and lifestyle changes. Looks at practical issues surrounding menopause and answers the most common questions. Part of an ongoing series to provide the in - depth medical information patients and their families need to know.
Health and Safety
Dist - TILIED **Prod** - TILIED 1995

Menopause - Facts and Myths 19 MIN
U-matic / VHS
Color (C)
$249.00, $149.00 purchase _ #AD - 1990
Explains away some of the popular misconceptions concerning menopause. Profiles two women - one who suffered the 'typical' symptoms including hot flashes, mild depression and fatigue, and one whose symptoms were quite mild. Emphasizes the need for estrogen therapy in both cases to alleviate the symptoms and help prevent osteoporosis and heart disease.
Health and Safety; Science - Natural; Sociology
Dist - FOTH **Prod** - FOTH

Menopause - guidelines to a healthy life 35 MIN
VHS
Women's health series
Color (G)
$49.00 purchase _ #WHV7
Offers the most - up - to - date medical information on menopause, reviewed and approved by a national panel of health care professionals. Features medical correspondent Dr Holly Atkinson of NBC News Today. Part of an eight - part series.
Health and Safety; Sociology
Dist - GPERFO **Prod** - AMEDCO

Menopause - How to Cope 29 MIN
U-matic
Woman Series
Color
Looks at ways to prevent acute depression during menopause.
Health and Safety; Psychology
Dist - PBS **Prod** - WNEDTV

Menopause - Myths and Realities 22 MIN
U-matic / VHS / 16mm
Color (A)
Deals with causes and consequences of menopause and shows that the symptoms are not usually as bad as anticipated, they are not painful and not permanent.
Health and Safety; Psychology; Science - Natural
Dist - PEREN **Prod** - BURN

Menopause - Our shared experience 29 MIN
VHS
Color (G)
$60.00 rental, $195.00 purchase
Explores the physical and psychological experience of menopause. Engages a range of professional experts and women who have gone through menopause to address hot flashes, osteoporosis, depression, hysterectomy, Hormone Replacement Therapy, diet and excercise. Emphasizes that although most women go through menopause there is a tremendous diversity in the way it is experienced by each individual. Produced by Suzanne Landau and Valerie Toizer.
Fine Arts; Sociology
Dist - WMEN

The Menopause Story 30 MIN
16mm / U-matic / VHS
Color (A)
Looks at the myths and realities of menopause. Discusses worries about aging, keeping fit and sexuality.
Health and Safety; Sociology
Dist - CF **Prod** - MOBIUS 1982

Menopause - Taking charge 90 MIN
VHS
Color (G)
$39.95 purchase
Takes a comprehensive up - to - date look at the experience of menopause. Features Veryl Rosenbaum, psychotherapist, fitness researcher and author, who guides the viewer through menopause by interviewing female health experts, women in different stages of menopause and by utilizing graphics. Covers hot flashes, vaginal dryness, hormones, diet, clothing, insomnia, stress and fitness.
Health and Safety
Dist - FCSINT

Menopause - taking charge 90 MIN
VHS
Color (G I J H)
$59.95 purchase _ #SD05
Reveals how women can take an active role in health choices. Looks at - menstrual fluctuations; lifetime estrogen levels; body changes; high calcium lowfat foods; hot flash triggers and solutions; breast health; exercise; menopausal phases; stress management; personal menstrual chart; nutrition; osteoporosis; female frienship; temporary symptoms; attitudes; books to read. Features Veryl Rosenbaum.
Social Science; Sociology
Dist - SVIP

Menotti's Amahl and the night visitors 52 MIN
VHS
Color (G)
$29.95 purchase
Features Teresa Stratas, Giorgio Tozzi, Willard White, and Nico Castal in a performance of 'Amahl And The Night Visitors' by Menotti, along with the Philharmonic Orchestra conducted by Jesus Lopez - Cobos.
Fine Arts
Dist - PBS **Prod** - WNETTV 1979

Men's and Women's Javelin 30 MIN
VHS / U-matic
Track & Field Event Videos Series
Color; B&W; Stereo; Mono; Silent (H C A)
#V86 11
Presents an extensive succession of performances by top athletes of the present and past, illustrating the technique

of the men's and women's javelin. Features many clips photographed from various angles and at various speeds.
Physical Education and Recreation
Dist - TRACKN **Prod** - TRACKN 1985

Men's Basketball Basics 56 MIN
VHS / BETA
Color (A)
Presents Marv Harshman, who demonstrates the drills he uses to school his teams on sound defensive principles. Begins with individual reaction drills and progresses to team defense, including both man - for - man and zone defensive strategy.
Physical Education and Recreation
Dist - RMIBHF **Prod** - RMIBHF

Men's Basketball Basics - Creating an Offense 57 MIN
VHS / BETA
Color (A)
Explains how to create an offense which takes advantage of what the opposition defense gives them. Discusses offensive strategy for man - for - man and zone defenses. Includes creating a lead, post play, the double stack, using the back door and the passing game. Features Marv Harshman, one of the outstanding coaches in college basketball.
Physical Education and Recreation
Dist - RMIBHF **Prod** - RMIBHF

Men's Basketball Basics - Offensive Drills 59 MIN
BETA / VHS
Color (A)
Demonstrates drills to help build an offense in basketball, including shooting, passing, dribbling, screening, rebounding and movement without the ball. Features Marv Harshman, University of Washington coach.
Physical Education and Recreation
Dist - RMIBHF **Prod** - RMIBHF

Men's Basketball Basics Series
Drills that get scoreboard results 59 MIN
Tough Defense - It'll Keep You in the Game 56 MIN
A Winning Offense 57 MIN
Dist - MOHOMV

Men's Championship Basketball Series
Championship Basketball - Defense
Championship Basketball - Offense
Dist - ATHI

Men's dance 11 MIN
U-matic / VHS / BETA
Pushtu tribe series
Color; PAL (G H C)
PdS30, PdS38 purchase
Points out that the Pushtu are dependent upon traditional dances to provide entertainment and pleasure. Without narration. Part of a four - part series.
Fine Arts; Geography - World; Sociology
Dist - EDPAT **Prod** - IFF
IFF

Men's Discus 4 MIN
16mm
Track & Field Technique Study Films Series
Color; Silent (H C A)
#85 7
Presents a succession of performances by the leading athletes in the men's discus event. Features live film footage.
Physical Education and Recreation
Dist - TRACKN **Prod** - TRACKN 1985

Men's Discus Throw 30 MIN
U-matic / VHS
Track & Field Event Videos Series
Color; B&W; Stereo; Mono; Silent (H C A)
#V86 7
Presents an extensive succession of performances by top athletes of the present and past, illustrating the technique of the men's discus throw. Features many clips photographed from various angles and at various speeds.
Physical Education and Recreation
Dist - TRACKN **Prod** - TRACKN 1985

Men's Glide Shot Put 4 MIN
16mm
Track & Field Technique Study Films Series
Color; Silent (H C A)
#85 6
Presents a succession of performances by the leading athletes in the men's glide shot put event. Features live film footage.
Physical Education and Recreation
Dist - TRACKN **Prod** - TRACKN 1985

Men's Golf with Al Geiberger 60 MIN
BETA / VHS
Color
Presents neuromuscular training using Al Geiberger as the model for an improved golf game. Includes four audiocassettes and personal training guide.
Physical Education and Recreation; Psychology
Dist - SYBVIS **Prod** - SYBVIS

Men's Hammer Throw 4 MIN
16mm
Track & Field Technique Study Films Series
Color; Silent (H C A)
#85 8
Presents a succession of performances by the leading athletes in the men's hammer throw event. Features live film footage.
Physical Education and Recreation
Dist - TRACKN **Prod** - TRACKN 1985

Men's High Jump 30 MIN
VHS / U-matic
Track & Field Event Videos Series
Color; B&W; Stereo; Mono; Silent (H C A)
#V86 1
Presents an extensive succession of performances by top athletes of the present and past, illustrating the technique of men's high jumping. Features many clips photographed from various angles and at various speeds.
Physical Education and Recreation
Dist - TRACKN **Prod** - TRACKN 1985

Men's High Jump 4 MIN
16mm
Track & Field Technique Study Films Series
Color; Silent (H C A)
#85 1
Presents a succession of performances by leading athletes in the men's high jump event. Features live film footage.
Physical Education and Recreation
Dist - TRACKN **Prod** - TRACKN 1985

Men's Hurdle Races 4 MIN
16mm
Track & Field Technique Study Films Series
Color; Silent (H C A)
#85 13
Presents a succession of performances by the leading athletes in men's hurdle racing. Features live film footage.
Physical Education and Recreation
Dist - TRACKN **Prod** - TRACKN 1985

Men's Hurdling Techniques 4 MIN
16mm
Track & Field Technique Study Films Series
Color; Silent (H C A)
#85 12
Presents a succession of performances by the leading athletes illustrating men's hurdling techniques. Features live film footage.
Physical Education and Recreation
Dist - TRACKN **Prod** - TRACKN 1985

Men's Javelin 4 MIN
16mm
Track & Field Technique Study Films Series
Color; Silent (H C A)
#85 9
Presents a succession of performances by the leading athletes in the men's javelin event. Features live film footage.
Physical Education and Recreation
Dist - TRACKN **Prod** - TRACKN 1985

Men's Liberation 29 MIN
U-matic
Woman Series
Color
Features Warren Farrell, author of Beyond Masculinity, explaining that men can be victims of stereotyping.
Sociology
Dist - PBS **Prod** - WNEDTV

Men's Lives 43 MIN
16mm
Color (I)
LC 75-701564
Shows by a series of candid interviews what American boys and men believe about the American concept of masculinity.
Psychology; Sociology
Dist - NEWDAY **Prod** - NEWDAY 1974

Men's Long Jump 30 MIN
U-matic / VHS
Track & Field Event Videos Series
Color; B&W; Stereo; Mono; Silent (H C A)
#V86 3
Presents an extensive succession of performances by top athletes of the present and past, illustrating the technique of the men's long jump. Features many clips photographed from various angles and at various speeds.
Physical Education and Recreation
Dist - TRACKN **Prod** - TRACKN 1985

Men's Long Jump 4 MIN
16mm
Track & Field Technique Study Films Series
Color; Silent (H C A)
#85 3
Presents a succession of performances by the leading athletes in the men's long jump event. Features live film footage.
Physical Education and Recreation
Dist - TRACKN **Prod** - TRACKN 1985

Men's Middle and Long Distance Races 4 MIN
16mm
Track & Field Technique Study Films Series
Color; Silent (H C A)
#85 14
Presents a succession of performances by the leading athletes in men's middle and long distance racing. Features live film footage.
Physical Education and Recreation
Dist - TRACKN **Prod** - TRACKN 1985

Men's Pole Vault 30 MIN
VHS / U-matic
Track & Field Event Videos Series
Color; B&W; Stereo; Mono; Silent (H C A)
#V86 2
Presents an extensive succession of performances by top athletes of the present and past, illustrating the technique of men's pole vaulting. Features many clips photographed from various angles and at various speeds.
Physical Education and Recreation
Dist - TRACKN **Prod** - TRACKN 1985

Men's Pole Vault 4 MIN
16mm
Track & Field Technique Study Films Series
Color; Silent (H C A)
#85 2
Presents a succession of performances by leading athletes in the men's pole vault event. Features live film footage.
Physical Education and Recreation
Dist - TRACKN **Prod** - TRACKN 1985

Men's Rotation Shot Put 4 MIN
16mm
Track & Field Technique Study Films Series
Color; Silent (H C A)
#85 5
Presents a succession of performances by the leading athletes in the men's shot put event. Features live film footage.
Physical Education and Recreation
Dist - TRACKN **Prod** - TRACKN 1985

Men's Shot Put 30 MIN
VHS / U-matic
Track & Field Event Videos Series
Color; B&W; Stereo; Mono; Silent (H C A)
#V86 6
Presents an extensive succession of performances by top athletes of the present and past, illustrating the technique of the men's shot put. Features many clips photographed from various angles and at various speeds.
Physical Education and Recreation
Dist - TRACKN **Prod** - TRACKN 1985

Men's skin care and make - up techniques 60 MIN
VHS
Make - up techniques with David Nicholas series
Color (H C G)
$48.00 purchase _ #BY205V
Teaches men how to take care of their skin, camouflage baldness, cover scars, trim and style beards, hide shaving nicks and many other grooming techniques. Part of a series featuring makeup artist David Nicholas.
Home Economics; Sociology
Dist - CAMV

Men's Sprint Races 4 MIN
16mm
Track & Field Technique Study Films Series
Color; Silent (H C A)
#85 11
Presents a succession of performances by the leading athletes in men's sprint racing. Features live film footage.
Physical Education and Recreation
Dist - TRACKN **Prod** - TRACKN 1985

Men's Sprinting Techniques 4 MIN
16mm
Track & Field Technique Study Films Series
Color; Silent (H C A)
#85 10
Presents a succession of performances by the leading athletes illustrating men's sprinting techniques. Features live film footage.
Physical Education and Recreation
Dist - TRACKN **Prod** - TRACKN 1985

Men's Sprints and Hurdles 30 MIN
U-matic / VHS
Track & Field Event Videos Series

Color; B&W; Stereo; Mono; Silent (H C A)
#V86 9
Presents an extensive succession of performances by top athletes of the present and past, illustrating the technique of the men's sprint and hurdles. Most show hurdle events. Features many clips photographed from various angles and at various speeds.
Physical Education and Recreation
Dist - TRACKN **Prod** - TRACKN 1985

Men's style - a practical guide for building your business wardrobe 40 MIN
VHS
Color (A)
$29.95 purchase _ #REG01V-H
Illustrates what to wear as well as how and when to wear it. Features the do's and don'ts of a business wardrobe which will fit the viewer's career objectives, personality, size, and budget. Shows how to choose classic business suits, sports coats, slacks, dress shirts, belts, ties, shoes, and formal wear. Describes different types of fabrics, colors, the fit of a suit, shirt, or slacks, and other essentials for putting together a business wardrobe appropriate for the individual viewer.
Home Economics
Dist - CAMV

Men's Track and Field Series no 1
Starting, Running and Finishing - Men's Track 17 MIN
Dist - ATHI

Men's Track and Field Series no 3
Long and High Jump, Pole Vaulting, Triple Jump 21 MIN
Dist - ATHI

Men's Track and Field Series no 4
Discus, Shot and Javelin 21 MIN
Dist - ATHI

Men's track and field series
Basic strategies 21 MIN
Dist - ATHI

Men's Triple Jump 4 MIN
16mm
Track & Field Technique Study Films Series
Color; Silent (H C A)
Presents a succession of performances by the leading athletes in the men's triple jump event. Features live film footage.
Physical Education and Recreation
Dist - TRACKN **Prod** - TRACKN 1985

Men's Triple Jump 30 MIN
U-matic / VHS
Track & Field Event Videos Series
Color; B&W; Stereo; Mono; Silent (H C A)
#V86 4
Presents an extensive succession of performances by top athletes of the present and past, illustrating the technique of the men's triple jump. Features many clips photographed from various angles and at various speeds.
Physical Education and Recreation
Dist - TRACKN **Prod** - TRACKN 1985

The Men's wear industry 20 MIN
VHS
Business of fashion series
Color (A H)
$120.00 purchase _ #DEP02V-H
Focuses on the different types of merchandise included in the men's wear industry. Interviews a manufacturer of fine suits, coats and trousers, as well as a well known designer. Examines production facilities plus the various routes taken in the marketing of men's wear. Visits a trade exposition and runway show.
Home Economics
Dist - CAMV

Mens weight training 60 MIN
VHS
Weight training series
Color (G)
$39.99 purchase _ #MFV004V
Demonstrates a series of weight training exercises that are designed for beginning male lifters. Presents two different workouts to choose from.
Physical Education and Recreation; Science - Natural
Dist - CAMV **Prod** - CAMV 1988

Men's work - video 60 MIN
VHS
Color (G)
$29.95 purchase _ #5850
Models alternatives to violence for men. Shows how to accept oneself but not one's violent behavior. Identifies violence and its roots, including the role of shame. Features Paul Kivel, co - founder of the Oakland Men's Project, Oakland, California, to help men develop alternatives to violence.
Psychology; Sociology
Dist - HAZELB

Men's Workable Wardrobe
VHS / 35mm strip
$69.00 purchase _ #LS52 filmstrip, $79.00 purchase _ #LS52V VHS
Provides instruction on how to develop a professional wardrobe on a limited budget. Portrays how haircuts, beards and wardrobe choices affect first impressions. Teaches about fabric, style and cost.
Home Economics
Dist - CAREER **Prod** - CAREER

Mensch Mutter 80 MIN
16mm
Color (GERMAN (ENGLISH SUBTITLES))
A German language film with English subtitles. Presents a study of the survival of Helga Fuchs, who with a minimal home job attempts to support her three children. Portrays Helga's futile fight to be a 'good mother,' although she does not possess the inner strength to succeed and lives in constant fear that her children might capsize her already barely floating boat.
Fine Arts; Foreign Language
Dist - WSTGLC **Prod** - WSTGLC 1977

Menschen Untereinander 90 MIN
16mm
B&W
A silent motion picture without subtitles. Presents a vivid picture of varying human emotions. Explores the lives of people with different fates, with arrogance, despondence, happiness and sorrow.
Fine Arts
Dist - WSTGLC **Prod** - WSTGLC 1926

Menses 4 MIN
16mm
Color (G)
$15.00 rental
Applies a wry comedy to the disagreeable aspects of menstruation where women act out their own dramas in a variety of places. Combines both imagery and politics of menstruation with comedy and drama.
Fine Arts
Dist - CANCIN **Prod** - BARHAM 1974

Menstruation 14 MIN
VHS / U-matic
Color
Explains menstruation, ovulation and menstrual flow. Discusses common symptoms related to menstruation and their management.
Health and Safety; Science - Natural
Dist - MEDFAC **Prod** - MEDFAC 1981

Menstruation and Premenstrual Tension 29 MIN
U-matic
Woman Series
Color
Examines the problems surrounding menstruation and premenstrual tension. Emphasizes the role of parents in determining how their daughters will react to menstruation.
Health and Safety
Dist - PBS **Prod** - WNEDTV

Menstruation and Sexual Development 28 MIN
16mm / U-matic / VHS
Inner Woman Series
Color (H C A)
LC 77-702979
Uses drawings to show the internal reproductive organs of the female. Discusses the signs of developing maturity, the development of sex organs, menstruation, ovulation and conception.
Health and Safety; Science - Natural
Dist - MGHT **Prod** - WXYZTV 1975

Menstruation - Hormones in Harmony 19 MIN
U-matic / VHS
Color (I J H)
Uses graphics and narration to explain the process of menstruation. Includes advice on hygiene and charting the cycle.
Health and Safety; Science - Natural
Dist - PEREN **Prod** - PPPO

Menstruation - understanding your body 35 MIN
VHS
Women's health series
Color (G)
$49.00 purchase _ #WHV1
Offers the most - up - to - date medical information on menstruation, reviewed and approved by a national panel of health care professionals. Features medical correspondent Dr Holly Atkinson of NBC News Today. Part of an eight - part series.
Health and Safety; Sociology
Dist - GPERFO **Prod** - AMEDCO

Mental and Emotional Damages 120 MIN
U-matic / VHS / Cassette
Color; Mono (PRO)
Discusses the development of legal theories permitting recovery for emotional damages, elements of the cause of action for emotional distress presenting evidence at trial.
Civics and Political Systems
Dist - CCEB **Prod** - CCEB

Mental and socioeconomic assessment 16 MIN
BETA / VHS / U-matic
Assessing the elderly series
Color (C PRO)
$280.00 purchase _ #617.5
Presents the assessment of mental status and socioeconomic factors that play a major role in the elderly person's ability to maintain an optimal level of functioning. Demonstrates how to assess the patient for cognitive and affective changes as well as socioeconomic status as part of a multidimensional assessment. Part of a five - part series on assessing the elderly produced by the School of Nursing, State University of New York at Stony Brook.
Health and Safety
Dist - CONMED

Mental aspects 30 MIN
VHS
Tennis with Van der Meer series
Color (C A)
$95.00 purchase, $55.00 rental
Features tennis player and instructor Dennis Van der Meer in a presentation on mental aspects of the game. Uses freeze - frame photography and repetition to stress skill development. Serves as part seven of a 10 - part telecourse.
Physical Education and Recreation; Psychology
Dist - SCETV **Prod** - SCETV 1989

The Mental athlete 30 MIN
VHS
Color (J H A)
$49.95 purchase _ #WES1614V
Examines the mental aspects of athletics. Suggests that mental conditioning can be used to improve athletic performance. Discusses establishment of realistic goals, positive self - affirmation, progressive relaxation, creative visualization, and more.
Physical Education and Recreation; Religion and Philosophy; Science - Natural
Dist - CAMV

Mental Computation - using Mental Computation for Addition 15 MIN
VHS / U-matic
Math Works Series
Color (I)
Demonstrates left - right method and plus - minus method of adding two - digit numbers.
Mathematics
Dist - AITECH **Prod** - AITECH

Mental Computation - using Mental Computation for Multiplication 15 MIN
U-matic / VHS
Mathematics for the '80s - Grade Six Series
(I)
$125.00 purchase
Suggests different strategies for a variety of problems that focus on money.
Mathematics
Dist - AITECH **Prod** - AITECH 1987

Mental Game 60 MIN
VHS
One on One Coaching Series
(J H C)
$39.95 _ #CVN1100V
Discusses issues concerning the football player. Features interviews with coaches who discuss positive attitudes, scholarships, academics, character, goal setting, drug problems, and more.
Physical Education and Recreation
Dist - CAMV **Prod** - CAMV

Mental handicap 25 MIN
VHS
Coping series
Color; PAL (G)
PdS25 purchase
Focuses on a family with a severly handicapped teenager. Shares their story to help others who are in the same situation. Part of a series on coping with illness or tragedy. Contact distributor about availability outside the United Kingdom.
Guidance and Counseling; Health and Safety; Psychology; Sociology
Dist - ACADEM

Mental Health 15 MIN
VHS / U-matic
Well, Well, Well with Slim Goodbody Series
Color (P)
Shows how to express feelings without losing control by thinking it over and talking to someone, if necessary.
Guidance and Counseling; Health and Safety
Dist - AITECH **Prod** - AITECH

Mental Health 30 MIN
U-matic / VHS
Health, Safety and Well - Being Series
Color
Health and Safety
Dist - CAMB **Prod** - MAETEL

Mental Health and the Family 66 MIN
VHS
Color (J H)
Examines the crucial role of the family in determining mental health, and documents the increasing effectiveness of family based therapy. Your students see how the family shapes personality through parent and child relationships, and how disorders can be traced to family experience. Psychologists clarify the characteristics of a healthy family.
Health and Safety; Sociology
Dist - HRMC **Prod** - HRMC 1980

Mental Health and the Family 66 MIN
VHS
Color (H)
Examines the role of the family in mental health, and documents the increasing effectiveness of family based therapy. Psychologists clarify the characteristics of a healthy family.
Guidance and Counseling; Health and Safety; Psychology; Sociology
Dist - IBIS **Prod** - IBIS 1980

Mental Health Care for Women, Pt 2 29 MIN
U-matic
Woman Series
Color
Discusses what qualities to look for in a therapist.
Psychology
Dist - PBS **Prod** - WNEDTV

Mental Health Challenges - Past and Future 16 MIN
16mm
Color
LC 75-700863
Uses animation to present a review of the progress in the field of mental health during the last 25 years. Features Drs Robert H Felix, Stanley F Yolles and Bertram S Brown, the first three directors of the U S National Institute of Mental Health.
Biography; Health and Safety; Psychology
Dist - USNAC **Prod** - NIMH 1971

Mental health concepts for nursing series
Introduction to the Nurse - Patient Relationship 30 MIN
Mental health concepts for nursing, Unit 2 - self - acceptance - a series
Self - Acceptance - Role of the Significant Other 30 MIN
Dist - GPN

Mental health concepts for nursing, Unit 2 - self - acceptance - a series
Mental health concepts for nursing series
B&W (PRO)
Self - Acceptance - Role Of The Significant - - ; Self - Acceptance - The Individual.
Health and Safety; Psychology
Dist - GPN **Prod** - GPN 1971

Mental health in nursing - caring for body and mind 28 MIN
VHS
Educational horizons videos series
Color (C PRO)
$250.00 purchase, $100.00 rental _ #42 - 2498, #42 - 2498R
Begins with a curriculum discussion for faculty where leading nurse educators debate a range of issues. Considers whether mental health should be integrated throughout the curriculum and how to overcome negative attitudes toward the mentally ill. Explores the delicate balance between mind and body and highlights the innovative mental health treatment models and student nurses' experiences in those settings. Includes a study guide with discussion questions, related articles, bibliography and definitions of key terms. .3 CEUs - certification education units - per program. Part of a series overviewing contemporary nursing issues.
Health and Safety
Dist - NLFN **Prod** - NLFN

The Mental Health Needs of Women with Medically High Risk Pregnancy
U-matic
Color (PRO)
LC 79-707726
Illustrates the emotional needs and reponses of women with medically high - risk pregancies, encouraging health - care professionals to be sensitive to their needs. Describes the role of the mental health nurse in obstetrics.
Health and Safety
Dist - UMMCML **Prod** - UMICHM 1978

Mental Health - New Frontiers of Sanity 22 MIN
U-matic / VHS / 16mm
Color (J)
Points out that mental health patients fill more than half of all hospital beds. Gives the statistics for mental sickness and interviews some leading psychiatrists. Claims that our society encourages schizoid personality and then calls it sanity.
Psychology
Dist - CNEMAG **Prod** - DOCUA 1971

Mental Hospital 20 MIN
U-matic / VHS / 16mm
B&W (C A)
Documents the daily experiences of a mental patient, from admission to the hospital to discharge. Follows the patient's viewpoint.
Health and Safety; Psychology
Dist - IFB **Prod** - UOKLA 1953

Mental Illness, Pt 2 - the Search 25 MIN
16mm
Color
Shows the research and treatment of the mentally ill conducted at Tulane University.
Health and Safety; Psychology
Dist - CCNY **Prod** - MGHT

Mental Patients' Association 29 MIN
16mm
Color (H C A)
Shows how ex - mental patients and their friends formed the Vancouver Mental Patients' Association, a democratically - organized, self - help group to assist people during the critical post - release period.
Geography - World; Health and Safety; Psychology
Dist - NFBC **Prod** - NFBC 1977

Mental Retardation and Social Work 18 MIN
U-matic / VHS
Color
Designed to increase the social worker's awareness of the needs of the mentally retarded and the facilities available. Discusses the trainable, moderately retarded, severely retarded and profoundly retarded.
Psychology; Sociology
Dist - UWISC **Prod** - LASSWC 1979

Mental Retardation Plus - the Twice Afflicted 20 MIN
16mm
Color
LC 74-705131
Focuses on mobility, sight and communication disorders among the profoundly retarded and on beginning efforts on institutions to assess, educate and train this population.
Education; Guidance and Counseling; Psychology
Dist - USNAC **Prod** - USHHS 1974

Mental Retardation, Pt 1 29 MIN
16mm
Color
Focuses upon the needs and progress made on behalf of the most severely and profoundly retarded. Emphasis is upon medical aspects, manpower needs, research efforts and activities within training centers.
Health and Safety; Psychology
Dist - UWISC **Prod** - UWISC 1966

Mental Retardation, Pt 2 29 MIN
16mm
Color
Deals with the needs and most recent breakthroughs in the training, education and habilitation of the moderately, mild and borderline groups of mentally retarded. Special education facilities, sheltered workshop and work adjustment services are featured.
Education; Health and Safety
Dist - UWISC **Prod** - UWISC 1966

Mental Retardation - the Hopeless 25 MIN
16mm / U-matic / VHS
Color (H C A)
LC 72-702671
Portrays the realistic view of the mentally retarded, in an effort to refute the popular prejudices and misconceptions that surround them. Shows how a vast majority of the retarded have the ability to relate to others and the proven potential for varying degrees of self - care, productivity and independence.
Education; Health and Safety; Psychology; Sociology
Dist - AIMS **Prod** - MONWIL 1972

Mental Status Exam
U-matic / VHS
Physical Assessment - Neurologic System Series
Color
Health and Safety; Psychology
Dist - CONMED **Prod** - CONMED

Mental Status Exam, the, Pt I 60 MIN
U-matic / VHS
B&W
Features a discussion by Dr Leonard Stein on the mental status exam he uses to judge a client's psychological state. Topics include general or immediate observation, one's capacity to abstract, mood and affect.
Psychology; Sociology
Dist - UWISC **Prod** - VRL

Mental Status Exam, the, Pt II 15 MIN
U-matic / VHS
B&W
Concludes discussion with Dr Leonard Stein on his mental status exam. Covers perception, memory and judgement.
Psychology; Sociology
Dist - UWISC **Prod** - VRL

The Mental Status Examination 34 MIN
16mm
B&W (PRO)
LC FIE63-288
Demonstrates techniques of initial or mental status interviews in psychiatric practice. Shows how information about behavior, appearance, intelligence, emotions and perceptions is compiled and analyzed to form the basis for subsequent psychiatric treatment. For professional use.
Psychology
Dist - USNAC **Prod** - USPHS 1962

The Mental status examination of the demented adult 16 MIN
VHS
Color (G C PRO)
$165.00 purchase, $40.00 rental
Teaches specific skills required for health - care professionals to evaluate mentally - impaired older patients. Explains the symptoms encountered and how to assess the patient's mental state.
Health and Safety
Dist - TNF **Prod** - JHU

Mental Wellness - Making it Happen 21 MIN
16mm / VHS
Color (J H A PRO)
$145.00, $480.00 purchase, $50.00 rental _ #8146
Shows teenagers how to increase their self - esteem through accepting responsibility, improving their competency in handling tasks and learning to balance commitments.
Guidance and Counseling; Health and Safety; Psychology
Dist - AIMS **Prod** - HRMC 1990

Mentally handicapped and epileptic 30 MIN
VHS
Color (G)
$149.00 purchase, $75.00 rental _ #UW4349
Discusses the combination of mental handicap and epilepsy, showing footage of seizures and discussing the psychosocial implications of this combination of problems. Looks at first - aid, risk - taking and prognosis. Concludes that, despite intractable seizures and limitations, even severe mental handicaps and epilepsy need not preclude a happy and fulfilling life.
Health and Safety; Psychology
Dist - FOTH

The Mentally Retarded and Slow Learning Child 30 MIN
VHS / U-matic
Promises to Keep Series Module 2
Color (T)
Reviews the characteristics of the slow learning and mentally retarded child, how the curriculum should be adapted and how the regular classroom can help this child experience success.
Education
Dist - LUF **Prod** - VPI 1979

Mentoring 20 MIN
VHS
Color (A PRO)
$495.00 purchase, $150.00 rental
Provides case studies and examples of mentoring and its benefits to an organization. Distinguishes several types of mentoring and explains how to plan for its effective application to an organization.
Business and Economics; Psychology
Dist - DHB **Prod** - CRISP 1993

Mentoring 20 MIN
VHS
Color (PRO IND A)
$495.00 purchase, $150.00 rental _ #CRI40
Describes mentoring as a skill to be learned. Guides mentors into examining the meaning of mentoring, how to understand the needs of individuals being mentored, do's and don'ts of mentoring and mentoring styles. Based on the book by Gordon Shea.
Business and Economics
Dist - EXTR

Mentoring - or take my hand, I'm a stranger in paradise and support systems - or united we stand, divided we freak out 30 MIN
VHS
First - year teacher series
Color (T)
$69.95 purchase, $45.00 rental
Discusses the unique challenges and rewards that first - year school teachers face. Serves as the second episode of a 12 - part telecourse. Features discussions between first - year teachers and Winthrop College professor Glen Walter on the importance of mentors and support systems for new teachers.
Education; Psychology
Dist - SCETV **Prod** - SCETV 1988

Menu for an Astronaut 15 MIN
16mm
Color
Focuses on the modern processing of food preparation for the astronauts.
Health and Safety; Home Economics; Psychology
Dist - FLADC **Prod** - FLADC

Menu for Space Flight 6 MIN
16mm
Color
Shows the preparation of nutritious and appetizing foods for space flight and demonstrates how foods can be eaten by space travelers.
Health and Safety; Industrial and Technical Education; Psychology; Science - Physical
Dist - NASA **Prod** - NASA

Menu makeovers - how to plan and prepare low - fat meals - 3 17 MIN
VHS
Cholesterol watch series
Color (G)
$195.00 purchase
Provides cooking tips, meal and snack suggestions, lunch alternatives and low - fat ethnic recipes. Features simple recipe secrets that transform paella, lasagna, pasta primavera, stir - fry chicken and beef curry into tasty, low - fat meals. Part three of a four - part series on cholesterol.
Health and Safety; Home Economics; Social Science
Dist - GPERFO

Menu planning for fast food addicts 15 MIN
VHS
Becoming independent series
Color (H G)
$79.00 purchase _ #CDHEC516V
Introduces the food groups and the importance of a balanced menu plan. Emphasizes that all fast food is not created equal, that, in a pinch, there are healthy choices available. Part of a 13 - part series featuring practical life and consumer skills for teens venturing out into independence.
Guidance and Counseling; Home Economics; Social Science
Dist - CAMV

Menura - the Lyrebird 22 MIN
16mm
Australian Wildlife Series
Color (I)
Describes the life cycle of the superb lyrebird, the cleverest of all bird mimics. Includes close - ups of the mating dance, nest building, female incubating her single egg and raising her young.
Science - Natural
Dist - AVEXP **Prod** - POLLCK

The Meo 53 MIN
VHS
Disappearing world series
Color (G C)
$99.00 purchase, $19.00 rental _ #51249
Reveals that the Vietnam War devastated the Meo of Indochina. Discloses that before the war, the Meo grew maize and opium and lived in villages with their extended families. When the war destroyed their peaceful environment, most males over the age of 14 went to join the fighting, while tens of thousands of Meos fled to refugee camps. Features anthropologist Jacques Lemoine. Part of a series working closely with anthropologists who lived for a year or more in societies whose social structures, beliefs and practices are threatened by the expansion of technocratic civilization.
Sociology
Dist - PSU **Prod** - GRANDA 1972

Meow, Meow 8 MIN
16mm
Color (K P I)
Presents a series of animated cut - out designs made by children.
Fine Arts; Literature and Drama
Dist - YELLOW **Prod** - YELLOW 1969

Mephisto's Little Film Plays 18 MIN
16mm
Color (K P I J H)
Presents a collection of short film plays by young filmmakers, aged 14 to 21. Includes the film plays Ethereal Voyage, POW, Subway, 27, Read 'Em and Weep, Skyway Drive - in and Cosmic Crystal.
Education; Fine Arts; Industrial and Technical Education
Dist - YELLOW **Prod** - YELLOW

Mer a Mer 25 MIN
16mm
Color (FRENCH)
LC 76-701478
A French language version of the 1975 film Sea To Sea. Views the Canadian fishing industry on both the east and west coasts of Canada and the way of life of those who work in the fishing industry.
Business and Economics; Foreign Language; Geography - World; Social Science; Sociology
Dist - WILFGP **Prod** - WILFGP 1975

Merce Cunningham 30 MIN
U-matic / VHS
Eye on Dance - Dance on TV and Film Series
Color
Focuses on the development of videodance.
Fine Arts
Dist - ARCVID **Prod** - ARCVID

Merce Cunningham, Charles Atlas and Chris Komar 30 MIN
U-matic / VHS
Eye on Dance - Dance on TV and Film Series
Color
Discusses collaborating on videodance.
Fine Arts
Dist - ARCVID **Prod** - ARCVID

The Mercenary Game 60 MIN
U-matic / VHS
Color (I)
LC 84-707171
Analyzes the international political implications of mercenary attempts to subvert foreign governments. Traces an ill - fated 1980 attempt by a group of American mercenaries to take over the small Caribbean island of Dominica. Shows how the plot, which involved members of the Ku Klux Klan, was foiled by the FBI.
Civics and Political Systems
Dist - CNEMAG **Prod** - IP 1983

Merchandise Control for Retailers 14 MIN
16mm / U-matic / VHS
Running a Small Business Series
Color (H C A)
Focuses on four main elements for proper control which are what to sell, getting the right supplier, good procedures for receiving, checking and storing merchandise, and proper control for merchandise in stock.
Business and Economics
Dist - BCNFL **Prod** - MVM 1983

Merchandising and sales 10 MIN
VHS
Skills - occupational programs series
Color (H C)
$49.00 purchase, $15.00 rental _ #316628; LC 91-712481
Discusses the skills needed for success in sales and merchandising. Feautures an assistant produce manager, a store manager and salespeople who deal in clothes, cars and stationery. Part of a series that features occupations in the skilled trades, in service industries and in business leading to careers in areas of demand and future growth. Includes teacher's guide with reproducible worksheets.
Business and Economics; Guidance and Counseling; Psychology
Dist - TVOTAR **Prod** - TVOTAR 1990

Merchandising - Food Services
U-matic / VHS
Color (J H)
Introduces your students to the basic principles of retail merchandising and food services.
Business and Economics; Social Science
Dist - CAREER **Prod** - CAREER

Merchant Marine Safety 28 MIN
16mm
Color (PRO)
Defines the responsibilities of the coast guard in Merchant Marine safety, such as inspection and approval of blueprints for vessel construction, safety requirements for construction and equipment of vessels, annual or periodic inspection thereafter and licensing and certification of the officers and crews of vessels.
Health and Safety; Social Science
Dist - USNAC **Prod** - USGEOS 1962

The Merchant of Four Seasons 88 MIN
16mm
Color (GERMAN)
Tells the story of Hans, a squat, cloddish fruit peddler whose mother despises him and whose sweetheart rejects him because his job is too dirty. Follows him through numerous episodes of almost unbelievable bad luck.
Fine Arts; Foreign Language
Dist - NYFLMS **Prod** - NYFLMS 1972

The Merchant of Los Angeles 26 MIN
U-matic / VHS
Color (G)
$249.00, $149.00 purchase _ #AD - 1950
Dramatizes the life of Harris Newmark, an immigrant who arrived in Los Angeles in 1853, became a successful merchant, was instrumental in bringing the railroad to the city, helped found its Chamber of Commerce, and, 60 years later, wrote the history of Los Angeles's dramatic growth. Stars Theodore Bikel in the role of Newmark.
Biography; Geography - United States; Geography - World; History - United States
Dist - FOTH **Prod** - FOTH

The Merchant of Venice 157 MIN
U-matic / VHS
Shakespeare Plays Series
Color (H C A)
LC 81-706561
Dramatizes William Shakespeare's play The Merchant Of Venice which strives to answer the question of whether the moneylender Shylock is an implacable villain, a comic buffoon, a tragic hero or a venomous monster.
Literature and Drama
Dist - TIMLIF **Prod** - BBCTV 1980

The Merchant of Venice 157 MIN
VHS
BBC Shakespeare series
Color (G C H)
$109.00 purchase _ #DL457
Fine Arts
Dist - INSIM **Prod** - BBC

Merchant of Venice 157 MIN
VHS / 16mm
BBC's Shakespeare Series
(H A)
$249.95
Retells Shakespeare's tragic comedy, The Merchant Of Venice, about the adventures of the complex character Shylock.
Literature and Drama
Dist - AMBROS **Prod** - AMBROS 1981

The Merchant of Venice - Act I, Scene III, Act IV, Scene I 26 MIN
U-matic / VHS / 16mm
Great Scenes from Shakespeare Series
Color (J)
LC 70-714375
Through a wide range of selection of scenes from Shakespeare, shows the great variety of Shakespeare's art and his understanding of man as an individual and as a member of society.
Literature and Drama
Dist - PHENIX **Prod** - SEABEN 1971

The Merchant of Venice - Shylock 27 MIN
VHS / U-matic
Shakespeare explorations with Patrick Stewart series
Color (J H C)
$210.00, $189.00 purchase _ #V230
Focuses on the role of Shylock in the play 'The Merchant of Venice,' by Shakespeare. Features a famous Shakespearean actor who discusses what he learned in his portrayal of the character. Patrick Stewart hosts.
Fine Arts; Literature and Drama
Dist - BARR **Prod** - BBC 1991

Merchants and masterpieces 87 MIN
VHS
Color (G)
$39.95 purchase _ #MER-01
Meets the persons of wealth who originally collected the masterpieces of the Metropolitan Museum of Art - J Pierpont Morgan, Robert Lehman, Benjamin Altman, the Rockefellers and the Webbs. Based on Calvin Tomkins' history of the museum.
Biography; Fine Arts
Dist - HOMVIS ARTSAM **Prod** - MMOA 1990

Merchants of Grain 57 MIN
U-matic / VHS
Color
LC 83-707212
Uses charts, animation and music to discuss the complexity of the grain trade and the large companies that control it. Presents spokesmen for one of the large companies who describe various aspects of the world's grain traffic. Demonstrates the growing importance of the grain trade as a instrument of foreign policy.
Business and Economics; Health and Safety
Dist - FLMLIB **Prod** - CANBC 1983

The Merchants of Peace 25 MIN
16mm / U-matic / VHS
Maclear Series
Color; Mono (J H C A)
$300.00 film, $250.00 video, $50.00 rental
Reports on the Canada - U.S. Defense Sharing Agreement and the problems suffered today by many Canadian workers as a result of this program.
Business and Economics; Civics and Political Systems; Geography - World
Dist - CTV **Prod** - CTV 1975

The Merchant's Tale 30 MIN
Videoreel / VT1
Canterbury Tales Series
B&W (A)
History - World; Literature and Drama
Dist - UMITV **Prod** - UMITV 1967

Mercury and Venus 29 MIN
U-matic
Project Universe - Astronomy Series Lesson 8
Color (C A)
Describes space explorations of Mercury and Venus since 1970. Uses animation to illustrate the unusual backtracking path the sun would appear to take when seen from Mercury's surface. Compares physical characteristics of Venus with the earth.
Science - Physical
Dist - CDTEL **Prod** - COAST

Mercury and Venus 26 MIN
U-matic / VHS
Planets Series
Color (C)
$249.00, $149.00 purchase _ #AD - 1143
Features Hal Mazursky who advises the Russians where to land their space craft as host. Explains what has been learned from the exploration of Venus, shows how the US Geological Survey maps planets and introduces Mercury. Heather Cooper explains how to determine the age of a planet. Part of a seven - part series on planets.
Industrial and Technical Education; Science - Physical
Dist - FOTH **Prod** - FOTH

Mercury - Exploration of a Planet 28 MIN
16mm
Color (J)
LC 77-700804
Uses animation and photography to illustrate the flight of Mariner X to Mercury and Venus.
Industrial and Technical Education; Science - Physical
Dist - USNAC **Prod** - NASA 1976

The Mercury Spacecraft Missions 30 MIN
BETA / VHS
Color
Relives the exciting first years of America's daring space program, including the first manned space flights with astronauts Shepard, Conrad, Glenn and others.
Science - Physical
Dist - CBSC **Prod** - CBSC

Mercury spacecraft missions and Legacy of Gemini 56 MIN
VHS
Color (G)
$29.95 purchase _ #V28
Relives the drama of the first years of the United States space program in two programs. Examines the 'firsts' in space accomplished by the Mercury and Gemini missions. Includes footage of astronauts John Glenn, Ed White, Virgil Grissom and others.
History - World; Industrial and Technical Education
Dist - INSTRU

Mercy 10 MIN
16mm
Color (G A)
$40.00 rental
Presents the work of filmmaker Abigail Child. Incorporates found footage from industrial, promotional and tourist films of the sixties into a glittering, kinetic bauble with images of machines moving and overlays of Asian voices in commemoration of America's wars in Asia.
Fine Arts; History - United States; History - World; Industrial and Technical Education; Sociology
Dist - PARART **Prod** - CANCIN 1989

Mercy Killing 28 MIN
U-matic / VHS
Color (C)
$249.00, $149.00 purchase _ #AD - 1441
Presents a Phil Donahue show which features a woman who helped her terminally ill mother end her own life, the daughter of a man who shot his crippled wife after she begged him to end her misery and the mother of Karen Ann Quinlan.
Civics and Political Systems; Health and Safety; Religion and Philosophy; Sociology
Dist - FOTH **Prod** - FOTH

Mercy - part 7 10 MIN
16mm
Is this what you were born for series
(G)
$40.00 rental
Explores public visions of technological and romantic invention. Dissects the game mass media plays with private perceptions.
Fine Arts
Dist - CANCIN **Prod** - CHILDA 1989

Merdeka Joy 19 MIN
16mm
B&W
Shows the joy felt by independence and the celebrations which were held throughout the country of Malaysia.
Civics and Political Systems; Geography - World; History - World
Dist - PMFMUN **Prod** - FILEM 1967

Meredith Monk 40 MIN
U-matic / VHS
B&W
Features an interview with Meredith Monk. Presented by Kate Horsfield and Lyn Blumenthal.
Fine Arts
Dist - ARTINC **Prod** - ARTINC

Meredith Monk and Laura Dean 30 MIN
U-matic / VHS
Eye on Dance - Dance on TV Series
Color
Discusses the experience of working with television. Shows dancers in excerpts from thier work. Includes a performance of 'Esoterica' with Kenneth Archer.
Fine Arts
Dist - ARCVID **Prod** - ARCVID

Merengue 60 MIN
VHS
Kathy Blake dance studios - let's learn how to dance series
Color (G A)
$39.95 purchase
Features dance instructors Kathy Blake and Gene Russo, who instruct viewers on the basics of the Merengue. First of two parts.
Fine Arts
Dist - PBS **Prod** - WNETTV

Merengue
VHS
Arthur Murray dance lessons series
Color (G)
$19.95 purchase _ #MC053
Offers lessons in classic ballroom dancing from instructors in Arthur Murray studios, focusing on the merengue. Part of a 12 - part series on various ballroom dancing styles.
Fine Arts; Physical Education and Recreation; Sociology
Dist - SIV

Merengue II 60 MIN
VHS
Kathy Blake dance studios - let's learn how to dance series
Color (G A)
$39.95 purchase
Features dance instructors Kathy Blake and Gene Russo, who instruct viewers on the basics of the Merengue. Second of two parts.
Fine Arts
Dist - PBS **Prod** - WNETTV

Mergers, Acquisitions and Other Corporate Transactions After TEFRA 180 MIN
Cassette / U-matic / VHS
Color (PRO)
$150.00, $30.00 purchase _ #P133, #M545
Examines income tax consequences for sale, purchase, redemption or liquidation of corporate business under 1982 tax legislation. Considers corporate election to a step - up basis, accumulated earnings tax and redemption transactions. Includes two audiocassettes or one video cassette and study material in complete three hour program.
Business and Economics; Civics and Political Systems; Social Science
Dist - ALIABA **Prod** - ALIABA 1987

Merging Control Systems 15 MIN
16mm
Color
LC 74-706145
Reports on a research study aimed at assisting the driver in entering the freeway traffic stream as smoothly and easily as possible. Shows how two merging control systems are developed and tested. Explains the racer system and the green band system to avoid rear - end and sidewipe accidents.
Health and Safety; Psychology; Social Science
Dist - USNAC **Prod** - USDTFH 1971

Merit Pay 18 MIN
U-matic
Launching Civil Service Reform Series
Color
LC 79-706268
Discusses merit pay under the system created by the Civil Service Reform Bill. Discusses a timetable for implementation of the system, employees covered by the system, the earning of pay based on performance, and distribution of merit pay funds.
Civics and Political Systems
Dist - USNAC **Prod** - USOPMA 1978

Merkaba 8 MIN
16mm
Color (A)
Presents an experimental film by Dennis Pies which explores light's emanations and hypnotic patterns.
Fine Arts
Dist - STARRC **Prod** - STARRC 1973

Merle Travis - rare performances 1946 - 1981 60 MIN
VHS
Color (G)
$24.95 purchase _ #VDZ - MT01
Shows Merle Travis playing 18 of his best - known songs, starting as a 29 - year - old and ending with a pair of duets with his grown son, Thomas Bresh. Includes booklet.
Fine Arts
Dist - HOMETA **Prod** - HOMETA

Merle Travis - the video collection 60 MIN
VHS
Color (G)
$22.50 purchase _ #VEST13012
Includes accompanying booklet.
Fine Arts
Dist - ROUNDR **Prod** - VESTAP 1994

Merlin's Magic of Learning 15 MIN
U-matic / VHS / 16mm
Color (P I)
LC 80-700251
Uses a story about a magician named Merlin to demonstrate the relevancy of studying and schoolwork.
Guidance and Counseling
Dist - JOU

Merlin's Magical Message 7 MIN
16mm / U-matic / VHS
Color
Presents an animated film, with Merlin and King Arthur as the characters, pointing out the importance of home dental care, especially brushing, in preserving good dental health.
Health and Safety
Dist - PRORE **Prod** - PRORE

Merlin's Magical Message 5 MIN
16mm
Color (I)
LC 74-706056
Uses animation to emphasize the importance of home dental care in preserving good dental health.
Health and Safety
Dist - MTP **Prod** - AMDA 1970

Merlo 16 MIN
VHS / U-matic
B&W
Deals with the perception of image and sound over varying distances.
Fine Arts
Dist - KITCHN **Prod** - KITCHN

The Mermaid Princess - a Hans Christian Andersen Tale 14 MIN
U-matic / VHS / 16mm
Color (P I)
LC 76-703582
Presents an adaptation of Hans Christian Anderson's story about a little mermaid and her love for a shipwrecked prince.
Literature and Drama
Dist - CORF **Prod** - CORF 1976

Mermaids and monsters 15 MIN
U-matic / VHS
Return to the magic library series
Color (P I)
#362408; LC 91-706823
Features a mermaid who tells the puppet characters a sea tale, The Voice in the Shell by Joan Aiken, about a boy who makes a deal with a mysterious creature on the seashore which comes back to haunt him. Part of a series using puppet mice and live storytellers to encourages students to read the featured story and respond with questions and comments. Includes teacher's guide and five readers.
Literature and Drama; Social Science
Dist - TVOTAR **Prod** - TVOTAR 1990

Mermaids, Frog Legs and Fillets 19 MIN
U-matic / VHS / 16mm
Color (H C G T A)
Documentary about a black man, Lincoln Rorie, a white man, Jerry Williams, and the unique way in which they earn their living at a seafood selling boat on a Washington, D C wharf, attracting customers with rhymes and 'cries.' Discusses both men's backgrounds, Lincoln's in the city streets and open air markets of Washington, and Jerry's among the fishing boats and country stores of rural Virginia, and the influence of each man's father in their choice of occupation and fast talking abilities.
Sociology
Dist - PSU **Prod** - PSU 1981

Merrill Ashley, Dr Joseph D'Amico and Dr Tom Novella 30 MIN
U-matic / VHS
Eye on Dance - Dancers' Health Series
Color
Looks at the repair and care of dancers' feet. Includes a performance of 'Esoterica' with Harvey Lichtenstein Hosted by Irene Dowd.
Fine Arts
Dist - ARCVID **Prod** - ARCVID

Merrill Brockway and Kinberg 30 MIN
VHS / U-matic
Eye on Dance - Dance on TV and Film Series
Color
Tells the story of 'Dance in America.' Looks at a performance of 'Esoterica' with Catrina Neiman. Hosted by Celia Ipiotis.
Fine Arts
Dist - ARCVID **Prod** - ARCVID

Merrily we roll along 51 MIN
VHS
Color (J H)
$119.00 _ #05164 - 026
Steers viewers through 70 years of automotive history, from the first 'horseless carriage' to the impact the automobile has had on the American economy. Includes teacher's guide and library kit.
Education; Industrial and Technical Education; Sociology
Dist - GA

Merrily We Roll Along, Pt 1 25 MIN
U-matic
B&W (H C)
Features Groucho Marx offering a 70 - year retrospective of automobile development.
Industrial and Technical Education
Dist - GA **Prod** - BENDIK

Merrily We Roll Along, Pt 2 26 MIN
U-matic
B&W (H C)
Features Groucho Marx offering a 70 - year retrospective of automobile development.
Industrial and Technical Education
Dist - GA **Prod** - BENDIK

A Merry Chase - Debussy's Afternoon of a Faun 10 MIN
16mm
Animations from Allegro Non Troppo Series
Color (C A)
Offers an animated story set to the music of Debussy's Afternoon Of A Faun. Tells the story of a squat and aging satyr who lusts for the sexual attention of the young nymphs of the serene woodland. Reveals that when the nymphs ignore him, he takes a forlorn walk through the desert, unaware that the desert is actually the body of a gigantic, beautiful woman.
Fine Arts
Dist - TEXFLM **Prod** - BOZETO 1978

Merry Christmas 14 MIN
VHS / U-matic
Stepping into Rhythm Series
Color (P)
Introduces hand bells and heralds the Christmas season with favorite holiday songs.
Fine Arts
Dist - AITECH **Prod** - WVIZTV

Merry - Go - Round 24 MIN
16mm
B&W (J)
A doctor, talking to patients, doctors and others, asks why tuberculosis has not yet been defeated.
Health and Safety
Dist - AMLUNG **Prod** - NTBA 1961

Merry go round 11 MIN
VHS
Ruth Heller language stories series
Color (P I)
$44.95 purchase _ #SAV9042
Offers a colorful program about nouns, possessives and more. Teaches English grammar. Part of a four - part series adapting picture books that teach grammar by Ruth Heller.
English Language
Dist - KNOWUN

Merry - go - round 90 MIN
16mm
B&W (G)
$100.00 rental
Portrays a young Austrian nobleman about to enter a loveless marriage who seeks freedom with a mistreated young woman from the carnival and the other denizens of her amusement park netherworld. Directed by Erich von Stroheim and Rupert Julian.
Fine Arts
Dist - KINOIC

Merry - Go - Round 45 MIN
16mm
Color (A)
LC 78-700005
Dramatizes three different family situations to describe the causes, effects and treatment of the problem of child abuse. Notes the cyclical nature of the problem in that abusive parents tend to have been abused as children.
Psychology; Sociology
Dist - USNAC **Prod** - WRAIR 1977

The Merry - Go - Round Horse 17 MIN
U-matic / VHS / 16mm
Color (P I)
LC 74-700604
Presents an art film without narration about the love of a little ragamuffin for an old wooden merry - go - round horse which is mistreated by a wealthy child for whom the horse was purchased at the flea market.
Guidance and Counseling; Literature and Drama
Dist - LCOA **Prod** - LCOA 1969

Merry - Go - Round, Pt 1 23 MIN
16mm
Color (A)
LC 78-700005
Dramatizes three different family situations to describe the causes, effects and treatment of the problem of child abuse. Notes the cyclical nature of the problem in that abusive parents tend to have been abused as children.
Sociology
Dist - USNAC **Prod** - WRAIR 1977

Merry - Go - Round, Pt 2 23 MIN
16mm
Color (A)
LC 78-700005
Dramatizes three different family situations to describe the causes, effects and treatment of the problem of child abuse. Notes the cyclical nature of the problem in that abusive parents tend to have been abused as children.
Sociology
Dist - USNAC **Prod** - WRAIR 1977

The Merry Widow 60 MIN
VHS
Color (G)
$39.95 purchase _ #1236
Presents the New York City Ballet production of 'The Merry Widow.' Stars Peter Martins and Patricia McBride.
Fine Arts; Physical Education and Recreation
Dist - KULTUR

The Merry wives of Windsor 140 MIN
VHS
Shakespearean drama series
Color (I J H C)
$59.95 purchase _ #US28
Presents one of a series in which the Bard's works are staged almost exactly as seen in the 16th century, but without unfamiliar English accents. Stars Leon Charles and Gloria Grahame. Directed by Jack Manning.
Literature and Drama
Dist - SVIP

The Merry Wives of Windsor 167 MIN
VHS / 16mm
BBC's Shakespeare Series
(H A)
$249.95
Depicts the Shakespearean comedy, The Merry Wives Of Windsor, about the character Falstaff seducing two affluent married women.
Literature and Drama
Dist - AMBROS **Prod** - AMBROS 1983

The Merry wives of Windsor 167 MIN
VHS
BBC Shakespeare series
Color (G C H)
$109.00 purchase _ #DL458
Fine Arts
Dist - INSIM **Prod** - BBC

The Merry Wives of Windsor 167 MIN
U-matic / VHS
Shakespeare Plays Series
Color (H C A)
Presents William Shakespeare's play The Merry Wives of Windsor which brings together an inept con man, a jealous husband with a mischievous wife, a pair of young lovers, a dose of disguise, considerable slapstick, an elopement and a concluding spectacle.
Literature and Drama
Dist - TIMLIF **Prod** - BBCTV 1984

Mersey Forth 14 MIN
16mm
Color
LC 80-700913
Explores the tourist attractions of the Mersey Forth area of Tasmania.
Geography - World
Dist - TASCOR **Prod** - TASCOR 1979

Merton 80 MIN
16mm
Color (G)
Presents an independent production by P Wilkes and A Glynn. Offers a biography of religious philosopher Thomas Merton.
Biography; Fine Arts; Religion and Philosophy
Dist - FIRS

Merton - a film biography 60 MIN
VHS
Color (R)
$39.95 purchase _ #493 - 7
Offers an intimate profile of Trappist mystic, spiritual writer and advocate for peace, Thomas Merton.
Religion and Philosophy
Dist - USCC **Prod** - USCC 1992

Merton - a film biography 60 MIN
VHS
Color (G)
$39.95 purchase _ #FRM
Focuses on Trappist monk Thomas Merton. Examines his life through interviews with those who knew him - the Dalai Lama, poet Lawrence Ferlinghetti, Ernesto Cardenal, Robert Giroux and Joan Baez. Interweaves passages from Merton's writings. Produced by Paul Wilkes and Audrey Glynn.
Religion and Philosophy
Dist - SNOWLI **Prod** - SNOWLI

Mesa Verde - Colorado, land of forgotten people and lost cities 22 MIN
BETA / U-matic / VHS
National park series
Color (G)
$29.95, $130.00 purchase _ #LSTF94
Visits Mesa Verde, site of one of the largest of the ancient pueblos of the Anasazi. Includes script and teachers' guide. Produced by Creative Vision, Inc.
Geography - United States; Social Science
Dist - FEDU

Mesa Verde - Mystery of the Silent Cities 14 MIN
U-matic / VHS / 16mm
Color (I)
LC 76-701128
Introduces students to an ancient North American Indian culture that thrived briefly in a plateau in what is now Mesa Verde National Park in Colorado. Shows how archaeologists are able to reach some conclusions about how they lived.
History - United States; Science - Physical; Social Science; Sociology
Dist - EBEC **Prod** - EBEC 1975

Mesa Verde National Park 23 MIN
BETA / VHS
Color
Visits the world famous cliff dwellings of Mesa Verde, ruins of an ancient Indian civilization that flourished for a thousand years then vanished forever.
Geography - United States
Dist - CBSC **Prod** - CBSC
UILL

The Mesencephalon 15 MIN
VHS / U-matic
Neurobiology Series
Color (PRO)
Identifies the macroscopic structures of the midbrain using brain specimens and diagrams. Discusses briefly the physiology and pathology of the midbrain.
Health and Safety; Science - Natural
Dist - HSCIC **Prod** - HSCIC

Mesenteric Caval Shunt for Extrahepatic Obstruction 21 MIN
16mm
Color (PRO)
Explains that mesenteric - caval anastomosis has proven to be an effective means of portal decompression in patients with extrahepatic portal obstruction. Illustrates operative technique and discusses patient care.

Health and Safety; Science
Dist - ACY **Prod** - ACYDGD 1966

Mesenteric Thrombosis and Adhesion Band Strangulation 18 MIN
16mm
Color (PRO)
Shows mesenteric thrombosis as seen at surgery and at autopsy, and examples of adhesion band strangulation with and without gangrene. Demonstrates the mechanism of strangulation by an experiment in animal surgery.
Health and Safety; Science
Dist - ACY **Prod** - ACYDGD 1951

Mesentric Vascular Insufficiency 24 MIN
U-matic
Color (PRO)
LC 76-706057
Discusses mesenteric vascular insufficiency, showing associated factors, etiology, arteriography and surgical management.
Health and Safety
Dist - USNAC **Prod** - WARMP 1969

Meshes of the Afternoon 14 MIN
16mm
B&W (C)
$300.00
Experimental film by Maya Daren.
Fine Arts
Dist - AFA **Prod** - AFA 1943

Meshie 28 MIN
16mm
B&W (C)
LC 75-702185
Studies a chimpanzee raised among humans and subjected to training designed to test the limits of a chimpanzee's ability to acquire human behavior patterns. Records some of Meshie's activities.
Psychology
Dist - PSUPCR **Prod** - AMNH 1975

The Mesolithic Society 18 MIN
U-matic / VHS / 16mm
Color (J)
Examines the known facts regarding the inhabitans of Northern Europe at the end of the last great Ice Age. Provides insight into the practical problems faced by people who bridged the period between the Paleolithic and Neolithic cultures.
History - World
Dist - LUF **Prod** - LUF 1980

Mesolithic Society 18 MIN
U-matic / VHS
Color (I J H C G)
Examines in detail the known facts regarding the inhabitants of Northern Europe at the end of the last great Ice Age. Utilizes two accepted methods of archaeological investigation, the traditional examination of period artifacts and the experimental in which students are seen living for long periods under conditions similar to those experienced by Mesolithic peoples.
History - World; Sociology
Dist - VIEWTH **Prod** - GATEEF

Mesopotamia - from bronze to iron - Parts 3 and 4 60 MIN
VHS / U-matic
Western tradition - part I series
Color (G)
$45.00, $29.95 purchase
Presents two thirty - minute programs tracing the history of ideas, events and institutions which have shaped modern societies hosted by Eugen Weber. Looks at settlements in the Fertile Crescent which gave rise to the great river civilizations in the Middle East in part 3. Part 4 examines the revolutionary development of tools and societies through the use of metal in the empires of Assyria, Persia and Neo - Babylonia. Parts 3 and 4 of a 52 - part series on the Western tradition.
Geography - World; History - World; Sociology
Dist - ANNCPB **Prod** - WGBH 1989

Mesopotamia - return to Eden 50 MIN
VHS
Lost civilizations video series
Color (G)
$19.99 purchase _ #0 - 7835 - 8271 - 4NK
Explores the earliest civilizations and pathways back to the original Garden of Eden. Visits lands of the Bible, the Torah and the Koran. Looks at the Jerusalem of judges and kings, the Babylon of Nebuchadnezzar, and Summarian cities thriving with culture and commerce. Part of a ten - part series incorporating the newest research, evidence and discoveries; orginal cinematography in 25 countries on 5 continents; dramatized recreations of scenes from the past; three - dimensional computer graphics to reconstruct ancient cities and monumental feats of engineering; historic footage; and computer - animated maps.
History - World
Dist - TILIED **Prod** - TILIED 1995

Mesothelioma and Malignant Effusion 27 MIN
U-matic
Color
Discusses the different types of mesothelioma and their relationship to asbestos.
Health and Safety
Dist - UTEXSC **Prod** - UTEXSC

Mesozoic and Cenozoic Eras 28 MIN
VHS
Grand Canyon Chronicles Series
Color
$69.95 purchase _ #9699
Tells the story of the Grand Canyon's 'recent' past, the last 225 million years, during which the dinosaurs reigned and the Age of Mammals began.
History - World; Science - Physical
Dist - AIMS **Prod** - AIMS

Mess Management - Conservation Control in the Management of a Mess 14 MIN
16mm
Color
LC FIE56-92
Explains the basic functions of mess management and the importance of meal planning. Discusses on - the - job training of mess personnel and the functions and responsibilities of the mess officer, food adviser and unit commanders.
Civics and Political Systems; Health and Safety; Home Economics; Industrial and Technical Education; Psychology; Social Science
Dist - USNAC **Prod** - USA 1956

A Message 5 MIN
VHS / U-matic
Color (S)
Presents an animated story to motivate hearing impaired children to read.
Fine Arts; Guidance and Counseling; Home Economics; Psychology
Dist - GALCO **Prod** - GALCO 1981

Message from Budapest 15 MIN
16mm
Color & B&W (G)
$30.00 rental
Records a trip to Budapest, its hustle and bustle and the annual May Day parade. Shares a fragmented diary of images and sounds. Produced by Moira Sweeney.
Fine Arts; Geography - World
Dist - CANCIN

A Message from Silence Dogwood 11 MIN
16mm
Color
LC 76-703138
Portrays the adage 'Time is money' from Ben Franklin's autobiography, emphasizing the cost effectiveness of the Xerox telecopier.
Business and Economics; Social Science
Dist - STOKB **Prod** - XEROX 1976

Message from Space 30 MIN
16mm
Color; B&W (I)
LC FIA67-5776
Tells the story of two young scientists who work at a remote radio astronomy monitoring station, where they are joined by a woman scientist and the father of one of the men. Examines basic issues of Christian faith against a background of new scientific thought.
Religion and Philosophy; Science
Dist - FAMF **Prod** - FAMF 1967

Message from the Stone Age - the Story of the Tasaday 16 MIN
U-matic / VHS / 16mm
Color (I A)
Describes how, in 1971, the Tasaday hiked 30 miles from their home in a Philippine rain forest to the forest's edge where they discovered and were discovered by the modern world, a transition of 30,000 years from the Stone Age to the Space Age. Looks at this self - contained social environment and encourages students to look at their own culture and beliefs.
Geography - World; Sociology
Dist - UNKNWN

Message from Women in Japan 25 MIN
Videoreel / VHS
B&W (JAPANESE)
Introduces women's spaces and events in Japan.
Foreign Language; Sociology
Dist - WMENIF **Prod** - WMV

Message in the Rocks 57 MIN
16mm / U-matic / VHS
Nova Series
Color (H C A)
LC 83-700015
Demonstrates how studying rock specimens may reveal clues to the age of the earth and how it was formed. Analyzes the geologic significance of the eruption of volcanoes such as Mt St Helens.
Science - Physical
Dist - TIMLIF **Prod** - WGBHTV 1982

The Message is the Medium 43 MIN
U-matic
Color
Provides detailed information about all aspects of video production as it applies to mental health. Presents basics for using television in medicine and pschiatry.
Fine Arts; Health and Safety; Psychology
Dist - UWASHP **Prod** - UWASHP

The Message is Yours - Don't Lose it 55 FRS
VHS / U-matic
New Supervisor Series Module 2
Color
Explains how the new supervisor can overcome the barriers to good communication, in writing, in face - to - face conversation and in a conference.
Business and Economics; Psychology
Dist - RESEM **Prod** - RESEM

A Message of hope 120 MIN
VHS
Color (G)
$39.95 purchase _ #P34
Features four individuals who share their compelling journeys beyond the boundaries of this life. Offers a production used extensively around the world for counseling. With Dr Raymond Moody.
Fine Arts; Sociology
Dist - HP

A Message of Life 26 MIN
16mm
Color
Portrays the impact of the Yom Kippur War on the people of Israel.
History - World; Sociology
Dist - ALDEN **Prod** - UJA

Message of Starlight 24 MIN
VHS / U-matic
Discovering Physics Series
Color (H C)
Explains how astronomers deduce the history of stars using observations of the stars from telescopes and related instruments. Shows how aspects of light are measured by spectrograph. Describes spectral curve and Hertzprung - Russell plot. Filmed at Britain's Royal Greenwich Observatory and Oxford.
Science; Science - Physical
Dist - MEDIAG **Prod** - BBCTV 1983

The Message of Starlight 29 MIN
U-matic
Project Universe - Astronomy Series Lesson 17
Color (C A)
Explains how measurements of magnitudes and spectroscopic analysis yield extensive information about the properties of individual stars. Reviews modern spectroscopic techniques.
Science - Physical
Dist - CDTEL **Prod** - COAST

Message of the Medium 30 MIN
U-matic
Realities
Color (A)
Delves into the political, social, economic and cultural trends of the 1980s. Probes a wide range of contemporary concerns. Each segment includes a guest speaker who is an expert in the field under discussion.
Business and Economics; Civics and Political Systems; Social Science; Sociology
Dist - TVOTAR **Prod** - TVOTAR 1985

The Message of the Myth 58 MIN
Cassette / VHS
Power of Myth Series
Color (G)
$29.95, $9.95 purchase _ #XVMTM, XAMTM
Compares creation stories from around the world. Suggests that today's people need new mythologies and metaphors that match modern needs. Part of the Power Of Myth series featuring Joseph Campbell.
Literature and Drama; Religion and Philosophy
Dist - GAINST **Prod** - PBS

Message of the myth
VHS
Power of myth series
Color (G)
$29.95 purchase
Presents 'The Message Of The Myth,' the second part of the 'Power Of Myth' series with the late Joseph Campbell and Bill Moyers.
Religion and Philosophy
Dist - PBS **Prod** - WNETTV

The Message of the Myth
VHS / Cassette
Power of Myth Series
(G)
$29.95, $9.95 purchase
Features Joseph Campbell and Bill Moyers.
Literature and Drama; Religion and Philosophy
Dist - BKPEOP **Prod** - MFV

The Message of the myth, vol 2 60 MIN
VHS
Power of Myth series
Color (G)
$29.95 purchase _ #683
Features storyteller Joseph Campbell who compares the creation story in Genesis with creation stories from around the world. Part of a six - part series on Joseph Campbell with introductions by Bill Moyers.
Literature and Drama; Religion and Philosophy
Dist - YELMON **Prod** - PBS

A Message to Our Parents 52 MIN
U-matic / VHS
Color (K)
$249.00, $149.00 purchase _ #AD - 1281
Airs the concerns of youngsters about the threat of nuclear war. Reveals that since Hiroshima many youngsters feel a compelling sense of impending and implacable doom. Shows the questions young people ask scientific and political experts.
Geography - World; History - United States; Literature and Drama; Psychology; Sociology
Dist - FOTH **Prod** - FOTH

Messages 15 MIN
VHS / 16mm
Native Imagery Series
Color (I)
$200.00 purchase _ #283502
Introduces the rich traditions as well as the new directions of Native North American imagery in contemporary visual art. Includes commentary from artists in the series. 'Messages' explores the way in which artists express feelings, create moods and convey ideas or issues. Profiles painters Alex Janvier and Joane Cardinal - Schubert, sculptor Brian Clark, Kim McLain who paints, creates photocollage and is a printmaker, and George Littlechild who combines bright colors, bold lines and other media to create expressive portraits.
Fine Arts; Social Science
Dist - ACCESS **Prod** - ACCESS 1988

Messages 6 MIN
16mm
Color (K P I)
Features a collection of five one - minute service spots on nutrition and consumerism, made by children, ages 11 to 19.
Fine Arts; Home Economics; Social Science
Dist - YELLOW **Prod** - YELLOW 1972

Messages 30 MIN
U-matic
Polka Dot Door Series
Color (K)
Presents a variety show for pre - school children. Includes songs, mime, stories, film sequences, talk, dance and fantasy figures. Each show emphasizes a particular theme such as numbers, feelings, exploring, music or time. Comes with parent teacher guide.
Fine Arts; Literature and Drama
Dist - TVOTAR **Prod** - TVOTAR 1985

Messages Along the Trail - Signes De Piste 10 MIN
16mm
How to do it Series
Color (G)
#1X25
Illustrates aspects of traditional Montagnis Indian life. Shows how they leave signs for other hunters along the trail in the bush. Not narrated.
Social Science
Dist - CDIAND **Prod** - ADCQ 1978

Messages by Hand 8 MIN
16mm / U-matic / VHS
Zoom Series
Color
LC 78-700139
Presents a deaf boy using sign language discussing his experiences at a special summer camp for deaf children.
Guidance and Counseling; Psychology; Sociology
Dist - FI **Prod** - WGBH 1977

Messages from Mother Mary for the 20th century 62 MIN
VHS
Color (G)
$29.95 purchase _ #P43
Follows Mother Mary and views her calls for urgency. Travels around the globe where her increasing visitations are being seen, including Fatima, Portugal; Belgium; Akita, Japan; Yugoslavia; Spain; and more. Also called Marian Apparitions of the 20th Century.
Fine Arts; Religion and Philosophy
Dist - HP

Messages from the birds 60 MIN
VHS
National Audubon Society specials series
Color; Captioned (G)
$49.95 purchase _ #NTAS - 304
Describes how the results of the annual International Shorebird Survey can reveal environmental problems. Focuses on the example of the Delaware Bay, where several shorebird species stop during their migration seasons. Also produced by Turner Broadcasting and WETA - TV. Narrated by Martin Sheen.
Science - Natural
Dist - PBS **Prod** - NAS 1988

Messages from the stars 26 MIN
VHS
Stars series
Color (I J H)
$195.00 purchase
Looks at the technology and tools used by astronauts to study stars. Shows how and why time is measured in light years. Interprets astrophotographs, what a star's color indicates and the way a star's spectrum indicates its composition. Part of a six - part series on astronomy.
History - World; Science - Physical
Dist - LANDMK **Prod** - LANDMK 1988

Messages in Media 15 MIN
VHS / 16mm
Junior High Ethics Resource Package Series
Color (J)
$200.00, $250.00 purchase _ #278406
Presents a comprehensive series on ethics for educators, junior high students and concerned adults. Describes an ethics course introduced in Alberta, Canada, schools and suggests teaching strategies for educators. The last five programs are dramas for students to teach key ethical concepts. 'Messages In Media' makes students aware of the power of media and some of the techniques used to influence audiences.
Business and Economics; Guidance and Counseling; Psychology; Religion and Philosophy; Sociology
Dist - AITECH **Prod** - ACCESS 1989

Messages, messages 30 MIN
16mm
B&W (G)
$35.00 rental
Weaves a tapestry that explores the phenomena of psychic life. Reveals a world of winged cloud creatures, insect women, underwater cities, gardens of lunar labyrinths, and grottoes of transparent levitating bodies. Stars The Joseph, Liam O'Gallagher, Ruth Weiss and a cast of fifty.
Fine Arts; Psychology
Dist - CANCIN **Prod** - WIESEM

Messenger from Violet Drive 30 MIN
16mm
American in the 70's, Pt 3 Series
B&W (H C A)
LC FIA68-1580
Interviews Elijah Muhammed, leader of the Black Muslims, who discusses the philosophy of total separation of Blacks and Whites in America. Discusses Muhammed's beliefs concerning the origins of the African and caucasian races, his prophesied destruction of America and his mission as the last messenger from Allah to the American Blacks.
Civics and Political Systems; History - United States; Religion and Philosophy
Dist - IU **Prod** - NET 1965

Messiah 90 MIN
U-matic
Color
Presents selections from George Handel's Messiah, performed by the combined choirs of the U S Naval Academy and Hood College. Offers background on Handel and the Naval Academy and draws parallels between 18th century London and Annapolis.
Fine Arts
Dist - MDCPB **Prod** - MDCPB

The Messiah 170 MIN
U-matic / VHS
Color (A)
Recreates George Frederick Handel's 'The Messiah' in its original setting. Utilizes Westminster Abbey's fine acoustics and visual setting.
Fine Arts
Dist - SRA **Prod** - SRA

The Messiah 150 MIN
VHS
Color (S)
$39.95 purchase _ #623 - 9792; $39.95 purchase _ #S01361
Recreates authentically 'The Messiah' by Handel. Presents the Academy of Ancient Music at Westminster Abbey playing period instruments. Features an impressive roster of soloists including Judith Nelson, Carolyn Watkinson, Emma Kirkby, Paul Elliot and David Thomas.
Fine Arts; Geography - World; Religion and Philosophy
Dist - FI **Prod** - NVIDC 1986
UILL

The Messiah
BETA / VHS
Color
Presents Handel's Messiah performed by the Westminster Abbey Choir.
Fine Arts
Dist - GA **Prod** - GA

The Messiah at Lindsborg 33 MIN
VHS / 16mm
Color (I J H G)
$550.00, $29.95 purchase
Combines several excerpts from Handel's Messiah with the landscape, the people and the Swedish tradition of Linsborg, Kansas.
Fine Arts; Geography - United States; History - United States
Dist - KAWVAL **Prod** - KAWVAL

The Messiah in the shadow of death 10 MIN
16mm
B&W (G)
$30.00 rental
Takes inventory of the logic of growing violence in contemporary Britain. Uses only photographs and the music of Handel to create a frame - by - frame animation production. A film by Richard Philpott.
Fine Arts; Geography - World; Sociology
Dist - CANCIN

Messiah of love - Volume 9 30 MIN
VHS
Jesus of Nazareth series
Color (I J H C G A R)
$29.95 purchase, $10.00 rental _ #35 - 8322 - 1502
Presents excerpts from the Franco Zeffirelli film on the life and ministry of Jesus. Surveys the events of Jesus' entry into Jerusalem, the incident at the Temple with the moneychangers, Jesus with the children, and Jesus' conflicts with the Pharisees.
Literature and Drama; Religion and Philosophy
Dist - APH **Prod** - BOSCO

The Messianic Idea in Jewish History 30 MIN
U-matic
Indiana University Discussion Series
Color
Discusses personalities and theology of Messiahs through Jewish history.
Religion and Philosophy
Dist - ADL **Prod** - ADL

Messy Sally 13 MIN
VHS / U-matic
Magic Pages Series
Color (P)
Literature and Drama
Dist - AITECH **Prod** - KLVXTV 1976

Meta Mayan II 20 MIN
U-matic
Color (C)
Experimental film by Edin Valez.
Fine Arts
Dist - AFA **Prod** - AFA 1981

Metabolic acidosis and alkalosis 27 MIN
VHS / U-matic
Fluids and electrolytes series
Color (PRO)
Describes acidosis and alkalosis resulting from problems related to metabolism. Shows signs and symptoms related to metabolic problems plus appropriate health - team actions and treatments.
Health and Safety; Science; Science - Natural
Dist - BRA **Prod** - BRA

Metabolic alkalosis and acidosis 29 MIN
BETA / VHS / U-matic
Acid base balance series
Color (C PRO)
$280.00 purchase _ #605.3
Focuses on the acid - base imbalances that occur as a result of metabolic dysfunction, covering in depth the causes, clinical manifestations and effects on arterial blood gases. Emphasizes nursing assessments, nursing diagnoses and the importance of initiating appropriate interventions. Produced by Golden West College.
Health and Safety; Science - Natural
Dist - CONMED

Metabolic Coma - an Overview 94 FRS
U-matic / VHS
Comatose Patient Series

Color (PRO)
Identifies metabolic conditions causing coma, abnormalities, and differentiation from other pathophysiologic categories.
Health and Safety; Science - Natural
Dist - BRA **Prod** - BRA

Metabolism 52 MIN
VHS
Introductory principles of nutrition series
Color (C PRO G)
$70.00 purchase, $16.00 rental _ #50707
Examines pathways for degrading fuel nutrients until they are incorporated into ATP, the regulatory role of vitamin and mineral coenzymes, the synthesis of protein at the ribosomes and the role of amino acids and energy in the anabolic process. Part of a 20 - part series on basic principles of nutrition, evaluation of dietary intake, nutritional status, nutrition through the life cycle and world food supplies.
Health and Safety; Social Science
Dist - PSU **Prod** - WPSXTV 1977

Metabolism and Activity of Lizards 12 MIN
16mm / U-matic / VHS
Aspects of Animal Behavior Series
Color
Shows patterns of energy metabolism in relation to locomotor activity in diversely adapted lizards. Shows animals running on a treadmill and feeding. Demonstrates methods of measuring gas exchange during activity and the ecology of each type of lizard.
Science - Natural
Dist - UCEMC **Prod** - UCLA 1981

Metabolism - Structure and Regulation 21 MIN
U-matic / 35mm strip
Color (H C)
$43.95 purchase _ #52 3126
Discusses the organization of metabolism from single reactions to to complex groups of pathways. Examines the principles of metabolic control including compartmentation and regulatory enzymes. Includes a teacher's guide.
Science - Natural
Dist - CBSC **Prod** - BMEDIA

Metabolism - the Fire of Life 36 MIN
VHS
Color (J)
LC 85-703880
Illustrates the biochemical process of metabolism. Tells how the body burns food, the role of key nutrients, and describes calories and the basal metabolic rate. Details cellular respiration, both aerobic and anaerobic.
Science - Natural
Dist - HRMC **Prod** - HRMC

Metabolism - the Fire of Life 36 MIN
VHS
Color (H C)
Illustrates the biochemical processes on which all life depends.
Science - Natural
Dist - IBIS **Prod** - IBIS 1982

Metafitness - Your Thoughts Taking Shape 60 MIN
Cassette / VHS
Color (G)
$19.95, $9.95 purchase _ #410, #221
Presents an exercise tape by Suzy Prudden with subliminal affirmations for reinforcement by Louise L Hay. Combines low - impact conditioning and toning with affirmations, visualizations and subliminals to change negative beliefs about the body.
Health and Safety; Physical Education and Recreation; Psychology
Dist - HAYHSE **Prod** - HAYHSE

The Metal
VHS
Edward Meier series
Color (G)
$39.95 purchase _ #GB002
Looks at metals some have claimed are 'not of Earth origin' from Edward Meier's over 100 claimed encounters with aliens.
Science - Physical; Sociology
Dist - SIV

Metal 29 MIN
Videoreel / VT2
Directions in Design Series
Color
Provides a glimpse of Hawaiian craftsmen working with metal.
Fine Arts; Geography - United States; Industrial and Technical Education
Dist - PBS **Prod** - HETV

Metal arc welding series
Gas metal arc welding 40 MIN
Gas tungsten arc welding 47 MIN
Stick metal arc welding - I 42 MIN
Stick metal arc welding - II 25 MIN
Dist - VEP

Metal collectibles 30 MIN
U-matic
Antiques series
Color
Fine Arts
Dist - PBS **Prod** - NHMNET

Metal Conditioning 7 MIN
VHS / BETA / 16mm
Color (A PRO)
$53.50 purchase _ #AB159
Explains reasons to use metal conditioners and their application.
Industrial and Technical Education
Dist - RMIBHF **Prod** - RMIBHF

Metal Cutting Chisels, Pt 6 5 MIN
16mm
B&W
LC FIE58-7
Describes the correct uses of the cold chisel, cape advection fog, ground fog and low ceiling clouds. Explains the cutting action of the chisel, diamond point and half - round chisel and how they are sharpened.
Industrial and Technical Education
Dist - USNAC **Prod** - USN 1954

Metal cutting machines series
Safety in drilling, milling and boring machines 17 MIN
Dist - ASMATE

Metal Dogs of India 3 MIN
16mm
Color (G)
Shows a collage of visual images drawn directly on the film, creating animation without the use of a camera, mixed with some fast paced music.
Fine Arts
Dist - MTOLP **Prod** - MTOLP 1985

Metal Fabrication - Different Types of Sheet Metals in Common Use Today Series
Cold rolled sheet metal theory 9 MIN
Hot Rolled Sheet Metal Theory 10 MIN
Dist - RMIBHF

Metal fabrication - different types of sheet metals in common use today series
Aluminum sheet metal theory 5 MIN
Galvanized sheet metal theory 10 MIN
Hot rolled pickled and oiled sheet metal theory 11 MIN
Dist - RMIBHF

Metal Fabrication - Duct End Cap Layout Series
Square and Rectangular Duct End Cap Layout Drive and Slip 9 MIN
Square and Rectangular Duct End Cap Layout Slip Pocket 10 MIN
Dist - RMIBHF

Metal fabrication - eight - foot hydraulic squaring shear series
Eight - foot hydraulic squaring shear operation - Pt I 45 MIN
Eight - foot hydraulic squaring shear operation - Pt II 10 MIN
Dist - RMIBHF

Metal fabrication - fitup and assembly series
Fitup and assembly tacking together - Pt I 37 MIN
Fitup and assembly tacking together - Pt II 24 MIN
Dist - RMIBHF

Metal Fabrication - Hand Tool Identification, Demonstration and Applications Series
General Hand Tools 15 MIN
Hammers used in Sheet Metal Work 4 MIN
Hand Snips and Shears 20 MIN
Use of Basic Layout Tools 7 MIN
Dist - RMIBHF

Metal Fabrication - Lock Former Machine Series
Lock Former Machine Acme or Pipelock Seam 11 MIN
Lock Former Machine Pittsburgh Seam 14 MIN
Dist - RMIBHF

Metal fabrication - parallel line development series
Five P C 90 degree round elbow 37 MIN
Introduction to Parallel Line Development Theory 24 MIN
Ninety Degree Round Elbow using Rise Method 10 MIN
Round Elbow Pattern Layout using End Gore Template 17 MIN
Round Pipe Different Diameters 45 Degree Intersection Offset 21 MIN
Round Pipe Different Diameters 90 Degree Intersection Offset 22 MIN
Round Pipe Intersected by Rectangular Pipe Centered at 45 Degree 20 MIN
Round Pipe Intersecting a Round Taper at 45 Degrees 13 MIN
Round Pipe Intersecting a Round Taper at 90 Degrees 18 MIN
Round Pipe Mitered End 32 MIN
Round Pipe same Diameter 45 Degree Intersection 24 MIN
Round Pipe same Diameter 90 Degree Intersection 40 MIN
Dist - RMIBHF

Metal Fabrication - Round Pipe Fabrication Series
Round Pipe Fabrication - Grooved Lock Seam 19 MIN
Round Pipe Fabrication - Machine Formed Seam 9 MIN
Dist - RMIBHF

Metal Fabrication - Round Tapers Series
Centered Round Taper - Triangulation Plan View Method - Openings Parallel 32 MIN
China cup - weather cap dimensioning and layout shortcuts 15 MIN
Gradual taper - shortcut, three - side view method 15 MIN
Offset Taper - Side View Method, Openings not Parallel 35 MIN
Offset Taper - Side View Rotational Subtraction Method, Openings not Parallel 32 MIN
Offset Taper - Triangulation Plan View Method, Openings Parallel 31 MIN
Radial Line - 180 Degree Shortcut Method 12 MIN
Radial Line Theory for Cone or Frustrum of Cone - Parallel Openings 20 MIN
Round Taper Intersecting a Round Pipe at 45 Degrees 32 MIN
Round Taper Intersecting a Round Pipe at 90 Degrees 14 MIN
Round Tapers - Internal or External Offset 19 MIN
Round Y - Branch Layout 57 MIN
Truncated Cone - Radial Line Method , Openings not Parallel 19 MIN
Dist - RMIBHF

Metal Fabrication - Square to Round Layout Series
Introduction to Square to Rounds 26 MIN
Rectangular to Larger Round Transition - Centered 15 MIN
Rectangular to Round Transition - Centered 20 MIN
Rectangular to Round Transition - Double Offset 37 MIN
Rectangular to Round Transition - Offset One - Way 34 MIN
Rectangular to Round Transition - Offset Two - Way 44 MIN
Square to Round - Offset One - Way Openings not Parallel 28 MIN
Square to Round Transition - Offset One - Way 32 MIN
Dist - RMIBHF

Metal Fabrication - Tap Collar Type of Fittings Series
Tap Collar Closed Corners Fabrication 9 MIN
Tap Collar Open Corners Fabrication 13 MIN
Dist - RMIBHF

Metal Fabrication - Transitional Elbows Series
Transitional Elbow - Flat Top or Bottom, Change Cheek 28 MIN
Transitional Elbow - Flat Top or Bottom, same Size Cheeks 37 MIN
Dist - RMIBHF

Metal fatigue - recent developments in probabilistic design - a series
Metal fatigue - recent developments in probabilistic design - a`series
B&W
Summarizes recent developments in fatigue analysis under random stress processes and recent developments in the application of probabilistic design theory to the metal fatigue problem. Focuses on research being conducted at the University of Arizona. Consists of two 50 - minute tapes.
Industrial and Technical Education; Mathematics
Dist - UAZMIC **Prod** - UAZMIC 1978

Metal fatigue - recent developments in probabilistic design - a series
Metal fatigue - recent developments in

probabilistic design - a series
Dist - UAZMIC

Metal Files 13 MIN
16mm
Metalwork - Hand Tools Series
Color (J H A)
Presents sizes, shapes and cuts, types of files, care of files, straight filing, draw filing and fine filing.
Industrial and Technical Education
Dist - SF **Prod** - MORLAT 1967

Metal Finishing, Large Dent 30.5 MIN
VHS / BETA
Color (A PRO)
$113.00 purchase _ #AB121
Deals with auto body repair.
Industrial and Technical Education
Dist - RMIBHF **Prod** - RMIBHF

Metal Finishing, Tool Identification and Minor Dent 33 MIN
32.5 MIN
VHS / BETA / 16mm
Color (A PRO)
$118.00 purchase _ #AB120
Discusses tool identification for the metal finishing of a minor dent.
Industrial and Technical Education
Dist - RMIBHF **Prod** - RMIBHF

Metal Forming 30 MIN
U-matic / VHS
Color
Demonstrates non - traditional metal forming techniques, including high energy rate forming that uses high explosives and other forces to create new parts for modern architecture and the space program.
Business and Economics; Industrial and Technical Education
Dist - SME **Prod** - CONNTV

Metal Lost in Rolling 10 MIN
BETA / VHS
Color (IND)
Demonstrates graphically the metal lost in rolling when forming a cylinder and having to maintain an accurate inside or outside diameter. Deals with the bend allowance theory.
Industrial and Technical Education; Psychology
Dist - RMIBHF **Prod** - RMIBHF

Metal patternmaker 5 MIN
U-matic
Good work series
Color (H)
Provides useful, up to date information on various occupations to aid high school students in career selection. Available in five series of ten jobs each.
Education; Guidance and Counseling; Industrial and Technical Education
Dist - TVOTAR **Prod** - TVOTAR 1981

Metal patternmaker 5 MIN
VHS / 16mm
Good works 2 series
Color (A PRO)
$40.00 purchase _ #BPN205601
Presents the occupation of a metal patternmaker. Gives a profile of a young person who is either undergoing an apprenticeship or has recently completed training in this field. Takes the viewer on a tour of this person's workplace and explains the practical skills and training offered by employers and schools. Gives a better understanding of the demand for skilled workers today and the potential for personal growth.
Guidance and Counseling
Dist - RMIBHF **Prod** - RMIBHF

Metal Punching 60 MIN
BETA / VHS
Color
Illustrates ways to make seasonal ornaments, wall hangings, wreaths and more. Shows a variety of methods and finishing techniques.
Fine Arts
Dist - HOMEAF **Prod** - HOMEAF

Metal shop & woodshop series
Arc welding - safety and operation 13 MIN
Oxyacetylene welding - safety and operation 75 MIN
Dist - EDPAT

Metal Shop Math
VHS / U-matic
Color (J H)
Teaches math skills needed in the metal shop.
Industrial and Technical Education; Mathematics
Dist - CAREER **Prod** - CAREER

Metal shop safety 20 MIN
VHS
Shop safety series
Color (H G IND)
$109.00 purchase _ #60482 - 027
Demonstrates the types of dangers that may occur and precautions that should be taken for any general industrial education shop. Illustrates the kinds of accidents that can happen and describes how to prevent them. Part of a four - part series.
Education; Health and Safety; Industrial and Technical Education
Dist - GA

Metal Shop Safety
VHS
Metalworking Industrial Arts Series
(H C G)
$59.00 _ CA221
Gives safety tips relating to clothing, eyes, use of hand tools, power machinery, and hot metal work.
Industrial and Technical Education
Dist - AAVIM **Prod** - AAVIM 1989

Metal Shop Safety 52 MIN
VHS / 35mm strip
(J H A IND)
#514XV7
Shows safety in the metal shop. Includes protective clothing & good hand tool practices, working with power tools & machines, working with a metal lathe, and working with a vertical milling machine (4 tapes). Includes a Study Guide.
Education; Health and Safety; Industrial and Technical Education
Dist - BERGL

Metal Shop - Safety and Operations Series
Arc welding - safety and operations 14 MIN
Facing on the lathe 11 MIN
Oxyacetylene Welding - Safety and Operations 14 MIN
Safety and basic fundamentals on the engine lathe - Pt 1 11 MIN
Safety and basic fundamentals on the engine lathe - Pt 2 13 MIN
Straight Turning between Centers on the Lathe 18 MIN
Dist - AIMS

Metal Spinning
VHS
Metalworking Industrial Arts Series
(H C G)
$59.00 _ CA216
Gives elementary techniques of metal spinning and related hand tools.
Industrial and Technical Education
Dist - AAVIM **Prod** - AAVIM 1989

Metal Stretch 13 MIN
BETA / VHS
Color (A PRO)
$68.50 purchase _ #KTI66
Deals with auto body repair. Defines metal stretch and demonstrates shrinking.
Industrial and Technical Education
Dist - RMIBHF **Prod** - RMIBHF

Metal trim and Chrome preparation - Volume 6 40 MIN
VHS
Collector car restoration home video libary series
Color (G)
$24.95 purchase
Shows how to select the right equipment, tools and supplies for metal trim and chrome preparation in collector cars. Demonstrates that many tools and equipment can be improvised at very little cost. Illustrates techniques. Part six of a six - part series on classic car restoration.
Industrial and Technical Education
Dist - COLLEC **Prod** - COLLEC 1993

Metal Working 10 MIN
U-matic / VHS / 16mm
Jewelry Making Series
Color (J)
Demonstrates various metalwork techniques including annealing, rolling mill, forging and finishing. Reveals how the pieces are soldered together, finished in an acid bath, sanded and brushed.
Industrial and Technical Education
Dist - LUF **Prod** - LUF 1978

Metal Working Industrial Arts Series
Intro to Metal Shop
Dist - AAVIM

Metal working liquids 14 MIN
BETA / VHS / U-matic
Hazard communication series
Color (IND G)
$395.00 purchase _ #600 - 37
Discusses the health and physical hazards associated with metalworking fluids. Identifies common routes of entry and describes potential acute and chronic health effects. Covers emergency procedures, proper protective equipment, storage, handling and disposal techniques. Part of a series on hazard communication.
Health and Safety; Industrial and Technical Education; Psychology
Dist - ITSC **Prod** - ITSC

Metallographic Interpretation 53 MIN
U-matic / BETA / VHS
Color
$400 purchase
Presents individual preparation techniques for cast irons, steels, aluminum, cobalt, copper, lead, nickel, titanium, refractory metals, precious metals, and others.
Science; Science - Physical
Dist - ASM **Prod** - ASM 1987

Metallographic Specimen Preparation I 59 MIN
BETA / VHS / U-matic
Color
$400 purchase
Covers cutoff and sectioning techniques and equipment, mounting techniques and equipment, and the effect of particle size and pressure on metal removal rate.
Science; Science - Physical
Dist - ASM **Prod** - ASM 1987

Metallographic Specimen Preparation II 59 MIN
U-matic / BETA / VHS
Color
$400 purchase
Shows grinding steps, cooling fluids, and patterns, rough and fine polishing, polishing cloths, abrasives and fluids, diamond and other polishing compounds, electropolishing and electroetching, and chemical etching.
Science; Science - Physical
Dist - ASM **Prod** - ASM 1987

Metallography - its History and Aims 56 MIN
VHS / BETA / U-matic
Color (IND)
$400.00 purchase
Defines basic terminology used in metallography. Reviews Henry Clifton Sorbys' pioneering work in metallography. Examines meaningful features of meteorite and Samurai sword microstructures.
Science; Science - Physical
Dist - ASM **Prod** - ASM 1987

Metallurgy - Oxyacetylene
VHS / 35mm strip
Metallurgy Series
Color
$42.00 purchase _ #LX99C filmstrip, $62.00 purchase _ #LX99V VHS
Introduces physical properties including stress, strain, elasticity, elastic limit, tensile strength, torsional strength, shear strength and fatigue strength.
Industrial and Technical Education
Dist - CAREER **Prod** - CAREER

Metallurgy Process - Electric Arc
VHS / 35mm strip
Metallurgy Series
$42.00 purchase _ #LX98C filmstrip, $62.00 purchase _ #LX98V VHS
Talks about how metallurgy applies to various welding processes and problems encountered with various kinds of steel.
Education; Industrial and Technical Education
Dist - CAREER **Prod** - CAREER

Metallurgy series
Basic metallurgy, Pt I
Basic metallurgy, Pt II
Metallurgy - Oxyacetylene
Metallurgy Process - Electric Arc
Dist - CAREER

Metalodeon trailer 3 MIN
16mm
Color (G)
$8.00 rental
Presents an apocalyptic preview from 'I am the Barbeque' originally done for the short - lived Metalodeon film series in San Francisco.
Fine Arts
Dist - CANCIN **Prod** - WENDTD 1972

Metals 22 MIN
VHS / 16mm
Manufacturing Materials Series
Color (I)
LC 90713864
Traces the development of metal from prehistoric times to the present. Focuses on the uses of iron and steel and how these materials helped change the way people live. Describes how metals and alloys are made.
Business and Economics; History - World; Industrial and Technical Education; Science - Physical
Dist - BARR

Metals and Alloys 11 MIN
VHS
Chemistry - from Theory to Application Series
Color (H)

$190.00 purchase
Illustrates the 'lattice' structure of the atoms of pure metals. Shows how pure metals bend easily but may be hardened by the addition of other types of particles.
Science; Science - Physical
Dist - LUF **Prod** - LUF 1989

Metals and Ionic Solids 10 MIN
U-matic
Electron Arrangement and Bonding Series
Color (H C)
Explains the common properties of metal, its conductivity and malleability. The properties of metals, which are covalent solids are contrasted with those of crystals which are ionic solids.
Science; Science - Physical
Dist - TVOTAR **Prod** - TVOTAR 1984

Metals and Non - Metals 13 MIN
U-matic / VHS / 16mm
Color (H C)
$325, $235 purchase _ #1538
Shows the differences between metals and non - metals and their chemical properties and talks about the periodic table.
Science - Physical
Dist - CORF

Metals and Non Metals - Visible, Atomic and Chemical Contrasts 18 MIN
U-matic
Chemistry 101 Series
Color (C)
Compares the properties of metals and nonmetals. Observable characteristics such as conductivity, lustre and malleability are discussed followed by a comparison of atomic properties.
Science; Science - Physical
Dist - UILL **Prod** - UILL 1973

Metals Frontier 22 MIN
16mm
Color (C A)
Portrays the development, at the Ames laboratory of the USAEC, of a process for the separation of tytrium from the rare earth metals and the production of high purity tytrium metal.
Business and Economics; Science - Physical
Dist - USERD **Prod** - IOWA 1961

Metals Information Center of Tomorrow 13 MIN
16mm
Color
Describes in lay terms the activities of the Western Reserve University in the field of metallurgy. Shows the potentials for mechanical computing machines in library research.
Science - Physical
Dist - CWRU **Prod** - CWRU

Metals - on the surface - Parts 19 and 20 60 MIN
U-matic / VHS
World of chemistry series
Color (C)
$45.00, $29.95 purchase
Presents parts 19 and 20 of the 26 - part World of Chemistry series. Examines the properties of metals - malleability, ductility and conductivity. Covers metal extraction from ores and the formation of alloys. Considers how the surface of a substance differs from its bulk. Reveals that surfaces react with each other at the molecular level and are unique in the way in which they behave catalytically in chemical reactions. Two thirty - minute programs hosted by Nobel laureate Roald Hoffmann.
Science - Physical
Dist - ANNCPB **Prod** - UMD 1990

Metalwork - Hand Tools Series
Forge and ornamental iron 13 MIN
Layout Tools for Metal Work 13 MIN
Metal Files 13 MIN
Snips and Shears 13 MIN
Soldering 13 MIN
Welding 13 MIN
Dist - SF

Metalwork - Machine Operation Series
The Drill Press 13 MIN
Lathe - Chuck Work 13 MIN
Lathe - Work between Centers 13 MIN
Machine Operations - Sheet Metal 13 MIN
Dist - SF

Metalwork - machine operations series
Fastening metals 13 MIN
Dist - SF

Metalwork series - aluminum and copper tooling with a mold 21 MIN
U-matic / VHS
Metalwork series
Color
Explains and demonstrates the procedures for tooling a design from a mold into sheet metal, for finishing the sheet, and for matting it for display. First of three - program unit on metalworking.
Fine Arts; Guidance and Counseling; Industrial and Technical Education
Dist - HSCIC **Prod** - HSCIC

Metalwork series - copper enameling 16 MIN
VHS / U-matic
Metalwork series
Color
Explains and demonstrates copper enameling.
Fine Arts; Guidance and Counseling; Industrial and Technical Education
Dist - HSCIC **Prod** - HSCIC

Metalwork series - freeform copper tooling 20 MIN
VHS / U-matic
Metalwork series - freeform copper tooling
Color
Teaches procedures for tooling a design into copper foil without the use of a mold, for finishing the piece, and for mounting it for display.
Fine Arts; Guidance and Counseling; Industrial and Technical Education
Dist - HSCIC **Prod** - HSCIC

Metalwork series - freeform copper tooling
Metalwork series - freeform copper tooling 20 MIN
Dist - HSCIC

Metalwork series
Metalwork series - aluminum and copper tooling with a mold 21 MIN
Metalwork series - copper enameling 16 MIN
Dist - HSCIC

Metalworking fluids 14 MIN
VHS
Specific material handling series
Color (IND)
$395.00 purchase, $95.00 rental _ #600 - 37
Addresses hazard communication information about metalworking fluids - routes of entry, health hazards, protective equipment, emergency procedures. Includes leader's guide.
Health and Safety; Psychology
Dist - ITSC **Prod** - ITSC

Metalworking Industrial Arts
VHS / U-matic
Color (J H)
Uses extensive graphics and informative lessons with quizzes to familiarize students with the many job opportunities available in welding.
Guidance and Counseling; Industrial and Technical Education
Dist - CAREER **Prod** - CAREER 1969

Metalworking industrial arts series
Bench metal work
The Crib foreman's assignment
The Engine lathe
The Engine lathe - Pt 2
How to Operate the Shaper
How to Operate the Vertical Milling Machine
How to Use the Oxyacetylene Welder
Metal Spinning
Operate the Foundry
Sheet Metal Work
Dist - AAVIM

Metalworking Industrical Arts Series
Metal Shop Safety
Dist - AAVIM

Metalworking Lathe
VHS / U-matic
Color (J H)
Teaches students how to carry out the various lathe operations.
Industrial and Technical Education
Dist - CAREER **Prod** - CAREER 1972

Metalworking - Precision Measuring Series
The Bevel protractor 13 MIN
The Combination set 13 MIN
The Combination square 13 MIN
The Outside Micrometer 13 MIN
Vernier Caliper 13 MIN
Vernier Height Gage 13 MIN
Dist - VISIN

Metalworking series
Arc welding - safety and operations 13 MIN
Dist - AAVIM

Metamorphic rock 15 MIN
U-matic / VHS
Discovering series; Unit 6 - Rocks and minerals
Color (I)
Science - Physical
Dist - AITECH **Prod** - WDCNTV 1978

Metamorphic rocks 12 MIN
VHS
Earth materials series
Color (H C)
$24.95 purchase _ #S9795
Discusses metamorphic rocks. Part of a ten - part series on the development of minerals, rocks and soil.
Science - Physical
Dist - HUBDSC **Prod** - HUBDSC

Metamorphic rocks 21 MIN
VHS
Color (J H C)
$39.95 purchase _ #IV135
Studies rocks which ahve been changed by pressure or heat or a combination of both. Examines common metamorphic rocks and how they have been changed. Looks at slate, schists, gneisses, granite, marble and quartzites.
Science - Physical
Dist - INSTRU

Metamorphism 30 MIN
U-matic / VHS
Earth, Sea and Sky Series
Color (C)
Explains the origin of many rocks and minerals.
Science - Physical
Dist - DALCCD **Prod** - DALCCD

Metamorphoses 3 MIN
16mm
Color (I)
The animation artist, Laurent Coderre, has created a clown so versatile in the art of juggling that, between times, he even juggles himself. One moment the clown stands tossing balls, the next he becomes dismembered, following the balls about on the screen but coming together again all in one piece to finish the act.
Fine Arts
Dist - NFBC **Prod** - NFBC 1969

Metamorphosis 8.5 MIN
16mm
Color (C)
$334.00
Experimental film by Lillian Schwartz.
Fine Arts
Dist - AFA **Prod** - AFA 1974

Metamorphosis 5 MIN
16mm
Color
LC 78-712036
An animated film, which poetically interprets the history of the evolution of man, plants and animals.
Science - Natural
Dist - RADIM **Prod** - ROSSED 1970

Metamorphosis 8 MIN
16mm
Color
LC 74-702489
An art film which presents computer - generated everchanging colors edited to the music of Saliere's Symphony in D major.
Fine Arts; Industrial and Technical Education
Dist - LILYAN **Prod** - LILYAN 1974

Metamorphosis 20 MIN
16mm / VHS
Development of the sea urchin series
Color (G C)
$110.00 purchase, $14.00 rental _ #11788
Uses time - lapse photography to show the 'dissolution' of the larval body. Explains the transition from the bilateral symmetry of the pluteus to the star - shaped radial symmetry in an animated sequence. Part of a series on development of the sea urchin.
Science - Natural
Dist - PSU **Prod** - IWIF 1982

Metamorphosis 15 MIN
16mm
Color (G)
$35.00 rental
Employs the quantizer, a piece of equipment which evaluates gray values in black and white videotape and transforms these values into intense colors. Pictures two nude females weaving together on a bed while the shadows of their bodies are broken down into distinct color fields. Produced by Roy Colmer.
Fine Arts
Dist - CANCIN

A Metamorphosis in logic 8 MIN
16mm
Color (G)
$20.00 rental
Combines live action with animation to create an absurd dark portrayal of a man who feels stuck and wonders how he got there. Plays with narrative form.A Brady Lewis production.

Fine Arts
Dist - CANCIN

Metamorphosis - man into woman 58 MIN
VHS / 16mm
Color (H C G)
$895.00, $445.00 purchase, $150.00, $85.00 rental
Reveals that as many as 60,000 people are uncomfortable with the sex they were born into - gender dysphoria. Focuses on Gary, 39, convinced since childhood that he is a woman trapped in a man's body. At age 36 Gary decided to begin the process of changing his sex. Follows the three - year transformation of Gary into Gabi, from initially proving that he can successfully live and work as a woman, 24 hours a day, for one year, to reconciliation with his mother and returning home to attend a 20th high school reunion. Observes Gary sorting out his gender traits, plastic surgery, electrolysis, hormone therapy, psychological counseling, mixed reactions from his co - workers, transsexual support groups, religious conflicts. Produced by Claudia Hoover.
Sociology
Dist - FLMLIB

The Metamorphosis - Nabokov on Kafka 30 MIN
VHS
Color; CC (I J H)
$24.95 purchase _ #33230
Stars Jeremy Plummer who portrays Vladimir Nabokov offering commentary on The Metamorphosis by Kafka.
Literature and Drama
Dist - KNOWUN

Metamorphosis of an Oncology Nurse 12 MIN
U-matic
Color
Discusses the different stages in an oncology nurse's career.
Health and Safety
Dist - UTEXSC **Prod** - UTEXSC

The Metamorphosis of Mr Samsa, from a Story by Franz Kafka 10 MIN
U-matic / VHS / 16mm
Color (H C A)
LC 80-700140
Presents a capsulized interpretation of Franz Kafka's story entitled Die Verwandlung, about a man who awakens one morning to find himself transformed into a beetle.
Fine Arts; Literature and Drama
Dist - TEXFLM **Prod** - NFBC 1979

Metamorphosis of the Butterfly 10 MIN
U-matic / VHS
Elements of Biology Series
Color (C)
$229.00, $129.00 purchase _ #AD - 1288
Follows the life cycle of the butterfly through the phases of egg, larva and chrysalis.
Science - Natural
Dist - FOTH **Prod** - FOTH

The Metamorphosis of the Cello 14 MIN
16mm
B&W (H C)
LC FIA65-1037
Pictures the construction and the performance of the Violoncello. Features the French virtuoso Maurice Gendron playing music by Haydn, Bach, Boccherini and Chopin.
Fine Arts
Dist - RADIM **Prod** - DELOUD 1965

Metanomen 8 MIN
16mm
B&W (G)
$15.00 rental
Presents 'two characters set in a flux of manipulated technology run wild.'
Business and Economics; Fine Arts
Dist - CANCIN **Prod** - BARTLS 1966

Metaphoric Thinking and Analogic Thought 30 MIN
VHS / U-matic
Teaching for Thinking - Creativity in the Classroom Series
Color (T PRO)
$180.00 purchase,$50.00 rental
Introduces methods and ideas that aid in utilizing metaphors and analogies in the teaching process.
Education; English Language
Dist - AITECH **Prod** - WHATV 1986

Metaphors of transformation 30 MIN
BETA / VHS
Transforming awareness series
Color (G)
$29.95 purchase _ #S070
Stresses the importance of metaphor in guiding and understanding development. Focuses on the many forms of the metaphor of death and rebirth and the journey. Features Dr Ralph Metzner, author of 'Opening to Inner Light.' Part of a four - part series on transforming awareness.
Psychology; Religion and Philosophy
Dist - THINKA **Prod** - THINKA

Metaphysical and Devotional Poetry 28 MIN
U-matic / VHS
Survey of English Verse Series
Color (C)
$249.00, $149.00 purchase _ #AD - 1298
Presents poetry by John Donne, George Herbert and Andrew Marvell.
Fine Arts; Literature and Drama; Religion and Philosophy
Dist - FOTH **Prod** - FOTH

Metastasizing Basal Cell Carcinoma 10 MIN
16mm
Color (PRO)
Presents a case study of basal cell carcinoma lesions on the skin of a 69 - year - old man which had metastasized from a single, ulcerative basal cell carcinoma present on the patient's leg for five years without being diagnosed or adequately treated.
Health and Safety; Science - Natural
Dist - SQUIBB **Prod** - SQUIBB

Metathesis 3 MIN
16mm
Color
Offers a blending of computer graphics and animation which makes use of exotic, flowing forms, colors and electronic music.
Fine Arts; Mathematics
Dist - LILYAN **Prod** - LILYAN

Metco / Oreo Cookie / Interracial Dating 29 MIN
U-matic
As We See it Series
Color
Describes a voluntary busing program in Boston which enriched the lives of city and suburban students. Presents students from Wichita, Kansas, examining pressures resulting from desegregation. Shows Portland, Oregon, students who indicate that attitudes are not as tolerant as many would like.
Sociology
Dist - PBS **Prod** - WTTWTV

Meteor 107 MIN
16mm
Color (H A)
Shows the diplomatic efforts of the American President with the Soviets who saves the world from a blazing comet hurtling toward earth. Stars Sean Connery, Natalie Wood and Henry Fonda.
Fine Arts
Dist - TIMLIF **Prod** - AIP 1979

Meteor 104 MIN
16mm
Color
Asks whether scientists can save the earth from a giant meteor. Stars Sean Connery, Natalie Wood and Karl Malden.
Fine Arts
Dist - SWANK **Prod** - AIP

Meteor craters and cliff dwellings 12 MIN
VHS
Scenes of the plateaulands and how they came to be series
Color (J H)
$19.95 purchase _ #IVSPL - 5
Studies meteor craters and cliff dwellings on the Colorado Plateau. Part of a five - part series which overview the geological forces that formed and are still working on the Colorado Plateau. Includes footage of Colorado, Utah and Arizona, Grand Canyon, Bryce Canyon, Zion National Park, Arches, Bridges, Dinosaur, Petrified Forest and Canyonlands National Parks.
Geography - United States
Dist - INSTRU

Meteorological Society film series
Convective clouds 27 MIN
Dist - MLA

Meteorology - Fog, a Terminal Problem 23 MIN
16mm
Color
LC 75-702892
Explains the theory of fog formation and dissipation. Discusses the effects of fog on aviation.
Science - Physical
Dist - USNAC **Prod** - USN 1971

Meteorology - Fog and Low Ceiling Clouds Advection Fog and Ground Fog 25 MIN
U-matic / VHS
Color (A)
Discusses in detail the characteristics and conditions conducive to fog with explanation of theory of fog formation.
Industrial and Technical Education; Science - Physical
Dist - AVIMA **Prod** - FAAFL 1962
USFAA

Meteorology - Fog and Low Ceiling Clouds - Advection Fog and Ground Fog 23 MIN
16mm
Color
LC 73-701253
Discusses the theory of fog formation, provididng examples of advection fog, ground fog and low ceiling clouds.
Science - Physical
Dist - USNAC **Prod** - USN 1961

Meteorology - Fog and Low Ceiling Clouds - Upslope Fog and Frontal Fog 10 MIN
16mm
Color
Illustrates how upslope fog, frontal fog and low straclouds generated. Compares warm front fog and cold front fog, analyzes their formation and discusses their effect on flying.
Science - Physical
Dist - USFAA **Prod** - FAAFL 1962

Meteorology - Fog and Low Ceiling Clouds, Upslope Fog and Frontal Fog 10 MIN
U-matic / VHS / 16mm
Color
Shows how upslope fog, frontal fog and low stratus clouds gather. Compares warm front fog and cold front fog and discusses their effect on flying.
Industrial and Technical Education; Science - Physical
Dist - USNAC **Prod** - USN

Meteorology - Ice Formation on Aircraft 20 MIN
16mm
B&W
LC 74-705132
Shows how structural ice interferes with normal flight procedures and how its hazard can be reduced. Discusses carburetor and pilot tube icing and turbo - jet engine icing problems.
Industrial and Technical Education; Science - Physical
Dist - USFAA **Prod** - FAAFL 1960

Meteorology series
Presents a six - part series using single - concept format. Incorporates NASA footage with actual experiments to demonstrate meteorological principles. Includes Temperature, Pressure and Wind; Atmospheric Circulation; Coriolis Effect; Evaporation and Condensation; Cloud Formation; Weather Fronts and Precipitation.
Meteorology series 65 MIN
Dist - HUBDSC **Prod** - HUBDSC 1960

Meteorology Series
Above the horizon 21 MIN
Solar Radiation, Sun and Earth's Rays 18 MIN
Wind Chill
Dist - MLA

Meteorology series
Atmospheric circulation 16 MIN
Cloud formation 8 MIN
Coriolis effect 8 MIN
Evaporation and condensation 8 MIN
Temperature, pressure and wind 16 MIN
Weather fronts and precipitation 9 MIN
Dist - WARDS

Meteorology - the Cold Front 15 MIN
16mm / U-matic / VHS
Color (A)
Explains formations, characteristics and dangers of cold fronts. Demonstrates how to avoid hazards of cold fronts by either high or low level flight.
Industrial and Technical Education; Science - Physical
Dist - USNAC **Prod** - USN

Meteorology - the Warm Front 20 MIN
16mm
Color
LC 74-705134
Explains the meeting boundaries of warm and cold air, dangerous stratified layers of clouds formed, how to plan a course around them, types of visibility precipitation and ceiling conditions, their location and cirrus, cirrostratus and altostratus clouds.
Industrial and Technical Education; Science - Physical; Social Science
Dist - USFAA **Prod** - FAAFL 1962

Meteorology - the Warm Front 17 MIN
16mm / U-matic / VHS
Color
Shows formation characteristics and dangers of warm fronts and how to recognize and deal with the flight problems involved.
Industrial and Technical Education; Science - Physical
Dist - USNAC **Prod** - USN

Meteorology Today 26 MIN
VHS / 16mm
Color (J)
$149.00 purchase, $75.00 rental _ #OD - 2233
Visits test facilities of the National Oceanic and Atmospheric Administration to explain how the latest meteorological forecasting and tracking apparatuses work.
Science - Physical
Dist - FOTH

Meteorology videos 65 MIN
VHS
Color (J H)
$175.00 purchase _ #193 W 0069
Presents a six - part single concept series which uses NASA footage to complement experimental devices and laboratory set - ups to demonstrate basic meteorological principles. Covers evaporation and condensation, cloud formation, coriolis effect, atmospheric circulation, temperature, pressure and wind, and weather fronts and precipitation.
Science - Physical
Dist - WARDS **Prod** - WARDS

Meter 15 MIN
U-matic / VHS
Music machine series
Color (P)
Discusses rhythmical structure in music.
Fine Arts
Dist - GPN **Prod** - INDIPS 1981

Meter, Liter and Gram 13 MIN
16mm / U-matic / VHS
Color (I)
Describes how the metric system uses related units of length, volume and mass - the meter, liter and kilogram and relates these units to real objects. Adds information on how temperature can be measured according to the decimal system.
Mathematics
Dist - PHENIX **Prod** - EDOGNC 1981

Meter, Liter, and Gram 13 MIN
16mm / U-matic / VHS
Color (I J H)
LC 81-701064
Relates units in the metric system to real objects. Shows how the system of tens in the metric system names different units through the use of prefixes such as deci - , centi - , milli - , and kilo - .
Mathematics
Dist - SALENG **Prod** - EDOGNC 1981

Meter Reader 15 MIN
VHS / U-matic
Music and Me Series
Color (P I)
Discusses meter in music.
Fine Arts
Dist - AITECH **Prod** - WDCNTV 1979

Metering and exposure controls - Volume 3 15 MIN
VHS
Classroom collection series
Color (H C A G)
$24.95 purchase _ #CLA - 03
Discusses metering and exposure controls. Part of a series on photography suitable for the classroom that provides the teacher with numerous topics for discussion in class. Uses basic techniques along with well - structured information which gives teachers the opportunity to expand course material.
Fine Arts; Industrial and Technical Education
Dist - ARTSAM **Prod** - BIP

A Methadone Treatment Program 25 MIN
16mm
Films and Tapes for Drug Abuse Treatment Personnel Series
Color (PRO)
LC 73-703452
Presents in detail the organization and operations of a methadone treatment program. Follows the progress of an addict through such a program. Emphasizes strict application of security procedures for urine surveillance and control of methadone dispensing.
Education; Health and Safety; Psychology; Sociology
Dist - NIMH **Prod** - NIMH 1973

Methamphetamines - Haight - Ashbury training series 163 MIN
VHS
Methamphetamines - Haight - Ashbury training series
Color (G)
$495.00 purchase
Presents a three - part series on methamphetamines. Includes the titles Pharmacology and Physiology, Treatment and Recovery, and Patient Module.
Guidance and Counseling; Psychology
Dist - FMSP

Method 60 MIN
U-matic / VHS
Computer Dialogue - the Key to Successful Systems Series
Color
Presents a new approach for the development of effective and powerful dialogues, a comprehensive methodology for the analysis, design and development of dialogues that are efficient from the computer perspective and psychologically effective for their end users.
Industrial and Technical Education
Dist - DELTAK **Prod** - DELTAK

A Method for Cleaning the Machida Flexible Bronchoscope 29 MIN
U-matic / VHS
Color
LC 80-707207
Demonstrates procedures for cleaning the Machida flexible bronchoscope and explains precautions required to avoid damaging the equipment during cleaning.
Health and Safety
Dist - USNAC **Prod** - USVACE 1979

A Method for Cleaning the Olympus Flexible Bronchoscope 29 MIN
U-matic / VHS
Color
LC 80-707208
Demonstrates procedures for cleaning the Olympus flexible bronchoscope and explains precautions required to avoid damaging the equipment during cleaning.
Health and Safety
Dist - USNAC **Prod** - USVACE 1979

Method for Rapid Electrophoresis 11 MIN
8mm cartridge / 16mm
Color
LC 75-702019;
Explains how to set up electrophoretic apparatus and describes the functions of its parts. Demonstrates a typical run, portraying the technique of applying serum samples to the membrane and the step - by - step procedure of clearing and staining the resulting image.
Science
Dist - USNAC **Prod** - USPHS 1966

Method of Galerkin 34 MIN
VHS / U-matic
Nonlinear Vibrations Series
B&W
Mathematics
Dist - MIOT **Prod** - MIOT

Method of Krylov - Bogliubov 24 MIN
U-matic / VHS
Nonlinear Vibrations Series
B&W
Mathematics
Dist - MIOT **Prod** - MIOT

A Method of Thoracoplasty for Chronic Empyema 20 MIN
16mm
Color (PRO)
Explains that when thoracoplasty is necessary in the treatment of a chronic empyema the ideal operation should provide for certain closure of the pleural space, should cause minimal damage to the anatomical components of the chest wall, should permit closure of bronchopleural fistulae, and should result in a stable chest wall.
Health and Safety; Science
Dist - ACY **Prod** - ACYDGD 1955

Method of Treatment for the Intrabony Pocket 14 MIN
16mm
Color
Demonstrates the surgical technique used in subgingival curettage.
Health and Safety; Science
Dist - USNAC **Prod** - USA 1962

The Method - Video II 45 MIN
VHS
Therapeutic touch - healing through human energy fields series
Color (C PRO)
$275.00 purchase, $75.00 rental _ #42 - 2486, #42 - 2486R
Joins a class of nurses as Janet Quinn teaches them, step - by - step, how to perform Therapeutic Touch. Includes a printed guide, How to Use the Method. Part of a three - part series featuring Janet Quinn with Dora Kunz, Janet Macrae and other experts.
Business and Economics; Health and Safety
Dist - NLFN **Prod** - NLFN

Methodist Hospital Psychiatric Patient Care Team, Pt I 60 MIN
VHS / U-matic
B&W
Offers a panel presentation from a psychiatric patient care team at a hospital in Madison, Wisconsin, and consists of talks with registered nurses, mental health workers and an occupational therapist, a social worker and a unit clerk. Discusses their philosophies, responsibilities, a typical day in the ward and maintaining a good working relationship with other staff members since many patients look to the team as role models.
Health and Safety; Sociology
Dist - UWISC **Prod** - UWISC 1979

Methodist Hospital Psychiatric Patient Care Team, Pt II 25 MIN
VHS / U-matic
B&W
Continues a panel discussion among personnel at a psychiatric ward in a Wisconsin hospital. Discusses how they take care of themselves and look out for each other in what sometimes can be a dangerous environment.
Health and Safety; Sociology
Dist - UWISC **Prod** - UWISC 1979

Methodology of Energy Audits for Industrial and Commercial Facilities 60 MIN
U-matic / VHS
(Fazzolare (from the How to Save Energy Dollars in Industrial and 'Commercial Facilities Series Pt 2; Pt 2
B&W
Business and Economics; Industrial and Technical Education; Social Science
Dist - UAZMIC **Prod** - UAZMIC 1978

Methodology - the Psychologist and the Experiment 31 MIN
U-matic / VHS / 16mm
Color (H C A)
LC 78-700767
Explores the basic rules or methods common to all psychological research by actual documentation of two different experiments. Includes Dr Stanley Schachter's 'fear and affiliation' social psychology experiment using human subjects and Dr Austin Riessen's experiment on the development of visual motor coordination using kittens as subjects.
Psychology
Dist - MGHT **Prod** - MGHT 1975

Methods 25 MIN
16mm / U-matic / VHS
Untamed World Series
Color; Mono (J H C A)
$400.00 film, $250.00 video, $50.00 rental
Explains the methods of survival and evolution within the animal kingdom.
Science - Natural
Dist - CTV **Prod** - CTV 1973

Methods and Instruments of Oceanography 18 MIN
U-matic / VHS / 16mm
Color (J H)
LC 71-706764
Defines oceanography, describes the basic instruments used in oceanographic research and shows the methods by which these instruments are employed.
Science - Natural; Science - Physical
Dist - MEDIAG **Prod** - WILEYJ 1970

Methods and Techniques 30 MIN
U-matic / VHS
Basic Education - Teaching the Adult Series
Color (T)
Explores the methods and techniques used to teach adult basic education students.
Education
Dist - MDCPB **Prod** - MDDE

Methods and values in science today 17 MIN
VHS
Color; CC (H C)
$79.00 purchase _ #915
Presents a clear picture of scientific methods and values. Uses examples from actual scientists working in the laboratory and in the field. Part 2 of the program Scientific Methods and Values. Includes a book of the same title from the Learning Power series.
Guidance and Counseling; Science
Dist - HAWHIL **Prod** - HAWHIL 1994

Methods for Assessing the Training - Development Needs of Managers 90 MIN
U-matic / VHS
(A PRO)
$180.00 purchase members, $200.00 purchase non - members, $50.00
Features Scott B. Parry, President of Training House Incorporated, as he discusses the five major areas of managerial behavior and ways to assess supervisory needs.
Business and Economics; Education
Dist - ASTD **Prod** - ASTD

Methods for Managing the Computer in the Classroom
VHS / Software / Kit / U-matic
New Horizons Series
(PRO)
$1595 series purchase
Shows how teachers can set up and use computers in different physical environments and for various instructional needs.
Computer Science
Dist - AITECH **Prod** - ALASDE 1986

Methods for Obtaining Anaerobiasis 12 MIN
16mm
Color
LC FIE67-44
Demonstrates the use of the anaerobe jar for culturing organisms that require an oxygen - free environment.
Health and Safety; Science
Dist - USNAC **Prod** - USPHS 1965

Methods for Teaching Information 30 MIN
VHS / U-matic
Training the Trainer Series
Color (T)
Explores methods for teaching information, including lectures, question - and - answer sessions and group discussions.
Education; Psychology
Dist - ITCORP **Prod** - ITCORP

Methods for Teaching Skills 30 MIN
U-matic / VHS
Training the Trainer Series
Color (T)
Deals with methods for teaching skills, including demonstrations, simulators and role playing.
Education; Psychology
Dist - ITCORP **Prod** - ITCORP

Methods improvement 45 MIN
U-matic / BETA / VHS
Color (A PRO)
$200.00 purchase
Details all the principles important to efficient machine operation and assembly performance. Uses an actual project to develop an efficient method for assembling a seven - part gate valve.
Business and Economics; Psychology
Dist - TAMMFG **Prod** - TAMMFG

Methods in Diagnostic Parasitology 34 MIN
U-matic / VHS
Color (PRO)
Presents an introduction to techniques used in the detection of intestinal and blood parasites. Covers proper method for submitting a stool specimen for parasitological study, performance of the ova - parasite (OP) test and the blood - ova - parasite (BOP) test, the trichrome staining method and the preparation and staining of blood films.
Health and Safety
Dist - HSCIC **Prod** - HSCIC

Methods of Applying Fertilizer, Set 10 22 FRS
VHS / Slide / Cassette
Western Fertilizer Handbook Series
Color (G)
$30.95, $40.00, $8.50 purchase _ #1 - 580 - 610P, #1 - 580 - 210P, #1 - 580 - 540P
Looks at methods of applying fertilzer. Part of a fourteen - part series based on the Western Fertilizer Handbook.
Agriculture
Dist - VEP **Prod** - VEP

Methods of Birth Control 13 MIN
U-matic / VHS
Color (SPANISH)
LC 78-730127
Discusses birth control pills, IUDs, Diaphragms, vasectomy, tubal ligation, condoms, contraceptive foam and theoretical and actual effectiveness rates. Describes natural birth controls as well, briefly.
Guidance and Counseling; Sociology
Dist - MEDCOM **Prod** - MEDCOM

Methods of Birth Control 21 MIN
VHS / U-matic
Color
Presents all available systems of birth control through artwork and cartoons. Discusses advantages and disadvantages.
Sociology
Dist - MEDFAC **Prod** - MEDFAC 1979

Methods of contraception
VHS
Color (J H C G T A PRO)
$79.50 purchase _ #AH46308
Portrays 10 different forms of birth control. Discusses their advantages, disadvantages, reliability and possible medical complications.
Health and Safety
Dist - HTHED **Prod** - HTHED

Methods of contraception 28 MIN
VHS / U-matic
Color (PRO)
$275.00 purchase, $60.00 rental _ #7343S, #7343V
Explains the latest techniques of contraception for women, along with the pros and cons of each method. Includes barrier methods such as the diaphragm, oral methods such as the pill, chemical methods such as spermicidal foam, intrauterine devices, and natural but unreliable methods such as basal body temperature to predict periods of fertility. Includes male contraceptive methods such as the surgical procedure of vasectomy. Teaches the pressing need for reliable contraceptive information.
Health and Safety; Sociology
Dist - AJN **Prod** - HOSSN 1984

Methods of Control - Coatings and Potential Modification 57 MIN
BETA / VHS / U-matic
Color
$400 purchase
Shows anodic and cathodic protection systems.
Science; Science - Physical
Dist - ASM **Prod** - ASM

Methods of Control - Design, Material Selection, Environment Modification 57 MIN
BETA / VHS / U-matic
Color
$400 purchase
Shows design methods and materials selection to control corrosion.
Science; Science - Physical
Dist - ASM **Prod** - ASM

Methods of Family Planning 18 MIN
U-matic / VHS / 16mm
Color (H C A) (SPANISH)
LC 72-702672;
Explains methods of contraception, including rhythm, pills, diaphragm, intrauterine device and condoms. Includes the surgical methods of vasectomy and tubal ligation.
Guidance and Counseling; Health and Safety; Sociology
Dist - AIMS **Prod** - MORLAT 1972

Methods of Forming Metals 45 MIN
U-matic / BETA / VHS
Color
$300 purchase
Shows film on methods of casting and mechanical forming operations.
Industrial and Technical Education; Psychology; Science - Physical
Dist - ASM **Prod** - ASM

Methods of Naso - Enteral Alimentation 11 MIN
16mm
Color (PRO)
LC 80-701414
Discusses the case of a patient with short - bowel syndrome on whom an ileostomy has been performed. Shows the patient at home as she functions with a nasoenteral tube.
Health and Safety
Dist - EATONL **Prod** - EATONL 1979

Methods of Processing Plastics Materials 25 MIN
16mm
Plastics Series no 2
B&W
LC FIE52-294
Discusses fundamentals of lamination and of the compression, transfer, extrusion and injection molding methods. Shows how to finish molded parts.
Industrial and Technical Education
Dist - USNAC **Prod** - USOE 1945

Methods to Section a Whole Chicken 20 MIN
BETA / VHS
Color (G PRO)
$59.00 purchase _ #QF21
Explains how to section, portion and cut up a whole chicken, and illustrates an easy method of working with poultry and how to utilize the by - products.
Home Economics
Dist - RMIBHF **Prod** - RMIBHF

Methyl ethyl ketone 10 MIN
U-matic / BETA / VHS
Hazard communication series
Color (IND G)
$295.00 purchase _ #830 - 07
Discusses the potential health and physical hazards of working with methyl ethyl ketone - MEK. Emphasizes the high flammability of MEK and how to reduce the risk of explosion or fire. Covers spill cleanup, handling, safety and first aid precautions. Part of a series on hazard communication.
Health and Safety; Industrial and Technical Education; Psychology
Dist - ITSC **Prod** - ITSC

The Metis 27 MIN
U-matic / VHS / 16mm
Color (J H)
LC 78-701262
Deals with the Metis people of North America who trace their ancestry to both Indian and European roots.
Social Science; Sociology
Dist - MGHT **Prod** - DEVGCF 1978

Metooshow Series
If I were an Animal 20 MIN
Water is Wet 20 MIN
Dist - TPTP

Metrazol Induced Convulsions in Normal and Neurotic Rats 16 MIN
16mm
B&W (C)
A neurotic strain of rats and a normal strain are both subjected to metrazol convulsion. In comparison to normal rats the neurotic strain exhibits a lower threshhold to the effect of metrazol, a delayed onset of convulsions, hops and excessive forepaw clonus following initial torsion and a succession of convulsive reactions following a single injection. Neurotic rats often show seizures from the auditory stimulation of the jingling of keys. Rats of the normal strain seldom respond so violently.
Psychology; Science - Natural
Dist - PSUPCR **Prod** - PSUPCR 1940

Metre 15 MIN
U-matic
Music Box Series
Color (K P)
Explains strong beats and weak beats and demonstrates different metres.
Fine Arts
Dist - TVOTAR **Prod** - TVOTAR 1971

Metre and Litre are Neater 45 MIN
16mm
Color (T)
LC 75-704371
Covers the history of the metric system, explaining the SI metric system. Studies problems encountered in teaching metrics to elementary school children. Shows a workshop for teachers being conducted by Robert Tardif.
Mathematics
Dist - SRSPRD **Prod** - SRSPRD 1975

Metres, Litres and Grams 11 MIN
16mm
Color
Uses animation to examine metrics.
Mathematics
Dist - GM **Prod** - GM

Metric America 32 MIN
VHS / U-matic
Metric Education Video Tapes for Pre and Inservice Teachers (K - 8 'Series
Color
Discusses the philosophy, rationale and utilization of metric education using SI units. Includes sample activities.
Mathematics
Dist - PUAVC **Prod** - PUAVC

A Metric America 16 MIN
16mm / U-matic / VHS
Color (J H C G T A)
$24 rental _ #9438
Introduces the metric system and answers the question 'Why change to metrics?'.
Mathematics
Dist - AIMS **Prod** - AIMS 1973

Metric America, a 16 MIN
U-matic / VHS / 16mm
Color (J)
Uses parables about people called 'Wimples' to show the process of metric conversion and the difficulties experienced with their own cumbersome measuring system. Highlights reasons for U S metric conversion and introduces the meter, liter, kilogram and Celsius. Emphasizes the prefixes centi, milli and kilo and stresses the decimal nature of the metric system.
Mathematics
Dist - AIMS **Prod** - AIMS 1974

Metric education video tapes for pre and inservice teachers (K - 8) series
Volume 27 MIN
Dist - PUAVC

Metric Education Video Tapes for Pre and Inservice Teachers - K - 8 Series
Length 25 MIN
Dist - PUAVC

Metric Education Video Tapes for Pre and Inservice Teachers (K - 8 Series
Area and perimeter 25 MIN
Consumer Metrics 26 MIN
History 25 MIN
Mass and Weight 24 MIN
Metric America 32 MIN
Metric Units 26 MIN
Pros and Cons 28 MIN
Temperature 25 MIN
Dist - PUAVC

The Metric Film 13 MIN
U-matic / VHS / 16mm
Color (J)
LC 75-702937
Discusses the history of the metric system, conversion to the metric system and how to solve measurement problems.
Mathematics
Dist - AMEDFL **Prod** - HALLL 1975

Metric Marvels Series
Eeny, meeny, miney milliliter 3 MIN
I'm Your Liter Leader 3 MIN
Mara - Mara - Marathon 3 MIN
Meet Meter Man 3 MIN
Super Celsius 3 MIN
Wonder Baby 3 MIN
Wonder Gram 3 MIN
Dist - GA

The Metric Matter 30 MIN
U-matic
Color
Focuses on the debate over converting America to the metric system. Points out that the metric system is accurate and easily learned.
Mathematics
Dist - NETCHE **Prod** - NETCHE 1975

Metric Measure made Easy 14 MIN
16mm
Color
Explains the basic units of metric measure for length, volume, mass and temperature. Illustrates the appropriate use of kilo, mili and centi with each of these measures.
Mathematics
Dist - MTP **Prod** - CALCHM

Metric Measure made Easy 14 MIN
U-matic / VHS / 16mm
Color (P I)
LC 75-700958
Explains the metric system, paying close attention to the process of measurement and how this process applies using meter, liters, kilograms and Celsius. Stresses the decimal nature of the metric system.
Mathematics
Dist - AIMS **Prod** - NULSEN 1974

Metric Measurement, Film 1 14 MIN
U-matic / VHS / 16mm
Beginning Mathematics Series
Color (P) (SPANISH)
Shows how the metric system is based on the number ten. Uses a variety of examples from everyday life in order to show how metric units are employed to measure weight, distance and temperature.
Foreign Language; Mathematics
Dist - JOU **Prod** - JOU 1974

Metric Measurement, Film 2 14 MIN
16mm / U-matic / VHS
Intermediate Mathematics Series
Color (P I) (SPANISH)
Compares each unit of the metric system with its multiples and divisions to familiar objects and situations. Examines the relationship of the gram and liter and reviews the Celsius system of temperature measurement.
Foreign Language; Mathematics
Dist - JOU **Prod** - JOU 1974

Metric Measurement I - Measurement and Why We Need a Standard Unit 14 MIN
16mm / U-matic / VHS
Beginning Mathematics Series
Color (P)
LC 75-700976
Shows how the metric system is based on the number ten. Uses a variety of examples from everyday life in order to show how metric units are employed to measure weight, distance and temperature.
Mathematics
Dist - JOU **Prod** - GLDWER 1974

Metric Measurement II - what is the Metric System and How is it used 15 MIN
U-matic / VHS / 16mm
Intermediate Mathematics Series
Color (P I)
LC 75-700977
Compares each unit of the metric system with its multiples and divisions to familiar objects and situations. Examines the relationship of the gram and liter and reviews the Celsius system of temperature measurement.
Mathematics
Dist - JOU **Prod** - GLDWER 1974

Metric Measurement - Length and Area 12 MIN
16mm
Color (I J)
Presents the meter and the various prefixes which accompany its various multiples. Shows how the meter is used to find area.
Mathematics
Dist - SF **Prod** - SF 1974

Metric Measurement - Mass 9 MIN
16mm
Color (I J)
Demonstrates the concept of mass for which the kilogram is the base unit. Shows how the various multiples of the gram are used to weigh different items.
Mathematics
Dist - SF **Prod** - SF 1974

Metric measurement - volume and capacity 9 MIN
16mm
Color (I J)
Explains the relationship of volume to linear measurement. Uses everyday experiences to illustrate the concepts of volume and the liter which is the basic unit used to measure it.
Mathematics
Dist - SF **Prod** - SF 1974

Metric Meets the Inchworm 10 MIN
U-matic / VHS / 16mm
Color (C H J A)
$49.95 purchase _ #Q10835; LC 74-703306
Features a story about Fred Inchworm to explore the basic components of the metric system and show the advantages of converting to this form of measurement. Presents Fred as he tries to find a job, only to be turned down because he does not know the metric system.
Mathematics
Dist - CF **Prod** - BOSUST 1974

The Metric Micrometer 9 MIN
16mm
Color (IND)
Shows how to use the metric micrometer.
Industrial and Technical Education
Dist - MOKIN **Prod** - MOKIN

The Metric Movie 15 MIN
16mm
Color (I)
LC 76-703718
Presents a brief, animated history of measurement. Introduces, compares, illustrates and clarifies the fundamental concepts of the SI metric system.
Mathematics
Dist - BESTF **Prod** - GRAP 1975

Metric Properties of Figures 30 MIN
16mm
Mathematics for Elementary School Teachers Series no 15
Color (T)
Discusses the metric properties of various geometric figures. Shows how to determine a measure by an arbitrary unit. To be used following 'POLYGONS AND ANGLES.'.
Mathematics
Dist - MLA **Prod** - SMSG 1963

The Metric System 13 MIN
16mm
Mathematical Relationships Series
Color (I J)
Presents an animated film on the metric system.
Mathematics
Dist - NBCTV **Prod** - OECA 1972

Metric System 15 MIN
U-matic / VHS / 16mm
Color (I J H)
LC 79-701801
Shows the basic principles of the metric system and explains the interrelationship of metric units. Shows how the metric system can simplify daily life and how it applies to sophisticated 20th - century technology.
Mathematics
Dist - MCFI **Prod** - FILCOM 1974

The Metric system 30 MIN
VHS
Basic mathematical skills series
Color (J H)
$125.00 purchase _ #M13
Teaches about the metric system. Features Elayn Gay. Part of a 15 - part series on basic math.
Mathematics
Dist - LANDMK **Prod** - MGHT

The Metric System 15 MIN
U-matic
Mathematical Relationship Series
Color (I)
Compares the metric system with the imperial and its uses are examined.
Education; Mathematics
Dist - TVOTAR **Prod** - TVOTAR 1982

Metric System - Linear Measure 15 MIN
U-matic / VHS
Math Matters Series Blue Module
Color (I J)
Identifies the terms kilometer, meter, centimeter and millimeter as referring to standards of length in the metric system of measurement and compares them as to their relative size.
Mathematics
Dist - AITECH **Prod** - STETVC 1975

Metric system of measurement - SI base units 17 MIN
VHS / U-matic
Color (C PRO)
$395.00 purchase, $80.00 rental _ #C861 - VI - 059
Introduces the metric system of measurements. Presents the seven base units and two supplemental units of the international system of measure. Explains the origin of each unit, its definition and proper symbol as well as common prefixes used to modify the units. Presented by Jack F Peterson and Jackie Waterhouse.
Health and Safety; Mathematics
Dist - HSCIC

Metric System of Measurement - SI Base Units 19 MIN
VHS / U-matic
Metric System of Measurements Series
Color
Discusses the conversion of standard scientific units into the Standard International System (Metric System).
Mathematics
Dist - USNAC **Prod** - USHHS

Metric system of measurement - SI radiation units 31 MIN
U-matic / VHS
Color (C PRO)
$395.00 purchase, $80.00 rental _ #C861 - VI - 060
Presents a system of measurement that makes performing radiographs calculations easier. Discusses the four fundamental quantities in the radiation sciences - exposure, absorbed dose, dose equivalent and activity. Compares the new units of measure for such quantities to the units in the old system and demonstrates how to measure the four quantities using the proper units from the international system - SI. Presented by Jack F Patterson and Jackie Waterhouse.
Health and Safety; Mathematics
Dist - HSCIC

Metric System of Measurement - SI Radiation Units 31 MIN
VHS / U-matic
Metric System of Measurements Series WASHINGTON, DC 20409
Color
Discusses the conversion from special or traditional radiation units to the SI or Metric system.
Mathematics; Science - Physical
Dist - USNAC **Prod** - USHHS

Metric System of Measurements Series WASHINGTON, DC 20409
Metric System of Measurement - SI Radiation Units 31 MIN
Dist - USNAC

Metric System of Measurements Series
Metric System of Measurement - SI Base Units 19 MIN
Dist - USNAC

Metric System, Pt 1 13 MIN
U-matic
Color (I)
Presents the history, advantages, decimal calculating and comparison of English and metric systems.
Mathematics
Dist - VISIN **Prod** - VISIN

Metric System, Pt 2 13 MIN
U-matic

Color (I)
Presents weights, volumes and short and long lengths.
Mathematics
Dist - VISIN **Prod** - VISIN

Metric System Series

Comparing lengths	20 MIN
Comparing units of volume	20 MIN
Comparing units of weight	20 MIN
Introducing the Metric System	20 MIN
It's all Based on the Meter	20 MIN
Metric Units of Length	20 MIN
Metric units of volume	20 MIN
Metric Units of Weight	20 MIN
Science and the Metric System	20 MIN
The System is Based on 10	20 MIN
Using the Metric System Every Day	20 MIN
What do We Know about the Metric System	20 MIN
What is the Metric System	20 MIN
You Can Use it Now	20 MIN

Dist - GPN

Metric System Series

Linear Measurement	10 MIN

Dist - SF

Metric System - Weight and Capacity 15 MIN
U-matic / VHS
Math Matters Series Blue Module
Color (I J)
Identifies the terms gram and kilogram as standards of weight in the metric system. Considers a liter as a measurement of capacity.
Mathematics
Dist - AITECH **Prod** - STETVC 1975

Metric Systems, Welding Terms and Symbols 82 MIN
U-matic / BETA / VHS
Color
$400 purchase
Contains two tapes.
Guidance and Counseling; Industrial and Technical Education; Psychology
Dist - ASM **Prod** - ASM

Metric Units 26 MIN
U-matic / VHS
Metric Education Video Tapes for Pre and Inservice Teachers (K - 8 'Series
Color
Reviews the common metric units of length, volume, mass and temperature. Gives instruction on how to construct metric measuring equipment. Suggests activities to familiarize students with these metric units.
Mathematics
Dist - PUAVC **Prod** - PUAVC

Metric Units of Length 20 MIN
U-matic
Metric System Series
Color (J)
Emphasizes the common units of metric length. Discusses the millimeter, centimeter, meter and kilometer.
Mathematics
Dist - GPN **Prod** - MAETEL 1975

Metric units of volume 20 MIN
VHS
Metric system series
Color (J)
Introduces the liter as the basic unit of volume.
Mathematics
Dist - GPN **Prod** - MAETEL 1975

Metric Units of Weight 20 MIN
U-matic
Metric System Series
Color (J)
Discusses the gram and kilogram and describes the use of the Celsius temperature scale.
Mathematics
Dist - GPN **Prod** - MAETEL 1975

Metrics for elementary series

Metrics - Length and Distance	10 MIN
Metrics - Mass	10 MIN
Metrics - volume and capacity	10 MIN

Dist - AIMS

Metrics for Measure 13 MIN
16mm / U-matic / VHS
Color (P)
LC 75-700203
Uses an animated story about an inchworm in order to introduce the background and characteristics of the metric system.
Mathematics
Dist - PHENIX **Prod** - PETAW 1975

Metrics for Primary - How Big is Big 11 MIN
16mm / U-matic / VHS
Metrics for Primary Series
Color (P) (SPANISH)
Explores nonstandard and standard units for measuring liquid and solid materials, illustrating that one cubic decimetre has the capacity of one litre.
Mathematics
Dist - AIMS **Prod** - CINEDU 1976

Metrics for Primary - How Heavy is Heavy 11 MIN
U-matic / VHS / 16mm
Metrics for Primary Series
Color (P) (SPANISH)
Introduces metric measures of mass, illustrating concepts of light and heavy and explaining the gram and kilogram as standard metric units.
Mathematics
Dist - AIMS **Prod** - CINEDU 1976

Metrics for Primary - How Hot is Hot 11 MIN
16mm / U-matic / VHS
Metrics for Primary Series
Color (P) (SPANISH)
Discovers that the terms hot, warm and cold are relative and investigates the Celsius scale as a standard metric measure.
Mathematics
Dist - AIMS **Prod** - CINEDU 1976

Metrics for Primary - How Long is Long 11 MIN
U-matic / VHS / 16mm
Metrics for Primary Series
Color (P) (SPANISH)
Emphasizes units of informal measurement and standard units of length, explores the relationship between the metre, decimetre and centimetre and compares length, height and distance.
Mathematics
Dist - AIMS **Prod** - CINEDU 1976

Metrics for Primary Series

Metrics for Primary - How Big is Big	11 MIN
Metrics for Primary - How Heavy is Heavy	11 MIN
Metrics for Primary - How Hot is Hot	11 MIN
Metrics for Primary - How Long is Long	11 MIN

Dist - AIMS

Metrics - Length and Distance 10 MIN
U-matic / VHS / 16mm
Metrics for Elementary Series
Color (I) (SPANISH)
Illustrates the subdivisions and extrapolations of metrication.
Mathematics
Dist - AIMS **Prod** - CINEDU 1974

Metrics - Mass 10 MIN
16mm / U-matic / VHS
Metrics for Elementary Series
Color (I) (SPANISH)
Presents units of mass as used in household activities, sports events and amusements. Illustrates the relationship between mass and other measures, such as the litre.
Mathematics
Dist - AIMS **Prod** - CINEDU 1974

Metrics, Pt 1 - History, Length and Decimals 12 MIN
16mm
Metrics Series
Color (I J H C)
Describes early measurement systems based on body parts. Shows how the meter is the base unit of length which is successively divided or multiplied by ten.
Mathematics
Dist - BNCHMK **Prod** - BNCHMK

Metrics, Pt 3 - Mass and Temperature 9 MIN
16mm
Metrics Series
Color (I J H C)
Describes the use of various metric units of mass such as the gram, milligram and kilogram to measure the weights of common objects.
Mathematics
Dist - BNCHMK **Prod** - BNCHMK

Metrics, Pt 2 - volume 11 MIN
16mm
Metrics series
Color (I J H C)
Describes the relationship between meters and grams which measure length and weight, and liters which measure volume.
Mathematics
Dist - BNCHMK **Prod** - BNCHMK

Metrics Series

Metrics, Pt 1 - History, Length and Decimals	12 MIN
Metrics, Pt 3 - Mass and Temperature	9 MIN
Metrics, Pt 2 - volume	11 MIN

Dist - BNCHMK

Metrics, Unit 1, Lesson 1 15 MIN
U-matic
Color (J)
Tells how to measure an object to the nearest whole number of units, given an appropriate nonstandard unit of length. Explains how to match metric units with their symbols.
Mathematics
Dist - NYSED **Prod** - AALC 1977

Metrics, Unit 1, Lesson 2 6 MIN
U-matic
Color (J)
Tells how to choose the metric unit of length that will give the most accurate measurement in a particular situation.
Mathematics
Dist - NYSED **Prod** - AALC 1977

Metrics, Unit 1, Lesson 3 11 MIN
U-matic
Color (J)
Presents a picture and a metric unit of length and then shows how to estimate the size of the real - life object.
Mathematics
Dist - NYSED **Prod** - AALC 1977

Metrics, Unit 1, Lesson 4 9 MIN
U-matic
Color (J)
Presents two standard metric units of length and an illustration. Tells how to state the length of that illustration in the larger and smaller units.
Mathematics
Dist - NYSED **Prod** - AALC 1977

Metrics, Unit 1, Lesson 5 12 MIN
U-matic
Color (J)
Explains how to convert linear measurements into measurements in another unit, changing into or from decimal notation.
Mathematics
Dist - NYSED **Prod** - AALC 1977

Metrics, Unit 2, Lesson 1 8 MIN
U-matic
Color (J)
Discusses how to change a metric distance into a measurement in two units.
Mathematics
Dist - NYSED **Prod** - AALC 1977

Metrics, Unit 2, Lesson 2 10 MIN
U-matic
Color (J)
Gives a situation and three measurements in different metric units, showing how to choose the measurement which best fits the situation.
Mathematics
Dist - NYSED **Prod** - AALC 1977

Metrics, Unit 2, Lesson 3 13 MIN
U-matic
Color (J)
Explains how to read a distance in meters and decimal parts of a meter, and then round off to the nearest whole number of meters. Tells how to estimate distance in meters.
Mathematics
Dist - NYSED **Prod** - AALC 1977

Metrics, Unit 3, Lesson 1 13 MIN
U-matic
Color (J)
Shows how to calculate perimeter with metric units.
Mathematics
Dist - NYSED **Prod** - AALC 1977

Metrics, Unit 3, Lesson 2 11 MIN
U-matic
Color (J)
Explains how to estimate a perimeter in metric units.
Mathematics
Dist - NYSED **Prod** - AALC 1977

Metrics, Unit 3, Lesson 3 14 MIN
U-matic
Color (J)
Presents a number of figures and their dimensions and tells how to calculate their perimeters and order them from greatest to least.
Mathematics
Dist - NYSED **Prod** - AALC 1977

Metrics, Unit 4, Lesson 1 11 MIN
U-matic
Color (J)
Shows how to calculate the area of a simple geometric figure in metric area units.
Mathematics
Dist - NYSED **Prod** - AALC 1977

Metrics, Unit 4, Lesson 2 10 MIN
U-matic

Color (J)
Discusses how to do metric problems involving the area of geometric figures.
Mathematics
Dist - NYSED **Prod** - AALC 1977

Metrics, Unit 5, Lesson 1 13 MIN
U-matic
Color (J)
Illustrates how to calculate volume in metric units.
Mathematics
Dist - NYSED **Prod** - AALC 1977

Metrics, Unit 5, Lesson 2 12 MIN
U-matic
Color (J)
Illustrates how to calculate volume in metric units.
Mathematics
Dist - NYSED **Prod** - AALC 1977

Metrics, Unit 5, Lesson 3 12 MIN
U-matic
Color (J)
Explains how to calculate capacity in metric units.
Mathematics
Dist - NYSED **Prod** - AALC 1977

Metrics, Unit 5, Lesson 4 7 MIN
U-matic
Color
Points out how to choose the best metric capacity unit for each situation.
Mathematics
Dist - NYSED **Prod** - AALC 1977

Metrics, Unit 6, Lesson 1 11 MIN
U-matic
Color (J)
Gives a measurement in one mass unit and explains how to convert it to a measurement in another mass unit.
Mathematics
Dist - NYSED **Prod** - AALC 1977

Metrics, Unit 6, Lesson 2 12 MIN
U-matic
Color (J)
Tells how to choose the unit of metric mass that best suits each object or situation.
Mathematics
Dist - NYSED **Prod** - AALC 1977

Metrics, Unit 6, Lesson 3 14 MIN
U-matic
Color (J)
Tells how to choose the unit of metric mass that best suits each object or situation.
Mathematics
Dist - NYSED **Prod** - AALC 1977

Metrics, Unit 7, Lesson 1 10 MIN
U-matic
Color (J)
Discusses body temperature, boiling points, and freezing points in Celsius measurement.
Mathematics
Dist - NYSED **Prod** - AALC 1977

Metrics, Unit 7, Lesson 2 7 MIN
U-matic
Color (J)
Explains how to estimate temperature in degrees Celsius.
Mathematics
Dist - NYSED **Prod** - AALC 1977

Metrics, Unit 7, Lesson 3 11 MIN
U-matic
Color (J)
Discusses Celsius temperature measurement.
Mathematics
Dist - NYSED **Prod** - AALC 1977

Metrics, Unit 8, Lesson 3 14 MIN
U-matic
Color (J)
Reviews linear metric measurement.
Mathematics
Dist - NYSED **Prod** - AALC 1977

Metrics, Unit 8, Lesson 4 11 MIN
U-matic
Color (J)
Reviews the use of metric units to calculate perimeters.
Mathematics
Dist - NYSED **Prod** - AALC 1977

Metrics, Unit 8, Lesson 5 11 MIN
U-matic
Color (J)
Reviews the use of metric units to calculate area.
Mathematics
Dist - NYSED **Prod** - AALC 1977

Metrics, Unit 8, Lesson 6 12 MIN
U-matic
Color (J)
Discusses the metric measurement of volume and capacity.
Mathematics
Dist - NYSED **Prod** - AALC 1977

Metrics, Unit 8, Lesson 7 12 MIN
U-matic
Color (J)
Discusses the metric measurement of mass.
Mathematics
Dist - NYSED **Prod** - AALC 1977

Metrics, Unit 8, Lesson 1 and 2 24 MIN
U-matic
Color (J)
Reviews linear metric measurement.
Mathematics
Dist - NYSED **Prod** - AALC 1977

Metrics - volume and capacity 10 MIN
U-matic / VHS / 16mm
Metrics for elementary series
Color (I) (SPANISH)
Provides a basis for judging volume through utilization of everyday situations. Demonstrates the litre and its companion volume measurement, the cubic centimeter.
Mathematics
Dist - AIMS **Prod** - CINEDU 1974

Metro - Mobility 22 MIN
16mm
Color (A)
Explores the need for the free movement of people and goods in our ever - expanding cities and satellite suburbs.
Social Science
Dist - GM **Prod** - GM

Metromatic 5 MIN
16mm
B&W (K P I J H C)
LC 72-700044
Emphasizes dehumanizing aspects of airport technology by showing crowd movements in a large metropolitan air terminal.
Business and Economics; Social Science; Sociology
Dist - PCHENT **Prod** - PCHENT 1971

Metropolis 90 MIN
VHS
Signature series
B&W (G)
$29.95 purchase
Presents a version of Metropolis mastered from a mint condition 35mm print. Features a huge cast and massive expressionist sets in a story about a workers' revolt in the 21st century. Directed by Fritz Lang.
Fine Arts; Literature and Drama
Dist - KINOIC

Metropolis 87 MIN
VHS
Color; B&W (G)
$79.95 purchase _ #S00254
Presents a reconstructed, colorized version of the 1926 silent film. Portrays the class conflict and societal confrontation that results from a romantic relationship in a futuristic society. Soundtrack, selected by composer Giorgio Moroder, features songs by Pat Benatar and Queen. Also available in the original silent, black - and - white version for a lower charge.
Fine Arts; Literature and Drama; Sociology
Dist - UILL

The Metropolis 57 MIN
U-matic / VHS / 16mm
Age of Uncertainty Series
Color (H C A)
LC 77-701491
Portrays problems of the industrial society as seen in the urban metropolis. Based on the book The Age Of Uncertainty by John Kenneth Galbraith.
Business and Economics; Sociology
Dist - FI **Prod** - BBCL 1977

Metropolis 115 MIN
U-matic / VHS
B&W
Science fiction film which depicts an incredible city of the future. Has an underlying story of love against a background of social conflict.
Fine Arts
Dist - IHF **Prod** - IHF

Metropolis 87 MIN
35mm / 16mm
B&W w/color tint (G)
Features a masterpiece of German expressionism, with spectacular sets and special effects. Looks at the mechanized world of 2026 which is interrupted by a clash between workers and industrialists, inspiring the mad scientist Rotwang to create a robot clone from a beautiful heroic laborer and send her to do the evil bidding of the overboss. Giorgio Moroder presents Fritz Lang's classic vision of the future, color - tinted and with a contemporary music score, restored as closely to its original conception as possible and containing several scenes that don't exist in any other prints. Contact distributor for price.
Fine Arts
Dist - OCTOBF

Metropolis 30 MIN
VHS
Tales from the map room
Color; PAL (H C A)
PdS65 purchase; Not available in the United States
Features actors who re - create significant events in the history of cartography. Presents maps as historical documents and uses London maps to provide a history of the city from 1745 onwards. First in a series of six programs.
Geography - World
Dist - BBCENE

Metropolis series
Traces the historical and technological evolution of six components of a modern city. Uses advanced graphics, video effects and dramatic recreation. Reveals the hidden mechanisms that enable the modern city to function.

A Big stink 30 MIN
Bright lights, big city 30 MIN
Going underground 30 MIN
Light, lines and heavy fines 30 MIN
Someone to watch over us 30 MIN
The Tower without ends 30 MIN
Dist - BBCENE

Metropolis, the, Pt 1 28 MIN
U-matic / VHS / 16mm
Age of Uncertainty Series
Color (H C A)
LC 77-701491
Portrays problems of the industrial society as seen in the urban metropolis. Based on the book The Age Of Uncertainty by John Kenneth Galbraith.
Sociology
Dist - FI **Prod** - BBCL 1977

Metropolis, the, Pt 2 29 MIN
16mm / U-matic / VHS
Age of Uncertainty Series
Color (H C A)
LC 77-701491
Portrays problems of the industrial society as seen in the urban metropolis. Based on the book The Age Of Uncertainty by John Kenneth Galbraith.
Sociology
Dist - FI **Prod** - BBCL 1977

Metropolitan Cats 24 MIN
U-matic / VHS / 16mm
Color (J)
Presents a tribute to the cat, as seen through 4,000 years of art and sculpture in the Metropolitan Museum Of Art.
Fine Arts
Dist - PERSPF **Prod** - ABCVID 1984
CORF

Metropolitan cats 16 MIN
VHS
Color (H)
Celebrates 4,000 years of cats as portrayed in the collection of the Metropolitan Museum of Art in New York. Features museum staff members who offer interpretations of the artwork based on their personal experiences with cats.
Fine Arts
Dist - VIEWTH **Prod** - VIEWTH

Metropolitan Museum Seminars in Art Series
The Artist as Social Critic - Visionary
Composition
Expressionism / abstraction
Techniques
What is a Painting / Realism
Dist - GA

Metropolitan opera series
Francesca da Rimini 148 MIN
Dist - FI
PBS

Metropolitan opera series
Don Carlo 214 MIN
Elektra 112 MIN
Ernani 142 MIN
Hansel and Gretel 104 MIN
Idomeneo 185 MIN
La boheme 142 MIN
L'elisir d'amore 132 MIN
Live from the Met highlights - Volume 1 70 MIN
Lucia di Lammermoor 128 MIN
Manon lescaut 135 MIN
Tannhauser 176 MIN
Tosca 127 MIN
Un ballo in maschera 150 MIN
Dist - PBS

Metropolitan Police Department 15 MIN
16mm / U-matic / VHS
Career Awareness
(I)
$130 VC purchase, $240 film purchase, $25 VC rental, $30 film rental
Presents an empathetic approach to career planning, showing the personal as well as professional qualities of metropolitan police personnel. Highlights the importance of career education.
Civics and Political Systems; Guidance and Counseling; Social Science
Dist - GPN

The Metropolitan Washington Heroin Test 46 MIN
16mm
Color
LC 74-700621
Helps develop an awareness of the drug problem by presenting a test regarding the key issues surrounding the heroin problem in the Washington, DC, metropolitan area.
Health and Safety; Psychology; Sociology
Dist - FORM **Prod** - FEDCC 1973

Metropolitanism 30 MIN
VHS / U-matic
American Government Series; 1
Color (C)
Uses greater Chicago as a focal point for examining the many governmental agencies involved in a major city. Looks at ways the states differ in their ability and willingness to deal with urban programs.
Civics and Political Systems
Dist - DALCCD **Prod** - DALCCD

Mexican 1000 (Twenty - Seven and One - Half Hours to La Paz) 26 MIN
16mm
Color (I)
LC 72-702087
Shows the championship car race of 'THE BAJA' from Ensenada to La Paz. Illustrates man's struggle with natural terrain consisting of cliffs, gulches, silt and sand.
Geography - World; Industrial and Technical Education; Physical Education and Recreation
Dist - SFI **Prod** - SFI 1970

Mexican - American Children 27 MIN
16mm
Play and Cultural Continuity Series Part 3
Color (H C T)
Covers the Rio Grande Valley, near Edinburg, Texas, an area where traditional cultural values are maintained and actively passed on to young children. Presents the importance of fiestas, dancing, music serenade and family. Observes children in numerous play episodes in the center and at home. Shows prescribed modes of interaction between boys and girls and emphasizes mutual respect and affection between the very old and the very young and perpetuating their bilingual heritage.
Fine Arts; Geography - United States; Physical Education and Recreation; Sociology
Dist - CFDC **Prod** - CFDC 1977

Mexican - American Culture - its Heritage 18 MIN
16mm
Uses of Music Series
Color (I)
LC 78-708130
Demonstrates visually and musically the origins and history of the Mexican - American culture.
Fine Arts; History - United States; Psychology; Sociology
Dist - CGWEST **Prod** - CGWEST 1970

Mexican - American Family 16 MIN
16mm
Color (P I J H)
LC 75-71137
Provides insight into the life of a Mexican - American family. Features warmth between members of the family, traditions they cherish, adjustment to a new language and society, efforts and sacrifices to maintain unity of the family.
History - United States; Psychology; Sociology
Dist - ATLAP **Prod** - ATLAP 1970

The Mexican - American - heritage and destiny 29 MIN
U-matic / VHS / 16mm
Americana series; no 7
Color (J) (SPANISH)
LC 78-701795
Tells how a Mexican - American who feels culturally deprived and unsure of his identity is shown his cultural heritage. Discusses Mexican history and shows how Spanish words, architecture and music have become part of American culture. Describes contributions of outstanding Mexican - Americans.
Biography; English Language; Fine Arts; History - World; Sociology
Dist - HANDEL **Prod** - HANDEL 1977

The Mexican - American Speaks - Heritage in Bronze 20 MIN
VHS / U-matic
Color (J C)
$79.00 purchase _ #3153
Focuses upon the Mexican - Americans and their history from the conquest of the Indians by Spanish conquistadors through the impact of 'Latino' culture of the 20th century.
Biography; Sociology
Dist - EBEC

Mexican Americans 30 MIN
VHS
Multicultural peoples of North America series
Color (J H C G)
$49.95 purchase _ #LVCD6683V - S
Celebrates the heritage of Mexican Americans. Traces the history of their emigration to North America and shows the unique traditions they brought with them. Discusses why and when they emigrated, where they settled, their occupations and their important leaders. Focuses on a Mexican American family and explains the importance of cultural identity. Part of a 15 - part series on multiculturalism in North America.
History - United States; Sociology
Dist - CAMV

Mexican - Americans - an Historic Profile 29 MIN
16mm
B&W
LC 72-700816
Presents Maclovio Barraza, Chairman of the Board of the southwest council of La Raza, who traces the history of the Mexican - American from the time of the Spanish Conquistadores to the present.
History - World
Dist - ADL **Prod** - ADL 1970

Mexican - Americans - the Invisible Minority 38 MIN
16mm / U-matic / VHS
Public Broadcast Laboratory Series
Color (H C)
LC 70-702700
Describes the struggle of Mexican - Americans for an identity within the protest movement, discussing their economic poverty, their employment as unskilled laborers and their education in a system designed for white English - speaking students.
Civics and Political Systems; Psychology; Sociology
Dist - IU **Prod** - NET 1969

Mexican - Americans - Viva La Raza 47 MIN
U-matic / VHS / 16mm
B&W (H C A)
LC 72-701374
Examines the rapidly growing movement of young militant Mexican - Americans, focusing on Los Angeles. Aims to measure the influence of the movement since its inception.
Geography - United States; Sociology
Dist - MGHT **Prod** - CBSTV 1972

Mexican Baja, Baja Sur and fishing Los Cabos
VHS
Color (G)
$19.80 purchase _ #0874
Explores the desert peninsula of the Mexican Baja. Fishes in the Pacific for marlin, sailfish, yellowtail, tuna and grouper. Visits the secluded shores of the 'Cabos' for swimming, surfing and wind surfing.
Geography - World; Physical Education and Recreation
Dist - SEVVID

Mexican Boy - the Story of Pablo 22 MIN
16mm / U-matic / VHS
Color; B&W (P I)
Tells of Pablo and his family who live in a small mountain village in Mexico. Pictures a one - room adobe house, school and church, market place and farm.
Geography - World; Psychology; Sociology
Dist - EBEC **Prod** - EBEC 1961

Mexican Bus Ride 73 MIN
16mm
B&W (H C)
Presents the misadventures of an innocent young man sent over the mountains to fetch a lawyer. Taking a bus in Mexico, he learns that buses have supernatural and surreal qualities.
Fine Arts
Dist - TRANSW **Prod** - CON 1951

Mexican Caribbean, Cancun and Cozumel
VHS
Color (G)
$19.80 purchase _ #0864
Visits the city of Cancun in Yucatan, Mexico, and the Mexican island of Cozumel in the Caribbean. Shows snorkeling, surfing and jet skiing.
Geography - World; Physical Education and Recreation
Dist - SEVVID

A Mexican colonial tour 35 MIN
VHS
Color (G) (SPANISH)
$39.95 purchase _ #W1402, #W1403
Visits cities and sites of Mexico including Mexico City, the floating gardens in Xochimilco and haciendas and shops. Takes a look at works of muralist Diogo Rivera.
Foreign Language; Geography - World; Sociology
Dist - GPC

Mexican Dances, Pt 1 18 MIN
U-matic / VHS / 16mm
Color (I) (SPANISH)
LC 77-714070
Features the ballet Folklorico Estudiantil Los Angeles, portraying famous Mexican dances dating back to Aztec times. Introduces Mexican - American students and their cultural contributions.
Fine Arts; Geography - World
Dist - AIMS **Prod** - ASSOCF 1971

Mexican Dances, Pt 2 18 MIN
U-matic / VHS / 16mm
Color (I) (SPANISH)
LC 70-714071; 77-714071
Features the ballet Folklorico Estudiantil Los Angeles, portraying Mexican dances and their place in history and culture, paralleling Mexican and American history.
Fine Arts; Geography - World
Dist - AIMS **Prod** - ASSOCF 1971

Mexican festivals 30 MIN
VHS
Color (G)
$39.95 purchase _ #W1464
Focuses on the days of fiesta held in each village and town in Mexico, celebrated with food and craft markets, bullfights, charreadas and rinas de gallos.
Foreign Language; Geography - World
Dist - GPC

Mexican Heritage Series
America's first city - Teotihuacan 18 MIN
Christmas in Oaxaca 14 MIN
Creative arts and crafts of mexico 16 MIN
Descubrir veracruz 16 MIN
Discover Veracruz 16 MIN
The Many Faces of Mexico 17 MIN
Monument to the Sun - the Story of the Aztec Calendar Stone 16 MIN
The Story of the Aztecs 19 MIN
These were the Maya 19 MIN
Dist - FI

Mexican Heritage - Spanish series
Artes Creativos De Mexico 16 MIN
Estos Fueron Los Mayas 19 MIN
La Historia De Las Aztecas 19 MIN
La Navidad En Oaxaca 14 MIN
Monumento Del Sol - La Historia De La Piedra Del Sol 16 MIN
Dist - FI

Mexican Heritage
La Primera Ciudad De Las Americas - Teotihuacan 18 MIN
Las Muchas Caras De Mexico 17 MIN
Dist - FI

Mexican Indian Legends 16 MIN
U-matic / VHS / 16mm
Color (I J H)
LC 76-702965
Dramatizes several Indian legends from Toltec, Mayan and Aztec cultures, pointing out different themes such as the explanation of natural phemomena, moral lessons, heroic adventures and stories of the gods.
Literature and Drama; Social Science
Dist - PHENIX **Prod** - PHENIX 1976

Mexican jail footage 18 MIN
16mm
Color (G)
$35.00 rental
Documents the imprisonment of the filmmaker, Gordon Ball, in a Mexican jail in 1968, along with 25 other Americans.
Fine Arts; History - World; Sociology
Dist - CANCIN

Mexican Market 10 MIN
U-matic / VHS / 16mm
Color (I J H) (SPANISH)
LC 76-701140
Presents a marketplace just outside Mexico City. Discusses the day - to - day activities there and the experience of taking part in a public market, a typical aspect of Latin American village life.
Geography - World; Social Science
Dist - AIMS **Prod** - ACI 1971

The Mexican muralists - painting with fire 29 MIN
35mm strip / VHS
Color (J H C T A)
$93.00 purchase _ #MB - 909734 - 0, #MB - 909471 - 6
Surveys the development of Mexican mural art. Focuses on the works of Diego Rivera, Clemente Orozco, and David Alfaro Siqueiros. Notes that the murals were viewed by the revolutionary Mexican government as a force for inspiring the Mexican people.
Fine Arts; History - World
Dist - SRA **Prod** - SRA 1990

Mexican Murals - a Revolution on the Walls 30 MIN
U-matic / VHS
Color
Examines the revolutionary mural paintings of Mexico. Looks at the murals, not only for their great aesthetic value, but also as an essential and fascinating part of Mexico's history. Focuses on the murals of the three major artists of the period, Diego Rivera, Jose Clemente Orozco and David Alfaro Siqueiros.
Fine Arts; History - World
Dist - OHUTC **Prod** - OHUTC

Mexican or American 17 MIN
16mm
Color (P I J H)
LC 79-711338
Gives insight into the problems of the Spanish - speaking minority of America, as seen through the eyes of an educated Mexican - American. Faces the fundamental issue of cultural conflict in the United States.
History - United States; Psychology; Sociology
Dist - ATLAP **Prod** - ATLAP 1970

Mexican people and culture 25 MIN
VHS
Hispanic culture video series
Color (J H)
$49.95 purchase _ #VK4537X
Focuses on the history, geography and historical development of Mexico and the role of Mexican - Americans in contemporary society. Presents part of a six - part series that examines the background and history of Spanish influences on the history, culture and society of different parts of the world.
History - World
Dist - KNOWUN

Mexican prehispanic cultures 30 MIN
VHS
Color (J H C G)
$39.98 purchase _ #IMX1001V
Offers a panoramic view of various prehispanic civilizations that existed in Mexico. Visits the mysteriously abandoned civilization created by the Tetehuacans. Admires the works of the Toltecs, the Aztecs and the astronomy, mathematics and art of the Mayans.
History - World
Dist - CAMV

Mexican pyramid tour 30 MIN
VHS
Color (G)
$29.95 purchase _ #S01053
Visits both ancient and modern sites in Mexico. Focuses on the ancient Aztec and Mayan ruins found throughout the nation.
Geography - World; History - World; Social Science
Dist - UILL

A Mexican pyramid tour 35 MIN
VHS
Color (G) (SPANISH)
$39.95 purchase _ #W1400, #W1401
Visits museums and historic sites of ancient Mexican civilizations, including the Museum of Anthropology in Mexico City and such locations as Teotihuacan and Chichen Itza.
Foreign Language; Geography - World; Sociology
Dist - GPC

Mexican Rebellion 20 MIN
16mm
B&W (C A)
Follows the initial stages of the Mexican student rebellion during the summer of 1968. Compiled from stills, films and film clips made by the students.
Civics and Political Systems; Education; Geography - World; Psychology; Sociology
Dist - CANWRL **Prod** - UNKNWN 1968

The Mexican tapes - a chronicle of life outside the law 270 MIN
VHS
Color (G)
$200.00 purchase
Weaves a narrative from the filmmaker's experience as a neighbor in a southern California colony of undocumented Mexicans. Records the community which reflects the covert, ubiquitous presence of millions of immigrants living and working in the shadow of United States law - the 'new' Americans. Follows three families over a five - year period, chronicling their movement back and forth across the border and within the changing neighborhood. Produced by Louis Hock. In four parts on two tapes; each episode is 55 minutes in length.
Fine Arts; Social Science; Sociology
Dist - CANCIN

The Mexican Tapes - a Chronicle of Life Outside the Law - Pt I - El Gringo 29 MIN
16mm / U-matic
Presente Series
Color (ENGLISH (ENGLISH SUBTITLES))
Presents a documentary on the lives of three families of illegal Mexican immigrants living covertly in a wealthy Southern Californian community. Reveals how they got there, how they feel about being there and their dreams about making it in the United States, living with the chronic fear of arrest by government authorities. In English and Spanish with English subtitles.
Civics and Political Systems; Sociology
Dist - KCET **Prod** - KCET

The Mexican Tapes - a Chronicle of Life Outside the Law - Pt II - El Rancho Grande 29 MIN
16mm / U-matic
Presente Series
Color (ENGLISH (ENGLISH SUBTITLES))
Documents the tension - filled life of undocumented Mexican immigrants who live mostly in cities and follow the American way of life but face the chronic hazards of deportation, unstable employment and a lack of fluency in English. Shows how this has become a major structural element in the socio - economic make - up of the United States. In English and Spanish with English subtitles.
Foreign Language; Guidance and Counseling; Sociology
Dist - KCET **Prod** - KCET

The Mexican Tapes - a Chronicle of Life Outside the Law - Pt III - the Winner's 29 MIN
16mm / U-matic
Presente Series
Color (ENGLISH (ENGLISH SUBTITLES))
Complete title is Mexican Tapes, The - A Chronicle Of Life Outside the Law - Pt III - The Winner's Circle. Looks at the women who live with their men and children as undocumented Mexican workers in San Diego. Reveals their ambivalent feelings about being working partners with the men as they are torn between loyalty to them and the new - found independence brought on by wage - earning. In English and Spanish with English subtitles.
Sociology
Dist - KCET **Prod** - KCET

The Mexican Tapes - a Chronicle of Life Outside the Law - Pt IV - La Migra 29 MIN
U-matic / 16mm
Presente Series
Color (ENGLISH (ENGLISH SUBTITLES))
Reveals the negative bias towards Latinos of the Immigration and Naturalization Services' arrest procedure and its effects on the children and parents. Shows the difference between life in the United States and Mexico for undocumented immigrants with scenes in the laundromat on both sides of the border. Shows these immigrants driven out of their apartments by redevelopment and immigration authority raids. In English and Spanish with English subtitles.
Civics and Political Systems; Geography - World; Sociology
Dist - KCET **Prod** - KCET

The Mexican Texans to 1865 10 MIN
U-matic / VHS / Slide
Hispanic Studies, Ranching and Farming Series
Color; Mono (I J H)
History - United States; Sociology
Dist - UTXITC **Prod** - UTXITC 1973

The Mexican Texans to 1865 10 MIN
U-matic / VHS / Slide
Texas Military History Series
Color; Mono (J H)
History - United States; Social Science; Sociology
Dist - UTXITC **Prod** - UTXITC 1976

Mexican Village in Transition - Tepoztlan 11 MIN
16mm
Color (I)
LC FIA66-553
Describes the Mexican village of Tepoztlan, long studied by archaeologists as an isolated folk village of pre - hispanic times. Shows how the old and new exist together as the village is slowly taking its place in the national life of Mexico.
Geography - World; Science - Physical
Dist - SF **Prod** - BOUWM 1965

The Mexican War and the Civil War 28 MIN
16mm
Glory and the Dream - Ohio's Response to War Series
Color
Describes Ohio's participation in and reactions to the Mexican and Civil Wars. Discusses the first military conscription during the Civil War.
History - United States
Dist - HRC **Prod** - OHC

The Mexican Way of Life 23 MIN
16mm / U-matic / VHS
Color (I J H C G T A)
$50 rental _ #9848
Describes lifestyle and typical week in life of students in these foreign countries.
Geography - World; History - World
Dist - AIMS **Prod** - SAIF 1986

The Mexicans - through their eyes 59 MIN
BETA / VHS / U-matic
Color (G)
$90.00 purchase _ #C51522
Examines the mosaic of modern Mexico through the eyes of its Indians, peasants, artists and philosophers. Shows how these Mexicans draw on the rich heritage of their pre - Hispanic past to shape their future.
Geography - World; History - World; Social Science
Dist - NGS **Prod** - NGS 1992

Mexico 29 MIN
Videoreel / VT2
International Cookbook Series
Color
Features home economist Joan Hood presenting a culinary tour of specialty dishes from around the world. Shows the preparation of Mexican dishes ranging from peasant cookery to continental cuisine.
Geography - World; Home Economics
Dist - PBS **Prod** - WMVSTV

Mexico 17 MIN
16mm
Latin American Series - a Focus on People Series
Color (I J H)
Illustrates Mexican heritage and customs, giving a contemporary view of Mexico today. Presents views on solutions to social and economic problems and indicates some directions the government is taking.
Business and Economics; Geography - World; Sociology
Dist - SF **Prod** - CLAIB 1973

Mexico 25 MIN
VHS / U-matic
Nations of the World Series
Color (I J H A)
Observes life in Mexico, a dynamic, growing, yet troubled country, in its factories and cities, on its farms, and along its border with the United States.
Geography - World
Dist - NGS **Prod** - NGS

Mexico
VHS
Dances of the world series
Color (G)
$39.95 purchase _ #FD600V
Presents performances of dances from Mexico. Interviews the dancers.
Fine Arts; Geography - World; Physical Education and Recreation
Dist - CAMV **Prod** - CAMV

Mexico 10 MIN
VHS
Color (G)
$20.00 rental, $35.00 purchase
Visits Mexico from the point of view of the women. Uses short takes. Produced by Silvianna Goldsmith.
Fine Arts; Geography - World
Dist - CANCIN

Mexico 35 MIN
VHS
Color (G) (SPANISH)
$39.95 purchase _ #W1418, #W1419
Focuses on the culture of Mexico as seen through the bullfights, charros and the Ballet Folklorico and in the ruins of ancient civilizations.
Foreign Language; Geography - World; Sociology
Dist - GPC

Mexico 15 MIN
U-matic / VHS
Families of the World Series
Color (I)
Takes the viewer to the birthday party of Alejandra de Prado, who has just turned thirteen. Alejandra's hometown, Puebla, is an industrial center with a colonial heritage located near Mexico City. Shows Alejandra's school and family life.
Geography - World
Dist - NGS **Prod** - NGS

Mexico 1 15 MIN
U-matic
It's Your World Series
Color (I)
Introduces students to the world around them. Segment titles are; What Is Archaeology, The Maya, The Aztec, The Spanish Conquest, Independence.
Education; Geography - World
Dist - TVOTAR **Prod** - TVOTAR 1984

Mexico 2 15 MIN
U-matic
It's Your World Series
Color (I)
Introduces students to the world around them. Segment titles are; Geography, The Climate, Plants And Animals, Agriculture And Industry.
Education; Geography - World
Dist - TVOTAR **Prod** - TVOTAR 1984

Mexico 3 15 MIN
U-matic
It's Your World Series
Color (I)
Introduces students to the world around them. Segment titles are; The People, The Food, Art And Handicrafts, Fiesta.
Education; Geography - World
Dist - TVOTAR **Prod** - TVOTAR 1984

Mexico 68 20 MIN
16mm
Color
Shows the student - worker mass actions of hundreds of thousands of people as they down the regime of Diaz Urdaz. Shows how the government answered with the military invasion of the university, the October 2nd Tlateloco Massacre.
Civics and Political Systems; Geography - World; Sociology
Dist - CANWRL **Prod** - CANWRL 1968

Mexico - a Changing Land 22 MIN
U-matic / VHS / 16mm
Color (I J)
LC 80-701738
Discusses the history and geography of Mexico. Looks at the development of land, oil and gas resources, the fishing industry, and the tourist trade.
Geography - World
Dist - HIGGIN **Prod** - HIGGIN 1980

Mexico - a Family - Style Menu 28 MIN
U-matic / VHS / 16mm
World of Cooking Series
Color (J)
Depicts the tasty creations of Mexican master chef Joaquin Guzman.
Geography - World; Home Economics
Dist - CORF **Prod** - SCRESC

Mexico - an Introduction 24 MIN
U-matic / VHS / 16mm
Color (I J)
Presents a view of a rapidly changing nation. Explains that Mexico is emerging as a strong nation because of its oil reserves and it is important for people in the United States to understand Mexico better.
Geography - World; Sociology
Dist - PHENIX **Prod** - PHENIX 1982

Mexico and the U S - Ambivalent Allies 30 MIN
VHS
World Beat - Great Decisions In Foreign Policy Series
Color (G)
$39.95 purchase _ #WDBT - 103
Examines issues that concern both the U S and Mexico. Considers the two nation's economic ties and common problems, which include drugs, debt, trade and immigration.
Business and Economics; Civics and Political Systems
Dist - PBS **Prod** - WETATV 1988

Mexico Before Cortez 14 MIN
16mm / U-matic / VHS
Color (I)
LC 72-700516
Uses the art and architecture of the Aztecs, Zapotecs, Mixtecs and Toltecs, combined with the murals of the modern Mexican artist, Diego Rivera, to reconstruct a picture of the life of the original inhabitants of the Americas.
History - World
Dist - AIMS **Prod** - HP 1972

Mexico City 3 MIN
16mm
Of all Things Series
Color (P I)
Discusses Mexico City, Mexico.
Geography - World
Dist - AVED **Prod** - BAILYL

Mexico City 20 MIN
16mm
Color (J)
Depicts art objects and architectural interiors and exteriors of Mexico City. Shows the progress that has been made in the city since the turn of the century.
Geography - World; Psychology; Social Science; Sociology
Dist - AVED **Prod** - BARONA 1957

Mexico City - Ole) 20 MIN
U-matic / VHS
Color (J)
LC 82-706774
Takes viewers to Mexico City and shows the bullfights, modern squares, buildings, streets and monuments. Visits the opera house and catches some of the city's old - world traditions.
Geography - World; History - World
Dist - AWSS **Prod** - AWSS 1980

Mexico earthquake, September 19, 1985 20 MIN
VHS
Color (J H C)
$24.95 purchase _ #IV182
Witnesses the devasation caused by the 1985 earthquake in Mexico City. Reveals that more than 400 buildings collapsed and another 700 buildings were seriously damaged. Uses aftermath cinematography and computer graphics to illustrate the failure of beam - to - column joint, 'slab punching,' the 'hammering' effect; and shows that slab shear failures accounted for 30 percent of the damage. Provokes questions about the probability of similar earthquake damage in the United States and how structures can be designed to withstand earthquake forces.
History - World
Dist - INSTRU **Prod** - USNBOS 1985

Mexico, England, Utah 27 MIN
16mm
Big Blue Marble - Children Around the World Series Program S; Program S
Color (P I)
LC 76-700631
Presents the sporting activities of children in Mexico, England and Utah. Retells a Greek folk tale about the gods who live on Mount Olympus.
Geography - United States; Geography - World; Literature and Drama; Social Science
Dist - VITT **Prod** - ALVEN 1975

Mexico - for sale
VHS
Color (G)
$39.95 purchase
Examines the Mexican perspective on free trade. Documents opposition to a trade pact from the PRI, academia, labor and the PRD. Produced by Dermot Belgley and Carla Fountain.
Business and Economics; Geography - World
Dist - MEXLIB

Mexico - Four Views 15 MIN
U-matic / VHS / 16mm
Color (I J H)
LC 74-703518
Revised edition of the 1955 film Mexico - Geography Of The Americas. Takes a look at Mexico through the eyes of four of its people, a farmer, a truck driver, a teacher and a housing contractor.
Geography - World; Social Science
Dist - CORF **Prod** - CORF 1975

Mexico - giant of Latin America 22 MIN
VHS
Color; PAL (P I J H)
Looks at the economic development of Mexico during the 1970s. Considers the effects of foreign capital, urbanization, agricultural revolution, expanded educational facilities and efficient system of mass transportation against the background of political aspirations and traditional culture.
Geography - World; History - World; Sociology
Dist - VIEWTH **Prod** - VIEWTH

Mexico - Giant of Latin America 23 MIN
U-matic / VHS / 16mm
Color (I J H C)
LC 70-713129
Portrays the geography, people, history, agriculture, industry, education and art of Mexico. Discusses the blend of Indian and hispanic culture, the economic boom and the one party democracy in Mexico.
Agriculture; Business and Economics; Geography - World; Social Science; Sociology
Dist - LUF **Prod** - LEMONT 1971

Mexico in the 70's - a City Family 18 MIN
16mm / U-matic / VHS
B&W (I J H)
LC 76-712712
Discusses how the fast growing industrial economy of Mexico is affecting the life style of its people. Takes a look at a family from Mexico City to show the traditional and family culture and the increased economic well - being which has accompanied Mexico's industrialization.
Geography - World; Psychology; Social Science
Dist - PHENIX **Prod** - GARDON 1971

Mexico in the 70's - Heritage and Progress 12 MIN
U-matic / VHS / 16mm
Color (I J H)
LC 72-712711
Examines Mexico's blend of old and new through the eyes of a farmer, a butcher and an architect. Explains how the National Museum of Anthropology symbolizes the Mexican's unique ability to blend centuries of tradition with modern technology.
History - World; Sociology
Dist - PHENIX **Prod** - GARDON 1971

Mexico - journey to the sun 60 MIN
VHS
Central and South American collection series
Color (J H C G)
$29.95 purchase _ #IVN558V-S
Teaches about the people, culture and history of Mexico. Visits historic buildings, monuments and landmarks. Examines the physical topography of the coutry. Part of a three-part series on Central and South America. Also part of a larger series entitled Video Visits that travels to six continents.
Geography - World; History - World
Dist - CAMV **Prod** - WNETTV

Mexico - Land in the Sun 20 MIN
U-matic / VHS
Color (J)
LC 82-706775
Visits Mexico, including the beaches and restaurants of Puerto Vallarta, Acapulco, Mazatlan, Guadalajara, Cozumel, Cuernavaca and the coastline of Baja California.
Geography - World; History - World; Home Economics; Sociology
Dist - AWSS **Prod** - AWSS 1980

Mexico - Land of Contrast 3 MIN
16mm
Of all Things Series
Color (P I)
Discusses the country of Mexico.
Geography - World
Dist - AVED **Prod** - BAILYL

Mexico - Land of Paradox 30 MIN
U-matic
Countries and Peoples Series
Color (H C)
Gives a portrait of Mexico as a mature, stable, progressive country with a rich heritage and a promising future.
Geography - World; History - World
Dist - TVOTAR **Prod** - TVOTAR 1982

Mexico - Land of Paradox 29 MIN
VHS / 16mm
Countries and Peoples Series
Color (H C G)
$90.00 purchase _ #BPN128128
Depicts Mexico as a mature, stable, progressive country with a rich heritage and a promising future. Discusses current issues such as overpopulation, vast poverty in a land of plenty, and utilization of the country's extensive oil reserves.
Geography - World; History - World
Dist - RMIBHF **Prod** - RMIBHF

Mexico Laura 30 MIN
16mm
Color (G)
$50.00 rental
Deals with the eroticism of memory in relation to 'Laura' and Mexico. Presents varying versions of the same material. Visuals are taken from a 1950s travelogue film interspersed with tango music and a voiceover.
Fine Arts; Geography - World; Psychology; Sociology
Dist - CANCIN **Prod** - SONDHE 1984

Mexico - our neighbor to the south 40 MIN
VHS
Color (I J)
$149.95 purchase _ #UL10089_#10089VL
Presents a two - part program which uses the narrative of a Mexican citizen to tell the story of Mexico. Examines the geography of Mexico, natural resources, industries, population problems and hopes for Mexico's future. Includes a brief history of Mexico and looks at the people, arts, festivals and more.
Geography - World; History - World; Sociology
Dist - KNOWUN
UNL

Mexico - Quatro Aspectos 15 MIN
U-matic / VHS / 16mm

Color (I J H) (SPANISH)
A Spanish language version of Mexico - Four Views. Offers four personal views of Mexico, from the eyes of a farmer, a truck driver, a teacher and a housing contractor. Shows the daily life of a farm family, the movement of farmers to Mexico City, the heritage of historic Mexico and construction for the future.
Foreign Language; Geography - World; Sociology
Dist - CORF **Prod** - CORF

Mexico Series
End of an Era - 1982 - 1988 - Pt 3 57 MIN
From boom to bust - 1940 - 1982 - pt 2 57 MIN
Revolution - 1910 - 1940 - Pt 1 57 MIN
Dist - FI

Mexico - the Frozen Revolution 65 MIN
16mm / VHS
Color (G)
$895.00, $595.00 purchase, $100.00 rental
Presents a socio - historical analysis of Mexico. Considers it as a society created by a revolution which failed to live up to its promises. Uses the Mexican Revolution of 1910 - 1917 as the point of reference. Depicts dominant social forces, ideologies and personalities.
Civics and Political Systems; History - United States; History - World
Dist - CNEMAG **Prod** - CNEMAG 1971

Mexico - the Frozen Revolution 5 MIN
U-matic / VHS / 16mm
Captioned; Color (A) (SPANISH (ENGLISH SUBTITLES))
Presents a socio - historical analysis of Mexico in view of continuing poverty and the failed hopes of the 1910 revolution. Spanish dialog with English subtitles.
Civics and Political Systems; Fine Arts; History - World
Dist - CNEMAG **Prod** - TRIFCW 1971

Mexico - the Land and the People 20 MIN
U-matic / VHS / 16mm
Color; B&W (I J H)
Illustrates the contrasts of Mexico between aristocrat and farmer, city and village and the old and new methods in industry and agriculture. Traces the cultural, religious and economic heritage of the people.
Geography - World
Dist - EBEC **Prod** - EBEC

Mexico - the Oil Boom 25 MIN
VHS / U-matic
Color (H C A)
States that the oil reserves of Mexico might prove greater than those of Saudi Arabia. Reviews the impact of oil on the Mexican people and charts the potential for the future.
Geography - World; Social Science
Dist - JOU **Prod** - UPI

Mexico Vivo 120 MIN
VHS
Color (S) (SPANISH SPANISH (ENGLISH SUBTITLES))
$535.00 purchase
Teaches Latin - American Spanish, its vocabulary, structure and context. Introduces various aspects of Mexican life and culture, from modern dance to the Mexican revolution, from life in the world's largest city to the problems of Mexico's indigenous groups. The five - part video series is based on authentic material specifically recorded in Mexico. Available with or without subtitles.
Foreign Language; Geography - World; History - World; Social Science
Dist - FI **Prod** - BBCTV 1990

Mexico Y Sus Contornos 20 MIN
16mm / U-matic / VHS
Color (H C) (SPANISH)
Revised edition of 'MEXICO CIUDAD ENCANTADORA.' Begins with an illustrated sequence on the origin of Mexico city and continues with views of the city and its environs. Includes a sequence on the bull fight.
Foreign Language
Dist - IFB **Prod** - IFB 1958

Mexico - yesterday and today
VHS
Color (P I J)
$55.00 purchase _ #5490VD
Looks at the history of Mexico and the problems and challenges the country faces in the early 1990s. Focuses on Mexico's relationship with the United States at a time when that relationship is undergoing major changes. Includes a teacher's guide.
Civics and Political Systems; Geography - World; History - World
Dist - KNOWUN **Prod** - KNOWUN 1993

Mexico's beach resorts 55 MIN
VHS
Color (G)
$29.95 purchase _ #S01479
Presents the Mexican beach resorts of Ixtapa, Acapulco and Cancun. Gives advice on how to get to the resorts, where to stay, what to do, and more.
Geography - World; History - World
Dist - UILL **Prod** - RMNC

Mexico's History 16 MIN
16mm / U-matic / VHS
Color (I J H)
LC FIA68-3172
Presents the history of Mexico within the framework of four great events, including the Spanish conquest of the Indians in 1519, the revolt against Spain in 1810, the Juarez revolt of 1857 and the social revolution of 1910.
Geography - World; History - World
Dist - CORF **Prod** - CORF 1969

Mexico's Sea of Cortes
16mm
Color (I)
LC FIA61-807
Presents a travel - documentary about the Gulf of California and the major ports on or near it. Emphasizes the wonderful fishing found near the gulf.
Geography - World; Physical Education and Recreation
Dist - CLI **Prod** - CLI 1959

Mezzo the musical mouse 15 MIN
U-matic / VHS
Music machine series
Color (P)
Discusses the concepts of high and low tones.
Fine Arts
Dist - GPN **Prod** - INDIPS 1981

Mgodo 1973 Series
The Mgodo Wa Mbanguzi, 1973 53 MIN
The Mgodo Wa Mkandeni, 1973 48 MIN
Dist - PSU

The Mgodo Wa Mbanguzi, 1973 53 MIN
U-matic / VHS
Mgodo 1973 Series
Color
Fine Arts; Geography - World
Dist - PSU **Prod** - PSU

The Mgodo Wa Mkandeni, 1973 48 MIN
VHS / U-matic
Mgodo 1973 Series
Color
Fine Arts; Geography - World
Dist - PSU **Prod** - PSU

Mi Amor Disperato 7 MIN
16mm
Color
LC 78-701561
Presents a spoof of Italian movies. Shows a protagonist reflecting on his sorrowful past as he mourns his lost and desperate love for a beautiful woman.
Fine Arts; Literature and Drama
Dist - KRUNIC **Prod** - KRUNIC 1978

Mi Casa Es Su Casa - 23 15 MIN
VHS
Amigos Series
Color (K) (SPANISH)
$125.00 purchase
Enables teachers with no knowledge of Spanish to introduce basic words to children in kindergarten through second grade. Uses simple concepts and music and features Perro Pepe, a six - foot orange dog, and Senorita Fernandez as instructors. Promotes awareness of and appreciation for Hispanic culture and sparks interest in the geography of Spanish - speaking countries. Part 23 is entitled 'Mi Casa Es Su Casa.'.
Foreign Language; Geography - World
Dist - AITECH

Mi Familia 15 MIN
VHS / U-matic
Saludos
(P I G) (ENGLISH AND SPANISH)
$130 purchase, $25 rental, $75 self dub
Designed to introduce Spanish to the English speaking student at primary through intermediate levels. Third in a 25 part series.
Foreign Language
Dist - GPN

Mi Mi, the Lazy Kitten 22 MIN
VHS / 16mm
Chinese Animations Series
Color (K)
Tells the story of Mi Mi, the prettiest cat in the village, but lazy with a house filled with mischievous mice. Created by He Yumen of the People's Republic of China.
Fine Arts; Geography - World; History - United States; Literature and Drama
Dist - LUF **Prod** - SAFS

Mi vida - The Three worlds of Maria Gutierrez 28 MIN
VHS / 16mm
Color; Open captioned (J H) (ENGLISH W/OPEN CAPTIONS)
Features Maria Gutierrez who tells how, against great odds, she crossed two worlds into the life of a college student. Recounts her life as the daughter of migrant farmworkers raised in rural Mexico; joining her family in Central Valley, California and living in a substandard labor camp infested with vermin. Beginning school at 14, she learned to speak English in 6 months and later won a Migrant Scholarship to the Univ of Calif. Follows Maria visiting relatives in Mexico; attending classes; counseling young people about the importance of education. Studying languages, politics and international economics, she hopes to work for the UN as an ambassador to a Latin American country. Produced and directed by Mark Schwartz and Geoffrey Dunn.
Education; Fine Arts; Psychology; Sociology
Dist - CHIPTA

Miami - a Snowman's Holiday 14 MIN
16mm
B&W
Portrays the fantasy journey of Mr and Mrs Snowman who succumb to the irresistible lure of a magical Miami vacation and who venture from snow - bound northern New England to a fatal, for snowpeople, sunswept Miami Beach.
Geography - United States
Dist - MIMET **Prod** - MIMET

Miami - Havana 60 MIN
VHS
Color (G) (ENGLISH & SPANISH W/ENG SUBTITLES)
$295.00 purchase, $95.00 rental
Portrays emotional family reunions at the Miami and Havana airports. Analyzes the painful effects of the long rupture in US - Cuban relations. Official policy has not only separated loved ones physically but has engendered heated ideological schisms revealed in interviews with members of the Cuban - American community in Miami and the residents of Havana. Miami immigrants have found the American Dream impossible to realize and express regret for leaving their Cuban homeland. Right - wing, anti - Castro organizations uphold the American blockade of the island and conflict with groups arguing for the end of sanctions and an opening of relations with Cuba. Produced by Sandy Balfour, Julio Alom; a Double Exposure - TV Latina coproduction.
Civics and Political Systems; Fine Arts; History - United States; History - World; Sociology
Dist - CNEMAG

Miami is for You 14 MIN
16mm
Color
Stresses the variety of events and attractions available to visitors throughout the year in Miami and why the area is an ideal place for a convention.
Geography - United States; Sociology
Dist - MIMET **Prod** - MIMET

Miami University
VHS
Campus clips series
Color (H C A)
$29.95 purchase _ #CC0086V
Takes a video visit to the campus of Miami University in Ohio. Shows many of the distinctive features of the campus, and interviews students about their experiences. Provides information on the composition of the student body, professors, academics, social life, housing, and other subjects.
Education
Dist - CAMV

Miao Year 61 MIN
U-matic / VHS / 16mm
Color (C A)
LC 70-709342
Presents the life of the Blue Miao of Northern Thailand. Covers a full year in the life of these people and deals with the subject of poppy cultivation and efforts to eliminate this crop.
Geography - World; Sociology
Dist - MGHT **Prod** - GEDDES 1970

Miao Year, Pt 1 30 MIN
U-matic / VHS / 16mm
Color (C A)
Presents the life of the Blue Miao of Northern Thailand. Covers a full year in the life of these people and deals with the subject of poppy cultivation and efforts to eliminate this crop.
Geography - World; Sociology
Dist - MGHT **Prod** - GEDDES 1970

Miao Year, Pt 2 31 MIN
16mm / U-matic / VHS
Color (C A)
Presents the life of the Blue Miao of Northern Thailand. Covers a full year in the life of these people and deals with the subject of poppy cultivation and efforts to eliminate this crop.
Geography - World; Sociology
Dist - MGHT **Prod** - GEDDES 1970

Mica Industry 11 MIN
16mm
B&W (J)
Explains that India supplies 80 percent of the world's requirements of mica, which is being increasingly used in the manufacture of industrial appliances. Introduces the various stages of production and testing of Mica.
Business and Economics; Science - Physical
Dist - NEDINF **Prod** - INDIA

Micah and Isaiah 30 MIN
U-matic / VHS
True and false prophecy series
Color (A)
Focuses on the messages of Old Testament prophets Micah and Isaiah. Features theologian Dr James A Sanders.
Religion and Philosophy
Dist - ECUFLM **Prod** - UMCOM 1982

The Micawber Equation 25 MIN
U-matic / VHS / 16mm
Finance for Managers Series
Color (A)
LC 81-701632
Dramatizes how a hi - fi equipment company averts disaster when sales of their best - selling equipment drop. Designed to promote discussion of general financial principles and specific problems related to roles of managers and the development of supporting skills and attitudes.
Business and Economics
Dist - IFB **Prod** - LOYDSB 1980

Mice and How they Live 11 MIN
16mm / U-matic / VHS
Color (P I) (SPANISH)
LC 71-703537
Shows mice, their habits and behavior as found in a deserted shack on the desert. Available with or without narration.
Science - Natural
Dist - AIMS **Prod** - CAHILL 1969

Mice are Nice 15 MIN
VHS / U-matic
Picture Book Park Series Green Module; Green module
Color (P)
Presents the children's stories Henry The Uncatchable Mouse by Sidney Simon and Frederick by Leon Lionni. Includes the poem The City Mouse And The Country Mouse by Christina Rossetti.
Literature and Drama
Dist - AITECH **Prod** - WVIZTV 1974

Mice in a mystery 15 MIN
U-matic / VHS
Return to the magic library series
Color (P I)
#362406; LC 91-706557
Presents smooth - talking Sadie McSleuth, who shows up to read 'Red Rocket' by Ian Ritchie. Part of a series that uses puppet mice and live storytellers to encourage students to read the featured story and respond with comments and questions. Includes teacher's guide and five readers.
Literature and Drama; Social Science
Dist - TVOTAR **Prod** - TVOTAR 1990

Mice Twice
VHS / 35mm strip
Caldecotts on Filmstrip Series
Color (K)
$35.00 purchase
Presents a children's story. Part of the Caldecott series.
English Language; Literature and Drama
Dist - PELLER

Michael 9 MIN
16mm
Rebop Series
Color (I J H)
LC 79-700476
Introduces Michael, a 12 - year - old boy who leaves his secluded farm life to undertake a grueling 3,000 - mile bike trip. Tells of the trials and rewards experienced in order to show the conflicts faced by individuals who attempt difficult and unusual undertakings.
Biography; Geography - United States; Guidance and Counseling
Dist - IU **Prod** - WGBHTV 1979

Michael, a Gay Son 27 MIN
16mm
Color (A)
LC 82-700029
Examines the experiences and emotions of homosexuals revealing to their families their chosen life - styles. Follows Michael Collins as he faces this with a peer support group and as he deals with the surfacing issues in a tense family discussion.
Psychology; Sociology
Dist - FLMLIB **Prod** - FLMLIB 1981

Michael - a Mongoloid Child 14 MIN
16mm
B&W (C T)
An intimate study of a mongoloid teenager living on a farm in England. Shows his acceptance by the community, his ordinary family life and his activities.
Psychology; Sociology
Dist - NYU **Prod** - BFI 1961

Michael Amnasan - 10 - 27 - 88
VHS / Cassette
Poetry Center reading series
Color (G)
$15.00, $45.00 purchase _ #828 - 650
Features the experimental writer reading from 5 Fremont at the Poetry Center, San Francisco State University, with an introduction by Robert Gluck.
Literature and Drama
Dist - POETRY **Prod** - POETRY 1988

Michael 'Badhair' Williams Video - Vol I 30 MIN
VHS
Tell Me a Story Series
Color (K)
$19.95 purchase _ #W181 - 051
Features Michael 'Badhair' Williams as storyteller in volume I of two volumes. Includes 'Muts Mag,' 'Old One - Eye' and 'Turkey In The Straw.' Part of an eight - unit series.
Literature and Drama
Dist - UPSTRT **Prod** - UPSTRT

Michael 'Badhair' Williams Video - Vol II 30 MIN
VHS
Tell Me a Story Series
Color (K)
$19.95 purchase _ #W181 - 054
Features Michael 'Badhair' Williams as storyteller in volume II of two volumes. Includes 'Wicked John' and 'Soap, Soap, Soap.' Part of an eight - unit series.
Literature and Drama
Dist - UPSTRT **Prod** - UPSTRT

Michael Brown and Joseph Goldstein - unlocking the secrets of cholesterol 15 MIN
VHS
Nobel prize series - biology
Color (J H C)
$49.00 purchase _ #2321 - SK
Features Michael Brown and Joseph Goldstein, Nobel Prize winners, who share their discoveries of the mechanism by which cholesterol levels are established and maintained in the bloodstream. Shows that there may be a genetic link to cholesterol metabolism. Includes student notebook and teacher resource book, with additional student workbooks available at an extra charge.
Education; History - World; Science - Natural
Dist - SUNCOM

Michael Brownstein - 10 - 8 - 75 37 MIN
VHS / Cassette
Poetry Center reading series
Color (G)
$15.00, $45.00 purchase, $15.00 rental _ #141 - 108
Features the writer reading from his works at the Poetry Center, San Francisco State University, with an introduction by Lewis MacAdams. Includes selections from Brainstorms and Strange Days Ahead.
Literature and Drama
Dist - POETRY **Prod** - POETRY 1975

Michael Caine 29 MIN
Videoreel / VT2
Elliot Norton Reviews II Series
Color
Presents exchanges and arguments between the dean of American theatre critics, Elliot Norton, and Michael Caine.
Fine Arts
Dist - PBS **Prod** - WGBHTV

Michael Card 60 MIN
VHS
Front row concert video series
Color (G R)
$14.95 purchase _ #VCV3108
Features the music of contemporary Christian artist Michael Card. Presented in an acoustic format.
Fine Arts; Guidance and Counseling; Literature and Drama; Religion and Philosophy
Dist - GF

Michael Cardew 29 MIN
VHS / 16mm / U-matic
Color (H C A)
Portrait of master potter Cardew filmed in Cornwall, England shortly before his death in February 1983.
Fine Arts
Dist - CEPRO **Prod** - VDO

Michael Davidson - 4 - 24 - 86 37 MIN
VHS / Cassette
Poetry Center reading series
Color (G)
$15.00, $45.00 purchase, $15.00 rental _ #701 - 567
Features the writer reading his works at the Poetry Center, San Francisco State University, with an introduction by Kathleen Fraser.
Literature and Drama
Dist - POETRY **Prod** - POETRY 1986

Michael Davidson - 4 - 10 - 75 28 MIN
VHS / Cassette
Poetry Center reading series
Color (G)
$15.00, $45.00 purchase, $15.00 rental _ #113 - 87
Features the writer reading his works at the Poetry Center, San Francisco State University, with an introduction by Kathleen Fraser.
Literature and Drama
Dist - POETRY **Prod** - POETRY 1975

Michael Dennis Browne - 2 - 19 - 86 30 MIN
VHS / Cassette
Poetry Center reading series
Color (G)
$15.00, $45.00 purchase, $15.00 rental _ #683 - 560
Features the writer reading from his works at the Poetry Center, San Francisco State University, with an introduction by Frances Phillips.
Literature and Drama
Dist - POETRY **Prod** - POETRY 1986

Michael Gottlieb - 9 - 22 - 83 34 MIN
VHS / Cassette
Poetry Center reading series
Color (G)
$15.00, $45.00 purchase, $15.00 rental _ #549 - 466
Features the writer reading his works, The Test of Time and Hey Taxi, at the Poetry Center, San Francisco State University.
Literature and Drama
Dist - POETRY **Prod** - POETRY 1983

Michael Hall, Sculptor 10 MIN
16mm
Color
LC 80-701242
Features sculptor Michael Hall discussing his work, which centers around large sheets of steel and I - beams.
Fine Arts
Dist - MARXHA **Prod** - MIFA 1980

Michael Jordan's playground
VHS
Color (G)
$19.95 purchase _ #FOX001
Combines footage of Jordan's career with an interview.
Physical Education and Recreation
Dist - SIV

Michael Josephson 30 MIN
VHS
World Of Ideas With Bill Moyers - Season I - series
Color (G)
$39.95 purchase _ #BMWI - 103
Interviews ethicist Michael Josephson, who discusses the importance of ethical standards. Suggests that the 'yuppie' culture of the 1980s was particularly lacking in ethical standards. Theorizes that individual selfishness is the root of many problems.
Business and Economics; Guidance and Counseling; Health and Safety; History - United States; Psychology; Religion and Philosophy; Social Science; Sociology
Dist - PBS

Michael Lax, Industrial Designer 29 MIN
Videoreel / VT2
Design 2000 Series
B&W
Fine Arts; Industrial and Technical Education; Sociology
Dist - PBS **Prod** - WITFTV

Michael McClure - 1 - 22 - 66 47 MIN
VHS / Cassette
NET Outtake series
B&W (G)
$15.00, $125.00 purchase, $15.00 rental _ #191 - 148
Features the writer in the lion house at the San Francisco Zoo, where he roars Ghost Tantra #49 to Tuffy the lion, and on the following day in his apartment, where he reads The Lion Fight; The Roar of Life Insurance; and sections from The Robe and The Mad Club. Discusses hallucinogens, self - consciousness and avoiding fixed categories. Part of a series of films composed of outtakes from the series USA - Poetry, which was produced in 1965 - 66 for National Educational Television, using all retrievable footage to provide rare glimpses of the poets in their own settings. Interviewed by Richard O Moore.
Guidance and Counseling; Literature and Drama; Science - Natural
Dist - POETRY **Prod** - KQEDTV 1966

Michael McClure - 10 - 4 - 87 120 MIN
VHS / Cassette

Poetry Center reading series
Color (G)
#933 - 629
Features the writer reading from his works at the Ruth Witt - Diamant Memorial Reading at the Poetry Center, San Francisco State University. Also includes readings by James Broughton, Robert Duncan, Rosalie Moore, Mark Linenthal, Shirley Taylor, Christy Taylor, Justine Fixel, Lawrence Fixel, Gail Layton, and Stephen Witt - Diamant. Introduction by Frances Phillips. Slides of Ruth Witt - Diamant courtesy of Caryl Mezey. Available for listening purposes only at the Center; not for sale or rent.
Literature and Drama
Dist - POETRY **Prod** - POETRY 1987

Michael Moorcock 40 MIN
VHS
Color (H C G)
$79.00 purchase
Features the writer talking with Colin Greenland about writing books involving moral questions and themes such as the misuse of power. Discusses his work including Byzantium Endures and Mother London.
Literature and Drama
Dist - ROLAND **Prod** - INCART

Michael, My Brother
16mm
Color
Tells the story of a 12 - year - old boy with Down's Syndrome and the difficulties encountered and progress made when he is tutored by his older brother.
Education; Guidance and Counseling; Psychology
Dist - SMTTPG **Prod** - SMTTPG

Michael Porter on competitive strategy 146 MIN
BETA / VHS
Proven strategies for competitive success series
Color; PAL (G)
$2000.00 purchase
Reveals the five forces which drive competition and determine profitability in any industry. Shows how to defend against these forces - or use them. Discusses cost and differentiation strategies within broadly or tightly focused markets. Features Michael Porter.
Business and Economics
Dist - NATTYL **Prod** - HBS 1990

Michael Powell 50 MIN
VHS
Color (H C G)
$79.00 purchase
Features the writer talking with Chris Peachment about writing for movies and about writing autobiography. Discusses his work including The Red Shoes; Black Narcissus; and the autobiographical A Life in Movies.
Fine Arts; Literature and Drama
Dist - ROLAND **Prod** - INCART

Michael Smith - Mike Builds a Shelter 25 MIN
U-matic / VHS
Color
Introduces Mike, a present day anti - hero.
Fine Arts
Dist - ARTINC **Prod** - ARTINC

Michael Stewart, Tommy Walsh and Ronald Dennis 30 MIN
U-matic / VHS
Eye on Dance - Broadway Series
Color
Features members of the original Chorus Line cast as they talk about where they've gone since then. Hosted by Celia Ipiotis.
Fine Arts
Dist - ARCVID **Prod** - ARCVID

Michael Wood on Henry VI - Pt 1 25 MIN
VHS
Shakespeare in perspective series
Color (A)
PdS45 purchase _ Unavailable in USA
Films Michael Wood and his commentary on location and includes extracts of the Shakespeare play Henry IV - part 1. Challenges many of the more traditional interpretations of Shakespeare's works. Part of a series produced between 1978 and 1985.
Literature and Drama
Dist - BBCENE

Michael Wood on Henry VI - Pt 2 25 MIN
VHS
Shakespeare in perspective series
Color (A)
PdS45 purchase _ Unavailable in USA
Films Michael Wood and his commentary on location and includes extracts of the Shakespeare play Henry IV - part 2. Challenges many of the more traditional interpretations of Shakespeare's works. Part of a series produced between 1978 and 1985.
Literature and Drama
Dist - BBCENE

Michael Wood on Henry VI - Pt 3 25 MIN
VHS
Shakespeare in perspective series
Color (A)
PdS45 purchase - Unavailable in USA
Films Michael Wood and his commentary on location and includes extracts of the Shakespeare play Henry IV - part 3. Challenges many of the more traditional interpretations of Shakespeare's works. Part of a series produced between 1978 and 1985. Not available in the United States.
Literature and Drama
Dist - BBCENE

Michaelangelo and His Art 16 MIN
16mm / U-matic / VHS
Color (J H C)
$385, $250 purchase _ #1524
Discusses the life and work of Michaelangelo, showing how his knowledge of the human body influenced his work.
Fine Arts; History - World
Dist - CORF

Michael's First Day 6 MIN
16mm
Exploring Childhood Series
Color (J)
LC 76-701889
Explains that it is the first day at school for both four - year - old Michael and his student helper. Follows the student's efforts to understand Michael's feelings when he becomes unhappy. Focuses on the different ways in which children and older people approach and handle unfamiliar situations.
Education; Psychology
Dist - EDC **Prod** - EDC 1975

Michagan Avenue 7 MIN
16mm
Color (G)
$35.00 rental
Narrates an investigation of two women in time and space to the point where the investigation becomes the narrative. Delves into an analysis of phenomena of perception of movement. Produced by Bette Gordon and James Benning.
Fine Arts
Dist - CANCIN

Michel Ander - Catastrophe 3 MIN
U-matic / VHS
Color
Deals with captivity.
Fine Arts
Dist - ARTINC **Prod** - ARTINC

Michel Ander - Flying Back from Europe 4 MIN
VHS / U-matic
B&W
Deals with captivity.
Fine Arts
Dist - ARTINC **Prod** - ARTINC

Michel Auder - Jesus 55 MIN
VHS / U-matic
Color
Highlights captivity and confession.
Fine Arts
Dist - ARTINC **Prod** - ARTINC

Michel Auder - made for Denise 4 MIN
U-matic / VHS
Color
Highlights confession of the captive.
Fine Arts
Dist - ARTINC **Prod** - ARTINC

Michel Auder - My Love 5 MIN
U-matic / VHS
Color
Deals with confession of the captive.
Fine Arts
Dist - ARTINC **Prod** - ARTINC

Michel Auder - Portrait of Hassan, Portrait of an Island 28 MIN
VHS / U-matic
B&W
Deals with confession and captivity.
Fine Arts
Dist - ARTINC **Prod** - ARTINC

Michel Auder - Seduction of Patrick 43 MIN
VHS / U-matic
Color
Deals with confession of the captive.
Fine Arts
Dist - ARTINC **Prod** - ARTINC

Michel Auder - the Games 28 MIN
U-matic / VHS
Color
Deals with confession of the captive.
Fine Arts
Dist - ARTINC **Prod** - ARTINC

Michel Auder - TV America 24 MIN
U-matic / VHS
Color
Examines confession of the captive.
Fine Arts
Dist - ARTINC **Prod** - ARTINC

Michel Tatu 29 MIN
U-matic
Foreign Assignment - U S a Series
Color
Features an interview with a Washington Correspondent for Le Monde of Paris.
Literature and Drama; Social Science; Sociology
Dist - UMITV **Prod** - UMITV 1978

Michelangelo 29 MIN
U-matic
Meet the Masters Series
B&W
Demonstrates Michelangelo's wet plaster painting technique, the same method the master used to paint the Sistine Chapel ceiling.
Fine Arts
Dist - UMITV **Prod** - UMITV 1966

Michelangelo (1475 - 1564) 65 MIN
16mm
Color
Presents the work of Michelangelo.
Fine Arts
Dist - ROLAND **Prod** - ROLAND

Michelangelo and His Art 16 MIN
U-matic / VHS / 16mm
Color (I)
Traces the life and career of Michelangelo - - sculptor, painter, architect, poet and leading figure of the Italian Renaissance. Among the original works photographed and analyzed are 'DAVID,' 'LA PIETA,' 'MOSES,' THE MEDICI CHAPEL AND 'THE DEPOSITION.'.
Biography; Fine Arts; History - World
Dist - CORF **Prod** - NETHIS 1963

Michelangelo at work 19 MIN
35mm strip / VHS
Color (J H C T A)
$93.00 purchase _ #MB - 909731 - 6, #MB - 909711 - 1
Focuses on the techniques and creative philosophy of Michelangelo.
Fine Arts
Dist - SRA **Prod** - SRA 1990

Michelangelo - the early years 29 MIN
VHS
Color; PAL (J H C G)
PdS29.50 purchase
Follows this remarkable Renaissance artist from his birth in an Italian village in 1475 to his apprenticeship to the painter Domenico Ghirlandajo. Features the Statue of David and the ceiling frecoes of the Sistine Chapel in the Vatican.
Fine Arts; History - World
Dist - EMFVL **Prod** - AIMS

Michelangelo - the Last Giant 67 MIN
16mm / U-matic / VHS
Color
LC FIA66-479
Shows the life, times and work of Michelangelo, and the relationship of the man and his work. Edited from the television program of the same name.
Biography; Fine Arts; History - World
Dist - MGHT **Prod** - NBCTV 1967

Michelangelo - the Last Giant, Pt 1 33 MIN
16mm / U-matic / VHS
Color (H C A)
Shows the life, times and work of Michelangelo, and the relationship of the man and his work. Edited from the television program of the same name.
Fine Arts
Dist - MGHT **Prod** - NBCTV 1967

Michelangelo - the Last Giant, Pt 2 34 MIN
U-matic / VHS / 16mm
Color (H C A)
Shows the life, times and work of Michelangelo, and the relationship of the man and his work. Edited from the television program of the same name.
Fine Arts
Dist - MGHT **Prod** - NBCTV 1967

Michelangelo - the later years 29 MIN
VHS
Color; PAL (J H C G)
PdS29.50 purchase
Follows this remarkable Renaissance artist during the period he worked for the Medici family. Shows that much of his energy was devoted to architecture and writing poetry. Includes St. Peter's Church, the Laurentian Library in Florence, the Medici sculptures and the Last Judgment in the Sistine Chapel.

Fine Arts; History - World
Dist - EMFVL **Prod** - AIMS

Michelangelo - the Medici Chapel 22 MIN
16mm
Treasures of Tuscany Series
Color (C)
LC FIA64-741
Examines the sculpture of Michelangelo in the new sacristy of the Basilica of San Lorenzo in Florence.
Fine Arts
Dist - RADIM **Prod** - WESTCB 1964

Michele Delgado and Kate Wojciechowski 30 MIN
VHS / U-matic
Somebody else's place series
Captioned (J H)
$65.00 purchase, $25.00 five day rental
Uses dramatization of a visit between two young people of different backgrounds to encourage appreciation of ethnic and geographic diversity. Ninth in a 12 part series.
Sociology
Dist - GPN **Prod** - SWCETV 1982

Michele Lee 1 MIN
VHS / U-matic
ADL celebrity spot series
Color (G)
$15.00 purchase _ #PPF - 637
Stars Michele Lee of 'Knot's Landing' who thinks that everyone should look deep within themselves to conquer their fears of people who are different. Part of a series against prejudice starring celebrities.
Sociology
Dist - ADL **Prod** - ADL

Michele Mouton Explains Rallying 30 MIN
VHS
Color; Stereo (G)
$19.98 purchase _ #TT8029
Features the world's top driving team as it challenges the most demanding racing and driving tests.
Literature and Drama; Physical Education and Recreation
Dist - TWINTO **Prod** - TWINTO 1990

Michele Roberts 39 MIN
VHS
Color (H C G)
$79.00 purchase
Features the writer talking with Giuliana Schiavi about drawing inspiration and ideas from other writers and from one's own life experiences. Discusses her work including The Wild Girl; A Piece of the Night; and The Book of Mrs Noah.
Literature and Drama
Dist - ROLAND **Prod** - INCART

Michelle at Home (Hi, Daddy) 10 MIN
16mm
Exploring Childhood Series
Color (J)
LC 76-701890
Demonstrates different family situations. Follows the family of a four - year - old girl through one afternoon showing her mother, father and her five - year - old brother.
Guidance and Counseling; Sociology
Dist - EDC **Prod** - EDC 1975

Michelle Cliff - 4 - 13 - 85 72 MIN
VHS / Cassette
Color (G)
$15.00, $45.00 purchase, $15.00 rental _ #640 - 535
Features the writer participating in a panel discussion on Women Writers and Literary Form during the Women Working in Literature conference at the Poetry Center, San Francisco State University.
Literature and Drama; Sociology
Dist - POETRY **Prod** - POETRY 1985

Michelle Cliff - 10 - 9 - 86 39 MIN
VHS / Cassette
Poetry Center reading series
Color (G)
$15.00, $45.00 purchase, $15.00 rental _ #714 - 575
Features the writer at the Poetry Center at San Francisco State University, reading from No Telephone To Heaven, with an introduction by Frances Phillips.
Literature and Drama
Dist - POETRY **Prod** - POETRY 1986

Michelob basic sailing instruction
VHS
Color (G A)
$24.80 purchase _ #0222
Teaches sailing to the novice sailor. Covers apparent wind, sail trim, safety and rules. Features Gary Jobson.
Health and Safety; Physical Education and Recreation
Dist - SEVVID **Prod** - MICLOB

Michelson Interferometer L - 4 3 MIN
16mm
Single - Concept Films in Physics Series
Color (H C)
Illustrates the adjustment of mirrors, monochromatic and white - light fringes, and displacement of fringes by insertion of thin film. Shows the Mach - zehnder interferometer.
Science; Science - Physical
Dist - OSUMPD **Prod** - OSUMPD 1963

The Michelson - Morley experiment - the Lorentz transformation - Parts 41 and 42 60 MIN
VHS / U-matic
Mechanical universe...and beyond - Part II series
Color (G)
$45.00, $29.95 purchase
Chronicles the most brilliant failure in scientific history, the Michelson - Morley experiment to measure earth's motion through the aether in Part 41. Observes that if the speed of light is to be the same for all observers, then the length of a meter stick, or the rate of a ticking clock, depends upon who measures it in Part 42. Parts of a 52 - part series on the mechanics of the universe.
Science; Science - Physical
Dist - ANNCPB **Prod** - SCCON 1985

Michigan 60 MIN
VHS
Portrait of America series
Color (J H C G)
$99.95 purchase _ #AMB22V
Visits Michigan. Offers extensive research into the state's history. Films key locations and presents segments on history, government, education, folklore, science, journalism, sociology, industry, agriculture and business. Shows what is unique about Michigan and distinctive about its regional culture and how it got to be that way. Includes study guide. Part of a 50 - part series.
Geography - United States; History - United States
Dist - CAMV

Michigan Perinatal Education, Instructional Unit B - Respiratory Distress Series
Initial Management of Respiratory Distress 12 MIN
Respiratory Distress Syndrome 15 MIN
Dist - UMICH

Michigan perinatal education _ Instructional Unit B - respiratory distress series
Clinical assessment of gestational age - Dubowitz method 17 MIN
Respiratory distress - clinical identification 15 MIN
Dist - UMICH

Michigan Perinatal Education, Instructional Unit C - Resuscitation Series
Emergency Care of the Newborn 19 MIN
Resuscitation - Bag and Mask Technique 15 MIN
Dist - UMICH

Michigan Perinatal Education, Instructional Unit D - Supportive Care Series
Gavage Technique 18 MIN
Intravenous Therapy, Pt 1 12 MIN
Dist - UMICH

Michigan perinatal education, instructional Unit F - blood gas studies series
Blood gas sampling 11 MIN
Dist - UMICH

Michigan State
VHS
Campus clips series
Color (H C A)
$29.95 purchase _ #CC0063V
Takes a video visit to the campus of Michigan State University. Shows many of the distinctive features of the campus, and interviews students about their experiences. Provides information on the composition of the student body, professors, academics, social life, housing, and other subjects.
Education
Dist - CAMV

Michigan State University Jazz Ensemble 29 MIN
Videoreel / VT2
People in Jazz Series
Color (G)
$55.00 rental _ #PIEJ - 106
Presents the music of the Michigan State University Jazz Ensemble. Features host Jim Rockwell interviewing band members.
Fine Arts
Dist - PBS **Prod** - WTVSTV

Michigan Year 28 MIN
16mm
Color
A fast paced tour of Michigan in which the beauty of the four seasons are shown as well as places of interest like Hollands Tulip Festival, Interlockens Music Camp, Traverse Citys Cherry Festival, and Dunes of the Upper Penninsula. Art fair at Ann Arbor, plus winter and summer sports.
Geography - United States
Dist - CONPOW **Prod** - CONPOW

Mick and the Moon 20 MIN
16mm
Color
LC 80-700824
Shows how the art of the Desert Nomads of Central Australia took the form of elaborate body decorations and sand mosaics painted with ochre on the ground. Tells how this art form evolved into many graphic symbols for various desert motifs and has now been transposed onto hardboard using acrylic and poster paints.
Fine Arts; Geography - World; Sociology
Dist - TASCOR **Prod** - BARDON 1978

Mickey 61 MIN
Videoreel / VT2
Toys that Grew Up II Series
Color
Fine Arts
Dist - PBS **Prod** - WTTWTV

Mickey Mantle 20 MIN
16mm
Sports Legends Series
Color (I J)
Presents Mickey Mantle talking about his boyhood in Oklahoma, how he signed a contract with the Yankees right out of high school and reviews film footage of many of the great moments in his playing days.
Biography; Physical Education and Recreation
Dist - COUNFI **Prod** - COUNFI

Mickey Mouse - safety belt expert 16 MIN
VHS / U-matic / 16mm
Color (P I J G)
$400.00, $280.00 purchase _ #JC - 67116
Witnesses the case of Mrs Horn, on trial for not wearing a safety belt. Stars Mickey Mouse as the judge and his safety clubhouse is the courtroom, where children present evidence in favor of safety belts. Demonstrates the proper way to wear a safety belt and shows a number of people buckling up. Includes music and animation.
Health and Safety; Industrial and Technical Education
Dist - CORF **Prod** - DISNEY 1988

Mickey Mouse - the early years series
The Band concert 8 MIN
Steamboat Willie 8 MIN
Thru the Mirror 8 MIN
Dist - CORF

Mickey Thompson's Off - Road Warriors 85 MIN
VHS
Color; Stereo (G)
$39.98 purchase _ #TT8020
Presents the sport of off - roading in Baja and beyond.
Literature and Drama; Physical Education and Recreation
Dist - TWINTO **Prod** - TWINTO 1990

Mickey's Christmas Carol 26 MIN
U-matic / VHS / 16mm
Color
Presents an adaptation of Charles Dickens' story A Christmas Carol with Mickey Mouse as overworked, underpaid Bob Cratchit and Scrooge McDuck as Ebenezer Scrooge.
Fine Arts; Literature and Drama; Social Science
Dist - CORF **Prod** - DISNEY 1983

Mickey's field trips series
Mickey's field trips - the United Nations 16 MIN
Dist - CORF

Mickey's field trips - the United Nations 16 MIN
U-matic / 16mm / VHS
Mickey's field trips series
Color (P)
$425.00, $280.00 purchase _ #JC - 67252
Visits the United Nations in New York City with Mickey Mouse and two children. Features several real tour guides from different countries who show them around the United Nations, explaining what the organization does. Looks at the flags from the 159 member countries, tours the Security Council and meets interpreters for each one of the six official languages of the UN - French, Spanish, Russian, English, Arabic and Chinese.
Civics and Political Systems; History - World
Dist - CORF **Prod** - DISNEY 1989

Mickey's safety club series
Halloween surprises 13 MIN
Playground fun 20 MIN
Street safe, street smart 13 MIN
What to do at home 16 MIN
Dist - CORF

Mickey's Trailer 8 MIN
U-matic / VHS / 16mm
Gang's all Here Series
Color
Portrays what happens when Goofy leaves a trailer driverless when he is called back to eat breakfast.
Fine Arts
Dist - CORF **Prod** - DISNEY

Micmac Scale Basket - Plateau De Balance Micmac En Vannerie 12 MIN
16mm
Color (G) (FRENCH)
#2X82 I
Discusses how the Micmac Indians of Canada have been making splint baskets out of black ash for hundreds of years. Illustrates the work of Rita and Noel Michael of Shubenacadie who have created many different styles to suit various needs. Demonstrates the procedure for making the basket.
Fine Arts; Social Science
Dist - CDIAND **Prod** - NAIFL 1977

Mico Video Learning Systems Series
DBase III
Dist - CAMV

Micor Video Learning Systems Series
Lotus 1 - 2 - 3
Dist - CAMV

Micro 70 23 MIN
16mm
Color
LC 75-700081
Shows the role of the microscope in modern technology and provides instruction in its use.
Science
Dist - BLSOPD **Prod** - BLSOPD 1974

Micro - Dermagrafting Procedure 10 MIN
16mm
Color (PRO)
LC FIA66-55
Illustrates the use of the meek - wall microdermatome in the treatment of patients with severe, extensive burns where there is a need to cover a large area of burn with a small amount of donor skin. Details the technique and the results.
Health and Safety; Science
Dist - EATONL **Prod** - EATONL 1963

Micro - Electronics 25 MIN
U-matic / VHS
Technical Studies Series
Color (H C A)
Discusses aspects of micro - electronics.
Industrial and Technical Education
Dist - FI **Prod** - BBCTV 1981

Micro Guide to Careers Series
Micro Guide to Careers Set Living with AIDS 24 MIN
Dist - CADESF

Micro Guide to Careers Set Living with AIDS 24 MIN
16mm / Software / VHS
Micro Guide to Careers Series
(H C A J H C G)
#MGS 126 $65 3 Day 16mm/3/4
Features an inventory profile that encourages students to compare their interests with those of a typical worker in nursing, teaching, counseling, liberal arts, self - employment, sales, fashion, office occupations, and high tech careers. Comes with eight disks and a manual. Chronicles the last six weeks in the life of 22 - year - old Todd Coleman, illustrating the agony of those afflicted with AIDS and those who must stand by helplessly and watch them die. Features interviews with Todd, his lover, his nurse, his social worker, and his hospice volunteers, showing the community support and unconditional love that Todd recieved as he grew weaker and less able to care for himself.
Guidance and Counseling; Health and Safety; Sociology
Dist - CADESF **Prod** - CADESF

The Micro - life resource - bacteria, flagellates, amoebas - Part I 26 MIN
VHS / BETA
Micro - life resource series
Color; PAL (J H C)
PdS58
Shows the behavior and ecological interactions of microorganisms. Discusses the Kingdoms of micro - life and focuses on bacteria, cyanobacteria, flagellates, euglena, termite sybionts, volvox and amoeba and heliozoans. Part one of two parts on species of microrganisms and part of a three - part series on micro - life.
Science - Natural
Dist - VIEWTH

The Micro - life resource - ciliates, algae, water molds - Part II 26 MIN
VHS / BETA
Micro - life resource series
Color; PAL (J H C)
PdS58
Shows the behavior and ecological interactions of microorganisms. Discusses the ecological niches of ciliates. Looks at paramedium, vorticella, the giant ciliates, micro algae and water molds. Part two of two parts on species of microorganisms and part of a three - part series on micro - life.
Science - Natural
Dist - VIEWTH

The Micro - life resource - Parts 1 - 2 26 MIN
VHS
Real time video micrography series
Color (I J H G)
$59.95 purchase _ #BV102
Offers full - motion segments on bacteria, cyanobacteria, kingdoms of micro - life, flagellates, euglena, termite symbionts, volvox, amoeba and heliozoans. Part of a nine - part series on the behavior and interactions of microorganisms.
Science - Natural
Dist - ENVIMC **Prod** - BIOMED 1991

The Micro - life resource - Parts 2 - 3 26 MIN
VHS
Real time video micrography series
Color (I J H G)
$59.95 purchase _ #BV103
Offers full - motion segments on ciliates, the ecological niches of ciliates, paramecia, vorticella, the giant ciliates, micro - algae and water molds. Part of a nine - part series on the behavior and interactions of microorganisms.
Science - Natural
Dist - ENVIMC **Prod** - BIOMED 1991

Micro - life resource series
Imaging a hidden world - microscopy and videomicroscopy 14 MIN
The Micro - life resource - bacteria, flagellates, amoebas - Part I 26 MIN
The Micro - life resource - ciliates, algae, water molds - Part II 26 MIN
Dist - VIEWTH

Micro moppets series
Communicating instructions to the computer 15 MIN
Computer - related terminology 15 MIN
History and Development of Computers 15 MIN
Use of the Computer as a Tool 15 MIN
Dist - GPN

Micro Moppets
Computer - related careers 15 MIN
History and Development of Computers 15 MIN
Dist - GPN

Micro - organisms 30 MIN
U-matic
Aspects of Ecology Series
(H)
Explores the microbiology of a freshwater stream, soil microbiology, nitrogen fixation and giardiasis.
Science - Natural
Dist - ACCESS **Prod** - ACCESS 1984

Micro Organisms - Beneficial Activities 14 MIN
16mm
Color (J H C G)
Uses microscope, live photography and animation to show ways in which micro organisms benefit mankind. Shows the nitrogen cycle, bacteria in sewage treatment, antibiotics, productions of useful chemicals and bacteria yeast in food production.
Science - Natural
Dist - VIEWTH **Prod** - GATEEF

Micro Organisms - Harmful Activities 16 MIN
16mm
Color (J H C G)
Uses microscope, live photography and animation to show how micro organisms cause disease and undesirable destruction. Deals with control of harmful micro organisms, undesirable activities and disease.
Science - Natural
Dist - VIEWTH **Prod** - GATEEF

The Micro revolution
U-matic / VHS
Audio visual library of computer education series
Color
Explains why silicon chips have become so important and why they are used. Provides a non - technical discussion of the new micro chip technology.
Business and Economics; Mathematics
Dist - PRISPR **Prod** - PRISPR

Micro - Techniques in Serology 8 MIN
16mm
Color (PRO)
LC 74-705139
Demonstrates the use of micro - equipment for performing serologic titration tests. Explains that the method is economical in the use of reagents and time - - it enables one technologist to test 144 Sera against three antigens in an eight hour day.
Science; Science - Natural
Dist - USNAC **Prod** - USPHS

Micro Video Learning System Series
Multi - Mate - Advantage
Dist - CAMV

Micro video learning systems - dBase III plus
VHS
Color (H C A)
$495.00 purchase _ #MV400V
Presents step - by - step instruction in the use of dBase III Plus software. Consists of one videocassette, a workbook, and a data diskette.
Computer Science
Dist - CAMV

Micro video learning systems - dBase IV
VHS
Color (H C A)
$495.00 purchase _ #MV410V
Presents step - by - step instruction in the use of dBase IV software. Consists of one videocassette, a workbook, and a data diskette.
Computer Science
Dist - CAMV

Micro video learning systems - dBase IV advanced
VHS
Color (H C A)
$495.00 purchase _ #MV420V
Presents more advanced step - by - step instruction in the use of dBase IV software. Consists of one videocassette, a workbook, and a data diskette.
Computer Science
Dist - CAMV

Micro video learning systems - IBM PC primer
VHS
Color (H C A)
$295.00 purchase _ #MV100V
Presents step - by - step instruction in the use of IBM PC Primer software. Consists of one videocassette, a workbook, and a data diskette.
Computer Science
Dist - CAMV

Micro video learning systems - Lotus 1 - 2 - 3
VHS
Color (H C A)
$495.00 purchase _ #MV200V
Presents step - by - step instruction in the use of Lotus 1 - 2 - 3 software. Consists of one videocassette, a workbook, and a data diskette.
Computer Science
Dist - CAMV

Micro video learning systems - MultiMate
VHS
Color (H C A)
$495.00 purchase _ #MV700V
Presents step - by - step instruction in the use of MultiMate software. Consists of one videocassette, a workbook, and a data diskette.
Computer Science
Dist - CAMV

Micro video learning systems - Pagemaker 3.0
VHS
Color (H C A)
$495.00 purchase _ #MV800V
Presents step - by - step instruction in the use of Pagemaker 3.0 software. Consists of one videocassette, a workbook, and a data diskette.
Computer Science
Dist - CAMV

Micro Video Learning Systems Series
DBase III Plus
Display - Write 3
IBM PC Primer
Symphony
Dist - CAMV

Micro video learning systems - Symphony
VHS
Color (H C A)

$495.00 purchase _ #MV500V
Presents step - by - step instruction in the use of Symphony software. Consists of one videocassette, a workbook, and a data diskette.
Computer Science
Dist - CAMV

Micro video learning systems - WordPerfect 5 advanced
VHS
Color (H C A)
$495.00 purchase _ #MV910V
Presents advanced step - by - step instruction in the use of WordPerfect 5 software. Consists of one videocassette, a workbook, and a data diskette.
Computer Science
Dist - CAMV

Micro video learning systems - WordPerfect 5 basic
VHS
Color (H C A)
$495.00 purchase _ #MV900V
Presents basic step - by - step instruction in the use of WordPerfect 5 software. Consists of one videocassette, a workbook, and a data diskette.
Computer Science
Dist - CAMV

Microanatomy Laboratory Orientation Series
Anatomy of the adult human tooth 10 MIN
Blood 9 MIN
Bone 9 MIN
Cardiovascular system I 13 MIN
Cardiovascular system II 7 MIN
Cartilage 10 MIN
Connective Tissues Proper 21 MIN
Dentin and pulp cavity 17 MIN
Ear 11 MIN
Enamel 15 MIN
Endocrine System I 6 MIN
Endocrine System II 6 MIN
Endocrine System III 10 MIN
Epithelia and glands 18 MIN
Eye 25 MIN
Female reproductive system I 12 MIN
Female reproductive system II 18 MIN
Gastrointestinal Tract I 21 MIN
Gastrointestinal Tract II 23 MIN
Gastrointestinal Tract III 12 MIN
Hemopoiesis 11 MIN
Integumentary System I 14 MIN
Integumentary System II 8 MIN
Introduction 6 MIN
Introduction to Oral Histology 8 MIN
The Living leukocyte 12 MIN
Lymphoid Organs 12 MIN
Male Reproductive System I 14 MIN
Male Reproductive System II 12 MIN
Maxillary Sinus 4 MIN
Muscle 11 MIN
Nervous Organs 15 MIN
Nervous Tissue - Stains 16 MIN
Nervous Tissue I 18 MIN
Nervous Tissue II 12 MIN
Nervous Tissue III 9 MIN
Odontogenesis - Early 11 MIN
Odontogenesis - Late 12 MIN
Oral Mucosa and Epithelial Attachment 19 MIN
The Palate 19 MIN
Periodontium 25 MIN
Respiratory Tract 11 MIN
Salivary Glands 19 MIN
The Tonsillar Ring 9 MIN
Urinary Tract I 13 MIN
Urinary Tract II 12 MIN
Dist - UOKLAH

Microanatomy of connective tissue proper 35 MIN
U-matic / VHS
Color (C PRO)
$395.00 purchase, $80.00 rental _ #C920 - VI - 035
Assists students in developing the skills needed to identify cells of connective tissue properly. Reviews the various types of connective tissue and examines subdivisions of connective tissue proper. Describes briefly the two methods for mounting slides and views a series of connective proper cells, photographs and drawings with specific cell structures labeled. Presented by Drs James A Hightower and Alice S Pakurar, University of South Carolina, School of Medicine.
Health and Safety; Science - Natural
Dist - HSCIC

Microbes and men series
Outlines the history of modern medicine. Describes the contributions by the pioneers of modern medicine. Covers the period from 1840 to 1900. Includes six episodes which are also available individually.
A germ is life 55 MIN
Dist - BBCENE

Microbes and men
Certain death 55 MIN
Invisible enemy 55 MIN
Men of little faith 55 MIN
Search for the magic bullet 55 MIN
Tuberculin affair 55 MIN
Dist - BBCENE

Microbes, Bacteria and Fungi 17 MIN
16mm / U-matic / VHS
Color (I J)
$50 rental _ #9775
Examined are the physical characteristics, the risky and beneficial applications, and ways to impede and prevent growth of microbes.
Science; Science - Natural
Dist - AIMS **Prod** - SAIF 1985

Microbial sampling of the operating room environment 20 MIN
16mm
AORN film series
Color (PRO)
LC 75-703021
Counsels all personnel concerned with infection control in hospitals of facts concerning microbial sampling of the operating room environment.
Health and Safety
Dist - ACY **Prod** - AORN 1975

Microbial Susceptibility 29 MIN
U-matic / VHS
Color (PRO)
Details the results of a nationwide study of microbial susceptibility.
Health and Safety
Dist - WFP **Prod** - WFP

Microbiological techniques 16 MIN
VHS
Color (J H)
$145.00 purchase _ #A5VH 1008
Demonstrates sterile techniques involved in the inoculation, transfer and growth of microorganisms. Addresses special procedures such as sterile transfers, streak plating, pour plating, serial dilution and pipetting.
Science - Natural
Dist - CLRVUE **Prod** - CLRVUE

Microbiological techniques
VHS
Science laboratory technique series
Color (J H)
$79.95 purchase _ #193 W 2202
Details various sterile techniques used in the inoculation, transfer and growth of microorganisms. Part of a series on laboratory technique, including proper use and handling of equipment, preparation of materials and recording observations. Includes a supplementary teaching guide.
Science
Dist - WARDS **Prod** - WARDS

Microbiology 48 MIN
U-matic / VHS
Color
Includes 48 half - hour videotape lessons on aspects of microbiology.
Science - Natural
Dist - TELSTR **Prod** - TELSTR

The Microbiology of AIDS 10 MIN
VHS
Color (G)
$59.95 purchase _ #UW2530
Examines the destructive effects of the AIDS virus on a microscopic level. Blends state - of - the - art computer graphics with live - action photography made possible by an electron microscope to show the virus in action. Produced in conjunction with the Pasteur Institute.
Health and Safety; Science - Natural; Sociology
Dist - FOTH

Microbiology Series
Classifying microorganisms 15 MIN
Imaging a Hidden World - the Light Microscope 15 MIN
Dist - CORF

Microbiology series
Imagining a hidden world - the light microscope 15 MIN
Dist - CORF
VIEWTH

Microbiology series
Classifying micro - organisms 15 MIN
Dist - VIEWTH

Microbiology teaching series
The Clinical aspects of leprosy 4 MIN
The Life Cycle of the Malaria Parasite 12 MIN
Dist - UCEMC

Microbiology technician 4.5 MIN
VHS / 16mm
Good works 5 series
Color (A PRO)
$40.00 purchase _ #BPN238003
Presents the occupation of a microbiology technician. Gives a profile of a young person who is either undergoing an apprenticeship or has recently completed training in this field. Takes the viewer on a tour of this person's workplace and explains the practical skills and training offered by employers and schools. Gives a better understanding of the demand for skilled workers today and the potential for personal growth.
Guidance and Counseling
Dist - RMIBHF **Prod** - RMIBHF

Microbiology technician 5 MIN
U-matic
Good work series
Color (H)
Provides useful, up to date information on various occupations to aid high school students in career selection. Available in five series of ten jobs each.
Education; Guidance and Counseling; Science - Natural
Dist - TVOTAR **Prod** - TVOTAR 1981

Microchip Technology 60 MIN
VHS / 35mm strip
(J H A IND)
#873XV7
Gives an in - depth explanation of the fundamentals of modern silicon chip technology including design, operation and application. Includes microchip development, manufacturing, identification and applications (4 cassettes). Study Guide included.
Industrial and Technical Education
Dist - BERGL

The Microcomputer - a Tool and a Challenge 34 MIN
U-matic / VHS
Color
Features computer experts John and Barbara McMullen showing friends a typical microcomputer system, including an Apple II with CRT screen, printer, and Visicalic software. Explains the usefulness to business of employing conventional telephone lines to gain access to databases throughout the country.
Industrial and Technical Education
Dist - STURTM **Prod** - STURTM 1982

Microcomputer application series
Computer Business - Microcomputers and Office Automation 29 MIN
Computer Calc - Electronic Spreadsheets and Microcomputers 29 MIN
Computer Careers - Workplace of the Future 29 MIN
Computer Crime - Ethics and Data Security 29 MIN
Computer Images - Computer Graphics 29 MIN
Computer Peripherals - Input, Output and Storage 29 MIN
Computer Sound - Microcomputers and Music 29 MIN
Computer Talk - Microcomputer Communications 29 MIN
Electronic words - word processing and microcomputers 29 MIN
Keeping Track - Database Management and Microcomputers 29 MIN
Dist - AIMS

Microcomputer at School Series Program Three
Planning and Decision Making 3 MIN
Dist - EDCORP

Microcomputer Basic
U-matic / VHS
Microprocessor Video Training Course Series
Color
Industrial and Technical Education
Dist - VTRI **Prod** - VTRI

Microcomputer Basics
VHS / U-matic
Microprocessor Series
Color
Industrial and Technical Education; Mathematics
Dist - HTHZEN **Prod** - HTHZEN

Microcomputer Circuits Explained 64 MIN
VHS / 35mm strip
(G A IND)
#874XV7
Describes system components, the microprocessor, memory and system timing, and input - output and circuit connection (4 tapes). Study Guide included.
Computer Science
Dist - BERGL

Microcomputer Circuits Explained
VHS / 35mm strip

$249.00 purchase _ #BX874 filmstrip, $224.00 purchase _ #BX874V VHS
Discusses system components, microprocessor, memory and system timing, and input - output and circuit connection.
Industrial and Technical Education
Dist - CAREER **Prod** - CAREER

Microcomputer Data Storage Devices - 1 60 TO 90 MIN
VHS
Microcomputer I - O Devices Module Series
Color (PRO)
$600.00 - $1500.00 purchase _ #MCDS1
Covers the concepts of data storage technology. Differentiates between floppy disk and hard disk drives. Part of a six - part series on microcomputer I - O devices. Includes five student guides, five workbooks and an instructor guide.
Computer Science; Education; Industrial and Technical Education; Psychology
Dist - NUSTC **Prod** - NUSTC

Microcomputer Data Storage Devices - 2 60 TO 90 MIN
VHS
Microcomputer I - O Devices Module Series
Color (PRO)
$600.00 - $1500.00 purchase _ #MCDS2
Looks at non - floppy and hard disk drive data storage devices. Describes optical disk drives, RAM disks, bubble memories, ferrite core memories and PROMS. Discusses interfacing between these types of storage devices. Part of a six - part series on microcomputer I - O devices. Includes five student guides, five workbooks and an instructor guide.
Computer Science; Education; Industrial and Technical Education; Psychology
Dist - NUSTC **Prod** - NUSTC

Microcomputer Example 30 MIN
U-matic / VHS
Pascal, Pt 3 - Advanced Pascal Series
Color (H C A)
LC 81-706049
Reviews basics of building parsers by considering a very tiny block - structured programming language for microcomputers. Concludes with demonstration of cross - Pascal compiler for the HP64000 and an example of a recursive function for factorial evaluation.
Industrial and Technical Education; Mathematics; Sociology
Dist - COLOSU **Prod** - COLOSU 1980

Microcomputer I - O Devices Module Series
Microcomputer Data Storage Devices - 1 — 60 TO 90 MIN
Microcomputer Data Storage Devices - 2 — 60 TO 90 MIN
Microcomputer Input Devices — 60 TO 90 MIN
Microcomputer Printing Devices — 60 TO 90 MIN
Microcomputer Visual Display Devices — 60 TO 90 MIN
Troubleshooting Microcomputer I - O Devices — 60 TO 90 MIN
Dist - NUSTC

Microcomputer Input Devices 60 TO 90 MIN
VHS
Microcomputer I - O Devices Module Series
Color (PRO)
$600.00 - $1500.00 purchase _ #MCKEY
Examines input devices used to interface with microcomputers. Looks at keyboards, optical readers, mice, light pens and touch screens. Part of a six - part series on microcomputer I - O devices. Includes five student guides, five workbooks and an instructor guide.
Computer Science; Education; Industrial and Technical Education; Psychology
Dist - NUSTC **Prod** - NUSTC

Microcomputer Manages Information, and some Do's and Don'ts 40 MIN
VHS / U-matic
Color
Features computer experts John and Barbara McMullen acquainting new user Chip Mann with microcomputer applications such as weather forecasting, inventory management, apartment rental indexing and mailing lists. Offers tips on the proper handling of hardware and software using the Apple II as a representative computer.
Industrial and Technical Education
Dist - STURTM **Prod** - STURTM 1982

The Microcomputer Memory 180 MIN
U-matic
Microprocessor Technical Fundamentals Series
Color (IND)
Discusses microcomputer memory partitioning, memory hardware design, and generating addresses in software. Includes RAM, ROM and EPROM devices, interfacing and chip selection circuitry.
Computer Science; Industrial and Technical Education
Dist - INTECS **Prod** - INTECS

Microcomputer memory design series
Advanced memory logic — 30 MIN
Design example of a complete memory system — 30 MIN
Direct Memory Access (DMA) — 30 MIN
Dynamic RAM — 30 MIN
Hierarchical Memories and some Physical Design Considerations — 30 MIN
Magnetic Bubble Memories - MBM — 30 MIN
Memory Array, the and the Decoding Logic of a Memory System — 30 MIN
Memory Technologies, Microcomputer Organization and Operation — 30 MIN
Microprocessor and Memory Timing — 30 MIN
More on Decoding Logic and Data and Address Bus Interfaces — 30 MIN
Semiconductor Memory Devices — 30 MIN
Dist - COLOSU

The Microcomputer Presents and Gathers Information 38 MIN
U-matic / VHS
Color
Features computer experts John and Barbara McMullen demonstrating how the Apple II can present visual comparisons by plotting graphs and by producing charts. Discusses word processing and explains the global search and vocabulary features. Emphasizes that microcomputers competitive with large word processors are available at a reasonable price.
Industrial and Technical Education
Dist - STURTM **Prod** - STURTM 1982

Microcomputer Printing Devices 60 TO 90 MIN
VHS
Microcomputer I - O Devices Module Series
Color (PRO)
$600.00 - $1500.00 purchase _ #MCPD1
Examines printing device functions. Discusses printer classification and their characteristics. Part of a six - part series on microcomputer I - O devices. Includes five student guides, five workbooks and an instructor guide.
Computer Science; Education; Industrial and Technical Education; Psychology
Dist - NUSTC **Prod** - NUSTC

Microcomputer Structure and Operation 180 MIN
U-matic
Microprocessor Technical Fundamentals Series
Color (IND)
Discusses microcomputer hardware, including memory, input - output and buses. Explains software and program fundamentals and describes operation of the microprocessor.
Computer Science; Industrial and Technical Education
Dist - INTECS **Prod** - INTECS

Microcomputer technician 5 MIN
U-matic
Good work series
Color (H)
Provides useful, up to date information on various occupations to aid high school students in career selection. Available in five series of ten jobs each.
Computer Science; Education; Guidance and Counseling
Dist - TVOTAR **Prod** - TVOTAR 1981

Microcomputer Visual Display Devices 60 TO 90 MIN
VHS
Microcomputer I - O Devices Module Series
Color (PRO)
$600.00 - $1500.00 purchase _ #MCMQ1
Introduces visual display devices used with microcomputers. Describes their operation. Part of a six - part series on microcomputer I - O devices. Includes five student guides, five workbooks and an instructor guide.
Computer Science; Education; Industrial and Technical Education; Psychology
Dist - NUSTC **Prod** - NUSTC

The Microcomputer, what it Can do and the Power of Visicalc 23 MIN
U-matic / VHS
Color
Features computer experts John And Barbara McMullen demonstrating to economist Chip Mann the graphics and word processing capabilities of the Apple II system using Visicalc. Shows the McMullens communicating with the databases of Dow Jones, Associated Press, and New York Times, as well as university, legal medical and insurance databases.
Industrial and Technical Education
Dist - STURTM **Prod** - STURTM 1982

Microcomputers
U-matic / VHS
Audio visual library of computer education series
Color
Explains the structure of microcomputers and includes pictures of the very latest equipment. Demonstrates how the different components of a microcomputer contribute to its operation, and location photographs represent the wide variety of devices available.
Business and Economics; Mathematics
Dist - PRISPR **Prod** - PRISPR

Microcomputers 30 MIN
VHS
Computers at work series
Color (H C G)
$150.00 purchase, $50.00 rental _ #37035
Illustrates the significance of the microcomputer in business and personal lives. Discusses the components of a microcomputer system and provides tips for selecting one. Part of a 10 - part series which illustrates the essential concepts of computer systems and their applications, produced by Mitchell Publishing - McGraw - Hill.
Computer Science; Home Economics
Dist - UCEMC

Microcomputers 30 MIN
VHS / U-matic
Making it Count Series
Color (H C A)
LC 80-707581
Describes the characteristics and applications of microcomputers starting with a simplified explanation of logic circuits and going on to describe their integration on small silicon chips. Discusses bus architecture in microcomputers, several types of memory, and the advantages of microcomputer size, price, speed, and capacity to numerous applications.
Business and Economics; Mathematics
Dist - BCSC **Prod** - BCSC 1980

Microcomputers - an Introduction 27 MIN
VHS / 16mm
#109016 - 9 3/4
Provides a basic introduction to microcomputers and explores how they can increase productivity.
Business and Economics; Computer Science
Dist - MGHT

Microcomputers - an Introduction 26 MIN
U-matic / VHS / 16mm
Color (C A)
LC 82-700864
Discusses what a microcomputer is, how it works and how it can be used.
Mathematics
Dist - CRMP **Prod** - ONEPAS 1982

Microcomputers - an Introduction or the Computer and the Crook 15 MIN
U-matic / VHS / 16mm
Simply Scientific Series
Color (K P I)
LC 82-700638
Shows Jeff learning how a microcomputer helps run his cousin's farm, assists in household matters and provides entertainment. Depicts how it can be used to catch a crook.
Guidance and Counseling; Literature and Drama; Mathematics
Dist - LCOA **Prod** - LCOA 1982

Microcomputers and electronic instrumentation - making the right connections 150 MIN
Kit / VHS
Color; PAL (C PRO)
$995.00, $895.00 purchase _ #V - 6000 - 28604, #V - 6001 - 2868X
Offers a sound working knowledge of electronic systems and devices to enhance technical abilities, increase effectiveness and productivity. Includes text of the same title, two videos, lab electronics kit and experiment manual for hands - on experience with key electronic devices, circuits and concepts in the kit. Videos also available separately. Captures real - life measurement and control instrumentation situations and reinforces key instrumentation concepts. Created through the collaboration of Drs Howard Malmstadt, Christie Enke and Stanley Crouch.
Computer Science; Industrial and Technical Education; Science - Physical
Dist - AMCHEM

Microcomputers and hydrologic analysis
Storm water management series; Pt 2
Color (PRO IND VOC)
Demonstrates how to use Apple or IBM microcomputers in conducting hydrologic studies. Uses classroom format in video taping two hours of lectures, and shows how to modify the program to fit local needs.
Industrial and Technical Education; Science - Physical
Dist - AMCEE **Prod** - GATECH

Microcomputers at School Series Program One
Using Microcomputers - an Introduction — 3 MIN
Dist - EDCORP

Microcomputers at School Series Program Two
Computer Literacy - the Fourth R 3 MIN
Dist - EDCORP

Microcomputers for Instruction 29 MIN
VHS / U-matic
On and about Instruction Series
Color (T)
Describes briefly the basics of microcomputer technology and its application in the school.
Education; Mathematics
Dist - GPN **Prod** - VADE 1983

Microcomputers for Learners - Program One 29 MIN
VHS / 16mm
Microcomputers for Learners Series
Color (A PRO)
$200.00 purchase _ #269901
Presents thirteen 30 - minute programs which investigate the role computers play in today's classrooms and educator's thoughts on the potential of the technology. Divides each program into four parts - ideas for educational use of microcomputers, hardware - related topics, basic concepts and a review of an educational software package. Program One introduces vocabulary from the 'new' computer literacy, shows how to put together a computer system, demonstrates 'keyboard technique' and demonstrates a junior high software package.
Computer Science; Industrial and Technical Education; Mathematics; Psychology
Dist - ACCESS **Prod** - ACCESS 1988

Microcomputers for Learners - Program Two 29 MIN
VHS / 16mm
Microcomputers for Learners Series
Color (A PRO)
$200.00 purchase _ #269902
Presents thirteen 30 - minute programs which investigate the role computers play in today's classrooms and educator's thoughts on the potential of the technology. Divides each program into four parts - ideas for educational use of microcomputers, hardware - related topics, basic concepts and a review of an educational software package. Program Two discusses how best to organize the classroom, investigates the disk drive, and features Dr Gene Romaniuk, University of Alberta, who looks at computer memory, and reviews an interactive text - adventure game software for junior high students.
Computer Science; Industrial and Technical Education; Mathematics; Psychology
Dist - ACCESS **Prod** - ACCESS 1988

Microcomputers for Learners - Program Three 29 MIN
VHS / 16mm
Microcomputers for Learners Series
Color (A PRO)
$200.00 purchase _ #269903
Presents thirteen 30 - minute programs which investigate the role computers play in today's classrooms and educator's thoughts on the potential of the technology. Divides each program into four parts - ideas for educational use of microcomputers, hardware - related topics, basic concepts and a review of an educational software package. Program Three visits the Apple Centre for Innovation, looks at the use and care of the 'mouse,' introduces word processing and reviews 'Superkey.'.
Computer Science; Industrial and Technical Education; Mathematics; Psychology
Dist - ACCESS **Prod** - ACCESS 1988

Microcomputers for Learners - Program Four 29 MIN
VHS / 16mm
Microcomputers for Learners Series
Color (A PRO)
$200.00 purchase _ #269904
Presents thirteen 30 - minute programs which investigate the role computers play in today's classrooms and educator's thoughts on the potential of the technology. Divides each program into four parts - ideas for educational use of microcomputers, hardware - related topics, basic concepts and a review of an educational software package. Program Four examines integration of computers into classrooms, highlights various types of computer monitors, discusses computer assisted instruction and reviews 'WordPerfect.'.
Business and Economics; Computer Science; Industrial and Technical Education; Mathematics; Psychology
Dist - ACCESS **Prod** - ACCESS 1988

Microcomputers for Learners - Program Five 29 MIN
VHS / 16mm
Microcomputers for Learners Series
Color (A PRO)
$200.00 purchase _ #269905
Presents thirteen 30 - minute programs which investigate the role computers play in today's classrooms and educator's thoughts on the potential of the technology. Divides each program into four parts - ideas for educational use of microcomputers, hardware - related topics, basic concepts and a review of an educational software package. Program Five shows how to use computers for class chores, looks at the IBM Personal System 2, demonstrates data bases and reviews a telecommunications software program for elementary children.
Computer Science; Industrial and Technical Education; Mathematics; Psychology
Dist - ACCESS **Prod** - ACCESS 1988

Microcomputers for Learners - Program Six 29 MIN
VHS / 16mm
Microcomputers for Learners Series
Color (A PRO)
$200.00 purchase _ #269906
Presents thirteen 30 - minute programs which investigate the role computers play in today's classrooms and educator's thoughts on the potential of the technology. Divides each program into four parts - ideas for educational use of microcomputers, hardware - related topics, basic concepts and a review of an educational software package. Program Six features the IBM Othello Project, presents a variety of printers, Dr Romaniuk explains how to use computers in a classroom, and a teacher reviews 'Mathematics Activities Courseware.'.
Computer Science; Industrial and Technical Education; Mathematics; Psychology
Dist - ACCESS **Prod** - ACCESS 1988

Microcomputers for Learners - Program Seven 29 MIN
VHS / 16mm
Microcomputers for Learners Series
Color (A PRO)
$200.00 purchase _ #269907
Presents thirteen 30 - minute programs which investigate the role computers play in today's classrooms and educator's thoughts on the potential of the technology. Divides each program into four parts - ideas for educational use of microcomputers, hardware - related topics, basic concepts and a review of an educational software package. Program Seven evaluates educational software, demonstrates laser printers and explores disk operating systems. 'Bank Street Writers 3,' an elementary word processor, is reviewed.
Business and Economics; Computer Science; Industrial and Technical Education; Mathematics; Psychology
Dist - ACCESS **Prod** - ACCESS 1988

Microcomputers for Learners - Program Eight 29 MIN
VHS / 16mm
Microcomputers for Learners Series
Color (A PRO)
$200.00 purchase _ #269908
Presents thirteen 30 - minute programs which investigate the role computers play in today's classrooms and educator's thoughts on the potential of the technology. Divides each program into four parts - ideas for educational use of microcomputers, hardware - related topics, basic concepts and a review of an educational software package. Program Eight examines software piracy, shows how one printer can be shared by several computers, looks at spreadsheets and reviews 'The Factory,' a problem solving software.
Computer Science; Industrial and Technical Education; Mathematics; Psychology
Dist - ACCESS **Prod** - ACCESS 1988

Microcomputers for Learners - Program Nine 29 MIN
VHS / 16mm
Microcomputers for Learners Series
Color (A PRO)
$200.00 purchase _ #269909
Presents thirteen 30 - minute programs which investigate the role computers play in today's classrooms and educator's thoughts on the potential of the technology. Divides each program into four parts - ideas for educational use of microcomputers, hardware - related topics, basic concepts and a review of an educational software package. Program Nine tours the Canadian Centre for Learning Systems in Calgary, demonstrates a modem and discusses the available types of telecommunications software. Reviews 'Early Learning Series' published by the Minnesota Educational Computing Corporation.
Computer Science; Industrial and Technical Education; Mathematics; Psychology; Social Science
Dist - ACCESS **Prod** - ACCESS 1988

Microcomputers for Learners - Program Ten 29 MIN
VHS / 16mm
Microcomputers for Learners Series
Color (A PRO)
$200.00 purchase _ #269910
Presents thirteen 30 - minute programs which investigate the role computers play in today's classrooms and educator's thoughts on the potential of the technology. Divides each program into four parts - ideas for educational use of microcomputers, hardware - related topics, basic concepts and a review of an educational software package. Program Ten surveys how computers have been integrated into the classroom and looks at the local area network. Dr Romaniuk demonstrates computer graphics, and 'Kidtalk,' a word processor that talks back designed for elementary students, is reviewed.
Business and Economics; Computer Science; Industrial and Technical Education; Mathematics; Psychology
Dist - ACCESS **Prod** - ACCESS 1988

Microcomputers for Learners - Program Eleven 29 MIN
VHS / 16mm
Microcomputers for Learners Series
Color (A PRO)
$200.00 purchase _ #269911
Presents thirteen 30 - minute programs which investigate the role computers play in today's classrooms and educator's thoughts on the potential of the technology. Divides each program into four parts - ideas for educational use of microcomputers, hardware - related topics, basic concepts and a review of an educational software package. Program Eleven discusses the use of computers for special education, continues the examination of local area networks, introduces the concept of integrated software, and reviews 'The Other Side,' a social studies simulation software.
Computer Science; Industrial and Technical Education; Mathematics; Psychology
Dist - ACCESS **Prod** - ACCESS 1988

Microcomputers for Learners - Program Twelve 29 MIN
VHS / 16mm
Microcomputers for Learners Series
Color (A PRO)
$200.00 purchase _ #269912
Presents thirteen 30 - minute programs which investigate the role computers play in today's classrooms and educator's thoughts on the potential of the technology. Divides each program into four parts - ideas for educational use of microcomputers, hardware - related topics, basic concepts and a review of an educational software package. Program Twelve highlights a joint venture between private industry and the education sector in British Columbia - the Saanich Project. Demonstrates the LCD projection system for computers, considers desktop publishing and reviews 'Appleworks.'.
Business and Economics; Computer Science; Geography - World; Industrial and Technical Education; Mathematics; Psychology
Dist - ACCESS **Prod** - ACCESS 1988

Microcomputers for Learners - Program Thirteen 29 MIN
VHS / 16mm
Microcomputers for Learners Series
Color (A PRO)
$200.00 purchase _ #269913
Presents thirteen 30 - minute programs which investigate the role computers play in today's classrooms and educator's thoughts on the potential of the technology. Divides each program into four parts - ideas for educational use of microcomputers, hardware - related topics, basic concepts and a review of an educational software package. Program Thirteen scrutinizes the use of computers in early childhood classrooms, demonstrates digital scanners, Dr Romaniuk looks at LOGO, and 'PageMaker,' a desktop publishing package, is reviewed.
Computer Science; Industrial and Technical Education; Mathematics; Psychology
Dist - ACCESS **Prod** - ACCESS 1988

Microcomputers for Learners Series
Microcomputers for Learners - Program Eight 29 MIN
Microcomputers for Learners - Program Eleven 29 MIN
Microcomputers for Learners - Program Five 29 MIN
Microcomputers for Learners - Program Four 29 MIN
Microcomputers for Learners - Program Nine 29 MIN
Microcomputers for Learners - Program One 29 MIN
Microcomputers for Learners - Program Seven 29 MIN
Microcomputers for Learners - 29 MIN

Program Six
Microcomputers for Learners - Program Ten 29 MIN
Microcomputers for Learners - Program Thirteen 29 MIN
Microcomputers for Learners - Program Three 29 MIN
Microcomputers for Learners - Program Twelve 29 MIN
Microcomputers for Learners - Program Two 29 MIN
Dist - ACCESS

Microcomputers in Your School
U-matic / VHS
School Inservice Videotape Series
Color (T)
Includes three videotapes on planning, implementing and using microcomputers in the school. Discusses grade - level increase, budgeting for computers and community support.
Education; Mathematics
Dist - SLOSSF **Prod** - TERRAS

Microcosmic orbit - meditation
VHS
Guided practice series
Color (G)
$55.00 purchase _ #V61 - M
Awakens and circulates healing energy from universal, cosmic and earth energy - Chi or prana - through the primary acupuncture channels to empower the body. Features Master Mantak Chia as instructor.
Health and Safety; Physical Education and Recreation; Religion and Philosophy
Dist - HTAOC **Prod** - HTAOC

Microcosmic orbit - theory
VHS
Guided practice series
Color (G)
$55.00 purchase _ #V61 - T
Discusses theory of the small heavenly cycle - the microcosmic orbit. Features Master Mantak Chia as instructor.
Health and Safety; Physical Education and Recreation; Religion and Philosophy
Dist - HTAOC **Prod** - HTAOC

Microcultural Incidents in Ten Zoos 34 MIN
16mm
Color (H C A)
$485.00, $160.00 purchase, $23.50 rental _ #33028; LC 71-711892
Shows Professor Ray L Birdwhistell demonstrating the context control method for comparative analysis of cross - cultural situations. Short film excerpts illustrate the interaction of families' members with each other and with animals in zoos in England, France, Italy, Hong Kong, India, Japan and the United States. An epilogue illustrates observer and, particularly, cameraman biases in recording interactional data.
History - World
Dist - PSUPCR **Prod** - COMPEN 1971
PSU

Microcultural Incidents in Ten Zoos 35 MIN
16mm
Color (C)
$504.00
Experimental film by R.L. Birdwhistell and J.D. Van Vlack.
Fine Arts
Dist - AFA **Prod** - AFA 1971

Microelectrodes in Muscle 19 MIN
U-matic / VHS / 16mm
Physiology Series
Color (PRO)
LC 73-713048
Shows the intracellular microelectrode technique being used to measure transmembrane potential changes. Uses a frog dissection to demonstrate that the electrical responses of an excitable cell depend upon the ionic composition of the external solution.
Science; Science - Natural
Dist - MEDIAG **Prod** - WILEYJ 1970

Microelectronic Revolution - Ready or not 30 MIN
U-matic
Color (A)
Details the effect of the microelectronics revolution on white collar, blue collar and service employees. Focuses on the response of some Canadian unions to the changes.
Business and Economics; Sociology
Dist - AFLCIO **Prod** - CANLAB 1983

Microelectronics Explosion Series
Business applications 40 MIN
The Changing Workforce 40 MIN
Microelectronics Technology 40 MIN
Dist - DELTAK

Microelectronics Technology 40 MIN
VHS / U-matic
Microelectronics Explosion Series
Color
Examines microelectronics technology and the impact it is having on products.
Industrial and Technical Education
Dist - DELTAK **Prod** - DELTAK

Microfiche, Microfilm and Other Minutiae 9 MIN
U-matic / VHS / 16mm
Color (H C A)
LC 81-701452
Illustrates the use of micrographics to facilitate storage and handling of printed and graphic material in libraries and other institutions. Compares the cumbersome and wasteful storage of hardcopy with the ease and compactness of microform use. Examines microfiche, ultrafiche, aperture cards, microcopying, and computer - generated micrographics. Includes a discussion of the lack of uniformity in microform indexing.
Education
Dist - IU **Prod** - IU 1981

Microfilariae of Wuchereria Bancrofti 4 MIN
16mm
Parasitology Series
Color
LC FIE52-2238
Uses cinemicrography to show activity of diurnally periodic microfilariae of wuchereria bancrofti from the blood of a soldier infected in the society islands. For professional use.
Health and Safety
Dist - USNAC **Prod** - USPHS 1947

Microgravity 13 MIN
VHS
Space education series
Color (J H G T A)
$49.00 purchase, $15.00 rental _ #335703; LC 91-706535
Explores gravity and its varying affects. Explains the concepts of free fall and zero gravity. Part of a series providing teachers and students with information regarding the latest experimentation with weightlessness. Includes teacher's guide.
History - World; Industrial and Technical Education; Science; Science - Physical
Dist - TVOTAR **Prod** - TVOTAR 1989

Microlights 30 MIN
VHS
Perspectives - transport and communication - series
Color; PAL; NTSC (G)
PdS90, PdS105 purchase
Shows how the addition of a tiny motor to a hang - glider makes a cheap plane for surveying, crop spraying and recreation.
Industrial and Technical Education
Dist - CFLVIS **Prod** - LONTVS

Micrologic 5500 - 5000 - 3000 60 MIN
VHS
Using Loran series
Color (G A)
$29.90 purchase _ #0173
Shows how to operate the Micrologic 5500, 5000 and 3000 Loran models. Includes installation tips, initialization, calibration, chain selection, notch filters, signal - to - noise ratio, time differentials, Lat - Lon functions, selecting and programming waypoints, setting anchor and waypoint alarm, cross - track error, determining course to steer and distance to go. Part of a series on the most popular Loran models.
Physical Education and Recreation; Social Science
Dist - SEVVID

Micrologic 7500 - 8000
VHS
Loran operation guide series
Color (G A)
$29.90 purchase _ #0914
Teaches Loran C programming for the Micrologic 7500 - 8000 in nautical navigation. Shows how to enter the correct Loran chain for specific positions, how to program positions, determine the accuracy of a Loran C 'fix' and how to deal with the intricacies of specific machines.
Physical Education and Recreation; Social Science
Dist - SEVVID

Micrologic 7500 - 8000 60 MIN
VHS
Using Loran series
Color (G A)
$29.90 purchase _ #0746
Shows how to operate the Micrologic 7500 - 8000 Loran models. Includes installation tips, initialization, calibration, chain selection, notch filters, signal - to - noise ratio, time differentials, Lat - Lon functions, selecting and programming waypoints, setting anchor and waypoint alarm, cross - track error, determining course to steer and distance to go. Part of a series on the most popular Loran models.
Physical Education and Recreation; Social Science
Dist - SEVVID

Micrologic - Explorer
VHS
Loran operation guide series
Color (G A)
$29.90 purchase _ #0786
Teaches Loran C programming for the Micrologic - Explorer in nautical navigation. Shows how to enter the correct Loran chain for specific positions, how to program positions, determine the accuracy of a Loran C 'fix' and how to deal with the intricacies of specific machines.
Physical Education and Recreation; Social Science
Dist - SEVVID

Micrologic - Explorer - Voyager 60 MIN
VHS
Using Loran series
Color (G A)
$29.90 purchase _ #0750
Shows how to operate the Micrologic - Explorer and Voyager Loran models. Includes installation tips, initialization, calibration, chain selection, notch filters, signal - to - noise ratio, time differentials, Lat - Lon functions, selecting and programming waypoints, setting anchor and waypoint alarm, cross - track error, determining course to steer and distance to go. Part of a series on the most popular Loran models.
Physical Education and Recreation; Social Science
Dist - SEVVID

Micrologic - Voyager
VHS
Loran operation guide series
Color (G A)
$29.90 purchase _ #0788
Teaches Loran C programming for the Micrologic - Voyager in nautical navigation. Shows how to enter the correct Loran chain for specific positions, how to program positions, determine the accuracy of a Loran C 'fix' and how to deal with the intricacies of specific machines.
Physical Education and Recreation; Social Science
Dist - SEVVID

The Micrometer 15 MIN
U-matic
Machine Shop Work - Precision Measurement Series no 2
B&W
LC 79-707076
Shows various types of micrometers, how to use and care for the instrument, how to read the barrel and thimble scales and how to check the accuracy of readings. Issued in 1941 as a motion picture.
Industrial and Technical Education; Mathematics
Dist - USNAC **Prod** - USOE 1979

The Micrometer 15 MIN
16mm
Machine Shop Work Series
B&W (SPANISH)
LC FIE62-71
Explains the care, use and maintenance of micrometers.
Foreign Language; Mathematics
Dist - USNAC **Prod** - USOE 1941

Micrometer (Telescope Gages, Caliper, Hole Gages)
VHS / U-matic
Basic Machine Technology Series
Color (SPANISH)
Industrial and Technical Education; Mathematics
Dist - VTRI **Prod** - VTRI

Micrometers 18 MIN
VHS / 16mm
Precision Mechanical Measuring Series
Color (H A)
$465.00 purchase, $110.00 rental
Demonstrates how to take and read measurements using an outside vernier micrometer.
Industrial and Technical Education
Dist - TAT **Prod** - TAT 1989

Microorganisms - Beneficial Activities 15 MIN
16mm / U-matic / VHS
Bacteriology Series
Color (H C A) (ARABIC)
Contrasts various related activities of microorganisms. Indicates by animation that only a small number of all all microorganisms are harmful while much greater numbers are beneficial. Shows the means whereby microorganisms produce change in their environment and cause the formation of new substances.
Science - Natural
Dist - IU **Prod** - IU 1958

Microorganisms - Harmful Activities 15 MIN
16mm / U-matic / VHS
Bacteriology Series
Color (H C A)
Presents some of the methods developed for protection against disease and against undesirable decomposition of foods. Through animation explains how bacteria produce enzymes and toxic waste products which may cause disease and decomposition.

Science - Natural
Dist - IU **Prod** - IU 1958

Microorganisms in the Health Care Setting 15 MIN
16mm
Basic Procedures for the Paramedical Employee Series
Color (H C A)
LC 80-701067
Defines microorganism, pathogen and non - pathogen, conditions for their existence and their major sources. Discusses means of dissemination, routes to and from the body, ways to prevent dissemination and methods of control.
Health and Safety
Dist - COPI **Prod** - COPI 1969

Microorganisms of Gas Gangrene 9 MIN
16mm
Color
LC FIE54-115
Shows species of clostridium causing gas gangrene, the morphological characteristics of these bacteria, and studies of the bacteria in various cultures.
Health and Safety
Dist - USNAC **Prod** - USPHS 1954

Microorganisms that Cause Disease 11 MIN
16mm / U-matic / VHS
Color (J H)
$270, $190 purchase _ #1205
Shows the five kinds of pathogenic microorganisms, that is, the ones that cause infectious diseases.
Health and Safety; Science - Natural
Dist - CORF

Micropack 10 MIN
16mm
Color
LC 77-702108
Uses closeups and microscope photography to show various aspects of design, manufacture and packaging of the new breed of integrated circuits. Shows the potential uses of these circuits in computers.
Business and Economics; Industrial and Technical Education
Dist - HONIS **Prod** - HONEYW 1977

MicroPatent APS '89 and '90 - monthly
CD-ROM
Color (PRO A)
$950.00 purchase _ #2971
Gives patent number, title, date of issue, application number and date, inventor, state, assignee, status, classification, references and abstract. Includes all of 1989 in 1990 subscription. For IBM PCs and compatibles. Requires 640K RAM, DOS Version 3.1 or greater, one floppy disk drive - hard disk drive recommended, one empty expansion slot, and an IBM compatible CD - ROM drive.
Computer Science; History - United States
Dist - BEP

MicroPatent APS '89 and '90 - weekly
CD-ROM
Color (PRO A)
$3150.00 purchase _ #2972
Gives patent number, title, date of issue, application number and date, inventor, state, assignee, status, classification, references and abstract. Includes all of 1989 in 1990 subscription. For IBM PCs and compatibles. Requires 640K RAM, DOS Version 3.1 or greater, one floppy disk drive - hard disk drive recommended, one empty expansion slot, and an IBM compatible CD - ROM drive.
Computer Science; History - United States
Dist - BEP

Microprocessor and Memory Timing 30 MIN
VHS / U-matic
Microcomputer Memory Design Series
Color (IND)
Discusses read and write cycle timing of memory devices, microprocessor memory cycle timing analysis, and timing examples for 8080 and 6800.
Industrial and Technical Education; Mathematics; Sociology
Dist - COLOSU **Prod** - COLOSU

Microprocessor Applications - Communications Design 30 MIN
U-matic / VHS
Designing with Microprocessors Series
Color (PRO)
Discusses problems of digital communications and describes cost - effective hardware solutions using microprocessors. Describes typical system using one of today's better known chip sets.
Industrial and Technical Education
Dist - TXINLC **Prod** - TXINLC

Microprocessor Applications - Other Terminal Functions 30 MIN
U-matic / VHS
Designing with Microprocessors Series
Color (PRO)
Uses general purpose video terminal to illustrate benefits of microprocessors in improving capabilities of interactive terminals.
Industrial and Technical Education
Dist - TXINLC **Prod** - TXINLC

Microprocessor Applications - Point of Sale Terminals 30 MIN
U-matic / VHS
Designing with Microprocessors Series
Color (PRO)
Defines requirements of POS terminal and discusses advantages of certain chip sets for this application. Analyzes design of a specific terminal using a microprocessor.
Industrial and Technical Education
Dist - TXINLC **Prod** - TXINLC

Microprocessor Architecture I 50 MIN
U-matic / VHS
Management of Microprocessor Technology Series
Color
Discusses software and hardware, conceptualizing buzz words, computer data structure, memory types, computer operations and system organization.
Industrial and Technical Education; Mathematics
Dist - MIOT **Prod** - MIOT

Microprocessor Architecture II 49 MIN
VHS / U-matic
Management of Microprocessor Technology Series
Color
Discusses instruction sets, interfacing to the real world input/output, interrupts, direct memory access, peripheral chips and hardware trends in microprocessor architecture.
Industrial and Technical Education; Mathematics
Dist - MIOT **Prod** - MIOT

Microprocessor Background Via Digital Computer System Architecture 30 MIN
VHS / U-matic
Designing with Microprocessors Series
Color (PRO)
Explores digital computer system architecture as a basis for understanding microprocessors. Discusses peripheral controllers, distributed networks, and direct memory access channels.
Industrial and Technical Education
Dist - TXINLC **Prod** - TXINLC

Microprocessor - Based Product Opportunities 56 MIN
U-matic / VHS
Management of Microprocessor Technology Series
Color
Discusses the low, medium and high volume product areas and active industrial and consumer product areas in microprocessor technology.
Industrial and Technical Education; Mathematics
Dist - MIOT **Prod** - MIOT

Microprocessor Bus Structures 60 TO 90 MIN
VHS
Microprocessors Module Series
Color (PRO)
$600.00 - $1500.00 purchase _ #MIMBS
Addresses microprocessor buses, a group of wires connecting various components. Reveals that a microprocessor has three buses - a control, data and an address bus. Part of an eleven - part series on microprocessors. Includes five student guides, five workbooks and an instructor guide.
Computer Science; Education; Industrial and Technical Education; Psychology
Dist - NUSTC **Prod** - NUSTC

Microprocessor Chip Architecture 30 MIN
U-matic / VHS
Designing with Microprocessors Series
Color (PRO)
Surveys chips and chip sets architectural types available. Groups architectural types to simplify selection process. Provides guidelines for selection of proper chip architecture for particular applications.
Industrial and Technical Education
Dist - TXINLC **Prod** - TXINLC

Microprocessor Chip Fabrication 30 MIN
U-matic / VHS
Designing with Microprocessors Series
Color (PRO)
Examines major fabrication technologies in use today, their advantages and disadvantages. Enables designer to acquire insight into selection of right technology for specific applications. Gives background on Schottky TTL, ECL, PMOS, NMOS, CMOS, SOS and revolutionary new I - squared L.
Industrial and Technical Education
Dist - TXINLC **Prod** - TXINLC

Microprocessor - Computer on a Chip 13 MIN
16mm / U-matic / VHS
Color
Traces the development of the microprocessor from early man's attempts to count and keep time. Discusses the key components, which are reviewed and compared to the computer.
Industrial and Technical Education
Dist - FORDFL **Prod** - FORDFL

The Microprocessor in Avionics 30 MIN
U-matic / VHS
Designing with Microprocessors Series
Color (PRO)
Develops general problems encountered in avionics and offers improved solutions through use of microprocessors. Studies a specific hardware and software problem using one of today's advanced bit - slice architecture.
Industrial and Technical Education
Dist - TXINLC **Prod** - TXINLC

Microprocessor Instruction Sets 30 MIN
U-matic / VHS
Designing with Microprocessors Series
Color (PRO)
Describes various instruction sets, grouped by categories. Studies examples to provide in - depth understanding of selection process. Enables engineers to develop a software package for their specific application.
Industrial and Technical Education
Dist - TXINLC **Prod** - TXINLC

Microprocessor Instructions 60 TO 90 MIN
VHS
Microprocessors Module Series
Color (PRO)
$600.00 - $1500.00 purchase _ #MIMPI
Describes how the registers of a microprocessor work with memory in processing an instruction. Identifies addressing modes. Explains how those modes are used to access data. Part of an eleven - part series on microprocessors. Includes five student guides, five workbooks and an instructor guide.
Computer Science; Industrial and Technical Education; Psychology
Dist - NUSTC **Prod** - NUSTC

Microprocessor Interface Design 30 MIN
U-matic / VHS
Designing with Microprocessors Series
Color (PRO)
Studies solutions to interface design problems. Explores problems encountered in interfacing microprocessors with equipments. Describes devices currently available to solve various interface problems.
Industrial and Technical Education
Dist - TXINLC **Prod** - TXINLC

Microprocessor interfacing series

Busing Pt 2	33 MIN
Grounding and Shielding, Pt 1	38 MIN
Grounding and Shielding, Pt 2	46 MIN
Magnetic Disc Interfacing, Pt 1	48 MIN
Magnetic Disk Interfacing, Pt 2	44 MIN
Magnetic Tape Interfacing, Pt 1	45 MIN
Magnetic Tape Interfacing, Pt 2	45 MIN
Parallel Interfacing, Pt 1	42 MIN
Parallel Interfacing, Pt 2	44 MIN
Serial Interfacing, Pt 1	48 MIN
Serial Interfacing, Pt 2	41 MIN

Dist - MIOT

Microprocessor Interrupts 60 TO 90 MIN
VHS
Microprocessors Module Series
Color (PRO)
$600.00 - $1500.00 purchase _ #MIMIN
Describes the different ways in which a microprocessor can handle interrupts. Explains the operation of a programmable interrupt controller IC. Part of an eleven - part series on microprocessors. Includes five student guides, five workbooks and an instructor guide.
Computer Science; Education; Industrial and Technical Education; Psychology
Dist - NUSTC **Prod** - NUSTC

Microprocessor Programming 180 MIN
U-matic
Microprocessor Technical Fundamentals Series
Color (IND)
Describes programming a microprocessor, including arithmetic, logic, branching, loops, subroutines and utility functions.
Computer Science; Mathematics
Dist - INTECS **Prod** - INTECS

Microprocessor real - time interfacing and control series

Designing real - time software	180 MIN

Dist - INTECS

Microprocessor real - time interfacing and control systems series
Actuator and display interfaces 180 MIN
Analog - digital conversion 180 MIN
Control software 180 MIN
Data communications and summary 180 MIN
Introduction 180 MIN
Introductory Hands - on Session 180 MIN
Sensor and transducer interfaces 180 MIN
Signal and Power Conditioning 180 MIN
Dist - INTECS

The Microprocessor Revolution 30 MIN
U-matic
Fast Forward Series
Color (H C)
Shows that the microprocessor chip can replace tons of old equipment. It has revolutionized information processing, storage and technology ranging from toys to computers.
Computer Science; Science
Dist - TVOTAR **Prod** - TVOTAR 1979

Microprocessor Series
Interfacing Basics
Interfacing Peripheral Adaptors
Interfacing RAMS, Displays
Interfacing Switches
Introduction to Programming - Algorithms
Introduction to Programming - Branching
Microcomputer Basics
Number Systems and Codes
Sixty - Eight Hundred I, O Operations, Interrupts
Sixty - Eight Hundred Microprocessor
Sixty - Eight Hundred Stack Operations, Subroutines
Dist - HTHZEN

Microprocessor System Design 180 MIN
U-matic
Microprocessors - a Comprehensive Introduction Series
Color (A)
Discusses microprocessor system design elements. Presents guidelines for key tradeoff decisions, structuring the design team and minimizing costs. Application case study looks at developing functional specifications, partitioning the system into modules, and planning for future expansion.
Computer Science
Dist - INTECS **Prod** - INTECS

Microprocessor Technical Fundamentals Series
Case study - anatomy of a microprocessor system design 180 MIN
Fundamental microprocessor concepts 180 MIN
Input and Output (I/O) 180 MIN
Interrupts and Direct Memory Access Techniques 180 MIN
The Microcomputer Memory 180 MIN
Microcomputer Structure and Operation 180 MIN
Microprocessor Programming 180 MIN
Software Languages and Systems 180 MIN
Dist - INTECS

Microprocessor technician 4.5 MIN
VHS / 16mm
Good works 5 series
Color (A PRO)
$40.00 purchase _ #BPN238001
Presents the occupation of a microprocessor technician. Gives a profile of a young person who is either undergoing an apprenticeship or has recently completed training in this field. Takes the viewer on a tour of this person's workplace and explains the practical skills and training offered by employers and schools. Gives a better understanding of the demand for skilled workers today and the potential for personal growth.
Guidance and Counseling
Dist - RMIBHF **Prod** - RMIBHF

Microprocessor Troubleshooting Series
Microprocessor Troubleshooting Techniques 360 MIN
Microprocessor Troubleshooting with Conventional Lab Equipment 540 MIN
Microprocessor Troubleshooting with Diagnostic Software and in - Circuit Emulation 720 MIN
Microprocessor Troubleshooting with Logic Analyzers 960 MIN
Microprocessor Troubleshooting with Signature Analysis 540 MIN
Dist - INTECS

Microprocessor Troubleshooting Techniques 360 MIN
U-matic
Microprocessor Troubleshooting Series
Color (IND)
Discusses basic and advanced microprocessor troubleshooting techniques and equipment.
Computer Science; Industrial and Technical Education
Dist - INTECS **Prod** - INTECS

Microprocessor Troubleshooting with Conventional Lab Equipment 540 MIN
U-matic
Microprocessor Troubleshooting Series
Color (PRO IND)
Discusses recognizing and locating manufacturing induced faults, field failures, design errors and software - related problems in microprocessors. Includes oscilloscope testing and data books.
Computer Science; Industrial and Technical Education
Dist - INTECS **Prod** - INTECS

Microprocessor Troubleshooting with Diagnostic Software and in - Circuit Emulation 720 MIN
U-matic
Microprocessor Troubleshooting Series
Color (IND PRO)
Tells how to use diagnostic software as an effective troubleshooting tool for microprocessors, and how to apply in - circuit emulation for chip - level diagnosis.
Computer Science; Industrial and Technical Education
Dist - INTECS **Prod** - INTECS

Microprocessor Troubleshooting with Logic Analyzers 960 MIN
U-matic
Microprocessor Troubleshooting Series
Color (IND PRO)
Tells how to use both state and timing logic analyzers to pinpoint hardware and software faults.
Computer Science; Industrial and Technical Education
Dist - INTECS **Prod** - INTECS

Microprocessor Troubleshooting with Signature Analysis 540 MIN
U-matic
Microprocessor Troubleshooting Series
Color (IND)
Tells how to apply signature analysis for rapid chip - level diagnosis of microprocessor problems.
Computer Science; Industrial and Technical Education
Dist - INTECS **Prod** - INTECS

Microprocessor Video Training Course Series
Interfacing Peripheral Adapters
Interfacing RAMS/Displays
Introduction to Programming /Algorithms
Introduction to Programming/Branching
Microcomputer Basic
Numbers Systems and Codes
Sixty - Eight Hundred MPU I/O Operations/Interrupts
Sixty - Eight Hundred MPU Stack Operation/Subroutines
Dist - VTRI

Microprocessors
16mm / U-matic
Instrumentation Maintenance Series
Color (IND)
Teaches digital control techniques, data transfer and direct digital control system maintenance and troubleshooting. Explains diagnostic software and troubleshooting a distributed system.
Mathematics
Dist - ISA **Prod** - ISA

Microprocessors - a Comprehensive Introduction Series
The Big picture - microprocessors 180 MIN
Hands - on Application Examples - Microprocessors 180 MIN
Hardware and Software Fundamentals 180 MIN
Introduction - Microprocessors 180 MIN
Key Decisions in Applying Microprocessors 180 MIN
Microprocessor System Design 180 MIN
Putting Microprocessors to Work 180 MIN
Writing and Executing Programs 180 MIN
Dist - INTECS

Microprocessors and Digital - Systems - Introduction
16mm / U-matic
Instrumentation Maintenance Series
Color (IND)
Introduces digital basics, memory devices and microprocessor programming. Explains digital logic - AND, OR, NOT, NAND, NOR and binary numbering systems. Presents digital test equipment, combinational and sequential logic. Deals with troubleshooting - test programs, single - stepping, timing diagrams, logic analyzers.
Mathematics
Dist - ISA **Prod** - ISA

Microprocessors for Monitoring and Control Series
The Algorithmic state machine chart 30 MIN
Class - 3 machines - class - 4 machines 30 MIN
Development of Boolean equations from ASM charts 30 MIN
A Frequency - Counter Design - State 000, State 010, State 011, Pt 1 30 MIN
A Frequency - Counter Design - State 000, State 010, State 011, Pt 2 30 MIN
Introduction - binary and octal numbers 30 MIN
Introduction to the 8080 - instructions for logic implementation, addressing modes 30 MIN
Logic Modules - Task Description using an Algorithm 30 MIN
Logical or Boolean Expressions - Table Representations, Map Representations 30 MIN
More on Algorithms 30 MIN
More on Map Representations - Map - Entered Variables, Don't - Care Map Terms 30 MIN
Program Execution - a Grey Code - Counter Implementation 30 MIN
Simple Time - Interval Measurement System, a, Pt 1 30 MIN
Simple Time - Interval Measurement System, a, Pt 2 30 MIN
The State Machine - Definition of Input and Output Signals 30 MIN
Table Representation of the Next State Function and Outputs - Class - 0 Machines, 30 MIN
Dist - COLOSU

Microprocessors in Automotive Applications 30 MIN
VHS / U-matic
Designing with Microprocessors Series
Color (PRO)
Explores unique requirements of automotive field. Describes how a microprocessor can be used in numerous applications requiring a comparatively sophisticated controller. Examines one subsystem in detail and relates the bit - slice architecture solution to four others.
Industrial and Technical Education
Dist - TXINLC **Prod** - TXINLC

Microprocessors in Controllers 30 MIN
U-matic / VHS
Designing with Microprocessors Series
Color (PRO)
Describes various forms of control systems and how microprocessors meet their needs. Shows by examples three types of applications ranging from a simplified controller to a complex programmable sequence, with feedback, that can be controlled by a central computer.
Industrial and Technical Education
Dist - TXINLC **Prod** - TXINLC

Microprocessors module series
Central Processing Units 60 TO 90 MIN
Fundamentals of digital computers 60 TO 90 MIN
Fundamentals of microprocessor systems 60 TO 90 MIN
Microprocessor Bus Structures 60 TO 90 MIN
Microprocessor Instructions 60 TO 90 MIN
Microprocessor Interrupts 60 TO 90 MIN
Parallel Data Transfer Devices 60 TO 90 MIN
Principles of Computer Memory - 1 60 TO 90 MIN
Principles of Computer Memory - 2 60 TO 90 MIN
Serial data transfer devices 60 TO 90 MIN
Troubleshooting Microprocessors 60 TO 90 MIN
Dist - NUSTC

Micropuncture of Cells by U V Microbeam 10 MIN
16mm
B&W (PRO)
Studies anatomy at the cellular level, using phase - contrast and time - lapse photo - microscopy. Examines the effect of irradiation at the cellular level and points out that the results obtained from controlled irradiation are of considerable help in furthering knowledge of cellular physiology.
Health and Safety; Science - Natural
Dist - SQUIBB **Prod** - SQUIBB

Micros and the Arts 30 MIN
U-matic / VHS
Ready or not Series
Color
Focuses on computer courseware available in the arts, especially music and the visual arts. Shows how computer skills can become an integral part of arts education.
Fine Arts; Industrial and Technical Education; Psychology
Dist - PCATEL **Prod** - NCSDPI

Micros and the Writing Process 30 MIN
U-matic / VHS
Ready or not Series
Color
Focuses on integrating the use of microcomputers and communications skills. Shows programs that teach writing rather than simple word processing.
English Language; Psychology
Dist - PCATEL **Prod** - NCSDPI

Micros for Managers - Software Series
Background and definitions 30 MIN
Intro Ada 30 MIN
Intro BASIC 30 MIN
Intro FORTRAN and Pascal 30 MIN
Intro LISP 30 MIN
Operating Systems 30 MIN
Structured Programming and Software Maintenance 30 MIN
Trade - Offs and Future Trends 30 MIN
Dist - COLOSU

The Microscope 15 MIN
16mm
Darkfield microscopy series
Color
LC 79-701850
Describes the theory of darkfield illumination, which involves diffraction of light around the edges of a backlighted object. Deals with the theory and use of special darkfield condensers to show how modern compound microscopes are adapted for darkfield observation of specimens. Shows the preparation of a microscope slide using an oral specimen containing the spirochete and procedures for setting up and focusing the microscope.
Science
Dist - USNAC **Prod** - USNHET 1978

The Microscope and its Incredible World 21 MIN
U-matic / VHS / 16mm
Color (J H)
$495, $345, $371 purchase _ #A432
Shows viewers proper techniques for using and maintaining a microscope and specimen slides. Offers a basic explanation as to how a microscope works. Explains there are two kinds of magnifying lenses on a typical microscope, the eyepiece lens and the objective lens which is located on a rotating nosepiece above the microscope stage. Presents a brief description of the microscope's history.
Health and Safety; Science; Science - Physical
Dist - BARR **Prod** - BARR 1987

The Microscope and its incredible world
Videodisc
Color; CAV (J H)
$189.00 purchase _ #8L432
Uses photomicrography extensively to demonstrate the range of the microscope. Shows step - by - step techniques for using and maintaining a microscope and specimen slides. Presents a brief description of the microscope's history and its importance to research. Barcoded for instant random access.
Industrial and Technical Education; Science - Natural
Dist - BARR **Prod** - BARR 1991

The Microscope and the Prayer Shawl 30 MIN
16mm
B&W
Tells the story of Waldemar Haffkine, a scientist who, because he refused to convert to Christianity, was not permitted to continue his research in his native Russia. Discusses his discovery to a vaccine against cholera when he was invited to France to work with Louis Pasteur. (Kinescope).
Religion and Philosophy; Science
Dist - NAAJS **Prod** - JTS 1954

Microscope - Making it Big 28 MIN
16mm
Color (H C A)
LC 83-700089
Traces the development of the microscope from the magnifying glass to the world's most powerful microscope. Shows how microscopes permit surgeons to perform delicate eye operations and neurosurgery, and a seven - ton electron microscope can take pictures of atomic structures.
Health and Safety; Science
Dist - FLMLIB **Prod** - CANBC 1982

The Microscope - Passport to the Miniworld 15 MIN
U-matic / VHS / 16mm
Color (I J H)
Describes the different types of microscopes and provides a step - by - step demonstration of proper care and use of these instruments. Explains the preparation of a sample and the process of staining.
Science
Dist - HANDEL **Prod** - HANDEL 1979

Microscopic Life in Soil 14 MIN
U-matic / VHS / 16mm
Color; B&W (I J H)
Explains that soil contains many microorganisms which are important to the balance of nature. Shows motile algae, protozoans and multicellular animals and depicts their importance in the food chain.
Agriculture; Science - Natural; Social Science
Dist - STANF VIEWTH **Prod** - STANF 1963

Microscopic Look at Digestion 21 MIN
U-matic / VHS
Color
Reveals the processes of digestion using time lapse and macrophotography, models and drawings. Includes examples of enzymes, fat particles, starch granules and protein fibers.
Science - Natural
Dist - BANDER **Prod** - BANDER

Microscopic pond life 15 MIN
U-matic / VHS
Animals and such series; Module blue - habitats
Color (I J)
Demonstrates that microscopic life is complex despite its smallness. Shows amoeba, paramecia and volvox.
Science - Natural
Dist - AITECH **Prod** - WHROTV 1972

Microscopic Vasovasotomy 30 MIN
16mm
Color
LC 76-702602
Presents Dr Sherman J Silber, who shows microsurgery techniques used to reanastomose the vas deferens. Features his answers to questions from a panel of three urologists and a moderator.
Health and Safety
Dist - EATONL **Prod** - EATONL

Microscopy prelab series
Compound microscope - structure and operation 13 MIN
Mitosis 10 MIN
Protozoans - Part One 10 MIN
Protozoans - Part Two 9 MIN
Slide preparation 12 MIN
Dist - HRMC

Microsecond 5 MIN
16mm
Color
Uses a variety of techniques, including the split screen, kinestasis film, time lapse photography and animation, to define the term microsecond.
Mathematics
Dist - SLFP **Prod** - SLFP

MicroSoft 2.0 for Windows 176 MIN
U-matic / VHS / BETA
Color; NTSC; PAL; SECAM (J H C G)
PdS99.95
Shows how to use MicroSoft's leading word processor. Features Shelagh Marsh of MicroSoft Ltd.
Computer Science
Dist - VIEWTH

MicroSoft Access 173 MIN
U-matic / VHS / BETA
Color; NTSC; PAL; SECAM (J H C G)
PdS99.95
Presents MicroSoft's easy - to - use database for Windows. Shows how to get the best from the most - used features of Access. Features Pamela Neville.
Computer Science
Dist - VIEWTH

Microsoft bookshelf
CD-ROM
(G)
$199.00 purchase _ #1341
Contains ten reference works on one disc - the American Heritage Dictionary, Roget's Electronic Thesaurus, World Almanac and Book of Facts, Bartlett's Familiar Quotations, the Chicago Manual of Style, Houghton Mifflin Spelling Verifier and Corrector, Forms and Letters, U.S. Zip Code Directory, Houghton Mifflin Usage Alert, and Business Information Sources. Provides access to useful sources for the writer. For IBM PCs and compatibles, requires 640K RAM, DOS 3.1 or later, one floppy disk drive - hard disk recommended, one empty expansion slot, and an IBM compatible CD - ROM drive.
Computer Science; Literature and Drama
Dist - BEP **Prod** - MICRSF

Microsoft Excel 120 MIN
VHS / U-matic
(A PRO)
$495.00, $595.00 purchase
Includes information on utilizing all capabilities of advanced spreadsheet, business graphics and database programs.
Computer Science
Dist - VIDEOT **Prod** - VIDEOT 1988

Microsoft Excel 140 MIN
VHS / Software / 16mm
Color (PRO)
$495.00 purchase, $40.00 preview
Instructs employees on the use of the Microsoft Excel spread sheet, business graphics, and database computer program. Explains how to start the program, help for users, the work sheet, choosing commands, the mouse and keyboard, formulas, names, charts, data tables, and macros. Includes workbook and practice disk.
Computer Science; Mathematics; Psychology
Dist - UTM **Prod** - UTM

Microsoft Excel 4.0
VHS / BETA / U-matic
Windows training videos series
Color (G)
$995.00 purchase, $250.00 rental
Offers introductory and advanced training in Microsoft Excel 4.0. Shows how to navigate through columns and rows of numbers.
Computer Science; Psychology
Dist - AMEDIA **Prod** - AMEDIA

MicroSoft Excel 4.0 for Windows 179 MIN
U-matic / VHS / BETA
Color; NTSC; PAL; SECAM (J H C G)
PdS99.95
Presents the key features of Excel 4.0. Shows how to build spreadsheets and harness a number of spreadsheet concepts. Features Oliver Roll of MicroSoft Ltd.
Computer Science
Dist - VIEWTH

MicroSoft Excel 5.0 for Windows 172 MIN
U-matic / VHS / BETA
Color; NTSC; PAL; SECAM (J H C G)
PdS99.95
Presents the key features of the latest version of Excel. Explains the most - used features and new features to typical users. Presented by Oliver Roll of MicroSoft Ltd.
Computer Science
Dist - VIEWTH

MicroSoft Excel 5.0 for Windows - II - advanced 169 MIN
U-matic / VHS / BETA
Color; NTSC; PAL; SECAM (J H C G)
PdS99.95
Shows how users can get more from Excel 5.0. Discusses selected advanced topics and tricks and tips with Stephen Berry of SoftVision. Features Nick McGrath of MicroSoft Ltd.
Computer Science
Dist - VIEWTH

Microsoft Excel 5.0 for Windows learning system - advanced 120 MIN
VHS
Microsoft Excel 5.0 for Windows learning system series
Color; CC (G H C IND PRO)
$595.00 purchase _ #MIC23
Trains in use of the spreadsheet software program. Contains part of a three - part series.
Computer Science
Dist - EXTR **Prod** - MICROV

Microsoft Excel 5.0 for Windows learning system - intermediate 120 MIN
VHS
Microsoft Excel 5.0 for Windows learning system series
Color; CC (G H C IND PRO)
$595.00 purchase _ #MIC23
Trains in use of the spreadsheet program. Contains part of a three - part series.
Computer Science
Dist - EXTR **Prod** - MICROV

Microsoft Excel 5.0 for Windows learning system - introduction 150 MIN
VHS
Microsoft Excel 5.0 for Windows learning system series
Color; CC (G C H IND PRO)
$595.00 purchase _ #MIC23
Trains in use of the spreadsheet program. Contains the first course in a three - part series.
Computer Science
Dist - EXTR **Prod** - MICROV

Microsoft Excel 5.0 for Windows learning system series
Shows how to use the spreadsheet program in three parts, introduction, intermediate, and advanced.
Microsoft Excel 5.0 for Windows learning system - advanced 120 MIN
Microsoft Excel 5.0 for Windows learning system - intermediate 120 MIN
Microsoft Excel 5.0 for Windows 150 MIN

learning system - introduction
Microsoft Excel 5.0 for Windows learning system series 330 MIN
Dist - EXTR **Prod** - MICROV

Microsoft office
CD-ROM
(G)
$539.00 purchase _ #1345
Includes four Macintosh programs on one disc - MS Word for word processing, MS Excel spreadsheet, MS PowerPoint presentations program, and MS Mail for electronic mail. Offers online documentation and a variety of additional software. For Macintosh Classic, Plus, SE and II computers. Requires 2MB RAM, floppy disk drive, Apple compatible CD - ROM drive.
Computer Science
Dist - BEP **Prod** - MICRSF

MicroSoft PowerPoint 3.0 Windows 156 MIN
U-matic / VHS / BETA
Color; NTSC; PAL; SECAM (J H C G)
PdS99.95
Shows a typical user around PowerPoint 3.0. Features presentation graphics specialist Natalie Mead, of MicroSoft Ltd.
Computer Science
Dist - VIEWTH

MicroSoft PowerPoint 4.0 156 MIN
U-matic / VHS / BETA
Color; NTSC; PAL; SECAM (J H C G)
PdS99.95
Shows a typical user how to use PowerPoint to create effective presentations. Covers the most - used features and offers tips and hints to increase the quality of presentations. Features Jackie Elleker, a presentation specialist at MicroSoft Ltd.
Computer Science
Dist - VIEWTH

Microsoft programmer's library
CD-ROM
(PRO)
$345.00 purchase _ #1342
Contains programming documentation and sample code for a variety of languages. Includes the Microsoft editions of C, QuickC, FORTRAN, BASIC, QuickBASIC, Pascal, Macro Assembler. Offers Windows SDK, OS - 2 Presentation Mgr Toolkit, MS - DOS References, MS SQL Server, MS LAN Manager, MS Systems Journal vols 1 - 5, and hardware references for Intel, Mouse, and CD - ROM extensions. Includes initial disc and subscription to three more discs from Microsoft. Network licenses available. For IBM PCs and compatibles, requires 640K RAM, DOS 3.1 or later, one floppy disk drive - hard disk recommended, one empty expansion slot, and an IBM compatible CD - ROM drive.
Computer Science
Dist - BEP **Prod** - MICRSF

MicroSoft Project 3.0 176 MIN
U-matic / VHS / BETA
Color; NTSC; PAL; SECAM (J H C G)
PdS149
Shows how to get the best from MicroSoft Project. Features consultant Paul Barons.
Computer Science
Dist - VIEWTH

Microsoft small business consultant
CD-ROM
(G)
$118.00 purchase _ #1344
Contains a complete library of more than 220 publications from the Small Business Administration, other government agencies, and the accounting firm of Deloitte, Haskins, and Sells. Provides an overview of important small business information - planning, financing, marketing, advertising, government agencies, accounting, management, personnel, employee safety, crime and liability protection, importing, and exporting. For IBM PCs and compatibles, requires at least 640K RAM, DOS 3.1 or later, one floppy disk drive - hard disk recommended, one empty expansion slot, and an IBM compatible CD - ROM drive.
Business and Economics; Social Science
Dist - BEP **Prod** - MICRSF

Microsoft stat pack
CD-ROM
(G)
$118.00 purchase _ #1343
Provides access to statistical facts and figures about people, industry, trade, agriculture, and business. Includes the following government publications - Statistical Abstract of the United States, Area Wage Survey, Business Statistics, Agricultural Statistics, and Public Land Statistics. For IBM PCs and compatibles, requires at least 640K RAM, DOS 3.1 or later, one floppy disk drive - hard disk recommended, one empty expansion slot, and an IBM compatible CD - ROM drive.
Agriculture; Sociology
Dist - BEP **Prod** - MICRSF

Microsoft Windows 3.0 or 3.1
BETA / U-matic / VHS
Windows training videos series
Color (G)
$995.00 purchase, $250.00 rental
Offers introductory and advanced training in Microsoft Windows 3.0 or 3.1. Shows how to manipulate Windows' desktop, arrange icons and exchange data between programs.
Computer Science; Psychology
Dist - AMEDIA **Prod** - AMEDIA

Microsoft Windows 3.1 49 MIN
VHS
Computer training series
Color (G)
$24.95 purchase _ #CI06
Offers the latest on Microsoft Windows 3.1. Part of a six - part series explaining PCs and software. Includes booklet. Produced by M - USA.
Computer Science
Dist - SVIP

Microsoft Windows 95 video guide 60 MIN
VHS
Color (G)
$29.95 purchase _ #GTIMES77226V-B
Introduces Windows 95. Includes stars of the TV comedy Friends, Jennifer Aniston and Matthew Perry, who lead a cast through the program. Shows features on Windows 95, including a new user interface; plug and play; the Microsoft network; recycle bins; multi-tasking; faster file and disk access; creating your own shotcuts; and more. Provides answers to 20 most-asked questions about Windows 95.
Computer Science
Dist - CAMV

Microsoft Word 3.01 introduction
VHS
Video professor Macintosh series
Color (J H C G)
$29.95 purchase _ #VP302V
Makes the most complex operations of Microsoft Word 3.01 easy to understand. Uses advanced production techniques which allow viewer to see keyboard and monitor simultaneously. Allows students to learn at their own pace, rewinding or pausing for any section they don't fully understand. Part of six - part series on Macintosh graphics.
Computer Science; Industrial and Technical Education
Dist - CAMV

MicroSoft Word 4.0 introduction 53 MIN
VHS
Word processing series
Color (J H C G)
$29.95 purchase _ #VP112V
Introduces concepts in MicroSoft Word 4.0. Allows viewer to see keyboard and monitor simultaneously so that students can see the result of every keystroke. Part of a series on word processing.
Business and Economics; Computer Science
Dist - CAMV

MicroSoft Word 4.0 level II 58 MIN
VHS
Word processing series
Color (J H C G)
$29.95 purchase _ #VP113V
Offers intermediate and advanced concepts in MicroSoft Word 4.0. Allows viewer to see keyboard and monitor simultaneously so that students can see the result of every keystroke. Part of a series on word processing.
Business and Economics; Computer Science
Dist - CAMV

MicroSoft Word 5.0 introduction 60 MIN
VHS
Word processing series
Color (J H C G)
$29.95 purchase _ #VP132V
Introduces concepts in MicroSoft Word 5.0. Allows viewer to see keyboard and monitor simultaneously so that students can see the result of every keystroke. Part of a series on word processing.
Business and Economics; Computer Science
Dist - CAMV

MicroSoft Word 6.0 for Windows 170 MIN
U-matic / VHS / BETA
Color; NTSC; PAL; SECAM (J H C G)
PdS99.95
Shows a typical user how to use Word. Includes new features as well as hints and tips. Features Julia Philpot of MicroSoft Ltd.
Computer Science
Dist - VIEWTH

MicroSoft Word 6.0 for Windows - II - advanced 173 MIN
U-matic / VHS / BETA
Color; NTSC; PAL; SECAM (J H C G)
PdS99.95
Shows an advanced user how to get more from Word 6.0. Discusses selected advanced topics and tricks and tips with Stephen Berry of SoftVision. Features Julia Philpot of MicroSoft Ltd.
Computer Science
Dist - VIEWTH

Microsoft Word 6.0 for Windows learning system 348 MIN
VHS
Microsoft Word 6.0 Windows learning system series
Color; CC (G H C PRO IND)
$1295.00 purchase _ #MIC22
Trains on the use of the word processing software program. Includes three parts, an introduction, intermediate and advanced tape, available separately.
Computer Science
Dist - EXTR **Prod** - MICROV

Microsoft Word 6.0 for Windows learning system - advanced 120 MIN
VHS
Microsoft Word 6.0 for Windows learning system series
Color (G H C IND PRO)
$595.00 purchase _ #MIC22
Trains in use of the word processing software program. Part of a three - part series.
Computer Science
Dist - EXTR **Prod** - MICROV

Microsoft Word 6.0 for Windows learning system - intermediate 93 MIN
VHS
Microsoft Word 6.0 for Windows learning system series
Color; CC (G H C IND PRO)
$595.00 purchase _ #MIC22
Trains in the use of the software. Part of a three - part series.
Computer Science
Dist - EXTR **Prod** - MICROV

Microsoft Word 6.0 for Windows learning system - introduction 135 MIN
VHS
Microsoft Word 6.0 Windows learning system series
Color; CC (G H C IND PRO)
$595.00 purchase _ #MIC22
Introduces use of the software program. Contains part of a three - part series.
Computer Science
Dist - EXTR **Prod** - MICROV

Microsoft Word 6.0 for Windows learning system series
Microsoft Word 6.0 for Windows learning system - advanced 120 MIN
Microsoft Word 6.0 for Windows learning system - intermediate 93 MIN
Dist - EXTR

Microsoft Word 6.0 Windows learning system series
Microsoft Word 6.0 for Windows learning system 348 MIN
Microsoft Word 6.0 for Windows learning system - introduction 135 MIN
Dist - EXTR

Microsoft Word 5 0 - Mastering Word Processing 60 MIN
U-matic / VHS
(A PRO)
$275.00
Includes creating documents, revising and formatting.
Computer Science
Dist - VIDEOT . **Prod** - VIDEOT 1988

MicroSoft Word 5 advanced learning system
U-matic / VHS
Color (H C G)
$595.00, $495.00 purchase _ #08 - MWA
Trains users of MicroSoft Word 5. Addresses new features such as customizing, macros, merging form letters, outline, table of contents, advanced formatting, graphics, glossaries and style sheets. Includes a videocassette, diskette and guide. Published by MicroVideo Learning Systems.
Business and Economics; Computer Science
Dist - VIDEOT

MicroSoft Word 5 learning system
U-matic / VHS
Color (H C G)
$595.00, $495.00 purchase _ #08 - MMW
Trains users of MicroSoft Word 5. Covers writing, editing, basic formatting, document handling, page formatting printing and reference capabilities. Includes a videocassette, a guide and a diskette. Published by MicroVideo Learning Systems.

Business and Economics; Computer Science
Dist - VIDEOT

MicroSoft Word 5 learning system - complete set
U-matic / VHS
Color (H C G)
$995.00, $895.00 purchase _ #08 - MMW - MWA
Presents two courses for training users of MicroSoft Word 5. Covers basic features of writing, editing, basic formatting, document handling, page formatting, printing and reference capabilities. Addresses new features such as customizing, macros, merging form letters, outline, table of contents, advanced formatting, graphics, glossaries and style sheets. Includes 2 videocassettes, 2 diskettes and 2 guides. Published by MicroVideo Learning Systems.
Business and Economics; Computer Science
Dist - VIDEOT

Microsoft Word for Windows
BETA / U-matic / VHS
Windows training videos series
Color (G)
$995.00 purchase, $250.00 rental
Offers introductory and advanced training in Microsoft Word for Windows. Shows how to enter text, edit documents and use utilities, through advanced formatting, macros, templates and more.
Computer Science; Psychology
Dist - AMEDIA **Prod** - AMEDIA

Microsoft word for Windows introduction 51 MIN
VHS
Windows applications series
Color (J H C G)
$29.95 purchase _ #VP144V
Introduces concepts in Microsoft Windows. Allows viewer to see keyboard and monitor simultaneously so that students can see the result of every keystroke. Part of an eight - part series on Windows.
Computer Science
Dist - CAMV

Microsoft word for Windows level II 43 MIN
VHS
Windows applications series
Color (J H C G)
$29.95 purchase _ #VP145V
Offers intermediate concepts in Microsoft Windows. Allows viewer to see keyboard and monitor simultaneously so that students can see the result of every keystroke. Part of an eight - part series on Windows.
Computer Science
Dist - CAMV

Microsoft Word - Mastering Word Processing 60 MIN
VHS / Software / 16mm
Color (PRO)
$325.00 purchase, $40.00 preview
Teaches skills for using the Microsoft Wordprocessing system. Includes practice diskette and personal training guide.
Business and Economics; Guidance and Counseling; Mathematics; Psychology
Dist - UTM **Prod** - UTM

Microsoft Word series
5.5 introduction
5.0 for Windows, introduction
Dist - SIV

Microsoft Works 2.0 - word processor
VHS
Video professor Macintosh series
Color (J H C G)
$29.95 purchase _ #VP306V
Makes the most complex operations of Microsoft Works 2.0 easy to understand. Uses advanced production techniques which allow viewer to see keyboard and monitor simultaneously. Allows students to learn at their own pace, rewinding or pausing for any section they don't fully understand. Part of six - part series on Macintosh graphics.
Computer Science; Industrial and Technical Education
Dist - CAMV

Microsoft Works word processing 1.05 50 MIN
VHS
Word processing series
Color (J H C G)
$29.95 purchase _ #VP125V
Offers information on Microsoft Works word processing 1.05. Allows viewer to see keyboard and monitor simultaneously so that students can see the result of every keystroke. Part of a series on word processing.
Business and Economics; Computer Science
Dist - CAMV

Microstructure and Classifications of Steels 59 MIN
BETA / VHS / U-matic
Color
$400 purchase
Details single phase constituents and their microstructures.
Science; Science - Physical
Dist - ASM **Prod** - ASM 1987

Microstructure of Steels - Ferrite, Pearlite and Bainite 50 MIN
U-matic / BETA / VHS
Color
$400 purchase
Shows structure property relationship in steel/carbon and alloying elements in heat treatment.
Science; Science - Physical
Dist - ASM **Prod** - ASM

Microsurgery 27 MIN
16mm / U-matic / VHS
Perspective Series
Color (C A)
Follows step - by - step the design of new microsurgical instruments, the training of surgeons to use them to make minute stitches and the performance of a life - prolonging operation upon a man's brain.
Health and Safety; History - World
Dist - STNFLD **Prod** - LONTVS

Microsurgery for Accidents 19 MIN
VHS / U-matic
Color
Gives a surgeon's eye - view of limb and digit replantations as well as microvascular free tissue transplantation.
Health and Safety
Dist - SPRVER **Prod** - SPRVER

Microteaching 28 MIN
16mm
Color (T)
Presents a preliminary teaching experience. Explores training effects under controlled conditions.
Education
Dist - EDUC **Prod** - EDUC

Microvascular Surgery - Clinical Case Examples 30 MIN
U-matic / VHS
Color (PRO)
Demonstrates of microvascular surgery experiences of surgeons throughout the world by Dr Harry J Buncke. Part two of a three part series.
Health and Safety
Dist - ASSH **Prod** - ASSH

Microvascular Surgery - Demonstration of Technique 60 MIN
U-matic / VHS
Color (PRO)
Shows the operating field as Dr Harry J Buncke conducts an experimental microvascular surgery. Final part of a three part series.
Health and Safety
Dist - ASSH **Prod** - ASSH

Microvascular Surgery - History and Technique 35 MIN
VHS / U-matic
Color (PRO)
Reviews the history and techniques of microvascular surgery as presented by Dr Harry J Buncke. Part one of a series.
Health and Safety
Dist - ASSH **Prod** - ASSH

Microwave Cooking
VHS / 35mm strip
$39.95 purchase _ #RPVT1128V ; $229.00 purchase _ #PX1239 filmstrip, $229.00 purchase _ #PX1239V VHS
Discusses different aspects of microwave cooking from advantages to disadvantages. Talks about how to cook using a microwave oven.
Health and Safety; Home Economics; Social Science
Dist - CAREER **Prod** - CAREER

Microwave cooking 60 MIN
VHS
Color (A)
$34.95 purchase _ #S00839
Features Pat Hutt in an exploration of microwave cooking. Includes cookbook with over 200 recipes.
Home Economics; Industrial and Technical Education; Social Science
Dist - UILL

Microwave Cooking 60 MIN
VHS / U-matic
$34.95 purchase
Gives a comprehensive course on this modern cooking method for today's busy homemaker.
Home Economics
Dist - BESTF **Prod** - BESTF

Microwave Cooking 61 MIN
VHS / 16mm
(G)
$39.95 purchase _ #VT1128
Teaches the techniques of microwave cooking. Covers the 'microwave shape', defrosting, shielding, 'sauteing' without cholesterol, when to cover food, utensils to use, converting a conventional recipe, and ways to cook meats, poultry, and vegetables by weight. Taught by Barbara Harris, author of 'Let's Cook Microwave'.
Home Economics
Dist - RMIBHF **Prod** - RMIBHF

Microwave cooking and safety
VHS
Kitchen video series
$79.00 purchase _ #FY101V
Teaches the importance of kitchen safety and following directions. Uses kitchen video transfers and graphic photography.
Home Economics; Industrial and Technical Education
Dist - CAREER **Prod** - CAREER

Microwave Cooking Series
Apples to zucchini
Entertaining extraordinaire
Fun food fast
Main Dish Delights
Microwave in - Service Training
Microwave Magic
Dist - AAVIM

Microwave cooking series
Teaches viewers the applications and techniques that make cooking with a microwave successful.
Microwave cooking series
Dist - CAREER **Prod** - CAREER

Microwave in - Service Training
VHS
Microwave Cooking Series
(C G)
$59.00_CA255
Overviews microwave mechanical and safety operations.
Home Economics; Industrial and Technical Education
Dist - AAVIM **Prod** - AAVIM 1989

Microwave Landing System 15 MIN
U-matic / VHS
Color (C)
Explains how a Microwave Landing System (MLS) functions, and highlights advantages over conventional Instrument Landing System (ILS). Provides explanation of MLS techniques known as Time Reference Scanning Beam (TRSB) which will serve all aviation well into the next century.
Industrial and Technical Education
Dist - AVIMA **Prod** - FAAFL

Microwave Landing Systems 16 MIN
16mm
Color (A)
LC 77-702203
Examines the functions of new microwave landing systems and highlights the advantages of these systems over conventional instrument landing systems.
Industrial and Technical Education
Dist - USNAC **Prod** - USFAA 1976

Microwave Magic
VHS
Microwave Cooking Series
(C G)
$59.00_CA256
Covers common misconceptions concerning microwave cooking and presents construction, operation, and safety items.
Home Economics
Dist - AAVIM **Prod** - AAVIM 1989

Microwave miracles
VHS
Video cooking library series
Color (J H G)
$19.95 purchase _ #KVC941V
Illustrates microwave cookery through step - by - step demonstrations. Covers everything needed from ingredients to equipment, with clear explanations of cooking techniques. Includes recipes. Part of a 22 - part series.
Home Economics
Dist - CAMV

Microwave Optics - an Introduction 13 MIN
16mm
College Physics Film Program Series
B&W (C)
LC FIA68-3022
Dr James Meyer, using a small tungsten filament lamp as a director, demonstrates the polarity of microwaves, determines the wavelength, and shows the interference pattern of 2 - slits and focusing effects of glass and pitch lenses. Describes a crystal detector, and illustrates how it is used to determine the polarization of radiation scattered from the tungsten lamp.

Science - Physical
Dist - MLA **Prod** - EDS 1968

Microwave Oscillators, Pt 1 - Reflex Klystrons 20 MIN
16mm
B&W
Describes the general characteristics, components and operation of reflex klystron tubes used as local oscillators in radar receiving systems.
Science - Physical
Dist - USNAC **Prod** - USA 1965

Microwave Oscillators - Reflex Klystrons 20 MIN
U-matic
B&W
LC 79-707775
Describes the characteristics, components, and operation of reflex klystron tubes used as local oscillators in radar receiving systems. Issued in 1965 as a motion picture.
Industrial and Technical Education
Dist - USNAC **Prod** - USA 1979

The Microwave oven 11 MIN
16mm / U-matic / VHS
Professional food preparation and service program series
Color (A)
Shows how a wide variety of foods can be heated quickly and efficiently in the microwave oven. Explains the differences between microwave heating and conventional oven heating. Covers all factors affecting microwave oven heating time, including food thickness, density, temperature, quantity, shape and oven power.
Industrial and Technical Education
Dist - NEM **Prod** - NEM

Microwaves and the Future 145 MIN
U-matic
University of the Air Series
Color (J H C A)
$750.00 purchase, $250.00 rental
Discusses the basic principles of microwave heating as well as safety aspects and biological effects. Program contains a series of five cassettes 29 minutes each.
Home Economics; Industrial and Technical Education
Dist - CTV **Prod** - CTV 1977

Microwaving secrets 27 MIN
VHS
Color (H C G)
$49.95 purchase _ #CDC100V
Takes the mystery out of microwaving and replaces it with reliable information. Shows how microwaves cook food, how to use covers and wraps for even more cooking, how to defrost frozen foods in minutes, achieve browned meats and poultry and how to use a conventional oven in combination with a microwave. Teaches how to successfully use temperature probes and cook complicated dishes using varied power settings. Illustrates how to test common kitchen utensils for microwave suitability. Presents step - by - step directions for eight microwave dishes and a print version of the recipes.
Home Economics
Dist - CAMV

Microworld 50 MIN
U-matic / VHS / 16mm
Color (H C A)
Discusses Britain's attempt to compete with America and Japan in microchip technology.
Industrial and Technical Education; Mathematics
Dist - FI **Prod** - BBCTV 1984

MICU - the ethics of intensive care 58 MIN
VHS / U-matic
Color (H A G)
$235.00 purchase, $100.00, $50.00 rental _ #059
Follows five patients, ranging from a 56 - year - old man with an unknown disease to a 90 - year - old woman who has spent nine months in a hospital's Medical Intensive Care Unit - MICU. Reveals that many of these people would die without the aggressive and often invasive treatment they receive around the clock, but the availability of medical treatment which can prolong life raises ethical questions about who should be treated, how much they should be treated and when treatment should stop. Profiles medical staff people who make decisions about these patients.
Health and Safety; Sociology
Dist - FANPRO **Prod** - FANPRO

Mid - Atlantic 60 MIN
VHS
AAA travel series
Color (G)
$24.95 purchase _ #NA09
Explores the Middle Atlantic states.
Geography - United States; Geography - World
Dist - SVIP

The Mid - Atlantic States 30 MIN
16mm / U-matic / VHS
Color (I J H C)
Edited from the motion picture These States. Features the battles, places of reverence and historical figures of New York, New Jersey, Pennsylvania, Delaware and Maryland. Includes scenes of Saratoga, Fort Ticonderoga, Valley Forge and Annapolis.
Geography - United States; History - United States
Dist - FI **Prod** - BCTOS 1975

The Mid - Atlantic States 27 MIN
16mm / U-matic / VHS
United States Geography Series
Color (I J)
Explores the states of New York, New Jersey, Pennsylvania, Delaware, Maryland and Washington, DC which contain mountains, valleys, rivers, harbors, bountiful farms and burgeoning metropolitan areas.
Geography - United States
Dist - NGS **Prod** - NGS 1983

The Mid - Atlantic - the eastern shore 55 MIN
VHS
On the waterways series
Color (G H)
$29.95 purchase _ #OW10
Travels with the crew of the Driftwood to explore the mid - Atlantic from Rhode Island to New Jersey, home to preservationists, yachtsmen, an entrepreneur who turned an East River barge into a hot music venue and a man racing a ferry - in a rowboat. Narrated by Jason Robards. Part of a 13 - part series on the history, geography, culture and ecology of North American waterways.
Social Science
Dist - SVIP

Mid - Summer Night's Dream 25 MIN
U-matic / VHS / 16mm
Mr Magoo in World Classics Series
Color
Magoo as Puck romps through Shakespeare's lyric tale of ancient Greece in which a queen is tricked and a King wears a donkey's head.
Literature and Drama
Dist - FI **Prod** - FLEET 1965

The Mid - Torso of Inez 26 MIN
U-matic / VHS
B&W
Portrays in a dreamlike manner mysterious incidents in the early life of Grandfather, as told to his grand - daughter, Lois Ann, at a family dinner at which he is apparently an unwelcome guest. An experimental film.
Fine Arts; Sociology
Dist - MEDIPR **Prod** - MEDIPR 1979

The Middle Age Blues 49 MIN
16mm
Color
LC 75-702655
Examines the lives, careers and attitudes of two men in middle age, pointing out that middle age can be a time for change and a reconsideration of life's goals.
Guidance and Counseling; Psychology; Sociology
Dist - SSC **Prod** - RKOTV 1975

The Middle ages 30 MIN
VHS
Western tradition series
Color; PAL (J H G)
PdS29.50 purchase
Relates how, in the midst of invasion and civil disorder, a military aristocracy dominates the kingdom of Europe. Presents part of an eight - part series that conveys the excitement of historical inquiry while stimulating critical thinking about the unique events of each major period of history.
Civics and Political Systems; History - World
Dist - EMFVL **Prod** - CORF

The Middle Ages 31 MIN
U-matic / VHS / 16mm
Outline History of Europe Series
Color (H C A) (SWEDISH)
LC 80-701110
Traces the social, economic and cultural development of western Europe, emphasizing the life of the people during the Middle Ages.
History - World
Dist - IFB **Prod** - IFB 1975

The Middle Ages 46 MIN
VHS
Color (I J)
$148.00 purchase _ #TK111
Presents three - parts on the Middle Ages which lasted for roughly 1,000 years and transformed Europe from a vast wilderness to a complex of nations with separate identities and political structures. Examines in - depth the Early, High and Late Middle Ages, focusing on the social, economic, religious and political highlights of each era.
History - World; Literature and Drama; Religion and Philosophy
Dist - KNOWUN **Prod** - KNOWUN

The Middle Ages 30 MIN
16mm
How Should We Then Live Series no 2; Episode 2
Color (DUTCH)
LC 77-702364
Traces the history of the Christian church during the Middle Ages, focusing on its corruption by political power and materialism. Based on the book How Should We Then Live by Francis A Schaeffer.
History - World; Religion and Philosophy
Dist - GF **Prod** - GF 1977

The Middle Ages - a wanderer's guide to life and letters 27 MIN
U-matic / BETA / 16mm / VHS
Western civilization - majesty and madness series
Color (J H C A)
$445.00, $89.00 purchase _ #JY - LEN506
Looks at the Middle Ages in Europe.
History - World; Literature and Drama; Religion and Philosophy; Sociology
Dist - CORF **Prod** - LCOA 1971

The Middle Ages - a Wanderer's Guide to Life and Letters 27 MIN
U-matic / VHS / 16mm
Color (J) (SPANISH)
LC 73-710038;
Features excerpts from such stories as Everyman, Dante's Love Sonnets and The Wife Of Bath.
History - World; Literature and Drama
Dist - LCOA **Prod** - SCNDRI 1971

The Middle Ages - Culture of Medieval Europe 24 MIN
U-matic / VHS / 16mm
Color (J H)
History - World
Dist - EBEC **Prod** - NBCTV 1966

The Middle Ages - Rise of Feudalism 20 MIN
16mm / U-matic / VHS
Color (J H)
History - World
Dist - EBEC **Prod** - NBCTV 1966

Middle Ages School Kit 120 MIN
VHS
Color (G)
$125.00 purchase _ #MESK - 000
Uses eight 15 - minute modules from the PBS programs "Castle" and "Cathedral" to teach about the Middle Ages. The first four modules, which are from "Castle," discuss daily life, technology and warfare during the Middle Ages. The remaining four modules, from "Cathedral," explore cathedrals, church - state relations, the beginning of the middle class and the end of the Middle Ages. Hosted by David Macaulay. Includes teacher's guide and instructional materials.
Fine Arts; History - World
Dist - PBS

Middle Ages series
The Castle - Pt 2 20 MIN
The Church - Pt 3 20 MIN
The Peasants' Revolt - Pt 1 20 MIN
The Town - Pt 4 20 MIN
The Traders - Pt 5 20 MIN
Dist - FI

The Middle Ages - the feudal order - Parts 19 and 20 60 MIN
U-matic / VHS
Western tradition - part I series
Color (G)
$45.00, $29.95 purchase
Presents two thirty - minute programs tracing the history of ideas, events and institutions which have shaped modern societies hosted by Eugen Weber. Looks at the military aristocracy which dominated the kingdoms of Europe amid invasion and civil disorder in part 19. Part 20 considers the social divisions of feudalism in the year 1000 AD, such as bishop, knight and peasant. Parts 19 and 20 of a 52 - part series on the Western tradition.
Civics and Political Systems; Geography - World; History - World; Sociology
Dist - ANNCPB **Prod** - WGBH 1989

Middle ages with missiles
VHS
The Great wall of iron series
Color (J H G)
$225.00 purchase
Presents part 3 of a four - part series that tells of the Chinese People's Liberation Army, known to the Chinese as the Great Wall of Iron. Looks at its funding and its methods, based on numbers rather than on weaponry. Also available in a set of four videos.
Geography - World; History - World
Dist - LANDMK

The Middle Atlantic Region 17 MIN
16mm / U-matic / VHS
U S Geography Series
Color (J)
LC 76-701772
Examines the people, industry, economy and landscape of the Middle Atlantic region of the United States.
Business and Economics; Geography - United States; Geography - World; Social Science
Dist - MGHT **Prod** - MGHT 1976

Middle distance running APPROXIMATELY 33 MIN
U-matic / VHS
Women's Track & Field Videos Series
Color; B&W; Silent; Stereo; Mono (H C A)
Demonstrates techniques and drills by famous athletes for the middle distance running events. Prepared and narrated by coach Ken Foreman.
Physical Education and Recreation
Dist - TRACKN **Prod** - TRACKN 1986

Middle Distance Running 12 MIN
U-matic / VHS / 16mm
Athletics Series
Color (H C A)
LC 80-700341
Opens with a 3000 - meter race featuring world - class middle distance runners. Shows middle distance training exercises demonstrated by athletes running on a variety of terrains at varying speeds.
Physical Education and Recreation
Dist - IU **Prod** - GSAVL 1980

Middle Distance Running 42 MIN
BETA / VHS
Women's Track and Field Series
Color
Physical Education and Recreation
Dist - MOHOMV **Prod** - MOHOMV

Middle distance running 42 MIN
VHS
Track and field series
Color (J H C A)
$39.95 purchase _ #MXS470V
Features Dr Ken Foreman, former U S Olympic women's track coach, in a comprehensive program to teach skills of middle distance running. Focuses on preparation and training, also discussing off - track training programs.
Physical Education and Recreation
Dist - CAMV

Middle distance running 30 MIN
VHS
Track and field techniques series
Color (H C G)
$29.95 purchase _ #WK1101V
Features runner Sebastian Coe who discusses middle distance running and improving performance. Part of a series.
Physical Education and Recreation
Dist - CAMV

Middle Ear Infection 8 MIN
U-matic / VHS
Take Care of Yourself Series
Color
Explains middle ear infections and counters misconceptions patients may have. Describes treatment and signs that indicate the need to call a doctor.
Health and Safety; Science - Natural
Dist - UARIZ **Prod** - UARIZ

Middle Ear Infections 11 MIN
U-matic / 8mm cartridge
Color (A) (SPANISH)
Describes the anatomy and function of the middle ear. Explains the cause and treatments of infections.
Health and Safety; Science - Natural
Dist - PRORE **Prod** - PRORE

Middle East 120 MIN
VHS
Color (J H G)
$495.00 purchase
Looks at events in the Middle East occurring during the 20th century, including periods of domination by France, Britain, the United States and Russia in turn. Brings out political and economic issues of importance in the region, such as the Arab - Israeli conflicts, the Suez Crisis, the Gulf War and the development of the oil fields. Set of two videos, part 1 covering from 1900 - 1956 and part 2 from 1956 - 1991. Available only as a set.
History - World; Sociology
Dist - LANDMK

The Middle East 27 MIN
16mm / U-matic / VHS
Seventies Series
Color (J)
LC 81-700251
Explores the Arab/Israeli conflict during the 1970's, focusing on various efforts to resolve it. Details step - by - step negotiations leading to the Begin - Sadat summits. Covers the civil wars in Jordan and Lebanon.
History - World
Dist - JOU **Prod** - UPI 1980

The Middle east 75 MIN
35mm strip / VHS
Color (J H C T A)
$162.00, $162.00 purchase _ #MB - 540336 - 6, #MB - 540030 - 8
Takes a comprehensive look at the people and nations of the Middle East. Discusses subjects including cultural heritage, historic conflicts, and the region's importance in world affairs.
History - World
Dist - SRA **Prod** - SRA 1989

Middle East - building a dream 22 MIN
VHS
Gulf crisis series
Color; PAL (H)
Focuses on Israel and its role in the Middle East.
Geography - World; History - World; Religion and Philosophy
Dist - VIEWTH

Middle East - cradle of conflict 40 MIN
VHS
Color (J H C G)
$29.95 purchase _ #BPG900V
Examines the history of the Middle East, the Cradle of Civilization, the place of origin of the alphabet, mathematics, literature, science and the arts for Western Civilization. Examines issues surrounding present controversies and the birth and development of Judaism, Christianity and Islam.
History - World; Sociology
Dist - CAMV

Middle East diary - Mac
CD-ROM
Color (G A)
$175.00 purchase _ #2855m
Contains a lengthy review of Middle East history, personalities and conflicts. Gives the background needed to make competent decisions on travel, business and relationships in the Middle East. For Macintosh Plus, SE and II computers. Requires at least one M of RAM, one floppy disk drive, and an Apple compatible CD - ROM drive.
Geography - World; Literature and Drama
Dist - BEP

Middle East diary - PC
CD-ROM
Color (G A)
$175.00 purchase _ #2855p
Contains a lengthy review of Middle East history, personalities and conflicts. Gives the background needed to make competent decisions on travel, business and relationships in the Middle East. For IBM PCs and compatibles. Requires 640K RAM, DOS Version 3.1 or greater, one floppy disk drive - a hard disk drive is recommended, one empty expansion slot, and an IBM compatible CD - ROM drive.
Geography - World; Literature and Drama
Dist - BEP

The Middle East - from Mohammed to Sadat
VHS / U-matic
Color (H)
Explores key events in Middle Eastern history, from the birth of Islam to the modern age. Illustrated with Islamic paintings, artifacts and location photography.
Geography - World; History - World
Dist - GA **Prod** - EAV

Middle East - leadership and identity 22 MIN
VHS
Gulf crisis series
Color; PAL (H)
Examines the governmental styles and leadership of the countries in the Middle East.
Civics and Political Systems; Geography - World; Guidance and Counseling; History - World; Religion and Philosophy
Dist - VIEWTH

Middle East - mosaic of peoples 22 MIN
VHS
Gulf crisis series
Color; PAL (H)
Examines the diverse ethnic population and the varieties of Islam in the Middle East.
Geography - World; History - World; Religion and Philosophy
Dist - VIEWTH

The Middle East - Mosaic of Peoples (an Overview) 28 MIN
U-matic / VHS / 16mm
Middle East Series
Color (I J H)
Surveys the diversified cultures of the Middle East, focusing on the ancient heritages of Sumer, Babylon and Persia, the lifestyles of ethnic minority groups and the coexistence of different religious sects.
Geography - World; History - World; Sociology
Dist - CORF **Prod** - BIBICF 1979

Middle East - oil and sudden wealth 22 MIN
VHS
Gulf crisis series
Color; PAL (H)
Looks at the economic impact of Middle Eastern oil reserves.
Business and Economics; Geography - World; History - World; Religion and Philosophy; Social Science
Dist - VIEWTH

The Middle East - Oil and Sudden Wealth (Gulf Countries) 28 MIN
16mm / U-matic / VHS
Middle East Series
Color (I J H)
Investigates the lives of the people of the Gulf countries of the Middle East as they are changed by the discovery and development of rich oil fields. Presents some long - range thinking of national policy makers concerning future direction and use of oil profits.
Geography - World; History - World; Social Science
Dist - CORF **Prod** - BIBICF 1979

Middle East Series
Nomads of Iran 13 MIN
Dist - AIMS

Middle East Series
The Middle East - Mosaic of Peoples (an Overview) 28 MIN
The Middle East - Oil and Sudden Wealth (Gulf Countries) 28 MIN
Dist - CORF

Middle East - the desert of God 15 MIN
VHS
Great deserts of the world series
Color; PAL (H)
Reveals that four great religions, born in the Middle Eastern deserts, called upon people to worship one god. Looks at the Egyptian king Amenhotep IV, Moses, Jesus and Mohammed, all inspired by visions in the desert. Visits locations and landscapes in the Middle East, and traces the history of religious tradition from the many gods of the Egyptians to the monotheistic doctrine and holy cities of the Christians, Jews and Muslims. Part of a six - part series on deserts of the world.
Geography - World; History - World; Religion and Philosophy; Science - Natural
Dist - VIEWTH **Prod** - VIEWTH
CORF

Middle English drama - A Game of soldiers 45 MIN
VHS
Middle English drama series
Color; PAL (I)
PdS30 purchase
Dramatizes a play by Jan Needle. Focuses on three children, living on the Falkland Islands during the recent conflict with Britain, who find a young, wounded Argentine conscript. Encourages children to consider the common ground that the Falklands war shares with violent conflicts everywhere. Contact distributor about availability outside the United Kingdom.
Literature and Drama; Psychology; Sociology
Dist - ACADEM

Middle English drama - Down and out 15 MIN
VHS
Middle English drama series
Color; PAL (I)
PdS20 purchase
Dramatizes the story of an old lady who befriends a young vagrant who reminds her of her dead son. Reveals that he does the gardening, but she hesitates to offer him a room for the night. She regrets her action when his promise to return fails to come about. Contact distributor about availability outside the United Kingdom.
Literature and Drama; Psychology
Dist - ACADEM

Middle English drama - Izzy 45 MIN
VHS
Middle English drama series
Color; PAL (I)
PdS30 purchase
Presents a specially - written three - part drama about the pressures of everyday life and the prejudices and misunderstandings that arise from them. Portrays Izzy, a latchkey child caught between adults who don't communicate and who somehow rises above the situation. Contact distributor about availability outside the United Kingdom.
Literature and Drama; Sociology
Dist - ACADEM

Middle English drama - Roald Dahl 15 MIN
VHS
Middle English drama series
Color; PAL (I)
PdS20 purchase
Focuses on children's author Roald Dahl. Features Sir Michael Horden who reads excerpts from Dahl's work, and illustrations by Quentin Blake. Interviews Dahl who examines the mysteries of writing and identifies what goes into making a good children's book - a strong plot, suspense and, above all, humor. Reveals the sources of inspiration for Dahl's unique stories, including drawing on his experiences as a child. Explains how his 'crazy' characters and events do have a moral sense behind them. Contact distributor about availability outside the United Kingdom.
Literature and Drama
Dist - ACADEM

Middle English drama series
Middle English drama - A Game of soldiers 45 MIN
Middle English drama - Down and out 15 MIN
Middle English drama - Izzy 45 MIN
Middle English drama - Roald Dahl 15 MIN
Middle English drama - The Chinese word for horse 15 MIN
Middle English drama - The Longest road 30 MIN
Middle English drama - The Secret 45 MIN
Middle English drama - The Shadow cage 30 MIN
Middle English drama - The Strangers 60 MIN
Dist - ACADEM

Middle English drama - The Chinese word for horse 15 MIN
VHS
Middle English drama series
Color; PAL (I)
PdS20 purchase
Presents John Lewis' story about the meeting between horse and man. Brings the story alive with the animation of Chinese characters for all elements of the story. Contact distributor about availability outside the United Kingdom.
Literature and Drama
Dist - ACADEM

Middle English drama - The Longest road 30 MIN
VHS
Middle English drama series
Color; PAL (I)
PdS30 purchase
Presents members of Greenwich Young People's Theatre and local school children in Britain who recreate a true wartime story. Portrays the hazardous journey of the children of Lvov, Poland, to Yugoslavia in 1939, on the outbreak of hostilities in World War II. In two parts. Contact distributor about availability outside the United Kingdom.
History - World; Literature and Drama; Sociology
Dist - ACADEM

Middle English drama - The Secret 45 MIN
VHS
Middle English drama series
Color; PAL (I)
PdS30 purchase
Portrays Mrs Mitchell who goes out for a day when unforseen circumstances prevent her return. Reveals that Nicky and Roy, her children, decide that they must keep their mother's disappearance a secret or they will be taken away by the authorities. In three parts of 15 minutes each. Contact distributor about availability outside the United Kingdom.
Guidance and Counseling; Literature and Drama; Sociology
Dist - ACADEM

Middle English drama - The Shadow cage 30 MIN
VHS
Middle English drama series
Color; PAL (I)
PdS30 purchase
Presents a mystery in two parts. Shows how a frightening event becomes even more terrifying when it occurs among familiar surroundings. Contact distributor about availability outside the United Kingdom.
Literature and Drama
Dist - ACADEM

Middle English drama - The Strangers 60 MIN
VHS
Middle English drama series
Color; PAL (I)
PdS35 purchase
Dramatizes the conflicts that develop between a group of school children from Belfast when they arrive in Donegal on the West Coast of Ireland. Contact distributor about availability outside the United Kingdom.
Civics and Political Systems; Literature and Drama
Dist - ACADEM

The Middle Manager as Innovator 30 MIN
VHS / 16mm
Harvard Business Review Video Series
(A PRO)
$650.00 purchase _ #AG - 4814M
Define's critical organizational needs and demonstrates techniques for handling them with solid practical management strategies.
Business and Economics; Psychology
Dist - CORF **Prod** - WGBH 1987
GOODMI

Middle managers and safety accountability 13 MIN
VHS / U-matic / BETA
Color; PAL (IND G)
$175.00 rental _ #ASF - 150
Teaches middle managers about the importance of their role in the safety environment of line workers. Reveals that their budgetary decisions, training programs, communication, safety audits and long - range planning have more impact on safety than they may realize. Includes leader's guide and 10 workbooks which are available in English only.
Business and Economics; Guidance and Counseling; Health and Safety; Psychology
Dist - BNA **Prod** - BNA

The Middle of Midnight 80 MIN
VHS
Color (S)
$29.95 purchase _ #833 - 9552
'Unravels the riddle' of India. Features controversial author Salmon Rushdie who interviews a city pavement dweller, an Indian yuppie, a peasant communist who still prays to Hindu gods, a fisherman who now lives in a poisoned paradise and a widow whose family was butchered in the name of religion.
Agriculture; Geography - World; History - World; Religion and Philosophy
Dist - FI

The Middle of the World 115 MIN
16mm
Color (FRENCH (ENGLISH SUBTITLES))
An English subtitle version of the French language film. Describes the love affair of a Swiss engineer and an Italian emigrant over a period of 112 days.
Fine Arts; Foreign Language; Sociology
Dist - NYFLMS **Prod** - NYFLMS 1974

Middle Passage 30 MIN
VHS / 16mm
Say Brother National Edition Series
Color (G)
$55.00 rental _ #SBRO - 109
Sociology
Dist - PBS **Prod** - WGBHTV

The Middle Path 29 MIN
VHS / U-matic
Journey into Thailand Series
Color (J S C A)
MV=$195.00
Visits the small market town of Chom Thong where a rare glimpse of life in a Buddhist monastery is seen. The monastery and monks play a vital part in the day - to - day life of the town.
Geography - World; History - World
Dist - LANDMK **Prod** - LANDMK 1986

The Middle phase of field instruction 107 MIN
U-matic / VHS
Core skills for field instructors series; Program 3
Color (C T)
LC 83-706440
Shows field instructors how they can deal with student defensiveness and resistance, help the student make more effective use of the field instructor, use effective teaching methods in field instruction conferences and deal with evaluation.
Education; Sociology
Dist - MCGILU **Prod** - MCGILU 1983

Middle Protest 30 MIN
U-matic / VHS
Afro - American Perspectives Series
Color (C)
Discusses the black protests for civil rights in America.
History - United States
Dist - MDCPB **Prod** - MDDE

Middle Road Traveler Series
Child Development, Family Living Styles, and Interpersonal Relationships 30 MIN
Communication, safety, and nutrition 30 MIN
Family living styles, legal rights and responsibilities, and economics 30 MIN
Health, Interpersonal Relationships and Discipline 30 MIN
Safety, Nurturance, and Expectations 30 MIN
Dist - GPN

The Middle School 30 MIN
VHS / U-matic
On and about Instruction Series
Color (T)
Explains the concept of the middle school and explores alternatives.
Education
Dist - GPN **Prod** - VADE 1983

Middle School Interview with Bernard Bragg 24 MIN
VHS / U-matic
Color (S)
Presents discussion and questions with young elementary students and Bernard Bragg. Signed.
Education; Guidance and Counseling; Psychology
Dist - GALCO **Prod** - GALCO

The Middle school years 36 MIN
VHS / U-matic
Coping with cancer series
Color (PRO)
$200.00 purchase, $70.00 rental _ #5262S, #5262V
Follows three young patients when their cancer is diagnosed and when they return to school; when peers asked questions; when fellow patients in the hospital died; when their treatments caused pain, hair loss and fear; and when they were teased or friends failed to understand. Part of four-part series that discusses and helps explain what children with cancers and their siblings are feeling.
Health and Safety; Sociology
Dist - AJN **Prod** - MSKCC 1983

The Middle School Years - Guidance for Transition 30 MIN
16mm
Color (C T)
LC 77-703459
Depicts guidance activities proven successful with middle school students, such as advisor - advisee programs, parent groups and various classroom guidance projects.
Education; Guidance and Counseling
Dist - EDMDC **Prod** - EDMDC 1977

The Middle Years 17 MIN
U-matic / VHS / 16mm
Color (J)
Deals with adulthood, the years of parenting and participating in society.
Social Science; Sociology
Dist - PFP **Prod** - HUBLEY

The Middle Years 50 MIN
U-matic / 16mm / VHS
Human Journey Series
Color; Mono (J H C A)
MV $350.00 _ MP $450.00 purchase, $50.00 rental
Presents a predictable veiw of the life cycle. Suggests that the best years of life are between age 43 and 50. This is a time when there is still youthfulness, but also experience and wisdom.This film offers an optimistic message.
History - World; Psychology; Science - Natural
Dist - CTV **Prod** - CTV

Middlemarch 350 MIN
VHS
Color (A)
PdS99 purchase _ Unavailable in USA
Presents the George Eliot epic saga of love, disillusionment and blackmail in 19th-century England, adapted by Andrew Davies, directed by Anthony Page. Stars Juliet Aubrey as Dorothea who misguidedly marries the Rev Edward Casaubon - Patrick Malahide, while Dr Lydgate - Douglas Hodge - finds his ideals thwarted by the insatiable financial demands of his shallow selfish wife, Rosamond - Trevyn McDowell. Offers footage filmed on location in Lincolnshire, Dorset and Rome, a cast including Robert Hardy, Peter Jeffrey and Michael Hardern. In seven segments.
Literature and Drama
Dist - BBCENE

Middleness Concept in Chimpanzees 7 MIN
16mm
B&W (C T)
Illustrates a research project to determine the extent to which a five - and - a - half year - old chimpanzee can perceive the middle object in varying arrays of objects. Uses the Wisconsin general test apparatus containing 25 food wells arranged in an arc. Circular plugs which fit into the wells are used as stimulus objects and food pellets are used as rewards.
Psychology; Science - Natural
Dist - PSUPCR **Prod** - KANSSU 1966

Middletown series
The Big game 60 MIN
The Campaign 90 MIN
Community of praise 60 MIN
Second Time Around 60 MIN
Seventeen 90 MIN
Dist - FI

Mideast - Arts, Crafts and Architecture 18 MIN
16mm / U-matic / VHS
Mideast Series
Color (J)
LC 78-700907
Views craftsmen at work and presents the role of the Islamic religion in shaping artistic activity and expression in the Middle East.
Fine Arts; Geography - World; History - World; Religion and Philosophy
Dist - PHENIX **Prod** - VOFI 1977

Mideast - Economic Development 18 MIN
16mm / U-matic / VHS
Mideast Series
Color (J)
LC 78-700909
Discusses the economic development of the Middle East. Explores the impact of oil on the region and examines the plans of Mideast nations to build a strong economic future.
Business and Economics; Geography - World; History - World
Dist - PHENIX **Prod** - VOFI 1977

Mideast - Economic Devlopment 18 MIN
16mm / U-matic / VHS
(French (from the Mideast Series
Color (J)
LC 78-700909
Discusses the economic development of the Middle East. Explores the impact of oil on the region and examines the plans of Mideast nations to build a strong economic future.
Business and Economics; Foreign Language; Geography - World; History - World
Dist - PHENIX **Prod** - VOFI 1977

Mideast - Islam, the Unifying Force 17 MIN
U-matic / VHS / 16mm
Mideast Series
Color (J)
LC 78-700908
Discusses the history, beliefs and practices of the Islamic religion and its role in the lives of Muslims all over the world.
Geography - World; History - World; Religion and Philosophy; Social Science; Sociology
Dist - PHENIX **Prod** - VOFI 1977

Mideast - Land and People 20 MIN
16mm / U-matic / VHS
Mideast Series
Color (J) (SWEDISH)
LC 78-700910
Shows the Middle East, located at the juncture of Asia, Africa and Europe. Illustrates the landscapes which vary from parched deserts to subtropical farming regions, as well as the ruins of ancient civilizations which coexist with traditional bazaars and modern skylines. Discusses the countries of Saudi Arabia, Egypt, Iran, Iraq, Morocco and the Gulf States.
Geography - World; Sociology
Dist - PHENIX **Prod** - VOFI 1977

Mideast - Pioneers of Science 20 MIN
16mm / U-matic / VHS
Mideast Series
Color (J)
LC 78-700911
Enumerates various contributions to modern civilization originating in the Middle East, including the wheel and axle, writing, the use of the decimal point, anesthetics and the number system.
Geography - World; History - World
Dist - PHENIX **Prod** - VOFI 1977

Mideast Series
Mideast - Arts, Crafts and Architecture 18 MIN
Mideast - Economic Development 18 MIN
Mideast - Islam, the Unifying Force 17 MIN
Mideast - Land and People 20 MIN
Mideast - Pioneers of Science 20 MIN
Dist - PHENIX

Mideastern Dance - an Introduction to Belly Dance 122 MIN
U-matic
Color (G)
Gives step by step instruction for learning to perform mideastern belly dances.
Fine Arts; Physical Education and Recreation
Dist - BASTET **Prod** - LLAMAV 1985

The Midgets 25 MIN
U-matic / VHS / 16mm
Untamed World Series
Color; Mono (J H C A)
$400.00 film, $250.00 video, $50.00 rental
Features the habits and behaviour of over 900,000 different kinds of anthropods.
Science - Natural
Dist - CTV **Prod** - CTV 1971

Midlife Career Change 30 MIN
VHS / 16mm
(PRO G)
$89.95 purchase _ #DGP59
Discusses the challenge of changing an established career and the impact it has on people's lives. Hosted by Dick Goldberg.
Business and Economics; Guidance and Counseling
Dist - RMIBHF **Prod** - RMIBHF

Midnight 151 MIN
VHS
Color (G) (MANDARIN CHINESE)
$45.00 purchase _ #1082A
Presents a Mandarin Chinese language movie produced in the People's Republic of China.
Fine Arts; Geography - World; Literature and Drama
Dist - CHTSUI **Prod** - CHTSUI

Midnight Cowboy 113 MIN
16mm
Color
Focuses on a Texan who arrives in New York City hoping to make his fortune by selling himself to lonely rich women. Tells how he meets a seedy, crippled con artist. Stars Dustin Hoffman and Jon Voight. Direct by John Schlesinger.
Fine Arts
Dist - UAE **Prod** - UNKNWN 1969

Midnight Express 120 MIN
16mm
Color
Dramatizes an escape from a horrifying Turkish prison.
Fine Arts
Dist - SWANK **Prod** - CPC

Midnight is a place 15 MIN
VHS
More books from cover to cover series
Color (I G)
$25.00 purchase _ #MBCC - 113
Describes how fourteen - year - old Lucas' boring life changes when an unusual little girl unexpectedly arrives. Shows how this event leads to other life - changing experiences. Based on the book 'Midnight Is a Place' by Joan Aiken. Hosted by John Robbins.
Education; English Language; Literature and Drama
Dist - PBS **Prod** - WETATV 1987

Midnight ramble 60 MIN
VHS
CC; Color (C H G A)
$59.95 purchase _ #AMEX-704-WC95
Describes the African American filmmakers that flourished during the early part of the twentieth century. Explains that directors such as Oscar Micheaux make hundreds of motion pictures that presented African Americans as people and not stereotypes. Includes information on the directors, actors, and producers that made these 'forgotten' movies.
Fine Arts
Dist - PBS **Prod** - NLP 1994

Midnight Ride of Paul Revere 11 MIN
U-matic / VHS / 16mm
Color (I J)
$270, $190 purchase _ #1138
Deals with American literature that is based on history, and describes the pre - Revolutionary period.
History - United States; Literature and Drama
Dist - CORF

The Midnight ride of Paul Revere 10 MIN
VHS / U-matic / 16mm
Color (I J H)
$290.00, $250.00 purchase _ #HP - 5929C
Adapts the poem of Henry Wadsworth Longfellow. Uses animation to give a sense of the historical circumstances of the crucialness of the ride of Paul Revere. Produced by Sharon Hoogstraten Productions.
Fine Arts; History - United States; Literature and Drama
Dist - CORF

Midnight songs 106 MIN
VHS
Color (G) (CHINESE)
$45.00 purchase _ #6065C
Presents a film from the People's Republic of China, a remake of a famous 1930s film.
Geography - World; Literature and Drama
Dist - CHTSUI

Midnight trailer 3 MIN
16mm
Color (G)
$10.00 rental
Features a collage and kinestasis commissioned by Mike Getz for his Midnight Movie circuit. Contains clips from Reefer Madness, Everready Hardon, Popcorn and countless others.
Fine Arts
Dist - CANCIN **Prod** - WENDTD 1974

Midsummer Mush 20 MIN
16mm
B&W (I J H C)
Presents the 1933 comedy film, 'MIDSUMMER MUSH,' featuring Charlie Chase as a New York scoutmaster who takes his troop of scouts from Broadway and 42nd street to the side of a lake for summer camping. Also features Betty Mack.
Fine Arts
Dist - RMIBHF **Prod** - ROACH 1933

A Midsummer Night's Dream 110 MIN
VHS / U-matic
Shakespeare Plays Series
Color (H C A)
LC 82-707359
Presents A Midsummer Night's Dream, William Shakespeare's play about devilish fairies, bedeviled lovers, and tradesmen - actors.
Literature and Drama
Dist - TIMLIF **Prod** - BBCTV 1982

A Midsummer Night's Dream 165 MIN
VHS / U-matic
Color
Presents an American production of the Shakespearean play A Midsummer Night's Dream, directed by Joseph Papp and starring William Hurt.
Literature and Drama
Dist - FOTH **Prod** - FOTH 1984

A Midsummer night's dream 112 MIN
VHS
BBC Shakespeare series
Color (G C H)
$109.00 purchase _ #DL459
Fine Arts
Dist - INSIM **Prod** - BBC

A Midsummer Night's Dream 156 MIN
VHS
Color (S)
$39.95 purchase _ #833 - 9274
Presents the Glyndebourne production of Bejamin Britten's 'A Midsummer Night's Dream.' Stars Ileano Cotrubas, James Bowman, Curt Apelgren, Cynthia Buchan and Felicity Lott. Sir Peter Hall directs.
Fine Arts; Geography - World
Dist - FI **Prod** - NVIDC 1987

A Midsummer Night's Dream 30 MIN
U-matic / VHS
Shakespeare in Perspective Series
Color (J)
LC 84-707155
Presents an adaptation of Shakespeare's A Midsummer Night's Dream, a classic comedy of the trials and errors of four lovers lost in a woods, of Oberon who seeks revenge on his wife Titania, and of a company of rustics rehearsing the story of Pyramus and Thisbe. Includes the plays King Lear, The Tempest and As You Like It on the same tape.
Literature and Drama
Dist - FI **Prod** - FI 1984

A Midsummer Night's Dream 124 MIN
U-matic / VHS / 16mm
Color
Stars Diana Rigg and David Warner in Shakespeare's comedy A Midsummer Night's Dream.
Fine Arts; Literature and Drama
Dist - FI **Prod** - UNKNWN 1968

A Midsummer night's dream 117 MIN
VHS
B&W (G)
$59.95 purchase _ #S00525; $79.00 purchase _ #05704 - 85
Features 11 - year - old Mickey Rooney as Puck in the 1935 film version of Shakespeare's 'A Midsummer Night's Dream.' Co - stars James Cagney, Joe E Brown, Victor Jory, Dick Powell and Olivia de Havilland. Uses the music of Mendelssohn during ballet sequences.
Literature and Drama
Dist - UILL
CHUMAN
UAE

A Midsummer Night's Dream - an Introduction 26 MIN
U-matic / VHS / 16mm
Shakespeare Series
Color (J)
LC 79-709295
Selects scenes performed by an English company to introduce Shakespeare's comedy A Midsummer Night's Dream.
Fine Arts; Literature and Drama
Dist - PHENIX **Prod** - SEABEN 1970

Midway 30 MIN
U-matic / VHS
World War II - GI Diary Series

Color (H C A)
History - United States; History - World
Dist - TIMLIF **Prod** - TIMLIF 1980

Midway is East 27 MIN
16mm / U-matic / VHS
Victory at Sea Series
B&W (J H)
Documents Japanese victories in the Pacific and the Battle of Midway.
Civics and Political Systems; History - United States; History - World
Dist - LUF **Prod** - NBCTV

Midwest - Heartland of the Nation 25 MIN
U-matic / VHS
Color (I J)
$49.00 purchase _ #2761
Provides an examination of the many factors responsible for the wealth of the Midwestern United States as well as the problems this same wealth has created.
Agriculture
Dist - EBEC

Midwest Holiday 26 MIN
16mm
Color (J)
Presents the Michigan Dunes to the Grand Tetons of Wyoming. Shows Mount Rushmore in South Dakota's Black Hills, Minnesota's Iron Range, Lincoln's home, Tom Sawyer's habitat and many other beautiful scenes in ten midwestern States.
Geography - United States
Dist - AMROIL **Prod** - AMROIL 1953

Midwest Old Threshers 29 MIN
16mm
Color
LC 80-701321
Shows the activities, displays and attractions at the annual reunion of the Midwest Old Settlers and Threshers Association. Depicts the sights and sounds of steam engines, locomotives, trolleys and handicrafts of a bygone era.
Social Science
Dist - UIOWA **Prod** - MOSAT 1980

Midwestern Farmer Cooperatives 18 MIN
VHS / 16mm
Color (H C A)
Reviews the history of the cooperative movement, describes the organizational structure of typical modern cooperatives and compares them to other forms of public and private enterprise.
Business and Economics
Dist - IOWA **Prod** - IOWA 1987

Midwife - with Woman 28 MIN
16mm / VHS
Color (G)
$240.00 purchase
Illustrates how the nurse - midwife profession has regained a foothold in American maternity care.
Health and Safety; Sociology
Dist - FANPRO **Prod** - FANPRO 1989

Midwifery - the Second Oldest Profession 26 MIN
VHS / U-matic
Color
Reveals how renewed interest in home birth has created a demand for lay mid - wives, the ageless art of women attending women in childbirth. Shows actual births.
Health and Safety
Dist - WCCOTV **Prod** - WCCOTV 1978

Midwives - Lullabies - And Mother Earth 52 MIN
VHS
Color (H C G)
$195.00 purchase, $75.00 rental
Relates how women can experience more fully the miracle of giving birth. Features Dr Michel Odent, pioneer of the natural childbirth movement, who promotes intimate birthing rooms and giving mothers and midwives more status. He has studied the long - term health impacts of his techniques and stipulates that life - long health is greatly influenced by the mother during pregnancy and birth. Insists that medicine should turn towards nurturing rather than preoccupied with the causes of disease. Produced by 220 Productions. A film by Julian Russell and Tony Gailey.
Fine Arts; Health and Safety
Dist - CANCIN

MIG and TIG Welding - Spanish Series
Butt joint, t-joint and lap joint with dual shielding
Butt joint, t-joint, lap joint and outside corner joints in the flat and horizontal position
Butt joint, t-joint, lap joint and outside corner joints in the vertical and overhead position
Multi Pass Welding with Dual Shielded
Safety and equipment for gas shielded arc welding
Safety in gas tungsten arc welding
Selection of Electrode, Gas, Cups and Filler Rod for Inert Gas Tungsten - TIG
Setting up aluminum wire feed and running butt, t, and lap joints
Setting up and padding of the inert - gas shielded metal - arc welding
Setting up flux cored wire and running continuous beads
Submerged arc welding
Welding Aluminum with Inert Gas Tungsten Arc
Welding Mild Steel with Inert Gas Tungsten Arc
Welding Stainless Steel with Inert Gas Tungsten Arc
Dist - VTRI

MIG Welding 70 MIN
VHS / 35mm strip
Color (H A IND)
#906XV7
Explains the equipment, procedures and applications of MIG welding. Includes gas metal arc welding process, wire feeders and torches, short circuit transfer, spray arc transfer, and troubleshooting (5 tapes). Prerequisite required. Includes a Study Guide.
Education; Industrial and Technical Education
Dist - BERGL

MIG Welding
VHS / 35mm strip
Welding Series
Color
$42.00 purchase _ #LX83C filmstrip, $62.00 purchase _ #LX83V VHS
Shows how to safely set up and operate a MIG welding unit. Reveals jobs suitable for this process.
Education; Industrial and Technical Education
Dist - CAREER **Prod** - CAREER

Might as Well Accept it, Everybody's Got One, Vol 4 22 MIN
VHS / 16mm
Friend Like Patty Series
Color (G)
$95.00 purchase
Focuses upon positive messages to teenage girls. Part of an eight - part series, 'A Friend Like Patty,' featuring Patty Ellis.
Health and Safety; Psychology; Sociology
Dist - PROSOR

The Might of the Pen 28 MIN
16mm
Color
LC 75-701349
Describes the work of the combat historians and combat artists who record the actions and faces of an army at war.
Civics and Political Systems; History - United States
Dist - USNAC **Prod** - USA 1965

Mightier than the sword 10 MIN
16mm / VHS
Color (G IND)
$5.00 rental
Teaches officers of local unions and central bodies the importance of regular communication with the membership, especially through newsletters and newspapers. Names available sources of help in starting and regularly publishing a newsletter or newspaper. Features Howard Hesseman. Produced by the International Labor Communications Association.
Business and Economics; Literature and Drama; Social Science
Dist - AFLCIO

Mightier than the Sword 52 MIN
U-matic / VHS
Testament - the Bible and History Series
Color (G)
$279.00, $179.00 purchase _ #AD - 1727
Looks at the historical context into which Jesus was born and the background against which the New Testament was written. Examines the period in which the Old Testament achieved its final shape. Part of a seven - part series on the Bible and history.
History - World; Literature and Drama; Religion and Philosophy
Dist - FOTH **Prod** - FOTH

The Mighty Battleship - Renaissance of the War Machine 20 MIN
VHS / U-matic
Color
$335.00 purchase
Civics and Political Systems
Dist - ABCLR **Prod** - ABCLR 1982

The Mighty Fistful 60 MIN
U-matic / VHS
James Galway's Music in Time Series
Color (J)
Presents flutist James Galway discussing the founding of the Russian style of music. Includes a performance of Osipov's Balalaika Orchestra, the Bolshoi Opera's grand production of the coronation scene from Mussorgsky's Boris Godunov and Tchaikovsky's Violin Concerto.
Fine Arts
Dist - FOTH **Prod** - POLTEL 1982

Mighty Hunters 15 MIN
U-matic / VHS
Picture Book Park Series Green Module; Green module
Color (P)
Presents the children's story Good Hunting Little Indian by Peggy Parish and The Mighty Hunter by Berta Bader. Includes the poem Indian Children by Annette Wynne from For Days And Days.
Literature and Drama
Dist - AITECH **Prod** - WVIZTV 1974

Mighty little shepherd and in all his glory - Volume 24 45 MIN
VHS
Superbook series
Color (K P I R)
$11.99 purchase _ #35 - 86805 - 979
Uses an animated format to tell the story of Chris and Joy and their time travels through Biblical places and events. 'Mighty Little Shepherd' tells the story of David, while 'In All His Glory' is an account of King Solomon.
Literature and Drama; Religion and Philosophy
Dist - APH **Prod** - TYHP

Mighty Moose and the Quarterback Kid 31 MIN
16mm / U-matic / VHS
Teenage Years Series
Color (I)
LC 80-700981
Shows how 12 - year - old Benny plays football only to placate his father, and how the new football coach emphasizes playing the game for fun instead of for competition. Explains how the coach manages to bring Benny and his father closer together.
Fine Arts; Guidance and Counseling; Physical Education and Recreation; Sociology
Dist - TIMLIF **Prod** - BERKAR 1977

The Mighty pawns 60 MIN
VHS
Wonderworks collection series
Color (I J H)
$29.95 purchase _ #MIG010
Portrays inner - city kids who are inspired by their teacher to stay off the streets and rechannel their energies using chessboards and chessmen.
Guidance and Counseling; Literature and Drama; Physical Education and Recreation
Dist - KNOWUN **Prod** - PBS 1987

The Mighty Volga 25 MIN
U-matic / VHS / 16mm
Color (H C A)
Follows the flagship Lenin of the Volga fleet on its cruise down the Volga River, the lifeline of European Russia and the longest river in Europe.
Geography - World
Dist - NGS **Prod** - NGS 1977

Mighty Warriors 30 MIN
16mm
Glory Trail Series
B&W (I)
LC FIA66-1239
Describes the white settlers' hard and costly victory over the plains Indians in the push westward, picturing such battles as the Little Big Horn, the Sand Creek Massacre and the Fetterman Massacre. Stresses knowledge the whites acquired from their contact with Indians.
History - United States; Social Science
Dist - IU **Prod** - NET 1964

Mignon 30 MIN
U-matic / VHS / 16mm
Who's Afraid of Opera Series
Color (J)
LC 73-703434
Presents Joan Sutherland singing the opera Mignon. Features puppets in an opera box acting as a reviewing audience conversing with the performers as they enter or leave front stage.
Fine Arts
Dist - PHENIX **Prod** - PHENIX 1973

Mignon, and, La Perichole - Vol 4 60 MIN
VHS
Who's Afraid of Opera Series
Color (K)

$29.95 purchase _ #1258
Presents Joan Sutherland and her puppet friends to make opera fun. Features excerpts from the operas 'Mignon' and 'La Perichole' in Volume 4 of four volumes.
Fine Arts; Sociology
Dist - KULTUR

Migraine and other headaches 30 MIN
VHS
At time of diagnosis series
Color (G)
$19.95 purchase _ #1 - 5757 - 7017 - 2NK
Provides patients who have just been diagnosed with migraine or other headache problems and their families with thorough, comprehensive and understandable information. Examines what is going on in the body and what might have caused the condition. Explains the type of medical professionals a patient may encounter and how the condition is monitored. Explores treatment options, including medication and lifestyle changes. Looks at practical issues surrounding the illness and answers the most common questions. Part of an ongoing series to provide the in - depth medical information patients and their families need to know.
Health and Safety
Dist - TILIED **Prod** - TILIED 1996

Migraine - Diagnosis and Management 30 MIN
U-matic
Color (PRO)
Focuses on the migraine. Interviews three prominent headache specialists. Includes the most common headache - symptom profiles, organic and nonorganic etiologic factors and patient counseling.
Health and Safety
Dist - AYERST **Prod** - AYERST

Migrant Farmworkers 20 MIN
U-matic / VHS
Color
Portrays the poor quality of life among migrant laborers. Focuses on illegal aliens, Haitians, cardboard housing, a successful Arizona Farmworker's Union strike and the hope for further improvements for migrant workers.
Business and Economics; Social Science; Sociology
Dist - DCTVC **Prod** - DCTVC

Migrant misery 30 MIN
VHS
All black series
Color; PAL (H C A)
PdS65 purchase; Available in the United Kingdom or Ireland only
Investigates economic opportunities for blacks and focuses specifically on the illegal labor market. Documents the hardships and conditions blacks must cope with when working as illegal migrant workers. Sixth in a series of seven programs.
Sociology
Dist - BBCENE

Migrant, Pt 1 27 MIN
16mm
Color (J)
LC 79-709051
Tells the story of the migrant workers who are still the unwilling victims of the cost and profit squeeze between the consumer and the producer. Points out that the migrants lack unemployment insurance, minimum wage laws and child labor laws.
Sociology
Dist - NBCTV **Prod** - NBCTV 1970

Migrant, Pt 2 27 MIN
16mm
Color (J)
LC 79-709051
Tells the story of the migrant workers who are still the unwilling victims of the cost and profit squeeze between the consumer and the producer. Points out that the migrants lack unemployment insurance, minimum wage laws and child labor laws.
Sociology
Dist - NBCTV **Prod** - NBCTV 1970

Migrants 51 MIN
16mm
Color (G)
$50.00 rental
Offers a landmark documentary by M Carr about the hardships experienced by farmworkers as they travel from one harvest to another.
Agriculture; Fine Arts; Sociology
Dist - KITPAR

The Migrants 1980 52 MIN
U-matic / VHS / 16mm
Color (H C A)
Examines the plight of the migrant farmworkers. Documents the use of child labor, the substandard housing, and the traffic in illegal aliens. Narrated by Chris Wallace.
Agriculture; Sociology
Dist - FI **Prod** - NBCTV 1980

The Migrating Monarch 11 MIN
U-matic / VHS / 16mm
Color
Shows how millions of monarch butterflies congregate on 'butterfly trees,' where they remain dormant through the winter months. Depicts their spring flight north, repopulating wide areas of North America and Canada. Covers the four life stages of the butterfly.
Science - Natural
Dist - STANF **Prod** - STANF

Migration 12 MIN
16mm
Color (G)
$20.00 rental
Makes full use of rear - projection rephotography, stop - framing and slow motion. Interprets the migration of a flight of a ghost bird through aeons of space and time.
Fine Arts
Dist - CANCIN **Prod** - RIMMER 1969

Migration and Accumulation 43 MIN
VHS / U-matic
Basic and Petroleum Geology for Non - Geologists - Hydrocarbons and '- - Series; Hydrocarbons
Color (IND)
Industrial and Technical Education; Science - Physical
Dist - GPCV **Prod** - PHILLP

Migration of Birds - the Canada Goose 11 MIN
16mm / U-matic / VHS
Color (I J H)
Maps show the migratory patterns of the Canadian goose. Habits and characteristics shown include nesting, raising the young, teaching them to fly and flocking.
Science - Natural
Dist - EBEC **Prod** - EBEC 1959

Migration of the primordial sex cells into the genital ridge 18 MIN
16mm
Development of the female reproductive system series
Color
LC 74-702456
Demonstrates the development of the female reproductive system with emphasis on migration of the primordial sex cells into the genital ridge.
Science - Natural
Dist - EATONL **Prod** - EATONL 1974

The Migrations of a Melody 30 MIN
16mm
Eternal Light Series
B&W (H C A)
LC 79-700955
Based on a story by Yitzhak Leib Peretz, 'THE FATHER OF YIDDISH LITERATURE,' and presented in commemoration of the 50th anniversary of his death. Dramatizes the history of a melody which for years remained lost, unsung and presumed dead, but which periodically returned to life in different situations. (Kinescope).
Fine Arts; Religion and Philosophy
Dist - NAAJS **Prod** - JTS 1966

Miguel 10 MIN
16mm
B&W
Tells the story of a Puerto Rican boy who rebels against his background in a failed attempt to escape his environment.
Fine Arts; Sociology
Dist - NYU **Prod** - NYU

Miguel Angel Asturias - Cadaveres Para La Publicidad 60 MIN
U-matic / VHS / 16mm
Color (SPANISH)
Presents an adaptations of Miguel Angel Asturias' work Cadaveres Para La Publicidad which depicts how the execution and mass burial of a group of labor organizers is hushed up until the government discovers a taste for publicity and decides that people love to read about murder.
Foreign Language; Literature and Drama
Dist - FOTH **Prod** - FOTH 1984

Miguel De Cervantes - El Licenciado Vidriera 60 MIN
U-matic / VHS / 16mm
Color (SPANISH)
Offers an adaptation of Cervantes' work El Licenciado Vidriera.
Foreign Language; Literature and Drama
Dist - FOTH **Prod** - FOTH

Miguel De Unamuno - Niebla 60 MIN
U-matic / VHS
Color (SPANISH)
Presents a version of Miguel de Unamuno's absurdist work Niebla.
Foreign Language; Literature and Drama
Dist - FOTH **Prod** - FOTH 1984

Miguel Muligan Y Su Pala De Vapor 11 MIN
U-matic / VHS / 16mm
Color (SPANISH)
LC 73-702772
A Spanish version of 'MIKE MULLIGAN AND HIS STEAM SHOVEL.' Explains that in his haste to dig the cellar for a town hall, Miguel Muligan forgets to leave a way out for his steam shovel. Shows how the problem is solved when the steam shovel is converted into a furnace for the new building.
Foreign Language; Literature and Drama
Dist - WWS **Prod** - WWS 1960

Miguel - Up from Puerto Rico 15 MIN
16mm / U-matic / VHS
Many Americans Series
Color (I J)
Portrays some events in the life of a boy born in Puerto Rico who must now cope with life in New York City. Tells of his dejection when he finds he cannot catch a fish in the city river and of his happiness when he discovers he can work as a translator for Spanish speaking customers at a neighborhood store. Shows the close family relationships and gives a lesson in resourcefulness and the advantages of bi - cul turalism.
Guidance and Counseling; Social Science; Sociology
Dist - LCOA **Prod** - LCOA 1970

Miguelin 63 MIN
16mm
Color; B&W (I J H C) (SPANISH)
A Spanish - language motion picture which tells of a small boy's effort to cope with poverty by taking the poor box from the church. Shows that when he realizes his mistake, he sells his burro to leave money in the poor box. Recounts that when the villagers discover what he has done, they help him recover his burro for the blessing of the animals.
Foreign Language; Religion and Philosophy; Social Science; Sociology
Dist - TRANSW **Prod** - IFB 1964
IFB

The Mikado 150 MIN
VHS
Color (H C G)
$59.00 purchase _ #DL234; $49.95 purchase _ #S01693
Presents a 1986 production of the Gilbert and Sullivan musical, The Mikado, which spoofs Victorian England disguised as a Japanese musical drama.
Fine Arts; Literature and Drama
Dist - INSIM
UILL

The Mikado 150 MIN
VHS
Color (G)
$49.95 purchase _ #S01693
Presents Gilbert and Sullivan's comic opera 'The Mikado,' a spoof of Victorian society disguised as a Japanese musical drama.
Fine Arts; Literature and Drama
Dist - UILL

The Mikado 88 MIN
VHS
Color (G)
$39.95 purchase _ #MIK030
Teams a cast from the D'Oyly Carte Opera Company with the London Symphony Orchestra for this screen adaptation of Gilbert and Sullivan's most popular operetta. Uses the guise of a Japanese musical drama to present a raucous comic spoof of Victorian society. Directed by Victor Schertzinger.
Fine Arts; Literature and Drama
Dist - HOMVIS **Prod** - JANUS 1939

Mike 11 MIN
16mm
B&W
LC FIA63-667
A story of Mike, a potential drop - out. Shows some of Mike's feelings about school and acceptance of authority. The case worker tries to help Mike understand the importance of school at his age.
Education; Guidance and Counseling; Psychology; Sociology
Dist - USC **Prod** - USC 1961

Mike and Kathy 28 MIN
16mm
Jason Films Portrait Series
Color
LC 73-700739
Presents a cinema verite portrait of Mike Burton, a blind Vietnam veteran, and his wife, Kathy, as they struggle to find a new life for themselves.
Guidance and Counseling; Psychology; Sociology
Dist - JASON **Prod** - JASON 1973

Mike and Lee Moore 28 MIN
16mm

Private Lives of Americans Series
Color
LC 72-700470
Portrays the aspirations, dreams, and frustrations of average Americans by presenting the private lives of a typical young couple who live in Oakland, California. Characterizes the husband, a former Marine and Vietnam veteran, as an automobile mechanic who enjoys the hobbies of drag racing and motorcycle riding while the wife is employed as a waitress.
Psychology; Sociology
Dist - KQEDTV **Prod** - KQEDTV 1972

Mike Fright 18 MIN
16mm
B&W
Describes what happens when the Little Rascals enter their International Silver String Submarine Band in a radio station contest.
Fine Arts
Dist - RMIBHF **Prod** - ROACH 1934

Mike Kolarov 12 MIN
16mm / U-matic / VHS
Color (H C A)
Presents Mike Kolarov sharing his traditional Yugoslav Macedonian music and dance with American enthusiasts in the California redwoods. Features Novo Selo playing gajda, kaval, tambura and tupan.
Fine Arts
Dist - AGINP **Prod** - AGINP

Mike Mulligan and His Steam Shovel 11 MIN
16mm / U-matic / VHS
Color (K P)
An iconographic film using the pictures and text of Virginia Lee Burton's story of the steam shovel that defied obsolescence by becoming the furnace in the Popperville Town Hall.
English Language; Literature and Drama
Dist - WWS **Prod** - WWS 1958

Mike Mulligan and His Steam Shovel 35 MIN
VHS / 16mm
Children's Circle Video Series
Color (K)
$18.88 purchase _ #CCV012
Also includes other children's stories - Burt Dow, Deep Water Man, Moon Man.
Literature and Drama
Dist - EDUCRT

Mike Rosen 40 MIN
VHS
Color (H C G)
$79.00 purchase
Features the children's writer talking about writing poetry and fiction for children, and about themes such as family and pets. Discusses his work including You Can't Catch Me; Nasty, Hairy Tales; and Nursery Crimes.
Literature and Drama
Dist - ROLAND **Prod** - INCART

Mike the Bike 11 MIN
U-matic / VHS / 16mm
Color (P I J)
LC 75-702206
Demonstrates correct ways to ride bikes on the streets and highways. Shows the importance of properly equipping bikes and checking their condition before taking them on the road.
Health and Safety
Dist - AIMS **Prod** - JRDNJR 1975

Mike the Bike 11 MIN
U-matic / VHS / 16mm
Color (I J H)
$25 rental _ #4176
Points out that bike riding is an enjoyable and healthy pastime that can be made even more so when safety, the rules of the road, and common sense are adhered to.
Health and Safety
Dist - AIMS **Prod** - AIMS 1973

Mike Wallace 60 MIN
VHS / U-matic
John Callaway Interviews Series
Color
LC 82-706690
Presents John Callaway interviewing Mike Wallace of the CBS television program 60 Minutes. Discusses journalistic ethics, techniques used by the 60 Minutes team and other journalistic insights and personal anecdotes.
Fine Arts
Dist - PBS **Prod** - WTTWTV 1981

Mike Wilks 30 MIN
VHS
Making their mark series
Color (A)
PdS65 purchase _ Unavailable in South Africa
Profiles Mike Wilks, who has a unique drawing style and way of working. Introduces the viewer to practical and aesthetic aspects of the skill of drawing. Part of a six-part series.
Fine Arts
Dist - BBCENE

Mikey and Nicky 205 MIN
16mm
Color
Looks at a friendship between two men that is falling apart. Illustrates the axiom that sometimes even paranoids have real enemies.
Fine Arts
Dist - TLECUL **Prod** - TLECUL

Mikhail Tahl 29 MIN
Videoreel / VT2
Koltanowski on Chess Series
Color
Physical Education and Recreation
Dist - PBS **Prod** - KQEDTV

Mikis Theodorakis 52 MIN
VHS / U-matic
Color (G) (FRENCH (ENGLISH NARRATION))
Presents a video portrait of the famous Greek composer; his ideas are juxtaposed with concert performances.
Fine Arts; Foreign Language; History - World
Dist - RIZACV **Prod** - RIZACV

Miklos Jansco series
My Way home 79 MIN
The Red and the white 92 MIN
Red psalm 88 MIN
Silence and cry 79 MIN
Dist - KINOIC

Mil - STD - 781C - Examples 30 MIN
U-matic / VHS
Reliability Engineering Series
Color (IND)
Describes procedures to select appropriate sampling plans.
Industrial and Technical Education
Dist - COLOSU **Prod** - COLOSU

Mila 23 - Simion's World 15 MIN
16mm / U-matic / VHS
Color (C A)
Describes a group of people living at the marshy delta of Europe's River Danube. Tells how they have adapted to this harsh way of life and how they have been strengthened by their traditions and beliefs.
Geography - World; Sociology
Dist - WOMBAT **Prod** - LESFMA

Milani Comparetti Motor Development Test 25 MIN
VHS / U-matic
Color (PRO)
Describes and demonstrates the Milani Comparetti test, a series of simple procedures designed to evaluate a child's motor development from birth to about two years.
Psychology
Dist - UNEBO **Prod** - UNEBO

Mild Salt - Restricted Diet
U-matic / VHS
Color
Shows a middle - aged man who is urged to cut back on his use of salt. Recommends examination of food labels, substitute spices and eliminating certain foods.
Health and Safety
Dist - MIFE **Prod** - MIFE

Mildred Cohn 30 MIN
VHS
Eminent chemists videotapes series
Color (H C G)
$60.00 purchase _ #VT - 028
Meets chemist Mildred Cohn. Part of a series glimpsing into the history of chemistry and offering insights into the successes, trials and tribulations of some of the most distinguished names in the world of chemistry.
Science
Dist - AMCHEM

Mildred Dilling - Memoirs of a Harp Virtuoso 60 MIN
VHS / U-matic
Color
Features Mildred Dilling, an 84 - year old harpist, as she combines performance with remembrances of her experiences with her teacher and with her own star pupil, Harpo Marx. Presented in two half - hour programs.
Fine Arts
Dist - OHUTC **Prod** - OHUTC

Mildred - the first 90 years 29 MIN
VHS
Color (G C)
$165.00 purchase, $45.00 rental
Focuses on an aging dance teacher and the impact of her life on the lives of others.
Fine Arts; Health and Safety
Dist - TNF

Mile zero - the sage tour 49 MIN
16mm / VHS
Color (J H C G T A)
$75.00 purchase, $35.00 rental
Profiles four Canadian high school students who decide to drive cross - country, speaking out for nuclear disarmament. Follows the four on their nine - month trip, in which they spoke to more than 120,000 students in 362 schools. Co - produced by DLI Productions.
Civics and Political Systems; History - World; Sociology
Dist - EFVP **Prod** - NFBC 1988

Miles of Smiles, Years of Struggle - the Untold Story of the Pullman Porter 59 MIN
16mm
Color (H C A)
LC 83-700123
Provides a history of the Black Pullman Porters, who during the 100 years after the Civil War were envied by some Blacks for the good jobs they had and reviled by others for being Uncle Toms. Reveals how they finally succeeded in forming their own Black Trade Union in 1925, which became a prime force behind the Civil Rights movement.
Business and Economics; History - United States; Social Science
Dist - BNCHMK **Prod** - BNCHMK 1982
AFLCIO

Miles to Go 80 MIN
VHS / U-matic
Color (H A)
LC 84-707156
Illustrates the good and bad experiences of eight neophyte female backpackers ranging in age from 27 to 72 who take a guided trek through the mountains of North Carolina and Georgia.
Physical Education and Recreation
Dist - MADDBP **Prod** - MADDBP 1984

Miles to Go 30 MIN
16mm
B&W
LC 77-702109
Tells about an independent Black trucker from rural Texas, who has been driving a truck for 25 years and a million miles. Shows the driver on a long solitary drive as he reminisces about his life, friends and work.
Guidance and Counseling; Social Science; Sociology
Dist - GORDNB **Prod** - GORDNB 1976

Miles to go - a women's wilderness journey 80 MIN
VHS / 16mm
Color (H C G)
$1100.00, $395.00 purchase, $150.00 rental
Follows eight women who undertake a two - week wilderness journey in the Smokey Mountains. Reveals that their ages range from 27 - 72, their economic and cultural backgrounds are disparate but they all have had no prior wilderness experience and are eager to meet and cope with new challenges in their lives. Studies group dynamics and how people exercise leadership, take risks and make decisions.
Guidance and Counseling; Psychology; Sociology
Dist - FLMLIB **Prod** - MADDBP 1983

Milestones 14 MIN
16mm
Color
Shows a program in which parents help their pre - school deaf children learn to speak by utilizing their residual hearing.
Education; Guidance and Counseling
Dist - FLMLIB **Prod** - FLMLIB

Milestones in Missilery 10 MIN
16mm
Color
LC FIE63-65
Describes outstanding milestones in missile development and testing accomplished at the White firings of the V2 rocket in 1945.
Industrial and Technical Education; Science
Dist - USNAC **Prod** - USA 1961

Milestones in Space 5 MIN
16mm
Screen news digest series; Vol 5; Issue 1
B&W (J H)
Describes Telstar out in orbit as a peaceful servant of mankind, helping nations to communicate through its relay system.
Psychology; Science; Social Science
Dist - HEARST **Prod** - HEARST 1962

Milisen - Articulation Testing 37 MIN
16mm
Videoclinical Series Series
B&W (C S)
LC 73-702603
Shows Dr Robert L Milisen of Indiana University testing the articulation of several young children. Includes a segment of an interview with the parents of one of the children.

Education
Dist - WMUDIC Prod - WMUDIC 1972

Military 30 MIN
U-matic / VHS
Clues to Career Opportunities for Liberal Arts Graduates Series
Color (C A)
LC 80-706238
Compares a career in the military to working for a large corporation. Discusses how students can gain training or further education while serving in the military. Examines travel opportunities, lifestyles, and benefits.
Civics and Political Systems; Psychology
Dist - IU Prod - IU 1979

Military 29 MIN
Videoreel / VT2
Commonwealth Series
Color
Guidance and Counseling; History - United States
Dist - PBS Prod - WITFTV

Military 30 MIN
U-matic
Fast Forward Series
Color (H C)
Explores computers, lasers, smart weaponry and sensors and their effects on the military.
Computer Science; Science
Dist - TVOTAR Prod - TVOTAR 1979

Military 14 MIN
U-matic / VHS
Tax tips on tape series
Color; Captioned (A PRO IND)
$20.00, $40.00 purchase _ #TCA17594, #TCA17593
Discusses taxation for service members. Differentiates between taxable and nontaxable pay and bonuses for active - duty military personnel. Reveals that service members can deduct mortage payments, in some cases, while receiving tax - free military housing allowances.
Business and Economics; Civics and Political Systems; Social Science
Dist - USNAC Prod - USIRS 1988

The Military and the environment 29 MIN
VHS
Color (J H C G T A)
$25.00 purchase
Reveals that the Pentagon is using and disposing of many deadly substances, often secretly and without any civilian oversight. Interviews Congressmen Mike Synar and Richard Ray, New York Times reporter Keith Schneider and others on the consequences of these practices. Produced by Sandy Gottlieb.
Sociology
Dist - EFVP Prod - CDINFO 1990

Military Budget - Dollars and Defense 28 MIN
U-matic / VHS
Issues in the News Series
Color (J H C)
LC 84-707122
Looks at differing views of military spending by the Reagan Administration. Includes the views of such experts as Admiral Eugene J Carrol, Jr, former Commanding Officer of the USS Midway, Congresswoman Pat Schroeder of Colorado, Admiral Stanley Fine, Pentagon budget analyst for three administrations and General David Jones, former Chairman of the Joint Chiefs of Staff.
Civics and Political Systems
Dist - CNEMAG Prod - FUNPC 1984

Military Civic Action 31 MIN
16mm
B&W
LC 74-706146
Reveals past and present roles of the U S Army in military civic action.
Civics and Political Systems; History - United States
Dist - USNAC Prod - USA 1964

Military Eyewear - Measurement, Fit and Adjustment 30 MIN
U-matic / VHS / 16mm
Color (A)
Demonstrates measurement methods and techniques for fitting a patient for eyewear.
Civics and Political Systems; Health and Safety
Dist - USNAC Prod - WRAIR 1983

Military Immunization - General Procedures 25 MIN
16mm
B&W
Depicts the procedures which enable a small team of medical personnel to immunize large groups of men safely and speedily. Stresses the proper planning and organization and the use of an individual sterile syringe and needle for each injection.
Civics and Political Systems; Health and Safety
Dist - USNAC Prod - USN

Military Immunization - Smallpox Vaccination 10 MIN
16mm
Color
LC FIE59-142
Depicts the procedures for smallpox vaccination and for observing and recording the effects of vaccination.
Civics and Political Systems; Health and Safety
Dist - USNAC Prod - USN 1954

The Military - Industrial Firm 55 MIN
VHS / U-matic
Briefings on Peace and the Economy - Converting from a Military to a Civilian Economy Series
Color (C)
Talks about the relationship between the Pentagon and military contractors. Produced by Office for East Asia and the Pacific and the NCCC.
Civics and Political Systems
Dist - CWS

Military Instruction Series no 1
Principles of Learning 23 MIN
Dist - USNAC

Military Instruction Series
Speech techniques 11 MIN
The Stages of Instruction - Application, Examination and Review or Critique 20 MIN
The Stages of Instruction - Preparation 12 MIN
The Stages of Instruction - Presentation 12 MIN
Training aids 23 MIN
Dist - USNAC

Military Medicine 19 MIN
16mm
B&W
LC FIE63-269
Reports on advances made in military medicine. Reviews the benefits to humanity as well as to military personnel. Deals with Major Walter Reed's fight against yellow fever. Covers accomplishments in tissue grafting and nuclear, submarine and aerospace medicine.
Civics and Political Systems; Health and Safety
Dist - USNAC Prod - USDD 1962

Military Oceanography - Bathythermograph Observations 16 MIN
16mm
Color
Explains the features and operation of a bathythermograph and demonstrates its lowering and recovery, removal of the slide and proper care of the bathythermograph.
Industrial and Technical Education; Science - Physical
Dist - USNAC Prod - USN 1950

Military Oceanography - Occupying an Oceanographic Station 29 MIN
16mm
Color
Shows the principal design features of nansen bottles as they are used in drawing water samples and in performing other procedures.
Industrial and Technical Education; Science - Physical
Dist - USNAC Prod - USN 1950

Military Pipeline System 24 MIN
16mm
B&W
LC FIE52-1692
Tells the story of a pipeline built by American troops in difficult terrain under hazardous conditions.
Civics and Political Systems; Industrial and Technical Education
Dist - USNAC Prod - USA 1948

Military Pipeline System - CBI Theater 24 MIN
U-matic
Historical Reports Series
B&W
LC 80-706768
Tells the story of a pipeline built by American troops in difficult terrain under hazardous conditions during World War II. Issued in 1948 as a motion picture.
Civics and Political Systems; History - United States; History - World
Dist - USNAC Prod - USA 1980

Military Police Operation, Pt 3 - Military Police Patrol Investigations 28 MIN
16mm
B&W
LC 74-705142
Outlines the mission of the individual military policeman in patrol investigations - shows a patrol in action investigating an assault.
Civics and Political Systems
Dist - USNAC Prod - USA 1971

The Military Police Story 33 MIN
16mm
B&W (GERMAN)
LC FIE54-238
Illustrates the training, duties and responsibilities of the Military Police Corps. Shows MP activities in Germany and Korea today.
Civics and Political Systems; Geography - World; Guidance and Counseling
Dist - USNAC Prod - USA 1954

Military Police Support in Amphibious Operations 14 MIN
16mm
B&W
LC FIE53-469
Explains the duties and functions of the U S Military Police in a combined amphibious assault.
Civics and Political Systems
Dist - USNAC Prod - USA 1953

Military Police Town Patrol, Pt 2 - Motor Patrols 16 MIN
16mm
B&W
Explains the responsibilities and techniques involved in motor patrolling, showing how motor patrols are organized and how patrol missions are performed.
Civics and Political Systems
Dist - USNAC Prod - USAF

Military Police Traffic Control, Pt 4 - Traffic Control Reconnaissance 27 MIN
16mm
Color
LC 74-705143
Depicts various aspects of traffic control reconnaissance under safe and occasional enemy action conditions.
Civics and Political Systems
Dist - USNAC Prod - USA 1970

Military Roads and Airfields, Pt 2 - Drainage 23 MIN
16mm
B&W
LC 75-703727
Shows the construction, application and maintenance of drainage devices, the crown or grade of road and airfield surfaces and side, intercepting and diversion ditches. Demonstrates how to check dams and culverts.
Civics and Political Systems; Industrial and Technical Education
Dist - USNAC Prod - USA 1968

Military Rock Climbing - Technique of Climbing 32 MIN
16mm
B&W
LC FIE52-1512
Shows the organization of two and three man 'CLIMBING TEAMS,' equipment and its use, climbing technique for various types of formations and types of holds and knots.
Civics and Political Systems; Physical Education and Recreation; Psychology
Dist - USNAC Prod - USA 1948

The Military Sea Transportation Service - Introduction 19 MIN
16mm
B&W
LC FIE54-101
Explains the functions, organization and operations of the military transportation service of the U S Navy.
Civics and Political Systems; Social Science
Dist - USNAC Prod - USN 1953

The Military Sea Transportation Service - Troop Transportation 20 MIN
16mm
B&W
LC FIE55-258
Illustrates the problems and procedures involved in the formation, functions and duties of the advance parties and voyage staffs aboard MSTS transports.
Civics and Political Systems; Psychology; Social Science
Dist - USNAC Prod - USN 1954

Military spending after the war with Iraq 30 MIN
VHS
America's defense monitor series; War with Iraq
Color (J H C G)
$29.95 purchase _ #ADM435V
Investigates United States military policy and spending after the war with Iraq. Part of a six - part series examining the United States war with Iraq, 1990 - 1991.
Civics and Political Systems; History - United States; Sociology
Dist - CAMV

Military Stevedoring, Pt 8 - Rigging Expedients for Heavy Lifts 24 MIN
16mm
Color
LC 74-706147
Shows several methods for using standard riggings to create a heavy lift capability for loading and unloading military cargo.
Civics and Political Systems; Industrial and Technical Education
Dist - USNAC **Prod** - USA 1971

Military Stevedoring, Pt 2 - Slings and Bridles 20 MIN
16mm
B&W
LC 74-705145
Shows several types of slings and bridles and their uses. Empahsizes the importance of using the right equipment for the job.
Industrial and Technical Education
Dist - USNAC **Prod** - USA 1971

Milk and beef 15 MIN
VHS
Color; PAL (P I J H)
Examines the use of cattle as food animals, both as sources of milk and meat. Uses diagrams to explore a cow's stomach. Visits a dairy farm and milk bottling plant. Shows beef cattle being sold and their carcasses.
Agriculture; Social Science
Dist - VIEWTH **Prod** - VIEWTH

Milk and Public Health 12 MIN
16mm
B&W
LC FIE53-208
Points out the dangers of haphazard milk production, the resultant public health problem and the need for regulatory legislation. Reviews steps taken to insure healthy cows and sanitary equipment and supplies. For professional use only.
Health and Safety; Home Economics
Dist - USNAC **Prod** - USPHS 1951

Milk and Republic Health 11 MIN
16mm
B&W (SPANISH)
LC 74-705147
Points out the dangers of haphazard milk production, the resultant public health problem, and the need for regulatory legislation. Reviews the steps taken to insure healthy cows, sanitary equipment and supplies, and other hygenic methods throughout the production and processing of milk.
Agriculture; Foreign Language; Health and Safety; Social Science
Dist - USNAC **Prod** - NMAC 1951

Milk Composition and Yield and Removal of Milk from the Udder 17 MIN
VHS / U-matic
Color
Identifies the various factors that influence milk yield in cattle. Looks at three main methods of removing milk from the udder.
Agriculture
Dist - HOBAR **Prod** - HOBAR

The Milk Ejection Reflex 21 MIN
16mm / U-matic / VHS
Physiology Series
Color
LC 73-703202
Shows how milk is secreted from the mammary gland and explains the chemical mechanism involved. Illustrates how electrical stimulation of the nerve supply to the posterior pituitary evokes a positive milk rejection response.
Science - Natural
Dist - MEDIAG **Prod** - WILEYJ 1972

Milk - from Farm to You 13 MIN
16mm / U-matic / VHS
Color (K P)
LC 73-700470
Follows the production of milk from the milking of the cows to the creamery to the home. Explains the processes of homogenization and pasteurization. Depicts the production of related dairy products, such as cheese and ice cream.
Agriculture; Social Science
Dist - EBEC **Prod** - EBEC 1972

Milk in the Computer Age 13 MIN
16mm
Color (I J)
Accompanies two sixth grade students as the visit a dairy farm and a milk processing plant. Follows milk production techniques from the time it leaves the cow until it is ready for delivery to consumers.
Agriculture; Health and Safety
Dist - NDC **Prod** - NDC 1983

The Milk makers - 32
VHS
Reading rainbow series
Color; CC (K P)
$39.95 purchase
Shows how milk travels from the dairy cow to the neighborhood supermarket. Visits the dairy country of California with LeVar, who gets a lesson on how to milk a cow by hand and an introduction to the modern way of milking and feeding 600 cows. Part of a series offering a multicultural approach to generating reading enthusiasm with cross - curricular applications, hosted by LeVar Burton.
Agriculture; English Language; Home Economics; Literature and Drama; Science
Dist - GPN **Prod** - LNMDP

Milk, Milk, Milk 1 MIN
U-matic / VHS
Color
Describes the goodness of milk and where you can find it. Uses two calves and their mother in this singing television spot.
Health and Safety; Home Economics
Dist - KIDSCO **Prod** - KIDSCO

Milk Products 5 MIN
U-matic / VHS / 16mm
How It's made Series
Color (K)
Business and Economics
Dist - LUF **Prod** - HOLIA

Milking Goats 15 MIN
VHS / U-matic
Encounter in the Desert Series
Color (I)
Deals with milking goats and making cheese and butter among the Bedouin nomads.
Geography - World; Social Science; Sociology
Dist - CTI **Prod** - CTI

The Milkman 10 MIN
16mm
Color (P I)
Shows the work necessary to get a bottle of milk to the consumer. Covers dairy farms and machine and hand milking. Describes milk delivery as it was when milkmen delivered bottles of milk to individual houses.
Agriculture; Home Economics
Dist - VIEWTH **Prod** - GATEEF

Milkweed - A Study in symbiosis 25 MIN
VHS / U-matic
Color (J H)
$270.00, $320.00 purchase, $50.00 rental
Studies a common plant which is part of a complex living network of interaction and interdependence. Explains how milkweed and its insect visitors provide an excellent model for ecological study.
Science - Natural
Dist - NDIM **Prod** - CANBC 1990

The Milky Way Discovered 29 MIN
U-matic
Project Universe - Astronomy Series Lesson 19
Color (C A)
Discusses effects of dust in space on astronomic observations. Reviews Herschel's method by which he determined possible shape of the galaxy.
Science - Physical
Dist - CDTEL **Prod** - COAST

The Milky Way Structure 29 MIN
U-matic
Project Universe - Astronomy Series Lesson 20
Color (C A)
Illustrates problems in obtaining an accurate picture of our galaxy. Recounts development of radio astronomy. Describes operation of radio telescope at Harvard University.
Science - Physical
Dist - CDTEL **Prod** - COAST

The Mill 15 MIN
U-matic / VHS / 16mm
Color (C A)
Presents a dramatization of women's lives in Yugoslavia, culminating with an abortion.
Fine Arts; Sociology
Dist - WOMBAT **Prod** - WOMBAT

The Mill Brothers story 56 MIN
VHS
Color; B&W; Hi-fi; Dolby stereo (G)
$29.95 purchase _ #1309
Documents the family saga of the Mills Brothers, spanning more than 50 years in show business. Tells their story from early innovations of vocally imitating musical instruments, through tragic career setbacks, to successes as performing artists and recording stars. Includes films clips dating back to 1932 and their final public appearance in 1981, and the Mills Brothers' renditions of American classics. Interviews Harry, Donald and Herbert Mills and offers clips of John Charles Mills and John Hutchinson Mills.
Fine Arts; History - United States
Dist - KULTUR **Prod** - KULTUR 1992

Mill - in 12 MIN
16mm
Color
Shows anti - war demonstrators as they take to the street in New York, Christmas 1967 and last minute Christmas shoppers who are hassled by the police.
Geography - United States; Sociology
Dist - CANWRL **Prod** - CANWRL

Millay at Steepletop 25 MIN
16mm / U-matic / VHS
Color (J)
History - United States; Literature and Drama
Dist - PHENIX **Prod** - PHENIX 1984

Millbrook 9 MIN
16mm
Color (G)
$18.00 rental
Depicts a young couple losing their individual identity and merging with rotting leaves as the universe decays and is regenerated by a mysterious stranger. Produced by Gordon Ball.
Fine Arts; Sociology
Dist - CANCIN

Millenia 5 MIN
VHS / U-matic
Color
Depicts the evolution of five aspects of physical life - geometry,men, animals, moons and the dead. Uses analog and digital imaging techniques.
Fine Arts
Dist - KITCHN **Prod** - KITCHN

Millenium - tribal wisdom and the modern world 120 MIN
VHS
Color (G)
$29.95 purchase _ #X007
Examines the lives of diverse tribal cultures to redefine thinking about the Earth and the people who inhabit it. Looks through the eyes of tribal people to gain new perspective about the most basic issues of life - love, work, family and spirituality. Features David Maybury - Lewis as host.
Sociology
Dist - STRUE **Prod** - PAV 1993

Millennia 5 MIN
U-matic
Color; Silent (C)
$150.00
Experimental film by Barbara Buckner.
Fine Arts
Dist - AFA **Prod** - AFA 1981

Miller a C Transformer 180 Amp Shielded Arc Machine Set - Up 3 MIN
VHS / BETA
Color (IND)
Shows the set - up for a Miller A C 180 amp shielded arc machine.
Industrial and Technical Education; Psychology
Dist - RMIBHF **Prod** - RMIBHF

Miller module method series

Shielded metal arc welding - Pt 01	14 MIN
Shielded metal arc welding - Pt 02	14 MIN
Shielded metal arc welding - Pt 03	14 MIN
Shielded metal arc welding - Pt 04	14 MIN
Shielded metal arc welding - Pt 05	14 MIN
Shielded metal arc welding - Pt 06	14 MIN
Shielded metal arc welding - Pt 07	14 MIN
Shielded metal arc welding - Pt 08	14 MIN
Shielded metal arc welding - Pt 09	14 MIN
Shielded metal arc welding - Pt 10	14 MIN
Shielded metal arc welding - Pt 11	14 MIN
Shielded metal arc welding - Pt 12	9 MIN
Shielded metal arc welding - Pt 13	14 MIN
Shielded metal arc welding - Pt 14	14 MIN
Shielded metal arc welding - Pt 15	17 MIN
Shielded metal arc welding - Pt 16	14 MIN

Dist - MILEL

Miller Moves Out 4 MIN
16mm
Color
LC 75-700324
Presents, without narration, the story of Miller Brewing Company's expansion program. Shows the company's new facilities under construction.
Business and Economics
Dist - MBC **Prod** - MBC 1975

Miller's Tale 45 MIN
U-matic / VHS
Survey of English Literature I Series
Color
Analyzes the British literary work Miller's Tale.
Literature and Drama
Dist - MDCPB **Prod** - MDCPB

Millersville State College - Guest Frank Fletcher, Program a 29 MIN
Videoreel / VT2
Sonia Malkine on Campus Series
Color
Features French folk singer Sonia Malkine and her special guest Frank Fletcher visiting Millersville State College in Pennsylvania.
Fine Arts; Foreign Language; Geography - United States
Dist - PBS **Prod** - WITFTV

Millersville State College - Guest Frank Fletcher, Program B 29 MIN
Videoreel / VT2
Sonia Malkine on Campus Series
Color
Features French folk singer Sonia Malkine and her special guest Frank Fletcher visiting Millersville State College in Pennsylvania.
Fine Arts; Foreign Language; Geography - United States
Dist - PBS **Prod** - WITFTV

Millhouse - a White Comedy 93 MIN
16mm
B&W
Questions the American electoral process and chronicles the public career of Richard Nixon. Documents Nixon's image - building through the media.
Biography; Civics and Political Systems; Fine Arts; Literature and Drama
Dist - NYFLMS **Prod** - NYFLMS 1971

Millicent 30 MIN
16mm
B&W
LC FIA67-5316
Presents a case study of a four - and - a - half - year - old girl who is mentally retarded, hyperactive, and distractible. Demonstrates the Else Haeussermann techniques for testing children with multiple handicaps.
Psychology
Dist - UCPA **Prod** - HAEUS 1965

Millicent Dillon - 5 - 9 - 80 60 MIN
VHS / Cassette
Poetry Center reading series
Color (G)
$15.00, $45.00 purchase, $15.00 rental _ #389 - 323
Features the writer participating at the Women Writers Union reading on the workplace at the Poetry Center, San Francisco State University, with an introduction by Tom Mandel. Includes Dillon talking about writing her biography of Jane Bowles, A Little Original Sin; the difficulty of getting biographical information; the biographer's problem with identity; and Bowles' difficulties with writer's block. Reads fragments from Bowles' journals and talks about her preoccupation with religion and sexuality.
Literature and Drama
Dist - POETRY **Prod** - POETRY 1980

Millicent Dillon - 4 - 2 - 87 45 MIN
VHS / Cassette
Poetry Center reading series
Color (G)
$15.00, $45.00 purchase, $15.00 rental _ #749 - 599
Features the writer reading the first act of her play, She Is In Tangier, at the Poetry Center, San Francisco State University, with an introduction by Frances Phillips.
Literature and Drama
Dist - POETRY **Prod** - POETRY 1987

Millicent Hodson and Annabelle Gamson 30 MIN
U-matic / VHS
Eye on Dance - Passing on Dance Series
Color
Features dancers recreating the earliest modern dance. Hosted by Julinda Lewis.
Fine Arts
Dist - ARCVID **Prod** - ARCVID

The Millikan Experiment 15 MIN
U-matic / VHS
Mechanical Universe - High School Adaptation Series
Color (H)
Science - Physical
Dist - SCCON **Prod** - SCCON 1986

Millikan Experiment 30 MIN
16mm
PSSC Physics Films Series
B&W (H)
Discusses the use of conservation of energy principles in analyzing the behavior of electrical systems. Shows a simplified Millikan experiment as photographed through a microscope.
Science - Physical
Dist - MLA **Prod** - PSSC 1959

The Millikan Experiment 30 MIN
16mm / U-matic / VHS
Mechanical Universe Series
Color (C A)
Describes how Robert Millikan, understanding the electric force on a charged droplet and viscosity, measured the charge of a single electron.
Science - Physical
Dist - FI **Prod** - ANNCPB

Millikan's Oil - Drop Experiment 15 MIN
U-matic / VHS
Experiment - Physics Level 2 Series
Color (C)
$249.00, $149.00 purchase _ #AD - 1078
Uses a modified version of the Millikan oil - drop apparatus to measure the radius and total charge of oil droplets. Part of a series of videos demonstrating physics experiments which are too impractical to perform in a classroom laboratory.
Education; Psychology; Science - Physical
Dist - FOTH **Prod** - FOTH

Milling 9 MIN
VHS / U-matic
Manufacturing Materials and Processes Series
Color
Covers types of milling machines, major components of a vertical milling machine, types of milling cutters and description of milling process.
Industrial and Technical Education
Dist - WFVTAE **Prod** - GE

Milling a Circular T - Slot 22 MIN
16mm
Machine Shop Work Series Operations on the Vertical Milling Machine,'no 5
B&W
LC FIE51-565
Shows how to mill a circular T - slot in solid metal, use a rotary table for continuous circular milling, use a two - lip end mill, end mill and T - slot cutter, and use a dial indicator with a test bar.
Industrial and Technical Education
Dist - USNAC **Prod** - USOE 1943

Milling a Helical Cutter 18 MIN
16mm
Machine Shop Work Series Operations on the Milling Machine, no 8
B&W
LC FIE51-599
Shows how to Mount Arbor, Cutter and Arbor support, mount workpiece between centers, set dividing head for specified number of divisions, position workpiece for first cut, and rough - and finish - mill the workpiece.
Industrial and Technical Education
Dist - USNAC **Prod** - USOE 1945

Milling a Helical Groove 28 MIN
16mm
Machine Shop Work Series Operations on the Vertical Milling Machine,'no 4
B&W
LC FIE51-566
Explains how to mill a helical groove in a cylindrical shaft, how to select and set the machine gears for milling a helical groove with any lead and how to use the dividing head. Explains lead and backlash.
Industrial and Technical Education
Dist - USNAC **Prod** - USOE 1943

Milling a Template 17 MIN
16mm
Machine Shop Work Series Operations on the Milling Machine, no 5
B&W
LC FIE51-606
Shows how to mount the end mill in the milling machine spindle, position the table and workpiece in relation to the cutter, rough - and finish - mill the piece and check for finished dimensions.
Industrial and Technical Education
Dist - USNAC **Prod** - USOE 1945

Milling and Tool Sharpening Series
Gouging of end mill 2 and 4 flute
Identification of Parts and Operation of a Horizontal Milling Machine
Identification of Parts and Operation of a Vertical Milling Machine
Reamer Sharpening between Centers
Setup for holding work to be milled
Sharpening ends of end mills
Sharpening Lathe Tools Including N /C Lathe Tools
Sharpening Side Milling Cutters, Slitting Saws and Staggered Tooth Cutters
Sharpening the periphery of end mills
Use of Dividing Head and Rotary Table
Use of Face Milling Cutters on the Horizontal Mill
Use of Plain and Side Milling Cutters on the Horizontal Milling Machine
Dist - VTRI

Milling and Tool Sharpening - Spanish Series
Cutters and machining operations for the vertical milling machine
Machine Keyways on the Vertical Milling Machine (Straight and Woodruff)
Setup for holding work to be milled
Dist - VTRI

Milling Cutters and Accessories 18 MIN
U-matic / VHS
Introduction to Machine Technology, Module 2 Series; Module 2
Color (IND)
Focuses on the types and uses of milling cutters.
Industrial and Technical Education
Dist - LEIKID **Prod** - LEIKID

Milling I and II 57 MIN
U-matic / BETA / VHS
Color
$400 purchase
Shows milling characteristics.
Industrial and Technical Education; Science
Dist - ASM **Prod** - ASM

The Milling Machine 8 MIN
16mm
B&W (IND)
LC FIE51-14
Shows types of jobs which can be done on the milling machine. Demonstrates how to mount the cutter on the arbor, adjust the overarm bracket and set cutter speeds and table feeds.
Industrial and Technical Education
Dist - USNAC **Prod** - USOE 1941

The Milling Machine 15 MIN
16mm
Machine Shop Work Series Basic Machines
B&W (SPANISH)
LC FIE51-571
Explains the functions, characteristics and basic operations of the milling machine.
Industrial and Technical Education
Dist - USNAC **Prod** - USOE 1944

Milling Machine Safety
VHS / 35mm strip
Skills Related Safety Series
Color
$28.00 purchase _ #TX1E3 filmstrips, $58.00 purchase _ #TX1E3V VHS
Teaches about milling machine safety.
Health and Safety; Industrial and Technical Education
Dist - CAREER **Prod** - CAREER

Milling Machines 16 MIN
VHS / U-matic
Introduction to Machine Technology, Module 2 Series; Module 2
Color (IND)
Covers verticle and horizontal mills, milling operations and the universal dividing head.
Industrial and Technical Education
Dist - LEIKID **Prod** - LEIKID

Million Acre Playground 15 MIN
16mm
Color
Surveys the one million acres maintained by the Florida Flood Control District for sports and recreation.
Geography - United States; Physical Education and Recreation; Science - Natural
Dist - FLADC **Prod** - FLADC

The Million Club 28 MIN
16mm
Color (C A)
LC FIA65-845
Dramatizes the threat of cancer and discusses its increasing curability.
Health and Safety; Psychology
Dist - AMCS **Prod** - AMCS 1964

The Million Dollar Customer 12 MIN
16mm
B&W (C A)
LC FI67-93
Shows that an alert and aggressive sales staff is a protection against shoplifting.
Business and Economics; Psychology; Sociology
Dist - FRAF **Prod** - LATOUR 1960

Million Dollar Dreams 30 MIN
U-matic / VHS / 16mm
Color (J)
Looks at six Americans who started with nothing but an idea and a commitment to hard work. Shows how they became millionaires who make cookies, suntan lotion, computer programs, herbal tea and cosmetics.
Business and Economics
Dist - CORF **Prod** - GANNET 1983

The Million Dollar Scan 30 MIN
U-matic / VHS / 16mm
Enterprise Series
Color (H C A)
Tells about the struggle of a company to hold its own in the marketplace after failing to move fast enough in the field of nuclear magnetic resonance scanning.
Business and Economics
Dist - CORF **Prod** - CORF

The Million Mile Driver Show 21 MIN
16mm
Color
LC 79-701329
Demonstrates the role and responsibilities of the driver and shows safe driving behavior for special education and mentally retarded students.
Education; Health and Safety; Psychology
Dist - PARPRO **Prod** - PARPRO 1979

Million pound prize 40 MIN
VHS
Adventurers series
Color (A)
PdS65 purchase
Examines the Docklands Arena which is in debt and receivership. Reveals that a management team wants to be given the opportunity to make the project work. Part of a six-part series on a year in the life of a venture capital house, Grosvenor Venture Managers Ltd, which is approached with up to 600 ideas annually - of which around 20 will receive backing. Explains how the successful ventures are selected, and the drama and conflicts that lie behind the deals.
Business and Economics
Dist - BBCENE

A Million Teenagers 23 MIN
U-matic / VHS / 16mm
Color (J H)
$480 purchase - 16 mm, $360 purchase - video
Discusses the different venereal diseases and their transmission, symptoms, treatment, and dangers. Directed by Judy Reidel with animation by Spencer Peel and Diane Franklin.
Health and Safety
Dist - CF **Prod** - CF 1988

A Million to One 5 MIN
16mm
PSSC Physics Films Series
B&W (H)
LC 75-702719
Shows a flea pulling a massive dry ice puck, thus demonstrating the small force needed to move a nearly frictionless body. Includes a short excerpt from the film 'INERTIA' which describes the dry ice puck.
Science - Physical
Dist - MLA **Prod** - EDS 1961

A Million Years of Man 24 MIN
16mm / U-matic / VHS
Smithsonian Series
Color (I J)
LC FIA67-730
Presents an introduction to anthropology, explaining how this science of man has contributed to knowledge of the ancestors of modern man.
History - World; Science - Natural; Sociology
Dist - MGHT **Prod** - NBCTV 1967

Millionaires of Poverty Gulch 30 MIN
16mm
Glory Trail Series
B&W (I)
LC FIA66-1241
Depicts the gold rush days in Colorado and the problems of a sudden increase in wealth and population. Traces the rise and fall of the small mining town of Cripple Creek.
Geography - United States; History - United States
Dist - IU **Prod** - NET 1964

Millions and Millions of Bubbles 11 MIN
16mm / U-matic / VHS
Color (P)
$195 purchase - 16 mm, $79 purchase - video
Shows the seashore, tidepool, and two children who are exploring it.
Science - Natural
Dist - CF

Millions of Cats 10 MIN
U-matic / Record / VHS / 16mm
Color; Mono; B&W (K P) (SPANISH)
An iconographic motion picture based on the children's book of the same title by Wanda Gag.
Science - Natural
Dist - WWS **Prod** - WWS 1958

Millones De Gatos 10 MIN
U-matic / VHS / 16mm
B&W (SPANISH)
LC 73-702773
A Spanish version of 'MILLIONS OF CATS.' Tells how a homely kitten, the lone survivor of a fight in which millions of cats devour each other, becomes the most beautiful cat in the world because of the loving care of an elderly couple.
Foreign Language
Dist - WWS **Prod** - WWS 1960

Millstone Sewing Center 10 MIN
16mm
Color (H A)
LC 74-702535
Shows the activities in the Millstone Sewing Center, a community center which uses the volunteer work of local widows and older women residents of the center in order to produce well - fitting, new clothes for the poor of Letcher County, Kentucky, free of charge.
Home Economics; Sociology
Dist - APPAL **Prod** - APPAL 1974

Milos Forman 32 MIN
VHS
Filmmakers on their craft series
Color (PRO G C)
$79.00 purchase, $29.00 _ #726
Features Czech director Milos Forman, director of Amadeus, Taking Off, One Flew Over the Cuckoo's Nest. Compares working in Czechoslovakia under communism with working in Hollywood under the studio systems and draws some surprising conclusions. Emphasizes the importance of the casting and building of a character, blending the personality of the actor with the written part. Features Peter Thompson as interviewer. Part of a six - part series on world famous filmmakers produced by the Australian Film, Television and Radio School.
Fine Arts; Industrial and Technical Education
Dist - FIRLIT

Milo's Journey 15 MIN
16mm
Peppermint Stick Selection Series
Color (P I)
LC 77-701719
An excerpt from the motion picture The Phantom Tollbooth. Tells the story of a boy who discovers the joys of living and the need for learning. Based on the book The Phantom Tollbooth by Norman Juster.
English Language; Literature and Drama
Dist - FI **Prod** - FI 1976

Milton 28 MIN
U-matic / VHS
Survey of English Verse Series
Color (C)
$249.00, $149.00 purchase _ #AD - 1299
Focuses on 'Paradise Lost' by John Milton. Includes his sonnet to his dead wife, Katherine.
Fine Arts; Literature and Drama
Dist - FOTH **Prod** - FOTH

Milton and 17th Century Poetry 35 MIN
VHS / U-matic
Color
Focuses on Milton's Paradise Lost and the work of Donne, Herbert and Marvell. Discusses the epic form and the characteristics of metaphysical poetry.
Literature and Drama
Dist - FOTH **Prod** - FOTH

Milton Berle - the second time around
VHS
Color (G)
$56.85 purchase _ #EK900 - - 3 tape set
Brings back Uncle Miltie in bits from his TV series photographed live. Guests include Phil Silvers, Elvis, Martin and Lewis, Red Skelton, Duke Ellington and more.
Fine Arts; Literature and Drama
Dist - SIV

Milton by Himself 27 MIN
U-matic / VHS
Color (C)
$249.00, $149.00 purchase _ #AD - 1032
Examines the life and times of John Milton through his major and autobiographical writings. Includes period art and location photography at London and Cambridge, music of the time and Milton's own words.
Fine Arts; Geography - World; Literature and Drama
Dist - FOTH **Prod** - FOTH

Milton Friedman on liberty and drugs 29 MIN
VHS
America's drug forum second season series
Color (G)
$19.95 purchase _ #223
Presents a one - on - one interview Nobel Laureate economist Milton Friedman. Discusses his ideas on liberty and drugs.
Civics and Political Systems; Psychology
Dist - DRUGPF **Prod** - DRUGPF 1992

Milton Friedman speaking - Lecture 14 series
Equality and freedom in the free enterprise system 84 MIN
Equality and freedom in the free enterprise system - Part 1 42 MIN
Dist - HBJ

Milton Friedman speaking series lecture 11
Putting Learning Back in the Classroom 45 MIN
Putting learning back in the classroom - Pt 1 23 MIN
Putting learning back in the classroom - Pt 2 22 MIN
Dist - HBJ

Milton Friedman Speaking Series Lecture 14
Equality and Freedom in the Free Enterprise System, Pt 2 42 MIN
Dist - HBJ

Milton Friedman Speaking Series Lecture 1
What is America 72 MIN
What is America, Pt 1 36 MIN
What is America, Pt 2 36 MIN
Dist - HBJ

Milton Friedman Speaking Series Lecture 2
Myths that Conceal Reality 82 MIN
Myths that Conceal Reality, Pt 1 41 MIN
Myths that Conceal Reality, Pt 2 41 MIN
Dist - HBJ

Milton Friedman Speaking Series Lecture 3
Is Capitalism Humane 69 MIN
Is Capitalism Humane, Pt 1 35 MIN
Is Capitalism Humane, Pt 2 34 MIN
Dist - HBJ

Milton Friedman Speaking Series Lecture 4
The Role of Government in a Free Society 76 MIN
Dist - HBJ

Milton Friedman Speaking Series Lecture 5
What is Wrong with the Welfare State 87 MIN
What is Wrong with the Welfare State, Pt 1 43 MIN
What is Wrong with the Welfare State, Pt 2 44 MIN
Dist - HBJ

Milton Friedman Speaking Series Lecture 6
Money and Inflation 81 MIN
Money and Inflation, Pt 1 40 MIN
Money and Inflation, Pt 2 41 MIN
Dist - HBJ

Milton Friedman Speaking Series Lecture 7
Is Tax Reform Possible 81 MIN
Is Tax Reform Possible, Pt 1 40 MIN
Is Tax Reform Possible, Pt 2 41 MIN
Dist - HBJ

Milton Friedman Speaking Series Lecture 8
Free Trade - Producer Versus Consumer 80 MIN
Free Trade - Producer Versus Consumer, Pt 1 40 MIN
Free Trade - Producer Versus Consumer, Pt 2 40 MIN
Dist - HBJ

Milton Friedman Speaking Series
The Economics of medical care 45 MIN
The economics of medical care - Pt 1 22 MIN
The economics of medical care - Pt 2 23 MIN
The Energy crisis - a human solution - Lecture 9 87 MIN
The Energy crisis - a human solution - Lecture 9, Pt 1 43 MIN
The Energy crisis - a human solution - Lecture 9, Pt 2 44 MIN
The Future of our free society 45 MIN
The Future of our free society, Pt 1 23 MIN
The Future of our free society, Pt 2 22 MIN
The Role of Government in a Free Society - Pt 1 38 MIN
The Role of Government in a Free Society - Pt 2 38 MIN
Who Protects the Consumer 85 MIN
Who Protects the Consumer, Pt 1 42 MIN
Who Protects the Consumer, Pt 2 43 MIN
Who Protects the Worker 82 MIN
Who Protects the Worker, Pt 1 41 MIN
Who Protects the Worker, Pt 2 41 MIN
Dist - HBJ

Mime 13 MIN
VHS / 16mm
Drama Reference Series
Color (C)
$150.00 purchase _ #268404
Implements elementary drama curriculum. Presents drama content, teaching strategies and resources, and demonstrated drama activities for the classroom. 'Mime' teaches that it is an art form which creates an awareness of body movement and nonverbal expression.
Education; Literature and Drama; Mathematics
Dist - ACCESS **Prod** - ACCESS 1987

Mime Control 9 MIN
16mm
Color
Presents a mime who performs in real time while an artist uses a computer to accent and control the mime's disciplined choreography.
Fine Arts; Mathematics
Dist - LILYAN **Prod** - LILYAN

The Mime of Marcel Marceau 23 MIN
U-matic / VHS / 16mm
Color (J H C)
LC 72-701012
Views the French pantomimist at work both on stage and behind the scenes.
Biography; Fine Arts; Geography - World
Dist - LCOA **Prod** - LCOA 1972

Mime One 27 MIN
U-matic / VHS
Color
Introduces five pieces performed by the Oregon Mime Theater, directed by Francisco Reynders. Includes The Bird.
Fine Arts; Geography - United States
Dist - MEDIPR **Prod** - MEDIPR 1980

Mime Over Matter 15 MIN
16mm
Color (J)
LC 70-711341
Examines the use of pantomime to explore ideas and provoke open - ended discussion of such topics as man's relationships to the material objects that make his life comfortable. Features Ladislav Fialka.
Fine Arts; Religion and Philosophy; Sociology
Dist - SIM **Prod** - KRATKY 1970

Mime over matter 101 MIN
VHS
Performance theatre series
Color (J H C G)
$95.00 purchase _ #DSV003V; $139.00 purchase _ #DL137
Leads one person or a full class through easy - to - follow mime exercises. Introduces mime, exaggerated action, sections of the body, isolations, breaking down movement and more. Includes teacher's guide. Part of a series on performance.
Fine Arts
Dist - CAMV
INSIM

Mime Talk 30 MIN
VHS / 16mm
First International Mime Clinic and Festival Series
Color (G)
$55.00 rental _ #FMFI - 007
Fine Arts
Dist - PBS **Prod** - KTCATV

Mime Technique, Pt 1 27 MIN
U-matic / VHS / 16mm
Color (H C A)
LC 81-700942
Introduces mime Paul Gaulin as he brings to life a story about an ape who is transformed into a man. Shows the new man experimenting with the art of mime when he finds a book on the basic techniques.
Fine Arts
Dist - PHENIX **Prod** - LIPPES 1977

Mime Time 10 MIN
VHS / U-matic
Book, Look and Listen Series
Color (K P)
Deals with the ability to interpret actions and expressions of a pantomimist as a storyteller.
English Language; Literature and Drama
Dist - AITECH **Prod** - MDDE 1977

Mimi 12 MIN
16mm
B&W (J)
LC 73-700891
Presents a young woman paralyzed from birth, talking about herself and her life, relating to 'NORMAL' people and how they relate to her.
Health and Safety; Psychology; Sociology
Dist - BBF **Prod** - BBF 1972

Mimi and Richard Farina 52 MIN
VHS / U-matic
Rainbow quest series
Color
Features many songs written by Richard Farina as he plays harmonica and dulcimer and Mimi Farina plays guitar.
Fine Arts
Dist - NORROS **Prod** - SEEGER

Mimicry
VHS
BSCS Classic Inquiries Series
Color (H C)
$59.95 purchase _ #193 W 2206
Poses questions, raises problems and presents experimental data on mimicry as a protective adaptation in the animal world. Part of a series on the life sciences.
Science - Natural
Dist - WARDS **Prod** - WARDS

Min have I Provence (My Garden in Provence) 18 MIN
16mm
Color (DANISH)
Presents the Danish sculptor Ib Schmedes' description of the insect fauna in Provence where he now lives.
Foreign Language; Science - Natural
Dist - STATNS **Prod** - STATNS 1963

Minbo - or the gentle art of Japanese extortion 123 MIN
VHS
Color (G)
$79.95 purchase _ #MIN030
Presents a daring satire of the Japanese mob. Blends realism and raucous farce to pit buffoonish criminals against a fearless lawyer. Directed by Juzo Itami. Produced by Northern Arts.
Fine Arts; Literature and Drama; Sociology
Dist - HOMVIS

Mind - altering drugs 30 MIN
16mm
Directions for education in nursing via technology series; Lesson 87
B&W (PRO)
LC 74-701866
Reviews the five major mind - altering drugs, amphetamines, barbiturates, hallucinogenics, heroin and pop drugs.
Health and Safety
Dist - WSUM **Prod** - DENT 1974

Mind and body 50 MIN
VHS
Healing arts series
Color; PAL (G)
PdS99 purchase
Presents the world of faith - healing and mind - body therapeutic techniques. Interviews patients who have turned to practitioners of holistic and mental healing to cure illnesses. Part eight of a nine - part series.
Health and Safety; Psychology
Dist - BBCENE

The Mind and Body in Crisis 16 MIN
VHS / 16mm
Conquering Cocaine Series
Color (H A PRO)
$245.00 purchase, $75.00 rental _ #8096
Considers the physiological and psychological consequences of excessive and continuous use of cocaine.
Guidance and Counseling; Psychology
Dist - AIMS **Prod** - AIMS 1988

Mind and body series
Presents an eight - part series featuring Dr Jonathan Freedman. Includes the titles Affirmative Action in the Medical Community, Assessment of Dementia, Introduction to Neurolinguistic Programming, Memory and the Elderly, The Parents Speak I and II, Stress and Suicide.

Affirmative action in the medical community	29 MIN
Assessment of dementia	18 MIN
Introduction to neurolinguistic programming	19 MIN
Memory and the elderly	20 MIN
The Parents speak I	29 MIN
The Parents speak II	18 MIN
Stress	31 MIN
Suicide	30 MIN

Dist - HSCIC

Mind and Hand 28 MIN
16mm
Color
Outlines the different views on the relationship between mind and body as seen by such disparate disciplines as Eastern philosophy and modern cybernetics. Explores psychosomatic illness, hypnosis, biofeedback and meditation and shows how these techniques are applied to such areas as pain control and the self - mastery of involuntary responses.
Psychology; Science - Natural
Dist - FLMLIB **Prod** - CANBC

Mind and Muscle Power 20 MIN
U-matic / VHS
Once upon a Town Series
Color (P I)
Explores literary selections that deal with physical health and discipline as crucial to achievements in many fields.
English Language; Literature and Drama
Dist - AITECH **Prod** - MDDE 1977

The Mind and Perception - Part Two 42.06 MIN
VHS
Using Your Creative Brain Series
Color (J H C)
LC 88-700272
Discusses the psychology, biology, and sociology related to the perceptiveness of the brain.
Psychology; Science - Natural
Dist - SRA **Prod** - SRA 1984

Mind as a myth 30 MIN
BETA / VHS
Does mind matter series
Color (G)
$29.95 purchase _ #S119
Asks if the mind exists as a distinct entity apart from an individual's thoughts about it. Features U G Krishnamurti, skeptic and author of 'Mind Is a Myth' and 'The Myth of Enlightenment,' who argues that 'mind' is a myth, as well as the notion of the 'self.' Part of a four - part series asking, does the mind matter.
Religion and Philosophy
Dist - THINKA **Prod** - THINKA

Mind at Large - Adler on Aristotle 60 MIN
VHS / U-matic
Bill Moyers' Journal Series
Color (A)
LC 79-708090
Presents an interview with Mortimer Adler in which he discusses philosophical issues, such as the nature of the good life, the role and attainment of virtue, the function of philosophy in modern society, and concepts of the rational and virtuous man.
Religion and Philosophy
Dist - PBS **Prod** - WNETTV 1979

The Mind awake and asleep - the mind hidden and divided - Parts 13 and 14 60 MIN
VHS / U-matic
Discovering psychology series
Color (C)
$45.00, $29.95 purchase
Presents parts 13 and 14 of the 26 - part Discovering Psychology series. Explores the nature of sleeping, dreaming and altered states of consciousness. Shows how consciousness enables the interpretation, analysis and direction of behavior in adaptive, flexible ways. Looks at how the events and experiences of the subconscious mind affect moods, actions and health. Two thirty - minute programs hosted by Professor Philip Zimbardo of Stanford University.
Health and Safety; Psychology
Dist - ANNCPB **Prod** - WGBHTV 1989

Mind, Body and Spirit 28 MIN
U-matic / VHS / 16mm
Human Face of China Series
Color (H C A)
LC 79-701737
Tells how barefoot doctors, drawn from local communities, are trained to attend to the basic health care needs of the rural people of China. Explains the emphasis of preventive medicine.
Geography - World; Health and Safety; History - World; Sociology
Dist - LCOA **Prod** - FLMAUS 1979

The Mind - body connection 30 MIN
BETA / VHS
Transformation and the body series
Color (G)
$29.95 purchase _ #S300
Suggests that understanding the mind - body connection can be approached through many disciplines - dance, massage, biofeedback, martial arts, yoga. Features Dr Eleanor Criswell, psychologist and managing editor of 'Somatics.' Part of a four - part series on transformation and the body.
Health and Safety; Psychology; Science - Natural
Dist - THINKA **Prod** - THINKA

The Mind - body problem 30 MIN
VHS / BETA
Does mind matter series
Color (G)

$29.95 purchase _ #S485
Disputes the materialistic view of the mind as an entity which will eventually be explained in terms of neurological functioning. Features Dr Julian Isaacs who suggests that evidence produced by parapsychology refutes the materialistic view. Part of a four - part series asking, does the mind matter.
Psychology; Religion and Philosophy
Dist - THINKA **Prod** - THINKA

Mind - body wellness 30 MIN
VHS
Insights - topics in contemporary psychology series
Color (H C G)
$89.95 purchase _ #ARG - 111
Examines the relationship between emotional and personal well - being and health. Features Dr Joan Borysenko, author of Minding the Body, Mending the Mind, her husband and a nationally recognized expert psychoneuroimmunology. Discusses how intertwined mental health, marriage, happiness and peace of mind are to health. Part of a four - part series on contemporary psychology.
Health and Safety; Psychology
Dist - INSTRU

Mind - brain classroom series
Aging 30 MIN
Depression 30 MIN
Development 30 MIN
The Two brains 30 MIN
Dist - PBS

Mind, brains and science 30 MIN
VHS / BETA
Does mind matter series
Color (G)
$29.95 purchase _ #S493
Challenges the notion that the human mind operates like a computer and that computers will achieve consciousness. Features Dr John Searle who points out that intentionality and other human faculties are not achievable through artificial intelligence. Part of a four - part series asking, does the mind matter.
Mathematics; Religion and Philosophy; Science - Natural
Dist - THINKA **Prod** - THINKA

Mind Control 33432 25 MIN
U-matic / VHS
Color (J)
Considers people's ability to develop additional psychic power. Demonstrates exercises which can enhance awareness of intuition.
Psychology; Sociology
Dist - SIRS **Prod** - SIRS

A Mind for music with Peter Sellars - Parts I and II 60 MIN
VHS
World of ideas with Bill Moyers - Season II - series
Color (G)
$59.95 purchase _ #WIWM - 208D
Interviews avant - garde theater director Peter Sellars, director of the Los Angeles Festival. Presents Sellars' views on his career, Shakespeare, Los Angeles and changes in American society. Hosted by Bill Moyers. Consists of two 30 - minute programs.
Fine Arts; Sociology
Dist - PBS

Mind games 30 MIN
VHS
Contenders series
Color (A)
PdS30 purchase
Looks at psychology and scientific gamesmanship. Part of a five-part series showing how scientific ideas have permeated almost every sporting event, bringing major advances in sports achievement. Follows some of the world's finest sportspeople in their struggle to succeed.
Physical Education and Recreation
Dist - BBCENE

Mind in Tibetan Buddhism 30 MIN
VHS / BETA
Does mind matter series
Color (G)
$29.95 purchase _ #S056
Describes the mind as a pure, limitless field where thoughts create various visions which appear objective to the individual in sleep and in death. Features Dr Ole Nydahl, philosopher and trained as a Tibetan Buddhist meditation master. Part of a four - part series asking, does the mind matter.
Psychology; Religion and Philosophy; Sociology
Dist - THINKA **Prod** - THINKA

The Mind Machines 59 MIN
U-matic / VHS / 16mm
Nova Series
Color (H C A)
LC 79-701907
Discusses research being done in Artificial Intelligence, a branch of computer science. Explores possible developments, such as computer controlled robots equipped with a sense of vision and the ability to respond flexibly to changing conditions.
Mathematics; Science; Science - Natural; Sociology
Dist - TIMLIF **Prod** - WGBHTV 1978

Mind of a Murderer, Pt 1 60 MIN
VHS / U-matic
Frontline Series
Color
LC 84-707627
Focuses on convicted murderer Kenneth Bianchо, known as the Hillside Strangler. Probes the complex area of criminal psychology.
Psychology; Sociology
Dist - PBS **Prod** - BARNEM

Mind of a Murderer, Pt 2 60 MIN
VHS / U-matic
Frontline Series
Color
LC 84-707627
Focuses on convicted murderer Kenneth Bianchо, known as the Hillside Strangler. Probes the complex area of criminal psychology.
Psychology; Sociology
Dist - PBS **Prod** - BARNEM

The Mind of Man 119 MIN
U-matic / VHS / 16mm
Color
LC 77-712774
Presents a survey of modern research on the mind in various countries of the world. Covers areas of mind development in children, effects of drugs, dreams, brain structure, chemical changes within the brain, the brain and sexuality, reasoning and the power of the mind in controlling bodily functions. Includes interviews with Sir John Eccles, Donald Hebb and B F Skinner.
Education; Psychology
Dist - IU **Prod** - NET 1971

The Mind of Music 29 MIN
16mm
Color (H C A)
LC 81-700106
Inquires into the link forged between an individual and music. Interviews composers, a musician, a musicologist and a biologist.
Fine Arts
Dist - LAWFI **Prod** - LAWFI 1980

The Mind of Patricia Churchland 30 MIN
VHS
World of ideas with Bill Moyers - Season II - series
Color; Captioned (G)
$39.95 purchase _ #WIWM - 203
Interviews philosophy professor Patricia Churchland. Examines her work with scientists and philosophers in gaining a better understanding of the human mind. Suggests that thoughts, decisions and choices may not be as dependent on free will as once thought. Hosted by Bill Moyers.
Psychology
Dist - PBS

Mind Over Body 49 MIN
U-matic / VHS / 16mm
Color (H C)
LC 73-701679
Shows recently developed techniques which teach patients to use their minds to produce bodily changes that can ward off or cure illness. Includes bizarre examples of the power of mind over body.
Psychology
Dist - TIMLIF **Prod** - BBCTV 1973

Mind over machine 30 MIN
VHS / BETA
Computers and the mind series
Color (G)
$29.95 purchase _ #S150
Considers human intuition and perception as basic and essential phenomena of consciousness and incapable of replication by computers. Features Dr Hubert Dreyfus, philosopher and archcritic of the artificial intelligence establishment and author of 'What Computers Can't Do' and coauthor of 'Mind over Machine.' Part of a four - part series on computers and the mind.
Computer Science; History - United States; Industrial and Technical Education; Literature and Drama; Mathematics; Sociology
Dist - THINKA **Prod** - THINKA

Mind Over Matter 10 MIN
16mm
Safety Management Series
Color
Business and Economics; Health and Safety
Dist - NSC **Prod** - NSC

Mind over matter 33 MIN
16mm
Color & B&W (G)
$100.00 rental
Records the filmmaker creating a new life for herself in the face of illness and failed romance by retaining the hope of redemption. Contrasts film stock with light and shadows while a woman moves within the atmosphere of lush plant life. Produced by Carmen Vigil.
Fine Arts
Dist - CANCIN

Mind over matter 30 MIN
VHS
Bodymatters series
Color (H C A)
PdS65 purchase
Discusses the mind and its effect on health. Part of a series of 26 30-minute videos on various systems of the human body.
Health and Safety; Psychology; Science - Natural
Dist - BBCENE

Mind over matter - six conceptual artists at the Whitney Museum 58 MIN
VHS / 16mm
Color (G)
Brings together recent work by artists in their thirties who share a strong predisposition to rationalized art making. Views their work on exhibit in the Whitney Museum and the artists discuss the exhibition with curator Richard Armstrong and critic Bruce Ferguson. Features Ashley Bickerton, Ronald Jones, Nayland Blake, Liz Larner, Tishan Hsu, Annette Lemieux.
Fine Arts
Dist - BLACKW **Prod** - BLACKW 1992

Mind over muscle 26 MIN
VHS
Color (G)
$39.95 purchase _ #TTI6200V
Explores the possibility that visualization may help improve sports performance. Interviews various athletes who have apparently used visualization successfully. Offers advice for implementing visualization in all areas of life, not just sports.
Physical Education and Recreation; Religion and Philosophy; Science - Natural
Dist - CAMV **Prod** - CAMV 1987

Mind power 30 MIN
BETA / VHS
Optimal performance series
Color (G)
$29.95 purchase _ #S215
Suggests some techniques - learning to monitor and change negative thought patterns, working with positive memories, visualizing goals, mental relaxation and working with mental advisors - for transforming and improving life. Features Dr Bernie Zilbergeld, clinical psychologist and author of 'Mind Power.' Part of a four - part series on optimal performance.
Health and Safety; Psychology
Dist - THINKA **Prod** - THINKA

The Mind - Pt 1 - the Search for the Mind 60 MIN
VHS / 16mm
Mind Series
Color (H)
$10.00 rental _ #60928
Traces the use of the mind historically, from the primitive cave paintings at Lascaux, France, through the golden age of philosphy in ancient Greece to the Vienna office of psychiatrist Sigmund Freud and his first attempts at psychoanalysis.
Education; Fine Arts; Psychology; Religion and Philosophy
Dist - PBS

The Mind - Pt 7 - Language 60 MIN
VHS / 16mm
Mind Series
Color (H)
$10.00 rental _ #60934
Considers the evolution of language and the special human phenomenon of speech. Identifies an innate drive to communicate and an existing linguistic capacity even without speech and hearing.
Education; English Language; Religion and Philosophy; Social Science
Dist - PBS

Mind Series
Explores the growing knowledge of the workings of the human mind. Considers the role of language, memory, the unconscious and other subjects. Nine - part series interviews scientists and researchers.
Addiction - Program 4 60 MIN
Addictions 60 MIN
Aging 60 MIN
Aging - program 3 60 MIN
Depression 60 MIN
Depression - program 6 60 MIN
Development 60 MIN

Development - Program 2 60 MIN
Language 60 MIN
Language - Program 7 60 MIN
The Mind - Pt 1 - the Search for the Mind 60 MIN
The Mind - Pt 7 - Language 60 MIN
Pain and Healing 60 MIN
Thinking 60 MIN
Thinking - Program 8 60 MIN
The Violent mind 60 MIN
Dist - PBS **Prod** - WNETTV 1988

Mind Series
Presents a nine - part series exploring the human mind. Covers subjects including psychological theories of mind, development, aging, addiction, pain and healing, depression, language, thinking, and the role of the mind in violent behavior.
Addiction - Program 4 60 MIN
Addictions 60 MIN
Aging 60 MIN
Aging - program 3 60 MIN
Depression 60 MIN
Depression - program 6 60 MIN
Development 60 MIN
Development - Program 2 60 MIN
Language 60 MIN
Language - Program 7 60 MIN
The Mind - Pt 1 - the Search for the Mind 60 MIN
The Mind - Pt 7 - Language 60 MIN
Pain and Healing 60 MIN
Thinking 60 MIN
Thinking - Program 8 60 MIN
The Violent mind 60 MIN
Dist - PBS **Prod** - WNETTV 1988

Mind series
The Search for mind - Part 1 60 MIN
Dist - PBS
PSU

Mind Series
Language, Pt 7 60 MIN
Dist - PSU

Mind that child - the horrors of child sexual abuse 25 MIN
VHS
Color (H C G)
$29.95 purchase _ #VVD0147V - K
Shows how to recognize the symptoms of and find healing for a child who has been sexually abused and frightened into silence. Offers practical guidance on how to prevent child sexual abuse.
Sociology
Dist - CAMV

Mind Your Back 17 MIN
U-matic / VHS / 16mm
Color (A)
LC 83-700583
Discusses bad lifting habits developed by men and women at home and at work. Presents experts on lifting and posture who show that with a little care and know - how it is possible for everyone to take care of their back, avoid pain and avoid losing days at work as well.
Health and Safety
Dist - IFB **Prod** - MILLBK 1982

Mind Your Back 13 MIN
16mm
Color (IND)
LC FIA68-1743
Shows how proper lifting methods can prevent back injuries to industrial workers and demonstrates the right and wrong way to handle and lift timber, steel rails, oil drums, gas cylinders and other heavy objects.
Business and Economics; Health and Safety; Physical Education and Recreation
Dist - AUIS **Prod** - ANAIB 1966

Mind your colour - a South African dilemma 27 MIN
VHS
Color; PAL (G)
PdS50 purchase
Explores the political ramifications of South Africa's racially - mixed population. Presents a Frank Klein, Netherlands, production.
Fine Arts; Geography - World; Sociology
Dist - BALFOR

Mind your manners
VHS
Color (S T PRO)
$399.00 purchase _ #1008
Presents a six - part video program which teaches manners to persons with developmental disabilities. Uses humorous dramatizations to show the destructive consequences of bad manners and how good manners promote respect and acceptance. Includes teacher's guide and teacher training video.
Education; Home Economics; Psychology; Social Science; Sociology
Dist - STANFI **Prod** - STANFI

Mind your own business 30 MIN
VHS
Business matters series
Color (A)
PdS65 purchase
Compares the share price performance of companies in which families own more than 25 percent of the stock against the FT All Share Index. Asks why family companies usually do better than their corporate rivals.
Business and Economics
Dist - BBCENE

Mind/Brain Classroom Series
Learning and Memory 30 MIN
Dist - FI

Mind/Brain Classroom Series
Addictions 30 MIN
Language 30 MIN
Madness 30 MIN
Pain and Healing 30 MIN
Thinking 30 MIN
Dist - PBS

The Minders 50 MIN
VHS / 16mm
Color (G)
$275.00 purchase, $75.00 rental
Imagines a celestial utopia ruled by benevolent, intergalactic women. Depicts the Minders, guardian angels watching over Earth, aware of the raw deal sometimes given women. When they find someone in trouble, telepathic mindlink intervenes to offer wisdom and comfort. Feminism meets Star Trek in this woman - ruled paradise. Produced by Judy Rymer from New Zealand.
Civics and Political Systems; Fine Arts; Literature and Drama; Sociology
Dist - WMEN **Prod** - EEMP 1985

Minding my own business series
Features women entrepreneurs who have developed businesses. Discusses the motivation for beginning and the success of their new businesses. Combines six videos that highlight the personal experiences of business owners in getting started.
Evaluating 27 MIN
Financing 27 MIN
Inspiration and motivation 27 MIN
Managing 27 MIN
Marketing 27 MIN
Planning 27 MIN
Dist - LANDMK

Minding your manners at school 12 MIN
VHS
Minding your manners series
Color (P I)
$79.95 purchase _ #1045VL
Presents four young 'good manners' reporters as they travel to schools to teach proper classroom and school behavior. Uses live - action footage and animation to show correct attitudes; sharing and cooperation; respecting others' feelings; and avoiding physical violence. Comes with a teacher's guide and discussion questions with script.
Guidance and Counseling; History - World; Home Economics; Social Science
Dist - UNL

Minding your manners series
Everyday etiquette 15 MIN
Minding your manners at school 12 MIN
Dist - UNL

Minding Your Own Business 24 MIN
U-matic / VHS
Color (G)
$249.00, $149.00 purchase _ #AD - 2016
Reports on the risks and rewards of entrepreneurship. Profiles one entrepreneur who is trying to get his company started and another whose business is showing a profit. Includes a panel with economist Uwe Reinhardt and the creators of the Tarrytown Conference Center and David's Cookies.
Business and Economics
Dist - FOTH **Prod** - FOTH

Minding Your Own Business - 124 30 MIN
U-matic
Currents - 1984 - 85 Season Series
Color (A)
Examines the growth of entrepreneurship in this country. Reveals why it is growing and who is able to make it work.
Business and Economics; Social Science
Dist - PBS **Prod** - WNETTV 1985

Minding your own business - 42 13 MIN
VHS / U-matic
Life's little lessons - self - esteem 4 - 6 series
Color (I)
$129.00, $99.00 purchase _ #V671
Follows Albert who is a passenger in a tour bus on the island of Jamaica. Reveals that he thinks he is being helpful, but he is only meddling in things that are none of his business. Part of a 65 - part series on self - esteem.
Guidance and Counseling; Home Economics; Psychology
Dist - BARR **Prod** - CEPRO 1992

Mindpower 39 MIN
VHS
Color (G)
$495.00 purchase, $150.00 rental _ #V1076 - 06
Presents a technique to improve memory, mind use and decision making for business success. Features Tony Buzan and his technique called 'mind mapping.'
English Language
Dist - BARR **Prod** - BBC

Minds and Machines 25 MIN
U-matic / VHS
Introduction to Philosophy Series
Color (C)
Religion and Philosophy
Dist - UDEL **Prod** - UDEL

Mind's Eye 28 MIN
16mm
Color
Shows the wide spectrum of job capabilities of rehabilitated blinded war veterans. Presents 12 blinded veterans in various sections of the country living as members of their communities and performing effectively in a wide variety of occupations.
Health and Safety; Social Science
Dist - USVA **Prod** - USVA 1963

The Mind's Eye 29 MIN
Videoreel / VT2
Museum Open House Series
Color
Fine Arts
Dist - PBS **Prod** - WGBHTV

The Mind's Eye 50 MIN
16mm / VHS / U-matic
Color (H C A)
Examines how the brain takes an upside down, distorted picture on the retina and interprets it using a vast battery of decoders. Looks at how the brain estimates distance and demonstrates that there are specific brain cells which respond to lines, edges, angles and colors.
Science - Natural
Dist - FI **Prod** - BBCTV 1981

The Mind's Eye 40 MIN
Cassette / VHS / CD
Color (G)
$19.95 $14.98, $9.98 purchase _ # MVP6001
Presents a computer animation odyssey. Features music by James Reynolds.
Fine Arts
Dist - MIRMP **Prod** - MIRMP 1991

The Mind's eye - the experience of learning 30 MIN
U-matic / VHS
Color (G)
$375.00 purchase _ #JC - 67272
Examines the learning disability dyslexia. Explores some interesting methods being used to treat this hard - to - diagnose perceptual disability. States the need for support, early diagnosis and alternative individualized learning programs. Features screenwriter Alvin Sargent, who has dyslexia, as narrator.
Health and Safety; Sociology
Dist - CORF **Prod** - DISNEY 1989

The Minds of Men 52 MIN
VHS / U-matic
Greeks Series
Color
Offers a detailed look at the life and teachings of Socrates and his pupil Plato, and the worlds of the first historians, Herodotus and Thucydides. Exemplifies the vital curiousity of the Greeks about the wellsprings of human behavior, the nature of man and his place in the world around him.
History - World
Dist - FOTH **Prod** - FOTH 1984

Minds or Eyeballs 29 MIN
U-matic
Children and Television Series
Color
Looks at the advertiser's role in determining children's programming. Discusses responses from the broadcast industry to lobbyists' pressures for more diversified programming.
Social Science; Sociology
Dist - UMITV **Prod** - UMITV

Mindscape 5 MIN
16mm
B&W (H C A)
LC 75-703210
Presents a visual interpretation of a youth's 'trip' after taking a drug. Follows him as he imagines he is in a slaughter house and then that he is being dragged underwater.
Fine Arts; Health and Safety; Psychology
Dist - USC **Prod** - USC 1967

Mindscape 8 MIN
VHS / 16mm / U-matic
Color (H C A)
LC 77-701096
Explores, through the use of pinscreen animation, creative processes of the mind. Shows a painter as he steps into the scene of the landscape that he is painting and travels the regions of the mind. Uses flowing images to show the interior landscape of the mind.
Fine Arts; Psychology
Dist - PFP **Prod** - NFBC 1976

Mindscape no 1 3 MIN
16mm
B&W (G)
$3.00 rental
Fills the screen with nightmares and madness. Marches obsessive, oppressive images against a background of droning sound. A David Ringo production.
Fine Arts
Dist - CANCIN

Mindscape no 2 3 MIN
16mm
Color (G)
$3.00 rental
Deals with specific periods in filmmaker's life in terms of images, not events. Continues the Mindscape series. A David Ringo production.
Fine Arts
Dist - CANCIN

The Mindset for winning 30 MIN
VHS
Color (G)
$39.95 purchase _ #ATV100V
Presents a four - step mental training program. Teaches athletes to maintain proper stress and arousal levels, improve concentration and self - image, and use mental rehearsal to visualize desired performance.
Physical Education and Recreation; Psychology; Science - Natural
Dist - CAMV **Prod** - CAMV 1988

The Mind/The Brain 300 MIN
U-matic / VHS
Color (H G)
$450.00, $650.00 purchase
Includes ten 30 - minute edited episodes from the two series, 'The Mind' and 'The Brain.' Considers topics such as madness, learning, memory, addictions, language and pain and healing. Intended for high school students.
Psychology
Dist - PBS **Prod** - WNETTV

MindWalk 110 MIN
VHS
Color; PAL (G C PRO)
$29.95 purchase _ #VMDK1
Takes a concept based on the book by Fritjof Capra, The Turning Point. Portrays a conversation among a physicist, a poet and a politician that covers the landscape of human history and thought as they explore the systemic, interdependent nature of the world. Stars Liv Ullmann, Sam Waterston and John Heard. Produced by Triton Pictures.
Business and Economics; Psychology; Sociology
Dist - PEGASU

Mindworks - How to be a more Creative and Critical Thinker 120 MIN
U-matic / VHS
Color (G)
$200.00, $175.00 purchase
Features Charleen Swansea who reveals new discoveries on how to release the mind's tremendous powers.
Psychology
Dist - SCETV **Prod** - SCETV 1990

The Mine and the Minotaur 59 MIN
16mm
Color (I J)
Tells about four youngsters who discover that local potters have hidden a priceless gold mythological figure in a disused Cornish tin mine. Describes how they prevent the figure from being smuggled out of the country.
Literature and Drama
Dist - LUF **Prod** - LUF 1981

Mine Emergency Operations - MEO 17 MIN
U-matic / VHS / 16mm
Color (IND)
Shows emergency rescue and recovery procedures for situations in which trapped miners cannot be reached through existing tunnels. Details the MEO system which includes seismic and electromagnetic communication and location equipment, drilling from the surface, and survival instructions for trapped miners.
Health and Safety; Industrial and Technical Education; Social Science
Dist - USNAC **Prod** - USDL 1982

Mine eyes have seen the glory 30 MIN
VHS
Color & B&W (G)
$29.99 purchase
Discusses the development of the Women's Army Corps.
History - United States; History - World
Dist - DANEHA **Prod** - DANEHA 1994

Mine Fire Control 26 MIN
16mm
Color (H C A)
Explains how the bureau of mines, in cooperation with state and local agencies, works to control underground mine fires, thereby saving coal resources and restoring the surface to constructible use.
Health and Safety; Science - Natural
Dist - USDIBM **Prod** - USDIBM

A Mine for Growth 16 MIN
16mm
Color (H C A)
Presents the story of the development and operation of The Griffith Mine, a modern iron ore mining and pelletizing complex at Bruce Lake in northwestern Ontario.
Geography - World; Industrial and Technical Education; Social Science
Dist - PICMAT **Prod** - PICMAT

Mine for Keeps 15 MIN
U-matic / VHS
Best of Cover to Cover 1 Series
Color (P)
Literature and Drama
Dist - WETATV **Prod** - WETATV

Mine Forces in Action 14 MIN
16mm
Color
LC 75-700864
Discusses mine laying as a defense system. Focuses on laying mines and mine countermeasures and describes strategic significance.
Civics and Political Systems
Dist - USNAC **Prod** - USN 1957

Mine of El Teniente 26 MIN
16mm
Color
LC 72-702198
Describes cooperative efforts between firms in North and South America to modernize a 200 - year - old copper mine in the Chilean Andes and move 13,000 miners from their mountainous isolation to a modern townsite.
Business and Economics; Industrial and Technical Education; Social Science; Sociology
Dist - BECHTL **Prod** - BECHTL 1972

Mine Rescue Contest Training 25 MIN
16mm
Color
LC 74-705149
Photographs participants going through a typical rescue - recovery problem, on a field course laid out to stimulate a working section in an underground mine. Shows step - by - step procedures that are taken by each member of a team in an actual mine rescue and gives an explanation for each action.
Health and Safety
Dist - USNAC **Prod** - USBM 1962

Mine War on Blackberry Creek 29 MIN
VHS / 16mm
Color (G)
$100.00 purchase _ #MWOBCVH
Documents a strike by mineworkers against a multinational coal company. Points out that the strike took place on the state line between West Virginia and Kentucky, where other strikes took place in the 1920s.
Geography - United States
Dist - APPAL

Mine, Yours, Ours - 13 30 MIN
VHS
English 101 - Ingles 101 Series
Color (H)
$125.00 purchase
Presents a series of thirty 30 - minute programs in basic English for native speakers of Spanish. Focuses on a specific topic in order to emphasize a particular grammatical point or set of idioms. English is used from the beginning as the primary language of instruction but Spanish translations are included to ensure understanding. Part 13 looks at possessive and reflexive pronouns, forms of possessive pronouns, forms of reflexive pronouns.
English Language; Foreign Language
Dist - AITECH **Prod** - UPRICO 1988

The Minefield 29 MIN
U-matic
Visions - the Critical Eye Series
Color (H C)
Explores modernist art and related subjects such as methods of marketing, drawbacks involved in adopting theories of mainstream art, the role of the critic and the ways in which art can express religious experience.
Fine Arts
Dist - TVOTAR **Prod** - TVOTAR 1985

The Mineral Challenge 28 MIN
16mm
Color
Explains the technological advances used to meet needs for fuels, metals and other minerals. Includes conservation of resources to take care of future needs.
Science - Natural
Dist - USDIBM **Prod** - USDIBM 1970

Mineral Curiosities 29 MIN
Videoreel / VT2
Observing Eye Series
Color
Science - Physical; Sociology
Dist - PBS **Prod** - WGBHTV

Mineral exploration 30 MIN
VHS
Color (J H C)
$21.95 purchase _ #IV803
Shows how aerial and satellite technology is used to explore the Earth for mineral resources. Discusses remote sensing and how geologists and mining engineers locate new mining sites. Reveals how remote sensing works by using satellites, areial photographs and infra - red photography. Includes a discussion guide with glossary.
Science - Physical; Social Science
Dist - INSTRU

Mineral identification 10 MIN
VHS
Earth materials series
Color (H C)
$24.95 purchase _ #S9793
Discusses the process of selective elimination in identifying minerals. Part of a ten - part series on the development of minerals, rocks and soil.
Science - Physical
Dist - HUBDSC **Prod** - HUBDSC

Mineral properties 11 MIN
VHS
Earth materials series
Color (H C)
$24.95 purchase _ #S9792
Discusses the properties of mineral specimens. Part of a ten - part series on the development of minerals, rocks and soil.
Science - Physical
Dist - HUBDSC **Prod** - HUBDSC

Mineral Resources 43 MIN
VHS / U-matic
Basic and Petroleum Geology for Non - Geologists - Earth's Interior '- - Series; Earth's interior
Color (IND)
Industrial and Technical Education; Science - Physical
Dist - GPCV **Prod** - PHILLP

Mineral Resources 30 MIN
U-matic / VHS
Oceanus - the Marine Environment Series Lesson 26
Color
Describes the minerals found in the oceans of the earth. Includes salt, magnesium, bromine and iodine. Discusses the origin of petroleum.
Science - Natural; Science - Physical
Dist - CDTEL **Prod** - SCCON
SCCON

Mineral structures 10 MIN
VHS
Earth materials series
Color (H C)
$24.95 purchase _ #S9791
Discusses the chemical composition of minerals. Part of a ten - part series on the development of minerals, rocks and soil.
Science - Physical
Dist - HUBDSC **Prod** - HUBDSC

Minerals 30 MIN
VHS
Nutrition in action series

Color (C T)
$200.00 purchase, $20.50 rental _ #34731
Highlights essential minerals and the functions they perform. Details calcium and iron. Part of a ten - part series preparing K - 6 educators to teach nutrition, each program covering a specific nutritional topic and demonstrating creative classroom activities for teaching the concepts. Includes self - help manual.
Education; Health and Safety; Social Science
Dist - PSU **Prod** - WPSXTV 1987

Minerals 23 MIN
VHS
Color (J H C)
$39.95 purchase _ #IV136
Looks at how minerals are classified and shows some of the major minerals which make up the Earth. Explores mineral characteristics such as color, crystal structure, luster, optical properties and cleavage.
Science - Physical; Social Science
Dist - INSTRU

Minerals 30 MIN
VHS / U-matic
Food for Life Series
Color
Home Economics; Social Science
Dist - MSU **Prod** - MSU

Minerals 15 MIN
U-matic / VHS
Discovering series; Unit 6 - Rocks and minerals
Color (I)
Science - Physical
Dist - AITECH **Prod** - WDCNTV 1978

Minerals 58 MIN
VHS
Introductory principles of nutrition series
Color (C A PRO)
$70.00 purchase, $16.00 rental _ #60369
Discusses minerals. Part of a 20 - part series on nutrition. Emphasizes controversial nutritional issues and the principle instructional objectives.
Health and Safety; Social Science
Dist - PSU **Prod** - WPSXTV 1978

Minerals
VHS
Robert Krampf's World Of Science Series
Color (J H T)
$79.95 purchase
Presents science educator Robert Krampf in a visit to a quartz mine, along road cuts, and in stream beds, as he explaines the propereties of minerals. Demonstrates a laboratory technique for identifying minerals. Shows how to prepare and organize specimens into a collection. Includes teacher guide, worksheets and quizzes.
Science - Physical; Social Science
Dist - BEARDW **Prod** - BEARDW 1991

Minerals 19 MIN
Videodisc / VHS
Earth science videolab series
Color (J H)
$179.95, $149.95 purchase _ #Q18517
Presents an interdisciplinary, multi - learning approach to the study of minerals. Demonstrates how to analyze physical properties such as hardness, luster, cleavage and fracture. Focuses on identification of minerals. Includes teacher's guide and enough materials to teach multiple sections of students. Part of a five - part series.
Science; Science - Physical
Dist - CF

Minerals and rocks 15 MIN
VHS
Color (J H) (SPANISH)
$99.00 _ #3619 - 026
Takes a look at the composition of minerals. Describes methods used to analyze mineral species. Includes teacher's guide.
Education; Science - Physical
Dist - GA **Prod** - EBEC
EBEC

Minerals - building blocks of the earth 19 MIN
Videodisc / VHS
Earth science library series
Color (J H)
$99.95, $69.95 purchase _ #Q18512; $99.95, $69.95 purchase _ #ES8510
Focuses on minerals as building blocks of the earth and investigates how geologists collect and identify them from the earth's crust. Explains how the arrangement of atoms determines the properties of minerals and how these resources provide us with raw materials for a variety of products. Includes teacher's guide.
Science; Science - Physical
Dist - CF
INSTRU

Minerals - Finds for the Future 24 MIN
VHS / 16mm
Earth's Physical Resources Series
Color (S)
$200.00 purchase _ #236216
Presents a global view of the earth's resource potential. Features footage filmed in Britain, Europe and North America. 'Minerals - Finds For The Future' discusses technological advancement in methods for searching for minerals in both new and existing mining areas. Highlights new, computerized geological mapping techniques, and new geochemical and geophysical exploration methods, with emphasis on airborne spectrospanner surveys.
History - World; Industrial and Technical Education; Psychology; Science - Physical; Social Science; Sociology
Dist - ACCESS **Prod** - BBCTV 1984
MEDIAG

Minerals from Iowa's Beautiful Land 20 MIN
16mm
Color (H C A)
LC 81-701623
Documents the joint efforts of state government and industry in achieving effective regulation of surface mining practices in Iowa. Describes how and why Iowa's mined - law reclamation law evolved, as well as the reasons for its success, using comments of governmental officials, mining industry representatives and the general public.
Geography - United States; Social Science
Dist - IOWA **Prod** - ISOCON 1981

Minerals in the Diet - Barbara Harland, PhD 35 MIN
U-matic
Food and Nutrition Seminars for Health Professionals Series 'WASHINGTON, DC 20409
Color
LC 78-706162
Introduces Dr Harland discussing the essential minerals, their functions, and their occurrences in foods. Tells how an excess of one or more minerals may cause an imbalance in the nutritional state.
Health and Safety
Dist - USNAC **Prod** - USFDA 1976

Minerals in the Earth's crust 20 MIN
VHS
Color (J H C)
$29.95 purchase _ #IV801
Looks at the major minerals which form sedimentary, metamorphic and igneous rocks. Organizes the most common minerals and shows how they become the building blocks for the different types of rocks.
Science - Physical; Social Science
Dist - INSTRU

Miners '88 - Gornicy '88
VHS
(G A) (POLISH)
$24.95 purchase _ #V111
Documents the strike of the Manifest Lipcowy Mine in August 1988, which led to the breakdown of old politics in Poland.
Fine Arts; History - World; Social Science
Dist - POLART

The Miner's Daughter 8 MIN
16mm
Color
Presents an animated story based on the song My Darling Clementine.
Fine Arts
Dist - TIMLIF **Prod** - TIMLIF 1982

Miners of Bolivia 15 MIN
U-matic / VHS / 16mm
Man and His World Series
Color (P I J H C)
LC 73-705482
Depicts the sub - marginal living of Indian miners digging for tin ore. Shows their daily life of work, chewing of coca leaf and then return to ghetto like huts.
Geography - World; Sociology
Dist - FI **Prod** - FI 1969

Ming Garden 29 MIN
VHS
Color (S)
$29.95 purchase _ #412 - 9016
Documents the first cultural exchange between the People's Republic of China and the United States - the installation at the Metropolitan Museum of Art of a Ming - style garden courtyard. Reveals the construction techniques of Suzhou gardens which have been created in China for hundreds of years.
Agriculture; Fine Arts; History - World; Social Science; Sociology
Dist - FI **Prod** - MMOA 1987

Ming garden 30 MIN
VHS
Color (G)
$29.95 purchase _ #S01950
Portrays the building of the Museum of Modern Art's Ming - style garden in the museum's Astor Court. Shows the collaboration that took place between Amnerican and Chinese workers in creating the garden. Notes the underlying philosophy of design.
Agriculture; Fine Arts; History - World
Dist - UILL

Ming - Oi the Magician 25 MIN
U-matic / VHS / 16mm
World Cultures and Youth Series
Color (I J A)
LC 80-700084
Introduces Ming - Oi, a girl of Hong Kong who is studying the secrets of ancient Chinese magic from one of that style's two remaining practitioners. Shows her practicing diligently to prepare for her opening night.
Geography - World; Sociology
Dist - CORF **Prod** - SUNRIS 1980

Minga - We Work Together 14 MIN
U-matic / VHS / 16mm
Just One Child Series
Color (I J)
Shows the lifestyle of an eight year old Quechuan Indian girl in the mountains of Ecuador. Traces her day spent carrying water and other supplies, sewing, weaving, marketing and farming, but without school since there is little need to learn what is not taught at home.
Geography - World; Psychology; Sociology
Dist - BCNFL **Prod** - REYEXP 1983

Mingus 60 MIN
16mm
B&W
Documents the turbulent night in November, 1966 as the internationally renowned bassist - composer, Mingus, and his five year old daughter, Carolyn, awaited the arrival of the city Marshal and police who were to evict them from their bowery loft for non - payment of rent.
Civics and Political Systems; Fine Arts
Dist - IMPACT **Prod** - IMPACT 1966

Mingus - Charlie Mingus 1968 58 MIN
16mm / VHS
B&W (G)
$29.95 purchase, $250.00 rental
Offers a frank and sometimes shocking portrait of jazz bassist - composer Charlie Mingus as he faces hard times. Intercuts scenes of Mingus on stage with scenes of the embittered musician as he awaits eviction from his cluttered New York loft and speaks candidly on topics ranging from music to sex to racism. Songs include 'Take the A Train' and 'Secret Love.'
Biography; Fine Arts; History - United States; Sociology
Dist - KINOIC **Prod** - RHPSDY 1968

Mini enterprises 40 MIN
VHS
Color; PAL (H)
PdS25 purchase
Presents two 40 - minute programs which serve as a manual for setting up mini industries in school. Guides teachers and students through the mechanics of setting up a school enterprise. Advises on ways to help youngsters grasp business and industrial skills. Includes a booklet. Contact distributor about availability outside the United Kingdom.
Business and Economics
Dist - ACADEM

Mini films on prejudice series
Presents a series of 14 thirty to sixty second public service shorts against prejudice. Includes titles 'Red, White and Blue', 'Ask My Father', 'I Am America', 'Flowers', 'Different Faces', and spots by Edward Asner, Linda Lavin, Larry Hagman, Erik Estrada, Judd Hirsch, Carroll O'Connor, Bonnie Franklin, Michele Lee and Angela Lansbury.
Mini films on prejudice series 8 MIN
Dist - ADL **Prod** - ADL

Mini Grammar Lesson 4 MIN
VHS / 16mm
English as a Second Language Series
Color (A PRO)
$165.00 purchase _ #290314
Demonstrates key teaching methods for English as a Second Language - ESL teachers. Features a teacher - presenter who introduces and provides a brief commentary on the techniques, then demonstrates the application of the technique to the students. 'Mini Grammar Lesson' illustrates how a student's grammatical error can be corrected in a concise, unobtrusive manner.
Education; English Language; Mathematics
Dist - ACCESS **Prod** - ACCESS 1989

Mini - Laparotomy 12 MIN
16mm
Color
Portrays the preparation, equipment and actual technique used in a mini - laparotomy, the most popular type of female interval sterilization.
Health and Safety; Sociology
Dist - PODY **Prod** - RMABDI 1976

Mini - Marathon 25 MIN
16mm / U-matic / VHS
Color
LC 79-701611
Follows the running of the 10,000 - meter Bonne Belle mini - marathon in New York City's Central Park. Includes interviews with many of the 2,500 women contestants who talk about their motivations, strategies and enthusiasm for running.
Physical Education and Recreation
Dist - WOMBAT **Prod** - HANMNY 1979

Mini movies - springboard for learning - unit 1, who are we - a series
Mini moview - springboard for learning series
Color (P I)
Body Talk; Hands And Feet; Summertime - Wintertime; Talking; Touching.
English Language; Guidance and Counseling
Dist - MORLAT **Prod** - MORLAT 1975

Mini Movies - Springboard for Learning - Unit 1, who are We Series
Body talk 4 MIN
Hands and Feet 4 MIN
Summertime - Wintertime 4 MIN
Talking 4 MIN
Dist - MORLAT

Mini movies - springboard for learning - Unit 2, what do we - a series
What do we series
Color (P I)
Cans; Chocolate; Glass; Toothpicks.
Fine Arts; Science - Physical
Dist - MORLAT **Prod** - MORLAT 1975

Mini movies - springboard for learning - unit 2, what do we do series
Chocolate 4 MIN
Dist - MORLAT

Mini movies - springboard for learning - unit 2, what do we series
Cans 4 MIN
Glass 4 MIN
Toothpicks 4 MIN
Dist - MORLAT

Mini Movies - Springboard for Learning - Unit 3, Why is it Series
Blow - ups 4 MIN
Flight 4 MIN
Growth 4 MIN
On - Off 4 MIN
Dist - MORLAT

Mini movies - springboard for learning - why is it series
Beans and seeds 4 MIN
Dist - MORLAT

Mini Movies, Unit 2 - what do We do Series
What do We - Cans 4 MIN
What do We - Chocolate 4 MIN
Dist - CORF

Mini moview - springboard for learning series
Mini movies - springboard for learning - unit 1, who are we - a series
Dist - MORLAT

Mini - Stretches 10 MIN
Videoreel / VT2
Janaki Series
Color
Physical Education and Recreation
Dist - PBS **Prod** - WGBHTV

Mini Terrariums 15 MIN
U-matic
Know Your World Series
(I J)
Explores the study of plants and ecosystems with the construction of a classroom terrarium.
Science
Dist - ACCESS **Prod** - ACCESS 1981

Miniature Geometry 20 MIN
U-matic / VHS
Shapes of Geometry Series Pt 3
Color (H)
LC 82-707389
Presents teachers Beth McKenna and David Edmonds encouraging the use of an intuitive approach in developing a geometric system. Shows them presenting the elements of a mathematical system, developing a four - point geometry and demonstrating five postulates by building a model. Urges the proposal of theorems based on observations.
Mathematics
Dist - GPN **Prod** - WVIZTV 1982

Miniature miracle - the computer chip 60 MIN
VHS
Color; Captioned (G)
$29.95 purchase _ #S01389
Documents the technological breakthroughs that have come with advances in computer and robot technology. Suggests that medicine, aviation and arts have benefitted most.
Computer Science
Dist - UILL **Prod** - NGS
NGS

Miniature miracle - the computer chip 60 MIN
VHS
National Geographic video series
Color (G)
$29.95 purchase
Portrays the significant advancements in computer technology in recent years. Shows how computers and robots have helped create significant breakthroughs in medicine, aviation, and the arts.
Computer Science
Dist - PBS **Prod** - WNETTV

The Miniature Theatre - Notes from an Unknown Source - a Science Fiction 30 MIN
U-matic
Color
Deals with the nature of bureaucracy, its technocratic layerings and basic anti - humanism. Presented as a continuous, rolling, character - generated script - over - image.
Fine Arts; Sociology
Dist - WMENIF **Prod** - WMENIF

Miniature Worlds 25 MIN
VHS / U-matic
Blizzard's Wonderful Wooden Toys Series
Color (H C A)
Teaches how to make a doll house.
Fine Arts
Dist - FI **Prod** - BBCTV

Miniatures 10 MIN
16mm
Color (G)
$30.00 rental
Features a series of very short collectibles produced 1985 - 1988.
Fine Arts
Dist - CANCIN **Prod** - AVERYC

The Miniatures Magnificent 19 MIN
16mm
Color (J)
Presents postage stamps of Papua and New Guinea.
Geography - World; Social Science
Dist - AUIS **Prod** - ANAIB 1971

Miniatures, Stylized - Sculptured - and Oriental Designs 60 MIN
VHS / 16mm
(G)
$49.00 purchase _ #FA1004
Instructs how to make miniature arrangements, sculptured and Oriental floral designs. Taught by Pat Quigley.
Fine Arts; Physical Education and Recreation
Dist - RMIBHF **Prod** - RMIBHF

Minigardens 13 MIN
16mm
Color
Shows that Americans are growing minigardens, little vegetable and flower gardens in all sorts of containers such as old shoes, pots, plastic bags and pails. Portrays their attractive effect on cities as they spring up in dark cellars, drab halls, back steps, schoolrooms and fire escapes.
Agriculture; Guidance and Counseling
Dist - KLEINW **Prod** - KLEINW 1971

Minilaparotomy 16 MIN
U-matic / VHS / 16mm
Color (A)
Provides important, comprehensive information to help obtain informed consent, how tubal sterilization prevents pregnancy, alternative methods, facts about how, when and where minilap can be performed, and possible complications.
Health and Safety
Dist - PRORE **Prod** - PRORE

Minilaparotomy Techniques 27 MIN
16mm
Color (PRO)
LC 77-702110
Presents clinical examples photographed in the Far East, Africa and South America to demonstrate techniques for performing tubal ligation by minilaparotomy.
Health and Safety; Sociology
Dist - PATHFU **Prod** - PATHFU 1977

Minimal Brain Dysfunction, Pt 1 6 MIN
VHS / U-matic
Color (PRO)
Science - Natural
Dist - PRIMED **Prod** - PRIMED

Minimal Brain Dysfunction, Pt 2 6 MIN
VHS / U-matic
Color (PRO)
Science - Natural
Dist - PRIMED **Prod** - PRIMED

Minimal Expectations for Health Supervision of Sports 19 MIN
U-matic / VHS
Sports Medicine Series
Color (C A)
$69.00 purchase _ #1451
Suggests a plan which seeks to ensure that injuries are transient including key components of sports participation which should help eradicate injuries.
Health and Safety; Physical Education and Recreation
Dist - EBEC

Minimizing Back Injury 24 MIN
U-matic / VHS
Color (IND)
Examines how back injuries occur. Addresses proper lifting techniques. Focuses on day - to - day strains of lifting, sitting, pushing and bending.
Health and Safety; Industrial and Technical Education
Dist - TAT **Prod** - TAT

Minimizing Back Strain on the Job
U-matic / VHS
Color
Demonstrates specific techniques to reduce back strain on the job.
Education; Health and Safety
Dist - TAT **Prod** - TAT

Minimizing long term complications of diabetes 13 MIN
VHS
Color (PRO A G)
$200.00 purchase _ #DB - 18
Helps patients understand that complications affecting vision, the circulatory system, the kidneys and the nervous system can be minimized if medical advice and self - care regimens are followed and tight control is maintained.
Health and Safety
Dist - MIFE **Prod** - MIFE

Minimizing radiation exposure of the breast during scoliosis radiography 27 MIN
VHS / U-matic
Color (PRO C)
$395.00 purchase, $80.00 _ #C880 - VI - 004
Discusses techniques that reduce breast exposure during scoliosis X - ray exam while improving the diagnostic quality of the films. Includes using a more sensitive film screen, using a compensating filter, using a PA projection and using protection devices such as metal shields. Presented by Drs John Boice and Edward F Downey, Jr, Priscilla F Butler, Dr Armand E Brodeur and Darrell Draughon.
Health and Safety; Science
Dist - HSCIC

Minimizing the risk 21 MIN
U-matic / VHS / BETA
Rightful discharge series
Color; PAL (IND PRO G)
Contact distributor about price
Shows managers the right way to discipline and discharge employees. Trains supervisors to handle discharges properly, to avoid legal liability and treat employees with dignity and respect. Shows how to properly handle problem employees for increased productivity and higher morale. Increases an organization's chance of successful defense should a discharge case go to court. Part of two parts on rightful discharge.
Business and Economics; Guidance and Counseling
Dist - BNA **Prod** - BNA

Minimizing the Stress of Surgery 28 MIN
VHS / U-matic
Color
Helps remove some of the mystery and fear about surgery and shows the usual activities and procedures that take place before and after surgery.
Health and Safety; Psychology
Dist - FAIRGH **Prod** - FAIRGH

Minimum Impact on Wilderness 15 MIN
U-matic / VHS
Color
LC 81-707148
Shows ways in which people should and should not treat the wilderness in order to preserve it.
Physical Education and Recreation; Science - Natural; Social Science
Dist - WESTWN **Prod** - WESTWN

Minimum Mean - Square Error Estimation 18 MIN
U-matic / VHS
Probability and Random Processes - Statistical Averages Series
B&W (PRO)
Reviews the idea of the minimum mean - square error estimation. Presents an example involving the joint Gaussian probability density.
Mathematics
Dist - MIOT **Prod** - MIOT

The Minimum Principle - Discrete Time Case 43 MIN
U-matic / VHS
Modern Control Theory - Deterministic Optimal Control Series
Color (PRO)
Discusses discrete optimal control problems and the associated minimum principles for their solutions.
Industrial and Technical Education; Mathematics
Dist - MIOT **Prod** - MIOT

The Minimum Principle of Pontryagin - Continuous Time Case 49 MIN
U-matic / VHS
Modern Control Theory - Deterministic Optimal Control Series
Color (PRO)
Industrial and Technical Education; Mathematics
Dist - MIOT **Prod** - MIOT

Minimum Principle Vs Dynamic Programming 50 MIN
VHS / U-matic
Modern Control Theory - Deterministic Optimal Control Series
Color (PRO)
Contrasts from a technical and algorithmic viewpoint the two methods for solving optimal control problems.
Industrial and Technical Education; Mathematics
Dist - MIOT **Prod** - MIOT

A Mining Community - Kimberley 14 MIN
16mm / U-matic / VHS
This is My Home Series
Color (P I)
Introduces one of the world's largest lead - zinc mines in operation since the beginning of the century. Shows how when the ore runs out, inhabitants have to depend on other ways to mabe a living. Describes development of the tourist industry in Kimberley.
Geography - World; Social Science
Dist - BCNFL **Prod** - BCNFL 1984

Mining Engineer 15 MIN
16mm / U-matic / VHS
Career Awareness
(I)
$130 VC purchase, $240 film purchase, $25 VC rental, $30 film rental
Presents an empathetic approach to career planning, showing the personal attributes of mining engineers as well as their professional qualifications. Highlights the importance of career education.
Guidance and Counseling; Industrial and Technical Education
Dist - GPN

Mining engineering technician 4.5 MIN
VHS / 16mm
Good works 3 series
Color (A PRO)
$40.00 purchase _ #BPN213905
Presents the occupation of a mining engineering technician. Gives a profile of a young person who is either undergoing an apprenticeship or has recently completed training in this field. Takes the viewer on a tour of this person's workplace and explains the practical skills and training offered by employers and schools. Gives a better understanding of the demand for skilled workers today and the potential for personal growth.
Guidance and Counseling
Dist - RMIBHF **Prod** - RMIBHF

Mining Engineering Technician 5 MIN
U-matic
Color (H)
Provides useful, up to date information on various occupations to aid high school students in career selection. Available in five series of ten jobs each.
Education; Guidance and Counseling; Industrial and Technical Education
Dist - TVOTAR **Prod** - TVOTAR 1981

Mining Nickel 35 MIN
16mm
Color
Shows modern methods used in the development of nickel mines and the excavation of ore.
Industrial and Technical Education; Social Science
Dist - MTP **Prod** - MTP

Mining Noise Hazards 21 MIN
16mm
Color
LC 74-705150
Promotes a general awareness of noise hazards in the coal mining industry. Defines the sound and its characteristics. Shows the actual underground mining scenes, on - the - job noise surveys, and laboratory tests and analysis. Demonstrates the preventive methods along with various forms of engineering controls and protective devices.
Health and Safety; Industrial and Technical Education; Science - Natural; Science - Physical
Dist - USNAC **Prod** - USBM 1973

Mining's Challenge 15 MIN
16mm
Color
Discusses the challenges and career opportunities that exist in the mining profession today.
Guidance and Counseling; Industrial and Technical Education; Psychology
Dist - CROMAR **Prod** - COLOMN

Minipi trout 30 MIN
VHS
Color (G)
$29.90 purchase _ #0391
Travels to the Minipi Basin of Newfoundland to fish for brook trout.
Geography - World; Physical Education and Recreation; Science - Natural
Dist - SEVVID

Minister of Hate - Josef Goebbels 27 MIN
U-matic / VHS / 16mm
Twentieth Century Series
B&W (J H C)
Examines the techniques of totalitarian control of communications evolved by the Nazi, Joseph Goebbels. Includes actual scenes of the burning of all books considered hostile to the Nazi regime. Trevor - Roper, author of 'THE LAST DAYS OF HITLER,' comments on Goebbels' career.
History - World; Psychology; Social Science
Dist - CRMP **Prod** - CBSTV 1959

Ministering to the spiritual needs of the patient and family 60 MIN
VHS
Hospice - living with dying series
Color (R G)
$49.95 purchase _ #HOLD3
Trains clergy and pastoral ministers, physicians and nurses, social workers and therapists, counselors and volunteers and others who provide care and outreach to seriously ill patients and their families. Informs those who want information about options for care of their seriously ill family members. Features the Visiting Nurse Service of New York's Hospice Care Team and some of the patients and families under their care, as well as Dr Patrick Del Zoppo. Part of three parts on hospice care.
Guidance and Counseling; Health and Safety; Religion and Philosophy
Dist - CTNA **Prod** - CTNA

Ministry of John the Baptist 20 MIN
16mm
Living Bible Series
Color; B&W (I)
Jesus comes to John to be baptized. John calls him 'THE LAMB OF GOD.' John continues to preach and to baptize until he is imprisoned by Herod. John sends two disciples to ask Jesus if the Christ has really come.
Religion and Philosophy
Dist - FAMF **Prod** - FAMF

Minna Von Barnhelm 114 MIN
16mm
Color (GERMAN)
Introduces the Prussian Major Von Tellheim, who after the Seven Year War is awaiting his reimbursement from the state treasury and his vindication from a false accusation. Concludes with Minna, his fiancee, winning Tellheim through a clever plot which takes advantage of his pride. A film presentation of the drama, 'Minna Von Barnhelm, ' by Lessing.
Foreign Language; Literature and Drama
Dist - WSTGLC **Prod** - WSTGLC

Minneapolis past 57 MIN
VHS
Color (G)
$29.95, $19.95 purchase _ #V - 008, #V - 007
Chronicles the history of Minneapolis, Minnesota from the early years at St Athony's Falls milling district to a young mayor named Hubert Humphrey who crusaded for civil rights. Offers a teaching kit including teaching materials and a guide or video alone.
Biography; History - United States
Dist - MINHS **Prod** - KTCATV

Minnesota 60 MIN
VHS
Portrait of America series
Color (J H C G)
$99.95 purchase _ #AMB23V
Visits Minnesota. Offers extensive research into the state's history. Films key locations and presents segments on history, government, education, folklore, science, journalism, sociology, industry, agriculture and business. Shows what is unique about Minnesota and distinctive about its regional culture and how it got to be that way. Includes study guide. Part of a 50 - part series.
Geography - United States; History - United States
Dist - CAMV

Minnesota Landscapes 60 MIN
VHS / U-matic
Color
Presents a collection of behind - the - camera video artworks commissioned by station KCTA - TV. A PBS affiliated station in St Paul. Includes works by video artists James Byrne, Steve Christiansen, Steina, Skip Blumberg, Cynthia Neal and Davidson and Gigliotti.
Fine Arts
Dist - EIF **Prod** - EIF

Minnesota soap series
Twelve skits focusing on counseling situations in which questions and concerns about sexuality can arise. Exemplifies good and bad ways of dealing with problems.
Minnesota soap series 21 MIN
Dist - MMRC **Prod** - NATSF

Minnesota Valley National Wildlife Refuge 16 MIN
16mm / U-matic / VHS
Color
Chronicles the evolution of the valley and floodplain of the Minnesota River in the Twin City metropolitan area from an ignored and abused bottomland to an area recognized for its unique cultural, environmental and recreational values.
Geography - United States; History - United States
Dist - USNAC **Prod** - USBSFW

Minnesotanos Mexicanos 61 MIN
16mm
Color
LC 79-701377
Examines Mexican Americans in Minnesota, dealing with their pre - Columbian heritage, their years spent in the American Southwest, and their arrival in Minnesota in the late 19th century. Explores 20th century issues, such as bilingual education, migrant workers and the Bakke case.
Geography - United States; Sociology
Dist - SPSP **Prod** - SPSP 1978

Minnesotanos Mexicanos, Pt 1 31 MIN
16mm
Color
LC 79-701374
Examines Mexican Americans in Minnesota, dealing with their pre - Columbian heritage, their years spent in the American Southwest, and their arrival in Minnesota in the late 19th century. Explores 20th century issues, such as bilingual education, migrant workers and the Bakke case.
Sociology
Dist - SPSP **Prod** - SPSP 1978

Minnesotanos Mexicanos, Pt 2 30 MIN
16mm
Color
LC 79-701374
Examines Mexican Americans in Minnesota, dealing with their pre - Columbian heritage, their years spent in the American Southwest, and their arrival in Minnesota in the late 19th century. Explores 20th century issues, such as bilingual education, migrant workers and the Bakke case.
Sociology
Dist - SPSP **Prod** - SPSP 1978

Minnie Black's Gourd Band 29 MIN
VHS / 16mm
Color (G)
$100.00 purchase _ #MBLACKV
Exhibits Minnie Black leading a tour of her gourd museum and performing with her band. Relates her techniques of gourd sculpture.
Fine Arts
Dist - APPAL

Minnie remembers 5 MIN
16mm
Color

LC 77-700204
Focuses on the reminiscences of an old woman about the past, contrasting the warmth and love which typified her youth and womanhood with the loneliness and isolation of old age.
Guidance and Counseling; Health and Safety; Sociology
Dist - ECUFLM **Prod** - UMCOM 1976

Minnie the Moocher 55 MIN
16mm
Color (G)
Presents an independent production by Manny Pittson. Takes a nostalgic tour through famous Harlem jazz clubs using archival footage and the use of 'soundies.' Features Cab Calloway as narrator.
Fine Arts; History - United States
Dist - FIRS

A Minor Altercation 30 MIN
16mm / VHS
Color (G)
$500.00, $225.00 purchase, $60.00 rental
Dramatizes a fight over placement in a computer class between a black girl and a white girl. Reveals that the families of the girls, after overcoming the basic racial prejudice in each, come together to confront institutional racism.
History - United States; Sociology
Dist - WMEN **Prod** - JASH 1977

A Minor Altercation 30 MIN
16mm / U-matic / VHS
Color (H C A)
$450.00 purchase, $300.00 purchase, $55 rental
Investigates racial conflict in public schools, viewing it from both black and white perspectives. Reveals the feelings underlying racial tensions. Produced by Jackie Shearer, Terry Signaigo, Mary Tiseo, and Jay Watkins.
Education; Sociology
Dist - CNEMAG **Prod** - CNEMAG 1988

Minor Burns 20 MIN
VHS / U-matic
Medical Cisis Intervention Series
Color (PRO)
Designed to provide the participant with the knowledge to care for minor burn injuries. Demonstrates how to determine when a particular burn should be referred to a specialist. Gives a description of the anatomical structure and normal function of the skin and the psysiological events associated with minor burns. Tells how to inform patient about the procedure for follow - up treatment.
Health and Safety
Dist - LEIKID **Prod** - LEIKID

Minor Burns
U-matic / VHS
Burns - Emergency Management Series
Color
Presents a program of discussion and illustration of the effect of burns on the skin, the skin's role in healing and emergency department procedures for treatment.
Health and Safety
Dist - VTRI **Prod** - VTRI

Minor crafts series - decoupage 10 MIN
VHS / U-matic
Minor crafts series
Color
Explains and demonstrates decoupage (a French term for decorating wood surfaces with pictures).
Fine Arts; Guidance and Counseling
Dist - HSCIC **Prod** - HSCIC

Minor crafts series
Minor crafts series - decoupage 10 MIN
Dist - HSCIC

Minor Electrical Repairs of Small Appliances 13 MIN
U-matic / VHS / 16mm
Home Repair Series
Color (J)
$315.00, $220.00 purchase _ #80534; LC 81-700043
Illustrates the basic tools needed to make simple electrical repairs. Shows several common problems and tells how to solve them.
Industrial and Technical Education
Dist - CORF **Prod** - CENTRO 1981

Minor Oral Surgery Technics in Dentistry 135 MIN
U-matic / VHS
Color (PRO)
Presents the surgical procedure for the correction of central incisor diastemas. Shows the removal of a torus palatinus by interrupting the circulation, leading to necrosis and the nontraumatic removal of the torus. Also shows method for uncovering embedded canines.
Health and Safety
Dist - USNAC **Prod** - CHIDEN

Minor Sport Injuries made Major 28 MIN
U-matic
Sports Medicine in the 80's Series
Color (G)
Teaches the role of sports medicine as it relates to athlete, coach, trainer, team and school. Covers most kinds of injuries encountered in sports.
Health and Safety; Physical Education and Recreation
Dist - CEPRO **Prod** - CEPRO 1989

Minorities 15 MIN
U-matic / VHS / 16mm
American Condition Series
Color (H C A)
LC 77-700631
Presents a documentary about a skilled Black worker and his economic problems. Shows that his efforts to find steady work in his craft as a firebrick mason typify many of the problems of Black workers. Examines the status of Blacks today, how far they have come and their prospects for the future.
History - United States; Sociology
Dist - MGHT **Prod** - ABCTV 1976

Minorities 30 MIN
VHS / U-matic
Focus on Society Series
Color (C)
Discusses the present status of minorities in society.
Sociology
Dist - DALCCD **Prod** - DALCCD

Minorities in Communications 30 MIN
16mm
Color (J)
Discusses career opportunities for minorities, giving direction and supplying answers to questions raised by minority members themselves.
Guidance and Counseling; Psychology; Social Science
Dist - NWMA **Prod** - NWMA 1974

Minorities in journalism - Making a difference 25 MIN
VHS
Color (G)
$19.95 purchase _ #MJMD - 000
Presents the myriad opportunities available to minorities in journalism. Traces the history of minority participation in media. Points out the personal and educational qualifications necessary for success in journalism. Interviews many professionals.
History - United States; Literature and Drama; Sociology
Dist - PBS **Prod** - KETCTV 1989

Minorities - What's a Minority 14 MIN
U-matic / VHS / 16mm
Color (J H C)
LC 72-701958
Interviews members of various groups to provide perspectives on the problems of prejudice and of different races, religions and ethnic groups living together.
Guidance and Counseling; Sociology
Dist - CORF **Prod** - CORF 1972

Minority Candidates 35 MIN
VHS / U-matic
Interview - EEO Compliance Series Pt 2; Pt 2
Color (A)
Focuses on avoiding illegal questions while conducting job interviews with minority candidates.
Business and Economics; Civics and Political Systems; Psychology; Sociology
Dist - XICOM **Prod** - XICOM

Minority Carriers in Semiconductors 26 MIN
Videoreel / VHS
B&W
Demonstrates the existence and behavior of injected excess minority carriers in semiconductors by repeating in modified form the Haynes - Shockley drift - mobility experiment.
Industrial and Technical Education
Dist - EDC **Prod** - NCEEF

Minority of One 28 MIN
U-matic / VHS / 16mm
Color (H C)
LC 77-701733
Discusses the neurological disorder known as autism, the children who suffer from it and the problems faced by their parents.
Psychology; Sociology
Dist - FI **Prod** - NBCTV 1977

Minority Report 29 MIN
U-matic / VHS / 16mm
Human Relations and School Discipline Series
Color (T)
Presents an in - depth look at two related concerns, the special problems of minorities in what many observers consider an alien educational environment and, secondly, the pros and cons of what has become known as 'RADICAL SCHOOL REFORM.' Discusses free and alternative schools.
Education; Sociology
Dist - FI **Prod** - MFFD

Minority Youth - Adam 10 MIN
U-matic / VHS / 16mm
Color (I J H)
LC 72-712336
Describes the problems of Adam, an Indian boy in a predominantly Anglo society. He shows pride in his cultural heritage as he chooses to retain the strengths of his own culture in the face of assimilation into the American way of life.
Guidance and Counseling; Sociology
Dist - PHENIX **Prod** - ROE 1971

Minority Youth - Akira 15 MIN
U-matic / VHS / 16mm
Color (I J H)
Describes Akira's frustrations and pride in having a different racial background from most of the people in his society. Relates his choice to adhere to the cultural heritage of his Japanese ancestry in the face of assimilation into the American way of life.
Guidance and Counseling; Sociology
Dist - PHENIX **Prod** - ROE 1971

Minority Youth - Angie 11 MIN
U-matic / VHS / 16mm
Color
LC 70-712338
A girl relates her personal feelings about being Mexican - American.
Sociology
Dist - PHENIX **Prod** - ROE 1971

Minority Youth - Felicia 12 MIN
16mm / U-matic / VHS
B&W (I J H)
Presents the problems of young black people and tells the story of a girl who has feelings of alienation from the predominately white American culture.
Guidance and Counseling; Sociology
Dist - PHENIX **Prod** - ROE 1971

Minority youth series
Adam - minority youth 10 MIN
Akira - minority youth 15 MIN
Angie - minority youth 11 MIN
Felicia 13 MIN
Dist - PHENIX

Minors 36 MIN
U-matic / VHS / 16mm
Color (J H A)
Features story of a minor - league baseball player and a young 14 - year - old girl who wants to coach him.
Fine Arts; Physical Education and Recreation; Psychology
Dist - LCOA **Prod** - LCOA 1985

Minors' Rights 29 MIN
U-matic
You and the Law Series Lesson 11
Color (C A)
Concentrates on laws that govern persons prior to age of majority. Discusses major areas where the law applies differently to adults. Examines juvenile deliquency.
Civics and Political Systems; Sociology
Dist - CDTEL **Prod** - COAST

The Minotaur 55 MIN
U-matic / VHS
Color (PRO)
Allows students to see how their own responses may affect the course of evaluation and treatment.
Health and Safety; Psychology
Dist - HSCIC **Prod** - HSCIC 1979

Minou - standing on your own
VHS
Key concepts in self - esteem
Color (K P)
$79.95 purchase _ #MF9341RA
Presents one of an 11 - part series teaching key curriculum concepts such as independence, freedom and responsibility, and peer pressure. Includes video, storybook and teaching guide with activities and games. In this video, a pampered cat suddenly finds herself alone on the streets of Paris, unprepared to fend for herself. Like Minou, youngsters can gain confidence in their growing ability to control their lives.
Education; Psychology
Dist - CFKRCM **Prod** - CFKRCM

The Mint 400 24 MIN
16mm
Color
Depicts the Mint 400, the richest off - road race in America held in Las Vegas, Nevada. Shows the planning and preparation, support crews, the exotic racing machines and the race itself.
Physical Education and Recreation
Dist - MTP **Prod** - GC

Minuet into Scherzo 28 MIN
U-matic / VHS
Beethoven by Barenboim Series

Color (C)
$249.00, $149.00 purchase _ #AD - 1222
Illustrates Beethoven's impatience with societal formality through his transformation of the most conventional musical form of the time, the minuet, into the scherzo, retaining the rhythm but using the movement in entirely new and revolutionary ways. Part of a thirteen - part series placing Beethoven, his music and his life within the context of his time and the history of music, Beethoven by Barenboim.
Fine Arts; History - World
Dist - FOTH **Prod** - FOTH

Minus One
16mm
Rats Series
Color
Health and Safety; Home Economics; Sociology
Dist - MLA **Prod** - MLA

Minus three miles 3 MIN
U-matic
Apollo digest series
Color
LC 79-706985
Analyzes the mobility concept of assembling a 36 - story rocket and moving it to the launch area. Issued in 1969 as a motion picture.
Industrial and Technical Education; Science - Physical
Dist - USNAC **Prod** - NASA 1979

Minus three miles 7 MIN
16mm
Apollo digest series
Color
LC 74-705151
Shows the movement of assembled rocket to launch pad.
Industrial and Technical Education; Social Science
Dist - USNAC **Prod** - NASAMS 1969

The Minus Tide 126 FRS
VHS / U-matic
Color (J H)
Details the movements of the waters, both violent and peaceful, that have carved the environment for plants and animals of the tidal regions on California's coast when the lowest of the low tides reveals sponges, starfish, anemones, kelp, algae, and various mollusks.
Science - Natural
Dist - CEPRO **Prod** - CEPRO

Minute and a Half Man 6 MIN
16mm
Color (P)
Introduces Hector Heathcote, a minute man who is always late. Show how his tardiness is rewarded when the enemy is routed.
Guidance and Counseling
Dist - SF **Prod** - SF 1975

Minute men of the American Revolution 35 MIN
VHS
Color (I J)
$29.95 purchase _ #ST - FF0133
Explores the issues dividing the colonies in North America from the government of England through the eyes of an American patriot.
History - United States
Dist - INSTRU

The Minute Saved 29 MIN
16mm
B&W
LC 74-705152
Concerns the element of haste that all too often acts as the catalyst of destruction in aviation.
Industrial and Technical Education
Dist - USNAC **Prod** - USA 1967

Minute Waltz 3 MIN
U-matic
Laurie McDonald Series
Color
Speeds up twenty minutes of actual dancing time to produce three minutes of hilarious video to Chopin's Minute Waltz.'.
Fine Arts
Dist - WMENIF **Prod** - WMENIF

Minuteman - Missile and Mission 20 MIN
16mm
Color (H)
LC FIA67-2336
Explains the role of the thiokel chemical corporation in the development and manufacture of the Minuteman Intercontinental Ballistic Missile. Features testing and live firing of the missile.
Civics and Political Systems; Industrial and Technical Education
Dist - THIOKL **Prod** - THIOKL 1962

Miracle 15 MIN
16mm
B&W (J)
Depicts the images of a city as they shift from dawn to noon.
Social Science; Sociology
Dist - UWFKD **Prod** - UWFKD

Miracle 26 MIN
16mm
Color (R)
Portrays the true story of a talented and wealthy musician, ruined by alcohol, who is transformed by receiving Jesus Christ as his savior.
Literature and Drama; Religion and Philosophy
Dist - UF **Prod** - UF

A Miracle 1 MIN
16mm
Color (G)
$10.00 rental
Presents a 30 - second collage in which Pope Pious XII does a juggling act in a Robert Breer production.
Fine Arts; Religion and Philosophy
Dist - CANCIN

Miracle at Moreaux 55 MIN
VHS
WonderWorks Series
Color (P)
$29.95 purchase _ #766 - 9013
Tells the story of a nun and her young charges who protect three Jewish children escaping from the Nazis. Stars Loretta Swit, Robert Joy. Based on the book 'Twenty And Ten' by Clare Huchet Bishop. Part of the WonderWorks Series which centers on themes involving rites of passage that occur during the growing - up years from seven to sixteen. Features young people as protagonists and portrays strong adult role models.
Fine Arts; History - United States; History - World; Literature and Drama; Psychology; Sociology
Dist - FI **Prod** - PBS 1990

Miracle at the Time 18 MIN
16mm
B&W
Shows how a bitter, alienated motel owner in a decadent urban situation discovers that his happiness can be provided by the very people who have been the source of his bitterness. Tells how one such person provides him with a miracle that opens up his small, enclosed world.
Fine Arts; Guidance and Counseling
Dist - USC **Prod** - USC

Miracle days 30 MIN
VHS
Color (K P I)
$22.95 purchase _ #837
Brings the Jewish calender to life with the help of Yoni, a magical minstrel who sings and dances his way from Rosh Hashanah to Hanukah to Shavuot, with his enthusiastic and energetic group of young friends. Dances with the Torah, buildings a sukkah, parties on Purim and bakes matzah. Introduces children to the Jewish holiday cycle.
Mathematics; Sociology
Dist - ERGOM

Miracle Drugs 26 MIN
U-matic / VHS
Color (C)
$249.00, $149.00 purchase _ #AD - 1721
Traces the roots of many miracle drugs that are being developed almost routinely. Examines the search for microorganisms that will produce tomorrow's antibiotics, the use of computers to model molecules and simulate experiments, the degree to which US society has become drug dependent, and the economic factors affecting the targets chosen for chemical and pharmaceutical research.
Health and Safety; Psychology; Science - Natural
Dist - FOTH **Prod** - FOTH

Miracle in Color 22 MIN
16mm
Color
Begins with the birth of latex in the Dow labs and carries through to the final application of latex in your home or office building.
Business and Economics; Industrial and Technical Education
Dist - DCC **Prod** - DCC

Miracle in Milan 96 MIN
VHS
B&W (G)
$39.95 purchase _ #MIR040
Features a classic of the Italian cinema renaissance. Uses fantasy, satire and humor to tell the story of Toto, an abandoned newborn who is raised by a kindly old lady to be a paragon of goodness. Directed by Vittorio De Sica. Remastered with new translation.
Fine Arts; Guidance and Counseling; Literature and Drama; Sociology
Dist - HOMVIS **Prod** - JANUS 1951

Miracle in the Desert - the Story of Hanford 29 MIN
16mm
Color
LC 74-705155
Tells the story of the development of the Hanford Engineer Works in southern Washington during World War II. Shows how the discovery of plutonium and the first successful nuclear chain reaction by Dr Enrico Fermi led to the construction of the billion dollar plant.
Industrial and Technical Education; Science; Science - Physical
Dist - USNAC **Prod** - USNRC 1966

Miracle in Tonga 16 MIN
16mm
Color
LC FIE67-45
Records the cooperative efforts of the Tongan Medical Department and the communicable disease center to protect against smallpox in Tonga. Explains and illustrates a new method for smallpox vaccination.
Geography - World; Health and Safety; Sociology
Dist - USNAC **Prod** - USPHS 1965

The Miracle Man 29 MIN
VHS / U-matic
(G PRO)
$595.00 purchase, $130.00 rental
Illustrates positive thinking and motivation through the story of Morris Goodman, who overcame total paralysis against all medical predictions.
Psychology
Dist - CREMED **Prod** - CREMED 1987

Miracle Man 30 MIN
16mm / VHS
Color (PRO)
$595.00 purchase, $130.00 rental, $35.00 preview
Presents the story of one man's triumph over impossible handicaps. Illustrates the power of positive thinking and motivation.
Psychology
Dist - UTM **Prod** - UTM

The Miracle Months
U-matic / VHS
Body Human Series
Color
Expresses the drama and the wonder of conception, gestation and birth. Covers human ovulation, the instant of penetration of the sperm into the egg, a living 40 - day embryo inside its mother's uterus, its two - chambered heart beating vigorously. Documents major medical advances including a hazardous intrauterine transfusion that pumps blood directly into a baby dying in its mother's womb of Rh disease, and a perfectly timed decision, based on sophisticated testing of amniotic fluid, that allows survival of mother and child, both threatened by a condition called placenta previa.
Health and Safety; Industrial and Technical Education
Dist - MEDCOM **Prod** - MEDCOM

The Miracle of birth 21 MIN
VHS
Color (PRO A)
$250.00 purchase _ #OB - 112
Gives parents realistic expectations of labor and delivery by following three expectant parents through individual birth experiences. Shows delivery using epidural and foreceps, caesarean section and natural delivery. Reviews the importance of prenatal care and shares the feelings of these three parents.
Health and Safety
Dist - MIFE **Prod** - AIMS 1991

The Miracle of birth 30 MIN
VHS
Color (C A PRO)
$395.00 purchase, $75.00 rental _ #9986
Focuses on three different births, showing the differing birthing procedures. Demonstrates epidural blocks and the use of forceps, Caesarean section, and natural childbirth. Interviews parents and members of the respective medical teams. Produced by the Brigham Young University College of Nursing.
Science - Natural
Dist - AIMS **Prod** - BYU 1988

Miracle of Birth 30 MIN
16mm
Color (C A)
LC 75-700308
Prepares expectant parents for childbirth. Shows the live birth of three infants. Captures the joy and beauty of the occasion as it is shared by the young couples.
Science - Natural; Sociology
Dist - BYU **Prod** - BYU 1974

The Miracle of change 7 MIN
16mm

Color (G)
$15.00 rental
Explores territoriality, paranoia and voyeurism while taking place in a laundromat. Watches the characters strive to define and maintain their individual semi - private spaces in this public place.
Fine Arts; Literature and Drama; Psychology
Dist - CANCIN **Prod** - PIERCE 1984

Miracle of Corn 8 MIN
VHS / 16mm
Color (H C A)
Shows through time lapse photography the tremendous productive capacity of the corn plant, from the time it is planted through germination, emergence, vegetative growth, reproduction and harvest. Features three complete growing seasons.
Agriculture; Science - Natural
Dist - IOWA **Prod** - IOWA 1989

Miracle of Czechoslovakia 29 MIN
Videoreel / VT2
Course of Our Times I Series
Color
History - World
Dist - PBS **Prod** - WGBHTV

The Miracle of Intervale Avenue 65 MIN
VHS
Color (G)
$59.95 purchase _ #430
Uses the research of Dr Jack Kugelmass to explore a once - thriving Jewish community in the South Bronx that somehow continues despite the decay that surrounds it. Shows a remarkable reality of Jews, blacks and Puerto Ricans interacting and helping each other.
History - United States; Sociology
Dist - ERGOM **Prod** - ERGOM

The Miracle of life 60 MIN
VHS
Color (J H)
$29.00 purchase _ #04791 - 126
Photographs the developing human fetus. Features the work of Swedish photographer Lennart Nilsson.
Psychology
Dist - GA **Prod** - GA

The Miracle of Life
VHS / U-matic
Color (J H)
Deals with the contemporary issues and all the facts of parenting and childbirth.
Home Economics; Sociology
Dist - CAREER **Prod** - CAREER 1980

Miracle of life 60 MIN
VHS
Color (G)
$24.95 purchase
Uses microscopic photography to reveal the inner workings of the human body as they relate to human conception. From the PBS series 'NOVA.'
Science - Natural
Dist - PBS **Prod** - WNETTV

The Miracle of Life 15 MIN
U-matic / VHS / 16mm
Color (J) (ARABIC, ENGLISH)
Explores the processes of fertilization, cell division and growth by means of microscope photography. Describes both human and animal fetus development focusing on the ways they differ.
Science - Natural
Dist - PFP **Prod** - CINSCI

The Miracle of Life 57 MIN
U-matic / VHS / 16mm
Nova Series
Color (H C A)
LC 83-700535
Describes the male and female productive organs, showing the formation of sperm and the passage of a fertile egg through the fallopian tubes. Uses a microscope to observe DNA, chromosomes and other minute body details.
Science - Natural
Dist - TIMLIF **Prod** - SVERTV 1983

The Miracle of life 60 MIN
VHS
Color (C A)
$24.95 purchase
Follows an egg after release by the ovary, sperm from its early development through ejaculation to fertilization of the egg, development of the egg into an embryo, a fetus and a full - term baby. Features the work of Swedish photographer Lennart Nilsson.
Health and Safety; Science - Natural
Dist - FCSINT **Prod** - FCSINT 1982

Miracle of Life 57 MIN
16mm / VHS
Nova Series
(J H C)
$99.95 each
Looks at conception and the following stages of reproduction in actual footage of living humans.
Science; Science - Natural; Sociology
Dist - AMBROS **Prod** - AMBROS 1985

Miracle of Morgan's Creek 98 MIN
U-matic / VHS / 16mm
B&W
Tells the story of a girl who frantically tries to learn which of a townful of soldiers was the father of her baby. Directed by Preston Sturges.
Fine Arts
Dist - FI **Prod** - PAR 1944

The Miracle of Reproduction 15 MIN
U-matic / VHS / 16mm
Color (P I)
LC 76-702173
Explains how plants, fish, animals and human beings reproduce their species.
Science - Natural
Dist - AIMS **Prod** - DAVP 1974

Miracle of Taxila 45 MIN
16mm
Color
Tells the story of the Christian Hospital Taxila, a small Christian hospital in Islamic Pakistan that restores sight to more than 12,000 blind people yearly.
Health and Safety; Religion and Philosophy
Dist - WHLION **Prod** - WHLION 1983

Miracle of the eagles - restoration of the American bald eagle - the windrifters -Part I 21 MIN
U-matic / VHS / BETA
Color (I J H)
$29.95, $130.00 purchase _ #LSTF82
Shows how biologists coaxed a pair of bald eagles into raising incubator chicks - part of a program to increase the eagle population. Explains the effects of DDT contamination on birds and their eggs. Includes teacher's guide. Produced by Nature Episodes assisted by the New York State Dept of Environmental Conservation.
Science - Natural
Dist - FEDU

Miracle of the eagles - restoration of the American bald eagle - second chance -Part II 20 MIN
U-matic / VHS / BETA
Color (I J H)
$29.95, $130.00 purchase _ #LSTF83
Shows mow biologists transplant young bald eagles from Alaska to the Northeastern states - part of a program to increase the eagle population. Includes teacher's guide. Produced by Nature Epidodes assisted by the New York State Dept of Environmental Conservation.
Science - Natural
Dist - FEDU

Miracle of the Helicopter 17 MIN
U-matic / VHS
Color
Traces the progress of Sikorsky helicopters from the first flight of Igor Sikorsky's VS - 300 to the early 1970s. Illustrates the range of military and civilian missions performed by Sikorsky models with worldwide operations including rescues, astronaut retrieval, airline service and timber harvesting.
Industrial and Technical Education
Dist - IHF **Prod** - IHF

Miracle of the Mind 30 MIN
Videoreel / VT1
Twenty - First Century Series
Color
Indicates how some day man may be able to control and manipulate his thoughts, memories and emotions.
Psychology; Science; Sociology
Dist - MTP **Prod** - UCC

Miracle of the Mind 26 MIN
U-matic / VHS / 16mm
Twenty - First Century Series
Color (J)
LC FIA68-2237
Describes the attempts made by man to understand the nature of the mind and surveys the contribution science has made to this understanding. Evaluates present knowledge of the brain and mental functions in terms of man's future.
Psychology
Dist - MGHT **Prod** - CBSTV 1968

Miracle of the Mind 19 MIN
16mm / U-matic / VHS
Twenty - First Century Series
Color (J)
LC 75-702563
Edited version of the 1968 motion picture 'Miracle of the Mind.' Describes the attempts made by man to understand the nature of the mind and surveys the contribution science has made to this understanding. Evaluates present knowledge of the brain and mental functions in terms of man's future.
Psychology; Science; Sociology
Dist - MGHT **Prod** - CBSTV 1975

Miracle of the Mud Pies 11 MIN
U-matic / VHS / 16mm
Color (P I)
Reveals that only plants are able to take nourishment directly from the soil.
Science - Natural
Dist - STANF **Prod** - STANF

Miracle of the Trees 10 MIN
U-matic / VHS / 16mm
Color (I)
Uses time - lapse photography to show the development of tree buds as winter merges into spring.
Science - Natural
Dist - IFB **Prod** - OTT 1950

Miracle of the White Stallions 115 MIN
16mm / U-matic / VHS
Color
Tells how the director of the famous Spanish riding school of Vienna evacuates the priceless Lipizzan stallions from bombarded Vienna during the critical months of the war.
Fine Arts
Dist - FI **Prod** - DISNEY 1967

Miracle of Vision 15 MIN
16mm
B&W
Covers structure of eye and its function for seeing. Discusses optical illusions, abnormal conditions of the eye which cause poor vision, and corrective measures for vision defects. Presents a brief history of optometry and the work of the optometrist.
Health and Safety; Science - Natural
Dist - FILAUD **Prod** - AOA

Miracle of water 25 MIN
VHS
Color (G)
$24.95 purchase _ #BOR - 8
Recalls the heritage of the Bureau of Reclamation. Explains the evolving program required for a prosperous land with an adequate water supply. Shows why the Bureau built multipurpose projects such as Central Valley Project in California and others.
Civics and Political Systems; Industrial and Technical Education; Science - Natural; Social Science
Dist - INSTRU **Prod** - USBR
USNAC

Miracle on Second Avenue 22 MIN
16mm
Color
LC 75-703287
Presents an account of the way in which the Bell System restored telephone service to a major central office switching center destroyed by the worst fire in its history.
Industrial and Technical Education
Dist - MGS **Prod** - ATAT 1975

Miracle planet - the life story of Earth series 360 MIN
VHS
Miracle planet - the life story of Earth series
Color (I J H)
$500.00 purchase _ #A5VH 1292
Presents a six - part series examining the intricate balance of systems known as planet Earth. Explores the origins of Earth in The Third Planet; examines Earth's interior in The Heat Within; shows how ocean life created the atmospheric balance necessary for land life in Life From the Sea; illustrates how the creation of the ozone layer allowed the emergence of plant life in Patterns in the Air; shows dramatic changes in Earth history in Riddles of Sand and Ice; and considers future prospects for Earth in The Home Planet.
Science - Physical; Sociology
Dist - CLRVUE

The Miracle resume - creating effective resumes 23 MIN
VHS
Color (H C G)
$99.00 purchase _ #JWMRV
Explains the basic of writing a resume through a colorful story about Wayne Miracle, the hopeless comedian. Shows how Wayne learns about the three kinds of resumes - chronological, skills and creative, and the advantages and disadvantages of each. Teaches the basic steps to writing each type of resume, such as how to phrase the job objective. Offers tips on length, typesetting and appearance that improve any resume. Includes the book Getting the Job You Really Want.

Business and Economics; Guidance and Counseling
Dist - CAMV **Prod** - JISTW 1990

The Miracle rider 25 MIN
VHS
Cliffhangers I series
B&W (G)
Features Tom Mix in his last screen appearance. Includes seven episodes.
Fine Arts
Dist - SCETV **Prod** - SCETV 1983

The Miracle rod and those amazing trumpets - Volume 3 45 MIN
VHS
Superbook series
Color (K P I R)
$11.99 purchase _ #35 - 86607 - 979
Uses an animated format to tell the story of Chris and Joy and their time travels through Biblical places and events. 'The Miracle Rod' tells the story of Moses and his miraculous rod, while 'Those Amazing Trumpets' tells the story of Joshua and the city of Jericho.
Literature and Drama; Religion and Philosophy
Dist - APH **Prod** - TYHP

The Miracle Seekers 25 MIN
VHS / U-matic / 16mm
Maclear Series
Color; Mono (J H C A)
MV $250 00, MP $300.00 purchase, $50.00 rental
Looks at Banguio in the Philippines and the surgical methods that use no knife or anaesthetic found there.
Health and Safety
Dist - CTV **Prod** - CTV 1974

The Miracle Woman 90 MIN
16mm
B&W
Tells how an embittered young woman (Barbara Stanwyck) opens a religious tabernacle in order to fleece the masses. Directed by Frank Capra.
Fine Arts
Dist - KITPAR **Prod** - CPC 1931

The Miracle worker 107 MIN
VHS
B&W (I J H)
$24.95 purchase _ #119033
Stars Anne Bancroft and Patty Duke in an adaptation of the William Gibson play about Helen Keller and her teacher, Ann Sullivan.
Biography; Guidance and Counseling; Literature and Drama
Dist - KNOWUN

The Miracle worker 98 MIN
VHS
Color (G)
$59.95 purchase _ #S00046
Tells the story of Helen Keller and her first encounters with teacher Anne Sullivan, who would eventually become her life - long companion. Stars Patty Duke Astin as Sullivan, with Melissa Gilbert as Keller. Remake of 1962 film, in which Duke won an Oscar playing Keller. Directed by Paul Aaron.
Fine Arts; Guidance and Counseling; History - World
Dist - UILL **Prod** - GA 1979
GA

Miracle workers 30 MIN
VHS
Business matters series
Color (A)
PdS65 purchase
Reveals that Hong Kong and Singapore are now the economic power houses of the Far East. Asks what lessons the British business community can learn from their success.
Business and Economics
Dist - BBCENE

Miracles from Agriculture 14 MIN
16mm / U-matic
Color
Reports on the farming and ranching, marketing, processing, storing, transporting, and merchandising of food and other agricultural products. Describes the role of research and agricultrual services from farm to market to home.
Agriculture; Social Science; Sociology
Dist - USDA **Prod** - USDA 1972

The Miraculous Arabian Steed - a Middle East Folk Tale 7 MIN
16mm
Folk Tales from Around the World Series
Color (K P I)
LC 80-700789
Presents an animated story about a wily police chief who tries to cheat Djoha out of his horse and is, in the end, outwitted himself.
Literature and Drama
Dist - SF **Prod** - ADPF 1980

The Miraculous Pool 28 MIN
16mm
Color
LC 70-707509
Portrays the story of medical research at the National Institutes of Health, emphasizing the role of the National Institute of Allergy and Infectious Diseases and its efforts to combat viral and other infectious diseases through a collaborative vaccine development program.
Health and Safety; Sociology
Dist - NMAC **Prod** - BECDIC 1967

Mirage at the Desert's Edge 22 MIN
16mm
Color (C A)
Shows that Islam, the spiritual mirage of the country of Senegal, can be dispelled only by the reality of Jesus Christ.
Geography - World; Religion and Philosophy
Dist - CBFMS **Prod** - CBFMS

Miranda and the Right to Counsel 50 MIN
U-matic / VHS
Criminal Procedure and the Trial Advocate Series
Color (PRO)
Distinguishes between the Miranda warning and the sixth amendment right to counsel. Explores eyewitness identification and its limitations and the subject of prior confessions.
Civics and Political Systems
Dist - ABACPE **Prod** - ABACPE

Mirele Efros 80 MIN
VHS
B&W (G) (YIDDISH WITH ENGLISH SUBTITLES)
$79.95 purchase _ #752
Features Berta Gersten as Mirele, a noble, dignified widow and successful businesswoman who comes into conflict with the daughter - in - law she chose for her eldest son. Reveals that her generosity and love for her son leads to her own undoing. Adapts the popular play by Jacob Gordin and is set in turn - of - the - century Grodno. Directed by Josef Berne.
Literature and Drama; Sociology
Dist - ERGOM **Prod** - ERGOM 1938

Miriam and baby Moses 25 MIN
VHS
Greatest stories ever told series
Color (K P I R)
$19.95 purchase, $10.00 rental _ #35 - 88 - 2020
Uses an animated format to tell the story of Miriam and her brother Moses. Presents the story from Miriam's point of view.
Literature and Drama; Religion and Philosophy
Dist - APH **Prod** - ANDERK

Miriam Fried - a Profile 30 MIN
VHS / U-matic
Color (H C A)
Features a closeup of Miriam Field, a violinist, as she discusses the balance she seeks between the critical elements of her life - performance and family.
Fine Arts
Dist - IU **Prod** - IU 1982

Mirna and Mario - Birth 3
VHS / U-matic
Video birth library series
Color (J H G)
$100.00 purchase
Follows the childbirth experiences of a Hispanic couple, Mirna and Mario, who are having their 4th child. Reveals that their obstetrician and nurse are also Hispanic. Mirna is induced with pitocin because she has a history of precipitous labors and is at 42 weeks. Mario discusses the fetal monitor printout with Mirna and the nurse, and is a good example of an active, committed coach during the labor. Part of a 15 - part series on childbirth education.
Health and Safety
Dist - POLYMR **Prod** - POLYMR

Mirny 14 MIN
U-matic
White Inferno Series
Color (H)
Examines the preparation necessary for an exedition of 2300 kilometers. Tells of the voyage from Le Harve to Mirny and the first contacts with the other scientific team.
Geography - World
Dist - TVOTAR **Prod** - TVOTAR 1971

The Mirror 106 MIN
35mm / 16mm
Color; B&W (G) (RUSSIAN WITH ENGLISH SUBTITLES)
$300.00, $400.00 rental
Juxtaposes nostalgic visions of the childhood of director Andrei Tarkovsky in war - torn exile with slow - motion dream sequences and stark World War II newsreels.
Fine Arts; History - World; Literature and Drama
Dist - KINOIC **Prod** - IFEX 1975

Mirror and Image 9 MIN
U-matic / VHS
Introductory Concepts in Physics - Light Series
Color (C)
$229.00, $129.00 purchase _ #AD - 1211
Explains the different images produced by parallel mirrors, half - mirrors and mirrors with curved surfaces through experiments with the nature of the relationship between the object, its image in a mirror and the mirror.
Science - Physical
Dist - FOTH **Prod** - FOTH

Mirror Images - Figures and Symmetry 20 MIN
U-matic
Let's Figure it Out Series
B&W (P)
Mathematics
Dist - NYSED **Prod** - WNYE 1968

Mirror, Mirror 11 MIN
16mm
Color
LC 77-702967
Deals with mystery, mythology and psychology.
Literature and Drama; Psychology; Religion and Philosophy
Dist - CANFDC **Prod** - ASTIRM 1972

Mirror mirror 17 MIN
VHS / U-matic / 16mm
Color (G)
$500.00, $250.00 purchase, $60.00 rental
Explores the relationship between a woman's body image and the quest for an idealized form. Interviews thirteen women of varying age, size and ethnicity who are ambivalent about their bodies. Their comments on the size and shape of specific body parts are underscored by archival footage depicting beauty contests from the 1930s which incisively illuminates the vagaries in the concept of an 'ideal' body type.
Sociology
Dist - WMEN **Prod** - KRAWZJ 1990

Mirror, mirror - facial disfigurement 27 MIN
VHS
Color (H C G)
$295.00 purchase, $55.00 rental
Examines the lives of several people of various ages with facial disfigurement - one of the most psychologically difficult disabilities because it tends to alienate others. Features psychiatrist Ariette Lefebvre who discusses the self - fulfilling prophecy that occur when disfigured people suffer rejectin from early childhood. They develop low self esteem and feel unlovable. Shows how many people featured in the program have broken the cycle and feel at home in the world and have relationships and careers.
Psychology
Dist - FLMLIB **Prod** - CANBC 1991

Mirror of a Child 30 MIN
VHS
Color (C H G PRO)
$525.00 purchase _ #8825; $75.00 rental _ #8230
Illustrates the feelings and characteristics common to adult children of alcoholics. Helps adult children realize how their past affects their lives. Offers hope for recovery through ACOA - Adult Children Of Alcoholics - and Al - Anon.
Guidance and Counseling; Health and Safety; Psychology; Sociology
Dist - HAZELB **Prod** - JOHNIN 1990
AIMS

Mirror of Gesture 21 MIN
U-matic / VHS / 16mm
Color
LC 74-702911
Focuses on the relationship between the sculpture and dance of India using sculpture from the Indian galleries of the Los Angeles County Museum of Art. Intercuts Indian sculpture with dance sequences to emphasize the artistic correspondences between the two media and to demonstrate how effectively the rhythms of the dancer have been translated into sculptural form.
Fine Arts
Dist - UCEMC **Prod** - LACMOA 1974

Mirror People 4 MIN
16mm
Color
LC 75-700149
An animated film in which elegant, goon - faced characters cavort with their double images.
Fine Arts
Dist - CFS **Prod** - ROSEK 1974

Mirror - reflection 21 MIN
16mm
Color & B&W (G)
$30.00 rental
Allows the camera to wander about in a mirror - labyrinth or maze looking for a place in the world. Induces a feeling in the viewer like that of the whirling dervish in dance by attaching a semi - transparent mirror in front of the lens. Produced by Andras Szirtes.

Fine Arts
Dist - CANCIN

Mirror with a memory 25 MIN
VHS
Pioneers of photography series
Color (A)
PdS65 purchase
Displays the earliest discoveries of Nicephore Niepce and his partnership with Daguerre. Part of an eight-part series that examines the contributions made by pioneers in photography.
Fine Arts; Industrial and Technical Education
Dist - BBCENE

Mirrors on the Universe - the MMT Story 29 MIN
16mm
Color
LC 79-701007
Uses animated segments to document the construction of the laser - and computer - controlled multiple mirror telescope at the Mt Hopkins Observatory, located atop an 8,500 - foot mountain in southern Arizona.
Science - Physical
Dist - UARIZ **Prod** - SMITHS 1979

Mirrors - Reflections of a Culture 16 MIN
U-matic / VHS / 16mm
Color (J)
LC 80-701646
Shows how the murals of three Mexican - Americans present images that help the Chicano see himself as the inheritor of a strong and important tradition.
Fine Arts; Sociology
Dist - CF **Prod** - PAULMI 1980

Misa Colombiana 20 MIN
16mm / VHS
B&W (G)
$400.00, $200.00 purchase, $45.00, $35.00 rental
Recalls that the beginning of the 20th century saw only four Latin American countries with ten percent of their population living in cities of more than 20,000. Reveals that fifty years later one quarter of Latin American populations lived in cities, in the second half of the 20th century urban population surged. Films a tugurio - squatter's community - at the edge of the Medellin, Colombia town dump. Shows the tugurio inhabitants gleaning the 'leftovers of the the rich', paper, glass and metal to be recycled to the city's factories, discarded clothing, firewood, food. Witnesses a mass where a dissident priest pleads 'How can there be love in Columbia when...100 children die daily of hunger.' By Anne Fischer and Glen McNatt.
Geography - World; Sociology
Dist - DOCEDR **Prod** - DOCEDR 1977

The Misadventures of Merlin Jones 91 MIN
16mm
Color
Presents Merlin Jones, an oddball college student whose weird mental experiments involve him and his beautiful girlfirend in an unending series of situations.
Fine Arts
Dist - UAE **Prod** - DISNEY 1965

Misbehavior - what You Could have Done but Didn't 30 MIN
U-matic / VHS
Coping with Kids Series
Color
Identifies the goals of disruptive behavior and how these relate to discouragement. Discusses the methods used to break the chain of events which contribute to disruptive behavior.
Guidance and Counseling; Sociology
Dist - OHUTC **Prod** - OHUTC

Misbehavior - what You Could have Done but Didn't 29 MIN
U-matic / VHS
Coping with Kids Series
Color (T)
Education
Dist - FI **Prod** - MFFD

Miscarriage and stillbirth 51 MIN
VHS
Understanding maternal grief series
Color (C G)
$195.00 purchase, $50.00 rental _ #38181
Portrays a woman who has had several miscarriages and a stillbirth. Illustrates the psychological needs of bereaved women and the effects on women's health when these needs are not met. Part of a five - part series produced by Margaret Nicol, an Australian clinical psycologist specializing in the effects of reproductive loss on women's physical and mental health.
Guidance and Counseling; Health and Safety; Sociology
Dist - UCEMC

Miscarriage and stillbirth 24 MIN
VHS
Color (G)
$149.00 purchase, $75.00 rental _ #UW5351
Reveals that approximately one in four pregnancies in the United States ends in miscarriage, and that many babies die at birth or shortly after. Looks at how bereaved parents come to terms with miscarriage and stillbirth, focusing on a special bereavement unit at a London hospital where parents are helped to cope with loss at any stage of pregnancy.
Health and Safety
Dist - FOTH

Miscellaneous and Arrhythmias of Cardiac Arrest 8 MIN
U-matic
EKG Interpretation and Assessment Series
Color (PRO)
Teaches the criteria for the identification of some miscellaneous arrhythmias and arrhythmias seen in cardiac arrest.
Science; Science - Natural
Dist - CSUS **Prod** - CSUS 1984

Miscellaneous Biochemical Tests - IMViC Reactions 29 MIN
U-matic / VHS
Color
Includes two presentations on tape numbered 6205. Shows ways of performing and reading tests for catalase, oxidase, nitrate reduction, ammonia production and urea hydrolysis and, in addition, explains the biochemical basis for each. Illustrates the usefulness of the LMViC ests in the identification of gram - negative bacilli. Information on the IMViC tests includes the biochemical basis, media and reagents usedmethod of innoculation and interpretation of results.
Science; Science - Natural
Dist - AVMM **Prod** - AMSM

Miscellaneous Devices 16 MIN
VHS / 16mm
Electronics Series
(C A IND)
$99.00 purchase _ #VCI15
Describes the operating principles and applications of a broad variety of uncommon solid state devices. Shows how the special characteristics of certain solid state components can be used in practical applications. Utilizes an additional workbook.
Industrial and Technical Education
Dist - RMIBHF **Prod** - RMIBHF

Miscellaneous Electrical Equipment 7 MIN
U-matic / VHS / 16mm
Basic Electricity Series
Color (H C A)
Deals with such pieces of electrical equipment as the relay, meters, the moving coil, the potentiometer in a circuit and the rheostat.
Science - Physical
Dist - IFB **Prod** - STFD 1979

Miscellaneous equations 30 MIN
VHS
College algebra series
Color (C)
$125.00 purchase _ #4009
Explains miscellaneous equations. Part of a 31 - part series on college algebra.
Mathematics
Dist - LANDMK **Prod** - LANDMK

Miscellaneous Equations 30 MIN
VHS
Mathematics Series
Color (J)
LC 90713155
Discusses miscellaneous equations. The 71st of 157 installments of the Mathematics Series.
Mathematics
Dist - GPN

Miscellaneous Pointers 30 MIN
VHS / U-matic
Drafting - Piping Pointers Series
Color (IND)
Industrial and Technical Education
Dist - GPCV **Prod** - GPCV

Miscellaneous Quadratic Equations Solved by Factoring 30 MIN
VHS
Mathematics Series
Color (J)
LC 90713155
Examines miscellaneous quadratic equations solved by factoring. The 55th of 157 installments of the Mathematics Series.
Mathematics
Dist - GPN

Miscellaneous quadratic equations solved by factoring
VHS
Intermediate algebra series
Color (J H)
$125.00 purchase _ #3024
Teaches basic concepts involved in solving quadratic equations by factoring. Part of a 31 - video series, each part 25 to 30 minutes long, that explains and reinforces concepts in intermediate algebra. Uses definitions, theorems, examples and step - by - step solutions to tutor the student. Videos also available in a set.
Mathematics
Dist - LANDMK

Miscellaneous Taping 30 MIN
VHS / U-matic
Athletic Trainer Series
Color
Covers the other joints of the body, which do not receive much attention but can cause problems, including the shoulder, elbow, fingers, thumb, feet, toes, arms, thighs and lower legs.
Health and Safety; Physical Education and Recreation
Dist - NETCHE **Prod** - NETCHE 1972

Miscellaneous test instruments 60 MIN
U-matic / VHS
Electrical maintenance training series; Module B - Test instruments
Color (IND)
Covers bridges, phase rotation, phase sequence and variable current tester.
Industrial and Technical Education
Dist - LEIKID **Prod** - LEIKID

Mischief 8 MIN
U-matic / VHS / 16mm
Color (P I J)
LC 74-702583
Presents the story about a naughty boy who is punished for his mischief by animals in the yard.
Sociology
Dist - PHENIX **Prod** - CZECFM 1974

Mischief 63 MIN
U-matic / VHS / 16mm
Color (P I)
Recounts that when a former circus pony becomes part of a stable, he leads young Davy to incidents full of excitement and suspense.
Literature and Drama
Dist - LUF **Prod** - LUF 1974

Mischievous Marks - ( )'s 15 MIN
16mm / U-matic / VHS
Punctuation Series
Color (I J)
$365.00, $250.00 purchase _ #76534
Shows how to insert comments in sentences with dashes and parentheses.
English Language
Dist - CORF

Miscommunications 5 MIN
16mm
Color (I)
LC 74-702118
Satirizes obstacles to individual communication in four animated vignettes.
English Language; Guidance and Counseling; Psychology
Dist - MMA **Prod** - MMA 1972

Misconception 42 MIN
VHS
Color (G)
$100.00 purchase, $80.00 rental
Focuses on juxtapositions such as indoors - outdoors, redecoration - destruction, exercises - actual birth and preparation - pain.
Fine Arts
Dist - CANCIN **Prod** - KELLEM 1977

Misconceptions Regarding Good Health Care 30 MIN
VHS / U-matic
Care and Feeding of Dancers Series
Color
Fine Arts; Health and Safety; Industrial and Technical Education
Dist - ARCVID **Prod** - ARCVID

Mise En Place
VHS / U-matic
Vegetable Cutting Series
Color
Home Economics; Industrial and Technical Education
Dist - CULINA **Prod** - CULINA

The Miseries of war - paintings by Felix Labisse 10 MIN
U-matic / VHS / 16mm
Color (C A)

LC 80-700661
Shows Felix Labisse's surrealistic paintings as a fierce protest against the threat of atomic warfare.
Fine Arts
Dist - IFB **Prod** - STORCH 1978

Misery in the Borinage 29 MIN
U-matic / VHS / 16mm
Color (H C A)
LC 80-700580
Depicts the 1933 coal miners' strike in the Borinage region of Belgium.
History - World; Social Science; Sociology
Dist - IFB **Prod** - STORCH 1932

Misery Merchants 29 MIN
16mm
B&W
Exposes the greed of quack remedy merchants who promote 'sitting in an abandoned uranium mine as a treatment for arthritis.' Includes simple explanations of arthritis and its accepted treatment. Features Dennis O'Keefe and Everett Sloan.
Health and Safety
Dist - WSTGLC **Prod** - WSTGLC

Misfit 63 MIN
16mm
Color
Exposes the truth about church - school - and home dropouts. Offers a Christian solution to the problem clearly presenting the drop - out's problem, misfit dynamically portrays his real need and the answer to it. A never - to - be - forgotten message that is realistically presented with teen - age appeal. Answers the question, 'IS THERE HOPE FOR THE DROP - OUT.'.
Psychology; Religion and Philosophy; Sociology
Dist - GF **Prod** - YOUTH 1965

Misha - recovery from a serious accident 40 MIN
VHS
Color (G)
$149.00 purchase, $75.00 rental _ #UW5690
Tells the story of 16 - year - old Misha Heselwood and her successful fight to regain her life after being seriously injured. Begins with Misha's hospitalization with severe brain injuries suffered in a car accident. Follows Misha, her family and the medical staff over a nine - month period, charting her recovery from coma as she relearns how to walk, talk, eat and eventually gain self - reliance and independence. Examines how the family of a recovering patient must cope with the emotional and financial pressures associated with the patient's recovery.
Health and Safety; Psychology
Dist - FOTH

Mishima 121 MIN
VHS
Color (G) (JAPANESE WITH ENGLISH SUBTITLES)
$79.95 purchase _ #WAR11530
Portrays the life of controversial writer Yukio Mishima and his fiery works. Produced by Paul Schrader.
Fine Arts
Dist - CHTSUI

Mislabeled and Unlabeled Deaths 236 MIN
U-matic
Forensic Medicine Teaching Programs Series no 11; No 11
Color (PRO)
LC 78-706054
Discusses mislabeled deaths.
Health and Safety
Dist - USNAC **Prod** - NMAC 1978

Mislabeled and Unlabeled Deaths, Pt 1 53 MIN
U-matic
Forensic Medicine Teaching Programs Series no 11; No 11
Color (PRO)
LC 78-706054
Discusses mislabeled deaths in general, using several cases to illustrate the danger of diagnosing without performing an autopsy. Emphasizes simulated heart attacks and discusses perimortem injuries.
Sociology
Dist - USNAC **Prod** - NMAC 1978

Mislabeled and Unlabeled Deaths, Pt 2 44 MIN
U-matic
Forensic Medicine Teaching Programs Series no 11; No 11
Color (PRO)
LC 78-706054
Stresses the importance of determining manner of death as well as cause.
Sociology
Dist - USNAC **Prod** - NMAC 1978

Mislabeled and Unlabeled Deaths, Pt 3 36 MIN
U-matic
Forensic Medicine Teaching Programs Series no 11; No 11
Color (PRO)
LC 78-706054
Shows examples of gunshot wounds.
Sociology
Dist - USNAC **Prod** - NMAC 1978

Mislabeled and Unlabeled Deaths, Pt 4 51 MIN
U-matic
Forensic Medicine Teaching Programs Series no 11; No 11
Color (PRO)
LC 78-706054
Shows examples of death resulting from cutting and stabbing.
Sociology
Dist - USNAC **Prod** - NMAC 1978

Mislabeled and Unlabeled Deaths, Pt 5 52 MIN
U-matic
Forensic Medicine Teaching Programs Series no 11; No 11
Color (PRO)
LC 78-706054
Presents a lecture on blunt force injury death and discusses poisoning deaths.
Sociology
Dist - USNAC **Prod** - NMAC 1978

Misplaced Goals 29 MIN
VHS / 16mm
Sonrisas Series
Color (T P) (SPANISH)
$46.00 rental _ #SRSS - 138
Shows that failing at something does not make someone a failure. In Spanish and English.
Sociology
Dist - PBS

Misrecognitions 20 MIN
16mm
Color (G)
$40.00 rental
Accumulates short works dealing with misrecognition and information and presented as psychoanalytical tableaus. Includes I am a Woman and Swamp Monolog.
Fine Arts; Psychology
Dist - CANCIN **Prod** - SONDHE 1990

Miss America 7 MIN
16mm
B&W
Shows how women's liberation groups attempted to disrupt the annual miss America pageant and make boardwalk and contestant spectators more aware of the insidious contest with its image of mindless womanhood.
Sociology
Dist - CANWRL **Prod** - CANWRL

Miss Amy and Miss May 40 MIN
VHS / U-matic
Color (G)
$350.00 purchase, $85.00 rental
Documents the history of the fight for social justice for women in Jamaica. Profiles Amy Bailey, daughter of an eminent Black family and leader of the Jamaican Women's Movement in the 1930s, and May Farguharson, daughter of a wealthy planter and fighter for reproductive rights for women and reforms to benefit the elderly. Combines contemporary interviews and dramatized scenes from their long friendship. Produced by Phase 3 and Sistren Research. Directed by Cynthia Wilmot.
History - World; Sociology
Dist - WMEN

Miss Clara Let Us be 29 MIN
Videoreel / VT2
Our Street Series
Color
Sociology
Dist - PBS **Prod** - MDCPB

Miss Esta Maude's Secret 10 MIN
U-matic / VHS / 16mm
Storybook Series
Color (K P I)
Tells the story of a school teacher's secret adventures in her racing car. An animated film.
English Language; Literature and Drama
Dist - MGHT **Prod** - MGHT 1964

Miss Ewa's follies - Szalenstwa panny Ewy 158 MIN
VHS
Color (P I J) (POLISH)
$24.95 purchase _ #V165
Offers a musical comedy for children based on a novel by Kornel Makuszynski, set in 1932. Describes how, following the departure for China of her physician father, 14 - year - old Ewa flees the house of her unfriendly guardians and embarks on a series of 'follies' - kindhearted and wise acts that bring happiness to those involved.
Fine Arts; Literature and Drama; Psychology; Sociology
Dist - POLART

Miss Fluci Moses 22 MIN
VHS
Color (G)
$60.00 rental, $195.00 purchase
Visits Louise Jane Moses, an African American poet who wrote her first poem as a child but was not published until after her retirement from a long career as a teacher and librarian. Combines interviews, archival footage and poetry readings from Fluci Moses - her pen name - who believed in the importance of African Americans recording their lives and feelings. By Alile Sharon Larkin.
Fine Arts; History - United States; Literature and Drama
Dist - WMEN

Miss Goodall and the Baboons of Gombe 52 MIN
16mm / U-matic / VHS
Color (I)
LC 75-703801
Examines the habits, inter - group relationships and leadership rivalries of the East African baboon.
Psychology; Science - Natural
Dist - FI **Prod** - METROM 1974

Miss Goodall and the Hyena Story 52 MIN
U-matic / VHS / 16mm
Color (J)
Depicts Jane Goodall's study of hyenas in East Africa's Ngorongoro Crater. Shows that hyenas live in a complex matriarchal society divided into clans. Reveals the difficulties one maverick hyena experienced in his attempts to become a member of a clan.
Geography - World; Science - Natural
Dist - FI **Prod** - METROM 1975

Miss Goodall and the Lions of Serengeti 52 MIN
U-matic / VHS / 16mm
Color (J H C)
LC 77-700931
Follows animal behaviorist Jane Goodall and photographer Hugo van Lawick on a trip to East Africa's Serengeti Plains, where they observe a pride of lions and record their behavior patterns, territorial and social habits, and relationships with other animals.
Geography - World; Psychology; Science - Natural
Dist - FI **Prod** - METROM 1976

Miss Goodall and the Lions of Serengeti, Pt 1 25 MIN
U-matic / VHS / 16mm
Color (J H C)
LC 77-700931
Follows animal behaviorist Jane Goodall and photographer Hugo van Lawick on a trip to East Africa's Serengeti Plains where they observe a pride of lions and record their behavior patterns, territorial and social habits and relationships with other animals.
Science - Natural
Dist - FI **Prod** - METROM 1976

Miss Goodall and the Lions of Serengeti, Pt 2 25 MIN
16mm / U-matic / VHS
Color (J H C)
LC 77-700931
Follows animal behaviorist Jane Goodall and photographer Hugo van Lawick on a trip to East Africa's Serengeti Plains where they observe a pride of lions and record their behavior patterns, territorial and social habits and relationships with other animals.
Science - Natural
Dist - FI **Prod** - METROM 1976

Miss Goodall and the Wild Chimpanzees 52 MIN
U-matic / VHS / 16mm
Color (J H C)
LC FIA68-970
The story of a young English girl who embarked on a five - year adventure in jungles of East Africa, observing the daily lives of wild chimpanzees in an attempt to understand the behavior of chimpanzee in relation to human realization.
Geography - World; Psychology; Science - Natural
Dist - NGS **Prod** - NGS 1966

Miss Goodall and the Wild Dogs of Africa 52 MIN
16mm / U-matic / VHS
Color (I)
LC 75-701619
Records an intimate study made by animal behaviorist Jane Goodall and her photographer husband Hugo van Lawick of a pack of wild dogs on the plains of the Serengeti in Africa. Follows one young pup who gets detached from the pack as he searches for a new family.
Geography - World; Psychology; Science; Science - Natural
Dist - FI **Prod** - METROM 1973

Miss Grouse 5 MIN
U-matic / VHS
Write on, Set 1 Series
Color (J H)
Deals with avoiding cliches in writing.
English Language
Dist - CTI **Prod** - CTI

Miss Jesus fries on grill 12 MIN
16mm
Color (G)
$15.00 rental
Interprets a newspaper story of a Miss Jesus, who was killed when a car smashed into the cafe where she was eating - the impact threw her on the grill, heated to 500 degrees. Looks at the sensations of living within the confines of impending death for us all, with the portrayal of a baby being bathed and crying, nursing, falling asleep, and references to parochial school stories full of black humor.
Fine Arts; Sociology
Dist - CANCIN **Prod** - WILEYJ 1973

Miss Julie 60 MIN
U-matic / VHS
Drama - play, performance, perception series
Color (H C A)
Conveys an understanding of the role of the director in blending dramatic elements and synthesizing the work of the artists. Uses the play Miss Julie as an example.
Fine Arts; Literature and Drama
Dist - FI **Prod** - BBCTV 1978

Miss Julie 100 MIN
VHS
Color (A)
PdS99 purchase
Presents a Strindberg play about the aristocratic daugher of a count - played by Janet McTeer - who breaks off her engagement to a weak fiance. Reveals that she seeks consolation with her father's virile valet, Jean - Patrick Malahide - but he seduces her and she soon finds herself completely in his power.
Literature and Drama
Dist - BBCENE

Miss Nelson is Back 30 MIN
VHS / U-matic
Reading Rainbow Series no 2
Color (P)
Presents Ruth Buzzi narrating the book Miss Nelson Is Back which is all about surprises. Shows LeVar Burton finding some surprises of his own as he embarks on a birthday treasure hunt.
English Language; Social Science
Dist - GPN **Prod** - WNEDTV 1982

Miss Nelson is Missing 14 MIN
U-matic / VHS / 16mm
Color (P I)
Tells what happens when Miss Nelson, an excellent but ignored teacher, decides to disappear for a day, leaving her class to cope with the poisonous personality of Miss Swamp, the odious substitute.
Guidance and Counseling; Literature and Drama
Dist - LCOA **Prod** - LCOA 1979

Miss Nelson is Missing 7 MIN
U-matic / VHS
(K P I)
Shows Miss Nelson the nicest teacher in the school. She was always smiling and cheery, even when her students cut up in class or would not open their math books nor pay attention during story hour. One day Miss Nelson did not come to school. A substitute teacher came instead. Miss Swamp promptly laid down the law - no talking, no goofing off in class, and loads of homework. Where was Miss Nelson? The students hunt for her high and low, with the dubious help of Detective McSmogg.
English Language; Literature and Drama; Social Science
Dist - WWS **Prod** - WWS 1984

Miss Newton's Trial 5 MIN
U-matic / VHS
Write on, Set 1 Series
Color (J H)
Teaches the use of commas in a series.
English Language
Dist - CTI **Prod** - CTI

Miss or Myth 60 MIN
VHS / 16mm
Color (G A)
$595.00 purchase, $100.00 rental
Features a study of beauty pageants and the images of women they promote, allowing both pageant supporters and protesters to express their viewpoints.
Sociology
Dist - CNEMAG **Prod** - CNEMAG

Miss Switch to the Rescue 48 MIN
VHS / U-matic
Color (K I P)
$455.00 purchase
Literature and Drama
Dist - ABCLR **Prod** - ABCLR

Miss Twiggley's Tree 13 MIN
16mm
Color (K P I)
LC 73-700519
Presents a lovable character living happily in her tree house who faces eviction by the townspeople because they do not understand her strange ways.
Fine Arts
Dist - SF **Prod** - SF 1971

Miss U S A 1965 15 MIN
16mm
Color
Shows the Miss U S A competition held in Miami Beach every year. Winner of the 1965 title is Sue Ann Downey, representing the state of Ohio.
Guidance and Counseling; Home Economics; Physical Education and Recreation
Dist - FDC **Prod** - FDC

Miss Universe 1965 15 MIN
16mm
Color
Shows the Miss Universe Contest in Miami and Miami Beach. Apasra Hongsakula, Miss Thailand, is selected as Miss Universe 1965.
Guidance and Counseling; Home Economics; Physical Education and Recreation
Dist - FDC **Prod** - FDC

Miss Universe in Peru 32 MIN
16mm / VHS
B&W (G) (SPANISH (ENGLISH SUBTITLES))
$250.00 purchase, $60.00 rental
Documents the Miss Universe contest in Peru in 1982. Juxtaposes the glamour of the pageant with the realities of Peruvian women's lives. Critiques multinational corporate interest in the universal commodification of women.
Business and Economics; Geography - World; Religion and Philosophy; Sociology
Dist - WMEN **Prod** - CHASKI 1986

Missile 115 MIN
VHS / 16mm
Color (G)
$350.00 purchase, $150.00 rental
Documents the U S Air Force's training program for its officers who control ICBM launching. Discusses the morality of nuclear war, military issues, and many other matters dealt with in training.
Civics and Political Systems; Fine Arts; Sociology
Dist - ZIPRAH **Prod** - WISEF

Missile experimental - Part 11 60 MIN
VHS / U-matic
War and peace in the nuclear age series
Color (G)
$45.00, $29.95 purchase
Explores the strategy, technology and politics behind the creation of the biggest and most powerful US weapons - the MX and Midgetman missiles. Part eleven of a thirteen - part series on war and peace in the nuclear age.
Civics and Political Systems; History - United States
Dist - ANNCPB **Prod** - WGBHTV 1989

Missile Explosive Device Safety 14 MIN
16mm
Color
LC FIE63-318
Demonstrates hazards involved when missile explosive devices are manhandled. Explains the purpose and nature of fuses, squibs, igniters and initiators. Outlines safety procedures for handling, installing and testing such devices.
Civics and Political Systems
Dist - USNAC **Prod** - USDD 1961

Missile Fuels, Propellants and Oxidizers - Liquid Oxygen 22 MIN
16mm
Color
LC 74-706148
Describes receipt, transfer, storage and disposal of liquid oxygen. Shows safety measures for transferring fuel from tank trucks to storage areas and procedures for disposing of contaminated fuel.
Health and Safety; Industrial and Technical Education
Dist - USNAC **Prod** - USAF 1961

Missile Safety at Vandenberg Air Force Base 23 MIN
16mm
Color
LC FIE62-72
Describes Vandenberg's physical layout and hazards peculiar to missile operations. Explains the need for rigid enforcement of safety practices. Illustrates safety requirements at missile complexes before, during and after a launching.
Civics and Political Systems; Health and Safety; Science - Physical
Dist - USNAC **Prod** - USDD 1960

The Missiles of October 155 MIN
VHS / U-matic
Captioned; Color (J)
Reenacts the 12 days in October 1962 that followed the U S discovery of Soviet missile bases in Cuba.
Biography; Fine Arts; History - United States
Dist - LCOA **Prod** - VIACOM 1974

The Missiles of October 150 MIN
VHS
Color (C G J H A)
$59.95 purchase _ #S00345; $79.00 purchase _ #0573094
Dramatizes the events of the 1962 Cuban missile crisis, in which the U S faced off with the Soviets after discovering Soviet missile bases in Cuba. Focuses on the inner workings of the US government during this crisis. Stars William Devane as President John Kennedy, Martin Sheen as Robert Kennedy, Ralph Bellamy as Adlai Stevenson, and Howard Da Silva as Nikita Khrushchev.
History - United States; History - World; Sociology
Dist - UILL
ASPRSS

Missiles of October - a Case Study in Decision Making Series

Data gathering - understanding the problem	15 MIN
Examining the Alternatives	20 MIN
Implementing the Decision	30 MIN
Managing the Decision	60 MIN
Power, Control, and Decision Making	40 MIN
The Waiting Game - Control or Confrontation	20 MIN

Dist - DELTAK

Missing 56 MIN
BETA / VHS / U-matic
Color; Mono (H C A G)
$75.00
Reports on the problem of missing children. Program is presented in three segments - children who have been abducted by a stranger, children who have been abducted by an estranged parent and runaway children. Focuses on veiws held by various police officers and social agencies who deal with these cases on a regular basis.
Sociology
Dist - CTV **Prod** - GLNWAR 1986

Missing
U-matic / VHS
Color (J H C A)
$59.00 purchase _ #04162 94
Tells the true story of a father's search for his son, who disappeared amidst political upheaval in Chile. Stars Jack Lemmon and Sissy Spacek.
Fine Arts; History - World
Dist - ASPRSS

The Missing Addends 15 MIN
U-matic / VHS
Math Mission 2 Series
Color (P)
Mathematics
Dist - GPN **Prod** - WCVETV 1980

Missing Children 28 MIN
16mm / U-matic / VHS
Color (H C A)
$425 purchase - 16 mm, $295 purchase - video, $55 rental
Portrays the struggles of Argentine mothers and grandmothers to locate their children and grandchildren who were victims of the junta's 'dirty war' against the opposition during the 1970s and early 1980s. Includes historical footage, statements from human rights activists and former government leaders, and interviews with the mothers and grandmothers. Directed by Estela Bravo.
Civics and Political Systems; Sociology
Dist - CNEMAG

Missing Hero 51 MIN
VHS / 16mm
Color (S)
$800.00, $79.00 purchase _ #548 - 9119
Gives an account of Swedish diplomat Raoul Wallenberg who risked his life to save 100,000 Hungarian Jews from the Nazi gas chambers, then disappeared mysteriously in 1945 under Soviet military escort. Reveals that although the Soviets have never fully explained his fate, evidence suggests that he may still be alive. Former Israeli Prime Minister Menachem Begin has called Wallenberg 'the greatest hero of World War II.'.
Foreign Language; History - United States; History - World; Sociology
Dist - FI **Prod** - BBCTV 1982

Missing in action 58 MIN
VHS
Color (G)
$29.95 purchase _ #S01500
Portrays a five - man Australian team sent to Vietnam to recover six countrymen. Shows how Vietnam is struggling to recover from the long war. Includes documentary footage and comments from Vietnamese, Australian and American participants in the war.

History - United States; Sociology
Dist - UILL

The Missing Person's Bureau 27 MIN
U-matic / VHS
Color (J A)
Tells the story of a Vietnam veteran who returns home to his son's death and his wife's infidelity and eventually learns forgiveness instead of hatred.
Fine Arts; Sociology
Dist - SUTHRB **Prod** - SUTHRB

Missing Person's Bureau 27 MIN
U-matic / VHS / 16mm
Insight Series
Color (H C A)
Describes a Vietnam veteran's return home to find his son dead and his wife unfaithful. Shows the veteran going to a Missing Person's Bureau where he learns the value of forgiveness instead of hate. Stars Hector Elizondo.
Guidance and Counseling; Psychology; Religion and Philosophy
Dist - PAULST **Prod** - PAULST

Missing Persons - the Drama of the Disappeared Political Prisoners in Chile 26 MIN
16mm
B&W (H C A)
LC 81-701527
Presents three spokeswomen who discuss the inexplicable disappearance of their husbands, their children, even a two - and - one - half - year - old grandchild and other terrorist practices of the post - Allende Chilean regime.
Civics and Political Systems; History - World
Dist - ICARUS **Prod** - ICARUS 1981

Missing persons - the drunk driving holocaust 30 MIN
VHS
Color (J H C G)
$69.95 purchase _ #CCP0076V
Shows the consequences of drinking driving. Unites bereaved parents and friends, permanently disabled victims and young inmates convicted of vehicular homicide to educate students about the direct connection between alcohol, death and prison. Features members of MADD - Mothers Against Drunk Driving' SADD - Students Against Drunk Driving and CAR - Convicts After Recovery, who talk about the drastic changes in their lives caused by someone drinking and driving. Dispels common myths on blood alchohol concentration and brings the real - life consequences of mixing alcohol and driving into the classroom.
Guidance and Counseling; Health and Safety; Psychology
Dist - CAMV **Prod** - CAMV 1992

Missing Pieces - Georgia Folk Art, 1770 - 1976 29 MIN
16mm
Color
LC 77-702278
Examines the work of five folk artists of Georgia, including potter Lanier Meaders, painter Mattie Lou O'Kelley, carver Ulysses Davis, painter Ed Martin and Rev Howard Finster, who created a paradise garden in his backyard.
Fine Arts; Industrial and Technical Education
Dist - GCAH **Prod** - GCAH 1976

Missing something somewhere 17 MIN
16mm
Color (G)
$35.00 rental
Celebrates that which can't be apprehended, battened down or burdened with specific meaning. Presents three visual chapters, each with its own rhythm and narrative.
Fine Arts
Dist - CANCIN **Prod** - STREEM 1992

Missing You in Southern California 31 MIN
U-matic / VHS / 16mm
Color
Points out that after almost colliding with a C - 141, a couple in a private plane learns more about civilian and military flying rules and procedures.
Industrial and Technical Education; Social Science
Dist - USNAC **Prod** - USAF 1982

The Mission 33 MIN
16mm
Color (C R)
Shows the activities of old missionaries throughout the federation of Nigeria in schools, training colleges, hospitals, maternity wards, a leper colony and an operating theater.
Geography - World; Religion and Philosophy
Dist - DKB **Prod** - DKB 1962

Mission and witness 30 MIN
VHS
Faith completed by works series
Color (R G)
$39.95 purchase _ #FCBW1
Witnesses the work of lay missionaries in several mission fields in the United States and abroad. Starts from the premise that all Christians are challenged to become missionaries, to bring the good news of Jesus to the poor and marginalized of the world. Part of six parts on evangelization in the Roman Catholic Church.
Religion and Philosophy
Dist - CTNA **Prod** - CTNA 1994

Mission Beyond Healing 20 MIN
U-matic
Color
Gives the history of the University of Texas System Cancer Center and its main goal of fighting cancer. Includes statistics about the average patient load and a description of some of the equipment in use.
Health and Safety
Dist - UTEXSC **Prod** - UTEXSC

Mission Dustoff - Helicopter Evacuation 12 MIN
16mm
Color
LC 74-706149
Depicts the role of the helicopter ambulance and its crew in evacuation of battlefield casualities in Vietnam.
Geography - World; Health and Safety; History - United States; Sociology
Dist - USNAC **Prod** - USA 1969

A Mission for Mariner 15 MIN
16mm
Color (I A)
LC 71-703344
Describes the results of the Mariner V mission to Venus and describes the continuing Mariner program for exploration of the other planets. Uses animation to show various theories about the nature of Venus and its capabilities for supporting life, and explains how these theories were affected by the Mariner Fly - by.
Science - Physical
Dist - NASA **Prod** - NASA 1969

Mission Houses 12 MIN
16mm
Color (J H)
Shows the homes and the people that comprised the first protestant missionaries to Hawaii in 1820.
Geography - United States; Geography - World; History - United States
Dist - CINEPC **Prod** - CINEPC

Mission in America 30 MIN
VHS
Faith completed by works series
Color (R G)
$39.95 purchase _ #FCBW6
Witnesses the work of lay missionaries in several mission fields in the United States and abroad. Starts from the premise that all Christians are challenged to become missionaries, to bring the good news of Jesus to the poor and marginalized of the world. Part of six parts on evangelization in the Roman Catholic Church.
Religion and Philosophy
Dist - CTNA **Prod** - CTNA 1994

Mission in Central America 28 MIN
VHS
Color (G)
$14.95 purchase
Voices the difficulties faced by American missionaries in violence - torn Central America.
Religion and Philosophy
Dist - MARYFA

A Mission in life 30 MIN
VHS
Faith completed by works series
Color (R G)
$39.95 purchase _ #FCBW5
Witnesses the work of lay missionaries in several mission fields in the United States and abroad. Starts from the premise that all Christians are challenged to become missionaries, to bring the good news of Jesus to the poor and marginalized of the world. Part of six parts on evangelization in the Roman Catholic Church.
Religion and Philosophy
Dist - CTNA **Prod** - CTNA 1994

Mission - meteorology 25 MIN
VHS
Active atmosphere series
Color (I J H)
$80.00 purchase _ #A2VH 4705
Examines the different fields of meteorology. Joins a teenage detective as she goes on assignment to find out about the following branches - broadcasting, the National Weather Service, pollution monitoring, private consulting, agriculture and aviation. Part of a nine - part series on weather.
Guidance and Counseling; Science - Physical
Dist - CLRVUE **Prod** - CLRVUE

Mission - Mind Control 52 MIN
U-matic / VHS / 16mm
Color (H C A)
LC 79-701635
Examines American intelligence activities after World War II involving the use of consciousness - altering drugs, often on unsuspecting subjects. Originally shown on the ABC Television program entitled Closeup.
Civics and Political Systems; Psychology
Dist - CORF **Prod** - ABCNEW 1979

Mission Nutrition 10 MIN
U-matic
Body Works Series
Color (P I J H)
Shows children searching for a secret formula for healthy eating.
Physical Education and Recreation; Social Science
Dist - TVOTAR **Prod** - TVOTAR 1979

Mission Oceanography 29 MIN
16mm
Color
LC FIE67-98
Tells of the research and discoveries by ocean scientists of the early 1800's and the Navy's involvement with the seas and oceanography. Shows the progress of oceanography from the early sailing days to the present time.
Civics and Political Systems; Science; Science - Physical
Dist - USNAC **Prod** - USN 1966

The Mission of Apollo - Soyuz 29 MIN
16mm
Color (J H A)
LC 76-701592
Stresses the spirit of cooperation and friendship that helped make the joint Soviet - American mission a success. Follows the mission timeline and uses flashbacks to show the period of development and training. Comments on future joint efforts, featuring the space shuttle and the European Development, Spacelab.
Civics and Political Systems; History - World; Science - Physical
Dist - USNAC **Prod** - NASA 1976

Mission of Discovery 27 MIN
16mm
B&W
LC 75-700865
Presents various aspects of the Peace Corps services, including the tedium and hardship, the pleasure and accomplishment. Shows volunteers on the job, at home and socializing with friends in the host countries where they serve.
Sociology
Dist - USNAC **Prod** - USPC 1963

Mission of Discovery 60 MIN
VHS
Color (G)
$49.95 purchase _ #MODS - 000
Gives a behind - the - scenes look at preparations for the Discovery space shuttle mission. Traces the stringent preparations to the Challenger shuttle disaster.
History - World; Industrial and Technical Education; Science - Physical
Dist - PBS **Prod** - WETATV 1988

The Mission of the twelve 30 MIN
VHS
Gospel of Mark series
Color (R G)
$39.95 purchase _ #GMAR5
Examines the structures and the key messages of the Gospel of Mark, as well as examining the life and times of Mark, according to the teachings of the Roman Catholic Church. Features Biblical scholar Father Eugene LaVerdiere, SSS. Part five of ten parts.
Literature and Drama; Religion and Philosophy
Dist - CTNA **Prod** - CTNA

Mission Possible - Bike Safety 15 MIN
16mm
Color
Examines rules of bike safety, courtesy, maintenance and theft prevention. Explains how to meet federal, state and local guidelines for bicycle safety.
Health and Safety
Dist - APS **Prod** - APS

Mission - Possible or Pepe's Angels - Articles and Demonstratives - 14 30 MIN
VHS
English 101 - Ingles 101 Series
Color (H)
$125.00 purchase
Presents a series of thirty 30 - minute programs in basic English for native speakers of Spanish. Focuses on a specific topic in order to emphasize a particular grammatical point or set of idioms. English is used from the beginning as the primary language of instruction but Spanish translations are included to ensure understanding. Part 14 looks at definite articles, indefinite articles, demonstrative adjectives and pronouns.

English Language; Foreign Language
Dist - AITECH Prod - UPRICO 1988

The Mission stop 18 MIN
16mm
Color (G)
$40.00 rental
Alternates between a meditative and chaotic portrait of San Francisco's Mission District.
Fine Arts
Dist - CANCIN Prod - STREEM 1988

Mission - Success 60 MIN
VHS / U-matic
Stereo (G)
Presents a young man's search for success.
Psychology; Religion and Philosophy
Dist - BANTAP Prod - BANTAP 1986

The Mission - Tape 4 20 MIN
VHS
Journeys in faith - Volume II
Color (J H C G A R)
$29.95 purchase, $10.00 rental _ #35 - 8121 - 2076
Examines the Lutheran doctrine of the priesthood of all believers. Produced by Seraphim.
Religion and Philosophy
Dist - APH

Mission Third Planet - Green Grow the Plants 13 MIN
16mm / U-matic / VHS
Mission Third Planet Series
Color (I J)
Tells how two young scientists and their robot journey to Earth from a distant planet to classify plant life. Shows how they learn the basic methods of plant classification, examine and compare the structures of various plants and relate form to function.
Science; Science - Natural
Dist - CORF Prod - CORF

Mission Third Planet Series
Mission Third Planet - Green Grow the Plants 13 MIN
Dist - CORF

Mission to Earth, Pt 2 - Life Forms and Resources 17 MIN
U-matic / VHS / 16mm
Mission to Earth Series
Color (I J H)
LC 77-703352
Uses the story of a spaceship from another galaxy exploring the Earth's life forms and natural resources to discuss the Earth's natural and cultivated plant life, animal life that gets its sustenance from plant life, humanoids that utilize and modify the planet's resources and the planet's heavy reliance on energy sources.
Science - Natural; Social Science
Dist - BARR Prod - BARR 1977

Mission to Earth Series
Mission to Earth, Pt 2 - Life Forms and Resources 17 MIN
Dist - BARR

Mission to planet Earth - 5 60 MIN
VHS
Space age series
Color (G)
$24.95 purchase _ #SPA100
Reveals that on the way to the Moon, humans discovered a new planet - their own. Discloses that the photo of Earth from space - perhaps the most important photograph of the 20th century - began the transformation of humanity's understanding of Earth as a living system. Shows how the technology developed to explore other planets is being used to monitor the system of Earth. Joins scientists as they chart a course for a healthy planet and reveal the Earth in ways that were never possible before the Space Age. Features Patrick Stewart as host. Part five of a six - part series.
History - World; Science - Physical
Dist - INSTRU Prod - NAOS
KNOWUN

Mission to the Moon - Report on Project Apollo 16 MIN
16mm
Screen news digest series; Vol 8; Issue 6
B&W (J)
LC 76-700504
Presents highlights of the space rendezvous between Geminis 6 and 7. Uses animation to explain how the manned flight to the moon will be carried out by 1970.
Science - Physical
Dist - HEARST Prod - HEARST 1966

Mission to Yenan 32 MIN
U-matic / VHS / 16mm
Color (J H A)
LC 73-701821
Presents an historical reevaluation of America's China policy.
Civics and Political Systems; History - United States; History - World
Dist - FI Prod - FI 1972

Mission videos series
Big Joe 18 MIN
Bringing Christ to the cities 25 MIN
Called out and sent back 23 MIN
Clemente 20 MIN
Dreams into reality 18 MIN
God's love reaching - through people to people 15 MIN
His word, our language 22 MIN
How will they know 15 MIN
In whom Christ lives 16 MIN
Jesus loves the little children 10 MIN
Keep on clapping 19 MIN
The Least of these 15 MIN
The Nations within 23 MIN
Our Hispanic friends 10 MIN
The Same Gospel - different disciples 15 MIN
The Stranger in our midst 18 MIN
That's why we're here 28 MIN
Thirsty people in thirsty lands 15 MIN
Whom shall I send 21 MIN
Dist - CPH

Missions 28 MIN
VHS
Illuminations series
Color (G R)
#V - 1037
Interviews Greek Orthodox missionaries on their work worldwide. Shows that they have built medical clinics, schools, and churches for those less fortunate. Features the work of the Greek Orthodox mission in Kenya.
Religion and Philosophy
Dist - GOTEL Prod - GOTEL 1989

Missions Abroad 37 MIN
16mm / U-matic / VHS
Christians Series Episode 11; Episode 11
Color (H C A)
LC 78-701660
Discusses one of the most dramatic examples of Christian revival in the 19th century, the spread of missionary activity in the slums of Europe's industrial cities and in the lands of the new colonial empires.
History - World; Religion and Philosophy
Dist - MGHT Prod - GRATV 1978

Mississippi 60 MIN
VHS
Portrait of America series
Color (J H C G)
$99.95 purchase _ #AMB24V
Visits Mississippi. Offers extensive research into the state's history. Films key locations and presents segments on history, government, education, folklore, science, journalism, sociology, industry, agriculture and business. Shows what is unique about Mississippi and distinctive about its regional culture and how it got to be that way. Includes study guide. Part of a 50 - part series.
Geography - United States; History - United States
Dist - CAMV

Mississippi blues 92 MIN
35mm / 16mm
Color (G)
$250.00, $300.00 rental
Explores the unique culture of the Mississippi Delta and the music played by the natives. Directed by Bertrand Tavernier and Robert Parrish.
Fine Arts; History - United States
Dist - KINOIC

Mississippi Delta Blues 28 MIN
16mm
B&W
Features the research done by Bill Ferris from 1968 to 1970 as he traveled from farms to books to homes to collect music he felt best expressed the richness of delta blues.
Fine Arts; Geography - United States; Sociology
Dist - SOFOLK Prod - SOFOLK

Mississippi Delta Blues 18 MIN
16mm
Color (J)
LC 74-701910
Presents selections of music that best represent the richness of Mississippi Delta blues.
Fine Arts; Geography - United States
Dist - SOFOLK Prod - SOFOLK 1974

Mississippi - is this America - 1962 - 1964 60 MIN
VHS / 16mm
Eyes on the Prize Series
Color; Captioned (G)
$59.95 purchase _ #EYPZ - 105
Looks at the 1962 to 1964 voting rights campaign in Mississippi. Features leaders in the campaign such as Medgar Evers, Michael Schwerner, Andrew Goodman, James Chaney, Robert Moses, Fannie Lou Hamer and others. Profiles the activities of the NAACP, SCLC, SNCC and CORE and highlights the activities of northern whites. Part of a six - part series on the civil rights struggle in America between 1954 and 1965.
Biography; Civics and Political Systems; History - United States
Dist - PBS Prod - BSIDE 1987

Mississippi mass choir 120 MIN
VHS
Color (G R)
$29.95 purchase _ #35 - 83 - 94
Presents the Mississippi Mass Choir in a performance of Gospel songs, including 'I Just Can't Tell You,' 'Near The Cross,' and others. Produced by Mercury Films.
Fine Arts; Religion and Philosophy
Dist - APH

Mississippi - Ol'Man River and the 20th Century 21 MIN
U-matic / VHS / 16mm
Color
Traces the history of the Mississippi River.
Geography - United States; History - United States
Dist - KAWVAL Prod - KAWVAL

The Mississippi - Prize and Pawn of Empires 22 MIN
16mm / U-matic / VHS
Color
Deals with the Mississippi River.
Geography - United States
Dist - KAWVAL Prod - KAWVAL

Mississippi River 17 MIN
U-matic / VHS / 16mm
Color (I J H)
Explains how the history of the United States has been influenced by the Mississippi River as it travels its course from Minnesota to the Gulf of Mexico. Examines the early settlements, transportation, farming, urbanization, and the serious problems of pollution and flooding along the Mississippi River.
Geography - United States; Geography - World; History - United States
Dist - LUF Prod - LUF 1979

Mississippi River 16 MIN
VHS / U-matic
Color (I J H)
Presents the role of the Mississippi River in U S history. Focuses on river transportation and farming along the river. Features Minneapolis, Saint Paul, Saint Louis and New Orleans as the most important cities along the Mississippi. Deals with climatic differences, pollution problems and spring flooding.
Geography - United States; Social Science
Dist - VIEWTH Prod - VIEWTH

Mississippi River Festival 20 MIN
16mm
Color
LC 75-711345
Discusses the factors that were necessary to make the Mississippi River Festival, a summer music program, an important cultural experience for the St Louis area. Shows the work of the many volunteers, civic and university leaders.
Fine Arts; Geography - United States; Sociology
Dist - SIUFP Prod - SILLU 1970

Mississippi River series
Ol' Man River and the 20th century 25 MIN
The Prize and pawn of empires 22 MIN
Steamboat a - comin' 25 MIN
Dist - REVID

The Mississippi - Steamboat a - Comin' 21 MIN
16mm / U-matic / VHS
Color (J)
Recounts the history and romance of the era of the steamboat. Focuses on the Mississippi River, tells how railroads supplanted riverboats.
History - United States; Social Science
Dist - KAWVAL Prod - KAWVAL 1981

Mississippi Suite 15 MIN
VHS
Music Experiences Series
Color
$69.95 purchase _ #1104
Features a full symphony orchestra. Explained are basic concepts such as melody, harmony, rhythm, form, and the suite.
Fine Arts
Dist - AIMS Prod - AIMS

Mississippi Suite 14 MIN
16mm / U-matic / VHS
Music Experiences Series
Color (I) (SPANISH)
LC 72-703355
Presents the Mississippi Suite, by Ferde Grofe, played by a symphony orchestra and directed by Grofe. Uses animation and live photography to convey basic music concepts.
Fine Arts
Dist - AIMS **Prod** - STEVNS 1969

Mississippi Summer 58 MIN
U-matic / VHS
Color (G)
$249.00, $149.00 purchase _ #AD - 1266
Combines documentary footage and interviews with participants to show some of the events leading up to the historic summer of 1964 - the 1954 Supreme Court ruling on the integration of public schools, the Civil Rights Act of 1957, the effort to keep James Meredith out of the University of Mississippi, the assassination of Medgar Evers, the Civil Rights Act of 1964, the murders of James Chaney, Michael Schwerner and Andrew Goodman.
Civics and Political Systems; History - United States; Sociology
Dist - FOTH **Prod** - FOTH

The Mississippi System - Waterway of Commerce 17 MIN
U-matic / VHS / 16mm
Color; B&W (I J H)
LC 77-708907
Traces the development of river traffic along the Mississippi from 1541 through the beginning of the steamboat era in 1812 and the first railroads, which put the river queens out of business after the Civil War. Continues with the neglect of the river, floods, congressional acts and today's revitalized river system.
Geography - United States; History - United States; Social Science
Dist - EBEC **Prod** - ADMFLM 1970

Missouri 60 MIN
VHS
Portrait of America series
Color (J H C G)
$99.95 purchase _ #AMB25V
Visits Missouri. Offers extensive research into the state's history. Films key locations and presents segments on history, government, education, folklore, science, journalism, sociology, industry, agriculture and business. Shows what is unique about Missouri and distinctive about its regional culture and how it got to be that way. Includes study guide. Part of a 50 - part series.
Geography - United States; History - United States
Dist - CAMV

Missouri - Gateway to the West 15 MIN
16mm
Color
Depicts Missouri's history from pioneer to modern times. Includes scenes of the Old Cathedral, St Genevieve, the capitol building in Jefferson City, Daniel's judgment Tree at Defiance, Grant's farm, Mark Twain's birthplace, the Old Courthouse in St Louis and Carver National Monument. Presents vignettes from the lives of famous Missourians such as Jesse James, General John J Pershing and Harry S Truman.
Biography; Geography - United States; History - United States
Dist - MODT **Prod** - MODT

Missouri - Seven Ways to Get Away 13 MIN
16mm
Color
Features Missouri's seven famous vacationlands, including the Big Springs Region of southeast Missouri, the St Louis Area, the Mark Twain Region centering on Hannibal, the Lake of the Ozarks Region, The Ozark Playground Region of southwest Missouri, the Kansas City area and the Pony Express Region of northwest Missouri.
Geography - United States; History - United States
Dist - MODT **Prod** - MODT

Mist of Death 29 MIN
U-matic
Iliad of Homer Series
Color
Focuses on the fighting and dying on the plains of Troy.
History - World; Literature and Drama
Dist - UMITV **Prod** - UMITV 1974

The Mistake 15 MIN
U-matic / VHS
La Bonne Aventure Series
Color (K P)
Deals with French - American children. Focuses on a learning experience.
Foreign Language; Guidance and Counseling; Home Economics; Psychology
Dist - GPN **Prod** - MPBN

Mistake - Proof Wallpapering 30 MIN
BETA / VHS
This Old House, Pt 2 - Suburban '50s Series
Color
Gives tips for wallpapering.
Industrial and Technical Education; Sociology
Dist - CORF **Prod** - WGBHTV

Mistaken Identity 20 MIN
16mm
Color (A)
LC 81-701272
Introduces a man and a woman who meet at a party and think in the first flush of their infatuation that they are right for each other. Shows them ending up in a motel and discovering that they are wrong for each other in every way.
Fine Arts
Dist - PARALX **Prod** - PARALX 1981

Mistassini for me
VHS
Color (G)
$29.90 purchase _ #0383
Travels to Mistassini Lake in Quebec, Canada to fish for the largest brook trout, lake trout and northern pike. Reveals that the area has been home to the Cree Indians for thousands of years.
Geography - World; Physical Education and Recreation; Science - Natural
Dist - SEVVID

Mister Gimme 28 MIN
U-matic / VHS / 16mm
Captioned; Color (P I) (SPANISH)
LC 79-701415
Tells the story of a boy who wants a set of drums and the trouble it causes him and his family when he tries to make money selling greeting cards.
Fine Arts; Sociology
Dist - LCOA **Prod** - LCOA 1979

Mister Johnson 92 MIN
35mm / 16mm
Color (G)
$300.00 rental
Portrays Mister Johnson, a young African who is obsessed with all things British and strives to emulate his boss, the local district commander. Reveals that Johnson, in order to prove his value to the British and impress the locals, supervises the construction of a road 100 miles through the bush to link up with the main trade route. Directed by Bruce Beresford.
Fine Arts; Geography - World; Sociology
Dist - KINOIC

Mister Klein Looks at Geometry 24 MIN
U-matic / VHS / 16mm
Color
Examines how different properties can be preserved under transformations of the plane. Focuses on affine geometry.
Mathematics
Dist - MEDIAG **Prod** - OPENU 1979

Mister Magoo Series
Grizzly Golfer 7 MIN
Magoo's Puddle Jumper 7 MIN
When Magoo Flew 7 MIN
Dist - CF

Mister Midwife 29 MIN
U-matic
Woman Series
Color
Offers an interview with a male midwife.
Health and Safety
Dist - PBS **Prod** - WNEDTV

Mister Roberts 123 MIN
U-matic / VHS / 16mm
Color (C A)
Stars Henry Fonda, James Cagney and Jack Lemmon in the classic comedy about life aboard a navy cargo ship in World War II. Tells of the men aboard the USS Reluctant, peacefully anchored off a small Pacific island while all the action passes them by. Introduces Mr Roberts who dreams only of transfer to combat duty and the authoritarian, relentlessly cruel captain.
Civics and Political Systems; Fine Arts; Sociology
Dist - FI **Prod** - WB 1955
UILL

Mister Rodgers talks with parents about day care 28 MIN
VHS
Mister Rodgers talks with parents series
Color (G)
$39.95 purchase _ #MRTD - 000
Considers how day care has become a necessity for many families. Explores the pressures of working and being a good parent. Suggests that the best day care involves a partnership between parents and caregivers. Hosted by Fred Rodgers.
Health and Safety; Psychology; Sociology
Dist - PBS **Prod** - FAMCOM 1980
FAMCOM

Mister Rodgers talks with parents series
Mister Rodgers talks with parents about day care 28 MIN
Dist - FAMCOM
PBS

Mister Rogers - Conceptual Behavior Series
A Visit to the Doctor 30 MIN
What is Love 30 MIN
Dist - BRENTM

Mister Rogers - Health and Safety Series
Going to the hospital 30 MIN
Having an Operation 30 MIN
A Visit to the Emergency Department 30 MIN
Wearing a Cast 30 MIN
Dist - BRENTM

Mister Rogers' home videos series
Dinosaurs and monsters 60 MIN
Music and feelings 60 MIN
Musical stories 60 MIN
What about love 60 MIN
When parents are away 60 MIN
Dist - FAMCOM

Mister Rogers Talks about Series
A Dentist and a toothfairy 30 MIN
Talking with Young Children about Death 30 MIN
Dist - FAMCOM

Mister Rogers talks about the environment 30 MIN
VHS
Color (K P G)
$16.50 purchase _ #V1617
Touches on many issues of recycling and caring for the environment. Visits a recycling center with Mister Rogers. Shows how to create toys from household castoffs. Looks at the Neighborhood of Make - Believe where the Neighbors cope with their garbage problem. Includes a 24 - page activities booklet.
Science - Natural
Dist - FAMCOM **Prod** - FAMCOM 1991

Mister Rogers Talks with Parents about Competition 58 MIN
VHS
Mister Rogers Talks With Parents Series
Color (G)
$59.95 purchase _ #MTPC - 000
Features Fred Rogers, who discusses the meaning of competition and how children are affected by it. Also hosted by psychologist Tom Cottle and Susan Stamberg of National Public Radio.
Business and Economics; Psychology; Sociology
Dist - PBS **Prod** - FAMCOM 1980
FAMCOM

Mister Rogers Talks with Parents about Discipline 28 MIN
VHS
Mister Rogers Talks With Parents Series
Color (G)
$39.95 purchase _ #MTTD - 000
Considers issues involved in disciplining children. Identifies limits for discipline. Comments on the need to convince children that discipline is in their best interests. Deals with fears parents may have. Hosted by Fred Rogers.
Psychology; Sociology
Dist - PBS **Prod** - FAMCOM 1980
FAMCOM

Mister Rogers Talks with Parents about Divorce 58 MIN
VHS
Mister Rogers Talks With Parents Series
Color (G)
$59.95 purchase _ #MTPD - 000
Discusses divorce and how it affects the various family members. Features Susan Stamberg of National Public Radio and author and counselor Dr Earl Grollman. Hosted by Fred Rogers.
Psychology; Sociology
Dist - PBS **Prod** - FAMCOM 1980
FAMCOM

Mister Rogers Talks with Parents about make - Believe 28 MIN
VHS
Mister Rogers Talks With Parents Series
Color (G)
$39.95 purchase _ #MRTC - 000
Features Fred Rogers, who discusses the importance of make - believe in children's play. Shows how parents can encourage imagination, playfulness and creativity in their children.
Psychology; Sociology
Dist - PBS **Prod** - FAMCOM 1980
FAMCOM

Mister Rogers Talks with Parents about Pets 28 MIN
VHS
Mister Rogers Talks With Parents Series
Color (G)
$39.95 purchase _ #MWPP - 000
Considers the benefits and limitations of family pets. Provides suggestions for dealing with a variety of situations. Explores the relationship between children and pets. Hosted by Fred Rogers.
Psychology; Science - Natural; Sociology
Dist - PBS **Prod** - FAMCOM 1980
FAMCOM

Mister Rogers Talks with Parents about School 58 MIN
VHS
Mister Rogers Talks With Parents Series
Color (G)
$59.95 purchase _ #MRTP - 000
Discusses attitudes and expectations children may have about going to school. Features broadcast journalist Sandy Hill and author and educator Ellen Galinsky. Hosted by Fred Rogers.
Health and Safety; Psychology; Social Science; Sociology
Dist - PBS **Prod** - FAMCOM 1980
FAMCOM

Mister Rogers Talks With Parents Series
Mister Rogers Talks with Parents about Competition 58 MIN
Mister Rogers Talks with Parents about Discipline 28 MIN
Mister Rogers Talks with Parents about Divorce 58 MIN
Mister Rogers Talks with Parents about make - Believe 28 MIN
Mister Rogers Talks with Parents about Pets 28 MIN
Mister Rogers Talks with Parents about School 58 MIN
Dist - FAMCOM
PBS

Mister, You made a Big Mistake on My Bill 17 MIN
16mm
Color (H C A)
LC 76-703958
Features Don Knotts playing a man who receives his hospital bill and thinks it is too much. Shows a series of different scenes at the hospital in which he is informed about why a hospital charges what it does.
Health and Safety; Social Science
Dist - BYU **Prod** - BYU 1976

Misty of Chincoteague
35mm strip / VHS / Cassette
Newbery Award - Winners Series
Color (I)
$66.00, $14.00 purchase
English Language; Literature and Drama
Dist - PELLER

Misty of Chincoteague 15 MIN
U-matic / VHS
Book bird series
Color (I)
Tells of the colt Misty, from the book by Marguerite Henry.
English Language; Literature and Drama
Dist - CTI **Prod** - CTI

Misty Wizards 30 MIN
Videoreel / VHS / 16mm
People in Jazz Series
Color (G)
$55.00 rental _ #PEIJ - 103
Biography; Fine Arts
Dist - PBS **Prod** - WTVSTV

Misunderstood monsters series
Features Stanley, who gets the reputation of being a 'monster' because he reacts to taunts in anger and frustration. Includes an understanding animated character, the Mouth, who counsels Stanley and presents three animated stories about misunderstood monsters, Creole by Stephen Cosgrove, The Reluctant Dragon by Kenneth Grahame and Beauty and the Beast retold by Mariana Mayer.
Beauty and the beast 12 MIN
Creole 8 MIN
Misunderstood monsters series 44 MIN
The Reluctant dragon 12 MIN
Dist - CF **Prod** - BOSUST

Mitakuye Oyasin - We are all related 60 MIN
VHS
Color (G)
$19.95 purchase
Social Science
Dist - CARECS

Mitch and Allen 48 MIN
VHS
Color (J H C G A R)
$39.99 purchase, $10.00 rental _ #35 - 83577 - 533
Presents Christian stand - up comedians Mitch and Allen. Uses nightclub - type sketches and one - liners to communicate a Biblical message.
Literature and Drama; Religion and Philosophy
Dist - APH **Prod** - WORD

Mitchell B - 25 Bomber
VHS
World War II planes series
Color; B&W (G)
$19.95 purchase _ #PP000
Recreates the flight of Doolittle's Raiders in the Mitchell B - 25 bomber. Incorporates the sound of the lift off of 1700 hp engines.
History - World; Industrial and Technical Education
Dist - SIV

Mitchell Kriegman - Always Late 10 MIN
VHS / U-matic
Color
Presented by Mitchell Kriegman.
Fine Arts
Dist - ARTINC **Prod** - ARTINC

Mitchell Kriegman - Bill Irwin, the Dancing Man 3 MIN
U-matic / VHS
Color
Introduces Bill Irwin.
Fine Arts
Dist - ARTINC **Prod** - ARTINC

Mitchell Kriegman - Heart to Heart 2 MIN
U-matic / VHS
Color
Presented by Mitchell Kriegman.
Fine Arts
Dist - ARTINC **Prod** - ARTINC

Mitchell Kriegman - My Neighborhood 27 MIN
U-matic / VHS
Color
Presents a comic story about a guy who loves his neighborhood and claims to know everyone in it and everything about it.
Fine Arts
Dist - ARTINC **Prod** - ARTINC

Mitchell Kriegman - Someone's Hiding in My Apartment 2 MIN
VHS / U-matic
Color
Presented by Mitchell Kriegman.
Fine Arts
Dist - ARTINC **Prod** - ARTINC

Mitchell Kriegman - the Marshall Klugman Show 29 MIN
VHS / U-matic
Color
Mirrors frustrations and anxieties in a comic story.
Fine Arts
Dist - ARTINC **Prod** - ARTINC

Mitchell, Parren 29 MIN
U-matic
Like it is Series
Color
Discusses problems faced by black politicians and how blacks are affected by unemployment and urban problems.
History - United States; Sociology
Dist - HRC **Prod** - OHC

Mitchell Vs Military Tradition 25 MIN
U-matic / VHS / 16mm
Men in Crisis Series
B&W (J H C)
LC 73-706743
Presents the story of Brig Gen Billy Mitchell, who crusades to prove that the airplane is our most effective combat weapon, runs a crucial bombing test in 1921 and clearly demonstrates the superiority of air attack over surface units.
Civics and Political Systems; Industrial and Technical Education
Dist - FI **Prod** - WOLPER 1964

The Miter Box Project 20 MIN
VHS
(G A IND)
$99.00 purchase _ #W24V7
Shows making a miter box. Study Guide included.
Industrial and Technical Education
Dist - BERGL

The Miter Box Project
VHS
Construction Technology Series
$69.00 purchase _ #BX24V
Industrial and Technical Education
Dist - CAREER **Prod** - CAREER

MITI - guiding hand of the Japanese economic miracle 30 MIN
VHS
Anatomy of Japan - wellsprings of economic power series
Color (H C G)
$250.00 purchase
Reveals that the Japanese government, industries and people have all worked to rebuild the Japanese economy out of the ruins of war. Focuses on MITI, the Ministry of International Trade and Industry and its industrial policies in the postwar period. Analyzes how MITI has tried to nurture Japanese industries and guide structural changes in Japan's economy. Part of a 10 - part series on the current relations between Japan and the world.
Business and Economics; Geography - World
Dist - LANDMK **Prod** - LANDMK 1989

Mitochondrial DNA and automated DNA sequencing 89 MIN
VHS
DNA technology in forensic science series
Color (A PRO)
$50.00 purchase _ #TCA17406
Presents two lectures on DNA technology in forensic science. Covers subjects including the structure and function of mitochondrial DNA, nuclear genome, evolutionary relations, the DuPont Genesis 2000 system for sequencing DNA.
Science - Natural; Sociology
Dist - USNAC **Prod** - FBI 1988

The Mitochondrion and ATP synthesis 14 MIN
VHS / BETA
Cell biology resource series
Color; PAL (J H C)
PdS58
Presents striking visualizations of cell processes. Examines the variety of cells and looks into cell structure. Includes modules on oxygen and animal evolution, aerobic respiration, mitochondria origins, the mitochondrion, ATP synthesis by chemiosis, electron transport chain, the Krebs cycle. Part of a six - part series covering how cells acquire energy, how cells are controlled and how genetic information is passed on, presented in bite - sized modules.
Science - Natural
Dist - VIEWTH

Mitos, Rituales Y Costumbres Aztecas 56 MIN
U-matic / VHS
Color (C) (SPANISH)
$279.00, $179.00 purchase _ #AD - 2174
Documents Aztez civilization, history, traditions and rituals - including human sacrifice. In Spanish.
Foreign Language; Geography - World; History - World; Religion and Philosophy; Social Science; Sociology
Dist - FOTH **Prod** - FOTH

Mitosis 15 MIN
U-matic / VHS / 16mm
Biology Series Unit 5 - Genetics; Unit 5 - Genetics
Color (J H) (SPANISH)
LC 80-701808
Uses microphotography, animation and artwork to show how the basic process of mitosis occurs in plants and animals. Explains the roles of the cell nucleus, DNA, chromosomes, chromatids and the centriole. Examines the issue of cloning.
Science - Natural
Dist - EBEC **Prod** - EBEC 1980

Mitosis 11 MIN
16mm / U-matic / VHS
Life Cycle of a Flowering Plant Series no 2
Color
LC 73-703035
Uses the apple tree to explain the process of mitosis.
Science - Natural
Dist - LUF **Prod** - SCHLAT 1971

Mitosis 14 MIN
VHS
Color (J H)
$99.00 purchase _ #3668 - 026
Uses microphotography to show how the basic process of mitosis takes place in plants and animals. Focuses on chromosome structure. Includes teacher's guide.
Education; Science - Natural
Dist - GA **Prod** - EBEC

Mitosis 10 MIN
VHS
Microscopy prelab series
Color (J H C)
$95.00 purchase _ #CG - 965 - VS
Shows the role of DNA replication in the process of mitosis. Uses graphs to explain the stages of a cell's life from interphase through the stages of mitosis. Compares onion root tip cells and white fish blastula cells to illustrate plant

and animal mitosis. Slide preparations guide students through their lab study. Part of a five - part series on microscopy prelab produced by Bill Pieper.
Science; Science - Natural
Dist - HRMC

Mitosis 14 MIN
16mm / U-matic / VHS
Color (J H) (SPANISH)
$59.95 purchase _ #193 W 2213
A Spanish language version of the film and videorecording Mitosis.
Science - Natural
Dist - WARDS **Prod** - WARDS

Mitosis 10 MIN
VHS
Color (J H)
$70.00 purchase _ #A5VH 1597
Uses an interactive format to help students to observe and describe the changes in the nucleus of a cell. Challenges them to anticipate the significance of these changes. Includes teacher's guide.
Science - Natural
Dist - CLRVUE **Prod** - BSCS

Mitosis
VHS
Basic science series
Color (J H) (ENGLISH AND SPANISH)
$39.95 purchase _ #MCV5019
Focuses on mitosis, presenting only basic concepts. Includes teacher's guide and review questions. Combines computer animation and the use of 'sheltered language' to help students acquire content vocabulary, become comfortable with scientific language and achieve success in science curriculum. Part of a series on basic science concepts.
Science; Science - Natural
Dist - MADERA **Prod** - MADERA

Mitosis 9 MIN
16mm / U-matic / VHS
Color (C)
Uses animation to show how cells divide and multiply.
Science - Natural
Dist - IFB **Prod** - IFB 1958

Mitosis and cytokinesis 30 MIN
VHS
Color (J H)
$49.95 purchase _ #193 W 0131
Demonstrates cell division in prepared microscope slides of onion root tip and whitefish blastodisc. Covers plant cell mitosis, animal cell mitosis, reviews plant and animal cell structures and includes two timed review quizzes of 15 questions each which cover mitotic stages and cell structures. Illustrates proper microsearch techniques. Produced by the University of New Brunswick.
Science - Natural
Dist - WARDS

Mitosis and genetics
Videodisc
Color; CAV (I J H)
$189.00 purchase _ #8L572
Reviews mitosis, the process by which genetic information is passed on during cell division. Explains clearly all five phases of mitosis using time - lapse photomicrography to capture the chromosomes duplicating along with the entire mitosis process. Barcoded for instant random access.
Industrial and Technical Education; Science - Natural
Dist - BARR **Prod** - BARR 1991

Mitosis and Genetics 17 MIN
16mm / VHS
Cell Series
Color (J)
LC 90708922
Outlines the process of mitosis. Focuses on the roles of chromosomes, genes and DNA in mitosis.
Science - Natural
Dist - BARR

Mitosis and Meiosis 17 MIN
U-matic / VHS / 16mm
Continuity of Life Series
Color; B&W (J H C)
Illustrates the life cycle of common organisms and the two basic types of cell division - - mitosis, accounting for growth from the fertilized egg to the adult - and meiosis, essential to the production of sex cells - by examining the life cycle of a starfish.
Science - Natural
Dist - IU **Prod** - IU 1956

Mitosis and Meiosis 17 MIN
16mm
Color (J H C G)
Compares mitosis and meiosis. Show onion root tip, whitefish embryo, salamander, epidermal and living Tradescantia staminal hair cells to present details of mitosis. Portrays the basic features of meiosis by using lily anther cells and living sperm cells of a grasshopper. Gives side by side comparison of two processes and shows how mitosis, meiosis and fertilization fit into the life cycle of common organisms.
Science - Natural
Dist - VIEWTH **Prod** - GATEEF

Mitosis and meiosis 23 MIN
VHS
Color (H)
$99 purchase _ #10304VG
Looks at the processes of mitosis and meiosis in two parts. Features microscopic images and animation to illustrate the cell cycles and division. Comes with an interactive video quiz, teacher's guide and seven blackline masters.
Science - Natural
Dist - UNL

Mitosis and Meiosis - How Cells Divide 45 MIN
Slide / U-matic / VHS
Color (J H)
$195.00 filmstrips, $209.00 sound slides purchase _ #01071 - 161
Uses photomicrographs and computer graphics to analyze the different phases of cell division.
Science - Natural
Dist - GA **Prod** - GA

Mitosis Y Miosis 20 MIN
U-matic / VHS / 16mm
Color (H C A) (SPANISH)
A Spanish language version of Cell Division - Mitosis And Meiosis. Presents an inside look at living cells, showing the processes of mitosis and meiosis.
Foreign Language; Science - Natural
Dist - MGHT **Prod** - KATTNS 1978

Mitsuye and Nellie, Asian American Poets 58 MIN
VHS / U-matic
Color
LC 82-706954
Shows how a common heritage as Asian - American women binds poets Mitsuye Yamada and Nellie Wong in this examination of oriental ethnicity in the United States. They recite poetry and discuss the impact of Japanese and Chinese cultures on their upbringing.
Literature and Drama; Sociology
Dist - SARLGT **Prod** - SARLGT 1981
WMEN

The Mitt 17 MIN
U-matic / VHS / 16mm
Color (P I)
LC 78-700114
Tells the story of a 12 - year - old boy who dreams of buying a new baseball mitt and who earns enough money to do so. Shows how he passes up the mitt to buy his mother something she has been secretly wanting.
Guidance and Counseling; Literature and Drama
Dist - LCOA **Prod** - CEDARF 1978

Mitzi a Da Si - a Visit to Yellowstone National Park 20 MIN
VHS / U-matic
Nature Episodes Series
Color
Shows Yellowstone Park, the wildlife and the thermal features found there.
Science - Natural
Dist - EDIMGE **Prod** - EDIMGE

Mitzi a da si - Yellowstone National Park 16 MIN
U-matic / VHS / BETA
Color (J H)
$29.95, $130.00 purchase _ #LSTF90
Tours Yellowstone, noting wildlife and their habitats and the various thermal features such as geysers. Includes teachers' guide. Produced by Nature Episodes assisted by Yellowstone National Park.
Geography - United States
Dist - FEDU

A Mitzvah to Serve 26 MIN
16mm
Color
LC 74-706150
Provides an orientation to the meaning, responsibilities and value of Jewish lay leadership in the U S armed forces.
Civics and Political Systems; Sociology
Dist - USNAC **Prod** - USA 1969

Mix a Material 25 MIN
16mm
Start Here - Adventures into Science Series
Color
Explains why materials bend, stretch and break. Shows experiments to demonstrate behavior of molecular lattices in everyday substances from chocolate fudge to rubber balloons.
Science - Physical
Dist - LANDMK **Prod** - VIDART 1983

Mix and Application 18 MIN
16mm
Color
Shows proper methods of mixing and applying polysulfide base sealants and caulking materials to a variety of building materials.
Industrial and Technical Education
Dist - THIOKL **Prod** - THIOKL 1970

Mix yarn with wheat paste 15 MIN
Videoreel / VT2
Art corner series
B&W (P)
Deal with manipulating yarn dipped in wheat paste to form designs and shapes.
Fine Arts
Dist - GPN **Prod** - CVETVC

A Mixed - ability fourth year GCSE examination group in a Roman Catholic school - Unit B 32 MIN
VHS
Religious education in secondary schools series
Color; PAL (T)
PdS35.00 purchase
Presents religious education in ways which are relevant to pupils in mixed - ability classes. Demonstrates a variety of approaches used by four teachers in very different situations. Part of an eight - part series.
Education; Religion and Philosophy
Dist - EMFVL

Mixed blood 20 MIN
VHS
Color (G)
$125.00 purchase, $50.00 rental
Takes a personal view of interracial relationships between Asian Americans and non - Asian Americans. Combines interviews with over 30 concerned individuals with clips from scientific films and classic miscegenation dramas. Explores the complexities of cross - cultural intimacy and whether such choices have public and political implications. Directed by Valerie Soe.
Guidance and Counseling; History - United States; Sociology
Dist - CROCUR

Mixed Double 5 MIN
16mm
Color
Presents a Pas De Deux performed by Sorella Englund and Eske Holm of the Royal Danish Ballet.
Fine Arts
Dist - AUDPLN **Prod** - RDCG

Mixed doubles 30 MIN
VHS
Tennis talk series
Color (J H A)
$24.95 purchase _ #PRO002V
Features tennis instructor Dennis Van der Meer teaching about mixed doubles.
Physical Education and Recreation
Dist - CAMV

Mixed Fruit and Yogurt 6 MIN
VHS / U-matic
Cooking with Jack and Jill Series
Color (P I)
$95.00
Portrays the skills of twins Jack and Jill as they cook nutritious and delicious snacks that are easy to prepare. Kitchen safety is emphasized. Animated.
Home Economics
Dist - LANDMK **Prod** - LANDMK 1986

Mixed - Gas Diving 13 MIN
VHS / U-matic
Diving Orientation for Offshore Personnel Series
Color (IND)
Explains the need for mixed - gas diving. Lists Coast Guard requirements. Discusses a pipe tie - in operation using mixed gas.
Industrial and Technical Education
Dist - UTEXPE **Prod** - UTEXPE 1980

Mixed - in - Place Soil - Cement Construction 18 MIN
16mm
Color
LC 82-700039
Shows how durable, low - cost pavements can be built with soil - cement. Includes scenes from a variety of soil - cement paving projects in the United States and Canada, illustrating the basics of mixed - in - place construction, current equipment and technology and successful practices.
Industrial and Technical Education
Dist - PRTLND **Prod** - PRTLND 1977

Mixed Media 15 MIN
VHS / U-matic

Expressions
(I J)
$130 purchase, $25 rental, $75 self dub
Designed to interest fifth through ninth graders in art. Emphasizes creativity and experimentation. Features the making of handmade paper and explains the value of mixed media. Seventeenth in an 18 part series.
Fine Arts; Sociology
Dist - GPN

Mixed messages and the media 30 MIN
VHS
Club connect series
CC; Color (J H G)
$59.95 purchase _ #CCNC-911-WC95
Describes how teenagers deal with the constant barrage of images and noises they experience from television, the movies, radio, and other sources. Explains how the younger generation views mass media and what the images they see mean to them. Includes information on how the media industry affects teens.
Fine Arts
Dist - PBS **Prod** - WTVSTV 1994

Mixed Numbers and Improper Fractions 23 MIN
U-matic
Basic Math Skills Series Fraction Understanding; Fraction understanding
Color
Mathematics
Dist - TELSTR **Prod** - TELSTR

Mixed Operation - Sums to Six 15 MIN
U-matic
Measure Up Series
Color (P)
Explains the use of plus, minus and equal signs in doing mathematic operations with sums up to six.
Mathematics
Dist - GPN **Prod** - WCETTV 1977

Mixed Operations to Sums of Ten 15 MIN
U-matic
Measure Up Series
Color (P)
Tells how to write two addition facts and two subtraction facts when given three numbers.
Mathematics
Dist - GPN **Prod** - WCETTV 1977

Mixed potentials - passivity - corrosion I 46 MIN
VHS / U-matic
Electrochemistry - Pt V - electrokinetics series
Color
Science; Science - Physical
Dist - MIOT **Prod** - MIOT

Mixed Potentials, Passivity, Corrosion, Pt 1 46 MIN
VHS / U-matic
Electrochemistry Series
Color
Science; Science - Physical
Dist - KALMIA **Prod** - KALMIA

Mixed Random Variables 30 MIN
VHS / U-matic
Probability and Random Processes - Random Variables Series
B&W (PRO)
Illustrates mixed random variables.
Industrial and Technical Education; Mathematics
Dist - MIOT **Prod** - MIOT

Mixed - Up 'Middles' 30 MIN
16mm
Growth and Development, the Adult Years Series
B&W (C)
LC 74-706817
Shows the problems and rewards as well as the responsibilities of middle age. Discusses the need for adjusting to problems of younger and older generations and planning for changes in a future life style.
Psychology; Sociology
Dist - AJN **Prod** - VDONUR 1969

Mixed up Mother Goose
CD-ROM
(G A)
$59.00 purchase _ #2691
Requires no reading skills and is perfect at home, in day care centers and elementary school classrooms. Presents characters who can speak and sing in five languages - English, Spanish, French, German and Japanese. For IBM and compatibles. Requires at least 640K RAM, DOS version 3.1 or greater, one floppy disk drive - a hard disk drive is recommended, one empty expansion slot, and and IBM compatible CD - Rom dirve.
Education; Foreign Language; Literature and Drama
Dist - BEP

Mixing Color, Color Analysis 60 MIN
VHS
Color, Perspective and Composition - Hal Reed Series
Color (J)
$29.95 purchase _ #HV - 687
Presents two 30 - minute lessons on mixing color and color analysis. Part of a six - part series on color, perspective and composition by Hal Reed.
Fine Arts
Dist - CRYSP **Prod** - CRYSP

Mixing dental cements 14 MIN
VHS / U-matic
Color (PRO C)
$395.00 purchase, $80.00 rental _ #C901 - VI - 021
Introduces dental students and technicians to the precise techniques for mixing various cements. Includes four segments which provide detailed instructions for the mixing of glass ionomer cements, polycarboxylate cement, zinc oxide - eugenol and non - eugenol cements and zinc phosphate cement. Presents the materials required for each technique and demonstrates procedures. Presented by Drs Madeline Borecki, John M Powers and Lon T Smith, the University of Texas Health Science Center at Houston.
Health and Safety
Dist - HSCIC

Mixing it Up with Colors and Paints 15 MIN
16mm
Fingermouse, Yoffy and Friends Series
Color (K P I)
LC 73-700444
Follows Yoffy and Fingermouse as they mix colors in order to paint a picture.
Guidance and Counseling; Literature and Drama
Dist - VEDO **Prod** - BBCTV 1972

Mixing Operations 60 MIN
VHS
Systems Operations Series
Color (PRO)
$600.00 - $1500.00 purchase _ #RCAGS
Covers the principles of industrial mixing for both liquid - liquid and liquid - solid processes. Addresses components and operation of various types of mixing equipment. Discusses operator responsibilities and typical mixing problems. Includes ten textbooks and an instructor guide to support four hours of instruction.
Education; Industrial and Technical Education; Psychology
Dist - NUSTC **Prod** - NUSTC

Mixing the Media 29 MIN
U-matic
Artist at Work Series
Color
Demonstrates drawing the traditional ballerina with chalks, pencils and pastels.
Fine Arts
Dist - UMITV **Prod** - UMITV 1973

Mixing Zinc Phosphate Cement, Final Cementation 6 MIN
BETA / VHS
Color (PRO)
Discusses dental cements.
Health and Safety
Dist - RMIBHF **Prod** - RMIBHF

Mixtures 10 MIN
U-matic
Take a Look Series
Color (P I)
Teaches the difference between two types of mixtures, suspension and solution and ways to safely experiment with them at home.
Science; Science - Physical
Dist - TVOTAR **Prod** - TVOTAR 1986

Mixtures and Mechanical Separation 60 MIN
U-matic / VHS
Chemistry Training Series
Color (IND)
Covers heterogeneous and homogeneous mixtures, constituents of mixtures in the air, filtration, sedimentation and centrifurging and deep - bed filtration of river water.
Science; Science - Physical
Dist - ITCORP **Prod** - ITCORP

Mizu shobai - water business 12 MIN
16mm / VHS
B&W/Color (G)
$50.00 rental, $195.00 purchase
Depicts a geisha's imaginary round the world sea voyage during the period of Japanese isolation as she drifts byond the prescribed bounds of her place in the world. Blends cultures of past and present, native and alien via her experience and memory. The title is the Japanese word for 'water business,' a term for the entertainment world.
Fine Arts; Geography - World; Sociology
Dist - WMEN **Prod** - LIN 1993

Mnemosyne mother of muses 18 MIN
16mm
Larry Gottheim series
Color (G A)
$60.00 rental
Presents the work of filmmaker Larry Gottheim. Links diverse materials, such as the stroke of Gottheim's father and other personal matters, with Tosconini conducting Wagner, film noir 'The Killers' by Siodmak, in a structure which goes backwards while continually moving forward.
Fine Arts; History - United States; Industrial and Technical Education
Dist - PARART **Prod** - CANCIN 1986

Moan and Groan, Inc 21 MIN
16mm
B&W
Tells how Jackie, Wheezer and Chubby dig for buried treasure in a mansion haunted by a codger intent on keeping intruders out. A Little Rascals film.
Fine Arts
Dist - RMIBHF **Prod** - ROACH 1929

Moani and the Sacred Prince 11 MIN
16mm
Color (J G)
Tells one of the legends of Hawaii in which a village boy, Moani, befriends a lame prince, and an ancient and cruel law prohibiting the talking to royalty was abolished.
Geography - United States; History - United States; Literature and Drama; Religion and Philosophy; Sociology
Dist - CINEPC **Prod** - TAHARA 1978

Moaning Minnie 19 MIN
VHS / 16mm
Managing Problem People Series
Color (A PRO)
$415.00 purchase, $195.00 rental
Shows how a chronic complainer becomes effective with help from John Cleese. Part of a series on managing 'problem' employees.
Business and Economics; Guidance and Counseling
Dist - VIDART **Prod** - VIDART 1990

The Moat Monster 12 MIN
16mm
Training Module on Role Enactment in Children's Play Three
Color (A)
LC 76-700935
Shows several young boys enacting a child's frightening dream of a sea monster. Shows through the role of the moat monster the children working out their ideas of rescue and escape and facilitates study and discussion for students and practitioners in child development, child psychology and other related disciplines.
Education; Psychology
Dist - CFDC **Prod** - UPITTS 1974

Mobile - by Alexander Calder 24 MIN
16mm / VHS / U-matic
Color (H C A)
$29.95 purchase _ #CAL-02
Takes a look at the last major work by sculptor Alexander Calder, the first work placed in the National Gallery's East Building and his last major piece, from idea through completion, and shows the craftsmanship used in meeting the challenges posed in the fabrication of this complex work of art. Takes viewers behind the scenes as Calder, architect I M Pei, artist - engineer Paul Matisse, and museum officials meet the challenge of building Calder's complex work.
Fine Arts
Dist - ARTSAM **Prod** - USNGA 1980
USNAC
CAMV
USNGA

Mobile Home Fire Safety 15 MIN
16mm
Color (H C A)
LC 77-701516
Depicts special fire hazards unique to mobile homes, including windows too small to crawl through, flammable walls and drapes and a lack of fire warning devices. Explains how to correct these problems. Reviews essentials of fire safety, such as escape planning, early detection, prevention and suppression.
Guidance and Counseling; Health and Safety
Dist - FILCOM **Prod** - FILCOM 1977

Mobile homes 30 MIN
U-matic / VHS
Consumer survival series; Homes
Color
Presents tips on the maintenance of mobile homes.
Home Economics
Dist - MDCPB **Prod** - MDCPB

Mobile Lab - Any Questions 6 MIN
16mm / U-matic / VHS
Color (I)

LC 74-703352
Describes the curriculum of a mobile science laboratory traveling from high school to high school in Washington, DC. Shows how the program demonstrates that science is relevant to urban living.
Education; Geography - United States; Science
Dist - AMEDFL **Prod** - NSF 1974

Mobile Programs 30 MIN
U-matic
Growing Old in Modern America Series
Color
Health and Safety; Sociology
Dist - UWASHP **Prod** - UWASHP

Mobile Videotape Production 30 MIN
VHS / U-matic
Video - a Practical Guide and more Series
Color
Presents a checklist for evaluating remote locations, considering the pysical needs of the production and crew. Illustrates problems encountered, including lighting, sound, power and mobility.
Fine Arts; Industrial and Technical Education
Dist - VIPUB **Prod** - VIPUB

Mobile Yoke 16 MIN
16mm
Color
LC FIE62-73
Pictures mobile yoke, a goodwill - training exercise in which a tactical air command composite air strike force is deployed to Thailand. Includes briefings, support activities, actual deployment and arrival.
Civics and Political Systems
Dist - USNAC **Prod** - USDD 1960

Mobiles - making art that moves 22 MIN
35mm strip / VHS
Color (J H C T A)
$93.00 purchase _ #MB - 512985 - X, #MB - 512972 - 8
Features mobiles from the most famous artists in that medium, most notably Alexander Calder. Teaches techniques in creating mobiles.
Fine Arts
Dist - SRA **Prod** - SRA 1988

Mobility 19 MIN
VHS / U-matic
Jobs - Seeking, Finding, Keeping Series
Color (H)
Traces the rise to success of a young photographer, pointing out where she made her major career decisions.
Guidance and Counseling
Dist - AITECH **Prod** - MDDE 1980

Mobility 15 MIN
16mm
B&W
LC FIE65-106
Pictures nato's operational material. Develops the theme that mobility is adaptation to any situation. Includes shots of modern maneuvers and action sequences from World Wars I and II.
Civics and Political Systems
Dist - USDS **Prod** - NATO

Mobility 37 MIN
16mm / VHS
Color (C A)
$400.00, $160.00 purchase, $30.00 rental _ #CC3952
Examines the plight of cities in Kenya, Brazil, India and Thailand. Focuses on transit systems.
Civics and Political Systems; Social Science; Sociology
Dist - IU **Prod** - NFBC 1986

Mobility - Life as a New Nomad 14 MIN
16mm / U-matic / VHS
Color
Points out that every year one in five North Americans change their addresses. Features Vance Packard, journalist, sociologist, social critic and author, Brian Ketchum, New York City planner, James Grold, Los Angeles psychiatrist and Martin Zitter, the spokesman and organizer of a commune, who discuss these North American nomads.
Guidance and Counseling; Sociology
Dist - CNEMAG **Prod** - DOCUA

Mobility - Life as a Nomad 14 MIN
U-matic / VHS / 16mm
Color
Points out that every year one in five North Americans changes his address. Looks at these American nomads, as well as New York City subway commuters, automobile users, mobile homes, and tent cities.
Sociology
Dist - CNEMAG **Prod** - DOCUA

Mobilization for Progress - the Story of International Development Service 29 MIN
16mm
Color
LC 75-700866
Shows international voluntarism in Kenya, Panama, Iran and Malaysia in 1970.
History - World; Social Science; Sociology
Dist - USNAC **Prod** - USPC 1970

Mobilization of the Stroke Patient 21 MIN
U-matic / VHS
Color (PRO)
Views techniques for the mobilization of the stroke patient from the first post - stroke days.
Health and Safety
Dist - UMICHM **Prod** - UMICHM 1975

The Mobin - Uddin Umbrella Filter 17 MIN
U-matic / VHS
Color (PRO)
Shows the implantation of an umbrella filter in the vena cava, below the left kidney. Discusses indications and contra - indications for this procedure.
Health and Safety
Dist - WFP **Prod** - WFP

Moby Dick
16mm / Cassette
Now Age Reading Programs, Set 1 Series
Color (I J)
$9.95 purchase _ #8F - PN681816
Brings a classic tale to young readers. The filmstrip set includes filmstrip, cassette, book, classroom materials and a poster. The read - along set includes an activity book and a cassette.
English Language; Literature and Drama
Dist - MAFEX

Moby Dick 26 MIN
U-matic / VHS / 16mm
Mr Magoo in World Classics Series
Color (P I)
Shows Magoo as Ishmael who sails the Pacific with vengeance - driven Captain Ahab, determined to kill the great white whale Moby Dick.
Fine Arts; Literature and Drama
Dist - FI **Prod** - FLEET

Moby Dick 116 MIN
VHS
Color (J H)
$39.00 purchase _ #05696 - 126
Stars Gregory Peck as Captain Ahab in Moby Dick by Herman Melville.
Literature and Drama
Dist - GA **Prod** - GA

Moby Dick 116 MIN
VHS
Color (G)
$49.98 purchase _ #S00526
Presents a version of the Herman Melville novel Moby Dick. Stars Gregory Peck as Captain Ahab, along with Richard Basehart, Orson Welles and others. Screenplay by John Huston and Ray Bradbury. Directed by Huston.
Literature and Drama
Dist - UILL

Moby Dick
U-matic / VHS
American Literature Series
Color (G C J)
$69 purchase _ #05696 - 85
Screens the film version of Melville's tale of Captain Ahab. Stars Gregory Peck. Directed by John Huston.
Fine Arts; Literature and Drama
Dist - CHUMAN

Moby Dick - the Great American Novel 25 MIN
U-matic / VHS / 16mm
Color (H C A)
Introduces an awareness of the timelessness of the novel MOBY DICK by Herman Melville and suggests that similar value lies in all great literature.
Literature and Drama
Dist - PHENIX **Prod** - CBSTV 1969

Mock Codes 26 MIN
VHS / 16mm
(C)
$385.00 purchase _ #850VJ017
Illustrates the importance of numerous interrelated procedures crucial to carrying out a successful life support effort in a 'code,' or cardiac, arrest.
Health and Safety
Dist - HSCIC **Prod** - HSCIC 1985

Mock Trial, Pt 2 60 MIN
BETA / VHS / U-matic
Court Preparation for Professionals Series
Color; Mono (A)
Civics and Political Systems; Guidance and Counseling; Social Science; Sociology
Dist - UCALG **Prod** - UCALG 1986

Mockingbird 4 MIN
16mm
B&W (G)
$8.00 rental
Approaches an abstract study of struggle. Uses flightless flapping of a plastic bird to illustrate struggle and loss.
Fine Arts
Dist - CANCIN **Prod** - FORTDE 1981

The Mockingbird 39 MIN
16mm
B&W
LC FIA68-3284
Based on the short story of the same title by Ambrose Bierce. Concerns a Union soldier in the Civil War who accidentally kills his Confederate twin brother.
Literature and Drama
Dist - FI **Prod** - BF 1968

Modai Huangdi 1230 MIN
VHS
Color (G) (CHINESE)
$390.00 purchase _ #5001
Presents a mini - series from the People's Republic of China. Includes 13 videocassettes.
Geography - World; Literature and Drama
Dist - CHTSUI

Mode, median, and midrange
VHS
Probability and statistics series
Color (H C)
$125.00 purchase _ #8005
Provides resource material about the meaning of mode, median and midrange for help in the study of probability and statistics. Presents a 60 - video series, each part 25 to 30 minutes long, that explains and reinforces concepts using definitions, theorems, examples and step - by - step solutions to tutor the student. Videos are also available in a set.
Mathematics
Dist - LANDMK

The Mode of Action of Tetracyclines 13 MIN
16mm
Color (PRO)
Uses animation to present the basic facts on tetracycline in this synthesis, the difference between bacteriostatic and bactericidal action and the development of resistance to tetracycline. Reviews the theory of how minocycline works and its differences from tetracycline as set forth in the approved minocycline circular.
Health and Safety
Dist - LEDR **Prod** - ACYLLD 1974

Mode Superposition Analysis - Time History 48 MIN
VHS / U-matic
Finite Element Methods in Engineering Mechanics Series
Color
Discusses solution of dynamic response by mode superposition and the basic idea of mode superposition.
Industrial and Technical Education; Mathematics
Dist - MIOT **Prod** - MIOT

Model 129 MIN
16mm / U-matic / VHS
B&W
LC 81-700419
Shows men and women models at work with photographers whose techniques illustrate different styles of fashion and product photography.
Business and Economics; Industrial and Technical Education
Dist - ZIPRAH **Prod** - WISEF 1980

The Model 22 MIN
16mm
Ford Marketing Institute Series
Color
LC 75-703288
Presents a motivation training film for Ford auto salesmen. Uses a dramatization involving a learning lesson between father and son to show the value of setting goals upon which to base actions.
Business and Economics
Dist - FORDFL **Prod** - COMICO 1975

Model Examination - I with Explanations 120 MIN
VHS / U-matic
PSAT and National Merit Scholarship Qualifying Test Preparation 'Series
Color
Education
Dist - KRLSOF **Prod** - KRLSOF

Model Examination I with Explanations 120 MIN
U-matic / VHS
SAT Exam Preparation Series
Color
Education
Dist - KRLSOF **Prod** - KRLSOF 1985

Model Examination - II with Explanations 120 MIN
VHS / U-matic
PSAT and National Merit Scholarship Qualifying Test Preparation 'Series
Color
Education
Dist - KRLSOF **Prod** - KRLSOF

Model Examination II with Explanations 120 MIN
U-matic / VHS
SAT Exam Preparation Series
Color
Education
Dist - KRLSOF **Prod** - KRLSOF 1985

Model Examination - III with Explanations 120 MIN
U-matic / VHS
PSAT and National Merit Scholarship Qualifying Test Preparation 'Series
Color
Education
Dist - KRLSOF **Prod** - KRLSOF

Model Examination III with Explanations 120 MIN
U-matic / VHS
SAT Exam Preparation Series
Color
Education
Dist - KRLSOF **Prod** - KRLSOF 1985

Model for continuous improvement 50 MIN
VHS
Color (PRO IND A)
$595.00 purchase, $195.00 rental _ #CON01
Presents a video workshop which visualizes the concepts of the continuous improvement system. Helps managers in the areas of interrelationships, quality improvement, productivity, and the elimination of waste. Features David Frost and Bill Conway. Support materials include The Model Workbook and Leader Delivery kit. By Conway Quality Inc.
Business and Economics
Dist - EXTR

A Model for oral hygiene in long term care facilities 25 MIN
VHS / U-matic
Color (PRO C)
$395.00 purchase, $80.00 rental _ #C901 - VI - 027
Offers a model plan for daily oral hygiene in institutions providing long term care for elderly patients. Presents techniques for both dentate and edentate patients who range in abilities from those who are able to provide self - care to those who need some assistance to those who are completely incapacitated. Presented by Dr E Earl Williams and Jessie O Brown, the Medical College of Georgia, School of Dentistry, Augusta.
Health and Safety
Dist - HSCIC

Model Houses 5 MIN
16mm / U-matic / VHS
Creative Hands Series
Color (P)
Shows the steps involved in making cardboard and paper models for a whole town project.
Fine Arts
Dist - IFB **Prod** - CRAF 1949

Model Negotiations 70 MIN
U-matic / VHS
Color (PRO)
Portrays two sets of lawyers attempting to resolve a dispute between their respective clients. Shows how lawyers employ different approaches and propose different potential solutions.
Civics and Political Systems; Social Science
Dist - ABACPE **Prod** - ABACPE

Model negotiations I 30 MIN
Cassette
Model negotiations series
Color (PRO)
$125.00, $30.00 purchase, $50.00 rental _ #SKL1-P04, #ASK1-P04
Features two sets of lawyers attempting to resolve a dispute between their respective clients. Shows that using the same fact situation, the lawyers employ very different approaches and propose different potential solutions. Part one of two parts. Includes transcript.
Civics and Political Systems
Dist - AMBAR **Prod** - AMBAR 1980

Model negotiations II 40 MIN
Cassette
Model negotiations series
Color (PRO)
$125.00, $30.00 purchase, $50.00 rental _ #SKL1-P05, #ASK1-P05
Features two sets of lawyers attempting to resolve a dispute between their respective clients. Shows that using the same fact situation, the lawyers employ very different approaches and propose different potential solutions. Part two of two parts. Includes transcript.
Civics and Political Systems
Dist - AMBAR **Prod** - AMBAR 1980

Model negotiations series
Model negotiations I 30 MIN
Model negotiations II 40 MIN
Dist - AMBAR

Model of equally likely outcomes
VHS
Probability and statistics series
Color (H C)
$125.00 purchase _ #8010
Provides resource material about probability laws and models of equally likely outcomes for help in the study of probability and statistics. Presents a 60 - video series, each part 25 to 30 minutes long, that explains and reinforces concepts using definitions, theorems, examples and step - by - step solutions to tutor the student. Videos are also available in a set.
Mathematics
Dist - LANDMK

Model oral argument - demonstration and critique 124 MIN
U-matic / VHS
Appellate advocacy and the appellate process series
Color (PRO)
Presents oral arguments in an appeal case. Concludes with a panel discussion of oral arguments focusing on the Griswold - Wright agreement.
Civics and Political Systems
Dist - ABACPE **Prod** - ABACPE

Model Railroading Unlimited 28 MIN
16mm
Color
LC 75-702752
Encourages the average individual to get involved with the hobby of model railroading.
Physical Education and Recreation
Dist - MORAIL **Prod** - MORAIL 1975

Model Railroading Unlimited 19 MIN
U-matic / VHS / 16mm
Color (J)
LC 78-701044
Presents a brief history of model railroading and a dramatization about a man who enters a hobby shop and comes out as the chief dispatcher of the world's largest model train layout.
Physical Education and Recreation; Social Science
Dist - PFP **Prod** - LIBERP 1978

A Model Recovery - the Story of Ivy Gunter 9 MIN
U-matic / VHS
Color
Follows model Ivy Gunter from diagnosis of bone cancer and loss of her lower right leg to recovery from surgery and resumption of her modeling career.
Health and Safety
Dist - AMCS **Prod** - AMCS 1984

Model Rocketry - the Last Frontier 15 MIN
16mm
Color
Explains the construction and launching of model rockets. Narrated by William Shatner.
Industrial and Technical Education; Physical Education and Recreation
Dist - MTP **Prod** - ESTES

The Model T Man from Michigan, America - Henry Ford and His Horseless Carriage 24 MIN
Videodisc / VHS
American Lifestyles II - Industrialists Series
Color (I)
$125.00, $70.00 purchase, $50.00 rental _ #9883
Tells of the complexities of Henry Ford, the industrialist and private man, as he tours many of the Ford homes. Touches on his creation of the Model T and his innovative ideas which essentially created the assembly line in factories. Hosted by E G Marshall.
Biography; Business and Economics; History - United States; History - World; Industrial and Technical Education
Dist - AIMS **Prod** - COMCO 1986

The Model T man from Michigan, America - Henry Ford and his horseless carriage 24 MIN
VHS
American lifestyle series; Politics and the military
Color (I J H C A)
$70.00 purchase, $50.00 rental _ #9883
Profiles Henry Ford, American industrialist. Shows that Ford's creation of the Model T automobile and innovative assembly ideas changed American industry forever. Tours many of the Ford homes, and looks into the private life of the man. Hosted and narrated by E G Marshall.
Business and Economics
Dist - AIMS **Prod** - COMCO 1986

Modeling 18 MIN
16mm
Search for Solutions Series
Color (J)
LC 79-701460
Demonstrates how it is possible to test scientific theories and predictions with the use of a model. Narrated by Stacy Keach.
Science
Dist - KAROL **Prod** - PLYBCK 1979

Modeling 10 MIN
VHS / U-matic
Protocol Materials in Teacher Education - the Process of Teaching, 'Pt 2 Series
Color (T)
Education; Psychology
Dist - MSU **Prod** - MSU

Modeling Photochemical Air Pollution by Computer 23 MIN
16mm
Color
LC 75-701307
Provides an overview of modeling for air pollution. Describes how the photochemical system is simulated and demonstrates the computer output for the particle - in - cell model.
Mathematics; Science; Science - Natural; Science - Physical
Dist - USNAC **Prod** - NERC 1974

Modeling the Universe 14 MIN
16mm / U-matic / VHS
Color (H C A)
LC 79-700965
Presents Buckminster Fuller discussing some of his ideas on mathematics, physics and structural design. Focuses on his design principles taken from nature.
Fine Arts; Mathematics; Religion and Philosophy; Science - Physical
Dist - PFP **Prod** - MM 1979

Modeling with Difference Equations 30 MIN
U-matic
Introduction to Mathematics Series
Color (C)
Mathematics
Dist - MDCPB **Prod** - MDCPB

Modeling with Light and Shadow 30 MIN
U-matic / VHS
Actor's Face as a Canvas Series
Color
Discusses modeling with light and shadow, the basic tool of the designer. Explains that by highlighting or dimming certain lines and surfaces, the face can be made to appear fat or thin, young or old, ruddy or callow.
Fine Arts
Dist - NETCHE **Prod** - NETCHE 1973

Modelling Basic Circuits
16mm
B&W
Discusses the mathematical modelling of simple electric circuits.
Mathematics
Dist - OPENU **Prod** - OPENU

Modelling Cranes 24 MIN
U-matic / VHS / 16mm
Color
Looks at the elementary statics behind crane design. Shows how modelling forces with vectors can predict instability.
Mathematics
Dist - MEDIAG **Prod** - OPENU 1979

Modelling Drug Therapy 24 MIN
U-matic / VHS / 16mm
Color
Explains how mathematical modelling was used to formulate the best use of the drug Theophylline, used to control asthma.
Health and Safety; Mathematics
Dist - MEDIAG **Prod** - OPENU 1979

Modelling Pollution 24 MIN
16mm / U-matic / VHS
Color
Shows how the interaction between sewage pollutant and oxygen can be described mathematically, using the polluted Thames as an example.
Mathematics; Sociology
Dist - MEDIAG **Prod** - OPENU 1979

Modelling Stock Control 24 MIN
16mm / U-matic / VHS
Color
Shows how the factors underlying stock control problems can be analyzed in terms of progressively more complicated mathematical models. Concentrates on the simplest model producing the famous square root formula for re - order quantities.

Mathematics
Dist - MEDIAG **Prod** - OPENU 1979

Modelling Surveys 24 MIN
U-matic / VHS / 16mm
Color
Looks at the idea of sampling and the variability in sampling. Develops the binomial distribution as a simple model of the sampling process.
Mathematics
Dist - MEDIAG **Prod** - OPENU 1979

Modelling with Vectors
16mm
B&W
Shows that forces, moments and angular velocities can be modelled by vectors, but that finite rotations cannot. Solves two physical problems using vectors.
Mathematics
Dist - OPENU **Prod** - OPENU

Models 25 MIN
U-matic / VHS
Blizzard's Wonderful Wooden Toys Series
Color (H C A)
Shows how to build a model of a Scania Truck, a Landrover and a huge forklift truck.
Fine Arts
Dist - FI **Prod** - BBCTV

Models for growth - describing relationships - Parts 7 and 8 60 MIN
U-matic / VHS
Against all odds - inside statistics series
Color (C)
$45.00, $29.95 purchase
Presents parts 7 and 8 of 26 thirty - minute programs on statistics hosted by Dr Teresa Amabile of Brandeis University. Explores linear and exponential growth, prediction and extrapolation. Looks at scatterplots and least squares regression lines. Produced by the Consortium for Mathematics and Its Applications - COMAP - and the American Statistical Association and American Society of Quality Control.
Mathematics; Psychology
Dist - ANNCPB

Models for Manpower Development in Education 28 MIN
16mm
Color (T)
Explains how institutional change might be enhanced in the field of education. Suggests the need for new transition strategies to implement alternatives as they are developed.
Education
Dist - EDUC **Prod** - EDUC

Models for Small Group Instruction 10 MIN
16mm
Emerging Educational Patterns Series
Color (H C A)
Utilizes the small group mode of instruction to modify learner behavior in accordance with educational goals.
Education
Dist - EDUC **Prod** - EDUC

Models in the mind 29 MIN
16mm / U-matic / VHS
Dimensions in science - Pt 2 series
Color (H C)
Shows how mathematics as a tool of physics enables scientists to construct elaborate, abstract models of physical events that sometimes reveal similarities to mathematics in underlying structure. Illustrates some physical applications of conic sections and the exponential law of growth and decay.
Science - Physical
Dist - FI **Prod** - OECA 1979

Models in the Mind 30 MIN
U-matic
Dimensions in Science - Physics Series
Color (H C)
Looks at the historic attempts to understand how things work.
Science; Science - Physical
Dist - TVOTAR **Prod** - TVOTAR 1979

Models of Development 30 MIN
U-matic / VHS
Developmental Biology Series
Color
Deals with the models sometimes used in place of embryonic research in order to make important generalizations about complex subjects.
Science - Natural
Dist - NETCHE **Prod** - NETCHE 1971

Models of enterprise - Kamsky Associates 30 MIN
U-matic
Adam Smith's money world 1985 - 1986 season series; 228
Color (A)
Attempts to demystify the world of money and break it down so that small as well as large businesses and it's people understand and adjust to new social and economic trends. Reports on the major economic stories and discoveries of 1985 and 1986.
Business and Economics
Dist - PBS **Prod** - WNETTV 1986

Modems and data bases
VHS
Computer series
Color (G)
$29.95 purchase _ #IV - 020
Explains computer communications.
Computer Science; Education; Industrial and Technical Education
Dist - INCRSE **Prod** - INCRSE

Moderate impact aerobics 30 MIN
VHS
Esquire great body series
Color (H C A)
$19.99 purchase _ #EQGB08V
Presents the eighth of a nine - part exercise series oriented to women. Combines stretches and a moderate - impact aerobic exercise program. Developed by Deborah Crocker.
Physical Education and Recreation; Science - Natural
Dist - CAMV

Moderate Retardation in Young Children 43 MIN
U-matic / VHS / 16mm
B&W
Describes a mentally retarded children's program for ages five through seven and shows how a group of these children react to classroom activities.
Education; Psychology
Dist - FEIL **Prod** - CWRUSM 1963

Moderation in eating 11 MIN
VHS / 16mm
Lifestyles in wellness series
Color (C A PRO)
Features a registered dietician who shares her expert knowledge on the problems of the traditional diet which is too rich in protein, fat and cholesterol, and loaded with salt and sugar but devoid of fiber. Gives specific life-saving advice. Part three of a five-part series.
Health and Safety; Home Economics; Psychology; Social Science
Dist - AIMS **Prod** - SANDE 1987
AJN

Modern agricultural methods 23
VHS
Color (H C G)
Looks at modern agricultural methods. Shows how increased production has been achieved while employment and working hours have been reduced.
Agriculture
Dist - VIEWTH **Prod** - VIEWTH

Modern American Drama - O'Neill, Long Day's Journey into Night 47 MIN
U-matic / VHS / 16mm
History of the Drama Series
B&W
Presents Eugene O'Neill's play Long Day's Journey Into Night which demonstrates the playwright's method of building a towering structure out of a simple story, without much action and in ordinary language. Stars Katharine Hepburn, Ralph Richardson, Jason Robards, Jr and Dean Stockwell.
Literature and Drama
Dist - FOTH **Prod** - FOTH 1984

Modern american literature eminent scholar - teachers video series

American literature and politics	30 MIN
American literature of the Thirties	30 MIN
American Literature of the Twenties	30 MIN
American Literature of World War II	30 MIN
Black American Literature	30 MIN
An Introduction to Edith Wharton's Fiction	30 MIN
An Introduction to Ernest Hemingway's Fiction	30 MIN
Introduction to F Scott Fitzgerald's Fiction	30 MIN
An Introduction to John Dos Passos' Fiction	30 MIN
An Introduction to John Steinbeck's Fiction	30 MIN
An Introduction to John Updike's Fiction	40 MIN
An Introduction to Postmodern Fiction	40 MIN
An Introduction to Richard Wright's Fiction	30 MIN
An Introduction to Robert Frost's Poetry	30 MIN
An Introduction to T S Eliot's Poetry	30 MIN
An Introduction to Theodore Dreiser's Fiction	30 MIN
An Introduction to Thomas Wolfe's Fiction	30 MIN
An Introduction to William Faulkner's Fiction	30 MIN
The Modern American Novel	30 MIN
Modern American Poetry	30 MIN
Profession of Authorship in America	30 MIN
Realism and Naturalism in American Literature	30 MIN
The Southern Literary Renaissance	30 MIN
Understanding Dos Passos' USA	30 MIN
Understanding Dreiser's Sister Carrie	30 MIN
Understanding Eliot's the Waste Land	30 MIN
Understanding Fitzgerald's the Great Gatsby	30 MIN
Understanding Hemingway's a Farewell to Arms	30 MIN
Understanding Shakespeare's Othello	40 MIN
Understanding Shakespeare's Romeo and Juliet	40 MIN
Understanding Steinbeck's Grapes of Wrath	30 MIN
Understanding Thomas Wolfe's Look Homeward, Angel	30 MIN
Understanding Wharton's House of Mirth	30 MIN
Understanding William Faulkner's as I Lay Dying	30 MIN

Dist - OMNIGR

The Modern American Novel 30 MIN
VHS
Modern American Literature Eminent Scholar - Teachers Video Series
Color (C)
$95.00 purchase
Provides an overview of American fiction from 1910 to 1950, identifying over 60 prominent novelists and commmenting on their work. Features Professor George Garrett. The 26th of 34 installments of the Modern American Literature Eminent Scholar - Teacher Video Series.
Literature and Drama
Dist - OMNIGR

Modern American Poetry 30 MIN
VHS
Modern American Literature Eminent Scholar - Teachers Video Series
Color (C)
$95.00 purchase
Surveys the ideas and explicates representative poems of the American internationalists and nationalists who came of age between the two world wars. The 26th of 34 installments of the Modern American Literature Eminent Scholar - Teacher Video Series.
Literature and Drama
Dist - OMNIGR

Modern American Tragedy - Hughes Aircraft 60 MIN
U-matic / VHS
Sixty Minutes on Business Series
Color (G)
Business and Economics
Dist - VPHI **Prod** - VPHI 1984

A Modern American Tragedy - Hughes Aircraft Co
U-matic / VHS
Sixty Minutes on Business Series
Color
One of ten segments selected from the realities of the business world, and chosen from key `60 Minutes' telecasts to provide insight into vital issues affecting business today. Includes sourcebook.
Business and Economics; Psychology
Dist - CBSFOX **Prod** - CBSFOX

Modern and Ancient Climates 30 MIN
VHS / U-matic
Earth, Sea and Sky Series
Color (C)
Points out how climate more than anything else determines where people live and work. Compares ancient climates with those of today and considers the future course of climatic changes.
Science - Physical
Dist - DALCCD **Prod** - DALCCD

Modern Ballet 29 MIN
U-matic / VHS / 16mm
Time to Dance Series
B&W (C A)
Discusses and illustrates trends in ballet which began in the 1940's. Describes the changes in subject and mood which accompany this dance form. Gives reasons for a retention of the traditional steps and positions of classical ballet. Presents excerpts from the ballet Pillar Of Fire.
Fine Arts
Dist - IU **Prod** - NET 1960

Modern bankruptcy practice series
Case administration - assets of the estate and their distribution 60 MIN
Chapter 11 - Reorganization 60 MIN
Court and Adminstrative Structures 60 MIN
Representing the Individual Debtor 60 MIN
Dist - ABACPE

Modern basics of classical cooking series
Baking - Lesson 10 7 MIN
Blanching - Lesson 2 7 MIN
Boiling - Lesson 3 7 MIN
Braising - glazing fish and vegetables - Lesson 13 9 MIN
Braising - glazing meat - Lesson 12 12 MIN
Broiling - grilling - Lesson 8 7 MIN
Casseroling - Lesson 14 7 MIN
Deep - fat frying - Lesson 6 7 MIN
Gratinating 5 MIN
Poaching 9 MIN
Roasting - Lesson 11 10 MIN
Sauteing - pan frying - Lesson 7 8 MIN
Steaming - Lesson 4 6 MIN
Stewing - simmering 5 MIN
The Theory of cooking, in brief - lesson 1 8 MIN
Dist - CONPRO

Modern biology series
The Five kingdom classification 20 MIN
From protistans to first multicellular animals 18 MIN
Fungi 18 MIN
Fungi and man 18 MIN
Genetic Engineering - the Bacterial Connection 21 MIN
Genetic engineering and protein synthesis 27 MIN
The Immune Response and Immunization 16 MIN
Mollusks - the Mussel, Respiration and Digestion 7 MIN
Monera - bacteria and cyanobacteria - classification, structure , reproduction - Part one 19 MIN
Monera - bacteria and cyanobacteria - nutrition and respiration - Part two 15 MIN
The Paramecium 12 MIN
Protista - Protozoa and Algae 14 MIN
Simple Multicellular Animals - Sponges, Coelenterates, and Flatworms 20 MIN
Slime molds - plasmodial and cellular 20 MIN
Dist - BNCHMK

Modern CAD Systems
VHS / 35mm strip
CAD - CAM Technology Series
$42.00 purchase _ #LX5505 filmstrip, $62.00 purchase _ #LX5505V VHS
Discusses modern computer aided design systems.
Computer Science
Dist - CAREER **Prod** - CAREER

Modern CAD Systems
VHS / 16mm
(A PRO)
$89.00 purchase _#CC05
Gives an overview of modern CAD systems, drafting and design systems, and future trends.
Computer Science; Education
Dist - RMIBHF **Prod** - RMIBHF

Modern Carbonates 17 MIN
VHS / 16mm
Sedimentary Processes and Basin Analysis Series
Color (C)
$150.00, $185.00 purchase _ #269507
Illustrates the key concepts, economic relevance and influence of measurement technology advances in palaeoenvironmental and basin analysis. Observes how large parts of the earth's crust subside and accumulate thick deposits of sediments, possible reservoirs for oil, gas and coal. Divides into four themes - Sedimentary Petrology, Sedimentary Environments, Basin Analysis and North Sea - Western Canada Case Studies. 'Modern Carbonates' identifies three distinctly different modern carbonate environments. Illustrates the characteristic carbonate environments produced in ramp settings with film from the Persian Gulf, while a film of the Bahamas shows shelf and platform settings.
Geography - World; Science - Physical
Dist - ACCESS **Prod** - BBCTV 1987

The Modern Chemist - Diamond Synthesis 12 MIN
16mm
Color (J H)
Shows how Dr H Tracy Hall discovered diamond synthesis and emphasizes the modern chemist's reliance on discoveries from the past. Points out the chemist's creative thinking and experimental method. Explains how chemistry contributes to the welfare of man.
Science; Science - Physical
Dist - SUTHLA **Prod** - SUTHLA 1962

Modern China Series
Care of the Young and Old in Modern China 6 MIN
The Old and the New in Modern China 7 MIN
Recreation in Modern China 7 MIN
Urban Life in Modern China 7 MIN
Dist - IFB

Modern Coastal Piloting
VHS
Better Boating Series
(H C A)
$225.00 purchase series of five _ #BM300SV
Teaches theory and practice of boat piloting. Explains how to read a chart, how to understand longitude and latitude, how to measure distances and how to use a compass.
Physical Education and Recreation
Dist - CAMV

Modern coastal piloting
VHS
Color (G A PRO)
$39.80 purchase _ #0291
Explains coastal piloting from theoretical concepts to practical execution. Examines the use of the Loran, radar and traditional methods of navigation.
Civics and Political Systems; Physical Education and Recreation; Social Science
Dist - SEVVID **Prod** - SEVVID

Modern Concepts in Diabetes 120 MIN
VHS / U-matic
Color
Presents a survey of current knowledge of the pathophysiology of diabetes and its major clinical classes. Discusses therapeutic modalities, complications, control, new trends in management and effective counseling techniques.
Health and Safety; Psychology
Dist - ADA **Prod** - ADA

Modern Control Theory - Deterministic Optimal Control Series
The Dynamic Programming Algorithm 60 MIN
General Discussion 49 MIN
The Minimum Principle - Discrete Time Case 43 MIN
The Minimum Principle of Pontryagin - Continuous Time Case 49 MIN
Minimum Principle Vs Dynamic Programming 50 MIN
Newton's Method 83 MIN
Numerical Example - Solution of a Minimum Fuel Problem in the Apollo Project 21 MIN
The Steepest Descent Method 45 MIN
Dist - MIOT

Modern control theory - deterministic optimal linear feedback - a series
Modern control theory series
Color (PRO)
Discusses deterministic optimal linear feedback in modern control theory which deals with specific analytical and algorithmic methods which can be used to control complex stochastic dynamic systems so as to optimize their performance. Air Traffic Control In The Near Terminal Area; Asymptotic Behavior Of Steady - State Linear - - ; Control Of Helicopter At Hover; Design Of Proportional - Derivative Integral - - ; Motivation For The Linear - Quadratic Problem; Motivation For The Steady - State Linear - - ; Optimal Control Of A Macroeconomic Model Of - - ; Programs - Helicopter Example; Solution Of The Linear - Quadratic Problem, The; Steady - State.
Industrial and Technical Education
Dist - MIOT **Prod** - MIOT

Modern Control Theory - Deterministic Optimal Linear Feedback Series
Air traffic control in the near terminal area 152 MIN
Asymptotic behavior of steady - state linear quadratic closed loop systems 77 MIN
Control of helicopter at hover 31 MIN
Design of proportional - derivative integral controllers for tracking step inputs 44 MIN
Motivation for the Linear - Quadratic Problem 73 MIN
Motivation for the Steady - State Linear Quadratic Problem 104 MIN
Optimal Control of a Macroeconomic Model of the US Economy 1957 - 1962 44 MIN
Programs - Helicopter Example 45 MIN
The Solution of the Linear - Quadratic Problem 47 MIN
The Steady - State Linear - Quadratic Problem - Continuous - Time Case 51 MIN
The Steady - State Linear - Quadratic Problem - Discrete Time Case 38 MIN
Steady - State Linear - Quadratic Problem with Deterministic Disturbances 41 MIN
The Steady - State Linear Regulator Problem for Constant Disturbances 70 MIN
Dist - MIOT

Modern control theory series
Deterministic optimal linear feedback 50 MIN
Dist - AMCEE

Modern control theory series
Modern control theory - deterministic optimal linear feedback - a series
Dist - MIOT

Modern Control Theory - Stochastic Control Series
The Continuous - Time Linear - Quadratic - Gaussian (LQG) Problem 87 MIN
Control of a nonlinear system about desired constant equilibrium 39 MIN
Control of a nonlinear system about desired time varying trajectory 52 MIN
The Discrete - Time Linear - Quadratic - Gaussian (LQG) Problem 83 MIN
The General Problem 89 MIN
Numerical Example of LQG Design for a Third - Order Continuous Time System 27 MIN
The Steady State LQG Problem - Continuous - Time Case 68 MIN
Steady State Theory Computer Programs - Helicopter Example 57 MIN
Systematic Procedures and Numerical Example 38 MIN
Dist - MIOT

Modern Control Theory - Stochastic Estimation Series
The Bayesian approach to parameter estimation 90 MIN
Computer Routines for Linear Stochastic Estimation 54 MIN
The Continuous - Time Kalman - Bucy Filter 48 MIN
Discrete - Time Kalman Filter 86 MIN
Effect of changing covariance matrix of measurement upon a Kalman filter 36 MIN
Introduction 47 MIN
Numerical Example - Estimation of Position, Velocity, and Ballistic Parameter for a 47 MIN
Numerical Example - Estimation of Positions Velocities, and Accelerations 32 MIN
Numerical Example - Sensor Trade - Offs 47 MIN
Response of Linear Systems to White Noise Inputs - Continuous Time Case 52 MIN
Response of Linear Systems to White Noise Inputs - Discrete Time Case 46 MIN
Review of Probablistic Concepts 50 MIN
Steady - State Kalman - Bucy Filter - Continuous - Time Case 48 MIN
Steady - State Kalman Filter - Discrete - Time Case 43 MIN
Suboptimal Nonlinear Filtering Algorithm - Discrete - Time 87 MIN
Dist - MIOT

Modern control theory - systems analysis series
Computer Routines for Linear System Analysis 38 MIN
Controllability and observability 50 MIN
Discrete - Time Dynamical Systems 40 MIN
Dynamic Linearization for Continuous Time Systems 27 MIN
From Transfer Functions to State Variable Representations 41 MIN
The General Notion of the State of a Dynamical System 45 MIN
Introduction to Optimal Control and Estimation Methods (1) 49 MIN
Introduction to Optimal Control and Estimation Methods (2) 36 MIN
Linear Continuous Time Dynamical Systems 42 MIN
Linear Time Invariant Dynamical Systems 52 MIN
The Relation of transfer functions and state variable representations 53 MIN
Dist - MIOT

The Modern Corporation 28 MIN
16mm
Color; B&W (H)
LC FIA67-1452
Deals with the structure and operation of a modern corporation and with the corporation's role in today's economic society.
Business and Economics
Dist - SUTHLA **Prod** - SLOAN 1967

Modern Counseling Program in North Carolina Elementary Schools 35 MIN
16mm
Color (A)
Presents techniques for promoting class participation in developing an understanding of personal behavior, feelings, sensory awareness, and assertiveness. Discusses the children's need for career awareness and social relations. Recommended for counselors, teachers, and principals.
Education; Guidance and Counseling
Dist - AACD **Prod** - AACD 1982

The Modern day humanitarians - Part 5 22 MIN
VHS
Cutting edge series
Color (G)
$150.00 purchase _ #8027
Examines research in the humanities - an automated system for eye and ear testing which would make the common eye chart and audio booth redundant, the lifestyle and living conditions of the people of Nepal, computer software which simulates real life experiences to teach high school students, and computer animation used to simulate stage lighting for theater technicians. Part of a five - part series on the latest research and technology developments in Western Canada.
Computer Science; Fine Arts; Geography - World; Health and Safety; History - World; Science
Dist - UCALG **Prod** - UCALG 1989

Modern Design 29 MIN
VHS / U-matic
Flower Show Series
Color
Features Mrs Ascher using exotic and unusual flowers and plant materials to create flower arrangements in a modern mood.
Fine Arts; Home Economics; Science - Natural
Dist - MDCPB **Prod** - MDCPB

The Modern Diabetic 15 MIN
VHS
Color (C A)
Deals with diabetes. Relates the story of a woman recently diagnosed as diabetic, who joins a group of other diabetics and learns how she can manage her disease while she maintains her normal activities.
Health and Safety; Psychology
Dist - WSTGLC **Prod** - WSTGLC

Modern Diagnosis and Control of the Epileptic Seizure
U-matic
Color (PRO)
Discusses current approaches to seizure diagnosis and management. Reviews current drug therapy.
Health and Safety
Dist - AYERST **Prod** - AYERST

Modern Egypt 11 MIN
16mm
Color (J)
LC 78-701200
Pictures Egypt today, commenting on government, EducaTion, industries and agriculture. Scenes include the suez canal, Cairo, Alexandria, the Nile, pyramids, sphinxes, Karnak, Luxor, Abu Simbil and the Aswan Dam.
Geography - World
Dist - AVED **Prod** - CBF 1967

A Modern Egyptian family 17 MIN
U-matic / VHS / BETA
Color; PAL (G H C)
Views changes which took place in Egypt through the eyes of a 78 year - old man. Looks at the Aswan Dam; a series of costly wars; the re - opened Suez Canal; oil exploration in the Red Sea; a movement to the cities and resulting urban problems.
Fine Arts; History - World; Sociology
Dist - EDPAT **Prod** - IFF

Modern Elementary Mathematics Series
Associativity 12 MIN
Commutativity 12 MIN
Equations 12 MIN
Sets and Numbers 12 MIN
Dist - MGHT

Modern Embalming Techniques 31 MIN
16mm
Color (C A)
Explains modern embalming techniques.
Health and Safety; Science; Sociology
Dist - WSUM **Prod** - WSUM 1968

Modern Engines and Energy Conversion 12 MIN
16mm / U-matic / VHS
Color (I J)
$305.00, $215.00 purchase _ #78503; LC 78-701784
Analyzes and compares several types of conventional engines in terms of the mechanical operation, heat cycle and energy efficiency of each. Deals with nuclear power plants on ships, ion engines for space travel and solar engines.
Industrial and Technical Education; Social Science
Dist - CORF **Prod** - CENTRO 1978

Modern Europe series
Austria 19 MIN
Belgium 18 MIN
Finland 19 MIN
Greece 19 MIN
Ireland 22 MIN
The Netherlands 19 MIN
Norway 17 MIN
Portugal 19 MIN
Scotland 21 MIN
Spain 16 MIN
Sweden 22 MIN
Switzerland 19 MIN
Yugoslavia 19 MIN
Dist - JOU

Modern Fertility Control 30 MIN
U-matic / VHS
Family Planning Series
Color
Discusses birth control pills, intra - uterine devices, sterilization and other contraceptive methods.
Science - Natural; Sociology
Dist - NETCHE **Prod** - NETCHE 1970

Modern Food Preservation
VHS / U-matic
Color (J H)
Provides step by step instructions for successful food preservation, from traditional to the latest procedures.
Home Economics; Social Science
Dist - CAREER **Prod** - CAREER 1980

Modern genetics 26 MIN
VHS
Color (J H)
$100.00 purchase _ #A5VH 1260
Challenges students to develop hypotheses as they observe the discoveries leading to modern genetics - sex chromosomes, location of genes and the structure of DNA. Teaches the concepts of replication and mutation. Describes the goals and possible consequences of the human genome project.
Science - Natural
Dist - CLRVUE **Prod** - CLRVUE 1992

Modern Geodetic Surveying 18 MIN
16mm
Color (C T)
LC 72-701471
Portrays the need, nature, and means of geodetic surveying as it exists today, with emphasis on the challenge of the future.
Geography - World; Industrial and Technical Education; Science; Social Science
Dist - USNAC **Prod** - USN 1967

Modern Golf Instruction in Motion Pictures Series Unit 2
How to Build a Golf Swing, Pt 1 16 MIN
How to Build a Golf Swing, Pt 2 16 MIN
Dist - NGF

Modern Golf Instruction in Motion Pictures Series Unit 5
Putting - Golf's End Game 12 MIN
Dist - NGF

Modern golf instruction in motion pictures series
Golf - a special kind of joy 16 MIN
How to Build a Golf Swing, Pt 1 17 MIN
How to Build a Golf Swing, Pt 2 17 MIN
Putting - Golf's End Game 13 MIN
The Short approach shots 9 MIN
Dist - NGF

Modern Israel 20 MIN
VHS / U-matic
Color (J)
LC 82-706776
Highlights Israel as an ancient but modern land. Includes visits to Haifa, Tel Aviv, Galilee, Jerusalem and Negev.
Geography - World; History - World
Dist - AWSS **Prod** - AWSS 1981

Modern Livestock Systems 22 MIN
16mm
Color
Shows new methods for feed - processing and waste - disposal. Describes an artificial environment with climate - controlled steel buildings and easily maintained steel equipment that results in smooth - running, labor - saving systems, thereby increasing productivity.
Agriculture
Dist - USSC **Prod** - USSC

A Modern look at ancient Greek civilization
VHS
Color (C A)
$149.95 purchase _ #AI - B421
Presents eight lectures which offer an panoramic view of the art, history and literature of ancient Greece. Features Prof Andrew Szegedy - Maszak of Wesleyan University as lecturer.
Fine Arts; History - World; Literature and Drama
Dist - TTCO **Prod** - TTCO

Modern main street, USA 120 MIN
VHS
March of time - post - war problems and solutions series
B&W (G)
$24.95 purchase _ #S02133
Presents the final installment of a five - part series of newsreel excerpts covering the post - World War II era in the US and abroad. Segments include 'Public Relations,' 'The Case of Mrs Conrad,' 'White Collar Girls.'
History - United States; Sociology
Dist - UILL

Modern man 5 MIN
16mm
B&W (G)
$10.00 rental
Questions the futures of pensive suburban boys in an industrial city. Features original soundtrack by members of Boy Dirt Car. Produced by Paul Heilemann.
Fine Arts
Dist - CANCIN

Modern Management of Multiple Births 20 MIN
16mm
Color (PRO)
Discusses the problems of multiple births and their increased risks. Reviews conditions such as prematurity, toxemia, anemia and stress and shows the use of the placentogram and obstetrical procedures involved in breech and transverse presentations. Presents sequences taken during the birth of identical quadruplets.
Health and Safety
Dist - LEDR **Prod** - ACYLLD 1964

The Modern Management of Tuberculosis 60 MIN
16mm
Color (PRO)
LC 73-702041
Explains modern theories regarding the diagnosis, transmission and treatment of tuberculosis.
Health and Safety; Science; Science - Natural
Dist - AMLUNG **Prod** - DCC 1973

Modern Management Series
Listen, Please 12 MIN
Dist - BNA

Modern Manufacturing - Command Performance 33 MIN
16mm
Color
LC FIE63-219
Illustrates the need for using modern methods in the production of aerospace vehicles and depicts many of the latest manufacturing techniques. Explains that the use of automation from programming to finished product can supersede conventional methods in speed, reliability and economy.
Business and Economics; Industrial and Technical Education
Dist - USNAC **Prod** - USAF 1963

Modern Manufacturing Systems 30 MIN
U-matic / VHS
Color
Demonstrates computer integrated manufacturing along with all the computerized products and services available to engineers who are automating their manufacturing operations.
Business and Economics; Industrial and Technical Education
Dist - SME **Prod** - SME

Modern Mapmakers 20 MIN
U-matic
Understanding Our World, Unit I - Tools We Use Series
Color (I)
Explains the entire process of mapmaking from aerial photography and ground control teams to the final inscribing.
Geography - World; Social Science
Dist - GPN **Prod** - KRMATV

Modern masters of Chinese martial arts - Volume 2 106 MIN
VHS
Color (G)
$49.95 purchase _ #1178
Explores internal aspects of T'ai chi ch'uan and push hands techniques with T T Liang, Yu Cheng - Hsiang, C K Chern, Don Miller, and Arthur Goodridge.
Physical Education and Recreation
Dist - WAYF

Modern masters of the Chinese martial arts - 1 130 MIN
VHS
Color (G)
$49.95 purchase _ #1114
Includes demonstrations and interviews with masters and judges from the 1991 U S National Chinese Martial Arts Competitions. Includes Tai Chi - Yang, Wu, and Chen standard and fast forms - plus Hsing I, Pa Kua, various applications and fighting forms for several styles, weapons forms and sword fencing, Praying Mantis, Wing Chun, and Shuai Chiao.
Physical Education and Recreation
Dist - WAYF

Modern Mathematics - Number Line 13 MIN
16mm / U-matic / VHS
Color (P I)
Introduces the number line and shows uses for it, such as addition, subtraction, comparison and measurement.
Mathematics
Dist - PHENIX **Prod** - BAILEY 1966

Modern Mathematics - Number Sentences 11 MIN
U-matic / VHS / 16mm
Color (P I) (SPANISH)
LC 70-711602
Children playing discover relationships between everyday objects and concepts explained by mathematical sentences or simple equations.
Mathematics
Dist - PHENIX **Prod** - PHENIX 1966

Modern Mathematics - Sets 13 MIN
U-matic / VHS / 16mm
Color (P I)
Uses animation to illustrate concepts of sets, one - toone correspondence, associative and commutative laws, cardinal numbers and numerals used in foreign language. Shows their relation to daily family activity.
Mathematics
Dist - PHENIX **Prod** - BAILEY 1966

Modern mavericks 15 MIN
VHS
Art history - century of modern art series
Color (I H A)
$125.00 purchase; $25.00 rental
Discusses art's modern mavericks, Gustav Klimt, Paul Klee, George Rouault, Amedeo Modigliani, Giacomo Balla and Oskar Kokoschka. Considers selected works, comments on the artists' personal histories and points out their distinctive styles and subjects.
Fine Arts
Dist - AITECH **Prod** - WDCNTV 1988

Modern Medicine 30 MIN
Videoreel / VT2
Investigating the World of Science, Unit 2 - Energy within Living 'Systems Series
B&W (J)
Science; Science - Natural
Dist - GPN **Prod** - MPATI

Modern Methods of Venous Blood Collection 25 MIN
16mm
Color (PRO)
LC 77-700389
Discusses proper venipuncture techniques, including preparation of equipment and patient, single and multiple specimen collection, handling of blood specimens and tube additives related to various laboratory tests.
Health and Safety; Science
Dist - SCITIF **Prod** - BECDIC 1976

Modern moves for pregnancy fitness 54 MIN
VHS
Color (G)
$19.95 purchase _ #PA05
Shows how to exercise safely, including modification of exercises throughout pregnancy. Describes Kegel exercises in a pelvic floor training routine for labor, delivery, and recovery. Two 20 - minute workouts provide body conditioning while stretching and firming key areas. Has a guided relaxation segment.
Health and Safety; Physical Education and Recreation
Dist - SVIP

Modern moves for pregnancy fitness 60 MIN
VHS
Color (C PRO G)
$29.95 purchase _ #5323S
Combines yoga with contemporary non - impact exercise in a fitness program for healthy pregnant patients. Divides into four modules - warmup; more demanding exercises; relaxation; and pelvic - floor exercises. Produced by Elize St Charles and Associates.
Health and Safety; Physical Education and Recreation
Dist - AJN

The Modern Navy 28 MIN
VHS / 16mm
Blue Revolution Series
Color (J)
$149.00 purchase, $75.00 rental _ #QD - 2290
Follows the development of ships for warfare. The tenth of 16 installments of the Blue Revolution Series.
Civics and Political Systems; Social Science; Sociology
Dist - FOTH

A Modern Newspaper Plant 20 MIN
U-matic
Newspaper in the Classroom Series
Color (I J H)
Social Science
Dist - GPN **Prod** - GPN

A Modern Newspaper Plant 15 MIN
U-matic
Newspaper - What's in it for Me Series
Color (I J)
Presents a tour through the Omaha World - Herald. Shows the steps in the production and dissemination of a newspaper.
Social Science
Dist - GPN **Prod** - MOEBA 1980

Modern Nutrition 45 MIN
16mm
Color
Discusses vitamin deficiencies.
Health and Safety; Social Science
Dist - SQUIBB **Prod** - SQUIBB 1952

Modern Obstetrics - Cesarean Section 21 MIN
U-matic / VHS
Color (PRO)
Details the history of Cesarean section as well as indications and diagnostic tests. Discusses and shows in actual deliveries the classical low cervical and extra - peritoneal types of Cesarean section.
Health and Safety
Dist - WFP **Prod** - WFP

Modern Obstetrics - Fetal Evaluation 25 MIN
U-matic / VHS
Color (PRO)
Describes the techniques that are available for evaluating gestational age, fetal growth, maturation, well being and malformations. Demonstrates amniocentesis, electronic heart monitoring, fetoscopy and ultrasonography.
Health and Safety
Dist - WFP **Prod** - WFP

Modern Obstetrics - Normal Labor and Delivery 22 MIN
VHS / U-matic
Color (PRO)
Details all the procedures the medical staff undertakes during the course of labor and safe delivery of the baby by following a mother in labor.
Health and Safety
Dist - WFP **Prod** - WFP

Modern Obstetrics - Postpartum Hemorrhage 25 MIN
VHS / U-matic
Color (PRO)
Illustrates the causes of postpartum hemorrhage and how to diagnose and manage such hemorrhages.
Health and Safety
Dist - WFP **Prod** - WFP

Modern Obstetrics - Pre - Eclampsia, Eclampsia 27 MIN
U-matic / VHS
Color (PRO)
Demonstrates by means of clinical cases, the diagnosis and treatment of eclampsia and pre - eclampsia. Animation is used to illustrate the etiology of toxemia and the changes which occur as the condition progresses.
Health and Safety
Dist - WFP **Prod** - WFP

Modern physics - Quad VII 60 MIN
VHS
Mechanical universe - high school adaptation series
Color (H)
$75.00 purchase _ #MU - Q7
Presents 4 parts on physics. Includes - The Wave of Natural Light - the properties that light shares with other kinds of waves, the unique characteristics of the electromagnetic spectrum and the fundamental nature of the interaction between light and matter; Wave - Particle Duality - explores in depth the wave characteristics of matter and the wave - particle duality of light and matter; Models of the Atom - examines the development of various models of the atom, starting with Dalton's chemically combining spheres through the Bohr model up to the current electron cloud model; Special Relativity - presents the postulates of special relativity and how they lead to the failure of simultaneity, time dilation, length contraction and relativistic mass.
Science - Physical
Dist - INSTRU

Modern Portable Fire Extinguishers - First Line of Defense Against Fire 29 MIN
16mm
Color (I)
LC 74-703690
Demonstrates the use of a variety of fire extinguishers, including the BC and ABC dry chemical types, the carbon dioxide gas type and the pressurized water type.
Health and Safety
Dist - SUMHIL **Prod** - SUMHIL 1974

The Modern Post Office 13 MIN
16mm / U-matic / VHS
Color; B&W (P I)
LC FIA68-1194
The movement of a single piece of mail - - a post card - is used to illustrate the work of the modern post office.
Psychology; Social Science
Dist - PHENIX **Prod** - WANDIA 1967

Modern presidency series
Interviews former Presidents Nixon, Ford, Carter and Reagan in five - part series. Focuses, in first part, on the history of the presidency as an institution, with particular emphasis on presidential authority. The remaining parts allow host David Frost to interview each of the former Presidents about their time in office.

The Challenge of the Presidency	60 MIN
Gerald Ford - the Healing of the Presidency	60 MIN
Jimmy Carter - the moralist president	60 MIN
Richard Nixon - Crisis in the Presidency	60 MIN
Ronald Reagan - the Presidency of Affirmation	60 MIN

Dist - PBS **Prod** - ENMED 1967

Modern President Series

Chief Administrator	15 MIN
Coalition Builder	15 MIN
Crisis manager	15 MIN
Party Leader	15 MIN
Priority Setter	15 MIN
Symbolic Leader	15 MIN

Dist - CORF

Modern Programming Practices 30 MIN
U-matic / VHS
MC68000 Microprocessor Series
Color (IND)
Focuses on position independent programs and coding instructions and program counter relative instructions. Describes LEA and PEA instructions.
Industrial and Technical Education; Mathematics; Sociology
Dist - COLOSU **Prod** - COLOSU

The Modern Prospector 15 MIN
16mm / U-matic / VHS
B&W (H C)
Shows electro - magnetic recording machines, gravity meters and other tools that aid the prospector in his search for mineral ore deposits. Describes the work of geologists, mineralogists and technicians in pinpointing commercially profitable deposits.
Guidance and Counseling; Psychology; Science; Science - Physical
Dist - IFB **Prod** - NFBC 1958

Modern Protest 30 MIN
VHS / U-matic
Afro - American Perspectives Series
Color (C)
Discusses the black protests for civil rights in America.
History - United States
Dist - MDCPB **Prod** - MDDE

Modern punting techniques and fundamentals 46 MIN
VHS
Color (H C A)
$69.50 purchase _ #PKS100V
Features NFL punter Brian Hansen instructing in the techniques of punting. Covers subjects including warm - up exercises, kicking techniques, and special alignment techniques and drills.
Physical Education and Recreation
Dist - CAMV

Modern Rack and Pinion Steering Systems 30 MIN
VHS
$189.00 purchase _ #017 - 157
Uses live action demonstrations, computer graphics, and cutaway models to provide an in - depth exploration of the basic operation and service procedures for manual and power assist rack and pinion steering systems.
Education; Industrial and Technical Education
Dist - CAREER **Prod** - CAREER

Modern soccer - style placekicking techniques and fundamentals 55 MIN
VHS
Color (H C A)
$69.50 purchase _ #PKS300V
Features Philadelphia Eagles placekicker Roger Ruzek instructing in the techniques of soccer - style placekicking. Covers subjects including stretching and flexibility exercises, kicking techniques, how to deal with kicking problems, and kickoff and on - side kick techniques.
Physical Education and Recreation
Dist - CAMV

Modern Steel Making 23 MIN
16mm
Color (H C A)
Shows basic steelmaking today in the blast, open hearth and electric furnaces. Uses animation and live photography with on - the - scene sound effects to illustrate the steelmaking operations.
Business and Economics
Dist - USSC **Prod** - SUTHP 1960

Modern Techniques in Language Teaching 32 MIN
16mm
Principles and Methods of Teaching a Second Language Series
B&W (H T)
Discusses the procedures involved in forming new language habits. Uses an English class for non - English speakers to show how the sound system, grammatical organization and lexicon of a language is taught.
Education; English Language; Foreign Language
Dist - IU **Prod** - MLAA 1962

Modern times 30 MIN
VHS
Hurray for today series
Color; PAL (G)
PdS25
Visits supermarkets and multi - level parking garages to examine changes in British architecture in recent years. Features Lucinda Lambton, an architectural photographer for over 20 years. Part of a six - part series studying architectural changes in Britain from the grim years of modernization, comprehensive redevelopment and concrete blocks to a new age of beautiful and exciting modern buildings.
Fine Arts; Geography - World; History - World
Dist - ACADEM

Modern Times 28 MIN
U-matic / VHS
Color
Explores a woman's experience in contemporary society. Emphasizes a non - linear narrative.
Fine Arts; Sociology
Dist - KITCHN **Prod** - KITCHN

Modern Times - Revisited - Alternatives to Assembly Lines 29 MIN
VHS / U-matic
Re - Making of Work Series
Color (C A)
Visits assembly plants in Sweden and Italy to reveal worker oriented production plants being used by more firms to stimulate employee creativity. Examines self - paced work teams at the Volvo truck division in Sweden and at the Olivetti factory near Turin. Contains employee interviews.
Business and Economics; Industrial and Technical Education; Sociology
Dist - EBEC

Modern U S History - from Cold War to Hostage Crisis Series
Nineteen Forty - Five to 1960
Nineteen Sixty - Nine to 1981
Nineteen Sixty - One to 1968
Dist - GA

Modern U S History - from Cold War to Hostage Crisis - Unit I - 1945 - 1960
U-matic / VHS / 35mm strip
(J H C)
$179.00 purchase _ #06804 94
Covers the Truman and Eisenhower years when America entered the Cold War. Explores the anticommunist hysteria of the McCarthy era and traces the course of the Koean War. Duscusses America's response to Sputnik and to the first atomic bomb. Features historical photography. In 4 parts.
History - United States; Sociology
Dist - ASPRSS **Prod** - GA

Modern U S History - from Cold War to Hostage Crisis - Unit II - 1961 - 1968
U-matic / VHS / 35mm strip
(J H C)
$179.00 purchase _ #06806 94
Focuses on the Kennedy and Johnson years when the struggle for Black civil rights reached its climax. Discusses America's response to the Cuban Missile Crisis, Kennedy's assassination, and internal conflict over the Vietnam war. In 4 parts.
History - United States
Dist - ASPRSS **Prod** - GA

Modern U S History - from Cold War to Hostage Crisis - Unit III - 1969 - 1981
U-matic / VHS / 35mm strip
(J H C)
$179.00 purchase _ #06807 94
Examines the Nixon, Ford, and Carter years, when relations with China were reopened. Discusses the effects of Watergate, the rise of OPEC, and the Iran hostage crisis. In 4 parts.
History - United States
Dist - ASPRSS **Prod** - GA

Modern Women - the Uneasy Life 60 MIN
U-matic / VHS / 16mm
N E T Journal Series
B&W (H C A)
LC FIA68-2499
Interviews college - educated women who are housewives, professional career women, and women who combine careers and homemaking about the various roles of educated women. Explores the attitudes of husbands and bachelors toward educated women.
Education; Guidance and Counseling; Psychology; Sociology
Dist - IU **Prod** - NET 1967

The Modern World, 1945 - 26 MIN
16mm / U-matic / VHS
World - a Television History Series
Color (J H C)
$475.00 purchase
Shows postwar reconstruction, East - West conflict, the Cold War, colonial wars in Southeast Asia, the Middle East and Africa. Ends with man's major achievements in the sciences and social systems.
History - World
Dist - LANDMK **Prod** - NETGOL 1985

The Modern world - 1945 - present 30 MIN
VHS
World - A Television history series
Color (C A T)
$55.00 rental
Covers the period from 1945 to the present day. Based on "The Times Atlas of World History." Serves as the final part of a 26 - part telecourse. Available only to institutions of higher education.
History - World; Sociology
Dist - SCETV **Prod** - SCETV 1986

The Modern World of Industrial Arts 13 MIN
16mm
Color (J H)
Stresses the need for a basic education in industrial arts in a world of modern technical complexities. Shows how industrial arts courses relate to the other subjects in the general education curriculum.
Education; Guidance and Counseling; Psychology
Dist - VADE **Prod** - VADE 1960

The Modern world - ten great writers series 580 MIN
VHS
The Modern world - ten great writers series
Color (G)
$949.00 purchase _ #S01961
Consists of ten programs, each examining a different early 20th century European author. Uses drama, documentary, and literary criticism to portray each author's experience, background and personal philosophy. Available for educational use only.
Literature and Drama
Dist - UILL

The Modern world - ten great writers series
Fyodor Mikhailovich Dostoevsky - Pt 1 58 MIN
Henrik Ibsen - Pt 2 58 MIN
Thomas Mann - Pt 6 58 MIN
Thomas Stearns Eliot - Pt 9 58 MIN
Dist - FI

Modern World - Ten Great Writers Series
Franz Kafka 58 MIN
Fyodor Dostoevsky 58 MIN
Henrik Ibsen 58 MIN
Joseph Conrad 58 MIN
Luigi Pirandello 58 MIN
Marcel Proust 58 MIN
T S Eliot 58 MIN
Thomas Mann 58 MIN
Dist - FI
PSU

Modern World - Ten Great Writers Series
James Joyce 58 MIN
Dist - FI
PSU
UILL

Modern World - Ten Great Writers Series
Virginia Woolf 58 MIN
Dist - PSU

Modern world - ten great writers series
Feodor Mikalovitch Dostoevsky - 1821 - 1881 - Volume I 58 MIN
Franz Kafka - 1893 - 1924 - Volume VII 58 MIN
Henrik Ibsen - 1826 - 1906 - Volume III 58 MIN
Joseph Conrad - 1857 - 1924 - Volume II 58 MIN
Luigi Pirandello - 1867 - 1936 - Volume IX 58 MIN
Marcel Proust - 1871 - 1922 - Volume IV 58 MIN
The Modern world - ten great writers series 580 MIN
Thomas Mann - 1875 - 1955 - Volume V 58 MIN
Thomas Stearns Eliot - 1888 - 1965 - Volume VIII 58 MIN
Dist - UILL

Modern World, the - 10 Great Writers Series
Franz Kafka - Pt 10 58 MIN
James Joyce - Pt 7 58 MIN
Joseph Conrad - Pt 3 58 MIN
Luigi Pirandello - Pt 4 58 MIN
Marcel Proust - Pt 5 58 MIN
Dist - FI

Modern X - Ray Generators, Pt 1, Three - Phase Rectification 29 MIN
U-matic / VHS
Modern X - Ray Generators Series
Color (PRO)
Explains interrogation time, kilowatt rating, conversion from fractional to decimal system, three - phase transformers and rectification.
Industrial and Technical Education; Science - Physical
Dist - USNAC **Prod** - USVA

Modern X - Ray Generators, Pt 2, Primary and Secondary Switching, Synchronous and 25 MIN
U-matic / VHS
Modern X - Ray Generators Series
Color (PRO)
Complete title is Modern X - Ray Generators, Pt 2, Primary And Secondary Switching, Synchronous And Nonsynchronous Timing. Discusses approaches to switching or contacting the high voltage to the X - ray tube.
Industrial and Technical Education; Science - Physical
Dist - USNAC **Prod** - USVA

Modern X - Ray Generators, Pt 3, Film Changers and Maximum Available Exposure Time 27 MIN
U-matic / VHS
Modern X - Ray Generators Series
Color (PRO)
Explains why a non - synchronous generator increases the amount of MAS.
Industrial and Technical Education; Science - Physical
Dist - USNAC **Prod** - USVA

Modern X - Ray Generators, Pt 4, Photospot and Cine Cameras, Phototimers 28 MIN
VHS / U-matic
Modern X - Ray Generators Series
Color (PRO)
Discusses photospot cine cameras, automatic brightness controls and phototimers.
Industrial and Technical Education; Science - Physical
Dist - USNAC **Prod** - USVA

Modern X - Ray Generators Series
Modern X - Ray Generators, Pt 1, Three - Phase Rectification 29 MIN
Modern X - Ray Generators, Pt 2, Primary and Secondary Switching, Synchronous and asynchronous 25 MIN
Modern X - Ray Generators, Pt 3, 27 MIN

Film Changers and Maximum Available Exposure Time
Modern X - Ray Generators, Pt 4, Photospot and Cine Cameras, Phototimers 28 MIN
Dist - USNAC

Modern X - Ray Tubes, Pt 1, Production of an X - Ray Tube 50 MIN
VHS / U-matic
Modern X - Ray Tubes Series
Color (PRO)
Describes the process of constructing and testing a rotating anode X - ray tube.
Industrial and Technical Education; Science - Physical
Dist - USNAC **Prod** - USVA

Modern X - Ray Tubes, Pt 2, Rotating Anode X - Ray Tubes, How they Function 25 MIN
U-matic / VHS
Modern X - Ray Tubes Series
Color (PRO)
Explains the development of rotating anode X - ray tubes, how they work, and factors that affect tube ratings.
Industrial and Technical Education; Science - Physical
Dist - USNAC **Prod** - USVA

Modern X - Ray Tubes, Pt 3, Heating and Cooling of X - Ray Tubes 20 MIN
U-matic / VHS
Modern X - Ray Tubes Series
Color (PRO)
Explains tube ratings, heat monitoring systems and heat dissipation systems.
Industrial and Technical Education; Science - Physical
Dist - USNAC **Prod** - USVA

Modern X - Ray Tubes, Pt 4, Use and Abuse of X - Ray Tubes 20 MIN
U-matic / VHS
Modern X - Ray Tubes Series
Color (PRO)
Explains how tubes are damaged by equipment malfunction and improper operation. Discusses how to protect the tubes.
Industrial and Technical Education; Science; Science - Physical
Dist - USNAC **Prod** - USVA

Modern X - Ray Tubes, Pt 5, How to Select an X - Ray Tube 18 MIN
U-matic / VHS
Modern X - Ray Tubes Series
Color (PRO)
Explains recent development, construction and operation of radiographic equipment, and considerations in X - ray tube selection.
Industrial and Technical Education; Science; Science - Physical
Dist - USNAC **Prod** - USVA

Modern X - Ray Tubes, Pt 6, Focal Spot Measurements 17 MIN
VHS / U-matic
Modern X - Ray Tubes Series
Color (PRO)
Discusses the importance of focal spot size in high - resolution photography.
Industrial and Technical Education; Science; Science - Physical
Dist - USNAC **Prod** - USVA

Modern X - Ray Tubes, Pt 7, Magnification Procedures and Biased Focal Spots 17 MIN
U-matic / VHS
Modern X - Ray Tubes Series
Color (PRO)
Discusses the principles, techniques and problems of magnification focal spot integrity, including biased focal spots.
Industrial and Technical Education; Science; Science - Physical
Dist - USNAC **Prod** - USVA

Modern X - Ray Tubes, Pt 8, Single - Phase Vs Three - Phase X - Ray Tube Ratings 19 MIN
U-matic / VHS
Modern X - Ray Tubes Series
Color (PRO)
Explains how a three - phase apparatus is more efficient than a single - phase apparatus.
Industrial and Technical Education; Science; Science - Physical
Dist - USNAC **Prod** - USVA

Modern X - Ray Tubes Series
Modern X - Ray Tubes, Pt 1, Production of an X - Ray Tube 50 MIN
Modern X - Ray Tubes, Pt 2, Rotating Anode X - Ray Tubes, How they Function 25 MIN
Modern X - Ray Tubes, Pt 3, Heating and Cooling of X - Ray Tubes 20 MIN
Modern X - Ray Tubes, Pt 4, Use and Abuse of X - Ray Tubes 20 MIN
Modern X - Ray Tubes, Pt 5, How to Select an X - Ray Tube 18 MIN
Modern X - Ray Tubes, Pt 6, Focal Spot Measurements 17 MIN
Modern X - Ray Tubes, Pt 7, Magnification Procedures and Biased Focal Spots 17 MIN
Modern X - Ray Tubes, Pt 8, Single - Phase Vs Three - Phase X - Ray Tube Ratings 19 MIN
Dist - USNAC

Modernization 5 MIN
U-matic
See, Hear - the Middle East Series
Color (J)
Looks at the kaleidoscope of life in the modern Middle East and the strains of urbanization, an exploding population and sudden prosperity.
Geography - World; History - World; Religion and Philosophy
Dist - TVOTAR **Prod** - TVOTAR 1980

The Modernization of American liberal thought 60 MIN
VHS
Europe and America in the modern age - 1776 to the present series
Color (H C PRO)
$95.00 purchase
Presents a lecture by David M Kennedy. Focuses on a critical period in European and American history and on leaders of the time. Part of a 20 - part series that looks at the last two centuries in Europe and America. Series presents lectures by David M Kennedy and James Sheehan of Stanford University on such figures as Adam Smith, Marx, Lincoln, Washington, Jefferson, Freud, Margaret Sanger, Susan B Anthony and Jane Adams and their impact on the events of their day. For history resource material and continuing education courses.
Civics and Political Systems; History - United States; History - World
Dist - LANDMK

The Modernization of Merit Brass
VHS
Color (C PRO G)
$150.00 purchase _ #92.06
Focuses on statistical forecasting, cellular manufacturing, manufacturing and purchasing resources and finished goods inventory management, which provide the four major components of a modernized, integrated management system. Shows how the Merit Brass Company has made major improvements in customer service at modest cost and in record time. A Dale Flowers.
Business and Economics
Dist - INMASC

Modes and Music
16mm
B&W
Illustrates that with the same fingering a flute can produce two distinct notes, eight tones apart, and a clarinet two distinct notes, twelve tones apart. Shows how to explain this difference mathematically.
Mathematics
Dist - OPENU **Prod** - OPENU

Modest Mussorgski - Pictures at an Exhibition 37 MIN
U-matic / VHS
Color
Focuses on Mussorgski's most popular composition, Pictures At An Exhibition. Includes a performance of the work and an examination of the biographical circumstances surrounding the composition.
Fine Arts
Dist - FOTH **Prod** - FOTH

Modification of Radiation Injury in Mice 10 MIN
16mm
Color
LC FIE63-169
Shows the effects on mice of chemical protection by mercaptoethylguanidane (MEG) before irradiation and bone - marrow transplant after exposure to lethal doses of 900 R, as well as possible implications regarding treatment of some human disease.
Science; Science - Physical
Dist - USNAC **Prod** - USNRC 1958

Modified Davis Intubated Ureterotomy 15 MIN
16mm
Surgical Correction of Hydronephrosis, Pt 1 - Non - Dismembering 'Procedures Series
Color
LC 75-702260
Depicts a case in which the modified Davis intubated ureterotomy was the only procedure that could successfully correct the obstruction. Shows how the operation results in the almost complete return of normal function in the kidney.
Science
Dist - EATONL **Prod** - EATONL 1968

Modified Denis - Browne Urethroplasty for Hypospadias 10 MIN
16mm
Color
LC 75-702278
Explains that the second stage modified Denis - Browne urethroplasty is performed after an interval of at least 12 months following the initial chordee correction. Shows how the technique differs from the basic Denis - Browne procedure.
Science
Dist - EATONL **Prod** - EATONL 1971

Modified Diets 15 MIN
16mm
Color (J H C)
Explains modified diets, showing food groups and exchange lists. Includes restricted calorie, residue, fat, sodium and diabetic diets. Points out the reasons diets are usually prescribed and stresses the necessity of following the doctor's directions and accurately measuring quantities.
Health and Safety
Dist - SF **Prod** - SF 1968

Modified Martienssen Method Subharmonic Resonance 32 MIN
U-matic / VHS
Nonlinear Vibrations Series
B&W
Mathematics
Dist - MIOT **Prod** - MIOT

Modified Neurological Examination 19 MIN
VHS / U-matic / 16mm
Color (PRO C)
$330.00 purchase _ #380VI005
Demonstrates a brief screening examination that can quickly differentiate normality from disorder. Covers all major categories of neurological function.
Health and Safety
Dist - HSCIC **Prod** - HSCIC 1977

Modified Radical Mastectomy 27 MIN
16mm
Color (PRO)
Demonstrates the technique of complete mastectomy with preservation of both pectoral muscles and sub - total axillary dissection for carcinoma. Explains that its advantages, cosmetic and function, make it more acceptable to patients, and evidence suggests that it is as efficacious as conventional radical mastectomy in the treatment of breast cancer.
Health and Safety; Science
Dist - ACY **Prod** - ACYDGD 1971

Modified Retropublic Prostatectomy 16 MIN
16mm
Color
Shows a surgical procedure which has been performed by numerous urologists in this country, but has not been widely adopted. Provides rapid access to the hyperplastic prostate under excellent vision.
Health and Safety; Science - Natural
Dist - USVA **Prod** - USVA 1955

Modified Turner - Warwick Urethroplasty for Management of Deep Urethral Strictures 18 MIN
16mm
Color
Points out that management of strictures in the proximal bulbous and membranous urethra in adults and children has always been an enigma to the urologist. Presents a modification of the Turner Warwick urethroplasty which has been used successfully in 20 patients without the use of special instruments by using a routine perineal prostatectomy incision and performing the urethral - scrotal inlay anastomosis under direct vision through this incision.
Science
Dist - EATONL **Prod** - EATONL 1973

Modified Widman Flap 14 MIN
16mm
Color (PRO)
LC 77-701396
Describes a modifed Widman flap procedure for the patient with extensive interproximal pockets. Demonstrates the principles of flap design, access to the involved sites, tissue removal, planing of exposed root surfaces, bone recontouring and flap adaptation.
Health and Safety; Science
Dist - USNAC **Prod** - VADTC 1977

Modifiers - Adjectives and Adverbs 8 MIN
U-matic / VHS / 16mm
Basic Grammar Series
Color (P I)
LC 81-706573
Uses an animated circus to illustrate various adjectives and adverbs while the people discuss what modifiers do and how they can be told apart.
English Language
Dist - AIMS **Prod** - LEVYL 1981

Modifying drawings 119 MIN
VHS
First step for AutoCAD LT series
Color (G H VOC C PRO)
$49.95 purchase _ #AVT204V-T
Provides instruction on operating AutoCAD LT and Release 12 for Windows for all level of user. Focuses on 13 lessons to help users understand the basics of Edit; Selection Sets; UNDO; MOVE; COPY; MIRROR; ROTATE; SCALE; STRETCH; TRIM; OFFSET; GRIPS; and Changing Properties.
Computer Science
Dist - CAMV

Modifying drawings
VHS
First step for AutoCAD 13 series
Color (G H VOC C PRO)
$49.95 purchase _ #AVT304V-T
Describes the basics of AutoCAD 13 in a seven-part series. Focuses on the basics of editing. Includes Selection sets; Changing properties; GRIPS; TRIM; STRETCH; EXTEND; SCALE; and ROTATE commands.
Computer Science
Dist - CAMV

Modifying Recipes to Control Saturated Fats and Calories 14 MIN
16mm
Eat Right to Your Heart's Delight Series
Color (J H)
Shows the principles of recipe modification, aiming to reduce saturated fats, calories and cholesterol through the elimination of problem ingredients or substitutes. Emphasizes such dishes as baked lasagna, pancakes, beef stews and entrees with white sauce, including an extra section on gelatin salad with tips for low - fat topping. Tests all dishes and confirms the calorie analysis.
Health and Safety; Home Economics; Psychology
Dist - IPS **Prod** - IPS 1976

Modifying the Weather - the Case of the Man - made Desert 26 MIN
VHS / 16mm
Climate & Man Series
Color (J)
$149.00 purchase, $75.00 rental _ #OD - 2404
Examines the roles migration, uncontrolled water usage and desert irrigation methods have played in the creation of climatic disasters. The fourth of six installments of the Climate & Man Series.
Geography - World; Science - Physical
Dist - FOTH

Modmath 15 MIN
16mm / U-matic / VHS
Color (I) (FRENCH)
LC 80-700118;
Introduces the properties of mathematical sets, including transitivity, associativity and commutativity. Defines reflexive and symmetrical relationships.
Mathematics
Dist - IFB **Prod** - IFB 1975

Modular Scheduling and Elementary Schools 29 MIN
16mm
Color (C T)
LC 70-710822
Shows the experience of students, teachers and principals under the new modular scheduling design, and stresses the theme of the learner as a free inquirer. Portrays ideas and practices such as non - structured time, the open laboratory concept, small group - large group instruction, cross - gradedness, resource centers and departmentalization.
Education
Dist - EDUC **Prod** - EDUC 1970

Modulation 29 MIN
U-matic
Beginning piano - an adult approach series; Lesson 24
Color (H A)
Explains modulation. Reviews A - flat major scales and chords. Introduces E - flat major scales and chords.
Fine Arts
Dist - CDTEL **Prod** - COAST

Module 1, Inspiration - the Composer 15 MIN
U-matic / VHS
Arts Abound Series
Color (I)
Takes fifth and sixth grade students on visual field trips to where the arts are made, displayed or performed. Helps them understand, value and enjoy theatre, dance, music and the visual arts by exposing them to the people, the process and the performance of all kinds of arts. In five modules containing 16 fifteen minute segments.
Fine Arts
Dist - GPN **Prod** - WVIZTV

Module 1, Inspiration - the Director 15 MIN
VHS / U-matic
Arts Abound Series
Color (I)
Takes fifth and sixth grade students on visual field trips to where the arts are made, displayed or performed. Helps them understand, value and enjoy theatre, dance, music and the visual arts by exposing them to the people, the process and the performance of all kinds of arts. In five modules containing 16 fifteen minute segments.
Fine Arts
Dist - GPN **Prod** - WVIZTV

Module 1, Inspiration - the Playwright 15 MIN
U-matic / VHS
Arts Abound Series
Color (I)
Takes fifth and sixth grade students on visual field trips to where the arts are made, displayed or performed. Helps them understand, value and enjoy theatre, dance, music and the visual arts by exposing them to the people, the process and the performance of all kinds of arts. In five modules containing 16 fifteen minute segments.
Fine Arts
Dist - GPN **Prod** - WVIZTV

Module 1, Inspriation - the Choreographer 15 MIN
VHS / U-matic
Arts Abound Series
Color (I)
Takes fifth and sixth grade students on visual field trips to where the arts are made, displayed or performed. Helps them understand, value and enjoy theatre, dance, music and the visual arts by exposing them to the people, the process and the performance of all kinds of arts. In five modules containing 16 fifteen minute segments.
Fine Arts
Dist - GPN **Prod** - WVIZTV

Module 2, Running the Show - the Curator 15 MIN
U-matic / VHS
Arts Abound Series
Color (I)
Takes fifth and sixth grade students on visual field trips to where the arts are made, displayed or performed. Helps them understand, value and enjoy theatre, dance, music and the visual arts by exposing them to the people, the process and the performance of all kinds of arts. In five modules containing 16 fifteen minute segments.
Fine Arts
Dist - GPN **Prod** - WVIZTV

Module 3, the Team Backstage - Sets, Lighting, Costumes, Design 15 MIN
U-matic / VHS
Arts Abound Series
Color (I)
Takes fifth and sixth grade students on visual field trips to where the arts are made, displayed or performed. Helps them understand, value and enjoy theatre, dance, music and the visual arts by exposing them to the people, the process and the performance of all kinds of arts. In five modules containing 16 fifteen minute segments.
Fine Arts
Dist - GPN **Prod** - WVIZTV

Module 4, in the Spotlight - Classical Ballet 15 MIN
VHS / U-matic
Arts Abound Series
Color (I)
Takes fifth and sixth grade students on visual field trips to where the arts are made, displayed or performed. Helps them understand, value and enjoy theatre, dance, music and the visual arts by exposing them to the people, the process and the performance of all kinds of arts. In five modules containing 16 fifteen minute segments.
Fine Arts
Dist - GPN **Prod** - WVIZTV

Module 4, in the Spotlight - Ethnic Dance 15 MIN
U-matic / VHS
Arts Abound Series
Color (I)
Takes fifth and sixth grade students on visual field trips to where the arts are made, displayed or performed. Helps them understand, value and enjoy theatre, dance, music and the visual arts by exposing them to the people, the process and the performance of all kinds of arts. In five modules containing 16 fifteen minute segments.
Fine Arts
Dist - GPN **Prod** - WVIZTV

Module 4, in the Spotlight - Modern Dance 15 MIN
U-matic / VHS
Arts Abound Series
Color (I)
Takes fifth and sixth grade students on visual field trips to where the arts are made, displayed or performed. Helps them understand, value and enjoy theatre, dance, music and the visual arts by exposing them to the people, the process and the performance of all kinds of arts. In five modules containing 16 fifteen minute segments.
Fine Arts
Dist - GPN **Prod** - WVIZTV

Module 4, in the Spotlight - the Actor 15 MIN
U-matic / VHS
Arts Abound Series
Color (I)
Takes fifth and sixth grade students on visual field trips to where the arts are made, displayed or performed. Helps them understand, value and enjoy theatre, dance, music and the visual arts by exposing them to the people, the process and the performance of all kinds of arts. In five modules containing 16 fifteen minute segments.
Fine Arts
Dist - GPN **Prod** - WVIZTV

Module 4, in the Spotlight - the Musician 15 MIN
VHS / U-matic
Arts Abound Series
Color (I)
Takes fifth and sixth grade students on visual field trips to where the arts are made, displayed or performed. Helps them understand, value and enjoy theatre, dance, music and the visual arts by exposing them to the people, the process and the performance of all kinds of arts. In five modules containing 16 fifteen minute segments.
Fine Arts
Dist - GPN **Prod** - WVIZTV

Module 4, in the Spotlight - the Painter 15 MIN
VHS / U-matic
Arts Abound Series
Color (I)
Takes fifth and sixth grade students on visual field trips to where the arts are made, displayed or performed. Helps them understand, value and enjoy theatre, dance, music and the visual arts by exposing them to the people, the process and the performance of all kinds of arts. In five modules containing 16 fifteen minute segments.
Fine Arts
Dist - GPN **Prod** - WVIZTV

Module 4, in the Spotlight - the Sculptor 15 MIN
VHS / U-matic
Arts Abound Series
Color (I)
Takes fifth and sixth grade students on visual field trips to where the arts are made, displayed or performed. Helps them understand, value and enjoy theatre, dance, music and the visual arts by exposing them to the people, the process and the performance of all kinds of arts. In five modules containing 16 fifteen minute segments.
Fine Arts
Dist - GPN **Prod** - WVIZTV

Module 5, Synthesis - Architecture 15 MIN
U-matic / VHS
Arts Abound Series
Color (I)
Takes fifth and sixth grade students on visual field trips to where the arts are made, displayed or performed. Helps them understand, value and enjoy theatre, dance, music and the visual arts by exposing them to the people, the process and the performance of all kinds of arts. In five modules containing 16 fifteen minute segments.
Fine Arts
Dist - GPN **Prod** - WVIZTV

Module 5, Synthesis - Opera 15 MIN
U-matic / VHS
Arts Abound Series
Color (I)
Takes fifth and sixth grade students on visual field trips to where the arts are made, displayed or performed. Helps them understand, value and enjoy theatre, dance, music and the visual arts by exposing them to the people, the process and the performance of all kinds of arts. In five modules containing 16 fifteen minute segments.
Fine Arts
Dist - GPN **Prod** - WVIZTV

Module A - Bipolar Transistor Fundamentals and Basic Amplifier Circuits 45 MIN
VHS / U-matic
Linear Analog Integrated Circuits Series
Color (IND)
Presents and discusses characterics of diodes and bipolar transistors. Cites low - frequency, small - signal, input and output transistor models, and measuring methods of models shown. Gives methods of obtaining input - and

output - equivalent circuits of transistor amplifiers. Show how common - emitter, common - base and common - collector amplifier large - as well as small - signal characteristics are obtained. Gives expressions showing dependence of gain on operating point.
Industrial and Technical Education
Dist - COLOSU **Prod** - COLOSU

Module A - Introduction to the Computer 41 MIN
U-matic
Nibbles Series
Color (J H)
Explains ROM, RAM, CPU, DOS, pixels, cassettes, disks, monitors, receivers, synthesizer chips, disk drives, plotters and the fusion of music and graphics.
Computer Science; Education
Dist - TVOTAR **Prod** - TVOTAR 1984

Module B - Current Sources and Applications 45 MIN
U-matic / VHS
Linear Analog Integrated Circuits Series
Color (IND)
Presents ideal and actual current - source characteristics and methods of output - characteristic measurement. Discusses in detail basic, widely used integrated circuit. Develops more accurate and versatile current sources, using modifications on basic circuit. The several current sources are compared. Shows use of current sources for getting large signal gains for the common emitter amplifier.
Industrial and Technical Education
Dist - COLOSU **Prod** - COLOSU

Module B - Programming 41 MIN
U-matic
Nibbles Series
Color (J H)
Examines the development of educational software and systems. Looks at high level language, machine language, compilers, interpreters and the fundamental concepts of repetition and decision.
Computer Science; Education
Dist - TVOTAR **Prod** - TVOTAR 1984

Module Blue - Body I 15 MIN
VHS / U-matic
Wordsmith Series
Color (I)
Discusses root words which relate to the body. Includes manu, ped, pod, pus and dent.
English Language
Dist - AITECH **Prod** - NITC 1975

Module Blue - Body II 15 MIN
U-matic / VHS
Wordsmith Series
Color (I)
Discusses root words which relate to the body. Includes opt, ops, derm, ocul, cap, capit and corp.
English Language
Dist - AITECH **Prod** - NITC 1975

Module Blue - Fire 15 MIN
VHS / U-matic
Wordsmith Series
Color (I)
Discusses root words which relate to fire. Includes sol, helio, pyr, torr, therm and ign.
English Language
Dist - AITECH **Prod** - NITC 1975

Module Blue - Looking 15 MIN
VHS / U-matic
Wordsmith Series
Color (I)
Discusses root words which relate to looking. Includes spec, vis, vid and orama.
English Language
Dist - AITECH **Prod** - NITC 1975

Module Blue - Sound 15 MIN
VHS / U-matic
Wordsmith Series
Color (I)
Discusses root words which relate to sound. Includes audi and son.
English Language
Dist - AITECH **Prod** - NITC 1975

Module Brown - Leading 15 MIN
VHS / U-matic
Wordsmith Series
Color (I)
Discusses root words which relate to leading. Includes reg, rect, duc, duct, cracy and agog.
English Language
Dist - AITECH **Prod** - NITC 1975

Module Brown - Nature 15 MIN
U-matic / VHS
Wordsmith Series
Color (I)
Discusses root words which relate to nature. Includes terr, geo, nat and eco.
English Language
Dist - AITECH **Prod** - NITC 1975

Module Brown - Position 15 MIN
U-matic / VHS
Wordsmith Series
Color (I)
Discusses root words which relate to position. Includes pos, sta, sed and sid.
English Language
Dist - AITECH **Prod** - NITC 1975

Module Brown - Transportation I 15 MIN
VHS / U-matic
Wordsmith Series
Color (I)
Discusses root words which relate to transportation. Includes mot, mob, mov and drom.
English Language
Dist - AITECH **Prod** - NITC 1975

Module Brown - Transportation II 15 MIN
VHS / U-matic
Wordsmith Series
Color (I)
Discusses root words which relate to transportation. Includes it, port and fug.
English Language
Dist - AITECH **Prod** - NITC 1975

Module C - Impact on Society 73 MIN
U-matic
Nibbles Series
Color (J H)
Examines why computers don't have human intelligence and how computer assisted instruction developed. Demonstrates the computer's current impact as a storage medium, a database, a teaching tool and a help in running homes and businesses.
Computer Science; Education
Dist - TVOTAR **Prod** - TVOTAR 1984

Module C - the Differential Amplifier 45 MIN
U-matic / VHS
Linear Analog Integrated Circuits Series
Color (IND)
Presents large and small - signal characteristics of the differential amplifier. Shows methods for obtaining input - and output - equivalent circuits. Give expressions for the common - mode and differential - mode gain. Shows effects of mismatches in saturation currents and resistor values. Defines and calculates offset voltage and offset current. Discusses an integrated - circuit differential amplifier with large signal gain and large common - mode rejection ratio.
Industrial and Technical Education
Dist - COLOSU **Prod** - COLOSU

Module D - Class A, B, and AB Output Stages and the MuA741 Operational Amplifier 45 MIN
U-matic / VHS
Linear Analog Integrated Circuits Series
Color (IND)
Gives large - and small - signal characterics of Class - A emitter - follower output stage. Shows power and efficiency relations. Discusses crossover distortion present in the Class - B emitter - follower output stage, and methods for eliminating it by using class - AB operations shown. Uses the muA741 operational amplifier as example to show how the differential, the intermediate, and output stages are put together to design an integrated circuit operational amplifier.
Industrial and Technical Education
Dist - COLOSU **Prod** - COLOSU

Module D - Electronics and Technology 13 MIN
U-matic
Nibbles Series
Color (J H)
Examines technological aspects of computers including the difference between analog and digital systems, binary code, and the computer as a logic machine.
Computer Science; Education
Dist - TVOTAR **Prod** - TVOTAR 1984

Module E - Information Processing 31 MIN
U-matic
Nibbles Series
Color (J H)
Examines the computer as information processor including data structures, modems, networks, word processors and spreadsheets.
Computer Science; Education
Dist - TVOTAR **Prod** - TVOTAR 1984

Module Eight - Current and Ammeters
VHS / U-matic
D C Electronics Series
Color
Includes The Ammeter (Theory) and Measuring Current (Lab Job).
Industrial and Technical Education
Dist - WFVTAE **Prod** - WFVTAE

Module Eight - R L Circuits
U-matic / VHS
A C Electronics Series
Color
Includes Inductive A C Circuits (Theory), Dual Trace Oscilloscope - Measuring Voltage and Dual Trace Oscilloscope - Measuring Phase Shift (Lab Jobs).
Industrial and Technical Education
Dist - WFVTAE **Prod** - WFVTAE

Module Eleven - Circuit Analysis
U-matic / VHS
D C Electronics Series
Color
Includes Kirchhoff's Law and Superposition/Network Theorems (Theory) and Resistance Bridge Circuits (Lab Job).
Industrial and Technical Education
Dist - WFVTAE **Prod** - WFVTAE

Module Eleven - R L C Circuits
U-matic / VHS
A C Electronics Series
Color
Includes R L C Circuits and Introduction To Resonance (Theory).
Industrial and Technical Education
Dist - WFVTAE **Prod** - WFVTAE

Module Five - Capacitive Circuits
VHS / U-matic
A C Electronics Series
Color
Includes Capacitive A C Circuits (Theory) and Capacitive Reactance and Impedance (Lab Job).
Industrial and Technical Education
Dist - WFVTAE **Prod** - WFVTAE

Module 5 - Getting Approval from Authorized Departments 12 MIN
VHS / 16mm
Manager - to - Manager Series
Color (PRO)
$300.00 purchase, $85.00 rental, $50.00 preview
Counsels on interactions between managers and subordinates. Uses vignettes to explain how to obtain approval for business projects. Includes a teacher's guide and workbook. Created by Jack Noon, Midi, Inc.
Business and Economics; Psychology; Sociology
Dist - UTM

Module Five - Resistance
U-matic / VHS
D C Electronics Series
Color
Includes Resistance, Series Parallel Resistive Circuits and the Ohmmeter (Theory), The Calculator - Prefixes and Resistance Problems (Skill Module), Measuring Resistance, Using the Lab Breadboard, Continuity, Opens and Shorts and Measuring Resistance Characteristics (Lab Jobs). With a diskette on Color Code.
Industrial and Technical Education
Dist - WFVTAE **Prod** - WFVTAE

Module Four - Batteries and Voltage Drops
U-matic / VHS
D C Electronics Series
Color
Includes Voltage Rises and Voltage Drops (Theory) and the Calculator - Getting Started (Skill Module).
Industrial and Technical Education
Dist - WFVTAE **Prod** - WFVTAE

Module 4 - Helping Colleagues Handle Problems 13 MIN
VHS / 16mm
Manager - to - Manager Series
Color (PRO)
$300.00 purchase, $85.00 rental, $50.00 preview
Counsels on interactions between managers and subordinates. Uses vignettes to show how to counsel and support colleagues dealing with difficult situations. Teaches diplomacy, communication skills, and objectivity. Includes a teacher's guide and workbook. Created by Jack Noon, Midi, Inc.
Business and Economics; Psychology; Sociology
Dist - UTM

Module 4 - Making a difference
VHS
Power of positive students series
Color (K P I T)
$150.00 purchase _ #B020 - V8
Encourages student acceptance and tolerance for those who are different or special, part a series giving children K - 5 the foundation for lasting self - esteem, self - awareness, confidence, and positive decision - making skills. Introduces students to real - life problems. Begins with the Positively Solving Problems segment, which guides through a problem - solving skills sequence.

Students practice this sequence to resolve the dilemma presented, and eventually apply it to their own problems. Includes two videos, two audiocassettes for teachers, a Teacher's Video Guide, and a Parent's Planner with 30 activities for parents and kids.
Guidance and Counseling; Psychology
Dist - ETRASS **Prod** - ETRASS

Module Four - Resistive Circuits and Introduction to Capacitors
VHS / U-matic
A C Electronics Series
Color
Includes A C Resistive Circuits and Introduction to Capacitors (Theory).
Industrial and Technical Education
Dist - WFVTAE **Prod** - WFVTAE

Module Fourteen - Capacitive Circuits
VHS / U-matic
D C Electronics Series
Color
Includes R C and L R Time Constants (Theory), R C Time Constants, Capacitors in Series and Parallel, and Using Capacitors (Lab Jobs).
Industrial and Technical Education
Dist - WFVTAE **Prod** - WFVTAE

Module Green - Numbers I 15 MIN
VHS / U-matic
Wordsmith Series
Color (I)
Discusses root words which relate to numbers. Includes uni, bi, tw and mono.
English Language
Dist - AITECH **Prod** - NITC 1975

Module Green - Numbers II 15 MIN
U-matic / VHS
Wordsmith Series
Color (I)
Discusses root words which relate to numbers. Includes hemi, semi, amphi, ambi, pan, panto, multi and poly.
English Language
Dist - AITECH **Prod** - NITC 1975

Module Green - Numbers III 15 MIN
U-matic / VHS
Wordsmith Series
Color (I)
Discusses root words which relate to numbers. Includes tri, quart, quadr, dec and cent.
English Language
Dist - AITECH **Prod** - NITC 1975

Module Green - Walk and Run 15 MIN
U-matic / VHS
Wordsmith Series
Color (I)
Discusses root words which relate to ambulation. Includes ambul, grad, gress and cur.
English Language
Dist - AITECH **Prod** - NITC 1975

Module Green - Water 15 MIN
VHS / U-matic
Wordsmith Series
Color (I)
Discusses root words which relate to water. Includes aqua, mar, hydr and flu.
English Language
Dist - AITECH **Prod** - NITC 1975

Module Nine - Transformer Theory
VHS / U-matic
A C Electronics Series
Color
Includes Transformers I (Theory) and Measuring Transformer Characteristics (Lab Job).
Industrial and Technical Education; Science - Physical
Dist - WFVTAE **Prod** - WFVTAE

Module Nine - Voltmeters and Ohmmeters
U-matic / VHS
D C Electronics Series
Color
Includes The Multimeter (Theory) and Loading Effects of Voltmeters(Lab Job).
Industrial and Technical Education
Dist - WFVTAE **Prod** - WFVTAE

Module One - Introduction to Alternating Current
U-matic / VHS
A C Electronics Series
Color
Includes Introduction To Alternating Current (Theory).
Industrial and Technical Education
Dist - WFVTAE **Prod** - WFVTAE

Module 1 - Overcoming Resistance to Change 12 MIN
VHS / 16mm
Manager - to - Manager Series
Color (PRO)
$300.00 purchase, $85.00 rental, $50.00 preview
Counsels on interactions between managers and colleagues and challenging situations which may arise in the business context. Uses vignettes to discuss how to overcome the fears that come with change. Includes a leader's guide and workbook. Created by Jack Noon, Midi, Inc.
Business and Economics; Psychology; Sociology
Dist - UTM

Module 1 - Self awareness
VHS
Power of positive students series
Color (K P I T)
$150.00 purchase _ #B017 - V8
Shows how to discover personal strengths and overcome weakenesses, part of a series giving children K - 5 the foundation for lasting self - esteem, self - awareness, confidence, and positive decision - making skills. Introduces students to real - life problems. Begins with the Positively Solving Problems segment, which guides through a problem - solving skills sequence. Students practice this sequence to resolve the dilemma presented, and eventually apply it to their own problems. Includes two videos, two audiocassettes for teachers, a Teacher's Video Guide, and a Parent's Planner with 30 activities for parents and kids.
Guidance and Counseling; Psychology
Dist - ETRASS **Prod** - ETRASS

Module Orange - Communication 15 MIN
U-matic / VHS
Wordsmith Series
Color (I)
Discusses root words which relate to communication. Includes tele, graph, gram, scrib, script, her and hes.
English Language
Dist - AITECH **Prod** - NITC 1975

Module Orange - Connection 15 MIN
U-matic / VHS
Wordsmith Series
Color (I)
Discusses root words which relate to connection. Includes con, com, co and syn.
English Language
Dist - AITECH **Prod** - NITC 1975

Module Orange - Measure and Metrics 15 MIN
VHS / U-matic
Wordsmith Series
Color (I)
Discusses root words which relate to measurement and the metric system. Includes meter and metr.
English Language
Dist - AITECH **Prod** - NITC 1975

Module Orange - Relatives 15 MIN
U-matic / VHS
Wordsmith Series
Color (I)
Discusses root words which relate to relatives. Includes mater, matr, pater, patr and ped.
English Language
Dist - AITECH **Prod** - NITC 1975

Module Orange - Twist and Turn 15 MIN
U-matic / VHS
Wordsmith Series
Color (I)
Discusses root words which relate to twisting and turning. Includes tor, trop, vert and vers.
English Language
Dist - AITECH **Prod** - NITC 1975

Module Red - Animals I 15 MIN
U-matic / VHS
Wordsmith Series
Color (I)
Discusses root words which relate to animals. Includes anim, zo, can, cyn and ine.
English Language
Dist - AITECH **Prod** - NITC 1975

Module Red - Animals II 15 MIN
VHS / U-matic
Wordsmith Series
Color (I)
Discusses root words which relate to animals. Includes bio, greg and drom.
English Language
Dist - AITECH **Prod** - NITC 1975

Module Red - Cutting 15 MIN
U-matic / VHS
Wordsmith Series
Color (I)
Discusses root words which relate to cutting. Includes cis, sect, tom and ec.
English Language
Dist - AITECH **Prod** - NITC 1975

Module Red - Serendipity 15 MIN
U-matic / VHS
Wordsmith Series
Color (I)
Presents an anecdotal program which emphasizes various word idioms.
English Language
Dist - AITECH **Prod** - NITC 1975

Module Red - Time 15 MIN
VHS / U-matic
Wordsmith Series
Color (I)
Discusses root words which relate to time. Includes chron, temp, ann, enn, pre and post.
English Language
Dist - AITECH **Prod** - NITC 1975

Module Seven - Inductive Circuits
VHS / U-matic
A C Electronics Series
Color
Includes Introduction to Inductors (Theory) and Inductive Reactance and Impedance (Lab Job).
Industrial and Technical Education
Dist - WFVTAE **Prod** - WFVTAE

Module Seven - Magnetism
VHS / U-matic
D C Electronics Series
Color
Includes Magnetism and A C And D C Generators (Theory), and Electromagnetism, and Magnetic and Electromagnetic Devices (Lab Jobs).
Industrial and Technical Education; Science - Physical
Dist - WFVTAE **Prod** - WFVTAE

Module Six - Math Applications in a C Circuit
VHS / U-matic
A C Electronics Series
Color
Includes Math Applications (Theory).
Industrial and Technical Education; Mathematics
Dist - WFVTAE **Prod** - WFVTAE

Module Six - Ohm's Law and Power
U-matic / VHS
D C Electronics Series
Color
Includes Ohm's Law and Power (Theory), The Calculator - Prefixes and Ohm's Law Problems (Skill Module), Verifying Ohm's Law and Power (Lab Jobs).
Industrial and Technical Education; Science - Physical
Dist - WFVTAE **Prod** - WFVTAE

Module Ten - Series, Parallel and Voltage Divider Circuits
U-matic / VHS
D C Electronics Series
Color
Includes Series - Parallel Resistive Circuits (Theory) and Voltage Dividers (Theory).
Industrial and Technical Education
Dist - WFVTAE **Prod** - WFVTAE

Module Ten - Transformer Applications
VHS / U-matic
A C Electronics Series
Color
Includes Transformers II (Theory), Transformer Loading Effects and Transformers In - Phase and Out - of - Phase (Lab Jobs).
Industrial and Technical Education
Dist - WFVTAE **Prod** - WFVTAE

Module Thirteen - Inductance and Capacitance
VHS / U-matic
D C Electronics Series
Color
Includes Inductors and Capacitors (Theory).
Industrial and Technical Education
Dist - WFVTAE **Prod** - WFVTAE

Module Thirteen - Parallel Resonance and Filters
U-matic / VHS
A C Electronics Series
Color
Includes Series Resonance/Parallel Resonance (Theory), Parallel Resonance, Band - Pass Band - Stop Filters and Low - Pass and High - Pass Filters (Lab Jobs).
Industrial and Technical Education
Dist - WFVTAE **Prod** - WFVTAE

Module Three - a C Measurements
U-matic / VHS
A C Electronics Series
Color
Includes Oscilloscopes (Theory), The Oscilloscope - Basic Operations and The Oscilloscope - Determining Period and Frequency (Skill Modules).

Industrial and Technical Education
Dist - WFVTAE **Prod** - WFVTAE

Module 3 - Dealing with Difficult People 11 MIN
VHS / 16mm
Manager - to - Manager Series
Color (PRO)
$300.00 purchase, $85.00 rental, $50.00 preview
Counsels on interactions between managers and subordinates. Uses vignettes to explain dealing with difficult people in the workplace. Includes a teacher's guide and workbook. Created by Jack Noon, Midi, Inc.
Business and Economics; Psychology; Sociology
Dist - UTM

Module Three - Electromotive Force
U-matic / VHS
D C Electronics Series
Color
Includes Electromotive Force (Theory), The Voltmeter (Theory), Meter Scales, The Analog Multimeter and The Digital Multimeter (Skill Modules), and Measuring Voltage (Lab Job).
Industrial and Technical Education
Dist - WFVTAE **Prod** - WFVTAE

Module 3 - Enthusiasm and coping skills
VHS
Power of positive students series
Color (K P I T)
$150.00 purchase _ #B019 - V8
Stresses the value of organization and communication skills, part of a series giving children K - 5 the foundation for lasting self - esteem, self - awareness, confidence, and positive decision - making skills. Introduces students to real - life problems. Begins with the Positively Solving Problems segment, which guides them through a problem - solving skills sequence. Students practice this sequence to resolve the dilemma presented, and eventually apply it to their own problems. Includes two videos, two audiocassettes for teachers, a Teacher's Video Guide, and a Parent's Planner with 30 activities for parents and kids.
Guidance and Counseling; Psychology
Dist - ETRASS **Prod** - ETRASS

Module Twelve - Series Resonance
VHS / U-matic
A C Electronics Series
Color
Includes Series Resonance/Parallel Resonance (Theory) and Series Resonance and Bandwidth Measurement (Lab Job).
Industrial and Technical Education
Dist - WFVTAE **Prod** - WFVTAE

Module Twelve - Thevenin's and Norton's Theorems
VHS / U-matic
D C Electronics Series
Color
Includes Superposition/Network Theorems (Theory).
Industrial and Technical Education; Science - Physical
Dist - WFVTAE **Prod** - WFVTAE

Module Two - Current Flow and Circuits
VHS / U-matic
D C Electronics Series
Color
Includes Scientific Notation and Metric Prefixes (Theory), Volts, Amps, Ohms, Watts (Skill Module) and a diskette on Prefixes.
Industrial and Technical Education
Dist - WFVTAE **Prod** - WFVTAE

Module 2 - Gaining Cooperation from Peers 11 MIN
VHS / 16mm
Manager - to - Manager Series
Color (PRO)
$300.00 purchase, $85.00 rental, $50.00 preview
Counsels on interactions between managers and subordinates. Uses vignettes to discuss how to structure cooperative management efforts. Includes a teacher's guide and workbook. Created by Jack Noon, Midi, Inc.
Business and Economics; Psychology; Sociology
Dist - UTM

Module 2 - Goals and expectations
VHS
Power of positive students series
Color (K P I T)
$150.00 purchase _ #B018 - V8
Helps children to set realistic goals and cope with temporary setbacks, part of a series giving children K - 5 the foundation for self - esteem, self - awareness, confidence, and positive decision - making skills. Introduces students to real - life problems. Begins with the Positively Solving Problems segment, which guides them through a problem - solving skills sequence. Students practice this sequence to resolve the dilemma presented, and eventually apply it to their own problems. Includes two videos, two audiocassettes for teachers, a Teacher's Video Guide, and a Parent's Planner with 30 activities for parents and kids.
Guidance and Counseling; Psychology
Dist - ETRASS **Prod** - ETRASS

Module Two - the Sine Wave and a C Values
U-matic / VHS
A C Electronics Series
Color
Includes Characteristics of the Sine Wave (Theory), and Measuring A C Voltage (Lab Job).
Industrial and Technical Education; Science - Physical
Dist - WFVTAE **Prod** - WFVTAE

Module Yellow - Food 15 MIN
U-matic / VHS
Wordsmith Series
Color (I)
Discusses root words which relate to food. Includes carn, coct, vor and sal.
English Language
Dist - AITECH **Prod** - NITC 1975

Module Yellow - Form 15 MIN
U-matic / VHS
Wordsmith Series
Color (I)
Discusses root words which relate to form. Includes form, lic, ly and morph.
English Language
Dist - AITECH **Prod** - NITC 1975

Module Yellow - Potpourri 15 MIN
VHS / U-matic
Wordsmith Series
Color (I)
Presents an anecdotal program which emphasizes various word idioms and homonyms.
English Language
Dist - AITECH **Prod** - NITC 1975

Module Yellow - Size 15 MIN
U-matic / VHS
Wordsmith Series
Color (I)
Discusses root words which relate to size. Includes magn, mega, megalo, equ and min.
English Language
Dist - AITECH **Prod** - NITC 1975

Module Yellow - Talking 15 MIN
U-matic / VHS
Wordsmith Series
Color (I)
Discusses root words which relate to talking. Includes dict, loqu and log.
English Language
Dist - AITECH **Prod** - NITC 1975

Mog - the Forgetful Cat - Pt 6 17 MIN
VHS
Words and Pictures Series
Color (P)
$49.00 purchase _ #548 - 9870
Uses animated stories to improve reading and vocabulary skills. Discusses the story content of each program and suggests several activities that relate to the story and the lessons learned. Part 6 of the seven part series features an intriguing twist - the author - illustrator is shown at home as she sketches Mog's story.
English Language; Fine Arts; Literature and Drama
Dist - FI **Prod** - BBCTV 1984

The Moghul Emperors 29 MIN
U-matic / VHS
Journey into India Series
Color (G)
MV=$195.00
Records the history of the Moghul dynasty from Babur, who conquered India, through Akbar, to Shah Jahan who built the Taj Mahal.
Geography - World; History - World
Dist - LANDMK **Prod** - LANDMK 1986

Mogul Mike Presents Ski Sense and Safety 22 MIN
U-matic / VHS / 16mm
Color
Outlines the responsibilities of a safe skier, the basic elements of ski courtesy and the major aspects of ski safety. Uses animation and live sequences of ski scenes to entertain and instruct every skier, beginner to advanced.
Health and Safety; Physical Education and Recreation
Dist - ATHI **Prod** - ATHI

Mohammed Reza Pahlavi - politics of oil 24 MIN
U-matic / VHS / 16mm
Leaders of the 20th century - portraits of power series
Color (H C A)
LC 80-700037
Deals with the rise and fall of the Shah of Iran. Tells how he succeeded his father in 1941 and was sent into exile after the return of the Ayatollah in 1979. Originally shown on the Canadian television program Portraits Of Power.
Biography; Civics and Political Systems; History - World; Social Science
Dist - LCOA **Prod** - NIELSE 1980

Mohawk 27 MIN
U-matic / VHS / 16mm
Insight Series
Color; B&W (J)
LC 75-700941
Presents a drama about an angry Mohawk Indian who decides to meditate before the doors of St Patrick's Cathedral. Deals with his confrontation with a policeman and with a priest and attempts to answer questions about meditation and prayer.
Guidance and Counseling; Religion and Philosophy; Social Science; Sociology
Dist - PAULST **Prod** - PAULST 1974

Mohawk 17 MIN
U-matic
Color
Discusses modification and updating of the Grumman Mohawk.
Civics and Political Systems
Dist - WSTGLC **Prod** - WSTGLC

Mohawk Basketmaking - a Cultural Profile 28 MIN
16mm / U-matic / VHS
Color (H C G T A)
Documents the art of basketmaking as practiced by Mary Adams, a nationally recognized Mohawk artist. Adams leads the viewer through the creation of a basket, from shaving and dying the black ash splints to weaving them into intricate designs, while narrating the story of her youth and of her people's struggle to survive.
Fine Arts; Social Science; Sociology
Dist - PSU **Prod** - PSU 1980

Moi Aussi Je Parle Francais - La Beauce 28 MIN
16mm
Color (FRENCH)
_ #106C 0278 950
Geography - World
Dist - CFLMDC **Prod** - NFBC 1978

Moi Aussi Je Parle Francais - L'Acadie 28 MIN
16mm
Color (FRENCH)
_ #106C 0278 950
Geography - World
Dist - CFLMDC **Prod** - NFBC 1978

Moi pilote - 1
VHS
French language for primary - pilote series
Color; PAL (I J)
PdS29.50 purchase
Provides an introduction to key vocabularies and structures for pupils beginnng French. Includes greetings, numbers, names, birthdays, ages, dates, family and pets. Part of a four - part series on French for beginners at key stage 2 and 3. Includes teacher's notes. Produced by KETV in the United Kingdom.
Foreign Language
Dist - EMFVL

The Moieties 9 MIN
16mm
Color (G)
$30.00 rental
Merges the filmmaker's heartbeat in contrapuntal rhythm with beads of light searching out the 'beloved.'
Fine Arts .
Dist - CANCIN **Prod** - DOBERG 1978

Moirage 8 MIN
16mm
Color
Presents a study in opticular illusions, pattern superimposition producing other patterns and illusions of three dimensionality.
Fine Arts; Industrial and Technical Education
Dist - VANBKS **Prod** - VANBKS

Moire 8 MIN
16mm
Color (H C A J) (SPANISH)
LC 75-700286
Shows kinetic works of Venezuelan artist J M Cruxent.
Fine Arts
Dist - MOMALA **Prod** - OOAS 1970

Moiseyev Ballet 120 MIN
VHS
Color (G)

$29.95 purchase_#1395
Displays colorful costumes, daring acrobatics and exciting Russian dance and folk music in performances by the Moiseyev Ballet. Features the ballet company's greatest works.
Fine Arts
Dist - KULTUR

Moiseyev dance company 70 MIN
VHS
Color (G A)
$39.95 purchase
Features the Moiseyev Dance Company in eight performances of Russian folk dancing.
Fine Arts
Dist - PBS **Prod** - WNETTV

The Moist Coniferous Forest 18 MIN
VHS / U-matic
Color (H C)
$43.95 purchase _ #52 2408B
Introduces the three main subdivisions of the moist coniferous forest biome, as Sitka Spruce Forest, Coastal Redwood Forest and Cascade Forest. Also discusses human use of the forest for wood products and techniques for forest management. Video version of 35mm filmstrip program, with live open and close.
Science - Natural
Dist - CBSC **Prod** - BMEDIA

Moisture Proofing Electrical and Type Connectors 20 MIN
16mm
Color
LC 74-705161
Tells how to apply synthetic rubber to electrical connections, and how to mix, test and store potting compound.
Industrial and Technical Education
Dist - USNAC **Prod** - USN 1957

Mojo and the Russians 15 MIN
VHS
Storybound series
Color (I)
#E375; LC 90-713284
Tells the story, 'Mojo and the Russians' by Walter Dean Myers, which follows a young boy and his gang from the streets of Harlem to the Russian consulate, the New York Police and the FBI. Part of a 16 - part series designed to lead viewers to the library to find and finish the stories they encounter in the series.
English Language; Literature and Drama; Social Science
Dist - GPN **Prod** - CTI 1980
CTI

Moko Jumbie - traditional stilt walkers 15 MIN
VHS / 16mm
Color (J H G)
$400.00, $195.00 purchase, $60.00, $50.00 rental
Shows the art, craft, dance and history of the moko jumbie - dancing spirit, 10 - foot - high stilt walkers who appear at street festivals in New York City, at Carnival celebrations in the Caribbean and during religious ceremonies in West Africa. Gives the background of the costume and dance movements and the origins of the moko jumbie in West Africa. Features two moko jumbies as narrators.
Fine Arts; Geography - World; History - United States; Sociology
Dist - FLMLIB **Prod** - KRAMRK 1991

Molala Harai 19 MIN
16mm
Color (J)
LC 72-702915
Uses animation to tell the story behind a set of stamps designed by the Reverend Bert Brown, missionary and part - time artist in the territory of papua and New Guinea.
Geography - World; Social Science
Dist - AUIS **Prod** - ANAIB 1971

Molar Mass by Elevation of the Boiling Point 20 MIN
U-matic / VHS
Experiment - Chemistry Series
Color (C)
$249.00, $149.00 purchase _ #AD - 1063
Teaches linear plotting of data to determine the proportionality constant in the linear relationship between boiling point elevation and solute concentration. Part of a series on experiments in chemistry.
Education; Psychology; Science; Science - Physical
Dist - FOTH **Prod** - FOTH

Molasses and the American Heritage 15 MIN
16mm
Color
LC 80-701041
Uses scenes from American history and recipes to tell the story of molasses in the United States and to show how its use has influenced many traditional foods.
Home Economics
Dist - KLEINW **Prod** - KLEINW 1979

Mold 7 MIN
U-matic / VHS
Color (C)
$229.00, $129.00 purchase _ #AD - 1283
Looks at the growth and reproduction of mold. Shows the introduction of spores into an agar medium, their germination and production of thin mycelia which spread in to branches, and the development of new mold colonies.
Science - Natural
Dist - FOTH **Prod** - FOTH

Mold maker 5 MIN
U-matic
Good work series
Color (H)
Provides useful, up to date information on various occupations to aid high school students in career selection. Available in five series of ten jobs each.
Education; Guidance and Counseling; Industrial and Technical Education
Dist - TVOTAR **Prod** - TVOTAR 1981

Mold making and casting of the face and foot 19 MIN
VHS
Color (G)
$225.00 purchase _ #6875
Uses two aspects of the human form - the face and the foot - to demonstrate fundamental mold making and casting procedures. Illustrates plaster bandages and sand casting. Emphasizes safety considerations as well as correct procedures.
Fine Arts
Dist - UCALG **Prod** - UCALG 1988

The Moldau 15 MIN
U-matic / VHS / 16mm
Color
Follows the Moldau River. Blends music with the towns, cities and countryside of Czechoslovakia.
Geography - World; History - World
Dist - KAWVAL **Prod** - KAWVAL

Molded Papier Mache 14 MIN
Videoreel / VT2
Living Better II Series
Color
Shows how to use papier mache to make bowls and vases.
Fine Arts; Home Economics
Dist - PBS **Prod** - MAETEL

Molder of dreams 96 MIN
VHS
Color (G A R)
$120.00 purchase _ #36 - 80 - 2025
Profiles the life of Guy Doud, a social outcast as a child. Shows that Doud achieved his goals and eventually was named National Teacher of the Year. Produced by Focus on the Family Ministries.
Education
Dist - APH

Molders of Troy 90 MIN
VHS / U-matic
Color
Centers on Brian Duffy, an Irish immigrant who overcame ethnic pressures to organize Troy's Iron Molders Union into one of the strongest unions in the country.
Business and Economics; History - United States; Sociology
Dist - PBS **Prod** - WMHTTV 1980

Molding a Horizontal Cored Part 22 MIN
16mm
Foundry Practice Series Floor Molding, No 4; Floor molding; No 4
B&W
LC FIE52-112
Shows how to use a horizontal core, a split pattern, chaplets and chaplet supports, how to gate a mold to pour a thin casting and how to clean a casting.
Industrial and Technical Education
Dist - USNAC **Prod** - USOE 1945

Molding a Valve Body 25 MIN
16mm
B&W
LC FIE52-113
Demonstrates use of a split pattern and multipart dry sand core, how to gate a mold for rapid, uniform distribution of clean metals, and how to locate a core and seal the core prints.
Industrial and Technical Education
Dist - USNAC **Prod** - USOE 1945

Molding and picture frame 30 MIN
VHS
Woodworking video series
Color (G)
$39.95 purchase _ #255
Explains constructing molding and picture frames. Shows how to choose stock, tools, materials, design, assemble and finish both projects.
Home Economics; Industrial and Technical Education
Dist - DIYVC **Prod** - DIYVC

Molding and Picture Frame - Molding
VHS
Woodworking Series
(G)
$19.95_SH405
Covers choosing stock, tools and materials, design preparation and installation of baseboard, chair rail and crown molding, cutting profiles, bevel cuts, finishing touches. Picture frames - Covers choosing stock, design cutting profiles, bevel cuts, assembly of frame, finishing touches.
Industrial and Technical Education
Dist - AAVIM **Prod** - AAVIM 1989

Molding on a Jolt Roll - Over Pattern Draw Machine 23 MIN
16mm
Foundry Practice Series Machine Molding; Machine molding
B&W
LC FIE52-116
Explains the jolt roll - over pattern draw machine. Shows how To fill the drag and jolt it, draw the Pattern, set the drag and cope pattern plates, fill the cope and jolt it, and finish and close the mold.
Industrial and Technical Education
Dist - USNAC **Prod** - USOE 1945

Molding on a Jolt Squeeze Machine 10 MIN
16mm
B&W
LC FIE52-114
Shows the principles of the jolt squeeze molding machine, how to roll the mold, fill the cope and apply pressboard, squeeze the mold, draw the pattern, and finish and close the mold.
Industrial and Technical Education
Dist - USNAC **Prod** - USOE 1945

Molding Part Having a Vertical Core 19 MIN
16mm
B&W
Demonstrates how to mold a gate and riser, make a pouring basin, vent a mold to permit the escape of core gases and locate a vertical core in a mold.
Industrial and Technical Education
Dist - USNAC **Prod** - USOE 1944

Molding Part with Deep Green Sand Core 25 MIN
16mm
B&W
LC FIE52-109
Explains the use of a follow board with a thin boxlike pattern. Shows how to reinforce a green sand core with nails, locate sprue and watch - up pins, use gaggers and ram and vent a green sand core.
Industrial and Technical Education
Dist - USNAC **Prod** - USOE 1945

Molding with a Gated Pattern 11 MIN
16mm
Foundry Practice Series Bench Molding, no 5; Bench molding; No 5
B&W
LC FIE52-111
Explains what a gated pattern is and why it is used. Shows how a match or follow board may simplify making a parting, how facing sand is prepared, and how and why some patterns are rapped through the cope.
Industrial and Technical Education
Dist - USNAC **Prod** - USOE 1944

Molding with a Loose Pattern 21 MIN
16mm
B&W
Explains how molding sand is prepared. Demonstrates how to face a pattern, ram and vent a mold, roll a drag, cut a sprue, runner, riser and gates, and swabs, and rap and draw a pattern. Uses animation to show what takes place inside a mold during pouring.
Industrial and Technical Education
Dist - USNAC **Prod** - USOE 1944

Molding with a Loose Pattern - Bench 21 MIN
16mm
Foundry Practice Series Bench Molding no 1; Bench molding; No 1
B&W
LC FIE52-108
Shows how to use bench molder's tools, prepare molding sand, face a pattern, ram and vent a mold, roll a drag and cut a sprue, runner, riser and gates. Depicts with animation the inside of a mold during pouring.
Industrial and Technical Education
Dist - USNAC **Prod** - USOE 1944

Molding with a Loose Pattern - Floor 24 MIN
16mm
Foundry Practice Series Floor Molding no 1; Floor molding; No 1

B&W
LC FIE52-110
Shows difference between bench and floor molding, how to face a deep pattern, ram a drag and walk it off, clamp a mold, locate sprues and risers, and tuck the crossbars of a large cope.
Industrial and Technical Education
Dist - USNAC **Prod** - USOE 1945

Molding with a Split Pattern 19 MIN
16mm
Foundry Practice Series Bench Molding, no 4; Bench molding; No 4
B&W
LC FIE52-105
Explains how split patterns aid in the molding of some castings. Shows how ramming affects the permeability of sand in a mold, how to reinforce a mold with nails and how to patch a mold.
Industrial and Technical Education
Dist - USNAC **Prod** - USOE 1944

Molding with a Three Part Flask 35 MIN
16mm
Foundry Practice Series Floor Molding, no 5; Floor molding; No 5
B&W
LC FIE52-115
Explains the use of a deep follow board and outlines techniques of facing, ramming and venting a deep green sand core. Shows how to use a cheek in a three - part flask. Gives the purpose and method of step - gating.
Industrial and Technical Education
Dist - USNAC **Prod** - USOE 1945

Molds and How they Grow 11 MIN
U-matic / VHS / 16mm
Color (I J)
$265.00 purchase; $185.00 purchase; LC 75-703337
Uses laboratory demonstrations, photomicrography, and time - lapse photography to show the conditions under which molds grow, their structure, spore production, colony formation and reproduction.
Science - Natural
Dist - CORF **Prod** - CORF 1969

Molds and Models - How they are used 28 MIN
Videoreel / VT2
Wheels, Kilns and Clay Series
Color
Features Mrs Peterson describing certain ceramic processes for her classroom at the University of Southern California. Discusses the use of molds and models.
Fine Arts
Dist - PBS **Prod** - USC

Molds and Models - Start to Finish 28 MIN
Videoreel / VT2
Wheels, Kilns and Clay Series
Color
Features Mrs Peterson describing certain ceramic processes for her classroom at the University of Southern California. Discusses the use of molds and models.
Fine Arts
Dist - PBS **Prod** - USC

The Mole 10 MIN
U-matic
Mole Concept Series
Color (H C)
Introduces the mole as the ultimate standard container for directly comparing large numbers of atoms. Extends the use of the mole to standardize gas volume comparison and introduces Avogadro's number.
Science; Science - Physical
Dist - TVOTAR **Prod** - TVOTAR 1986

The Mole and the Bulldozer 7 MIN
U-matic / VHS / 16mm
Mole Series
Color (K P I)
LC 77-703335
Presents an animated film about a mole who decides to prevent the construction of a highway on his territory.
Fine Arts; Literature and Drama
Dist - PHENIX **Prod** - SFSP 1977

The Mole and the Camera 7 MIN
U-matic / VHS / 16mm
Mole Series
Color (K P I)
LC 77-703336
Presents an animated film about a mole whose new camera is broken during a fight with his friend Mouse.
Fine Arts; Literature and Drama
Dist - PHENIX **Prod** - SFSP 1977

The Mole and the Car 16 MIN
U-matic / VHS / 16mm
Mole Series
Color (K P I)
LC 77-703337
Presents an animâted film about a mole who becomes so fascinated by the cars whizzing past his molehill that he decides to get one of his own.
Fine Arts; Literature and Drama
Dist - PHENIX **Prod** - SFSP 1977

The Mole and the Chewing Gum 9 MIN
16mm / U-matic / VHS
Mole Series
Color (K P I)
LC 72-700651
An animated cartoon in which a mole is unable, even with the help of other animals, to get rid of the piece of chewing gum that is stuck on him.
Literature and Drama
Dist - PHENIX **Prod** - CFET 1972

The Mole and the Christmas Tree 6 MIN
16mm / U-matic / VHS
Mole Series
Color (K P I)
LC 77-703339
Presents an animated film about a mole who brings a Christmas tree home and invites his friend Mouse to Christmas dinner.
Fine Arts; Literature and Drama
Dist - PHENIX **Prod** - SFSP 1977

The Mole and the Egg 6 MIN
U-matic / VHS / 16mm
Mole Series
Color (K P I)
LC 77-703341
Presents an animated film about a mole who finds a hen's abandoned egg and sets out to find the egg's mother.
Fine Arts; Literature and Drama
Dist - PHENIX **Prod** - SFSP 1977

The Mole and the Flying Carpet 6 MIN
U-matic / VHS / 16mm
Mole Series
Color (K P I)
LC 76-702491
Presents the story about the Mole finding a flying carpet in a dustbin and after cleaning the carpet, the Mole is rewarded by the carpet becoming his friend.
Literature and Drama
Dist - PHENIX **Prod** - CFET 1976

Mole and the Green Star 8 MIN
U-matic / VHS / 16mm
Mole Film Series
Color (K P I)
LC 75-707596
Follows little Mole as he spring cleans his house and discovers a shining green stone that he is sure must be a star. Tells how Mole and his friends try to put it back into the heavens.
Education; Science - Natural
Dist - PHENIX **Prod** - CFET 1970

The Mole and the Hedgehog 10 MIN
16mm / U-matic / VHS
Mole Series
Color (K P I)
LC 82-700542
Presents an animated story about how Mole and his friend Mouse rescue the hedgehog who has been captured and taken to a school laboratory.
Fine Arts; Literature and Drama
Dist - PHENIX **Prod** - KRATKY 1981

The Mole and the Lollipop 9 MIN
16mm / U-matic / VHS
Mole Film Series
Color (K P I)
LC 71-713992
Uses animation to tell the story about a mole who finds a lollipop but does not know what to do with it.
Literature and Drama
Dist - PHENIX **Prod** - SFSP 1971

The Mole and the Matchbox 6 MIN
U-matic / VHS / 16mm
Color (P I)
LC 83-700377
Relates what happens when the Mole and the Mouse discover a matchbox and gradually discover the true purpose of the matches.
Literature and Drama
Dist - PHENIX **Prod** - KRATKY 1982

The Mole and the Music 6 MIN
U-matic / VHS / 16mm
Mole Series
Color (K P I)
LC 76-702492
Tells the story about the Mole's love for music which helps sustain him when he has to make a new record from scratch after breaking his favorite one.
Literature and Drama
Dist - PHENIX **Prod** - CFET 1976

The Mole and the Rocket 10 MIN
16mm / U-matic / VHS
Mole Series
Color (K P I)
LC 74-700406
Tells a story about a little mole who is carried by a rocket to a deserted island in the middle of the ocean. Shows how the sea animals help repair the ruined rocket and go off in it with the mole.
Fine Arts; Literature and Drama
Dist - PHENIX **Prod** - CFET 1973

The Mole and the Telephone 7 MIN
16mm / U-matic / VHS
Mole Series
Color (K P I)
LC 76-702493
Tells the story about the Mole discovering a telephone receiver and giving it a cold as he tries to get a response from it.
Literature and Drama
Dist - PHENIX **Prod** - CFET 1976

The Mole and the TV Set 8 MIN
U-matic / VHS / 16mm
Mole Series
Color (K P I)
LC 72-700591
Presents an animated story in which little Mole breaks the television aerial in order to keep the gardener from hearing a television program discussing the necessity of exterminating moles.
Literature and Drama; Sociology
Dist - PHENIX **Prod** - CFET 1972

The Mole and the Umbrella 9 MIN
U-matic / VHS / 16mm
Mole Film Series
Color (K P I)
LC 73-700413
Tells the story of a mole who finds an umbrella on a scrap heap. Explains that the wind carries him, hanging on the umbrella, over the lake and the mole lands on its bank where a melon - dealer has his stand. Tells how the umbrella saves the mole from this precarious situation.
Literature and Drama
Dist - PHENIX **Prod** - SFSP 1973

The Mole as a Chemist 7 MIN
U-matic / VHS / 16mm
Mole Series
Color (K P)
Describes how the Mole, while digging a hole, finds a box containing a chemistry set and begins to play with it. Things get out of control until finally the resourceful Mole restores peace and quiet.
Fine Arts
Dist - PHENIX **Prod** - KRATKY

The Mole as a Gardener 8 MIN
16mm / U-matic / VHS
Mole Series
Color (K P I)
LC 72-700650
An animated cartoon in which a mole and a gardener eventually come to an agreement after they quarrel.
Guidance and Counseling; Literature and Drama
Dist - PHENIX **Prod** - CFET 1972

The Mole as a Painter 11 MIN
U-matic / VHS / 16mm
Mole Series
Color (K P I)
LC 74-701569
Describes how a mole's friends help him frighten away their common enemy, the fox, by dramatizing themselves in colorful paints left by a painter.
Fine Arts; Literature and Drama
Dist - PHENIX **Prod** - CFET 1974

The Mole as a Watchmaker 6 MIN
U-matic / VHS / 16mm
Mole Series
Color (K P I)
LC 76-702494
Tells a story about the Mole who gets mixed up with a game of marbles and a cuckoo clock.
Literature and Drama
Dist - PHENIX **Prod** - CFET 1976

The Mole at the Carnival 6 MIN
U-matic / VHS / 16mm
Mole Series
Color (K P I)
LC 77-703338
Uses animation to tell the story of a mole who goes to a carnival and encounters a large bulldog.
Fine Arts; Literature and Drama
Dist - PHENIX **Prod** - SFSP 1977

The Mole concept 60 MIN
VHS
Concepts in science - chemistry series
Color; PAL (J H)
PdS29.50 purchase
Clarifies the reasoning behind the historical development of the mole concept and opens the way to understanding chemical reactions at a molecular level. Divided into six

10 - minute concepts - Relative Mass; Gas Volumes; Combining Gas Volumes; Avogadro's Hypothesis; Relative Atomic Mass; and The Mole. Part of a six - part series.
Science; Science - Physical
Dist - EMFVL **Prod** - TVOTAR

Mole concept series

Avogadro's hypothesis	10 MIN
Combining gas volume	10 MIN
Gas volume	10 MIN
The Mole	10 MIN
Relative Atomic Mass	10 MIN
Relative Mass	10 MIN

Dist - TVOTAR

Mole Film Series

Mole and the Green Star	8 MIN
The Mole and the Lollipop	9 MIN
The Mole and the Umbrella	9 MIN

Dist - PHENIX

The Mole in the Desert 7 MIN
16mm / U-matic / VHS
Mole Series
Color (K P I)
LC 77-703342
Presents an animated film about a mole who journeys to the desert and helps the desert animals find water.
Fine Arts; Literature and Drama
Dist - PHENIX **Prod** - SFSP 1977

Mole in the Town 30 MIN
U-matic / VHS / 16mm
Mole Series
Color (P I J H C)
LC 84-707080
Fine Arts; Guidance and Counseling
Dist - PHENIX **Prod** - KRATKY 1984

The Mole in the Zoo 10 MIN
U-matic / VHS / 16mm
Mole Series
Color (K P I)
LC 73-703441
Tells how the mole goes where angels fear to tread. Shows how he seeks to give help to an ailing lion by pulling the lion's throbbing tooth.
Fine Arts; Literature and Drama
Dist - PHENIX **Prod** - CFET 1973

The Mole - its digging behaviour and movements 5 MIN
VHS
Color; PAL (H)
Observes the use of the fore - limbs for digging in the mole, and the two - speed locomotion which results from the differences in length of the fore - limbs and the hind - limbs.
Psychology; Science - Natural
Dist - VIEWTH

Mole Poblano Con Pollo 17 MIN
U-matic / VHS
Color (PRO)
Demonstrates the preparation of chicken in a chocolate - chili sauce.
Home Economics; Industrial and Technical Education
Dist - CULINA **Prod** - CULINA

Mole Series

How the Mole Got His Trousers	14 MIN
The Mole and the Bulldozer	7 MIN
The Mole and the Camera	7 MIN
The Mole and the Car	16 MIN
The Mole and the Chewing Gum	9 MIN
The Mole and the Christmas Tree	6 MIN
The Mole and the Egg	6 MIN
The Mole and the Flying Carpet	6 MIN
The Mole and the Hedgehog	10 MIN
The Mole and the Music	6 MIN
The Mole and the Rocket	10 MIN
The Mole and the Telephone	7 MIN
The Mole and the TV Set	8 MIN
The Mole as a Chemist	7 MIN
The Mole as a Gardener	8 MIN
The Mole as a Painter	11 MIN
The Mole as a Watchmaker	6 MIN
The Mole at the Carnival	6 MIN
The Mole in the Desert	7 MIN
Mole in the Town	30 MIN
The Mole in the Zoo	10 MIN

Dist - PHENIX

The Mole - water - Parts 11 and 12 60 MIN
VHS / U-matic
World of chemistry series
Color (C)
$45.00, $29.95 purchase
Presents parts 11 and 12 of the 26 - part World of Chemistry series. Examines the concept of the mole and the use of Avogodro's law. Explores the special chemical properties of water and reviews the protection and conservation of water as a natural resource. Two thirty - minute programs hosted by Nobel laureate Roald Hoffmann.
Science - Physical; Social Science
Dist - ANNCPB **Prod** - UMD 1990

Molecular Architecture 16 MIN
VHS
Chem 101 - Beginning Chemistry Series
Color (C)
$50.00 purchase, $21.00 rental _ #58247
Introduces Valence Shell Electron Pair Repulsion - RSEPR. Explains that ion molecular structure can be predicted by counting the regions of electron density around an atom and arranging them as far apart as possible. Shows that if polar bonds in a molecule are arranged so their dipole moments cancel each other, the molecule will be nonpolar.
Science - Physical
Dist - UILL **Prod** - UILL 1987

Molecular architecture - signals from within - Parts 9 and 10 60 MIN
U-matic / VHS
World of chemistry series
Color (C)
$45.00, $29.95 purchase
Presents parts 9 and 10 of the 26 - part World of Chemistry series. Shows that the shape and physical properties of a molecule are determined by the electronic structure of its elements and its bonds. Reveals how living organisms distinguish beteween similar molecules - isomers. Considers that atoms and molecules can be made to communicate and scientists have learned to interpret atomic level language. Two thirty - minute programs hosted by Nobel laureate Roald Hoffmann.
Science - Physical
Dist - ANNCPB **Prod** - UMD 1990

Molecular Biology 15 MIN
U-matic / VHS / 16mm
Biological Sciences Series
Color (J H C)
$380.00, $250.00 purchase _ #3983
Tells how molecular biologists are trying to understand how the molecules of life first formed and began their control of biological processes using energy - rich molecules of ATP that drive the life functions, and DNA, information molecules that guide the cell to produce the needed materials and then are duplicated and passed on.
Science - Natural
Dist - CORF **Prod** - CORF 1981

Molecular Biology - an Introduction 15 MIN
16mm
Color
LC 75-703329
Presents an introductory discussion of the new science of molecular biology, including a review of technological advances, such as the improved resolution of the electron microscope, the isolation of cell parts by ultracentrifugation, the separation capabilities of chromatography, the localization of autoradiography, and the sensitivity of liquid scintillation counting.
Science - Natural
Dist - USNAC **Prod** - ANL 1969

Molecular Biology Films Series

Alpha helix formation	3 MIN
Amino acids and proteins	6 MIN
Biosynthesis of steroids	6 MIN
Catalysis by a co - enzyme	5 MIN
Chempak	9 MIN
Small Molecules	4 MIN
Structure of Proteins	10 MIN

Dist - EDC

Molecular Bonding - a Union of Atoms 13 MIN
VHS
Chemistry - from Theory to Application Series
Color (H)
$190.00 purchase
Demonstrates that mercury, a liquid, and chlorine, a gas, can both be solidified at low temperatures. Shows through a series of experiments that the atomic nucleus and surrounding electrons of chlorine are tightly bound together.
Science; Science - Physical
Dist - LUF **Prod** - LUF 1989

The Molecular building blocks of life 18 MIN
VHS / BETA
Cell biology resource series
Color; PAL (J H C)
PdS58
Presents striking visualizations of cell processes. Examines the variety of cells and looks into cell structure. Includes modules on carbon chemistry, polymers, carbohydrates, testing for sugar and starch, protein structure, nucleic acids overview, energy storage, fats and how enzymes promote reactions. Part of a six - part series covering how cells acquire energy, how cells are controlled and how genetic information is passed on, presented in bite - sized modules.
Science - Natural; Science - Physical
Dist - VIEWTH

Molecular Formulas Confirm One Another
VHS
Chemistry - from Theory to Application Series
Color (H)
$190.00 purchase
Reveals that equal volumes of hydrogen and chlorine react together to form gaseous hydrogen chloride. Evaluates the results using Avogadro's law. The molecular formulas H2, Cl2, HCl, and H2O confirm one another.
Science; Science - Physical
Dist - LUF **Prod** - LUF 1989

Molecular Genetics - the Heritage of Robert Koch 24 MIN
U-matic / VHS
Elements of Biology Series
Color (C)
$249.00, $149.00 purchase _ #AD - 2198
Shows the groundbreaking work of Robert Koch, who isolated the tuberculin bacillus over the opposition of an establishment which believed poverty to be the cause of TB. Demonstrates new methods and techniques such as electron microscopy which are constantly providing new knowledge about the structures of microorganisms.
Science; Science - Natural
Dist - FOTH **Prod** - FOTH

Molecular modeling for biological systems 240 MIN
VHS
Color (C PRO)
$400.00 purchase _ #V - 4500 - 17122
Examines developments and applications for hardware and software packages. Shows how to search for conformations and use modeling to predict the geometry and molecular interactions of large biological molecules and how to choose programs for use in solving research problems. Illustrates unique ways to use molecular modeling. Features David A Case, Jeffrey Blaney, Will L Jorgensen, Peter A Kollman and Arthur J Olson as instructors. Includes four videos and a course study guide.
Science - Physical
Dist - AMCHEM **Prod** - AMCHEM 1990

Molecular modeling in the discovery of new drugs 180 MIN
VHS
Color; PAL (C PRO)
$2200.00 purchase _ #V - 5900 - 26709
Examines the role of computer - aided modeling in the discovery of new drugs. Looks at the interaction of the major histocompatibility complex protein with peptides. Shows how structual information is used in the discovery of new drugs and the use of elastase crystal information and molecular modeling techniques in the design of novel, non - peptidic, competitive and reversible HLE inhibitors. Observes the interaction of MHC molecules with antigenic peptides described by computer - aided molecular design and how it may lead to the design of potential synthetic vaccines - especially in the field of autoimmune disease. John J Baldwin, John W Erickson, Gerd Folkers, Helen Free, Jonathan Greer, Michael D Varney and Peter Warner instruct.
Science - Physical
Dist - AMCHEM **Prod** - AMCHEM 1993

Molecular modeling - the small molecule approach 180 MIN
VHS
Color; PAL (C PRO)
$2200.00 purchase _ #V - 6300 - 28620
Shows how to analyze the structures of small - molecule inhibitors themselves - in the absence of a receptor site - to arrive at novel, more potent ligands. Requires a basic knowledge of medicinal chemistry; molecular modeling techniques; basic biochemistry as it relates to drug - receptor interactions; and common biological testing techniques used in the discovery of new drugs. Features J Phillip Bowen, Univ of Georgia; Prof Garland R Marshall, Washing Univ; Yvonne Connolly Martin, Abbott Laboratories; and Daniel F Ortwine, Warner - Lambert Co. Includes two videos and a course guide.
Science - Physical
Dist - AMCHEM **Prod** - AMCHEM 1994

Molecular motions 13 MIN
VHS / 16mm
Chem study video - film series
Color (H C)
$208.00, $99.00 purchase, $23.00 rental _ #192 W 0805, #193 W 2037, #140 W 4115

Considers that many properties of matter - fluidity, vaporization and rates of chemical reactions - indicate that molecular motion must be occurring and that the freedom of motion increases in going from the solid to the liquid to the gaseous state. Looks at the concepts of translational, rotational, and vibrational molecular motions which allow the interpretation of the observed properties. Part of a series for teaching chemistry to high school and college students.
Science - Physical
Dist - WARDS **Prod** - WARDS 1990

Molecular Motions 13 MIN
16mm
CHEM Study Films Series
Color (H)
Explores the properties of matter, such as fluidity, vaporization and rates of chemical reactions, which indicate that molecular motion must be occurring. Describes the solid, liquid and gaseous States and presents the concepts of translational, rotational and vibrational molecular motions.
Science - Physical
Dist - MLA **Prod** - CHEMS 1962

Molecular Orbitals - Rules of the Road 13 MIN
U-matic
Chemistry 101 Series
Color (C)
Describes the wave function of an atomic orbital. After in phase, out of phase and node have been defined, shows how sigma bonding and antibonding orbitals result from combining atomic orbitals.
Science; Science - Physical
Dist - UILL **Prod** - UILL 1973

Molecular Reactivity 270 MIN
U-matic / VHS
Color
Uses an integrated thermodynamic - kinetic approach to the study of molecular processes. Presents the important elements to describe molecular reactivity, techniques used for evaluating kinetic data, factors that govern rates of chemical processes and thermodynamic concepts that apply to molecular reactions.
Science - Physical
Dist - AMCHEM **Prod** - AMCHEM

Molecular spectroscopy 23 MIN
VHS / 16mm
Chem study video - film series
Color (H C)
$368.00, $99.00 purchase, $33.00 rental _ #192 W 0850, #193 W 2038, #140 W 4142
Shows the infrared light absorption process and its relation to molecular properties using laboratory experiments, molecular models and animation. Stresses the concept of natural molecular vibrations. Shows how infrared spectrum is used to identify molecules and determine their structures. Part of a series for teaching chemistry to high school and college students.
Science - Physical
Dist - WARDS **Prod** - WARDS 1990

Molecular Spectroscopy 23 MIN
16mm
CHEM Study Films Series
Color (H C)
LC FIA63-379
Uses laboratory experiments, molecular models and animation to show details of the infrared light absorption process and its relation to molecular properties. Presents the concept of natural vibration frequencies in molecules.
Science; Science - Physical
Dist - MLA **Prod** - CHEMS 1962

Molecular Speeds and the Non - Ideality of Gases 11 MIN
U-matic
Chemistry 101 Series
Color (C)
Discusses effect of the transfer of kinetic energy in the molecular motion of gases, comparing the speed of oxygen molecules in air with that of hydrogen which is much greater.
Science; Science - Physical
Dist - UILL **Prod** - UILL 1976

Molecular structure and health 22 MIN
16mm / VHS
Chem study video - film series
Color (H C)
$352.00, $99.00 purchase, $32.00 rental _ #192 W 0915, #193 W 2019, #140 W 4181
Identifies the role of molecular structure in determining biological activity. Shows that the correlation of the structure and biological activity of sulfanilamide with a vitamin essential for bacterial growth leads to a more general presentaion of the biochemical nature of growth. Uses time - lapse photomicrography to show laboratory demonstrations. Part of a series for teaching chemistry to high school and college students.
Science - Natural; Science - Physical
Dist - WARDS **Prod** - WARDS 1990

Molecular structure and health
VHS
Chem study videos for biology teachers series
Color (T)
$99.00 purchase _ #193 Y 2019
Identifies the role of molecular structure in determining biological activity. Shows that the correlation of the structure and biological activity of sulfanilamide with a vitamin essential for bacterial growth leads to a more general presentation of the biochemical nature of growth. Uses time - lapse photomicrography to show the laboratory demonstrations. Includes a teacher's guide. Part of a five - part series to teach chemical concepts to biology teachers.
Science - Natural; Science - Physical
Dist - WARDS **Prod** - WARDS 1990

Molecular Substance and Covalent Crystals 10 MIN
U-matic
Electron Arrangement and Bonding Series
Color (H C)
Explains stable and unstable atomic bonds.
Science; Science - Physical
Dist - TVOTAR **Prod** - TVOTAR 1984

The Molecular Theory of Matter 11 MIN
U-matic / VHS / 16mm
Color (H C) (SPANISH)
Demonstrates kinetic molecular theory of matter by showing the diffusion of gases in air, the condensation of steam, the evaporation of liquids and the transformation of liquids into solids. Demonstrates brownian movement.
Foreign Language; Science - Physical
Dist - EBEC **Prod** - EBEC

Molecular Weight Distributions, Determination of Average Molecular Weight by Osmotic 42 MIN
VHS / U-matic
Colloid and Surface Chemistry - Lyophilic Colloids Series
Color
Discusses molecular weight distributions, determination of average molecular weight by osmotic pressure, chemical analysis and viscosity.
Science; Science - Physical
Dist - KALMIA **Prod** - KALMIA

Molecular Weight Distributions - Determination of Average Molecular Weight by Osmotic - 42 MIN
VHS / U-matic
Colloids and Surface Chemistry - Lyophilic Colloids Series
B&W
Discusses molecular weight distributions and determination of average molecular weight by osmotic pressure, chemical analysis and viscosity.
Science - Physical
Dist - MIOT **Prod** - MIOT

The Molecule mine 30 MIN
VHS
Perspective - biotechnology - series
Color; PAL; NTSC (G)
PdS90, PdS105 purchase
Shows how the plants in tropical rain forests can be sources of medicines, dyes and foodstuffs.
Science - Natural
Dist - CFLVIS **Prod** - LONTVS

The Molecule of Management 22 MIN
U-matic / VHS
Time Management for Managers and Professionals Series
Color
Business and Economics; Psychology
Dist - DELTAK **Prod** - DELTAK

Molecules
VHS
Basic science series
Color (J H) (ENGLISH AND SPANISH)
$39.95 purchase _ #MCV5022
Focuses on molecules, presenting only basic concepts. Includes teacher's guide and review questions. Combines computer animation and the use of 'sheltered language' to help students acquire content vocabulary, become comfortable with scientific language and achieve success in science curriculum. Part of a series on basic science concepts.
Science; Science - Physical
Dist - MADERA **Prod** - MADERA

Molecules - a First Film 10 MIN
16mm / U-matic / VHS
Color (I J)
LC 72-700796
Suggests that there is a similarity in the structure of solid matter, liquids and gases. Uses a molecular model to help explain why a liquid that has changed to a gas occupies a much larger volume than the original liquid.
Science - Physical
Dist - PHENIX **Prod** - IWANMI 1972

Molecules and Life 20 MIN
16mm / U-matic / VHS
Color (H)
LC 76-710639
Outlines achievements in molecular biology which have revolutionized understanding of the chemical and physical basis of life. Discusses the molecules vitamin B12, hemoglobin, myoglobin and proteins in general.
Science - Natural
Dist - MGHT **Prod** - EFVA 1971

Molecules and matter 15 MIN
U-matic / VHS
Discovering series; Unit 3 - Chemistry
Color (I)
Science - Physical
Dist - AITECH **Prod** - WDCNTV 1978

Molecules at Work, Pt 1 15 MIN
Videoreel / VT2
Science is Everywhere Series no 4
B&W (P)
Explains that heat makes molecules move faster, increased molecular motion causes matter to expand and expansion exerts a force that does work.
Science - Physical
Dist - GPN **Prod** - DETPS

Molecules at Work, Pt 2 15 MIN
Videoreel / VT2
Science is Everywhere Series no 5
B&W (P)
Explains that heat makes molecules move faster, increased molecular motion causes matter to expand and expansion exerts a force that does work.
Science - Physical
Dist - GPN **Prod** - DETPS

Molecules at Work, Pt 3 15 MIN
Videoreel / VT2
Science is Everywhere Series no 6
B&W (P)
Explains that heat makes molecules move faster, increased molecular motion causes matter to expand and expansion exerts a force that does work.
Science - Physical
Dist - GPN **Prod** - DETPS

Molecules in Liquids 5 MIN
U-matic
Eureka Series
Color (J)
Shows that as molecules in a solid get hotter, they vibrate faster and slip out of their latticework pattern. When this occurs the substance melts, changing from a solid to a liquid state.
Science; Science - Physical
Dist - TVOTAR **Prod** - TVOTAR 1980

Molecules in Solids 5 MIN
U-matic
Eureka Series
Color (J)
Defines the three states of matter and illustrates the latticework pattern of molecules in solids.
Science; Science - Physical
Dist - TVOTAR **Prod** - TVOTAR 1980

Molecules with sunglasses 50 MIN
VHS
Horizon series
Color (A PRO C)
PdS99 purchase _ Unavailable in USA
Describes the attempts of two scientists, in 1985, to create a star's surface in a laboratory setting. Tells about their glimpse of a third form of solid carbon. Could this be the solution to a great mystery of the universe?
Science - Physical
Dist - BBCENE

Moleshow and Whatever happened to vileness fats
VHS
Color & B&W (G)
$35.00 purchase
Follows The Moleshow, a troupe of dancers, prop movers and performers, who toured the United States West Coast and extensive regions of Europe, between 1992 and 1983, with an elaborate stage presentation of live - on - stage storytelling, considered one of the most primitive yet technologically advanced displays in the genre. Features a collage presentation of the show combining computer - generated animation and live footage, with The Residents providing music. Whatever Happened To Vileness Fats combines a passionate love affair, twisted nightclub and

the tortured relationship between frightening Siamese twins. Originally conceived as a full - length video in 1972, this compilation of footage remains true to form. Produced by Ralph Records.
Fine Arts; Industrial and Technical Education
Dist - CANCIN

Moliere and the comedie Francaise 17 MIN
VHS
Color (H C G)
$129.00 purchase _ #DL361
Provides an overview of the many facets of the Comedie Francaise. Features Jacques Charon who directs brief excerpts from Moliere's The Misanthrope and Le Tartuffe which highlight the playwright's comic style as well as the style of the comedie.
Fine Arts; History - World; Literature and Drama
Dist - INSIM

Moliere - Dom Juan 106 MIN
U-matic / VHS
B&W (C) (FRENCH)
$349.00, $199.00 purchase _ #AD - 1616
Presents 'Dom Juan' by Moliere who turned the Spanish Don Juan, an unscrupulous seducer, into a man of overweening, pride, cynacism and disdain. In French.
Foreign Language; History - World; Literature and Drama; Sociology
Dist - FOTH **Prod** - FOTH

Moliere - Le Bourgeois Gentilhomme 131 MIN
U-matic / VHS
Color (C) (FRENCH)
$399.00, $249.00 purchase _ #AD - 1514
Presents 'Le Bourgeois Gentilhomme' by Moliere. In French.
Foreign Language; History - World; Literature and Drama; Sociology
Dist - FOTH **Prod** - FOTH

Moliere - Le Malade Imaginaire 105 MIN
U-matic / VHS
Color (C) (FRENCH (ENGLISH SUBTITLES))
$399.00, $249.00 purchase _ #AD - 939
Presents 'Le Malade Imaginaire' by Moliere, produced by the Societe des Comediens Francais. In French with English subtitles.
Foreign Language; Geography - World; History - World; Literature and Drama
Dist - FOTH **Prod** - FOTH

Moliere - Le Medicin Malgre Lui 60 MIN
U-matic / VHS
Color (C) (FRENCH (ENGLISH SUBTITLES))
$299.00, $199.00 purchase _ #AD - 938
Presents 'Le Medicin Malgre Lui' by Moliere, produced by the Societe des Comediens Francais. In French with English subtitles.
Foreign Language; Geography - World; History - World; Literature and Drama
Dist - FOTH **Prod** - FOTH

Moliere - Le Misanthrope 140 MIN
U-matic / VHS
Color (C) (FRENCH (ENGLISH SUBTITLES))
$399.00, $249.00 purchase _ #AD - 937
Presents 'Le Misanthrope' by Moliere, produced by the Societe des Comediens Francais. In French with English subtitles.
Foreign Language; Geography - World; History - World; Literature and Drama
Dist - FOTH **Prod** - FOTH

Moliere - L'Ecole Des Femmes 120 MIN
U-matic / VHS
Color (C) (FRENCH)
$399.00, $249.00 purchase _ #AD - 1615
Presents 'L'Ecole des Femmes' by Moliere. In French.
Foreign Language; Geography - World; History - World; Literature and Drama
Dist - FOTH **Prod** - FOTH

Moliere - Les Fourberies De Scapin 100 MIN
U-matic / VHS
Color (C) (FRENCH (ENGLISH SUBTITLES))
$399.00, $249.00 purchase _ #AD - 1490
Presents 'Les Fourberies De Scapin' by Moliere. In French with English subtitles.
Foreign Language; History - World; Literature and Drama; Sociology
Dist - FOTH **Prod** - FOTH

Moliere - Tartuffe 119 MIN
U-matic / VHS
Color (C) (FRENCH (ENGLISH SUBTITLES))
$399.00, $249.00 purchase _ #AD - 940
Presents 'Tartuffe' by Moliere, produced by the Societe des Comediens Francais. In French with English subtitles.
Foreign Language; Geography - World; History - World; Literature and Drama
Dist - FOTH **Prod** - FOTH

Molissa Fenley, Dana Reitz and Marta Renzi 30 MIN
VHS / U-matic
Eye on Dance - the Experimentalists Series
Color
Fine Arts
Dist - ARCVID **Prod** - ARCVID

Molluscs 10 MIN
16mm / VHS
Inhabitants of the planet Earth series
Color (H C) (FRENCH)
$160.00, $120.00 purchase, $25.00 rental _ #194 W 2035, #193 W 2064, #140 W 2035
Looks at chitons which cling to rocks with a muscular foot. Examines their anatomy. Displays the waves of muscular activity of a snail moving over a windowpane. Illustrates nudibranches. Explores a clam's water circulatory mechanism. Exhibits a hatching octopus. Part of a series on invertebrates.
Science - Natural
Dist - WARDS **Prod** - WARDS

Molluscs 10 MIN
16mm
Inhabitants of the Planet Earth Series
Color (J H C)
LC 76-701108
Begins with the most generalized life forms, showing how the basic molluscan body plan has become modified to produce a great diversity of specialized life forms. Examines the basic cephalopod features on a hatching octopus and illustrates the locomotion of a land snail and the circulatory mechanism of a clam through use of a die.
Science - Natural
Dist - MLA **Prod** - RUSB 1976

Mollusks 15 MIN
Videoreel / VT2
Let's Go Sciencing, Unit III - Life Series
Color (K)
Illustrates the life of a mollusk both in the water and on land.
Science - Natural
Dist - GPN **Prod** - DETPS

The Mollusks - 6 12 MIN
VHS
Real time video micrography series
Color (I J H G)
$59.95 purchase _ #BV106
Examines chitons, gastropods, including close - ups of snails, nudibranchs, bivalves, squid and the octupus. Part of a nine - part series on the behavior and interactions of microorganisms.
Science - Natural
Dist - ENVIMC **Prod** - BIOMED 1991

Mollusks - Snails, Mussels, Oysters, Octopuses and their Relatives 14 MIN
16mm / U-matic / VHS
Color (J H C)
Discusses the distinguishing characteristics and habitats of the five classes of mollusks showing some of the ways in which they are useful to man.
Science - Natural
Dist - EBEC **Prod** - EBEC 1955

Mollusks - the Mussel 7 MIN
16mm
Color (H C)
Observes the living mussel's interior vital processes through the use of live photography and animation.
Science - Natural
Dist - BNCHMK **Prod** - BNCHMK 1983

Mollusks - the Mussel, Respiration and Digestion 7 MIN
VHS / U-matic
Modern Biology Series
Color (H C)
Observes the mussel's interior processes. Reviews mussel's respiration, digestion and filter feeding. Dissections identify usually hard - to - see structures.
Science - Natural
Dist - BNCHMK **Prod** - INFB 1985

Molly 83 MIN
16mm
B&W (G)
$150.00 rental
Looks at life with the Goldbergs, as Molly's former suitor pays the family a visit. Stars Gertrude Berg and Philip Loeb. Directed by Walter Hart.
Fine Arts; Religion and Philosophy; Sociology
Dist - NCJEWF

Molly Harrower - writing in the upward years 23 MIN
VHS
Writing in the upward years series
Color (G C)
$195.00 purchase, $55.00 rental
Focuses on the effect of aging on the creative process as demonstrated in the life and writings of poet Molly Harrower. Features readings by and interviews with the poet.
Fine Arts; Health and Safety; Literature and Drama
Dist - TNF

Molly O'Mally 15 MIN
VHS / U-matic
Teletales Series
Color (P)
$125.00 purchase
Depicts a child's tale that originates from Wales/England.
Education; Literature and Drama
Dist - AITECH **Prod** - POSIMP 1984

Molly Rush - Turning Swords into Plowshares 28 MIN
U-matic
Color
Examines the motives and convictions of Molly Rush who joined with the Plowshare activists in their nonviolent protest of the nuclear arms race when they entered a missile assembly plant in Fall, 1980.
Sociology
Dist - GMPF **Prod** - GMPF

Mollye and Max 24 MIN
VHS
Color (G C)
$185.00 purchase, $55.00 rental
Depicts a married couple who age gracefully together, giving a model of a cheerful old age. Filmed and narrated by their granddaughter.
Health and Safety; Psychology; Sociology
Dist - TNF

Molly's Pilgrim 24 MIN
U-matic / VHS / 16mm
Color (P I)
Tells the story of a newly arrived Russian immigrant, Molly. Shows her being ostracized at school for being different, but finally gaining acceptance.
Sociology
Dist - PHENIX **Prod** - PELZRC 1985

Molly's pilgrim 24 MIN
U-matic / 16mm / VHS
Color (I J G)
$485.00, $300.00 purchase, $50.00 rental _ #APF - 693, #AVC - 693, #AHC - 693, #ARP - 693
Portrays nine - year - old Molly, a Russian - Jewish girl whose foreign accent, strange ways and peculiar clothes make her the object of her classmates' taunts. Reveals that when the children make dolls for a display of the first Thanksgiving, Molly brings in a Russian - Jewish figure which leads the children to understand Molly and her family's search for religious freedom.
Social Science; Sociology
Dist - ADL **Prod** - ADL

Molson Lake Fishing Lodge 14.5 MIN
16mm
Color (G)
#2X29 I
Documents how an economic development fund in Canada enabled band members of Norway House to lease land and build a fishing lodge at Molse Lake, Manitoba, Canada. Shows how accommodations were built for fishermen with local Indian people as guides.
Social Science
Dist - CDIAND **Prod** - AINC 1973

Molten Salt Reactor Experiment 20 MIN
16mm
Color
LC FIE68-67
Uses animation to describe the design, construction and operation of the molten salt reactor experiment. Discusses the possibility of using molten - salt reactors as thermal breeders.
Science - Physical
Dist - USNAC **Prod** - ORNLAB 1968

Mom 15 MIN
16mm
Color (G)
$25.00 rental
Presents a memory of filmmaker's mother smiling, eating and walking around nice places.
Fine Arts; Sociology
Dist - CANCIN **Prod** - KUCHAR 1983

Mom and Dad Can't Hear Me 47 MIN
U-matic / VHS / 16mm
Teenage Years Series
Color
LC 78-701400
Presents the story of a 14 - year - old girl who has just moved to a new town. Shows how she is afraid that her friends will reject her if they discover that her parents are deaf.
Guidance and Counseling; Sociology
Dist - TIMLIF **Prod** - WILSND 1978

Mom Deserves some Thanks 14 MIN
U-matic / 16mm
Fat Albert and the Cosby Kids IV Series
Color (K P I J)
Shows Fat Albert discovering how many things mothers do when he takes care of the house while his mother is away.
Fine Arts; Home Economics; Sociology
Dist - BARR **Prod** - BARR

The Mom Tapes 27 MIN
VHS / U-matic
B&W
Portrays a typical mother - daughter relationship. Spans four years. Includes Mom, I'm Bored, Skin Cancer and Household Questions.
Fine Arts; Sociology
Dist - KITCHN **Prod** - KITCHN

Mom, the Wolfman and Me 100 MIN
U-matic / VHS
Color (H C A)
Explains how a little girl overcomes her mother's hesitancy to marry a man who loves her very much. Stars Patty Duke Astin, David Birney and Danielle Brisebois.
Fine Arts; Sociology
Dist - TIMLIF **Prod** - TIMLIF 1982

Moment 13 MIN
16mm
Color (A)
$30.00 rental
Presents a continuous fixed gaze by the camera at a girl's face before, during and after orgasm. Concentrates on the subtle changes within her face. The camera moves from an objective look into a subjective one and then back out. Produced by Steve Dwoskin.
Fine Arts
Dist - CANCIN

Moment 25 MIN
16mm
B&W (G)
$50.00 rental
Offers a demonstration - exploration of the line between human information and machine information - a dynamic revelation of film's basic unit, the frame. Produced by Bill Brand.
Fine Arts
Dist - CANCIN

Moment for a gorilla 55 MIN
VHS
Color (H C G)
$445.00 purchase, $75.00 rental
Records the behavior of the Lowland Gorilla as a group settles into a specialy built habitat at a Dutch zoo. Reveals that their adaptation was so successful that a baby gorilla was born in captivity. Travels to their natural habitat in Cameroon where they are pursued by Pygmy hunters who consider the gorilla their arch enemy.
Psychology; Science - Natural
Dist - FLMLIB **Prod** - HA 1990

Moment for Decision 8 MIN
U-matic / VHS
Take Ten for Safety Series
Color (IND)
Stresses the importance of accepting personal responsibility for protecting oneself and others from work - related injury.
Health and Safety; Industrial and Technical Education
Dist - CORF **Prod** - OLINC

Moment for decision 13 MIN
BETA / VHS / U-matic
Color; PAL (IND G)
$175.00 rental _ #AEB - 103
Teaches the value of developing safe work habits. Examines skill deficiencies and motivational problems and provides solutions for these two sources of accidents. Includes leader's guide and 10 workbooks.
Business and Economics; Health and Safety; Psychology
Dist - BNA **Prod** - BNA

A Moment in History 14 MIN
16mm
Color (J H C)
LC 74-705163
Shows the events leading to the presentation of honorary U S citizenship to Winston Churchill by President Kennedy on April 6, 1963. Includes the ceremony which was transmitted live by relay satellite from the White House to England.
History - United States; History - World; Psychology; Social Science
Dist - NASA **Prod** - NASA 1964

A Moment in Time 55 MIN
16mm / U-matic / VHS
American Documents Series
Color (J)
Traces the history of America by using old photographs, newsreel film and archival recordings.
History - United States
Dist - LUF **Prod** - LUF

A Moment in Time 25 MIN
16mm
Color (J)
LC 74-705164
Depicts the scope of Navy photography and the mission of major photographic field activities.
Civics and Political Systems; Industrial and Technical Education
Dist - USNAC **Prod** - USN 1968

A Moment in time 30 MIN
VHS
Color (G)
$29.95 purchase _ #S00989
Portrays photographers and their subjects from the 19th century to the present day. Features photographers Mathew Brady, Dorothea Lange and Ansel Adams. Narrated by Gordon Parks.
Fine Arts; Industrial and Technical Education
Dist - UILL

A Moment in Time 22 MIN
U-matic / VHS / 16mm
American Documents Series
Color (J)
A shortened version of the motion picture A Moment In Time. Traces the history of America by using old photographs, newsreel film and archival recordings.
History - United States
Dist - LUF **Prod** - LUF 1979

Moment of Crisis - Berlin Airlift 20 MIN
VHS / U-matic
Color
$335.00 purchase
Civics and Political Systems
Dist - ABCLR **Prod** - ABCLR 1983

Moment of Decision 11 MIN
16mm
Professional Selling Practices Series I Series
Color (H C A)
LC 77-702361
Presents techniques for bringing a sale to a successful close in a minimum amount of time. Shows how salespersons can help the indecisive customer reach an affirmative and satisfying buying decision.
Business and Economics
Dist - SAUM **Prod** - SAUM 1967

Moment of Decision 12 MIN
U-matic / VHS / 16mm
Color (J H)
LC 81-700718
Examines the decisions of four boys to steal or not to steal a sports car.
Psychology; Sociology
Dist - AIMS **Prod** - CAHILL 1979

Moment of light - The Dance of Evelyn Hart 48 MIN
VHS
Color (H C G)
$195.00 purchase, $75.00 rental
Portrays one of the world's greatest interpreters of classical ballet. Creates a glimpse into the inner spirit and motivation of Evelyn Hart. Part documentary and part biography, filmed during 1991 when Hart split her time between her home company in Winnipeg and the Munich Ballet. Produced by Blue Morpho Films. A film by Gordon Reeve.
Biography; Fine Arts
Dist - CANCIN **Prod** - NFBC 1993

Moments and Centroids 20 MIN
VHS
Calculus Series
Color (H)
LC 90712920
Discusses moments and centroids. The 44th of 57 installments of the Calculus Series.
English Language; Mathematics
Dist - GPN

A Moment's Glory 23 MIN
16mm
Color
Provides a documentary record of a world catamaran race held in Hawaii.
Physical Education and Recreation
Dist - ALLNRP **Prod** - ALLNRP 1977

A Moment's Life 18 MIN
16mm
Color
LC 78-701562
Tells the story of a beggarwoman who pawns her only possession of any value to buy a funeral for an infant that she found in a garbage can.
Fine Arts
Dist - BRADAV **Prod** - BRADAV 1978

Moments of a Random Variable 18 MIN
U-matic / VHS
Probability and Random Processes - Statistical Averages Series
B&W (PRO)
Defines moments and central moments.
Mathematics
Dist - MIOT **Prod** - MIOT

Moments of Joy 24 MIN
U-matic / VHS / 16mm
Color (J)
LC 76-701155
Shows the effect of new humanization programs now being used in some state mental institutions to promote the development and independence of mental patients.
Health and Safety; Psychology
Dist - WOMBAT **Prod** - DRAKED 1975

Moments of love 40 MIN
VHS
Everyman series
Color (A)
PdS65 purchase
States that people with severe learning difficulties can suffer extreme isolation and an impaired sense of self. Reveals that health workers are frequently defeated in attempts to reach them in order to provide access to experiences and other people. Examines the pioneering ways of Phoebe Caldwell, who is breaking down the barriers in simple, imaginative, and, above all, human ways.
Health and Safety; Psychology
Dist - BBCENE

Moments of the Runner 28 MIN
16mm
Color
LC 79-701378
Examines the popularity of running in the United States and traces the roots of long - distance running from ancient Greece. Shows America's most popular road races.
Physical Education and Recreation
Dist - DARRAH

Momentum 10 MIN
16mm
Color
LC 79-701179
Uses experimental techniques to offer a glimpse of the world of an auto mechanic.
Fine Arts; Industrial and Technical Education
Dist - DAYRAY **Prod** - DAYRAY 1979

Momentum 9 MIN
U-matic / VHS
Introductory Concepts in Physics - Dynamics Series
Color (C)
$229.00, $129.00 purchase _ #AD - 1190
Reveals that when bodies in motion collide, the impact on one is determined by the mass and speed of the other. Examines momentum before and after collision.
Science - Physical
Dist - FOTH **Prod** - FOTH

Momentum - 8 50 MIN
VHS
Conceptual physics alive series
Color (H C)
$45.00 purchase
Rearranges Newton's 2nd law to the form - impulse equals change in momentum. Uses a variety of everyday examples, such as bouncing, to illustrate the concept. Demonstrates conservation of motion with colliding cars on an air track. Part 8 of a 35 - part series adapted from the college and high school textbook Conceptual Physics by Professor Paul Hewitt.
Science - Physical
Dist - MMENTE **Prod** - HEWITP 1992

Momma Never Told Me about VD 25 MIN
U-matic / VHS
Color
Shows high school students of the Youth Gives A Dam Health Club staging a health happening to present the facts about the venereal disease epidemic. Features skits, student - on - the - street interviews, a 'talking bus', a tour of a VD clinic and a rap session with health officials.
Health and Safety
Dist - MEDCOM **Prod** - MEDCOM

Momma Violet's Wish 30 MIN
U-matic
Gettin' to Know Me Series
Color (I J H)
History - United States; Sociology
Dist - GPN **Prod** - CTI 1979

Mommies - are You My Mother - the Way Mothers are 15 MIN
U-matic
Tilson's Book Shop Series

Color (P)
Presents the children's stories Mommies by Lonnie Carton, Are You My Mother by P D Eastman, and The Way Mothers Are by Miriam Schlein.
Literature and Drama
Dist - GPN **Prod** - WVIZTV 1975

Mommy, Daddy and Me 30 MIN
VHS / U-matic
Color (I)
Examines changes in the family over the past quarter - century. Looks at single - parent households and homes in which both parents work. Features Dr Benjamin Spock introducing a discussion of these changes.
Psychology; Sociology
Dist - WETATV **Prod** - WETATV

Momokko Taro - the Story of a Boy who was Born from a Peach 17 MIN
16mm
Color
Tells a Japanese folk tale.
Literature and Drama
Dist - UNIJAP **Prod** - UNIJAP

Moms, dads and other endangered species 30 MIN
VHS
Stop, look, and laugh series
Color (J H R)
$19.95 purchase, $10.00 rental _ #35 - 821 - 19
Explores the question of what parents expect from their children. Uses humor, comic vignettes and a question - and - answer session to present a Christian perspective. Hosted by Pat Hurley.
Literature and Drama; Religion and Philosophy
Dist - APH **Prod** - CPH
CPH

Mon Bras, Ton Nez 10 MIN
U-matic / VHS
Salut - French Language Lessons Series
Color
Focuses on parts of the body and possessive adjectives.
Foreign Language
Dist - BCNFL **Prod** - BCNFL 1984

Mon oncle 116 MIN
VHS
Color (G) (FRENCH (ENGLISH SUBTITLES) FRENCH (ENGLISH DUBBING))
$29.95 purchase _ #S00919A, #S00919
Tells the story of Mr Hulot and his constant mishaps while living with his sister and brother - in - law. Stars Jacques Tati, Jean - Pierre Zola, Adrienne Servantie, and Alain Bercourt. Written and directed by Tati.
Fine Arts
Dist - UILL

Mon oncle 87 MIN
VHS
Color (H G) (FRENCH)
$39.00 purchase _ #05825 - 126
Portrays a man's comic battle again a high technology life in an automated building. Directed by Jacques Tati.
Fine Arts; Literature and Drama
Dist - GA **Prod** - GA

Mon oncle Antoine 104 MIN
VHS
Color (G)
$39.95 _ #MON050
Explores the coming - of - age of a 15 - year - old boy in a small, economically depressed mining town in the backwoods of Quebec. Deals with universal truths about life, death, fear, love and desire. Directed by Claude Jutra.
Fine Arts; Psychology; Sociology
Dist - HOMVIS **Prod** - JANUS 1971

Mon Pays Est Ma Vie 27 MIN
16mm
Color (G)
#3X49N
Docements the November 13, 1967 move of the Northwest Territory from Ottawa to Yellowknife. Explains how the responsibility for the North is now on the shoulders of the new elected government body.
Civics and Political Systems; History - World
Dist - CDIAND **Prod** - DWMP 1975

Mon Pere Est Electricien 16 MIN
16mm / U-matic / VHS
Color (P I J H) (FRENCH)
A French - language version of the motion picture My Pop's A Lineman. Shows a lineman who sees his son trying to retrieve a kite tangled in a high voltage line and takes the boy to work with him. Dramatizes several dangerous situations involving high tension wires. Includes flashbacks to a high - voltage demonstration by H C Potthast.
Foreign Language; Health and Safety; Social Science
Dist - IFB **Prod** - STSC 1957

Mon ticket s'il vous plait 13 MIN
16mm
Les Francais chez vous series
B&W (I J H)
Foreign Language
Dist - CHLTN **Prod** - PEREN 1967

Mona Lisa descending a staircase 8 MIN
VHS / Videodisc
Color (H C A)
$195.00 purchase
Uses animation to take the viewer on a tour of various schools of art, from post - impressionism to pop - art, covering the works of 35 artists ranging from Van Gogh to Warhol. Produced by Joan Gratz.
Fine Arts
Dist - PFP

Monarch 15 MIN
16mm
Color (I)
LC 79-700962
Traces the life cycle of the monarch butterfly.
Science - Natural
Dist - CANFDC **Prod** - MELFIL 1979

The Monarch and the Milkweed 11 MIN
16mm / U-matic / VHS
Many Worlds of Nature Series
Color
LC 77-700173
Shows the unique life histories of both the monarch butterfly and the milkweed plant and their relationship to each other.
Science - Natural
Dist - CORF **Prod** - MORALL 1975

The Monarch Butterfly Story 11 MIN
16mm / U-matic / VHS
Color (P I J H C)
LC FIA68-1142
Pictures the geographical range of the monarch butterfly and shows close - up detail of its structure during various stages of its life cycle - - egg, larva, chrysalis and imago. Shows a larva developing within an egg, the larva hatching and molting several times, the spinning of a cocoon and emergence of the adult. Investigates the migratory Habit.
Science - Natural
Dist - EBEC **Prod** - EBEC 1967

Monarch Magic 20 MIN
VHS / U-matic
Color (J)
Shows the metamorphosis of a caterpillar into a beautiful Monarch butterfly.
Science - Natural
Dist - AWSS **Prod** - AWSS 1981

A Monarchy of trees - New Forest, Hampshire, England 24 MIN
VHS / 16mm
Amateur naturalist series
Color (I J H C G)
$495.00, $195.00 purchase
Observes autumn and spring in 800 - year - old woodlands. Looks at the strategies of squirrels, voles, adders, bats and dormice for the approaching winter. Shows the the emergence of badgers and the singing of birds in the spring. Part of a 13 - part series featuring a naturalist and a zoologist, Gerald and Lee Durrell, on field trips to different habitats.
Geography - World; Science - Natural
Dist - LANDMK **Prod** - LANDMK 1988

The Monastery (1981 Version) 72 MIN
VHS
Color
From the ABC TV program, Close Up.
Religion and Philosophy
Dist - ABCLR **Prod** - ABCLR 1981

The Monastery (1982 Version) 60 MIN
VHS
Color
From the ABC TV program, Close Up.
Religion and Philosophy
Dist - ABCLR **Prod** - ABCLR 1982

Monasticism 30 MIN
VHS
Saints and legions series
Color (H)
$69.95 purchase
Looks at monasticism. Part 11 of a twenty - six part series which introduces personalities, movements and events in ancient history responsible for the beginnings of Western Civilization.
History - World; Religion and Philosophy
Dist - SCETV **Prod** - SCETV 1982

The Moncada Program 51 MIN
16mm / U-matic / VHS
Captioned; Color (A) (SPANISH (ENGLISH SUBTITLES))
Discusses the programs and accomplishments of the Cuban Revolution, including agrarian reform, nationalization of foreign - owned businesses, and improvements in housing, education and health care for the Cuban people. Spanish dialog with English subtitles.
Fine Arts; History - World
Dist - CNEMAG **Prod** - CUBAFI 1973

Mondale - Presidential Candidate 17 MIN
U-matic / VHS
Color (H C A)
Presents an in - depth look at Walter Mondale, former Vice - President and Presidential nominee of the Democratic Party. Examines his past political affiliations, their likely effects and possible challengers.
Biography; Civics and Political Systems
Dist - JOU **Prod** - JOU

The Monday morning absentee 21 MIN
16mm
Color (G IND)
$5.00 rental
Follows an arbitration hearing for an employee with a drinking problem who is discharged when he fails to appear for work and does not call in. Reveals that later he is able to produce a valid reason for his absence. Determines if the dismissal was justified.
Business and Economics; Psychology; Social Science
Dist - AFLCIO **Prod** - AARA 1978

Monday's girls 50 MIN
VHS
Color (G)
$75.00 rental, $295.00 purchase
Follows two young Nigerian women's different experiences of a traditional rite of passage. Reveals how the young virgins, 'irabo,' spend five weeks in 'fattening rooms,' with heavy copper coils on their legs to enforce inactivity as they are waited on and honored by their families, finally emerging to dance before the villagers and to be married. Portrays Florence, from the village and eager to take part, and Akisiye, who returns from the city at her father's behest and uncertain about participating. Combines voice - over and interviews to document tradition, modernity, dissent and contradiction in African women's lives.
Fine Arts; Religion and Philosophy; Sociology
Dist - WMEN **Prod** - NGON 1993

Mondo Cane 105 MIN
16mm / U-matic / VHS
Color (C A)
Displays the weird, the bizarre and the grotesque customs of 'CIVILIZED' man the world over. Combines with a striking musical score and a witty and often ironic commentary on man's foibles.
Fine Arts; Psychology; Sociology
Dist - FI **Prod** - UNKNWN 1963

Mondo cane 1
VHS
Color (G)
$39.95 purchase _ #VF004
Presents a look at bizarre - tree climbing fish, self mutilations, a tribe of plane worshippers, etc. Part of two parts.
Science - Natural; Sociology
Dist - SIV

Mondo cane 2
VHS
Color (G)
$39.95 purchase _ #VF005
Presents the bizarre world of tree - climbing fish, self - mutilations, a tribe of plane worshippers and more human and natural oddities.
Religion and Philosophy
Dist - SIV

The Mondragon Experiment 50 MIN
U-matic / VHS / 16mm
Color (C A)
Studies the economic health of Mondragon, Spain where more than 80 factories are cooperatively owned by the workers. Shows that the 18,000 workers appoint the managers and make the decisions, thereby creating the most efficient factories in all of Spain.
Business and Economics; History - World
Dist - FI **Prod** - BBCTV 1981

Mondrian 29 MIN
U-matic
Meet the Masters Series
B&W
Presents the technique and profound influence of contemporary painter Mondrian.
Fine Arts
Dist - UMITV **Prod** - UMITV 1966

Mondrian 30 MIN
VHS
Color (G)

$29.95 purchase _ #ACE11V - F
Highlights the development of artist Piet Mondrian's abstract style of painting that focused on basic colors and perpendicular lines.
Fine Arts
Dist - CAMV

Monera - bacteria and cyanobacteria - classification, structure , reproduction - Part one 19 MIN
VHS / U-matic
Modern biology series
Color (H C)
LC 90-708075
Explores the Kingdom Monera which contains single - celled organisms not having a nucleus. Looks at the systems of classifications by size, shape, external and internal structures, methods of reproduction. Part one of two parts on Monera.
Science - Natural
Dist - BNCHMK **Prod** - BNCHMK 1990

Monera - bacteria and cyanobacteria - nutrition and respiration - Part two 15 MIN
VHS / U-matic
Modern biology series
Color (H C)
LC 90-708076
Explores the Kingdom Monera which contains single - celled organisms not having a nucleus. Looks at methods of consuming energy and respiration of Monera. Part two of two parts on Monera.
Science - Natural
Dist - BNCHMK **Prod** - BNCHMK 1990

Monet 4 MIN
16mm
Color
Employs the comments of artist Claude Monet which underscore the development of his style as seen in paintings dating from the 1870s to the early years of the 20th century.
Fine Arts
Dist - USNGA **Prod** - USNGA

Monet 27 MIN
VHS
Color (J)
$29.95 purchase _ #HV - 936
Presents Monet's story as an Impressionist artist using his own words from journal excerpts. Includes personal interviews, his paintings and views of his home and scenes he painted.
Fine Arts; History - World
Dist - CRYSP **Prod** - CRYSP

Monet - legacy of light 27 MIN
VHS
Color (I J H)
$29.95 purchase _ #771 - 9002
Uses letters, journals, interviews and the works of Monet to tell of his quest to capture light and color.
Fine Arts
Dist - KNOWUN

Monetary and Fiscal Policy 45 MIN
U-matic / VHS
Economic Perspectives Series
Color
Discusses aspects of monetary and fiscal policy.
Business and Economics
Dist - MDCPB **Prod** - MDCPB

Monetary policy - differing views 60 MIN
VHS
Macroeconomics series
Color (H C G)
$89.00 purchase _ #GSU - 322
Examines the effects of monetary policy in part of a 24 - part series instructed by Dr Edward F Stuart, Northwestern University, which focuses on a description of the major economic policy - making bodies in the United States and their interrelationships.
Business and Economics
Dist - INSTRU

Monetary Policy - How Well Does it Work 30 MIN
U-matic / VHS
Economics USA Series
Color (C)
Business and Economics
Dist - ANNCPB **Prod** - WEFA

Monetary Policy I 45 MIN
VHS / U-matic
Economic Perspectives Series
Color
Discusses aspects of American monetary policy.
Business and Economics
Dist - MDCPB **Prod** - MDCPB

Monetary Policy II 45 MIN
U-matic / VHS
Economic Perspectives Series
Color
Discusses aspects of American monetary policy.
Business and Economics
Dist - MDCPB **Prod** - MDCPB

Monex - the Monsoon Experiment 20 MIN
U-matic / VHS / 16mm
Color (H A)
Documents a scientific venture undertaken by the United States andSoutheast Asia. It is an attempt to understand the mechanism of monsoons in hope of improving short - range predictions of monsoon rainfall, cyclones and other related events.
History - World; Science; Science - Physical
Dist - USNAC **Prod** - NSF 1981

Money 15 MIN
16mm / U-matic / VHS
Color (I J H)
LC 78-700966
Highlights the history of money from cows and elephant tails to credit cards and computers.
Business and Economics; Social Science
Dist - GA **Prod** - WMD 1978

Money 15 MIN
U-matic
Math Makers One Series
Color (I)
Presents the math concepts of budgeting, the history of money, change making problems, money problems up to $10, rate problems, time approximations involving weeks and months and interest.
Education; Mathematics
Dist - TVOTAR **Prod** - TVOTAR 1979

Money 30 MIN
VHS / 16mm
Growing a Business Series
(H C)
$99.95 each, $1,295.00 series
Looks at the role captial plays in building a new business.
Business and Economics
Dist - AMBROS **Prod** - AMBROS 1988

Money 29 MIN
U-matic
Woman Series
Color
Discusses the extent of women's economic clout and warns of the need for women to avoid exploitation by marketing specialists.
Home Economics; Sociology
Dist - PBS **Prod** - WNEDTV

Money 15 MIN
VHS
Color (G)
$40.00 rental, $25.00 purchase
Centers around a discussion of economic problems facing avant - garde artists in the Reagan era. Fragments the discussion into words and phrases to resemble writing. Filmed mostly on the Manhattan streets. Produced by Henry Hills.
Fine Arts
Dist - CANCIN

Money 20 MIN
U-matic / VHS
Contract Series
Color (J H)
English Language
Dist - AITECH **Prod** - KYTV 1977

Money 45 MIN
16mm
B&W (G)
$50.00 rental
Presents a silent - screen type comedy starring Edwin Denby as mean old billionaire Hemlock Stinge, along with a variety of other nasty characters rich and poor.
Fine Arts
Dist - CANCIN **Prod** - BURCKR 1968

Money 16 MIN
VHS / U-matic
Math Cycle Series
Color (P)
Discusses valutes of U S currency.
Mathematics
Dist - GPN **Prod** - WDCNTV 1983

Money and Banking 28 MIN
16mm
Color (H C)
LC 75-702723
Explains the American monetary and fiscal policies. Includes how the Federal Reserve exercises control in expanding and contracting bank credit.
Business and Economics
Dist - SUTHLA **Prod** - SPI 1968

Money and banking 30 MIN
VHS
Introductory economics series
Color; PAL (J H C G)
PdS29.50 purchase
Examines government attempts to stabilize the economy, focusing on monetary policy. Teaches about fractional reserve banking. Features Ellen Roseman and Professor John Palmer describing three methods. Part of a four - part series.
Business and Economics
Dist - EMFVL **Prod** - TVOTAR

Money and How it Works 20 MIN
U-matic
Exploring Our Nation Series
Color (I)
Shows how money is made and discusses its distribution.
Business and Economics
Dist - GPN **Prod** - KRMATV 1975

Money and Inflation 81 MIN
U-matic / VHS
Milton Friedman Speaking Series Lecture 6
Color (C)
LC 79-708065
Presents economist Milton Friedman examining the causes and possible cures of inflation.
Business and Economics
Dist - HBJ **Prod** - HBJ 1980

Money and Inflation, Pt 1 40 MIN
U-matic / VHS
Milton Friedman Speaking Series Lecture 6
Color (C)
LC 79-708065
Presents economist Milton Friedman examining the causes and possible cures of inflation.
Business and Economics
Dist - HBJ **Prod** - HBJ 1980

Money and Inflation, Pt 2 41 MIN
VHS / U-matic
Milton Friedman Speaking Series Lecture 6
Color (C)
LC 79-708065
Presents economist Milton Friedman examining the causes and possible cures of inflation.
Business and Economics
Dist - HBJ **Prod** - HBJ 1980

Money and Interest 145 MIN
U-matic
University of the Air Series
Color (J H C A)
$750.00 purchase, $250.00 rental
Examines simples and compound interest calculations, concepts of annuities and mortgages, and their percentage payments of principal and interest. Program contains a series of five cassettes 29 minutes each.
Business and Economics
Dist - CTV **Prod** - CTV 1978

Money and monetary policy 28 MIN
VHS
Color; PAL (J H)
PdS29.50 purchase
Facilitates the understanding of money and monetary policy. Provides viewers with the opportunity to hear experts making decisions, usually done behind closed doors. Includes notes. Intended as a teaching and learning aid for students of economics and business at the GCSE and advanced level, and for those in the first year of a degree course.
Business and Economics; Psychology
Dist - EMFVL **Prod** - GLAMOR

Money and Politics 60 MIN
U-matic / VHS
Bill Moyers' Journal Series
Color
Looks at the rising number and increasing influence of corporate and political action committees, citing the influence their money has on legislation.
Civics and Political Systems
Dist - PBS **Prod** - WNETTV 1980

Money and the banking system - the Fed acts, banks react 12 MIN
35mm strip / VHS
Our economy - how it works series
Color (J H C A)
$39.00, $39.00 purchase _ #MB - 510678 - 7, #MB - 508872 - X
Presents the fifth segment of a six - part series on basic concepts of economics. Focuses on the banking system, including savings institutions, as well as on the importance of the money that drives the system.
Business and Economics
Dist - SRA **Prod** - SRA

Money and the economy 60 MIN
VHS
Macroeconomics series
Color (H C G)
$89.00 purchase _ #GSU - 321
Discusses classic Keynesian and monetarist views of the role of money in income determination. Interviews Charles Furbee, Senior VP, Federal Reserve Bank of Chicago. Part of a 24 - part series instructed by Dr Edward F Stuart, Northwestern University, which focuses on a description of the major economic policy - making bodies in the United States and their interrelationships.
Business and Economics
Dist - INSTRU

Money and Work - Living it Your Way 16 MIN
U-matic / VHS / 16mm
Color (J H C)
Depicts a young woman who, having just finished school, has to decide whether or not to opt for dollars in traditional careers, or for small cash but big enjoyment at a career she loves.
Guidance and Counseling
Dist - BCNFL **Prod** - HARDAP 1983

Money business 22 MIN
U-matic / 16mm / VHS
Color (K P I)
$495.00, $375.00, $345.00 purchase _ #A369
Tells about Barney the little bear who learns about money and the responsibilities that come along with it. Reveals that Barney wants a saxophone but he doesn't have enough money. Then Barney gets a job at the Paradise Cafe and discovers that working can be fun. Produced by Timothy Armstrong.
Business and Economics; Guidance and Counseling
Dist - BARR **Prod** - SANCIN 1985

Money Business 15 MIN
U-matic
Math Factory, Module VI - Money Series
Color (P)
Presents money problems that require the use of two - place subtraction with regrouping of tens and ones.
Business and Economics; Mathematics
Dist - GPN **Prod** - MAETEL 1973

The Money Can 10 MIN
16mm
Color
LC 76-702319
Points out the benefits of recycling aluminum cans.
Industrial and Technical Education; Science - Natural
Dist - REYMC **Prod** - REYMC 1974

Money - earning, saving and investing it 24 MIN
VHS
Color (H)
$39.95 purchase _ #LF903V-H
Helps teens learn about how money works in our society - how it is earned, saved, invested and wisely spent. Topics include saving as a goal, the cycle of money, the differences among investing in savings, checking, money market accounts, or stocks and bonds, summer jobs and mentoring successful professionals.
Business and Economics; Home Economics
Dist - CAMV

Money for Sale 13 MIN
16mm / U-matic / VHS
Captioned; Color (J) (SPANISH)
LC 75-700959
Presents an animated film which uses the character of a kindly pawnbroker to show how to borrow money intelligently. Suggests sources for borrowed money, stressing the importance of shopping for a loan and restraint in borrowing. Explains in detail Federal truth in lending legislation.
Business and Economics; Home Economics; Social Science
Dist - AIMS **Prod** - NULSEN 1974

The Money Game 16 MIN
U-matic / VHS
Color (H C A)
Tells the story of a young Canadian golfer who is still seeking his first tour victory. Discusses the intense competition and frustration in golf.
Physical Education and Recreation
Dist - JOU **Prod** - CANBC

Money - How its Value Changes 14 MIN
U-matic / VHS / 16mm
Color (J H C)
LC 73-713119
Explains how changes in the value of money are related to concepts such as cost of living, recession, depression, supply and demand and inflation.
Business and Economics; Social Science
Dist - CORF **Prod** - CORF 1971

Money in the Marketplace 15 MIN
U-matic / VHS / 16mm
Marketplace Series
Color (P I)
$59.00 purchase _ #3494
Provides an introduction to economics and basic money concepts. Uses a trip through a flea market to examine the ideas of marketplace, consumer, demand and value. Shows that money must be durable, portable and acceptable.
Business and Economics; Home Economics; Social Science
Dist - EBEC **Prod** - EBEC

Money laundering and currency violations - Traps for the unwary attorney and client 50 MIN
VHS
Color (C PRO A)
$95.00 purchase _ #Y136
Examines various civil and criminal penalties attached to monetary transactions aimed at changing the form of money or concealing the ownership of 'dirty' money. Includes specific topics such as legal mechanisms dealing with criminal money laundering, reports to the IRS, evasive schemes and devices commonly used by violators, ways in which lawyers can handle the proceeds of crime and sensible cash receipt policies for law practices.
Business and Economics; Civics and Political Systems; Sociology
Dist - ALIABA **Prod** - CLETV 1990

Money Magic 11 MIN
16mm
Kids and Cash Series
Color (P I J)
Addresses the basic principles of money management and how to spend wisely. Includes some consumer math and good buying practices. Seeks to improve skills of buying through a variety of educational and cinematic techniques including live action, special effects and simple animation combined in a short, fast - paced presentation.
Business and Economics; Fine Arts; Home Economics; Social Science
Dist - COUNFI **Prod** - COUNFI

Money makers series
Profiles Sir John Harvey - Jones of the United Kingdom, Giovanni Agnelli of Italy, Akio Morita of Japan, Robert Orville Anderson of the United States, Stanley Ho of Macau and Russi Mody of India. Examines the background history and vicissitudes of their business empires and uses interviews to determine the practicality and fallibility of their commercial philosophies. Part of a series featuring six of the world's leading entrepreneurs.

Betting on a certainty	30 MIN
The Company man	30 MIN
India's steel man	30 MIN
Italy's uncrowned king	30 MIN
Japan's super salesman	30 MIN
The Oil tycoon	30 MIN

Dist - BBCENE

The Money making merger of music and video 30 MIN
U-matic
Adam Smith's money world series; 149
Color (A)
Attempts to demystify the world of money and break it down so that small as well as large businesses and it's people understand and adjust to new social and economic trends. Reports on the major economic stories and discoveries of the day.
Business and Economics
Dist - PBS **Prod** - WNETTV 1985

Money man 60 MIN
VHS
Color (G)
$39.95 purchase _ #MON - 05
Portrays J S G Boggs who makes money the old - fashioned way, and the government is out to stop him. Reveals that Boggs is an artist whose medium is money, and his 'dollars' have been confiscated as counterfeit by the US Treasury. Follows Boggs as he heads to Washington on a mission to convince the giant bureaucracy of the Treasury to return his confiscated notes, while along the way he uses his art to spread his 'subversive' message and to buy a variety of things, including a motorcycle and a stay in a posh hotel.
Industrial and Technical Education; Literature and Drama
Dist - ARTSAM **Prod** - HAASPH

Money Management
VHS
Marriage, Family Living and Counseling Series
(C G)
$59.00_CA233
Discusses family money management.
Business and Economics; Guidance and Counseling
Dist - AAVIM **Prod** - AAVIM 1989

Money Management 20 MIN
U-matic / VHS
Consumer Squad Series
Color
Shows how to develop a budget and start a savings account as Squad member Karen helps a friend who is constantly running out of money.
Business and Economics; Home Economics
Dist - PBS **Prod** - MSITV 1982

Money Management and Family Financial Planning Series

Banking	18 MIN
Budgeting	12 MIN
Buying	13 MIN
Credit	18 MIN
Insurance	17 MIN
Securities	19 MIN

Dist - AETNA

Money Management in Troubled Times 25 MIN
VHS / U-matic
Your Money Matters Series
Color
Gives quiz to determine possible financial pitfalls. Presents hints on better money management.
Business and Economics; Social Science
Dist - FILMID **Prod** - FILMID

Money managers 30 MIN
U-matic
Adam Smith's money world series; 112
Color (A)
Attempts to demystify the world of money and break it down so that small as well as large businesses and it's people understand and adjust to new social and economic trends. Reports on the major economic stories and discoveries of the day.
Business and Economics
Dist - PBS **Prod** - WNETTV 1985

The Money Market 28 MIN
VHS / U-matic
Personal Finance and Money Management Series
Color (C A)
Business and Economics; Civics and Political Systems
Dist - SCCON **Prod** - SCCON 1987

The Money Market 30 MIN
U-matic / VHS
Personal Finance Series Lesson 16
Color (C A)
Introduces money market investments such as savings accounts, certificates of deposit, bonds, mutual funds and individual retirement accounts. Defines several terms.
Business and Economics
Dist - CDTEL **Prod** - SCCON

The Money Masters - the Federal Reserve System 48 MIN
U-matic / VHS
Color
$455.00 purchase
Business and Economics
Dist - ABCLR **Prod** - ABCLR 1982

Money Matters 15 MIN
U-matic / VHS
Math Mission 2 Series
Color (P)
LC 82-706330
Tells how a space robot's puppet assistant learns about money, including the names of U S coins, the value of each in cents, and their values as fractional parts of the dollar. Shows how she finds out that items other that coins were used in colonial times.
Business and Economics; Mathematics
Dist - GPN **Prod** - WCVETV 1980

Money Matters - Introduction 15 MIN
VHS / U-matic
Money Matters Series Pt 1
Color (I)
LC 83-706012
Presents a cast of three ten - year - old children interacting with adults to demonstrate various economic concepts and business activities.
Business and Economics
Dist - GPN **Prod** - KEDTTV 1982

Money Matters Series Pt 1
Money Matters - Introduction 15 MIN
Dist - GPN

Money, Money, Money 14 MIN
16mm
Screen news digest series; Vol 25; Issue 5
Color
Reviews the American banking system and its effect on government and fiscal policy.
Business and Economics
Dist - AFA **Prod** - AFA 1983

Money on the land 100 FRS
35mm strip / 16mm / VHS / U-matic
America - a personal history of the United States series
Color (H C A) (SPANISH)
LC 74-734119; 77-701681
Deals with the industrialization of the United States at the beginning of the 20th century. Discusses the American inventors whose newly discovered methods and resources were exploited by the Rockefellers, Carnegies and other industrialists for business purposes.
Business and Economics; History - United States; Social Science
Dist - TIMLIF **Prod** - BBCTV 1973

Money on the Land 52 MIN
16mm / VHS
America Series
(J H C)
$99.95 each, $595.00 series
Discusses the rise of industrialism in the United States, focusing on inventions and entrepeneurs.
Geography - United States; History - United States
Dist - AMBROS **Prod** - AMBROS 1973

Money on the land - Pt 1 26 MIN
16mm / U-matic
America - a personal history of the United States series; No 8
Color (J)
LC 74-701578
Depicts how the focus of America is given over from the farmer to the cities. Describes how the early inventors, like Edison, find the methods and resources and then the Rockefellers, Carnegies and Vanderbilts move in. Narrated by Alistair Cooke.
Social Science
Dist - TIMLIF **Prod** - BBCTV 1972

Money on the land - Pt 2 26 MIN
16mm / U-matic
America - a personal history of the United States series; No 8
Color (J)
LC 74-701578
Depicts how the focus of America is given over from the farmer to the cities. Describes how the early inventors, like Edison, find the methods and resources and then the Rockefellers, Carnegies and Vanderbilts move in. Narrated by Alistair Cooke.
Social Science
Dist - TIMLIF **Prod** - BBCTV 1972

Money, power, status - can women have it all with an MBA 30 MIN
U-matic
Adam Smith's money world 1985 - 1986 season series; 210
Color (A)
Attempts to demystify the world of money and break it down so that small as well as large businesses and it's people understand and adjust to new social and economic trends. Reports on the major economic stories and discoveries of 1985 and 1986.
Business and Economics
Dist - PBS **Prod** - WNETTV 1986

Money, Pt 1 15 MIN
U-matic
Studio M Series
Color (P)
Tells how to name coins needed for sums less than one dollar and how to name the smallest amount of coins for a given amount.
Business and Economics
Dist - GPN **Prod** - WCETTV 1979

Money, Pt 2 15 MIN
U-matic
Studio M Series
Color (P)
Explains how to use money to show how to rename ten as ten ones.
Business and Economics
Dist - GPN **Prod** - WCETTV 1979

Money Puzzle - the World of Macroeconomics Series Module 11
A Run for Your Money 30 MIN
Dist - MDCC

Money Puzzle - the World of Macroeconomics Series Module 13
Slippin' away 30 MIN
A Steep and Thorny Path 30 MIN
Dist - MDCC

Money Puzzle - the World of Macroeconomics Series Module 15
The Investors 30 MIN
Dist - MDCC

Money Puzzle - the World of Macroeconomics Series Module 1
The Pieces of the Puzzle 30 MIN
Dist - MDCC

Money Puzzle - the World of Macroeconomics Series Module 2
The Invisible Hand 30 MIN
You Can't Always Get what You Want 30 MIN
Dist - MDCC

Money Puzzle - the World of Macroeconomics Series Module 3
The Free Rider 30 MIN
Dist - MDCC

Money Puzzle - the World of Macroeconomics Series Module 4
Familiar Fallacies 30 MIN
Loopholes 30 MIN
Dist - MDCC

Money Puzzle - the World of Macroeconomics Series Module 6
Measuring My Success 30 MIN
Dist - MDCC

Money Puzzle - the World of Macroeconomics Series Module 7
Withdrawal Symptoms 30 MIN
Dist - MDCC

Money Puzzle - the World of Macroeconomics Series Module 9
The Inspectors 30 MIN
Dist - MDCC

Money puzzle - the world of macroeconomics series
All of the people, all of the time 30 MIN
All that glitters is gold 30 MIN
Balancing act 30 MIN
Blowing the whistle 30 MIN
Don't let them take my job away 30 MIN
Economic roller coaster 30 MIN
Fast food economics 30 MIN
Getting and spending 30 MIN
Go with the flow - Module 6 30 MIN
Income, go forth and multiply 30 MIN
Karen goes political 30 MIN
Karen's magic flute 30 MIN
The Man who Needed Nobody 30 MIN
The Shrinking dollar 30 MIN
Thomas and the fiscal fighters 30 MIN
The Tightrope walkers 30 MIN
Dist - MDCC

The Money Shuttle 60 MIN
U-matic / VHS
Sixty Minutes on Business Series
Color (G)
Business and Economics
Dist - VPHI **Prod** - VPHI 1984

The Money Shuttle - Rockwell International Corp
U-matic / VHS
Sixty Minutes on Business Series
Color
One of ten segments selected from the realities of the business world, and chosen from key `60 Minutes' telecasts to provide insight with vital issues affecting business today. Includes sourcebook.
Business and Economics; Psychology
Dist - CBSFOX **Prod** - CBSFOX

Money Smart - a Guide to Personal Finance Series
Buying a house 25 MIN
Designing your financial plan 25 MIN
Effective buying 25 MIN
Insuring Your Life 25 MIN
Investing in Stocks 25 MIN
Planning for Financial Success 25 MIN
Planning for Retirement 25 MIN
Principles of Investment 25 MIN
Property and Liability Insurance 25 MIN
Putting Your Financial Plan into Action 25 MIN
Renting Your Money for Profit 25 MIN
Using Credit Wisely 25 MIN
Your will and Estate 25 MIN
Dist - BCNFL

Money - Summing it Up 23 MIN
16mm / U-matic / VHS
Color (I)
LC 82-700718
Chronicles the use of barter and commodity money, then gold and silver, and finally paper money. Describes the function of the Federal Reserve System in regulating the supply of money and shows new money being printed and old money being destroyed.
Business and Economics
Dist - NGS **Prod** - NGS 1982

Money Talk 6.33 MIN
VHS
Spanish Plus Series
(J H A) (SPANISH)
Explains the numbers in the hundreds and thousands and then possesive adjectives in the Spanish Language.
Foreign Language
Dist - AITECH **Prod** - LANGPL 1985

Money Talk 4.41 MIN
VHS
English Plus Series
(J H A)
Covers contractions, pronouns and numbers in the hundreds and thousands.
English Language
Dist - AITECH **Prod** - LANGPL 1985

Money Talks 26 MIN
16mm
Color
LC 74-702873
Traces the history of taxation in the United States from its beginning to the present.
Civics and Political Systems; History - United States; Social Science
Dist - PTRHG **Prod** - PTRHG 1974

Money - the Bottom Line - Financial Decisions Faced by the Small Business Person
VHS
Entrepreneurs - the Risk Takers Series
$70.00 purchase _ #RPS3V
Demonstrates how financial decision making affects the day to day business of entrepreneurs and the profits and losses of their companies.
Business and Economics
Dist - CAREER **Prod** - CAREER

Money - the Nature of Money 10 MIN
U-matic / VHS / 16mm
Foundations of Wealth Series
Color
Explains how money developed to meet the need for a readily acceptable medium of exchange. Discusses the characteristics of money as a measure of worth.
Business and Economics
Dist - FOTH **Prod** - FOTH

Money to Burn 12 MIN
16mm
Color
Shows how to conserve natural gas and save money.
Science - Natural; Social Science
Dist - BUGAS **Prod** - BUGAS

The Money Tree 21 MIN
16mm / U-matic / VHS
Color (J)
LC 83-700197
Stresses the importance of good money sense, telling the story of a young married couple who are in deep financial trouble. Shows how they are misled by societal and economic pressures as well as their own lack of sophistication in dealing with those pressures.
Home Economics
Dist - AIMS **Prod** - AIMS 1983

Money - what It's Worth 16 MIN
U-matic / VHS / 16mm
Color (I J)
LC 76-700063
Uses animated explanations of a computer to define money, describe its convenience and show why its various forms evolved.
Business and Economics; Home Economics
Dist - ALTSUL **Prod** - ALTSUL 1975

Money with Jacob Needleman 30 MIN
U-matic / VHS
World of ideas with Bill Moyers - season 2 series
Color; Captioned (A G)
$39.95, $59.95 purchase _ #WIWM - 222
Features Jacob Needleman, author and professor of philosophy and comparative religion at San Francisco State University. Discusses money and its power to shape life's meaning. Addresses the dilemma of how to make a living and still keep one's soul. Reveals that after 100 years of time saving inventions, people have lots of material things, but no time. Part of a series with Bill Moyers that explores the ideas and values shaping our future, and featuring scientists, writers, artists, philosophers, historians and others.
Business and Economics; Sociology
Dist - PBS

The Money X - Change 35 MIN
16mm
Color

LC 78-701437
Offers an introduction to the mechanics of the world money market and foreign exchange transactions. Traces the historical development of market concepts and explains how socio - political changes affect the values of foreign and domestic currencies.
Business and Economics; Social Science
Dist - COUNFI **Prod** - AMCOL 1977

Moneywatchers Series
The High Cost of Healing 59 MIN
Inflation - the Money Merry - Go - Round 59 MIN
The Quality of Life 58 MIN
Dist - PBS

Mongane Serote 35 MIN
VHS
Color (H C G)
$79.00 purchase
Features the writer Mongane Serote talking with Edward Blishen about South Africa's society as a spur to writing and the role of writers in expressing the people's concerns. Discusses his works including Yakhal'Inkomo; Tsetlo; No Baby Must Weep; and his novel, To Every Birth Its Blood.
Literature and Drama
Dist - ROLAND **Prod** - INCART

The Mongol Empire - November 18, 1247 30 MIN
VHS / 16mm
Timeline Video Series
Color (J)
$69.95 purchase _ #ZF303VTM
Focuses on the Mongol army, fully mobilized and moving west. Considers the proverb 'The enemy of my enemy is my friend' as Catholics look for Mongol support against Islam, and some Moslems look for Christian support against the Mongols. Portrays Brother Carpini, the Pope's peace envoy, whose message from the Mongols is ignored by Europeans. These events create a lasting belief pattern. Centuries later, when Europe looks east at Russia, it recalls the horror of the Mongol hordes.
Geography - World; History - World; Social Science
Dist - ZENGER **Prod** - MPTPB 1989

Mongol Onslaught, 850 - 1500 26 MIN
16mm / U-matic / VHS
World - a Television History Series
Color (J H C)
MV=$400
Describes the terrorizing campaigns of the Mongols led by Genghis Khan. The Mongols were legendary for their military skills and superb horsemanship. They went on to create one of the largest empires in world history.
History - World
Dist - LANDMK **Prod** - NETGOL 1985

The Mongol onslaught - 850 - 1500 30 MIN
VHS
World - A Television history series
Color (C A T)
$55.00 rental
Covers the Mongols and their role in the period from 850 to 1500. Based on "The Times Atlas of World History." Serves as part 10 of a 26 - part telecourse. Available only to institutions of higher education.
History - World; Sociology
Dist - SCETV **Prod** - SCETV 1986

Mongolia - on the edge of the Gobi 52 MIN
VHS
Disappearing world series
Color (G C)
$99.00 purchase, $19.00 rental _ #51216
Tours the great plains of Mongolia, contrasting the ancient skills of Mongolian horse people with new socialist methods. Reveals that the revolution brought collective farming to the steppes of a nation the size of Western Europe with a population of only 1.5 million. Features anthropologist Owen Lattimore. Part of a series working closely with anthropologists who lived for a year or more in societies whose social structures, beliefs and practices are threatened by the expansion of technocratic civilization.
Civics and Political Systems; Sociology
Dist - PSU **Prod** - GRANDA 1975

Mongolia - the city on the steppes 52 MIN
VHS
Disappearing world series
Color (G C)
$99.00 purchase, $19.00 rental _ #51217
Visits Ulan Bator, the capital city of Mongolia and home to a quarter of its people. Focuses on the city's celebration of the 53rd anniversary of the revolution. Shows parades, festivals, wrestling and archery contests, and one of the world's most remarkable horse races. Features anthropologist Owen Lattimore. Part of a series working closely with anthropologists who lived for a year or more in societies whose social structures, beliefs and practices are threatened by the expansion of technocratic civilization.
Civics and Political Systems; Sociology
Dist - PSU **Prod** - GRANDA 1975

Mongoloid 4 MIN
16mm
B&W (G)
$10.00 rental
Explores the manner in which a determined young man overcame a basic mental defect and became a useful member of society. Reveals the dreams, ideals and problems that face a large segment of the American male population. Background music written and performed by the DEVO orchestra.
Fine Arts; Psychology
Dist - CANCIN **Prod** - CONNER 1978

Mongoloid and America is waiting 8 MIN
16mm
B&W (G)
$30.00 rental
Presents two short films. Explores the manner in which a young mongoloid man overcame a mental defect and became a useful member of society in Mongoloid, 1978, four minutes, music by the DEVO orchestra. Also reveals the dreams and problems facing a large segment of American male population. America Is Waiting, 1982, four minutes, examines ideas of loyalty, power, patriotism and paranoia through interlocking visual connections, emblematic content and ambiguity of the human condition. Includes music by David Byrne and Brian Eno. Available for rental in group packages only.
Fine Arts; Psychology
Dist - CANCIN **Prod** - CONNER 1982

The Mongreloid 10 MIN
16mm / VHS
Color (G)
$10.00 rental, $25.00 purchase
Journeys with a man and his dog through the regions they traverse.
Fine Arts; Science - Natural
Dist - CANCIN **Prod** - KUCHAR 1978

Monica Dickens 40 MIN
VHS
Color (H C G)
$79.00 purchase
Features the British writer with David Cook, discussing her literary heritage from Charles Dickens, and how to research for a writing project. Talks about her work including One Pair of Feet; Flowers on the Grass; and The Winds of Heaven.
Literature and Drama
Dist - ROLAND **Prod** - INCART

Monika 96 MIN
VHS
B&W (G)
$29.95 purchase _ #MON190
Features a sensual, bittersweet portrait of a tragic romantic interlude. Chronicles the coming - of - age of a young woman, Monika, an impoverished, self - centered but sensuous teenager smitten with Harry, the boy next door. Captures the characters' awakening to passion and the human body.
Fine Arts; Psychology; Sociology
Dist - HOMVIS **Prod** - JANUS 1952

Monilial Vaginitis 7 MIN
U-matic / VHS
Take Care of Yourself Series
Color
Explains the symptoms and treatment for monilial vagnitis and encourages patient compliance in treatment.
Health and Safety; Science - Natural
Dist - UARIZ **Prod** - UARIZ

Monique of Amsterdam 15 MIN
U-matic / VHS
Other families, other friends series; Red module; Holland
Color (P)
Visits the Anne Frank home and shows a diamond polisher at work in Holland.
Geography - World; Social Science
Dist - AITECH **Prod** - WVIZTV 1971

The Monitor and the Merrimac 14 MIN
16mm
Color (I)
LC 75-701527
Shows the first encounter between the Monitor and the Merrimack, Explains how this encounter may have changed the course of the Civil War in the United States.
Civics and Political Systems; History - United States
Dist - FFORIN **Prod** - FRITH 1973

Monitoring and reporting vital signs 25 MIN
VHS
Home care training videos - HCTV - series
Color (C PRO)
$125.00 purchase, $60.00 rental _ #42 - 2417, #42 - 2417R
Covers how to monitor TPR - temperature, pulse and respiration. Discusses the detection of unusual symptoms and the evaluation of mood as an indicator of health problems. Shows how to handle emergency situations. Includes instructional guide for review and testing and meets OBRA federal regulations. Part of a five - part series training home health aides in essential skills and teaching basic skills to nursing students.
Health and Safety; Psychology
Dist - NLFN **Prod** - NLFN

Monitoring Classroom Behavior, Pt 1 9 MIN
16mm / U-matic / VHS
Monitoring Classroom Behavior Series
Color (C A)
LC 83-700036
Explains the concept of monitoring and provides examples of five student behavior categories. Shows these behaviors in both secondary and elementary settings.
Education
Dist - IU **Prod** - IU 1982

Monitoring Classroom Behavior, Pt 2 12 MIN
16mm / U-matic / VHS
Monitoring Classroom Behavior Series
Color (C A)
LC 83-700036
Monitors two classroom situations identifying scenes in which the differenct categories of behavior occur. Provides material for practicing behavior categorization and presents correct categorizations of student behavior based on experts' judgments.
Education
Dist - IU **Prod** - IU 1982

Monitoring Classroom Behavior, Pt 3 6 MIN
U-matic / VHS / 16mm
Monitoring Classroom Behavior Series
Color (C A)
LC 83-700036
Simulates a situation in which the teacher monitors the behavior of more than one group of students at a time. Develops the ability to identify categories of student behavior while quickly scanning different groups.
Education
Dist - IU **Prod** - IU 1982

Monitoring Classroom Behavior Series
Monitoring Classroom Behavior, Pt 1 9 MIN
Monitoring Classroom Behavior, Pt 2 12 MIN
Monitoring Classroom Behavior, Pt 3 6 MIN
Dist - IU

Monitoring the Anesthetized Patient 22 MIN
16mm
Color (PRO)
LC 72-700365
Demonstrates and explains to medical students the principles of monitoring the resiratory, cardiovascular, and other body systems. Uses dramatizations during which the viewer is asked to interpret monitoring findings and to decide on remedial measures.
Health and Safety; Science
Dist - AYERST **Prod** - AYERST 1973

Monitoring the Masses - 206 30 MIN
U-matic
Currents - 1985 - 86 Season Series
Color (A)
Explores the growing concern about computer data banks and the invasion of personal privacy.
Civics and Political Systems; Computer Science; Social Science
Dist - PBS **Prod** - WNETTV 1985

Monitoring the unstable earth 20 MIN
VHS / 16mm
Color (G)
$30.00 rental, $40.00 purchase
Collects and reorders the elements of the external world during travels in California, Nevada, Utah and Colorado. Uses shape and texture, color and light to overcome meaning to affect perception on a primary, visceral level. Music by Jon Gibson.
Fine Arts; Geography - United States; Psychology; Science - Physical
Dist - CANCIN **Prod** - WALLIN 1980

Monitos - Portrait of an Artisan Family 11 MIN
16mm / U-matic / VHS
Color (P I J)
LC 74-702349
Portrays a typical summertime day in the life of the Garcia Aguilar family showing farming and household chores and the making of the Monitos people, small clay figures that have brought the mother fame in the world of popular folk art.
Fine Arts; Guidance and Counseling; Literature and Drama; Social Science
Dist - ALTSUL **Prod** - PEREZ 1974

The Monk, the trees and the concrete jungle 26 MIN
VHS
How to save the Earth series
Color (J H C G)
$175.00 purchase, $45.00 rental
Focuses on southeast Asia and what is being done in Thailand to stop deforestation and the trade in endangered species. Visits Japan to see how action is being taken to reduce the consumption of tropical hardwoods.
Fine Arts; Science - Natural; Social Science
Dist - BULFRG **Prod** - CITV 1993

The Monk, the Village, and the Bo Tree - Pt 11 28 MIN
VHS
Only One Earth Series
Color (S)
$79.00 purchase _ #227 - 9011
Explores and demystifies the links between environment and development and illustrates the detrimental clashes between economics and ecology in the first three programs. Presents positive examples of how development can be achieved without harming the environment in the last eight half - hour programs. Part 11 of eleven reveals that in the remote village of Galahitiya, Sri Lanka, a Buddhist monk has launched a crusade against misuse of the land and unsafe farming practices.
Agriculture; Religion and Philosophy; Science - Natural
Dist - FI **Prod** - BBCTV 1987

The Monkey 11 MIN
U-matic / VHS / 16mm
Animal Families Series
Color (K P I)
$275, $195, $225 purchase _ #B420
Examines the family structures, basic anatomy, feeding habits, and natural habitats of monkeys. Shows monkeys using their hands to remove fleas from their hair.
Science - Natural
Dist - BARR **Prod** - BARR 1986

The Monkey and the Crocodile 15 MIN
U-matic
Magic Carpet Series
Color (P)
Presents a folk tale from India.
Literature and Drama
Dist - GPN **Prod** - SDCSS 1977

The Monkey and the Crocodile - Pt 1 15 MIN
VHS
Words and Pictures Series
Color (P)
$49.00 purchase _ #548 - 9689
Uses animated stories to improve reading and vocabulary skills. Discusses the story content of each program and suggests several activities that relate to the story and the lessons learned. Part 1 of the seven part series recreates the classic East Indian tale of the monkey and the crocodile and emphasizes the consonant blend 'cr.'.
English Language; Fine Arts; Literature and Drama
Dist - FI **Prod** - BBCTV 1984

Monkey Business 70 MIN
16mm
B&W
Tells how the Marx Brothers stow away on a transatlantic ocean linter.
Fine Arts
Dist - SWANK **Prod** - UPCI

Monkey Business 14 MIN
16mm
American Film Genre - the Comedy Film Series
B&W (H C A)
LC 77-701141
Presents an excerpt from the motion picture Monkey Business, issued in 1952. Tells the story of a research chemist seeking a formula to restore youth. Shows how an experimental chimp gets out of his cage and how the magic formula inadvertently ends up in the lab's water cooler, resulting in a series of wild adventures. Exemplifies the comic film genre.
Fine Arts
Dist - FI **Prod** - TWCF 1975

Monkey business - the key to service excellence 22 MIN
VHS
Color (IND)
$495.00 purchase, $165.00 rental _ #PAC02
Uses humorous vignettes with live monkeys to illustrate customer service techniques. Features Rick Tate, of Legendary Service, and Bill Oncken III, known for his work with Monkey Management. Includes a leader's guide and 10 workbooks.
Business and Economics; Literature and Drama; Psychology
Dist - EXTR **Prod** - ONCKEW

Monkey grip 101 MIN
35mm
Color; PAL (G)
Portrays Nora, divorced with a young daughter to raise and trying to live outside the world of conventional domesticity and dependence upon men. Views her obsessive relationship with an addict who draws her into the world of writers, actors and musicians as she struggles for control over her own life. Produced by Pavilion Films, Australia. Contact distributer about price and availability outside the United Kingdom.
Fine Arts; Psychology; Sociology
Dist - BALFOR

Monkey king looks west 42 MIN
VHS / 16mm
Color (H C G)
$750.00, $350.00 purchase, $100.00, $65.00 rental
Contrasts the heritage of Chinese opera with the day - to - day realities of its emigre performers in New York's Chinatown. Depicts the efforts of three classically - trained opera artists to keep their art form alive in an alien culture. Interviews I Peng Chang, Lisa Lu and Alan Chow who work at grinding jobs but continue to perform and teach Chinese opera. Produced by Renee Tajima.
Fine Arts; Sociology
Dist - FLMLIB

Monkey man 30 MIN
VHS
Business matters series
Color (A)
PdS65 purchase
Focuses on Michael Hartley - Brewer, a PdS400-a-day negotiation consultant in great demand in the City. Shows how he adopts a practical hands-on approach involving role-playing and plenty of brutally honest analysis. Follows Hartley - Brewer to Hewlett Packard for a two-day seminar.
Business and Economics
Dist - BBCENE

Monkey of the clouds 18 MIN
VHS
Wildlife environment series
Color (P I J H)
$195.00 purchase
Portrays the yellow - tailed woolly monkey and its habitat in the Peruvian Andes. Shows the work of local Peruvians to protect the yellow - tail and its cloud forest home for future generations. Part of a three - part series on wildlife in South America.
Geography - World; Science - Natural
Dist - LANDMK **Prod** - LANDMK 1992

The Monkey people 30 MIN
VHS
Rabbit ears collection series
Color (K P I J)
$12.95 purchase _ #479142
Features Raul Julia who narrates a fable from the Amazon rainforest.
Literature and Drama
Dist - KNOWUN **Prod** - RABBIT

Monkey rain forest 10 MIN
U-matic / 16mm / VHS
Wild places series
Color (P)
$290.00, $250.00 purchase _ #HP - 6075C
Shows that the tropical rain forest is damp, dark, warm, extremely colorful and filled with a diversity and abundance of living things. Identifies a number of rain forest plants and animals living at various levels of the rain forest, from high in the trees to the ground. Part of a series teaching about different kinds of habitats which show how living things adapt to varying environments and how each creature depends upon others for existence. Produced by Partridge Film and Video, Ltd.
Science - Natural
Dist - CORF

Monkey see monkey do 25 MIN
VHS
Big comfy couch series
Color (K P)
$14.99 purchase _ #0 - 7835 - 8309 - 5NK
Watches as Loonette gets carried away playing copycat. Shows how she decides to imiate everything and everyone. Stimulates physical, mental and emotional growth. Shows youngsters how to deal with typical feelings and fears. Offers movement games and activities for developing coordination and motor skills. Builds positive attitudes toward books and reading. Part of a series.
English Language; Guidance and Counseling; Literature and Drama; Social Science
Dist - TILIED **Prod** - PBS 1995

Monkey See, Monkey do - Verbs 10 MIN
U-matic / VHS / 16mm
Reading Motivation Series
Color (P I)
LC 79-712710
Deals with word classification, emphasizing action words from basic vocabulary lists. Shows monkeys illustrating verbs such as play, ride, swing, jump and eat. Enables children to see objects and actions, hear the words, read them in simple sentences and review them in rhyme.
Education; English Language
Dist - PHENIX **Prod** - BEANMN 1971

Monkey Taming - Adaptation to Humans 19 MIN
16mm
B&W (PRO)
LC 74-702784
Shows pigtail and rhesus monkeys in a training program designed to adapt them to contact with researchers. Explains that the process involves a series of 11 graduated steps.
Psychology; Science
Dist - PSUPCR **Prod** - AARONL 1972

Monkey Tricks 15 MIN
16mm
Color (P I)
Shows what occurs when a thunderstorm scares Alice the chimp out of her usual treehouse home and into Mr Graham's bed.
Literature and Drama
Dist - LUF **Prod** - LUF 1977

The Monkey who would be King 11 MIN
16mm / U-matic / VHS
Color (P) (SPANISH)
Tells how the mighty lion decides he's tired of being king and how a monkey snatches his crown. Explains that the monkey learns it takes more than a crown to make a king.
Foreign Language; Literature and Drama
Dist - EBEC **Prod** - EBEC

Monkeys 9 MIN
U-matic / VHS / 16mm
Color (P I)
Compares and contrasts monkeys and apes. Gives some examples of old world and of American monkeys.
Science - Natural
Dist - IFB **Prod** - BHA 1966

Monkeys 5 MIN
16mm / U-matic / VHS
Zoo Animals in the Wild Series
Color (K P)
$135.00, $95.00 purchase _ #3995
Shows various types of monkeys, their habits and the environments in which they live.
Science - Natural
Dist - CORF **Prod** - CORF 1981

Monkeys and Apes - an Introduction to the Primates 11 MIN
U-matic / VHS / 16mm
Color; B&W (P I J) (SPANISH)
LC FIA65-332
Discusses the group of primates, of which the monkeys, apes and their relatives are all a member. Illustrates the characteristics of the primates and their habits.
Foreign Language; Science - Natural
Dist - PHENIX **Prod** - BURN 1965

Monkeys, Apes and Man 52 MIN
U-matic / VHS / 16mm
Color (H C A)
LC 73-714341
Points out that man is learning that the similarity between monkeys and himself is not superficial and explains that man is a primate, bound in evolution to monkeys and apes.
Science - Natural
Dist - NGS **Prod** - NGS 1971

Monkeys Fishing the Moon 11 MIN
16mm / VHS
Color (K)
$300.00, $240.00 purchase
Tells the story of a group of monkeys who chase the bright, full moon until they trap its image in a pool at the foot of a dramatic cliff. Reveals that after they fish it out with a bowl they quarrel over who should have it. The bowl breaks and the moon takes its place in the sky once again.
Health and Safety; Literature and Drama; Psychology; Sociology
Dist - LUF **Prod** - LUF

Monkeys, Go Home 100 MIN
U-matic / VHS / 16mm
Color
Stars Maurice Chevalier, Dean Jones and Yvette Mimieux. Describes the adventures of a young American who has inherited a small farm in France and receives the help of four chimps who become olive pickers.
Literature and Drama
Dist - FI **Prod** - DISNEY

Monkeys is the cwaziest people
16mm
Fox Movietone news series
B&W (G)
$15.00 rental
Features Lew Lehr narrating a series of vignettes with monkeys performing human tasks in various comic situations. Presents part of a series of special Movietone issues, 6 - 11 minutes.
Fine Arts; Literature and Drama
Dist - KITPAR **Prod** - FOXNEW 1939

The Monkey's Paw 19 MIN
U-matic / VHS / 16mm
Color (J)
LC 78-700913
Adapted from the short story The Monkey's Paw by W W Jacobs. Tells the story of an old couple whose wish to have their dead son returned to them is granted by a mysterious monkey's paw.
Fine Arts; Literature and Drama
Dist - PHENIX **Prod** - MORANM 1978

The Monkey's Paw 27 MIN
16mm / U-matic / VHS
LCA Short Story Library Series
Color (I)
LC 83-700543
Introduces the White family, who finds itself in possession of a monkey's paw which is purported to give them three wishes. Relates that after using the three wishes, the Whites are in worse shape, having lost their son. Based on the short story The Monkey's Paw by W W Jacobs.
Literature and Drama
Dist - LCOA **Prod** - LCOA 1983

The Monkey's Uncle 90 MIN
16mm / U-matic / VHS
Color
Adds to the misadventures of Merlin Jones, as Merlin invents a screwball learn - while - you sleep device and perfects an antique man - powered glider.
Fine Arts
Dist - FI **Prod** - DISNEY 1965

Monocular Experiences 10 MIN
U-matic / VHS
Color
Health and Safety; Science - Natural
Dist - PRIMED **Prod** - PRIMED

Monolayers, surfaces and thin films series
Presents a seven - part series on monolayers, surfaces and thin films. Discusses the behavior of liquids near boundaries; self - assembled monolayer films; proteins at interfaces; protein caught in action; molecular structure and interface properties of surfactant - coated surfaces; transistors and diodes based on redox active thin film polymers; and technological application of biologically derived microstructures. Recorded live at the Eastman Kodak Company, Rochester.
Monolayers, surfaces and thin films - Tape 1
Monolayers, surfaces and thin films - Tape 2
Monolayers, surfaces and thin films - Tape 3
Monolayers, surfaces and thin films - Tape 4
Monolayers, surfaces and thin films - Tape 5
Monolayers, surfaces and thin films - Tape 6
Monolayers, surfaces and thin films - Tape 7
Dist - AMCHEM

Monolayers, surfaces and thin films - Tape 1
VHS
Monolayers, surfaces and thin films series
Color (C PRO)
$100.00 purchase _ #V - 4701 - 1753X
Features a discussion of the behavior of liquids near boundaries by Carl Frank, Cornell Univ. Part one of a seven - part series recorded live at the Eastman Kodak Company in Rochester.
Industrial and Technical Education
Dist - AMCHEM

Monolayers, surfaces and thin films - Tape 2
VHS
Monolayers, surfaces and thin films series
Color (C PRO)
$100.00 purchase _ #V - 4702 - 17548
Discusses self - assembled monolayer films - organic sulfur compounds on gold and related systems. Features George Whitesides, Harvard Univ. Part two of a seven - part series recorded live at the Eastman Kodak Company, Rochester.
Industrial and Technical Education
Dist - AMCHEM

Monolayers, surfaces and thin films - Tape 3
VHS
Monolayers, surfaces and thin films series
Color (C PRO)
$100.00 purchase _ #V - 4703 - 17556
Discusses proteins at interfaces - principles and applications. Features Joseph Andrade, Univ of Utah. Part three of a seven - part series recorded live at the Eastman Kodak Company, Rochester.
Industrial and Technical Education
Dist - AMCHEM

Monolayers, surfaces and thin films - Tape 4
VHS
Monolayers, surfaces and thin films series
Color (C PRO)
$100.00 purchase _ #V - 4704 - 17564
Discusses protein caught in action - specific surface recognition and enzyme function in monolayers. Features Helmut Ringsdorf, Univ of Mainz, Germany. Part four of a seven - part series recorded live at the Eastman Kodak Company, Rochester.
Industrial and Technical Education
Dist - AMCHEM

Monolayers, surfaces and thin films - Tape 5
VHS
Monolayers, surfaces and thin films series
Color (C PRO)
$100.00 purchase _ #V - 4705 - 17572
Discusses molecular structure and interface properties of surfactant - coated surfaces. Features Steve Garoff, Carnegie - Mellon Univ. Part five of a seven - part series recorded live at the Eastman Kodak Company, Rochester.
Industrial and Technical Education
Dist - AMCHEM

Monolayers, surfaces and thin films - Tape 6
VHS
Monolayers, surfaces and thin films series
Color (C PRO)
$100.00 purchase _ #V - 4706 - 1750
Discusses transistors and diodes based on redox active thin film polymers. Features Mark Wrighton, MIT. Part six of a seven - part series recorded live at the Eastman Kodak Company, Rochester.
Industrial and Technical Education
Dist - AMCHEM

Monolayers, surfaces and thin films - Tape 7
VHS
Monolayers, surfaces and thin films series
Color (C PRO)
$100.00 purchase _ #V - 4707 - 17599
Discusses the technological application of biologically derived microstructures. Features Joel Schnur, Naval Research Laboratory. Part seven of a seven - part series recorded live at the Eastman Kodak Company, Rochester.
Industrial and Technical Education
Dist - AMCHEM

Mononucleosis 40 MIN
16mm
Boston Medical Reports Series
B&W (PRO)
Discusses epidemiologic studies needed in mononucleosis, along with its unknown but probable viral etiology. Emphasizes its varied hematologic and immunologic aspects. Covers treatment of the disease.
Health and Safety; Science - Natural
Dist - NMAC **Prod** - NMAC 1966

Monopoly - Who's in Control 30 MIN
U-matic / VHS
Economics USA Series
Color (C)
Business and Economics
Dist - ANNCPB **Prod** - WEFA

Monoprints 30 MIN
U-matic
Media and Methods of the Artist Series
Color (H C A)
Demonstrates techniques for creating monoprints.
Fine Arts
Dist - TVOTAR **Prod** - TVOTAR 1971

Monroe 6 MIN
U-matic / VHS / 16mm
Color (C A)
Presents a comedy in which overworked Monroe meets what he wants copied when it materializes.
Literature and Drama
Dist - CORF **Prod** - CORF

The Monroe Doctrine
U-matic / VHS / 35mm strip
(J H C) (LATIN)
$97.00 purchase _ #31157 94
Describes the impact of the Monroe Doctrine and the 1904 Roosevelt Corollary which declared the authority of the U S to intervene in Latin American affairs. Discusses the subsequent involvement in the Dominican Republic, Cuba, Panama, Haiti, and Nicaragua and illustrates how the doctrine continues to influence U S and Latin American relations today. In 2 parts.
Civics and Political Systems; History - United States
Dist - ASPRSS **Prod** - ASPRSS

The Monroe Doctrine applied - US policy toward Latin America 16 MIN
VHS
Color (I J H)
$99.00 purchase _ #31157 - 026
Focuses on the impact of the Monroe Doctrine and the 1904 Corollory upon Latin America. Describes how interventionism came about and what happened as a result. Considers the present relations of the United States with its neighbors to the south. Includes teachers' guide and library kit.
Civics and Political Systems; Geography - World; History - World
Dist - INSTRU
GA

Monsieur Pointu 13 MIN
16mm / U-matic / VHS
Color (K P I)
LC 77-700699
Features Quebecois country style violinist Paul Cormier as Monsieur Pointu, whose efforts to play his instrument are thwarted when the violin begins to have a mind of its own. Uses trick cinematography and pixillation to show how the violin continually eludes his grasp, shrinks and grows, attacks him and shatters into small pieces which fly menacingly at him.
Fine Arts; Industrial and Technical Education; Literature and Drama
Dist - PFP **Prod** - NFBC 1976

Monsieur Rene Magritte 50 MIN
VHS
Color (C A H S)
$39.95 purchase _ #833 - 9012
Illuminates the work of Surrealist Rene Magritte through archival film featuring conversations with the artist and location footage of his home in Belgium and the other places which inspired him - Brussels, Paris, the casino, the racecourse. Shows an artist who chose to lead a quiet life, influenced artistically by his everyday surroundings.
Fine Arts; Geography - World
Dist - FI **Prod** - RMART 1986
ARTSAM

Monsieur Rene Magritte 60 MIN
VHS
Color (H C G T A)
$39.95 purchase _ #S01443
Portrays many of the places which inspired artist Monsieur Rene Magritte's work. Focuses on Magritte's style, which was to give new and strange portrayals of familiar scenes.
Fine Arts
Dist - UILL **Prod** - UILL

Monsieur Vincent 115 MIN
16mm
Color
Tells of the humbly born priest who fled from the ease and luxury of a noble household in 17th century Paris to devote himself to an unceasing battle against disease, hunger, cruelty and prejudice, always spreading his teaching of spiritual love, brotherhood and peace. Stars Pierre Fresnay.
Biography; Fine Arts; History - World; Religion and Philosophy
Dist - TWYMAN **Prod** - UNKNWN

The Monster 15 MIN
16mm / U-matic / VHS
Color (C J H I A)
$365.00, $250.00 purchase _ #76506; LC 77-703614
Examines the legend of the Loch Ness monster through the reported experiences of a group of people who live on the shores of Loch Ness, Scotland.
Geography - World; Psychology; Religion and Philosophy
Dist - CORF **Prod** - CENTRO 1976

The Monster and the tailor 11 MIN
VHS
Paul Galdone's illustrated spooky stories series
Color (K P I)
$44.95 purchase _ #SAV9027
Tells about a Grand Duke who orders a tailor to make a pair of trousers in a graveyard where a monster lives. Presents part of a four - part series of spooky stories by Paul Galdone.
Literature and Drama
Dist - KNOWUN

A Monster Concert 30 MIN
VHS / U-matic
(G)
Features ten grand pianos and 20 pianists, including Eugene List. George Koutzen conducts the music of Stephen Foster, John Phillip Sousa and Scott Joplin. Participants are costumed to evoke the periods in which the pieces were written.
Fine Arts
Dist - GPN **Prod** - NETV 1987

A Monster Concert 28 MIN
U-matic
Color
Presents a concert in which 20 pianists play 10 pianos in unison. Includes works by Gottschalk, Stephen Foster, Sousa, and Joplin.
Fine Arts
Dist - PBS **Prod** - NETCHE

Monster Hits 30 MIN
VHS / 16mm
Sesame Street Home Video Series
Color; Captioned (K)
$14.44 purchase _ #RH 9 - 805176
Features Sesame Street characters singing hit songs.
Fine Arts
Dist - EDUCRT **Prod** - RH

The Monster Inside Me - Child Abuse 25 MIN
U-matic / VHS
Color
Explores new approaches to the problem of child abuse. Features a discussion among parents who have physically abused their children but have found help. Discusses new trends in clinical aid with Drs Morris Paulson and James Apthorp.
Home Economics; Psychology; Sociology
Dist - MEDCOM **Prod** - MEDCOM

The Monster Machine 30 MIN
U-matic
Paths of Development Series
Color (H C A)
Shows that some Third World countries utilize external help in order to gain greater control of their development destiny.
Sociology
Dist - ACCESS **Prod** - ACCESS 1985

The Monster of Highgate Pond 59 MIN
16mm
B&W (K P I)
Tells the story of three children who help their uncle unpack specimens from Malaya. They are rewarded by being given an unidentified egg. When it hatches into a baby monster the adventure begins and when the growing monster takes up residence in the town pond, the results are hilarious.
Literature and Drama
Dist - LUF **Prod** - CHILDF 1968

The Monster Ox 52 MIN
16mm
Color (JAPANESE)
A Japanese language film. Tells the story of poor villagers who were long forced to offer a large quantity of rice to their monster God. Explains that, led by a courageous boy, whose girl was locked in a cave by their evil headman, the villagers finally succeed in exposing the headman's treachery and capture the ox God. Points out that the headman has stored for himself the crop supposedly given to the God, and the God was found to be just a mild field ox disguised as a monster.
Foreign Language; Literature and Drama
Dist - UNIJAP **Prod** - UNIJAP 1970

Monster Under My Bed 8 MIN
U-matic / VHS
Giant First Start Series
Color (K P)
$29.95 purchase _ #VM020
Presents an adaptation of the book Monster Under My Bed. Contains a 32 page hardcover book and a video.
English Language; Literature and Drama
Dist - TROLA

Monstermania 30 MIN
VHS
Color; Stereo (K)
$14.98 purchase _ #TT8022
Shows world champion monster trucks in action.
Physical Education and Recreation
Dist - TWINTO **Prod** - TWINTO 1990

Monsters and Magic 19 MIN
U-matic / VHS
Folk Book Series
Color (P)
Presents folktales from Russia and Appalachia which revolve around monsters and magic.
Literature and Drama
Dist - AITECH **Prod** - UWISC 1980

Monsters and Other Scary Things 30 MIN
VHS / U-matic
Color
Explores the dark places where monsters lurk and examines the evidence for and against their existence. Describes sightings of the Loch Ness monster, Big Foot, and the Abominable Snow Man.
Sociology
Dist - JOU **Prod** - CANBC

Monsters and Things that Go Bump 30 MIN
U-matic
Hooked on Reading Series
Color (PRO)
Portrays a father who encourages the shared reading of books. He reads scary stories to his children, they read to him and to each other.
English Language; Literature and Drama
Dist - TVOTAR **Prod** - TVOTAR 1986

The Monsters Christmas 48 MIN
16mm / VHS
Color (J)
$520.00, $310.00 purchase
Tells the story of a little girl who tries to help her friends, the monsters, recover their voices from a bad witch. Reveals that the girl is captured, but the monsters rescue her and get their voices back. New Zealand is used as a setting.
Literature and Drama; Social Science
Dist - FLMWST

Monsters We've Known and Loved 26 MIN
16mm
B&W (GERMAN)
LC FI68-179
Traces the development of the horror film from its beginning in Germany in the twenties through mad doctors, graveyard monsters, creatures from underworld regions and outer space, to the comic - horror attempts of Vincent Price and Peter Lorre. Presents John Barrymore, Lon Chaney, Bela Lugosi and Boris Karloff in their monster roles.
Fine Arts
Dist - WOLPER **Prod** - WOLPER 1964

Mont Saint Michel 55 MIN
VHS
Treasures of France on Video Series
Color (G)
$34.50 purchase _ #V72170
Displays the beauty and unique character of the famed architectural masterpiece.
Geography - World
Dist - NORTNJ

Montage - what is it Out There 20 MIN
16mm
B&W (C)
Uses elaborate play test instruments to test and record responses of infants to their environment. Shows applications for helping handicapped children enrich their experiences.
Education; Psychology
Dist - PSUPCR **Prod** - PSUPCR 1967

Montana 60 MIN
VHS
Portrait of America series
Color (J H C G)
$99.95 purchase _ #AMB26V
Visits Montana. Offers extensive research into the state's history. Films key locations and presents segments on history, government, education, folklore, science, journalism, sociology, industry, agriculture and business. Shows what is unique about Montana and distinctive about its regional culture and how it got to be that way. Includes study guide. Part of a 50 - part series.
Geography - United States; History - United States
Dist - CAMV

Montana 76 MIN
16mm
Color
Presents the saga of the battle of the sheepmen against the cattlemen for grazing rights. Stars Errol Flynn.
Fine Arts
Dist - TWYMAN **Prod** - WB 1950

Montana Aeronautics Films Series
Montana and the Sky 18 MIN
Dist - FO

Montana and its Aircraft 28 MIN
16mm
Aeronautics Films Series
Color; B&W (I J H C G T A)
Uses of airplanes and helicopters in the state of Montana presented as it was in the late sixties. Confident and extensive use in forest fire control, the use of growth regulators in wheat production, the birth of the communter airline, expansion of charter and air taxi services, flying farmers, doctors, professional people, and the opportunity for careers in general aviation are the situations depicted.
Guidance and Counseling; History - United States; Industrial and Technical Education; Social Science
Dist - FO **Prod** - FO 1969

Montana and the Sky 18 MIN
16mm
Montana Aeronautics Films Series
Color; B&W (I J H C G T A)
Identifies the state of Montana with the world's air space, the sky. In the early fifties there was a growing ecstatic realization that the air that surrounds the globe was going to be even better than the ocean for universal travel. This was known as 'air age education.' For students and teachers alike this learning held an 'awe' which gave new meaning to the air masses that move across Montana each day.
History - United States; Industrial and Technical Education; Social Science
Dist - FO **Prod** - FO 1952

Montana - as Science Sees it Series
We are Water 27 MIN
Dist - CONICO

Montana Indian Children 27 MIN
16mm
Play and Cultural Continuity Series Part 4
Color (H C T)
Covers the Flathead Indian Reservation and the surrounding countryside, including the Arlee Pow Wow grounds and Missoula, Montana. Shows children and adult members of numerous Indian tribes, including the Salish speaking people, the Black Foot and the Cherokee. Presents the importance of hunting, story telling and traditional teachings as well as the repeated emphasis on reinstating Indian values and pride.
Fine Arts; Geography - United States; Physical Education and Recreation; Sociology
Dist - CFDC **Prod** - CFDC 1977

Montana on my mind 54 MIN
VHS
Color (G)
$24.95 purchase
Presents images of Glacier and Yellowstone, wildflowers and wildlife, harvest time, cowboys and rodeos, skiing, flyfishing and more from Montana. Includes scenes from the Governor's Cup Run, Helena's Race to the Sky, Billings Night Rodeo and Native American powwows. Includes quotes from A B Guthrie, Norman McLean, Charlie Russell, John Steinbeck.
Geography - United States
Dist - FALPRE **Prod** - FALPRE 1994

Montana, Pt 1 30 MIN
U-matic
South by Northwest Series
Color
Describes how black cowboys drove cattle from Texas to Montana.
History - United States
Dist - GPN **Prod** - KWSU 1977

Montana, Pt 2 30 MIN
U-matic
South by Northwest Series
Color
Presents the story of Cattle Kate and Mary Fields, two black frontierswomen.
History - United States; History - World
Dist - GPN **Prod** - KWSU 1977

Monte Alban 56 MIN
U-matic / VHS
Color (C) (SPANISH)
$279.00, $179.00 purchase _ #AD - 2191
Looks at Monte Alban, sacred capital of Oaxaca's ancient people whose culture gave rise to Zapotec civilization. Examines its symetrical urban design and its enigmatic religious practices. In Spanish.
Fine Arts; Foreign Language; Geography - World; History - World; Religion and Philosophy; Social Science; Sociology
Dist - FOTH **Prod** - FOTH

Monterey Bay Aquarium 30 MIN
VHS
VideoTours history series
Color (G I J H)
$19.95 purchase _ #ZA03
Visits the Monterrey Bay Aquarium.
Geography - United States; Geography - World; Science - Natural
Dist - SVIP

The Monterey Historic 28 MIN
16mm
Color
Looks at the Monterey Historic Race in which some of the classic racing cars of yesteryear are driven in competition by racing luminaries.
Physical Education and Recreation
Dist - MTP **Prod** - MTP

Monterey Pop 82 MIN
16mm
Color
Features the Monterey International Pop Festival with Jimi Hendrix, Janis Joplin, Big Brother and the Holding Company, Otis Redding, Jefferson Airplane, Ravi Shankar, The Who, Country Joe and the Fish, Scott McKenzie, Mamas and Papas, Hugh Maskela, Canned Heat, Eric Burden and the Animals.
Fine Arts
Dist - PENNAS **Prod** - PENNAS

Monterey's boat people 29 MIN
VHS / U-matic
Color (G)
$99.00 purchase, $40.00 rental
Examines the continuing tension between the established Italian fishing community and the recently - arrived Vietnamese fisherman in California's Montery Bay peninsula. Documents a specific fact of anti - Asian sentiment and the conflicts faced by an industry that is also fighting for survival. Produced by Spencer Nakasako and Vincent DiGirolamo.
History - United States; Industrial and Technical Education; Sociology
Dist - CROCUR

Montessori 21 MIN
16mm
Color
LC 74-705168
Illustrates expansion of the Montessori core curriculum through application of principles of learning linguistic theory, child development, educational technology and cybernetic principles. Shows how adaptations have resulted in a highly individualized program for the hearing impaired child with learning disabilities.
Education; English Language; Guidance and Counseling; Psychology
Dist - USNAC **Prod** - USBEH

Montessori - a Way to Grow 32 MIN
16mm
Color
Overviews the Montessori method of childhood education, revealing how the programs provide for individual differences in learning style and pace, social development and creativity. Shows children from two and a half to six years.
Education; Psychology
Dist - PROMET **Prod** - PROMET

Montessori in Your Home 35 MIN
VHS / U-matic
$19.95 purchase
Gives examples of techniques and exercises used in the Montessori principles of education that can be applicable at home.
Education
Dist - BESTF **Prod** - BESTF

Monteverdi in Mantua 53 MIN
U-matic / VHS
Man and Music Series
Color (C)
$279.00, $179.00 purchase _ #AD - 1763
Considers the patronage of composers. Focuses on Monteverdi, late 16th - century Italy, brought to the court of the Gonzaga. Part of a 22 - part series that sets Western music into the historial and cultural context of its time.
Civics and Political Systems; Fine Arts; History - World
Dist - FOTH **Prod** - FOTH

Montgomery to Memphis 103 MIN
VHS
Color (J H C)
$49.00 purchase _ #03881 - 126
Records the civil rights battle of Dr Martin Luther King, Jr, and discusses his philosophy of nonviolence.
Biography; Civics and Political Systems; History - United States
Dist - GA **Prod** - GA

Montgomery to Memphis 103 MIN
VHS
Color (G)
$69.95 purchase
Documents the activities of Dr Martin Luther King, Jr, in the Civil Rights Movement.
Biography; Civics and Political Systems; History - United States; Religion and Philosophy
Dist - KINGML **Prod** - KINGML 1971

A Month for the entertainment of spirits 30 MIN
VHS
Color (C G)
$250.00 purchase, $50.00 rental _ #38143
Examines the ceremonies of African - Guyanese who continue African,traditions of making contact with the spirit world. Reveals that rituals are performed year - round, but they are most frequent in August, the month in which slavery was abolished in 1838. Begins with a libation ceremony celebrating emancipation, performed to make contact with their ancestors by descendants of slaves. Studies four Comfa ceremonies and explores their similarities which access the spirit world. Produced by Dr Kean Gibson, Dept of Linguistics, University of the West Indies, Barbados.
Geography - World; Religion and Philosophy; Sociology
Dist - UCEMC

Monthly Ancestral Offerings in Hinduism 8 MIN
16mm
Hindu Religion Series no 4; No 4
Color (C)
Presents a Hindu householder of Madreas City making offerings of seasame - seeds and water onto a special burca - grid of sacred grass.
Religion and Philosophy; Sociology
Dist - SYRCU **Prod** - SMTHHD

Montserrat 30 MIN
VHS
John Stobart's WorldScape series
Color (A G)
$19.95 purchase _ #STO - 05
Features Montserrat, the 'Emerald isle of the Carribbean.' Follows artist John Stobart as he travels the globe, painting directly from life, and demonstrates the simplicity of the method that has made him the foremost living maritime artist. Demonstrates Stobart's classical maritime style in numerous evocative settings around the world. Part of a series on painting outdoors.
Fine Arts
Dist - ARTSAM **Prod** - WORLDS

Montserrat Caballe and Jose Carreras in Moscow 120 MIN
VHS
Color (G)
$24.95 purchase_#1368
Blends the voices of Montserrat Caballe and Jose Carreras in concert at the Bolshoi Theatre in Moscow. Includes favorite arias and duet by a variety of composers - Puccini, Verdi, Rossini, Bellini and others.
Fine Arts
Dist - KULTUR

Montserrat Caballe - the Woman, the Diva 67 MIN
VHS
Color (G)
$19.95 purchase _ #1143
Presents Montserrat Caballe performing arias from ten selections from performances around the world. Includes her brief comments.
Fine Arts; Geography - World
Dist - KULTUR

The Monument of Chief Rolling Mountain Thunder 29 MIN
VHS / U-matic
Visions of Paradise Series
Color
Shows Chief Thunder, American folk artist, who created the Monument on the Nevada Desert. Captures the tragedy of his life, his painful isolation, the beauty of his work and his creative process.
Fine Arts
Dist - SARLGT **Prod** - SARLGT

Monument to the dream 27 MIN
VHS
Color (G)
$69.95 purchase _ #S01416
Documents the construction of St Louis' Gateway Arch, designed by Eero Saarinen. Reveals the many challenges involved in the process.
Fine Arts; Geography - United States
Dist - UILL

Monument to the Dream 30 MIN
U-matic / VHS
Color
Presents the Gateway Arch of the Jefferson National Expansion Memorial as a testament to modern man's pioneering accomplishments.
Industrial and Technical Education
Dist - MPS **Prod** - AIAS

Monument to the Sun - the Story of the Aztec Calendar Stone 16 MIN
16mm / U-matic / VHS
Mexican Heritage Series
Color
LC 76-703905
Explains the meaning and history of the monumental carving known as the Aztec calendar stone. Tells how the ancient calendar of the Mayas was handed down through the centuries and how the Aztec astrologers and mathematicians devised their calendar from their ancient ancestors.
Geography - World; History - World; Mathematics; Science - Physical
Dist - FI **Prod** - STEXMF 1976

Monument Valley - Land of the Navajo 22 MIN
U-matic / VHS / 16mm
Color
Presents a brief look at the life of a Navajo who lives in the four - corner country of Arizona, Colorado, New Mexico and Utah.
Geography - United States; Social Science
Dist - MCFI **Prod** - HOE 1959

A Monumental landscape 5 MIN
16mm
Color (G)
$15.00 rental
Tours a hometown of personal landmarks to show how individuals identify with or are made to feel disconnected from everyday places in a Marina McDougall production.
Fine Arts; Sociology
Dist - CANCIN

Monumento Del Sol - La Historia De La Piedra Del Sol 16 MIN
16mm / U-matic / VHS
Mexican Heritage - Spanish Series
Color (SPANISH)
LC 76-703906
A Spanish language version of Monument To The Sun - The Story Of The Aztec Calendar Stone. Explains the meaning and history of the monumental carving known as the Aztec calendar stone. Tells how the ancient calendar of the Mayas was handed down through the centuries and how the Aztec astrologers and mathematicians devised their calendar from their ancient ancestors.
Foreign Language; Geography - World; History - World; Mathematics; Science - Physical
Dist - FI **Prod** - STEXMF 1976

Monuments 28 MIN
16mm
Color
LC 77-701818
Demonstrates that builders have the skill and tools to improve the quality of life for much of the world's population. Shows man's architectural efforts through the ages and examples of construction masterpieces.
Fine Arts; Industrial and Technical Education
Dist - MTP **Prod** - CTRACT 1977

Monuments to Erosion 11 MIN
U-matic / VHS / 16mm
Color (I J H C)
LC 74-702595
Presents a pictorial study of monuments as unique, colorful and dramatic landforms created over the ages by the eroding action of wind and water.
Agriculture; History - United States; Science - Physical
Dist - EBEC **Prod** - EBEC 1974

Monuments to Failure - America's Prison Crisis 60 MIN
VHS
Color (G)
$150.00 purchase _ #MNTF - 000
Concludes that the American prison system is failing at its job. Documents the growing prison population and the rising costs of incarceration. Submits that prisons are failing to deter crime and rehabilitate criminals.
Sociology
Dist - PBS **Prod** - KNMETV 1988

Monuments to man 52 MIN
VHS
Color (J H C)
$195.00 purchase
Documents the history of concrete, the humble substance responsible for the creation of modern cities. Discusses its discovery, its disappearance for 15 centuries and its re - emergence into a versatile and effective building material. Looks at the concrete structures of architects Le Corbusier, Frank Lloyd Wright and Antonio Gaudi.
Industrial and Technical Education
Dist - LANDMK **Prod** - LANDMK 1992

Monuments to progress 50 MIN
VHS
Triumph of the West series
Color; PAL (H C A)
PdS99 purchase; Not available in the United States
Documents the rise of Western civilization and its continuing impact on the rest of the world. Focuses specifically on the progression of political ideas in Western history. Ninth in a series of 13 programs written and presented by J M Roberts.
Civics and Political Systems; History - World
Dist - BBCENE

Moo - Shi Pork 29 MIN
Videoreel / VT2
Joyce Chen Cooks Series
Color
Features Joyce Chen showing how to adapt Chinese recipes so they can be prepared in the American kitchen and still retain the authentic flavor. Demonstrates how to prepare moo - shi pork.

Geography - World; Home Economics
Dist - PBS **Prod** - WGBHTV

Mood Altering Drugs - no Need to Get MAD 30 MIN
U-matic
Action Options - Alcohol, Drugs and You Series
(H C A)
Examines patterns of behaviour that can lead to dependency, how people exhibit dependent behavior and their denial of addiction.
Psychology; Sociology
Dist - ACCESS **Prod** - ACCESS 1986

Mood indigo - Blacks and Whites 30 MIN
VHS
America in World War II - The home front series
Color (G)
$49.95 purchase _ #AWWH - 107
Highlights the accomplishments and lives of black American servicemen. Shows that :acial segregation within the U.S. forces reflected the racial divisions of society. Reveals that conditions for black Americans at home were poor. Narrated by Eric Sevareid.
History - United States
Dist - PBS

Mood Music 15 MIN
U-matic
It's Mainly Music Series
Color (I)
Teaches children how music can easily create an atmosphere or feeling.
Fine Arts
Dist - TVOTAR **Prod** - TVOTAR 1983

Mood of Zen 13 MIN
16mm
Color (J H C)
LC FIA67-1806
Discusses Zen philosophy with Alan Watts. Depicts scenes of the Japanese countryside that are set against Kyoto music and the chanting of Buddhist monks.
Geography - World; Religion and Philosophy
Dist - HP **Prod** - HP 1967

Mood of Zen 14 MIN
U-matic / VHS
Color
Explains some of the basic teachings of Zen, including the role and goals of meditation, need to flow with the current of life to release creative energy, not to oppose cosmic forces but to conquer them by going with them, and to wake up from illusions under which we suffer.
Religion and Philosophy
Dist - HP **Prod** - HP

Moods in Safety 21 MIN
16mm
Color
LC 74-705169
Demonstrates how various types of moods and emotions can be detrimental to personal safety on and off the job. Shows how over - confidence, cockiness, anger, depression and tension cause accidents through distortion of intelligence, logic and sense of reason. Stresses the importance of following safety rules on the flight line, in flight, at the missile site and behind the wheel.
Guidance and Counseling; Health and Safety; Industrial and Technical Education; Psychology
Dist - USNAC **Prod** - USAF 1966

The Moods of Surfing 15 MIN
U-matic / VHS / 16mm
B&W (I)
LC FIA68-152
A poetic interpretation of the sights, sounds, beauty, rhythm and changing moods of the ocean.
Physical Education and Recreation
Dist - PFP **Prod** - PFP 1968

Moods of the Amazon 18 MIN
16mm
Color
LC 75-706371
Gives impressions of the way of life in the region of the Amazon.
Geography - World; Social Science
Dist - PACEF **Prod** - INFORF 1969

Moods of the Arctic 10 MIN
U-matic / VHS / 16mm
Color (J H C)
LC 73-700892
Explains that one of the last frontiers remaining to man is the vast reaches which lie north of the Arctic Circle. Points out that the popular idea that this area is merely a large area of perpetual ice and snow is a misconception.
Geography - World; Science - Natural
Dist - AIMS **Prod** - COUKLA 1973

Moody 55 MIN
VHS
Color (J H C G A R)
$59.95 purchase, $10.00 rental _ #35 - 82023 - 8936
Portrays the life of Dwight Moody, the 19th century evangelist and lay leader.
Computer Science; Religion and Philosophy
Dist - APH **Prod** - QUADCO

Moody science adventures series
The Clown - faced carpenter - Journey to the stars - Water, water everywhere 30 MIN
The Power in plants - Busy as a bee - It's a small world 30 MIN
Treasure hunt - Animals move - Eight - legged engineer 30 MIN
The Wonder of you - A Mystery story - A Matter of taste 30 MIN
Dist - MOODY

Moody science classics series
City of the bees 28 MIN
Dust or destiny 28 MIN
Empty cities 28 MIN
Facts of faith 28 MIN
God of creation 28 MIN
Hidden treasures 28 MIN
Prior claim 28 MIN
Red river of life 28 MIN
Signposts aloft 28 MIN
Where the waters run 28 MIN
Dist - MOODY

Moody's 5000 plus on CD - ROM
CD-ROM
(G)
Presents Moody's business and financial information on publicly - held corporations on CD - ROM with an easy - to - use menu. Allows screening of companies by either textual or financial information. Gives in - depth analyses of detailed financial - stock performance data and history, including mergers and acquisitions, income accounts and balance sheets and comparative financial records. Updated quarterly, including year - to - date Moody's News Reports.
Business and Economics
Dist - MOODIS **Prod** - MOODIS

Moomoons 25 MIN
16mm
Color (G)
$25.00 rental
Informs the viewer about modern technology and the processing of cows with part documentary and part experimental collage. Creates more of a poetic barrage than journalistic examination of the nature of meat - eating reality. Produced by Kon Petrochuk.
Fine Arts; Health and Safety; Sociology
Dist - CANCIN

The Moon 10 MIN
U-matic
Take a Look Series
Color (P I)
Shows the four phases of the moon, how to make a calendar to chart the moon's progress and the astronauts on the surface of the moon.
Science; Science - Physical
Dist - TVOTAR **Prod** - TVOTAR 1986

Moon 1969 15 MIN
16mm
Color (J)
LC 79-709315
Uses various film techniques to take the viewer on a trip into the human soul. Says that clues to man's essence lie somewhere between the spiritual and the mathematical, between the incomprehensible magnitude of the universe and the knowledge that one day the frontier will be conquered. Uses footage showing man walking in space and landing on the moon, clouds drifting, ocean waves pounding, sunsets and all else that symbolizes the current joy - fear anxiety of a nation in a state of transformation.
Fine Arts; Religion and Philosophy
Dist - SERIUS **Prod** - BARTLS

Moon 1969 15 MIN
16mm
Color (C)
$392.00
Experimental film by Scott Bartlett.
Fine Arts
Dist - AFA **Prod** - AFA 1969

The Moon - a Giant Step in Geology 24 MIN
U-matic / VHS / 16mm
Earth Science Program Series
Color (J H)
LC 76-703646
Uses scenes of scientists at work in Houston's Lunar Receiving Laboratory and animated segments of the moon's surface to indicate what is being done with the scientific information received from lunar rock samples.
Science - Physical
Dist - EBEC **Prod** - EBEC 1976

The Moon - an Emerging Planet 13 MIN
U-matic / VHS / 16mm
Color
LC 75-701275
Reviews in nontechnical terms what has been learned of the early events in the history of the Moon. Details accretion, structural formation, volcanic activity and bombardment. Compares the geology of the Moon with that of Earth and other planets.
Science - Physical
Dist - USNAC **Prod** - NASA 1973

The Moon and How it Affects Us 18 MIN
U-matic / VHS / 16mm
Exploring Space Series
Color (I J H C A)
$425, $250 purchase _ #3551
Discusses the moon's movements, phases, and effects on the earth.
Science - Physical
Dist - CORF

The Moon and the Sledgehammer 65 MIN
16mm
B&W
Presents a real life portrait of a family, their bizarre habits and estranged attitudes.
Psychology; Sociology
Dist - IMPACT **Prod** - IMPACT 1971

Moon Buggy 25 MIN
U-matic / VHS
Color
Documents the technology theory and experimentation behind a trip to the moon.
Fine Arts; Science - Physical
Dist - IHF **Prod** - IHF

Moon Creatures 14 MIN
VHS / U-matic
Young at Art Series
Color (P I)
Fine Arts
Dist - AITECH **Prod** - WSKJTV 1980

Moon Eyes 15 MIN
VHS / U-matic
Best of Cover to Cover 2 Series
Color (I)
Literature and Drama
Dist - WETATV **Prod** - WETATV

Moon goddess 15 MIN
16mm
Color (G)
$35.00 rental
Couples a Native American woman with a stark desert landscape. Searches for the feminine creative spirit guided by moon power. Made with Gloria Churchwoman.
Fine Arts; Sociology
Dist - CANCIN **Prod** - BARHAM 1976

The Moon is Coming Out 14 MIN
U-matic / VHS
Stepping into Rhythm Series
Color (P)
Features Japanese music and introduces the music staff.
Fine Arts
Dist - AITECH **Prod** - WVIZTV

Moon Jelly - the Cycle of Aurelia Aurita 33 MIN
U-matic / VHS
Color (H C G T A)
Detailed time lapse, cine macro, and cine microphotography show the life cycle of the jellyfish, Aurelia aurita, from embryonal development, metamorphosis of planulae, colony formation of polyps, and strobilation, to the adult medusa.
Science; Science - Natural
Dist - PSU **Prod** - PSU 1977

Moon Man 8 MIN
16mm / U-matic / VHS
Color (K P)
LC 81-700280
Tells how the man in the moon becomes bored with his life and rockets down to Earth. Based on the children's story Moon Man by Tomi Ungerer.
Literature and Drama
Dist - WWS **Prod** - WWS 1981

Moon Mask - Un Masque De Lune 10 MIN
16mm
Color (G) (FRENCH)
#1X58 I
Illustrates the design and craftsmanship of Northwest Coast Indian art. Demonstrates the making of a moon mask by a female Haida Indian of the Eagle Clan.
Fine Arts; Social Science
Dist - CDIAND **Prod** - NAIFL 1977

Moon Motel 30 MIN
U-matic
Color (I J)
Shows how a boy from a special education class can do a good job.
Psychology; Sociology
Dist - TVOTAR **Prod** - TVOTAR 1986

Moon Motion and Phases 7 MIN
16mm / VHS
Color (C)
$80.00, $34.95 purchase _ #194 E 0080, 193 E 2080
Examines the rotation and revolution of the moon about the spinning earth andthe continuous progression of moon phases as seen from the earth's surface.
Science - Physical
Dist - WARDS **Prod** - AAS

Moon - motion and phases 8 MIN
VHS
Astronomy series
Color (J H)
$24.95 purchase _ #S9101
Focuses on the moon and its motion and phases. Part of a six - part series on astronomy using single - concept format and incorporating NASA footage.
Science - Physical
Dist - HUBDSC **Prod** - HUBDSC

Moon - motion and phases 8 MIN
VHS
Astronomy series
Color (J H)
$34.95 purchase _ #193 W 0052
Shows revolutions of the Moon around the Earth. Includes a continuous progression of Moon phases as seen from the Earth. Part of a six - part series presenting a single concept about astronomy.
Mathematics; Science - Physical
Dist - WARDS **Prod** - WARDS

The Moon Old and New 26 MIN
16mm
Color
LC 70-710254
Gives a brief history of lunar studies before the Apollo 11 mission. Covers the major findings and questions that have emerged from studying Apollo 11 and 12 lunar samples and the data returned from scientific instruments left on the surface. Closes with a brief resume of investigations that scientists would like to undertake in the future.
History - World; Industrial and Technical Education; Science; Science - Physical
Dist - USNAC **Prod** - NASA 1980

The Moon - Old and New 25 MIN
16mm
Color
Gives a brief history of lunar studies before the Apollo 11 mission. Covers the major things we have learned and the major questions that have emerged from studying Apollo 11 and 12 lunar samples and the data returns from scientific instruments left on the surface of the moon.
Industrial and Technical Education; Science; Science - Physical
Dist - NASA **Prod** - NASA 1970

Moon Shadows 29 MIN
16mm / U-matic
Presente Series
Color
Looks at the controversial political maneuverings of Reverend Sun Myung Moon's Unification Church and a coalition of Latin American right - wing 'contra' groups. Focuses on exiles from Latin American countries overthrown by Communism, their attempts to fight against Communism and their link to Moon's church. Includes interviews with an ex - Moonie, ex - Black Panther Eldridge Cleaver, an anti - communist backed by a moonie group, a Latin American newspaper editor in San Francisco and Senator Jim Leach of Iowa.
Civics and Political Systems; History - World; Religion and Philosophy; Sociology
Dist - KCET **Prod** - KCET

Moon shot - the inside story of America's race to the Moon 30 MIN
VHS
Author's night at the Freedom Forum series
Color (G)
$15.00 purchase _ #V94 - 11
Focuses on former astronaut Alan B Shepard, Jr, author of the book of the same title, in part of a series on freedom of the press, free speech and free spirit.
History - World; Industrial and Technical Education; Social Science; Sociology
Dist - FREEDM **Prod** - FREEDM 1994

Moona Luna 10 MIN
16mm
Color (G)
$30.00 rental
Portrays filmmaker Emily Breer's 'first trip to the moon.'
Fine Arts
Dist - CANCIN

The Moonbeam princess 18 MIN
VHS
Color (P)
Presents an animated version of 'The Moonbeam Princess.' Tells of a little princess sent to Earth on a moonbeam. Reveals that the princess is raised by a woodcutter and his wife, and wooed by three princes who fail in their courtship. Recalled to her original home, the princess leaves a gift of magical flowers for the ones she loved on Earth.
Fine Arts; Literature and Drama
Dist - VIEWTH **Prod** - VIEWTH

The Moonbeam Princess - a Japanese Fairy Tale 19 MIN
U-matic / VHS / 16mm
Color (P)
$425.00, $250.00 purchase _ #1819; LC FIA67-1263
Tells the story of a princess who is sent to earth on a moonbeam as a baby and raised by a woodcutter and his wife. Although sought by three princes, she returns to the moon leaving magical flowers on earth for her loved ones. An animated film.
English Language; Literature and Drama
Dist - CORF **Prod** - GAKKEN 1967

Moonchild 49 MIN
16mm / U-matic / VHS
Color (H C A)
LC 82-700286
Shows a young man, Chris Carlson, who became a member of Rev Moon's Unification Church, and how his parents were able to extricate him from that group through legal deprogramming. Includes recollections of other ex - Moonies.
Psychology; Religion and Philosophy
Dist - PFP **Prod** - MAKPEC 1982

Moondance 4 MIN
16mm
Color (G)
$10.00 rental
Invokes night and nature, magic and the dark mystery of daydream. Examines how creatures - even humans - emerge at nightfall with the moon and lurk alone in the cool of the daytime. Produced by Phil Costa Cummins.
Fine Arts
Dist - CANCIN

Mooney Vs Fowle 55 MIN
16mm
B&W (C A)
Depicts the trials of competition between two high school football coaches in a film style making the film entertaining as well as a biting commentary on contemporary life.
Fine Arts; Sociology
Dist - DIRECT **Prod** - DREW 1970

Moonflights and Medicine 26 MIN
16mm
Color
LC 73-700598
Shows some of the advances made in medicine through projects which were initiated and sponsored by the National Aeronautics and Space Administration.
Health and Safety
Dist - NASA **Prod** - MESHDO 1972

Moongates - Marnee Morris - Rocking Orange III 30 MIN
U-matic / VHS
Doris Chase Dance Series
Color
Features Staton Dance Ensemble. Shows footwork of Marnee Morris, and Kinetic sculptures.
Fine Arts; Physical Education and Recreation
Dist - ARTINC **Prod** - CHASED

Moonglow 10 MIN
U-matic / VHS
Color (K A)
Presents an animated fairy tale.
Fine Arts; Literature and Drama
Dist - SUTHRB **Prod** - NETHIS

Moonies and Mormons - a comparative study 30 MIN
VHS
Challenge of the cults series
Color (J H C G A R)
$39.95 purchase, $10.00 rental _ #35 - 845 - 2076
Compares the beliefs and practices of the Unification Church, also known as the 'Moonies,' and the Church of Jesus Christ of Latter - Day Saints, otherwise known as the 'Mormons.' Suggests that both groups are cults and out of the mainstream of Christianity. Hosted by Dr Trygve Skarsten. Produced by Seraphim.
Religion and Philosophy
Dist - APH

The Moonlight in Vermont Show 30 MIN
U-matic / VHS
Cookin' Cheap Series
Color
Presents basically crazy cooks Larry Bly and Laban Johnson who offer recipes, cooking and shopping tips.
Home Economics
Dist - MDCPB **Prod** - WBRATV

Moonlight revenge - Volume 5 45 MIN
VHS
Bubblegum crisis series
Color (A) (JAPANESE WITH ENGLISH SUBTITLES)
$34.95 purchase _ #CPM91005
Presents a Japanese animated film. Viewer discretion is advised as some films contain strong language or violence.
Fine Arts
Dist - CHTSUI

Moonlight sonata 5 MIN
16mm
Color (G)
$15.00 rental
Interprets the rhythms of Eric Satie's Gnossienne V with moonlight and soft greens and blues in the background. Refines his techniques with simple movements to evoke the poetry of animation.
Fine Arts
Dist - CANCIN **Prod** - JORDAL 1979

Moonlighters 14 MIN
VHS
Tax tips on tape series
Color; Captioned (A PRO IND)
$20.00, $40.00 purchase _ #TCA17618, #TCA17617
Covers tax law for 'moonlighters.' Discusses the different ways in which 'moonlighters' are paid and how the law determines taxation for each type.
Business and Economics; Civics and Political Systems; Social Science
Dist - USNAC **Prod** - USIRS 1988

Moonplay 18 MIN
16mm / U-matic / VHS
Color (P I)
LC 77-700124
Stimulates imaginative thinking in children with a story about a small girl who wishes for the moon and experiences delightful adventures when it materializes as a bright golden ball on her window ledge and leads her on a fantastic chase.
English Language; Guidance and Counseling; Literature and Drama
Dist - CF **Prod** - SVEK 1977

Moons pool 15 MIN
16mm
Color (G)
$35.00 rental
Portrays the search for identity and resolution of self. Uses underwater photography. Live bodies are intercut with natural landscapes. Shown on BBC TV - London.
Fine Arts; Industrial and Technical Education; Psychology
Dist - CANCIN **Prod** - NELSOG 1973

Moonspell 25 MIN
16mm / VHS / BETA
Color
LC 77-702517
Examines the experience of space travel and the profound effect that it has had on Apollo astronauts, such as James Irwin and Edwin E Aldrin. Finds these men turning to self - worship, or to self - doubt and depression.
Industrial and Technical Education; Psychology; Science - Physical
Dist - CTV **Prod** - CTV 1976

Moonstones 76 MIN
U-matic / VHS
Color (PRO)
Traces progress of a relationship between a male psychiatry resident and his thirteen - year - old patient over a three - month period. Comes on two tapes.
Health and Safety; Home Economics; Psychology
Dist - HSCIC **Prod** - HSCIC 1985

Moonstruck 26 MIN
VHS / U-matic
Color (H C A)
Looks at Sun Myung Moon and his followers.
Religion and Philosophy; Sociology
Dist - JOU **Prod** - CANBC

Moonwalk 40 MIN
16mm / VHS / U-matic

Color; Captioned (P J I) (DANISH SPANISH)

LC 76-700287; 76-700286
Documents almost every aspect of the historic voyage of spaceship Apollo 11 in July 1969. Full version.
History - United States; History - World; Science; Science - Physical
Dist - LCOA **Prod** - NASA 1976

The Moonwalk - a Look Back 25 MIN
VHS / U-matic
Color
Provides footage of the moon missions flown by the United States between July 1969 and December 1972.
History - World; Industrial and Technical Education; Science - Physical
Dist - JOU **Prod** - UPI

Moore report series
Farewell to freedom 60 MIN
Fear and present danger 55 MIN
The Quiet Crisis 55 MIN
You've come a long way, maybe 55 MIN
Dist - IU

Moose Jaw 55 MIN
16mm
Color (G)
$120.00 rental
Delves into political history, personal memory and the prehistoric. Exposes the complicity of the filmmaker in an ironically humorous and disturbing view of his hometown, with its motto 'There's a Future in our Past' as a faded symbol of Empire and 'storm center' in the crash of technological nationalism. Mixes experimental and documentary techniques.
Fine Arts; Literature and Drama; Sociology
Dist - CANCIN **Prod** - HANCXR 1992

The Moose - Our Largest Deer 11 MIN
VHS
A Closer Look Series
Color
$69.95 purchase _ #9677
Teaches about one of North America's most spectacular animals, the moose. Gives viewers a lesson in observing and gathering data about the animal's structure and function, behavior, adaptation, and environment.
Science - Natural
Dist - AIMS **Prod** - AIMS 1981

Moowis, Where are You, Moowis 26 MIN
16mm / U-matic / VHS
Color
Dramatizes an Algonquin Indian legend about a young warrior spurned by the chief's daughter.
Literature and Drama; Social Science
Dist - FOTH **Prod** - FOTH

Mop top 10 MIN
VHS
Color (K P)
$34.95 purchase
Presents a video version of the Don Freeman book 'Mop Top.' Tells the story of Moppy, a boy whose head is often mistaken for a mop - in appearance - and how he adopts a more clean - cut appearance.
Literature and Drama; Psychology
Dist - LIVOAK **Prod** - LIVOAK

Mop Top
35mm strip / VHS / Cassette
Storybook Library Series
Color (K)
$34.95, $32.00, $29.95 purchase
Offers another Corduroy, the favorite teddy bear, story by Don Freeman.
English Language; Literature and Drama
Dist - PELLER

Mopac Delivers 25 MIN
16mm
Color
LC 75-702822
Shows the kinds of technology and services the Missouri Pacific Railroad can offer its customers.
Social Science; Sociology
Dist - MOPAC **Prod** - MOPAC 1975

Moped Safety 15 MIN
U-matic / VHS / 16mm
Color (J)
Emphasizes the excellent fuel economy of the moped and discusses the special safety precautions to be used when riding this vehicle.
Health and Safety
Dist - HANDEL **Prod** - HANDEL 1979

Moped Safety - the Facts of Life 18 MIN
16mm / U-matic / VHS
Color (J)
LC 81-701545
Presents basic information on applicable traffic laws, required safety equipment, and safe riding techniques for beginning mopedalists. Stresses the unique capabilities as well as the limitations of the moped. Shows teenagers, parents and grandparents operating mopeds.
Health and Safety
Dist - CORF **Prod** - CENTRO 1981

Mops and brooms and things
VHS
Equipment maintenance series
Color (H A G T)
$225.00 purchase _ #BM135
Shows how to make mops, brooms and other cleaning items last two to five to possibly even 10 times longer. Part of a series on equipment maintenance.
Home Economics; Industrial and Technical Education; Psychology
Dist - AAVIM **Prod** - AAVIM 1992

Moral Conflicts - the same for Men and Women 30 MIN
U-matic
Realities
Color (A)
Delves into the political, social, economic and cultural trends of the 1980s. Probes a wide range of contemporary concerns. Each segment includes a guest speaker who is an expert in the field under discussion.
Business and Economics; Civics and Political Systems; Social Science; Sociology
Dist - TVOTAR **Prod** - TVOTAR 1985

Moral decision making series
Aggression - assertion 8 MIN
Anger 8 MIN
Cheating 9 MIN
Envy 7 MIN
Frustration 8 MIN
Response to Misbehavior 9 MIN
Sharing 9 MIN
Stealing 12 MIN
Dist - AIMS

Moral Development 28 MIN
U-matic / VHS / 16mm
Developmental Psychology Today Film Series
Color (C A)
LC 73-700599
Presents Dr Lawrence Kohlberg's theory on moral development. States that all people develop morality in consistent and unchanging ways and that behavior is determined by the state of moral development that has been reached. Contrasts Kohlberg's theory with the social learning theory.
Psychology; Sociology
Dist - CRMP **Prod** - CRMP 1973

Moral Development 30 MIN
U-matic
Growing Years Series
Color
Presents the various theories and the stages of moral development in childhood.
Psychology
Dist - CDTEL **Prod** - COAST

Moral Dimension 30 MIN
16mm
Eternal Light Series
B&W (H C A)
LC 74-700951
A memorial program presented on the second anniversary of the death of Herbert H Lehman, former U S Senator and governor of the state of New York. Includes an interview of Vice - President Hubert H Humphrey. (Kinescope).
Religion and Philosophy
Dist - NAAJS **Prod** - JTS 1966

Moral Education for Children 30 MIN
U-matic / VHS
Moral Values in Contemporary Society Series
Color (J)
Shows James W Prescott, of the National Institute of Child Health and Human Development at HEW, and Roy Fairfield, of the Union For Experimenting Colleges and Universities, talking about moral education for children.
Education; Religion and Philosophy; Sociology
Dist - AMHUMA **Prod** - AMHUMA

Moral Education in Our Schools, Pt 1 - Values Clarification 30 MIN
U-matic / VHS
Ethics in America Series
Color (H C A)
Describes aims and techniques of innovative values, clarification methods. Discussion by Louis Raths and Joel Goodman. Graphic film sequences with Dr. Sidney Simon.
Education; Religion and Philosophy
Dist - AMHUMA **Prod** - AMHUMA

Moral Education in Our Schools, Pt 2 - Moral Development 30 MIN
U-matic / VHS
Ethics in America Series
Color (H C A)
Presents Dr. Lawrence Kohlberg, Professor of Psychology and Social Education at Harvard, explaining moral development methodology, which he pioneered.
Education; Religion and Philosophy
Dist - AMHUMA **Prod** - AMHUMA

Moral Education in Our Schools, Pt 3 - Moral Development 30 MIN
VHS / U-matic
Ethics in America Series
Color (H C A)
Shows Ralph Mosher, Professor Lisa Kuhmerke and Thomas Ladenburg discussing practical application of Dr. Lawrence Kohlberg's theories of moral development methodology. Includes on - location classroom discussions and student, teacher and administrator evaluations.
Education; Religion and Philosophy
Dist - AMHUMA **Prod** - AMHUMA

Moral Integration 45 MIN
BETA / VHS
Psychological Growth and Spritual Development Series
Color (G)
Psychology; Religion and Philosophy
Dist - DSP **Prod** - DSP

Moral Judgment and Reasoning 17 MIN
16mm / U-matic / VHS
Color (H C A)
LC 78-701011
Examines concepts of moral development and points out that moral knowledge comes to a child from many sources, including parents, older siblings and playmates.
Guidance and Counseling; Psychology; Sociology
Dist - MGHT **Prod** - UCSD 1978

Moral philosophy 45 MIN
VHS
Men of ideas series
Color; PAL (H C A)
PdS99 purchase; Not available in Canada.
Explains in simple terms the main developments in Western philosophy from the 19th century to the present day. Features a contemporary thinker discussing his ideas and beliefs on moral philosophy with Bryan Magee. Part eight of a fifteen part series.
Psychology; Religion and Philosophy
Dist - BBCENE

Moral question series
Abortion - a question of life 59 MIN
Killing and dying 29 MIN
The Last hanging in Canada 29 MIN
The Moral question with Jonathan Glover 29 MIN
Philosophers at work - capital punishment 29 MIN
Philosophers at work - moral philosophy 29 MIN
Philosophers at work - poverty and affluence 29 MIN
Philosophers at work - suicide and euthanasia 29 MIN
Philosophers at work - the morality of war 29 MIN
The Right to die 29 MIN
Dist - RMIBHF

Moral question series
Better off dead - who decides 29 MIN
Dist - RMIBHF
TVOTAR

The Moral question with Jonathan Glover 29 MIN
VHS / 16mm
Moral question series
Color (C A G)
$90.00 purchase _ #BPN177913
Looks at moral philosophy, discusses its components and formulations. Hosted by Jonathan Glover.
Religion and Philosophy; Sociology
Dist - RMIBHF **Prod** - RMIBHF

The Moral Question with Jonathan Glover 30 MIN
U-matic
Color (A)
Provides a documentary examination of moral philosophy and its components and formulations.
Religion and Philosophy; Sociology
Dist - TVOTAR **Prod** - TVOTAR 1985

Moral Responsibility of Safety 6 MIN
16mm
B&W

LC FIE60-163
Tells of four people directly and indirectly involved in a traffic accident facing the issue of who was morally responsible for the accident.
Health and Safety; Social Science; Sociology
Dist - USNAC **Prod** - USA 1959

The Moral Revolution 30 MIN
U-matic / VHS
Moral Values in Contemporary Society Series
Color (J)
Shows Charles Frankel of Columbia University talking about the moral revolution.
Psychology; Religion and Philosophy; Sociology
Dist - AMHUMA **Prod** - AMHUMA

The Moral Value of Health 16 MIN
U-matic
Bioethics in Nursing Practice Series Module 5; Module 5
Color (PRO)
LC 81-707063
Health and Safety
Dist - BRA **Prod** - BRA 1981

Moral values in comtemporary society series
The Future of the university, Pt 1 30 MIN
Dist - AMHUMA

Moral values in contemporary society series
Beneficent euthanasia 30 MIN
Beyond the Sexual Revolution 30 MIN
Biology and the future of humankind, Pt 1 30 MIN
Biology and the future of humankind, Pt 2 30 MIN
Boredom - it's epidemic 30 MIN
The Church, the State, and the First Amendment 30 MIN
The Disillusioned Americans 30 MIN
Divorce and alimony - the American tragedy 30 MIN
Does God exist 30 MIN
Ethics and the Law 30 MIN
Ethics Without Religion 30 MIN
Fear of eroticism and its human implications 30 MIN
Free Thought and the Mass Media 30 MIN
The Future of the university, Pt 2 30 MIN
Growing Old - the Prospects for Happiness 30 MIN
How to enjoy your first one hundred years 30 MIN
Humanism and Democracy 30 MIN
Humanism and Feminism - New Directions 30 MIN
Humanism and its Enemies 30 MIN
Humanism and Science 30 MIN
Humanism and the Frontiers of Education 30 MIN
Humanism in the Churches 30 MIN
Humanizing the Workplace 30 MIN
Immortality - a Debate 30 MIN
Involuntary Commitment 30 MIN
Is the Family Dead? 30 MIN
Moral Education for Children 30 MIN
The Moral Revolution 30 MIN
New Concepts in Marriage 30 MIN
The New Cults as a Social Phenomenon 30 MIN
The New Sexual Revolution 30 MIN
On Black America 30 MIN
Our Disintegrating Public Schools 30 MIN
Paranormal Phenomena - Reality or Illusion 30 MIN
Religious liberty 30 MIN
Science and the Free Mind 30 MIN
Situation Ethics 30 MIN
What is Humanism? 30 MIN
Dist - AMHUMA

Morale and the Team Effort 4 MIN
VHS / 16mm
Patton Series
Color (PRO)
$150.00 purchase, $100.00 rental
Presents the character of General George Patton who motivates employees to work together as a team and raise morale. Free preview cassette available.
Education; Psychology
Dist - UTM **Prod** - UTM

Morale and the Team Effort 4 MIN
VHS / 16mm
Spirit of Patton Series
Color (G)
$150.00 purchase, $100.00 rental
Spoofs General George Patton. Motivates team spirit in an organization.
Business and Economics; Guidance and Counseling
Dist - PROSOR

The Morality of Collaboration 29 MIN
Videoreel / VT2
Course of Our Times I Series
Color
History - World
Dist - PBS **Prod** - WGBHTV

The Morality of Geopolitics 30 MIN
U-matic
Realities
Color (A)
Delves into the political, social, economic and cultural trends of the 1980s. Probes a wide range of contemporary concerns. Each segment includes a guest speaker who is an expert in the field under discussion.
Business and Economics; Civics and Political Systems; Social Science; Sociology
Dist - TVOTAR **Prod** - TVOTAR 1985

Morality - the Process of Moral Development 28 MIN
16mm
Piaget's Developmental Theory Series
Color
LC 78-700201
Shows Dr Susan De Merrsemen - Warren and Dr Elliot Turiel interviewing and testing children ranging from four years of age into early adulthood in order to examine their concepts of sharing, fairness, justice and other attitudes linked to the process of moral development.
Guidance and Counseling; Psychology; Sociology
Dist - DAVFMS **Prod** - DAVFMS 1977

Morals, Manners and Varmints 10 MIN
U-matic / VHS / 16mm
Color (P)
LC 75-704013
Presents a tale about morals, manners and varmints in order to point out several human traits which are considered to be rude or impolite. Emphasizes that rude people are not popular.
Guidance and Counseling; Literature and Drama
Dist - BARR **Prod** - SAIF 1975

Moratorium 11 MIN
16mm
Color
LC 77-706062
Portrays the nationwide protest regarding the involvement of the United States in the Vietnam War which occurred on October 15, 1969. Shows students, teachers and administrators, in harmony and in conflict, as they participated in the demonstration at Southern Illinois University.
Education; Sociology
Dist - SIUFP **Prod** - SILLU 1970

More 4 MIN
VHS
Color (P I J H G)
$49.95 purchase _ #8379
Presents an animiated program which reminds viewers that world resources arefinite and that greed may destroy the world.
Guidance and Counseling; Science - Natural; Social Science; Sociology
Dist - AIMS **Prod** - DAVFMS 1991

More about Dinosaurs 8 MIN
U-matic / VHS
Now I Know Series
Color (K P)
$29.95 purchase _ #VM132
Presents an adaptation of the book More About Dinosaurs. Contains a 32 page hardcover book and a video.
English Language; Literature and Drama; Science - Natural
Dist - TROLA

More about LOTUS 1 - 2 - 3 commands 90 MIN
U-matic
Color (A)
Instructs experienced user on use of advanced commands for LOTUS 1 - 2 - 3 and LOTUS 1 - 2 - 3 Release 2. Includes tape, workbook, practice data diskette, quick reference guide, keyboard reference guide and command chart.
Computer Science
Dist - ITTST **Prod** - ITTST 1986

More about program construction 29 MIN
U-matic / VHS
Programming for microcomputers series; Unit 20
Color (J)
LC 83-707138
Checks the program designed in the videocassette Nested Loops And More About Program Design in terms of sequence, repetition, alternation or conditional flow, and logical groups. Uses a planning grid to formalize subroutines, along with a top - down approach to implement block structure and for coding and testing.
Mathematics
Dist - IU **Prod** - IU 1983

More about Quotient Rings
16mm
B&W
Shows how the isomorphism theorems follow naturally if one ring homomorphism is extended to a second. Demonstrates the one - to - one correspondence between ideals in the quotient ring and ideals which contain the kernel of the original homomorphism. Constructs a chain for the integers and uses this chain to introduce new ideas of integral domain, zero divisors, and field.
Mathematics
Dist - OPENU **Prod** - OPENU

More about Rhythm, Pt 1 15 MIN
U-matic / VHS
Song Sampler Series
Color (P)
LC 81-707061
Reviews the rhythm symbols ta, ti and toe and shows how to accompany a song with rhythm instruments. Relates how to recognize a familiar song by listening to the rhythm of the melody.
Fine Arts
Dist - GPN **Prod** - JCITV 1981

More about Rhythm, Pt 2 15 MIN
VHS / U-matic
Song Sampler Series
Color (P)
LC 81-707061
Reviews the rhythm symbols ta, ti and toe and shows how to accompany a song with rhythm instruments. Relates how to recognize a familiar song by listening to the rhythm of the melody.
Fine Arts
Dist - GPN **Prod** - JCITV 1981

The More abundant life 52 MIN
16mm / U-matic
America - a personal history of the United States series; No 13
Color (J) (SPANISH)
LC 74-701584;
Presents a potpourri of impressions by Alistair Cooke. Discusses what in America's experience has been fulfilled and what has been betrayed. Includes the Hoover Dam from the confident 30's and Hawaii, showing racial harmony amid pollution and overdevelopment.
History - United States
Dist - TIMLIF **Prod** - BBCTV 1972

The More abundant life - Pt 1 26 MIN
16mm / U-matic
America - a personal history of the United States series; No 13
Color (J)
LC 74-701584
Presents a potpourri of impressions by Alistair Cooke. Discusses what in America's experience has been fulfilled and what betrayed. Views Hoover Dam from the confident '30's. Pictures Hawaii showing racial harmony amid pollution and overdevelopment.
Literature and Drama
Dist - TIMLIF **Prod** - BBCTV 1972

The More abundant life - Pt 2 26 MIN
U-matic / 16mm
America - a personal history of the United States series; No 13
Color (J)
LC 74-701584
Presents a potpourri of impressions by Alistair Cooke. Discusses what in America's experience has been fulfilled and what betrayed. Views Hoover Dam from the confident '30'S. PICTURES HAWAII SHOWING RACIAL HARMONY AMID POLLUTION AND OVERDEVELOPMENT.
Literature and Drama
Dist - TIMLIF **Prod** - BBCTV 1972

More Alike than Different 29 MIN
U-matic
Color
Looks at a special program for visually impaired infants and pre - school youngsters.
Education; Psychology
Dist - PBS **Prod** - WKARTV

More and Less 10 MIN
16mm / U-matic / VHS
Color (P I)
LC FIA66-860
Illustrates the meaning of the equality and inequality of numbers by matching objects from two sets. Indicates the symbols used to show these relationships.
Mathematics
Dist - PHENIX **Prod** - BOUNDY 1966

More and Louder 11 MIN
16mm
Color (P I J H)
Combines animation and live action to tell about the new United States Postal Service, what it means and how it will work.

Social Science
Dist - USNAC **Prod** - USNAC 1971

More and more 27 MIN
16mm / U-matic / VHS
Five Billion People Series
Color
Examines the concept of economic growth, challenging the conventional wisdom that the constant proliferation of an already considerable flow of goods and services is a desirable goal.
Business and Economics
Dist - CNEMAG **Prod** - LEFSP

More Awkard Customers 30 MIN
VHS / U-matic
Color
Shows the proper and improper ways of handling difficult customers. Emphasizes the importance of professional knowledge when dealing with customers.
Business and Economics
Dist - VISUCP **Prod** - VIDART

More Awkward Customers 31 MIN
VHS / U-matic
Color (A)
Shows additional types of awkward customers, including the snob, the person who won't say what he wants and the finicky person. Presents techniques for handling these customers.
Business and Economics; Psychology
Dist - XICOM **Prod** - XICOM

More Baby Songs 30 MIN
VHS
Baby Songs Series
Color (K)
$14.95 purchase _ #XVMBS
Offers live action and animated music for infants and young children. Includes book of lyrics.
Fine Arts; Health and Safety; Literature and Drama; Sociology
Dist - GAINST

More basic maneuvers
VHS
You and your horse series
Color (G)
$49.95 purchase _ #6 - 027 - 107A
Shows how to train a horse about leg pressure, side passing and two track maneuvers. Part of a six - part series on training the western horse featuring B F Yeates, Extension Horse Specialist Emeritus of Texas A&M University.
Physical Education and Recreation
Dist - VEP **Prod** - VEP

More Bloody Meetings
VHS / U-matic
Color
Moves from the organizational aspects of a meeting to the human side of actually running a meeting.
Psychology
Dist - VISUCP **Prod** - VIDART

More Bloody Meetings
VHS / 16mm
(C PRO)
Concentrates on handling the people attending a meeting. Shows how to unite the group, focus the group and mobilize the group. Sequel to Meetings, Bloody Meetings.
Education
Dist - VLEARN

More books from cover to cover series
Presents 17 children's books in video form. Tells the story up to a critical point, then encourages the children to read the book to find out how the story turned out. Series is hosted by John Robbins.

The agony of Alice	15 MIN
Baby - sitting is a dangerous job	15 MIN
The Castle in the attic	15 MIN
Come sing Jimmy Jo	15 MIN
The Dark is rising	15 MIN
The ghost squad breaks through and who kidnapped the sheriff - Tales from Tickfaw	15 MIN
Mama's going to buy you a mockingbird	15 MIN
Midnight is a place	15 MIN
The Not - just - anybody family	15 MIN
The Root cellar	15 MIN
Stone fox	15 MIN
Tom's midnight garden	15 MIN
The Whipping boy	15 MIN
The Wish giver	15 MIN
Won't know till I get there	15 MIN

Dist - PBS **Prod** - WETATV

More Commands
U-matic / VHS
UNIX Fundamentals Series
Color
Explains how to execute the pr, grep, sort, wc, tail and stty commands.
Industrial and Technical Education; Mathematics; Sociology
Dist - COMTEG **Prod** - COMTEG

More Complicated Weaves 29 MIN
Videoreel / VT2
Exploring the Crafts - Weaving Series
Color
Fine Arts; Home Economics
Dist - PBS **Prod** - NHN

More Control Statements
VHS / U-matic
'C' Language Programming Series
Color
Describes the syntax and use of the switch control statement, specifying the rules for the switch expression, case constants and switch execution flow. Describes the use of the default case, break control, continue control statement and the goto and return statements.
Industrial and Technical Education; Mathematics; Sociology
Dist - COMTEG **Prod** - COMTEG

More Creativity Behind the Scenes 30 MIN
U-matic / VHS
Behind the Scenes Series
Color
Fine Arts
Dist - ARCVID **Prod** - ARCVID

More Cuttings 29 MIN
Videoreel / VT2
Making Things Grow III Series
Color
Agriculture
Dist - PBS **Prod** - WGBHTV

More Deadly than War - the Communist Revolution in America, Pt 1 38 MIN
16mm
B&W
LC 73-700813
Presents a lecture by G Edward Griffin on the communist theory and practice of revolution, particularly as applied to the United States.
Civics and Political Systems; History - United States
Dist - AMMED **Prod** - AMMED 1969

More Deadly than War - the Communist Revolution in America, Pt 2 38 MIN
16mm
B&W
LC 73-700813
Presents a lecture by G Edward Griffin on the communist theory and practice of revolution, particularly as applied to the United States.
Civics and Political Systems; History - United States
Dist - AMMED **Prod** - AMMED 1969

A More Difficult Solo 29 MIN
Videoreel / VT2
Playing the Guitar II Series
Color
Fine Arts
Dist - PBS **Prod** - KCET

More dinosaurs 30 MIN
VHS
Color (K P I T)
$19.95 purchase _ #S01350
Uses a variety of formats to present a documentary on dinosaurs. Includes animation, live action footage, clips from classic Hollywood films, and interviews. Hosted by Los Angeles disc jockey Gary Owens and television emcee Eric Boardman.
Science; Science - Natural
Dist - UILL

More Dinosaurs 30 MIN
VHS
Color; Stereo (K)
$14.98 purchase _ #TT8031
Journeys across the globe and through time in search of prehistoric monsters.
History - World; Science - Natural
Dist - TWINTO **Prod** - TWINTO 1990

More duple rhythm 29 MIN
U-matic
Beginning piano - an adult approach series; Lesson 6
Color (H A)
Tests student comprehension of, and facility with, intervals up to the fifth, pitch notations and keyboard letter names. Introduces a new piece.
Fine Arts
Dist - CDTEL **Prod** - COAST

More exponents and introduction to radicals
VHS
Basic mathematical skills series
Color (J H)
$125.00 purchase _ #1016
Teaches the concepts involved in using exponents and radicals in mathematical expressions. Presents part of a series that provides 27 videos, each between 25 and 30 minutes long, that explain and reinforce basic mathematical concepts. Tutors the student through definitions, theorems, step - by - step solutions and examples. Videos are also available in a set.
Mathematics
Dist - LANDMK

More Exponents and Introduction to Radicals 30 MIN
VHS
Mathematics Series
Color (J)
LC 90713155
Discusses exponents and radicals. The 16th of 157 installments in the Mathematics Series.
Mathematics
Dist - GPN

More Expressions
U-matic / VHS
'C' Language Programming Series
Color
Discusses the relationship between bits and bytes for each fundamental storage type and describes the use and application of the four bitwise operators. Illustrates the use and application of the two shift operators, the use of the compound assignment operators and the syntax.
Industrial and Technical Education; Mathematics; Sociology
Dist - COMTEG **Prod** - COMTEG

More food 15 MIN
VHS
Zardips search for healthy wellness series
Color (P I)
LC 90-707983
Presents an episode in a series which help young children to understand basic health issues and the value of taking good care of their bodies. Explains the importance of good eating habits. Includes teacher's guide.
Education; Health and Safety
Dist - TVOTAR **Prod** - TVOTAR 1989

More for Peace 45 MIN
16mm
Color (J A)
Presents a veteran returning from Korea, disillusioned by the seeming contentedness of his community, who finally discovers what his little church is actually doing and decides to support it wholeheartedly.
Guidance and Counseling; Religion and Philosophy
Dist - YALEDV **Prod** - YALEDV

More French for children 40 MIN
VHS
Color (K P I)
PdS15 purchase _ #ML-LML0143
Teaches young viewers the basics of the French language through the further adventures of Marcus the Mole. Takes viewers into a restaurant, Moleville, and more. Helps viewers understand how the body works by watching Marcus handle illness. Introduces children to everyday words and phrases. Bases adventures on a computer game format, and places Marcus in surroundings that should seem familiar and comfortable for children.
Foreign Language
Dist - AVP **Prod** - LABFLM

More from Less 28 MIN
16mm
Color
Explains the practice of planting a crop without prior conventional tillage. Shows work being done to improve the environment by control of erosion.
Agriculture
Dist - IDEALF **Prod** - ALLISC

More fun with finger paints 15 MIN
Videoreel / VT2
Art corner series
B&W (P)
Explores the possibilities of monoprints.
Fine Arts
Dist - GPN **Prod** - CVETVC

More Gag - Gathering Methods 15 MIN
Videoreel / VT2
Charlie's Pad Series
Color
Fine Arts
Dist - PBS **Prod** - WSIU

More germs 15 MIN
VHS
Zardips search for healthy wellness series
Color (P I)
LC 90-707989
Presents an episode in a series which help young children to understand basic health issues and the value of taking good care of their bodies. Explains how germs cause disease. Includes teacher's guide.
Education; Health and Safety; Science - Natural
Dist - TVOTAR **Prod** - TVOTAR 1989

More Income Per Acre 30 MIN
16mm
Color (H C A)
Presents face - to - face interviews with actual users of sprinkler irrigation who explain its advantages on the farm.
Agriculture
Dist - REYMC **Prod** - REYMC 1957

More initial consonant clusters 15 MIN
U-matic / Kit / VHS
Space station readstar series
(P)
$130 purchase, $25 rental, $75 self dub
Teaches phonics in a series designed to supplement second grade reading programs. Discusses more initial consonant clusters. Twelfth in a 25 part series.
English Language
Dist - GPN

More I/O 30 MIN
VHS / U-matic
Pascal, Pt 3 - Advanced Pascal Series
Color (H C A)
LC 81-706049
Reviews the sequential file aspects of Pascal and introduces file buffers of the GET and PUT procedures. Describes problem of using Pascal as an interactive language, and discusses a file - merge program and other file - utility programs.
Industrial and Technical Education; Mathematics; Sociology
Dist - COLOSU **Prod** - COLOSU 1980

More is better - the bio - diversity story 20 MIN
VHS
CC; Color (I J H)
$89.95 purchase _ #10324VG
Discusses the current loss of species and endangered species around the world. Looks at the need for biodiversity and how scientists are trying to maintain it. Comes with a teacher's guide, discussion questions and five blackline masters.
Science - Natural
Dist - UNL

More Italian places 13 MIN
VHS / 8mm cartridge
Color (G)
$25.00 rental
Contains three shorts. Includes - Selinunte, Greek ruins in Sicily; Verona, Guisti Gardens, castelvecchio, the Adige, Piazza delle Erbe; Bay of Naples, serene blue bay with Vesuvio looming.
Fine Arts; Geography - World
Dist - CANCIN **Prod** - ADLEST 1989
FLMKCO

More Meat for Your Money 25 MIN
VHS / U-matic
Consumer Education for the Deaf Adult Series
Captioned; Color (S)
Presents Catherine Rhoads showing how to balance budget and nutrition. Demonstrates selection and use of economical cuts of meat.
Guidance and Counseling; Home Economics; Psychology
Dist - GALCO **Prod** - GALCO 1975

More Music from Aspen 59 MIN
U-matic
Color
Covers the annual three - day Aspen, Colorado, Music Festival, which brings together famous musicians and gifted students.
Fine Arts
Dist - PBS **Prod** - KQEDTV

More Non - Fiction 30 MIN
VHS / U-matic
Communicating through Literature Series
Color (C)
Literature and Drama
Dist - DALCCD **Prod** - DALCCD

More Nuclear Power Stations 48 MIN
U-matic / VHS
Color
Offers a glimpse into the workings of the nuclear power industry.
Social Science
Dist - GMPF **Prod** - GMPF 1977

More on Algorithms 30 MIN
VHS / U-matic
Microprocessors for Monitoring and Control Series
Color (IND)
Develops two algorithms, the first describing a simple decoder for events such as an alarm system and the second for a timer to generate desired time interval. Notes latter has many commercial applications.
Industrial and Technical Education; Mathematics; Sociology
Dist - COLOSU **Prod** - COLOSU

More on Decoding Logic and Data and Address Bus Interfaces 30 MIN
U-matic / VHS
Microcomputer Memory Design Series
Color (IND)
Discusses design examples of address decoding logic, dynamic mapping of a memory space, address bus interface and data bus interface.
Industrial and Technical Education; Mathematics; Sociology
Dist - COLOSU **Prod** - COLOSU

More on Map Representations - Map - Entered Variables, Don't - Care Map Terms 30 MIN
VHS / U-matic
Microprocessors for Monitoring and Control Series
Color (IND)
Provides more material on map use to represent logical expressions.
Industrial and Technical Education; Mathematics; Sociology
Dist - COLOSU **Prod** - COLOSU

More Patterns I 29 MIN
Videoreel / VT2
Busy Knitter II Series
Color
Fine Arts; Home Economics
Dist - PBS **Prod** - WMVSTV

More Patterns II 29 MIN
Videoreel / VT2
Busy Knitter II Series
Color
Fine Arts; Home Economics
Dist - PBS **Prod** - WMVSTV

More perfect union series
Explains the workings of the federal government, by introducing in a dramatic way the basic civics concepts needed to understand how the three branches of government work and interact. Covers the Presidency, the Congress, and the Supreme Court.
The Supreme Court 15 MIN
Dist - CAMV

More perfect union series
The Congress 18 MIN
Dist - CAMV
KNOWUN

More perfect union series
Presents a three - part series on the three branches of the federal government. Includes The Presidency, The Congress and The Supreme Court with a resource guide.
The Presidency 17 MIN
The Supreme Court 15 MIN
Dist - KNOWUN **Prod** - KNOWUN

More perfect union - the three branches of the federal goverment series
A More perfect union - the three branches of the federal government series 50 MIN
The Supreme Court 15 MIN
Dist - CAMV

A More perfect union - the three branches of the federal government series 50 MIN
VHS
More perfect union - the three branches of the federal goverment 'series
Color (J H C G)
$150.00 purchase _ #KUN4013SV
Presents a three - part series on the branches of the federal government. Includes The Presidency, The Congress, and The Supreme Court.
Civics and Political Systems
Dist - CAMV

More perfect union - the three branches of the federal government series
The Presidency 17 MIN
Dist - CAMV

More Power for the Job 19 MIN
U-matic / VHS / 16mm
Color (A)
LC FIA65-1882
Explores the changing patterns of career opportunities in the 1960's. Emphasizes the importance of an early choice of a career and reviews the planning and training necessary for a variety of jobs and professions.
Education; Guidance and Counseling; Psychology
Dist - IFB **Prod** - IFB 1965

More Power on the Ground 13 MIN
16mm
Color
Presents the 'World Series' of tractor - pulls in Louisville, Kentucky. Describes the rules, weight classes and degrees of competition. Shows how pull power means more power on the ground, less man power and less man hours.
Agriculture
Dist - IDEALF **Prod** - ALLISC

More Power to You 10 MIN
16mm
Color
Describes the use of the Euclid Twin Power Scraper in coal stock - piling.
Industrial and Technical Education; Psychology
Dist - GM **Prod** - GM

More Precious than Gold 30 MIN
BETA / VHS
On the Money Series
Color
Explores investing in gold. Discusses choosing a guardian for children. Describes what to look for in a personal computer.
Business and Economics; Home Economics; Industrial and Technical Education; Mathematics; Sociology
Dist - CORF **Prod** - WGBHTV

More pronouns - more sub material 18 MIN
VHS
Language construction company series
Color (H C G)
$50.00 purchase _ #LCC - 5
Assists students in improving their written and spoken English grammar skills. Bases all programs on a 'construction theme.' Includes review tests as an integral part of each lesson. Students may stop, start and repeat any part of the lesson. Visual cues are given for review purposes. Part of a 15 - part series.
English Language
Dist - INSTRU

More Safely Tomorrow 10 MIN
16mm
Color
Depicts the need for accident prevention in the years ahead. Stresses the need for safety to a growing economy and improved social order.
Health and Safety
Dist - NSC **Prod** - NSC

More signs you already know 30 MIN
VHS / U-matic
Say it with sign series; Pt 2
Color (H C A) (AMERICAN SIGN)
LC 83-706359
Presents Lawrence Solow and Sharon Neumann Solow introducing American Sign Language used by the hearing - impaired. Emphasizes signs that resemble gestures already used by many people in spoken conversation.
Education
Dist - FI **Prod** - KNBCTV 1982

More Solutions of Linear Equations 30 MIN
16mm
Intermediate Algebra Series
B&W (H)
Presents four steps to use in solving word problems correctly. Obtains solutions to a problem about the relations in the rational number system, a problem in uniform motion, a mixture problem and a river - boat problem involving combined velocities.
Mathematics
Dist - MLA **Prod** - CALVIN 1959

More Storage Space in the Kitchen 13 MIN
Videoreel / VT2
Living Better I Series
Color
Fine Arts; Home Economics
Dist - PBS **Prod** - MAETEL

More stories for the very young 35 MIN
VHS
Children's circle collection series
Color (K P I)
$14.95 purchase _ #WK1194
Offers Max's Christmas; The Little Red Hen; Petunia; Not So Fast; Songololo; and The Napping House.
Fine Arts; Literature and Drama
Dist - KNOWUN

More swing bass 29 MIN
U-matic
Beginning piano - an adult approach series
Color (H A)
Applies swing bass to a familiar melody. Reviews earlier lessons and adds chords in B - flat major.
Fine Arts
Dist - CDTEL **Prod** - COAST

More telephone communication skills 26 MIN
VHS / BETA / U-matic
Color (G)
$395.00 purchase, $150.00 rental
Trains bank employees in telephone communication skills.
Business and Economics; Psychology; Social Science
Dist - AMEDIA **Prod** - AMEDIA

More ten easy lessons - Video Two 75 MIN
VHS
Kid's guitar series

Color (K P I J)
$24.95 purchase _ #VD - MAX - KI02
Teaches more chords, strums and songs for children on an easy - to - follow video. Features Marcy Marxer as instructor. Covers simple fingerpicking arpeggios, the use of the capo and simple chord theory. Includes the songs Won't It Be Joyful; Shortenin' Bread; Hey, Ho, Nobody Home; This Old Man; Twinkle, Twinkle, Little Star; I've Been Working on the Railroad; Heart and Soul; Hush Little Baby. Includes chords. Part two of a two - part series.
Fine Arts
Dist - HOMETA **Prod** - HOMETA

More than a Breakfast Cereal 10 MIN
16mm
Color
Shows that it is possible for even the beginning student to prepare a variety of dishes with breakfast cereals. Stresses basic cooking skills as demonstrated by a zany gourmet chef and his class of teenage cooks.
Home Economics
Dist - MTP **Prod** - CHEX

More than a Carpenter 58 MIN
16mm / VHS
Color (J H A)
$49.95 video purchase, $56.00 film rental
Portrays a skeptical archaeologist who finds the faith of Christianity in the Holy Land.
Religion and Philosophy
Dist - CAFM **Prod** - CAFM 1977

More than a Carpenter 58 MIN
16mm
Color (R)
Reveals how Josh McDowell visits an archaeological dig and finds compelling evidence concerning the identity of Jesus of Nazareth which challenges a professor, nearly explodes a romance and drives a young archaeologist to the breaking point.
Guidance and Counseling; Religion and Philosophy
Dist - OUTRCH **Prod** - OUTRCH

More than a Contract 29 MIN
U-matic
Life, Death and Taxes Series
Color
Investigates some of the problems that occur in the settlement of divorce and remarriage.
Business and Economics; Sociology
Dist - UMITV **Prod** - UMITV 1977

More than a game series
mresents an eight-part series that looks at sports as an integral part of every civilization, offering participation, the opportunity to excel and to belong. Asks if this is a romantic view of sport. Examines the importance of winning, amateur vs professional status in sports, drug use in sports, the commercialization of sports, the collapse of the USSR and its effect on sports, the impact of television upon sports, sportsmanship, and whether or not everyone can participate in sports.

Amateurs or shamateurs	50 MIN
Brotherhood of the needle	50 MIN
The Dynamo runs down	50 MIN
Is sportsmanship dead	50 MIN
Sold on sport	50 MIN
Who's in the control room	50 MIN
Whose game is it anyway	50 MIN
Winning	50 MIN

Dist - BBCENE

More than a game - sexual decision making for boys 19 MIN
VHS
Color (P I J H)
$119.00 purchase _ #CG - 927 - VS
Helps boys to think about the consequences of sexual activity. Portrays Victor, his baseball coach and his brother Tony, who is dating Teresa. Reveals that Victor is confused about many aspects of dating, sexuality, pregnancy and sexual decision - making. Shows that Victor, through discussions with his coach and his coach's wife Tracy, learns about the many facets of sexual relationships and the importance of knowledge, communication and responsible choices between partners. Includes a fantasy TV game, Let's Make a Choice, whose object is to answer questions correctly about sex and dating or risk becoming a father. Offers an optional demonstration of proper condom use.
Guidance and Counseling; Health and Safety; Sociology
Dist - HRMC **Prod** - HRMC

More than a Gut Feeling 28 MIN
U-matic / VHS
(PRO)
$550.00 purchase, $110.00 rental.
Presents Dr. Paul Green's theory of 'Behavioral Interviewing.'.
Business and Economics; Guidance and Counseling
Dist - CREMED **Prod** - CREMED 1987

More than a Gut Feeling 28 MIN
U-matic / VHS
Color (A)
Describes a selection interviewing process designed to train supervisors, managers and personnel employees. Presents ideas in a story format using two characters.
Guidance and Counseling; Psychology
Dist - AMEDIA **Prod** - AMEDIA

More than a gut feeling course
VHS
Color (A PRO IND)
$849.00 purchase
Covers how to prepare for and conduct a job selection interview. Discusses what questions should and should not be asked, and gives examples of how to ask questions and evaluate the answers. Includes leader's guide, participant handbooks, and materials which summarize legal and illegal questions.
Business and Economics; Guidance and Counseling; Psychology
Dist - VLEARN **Prod** - AIMS

More than a gut feeling II 28 MIN
BETA / U-matic / VHS
Color; CC (G)
$695.00 purchase, $165.00 rental
Updates a previous video on interviewing. Shows how to obtain examples of past behavior, both personal and on the job, obtain 'contrary' evidence, use silence as an effective interviewing tool, objectively evalute skills, plan an interview and build rapport. Uses behavioral - style interviewing developed by industrial psychologist Dr Paul C Green.
Business and Economics; Guidance and Counseling; Psychology; Sociology
Dist - AMEDIA **Prod** - AMEDIA

More than a Memory 15 MIN
16mm
Growing Up - Growing Older Series
Color
Shows scenes from the 1920's to demonstrate that the experiences of children then are similar to the experiences of children in the 1980's.
Guidance and Counseling; Health and Safety; Sociology
Dist - MTP **Prod** - SEARSF 1982

More than a Paycheck 28 MIN
16mm
Color
LC 78-701799
Deals with cancer which is caused by exposure to cancerous agents found in work environments. Describes types of work situations in which exposure can occur and discusses methods of protecting employees. Narrated by John Wayne.
Health and Safety
Dist - USNAC **Prod** - GWASHU 1978

More than a Place to Die 59 MIN
U-matic / VHS
To Age is Human Series
B&W (H C G T A)
Shows the problems of a nonprofit nursing home as seen from the administrator's point of view. Administrator David Reed discusses his philosophy, his relationship with the home's board of directors, the problems of residents and staff, and government regulations.
Health and Safety; Sociology
Dist - PSU **Prod** - PSU 1977

More than a Promise 14 MIN
16mm
Exceptional Learners Series
Color (T S)
LC 79-700708
Presents an overview of the spirit and implementation of some of the provisions of P L 94 - 142 and the promises this law makes to handicapped people.
Civics and Political Systems; Education; Psychology
Dist - MERILC **Prod** - MERILC 1978

More than a School 56 MIN
16mm
Color (H C A)
Portrays an alternative community high school within the regular school and shows its positive effects on students, parents and the community.
Education
Dist - NYU **Prod** - NYU

More than a Snapshot 10 MIN
16mm / U-matic / VHS
Zoom Series
Color
LC 78-700141
Presents two young people who talk about their interest in and approach to photography.
Industrial and Technical Education; Sociology
Dist - FI **Prod** - WGBHTV 1977

More than an Investment 14 MIN
VHS
Color (H)
Presents South Africa as a potential center for investment. Includes a presentation on South Africa's infrastructure, resources and information for the foreign investor about the country's regional development plan. Available for free loan from the distributor.
Business and Economics; Geography - World
Dist - AUDPLN

More than Anger 27 MIN
16mm
Color (I J H)
Presents the animated story of the Christmas Seal.
Literature and Drama; Religion and Philosophy
Dist - AMLUNG **Prod** - NTBA 1968

More than bows and arrows
VHS
Color (G)
$24.95 purchase _ #CA002
Examines the little - known but crucial role of Native Americans in the development of the United States.
History - United States; Social Science; Sociology
Dist - SIV

More than Bows and Arrows 56 MIN
16mm
Color
LC 78-701467
Deals with the role of the American Indian in shaping various aspects of American culture, ranging from food and housing to philosophy.
Social Science; Sociology
Dist - CIASP **Prod** - CIASP 1978

More than Bows and Arrows, Pt 1 28 MIN
16mm
Color
LC 78-701467
Deals with the role of the American Indian in shaping various aspects of American culture, ranging from food and housing to philosophy.
Sociology
Dist - CIASP **Prod** - CIASP 1978

More than Bows and Arrows, Pt 2 28 MIN
16mm
Color
LC 78-701467
Deals with the role of the American Indian in shaping various aspects of American culture, ranging from food and housing to philosophy.
Sociology
Dist - CIASP **Prod** - CIASP 1978

More than bows and arrowss 60 MIN
VHS
Ancient America series
Color (J H)
$24.95 purchase _ #WK1225V-S
Reveals the marvels, wonders, and rituals of the world of the American Indians. Explores in detail the characteristics of Native American cultures. Details the achievements of Native Americans before the arrival of Europeans. Traces the contributions of Indians to the culture that has developed on this continent today. Describes the League of Five Nations, the ceremonial mounds of the Hopewells and the Mississippians, and the architectural feats of the Anasazis.
Social Science
Dist - CAMV

More than broken glass - memories of Kristallnacht 57 MIN
VHS
B&W; Color (G)
$39.95 purchase _ #616, #616C
Recalls the night of November 9, 1938, when the Nazis publicly announced that they had declared open war on Jewish people. Uses archival footage, photographs and interviews with witnesses. Narrated by Ken Olin.
Civics and Political Systems; History - World; Sociology
Dist - ERGOM **Prod** - ERGOM

More than Color 30 MIN
VHS / U-matic
Color
Explores several of the issues and problems confronting the black artist in America today. Examines the relationship between black culture and black aesthetics to contemporary mainstream art. Features several black artists.
Fine Arts
Dist - OHUTC **Prod** - OHUTC

More than Dance 15 MIN
16mm
B&W
LC 76-703786
Presents an impressionistic view of a dance studio.
Fine Arts
Dist - RYERI **Prod** - RYERI 1976

More than enough - literacy for the hearing impaired 28 MIN
VHS
Color (H C G)
$295.00 purchase, $55.00 rental
Demands that the hearing impaired be given equal educational opportunity. Advocates the use of ASL, American Sign Language. Dr Jerome Schein, Chair of Deaf Studies at the University of Alberta believes that hearing disabled have been overlooked by educators - many cannot read beyond a fourth grade level. Shows young adults learning life skills, ordering from menus, communicating via telephone, discussing current events from the newspaper.
Education; English Language; Guidance and Counseling
Dist - FLMLIB **Prod** - CANBC 1992

More than Friends 21 MIN
16mm
Color (J H C)
Introduces a couple who like each other but are confused about how to show it. Shows each person getting conflicting advice from different people and learning how hard it is to express true feelings.
Guidance and Counseling; Psychology
Dist - ODNP **Prod** - ODNP 1983

More than Gut Feeling 28 MIN
VHS / 16mm
(C PRO)
$550.00 purchase, $110.00 rental
Demonstrates how - to techniques for interviewing through a series of vignettes. Includes evaluation of skills instead of behavior, use of past behavior to predict future success, and how to look at contrary evidence.
Education
Dist - VLEARN

More than Gut Feeling Course
VHS / 16mm
(C PRO)
$849.00 purchase
Shows how to prepare and conduct a selection interview. Supports the videocassette More Than Gut Feeling and includes ten participant handbooks, sliderules of lawful and unlawful questions and desk reminder cards.
Education
Dist - VLEARN

More than Hugs and Kisses - Affective Education in a Mainstreamed Classroom 23 MIN
16mm
Color (T)
LC 81-700040
Demonstrates how teacher Alice Brogan, a victim of spina bifida, teaches her students at Jowonio School in Syracuse, NY, where one - third of the students are developmentally delayed. Illustrates activities and attitudes which further the development of the whole child and an approach to affective education which can be used in more traditional school environments.
Education; Psychology
Dist - FLMLIB **Prod** - VIDDA 1980

More than just a body 16 MIN
VHS
Price tag of sex series
Color (J H T)
$89.95 purchase _ #UL903V; $89.95 purchase _ #10379VG
Addresses teen sexuality and the consequences of sexual indulgence. Features a speaker who stresses the advantages of abstinence and promotes positive interaction and discussion. Looks at sex and self-esteem and virginity. Part of a four-part series.
Health and Safety; Psychology; Sociology
Dist - CAMV
UNL

More than M and M's 30 MIN
U-matic / VHS
Dealing in Discipline Series
Color (T)
Education; Psychology
Dist - GPN **Prod** - UKY 1980

More than meets the eye 30 MIN
VHS
Bodymatters series
Color (H C A)
PdS65 purchase
Discusses vision and how eyes work. Part of a series of 26 30-minute videos on various systems of the human body.
Science - Natural
Dist - BBCENE

More than Meets the Eye 30 MIN
16mm
Life Around Us - Spanish Series
Color (SPANISH)
LC 78-700082
Examines the process of seeing and the role light plays in seeing. Discusses the difference between seeing and perception and shows how experience, memory and prejudice influence people's view of their surroundings.
Foreign Language; Psychology; Science - Natural; Sociology
Dist - TIMLIF **Prod** - TIMLIF 1971

More than Meets the Eye 30 MIN
16mm / VHS
Life Around Us Series
(J H C)
$99.95 each, $695.00 series
Covers the complex workings of the human eye.
Science - Natural; Science - Physical; Sociology
Dist - AMBROS **Prod** - AMBROS 1971

More than Meets the Eye 30 MIN
16mm / U-matic / VHS
Life Around Us Series
Color (I J H)
Investigates the difference between seeing and perception. Shows how experience, memory and prejudice influence man's view of his surroundings.
Psychology; Sociology
Dist - TIMLIF **Prod** - TIMLIF

More than Money 30 MIN
VHS / 16mm
(C PRO)
$630.00 purchase, $150.00 rental
Shows managers how to motivate employees by communicating high standards that spur involvement. Covers important motivational areas, including expectation, goal setting, feedback, and reinforcement.
Education
Dist - VLEARN

More than Money 23 MIN
U-matic / VHS / 16mm
Color (A)
Discusses motivation and managerial expectations in relation to employee production, 'Theory X' and 'Theory Y' managerial styles, and leadership, supervision and interpersonal skills.
Business and Economics; Psychology
Dist - RTBL **Prod** - RTBL

More than one way 10 MIN
U-matic
Body works series
Color (J H)
Gives exercise demonstrations and a nutritious cookie recipe.
Physical Education and Recreation; Social Science
Dist - TVOTAR **Prod** - TVOTAR 1979

More than Retirement 15 MIN
U-matic / VHS / 16mm
Color
Discusses the rights and benefits workers have under Social Security.
Business and Economics; Sociology
Dist - USNAC **Prod** - USSSA 1981

More than shelter - the public life of buildings 28 MIN
VHS
Color (H C G)
$195.00 purchase, $35.00 rental _ #37793
Explores the postmodernism movement in contemporary architecture. Examines the impact and accomplishments of the movement and evaluates many of the most famous postmodernist buildings around the United States, including the Portland Building by Michael Graves, the AT&T Building by Philip Johnson, the Museum of Contemporary Art in Los Angeles by Arrata Isosaki. Provides commentary by prominent architecture critics, historians and designers. Produced by the Rutgers University Office of TV and Radio.
Fine Arts
Dist - UCEMC

More than skin deep 9 MIN
VHS / U-matic
Cancer education series
Color (G C PRO)
$195.00 purchase _ #C920 - VI - 044
Describes skin cancer, possible causes of the disease, early signs and ways to reduce the chances of contracting skin cancer. Emphasizes prevention and early detection of the disease. Part of a four - part series presented by the University of Texas, MD Anderson Center.
Health and Safety; Science - Natural
Dist - HSCIC

More than Skin Deep 25 MIN
16mm
B&W
Discusses the problems of personal cleanliness for both patients and personnel in nursing homes. Shows how and why such cleanliness is essential.
Health and Safety
Dist - HF **Prod** - UHOSF 1966

More than Speed 12 MIN
16mm
Color
LC 80-700213
Illustrates driving safety techniques through interviews with professional race drivers at Indianapolis Motor Speedway and tips from professional driving instructors.
Health and Safety
Dist - CREATC **Prod** - CHSPC 1979

More than the Music 28 MIN
VHS / 16mm
Color (J)
$325.00, $250.00 purchase
Documents a classical piano concert given by Norma Golabek in a California women's prison.
Fine Arts; Sociology
Dist - UNKNWN

More than Words 14 MIN
16mm
Color (A)
Outlines basic methods for successful communication. Analyzes factors involved in thinking out what you want to accomplish and then selecting the most useful methods to communicate what needs to be done.
Psychology
Dist - AFLCIO **Prod** - STRAUS 1969

More than Words - the Official Languages Act 15 MIN
16mm
Color (G)
_ #106C 0180
Describes the Official Languages Act and what it means in practical terms for Canada. Includes an outline of the role of the Commissioner of Official Languages in overseeeing the Act, and promoting the use of English and French, when required, in the services of the Government of Canada.
Civics and Political Systems
Dist - CFLMDC **Prod** - NFBC 1980

More they learn 47 MIN
U-matic / VHS / BETA
Color; PAL (J H C G PRO T)
PdS175, PdS183 purchase
Takes the viewer through the everyday life of David McPherson, a young paraplegic of exceptional will and outlook. Shows that physically disabled does not mean 'mentally retarded' without relying on tear - jerking statements.
Health and Safety
Dist - EDPAT

More Time to Live - Flexible Working Time 30 MIN
VHS / U-matic
Re - Making of Work Series
Color (C A)
Exemplifies growing trend among industrialized nations to eliminate conventional work routines. Features the Dutch national postal service and a German department store.
Business and Economics; Sociology
Dist - EBEC

The More we get together - helping disoriented old people 44 MIN
VHS
Color (H C G)
$335.00 purchase, $55.00 rental
Gives insights into working with very old, disoriented nursing home residents. Features Naomi Feil who demonstrates her techniques for restoring dignity, awakening social responses and making sense out of confused behavior. In The Three Stages of Disorientation, Feil shows how to work with individuals suffering from malorientation, time confusion and repetitive movement. In The Three Phases of a Validation Group she shows how to create a group for reducing anxiety, regaining social controls and recovering a sense of well being.
Social Science; Sociology
Dist - FLMLIB **Prod** - FEIL 1986

The More you know 55 MIN
VHS / U-matic / BETA
Color (J H)
$99.00 purchase _ #JR - 6196M
Responds to the September, 1989 anti - drug address of George Bush. Features students from high schools in Flossmoor, Illinois, Washington, DC, and Glendale, California. Tom Brokaw hosts with support from Malcolm Jamal Warner, Dave Winfield, DJ Jazzy Jeff and Fresh Prince, and John Larroquette.
Guidance and Counseling; Psychology; Sociology
Dist - CORF **Prod** - NBCNEW 1989

Morelos
VHS
Color (J H G) (SPANISH)
$44.95 purchase _ #MCV5013, #MCV5014
Presents a program on the history of Mexico.

History - World
Dist - MADERA **Prod** - MADERA

Morgan Fairchild - stress management
VHS
Color (G)
$19.95 purchase _ #EK035
Presents actress Morgan Fairchild and Dr Anthony Reading of UCLA School of Medicine, with a mix of massage, low - impact aerobics, Tai Chi and relaxation techniques for reducing stress.
Health and Safety; Psychology
Dist - SIV

Morgan the pirate 96 MIN
VHS
Color (G)
$39.80 purchase _ #0179
Presents a drama about Morgan the pirate. Portrays Morgan's enslavement in the gold mines of Panama, his escape and capture of a Spanish galleon. He sets sail for Tortuga, headquarters of Caribbean pirates, becoming the most feared name on the high seas.
Geography - World; Literature and Drama
Dist - SEVVID **Prod** - IDEAL

Morgan's treasure hunt 25 MIN
VHS
Color (P I J)
$19.95 purchase
Features two mountain - dwelling 14 - year - olds, Morgan and Donnie, who share with a city friend, Donnie, what it's like to be a gold miner. Tells about the adventures of Morgan, who has been hard rocking mining since he was eight years old.
Geography - United States
Dist - DICOM **Prod** - DICOM 1994

Morgenrot 75 MIN
VHS / U-matic
B&W (GERMAN)
A German language film. Depicts a World War I submarine drama.
Fine Arts; Foreign Language; History - World
Dist - IHF **Prod** - IHF

The Mormon dilemma 67 MIN
VHS
Color (H C G A R)
$49.95 purchase, $10.00 rental _ #35 - 83 - 2504
Compares and contrasts Mormonism and orthodox Christianity. Simulates a discussion between a Mormon couple and an orthodox Christian.
Religion and Philosophy
Dist - APH

Mormon Foods 28 MIN
Videoreel / VT2
Frying Pans West Series
Color
Presents host Sam Arnold presenting recipes for preparing Mormon foods.
Home Economics
Dist - PBS **Prod** - KRMATV

Mormonism - Christian or cult
VHS
Counterfeits series
Color (H C G A R)
$10.00 rental _ #36 - 83 - 2024
Examines the history and theology of Mormonism. Compares Mormon theology with orthodox Christianity. Suggests strategies for evangelism. Hosted by Ron Carlson. Produced by Cinema Associates and Film Educators.
Religion and Philosophy
Dist - APH

Morning 16 MIN
16mm
PANCOM Beginning Total Communication Program for Hearing Parents of 'Series Level 2
Color (K)
LC 77-700504
Education; Guidance and Counseling; Psychology; Sociology
Dist - JOYCE **Prod** - CSDE 1977

Morning 5 MIN
16mm
Color (G)
$10.00 rental
Pictures a quiet narrative in which two people are sitting in a room and nothing seemingly happens. Tells a story by way of action between the frames and light setting the tone. Produced by Ernie Gehr.
Fine Arts
Dist - CANCIN

Morning After 17 MIN
16mm
Color
Shows the vulnerability of a seemingly cool, sophisticated man to the breakup of a long - standing relationship.
Fine Arts; Psychology
Dist - FLMLIB **Prod** - TRAMNC 1982

The Morning After - a Story of Vandalism 27 MIN
VHS / U-matic
Color (J)
$375.00, $325.00 purchase, $75.00 rental
Tells of four high school boys who went out for a night of fun and alcohol and did a million dollars worth of damage, destroying a school, creating a nightmare for a town. Reveals that now the boys are paying - with jail time, alienation and clouded futures. Discusses the consequences of actions and dealing with impulsive behavior.
Health and Safety; Psychology; Sociology
Dist - PFP

Morning Airport 11 MIN
16mm / U-matic / VHS
Color (P I) (SPANISH)
LC 72-703428;
Shows the many people who work at the airport throughout the night and early morning to prepare planes for their departure.
Industrial and Technical Education; Social Science
Dist - ALTSUL **Prod** - MICLSM 1972

Morning care 27 MIN
16mm
Directions for education in nursing via technology series; Lesson 4
B&W (PRO)
LC 74-701777
Discusses and demonstrates activities of daily living related to the hospitalized patient.
Health and Safety
Dist - WSUM **Prod** - DENT 1974

Morning comes 20 MIN
VHS / U-matic
We are one series
Color (G)
Presented in May, 'the moon in which they plant.' We are introduced to the members of an Omaha family as they begin the day. Following the father's morning prayer the family sits for their morning meal in an earth lodge. Included in the family are the father, mother, daughter, son, and grandmother. Discussion at the meal centers around the tasks of all of the members of the family and the two most important events for the Omaha - the planting of the corn and the summer buffalo hunt.
Social Science
Dist - NAMPBC **Prod** - NAMPBC 1986

The Morning during 11 MIN
16mm
Color
LC 80-700274
Shows a woman on her wedding night fantasizing about the lovers she will never have. Explains that when morning comes she gains a renewed conviction about the choice she has made.
Fine Arts; Sociology
Dist - BATB **Prod** - BATB 1979

Morning Glory 20 MIN
16mm
Color (A)
LC 81-700397
Offers a portrait of a summer day as seen through the eyes of a woman.
Fine Arts
Dist - SMITHD **Prod** - SMITHD 1980

Morning glory - 3 10 MIN
VHS / U-matic / 16mm
How plants grow series
Color (K P I)
$265.00, $215.00, $185.00 purchase _ #B595
Presents close - up photography of the life cycle of the morning glory. Shows roots, leaves, flowers and seed pods as the morning glory grows from seed, matures and dies. Examines the role of chlorophyll, the ability of the morning glory to climb and its reaction to heat. Part of a seven - part series on how plants grow.
Science - Natural
Dist - BARR **Prod** - GREATT 1990

Morning Harbor 11 MIN
U-matic / VHS / 16mm
Color; Captioned (P I) (SPANISH)
LC 73-702931
Shows the many people who work to maintain a harbor as a center for the shipping and receiving of goods.
Business and Economics; Geography - United States; Social Science
Dist - ALTSUL **Prod** - HEDENC 1973

Morning in the Grass 5 MIN
16mm
Adventures in the High Grass Series
Color (K P I)
LC 74-702123
Portrays an insect community in puppet animation. Shows how human beings appear and cause the community problems and dangers, which the insects cope with.
Guidance and Counseling; Literature and Drama
Dist - MMA **Prod** - MMA 1972

Morning - June - August 1944 52 MIN
16mm / U-matic / VHS
World at War Series
Color (H C A)
Documents D - Day, June 6, 1944, when the Allies under the command of General Dwight D. Eisenhower began an advance on Normandy at Cherbourg, a German fortification that later became a major Allied supply base. Preparations insured an oil supply, harbor facilities and accurate weather predictions.
History - World
Dist - MEDIAG **Prod** - THAMES 1973

Morning - June to August, 1944 60 MIN
16mm
World at War Series
Color (H C A)
LC 76-701778
History - World; Sociology
Dist - USCAN **Prod** - THAMES 1975

Morning Light 15 MIN
16mm
B&W
LC 79-700248
Shows how a middle - aged woman confronts the unfulfillment in her life and then finds that there is still much life ahead to be lived.
Fine Arts; Guidance and Counseling; Sociology
Dist - DISTER **Prod** - DISTER 1979

Morning Line 18 MIN
16mm
Color
LC 74-703425
Examines the world of gamblers and ponies.
Sociology
Dist - CFDEVC **Prod** - BRYNTP 1973

Morning, Noon and Evening 14 MIN
16mm / U-matic / VHS
Color (P I)
LC 74-704201
Contrasts the daily lives of a rural family and of an urban family.
Psychology; Social Science; Sociology
Dist - ALTSUL **Prod** - FILMSW 1969

Morning on the Lievre 13 MIN
16mm
Color (G)
_ #106c 0177 518
Shows the beauty of the Lievre River in Quebec as it winds past hills in late September. Accompanied by the reading of a poem by Archibald Lampman describing the river and specially composed music.
Geography - World; Literature and Drama
Dist - CFLMDC **Prod** - NFBC 1977

Morning procession in Yangchow 4 MIN
16mm
Color (G)
$70.00 rental
Depicts a girl drying her hair, a woman wringing a cloth washed in the river, a funeral in the early yellow light. Must be rented with 'The Chinese Typewriter.'
Fine Arts; Geography - World
Dist - CANCIN **Prod** - BARND 1981

Morning Scene 29 MIN
U-matic
Magic of Oil Painting Series
Color
Fine Arts
Dist - PBS **Prod** - KOCETV

Morning service at Throssel Hole Priory 22 MIN
VHS / BETA
Color; PAL (G)
PdS10, $20.00 purchase
Features the Venerable Lama Thubten Zopa. Shows an early morning ceremony in which the entire community comes together. Takes place at a Soto Zen Buddhist monastery and retreat centre in England. Produced by Wessex Education Television Consortium.
Fine Arts; Religion and Philosophy
Dist - MERIDT

Morning sickness - all day and all night 27 MIN
VHS
Color (PRO C G H)
$99.00 purchase, $40.00 rental _ #4418
Discusses the timeless problem of morning sickness during pregnancy. Combines years of documented research and features two dieticians discussing the latest strategy for controlling the nausea and vomiting associated with morning sickness. Examines the variations in different

pregnancies and explains what morning sickness is and what to do to control it. Looks at the myths and false beliefs associated with morning sickness, combining practical knowledge and interesting facts. Produced by Lemon - Aid Films Inc.
Health and Safety
Dist - AJN

A Morning Song 23 MIN
16mm
Color (A R)
LC 79-700940
Focuses on a Mennonite farmer and his family living near Lancaster, Pennsylvania. Discusses the history and beliefs of the Mennonites and problems caused by the changing world around them.
Religion and Philosophy; Sociology
Dist - EMBMC **Prod** - MARTC 1978

The Morning Spider 22 MIN
VHS / 16mm / U-matic
Color (J)
LC 77-701098
Presents, without narration, a humorous children's tale in mime which depicts the life of a hard - working, but often inept, morning spider.
Literature and Drama; Science - Natural
Dist - PFP **Prod** - CHGRIN 1976

Morning Star 36 MIN
16mm / U-matic / VHS
Color (I J H)
$89.00 purchase _ #573
Shows spring migration of a herd of sheep across the wildest, most inaccessible area of the United States - the Tonto Basin near Phoenix, Arizona.
Agriculture; English Language; Geography - United States; Science - Natural; Social Science
Dist - EBEC **Prod** - LINE 1951

Morning Star Painter 30 MIN
16mm
Color
LC 80-700825
Introduces Jack Wunuwun, an aboriginal bark painter who lives near Maningrida in Arnhemland.
Fine Arts; Geography - World
Dist - TASCOR **Prod** - TASCOR 1979

Morning Zoo 10 MIN
16mm / U-matic / VHS
Color (P I J)
LC 72-701730
Explores what goes in the zoo when the public is not present. Portrays the routine care of the animals.
Science - Natural; Social Science
Dist - ALTSUL **Prod** - MICLSM 1972

Morning Zoo 11 MIN
16mm / U-matic / VHS
Color (P I J)
Looks at the early morning, pre - opening chores at a large zoo seen through the eyes of a young girl zooworker who arrives for her tasks at the children's section. Shows the routines of feeding and cleaning and closeups of various animals.
Science - Natural
Dist - ALTSUL **Prod** - ALTSUL

Morocco 10 MIN
16mm
Color
LC 73-701117
Shows the geographic features, life - style, handicrafts, architecture and festive celebrations of Morocco.
Fine Arts; Geography - World; Sociology
Dist - PICNIC **Prod** - PICNIC 1972

Morocco 25 MIN
U-matic / VHS / 16mm
Untamed World Series Series
Color; Mono (J H C A)
$400.00 film, $250.00 video, $50.00 rental
Presents the people, culture and history of Morocco.
Geography - World; History - World
Dist - CTV **Prod** - CTV 1969

Morocco 3 MIN
16mm
Of all Things Series
Color (P I)
Discusses the country of Morocco in Africa.
Geography - World
Dist - AVED **Prod** - BAILYL

Morocco - Berber Profile 30 MIN
U-matic
Countries and Peoples Series
Color (H C)
Looks at Morocco and its original inhabitants, the Berbers.
Geography - World; History - World
Dist - TVOTAR **Prod** - TVOTAR 1982

Morocco - Berber Profile 29 MIN
VHS / 16mm
Countries and Peoples Series
Color (H C G)
$90.00 purchase _ #BPN128116
Takes a look a Morocco and its original inhabitant, the Berbers. Includes scenes of Islamic architecture, colorful costumes, new agricultural developments, and Casablanca, Fez, and Marrakesh.
Geography - World; History - World
Dist - RMIBHF **Prod** - RMIBHF

Morocco Body and Soul 80 MIN
16mm
Color (G)
Presents an independent production by I Genini. Illuminates the beauty and diversity of Moroccan custom through its music.
Fine Arts; Geography - World; History - World; Religion and Philosophy
Dist - FIRS

Morocco, body and soul series
Aita 26 MIN
Hymns of praise 26 MIN
Lutes and delights 26 MIN
Dist - FIRS

Morocco for all Seasons 26 MIN
16mm
Color (FRENCH ARABIC PORTUGUESE)
LC 76-702853
Shows cultural and tourist attractions in Morocco.
Geography - World
Dist - WELBIT **Prod** - WELBIT 1976

Morocco - the music of Moroccan Jews 28 MIN
VHS
Jewish music heritage library series
Color (G)
$39.95 purchase _ #795
Reveals that the Moroccan Jews of North Africa created their own unique musical form of expression by borrowing tunes from their Arab neighborsa and adding Hebrew texts to them. Records on - location footage in Morocco and Israel to focus on the unique character and flavor of the poetry, messianic songs and tunes that evolved into Moroccan Jewish music. Features Shlomo Bar and Habrera Hativit Ensemble. Part of a series on Jewish music from around the world, featuring Martin Bookspan as narrator.
Fine Arts; Sociology
Dist - ERGOM **Prod** - IMHP

Moron movies 90 MIN
VHS / 16mm
Color (G)
$150.00 rental
Presents an independent movie directed by Len Cella.
Fine Arts
Dist - KINOIC

Morris 9 MIN
16mm
Color (H C A)
LC 79-700123
Presents a humorous look at an undersea society.
Fine Arts
Dist - USC **Prod** - USC 1979

Morris Craft Series
Applique - mola design 55 TO 60 MIN
Bread Dough Folk Art 55 TO 60 MIN
Country Crafts 55 TO 60 MIN
Crafting with Discards 55 TO 60 MIN
Eggery and gold leafing 60 MIN
Gift - Bazaar Projects 1 55 TO 60 MIN
Gift - Bazaar Projects 2 55 TO 60 MIN
Hairpin - Broomstick Lace 55 TO 60 MIN
Making Soft Dolls 55 TO 60 MIN
Patchwork Projects 55 TO 60 MIN
Weaving Without a Loom 55 TO 60 MIN
Dist - CAMV

Morris Dances - Ancient Ritual English Dances 30 MIN
U-matic / VHS
Shaping Today with Yesterday Series
Color
Fine Arts; Industrial and Technical Education
Dist - ARCVID **Prod** - ARCVID

Morris Flower Series
The Art of Flower Arranging - Part 1 - Basic Arranging 60 MIN
The Art of Flower Arranging - Part 2 - Material Selections and Arrangement Styles 60 MIN
Driftwood and other naturals 58 MIN
Flower arranging - a step further 60 MIN
Flower arranging - the basics 60 MIN
Preserving Flowers and Foliages 61 MIN
Silk Flower Making - Part 2 60 MIN
Silk Flower Making - Part One 60 MIN
Dist - CAMV

Morris goes to school 15 MIN
VHS / 16mm
Color (K P)
$59.95 purchase _ #P10386
Presents the animated experience of a moose named Morris who goes to school to learn how to read and count. Depicts his first day of school where his antics, mistakes and successes correlate with those of young children who, like Morris, are just beginning their school careers. Emphasizes the value of learning. A film by John Matthews. Based on the book by Bernard Wiseman.
Education; English Language; Mathematics
Dist - CF

Morris, the Midget Moose 8 MIN
16mm / U-matic / VHS
Color (P I)
LC 74-700272
Explains that Morris, the midget moose with the magnificent antlers, teams up with Brawny Balsam, the possessor of a puny set of horns, to prove that two heads are better than one.
Literature and Drama
Dist - CORF **Prod** - DISNEY 1973

Morris's Disappearing Bag 10 MIN
U-matic / VHS / 16mm
Color (K P)
LC 82-701217
Relates that on Christmas morning, Morris finds himself too little to play with his brother's hockey outfit and too young to play with his sister's chemistry set. Reveals that he finds one more present under the tree - a disappearing bag. Based on the book Morris's Disappearing Bag by Rosemary Wells.
Literature and Drama
Dist - WWS **Prod** - WWS 1982

The Morrow plots 3 MIN
16mm
B&W (G)
$5.00 rental
Looks at the nation's oldest experimental farm.
Fine Arts; Social Science
Dist - CANCIN **Prod** - OSBONS 1983

The Mortal Body 12 MIN
16mm
B&W
Projects such images as the birth of a child, a couple making love and an old man contemplating eternity to encapsulize the human life cycle.
Sociology
Dist - FLMLIB **Prod** - ZAGREB

Mortal choices with Ruth Macklin - Part 1; Public policy, private choices with Ruth Macklin - Part 2 60 MIN
U-matic / VHS
World of ideas with Bill Moyers - season 2 series
Color; Captioned (A G)
$59.95, $79.95 purchase _ #WIWM - 234D
Features Dr Ruth Macklin, a philosopher and professor of bioethics at Albert Einstein College of Medicine in New York City. Explores philosophical problems that can confront anyone - patient and family, parent and child, the living and the dying - at any time. Discusses the difficult decisions involved in medical care today. Part 2 offers eithical insights into the emotional and morally difficult issues surrounding pregnancy. Part of a series with Bill Moyers that explores the ideas and values shaping our future, and featuring scientists, writers, artists, philosophers, historians and others.
Health and Safety; Religion and Philosophy
Dist - PBS

Mortgage on my body - Part I 23 MIN
16mm
Breaking time series
Color (G)
$60.00 rental
Looks at gas stations throughout Connecticut and New York City and rides around with the filmmaker's father. Part of a series, made between 1978 - 1983, that describes Levine's return to his hometown of New Haven in 1977 where he resumes working in his father's gas station. Confronts his past by looking back on the working people and places of his childhood and the automotive and petroleum base of that culture. Each film is a complete work and may be viewed separately.
Fine Arts; Geography - United States; Literature and Drama; Sociology
Dist - CANCIN **Prod** - LEVINE 1983

Mortgages 29 MIN
U-matic
You and the Law Series Lesson 18

Color (C A)
Discusses where mortgages originate, the two major elements of a mortgage and some important clauses found in a mortgage. Defines terms such as amortization, escalation privileges and reserve accounts. Gives examples of types of interest rates.
Business and Economics; Civics and Political Systems
Dist - CDTEL **Prod** - COAST

Mortice and Tenon - Dados 56 MIN
Videoreel / VHS
Woodworking Series
Color
Shows how to do the important woodworking step of joining with the mortice and tenon joint. Goes on to instruction for making a through dado.
Industrial and Technical Education
Dist - ANVICO **Prod** - ANVICO

Mortimer Adler - teaching the Consitution 60 MIN
U-matic / VHS
In search of the Constitution series
Color (A G)
$59.95, $79.95 purchase _ #MOYR - 103
Features students at St. John's College in Annapolis, Maryland, who challenge Mortimer Adler, philosopher, author and educator, on his view about fundamental ideas in the Constitution and their relevance today. Part of an 11 - part series in which Bill Moyers examines the vitality of our nation's most important document by listening to people who interpret and teach it and people whose lives have been changed by it.
Civics and Political Systems
Dist - PBS

The Mortise and Tenon Joint Project
VHS
Construction Technology Series
$99.00 purchase _ #BX25V
Industrial and Technical Education
Dist - CAREER **Prod** - CAREER

The Mortise and Tenon Joint Project 39 MIN
VHS
(G A IND)
$179.00 purchase _ #W22V7
Shows stock preparation and layout procedures, and cutting joint and molding installation (2 tapes). Study Guide included.
Industrial and Technical Education
Dist - BERGL

Morton Schindel - from Page to Screen 27 MIN
U-matic / VHS / 16mm
Color (J)
LC 81-700771
Offers a tour of the Weston Woods studios and explains how children's books are adapted to motion pictures and filmstrips.
Fine Arts; Literature and Drama
Dist - WWS **Prod** - WWS 1981

Morwen of the Woodlands 27 MIN
U-matic / VHS / 16mm
Storybook International Series
Color
Tells the Welsh tale of a Prince who grows bored with his wife who was once young and beautiful and falls in love with a beautiful maiden whom he finds in the woods. Reveals that she returns to the castle with him on the condition that once a week she return to the forest and he not follow her. Relates that a monk - magician finally reveals that the girl is really the Prince's wife in disguise.
Guidance and Counseling; Literature and Drama
Dist - JOU **Prod** - JOU 1982

MOS and Linear Integrated Circuits 60 MIN
Videoreel / VT1
Understanding Semiconductors Course Outline Series no 12
Color (IND)
Tells how MOS integrated circuits differ from others, enabling them to be more complex. Describes the operation of the key element in MOS integrated circuits, the Field Effect Transistor (FET.) Explains how Field Effect Transistors are used and surveys linear integrated circuits.
Industrial and Technical Education
Dist - TXINLC **Prod** - TXINLC

MOS Device Physics 30 MIN
U-matic / VHS
MOS Integrated Circuit Series
Color (PRO)
Examines the MOSFET, emphasizing the solid - state physics of materials used in production of the metal - oxide silicon - field effect transistor.
Industrial and Technical Education
Dist - TXINLC **Prod** - TXINLC

MOS - from Design to Product 30 MIN
U-matic / VHS
MOS Integrated Circuit Series
Color (PRO)
Illustrates tour of a MOS production facility, tracing MOS device of alrication from circuit specifications to final product. Shows actual facilities needed to produce MOS.
Industrial and Technical Education
Dist - TXINLC **Prod** - TXINLC

MOS, I2L Logic Circuits
VHS / U-matic
Digital Techniques Series
Color
Industrial and Technical Education
Dist - HTHZEN **Prod** - HTHZEN

MOS integrated circuit series
Basic mOS shift registers 30 MIN
Bipolar - mos interface 30 MIN
CMOS and SOS Inverter Characteristics 30 MIN
CMOS Capabilities, Advantages and Applications 30 MIN
D and N - channel inverter characteristics 30 MIN
Four - Phase, CMOS and CCD Shift Registers 30 MIN
High Functional Density Design with PLA - I 30 MIN
High Functional Density Design with PLA - II 30 MIN
MOS - from Design to Product 30 MIN
MOS Device Physics 30 MIN
MOS Random - Access Memory Applications 30 MIN
MOS Random - Access Memory Design 30 MIN
MOS ROMS 30 MIN
MOS Special Devices and Chip Layout 30 MIN
MOS Transistor Characteristics 30 MIN
MOS Transistor Characteristics Related to MOS Process 30 MIN
MOS/LSI Economics 30 MIN
MOS/LSI Reliability 30 MIN
N - Channel, CMOS, SOS and Ion Implantation Technology 30 MIN
An Overview of MOS 30 MIN
Dist - TXINLC

MOS Memory 55 MIN
VHS / U-matic
Introduction to VLSI Design Series
Color (PRO)
Covers the topic of flip - flops and shift register memory. Treats, also, logic symbolism, circuit diagrams, detailed timing of clock structures.
Industrial and Technical Education
Dist - MIOT **Prod** - MIOT

MOS Processing 55 MIN
U-matic / VHS
Introduction to VLSI Design Series
Color (PRO)
Covers silicon - gate fabrication sequence, HMOS improvements, bulk CMOS Processing, and IC fabrication yields.
Business and Economics; Industrial and Technical Education
Dist - MIOT **Prod** - MIOT

MOS Random - Access Memory Applications 30 MIN
U-matic / VHS
MOS Integrated Circuit Series
Color (PRO)
Charts performance of available MOS RAMs. Discusses signal interface and shows specific applications of D and N - channel MOS RAMS for use in !arger memory systems.
Industrial and Technical Education
Dist - TXINLC **Prod** - TXINLC

MOS Random - Access Memory Design 30 MIN
U-matic / VHS
MOS Integrated Circuit Series
Color (PRO)
Looks at design details of random - access storage elements necessary to achieve cost - effective performance required when using MOS.
Industrial and Technical Education
Dist - TXINLC **Prod** - TXINLC

MOS Random Access Semiconductor Storage Design 60 MIN
Videoreel / VT1
Semiconductor Memories Course Series no 5
Color (IND)
Discusses static and dynamic storage cells and their design. Covers 8 - , 6 - , 4 - , 3 - and 1 - transistor cells.
Industrial and Technical Education
Dist - TXINLC **Prod** - TXINLC

MOS ROMS 30 MIN
VHS / U-matic
MOS Integrated Circuit Series
Color (PRO)
Analyzes design of MOS read - only storage elements. Outlines the process technology and performance characteristics of these MOS devices.
Industrial and Technical Education
Dist - TXINLC **Prod** - TXINLC

MOS Special Devices and Chip Layout 30 MIN
VHS / U-matic
MOS Integrated Circuit Series
Color (PRO)
Discusses special devices such as floating gate MOS, CCDs, and important factors required for implementing an MOS/LSI chip layout.
Industrial and Technical Education
Dist - TXINLC **Prod** - TXINLC

The MOS Transistor 55 MIN
VHS / U-matic
Introduction to VLSI Design Series
Color (PRO)
Treats physical structure of the Metal - Oxide - Semiconductor (MOS), doping of semiconductors, PN junction, diffusion and drift, and diodes.
Industrial and Technical Education
Dist - MIOT **Prod** - MIOT

MOS Transistor Characteristics 30 MIN
U-matic / VHS
MOS Integrated Circuit Series
Color (PRO)
Analyzes basic solid - state action that occurs to produce canier current conduction in a metal - oxide - silicon field effect transistors.
Industrial and Technical Education
Dist - TXINLC **Prod** - TXINLC

MOS Transistor Characteristics Related to MOS Process 30 MIN
VHS / U-matic
MOS Integrated Circuit Series
Color (PRO)
Discusses the interrelationships of MOS transistor V - I characteristics, characteristics that depend on variations of subsrate material, gate material and source and drain diffusions.
Industrial and Technical Education
Dist - TXINLC **Prod** - TXINLC

Mosaic 6 MIN
16mm / U-matic / VHS
Color (J)
LC 73-701705
Superimposes films 'LINES VERTICAL' and 'LINES HORIZONTAL' to give a geometric and non - figurative example of cinematographic 'OP' art.
Fine Arts
Dist - IFB **Prod** - NFBC 1965

Mosaic Experiments 20 MIN
U-matic / VHS / 16mm
Color (J H C)
Presents the work of students from Immaculate Heart College. Panels and sculptures are shown. Various materials and ways of using them are explained.
Fine Arts
Dist - IFB **Prod** - VEF 1958

Mosaic - Hobart Smith 30 MIN
16mm
B&W
LC FI67-92
Folksinger Hobart Smith discusses his life and his songs and performs several selections on the banjo, guitar and fiddle.
Fine Arts
Dist - WTTWTV **Prod** - WTTWTV 1966

Mosaic series
All in the mind 30 MIN
Just the job 30 MIN
Recruitment interviewing across cultures 40 MIN
Dist - BBCENE

Mosaics 15 MIN
U-matic / VHS
Art cart series
Color (P I)
Shows how to design a paper mosaic and a mosaic using seeds, pasta and buttons.
Fine Arts
Dist - AITECH **Prod** - WBRATV 1979

Mosaics 30 MIN
VHS / U-matic
Arts and Crafts Series
Color (H A)

LC 81-706357
Shows Dr George Baker decorating objects of aesthetic and utilitarian value through the use of mosaic techniques. Explores ceramic tile, natural materials, and seed mosaic techniques for children.
Fine Arts
Dist - GPN **Prod** - GPN 1981

Mosaics - Works of Jeanne Reynal 20 MIN
16mm
Color
LC FIA68-3065
Artist Jeanne Reynal explains and demonstrates her process for creating a mosaic mural. Includes scenes of the preparation of the tesserae, the proper use of cement mix, acid baths, tools and other requirements needed to create a mosaic.
Fine Arts
Dist - RADIM **Prod** - FALKBG 1968

Mosaik im Vertrauen 17 MIN
16mm
Color; B&W (G)
$35.00 rental
Presents a production by Peter Kubelka, an independent filmmaker since 1952 and founder and curator of the Oesterreichisches Filmmuseum.
Fine Arts
Dist - CANCIN

Mosby cameo series
Presents three volumes of a series featuring the work of outstanding nurse researchers. Includes the titles Adaptation to Epilepsy in children featuring Dr Joan Kessner Austin; AIDS and Minority Women, Dr Jacqueline H Flaskerud; Urinary Incontinence in Women, Dr Thelma J Wells.
Adaptation to epilepsy in children
Addiction among nurses
AIDS and minority women
Battered women
Child development
Low birth weight infants
Premenstrual syndrome
Psychiatric mental health
Urinary incontence in women
Dist - MOSBY **Prod** - SITHTA 1955

Mosby cameo series
Presents three volumes of a series featuring the work of outstanding nurse researchers. Includes the titles Low Birth Weight Infants featuring Dr Dorothy Brooten; Premenstrual Syndrome and Dr Nancy Fugate Woods; Addiction Among Nurses and Drs Elizabeth M Burns and Eleanor J Sullivan.
Adaptation to epilepsy in children
Addiction among nurses
AIDS and minority women
Battered women
Child development
Low birth weight infants
Premenstrual syndrome
Psychiatric mental health
Urinary incontence in women
Dist - MOSBY **Prod** - SITHTA 1955

Moscow
VHS
(J H C)
Gives viewers a basic description of the Soviet political system. Provides a look at the people and their lives in modern day Moscow. Introduces the history and culture of Russia and the entire Soviet Union through a look at places such as the Kremlin, Red Square, and other sights.
Geography - World; History - World
Dist - BARR **Prod** - BARR 1988

Moscow and Leningrad 14 MIN
U-matic / VHS / 16mm
Russian Language Series
Color (H C) (RUSSIAN)
A Russian language film. Views Red Square, the Kremlin, the Pokrovskiy Cathedral and aspects of modern urban life in the USSR.
Foreign Language
Dist - IFB **Prod** - IFB 1963

Moscow and Leningrad 50 MIN
VHS
Color (G)
$29.95 purchase _ #ST - IV1798
Visits the Kremlin, a walled city within a city and seat of government. Views the pageantry of Red Square, St Basil's Cathedral and Gorky Park. Travels to Leningrad, the cultural capital of the Soviet Union, to tour Palace Square, view the Alexander Column and the Winter Palace, home of the Hermitage Museum, and Palace Petrodvorets with miles of waterfall and fountains.
Geography - World; History - World
Dist - INSTRU

Moscow and Leningrad - the crown jewels of Russia 60 MIN
VHS
European collection series
Color (J H C G)
$29.95 purchase _ #IVN120V-S
Teaches about the people, culture and history of the cities of Moscow and Leningrad in the Soviet Union. Visits historic buildings, monuments and landmarks. Examines the physical topography of each city. Part of a 16-part series on European countries. Also part of a larger series entitled Video Visits that travels to six continents.
Geography - World
Dist - CAMV **Prod** - WNETTV

Moscow, City of Contrasts 20 MIN
VHS / U-matic
Color (J)
LC 82-706778
Geography - World; History - World
Dist - AWSS **Prod** - AWSS 1981

Moscow clad in snow 3 MIN
16mm
B&W (G)
$15.00 rental
Features the forerunner of the documentary with its evocatively beautiful scenery of a former era. Includes added narration.
Fine Arts; Geography - World; Literature and Drama
Dist - KITPAR **Prod** - PATHEF 1909

Moscow Does not Believe in Tears 150 MIN
16mm
Color (H C A) (RUSSIAN)
LC 82-700456
Presents a romantic comedy about three young, working - class country girls who go to Moscow in 1958 to seek work, men and success. Looks at the results of their expedition in 1978.
Fine Arts; Foreign Language
Dist - IFEX **Prod** - MOSFLM 1981

Moscow Does not Believe in Tears, Pt 1 38 MIN
16mm
Color (H C A) (RUSSIAN)
LC 82-700456
Presents a romantic comedy about three young, working - class country girls who go to Moscow in 1958 to seek work, men and success. Looks at the results of their expedition in 1978.
Fine Arts
Dist - IFEX **Prod** - MOSFLM 1981

Moscow Does not Believe in Tears, Pt 2 38 MIN
16mm
Color (H C A) (RUSSIAN)
LC 82-700456
Presents a romantic comedy about three young, working - class country girls who go to Moscow in 1958 to seek work, men and success. Looks at the results of their expedition in 1978.
Fine Arts
Dist - IFEX **Prod** - MOSFLM 1981

Moscow Does not Believe in Tears, Pt 3 37 MIN
16mm
Color (H C A) (RUSSIAN)
LC 82-700456
Presents a romantic comedy about three young, working - class country girls who go to Moscow in 1958 to seek work, men and success. Looks at the results of their expedition in 1978.
Fine Arts
Dist - IFEX **Prod** - MOSFLM 1981

Moscow Does not Believe in Tears, Pt 4 37 MIN
16mm
Color (H C A) (RUSSIAN)
LC 82-700456
Presents a romantic comedy about three young, working - class country girls who go to Moscow in 1958 to seek work, men and success. Looks at the results of their expedition in 1978.
Fine Arts
Dist - IFEX **Prod** - MOSFLM 1981

Moscow Doesn't Answer 12 MIN
16mm
Color
Relates the plight of Soviet Jews wishing to immigrate to Israel. Traces the case histories of leading Jewish scientists not allowed to leave Russia.
Civics and Political Systems; History - World; Sociology
Dist - ALDEN **Prod** - UJA

Moscow Life 26 MIN
U-matic / VHS
Color
Examines the daily life of the average Soviet citizen. Focuses on housing, transportation, work opportunity and consumer goods.
Geography - World
Dist - JOU **Prod** - UPI

Moscow parade 103 MIN
VHS / 16mm
Color (A)
$490.00 purchase, $125.00 rental
Features a dramatic film set in Stalin's Russia. Stars Ute Lemper as the wife of a chief in the NKVD, Stalin's brutal secret police, in a tale of terror, passion and eroticism. Produced by Ivan Dykhovichny.
Civics and Political Systems; Fine Arts; History - World; Literature and Drama
Dist - FIRS

Moscow to Peking 17 MIN
16mm
Color (J H C G)
Takes the viewers as passengers in a train across Asia from west to east. Covers 5,000 miles of Asia from Moscow through Siberia and Mongolia to China.
Geography - World; Social Science
Dist - VIEWTH **Prod** - GATEEF

Moscow's man 55 MIN
VHS / U-matic
Color (H C G)
$225.00, $195.00 purchase _ #V437
Profiles double - agent operative Kim Philby who rose to the highest ranks of the British Secret Service while an agent for the Kremlin. Includes interviews, rare films and footage of Philby in retirement in Moscow.
Civics and Political Systems; History - World
Dist - BARR **Prod** - CEPRO 1988

Moscow's Red Square 20 MIN
VHS / U-matic
Color
Tells the history of Red Square which has witnessed eight centuries of heroic events in the history of Russia and the Soviet Union.
Civics and Political Systems; History - World
Dist - IHF **Prod** - IHF

Moses 20 MIN
VHS
Children's heroes from the Bible series
Color (K P I R)
$14.95 purchase _ #35 - 853 - 8516
Uses an animated format to tell the Old Testament story of Moses.
Literature and Drama; Religion and Philosophy
Dist - APH **Prod** - VISVID

Moses 63 MIN
16mm / U-matic / VHS
Greatest Heroes of the Bible Series
Color (I)
Presents the story of Moses, who is instructed by God to deliver his people from bondage. Reveals that when the Pharoah resists, Moses calls down a series of plagues on Egypt until the Pharoah agrees to set the Hebrews free. Stars John Marley and Julie Adams.
Religion and Philosophy
Dist - LUF **Prod** - LUF 1979

Moses 20 MIN
16mm
Fant Anthology of AMESLAN Literature Series
Color (S R) (AMERICAN SIGN)
LC 74-701463
Shows the Moses story from Genesis told by Mr Louie J Fant in AMESLAN (American Sign Language.).
Guidance and Counseling; Literature and Drama
Dist - JOYCE **Prod** - JOYCE 1973

Moses 30 MIN
VHS
Greatest adventure series
Color (P I R)
$14.95 purchase _ #35 - 830002 - 1518
Uses animation format to present the Biblical story of Moses. Features the voices of James Whitmore as Moses and James Earl Jones as Pharaoh.
Literature and Drama; Religion and Philosophy
Dist - APH **Prod** - HANBAR

Moses 30 MIN
VHS
Great Bible stories series
Color (P I R)
$15.95 purchase, $10.00 rental _ #35 - 8282 - 8936
Tells the Old Testament story of Moses. Shows that, as a baby, Moses was placed on the river in a basket, found by Pharaoh's daughter, and raised to eventually become the leader of his people.
Literature and Drama; Religion and Philosophy
Dist - APH

Moses and Aaron 110 MIN
16mm
Color
Offers an adaptation of Schonberg's opera Moses and Aaron. Directed by Jean - Marie Straub and Daniele Huillet.
Fine Arts
Dist - NYFLMS **Prod** - UNKNWN

Moses and His People 15 MIN
16mm
Color (P I J)
Presents the story of Moses told using puppets. Covers Moses' return to Egypt to the crossing of the Red Sea.
Literature and Drama
Dist - YALEDV **Prod** - YALEDV

Moses and plagues and Moses and Israelites - Volume 23 45 MIN
VHS
Superbook series
Color (K P I R)
$11.99 purchase _ #35 - 86804 - 979
Uses an animated format to tell the story of Chris and Joy and their time travels through Biblical places and events. 'Moses and Plagues' and 'Moses and Israelites' both deal with the efforts by Moses to get the Israelites out of slavery in Egypt.
Literature and Drama; Religion and Philosophy
Dist - APH **Prod** - TYHP

Moses and the Lime Kiln 27 MIN
16mm / U-matic / VHS
Storybook International Series
Color
Tells the Israeli tale of Moses, who is called to a great city to impart knowledge to a Caliph. Reveals that when a courtier plots to murder Moses at a lime - kiln, God saves him for being so righteous.
Guidance and Counseling; Literature and Drama
Dist - JOU **Prod** - JOU 1982

Moses and the Mountain of Fire 30 MIN
16mm
Color (R)
Portrays leadership qualities exhibited by Moses as he brings the people back to a right relationship with God after finding them worshiping a golden idol. Shows Moses to be a man of strong leadership qualities, qualities which church leaders need today.
Guidance and Counseling; Literature and Drama; Religion and Philosophy
Dist - BROADM **Prod** - BROADM 1964

Moses and the Ten Commandments 15 MIN
16mm
Color (P I J)
Presents the story of Moses told using puppets. Covers the wilderness journeys, the golden calf and the giving of the Ten Commandments.
Literature and Drama
Dist - YALEDV **Prod** - YALEDV

Moses Coady 58 MIN
U-matic / VHS / 16mm
Color (H C A)
LC 77-700249
Presents the story of Moses Coady, a zealous Cape Breton priest, who was responsible for the foundation of the cooperative education movement in the Maritimes.
Biography; Education; Geography - World; Religion and Philosophy; Sociology
Dist - BULFRG **Prod** - NFBC 1976

Moses - Creation of a Heroic Sculpture 19 MIN
U-matic / VHS / 16mm
Color (J H C A)
Traces the 15 year creation of a sculpted figure of Moses. Shows sculptor Elden C Tefft at work during the stages of the project, from consideration of the architectural setting through the lost wax casting of the finished work.
Fine Arts
Dist - IFB

Moses in Egypt 15 MIN
16mm
Color (P I J)
Presents the story of Moses told using puppets. Covers Moses' birth to his call to lead his people out of bondage.
Literature and Drama
Dist - YALEDV **Prod** - YALEDV

Moses Pendleton Presents Moses Pendleton 60 MIN
VHS / U-matic
Color
Fine Arts
Dist - ABCLR **Prod** - ABCLR

The MOSFET and the Inverter 55 MIN
VHS / U-matic
Introduction to VLSI Design Series
Color (PRO)
Treats the shape of the current - voltage curve and design implications. Deals with the inverter and inverter loads - resistor, linear, saturated, and depletion.
Industrial and Technical Education
Dist - MIOT **Prod** - MIOT

The MOSFET Inverter and Simple Gates 55 MIN
VHS / U-matic
Introduction to VLSI Design Series
Color (PRO)
Treats the sizings of the generalized inverter structure - pull - up / pull - down ratio for inverter pass transistor in the gate circuit. Considers the NAND and NOR structures.
Industrial and Technical Education
Dist - MIOT **Prod** - MIOT

The Moshav - Israel's Middle Way 25 MIN
16mm
Color
Shows Israel's successful experiment with agricultural and regional planning. Points out that the Moshav, a cooperative settlement, is a middle way between the closely - knit communal kibbutz and the independent farmer.
Agriculture; Geography - World
Dist - ALDEN **Prod** - ALDEN

Moshe Dayan - a portrait 50 MIN
VHS
Color (G)
$29.95 purchase _ #913
Traces the life of Moshe Dayan, considered an outstanding but controversial leader of Israel. Looks at his childhood, military service and rise to power in Israel, his fall because he was held responsible for Israel's lack of preparedness in the Yom Kippur War, and his critical role in the peace process that brought Anwar Sadat to Jerusalem.
History - World
Dist - ERGOM **Prod** - ERGOM

Mosholu holiday 10 MIN
16mm
B&W (G)
$10.00 rental
Features a guest appearance by Canadian TV star Bill Ronald and Frances Leibowitz with her girlfriend Iris. Describes this production as a 'must - see for travel enthusiasts and horror fans.'
Fine Arts; Geography - United States; Literature and Drama
Dist - CANCIN **Prod** - KUCHAR 1966

MOS/I L Logic Circuits
U-matic / VHS
Digital Techniques Video Training Course Series
Color
Industrial and Technical Education
Dist - VTRI **Prod** - VTRI

Moskusoksen - the Musk Ox 10 MIN
16mm
Color
Presents the musk ox in its natural surroundings in Greenland, among reindeer and Arctic foxes. Includes sound effects.
Geography - World; Science - Natural
Dist - STATNS **Prod** - STATNS 1967

Moskva I Leningrad - Moscow and Leningrad 14 MIN
16mm / U-matic / VHS
Color (H C) (RUSSIAN)
LC FIA65-1536
A Russian language film. Pictures urban life in Moscow and Leningrad, showing traffic patterns and the interior of a large department store. Views Red Square, the Kremlin and Polrovskiy Cathedral. Shows the construction of an apartment house on the outskirts of Moscow.
Foreign Language
Dist - IFB **Prod** - IFB 1963

Moslems in Spain 39 MIN
U-matic / VHS / 16mm
Color (J)
LC 79-700500
Depicts the Muslim and Christian struggle for control of southern Spain between 756 and 1492 A D. Summarizes the major events of this era and points out Muslim contributions to all aspects of Spanish culture.
History - World; Religion and Philosophy
Dist - IFB **Prod** - PILPRO 1978

The Moslems in Spain 39 MIN
16mm / U-matic / VHS
Color (H C)
Recounts the 781 years in which Moslems and Spaniards merged two cultures into a distinctive Hispano - Moorish civilization.
History - World
Dist - IFB **Prod** - KIRBY 1979

MOS/LSI Economics 30 MIN
U-matic / VHS
MOS Integrated Circuit Series
Color (PRO)
Looks at the cost - effective process of MOS in large scale integration of high functional density digital systems designs and traces this effectiveness through time.
Industrial and Technical Education
Dist - TXINLC **Prod** - TXINLC

MOS/LSI Reliability 30 MIN
U-matic / VHS
MOS Integrated Circuit Series
Color (PRO)
Examines reliability of MOS/LSI devices showing their progress with time compared to other IC technologies.
Industrial and Technical Education
Dist - TXINLC **Prod** - TXINLC

Mosori Monika 20 MIN
VHS / 16mm
Color (G)
$35.00 rental, $50.00 purchase
Presents an ethnographic production about two cultures encountering one another, the Warao Indians of Venezuela and Spanish Franciscan missionaries. Looks at the acculturation of the Warao women.
Fine Arts; Religion and Philosophy; Social Science; Sociology
Dist - CANCIN **Prod** - STRANC 1970

Mosque 30 MIN
VHS
Maryknoll video magazine presents series
Color (G)
$14.95 purchase
Provides a look at beliefs and practices of Islam for non - Muslims.
Religion and Philosophy
Dist - MARYFA

The Mosquito - 21 11 MIN
VHS / U-matic / 16mm
Animal families series
Color (K P I)
$275.00, $225.00, $195.00 purchase _ #B600
Shows that the male mosquito lives on the juice of fruit and is rarely seen. Reveals that female mosquitoes live on blood and are quite visble. Explains how the female mosquito lays her eggs in pond water, how the eggs hatch larvae which live beneath the surface of the water and breath through tubes at the rear of their bodies. Illustrates the life cycle of mosquitoes from larvae to flying insect, and their anatomy. Part of a series on animal families.
Science - Natural
Dist - BARR **Prod** - GREATT 1989

The Mosquito - a Bite for Survival 29 MIN
U-matic / VHS / 16mm
Color (P I J H)
Relates the effects of mosquito bites.
Health and Safety; Science - Natural
Dist - EBEC **Prod** - EBEC 1984

Mosquito Fighters 21 MIN
16mm
Color (J A)
LC 76-711348
Tells how the citizens of a small rural community in the Bayou country of south Louisiana, despite their original skepticism, cooperate in a modern mosquito control program to fight the mosquito - borne disease, encephalitis.
Health and Safety; Science - Natural
Dist - FINLYS **Prod** - STOKES 1970

Mosquito Prevention in Irrigated Areas 7 MIN
16mm
B&W
LC FIE55-234
Shows how to control mosquitoes in irrigated areas by good design and careful maintenance of the irrigation system, accurate preleveling of fields, and adequate provision for run - off drains to avoid standing water.
Agriculture; Health and Safety; Science - Natural
Dist - USNAC **Prod** - USPHS 1955

Mosquito Stages of Plasmodium Falciparum 11 MIN
16mm
B&W
LC FIE55-351
Uses cinemacrography, cinemicrography and graphics to show mouth parts within tissues as a female anopheles quadrimaculatus feeds on blood. Depicts gamete formation and fertilization. Traces ookinete, oocyst and sporozoites development. Shows sporozoites transfer to salivary glands and inoculation into host tissues.
Health and Safety; Science - Natural
Dist - USNAC **Prod** - USPHS 1954

Mosquito Survey Techniques 15 MIN
16mm
Color
LC FIE58-83
Shows mosquito survey methods under a variety of circumstances and for various mosquito species. Explains the proper way to collect larvae and adult mosquitoes, to keep accurate records and to evaluate results.
Health and Safety
Dist - USNAC **Prod** - USPHS 1954

Mosquitoes and High Water 25 MIN
U-matic / VHS
Captioned; Color (A) (SPANISH (ENGLISH SUBTITLES))
Portrays the history and culture of the Spanish - speaking 'Islenos' of St Bernard Parish, Louisiana. Presents their customs and traditions, and discusses some of their problems. Spanish language with English subtitles.
Fine Arts
Dist - CNEMAG **Prod** - CNAM 1983

Mosquitos - Effect on Cattle 9 MIN
16mm
Color (IND)
LC 77-701958
Investigates the problems of mosquito - caused irritations, weight loss and damage to cattle herds and shows how good management can help solve some of these problems.
Agriculture; Science - Natural
Dist - CENTWO **Prod** - ADAIB 1977

Moss life cycle 10 MIN
VHS
Color (J H)
$60.00 purchase _ #A5VH 1046
Explains thoroughly the life cycle of moss, using Mnium, Polytrichum and Sphagnum. Emphasizes gametophytic and sporophytic development, the sexual and asexual phases of moss reproduction.
Science - Natural
Dist - CLRVUE **Prod** - CLRVUE

Moss life cycle 15 MIN
VHS
Color (H C)
$39.95 purchase _ #49 - 8486 - V
Presents a general introduction to the mosses with emphasis on gametophytic and sporophytic development. Presents the life cycle of a typical moss using Mnium, Polytrichum and Spaghnum. Still frame.
Science - Natural
Dist - INSTRU **Prod** - CBSC

Moss, Reverend Otis 29 MIN
U-matic
Like it is Series
Color
Presents Rev Otis Moss, who discusses the church's role in developing black leaders and its relationship to the contemporary black family.
History - United States
Dist - HRC **Prod** - OHC

Mosses, Liverworts and Ferns 14 MIN
16mm / U-matic / VHS
Major Phyla Series
Color (J H C)
$315.00, $220.00 purchase _ #1482; LC 79-704134
Uses close - ups, microphotography and animation to show how mosses, liverworts and ferns grow and reproduce and how they are adapted for survival on land.
Science - Natural
Dist - CORF **Prod** - CORF 1969

The most 28 MIN
16mm
B&W (H C A)
LC 78-738824
Presents a fascinating documentary of 'PLAYBOY' Hugh Hefner. Takes place at a Bacchanalian party at Hefer's mansion, where the 'PLAYBOY PHILOSOPHY' is candidly and ironically revealed.
Biography; History - World
Dist - VIEWFI **Prod** - BALSHE 1971

The Most Adult Game, Pt 1 25 MIN
16mm
Color
LC 79-707704
Explores the history of the Synanon game and why it has become popular.
Health and Safety; Psychology; Sociology
Dist - KRONTV **Prod** - KRONTV 1967

The Most Adult Game, Pt 2 25 MIN
16mm
Color
LC 79-707704
Illustrates the Synanon game in action with children, teenagers and adults pointing out the potential of the game.
Health and Safety; Psychology; Sociology
Dist - KRONTV **Prod** - KRONTV 1967

The Most Beautiful Home 15 MIN
16mm
Color (J)
Shows how to clean carpets and how to keep them attractive, fresh and useful for extended numbers of years. Illustrates the rights and wrongs of carpet care, describing how to remove surface dirt, deep dirt and unpleasant odors.
Home Economics
Dist - KLEINW **Prod** - KLEINW

The Most Beautiful Place on Earth 28 MIN
U-matic / VHS / 16mm
Color (J)
LC 74-701768
Discusses several facets of the continent of Antarctica, including its climate, wildlife, topography and geology.
Geography - World; Science - Physical
Dist - JOU **Prod** - UN 1974

The Most Brilliant Game of the Year 28 MIN
Videoreel / VT2
Grand Master Chess Series
Color
Physical Education and Recreation
Dist - PBS **Prod** - KQEDTV

The Most common areas of management failure 40 MIN
VHS
Color (A PRO IND)
$129.00 purchase _ #S01129
Advises managers on how to avoid common areas of managerial failure. Covers subjects including use of motivational and reward techniques and how and when to use outside consultants. Hosted by Ken Blanchard.
Business and Economics; Guidance and Counseling; Psychology
Dist - UILL

Most common procedural mistakes which schools make - Tape 10 38 MIN
VHS
Legal challenges in special education series
Color (G)
$90.00 purchase
Reviews mistakes which courts are finding in the way school provide evaluation - what is evaluation, when, by whom; independent evaluation - when must a school reimburse a parent; written notice to parents - what goes into the notice; and record access and confidentiality - can parents see the psychologist's records and protocols. Explains how to avoid those mistakes. Features Reed Martin, JD. Includes resource materials. Part of a 12 - part series on Public Law 94 - 142.
Education
Dist - BAXMED

Most Efficient Instrument 29 MIN
U-matic
Life, Death and Taxes Series
Color
Gives examples of special trust devices for reducing taxes.
Business and Economics
Dist - UMITV **Prod** - UMITV 1977

The Most Famous Forgotten Writer in America 60 MIN
VHS / U-matic
World of F Scott Fitzgerald Series
Color (C)
Depicts Fitzgerald's turn to alcohol and despair, while everyone else it seemed to him turned to Marxism in this dramatization of a Fitzgerald story.
Literature and Drama
Dist - DALCCD **Prod** - DALCCD

The Most for Your Money 28 MIN
U-matic / VHS / 16mm
Learning to Live on Your Own Series
Color (S) (SPANISH)
LC 80-700259;
Explores the concepts of wise consumer shopping, including planning a shopping trip, tips on how to make the best buys and suggested questions for receiving helpful information from salespeople.
Home Economics
Dist - JOU **Prod** - LINCS 1979

Most Frequently Asked Tennis Questions 29 MIN
VHS / U-matic
Vic Braden's Tennis for the Future Series
Color
Physical Education and Recreation
Dist - PBS **Prod** - WGBHTV 1981

The Most Important Person 4 MIN
16mm / U-matic / VHS
Most Important Person - Identity Series
Color (K P I) (ENGLISH & SPANISH)
Presents Fumble, Bird and their friends who realize that each individual is, to himself or herself, the most important person.
Guidance and Counseling
Dist - EBEC **Prod** - EBEC 1972

Most Important Person - Attitudes Series
I'm Lonely 4 MIN
It's not Much Fun Being Angry 4 MIN
Nothing Ever Seems to Work Out for Me 4 MIN
Oops, I made a Mistake 4 MIN
We Can do it 4 MIN
Why not Try 4 MIN
Dist - EBEC

Most Important Person - Body Movement Series
How Big is Big 4 MIN
Put your hands on the top of your head 4 MIN
Dist - EBEC

Most Important Person - Creative Expression Series
Be Curious 4 MIN
Rhythm Around You 4 MIN
This is me 4 MIN
Use Your Imagination 4 MIN
When You're Waking Up 4 MIN
Without Saying a Word 4 MIN
Dist - EBEC

Most Important Person - Feelings Series
Feeling good, feeling happy 4 MIN
I used to be Afraid 4 MIN
Dist - EBEC

Most Important Person - Getting Along with Others Series
Doing something nice 4 MIN
Living Things are all Around Us 4 MIN
Share it with Someone 4 MIN
Thinking of Others 4 MIN
What do You Mean 4 MIN
What is a Friend 4 MIN
Dist - EBEC

Most Important Person - Health and Your Body Series
Tell Us How You Feel 4 MIN
Visiting the Doctor 4 MIN
The Voice Box 4 MIN
When You Get Hurt 4 MIN
Where Does Food Go 4 MIN
Dist - EBEC

Most Important Person - Identity Series
Every family is special 4 MIN
I'm the Only Me 4 MIN
The Most Important Person 4 MIN
What do You Think You Want to be 4 MIN
Where are You in Your Family 4 MIN
Dist - EBEC

Most Important Person - Identity (Spanish Series
I'm the only me 4 MIN
What do You Think You Want to be 4 MIN
Dist - EBEC

Most important person - nutrition series
Foods around us 4 MIN
Have a Snack 4 MIN
Tasting Party 4 MIN
What's for Breakfast 4 MIN
Dist - EBEC

Most Important Person - Senses Series
The Five senses 4 MIN
Hearing 4 MIN
Seeing 4 MIN
Dist - EBEC

The Most Marvelous Cat 11 MIN
U-matic / VHS / 16mm
Color (I)
Follows the adventures of a conscientious cat who hires out as a duster, an actor and a mouse catcher to earn money to pay his rent. Shows how the cat finally puts his musical background to work when he becomes the conductor of a symphony orchestra.
English Language
Dist - GA **Prod** - XEROX 1973

Most Precious Resource 29 MIN
16mm
Color (I)
LC 76-700015
Views the organization for rehabilitation through training Israel network, the largest single ORT operation in 22 countries, and shows its role in building the future of Israel.
Geography - World; Guidance and Counseling; Psychology
Dist - WAORT **Prod** - WAORT 1968

The Most Remarkable Cat 15 MIN
U-matic
Storytime Series
Color (K P)
Literature and Drama
Dist - GPN

Most Secret Source 30 MIN
U-matic
Best Kept Secrets Series
Color (H C A)
Shows historical footage of Churchill's war room and a captured German Enigma coding machine which was an early computer. The use of the coding machine meant the Allies could anticipate major German moves.
Civics and Political Systems; History - World
Dist - TVOTAR **Prod** - TVOTAR 1985

The Most Thankless Job on Earth 25 MIN
16mm / U-matic
Maclear Series
Color; Mono (J H C A)
$300.00 film, $250.00 video, $50.00 rental
Features an interview with Kurt Waldeim, Secretary General of the United Nations, and give some history and description of his position and duties.
Civics and Political Systems
Dist - CTV **Prod** - CTV 1976

The Most Wonderful Egg in the World 6 MIN
VHS / U-matic
(K P I)
Shows three hens quarreling about which of them was most beautiful. And, since they could not settle the quarrel, they decided to ask the King. The way in which the King resolved this dilemma makes a perfect and peaceable ending to an amusing tale that points up in a new way the wise old adage, Beauty is as beauty does.
English Language; Guidance and Counseling; Literature and Drama
Dist - WWS **Prod** - WWS 1984

Motel 18 MIN
16mm
Color
LC 76-703140
Presents an adaptation of Jean Claude van Itallie's play Motel. Concerns three characters in oversized puppet heads and a man and a woman who arrive in a motel room, seemingly prepared for an evening of sex, while a grotesque motel keeper delivers a monologue of platitudes about America and the homey quality of her motel. Shows how the monologue changes from nonsense to chaos and the couple proceed to wreck the room.
Literature and Drama; Psychology; Sociology
Dist - EQINOX **Prod** - EQINOX 1976

The Moth - eyed man 9 MIN
16mm
Color (G)
$30.00 rental
Questions meditation by talking in someone else's tongue while maintaining its own ontology. Delves into boundary distinctions. A portrait of Brakhage in Brakhage's style.
Fine Arts; Religion and Philosophy
Dist - CANCIN **Prod** - DOBERG 1978

Mother 87 MIN
16mm
Soviet Union - the pioneers series
B&W (G)
$150.00 rental
Portrays a peasant woman who embraces revolutionary ideals when her son is arrested for political activities. Includes a musical score as sound background. Directed by Vsevolod Pudovkin.
Fine Arts; History - World
Dist - KINOIC

Mother 98 MIN
VHS
Japan Film Collection from SVS Series
B&W (G) (JAPANESE (ENGLISH SUBTITLES))
$59.95 purchase _ #K0658
Presents a movie produced in Japan. Features Mikio Naruse as director. Stars Kinuyo Tanaka and Kyoko Kagawa. Also called 'Okaasan' in Japanese.
Fine Arts; Geography - World
Dist - CHTSUI **Prod** - SONY 1952

Mother 70 MIN
U-matic / VHS
B&W
Tells the story of a Russian family during the 1905 uprising.
Fine Arts
Dist - IHF **Prod** - IHF

Mother 30 MIN
BETA / VHS
American Professionals Series
Color
Describes the life of Ann Sweeney of Greenwich, Connecticut, who is 'Mom' to eighteen children. Seven are by her husband, a music publisher, plus eleven multi - national, multi - racial adopted children, ranging in age from eight to thirty.
Guidance and Counseling; Social Science; Sociology
Dist - RMIBHF **Prod** - WTBS

Mother 4 MIN
16mm
Color (G)
$15.00 rental
Exposes some words and pictures on metaphysics and individuation in a film by Todd Herman.
Fine Arts
Dist - CANCIN

Mother and Child 25 MIN
16mm / U-matic / VHS
Children Growing Up Series
Color (H C A)
Examines the importance of the physical and psychological relationship existing between mother and child. Discusses the difficulties that can arise with separation or with the arrival of a new baby.
Psychology; Sociology
Dist - FI **Prod** - BBCTV 1981

Mother and Child 15 MIN
16mm
Color
LC 75-702753
Features actresses Susan St James and Natalie Wood and the president of La Leche League International, Marian Tompson, in a discussion about the values and techniques of breast feeding.
Health and Safety; Home Economics; Sociology
Dist - KLEINW **Prod** - MAJAC 1975

The Mother and the Whore 215 MIN
16mm
B&W (FRENCH)
Presents Alexandre who reads Proust in cafes and wears long flowing silk scarves. Portrays him as an accomplished mock - philosophical raconteur who has no visible means of support at age 30. Surveys the social and sexual lives of Alexandre and the women he meets.
Fine Arts; Foreign Language
Dist - NYFLMS **Prod** - NYFLMS 1973

Mother and Toddlers - Humanizing the Growth Experience 18 MIN
16mm / U-matic / VHS
B&W
LC 79-712875
Documents the experiences of the Dr Martin Luther King Family Center with toddler's lab, a program in which children, from 18 months to three years are accepted for what they are and are engaged individually so that each child's special ways of coping with his world are not threatened. Demonstrates what it means to work with a person's strengths rather than his deficiences.
Psychology; Sociology
Dist - JOU **Prod** - JOU 1971

Mother Cat and Her Baby Skunks 11 MIN
U-matic / VHS / 16mm
Color (P)
The story of a mother cat and three orphaned baby skunks which she rescues and raises with her own kittens.
Literature and Drama; Science - Natural
Dist - EBEC **Prod** - EBEC 1958

Mother Deer and Her Twins 11 MIN
16mm / U-matic / VHS
Color (P)
The story of twin fawns. Shows how the mother protects them at first but later teaches them to care for themselves.
Literature and Drama; Science - Natural
Dist - EBEC **Prod** - EBEC 1959

Mother Earth, Father Sky 13 MIN
16mm
Color
LC 74-702492
Shows people of various ages and ethnic backgrounds as they participate in a wide variety of outdoor activities in mountain, beach, urban and desert environments.
Physical Education and Recreation; Psychology; Sociology
Dist - FORDFL **Prod** - FMCMP 1974

Mother Goose 4 MIN
16mm
Color
LC 79-700124
Examines the lyrics and meanings of three Mother Goose favorites.
Literature and Drama
Dist - USC **Prod** - USC 1978

Mother Goose 11 MIN
16mm / U-matic / VHS
Bank Street Reading Incentive Film Series
Color (P)
LC FIA68-2228
Based on the book of nursery rhymes, Mother Goose, illustrated by Brian Wildsmith. Pictures Mother Goose nursery rhymes, which are read by Betsy Palmer.
Literature and Drama
Dist - MGHT **Prod** - BANKSC 1968

Mother Goose Musical Rhymes 30 MIN
VHS / 16mm
Music Stories Series
Color (P)
$39.95 purchase _ #CL6901
Presents musical versions of Mother Goose rhymes.
Literature and Drama
Dist - EDUCRT

Mother Goose Rhymes - Background for Reading and Expression 11 MIN
U-matic / VHS / 16mm
Color (P)
Provides an excursion to Mother Goose Land. Pictures such famous characters and places as Little Bo - Peep, Jack - Be - Nimble, the Old Woman Who Lived in a Shoe, Little Boy Blue, Little Miss Muffet, Mother Goose and the London Bridge.
English Language; Literature and Drama
Dist - CORF **Prod** - CORF 1957

Mother Goose Stories 11 MIN
U-matic / VHS / 16mm
Color; B&W (P I A)
LC FIA52-4364
Mother Goose steps out of the nursery rhyme book and brings some of her favorite characters to life, including Little Miss Muffet and Humpty Dumpty. Portrayed by animated figures.
English Language; Literature and Drama
Dist - PHENIX **Prod** - HARRY 1961

Mother Goose Stories 11 MIN
U-matic / VHS / 16mm
Captioned; Color (P I A)
Mother Goose steps out of the nursery rhyme book and brings some of her favorite characters to life, including Little Miss Muffet and Humpty Dumpty. Portrayed by animal figures.
English Language; Literature and Drama
Dist - PHENIX **Prod** - HARRY 1961

Mother Goose video treasury - Volume 1
VHS
Color (K P I)
$14.95 purchase
Presents the first of a four - part series on the fairy tales of Mother Goose. Includes the stories of Old King Cole, Humpty Dumpty, Peter Piper, and more. Combines puppets, actors, lavish costumes and sets, and special music. Produced by Frank Brandt of the Disney Channel.
Literature and Drama
Dist - PBS **Prod** - WNETTV

Mother Goose video treasury - Volume 2
VHS
Color (K P I)
$14.95 purchase
Presents the second of a four - part series on the fairy tales of Mother Goose. Includes the stories of London Bridge, Simple Simon, Mary, Mary, and more. Combines puppets, actors, lavish costumes and sets, and special music. Produced by Frank Brandt of the Disney Channel.
Literature and Drama
Dist - PBS **Prod** - WNETTV

Mother Goose video treasury - Volume 3
VHS
Color (K P I)
$14.95 purchase
Presents the third of a four - part series on the fairy tales of Mother Goose. Includes the stories of Little Bo Peep, The House That Jack Built, and more. Combines puppets, actors, lavish costumes and sets, and special music. Produced by Frank Brandt of the Disney Channel.
Literature and Drama
Dist - PBS **Prod** - WNETTV

Mother Goose video treasury - Volume 4
VHS
Color (K P I)
$14.95 purchase
Presents the fourth of a four - part series on the fairy tales of Mother Goose. Includes the stories of Jack and Jill, Itsy Bitsy Spider, and more. Combines puppets, actors, lavish costumes and sets, and special music. Produced by Frank Brandt of the Disney Channel.
Literature and Drama
Dist - PBS **Prod** - WNETTV

Mother Holle 11 MIN
VHS / U-matic
Fairy Tale Series
Color (K P I)
Relates the story of the girl who enters an enchanted world and is showered with gold by Mother Holle for her industriousness. Comes with teacher materials.
Literature and Drama
Dist - BNCHMK **Prod** - BNCHMK 1985

Mother Infant Interaction - Feeding and Function Pleasure in the First Year of Life 42 MIN
16mm
B&W
LC 70-712696
Describes relationships between types of maternal behavior and maturity of function pleasure in infants. Shows a mother and infant pair from each of seven maternal types. Includes a record of the psychological test performance of an infant.

Psychology; Sociology
Dist - NYU Prod - BROAXE 1970

Mother - Infant Interaction, Pt 5 - Maternal Behavior and the Infant's Cathexis in the first year of life 41 MIN
16mm
Color
Illustrates the relationship between the way an infant is mothered (FED) and the development of his object cathexis - the quality and quantity of investment in the outer world. Shows seven types of mother - infant interaction at six weeks, six months and one year, followed by selections from the infants' test performances.
Guidance and Counseling; Psychology; Sociology
Dist - NYU **Prod** - BROAXE

Mother - Infant Interaction, Pt 4 - Feeding and Function - Pleasure in the First Year of Life 42 MIN
16mm
Color
Presents a small longitudinal study with samples of interaction in the feeding situation taken at six weeks, six months and one year. Illustrates seven types of mother - infant behavior and their relation to function - pleasure through seven mother - infant pairs.
Guidance and Counseling; Psychology; Sociology
Dist - NYU **Prod** - BROAXE

Mother - Infant Interaction, Pt 1 - Forms of Interaction at Six Weeks 49 MIN
16mm
Color
Shows variations in mothers' ways of touching, holding, looking at and talking to their babies during feeding and the immediate effects of differences in handling on the infant, based on a longitudinal study of behavioral and emotional interactions during the first year of life.
Guidance and Counseling; Psychology; Sociology
Dist - NYU **Prod** - BROAXE

Mother - Infant Interaction, Pt 6 - Resemblances in Expressive Behavior 41 MIN
16mm
Color
Shows a variety of examples of mother - infant interaction in which particular modes of maternal behavior have been repeatedly available to the infant's experience during feeding. Suggests that the expressive behavior of the infant is derived largely from the maternal behavior to which he has become accustomed and accommodated himself.
Guidance and Counseling; Psychology; Sociology
Dist - NYU **Prod** - BROAXE

Mother - Infant Interaction, Pt 3 - Feeding and Object Relations at One Year 40 MIN
16mm
Color
Shows connections between the modes of infants' experiences with their mothers and the infants' relationships to persons and things when he is one year old. Portrays the amount of independence the mothers allow their infants and how the infants strive to enjoy feedings.
Guidance and Counseling; Psychology; Sociology
Dist - NYU **Prod** - BROAXE

Mother - Infant Interaction, Pt 2 - Forms of Interaction at Six Months 42 MIN
16mm
Color
Shows relationships between infantile experience during feeding at six months and the development of tension tolerance. Illustrates ways in which the infant is helped to wait for food, the ways in which the mother notes his wish to take the initiative and responds to it and the ways he can be satisfied or frustrated by his feeding.
Guidance and Counseling; Psychology; Sociology
Dist - NYU **Prod** - BROAXE

Mother - infant interaction series 256 MIN
VHS
Mother - infant interaction series
B&W (C G A)
$995.00 purchase
Offers six videos illustrating in striking detail the influence that a mother can have on the emotional and cognitive development of her infant. Produced the Drs Sylvia Brody and Sidney Axelrad at the City University of New York's Child Development Research Project.
Psychology; Sociology
Dist - UCEMC

Mother Ireland 52 MIN
VHS / 16mm
Color (G)
$350.00 purchase, $90.00 rental; LC 89715584
Explores the historical imagery which portrayed Ireland as a woman. Discusses the social functions of the romantic stereotyping of Irish womanhood. Examines the relationship between nationalism, feminism and Catholicism. Reveals the largely unrecorded role of women in Irish history.
Civics and Political Systems; Geography - World; History - World; Religion and Philosophy; Sociology
Dist - CNEMAG **Prod** - DERRY 1988

A Mother is a Mother 27 MIN
U-matic
Color
Documents the lives of seven black teenage mothers. Features these young women discussing their lives and shows what teenage parenting is like.
Sociology
Dist - BLKFMF **Prod** - BLKFMF 1982
UCV

Mother Kusters Goes to Heaven 108 MIN
16mm
Color (GERMAN (ENGLISH SUBTITLES))
Tells how a murderer's widow tries to make sense out of her husband's seemingly pointless act. Directed by Rainer Werner Fassbinder. With English subtitles.
Fine Arts; Foreign Language
Dist - NYFLMS **Prod** - UNKNWN 1975

Mother load 15 MIN
16mm
Color; B&W (G)
$30.00 rental
Weaves together diverse images and voices to explore the decision whether or not to bear life. Reflects on the expansion of women's roles in society and the complexity of this issue in modern times. Reveals various perspectives on childbirth and motherhood and offers an alternative approach to the traditional documentary. Combines live action with stock footage to illuminate the irony implicit in the life choices women today must face. Produced by Betsy Weiss.
Fine Arts; Sociology
Dist - CANCIN

Mother Love 20 MIN
16mm
Film Studies of the Psychoanalytic Research Project on Problems in 'Infancy Series
B&W (C T)
Shows the relationship between Johnny and his mother from his birth. Points out that the absence or presence of mother love influences the child's adjustment.
Psychology; Sociology
Dist - NYU **Prod** - SPITZ 1952

Mother Love 26 MIN
16mm / U-matic / VHS
Conquest Series
B&W (J)
Tests the reactions of a large colony of new - born rhesus monkeys to a variety of unusual and inanimate mother substitutes. These experiments show that the single most important factor is body contact, holding and nestling, and that deprivation of this can cause deep emotional disturbances, even death.
Psychology; Science - Natural; Sociology
Dist - CAROUF **Prod** - CBSTV 1960

Mother may I? 24 MIN
16mm / U-matic / VHS
Color (J H C A)
$440 purchase - 16 mm, $310 purchase - video
Talks about a young girl's anxiety when she thinks that she is pregnant. A Shared Futures film. Directed by Linda Feferman.
Health and Safety
Dist - CF

Mother may I 28 MIN
U-matic / VHS / 16mm
Color (J H C A)
LC 82 - 706513; 82-700006
Deals with sexuality and teenage pregnancy as seen through the eyes of an 11 - year - old girl and her 16 - year - old sister who thinks she is pregnant. Shows how they learn to communicate about sexuality and to act responsibly on sexual issues.
Health and Safety
Dist - CF **Prod** - SHRFUT 1982

Mother may I 9 MIN
16mm
Color
LC 74-702475
A fantasy which portrays changing attitudes towards love and violence and the lack of communication between generations.
Guidance and Counseling; Psychology; Social Science
Dist - MMM **Prod** - PHOCI 1968

Mother may I - School Version 24 MIN
U-matic / VHS / 16mm
Color (J)
LC 82-700006
Deals with sexuality and teenage pregnancy as seen through the eyes of an 11 - year - old girl and her 16 - year - old sister who thinks she is pregnant. Shows how they learn to communicate about sexuality and to act responsibly on sexual issues.
Health and Safety
Dist - CF **Prod** - SHRFUT 1982

The Mother - mitos maternos 69 MIN
VHS
Color (G)
$75.00 rental, $250.00 purchase
Explores the mythical figure of the mother from multiple viewpoints - documentary and fiction; Spanish and English; theory and experience. Interviews people on the street, views Hollywood stalwarts of maternal sentiment like Stella Dallas, reads what feminist thinkers say on the subject, and copes with life as a single Latina mother. Challenges popular beliefs about the mother's place and traditional representations of sacrifice and guilt.
Fine Arts; History - World; Sociology
Dist - WMEN **Prod** - BAUTIS 1994

Mother, Mother 30 MIN
VHS / 16mm
Color (G)
Explores the relationship between a young man with AIDS and his estranged mother. Provided as a complimentary copy with every purchase of Too Little, Too Late.
Health and Safety; Sociology
Dist - FANPRO **Prod** - FANPRO 1989

Mother Necessity 3 MIN
U-matic / VHS
America Rock Series
Color (P I)
Deals with common, everyday inventions, such as the light bulb, radio and television, and with their inventors.
History - United States; Social Science
Dist - GA **Prod** - ABCTV 1978

Mother of five 7 MIN
16mm
Color (G)
$15.00 rental
Describes a day in the life of American TV culture. Looks at television commercials turned inside out. A David McLaughlin production.
Fine Arts
Dist - CANCIN

Mother of invention 30 MIN
VHS
Perspective 10 series
Color; PAL; NTSC (G)
PdS90, PdS105 purchase
Examines the modern trend of movement of population from rural areas into urban areas for employment. Reveals that in England, the Rural Development Commission hopes to halt this trend and works to design simple, inexpensive, innovative technology which will assist small firms to improve productivity, create jobs and aid expansion.
Sociology
Dist - CFLVIS **Prod** - LONTVS 1993

Mother of many Children 58 MIN
16mm
Color (H C A)
Presents Agatha Marie Goodine, an 108 - year - old member of the Hobbema tribe. Contrasts her memories with the conflicts that most Indian and Inuity women face today. Traces the cycle of their lives from birth to old age in a series of sensitive vignettes.
Social Science; Sociology
Dist - NFBC **Prod** - NFBC 1977

Mother of many children 58 MIN
VHS
Color (G)
$75.00 rental, $195.00 purchase
Features a series of vignettes by an Abenaki filmmaker of Native women from different first nations. Reflects a proud matriarchal culture that for centuries has been pressured to adopt the values and traditions of white society. Traces the cycle of these Native women's live from birth to childhood, puberty, young adulthood, maturity and old age to show how they have struggled to regain a sense of equality, instill cultural pride in their children and pass on their stories and language to younger generations.
Fine Arts; Social Science; Sociology
Dist - WMEN **Prod** - OBOMSA 1977

Mother of the megacities 50 MIN
VHS
Nature series
Color; PAL (G)
PdS99 purchase
Focusses on Cairo, Egypt and its successful urban development that limits homelessness and crime while maintaining traditional cultural values. Examines the plight of many of the world's cities and whether they could apply the methods used by Cairo.

Geography - World; History - World; Sociology
Dist - BBCENE

Mother of the Year 30 MIN
U-matic / VHS
Color
Tells the story of 80 - year - old Ruth Youngdahl Nelson who was arrested along with others during the Seattle blockade of the first Trident submarine in Puget Sound. Strikes a course for civil disobedience.
Civics and Political Systems; Sociology
Dist - NFPS **Prod** - PLOW 1984
UCV

Mother - prison visit 6 MIN
16mm
Film study extracts series
B&W (J)
Presents an excerpt from the 1926 motion picture Mother. Shows the mother visiting her son in prison, passing him a note which reveals plans made for his escape. Directed by Vsevolod Pudovkin.
Fine Arts
Dist - FI **Prod** - UNKNWN

Mother Russia 60 MIN
VHS / 16mm
Portrait of the Soviet Union Series
(H C)
$99.95 each, $595.00 series
Details the Russian Republic and its people, and the histories of both.
Geography - World; History - World
Dist - AMBROS **Prod** - AMBROS 1988

Mother Teresa 82 MIN
VHS
Color (G)
$22.00 purchase _ #P38; $59.95 purchase _ #S02169
Portrays Mother Teresa in ten countries on four continents. Shows how she transcends political, religious and social barriers with her works of love based on deep faith. Shot over a period of five years.
Fine Arts; Religion and Philosophy; Sociology
Dist - HP
UILL

Mother Teresa and Her World 55 MIN
BETA / VHS
Color (J H A)
Takes the viewer through the streets of Calcutta where Mother Teresa and her Missionaries of Charity daily serve those whom society has forsaken.
Biography; Religion and Philosophy
Dist - DSP **Prod** - DSP 1986

Mother Teresa - mother of mercy 30 MIN
VHS
Color (J H G)
$250.00 purchase
Portrays Mother Teresa who leads nearly 4,000 missionaries - mostly nuns - in 180 countries, feeds 50,000 people every day and cares for 15,000 terminally ill people every year. Reveals that Mother Teresa possesses only two articles of clothing and a hymnal and still cleans bathrooms. Recalls Mother Teresa's birth to Albanian parents in Skopje, Yugoslavia and joining the Loreto Nuns of Dublin to work in India as a teacher in the 1930s. She opened a mission in Calcutta in 1948 in order to work with the poor. She has worked with refugees from Pakistan, in the war zones of Beirut, India, Nicaragua and South Africa, and given aid to victims of disasters in Bhopal, Ethiopia, the Sudan, Armenia and Bangladesh.
History - World; Religion and Philosophy
Dist - LANDMK **Prod** - LANDMK 1993

Mother Teresa of Calcutta 51 MIN
16mm / U-matic / VHS
Color (J H A)
LC 72-700658
Malcolm Muggeridge interviews an Indian nun who through her life and her dedication to rescuing abandoned babies exemplifies, for people of all religious beliefs, the power for good in the individual.
Guidance and Counseling; Religion and Philosophy
Dist - FI **Prod** - BBCTV 1971

Mother, this Isn't Your Day 21 MIN
16mm
B&W (T)
LC 75-701394
Emphasizes the importance of children being given a choice of subject matter for their writing.
Education; English Language; Psychology
Dist - EDC **Prod** - EDC 1972

Mother Tiger, Mother Tiger 11 MIN
16mm
Contemporary Family Series
Color
LC 75-700458
Explores a mother's struggle, despair and eventual acceptance of her multi - handicapped child.
Education; Psychology; Sociology
Dist - FRACOC **Prod** - FRACOC 1975

Mother to Daughter 18 MIN
U-matic / VHS / 16mm
Color (A) (SPANISH)
LC 81-700300;
Presents a mother's personal statement of love for her daughter and her hope that the child will grow up in a better world.
Sociology
Dist - PHENIX **Prod** - MARRUS 1980

Mother tongue 4 MIN
16mm
Color (G)
$20.00 rental
Juxtaposes textured layers of imagery and sound to call forth the generational and cultural conflict in a mother - daughter relationship. Interweaves manipulated home movie footage of the child with the mother's voice. A childhood experience of a first - generation American. Produced by Irina Leimbacher.
Fine Arts; Sociology
Dist - CANCIN

Motherhood in Mid Life 24 MIN
VHS
Color
From an AB TV program.
Health and Safety; Sociology
Dist - ABCLR **Prod** - KGOTV 1980

Motherhood in Mid - Life 24 MIN
U-matic / VHS
$335.00 purchase
Fine Arts; Health and Safety
Dist - ABCLR **Prod** - ABCLR 1980

Motherlove 20 MIN
VHS / 16mm
Color; B&W (G)
$60.00 rental, $225.00 purchase
Captures the spirit of the classic feminist short story 'I Stand Here Ironing' by Tillie Olsen. Uses flashbacks to the Depression era while a woman quietly reminisces about the struggles of raising a daughter alone. Illuminates the inner lives of women conveying the pain and joy of motherhood.
Literature and Drama; Religion and Philosophy
Dist - WMEN **Prod** - MKNZM 1980

Mothers After Divorce 20 MIN
16mm
Color (H C A)
LC 76-703857
Presents several divorced suburban women with children in high school talking of their lives before and after divorce and their concerns as parents.
Guidance and Counseling; Sociology
Dist - POLYMR **Prod** - POLYMR 1976

Mothers Always have a Reason to be 7 MIN
U-matic
Color
Shows a mother reflecting on her children and her work.
Sociology
Dist - WMEN **Prod** - WMEN

Mothers and Daughters 29 MIN
U-matic
Woman Series
Color
Looks at mother - daughter relationships.
Sociology
Dist - PBS **Prod** - WNEDTV

Mothers are People 7 MIN
16mm
Working Mother Series
Color (H C A)
LC 75-701046
Features a research biologist, a widow with two school - age children, expressing her own dilemmas about on - the - job discrimination and the absense of universal day care.
Home Economics; Sociology
Dist - NFBC **Prod** - NFBC 1974

Mother's Bumblebees 4 MIN
16mm
Color (P) (AMERICAN SIGN)
LC 76-701694
Tells in American sign language a tale of farm life in 1930 involving a mother who discovers bumblebees in the family's backhouse. Signed for the deaf by Sharon Tate.
Fine Arts; Guidance and Counseling
Dist - JOYCE **Prod** - JOYCE 1975

Mother's Day
16mm
B&W (G)
$30.00 rental
Presents a painfully humorous recollection of childhood in which a family of adults recreate their infancy by behaving as they did when growing up.
Fine Arts; Sociology
Dist - CANCIN **Prod** - BROUGH 1948

Mother's Day 23 MIN
16mm
B&W (C)
$353.00
Experimental film by James Broughton.
Fine Arts
Dist - AFF **Prod** - AFA 1948

Mother's Day 1977 60 MIN
VHS / U-matic
Color
Recounts parents' experiences with the children's involvement with Yoga.
Religion and Philosophy
Dist - IYOGA **Prod** - IYOGA

Mother's Day 1979 60 MIN
VHS / U-matic
Color
Shows the ceremonies at Satchidananda Ashram - Yogaville East on Mother's Day. Shows children and adults and the Ashram guests.
Religion and Philosophy
Dist - IYOGA **Prod** - IYOGA

Mother's Day, 1980 30 MIN
U-matic
Color
Shows the celebration on Mother's Day, 1980 when women gathered under one banner 'every Mother is a working Mother.'.
Sociology
Dist - WMENIF **Prod** - AMELIA

Mother's Day 1981 30 MIN
VHS / U-matic
Color
Presents Sri Swami Satchidananda giving a special Mother's Day satsang on the Divine Mother.
Religion and Philosophy
Dist - IYOGA **Prod** - IYOGA

Mother's day and the beauty queen - Volume 8 45 MIN
VHS
Superbook series
Color (K P I R)
$11.99 purchase _ #35 - 86613 - 979
Uses an animated format to tell the story of Chris and Joy and their time travels through Biblical places and events. 'Mother's Day' tells the story of Ruth, while 'The Beauty Queen' tells the story of Esther.
Literature and Drama; Religion and Philosophy
Dist - APH **Prod** - TYHP

Mother's day - new reproductive technology 52 MIN
VHS
Color (H C G)
$445.00 purchase, $75.00 rental
Examines the technology of in vitro fertilization pioneered by Dr Patrick Steptoe. Reveals that doctors can implant eggs from a donor into infertile women, producing babies with two mothers, a genetic mother who donated the egg and a carrying or birth mother. Raises the issue of which mother will have the greater claim on the infant. Shows that childbearing years can be extended with implantation and meets a happy mother who gave birth at age 50. One doctor feels that women could bear children until the age of 65 but questions whether this is desirable for society. Asks who should make the decisions like these. Produced by Jane Walmsley Productions.
Health and Safety
Dist - FLMLIB

Mother's Diet and Her Baby's Future 23 MIN
16mm
Color
LC 74-706499
Shows what effect the lack of protein in the diet of pregnant rats has on their offspring. States that favorable and far - reaching results of the experiment have promoted similar research in humans.
Health and Safety; Psychology; Science; Science - Natural
Dist - USNAC **Prod** - USN 1969

Mother's - Father's Day 15 MIN
U-matic
Celebrate Series
Color (P)
Social Science
Dist - GPN **Prod** - KUONTV 1978

A mother's love 30 MINS.
VHS
Lifestories
Color; PAL (A F)
PdS50 purchase
Documents a real life family as they confront the challenges of raising an adopted child and the child's concerns about being part of an adopted family. Covers how the family works to overcome their obstacles. Third in the six - part Lifestories series.

Sociology
Dist - BBCENE

Mothers of invention 50 MIN
VHS
White heat series
Color; PAL (G)
PdS99 purchase; Not available in the United States or Canada
Presents the connections between culture and human innovation. Looks at the role of inventions in society and how societal influences change technology to suit its needs. Part two of an eight - part series.
History - World; Sociology
Dist - BBCENE

A Mother's Perspective on Spinal Cord Injury 55 MIN
U-matic / VHS
Color (G)
$100.00 VHS purchase, $130.00 3/4 INCH purchase, $50.00 VHS rental,
Presents an interview between a rehabilitation counselor and the mother of a 20 year old spinal cord injury patient. Describes the mother's feelings and reactions toward each step in her son's injury and rehabilitation.
Guidance and Counseling; Health and Safety
Dist - BUSARG **Prod** - ARTORT 1986

Mothers' perspectives - Video 1
VHS
Neither damned nor doomed series
Color (T PRO A G)
$95.00 purchase
Focuses on mothers, many recovering addicts, who tell of their drug addiction and the lasting psychological, physical and emotional effects parental drug addiction has had on their children. Part 1 of a three - part series on children prenatally exposed to drugs and alcohol produced by the Elementary School Center - ESC.
Guidance and Counseling; Psychology; Sociology
Dist - SELMED

Mothers - what they do 11 MIN
U-matic / VHS / 16mm
Color (K P I)
LC FIA67-5811
Presents the economics of mothers who work in order to provide goods and services for their families.
Business and Economics; Guidance and Counseling; Psychology; Social Science; Sociology
Dist - ALTSUL **Prod** - FILMSW 1968

Mothers who are part of supportive day care 29 MIN
U-matic
Are you listening series
Color (J H C)
LC 81-706008
Features mothers from various social, economic and ethnic backgrounds discussing their efforts to combine motherhood and jobs outside the home.
Sociology
Dist - STURTM **Prod** - STURTM 1980

Mothers who Leave Home 29 MIN
U-matic
Woman Series
Color
Offers an interview with Judy Sullivan, who walked out on her marriage and wrote about it in her book. Examines the conflicts of having a home, a career, and an ambition to write.
Sociology
Dist - PBS **Prod** - WNEDTV

A Mother's worry 33 MIN
16mm / VHS
Emotional factors affecting children and parents in the hospital series
Color (C A)
LC 81-701486
Presents an account of a mother as she experiences the hospitaliztion of her two - year - old son who undergoes tests with inconclusive results. Shows the emergence of the mother's anxiety and the stress which both parents and physcians feel as they struggle to communicate about the child's illness.
Health and Safety; Sociology
Dist - LRF **Prod** - LRF 1979

Motherwell - a medically proven program for expectant and new mothers 90 MIN
VHS
Color (J H C G)
$29.95 purchase _ #SBI100V - K
Presents an exercise program for pregnant women. Covers exercise routines, relaxation and stretching techniques, questions and answers, dietary tips and abdominal exercises for after delivery.
Physical Education and Recreation
Dist - CAMV

Motherwell - Alberti - a La Pintura 15 MIN
16mm / VHS
Color (H C)
$475.00, $190.00 purchase, $75.00 rental
Represents the collaborative efforts of the poet Rafael Alberti and the painter Robert Motherwell.
Fine Arts; Industrial and Technical Education
Dist - BLACKW **Prod** - BLACKW 1973

Mothlight 4 MIN
16mm
Color; Silent (C)
$179.00
An experimental film by Stan Brakhage.
Fine Arts
Dist - AFA **Prod** - AFA 1963

Mothlight 4 MIN
16mm
Color
LC 76-712467
An experimental film which presents a fluttering light collage created by pasting moth wings and bits of plants between strips of Mylar tape and running the tape through an optical printer.
Fine Arts; Industrial and Technical Education
Dist - FMCOOP **Prod** - BRAKS 1971

Moths and how they live 17 MIN
16mm / VHS
Animals and how they live series
Color (I J)
$425.00, $295.00 purchase, $50.00 rental _ #8395
Uses microphotography to portray the life cycle of the moth.
Science - Natural
Dist - AIMS **Prod** - VATV 1991

Motility in Parent - Child Relationships 40 MIN
16mm
B&W (C T)
Focuses on the important role of motility in the development of personal relationships in the first year and a half of life. Stresses reciprocity between parent and child as the main theme.
Psychology; Sociology
Dist - NYU **Prod** - MITM 1959

Motility of Entamoeba Histolytica 4 MIN
16mm
Color
LC 74-705171
Presents a photomicrography of scrapings from rectal lesion of a case of amebiasis showing movement of parasites.
Health and Safety; Science - Natural
Dist - USNAC **Prod** - USPHS

Motion and Emotion - Baroque Sculpture 29 MIN
Videoreel / VT2
Museum Open House Series
Color
Fine Arts
Dist - PBS **Prod** - WGBHTV

Motion and Time - an Introduction to Einstein's Theory of Relativity 11 MIN
16mm
Color; B&W (I)
Describes how the concepts of time, motion and space have changed from the time of Copernicus to that of Einstein. Explains the principles of the theory of relativity, and demonstrates that measurements of both time and space are not absolute, but are functions of motion.
Mathematics; Science; Science - Physical
Dist - SF **Prod** - SF 1960

Motion and Time Study 9 MIN
16mm
B&W
LC FIA52-303
Several different motions common to industrial production are presented and analyzed by motion and time study techniques.
Business and Economics
Dist - USC **Prod** - USC 1948

Motion Compensators 17 MIN
VHS / U-matic
Color (IND)
which heave compensators for floating drilling units operate. Features the Vetco single - and dual - cylinder systems.
Industrial and Technical Education
Dist - UTEXPE **Prod** - UTEXPE 1978

Motion Geometry 20 MIN
U-matic
Mainly Math Series
Color (H C)
Introduces congruence, similarity, motion geometry and symmetry.
Mathematics
Dist - GPN **Prod** - WCVETV 1977

Motion Offense 11 MIN
16mm
B&W (H)
LC 78-701962
Presents the fundamentals of motion offense in basketball, including the development of both individual and team skills.
Physical Education and Recreation
Dist - BKBA **Prod** - BKBA 1975

Motion painting I 11 MIN
VHS
Color (G)
$27.50 rental
Stands in length and complexity as filmmaker's major work. Uses oil - on - plexiglass technique to accomplish a purely abstract work.
Fine Arts
Dist - CANCIN **Prod** - FISCHF 1947

Motion Painting, no 1 11 MIN
16mm
Color (J)
LC 72-703164
Shows a painting in continuous change as it is being painted, from the first stroke to the fully developed sequence of successive overlying compositions that fulfill the concept of the work.
Fine Arts
Dist - CFS **Prod** - PFP 1972

Motion Perception, Pt 1 - Two - Dimensional Motion Perception 7 MIN
16mm
Films at the Frontiers of Psychological Inquiry Series
Color (H C A)
LC 72-702269
Presents Professor Gunnar Johansson who demonstrates how stimuli moving in two - dimensional space are perceived by the viewer. Uses computer generated stimuli and movements of human subjects to show how motions are seen and analyzed in terms of groups and subgroups.
Psychology
Dist - HMC **Prod** - HMC 1971

Motion Perception, Pt 2 - Three - Dimensional Motion Perception 11 MIN
16mm
Films at the Frontiers of Psychological Inquiry Series
Color (H C A)
LC 72-702270
Presents Professor Gunnar Johansson who uses computer generated stimuli and movements of human subjects to shows the information necessary to give rise to the perception of three - dimensionality. Illustrates motion patterns, changes of size and length and specifies their resulting effects.
Psychology
Dist - HMC **Prod** - HMC 1971

Motion Picture 18 MIN
16mm
Color
Presents Torben Ulrich, the Danish tennis player, who practices his strokes, his serve, his running and his jumps.
Physical Education and Recreation
Dist - STATNS **Prod** - STATNS 1970

The Motion Picture History of the Korean War 58 MIN
U-matic / VHS
B&W
Shows Korean War fighting and problems encountered by American and U N forces during the major phases of the battle from the initial gunfire on June 25, 1950, to the armistice on July 27, 1953.
History - United States; History - World
Dist - IHF **Prod** - IHF

Motion Picture History of the Korean War 58 MIN
16mm
B&W
Reviews the Korean War, showing the fighting and discussing the problems encountered by American and United Nations forces during the major phases of battle. Traces events, from the initial gunfire on June 25, 1950, to the armistice on July 27, 1953.
Civics and Political Systems; History - World
Dist - USNAC **Prod** - USDD 1958

Motion Pictures and the Navy 24 MIN
16mm
Color
LC 74-706500
Shows the operation and responsibilities of the people concerned with the annual Navy motion picture program.
Civics and Political Systems; Fine Arts
Dist - USNAC **Prod** - USN 1971

Motion Study Applications 22 MIN
16mm
B&W (C)
Shows old and improved methods of performing such jobs as filling the pin - board, inserting papers in mailing envelopes, folding paper cartons and assembling refrigerator grids.
Business and Economics
Dist - UIOWA **Prod** - UIOWA 1952

Motion Study in Action 18 MIN
16mm
B&W (C)
Shows that principles of motion economy can be applied to almost any kind of manual work.
Business and Economics
Dist - UIOWA **Prod** - UIOWA 1949

Motion Study on the Job 25 MIN
16mm
B&W (C)
Examines, in detail, work methods of 12 jobs and shows how production was increased in each case by the application of method - improvement techniques.
Business and Economics
Dist - UIOWA **Prod** - UIOWA 1958

Motion Study Principles 22 MIN
16mm
B&W (C)
Presents 11 principles of motion economy using three applications to illustrate the principles - - bolt and washer assembly, refrigerator doorknob assembly and folding X - ray film packing papers.
Business and Economics
Dist - UIOWA **Prod** - UIOWA 1952

Motions during and After Trial 120 MIN
VHS / U-matic / Cassette
Color; Mono (PRO)
Discusses techniques and strategies for making and opposing motions in limine, motions during trial for continuance or stay and motions at conclusion of trial for judgment notwithstanding the verdict or for new trial. Emphasizes how motion practice and strategy in the trial courtroom differs from pretrial law and motion practice.
Civics and Political Systems
Dist - CCEB **Prod** - CCEB
ABACPE

Motions for protective order and discovery abuse 35 MIN
Cassette
Effective discovery techniques series
Color (PRO)
$100.00, $20.00 purchase, $50.00 rental _ #EDT1-003, #AEDT-003
Provides a basic understanding of all aspects of discovery prior to depositions. Designed to provide practical information for the attorney with minimal litigation experience. Covers motions for protective order, and discovery abuse. Includes study guide.
Civics and Political Systems
Dist - AMBAR **Prod** - AMBAR 1985

The Motions of Attracting Bodies 8 MIN
16mm
Explorations in Space and Time Series
Color (H C A)
LC 75-703976
Uses computer animation to investigate Newton's laws of motion and universal gravitation. Applies these principles to specific instances of Earth satellites and binary star systems.
Science - Physical
Dist - HMC **Prod** - HMC 1974

The Motions of Stars 8 MIN
16mm
Explorations in Space and Time Series
Color (H C A)
LC 75-703978
Uses computer animation to examine the motions of stars in various constellations, showing the changes that will occur in periods up to 200,000 years.
Science - Physical
Dist - HMC **Prod** - HMC 1974

Motivate people to peak performance 60 MIN
VHS
Effective manager seminar series
Color (H C A)
$95.00 purchase _ #NGC749V
Presents a multimedia seminar on motivating people to peak performance. Consists of a videocassette, a 60 - minute audiocassette, and a study guide.
Psychology
Dist - CAMV

Motivating at work 17 MIN
VHS
Color (A PRO)
$495.00 purchase, $150.00 rental
Provides managers simple and effective ways to encourage and motivate those under them. Promotes helping employees meet their goals in ways that benefit the organization.
Business and Economics; Psychology
Dist - DHB **Prod** - CRISP 1993

Motivating Children to Learn Series
Group Discussions 30 MIN
Dist - GPN

Motivating, directing, leading - the basics of winning with people 30 MIN
VHS
Color (A PRO)
$79.00 purchase _ #S01539
Proposes that there are four basic personality types, each of which must be handled differently by managers. Suggests that managers should treat people as they prefer to be treated. Hosted by Jim Cathcart.
Business and Economics; Guidance and Counseling; Psychology
Dist - UILL

Motivating employees trapped on a plateau 18 MIN
VHS
Managing people problems series
Color (A PRO IND)
$495.00 purchase, $150.00 rental
Discusses how to help 'plateaued' employees - those who will not advance to higher positions - maintain their motivation for personal and professional growth. Explains the reasons plateauing can occur and gives guidelines to help employees.
Business and Economics; Guidance and Counseling; Psychology
Dist - VLEARN **Prod** - EBEC

Motivating four American generations 60 MIN
VHS
Color (A PRO)
$69.95 purchase _ #S01548
Examines the four main generations present in the US work force. Traces the influence of each generation's values to show how motivation differs from group to group.
Business and Economics; Guidance and Counseling; Psychology
Dist - UILL

Motivating high performance - Mary Lippett 90 MIN
VHS
Color; PAL (C G PRO)
$89.95, $69.95 purchase _ #91AST - V - W39
Analyzes how reward systems and motivational practices can either support or subvert organizational goals. Assesses how five motivational traps limit the scope of managerial behavior. Examines the perceived messages or priorities in organizational reward systems. Allows participants to analyze their own personal motivational preferences and the impact on their organizations. Features Mary Lippitt, President, Enterprise Management Ltd, Bethesda MD.
Business and Economics; Psychology
Dist - MOBILE **Prod** - ASTD 1991

Motivating others 30 MIN
VHS
Color (G PRO)
$79.95 purchase _ #741 - 67
Demonstrates a concrete set of guidelines to elicit superior performance. Pinpoints top - rated employee motivators.
Business and Economics; Guidance and Counseling; Psychology
Dist - MEMIND **Prod** - AMA 1993

Motivating others
VHS
FYI video series
Color (J H C G)
$79.95 purchase _ #AMA84011V
Shows what the proven, top - rated employee motivators are and how to use them. Part of a 12 - part series on professional and personal skills for the work place.
Business and Economics; Guidance and Counseling; Psychology
Dist - CAMV **Prod** - AMA

Motivating People
VHS / 16mm
Management Skill Development Series
(PRO)
$89.95 purchase _ #MDS2
Presents concepts derived from organizational psychology to use in motivating people. Shows different bases for motivation and when to apply motivational techniques.
Business and Economics
Dist - RMIBHF **Prod** - RMIBHF

Motivating People toward Peak Performance 60 MIN
Cassette / VHS
Effective Manager Series
Color (G)
$95.00 purchase _ #6419
Features Brian Tracy who shows how to get extraordinary performance from ordinary people. Includes a 60 - minute video, two audiocassettes and two workbooks. Part of a fourteen - part series.
Business and Economics; Civics and Political Systems; Guidance and Counseling; Psychology
Dist - SYBVIS

Motivating people toward peak performance 60 MIN
Cassette / VHS
Color (G)
$95.00 purchase _ #6 - 401 - 113Q
Features sales and management consultant Brian Tracy. Illustrates proven strategies for getting extraordinary performance from ordinary people. Includes videocassette, two audiocassettes and two workbooks.
Business and Economics; Psychology
Dist - VEP

Motivating Scientists and Engineers 45 MIN
U-matic / VHS
Management of Technological Innovation Series
Color
Business and Economics; Industrial and Technical Education
Dist - MIOT **Prod** - MIOT

Motivating the Conservative and the Cautious Personality, Case Examples - Personalities 35 MIN
VHS / U-matic
Personality Styles Series
Color
Looks at the underlying motivational forces at work in people who are of the 'steadiness' style and the 'complaint' style. Presents two vignettes which demonstrate the interaction of personalities in the four behavioral styles.
Psychology; Sociology
Dist - AMA **Prod** - AMA

Motivating the Disadvantaged 10 MIN
U-matic / 35mm strip
Supervising the Disadvantaged Series Module 2
Color
Considers the alternatives of reward and punishment and the use of psychological rewards in motivating disadvantaged workers.
Business and Economics; Psychology
Dist - RESEM **Prod** - RESEM

Motivating the Dominant and the 'People - Oriented' Personality 25 MIN
VHS / U-matic
Personality Styles Series
Color
Presents data on how to manage, motivate and direct a personality style that is very dominant or very high on the persuasion - people oriented factor of 'inducement.'.
Psychology
Dist - AMA **Prod** - AMA

Motivating the team 30 MIN
VHS
Color (A PRO IND)
$795.00 purchase, $185.00 rental
Explores how to motivate a group of employees. Stresses the idea that the team leader will have to motivate each employee individually as well.
Business and Economics; Guidance and Counseling; Psychology
Dist - VLEARN **Prod** - MELROS

Motivating the team 30 MIN
VHS
Color (PRO IND A)
$795.00 purchase, $185.00 rental _ #VLS08
Motivates employees to give their best and experience stimulation from theirjobs. Enables team leaders to address the task of motivation and face the reality that employees must find work to be self - determined, purposeful, useful and rewarding. Includes Trainer's Guide. By VideoLearning Resource Group.
Business and Economics; Guidance and Counseling; Psychology
Dist - EXTR

Motivating the Unmotivated 88 MIN
VHS / U-matic
JIST Conference Presentations
(C A P)
$60 _ #JWCV62V
Highlights David Swanson, professional development expert, as he speaks on career issues.

Business and Economics
Dist - JISTW **Prod** - JISTW

Motivating the Unmotivated 48 MIN
VHS / 16mm
Color (A PRO)
$95.00 purchase _ #CR101V
Answers questions most often asked by unemployed or disadvantaged employment seekers. Suggests a variety of possible answers. Targeted to the needs of social services personnel.
Psychology; Sociology
Dist - JISTW

Motivating to Achieve Results
U-matic / VHS
Management Training Series
Color
Business and Economics; Psychology
Dist - DELTAK **Prod** - THGHT

Motivating Underachievers 28 MIN
U-matic / VHS
Color (G)
$249.00, $149.00 purchase _ #AD - 1592
Explores the problem of underachieving children. Examines why so many schools fail to deal with the problem effectively. Features Dr Linus Pecaut, Larry Hawkins and parents.
Health and Safety; Psychology
Dist - FOTH **Prod** - FOTH

Motivating volunteers and staff - Tape 3 60 MIN
VHS
Management skills for church leaders series
Color (G R PRO)
$10.00 rental _ #36 - 83 - 223
Gives strategies for motivating both volunteers and paid church staff. Covers motivation principles, selecting approaches and achieving team participation.
Business and Economics; Religion and Philosophy
Dist - APH

Motivation 9 MIN
16mm
Safety and You Series
Color
Shows that there is a reason or motive for all human behavior. Points out that understanding motives can lead to a safer, more rewarding life.
Psychology; Sociology
Dist - FILCOM **Prod** - FILCOM

Motivation 41 MIN
U-matic / VHS
Learning and Liking it Series
Color (T)
Examines and demonstrates the six cognitive principles of motivation. Includes cognitive dissonance, open communication and meaningfulness.
Education; Psychology
Dist - MSU **Prod** - MSU

Motivation 29 MIN
16mm
Corporation Series
B&W
LC 74-702400
Depicts the driving force behind Sam Steinberg, a supermarket corporation's founder and chief executive officer. Shows how Steinberg's drive affects the more than 20,000 employees who work for the corporation.
Business and Economics; Geography - World; Psychology
Dist - NFBC **Prod** - NFBC 1973

Motivation 26 MIN
VHS / U-matic
Interpersonal Competence, Unit 03 - Motivational Series; Unit 3 - Motivation
Color (C A)
Features a humanistic psychologist whi, by analysis and examples, discusses motivations involved in interpersonal relationships.
Psychology; Sociology
Dist - TELSTR **Prod** - MVNE 1973

Motivation 30 MIN
VHS / 16mm
Psychology - the Study of Human Behavior Series
Color (C A)
$99.95, $89.95 purchase _ 24 - 12
Describes what motivates people to think, behave, and make choices.
Psychology
Dist - CDTEL **Prod** - COAST 1990

Motivation 16 MIN
16mm
Basic Psychology Series
Color (H C A)
LC 76-702922
Considers various topics as they apply to the psychology of motivation, including instincts, motives and the major theories of motivation of Freud, Hull and Maslow.
Psychology
Dist - EDMDC **Prod** - EDMDC 1973

Motivation 25 MIN
U-matic / VHS
Effective Manager Series
Color
Business and Economics; Guidance and Counseling; Psychology
Dist - DELTAK **Prod** - DELTAK

Motivation 17 MIN
VHS
Color (PRO IND A)
$595.00 purchase, $150.00 rental _ #VCO06
Demonstrates how to motivate employees to enable them to feel part of the work team. Helps supervisors get the best out of their staff by meeting needs related to self - concept, recognition, feelings of progress and job satisfaction. Includes Leader's Guide. By Video Communicators.
Business and Economics; Psychology
Dist - EXTR

Motivation 33 MIN
Videoreel / VHS
One Strong Link Series
B&W
Guidance and Counseling; Social Science
Dist - CORNRS **Prod** - CUETV 1971

Motivation - a Means to Accident Prevention 11 MIN
16mm
Foremanship Training Series
Color
LC 74-705172
Shows how proper motivation prevents accidents at home and on the job. Presents the reasoning that motivates the workmen in a visually interesting manner.
Health and Safety; Psychology
Dist - USNAC **Prod** - USBM 1969

Motivation and Goals 27 MIN
Videoreel / VT2
Interpersonal Competence, Unit 03 - Motivation Series; Unit 3 - Motivation
Color (C A)
Features a humanistic psychologist who, by analysis and examples, discusses motivations and goals involved in human relationships.
Psychology; Sociology
Dist - TELSTR **Prod** - MVNE 1973

Motivation and Hunger 29 MIN
U-matic
Understanding Human Behavior - an Introduction to Psychology Series 'Lesson 12
Color (C A)
Details factors that influence motivation. Defines concept of motivation and discusses uses of the term by psychologists.
Psychology
Dist - CDTEL **Prod** - COAST

Motivation and Incentives, Pt 1 30 MIN
U-matic / VHS
Business of Managing Professionals Series
Color
Discusses the use of motivation and incentives as applied to managing professionals.
Business and Economics
Dist - KYTV **Prod** - KYTV 1983

Motivation and Incentives, Pt 2 30 MIN
VHS / U-matic
Business of Managing Professionals Series
Color
Discusses motivation and incentives as applied to managing professionals.
Business and Economics
Dist - KYTV **Prod** - KYTV 1983

Motivation and Needs 30 MIN
Videoreel / VT2
Interpersonal Competence, Unit 03 - Motivation Series; Unit 3 - Motivation
Color (C A)
Features a humanistic psychologist who, by analysis and examples, discusses motivations and needs involved in interpersonal relationships.
Psychology; Sociology
Dist - TELSTR **Prod** - MVNE 1973

Motivation and Productivity Series
Behavioral Modeling 22 MIN
Effective leadership 27 MIN
Managing Employee Morale 25 MIN
Motivation - Myths and Realities 18 MIN
Dist - BNA

Motivation and Reinforcement in the Classroom 30 MIN
16mm
Aide - Ing in Education Series
Color (T)
Presents two annotated lessons which demonstrate the use of the principles of motivation and reinforcement in typical classrooms.

Education; Psychology
Dist - SPF **Prod** - SPF

Motivation and Reward in Learning 15 MIN
16mm
B&W (C)
A photographic story of experimental demonstration with white rats to illustrate the importance of motivation and reward in the learning process. Trial and error learning behavior is shown.
Education; Psychology
Dist - PSU **Prod** - PSUPCR 1948

Motivation and Team Building, Susan Pistone
U-matic / VHS
Management Skills Series
Color (PRO)
Business and Economics; Psychology
Dist - AMCEE **Prod** - AMCEE

Motivation, coaching and team - building 60 MIN
VHS / U-matic
Dynamics of sales management series; Session 5
Color
Demonstrates how managers can influence positive behavior for improved sales results. Includes a spectrum of five motivation types, needs and performance, goals and rewards and community and motivation.
Business and Economics; Psychology
Dist - PRODEV **Prod** - PRODEV

Motivation for Behavior 30 MIN
VHS / U-matic
Developing Discipline Series
Color (T)
Discusses the rationale behind specific behavior.
Education; Guidance and Counseling; Psychology; Sociology
Dist - GPN **Prod** - SDPT 1983

Motivation for Living 29 MIN
16mm
Color (H C)
Presents a speech by Bob Richards, twice Olympic pole vault champion. Uses excerpts and events from the worlds of sports and religion as examples of things that motivation and dedication can accomplish. Delivers a message on the urgency of these qualities in young people.
Guidance and Counseling; Physical Education and Recreation; Religion and Philosophy
Dist - NINEFC **Prod** - GEMILL

Motivation for the Linear - Quadratic Problem 73 MIN
U-matic / VHS
Modern Control Theory - Deterministic Optimal Linear Feedback Series
Color (PRO)
Industrial and Technical Education; Mathematics
Dist - MIOT **Prod** - MIOT

Motivation for the Steady - State Linear Quadratic Problem 104 MIN
U-matic / VHS
Modern Control Theory - Deterministic Optimal Linear Feedback Series
Color (PRO)
Industrial and Technical Education; Mathematics
Dist - MIOT **Prod** - MIOT

Motivation in the Classroom 27 MIN
VHS / U-matic
Successful Teaching Practices Series
Color (C A)
$75.00 purchase _ #1489
Provides information on how teachers can maximize the learning in their classrooms through motivators. Presented by Dr Raymond J. Wlodkowski, University of Wisconsin.
Education; Psychology
Dist - EBEC

Motivation - It's not Just the Money 26 MIN
U-matic / VHS / 16mm
Human Resources and Organizational Behavior Series
Color (C A)
Examines the factors which contribute to job satisfaction and productivity by interviewing employees, managers and behavioral scientists. Looks at a Swedish Volvo plant's efforts to increase participation in decision - making, reduce systematization and specialization, shorten working hours for those with boring jobs and extend the autonomy of the individual worker. Discusses the ideas of Abraham Maslow and Douglas McGregor.
Business and Economics; Psychology
Dist - CNEMAG **Prod** - DOCUA

Motivation - Leadership in Action 18.20 MIN
VHS / U-matic / BETA
Supervisory Series
(PRO A)
$225 _ #1021
Presents examples of skills in motivation used at various levels of an organization to the end of increasing productivity, imporving employee self - esteem and raising the morale of the work force.
Education; Guidance and Counseling
Dist - CTT **Prod** - CTT

Motivation - leadership in action 19 MIN
VHS
Color (H A G T)
$225.00 purchase _ #BM121
Provides examples of motivation skills used with personnel at different levels in an organization - from entry - level workers to managers.
Business and Economics; Guidance and Counseling; Psychology
Dist - AAVIM **Prod** - AAVIM

Motivation - Myths and Realities 18 MIN
U-matic / VHS
Motivation and Productivity Series
Color
Illustrates various approaches to motivating people. Explores inspiration, initiative, following orders and cooperation.
Psychology
Dist - BNA **Prod** - BNA

The Motivation, Pt 1 15 MIN
BETA / VHS / U-matic
Fit for the Final Series
Color (J H C G)
Health and Safety; Physical Education and Recreation
Dist - UCALG **Prod** - UCALG 1986

Motivation - sparking students' interest
VHS
Strategies for effective instruction series
(T PRO)
$100.00 purchase _ #V3 - 4
Features Pat Wolfe who discusses student motivational strategies. Includes demonstrations by actual teachers in actual classrooms and a leader's guide. Part of a series based on research - proven techniques for improving student achievement.
Education; Psychology
Dist - NSDC **Prod** - NSDC 1990

Motivation - the Test of Leadership 20 MIN
U-matic / VHS
Supervisory Management Course, Pt 1 Series Unit 7
Color
Familiarizes supervisors with motivation as a qualification for sound leadership. Reviews current thinking on various theoretical and practical factors relating to motivating employees.
Business and Economics; Psychology
Dist - AMA **Prod** - AMA

Motivation Theory for Teachers 28 MIN
16mm
Translating Theory into Classroom Practices Series
B&W (C)
Features Dr Madeline Hunter discussing the six variables, subject to control, which influence motivation. Suggests how to apply theory in daily classroom practice.
Education
Dist - SPF **Prod** - SPF

Motivation to learn series
Shows how parents and teachers can team up to improve student attitude toward learning. Discovers the common issues surrounding academically unmotivated students. Demonstrates how to conduct effective parent - teacher conferences on motivational concerns. Includes two videos, How Parents and Teachers Can Help and Guidelines for Parent - Teacher Conferences, leader's manual and the book, Eager to Learn - Helping Children Become Motivated and Love Learning, by Raymond Wlodkowski and Judith Jaynes.

Guidelines for parent - teacher conferences - Tape Two	28 MIN
How parents and teachers can help - Tape One	25 MIN
Motivation to learn series	53 MIN

Dist - AFSCD **Prod** - AFSCD

Motivation Unit
U-matic / VHS
Management Skills for Supervisors Series
Color (A)
Depicts common work incidents in which motivation, or the lack of it, affects employees' behaviors and attitudes. Shows the use of feedback, reward and reinforcement as motivators and illustrates the effects of perception and expectation on behavior.
Business and Economics; Psychology
Dist - TIMLIF **Prod** - TIMLIF 1984

Motivation - Why Employees Work
U-matic / VHS
Principles of Management Series
Color (PRO)
$150.00 purchase _ #P5112
Discusses the manager's role in motivation and the creation of an environment in which people can motivate themselves. Shows how a manager must work with employee needs, values and expectations.
Business and Economics; Psychology
Dist - RMIBHF **Prod** - RMIBHF

Motivational Selling - What Motivates You
U-matic / VHS
Making of a Salesman Series Session 6, Parts 1 and 2
Color
Focuses on motivational selling and maintaining personal motivation in order to be a better salesperson. Includes clues to buyer needs, buyer's group behavior, identifying motivational slumps, personal goal setting and motivational chemistry and processes.
Business and Economics; Psychology
Dist - PRODEV **Prod** - PRODEV

Motivational Sports - Positive Vibes 10 MIN
U-matic / VHS / 16mm
Motivational Sports Series
Color (H C A)
Demonstrates how to keep the momentum in a game going. Presents Coach Bill Foster showing how he does it on and off the basketball court.
Physical Education and Recreation
Dist - ATHI **Prod** - ATHI 1981

Motivational Sports - Program for Victory 10 MIN
U-matic / VHS / 16mm
Motivational Sports Series
Color (H C A)
Presents Coach Tom Osborne discussing the general motivational principles of care, understanding and the sharing of mutual goals when playing sports.
Physical Education and Recreation
Dist - ATHI **Prod** - ATHI 1981

Motivational Sports Series

Motivational Sports - Positive Vibes	10 MIN
Motivational Sports - Program for Victory	10 MIN
Motivational Sports - the Winning Edge	10 MIN

Dist - ATHI

Motivational Sports - the Winning Edge 10 MIN
16mm / U-matic / VHS
Motivational Sports Series
Color (H C A)
Presents former U S Olympic Hockey Coach Herb Brooks discussing what it takes to lead a team to success, even against great odds.
Physical Education and Recreation
Dist - ATHI **Prod** - ATHI 1981

Motivational Techniques for Engineers 30 MIN
U-matic / VHS
Management for Engineers Series
Color
Business and Economics; Industrial and Technical Education; Psychology
Dist - SME **Prod** - UKY

Motivations 13 MIN
16mm
Cuba - a view from inside series
Color (G)
$200.00 purchase, $25.00 rental
Interviews painter Manuel Mendive who discusses the African themes in his art. Features part of a 17 - part series of shorts by and about Cuban women. Directed by Marisol Trujillo. Illustrated catalog available. Contact distributor for programming advice and discount package rental fees.
Fine Arts
Dist - CNEMAG

The Motives in Our Lives 30 MIN
U-matic / VHS
Psychology of Human Relations Series
Color
Presents Dr David McClelland on his studies of human motives for achievement, power and affiliation. Presents steps for developing certain types of motivation in an individual.
Psychology
Dist - WFVTAE **Prod** - MATC

Moto - Gaz 8 MIN
16mm
Color
LC FIA65-1875
Uses animation and music to comment on air pollution, emphasizing the effect of automobile exhaust.
Industrial and Technical Education; Psychology; Science - Natural; Sociology
Dist - SF **Prod** - RADIM 1964

Moto - Insanity - Supercross Racing USA 30 MIN
VHS
Motocross Series
Color (G)
$14.98 purchase _ #TT8119
Presents the most exciting motocross ever filmed.
Industrial and Technical Education; Literature and Drama; Physical Education and Recreation
Dist - TWINTO **Prod** - TWINTO 1990

Moto - X 29 MIN
Videoreel / VT2
Bayou City and Thereabouts People Show Series
Color
Explains that motocross is a sport for both amateurs and professionals and consists of competitive motorcycle trail riding.
Physical Education and Recreation
Dist - PBS **Prod** - KUHTTV

Motocross Series

The Best of supercross	60 MIN
Crash and Burn - Hot Music - Hot Biking	30 MIN
Moto - Insanity - Supercross Racing USA	30 MIN
Rick Johnson - Profile of a Champion	90 MIN
Rick Johnson's Motivation	60 MIN
Riding Motocross Glover Style	60 MIN
World's Greatest Supercross Races	60 MIN

Dist - TWINTO

Motor Activity Disabilities 30 MIN
U-matic / VHS
Characteristics of Learning Disabilities Series
Color (C A)
Discusses motor activity disabilities in children.
Education; Psychology
Dist - FI **Prod** - WCVETV 1976

Motor Aptitude Tests and Assembly Work 22 MIN
16mm
B&W (C T)
Compares a subject with good motor ability with a subject of average capacity. Pictures performance on dynamoter, whipple steadiness, slot - board steadiness, metal - stylus tapping, peg - board, bolt - block and O'Connor Wiggley - block tests. Pictures the two men, after test series, at an assembly work job in which good motor ability is needed.
Business and Economics; Psychology
Dist - PSUPCR **Prod** - PSUPCR 1941

Motor Bike Safety Tips 15 MIN
16mm
Color (J)
LC 74-700623
Presents the basic safety rules for motorcycle riders, correlated with the safety guidelines of the National Safety Council, the National Highway Traffic Safety Administration and the Motorcycle Industry Safety Council and Education Foundation.
Health and Safety
Dist - PF **Prod** - PF 1973

Motor Boat Racing 3 MIN
16mm
Of all Things Series
Color (P I)
Discusses the sport of motor boat racing.
Physical Education and Recreation
Dist - AVED **Prod** - BAILYL

Motor Branch Circuit Protection 60 MIN
VHS
Motors and Motor Controllers Series
Color (PRO)
$600.00, $1500.00 purchase _ #EMMBC
Focuses on the basics of motor branch protection, motor branch circuits and components. Covers safety switch, fuse, molded - case circuit breaker and motor controller operation. Part of a ten - part series on motors and motor controllers, which is part of a 29 unit set on electrical maintenance. Includes 10 textbooks and an instructor guide which provide four hours of instruction.
Education; Industrial and Technical Education; Psychology
Dist - NUSTC **Prod** - NUSTC

Motor Conduction Velocity Studies of the Median and Ulnar Nerves 8 MIN
16mm
Color
LC 74-705173
Defines the character of neuropathic lesions. Presents a method of determining the velocity in motor fibers of the median nerve in the forearm.
Psychology; Science - Natural
Dist - USNAC **Prod** - USPHS 1966

Motor Control Centers 8 MIN
U-matic / VHS
Electrical Safety Series
Color (IND)
Demonstrates recommended safety procedures for maintaining MCCs. Emphasizes need for communication among all operating and maintenance personnel.
Health and Safety; Industrial and Technical Education
Dist - GPCV **Prod** - GPCV

Motor Develoopment Patterns Series
Motor Development Series - Catching
Dist - SDSC

Motor Development - Assessment and Intervention 159 MIN
U-matic / VHS
Meeting the Communication Needs of the Severely - Profoundly˙Handicapped 1981 Series
Color
Presents a basic format by which deviations in primary and secondary motor dimensions can be quantitatively assessed for selecting a motor form of communication for children exhibiting deviant motor patterns.
Psychology; Social Science
Dist - PUAVC **Prod** - PUAVC

Motor Development Pattenrs Series
Motor Development Series - Jumping
Dist - SDSC

Motor Development Patterns Series
Motor Development Series - Kicking
Motor Development Series - Running
Motor Development Series - Striking
Motor Development Series - Throwing
Dist - SDSC

Motor Development Series - Catching
U-matic
Motor Develoopment Patterns Series
Color (J C)
Shows part one, Catching, a videotape in which selected patterns of motor development of children are examined. Each lesson includes both normal speed and slow motion segments illustrating the developmental and mature forms of each motor pattern. The presentations are made by Dr. Robert Carlson of the Department of Physical Education at SDSU.
Physical Education and Recreation; Science - Natural
Dist - SDSC **Prod** - SDSC 1980

Motor Development Series - Jumping
U-matic
Motor Development Pattenrs Series
Color (J C)
Shows part two, Jumping, a videotape in which selected patterns of motor development of children are examined. Each lesson includes both normal speed and slow motion segments illustrating the developmental and mature forms of each motor pattern. The presentations are made by Dr. Robert Carlson of the Department of Physical Education at SDSU.
Physical Education and Recreation; Science - Natural
Dist - SDSC **Prod** - SDSC 1980

Motor Development Series - Kicking
U-matic
Motor Development Patterns Series
Color (J C)
Shows part three, Kicking, a videotape in which selected patterns of motor development of children are examined. Each lesson includes both normal speed and slow motion segments illustrating the developmental and mature forms of each motor pattern. The presentations are made by Dr. Robert Carlson of the Department of Physical Education at SDSU.
Physical Education and Recreation; Science - Natural
Dist - SDSC **Prod** - SDSC 1980

Motor Development Series - Running
U-matic
Motor Development Patterns Series
Color (J C)
Shows part four, Running, a videotape in which selected patterns of motor development of children are examined. Each lesson includes both normal speed and slow motion segments illustrating the developmental and mature forms of each motor pattern. The presentations are made by Dr. Robert Carlson of the Department of Physical Education at SDSU.
Physical Education and Recreation; Science - Natural
Dist - SDSC **Prod** - SDSC 1980

Motor Development Series - Striking
U-matic
Motor Development Patterns Series
Color (J C)
Shows part five, Striking, a videotape in which selected patters of motor development of children are examined. Each lesson includes both normal speed and slow motion segments illustrating the developmental and mature forms of each motor pattern. The presentations are made by Dr. Robert Carlson of the Department of Physical Education at SDSU.
Physical Education and Recreation; Science - Natural
Dist - SDSC **Prod** - SDSC 1980

Motor Development Series - Throwing
U-matic
Motor Development Patterns Series
Color (J C)
Shows part six, throwing, a videotape in which selected patterns of motor development of children are examined. Each lesson includes both normal speed and slow motion segments illustrating the developmental and mature forms of each motor pattern. The presentations are made by Dr. Robert Carlson of the Department of Physical Educ.
Physical Education and Recreation
Dist - SDSC **Prod** - SDSC 1980

Motor Disorders of Speech 100 MIN
VHS / U-matic
Color
Reviews neuroanatomy and the hierarchies of oral communication. Discusses the diagnosis and management of persons with motor disorders.
Education; Psychology
Dist - PUAVC **Prod** - PUAVC

Motor evaluation and treatment of patient with rupture of A - V malformation 56 MIN
VHS
Color (PRO)
$140.00 purchase, $75.00 rental
Presents two parts on stroke patient evaluation and rehabilitation. Offers a physical therapist's evaluation of a 25 - year - old stroke patient 2.5 weeks after the stroke in part 1. Part 2 observes the physical therapist interviewing the patient 15 months after the initial stroke and assessing current motor status. Discusses the goals of the patient and demonstrates treatment techniques. Produced by Prudy Markos.
Health and Safety
Dist - BUSARG

Motor Evaluation of an Adult with Limb - Girdle Muscular Dystrophy 35 MIN
50 MIN
VHS / U-matic
B&W
Demonstrates gait, abnormalities and presents discussions of causative factors. Shows a gross motor muscle exam with the patient sitting, side - lying, supine and prone.
Health and Safety
Dist - BUSARG **Prod** - BUSARG

Motor Learning 11 MIN
16mm
Coaching Development Programme Series no 4; No 4
Color
LC 76-701028
Teaches basic motor learning and development.
Physical Education and Recreation
Dist - SARBOO **Prod** - SARBOO 1974

Motor Mania 8 MIN
U-matic / VHS / 16mm
Color (H) (GERMAN FRENCH GREEK JAPANESE)
Examines the tendency to drive aggressively. Encourages driving safely.
Foreign Language; Industrial and Technical Education; Social Science
Dist - CORF **Prod** - DISNEY 1953

Motor Mania 8 MIN
U-matic / VHS / 16mm
Color (H C A) (ARABIC DANISH FLEMISH FRENCH GERMAN GREEK JAPANESE PORTUGUESE SWEDISH)
Examines the tendency to drive aggressively. Encourages driving safely.
Industrial and Technical Education; Social Science
Dist - CORF **Prod** - DISNEY 1953

Motor Nameplates 19 MIN
VHS / 16mm
Maintaining & Troubleshooting Electric Motors Series
Color (H A)
$465.00 purchase, $110.00 rental
Explains specifications and terms found on a motor nameplate.
Industrial and Technical Education
Dist - TAT **Prod** - TAT 1989

Motor Neuron Biology in Health and Disease
U-matic
Color (PRO)
LC 79-707394
Discusses age of onset, symptoms and progression rate of amyotrophic lateral sclerosis. Explains lower and upper motor neuron involvement in ALS, illustrates its pathology, examines muscle fiber to determine what is happening in motor neurons and gives the value of muscle biopsy in ALS. Discusses therapeutic trials of the ALS patient and presents studies describing its possible causes.
Health and Safety; Science - Natural
Dist - USNAC **Prod** - NINDIS 1978

Motor Oils - Paying for College Education - Small Claims Courts
U-matic / VHS
Consumer Survival Series
Color
Discusses various aspects of motor oils, paying for a college education and small claims courts.
Civics and Political Systems; Education; Home Economics; Industrial and Technical Education
Dist - MDCPB **Prod** - MDCPB

Motor Operators 60 MIN
VHS
Motors and Motor Controllers Series
Color (PRO)
$600.00, $1500.00 purchase _ #EMMOP
Introduces motor operators and associated equipment such as limit and torque switches. Part of a ten - part series on motors and motor controllers, which is part of a 29 unit set on electrical maintenance. Includes 10 textbooks and an instructor guide which provide four hours of instruction.
Education; Industrial and Technical Education; Psychology
Dist - NUSTC **Prod** - NUSTC

Motor Operators 60 MIN
VHS
Piping and Valves Series
Color (PRO)
$600.00, $1500.00 purchase _ #GMMOP
Introduces motor operators and associated equipment such as limit and torque switches. Describes the parts and operation of a motor operators, limit and torque switches and maintenance and adjustment. Part of a six - part series on piping and valves, which is part of a set on general and mechanical maintenance. Includes 10 textbooks and an instructor guide which provide four hours of instruction.
Education; Industrial and Technical Education; Psychology
Dist - NUSTC **Prod** - NUSTC

Motor Patterns of Polar Bears 12 MIN
16mm
Color (H C T)
LC 76-703729
Illustrates the typical motor patterns of polar bears, including swimming, walking, trotting, galloping, diving and wading. Shows the bears in their natural habitat in the Spitzbergen Island group in the Arctic near Norway. Demonstrates, through scenes photographed underwater, that the hind legs act only as a rudder while the forelegs are used for propulsion.
Geography - World; Psychology; Science - Natural
Dist - PSUPCR **Prod** - SCHEIN 1965

Motor skill acquisition 19 MIN
VHS
Sports science series
Color; PAL (T J H)
PdS29.50 purchase
Defines and discusses open and closed motor skills; the three mechanisms involved in performing a skilled action; and the three stages of learning a motor skill. Features part of a seven - part series on the science behind sports and physical activity, suitable for health and physical education courses, coaching and fitness programs.
Physical Education and Recreation
Dist - EMFVL

Motor Skill Acquisition - 5 8 TO 37 MIN
VHS
Sports Science Series
Color (H)
$75.00 purchase
Presents the science behind sports and physical activity, including training, acquiring new motor skills and preventing injuries. Alternates scenes of athletes in practice and competition with views of anatomical models, commentary and graphics that explain the science and physiology behind movements. Program 5 defines and discusses motor skills, including open and closed skills, the three mechanisms involved in performing a skilled action, and the three stages of learning a motor skill.
Health and Safety; Physical Education and Recreation; Science - Natural
Dist - AITECH

Motor starters - combination and reversing 60 MIN
U-matic / VHS
Electrical maintenance training series; Module 1 - Control equipment
Color (IND)
Industrial and Technical Education
Dist - LEIKID **Prod** - LEIKID

Motor Systems and Reflexes 29 MIN
VHS / U-matic
Color (PRO)
Provides a background for diagnosing hyperkinetic and hypokinetic patients. Shows the procedures for examining patients for motor system disorders and lists the clues which can be found during a thorough physical examination.
Science - Natural
Dist - PRIMED **Prod** - PRIMED

Motor Testing
U-matic / 35mm strip
Physical Assessment - Neurologic System Series
Color
Health and Safety; Psychology
Dist - CONMED **Prod** - CONMED

Motor Training - Phase A 11 MIN
U-matic / VHS / 16mm
Aids for Teaching the Mentally Retarded Series
Color (C T S)
Uses unique devices and special exercises to stimulate the passive child to initate activity and to help him understand cause and effect relationships.
Education
Dist - IFB **Prod** - THORNE 1964

Motor vehicle engineering crafts - workshop practice series
Checking steering geometry - Unit E 58 MIN
Overhauling a mechanical petrol pump - Unit A 40 MIN
Overhauling an S U carburettor - Unit B 31 MIN
Removing, examining and refitting a clutch - Unit C 36 MIN
Spill timing an inline diesel fuel pump - Unit D 54 MIN
Dist - EMFVL

Motor Vehicle Laws 28 MIN
16mm
Sportsmanlike Driving Series no 9
B&W (H A)
LC FIA68-919
Presents questions and answers concerning driver licensing, vehicular equipment, speed laws, road racing reckless driving, signaling, traffic control devices, and various driver violations which can result from lack of knowledge or understanding.
Health and Safety; Social Science
Dist - GPN **Prod** - AAA 1967

Motorcycle 4 MIN
16mm
Color (H C)
Presents a subjective documentary cinepoem on the female's sexual attraction to motorcycles.
Psychology; Sociology
Dist - CFS **Prod** - CFS 1968

Motorcycle Challenges - Riding Techniques
16mm
Color
LC 76-702697
Shows basic motorcycle riding techniques.
Physical Education and Recreation
Dist - USNAC **Prod** - USAF 1975

Motorcycle Driving Tactics 15 MIN
U-matic / VHS / 16mm
Color (J) (SPANISH)
Features pointers for motorcyclists involving excesses of speed. Includes staged collisions of motorcycles and automobiles.
Health and Safety; Physical Education and Recreation
Dist - AIMS **Prod** - CAHILL 1971

The Motorcycle Experience 15 MIN
16mm
Color (H C A)
LC 76-700513
Dramatizes the importance of maintaining a constant awareness while riding a motorcycle.
Health and Safety; Physical Education and Recreation
Dist - FFORIN **Prod** - STNLYL 1976

Motorcycle Maintenance 59 MIN
U-matic / VHS / 16mm
(A PRO)
#VT1058
Shows the viewer how to service a motorcycle and perform the common minor repairs necessary to keep a motorcycle running safely and well. Includes such topics as tools, chain care and replacement, cable adjustment, oil change, electrical system, grakes, points, plugs and timing, filters, fork maintenance and troubleshooting. Explains each procedure in detail. Instructed by Steve Kimball, Managing Editor, 'Cycle World' magazine.
Industrial and Technical Education
Dist - RMIBHF **Prod** - RMIBHF

Motorcycle Maintenance - EZ4U 59 MIN
BETA / VHS
Color
Demonstrates servicing a motorcycle and taking care of common minor repairs. Features Steve Kimball, managing editor of Cycle World Magazine.
Industrial and Technical Education
Dist - MOHOMV **Prod** - MOHOMV

Motorcycle Maintenance - EZUU 59 MIN
VHS
Color (H C A PRO)
$20.00 purchase _ #TA228
Shows how to service a motorcycle and take care of minor repairs.
Industrial and Technical Education
Dist - AAVIM **Prod** - AAVIM 1990

Motorcycle Safety 11 MIN
16mm
Color (H C A)
LC 81-701537
Uses interviews and simulated crashes to address the issue of motorcycle safety. First shown on the CBS program 30 Minutes.
Health and Safety
Dist - MOKIN **Prod** - CBSTV 1981

Motorcycle Safety 23 MIN
16mm / U-matic / VHS
Color (J)
$515.00, $250.00 purchase _ #80515; LC 81-700049
Describes safety rules to follow when riding a motorcycle. Discusses inspection and maintenance of cycle safety equipment and illustrates protective clothing.
Health and Safety
Dist - CORF **Prod** - CENTRO 1981

Motorcycle safety 19 MIN
16mm / VHS / BETA / U-matic
Color; PAL (G)
PdS125, PdS133 purchase
Discusses clothing, bike maintenance, breaking techniques and handling in traffic and open roads.
Health and Safety; Industrial and Technical Education
Dist - EDPAT

Motorcycle Safety - Helmet Effectiveness 22 MIN
16mm
Color
LC 80-701862
Presents traffic accident experts discussing the role of helmets in reducing the severity of motorcycle injuries. Shows that, although some bikers complain that the helmets are inconvenient, uncomfortable and expensive, they can prevent a minor injury from turning into a fatality.
Health and Safety
Dist - USNAC **Prod** - NHTSA 1980

Motorcycle Safety - Sharing the Road 14 MIN
U-matic / VHS / 16mm
Color (J)
LC 78-700836
Dramatizes urban and rural traffic scenes and outlines rules for safe operation of motorcycles in traffic. Describes proper clothing and protective gear to wear while riding, reviews procedures for examining a motorcycle before riding and illustrates several potentially hazardous traffic situations.
Guidance and Counseling; Health and Safety; Physical Education and Recreation
Dist - EBEC **Prod** - EBEC 1977

Motorcycle Safety Tips 14 MIN
16mm / U-matic / VHS
Color
LC 74-700623
Demonstrates a variety of basic safety rules for motorcycle riders using live - action enactments of various traffic situations.
Health and Safety; Physical Education and Recreation; Social Science
Dist - PFP **Prod** - PFP 1973

Motorcycles 29 MIN
U-matic / VHS
Right Way Series
Color
Describes basic operating procedures and traffic interaction.
Health and Safety
Dist - PBS **Prod** - SCETV 1982

Motorcycles and Helmets 30 MIN
BETA / VHS
Last Chance Garage Series
Color
Features motorcycles, helmets and cycles. Shows how to assemble a clutch. Explains the gears and flywheel.
Industrial and Technical Education
Dist - CORF **Prod** - WGBHTV

Motorcycling - Britain's golden years 54 MIN
VHS
Color (G)
$29.95 purchase _ #405
Traces the history of the motorcycle industry in Great Britain from its inception to its demise in the late 1970s. Features British motorsports commentator Murray Walker. Include archival footage of 80 years of British racing and close - up shots of restored BSAs, Matchlesses, Nortons, Triumphs, taken at one of Britain's largest motorcycle museums.
Business and Economics; Geography - World; History - World; Industrial and Technical Education; Physical Education and Recreation
Dist - IHF

Motors and Generators 7 MIN
U-matic / VHS / 16mm
Basic Electricity Series
Color (H C A)
Deals with dart notation and direction of current. Presents an experiment with a free - moving wire in a magnetic field. Provides a diagrammatic explanation of the motor effect. Describes the right - hand rule, the left - hand rule and the commutator.
Science - Physical
Dist - IFB **Prod** - STFD 1979

Motors and Generators, Pt 1 - DC Motors and Generators 35 MIN
16mm
B&W
LC FIE63-66
Describes the construction, uses and principles governing the operation of DC motors and generators.
Industrial and Technical Education
Dist - USNAC **Prod** - USA 1961

Motors and Generators, Pt 2 - AC Motors and Generators 25 MIN
16mm
B&W
LC FIE63-67
Describes the design, characteristics and operation of AC generators and motors.
Industrial and Technical Education
Dist - USNAC **Prod** - USA 1961

Motors and Motor Controllers Series
AC motor controller maintenance - 1 60 MIN
AC motor controller maintenance - 2 60 MIN
DC Motor Controller Maintenance - 1 60 MIN
DC Motor Controller Maintenance - 2 60 MIN
Motor Branch Circuit Protection 60 MIN
Motor Operators 60 MIN
Single - Phase AC Induction Motor Maintenance 60 MIN
Synchronous Motors and Controller Maintenance 60 MIN
Three - Phase AC Induction Motor Maintenance 60 MIN
Dist - NUSTC

Motors, Pt 1 22 MIN
VHS / U-matic
Color (IND) (SPANISH)
Gives a history of motors. Explains the differences between AC and DC currents. Gives nine items required to completely identify a motor.
Education; Foreign Language; Industrial and Technical Education
Dist - TAT **Prod** - TAT

Motors, Pt 2 22 MIN
U-matic / VHS
Color (IND) (SPANISH)
Defines NEMA. Covers three phase current and induced current in a rotor. Discusses enclosures, mountings, and insulations.
Education; Foreign Language; Industrial and Technical Education
Dist - TAT **Prod** - TAT

Motors, Tape 5 - Troubleshooting 60 MIN
U-matic / VHS
Electrical Equipment Maintenance Series
Color (IND) (SPANISH)
Industrial and Technical Education
Dist - ITCORP **Prod** - ITCORP

Motors, Tape 4 - DC Motors Commutator Maintenance, Brushes, Brush Holders 60 MIN
VHS / U-matic
Electrical Equipment Maintenance Series
Color (IND) (SPANISH)
Industrial and Technical Education
Dist - ITCORP **Prod** - ITCORP

Motors, Tape 1 - Introduction, Motor Disassembly, Testing Bearings 60 MIN
VHS / U-matic
Electrical Equipment Maintenance Series
Color (IND) (SPANISH)

Industrial and Technical Education
Dist - ITCORP **Prod** - ITCORP

Motors, Tape 3 - Slip Rings, Brushes, Single Phase, Centrifugal Switch and Capacitor 60 MIN
U-matic / VHS
Electrical Equipment Maintenance Series
Color (IND) (SPANISH)
Industrial and Technical Education
Dist - ITCORP **Prod** - ITCORP

Motors, Tape 2 - Bearing Replacement, 60 MIN
VHS / U-matic
Electrical Equipment Maintenance Series
Color (IND) (SPANISH)
Industrial and Technical Education
Dist - ITCORP **Prod** - ITCORP

Mots difficiles 16 MIN
VHS
Color (I J H) (FRENCH)
$39.95 purchase _ #W3462
Presents native speakers of French in practical situations, using idiomatic expressions. Helps students develop understanding of French use of language, intonation and gesture and increase skill in conversation. Includes script.
Foreign Language
Dist - GPC

Motu, the Sentinel 11 MIN
16mm
Color (I J H)
LC FIA67-501
Tells the story of a young boy who, in trying to defend his land from the hated enemy, comes to realize the strength of friendship.
Guidance and Counseling; Psychology
Dist - CINEPC **Prod** - TAHARA 1967

Mouches Volantes 68 MIN
16mm
Color; B&W (C)
$1680.00
Experimental film by Larry Gottheim.
Fine Arts
Dist - AFA **Prod** - AFA 1976

Moulay Idriss 11 MIN
16mm
B&W
Records the journey of the Moslem pilgrims who were unable to travel to Mecca as they converge on this holy meeting place in Morocco where the faithful may come and receive exoneration.
Geography - World; Religion and Philosophy
Dist - RADIM **Prod** - FILIM

Mould maker 4.5 MIN
VHS / 16mm
Good works 1 series
Color (A PRO)
$40.00 purchase _ #BPN195804
Presents the occupation of a mould maker. Gives a profile of a young person who is either undergoing an apprenticeship or has recently completed training in this field. Takes the viewer on a tour of this person's workplace and explains the practical skills and training offered by employers and schools. Gives a better understanding of the demand for skilled workers today and the potential for personal growth.
Guidance and Counseling
Dist - RMIBHF **Prod** - RMIBHF

Mould, the myth and the microbe 50 MIN
VHS
Horizon series
Color (C PRO H A)
PdS99 purchase
Examines the work of Howard Florey and Norman Heatley in the development of penicillin. Includes footage shot by Florey showing the administration of penicillin for the first time, in 1943, to soldiers in Africa.
Science - Natural
Dist - BBCENE

The Moulds We Live with 22 MIN
16mm
Color
Provides examples of common moulds to which people are exposed constantly, such as aspergillus, penicillium and fusarium which can be both benefactor and enemy.
Science - Natural
Dist - UTORMC **Prod** - UTORMC

Mount Desert 21 MIN
16mm
Color (H)
LC 77-703228
Documents activities on Mount Desert, a resort island off the coast of Maine.
Geography - United States; Sociology
Dist - USNAC **Prod** - USNPS 1969

Mount Holyoke
VHS
Campus clips series
Color (H C A)
$29.95 purchase _ #CC0055V
Takes a video visit to the campus of Mount Holyoke College in Massachusetts. Shows many of the distinctive features of the campus, and interviews students about their experiences. Provides information on the composition of the student body, professors, academics, social life, housing, and other subjects.
Education
Dist - CAMV

Mount Mc Kinley - the Land Eternal 24 MIN
16mm
Color (A)
LC 77-703154
Traces the interdependence of life through the seasons in the subarctic region of Alaska.
Geography - United States; Science - Natural
Dist - USNAC **Prod** - USNPS 1975

Mount McKinley Hang Glide 19 MIN
16mm / U-matic / VHS
Color (J H A)
Joins four young Americans as they attempt to hang glide from the top of Mount McKinley.
Physical Education and Recreation
Dist - CORF **Prod** - ABCSRT 1978

Mount Rainier 28 MIN
VHS
Color (G)
$29.95 purchase _ #V42
Discovers the scenic and geological wonders plus early pioneer history of Mount Rainier.
Geography - United States
Dist - INSTRU **Prod** - USNPS

Mount Rainier National Park, WA 28 MIN
BETA / VHS
Color
Shows life in its most beautiful forms as one explores the majestic beauty of Mount Rainier and its surrounding national park.
Geography - United States
Dist - CBSC **Prod** - CBSC

Mount Rainier - Olympic - northwest treasures 60 MIN
VHS
Great national parks - Set II series
Color; CC (G)
$24.95 purchase _ #996
Witnesses Mount Rainer's great flash floods called 'jokulhlaups.' Looks at the effects of Rainier's twin forces - volcanic heat and glacial cold. Discovers Olympic's three distinct landscapes. Views Olympic's Hoh Rain Forest and hikes glacier - sculpted mountains. Examines massive coastal rocks and delicate tide pools teeming with life. Part of a series on national parks.
Geography - United States
Dist - APRESS **Prod** - READ

Mount Rushmore
U-matic / VHS
Color (P I J)
Introduces children to one of man's artworks on nature. Narrated by Burgess Meredith.
Geography - United States; History - United States
Dist - KTVID **Prod** - CNVID

Mount Rushmore - Four Faces on a Mountain 30 MIN
BETA / VHS
B&W
Reveals the faces of Presidents Washington, Jefferson, Lincoln, and Theodore Roosevelt being carved from Mount Rushmore. Includes a recounting of the struggles and challenges each of these four great presidents overcame to help make our nation what it is today.
Geography - United States; History - United States
Dist - CBSC **Prod** - CBSC

The Mount Snow Ski Week 19 MIN
U-matic
Color
Illustrates a week of skiing and nightlife at Mount Snow, a Vermont winter resort. Shows both skiing lessons and entertainment.
Geography - United States; Physical Education and Recreation
Dist - MTP **Prod** - MSSKI

The Mount St Helens volcano - Fire and life
CD-ROM
Color; CAV (J H C G)
$249.00 purchase
Uses the May 1980 dramatic eruption of Mount St Helens and its aftermath to show students that geologic events and processes actively shape the Earth. Features 20 minutes of video clips and over 3,000 slides in an interactive tour of volcanoes, the eruption, plants, animals, people and the land around Mount St Helens. Interactive computer software includes database of slides and clips and a 'documentary maker' feature. Print materials and study guide also enclosed.
Fine Arts; Geography - World; Science - Physical
Dist - BULFRG

Mount St Helens - what Geologists Learned 40 MIN
VHS
Color (H)
$79.95 purchase _ #ES 8200
Incorporates footage of the eruption of Mt St Helens and subsequent eruptions to explore the causes of volcanism. Interviews scientists who explain what new knowledge has been gained from the studies of the Mt St Helens eruption.
Geography - World; Science; Science - Physical
Dist - SCTRES **Prod** - SCTRES

Mount Trashmore 4 MIN
16mm
Color
LC 75-700687
Discusses the solid - waste disposal problem facing many communities. Shows how Virginia Beach, Virginia, solved it by combining its trash with that from neighboring communities to build a large sanitary landfill on top of the ground. Shows how the landfill will be used as a recreational area when completed.
Health and Safety; Physical Education and Recreation; Social Science
Dist - USNAC **Prod** - USEPA 1974

Mount Up, Vol III 60 MIN
VHS
Basic Horsemanship Series
Color (G)
$65.00 purchase _ #6 - 035 - 105P
Teaches English and Western riding skills. Part three of three parts on horse training.
Agriculture; Physical Education and Recreation
Dist - VEP **Prod** - VEP

Mount Vernon Blacks 30 MIN
U-matic / VHS
Color
History - United States; Sociology
Dist - SYLWAT **Prod** - RCOMTV 1983

Mount Washington among the clouds 30 MIN
VHS
Color (G)
$19.95 purchase
Portrays 1852 - 1908 era life in the resort community at the top of Mount Washington in New Hampshire, at the end of the newly - built cog railway. Views the town's newspaper, hotels and the railway construction.
Geography - United States; History - United States
Dist - NEFILM

The Mountain 15 MIN
VHS
Color (K P I J H)
$249.00 purchase
Presents an animated film narrated by Dick Van Dyke which offers the allegory of the mountain. Reveals that the mountain, beautiful and enticing, lures climbers to its slopes, but a series of accidents on the mountain leads the villagers to over - react to the problem using simplistic and ineffective solutions. Shows how reason ultimately prevails and illustrates problem solving skill for a number of situations ranging from substance abuse to other social issues.
Fine Arts; Literature and Drama; Psychology
Dist - FMSP **Prod** - FWP 1979

The Mountain 15 MIN
U-matic / VT1 / VHS
Walking with Grandfather series
Color (G)
$39.95 purchase, $35.00 rental
Tells of Great Wolf crying because he has lost his eyes through his own foolishness. Reveals that Little Mouse Sister gives him her eyes and they journey to Sacred Lake to ask for help for the blind mouse. The journey is difficult and they overcome many obstacles to reach Sacred Lake on a high mountain. Great Wolf makes offerings and leaves the mouse to discover the promise of Sacred Lake. She is told to jump higher and higher and she obeys, opening her eyes to discover that she has become a mighty eagle. Part of a series on storytelling by elders produced by Phil Lucas Productions, Inc.
Guidance and Counseling; Literature and Drama; Social Science
Dist - NAMPBC

Mountain and Desert Survival - Desert Survival 31 MIN
16mm
Color
LC FIE63-66
Outlines principles of desert survival. Shows procedures for promoting rescue and maintaining personnel health and comfort. Points out sources of food and water, explains shelter construction and discusses use of signal fires and mirrors. Emphasizes the importance of calmness and clear thinking.
Guidance and Counseling; Health and Safety; Social Science; Sociology
Dist - USNAC **Prod** - USAF 1963

Mountain and Desert Survival - Mountain Survival 28 MIN
16mm
Color
LC 75-700795
Outlines principles of survival in mountainous regions, describing procedures for promoting rescue and maintaining personal health and comfort. Shows how to obtain food and water, construct a shelter and build signal fires. Emphasizes the necessity of calmness and clear thinking.
Geography - World; Health and Safety; Physical Education and Recreation
Dist - USNAC **Prod** - USAF 1963

The Mountain Awakens 30 MIN
U-matic / VHS
Alpine Ski School Series
Color
Highlights the sport of down - hill skiing, the selection and use of equipment and apparel. Demonstrates the basics of starting, steering and stopping on skis.
Physical Education and Recreation
Dist - PBS **Prod** - PBS 1983

Mountain building in the Western Himalayas 25 MIN
U-matic / VHS
Plate tectonics series
Color (H C)
$250.00 purchase _ #HP - 5779C
Examines the structural and mineralogic evidence which explains the geologic events of the Himalayan Mountains. Reveals that most such mountains result from two geologic processes - magmatism at continental margins and crustal uplift after continents collide. The Himalayas appear to have been formed with unusual speed and continue to grow through the folding and thrusting caused by the collision of the Indian subcontinent with Asia. Part of the Plate Tectonics series.
Geography - World; Science - Physical
Dist - CORF **Prod** - BBCTV 1989

Mountain Community of the Himalayas 11 MIN
16mm
Communities and Families of Our World Series
Color (P I J)
LC FIA65-524
Depicts life styles in a Himalayan village. Shows how trade with the lowland peoples is accomplished.
Geography - World; Social Science
Dist - ATLAP **Prod** - ATLAP 1964

Mountain Dance 12 MIN
16mm
Color
LC 76-703248
Attempts to fuse dancing and nature and fit the choreography and filming to the natural element.
Fine Arts
Dist - CANFDC **Prod** - CANFDC 1975

The Mountain Does it for Me 12 MIN
16mm
Color (I)
LC 81-700473
Shows how children with cerebral palsy are given skiing lessons in Colorado.
Psychology
Dist - CRYSP **Prod** - OAKCRK 1981

Mountain Driving 20 MIN
16mm
Color (J)
LC FIA66-1686
Uses cartoon sequences and scenes of narrow, winding roads to demonstrate problems of mountain driving. Discusses acceleration, passing, turnouts, overheating, parking, high altitude, soft shoulders, deceleration and curves.
Health and Safety
Dist - AVED **Prod** - MCKINY 1964

Mountain Family in Europe 9 MIN
U-matic / VHS / 16mm
Color (K P)
LC 73-715381
Contrasts farming in the United States with the traditional style of farming carried on by an Alpine family. Includes scenes of the family members as they milk, make butter and cheese, bake bread, and reap and dry the hay.
Agriculture; Geography - World; Social Science; Sociology
Dist - FI **Prod** - IFFB 1972

Mountain Farm 32 MIN
16mm / U-matic / VHS
Color (H)
Artist Paul Sample demonstrates and discusses his approach to painting.
Fine Arts
Dist - IFB **Prod** - DARTC 1960

Mountain Farmer 12 MIN
16mm
Color (J)
LC 79-700975
Presents a tribute to a strong, independent man who tills the soil on his small farm with a horse and a wooden plow, finding joy in his work and harmony with the land.
Agriculture; Geography - United States; Social Science; Sociology
Dist - APPAL **Prod** - APPAL 1971

Mountain Farmer 9 MIN
U-matic
B&W
Pays tribute to a strong and independent mountaineer, Lee Banks, on his small mountain farm.
Agriculture; Geography - United States; Social Science
Dist - APPAL **Prod** - APPAL 1973

Mountain Flowers 14 MIN
16mm
Color
LC 77-700056
Shows wildflowers in various environments, from the prairies to the alpine tundra of the highest peaks. Notes the ecological conditions under which various plants grow.
Science - Natural
Dist - WESTWN **Prod** - WESTWN 1976

Mountain Flying 23 MIN
16mm / U-matic / VHS
Color
Explains that flying around or over mountains can be hazardous, with fast - changing weather and unpredictable air currents. Pilots should also know the capabilities of their aircraft and peculiarities of local terrain and weather.
Industrial and Technical Education; Science - Physical; Social Science
Dist - USNAC **Prod** - FAAFL

Mountain Forests 15 MIN
16mm / U-matic / VHS
Mountain Habitat Series
Color (I J H)
Portrays a variety of mountain forests, from straggling spruce at timberline to dense stands of both coniferous and deciduous trees in the valleys below. Shows how the forests harbor the greatest number of plants and animals to be found in the Rockies.
Geography - United States; Science - Natural
Dist - BCNFL **Prod** - KARVF 1982

Mountain Fun 13 MIN
16mm
Travelbug Series
Color
Shows the famous Cog railway to the top of Pike's Peak with the Manitou Incline, the Royal Gorge and Garden of the Gods.
Geography - United States
Dist - SFI **Prod** - SFI

Mountain Glaciers 19 MIN
16mm
Color (C A)
LC FIA67-502
Shows the formation and composition of mountain glaciers. Discusses movement patterns and glacial effects on land surfaces. Pictures Glacier Bay in Alasska, the Tasman Valley in New Zealand and the Victoria Mountains in America.
Science - Physical
Dist - OSUMPD **Prod** - OSUMPD 1966

Mountain Gorilla 16 MIN
16mm
Color (C T)
LC 76-701855
An intensive year - long behavior study shows the environment, behavior characteristics and social organizations of the mountain gorilla in his natural habitat in central Africa.
Geography - World; Science - Natural
Dist - PSUPCR **Prod** - NSF 1959

Mountain Habitat Series
Glacier country 16 MIN
High Country 16 MIN
Mountain Forests 15 MIN
Rivers of the Rockies 16 MIN
Timberline 16 MIN
Dist - BCNFL

Mountain Heritage - the Appalachians 29 MIN
U-matic / VHS / 16mm
Planet of Man Series
Color (H C)
Presents theories for the creation of the Appalachian mountain belt, suggesting that the collision of two earlier continents and the shrinking of an earlier ocean is inscribed and preserved in the rocks of Appalachia.
Geography - United States; Science - Physical
Dist - FI **Prod** - OECA 1978

Mountain in the Mist 29 MIN
U-matic
Artist at Work Series
Color
Demonstrates painting a landscape to teach aerial perspective.
Fine Arts
Dist - UMITV **Prod** - UMITV 1973

The Mountain is Yours 30 MIN
VHS / U-matic
Alpine Ski School Series
Color
Presents instruction in down - hill skiing techniques. Shows the step turn and gives a brief review of the Alpine Ski School series.
Physical Education and Recreation
Dist - PBS **Prod** - PBS 1983

Mountain lady 59 MIN
VHS
Color (I J H C G A R)
$29.95 purchase, $10.00 rental _ #35 - 8520 - 1518
Features country - and - western music star Stuart Hamblen, who tells the story of Old Tom, his Alaskan hunting and fishing companion whose granddaughter Heidi joined him for a summer of camping in the Alaska wilderness.
Physical Education and Recreation; Religion and Philosophy
Dist - APH **Prod** - SPAPRO

Mountain Life Zone Communities 21 MIN
16mm / VHS / U-matic
Color (I J H C A)
LC 81-706473; 81-700671
A revised version of Life Zones Of The Central Rockies. Examines the grassland, forest and alpine zones of the Rocky Mountains. Investigates the plants and animals that have adapted to each region.
Geography - United States; Science - Natural
Dist - IFB **Prod** - BERLET 1976

Mountain Life Zones 20 MIN
U-matic / VHS
Color (J)
LC 82-706780
Demonstrates how a series of distinct life zones are passed in travelling up the side of a tall mountain. Explains that temperatures, soil moisture and rainfall govern the life zones and provide insights into determining the effects of the physical environment.
Science - Natural; Science - Physical
Dist - AWSS **Prod** - AWSS 1982

Mountain Man 98 MIN
16mm / U-matic / VHS
Color (P I J)
Documents the story of Palan Clark's successful fight to save a magnificent wilderness and its animals. Reveals that he learns from naturalist John Muir the need to save the land from ruthless destruction and goes to Washington to win President Lincoln's support for his momentous cause.
History - United States; Science - Natural
Dist - LUF **Prod** - LUF 1979

Mountain man go home 30 MIN
VHS
Color (J H C G A R)
$24.95 purchase, $10.00 rental _ #35 - 8805 - 19
Portrays an educated woman who is ashamed of her 'hillbilly' father. Shows that her opinion changes when she learns how her father sacrificed so that she could attend college. Stars Buddy Ebsen as the father.
Sociology
Dist - APH **Prod** - CPH

Mountain man, go home 30 MIN
VHS
Crossroads of life series
Color (G R)
$24.95 purchase _ #87EE0805
Tells the story of an educated woman who is ashamed of her 'hillbilly' father until she learns of the sacrifices he made to send her to college.
Guidance and Counseling; Literature and Drama; Religion and Philosophy
Dist - CPH **Prod** - CPH

The Mountain Men 100 MIN
16mm
Color
Follows two trappers who try to survive natural dangers and the dwindling beaver trade. Stars Charlton Heston.
Fine Arts
Dist - SWANK **Prod** - CPC

The Mountain Men 15 MIN
U-matic / VHS / 16mm
B&W (I J)
Dramatizes the role of the fur trappers as explorers and trailblazers in the Westward Expansion of the United States. Shows early water routes, winter camp, spring trapping and trading activities. A short version of 'FUR TRAPPERS WESTWARD.'.
History - United States
Dist - BARR **Prod** - BARR 1964

Mountain Men 15 MIN
16mm / U-matic / VHS
American Scrapbook Series
Color (I)
Studies the people who roamed the wilderness in the mid - 1800's. Compares the lives of white trappers and hunters with those of the Indians. Re - creates scenes from the trappers' annual get - together.
History - United States; Social Science
Dist - GPN **Prod** - WVIZTV

The Mountain Men 16 MIN
U-matic / VHS / 16mm
Growth of America's West Series
Color (I J H)
LC 79-701277
Discusses the mountain men as an important force in the growth and development of America's West. Explains how these trappers learned to survive in the wilderness, discovered trails through the Rocky Mountains, trapped beaver and helped pioneers cross over to the farmland of Oregon and California. Examines the circumstances that led to the movement of trappers to the wilderness.
History - United States
Dist - PHENIX **Prod** - CAPFLM 1979

Mountain Monarchs 26 MIN
16mm
Color
Looks at the ways creatures like mountain goats, Alaskan Dall sheep and golden eagles survive the severe mountain environment.
Science - Natural
Dist - STOUFP **Prod** - STOUFP 1982

Mountain Music 9 MIN
U-matic / VHS / 16mm
Color (J)
LC 76-700707
Considers the struggle between technology and nature using three - dimensional clay figures and stop - motion photography.
Fine Arts; Sociology
Dist - PFP **Prod** - VINTN 1975

Mountain Music of Peru 60 MIN
U-matic / VHS / 16mm
Color (A)
Portrays the musical culture of the Andes, its importance to its people, its origin, and its function in preserving Indian cultural identity.
Fine Arts; Social Science
Dist - CNEMAG **Prod** - CNEMAG 1984

Mountain of the Goddess 25 MIN
16mm
Land of the Dragon Series
Color (H C A)
Describes how Dawa, a Yak herder and his family live in the region of Bhutan known as Chomolhari. Explains how Chomolhari, a sacred mountain, is considered a throne of the gods.
Geography - World
Dist - LANDMK **Prod** - NOMDFI 1983

Mountain Park 14 MIN
16mm
Journal Series
Color
LC 75-704324
Considers the history of the area surrounding Banff National Park in Alberta, Canada.
Geography - World; Science - Natural
Dist - FIARTS **Prod** - FIARTS 1973

The Mountain People 24 MIN
U-matic / VHS / 16mm
Color (J A)
LC 75-702898
Presents a documentary on the people of the Southern Appalachian region which includes parts of Alabama, Georgia, Mississippi, North Carolina, South Carolina, Tennessee and Virginia. Tells of their poverty and their exploitation by timber and coal speculators beginning in the early 20th century. Discusses self - help efforts and government projects designed to relieve social problems of the area.
Geography - United States; Sociology
Dist - WOMBAT **Prod** - GRATV 1975

Mountain People 52 MIN
16mm
Color
LC 78-701268
Documents the lifestyle of older mountain farmers in rural West Virginia.
Geography - United States; Sociology
Dist - CINEMV **Prod** - FIRESC 1978

Mountain People 14 MIN
16mm
Places People Live Series
Color (I)
LC 76-713011
Describes the force of tradition in the Swiss village of Guarda. Tells how a hardworking group of people, insulated from the outside world, have shaped and retained their harmonious way of life in the steep mountains. Compares the Gurungs of Nepal, living on the slopes of the Himalaya Mountains, whose culture has endured with little change for centuries.
Psychology; Science - Natural; Social Science; Sociology
Dist - SF **Prod** - CLAIB 1970

Mountain People, Pt 1 26 MIN
16mm
Color
LC 78-701268
Documents the lifestyle of older mountain farmers in rural West Virginia.
Sociology
Dist - CINEMV **Prod** - FIRESC 1978

Mountain People, Pt 2 26 MIN
16mm
Color
LC 78-701268
Documents the lifestyle of older mountain farmers in rural West Virginia.
Sociology
Dist - CINEMV **Prod** - FIRESC 1978

The Mountain people - the Caucasian Republic of Georgia 52 MIN
VHS
Icebreaker - family life in the Soviet Union series
Color (I J H)
$295.00 purchase
Visits the Guraspishvili family which lives in the village of Gremi, a small settlement in the foothills of the Caucasus Mountains of Georgia, where people commonly live beyond 100 years. Observes a family of five generations spread through a number of stone houses in the village. The village is an ancient Christian community built on grapes and wine and the crafts of the past - textiles, music, metalwork and woodwork. Part of a six - part series on ethnically different families in the Soviet Union.
Geography - World; Religion and Philosophy; Sociology
Dist - LANDMK **Prod** - LANDMK 1989

Mountain Peoples of Central Asia - Afghanistan Series
Casting iron plow shares - Tajik 11 MIN
Grinding Wheat - Tajik 7 MIN
Threshing Wheat - Tajik 9 MIN
Weaving Cloth - Pushto 9 MIN
Dist - IFF

Mountain peoples of Central Asia series
Baking oven bread - tajik 11 MIN
Baking unleavened bread - pushtu 10 MIN
Boy's Games - Pushtu 5 MIN
Building a bridge - Tajik 10 MIN
Buzkashi - Afghan tribes 8 MIN
Casting iron plow shares - Tajik 11 MIN
Making Felt Rugs - Pushtu 9 MIN
Making Gunpowder - Tajik 10 MIN
Pottery making - Tajik 15 MIN
Shearing Yaks - Tajik 9 MIN
Threshing Wheat 9 MIN
Weaving Cloth - Pushtu 9 MIN
Dist - IFF

Mountain Rescue 14 MIN
16mm
Outdoor Education Mountaineering Series
Color
LC 74-703426
Demonstrates basic mountain rescue techniques.
Physical Education and Recreation
Dist - SF **Prod** - MORLAT 1973

Mountain Rescue Workers 5 MIN
16mm / U-matic / VHS
European Studies - Germany Series
Color (H C A)
LC 76-700761
Shows the operation of a typical German rescue effort following an avalanche.
Geography - World
Dist - IFB **Prod** - MFAFRG 1973

Mountain Silence 18 MIN
16mm
Color (I)
Shows hearing - impaired people participating in many outdoor summer and winter activities at Mountain Silence, a camp school for the deaf in the Rocky Mountains. Shows them skiing, rafting, horseback riding, dancing, miming and generally gaining the confidence they need to become successful adults.
Education
Dist - CRYSP **Prod** - FLMRAN

Mountain Songs, Pt 1 15 MIN
VHS / U-matic
Song Sampler Series
Color (P)
LC 81-707029
Reviews the meaning of the terms refrain and ballad. Presents the songs She'll Be Coming Round The Mountain, Springfield Mountain and Down In The Valley.
Fine Arts
Dist - GPN **Prod** - JCITV 1981

Mountain Songs, Pt 2 15 MIN
VHS / U-matic
Song Sampler Series
Color (P)
LC 81-707029
Reviews the meaning of the terms refrain and ballad. Presents the songs She'll Be Coming Round The Mountain, Springfield Mountain and Down In The Valley.
Fine Arts
Dist - GPN **Prod** - JCITV 1981

Mountain Springtime 25 MIN
16mm
Color
LC 76-702450
Features the Canadian Rockies, showing the game and flowers of the area.
Geography - World; Physical Education and Recreation
Dist - MACBLO **Prod** - MACBLO 1975

The Mountain States 25 MIN
U-matic / VHS / 16mm
United States Geography Series
Color (I J)
Looks at the characteristics of the mountain states - Colorado, Idaho, Montana, Nevada, Utah and Wyoming which make up one - fourth of the continental United States, yet contain less than four percent of the population.
Geography - United States
Dist - NGS **Prod** - NGS 1983

Mountain Tops 27 MIN
16mm / U-matic / VHS
Color (I)
LC 81-700308
Presents the story of a paraplegic who adapts traditional mountain - climbing gear in order to scale a 13,000 - foot peak in the High Sierras.
Physical Education and Recreation; Psychology
Dist - PFP **Prod** - STNLYL 1981

Mountain Water - a Key to Survival 16 MIN
U-matic / VHS
Natural Science Specials Series Module Blue
Color (I)
Deals with the management of water in mountain regions, including dams, reservoirs, treatment plants and the process of terracing.
Geography - World; Science - Natural
Dist - AITECH **Prod** - COPFC 1973

Mountain Waters 16 MIN
16mm
Color (I J)
Shows how lakes are formed in the high mountains of the northwestern United States.
Geography - United States; Science - Natural; Science - Physical
Dist - MMP **Prod** - MMP 1958

Mountain Wolf Woman - 1884 - 1960 17 MIN
Cassette / U-matic / BETA / VHS
Women's history and literature media series
Color (P I J H G)
$95.00 purchase, $40.00 rental
Presents the story of a Winnebago woman, Mountain Wolf Woman, narrated by her granddaughter Naomi Russell. Photographs Winnebago beadwork, ribbon applique, moccasins, baskets, scenes from a Winnebago powwow and landscape views from around Black River Falls, Wisconsin, where Mountain Wolf Woman was born. Irene

Thundercloud, a Winnebago elder, speaks Winnebago at the beginning and end of the tape and sings a Winnebago wedding song. Part of a series on women's history and literature created by Jocelyn Riley. Resource guide available separately.
History - United States; History - World; Social Science
Dist - HEROWN **Prod** - HEROWN 1990

Mountaineering 10 MIN
16mm
Color (J H)
LC FIA67-5614
Stresses safety precautions in rock climbing at a Rocky Mountain camp.
Health and Safety; Physical Education and Recreation
Dist - SCHMUN **Prod** - MANSPR 1967

Mountainous Land 20 MIN
U-matic
Understanding Our World, Unit II - Geography We Should Know Series
Color (I)
Presents a study of peaks, timberline, mountain passes and valleys. Looks at a zinc mine deep in the Rockies, a ski resort and climbers on Mt Everest.
Geography - United States; Geography - World; Science - Physical
Dist - GPN **Prod** - KRMATV

Mountains 30 MIN
U-matic / VHS
Land and the People Series
Color
Explores the relationship between what people know, see and do and the mountains around them.
Science - Natural
Dist - MDCPB **Prod** - EKC

Mountains 60 MIN
VHS
Workshop in oils with William Palluth series
Color (J H C G)
$29.95 purchase _ #FHF143V
Shows how color is mixed and applied with brush and knife. Teaches how to achieve the illusion of depth in landscapes. Part of a series on oil painting by landscape artist William Palluth.
Fine Arts
Dist - CAMV

The Mountains 50.30 MIN
VHS / U-matic / 16mm
Canada - Five Portraits Series
Color; Mono (G) (FRENCH)
MV $350.00 _ MP $475.00 purchase, $50.00 rental
Features the rugged mountains of Western Canada. Six ranges are explored for the challenges they pose to men, for their streams of gold and for the secluded life offered to those who choose to live on the highest slopes or in distant valleys.
Geography - World
Dist - CTV **Prod** - CTV 1973

The Mountains 30 MIN
VHS / 16mm
Our Natural Heritage Series
Color (G)
$14.44 purchase _ #HSV4026
Explores mountains.
Psychology; Science - Natural
Dist - EDUCRT

The Mountains 14 MIN
VHS / 16mm / U-matic
Color (I J)
$240, $170, $200 purchase _ #A153
Explores the variety of mountain forms and the forces that created them. Shows some of the typical plants and animals that live in the forests, meadows, and rocky slopes of the mountain region.
Psychology; Science - Natural
Dist - BARR **Prod** - BARR 1970

Mountains 9 MIN
16mm / U-matic / VHS
Color (P I J)
Presents the geography of mountains - - differences between mountain peaks, ranges and systems, map symbols for mountains, the effect of mountains on the weather and mountain plant and animal life.
Science - Natural; Science - Physical
Dist - IU **Prod** - IU 1967

Mountains - a First Film 9 MIN
16mm / U-matic / VHS
Color (P I) (FRENCH)
LC 79-711110
Shows the variety of relationships between altitude, climate and life forms that exists as we descend from desert at the mountain base through forests and meadows to the tops of high mountains covered with snow and ice. Includes an introduction to the basic causes and effects of erosion and shows how mountain snows and streams help to provide our water supply.
Agriculture; Science - Natural; Science - Physical
Dist - PHENIX **Prod** - PHENIX 1969

Mountains and Mountain Building 15 MIN
16mm / U-matic / VHS
Natural Phenomena Series
Color (J)
LC 81-700682
Examines the forces that shape mountains.
Science - Physical
Dist - JOU **Prod** - JOU 1981

Mountains and Mountain Building - Nature's High Rise 19 MIN
U-matic / VHS
Natural Science Specials Series Module Green
Color (I)
Explores various kinds of mountain building and considers the theories of isostasy and continental drift.
Geography - World; Science - Physical
Dist - AITECH **Prod** - COPFC 1973

Mountains are for Painting 29 MIN
U-matic
Artist at Work Series
Color
Demonstrates how to draw landscapes by the highlighting of shadows, lights and texture.
Fine Arts
Dist - UMITV **Prod** - UMITV 1973

A Mountain's Domain 20 MIN
16mm
Color (J)
LC 78-701232
Shows the attractions of the area in Northeastern Australia known as the Gold Coast. Highlights the natural beauty of the coast as well as the inland rain forests. Features interviews with farmers, fishermen and those who serve the needs of the numerous tourists.
Geography - World; Sociology
Dist - AUIS **Prod** - FLMAUS 1976

Mountains Don't Care 20 MIN
16mm
Color (J A)
Two young people go on a mountain climbing expedition with an experienced older couple and learn many rules for safety in the mountains.
Health and Safety; Physical Education and Recreation
Dist - RARIG **Prod** - MTRES 1958

The Mountains - Headwaters 30 MIN
U-matic
Landscapes Series
(A)
Explains the mountain building process and shows the subalpine, timberline and alpine levels.
Science - Natural; Science - Physical
Dist - ACCESS **Prod** - ACCESS 1984

Mountains of gold 54 MIN
VHS
Decade of destruction series
Color (H C G)
$175.00 purchase, $75.00 rental
Depicts Brazil's untapped gold reserves where roughly 70 percent of its production is mined by freelance prospectors, who pan and dredge gold all over the forest on land licensed by the government to huge companies. Follows Jova, a prospector famous among his colleagues for his illegal gold strikes, as he plays hide and seek with the security forces of Brazil's largest mining multinational company.
Fine Arts; Industrial and Technical Education; Science - Natural
Dist - BULFRG **Prod** - COWELL 1990

Mountains, the 14 MIN
U-matic / VHS / 16mm
Color (I J)
LC 79-705052
Live action photography and graphics show mountain formations and the effects of glacial erosion. Close - up photography pictures cascading streams and flowered meadows, and the plants and animals found in forests, rock slides, slopes and other mountain habitats.
Science - Natural; Science - Physical
Dist - BARR **Prod** - BARR 1970

Mounting a Hubless Rotor on the FMC Brake Lathe 5 MIN
VHS / 16mm
Auto Mechanics Series
(G PRO)
$48.00 purchase _ #AM17
Shows how to mount a hubless rotor on the F.M.C. brake lathe.
Industrial and Technical Education
Dist - RMIBHF **Prod** - RMIBHF

Mounting a Rotor with Hub on the FMC Brake Lathe 5 MIN
VHS / 16mm
Auto Mechanics Series
(G PRO)
$48.00 purchase _ #AM18
Shows how to mount a rotor with a hub on the FMC brake lathe.
Industrial and Technical Education
Dist - RMIBHF **Prod** - RMIBHF

Mounting an Electrocardiogram 6 MIN
BETA / VHS
Color
Explains how to mount EKG strips for reading.
Health and Safety
Dist - RMIBHF **Prod** - RMIBHF

Mounting and Dressing of Grinding Wheels 14 MIN
16mm / U-matic / VHS
Vocational Skillfilms - Machine Shop Skills Series
Color (IND) (SPANISH PORTUGUESE)
Demonstrates correct procedures for mounting, truing, balancing and dressing of grinding wheels.
Industrial and Technical Education
Dist - RTBL **Prod** - RTBL 1982

Mounting and Truing Work in the 4 - Jaw Independent Chuck
VHS / U-matic
Basic Engine Lathe Series
Color (SPANISH)
Industrial and Technical Education
Dist - VTRI **Prod** - VTRI

Mounting and Truing Work in the 4 - Jaw Independent Chuck 15 MIN
U-matic / VHS
Machining and the Operation of Machine Tools, Module 2 - Engine 'Lathe Series
Color (IND)
Industrial and Technical Education
Dist - LEIKID **Prod** - LEIKID

Mounting cylindrical work in a four - jaw chuck 13 MIN
BETA / VHS
Machine shop - engine lathe series; No 19
Color (IND)
Explains methods of centering rough castings and of dialing in machined cylindrical work. Emphasizes accuracy and speed, using dial indicator and micrometer dials.
Industrial and Technical Education; Mathematics; Psychology
Dist - RMIBHF **Prod** - RMIBHF

Mounting, Facing, and Turning 20 MIN
U-matic / VHS
Introduction to Machine Technology, Module 2 Series; Module 2
Color (IND)
Discusses the procedure to mount with a universal chuck and collets. Gives the method for straight turning with a universal chuck.
Industrial and Technical Education
Dist - LEIKID **Prod** - LEIKID

Mounting Hubless Rotors and Drums on Ammco Brake Lathe 14 MIN
VHS / 16mm
Auto Mechanics Series
(G PRO)
$71.00 purchase _ #AM14
Shows how to mount hubless rotors and drums on the Ammco brake lathe.
Industrial and Technical Education
Dist - RMIBHF **Prod** - RMIBHF

Mounting of Casts in Semi - Adjustable Articulator and Use of Bite Planes 14 MIN
16mm
Color
LC 74-705175
Shows a step - by - step procedure for mounting a cast in a hanau semi - adjustable articulator using a conventional face bow and cheek bites. Demonstrates adjustment and function of a maxillary bite plane since the use of such appliances often is indicated prior to determination of optimal jaw relations.
Science
Dist - USNAC **Prod** - USVA 1970

Mounting rectangular and irregular work in a four - jaw chuck 16 MIN
VHS / BETA
Machine shop - engine lathe series; No 20
Color (IND)
Continues Engine Lathe No. 19, emphasizing speed and accuracy in dialing - in rectangular work. Includes the technique for dialing - in a center punch mark.

Industrial and Technical Education; Psychology
Dist - RMIBHF Prod - RMIBHF

Mounting Rotor and Drums with Hubs Ammco Brake Lathe 11.5 MIN
VHS / 16mm
Auto Mechanic Series
(G PRO)
$65.00 purchase _ #AM13
Shows how to mount rotor and drums with hubs on the Ammco brake lathe.
Industrial and Technical Education
Dist - RMIBHF Prod - RMIBHF

Mounting Techniques 30 MIN
VHS / 16mm
Chinese Brush Painting Series
Color (C A)
$85.00, $75.00 purchase _ 20 - 20
Shows how to protect color and surface and stabilize for hanging.
Fine Arts
Dist - CDTEL Prod - COAST 1987

The Mourides - Africa's Black Muslims 30 MIN
U-matic
Africa File Series
Color (J H)
Reveals that when pagan Senegal was conquered by the French, it turned to the Islamic Mouride brotherhood. Their blend of exploitation and cooperation illustrates problems of development and social change.
Business and Economics; Geography - World; History - World; Religion and Philosophy
Dist - TVOTAR Prod - TVOTAR 1985

Mourning for Mangatopi 56 MIN
16mm / U-matic / VHS
Australian Institute of Aboriginal Studies Series
Color
Details a pukamani mortuary ceremony held by the Tiwi tribe of Melville Island - one of the grandest and most colorful Aboriginal ceremonies.
History - World
Dist - UCEMC Prod - AUSIAS 1977

The Mouse - Activated Candle Lighter 5 MIN
16mm
Color (J)
Shows an amusing Rube Goldberg device consisting of a mouse trap, fishing pole, alarm clock, ice pack, train motor, rubber band, match and candle which illustrates various forms of potential and kinetic energy.
Science - Physical
Dist - SF Prod - SF 1973

The Mouse and the Motorcycle 41 MIN
16mm / U-matic / VHS
Color (P I)
$495 purchase - 16 mm, $195 purchase - video
Discusses how a boy and a mouse learn about friendship. Based on a novel by Beverly Cleary. Dimensional animation by John Matthews.
Literature and Drama; Psychology
Dist - CF

The Mouse and the motorcycle 15 MIN
U-matic / VHS
Book bird series
Color (I)
Tells the story of a mouse who craves adventure and danger. From the story by Beverly Cleary.
English Language; Literature and Drama
Dist - CTI Prod - CTI

Mouse Morning 7 MIN
U-matic / VHS / 16mm
Color (K P)
Presents an animated film featuring mice colored improbable shades of blue, green and red, who have difficulty waking a friend. Tells how it requires a group effort to solve their problems.
Fine Arts; Guidance and Counseling
Dist - PHENIX Prod - PANOWA

The Mouse on the Mayflower 57 MIN
16mm
Color (K P I)
LC 74-700684
Depicts, through animation, how the pilgrims came to America, incorporating the voices of Tennessee Ernie Ford, Eddie Albert, John Gary, Joanie Sommers and Paul Frees.
Fine Arts; History - United States
Dist - TWYMAN Prod - UPA 1969

The Mouse Takes a Chance 9 MIN
16mm / U-matic / VHS
Primary Language Development Series
Color (K P I)
LC 75-703674
Uses a story about a mouse who leaves her safe home for adventures in the world to show that it is sometimes necessary to take a chance.
Guidance and Counseling; Literature and Drama
Dist - AIMS Prod - PEDF 1975

Mouse Tales by Rumer Godden 30 MIN
Videoreel / VT2
Color
Presents a reading of two of British novelist Rumer Godden's most appealing works for children, The Mouse House and The Mouse Wife.
Literature and Drama
Dist - PBS Prod - WETATV

The Mouse that Roared 85 MIN
16mm
Color
Shows a world crisis developing when a small country steals a secret weapon and blackmails the rest of the world. Stars Peter Sellers.
Fine Arts
Dist - TIMLIF Prod - CPC 1959

Mouseland 6 MIN
16mm
Color (A)
Presents a fable about a land where mice always elected cats to govern them. Illustrates a speech given by the leader of the new Democratic Party in Canada.
Civics and Political Systems
Dist - AFLCIO Prod - CANLAB 1980

The Mouseman 14 MIN
U-matic / VHS / 16mm
Bloomin' Human Series
Color (P I)
LC 76-701507
Tells the story of a boy whose only friends are his pet mice. Shows how the other kids think he's weird until he gets an opportunity to make new friends. Explains that he must hurt someone else in order to do so.
Guidance and Counseling
Dist - MEDIAG Prod - PAULST 1975

The Mouse's Tale 25 MIN
16mm / U-matic / VHS
Color
Looks at the behavior and habitats of four species of mice - house mice, dormice, wood mice and harvest mice - in and around a country cottage in Wiltshire, England. Narrated by David Attenborough.
Science - Natural
Dist - FI Prod - BBCTV

The Mouse's tale 11 MIN
VHS
Color (R J H)
$17.95 purchase _ #605 - 0
Uses animation to explore the issues surrounding international food production and its relationship to hunger and famine around the world. Includes discussion guide. Produced by Australian Catholic Aid.
Health and Safety; Religion and Philosophy; Sociology
Dist - USCC

Mousie Baby 25 MIN
U-matic / VHS / 16mm
Color
LC 78-700202
Presents an adaptation of Tess Slesinger's short story entitled The Mouse - Trap about a young secretary in an advertising agency. Shows how the employees go on strike, but the secretary's handsome boss manipulates them and the strike is abandoned. Portrays the secretary rejecting his overtures and emerging alone.
Business and Economics; Literature and Drama; Sociology
Dist - PHENIX Prod - COMCO 1977

Mousie Party 6 MIN
U-matic / VHS / 16mm
Color (P)
LC 83-706008
Presents a puppet animation look at the efforts of a group of determined young mice to attain a goal of seemingly impossible proportions, both literally and figuratively. They try to reach a set of rings dangling from the ceiling.
Fine Arts
Dist - PHENIX Prod - FILBUL 1982

Mousse Au Chocolat 29 MIN
Videoreel / VT2
French Chef - French Series
Color (FRENCH)
A French language videotape. Features Julia Child of Haute Cuisine au Vin demonstrating how to prepare mousse au chocolate. With captions.
Foreign Language; Home Economics
Dist - PBS Prod - WGBHTV

Moussorgsky - Pictures at an exhibition
VHS
Music in motion series
Color (J H C G)
$75.00 purchase _ #MUS04V
Expresses visually what is heard in Pictures at an Exhibition by Moussorgsky. Teaches classical music appreciation, develops interest and enhances listening enjoyment. Includes manual with suggestions for presenting the video, questions for discussion, research projects, correlations with other subject areas and listening and reading lists. Part of an eight - part series.
Fine Arts
Dist - CAMV Prod - MUSLOG

Moutabel and Hummus Bi Tahini 19 MIN
U-matic / VHS
Color (PRO)
Demonstrates the preparation of two Arabic appetizers, Moutabel, with eggplant, and Hummus bi Tahini, with chick peas.
Home Economics; Industrial and Technical Education
Dist - CULINA Prod - CULINA

The Mouth, nose and pharynx 32 MIN
VHS / U-matic
Anatomy of the head and neck series
Color (PRO C)
$395.00 purchase, $80.00 rental _ #C901 - VI - 068
Demonstrates features of the oral and nasal cavities and of the pharynx. Covers relevant osteology includes the teeth and ethnoic sinuses. Describes the anatomy of the vestibule and oral cavity and tongue musculature. Examines the palatine tonsil, the nasal septum and lateral nasal wall, openings of the paranasal air sinuses, the lacrimal duct and the auditory tube. Part of a series on head and neck anatomy produced by Shakti Chandra, Faculty of Medicine, University of Newfoundland.
Health and Safety; Science - Natural
Dist - HSCIC

Mouth Preparation for Removable Partial Dentures 35 MIN
16mm
Color
LC 74-705176
Shows principles and procedures for diagnosing and treating the patient's mouth prior to receiving prosthesis.
Science
Dist - USNAC Prod - USVA 1964

The Mouth that Roared 5 MIN
16mm / U-matic / VHS
Color (J)
LC 84-706798
Presents an animated, avant - garde interpretation of the coming together of a single, self - sufficient component to make a larger, stronger whole, using the parts of the face to make its point.
Fine Arts; Psychology
Dist - PHENIX Prod - PHENIX 1983

Mouth - to - Mouth Breathing 15 MIN
U-matic / VHS / 16mm
REACT - Review of Emergency Aid and CPR Training Series
Color (H C A)
Health and Safety
Dist - CORF Prod - CORF

The Mouths of babes 15 MIN
VHS
Color (K P A R)
$10.00 rental _ #36 - 87 - 1521
Features children answering questions about God. Includes study guide.
Religion and Philosophy; Sociology
Dist - APH Prod - MMM

Mouthwatering meatless meals
VHS
Video cooking library series
Color (J H G)
$19.95 purchase _ #KVC937V
Illustrates vegetarian cookery through step - by - step demonstrations. Covers everything needed from ingredients to equipment, with clear explanations of cooking techniques. Includes recipes. Part of a 22 - part series.
Home Economics
Dist - CAMV

Movable Bridges 29 MIN
16mm
Color (J)
Depicts the history and development of the movable bridge and shows how one of the largest of all movable bridges was built at Houghton, Michigan.
Industrial and Technical Education
Dist - USSC Prod - HANDY 1960

Move Along - Enjoy Golf 28 MIN
16mm
Color
Presents Arnold Palmer, Amy Alcott and two average golfers playing golf in Hawaii and reviewing the rules of etiquette and courtesy.
Geography - United States; Physical Education and Recreation
Dist - MTP Prod - UAL

Move and do 15 MIN
U-matic / VHS
Children in Action Series
Color
Psychology
Dist - LVN **Prod** - LVN

Move - Artist in Schools Program 28 MIN
16mm
Color
LC 74-700356
Shows how dancers are helping open new horizons in education by means of the artists in school program sponsored by the National Endowment for the Arts.
Education; Fine Arts
Dist - NENDOW **Prod** - NENDOW 1973

Move Em Out 30 MIN
16mm
Color
LC 73-700378
Shows how Dick Sparrow, an Iowa farmer, organized and trained a 40 - horse hitch to re - create a spectacle from the great circus parades of the past. Includes the training of the horses and men, the circus parade and the homecoming parade.
Agriculture; Sociology
Dist - WMVSTV **Prod** - WMVSTV 1973

A Move in the Right Direction 14 MIN
16mm
Color
LC 72-701956
Shows the employee his individual role in cost reduction through correct material handling. Points out the results of employee carelessness, and gives an example of tangible results of proper motivation.
Business and Economics; Guidance and Counseling; Psychology
Dist - VOAERO **Prod** - VOAERO 1971

Move it 19 MIN
16mm
Color (A)
LC 79-700918
Presents the Ririe - Woodbury Dance Company satirizing everyday life in Salt Lake City, Utah, through modern dance.
Fine Arts
Dist - RADIM **Prod** - FILIM 1977

Move those Muscles 15 MIN
VHS / U-matic
All about You Series
Color (P)
Emphasizes the importance of exercising every day to develop strong muscles. Illustrates good posture and suggests that it should become a lifetime habit.
Health and Safety; Physical Education and Recreation; Science - Natural
Dist - AITECH **Prod** - WGBHTV 1975

Move to Intermediate Level 29 MIN
Videoreel / VT2
Skiing Series
Color
Physical Education and Recreation
Dist - PBS **Prod** - KTCATV

A Moveable Feast 60 MIN
VHS
Smithsonian World Series
Color (G)
$49.95 purchase _ #SMIW - 502
Suggests that changes in transportation have affected what foods Americans choose to eat. Gives examples from the era of the Pilgrims to the present day.
Social Science
Dist - PBS **Prod** - WETATV

A Moveable Feast - a Film about Breastfeeding 22 MIN
16mm / U-matic / VHS
Prepared Childbirth and Parenting Series
Color (H C A)
Looks at many of the most common myths, questions, concerns and problems encountered by parents about breastfeeding using documentary footage, animation and dramatization.
Health and Safety; Home Economics; Sociology
Dist - JOU **Prod** - JOU 1982

Movement 20 MIN
16mm
All that I Am Series
B&W (C A)
Fine Arts; Guidance and Counseling
Dist - NWUFLM **Prod** - MPATI

Movement 14 MIN
U-matic / VHS
Hands on, Grade One Series Unit 1 - Observing; Unit 1 - Observing
Color (P)
Science; Science - Physical
Dist - AITECH **Prod** - VAOG 1975

Movement 25 MIN
VHS
Exploring photography series
Color (A)
PdS65 purchase
Demonstrates how photography can record movement and interpret it imaginatively. Includes an interview with Ernst Haas. Explores the creative possibilities of still photography. Covers the major topics of interest to any photographer. Part of a six-part series hosted by Bryn Campbell.
Fine Arts; Industrial and Technical Education
Dist - BBCENE

Movement 10 MIN
U-matic / VHS / 16mm
Art of Seeing Series
Color
LC 71-702477
Illustrates the importance of movement as an element of art by means of a series of striking parallels. Shows how movement in the world of nature has been translated into paintings.
Fine Arts
Dist - FI **Prod** - AFA 1968

Movement and moving the camera 11 MIN
VHS
Lessons in visual language series
Color (PRO G C)
$99.00 purchase, $39.00 rental _ #751
Examines the way the human eye moves as it interacts with a visual scene. Demonstrates how movement of the camera must accommodate but not duplicate the movement of the eye. Analyzes three types of movement - movement within the frame, movement of the frame and movement of the camera itself through space. Features Peter Thompson as creator and narrator of a ten - part series on visual language. Produced by the Australian Film, Television and Radio School.
Industrial and Technical Education; Social Science
Dist - FIRLIT

Movement and the Center of Gravity 9 MIN
U-matic / VHS
Introductory Concepts in Physics - Dynamics Series
Color (C)
$229.00, $129.00 purchase _ #AD - 1194
Demonstrates how the movement of any object can be analyzed by determining its center of gravity.
Science - Physical
Dist - FOTH **Prod** - FOTH

Movement Disorders in Children 18 MIN
U-matic / VHS
Color (PRO)
Demonstrates several central nervous system disorders in children. Emphasizes observation of movements and their description.
Health and Safety; Psychology
Dist - UARIZ **Prod** - UARIZ

Movement Education 28 MIN
16mm / U-matic / VHS
Color (T) (SPANISH)
Demonstrates movement education activities in a variety of circumstances. Shows children at the Frostig Center of Educational Therapy in specific activities calculated to improve coordination, flexibility, strength, agility, static and dynamic balance and endurance.
Education; Physical Education and Recreation
Dist - AIMS **Prod** - MAFC 1976

Movement experience series
Dance design - motion 19 MIN
Dance design - shape and time 16 MIN
Dance design - space 19 MIN
Dist - AAHPER

Movement Exploration - what Am I 12 MIN
U-matic / VHS / 16mm
Color; B&W (P I) (SPANISH)
LC FIA68-2108
Presents an exercise in movement exploration in which children learn that they can not only move like themselves, but can mimic the movements of birds, animals and machines. Pictures the children developing perceptual abilities and refining concepts which are gateways to improved coordination and reading ability.
English Language; Physical Education and Recreation; Psychology
Dist - PHENIX **Prod** - FA 1968

Movement for the actor 75 MIN
VHS
Color (G C H)
$139.00 purchase _ #DL493
Teaches a series of exercises that focus on body positions coresponding to emotional states. Demonstrates types of walks, dynamics of movement, creation of a safe space, and effective gesturing. With Dawn Mora of Northwestern Univ.
Fine Arts
Dist - INSIM

Movement Improvisations 19 MIN
16mm
Color (C T)
LC FIA67-5558
Presents four different areas of movement expression in dance - - free movement of separate body parts, three duets and a trio, designs in movement, and heads, hands and feet.
Fine Arts; Physical Education and Recreation
Dist - METT **Prod** - METT 1957

Movement in Classical Dance - the Pelvic Area 11 MIN
16mm / U-matic / VHS
Color (J H C)
LC 80-701928
Explains safe and correct principles of position in classical dance.
Fine Arts; Physical Education and Recreation
Dist - IU **Prod** - IU 1980

Movement no 1 29 MIN
VHS / 16mm
Villa Alegre Series
Color (P T)
$46.00 rental _ #VILA - 105
Presents educational material in both Spanish and English.
Education
Dist - PBS

Movement no 2 29 MIN
VHS / 16mm
Villa Alegre Series
Color (P T)
$46.00 rental _ #VILA - 110
Presents educational material in both Spanish and English.
Education
Dist - PBS

Movement Possibilities 30 MIN
U-matic / VHS
In Our Own Image Series
Color (C)
Fine Arts
Dist - DALCCD **Prod** - DALCCD

Movement style and culture series
Presents four programs which demonstrate the pioneering work of Alan Lomax and Forrestine Paulay in developing choreometrics, a cross - cultural method of studying the relationship of dance style to culture and social structure. Employs dance and ethnographic footage from all over the world to show how aspects of movement vary regularly and predictably with aspects of social structure. Includes the titles Dance and Human History, The Longest Trail, Palm Play and Step Style.
Dance and human history 40 MIN
The Longest trail 58 MIN
Movement style and culture series 158 MIN
Palm play 30 MIN
Step style 30 MIN
Dist - UCEMC **Prod** - CHORP

Movement Techniques 17 MIN
U-matic / VHS
Color
LC 81-706251
Demonstrates field and sand table techniques developed by the Army to respond to enemy action. Shows movement techniques designed to make maximum use of terrain, obscure enemy vision, and assure maximum use of fire power. .
Civics and Political Systems
Dist - USNAC **Prod** - USA 1981

Movement Techniques - the Rifle Platoon 15 MIN
16mm
Color
LC 80-701837
Presents three standard movement techniques used by squads under direction of the platoon leader. Uses simulated battle action to show the benefit of employing cover and concealment of troops.
Civics and Political Systems
Dist - USNAC **Prod** - USA 1980

Movement within life 15 MIN
VHS / U-matic
Animals and such series; Module red - life processes
Color (I J)
Studies internal movement and how it is accomplished in both plants and animals.
Science - Natural
Dist - AITECH **Prod** - WHROTV 1972

Movements 18 MIN
16mm
Color; Silent (C)
$100.00
Experimental film by Barry Gerson.
Fine Arts
Dist - AFA **Prod** - AFA 1971

Movements 25 MIN
16mm
Color
Depicts the performing arts in Israel.
Fine Arts; Geography - World
Dist - ALDEN **Prod** - ALDEN

Movements of Endamoeba Histolytica 2 MIN
16mm
Parasitology Series
Color
LC FIE52-2235
Uses cinemicrography to show typical motility and ingested red cells of trophozoite of endamoeba histolytica from a clinical case of amoebic dysentery.
Health and Safety; Science - Natural
Dist - USNAC **Prod** - USPHS 1947

Movements of Organelles in Living Nerve Fibers 12 MIN
16mm
Color (PRO)
LC 77-700459
Illustrates the movements of organelles inside living axons from frog nerves in time - lapse cinematography.
Science - Natural
Dist - USNAC **Prod** - NMAC 1975

Movements of power 120 MIN
VHS
Color (G)
$29.95 purchase _ #1123
Presents a 60 - movement short form designed by William Chen and taught here by Robert Klein. Emphasizes health and body mechanics, not self defense aspects. Step by step instruction in detail, with multiple angles and repetition.
Physical Education and Recreation
Dist - WAYF

Movements of the Eyes and Tongue - Somatic Motor System 18 MIN
U-matic / VHS / 16mm
Anatomical Basis of Brain Function Series
Color (PRO)
Science - Natural
Dist - TEF **Prod** - AVCORP

Movements of the Jaw and Throat - Branchial Motor System 18 MIN
U-matic / VHS / 16mm
Anatomical Basis of Brain Function Series
Color (PRO)
Science - Natural
Dist - TEF **Prod** - AVCORP

Movements of the Shoulder Girdle 47 MIN
U-matic / VHS
B&W
Teaches the interrelationships of the movements of the shoulder girdle during functional activities.
Health and Safety
Dist - BUSARG **Prod** - BUSARG

Movements on the surface of social consciousness 37 MIN
16mm
Color (G)
$122.00 rental
Features a collection of four experimental films that utililize surface manipulation as social criticism. Challenges the boundaries of the frame by the use of optical printing. Universal in theme, yet distinct personal works, titles are - Visible Man - 1989 - 1990 - by Jerome Cook; Cowboys Were Not Nice People - 1990 - by Larry Kless; Quixote Dreams - 1991 - by Alfonso Alvarez; Symphonia de Erosus - 1991 - by Kevin Deal. Films also available separately.
Fine Arts; Sociology
Dist - CANCIN

Movers and Shakers 30 MIN
VHS / 16mm
Marketing Series
Color (C A)
$130.00, $120.00 purchase _ 15 - 25
Identifies market mix, environment, and target customers.
Business and Economics
Dist - CDTEL **Prod** - COAST 1989

Movie 10 MIN
16mm
Color (G)
$25.00 rental
Presents a 'hand - held' diary in the form of a Super 8 camera shooting only at night. Travels from Paris to Berlin, Amsterdam to Rio, Jerusalem to New York.
Fine Arts; Geography - World
Dist - CANCIN **Prod** - OSTROV 1982

A Movie 12 MIN
16mm
B&W (G)
$600.00 purchase
Collects a montage of found materials from newsreels and old movies. Explores destruction and sex, and juxtaposes Cowboys and Indians, elephants and tanks as metaphors for the apocalypse.
Fine Arts
Dist - CANCIN **Prod** - CONNER 1958

The Movie at the End of the World 57 MIN
U-matic / VHS
Documentaries on Art Series
Color (G)
$120.00, $80.00 purchase, $45.00, $30.00 rental
Features poet Thomas McGrath. Puns ironically on multiple levels about the remoteness of North Dakota, the meaning of human existence, that each moment ends one world and begins a new one, and the consideration that the excesses of humanity could destroy the world. Bares the angst and misery of the isolation and long winters of the land and people of North Dakota. Produced by the Center for International Education.
Biography; Education; Geography - United States; Literature and Drama
Dist - IAFC **Prod** - UCV 1981
UCV

Movie database and software potpourri
CD-ROM
(G)
$69.00 purchase _ #3002
Contains a database of 1000 movies, the full text of the King James Bible, and hundreds of shareware and public domain software programs. Provides access to the films by title, release date, studio, genre, producer, director, cast, and plot, and to the Bible by book, chapter, verse and concordance. The shareware and demo programs cover architecture, business, communications, databases, education, entertainment, graphics, languages, religion, spreadsheets, utilities and word processing. For IBM PCs and compatibles, requires at least 640K RAM, DOS 3.1 or later, one floppy disk drive - hard disk recommended, one empty expansion slot, and an IBM compatible CD - ROM drive.
Computer Science; Fine Arts; Literature and Drama
Dist - BEP

Movie Factory 15 MIN
U-matic / VHS
Explorers Unlimited Series
Color (P I)
Tours Universal City Studio to learn about some of the illusions used in making movies.
Fine Arts; Geography - United States; Industrial and Technical Education; Physical Education and Recreation
Dist - AITECH **Prod** - WVIZTV 1971

The Movie footage
VHS
Edward Meier series
Color (G)
$49.95 purchase _ #GB003
Presents Edward Meier's films of possible alien 'beamships.'
Science - Physical; Sociology
Dist - SIV

Movie Memories 30 MIN
16mm
Color
LC 73-700801
Presents a documentary showing the floats, bands and horses of the Rose Parade held in Pasadena, California, New Years Day, 1973.
Sociology
Dist - TRA **Prod** - TRA 1973

Movie Milestones no 1 10 MIN
16mm
B&W
Highlights sequences from the feature films of the silent days, including 'Blood And Sand' (1922) with Rudolph Valentino, Nita Naldi and Lilo Lee, 'The Covered Wagon' (1923) with Ernest Torrence, J Warren Kerrigan and Alan Hale, 'The Miracle Man' (1919) with Lon Chaney, Thomas Meighan, Betty Compson and Joseph Dowling and 'Beau Geste' (1926) with Ronald Coleman, Ralph Forbes, Noah Beery and William Powell.
Fine Arts
Dist - CFS **Prod** - CFS

Movie Movie 105 MIN
16mm
Color
Offers a spoof of the old Hollywood double feature. Includes a black and white boxing melodrama and a lavish musical story.
Fine Arts
Dist - SWANK **Prod** - WB

The Movie movie 36 MIN
VHS
Visual literacy series
Color; PAL (P I)
PdS29.50 purchase
Deals directly with the way in which viusal images can be manipulated to influence our thoughts and emotions. Part five of a five - part series.
Psychology; Religion and Philosophy; Sociology
Dist - EMFVL

The Movie reel Indians 29 MIN
VHS / U-matic / VT1
Images of Indians series
Color (G)
$49.95 purchase, $35.00 rental
Shows images of Indians as savage murderers in opening film clips. Features commentary by Indian spokespersons Dennis Banks and Vine Deloria who observe intentional viciousness against Indians in an industry where filmmaker fantasies govern the final imagery of the movies. Looks at Winterhawk, Chato's Land and A Man Called Horse which appear to be interested in accuracy, but act out white fantasies of Indian leadership as in the role of Richard Harris as a white man who becomes an Indian chief. By Robert Hagopian and Phil Lucas. Will Sampson narrates. Part of a five - part series on images of Indians.
Fine Arts; Religion and Philosophy; Social Science
Dist - NAMPBC **Prod** - KCTSTV

A Movie Star's Daughter 30 MIN
16mm / VHS / U-matic
Color (I J H P) (SPANISH)
LC 79-710418; 79-701417
Tells the story of a young junior high girl, the daughter of a movie idol, who encounters difficult choices upon arriving at a new school. Edited.
Guidance and Counseling
Dist - LCOA **Prod** - HGATE 1979

Movie stills 45 MIN
16mm
B&W (G)
$50.00 rental
Explores the relationship between still photography and cinema. Consists of 16 images taken from a frame - by - frame analysis of 200 feet of recorded footage. Produced by J J Murphy.
Fine Arts; Industrial and Technical Education
Dist - CANCIN

Movie Stuntmen 28 MIN
U-matic / VHS / 16mm
Color
LC 75-701070
Reveals the skill and courage demanded of motion picture stuntmen and shows how they can perform such stunts as flaming car crashes and leaps from cliffs.
Fine Arts; Guidance and Counseling
Dist - LCOA **Prod** - TRENCH 1975

Movie Words - 2 15 MIN
VHS
Wordscape Series
Color; Captioned (I)
$125.00 purchase
Uses the word 'cell' approach to teach vocabulary, opening each program - sixteen 15 - minute programs - with several word cells familiar to fourth graders and using these 'cells' to form compound words, birdhouse, girlfriend. Employs animated graphics to dramatize how compounds are 'built' of cells that form a seemingly endless series of new words and to teach that understanding cell words can help to understand the new words composed of them. Program 2 deals with words about motion and action. Stresses pronunciation and usage and the idea that words can have different meanings in different contexts.
English Language; Psychology
Dist - AITECH **Prod** - OETVA 1990

Movies 30 MIN
U-matic
Today's Special Series
Color (K P)
Develops language arts skills in children. Programs are thematically designed around subjects of interest to youngsters. Action takes place in a department store where people, mannequins, puppets, comic characters and special guests present a light hearted approach to language arts.
Fine Arts; Literature and Drama; Psychology
Dist - TVOTAR **Prod** - TVOTAR 1985

Movies 29 MIN
U-matic / VHS / 16mm
American Memoir Series
B&W (H C A)
Dr Dodds examines the movies of the 20th century for clues about changes and constancies in American taste.
Fine Arts
Dist - IU **Prod** - WTTWTV 1961

Movies and You Series
The Art Director 10 MIN
Dist - IU

The Movies Go West 14 MIN
U-matic / VHS / 16mm
Color (H C A)
LC 74-702912
Hal Angus, of the original Essanay Film Manufacturing Company western unit, revisits the studio and location sites and reminisces about the early days between 1909 - 1916 when Gilbert M Anderson produced and starred in hundreds of westerns. He points out that in the role of Bronco Billy, Gilbert Anderson created the prototype of the movie cowboy hero and established the format of the classic American movie western.
Fine Arts
Dist - UCEMC **Prod** - BELLG 1974

The Movies Learn to Talk 26 MIN
U-matic / VHS / 16mm
Twentieth Century Series
B&W (J H A)
Follows the development of sound movies from early experiments at the turn of the century to the 'JAZZ SINGER' in 1927 and the polished sound film of today. Provides glimpses of 34 personalities and excerpts from 12 silent and sound movies.
Fine Arts; History - United States; Physical Education and Recreation
Dist - MGHT **Prod** - CBSTV 1960
CRMP

The Movies March on 20 MIN
U-matic / VHS / 16mm
March of Time Series
B&W (J)
Uses film clips to present a history of the movies, from silent pictures to swashbucklers. Includes scenes of Theda Bara, Rudolph Valentino, Mary Pickford, Greta Garbo and Douglas Fairbanks, Sr.
Fine Arts; History - United States
Dist - TIMLIF **Prod** - TIMLIF 1974

Movies, movies series
Cheap it isn't 15 MIN
G, PG, R and X 15 MIN
Say it Again, Sam 15 MIN
So You Want to be a Star 15 MIN
There's no Business Like Show Business 15 MIN
Which End do I Look in 15 MIN
Dist - CTI

Movies - Our Modern Art Series
The Lost World Revisited 28 MIN
Dist - SF

Movies - our modern art series
The Gold rush '68 60 MIN
Let Katie do it 28 MIN
Svengali 45 MIN
Dist - STRFLS

The Movies' Story 25 MIN
16mm
B&W (J H C)
Depicts the pioneering days of the film as seen in the films of Edison, Melies, D W Griffith, Chaplin and others.
Fine Arts; Industrial and Technical Education
Dist - SLFP **Prod** - SLFP 1970

The Movies Today - a New Morality 37 MIN
U-matic / VHS / 16mm
Life Goes to the Movies Series Pt 5
Color
LC 79-707672
Takes a look at the life and career of Marilyn Monroe. Examines the movies of the 1960's which became subjects of controversy because of their language, sexuality and violence.
Biography; Fine Arts; Sociology
Dist - TIMLIF **Prod** - TIMLIF 1976

Movietone no. 400 26 MIN
16mm
Fox Movietone news series
B&W (G)
$30.00 rental
Contains The Normandie, 1935 - 1942, a chronicle of the luxury liner; Mississippi Showboat, 1933, paddlewheel theatrics with a minstrel show; and The Queen Mary, 1933 - 1940, luxury liner as a WWII troop carrier. Covers worldwide events with commentary by ace radio voices. Features part of a series consisting of two or three classic newsreels on one reel, 20 - 30 minutes in length.
Civics and Political Systems; Fine Arts; History - World; Literature and Drama
Dist - KITPAR **Prod** - FOXNEW

Movietone no. 401 20 MIN
16mm
Fox Movietone news series
B&W (G)
$30.00 rental
Contains Sir Arthur Conan Doyle, 1927, discussing his creation of Sherlock Holmes; and Authors in the News, 1930 - 1962, with Kipling, Shaw, Sax Rohmer, Wells, Steinbeck, Sinclair Lewis, Hemingway. Features part of a series consisting of two or three classic newsreels on one reel, 20 - 30 minutes in length.
Fine Arts; Literature and Drama
Dist - KITPAR **Prod** - FOXNEW

Movietone no. 402
16mm
Fox Movietone news series
B&W (G)
$30.00 rental
Contains Filming the Great, 1934, from Hitler to Hirohito, King George to Ghandi; Sports Immortals, 1938, Red Grange, Susanne Lenglen, Helen Mills, Barney Oldfield, Babe Ruth, Man O' War, Jack Dempsey, and others; and Personalities of the 1950s with Ike, Truman, Newman and Woodward, Nixon, Rainier and Kelly, and others. Features part of a series consisting of two or three classic newsreels on one reel, 20 - 30 minutes in length.
Biography; Civics and Political Systems; Fine Arts; History - World; Literature and Drama; Physical Education and Recreation
Dist - KITPAR **Prod** - FOXNEW

Movietone no. 403
16mm
Fox Movietone news series
B&W (G)
$30.00 rental
Contains When Disaster Strikes, 1933, with footage of floods, volcanic eruptions, fiery holocausts and earthquake aftermaths; Filming the Fashions, 1933, with prism and trick effects to show off the latest fashions; and Filming the Big Thrills, 1938, scenes of nature and man on the rampage, assassination of the king of Yugoslavia, the Hindenberg and more. Features part of a series consisting of two or three classic newsreels on one reel, 20 - 30 minutes in length.
Civics and Political Systems; Fine Arts; History - United States; History - World; Home Economics; Literature and Drama
Dist - KITPAR **Prod** - FOXNEW

Movietone no. 404
16mm
Fox Movietone news series
B&W (G)
$30.00 rental
Contains Mussolini's Decade of Progress, 1932, illustrates how Il Duce knew the value of projecting a good newsreel image; and Hitler's Ascent to Power, 1933, which has rare scenes, speeches and, in retrospect, many ironies. Features part of a series consisting of two or three classic newsreels on one reel, 20 - 30 minutes in length.
Civics and Political Systems; Fine Arts; History - World; Literature and Drama
Dist - KITPAR **Prod** - FOXNEW

Movietone no. 405
16mm
Fox Movietone news series
B&W (G)
$30.00 rental
Contains Appeasement at Munich, 1938, which looks at the Czechoslovakian disaster, Chamberlain's visits and appeasement of Hitler; FDR Declaration of War Against Japan, 1941, showing FDR at his eloquent best; and Pearl Harbor, 1943, which is narrated by Lowell Thomas. Features part of a series consisting of two or three classic newsreels on one reel, 20 - 30 minutes in length.
Biography; Civics and Political Systems; Fine Arts; History - World; Literature and Drama
Dist - KITPAR **Prod** - FOXNEW

Movietone no. 406
16mm
Fox Movietone news series
B&W (G)
$30.00 rental
Contains MTN October, 11, 1919, with a coast to coast air race, women fencers, Who's Who in America, Prince Albert in Toledo and more; and The Lone Eagle, Charles A Lindbergh, 1927, an early sound film of Lindy's takeoff and his speech in Washington, DC. Features part of a series consisting of two or three classic newsreels on one reel, 20 - 30 minutes in length.
Civics and Political Systems; Fine Arts; History - World; Industrial and Technical Education; Literature and Drama
Dist - KITPAR **Prod** - FOXNEW

Movietone Sports Series
Lady of the Rapids 11 MIN
Dist - TWCF

Movimiento creativo en Costa Rica 31 MIN
VHS
Color (G) (SPANISH)
$40.00 purchase
Presents La Pequena Compania of the Escuela Ciencias del Deporte, Universidad Nacional, Costa Rica. Demonstrates creative movement with their teacher, Barbara Mettler, who narrates in Spanish.
Fine Arts; Physical Education and Recreation; Social Science
Dist - METT **Prod** - METT 1989

Movin' Around, Movin' Out 29 MIN
VHS / U-matic
Bean Sprouts Series
Color (P I)
Shows a group of school friends in San Francisco's Italian, Latino and Chinese neighborhood shops. Includes incidents of thoughtless racism.
Sociology
Dist - GPN **Prod** - CTPROJ

Moving 30 MIN
U-matic
Today's Special Series
Color (K P)
Develops language arts skills in children. Programs are thematically designed around subjects of interest to youngsters. Action takes place in a department store where people, mannequins, puppets, comic characters and special guests present a light hearted approach to language arts.
Fine Arts; Literature and Drama; Psychology
Dist - TVOTAR **Prod** - TVOTAR 1985

Moving 10 MIN
VHS / U-matic
You - parents are special series
Color
Presents Fred Rogers on the subject of moving.
Psychology; Sociology
Dist - FAMCOM **Prod** - FAMCOM

Moving 15 MIN
U-matic / VHS
Safer You Series
Color (P I)
Shows how the act of moving affects a family. Explains how to prepare for the move, how to move and how to get settled in your new home. Offers advice on how to make the move safely and with as little stress as possible.
Health and Safety
Dist - GPN **Prod** - WCVETV 1984

Moving 50 MIN
VHS
Human brain series
Color (H C A)
PdS99 purchase
Highlights recent advances in knowledge about the brain and its functions relative to movement. Uses case histories to illustrate individuals' triumphs over brain injury. Part of a seven-video set focusing on the self, memory, language, movement, sight, fear, and madness.
Psychology
Dist - BBCENE

Moving a hippo 15 MIN
VHS / U-matic
Dragons, wagons and wax - Set 1 series
Color (K P)
Examines uses of the wheel, axle and pulley.
Science; Science - Physical
Dist - CTI **Prod** - CTI

Moving a mountain 30 MIN
VHS
Perspectives - industrial design - series
Color; PAL; NTSC (G)
PdS90, PdS105 purchase
Looks at the problem of hiding the biggest quarry in the world.
Science - Natural
Dist - CFLVIS **Prod** - LONTVS

Moving a Patient in Bed 16 MIN
8mm cartridge / 16mm
Nurse's Aide, Orderly and Attendant Series
Color (A)
LC 72-704825
Assesses the reasons for moving a patient in bed and demonstrates the proper procedures.
Guidance and Counseling; Health and Safety
Dist - COPI **Prod** - COPI 1969

Moving about 30 MIN
U-matic
Polka Dot Door Series

Color (K)
Presents a variety show for pre - school children. Includes songs, mime, stories, film sequences, talk, dance and fantasy figures. Each show emphasizes a particular theme such as numbers, feelings, exploring, music or time. Comes with parent teacher guide.
Fine Arts; Literature and Drama
Dist - TVOTAR **Prod** - TVOTAR 1985

Moving Air Affects the Weather 15 MIN
U-matic / VHS
Why Series
Color (P I)
Discusses how moving air affects the weather.
Science - Physical
Dist - AITECH **Prod** - WDCNTV 1976

The Moving and the Stuck 20 MIN
VHS / U-matic
Productivity - Quality of Work Life Series
Color
Business and Economics; Psychology
Dist - DELTAK **Prod** - GOODMI

Moving and Turning the Patient 7 MIN
U-matic / VHS
Color (PRO) (SPANISH)
LC 77-731353
Provides the rationale for frequently moving and turning the patient and explains the importance of enlisting the patient's cooperation. Demonstrates the steps to follow to safely turn and move the patient. Emphasizes the techniques that the home nurse should employ to avoid straining or injuring herself as she turns and moves the patient.
Health and Safety
Dist - MEDCOM **Prod** - MEDCOM

Moving easy - lift - free patient transfers 90 MIN
VHS
Color (G PRO)
$590.00 purchase, $125.00 rental
Demonstrates safe methods for moving patients that prevent stress or injury to the caregivers and the patients. Helps avoid back injuries. Consists of six 15 - minute videotapes.
Health and Safety
Dist - TNF **Prod** - DANAM

The Moving Experience
BETA / VHS
Adult Years - Continuity and Change Series
Color
Deals with moving, an unexpected part of life, and examines one family's move and the reactions of the family members to the adjustments in their lives.
Psychology; Sociology
Dist - OHUTC **Prod** - OHUTC

Moving from criticism - Part 2 14 MIN
VHS
The Employee development series
Color (PRO IND A)
$495.00 purchase, $150.00 rental _ #ITC28
Presents part two of a ten - part series designed to prepare employees for coping with workplace demands in a skillful and confident manner. Enables supervisors and managers to improve their skills and abilities as they work with their peers. Includes a leader's guide, instructions for self - study and a participant's booklet.
Business and Economics; Guidance and Counseling
Dist - EXTR **Prod** - ITRC

Moving gives me a stomach ache
CD-ROM
Discis Books on CD - ROM
(P) (SPANISH)
$84.00 purchase _ #2561
Contains the original text and illustrations of Moving Gives Me a Stomach Ache by Heather McKend. Enhances understanding with real voices, music, and sound effects. Every word in the text has an in - context explanation, pronunciation and syllables, available through a click of the mouse. Spanish - English version available for an extra $5 per disc. For Macintosh Classics, Plus, II and SE computers, requires 1MB of RAM, one floppy disk drive, and an Apple compatible CD - ROM drive.
English Language; Literature and Drama
Dist - BEP

The Moving Image - Super - 8 27 MIN
U-matic / VHS / 16mm
Color (J H C)
LC 76-703476
Shows steps involved in making super 8 mm films. Focuses on a high school filmmaking class and its experiences in using various filmmaking procedures and processes.
Education; Fine Arts
Dist - IU **Prod** - IU 1976

Moving in 18 MIN
16mm
B&W (G)
$25.00 rental
Begins as a testimony on the growing problem of homelessness in San Francisco in the wake of Reagan - era budget cuts and ends as a meditation on the filmmaker's own relationship to the situation. Uses his 'liberal guilt' regarding his privilege to raise questions about whether or not it is possible to represent a world that the filmmker has had little connection with without further exploiting, sentimentalizing or reinforcing the dehumanizaion of people who are victims of a political system that privileges greed over poverty. Produced by Jeffrey Skoller.
Fine Arts; Sociology
Dist - CANCIN

Moving in 15 MIN
VHS / U-matic
Consumer Education Series
Color
Home Economics
Dist - CAMB **Prod** - MAETEL

Moving in and Out of Your Wheelchair 5 MIN
U-matic
Spinal Cord Injury - Patient Education Series
Color
Presents an over - view of the physical preparation and equipment that is generally needed for wheelchair living.
Health and Safety
Dist - PRIMED **Prod** - PRIMED

Moving in Circles 7 MIN
VHS / U-matic
Mechanical Universe - High School Adaptation Series
(H)
Science - Physical
Dist - SCCON **Prod** - SCCON 1986

Moving in Circles 30 MIN
16mm / U-matic / VHS
Mechanical Universe Series
Color (C A)
Explains Plato's idea that stars are heavenly beings orbiting the earth with uniform perfection - uniform speed and perfect circles.
Science - Physical
Dist - FI **Prod** - ANNCPB

Moving in circles - fundamental forces - Parts 9 and 10 60 MIN
VHS / U-matic
Mechanical universe...and beyond - Part I series
Color (G)
$45.00, $29.95 purchase
Looks at the Platonic theory of uniform circular motion in Part 9. Explains all physical phenomena of nature with four forces - two nuclear forces, gravity and electricity - in Part 10. Parts of a 52 - part series on the mechanics of the universe.
Science; Science - Physical
Dist - ANNCPB **Prod** - SCCON 1985

Moving in the material world 30 MIN
VHS
Nature by design series
Color (A PRO C)
PdS65 purchase _ Unavailable in USA and Canada
Aims to create understanding of how design evolves, particularly as it relates to living in the material world. Part of a series which utilizes a visual style blending natural history footage, graphics and video effects - moving back and forth between science and nature. Emphasizes that good design is essential for the success of any product, in the natural world and today's high-tech world.
Psychology
Dist - BBCENE

Moving is Learning - Perceptual Motor Training 18 MIN
16mm
Color (S)
LC FIA68-2431
Shows teachers and parents of perceptually handicapped children a new method of assisting the children through physical methods of retraining at a visual learning center. Describes the method of training which was developed by Professor Brian Cleary.
Education
Dist - CRAF **Prod** - BRIANC 1967

Moving machines - kids at play, big machines at work 25 MIN
VHS
Color (G K)
$14.95 purchase _ #AC08
Shows 12 big machines at work, contrasted with kids using similar toys.
Health and Safety; Psychology
Dist - SVIP

Moving Mountains 27 MIN
16mm
Color (A)
LC 82-700543
Shows the successful integration of women into the outdoor crew at the Fording Coal Mine Company's open pit mine in Elkford, British Columbia.
Social Science; Sociology
Dist - MOBIUS **Prod** - USTLW 1981

Moving mountains 30 MIN
16mm
Color (G IND)
$5.00 rental
Looks at women working beside men in open pit mines in Elkford, British Columbia, driving mammoth bulldozers and loaders and working in blasting crews. Reveals that the company resisted hiring women for this work until the union took legal steps to force the company's hand. The women talk about why they want to do this work, the men's attitudes toward them, and the support they received from their union.
Business and Economics; Industrial and Technical Education; Social Science; Sociology
Dist - AFLCIO **Prod** - USTLW 1981

Moving mountains - the Montreal Yiddish theatre in the USSR 28 MIN
VHS
Color (G)
$34.95 purchase _ #915
Follows Dora Wasserman, director of the Montreal Yiddish Theatre, and her talented troupe of performers to a 1990 reunion - after a 40 year separation - with her sister and her birthplace. Travels to Moscow, Odessa, Kiev to bring the Yiddish play, Sages of Chelm, to the Jews living there.
Geography - World; Literature and Drama; Sociology
Dist - ERGOM **Prod** - ERGOM 1992

Moving mountains - the story of the Yiu Mien 58 MIN
16mm / VHS
Color (H C G)
$895.00, $445.00 purchase, $100.00, $75.00 rental
Looks at the Yiu Mien, a group of Southeast Asian refugees from the mountains of Laos whose involvement with the CIA during the Vietnam War forced the Mien to lose their homeland. Portrays their struggle to adapt to life in the United states using footage of the Miens in their mountain homeland, their present day rituals in city apartments, and the contrast of their culture with the mainstream American culture. Produced and directed by Elaine Velazquez.
History - United States; History - World; Sociology
Dist - FLMLIB

Moving Myths 52 MIN
VHS / 16mm
Color (G)
$295.00 purchase, $85.00 rental; LC 89715586
Looks at Protestant and Catholic churches in Ireland. Examines the myths and realities of their influence. Considers that a majority of both Protestamts and Catholics are not practicing Christians and do not attend church regularly. Churches continue to wield tremendous educational and legislative influence on issues such as abortion, contraception, homosexuality and women's rights.
Geography - World; Health and Safety; History - World; Religion and Philosophy; Sociology
Dist - CNEMAG **Prod** - BELIV 1989

Moving North to Chicago - 1900 - 1945 - 8 20 MIN
VHS
Geography in US History Series
Color (H)
Highlights the geographic concept of movement. Centers on a black family moving to Chicago from the South early in the 20th century to represent the rural to urban migration that occurred at that time. Part 8 of a ten - part series which emphasizes the study of American geography within the context of American history courses using geographic concepts.
Geography - United States; History - United States; Sociology
Dist - AITECH **Prod** - AITECH 1991

Moving Oil 21 MIN
16mm / U-matic / VHS
Color (IND)
Documents the operation of a crude oil pipeline company from the wellhead to the products terminal. Shows functions of the gauger, operations coordinator, terminal supervisor and other employees as oil and products are moved through the pipeline.
Business and Economics; Industrial and Technical Education; Social Science
Dist - UTEXPE **Prod** - UTEXPE 1981

Moving on 15 MIN
VHS
Art's place series
Color (K P)

$49.00 purchase, $15.00 rental _ #295813
Reveals that Leo has decided to leave Art's place to become a great artist, so his friends sadly prepare a going - away party for him. Everyone makes presents involving motion - an action picture, a flip book, a puppet and a mobile - and Leo has second thoughts about his move. Part of a series combining songs, stories, animation, puppets and live actors to convey the pleasure of artistic expression. Includes an illustrated teacher's guide.
Fine Arts
Dist - TVOTAR **Prod** - TVOTAR 1989

Moving on 15 MIN
U-matic / VHS
Work - the inside story series
Color (H C)
#389103; LC 91-706543
Focuses on how to leave a job without burning your bridges, and how to transfer skills and experience to a new workplace. Part of a series that offers practical advice to teens entering the workforce.
Business and Economics; Guidance and Counseling; Psychology
Dist - TVOTAR **Prod** - TVOTAR 1991

Moving on 27 MIN
VHS / 16mm
Color (H C A)
Leads students through a skill building program and concentrates on changing self - attitudes as a way of dealing with misconceptions of blindness.
Education; Psychology
Dist - IOWA **Prod** - IOWA 1984

Moving on 29 MIN
Videoreel / VT2
Making Things Grow III Series
Color
Agriculture
Dist - PBS **Prod** - WGBHTV

Moving on 15 MIN
U-matic
Job Skills Series
(H C A)
Deals with terminating employment in a positive way. Also looks at budgeting income and understanding the payslip and deductions.
Business and Economics; Guidance and Counseling; Science - Physical
Dist - ACCESS **Prod** - ACCESS 1982

Moving on series
Awkward loads 12 MIN
Awkward places 9 MIN
Helping hands 9 MIN
Dist - IFB

Moving on - the Hunger for Land in Zimbabwe 52 MIN
16mm
Color
Uses rare archival footage to recount the history of Zimbabwe, from before the arrival of the Europeans to the post - independence era. Contrasts a wealthy white family with the plight of a poor black family which barely scrapes a subsistence from poor land. Studies the complex legacy of colonialism.
History - United States; History - World
Dist - CANWRL **Prod** - CANWRL 1982

Moving on - the Hunger for Land Zimbabwe 52 MIN
U-matic / VHS / 16mm
Color (A)
LC 84-707115
Contrasts a black community barely eking out an existence on subpar land and an affluent white family employing modern farming techniques on lush acres in the African nation of Zimbabwe.
Agriculture; Geography - World; Sociology
Dist - CANWRL **Prod** - BELZIM 1983

A Moving Picture 54 MIN
16mm / U-matic / VHS
Color; Stereo (J H A)
$795.00, $300.00 purchase, $80.00 rental
Presents a National Ballet of Canada performance of an Ann Ditchburn dance which incorporates animation and optical effects.
Fine Arts
Dist - BULFRG **Prod** - RHOMBS 1989

Moving pictures 25 MIN
U-matic / VHS / 16mm
Making the most of the micro series; Episode 9
Color (J)
Uses portions of the feature films TRON and The Works to show what can be done by the computer in animation of motion pictures. Demonstrates a Computer Aided Design System that allows experimentation and interior design without moving furniture.
Mathematics
Dist - FI **Prod** - BBCTV 1983

Moving pictures 100 MIN
VHS
B&W (G)
$150.00 rental, $90.00 purchase
Features dream - images captured in slow, horizontal tracking shots. Meditates on and exposes the unconscious mind by using a variety of techniques from collage imagery, free association, lights and shadows to striking compositions, fragments of speech and music and catchy rhythms.
Fine Arts; Psychology
Dist - CANCIN **Prod** - MYERSR 1990

Moving Pictures - the Art of Jan Lenica 19 MIN
U-matic / VHS / 16mm
Color (J)
LC 76-701940
Shows Jan Lenica creating his latest animated film, Landscape. Attempts to distill the essence of the creative process in showing how the animator works.
Fine Arts
Dist - PHENIX **Prod** - PHENIX 1975

Moving - Product Liability - Tots
VHS / U-matic
Consumer Survival Series
Color
Presents tips on moving, product liability and child care.
Home Economics
Dist - MDCPB **Prod** - MDCPB

Moving Right Along Series
Bro 30 MIN
Diana's Big Break 30 MIN
Everybody's Doing it 30 MIN
It's a Family Matter 30 MIN
Jennifer's Choice 30 MIN
A Matter of Life and Death 30 MIN
Mr Juanderful 30 MIN
Smotherly Love 30 MIN
Stop the World - Maggie Wants to Get Off 30 MIN
Trust Brenda 30 MIN
Dist - CORF

Moving Spaces - 3 to the 4th power 16 MIN
16mm
B&W (G)
$20.00 rental
Explores the ways in which temporal and spatial equations are simulated by the filming and projection of 24 still photographs per second onto a white screen. Presents a film by David Gerstein.
Fine Arts
Dist - CANCIN

Moving Still 57 MIN
U-matic / VHS
Nova Series
Color (H C A)
LC 81-706778
Traces the history of photography from the early camera obscura to cinematic revelations of behavior and processes too slow or too fast for the human eye to perceive.
Fine Arts; History - World; Industrial and Technical Education
Dist - TIMLIF **Prod** - WGBHTV 1981

Moving still 14 MIN
16mm
B&W (G)
$56.00 rental
Deals with the space of many levels within a single movement, which has a circular form, in a production which lasted for one and a half years.
Fine Arts
Dist - CANCIN **Prod** - WONGAL 1974

Moving Target 32 MIN
16mm
Color
LC 78-701316
Documents the various uses of electro - motive diesel power. Shows the diesel engine in use in the Far East, Europe, Mexico and the United States. Includes scenes of factory assembly of the diesel engine.
Industrial and Technical Education
Dist - GM **Prod** - GM 1978

Moving the Earth 15 MIN
U-matic / VHS
Explorers Unlimited Series
Color (P I)
Explains that three steps in manufacturing earth - moving equipment are fabricating, machining and assembly.
Business and Economics; Social Science
Dist - AITECH **Prod** - WVIZTV 1971

Moving the mountain 83 MIN
35mm / 16mm
Color (G)
$200.00 rental
Re - examines the Tiananmen Square massacre in May 1989 from the perspective of four student leaders who escaped and now live in the United States. Records their personal experiences, their hopes for China and the responsibility they feel for the hundreds, possibly thousands, who died when the government ordered the military to crush the protests. Focuses on Li Lu, one of the movement's most charismatic leaders. Consists mainly of footage shot during the demonstrations and massacre and interviews with the student leaders, some still in China. Produced by Trudie Styler; directed by Michael Apted.
Civics and Political Systems; Fine Arts; History - World; Sociology
Dist - OCTOBF

Moving toward health 28 MIN
VHS
Color (C G)
$195.00 purchase, $50.00 rental _ #38159
Demonstrates the use of Authentic Movement - dance and movement therapy - in a support group for survivors of breast cancer. Shows that Authentic Movement can be a powerful therapeutic tool enabling women to cope with the experience of cancer and its impact on their body - image and self - esteem. Produced by psychotherapist and dance therapist Sandy Dibbell - Hope.
Fine Arts; Health and Safety; Psychology; Sociology
Dist - UCEMC

Moving toward Parallel Skiing 29 MIN
Videoreel / VT2
Skiing Series
Color
Physical Education and Recreation
Dist - PBS **Prod** - KTCATV

Moving Unseen Energy 26 MIN
16mm
Color
LC 72-712178
Shows farmers the use of anhydrous ammonia and how it is delivered by pipeline. A university professor also explains the function of nitrogen in plant growth.
Agriculture
Dist - STAFER **Prod** - STAFER 1970

Moving Up 15 MIN
U-matic
Keys to the Office Series
Color (H)
Gives advice on means to advancement in business such as achievement logs, portfolios, performance evaluations, networking and attitude.
Business and Economics
Dist - TVOTAR **Prod** - TVOTAR 1986

Moving Up - Making the Transition to Head Nurse 31 MIN
U-matic / VHS
Management Skills for Nurses Series
Color
Presents an overview of a nurse's transition from staff nurse to management. Focuses on specific leadership skills required in first - line nursing managers, such as the ability to communicate, make decisions, solve problems and manage stress.
Business and Economics; Guidance and Counseling; Health and Safety
Dist - AJN **Prod** - INTGRP

Moving west 15 MIN
VHS / U-matic
America past series
Color (J H)
$125.00 purchase
Relates the westward movement and territorial expansion of the United States.
History - United States
Dist - AITECH **Prod** - KRMATV 1987

Moving with the Center of Mass 26 MIN
16mm
PSSC Physics Films Series
B&W (H)
LC FIA67-503
Demonstrates the conservation of energy and momentum of several magnetic dry ice puck interactions. Discusses and illustrates the partition of energy into two parts - - one associated with the motion of the center of mass and the other associated with the motion of the parts with respect to the center of the mass.
Science - Physical
Dist - MLA **Prod** - PSSC 1966

Moving with the Times 24 MIN
16mm
Color
Describes how Sears grew to be the world's largest retailer from a modest beginning selling mail order watches.
Business and Economics
Dist - MTP **Prod** - SEARS

Moving Wool 17 MIN
16mm
Color (H C A)
LC 76-701869
Describes new and revolutionary methods of wool handling, from shearing and grading to baling and shipping.
Business and Economics; Geography - World; Social Science
Dist - AUIS **Prod** - AUSTWB 1974

Motivation - the Classic Concepts 21 MIN
16mm / VHS
#109045 - 2 3/4
Illustrates five classic theories of motivation with several job - the - job scenarios. Shows how employees can be influenced by appeals to their wants and needs.
Business and Economics; Guidance and Counseling
Dist - MGHT

Mowgli's Brothers 26 MIN
U-matic / VHS / 16mm
Color (P I)
LC 76-703279
Based on the story Mowgli's Brothers by Rudyard Kipling about a human baby called Mowgli who is adopted by wolves, from whom he learns about love, justice and the jungle code of loyalty.
Guidance and Counseling; Literature and Drama
Dist - GA **Prod** - CJE 1977

Moyers - Facing evil 90 MIN
VHS
Color; Captioned (G)
$79.95 purchase _ #BMSP - 000
Explores the problem of human evil. Questions whether evil can be eliminated from human experience. Interviews Maya Angelou, Raul Hilberg, Barbara Jordan and others. Hosted by Bill Moyers.
History - World; Sociology
Dist - PBS **Prod** - KERA 1988

Moyers - God and politics series 210 MIN
VHS
Moyers - God and politics series
Color; Captioned (G)
$170.00 purchase _ #MYGP - 000
Explores the relationship between religious belief and political action both in the U S and abroad. Examines such topics as Central America, the battle for control among Southern Baptists, and the Christian 'Reconstructionist' movement. Three - part series hosted by Bill Moyers.
Civics and Political Systems; Religion and Philosophy
Dist - PBS **Prod** - WNETTV 1987

Moyers - God and politics series
The Kingdom divided 90 MIN
Moyers - God and politics series 210 MIN
On earth as it is in heaven 60 MIN
Dist - PBS

Moyers - in search of the Constitution series 660 MIN
VHS
Moyers - in search of the Constitution series
Color (G)
$495.00 purchase _ #MOYR - 000
Gives an 11 - part look at the United States Constitution. Interviews Supreme Court justices, philosophers, legal scholars and historians. Considers Constitutional history and implications for the present day. Hosted by Bill Moyers.
Civics and Political Systems
Dist - PBS

Moyers - in search of the Constitution series
For the people 60 MIN
God and the Constitution 60 MIN
In the Beginning 60 MIN
Justice Lewis F Powell, Jr 60 MIN
Justice Sandra Day O'Connor 60 MIN
Moyers - in search of the Constitution series 660 MIN
Nineteen Eighty - Seven Versus the Constitution 60 MIN
Dist - PBS

Moyers - Joseph Campbell and the power of myth series 360 MIN
VHS
Moyers - Joseph Campbell and the power of myth series
Color (G)
$188.70 purchase _ #TWOM - 000
Interviews the late mythological scholar Joseph Campbell. Presents Campbell's observations about mythical themes such as the hero's journey, creation, storytelling, sacrifice, and gods and goddesses. Six - part series is hosted by Bill Moyers. Produced by Apostrophe S Productions, Public Affairs Television, and Alvin H Perlmutter, Inc.
Religion and Philosophy; Social Science; Sociology
Dist - PBS

Moyers - the power of the word series 360 MIN
VHS
Moyers - the power of the word series
Color; Captioned (G)
$300.00 purchase _ #MOPW - 000
Focuses on poetry and poets. Interviews modern poets such as Robert Bly, Octavio Paz, Lucille Clifton and W S Merwin. Includes a visit to the 1988 Geraldine R Dodge Poetry Festival in New Jersey. Six - part series is hosted by Bill Moyers. Produced by Public Affairs Television and David Grubin Productions. Teachers' guide available.
English Language; Literature and Drama
Dist - PBS

Moyers - the public mind series 240 MIN
VHS
Moyers - the public mind series
Color; Captioned (G)
$200.00 purchase _ #MPUM - 000
Considers, in a four - part series, how public opinion can be shaped by image makers, pollsters, media and propaganda. Suggests that visual images have largely replaced the printed word. Questions whether politicians have successfully manipulated the media. Explores how deception has influenced major events such as Watergate and the Vietnam War. Hosted by Bill Moyers.
Civics and Political Systems; Psychology; Sociology
Dist - PBS

Moyno Processing Cavity Pumps for Waste Treatment - Guest Lecture by Bill McGraw 19 MIN
VHS / BETA
Color
Discusses sewage disposal plants, needed equipment and supplies, and water and wastewater technology.
Health and Safety; Industrial and Technical Education; Social Science
Dist - RMIBHF **Prod** - RMIBHF

Moyshe Oysher film classics series
Presents three Yiddish theater films starring Moyshe Oysher. Includes The Cantor's Son, Overture to Glory and The Singing Blacksmith.
The Cantor's son - Dem Khazn's Zindl 90 MIN
Overture to glory - Der Vilner shtot Khazn 85 MIN
The Singing blacksmith - Yankl der schmid 95 MIN
Dist - ERGOM **Prod** - ERGOM

Mozambique - the Struggle for Survial 57 MIN
VHS / 16mm
Color (G)
$350.00 purchase, $90.00 rental; LC 90709581
Examines Mozambique, Africa's poorest nation. Reveals that its civilian population is threatened by famine and is under siege from RENAMO, a terrorist army supported by South Africa. Chronicles the history of the Mozambique National Resistance - RENAMO - from its founding by the white government of Rhodesia. Interviews ex - Rhodesian intelligence chief Ken Flower who reveals how and why he founded RENAMO and later turned it over to the South Africans.
History - World; Sociology
Dist - CNEMAG **Prod** - CNEMAG 1988

Mozart - a childhood chronicle 224 MIN
VHS / 35mm / 16mm
B&W (G) (GERMAN WITH ENGLISH SUBTITLES)
$200.00, $300.00 rental
Uses the correspondence of Mozart, his father, mother and older sister to trace the development of the prodigy from age seven to adulthood at 20. Directed by Klaus Kirschner.
Fine Arts; History - World
Dist - KINOIC

Mozart - a Genius in His Time 53 MIN
U-matic / VHS
Man and Music Series
Color (C)
$279.00, $179.00 purchase _ #AD - 1775
Focuses on Classical Vienna. Considers the last five difficult years of Mozart's life. War in many parts of Austria impoverished the capital. People found Mozart's music difficult to listen to and perform. He died destitute just as 'The Magic Flute' was beginning to receive great acclaim. Part of a 22 - part series that sets Western music into the historial and cultural context of its time.
Biography; Fine Arts; Geography - World; History - World
Dist - FOTH **Prod** - FOTH

Mozart and Handel - Israel Philharmonic Orchestra conducted by Zubin Mehta 45 MIN
VHS
Huberman Festival series
Color (G)
$19.95 purchase_#1357
Features violinist Itzhak Perlman and Pinchas Zukerman with Zubin Mehta and the Israel Philharmonic Orchestra. Includes performances of Mozart's Sinfonia Concertante for Violin, Viola and Orchestra in E Flat Major, K.364, and Passacaglia by Handel.
Fine Arts
Dist - KULTUR

Mozart and Haydn - Polish Chamber Orchestra, Conducted by Jerzy Maksymiuk 60 MIN
VHS
Color (G)
$29.95 purchase _ #1129
Presents 'Eine Kleine Nachtmusik Divertimento K136,' first movement, by Mozart, and the Farewell of 'Symphony No 45' by Haydn. Features Jerzy Masymiuk conducting the Polish Chamber Orchestra in the Haydnsaal of the Schloss Esterhazy.
Fine Arts; Geography - World
Dist - KULTUR

Mozart and His Music 13 MIN
16mm / U-matic / VHS
Color (I J H C A)
$315.00, $220.00 purchase _ #761
Shows scenes of Mozart's life against the backgrounds of Salzburg and Vienna.
Fine Arts
Dist - CORF **Prod** - CORF 1954

Mozart - Aufzeichnung Einer Jugend 230 MIN
16mm
B&W (GERMAN (ENGLISH SUBTITLES))
A German language motion picture available with or without English subtitles. Portrays Wolfgang Amadeus Mozart and his artistic development at the ages of 7, 12, and 20. Based on his and his family's authenticated letters and documents.
Fine Arts; Foreign Language; Literature and Drama
Dist - WSTGLC **Prod** - WSTGLC 1976

The Mozart Brothers 98 MIN
16mm
Color (G)
Presents an independent production by Suzanne Osten. Portrays a Swedish opera director, an enfant terrible anguished and divorce - wracked, who has a bizarre vision of a production of 'Don Giovanni' by Mozart. Features comic performances by stars of the Stockholm Opera and the musical score of Mozart's opera. Also available in 35mm film format.
Fine Arts; Literature and Drama
Dist - FIRS

Mozart - Concert in Tarascon Castle 60 MIN
VHS
Color (G)
$19.95 purchase _ #1249
Presents a concert of music by Mozart, including his 'Piano Concerto No 9,' 'Flute Concerto No 2' and 'Andante For Flute.' Features Jerzy Maksymiuk conducting the Polish Chamber Orchestra.
Fine Arts
Dist - KULTUR

Mozart - Dropping the Patron 53 MIN
U-matic / VHS
Man and Music Series
Color (C)
$279.00, $179.00 purchase _ #AD - 1774
Focuses on Classical Vienna. Considers Mozart who left his patron after physical abuse by his employer's steward. Shows Mozart's career before and after this point. Part of a 22 - part series that sets Western music into the historial and cultural context of its time.
Fine Arts; Geography - World; History - World
Dist - FOTH **Prod** - FOTH

Mozart ensemble - Salzburg 65 MIN
VHS
Color (G)
$19.95 purchase_#1316
Portrays two of Mozart's divertimenti - KV 247 & KV334 - set to scenes of Salzburg, where he was born and raised. Provides a blend of music and imagery. Includes dancers from LaScala, dressed in historical costumes, expressing the essence of Mozart's music.
Fine Arts
Dist - KULTUR

Mozart in Love 100 MIN
16mm
Color (G)
Presents an independent production by Mark Rappaport. Offers a witty cinematic collage.
Fine Arts
Dist - FIRS

Mozart - Le Nozze di Figaro
VHS

Color (G)
$54.98 purchase _ #SON46406V - F
Presents Mozart's opera telling the story of Figaro as interpreted by Claudio Abbado and Jonathan Miller. Stars Marie McLaughlin, Lucio Gallo, Cheryl Studer and Ruggero Raimondi. Includes two videocassettes.
Fine Arts
Dist - CAMV

Mozart piano quartets K.478 and K.493 60 MIN
VHS
Color (G)
$19.95 purchase_#1435
Presents two of Mozart's piano quartets - K.478 and K.493 - featuring Christian Zacharia on the piano with violinist Frank-Peter Zimmerman, violist Tabea Zimmermann and Tilman Wick on the violincello. Takes place at the Ludwigsburg Palace
Fine Arts
Dist - KULTUR

Mozart - Requiem 57 MIN
VHS
Color (G)
$19.95 purchase_#1319
Presents a performance of Mozart's Requiem with the London Symphony, Sir Colin Davis conducting. Features the choir and soloists Ileana Cotrubas, Helen Watts, Gwynne Howell and Stuart Burrows.
Fine Arts
Dist - KULTUR

Mozart, Smetana, Dvorak and Janacek 48 MIN
VHS
Color (G)
$19.95 purchase _ #1241
Presents a concert of music by Mozart, Smetana, Dvorak and Janacek. Features Vaclav Neumann conducting the Czech Philharmonic Orchestra. Includes 'The Moldeau' and 'Slavonic Dances.'.
Fine Arts
Dist - KULTUR

Mozart, the Clarinet, and Keith Puddy 26 MIN
U-matic / VHS / 16mm
Musical Triangle Series
Color (J)
Presents Wolfgang Amadeus Mozart (1756 - 1791), who was famous for symphonies, operas, chamber music, sonatas and concertos for piano, violin, flute and horn. Features professional musicians Keith Puddy and the Gabriel Quartet playing Mozart's music on the clarinet.
Fine Arts
Dist - MEDIAG **Prod** - THAMES 1975

Mozart - The Magic Flute 156 MIN
VHS
Color (G)
$39.95 purchase _ #VU1408V - F
Presents Mozart's opera involving Tamino and Pamina and the obstacles to their love.
Fine Arts
Dist - CAMV

Mozart's Jupiter symphony, third movement
VHS
Music in motion series
Color (J H C G)
$75.00 purchase _ #MUS02V
Expresses visually what is heard in the third movement of Mozart's Jupiter Symphony. Teaches classical music appreciation, develops interest and enhances listening enjoyment. Includes manual with suggestions for presenting the video, questions for discussion, research projects, correlations with other subject areas and listening and reading lists. Part of an eight - part series.
Fine Arts
Dist - CAMV **Prod** - MUSLOG

Mozart's Magic Flute - Ingmar Bergman
VHS / U-matic
Color
Fine Arts
Dist - MSTVIS **Prod** - MSTVIS

Mozart's Mass in C minor - K.427 60 MIN
VHS
Color (G)
$19.95 purchase_#1390
Offers a fine musical setting of the Mass liturgy. Presents conductor Helmuth Rilling rehearsing and performing Mozart's C minor Mass at the Knight's Hall in Wolfegg.
Fine Arts
Dist - KULTUR

Mozart's Requiem with Colin Davis 57 MIN
VHS
Color (S)
$29.95 purchase _ #101 - 9075
Presents Mozart's last work 'Requiem' performed by the Bavarian Radio Symphony Orchestra. Features Colin Davis as conductor and solists Edith Mathis, Trudeliese Schmidt, Peter Schreier and Gwynne Howell.
Fine Arts; Geography - World; Religion and Philosophy
Dist - FI **Prod** - RMART 1989

MPBC and the Roots of Yoga 60 MIN
U-matic / VHS
Color
Interviews Sri Gurudev at the International Vegetarian Conference in Maine, 1975. Presents several unique schools from India and documents the origins of Yoga.
Religion and Philosophy
Dist - IYOGA **Prod** - TIMLIF

Mr and Mrs Maternity 22 MIN
16mm
Color (H C A)
LC FIA61-804
Provides pre - natal training and information. Discusses the physiological and psychological events of normal pregnancy, labor and delivery.
Health and Safety; Science - Natural
Dist - CLI **Prod** - CLI

Mr and Mrs Pig's Evening Out 9 MIN
U-matic / 35mm strip
Color (K P I)
LC 85-700509
Reveals the perils of ten little piglets when, as it turns out, the new babysitter is a wolf in babysitter clothing, as Mr and Mrs Pig have an evening out. Provides chills and thrills for young viewers as all turns out for the good.
English Language; Literature and Drama
Dist - WWS **Prod** - WWS 1984

Mr and Mrs Robin's Family 10 MIN
U-matic / VHS / 16mm
Color (P I)
$255.00, $180.00 purchase _ #3888; LC 78-700508
Tells about a family of robins who arrive in a young girl's backyard in spring. Explains how the mother robin lays her eggs and how the baby robins eat, learn to fly and leave the nest.
Science - Natural
Dist - CORF **Prod** - CORF 1977

Mr Bean's Special Day 15 MIN
U-matic
Two Plus You - Math Patrol One Series
Color (K P)
Presents a review of the basic mathematical concepts of the series.
Education; Mathematics
Dist - TVOTAR **Prod** - TVOTAR 1976

Mr Beans's New Games 15 MIN
U-matic
Two Plus You - Math Patrol One Series
Color (K P)
Presents the mathematical concepts of operation of subtraction and the construction of subtraction number sequences.
Education; Mathematics
Dist - TVOTAR **Prod** - TVOTAR 1976

Mr Big 30 MIN
16mm
Color; B&W
Features a businessman from the city finding himself locked up in a small town jail after an auto accident in which he seriously injured an elderly woman.
Guidance and Counseling
Dist - FAMF **Prod** - FAMF

Mr Blandings Builds His Dream House 93 MIN
BETA
B&W
Stars Cary Grant and Myrna Loy as a couple who decide to move from their New York City apartment to an old home in the Connecticut countryside. Shows how their attempts to remodel the house result in chaos.
Fine Arts
Dist - RMIBHF **Prod** - UNKNWN 1948

Mr Boogie Woogie 30 MIN
U-matic
Color (G)
$39.95 purchase
Takes a look at blues pianist Mose Vinson from the early days of portable color video. Features Memphis Slim and Ma Rainey II, with informal performances by Mr Boogie Woogie and interviews from his boyhood home in Mississippi. Produced by Ann Rickey.
Biography; Fine Arts
Dist - CANCIN **Prod** - KRASIL 1978

Mr Business 3 MIN
VHS / 16mm
Color (PRO)
$245.00 purchase, $125.00 rental, $30.00 preview
Uses puppets to humorously comment on business terms and procedures. Introduces a bread during businesss meetings.
Business and Economics; Psychology
Dist - UTM **Prod** - UTM

Mr Chairman - the Fundamentals of Parliamentary Law 13 MIN
16mm / U-matic / VHS
Color; B&W (H C)
$49.00 purchase _ #1758
Uses animated sequences to show why rules of order are essential to democratic debate and decision - making. Suggests ways parliamentary procedures can be adapted to various groups.
Business and Economics; Civics and Political Systems; English Language
Dist - EBEC **Prod** - EBEC 1959

Mr Chimp Goes to the Circus 11 MIN
16mm
Color (P I A)
Presents a hilarious role for the jungle compound chimpanzee, Tamba, star of the Bonzo pictures. Dubbed in voices for the chimpanzees add to the comic effect.
Literature and Drama
Dist - AVED **Prod** - AVED 1958

Mr Clean 1 MIN
U-matic / VHS
Color
Shows a classic animated television commercial which the original theme song.
Business and Economics; Psychology; Sociology
Dist - BROOKC **Prod** - BROOKC

Mr Corbett's ghost 45 MIN
VHS
Heritage stories collection series
Color (J H)
$49.00 purchase _ #60307 - 126
Presents a story written in the style of British author Charles Dickens.
Literature and Drama
Dist - GA **Prod** - GA 1992

Mr Curry Takes a Bath - Fortune Telling 11 MIN
U-matic / VHS / 16mm
Paddington Bear, Series 1 Series
Color (K P I)
LC 77-700675
Presents an animated version of two episodes from an unpublished children's book by Michael Bond. Tells about the small bear, Paddington, and his adventures with a neighbor and a fortune - teller.
Fine Arts; Literature and Drama
Dist - ALTSUL **Prod** - BONDM 1977

Mr Dead and Mrs Free 50 MIN
VHS / U-matic
Color
Juxtaposes disparate elements of American culture such as sex, soft music, violence and power. Emphasizes the brutal and grotesque.
Fine Arts
Dist - KITCHN **Prod** - KITCHN

Mr Deeds Goes to Town 118 MIN
16mm
B&W (J)
Stars Gary Cooper as a small - town greeting - card verse writer who inherits an unwanted 20 million dollars and goes on trial for his sanity when he tries to give it all away.
Fine Arts
Dist - TIMLIF **Prod** - CPC 1936

Mr Edison's Dilemma - the Perplexing Problem of Keeping Our Lights on 18 MIN
16mm
Color (J H)
Analyzes the electric power business. Provides basic information about the production of electricity in power plants and the fuels used in the process. Explores its distribution in homes, businesses and industry.
Home Economics; Industrial and Technical Education; Social Science
Dist - CONPOW **Prod** - CENTRO

Mr Eichhorn's Golfball 5 MIN
16mm
Color (J)
Presents a probing examination of a golfball's most inner self.
Literature and Drama; Physical Education and Recreation
Dist - UWFKD **Prod** - UWFKD

Mr Fixit - My Dad 9 MIN
16mm
Color (J)
Presents a dramatization about the problems confronting a father when his son is arrested on a marijuana charge. Shows how he must decide to let justice take its course or intercede on his son's behalf.
Guidance and Counseling; Psychology; Sociology
Dist - AUIS **Prod** - FLMAUS 1976

Mr Flanagan, the Chaplain and Mr Lincoln 30 MIN
16mm

B&W
Dramatizes a Civil War incident which led to the repeal of discriminatory legislation limiting chaplaincy appointments in the armed services to 'ORDAINED MINISTERS OF THE CHRISTIAN FAITH.' Explains that the ultimate result was the commissioning of a Jewish chaplain in the Union army. (Kinescope).
History - United States; Religion and Philosophy
Dist - NAAJS **Prod** - JTS 1962

Mr Freedom 95 MIN
16mm
Color (C A)
Presents a cartoon on American intervention abroad in the name of freedom.
Fine Arts
Dist - GROVE **Prod** - GROVE

Mr Frenhoffer and the Minotaur 21 MIN
16mm
B&W (C)
$260.00
Experimental film by Sidney Peterson.
Fine Arts
Dist - AFA **Prod** - AFA 1948

Mr Frog Went a - Courtin' 5 MIN
16mm
Color (K P I)
LC 76-703371
Depicts, through the use of animation, the Scottish folksong Mr Froggie Went A - Courtin,' which tells about a frog who courts and marries a mouse. Shows how nature intervenes at the wedding feast when a large snake preys on the wedding party.
Fine Arts; Literature and Drama
Dist - NFBC **Prod** - NFBC 1976
FI

Mr Goshu, the Cellist 19 MIN
16mm / U-matic / VHS
Color (P I)
LC 72-707275
Presents the story of a young cellist in a symphony orchestra through animated puppets.
Fine Arts
Dist - IFB **Prod** - GAKKEN 1969

Mr Hayashi 3 MIN
16mm
B&W (C)
$168.00
Experimental film by Bruce Baillie.
Fine Arts
Dist - AFA **Prod** - AFA 1961

Mr Horse 26 MIN
16mm / U-matic / VHS
Color (H C A)
LC 83-700378
Views an old man's life, his displacement in the world and his decision to remain in control of his destiny.
Health and Safety; Sociology
Dist - PHENIX **Prod** - HARK 1981

Mr Hulot's holiday 86 MIN
VHS
B&W (G)
$24.95 purchase _ #HUL030
Introduces Mr Hulot in this wildly funny satire of middle - class vacationers on a summer holiday. Features the director Jacques Tati as the eccentric Hulot, whose presence at a very proper French seaside resort provokes one outrageous catastrophe after another. Pays homage to the classic silent comedies by blending colorful characters, sparse dialogue, impeccably timed sight gags and an innovative sound track.
Fine Arts; Literature and Drama
Dist - HOMVIS **Prod** - JANUS 1953

Mr Hyde 5 MIN
16mm
Color (J H C)
Presents a cartoon twist to the Jekyll and Hyde story, involving the chicken and the egg question as to who came first - Dr Jekyll or Mr Hyde.
Literature and Drama
Dist - CFS **Prod** - CFS

Mr Jefferson and his university 52 MIN
VHS
Color (C G H)
$149.00 purchase _ #EX4108
Focusses on the places designed and built by Thomas Jefferson. Examines Jefferson's thought and achievements.
Biography; Fine Arts
Dist - FOTH

Mr Jefferson's Legacy 29 MIN
16mm
Color
LC 77-700557
Uses 18th - century homes, taverns, meeting places and artifacts, as well as Monticello and the University of Virginia to provide a historical background in documenting the influence of Thomas Jefferson's birthplace, Albemarle County, Virginia, on his life.
Biography; History - United States
Dist - GUG **Prod** - CHARLT 1976

Mr Johnson's Had the Course 28 MIN
U-matic / VHS / 16mm
Insight Series
Color; B&W (H A)
LC 78-705427
Features a failing college student, who is afraid of losing his draft deferment, invading a professor's home and demanding a passing grade at gun point.
Civics and Political Systems; Guidance and Counseling; Psychology; Sociology
Dist - PAULST **Prod** - PAULST 1969

Mr Juanderful 30 MIN
16mm / U-matic / VHS
Moving Right Along Series
Color (J H A)
Reveals that when Juan's dream date for the school dance suddenly turns him down, he doesn't cope well with the rejection, especially because he feels he's letting his father down.
Psychology; Sociology
Dist - CORF **Prod** - WQED 1983

Mr Justice Blackmun 60 MIN
VHS / U-matic
In search of the Constitution series
Color (A G)
$59.95, $79.95 purchase _ #MOYR - 102
Interviews the Supreme Court Justice who wrote the majority opinion in Roe v Wade, the case that legalized abortion. Discusses the moral challenge of interpreting the Constitution. Part of an 11 - part series in which Bill Moyers examines the vitality of our nation's most important document by listening to people who interpret and teach it and people whose lives have been changed by it.
Civics and Political Systems; Sociology
Dist - PBS

Mr Justice Brennan 60 MIN
U-matic / VHS
In search of the Constitution series
Color (A G)
$59.95, $79.95 purchase _ #MOYR - 104
Visits with the senior justice of the present Supreme Court, who has been called America's most unyielding defender of individual rights. Part of an 11 - part series in which Bill Moyers examines the vitality of our nation's most important document by listening to people who interpret and teach it and people whose lives have been changed by it.
Civics and Political Systems
Dist - PBS

Mr Justice Douglas 52 MIN
16mm / U-matic / VHS
Color (J)
LC 73-700003
Presents a conversation with Justice Douglas ranging from old Supreme Court decisions, and the court's frame of reference, to FDR, the Kennedys, Harry Truman, electronic surveillance, busing, army spying and civil protest.
Biography; Civics and Political Systems
Dist - CAROUF **Prod** - CBSTV 1972

Mr Kennedy and Mr Krushchev 20 MIN
U-matic / VHS / 16mm
Twentieth Century History Series
Color (H C A)
Documents Fidel Castro's overthrow of the Cuban dictatorship of Fulgencio Batista. Discusses the rise to power of Nikita Krushchev in the Soviet Union and John Kennedy's election. Tells how these two powerful leaders confronted each other in 1963 over the establishment of Soviet rocket sites in Cuba.
Biography; History - United States; History - World
Dist - FI **Prod** - BBCTV 1981

Mr Klein 124 MIN
16mm
Color (FRENCH (ENGLISH SUBTITLES))
Tells about Robert Klein, a gentile art dealer in Nazi - occupied Paris, whose identity becomes confused with that of a Jew with the same name. Includes English subtitles.
Fine Arts; Foreign Language
Dist - TLECUL **Prod** - TLECUL

Mr Koumal Battles His Conscience 2 MIN
16mm
Mr Koumal Series
Color (J)
LC 72-713680
A satirical cartoon featuring Mr Koumal, an idea man who is thwarted at every turn. Designed to stimulate discussion on the realities of life and to help each individual develop acceptable patterns of behavior.
Guidance and Counseling; Literature and Drama; Psychology; Social Science; Sociology
Dist - SIM **Prod** - KRATKY 1971

Mr Koumal Carries the Torch 2 MIN
16mm
Mr Koumal Series
Color (J)
LC 72-704703
Presents Mr Koumal, an idea man, who is stumped at every turn. Stimulates discussion focused on the realities of life and helps each individual develop acceptable patterns of behavior.
Guidance and Counseling; Psychology; Sociology
Dist - SIM **Prod** - KRATKY 1969

Mr Koumal Crusades for Love 2 MIN
16mm
Mr Koumal Series
Color (J)
LC 78-705277
A satirical cartoon featuring Mr Koumal, an idea man who is stumped at every turn. Designed to stimulate discussion on the realities of life and to help each individual develop acceptable patterns of behavior.
Guidance and Counseling; Psychology; Sociology
Dist - SIM **Prod** - KRATKY 1969

Mr Koumal Discovers Koumalia 2 MIN
16mm
Mr Koumal Series
Color (J)
LC 74-713678
A satirical cartoon featuring Mr Koumal, an idea man who is thwarted at every turn. Designed to stimulate discussion on the realities of life and to help each individual develop acceptable patterns of behavior.
Guidance and Counseling; Literature and Drama; Psychology; Social Science; Sociology
Dist - SIM **Prod** - KRATKY 1971

Mr Koumal Faces Death 2 MIN
16mm
Mr Koumal Series
Color (J)
LC 74-705276
A satirical cartoon featuring Mr Koumal, an idea man who is stumped at every turn. Designed to stimulate discussion on the realities of life and to help each individual develop acceptable patterns of behavior.
Guidance and Counseling; Psychology; Sociology
Dist - SIM **Prod** - KRATKY 1969

Mr Koumal Flies Like a Bird 2 MIN
16mm
Mr Koumal Series
Color (J)
LC 70-705275
A satirical cartoon featuring Mr Koumal, an idea man, who is stumped at every turn. Stimulates discussion focused on the realities of life and helps each individual develop acceptable patterns of behavior.
Guidance and Counseling; Psychology; Sociology
Dist - SIM **Prod** - KRATKY 1969

Mr Koumal Gets Involved 2 MIN
16mm
Mr Koumal Series
Color (J)
LC 78-713679
A satirical cartoon featuring Mr Koumal, an idea man who is thwarted at every turn. Designed to stimulate discussion on the realities of life and to help each individual develop acceptable patterns of behavior.
Guidance and Counseling; Literature and Drama; Psychology; Social Science; Sociology
Dist - SIM **Prod** - KRATKY 1971

Mr Koumal Invents a Robot 1 MIN
16mm
Mr Koumal Series
Color (J)
LC 77-705274
A satirical cartoon featuring Mr Koumal, an idea man, who is stumped at every turn. Stimulates discussion focused on the realities of life and helps each individual develop acceptable patterns of behavior.
Guidance and Counseling; Psychology; Sociology
Dist - SIM **Prod** - KRATKY 1969

Mr Koumal Moves to the Country 2 MIN
16mm
Mr Koumal Series
Color (J H A)
LC 71-705278
A satirical cartoon featuring Mr Koumal, an idea man who is stumped at every turn. Designed to stimulate discussion on the realities of life and to help each individual develop acceptable patterns of behavior.

Guidance and Counseling; Psychology; Sociology
Dist - SIM **Prod** - KRATKY 1969

Mr Koumal Series
Mr Koumal Battles His Conscience 2 MIN
Mr Koumal Carries the Torch 2 MIN
Mr Koumal Crusades for Love 2 MIN
Mr Koumal Discovers Koumalia 2 MIN
Mr Koumal Faces Death 2 MIN
Mr Koumal Flies Like a Bird 2 MIN
Mr Koumal Gets Involved 2 MIN
Mr Koumal Invents a Robot 1 MIN
Mr Koumal Moves to the Country 2 MIN
Dist - SIM

Mr Lincoln and the Bible, Pt 1 30 MIN
16mm
B&W (R)
Maurice Samuel and Mark Van Doren discuss the influence of the Bible on the life and writings of Abraham Lincoln. (Kinescope).
Biography; History - United States; Religion and Philosophy
Dist - NAAJS **Prod** - JTS 1960

Mr Lincoln and the Bible, Pt 2 30 MIN
16mm
B&W (R)
Maurice Samuel and Mark Van Doren discuss the influence of the Bible on the life and writings of Abraham Lincoln. (Kinescope).
Biography; Religion and Philosophy
Dist - NAAJS **Prod** - JTS 1960

Mr Lincoln of Illinois 30 MIN
U-matic / VHS
Color (G)
$249.00, $149.00 purchase _ #AD - 2024
Recreates Abraham Lincoln's Illinois. Uses period photographs, art and memorabilia. Visits Lincoln sites in and around New Salem and Springfield. Recalls the words of Lincoln and his friends and associates and commentary by Lincoln scholars.
Biography; History - United States
Dist - FOTH **Prod** - FOTH

Mr Lincoln's Springfield 25 MIN
16mm
Color
LC 77-703227
Uses dramatizations and old photographs to trace the 20 - year career of Abraham Lincoln in Springfield, Illinois.
Biography; History - United States
Dist - USNAC **Prod** - USNPS 1977

Mr Lincoln's Springfield 30 MIN
VHS
National park series
Color (J H C G)
$34.95 purchase _ #FHF57V
Visits the town, Springfield, Illinois, and the beautifully restored home where Abe Lincoln lived for nearly 25 years before he became President. Part of a five - part series on United States' national parks.
Biography; Geography - United States; History - United States
Dist - CAMV

Mr Magoo at Sea 112 MIN
16mm
Color (P I)
Fine Arts
Dist - FI **Prod** - FI

Mr Magoo in Charles Dickens' 'Christmas Carol' 60 MIN
U-matic / VHS / 16mm
Color
Jim Backus is the voice of Magoo and leads the other star voices in an interpretation of Charles Dickens' classic.
Fine Arts; Literature and Drama
Dist - FI **Prod** - FLEET

Mr Magoo in Great World Classic Series
Paul Revere 30 MIN
Dist - FI

Mr Magoo in great world classics series
Captain Kidd 25 MIN
The Count of Monte Cristo 25 MIN
Cyrano 25 MIN
Dick Tracy with Mr Magoo 25 MIN
Dr Frankenstein and Mr Magoo 25 MIN
King Arthur 26 MIN
Rip Van Winkle 26 MIN
Sherlock Holmes with Mr Magoo 26 MIN
William Tell 26 MIN
Dist - FI

Mr Magoo in Sherwood Forest 105 MIN
16mm
Color (P I)
Fine Arts
Dist - FI **Prod** - FI

Mr Magoo in World Classics Series
Gunga Din 25 MIN
Mid - Summer Night's Dream 25 MIN
Moby Dick 26 MIN
Dist - FI

Mr Magoo's Christmas Carol 52 MIN
16mm / VHS / U-matic
Color (P I)
LC 79-701807; 79-701780
A shortened version of the motion picture Mr Magoo's Christmas Carol. Presents an animated adaptation of Charles Dickens' story A Christmas Carol with the cartoon character Mr Magoo in the role of Ebenezer Scrooge.
Fine Arts
Dist - MCFI **Prod** - UPA

Mr Magoo's Christmas Carol, Pt 1 26 MIN
16mm / U-matic / VHS
Color (P I)
LC 79-701807
Presents an animated adaptation of Charles Dickens' story A Christmas Carol with the cartoon character Mr Magoo in the role of Ebenezer Scrooge.
Fine Arts
Dist - MCFI **Prod** - UPA

Mr Magoo's Christmas Carol, Pt 2 26 MIN
U-matic / VHS / 16mm
Color (P I)
LC 79-701807
Presents an animated adaptation of Charles Dickens' story A Christmas Carol with the cartoon character Mr Magoo in the role of Ebenezer Scrooge.
Fine Arts
Dist - MCFI **Prod** - UPA

Mr Magrooter's Marvelous Machine 8 MIN
U-matic / VHS / 16mm
Color (P I J H C)
LC 74-712926
Tells the story of a man who proposes to add one more mechanized boon to man's creature comforts - a marvelous machine to remove the seeds from watermelons. Points out some things about the consumer market and our own truly marvelous machines.
Home Economics; Sociology
Dist - PHENIX **Prod** - KINGSP 1971

Mr Marfil's last will and testament 40 MIN
VHS
Detective stories for math problem solving series
Color (I J H)
$175.00 purchase _ #CG - 881 - VS
Follows Jerry and Jennie who are helping Constance and her husband Seymour solve the mystery of a 'treasure hunt' from the will of Constance's eccentric uncle so that Constance can get her inheritance. Involves watching students to formulate problems, finding needed data in the video and in the maps and materials in student kits. Develops number concepts, spatial concepts and sharpens problem - solving skills. Part of a series.
Literature and Drama; Mathematics; Psychology; Social Science
Dist - HRMC **Prod** - HRMC

Mr Microchip Series
Ask the teacher 30 MIN
Bits of Programming 30 MIN
Computer has a Code 30 MIN
Computers Don't do Windows 30 MIN
Does that compute 30 MIN
Flights of fancy 30 MIN
Games Computers Play 30 MIN
Information Please 30 MIN
Memory is made of this 30 MIN
Music on Key 30 MIN
A Pixel is Worth a Thousand Words 30 MIN
Problems, Problems, Problems 30 MIN
You Can Count on Computers 30 MIN
Dist - JOU

Mr Money 4 MIN
16mm / U-matic / VHS
Color
Presents a humorous tale of a man trying to cope with an automated teller machine that has a personality.
Business and Economics; Fine Arts; Literature and Drama
Dist - CORF **Prod** - FLMCOM

Mr Morita's mission 30 MIN
VHS
Business matters series
Color (A)
PdS65 purchase
Profiles one of the world's most successful business people in the 20th century - Akio Morita, chair and co-founder of SONY.
Business and Economics
Dist - BBCENE

Mr Moto Takes a Walk 13 MIN
16mm
Color (K P I)
LC FIA65-1698
Mr Moto, a macaque monkey, introduces the animals of the zoo in an alphabetical tour from aardvark to zebra.
English Language; Science - Natural
Dist - SF **Prod** - NYZS 1965

Mr Nobody 35 MIN
VHS / 16mm
Elderly at risk series
Color (H C G)
$650.00, $350.00 purchase, $65.00 rental
Features Lyn Wright as producer. Asks if mentally competent seniors have the right to neglect themselves and their surroundings to the extent that they offend the community. Focuses on quirky 65 - year - old Jack Huggins who has lived in his family's house every since the death of his parents. A bachelor, Huggins lavishes affection upon a menagerie of cats and the house is crammed with discarded appliances collected from garbage cans. His neighbors complained and health officials came and carted away his 'junk,' and for a while Huggins was declared incompetent and his financial affairs monitored by a state - appointed trustee. A senior advocacy group had him re - assessed by a psychiatrist.
Civics and Political Systems; Health and Safety
Dist - FLMLIB **Prod** - NFBC 1988

MR-1 Launch 14 MIN
16mm
Color
Examines the flight of the unmanned MR - 1.
History - World; Industrial and Technical Education; Science - Physical
Dist - NASA **Prod** - NASA

Mr Peanut's Guide to Nutrition 30 MIN
16mm
Color (P I)
Presents Mr Peanut, a cartoon character who takes the viewer through the ABC'S of vitamins, proteins, carbohydrates, fats and minerals. Illustrates the importance of balanced diet and good eating habits.
Fine Arts; Health and Safety; Home Economics; Social Science
Dist - MTP **Prod** - SBRAND

Mr Popper's Penguins
35mm strip / VHS / Cassette
Newbery Award - Winners Series
Color (I)
$66.00, $14.00 purchase
English Language; Literature and Drama
Dist - PELLER

Mr Potter Takes a Rest Cure 30 MIN
VHS / U-matic
Wodehouse Playhouse Series
Color (C A)
Presents an adaptation of the short story Mr Potter Takes A Rest Cure by P G Wodehouse.
Literature and Drama
Dist - TIMLIF **Prod** - BBCTV 1980

Mr Preble Gets Rid of His Wife 17 MIN
16mm
Color (J)
LC 81-700539
Tells how Mrs Preble thwarts her husband's tactics to murder her in the basement. Based on the short story Mr Preble Gets Rid Of His Wife by James Thurber.
Fine Arts; Literature and Drama
Dist - DIRECT **Prod** - MIDMAR 1981

Mr President, Mr President 58 MIN
U-matic / VHS
Inside Story Series
Color
Examines press coverage of the Reagan Administration. Shows cameras covering the White House press corps, before, during and after a Presidential press conference and gives the viewer a rare inside look at the problems of access and restrictions which those reporters face every day when covering the most important beat in the country.
Biography; Civics and Political Systems; Fine Arts; Literature and Drama; Social Science; Sociology
Dist - PBS **Prod** - PBS 1981

Mr Punch vs the drug alcohol 25 MIN
VHS
Color (P I J)
$30.00 purchase _ #578
Uses a Punch and Judy format to teach about alcohol use. Uses magic to introduce the concept of illusion to show that the drug alcohol has illustionary effects upon drivers and their judgment. Discusses alcohol as a drug, that beer, wine and whiskey all contain about the same amount of the drug alcohol, and the effects of alcohol on the body and mind.
Guidance and Counseling; Health and Safety; Psychology
Dist - AAAFTS **Prod** - AAAFTS 1983

Mr Roberts 123 MIN
U-matic / VHS / 16mm
Color
Based on the Broadway play Mr Roberts. Recreates the activities of a Navy officer and his crew during World War II in the South Pacific as they take their supply vessel 'between the islands of tedium and apathy with side trips to monotony.' Stars Henry Fonda, James Cagney and Jack Lemmon.
Fine Arts
Dist - FI **Prod** - HAYLE 1955

Mr Robinson Crusoe 76 MIN
16mm
B&W
Tells the story of a man who argues while on a yacht that he too could survive on a primitive paradise like Robinson Crusoe. Details what happens when he is left on the island and is later joined by a girl. Stars Douglas Fairbanks, Sr and Alfred Newman.
Fine Arts
Dist - KILLIS **Prod** - UNKNWN 1932

Mr Rooney Goes to Work 51 MIN
16mm / U-matic / VHS
Color (H C A)
LC 78-700912
Shows news commentator Andy Rooney talking to workers, company managers and union officials in an effort to determine if American productivity has declined. Concludes that Americans are far more productive than they believe themselves to be.
Business and Economics
Dist - PHENIX **Prod** - CBSTV 1978

Mr Rooney Goes to Work, Pt 1 26 MIN
U-matic / VHS / 16mm
Color (H C A)
LC 78-700912
Shows news commentator Andy Rooney talking to workers, company managers and union officials in an effort to determine if American productivity has declined. Concludes that Americans are far more productive than they believe themselves to be.
Business and Economics; Sociology
Dist - PHENIX **Prod** - CBSTV 1978

Mr Rooney Goes to Work, Pt 2 25 MIN
U-matic / VHS / 16mm
Color (H C A)
LC 78-700912
Presents news commentator Andy Rooney who explores alternatives to conventional work patterns.
Business and Economics; Sociology
Dist - PHENIX **Prod** - CBSTV 1978

Mr Rossi at the Beach 11 MIN
16mm
Color
LC 74-702132
Traces the misadventures of a man trying to have a good time at the beach.
Physical Education and Recreation; Science - Natural
Dist - CONNF **Prod** - CONNF 1973

Mr Rossi Goes Camping 11 MIN
16mm
Color (I J H C)
LC 74-702133
Shows how a search for a peaceful camping site turns into a series of confrontations with bulldozers, cows and mountain - climbing motorcycles.
Physical Education and Recreation; Science - Natural
Dist - CONNF **Prod** - CONNF 1973

Mr Rossi in Venice 16 MIN
16mm / U-matic / VHS
Color (I J H)
LC 79-700917
Describes the adventures of the mad Mr Rossi in Venice, where he tries to impress a pretty tourist by fighting pollution.
Fine Arts
Dist - TEXFLM **Prod** - BOZETO 1977

Mr Sandman 2 MIN
16mm
B&W (G)
$10.00 rental
Consists of an animated drawing in desert sand, Lake Pyramid, Nevada, by Victor Faccinto.
Fine Arts
Dist - CANCIN

Mr Saturday Night
VHS
Color (G)
$94.98 purchase
Shows Billy Crystal's comic genius at work in a sensitive portrayal of the most famous Jewish comic nobody has ever heard of.
Fine Arts
Dist - ERGOM

Mr Sears' Catalogue 60 MIN
VHS
American Experience Series
Color; Captioned (G)
$59.95 purchase _ #AMEX - 207
Suggests that the Sears Roebuck catalogue of the late 1800s was a symbol of the changes in American society. Shows how Sears went from a small business to become the world's largest merchandising firm. Emphasizes the importance of the Sears catalogue to rural Americans.
History - United States
Dist - PBS

Mr Shepard and Mr Milne 29 MIN
U-matic / VHS / 16mm
Color (H C A)
LC 73-701549
Tells about the collaboration of Ernest Shepard and A A Milne and the story behind their classic children's books through visits to the actual locales which were the scenes of the Pooh stories and poems.
Literature and Drama
Dist - WWS **Prod** - WWS 1972

Mr Sherlock Holmes of London 43 MIN
U-matic / VHS / 16mm
Color (C A)
LC 76-702947
Presents Anthony D Howlett, a noted London barrister and founding member of the Sherlock Holmes Society of London, who leads the viewer to the sites that figured prominently in Sir Arthur Conan Doyle's books. Recounts the beginning of the Sherlock Holmes mythology and reviews the publishing and film history of Doyle's works.
Fine Arts; Geography - World; Literature and Drama
Dist - UCEMC **Prod** - TAYLWF 1976

Mr Simplex Saves the Aspidistra 32 MIN
16mm
MAA Individual Lecturers Series
Color (H C T)
LC FIA65-848
Uses stop motion model photography to tell a story about Mr Simplex who introduces various maze problems and suggests possible mathematical solutions.
Mathematics
Dist - MLA **Prod** - MAA 1966

Mr Smith and Other Nonsense 29 MIN
Videoreel / VT2
Synergism - Encore Series
Color
Presents an international performance of mime, poetry, puppetry, dance, art and music.
Fine Arts; Literature and Drama
Dist - PBS **Prod** - WETATV

Mr Smith Goes to Washington 130 MIN
16mm
B&W (C I J H A)
$79.00 purchase _ #05741 94
Stars Jimmy Stewart and Jean Arthur in the story of an idealistic young senator who tangles with a political machine and a cynical Washington - wise young woman.
Civics and Political Systems; Fine Arts
Dist - TIMLIF **Prod** - CPC 1939
ASPRSS

Mr Speaker - Tip O'Neill 58 MIN
U-matic / VHS / 16mm
Color (H C A)
Looks at the day - to - day life and work of House Speaker Thomas P (Tip) O'Neill as he meets with the congressional elite, glad - hands voters back home, relaxes with his family and confers with President Jimmy Carter in the Oval Office.
Biography; Civics and Political Systems
Dist - FI **Prod** - WGBHTV 1978

Mr Story 28 MIN
U-matic / VHS / 16mm
Color (J)
Tells of an older man, Albert Story, whose life has produced no exceptional achievements, but who looks back with pride on a good life.
Guidance and Counseling
Dist - PHENIX **Prod** - PHENIX

Mr Symbol Man 50 MIN
16mm
Color (C A)
LC 76-701026
Presents a documentary on Charles K Bliss, an Austrian - australian who invented Blissymbols, a means of communication which enables a person to overcome the barriers to understanding posed by differing languages or physical handicap.
Education; Psychology
Dist - BNCHMK **Prod** - NFBC 1976

Mr Tense
U-matic / VHS
Color
Discusses treatment and prevention of cardiovascular problems. Focuses on stress.
Health and Safety; Psychology; Science - Natural
Dist - MEDFAC **Prod** - MEDFAC

Mr Thoreau Takes a Trip - a Week on the Concord and Merrimack 27 MIN
Videoreel / VT2
Synergism - Profiles, People Series
Color
Biography; Fine Arts; Literature and Drama; Religion and Philosophy
Dist - PBS **Prod** - WENHTV

MR-3 Onboard Pilot Observer 21 MIN
16mm
Color
Examines America's first manned journey into space with pre - flight preparations, readying of tracking stations and the launch of Freedom 7.
History - World; Industrial and Technical Education; Science - Physical
Dist - NASA **Prod** - NASA

Mr Tompkins in Wonderland - an Adventure on the Frontiers of Physics 31 MIN
16mm
Color (H C)
LC 76-700515
Communicates the concepts of relativistic mechanics as they affect space, time and gravitation by altering the numerical value of physical constants. Based on the book Mr Tompkins In Wonderland - An Adventure On The Frontier Of Physics by George Gamow.
Science - Physical
Dist - UAKRON **Prod** - NSF 1972

Mr Tri - State 12 MIN
16mm
Color (G)
$15.00 rental
Records a body building contest held in Chicago and featuring some of the best bodies in the Midwest. Zeroes in on one of the contestants and owner of a health club who explains the 'why' and 'what for.'
Fine Arts; Physical Education and Recreation
Dist - CANCIN **Prod** - PALAZT

MR-2 Launch 14 MIN
16mm
Color
Presents the flight of the MR - 2 and follows Ham, America's first space chimpanzee.
History - World; Industrial and Technical Education; Science - Physical
Dist - NASA **Prod** - NASA

Mr Vanik Leaves Washington 28 MIN
U-matic / VHS
Color (J)
LC 81-707017
Presents a portriat of United States Congressman Charles Vanik leaving office. Discusses the process of writing legislation and getting acts passed. Includes scenes of Vanik at a press conference, at subcommittee hearings and having lunch. Highlights the role of today's Congressman in relation to lobbyists.
Civics and Political Systems
Dist - WJKWTV **Prod** - STORBC 1980

Mr Winlucky 7 MIN
16mm
Color
LC 77-707173
An animated cartoon about James Hound, super agent, who is sent to break the bank of the crooked gambling casino.
Literature and Drama
Dist - TWCF **Prod** - TERTON 1967

Mr Wizard series

Breathing	28 MIN
Buoyancy	28 MIN
Communication theory	28 MIN
Errors in measurement	28 MIN
Fluids in motion	28 MIN
Hidden Salts	28 MIN
How to Change a Chemical Reaction	28 MIN
How Your Blood Circulates	28 MIN
Science of Orbiting	28 MIN
Scientific noise	28 MIN

Dist - MLA

Mr Wolenski, the treasure, the rescue - Tape 3
VHS
Oak Street chronicles and the good news series
Color (K P I R)

$29.95 purchase, $10.00 rental _ #35 - 860291 - 1
Features Mr Wolenski and a group of middle elementary children. Includes four modern video parables. 'Mr Wolenski' shows the kids visiting Mr Wolenski in the hospital. 'The Treasure' tells how the kids used Mr Wolenski's treasure map to find their way to the ice cream parlor, while 'The Rescue' features D J, who must enlist the kids' help to save his job.
Literature and Drama; Religion and Philosophy
Dist - APH **Prod** - ABINGP

MRI - magnetic resonance imaging 7 MIN
U-matic / VHS
Color (PRO)
$200.00 purchase, $60.00 rental _ #5285S, #5285V
Explains and illustrates what happens during magnetic resonance imaging. Uses animated computer graphics to illustrate how magnetic resonance images are obtained and recorded. Discusses the procedure with a patient - including preparation for the test, length of the procedure, and the equipment and noises the patient will see and hear.
Health and Safety
Dist - AJN **Prod** - LPRO 1989

MRI - magnetic resonance imaging 11 MIN
U-matic / VHS
Color (PRO C)
$395.00 purchase, $80.00 rental _ #C870 - VI - 048
Introduces medical, nursing and radiology students and personnel to the techniques of magnetic resonance imaging. Uses MRI images to detect and diagnose disease by providing detailed pictures of organs, bones and tissue. Cites two cases - diagnosing a brain tumor and a slipped disk. Presented by Dr Errol Levine.
Health and Safety
Dist - HSCIC

MRO Inventory Forecasting Techniques
U-matic / VHS
Effective Inventory Control Series
Color (IND)
Discusses Exponential Smoothing as most popular technique for forecasting as age rates for maintenance, repair and operations inventory. Talks about forecast error and general forecasting considerations as well as general guiding principles.
Business and Economics
Dist - GPCV **Prod** - GPCV

Mrs Amworth 29 MIN
U-matic / VHS / 16mm
Classics Dark and Dangerous - Captioned Series
Captioned; Color (P)
Stars Glynis Johns in this tale of vampires and the occult. Based on a story by E F Benson.
Literature and Drama; Sociology
Dist - LCOA **Prod** - LCOA 1977

Mrs Amworth 28 MIN
16mm / U-matic / VHS
Classics, Dark and Dangerous Series
Color (H C A) (SPANISH)
LC 76-703935
Presents an adaptation of the short story 'Mrs Amworth' by E F Benson, about modern vampirism in a small English village.
Literature and Drama; Sociology
Dist - LCOA **Prod** - LCOA 1977

Mrs Baker's House 10 MIN
16mm
Color
Presents a fun mystery story without an ending about Mrs Barker, a sweet old lady who lives alone in a Hansel and Gretel - type house in which all sorts of mysterious things happen. Describes the humorous antics of Mr Crochety, a nosy neighbor, and the mysterious happenings inside the house in order to spark creative thinking and storytelling.
English Language; Literature and Drama
Dist - ECI **Prod** - ECI

Mrs Breadwinner 12 MIN
U-matic / VHS / 16mm
Color (J)
LC 83-700171
Explores the growing number of women who earn more than their husbands and the effects this has on families. Narrated by Harry Reasoner and originally show on the CBS program 60 Minutes.
Sociology
Dist - CORF **Prod** - CBSTV 1982

Mrs Cabobble's caboose series

Apple cider time 15 MIN
Butterflies and fishing poles 15 MIN
Decorate and celebrate 15 MIN
Remember when 15 MIN
Dist - GPN

Mrs Cabobble's Caboose

April showers 15 MIN
Arrows and Tomahawks 15 MIN
Blast Off 15 MIN
Caboose caroling 15 MIN
Coats and Mittens 15 MIN
Doing the turkey trot 15 MIN
February holidays 15 MIN
Fiddle - dee - dee 15 MIN
Happy Hearts 15 MIN
Hoppin' Down the Bunny Trail 15 MIN
Keep it Movin' 15 MIN
Let's Go for a Hike 15 MIN
A Lot of Brass 15 MIN
Make a Wish 15 MIN
Making New Friends 15 MIN
The Music Man 15 MIN
Raindrops and Frog Hops 15 MIN
Rhythm and Rhymes 15 MIN
Round and Round 15 MIN
Spook in the Pumpkin Patch 15 MIN
Strike up the band 15 MIN
Summer Fun 15 MIN
Up, Down, and all Around 15 MIN
Windy Days 15 MIN
Dist - GPN

Mrs Frisbee and the Rats of NIMH
35mm strip / VHS / Cassette
Newbery Award - Winners Series
Color (I)
$66.00, $14.00 purchase
English Language; Literature and Drama
Dist - PELLER

Mrs Harding teaches resourcefully 20 MIN
U-matic / VHS / BETA
Color; PAL (T PRO)
PdS50, PdS58 purchase
Ask about the millions of dollars spent on teaching resources and if they are effective in the form of a story of Mrs Harding, who arrives at her new school to find it needs a big shake - up.
Education
Dist - EDPAT **Prod** - TASCOR

Mrs Katz and Tush
VHS
Reading rainbow series
Color; CC (K P)
$39.95 purchase
Portrays a relationship that transcends age and cultural differences in a story by Patricia Polacco and narrated by Reizl Boyzk and Rick English. Celebrates with LeVar the beauty and value of cross - cultural relationships as he visits his very own 'bubee' and learns to make challah. Part of a series offering a multicultural approach to generating reading enthusiasm with cross - curricular applications, hosted by LeVar Burton.
English Language; Literature and Drama; Psychology; Sociology
Dist - GPN **Prod** - LNMDP 1993

Mrs Mary Norton - Socialist Suffragette 30 MIN
U-matic
Color
Features Mary Norton, Vancouver Suffragette, reminiscing about the Canadian Womens' struggle for the vote.
Civics and Political Systems; History - World; Sociology
Dist - WMENIF **Prod** - WMENIF

Mrs Mixon 59 MIN
16mm
B&W (C A)
LC 71-702469
An account of the problems of a middle - aged negro woman from the rural South, her rehabilitation in a midwestern university hospital after diabetes had taken her legs and blinded her and her unresolved conflicts with white therapists.
Geography - United States; Health and Safety; History - United States; Psychology; Sociology
Dist - OSUMPD **Prod** - OHIOSU 1969

Mrs Murphy's Chowder 28 MIN
Videoreel / VT2
Environment - Today and Tomorrow Series
Color
Views water pollution not as an aesthetic issue but as a threat to man's survival. Looks at two areas of concern, an increasing demand by an ever - growing population and worsening pollution.
Science - Natural; Sociology
Dist - PBS **Prod** - KRMATV

Mrs Peabody's Beach 24 MIN
16mm / U-matic / VHS
Color (I J H)
LC 72-700150
Tells the story of a teenager who discovers a beach which is ideal for surfing, only to learn that the owner, Mrs Peabody, will permit surfing, only if he helps her develop it as a profitable business. Covers aspects of the law of supply and demand, capital investment and depreciation, diminishing returns and other aspects of basic economics.
Business and Economics; Social Science
Dist - CORF **Prod** - BELLDA 1971

Mrs Perlberg's Partner in Heaven 30 MIN
16mm
B&W (R)
Formerly titled 'MRS STEINBERG'S PARTNER IN HEAVEN.' Presents a fantasy about Mrs Perlbery on New York's East Side who, despite her own modest circumstances, is always doing good deeds - - she exemplifies the truly pious person, who practices charity as a partner of God. (Kinescope).
Religion and Philosophy
Dist - NAAJS **Prod** - JTS 1961

Mrs Ripley's trip 15 MIN
VHS
Short story series
Color (J H)
#E373; LC 90-713145
Tells a story of spiritual and economic poverty in the American Midwest in 'Mrs Ripley's Trip' by Hamlin Garland. Part of a 16 - part series which introduces American short story writers and discusses the technical aspects of short story structure.
Literature and Drama; Sociology
Dist - GPN **Prod** - CTI 1978

Mrs Ripley's Trip by Hamlin Garland 15 MIN
16mm / U-matic / VHS
Short Story Series
Color (J H C A)
LC 83 - 706130; 83-700047
Describes how a poor farm woman realizes a 23 - year - old ambition by leaving the farm for a trip to experience the civilized wonders of New York. Shows how the fulfillment of her ambition leaves her reconciled to her life of rural poverty upon her return. Based on the short story Mrs Ripley's Trip by Hamlin Garland.
Literature and Drama
Dist - IU **Prod** - IITC 1982

Mrs Ryder has the Blues 29 MIN
Videoreel / VT2
Our Street Series
Color
Sociology
Dist - PBS **Prod** - MDCPB

Mrs Tate's crusade 16 MIN
U-matic / VHS
Color (H C)
$250.00 purchase _ #HH - 6325M
Shows how crime can be reduced by sensitizing even the most violent criminals to the emotional impact of their crimes and by confronting them with the pain of the victim's surviving family members. Chronicles the involvement of Doris Tate, mother of Sharon Tate who was a victim of the Charles Manson murders in 1969.
Sociology
Dist - CORF **Prod** - ABCNEW 1990

Mrs Warren's Profession 115 MIN
16mm / U-matic / VHS
Classic Theatre Series
Color
LC 79-706925
Offers a production of George Bernard Shaw's play Mrs Warren's Profession. Explains how Mrs Warren works as a madam so that she can afford to educate her daughter.
Literature and Drama
Dist - FI **Prod** - BBCTV 1976

MS - DOS 6.0 49 MIN
VHS
Computer training series
Color (G)
$24.95 purchase _ #CI05
Teaches DOS commands such as copying files, formatting disks, undeleting files. Covers DoubleSpace, MemMaker and DeFrag. Part of a six - part series explaining PCs and software. Explains basic DOS commands, plus features new to version 6.0. Includes booklet. Produced by M - USA.
Computer Science
Dist - SVIP

MS - DOS 6.0 179 MIN
U-matic / VHS / BETA
Color; NTSC; PAL; SECAM (J H C G)
PdS99.95
Reveals that the new MS - DOS 6.0 offers a host of new utilities so that the user can get more from a PC. Features Anne Mitchard.
Computer Science
Dist - VIEWTH

MS - DOS 6.0 new features learning system 182 MIN
VHS
Color; CC (G H C IND PRO)
$595.00 purchase _ #MIC25
Trains new users and those upgrading the software.
Computer Science
Dist - EXTR **Prod** - MICROV

MS-DOS literacy
VHS
Computer software training series
Color (PRO G)
$49.95 purchase _ #AAT01V
Shows viewers how to use computer software. Provides information on commands and time-saving techniques used with MS-DOS through showing the viewer both the computer screen and keyboard. Uses simple, straightfoward techniques to help the viewer tackle the sometimes difficult task of learning a new computer software program.
Computer Science
Dist - CAMV

MS - DOS literacy - version 1 thru 3.3
VHS
Excellence in computer literacy series
Color (G)
$49.95 purchase
Covers the MS - DOS system, version 1 through 3.3. Shows how to 'bootup' computers. Looks at what files are and how computers use them, how to move and copy files to avoid time - consuming rekeying. Discusses the advantages of hard disks and how to use special commands and shortcuts.
Computer Science
Dist - SMPUB **Prod** - SMPUB

MS-DOS - the latest and greatest
VHS
Computer software training series
Color (PRO G)
$49.95 purchase _ #AAT11V
Teaches viewers how to use computer software. Provides information on commands and time-saving techniques used with MS-DOS through showing the viewer both the computer screen and keyboard. Focuses on the latest innovations within the MS-DOS program. Uses simple, straightfoward techniques to help the viewer tackle the sometimes difficult task of learning a new computer software program.
Computer Science
Dist - CAMV

MS - DOS - the latest and greatest - version 4 thru 5.0
VHS
Excellence in computer literacy series
Color (G)
$49.95 purchase
Covers MS - DOS, version 4 through 5.0. Views the menu - driven MS - DOS and its features. Explores the DOS shell. Shows how to combine and manipulate files, display more file information and master the built - in utilities program.
Computer Science
Dist - SMPUB **Prod** - SMPUB

MS - DOS training video series
Harvard graphics
Lotus 1 - 2 - 3 Release 2.2 and 3.0
Quattro pro
WordPerfect
Dist - AMEDIA

MS - DOS/PC - DOS
Videodisc
(H A)
$1995.00
Teaches the basics of MS - DOS/PC - DOS, the disk operating system of the computer. Focuses on operations by computer users and managers. Six to eight hours.
Computer Science; Education
Dist - CMSL **Prod** - CMSL

MS PC DOS - Advanced DOS Commands for Hard Disk Systems 120 - 180 MIN
VHS / U-matic
(A PRO)
$275.00 purchase
Explains DOS capabilities to make maximum use of hard disk drive computer systems. Teaches root directory trees, organization of files, path and tree commands.
Computer Science
Dist - VIDEOT **Prod** - VIDEOT 1988

MS PC DOS for Hard Disk System - Complete Anderson Set 360 MIN
U-matic / VHS
(A PRO)
$495.00 purchase
Combination of two hard disk drive instructional videotapes to provide advanced training on hard drive DOS techniques.
Computer Science
Dist - VIDEOT **Prod** - VIDEOT 1988

MS - PC DOS - using Advanced DOS with Hard Disk Systems 120 - 180 MIN
VHS / U-matic
(A PRO)
$275.00 purchase
Expands user's knowledge of MS or PC DOS for computers with hard disk drives. Explains DOS concepts, directories and commands.
Business and Economics; Computer Science
Dist - VIDEOT **Prod** - VIDEOT 1988

MS - PC DOS - using DOS with Hard Disk Systems 120 - 180 MIN
VHS / U-matic
(A PRO)
$275.00 purchase
Expands user's knowledge of MS or PC DOS to use computers with hard disk drives. Provides explanation of DOS concepts, directories and commands.
Computer Science
Dist - VIDEOT **Prod** - VIDEOT 1988

Ms - the Struggle for Women's Rights 14 MIN
16mm
Screen news digest series; Vol 15; Issue 2
B&W (I)
LC 73-701268
Depicts the people, places and events that have given impetus and leadership to the struggle for women's rights.
Civics and Political Systems; History - United States; Social Science; Sociology
Dist - HEARST **Prod** - HEARST 1972

The MSDS and you 15 MIN
U-matic / VHS
Color (IND A)
LC 90-708134
Covers the eight sections of the Material Safety Data Sheet. Produced by Business and Legal Reports.
Health and Safety; Industrial and Technical Education; Psychology
Dist - IFB

MSDS and you series
The Physical Hazards We Face 12 TO 18 MIN
Dist - IFB

MSDS - and you
Chemicals and common sense 12 TO 18 MIN
Dist - IFB

The MSDS - cornerstone of chemical safety - La MSDS - la piedra angular de la seguridad quimica 14 MIN
BETA / VHS / U-matic
Hazard communication - live - action video series
Color (IND G) (SPANISH)
$495.00 purchase _ #820 - 05, #820 - 17
Trains on the importance of Material Safety Data Sheets - MSDSs. Defines many terms - Threshold Limit Value, Permissible Exposure Limit, flash point, vapor density. Part of a series on hazard communication.
Business and Economics; Health and Safety; Industrial and Technical Education; Psychology
Dist - ITSC **Prod** - ITSC

The MSDS - first step to chemical safety - La FTSS - premiere etape vers la securite des produits chimiques 14 MIN
BETA / VHS / U-matic
Canadian specific programs series
Color (IND G) (FRENCH)
$495.00 purchase _ #821 - 13, #827 - 14
Informs employees on the components of the Canadian Material Safety Data Sheet - MSDS. Provides a basic overview of the information found on the MSDS. Instructs employees to consult MSDSs when working with hazardous materials. Produced by Innovative Video Training, Inc, of Candada.
Health and Safety; Industrial and Technical Education; Psychology
Dist - ITSC

MSDS - roadmap to safety
VHS
Right - to - know series
Color (H A G T)
$225.00 purchase _ #BM505
Trains educational market personnel about the potential chemical hazards they might encounter on the job. Discusses Material Safety Data Sheets - MSDS.
Business and Economics; Education; Health and Safety; Psychology
Dist - AAVIM **Prod** - AAVIM 1992

MSDS...and You
Health Hazards - Our Need to Know 12 TO 18 MIN
Dist - IFB

The MT - 80Z Fox Microcomputer Explained - the First Steps 32 MIN
VHS / 35mm strip
(H A IND)
#871XV7
Explains the fundamentals of assembly language programming and the Z80 based MT - 80Z Fox Microcomputer trainer. Includes the grand tour and fundamental programming (2 tapes). Prerequisite required. Includes a Study Guide.
Computer Science
Dist - BERGL

Mt Mc Kinley Hang Gliding 16 MIN
U-matic / VHS / 16mm
American Sportsman Series
Color (J)
LC 78-701395
Focuses on hang gliding off Mt Mc Kinley. Points out the risks involved in this sport.
Health and Safety; Physical Education and Recreation
Dist - CORF **Prod** - ABCSRT 1978

Mt Rainier national park 28 MIN
VHS
Color (G)
$29.95 purchase _ #S00641
Explores Mt Rainier National Park in the state of Washington.
Geography - United States
Dist - UILL

Mt Rushmore and The Black Hills of South Dakota 30 MIN
VHS
Color (G)
$29.95 purchase _ #V58
Explores Mount Rushmore and the surrounding Black Hills of South Dakota. Includes natural wonders and history of the old west in the stomping grounds of Will Bill Hickok, Calamity Jane, Poker Alice, Deadwood Dick and others. Visits the Badlands, Custer State Park, Wind Cave. Includes the story of Rushmore.
Geography - United States; History - United States
Dist - INSTRU **Prod** - USNPS

Mt Rushmore - four faces on a mountain 30 MIN
VHS
Color (G)
$29.95 purchase _ #S00642
Presents original footage of the carving of Mount Rushmore. Reviews the historical background.
Geography - United States; History - United States
Dist - UILL

Mt St Helens - Road to Recovery 29 MIN
16mm / U-matic / VHS
Color (J)
Focuses on the devastation wrought by the Mount St Helens eruption and the efforts of the USDA, Forest Service and State agencies to bring life back to the area.
Civics and Political Systems; Geography - United States; History - United States
Dist - USNAC **Prod** - USDA 1982

Mt Trashmore 7 MIN
U-matic / VHS / BETA
Color (G)
$29.95, $130.00 purchase _ #LSTF14
Shows how a community not only solved solid waste problems, but created parkland in place of a garbage dump.
Science - Natural
Dist - FEDU **Prod** - USEPA 1982

Mt Washington valley 25 MIN
VHS
Color (G)
$29.95 purchase
Presents a four - season look at the Mt Washington Valley of New Hampshire. Portrays small - town life there, and shows how outdoor activities are popular all year.
Geography - United States
Dist - PBS **Prod** - WNETTV

Mt Zao 25 MIN
16mm
Color
Points out that Mt Zao in North Japan is well - known for its juhyo, the frozen snow which makes the trees resemble flowers. Shows Yuichiro Miura, a pro - skier, and his teammates ski - rumming thought the Juhyo, together with scenes of the festivals.
Geography - World; Physical Education and Recreation
Dist - UNIJAP **Prod** - UNIJAP 1968

MTN August 17, 1932
16mm
Fox Movietone news series
B&W (G)
$15.00 rental
Features President Hoover's re - election campaign; tribute to the late Rin Tin Tin; speedboat Gold Cup race; Crown Prince of Germany interviewed; Roosevelt and teammate John Nance Garner discuss game plan; and West Point parade. Presents part of a series of authentic vintage newsreels in their entirety, 7 - 12 minutes in length.

Biography; Civics and Political Systems; Fine Arts; History - World; Literature and Drama; Physical Education and Recreation
Dist - KITPAR **Prod** - FOXNEW 1932

MTN August 24, 1929
16mm
Fox Movietone news series
B&W (G)
$15.00 rental
Features sound films of a Mexican border battle; Dutch craftsman making wooden shoes; US Mother beauty contest; opening session of Congress; English yacht race; and Feds busting up a hooch. Presents part of a series of authentic vintage newsreels in their entirety, 7 - 12 minutes in length.
Civics and Political Systems; Fine Arts; History - World; Literature and Drama
Dist - KITPAR **Prod** - FOXNEW 1929

MTN February 26, 1930
16mm
Fox Movietone news series
B&W (G)
$15.00 rental
Features Coolidge welcomed to Hollywood by Mary Pickford and Douglas Fairbanks, Sr; models displaying the latest hats; Aimee Semple MacPherson visiting the Los Angeles Zoo; rum rationing for sailors; and scientists discussing magnetism. Presents part of a series of authentic vintage newsreels in their entirety, 7 - 12 minutes in length.
Civics and Political Systems; Fine Arts; Home Economics; Literature and Drama; Science - Physical
Dist - KITPAR **Prod** - FOXNEW 1930

MTN January 10, 1930
16mm
Fox Movietone news series
B&W (G)
$15.00 rental
Features Mussolini declaring that Italy will not provoke war; native war dance in South Africa; woman flyer takes off from New York to Paris; trial of Soviet traitors; and Sinclair Lewis talks about his Nobel Prize. Presents part of a series of authentic vintage newsreels in their entirety, 7 - 12 minutes in length.
Civics and Political Systems; Fine Arts; Geography - World; History - World; Literature and Drama; Sociology
Dist - KITPAR **Prod** - FOXNEW 1930

MTN January 26, 1929
16mm
Fox Movietone news series
B&W (G)
$15.00 rental
Features a plane snatching mail from the ground without landing; Columbia University oarsmen; flooding in New York; Texas Guinan's speakeasy; and the publishing business. Presents part of a series of authentic vintage newsreels in their entirety, 7 - 12 minutes in length.
Civics and Political Systems; Fine Arts; History - United States; History - World; Literature and Drama; Physical Education and Recreation; Social Science
Dist - KITPAR **Prod** - FOXNEW 1929

MTN November 19, 1930
16mm
Fox Movietone news series
B&W (G)
$15.00 rental
Features Germans flying largest airliner built to date; Chicago's Felony Court; youngest Southern belles dance; Haile Selassie crowned King of Ethiopia; help boost the economy by spending your Christmas Club savings. Presents part of a series of authentic vintage newsreels in their entirety, 7 - 12 minutes in length.
Business and Economics; Civics and Political Systems; Fine Arts; History - World; Literature and Drama; Social Science
Dist - KITPAR **Prod** - FOXNEW 1930

MTN November 30, 1929
16mm
Fox Movietone news series
B&W (G)
$15.00 rental
Features fans braving a snowstorm to witness horse race; Mrs Coolidge at Christmas Seal campaign; New York from the Chrysler Building; chimp throwing tantrum upon meeting an ocelot; and a couple are wed in a plane and jump to their honeymoon. Presents part of a series of authentic vintage newsreels in their entirety, 7 - 12 minutes in length.
Civics and Political Systems; Fine Arts; Literature and Drama; Physical Education and Recreation; Science - Natural
Dist - KITPAR **Prod** - FOXNEW 1929

MTN October 27, 1928
16mm
Fox Movietone news series
B&W (G)
$15.00 rental
Features Presidential nominees Smith and Hoover; calisthenics aboard a Navy carrier; horse - drawn milk cart; and more. Presents part of a series of authentic vintage newsreels in their entirety, 7 - 12 minutes in length.
Biography; Civics and Political Systems; Fine Arts; History - World; Literature and Drama
Dist - KITPAR **Prod** - FOXNEW 1928

MTV - it's your right to say 'no' 4 MIN
VHS / 16mm
Starting early series
Color (I J H)
$35.00, $25.00 purchase _ #135, #445
Uses an MTV format to show youngsters that it's OK to say NO to alcohol. Investigates resisting peer pressure and urges kids not to ride with drivers who have been drinking. Part of a series on alcohol education.
Guidance and Counseling; Health and Safety; Psychology
Dist - AAAFTS **Prod** - AAAFTS 1985

Much Ado about DDD and One - Frog Bands 12 MIN
16mm
Color (H A)
LC 76-705614
Employs puppets to demonstrate how to use direct distance dialing. Describes the new wide scope of DDD service.
Psychology; Social Science
Dist - SWBELL **Prod** - SWBELL 1969

Much Ado about Golf 9 MIN
16mm
W C Fields Comedy Series
B&W
LC 76-700502
Tells the story of a hapless golfer who has many problems as he tries to drive the first ball in opening the links at a new country club.
Fine Arts; Literature and Drama
Dist - RMIBHF **Prod** - PARTOR

Much ado about nothing 150 MIN
VHS
Shakespeare series
Color (A)
PdS25 purchase
Stars Michael Elphick, Robert Lindsay and Cherie Lunghi. Part of a series of plays by Shakespeare performed by leading stage and screen actors and interpreted by directors and producers such as Jonathan Miller, Elijah Mohinsky and Jack Gold.
Literature and Drama
Dist - BBCENE

Much Ado about Nothing 120 MIN
U-matic / VHS
Shakespeare Plays Series
Color (H C A)
Presents William Shakespeare's play Much Ado About Nothing which involves Hero, an innocent slandered heroine, who is denounced for unchastity by her intended bridegroom, Claudio, at the wedding itself. Reveals that Hero faints and is presumed dead.
Literature and Drama
Dist - TIMLIF **Prod** - BBCTV 1984

Much Ado about Nothing 12 MIN
U-matic / VHS / 16mm
Shakespeare Series
Color (H C A)
An excerpt from the play of the same title. Shows Benedick and Beatrice in Act IV, Scene 1 as they declare their love for each other and Act V, Scene 2 in whihc Benedick attempts to write a love sonnet, but is interrupted by Beatrice.
Fine Arts; Literature and Drama
Dist - IFB **Prod** - IFB 1974

Much Ado about Nothing 120 MIN
VHS / 16mm
BBC's Shakespeare Series
(H A)
$249.95
Presents the romantic play Much Ado About Nothing, by Shakespeare.
Literature and Drama
Dist - AMBROS **Prod** - AMBROS 1984

Much ado about nothing 120 MIN
VHS
BBC Shakespeare series
Color (G C H)
$109.00 purchase _ #DL460
Fine Arts
Dist - INSIM **Prod** - BBC

Much Ado about Nut Things - Problem Solving, Estimation 13 MIN
U-matic / VHS / 16mm
Color (I)
Explains that Pistachio has only three days to collect and count 21,000 nuts to feed the gluttonous Nutmunch giant. Shows how he is saved when Captain Calculator arrives and demonstrates how estimation can help solve the counting problem and how the calculator can be used to estimate solutions.
Mathematics
Dist - EBEC **Prod** - EBEC

Much Ado about Nut Things - Problem Solving - Estimation 13 MIN
VHS / U-matic
Expanding Math Skills with the Minicalculator Series
Color (I)
$59.00 purchase _ #3500
Shows how estimation can help solve counting problem and how to use the calculator to estimate solutions. Animated story.
Mathematics
Dist - EBEC

The Much loved friend - a portrait of the National Gallery 47 MIN
VHS
Color (G)
PdS15.50 purchase _ #A4-300426
Examines the history and the role of the National Gallery through the eyes of those who work in it and visit it, including trustees such as the Prince of Wales, artist Howard Hodgkin, humorist Terry Gilliam, art historian Sister Wendy Beckett, author Julian Barnes, and members of the public. Combines archive footage with a look at the Gallery's work behind the scenes, especially in the Conservation and Scientific departments.
Fine Arts
Dist - AVP **Prod** - NATLGL

Much more's marvelous machine 7 MIN
VHS
Children's encyclopedia of mathematics - meeting numbers series
Color (K P I)
$49.95 purchase _ #8347
Illustrates the importance of place value. Part of a six - part series on numbers.
Mathematics
Dist - AIMS **Prod** - DAVFMS 1991
DAVFMS

The Muck and the Mystery Men - Pt 10 28 MIN
VHS
Only One Earth Series
Color (S)
$79.00 purchase _ #227 - 9010
Explores and demystifies the links between environment and development and illustrates the detrimental clashes between economics and ecology in the first three programs. Presents positive examples of how development can be achieved without harming the environment in the last eight half - hour programs. Part 10 of eleven looks at the organic farming movement, the increasing demand for organically grown produce, and farmers who are beginning to give up synthetic fertilizers and pesticides in favor of natural compost and pest management.
Agriculture; Home Economics; Science - Natural
Dist - FI **Prod** - BBCTV 1987

Mud 23 MIN
16mm
Color (J)
LC FIA68-3286
Studies urban erosion and sedimentation. Explains how engineering skills and conservation practices often applied to rural areas can be used in cities to prevent flooding and other drainage difficulties.
Psychology; Science - Natural; Science - Physical; Sociology
Dist - FINLYS **Prod** - FINLYS 1968

Mud and salt - the world of the estuary 20 MIN
VHS
Biology of water series
Color (J H)
$90.00 purchase _ #A5VH 1335; $89.00 purchase _ #1993VG
Looks at the unique environments created when freshwater returns to the sea. Presents two typical estuaries - the first in a temperate climate, the second a tropical mangrove lagoon. Examines tides and how they affect estuary dwellers and explores adaptations to constantly changing environments. Part of a four - part series on the role of water.
Science - Natural; Science - Physical
Dist - CLRVUE **Prod** - CLRVUE
UNL

Mud and Water Man 50 MIN
U-matic / VHS / 16mm
Color (H C)

LC 76-703566
Presents the life and work of contemporary English potter, Michael Cardew. Traces his working life as potter, teacher and writer in Africa and Cornwall, England. Features Cardew discussing his personal philosophy and his interest in reviving the craft of pottery - making in England.
Fine Arts
Dist - FI **Prod** - BCACGB 1976

Mud and Water Man 50 MIN
16mm
Color (H A)
$800.00 purchase, $75.00 rental
Features Cornwall potter Michael Cardew who has gone to villages in Ghana and Nigeria to train potters to create with native materials and modern machinery.
Fine Arts
Dist - AFA **Prod** - ACGB 1974

Mud and Water Man, Pt 1 25 MIN
U-matic / VHS / 16mm
Color (H C)
LC 76-703566
Presents the life and work of contemporary English potter, Michael Cardew. Traces his working life as potter, teacher and writer in Africa and Cornwall, England. Features Cardew discussing his personal philosophy and his interest in reviving the craft of pottery - making in England.
Fine Arts
Dist - FI **Prod** - BCACGB 1976

Mud and Water Man, Pt 2 25 MIN
U-matic / VHS / 16mm
Color (H C)
LC 76-703566
Presents the life and work of contemporary English potter, Michael Cardew. Traces his working life as potter, teacher and writer in Africa and Cornwall, England. Features Cardew discussing his personal philosophy and his interest in reviving the craft of pottery - making in England.
Fine Arts
Dist - FI **Prod** - BCACGB 1976

Mud Creek Clinic 29 MIN
VHS / 16mm
Color (G)
$100.00 purchase _ #MUDCRVH
Describes how the residents of Floyd County, Kentucky, established a rural health clinic against long odds. Focuses on the efforts of Eula Hall, who led the effort.
Geography - United States; Health and Safety; Sociology
Dist - APPAL

Mud House 29 MIN
16mm
Color
LC 75-700904
Examines the design and construction of an all - concrete house using the latest concrete technology.
Industrial and Technical Education; Social Science
Dist - STUDO **Prod** - ALEXP 1975

Mud pit volume recorders 19 MIN
U-matic / VHS
Color (IND)
Explains installation, maintenance and operation of Dresser Swaco pit - level indicators.
Industrial and Technical Education; Social Science
Dist - UTEXPE **Prod** - UTEXPE 1966

Mud puddle
CD-ROM
Discis Books on CD - ROM
(K P) (SPANISH)
$74.00 purchase _ #2555
Contains the original text and illustrations of Mud Puddle by Robert Munsch. Enhances understanding with real voices, music, and sound effects. Every word in the text has an in - context explanation, pronunciation and syllables, available through a click of the mouse. Spanish - English version available for an extra $5 per disc. For Macintosh Classics, Plus, II and SE computers, requires 1MB RAM RAM, one floppy disk drive, and an Apple compatible CD - ROM drive.
English Language; Literature and Drama
Dist - BEP

Mud Pumps 33 MIN
U-matic / VHS
Color (A PRO IND)
$175.00 purchase _ #11.1094, $185.00 purchase _ #51.1094
Shows operation, maintenance and installation of the power and fluid ends of duplex and triplex slush pumps used in drilling.
Industrial and Technical Education; Social Science
Dist - UTEXPE **Prod** - UTEXPE 1980

Mud, Sand, Clay and Cake 30 MIN
U-matic
Magic Ring I Series
(K P)
Playing with mud and experimenting with clay lead to learning the basics of the potter's craft and a visit to the beach.
Education; Literature and Drama
Dist - ACCESS **Prod** - ACCESS 1984

Mudflat Art 16 MIN
U-matic
Color
Concentrates on the unique driftwood art which is found on the Emeryville mudflat. Explores the meaning of 'junk' sculptures.
Fine Arts
Dist - RDR **Prod** - RDR

Mudhorse 12 MIN
16mm
B&W
Presents a statement on social conditions in Egypt. Describes Nile River workers and horses who mingle in an open - air brick factory, using a method thousands of years old.
Geography - World; Sociology
Dist - ICARUS **Prod** - ICARUS 1971

Mudpies and feathers - Volume 3 25 MIN
VHS
Filling station series
Color (K P I R)
$11.99 purchase _ #35 - 811327 - 979
Combines live action and animated sequences to teach the message that God loves people more than a flock of sparrows.
Literature and Drama; Religion and Philosophy
Dist - APH **Prod** - TYHP

Mudras - hand gestures of Sanskrit drama 38 MIN
VHS
Color (G C H)
$169.00 purchase _ #DL508
Features Mrinalini Sarabhai, founder of the Darpana Academy of Performing Arts in Ahmedabad, India.
History - World; Religion and Philosophy
Dist - INSIM

Mufaro's Beautiful Daughters 14 MIN
16mm / VHS
Color (K P I)
$120.00, $255.00 purchase, $25.00 rental _ #VC334V, #MP334
Presents the story from the book Mufaro's Beautiful Daughters by John Steptoe. Mufaro's two daughters are tested to reveal which is worthy enough to marry the king.
Geography - World; Health and Safety; Literature and Drama; Psychology
Dist - WWS **Prod** - WWS 1989

Mufaro's beautiful daughters - 55
VHS
Reading rainbow series
Color; CC (K P)
$39.95 purchase
Tells an African tale by John Steptoe, narrated by Phylicia Rashad, about two very different sisters. Celebrates the culture of Africa in New York City's Central Park where LeVar learns how to play authentic African musical instruments and joins in the fun with an African dance troupe, Forces of Nature. Part of a series offering a multicultural approach to generating reading enthusiasm with cross - curricular applications, hosted by LeVar Burton.
English Language; Literature and Drama
Dist - GPN **Prod** - LNMDP

Muffin Method 8 MIN
VHS / 16mm
Food Preparation Techniques Series
Color (H C A)
Shows step by step preparation of a basic muffin recipe. Illustrates also the results of common mistakes with this method, enabling the viewer to diagnose product failures.
Home Economics; Psychology
Dist - IOWA **Prod** - IOWA 1989

Muffinland - Holiday Specials Series
Christmas 14 MIN
Halloween 14 MIN
Thanksgiving - the Pilgrims 14 MIN
Thanksgiving - the Things I Like Best 14 MIN
Dist - PBS

Muffinland series
Autumn World - Pt 1 14 MIN
Autumn World, the, Pt 2 14 MIN
The City - Pt 1 14 MIN
The City - Pt 2 14 MIN
Columbus 14 MIN
Community helpers, Pt 1 14 MIN
Community helpers, Pt 2 14 MIN
The Farm 14 MIN
The Jungle 14 MIN
The Ranch - Pt 1 14 MIN
The Ranch - Pt 2 14 MIN
Smoky Mountains, Pt 1 14 MIN
Smoky Mountains, Pt 2 14 MIN
A Trip to the University 14 MIN
Visit to the World of the Muffins, Pt 1 14 MIN
Visit to the World of the Muffins, Pt 2 14 MIN
Winter World, Pt 1 14 MIN
Winter World, Pt 2 14 MIN
World of Muffins 14 MIN
World of the forest - Pt 1 14 MIN
World of the forest - Pt 2 14 MIN
Dist - PBS

Muffins 27 MIN
VHS
Cookbook videos series
Color (G)
$19.95 purchase _ #ALW102
Shows how to prepare muffins in short, easy - to - learn segments. Lists each ingredient as it is added in subtitles and visually reinforces spoken instructions. Gives recipe background and nutritional facts. Part of the Cookbook Videos series.
Home Economics; Social Science
Dist - CADESF **Prod** - CADESF

Muffy and Sylvester 30 MIN
VHS
Color (K P R)
$9.99 purchase _ #SPCN 85116.00337
Presents a story by Ethel Barrett which teaches children the values of honesty, truthfulness and the importance of being unselfish.
Religion and Philosophy
Dist - GOSPEL **Prod** - GOSPEL

Mugged 12 MIN
16mm / U-matic / VHS
Color
Examines what people, especially seniors, can do if they are mugged. Shows reformed muggers in New York City explaining to senior citizens in workshops what a mugger looks for in a victim.
Health and Safety; Sociology
Dist - CORF **Prod** - CBSTV

Muggers 15 MIN
U-matic / VHS / 16mm
Under the Law Series
Color (J H C)
LC 74-703797
Tells the story of Andy, a youth with no arrest record, who promised his mother he would watch over his older brother, a paroled drug addict. Portrays how Charlie, despite Andy's efforts, returns to his old habits. Shows how the police subsequently capture both of them and they are found guilty of robbery and grand theft. Depicts how they are sentenced individually in a manner that reflects the personalities of the offenders.
Civics and Political Systems; Sociology
Dist - CORF **Prod** - USNEI 1974

Mugging - You Can Protect Yourself 31 MIN
U-matic / VHS / 16mm
Color (J)
LC 77-702001
Offers guidelines on how to avoid threatening situations. Demonstrates specific methods by which a mugging victim can deal with an assailant, even at the point of a knife or gun.
Guidance and Counseling; Health and Safety; Sociology
Dist - LCOA **Prod** - JASON 1977

Muggins 11 MIN
16mm
Color (J H C)
Presents a semi - surrealistic study of the emotional conflict between a shrewish wife and a romantic husband.
Fine Arts; Sociology
Dist - CFS **Prod** - CFS 1968

Mughal Glory 19 MIN
16mm
Color (I)
Shows the architectural beauty of the monuments of Agra and Fatehpur Sikri - the Taj, Jumma Masjid and Dewan - i - khas.
Fine Arts; History - World
Dist - NEDINF **Prod** - INDIA

Muhammad Ali 30 MIN
VHS
Black Americans of achievement collection II series
Color (J H C G)
$49.95 purchase _ #LVCD6614V - S
Provides interesting and concise information on heavyweight boxing champion Muhammad Ali. Part of a 10 - part series on African - Americans.
History - United States; Physical Education and Recreation
Dist - CAMV

Muhammad - pbuh - the honest
VHS
Video lectures of Hamza Yusuf series

Color (G)
$12.00 purchase _ #110 - 075
Features Islamic lecturer Hamza Yusuf who reflects upon the remarkable qualities of honesty and trustworthiness of the Prophet. Presents statistics on Muslims in North America, and brother NeQunsio Abdullah discusses community needs and career choices.
Guidance and Counseling; Religion and Philosophy
Dist - SOUVIS **Prod** - SOUVIS 1995

Mujer de milfuegos - Woman of a thousand fires 15 MIN
VHS / 16mm
Color (G)
$30.00 rental
Presents a surrealistic portrayal of a Latin American woman. Evokes the consciousness of women in rural parts of such countries as Spain, Greece and Morocco. Uses dramatic action to express the thoughts and feelings of a woman in this culture.
Fine Arts; Sociology
Dist - CANCIN **Prod** - STRANC 1976

Mujeres Colombianas 20 MIN
U-matic
Are you listening series
Color (J H C)
LC 80-707404
Presents a group of Colombian women giving personal testimony to the advantages of using birth control. Discusses the new economic security, stabilized home life, and release from the fear of pregnancy. Discusses how they have dealt with disapproval from husbands and family members.
Sociology
Dist - STURTM **Prod** - STURTM 1973

Mujeria 20 MIN
VHS
Color (G) (SPANISH)
$50.00, $250.00 purchase
Combines two of filmmaker Teresa 'Osa' Hidalgo de la Riva's animations - Olmeca Rap, 1991 and Primitive and Proud, 1992. Focuses on the influence of the Olmeca culture on de la Riva, who attempts to go beyond the traditionally stereotypical use of Aztec iconography to represent Chicano and Mexican cultural identity by choosing a lesser - known but equally important culture in Mexico. Celebrates the beauty and strength of this culture, particularly as it relates to women and lesbians.
Fine Arts; Geography - World; History - World
Dist - WMEN

Mule Days 20 MIN
VHS / BETA
Color
Highlights the 1983 Mule Days Celebration in Bishop, California.
Physical Education and Recreation
Dist - EQVDL **Prod** - SMIFT

Mules 25 MIN
U-matic / VHS / 16mm
Color (I)
Looks at the history of the mule. Discusses the animal's intelligence and strength.
Agriculture; Physical Education and Recreation
Dist - CORF **Prod** - KAWVAL

Muleskinner live - the video 30 MIN
VHS
Color (G)
$22.95 purchase _ #VDZ - ML01
Records a group of fine young bluegrass pickers who convened in 1973 to pay a tribute to their 'father,' Bill Monroe. Features Clarence White - lead guitar, vocals; Richard Greene - fiddle; David Grisman - mandolin, vocals; Stuart Shulman - bass. Includes the songs New Camptown Races; Dark Hollow; Land of the Navajo; Blackberry Blossom; Knockin' On Your Door; Opus 57 in G Minor; Red Rocking Chair; The Dead March; and Orange Blossom Special. Bill Monroe never made it to the show - his bus broke down - but it was a fine show anyway.
Fine Arts
Dist - HOMETA **Prod** - HOMETA

Mulligan stew series

Count Down 4 - 4 - 3 - 2	28 MIN
Countdown - 4 4 3 2	30 MIN
The Flim flam man	30 MIN
Getting it all Together	30 MIN
The Great nutrition turn on	30 MIN
Look inside yourself	30 MIN
The Racer that Lost His Edge	30 MIN

Dist - GPN

Mulliner's Buck - U - Uppo 30 MIN
U-matic / VHS
Wodehouse Playhouse Series
Color (C A)
Presents an adaptation of the short story Mulliner's Buck - U - Uppo by P G Wodehouse.
Literature and Drama
Dist - TIMLIF **Prod** - BBCTV 1980

Multi 1250 service guide 120 MIN
VHS
Color (H C)
$79.95 purchase _ #SE - 21
Shows how to service a multi 1250 and save money. Covers ink unit, water unit - new and old, master cylinder, blanket cylinder, impression cylinder, impression trip, stop fingers, feed rolls, ejection rolls, speed control, cleaning clutch, conveyer board, vacuum pump, chain delivery, feeder timing, oiling and greasing and more.
Industrial and Technical Education
Dist - INSTRU

Multi - casualty ICS 10 MIN
VHS
Color (IND)
$60.00 purchase _ #35462
Shows how the ICS positions function and integrate at a multi - casualty incident. Illustrates responsibilities and procedures. Includes a 20 - page reproducible booklet containing a responsibility checklist for each position.
Health and Safety; Science - Physical; Social Science
Dist - OKSU **Prod** - UPLAND

A Multi - cultural Christmas 22 MIN
VHS
Color (K P I)
$69.95 purchase _ #10103VG
Explains Christmas customs among Northern Europeans, African - Americans, Native Americans, and Asians. Shows traditional foods, customs, songs, games, and costumes for different ethnic groups. Includes a guide.
Civics and Political Systems; Religion and Philosophy
Dist - UNL

Multi - Cultural Education - a Teaching Style 29 MIN
U-matic / VHS / 16mm
Survival Skills for the Classroom Teacher Series
Color (T)
Looks at the changes from the traditional melting pot theory to an appreciation of cultural pluralism. Demonstrates several classroom approaches which encourage ethnic groups to maintain their identity and pride while developing mutual respect for others.
Education
Dist - FI **Prod** - MFFD

Multi - Element Pneumatic Control Systems 60 MIN
VHS
Pneumatic Systems and Equipment Series
Color (PRO)
$600.00 - $1500.00 purchase _ #ICMEP
Covers the operating principles of ratio, cascade, auctioneering and three - element feedwater control systems. Part of an eleven - part series on pneumatic systems and equipment, which is part of a 49 - unit set on instrumentation and control. Includes five workbooks and an instructor guide to support four hours of instruction.
Education; Industrial and Technical Education; Psychology
Dist - NUSTC **Prod** - NUSTC

Multi - handicapped 126 MIN
VHS / 16mm
Color (G H)
$350.00 purchase, $150.00 rental
Documents the daily activities of multi - handicapped and sensory - impaired students and their teachers, dormitory parents, and counselors at the Helen Keller School. Directed by Frederick Wiseman.
Fine Arts; Guidance and Counseling; Health and Safety
Dist - ZIPRAH **Prod** - WISEF

Multi - Mate - Advantage
U-matic / VHS
Micro Video Learning System Series
(A IND)
$495.00 purchase _ #MV700
Demonstrates the use of the Multi Mate Advantage computer system.
Computer Science
Dist - CAMV

Multi - media 30 MIN
VHS
Computing for the less terrified series
Color (A)
PdS65 purchase
Shows how a PC helps bring archaeological sites to life and how a multimedia arcade game can raise HIV awareness. Part of a seven-part series which aims to allay everyone's fear of the computer, whether an individual is an experienced user or relative novice. Explores the numerous applications of the computer and illustrates some of the pitfalls.
Computer Science; Guidance and Counseling
Dist - BBCENE

Multi - Media Audubon's mammals - Mac
CD-ROM
Color (G A)
$79.00 purchase _ #1872m
Offers the 1840 edition of John James Audubon's Quadrupeds of North America on CD - ROM with plates in full color, text, as well as CD quality souunds from Cornell University's Library of Natural Sounds for many of the mammals. For Macintosh Plus, SE and II computers. Requires at least one M of RAM, one floppy disk drive, and an Apple compatible CD - ROM drive.
Literature and Drama; Science - Natural
Dist - BEP

Multi - Media Audubon's mammals - network
CD-ROM
Color (G A)
$158.00 purchase _ #1872n
Offers the 1840 edition of John James Audubon's Quadrupeds of North America on CD - ROM with plates in full color, text, as well as CD quality souunds from Cornell University's Library of Natural Sounds for many of the mammals. Network version.
Literature and Drama; Science - Natural
Dist - BEP

Multi - Media Audubon's mammals - PC
CD-ROM
Color (G A)
$79.00 purchase _ #1872p
Offers the 1840 edition of John James Audubon's Quadrupeds of North America on CD - ROM with plates in full color and text. Includes CD quality sounds from Cornell University's Library of Natural Sounds for many of the mammals. For IBM PCs and compatibles. Requires 640K RAM, DOS Version 3.1 or greater, one floppy disk drive - a hard drive is recommended, one empty expansion slot, and an IBM compatible CD - ROM drive.
Literature and Drama; Science - Natural
Dist - BEP

Multi - pass electric arc welding
U-matic / VHS
Shielded metal arc welding - Spanish series
Color (SPANISH)
Foreign Language; Industrial and Technical Education
Dist - VTRI **Prod** - VTRI

Multi - Pass Fillet 4 MIN
BETA / VHS
Welding Training - Comprehensive - Metal Inert Gas - M I G Welding Series
Color (IND)
Industrial and Technical Education; Psychology
Dist - RMIBHF **Prod** - RMIBHF

Multi - Pass Fillet Flat - Steel 5 MIN
VHS / BETA
Welding Training - Comprehensive - Metal Inert Gas - M I G Welding Series
Color (IND)
Industrial and Technical Education; Psychology
Dist - RMIBHF **Prod** - RMIBHF

Multi - Pass Fillet V - Up 3 MIN
BETA / VHS
Welding Training - Comprehensive - Metal Inert Gas - M I G Welding Series
Color (IND)
Industrial and Technical Education; Psychology
Dist - RMIBHF **Prod** - RMIBHF

Multi Pass Welding with Dual Shielded
U-matic / VHS
MIG and TIG Welding - Spanish Series
Color (SPANISH)
Foreign Language; Industrial and Technical Education
Dist - VTRI **Prod** - VTRI

Multi - piece wheel rims 16 MIN
BETA / VHS / U-matic
Driving safety series
Color (G)
$589.00 purchase, $125.00 rental _ #MUL002
Demonstrates the proper and safe method of changing a tire on a multi - piece wheel rim. Points out the possible dangers when changing a rim on such a wheel. Explains regulations pertaining to changing multi - piece wheel rim tires.
Health and Safety; Industrial and Technical Education
Dist - ITF **Prod** - GPCV

MultiBible
CD-ROM
Color (G A)
$125.00 purchase _ #2002
Contains six Bible databases. Includes Strong's Number, The New International Version, The Revised Standard Version, The New Revised Standard, The King James - Authorised - Version and The New King James Version. For IBM PCs and compatibles. Requires at least 640K RAM, DOS Version 3.1 or greater, one floppy disk drive - a hard drive is recommended, one empty expansion slot, and an IBM compatible CD - ROM drive.

Computer Science; Literature and Drama; Religion and Philosophy
Dist - BEP

Multicamera direction planning 30 MIN
VHS
Color (PRO G)
$149.00 purchase, $49.00 rental _ #704
Watches the planning and production of a multicamera video shoot. Observes the first read - through , the design meeting, setup of the rehearsal space, rehearsal, planning of camera coverage, final camera scripting, the production meeting, the technical run - through, the shoot day and the finished dramatic scene. Produced by the Australian Film, Television and Radio School.
Fine Arts; Industrial and Technical Education
Dist - FIRLIT

Multicultural America 30 MIN
VHS
Color (G)
$79.00 purchase
Explains the meaning of multiculturalism through the opinions of nationally - recognized authorities on the subject and the experiences of children in a school that emphasizes cultural awareness and cooperation.
History - United States; Sociology
Dist - DANEHA **Prod** - DANEHA 1994

Multicultural history series
Black is my color - the African American experience 15 MIN
From East to West - the Asian - American experience 22 MIN
One world, many worlds - Hispanic diversity in the United States 22 MIN
Dist - REVID

Multicultural peoples of North America series
Presents a 15 - part series on multiculturalism in North America. Examines the Amish, African, Arab and Central Americans, Chinese, German, Greek, Irish, Italian, Japanese, Jewish, Korean, Mexican and Polish Americans and Puerto Ricans.
African Americans 30 MIN
The Amish 30 MIN
Arab Americans 30 MIN
Central Americans 30 MIN
Chinese Americans 30 MIN
German Americans 30 MIN
Greek Americans 30 MIN
Irish Americans 30 MIN
Italian Americans 30 MIN
Japanese Americans 30 MIN
Jewish Americans 30 MIN
Korean Americans 30 MIN
Mexican Americans 30 MIN
Polish Americans 30 MIN
Puerto Ricans 30 MIN
Dist - CAMV

Multidisciplinary issues in IV therapy - therapeutic and clinical trends
VHS
Color (PRO)
#TU - 272
Presents a free - loan program which trains medical professionals. Contact distributor for details.
Health and Safety; Science - Natural
Dist - WYAYLA **Prod** - WYAYLA

Multihull fever
VHS
Color (G)
$39.90 purchase _ #0079
Shows the big French catamarans and trimarans that achieve speeds of up to 35 knots.
Physical Education and Recreation
Dist - SEVVID

Multilayer Printed Circuit Board Repair 8 TO 15 MIN
VHS
High - Reliability Soldering Series
Color (PRO)
$600.00 - $1500.00 purchase _ #TRMPC
Explains how multilayer printed circuit boards are manufactured. Describes damage that can occur to the boards. Shows how to repair a blister on a multilayer PCB substrate. Part of an eighteen - part series on high - reliability soldering. Requires a solid understanding of digital electronics. Includes one textbook and an instructor guide to support 45 minutes of instruction.
Education; Health and Safety; Industrial and Technical Education; Psychology
Dist - NUSTC **Prod** - NUSTC

Multilevel Teaching for Normal and Handicapped Children 29 MIN
16mm
Color (C T S)
LC 78-701601
Demonstrates techniques for providing individualized instruction while working with both handicapped and normal children who vary greatly in their skill levels.
Education; Psychology
Dist - UKANS **Prod** - UKANS 1977

Multilumen central venous catheters 28 MIN
U-matic / VHS
Color (PRO)
$275.00 purchase, $60.00 rental _ #7615S, #7615V
Shows how to provide safe, competent care when using the newly designed multilumen catheters. Reveals that these catheters require only one access site and are intended for patients who require multiple intravenous lines and may eventually lack usable veins. Describes the components of a multilumen catheter, types, uses and correct nursing care.
Health and Safety
Dist - AJN **Prod** - HOSSN 1986

Multimate 600 MIN
CD-ROM
(A PRO)
$1,195.00
Covers fundamentals of word processing using MultiMate.
Computer Science
Dist - VIDEOT **Prod** - VIDEOT 1988

MultiMate
Videodisc
(H A)
$1195.00
Teaches use of MultiMate word processing software. Recreates typical job tasks to demonstrate key features and allow practice in creating documents, entering, editing, printing, and merge printing. Also demonstrates use of the math functions. Six to eight hour course.
Computer Science; Education
Dist - CMSL **Prod** - CMSL

MultiMate Advantage II
Videodisc
(H A)
$2195.00
Explains fundamentals of word processing using demonstrations of job - related tasks. Teaches formatting, revising, editing, and printing text as well as using special features of the software. Ten to twelve hour course.
Computer Science; Education
Dist - CMSL **Prod** - CMSL

MultiMate Advantage II
VHS
Color (G)
$179.95 purchase _ #MMII
Provides video PC software training in MultiMate Advantage II. Includes training guide.
Computer Science
Dist - HALASI **Prod** - HALASI

Multimate Advantage II introduction 60 MIN
VHS
Color (J H C G)
$29.95 purchase _ #VP119V
Introduces concepts in Multimate Advantage II. Allows viewer to see keyboard and monitor simultaneously so that students can see the result of every keystroke. Part of a series on word processing.
Business and Economics; Computer Science
Dist - CAMV

Multimate Advantage Learning System 120 MIN
VHS / U-matic
(A PRO)
$495.00, $595.00
Covers all versions of the software. Also includes creating documents, correcting and revising and formatting.
Computer Science
Dist - VIDEOT **Prod** - VIDEOT 1988

Multimate - an Introduction to Word Processing 30 MIN
U-matic / VHS
Color
Describes fully how MULTIMATE is used in making an IBM PC emulate a Wang word processor. Details step - by - step procedure for booting - up, utilizing and creating hard copy from IBM PC. Includes written text.
Industrial and Technical Education
Dist - BERGL **Prod** - MICROV

MultiMate - Introduction to the Word Processor
U-matic / VHS
Color (A)
Introduces the concepts and applications of work processing. Includes creating, changing, copying and deleting documents; inserting, moving, copying and deleting words, paragraphs and pages; merging documents; and formatting. Explains automatic search and replace, math functions how to print selected pages and creating mailing lists with form letters.
Business and Economics
Dist - DSIM **Prod** - DSIM

The Multimedia design team 30 MIN
VHS
Multimedia series
Color (C T PRO)
$79.95 purchase
Informs on designing individual interactive multimedia material vs using a design team. Shows how to identify members of a design team to help instructors develop multimedia curriculum materials by either adapting existing materials or generating entirely new multimedia courseware. Examines the issue of copyright. Part of a five - part series on multimedia technology as a new learning tool hosted by news anchor Joan Stafford.
Computer Science; Education
Dist - AECT

Multimedia Instructional System for Coronary Care Unit Nurses Series
The Warning Arrhythmias 22 MIN
Dist - SUTHLA

Multimedia series
Presents a five - part series on multimedia technology as a new learning tool, hosted by news anchor Joan Stafford. Includes the titles Orientation to Multimedia; Hardware Instruction; Software Introduction; Accessing Data Networks; and The Multimedia Design Team.
Accessing data networks 30 MIN
Hardware instruction 30 MIN
The Multimedia design team 30 MIN
Orientation to multimedia 30 MIN
Software introduction 30 MIN
Dist - AECT

Multimedia World Factbook
CD-ROM
(G)
$99.00 purchase _ #3005
Profiles 248 nations, with details on geography, maritime claims, natural resources, climate, people, population, language, religion, government, agriculture, economy, and the military. Includes color flags, national anthem sound clips, and maps. Produced from non - classified CIA information. For Macintosh Plus, SE, and II computers. Requires 1MB RAM, floppy disk drive, Apple compatible CD - ROM drive. IBM PCs and compatibles require 640K RAM, DOS 3.1 or later, floppy disk drive - hard disk recommended, one empty expansion slot, IBM compatible CD - ROM drive.
Agriculture; Business and Economics; Geography - World; Literature and Drama
Dist - BEP

Multimeter use 60 MIN
VHS / U-matic
Electrical maintenance training series; Module B - Test instruments
Color (IND)
Industrial and Technical Education
Dist - LEIKID **Prod** - LEIKID

Multimeters - basic circuits - movements 60 MIN
VHS / U-matic
Electrical maintenance training series; Module B - Test instruments
Color (IND)
Industrial and Technical Education
Dist - LEIKID **Prod** - LEIKID

Multimeters Explained
VHS
$229.00 purchase _ #BX10V
Uses full motion video photography to introduce the fundamental features of analog and digital multimeters. Demonstrates the set up and use of multimeters.
Industrial and Technical Education
Dist - CAREER **Prod** - CAREER

Multimeters Explained 60 MIN
VHS / 16mm
Color (H A IND)
$239.00 purchase _ #E10
Details the basic features of analog and defines continuity and voltage - current.
Industrial and Technical Education
Dist - BERGL **Prod** - BERGL 1987

Multimodal Behavior Therapy 48 MIN
U-matic
Three Approaches to Psychotherapy II Series
Color
Jpresents Arnold A Lazarus, PhD, Professor, Graduate of Applied and Professional Psychology, Rutgers University, New Brunswick, NJ.
Psychology
Dist - PSYCHF **Prod** - PSYCHF

Multimodal Marital Therapy 22 MIN
U-matic / VHS
Multimodal Therapy Series

Color
Illustrates effective ways husband and wife can respond to each other's needs and feelings.
Psychology; Sociology
Dist - RESPRC **Prod** - RESPRC

Multimodal Therapy Series
Assessment - therapy connection 29 MIN
Multimodal Marital Therapy 22 MIN
Use of Bridging and Tracking to Overcome Apparent Resistance 17 MIN
Dist - RESPRC

Multiplan
Videodisc
(H A)
$1995.00
Discusses all major features of Multiplan's electronic spreadsheet including how to develop a cash flow worksheet, change formats, and use functions and formulas. Course is suitable for both experienced and first - time users. Five to eight hours.
Computer Science; Education
Dist - CMSL **Prod** - CMSL

MultiPlan
U-matic / VHS
Color
Illustrates the overall concept of an electronic spreadsheet and the basic model - building tools of MultiPlan. Shows how to build a financial model using basic MultiPlan commands and offers an introduction to the 'what if' game.
Industrial and Technical Education; Mathematics
Dist - ANDRST **Prod** - LANSFD

Multiple Aortocoronary Saphenous Vein Bypass Grafts 28 MIN
VHS / U-matic
Cardiovascular Series
Color
Health and Safety; Science - Natural
Dist - SVL **Prod** - SVL

Multiple Choice 20 MIN
16mm
Color (J)
LC 73-701193
Portrays the library trustee as he carries out the duties and responsibilities of his position in board meetings and in the community. Emphasizes certain responsibilities in the areas of policy - making, finance and public relations.
Business and Economics; Education; Guidance and Counseling; Psychology; Social Science
Dist - INDSLI **Prod** - INDSLI 1972

Multiple drug resistant organisms - a growing concern 20 MIN
VHS
Color (PRO C)
$285.00 purchase, $70.00 rental _ #4395
Provides the necessary information all healthcare workers must know in order to forestall the spread of methicillin resistant staphylococcus aureus - MRSA, one of the most prevalent forms of multiple drug resistant organisms. Discusses modes of transmission and strategies to prevent transmission. Explains the differences between virulence and resistence, and colonization and infection, and the drug treatment regime using Vancomycin. Includes information particular to Vancomycin resistant enterococci - VRE.
Health and Safety; Science - Natural
Dist - AJN **Prod** - AJN 1995

Multiple fractures to the arm 8 MIN
U-matic / VHS
EMT video - group two series
Color (PRO)
LC 84-706480
Shows methods for applying a sling, a wireladder splint, and cravats for fractures of both humerus and radial bones.
Health and Safety
Dist - USNAC **Prod** - USA 1983

Multiple Gastric Polyps 20 MIN
16mm
Color (PRO)
Deals with the diagnosis, pathology and surgical technique of subtotal gastrectomy for multiple gastric polyps. Emphasizes roentgenological diagnosis and pathological characteristics.
Health and Safety; Science
Dist - ACY **Prod** - ACYDGD 1964

The Multiple Handicapped 23 MIN
16mm
Color
LC 74-705179
Shows mentally retarded, cerebral palsied, dysmelia, deaf - blind and emotionally disturbed deaf children in Sweden, Germany, the Netherlands and England.
Education; Guidance and Counseling; Psychology
Dist - USNAC **Prod** - USBEH 1970

Multiple Integration and the Jacobian 33 MIN
VHS / U-matic
Calculus of several Variables - Multiple - Integration Series; Multiple integration
B&W
Mathematics
Dist - MIOT **Prod** - MIOT

Multiple orgasm 10 MIN
16mm
Color (A)
$20.00 rental
Discloses sensuality explicitly and employs visual overlays of erotic rock and cave formations.
Fine Arts
Dist - CANCIN **Prod** - BARHAM 1977

Multiple - pass fillet weld - 4 - F position 15 MIN
VHS / U-matic
Arc welding training series
Color (IND)
Industrial and Technical Education
Dist - AVIMA **Prod** - AVIMA

Multiple - pass fillet weld - 1 - F position 15 MIN
U-matic / VHS
Arc welding training series
Color (IND)
Industrial and Technical Education
Dist - AVIMA **Prod** - AVIMA

Multiple - pass fillet weld - 3 - F position 15 MIN
VHS / U-matic
Arc welding training series
Color (IND)
Industrial and Technical Education
Dist - AVIMA **Prod** - AVIMA

Multiple - pass fillet weld - 2 - F position 15 MIN
U-matic / VHS
Arc welding training series
Color (IND)
Industrial and Technical Education
Dist - AVIMA **Prod** - AVIMA

Multiple Random Variables - Discrete 34 MIN
VHS / U-matic
Probability and Random Processes - Random Variables Series
B&W (PRO)
Discusses the properties of joint probability distribution functions and marginal probability distribution functions.
Industrial and Technical Education; Mathematics
Dist - MIOT **Prod** - MIOT

Multiple Sclerosis 19 MIN
U-matic / VHS
Color (C)
$249.00, $149.00 purchase _ #AD - 1459
Explains the progression of multiple sclerosis, an unpredictable and frequently disabling disease. Profiles a young business analyst who learned recently that she has MS. Describes her fears and the adjustments in her life necessitated by the disease.
Health and Safety; Psychology; Science - Natural
Dist - FOTH **Prod** - FOTH

Multiple Sclerosis 28 MIN
16mm
Color
Dramatizes the episodic course of multiple sclerosis, following patients from the very earliest signs through characteristic periods of exacerbation and remission. Reviews muscular incoordination visual difficulties and problems of hearing and speech while illustrating the pathological changes that produced these deficits.
Health and Safety; Science - Natural
Dist - NMSS **Prod** - FLEMRP 1966

Multiple Sclerosis 32 MIN
VHS / 16mm
(C)
$385.00 purchase _ #850VI056
Presents an overview of multiple sclerosis - MS - . Discusses the various laboratory studies that assist in the diagnosis of multiple sclerosis, bases on medical history and physical examination.
Health and Safety
Dist - HSCIC **Prod** - HSCIC 1985

Multiple sclerosis - update and management 28 MIN
VHS / U-matic
Color (PRO)
$275.00 purchase, $60.00 rental _ #7511S, #7511V
Covers the various types of multiple sclerosis - benign, relapsing - remitting, remitting - progressive, and progressive. Explores the diagnostic process and its inherent difficulties, emphasizing the neurological examination, patient history, primary, secondary and tertiary symptoms, drug treatments for specific symptoms and nursing interventions.
Health and Safety
Dist - AJN **Prod** - HOSSN 1986

A Multiple Star System - Xi Ursae Majoris 8 MIN
16mm
Explorations in Space and Time Series
Color (H C A)
LC 75-703981
Uses computer animation to examine the multiple star system, Xi Ursae Majoris, a four - star system.
Science - Physical
Dist - HMC **Prod** - HMC 1974

Multiple - System Trauma - a Matter of Minutes 70 MIN
U-matic / VHS
Continuing Medical Education Emergency Care Programs Series
Color (PRO)
Presents techniques for treating medical emergencies consisting of multiple - system traumas. Dramatically enacts typical cases. Provides actual documentary footage.
Education; Health and Safety
Dist - CONTED **Prod** - CONTED

Multiple - Systems Trauma - a Matter of Minutes 70 MIN
U-matic / VHS
Color
Examines vital principles and priorities of emergency nursing care. Discusses critical assessment priorities, the ABC approach, recognition of shock and placement fluids. Offers a comprehensive, head - to - toe approach to examination of the patient.
Health and Safety; Psychology
Dist - AJN **Prod** - CONTED

Multiple trauma - assessment and interventions 31 MIN
VHS
Color (C PRO G)
$395.00 purchase _ #R861 - VI - 032
Presents two typical multiple trauma patients. Reveals that one patient is rushed to surgery immediately after preliminary assessment, while the other remains in the emergency room for a complete secondary examination. Reviews assessments and responses both in the field and in the emergency room. Demonstrates techniques for stabilizing a trauma patient, such as performing a head - to - toe secondary survey, and preparing the patient for surgery. Discusses the importance of good communication because the emergency room staff must be able to collect information from field personnel, disseminate results of their assessment to other hospital staff members and approach the patient's family in a frank and empathetic way.
Health and Safety; Social Science
Dist - HSCIC **Prod** - UNEBO 1987

Multiple Trauma - Assessments and Interventions 31 MIN
VHS / 16mm
(C)
$385.00 purchase _ #861VJ032
Reviews assessment of trauma victims and how to respond to their condition both in the field and in the emergency room. Demonstrates techniques for stabilizing a trauma patient, including performing a head - to - toe secondary survey and preparing the patient for surgery.
Health and Safety
Dist - HSCIC **Prod** - HSCIC 1987

Multiple Visceral Arterial Aneurysms 6 MIN
16mm
Color (PRO)
Shows how the workup of a 51 - year - old female with complaint of upper abdominal pain includes an arteriography which reveals an aneurysm of the celiac exis and of the superior mesenteric artery. Discusses the anatomy and pathology of the lesions in the course of the operative resection of the lesions and reconstruction of the visceral arterial tree.
Health and Safety; Science - Natural
Dist - UCLA **Prod** - UCLA 1970

Multiplexing 44 MIN
U-matic / VHS
Telecommunications and the Computer Series
Color
Discusses multiplexing techniques.
Industrial and Technical Education; Mathematics
Dist - MIOT **Prod** - MIOT

Multiplexing 45 MIN
VHS / U-matic
Telecommunications and the Computer Series
Color (C)
LC 81-707502
Discusses bandwidth and motivation for sharing, multiplexing techniques including frequency division multiplexing (FDM), time division multiplexing (TDM), concentration and Shannon's theorem for channel capacity.
Industrial and Technical Education; Mathematics
Dist - AMCEE **Prod** - AMCEE 1981

Multiplication 14 MIN
U-matic / VHS / 16mm
Beginning Mathematics Series
Color (P) (SPANISH)
LC 73-600981
Introduces the idea of multiplication as repeated addition.
Mathematics
Dist - JOU **Prod** - GLDWER 1973

Multiplication 30 MIN
16mm
Mathematics for Elementary School Teachers Series no 8
Color (T)
Uses model sets to point up the properties of multiplication. To be used following 'ADDITION AND SUBTRACTION TECHNIQUES.'.
Mathematics
Dist - MLA **Prod** - SMSG 1963

Multiplication 12 MIN
U-matic / VHS / 16mm
Math for Beginners Series
Color (P)
$305, $215 purchase _ #4193
Shows the methods that can be used to solve multiplication problems.
Mathematics
Dist - CORF

Multiplication 15 MIN
U-matic
Math Makers 1 Series
Color (I)
Presents the concepts of multiplication arrays, two digit by one digit multiplication, repeated addition, regrouping, two step problems and approximation.
Education; Mathematics
Dist - TVOTAR **Prod** - TVOTAR 1979

Multiplication 15 MIN
16mm / U-matic / VHS
Beginning Mathematics Series
Color (P)
Introduces the idea of multiplication as repeated addition. Develops the multiplication table up to the tens. Introduces the simplest form of multiplication computation.
Mathematics
Dist - JOU **Prod** - JOU

Multiplication 16 MIN
U-matic / VHS
Math Cycle Series
Color (P)
Introduces multiplication facts through 5 X 5.
Mathematics
Dist - GPN **Prod** - WDCNTV 1983

Multiplication 1, using the Cuisenaire Rods 9 MIN
16mm
Using Cuisenaire Rods Series no 3
Color (P I T)
LC FIA67-37
Demonstrates the use of cuisenaire colored rods in teaching multiplication.
Mathematics
Dist - MMP **Prod** - MMP 1966

Multiplication and Division 7 MIN
16mm
MAA Elementary Arithmetic Series
Color (P T)
Mathematics
Dist - MLA **Prod** - MAA 1967

Multiplication and division of fractions 30 MIN
VHS
Basic mathematical skills series
Color (J H)
$125.00 purchase _ #M6
Teaches the multiplication and division of fractions. Features Elayn Gay. Part of a 15 - part series on basic math.
Mathematics
Dist - LANDMK **Prod** - MGHT

Multiplication and division of radical expressions
VHS
Intermediate algebra series
Color (J H)
$125.00 purchase _ #3022
Teaches the concepts involved in multiplying and dividing radical expressions. Part of a set of 31 videos, each between 25 and 30 minutes long, that explain and reinforce concepts in intermediate algebra. Videos are also available in a set.
Mathematics
Dist - LANDMK

Multiplication and Division of Radical Expressions 30 MIN
VHS
Mathematics Series
Color (J)
LC 90713155
Discusses multiplication and division of radical expressions. The 53rd of 157 installments of the Mathematics Series.
Mathematics
Dist - GPN

Multiplication and division of rational expressions
VHS
Intermediate algebra series
Color (J H)
$125.00 purchase _ #3013
Teaches the concepts involved in multiplying and dividing rational expressions. Part of a set of 31 videos, each between 25 and 30 minutes long, that explain and reinforce concepts in intermediate algebra. Videos are also available in a set.
Mathematics
Dist - LANDMK

Multiplication and division of rational expressions 30 MIN
VHS
Beginning algebra series
Color (J H)
$125.00 purchase _ #M25
Explains multiplication and divison of rational numbers. Features Elayn Gay. Part of a 19 - part series on beginning algebra.
Mathematics
Dist - LANDMK **Prod** - MGHT

Multiplication and Division of Rational Expressions 30 MIN
VHS
Mathematics Series
Color (J)
LC 90713155
Demonstrates multiplication and division of rational expressions. The 44th of 157 installments of the Mathematics Series.
Mathematics
Dist - GPN

Multiplication, division and fractions - Part 2 36 MIN
VHS
Mathematics learning activities series
Color (T)
$175.00 purchase _ #6806 - 2
Demonstrates structured mathematics learning activities developed by professor Richard Skemp. Shows Skemp and teacher Marilyn Harrison interacting with small groups of elementary children in Make a Set - Make Others Which Match, Sets Under Our Hands, My Share Is..., The Rectangular Numbers Game, Match and Mix - Parts. Part of a two - part series. Additional sets of learning activities will be available in early 1991.
Education; Mathematics
Dist - UCALG **Prod** - UCALG 1990

Multiplication Facts 15 MIN
VHS / U-matic
Math Cycle Series
Color (P)
Introduces seven strategies that simplify learning the 100 basic multiplication facts.
Mathematics
Dist - GPN **Prod** - WDCNTV

Multiplication facts
VHS
Lola May's fundamental math series
Color (P I)
$45.00 purchase _ #10274VG
Reviews easy multiplication facts and then builds on known facts to find the more difficult ones. Teaches a pattern for the nine table and the difficult families of six, seven, and eight. Comes with a teacher's guide and blackline masters. Part 24 of a 30 - part series.
Mathematics
Dist - UNL

Multiplication of Rational Numbers 31 MIN
16mm
Intermediate Algebra Series
B&W (H)
Shows properties for the multiplication and division of signed numbers, using the idea that (- 1)(a) equals (- a) and (- B)(1/ - B) equals 1. Applies these concepts to the addition, subtraction, multiplication and division of multiple - term expressions involving powers.
Mathematics
Dist - MLA **Prod** - CALVIN 1959

Multiplication of several digits
VHS
Lola May's fundamental math series
Color (I)
$45.00 purchase _ #10277VG
Teaches how to multiply several digits by one digit and how to multiply two - digit by one - digit numbers. Uses models to practice without pencil and paper. Comes with a teacher's guide and blackline masters. Part 27 of a 30 - part series.
Mathematics
Dist - UNL

Multiplication of whole numbers 30 MIN
VHS
Basic mathematical skills series
Color (J H)
$125.00 purchase _ #M2
Teaches multiplication of whole numbers. Features Elayn Gay. Part of a 15 - part series on basic math.
Mathematics
Dist - LANDMK **Prod** - MGHT

Multiplication One 15 MIN
U-matic
Math Patrol Three Series
Color (P I)
Presents mathematical concepts of methods for multiplication.
Education; Mathematics
Dist - TVOTAR **Prod** - TVOTAR 1978

Multiplication principle for counting
VHS
Probability and statistics series
Color (H C)
$125.00 purchase _ #8014
Provides resource material about counting using the multiplication principle for help in the study of probability and statistics. Presents a 60 - video series, each part 25 to 30 minutes long, that explains and reinforces concepts using definitions, theorems, examples and step - by - step solutions to tutor the student. Videos are also available in a set.
Mathematics
Dist - LANDMK

Multiplication, Pt 1 15 MIN
U-matic
Studio M Series
Color (P)
Shows the meaning of multiplication in adding equal addends.
Mathematics
Dist - GPN **Prod** - WCETTV 1979

Multiplication, Pt 2 15 MIN
U-matic
Studio M Series
Color (P)
Tells how to solve multiplication facts through the product of 45. Emphasis is on threes and fours.
Mathematics
Dist - GPN **Prod** - WCETTV 1979

Multiplication Rock
16mm / U-matic / VHS
Color
Uses beats and lyrics to teach multiplication tables.
Mathematics
Dist - GA **Prod** - ABCTV

Multiplication Rock Series

Elementary, my dear (twos)	46 FRS
Figure eight	4 MIN
The Four - Legged Zoo	41 FRS
The Good eleven	4 MIN
I Got Six	4 MIN
Little Twelvetoes	4 MIN
Lucky Seven Sampson	4 MIN
My Hero Zero	4 MIN
Naughty Number Nine	4 MIN
Ready or not, here i come	4 MIN
Three is a Magic Number	41 FRS

Dist - GA

Multiplication Techniques 30 MIN
16mm
Mathematics for Elementary School Teachers Series no 10
Color (T)
Shows the existence of a multiplicative inverse, and introduces the distributive property. Develops algorithms consistent with the properties. To be used following division.
Mathematics
Dist - MLA **Prod** - SMSG 1963

Multiplication Two 15 MIN
U-matic
Math Patrol Three Series
Color (P I)
Presents mathematical concepts of arrays used to demonstrate the conmmutative property of multiplication.
Education; Mathematics
Dist - TVOTAR **Prod** - TVOTAR 1978

Multiplication Without Renaming 15 MIN
U-matic / VHS
Math Cycle Series
Color (P)
Shows two methods of finding the product of a two or three digit factor and a one digit factor, without renaming.
Mathematics
Dist - GPN **Prod** - WDCNTV

The Multiplier Effect 45 MIN
U-matic / VHS
Economic Perspectives Series
Color
Discusses the multiplier effect in economics.
Business and Economics
Dist - MDCPB **Prod** - MDCPB

Multiply and Subdue the Earth 70 MIN
U-matic / VHS / 16mm
Color (H C A)
LC 70-703708
Analysis of man's relationship to his environment with great emphasis on the need to maintain the ecological balance when opening up new areas.
Psychology; Science - Natural; Sociology
Dist - IU **Prod** - NET 1969

Multiply and Subdue the Earth, Pt 1 34 MIN
16mm / VHS / U-matic
Color (H C A)
LC 80-707088; 70-703708
Presents an analysis of man's relationship to his environment with great emphasis on the need to maintain the ecological balance with opening up new areas.
Psychology; Science - Natural; Sociology
Dist - IU **Prod** - NET 1969

Multiply and Subdue the Earth, Pt 2 33 MIN
U-matic / 16mm / VHS
Color (H C A)
LC 80-707088; 70-703708
Presents an analysis of man's relationship to his environment with great emphasis on the need to maintain the ecological balance with opening up new areas.
Psychology; Science - Natural; Sociology
Dist - IU **Prod** - NET 1969

The Multiply Handicapped 23 MIN
VHS / U-matic
International Education of the Hearing Impaired Child Series
Color
LC 80-707438
Shows mentally retarded, cerebral palsied, deaf - blind, and emotionally disturbed children in Sweden, Germany, the Netherlands, and England.
Education; Psychology
Dist - USNAC **Prod** - USBEH 1980

Multiplying and dividing radicals
VHS
Beginning algebra series
Color (J H)
$125.00 purchase _ #2025
Teaches basic concepts of multiplying and dividing radical expressions. Part of a 31 - video series, each part between 25 and 30 minutes long, that explains and reinforces fundamental concepts of beginning algebra. Uses definitions, theorems, examples and step - by - step solutions to instruct the student.
Mathematics
Dist - LANDMK

Multiplying Decimals 10 MIN
U-matic
Basic Math Skills Series Adding, Subtracting, Multiplying Decimals; Adding - subtracing - multiplying decimals
Color
Mathematics
Dist - TELSTR **Prod** - TELSTR

Multiplying Fractions 19 MIN
U-matic 9 MIN
Basic Math Skills Series Multiplying Fractions and Reducing; Multiplying fractions and reducing
Color
Mathematics
Dist - TELSTR **Prod** - TELSTR

Multiplying Mixed Numbers 11 MIN
U-matic
Basic Math Skills Series Multiplying and Dividing Fractions; Multiplying and dividing fractions
Color
Mathematics
Dist - TELSTR **Prod** - TELSTR

Multiplying real numbers 37 MIN
16mm
Teaching high school mathematics - first course series; No 6
B&W (T)
Mathematics
Dist - MLA **Prod** - UICSM 1967

Multiplying with decimals 8 MIN
VHS
Children's encyclopedia of mathematics - decimals series
Color (I)
$49.95 purchase _ #8364
Looks at multiplying with fractions. Part of a five - part series on decimals.
Mathematics
Dist - AIMS **Prod** - DAVFMS 1991

Multiplying with fractions 8 MIN
VHS
Children's encyclopedia of mathematics - multiplication and division of fractions series
Color (I)
$49.95 purchase _ #8355
Illustrates multiplication with fractions. Part of a seven - part series on multiplication and division with fractions.
Mathematics
Dist - AIMS **Prod** - DAVFMS 1991

Multiplying with fractions - distributivity 7 MIN
VHS
Children's encyclopedia of mathematics - multiplication and division of fractions series
Color (I)
$49.95 purchase _ #8357
Discusses the concept of distributivity in multiplication with fractions. Part of a seven - part series on multiplication and division with fractions.
Mathematics
Dist - AIMS **Prod** - DAVFMS 1991

Multiprogramming and Multiprocessing 30 MIN
U-matic / VHS
Making it Count Series
Color (H C A)
LC 80-707576
Introduces advanced computer systems by discussing differences in hardware operating speeds and the problems caused by disparities. Describes multiprogramming and multiprocessing, plus associated techniques such as timesharing, timeslicing and interrupt handling.
Business and Economics; Mathematics
Dist - BCSC **Prod** - BCSC 1980

Multiprogramming and Time Sharing 30 MIN
U-matic
Computing for Every Man Series
Color (H A)
Looks at the techniques of using combinations of hardware and software to permit several programs or users to share a common computer.
Mathematics
Dist - NYSED **Prod** - NYSED 1973

Multistage Centrifugal Pumps 60 MIN
VHS
Pumps Series
Color (PRO)
$600.00, $1500.00 purchase _ #GMMSC
Identifies the major components of a multistage centrifugal pump. Explains how the pump works. Shows how to troubleshoot some common pump problems. Teaches how to disassemble and reassemble axially split and radially split multistage centrifugal pumps. Part of a seven - part series on pumps, which is part of a set on general and mechanical maintenance. Includes 10 textbooks and an instructor guide which provide four hours of instruction.
Education; Health and Safety; Industrial and Technical Education; Psychology
Dist - NUSTC **Prod** - NUSTC

The Multistage Decision Model - further Considerations 51 MIN
U-matic / VHS
Decision Analysis Series
Color
Industrial and Technical Education; Mathematics
Dist - MIOT **Prod** - MIOT

The Multistage Model - a First Example 55 MIN
VHS / U-matic
Decision Analysis Series
Color
Discusses structure of the multistage decision model, decision trees and the sequencing of events within a decision tree representation of a decision problem and Al's problem and its solution to maximize monetary value.
Industrial and Technical Education; Mathematics
Dist - MIOT **Prod** - MIOT

Multivariable Control of Batch Processes
VHS / 16mm
Batch Control Series
Color (PRO)
$300.00 purchase, $90.00 rental
Includes Sequencing, Programmable Control for Batch Processes, Batch Process Control Using Digital Technology, Appropriate Expert System Batch Processes and Intermediate Raw Materials Handling. Part of a four - part series on batch control.
Home Economics; Industrial and Technical Education
Dist - ISA **Prod** - ISA

Multiview Drawing 32 MIN
16mm
B&W (C A)
Demonstrates with models and drawings how to represent an object by means of three orthographic views.
Industrial and Technical Education
Dist - PUAVC **Prod** - PUAVC 1959

Multiview Drawing
VHS
Engineering Drawing Videos Series
$69.95 purchase _ #017 - 072
Discusses work habits, orthographic projection concepts, missing line and missing view problems.
Industrial and Technical Education
Dist - CAREER **Prod** - CAREER

Mum Deoderant 1 MIN
U-matic / VHS
Color
Shows a classic television commercial.
Business and Economics; Psychology; Sociology
Dist - BROOKC **Prod** - BROOKC

Mummies and Maya - Pt 5 30 MIN
VHS
Wonderstruck Presents Series
Color (I)
$99.00 purchase _ #386 - 9059
Organizes science programs thematically for classroom use. Features Bob McDonald as host who makes learning fun with amazing science information and engaging activities. Part 5 of the eight part series introduces the fascinating world of archaeology in programs on the Maya, Mayan architecture, the crystal skull and the mummies of San Pedro.
Geography - World; History - World; Science - Physical; Social Science
Dist - FI **Prod** - CANBC 1989

Mummies and Mayas 26 MIN
VHS
Wonderstruck presents series
Color (I J)
$99.95 purchase _ #Q11173
Focuses on ancient burial rites and lost civilizations to illustrate archaeological methods that re - create the past. Investigates the significance and authenticity of the crystal skull found in 1923 by a child in Belize. Part of a series of 11 programs produced by the Canadian Broadcasting Corporation and hosted by Bob McDonald.
History - World; Science - Physical
Dist - CF

Mummies made in Egypt 15 MIN
U-matic / VHS
Through the Pages Series no 5
Color (P)
LC 82-707373
Introduces librarian Phyllis Syracuse reading from the book Mummies Made In Egypt by Aliki. Shows relics from the ancient Egyptian civilization through visits to two museums.
English Language
Dist - GPN **Prod** - WVIZTV 1982

Mummies made in Egypt - 54
VHS
Reading rainbow series
Color; CC (K P)
$39.95 purchase
Takes an in - depth look at the fascinating world of mummies in the book by Aliki. Visits the Museum of Fine Arts Boston with LeVar where the art of conserving Egyptian artifacts is explored. Shows what a mummy looks like after thousands of years using CAT scan technology. Part of a series offering a multicultural approach to generating reading enthusiasm with cross - curricular applications, hosted by LeVar Burton.
English Language; History - World; Literature and Drama; Science
Dist - GPN **Prod** - LNMDP

Mummies made in Egypt - Bringing the rain to Kapiti Plain
VHS
Reading rainbow treasury series
Color (K P)
$12.95 purchase _ #516456
Presents two animated stories. Features Levar Burton as host. Part of a six - part series.
English Language; Fine Arts; Literature and Drama
Dist - KNOWUN **Prod** - PBS

Mummy 27 MIN
U-matic / VHS / 16mm
Insight Series
B&W (H C A)
LC 71-705428
A dramatization about a daydreaming housewife who cannot accept the everyday limitations of being a wife and mother.
Guidance and Counseling; Psychology
Dist - PAULST **Prod** - PAULST 1968

The Mummy Mosaic 30 MIN
16mm
B&W
Presents highlights from Mummy features films, including 'The Mummy,' 'The Mummy's Tomb' and 'The Mummy's Ghost'.
Fine Arts; Literature and Drama
Dist - CFS **Prod** - CFS

The Mummy Strikes 8 MIN
16mm
B&W
Illustrates the Superman cartoon from the famed Fleischer studios.
Fine Arts
Dist - FCE **Prod** - FCE

The Mummy's blessing 30 MIN
VHS
Perspectives - health and medicine - series
Color; PAL; NTSC (G)
PdS90, PdS105 purchase
Shows how studying an Egyptian mummy helped a surgeon reconstruct a young girl's face.
Health and Safety
Dist - CFLVIS **Prod** - LONTVS

Mum's the word - PC and LAN data security 20 MIN
VHS
Color (A)
$525.00 purchase
Focuses on security issues for personal and laptop computer users and LAN network users in business settings. Explains how data is vulnerable to unauthorized access or corruption and how it can be protected, emphasizing security precautions, backup procedures, and general storage and handling principles essential for business computer use.
Business and Economics; Computer Science; Education
Dist - COMFLM **Prod** - COMFLM

Munch and Ensor - fathers of expressionism 21 MIN
VHS
Color (G)
$29.95 purchase _ #ACE04V - F
Looks at the works of European artists Edward Munch and James Ensor and their lives, showing how their themes were later expanded in German Expressionism.
Fine Arts
Dist - CAMV

Munchen 15 MIN
U-matic / VHS / 16mm
German Cities Series
Color (H C) (GERMAN)
LC 76-707312
A German language film. Presents various monuments of the city of Munich - - the Hofbrauhaus, the Residenz, the National Theater, the Lukas Church, the English Garden, the Frauen Church, old Munich with its Baroque architecture and the old and new Rathaus.
Foreign Language
Dist - IFB **Prod** - IFB 1969

The Munchers - a Fable - 010mpamda 10 MIN
16mm
Color
LC 74-700534
Uses animation techniques in order to examine the interaction of teeth and tooth decay in the mouth. Shows how different food groups have different effects on tooth decay and tooth growth.
Health and Safety
Dist - MTP **Prod** - AMDA 1973

Munchhausen 100 MIN
16mm
Color (GERMAN (ENGLISH SUBTITLES))
A German language film with English subtitles, adapted from Erich Kastner's novel, MUNCHHAUSEN. Relates the adventures of Baron Munchhausen, known for his unbelievable stories.
Fine Arts; Foreign Language
Dist - WSTGLC **Prod** - WSTGLC 1943

Munich 30 MIN
VHS
Color (G)
$29.95 purchase _ #S02027
Tours the Bavarian city of Munich. Features the Glockenspiel, Oktoberfest, and the many gardens and museums of the area.
Geography - World
Dist - UILL

Munich - Berlin walking trip 4 MIN
16mm
B&W (G)
$16.50 rental
Journeys with the filmmaker in the summer of 1927 when he walked from Munich to Berlin carrying his film equipment. Captures single - frame images of certain people and landscapes he encountered.
Fine Arts
Dist - CANCIN **Prod** - FISCHF 1927

The Munich crisis
16mm / VHS
British Universities historical studies in film series
B&W; PAL (G)
PdS495, PdS80 purchase
Examines the origins of the Munich crisis which occurred in 1938. Looks at the situation in Czechoslovakia and the role of Neville Chamberlain in appeasing Nazi Germany by agreeing to the German occupation of Sudetenland in Czechoslovakia. Focuses primarily on the crisis itself and its presentation. Uses material selected, edited and scripted by John Grenville and Nicholas Pronay.
History - World
Dist - BUFVC **Prod** - BUFVC

The Munich Crisis 58 MIN
16mm
British Universities Historical Studies in Film Series
Color (C)
LC 72-701256
Shows a detailed examination of the assumptions behind British policy which led to a great power settlement at the expense of Czechoslovakia.
History - World
Dist - KRAUS **Prod** - BUFVC 1975

The Munich Seasons 28 MIN
16mm
Color (C A)
Describes a 'Munich year,' a color - and - sound panorama of the varied lifestyles of the city set to the rhythms of the four seasons.
History - World
Dist - WSTGLC **Prod** - WSTGLC

Municipal and civil servants 14 MIN
VHS / U-matic
Tax tips on tape series
Color; Captioned (A PRO IND)
$20.00, $40.00 purchase _ #TCA17606, #TCA17605
Explains the rules for computing taxation of government or civil service retirement annuities. Covers taxation of Veterans' Administration disability benefits.
Business and Economics; Civics and Political Systems; Social Science
Dist - USNAC **Prod** - USIRS 1988

The Municipal garden 3 MIN
16mm
Color (G)
$15.00 rental
Tells a love story in living color.
Fine Arts; Religion and Philosophy
Dist - CANCIN **Prod** - OSBONS 1984

Municipal Government 30 MIN
U-matic / VHS
Making Government Work
(H)
Uses dramatization and interviews to familiarize high school students with the functions of government. Focuses on three forms of municipal government.
Civics and Political Systems
Dist - GPN

Municipal Water Treatment 16 MIN
U-matic
Chemistry 102 - Chemistry for Engineers - Series
Color (C)
Lists steps necessary in the purification of water, concentrating particularly on the removal of toxic cations. Illustrates three major methods used to remove unwanted ions from water; precipitation, ion exchange and chelation.
Industrial and Technical Education; Science - Physical
Dist - UILL **Prod** - UILL 1982

Munro 9 MIN
U-matic / VHS / 16mm
Color (A)
Portrays the trials of Munro, a four - year - old drafted into the army, when no one will believe he is only four.
Civics and Political Systems; Fine Arts
Dist - FI **Prod** - AUDBRF

Muppet break out 11 MIN
VHS
Color (IND PRO COR A)
$575.00 purchase, $315.00 rental, $50.00 preview
Presents 3 vignettes with Jim Henson's muppets which humorously make sales meetings motivational events. The muppets act out the importance of knowing everything about customers and how to sell, and how to end a meeting.
Business and Economics; Fine Arts; Psychology
Dist - VIDART

Muppet breakaway 8 MIN
VHS / U-matic
Color (G)
$550.00 purchase, $300.00 rental
Uses the Muppets of Jim Henson to kick off, break up and add humor to meetings. Includes the topics of 'Sales Savvy,' 'The Art of Negotiation,' and 'Break'n the Rules.'
Business and Economics; Guidance and Counseling; Literature and Drama; Psychology
Dist - VLEARN **Prod** - RTBL

The Muppet Breakaway 8 MIN
VHS / 16mm
Muppet Meeting Films Series
Color (PRO)
$550.00 purchase, $300.00 rental, $30.00 preview
Presents Jim Henson's muppets who introduce and humorously comment on business meetings and breaks. Consists of three to four segments each approximately two and a half minutes.
Business and Economics; Psychology; Sociology
Dist - UTM

Muppet breaker upper 9 MIN
U-matic / VHS
Color (G)
$550.00 purchase, $300.00 rental
Uses the Muppets of Jim Henson to kick off, break up and add humor to meetings. Includes the topics of 'Introduction with a Slight Snare,' 'Five Basic Rules of Selling,' 'Wheels of Progress,' and 'The Secret of Success.'
Business and Economics; Guidance and Counseling; Literature and Drama; Psychology
Dist - VLEARN **Prod** - RTBL

Muppet breaking point 10 MIN
Videoreel
Color (IND PRO COR A)
$575.00 purchase, $315.00 rental, $50.00 preview
Presents 3 vignettes with Jim Henson's muppets which pokes fun at the corporate world. Helps focus staff's attention by adding laughter to a meeting.
Business and Economics; Fine Arts; Psychology
Dist - VIDART

Muppet breakout 3 MIN
VHS
Muppet meeting films
Color (IND)
$575.00 purchase, $315.00 rental _ #VAR155
Contains three sketches involving Leo and Grump in the business world.
Business and Economics; Literature and Drama
Dist - EXTR **Prod** - VIDART

The Muppet Breaks - Call - it - Quits
VHS / 16mm
Muppet Meeting Films Series
Color (PRO)
$750.00 purchase, $300.00 rental, $30.00 preview
Presents five vignettes with Jim Hensen's muppets which humorously comment on office breaks.
Business and Economics; Psychology; Sociology
Dist - UTM

Muppet breakthrough 10 MIN
U-matic / VHS
Color (G)
$550.00 purchase, $300.00 rental
Uses the Muppets of Jim Henson to kick off, break up and add humor to meetings. Includes the topics of 'What's This Meeting All About,' 'The B I G Plan,' 'Who Needs a Break,' and 'The Sky's the Limit.'
Business and Economics; Guidance and Counseling; Literature and Drama; Psychology
Dist - VLEARN **Prod** - RTBL

Muppet coffee break 6 MIN
VHS / U-matic
Color (G)
$550.00 purchase, $300.00 rental
Uses the Muppets of Jim Henson to kick off, break up and add humor to meetings. Includes the topics of 'Explosion - Leo and the Monster' and 'The Coffee Break Machine.'
Business and Economics; Guidance and Counseling; Literature and Drama; Psychology
Dist - VLEARN **Prod** - RTBL

The Muppet Coffeebreak 8 MIN
VHS / 16mm
Muppet Meeting Films Series
Color (PRO)
$550.00 purchase, $300.00 rental, $30.00 preview
Presents Jim Henson's muppets who introduce and humorously comment on business meetings and breaks. Consists of three to four segments each approximately two and a half minutes.
Business and Economics; Psychology; Sociology
Dist - UTM

Muppet gimme a break 6 MIN
VHS / U-matic
Color (G)
$550.00 purchase, $300.00 rental
Uses the Muppets of Jim Henson to kick off, break up and add humor to meetings. Includes the topics of 'Meal Break,' 'Grump Critic,' and 'Let's Have the Dam Break.'
Business and Economics; Guidance and Counseling; Literature and Drama; Psychology
Dist - VLEARN **Prod** - RTBL

Muppet know how 3 MIN
VHS
Muppet meeting films
Color (IND)
$575.00 purchase, $315.00 rental _ #VAR148
Contains three sketches with Leo and Grump.
Business and Economics; Literature and Drama
Dist - EXTR **Prod** - VIDART

Muppet lift off 8 MIN
VHS / U-matic
Color (G)
$550.00 purchase, $300.00 rental
Uses the Muppets of Jim Henson to kick off, break up and add humor to meetings. Includes the topics of 'Super Salesperson,' 'The Safety Zone,' and 'The Rap.'
Business and Economics; Guidance and Counseling; Literature and Drama; Psychology
Dist - VLEARN **Prod** - RTBL

Muppet mayhem 9 MIN
VHS
Color (IND PRO COR A)
$575.00 purchase, $315.00 rental, $50.00 preview
Presents 3 humorous sketches for lightening up business meetings. These vignettes trace the beginnings of modern business, reveal what can go wrong when you depend on research alone to bring a new product to market, and show how taking credit for someone else's idea can have explosive results.
Fine Arts; Psychology
Dist - VIDART

Muppet meeting films 10 MIN
VHS / U-matic
Color (G)
$550.00 purchase, $300.00 rental
Uses the Muppets of Jim Henson to kick off, break up and add humor to meetings.
Business and Economics; Guidance and Counseling; Literature and Drama; Psychology
Dist - VLEARN **Prod** - RTBL

Muppet Meeting Films Series
Gimme a Break 8 MIN
Dist - HENASS
UTM

Muppet Meeting Films Series
Breakthrough 8 MIN
Lift off 8 MIN
The Muppet Breakaway 8 MIN
The Muppet Breaks - Call - it - Quits
The Muppet Coffeebreak 8 MIN
The Muppet Office - Operation Delegation
Perk Up 8 MIN
Picker Upper 8 MIN
Side splitter 8 MIN
Dist - UTM

Muppet meeting films
Muppet breakout 3 MIN
Muppet know how 3 MIN
Dist - EXTR

Muppet Meeting Openers 7 MIN
U-matic / VHS / 16mm
Color (G)
Presents sales, management, employee relations techniques, brief meeting openers or closers, and fillers for meeting breaks.
Business and Economics
Dist - VPHI **Prod** - VPHI 1986

The Muppet Meeting Openers - the Kick Off
VHS / 16mm
Color (PRO)
$750.00 purchase, $300.00 rental, $30.00 preview
Presents four vignettes with Jim Hensen's muppets which humorously introduce a business meeting.
Business and Economics; Psychology; Sociology
Dist - UTM

Muppet meeting series
Coffee break 6 MIN
Picker - Upper 8 MIN
Dist - HENASS

Muppet Meeting Series
Breaker - Upper 9 MIN
Dist - HENASS
UTM

The Muppet Motivational - Blast Off
VHS / 16mm
Color (PRO)
$750.00 purchase, $300.00 rental, $30.00 preview
Presents four vignettes with Jim Hensen's muppets which humorously motivate employees to succeed.
Business and Economics; Psychology; Sociology
Dist - UTM

The Muppet Movie 98 MIN
16mm
Color
Shows what happens when the Muppets seek stardom in Hollywood.
Fine Arts
Dist - SWANK **Prod** - UNKNWN

The Muppet Office - Operation Delegation
VHS / 16mm
Muppet Meeting Films Series
Color (PRO)
$750.00 purchase, $300.00 rental, $30.00 preview
Presents four vignettes with Jim Hensen's muppets which humorously comment on various apects of working in an office, including computers, benefits, time management, safety, and filing responsibilities.
Business and Economics; Psychology; Sociology
Dist - UTM

Muppet picker upper 8 MIN
U-matic / VHS
Color (G)
$550.00 purchase, $300.00 rental
Uses the Muppets of Jim Henson to kick off, break up and add humor to meetings. Includes the topics of 'Introduction - Just a Few Announcements' and 'Sell, Sell, Sell.'
Business and Economics; Guidance and Counseling; Literature and Drama; Psychology
Dist - VLEARN **Prod** - RTBL

Muppet Picker - Upper Films Series
Final Speech 2 MIN
Dist - HENASS

The Muppet Sales - make - a - Buck
VHS / 16mm
Color (PRO)
$750.00 purchase, $300.00 rental, $30.00 preview
Presents four vignettes with Jim Hensen's muppets which humorously comment on various apects of being a salesperson.
Business and Economics; Psychology; Sociology
Dist - UTM

Muppet sales sensation 15 MIN
Videoreel
Color (IND PRO COR A)
$795.00 purchase, $435.00 rental, $50.00 premium
Combines 4 vignettes on how to sell, great salespeople through history, sales savvy, and winning is everything. These segments from The Muppets Original Programs target topic-specific groups such as sales, motivation and management.
Business and Economics; Psychology
Dist - VIDART

Muppet side splitter 9 MIN
VHS / U-matic
Color (G)
$550.00 purchase, $300.00 rental
Uses the Muppets of Jim Henson to kick off, break up and add humor to meetings. Includes the topics of 'The Ideal Sales Rep,' 'Computer,' and 'Take This Form and File It.'
Business and Economics; Guidance and Counseling; Literature and Drama; Psychology
Dist - VLEARN **Prod** - RTBL

The Muppets Go Hollywood 50 MIN
VHS
Muppets Series
Color (K)
$49.00 purchase _ #064 - 9002
Features Kermit, Miss Piggy and the whole Muppet gang joining with hosts Dick Van Dyke and Rita Moreno in a silly send - up of Tinseltown. Offers this program as part of 'The Muppets' series.
Fine Arts; Health and Safety; Literature and Drama; Sociology
Dist - FI **Prod** - HENASS 1988

Muppets Go to the Movies 50 MIN
VHS
Muppets Series
Color (K)
$49.00 purchase _ #064 - 9003
Presents Kermit, Miss Piggy and the whole Muppet gang who decide to remake Hollywood classics such as 'The Wizard Of Oz,' 'Casablanca' and 'Frankenstein.' Offers this program as part of 'The Muppets' series.
Fine Arts; Health and Safety; Literature and Drama; Sociology
Dist - FI **Prod** - HENASS 1988

Muppets Series
Down at Fraggle Rock - Behind the Scenes 48 MIN
The Fantastic Miss Piggy show 51 MIN
Frog prince 51 MIN
Henson's place - the man behind the muppets 52 MIN
The Muppets Go Hollywood 50 MIN
Muppets Go to the Movies 50 MIN
Of Muppets and Men 52 MIN
Dist - FI

Mura Dehn, Sally Sommer and Sule Wilson 30 MIN
U-matic / VHS
Eye on Dance - Glance at the Past Series
Color
Presents a documentary on jazz dance. Hosted by Julinda Lewis.
Fine Arts
Dist - ARCVID **Prod** - ARCVID

The Mural 22 MIN
16mm
Classroom as a Learning Community Series
B&W (I)
LC 79-714104
A teacher - training film. Shows students in a sixth grade New York City classroom who, following a study of the Netsilik Eskimos, are making a mural about the winter migration of Eskimos.
Education; Fine Arts
Dist - EDC **Prod** - EDC 1971

Mural 5 MIN
16mm
Color
LC 78-700293
Shows the creation of a mural by sculptor Glen Michaels. Uses animation of tile, stone, wood, wax, bronze and brass to show the growth of segments of a mural piece by piece without the intrusion of hands. Shows the finished mural in its architectural setting.
Fine Arts
Dist - PAJON **Prod** - PAJON 1977

Mural in the Making 15 MIN
16mm
Color
Presents the story of the mural by artist Fred Conway painted in the lobby of Brown Shoe Company's office in St Louis, Missouri.
Fine Arts
Dist - SWANK **Prod** - BRNSHO 1956

Mural Making 6 MIN
U-matic / VHS / 16mm
Creative Hands Series
Color (P I)
Explains that the urge to draw and paint can be encouraged along constructive lines in the classroom. Shows the making of a mural as a class project with everyone participating.
Education; Fine Arts
Dist - IFB **Prod** - CRAF 1956

Mural Techniques 1 30 MIN
U-matic
Media and Methods of the Artist Series
Color (H C A)
Demonstrates techniques for mural painting.
Fine Arts
Dist - TVOTAR **Prod** - TVOTAR 1971

Mural Techniques 2 30 MIN
U-matic
Media and Methods of the Artist Series
Color (H C A)
Demonstrates techniques for mural painting.
Fine Arts
Dist - TVOTAR **Prod** - TVOTAR 1971

Murals 15 MIN
U-matic / VHS
Expressions
(I J)
$130 purchase, $25 rental, $75 self dub
Designed to interest fifth through ninth graders in art. Emphasizes creativity and experimentation. Features muralist Martin Charlot. Thirteenth in an 18 part series.
Fine Arts
Dist - GPN

Murals and celebrations - 8 22 MIN
VHS / U-matic
Think new series
Color (C G)
$129.00, $99.00 purchase _ #V583
Gives theoretical motivation and practical ideas about murals and their relationship with celebrations and other historical events. Draws content from mathematics, science, history, human feelings, every human endeavor. Part of an 11 - part series that treats art as an essential mode of learning.
Fine Arts
Dist - BARR **Prod** - CEPRO 1991

Murals and China Repairs - Wallpaper Murals, Gold Leaf and China Repairs 30 MIN
VHS / BETA
Wally's Workshop Series
Color
Fine Arts; Home Economics
Dist - KARTES **Prod** - KARTES

The Murals of Atzlan 23 MIN
VHS / U-matic
Color (J A)
Looks at an art show by Chicano artists in Los Angeles. Shows artists painting murals as the public watches.
Fine Arts; Sociology
Dist - SUTHRB **Prod** - SUTHRB

The Murals of East Los Angeles - a Museum Without Walls 46 MIN
16mm
Color
LC 77-700559
Deals with the visual and artistic revolution in the Barrio of East Los Angeles. Shows how Chicano artists are changing the environment with a multitude of murals that express Chicano concerns and aspirations.
Fine Arts; Geography - United States; Sociology
Dist - RKOGEN **Prod** - RKOGEN 1977

Murals of East Los Angeles - a Museum Without Walls - Pt 1 23 MIN
16mm
Color
LC 77-700559
Deals with the visual and artistic revolution in the Barrio of East Los Angeles. Shows how Chicano artists are changing the environment with a multitude of murals that express Chicano concerns and aspirations.
Fine Arts
Dist - RKOGEN **Prod** - RKOGEN 1977

Murals of East Los Angeles - a Museum Without Walls - Pt 2 23 MIN
16mm
Color
LC 77-700559
Deals with the visual and artistic revolution in the Barrio of East Los Angeles. Shows how Chicano artists are changing the environment with a multitude of murals that express Chicano concerns and aspirations.
Fine Arts
Dist - RKOGEN **Prod** - RKOGEN 1977

Muratti Greift Ein 4 MIN
16mm
Color
Presents a variation on dancing cigarettes.
Fine Arts
Dist - CFS **Prod** - PFP 1934

Muratti greift ein 3 MIN
16mm
Color (G)
$22.00 rental
Depicts a commercial for Muratti cigarettes with Bayer's Doll Fairy providing the music.
Fine Arts
Dist - CANCIN **Prod** - FISCHF 1934

Muratti privat 3 MIN
16mm ·
B&W (G)
$16.50 rental
Looks at a commercial for Muratti cigarettes with Mozart's Turkish Rondo. .
Fine Arts
Dist - CANCIN **Prod** - FISCHF 1935

Muratti Private 4 MIN
16mm
Color
Presents the object - animation of marching cigarettes and packets, as 'PRIVATE MURATTI' steps to Mozart's 'RONDO.'.
Fine Arts
Dist - CFS **Prod** - PFP 1934

Murder 102 MIN
16mm
B&W
Focuses on a jurist who becomes sure that a young woman convicted of murder is really innocent. Directed by Alfred Hitchcock.
Fine Arts
Dist - KITPAR **Prod** - UNKNWN 1930

Murder by Death 94 MIN
16mm
Color
Offers a satire of mystery movies, telling how an eccentric millionaire sends for five world - famous detectives and tests their investigative prowess.
Fine Arts
Dist - SWANK **Prod** - CPC

Murder by Television 55 MIN
VHS / BETA
B&W
Shows how a master electronics wizard and television inventor is murdered during a demonstration of the new marvel. Stars Bela Lugosi.
Fine Arts
Dist - VIDIM **Prod** - UNKNWN 1935

Murder in the Amazon 51 MIN
U-matic / VHS / 16mm
Color (H)
$275.00, $250.00 purchase $75.00 rental
Tells of the assassination of Chico Mendes, the Brazilian rubber - tappers union leader who resisted cattle ranching and slash and burn agriculture in the rainforest.
Agriculture; Biography; Business and Economics; Civics and Political Systems; Science - Natural; Social Science; Sociology
Dist - BULFRG **Prod** - COWELL 1990

Murder in the Cathedral 140 MIN
16mm / U-matic / VHS
B&W (I)
Stars Father John Groser as Thomas Becket in the T S Eliot play about the conflict between Becket and King Henry II. Introduces Becket when he returns to England from his seven year exile in France and Rome. Describes his conflict when he refuses the tempting offers by barons and bishops and instead succumbs to a fourth tempter who tries to corrupt him with presumptive and vengeful pride disguised as holy martyrdom.
Fine Arts; Literature and Drama
Dist - FI **Prod** - UNKNWN 1952

Murder in the Family 28 MIN
16mm / U-matic / VHS
Insight Series
B&W (H C A)
LC 75-705429
Tells of a young man faced with financial problems who orders his wife to have an abortion.
Guidance and Counseling; Psychology
Dist - PAULST **Prod** - PAULST 1965

Murder, My Sweet 12 MIN
16mm
American Film Genre - the Gangster Film Series
B&W (H C A)
LC 77-701142
Presents an excerpt from the motion picture Murder, My Sweet, issued in 1945. Tells the story of a private detective who gets drawn into a complex web of murder, blackmail and double - dealing while searching for a missing jade necklace. Exemplifies the gangster film genre.
Fine Arts
Dist - FI **Prod** - RKOP 1975

Murder - no Apparent Motive 60 MIN
VHS / 16mm
Color (G)
$350.00 purchase, $95.00 rental
Examines the growing phenomenon of serial murders in the US. Discusses such serial killers as David Berkowitz, John Wayne Gacy, Albert de Salvo, Kenneth Bianchi and Wayne Williams. Presents detailed studies of Ted Bundy and Edmund Kemper.
Sociology
Dist - CNEMAG **Prod** - HORVI 1984

The Murder of Fred Hampton 88 MIN
VHS
B&W (G)
$50.00 rental, $50.00, $150.00 purchase
Documents the murder of Fred Hampton, a Black Panther leader, by the United States government's COINTELPRO operations, which aimed to suppress domestic rebellions. Investigates the execution by Chicago police and relentlessly pursues the official spokesmen and traps them in their own lies and coverup. Produced by Michael Gray, scriptwriter for 'The China Syndrome.'
History - United States
Dist - CANCIN

Murder on the Orient Express 128 MIN
16mm / U-matic / VHS
Color
Tells the story of a murder committed on the Orient Express and shows how it is solved by Belgian detective Hercule Poirot. Stars Ingrid Bergman, Lauren Bacall and Albert Finney. Based on the novel MURDER ON THE ORIENT EXPRESS by Agatha Christie.
Fine Arts
Dist - FI **Prod** - PAR

Murder One 46 MIN
16mm
Color (G)
LC 77-703379
Examines the crime of murder, using interviews with murderers, witnesses and accomplices and by examining the background of the murders.
Sociology
Dist - BESTF **Prod** - WNETTV 1977

Murder psalm 16 MIN
16mm
Color (G)
$673.00 purchase, $37.00 rental
Meditates upon debauchery, and man as a filthy, cowardly, cruel, vicious reptile.
Fine Arts; Religion and Philosophy
Dist - CANCIN **Prod** - BRAKS 1981

Murder - those left behind 18 MIN
VHS
Color (H C G)
$150.00 purchase, $50.00 rental
Examines the situation of family survivors of a murder victim. Reveals that such families must contend with sensationalist media, a confusing and impersonal criminal system and a lack of privacy. Features Rosemary Masters, a post - traumatic stress disorder specialist who explains the emotional difficulties following such painful events. Produced by Donna Steiner Buttlaire.
Sociology
Dist - FLMLIB

The Murderer 28 MIN
16mm / U-matic / VHS
Color (H C A)
LC 76-703955
An adaptation of the short story, The Murderer by Ray Bradbury, about an individual who decides to liberate a futuristic society from its communication devices.
Literature and Drama; Psychology
Dist - PHENIX **Prod** - SILVEA 1976

Murderers are among us 84 MIN
35mm / 16mm
B&W (G) (GERMAN WITH ENGLISH SUBTITLES)
$250.00, $300.00 rental
Portrays a woman who returns from a concentration camp to find a drunken, shell - shocked doctor hiding in her apartment. Directed by Wolfgang Staudte.
Civics and Political Systems; Fine Arts; History - World; Literature and Drama
Dist - KINOIC **Prod** - IFEX 1946

The Muria 55 MIN
16mm / U-matic / VHS
Worlds Apart Series
Color (H C A)
Visits the Muria of Central India where children live in a central dormitory apart from the parents and marriages are arranged by the families independent of the child's wishes. Follows a girl who discovers she is pregnant by friend in the dormitory, but must carry out an arranged marriage anyway.
History - World; Sociology
Dist - FI **Prod** - BBCTV 1982

Muriel Cigars 1 MIN
U-matic / VHS
Color
Shows a classic television commercial with dancing cigars.
Business and Economics; Psychology; Sociology
Dist - BROOKC **Prod** - BROOKC

Muriel Rukeyser, poet 20 MIN
U-matic / VHS
3 portraits series
Color (G)
$125.00, $95.00 purchase
Portrays poet Muriel Rukeyser, whose art mirrors the challenges of her life and times. Part of a three - part series portraying women artists.
Biography; History - World; Literature and Drama; Sociology
Dist - RHOPRO **Prod** - RHOPRO

Muriel Topaz, Tom Brown and Phoebe Neville 30 MIN
VHS / U-matic
Eye on Dance - Passing on Dance Series
Color
Fine Arts
Dist - ARCVID **Prod** - ARCVID

Murini Window 28 MIN
16mm
Color (H C A)
LC 80-701817
Describes how glassblower Dudley Giberson creates a stained glass window for the University of Connecticut.
Fine Arts
Dist - IMAGER **Prod** - IMAGER 1980

Murita Cycles 28 MIN
16mm
Color
LC 79-701110
Presents a portrait of the filmmaker's father, Muray Braverman, a part - time philosopher who runs an unconventional bicycle shop in a New York City suburb.
Biography; Fine Arts
Dist - DIRECT **Prod** - BRAVE 1979

Murky Shadow Over the Gorges 97 MIN
VHS
Color (G) (MANDARIN CHINESE)
$45.00 purchase _ #1069B
Presents a Mandarin Chinese language movie produced in the People's Republic of China.
Fine Arts; Geography - World; Literature and Drama
Dist - CHTSUI **Prod** - CHTSUI

The Murmuring Heart 15 MIN
16mm
Doctors at Work Series
B&W (H C A)
LC FIA65-1352
Demonstrates corrective surgery for a heart murmur in an infant. Shows closeup views of the exposed heart and major blood vessels during surgery. Includes a discussion on the basic anatomy and physiology of the heart.
Health and Safety
Dist - LAWREN **Prod** - CMA 1961

Murphy's law 2 MIN
VHS / U-matic
Color (G)
$250.00 purchase, $125.00 rental
Uses NFL bloopers to demonstrate the truth of the old tenet 'If it can go wrong it will, and at the worst possible time,' relating it to business situations. Produced by NVC.
Business and Economics; Guidance and Counseling; Literature and Drama; Psychology
Dist - VLEARN

The Murray 57 MIN
U-matic / VHS
River Journeys
Color (H C A)
$1225 purchase (entire series), $285 purchase (each)
Discusses Russell Braddon's journey down the Murray River of Australia. Produced by BBC - TV and RKO Pictures for public television.
Geography - World
Dist - CF

Murray Avenue - a community in transition 28 MIN
VHS / U-matic / 16mm
Color (G)
Offers a personal portrait of Murray Avenue in Pittsburgh's Squirrel Hill. Captures a traditional Jewish neighborhood centered on its major commercial street. Produced by Sheila Chamovitz.
Geography - United States; History - United States; Sociology
Dist - NEWDAY

Murray Bowen, MD - assessment counsultation 4 16 MIN
VHS / 16mm
Hillcrest family - studies in human communication, assessment series
Color (C G PRO)
$220.00, $120.00 purchase, $16.50, $15.00 rental _ #22709
Features Murray Bowen, MD, in the fourth assessment consultation on the Hillcrest family. Covers the dynamics of the assessment interview and the rationale for the interviewing approach. Part of an eight - part series focusing on one family. Produced by R L Birdwhistell and J D Van Vlack.
Guidance and Counseling; Psychology; Sociology
Dist - PSU

Murray Bowen, MD - assessment interview 4 28 MIN
VHS / 16mm
Hillcrest family - studies in human communication, assessment series
Color (C G PRO)
$400.00, $205.00 purchase, $22.00, $19.50 rental _ #33025
Features Murray Bowen, MD, in the fourth assessment interview of the Hillcrest family. Emphasizes the causative factors in the family's problems. Part of an eight - part series focusing on one family. Produced by R L Birdwhistell and J D Van Vlack.
Guidance and Counseling; Psychology; Sociology
Dist - PSU

Murray Louis 30 MIN
VHS / U-matic
Eye on Dance - Dance on TV and Film Series
Color
Fine Arts
Dist - ARCVID **Prod** - ARCVID

Murray Louis in concert 52 MIN
VHS
Dance solos - Volume 1 series
Color (J H C)
LC 89-700201
Documents the career of Murray Louis as a dance soloist. Chronicles his choreography from his first concert in 1953 to present.
Fine Arts
Dist - DANCOR **Prod** - DANCOR 1989

Murs Et Appareils 12 MIN
16mm
Hand Operations - Woodworking - French Series
Color
LC 75-704355
A French languare version of Walls And Bonds. Demonstrates different kinds of wood bonds.
Foreign Language; Industrial and Technical Education
Dist - MORLAT **Prod** - MORLAT 1974

The Mursi 58 MIN
VHS
Disappearing world series
Color (G C)
$99.00 purchase, $19.00 rental _ #61402
Reveals that a shortage of grazing during a drought forced the Mursi of Ethiopia into conflict with their neighbors, the Bodi. Discloses that after many Mursi died fighting, they responded to Bodi peace proposals. Shows the extraordinary democratic process of the Mursi, as they came together to make life - and - death decisions. Features anthropologist David Turton. Part of a series working closely with anthropologists who lived for a year or more in societies whose social structures, beliefs and practices are threatened by the expansion of technocratic civilization.
Sociology
Dist - PSU **Prod** - GRANDA 1974

MURUGA 25 MIN
U-matic
Color (C A)
Documents the Nallur Temple Festival in the Northern section of Sri Lanka. Covers the events during a 26 - night period.
Geography - World; Sociology
Dist - HANMNY **Prod** - HANMNY 1973

Musa paradisiaca sapientum 5 MIN
16mm
Color (G)
$10.00 rental
Presents a surrealistic bunch of bananas running like lemmings to the sea. Features live action and 'banananimation' or object animation. Musical score by Handel and Balinese natives. The title is the botanical name for bananas. A Steve Klocksiem production.
Fine Arts
Dist - CANCIN

Muscle 11 MIN
U-matic
Microanatomy Laboratory Orientation Series
Color (C)
Demonstrates all three muscle forms, the smooth, skeletal and cardiac in both cross and longitudinal sections.
Health and Safety; Science - Natural
Dist - UOKLAH **Prod** - UOKLAH 1986

Muscle 20 MIN
VHS / U-matic
Histology review series; Unit 4
Color (PRO)
Introduces students to the structure, characteristics, and histological organization of skeletal, cardiac, and smooth muscle.
Health and Safety; Science - Natural
Dist - HSCIC **Prod** - HSCIC

Muscle 12 MIN
U-matic / VHS / 16mm
Color (J)
Shows Pat Perris lifting weights, training for the Manitoba Women's Provincial Body Building Championship. Contains body building sequences as well as footage from the competition.
Physical Education and Recreation
Dist - LUF **Prod** - NFBC

Muscle 38 MIN
VHS / U-matic
Biological Aspects of Aging - Rehabilitation Considerations Series
Color
Health and Safety
Dist - UMDSM **Prod** - UMDSM

Muscle 20 MIN
VHS / 16mm
Histology review series; Unit IV
(C)
$330.00 purchase _ #821VI037
Introduces students to the structure, characteristics and histological organization of skeletal, cardiac, and smooth muscle.
Health and Safety
Dist - HSCIC **Prod** - HSCIC 1983

Muscle 25 MIN
U-matic / VHS / 16mm
Color (H C A)
LC 72-701537
Shows the dynamics of muscle tissue and the amazing processes involved in muscle contraction. Examines the roles of membrane potential and chemical pumps as well as the sliding filament theory of muscle contraction.
Science - Natural
Dist - CRMP **Prod** - CRMP 1972

Muscle and Culture 7 MIN
16mm
Color
LC 72-711241
Uses animated sequences with accompanying text to analyze the evolutionary changes in the culture of man as represented by the Olympic Games.
Physical Education and Recreation; Social Science; Sociology
Dist - AMEDFL **Prod** - GENOVE 1972

Muscle Beach Party 95 MIN
16mm
Color (J)
Stars Frankie Avalon, Annette Funicello and Buddy Hackett. Presents the conflict between the surfers and a group of muscle - bound physical culturists, with further complications resulting with the arrival of a countess and her business manager.
Fine Arts
Dist - TWYMAN **Prod** - AIP 1964

Muscle Breathing Patterns in Poliomyelitis 19 MIN
16mm
Color
Describes the physical examination findings in patients when respiratory muscles are weakened by paralyzing diseases.
Health and Safety
Dist - RLAH **Prod** - RLAH

Muscle building series
Presents the 'Supersets' and 'Pyramids' body building workout programs. 'Supersets' develops both the cardiovascular and muscular systems by not allowing rest periods between sets, while 'Pyramids' uses the Oxford Method of weight training. Recommends at least six months of previous weight lifting experience due to the strenuousness of the programs. Consists of two videocassettes.
Muscle building series 120 MIN
Pyramids 60 MIN
Supersets 60 MIN
Dist - CAMV **Prod** - CAMV

Muscle - Chemistry of Contraction 15 MIN
U-matic / VHS / 16mm
Color (H C) (SPANISH)
A Spanish language version of the film and videorecording Muscle - Chemistry Of Contraction.
Foreign Language; Science - Natural
Dist - EBEC **Prod** - EBEC 1969

Muscle conditioning - metabolic booster
VHS

Spa workout series
Color (G H A)
$24.98 purchase _ #VEG02V-P
Offers viewers movements that firm and shape muscles using free weights and dynabands, which are included with video. Presents Canyon Ranch Fitness Director Rebecca Gorrell and Wellness Coordinator Jodina Scazzola-Pozo, who demonstrate modifications for all movements, including spinal, arm, and shoulder rotations. One of a set of three videos, ranging from 47 to 57 minutes, available individually or as a set.
Physical Education and Recreation
Dist - CAMV

Muscle - Dynamics of Contraction 22 MIN
16mm / U-matic / VHS
Color (H C) (SPANISH)
A Spanish language version of the film and videorecording Muscle - Dynamics Of Contraction.
Foreign Language; Science - Natural
Dist - EBEC **Prod** - EBEC 1969

Muscle - Dynamics of Contraction 21 MIN
U-matic / VHS / 16mm
Biology Series Unit 8 - Human Physiology; Unit 8 - Human physiology
Color; B&W (J H C)
LC 77-704147
Presents views of people engaged in various activities to show the dynamics of muscle contraction. Includes rare electron micrographs which reveal that the contractile properties of the whole muscle can be explained in terms of the properties of a single muscle cell, the basic unit of contraction.
Science - Natural
Dist - EBEC **Prod** - EBEC 1969

Muscle - Electrical Activity of Contraction 9 MIN
16mm / U-matic / VHS
Color (H C) (SPANISH)
A Spanish language version of the film and videorecording Muscle - Electrical Activity Of Contraction.
Foreign Language; Science - Natural
Dist - EBEC **Prod** - EBEC 1969

Muscle Evaluation - Common Peroneal Nerve 30 MIN
16mm
Color
LC 75-703056
Demonstrates tendons, muscle bellies, surface anatomy and areas of sensory supply on the human leg. Includes a voluntary muscle test on a patient with common peroneal nerve injury and substitution patterns used by patients to compensate for the loss of function.
Health and Safety; Science; Science - Natural
Dist - USNAC **Prod** - AMFSS 1968

Muscle Evaluation - Common Peroneal Nerve - Quiz Version 15 MIN
16mm
Color
LC 75-703058
Presents review and quiz material on muscle evaluation of the common peroneal nerve of the human leg. Covers physiology, injury and compensation for loss of function.
Health and Safety; Science; Science - Natural
Dist - USNAC **Prod** - AMFSS 1968

Muscle Evaluation - Hip and Knee, Normal 10 MIN
16mm
Color
LC 75-703059
Demonstrates tendons, muscle bellies, surface anatomy and areas of sensory supply on the human hip and lower limb.
Health and Safety; Science; Science - Natural
Dist - USNAC **Prod** - AMFSS 1968

Muscle Evaluation - Median Nerve 40 MIN
16mm
Color
LC 75-703060
Discusses tendons, muscle bellies, surface anatomy and areas of sensory supply on the human forearm. Includes a voluntary muscle test on a patient with a median nerve injury and substitution patterns used by patients to compensate for the loss of function.
Health and Safety; Science; Science - Natural
Dist - USNAC **Prod** - AMFSS 1968

Muscle Evaluation - Median Nerve - Quiz Version 20 MIN
16mm
Color
LC 75-703061
Presents review and quiz material on muscle evaluation of the human median nerve. Covers physiology, injury and compensation for loss of function.
Health and Safety; Science; Science - Natural
Dist - USNAC **Prod** - AMFSS 1968

Muscle Evaluation - Neck and Shoulder 49 MIN
16mm
Color
LC 75-703062
Depicts tendons, muscle bellies, surface anatomy and areas of sensory supply on the human neck and shoulder. Includes a voluntary muscle test on a patient with left shoulder and upper left limb injury and substitution patterns used by patients to compensate for the loss of function.
Health and Safety; Science; Science - Natural
Dist - USNAC **Prod** - AMFSS 1968

Muscle Evaluation - Neck and Shoulder - Quiz Version 17 MIN
16mm
Color
LC 75-703063
Presents review and quiz material on muscle evaluation of the human neck and shoulder. Covers physiology, injury and compensation for loss of function.
Health and Safety; Science; Science - Natural
Dist - USNAC **Prod** - AMFSS 1968

Muscle Evaluation - Radial Nerve 31 MIN
16mm
Color
LC 75-703064
Discusses tendons, muscle bellies, surface anatomy and areas of sensory supply on the human forearm. Includes a voluntary muscle test on a patient with a radial nerve injury and substitution patterns used by patients to compensate for the loss of function.
Health and Safety; Science; Science - Natural
Dist - USNAC **Prod** - AMFSS 1968

Muscle Evaluation - Radial Nerve - Quiz Version 16 MIN
16mm
Color
LC 75-703066
Presents review and quiz material on muscle evaluation of the human radial nerve. Covers physiology, injury and compensation for loss of function.
Science - Natural
Dist - USNAC **Prod** - AMFSS 1968

Muscle Evaluation - Sciatic and Posterior Tibial Nerve 35 MIN
16mm
Color
LC 75-703067
Demonstrates the normal sciatic and posterior tibial nerves of the human body. Includes a voluntary muscle test on a poliomyelitis patient and substitution patterns used by patients to compensate for the loss of nerve function.
Health and Safety; Science; Science - Natural
Dist - USNAC **Prod** - AMFSS 1968

Muscle Evaluation - Sciatic and Posterior Tibial Nerve - Quiz Version 14 MIN
16mm
Color
LC 75-703068
Presents review and quiz material on muscle evaluation of the human sciatic and posterior tibial nerve. Covers physiology, injury and compensation for loss of function.
Health and Safety; Science; Science - Natural
Dist - USNAC **Prod** - AMFSS 1968

Muscle Evaluation - Ulnar Nerve 49 MIN
16mm
Color
LC 75-703069
Discusses tendons, muscle bellies, surface anatomy and areas of sensory supply on the human forearm. Includes a voluntary muscle test on a patient with an ulnar nerve injury and substitutional patterns used by patients to compensate for the loss of function.
Health and Safety; Science; Science - Natural
Dist - USNAC **Prod** - AMFSS 1968

Muscle Evaluation - Ulnar Nerve - Quiz Version 17 MIN
16mm
Color
LC 75-703070
Presents review and quiz material on muscle evaluation of the human ulnar nerve. Covers physiology, injury and compensation for loss of function.
Health and Safety; Science; Science - Natural
Dist - USNAC **Prod** - AMFSS 1968

Muscle fiber 23 MIN
VHS / U-matic
Color (H G)
$295.00, $345.00 purchase, $50.00 rental
Explains the different kinds of muscle fibers in the body and how they influence muscular performance - speed, endurance and strength. Traces knowledge about muscles from the Renaissance to the present and how psysiology, sports training and medicine have benefited from new awareness.
Science - Natural
Dist - NDIM **Prod** - CANBC 1986

The Muscle Spindle 19 MIN
U-matic / VHS / 16mm
Physiology Series
Color (PRO)
LC 70-713047
Shows how the electrical impulses produced by movement and tension of a muscle are transmitted to and received from the nervous system. Demonstrates the techniques for isolating a muscle spindle and keeping it alive outside the body.
Science - Natural
Dist - MEDIAG **Prod** - WILEYJ 1970

Muscles 28 MIN
VHS
Human body - muscles and bones - series
Color (J H G)
$89.95 purchase _ #UW4169
Shows what muscle tissue is and how different types of muscles operate individually and together. Uses the example of athletic training to show how muscle power can be controlled and guided. Part of a 39 - part series featuring computer animation, medical photography, electron micrography, full - color drawings and diagrams and three - dimensional working models to cover the workings of the human body from head to toe and inside out.
Science - Natural
Dist - FOTH

The Muscles 8 MIN
16mm
Color
Features two puppets, Orsen the dog and Webster the owl, who introduce concepts about the muscles of the body. Covers concepts, such as brain impulses to the muscles, admitting one's mistakes, group activities, colors, right and left and numbers.
Science - Natural
Dist - ECI **Prod** - ECI

Muscles and Bones of the Body 11 MIN
U-matic / VHS / 16mm
Color (I)
$270.00, $190.00 purchase _ #1291
Emphasizes the importance of the muscles and bones to the internal and external functioning of the human body by showing how tendons, joints, muscles and the bones of the skeleton work smoothly together as one unit.
Science - Natural
Dist - CORF **Prod** - CORF 1960

Muscles and Energy 10 MIN
U-matic / VHS / 16mm
Active Body Series
Color (I)
$290 purchase - 16 mm, $250 purchase - video _ #5181C
Shows how muscles move large and small body parts. Shows differences between voluntary and involuntary muscles. Produced by Bill Walker Productions, Inc.
Science - Natural
Dist - CORF

Muscles and exercise 29 MIN
U-matic
Introducing biology series; Program 13
Color (C A)
Examines the muscles as active partners in movement. Identifies and describes three basic types of muscle tissue. Discusses two basic types of exercise, isometric and isotonic.
Physical Education and Recreation; Science - Natural
Dist - CDTEL **Prod** - COAST

Muscles and flowers 90 MIN
16mm
Color (G)
$90.00 rental
Approaches the mystery of woman contrasted to the mystery of man. Formulates the theory that a woman who has the muscular capability of a man is more feminine when her strength is used to express the tenderness of a woman. An audio - visual film which includes 90 minutes of audio and 45 minutes of visual. There are four periods during which the audience sits in the dark. Directed by Walter Gutman and produced by Hawk Serpent Productions, Ltd.
Fine Arts; Sociology
Dist - CANCIN

Muscles and Joints - Moving Parts 26 MIN
U-matic / VHS / 16mm
Living Body - an Introduction to Human Biology Series
Color
Shows how muscle activity is coordinated by the cerebellum and how position sensors in the muscles and joints and the balancing mechanism of the inner ear enable people to control their bodies. Follows the activities of a waterskier to demonstrate how muscles, joints and organs link up. Looks at the interior of the human knee to provide a clear view of how lubricating fluid is produced.

Science - Natural
Dist - FOTH **Prod** - FOTH 1985

Muscles and Joints - Muscle Power 26 MIN
U-matic / VHS / 16mm
Living Body - an Introduction to Human Biology Series
Color
Uses a scene in a movie theater to contrast the on - screen strength of a kung fu master with the audience slumped in its seats. Shows how muscles work, how two types of molecule collapsing against each other like a telescope produce enormous strength as they operate in large numbers. Demonstrates how much muscular activity takes place without our being aware of it, as the heart muscle contracts and the digestive tract is in motion.
Science - Natural
Dist - FOTH **Prod** - FOTH 1985

Muscles and Movement 15 MIN
U-matic / VHS / 16mm
Human Body Series
Color (I J H)
Shows how the skeleton acts as a system of levers and works in conjunction with the muscles to provide movement.
Science - Natural
Dist - LUF **Prod** - LUF 1980

Muscles of Facial Expression 16 MIN
U-matic / VHS
Color (C A)
Presents the anatomy of the facial muscles of expression.
Health and Safety; Science - Natural
Dist - TEF **Prod** - UWO

Muscles of Mastication and the Infratemporal Fossa 15 MIN
U-matic / VHS / 16mm
Cine - Prosector Series
Color (PRO)
Shows in detail, with a specimen and animation, how the temporal bone and the mandible work together at the temporomandibular joint.
Science - Natural
Dist - TEF **Prod** - AVCORP

Muscles of the Anterior Forearm 14 MIN
U-matic / VHS / 16mm
Cine - Prosector Series
Color (PRO)
Points out skeletal features of the upper limb and landmarks of the ulna and radius.
Science - Natural
Dist - TEF **Prod** - AVCORP

Muscles - their structure and function 25 MIN
VHS
Color (J H)
$99.00 purchase _ #4108 - 026
Defines the three types and functions of muscles. Demonstrates how to develop endurance, flexibility and cardiorespiratory fitness. Includes teacher's guide.
Education; Science - Natural
Dist - GA **Prod** - EBEC

Muscling in 30 MIN
VHS
Bodymatters series
Color (H C A)
PdS65 purchase
Discusses muscles of the body and how they work. Part of a series of 26 30-minute videos on various systems of the human body.
Health and Safety; Science - Natural
Dist - BBCENE

Muscular and skeletal systems 20 MIN
VHS
Your body series
Color (I)
$80.00 purchase _ #A51612
Teaches the importance of the human skeleton for support and protection of other parts of the body. Shows how the muscles and the bones and tendons work together for voluntary movement and demonstrates involuntary processes such as breathing and digestion. Makes use of both animation and live - action photography. Includes a teacher's guide.
Science - Natural
Dist - NGS **Prod** - NGS 1994

Muscular and Skeletal Systems 20 MIN
VHS / U-matic
Human Body Series
Color (J H C A G)
$216.00 purchase _ #51307
Explores the makeup of the human body, from the skeleton to the muscles.
Science - Natural
Dist - NGS

Muscular Coordination, Pt 1 - Cerebellar Cortex and Topography 18 MIN
16mm / U-matic / VHS
Anatomical Basis of Brain Function Series
Color (PRO)
Science - Natural
Dist - TEF **Prod** - AVCORP

Muscular Coordination, Pt 2 - Cerebellar Conducting Systems 18 MIN
16mm / U-matic / VHS
Anatomical Basis of Brain Function Series
Color (PRO)
Science - Natural
Dist - TEF **Prod** - AVCORP

Muscular dystrophy 26 MIN
VHS
Color (G)
$149.00 purchase, $75.00 rental _ #UW2371
Reveals how sufferers of muscular dystrophy deal with the incurable disease. Shows a young boy with the fatal form of the disease being treated at an Easter Seals Center, a six - year - old girl with spinal muscular dystrophy using braces and a young mother with myasthenia gravis getting help from surgery and medication. Covers the search for a cure and the available treatments.
Health and Safety
Dist - FOTH

Muscular Dystrophy - the Race for the Gene 50 MIN
U-matic / VHS / 16mm
Genetics Series
Color (C)
$775 purchase - 16 mm, $250 purchase - video
Talks about the gene that causes muscular dystrophy. Produced by the BBC for the Open University.
Health and Safety; Science - Natural
Dist - CORF

Muscular System 11 MIN
U-matic / VHS / 16mm
Human Body Series
Color (J H C)
$275, $195 purchase _ #3958
Shows how the muscles move the bones, pump blood through arteries and veins, and push food through the digestive system.
Science - Natural
Dist - CORF

Musculo 25 MIN
U-matic / VHS / 16mm
Color (H C A) (SPANISH)
A Spanish language version of Muscle. Discusses the three kinds of muscle in the human body and describes the unique properties of each kind of muscle tissue. Shows how different muscle systems are coordinated, how body activity affects the activity of cardiac muscle and how involuntary muscles work. Examines the role of the nervous system in muscular activity.
Foreign Language; Psychology; Science - Natural
Dist - MGHT **Prod** - LAZRST 1978

Musculoskeletal 17 MIN
16mm
Visual Guide to Physical Examination (2nd Ed Series
Color (PRO)
LC 81-701522
Demonstrates the physical examination of the musculoskeletal system, showing necessary procedures, manipulations, pacing, positions and patient - examiner interaction.
Health and Safety
Dist - LIP **Prod** - LIP 1981

Musculoskeletal examination 20 MIN
VHS / U-matic / BETA
Techniques of physical diagnosis - a visual approach series
Color (PRO)
$950.00 purchase
Reveiws the techniques of a screening musculoskeletal examination. Part of a series by Dr Donald W Novey teaching the basic skills of physical examination as seen through the eyes and ears of the examiner.
Health and Safety; Science - Natural
Dist - MEDMDS

A Muse of Fire 60 MIN
VHS / 16mm
Story of English Series
Color (C)
PdS99 purchase
Illustrates how Shakespeare enriched the English language with startling new works and phrases, examines the making of the King James version of the Bible, and follows the language's spread to the British colonies in America. Part 3 of the series.
English Language
Dist - BBCENE **Prod** - BBCTV 1986
FI
PSU

Museum 39 MIN
U-matic / VHS / 16mm
Color (J)
LC 80-701451
Looks behind the scenes at four museums as they prepare for four exhibitions including the Treasures of Tutankhamun at the Metropolitan Museum.
Fine Arts; History - World
Dist - FI **Prod** - JANUS 1981

Museum 30 MIN
16mm / U-matic / VHS
Color (I)
LC 80-700069
Investigates the inner workings of a museum by eavesdropping on its employees and following various activities. Covers issues such as preservation, education and fundraising.
Fine Arts
Dist - CAROUF **Prod** - GOODF 1980

The Museum at Work 30 MIN
VHS / U-matic
In Our Own Image Series
Color (C)
Fine Arts
Dist - DALCCD **Prod** - DALCCD

Museum Backroom 29 MIN
U-matic
Color
Shows how two children learn what goes on behind the scenes of a natural history museum.
Science - Natural
Dist - PBS **Prod** - KAETTV

Museum - Behind the Scenes at the Art Institute of Chicago 28 MIN
16mm
Color
LC 80-700304
Offers a behind - the - scenes look at the Art Institute of Chicago, introducing the curators who organize the exhibitions, the installers who handle the works of art, and the conservators who care for and preserve the paintings and prints.
Fine Arts; Geography - United States
Dist - AFA **Prod** - ARTINC 1979

The Museum Curator 15 MIN
VHS / 16mm
Harriet's Magic Hats IV Series
Color (P)
$175.00 purchase _ #207151
Presents thirteen new programs to familiarize children with more workers and their role in community life. Features Aunt Harriet's bottomless trunks of magic hats where Carrie has only to put on a particular hat to be whisked off to investigate the person and the role represented by the hat. 'The Museum Curator' reveals that Ralph is looking through a box of antiques and wondering what a particular item is. He suggests that Carrie visit Kevin, a museum curator. Kevin explains that his job is to identify objects from the past and who used them.
Business and Economics; Fine Arts; Guidance and Counseling; Psychology; Sociology
Dist - ACCESS **Prod** - ACCESS 1986

The Museum - Gateway to Perception 16 MIN
16mm
Color (I)
LC FIA65-527
Introduces the museum and indicates how its many materials relate to each other and to the museum visitor. Shows how museums contain the story of history.
Education; English Language; Social Science; Sociology
Dist - ATLAP **Prod** - ATLAP 1964

Museum Means People 30 MIN
16mm
B&W (R) .
Presents Jewish ceremonial objects from the Jewish Museum in New York City - - a ketubah, otrah curtain, mezuzah, tefillin case, haggadah, kiddush cup, etrog box, spice box and Torah crown. (Kinescope).
Religion and Philosophy
Dist - NAAJS **Prod** - JTS 1963

The Museum of Modern Art of Latin America 14 MIN
16mm
Color (SPANISH)
Offers a documentary on the collection of the Museum of Modern Art of Latin America.
Fine Arts
Dist - MOMALA **Prod** - OOAS 1983

Museum of Modern Art of Latin America 14 MIN
VHS / U-matic
Color (SPANISH)
Documents the collection of the Museum of Modern Art of Latin America.

Fine Arts
Dist - MOMALA **Prod** - MOMALA

Museum of the Solar System 23 MIN
16mm
Color (J A)
LC 78-711351
Documents the analysis of the moon rocks and soil brought to earth by the Apollo voyagers. Presents insights into the methods of modern science by visiting the laboratories of seven lunar scientists to learn how they sought answers to lunar mysteries such as the age of the moon, the composition of its elements, its origin and history and the nature of its minerals.
Science - Physical
Dist - FINLYS **Prod** - FINLYS 1970

Museum open house series
African art 29 MIN
American primitive masterpieces 29 MIN
The Artist and the City 29 MIN
The Artist and the Mirror 29 MIN
Artists and Atoms 29 MIN
The Book of tea 29 MIN
A Contemporary collection 29 MIN
The Cooking of French art 29 MIN
The Face of Rome 29 MIN
Figure this 29 MIN
The Gift of India 29 MIN
Japanese Temple Sculpture 29 MIN
Lautrec in Paris 29 MIN
Light, Dark and Daumier 29 MIN
Made in Japan - Ukiyo - E Prints 29 MIN
The Mind's Eye 29 MIN
Motion and Emotion - Baroque Sculpture 29 MIN
My Son the Artist 29 MIN
Of Time and the Artist 29 MIN
The Other Side of the Canvas 29 MIN
Painters and Pioneers 29 MIN
Piranesi 29 MIN
Portraits of Eternity 29 MIN
The Sight of Sound 29 MIN
A Spanish Gallery 29 MIN
Surrealism - Inner Space 29 MIN
Surrealism - Seekers of the Dream 29 MIN
A Thousand Words 29 MIN
Tribal Carvings from New Guinea 29 MIN
The Vocabulary of Art 29 MIN
Dist - PBS

Museum People 21 MIN
16mm
Color (I)
LC 75-700109
Relates the works of art and sculpture seen in a museum with art, music and everyday life outside the museum.
Fine Arts
Dist - KERA **Prod** - KERA 1974
PBS

Museum Without Walls Series
Giotto and the Pre - Renaissance 47 MIN
Dist - ARTSAM
GPN

Museum Without Walls Series
Crete and Mycenae 50 MIN
The Cubist Epoch 50 MIN
Germany - Dada 50 MIN
The Greek Temple 50 MIN
Hoya - Goya 50 MIN
Le Corbusier 50 MIN
Picasso - War, Peace, Love 50 MIN
Dist - GPN

Museums, Where Fun is Learning 17 MIN
16mm
Color (T)
LC 78-701985
Shows examples of model programs centering around art, history and science exhibitions. Offers suggestions for class trips, including pre - and post - trip activities.
Education; Fine Arts
Dist - USNAC **Prod** - SMITHS 1978

Museums without walls series
Outlines an eight - part series that introduces the world of art from three continents and 4,000 years. Includes segments on Crete and Mycenae, the Cubist Epoch, Germany - Dada, Giotto and the Pre-Renaissance, Goya, the Greek Temple, LeCorbusier, and Picasso - War, Peace, Love. Notes each tape delves into the specifics of its subject, focusing on the art and artists of its time and place. Covers some of the best - known works of art in world history.
Museums without walls series 374 MIN
Dist - CAMV

Mush! Alaskan grit and the winning spirit 23 MIN
VHS
Color (COR)
$495.00 purchase, $175.00 rental _ #DMA/DPI
Presents Susan Butcher, winner of the Iditerod sled race, offering personal and motivational advice on goal - setting. Draws parallels between business and sled - dog racing. Emphasizes commitment to a goal, positioning oneself to succedd, being ready to prepare and train, and carrying out the work. Includes footage showing Susan and her dogs in competition. Includes a Leader's Guide. Also available in a nine - minute version ($295 purchase, $145 rental).
Business and Economics; Guidance and Counseling; Psychology
Dist - ADVANM

Mush - Alaskan grit and the winning spirit - goal setting 23 MIN, 9 MIN
VHS
Color (I J H A)
$125.00, $95.00 purchase _ #10131VG, #10132VG
Features Susan Butcher, a leading dog sled racer, as she motivates students to set goals, fight adversity and learn the winning spirit. Explains the arduous training for dogsledding and the need for goals to achieve success. Intersperses footage from Alaska's Iditarod trail with Butcher teaching steps to finding success.
Guidance and Counseling; Psychology
Dist - UNL

Mushroom Carving 13 MIN
U-matic / VHS
Color (PRO)
Demonstrates the techniques of fluting, reliefing and impression.
Home Economics; Industrial and Technical Education
Dist - CULINA **Prod** - CULINA

Mushroom Gathering 10 MIN
16mm
Color
Shows thousands of people streaming out into the woods to gather mushrooms in Sweden in September and October.
Agriculture; Geography - World
Dist - AUDPLN **Prod** - ASI

Mushrooms 8 MIN
U-matic / VHS
Color (C)
$229.00, $129.00 purchase _ #AD - 1285
Shows the growth and reproductive cycles of cortinellus Shitake. Views spores released into the wind when they ripen. When they find a good medium for growth, they put forth buds and stretch their mycelium into branches, repeat adhesion and produce cotton like bodies of mycelia.
Science - Natural
Dist - FOTH **Prod** - FOTH

Mushrooms and Fungi 28 MIN
U-matic / VHS
Life of Plants Series
Color (C)
$249.00, $149.00 purchase _ #AD - 1678
Considers mushrooms, a term that covers a range of shapes and sizes from truffles to toadstools, delicacy to antibiotic, parasite to symbiont. Shows their structure, habitat, sexual and reproductive life. Part of a series on plants.
Science - Natural
Dist - FOTH **Prod** - FOTH

Music 15 MIN
VHS / U-matic
Arts Express Series
Color (K P I J)
Fine Arts
Dist - KYTV **Prod** - KYTV 1983

Music 16 MIN
VHS
Lessons in visual language series
Color (PRO G C)
$99.00 purchase, $39.00 rental _ #756
Studies the wide - ranging forms and functions of music for the screen. Uses a series of compelling dramatized scenes to highlight the evocative and emotive power of music. Composer Bruce Smeaton discusses the structure and purpose of the score he created for each scene. Features Peter Thompson as creator and narrator of a ten - part series on visual language. Produced by the Australian Film, Television and Radio School.
Fine Arts; Industrial and Technical Education; Social Science
Dist - FIRLIT

Music 20 MIN
U-matic / VHS
Contract Series
Color (J H)
English Language
Dist - AITECH **Prod** - KYTV 1977

Music 30 MIN
U-matic
Polka Dot Door Series
Color (K)
Presents a variety show for pre - school children. Includes songs, mime, stories, film sequences, talk, dance and fantasy figures. Each show emphasizes a particular theme such as numbers, feelings, exploring, music or time. Comes with parent teacher guide.
Fine Arts; Literature and Drama
Dist - TVOTAR **Prod** - TVOTAR 1985

Music 16 MIN
VHS / U-matic
En Francais series
Color (H C A)
Shows a traditional dance in a country town and tours a recording studio at the Office de Radio et Television Francaise.
Foreign Language; Geography - World
Dist - AITECH **Prod** - MOFAFR 1970

Music 15 MIN
U-matic / VHS / BETA
Career Success Series
Color (H C A)
$29.95 purchase _ #MX141 ; $29.95 _ #MX141
Portrays occupations in music by reviewing required abilities and interviewing people employed in this field. Shows anxieties and rewards involved in pursuing a career as a musician.
Education; Fine Arts
Dist - CAMV **Prod** - CAMV

Music 15 MIN
VHS / 16mm
(H C A)
$24.95 purchase _ #CS141
Describes the skills required for a career in music. Features interviews with people working in this field.
Guidance and Counseling
Dist - RMIBHF **Prod** - RMIBHF

Music 60 MIN
VHS
Liturgy and the arts - Word, work and worship series
Color (R G)
$49.95 purchase _ #LAWW3
Includes examples of liturgical life and worship from across the United States. Examines current suppositions which prevail regarding liturgical life. Examines the rich drama of life unfolded in sign and symbols in the Roman Catholic Church. Traces the development of the liturgy in the history of the Church, the evolution of Church architecture and art, music and the 'appointments' used in worship, and discusses the language of the liturgy as well as the use of gesture and other modalities of expression in worship. Features Melanie Donohugh. Part of four parts on worship in the Roman Catholic Church.
Fine Arts; Religion and Philosophy
Dist - CTNA **Prod** - CTNA

Music - Age - Old Search for Meaning 30 MIN
U-matic
Humanities through the Arts with Maya Angelou Series Lesson 10; Lesson 10
Color (C A)
Surveys history of music over a six - thousand year period. Offers excerpts from Beethoven's Third Symphony. Traces development of today's varied forms of music.
Fine Arts
Dist - CDTEL **Prod** - COAST

Music and Art - Germany 30 MIN
16mm
Music and the Renaissance Series
B&W
Compares German paintings and engravings of the Renaissance with contemporary music of the period.
Fine Arts; Geography - World; History - World
Dist - WQED **Prod** - NET 1957

Music and Art - Italy 30 MIN
16mm
Music and the Renaissance Series
B&W
Compares Italian paintings on musical subjects with music of contemporary composers of Italy during the Renaissance. Includes musical performances provided by the Saturday Consort.
Fine Arts; Geography - World; History - World
Dist - WQED **Prod** - NET 1957

Music and Art - the Netherlands 30 MIN
16mm
Music and the Renaissance Series
B&W
Compares Flemish and Dutch paintings dealing with musical subjects with contemporary music of the Renaissance.
Fine Arts; Geography - World; History - World
Dist - WQED **Prod** - NET 1957

Music and Cinema 29 MIN
U-matic
Color
Looks at how music enhances or changes a viewer's perception of a film. Features Professor James Dapogny, pianist and authority on American Jazz of the 20's and 30's, as he plays music from some of the classic films.
Fine Arts
Dist - UMITV **Prod** - UMITV 1978

Music and culture 40 MIN
VHS
Color (G J H C)
$60.00, $180.00 purchase _ #CLE6123CD - F, #CLE6123L - F ; $140.00 purchase _ #CLE0039V
Relates musical traditions from Polynesian, African and North American Indian peoples by comparing the vocal, instrumental and dance forms of their cultures' music. Provides a CD - ROM with audiovisual presentations, an encyclopedia and a glossary for resource material, based on a question - multiple - choice answer format. Can be used to create exams or quizzes. CD - ROM is compatible with Macintosh, Windows and MS - DOS formats, but the DOS version does not support sound play. Contact distributor for information about hardware requirements.
Fine Arts; Social Science
Dist - CAMV

Music and Dance 30 MIN
U-matic / VHS
Afro - American Perspectives Series
Color (C)
Discusses black trends in music and dance.
History - United States
Dist - MDCPB **Prod** - MDDE

Music and dance 76 MIN
VHS
Color; PAL (I)
PdS29.50 purchase
Offers two cassettes, Making Merry, which gives children an experience of medieval music and dance; and Pleasures and Pastimes, which introduces the music and dance of the Elizabethan age. Teaches children the carole, farandole, pavans and allemande dances.
Fine Arts
Dist - EMFVL

Music and Dance from Mindanao, the Philippines 23 MIN
16mm
Ethnic Music and Dance Series
B&W (J)
LC 72-700254
Presents instrumental and dance performances by the Tirurai of the area around Cotabato, Mindanao, the Philippines, and by two main Muslim peoples, the Maguindanao and the Maranao.
Fine Arts; Geography - World
Dist - UWASHP **Prod** - UWASH 1971

Music and Dance from the Sulu Islands, the Philippines 17 MIN
16mm
Ethnic Music and Dance Series
B&W (J)
LC 72-700253
Gives examples of dances of the Bajau peoples of the southern part of the Sulu Archipelago, and presents a gong ensemble of the Samal people from the northern end of the island area. Shows Samal dancing from the islands near Borneo.
Fine Arts; Geography - World
Dist - UWASHP **Prod** - UWASH 1971

Music and Dance of the Bagobo and Manobo Peoples of Mindanao, the Philippines 12 MIN
16mm
Ethnic Music and Dance Series
Color (J)
LC 72-700252
Presents a performance of the gong ensemble of the Bagobo and Manobo peoples of Mindanao, the Philippines. Includes a dancing performance by Manobo women.
Fine Arts; Geography - World
Dist - UWASHP **Prod** - UWASH 1971

Music and Dance of the Hill People of the Northern Philippines, Pt 1 29 MIN
16mm
Ethnic Music and Dance Series
Color (J)
LC 72-700251
Presents performances of various types of gong playing, singing and dancing by the people of the central part of Luzon. Explains that these individuals did not succumb to the Hispanic culture that influenced the coastal people of the Philippines.
Fine Arts; Geography - World
Dist - UWASHP **Prod** - UWASH 1971

Music and Dance of the Hill People of the Northern Philippines, Pt 2 12 MIN
16mm
Ethnic Music and Dance Series
B&W (J)
LC 72-700250
Shows how old and varied dance and musical styles have been preserved by the hill people of the Northern Philippines. Includes a performance on the pakkong, a bamboo instrument, and shows various styles of gong playing.
Fine Arts; Geography - World
Dist - UWASHP **Prod** - UWASH 1971

Music and Dance of the Ibaloy Group of the Northern Philippines 12 MIN
16mm
Ethnic Music and Dance Series
B&W (J)
LC 72-700249
Examines various group dances of the Ibaloy peoples of the Philippines. Shows a performance of a healing dance, and presents a gong and drum ensemble.
Fine Arts; Geography - World
Dist - UWASHP **Prod** - UWASH 1971

Music and Dance of the Maranao People of Mindanao, the Philippines 21 MIN
U-matic / VHS
Color (J)
Features two group dances by young girls to traditional gong orchestra music from one of the two main Muslim groups on the island of Mindanao, the Philippines.
Fine Arts; History - World
Dist - UWASHP **Prod** - UWASHP 1971

Music and Dance of the Yakan People of Basilian Island, the Philippines 12 MIN
U-matic / VHS
Color (J)
Depicts a variety of the music of the people living on Basilian, the northernmost island of the Sulu Archipelago, the Philippines.
Fine Arts; History - World
Dist - UWASHP **Prod** - UWASHP 1971

Music and feelings 60 MIN
VHS
Mister Rogers' home videos series
Color; Captioned (K P)
$14.95 purchase _ #HV102
Stars Mister Rogers who explores the many ways music touches and enriches life. Part of a series featuring favorite Mister Rogers Neighborhood programs.
Fine Arts; Guidance and Counseling; Health and Safety
Dist - FAMCOM **Prod** - FAMCOM 1990

Music and Me 15 MIN
VHS / U-matic
Music and Me Series
Color (P I)
Presents contemporary music and introduces musical instruments, concepts and traditions.
Fine Arts
Dist - AITECH **Prod** - WDCNTV 1979

Music and Me Series

The Ballad - 11	15 MIN
The Best of me	14 MIN
The Brass Family - 12	15 MIN
The Folk song	14 MIN
I Got the Beat	14 MIN
Intervals	14 MIN
The Keyboard Family	14 MIN
Makin' sweet harmony	14 MIN
Melodies	14 MIN
Meter Reader	15 MIN
Music and Me	15 MIN
Music of Afro - America	15 MIN
Music of Inspiration	15 MIN
Music of South America	15 MIN
Music of the First Americans	15 MIN
Music of the USA I	15 MIN
Music of the USA II	14 MIN
Music of the USA III	14 MIN
Note Value	15 MIN
The Percussion Family - 6	15 MIN
Songs of Christmas and Hanukkah I	14 MIN
Songs of Christmas and Hanukkah II	15 MIN
Songs of Halloween	15 MIN
Songs of Thanksgiving	15 MIN
The String Family - 13	15 MIN
Tempo and Dynamics	15 MIN
Use Your Voice to Sing	15 MIN
The Woodwind Family - 16	15 MIN

Dist - AITECH

Music and Performance 58 MIN
U-matic / VHS
Shared Realities Series
Color (A)
Features a tribute to the late musician Peter Ives, who died at age 36. Includes a compilation of the performance series held at Los Angeles Contemporary Exhibitions.
Fine Arts
Dist - LBMART **Prod** - LBMART 1983

Music and sound 21 MIN
U-matic / VHS / 16mm
Art of film series
Color
LC 75-703765
Uses selections from the motion pictures Wild Strawberries, Alexander Nevsky, Dodes Ka - den, M, Dead Of Night, and Valerie to illustrate the aural elements of film, including dialogue, music and sound effects.
Fine Arts
Dist - CORF **Prod** - JANUS 1975

Music and the Renaissance Series

Music and Art - Germany	30 MIN
Music and Art - Italy	30 MIN
Music and Art - the Netherlands	30 MIN

Dist - WQED

Music and Your Mind - a Key to Creative Potential 21 MIN
16mm
Color (H C A)
LC 75-702600
Examines the guided imagery and music technique. Explains the procedure and shows what happens when selected music stimuli are administered to relaxed subjects.
Fine Arts; Psychology
Dist - CRTVLC **Prod** - CINEMN 1975

Music at the Court of Louis XIV 53 MIN
U-matic / VHS
Man and Music Series
Color (C)
$279.00, $179.00 purchase _ #AD - 1764
Focuses on the patronage of composers in court. Considers the principal composers at Versailles in the court of Louis XIV, Jean - Baptiste Lully, composer of court dance music and music for playwright Moliere, religious composer Michel - Richard de Lalande and miniaturist Francois Couperin. Part of a 22 - part series which sets Western music into the historial and cultural context of its time.
Civics and Political Systems; Fine Arts; Foreign Language; History - World
Dist - FOTH **Prod** - FOTH

Music box
CD-ROM
(G)
$59.00 purchase _ #1801
Brings graphical control of audio compact discs to any CD - ROM installation using Microsoft CD - ROM extensions. Provides a graphical interface including a full digital display of audio track information. Both 3.5 and 5.25 diskettes are included. For IBM PCs and compatibles, requires 640K RAM, DOS 3.1 or later, MS CD - ROM Extensions 2.1 or later, one floppy disk drive - hard disk recommended, one empty expansion slot, and an IBM compatible CD - ROM drive. Not all CD - ROM drives support left and right channel selections.
Computer Science; Fine Arts
Dist - BEP

Music Box 28 MIN
16mm
Color (R)
LC 81-700423
Presents a parable about the rewards of Christian life. Explores the joy of the believer in a story about an ordinary factory worker, five gospel - singing angels and a special music box.
Religion and Philosophy
Dist - WHLION **Prod** - WHLION 1980

Music Box Series

Beat and tempo	15 MIN
Instruments	15 MIN
Listen to the Music	15 MIN
Melody	15 MIN
Metre	15 MIN
Music through the Ages	15 MIN
Musical Design	15 MIN
Pitch	15 MIN
Rhythm	15 MIN
Storytelling with Music	15 MIN
Style	15 MIN
Tone Color	15 MIN
World of Music	15 MIN

Dist - TVOTAR

Music boxes 30 MIN
U-matic
Antiques series
Color
Fine Arts
Dist - PBS **Prod** - NHMNET

The Music Child 45 MIN
16mm
B&W
LC 76-702855
Discusses the use of music therapy in the treatment of nonverbal handicapped children. Includes a wide variety of disabilities and improvizational music techniques.
Education; Fine Arts; Psychology
Dist - BNCHMK **Prod** - PARRYD 1976

Music computer programs 58 MIN
VHS
Key changes - a seminar for music educators series
Color (T A PRO)
$69.95 purchase _ #1263 - 0013
Presents part eleven of a 13 - part telecourse for music educators seeking renewal of their certification. Combines lecture and discussion on music computer programs.
Education; Fine Arts
Dist - SCETV **Prod** - SCETV 1990

Music, dance and festival among the Waiapi Indians of Brazil 39 MIN
VHS / U-matic
Waiapi Indians of Brazil series
Color (C G)
$160.00 purchase, $25.00 rental _ #CC3779VU, #CC3779VH
Examines five festivals of the Waiapi Indians of Brazil. Looks at the structure of the festivals, the importance of caxiri, or manioc beer, to the festivals, the variety of musical instruments and songs, and how Waiapi identity and culture are reinforced by the communal celebrations. Part of a five - part series on the Waiapi. Produced by Victor Fuks.
Geography - World; Social Science; Sociology
Dist - IU

Music - Emotion and Feeling in Sound 30 MIN
U-matic
Humanities through the Arts with Maya Angelou Series Lesson 11; Lesson 11
Color (C A)
Illustrates through a Brahms symphony that what is heard as music is a blend of carefully chosen elements. Demonstrates the 'look' of sound by showing waves recorded on an electronic apparatus.
Fine Arts
Dist - CDTEL **Prod** - COAST

Music experiences series
Bach is beautiful 15 MIN
Edvard Grieg - the man and his music 17 MIN
Grand Canyon suite 17 MIN
The Little Train of the Caipira 13 MIN
Mississippi Suite 14 MIN
Dist - AIMS

Music for a Nation 53 MIN
U-matic / VHS
Man and Music Series
Color (C)
$279.00, $179.00 purchase _ #AD - 2067
Focuses on Tsarist Russia. Begins in 1881 when Tsar Alexander II was assassinated and Tchaikovsky's Violin Concerto premiered. Part of a 22 - part series that sets Western music into the historial and cultural context of its time.
Civics and Political Systems; Fine Arts; Foreign Language; History - World
Dist - FOTH **Prod** - FOTH

Music for film 55 MIN
VHS
Color (PRO G)
$149.00 purchase, $49.00 rental _ #762
Features British composer Ron Goodwin who demonstrates film music production procedures emphasizing time and synchronization. Shows how timings for a scene are taken by the music editor and translated onto a score by the composer. Demonstrates the use of click tracks and discusses their pros and cons. Uses excerpts from Goodwin's scores for The Trap and Where Eagles Dare to show how a basic theme can be developed and used in a wide range of ways throughout a film. Produced by the Australian Film, Television and Radio School.
Fine Arts; Industrial and Technical Education
Dist - FIRLIT

Music for Metrics 29 MIN
U-matic
Color
Introduces the metric system through song and animation.
Mathematics
Dist - UMITV **Prod** - UMITV 1976

Music fol Prague 1968 28 MIN
U-matic / VHS / 16mm
Color (I)
LC 75-703601
Shows the Baltimore Symphony's performance of Karel Husa's Music For Prague 1968. Includes visual images which weave together the performance and Czech themes.
Fine Arts
Dist - PFP **Prod** - MUSICP 1975

Music for the Eyes 18 MIN
U-matic
Color
Focuses on the work and artistic vision of contemporary American sculptor James Rosati. Documents the creation ofa Rosati sculpture from foundry fabrication to installation in corporate headquarters. Shows the artist discussing the creative process and how he became a a sculptor.
Fine Arts; Industrial and Technical Education
Dist - MTP **Prod** - STEEL

Music for the Piano 145 MIN
U-matic
University of the Air
Color (J H C A)
$750.00 purchase, $250.00 rental
Presents a study of music for the piano, including the works of the Spanish composers, Mompou and Turina, as well as Chopin, Handel, Mendelssohn and Brahms. Program contains a series of five cassettes 29 minutes each.
Fine Arts
Dist - CTV **Prod** - CTV 1978

Music for the World 53 MIN
U-matic / VHS
Man and Music Series
Color (C)
$279.00, $179.00 purchase _ #AD - 2068
Focuses on Tsarist Russia. Begins with the turn of the century, an era of turbulent change and a flood of genius, including performers Scriabin and Heifetz, composers Glinka, Borodin, Mussorgsky, Tchaikovsky, Rimsky - Korsokov, Rachmoninov, Stravinsky and Schoenberg. Part of a 22 - part series that sets Western music into the historial and cultural context of its time.
Fine Arts; Foreign Language; History - World
Dist - FOTH **Prod** - FOTH

Music for Wilderness Lake 28 MIN
16mm
Color (G)
_ #106c 0180 084
Shows trombonists around the shores of a lake playing meditative music to one another at dusk and dawn. Canadian composer Murray Schafer cues trombonists from a raft in the middle of the lake while the wildlife responds.
Fine Arts; Geography - World; Science - Natural
Dist - CFLMDC **Prod** - NFBC 1980

Music for Wilderness Lake 29 MIN
16mm / U-matic / VHS
Color; Stereo (J H C A)
$515.00, $185.00 purchase, $50.00 rental
Performs a musical piece by Canadian composer R. Murray Schafer. Features twelve trombonists along the shores of a lake, conducted by Schafer from a raft in the middle of the lake.
Fine Arts; Sociology
Dist - BULFRG **Prod** - RHOMBS 1989

Music from Africa 15 MIN
VHS / U-matic
Music machine series
Color (P)
Discusses and gives examples of music from Africa.
Fine Arts
Dist - GPN **Prod** - INDIPS 1981

Music from Ghana 29 MIN
U-matic
Color
Features Kwasi Aduonum, musician, drummer and music teacher, as he leads viewers into Ghanian folk music. Analyzes the music and describes the story of the dances performed on the program.
Fine Arts; History - World
Dist - UMITV **Prod** - UMITV 1978

Music from Japan 15 MIN
U-matic / VHS
Music machine series
Color (P)
Discusses and gives examples of music from Japan.
Fine Arts
Dist - GPN **Prod** - INDIPS 1981

Music - from Popular to Concert Stage 15 MIN
16mm
Uses of Music Series
Color (I J H)
LC 77-715019
Shows how the concert music of the present began as the popular music of another day, using as examples the minuet, the square dance, and the Blue Danube Waltz. Discusses popular music, including the big bands and jazz, and concludes with concert versions of 'I WANT TO HOLD YOUR HAND,' 'SHE LOVES YOU,' and 'YESTERDAY' by the Beatles.
Fine Arts; History - World
Dist - CGWEST **Prod** - CGWEST 1969

Music in Early Childhood 28 MIN
16mm
Color (P I)
LC 73-703093
Features Bob Smith, a noted music educator, sharing some of his ideas and methods for teaching pre - school and primary children to appreciate music. Shows three different age groups of children enthusiastically enjoying music, through singing and through physical response.
Fine Arts
Dist - UILL **Prod** - UIME 1973

Music in early childhood 58 MIN
VHS
Key changes - a seminar for music educators series
Color (T A PRO)
$69.95 purchase _ #1263 - 0002
Presents part one of a 13 - part telecourse for music educators seeking renewal of their certification. Combines lecture and discussion of the role of music in early childhood education.
Education; Fine Arts
Dist - SCETV **Prod** - SCETV 1990

Music in Jerusalem 60 MIN
VHS
B&W (G)
$34.95 purchase _ #230
Records musical performances by Isaac Stern, Pablo Casals, Alexander 'Sasha' Schneider, Gina Bachauer and a young Yefim Bronfman at the Jerusalem Music Center. Visits with Golda Meir, David Ben - Gurion and Artur Rubenstein.
Fine Arts; History - World; Sociology
Dist - ERGOM **Prod** - ERGOM

Music in motion series
Expresses visually what is heard in nine selections of classical music by well known composers. Teaches classical music appreciation, develops interest and enhances listening enjoyment. Includes manual with suggestions for presenting the video, questions for discussion, research projects, correlations with other subject areas and listening and reading lists. Includes Purcell, Bach, Mozart, Beethoven, Moussorgsky, Rimsky - Korsakov, Liadov, Respighi and Aaron Copland.
Beethoven's Symphony no 8, third movement
Copland's Open Prairie from Billy the Kid
Liadov's The Enchanted lake
Moussorgsky - Pictures at an exhibition
Mozart's Jupiter symphony, third movement
Purcell's Fanfare in C - Bach's Toccata in D minor
Respighi's The Fountains of Rome
Rimsky - Korsakov's The Golden cockerel
Dist - CAMV **Prod** - MUSLOG

Music in Progress - Mike Westbrook - Jazz Composer 44 MIN
16mm
Color (H A)
$960.00 purchase, $80.00 rental
Features Mike Westbrook, a contemporary and innovative British jazz composer.
Fine Arts
Dist - AFA **Prod** - ACGB 1977

Music in special education 58 MIN
VHS
Key changes - a seminar for music educators series
Color (T A PRO)
$69.95 purchase _ #1263 - 0006
Presents part five of a 13 - part telecourse for music educators seeking renewal of their certification. Combines lecture and discussion of the role of music in special education.
Education; Fine Arts
Dist - SCETV **Prod** - SCETV 1990

Music in the age of Alfonso el Sabio 19 MIN
VHS
Color (G C)
$149.00 purchase _ #EX2331
Centers on the 'Cantigas de Santa Maria.' Describes the cultural currents of the 13th - century Spain of Alfonso el Sabio.
Fine Arts; History - World
Dist - FOTH

Music in the Art of the Renaissance 28 MIN
16mm
Color
Offers a collage of art works which depicts musical activity in a variety of settings, both religious and secular during the Renaissance.
Fine Arts; History - World; Religion and Philosophy
Dist - CCNCC **Prod** - CCNCC

Music in the Midnight Sun 29 MIN
16mm / U-matic / VHS
Color; Stereo (J)
$550.00, $275.00 purchase, $50.00 rental; $795.00, $300.00 purchase, $80.00 rental
Presents the one hour version of the Toronto Symphony's vist to the Canadian Arctic and a joint performance with native drummers, dancers and fiddlers. Also available in half hour version.
Fine Arts; Science - Natural
Dist - BULFRG **Prod** - RHOMBS 1989

Music in the Midnight Sun 29 MIN
16mm / VHS
(J A)
$50.00 rental
Features the Toronto Symphony's visit to the Canadian Arctic, and the combined performance with native drummers and dancers. Also available in a one hour version.
Fine Arts; Social Science
Dist - BULFRG

Music in the twelfth century 55 MIN
VHS
Color (G)
$350.00 purchase, $50.00 rental
Traces the development of the musical forms of twelfth century Europe. Presents The Folger Consort, resident early music ensemble of the Folger Shakespeare Library, performing the music in authentic costume on location in France. Presents several scenes from 'The Play of Daniel,' Benedictine monks singing plainchant, scenes from the Crusades, universities, manor house parties. Features Fritz Weaver as host who explains the musical concept of polyphony as composed by Leonin and Perotin. Produced by Millenium, Inc.
Fine Arts; History - World
Dist - IFB

Music in Therapy 30 MIN
VHS / U-matic
Sounds they make Series
Color
Offers a comprehensive look at the role of the Registered Music Therapist in the treatment of the mentally retarded and the mentally ill. Uses simulated therapy sessions to demonstrate the effect of music therapy in treating a behaviorally disordered adolescent, in teaching social/academic skills to a trainable mentally retarded girl and in promoting transferable music skills with a community mental health center patient.
Fine Arts; Psychology
Dist - OHUTC **Prod** - OHUTC

Music in Two Parts 29 MIN
Videoreel / VT2
Playing the Guitar I Series
Color
Fine Arts
Dist - PBS **Prod** - KCET

Music is 28 MIN
16mm
Music Series
Color
LC 78-701361
Examines the way music has been used by man as a means of communicating and expressing feeling. Points out that there are many different kinds of music and that music plays a significant part in many aspects of life.
Fine Arts
Dist - USNAC **Prod** - WETATV 1977

Music is 30 MIN
VHS / U-matic
Music is Series
Color (I)
Fine Arts
Dist - GPN **Prod** - WETATV

Music is Composed 28 MIN
16mm
Music Series no 7
Color
LC 78-701360
Examines the process of composing music, putting together the elements of rhythm, harmony, tone, color and form. Focuses on the stylistically revolutionary nature of composers such as Mozart, Berlioz and Beethoven.
Fine Arts
Dist - USNAC **Prod** - WETATV 1977

Music is Composed 30 MIN
VHS / U-matic
Music is Series
Color (I)
Fine Arts
Dist - GPN **Prod** - WETATV

Music is Conducted 30 MIN
U-matic / VHS
Music is Series
Color (I)
Fine Arts
Dist - GPN **Prod** - WETATV

Music is Conducted 28 MIN
16mm
Music Series no 8
Color
LC 78-701362
Explores the art of conducting music, pointing out that it is the conductor's role to keep a group of musicians together as they play. Explains that he encourages the musicians to play a piece as the composer intended it to be played. Examines a musical score.
Fine Arts
Dist - USNAC **Prod** - WETATV 1977

Music is Form 28 MIN
16mm
Music Series no 6
Color
LC 78-701363
Explains that through the use of various themes, melodies and variations music can be organized to make different compositions. Shows how distinguishing form can be accomplished by recognizing musical patterns.
Fine Arts
Dist - USNAC **Prod** - WETATV 1977

Music is Form 30 MIN
VHS / U-matic
Music is Series
Color (I)
Fine Arts
Dist - GPN **Prod** - WETATV

Music is Harmony 28 MIN
16mm
Music Series no 4
Color
LC 78-701364
Explains that harmony occurs when two or more sounds played together lose their separateness and produce a new sound. Illustrates the difference in sound between a single melody line and the same melody with harmonic accompaniment. Examines chords in the context of harmonic sound.
Fine Arts
Dist - USNAC **Prod** - WETATV 1977

Music is Harmony 30 MIN
U-matic / VHS
Music is Series
Color (I)
Fine Arts
Dist - GPN **Prod** - WETATV

Music is Improvised 28 MIN
16mm
Music Series no 9
Color
LC 78-701366
Employs a jazz band to demonstrate musical improvisation. Shows how a performer chooses from alternative paths to get from one musical place to another.
Fine Arts
Dist - USNAC **Prod** - WETATV 1977

Music is Improvised 30 MIN
VHS / U-matic
Music is Series
Color (I)
Fine Arts
Dist - GPN **Prod** - WETATV

Music is Melody 28 MIN
16mm
Music Series no 3
Color
LC 78-701367
Explains that melody is the basic idea of a song, those notes which give a song its sound and direction. Shows the different musical elements which can be changed to vary a melody and how such changes give a song an easily recognized sound.
Fine Arts
Dist - USNAC **Prod** - WETATV 1977

Music is Melody 30 MIN
VHS / U-matic
Music is Series
Color (I)
Fine Arts
Dist - GPN **Prod** - WETATV

Music is Rhythm 30 MIN
U-matic / VHS
Music is Series
Color (I)
Fine Arts
Dist - GPN **Prod** - WETATV

Music is Rhythm 28 MIN
16mm
Music Series
Color
LC 78-701368
Deals with different elements of rhythm, such as rests, duration, tempo and accent, pointing out that rhythm is the most immediately recognizable element in music because it can be felt.
Fine Arts
Dist - USNAC **Prod** - WETATV 1977

Music is Series

Music is	30 MIN
Music is Composed	30 MIN
Music is Conducted	30 MIN
Music is Form	30 MIN
Music is Harmony	30 MIN
Music is Improvised	30 MIN
Music is Melody	30 MIN
Music is Rhythm	30 MIN
Music is Style	30 MIN
Music is Tone Color	30 MIN

Dist - GPN

Music is Style 28 MIN
16mm
Music Series no 10
Color
LC 78-701369
Explains that style is the mode of expression or the characteristic mood that music assumes. Looks at various styles of Western music after 1600, including baroque, classical, romantic, impressionistic and modern.
Business and Economics; Fine Arts
Dist - USNAC **Prod** - WETATV 1977

Music is Style 30 MIN
VHS / U-matic
Music is Series
Color (I)
Fine Arts
Dist - GPN **Prod** - WETATV

Music is Tone Color 28 MIN
16mm
Music Series no 5
Color
LC 78-701370
Explains that tone color is the particular sound characteristic to each musical instrument. Points out that the elements of tone color are register, texture, range and dynamics.
Fine Arts
Dist - USNAC **Prod** - WETATV 1977

Music is Tone Color 30 MIN
U-matic / VHS
Music is Series
Color (I)
Fine Arts
Dist - GPN **Prod** - WETATV

The Music Lesson 30 MIN
16mm
World of Music Series
B&W (C A)
Shows a teacher at the Hoff Barthelson Music School as she leads a group of seven - year - olds through a series of musical games and exercises which enables them to learn how to read rhythm and tone from written notes.
Education; Fine Arts
Dist - IU **Prod** - NET 1967

Music Lessons 40 MIN
16mm
Color
LC 82-700228
Describes the Kodaly method of music training for children. Depicts music training in American public elementary schools that leads to extraordinary musical competence in fifth and sixth graders.
Fine Arts
Dist - KAROL **Prod** - FDF 1982

Music - Listening for the Unexpected 30 MIN
U-matic
Humanities through the Arts with Maya Angelou Series Lesson 13; Lesson 13
Color (C A)
Discusses criticism with Maya Angelou and a music critic and a director. Debates the qualifications, responsibilities and importance of the music critic.
Fine Arts
Dist - CDTEL **Prod** - COAST

A Music Loving Dog 11 MIN
U-matic / VHS / 16mm
Color (J H C)
LC 77-701528
Presents an animated story about a crazy scientist who invents a highly explosive ultrasonic violin, only to have it stolen by his pet dog, who first uses it to make music and later to rebel against his master.
Fine Arts; Literature and Drama; Science - Natural
Dist - TEXFLM **Prod** - LESFG 1977

Music machine 26 MIN
VHS
Color (K P I G R)
$19.95 purchase, $10.00 rental _ #35-804020-1345
Uses an action and adventure format to teach children about the Christian life. Takes viewers on a visit to the garden kingdom of Agapeland, where Majesty the King rules and the Music Machine brings joy to the people.
Literature and Drama; Religion and Philosophy
Dist - GF
APH

The Music machine - introduction 15 MIN
VHS / U-matic
Music machine series
Color (T)
Introduces the Music Machine Series which is designed to teach musical concepts through singing, moving and listening.
Fine Arts
Dist - GPN **Prod** - INDIPS 1981

Music machine series
The Barnyard 15 MIN
Beat no beat 15 MIN
Boo it's Halloween 15 MIN
The Brass family 15 MIN
Cadences 15 MIN
Duration 15 MIN
Fluff - an electronic musical story 15 MIN
Harmony 15 MIN
How fast to to - tempo 15 MIN
How loud to sing - dynamics 15 MIN
Hurray - we're American 15 MIN
I live in a city 15 MIN
Intervals 15 MIN
Meter 15 MIN
Mezzo the musical mouse 15 MIN
Music from Africa 15 MIN
Music from Japan 15 MIN
The Music machine - introduction 15 MIN
Musical stories 15 MIN
The Percussion family 15 MIN
The String family 15 MIN
Styles 15 MIN
Tone color 15 MIN
Valentine wishes 15 MIN
Which way did the melody go 15 MIN
The Woodwind family 15 MIN
Dist - GPN

Music Machines 15 MIN
16mm / U-matic / VHS
Color (P I J H)
Explores today's musical technology - the oscilloscope, synthesizer, mixing panel and tape recorder. Presents the blending of pitch, tonal quality and duration into various musical shapes.
Fine Arts; Science - Physical
Dist - MEDIAG **Prod** - THAMES 1984

Music madness volume II
CD-ROM
(J H C G)
$99.00 purchase _ #WTHI121
Shows students the magic of music through computer application. Features 640MB of music, tools and effects. Offers 318 music and effect clips to build tunes, add sound to Macintosh computers, create sound files, add sound to multimedia projects or applications, create music effects, learn about sound or become sound managers. Covers six music topics - jazz, rock, funk, multimedia, phrases and effects. Sounds are in 11Hz, 22Hz and 44Hz format. Requires a Mac with 1MB of free RAM, hard and CD - ROM drives.
Fine Arts
Dist - CAMV

Music Makers of the Blue Ridge 48 MIN
U-matic / VHS / 16mm
B&W (J)
LC FIA7-504
Studies life in Eastern mountain areas by examining folk music and dance. Includes scenes of isolated areas in western North Carolina. Shows the filmmakers guided to the homes of friends and neighbors of folksinger Bascom Lamar Lunsford.
Fine Arts; Geography - United States; Sociology
Dist - IU **Prod** - NET 1966

Music Makers of the Blue Ridge, Pt 1 24 MIN
U-matic / VHS / 16mm
B&W (J)
LC FIA7-504
Studies life in Eastern mountain areas by examining folk music and dance. Includes scenes of isolated areas in western North Carolina. Shows the filmmakers guided to the homes of friends and neighbors of folksinger Bascom Lamar Lunsford.
Fine Arts
Dist - IU **Prod** - NET 1966

Music Makers of the Blue Ridge, Pt 2 24 MIN
16mm / U-matic / VHS
B&W (J)
LC FIA7-504
Studies life in Eastern mountain areas by examining folk music and dance. Includes scenes of isolated areas in western North Carolina. Shows the filmmakers guided to the homes of friends and neighbors of folksinger Bascom Lamar Lunsford.
Fine Arts
Dist - IU **Prod** - NET 1966

The Music Man 15 MIN
VHS / U-matic
Mrs Cabobble's Caboose
(P)
Designed to teach primary grade students basic music concepts. Highlights melody, rhythm, harmony, and the different families of musical instruments. Features Mrs. Fran Powell.
Fine Arts
Dist - GPN **Prod** - WDCNTV 1986

The Music Man 151 MIN
16mm
Color
Presents Meredith Wilson's hit musical brought to the screen with all the great music and fun which earned it over 1500 performances on Broadway.
Fine Arts
Dist - SWANK **Prod** - SWAMD

Music - Meaning through Structure 30 MIN
U-matic
Humanities through the Arts with Maya Angelou Series Lesson 12; Lesson 12
Color (C A)
Probes the life and work of Johann Sebastian Bach. Discusses the importance of form to music and the meaning that the artist imparts in his work.
Fine Arts
Dist - CDTEL **Prod** - COAST

Music, Memories and Milestones Series
The Nineteen Fifties 60 MIN
The Nineteen Forties 60 MIN
The Nineteen Sixties 60 MIN
The Nineteen Thirties 60 MIN
Dist - KULTUR

Music mountain - a series 3 MIN
U-matic / VHS
Music mountain - a series
Color
Honors singer Carole (Karuna) King for the land she donated.
Religion and Philosophy
Dist - IYOGA **Prod** - IYOGA

Music mountain - a series
Music mountain - a series 3 MIN
Dist - IYOGA

Music movement with young children - Part I 30 MIN
VHS
Calico pie series
Color (C A T)
$69.95 purchase
Presents part five of a 16 - part telecourse for teachers who work with children ages three to five. Discusses how music can be used in the classroom. Hosted by Dr Carolyn Dorrell, an early childhood specialist.
Education; Psychology
Dist - SCETV **Prod** - SCETV 1983

Music movement with young children - Part II 30 MIN
VHS
Calico pie series
Color (C A T)
$69.95 purchase
Presents part six of a 16 - part telecourse for teachers who work with children ages three to five. Discusses how music can be used in the classroom. Hosted by Dr Carolyn Dorrell, an early childhood specialist.
Education; Psychology
Dist - SCETV **Prod** - SCETV 1983

Music, Music, Music 29 MIN
VHS / 16mm
Villa Alegre Series
Color (P T)
$46.00 rental _ #VILA - 164
Presents educational material in both Spanish and English.
Education; Fine Arts
Dist - PBS

Music of Africa 30 MIN
16mm
B&W (G)
LC 77-703288
Features Fela Sowande of Nigeria, African musicologist, composer, and organist, who explains how contemporary African music has mingled traditional African and Western idioms to create new forms.
Fine Arts
Dist - IU **Prod** - NET 1964

Music of Afro - America 15 MIN
VHS / U-matic
Music and Me Series
Color (I)
LC 80-706872
Introduces Afro - American music, from traditional African drum calls to Dixieland. Shows a field holler and a spiritual, and concludes with a sing - along.
Fine Arts; History - United States
Dist - AITECH **Prod** - WDCNTV 1979

Music of America Series
What Does Music do 20 MIN
Dist - GPN

Music of an Empire 53 MIN
U-matic / VHS
Man and Music Series
Color (C)
$279.00, $179.00 purchase _ #AD - 1773
Focuses on Classical Vienna. Reveals that for fifty years around 1800, it was the site of compositions by Haydn, Mozart, Beethoven and Schubert. Examines the historical circumstances that made Vienna the musical capital of Europe. Part of a 22 - part series that sets Western music into the historial and cultural context of its time.
Fine Arts; Geography - World; History - World
Dist - FOTH **Prod** - FOTH

The Music of Auschwitz 16 MIN
U-matic / VHS / 16mm
Color (J)
LC 78-701771
Features Holocaust survivor Fania Fenelon as she recalls her experiences as a musician at the Auschwitz concentration camp during World War II. Includes film footage and photographs taken at the camp. Originally shown on the CBS television program 60 Minutes.
History - World; Sociology
Dist - CAROUF **Prod** - CBSTV 1978

Music of China - Thirty Years of Change 110 MIN
U-matic
Color
Studies the music of China since 1949. Describes political setting, Western influences and traditional Chinese instruments.
Fine Arts; History - World
Dist - HRC **Prod** - OHC

The Music of Erich Zann 17 MIN
U-matic / VHS / 16mm
Color (J H)
Presents H P Lovecraft's story The Music Of Erich Zann, about a young 19th century American who is fascinated by Erich Zann, a mute violinist who plays wondrous music only at night.
Literature and Drama
Dist - MCFI **Prod** - MCFI

The Music of Harry Partch 30 MIN
Videoreel / VT2
Synergism - Variations in Music Series
Color
Fine Arts
Dist - PBS **Prod** - KPBS

Music of India - Classical 16 MIN
16mm
B&W (I)
Introduces the two time - honored systems of music in India and explains the traditions associated with them. Features a few of the well - known vocalists who sing some 'RAGAS' according to traditon.
Fine Arts
Dist - NEDINF **Prod** - INDIA

Music of India - Drums 12 MIN
16mm
B&W (I)
Shows the variety of drums used in the music and dance of India. Presents the intricate 'BOLS' played on the pakhawaj, mridang and tabla by renowned artists and shows all the other types of drums used in the villages.
Fine Arts
Dist - NEDINF **Prod** - INDIA

Music of India - Instrumental 11 MIN
16mm
B&W (I)
Introduces the rich variety of instruments used in Indian music. Features the been of North India, the veena of South India, the sarod and the sitar.
Fine Arts
Dist - NEDINF **Prod** - INDIA

Music of Inspiration 15 MIN
U-matic / VHS
Music and Me Series
Color (P I)
Presents music of inspiration.
Fine Arts
Dist - AITECH **Prod** - WDCNTV 1979

The Music of Japan - Koto Music 29 MIN
Videoreel / VT2
Synergism - Encore Series
Color
Presents an international performance of mime, poetry, puppetry, dance, art and music. Includes Koto music of Japan.
Fine Arts; Geography - World; Literature and Drama
Dist - PBS **Prod** - WKARTV

Music of Man Series
The Age of the composer 57 MIN
The Age of the individual 57 MIN
The Flowering of harmony 57 MIN
The Known and the Unknown 57 MIN
New Voices for Man 57 MIN
The Parting of the Ways 57 MIN
The Quiver of Life 57 MIN
Sound or Unsound 57 MIN
Dist - TIMLIF

Music of man
The Age of the individual 58 MIN
The Quiver of Life 58 MIN
Dist - CANBC

Music of Shakespeare's Time 30 MIN
16mm
World of Music Series
B&W (J)
Presents the New York Pro Musica playing music of Shakespeare's time with the original compositions and reproductions of the original instruments. Presents short talks on the nature of a particular selection, or the composer or instrument used, between numbers.
Fine Arts
Dist - IU **Prod** - NET 1965

Music of South America 15 MIN
VHS / U-matic
Music and Me Series
Color (P I)
Discusses the music of South America.
Fine Arts; Geography - World
Dist - AITECH **Prod** - WDCNTV 1979

The Music of Speech - Pitch and Poetry 29 MIN
U-matic
Pike on Language Series
Color
Shows how one word or sentence may imply several different meanings, just by varying pitch, stress and voice quality.
English Language; Psychology
Dist - UMITV **Prod** - UMITV 1977

The Music of the Devil, the Bear, and the Condor 52 MIN
VHS / 16mm
Color (G)
$350.00 purchase, $90.00 rental
Documents music festivals held in the heart of the Andes annually. Includes some of the most sacred, magical ceremonies of the Aymara Indians, those which feature elaborately costumed dancers clad as devils, bears and sacred spirits who come to life at carnival time. Also features the music of Inti - Raymi, K'Jarkas, Kollamarka, Rumilllajta and Jenny Cardenas.
Fine Arts; Geography - World; Religion and Philosophy; Social Science
Dist - CNEMAG **Prod** - CNEMAG 1989

Music of the First Americans 15 MIN
U-matic / VHS
Music and Me Series
Color (P I)
Discusses the music of the First Americans.
Fine Arts; Social Science
Dist - AITECH **Prod** - WDCNTV 1979

Music of the Spheres - Pt 1 26 MIN
16mm / U-matic
Ascent of Man Series
Color (H C A)
LC 74-702257
Presents the evolution of mathematics and its relationship to musical harmony, early astronomy and perspectives in painting. Narrated by Dr Jacob Bronowski of the Salk Institute.
Mathematics
Dist - TIMLIF **Prod** - BBCTV 1973

Music of the Spheres - Pt 2 26 MIN
16mm / U-matic
Ascent of Man Series
Color (H C A)
LC 74-702257
Presents the evolution of mathematics and its relationship to musical harmony, early astronomy and perspectives in painting. Narrated by Dr Jacob Bronowski of the Salk Institute.
Mathematics
Dist - TIMLIF **Prod** - BBCTV 1973

Music of the spirits 30 MIN
U-matic / VHS
Color (G)
$350.00, $250.00 purchase
Focuses on Stella Nekati - Chiweshe of Zimbabwe, a musical genius and virtuoso of the mbira - the African 'thumb piano' used in the invocation of the ancestral spirits in Shona religious rituals. Speaks of Nekati - Chiweshe's struggle to learn her craft, traditionally dominated by men. She sings and plays to illustrate, 'the spirit comes and talks to you, and does the work.' Produced by Ron and Ophera Hallis of Canada.
Fine Arts; History - World; Sociology
Dist - FLOWER

The Music of the Spoken Word 6 MIN
U-matic / VHS / 16mm
Communicating from the Lectern Series
Color (H C A)
Points out the little - realized importance of music in the English language.
English Language
Dist - AIMS **Prod** - METAIV 1976

Music of the USA I 15 MIN
VHS / U-matic
Music and Me Series
Color (P I)
Discusses the music of America.
Fine Arts
Dist - AITECH **Prod** - WDCNTV 1979

Music of the USA II 14 MIN
U-matic / VHS
Music and Me Series
Color (P I)
Discusses the music of America.
Fine Arts
Dist - AITECH **Prod** - WDCNTV 1979

Music of the USA III 14 MIN
U-matic / VHS
Music and Me Series
Color (P I)
Discusses the music of America.
Fine Arts
Dist - AITECH **Prod** - WDCNTV 1979

Music of Vietnam 6 MIN
16mm
Ethnic Music and Dance Series
Color (J)
LC 72-700245
Presents a performance of the traditional music of Vietnam played on the 16 - stringed zither, dan tranh, by the musician and musicologist, Tran Van Khe. Shows techniques used for the subtle ornament and tone changes that are characteristic of this music.
Fine Arts; Geography - World
Dist - UWASHP **Prod** - UWASH 1971

Music of Williamsburg 29 MIN
16mm / U-matic / VHS
Color (I J H C)
Re - creates the music of Colonial times, ranging from the simplest folk songs to music performed by instrumental ensemble and a professional opera company.
Fine Arts; History - United States
Dist - MGHT **Prod** - CWMS 1962

Music on Key 30 MIN
U-matic / VHS / 16mm
Mr Microchip Series
Color (I J H)
Takes an introductory look at the new technology of computer music and how computers can be used to teach or make music. Discusses software programs for teaching and arranging and creating music as well as portable pre - programmed keyboards.
Mathematics
Dist - JOU **Prod** - JOU

Music Reading 20 MIN
16mm
B&W (I T)
Uses a series of demonstrations to show how music experiences in kindergarten and lower elementary grades can help provide a foundation for music reading. Shows how a fifth grade class learns to read music.
Education; Fine Arts
Dist - MLA **Prod** - JHP 1952

Music Research 24 MIN
16mm
Communication Theory and the New Educational Media Series
B&W
LC 75-700564
Shows the application of educational technology to music. Examines a program which employs a keyboard - oriented teaching machine in order to teach elementary school children the basic skills of music.
Fine Arts
Dist - USNAC **Prod** - USOE 1966

The Music School 30 MIN
U-matic / VHS / 16mm
American Short Story Series
Color (J H C A)
$585, $250 purchase _ #3910
Tells the story of a writer who wishes to find a particular thing to focus on in his life. Shows how he enjoys taking his daughter to music school. Teleplay written and directed by John Korty. Based on the story by John Updike.
Literature and Drama
Dist - CORF **Prod** - LEARIF 1977
CDTEL

The Music school
VHS
American short story collection series
Color (J H)
$49.00 purchase
Tells of a struggling writer and his attempt to find order and harmony in his life, who finds great joy in taking his daughter to her music school. Written by John Updike.
History - United States; Literature and Drama; Sociology
Dist - GA **Prod** - GA

Music Sequence 10 MIN
16mm / U-matic / VHS
Color
Presents a collection of the popular music hits of the 1950's and illustrates the music with a quick - cutting montage.
Fine Arts
Dist - PFP **Prod** - EAMES 1960

Music Series no 10
Music is Style 28 MIN
Dist - USNAC

Music Series no 3
Music is Melody 28 MIN
Dist - USNAC

Music Series no 4
Music is Harmony 28 MIN
Dist - USNAC

Music Series no 5
Music is Tone Color 28 MIN
Dist - USNAC

Music Series no 6
Music is Form 28 MIN
Dist - USNAC

Music Series no 7
Music is Composed 28 MIN
Dist - USNAC

Music Series no 8
Music is Conducted 28 MIN
Dist - USNAC

Music Series no 9
Music is Improvised 28 MIN
Dist - USNAC

Music Series
Music is 28 MIN
Music is Rhythm 28 MIN
Dist - USNAC

Music Shop Series
Back to Bach 29 MIN
Backstage Beethoven 29 MIN
Creating the Commercial 29 MIN
The Drums Go Bang 29 MIN
Faking it 29 MIN
For the record 29 MIN
Gilbert and Sullivan 29 MIN
Half - Time 29 MIN
In the Mood 29 MIN
Jazz is a Personal Thing 29 MIN
Let's make a Musical 29 MIN
Making Movie Music 29 MIN
Rehearsal 29 MIN
Rock - Tilt with a Lilt 29 MIN
Search for Sounds 29 MIN
Selling a Song 29 MIN
Songs and Symphony 29 MIN
Soul to Soul 29 MIN
Twinkle, Twinkle, Little Star 29 MIN
Writing it Down 29 MIN
Dist - UMITV

Music Stories Series
Let's make Music Volume 1 30 MIN
Mother Goose Musical Rhymes 30 MIN
My Favorite Music Stories 30 MIN
Nursery Rhymes in Song Volume 1 30 MIN
Nursery Rhymes in Song Volume 2 30 MIN
Songs of Childhood 30 MIN
Dist - EDUCRT

The Music Student 30 MIN
16mm
B&W
LC FIA64-1144
A story of an opera singer who serves as cantor in a small synagogue. Discusses the background of the custom of Yahrzeit and Kaddish.
Religion and Philosophy
Dist - NAAJS **Prod** - JTS 1957

Music that won't stand still
Videodisc
Laser learning set 2 series; Set 2
Color; CAV (P I)
$375.00 purchase _ #8L5408
Traces the development of American jazz music from its African roots through the mixing of blues and ragtime and into a rich variety of jazz styles. Looks at literal and figurative language. Part of a series of six theme - based interactive videodisc lessons. Requires a Pioneer LD - V2000 or 2200, with barcode reader and adapter, or a Pioneer LD - V4200 or higher. Includes user's guide, two readers.
Fine Arts; Literature and Drama
Dist - BARR **Prod** - BARR 1992

Music - the Electronic Edge 20 MIN
16mm
Color (H C A)
$365 purchase, $50 rental
Explores the new wave of electronically produced sound, and tells how concert - goers become involved with what the musicians are doing, and take part in the event. Features interviews with rock musicians and 'progressive rock' disc jockeys.
Fine Arts
Dist - CNEMAG **Prod** - DOCUA 1988

Music, the Expressive Language 11 MIN
16mm
Color (K P)
LC FIA62-1679
Demonstrates the musical score as a graphic representation of melody and rhythm.
Fine Arts
Dist - SUTHLA **Prod** - SUTHLA 1962

Music Therapy - Preclinical Fieldwork 30 MIN
VHS / U-matic
Color
Presents the process used at the Ohio University School of Music to set up and carry out student field work experience in music therapy. Shows student therapists involved in group and individual sessions, working with a mentally retarded child, a geriatric patient and the pre - school developmentally delayed child.
Fine Arts; Psychology
Dist - OHUTC **Prod** - OHUTC

Music through the Ages 15 MIN
U-matic
Music Box Series
Color (K P)
Gives some different types of music that have been popular in other times; baroque, classical, romantic.
Fine Arts
Dist - TVOTAR **Prod** - TVOTAR 1971

Music to Express Ideas 12 MIN
16mm / U-matic / VHS
Color (I J) (SPANISH)
LC 77-704766
A class which is vitally interested in aviation, creates a full symphony, involving every student in research and individual creative expression.
English Language; Fine Arts
Dist - AIMS **Prod** - BRADLY 1970

Music to Learn about People 11 MIN
16mm / U-matic / VHS
Color (P I)
LC 70-704767
Presents six children in the class who are having birthdays. Shows their different ethnic origins, and how their customs, traditions and music become a focal point of study and creativity.
Fine Arts; History - United States; Psychology; Sociology
Dist - AIMS **Prod** - BRADLY 1970

Music to Live by 19 MIN
16mm / U-matic / VHS
Humanities Series
Color (H C A)
LC 75-713374
Illustrates that man throughout history has organized sounds to please him in a variety of ways and has listened to music. Presents music and visuals from several periods and cultures, rock - calypso, oriental, religious, jazz, folk and opera. Portrays the universal need for musical expression.
Fine Arts; Social Science
Dist - MGHT **Prod** - MGHT 1971

Music to Tell a Story 9 MIN
U-matic / VHS / 16mm
Color (K P) (SPANISH)
LC 74-704768
Shows children in a class and how they interpret their own story creatively in music and other expression, utilizing science, langauge arts and rhythms.
English Language; Fine Arts; Literature and Drama
Dist - AIMS **Prod** - BRADLY 1970

Music to Your Eyes 26 MIN
VHS / 16mm
Color (H)
$205.00 purchase
Explains the relationship between market demand and creative innovations in the production of music videos. Reports that music videos are made for a wide variety of tastes and are essential to the music business.
Business and Economics; Fine Arts
Dist - FLMWST

Music Video - Jim Yukich 23 MIN
VHS / 16mm
Action - a Day with the Directors Series
Color (H)
$39.95 purchase, $15.00 rental _ #86465
Interviews Jim Yukick who describes his beginnings at Purdue University where he minored in music composition and majored in film. Points out that his professional start was in the mail room at Capitol Records. Reveals, however, that he has been doing music videos for six years and has branched out into the Father Guido Sarducci comedy presentations. Offers valuable professional hints on cameras, budgets and methods.
Fine Arts; Industrial and Technical Education; Psychology
Dist - UILL **Prod** - SSN 1987

Music video, Rainbow Warriors No 1 5 MIN
VHS
Color (G)
$19.95 purchase
Intercuts images of Greenpeace activists in their most daring efforts to protect the environment with footage of the artists who donated music on this video to Greenpeace - the Pretenders, the Eurythmics, Sade and others.
Fine Arts; Science - Natural; Sociology
Dist - GRNPCE **Prod** - GRNPCE

Music video, Rainbow Warriors No 2 5 MIN
VHS
Color (G)
$19.95 purchase
Intercuts images of nature with footage of the artists who donated music on this video to Greenpeace - John Cougar Mellencamp, Sting, Bruce Hornsby, Terence Trent D'Arby.
Fine Arts; Science - Natural; Sociology
Dist - GRNPCE **Prod** - GRNPCE

Music with Balls 10 MIN
16mm
Color (H C A)
Presents a new kind of music with moving sculpture - gigantic, swinging spheres whose orbits make magical music.
Fine Arts
Dist - UWFKD **Prod** - UWFKD

Music Word Fire and I would do it Again, Coo - Coo - the Lessons 30 MIN
VHS / U-matic
Color
Introduces four principal characters - Isolde, Raoul de Noget, Buddy and Donnie. Features variations on the theme song from Episode Three of the television opera, Perfect Lives.
Fine Arts
Dist - KITCHN **Prod** - KITCHN

Musica 60 MIN
U-matic
Color
Traces the history and development of Latin American music in the United States. Tells the story through the words and music of artists such as Mario Bauza and Paquito D'Rivera.
Fine Arts; History - World; Sociology
Dist - BLKFMF **Prod** - BLKFMF

Musica En La Noche 85 MIN
16mm
B&W (A) (SPANISH)
A Spanish language film. Interprets the songs and dances of different countries with typical costumes and appropriate sets.
Fine Arts; Foreign Language; Social Science
Dist - TRANSW **Prod** - TRANSW

Musical Design 15 MIN
U-matic
Music Box Series
Color (K P)
Demonstrates how composers design a song.
Fine Arts
Dist - TVOTAR **Prod** - TVOTAR 1971

Musical Encounter Series
The Bassoon - piano show 30 MIN
The Clarinet - flute show 30 MIN
Musical Families 30 MIN
The Orchestra 30 MIN
The Piano Show 30 MIN
A Record Show 30 MIN
A Team Show 30 MIN
Dist - GPN

Musical Families 30 MIN
VHS / U-matic
Musical Encounter Series
Color (P I)
Presents musical families, including the Chiu brothers who keep busy with their fiddles and the Argosino brothers who do likewise with a piano and a penchant for musical composition. Features composer - conductor - pianist Lalo Schifrin. Hosted by Florence Henderson.
Fine Arts
Dist - GPN **Prod** - KLCSTV 1983

Musical families - strings, woodwinds and brass 22 MIN
U-matic / VHS
Color (I)
$350.00 purchase, $50.00 rental; LC 90710560
Features Alan Balter, Conductor and Director of the Memphis Symphony Orchestra, who describes and discusses three families of musical instruments - strings, woodwinds and brass. Illustrates the design and functioning of each instrument from playing techniques to how the instruments actually work, including the variety of sounds possible from each musical family.
Fine Arts
Dist - FIESTF **Prod** - FIESTF 1990

Musical Forms - the Canon 18 MIN
U-matic / VHS / 16mm
Color (I J H C)
$415, $250 purchase _ #73051
Shows how to recognize counterpoint melodic repetition, identify sounds of instruments, and time intervals.
Fine Arts
Dist - CORF

Musical Forms - the Fugue 19 MIN
U-matic / VHS / 16mm
Color (I J H C)
$435, $250 purchase _ #73053
Shows Bach's Fugue In G Minor performed accompanied by animation.
Fine Arts
Dist - CORF

Musical Genes 7 MIN
16mm / U-matic / VHS
Color (H C A)
Presents CBS news correspondent Charles Osgood, who interviews a scientist who has put the DNA chemistry to music. Shows how he uses this music and the state of the art in computer animation to make the 'melody of man' visible to all. Originally shown on the CBS television program Universe.
Fine Arts; Industrial and Technical Education; Science - Natural
Dist - CAROUF **Prod** - CBSTV

Musical Holdouts 51 MIN
U-matic / VHS / 16mm
Color (H C A)
LC 76-702495
Examines the music of Americans who have maintained their ethnic and individual identities in their music.
Fine Arts; Sociology
Dist - PHENIX **Prod** - COHNJ 1975

Musical Holdouts 47 MIN
U-matic / VHS / 16mm
Color (A)
Portrays musicians outside the mainstream American tradition, from blacks of the Carolina Sea Islands, to Appalachian Bluegrass players, to Berkeley Street musicians.
Fine Arts
Dist - CNEMAG **Prod** - CNEMAG 1976

Musical Horses 10 MIN
U-matic / VHS / 16mm
Color (P I J)
Features the training and care of the horses who star in the famous Royal Canadian Mounted Police Musical Ride. Shows what kind of training goes into teamwork between people and animals to produce this delightful example of non verbal communication.
Agriculture; English Language; Guidance and Counseling; Psychology; Science - Natural; Social Science
Dist - BULFRG Prod - YNF 1986

The Musical Instrument Maker of Williamsburg 54 MIN
16mm
Color
LC 76-700385; 76 - 700385
Shows George Wilson, master medical instrument maker, and his journeymen construct a spinet and a violin commencing with raw materials and ending with the completed instruments.
Fine Arts; Industrial and Technical Education
Dist - CWMS Prod - CWMS 1976

Musical Instruments Series
Classical percussion - Pt 1 18 MIN
Classical percussion - Pt 2 16 MIN
Colorful woodwinds, Pt 1 18 MIN
Colorful woodwinds, Pt 2 13 MIN
Early instruments - Pt 1 19 MIN
Early instruments - Pt 2 19 MIN
East African instruments - Pt 1 17 MIN
East African instruments - Pt 2 16 MIN
Majestic Brass, Pt 1 15 MIN
Majestic Brass, Pt 2 16 MIN
South American Instruments - Pt 1 17 MIN
South American Instruments - Pt 2 19 MIN
Vibrant Strings, Pt 1 16 MIN
Vibrant Strings, Pt 2 19 MIN
West African Instruments 17 MIN
Dist - GPN

Musical Instruments Series
Cymbal techniques 16 MIN
Timpani Techniques 20 MIN
Dist - MCFI

A Musical Journey through Eight Centuries with Carl Dolmetsch and Joseph Saxby 30 MIN
U-matic
B&W
Comprised of two programs which introduce a variety of instruments, including recorder, viol, rebec and others. Comments on works composed from the 13th to the 20th centuries.
Fine Arts
Dist - UWASHP Prod - UWASHP

Musical masterpieces series
The Baroque ensemble 29 MIN
Dist - PBS

Musical Masterpieces Series
The Master Singers of Nuremberg 20 MIN
Mendelssohn's Midsummer Night's Dream 20 MIN
Dist - SG

Musical masterpieces
Collegium musicum 29 MIN
Dist - PBS

Musical Mosaic Series
Musical Mosaic - South America 29 MIN
Dist - PBS

Musical Mosaic - South America 29 MIN
VHS / 16mm
Musical Mosaic Series
Color (G)
$55.00 rental _ #MUMO - 004
Features Phil Faini conducting the West Virginia University Percussion Ensemble in a program of South American music.
Fine Arts
Dist - PBS Prod - WWVUTV

Musical passage 73 MIN
16mm
Color (G)
$225.00 rental
Depicts one of the more successful Jewish emigree stories from the ongoing saga of the Soviet Emigre Orchestra, a highly successful ensemble comprised mostly of Soviet Jews who left their motherland to pursue their individual needs for freedom. Focuses on three musicians - the founder, Lazar Gosman, and violinists Grigory Zaritsky and Elmira Belkin. Looks at the actions of the Jews in Russia, in the late 1960s and early '70s, who began to study, reassert their Jewish identities and demand the right to leave a country that denied them full - expression - often at extreme personal cost. Selections from Haydn, Tchaikovsky and Shostakovitch. Produced, directed and photographed by Jim Barnes.
Fine Arts; History - World; Sociology
Dist - NCJEWF

Musical Possibilities 30 MIN
U-matic / VHS
In Our Own Image Series
Color (C)
Fine Arts
Dist - DALCCD Prod - DALCCD

Musical prodigy 26 MIN
VHS
Color (G)
$149.00 purchase _ #EX3330
Examines the impact of parents withdrawing a child from school to focus on musical study.
Education; Fine Arts; Psychology
Dist - FOTH

Musical Sound Series
Wind Instruments - Sound Emission 30 MIN
Dist - NETCHE

Musical stories 15 MIN
VHS / U-matic
Music machine series
Color (P)
Discusses program music.
Fine Arts
Dist - GPN Prod - INDIPS 1981

Musical stories 60 MIN
VHS
Mister Rogers' home videos series
Color; CC (K P)
$14.95 purchase _ #HV105
Presents two Mister Rogers' Neighborhood 'operas' for children and their families. Part of a series featuring favorite Mister Rogers Neighborhood programs.
Fine Arts; Literature and Drama; Sociology
Dist - FAMCOM Prod - FAMCOM 1990

A Musical Terms Melodrama 11 MIN
16mm
Color (J)
Depicts a presentation by a junior high group of a 'SILLY OPERA' designed to teach musical terminology.
Fine Arts
Dist - WSUM Prod - WSUM 1960

Musical Triangle Series
Bach, the organ, and Simon Preston 26 MIN
Britten, the Voice, and Peter Pears 26 MIN
Dowland, the Lute, and Julian Bream 26 MIN
Mozart, the Clarinet, and Keith Puddy 26 MIN
Purcell, the Trumpet and John Wilbraham and Michael Laird 26 MIN
Rameau, the Harpsichord, and George Malcolm 26 MIN
Schubert, the Piano Trio, and Peter Frankl, Gyorgy Pauk and Ralph Kirshbaum 26 MIN
Stockhausen, the percussion, and Tristan Fry 26 MIN
Villa - Lobos, the Guitar, and Julian Byzantine 26 MIN
Vivaldi, the Flute and James Galway 26 MIN
Dist - MEDIAG

Musical Triangles Series
Liszt, the Piano, and Craig Sheppard 26 MIN
Paganini, the Violin, and Desmond Bradley 26 MIN
Dist - MEDIAG

Musicanada 58 MIN
16mm
Color (G)
_ #106C 0175 120
Shows, among others, Edith Butler, Beau Dommage, Maureen Forrester, Glenn Gould, Paul Horn, the Huggett Family and Gilles Bigneault in concer in Canada.
Fine Arts
Dist - CFLMDC Prod - NFBC 1975

Musician 15 MIN
U-matic / 16mm / VHS
Career Awareness
(I)
$130 VC purchase, $240 film purchase, $25 VC rental, $30 film rental
Presents an empathetic approach to career planning, showing the personal as well as the professional attributes of musicians. Highlights the importance of career education.
Fine Arts; Guidance and Counseling
Dist - GPN

The Musician and the General 29 MIN
Videoreel / VT2
Koltanowski on Chess Series
Color
Physical Education and Recreation
Dist - PBS Prod - KQEDTV

The Musician's guide to publicity and promotion 60 MIN
VHS
Color (PRO G C)
$119.00 purchase, $39.00 rental _ #609P
Shows how to assemble an effective press kit, create advertising, write press releases and bios, build an effective mailing list, make the most of free publicity. Advises on how to find and work with designers and photographers at modest cost. Features Diane Rapaport, formerly an artist's manager for Bill Graham's Fillmore Management, who illustrates her presentation with materials from successful promotion campaigns. Includes a detailed written strategy outline to serve as a checklist for publicity campaigns. Produced by Workshop Arts.
Business and Economics; Fine Arts
Dist - FIRLIT

The Musician's guide to the music business 60 MIN
VHS
Color (J H C G)
$39.95 purchase _ #RMD01V
Offers information from music insiders who reveal what every songwriter, musician and performer needs to know to 'break in' and succeed in the music business. Shows how to get club owners to give a musical group a shot at performance, how to become part of the scene and create a buzz, when to get a manager or a lawyer, how much a group can do on its own and more.
Business and Economics; Fine Arts; Guidance and Counseling
Dist - CAMV

Musicians in exile 75 MIN
VHS
Color; Stereo (G)
$29.95 purchase
Offers some jazz musical renditions from Hugh Masekela, Qualapayun.
Fine Arts
Dist - KINOIC Prod - RHPSDY

Musicians in the Woods 14 MIN
16mm / U-matic / VHS
Color (P)
$340.00, $240.00 purchase _ #1499
Relates a story of a group of animals who set out to find their fortune together.
Literature and Drama
Dist - CORF Prod - GAKKEN 1962

Musicians of the Ages 18 MIN
16mm
Color
Presents the many outstanding musicians featured at Potter's Wax Museum in St Augustine, Florida.
Fine Arts; Physical Education and Recreation; Sociology
Dist - FLADC Prod - FLADC

A Musician's Tale 11 MIN
U-matic / VHS / 16mm
Color (H C A)
LC 83-700379
Presents the animated story of an old musician and a whistling beaver. Reveals how they attain fame and fortune, only to lose both as well as their friendship.
Fine Arts
Dist - PHENIX Prod - CFET 1982

Musicmakers 26 MIN
U-matic / VHS / 16mm
Color (P I J)
LC 81-700889
Presents famous singers, songwriters and instrumentalists showing how to create music. Encourages looking for musical possibilities in commonplace objects.
Fine Arts
Dist - PHENIX Prod - MARKS 1978

Musk oxen 10 MIN
VHS
Animal profile series
Color (P I)
$59.95 purchase _ #RB8106
Studies musk oxen. Examines their habitat in the barren lands of the Alaskan tundra. Reveals that a single animal can produce $600,000.00 worth of wool in a lifetime. Part of a series on animals which looks at examples from the mammal, snake and bird classes, filmed in their natural habitat.
Science - Natural
Dist - REVID Prod - REVID 1990

Musketeers 6 MIN
16mm / U-matic / VHS
Color (H C A)

LC 83-700380
Uses the framework of the novel THE THREE MUSKETEERS by Alexander Dumas to present a surrealistic adventure with a series of characters whose movements and expressions both imitate and mock their real - life counterparts.
Fine Arts
Dist - PHENIX **Prod** - KRATKY 1982

Muskie 22 MIN
16mm
Color (G)
Offers an underwater look at the fighting muskie and his habitat capped by a study of the contrasting techniques used in landing this elusive prey.
Physical Education and Recreation; Science - Natural
Dist - KAROL **Prod** - BRNSWK

Muskie Fishing Magic 55 MIN
BETA / VHS
From the Sportsman's Video Collection Series
Color
Presents the techniques that America's best muskie fishing guides use to consistently catch muskie, big muskie, on North America's finest muskie waters.
Physical Education and Recreation
Dist - CBSC **Prod** - CBSC

Muskwachees Community - Jason Visits the Reserve 30 MIN
U-matic
(P I)
Investigates lifestyles in culturally distinct communities. Shows some of the customs and traditions found on a Cree Indian reserve.
Social Science
Dist - ACCESS **Prod** - ACCESS 1985

The Muslim Family 5 MIN
U-matic
See, Hear - the Middle East Series
Color (J)
Discusses the traditional family relationships in the Middle East.
Geography - World; History - World; Religion and Philosophy
Dist - TVOTAR **Prod** - TVOTAR 1980

Muslims in the Americas before Columbus
VHS
Color (G)
$15.00 purchase _ #110 - 065
Tells of Muslims in the Americas from the oldest Arabic sources and recent findings. Describes how Muslims traveled and settled throughout the Americas. Claims that they fought against slavery. Looks at a revival of Islam in many parts of the Caribbean. Shot in Barbados.
Religion and Philosophy
Dist - SOUVIS **Prod** - SOUVIS

Mussau 32 MIN
16mm
Color (DANISH)
A Danish language film. Portrays life on the coral island of Mussau which lies in the Bismarck Sea. Points out that even if there has been a certain outside influence, everyday life goes on as it did a hundred years ago.
Foreign Language; Geography - World; Sociology
Dist - STATNS **Prod** - STATNS 1963

The Mussel Specialist 25 MIN
U-matic / VHS / 16mm
Behavior and Survival Series
Color (H C A)
LC 73-700426
Studies the behavior of oystercatchers on the coasts of Britain. Points out that these birds are experts in the complicated technique of opening mussels. Asks the question of what is innate and what has been learned.
Science - Natural
Dist - MGHT **Prod** - MGHT 1973

Mussolini 40 MIN
VHS
Heroes and tyrants of the twentieth century series
Color (J H C G)
$29.95 purchase _ #MH6026V
Portrays Benito Mussolini, a misguided dictator who went from being a womanizer, a casualty of war, to Fascist leader and a victim at the hands of his own people. Witnesses his theatrical personality, his egocentric oratory, his march on Rome, his private war with Adolph Hitler and his crushing defeats on the battlefield. Includes war footage. Part of a six - part series on 20th - century leaders.
Civics and Political Systems; History - World
Dist - CAMV

Mussolini 26 MIN
U-matic / VHS / 16mm
Biography Series
B&W (J)
Traces the life of Mussolini from his youth to the development of his own party and the Munich conference with Hitler. Shows his capture and death.
Biography; Civics and Political Systems; History - World
Dist - MGHT **Prod** - WOLPER 1963

Mussolini Visits Hitler 31 MIN
VHS / U-matic
B&W (GERMAN)
Shows Adolf Hitler and Benito Mussolini speaking at Berlin's Olympic Stadium in September 1937. Reports on the Italian dictator's state visit to Germany. Includes scenes of the Axis leaders' meeting in Munich.
Foreign Language; History - World
Dist - IHF **Prod** - IHF

Mussolini's Italy 29 MIN
Videoreel / VT2
Course of Our Times I Series
Color
History - World
Dist - PBS **Prod** - WGBHTV

Mussorgsky 78 MIN
VHS
Color (G C)
$149.00 purchase _ #EX4006
Examines Russian composer Mussorgsky's development from conventional Romantic to proto - impressionist.
Biography; Fine Arts; History - World
Dist - FOTH

Must I, may I 15 MIN
VHS / 16mm / U-matic
Inside-out series
Color
Presents parallel episodes which Debbie and Bobby try to deal with in situations that give them too much or not enough responsibility. Shows how to cope with the feelings caused by the tension between freedom and responsibility.
Guidance and Counseling; Psychology
Dist - AITECH

Must We Fall 17 MIN
16mm
Color (A)
Presents a stuntman who reenacts several dramatic accidents, then describes how he avoids slipping, tripping and falling during the execution of stunts. Shows how to use the same techniques to avoid falling in industrial and office situations.
Health and Safety
Dist - VISUCP **Prod** - VISUCP 1982

Must We have Noise 11 MIN
U-matic / VHS / 16mm
Caring about Our Community Series
Color (P I) (SPANISH)
LC 76-702244;
Presents sounds, both natural and artificial, that have become part of our daily existence. Focuses attention on noises that are rarely heard consciously. Results in a censure of one of the major pollutants of modern society.
Science - Natural
Dist - AIMS **Prod** - GORKER 1972

Mustang - Managing a Misfit 29 MIN
BETA / VHS
Color
Explores the American mustang's history. Pictures wild horses in their natural habitats.
Physical Education and Recreation
Dist - EQVDL **Prod** - USFS

Mustard - the Spice of Nations 26 MIN
VHS / U-matic
Spice of Life Series
Color (J A)
Identifies how and what kind of mustard is used in various countries.
Health and Safety; Home Economics
Dist - BCNFL **Prod** - BLCKRD 1985

Musvagen - Buteo Buteo - the Common Buzzard 10 MIN
16mm
B&W (DANISH)
A Danish language film. Describes the life of the common buzzard in the nest, in the forest and the fields.
Foreign Language; Science - Natural
Dist - STATNS **Prod** - STATNS 1962

Mutation 15 MIN
VHS / Software / U-matic
Gentetics
Color (J H)
$125.00 purchase,$95.00 software purchase
Probes the alteration of the DNA and its effects on future generations in the form of mutations.
Industrial and Technical Education; Science - Natural
Dist - AITECH **Prod** - WETN 1985

Mutation and all that 10 MIN
U-matic
Organic Evolution Series
Color (H C) (FRENCH)
Traces the development of various theories of evolution beginning with the Biblical account of creation and going on to discuss Darwin, Mendel and others. Ties together the microscopic and macroscopic, genetics and heredity, cell reproduction and breeding populations. Available in French. Comes with teacher's guide.
Science
Dist - TVOTAR **Prod** - TVOTAR 1986

The Mutation Machine 26 MIN
U-matic / VHS
Origins Series
Color (C)
$249.00, $149.00 purchase _ #AD - 1160
Covers the rise and decline of species like the dinosaurs, the role of mutation in the evolutionary process and environmental pressures such as the Ice Age which spurred human efforts to adapt.
Psychology; Science - Natural; Science - Physical
Dist - FOTH **Prod** - FOTH

Mutations 8 MIN
16mm
Color
Presents the changing dots, ectoplasmic shapes and electronic music of L Schwartz's Mutations, which has been shot with the aid of computers and lasers.
Fine Arts; Mathematics
Dist - LILYAN **Prod** - LILYAN

Mute 14 MIN
16mm
Color (G)
$45.00 rental
Tells a malevolent bedtime story in which the focal character firmly maintains her ambivalence towards her state of menace. Uses layers of allegory and true - crime stories along with subtitled information, which is the contrapuntal perspective of the 'other,' the mute. Produced by Greta Snider.
Fine Arts; Literature and Drama; Psychology
Dist - CANCIN

The Mute Swan 17 MIN
U-matic / VHS / 16mm
Color (I J H)
Presents the life cycle of the mute swan in Britain. Includes such aspects as the courtship dance, nesting, the cygnets, and the swan's aggressive nature.
Science - Natural
Dist - VIEWTH **Prod** - GATEEF

Mutiny on the Bounty 40 MIN
16mm
B&W (I J H)
LC FIA52-4973
Presents Charles Laughton and Clark Gable in the leading roles of the classic 'MUTINY ON THE BOUNTY.'.
Literature and Drama
Dist - FI **Prod** - PMI 1935

Mutiny on the bounty 132 MIN
VHS
B&W (G)
Features Charles Laughton as the tyrannical Captain Bligh, who drives his crew on the HMS Bounty to mutiny. Co - stars Clark Gable, Franchot Tone, Donald Crisp and Spring Byington. Filmed in 1935.
Fine Arts; Literature and Drama
Dist - UILL **Prod** - GA 1935
GA
SEVVID

Mutiny on the Western Front - WW I
U-matic / VHS
Color
History - United States; History - World
Dist - MSTVIS **Prod** - MSTVIS

Mutiny - part 3 11 MIN
VHS
Color (G)
$35.00 rental
Invents the machine - gun sound of explosives and composed sentences with speed - up speech, wild singing, laughter, violins screeching. Interviews women, documents dancers, street performers, all races and styles. Third in the loosely defined series Is this what you were born for by Abigail Child.
Fine Arts
Dist - CANCIN **Prod** - CHILDA 1983

The Mutiple Traumatized Patient
U-matic / VHS
Color
Presents an approach to the problems of the multiple traumatized patient. Emphasizes procedures applicable to all forms of trauma.
Health and Safety
Dist - AMEDA **Prod** - AMEDA

Mutter Krausens Fahrt Ins Gluck 106 MIN
16mm
B&W (GERMAN (GERMAN SUBTITLES))
A silent motion picture with German subtitles. Tells the story of Mother Krause, who lives poorly in a Berlin backyard, her son Paul who is arrested for burglary, and her daughter Erna, who is friends with a communist worker and who wants to fight for a better future. The first proletarian film in Germany.
Fine Arts; Foreign Language
Dist - WSTGLC **Prod** - WSTGLC 1929

Mutual Aid - the 'US' in Industry 25 MIN
16mm
Color
LC 74-705181
Explains the procedures of organizing and conducting an industrial mutual aid association, and its importance in civil defense.
Business and Economics; Civics and Political Systems; Health and Safety
Dist - USNAC **Prod** - USOCD 1965

Mutual Funds 51 MIN
BETA / VHS
Investing Series
Color
Deals with investing in mutual funds. Discusses such subjects as how a mutual fund works, the types available and the protections the industry provides the investor.
Business and Economics
Dist - MOHOMV **Prod** - MOHOMV

Mutual Funds 51 MIN
U-matic / VHS
Your Money Series
(C H A)
$29.95 _ #MX1221V
Focuses on the small investor's role in the stockmarket. Instructs viewers on mutual funds, types and features of mutual funds, and the vocabulary of funds.
Business and Economics
Dist - CAMV **Prod** - CAMV

Mutual Funds 51 MIN
VHS / 16mm
(G)
$39.95 purchase _ #VT1076
Teaches how a mutual fund works, the types and features available, the vocabulary of funds, and the protections the industry offers the investor.
Business and Economics
Dist - RMIBHF **Prod** - RMIBHF

Mutual of Omaha's Wild Kingdom series
Chase by copter 25 MIN
Dist - NBCTV

Mutual Respect Behavior Management, Pt 1 34 MIN
VHS / 16mm
(PRO)
$59.95 purchase _ #MA1
Presents principles which can be used to bring out the best in all employees. Discusses business culture, reprimand, attitude, management disloyalty, and communication. Features William Meisterfeld, expert in humanistic management.
Business and Economics
Dist - RMIBHF **Prod** - RMIBHF

Mutual Respect Behavior Management, Pt 2 34 MIN
VHS / 16mm
(PRO)
$59.95 purchase _ #MA2
Illustrates the principles of communication, timing, mutual respect, fear, and praise. Featuring William Mesterfeld, expert in humanistic management.
Business and Economics
Dist - RMIBHF **Prod** - RMIBHF

Mutual weekly no. 109 10 MIN
16mm
Original issue newsreel series
B&W (G)
$15.00 rental
Features the Serbs returning to Serbia; Serbian army in the Balkans; Bulgars blow up two bridges; Battle of the Czerna Reka; Irish rangers and more. Presents part of a series of original issue silent newsreels in their entirety.
Civics and Political Systems; Fine Arts; History - World; Literature and Drama
Dist - KITPAR

Mutuality Series
Oral Love 10 MIN
Self - Pleasuring 5 MIN
Susan and David 28 MIN
Dist - MMRC

The Muvver Tongue 60 MIN
VHS / 16mm
Story of English Series
Color (C)
PdS99 purchase
Studies the spread of English throughout the British Empire during the 19th century when seven million people emigrated from Great Britain, bound for its colonial outposts and speaking a variety of regional dialects. Part 7 of the series.
English Language
Dist - BBCENE **Prod** - BBCTV 1986
FI
PSU

Muzzy in Gondoland 75 MIN
Cassette / VHS
Color (P) (ENGLISH AND SPANISH)
$149.00 purchase _ #SV7285
Introduces English to young children through a six - episode cartoon video about Big Muzzy who comes from outer space to Gondoland. Includes six activity books, a thirty - minute audio cassette of songs, language jingles and dictionary, teacher - parent guide and workbook. Printed materials available in English only or in Spanish - English. A teacher's manual for school use is available separately.
English Language; Literature and Drama
Dist - NORTNJ

MV Cayman Aggressors I and II - the dynamic duo 30 MIN
VHS
Scuba World series
Color (G)
$24.90 purchase _ #0454
Experiences liveaboard dive travel on Aggressors I and II near the Cayman Islands. Includes a photo lab, top notch crew and comfortable cabins.
Geography - World; Industrial and Technical Education; Physical Education and Recreation
Dist - SEVVID

MVS - SP Conversion Considerations Series
JES2 in the MVS - SP Environment 30 MIN
JES3 in the MVS - SP Environment 30 MIN
Dist - DELTAK

MVS/SP Conversion Considerations Series
The Impact of MVS/SP 30 MIN
Dist - DELTAK

MX Debate 120 MIN
U-matic / VHS
Bill Moyers' Journal Series
Color
Bill Moyers serves as the moderator of a 'town meeting' on the Pentagon's plans to put 200 mobile intercontinental ballisitic missiles in the deserts of Utah and Nevada. Includes a discussion of the necessity of the MX system, a critical look at the efficiency of the system, an examination of the economic and environmental effects of the MX system, and feedback from the audience.
Civics and Political Systems
Dist - PBS **Prod** - WNETTV 1980

My 5th Super Bowl 29 MIN
VHS / U-matic
Color (A)
Features former professional football star Carl Eller telling the story of his struggle and eventual triumph over dependency on drugs and alcohol. Details his losses as well as his victory.
Health and Safety; Physical Education and Recreation; Psychology; Sociology
Dist - SFTI **Prod** - SFTI

My Aching Back 8 MIN
U-matic / VHS / 16mm
Color (H C A)
$205.00, $145.00 purchase
Discusses that effect that soft mattresses, obesity, lifting, posture, and stress have on people's backs. Directed by John Haugse.
Health and Safety
Dist - CF **Prod** - CF 1988

My amazing garden 30 MIN
VHS
Color (T K P)
$19.95 purchase _ #MHG200V
Offers children instruction in gardening. Uses step-by-step method to present ideas and projects for growing vegetables, flowers, and plants. Narrated by Peggy Knapp of the PBS series Newton's Apple. Comes with seed packet.
Agriculture; Health and Safety
Dist - CAMV

My Art is Me 21 MIN
16mm / U-matic / VHS
Color (C A)
LC 70-705615
A view of children in an experimental nursery school program. Shows them painting, drawing, sewing, mixing playdough, manipulating clay and constructing wood and scrap sculpture. Explains to teachers the benefits of encouraging creativity rather than providing assignments.
Education; Fine Arts
Dist - UCEMC **Prod** - UCEMC 1969

My ball 6 MIN
VHS / 16mm
Color (P I J H G)
$195.00, $89.00 purchase
Follows the adventures of a red runaway ball as its bounces through the city and causes confusion. Based on the song by Ib Spang Olsen.
Fine Arts; Literature and Drama
Dist - LANDMK **Prod** - LANDMK 1991

My beloved country 50 MIN
VHS / 16mm
Color (G)
$390.00 purchase, $75.00 rental
Takes a provacative look from within at Afrikaner extremists who cling to the belief that they are the chosen 'super race' of Africa. Exposes the fear Boers have for their future with the demise of white rule and reveals their formation of paramilitary groups training for an armed showdown with the new South African government. Produced by Sadkia Vredeveld.
Fine Arts; History - World
Dist - FIRS

My best friend's a computer 30 MIN
VHS
QED series
Color (A)
PdS65 purchase
Reveals that computer addiction has become a fast-growing phenomenon. States that some individuals fear that machines might replace important relationships with family and friends at crucial stages in a child's development.
Psychology
Dist - BBCENE

My Brother David 25 MIN
U-matic / VHS / 16mm
Color (H C A)
Presents Karen Fairman, aged twelve, who looks at the life of her brother David. David is micro - cephalic and partially spastic and is four years of age. David and Karen live with their parents in London, where this documentary was filmed.
Education; Psychology
Dist - MEDIAG **Prod** - THAMES 1971

My Brother Fidel 17 MIN
VHS / 35mm strip / U-matic
Color (H C A) (SPANISH (ENGLISH SUBTITLES))
$150 purchase, $35 rental
Features an interview with a campesion who met Cuban heroes Jose Marti and Maximo Gomez in 1895. Directed by Santiago Alvarez.
History - World; Sociology
Dist - CNEMAG

My Brother is Afraid of Just about Everything 11 MIN
16mm / VHS
Color (P)
$285.00, $250.00 purchase, $50.00 rental
Tells the story of Martin and his brother, Timmy, who is afraid of thunderstorms, scary movies, bearded men, and even mother's vacuum cleaner. Based on the Lois Osborn book, the story encourages children to share experiences and fears, thereby developing a greater sensitivity towards others.
Guidance and Counseling; Literature and Drama; Psychology
Dist - HIGGIN **Prod** - HIGGIN 1990

My Brother is Sick 13 MIN
16mm / VHS
Color (P I)
$125.00, $270.00 purchase, $30.00 rental _ #9782
Helps kids understand and talk about their complex but normal feelings. Tells about Jennifer who worries because sometimes she is angry at her brother Jason. Jason is sick and Jennifer worries that it could be her fault. Grandmother listens to Jennifer's concerns and reassures her.
Guidance and Counseling; Psychology
Dist - AIMS **Prod** - AIMS 1984

My Brother is Sick 12 MIN
U-matic / VHS
Color
Focuses on the emotional response of a well sibling to the hospitalization of her brother. Deals with the disruption of family and relationships when a child is hospitalized. Explores the feelings of the well sibling at home.
Health and Safety; Home Economics; Social Science
Dist - KIDSCO **Prod** - KIDSCO

My Brother is Sick 17 MIN
U-matic / VHS
Color
Focuses on the emotional response of a well sibling to the hospitalization of her brother. Deals with the disruption of family lifestyles and relationships when a child is hospitalized.
Health and Safety; Sociology
Dist - MIFE **Prod** - MIFE

My Brother, the Guru 24 MIN
16mm
Color (J H)
Impresses upon the viewer the kind of pain and suffering which may result from an irresponsible life - style such as that of using drugs. Tells the story of Warren and Marcia who are living together in an apartment near the university and who are both very much involved with the campus drug scene and have adopted a rather casual life - style that requires no long - term promises or commitments to one another.
Guidance and Counseling; Health and Safety; Psychology; Sociology
Dist - FAMF **Prod** - FAMF 1972

My brother's wedding 120 MIN
16mm
Color (G)
Portrays a man caught between aspiring middle - classness and a romanticized view of the poor. Presents Charles Burnett, director, Charles Burnett Productions, USA. Contact distributor about price and availability outside the United Kingdom. Also available in 90 - minute version.
Civics and Political Systems; Literature and Drama
Dist - BALFOR

My Brush is My Bait 29 MIN
U-matic
Artist at Work Series
Color
Demonstrates the use of Japanese brushes. Shows how to create an imaginary fish.
Fine Arts
Dist - UMITV **Prod** - UMITV 1973

My career plan series
How to get along with people on the job
How to match interests with jobs
How to Relate Needs, Interests, and Aptitudes to Jobs
Dist - AAVIM

My career plans series
Outlines 5 objectives based on decision making processes.
My career plans series
Dist - CAREER **Prod** - CAREER 1973

My Child is Blind 22 MIN
16mm
B&W
LC FIE52-1942
Shows how a blind child, given patient treatment and proper training at a special nursery school for the blind, can be taught many things normal children do.
Education; Psychology; Sociology
Dist - USNAC **Prod** - USA 1951

My Childhood 51 MIN
16mm
B&W (J)
LC FI67-2261
Studies the contrasts in the childhoods of Hubert Humphrey and James Baldwin. Emphasizes the effect of parental influence and environment in the forming of a man.
History - United States; Psychology; Sociology
Dist - BNCHMK **Prod** - METROM 1967

My Childhood, Pt 1 - Hubert Humphrey's South Dakota 25 MIN
16mm
B&W
Reveals Hubert Humphrey's happy memories in Doland, South Dakota, as he recreates a boy's admiration for his father and other constructive elements that influenced him.
Biography; Geography - United States; Sociology
Dist - BNCHMK **Prod** - METROM 1967

My Childhood, Pt 2 - James Baldwin's Harlem 25 MIN
16mm
B&W
James Baldwin reminisces about his childhood in Harlem.
History - United States; Literature and Drama
Dist - BNCHMK **Prod** - METROM 1967

My Choice - Drug Free 30 MIN
VHS
Color (I)
LC 89700230
Features teens talking to teens about concrete strategies for resisting peer pressure and refusing drugs and alcohol.
Guidance and Counseling; Psychology
Dist - AIMS **Prod** - HRMC 1989

My City 22 MIN
16mm
Urban Focus Series
Color (I J)
LC 79-702479
Provides insights into the world of urban children. Shows how they interpret and react to their environment.
Psychology; Science - Natural; Social Science; Sociology
Dist - MLA **Prod** - PEPSI 1969

My City - Toronto 15 MIN
U-matic
It's Your World Series
Color (I)
Introduces students to the world around them. Segment titles are; Toronto, Museums, CNE.
Education; Geography - World
Dist - TVOTAR **Prod** - TVOTAR 1984

My country - a Navajo boy's story 25 MIN
VHS / U-matic
Color (P I J)
$325.00, $295.00 purchase _ #V137
Visits a Navajo boy, Bruce, and his family where they live, in the heart of Monument Valley. Shows how Bruce respects his family's traditions, but finds them harder and harder to understand. Produced by David Bowyer Productions.
Geography - United States; Social Science
Dist - BARR

My Country Right or Wrong 15 MIN
16mm / U-matic / VHS
Searching for Values - a Film Anthology Series
Color (J)
LC 72-703089
Tells how rejection of the Vietnam war and of parental and societal pressures force a crisis in the life of a college student, impelling him to make crucial decisions about his values and his future.
Civics and Political Systems; Guidance and Counseling; History - World; Psychology; Sociology
Dist - LCOA **Prod** - LCOA 1972

My Country Right or Wrong 14 MIN^16 MIN
16mm / VHS
Searching for Values - a Film Anthology Series
Color (PRO J H C A)
$295.00, $250.00 purchase _ #LEK525
Talks about patriotism and the vietman war.
Civics and Political Systems; Guidance and Counseling; Health and Safety; History - United States; Psychology; Sociology
Dist - CORF **Prod** - BAXMED 1972

My dad can't be crazy, can he 46 MIN
VHS / U-matic
Color (J H C G)
$250.00 purchase _ #HH - 6251L, #HH6252L
Examines the seriousness and scope of mental health in American society. Takes a look at one family's struggle to come to terms with schizophrenia. Dramatizes the Karpinski family, Jack, Wanda and their son Nick, and their struggle to cope with Jack's schizophrenia. Stars Loretta Swit, Don Murray and Wil Wheaton. Also available in a 30 - minute version.
Health and Safety; Psychology; Sociology
Dist - LCA **Prod** - LCA 1990

My Daddy's ears are broken 27 MIN
VHS
Color (H C G)
$295.00 purchase, $55.00 rental
Tells the story of three hearing - impaired people who reveal the difficulties and triumphs of their adjustments to their disability. Reveals that Heather, the mother of two children, became deaf after an illness. Michael grew up deaf in a family that would not recognize his disability and went through childhood feeling like an outsider at home and in school. Catherine was born deaf and her lip - reading skills enable her to live successfully in the hearing world, but finds sign language a useful tool at work and in her social life.
Education; Guidance and Counseling; Social Science
Dist - FLMLIB **Prod** - CANBC 1990

My Dad's a Cop 18 MIN
16mm
Urban Crisis Series
Captioned; Color (P I J)
Illustrates how a person's work can affect family relations and attitudes.
Guidance and Counseling; Social Science; Sociology
Dist - BROSEB **Prod** - BROSEB 1975

My Dad's Given Up 14 MIN
16mm / U-matic / VHS
Just One Child Series
Color (I J)
Depicts the life of the twelve - year - old son of earthquake victims living in a crowded Guatemala City ghetto. Shows how his day is spent at school until noon, playing with friends, helping with chores and dreaming of a better future. Illustrates how his unemployed father is ready to leave the family and find a job elsewhere, leaving the son with responsibilities he is unprepared to deal with.
Geography - World; Psychology; Sociology
Dist - BCNFL **Prod** - REYEXP 1983

My Darling Clementine 15 MIN
16mm
American Film Genre - the Western Film Series
B&W (J)
LC 75-702625
An excerpt from the 1950 film of the same title. Presents a story based on the life of Wyatt Earp, frontier marshall.
Fine Arts
Dist - FI **Prod** - TWCF 1975

My day
16mm
Talking films series
Color (G)
$16.00 rental
Presents the Talking Films series which employs non - camera animation, associative editing and text written or scratched into the emulsion. Joins words with images to tell the story or with the audience to promote direct interaction. This production is a collaborative performance created by Irwin, comedian Robert Arriola and sculptor Bruce Hogeland. Delves into the ironic contradictions between an artist's creative life and the mundance daily existence he endures to pay the bills.
Fine Arts
Dist - CANCIN **Prod** - IRWINJ 1987

My Dear Uncle Sherlock 24 MIN
16mm / U-matic / VHS
Color (I J)
LC 78-701061
Adapted from the story My Dear Uncle Sherlock by Hugh Pentecost. Presents the story of a 12 - year - old boy who solves a mystery in his community using deductive reasoning skills he developed while playing Sherlock Holmes games with his uncle.
Literature and Drama; Religion and Philosophy
Dist - CORF **Prod** - ABCF 1978

My dinner with Abbie 57 MIN
VHS / 16mm
Color (G A)
$895.00, $350.00 purchase, $100.00 rental
Interviews 1960s radical emeritus Abbie Hoffman two years before his suicide in April, 1989. Features Nancy Cohen as interviewer. Discusses cultural changes during the sixties, seventies and eighties, the roles of men and women, food and sex, life underground and in prison, fleeting fame, midlife crisis and death. Produced by Howard Katzman and Nancy Cohen.
Biography; History - United States; Sociology
Dist - CNEMAG

My Dog is Lost 10 MIN
16mm / U-matic / VHS
Bank Street Reading Incentive Film Series
Color (P I)
Introduces Juanito, who doesn't speak English and has just arrived in New York City from Puerto Rico. Describes the people he meets who help him find his lost dog and who become his friends. Read by Harry Belafonte.
English Language; Social Science
Dist - MGHT **Prod** - BANKSC 1967

My Dog, the Teacher 26 MIN
16mm
Color (K)
LC 73-702480
Demonstrates how a handicapped child learns to care for his pet dog.
Education; Guidance and Counseling; Psychology
Dist - KLEINW **Prod** - HSUS 1968

My Dozen Fathers 12 MIN
U-matic / VHS / 16mm
Color (P I)
LC 81-701006
Offers an animated tale about a young girl whose parents are separated and her attempt's to get her mother's attention, while her mother is too busy attracting and discarding men.
Fine Arts; Guidance and Counseling; Sociology
Dist - PHENIX **Prod** - CFET 1981

My Fair Lady
VHS / BETA
Color
Presents Lerner and Lowe's musical adaptation of G B Shaw's play Pygmalion, starring Rex Harrison and Audrey Hepburn.
Fine Arts; Literature and Drama
Dist - GA **Prod** - GA

My Father Calls Me Son - Racism and Native Americans 29 MIN
VHS / 16mm
Color (G)

$55.00 rental _ #MFCS - 000
Looks at the Native American of California. Presents Native American history, present dilemmas and prospects for the future. Considers the poverty of reservation life and difficulties in assimilating into society.
Social Science; Sociology
Dist - PBS **Prod** - KOCETV 1976

My father, my brother, and me 24 MIN
U-matic / VHS
Young people's specials series
Color
Tells a young girl's story of her migrant worker father's devotion to her and her mentally retarded brother.
Fine Arts; Psychology; Sociology
Dist - MULTPP **Prod** - MULTPP

My Father, My Son 480 MIN
U-matic / VHS
Color (G)
$16.50 rental _ #2160
Shows how one family has dealt with tragedy. Told in the voices of father and son, it is about people who believe they can triumph over any adversity.
Health and Safety; Sociology
Dist - BKSOTP **Prod** - BKSOTP 1988

My Father Sun - Sun Johnson 28 MIN
U-matic / VHS / 16mm
Color; Captioned (I J) (SPANISH)
LC 76-701757
Presents the story of a young Jamaican boy trying to adjust to his parents' divorce and to his mother's remarriage to his father's business rival.
Geography - World; Guidance and Counseling; Social Science; Sociology
Dist - LCOA **Prod** - BBCTV 1977

My Father the Clown 24 MIN
16mm / U-matic / VHS
Color (K)
$495.00, $349.00, $249.00 purchase _ #AD - 1790
Tells the story of a thirteen - year - old's efforts to grow up even though her father continues to treat her like a child.
Literature and Drama; Psychology; Sociology
Dist - FOTH **Prod** - FOTH

My Father, the Doctor 18 MIN
16mm
Color (I J H C)
LC 74-702018
Examines the relationship between two people as the filmmaker, at age 25, shows the relationship she has had with her father during her life.
Guidance and Counseling; Health and Safety; Sociology
Dist - WEINSM **Prod** - WEINSM 1972

My Father the President 23 MIN
U-matic / VHS / 16mm
Color (I)
Presents a tour of President Theodore Roosevelt's homes at Sagamore Hill and Oyster Bay. Shows the man in the context of his family and his times.
Biography
Dist - PFP **Prod** - KIRKPS

My Father's Dragon 15 MIN
U-matic / VHS
Readit Series
Color (P I)
LC 83-706844
Introduces the story of a young boy who runs away and outsmarts wild animals to rescue a little dragon. Based on the book My Father's Dragon by Ruth Stiles Gannett.
English Language; Literature and Drama
Dist - AITECH **Prod** - POSIMP 1982

My Father's Dragon and the Hundred Dresses 15 MIN
U-matic / VHS
Magic Pages Series
Color
Literature and Drama
Dist - AITECH **Prod** - KLVXTV

My father's house 28 MIN
16mm
Color (G)
$30.00 rental _ #ZRF - 695
Looks at young Americans in the old city of Jerusalem who have come to study the Torah following the Yom Kippur War. Reveals that the search for peace is uppermost in their concerns. Discusses ethics and morality in Western society, personal freedom within moral responsibility and how to live life to its fullest potential.
Geography - World; Guidance and Counseling; Religion and Philosophy
Dist - ADL **Prod** - ADL

My Father's House 10 MIN
16mm
Color
LC 79-701331
Follows a young girl as she explores her parish church as God's house and sees in her mind's eye all that she has been told about the celebration of the liturgy.
Religion and Philosophy
Dist - FRACOC **Prod** - FRACOC 1979

My Father's names 103 MIN
VHS
Color (R)
$49.99 purchase _ #SPCN 85116.00124
Gives an understanding of the 80 names and descriptions of God the Father. Includes the book of the same name by Elmer L Towns, a group study guide and two videos. Videos also available separately.
Religion and Philosophy
Dist - GOSPEL **Prod** - GOSPEL

My Father's Son 33 MIN
VHS / U-matic
Color
Portrays the legacy of chemical dependency. Follows a 16 - year old, son of an alcoholic, trying to lead a normal life amidst the chaos of a dysfunctioning family.
Health and Safety; Psychology; Sociology
Dist - UNKNWN **Prod** - ROGGTP HAZELB

My Favorite Brunette 88 MIN
16mm
Color
Presents a comedy about an ex - private eye awaiting execution for murder. Stars Bob Hope and Dorothy Lamour.
Fine Arts
Dist - KITPAR **Prod** - PAR 1947

My Favorite Music Stories 30 MIN
VHS / 16mm
Music Stories Series
Color (P)
$39.95 purchase _ #CL6906
Presents Peter and the Wolf, and The Sorcerer's Apprentice.
Fine Arts; Literature and Drama
Dist - EDUCRT

My favorite opera series
Don Giovanni - Ruggero Raimondi 60 MIN
Don Pasquale - Barbara Hendricks 60 MIN
Guglielmo Tell - Nello Santi 60 MIN
I Capuleti e i Montecchi - Katia Ricciarelli 60 MIN
Werther - Alfredo Kraus 60 MIN
Dist - KULTUR

My Favorite Stories Volume 1 30 MIN
VHS / 16mm
Children's Stories Series
Color (P)
$39.95 purchase _ #CL8806
Presents Jack and the Beanstalk and The Three Bears.
Literature and Drama
Dist - EDUCRT

My Favorite Stories Volume 2 30 MIN
VHS / 16mm
Children's Stories Series
Color (P)
$39.95 purchase _ #CL8811
Presents Beauty and the Beast and Three Little Pigs.
Literature and Drama
Dist - EDUCRT

My Feelings 29 MIN
VHS / 16mm
Villa Alegre Series
Color (P T)
$46.00 rental _ #VILA - 146
Presents educational material in both Spanish and English.
Education; Psychology
Dist - PBS

My filmmaking, my life - Matilde Landeta 30 MIN
U-matic / VHS
Color (G)
$250.00 purchase, $75.00 rental
Documents the life of Mexican filmmaker Matilde Landeta. Follows her entry into the flourishing Mexican film industry in the 1930s through her working her way up from script girl to director of 110 short subjects and 3 feature films - 'Lola Casanova,' 'La Negra Angustias,' and 'Trotacalles.' Includes interviews with contemporary directors Marcela Fernandez - Violante and Maria Novarro. Produced by Patricia Diaz and Jane Ryder.
Fine Arts; History - World; Industrial and Technical Education; Sociology
Dist - WMEN

My Financial Career 7 MIN
16mm
Color
Animated version of the essay by Canadian humorist, Stephen Leacock, about a young man who is prospering and decides he should open a bank account, only to become over - awed and withdraw every penny he deposited.
Business and Economics; Guidance and Counseling; Literature and Drama; Psychology
Dist - SF **Prod** - NFBC 1962

My first activity video 50 MIN
VHS
My first activity video series
Color (K P)
$14.98 purchase _ #LV49554
Shows how to make pasta jewelry, shiny robot puppets, crazy wrapping paper and more. Features easy - to - understand demonstrations and an instruction card with a list of needed materials. Part of a four - part series based on best - selling activity books.
Fine Arts; Physical Education and Recreation
Dist - KNOWUN

My first activity video series
My first activity video 50 MIN
My first cooking video 50 MIN
My first nature video 50 MIN
My first science video 50 MIN
Dist - KNOWUN

My first cooking video 50 MIN
VHS
My first activity video series
Color (K P)
$14.98 purchase _ #LV49555
Shows children how to make simple, healthy and delicious food - including brad animals, pizza pizzas and more. Features easy - to - understand demonstrations and an instruction card with a list of needed materials. Part of a four - part series based on best - selling activity books.
Fine Arts; Home Economics; Physical Education and Recreation; Social Science
Dist - KNOWUN

My first nature video 50 MIN
VHS
My first activity video series
Color (K P)
$14.98 purchase _ #LV4955y
Shows how to build simple bird feeders, start a garden in a bottle and more. Features easy - to - understand demonstrations and an instruction card with a list of needed materials. Part of a four - part series based on best - selling activity books.
Agriculture; Science - Natural
Dist - KNOWUN

My first science video 50 MIN
VHS
My first activity video series
Color (K P)
$14.98 purchase _ #LV4955
Offers creative science projects that present the basics of light, sound, color, chemistry, magnetism and electricity. Features easy - to - understand demonstrations and an instruction card with a list of needed materials. Part of a four - part series based on best - selling activity books.
Science; Science - Physical
Dist - KNOWUN

My first skates 23 MIN
VHS
Color (K P I)
$19.95 purchase
Features professional skating instructor Leslie Heffron and Maximillian, the skating St Bernard. Teaches basic recreational skating skills and emphasizes having fun.
Physical Education and Recreation
Dist - INDPRO **Prod** - INDPRO 1991

My first time 28 MIN
VHS / 16mm
Color (H C G)
$550.00, $295.00 purchase, $55.00 rental
Breaks a taboo and asks a diverse group of Americans about their first experience of sex. Reveals that some are funny, some sad, some disappointing, some ecstatic. Provides new insights through reflections on sexual curiosity, anxiety over the act's aftermath, its exhilirating psychological effect and the retrospectively comic ignorance that often precedes the moment. Produced by Jessie Nelson.
Health and Safety; Psychology
Dist - FLMLIB

My Four Sons 5 MIN
16mm
Color
Presents Ross Allen's sons, of Silver Springs Reptile Land, who have followed in their father's footsteps and find excitement working with reptiles.
Geography - United States; Science - Natural
Dist - FLADC **Prod** - FLADC

My Friend Edi - Juvenile Diabetes
VHS / U-matic
Color (FRENCH)
Shows a young boy and his mother as they learn he has diabetes and try to cope with it.

Health and Safety
Dist - MIFE **Prod** - MIFE

My Friend Freddy 29 MIN
VHS / 16mm
Sonrisas Series
Color (T P) (SPANISH)
$46.00 rental _ #SRSS - 125
Shows how a little girl finds it difficult to let a wild bird go free after she has healed its wounds. In Spanish and English.
Sociology
Dist - PBS

My friend Ivan Lapshin 100 MIN
35mm / 16mm
Color; B&W (G) (RUSSIAN WITH ENGLISH SUBTITLES)
$250.00, $300.00 rental
Dramatizes one of the darkest periods in Soviet history in provincial Russia, 1935. Portrays a police investigator relentlessly and mercilessly pursues a gang of criminals, but in the process comes to realize the distance between the idealism of the revolutionaries and the grim, frightening reality of the Stalinist era. Directed by Alexei Gherman.
Fine Arts; History - World
Dist - KINOIC **Prod** - IFEX 1985

My Friend Joe 15 MIN
16mm
Color (J)
LC FIA65-1753
A study of multiple sclerosis, showing its effects on a young father of two children who is stricken. Describes the physical, emotional and financial problems which affect the entire family. Discusses what is being done to uncover the mystery of the disease, explaining that there is hope that the cause, prevention and cure will be found.
Health and Safety; Sociology
Dist - NMSS **Prod** - FLEMRP 1964

My Friend the Robin 10 MIN
U-matic / VHS / 16mm
Color (P)
Presents a young boy who tells in his own words his story of watching a pair of robins build a nest and raise a family.
Science - Natural
Dist - JOU **Prod** - JOU 1972

My Friend Wants to Die - Understanding Teenage Suicide 30 MIN
VHS
Color (J H)
Examines reasons for increase in teen suicide, and the underlying psychological and social factors contributing to the problem. Addresses problem of recongnizing warning signals, and tells what you can do to help.
Health and Safety; Sociology
Dist - HRMC **Prod** - HRMC 1986

My Friends Call Me Tony 12 MIN
16mm / U-matic / VHS
Color (I J)
LC 77-700231
Tells a story about a boy learning to cope with his blindness.
Guidance and Counseling; Psychology
Dist - MEDIAG **Prod** - NFBC 1975

My friends, my friends - alcohol and automobiles 22 MIN
VHS
Color (I J H C G)
$295.00 purchase, $60.00 rental
Tells the true story of three survivors - teens who killed people by drinking and driving. Reveals that all three have gone on trial - one is still in jail - and will be haunted by the pain of their acts for the rest of their lives. Each is obliged to tells his or her story over and over again to convey the horror of it to other youth.
Health and Safety; Sociology
Dist - CF **Prod** - CF 1990

My Friends, the Philodendrons 29 MIN
U-matic
House Botanist Series
Color
Answers common questions about philodendrons.
Agriculture; Science - Natural
Dist - UMITV **Prod** - UMITV 1978

My generation 60 MIN
VHS
History of rock 'n' roll series
Color (G)
$19.99 purchase _ #0 - 7907 - 2430 - 8NK
Experiences the counterculture, peace and love in the late 1960s. Features Santana, Jefferson Airplane and the Grateful Dead jamming live. Includes Janis Joplin and Jimi Hendrix, the Doors, Cream, Joni Mitchell, more of the Beatles and the Rolling Stones. Part of a ten - part series unfolding the history of rock music. May contain mature subject matter and explicit song lyrics.
Fine Arts
Dist - TILIED

My Girlfriend's Wedding 60 MIN
16mm
Color
Uses documentary footage to relate the fictional story of a girl who desperately wants to be modern. Explains how she wants to become involved in radical political causes.
Fine Arts; Guidance and Counseling; Sociology
Dist - NYFLMS **Prod** - NYFLMS 1970

My Government USA 10 MIN
16mm
Color (I J)
LC FIA67-1449
Discusses the relationship between city, state and federal governments. Reviews the responsibilities of each.
Civics and Political Systems; Psychology; Social Science
Dist - SF **Prod** - FINA 1966

My Grandpa Died Today 8 MIN
VHS / U-matic
Color
Deals with a young boy's relationship to his grandfather and how he responds to the death of this beloved family member. Uses the story and illustrations from the book of the same title.
Psychology; Sociology
Dist - PRIMED **Prod** - PRIMED

My grandparents had a hotel 30 MIN
VHS
Color (H C G)
$195.00 purchase, $55.00 rental
Recalls a family resort that flourished in the 1930s and 1940s in response to policies of many resorts which excluded Jews and other minorities. Uses home movies and reminiscences of guests and staff to recall the innocent pleasures of a gentler era at the Monteith Inn in Canada - the first job, the first summer away from home, first taste of romance. The hotel was destroyed by a fire in 1949 and rebuilt, but its memories survive.
History - World; Physical Education and Recreation; Sociology
Dist - FLMLIB

My grandson Lew 13 MIN
VHS / U-matic / 16mm
Color (K P I)
$270.00, $220.00, $190.00 purchase _ #A206
Portrays a young boy who misses his grandfather after he learns that he has died. Reveals that the boy and his mother share their memories of the old man, and this helps them both overcome the loneliness of being without him.
Guidance and Counseling; Literature and Drama; Sociology
Dist - BARR **Prod** - DONMAC 1976

My hair's falling out - am I still pretty 22 MIN
VHS / U-matic
Color; PAL (P I J)
$129.00 purchase
Combines live action, dance, animation and music to tell about two hospitalized children who are roommates living with the uncertainty of childhood cancer. Considers the story from the viewpoint of a physician who has had cancer as a child. Explains diagnostic tests and the effects of chemotherapy and hair loss. Supports the view that cancer does not discriminate and can be conquered.
Health and Safety
Dist - NEWGEN **Prod** - NEWGEN 1992

My Hands are the Tools of My Soul, Pt 1 27 MIN
U-matic / VHS / 16mm
Color
LC 77-702114
Shows American Indian artists at work and examines their carvings, pottery, song and dance in relation to their society.
Social Science
Dist - TEXFLM **Prod** - SWANN 1977

My Hands are the Tools of My Soul, Pt 2 27 MIN
U-matic / VHS / 16mm
Color
LC 77-702114
Shows American Indian artists at work and examines their carvings, pottery, song and dance in relation to their society.
Social Science
Dist - TEXFLM **Prod** - SWANN 1977

My Happiest Years - Unknown Chaplin 52 MIN
16mm / U-matic / VHS
Color (H C A)
Focuses on the comic shorts produced by Charlie Chaplin in 1916 and 1917, highlighting previously unseen outtakes and rushes. Narrated by James Mason.
Fine Arts; Industrial and Technical Education
Dist - MEDIAG **Prod** - THAMES 1983

My Hawaii 23 MIN
16mm
Color (A)
LC 80-701323
Showcases the tropical splendor of Hawaii, emphasizing the unspoiled beauty, serenity and adventures that await visitors to the islands.
Geography - United States
Dist - MILP **Prod** - MILP 1980

My Heart Attack 16 MIN
U-matic / Slide
Health Information Series
Color (C A)
LC 72-736647; 78-720423
Provides helpful information for the patient who is recovering from a myocardial infarction. Recounts story by a patient who had a heart attack over a year ago, and alerts viewers to problems he encountered during his recovery period as well as the practical aspects of adjustments necessary after a heart attack.
Health and Safety; Science - Natural
Dist - MEDCOM **Prod** - MEDCOM 1978

My Heart, Your Heart 60 MIN
VHS / U-matic
Color
Offers an informative look at heart attacks and heart disease and focuses on Jim Lehrer's personal heart attack experience, the symptoms, attack, surgery, treatment and continuing rehabilitation.
Health and Safety; Science - Natural; Sociology
Dist - PBS **Prod** - PBS

My heart, your heart
VHS
(G)
$275.00 purchase _ #K45171
Explains basic facts about heart disease and heart attacks. Follows story of heart attack, surgery, treatment and rehabilitation of MacNeill - Lehrer News Hour co - anchor Jim Lehrer.
Health and Safety
Dist - HTHED **Prod** - HTHED

My Heritage 27 MIN
16mm
Color (C A)
LC 74-702138
Describes the appreciation and use of natural and created teaching aids in the Head Start program on the Marshall Islands in Micronesia. Explains how the five senses are affected by the aids and how the senses are used creatively in the daily life and culture.
Education; Psychology; Science - Natural
Dist - CFOP **Prod** - USHHS 1973

My Hero Zero 4 MIN
U-matic / 35mm strip
Multiplication Rock Series
Color (P I)
LC 75-733957
Uses an original rock song illustrated by cartoon characters to demonstrate the use of the number zero.
Mathematics
Dist - GA **Prod** - ABCTV 1974

My home is Copacabana 48 MIN
16mm
B&W (G)
$75.00 rental
Studies the moral decline of four indigent Brazilian youngsters. Combines documentary footage with a hard - hitting story line.
Fine Arts; Geography - World; Sociology
Dist - KITPAR **Prod** - SUC 1965

My home, my prison 66 MIN
VHS / 16mm
Color (G) (ARABIC WITH ENGLISH SUBTITLES)
$90.00, $140.00 rental, $295.00 purchase
Documents the life of Palestinian peace activist and journalist, Raymonda Hawa Tawil, set against the backdrop of of the last fifty years of Israeli - Palestinian conflict. Interweaves documentary footage shot in Israel, the West Bank and Gaza Strip, archival footage and dramatized reenactments of scenes from Tawil's life. Directors, Erica Marcus and Susana Blaustein Munoz, are both Jewish women and activists for social justice.
Civics and Political Systems; Fine Arts; History - World
Dist - WMEN

My house 23 MIN
VHS
Bright sparks series
Color (P I)
$280.00 purchase
Looks at housing around the world. Examines building materials such as brick, glass, timber, earth, concrete and steel and structures built to withstand fire, earthquake and nuclear fallout. Part of a 12 - part animated series on science and technology.
Sociology
Dist - LANDMK **Prod** - LANDMK 1989

My Hug - A - Bear friend
VHS
Color (K P I)
Educates children with leukemia and their parents about the disease and about what to expect in treatment. Features an animated character, Hug - A - Bear, and Dr Samuel Gross.
Health and Safety
Dist - LEUSA **Prod** - LEUSA 1992

My husband hit me - a public service announcement 1 MIN
Videoreel / VT1
Color (G)
$150.00 purchase
Presents a 30 - second public service announcement for use by domestic violence projects. Delivers the message - My husband hit me. He said it was all my fault. I felt ashamed and scared. I needed someone to talk to....Finally I called the hotline and help is what I got.
Guidance and Counseling; Sociology
Dist - SELMED

My husband is going to kill me 60 MIN
VHS
Frontline series
Color; Captioned (G)
$59.95 purchase _ #FRON - 619K
Tells the story of how a Denver woman, Pamela Guenther, was murdered by her husband after she failed to find protection from friends, social workers, police or the courts. Suggests that the murder was the result of an overall failure to treat domestic abuse as a serious crime.
Guidance and Counseling; Sociology
Dist - PBS **Prod** - DOCCON 1988

My Husband Left Out on Us 23 MIN
16mm
Essential Elements of Interviewing Series
Color
LC 75-703836
Presents an interview situation in which an eligibility worker must determine whether desertion has actually occurred in the case of a mid - 30's woman with six children and a husband who has left them before for periods of time.
Guidance and Counseling; Sociology
Dist - USNAC **Prod** - USSRS 1975

My Husband Stopped Support Payments 22 MIN
16mm
Essential Elements of Interviewing Series
Color
LC 76-703713
Follows an interview by an intake worker of a woman with six children whose husband has deserted his family. Shows the responsibility of the Assistance Payments Administration and its clients in establishing eligibility for child support assistance.
Guidance and Counseling; Sociology
Dist - USNAC **Prod** - USSRS 1976

My idea of a good time 30 MIN
VHS
Called - the ministry of teaching series
Color (G A R)
$39.95 purchase, $10.00 rental _ #35 - 862 - 2076
Offers tips in classroom instruction for teachers. Includes study guide. Hosted by Sharon Lee. Produced by Seraphim.
Education; Religion and Philosophy
Dist - APH

My Interests 29 MIN
VHS / 16mm
Villa Alegre Series
Color (P T)
$46.00 rental _ #VILA - 136
Presents educational material in both Spanish and English.
Education; Psychology
Dist - PBS

My Jack London - a Daughter Remembers 25 MIN
VHS / U-matic
Color
Presents Jack London's daughter Becky tracing her celebrated father's life through personal remembrance, archival family photos and rare motion picture footage.
Biography; Literature and Drama
Dist - FOTH **Prod** - BELLG 1984

My Kind of place 24 MIN
VHS
Color (H C A)
$89.00 purchase _ #2044VG
Gives expert behind - the - scenes looks at infant and toddler care. Features parents talking about experiences in choosing child care and child care providers sharing the ingredients of quality child care. Includes a facilitator's guide and a brochure on choosing infant and toddler care.
Home Economics; Sociology
Dist - UNL

My Life 4 MIN
16mm
Color (I) (AMERICAN SIGN)
LC 76-701695
Presents Florian Caligiuri relating to the deaf in American sign language his personal experiences of what it was like to be a sick deaf boy in New York City, moving to the South and growing up in the depression years. He recounts his education at Gallaudet College and his work and career experiences as teacher and newspaperman.
Education; Guidance and Counseling; Psychology
Dist - JOYCE **Prod** - JOYCE 1975

My life as a bully 30 MIN
VHS
Color; PAL (I J H)
PdS29.50 purchase
Dramatizes a story about a bully named The Leader, and Booker, fed up with being bullied, who turns to books for guidance on how to deal with her situation. Emphasizes that no child deserves to be harassed and that a bully is a child to be pitied rather than feared. Shot in Grange Hill style at a school in East Sussex. Includes an education handbook on bullying. Produced by Firehorse.
Guidance and Counseling; Psychology
Dist - EMFVL

My life - east and west 60 MIN
VHS / BETA
Color; PAL (G)
PdS25 purchase
Features the Venerable Geshe Lhundrub Sopa who has been living in America since the mid 1960s and is a professor at the University of Wisconsin, Madison, where he has established a department of Tibetan and Buddhist studies. Answers questions concerning his early training in Tibet and the changes he has seen take place as Buddhism moves into a Western environment. Co - author of several books and translations of Buddhist philosophy texts, he is renowned for his deep understanding of the Madhyamika or Middle Way view of reality. Recorded at the Manjushri Centre, London. Interviewed by Geoff Jukes.
Fine Arts; Religion and Philosophy
Dist - MERIDT

My life in art 40 MIN
16mm
Color (G)
$40.00 rental
Offers a special package of films by Freude produced from 1968 through 1974. Includes Sacred Heart of Jesus, Promise Her Anything but Give Her the Kitchen Sink, Shooting Star, Stand Up and Be Counted, Adam's Birth, Sweet Dreams, Folly, Women and Children at Large and One and The Same. Please note - Sacred Heart of Jesus and Adam's Birth are available only in this package. The other films are available in package or separately.
Fine Arts; Sociology
Dist - CANCIN

My life in brief 45 MIN
VHS / BETA
Color; PAL (G)
PdS20 purchase
Features the former abbot of Drepung Monastery, the late Pema Gyaltsen Rinpoche, at the end of his eight - month visit to Great Britain. Recounts his life story, from his classical Buddhist education in Tibet, to his escape and subsequent responsibilities as the main spiritual teacher of Drepung. Recorded at the Lam Rim Centre, Wales. Translated by the Ven Geshe Namgyal Wangchen.
Fine Arts; Literature and Drama; Religion and Philosophy
Dist - MERIDT

My life, my times 11 MIN
16mm
Color (G)
$10.00 rental
Features a slide show from a lifetime of snapshots made by Lenny Lipton. Features family, girlfriends and big - city scenic eyesores. Music includes a Stephen Foster medley.
Biography; Fine Arts; Psychology; Sociology
Dist - CANCIN **Prod** - LIPTNL 1970

My life - Programme Five 26 MIN
VHS
My life series
Color; PAL (G)
PdS20 purchase
Presents a program focusing on a youth who has spent most of his life in foster care. Features former social worker and marriage counselor Colin Morris as moderator. Part of a six - part series talking with six very different young people about their most intimate and personal feelings. Contact distributor about availability outside the United Kingdom.
Guidance and Counseling; Sociology
Dist - ACADEM

My life - Programme Four 26 MIN
VHS
My life series
Color; PAL (G)
PdS20 purchase
Presents a program focusing on a young lesbian who has become pregnant. Features former social worker and marriage counselor Colin Morris as moderator. Part of a six - part series talking with six very different young people about their most intimate and personal feelings. Contact distributor about availability outside the United Kingdom.
Guidance and Counseling; Sociology
Dist - ACADEM

My life - Programme One 26 MIN
VHS
My life series
Color; PAL (G)
PdS20 purchase
Presents a program focusing on a 17 - year - old girl whose addiction to glue sniffing led to a suicide attempt. Features former social worker and marriage counselor Colin Morris as moderator. Part of a six - part series talking with six very different young people about their most intimate and personal feelings. Contact distributor about availability outside the United Kingdom.
Guidance and Counseling; Psychology; Sociology
Dist - ACADEM

My life - Programme Six 26 MIN
VHS
My life series
Color; PAL (G)
PdS20 purchase
Presents a program focusing on a young, unmarried mother. Features former social worker and marriage counselor Colin Morris as moderator. Part of a six - part series talking with six very different young people about their most intimate and personal feelings. Contact distributor about availability outside the United Kingdom.
Guidance and Counseling; Sociology
Dist - ACADEM

My life - Programme Three 26 MIN
VHS
My life series
Color; PAL (G)
PdS20 purchase
Presents a program focusing on a young anorexic who gives an articulate first - hand account of a disease which afflicts one percent of adolescent girls. Features former social worker and marriage counselor Colin Morris as moderator. Part of a six - part series talking with six very different young people about their most intimate and personal feelings. Contact distributor about availability outside the United Kingdom.
Guidance and Counseling; Sociology
Dist - ACADEM

My life - Programme Two 26 MIN
VHS
My life series
Color; PAL (G)
PdS20 purchase
Presents a program focusing on a black teenager from Brixton who tells how he is 'going straight' after a life of juvenile crime. Features former social worker and marriage counselor Colin Morris as moderator. Part of a six - part series talking with six very different young people about their most intimate and personal feelings. Contact distributor about availability outside the United Kingdom.
Guidance and Counseling; Sociology
Dist - ACADEM

My life series
Presents six 26 - minute programs focusing on six young people who reveal their most intimate and personal feelings to former social worker and marriage counselor Colin Morris. Includes a 17 - year - old girl whose addiction to glue sniffing led to a suicide attempt; a black teenager from Brixton who tells how he's 'going straight' after a life of juvenile crime; a young anorexic gives an articulate first - hand account of a disease which afflicts one percent of adolescent girls; a lesbian who has become pregnant; a teenager who has spent most of his life in care; and a young, unmarried mother. Contact distributor about availability outside the United Kingdom.
My life - Programme Five 26 MIN
My life - Programme Four 26 MIN
My life - Programme One 26 MIN
My life - Programme Six 26 MIN
My life - Programme Three 26 MIN
My life - Programme Two 26 MIN
Dist - ACADEM

My little island - 45
VHS
Reading rainbow series
Color; CC (K P)

$39.95 purchase
Tells about a little boy who takes his best friend to visit the Caribbean island where he was born, in the story by Frane Lessac. Visits the very same island, Montserrat, with LeVar, in the West Indies. As he tours the island, viewers experience the many colors and sights - including unique flowers and unusual fruits - pawpaws, mangoes and breadfruit. Part of a series offering a multicultural approach to generating reading enthusiasm with cross - curricular applications, hosted by LeVar Burton.
English Language; Geography - World; Literature and Drama
Dist - GPN **Prod** - LNMDP

My Little Margie
VHS / U-matic
Color
Features two episodes from the comdey TV series starring Gale Storm, Charles Farrell and Don Hayden.
Fine Arts; Sociology
Dist - IHF **Prod** - IHF

My Love, Flying Back from Europe, Disaster 11 MIN
VHS / U-matic
Color
Combines personal diaries with scripted fragments.
Fine Arts; Literature and Drama
Dist - KITCHN **Prod** - KITCHN

My Love has been Burning 84 MIN
16mm
B&W (JAPANESE (ENGLISH SUBTITLES))
Depicts the struggles of a 19th century feminist. Directed by Kenji Mizoguchi. With English subtitles.
Fine Arts; Foreign Language
Dist - NYFLMS **Prod** - UNKNWN 1949

My Main Man 14 MIN
U-matic / VHS / 16mm
Bloomin' Human Series
Color (P I)
LC 76-700386
Tells the story of a black father and son's struggle to relate to each other. Follows an argument they have and their eventual reconciliation.
Guidance and Counseling
Dist - MEDIAG **Prod** - PAULST 1975

My Majorca 17 MIN
16mm
Color
Presents a modest history of Majorca, one of the islands of the Balearics. Shows a native girl visiting relatives all over the island to whom she brings fish from the family catch.
Geography - World; Social Science
Dist - RADIM **Prod** - CHISH

My Man Godfrey 90 MIN
U-matic / VHS / 16mm
B&W
Presents the classic 1936 'screwball' comedy, starring Carole Lombard and William Powell, in which a hobo is hired by a daffy socialite to be a butler. Directed by Gregory La Cava.
Fine Arts
Dist - FI **Prod** - UPCI 1936
VIDIM

My Memories of Old Beijing 96 MIN
VHS
Color (G) (MANDARIN CHINESE)
$45.00 purchase _ #1030A
Presents a Mandarin Chinese language movie produced in the People's Republic of China.
Fine Arts; Geography - World; Literature and Drama
Dist - CHTSUI **Prod** - CHTSUI

My Michael
VHS
Color (A) (HEBREW WITH ENGLISH SUBTITLES)
$79.95 purchase _ #539
Portrays the marriage of Michael, a scientist, and Henna in Jerusalem in the late 1950s. Reveals that Henna is unfulfilled by her petit - bourgeois existence. Adapts the novel by Amos Oz. Stars Oded Kotler and Efrat Lavie. Directed by Dan Wolman. Recommended for mature audiences.
Fine Arts; History - World; Literature and Drama; Sociology
Dist - ERGOM **Prod** - ERGOM 1975

My mime 30 MIN
VHS
Color (G)
$40.00 purchase
Surveys the artist's work in pantomime as captured on film and video using experimental technologies. Includes shorts Walking Down Stairs and Balloonatics. Concludes with a demonstration of Pantomation, a machine - vision computer explicitly designed to integrate mime and dance with video and computer graphics.
Fine Arts
Dist - CANCIN **Prod** - DEWITT 1980

My Mind was a Chaos of Delight 52 MIN
U-matic / VHS / 16mm
Voyages of Charles Darwin Series
Color (H C A)
LC 80-700475
Describes the voyage of the HMS Beagle including a carnival in Salvador and a journey into the Brazilian rain forests. Recounts Charles Darwin's decision to pursue science and his first quarrel with Fitzroy.
Biography; Science; Science - Natural
Dist - TIMLIF **Prod** - BBCTV 1980

My Mom still loves me - video - and Good weather or not - book 20 MIN
VHS
Color (P I J)
$290.00 purchase
Helps children with a mentally ill parent cope with the situation. Includes the video My Mother Still Loves Me which tells the story of a puppet character Cat - a - lion who learns to deal with his feelings about his mother's illness and healthy ways he can cope, two copies of Good Weather or Not by Fred Rogers and a resource manual.
Health and Safety; Psychology; Sociology
Dist - TURCRV **Prod** - TURCRV

My Mom's Having a Baby 47 MIN
U-matic / VHS / 16mm
Teenage Years Series
Color
LC 77-702487
Presents Dr Lendon Smith explaining the events leading to pregnancy and birth to an anxious nine - year - old boy whose mother is pregnant.
Health and Safety; Sociology
Dist - TIMLIF **Prod** - DEPFRE 1977

My Mother is the most Beautiful Woman in the World 9 MIN
U-matic / VHS / 16mm
Color (P I)
LC FIA68-2109
Presents an Ukranian folk tale about Tanya, a lost little girl who cannot find her mother during the hustle and bustle of harvest time. Points out that her mother is the most beautiful woman in the world, if only in the eyes of her small daughter.
English Language; Literature and Drama
Dist - PHENIX **Prod** - BOSUST 1968

My Mother, My Daughter, My Self
VHS / BETA
Adult Years - Continuity and Change Series
Color
Presents grandmothers, mothers, and daughters from different ethnic backgrounds, who discuss themselves, each other, and their relationships. Explores the impact of community and ethnicity.
Psychology; Sociology
Dist - OHUTC **Prod** - OHUTC

My Mother, My Father
16mm
Color
Shows four different families, each faced with the need to provide care for a frail parent.
Sociology
Dist - TNF **Prod** - TNF

My mother, my father - seven years later 42 MIN
VHS
Color (G C)
$295.00 purchase, $55.00 rental
Visits a four - family group in a follow - up to consider the parents' needs and to look at ways the family members are dealing with their own needs as they grow older. Shows how caregiving is changing in the family and points out how family members deal with their future needs for care.
Health and Safety; Sociology
Dist - TNF **Prod** - TNF

My mother, the witch 24 MIN
U-matic / 16mm / VHS
Young people's specials series
Color (K)
$495.00, $349.00, $249.00 purchase _ #AD - 1533
Dramatizes the role of ignorance and intolerance during the Salem witch trials. Portrays Betsy who lives an ordinary life with her widowed mother until local children become convinced that a friend of Betsy's mother and then Betsy's mother are witches. As the two women are about to be burned at the stake, Betsy's mother turns the mob's ignorance into shame as she reveals the truth about the events that brought her under suspicion. Part of the Young People's Specials series.
Literature and Drama; Psychology; Religion and Philosophy; Sociology
Dist - FOTH **Prod** - FOTH

My mother thought she was Audrey Hepburn 20 MIN
VHS
Color (H C G)
$225.00 purchase, $50.00 rental
Offers a personal statement about growing up Asian - American in a white society. Reveals that Suzanne was brought up 'not to be Chinese' and her mother imitated Audrey Hepburn and Jackie Kennedy in dress. Produced by Sharon Jue.
History - United States; Sociology
Dist - FLMLIB

My Mother was Never a Kid 46 MIN
16mm / VHS / U-matic 30 MIN

Color; Captioned (J I H) (FRENCH)
LC 81-700001; 80-701633
Tells the story of a teenage girl at odds with her mother, until she travels back in time to see her mother's adolescence. Full version.
Foreign Language; Literature and Drama; Psychology
Dist - LCOA **Prod** - HGATE 1981

My mother's house in Albertville 11 MIN
16mm
B&W (G)
$20.00 rental
Explores new meaning of the extended family. Traces one family's history from 1951 to 1981 through the soundtrack.
Fine Arts
Dist - CANCIN **Prod** - FORTDE 1981

My Motor's Missing 3 MIN
16mm
Color (I) (AMERICAN SIGN)
LC 76-701696
Tells a humorous anecdote in American sign language of a hearing - impaired woman who misunderstands a gas attendant's message concerning her car. Signed for the deaf by Carolyn Larson.
Guidance and Counseling; Literature and Drama; Psychology
Dist - JOYCE **Prod** - JOYCE 1975

My, My Brooklyn U S A 20 MIN
16mm
Color
Presnets a tour of Brooklyn and its revived brownstone communities and other architectural highlights, such as a 17th century Dutch Reform Church, a neo Japanese house, and a Southern Colonial home.
Sociology
Dist - BUGAS **Prod** - BUGAS

My Name is Abbie, Orphan of America 28 MIN
U-matic / VHS / 16mm
Color
Presents Abbie Hoffman recounting his involvement in the civil rights movement, how he became a Yippie and an organizer and speaker at many anti - Vietnam War demonstrations, the famous Chicago Seven trial, why the movement fell apart, his drug arrest, his eventual flight and underground life.
Biography; Civics and Political Systems; History - United States; Sociology
Dist - ICARUS **Prod** - ICARUS 1981

My Name is David - and I'm an Alcoholic 24 MIN
U-matic / VHS / 16mm
Color (J)
LC 78-700641
Follows the progress of a middle - aged alcoholic who agrees to counseling and group therapy after being threatened with dismissal from his job. Explains the physiological facts of alcoholism and reasons for excessive drinking.
Health and Safety; Psychology; Sociology
Dist - AIMS **Prod** - GORKER 1977

My name is Ivan - Ivan's childhood 84 MIN
16mm / 35mm
B&W (G) (RUSSIAN WITH ENGLISH SUBTITLES)
$250.00, $300.00 rental
Presents the first film of director Andrei Tarkovsky. Tells of a 12 - year - old Russian boy during World War II.
Fine Arts; History - World; Sociology
Dist - KINOIC **Prod** - CORINT 1962

My Name is Oona 10 MIN
16mm
Color
Presents an experimental film by Gunvor Nelson.
Fine Arts; Industrial and Technical Education
Dist - CANCIN **Prod** - CANCIN 1969

My Name is Oona 10 MIN
16mm
B&W (C)
$242.00
Experimental film by Gunvor Nelson.
Fine Arts
Dist - AFA **Prod** - AFA

My name is Stanley Newman 6 MIN
VHS
Color (G C)
$135.00 purchase, $40.00 rental
Stimulates discussion of the end of life and its meaning for elders whose friends are gone and who feel they have no purpose in living longer. Presents the views of one man who feels he has lived long enough.
Health and Safety
Dist - TNF

My Name is Susan Yee 12 MIN
U-matic / VHS / 16mm
Color (P I)
LC 77-703011
Features a young Chinese - Canadian schoolgirl describing her life in Montreal in order to provide a glimpse of the life of someone in another area and in different circumstances.
Geography - World; Social Science; Sociology
Dist - MEDIAG **Prod** - NFBC 1977

My Neighbor and Me 15 MIN
U-matic / VHS
Neighborhoods Series
Color (P)
Discusses the characteristics of neighborhoods.
Sociology
Dist - GPN **Prod** - NEITV 1981

My Neighborhood 30 MIN
VHS / U-matic
Color
Portrays M, who claims to be friendly with everybody in his neighborhood. Shifts from humor to pathos.
Fine Arts
Dist - KITCHN **Prod** - KITCHN

My new body - boys
VHS
Color (I J T A PRO)
$79.50 purchase _ #AH46343
Deals with the physical and emotional changes of puberty.
Health and Safety; Science - Natural
Dist - HTHED **Prod** - HTHED

My new body - girls
VHS
Color (I J T A PRO)
$79.50 purchase _ #AH46344
Deals with the physical and emotional changes of puberty.
Health and Safety; Science - Natural
Dist - HTHED **Prod** - HTHED

My new film 5 MIN
16mm
B&W (A)
$10.00 rental
Investigates the 'hysteria' of hysterical writing; an overwrought text dealing with explicit sexuality and politics scrolls throughout after an abnormally long leader.
Fine Arts; Psychology
Dist - CANCIN **Prod** - SONDHE 1991

My New Home 14 MIN
U-matic / VHS
Under the Yellow Balloon Series
Color (P)
Shows that while in Greenfield Village, Thomas and Anita see the daily life of long ago.
Geography - United States
Dist - AITECH **Prod** - SCETV 1980

My Niagara 40 MIN
VHS / 16mm
Color (G)
$90.00,$125.00 rental, $295.00 purchase
Probes the emotional undercurrents of a third - generation Japanese woman. Looks at her life, after her mother's death, with her father, which is marked by painful, turbulent exchanges. Follows her finding refuge at work and meeting a young Korean man. Ends with ambivalence; together they find no easy resolutions. By Helen Lee. Made in the US and Canada.
Fine Arts; Sociology
Dist - WMEN

My old man 102 MIN
VHS
Color (H C)
$97.00 purchase _ #04459 - 126
Presents an expanded version of the short story by Ernest Hemingway about racetrack people.
Literature and Drama
Dist - GA **Prod** - GA

My papa - Moj papiez 84 MIN
VHS
Color (G A) (POLISH)
$19.95 purchase _ #V121
Features Adam Bujak, a photographer of Pope John Paul II, who recollects his work in Krakow and the Vatican. Presents over 250 photos which make up an interesting biography of Karol Wojtyla.
Fine Arts; History - World; Religion and Philosophy
Dist - POLART

My Parents are Getting a Divorce 26 MIN
VHS
Color (J H)
Looks at divorce in today's society and some of the reasons behind the high divorce rate. Helps your students confront the problems teenagers and other family members may encounter when divorce seems imminent.
Guidance and Counseling; Health and Safety; Sociology
Dist - HRMC **Prod** - HRMC 1976

My Parrot, Brewster 17 MIN
16mm / U-matic / VHS
Color (P I)
LC 80-700742
Tells the story of Dennis, who carelessly leaves his parrot Brewster's cage unlocked, allowing the pet to wander off. Describes how Dennis, during his search for Brewster, remembers the special qualities and needs of his pet and his responsibility to the animal.
Guidance and Counseling; Science - Natural
Dist - HIGGIN **Prod** - HIGGIN 1980

My Partner, Officer Smokey 17 MIN
16mm
Six to Remember Series
Color
LC 74-700853
Shows how a policeman and his partner, a German shepherd named Smokey, work together in patrolling streets and neighborhoods in Washington, DC.
Civics and Political Systems; Geography - United States; Social Science
Dist - AMEDFL **Prod** - AMEDFL 1973

My People are My Home 45 MIN
16mm
Color (C A)
LC 79-700919
Deals with the political and poetic odyssey of writer Meridel Le Sueur, spokeswoman for workers, the unemployed, women and American Indians.
Biography; Literature and Drama
Dist - SERIUS **Prod** - SERIUS 1977

My Perfect Child is Deaf 30 MIN
U-matic / VHS / 16mm
Children and Deafness Series
Color (C A)
Explores family reactions to the diagnosis, that lead to eventual acceptance.
Education; Guidance and Counseling
Dist - PFP **Prod** - YASNYP

My Pet Pelican 11 MIN
16mm
Nature Guide Film Series
Color (K P)
Presents the story of Snapper, a lame pelican and his home with a young girl. Explains that Snapper quickly adapts himself to this new life as the two become good friends and that Kelley's interest in her pet leads her to the world books where she finds many stories about pelicans and other interesting birds.
Science - Natural
Dist - AVEXP **Prod** - AVEXP

My Pop's a Lineman 16 MIN
16mm / U-matic / VHS
Color (P I J H)
LC FIA65-369
Shows a lineman who sees his son trying to retrieve a kite tangled in a high voltage line and takes the boy to work with him. Dramatizes several dangerous situations involving high tension wires. Includes flashbacks to a high - voltage demonstration by H C Potthast.
Health and Safety; Social Science
Dist - IFB **Prod** - STSC 1957

My Robot Buddy and My Trip to Alpha I 14 MIN
U-matic / VHS
Readit Series
Color (P I)
LC 83-706835
Presents two stories about a young boy and his robot buddy. Explains in the first story that the boy asks for a robot for his tenth birthday so he will have someone to play with, while in the second story the boy finds that interplanetary travel is not without dangers. Based on the books My Robot Buddy and My Trip To Alpha I by Alfred Slote.
English Language; Literature and Drama
Dist - AITECH **Prod** - POSIMP 1982

My Russian friends 58 MIN
VHS
Color (H C G T A)
$85.00 purchase, $40.00 rental
Features film maker and producer Steven Schecter and his Soviet friends in a personal look at the changes taking place in the Soviet Union in the late 1980s. Reveals that Soviets feel cautiously hopeful and excited about the changes. Deals with political, ideological, religious, and even "new age" issues.
Civics and Political Systems; Geography - World; Sociology
Dist - EFVP

My self esteem 18 MIN
VHS
Color (P I J) (SPANISH)
$295.00 purchase
Portrays 11 - year - old Molly Kramer who doesn't think much of herself. Reveals that suddenly her self - esteem comes to life - a mirror image of Molly who looks as bad as Molly feels. Molly's alter ego teaches her important techniques for developing self - esteem - liking oneself, respectful communicating and developing individual expertise.
Health and Safety; Psychology
Dist - PFP **Prod** - ARMPIC

My Side of the Mountain 38 MIN
VHS
Color
$69.95 purchase _ #4018
Intents on imitating Thoreau and learning about nature firsthand, thirteen year old Sam Gribley sets out on a once in a lifetime adventure in the wilderness.
Literature and Drama
Dist - AIMS **Prod** - AIMS

My Side of the Mountain 38 MIN
16mm / U-matic / VHS
Color (I J)
Tells the story of a boy's life alone in the wilderness and his Thoreau - like reactions to that experience. Based on the book My Side Of The Mountain by Jean George.
Literature and Drama
Dist - AIMS **Prod** - PAR 1979

My side of the mountain 100 MIN
VHS
Color (J H C)
$39.00 purchase _ #03923 - 126
Presents an adventure story about a young boy who leaves home for the challenge of wilderness living.
Literature and Drama
Dist - GA **Prod** - GA

My Side of the Mountain 100 MIN
U-matic / VHS / 16mm
Color
Tells the story of a 12 - year - old boy who sets out to live by himself in the Canadian wilderness.
Fine Arts
Dist - FI **Prod** - PAR 1969

My Son, Kevin 24 MIN
U-matic / VHS / 16mm
Color (H C A)
LC 75-700651
Shows the daily activities at home, play and school, of an 11 - year - old English boy who was born without arms or legs as a result of his mother's use of the drug thalidomide. Emphasizes the need for knowledge, hope and dignity in relating to the handicapped.
Guidance and Counseling; Health and Safety; Psychology; Science - Natural; Sociology
Dist - WOMBAT **Prod** - GRATV 1975

My son, my son 14 MIN
VHS
Color (H C G A R)
$59.95 purchase, $10.00 rental _ #35 - 87156 - 460
Tells the story of two fathers and their sons. Stresses the importance of maintaining respect and love for one another regardless of differences. Touches on issues suurounding AIDS and homosexuality.
Health and Safety; Sociology
Dist - APH **Prod** - FRACOC

My Son the Artist 29 MIN
Videoreel / VT2
Museum Open House Series
Color
Fine Arts
Dist - PBS **Prod** - WGBHTV

My Son, the Merchandise Manager 9 MIN
16mm
Color
Presents Elaine May and Mike Nichols who illustrate a brand new approach to merchandising a new product.
Business and Economics; Psychology
Dist - CCNY **Prod** - TALON

My Son the Vampire 75 MIN
16mm / U-matic / VHS
B&W (J)
Stars Bela Lugosi as the vampire who came to England to complete experiments in his mad bid to gain control of the world.
Fine Arts; Literature and Drama
Dist - FI **Prod** - UNKNWN 1952

My soul proclaims 60 MIN
VHS
Color (R)
$29.95 purchase _ #609 - 3
Examines the historical and contemporary contributions of Catholic women in the Church and in society. Includes discussion guide.
Religion and Philosophy; Sociology
Dist - USCC **Prod** - USCC

My special world 24 MIN
U-matic / VHS
Young people's specials series
Color
Features life of child television star Adam Rich. Explores behind the scenes of the television production.
Biography; Fine Arts
Dist - MULTPP **Prod** - MULTPP

My sweet little village 100 MIN
VHS / 35mm / 16mm
Films by Jiri Menzel series
Color (G) (CZECH WITH ENGLISH SUBTITLES)
$250.00, $300.00 rental
Unravels the story of an irascible truckdriver and his bumbling assistant who is in danger of losing his ancestral home to scheming bureacrats. Directed by Jiri Monzel.
Fine Arts
Dist - KINOIC

My Three Year Old 3 MIN
16mm
Color (I) (AMERICAN SIGN)
LC 76-701697
Presents Sharon L Tate relating in American sign language for the deaf her personal experiences as a deaf mother traveling across the United States with her 3 - year - old child.
Education; Guidance and Counseling; Sociology
Dist - JOYCE **Prod** - JOYCE 1975

My town - Mio paese 26 MIN
VHS
Color (J)
$195.00 purchase, $40.00 rental _ #37735
Demonstrates the strength and vitality of Italian - American traditions by showing the ongoing cultural similarities between residents of Palermiti in southern Italy, and the descendents of immigrants from Palmiti living in eastern Massachussetts. Shows the emotion - filled retelling of the Palermiti patron saint's legendary miracles by three generations of Italians and Italian - Americans. Produced by Katherine Gulla.
Geography - United States; History - United States; History - World; Religion and Philosophy; Sociology
Dist - UCEMC

My Turtle Died Today 8 MIN
U-matic / VHS / 16mm
Color (P I)
LC FIA68-2110
Tells a story about a boy whose pet turtle died and who later discovered that a pet cat had given birth to a litter of kittens. Designed to stimulate discussion on the inevitability of death and the continuity of life.
English Language; Guidance and Counseling; Literature and Drama; Psychology
Dist - PHENIX **Prod** - BOSUST 1968

My Twenty Pennies 14 MIN
U-matic / VHS
Stepping into Rhythm Series
Color (P)
Introduces the eighth note as a beat and teaches a song with Spanish words in it.
Fine Arts
Dist - AITECH **Prod** - WVIZTV

My Version of the Fall 8 MIN
16mm
Color (A)
Presents a hand colored silent experimental film by Diana Barrie where nothing remains fixed or permanent. Landscape, sky, clothes change colors and the film itself changes direction at mid - point and runs backwards.
Fine Arts
Dist - STARRC **Prod** - STARRC 1978

My very own book about me 20 MIN
VHS
Color (K P I)
$24.95 purchase _ #200
Demonstrates simple and effective techniques for teaching safety skills to young children. Guides students through the different kinds of touches. Includes an open and honest discussion about sexual abuse.
Health and Safety; Sociology
Dist - ACTFKI **Prod** - ACTFKI

My war years - Arnold Schoenberg 83 MIN
16mm / VHS
Color (H C G)
$1200.00, $275.00 purchase, $90.00 rental
Centers on the controversial composer and the explosive years, 1906 to 1923, when Schoenberg transformed the language of music itself. Looks at his poverty and isolation, then at his concerts which resulted in riots, fist - fights and challenges to duels, and to the declaration that Schoenberg composed some of the greatest music of all time. Archival footage and 're - enacted' home movies, combined with Vienna and the Austrian countryside, are interwoven to reveal that so composer has been at once more despised, revered and ultimately more influential. Produced with ZDF - German television.
Fine Arts
Dist - CANCIN **Prod** - RHOMBS 1993

My Way home 79 MIN
16mm / VHS
Miklos Jansco series
B&W (G) (HUNGARIAN WITH ENGLISH SUBTITLES)
$175.00 rental
Portrays a schoolboy captured by Russians in 1945 Hungary who slowly develops a warm friendship with a young soldier. Directed by Miklos Jansco.
Fine Arts; History - World
Dist - KINOIC

My way Sally - learning to be a leader
VHS
Key concepts in self - esteem
Color (K P)
$79.95 purchase _ #MF9352RA
Presents one of an 11 - part series teaching key curriculum concepts such as independence, freedom and responsibility, and peer pressure. Includes video, storybook and teaching guide with activities and games. In this video, a foxhound puppy learns that you have to be clever to be a leader, but you also have to study, practice, and work hard to gain the respect of others.
Education; Psychology
Dist - CFKRCM **Prod** - CFKRCM

My way to Islam - a personal story
VHS
Color (G)
$15.00 purchase _ #110 - 036
Features Rafael Narbaez, Greg Noakes and Imam Al - Amin Abdul Lateef who share their individual quests for the Truth.
Religion and Philosophy
Dist - SOUVIS **Prod** - SOUVIS

My Wife's Relations 23 MIN
16mm
B&W (J)
Stars Buster Keaton.
Fine Arts
Dist - TWYMAN **Prod** - MGM 1922

My Wise Daddy 4 MIN
16mm
B&W (I)
Presents a happy family with a couple of children, who are well looked after with love and affection from the parents.
Guidance and Counseling; Sociology
Dist - NEDINF **Prod** - INDIA

My World 20 MIN
U-matic / VHS
Readers' Cube Series
Color (I)
Presents dramatizations of literary works that deal with the community and how it influences the lives of its people.
English Language; Literature and Drama
Dist - AITECH **Prod** - MDDE 1977

My World, My Choice 20 MIN
U-matic / VHS / 16mm
Color (H C)
LC 84-706799
Describes the misguided decisions and events that lead a young man to the death sentence and serves as both an example and a warning for today's youth on the edge of trouble.
Guidance and Counseling; Sociology
Dist - PHENIX **Prod** - WECARP 1984

My world stories
VHS
Color; PAL (K P)
PdS20 purchase
Presents a ten - part series of programs from 7 - 9 minutes each adapted from the popular Little Yellow Van Series. Features youngsters on screen who tell the stories while printed scripts in the classroom encourage small groups of children to read the stories for themselves. Contact distributor about availability outside the United Kingdom and individual titles in the series.
Education; English Language; Literature and Drama
Dist - ACADEM

My world summer in the countryside 80 MIN
VHS
Color; PAL (K P)
PdS20 purchase
Presents a series of eight 10 - minute programs to accompany summer field - trip projects. Visits a farm in the Yorkshire Dales, a fishing village, a country veterinarian's practice, an exotic garden and more. Includes a curriculum of follow - up activities. Gives children an increased awareness of the world around them. Contact distributor about availability outside the United Kingdom.
Education; Geography - World; Sociology
Dist - ACADEM

My world - water 11 MIN
VHS
Color (K P)
$49.95 purchase _ #Q10730; LC 74-702244
Explores the wonders of water - its origins, its uses, and its pleasures. Points out the social implications of using and wasting water and the importance of water conservation.
Science - Natural; Sociology
Dist - CF

My Yiddish Momme McCoy 20 MIN
VHS
Color (G)
$195.00 purchase, $40.00 rental
Focuses on the filmmaker's spirited 90 - year - old grandmother, Belle Demner McCoy. Paints an intimate portrait of one woman's struggle with the conflicts between family, religion and love. Period photos and Yiddish and American songs sung by Belle herself help to see her attempt to reconcile tradition with assimilation. Directed by Bob Giges.
Fine Arts; Religion and Philosophy; Sociology
Dist - CNEMAG

Myasthenia Gravis 52 MIN
U-matic
Intensive Course in Neuromuscular Diseases Series
Color (PRO)
LC 76-706058
Presents a lecture by Dr John R Warmolts on myasthenia gravis.
Health and Safety; Science - Natural
Dist - USNAC **Prod** - NINDIS 1974

Myasthenia Gravis, Diagnosis and Treatment by Thymectomy 27 MIN
16mm
Color (PRO)
Shows a young woman with the characteristic findings of myasthenia gravis, weakness of the facial, pharyngeal and respiratory muscles. Demonstrates the technique of operation and the course of a specific patient.
Health and Safety; Science
Dist - ACY **Prod** - ACYDGD 1958

Mycological Slide Culture Technique 7 MIN
16mm
Color
LC FIE67-48
Demonstrates a method of growing fungi on microscope cover slips to preserve mycelia and spores intact.
Science; Science - Natural
Dist - USNAC **Prod** - USPHS 1965

Myelination of the Central Nervous System or Myelogenesis 60 MIN
U-matic
Nonbehavioral Sciences and Rehabilitation Series Part III
Color (PRO)
Discusses structures of the spinal cord and brain stem where myelination begins in the fourth to fifth month in utero. Outlines critical periods of myelination of certain nuclei, fiber tracts and nerves during fetal development and postnatal life. Uses parts of the central nervous system as examples.
Psychology; Science - Natural
Dist - AOTA **Prod** - AOTA 1980

Myles Horton - Adventures of a Radical Hillbilly, Pt 1 60 MIN
U-matic / VHS
Color
Presents an interview with Myles Horton, lifelong crusader for the rights of the poor and the weak.
Biography; Sociology
Dist - PBS **Prod** - WNETTV 1981

Myles Horton - Adventures of a Radical Hillbilly, Pt 2 60 MIN
U-matic / VHS
Color
Presents an interview with Myles Horton, lifelong crusader for the rights of the poor and the weak.
Biography; Sociology
Dist - PBS **Prod** - WNETTV 1981

Myocardial Infarction 94 MIN
U-matic / VHS
Electrocardiogram Series

Color (PRO)
Stresses the importance of the ECG diagnosis of myocardial infarction and emphasizes need for sequential and comparison ECGs.
Health and Safety; Science; Science - Natural
Dist - HSCIC **Prod** - HSCIC 1982

Myocardial Infarction 13 MIN
VHS / U-matic
Color (PRO)
Describes the usual clinical course of a patient with a myocardial infarction. Explains signs, symptoms and how the disease will affect life - style.
Health and Safety; Science - Natural
Dist - MEDFAC **Prod** - MEDFAC 1974

The Myocardial Infarction Patient 24 MIN
U-matic / VHS
Simulated Home Visits Series
Color
Presents a simulated home visit of nurse to a client recovering from a myocardial infarction. Discusses effects of patient's pathology, diet, medications, exercise, stress and other factors.
Health and Safety
Dist - AJN **Prod** - UTEXN

Myocardial perfusion imaging 7 MIN
VHS
Color (C PRO G)
$250.00 purchase
Helps prepare the patient by explaining the procedure and allaying the fears related to injection of radioactive compounds.
Health and Safety
Dist - LPRO **Prod** - LPRO

Myocardial Revascularization for Coronary Artery Disease 34 MIN
16mm
Color (PRO)
Illustrates diagnostic coronary arteriography as developed by Dr Sones at the Cleveland clinic. Illustrates the operative procedures which indicate implantation of the internal mammary artery, direct coronary endarterectomy and implantation of the splenic artery.
Health and Safety; Science
Dist - ACY **Prod** - ACYDGD 1967

Myocardial Revascularization - Vineberg Procedure 20 MIN
16mm
Upjohn Vanguard of Medicine Series
Color
LC FIA67-507
Explains a surgical procedure for rehabilitation of cardiac invalids. Includes highlights of actual surgery and utilizes three - dimensional animation to explain why no hematoma occurs, offers before - and - after cine coronary arteriography to prove it works. Summarizes clinical results achieved, and lists indications and contraindications for this procedure.
Health and Safety
Dist - UPJOHN **Prod** - UPJOHN 1966

Myopia 30 MIN
VHS
Doc Martin's casebook series
Color; PAL (G)
PdS40 purchase; Available only in the United Kingdom and Ireland
Presents the case of David, a firefighter who is in danger of losing his job due to failing eyesight. Examines the option of laser surgery for myopia and its risks and benefits. Dr. Martin Hughes narrates. Part eight of an eight - part series.
Health and Safety; Science - Natural
Dist - BBCENE

Myra 3 MIN
16mm / U-matic / VHS
Color (P I)
LC 80-701655
Uses animation to describe a little girl who disrupts her dancing class by turning into the animals the other children are imitating. Based on the children's story Myra by Barbara Bottner.
Fine Arts; Literature and Drama
Dist - CF **Prod** - BOSUST 1980

Myriads of Lights 122 MIN
VHS
Color (G) (MANDARIN CHINESE (ENGLISH SUBTITLES))
$45.00 purchase _ #6002A
Presents a Mandarin Chinese language movie produced in the People's Republic of China.
Fine Arts; Geography - World; Literature and Drama
Dist - CHTSUI **Prod** - CHTSUI

Myriam's gaze - la mirada de Myriam 28 MIN
U-matic / 16mm / VHS
Color (G) (SPANISH (ENGLISH SUBTITLES))
$225.00 purchase, $75.00 rental
Portrays Myriam, a single mother, who is building a life as a squatter on the outskirts of Bogota, Colombia. Uses drama to recreate her childhood memories of poverty, abuse and her conviction that she had the 'evil eye.' Reveals that today she has become a community leader and a teacher in the school she helped to build. Directed by Clara Riascos.
History - World; Sociology
Dist - WMEN **Prod** - CINMUJ 1987

Myringoplasty 15 MIN
16mm
Color (PRO)
Shows the repair of a perforated ear drum by the use of ear canal skin.
Health and Safety
Dist - EAR **Prod** - EAR

Myself, Yourself 30 MIN
16mm
Color
LC 81-700663
Presents three adults and two teenagers discussing growing up. Reveals how social attitudes affected their outlook on life.
Psychology
Dist - MOBIUS **Prod** - JENF 1981

Mysore 17 MIN
16mm
Color (I)
Presents the mysore state with its physical features, natural resources, economic developments and places of historic importance. Highlights the colorful Dasserah Festival.
Geography - World; History - World
Dist - NEDINF **Prod** - INDIA

The Mysteries of Harris Burdick
VHS
Color (P)
$45.00 purchase
Relates how Harris Burdick illustrated and wrote fourteen stories. Provides clues and visuals to help decipher the only remains of his work, foourteen black - and - white captioned illustrations. By Chris Van Allsburg.
English Language; Literature and Drama
Dist - PELLER

Mysteries of Mankind 59 MIN
VHS / U-matic
Color (G)
$79.95 purchase _ #51339
Follows famous scientists as they probe the past and search for fossils.
History - World; Science; Science - Physical
Dist - NGS

The Mysteries of motion and power - Video 10 47 MIN
VHS
Physical science - secrets of science series
Color (I J H C)
$49.95 purchase
Presents two parts in two segments each, looking at the science of motion, the three laws of Newton that govern the motion of all bodies, electricity and how it is produced and the forces that produce movement. Includes Considering Kinematics and Newton's Laws in Part I, Electricity - a Current Affair and The Physics of Force in Part II. Hosted by Discover Magazine Editor in Chief Paul Hoffman. First of four parts on physical science.
Science - Physical
Dist - EFVP **Prod** - DSCOVM 1994

Mysteries of Natrium and Chlorine 20 MIN
16mm
Color
Describes the use of natrium and chlorine which are as powerful as poisons, to help students correctly realize the idea of substance and chemical reaction.
Science - Physical
Dist - UNIJAP **Prod** - IWANMI 1969

Mysteries of Peru series
Presents two parts on Peruvian civilization. Includes the titles Nazca Lines and Enigma of the Ruins.
Enigma of the ruins 60 MIN
Nazca lines 60 MIN
Dist - INSTRU

Mysteries of the Deep 24 MIN
16mm / U-matic / VHS
Color (I J H) (FRENCH AFRIKAANS GERMAN DUTCH GREEK SWEDISH)
Explores the lower depths of the sea. Highlights the evolution of life and the struggle for survival.
Foreign Language; Science - Natural
Dist - CORF **Prod** - DISNEY 1961

Mysteries of the Great Pyramid 50 MIN
16mm / U-matic / VHS
Color (H C A)
LC 77-703349
Focuses on the Great Pyramid of Egypt. Uses maps and drawings to describe the beginnings of the ancient Egyptian culture and moves on to the conflicting theories of experts from various disciplines, who discuss why and how such an engineering feat was accomplished.
Geography - World; History - World; Sociology
Dist - FI **Prod** - WOLPER 1977

Mysteries of the Hidden Reefs 22 MIN
U-matic / VHS / 16mm
Undersea World of Jacques Cousteau Series
Color (G)
$5995 purchase - 16 mm (entire series), $1895 purchase - video
Examines interdependency, protective mechanisms, and adaptation of the life forms on a reef.
Science - Natural; Science - Physical
Dist - CF

Mysteries of the hidden reefs 23 MIN
16mm / U-matic / VHS
Undersea world of Jacques Cousteau series
Color (G)
$49.95 purchase _ #Q10629; LC 78-701096
A shortened version of The Mysteries Of The Hidden Reef. Features Jacques Cousteau as he explores the interdependency, adaptation, protective mechanisms and symbiotic relationships of the multitude of life in a reef both day and night.
Science - Natural
Dist - CF **Prod** - METROM 1977

Mysteries of the Mind 59 MIN
U-matic / VHS / 16mm
Color
LC 80-700265
Examines the brain's structures in an attempt to unravel some of its mysteries. Uses an artist's sculpture to show the brain's chemical and electrical processes while computer graphics relate human behavior and blood flow to particular parts of the brain. Documents feats of mind control.
Psychology; Science - Natural
Dist - NGS **Prod** - NGS 1980

Mysteries of the Mind 58 MIN
U-matic / VHS
Color (G)
$279.00, $179.00 purchase _ #AD - 2029
Presents a Lifequest special which explores manic - depression, obsessive - compulsive disorder, alcoholism and other mood disorders whose victims show a lack of control over their behavior and their lives. Examines the neuro - chemical and genetic components in these disorders. Shows some of the latest physiological, neurological and biomedical research into the mysteries of the brain.
Health and Safety; Psychology; Science - Natural; Sociology
Dist - FOTH **Prod** - FOTH

Mysteries of the pyramids 60 MIN
VHS
Color (J H C G)
$19.95 purchase _ #WK223V, #EK017
Looks into the secret passageways and chambers of the Great Pyramids of Egypt and discusses their history. Features Omar Sharif.
History - World
Dist - CAMV
SIV

Mysteries of the sphinx 95 MIN
VHS
Color (G)
$29.95 purchase _ #P48
Reveals new compelling evidence that the Sphinx is at least 10,000 years old. Explores the legends of Atlantis, the hidden room in the Sphinx, how the 200 ton blocks were lifted into place, the extraterrestrial Sphinx on Mars and Edgar Cayce predictions. Narrated by Charlton Heston.
Fine Arts; History - World; Religion and Philosophy
Dist - HP

Mysteries of Villacabamba 30 MIN
VHS
Color (G C)
$195.00 purchase, $55.00 rental
Focuses on the community life and serene activity of older people of Villacabamba, Guatemala where many live into their 100s. Looks at characteristics that may contribute to long life.
Health and Safety
Dist - TNF

Mysteries revealed - basic research skills 17 MIN
VHS
Color (I J)
$95.00 purchase _ #10336VG
Demonstrates the use of research materials in the library to find information on the mysterious disappearance of the Anasazi Indians of the Southwest. Focuses on library computer catalog systems; card catalogs; Reader's Guide to Periodical Literature; and data bases. Comes with a teacher's guide, student activities, discussion questions, and blackline masters.

Education; History - World; Science
Dist - UNL

The Mysterious Bee 50 MIN
U-matic / VHS / 16mm
Color (H C A)
Travels inside a beehive and shows the queen laying eggs, the worker bees air - conditioning the hive by fanning their wings and others preparing to gather pollen and nectar.
Science - Natural
Dist - FI **Prod** - FI 1981

The Mysterious black - footed ferret 60 MIN
VHS
National Audubon Society specials series
Color; Captioned (G)
$49.95 purchase _ #NTAS - 102
Describes efforts to breed black - footed ferrets in captivity to preserve their existence. Shows that the ferrets were thought extinct until a colony of them were discovered in Wyoming in 1981. Includes rare footage of the ferrets in the wild. Also produced by Turner Broadcasting and WETA - TV. Narrated by actress Loretta Swit.
Science - Natural
Dist - PBS **Prod** - NAS 1988

The Mysterious Fact - Critical Reading and Thinking 9 MIN
U-matic
Alexander Hawkshaw's Language Arts Skills Series
Color (I J)
Tells how Alexander Hawkshaw utilizes critical reading and thinking skills to solve a school vandalism problem.
English Language
Dist - GA **Prod** - LUMIN

The Mysterious Fruit Tree 20 MIN
VHS
Gentle Giant Series
Color (H)
LC 90712920
Uses story to teach children certain universal truths and morals. The 15th of 16 installments in The Gentle Giant Series, which takes stories from cultures throughout the world.
Health and Safety; Literature and Drama; Psychology
Dist - GPN

Mysterious Island 18 MIN
16mm
Color
An abridged version of the motion picture Mysterious Island. Tells the story of the escape of five men from a Confederate prison in an observation balloon and their landing on a strange South Sea island. Stars Michael Craig and Gary Merrill.
Fine Arts
Dist - TIMLIF **Prod** - CPC 1982

The Mysterious Island
Cassette / 16mm
Now Age Reading Programs, Set 2 Series
Color (I J)
$9.95 purchase _ #8F - PN68193x
Brings a classic tale to young readers. Filmstrip set includes filmstrip, cassette, corresponding book, classroom exercise materials and a poster. The read - along set includes student activity book, cassette, and paperback.
English Language; Literature and Drama
Dist - MAFEX

Mysterious Island 101 MIN
16mm
Color (J)
Stars Michael Craig and Joan Greenwood in Jules Verne's story of castaways on a Pacific island prowled by the inconceivable terrors of a fierce new animal world.
Fine Arts
Dist - TIMLIF **Prod** - CPC 1961

The Mysterious Mascot - using Context Analysis 8 MIN
U-matic
Alexander Hawkshaw's Language Arts Skills Series
Color (I J)
Tells how Alex and his friends put together the parts of a puzzle using context analysis skills.
English Language
Dist - GA **Prod** - LUMIN

The Mysterious Mechanical Bird - Reading for Comprehension 10 MIN
U-matic
Alexander Hawkshaw's Language Arts Skills Series
Color (I J)
Uses Alexander's search for a missing book page to illustrate aspects of reading comprehension.
English Language
Dist - GA **Prod** - LUMIN

The Mysterious Message 12 MIN
U-matic / VHS / 16mm
Color (P I)
LC 81-701577
Shows the importance of clear, readable handwriting through a humorous suspense story about a mail carrier and two young children, who deal with mysterious messages that are actually unreadable notes. Shows how to improve one's handwriting and illustrates jobs and professions in which handwriting is important.
English Language
Dist - ALTSUL **Prod** - ALTSUL 1981

The Mysterious Message - Phonics Analysis 9 MIN
U-matic
Alexander Hawkshaw's Language Arts Skills Series
Color (I J)
Shows Alexander and his news sleuths demonstrating the importance of phonics analysis skills.
English Language
Dist - GA **Prod** - LUMIN

The Mysterious Monsters 92 MIN
U-matic / VHS / 16mm
Color (I)
Investigates the existence of giant creatures such as Bigfoot, the Abominable Snowman and the Loch Ness monster with commentary from scientific experts.
Sociology
Dist - LUF **Prod** - LUF 1979

The Mysterious Mr Eliot 62 MIN
16mm / U-matic / VHS
Color (H C A)
LC 73-701580
Provides a historical framework for the work of T S Eliot. Correlates the complexity of 20th century western society to 20th century poetry. Relates the imagery of Eliot's poetry to his life.
Literature and Drama
Dist - MGHT **Prod** - BBCTV 1975

Mysterious Mr Eliot, the, Pt 1 30 MIN
16mm / U-matic / VHS
Color (H C A)
LC 73-701580
Provides a historical framework for the work of T S Eliot. Correlates the complexity of 20th century western society to 20th century poetry. Relates the imagery of Eliot's poetry to his life.
Literature and Drama
Dist - MGHT **Prod** - BBCTV 1975

Mysterious Mr Eliot, the, Pt 2 32 MIN
16mm / U-matic / VHS
Color (H C A)
LC 73-701580
Provides a historical framework for the work of T S Eliot. Correlates the complexity of 20th century western society to 20th century poetry. Relates the imagery of Eliot's poetry to his life.
Literature and Drama
Dist - MGHT **Prod** - BBCTV 1975

The Mysterious Note - Building Word Power 9 MIN
U-matic
Alexander Hawkshaw's Language Arts Skills Series
Color (I J)
Tells how Alexander Hawkshaw and his friends analyze a mysterious note with 'word power' and help avert the shutdown of the school newspaper.
English Language
Dist - GA **Prod** - LUMIN

Mysterious star 10 MIN
VHS
Color (K P R)
$10.00 rental _ #36 - 81011 - 19
Tells how Jamie's search for the Christmas star is unsuccessful until he helps six other people, who see the star in Jamie.
Literature and Drama; Religion and Philosophy
Dist - APH **Prod** - CPH

The Mysterious stranger 20 MIN
VHS
Goosehill gang adventure series
Color (K P I R)
$14.95 purchase _ #87EE0436
Features the five members of the Goosehill Gang in adventures with a Christian message. Portrays the gang as they accidentally become involved in a jewelry theft, but end up helping the thief become a Christian.
Guidance and Counseling; Literature and Drama; Religion and Philosophy
Dist - CPH **Prod** - CPH

The Mysterious stranger 89 MIN
VHS
(G)
$39.95 purchase _ #S00528
Dramatizes the magical Mark Twain story of a Missouri printer's apprentice who dreams himself in Europe in the Middle Ages. Stars Fred Gwynne, Chris Makepeace, and Lance Kerwin. Filmed in Austria.
Literature and Drama
Dist - UILL

Mysterious stranger 20 MIN
VHS
Goosehill gang series
Color (P I R)
$14.95 purchase, $10.00 rental _ #35 - 8436 - 19
Features the Goosehill Gang as they stumble upon a jewelry store robbery. Shows that the young thief has a change of heart in the end.
Literature and Drama; Religion and Philosophy
Dist - APH **Prod** - FAMF

The Mysterious Tadpole 5 MIN
VHS / U-matic
Color; Mono (K P I)
Shows Louis's best birthday present, from his Uncle McAlister in Scotland, a tadpole. Louis names his new pet Alphonse and can hardly wait to take him to school for show and tell. His class looks forward to watching Alphonse turn into a frog, but it soon becomes clear that Alphonse is not turning into an ordinary frog.
English Language; Literature and Drama; Psychology; Science - Natural
Dist - WWS **Prod** - WWS 1987

The Mysterious Tadpole 35 MIN
VHS / 16mm
Children's Circle Video Series
Color (K)
$18.88 purchase _ #CCV016
Also includes other stories - The 5 Chinese Brothers, Jonah and the Great Fish, The Wizard.
Literature and Drama
Dist - EDUCRT

Mysterious White Land 27 MIN
16mm
Color (FRENCH)
Presents a documentary about skiing on Mt Cook, the peak of the southern Alps in the south island of New Zealand. Covers the landing at the ski - base, the hermitage, with skiers Yuichiro Miura and Mitsuhiro Tachibana on the slopes of Mt Cook.
Geography - World; Physical Education and Recreation
Dist - UNIJAP **Prod** - UNIJAP 1967

The Mysterious World 390 MIN
VHS
Color (G)
$99.95 purchase _ #XVMW6
Presents a series of six videos by Arthur C Clarke which examine mysterious phenomena. Includes UFOs, water monsters, ancient monsters - real and imagined, the huge meteorite that crashed on Siberia, ancient teachings and other oddities.
Literature and Drama
Dist - GAINST

Mystery and detective fiction 31 MIN
VHS
Color (J H)
$99.00 purchase _ #06271 - 026
Demonstrates the development, basic elements and literary value of an exciting genre with roots in the works of Edgar Allan Poe. Surveys different styles by various authors. Includes teacher's guide and library kit.
Education; Literature and Drama
Dist - GA

Mystery at Johnson Farm 49 MIN
VHS
Color (P I R)
$12.99 purchase _ #35 - 867985 - 979
Portrays a mistrustful foster child, Libby, whose life changes when she learns to trust her new family and finds faith in God.
Literature and Drama; Religion and Philosophy
Dist - APH **Prod** - TYHP

Mystery at Smoky Hollow 28 MIN
16mm
Color
LC 74-705183
Traces the origin of a woods fire by questioning several members of a community about their activities in or near the woods at the time the fire started. Shows how each person is impressed with the need for careful attention whenever fire is used in or near a forested area.
Health and Safety; Science - Natural; Social Science
Dist - USNAC **Prod** - USDA 1968

The Mystery at Willoughby Castle 45 MIN
VHS
Color (P I R)
$49.95 purchase, $10.00 rental _ #35 - 83028 - 8936
Uses an adventure and mystery format to tell the story of three children who respond to a call for help and discover a haunted castle. Shows how the bully, Raymond, becomes a Christian.
Literature and Drama; Religion and Philosophy
Dist - APH **Prod** - QUADCO

Mystery Books 15 MIN
U-matic / VHS
Word Shop Series
Color (P)
Literature and Drama
Dist - WETATV **Prod** - WETATV

The Mystery Crash 8 MIN
16mm
Techniques of Defensive Driving Film Series
Color (I J H)
Deals with the one - vehicle accident, which is called the 'MYSTERY CRASH' because often there is no reason for it.
Health and Safety
Dist - NSC **Prod** - NSC

Mystery Map 16 MIN
U-matic / VHS / 16mm
Color (P I)
$59.00 purchase _ #3126; LC 75-715415
Teaches children to draw logical conclusions, as well as to be imaginative, by telling the story of four children who follow a treasure map. Presents three different endings to the story.
English Language; Guidance and Counseling; Psychology; Religion and Philosophy
Dist - EBEC **Prod** - MORLAT 1972

Mystery Meal 27 MIN
U-matic / VHS / 16mm
Ramona Series
Color (P I)
$3795 purchase - 16 mm (entire set), $435 purchase - 16 mm (per
Tells how Ramona and Beezus have to prepare the family dinner themselves the evening after they refuse to eat the "mystery meat" their mother cooks for them. From Ramona Quimby, Age 8. A production of Atlantis Films, Ltd. in association with Lancit Media Productions, Ltd. and Revcom Television.
Literature and Drama
Dist - CF

Mystery meal - Rainy Sunday 60 MIN
VHS
Beverly Cleary's Ramona series
Color; CC (K P I)
$29.95 purchase _ #KA434
Presents a Ramona story by Beverly Cleary.
Literature and Drama
Dist - KNOWUN

Mystery, Mr Ra 51 MIN
VHS
Color (G)
$29.95 purchase
Records the music of Sun Ra and his group.
Fine Arts
Dist - KINOIC **Prod** - RHPSDY

Mystery Murals of Baja California - as Told by Harry Crosby 30 MIN
VHS / 16mm
Color (G)
$55.00 rental _ #MMBL - 000
Explores the ancient cave paintings found on the Baja. Traces the travels and discoveries of chemistry teacher Harry Williams Crosby, who discovered over 100 caves containing the paintings.
Fine Arts
Dist - PBS **Prod** - KPBS

The Mystery of Amelia Earhart 22 MIN
U-matic / VHS / 16mm
You are There Series
Color (I J H)
LC 74-714892
Covers the immediate events surrounding the mysterious disappearance of aviatrix Amelia Earhart and the elements that have contributed to that mystery.
Biography; History - United States; Industrial and Technical Education
Dist - PHENIX **Prod** - CBSTV 1971

Mystery of Animal Behavior 51 MIN
16mm / U-matic / VHS
Color (I) (GERMAN)
LC 77-705617
Examines the world of animals and their interesting behavior. Visits the animal behavior institute in Germany where researchers study imprinting in birds, coloration in fish and ways animals care for their young.
Science - Natural
Dist - NGS **Prod** - NGS 1969

The Mystery of creation 30 MIN
VHS / BETA
Life in the universe series
Color (G)
$29.95 purchase _ #S494
Views the scientific worldview as incomplete without the imaginative imput from ancient and modern mythologies. Features Dr Richard Grossinger, author of 'Planet Medicine' and 'The Night Sky.' Part of a four - part series on life in the universe.
Religion and Philosophy; Science
Dist - THINKA **Prod** - THINKA

The Mystery of electricity 18 MIN
VHS
Color; CC (H C)
$79.00 purchase _ #922
Explains the three sides of electricity - as power, as information and as a glue that holds things together. Shows how electricity was first investigated in the 19th century, as well as presenting an overview of its wonder and power in the 20th century. Includes a guide.
Science - Physical
Dist - HAWHIL **Prod** - HAWHIL 1994

The Mystery of Henry Moore 83 MIN
VHS
Color (H C A)
$39.95
Interviews sculptor Henry Moore shortly before his death in 1986. Captures the emotional impact of his work as he discusses many aspects of life that influenced his creations. Brings out his thoughts about his stone and bronze sculptures.
Fine Arts
Dist - ARTSAM

A Mystery of Heroism 20 MIN
U-matic / VHS
B&W
Presents a reconstruction of a Civil War background. Based on a Stephen Crane short story about a young Southern soldier who braves hostile fire to bring a bucket of water to his comrades.
History - United States; Literature and Drama; Sociology
Dist - MEDIPR **Prod** - MEDIPR 1979

The Mystery of Howling Woods 20 MIN
VHS
Goosehill gang adventure series
Color (K P I R)
$14.95 purchase _ #87EE0426
Features the five members of the Goosehill Gang in adventures with a Christian message. Shows the gang on a camping trip, where they hear eerie noises and encounter an escaped prisoner.
Guidance and Counseling; Literature and Drama; Religion and Philosophy
Dist - CPH **Prod** - CPH

The Mystery of incarnation 30 MIN
BETA / VHS
Number, form and life series
Color (G)
$29.95 purchase _ #S512
States that social and environmental problems are the inevitable result of human biology. Features Dr Richard Grossinger, author of 'Planet Medicine' and 'Embryogenesis,' who feels, however, that the new factor of consciousness in human evolution may lead to new options and possiblities. Part of a four - part series on number, form and life.
Religion and Philosophy; Science - Natural; Sociology
Dist - THINKA **Prod** - THINKA

The Mystery of life - as discovered in Los Angeles 3 MIN
VHS / 16mm
B&W (G)
$20.00 rental
Shares first impressions of Los Angeles, Forest Lawn Cemetery, the Tropicana Motel. Includes the sandy beaches of Venice and Long Beach.
Fine Arts; Geography - United States
Dist - CANCIN **Prod** - ANGERA 1982
FLMKCO

The Mystery of light 19 MIN
VHS
Color; CC (H C)
$79.00 purchase _ #921
Explores the mystery of light as both a wave and a particle. Covers the concepts of electromagnetic spectrum, quanta, wavelength, frequency, speed of light, color, refraction, reflection, diffraction, conservation of matter, information, fiber optics and more. Includes a guide.
Science - Physical
Dist - HAWHIL **Prod** - HAWHIL 1994

The Mystery of Mesa Verde 22 MIN
U-matic / VHS
Phenomenal World Series
Color
$129.00 purchase _ #3976
Probes the mystery of the disappearance of the Anasazi, an ancient North American civilization that built great stone cities and then suddenly disappeared.
Social Science; Sociology
Dist - EBEC

The Mystery of Nefertiti 46 MIN
16mm / U-matic / VHS
Color (H C A)
LC 75-703968
Follows the six - year efforts of a team of archeologists to reconstruct on paper the Egyptian temple of Nefertiti. Shows how computer techniques were used to match building blocks with the plan to develop an impression of the temple's appearance.
History - World; Science - Physical
Dist - IU **Prod** - BBCL 1975

Mystery of Picasso 77 MIN
VHS
Color (H C A)
$39.95 purchase
Features Pablo Picasso creating more than 15 works never seen previously - or since, as all were destroyed after filming. Includes bullfighting scenes, nudes, collages, and other works.
Fine Arts
Dist - PBS **Prod** - WNETTV

Mystery of Plant Movement 11 MIN
16mm
Science Close - Up Series
B&W
LC FIA67-5015
Shows a four month time - lapse record of the growth of a seed in a 14 - foot vine, emphasizing the movement of various parts of the plant. Explains the role of auxin in the movement of the leaves, growing tip, tendrils and flowers.
Science - Natural
Dist - SF **Prod** - PRISM 1967

The Mystery of Stonehenge 57 MIN
U-matic / VHS / 16mm
Color; B&W (H C A)
LC FIA66-1488
Presents an account of Stonehenge, a prehistoric stone monument in England. Tests the theory that it was built as an observatory and computer.
Geography - World; History - World; Mathematics; Science - Physical; Sociology
Dist - MGHT **Prod** - CBSTV 1965

Mystery of Stonehenge, the, Pt 1 27 MIN
U-matic / VHS / 16mm
Color (H C)
Provides a clear, factual account of Stonehenge, the prehistoric stone monument on Salisbury Plain in England, and tests the theory that it was built as an observatory and as a computer.
History - World
Dist - MGHT **Prod** - CBSTV 1965

Mystery of Stonehenge, the, Pt 2 28 MIN
U-matic / VHS / 16mm
Color (H C)
Provides a clear, factual account of Stonehenge, the prehistoric stone monument on Salisbury Plain in England, and tests the theory that it was built as an observatory and as a computer.
History - World
Dist - MGHT **Prod** - CBSTV 1965

The Mystery of the Anasazi 59 MIN
16mm / U-matic / VHS
Nova Series
Color (H C A)
LC 78-700609
Inquires into the mysteries surrounding the Anasazi, the pueblo - builders of America's Southwest. Considers who these people were, why they disappeared and where they went.
Geography - United States; History - World; Social Science; Sociology
Dist - TIMLIF **Prod** - WGBHTV 1976

The Mystery of the Animal Pathfinders 58 MIN
VHS / U-matic
Nova Series
Color (H C A)
$250 purchase _ #5126C
Talks about animal migration, and how animals get to another habitat thousands of miles away. Produced by WGBH Boston.
Science - Natural
Dist - CORF

The Mystery of the bends 30 MIN
VHS
Return to the sea series
Color (I J H G)
$24.95 purchase _ #RTS203
Reveals that even divers who follow all the rules can be stricken with decompression sickness, commonly called 'the bends.' Takes a look at ongoing research into reducing the risks of diving. Part of a 13 - part series on marine life produced by Marine Grafics and University of North Carolina Public TV.
Science - Physical
Dist - ENVIMC

The Mystery of the full moon 51 MIN
VHS
Color (G)
$24.95 purchase _ #MYS01, #807-9002
Explores the impact of the moon upon nature and its influence on the daily lives of humans. Looks at the mythology and legends surrounding the moon and its cycles. Produced by Golden Dolphin Productions.
Psychology; Religion and Philosophy; Science - Physical
Dist - HOMVIS
FI

The Mystery of the Hidden Pronouns - 11 30 MIN
VHS
English 101 - Ingles 101 Series
Color (H)
$125.00 purchase
Presents a series of thirty 30 - minute programs in basic English for native speakers of Spanish. Focuses on a specific topic in order to emphasize a particular grammatical point or set of idioms. English is used from the beginning as the primary language of instruction but Spanish translations are included to ensure understanding. Part 11 looks at object pronouns, forms of object pronouns, pronouns as objects of prepositions, pronouns as objects of verbs.
English Language; Foreign Language
Dist - AITECH **Prod** - UPRICO 1988

Mystery of the Holy Land - secrets of the pyramids 26 MIN
VHS
Color (J H C G A R)
$10.00 rental _ #36 - 844 - 8579
Focuses on the more than 80 pyramids of the Holy Land. Shows how these 6000 - year - old structures have inspired human culture.
History - World; Religion and Philosophy
Dist - APH **Prod** - VIDOUT

Mystery of the howling woods 20 MIN
VHS
Goosehill gang series
Color (P I R)
$14.95 purchase, $10.00 rental _ #35 - 8426 - 19
Features the Goosehill Gang on a camping trip. Portrays the Gang as they follow a mysterious howling sound, eventually discovering it to be an author who is writing about wolves.
Literature and Drama; Religion and Philosophy
Dist - APH **Prod** - FAMF

The Mystery of the Lost Red Paint People 59 MIN
16mm / U-matic / VHS
Color (H)
$895.00, $520.00 purchase, $90.00 rental
Tells how American archeologists and anthropologists discovered the remains of a previously unknown advanced pre - historic culture on North America's Atlantic Coast.
History - World; Social Science; Sociology
Dist - BULFRG **Prod** - TWTIM 1987

The Mystery of the Master Builders 58 MIN
VHS / U-matic
Nova Series
Color (H C A)
$250 purchase _ #5269C
Discusses how ancient architectural masterpieces were constructed and how these structures influence modern architecture. Produced by WGBH Boston.
Industrial and Technical Education
Dist - CORF

The Mystery of the million seals 29 MIN
VHS / U-matic
Survivors series
Color (H C)
$250.00 purchase _ #HP - 6107C
Tracks the migration of a herd of fur seals from the waters off southern California to an Alaskan breeding ground with biologist Roger Gentry. Focuses on a female seal's migration for thousands of miles to breed, birth, socialize and rear her progeny - processes that are becoming more and more hazardous because of human activities. Part of a series on the issue of wildlife conservation and the enormity of the task of protecting wildlife and wilderness.
Science - Natural
Dist - CORF **Prod** - BBCTV 1990

Mystery of the Missing Fuzzy 9 MIN
U-matic / VHS
Happy Time Adventure Series
Color (K P)
$29.95 purchase _ #VM116
Presents an adaptation of the book Mystery Of The Missing Fuzzy. Contains a 32 page hardcover book and a video.
English Language; Literature and Drama
Dist - TROLA

The Mystery of the missing goldfish 20 MIN
U-matic / VHS
Color (P I)
$325.00, $295.00 purchase _ #V538
Dramatizes the story of Matt Robins who loves to read Sherlock Holmes mysteries. Shows how he decides to track down his birthday presents when he finds a note on his mother's calendar for a surprise on his birthday. Also shows his family searching for clues left by Matt about what he wants for his birthday.
Literature and Drama
Dist - BARR **Prod** - CEPRO 1991

The Mystery of the Pyramids 23 MIN
VHS / 16mm
Color (I)
LC 90713813
Examines how and why the pyramids of Egypt were built. Deals with the pyramids' design, construction and materials.
History - World; Industrial and Technical Education
Dist - BARR

Mystery of the Sphinx 95 MIN
VHS
Color (J H A)
$29.95 purchase _ #GHM025V-S
Surveys the history and legends of the Sphinx, one of the world's most recognized monuments and incredible mysteries. Describes new evidence assembled by a team of scientists and experts to offer interesting answers to the mysteries. Uses computer-generated reenactments, close-up views of the Sphynx, and interviews.
History - World
Dist - CAMV

The Mystery of the treehouse ghost 20 MIN
VHS
Goosehill gang adventure series
Color (K P I R)
$14.95 purchase _ #87EE0441
Features the five members of the Goosehill Gang in adventures with a Christian message. Portrays the boys of the gang, who find themselves tormented by a 'ghost' in their treehouse. Reveals that the 'ghost' is actually a friend who has run away from home, and the boys help him work things out. Teaches tthe importance of honoring one's parents.
Guidance and Counseling; Literature and Drama; Religion and Philosophy
Dist - CPH **Prod** - CPH

Mystery of the treehouse ghost 20 MIN
VHS
Goosehill gang series
Color (P I R)
$14.95 purchase, $10.00 rental _ #35 - 8441 - 19
Follows the Goosehill Gang as they discover the solution to the mysterious disappearance of food. Shows how they discover that a runaway boy was responsible.
Literature and Drama; Religion and Philosophy
Dist - APH **Prod** - FAMF

Mystery of Time 28 MIN
VHS / 16mm
Color (J)
Shows how high - speed and time - lapse photography help us escape our 'TIME COMPARTMENT.' Samples some of the elemental concepts of the theory of relativity as yardsticks shorten, clocks and heartbeats slow down as the laboratory is 'ACCELERATED' to almost the speed of light to portray the interdependence of time, space and matter.
Business and Economics; Mathematics; Science - Physical
Dist - MIS **Prod** - MIS 1968

Mystery on the docks - 19
VHS
Reading rainbow series
Color; CC (K P)
$39.95 purchase
Captures the mystery and ambiance of the sights, smells and sounds of the waterfront at night, the setting for a 'thriller' narrated by Raul Julia. Follows LeVar Burton back to the 'scene of the crime' to investigate and - at the end of the program - solve the mystery. Part of a series offering a multicultural approach to generating reading enthusiasm with cross - curricular applications, hosted by LeVar Burton.
English Language; Literature and Drama
Dist - GPN **Prod** - LNMDP

Mystery Pass 20 MIN
U-matic / VHS
Color
$335.00 purchase
Presents a program on Chief Joseph and the Nez Perce Indians. From the ABC TV program, 20 20.
Social Science
Dist - ABCLR **Prod** - ABCLR 1984

Mystery religions 30 MIN
VHS
Saints and legions series
Color (H)
$69.95 purchase
Examines mystery religions. Part 2 of a twenty - six part series which introduces personalities, movements and events in ancient history responsible for the beginnings of Western Civilization.
Geography - World; History - World; Religion and Philosophy
Dist - SCETV **Prod** - SCETV 1982

Mystery Stories 15 MIN
U-matic / VHS
Word Shop Series
Color (P)
English Language; Literature and Drama
Dist - WETATV **Prod** - WETATV

The Mystery that Heals 30 MIN
16mm / U-matic / VHS
Story of Carl Gustav Jung Series no 3
Color (H C A)
LC 72-702065
Deals with the life and philosophy of Carl Gustav Jung in his later years. Discusses the concept of the 'SHADOW' and his attitudes toward Christianity and death.
Biography; Psychology; Religion and Philosophy
Dist - FI **Prod** - BBCTV 1972

Mystery tour - part 1 30 MIN
VHS
Color (H C)
$139.00 purchase _ #458237 - X
Supports a mystery thriller course which follows the format of a television detective story in ten episodes, each lasting five to six minutes. Uses atmospheric locations in and around Oxford, England to provide a scenic background to the suspense and involve students. Part 1 of 2 parts. Written by Bob Baker. ESL adaption by Peter and Karen Viney.
English Language; Literature and Drama
Dist - OUP

Mystery tour - part 2 30 MIN
VHS
(H C)
$139.00 purchase _ #458246 - 9
Supports a mystery thriller course which follows the format of a television detective story in ten episodes, each lasting five to six minutes. Uses atomspheric locations in and around Oxford, England to provide a scenic background to the suspense and involve students. Part 2 of 2 parts. Written by Bob Baker. ESL adaption by Peter and Karen Viney.
English Language; Literature and Drama
Dist - OUP

Mystery Words - 7 15 MIN
VHS
Wordscape Series
Color; Captioned (I)
$125.00 purchase
Uses the word 'cell' approach to teach vocabulary, opening each program - sixteen 15 - minute programs - with several word cells familiar to fourth graders and using these 'cells' to form compound words, birdhouse, girlfriend. Employs animated graphics to dramatize how compounds are 'built' of cells that form a seemingly endless series of new words and to teach that understanding cell words can help to understand the new words composed of them. Program 7 reveals 'mystery words' about hiding, seeing and not seeing.
English Language; Psychology
Dist - AITECH **Prod** - OETVA 1990

Mystic arts special package
VHS
Color (G)
$85.35 _ #VDG100
Offers all three videos, The Art of the Tarot, Basic Witchcraft and Reading Chinese Horoscopes, for a special price.
Religion and Philosophy; Sociology
Dist - SIV

Mystic seaport 30 MIN
VHS
Color (G)
$24.95, $19.95 purchase _ #0796, #SS-S
Visits Mystic Seaport, a multi - dimensional maritime museum with a collection of original structures, authentic reproductions and historic vessels maintained at berth there. Views a showcase of 19th century maritime crafts, industries and lifestyles.
Fine Arts; History - United States; Physical Education and Recreation
Dist - SEVVID **Prod** - MYSTIC
MYSTIC

Mystical Malaysia 45 MIN
VHS
Color (G)
$29.95 purchase _ #ST - IV1799
Views Kuala Lumpur, gilded minarets, opulent temples, arabesque domes and sleek high rises in Malaysia. Visits the interior of the Batu Caves where Hindu shrines are tucked away in limestone recesses.

Geography - World; Religion and Philosophy
Dist - INSTRU

Mystical Malaysia - land of harmony 60 MIN
VHS
Asian collection series
Color (J H C G)
$29.95 purchase _ #IVN355V-S
Teaches about the people, culture and history of Malaysia. Visits historic buildings, monuments and landmarks. Examines the physical topography of the country. Part of a seven-part series on Asian countries, cities and islands. Also part of a larger series entitled Video Visits that travels to six continents.
Geography - World; History - World
Dist - CAMV **Prod** - WNETTV

Mystical paths quartet 120 MIN
VHS / BETA
Color (G)
$69.95 purchase _ #Q244
Presents a four - part series on mystical paths. Includes 'The Guru Principle' with Joseph Chilton Pearce, 'Approaches to Growth - East and West' with Dr Claudio Naranjo, 'Common Threads in Mysticism' with Dr Robert Frager and 'The Sufi Path' with Irina Tweedie.
Psychology; Religion and Philosophy
Dist - THINKA **Prod** - THINKA

Mystical paths series
Approaches to growth - East and West 30 MIN
Common threads in mysticism 30 MIN
The Guru principle 30 MIN
The Sufi path 30 MIN
Dist - THINKA

The Mystics 40 MIN
VHS
Color (J H C G A R)
$24.95 purchase, $10.00 rental _ #35 - 82025 - 8936
Takes a look at the world of eastern mysticism. Produced by Bridgestone Films.
Religion and Philosophy
Dist - APH

Myth and metaphor in society - a conversation with Joseph Campbell and Jamake Highwater 70 MIN
VHS
Color (G)
$350.00 purchase, $95.00 rental
Documents Campbell, the world's foremost authority on mythology and author of numerous books, addressing a wide variety of subjects, including the relationship of myth and the arts and the ways that myths differ from culture to culture while retaining a common human theme. Captures Campbell at a public presentation in Houston, 1986 answering inquiries from writer Jamake Highwater. Produced by the Native Arts Festival, Rice University.
Fine Arts; Literature and Drama; Religion and Philosophy
Dist - CNEMAG

Myth as History 29 MIN
U-matic
Of Greeks and Gods Series
B&W
History - World; Literature and Drama
Dist - UMITV **Prod** - UMITV 1971

Myth - Conceptions - a Teenage Sex Quiz 18 MIN
U-matic / VHS
Color (J)
Portrays a peer group education program for junior high and high school age youth. Explores traditional questions about sex and parenting.
Health and Safety; Psychology; Sociology
Dist - MMRC **Prod** - MMRC

Myth, History and Drama 22 MIN
U-matic / VHS
Color (C)
$249.00, $149.00 purchase _ #AD - 1636
Looks at the intertwining of myth and history in classic Greek tragedy. Traces the development of theatre from archaic Greek, to Hellenistic, to Roman.
History - World; Literature and Drama; Religion and Philosophy
Dist - FOTH **Prod** - FOTH

Myth in the electric age 14 MIN
16mm
Color (G)
$30.00 rental
Combines themes of earth, air, fire, and water amidst the rhythms and sensations of modern life. Produced by Alan Berliner, commentary by Marshall McLuhan.
Fine Arts; Religion and Philosophy
Dist - CANCIN

Myth of Naro as told by Dedeheiwa 22 MIN
16mm / VHS
Yanomamo series
Color (G) (YANOMAMO WITH ENGLISH VOICE OVER)
$420.00, $210.00 purchase, $35.00, $25.00 rental
Records the myth of Naro as told by Dedeheiwa. Tells about the jealousy of Naro the ugly toward his beautiful and fragrant brother Yanomamo who has two wives. Naro desires the wives and kills his brother by blowing magical charms, and is in turn killed by a third brother and some ancestors. This is the origin of harmful magic. Part of a series on the Yanomamo Indians of Venezuela by Timothy Asch and Napoleon Chagnon.
Geography - World; Religion and Philosophy; Social Science; Sociology
Dist - DOCEDR **Prod** - DOCEDR 1975

Myth of Naro as Told by Kaobawa 22 MIN
16mm
Yanomamo Series
Color (H C A)
Presents a headman of the Yanomamo Indians of South America 'acting out' his version of the Myth of Naro. Explains the origin of harmful magic stems from jealousy among brothers.
Social Science; Sociology
Dist - DOCEDR **Prod** - DOCEDR 1975

The Myth of Nationalism 30 MIN
U-matic / VHS / 16mm
Outline History of Europe Series
Color (H C A)
LC 80-701112
Suggests that the end of the 19th - century was a time when political idealists dreamed of democratic nationalism and statesmen, believing that war brought revolution, strove for peace. Details the period between the Franco - Prussian and the First World Wars.
History - World
Dist - IFB **Prod** - POLNIS 1975

Myth of the Pharaohs 13 MIN
16mm / U-matic / VHS
Color (I J H C)
LC 76-702235
Recounts the Egyptian myth of creation and follows one typical pharaoh, examining his conception, birth, childhood, crowning, feats in war and peace, death and the final judgment before osiris.
History - World; Religion and Philosophy; Sociology
Dist - AIMS **Prod** - ACI 1971

Myth, Superstition and Science 13 MIN
U-matic / VHS / 16mm
Color (J H C)
LC FIA65-344
Introduces the scientific method by presenting the story of a superstitious grammar school student and her more scientific brother. Follows the students as they tour a weather bureau to see how meteorologists forecast weather.
Science; Science - Physical
Dist - IFB **Prod** - VEF 1963

The Mythic Hitler 30 MIN
VHS
Color (G)
$14.98 purchase _ #TT8123
Provides film footage of Adolf Hitler's early years, his private life, and the horrors of World War II. Produced by Midwich Entertainment.
History - United States; History - World; Psychology
Dist - TWINTO **Prod** - TWINTO 1990

Mythical Cartoon Beasts 14 MIN
Videoreel / VT2
Charlie's Pad Series
Color
Fine Arts
Dist - PBS **Prod** - WSIU

Mythical Monsters of the Deep 25 MIN
16mm / U-matic / VHS
Color (H C A)
Looks at the legends attached to some underwater creatures. Dispels myths about mermaids, sea snakes, humpback whales and others.
Science - Natural
Dist - CORF **Prod** - CTV

Mythical Monsters of the Deep 25 MIN
U-matic / 16mm / VHS
Color; Mono (G)
MV $185.00 _ MP $530.00 purchase, $50.00 rental
Shatters popular myths about many of the creatures of the sea. The manatee, octupus, squid, whale, jelly fish and other creatures are honestly evaluated.
Science - Natural
Dist - CTV **Prod** - MAKOF 1982

Mythmakers 52 MIN
VHS
Planet for the taking series
Color (H C T G)
$198.00 purchase
Visits societies in the Kalahari Desert, a southern Indian Hindu village and modern urban areas to find out how each group answers the question, 'Where do humans fit in nature?' Features David Suzuki who explains that mythology is a necessary and natural form of explanantion in unspecialized societies and that the development of Western philosophy grew out of the belief that all things observed can be measured. Part of an eight - part series.
History - World; Religion and Philosophy; Sociology
Dist - FI **Prod** - CANBC 1988

Mythology - Gods and Goddesses 41 MIN
U-matic / 35mm strip
Color (H C J)
$119.00 filmstrips, $195.00 sound slides purchase _ #07173 - 161
Teaches students to recognize refernces to the classical myths. Includes a discussion of the 'Second Generation' of Olympians and characters such as Medusa, King Midas, and Romulus and Remus. In two parts.
History - World; Literature and Drama
Dist - GA **Prod** - GA

Mythology is alive and well
VHS
Color (J H C)
$109.00 purchase _ #06216 - 126
Relates Olympian gods and legends to modern music, poetry, science and cultural images. Shows how the ancient deities of Greece have influenced current myths and realities - from science fiction and space probes to Peter Pan and rock festivals. Explores the archetypal images and humanity and society through the stories of the Greek gods. Includes teacher's guide and library kit. In two parts.
History - World; Religion and Philosophy
Dist - GA **Prod** - GA

Mythology Lives - Ancient Stories and Modern Literature
U-matic / VHS
Color (H C)
Presents stories from the past, points out their recurring themes and characters, and looks at their modern - day counterparts, such as Orpheus and Eurydice - Romeo and Juliet.
History - World; Literature and Drama
Dist - GA **Prod** - GA

Mythology Lives - Ancient Stories and Modern Literature
VHS / Slide / 35mm strip / U-matic
Mythology Series
(G C J)
$197 purchase _ #00307 - 85
Surveys many of the famous myths and legends of the past. Follows their integration into the literature of today, and examines their modern counterparts.
Literature and Drama
Dist - CHUMAN

Mythology of Greece
U-matic / 16mm / VHS
Mythology of Greece Series
Color (I J H)
$2095, $1470, $1650
Recounts Greek myths used in literature textbooks at the elementary and junior high levels using animated film.
Education; Fine Arts; Religion and Philosophy
Dist - BARR **Prod** - BARR

Mythology of Greece and Rome 16 MIN
16mm / U-matic / VHS
Captioned; Color (I J H) (SPANISH)
LC 78-700191
Examines the myths of Ancient Greece and Rome as stories about gods and man invented in an attempt to explain natural phenomena and man's behavior. Includes stories of Ceres and Proserpina, Apollo and Daphne, Pegasus and Bellerophon.
History - World; Literature and Drama; Religion and Philosophy
Dist - PHENIX **Prod** - FA 1969

Mythology of Greece series
Hercules' return from Olympus 13 MIN
Jason and the Argonauts 20 MIN
Mythology of Greece
Perseus 20 MIN
Phaethon 5 MIN
Phaeton 5 MIN
Prometheus 10 MIN
Theseus and the Labyrinth 20 MIN
Dist - BARR

Mythology Series
Mythology Lives - Ancient Stories and Modern Literature
Dist - CHUMAN

Myths about motivation - or is it possible to overcome the who cares syndrome 30 MIN
VHS
First - year teacher series
Color (T)
$69.95 purchase, $45.00 rental
Discusses the unique challenges and rewards that first - year school teachers face. Serves as the final episode of a 12 - part telecourse. Features discussions between first - year teachers and Winthrop College professor Glen Walter on motivation and overcoming apathy.
Education; Psychology
Dist - SCETV **Prod** - SCETV 1988

Myths and Fables 15 MIN
VHS / U-matic
Zebra Wings Series
Color (I)
Considers the role of culture and imagination in the evolution of myths and fables.
English Language; Literature and Drama
Dist - AITECH **Prod** - NITC 1975

Myths and identity 60 MIN
U-matic / VHS
Art of being human series
Color (H C A)
Psychology; Religion and Philosophy
Dist - FI **Prod** - FI 1978

Myths and Legends - Mirrors of Mankind 46 MIN
U-matic / VHS
Color
LC 81-706687
Uses examples of art, literature and music to discuss the myths and legends man has created to explain the nature of the universe and his place in it.
Literature and Drama; Religion and Philosophy
Dist - GA **Prod** - CHUMAN 1981

Myths and Legends of Ancient Greece 56 MIN
VHS / U-matic
Myths and Legends of Ancient Greece Series
Color (I J)
Consists of 1 videocassette.
English Language; Religion and Philosophy
Dist - TROLA **Prod** - TROLA 1987

Myths and legends of ancient Greece
VHS
Color (I J H)
$110.00 purchase _ #0187
Presents five myths and legends from ancient Greece. Includes Jason and the Golden Fleece, Pegasus the Winged Horse, Perseus and Medusa, Prometheus and the Gift of Fire, and Theseus and the Minotaur.
History - World; Literature and Drama; Religion and Philosophy
Dist - SEVVID

Myths and legends of ancient Greece 20 MIN
VHS
Color (I J)
$89.95 purchase _ #10347VL
Offers three tales of ancient Greece in animated form. Includes Daedalus and Icarus; Pandora's Box; and Jason and the Golden Fleece. Comes with a guide.
History - World; Literature and Drama; Religion and Philosophy
Dist - UNL

Myths and Legends of Ancient Greece Series
Myths and Legends of Ancient Greece 56 MIN
Dist - TROLA

Myths and legends of ancient Greece - Volume one 43 MIN
VHS
Color (I J)
LC 89-700197
Presents a selection of ancient Greek myths and legends.
History - World; Literature and Drama; Religion and Philosophy
Dist - EAV **Prod** - EAV 1989

Myths and legends of ancient Greece - Volume two 42 MIN
VHS
Color (I J)
LC 89-700198
Presents a selection of ancient Greek myths and legends.
History - World; Literature and Drama; Religion and Philosophy
Dist - EAV **Prod** - EAV 1989

Myths and legends of ancient Rome 20 MIN
VHS
CC; Color (I J)
$89.95 purchase _ #1047VL
Presents a trilogy of ancient Roman tales of mythology in animated form. Shows Romulus and Remus; Perseus and Medusa; and Psyche and Cupid. Uses a full musical score and multi - track sound effects to enhance the stories. Comes with a teacher's guide, discussion questions and a script.
History - World; Religion and Philosophy
Dist - UNL

Myths and Manifest Destiny 20 MIN
U-matic
Silent Heritage - the American Indian Series
B&W
Social Science; Sociology
Dist - UMITV **Prod** - UMITV 1966

Myths and Mistakes of Financial Aid 25 MIN
U-matic / VHS
(J H A)
$98.00 _ #CD6100V
Uses live action to forwarn students of the common traps and obstacles that they may run into when seeking financial aid. These myths include believing that all colleges cost the same, that everything can be done alone, and others. Includes accompanying reproducible exercises.
Education
Dist - CAMV **Prod** - CAMV

Myths and Mistakes of Financial Aid
BETA / VHS / U-matic
Paying for College Series
Color (H G)
#MFV 102
Identifies the major traps students fall into when looking for financial aid. Explores the eight most common problems students encounter when securing a financial aid package. Comes with worksheets.
Business and Economics; Guidance and Counseling
Dist - CADESF **Prod** - CADESF 1988

Myths and Moundbuilders 59 MIN
16mm
Odyssey Series
Color (J H A)
Reconstructs the history of ideas associated with the mounds and their builders, from the mid nineteenth century explorations of curious citizens, to contemporary archaeologists research in the Illinois River Valley.
Social Science; Sociology
Dist - DOCEDR **Prod** - DOCEDR 1981

Myths and Moundbuilders 58 MIN
VHS / U-matic
Odyssey Series
Color
Features archaeologists who probe mysterious mounds in the eastern United States uncovering clues about a lost Indian civilization.
History - World; Science - Physical; Social Science
Dist - PBS **Prod** - PBA

Myths and moundbuilders
VHS
American Indian collection series
Color (J H C G)
$29.95 purchase _ #PAV263V
Illustrates that as far back as 300 BC huge mounds were engineered and built across America's heartland. Follows clues left by past civilizations to uncover the mysteries associated with these phenomena. Part of a five - part series on American Indians.
Social Science
Dist - CAMV

The Myths of Greece 90 MIN
VHS / U-matic
Color (I J)
Presents a six - part series on the mythical adventures of the Greek gods and the warrior - king Odysseus and the fables of Aesop. Adapts from the Iliad and the Odyssey by Homer. Includes the titles The Trojan War, The Cyclops, The Ant and the Grasshopper, Circe, The Fox and the Goat, The Fox and the Grapes, Odysseus and the Terrible Sea, The Lion and the Mouse, Telemachus, Son of Odysseus, The Lion and the Statues, anad The Homecoming.
History - World; Literature and Drama; Religion and Philosophy
Dist - GPN **Prod** - CTI 1990

The Myths of Shoplifting 16 MIN
U-matic / VHS / 16mm
Color (J H C)
$335 purchase - 16 mm, $89 purchase - video
Talks about the consequences of shoplifting.
Sociology
Dist - CF

The Myths of Shoplifting 16 MIN
U-matic / VHS / 16mm
Color (J H C)
LC 79-701860
Presents a series of vignettes which dramatize the serious consequences of shoplifting.
Sociology
Dist - CORF **Prod** - NRMA 1979

Myths of Technology 30 MIN
VHS / U-matic
Living Environment Series
Color (C)
Explores the impact of technology on the biosphere and other aspects of planet earth.
Science - Natural
Dist - DALCCD **Prod** - DALCCD

Myths of the pharoahs 12 MIN
VHS
Color (I J H C G T A)
$49.95 purchase, $25.00 rental _ #B4120, #4120
Uses animated illustrations based on Egyptian tomb paintings to introduce the mythology of the ancient Egyptians. Explains the life story of a Pharoah, from birth, to triumph over his kingdom, to death and final judgment before the gods.
History - World
Dist - KNOWUN **Prod** - AIMS 1971
AIMS

Myths that Conceal Reality 82 MIN
VHS / U-matic
Milton Friedman Speaking Series Lecture 2
Color (C)
LC 79-708060
Presents economist Milton Friedman discussing economic myths in American history which have accompanied a shift away from the belief in individual responsibility to an emphasis on social responsibility.
Business and Economics; History - United States
Dist - HBJ **Prod** - HBJ 1980

Myths that Conceal Reality, Pt 1 41 MIN
VHS / U-matic
Milton Friedman Speaking Series Lecture 2
Color (C)
LC 79-708060
Presents economist Milton Friedman discussing economic myths in American history which have accompanied a shift away from the belief in individual responsibility to an emphasis on social responsibility.
Business and Economics
Dist - HBJ **Prod** - HBJ 1980

Myths that Conceal Reality, Pt 2 41 MIN
VHS / U-matic
Milton Friedman Speaking Series Lecture 2
Color (C)
LC 79-708060
Presents economist Milton Friedman discussing economic myths in American history which have accompanied a shift away from the belief in individual responsibility to an emphasis on social responsibility.
Business and Economics
Dist - HBJ **Prod** - HBJ 1980

Myths, the collective dreams of mankind 30 MIN
VHS / U-matic
Art of being human series; Module 4
Color (C)
History - World; Literature and Drama; Religion and Philosophy
Dist - MDCC **Prod** - MDCC

Myths vs facts 57 MIN
BETA / VHS / U-matic
Color; CC (G IND PRO C)
Trains personnel in the skills and awareness necessary to recognize, prevent and resolve sexual harassment situations before they result in lawsuits. Uses video scenarios to dramatize a wide variety of sexual harassment situations. Teaches the difference between social interaction and sexual harassment, how to stop unwelcome behavior and defines the 'Reasonable Woman' standard. Shows managers how to interview alleged recipients of sexual harassment and how to respond, how to document facts, avoid common mistakes in handling complaints, how to resolve complaints, and intervene when subtle harassment is observed but nobody has complained. Includes two videos, trainer's manual and 20 participant manuals.
Business and Economics; Psychology; Sociology
Dist - BNA **Prod** - BNA 1993

Myths vs facts - employee version 27 MIN
U-matic / VHS / BETA
Color; CC; PAL (PRO G IND)
$895.00 purchase
Teaches employees the difference between making a sexual comment and giving a compliment. Offers a practical and objective five - step method for identifying subtle sexual harassment. Presents specific ways to confront the harasser and personally put a stop to unwelcome behaivior. Defines the 'Reasonable Woman' stnadard. Covers female to male, male to female, same -

sex, failed relationship, third - party and other unwelcome workplace behaviors. Includes a trainer's manual and 20 participant manuals with pre - and post - tests. Canadian version available in English or French.
Psychology; Social Science; Sociology
Dist - BNA **Prod** - BNA

Myths vs facts - management and employee versions 57 MIN
U-matic / VHS / BETA
Color; CC; PAL (PRO G IND)
$1595.00 purchase
Presents two videos, management and employee versions, on dealing with sexual harassment and stopping it before it starts. Illustrates a wide variety of harassment situations. Shows employees how to recognize harassing behavior. Demonstrates to managers strategies for interviewing alleged recipients and responding to victims and documenting facts. Includes a trainer's manual and 20 participant manuals with pre - and post - tests with each video, as well as 342 - page resource book, How to Effectively Manage Sexual Harassment Investigations, 2nd Ed by Stephen Anderson. Canadian version available in English or French.
Psychology; Social Science; Sociology
Dist - BNA **Prod** - BNA

Myths vs facts - management version 30 MIN
U-matic / VHS / BETA
Color; CC; PAL (PRO G IND)
$895.00 purchase
Helps managers recognize and put a stop to subtle sexual harassment. Illustrates a wide variety of harassment situations. Shows managers how to interview alleged recipients of harassment, respond if the victim wants to personally resolve the matter, respond if the victim insists that nothing be done, document facts, avoid common mistakes in handling complaints, use resource personnel to resolve complaints, intervene when subtle harassment is observed but no one has complained. Covers female to male, male to female, same - sex, failed relationship, third - party and other unwelcome workplace behaviors. Includes a trainer's manual and 20 participant manuals with pre - and post - tests. Canadian version available in English or French.
Psychology; Social Science
Dist - BNA **Prod** - BNA

Myxoma of Right Atrium - Surgical Removal during Cardiopulmonary Bypass 10 MIN
16mm
Color
LC FIA66-56
Shows step by step the procedures followed in an operation on 48 - year - old patient for the surgical removal during cardio - pulmonary bypass of a myxoma of the right atrium.
Health and Safety
Dist - EATONL **Prod** - EATONL 1961

Myxomas of the Heart 13 MIN
U-matic / VHS
Color (PRO)
Shows myxomas of the heart.
Health and Safety
Dist - WFP **Prod** - WFP

Mzima - Portrait of a Spring 30 MIN
16mm
Color (I)
LC 83-700160
A shortened version of Mzima - Portrait Of A Spring. Shows scenes of big and small wildlife in Kenya, including hippopotami, elephants, crocodiles and snakes.
Geography - World; Science - Natural
Dist - BNCHMK **Prod** - ROOTA 1983

Mzima - Portrait of a Spring 53 MIN
U-matic / VHS / 16mm
Color (H)
LC 70-713914
Shows scenes of big and small wildlife in Kenya, including hippopotami, elphants, crocodiles and snakes.
Geography - World; Science - Natural
Dist - MGHT **Prod** - ROOTA 1971

Mzima - Portrait of a Spring, Pt 1 27 MIN
U-matic / VHS / 16mm
Color (H)
Shows scenes of big and small wildlife in Kenya, including hippopotami, elephants, crocodiles and snakes.
Geography - World; Science - Natural
Dist - MGHT **Prod** - ROOTA 1971

Mzima - Portrait of a Spring, Pt 2 26 MIN
16mm / U-matic / VHS
Color (H)
Shows scenes of big and small wildlife in Kenya, including hippopotami, elephants, crocodiles and snakes.
Geography - World; Science - Natural
Dist - MGHT **Prod** - ROOTA 1971

N

N - A - I - L 20 MIN
VHS
Color (J H C G A R)
$19.95 purchase, $10.00 rental _ #35 - 87 - 8579
Reveals how a shiny nail found on the street transforms the lives of a lonely city woman, an alcoholic and many others.
Religion and Philosophy
Dist - APH **Prod** - VIDOUT

N A S A collector's edition 170 MIN
VHS
Color (G)
$69.95 purchase
Presents a five - part collection covering the highlights of the NASA space program. Includes 'Voyage Of Friendship 7,' which covers John Glenn's historic flight, 'The Eagle Has Landed,' covering the first man on the moon, 'On The Shoulders Of Giants,' covering the last lunar mission, 'Opening New Frontiers,' covering the first four space shuttle missions, and 'NASA - The 25th Year,' which reviews the history of the space program.
History - United States; History - World
Dist - PBS **Prod** - WNETTV

N C A A instructional video series
Baserunning
Basic fundamentals of the swing
Basic skills
Catching
Checking
Crew
Defensive ice hockey series
Diving techniques
Escapes and reverses
Fencing
Freestyle techniques
Goal tending
Goalkeeper play
Golf series
Gymnastics series
Hitting
The Horizontal bars
Individual defense
Individual offense
Individual offensive moves
Lacrosse series
Offensive baseball series
Offensive ice hockey series
The Parallel bars
Passing and receiving
Pitching
Pitching, chipping and bunker play
Pitching essentials
The Pommel horse
Post moves
The Putting game
Riding and pinning
The Rings
The Set - up - address position
Shooting
Shooting techniques
Skating techniques
Soccer series
Softball series
Starts, turns and individual medley
Stickhandling
Swimming and diving series
Takedowns
Water polo
Women's basketball series
Wrestling series
Dist - CAMV

N C A A volleyball instructional video series
Features Dr Marv Dunphy in a two - part series on basic volleyball skills. Covers the skills of serving, blocking, individual defense, passing, setting, and spiking.
Passing, setting and spiking
Serving, blocking and individual defense
Dist - CAMV **Prod** - NCAAF

N - C machine tool programmer 4.5 MIN
VHS / 16mm
Good works 3 series
Color (A PRO)
$40.00 purchase _ #BPN213901
Presents the occupation of a N - C machine tool maker. Gives a profile of a young person who is either undergoing an apprenticeship or has recently completed training in this field. Takes the viewer on a tour of this person's workplace and explains the practical skills and training offered by employers and schools. Gives a better understanding of the demand for skilled workers today and the potential for personal growth.
Guidance and Counseling
Dist - RMIBHF **Prod** - RMIBHF

N - Channel, CMOS, SOS and Ion Implantation Technology 30 MIN
U-matic / VHS
MOS Integrated Circuit Series
Color (PRO)
Describes variation in MOS V - I characteristics and basic process steps that result when N - channel, CMOS, SOS, and Ion Implantation structures are used.
Industrial and Technical Education
Dist - TXINLC **Prod** - TXINLC

N - Dimensional Vector Spaces 32 MIN
U-matic / VHS
Calculus of several Variables - Partial Derivatives Series; Partial derivatives
B&W
Mathematics
Dist - MIOT **Prod** - MIOT

N E T Journal Series
Modern Women - the Uneasy Life 60 MIN
Dist - IU

N F L follies go Hollywood
VHS
NFL series
Color (G)
$19.95 purchase _ #NFL1164V
Presents a collection of humorous 'bloopers' from the National Football League. Produced by NFL Films.
Literature and Drama; Physical Education and Recreation
Dist - CAMV

N is for nuclear - with Robert Jay Lifton, MD 25 MIN
VHS / 16mm
Color (H C G PRO)
$650.00, $295.00 purchase, $100.00, $55.00 rental
Documents children's views on nuclear war through their drawings and play. Films two elementary schools to show psychologists, teachers and parents allowing children to express their anxieties about nuclear warfare. Psychiatrist Robert Jay Lifton points out that it helps children to air these issues in a caring environment. Produced by Brian Danitz.
Fine Arts; Psychology
Dist - FLMLIB **Prod** - QUESTV 1992

N - O - T - H - I - N - G 36 MIN
16mm
Color (C)
$807.00
Experimental film by Paul Sharits.
Fine Arts
Dist - AFA **Prod** - AFA 1968

N O W Now 29 MIN
U-matic
Woman Series
Color
Looks at the goals of the National Organization for Women.
Sociology
Dist - PBS **Prod** - WNEDTV

The N - town passion play - Ludus Coventriae 68 MIN
VHS
Color (G C H)
$149.00 purchase _ #DL264
Presents a rendering of part of a Corpus Christi cycle performed in the city of Lincoln in the 15th and 16th centuries. Uses authentic costumes, a set based on a drawing from the time, and period music.
Fine Arts
Dist - INSIM

N Y, N Y 16 MIN
U-matic / VHS / 16mm
Color (J)
LC FIA68-64
Shows the rhythmic impression of New York City through shifting patterns of semi - abstract images of its people, building and traffic.
Fine Arts; Geography - United States; Social Science; Sociology
Dist - PFP **Prod** - THOMPN 1958

Naaman the leper - Samson 26 MIN
VHS
Color (R P I)
$14.95 purchase _ #6169 - 7
Presents two Bible stories with still illustrations and Mr Fixit and friends who show how scripture applies to daily life.
Literature and Drama; Religion and Philosophy
Dist - MOODY **Prod** - MOODY

Nabucco 140 MIN
VHS
Color (S) (ITALIAN)
$39.95 purchase _ #833 - 9310
Presents the La Scala production of 'Nabucco' by Verdi. Stars Renato Bruson, Ghena Dimitrova and Paata Burchuladze. Riccardo Muti conducts.

Fine Arts; Geography - World
Dist - FI **Prod** - NVIDC 1987

Nabucco 145 MIN
U-matic / VHS
Color (A)
Portrays the reign of Nabucco (Nebuchadnezzar, King of Babylon) in an opera whose theme of a repressed people's yearning for freedom made Verdi the political voice of his own country.
Fine Arts; Foreign Language
Dist - SRA **Prod** - SRA

Nace Una Nacion 52 MIN
U-matic / VHS
Espana Estuvo Alli Series
Color (C) (SPANISH)
$249.00, $149.00 purchase _ #AD - 1028
Looks at the American Revolution and the establishment of a new nation. In Spanish.
Geography - World; History - United States; History - World
Dist - FOTH **Prod** - FOTH

Nachrede Auf Klara Heydebreck 65 MIN
16mm
B&W (GERMAN)
Reconstructs the life of a 72 - year - old spinster who has died from an overdose of sleeping pills.
Foreign Language; Sociology
Dist - WSTGLC **Prod** - WSTGLC 1969

Nachtdienst 64 MIN
16mm
Color (GERMAN (ENGLISH SUBTITLES))
A German language motion picture with English subtitles. Tells the story of a sort of a verbal duel that takes place nightly between a critical young nurse and her elderly patient, who is quite versed in the entire repertoire of social oppression.
Foreign Language; Sociology
Dist - WSTGLC **Prod** - WSTGLC 1975

Nachtschatten 100 MIN
16mm
(GERMAN (ENGLISH SUBTITLES))
A German language motion picture with English subtitles. Unravels the mysterious events which take place when Jan Eckmann visits a country estate he is considering buying.
Foreign Language; Literature and Drama
Dist - WSTGLC **Prod** - WSTGLC 1971

Nadar the great 25 MIN
VHS
Pioneers of photography series
Color (A)
PdS65 purchase
Looks at the work of Felix Tournachon, whose portraits recorded famous people of his time and who used photography to explore his world. Part of an eight-part series that examines the contributions made by pioneers in photography.
Fine Arts; Industrial and Technical Education
Dist - BBCENE

Nadine Gordimer 40 MIN
VHS
Color (H C G)
$79.00 purchase
Features the writer discussing with Margaret Walters how to describe scenery and how to work while not in one's own country. Talks about her works that include Burger's Daughter; A Soldier's Embrace; and A Sport of Nature.
Literature and Drama; Sociology
Dist - ROLAND **Prod** - INCART

Nadja 94 MIN
35mm / 16mm
B&W (G)
$200.00 rental
Brings fresh blood to the vampire film genre. Concocts a brew of droll comedy, hallucinatory fantasy and lush eroticism. Elina Lowensohn stars in the title role as a seductive vampire who lives in the netherworld of New York City with her twin brother, played by Jared Harris. The vampire unconscious is seen as a misty, romantic domain of inhuman need, lust and cruelty. Simon Fisher Turner composed the haunting music and Portishead provides additional tracks. Produced by David Lynch; written and directed by Michael Almereyda. Stars Peter Fonda as Dr Van Helsing.
Fine Arts; Sociology
Dist - OCTOBF

Naer Himlen - Naer Jorden - Near the Sky - Near the Earth 26 MIN
16mm
Color; B&W (DANISH)
A Danish language film. Presents European and American hippies in Nepal. Observes the way of life these hippies have chosen to live 'OUTSIDE OF SOCIETY' in the light of the everyday rites and ceremonies of the Nepalese. Explains that the hippie movement is not just a caprice of fashion, but a religion.
Foreign Language; Religion and Philosophy; Social Science
Dist - STATNS **Prod** - STATNS 1968

Nagasaki - One Man's Return 55 MIN
16mm
Color
LC 76-700388
Tells the story of Buckner Fanning, a marine who lived in Nagasaki after the atomic bomb, who was invited to return to Nagasaki in order to relate his feelings and to get the reactions of the Japanese people 30 years after the bombing of that city.
History - World; Sociology
Dist - MILPRO **Prod** - MILPRO 1976

Nags 26 MIN
16mm / VHS
Color (PRO G)
$249.00, $349.00, $495.00 purchase _ #AD - 1371
Tells the story of one young girl's efforts to help her father give up smoking. Despite all her efforts, her father resists kicking the habit that is undermining his health. A near family tragedy makes him realise the dangers of his habit and he finally quits.
Guidance and Counseling; Health and Safety; Psychology
Dist - FOTH **Prod** - FOTH 1990

Nahal 10 MIN
16mm
Color
Shows how Israel's nahal (pioneer fighting youth) combines farming and soldiering.
Agriculture; Civics and Political Systems; Geography - World
Dist - ALDEN **Prod** - ALDEN

Nahanni 25 MIN
16mm
Color (FRENCH)
LC 72-701241
Covers an expedition by speleologist Jean Porirel and his crew who parachute near the headwaters of the South Nahanni River in western Canada, travel downstream by inflatable boats, scale the canyon walls above the river and explore Nahanni's caves.
Geography - World; Science - Physical
Dist - CDIAND **Prod** - CDIAND 1972

Nahanni 19 MIN
16mm
B&W (J A)
Follows Albert Faille, an aging prospector from Fort Simpson, on his journey down the Nahanni River, through forbidding wilderness and dark canyons.
Geography - World
Dist - NFBC **Prod** - NFBC 1962

Nahanni - Two Weeks of the River 16 MIN
16mm
Color (G)
_ #106C 0178 471
Shows six young men on their two week canoe trip down the Nahanni River in the Northwest Territories. Shares the fears and joys of the wilderness expedition.
Geography - World; Physical Education and Recreation; Science - Natural
Dist - CFLMDC **Prod** - NFBC 1980

Nai - the Story of a Kung Woman 58 MIN
16mm
Color
LC 80-701249
Presents a compilation of footage of the Kung people of Namibia from 1951 to 1978. Focuses on the changes in the lives of these people as seen through the reflections of one woman, Nai.
Geography - World; Sociology
Dist - DOCEDR **Prod** - DOCEDR 1980

Nai - the Story of a Kung Woman, Pt 1 29 MIN
16mm
Color
LC 80-701249
Presents a compilation of footage of the Kung people of Namibia from 1951 to 1978. Focuses on the changes in the lives of these people as seen through the reflections of one woman, Nai.
History - United States
Dist - DOCEDR **Prod** - DOCEDR 1980

Nai - the Story of a Kung Woman, Pt 2 29 MIN
16mm
Color
LC 80-701249
Presents a compilation of footage of the Kung people of Namibia from 1951 to 1978. Focuses on the changes in the lives of these people as seen through the reflections of one woman, Nai.
History - United States
Dist - DOCEDR **Prod** - DOCEDR 1980

Naia and the Fishgod 9 MIN
16mm
Color (J G) (HAWAIIAN)
Tells the Hawaiian legend of how the first porpoise appeared in Hawaiian waters.
Geography - United States; History - United States; Literature and Drama; Religion and Philosophy; Sociology
Dist - CINEPC **Prod** - TAHARA 1985

Nail 20 MIN
16mm / U-matic / VHS
Color
LC 73-702339
Tells of a lonely secretary who finds a large shiny nail, which proves to be the catalyst that brings her alienated fellow tenants together in a spontaneous celebration of love and fellowship.
Psychology; Sociology
Dist - AIMS **Prod** - FAMF 1973

Nails 13 MIN
16mm
Color (J)
LC 80-701154
Contrasts the blacksmith's slow craftsman's approach with the mass production methods of the 80's, using the ordinary nail as a symbol of industrial growth.
Sociology
Dist - NFBC **Prod** - NFBC 1980

Nails 4 MIN
U-matic / VHS / 16mm
Color (H C A)
LC 73-701829
Uses thousands of 'MULTIPLYING' nails to present an abstract statement on the problem of over - population.
Sociology
Dist - IFB **Prod** - IFB 1973

Nails - the Impact of Technological Change on One Industry 13 MIN
16mm / VHS
Color (H C A)
$535.00 purchase, $150.00 rental _ #170
Examines the process of nail - making from handicraft skill to mass production, exploring impact of change on modern industry. No narrative. Includes Leader's Guide.
Business and Economics; Psychology
Dist - SALENG **Prod** - NFBC 1980

Naim and Jabar 50 MIN
16mm
Faces of Change - Afghanistan Series
Color
Analyzes the friendship of two Afghan boys, emphasizing the hopes, fears and aspirations of adolescence.
Geography - World
Dist - WHEELK **Prod** - AUFS

The Naked breast 55 MIN
VHS
Color (C A)
$99.00 purchase, $50.00 rental
Studies the female breast, its evolution, physiology and role in sexuality. Uses lactation research from Perth, Australia, Cambridge and Edinburgh. Discusses the contraceptive effects of breastfeeding, the debate over breastfeeding v bottle feeding babies, breast cancer and breast enhancing fashions.
Health and Safety; Home Economics; Science - Natural; Sociology
Dist - FCSINT **Prod** - FCSINT

Naked Chicago - three films 55 MIN
VHS
Color (G)
$50.00 purchase
Includes Sneakin' and Peakin'; I was a Contestant at Mother's Wet T - Shirt Contest; and Hot Nasty, made between 1975 - 1977. See individual titles for description and availability for rental in 16mm format.
Fine Arts; Sociology
Dist - CANCIN **Prod** - PALAZT

Naked Civil Servant 78 MIN
U-matic / VHS / 16mm
Color (C A)
Presents the autobiography of flamboyant British homosexual Quentin Crisp. Dramatizes the story of courage in spite of years of intolerance, misunderstanding, ostracism and violence. Discusses his boyhood, ill - fated friendships, encounters with the law and rare moments of real happiness, interpreted masterfully by actor John Hurt.
Sociology
Dist - MEDIAG **Prod** - THAMES 1975

The Naked Gershwin 60 MIN
U-matic
Color (J C)
Blends the music of composer George Gershwin and the words written about him by his celebrated friends and admirers. This unique 60 - minute program was created by Cecil Lytle, a professor of music at UCSD, to reveal the relationship between the personal and artistic sides of Gershwins's life, as well as the jazz and classical aspects of his music. Featured in the performance are such

favorites as 'S'Wonderful,' 'A Fogy Day,' 'The Man I Love,' and excerpts from 'Porgy & Bess,' in addition to such lesser - known pieces as 'Piano Preludes' and 'The Two Waltzes.'.
Fine Arts
Dist - SDSC **Prod** - SDSC

The Naked Kiss 90 MIN
16mm
B&W (C A)
Presents a drama starring Constance Towers, Tony Eisley and Michael Dante.
Fine Arts
Dist - CINEWO **Prod** - CINEWO 1964

The Naked kiss 90 MIN
VHS
B&W (G)
$59.95 _ #NAK010
Features a sultry story of a prostitute's redemption in small - town America - where everything is not as it seems. Presents the quintessential Samuel Fuller, director, with an emotion - packed melodrama. Digitally remastered.
Fine Arts; Psychology; Sociology
Dist - HOMVIS **Prod** - JANUS 1964

Naked Spaces - Living is Round 135 MIN
16mm / VHS
Color (G)
$1600.00, $495.00 purchase, $225.00 rental
Explores the rhythm and ritual of life in the rural environments of six West African countries. Features nonlinear structure in the documentary form.
Agriculture; Fine Arts; Geography - World; History - United States; History - World
Dist - WMEN **Prod** - JPBOU 1985

The naked trees 97 MIN
VHS
Color; PAL (G)
PdS100 purchase
Raises questions concerning collective responsibility and individual aspirations through the affair between a small - time saboteur and a resistance group leader in World War II Denmark. Presents a Morten Henriksen, Danish Film Institute production.
History - World; Literature and Drama
Dist - BALFOR

Nakuru 25 MIN
16mm / U-matic / VHS
Untamed World Series
Color; Mono (J H C A)
$400.00 film, $250.00 video, $50.00 rental
Features the Lake Nakuru National Park in Africa that was established for the protection of birdlife.
Science - Natural
Dist - CTV **Prod** - CTV 1973

Nal Sarovar 10 MIN
16mm
B&W (I)
Shows the bird watchers' paradise at Nal Sarovar in Gujarat in India. Explains that it is a sanctuary for migrating birds from as far away as Europe and Siberia.
Science - Natural
Dist - NEDINF **Prod** - INDIA

Namaqualand - Diary of a Desert Garden 50 MIN
VHS / U-matic
Color (H C A)
Explores the Namaqualand region of South Africa, a vast area of desert, rocks and mountains supporting over 4,000 species of flowers. Explains that the little rain that falls comes in winter and evaporates slowly and how a delicate ecosystem has developed between the plants and animals.
Geography - World; Science - Natural
Dist - FI **Prod** - WNETTV

Namatjira, the Painter 18 MIN
16mm
Color
Studies Albert Namatjira, Australia's best - known Aboriginal artist and master of vivid watercolor landscape scenes.
Fine Arts; Geography - World; Sociology
Dist - AUIS **Prod** - FLMAUS

Name Designs 15 MIN
VHS / U-matic
Young at Art Series
Color (P I)
Discusses name designs in art.
Fine Arts
Dist - AITECH **Prod** - WSKJTV 1980

Name Game 240 - 360 MIN
Videodisc
(A PRO)
$2,595.00
Teaches students how to remember people and their names.
Computer Science
Dist - VIDEOT **Prod** - VIDEOT 1988

The Name Game 20 MIN
VHS / U-matic
Color
$335.00 purchase
Business and Economics
Dist - ABCLR **Prod** - ABCLR 1983

Name it 15 MIN
VHS / U-matic
Magic Shop Series no 6
Color (P)
LC 83-706151
Employs a magician named Amazing Alexander and his assistants to explore the use of nouns.
English Language
Dist - GPN **Prod** - CVETVC 1982

The Name of the Age - James Boswell and Samuel Johnson 45 MIN
U-matic / VHS
Survey of English Literature I Series
Color
Analyzes the work of James Boswell and Samuel Johnson.
Literature and Drama
Dist - MDCPB **Prod** - MDCPB

The Name of the Game 30 MIN
VHS / U-matic
Managerial Game Plan - Team Building through MBO Series
Color
Stresses the importance of identifying the managerial process. Covers common roadblocks to planning.
Business and Economics; Psychology
Dist - PRODEV **Prod** - PRODEV

Name of the Game 30 MIN
U-matic / VHS / 16mm
Powerhouse Series
Color (I J)
Discusses competition and drug use through the story of the Powerhouse soccer team's use of a ringer to win a match. Shows how the team is caught in a web of deception.
Health and Safety
Dist - GA **Prod** - EFCVA 1982

The Name of the Game 27 MIN
16mm
Color (J)
LC FIA68-1408
Highlights the 1966 professional football season, featuring team and individual performances of the Minnesota Vikings.
Physical Education and Recreation
Dist - NFL **Prod** - NFL 1967

The Name of the Game 28 MIN
16mm
B&W
Presents a function of the fellowship of Christian athletes. During the weekend of champions in Dallas, Tom Landry had the prayer, Dallas Cowboy tight end Pettis Norman read scripture and Bart Starr delivered the sermon during a Sunday morning worship service.
Physical Education and Recreation; Religion and Philosophy
Dist - FELLCA **Prod** - FELLCA

The Name of the Game is - Baseball 29 MIN
Videoreel / VT1
Color
Little Leaguers and Big Leaguers - all young players learn the fundamentals of baseball from Big League stars. Includes lots of baseball action. Narrated by Curt Gowdy.
Physical Education and Recreation
Dist - MTP **Prod** - PICA

The Name of the Game is - Fun 28 MIN
Videoreel / VT1
Color
Follows the evolution of a baseball season from spring training, coaching of rookies and the Grape Fruit League to regular season with a recap of great moments in American League history. Studies the American League.
Physical Education and Recreation
Dist - MTP **Prod** - CRYSLR

Name of the game is golf series
Hazard shots 55 MIN
Long irons 55 MIN
Putting - Volume 1 55 MIN
Short irons - Volume 2 55 MIN
Dist - CAMV

The Name of the Game is P and L 4 MIN
U-matic / VHS
Color (PRO)
Uses game show format to highlight possible antitrust liabilities. Contestants answer questions which determine whether they incur antitrust liabilities.
Civics and Political Systems
Dist - ABACPE **Prod** - ABACPE

The Name of the Game is Soccer 28 MIN
16mm
Color
LC 80-701247
Provides information about the basic elements of soccer. Highlights professional players on the field and during interviews.
Physical Education and Recreation
Dist - MTP **Prod** - PICA 1980

Name of the Gme is Golf Series
Wood and Tee Shots 55 MIN
Dist - CAMV

The Name Principle 15 MIN
VHS / U-matic
Color (H C G) (FRENCH)
$245, $275 _ #V127
Shows viewers that using a customer's name fosters a positive feeling and makes customers feel more comfortable in a place of business. Demonstrates that customers appreciate being asked for correct pronunciation of their name. Reinforces the point that being addressed by one's name is much appreciated by today's customer in our service oriented economy.
Business and Economics; Psychology
Dist - BARR **Prod** - BARR 1988

Name that Label 15 MIN
U-matic / VHS
TNRC Presents - Health and Self Series
Color (J H)
Presents members of the Twelfth Night Repertory Company using humor, satire, music, dance and drama to focus attention on attitudes regarding prejudices and stereotypes. Shows that Big Guy finds out that almost as soon as he creates Man and Woman, prejudice and stereotyping are born. Reveals that when groups that form to combat these problems don't communicate, the problems increase. Presents student leaders who use communication skills to mediate differences, to separate gossip from truth, and to make the world a better place for themselves and others.
Psychology; Sociology
Dist - AITECH **Prod** - KLCSTV 1984

Name that Publication - an Introduction to the VA Publication System 39 MIN
U-matic
Color
LC 79-707303
Deals with a variety of Veterans Administration publications, such as circulars, information letters, hospital bulletins and Title 38 of the Veterans Adminstration manual, part 1 and interim issues. Focuses on the use of these publications by the employees of the Medical Administration Service.
Guidance and Counseling
Dist - USNAC **Prod** - VAHSL 1978

Namekas - Music in Lake Chambri 53 MIN
16mm
Color (H A)
Reveals a wealth of musical tradition in Lake Chambri. Music is produced by carved wooden drums, sacred bamboo flutes, the panpipe, jew's harps, buzzing beetles and the human voice in a wide variety of songs.
Fine Arts; Geography - World; Social Science; Sociology
Dist - DOCEDR **Prod** - DOCEDR 1979

Names 15 MIN
VHS / U-matic
Pass it on Series
Color (K P)
Discusses first and last names and nicknames.
Education
Dist - GPN **Prod** - WKNOTV 1983

Names and origins - physical characteristics - Parts 5 and 6 60 MIN
VHS / U-matic
French in action - part I series
Color (C) (FRENCH)
$45.00, $29.95 purchase
Covers numbers, expressing age, necessity, negation, the imperatives of ' - er' verbs, 'il faut' and infinitives in Part 5. Looks at the expression of reality and appearance, describing oneself, talking about sports, numbers, questions in Part 6. Parts of a 52 - part series teaching the French language, all in French, written by Pierre Capretz, Director of the Language Laboratory at Yale.
Foreign Language; History - World
Dist - ANNCPB **Prod** - YALEU 1987

Names for Numbers 30 MIN
16mm
Mathematics for Elementary School Teachers Series no 3
Color (T)
Describes the concept of set, and introduces the number properties of sets. Discusses the properties of order for numbers as well as for sets. To be used following 'WHOLE NUMBERS.'.
Mathematics
Dist - MLA **Prod** - SMSG 1963

Names, Names, Names and Why We Need Them 10 MIN
16mm / U-matic / VHS
Color (K P)
LC 75-704014
Points out to children the importance of names for people, places and things. Shows how people could not communicate without names.
Guidance and Counseling; Social Science
Dist - BARR **Prod** - SAIF 1975

The Names of the Holy Spirit
VHS
Color (R)
$49.99 purchase _ #SPCN 85116.00701
Gives an understanding of the over 100 names and descriptions of the Holy Spirit. Includes the book of the same name by Elmer L Towns, a group study guide and two videos.
Religion and Philosophy
Dist - GOSPEL **Prod** - GOSPEL

Names We Never Knew 27 MIN
16mm
Spectrum Series
Color
LC 75-703111
Documents the quest of Oklahoman artist Charles Banks Wilson in order to portray the history of the common man.
Biography; Fine Arts
Dist - WKYTV **Prod** - WKYTV 1975

Namibia 26 MIN
U-matic / VHS
Color (H C A)
Examines the culture, ecology and government of Namibia.
Geography - World
Dist - JOU **Prod** - UPI

Namibia - Africa's Last Colony 52 MIN
VHS / U-matic
Third Eye Series
Color (J H C A)
Describes the South African occupation of Namibia, the last territory in Africa still to gain its independence.
Civics and Political Systems; Geography - World; History - World
Dist - CANWRL **Prod** - CANWRL 1984

Namibia - no easy road to freedom 58 MIN
VHS
Color (G)
$350.00 purchase, $90.00 rental
Examines Namibia's long history of colonial occupation by South Africa, including the armed conflict between South African troops and the Namibian resistance organization SWAPO. Looks at peace plan negotiations in 1978 and disucussions of the nation's independence in 1990. Directed by Kevin Harris.
Civics and Political Systems; Fine Arts; History - World; Sociology
Dist - CNEMAG

Namibia - rebirth of a nation 45 MIN
VHS
Color (G)
$295.00 purchase, $75.00 rental
Documents the challenges which face the citizens of Namibia after 23 years of struggle against South African forces of occupation. Reveals that after their independence on March 21, 1990, the Namibians must rebuild a nation dispossessed by a lifetime of colonial possession, including the assimilation of 44,000 exiled returnees, a shortage of housing and a 50 percent unemployment rate.
Geography - World; History - World; Sociology
Dist - CNEMAG

Naming sets - the set abstractor 33 MIN
16mm
Teaching high school mathematics - first course series; No 37
B&W (T)
Mathematics
Dist - MLA **Prod** - UICSM 1967

Naming the Parts 60 MIN
U-matic / VHS
Body in Question Series Program 1; Program 1
Color (H C A)
LC 81-706224
Argues that man's ignorance of basic physiology leads to unusual attitudes toward the body. Establishes what happens when a person becomes ill. Based on the book The Body In Question by Jonathan Miller. Narrated by Jonathan Miller.
Health and Safety; Science - Natural
Dist - FI **Prod** - BBCTV 1979

Nan kakkugi
VHS
Color (G)
$80.00 _ #42091
Features flower culture.
Fine Arts
Dist - PANASI

Nana, Mom and Me 47 MIN
16mm
Color (H C A)
LC 74-702495
Features a filmmaker, who is considering having a child. Examines interrelationships between herself, her mother and her grandmother. Raises questions about the nature and substance of family relationships.
Psychology; Sociology
Dist - NEWDAY **Prod** - ANOMFM 1974

Nana - Un Portrait 25 MIN
16mm
Color (FRENCH)
LC 74-700102
A French language film. Presents a portrait of 80 - year - old Nana Zilkha who was born in Bagdad and now lives in an apartment in New York. Tells of her life with her husband and seven children and of the people and places she has known.
Foreign Language
Dist - SIMONJ **Prod** - SIMONJ 1973

Nanami, first love 104 MIN
VHS
Color (G) (JAPANESE WITH ENGLISH SUBTITLES)
$35.95 purchase _ #TME1091
Offers a tale of passionate desire and psychological turbulence. Directed by Susumu Hani.
Fine Arts
Dist - CHTSUI

Nancy Acosta 28 MIN
U-matic / VHS
Old Friends - New Friends Series
Color
Features Nancy Acosta, a 21 year - old teacher in the barrios of La Puente outside of Los Angeles, where crime and violence are common. Tells how she is providing an alternative, a school for dropouts where the atmosphere offers uncompromising love and respect.
Education
Dist - PBS **Prod** - FAMCOM 1981

Nancy and Her Friends 28 MIN
16mm
Color (C A)
Presents a study of three divorced women who gave up custody of their children and set out on new paths.
Sociology
Dist - VIERAD **Prod** - VIERAD 1977

Nancy, Henri and Elizabeth 16 MIN
16mm
Color
LC 74-702874
Demonstates that an attempt to humanize Nancy, Henri and Elizabeth on one level while their actions and words function metaphorically, raises questions and stimulates emotions concerning the development and stability of sexual identity.
Guidance and Counseling; Psychology; Sociology
Dist - ANNSC **Prod** - AIBELR 1973

Nancy Holt - Locating no 2 14 MIN
U-matic / VHS
B&W
Focuses on the native turf of Nancy Holt.
Fine Arts
Dist - ARTINC **Prod** - ARTINC

Nancy Holt - Revolve 77 MIN
U-matic / VHS
B&W
Tells about a struggle for life.
Fine Arts
Dist - ARTINC **Prod** - ARTINC

Nancy Holt - Underscan 8 MIN
VHS / U-matic
B&W
Features a domestic drama.
Fine Arts; Sociology
Dist - ARTINC **Prod** - ARTINC

Nancy Schimmel Video 30 MIN
VHS
Tell Me a Story Series
Color (K)
$19.95 purchase _ #W181 - 048
Features Nancy Schimmel as storyteller. Includes 'The Handsome Prince,' 'Clever Monka,' 'The Peddler of Swaftham' and 'The Lionmakers.' Part of an eight - unit series.
Literature and Drama
Dist - UPSTRT **Prod** - UPSTRT

Nanduti - a Paraguayan Lace 18 MIN
16mm
Color
LC 78-701318
Introduces the origin of nanduti lace through one of its many legends. Juxtaposes the symbolic and representational patterns of nanduti with natural and manmade objects and documents the process of making nanduti.
Fine Arts; Sociology
Dist - CK **Prod** - CK 1978

Nanes Holocaust Symphony No. 3 160 MIN
VHS
Color (G)
$19.95 purchase_#1399
Presents a new symphony, entitled Holocaust Symphony No. 3, by American composer Richard Nanes. Presents a powerful musical statement about the World War II Holocaust. Taped at the Kiev Opera House during the Kiev International Music Festival and performed by the Kharkiv Festival Orchestra.
Fine Arts
Dist - KULTUR

Nanette - an Aside 44 MIN
16mm
Color
LC 78-700204
Presents an adaptation of a short story by Willa Cather in which a famous ballerina and her young secretary discover that their ideas and modes of living have become radically different.
Literature and Drama; Sociology
Dist - VANGLE **Prod** - WHITOM 1977

Nanette - an Aside, Pt 1 22 MIN
16mm
Color
LC 78-700204
Presents an adaptation of a short story by Willa Cather in which a famous ballerina and her young secretary discover that their ideas and modes of living have become radically different.
Literature and Drama
Dist - VANGLE **Prod** - WHITOM 1977

Nanette - an Aside, Pt 2 22 MIN
16mm
Color
LC 78-700204
Presents an adaptation of a short story by Willa Cather in which a famous ballerina and her young secretary discover that their ideas and modes of living have become radically different.
Literature and Drama
Dist - VANGLE **Prod** - WHITOM 1977

Nanny and Isaiah adventure series
The Care - filled caper
Care for God's children - teaching children to help others 45 MIN
Easter today, Easter forever 33 MIN
Friends in need, friends in deed
Grow in God's family 45 MIN
Learn to follow Jesus - teaching children to put faith into action 50 MIN
Learn to share Jesus - teaching children how to witness 40 MIN
The Secret of the second basement 30 MIN
The Winning combination
Wonder witness and mighty mouth
Dist - CPH

Nanny and Isaiah - Care for God's children 45 MIN
VHS
Nanny and Isaiah series
Color (K P I R)
$24.95 purchase, $10.00 rental _ #35-8511-19, #87EE0511
Features the characters Nanny and Isaiah as they visit an inner - city outreach center and learn how many people must struggle to make ends meet. Emphasizes the idea that kids can support such efforts.
Literature and Drama; Religion and Philosophy
Dist - APH **Prod** - CPH
CPH

Nanny and Isaiah - Grow in God's family 45 MIN
VHS
Nanny and Isaiah series
Color (K P I R)
$24.95 purchase, $10.00 rental _ #35-8521-19, #87EE0521
Features the characters Nanny and Isaiah as they learn how God can help families to grow closer together. Emphasizes the idea that, one day, all will be part of God's heavenly family.
Literature and Drama; Religion and Philosophy
Dist - APH **Prod** - CPH
CPH

Nanny and Isaiah learn to follow Jesus 50 MIN
VHS
Nanny and Isaiah series
Color (K P I R)

$24.95 purchase, $10.00 rental _ #35 - 8141 - 19
Portrays the characters Nanny and Isaiah as they attempt to show love and concern for other people while forming a church softball team. Includes leader's guide.
Literature and Drama; Religion and Philosophy
Dist - APH **Prod** - CPH

Nanny and Isaiah learn to share Jesus 40 MIN
VHS
Nanny and Isaiah series
Color (K P I R)
$24.95 purchase, $10.00 rental _ #35 - 8241 - 19
Teaches children basic skills in evangelism to their peers. Includes leader's guide.
Literature and Drama; Religion and Philosophy
Dist - APH **Prod** - CPH

Nanny and Isaiah series
Nanny and Isaiah learn to follow Jesus 50 MIN
Nanny and Isaiah learn to share Jesus 40 MIN
Dist - APH

Nanny and Isaiah series
Nanny and Isaiah - Care for God's children 45 MIN
Nanny and Isaiah - Grow in God's family 45 MIN
Dist - APH
CPH

Nanook of the North 69 MIN
VHS
B&W; Silent (H C G)
$29.95 purchase _ #NANO10
Follows the Eskimo Nanook and his family as they pit their human frailties against the vast and inhospitable Arctic. Captures the rhythms of the natural world and the presence of humans within its cycles.
Fine Arts; Literature and Drama
Dist - INSTRU **Prod** - FLAH 1922

Nanook of the North 60 MIN
U-matic / VHS
B&W
Presents a documentary about the Eskimo's struggle against the harsh elements. Directed by Robert Flaherty.
Geography - United States; Science - Physical; Sociology
Dist - IHF **Prod** - IHF

Naosaki 8 MIN
16mm
Color
LC 77-702988
Presents an aesthetic study of gymnastic movement, emphasizing its visual and kinesthetic elements.
Physical Education and Recreation
Dist - CANFDC **Prod** - HUNNL

The Nap 13 MIN
16mm
Color
LC 79-700846
Tells how a well - deserved afternoon nap turns into a nightmare.
Fine Arts
Dist - ROSENJ **Prod** - ROSENJ 1979

Nape and the Mice - Nape and the Rock 14 MIN
VHS / 16mm
Ukrainian Shadow Puppets Series
Color (I) (ENGLISH AND UKRAINIAN)
$175.00 purchase _ #277105
Introduces some of the cultural heritage of the Cree and Blackfoot people of Alberta, Canada, through a Ukrainian bilingual program to reach the Ukrainian commmunity. Contains a unique blend of myths and legends and original music and artwork commissioned from Cree and Blackfoot artists with Ukrainian silhouette puppets. 'Nape And The Mice - Nape And The Rock' recounts the Nape cycle of the Cree trickster. Nape loses his hair after joining a bunch of mice partying in an elk's skull in the first story. The second story explains how the kit fox got its black coat, the buffalo got its hump and how the large rock formation near Okotoks, Alberta, came into existence. Includes a booklet with Ukrainian language transcripts.
Geography - World; History - World; Literature and Drama; Religion and Philosophy; Social Science; Sociology
Dist - ACCESS **Prod** - ACCESS 1987

Napkins - the perfect accent 30 MIN
VHS
Color (J H C G)
$29.95 purchase _ #PG100V
Features over 23 different napkin sculptures for creating just the right ambiance, from formal elegance to rustic charm.
Fine Arts; Home Economics
Dist - CAMV

Naples to Cassino 26 MIN
U-matic
Historical Reports Series
B&W
LC 80-706774
Shows scenes of fighting during the drive of Allied forces from Naples to Cassino, Italy, during World War II. Issued in 1948 as a motion picture.
Civics and Political Systems; History - United States; History - World
Dist - USNAC **Prod** - USA 1980

Naples to Cassino 24 MIN
16mm
Historical Reports Series
B&W
LC FIE52-1691
Presents scenes of fighting during the drive of Allied forces from Naples to Cassino, Itlay.
Civics and Political Systems; History - World
Dist - USNAC **Prod** - USA 1949

Napoleon Bonaparte 12 MIN
U-matic / VHS
Color (C)
$229.00, $129.00 purchase _ #AD - 1853
Presents the life of Napoleon Bonaparte. Portrays him as a military genius and enormously capable organizer and administrator in his roles as empire builder, champion of the people and their revolution and codifier of French law.
Biography; Civics and Political Systems; Foreign Language; History - World
Dist - FOTH **Prod** - FOTH

Napoleon - the End of a Dictator 26 MIN
U-matic / VHS / 16mm
Western Civilization - Majesty and Madness Series
Color (J A)
LC 73-305738
Explores the causes of Napoleon's downfall which includes the weariness of war and tyranny in France and the new nationalism throughout Europe.
Biography; Civics and Political Systems; History - World
Dist - LCOA **Prod** - LCOA 1970

Napoleon - the End of a Dictator 26 MIN
16mm / U-matic / VHS
Color (J) (SPANISH)
Dramatizes Napoleon's return from Elba and his defeat at Waterloo.
Foreign Language; History - World
Dist - LCOA **Prod** - LCOA 1970

Napoleon - the Making of a Dictator 27 MIN
U-matic / VHS / 16mm
Color (J) (SPANISH)
Explores the first modern coup d'etat, the rise to power of Napoleon Bonaparte.
Foreign Language; History - World
Dist - LCOA **Prod** - LCOA 1970

Napoleon - the Making of a Dictator 27 MIN
U-matic / VHS / 16mm
Western Civilization - Majesty and Madness Series
Color (J A)
LC 77-705739
Examines the problem of freedom versus stability through the coup d'etat of 1799. Shows how military victories built Napoleon's popularity and how a corrupt government can be overpowered by a dictator.
Biography; Civics and Political Systems; History - World
Dist - LCOA **Prod** - LCOA 1970

The Napoleonic Era 14 MIN
U-matic / VHS / 16mm
Color (J H C)
Describes the Napoleonic era of 1796 - 1815 and its effects upon France and Europe. Includes scenes typifying Napoleon's rise to power, his governmental reforms in France, his conquests and the disintegration of the Grand Empire.
Biography; History - World
Dist - CORF **Prod** - CORF 1957

The Napoleonic era 40 MIN
VHS
Color (H C)
LC 89-700169
Examines Napoleon, his rise to power and his downfall.
History - World
Dist - EAV **Prod** - EAV 1989

Napoleon's last battle 65 MIN
VHS
Timewatch
Color; PAL (C H)
PdS99 purchase
Covers the last years of Napoleon Bonaparte's life. Focuses on Bonaparte as a self - propagandist. Dramatizes exchanges between Bonaparte (Kenneth Colley), his doctor and his biographer.
History - World
Dist - BBCENE

Napoleon's Last Great War 30 MIN
U-matic / VHS
How Wars End Series
Color (G)
$249.00, $149.00 purchase _ #AD - 910
Looks at Napoleon's invasion of Russia and his loss of military mastery through unclear aims, miscalculations of the enemy's intentions and intractability in negotiation. Examines the turning point in modern European history. Part of a six - part series on how wars end, hosted by historian A J P Taylor.
History - World; Sociology
Dist - FOTH **Prod** - FOTH

Napoli 98 MIN
VHS
Color (S)
$39.95 purchase _ #833 - 9276
Evokes a gloriously sunny Italian atmosphere to tell the story of Gennaro, a young fisherman, and his beloved Teresina. Features music by Helsted, Rossini, Gade, Paulli and Lumbye, choreography by August Bournonville of the 19th century. Danced by Linda Hindberg, Arne Villumsen and the Royal Danish Ballet.
Fine Arts; Physical Education and Recreation
Dist - FI **Prod** - NVIDC 1987

The Napping House 5 MIN
16mm / VHS
Color
Presents a simple tale of family members and the snuggling heap they make on a rainy day, until a wakeful flea causes the drowsing pyramid to erupt into wakefulness as the sun suddenly appears. Based on the book by Audrey Wood.
Literature and Drama
Dist - WWS **Prod** - SCHNDL

The Napping House 4 MIN
VHS / U-matic
(K P I)
Shows cool blue colors and wistful wood winds set the mood, as sleepy bodies accumulate on a sagging bed, one by one, each to its particular musical theme and narrative tone. The repetitive text invites young viewers to join in describing the wakeful flea on a slumbering mouse on a snoozing cat on a dozing dog on a dreaming child on a snoring grandma. All is calm until a fateful itch throws the pyramid into an eruptive reverie.
English Language; Literature and Drama
Dist - WWS **Prod** - WWS 1985

Nara - a Stroll through History 20 MIN
16mm
Color (H C A)
LC 77-702436
Presents a tour of the Japanese city of Nara, visiting its historical sites and showing examples of its eighth - century Buddhist art.
Fine Arts; Geography - World; History - World
Dist - JNTA **Prod** - JNTA 1973

Narayama bushi - ko 97 MIN
16mm / VHS
Color (G) (JAPANESE WITH ENGLISH SUBTITLES)
$250.00 rental
Depicts the Japanese legend of a son who must follow the custom of abandoning his mother on a mountain when she turns 70. Directed by Keisuke Kinoshita.
Fine Arts; Literature and Drama; Religion and Philosophy
Dist - KINOIC

Narc 26 MIN
VHS / 16mm
Color (J H G)
$249.00, $349.00 purchase, $50.00 rental _ #AD-1632, #95120116J
Presents the dilemma that arises when a popular high school student tries to prevent her friend, an accomplished football player, from driving while drunk. Reveals that, as a result, he is dismissed from the team and she becomes the target of alienation and ridicule. Discusses alcohol abuse, the temptation to follow the crowd, and the value of remaining true to one's own beliefs.
Guidance and Counseling; Health and Safety; Psychology
Dist - FOTH **Prod** - FOTH 1990
HAZELB

Narcissistic Personality Disorder - an Interview with a Senior Adult 30 MIN
U-matic / VHS
Color (PRO)
Illustrates some of the characteristic manifestations of a narcissistic personality disorder in an older adult.
Health and Safety
Dist - HSCIC **Prod** - HSCIC 1985

Narcissus 59 MIN
16mm
B&W (C)
$1064.00
Experimental film by Willard Maas.
Fine Arts
Dist - AFA **Prod** - AFA 1956

Narcissus 22 MIN
U-matic / VHS
Color (J)
LC 84-707133
Expands upon the beauty of ballet by showing the sensual movements of dancers from a distance and the passionate emotions conveyed by their unique interpretation of the Greek myth of Narcissus.
Fine Arts
Dist - NFBC **Prod** - VERRAD 1983

Narcissus and Echo
VHS / 35mm strip
Timeless Tales - Myths of Ancient Greece - Set II
Color (I)
$39.95, $28.00 purchase
Recreates the myth of Narcissus and Echo. Part of a five - part series on Greek mythology.
English Language; History - World; Literature and Drama; Religion and Philosophy
Dist - PELLER

Narcissus - Narcisse 22 MIN
16mm
Color
_ #106C 0083 008
Geography - World
Dist - CFLMDC **Prod** - NFBC 1983

Narcolepsy 12 MIN
16mm
Color
Presents Dr William C Dement of Stanford University who describes the symptoms and diagnosis of narcolepsy, a disease of deep sleep. Shows narcoleptic patients having sleep attacks, cataleptic attacks and hypnogogic hallucinations. Describes Dr Dement's research which has provided a definitive method of diagnosing narcolepsy using sleep recordings.
Health and Safety; Psychology; Science
Dist - AMEDA **Prod** - HOFLAR

Narcosynthesis 22 MIN
16mm
B&W (PRO)
Demonstrates the injection of ultra - short - acting barbiturates to the point of very light narcosis in various cases. Case one shows the movements. Case two shows the effect of reassurance and suggestion in hysteria with hemiparesis. Case three shows the production of emotional responsiveness in a schizophrenialike state. Case four shows the result of treatment of major hysteria in an 11 - year - old girl. restricted.
Health and Safety; Psychology
Dist - PSUPCR **Prod** - PSUPCR 1944

Narcotic and Non - Narcotic Analgesics 30 MIN
16mm
Pharmacology Series
Color (C)
LC 73-703335
Health and Safety; Psychology
Dist - TELSTR **Prod** - MVNE 1971

Narcotic Deaths, Pt 1 27 MIN
16mm
Clinical Pathology - Forensic Medicine Outlines Series
B&W (PRO)
LC 74-705184
Describes types of narcotic deaths, types of drugs used and symptomatic changes found externally as well as internally. Discusses and demonstrates the implements used to take narcotic drugs and shows slides of overdose victims and the effects of narcotic intravenous infections on veins and subcutaneous tissue. (Kinescope).
Health and Safety; Psychology; Sociology
Dist - USNAC **Prod** - NMAC 1970

Narcotic Deaths, Pt 1 30 MIN
VHS / U-matic
Narcotic Deaths Series
Color (PRO)
Health and Safety
Dist - PRIMED **Prod** - PRIMED

Narcotic Deaths, Pt 2 21 MIN
16mm
Clinical Pathology - Forensic Medicine Outlines Series
B&W (PRO)
LC 74-705185
Describes types of narcotic deaths, types of drugs used and symptomatic changes found externally as well as internally. Discusses and demonstrates the implements used to take narcotic drugs and shows slides of overdose victims and the effects of narcotic intravenous infections on veins and subcutaneous tissue. (Kinescope).
Health and Safety; Psychology; Science; Sociology
Dist - USNAC **Prod** - NMAC 1970

Narcotic Deaths, Pt 2 30 MIN
U-matic / VHS
Narcotic Deaths Series
Color (PRO)
Health and Safety
Dist - PRIMED **Prod** - PRIMED

Narcotic Deaths Series
Narcotic Deaths, Pt 1 30 MIN
Narcotic Deaths, Pt 2 30 MIN
Dist - PRIMED

Narcotics
VHS
Substance abuse video library series
Color (T A PRO)
$125.00 purchase _ #AH45145
Presents information on the abuse of narcotics. Details the history of narcotics, how they are abused, short - term physical and psychological effects, dependency and overdose risks, and treatment. Developed by Brock Morris and Kevin Scheel.
Guidance and Counseling; Health and Safety; Psychology; Sociology
Dist - HTHED **Prod** - HTHED

Narcotics 10 MIN
16mm / U-matic / VHS
Drug Information Series
Color
Discusses the characteristics of narcotics. Identifies the signs of use and abuse, the pharmacological and behavioral effects, and the short - and long - term dangers.
Health and Safety
Dist - CORF **Prod** - MITCHG 1982

Narcotics 113 FRS
VHS / U-matic
Assessment and Management of Acute Substance Abuse Series
Color (PRO)
Discusses pharmacologic properties and effects, cross - tolerance, seizures, acute intoxification, and treatment of narcotics.
Health and Safety; Psychology; Sociology
Dist - BRA **Prod** - BRA

Narcotics - a Challenge to Youth - Teachers 24 MIN
16mm
Color (H A)
Shows a troubled boy with emotional difficulties with which he cannot cope and how he becomes addicted to drugs, which release his frustrations. Explains the teacher's responsibility of preventing this through proper education.
Education; Guidance and Counseling; Health and Safety; Psychology; Social Science; Sociology
Dist - NEFA **Prod** - NEFA 1956

Narcotics File Series
Narcotics File - the Challenge 28 MIN
Narcotics File - the Connection 28 MIN
Narcotics File - the Source 28 MIN
Narcotics File - the Victims 28 MIN
Dist - JOU

Narcotics File - the Challenge 28 MIN
U-matic / VHS / 16mm
Narcotics File Series
Color (H C A)
LC 76-703930
Describes the life of the Meo hilltribes of northern Thailand and of their cultivation of the poppy and production of opium. Tells of the attempt being made to have these people change their occupation as a means of checking the source of illicit opium.
Geography - World; Health and Safety; Psychology; Sociology
Dist - JOU **Prod** - UN 1976

Narcotics File - the Connection 28 MIN
U-matic / VHS / 16mm
Narcotics File Series
Color (J)
LC 74-701913
Details efforts being made throughout the world to stem the criminal flow of drugs. Follows the poppy from cultivation, harvesting, smuggling, processing into morphine, processing into heroin and final sale on the streets of New York.
Health and Safety; Sociology
Dist - JOU **Prod** - UN 1974

Narcotics File - the Source 28 MIN
U-matic / VHS / 16mm
Narcotics File Series
Color (J)
LC 74-701914
Introduces measures that can be taken to eliminate the illicit opium supply at the point of origin. Tells what the United Nations and the rest of a concerned world are doing about drug abuse. Deals with Thailands's part in the Golden Triangle which originates about half of the world's illicit opium supply.
Health and Safety; Sociology
Dist - JOU **Prod** - UN 1974

Narcotics File - the Victims 28 MIN
16mm / U-matic / VHS
Narcotics File Series
Color (J)
LC 74-701915
Describes various treatment programs aimed at rehabilitating the heroin addict. Includes sequences filmed at Hong Kong, Tokyo, Stockholm, London and New York dealing with drug free communes, methadone maintenance, heroin maintenance, harsh jail sentences, one - to - one psychological treatment and prison - cum - treatment centers.
Health and Safety; Psychology; Sociology
Dist - JOU **Prod** - UN 1974

Narcotics - the Inside Story 12 MIN
U-matic / VHS / 16mm
Color (I J) (ARABIC SPANISH)
LC FIA68-1102
Presents positive applications of narcotics and drugs when administered by doctors for medical purposes. Shows how experimenting with drugs and narcotics can seriously upset the central nervous system.
Foreign Language; Health and Safety; Psychology; Science - Natural
Dist - AIMS **Prod** - CAHILL 1967

Narcotics trafficking - Part 1
VHS
Roundtables discussions series
Color (G A)
$20.00 purchase
Presents a roundtable discussion of drug trafficking in the US and abroad by religious leaders, treatment specialists, former DEA agents, former gang members, physicians and policy makers. Features Harvard Law Professors Charles Nesson and Charles Ogletree as moderators. Part one of three parts produced by 'Causes and Cures,' a national campaign on the narcotics epidemic.
Civics and Political Systems; Guidance and Counseling; Health and Safety; Sociology
Dist - CRINST **Prod** - CRINST

Narcotism 23 MIN
U-matic
Forensic Medicine Teaching Programs Series no 10; No 10
Color (PRO)
LC 78-706055
Gives an overview of narcotism. Describes various drugs and shows examples of drug - associated deaths, explaining signs commonly associated with drug addiction.
Health and Safety
Dist - USNAC **Prod** - NMAC 1978

Narmada 17 MIN
16mm
B&W (I)
Traces the entire course of the Narmada River from its source at Amarkantak in Central India, through the hills and forests to the historic town of Broach, where it ends its long journey by joining the Arabian Sea at the Gulf of Cambay.
Geography - World
Dist - NEDINF **Prod** - INDIA

The Narragansetts 30 MIN
U-matic
People of the First Light Series
Color
Social Science; Sociology
Dist - GPN **Prod** - WGBYTV 1977

The Narragansetts - Tradition 29 MIN
VHS / U-matic
People of the First Light Series
Color (G)
Focuses on ways Narragansetts strive to maintain their traditional heritage and to pass traditions from one generation to the next. Shows how the old use folklore and legend to pass on values and traditions to the young. And family members teach each other skills such as carpentry, animal husbandry, hunting, and making traditional clothing.
Social Science; Sociology
Dist - NAMPBC **Prod** - NAMPBC 1979

Narration and Description
VHS / U-matic
Write Course - an Introduction to College Composition Series
Color (C)
Shows one of four lessons studying traditional rhetorical patterns, using a pragmatic approach. Emphasizes the use of traditional patterns to develop individual writing patterns.
Education; English Language
Dist - DALCCD **Prod** - DALCCD

Narration and Description 30 MIN
U-matic / VHS

Write Course - an Introduction to College Composition Series
Color (C A)
LC 85-700980
Discusses the use of traditional patterns to develop individual writing patterns. Studies traditional rhetorical patterns, using a programmatic approach.
English Language
Dist - FI **Prod** - FI 1984

Narrow Gauge Train to Silverton 21 MIN
16mm
B&W
Presents the story of 'THE SILVERTON,' the summer passenger train on the Denver and Rio Grande Western's Durango - Silverton branch.
Social Science
Dist - RMIBHF **Prod** - RMIBHF

The Narrow margin 70 MIN
VHS
B&W; CC (G)
$19.95 purchase _ #6237
Stars Charles McGraw and Marie Windsor in a tight thriller in which police try to guard a prosecution witness on a train between Chicago and Los Angeles. Features Jacqueline White and Queenie Leonard. Directed by Richard Fleischer.
Fine Arts; Literature and Drama
Dist - APRESS

Narrowcasting Dance for Cable Television 30 MIN
U-matic / VHS
Dance on Television - Lorber Series
Color
Fine Arts; Industrial and Technical Education
Dist - ARCVID **Prod** - ARCVID

NASA - airmen and the weather
VHS
Color (G)
$39.80 purchase _ #0468
Shows how weather observations are made from space. Tells about hurricanes and tornadoes and how satellite information relates to severe storms. Includes Aeronautical Life Sciences at Ames, and Flying Machines for pilots.
Industrial and Technical Education; Science - Physical
Dist - SEVVID

The NASA Biosatellite Program - between the Atom and the Star 28 MIN
16mm
Color (J H C)
Biologists explain experiments concerning gravity that will be conducted in an earth - orbiting satellite, how they will be carried out, and the importance of seeking information about weightless atmospheres on life for scientific research and the manned space program.
Science; Science - Physical
Dist - NASA **Prod** - NASA 1965

NASA - Journey into Space 20 MIN
VHS / U-matic
Color (J)
LC 82-706779
Highlights America's journey into space, including the lift - off and recovery of Apollo 14, the first step on the moon and exploration of the moon's surface. Shows how NASA astronauts lived in space and tours the NASA Kennedy Space Center from within.
Science - Physical
Dist - AWSS **Prod** - AWSS 1980

NASA Tapes Series
Conclusion of Apollo Program 56 MIN
Lunar Landing 1 - the Eagle has Landed 55 MIN
Dist - ASTROV

Nasal and septal surgery 12 MIN
VHS
Color (PRO G)
$250.00 purchase _ #OT - 11
Teaches patients that surgery designed to correct structural defects in the nose can often alleviate discomfort and annoying nasal symptoms. Details procedures that may be performed during surgery such as septoplasty, partial turbinectomy, osteotomy and possibly rhinoplasty. Discusses risks and explains the recovery process, including possible use of an internal splint. Developed in cooperation with and endorsed by the American Academy of Otolaryngology - Head and Neck Surgery.
Health and Safety; Science - Natural
Dist - MIFE **Prod** - MIFE 1991

Nasal Cavities 12 MIN
VHS / U-matic
Skull Anatomy Series
Color (C A)
Describes the boundaries, demonstrates the bones and identifies the bony regions of the nasal cavities.
Health and Safety; Science - Natural
Dist - TEF **Prod** - UTXHSA

Nashville 159 MIN
16mm / U-matic / VHS
Color
Traces five days in Nashville, the country music capital of the world. Directed by Robert Altman.
Fine Arts
Dist - FI **Prod** - PAR 1975

Nashville - the View from '82 60 MIN
U-matic / VHS
Color
LC 83-706882
Uses interviews on various topics with leaders in Nashville, Tennessee, to forecast trends for the city in 1983 based on events and happenings in 1982.
Geography - United States
Dist - WNGETV **Prod** - WNGETV 1983

Nasogastric Intubation 9 MIN
VHS / U-matic
Medical Skills Films Series
Color (PRO)
Health and Safety
Dist - WFP **Prod** - WFP

Nasogastric Intubation 27 MIN
U-matic / VHS
Emergency Management - the First 30 Minutes, Vol I Series
Color
Demonstrates techniques of nasogastric intubation.
Health and Safety; Science - Natural
Dist - VTRI **Prod** - VTRI

Nasogastric Intubation 7 MIN
U-matic / VHS
Color (PRO)
Reviews essential equipment and illustrates the step - by - step analysis of the technique as well as demonstrating the actual procedure on two trauma victims. Shows procedure done for detection of upper GI bleeding and for a patient with head and neck injuries.
Health and Safety; Psychology; Science - Natural
Dist - UWASH **Prod** - UWASH

Nasolaryngoscopy - the inside view 12 MIN
VHS / U-matic
Color (PRO C)
$395.00 purchase, $80.00 rental _ #C890 - VI - 043
Explains the procedure for performing a nasolaryngoscopy, highly accepted by patients because it is fast and painless. Presented by Dr Donald DeWitt.
Health and Safety; Science - Natural
Dist - HSCIC

Nasser and the Middle East 180 MIN
VHS / 16mm
Color (J)
$299.00 purchase, $75.00 rental _ #OD - 2243
Documents the life of Gamal Abdel Nasser and the history of Egypt from the 1920s to the 1960s and Nasser's death. Examines Egypt's rule by a king in the 1920s and by the British in the 1940s and the 1950s. Charts Nasser's ascent to power and looks at the Arab - Israeli War of 1967.
Biography; History - World
Dist - FOTH

Nasser and the Resurgence of Egypt 29 MIN
Videoreel / VT2
Course of Our Times II Series
Color
History - World
Dist - PBS **Prod** - WGBHTV

Nasser - People's Pharoah 24 MIN
U-matic / VHS / 16mm
Leaders of the 20th century - portraits of power series
Color (H C A)
LC 80-700520
Documents President Nasser's role in Egypt from the Suez Canal crisis to the Middle East conflict. Narrated by Henry Fonda.
Biography; Civics and Political Systems; Guidance and Counseling; History - World; Psychology
Dist - LCOA **Prod** - NIELSE 1980

NASTAR - Go for Gold 14 MIN
16mm
Color (I)
Presents former Olympic ski coach Bob Beattie explaining basic ski racing techniques including ski preparation, the start, running the gates and the finish. Shows scenes from the National Standard Race (NASTAR).
Physical Education and Recreation
Dist - CRYSP **Prod** - CRYSP

The Nasty girl 92 MIN
16mm
Color (G) (GERMAN WITH ENGLISH SUBTITLES)
$250.00 rental
Depicts a determined student who tries to write an essay detailing her town's behavior during the Second World War period. Looks at the outraged townspeople who are determined that only their version of the truth will be accepted and who try to prevent her investigations. A cutting satire of German denial. Based on a true story.
Fine Arts; History - World; Literature and Drama; Psychology; Religion and Philosophy; Social Science
Dist - NCJEWF

Nat Horne and Mabal Robinson 30 MIN
U-matic / VHS
Eye on Dance - Broadway Dance Series
Color
Shows how theatre dance productions are prepared.
Fine Arts
Dist - ARCVID **Prod** - ARCVID

Natalie Wood - Hollywood's Child 26 MIN
16mm
Hollywood and the Stars Series
B&W
LC FI68-184
Traces the career of Natalie Wood, describing her successful transition from a child star to an adult actress. Includes clips from West Side Story and Love with a Proper Stranger.
Biography; Fine Arts
Dist - WOLPER **Prod** - WOLPER 1964

Natasha 70 MIN
VHS
Color (G)
$39.95 purchase _ #1146
Stars Natasha Makarova in excerpts from 'On Your Toes,' 'Romeo And Juliet,' 'Manon,' 'A Month In The Country,' 'Carmen,' 'Proust Remembered,' 'Bach Sonata' and 'Begin The Beguine.' Features Tim Flavin, Anthony Dowell, Denys Ganio and Gary Chryst as her partners in those pieces. Makarova solos in 'Dying Swan' and 'Les Sylphides.'.
Fine Arts; Physical Education and Recreation
Dist - KULTUR

Nate the Great and the Sticky Case 19 MIN
16mm / U-matic / VHS
Color (K P)
Reveals how Nate the Great, the sharpest sleuth since Sherlock Holmes, solves the mystery of his friend Claude's missing stegosaurus stamp aided by clear - headed logic, keen memory and strong powers of observation.
Fine Arts; Literature and Drama
Dist - EBEC **Prod** - EBEC 1983

Nate the Great Goes Undercover 10 MIN
16mm / U-matic / VHS
Contemporary Children's Literature Series
Color (K P I)
$240.00 purchase; LC 79-700043
Tells about Nate the Great, a 10 - year - old who tries to solve the mystery of the garbage snatcher. Based on the book Nate The Great Goes Undercover by Marjorie Weinman Sharmat.
Literature and Drama
Dist - CF **Prod** - BOSUST 1978

Nathalie 32 MIN
U-matic / VHS / 16mm
B&W (H C A) (FRENCH (ENGLISH SUBTITLES))
Introduces a girl who is confronting her blossoming maturity. Shows her and a girlfriend engaging in unconscious homosexual caresses, becoming aware of the stares of a man on a subway and fantasizing about being a young woman. Includes English subtitles.
Foreign Language; Health and Safety; Psychology
Dist - TEXFLM **Prod** - FI 1970

Nathalie Krebs 12 MIN
16mm
Color
Follows Nathalie Krebs, chemical engineer and creator of unique stoneware glazes, in her workshop where the glazes are mixed according to her own secret formulas.
Fine Arts
Dist - AUDPLN **Prod** - RDCG

Nathalie Sarraute - C'Est Beau 71 MIN
U-matic / VHS
Color (C) (FRENCH)
$299.00, $199.00 purchase _ #AD - 1489
Presents 'C'est Beau' by Nathalie Sarraute in French. Discourses eloquently on l'existence torpide.
Fine Arts; Foreign Language; History - World; Literature and Drama
Dist - FOTH **Prod** - FOTH

Nathan Ackerman, MD - assessment counsultation 1 12 MIN
VHS / 16mm
Hillcrest family - studies in human communication, assessment series

Color (C G PRO)
$150.00, $105.00 purchase, $14.00, $14.50 rental _ #22707
Features Nathan Ackerman, MD, in an assessment consultation on the Hillcrest family. Covers the dynamics of the assessment interview and the rationale for the interviewing approach. Part of an eight - part series focusing on one family. Produced by R L Birdwhistell and J D Van Vlack.
Guidance and Counseling; Psychology; Sociology
Dist - PSU

Nathan Ackerman, MD - assessment interview 1 32 MIN
16mm / VHS
Hillcrest family - studies in human communication, assessment series
Color (C G PRO)
$435.00, $235.00 purchase, $23.50, $21.00 rental _ #33023
Features Nathan Ackerman, MD, in an assessment interview of the Hillcrest family. Emphasizes the causative factors in the family's problems. Part of an eight - part series focusing on one family. Produced by R L Birdwhistell and J D Van Vlack.
Guidance and Counseling; Psychology; Sociology
Dist - PSU

Nathan Der Weise 148 MIN
16mm
B&W (GERMAN (ENGLISH SUBTITLES))
A German language motion picture, available with or without English subtitles. Demonstrates, through a comical and sometimes complicated plot, that what really matters is not religious persuasion but personal attitudes and moral principles. A film presentation of the famous play by Gotthold Ephraim Lessing.
Foreign Language; Literature and Drama
Dist - WSTGLC **Prod** - WSTGLC 1967

Nathaniel Dorsky series
Alaya 28 MIN
Seventeen reasons why 20 MIN
Dist - PARART

Nathaniel Hawthorne and Herman Melville 20 MIN
VHS / U-matic
American Literature Series
Color (H C A)
LC 83-706254
Offers a dramatization of a visit from Herman Melville to Nathanel Hawthorne, with introductions by Mrs Hawthorne, while Moby Dick and The House of Seven Gables are in progress.
Literature and Drama
Dist - AITECH **Prod** - AUBU 1983

Nathaniel Hawthorne - Light in the Shadows 23 MIN
16mm / U-matic / VHS
Color (H)
LC 82-700618
Presents a biography of writer Nathaniel Hawthorne using words from his novels to re - create the world and society which he knew.
Biography; History - United States; Literature and Drama
Dist - IFB **Prod** - UNIPRO 1982

Nathaniel Hawthorne - the World of the Scarlet Letter and its Structure 30 MIN
Videoreel / VT2
Franklin to Frost Series
B&W (J H)
Literature and Drama
Dist - GPN **Prod** - GPN

Nathaniel, the Grublet 30 MIN
VHS
Color (K P I R)
$14.95 purchase _ #35 - 83004 - 8936
Features Nathaniel, the youngest of six Grublet children. Shows how Nathaniel must resist peer pressure from his brothers, who are encouraging him to steal. Produced by Bridgestone.
Literature and Drama; Religion and Philosophy
Dist - APH

A Nation among Equals 30 MIN
U-matic / VHS
Japan - the Changing Tradition Series
Color (H C A)
History - World
Dist - GPN **Prod** - UMA 1978

A Nation at Risk - 217 30 MIN
U-matic
Currents - 1985 - 86 Season Series
Color (A)
Views with alarm the shrinking amount of liability insurance available to business, industry and the individual and the changes this is causing.
Business and Economics; Social Science
Dist - PBS **Prod** - WNETTV 1985

Nation Builds Under Fire 40 MIN A
U-matic / VHS
Color
Tells the story of the struggle of the people of the Republic of Vietnam to build a nation while war rages around them. Documents the role of the American Serviceman in helping these people. Narrated by John Wayne.
History - United States; History - World
Dist - IHF **Prod** - IHF

The Nation Family 51 MIN
U-matic / VHS / 16mm
Color (I)
LC 84-706131
Outlines why the traditional customs of social consensus and loyalty are the backbone of Japan's postwar success. Illustrates the national penchant for long - term business planning by focusing on a shipping manufacturer who met the oil crisis head on.
Business and Economics; History - World
Dist - WOMBAT **Prod** - CANBC 1983

A Nation in crisis 16 MIN
VHS
Color (G)
$69.95 purchase _ #S01501, #1806
Reveals the factors that led to the US Constitutional Convention. Shows that although the states approved the Articles of Confederation, they refused to grant the new Congress its powers. Documents Shay's Rebellion, which promoted the need for a stronger central government.
Civics and Political Systems; History - United States
Dist - UILL **Prod** - AIMS
AIMS

A Nation in crisis 16 MIN
16mm / U-matic / VHS
American history - birth of a nation series; No 6
Color (I)
LC FIA68-1149
Discusses the state legislatures' approval of the Articles of Confederation. Describes the quarrelling between Congress and the states as the western territory opened for settlement. Reviews Shay's Rebellion as evidence to the people of their lack of unity, resulting in the calling of a constitutional convention.
History - United States
Dist - AIMS **Prod** - CAHILL 1967

A Nation in Touch 26 MIN
16mm
Color
Describes the construction of the world's longest microwave system.
Industrial and Technical Education; Psychology; Social Science
Dist - CFI **Prod** - CFI

A Nation is Born Series
The Boston Tea Party 10 MIN
Columbus 8 MIN
How the Colonies Grew 8 MIN
The Pilgrims 8 MIN
The Ragged Ragamuffins of the Continental Army 8 MIN
Dist - LUF

A Nation of Immigrants 53 MIN
U-matic / VHS / 16mm
B&W (I)
LC 71-708978
Presents the history of immigration of America, based on John F Kennedy's book A Nation Of Immigrants. Tells of the difficult adjustments the immigrants have had to make in the new land. Covers individuals who have achieved greatness in the period known as the 'great wave,' between 1880 and 1910, when 23 million people left their homelands to come to America.
Biography; History - United States; Literature and Drama; Psychology; Sociology
Dist - FI **Prod** - FI 1967

A Nation of immigrants 16 MIN
VHS
Color (J H)
$99.00 purchase _ #06007 - 026
Traces the history of immigration and the contributions of immigrants to our society. Includes teacher's guide and library kit.
Education; History - United States; Sociology
Dist - GA

Nation of Immigrants 52 MIN
16mm / U-matic / VHS
Destination America Series
Color (J)
Compares and contrasts the immigrant experience in America for older, European - based immigrants with the modern immigrant experience for blacks, Puerto Ricans, Asians and Mexicans. Explains that they may be seen as a threat by descendents of earlier immigrants. Many are rediscovering their heritage.
History - United States; Sociology
Dist - MEDIAG **Prod** - THAMES 1976

A Nation of Immigrants - 1900 - 1990 -7 20 MIN
VHS
Geography in US History Series
Color (H)
Centers on the geographic concept of movement. Focuses on the new immigration of the 1980s and on a recent immigrant family which has settled in the Western US, with specific examples of immigration as an ongoing theme in US history. Part 7 of a ten - part series which emphasizes the study of American geography within the context of American history courses using geographic concepts.
Geography - United States; History - United States; Sociology
Dist - AITECH **Prod** - AITECH 1991

A Nation of Law - 1968 - 1971 60 MIN
VHS
Eyes On The Prize - Part II - Series
Color; Captioned (G)
$59.95 purchase _ #EYES - 206
Depicts the growth of the Black Panther Party in Chicago and police surveillance of the group. Shows how local and federal law enforcement agencies took action against the Black Panthers and other groups. Reviews the Attica prison takeover. Part of a series on the black civil rights movement.
History - United States; Sociology
Dist - PBS **Prod** - BSIDE 1990

A Nation of painters 7 MIN
16mm / U-matic / VHS
Art awareness collection series
Color (J H C)
LC 78-701205
Presents various painters and their works.
Fine Arts
Dist - EBEC **Prod** - USNGA 1973

A Nation of Spoilers 13 MIN
16mm / U-matic / VHS
Color (I J H)
LC 77-703318
Explores the growing problem of vandalism and illustrates some of the constructive ways in which young people can improve their communities.
Guidance and Counseling; Social Science; Sociology
Dist - HIGGIN **Prod** - HIGGIN 1978

A Nation ofImmigrants - Pt 1 29 MIN
16mm / U-matic / VHS
B&W (I)
LC 71-708978
Presents the history of immigration of America, based on John F Kennedy's book A Nation Of Immigrants. Tells of the difficult adjustments the immigrants have had to make in the new land. Covers individuals who have achieved greatness in the period known as the 'great wave,' between 1880 and 1910, when 23 million people left their homelands to come to America.
Sociology
Dist - FI **Prod** - FI 1967

A Nation ofImmigrants - Pt 2 23 MIN
16mm / U-matic / VHS
B&W (I)
LC 71-708978
Presents the history of immigration of America, based on John F Kennedy's book A Nation Of Immigrants. Tells of the difficult adjustments the immigrants have had to make in the new land. Covers individuals who have achieved greatness in the period known as the 'great wave,' between 1880 and 1910, when 23 million people left their homelands to come to America.
Sociology
Dist - FI **Prod** - FI 1967

Nation State - Dutch - Russian 30 MIN
U-matic / VHS
Historically Speaking Series Part 8; Pt 8
Color (H) (RUSSIAN)
Shows how the Netherlands and Russia struggled to become nation states. Documents the struggles of the Netherlands against Spanish control, the Dutch trading empire, and Russia's unification and attempts to westernize. Looks at the roles of Ivan II, Ivan IV, Peter The Great and Catherine the Great in Russian history.
History - World
Dist - AITECH **Prod** - KRMATV 1983

Nation State - England 30 MIN
U-matic / VHS
Historically Speaking Series Part 7; Pt 7
Color (H)
Shows the development of nation - state characteristics in England. Discusses William the Conqueror, Henry II, royal courts, common law and the jury system.
History - World
Dist - AITECH **Prod** - KRMATV 1983

Nation State - France 30 MIN
VHS / U-matic
Historically Speaking Series Part 6; Pt 6
Color (H)
Discusses the growth of absolute monarchy in France, the centralized tax system, the Hundred Years' War, Louis XIII and Richelieu, and Louis XIV and divine right.
History - World
Dist - AITECH **Prod** - KRMATV 1983

Nation State - Spain 30 MIN
VHS / U-matic
Historically Speaking Series Part 5; Pt 5
Color (H)
Presents the commonly accepted traits of a nation - state and the pattern of national development. Discusses the reconquista movement in Spain, the role of Ferdinand and Isabella, Charles V and Philip II. Gives examples of the art of El Greco and Velasquez.
Fine Arts; History - World
Dist - AITECH **Prod** - KRMATV 1983

A Nation Uprooted - Afghan Refugees in Pakistan 30 MIN
U-matic / VHS
Color (C)
Documents the work, education, play and worship of the Afghans in exile in Pakistan. Reveals their situation and determination to maintain their culture and traditions. Education edition of a previously released, longer film.
History - World
Dist - CPEA **Prod** - CPEA 1986

A Nation Uprooted - Afghan Refugees in Pakistan 58 MIN
U-matic / VHS
Color
Documents the work, education, play and worship of the Afghans in exile in Pakistan. Reveals their situation and determination to maintain their endangered culture and traditions.
Geography - World; History - World
Dist - CPEA **Prod** - DNKMAN

A Nation within a Nation 14 MIN
16mm
Screen news digest series; Vol 15; Issue 1
B&W (I)
LC 73-701267
Examines the winds of change that are sweeping across the lives of 140,000 Navajos on the largest Indian reservation in the world.
Social Science; Sociology
Dist - HEARST **Prod** - HEARST 1972

The National Aboretum 14 MIN
U-matic
Color
Presents a tour of the National Arboretum in Washington, D C, picturing the four seasons of the year. Pictured are the scientists who work there and the many varieties of plants.
Geography - United States; Science - Natural
Dist - USDA **Prod** - USDA 1972

The National AIDS Awareness Test 64 MIN
VHS / 16mm
Color (PRO)
$295.00 purchase, $150.00 rental, $50.00 preview
Features celebrities and medical experts who give answers to questions about AIDS. Discusses what causes the virus and how it is transmitted. Includes a viewer's guide and score sheet for a test on AIDS awareness.
Business and Economics; Health and Safety; Psychology; Sociology
Dist - UTM **Prod** - UTM

National and International Information Systems
VHS / 16mm
Color (PRO)
$350.00 purchase
Examines national and international information systems and how to use them. Features Dr Jerry Kidd, University of Maryland.
Education
Dist - LIBRAY **Prod** - LIBRAY 1977

National Anthem 3 MIN
U-matic / VHS / 16mm
Color (I)
Uses more that 100 engravings, cartoons, paintings and photographs to present a montage of American history from the early days of exploration to the space age.
History - United States
Dist - AIMS **Prod** - SGA 1975

National Audubon Society specials series
Ancient forests - rage over trees 60 MIN
Arctic refuge - a vanishing wilderness 60 MIN
Common ground - farming and wildlife 60 MIN
Condor 60 MIN
Crane river 60 MIN
Ducks under siege 60 MIN
Galapagos - my fragile world 60 MIN
Greed and wildlife - poaching in America 60 MIN
Grizzly and man - Uneasy truce 60 MIN
If dolphins could talk 60 MIN
Messages from the birds 60 MIN
The Mysterious black - footed ferret 60 MIN
On the edge of extinction - Panthers and cheetahs 60 MIN
Sea turtles - Ancient nomads 60 MIN
Sharks 60 MIN
Whales 60 MIN
Wolves 60 MIN
Wood stork - Barometer of the Everglades 60 MIN
Dist - PBS

National Audubon video series
Presents a five part series of nature documentaries featuring well - known professional actors. Includes If Dolphins Could Talk with Michael Douglas; Danger at the Beach with Ted Danson; Arctic Refuge with Meryl Streep; Wildfire with James Woods; and Wolves with Robert Redford.
Danger at the beach 60 MIN
Wildfire 60 MIN
Dist - CAMV **Prod** - NAS 1975

The National Bible Quiz 28 MIN
16mm
Color
LC 81-701075
Presents a variety of questions and answers about the Bible.
Literature and Drama; Religion and Philosophy
Dist - KLEINW **Prod** - KLEINW 1981

National Black History Landmarks 20 MIN
U-matic / VHS
B&W
History - United States
Dist - SYLWAT **Prod** - RCOMTV 1978

National Cancer Quiz 60 MIN
U-matic / VHS
Color
Shows the 1984 Cable TV Special produced by the American Cancer Society National Cable TV Association and Tumor Broadcasting System. Focuses on three cancer sites - lung, breast, and colorectal, and addresses risk - assessment question posed in quiz - style.
Fine Arts; Health and Safety
Dist - AMCS **Prod** - AMCS 1984

National Center for Atmospheric Research 29 MIN
VHS / U-matic
Creativity with Bill Moyers Series
Color (H C A)
LC 83-707213
Presents atmospheric researchers in eastern Montana who are challenged by the fact that natural changes occurring in our climate may be further enhanced by new changes caused through human activity.
Fine Arts; Psychology; Science - Physical
Dist - PBS **Prod** - CORPEL 1982

National committee for electrical engineering film series
Complex waves, Pt 1 - propagation, evanescence and instability 26 MIN
Harmonic phasors 7 MIN
Introduction to the General - Purpose Oscilloscope 24 MIN
Response of a Resonant System to a Frequency Step 12 MIN
Wave Velocities, Dispersion and the Omega - Beta Diagram 28 MIN
Dist - EDC

National committee for electrical engineering films series
Harmonic phasors - II 18 MIN
Dist - EDC

National committee for fluid mechanics films series
Aerodynamic generation of sound 44 MIN
Dist - EBEC

National Crime and Violence Test Series
What would You do if a Robber Stuck a Gun in Your Ribs 40 MIN
What would You Really do if Accosted by a Rapist 40 MIN
Dist - CORF

The National crime prevention test - Pt 1 - before it happens 30 MIN
16mm / U-matic / VHS
Color (J)
LC 79-700011
Discusses methods of preventing crimes in and around the home and neighborhood. Focuses on burglary, child abuse, battered wives, locks and safety devices, and Project Identification and Neighborhood Watch programs.
Sociology
Dist - CORF **Prod** - HAR 1978

The National crime prevention test - Pt 2 - the odds against yesterday 30 MIN
U-matic / VHS / 16mm
Color (J)
LC 79-700012
Discusses methods of preventing crime on the street and in businesses. Focuses on juvenile crime, shoplifting, white collar crimes, auto theft, crimes against the elderly and general street safety.
Sociology
Dist - CORF **Prod** - HAR 1978

The National Crime Test 30 MIN
U-matic / 16mm / VHS
(G) (FRENCH)
MV $185.00 _ MP $530.00 purchase, $50.00 rental
Reveals startling facts about crime in Canada. Discusses what can be done to prevent crime against property.
Sociology
Dist - CTV **Prod** - CTV

National Crisis - the Limits of Politics 29 MIN
Videoreel / VT2
Black Experience Series
Color
Civics and Political Systems; History - United States
Dist - PBS **Prod** - WTTWTV

National Day 1971 20 MIN
16mm
Color
Shows the National Day celebrations during 1971 in the Malaysian city of Kuala Lumpur with the focus on the youth of the country.
Geography - World; History - World; Sociology
Dist - PMFMUN **Prod** - FILEM 1971

The National Dental Care Quiz 14 MIN
16mm
Color (P I J H)
LC 81-701076
Uses an exchange between a studio audience and television star Don Wescott to raise questions and answers about dental care.
Health and Safety
Dist - KLEINW **Prod** - KLEINW 1981

The National Diet Quiz 28 MIN
16mm
Color (H C A)
LC 81-701077
Presents a quiz about dieting and obesity.
Health and Safety
Dist - KLEINW **Prod** - KLEINW 1981

National Diffusion Network - an Overview of Educational Programs that Work 39 MIN
U-matic / VHS
National Diffusion Network Series
Color
Shows what the National Diffusion Network is, what it does and how, and with what success. Describes its elements and its role and relationship to the NDH and the Joint Dissemination Review Panel.
Civics and Political Systems; Education
Dist - USNAC **Prod** - FWLERD 1982

National Diffusion Network - Educational Programs that Work 28 MIN
VHS / U-matic
National Diffusion Network Series
Color
Shows the needs, problems, resources, false starts and procedures involved in a school's adoption of a program approved by the Joint Dissemination Review Panel.
Civics and Political Systems; Education
Dist - USNAC **Prod** - FWLERD 1982

National Diffusion Network Series
Joint Dissemination Review Panel - Transferring Educational Programs 39 MIN
National Diffusion Network - an Overview of Educational Programs that Work 39 MIN
National Diffusion Network - Educational Programs that Work 28 MIN
Dist - USNAC

National directory
CD-ROM
Color (G A)
$195.00 purchase _ #1322
Gives a comprehensive listing of the most useful and important addresses, telephone, fax and telex numbers in the US and the world - 120,000 entries. Users can automatically dial or fax numbers, print lists and export to

other programs. For Macintosh Plus, SE and II computers. Requires at least one M of RAM, one floppy disk drive, and an Apple compatible CD - ROM drive.
Computer Science; Literature and Drama
Dist - BEP

The National Disaster Survival Test 45 MIN
16mm / U-matic / VHS
Color
Discusses public, home, industry and traffic safety within the context of such disasters as fires, floods, tornadoes, hurricanes, earthquakes and other potentially life - threatening situations.
Guidance and Counseling; Health and Safety
Dist - CORF **Prod** - CORF

The National driving test 29 MIN
VHS / 16mm
Color (H G)
$495.00, $195.00 purchase, $75.00 rental _ #8323
Features TV and sports personalities who discuss a wide range of automobile driving rules and tactics using a question and answer test format.
Health and Safety; Psychology
Dist - AIMS **Prod** - BANDBP 1991

The National Driving Test 29 MIN
U-matic / VHS / 16mm
Color (J H A) (FRENCH)
$185.00, $530.00 purchase, $50.00 rental
Reconstructs traffic accidents to show who was wrong and how the accidents could have been avoided. Offers true/false questions relating to the reenactments and to other basic driving habits.
Health and Safety
Dist - CORF **Prod** - CTV 1981
CTV

National driving test II 31 MIN
VHS
Color (COR)
$195.00 purchase, $125 rental _ #ANA/AIM
Presents driving situations to help drivers determine their levels of skills and knowledge when behind the wheel of a car. Tests drivers' ability to drive safely in a variety of scenarios ranging from the everyday situations to special circumstances. Includes a Leader's Guide.
Health and Safety; Psychology
Dist - ADVANM

The National Economy Quiz 28 MIN
16mm
Color (H)
Explores key elements of the American economy in the form of a quiz.
Business and Economics
Dist - AETNA **Prod** - AETNA 1976

National Family Planning Programs - Restoring the Balance 28 MIN
16mm
International Population Programs Series
Color (SPANISH)
LC 75-704431
Presents family planning program leaders from several countries in Asia, Africa, Latin America and the Middle East as they discuss their feelings, experiences and hopes for family planning in their regions.
Civics and Political Systems; Sociology
Dist - USNAC **Prod** - USOPOP 1974

National Federation Sports Films Series
Basketball at its best 28 MIN
The Challenge of Track and Field 28 MIN
Goal to go - the rules of football 27 MIN
The Key Goals to Winning Soccer 17 MIN
One Step Ahead - a Guide to Better Football Officiating 17 MIN
Ready, Wrestle - the Rules of Wrestling 17 MIN
Volleyball - the Winning Points 17 MIN
Winning Ways - the Rules of Basketball 28 MIN
Dist - NFSHSA

The National Fire Drill 29 MIN
U-matic / VHS / 16mm
Color (I)
Re - enacts case studies of fire situations to demonstrate the safest course of action.
Health and Safety
Dist - CORF **Prod** - CTV 1981

National Fisheries Center and Aquarium 11 MIN
16mm / U-matic / VHS
Color
Shows the architecture, content, general philosophies and disciplines of the National Aquarium.
Fine Arts; Science - Natural
Dist - PFP **Prod** - EAMES 1967

National Folk Festival, Pt 1 10 MIN
16mm
B&W
LC FIE52-2099
Includes Western German and Philippine dances, a New England barn dance and the Scottish Highland fling.
Fine Arts
Dist - USNAC **Prod** - USA 1950

National Folk Festival, Pt 2 10 MIN
16mm
B&W
LC FIE52-2100
Includes Polish, English, Croatian, American Indian, Lithuanian, Ukrainian, Texas and Tennessee dances and Negro and Yugoslav songs.
Fine Arts
Dist - USNAC **Prod** - USA 1950

National Folk Festival, Pt 3 10 MIN
16mm
B&W
LC FIE52-2101
Includes Israeli, Russian, Czechoslovakian and American dances, Ozark ballads, songs of Pennsylvania coal miners, Spanish American songs and 'CASEY JONES.'.
Fine Arts
Dist - USNAC **Prod** - USA

The National Gallery Builds 13 MIN
16mm
Color
Illustrates highlights of conception and construction of the East Building of the National Gallery, beginning with the challenge initially faced by architect I M Pei. Continues through various phases of construction and includes footage on the special works of art commissioned for the building from artists of international reputation such as Henry Moore and Alexander Calder.
Fine Arts
Dist - USNGA **Prod** - USNGA

National Gallery of Art 50 MIN
VHS
Color (J)
$39.95 purchase _ #HV - 905
Explores the artistic treasures of the National Gallery of Art. Provides an informative history of the gallery and a guided tour of the collection's finist works.
Fine Arts
Dist - CRYSP **Prod** - CRYSP

National gallery of art 50 MIN
VHS
Color (H C A)
$49.95 purchase
Tours the National Gallery of Art in Washington, D C. Features the best items from the museum's collection, including DaVinci, Vermeer, Holbein, Van Gogh, and others. Tells the history of the museum. Hosted by museum director J Carter Brown.
Fine Arts
Dist - PBS **Prod** - WNETTV

National Gallery of Art 50 MIN
VHS
Color (S)
$49.95 purchase _ #049 - 9001
Displays the artistic treasures of the National Gallery of Art in a two - part program hosted by gallery director J Carter Brown. Includes a concise history of the gallery and a private tour of some of the finest works in the collection.
Fine Arts; Geography - World
Dist - FI **Prod** - CORINT 1988

The National Gas Saver's Quiz 28 MIN
16mm
Color (J)
LC 81-701078
Features television stars McLean Stevenson and JoAnn Pflug in a quiz show which tells how to save on fuel expenses.
Home Economics; Social Science
Dist - KLEINW **Prod** - KLEINW 1981

National Geographic video series
Secrets of the Titanic 60 MIN
Dist - NGS
PBS
SEVVID
UILL

National Geographic video series
Among the wild chimpanzees 59 MIN
Atocha - quest for treasure 60 MIN
Ballad of the Irish horse 59 MIN
Born of fire 60 MIN
Creatures of the Namib desert 60 MIN
Egypt - quest for eternity 60 MIN
The Explorers - a century of discovery 60 MIN
The Gorilla 60 MIN
The Great whales 60 MIN
The Grizzlies 60 MIN
Himalayan river run 60 MIN
Iceland river challenge 60 MIN
In the shadow of Vesuvius 60 MIN
Incredible human machine 60 MIN
Jerusalem - within these walls 60 MIN
Man - eaters of India 60 MIN
Miniature miracle - the computer chip 60 MIN
Polar bear alert 60 MIN
Rain forest 60 MIN
Realm of the alligator 60 MIN
Save the panda 60 MIN
Search for the great apes 60 MIN
Sharks 60 MIN
Tropical kingdom of Belize 60 MIN
White wolf 60 MIN
Yukon passage 60 MIN
Dist - PBS

National Geographic video series
African wildlife 60 MIN
Land of the tiger 60 MIN
Dist - PBS
UILL

National Health Insurance - Should the Federal Government Provide Comprehensive Insurance 59 MIN
U-matic
Advocates Series
Color
Asks whether the federal government should provide comprehensive health insurance for every citizen. Features debaters Patricia Butler and William Rusher.
Business and Economics; Civics and Political Systems; Social Science
Dist - PBS **Prod** - WGBHTV

National health service 30 MIN
VHS
Inside Britain 1 series
Color; PAL; NTSC (G) (BULGARIAN CZECH HUNGARIAN SPANISH POLISH ROMANIAN RUSSIAN SLOVAK UKRAINIAN ENGLISH WITH ARABIC SUBTITLES)
PdS65 purchase
Joins patients, doctors, nurses, administrators and health visitors at a north London general practice. Shows how the Medical Practices offers a wide range of services and are enjoying increased autonomy. Encourages patients to live healthier lifestyles.
Health and Safety
Dist - CFLVIS **Prod** - INFVIS 1991

The National Hearing Quiz 30 MIN
16mm
Color (J)
Discusses hearing loss, covering what noise is, how it threatens health, which noises are the most dangerous, other contributions to hearing loss, and how to protect oneself from excessive noise.
Health and Safety; Sociology
Dist - KLEINW **Prod** - KLEINW

The National High Blood Pressure Quiz 30 MIN
16mm
Color (J)
LC 80-700121
Presents newscaster Peter Hackes asking questions about the disease of hypertension. Discusses how to detect high blood pressure, what causes it, how to treat it, who gets it and why it is called a silent disease.
Health and Safety
Dist - KLEINW **Prod** - KLEINW 1979

National income and its components 60 MIN
VHS
Macroeconomics series
Color (H C G)
$89.00 purchase _ #GSU - 310
Discusses national income, expenditure analysis, consumption, investment, government spending and net exports. Features Roger Waud, author of 'Macroeconomics' textbook. Part of a 24 - part series instructed by Dr Edward F Stuart, Northwestern University, which focuses on a description of the major economic policy - making bodies in the United States and their interrelationships.
Business and Economics; Social Science
Dist - INSTRU

The National Income Tax Quiz 28 MIN
16mm
Color (H C A)
LC 81-701079
Presents a quiz which reveals information about income tax.
Business and Economics; Social Science
Dist - KLEINW **Prod** - KLEINW 1981

National Kids' Quiz 30 MIN
U-matic
Color (I J)
Features Michael Landon in a discussion about the problems that trouble many teenagers. Offers re - created scenes of family and school dilemmas, involving such values as honesty, the right to privacy, and loyalty.
Guidance and Counseling; Psychology; Sociology
Dist - GA **Prod** - BANPRO

National lake survey 17 MIN
BETA / U-matic / VHS
Color (G)
$29.95, $130.00 purchase _ #LSTF15
Explains how the United States Environmental Protection Agency studies the acidification of fresh water lakes. Intended for audiences in areas where acidification is a serious problem.
Science - Natural; Sociology
Dist - FEDU **Prod** - USEPA 1984

The National LP Gas Energy Quiz 30 MIN
16mm
Color
Discusses liquified petroleum gas, comparing LP gas with electricity, natural gas, fuel oil and coal.
Social Science
Dist - KLEINW **Prod** - KLEINW

National monuments of southern Arizona 30 MIN
VHS
Color (G)
$29.95 purchase _ #V26
Explores the scenery and natural and cultural history of eight National Park Service locations in Southern Arizona. Visits Saguaro, Organ Pipe Cactus, Tonto, Tumacacori, Chiricahua, Casa Grande, Coronado and Fort Bowie.
Geography - United States
Dist - INSTRU **Prod** - USNPS

National Naval Medical Center 28 MIN
16mm
Color
LC 74-706155
Illustrates the nationwide mission of the National Naval Medical Center at Bethesda, Maryland, in personnel training, patient treatment and research projects.
Civics and Political Systems; Health and Safety
Dist - USNAC **Prod** - USN 1966

The National Nuclear Debate 120 MIN
VHS / 16mm
Color (G)
$120.00 rental _ #NLND - 000
Presents a debate commemorating the first anniversary of the Three Mile Island nuclear accident. Portrays experts from both sides of the controversy meeting in Harrisburg, Pennsylvania to discuss nuclear safety. Reports on the impact the accident had on residents of Central Pennsylvania.
Social Science; Sociology
Dist - PBS **Prod** - WITFTV

National Nutrition Quiz 60 MIN
VHS / U-matic
Color
Leads viewers through the bewildering maze of foodstuffs, and explores facts and fantasies about nutrition. Provides up - to - date scientific data on the protective and destructive properties of food eaten during a given day and its relationship to obesity, diabetes, heart disease and cancer. Hosted by health advocates Jane Brody and David Watts MD.
Health and Safety; Social Science; Sociology
Dist - PBS **Prod** - PBS

National origin - age issues - discipline - discharge - documentation - 3 ; 2nd ed.
U-matic / VHS / BETA
Choices - a management training program in equal opportunity series
Color; CC; PAL (IND PRO G)
Contact distributor about price
Shows managers how to deal with issues of age and national origin with regard to employee discipline, discharge and documentation of both procedures. Trains both new managers and those with previous EEO training. Part of a 12 - part program providing managers with essential knowledge of EEO and enhancing their skills in in such areas as hiring, interviewing, selecting, performance appraisals and more.
Business and Economics; Guidance and Counseling; Social Science
Dist - BNA **Prod** - BNA

National origin issues - selection - 8 ; 2nd ed.
U-matic / VHS / BETA
Choices - a management training program in equal opportunity series
Color; CC; PAL (IND PRO G)
Contact distributor about price
Shows managers how to deal with national issues issues and the employee selection. Trains both new managers and those with previous EEO training. Part of a 12 - part program providing managers with essential knowledge of EEO and enhancing their skills in in such areas as hiring, interviewing, selecting, performance appraisals and more.
Business and Economics; Guidance and Counseling; Social Science
Dist - BNA **Prod** - BNA

National park ranger
VHS
Vocational visions career series
Color (H A)
$39.95 purchase _ #CDS512
Interviews people who are national park rangers. Answers questions about the educational requirements and necessary skills for the occupation, as well as its career opportunities, salary range and outlook for the future. Part of a series which examines the potential of various occupations.
Business and Economics; Geography - United States; Guidance and Counseling; Psychology
Dist - CADESF **Prod** - CADESF 1989

National park series
Presents a five - part series on United States' national parks. Includes the titles Virginia's Civil War Parks; Mr Lincoln's Springfield; Gettysburg Battlefield Tour; To Keep Our Liberty - the Minute Men of the American Revolution; Independence - Philadelphia - 1774 - 1800.

Gettysburg battlefield tour 35 MIN
Independence - Philadelphia - 1774 - 1800 28 MIN
Mr Lincoln's Springfield 30 MIN
To keep our liberty - the Minute Men of the American Revolution 35 MIN
Virginia's Civil War parks 55 MIN
Dist - CAMV

National park series
Arches and bridges - Utah desert 12 MIN
Bryce Canyon and Kodachrome Basin 30 MIN
Discover Timpanogos Cave - Utah 22 MIN
Experience Utah 60 MIN
Experience Wyoming 60 MIN
A Forest of stone - Arizona 43 MIN
Freemont Indian State Park 30 MIN
The Grand staircase 60 MIN
Grand Teton National Park - Wyoming 32 MIN
Hoover Dam - Lake Mead 30 MIN
Mesa Verde - Colorado, land of forgotten people and lost cities 22 MIN
Over the rim - the Grand Canyon story 29 MIN
Sinopah trails - Glacier National Park along Canadian Border with Montana, USA 15 MIN
South Dakota's Black Hills, Badlands and lakes 60 MIN
Zion - Nature's Garden - Utah 29 MIN
Dist - FEDU

National Parks 1 30 MIN
VHS / U-matic
Earth, Sea and Sky Series
Color (C)
Shows national parks as outdoor laboratories in which the effects of weathering, erosion, deposition, volcanic activity and metamorphism can be observed and studied firsthand. Uses Yellowstone, the Petrified Forest and Padre Island National Parks as examples.
Science - Physical
Dist - DALCCD **Prod** - DALCCD

National Parks 2 30 MIN
U-matic / VHS
Earth, Sea and Sky Series
Color (C)
Examines Mesa Verde, Platt and Big Bend, three unique national parks.
Science - Physical
Dist - DALCCD **Prod** - DALCCD

The National parks of Utah 34 MIN
16mm / VHS
Color (I J H G)
$550.00, $29.95 purchase
Tours Zion, Bryce, Capitol Reef, the Canyonlands, the Arches National Parks in Utah.
Geography - United States
Dist - KAWVAL **Prod** - KAWVAL

National Parks - Our Treasured Lands 28 MIN
U-matic / VHS / 16mm
Color
Outlines the geographic scope and diversity of sites within the U S National Park system and explains how use of these areas is people - oriented. Narrated by Wally Schirra.
Geography - United States; Physical Education and Recreation
Dist - USNAC **Prod** - USNPS 1983

National Parks - Playground or Paradise 59 MIN
16mm / U-matic / VHS
Color
LC 81-700304
Presents both sides of the ongoing debate between conservationists and environmentalists over the use of the national parks. Uses views of Yellowstone, Yosemite and the Grand Canyon to point out the dilemma as attorney Eric Julber and professor of history and environmental studies Roderick Nash debate the issue.
Geography - United States
Dist - NGS **Prod** - WQED 1981

National Parks, Promise and Challenge 23 MIN
U-matic / VHS / 16mm
Color (J)
LC 82-700016
Examines the dual purposes of U S national parks to preserve natural wonders and to serve as recreation areas for the public. Visits Yosemite, Yellowstone and the Grand Canyon, discussing the conflict between developers and conservationists.
Geography - United States; Physical Education and Recreation; Science - Natural
Dist - NGS **Prod** - NGS 1981

National Party Conventions 145 MIN
U-matic
University of the Air Series
Color (J H C A)
$750.00 purchase, $250.00 rental
Discusses the impact of conventions on political leadership and on the political system itself. Program contains a series of five cassettes 29 minutes each.
Civics and Political Systems
Dist - CTV **Prod** - CTV 1977

National petroleum reserve in Alaska 16 MIN
VHS
Color (J H)
$18.95 purchase _ #IV178
Describes the role of the US Geological Survey in finding new sources of oil and gas on Alaska's North Slope. Stresses the need for providing new energy resources while preserving the area's ecology.
Geography - United States; Social Science
Dist - INSTRU **Prod** - USGEOS

National portrait gallery VGA
Videodisc
Color (G A)
$495.00 purchase _ #1856v
Contains 3,093 full - color and black and white fine art portraits from the Smithsonian Institution's National Portrait Gallery collection of notable Americans. Covers the span from the late 16th century to the present. For IBM PCs and compatibles. Requires 640K RAM, DOS Version 3.1 or greater, one floppy disk drive - a hard drive is recommended, one empty expansion slot, and an IBM compatible CD - ROM drive.
Fine Arts
Dist - BEP

National Pro - Am Racquetball 59 MIN
VHS / 16mm
Color (G)
$70.00 rental
Covers the November 13, 1977 racquetball tournament in Westminster, California. Includes commentary, interviews with participants and instruction demonstration.
Physical Education and Recreation
Dist - PBS **Prod** - KOCETV

A National Remembrance 15 MIN
16mm
Color
LC 81-701094
Shows the placing of the presidential wreath at the Tomb of the Unknown Soldier by Max Cleland, Administrator of Veteran Affairs, personal representative of President Carter.
Guidance and Counseling; History - United States
Dist - USNAC **Prod** - USVA 1979

The National Save - a - Life Test 52 MIN
U-matic / VHS / 16mm
Color (J)
Offers a TV quiz with multiple choice and true - false questions covering such topics as choking, chemical poisoning, automobile accidents, heart attacks, drowning, mugging, driving while intoxicated and home fires. Hosted by Michael Learned and Bernie Kopell.
Health and Safety
Dist - FI **Prod** - DBA 1984

The National Schiller Museum in Marbach 5 MIN
16mm / U-matic / VHS
European Studies - Germany Series
Color (H C A)
LC 76-700746
Gives a description of Marbach and of the museum erected there to commemorate Friedrich Schiller.
Geography - World; History - World
Dist - IFB **Prod** - MFAFRG 1973

The National Scream 28 MIN
16mm
Color (J G)
Offers a tongue - in - cheek look at Canada and Canadians. Explains how and why the beaver became the country's symbol. Uses animation and pseudo - documentary style to depict Canada's search for a national identity.

Geography - World; History - World; Social Science; Sociology
Dist - NFBC Prod - NFBC 1980
CFLMDC

National security and freedom of the press - Part 8 60 MIN
VHS / U-matic
Constitution - that delicate balance series
Color (G)
$45.00, $29.95 purchase
Presents a panel with former CIA Director and Secretary of Defense James Schlesinger, former Attorney General Griffin Bell and others. Debates the right of the public to know about national security issues. Part of a thirteen - part series on the United States Constitution created by journalist Fred Friendly.
Civics and Political Systems; Literature and Drama
Dist - ANNCPB Prod - WNETTV 1984
FI

National security in the 1990s 29 MIN
VHS
America's defense monitor series
Color (J H C G T A)
$25.00 purchase
Describes the debate over what constitutes "national security" in a post - Cold War age. Explores how America can be strong - economically, socially, and militarily. Interviews Lester Brown, Jessica Tuchman Mathews, Charles Schultze, John Jacobs, Keith Geiger, and William Webster. Produced by Sandy Gottlieb.
Civics and Political Systems; History - World; Sociology
Dist - EFVP Prod - CDINFO 1990

National Socialism in the 1920's 30 MIN
VHS / U-matic
Color (GERMAN)
Presents Dr. Otto Strasser, a member of the National Socialist Party in Germany during the 1920's, and later an outspoken opponent of Hitler. Explores the social and psychological events which allowed the rise of the Nazi Party.
Civics and Political Systems; History - World
Dist - NETCHE Prod - NETCHE 1971

The National Soul
VHS / Cassette
(G)
$29.95, $9.95 purchase
Features Bill Moyers who talks with Barbara Tuchman, E L Doctorow, Louise Erdrich and others.
Civics and Political Systems; History - United States; Sociology
Dist - BKPEOP Prod - MFV

The National Student Fire Safety Test 12 MIN
U-matic / VHS / 16mm
National Student Safety Test Series
Color (P)
LC 79-701256
Introduces questions concerning fire safety, dealing with such issues as the dangers of electrical heating and flammable clothing.
Health and Safety
Dist - CORF Prod - BELCHJ 1979

The National Student First Aid Safety Test 12 MIN
U-matic / VHS / 16mm
National Student Safety Test Series
Color (P)
LC 79-701257
Introduces questions concerning first aid safety, dealing with such problems as severe bleeding and serious sunburn.
Health and Safety
Dist - CORF Prod - BELCHJ 1979

The National Student Recreational Safety Test 12 MIN
U-matic / VHS / 16mm
National Student Safety Test Series
Color (P)
LC 79-701258
Introduces questions concerning recreational safety. Describes the appropriate clothing for active sports and discusses injuries received in play activities.
Health and Safety
Dist - CORF Prod - BELCHJ 1979

National Student Safety Test Series
The National Student Fire Safety Test 12 MIN
The National Student First Aid Safety Test 12 MIN
The National Student Recreational Safety Test 12 MIN
The National Student School Safety Test 12 MIN
The National Student Traffic Safety Test 12 MIN
Dist - CORF

The National Student School Safety Test 12 MIN
U-matic / VHS / 16mm
National Student Safety Test Series
Color (P)
LC 79-701259
Introduces questions concerning school safety, including such issues as school accidents and school fights.
Health and Safety
Dist - CORF Prod - BELCHJ 1979

The National Student Traffic Safety Test 12 MIN
16mm / U-matic / VHS
National Student Safety Test Series
Color (P)
LC 79-701260
Introduces questions concerning traffic safety. Discusses crossing streets, selecting a route, and being concerned with people's safety.
Health and Safety
Dist - CORF Prod - BELCHJ 1979

National Theater of the Deaf 44 MIN
U-matic / VHS
Color (I A)
Shows the National Theater Of The Deaf from New York as it tours Holland.
Education; Fine Arts; Guidance and Counseling; Psychology
Dist - SUTHRB Prod - SUTHRB

National Theatre School 13 MIN
16mm
Color
LC 77-702991
Depicts the day - to - day activities at the National Theatre School of Canada, including voice training, improvisations and fencing, as well as makeup, costume and set design classes.
Fine Arts; Geography - World
Dist - INCC Prod - CBCLS 1975

National town meeting - how is our democracy doing 55 MIN
VHS
Color (C G)
$70.00 purchase, $12.50 rental _ #61161
Examines the issues and institutions that affect the American democratic system and its future - lobbyists, special - interest groups, the media, citizen involvement and education. Shows how the system was nurtured and treasured, and how it has been assaulted and challenged. Features Hodding Carter as host.
Civics and Political Systems; Sociology
Dist - PSU Prod - KF 1989

National UFO reporting center - volume 1 30 MIN
VHS
Color (G)
$24.95 purchase _ #P27
Discusses sightings, evidence, types of UFOs and UFO activity throughout the United States with Brenda Roberts and Peter Davenport.
Fine Arts
Dist - HP

National velvet 124 MIN
VHS
Color (G)
$24.95 purchase _ #S01580
Presents the 1944 tale of kids training a horse to win England's Grand National Steeplechase. Stars Mickey Rooney, Donald Crisp, and 12 - year - old Elizabeth Taylor. Features scenes from the actual steeplechase.
Fine Arts; Literature and Drama
Dist - UILL Prod - GA
GA

National Velvet
VHS / BETA
Color
Presents Enid Bagnold's story of a girl striving to win a riding championship, starring Elizabeth Taylor and Mickey Rooney.
Fine Arts; Literature and Drama
Dist - GA Prod - GA

National voluntary laboratory accreditation program 9 MIN
U-matic / VHS
Color (A PRO)
$35.00, $80.00 purchase _ #TCA17904, #TCA17903
Describes the procedures used in determining accreditation of testing laboratories. Produced by the US Department of Commerce's National Institute of Standards and Technology.
Industrial and Technical Education; Science - Physical
Dist - USNAC

National Water Safety Test 29 MIN
16mm
Color (P)
LC 78-713269
Features comedian Pat Paulsen in a series of multiple choice vignettes illustrating the correct and incorrect things to do in 12 basic water safety situations.
Health and Safety; Physical Education and Recreation
Dist - AMRC Prod - AMRC 1971

National Youth Day 10 MIN
16mm
B&W
Covers the activities of the 1970 National Youth Day in Malaysia including a parade at the Merdeka Stadium.
Geography - World; Sociology
Dist - PMFMUN Prod - FILEM 1970

The National zoo 51 MIN
VHS
Color (I J H)
$35.00 purchase _ #A5VH 1131
Visits the living animal collection of the Smithsonian. Features the giant pandas Ling - Ling and Hsing - Hsing, exotic animals at the nonpublic Conservation and Research Center. Shows experts working to save endangered species and follows historic hunting expeditions around the world.
Science - Natural
Dist - CLRVUE Prod - CLRVUE

The National zoo 50 MIN
VHS
Smithsonian collection series
Color (P I J)
$39.95 purchase _ #PMV004V
Features seven - year - old Jenny and her friend Max who take viewers on a private tour of the Smithsonian Institution's living animal collection. Shows how zoos came into being, how zoos work and how native habitats of exotic animals from around the world are simulated. Explains the concepts of preservation and conservation so that viewers can appreciate their relevancy. Offers simple exlanations about procurement, nutrition and research and the on - going scientific study at the National Zoo. Part of a three - part series on Smithsonian collections.
Science - Natural
Dist - CAMV Prod - SMITHS

Nationalism 50 MIN
U-matic / 16mm / VHS
Window on the World Series
Color; Mono (J H C A)
MV $350.00 _ MP $600.00 purchase $50.00 rental
Traces the paths of three of Western history's most remembered nationalistic movements. The rebel soldiers of the American South during the War Between the States, the Irish insurgents of 1916,and the storm troopers of the Third Reich are examples of movements which carried their followers into the throes of war.
History - World
Dist - CTV Prod - CTV 1973

Nationalism 30 MIN
VHS / U-matic
American story - the beginning to 1877 series
Color (C)
History - United States
Dist - DALCCD Prod - DALCCD

Nationalism 27 MIN
VHS
Color (J H)
$99.00 purchase _ #06050 - 026
Highlights the political, economic and cultural aspects of American nationalism during the 19th and 20th centuries. Compares the phenomenon to that of Third World countries. Includes teacher's guide and library kit.
Civics and Political Systems; Education; History - United States; Social Science
Dist - GA

Nationalism and liberalism 60 MIN
VHS
Europe and America in the modern age - 1776 to the present series
Color (H C PRO)
$95.00 purchase
Presents a lecture by James Sheehan. Focuses on a critical period in European and American history and on leaders of the time. Part of a 20 - part series that looks at the last two centuries in Europe and America. Series presents lectures by David M Kennedy and James Sheehan of Stanford University on such figures as Adam Smith, Marx, Lincoln, Washington, Jefferson, Freud, Margaret Sanger, Susan B Anthony and Jane Adams and their impact on the events of their day. For history resource material and continuing education courses.
Civics and Political Systems; History - United States; History - World
Dist - LANDMK

Nationalism and Revolution 60 MIN
U-matic / VHS

James Galway's Music in Time Series
Color (J)
Presents flutist James Galway discussing the classical composers who sought to express political causes in music. Includes music from Berlioz' Requiem, Liszt's Fantasia on Hungarian Folk Themes and Wagner's Siegfried Idyll.
Fine Arts
Dist - FOTH **Prod** - POLTEL 1982

The Nationalists 28 MIN
16mm / U-matic / VHS
Captioned; Color (A) (SPANISH (ENGLISH SUBTITLES))
Discusses the Puerto Rican independence movement and the activities of the Puerto Rican Nationalist Party in the 1950's. Discusses the shooting incident by four nationalists in March 1954 which resulted in the wounding of two U S Congressmen, and portrays the movements's leading figure, Don Pedro Albizy Campos. Spanish dialog with English subtitles.
Fine Arts; History - United States
Dist - CNEMAG **Prod** - TORREJ 1973

Nations of the world series
Presents a ten - part series which studies the geography, cultures, economics and politics of nations around the world. Includes the titles Egypt, Yugoslavia, Mexico, East Germany, West Germany, Australia, Japan, Soviet Union, Israel, Central America.
Australia 26 MIN
Central America 25 MIN
East Germany 28 MIN
Egypt 25 MIN
Israel 25 MIN
Japan 25 MIN
Mexico 25 MIN
Soviet Union 25 MIN
West Germany 27 MIN
Yugoslavia 27 MIN
Dist - NGS **Prod** - NGS 1973

The Nations within 23 MIN
VHS
Mission videos series
Color (G R)
$12.50 purchase _ #S12351
Describes the ministry of the Lutheran Church - Missouri Synod to Native Americans.
Guidance and Counseling; Literature and Drama; Religion and Philosophy
Dist - CPH **Prod** - LUMIS

Nations within a nation 59 MIN
VHS / U-matic / VT1
Color (G)
$59.95 purchase, $35.00 rental
Examines the historical, legal and social background of the issue of sovereignty and Native American communities. Looks at the right to self government, the right to provide services to tribal members, the right to generate income for tribal programs and activities, the right to plan and direct economic development on tribal lands and the right to maintain the traditional activities of the community. Draws examples of tribal governments in operation from Taos Pueblo, the Mescalero Apache Tribe, the Muscogee - Creek - Nation and the Sac and Fox Tribe. Produced by the Dept of Sociology, Oklahoma State University.
Social Science
Dist - NAMPBC

The Native Aliens 22 MIN
U-matic / VHS
Color
Discusses the problems and needs of the Hispanic community relating to federal employment.
Civics and Political Systems; Guidance and Counseling; Social Science; Sociology
Dist - USNAC **Prod** - VAMCSL

Native American Art - Lost and found 22 MIN
VHS / 16mm
Color (H A)
$250.00 purchase, $50.00 rental
Features fourteen American Indian artists who are currently active.
Fine Arts; Social Science
Dist - AFA **Prod** - AMCAN 1986

Native American Arts 20 MIN
U-matic / VHS / 16mm
Color
Surveys native American art, including that of the Indian, Eskimo and Aleut. Shows how efforts in education, community cultural organizations and governmental encouragement are helping native American artists achieve important economic goals and new concepts of cultural identity.
Fine Arts; Social Science
Dist - USNAC **Prod** - USIACB

Native American Arts 19 MIN
16mm
Color (G)
#2X1 I
Tells the story of how the first settlers in America crossed the Bearing Straits. Discusses their culture, arts, weapons, and tools. Explains how the first white settlers exploited the Indian cultural heritage. Documents the 1935 formation of the United States Indian Arts and Crafts Board and how this encouraged new carving, basketweaving, and metal work.
Social Science
Dist - CDIAND **Prod** - DESCEN

Native - American cultures in the USA - Part one 60 MIN
VHS
Dealing with diversity series
Color (H C G)
$99.00 purchase _ #GSU - 107
Studies the early populations of Native Americans. Examines the rights of and stereotypes about Native Americans. Discusses treaty disputes, the Colville land allotments. Includes studio guest Paul Schranz, Governor's State University and Jerry Lewis, Historian, Potawatomis. Part one of two parts on Native Americans and part of a 23 - part series hosted by Dr J Q Adams, Western Illinois University, which helps students to develop the awareness that society is strengthened by a free and unfettered expression of individuality in all its diverse manifestations.
Social Science; Sociology
Dist - INSTRU

Native - American cultures in the USA - Part two 60 MIN
VHS
Dealing with diversity series
Color (H C G)
$99.00 purchase _ #GSU - 108
Studies the controversy surrounding the display of the remains of ancient Native Americans at Dickson Mounds Museum Burial Grounds, Lewiston, Illinois. Considers Native Americans and respect for the environment. Studio guests include James Yellowbank, coordinator of the Indian Treaty Rights Committee and Roxie Grignon, TEARS. Part two of two parts on Native Americans and part of a 23 - part series hosted by Dr J Q Adams, Western Illinois University, which helps students to develop the awareness that society is strengthened by a free and unfettered expression of individuality in all its diverse manifestations.
Civics and Political Systems; Social Science; Sociology
Dist - INSTRU

Native American Day 15 MIN
VHS
America's special days series
Color (K P) (SPANISH)
$23.95 purchase
Focuses on Native Americans and how they have contributed to life in the United States. Visits a store to learn names of foods and other words included in US language. Shows how the Native Americans helped early settlers survive and looks at the heritage of these people. Includes a visit for a day with a boy, Red Wing.
Civics and Political Systems; Social Science
Dist - GPN **Prod** - GPN 1993

Native American folk tales series
The Badger and the coyote
Star dancer
The Sun boy
The Turtle story
Dist - DANEHA

Native American folktales series
How the bear became white 30 MIN
Dist - DANEHA

Native American Images 29 MIN
VHS / U-matic
Color (J H C)
Profiles the lives, philosophies, and works of Paladine H. Roye , Ponca, Donald Vann, Cherokee, and Steve Forbes.
Fine Arts; Social Science
Dist - NAMPBC **Prod** - NAMPBC 1984

Native American images 29 MIN
VHS / U-matic / VT1
Color (G)
$25.00 rental
Profiles the lives, philosophies and works of Paladine H Roye - Ponca, Donald Vann - Cherokee and Steve Forbes, three artists living in Austin, Texas. Reveals that Roye and Vann are American Indians transplanted from their native Oklahoma and Forbes is a non - Indian who has devoted himself through anthropological study and artistry to the portrayal of contemporary Native Americans. Produced by Carol Patton Cornsilk.
Fine Arts; Social Science
Dist - NAMPBC **Prod** - SWTXPB 1984

Native American Myths 24 MIN
16mm / U-matic / VHS
Wide World of Adventure Series
Color (I J H)
Presents five animated myths that tell stories of demons, sorcery and the Indian's love for Mother Earth.
Literature and Drama; Religion and Philosophy; Social Science
Dist - EBEC **Prod** - AVATLI 1977

Native American series
Presents a three - part series on native Americans. Includes the titles 'Indians of California, Revised Edition,' 'Indians of the Plains,' and 'Indians of the Southeast.'
Indians of California - 1 23 MIN
Indians of the Plains - 2 17 MIN
Indians of the Southeast - 3 20 MIN
Dist - BARR **Prod** - BARR 1977

Native American series
Indian country 26 MIN
Dist - CNEMAG

Native American series
Indian cultures - from 2000 BC to 1500 AD 19 MIN
The Indian experience - after 1500 AD 19 MIN
Dist - JOU

Native American series
Native Americans - people of the desert 24 MIN
Native Americans - people of the forest 24 MIN
Native Americans - people of the plains 24 MIN
Dist - REVID

Native American Topics Series
Hopiit 15 MIN
Itam Hakim, Hopiit 58 MIN
Warriors 58 MIN
Dist - IAFC

Native American Topics Series
The Drum is in the Heart 29 MIN
Dist - IAFC
UCV

The Native Americans 26 MIN
U-matic / VHS / 16mm
Color (H C A)
$400 purchase - 16mm, $340 purchase - video, $55 rental
Examines the history of the North American Indian. Provides accounts of the struggle between the white men and Native Americans. Coproduced with the British Broadcasting Corporation.
History - United States; Social Science
Dist - CNEMAG **Prod** - DOCUA 1988

The Native Americans - first encounter 8 MIN
VHS
Columbus legacy series
Color (J H C G)
$40.00 purchase, $11.00 rental _ #12327
Looks at the lifestyle and the first contacts with Europeans of the Lenape, who lived in Pennsylvania before the arrival of Columbus. Features James 'Lone Bear' Revey who recounts the Lenape creation myth and describes the Walking Purchase deed of 1737, a land hoax perpetrated by the sons of William Penn. Part of a 15 - part series commemorating the 500th anniversary of Columbus' journeys to the Americas - journeys that brought together a constantly evolving collection of different ethnic groups and examining the contributions of 15 distinct groups who imprinted their heritage on the day - to - day life of Pennsylvania.
History - United States; Social Science; Sociology
Dist - PSU **Prod** - WPSXTV 1992

Native Americans - people of the desert 24 MIN
VHS
Native American series
Color (I J)
$99.00 purchase _ #RB865
Recreates an Anasazi cliff dwelling village to show how these ancestors of the modern Hopi adapted to their environment. Portrays their lifestyle and culture through the everyday experiences of a family. Watches the mother and daughter growing and preparing food, making clothes and creating pottery, the father and son making weapons, hunting and trading with other tribes. Reveals that the Anasazi achieved the highest level of cultural development in the Southwest and were among the first farmers, growing corn and beans. Part of a series on Native Americans.
History - United States; Social Science
Dist - REVID **Prod** - REVID 1993

Native Americans - people of the forest 24 MIN
VHS
Native American series
Color (I J)

$99.00 purchase _ #RB864
Portrays a Chippewa family to illustrate the typical life of Eastern Woodland Indians. Shows that they hunted deer and other forest game, fished and trapped in the rivers and lakes and made their homes from forest products. Looks at Acts Like a Brave, a young girl who is frustrated at being allowed only to do 'women's' work - cooking, sewing, basket making, farming - when she really wants to hunt, fish and trap. Part of a series on Native Americans.
Social Science; Sociology
Dist - REVID **Prod** - REVID 1993

Native Americans - people of the Northwest 24 MIN
VHS
Native Americans video series
Color (I J)
$99.00 purchase _ #RB866
Looks at the day - to - day life and customs of Native Americans in the Northwest United States prior to contact with Europeans. Teaches about the natural environment of the region and how tribes adapted to it in their choice of habitat, food, clothing, tools, weapons, art, family structure and basic economy. Utilizes historic photographs, graphics and authentic reenactments, using native people and narrators. Part of a four - part series on Native Americans.
Social Science
Dist - KNOWUN

Native Americans - people of the plains 24 MIN
VHS
Native American series
Color (I J)
$99.00 purchase _ #RB863
Looks at Indian tribes of the plains - the Commanche, the Blackfeet, the Chenyenne, the Sioux. Reveals that they all hunted buffalo. Follows a Sioux family to see how daily tasks are divided between the sexes - women and girls gathering and cooking food, making clothing and setting up the tipi, men and boys taking care of weaponry and hunting. Part of a series on Native Americans.
Social Science; Sociology
Dist - REVID **Prod** - REVID 1993

Native Americans Series
Examines the history of the North American Indians in ten episodes, 26 minutes each. Includes - Trail of Broken Treaties - injustices and attempts by Indian leaders to improve their situation; How the West was Won - efforts by Plains Indians to maintain cultural identity; They Promised to Take our Land - United States government's encroachment on Indian - owned land; Civilized Tribes - revolution of militant attitudes among younger Indians; Navajo - Race for Prosperity - modern life on the reservation; Cherokee - preserving ancient ceremonies; The Six Nations - Iroquois League of upstate New York; Pueblo Resistance - sacred traditions; Indian Country, southeastern United States' tribes; and Potlatch People - Pacific Northwest Indians and the potlatch.

Cherokee 26 MIN
Civilized tribes 26 MIN
How the West was Lost 26 MIN
Navajo, Race for Prosperity 26 MIN
Potlatch people 26 MIN
Pueblo Renaissance 26 MIN
The Six Nations 26 MIN
They Promised to Take Our Land 26 MIN
Trail of Broken Treaties 26 MIN
Dist - CNEMAG **Prod** - DOCUA 1993

Native Americans series
Indian cultures - from 2000 BC to 1500 a D 19 MIN
The Indian experience - after 1500 AD 18 MIN
Indian origins - the first 50,000 years 18 MIN
Dist - JOU

Native Americans - the history of a people 25 MIN
VHS
Color (P I J)
$55.00 purchase _ #5482VD
Introduces the numerous Native American cultures that developed before the arrival of the Europeans. Explores what was unique about each culture and what they shared in common. Offers a brief summary of the history of contact and conflict with Europeans societies after 1500 which precedes discussion of on - going issues in the lives of Native Americans in the 1990s. Includes teacher's guide.
Social Science
Dist - KNOWUN **Prod** - KNOWUN 1992

Native Americans video series
Native Americans - people of the Northwest 24 MIN
Dist - KNOWUN

A Native American's view - Columbus and European settlement 8 MIN
VHS / U-matic
Color (I J)
$220.00, $270.00 purchase, $50.00 rental
Features Native American storyteller, Helen Herrara Anderson, answering questions about Columbus and European explorers commonly asked her by young students. Gives a Native American perspective to encourage discussion about Columbus and the settling of America by European migration westward. Produced by ODOL Video.
History - United States; History - World; Social Science
Dist - NDIM

Native Awareness - Behind the Mask 29 MIN
VHS / 16mm
Color (C)
$250.00 purchase _ #278501
Increases awareness of Native culture and heritage in Canada. Shares information, activities, resource materials and discussion in an inservice workshop setting for educators.
Education; Geography - World; History - World; Social Science; Sociology
Dist - ACCESS **Prod** - ACCESS 1989

Native grace - prints of the New World, 1550 - 1876 30 MIN
VHS
Color (G)
$29.95 purchase
Presents a 300 - year survey of the impact of European civilization on the New World. Focuses on the tragic effect on the lives and culture of native Americans. Features Audobon birds and mammals, de Bry engravings - the first to depict native Americans of the Southeast, and 18th - century color prints of American plants and animals by Catesby. Includes romantic Western landscapes by Moran and authentic Indian prints from McKenny, Catlin and Bodmer.
Fine Arts; History - United States; Social Science
Dist - ARTSAM **Prod** - HOLDAY

Native Hawaiian Plants 30 MIN
VHS / BETA
Victory Garden Series
Color
Explores Waimea Falls Park at Oahu, Hawaii. Shows how to make cucumber soup.
Agriculture; Physical Education and Recreation
Dist - CORF **Prod** - WGBHTV

Native Imagery Series
Echoes 15 MIN
Messages 15 MIN
Paint Me a Story 15 MIN
Dist - ACCESS

Native Indian Treasures - Adapting Indian Art 20th Century Needlecraft 30 MIN
U-matic / VHS
Erica Series
Color
Demonstrates how to adapt Indian art to needlework in ponchos, and the use of silver thread embroidery in making Indian jewelry.
Fine Arts
Dist - KINGFT **Prod** - WGBHTV

The Native Land 17 MIN
16mm
Color
LC 77-700392
Shows a North American Indian mother, living on a reservation, who discusses her family and tribal problems, her past and her dreams for the future.
Social Science; Sociology
Dist - ATLAP **Prod** - ATLAP 1977

Native Land - Nomads of the Dawn 58 MIN
U-matic / VHS
Color (H C A)
$495 purchase, $95 rental
Describes the history and culture of the Native Americans who civilized the North and South American continents. Describes how a society changes when its mythology changes. Covers a time period from 65000 years ago to the rise of great civilizations. Written by Jamake Highwater. Produced by Alvin H. Perlmutter.
Social Science; Sociology
Dist - CNEMAG

Native Medicine 60 MIN
VHS / U-matic
Body in Question Series Program 9; Program 9
Color (H C A)
LC 81-706953
Contrasts the practice of modern medicine in an English town with the traditional magical system of the Azande tribe. Based on the book The Body In Question by Jonathan Miller. Narrated by Jonathan Miller.
Health and Safety; Sociology
Dist - FI **Prod** - BBCTV 1979

Native Music of the North - West Series
Sla - Hal, the Bone Game 27 MIN
Dist - WASU

Native Religious Traditions Series
The Sacred Circle 30 MIN
The Sacred Circle - Recovery 30 MIN
Dist - ACCESS

Native Self Reliance 20 MIN
U-matic / VHS
Color (J H A)
Documents technology projects underway in six different American Indian tribes involved in building windmills, solar crop dryer, solar greenhouses and collectors, small scale farming, and aqua culture. Offers tools for native peoples to act on their commitment to self determination and to maintain a healthy relationship with the earth.
Psychology; Science - Physical; Social Science; Sociology
Dist - BULFRG **Prod** - RINGRC 1980

Native son 111MIN
VHS
Color (J H C)
$89.00 purchase _ #04045 - 126
Tells the Richard Wright story of a poor black youth who inadvertently kills a white woman. Stars Oprah Winfrey, Matt Dillon and Geraldine Page.
History - United States; Literature and Drama; Sociology
Dist - GA **Prod** - GA

Native Transplants and Crude Drugs 18 MIN
16mm
Man and the Forest Series Part 4
Color (P I)
Illustrates how certain species of native trees and shrubs are identified in the forest, commercially dug and prepared for shipment to commercial nurseries. Shows how raw drug products are identified, and also gathered for sale to pharmaceutical companies.
Business and Economics; Health and Safety; Science - Natural
Dist - MMP **Prod** - MMP 1972

Natives - immigrant bashing on the border 28 MIN
VHS
B&W (H C G)
$295.00 purchase, $55.00 rental
Captures the xenophobia of many Americans living in California along the United States - Mexican border who are reacting to the influx of undocumented aliens they believe are draining community resources and committing crimes. Contrasts the professed love of these people for their country with their racist and anti - democratic attitudes. Produced by Jesse Lerner and Scott Sterling.
Geography - United States; History - United States; Sociology
Dist - FLMLIB

Natives of East Africa 11 MIN
16mm
Color (H C A)
Depicts the cultures, customs and activities of the East African natives with emphasis on the Masai, Galla and Secuma tribes. Describes the history and economic importance of Kenya, Tanganyika, Mombasa, Nairobi and Uganda.
Geography - World; History - United States; Sociology
Dist - AVED **Prod** - CBF 1960

Nativity 30 MIN
VHS
Greatest adventure series
Color (P I R)
$14.95 purchase _ #35 - 830008 - 1518
Uses animation format to present the Biblical story of the birth of Jesus.
Literature and Drama; Religion and Philosophy
Dist - APH **Prod** - HANBAR

The Nativity 30 MIN
VHS
Color (K P I G R)
$12.95 purchase _ #366VSV
Uses an animated format to tell the story of the birth of Jesus.
Literature and Drama; Religion and Philosophy
Dist - GF **Prod** - HANBAR

The Nativity - Piero Della Francesca 13 MIN
16mm
Color (H A)
$450.00 purchase, $45.00 rental
Examines elements of form, color and light in The Nativity, a late work of Piero della Francesca, 1446 - 1492.
Fine Arts; Industrial and Technical Education
Dist - AFA **Prod** - ACGB 1966

NATO - After 25 Years 13 MIN
U-matic / VHS
Color
Analyzes the first quarter century of the North Atlantic Treaty Organization.

Civics and Political Systems; History - World
Dist - JOU **Prod** - UPI

NATO - Past, Present, Future 20 MIN
16mm
Screen news digest series; Vol 9; Issue 2
B&W
Presents an exclusive report on the fate and future of the North Atlantic Treaty Organization.
Civics and Political Systems; History - United States; History - World
Dist - HEARST **Prod** - HEARST 1966

NATO Seapower for Peace 28 MIN
16mm
B&W
Reviews the activities and functions of SACLANT (Supreme Allied Command Atlantic) and its capabilities for the defense of NATO.
Civics and Political Systems; History - United States
Dist - USNAC **Prod** - USN 1957

Natsik Hunting 8 MIN
16mm
Color
LC 76-702091
Presents a documentary of a seal hunt on Baffin Island, photographed by an Inuit filmmaker.
Geography - World; Social Science
Dist - CDIAND **Prod** - CDIAND 1975

The Natural 134 MIN
VHS
Color (H C)
$79.00 purchase _ #04177 - 126
Stars Robert Redford and Glenn Close in an adaptation of the play by Bernard Malamud. Tells of an aging ballplayer dealing with his past demons.
History - United States; Literature and Drama; Physical Education and Recreation
Dist - GA **Prod** - GA

The Natural Balance 15 MIN
VHS / U-matic
Bioscope Series
Color (I J)
Describes the natural balance of plants and animals. Explains how weather, overpopulation, lack of food, and human interference can upset the natural balance.
Science - Natural
Dist - AITECH **Prod** - MAETEL 1981

The Natural balance of ecosystems 15 MIN
VHS
Color (J H C)
$39.95 purchase _ #49 - 8142 - V
Shows how the components of ecosystems interact with each other to maintain a natural balance. Still frame.
Science - Natural
Dist - INSTRU **Prod** - CBSC

Natural childbirth 25 MIN
VHS
Where there's life series
Color; PAL (G)
PdS25 purchase
Discusses the pros and cons of natural childbirth vs birth procedures in hospitals. Features Dr Miriam Stoppard as host in a series of shows making sense of science and treating controversial subjects in an informed way. Contact distributor about availability outside the United Kingdom.
Health and Safety
Dist - ACADEM

Natural Childbirth 10 MIN
16mm
Obstetrics and Gynecology Series
Color (H C A)
LC 75-700050
Presents a patient counseling film on natural childbirth.
Health and Safety; Science - Natural
Dist - MIFE **Prod** - MIFE 1974

Natural Childbirth
VHS / U-matic
Color (FRENCH SPANISH)
Presents a natural childbirth stressing the participation of both husband and wife. Concludes in the delivery room when they both respond to their newborn.
Health and Safety
Dist - MIFE **Prod** - MIFE

Natural connections 48 MIN
VHS / U-matic
Color (H G)
$250.00, $300.00 purchase, $50.00 rental
Traces the evolution of life from the big bang to homo sapiens. Shows the interrelations of all life forms, their common ancestry and chemical makeup. New experiments are providing a link to prove that both microbes and people are made of atoms that originated in the stars. Available in two parts.
Science - Natural; Science - Physical
Dist - NDIM **Prod** - CANBC 1989

A Natural Curriculum 29 MIN
U-matic / VHS
Authoring Cycle - Read Better, Write Better, Reason Better Series
Color (T)
Presents an overview of theoretical alternatives that may be used to teach reading and writing.
Education; English Language
Dist - HNEDBK **Prod** - IU

Natural Cycles and the Non Metallic Elements 17 MIN
U-matic
Chemistry 101 Series
Color (C)
Discusses the formation and breakdown of nitric oxide and nitrogen dioxide by natural and industrial methods.
Science; Science - Physical
Dist - UILL **Prod** - UILL 1974

Natural Disasters, Man - made Catastrophes 46 MIN
VHS
Color; Stereo (G)
$21.98 purchase _ #TT8052
Features George Kennedy narrating a documentary of the destruction man has endured throughout history.
History - United States; History - World; Literature and Drama
Dist - TWINTO **Prod** - TWINTO 1990

Natural Domain - Birds and Animals in Japan 30 MIN
16mm
Color
Introduces some of the rare and fascinating birds and animals found in Japan, such as the rare serow and the wild monkeys of Kyushu. Shows how the Japanese have taken steps to reverse some of the damage caused by pollution and rapid urbanization.
Geography - World; Science - Natural
Dist - MTP **Prod** - MTP

Natural enemies of forest insect pests 23 MIN
VHS / U-matic
Color (C PRO G)
$75.00 purchase, $25.00 rental _ #952
Explores the beneficial impact of some diseases, parasites and predators in dampening potential outbreaks of defoliatory insect pests in forests. Interviews forest scientists and researchers to explain the importance of natural enemies of insect pests such as viruses, wasps, ants and birds in natural regulatory processes.
Agriculture; Science - Natural; Social Science
Dist - OSUSF **Prod** - OSUSF 1989

Natural enemies - the deer and the wolf 24 MIN
VHS
Wild refuge series
Color (G)
$39.95 purchase
Looks at deer, moose and antelope as they forage, mate and breed under the watchful eye of coyotes and wolves. Presents part of a thirteen - part series on the North American wilderness. Each episode documents a different area and shows how animal species cope with their surroundings to survive.
Geography - World; Science - Natural
Dist - CNEMAG **Prod** - HOBELP 1976

Natural environment series

Amazon	25 MIN
Antarctica - the unowned land	28 MIN
The Desert southwest	15 MIN
The Florida Everglades	15 MIN
Galapagos - the enchanted islands	25 MIN
The Great Lakes	14 MIN
The Northern Lakes	14 MIN
Voyage to the Arctic	25 MIN
The Yukon Territory	15 MIN

Dist - JOU

Natural Environment Series

The High Plains - Caribou Country	18 MIN
The Northwest - Mountains to the Sea	23 MIN

Dist - JOU
UILL

Natural factory 30 MIN
VHS
Perspective - biotechnology - series
Color; PAL; NTSC (G)
PdS90, PdS105 purchase
Shows how animals and other organisms are miniature chemical factories.
Science - Natural
Dist - CFLVIS **Prod** - LONTVS

Natural features 30 MIN
16mm
Field studies series
Color (G)
$60.00 rental
Uses cut - outs, photographs, mirrors, water, toys, paint and ink in different combinations. Mingles still images with 3 - D objects and real images photographed through glass layerings into a bizarre form of animation. Fifth in the series of collage films 'Field Studies.'
Fine Arts
Dist - CANCIN **Prod** - NELSOG 1990

Natural force 30 MIN
VHS
Perspective - energy resources - series
Color; PAL; NTSC (G)
PdS90, PdS105 purchase
Examines the possibility of extracting power from the sea and directing its tides and currents to protect the coastlines.
Social Science
Dist - CFLVIS **Prod** - LONTVS

Natural Forces and the Motorcycle 14 MIN
16mm
American Honda Series
Color (H A)
Demonstrates the forces of gravity, inertia, friction and impact and the fact that a thorough knowledge of these forces is necessary for the safe operation of motorcycles. Shows the correct wearing apparel.
Health and Safety; Social Science
Dist - AHONDA **Prod** - AHONDA

Natural Gas and Clean Air 22 MIN
16mm
B&W
LC 70-711357
Examines the major types and sources of air pollution and shows how pollution is measured. Explains that natural gas can eliminate dangerous pollutants entirely where it replaces other fuels.
Physical Education and Recreation; Science - Natural; Social Science
Dist - BUGAS **Prod** - UGC 1970

Natural Gas and Clean Air 22 MIN
16mm
Color (J H A)
Examines the major types and sources of air pollution. Illustrates how they are measured and how natural gas can eliminate most dangerous pollutants entirely when it replaces other feuls.
Science - Physical; Social Science; Sociology
Dist - BUGAS **Prod** - BUGAS

Natural Gas Fuel Cell 20 MIN
16mm
Color (J H A)
Traces the development of the natural gas feul cell from the discovery of its basic principles to its application as a self contained power plant for home and industrial use. Shows how natural gas is converted into electricity through chemistry without any heat or mechanical devices whatsoever. Describes the many uses of the feul cell including providing energy, reducing pollution, and conserving natural resources.
Home Economics; Social Science
Dist - BUGAS **Prod** - BUGAS 1972

Natural Gas Industry's the Blue Flame 5 MIN
16mm
Color
LC 70-710884
Shows the world land speed record being broken at Bonneville, Utah by the Blue Flame, a vehicle using liquid natural gas as its fuel.
Physical Education and Recreation; Social Science
Dist - PROGRP **Prod** - IGT 1970

Natural Gas - Supply and Demand 28 MIN
16mm
Energy - an Overview Series
Color (J H)
Presents the problem facing the natural gas industry of increasing demand and dwindling supplies. Traces the formation of natural gas over millions of years and explores various steps being taken to increase gas reserves.
Home Economics; Industrial and Technical Education; Social Science
Dist - CONPOW **Prod** - CENTRO

Natural Habitat
16mm
B&W (A C)
Offers a commentary on the dehumanization of human life that takes place in the modern urban context. Award - winning documentary montage by Ralph Arlyck.
Psychology; Social Science; Sociology
Dist - ARRA **Prod** - ARRA 1970

Natural Healing Forces 30 MIN
VHS
Video Reflections Series
Color (G)
$29.95 purchase _ #VHEL
Combines images of nature with music and soothing environmental sounds. Uses visual and auditory subliminal messages for enhancing healing.
Health and Safety; Psychology
Dist - GAINST **Prod** - GAINST

Natural Highs and How to Get Them
VHS / U-matic
Color (J H)
Recognizes that everyone has the potential for getting high naturally and experiencing jubilant feeling without drugs. Designed as a drug education program. Includes teacher's guide.
Guidance and Counseling; Psychology
Dist - SUNCOM **Prod** - SUNCOM

Natural history 13 MIN
16mm
Color (G)
$30.00 rental
Says filmmaker Alan Berliner, '...from there to here, from then to now.'
Fine Arts; Science - Natural
Dist - CANCIN

Natural History in the Classroom Series
No Substitute for Experience - Pt 1 30 MIN
Dist - FI

Natural History in the Classroom Series
Changing Perspectives - Pt 3 30 MIN
Dist - FI
SCETV

Natural history in the classroom series
Presents a three - part series on ways to improve teaching of natural history. Stresses creative activities such as collecting insects, building terrariums, using attractants, and reassembling skeletons. Hosted by Rudy Mancke.
The Stories they tell 30 MIN
The Stories they tell - Pt 2 30 MIN
Dist - SCETV **Prod** - FI 1983

The Natural History of Hepatocellular Carcinoma 51 MIN
U-matic
Color
Discusses research on tumor initiation and promotion in rats by injecting drugs at specified times.
Health and Safety
Dist - UTEXSC **Prod** - UTEXSC

The Natural History of Our World - the Time of Man 50 MIN
16mm / U-matic / VHS
Color (J)
Traces a series of case studies of animal populations and primitive human cultures that have survived or perished according to their ability to adapt to their environment. Emphasizes that if man is to survive, he must maintain the environment that sustains him. Narrated by Richard Basehart.
Science - Natural; Sociology
Dist - PHENIX **Prod** - EALING 1970

The Natural History of Our World - the Time of Man, Pt 1 25 MIN
16mm / U-matic / VHS
Color (J)
Traces a series of case studies of animal populations and primitive human cultures that have survived or perished according to their ability to adapt to their environment. Emphasizes that if man is to survive, he must maintain the environment that sustains him. Narrated by Richard Basehart.
Science - Natural
Dist - PHENIX **Prod** - EALING 1970

The Natural History of Our World - the Time of Man, Pt 2 25 MIN
U-matic / VHS / 16mm
Color (J)
Traces a series of case studies of animal populations and primitive human cultures that have survived or perished according to their ability to adapt to their environment. Emphasizes that if man is to survive, he must maintain the environment that sustains him. Narrated by Richard Basehart.
Science - Natural
Dist - PHENIX **Prod** - EALING 1970

Natural History of Psychotic Illness in Childhood 19 MIN
16mm
B&W (C T)
Describes the evolution of a psychotic child from infancy to adolescence.
Psychology
Dist - NYU **Prod** - IPSY 1960

Natural History of the Water Closet 29 MIN
VHS / U-matic
Color
LC 82-706620
Utilizes a creative combination of documentary, animation and original music to survey the evolution of the modern - day toilet, complete with detailed descriptions of its actions.
Industrial and Technical Education
Dist - PBS **Prod** - WITFTV 1980

Natural history series
An Inkling of beetles 13 MIN
Dist - CBSC
CLRVUE

Natural history series
Carnivorous plants 21 MIN
The Caterpillar's psyche 20 MIN
A Double life 20 MIN
Dwellings 15 MIN
The Humming economies of bees and wasps 17 MIN
Hunters in the grass 15 MIN
Intimate strangers - symbiosis 9 MIN
Ladybug, ladybug 12 MIN
Ocean desert - the Sargasso Sea 10 MIN
Pollination - the insect connection 15 MIN
The Portuguese man - of - war 10 MIN
Rivals - the mating game 16 MIN
There's no such thing as an aunt in an ant colony 13 MIN
Weave and spin 13 MIN
Dist - CLRVUE

Natural home remedies 90 MIN
VHS
Color (G)
$29.95 purchase _ #P19
Demonstrates how to treat more than 50 common health conditions, from A to Z, and contains an alphabetical index. Features Jay Gordon. Includes a booklet.
Health and Safety
Dist - HP

Natural Ingredients - Development of the Preschool and School - Age Child 22 MIN
VHS / U-matic
Spoonful of Lovin' Series no 3
Color (H C A)
LC 82-706063
Presents journalist Reynelda Muse explaining why play may be the most important of all learning activities. Shows child - care providers summarizing how they handle the questions, doubts and fears of preschool to school - age children and discussing how the needs and behavior of school - age children differ from those of younger ones.
Home Economics; Psychology
Dist - AITECH **Prod** - KRMATV 1981

Natural Laws 29 MIN
U-matic / VHS
Right Way Series
Color
Tells how to maintain equilibrium between the vehicle and the roadway.
Health and Safety
Dist - PBS **Prod** - SCETV 1982

Natural light essay number 1 3 MIN
VHS / 16mm
B&W; Silent (G)
$10.00 rental
Meditates on natural light, filmed in a controlled setting of reflection and movement. Available for purchase in video format with a group package entitled Six Films.
Fine Arts
Dist - CANCIN **Prod** - BAINCL 1986

Natural Light Portraits 5.34 MIN
VHS / U-matic
Photo Tips Series
Color (J H A)
Employs a variety of subjects and settings to demonstrate the use of natural light in photography.
Fine Arts; Industrial and Technical Education
Dist - AITECH **Prod** - TURR 1986

Natural Liquified Gas 14 MIN
16mm
Color (PRO)
Describes the storage and handling of methane in its liquified state.
Health and Safety; Science - Physical; Social Science
Dist - LAFIRE **Prod** - LAFIRE

The Natural Logarithm - Graph of Y Inx
U-matic
Calculus Series
Color
Mathematics
Dist - MDCPB **Prod** - MDDE

Natural Mysteries 60 MIN
VHS / U-matic
Discovery of Animal Behavior Series
Color (H C A)
Explores medieval superstitions of ancient naturalists. Reveals that Frederick II of Hohenstaufen had a passion of falconry that resulted in the book On The Art Of Hunting With Birds.
Science; Science - Natural
Dist - FI **Prod** - WNETTV 1982

Natural Numbers, Integers and Rational Numbers 29 MIN
16mm
Intermediate Algebra Series
B&W (H)
Reviews properties of natural numbers, discussing the closure, associative, commutative and distributive laws. Shows why zero and negative numbers are essential to the integer system. Introduces the reciprocal as a means of developing the rational number system.
Mathematics
Dist - MLA **Prod** - CALVIN 1959

Natural Outside Cartoon Objects 15 MIN
Videoreel / VT2
Charlie's Pad Series
Color
Fine Arts
Dist - PBS **Prod** - WSIU

Natural Phenomena Series
Geysers, Lava and Hot Spots 16 MIN
Lakes, Rivers and Other Water Sources 17 MIN
Life between the Tides 20 MIN
Mountains and Mountain Building 15 MIN
Rocks, Fossils and Earth History 17 MIN
Spectacular Canyons 17 MIN
Trees, the Biggest and the Oldest Living Things 19 MIN
Volcanoes, Earthquakes and Other Earth Movements 17 MIN
Dist - JOU

Natural Phenomenon Series
Hurricanes, Tornadoes and Other Weather 17 MIN
The Land that Came in from the Cold 13 MIN
Dist - JOU

Natural process of aging 30 MIN
VHS
Color (PRO C)
$199.00 purchase, $70.00 rental _ #4379
Explains how aging affects the integumentary system, musculoskeletal system, respiratory system, gastrointestinal system, genitourinary system, central nervouse system, cardiovascular system and the senses. Uses dramatic scenes and graphic art to illustrate the changes - a voice - over narration adds further explanation. Covers some disease conditions that are common among the elderly. Presents suggested interventions and responses to natural changes and signs of disease.
Health and Safety
Dist - AJN **Prod** - MEDCOM

Natural products - 2 30 MIN
VHS / U-matic
Chemotherapy series
Color (PRO)
$275.00 purchase, $60.00 rental _ #7126S, #7126V
Presents a program on natural products used in cancer chemotherapy. Includes a 50 - question post - test. Part of a twelve - part series on chemotherapy.
Health and Safety
Dist - AJN **Prod** - HOSSN 1988

Natural resources 37 MIN
VHS
Color (I J H)
$130.00 purchase _ #A5VH 1380
Presents two parts which describe the role natural resources have played in the past and help students to make informed decisions about the role of natural resources in the future. Reveals that whale oil was once a much sought - after natural resource and that gold was once considered the most important natural resource. Shows how the concept of 'natural resource' has changed through the ages. Part 2 asks if the world's resources are limited and presents conflicting expert views, challenging students to investigate further and form their own opinions. Includes supplemental book.
Science - Natural; Social Science
Dist - CLRVUE **Prod** - CLRVUE

Natural Resources 10 MIN
U-matic
Color (P)
Examines the many responsibilities of a park ranger. Shows how foresters do everthing from keeping parks clean to planning new parks.

Guidance and Counseling; Science - Natural
Dist - GA **Prod** - MINIP

Natural resources engineering technician 5 MIN
U-matic
Good work series
Color (H)
Provides useful, up to date information on various occupations to aid high school students in career selection. Available in five series of ten jobs each.
Education; Guidance and Counseling; Science - Natural
Dist - TVOTAR **Prod** - TVOTAR 1981

Natural resources - future quest 33 MIN
VHS
Future quest series
Color (J H C)
$79.00 purchase _ #312
Debates the future of natural resources. Features Thomas Lovejoy, Julian Simon, Amory Lovins, Howard Odum and others. Asks if natural resources are limited or if human ingenuity can be counted upon to multiply them indefinitely. Includes a guide. Part of ten parts.
Science - Natural
Dist - HAWHIL **Prod** - HAWHIL

Natural Science Reading 120 MIN
VHS / U-matic
A C T Exam Preparation Series
Color
Education; Science - Natural
Dist - KRLSOF **Prod** - KRLSOF 1985

Natural Science Series
Presents a three - part series on natural history. Includes the titles 'The Prairie - 3rd Edition,' 'The Rocky Mountains - Revised Edition,' and 'The Desert - 3rd Edition.'
The Desert 16 MIN
The Desert - 3 16 MIN
The Prairie - 1 15 MIN
The Rocky Mountains 17 MIN
The Rocky Mountains - 2 17 MIN
Dist - BARR **Prod** - CASDEN 1985

Natural science specials Module blue series
Fossils - a book from the past 18 MIN
The Great Salt Lake - America's inland sea 18 MIN
Dist - AITECH

Natural science specials module green series
Dinosaurs - the thunder lizards 20 MIN
Dist - AITECH

Natural Science Specials Series Module Blue
Mountain Water - a Key to Survival 16 MIN
Volcanoes - Vulcan's Forge 18 MIN
The West - Land of many Faces 13 MIN
Dist - AITECH

Natural Science Specials Series Module Green
Lake Bonneville - History's High - Water Mark 19 MIN
Marshlands - Where the Action is 20 MIN
Mountains and Mountain Building - Nature's High Rise 19 MIN
Dist - AITECH

Natural science specials series
Canyonlands 19 MIN
The Desert bighorn sheep 14 MIN
Glaciers - nature's big bulldozers 18 MIN
Plant and animal life distribution - the natural world 18 MIN
Pond succession - a circle of life 17 MIN
Dist - AITECH

Natural Science, Tape 1 45 MIN
VHS / U-matic
CLEP General Examinations Series
Color (H A)
Prepares students for the College Level Examination Program (CLEP) tests in Natural Science. Explores astronomy.
Education; Science - Physical
Dist - COMEX **Prod** - COMEX

Natural Science, Tape 2 45 MIN
U-matic / VHS
CLEP General Examinations Series
Color (H A)
Prepares students for the College Level Examination Program (CLEP) test in Natural Science. Focuses on aspects of earth science such as plate tectonics and earth's formation.
Education; Science - Physical
Dist - COMEX **Prod** - COMEX

Natural Science, Tape 3 45 MIN
U-matic / VHS
CLEP General Examinations Series
Color (H A)
Prepares students for the College Level Examination Program (CLEP) tests in Natural Science. Explores the atmosphere, chemistry, atoms, molecules and radioactivity.
Education; Science - Physical
Dist - COMEX **Prod** - COMEX

Natural Science, Tape 4 45 MIN
VHS / U-matic
CLEP General Examinations Series
Color (H A)
Prepares students for the College Level Examination Program (CLEP) tests in Natural Science. Focuses on biology.
Education; Science - Natural
Dist - COMEX **Prod** - COMEX

Natural Science, Tape 5 45 MIN
U-matic / VHS
CLEP General Examinations Series
Color (H A)
Prepares students for the College Level Examination Program (CLEP) tests in Natural Science. Focuses on living things. Includes the plant and animal kingdoms.
Education; Science - Natural
Dist - COMEX **Prod** - COMEX

Natural Selection 30 MIN
VHS
Color (H C)
Examines how Darwin's ideas have been integrated with the growing understanding of genetics.
Science - Natural
Dist - IBIS **Prod** - IBIS 1984

Natural Selection 16 MIN
16mm / U-matic / VHS
Biology - Spanish Series Unit 10 - Evolution; Unit 10 - Evolution
Color (H) (SPANISH)
Reports on three experiments concerning the role of natural selection in evolution. Describes a study of bird predation, a study of natural selection among plant populations and an investigation of insecticide - resistant mosquitoes.
Foreign Language; Science - Natural
Dist - EBEC **Prod** - EBEC

Natural Selection 20 MIN
U-matic / VHS
Evolution Series
Color
Explains how drifting continents, island populations and genetic variability affect natural selection. Deals with the nature of clines.
Science - Natural; Science - Physical
Dist - FOTH **Prod** - FOTH 1984

Natural selection 30 MIN
VHS
Color (J H)
$145.00 purchase _ #A5VH 1278
Shows how the ideas of Darwin have been incorporated into the growing understanding of genetics. Covers the development of Darwin's theories, genetic foundations for natural selection, genotypes and phenotypes, and the Hardy - Weinberg law. Shows how the punctuated theory of evolution challenges the gradulism theory that species evolve in a gradual, orderly manner, leading paleontologists to reexamine fossil records.
Science - Natural; Science - Physical
Dist - CLRVUE **Prod** - CLRVUE

Natural selection 60 MIN
VHS
Ark series; Episode 2
Color (G)
$290.00 purchase, $50.00 rental
Continues with the story of Regent's Park Zoo in London and the necessity of weeding out which animals will remain - those popular with visitors will be kept, hundreds of others will go. Lists the birds, then the orangutans, reindeer, lemurs, etc. Fellows of the Zoological Society are up in arms at the dispersal of the zoo's collection and revolt is in the air. Part of a series on the Zoo which has been told, that due to the market economy, it must now pay its own way. Records events at the Ark for over a year as a cost conscious management team moves in, slashing expenditures, including 90 people and 1200 animals - 40 percent of the zoo's stock. Founded in 1822, the zoo's scientific research has received world wide acclaim.
Business and Economics; Fine Arts; Science - Natural
Dist - FIRS **Prod** - DINEEN 1993

Natural selection
VHS / 35mm strip
Color (J H)
$129.00, $145.00 purchase _ #CG - 782 - VS, #CG - 7820 - VS
Examines how the ideas of Darwin have been integrated into the growing understanding of genetics. Uses clear, scientifically accurate narration and a combination of color photographs and archival prints to show how one of the basic tenets of natural selection has recently been challenged by the new 'punctuated equilibrium theory' of evolution. In two parts - Natural Selection and Microevolution, and Gradualism vs the Punctuated Equilibrium Theory of Evolution.
Science - Natural
Dist - HRMC **Prod** - HRMC

Natural Selection 35 MIN
16mm
Color
Presents Lang Gottheim's film entry selected from the 1985 Whitney Biennial Film and Video Exhibition.
Fine Arts
Dist - AFA **Prod** - AFA 1986

Natural Selection - Evolution at Work 24 MIN
16mm / U-matic / VHS
Color (H C)
Shows how evolution depends on the availability of genetic variation. Uses as examples rats resistant to Warfarin and a copper - tolerant species of grass.
Science - Natural
Dist - MEDIAG **Prod** - BBCTV 1981

Natural States 45 MIN
VHS
Color (G)
$29.95 purchase _ #MVP8401
Tours the lush Pacific Northwest with music by David Lanz and Paul Speer.
Fine Arts; Geography - United States; Industrial and Technical Education; Science - Natural
Dist - MIRMP **Prod** - MIRMP 1991

Natural states 45 MIN
VHS
Color; Stereo (G)
$29.95 purchase _ #S01830
Combines footage of Big Sur, Mount Rainier and other areas of the Pacific Northwest with the New Age music of David Lanz and Paul Speer.
Fine Arts; Geography - United States
Dist - UILL

The Natural Tan 14 MIN
16mm
Color (J)
LC 81-701084
Presents pantomimes of a frustrated hero, trying vainly to gain a natural tan, to introduce information about proper exposure to the sun and sunlamps.
Health and Safety; Home Economics
Dist - KLEINW **Prod** - KLEINW 1980

Natural Transmutations 10 MIN
U-matic
Nuclear Physics Series
Color (H C)
Demonstrates at the atomic level how elements are transformed into new elements or isotopes through the process of decay. Three types of radioactive decay are explained and the concept of half life is discussed.
Science; Science - Physical
Dist - TVOTAR **Prod** - TVOTAR 1986

Natural Waste Water Treatment 29 MIN
VHS
Ecology Workshop Series
Color (J H C G) (GERMAN)
$195.00 purchase, $50.00 rental
Discusses small decentralized sewage treatment plants that use the natural purifying characteristics of marsh plants. Points out that such plants are operating in Germany, Switzerland, and the Netherlands.
Science - Natural; Science - Physical
Dist - BULFRG **Prod** - BULFRG 1987

Natural Waters 10 MIN
U-matic
Chemistry 102 - Chemistry for Engineers - Series
Color (C)
Examines the roles of water in the climate of earth and the life of man. Introduces some ways in which water can be treated and reviews selective precipitation.
Industrial and Technical Education
Dist - UILL **Prod** - UILL 1981

Natural Wonders of Virginia 20 MIN
16mm
Color (I)
Pictures Virginia's natural wonders, such as the caverns, natural bridge, natural tunnel and natural chimneys. Points out their locations and their geological and historical significance.
Geography - United States; Science - Natural; Science - Physical
Dist - VADE **Prod** - VADE 1961

Natural World 29 MIN
U-matic

Creation of Art Series
Color
Focuses on different points of view and styles of landscape painting.
Fine Arts
Dist - UMITV **Prod** - UMITV 1975

Natural world series
Big oil - in the wake of the Exxon Valdez 50 MIN
Echo of the elephants 60 MIN
Even the animals must be free 50 MIN
Fire bird 50 MIN
Gorillas in the midst of man 50 MIN
Island of the ghost bear 50 MIN
Pandas of the sleeping dragon 50 MIN
Prisoners of the sun 150 MIN
Snowdonia - realm of ravens 50 MIN
Toadskin spell 50 MIN
Vampires, devilbirds and spirits 50 MIN
Volcano watchers 50 MIN
Dist - BBCENE

The Naturalist 15 MIN
VHS / 16mm
Harriet's Magic Hats IV Series
Color (P)
$175.00 purchase _ #207140
Presents thirteen new programs to familiarize children with more workers and their role in community life. Features Aunt Harriet's bottomless trunks of magic hats where Carrie has only to put on a particular hat to be whisked off to investigate the person and the role represented by the hat. 'The Naturalist' shows Ralph the parrot munching on seeds and Carrie wondering whether birds will nest on the roof during spring. She visits Carolann who explains the role of naturalists and shows Carrie the types of birds and animals common to the park.
Business and Economics; Guidance and Counseling; Psychology; Science - Natural
Dist - ACCESS **Prod** - ACCESS 1986

Naturalists Series
The Captain of a Huckleberry Party - Henry Thoreau 29 MIN
Earth - planet, universe - John Muir 29 MIN
He who has Planted will Preserve - Theodore Roosevelt 28 MIN
How far are we from home - John Burroughs 29 MIN
Dist - IU

Naturalists Series
Henry David Thoreau - the captain of a huckleberry party 28 MIN
John Burroughs - How Far are We from Home 28 MIN
John Muir - Earth - Planet, Universe 28 MIN
Theodore Roosevelt - He who has Planted will Preserve 28 MIN
Dist - PBS

Naturally 10 MIN
16mm
B&W
Presents a documentary about a beauty school. Shows a group of girls learning how to walk, talk, 'DO' their hair and faces, and control their figures. Features the head of the school describing her aims, methods and values in relation to teaching girls how to be 'NATURAL,' and why such teaching is necessary.
Education; Guidance and Counseling; Home Economics
Dist - UPENN **Prod** - UPENN 1970

Naturally Better Way - the Application of Firefly Bioluminescence in the Microbiology Lab 10 MIN
U-matic
Color (PRO)
Provides an overview of the bioluminescent assay of adenosine triphosphate (ATP) and discusses its applications in the microbiology laboratory focusing on urine screening.
Health and Safety
Dist - MMAMC **Prod** - MMAMC

Nature and development of affection 19 MIN
16mm / VHS
Color (C G PRO)
$270.00, $130.00 purchase, $20.50 rental _ #22664
Documents the experiments of H E Harlow analyzing the nature and development of affection in primates. Follows rhesus monkeys separated from their mothers at birth who were raised nursing or non - nursing on cloth or wire surrogate mothers, and were tested for mother preferences under a variety of conditions. Produced by Harlow and R Zimmerman.
Psychology
Dist - PSU **Prod** - PSU 1959
PSUPCR

Nature and Nurture 52 MIN
U-matic / VHS
Human Animal Series
Color (G)
$279.00, $179.00 purchase _ #AD - 1134
Asks why a person becomes a stuntwoman or a librarian, a criminal or a clergyman, a warrior or a pacifist. Considers which behaviors might be inborn and which might be learned. Examines identical twins separated at birth and finds that some 10 - 15 percent of children are born with a slight tendancy to be outgoing or apprehensive, that there may be a chemical predisposition to seeking danger or high risk. Reveals also that a supportive environment produces well - adjusted adults while a hostile home can produce the opposite. Part of a series by Phil Donahue on the Human Animal.
Education; Psychology; Science - Natural; Sociology
Dist - FOTH **Prod** - FOTH

The Nature and Source of Demand 60 MIN
BETA / VHS
Manufacturing Series
(IND)
Identifies and describes the demand elements found in a master schedule plan.
Business and Economics
Dist - COMSRV **Prod** - COMSRV 1986

The Nature and Structure of the Hair
U-matic / VHS
Color
Provides an understanding of the nature of human hair for those who will go on to study the chemical and physical processes used in professional hair care. Explains the cuticle, cortex, medulla, macrofibrils, polypeptide chains, amino acids and melanin.
Education; Home Economics
Dist - MPCEDP **Prod** - MPCEDP 1984

The Nature and Transmission of AIDS 20 MIN
VHS / 16mm
Color (PRO G)
$149.00, $249.00, purchase _ #AD - 1798
Explains how venereal disease is transmitted and what kinds of sexual activity can transmit infection. Notes that, although many STD's (sexually transmitted diseases) can be treated and cured medically, AIDS is the fatal exception. Explains how the AIDS viruses lay their victims open to opportunistic infections and what these are. Discusses the problem of long incubation period, how HIV affects the immune system, and how AIDS can be caught.
Health and Safety; Psychology; Sociology
Dist - FOTH **Prod** - FOTH 1990

Nature Boy 18 MIN
VHS / U-matic
Color
Shows a young Japanese boy at the Kwannon festival who is told by a mysterious voice to grasp happiness with his own hands. Depicts how, after first grasping only a straw, and through kindness to others, he receives fine fruit, rich cloth, a horse and, finally, his own land to cultivate.
Fine Arts; Geography - World; History - World; Industrial and Technical Education
Dist - EDMI **Prod** - GAKKEN 1983

Nature Boy 18 MIN
16mm / VHS
Folktales from Japan Series
Color (K P I)
$295.00, $380.00 purchase, $50.00 rental _ #8002
Tells a Japanese folk story about generosity rewarded when Nature Boy, through his kindness to others, receives many rich benefits.
Geography - World; Literature and Drama
Dist - AIMS **Prod** - EDMI 1983

Nature by design series
Aims to create understanding of how design evolves. Utilizes a visual style which blends natural history footage, graphics and video effects - moving back and forth between science and nature. Emphasizes that good design is essential for the success of any product, in the natural world and today's high-tech world.
Driven by design 30 MIN
Image intensifiers 30 MIN
Moving in the material world 30 MIN
On the move 30 MIN
The protection racket 30 MIN
The shape of things to come 30 MIN
Dist - BBCENE

Nature Craft - an Introduction 13 MIN
16mm / U-matic / VHS
Color (I)
Discusses how to create art from natural objects like sea shells, leaves, flowers and stones.
Fine Arts
Dist - LUF **Prod** - LUF 1979

Nature Episode Series
Endangered Species - Massasauga Rattler and Bog Turtle 20 MIN
Guardians of the Cliff - the Peregrine Falcon Story 20 MIN
Dist - EDIMGE

Nature Episodes Series
Flag - the story of the white - tailed deer 20 MIN
I Walk in the Desert 20 MIN
Mitzi a Da Si - a Visit to Yellowstone National Park 20 MIN
A Visit to St Helens 20 MIN
Windrifters - the Bald Eagle Story 20 MIN
Dist - EDIMGE

Nature Guide Film Series
The Great white pelican 19 MIN
My Pet Pelican 11 MIN
Pelican Island 28 MIN
Dist - AVEXP

Nature in the City 13 MIN
U-matic / VHS / 16mm
Color (K P I)
LC 79-712692
Shows how grackles, pigeons, house mice, cockroaches, spiders, ants, bees, butterflies, gray squirrels, robbins and earth worms live, develop and adapt to their environment in the city.
Science - Natural
Dist - JOU **Prod** - WER 1971

Nature is Corrupt, Baby Master 6 MIN
U-matic / VHS
Color
Brings together weather, suprematism, death and swimming, for a soothing effect.
Fine Arts
Dist - KITCHN **Prod** - KITCHN

Nature next door 28 MIN
VHS
Color (P I J H)
$350.00 purchase, $15.00 rental
Shows how insects, reptiles, birds, plants and mammals relate to one another in a common area.
Industrial and Technical Education; Science - Natural
Dist - CMSMS **Prod** - SIERRA 1962

Nature of a continent 55 MIN
VHS
Africans series
Color (A)
PdS99 purchase _ Unavailable in USA or Canada
Features Ali Mazuri examining the history and peoples of Africa. Explores the influences of Islam and the West on the African continent. Part of an eight-part series.
History - World; Religion and Philosophy
Dist - BBCENE

The Nature of a continent - Pt 1 60 MIN
VHS / U-matic
Africans series
Color (G)
$45.00, $29.95 purchase
Looks at the influence of geography upon history. Explores the roles of water, desert and equatorial climate in the development of African culture and civilization. Part of a nine - part series hosted by Dr Ali Mazrui, Cornell University and University of Michigan.
Geography - World; History - United States; History - World; Social Science
Dist - ANNCPB **Prod** - WETATV 1988
BBCENE

The Nature of addiction 22 MIN
U-matic / VHS
Color (H C G)
$425.00, $395.00 _ #V150
Discloses the latest research on addiction. Focuses on the unique addictive properties of cocaine and crack.
Guidance and Counseling; Health and Safety; Psychology
Dist - BARR **Prod** - ABCNEW 1990

The Nature of Anthropology 30 MIN
U-matic
Faces of Culture - Studies in Cultural Anthropology Series Lesson 1; Lesson 1
Color (C A)
Reviews the interdisciplinary nature of anthropology. Looks briefly at the history of the discipline. Includes comments of anthropologists regarding anthropology as a science.
Sociology
Dist - CDTEL **Prod** - COAST

The Nature of Breast Cancer 10 MIN
VHS / 16mm
Understanding Breast Cancer Series
Color (H C A PRO)
$195.00 purchase, $75.00 rental _ #8068
Investigates the nature of breast cancer.
Guidance and Counseling; Health and Safety
Dist - AIMS **Prod** - HOSSN 1988

Nature of business
VHS
Dynamics of business series
Color (H C A)
$139.00 purchase _ #MAS01V
Explores basic business concepts. Considers subjects including economic systems, forms of business ownership, organizational structures, and scope of business.
Business and Economics
Dist - CAMV

The Nature of Children's Books 145 MIN
U-matic
University of the Air Series
Color (J H C A)
$750.00 purchase, $250.00 rental
Examines popular children's books from various countries and periods and studies the qualities of literature for children in relation to the society from which it springs. Program contains a series of five cassettes 29 minutes each.
Literature and Drama
Dist - CTV **Prod** - CTV 1978

The Nature of colour 11 MIN
VHS
Color; PAL (H)
Explains the physical phenomena of color and the principles by which colors are reproduced. Shows white light passing through a prism. Conducts experiments to show color reflection and absorption. Combines primary colors to produce secondary colors and uses colored spotlights to demonstrate color mixture by addition and subtraction of colors.
Fine Arts; Industrial and Technical Education; Science - Physical
Dist - VIEWTH **Prod** - VIEWTH

The Nature of Communication 30 MIN
VHS / U-matic
Writing for a Reason Series
Color (C)
English Language
Dist - DALCCD **Prod** - DALCCD

The Nature of Crude Oil and Natural Gas 11 MIN
VHS / U-matic
Overview of the Petroleum Industry Series
Color (IND)
Shows how oil and gas are measured, molecular structure of hydrocarbon change, and which contaminants occur naturally in oil and gas deposits.
Business and Economics; Industrial and Technical Education; Science - Physical; Social Science
Dist - GPCV **Prod** - GPCV

The Nature of Culture 30 MIN
U-matic
Faces of Culture - Studies in Cultural Anthropology Series Lesson 2; Lesson 2
Color (C A)
Presents basic aspects of the concept of culture. Defines ethnocentrism and cultural relativism. Gives examples of the aspects of culture in a variety of cultures and societies.
Sociology
Dist - CDTEL **Prod** - COAST

The Nature of Digital Computing
16mm
B&W
Deals with the fundamental ideas underlying the computing process.
Mathematics
Dist - OPENU **Prod** - OPENU

The Nature of Drug Dependency 32 MIN
VHS / 16mm
Color (G)
$165.00 purchase, $40.00 rental _ #0407H, 0607H, 0562J, 0627J
Describes the characteristics of chemical dependency and treatment. Features Dr Richard O Heilman.
Guidance and Counseling; Health and Safety; Psychology
Dist - HAZELB **Prod** - HAZELB

Nature of Energy Series
The Nature of light 17 MIN
The Nature of sound 14 MIN
Dist - CORF

The Nature of ethical problems 24 MIN
BETA / VHS / U-matic
Ethics, values and health care series
Color (C PRO)
$150.00 purchase _ #132.1
Presents a video transfer from slide program which introduces and defines ethics and ethical dilemmas. Presents two major ethical theories - the teleological and deontological - which can be useful in helping to think through ethical issues. Presents a six - step model for analyzing ethical problems. Features commentary by Leah Curtin, Director and Founder of the National Center for Nursing Ethics. Part of a series on ethics, values and health care.
Health and Safety; Religion and Philosophy
Dist - CONMED **Prod** - CONMED

The Nature of Foaling Video
VHS
Color (G)
$49.95 purchase _ #6 - 022 - 100P
Overviews the gestation and foaling periods of a bred mare. Shows how to observe and note the various subtle signs of the foaling mare. Emphasizes the importance of routine veterinary exams. Illustrates the proper approach of the foal in delivery so that students know when something is going wrong with the birth process.
Agriculture; Physical Education and Recreation
Dist - VEP **Prod** - VEP

The Nature of Human Attachments in Infancy 56 MIN
VHS / 16mm
Awakening and Growth of the Human - Studies in Infant Mental Health 'Series
Color (C A)
$150.00, $170.00 purchase _ #85849
Presents a summary of the 100 years of research in infant psychology which forms the basis of current understandings. Discusses how bonds are formed, why they sometimes fail to form, and what differences this makes to the child's development. Emphasizes the child's role as socially and psychologically active rather than passive, and his need of a basic emotional bond with a primary caregiver before he can develop.
Health and Safety; Psychology; Sociology
Dist - UILL **Prod** - IPIN 1986

The Nature of Human Color Change - Genetic, Hormonal and Neoplastic 90 MIN
16mm
Boston Medical Reports Series
B&W (PRO)
LC 74-705190
Depicts the importance of melanin pigmentation and its relationship to systemic disease. Uses patients, marine animals, mice, film, charts and slides to demonstrate the basic science aspects.
Health and Safety; Science - Natural
Dist - NMAC **Prod** - NMAC 1968

The Nature of Language 28 MIN
16mm
Language - the Social Arbiter Series
Color (H C T)
LC FIA67-5261
Examines current knowledge about language from the viewpoint of the scientific linguist. Features staff members of the Center for Applied Linguistics.
English Language
Dist - FINLYS **Prod** - FINLYS 1966

The Nature of Language and How it is Learned 32 MIN
16mm
Principles and Methods of Teaching a Second Language Series
B&W (H T)
Discusses the nature of language, how it is learned and the validity of the oral approach to teaching. Presents examples of speech from all over the world.
Education; English Language; Foreign Language
Dist - IU **Prod** - MLAA 1962

The Nature of Language - Brain and Mind 30 MIN
U-matic / VHS
Language and Meaning Series
Color (C)
English Language; Psychology
Dist - GPN **Prod** - WUSFTV 1983

The Nature of Lanuage - the Linguistic Perspective 30 MIN
U-matic / VHS
Language and Meaning Series
Color (C)
English Language; Psychology
Dist - GPN **Prod** - WUSFTV 1983

The Nature of Leadership 56 FRS
VHS / U-matic
Leadership Series Module 1
Color
Shows that leadership - follower relationships are found everywhere and that a leader is nothing without followers. Reveals that wise leaders understand, appreciate and motivate their followers.
Business and Economics; Psychology
Dist - RESEM **Prod** - RESEM

The Nature of Life - Cells, Tissue and Organs 11 MIN
U-matic / VHS / 16mm
Nature of Life Series
Color (J H)
Examines cell differentiation, the process that makes possible countless variations in kinds and species, in microscopic and normal scenes of living organisms.
Science - Natural
Dist - CORF **Prod** - CORF 1974

The Nature of Life - Energy and Living Things 13 MIN
16mm / U-matic / VHS
Nature of Life Series
Color (J H)
LC 74-706711
Demonstrates the importance of sunlight, photosynthesis, enzyme action and ATP in energy conversion.
Science - Natural
Dist - CORF **Prod** - CORF 1970

The Nature of Life - Living Things Interact 12 MIN
16mm / U-matic / VHS
Nature of Life Series
Color (J H)
LC 73-702898
Shows how a stray calf, lost in the desert, introduces interaction among organisms, occurring in the nitrogen cycle, the carbon cycle, the calcium cycle, parasitism and predation.
Science - Natural
Dist - CORF **Prod** - CORF 1973

The Nature of Life - Respiration in Animals 11 MIN
16mm / U-matic / VHS
Nature of Life Series
Color (J H)
LC 76-706709
Illustrates respiration throughout the animal kingdom, demonstrating relationships between respiration, blood circulation and feeding.
Science - Natural
Dist - CORF **Prod** - CORF 1970

Nature of Life Series
The Nature of Life - Cells, Tissue and Organs 11 MIN
The Nature of Life - Energy and Living Things 13 MIN
The Nature of Life - Living Things Interact 12 MIN
The Nature of Life - Respiration in Animals 11 MIN
The Nature of Life - the Living Cell 13 MIN
The Nature of Life - the Living Organism 12 MIN
Dist - CORF

The Nature of Life - the Living Cell 13 MIN
U-matic / VHS / 16mm
Nature of Life Series
Color (J H)
LC 70-706710
Shows how cells obtain food, convert food to energy, respond to the environments and reproduce.
Science - Natural
Dist - CORF **Prod** - CORF 1970

The Nature of Life - the Living Organism 12 MIN
U-matic / VHS / 16mm
Nature of Life Series
Color (J H)
LC 73-702897
Explores how organisms exchange substances with their environment, move materials about within their bodies, direct and coordinate their activities, feed and reproduce.
Science - Natural
Dist - CORF **Prod** - CORF 1973

The Nature of light 9 MIN
VHS
Color; PAL (H)
Oberves the principles of light and optics in natural situations.
Science - Physical
Dist - VIEWTH **Prod** - VIEWTH

The Nature of light 17 MIN
U-matic / VHS / 16mm
Nature of Energy Series
Color (I J)
LC 73-701783
Traces the work of scientists of the past three centuries to aid in an explanation of the properties and characteristics of light.
Science - Physical
Dist - CORF **Prod** - CORF 1973

Nature of Logarithms 31 MIN
16mm
Advanced Algebra Series

B&W (H)
Develops the nature of logarithms on the basis of powers of ten and the properties of exponents. Explains the differences between the mantissa and the characteristic and discusses the logarithm of fractional numbers. Shows the use of logs in computation.
Mathematics
Dist - MLA **Prod** - CALVIN 1960

The Nature of Management
VHS / U-matic
Essentials of Management Series Unit I; Unit I
Color
Defines the management work and the management cycle as well as the relationship between the individual, the team and the organization's objectives. Emphasizes building a team of professionally oriented managers and supervisors.
Business and Economics; Psychology
Dist - AMA **Prod** - AMA

The Nature of Management 20 MIN
VHS / U-matic
Supervision Management Course, Pt 1 Series Unit 1
Color
Acquaints supervisors with the basic concepts of management.
Business and Economics; Psychology
Dist - AMA **Prod** - AMA

The Nature of Marriage
VHS
Marriage, Family Living and Counseling Series
(C G)
$59.00_CA227
Discusses the nature of marriage.
Guidance and Counseling
Dist - AAVIM **Prod** - AAVIM 1989

The Nature of Matter - an Atomic View 24 MIN
U-matic / VHS / 16mm
Physical Science Film Series
Color (C A)
LC 73-700600
Visits the Dr Erwin Meuller Laboratory at Pensylvania State University to demonstrate the field - ion microscope. Discusses wave - particle duality and spectroscopy.
Science; Science - Physical
Dist - CRMP **Prod** - CRMP 1973

The Nature of Matter and Living Things
U-matic / VHS
Color
Provides an introduction to gaseous, solid and liquid forms of matter. Introduces the atom as the basic building block of all matter. Demonstrates how molecules of various substances are formed. Explains cell division and cell specialization with particular emphasis on the creation of hair and skin.
Science - Natural; Science - Physical
Dist - MPCEDP **Prod** - MPCEDP 1984

The Nature of Memory 26 MIN
U-matic / VHS
Color (G)
$249.00, $149.00 purchase _ #AD - 2137
Asks what memory is and how it works. Considers whether memory is reality or a creation of the subconscious and whether memory can be manipulated by dreams or hypnosis. Shows computer models mimicking the functions of human memory. Introduces studies of amnesiacs to determine how and where memories are made and stored. Probes the effect of emotions on memory and how memory can be altered.
Guidance and Counseling; Psychology; Science - Natural; Sociology
Dist - FOTH **Prod** - FOTH

The Nature of mental retardation 40 MIN
16mm
Counseling the mentally retarded series; No 1
Color (PRO)
LC 72-702028
Includes clinical examples of eight different etiologies of mental retardation and explains the rehabilitation potential of the five different adaptive behavior levels of mental retardation.
Education; Psychology
Dist - NMAC **Prod** - UKANS 1968

Nature of Mental Retardation 25 MIN
16mm
Color (C A)
Relates vocational counseling to the various adaptive behavior levels of retarded children. Contains examples of the various causes of mental retardation and defines the rehabilitation potential of the different levels.
Education; Guidance and Counseling; Psychology
Dist - UKANS **Prod** - UKANS 1968

The Nature of Mental Retardation 21 MIN
VHS / U-matic
Color (PRO)
Shows graphically what mental retardation means and that it doesn't mean idiocy. Displays that, depending upon the profundity of the retardation, much can be done to create useful lives.
Education; Psychology
Dist - PRIMED **Prod** - PRIMED

The Nature of mind 150 MIN
VHS / BETA
Color; PAL (G)
PdS40, $80.00 purchase
Features a speech by the Venerable Kalu Rinpoche in London, November 1987.
Fine Arts; Religion and Philosophy
Dist - MERIDT **Prod** - HP 1987

The Nature of mind 90 MIN
VHS / BETA
Color; PAL (G)
PdS31 purchase
Features His Eminence Sakya Trizin giving a lucid and profound explanation of the practice of Mahamudra from the lineage of Drogmi Lotsawa. Defines Mahamudra or the Great Symbol as the ultimate realization attained through tantric practice. Explains the progressive stages involved in this meditation and draws upon a classic series of analogies to describe the states of experience that a mahamudra practitioner encounters while bringing his or her mind to rest in its natural condition. Taped at Rigpa in London.
Fine Arts; Religion and Philosophy
Dist - MERIDT

The Nature of money 60 MIN
VHS
Macroeconomics series
Color (H C G)
$89.00 purchase _ #GSU - 319
Discusses money, banking and the federal reserve system. Reviews banks and money creation. Part of a 24 - part series instructed by Dr Edward F Stuart, Northwestern University, which focuses on a description of the major economic policy - making bodies in the United States and their interrelationships.
Business and Economics
Dist - INSTRU

The Nature of music 141 MIN
VHS
Color (G)
$49.95 purchase _ #NAT03
Presents a three part series by Jeremy Marre, The Nature of Music. Includes Sources and Sorcery, which examines Balinese exorcism rites and the throat songs of the Inuits, Songs and Symbols, which examines the use of animal sounds in music - singing monkeys, Arab exoricism, ancient Greek rituals, the operas of Richard Wagner, and Legends and Labels, which examines how society transforms musical tastes as shown by flamenco dancing, the piano concertos of Mozart, and Brazilian samba, as well as opera buffs and punk rockers.
Fine Arts; History - World; Psychology
Dist - HOMVIS **Prod** - RMART 1990

Nature of Pain, Pt 1 17 MIN
U-matic / VHS
Pain - Sleep Series
Color (PRO)
Health and Safety; Psychology
Dist - CONMED **Prod** - CONMED 1971

Nature of Pain, Pt 2 19 MIN
VHS / U-matic
Pain - Sleep Series
Color (PRO)
Health and Safety; Psychology
Dist - CONMED **Prod** - CONMED 1971

The Nature of Radioactivity 20 MIN
U-matic / VHS
Too Hot to Handle Series
Color (C)
$249.00, $149.00 purchase _ #AD - 1552
Examines the forty - plus years between Hiroshima and Chernobyl. Explains the four kinds of radiation and why heavier chemical elements are unstable, why radon is dangerous. Part of a series on radioactivity.
Health and Safety; Industrial and Technical Education; Social Science; Sociology
Dist - FOTH **Prod** - FOTH

Nature of Sea Water 29 MIN
16mm
Color
LC 74-705191
Describes physical and chemical properties of sea water. Explains how man's understanding of the sea is basic to making use of ocean resources.
Science - Physical; Social Science
Dist - USNAC **Prod** - USN 1967

The Nature of Signs 30 MIN
VHS / U-matic
Language and Meaning Series
Color (C)
English Language; Psychology
Dist - GPN **Prod** - WUSFTV 1983

The Nature of Sleep 89 FRS
VHS / U-matic
Pain - Sleep Series
Color (PRO)
LC 71-739167
Psychology; Science
Dist - CONMED **Prod** - CONMED 1971

The Nature of sound 13 MIN
VHS
Color; PAL (H)
Uses high - speed photography and demonstrations of air molecules with powdered plastic and magnets to establish sound as a form of wave energy. Illustrates sound waves in terms of amplitude, loudness, frequency, pitch, quality and Doppler effect and shows the uses of sound in oceanography and geology.
Fine Arts; Science - Physical
Dist - VIEWTH **Prod** - VIEWTH

The Nature of sound 14 MIN
U-matic / VHS / 16mm
Nature of Energy Series
Color (J)
LC 74-709425
Establishes sound as a form of wave energy and illustrates sound waves in terms of amplitude, loudness, frequency, pitch, quality and Doppler effect.
Science - Physical
Dist - CORF **Prod** - CORF 1971

The Nature of Symbols 30 MIN
U-matic / VHS
Language and Meaning Series
Color (C)
English Language; Psychology
Dist - GPN **Prod** - WUSFTV 1983

The Nature of the Film Medium 27 MIN
U-matic / VHS / 16mm
Color
Demonstrates the great flexibility of the motion picture medium. Discusses symbols, the effect of various camera speeds on the emotions, the psychology of subjective camera and the infinite possibilities of film editing. Includes clips from 'CITIZEN KANE,' 'HAND IN HAND,' 'REQUIEM FOR A HEAVYWEIGHT' and other films.
Fine Arts; Industrial and Technical Education
Dist - PAULST **Prod** - PAULST

The Nature of the Nerve Impulse 15 MIN
U-matic / VHS
Experiment - Biology Series
Color (C)
$249.00, $149.00 purchase _ #AD - 1091
Uses adult locusts to demonstrate the relationship between frequency and intensity of stimulus and respose. Part of a series on biology experiments.
Education; Psychology; Science - Natural
Dist - FOTH **Prod** - FOTH

The Nature of the Problem 66 MIN
U-matic
Preventing Sexual Harrassment in the Workplace Series
Color (A)
Explains the magnitude and the subtle nature of the problem. Uses role playing to explain who can be victimized and who can be charged with sexual harrassment.
Business and Economics; Sociology
Dist - VENCMP **Prod** - VENCMP 1986

Nature of things series
No spare parts 25 MIN
Dist - ASTRSK

Nature of things series
And god created whales 28 MIN
The Differences are inherited 28 MIN
The Evolution of Flight 28 MIN
The First inch 28 MIN
Grouse Country 28 MIN
The Invisible Reef 28 MIN
Left Brain, Right Brain 56 MIN
Out of the mouth of babes - the acquisition of language 28 MIN
Puffins, Predators and Pirates 28 MIN
Tipping the Scales 55 MIN
Water's Edge, the, Pt 1 - the Unseen World 28 MIN
Water's Edge, the, Pt 2 - the Silent Explosion 28 MIN
Dist - FLMLIB

The Nature of transactions
VHS
Color (H C A)
$98.00 purchase _ #CV0710V
Uses the start - up of a business to teach basic accounting principles. Includes support materials.
Business and Economics
Dist - CAMV

The Nature of Waves 11 MIN
U-matic / VHS
Introductory Concepts in Physics - Wave Motion Series
Color (C)
$229.00, $129.00 purchase _ #AD - 1201
Examines what a wave is and how to see and think about the concept of waves. Observes wave phenomena from various viewpoints - time waves, space waves and propagating waves.
Science - Physical
Dist - FOTH **Prod** - FOTH

Nature Photography 30 MIN
U-matic / VHS
Taking Better Pictures series
(G)
$180.00 purchase, $30.00 five day rental, $110.00 self dub
Designed to help beginning and intermediate photographers use 35 mm equipment effectively. Highlights nature photography techniques. Eighth in a ten part series.
Fine Arts; Industrial and Technical Education
Dist - GPN **Prod** - GCCED 1984

Nature photography 30 MIN
VHS
Color (G)
$24.95 purchase _ #S00936
Tells how to select and photograph nature scenes.
Industrial and Technical Education
Dist - UILL **Prod** - EKC

Nature Photography 30 MIN
U-matic / VHS
Roughing it Series
Color
Discusses nature photography while 'roughing it.'.
Industrial and Technical Education; Physical Education and Recreation
Dist - KYTV **Prod** - KYTV 1984

Nature photography 30 MIN
VHS
Kodak video programs - the advanced photography series
Color (H C A)
$14.95 purchase
Teaches photographic techniques for nature settings.
Industrial and Technical Education
Dist - PBS **Prod** - WNETTV

Nature series
Death on the St Lawrence 30 MIN
Devil's element 30 MIN
Exhausted 30 MIN
The Fourth hurdle 30 MIN
Look who's talking 30 MIN
Malaysian take - away 30 MIN
Mother of the megacities 50 MIN
Rain plague 30 MIN
Wish you weren't here 30 MIN
Dist - BBCENE

Nature story series
Chucky Lou - the story of a woodchuck 11 MIN
Dist - IU

Nature Walk 15 MIN
16mm
B&W
LC 79-700250
Tells the story of a hospital worker and an autistic boy who go for a walk in the woods. Describes their different perceptions of the world around them and shows how they relate to one another.
Education; Fine Arts; Psychology
Dist - CARMAG **Prod** - CARMAG 1976

Nature Walk at Low Tide 12 MIN
U-matic / VHS / 16mm
Nature's Sights and Sounds Series
Color (P I)
Guides a small group of children along a Pacific Ocean beach examining rocks and tidal pools, discovering many forms of plant and animal life.
Science - Natural
Dist - BCNFL **Prod** - MASLKS 1984

Nature watch series
Presents a series of 20 programs that explores the curious and uncommon characteristics of a variety of mammals, insects, birds and sea creatures, using state - of - the - art technology. Teacher's guide available.
Baby Koko 25 MIN
Chipmunk 25 MIN
City dwellers 25 MIN
Crayfish and coneshells 25 MIN
Crow and black headed gull 25 MIN
Cuckoo 25 MIN
Dragonfly 25 MIN
Mantis and wasp 25 MIN
Octopus 25 MIN
Otter, seal, and penguin 25 MIN
Rock ptarmigan 25 MIN
Ruddy kingfisher 25 MIN
Salamander 25 MIN
Shrike 25 MIN
Sika and sambar 25 MIN
Tern 25 MIN
Waterbirds 25 MIN
Wild boar 25 MIN
Woodpecker 25 MIN
Dist - TVOTAR **Prod** - TVOTAR 1984

Nature's builders 8 MIN
VHS / 16mm
Color (P I PRO)
$180.00, $145.00 purchase, $30.00 rental _ #8009
Teaches children that animals are born builders as they observe them building complex structures for reproduction, capturing food, and protection.
Science - Natural
Dist - AIMS **Prod** - EDMI 1984

Nature's Builders 8 MIN
U-matic / VHS
Color (K P I)
Shows a swallow building its nest with mouthfuls of mud, a spider spinning its web and cocooning captured insects, and a caterpillar building its cocoon, later emerging as a moth.
Science - Natural
Dist - EDMI **Prod** - AFTS 1984

Nature's Camouflage 13 MIN
U-matic / VHS / 16mm
Color (I)
LC 78-707910
Studies the ways in which form and color adaptation can conceal or distort the shapes of living creatures to protect them from their enemies. Uses close - up photography of insects and reptiles to demonstrate the ways in which they are camouflaged.
Science - Natural
Dist - AIMS **Prod** - ACI 1970

Nature's Colors - the Craft of Dyeing with Plants 10 MIN
VHS / U-matic
Color (A)
Explores a wide range of plant sources for dyes and shows the process of treating yarn.
Home Economics; Science - Natural
Dist - BBG **Prod** - BBG 1975

Nature's cure 30 MIN
VHS
Perspectives - health and medicine - series
Color; PAL; NTSC (G)
PdS90, PdS105 purchase
Visits the world of natural medicine.
Health and Safety
Dist - CFLVIS **Prod** - LONTVS

Nature's Engineer - the Beaver 10 MIN
U-matic / VHS / 16mm
Color (P I J)
LC FIA55-659
Shows how beavers build dams. Points out the benefits we derive from beavers.
Science - Natural
Dist - IFB **Prod** - WLF EBER 1947

Nature's Ever - Changing Communities 14 MIN
U-matic / VHS / 16mm
Color (I J)
LC 73-701349
Discovers the concepts of renewal, change and interdependence in the natural world. Shows how the living and non - living elements in an area are really an interdependent natural community.
Science - Natural
Dist - JOU **Prod** - GLDWER 1973

Nature's Food Chain 14 MIN
16mm
Color (J H)
LC 79-700462
Examines the hierarchical ordering of predators and prey in natural environment.
Science - Natural
Dist - BNCHMK **Prod** - NFBC 1978

Nature's Forge 29 MIN
16mm
Color
LC 74-703083
Examines the ecological effects of the release of excess heat from power plants, showing research by Government and commercial operators of nuclear plants on the effects of this heat on fish, plants and animals.
Science - Natural; Science - Physical; Social Science
Dist - USNAC **Prod** - USNRC 1974

Nature's Half Acre 33 MIN
16mm / U-matic / VHS
Color (I J H) (GERMAN AFRIKAANS DANISH FRENCH ITALIAN NORWEGIAN SPANISH SWEDISH)
LC 78-714972
Follows the never - ending cycle of life through the four seasons of the year, concentrating on birds, plants and insects. Portrays nature's plan of providing and caring for all.
Foreign Language; Science - Natural
Dist - CORF **Prod** - DISNEY 1955

Natures keeper - West Coast Africa - Part 25 8 MIN
VHS
Natures kingdom series
Color (P I J)
$125.00 purchase
Watches 5,000 gulls gathering - grayheads, laughing gull, wind gulls - as well as fiddler crabs. Part of a 26 - part series on animals showing the traits and habitats of various species.
Geography - World; Science - Natural
Dist - LANDMK **Prod** - LANDMK 1992

Nature's kingdom series
Presents a 26 - part series showing the traits and habitats of various species. Visits Canada, parts of Africa, Europe, South America, the Pacific Ocean and the Philippines to film marine animals, jungle animals, prairie animals and the French wild boar.
Animals of the forest - Ivory Coast - Part 2 8 MIN
Balloons over Africa - Kenya - Part 3 8 MIN
Barbary sea birds - Senegal - Part 21 8 MIN
Beaks and tails - Senegal - Part 14 8 MIN
Call of the sea - Pacific Ocean - Part 6 8 MIN
Claw and wing - Senegal - part 16 8 MIN
The Elephant family - Kenya - Part 26 8 MIN
Fierce nature - France - Part 12 8 MIN
Giants of the sea - Valdes Peninsula - Part 20 8 MIN
Hunters of the forest - Mindaneo - Part 7 8 MIN
Ivory Coast wildlife - West Coast Africa - Part 15 8 MIN
Law of nature - East Africa - Part 13 8 MIN
Lords of the bush - Kenya - Part 18 8 MIN
Lords of the prairie - Venezuela - Part 24 8 MIN
Natures keeper - West Coast Africa - Part 25 8 MIN
Pacific paradise - Philippines - Part 23 8 MIN
Pampas wildlife - Argentina - Part 9 8 MIN
A Ranch in South America - Venezuela 8 MIN
River bank home - Kenya - Part 5 8 MIN
The River horse - Kenya - Part 17 8 MIN
Seal beach - Argentina - Part 10 8 MIN
Triangle Island - British Columbia - Part 1 8 MIN
Tropical creatures - Philippines - Part 8 8 MIN
The Wild boar - France - Part 4 8 MIN
Wings of the tropics - Senegal - Part 11 8 MIN
Young red beasts - France - Part 22 8 MIN
Dist - LANDMK **Prod** - LANDMK 1992

Nature's Laws 60 MIN
U-matic
Nonbehavioral Sciences and Rehabilitation Series Part V
Color (PRO)
Presents certain trends concerning structure and function which appear to be enhanced as the physlogenetic scale is ascended, such as cephalization, the trend of 'stereomorphophysiology,' the increase in commissural systems, and the importance of multisensory input, multipotential receptors, and polysensory neurons in relation to function and plasticity.
Psychology; Science - Natural
Dist - AOTA **Prod** - AOTA 1980

Nature's pharmacy series
Presents a three - part series on nature's pharmacy. Includes Cooking with Edible Flowers and Culinary Herbs; Edible Wild Plants; and Trees, Shrubs, Nuts and Berries.
Cooking with edible flowers and culinary herbs 60 MIN
Edible wild plants 60 MIN
Nature's pharmacy series 180 MIN
Trees, shrubs, nuts and berries 60 MIN
Dist - CAMV

Nature's Rhythms 30 MIN
U-matic / VHS
Y E S Inc Series
Color (J H)
Demonstrates that adults, as well as young people can experience feelings of threat and insecurity when confronted with a situation that requires new learning. Leads viewers to consider ways of coping successfully in such situations.
Guidance and Counseling; Psychology
Dist - GPN **Prod** - KCET 1983

Nature's Sights and Sound Series
Spring - Nature's Sights and Sounds 14 MIN
Dist - BCNFL

Nature's Sights and Sounds Series
Autumn - nature's sights and sounds 14 MIN
Nature Walk at Low Tide 12 MIN
Summer - Nature's Sights and Sounds 14 MIN
Winter - Nature's Sights and Sounds 14 MIN
Dist - BCNFL

Nature's Strangest Creatures 16 MIN
U-matic / VHS / 16mm
Color (I J H) (AFRIKAANS GERMAN FRENCH GREEK NORWEGIAN)
Studies some of the rarest wildlife from the bush country of Australia and Tasmania.
Foreign Language; Science - Natural
Dist - CORF **Prod** - DISNEY 1963

Nature's Superlatives 29 MIN
Videoreel / VT2
Observing Eye Series
Color
Science - Natural; Sociology
Dist - PBS **Prod** - WGBHTV

Nature's Way 15 MIN
U-matic / VHS / 16mm
Craft, Design and Technology Series
Color (I J)
Explains that overcoming some of the problems faced by the handicapped through the design and manufacture of artificial limbs combines past knowledge and experience with space - age technology. Combines requirements for function, comfort and appearance with considerations of performance, reliability and weight.
Business and Economics; Sociology
Dist - MEDIAG **Prod** - THAMES 1983

Nature's Way 20 MIN
16mm
Color (H C A)
LC 74-702534
Shows a variety of Appalachian folk people and their various methods for curing maladies using remedies, such as herbs, lamb's tawder and wild tansy tea.
Geography - United States; Health and Safety; Social Science; Sociology
Dist - APPAL **Prod** - APPAL 1974

Nature's ways 26 MIN
16mm
Audubon wildlife theatre series
Color (I)
Presents an inquisitive look at an imposing array of birds, insects, fish and other wild creatures living close to human suburbia in Connecticut, yet easily overlooked community in the world around us.
Geography - United States; Science - Natural; Social Science
Dist - AVEXP **Prod** - AVEXP

Naturescene series
Features nature walks at various sites throughout the U S. Examines and discusses the plants, trees, insects, animals and other things seen at each site. Hosted by Rudy Mancke and Jim Welch. Consists of 65 episodes in an ongoing series begun in 1986.
Naturescene series 1833 MIN
Dist - SCETV **Prod** - SCETV

Natwaniwa - a Hopi philosophical statement 27 MIN
U-matic / VHS
Words and place series
Color (HOPI (ENGLISH SUBTITLES))
Hopi with English subtitles. Shows the significance of cultivation of the land to the Hopi. Shows many of the Hopi turning from the old ways.
Literature and Drama; Social Science
Dist - NORROS **Prod** - NORROS

Naughts 6 MIN
16mm
Color (G)
$20.00 rental
Features a series of five hand - painted, step - printed productions, each of which is a textured, thus tangible 'nothing' - a series of 'nots' in pun or knots of otherwise invisible energies. Includes fog clouds rising vertically; a progression of blue surreal shapes; a gathering of crystalline forms in primary colors; an orange rock - beseeming wall of lights; and a mixture of crystal and cellular shapes.
Fine Arts; Science - Physical
Dist - CANCIN **Prod** - BRAKS 1994

Naughty Number Nine 4 MIN
U-matic / 35mm strip
Multiplication Rock Series
Color (P I)
LC 75-733965
Uses an original rock song illustrated by cartoon characters to demonstrate multiplication by nine.
Mathematics
Dist - GA **Prod** - ABCTV 1974

Naughty nurse 9 MIN
16mm
Color (G)
Presents a short film directed by Paul Bartel.
Fine Arts
Dist - KINOIC

The Naughty Owlet 7 MIN
16mm / U-matic / VHS
Color (P I)
Uses animation to tell the story of three baby owls who live in a hollow tree and are instructed by their parents in the art of flying.
Literature and Drama
Dist - AIMS **Prod** - UILL 1971

Naughty words 3 MIN
16mm
B&W (G)
$15.00 rental
Covers the gamut of cinematic profanity.
Fine Arts; Psychology
Dist - CANCIN **Prod** - MCDOWE 1974

Nautical Astronomy 23 MIN
16mm
Navigation Series
B&W
LC FIE52-975
Explains how the celestial coordinates are placed in relation to the earth and how declination, Zenith point, Nadir line and the June and September solstices are used in celestial navigation.
Civics and Political Systems; Science - Physical; Social Science
Dist - USNAC **Prod** - USN 1943

Nautical chart interpretation 120 MIN
VHS
Color (G A)
$29.95 purchase _ #0949
Contains seven United States Coast Guard instructional films on interpreting nautical charts. Includes Understanding a Chart, Reading the Chart, Using the Chart, Aids to Navigation for Boatmen, Useful Knots for Boatmen, Visual Distress Signals, and Capsizing, Sinking and Falls Overboard.
Physical Education and Recreation
Dist - SEVVID

Navajo 21 MIN
16mm / U-matic / VHS
Color (I)
LC 73-702268
Describes the history, customs and life of the Navajo Indian nation, 15 million acres within the southwestern part of the United States. Explains that while much of Navajo life remains the same, other aspects of life have changed drastically.
Geography - United States; Social Science
Dist - IU **Prod** - PAINF 1972

Navajo 15 MIN
VHS
Color; PAL (G)
$19.95 purchase
Social Science; Sociology
Dist - CARECS

The Navajo 30 MIN
VHS
Indians of North America video series
Color; B&W; CC (P I J)
$39.95 purchase _ #D6658
Overviews the history of the Navajo. Combines interviews with leading authorities on Native American history with live footage and historic stills. Part of a ten - part series.
Social Science
Dist - KNOWUN

The Navajo - a Study in Cultural Contrast 15 MIN
U-matic / VHS / 16mm
Color (P I J H)
Views the environment, family structure, traditions, ceremonials and art of the Navajo Indians.
Social Science; Sociology
Dist - JOU **Prod** - JOU 1969

Navajo Canyon Country 13 MIN
16mm
Color (I)
Shows Navajo people in their native country and gives a brief description of their way of life today.
Geography - United States; Social Science; Sociology
Dist - MLA **Prod** - DAGP 1954

Navajo Code Talkers 28 MIN
VHS / U-matic
Color (G)
Uses 1940's archival footage of Navajo life as well as scenes of World War II to show the vital role a small group of Navajo Marines played in the South Pacific during the 2nd World War. Featured are interviews with Navajo Chairman Peter MacDonald, artist and scholar Carl Gorman, Taos artist R.C. Gorman and a special Presidential commendation by Ronald Reagan.
Sociology
Dist - NAMPBC **Prod** - NAMPBC 1986

Navajo Code Talkers 27 MIN
16mm / U-matic / VHS
Color
Deals with the contributions of Navajo Indians to World War II intelligence activities. Interviews some of the surviving Code Talkers. Utilizes Army films taken at Saipan, Guadalcanal and Iwo Jima and archival footage of Navajo reservation life during the 1940's.
History - United States; Social Science
Dist - ONEWST **Prod** - NMFV

Navajo Country 10 MIN
U-matic / VHS / 16mm
Color (I J)
Shows the dependence of the nomadic Navajos upon sheep and goats to supply their food as well as the wool for clothing and for marketable rugs and blankets. Depicts carding, spinning, weaving and jewelry making.
Geography - United States; Social Science; Sociology
Dist - IFB **Prod** - UMINN 1951

Navajo Coyote Tales 18 MIN
16mm
Navajo Folktales Series
Color (T)
Presents animated tales of the Coyote.
Education; Foreign Language; Social Science
Dist - BIECC **Prod** - BIECC 1972

Navajo Coyote Tales - Legend to Film 18 MIN
16mm
Color (I J H G) (ENGLISH AND NAVAJO)
$260.00 purchase, $11.00 rental
Shows how Coyote films were animated on computer. Animated.
Fine Arts
Dist - BIECC **Prod** - BIECC

The Navajo - Dine 30 MIN
VHS
Indians of North America series
Color (J H C G)
$49.95 purchase _ #LVCD6658V - S
Interviews Navajo leaders who discuss their nation's history. Includes location footage at reservations where children and elders discuss what it means to be Native American today. Part of a 10 - part series on Indian culture.
History - United States; Social Science
Dist - CAMV

Navajo Folktales Series
Coyote and Beaver 6 MIN
Coyote and Horned Toad 8 MIN
Coyote and Lizard 7 MIN
Coyote and Rabbit 7 MIN
Coyote and Skunk 9 MIN
Navajo Coyote Tales 18 MIN
Dist - BIECC

Navajo Girl 21 MIN
16mm / U-matic / VHS
Color (I J H)
LC 74-703490
Presents the environmental and cultural characteristics of an Indian reservation in the northeastern corner of Arizona. Tells about a young Navajo girl and the part she plays in the care of the sheep and goats that provide food and clothing.
Social Science; Sociology
Dist - GA **Prod** - XEROX 1973

Navajo Health Care Practices 40 MIN
VHS / U-matic
Color (PRO)
Interviews a Navajo practical nurse about the traditions and healing practices of her family. Describes the ways Navajos choose between modern and traditional healing.
Health and Safety; Social Science; Sociology
Dist - UARIZ **Prod** - UARIZ

The Navajo Indian 10 MIN
VHS
Color (P I)
$59.00, $265.00, $185.00 purchase _ #MF-3394
Reveals that the Navajo tribe is one of the few Indian tribes still increasing in population, and that they have adapted from modern life only what is useful and what fits into their traditional ways of living. Shows that as they adjust to the changes coming gradually to their homeland, they continue their lives as animal herders, skilled weavers and silversmiths.
Social Science
Dist - INSTRU **Prod** - CORF 1975
CORF

Navajo Land Issue 12 MIN
U-matic / VHS
Color (H C A)
Discusses the land issue that exists between the Navajo and the Hopi Indians. Interviews participants in the conflict and projects a potential outcome.
Geography - World; Social Science
Dist - JOU **Prod** - UPI

Navajo moon 24 MIN
U-matic / VHS
Young people's specials series
Color
Examines the view of changing reservation life through the eyes of three Navajo children.
Social Science
Dist - MULTPP **Prod** - MULTPP

Navajo Night Dances 11 MIN
16mm
Color (H C A)
#1X55 I
Documents seldom seen facets of Navajo Indian life during a nine day Healing Chant, Fire, Arrow and Feather Dances.
Social Science
Dist - CDIAND **Prod** - LEWISO 1966

Navajo, Race for Prosperity 26 MIN
16mm / U-matic / VHS
Native Americans Series
Color
Offers a view of life on the Navajo reservation and focuses upon the development of industries on the reservation. Investigates the possibility of a prosperous Navajo future dependent upon the Indian's management of the reservation's reserves of coal, uranium and oil.
Social Science; Sociology
Dist - CNEMAG **Prod** - BBCTV

Navajo Rain Chant 3 MIN
16mm
Color (J H C)
An animated collage in which an Arizona mesa is transformed into authentic Indian designs, accompanied by a Navajo rain chant.
Fine Arts; Social Science
Dist - CFS **Prod** - CFS

Navajo Rain Chant 2 MIN
16mm
Color (C)
$112.00
Experimental film by Susan Dyal.
Fine Arts
Dist - AFA **Prod** - AFA 1971

Navajo talking picture 40 MIN
VHS / 16mm
Color (G)
$85.00, $125.00 rental, $295.00 purchase
Portrays an urban - raised Navajo film student, the filmmaker Arlene Bowman, who travels to the Reservation to document the traditional ways of her grandmother. Persists in spite of her grandmother's forceful objections to this invasion of her privacy and emerges as a thought - provoking work. Calls into question issues of 'insider - outsider' status as an assimilated Navajo struggles to use as a 'white man's' medium to capture the remnants of her cultural past. By Arlene Bowman.
Fine Arts; Social Science
Dist - WMEN

Navajo - the Last Red Indians 50 MIN
U-matic / 16mm / VHS
Color (H C A)
LC 79-707438
Tells about the Navajo Indians' fight to preserve their way of life against the inroads of the white man's culture. Contains exclusive and uncensored scenes of Navajo rituals and ceremonies.
Social Science; Sociology
Dist - TIMLIF **Prod** - BBCTV 1972

The Navajo Way 52 MIN
U-matic / VHS / 16mm
Color (H C A)
LC 75-701560
Tells the story of the Navajo people, showing how they have survived within the white man's society because of their complete involvement with tradition.
Social Science; Sociology
Dist - FI **Prod** - NBCTV 1975

The Navajo - with Beauty all Around Me 22 MIN
U-matic / VHS
Color (J H)
Examines the traditional ways of the Navajos - their art, religion, medicine and deep connection to the land. Also covers the new ways and their blending with the old.
Social Science
Dist - CEPRO **Prod** - CEPRO

Naval Aviation - a Personal History - the Weapon is Tested 29 MIN
U-matic / VHS
B&W
Depicts the development of naval aviation during the 1920s. Discusses the experiences of pioneers in naval aviation.
Civics and Political Systems
Dist - IHF **Prod** - IHF

The Naval battle of 1894 110 MIN
VHS
Color (G) (CHINESE WITH ENGLISH SUBTITLES)
$45.00 purchase _ #1004C
Presents a film from the People's Republic of China.
Geography - World; Literature and Drama
Dist - CHTSUI

Naval Research Laboratory Reactor 21 MIN
16mm
B&W
LC FIE59-193
Explains the construction, operation and uses to which the naval research laboratory reactor is adapted.
Civics and Political Systems; Science; Science - Physical
Dist - USNAC **Prod** - USN 1958

Naval Steam Turbines - How Turbines Work 17 MIN
16mm
B&W
LC FIE56-124
Discusses the basic principles and design of main propulsion and auxiliary steam turbines in navy use. Explains differences between impulse and reaction thrust, how turbines work on steam velocity produced by drops in pressure and complexities of the marine steam turbine.
Civics and Political Systems; Industrial and Technical Education
Dist - USNAC **Prod** - USN 1951

Naval Steam Turbines - Turbine Casualties 12 MIN
16mm
B&W
LC FIE56-241
Explains the delicate nature of turbine equipment and the care which should be observed in its oiling, cleaning and maintenance.
Civics and Political Systems; Industrial and Technical Education
Dist - USNAC **Prod** - USN 1950

Navaratri Festival 60 MIN
U-matic / VHS
Color
Explains Mother Worship and how everything is done by the divine Mother. Talks about suffering, vain beauty, Romalinga Swamigal and more on the Mother.
Religion and Philosophy
Dist - IYOGA **Prod** - IYOGA

Navigating in Space 30 MIN
U-matic / VHS / 16mm
Mechanical Universe Series
Color (C A)
Explains how the amount of energy expended in voyages to other planets can be minimized by using the same force that drives the planets around the solar system.
Science - Physical
Dist - FI **Prod** - ANNCPB

Navigating the Space 18 MIN
U-matic / VHS
Mechanical Universe - High School Adaptation Series
Color (H)
Science - Physical
Dist - SCCON **Prod** - SCCON 1986

Navigation
VHS
Color (G A)
$39.90 purchase _ #0473
Presents a basic introduction to navigation for the yachtsman and amateur sailor. Covers planning, chartwork, tides and tidal streams, plotting and updating a course and navigational aids.
Physical Education and Recreation; Social Science
Dist - SEVVID **Prod** - SEVVID

Navigation by Transit Satellite 28 MIN
16mm
Color
LC 74-706501
Deals with navigation by transit satellite. Describes principles of operation, launch sequence, ground support system and basic user requirements.
Industrial and Technical Education
Dist - USNAC **Prod** - USN 1969

Navigation - Sail magazine
VHS
Color (G A)
$39.95 rental _ #0109
Presents a practical on - the - water approach to basic navigation. Covers charts, course plotting, dead reckoning, variation, deviation, bearings, fixes, tides, currents and aids to navigation. Produced by Sail Magazine.
Physical Education and Recreation; Social Science
Dist - SEVVID

Navigation series
Charts 18 MIN
The Earth 17 MIN
Nautical Astronomy 23 MIN
Dist - USNAC

Navigation - tool of discovery 18 MIN
VHS
Color; PAL (P I J H)
Traces the history of development of navigational instruments from the Phoenicians to the present day. Shows the effect on exploration by devices such as the compass, the leadline, the log, the quadrant, the sextant and the chronometer. Relates these inventions to navigators such as Magellan, Columbus and Captain Cook.
History - World; Social Science; Sociology
Dist - VIEWTH **Prod** - VIEWTH
STANF

The Navigator 92 MIN
35mm / 16mm / VHS
Color; B&W (G)
$300.00, $400.00 rental
Portrays a small mining village in medieval England which is approached by the plague - and only a nine - year - old boy's prophetic dreams provide a clue to the community's survival. Reveals that he leads a band of miners on a holy quest - across 10,000 miles and 650 years - to place a cross atop the world's highest mountain as a tribute to God. Directed by Vincent Ward.
Fine Arts; Literature and Drama; Religion and Philosophy
Dist - KINOIC

The Navigator
VHS
Color (G)
$49.90 purchase _ #0494
Examines the secrets of Polynesian navigation. Interviews Mau Piailug and a handful of others who may be the last keepers of the ancient skills.
Geography - World; Physical Education and Recreation
Dist - SEVVID

The Navigator 63 MIN
16mm
B&W (J)
Stars Buster Keaton as a rich boy who has never had to lift a finger, marooned on a huge ocean liner adrift at sea with only one other person aboard, an equally rich and helpless young girl.
Fine Arts
Dist - TWYMAN **Prod** - MGM 1924

The Navigators 17 MIN
16mm / U-matic / VHS
Cultures of the Southern Seas Series
Color (I J)
LC FIA68-940
Tells how Magellan sailed through the straits that bear his name and discovered the Pacific Ocean. Recounts how other explorers, following Magellan's route, sighted Hawaii and Australia.
History - World
Dist - MCFI **Prod** - HOE 1967

The Navigators - Pathfinders of the Pacific 59 MIN
U-matic
Color
Illustrates the methods used by ancient Polynesians to navigate the Pacific Ocean. Interviews Mau Piailug, the last navigator to be initiated on Satawal, a coral island in Micronesia. Demonstrates traditional techniques for building double - hulled canoes and navigating with a 'star compass.' Follows the voyage of a replica canoe from Hawaii to Tahiti without modern navigational aids. Produced by Sanford Low.
Geography - World; Sociology
Dist - DOCEDR **Prod** - DOCEDR

Navratilova on Nutrition, Sports and Fitness 28 MIN
U-matic / VHS
Color (C)
$249.00, $149.00 purchase _ #AD - 1512
Discusses the timing, content, quantity and method of eating for peak performance in athletics and other endeavors. Features tennis star Martina Navrtilova and her personal sports nutritionist Robert Haas, author of 'Eat To Win.' From a Phil Donahue show.
Business and Economics; Health and Safety; Physical Education and Recreation; Psychology; Social Science
Dist - FOTH **Prod** - FOTH

Navy Advisor in Vietnam - the River Force
VHS / U-matic
Color
Emphasizes the role of the U S Navy advisor working with Vietnamese river forces.
Civics and Political Systems; History - United States; History - World
Dist - IHF **Prod** - IHF

The Navy and Science 12 MIN
16mm
B&W
LC FIE52-1304
Highlights some of the scientific research programs being conducted by the Navy.
Civics and Political Systems; Industrial and Technical Education; Science
Dist - USNAC **Prod** - USN 1951

Navy Bobsled Racing Team 15 MIN
16mm
Color
LC 74-705194
Shows phases of bobsled racing and activities of the navy team in both domestic and international competitions.
Physical Education and Recreation
Dist - USNAC **Prod** - USN 1969

The Navy - Decisions 19 MIN
16mm
Color
LC 76-702714
Presents a story designed to create a favorable impression of Navy life on the general public, expecially high school students.
Civics and Political Systems; Guidance and Counseling
Dist - USNAC **Prod** - USN 1975

Navy Meteorology for College Graduates 15 MIN
16mm
Color
LC 74-705195
Shows opportunities for meteorologists as officers in the naval weather service.
Civics and Political Systems; Guidance and Counseling; Psychology; Science - Physical
Dist - USNAC **Prod** - USN 1967

Navy Officer Orientation 6 MIN
16mm
Color
LC 76-702713
Describes and illustrates the duties of the Civil Engineer Corps officer.
Civics and Political Systems; Guidance and Counseling; Industrial and Technical Education
Dist - USNAC **Prod** - USN 1975

Navy Officer Orientation - Aeronautical Maintenance Duty Officer 12 MIN
16mm
Color
LC 76-703872
Describes the demanding, complex and detailed work required of an aeronautical maintenance duty officer in the U S Navy.
Civics and Political Systems; Guidance and Counseling; Industrial and Technical Education
Dist - USNAC **Prod** - USN 1975

Navy Officer Orientation - Combat Scholar, Intelligence Officer 10 MIN
16mm
Color
LC 76-703873
Shows the duties of an intelligence officer in the U S Navy by following a young officer on his daily work routine with his squadron aboard an aircraft carrier.
Civics and Political Systems; Guidance and Counseling
Dist - USNAC **Prod** - USN 1975

Navy Officer Orientation - Cryptological Officer 7 MIN
16mm
Color
LC 76-703874
Provides a generalized description of the skills required for work as a cryptological officer in the U S Navy.
Civics and Political Systems; Guidance and Counseling
Dist - USNAC **Prod** - USN 1975

Navy Officer Orientation - Helo Flight 5 MIN
16mm
Color
LC 76-703875
Describes the work of helicopter flight officers in the U S Navy.
Civics and Political Systems; Guidance and Counseling; Industrial and Technical Education
Dist - USNAC **Prod** - USN 1975

Navy Officer Orientation - Jet Flight 5 MIN
16mm
Color
LC 76-703876
Describes the work of jet flight officers in the U S Navy.
Civics and Political Systems; Guidance and Counseling; Industrial and Technical Education
Dist - USNAC **Prod** - USN 1975

Navy Officer Orientation - Medical Corps 18 MIN
16mm
Color
LC 76-703877
Presents the challenges and advantages of a career as a doctor in the U S Navy.
Civics and Political Systems; Guidance and Counseling; Health and Safety; Science
Dist - USNAC **Prod** - USN 1975

Navy Officer Orientation - Medical Service Corps 14 MIN
16mm
Color
LC 76-703878
Presents the work of hospital and other medical administrative personnel of the U S Navy's Medical Service Corps.
Civics and Political Systems; Guidance and Counseling; Health and Safety; Science
Dist - USNAC **Prod** - USN 1975

Navy Officer Orientation - Naval Flight Officer 4 MIN
16mm
Color (PRO)
LC 77-700123
Shows the duties and responsibilities of a flight officer in the U S Navy.
Civics and Political Systems
Dist - USNAC **Prod** - USN 1975

Navy Officer Orientation - Navy Lawyer 10 MIN
16mm
Color
LC 76-703879
Presents career opportunities for a lawyer in the U S Navy.
Civics and Political Systems; Guidance and Counseling
Dist - USNAC **Prod** - USN 1975

Navy Officer Orientation - Navy Nurse Corps 14 MIN
16mm
Color
LC 76-703880
Presents career opportunities as a nurse in the U S Navy Nurse Corps.
Civics and Political Systems; Guidance and Counseling; Health and Safety; Science; Sociology
Dist - USNAC **Prod** - USN 1975

Navy Officer Orientation - Nuclear Language 10 MIN
16mm
Color
LC 76-703881
Describes a two - year nuclear training program offered by the U S Naval Reserve Officers' Training Corps for selected qualified college juniors and seniors.
Civics and Political Systems; Guidance and Counseling; Industrial and Technical Education
Dist - USNAC **Prod** - USN 1975

Navy Officer Orientation - Nuclear Navy 14 MIN
16mm
Color
LC 76-703882
Describes the provisions for young officers in the U S Navy to be trained under the Nuclear Propulsion Officer Candidate Program.
Civics and Political Systems; Industrial and Technical Education
Dist - USNAC **Prod** - USN 1975

Navy Officer Orientation - Officer Candidate School, to be an Ensign 18 MIN
16mm
Color
LC 76-703883
Describes the training program for an ensign at the U S Navy's Officer Candidate School, Newport, Rhode Island.
Civics and Political Systems; Guidance and Counseling
Dist - USNAC **Prod** - USN 1975

Navy Officer Orientation - People - People 10 MIN
16mm
Color
LC 76-703884
Features the humanitarian, compassionate work performed by the U S Navy's Medical Service Corps specialists.
Civics and Political Systems; Health and Safety
Dist - USNAC **Prod** - USN 1975

Navy Officer Orientation - Prop Flight 4 MIN
16mm
Color (PRO)
LC 77-700081
Shows the duties of a prop flight officer in the U S Navy.
Civics and Political Systems
Dist - USNAC **Prod** - USN 1975

Navy Officer Orientation - Sea Fever, Line Officer 12 MIN
16mm
Color
LC 76-703885
Presents career opportunities for line officers in the U S Navy, emphasizing command at sea as the primary goal.
Civics and Political Systems; Guidance and Counseling
Dist - USNAC **Prod** - USN 1975

Navy Officer Orientation - the Way to the Line 7 MIN
16mm
Color
LC 76-703886
Shows the U S Naval Reserve Officers' Training Corps as an excellent way of becoming an officer in the U S Navy or U S Marine Corps.
Civics and Political Systems; Guidance and Counseling
Dist - USNAC **Prod** - USN 1975

Navy Officer Orientation - U S Naval Academy, not for all to Share 10 MIN
16mm
Color
LC 76-703887
Shows the life of a midshipman at the U S Naval Academy, presenting the strong challenge and high standards that can only be met by men equal to the task.
Civics and Political Systems; Education; Guidance and Counseling
Dist - USNAC **Prod** - USN 1975

Navy Officer Orientation - Wind and Sea 13 MIN
16mm
Color
LC 76-703667
Depicts the daily life of a meteorologist and an oceanographer in the U S Navy during sea duty.
Civics and Political Systems; Guidance and Counseling; Science; Science - Physical
Dist - USNAC **Prod** - USN 1974

Navy Officer Orientation - Woman 12 MIN
16mm
Color
LC 76-703889
Presents the opportunities for a career as a woman officer in the U S Navy.
Civics and Political Systems; Guidance and Counseling; Sociology
Dist - USNAC **Prod** - USN 1975

Navy Participation in Atomic Tests 14 MIN
U-matic / VHS / 16mm
Color
Describes the work of the Navy in atomic ordnance experiments.
Civics and Political Systems
Dist - USNAC **Prod** - USDD

Navy Photography in Science 28 MIN
16mm
Color
LC FIE52-1344
Shows uses of photography in scientific research, including time - lapse, high - speed, slow - motion, stroboscopic, microscopic and under - water techniques.
Industrial and Technical Education; Science
Dist - USNAC **Prod** - USN 1948

Navy Sings it Like it is 26 MIN
16mm
Color
LC 74-706544
Describes the experiences of underwater demolition team personnel, pilots, submariners, corpsmen, nurses and other Navy personnel through the medium of folk ballads.
Civics and Political Systems; Fine Arts
Dist - USNAC **Prod** - USN 1970

Navy Standard Swimming Tests and Abandoning Ship Drills 18 MIN
16mm
B&W
LC FIE52-1099
Shows various tests given to navy personnel to determine swimming abilities and illustrates abandoning ship drills.
Civics and Political Systems; Health and Safety; Physical Education and Recreation
Dist - USNAC **Prod** - USN 1944

The Navy's Big Top 18 MIN
16mm
Color
LC 74-706503
Shows the preparation of a Navy vessel for a new method of topside encapsulation, focusing on fabrication of the encapsulating cover and installation of the cover on the vessel.
Civics and Political Systems; Industrial and Technical Education
Dist - USNAC **Prod** - USN 1973

Nawi 22 MIN
U-matic / VHS / 16mm
Color (I J H C)
LC 70-708274
A documentary which depicts the drive of the Jie of Uganda during the dry season when they take their cattle to temporary camps or Nawi, where fresh grass is abundant. Portrays the life of the Jie at the cattle camp. With subtitles.
Geography - World; Sociology
Dist - UCEMC **Prod** - MCDGAL 1970

Naye Masterji 23 MIN
16mm
B&W (I)
Emphasizes the important role a teacher plays in the life of the student community. Points out how the problem of student discipline can be solved by developing the right type of relationship between the teacher and the student.
Education
Dist - NEDINF **Prod** - INDIA

Nazca lines 60 MIN
VHS
Mysteries of Peru series
Color (G)
$24.95 purchase _ #ST - AT9001
Examines the Nazca lines in the Peruvian desert and puzzles over how the ancient people there achieved such geometrical precision and the meaning of their creation. Part of two parts.
History - World
Dist - INSTRU

Nazi Concentration Camps 59 MIN
16mm
B&W
$35.00 rental
Presents the official film record of the Nazi death camps as photographed by Allied forces advancing into Germany. Shows surviving prisoners, victims of medical experiments, gas chambers, and open mass graves.
History - World
Dist - USNAC **Prod** - USCPAC 1945
NCJEWF

The Nazi Connection 58 MIN
VHS
Color (S)
$79.00 purchase _ #083 - 9001
Reveals that wartime records of some German scientists were deliberately sanitized by American officials to prevent questions about the scientists' Nazi war crime activities. Uses interviews and newly released government documents as documentation. Features Judy Woodruff as narrator.
Civics and Political Systems; History - United States; History - World; Science - Physical
Dist - FI **Prod** - WGBHTV 1987

Nazi Germany - Years of Triumph 28 MIN
U-matic / VHS / 16mm
Rise and Fall of the Third Reich Series
B&W (H C A)
LC 74-702558
Traces the career of Hitler, from Chancellor in 1933, when he leads a shaky coalition in the German government, until his total dictatorship of the country. Describes how his lust for power turns outward and Austria, Czechoslovakia and Poland are swallowed up.
Biography; History - World; Sociology
Dist - FI **Prod** - MGMD 1972

Nazi Germany - years of triumph - Part II 30 MIN
16mm
Rise and fall of the Third Reich series
B&W (G)
$40.00 rental _ #HRF - 723
Chronicles the history of Germany between 1933 and 1939, when approximately 67 million people permitted themselves to become puppets of the Third Reich. Part two of a four - part series on Hitler.
Civics and Political Systems; History - World; Sociology
Dist - ADL **Prod** - ADL

Nazi Germany - Years of Triumph - Pt 2 28 MIN
16mm / VHS
Rise and Fall of the Third Reich Series
B&W (S)
$400.00, $79.00 purchase _ #135 - 9008
Answers the question that haunts us to this day - why did the Germans, supposedly a deeply religious and cultured people, degenerate into barbarous savagery in the 20th century? Features Richard Basehart as narrator, based on the book by William L Shirer. Part 2 reveals that Nazism flourished in the 1930s as Hitler's forces subverted the freedom of 67 million people. Austria and Czechoslovakia were taken in 'bloodless conquests.' Poland's fall sparked resistance from the Allies.
Civics and Political Systems; Foreign Language; Geography - World; History - United States; History - World
Dist - FI **Prod** - MGM 1972

The Nazi Strike 41 MIN
U-matic / VHS / 16mm
Why We Fight Series
B&W
Documents Germany's preparation for war, the conquest of Austria and Czechoslovakia and the attack upon Poland. Issued in 1943 as a motion picture.
History - World
Dist - USNAC **Prod** - USOWI 1979

The Nazi strike - blitzkrieg 50 MIN
VHS
B&W (G)
$19.95 purchase _ #S00379
Features captured German film footage of their early triumphs in World War II. Focuses on the Nazi quick strike - 'blitzkrieg' - tactics against Austria and Czechoslovakia.
History - World; Sociology
Dist - UILL

Nazi war crimes
VHS
Nazis series
Color (J H C G)
$29.95 purchase _ #MH1874V
Chronicles the Nazi slaughter of 200,000 civiliians at Babi Yar ravine in the Ukraine. Part of a five - part series on the Nazis.
Civics and Political Systems; History - World; Sociology
Dist - CAMV

Nazis series
Presents a five - part series on the Nazis. Includes Blitzkrieg - the Lightning War; Rommel - the Desert Fox; Nazi War Crimes; Witness to Genocide; Hitler.
Blitzkrieg - the lightning war
Hitler
Nazi war crimes
Rommel - the desert fox
Witness to genocide
Dist - CAMV

NBA Basketball Championship 30 MIN
16mm
B&W
Presents the championship playoff between Boston and Los Angeles.
Physical Education and Recreation
Dist - SFI **Prod** - SFI

NBC Proficiency Testing 17 MIN
16mm
Color
LC 81-700598
Illustrates the round robin procedure for testing trainees in their individual ability to survive a nuclear, biological or chemical attack.
Civics and Political Systems
Dist - USNAC **Prod** - USA 1981

NBC White Paper - China 100 MIN
U-matic / VHS
Color (H C A)
Shows what life in China is like by interviewing people in real - life situations, inside prisons, psychiatric institutions, criminal and divorce courts. Profiles factory towns and villages and offers the voices of workers, artists, teen - agers and victims of the Cultural Revolution.
Geography - World; History - World
Dist - TIMLIF **Prod** - NBCTV 1984

NBS into NIST 39 MIN
U-matic / VHS
Color (A PRO)
$65.00, $125.00 purchase _ #TCA17889, #TCA17888
Focuses on the changes that took place when the National Institute of Standards and Technology was created to expand the mission of the former National Bureau of Standards. Includes insights from Secretary of Commerce C William Verity, Dr Ernest Amber, and several members of Congress.
Business and Economics; Industrial and Technical Education; Sociology
Dist - USNAC

NCAA baseball series
Presents seven baseball instructional programs on two videocassettes. Includes the titles Hitting, Baserunning and Catching in the Baseball Offensive Series, and Pitching Essentials, Pitching Drills, Infield Play, and Outfield Play in the Baseball Defensive Series.
NCAA baseball series
Dist - CAMV **Prod** - NCAA 1988

NCAA basketball instructional video series
Ball handling and dribbling
Defensing the pivot man
Individual defense
Offensive post play
Passing techniques
Rebounding
Shooting
Dist - CAMV

NCAA basketball videos series
Defensive series
Offensive series
Dist - CAMV

NCAA football instructional videos series
Defensive back drills
Defensive line techniques
Offensive line techniques
Punting and kicking
The Quarterback
Running back techniques
Dist - CAMV

NCAA football videos - defensive series
VHS
NCAA football videos - defensive series
Color (A G T)
$89.95 purchase _ #KAR1310V-P
Presents instruction on skills and drills given by NCAA coaches. Features Paul Wiggin, Foge Fazio, Bobby Proctor, and Lou Holtz explaining defensive line techniques, linebacker play, defensive back drills, and punting and kicking. One of a set of videos that provide coaching tips to offensive and defensive players and coaches. Series is available as individual cassettes, a set of offensive series, a set of defensive series, or both series combined.
Physical Education and Recreation
Dist - CAMV

NCAA football videos - offensive series
Football offensive series
Offensive line techniques
Pass receiving
The Quarterback
Running back techniques
Dist - CAMV

NCAA football videos series
Presents instruction on skills and drills given by NCAA coaches. Features Paul Wiggin, Foge Fazio, Bobby Proctor, and Lou Holtz explaining defensive line techniques, linebacker play, defensive back drills, and punting and kicking. Also features Earle Bruce, Doug Scovil, Bobby Bowden, and Mervin Johnson explaining running back, quarterback, pass recieving, and offensive line techniques. Series is also available as individual cassettes, a set of offensive series, or a set of defensive series.
NCAA football videos series
Dist - CAMV

NCAA instructional video series
Presents a 68 - tape series of instructional programs in various sports. Features such coaches as Lou Holtz, Earle Bruce, Denny Crum, Jim Valvano, and many others. Covers sports including football, basketball, baseball, track and field, and more.
The Backhand
Defensive baseball series
The Discus
Field event series
The Forehand
Hurdling techniques
Infield play
The Long jump
Outfield play
Pitching drills
Serve and return of serve
Sprinting techniques
Tennis series
Track event series
The Triple jump
The Volley
Dist - CAMV **Prod** - NCAAF

NCAA soccer instructional video series
Goal keeping
Juggling, dribbling and passing
Shooting
Dist - CAMV

NCAA swimming - diving videos series
VHS
NCAA swimming - diving videos series
Color (G T)
$79.95 purchase _ #KAR2204V-P
Offers swimming and diving instruction from coaches Eddie Reese, Don Gambril, and Bob Webster in a series of three programs. Includes freestyle; diving; and starting, turning, and medley techniques. Provides drills for each area. Videos available individually.
Physical Education and Recreation
Dist - CAMV

NCAA swimming - diving videos series
NCAA swimming - diving videos series
Dist - CAMV

Ndando Yawusiwana - Song of Sadness 18 MIN
U-matic / VHS
Color
Records a performance of a ndando by Chopi composer Venancio Mbande. Looks at the ndando, a musical oral history of ancestors and friends which can serve as a release from unhappy past events or as a purely pleasurable experience. Narrated and interpreted by Champ Ramohuebo.
Fine Arts; Geography - World
Dist - PSU **Prod** - PSU

Ne Bougeons Plus 13 MIN
16mm
En Francais, set 1 series
Color (J A)
Foreign Language
Dist - CHLTN **Prod** - PEREN 1969

NEA 1 MIN
16mm
Color
LC 77-700391
Presents the opening title for the Independent Filmmakers Showcase, a number of short subject motion pictures. Uses animation to convey the progression and variety of film forms since the conception of the motion picture.
Fine Arts
Dist - NENDOW **Prod** - NENDOW 1976

The Neanderthal Man 28 MIN
VHS / U-matic
Once upon a Time - Man Series
Color (P I)
MV=$99.00
Shows the rise, distributions and disappearance of the Neanderthal along with a guess as to the culture enjoyed by them.
History - World; Sociology
Dist - LANDMK **Prod** - LANDMK 1981

Near and Far 14 MIN
U-matic / VHS
Young at Art Series
Color (P I)
Discusses depth in art.
Fine Arts
Dist - AITECH **Prod** - WSKJTV 1980

Near death 358 MIN
16mm / VHS
Color (G PRO)
$600.00 purchase, $150.00 rental, $650.00 purchase _ #42-2432T
Documents the workings of the intensive care unit at Boston's Beth Israel Hospital. Focuses on how people face death, exploring the issues involved.
Fine Arts; Health and Safety; Sociology
Dist - ZIPRAH **Prod** - WISEF
NLFN

Near death experience 105 MIN
VHS
Color (G)
$29.00 purchase _ #V - NDE
Features experts and ordinary people who have been declared clinically dead for minutes, hours, even days, who share their experiences. Discusses whether individuals can choose their time of death, what happens at the time of death, whether or not one is judged after death, the reason for existence.
Religion and Philosophy; Sociology
Dist - PACSPI
WHOLEL

The Near North 16 MIN
16mm
Color
Looks at the scenic highlights and recreational activities of the Almaquin Highlands in Ontario. Views such pastimes as canoeing, horseback riding, hiking, camping, fishing and skiing.
Geography - World
Dist - MTP **Prod** - OMITOU

Near the Big Chakra 5 MIN
U-matic / 16mm
Color (C A)
Explores a portion of the infinite variability of the human body. Views 36 female genitalia, ranging in age from six months to 56 years.
Health and Safety; Psychology; Sociology
Dist - MMRC **Prod** - MMRC

Nearly no Christmas 48 MIN
16mm / VHS
Color (K)
$595.00, $340.00 purchase
Tells the story of the year Santa Claus had to get a job to fix the machines in his factory. Reveals that while he is working, Mrs. Claus must handle the evil King of the Penguins. Uses the New Zealand Alps as a setting.
Literature and Drama; Social Science
Dist - FLMWST

Neat in the Street 18 MIN
16mm
Good Life Series
Color (S)
LC 81-700267
Uses a TV game show format to demonstrate appropriate appearance of clothes.
Education; Home Economics
Dist - HUBDSC **Prod** - DUDLYN 1981

The Neatos and the Litterbugs 7 MIN
U-matic / VHS / 16mm
Color (P)
Presents the concept of keeping the environment clean and free of trash that ultimately becomes pollution. Points out the value of taking care of the home environment before going out into other parts of the community.
Guidance and Counseling; Science - Natural; Social Science
Dist - BARR **Prod** - SAIF 1974

Nebraska 60 MIN
VHS
Portrait of America series
Color (J H C G)
$99.95 purchase _ #AMB27V
Visits Nebraska. Offers extensive research into the state's history. Films key locations and presents segments on history, government, education, folklore, science, journalism, sociology, industry, agriculture and business. Shows what is unique about Nebraska and distinctive about its regional culture and how it got to be that way. Includes study guide. Part of a 50 - part series.
Geography - United States; History - United States
Dist - CAMV

Nebraska for the People - Executive Branch 23 MIN
16mm
Color
LC 76-700923
Describes the authority and responsibility of the office of the Governor of Nebraska, including its limitations.
Civics and Political Systems; Geography - United States
Dist - NTCN **Prod** - NEBSL 1974

Nebraska for the People - Judicial Branch 20 MIN
16mm
Color
LC 76-700924
Explains the organization and services of the State of Nebraska's judicial branch of government, describing types of courts and what they do and the impact of the judiciary on the lives of Nebraskans.
Civics and Political Systems; Geography - United States
Dist - NTCN **Prod** - NEBSL 1974

Nebraska for the People - Legislative Branch 33 MIN
16mm
Color
LC 76-700921
Describes the functions and services of the Nebraska State Legislature, showing how a legislative bill is passed and how the use of a computer at the University of Nebraska has improved the legislative process.
Civics and Political Systems; Geography - United States; Industrial and Technical Education
Dist - NTCN **Prod** - NEBSL 1974

Nebraska Territory - Boom and Bust 30 MIN
16mm
Great Plains Trilogy, 3 Series Explorer and Settler - the White Man 'Arrives; Explorer and settler - the white man arrives
B&W (H C A)
Discusses the abandonment of the permanent Indian frontier, the organization of Nebraska Territory, the slave question, the establishment of government, the capital controversy, the economic development, the boom of towns and the panic of 1857. Traces the development of agriculture and schools.
History - United States; Social Science
Dist - UNEBR **Prod** - KUONTV 1954

Nebraska Water Resources Series
Living with Nebraska's Water 27 MIN
Nebraska's Water - its Future 29 MIN
Working with Nebraska's Water 29 MIN
Dist - UNEBR

Nebraska Water Resources Series
Water - Nebraska's Heritage 29 MIN
Dist - UNL

Nebraska - Where the Cornbelt Meets the Range 29 MIN
16mm
Color (J)
Presents Nebraska's agricultural and livestock enterprises as major contributions to the national economy by studying its past, present and future.
Agriculture; Geography - United States; Geography - World
Dist - UNL **Prod** - KUONTV 1967

Nebraska's Water - its Future 29 MIN
16mm
Nebraska Water Resources Series
Color (H C A)
LC 74-700164
Outlines possibilities for redistributing water supplies in Nebraska by engineering new systems and by altering management practices. Presents development and management methods within a framework of economics, social structure and ideas that may be applicable throughout the entire state. Stresses individual awareness of the water environment and man's responsibility for its management.
Geography - United States; Science - Natural
Dist - UNEBR **Prod** - UNL 1971

Nebula 1 6 MIN
16mm
Color (J H C)
Presents an abstract film exercise.
Fine Arts; Industrial and Technical Education
Dist - CFS **Prod** - CFS 1969

Nebula 2 7 MIN
16mm
Color (J H C)
LC 72-701344
An experimental film which concentrates on the various pulsations made by concentric circles of dots, while incorporating subliminal effects, radiating lines, glowing coloration, and classical and rock music.
Fine Arts; Industrial and Technical Education
Dist - CFS **Prod** - FRERCK 1971

Nebule 10 MIN
U-matic / VHS / 16mm
Color (P I J)
LC 80-701637
Presents the tale of Nebule, a child who uses his imagination to create dozens of shapes from a simple straight black line. Uses animation to portray a world of children's fantasy and to point out the joy of imagining.
Fine Arts
Dist - IFB **Prod** - NFBC 1975

NEC clip art 3D
CD-ROM
Color (G)
$355.00 purchase _ #1761p
Contains over 2500 three - dimensional images and typefaces for desktop publishing and presentation graphics. Produced by NEC. The position, perspective, size, lighting and colors of the images can be changed. Subjects include geography, human figures, buildings, food, and many other topics. For Macintosh Classic, Plus, SE and II computers, requires 1MB of RAM, one floppy disk drive, and an Apple compatible CD - ROM drive.
Computer Science
Dist - BEP

NEC image folio
CD-ROM
Color (G)
$355.00 purchase _ #1762
Includes over 4000 VGA quality images on one disc for use in desktop publishing, design, and presentation graphics. Produced by NEC. Subjects range from nature to industry. For IBM PCs and compatibles, requires 640K RAM, DOS 3.1 or later, one floppy disk drive - hard disk recommended, one empty expansion slot, and an IBM compatible CD - ROM drive.
Computer Science
Dist - BEP

NEC image gallery
CD-ROM
(G)
$349.00 purchase _ #1765
Contains 2800 professionally hand - drawn line art images on one disc produced by NEC. Includes categories from Art Deco and Business Graphics to Fashion and Travel. Customers can call NEC to purchase six additional categories. For IBM PCs and compatibles, requires at least 640K RAM, DOS 3.1 or later, one floppy disk drive -

hard disk recommended, one empty expansion slot, and an IBM compatible CD - ROM drive. For Macintosh Classic, Plus, SE and II computers, requires 1MB of RAM, one floppy disk drive, and an Apple compatible CD - ROM drive.
Computer Science; Industrial and Technical Education
Dist - BEP

NEC photo gallery
CD-ROM
(G)
$355.00 purchase _ #1766m
Includes over 1500 digitized black and white photos on one CD - ROM produced by NEC. Featres photos by UNIPHOTO Picture Agency. Categories include abstract, agriculture, animals, buildings, corporate, industry, lifestyles, occupations, medicine, people, sports, USA, and others. For IBM PCs and compatibles, requires at least 640K RAM, DOS 3.1 or later, one floppy disk drive - hard disk recommended, one empty expansion slot, and an IBM compatible CD - ROM drive. For Macintosh Classic, Plus, SE and II computers, requires 1MB of RAM, one floppy disk drive, and an Apple compatible CD - ROM drive.
Computer Science
Dist - BEP

NEC type gallery LJ - PC
CD-ROM
(G)
$279.00 purchase _ #1764
Provides access to 76 typefaces, including popular serif, sans serif and decorative typefaces such as Times and Futura, all designed for HP LaserJet printers and compatibles, produced by NEC. Customers can register to purchase three additional typeface families. For IBM PCs and compatibles, requires 640K RAM, DOS 3.1 or later, one floppy disk drive - hard disk recommended, one empty expansion slot, and an IBM compatible CD - ROM drive.
Industrial and Technical Education
Dist - BEP

NEC type gallery PS - Mac
CD-ROM
(G)
$299.00 purchase _ #1763m
Provides access to 470 Adobe Postscript language typefaces, from Aachen Bold to Helvetica to Zapf Chancery, produced by NEC. Comes with screen and printer fonts, kerning information, and a 100 page typeface catalog. Customers can register to purchase three additional typeface families. For Macintosh Classic, Plus, SE and II computers, requires 1MB of RAM, one floppy disk drive, and an Apple compatible CD - ROM drive.
Industrial and Technical Education
Dist - BEP

NEC type gallery PS - PC
CD-ROM
(G)
$355.00 purchase _ #1763p
Provides access to 470 Adobe Postscript language typefaces, from Aachen Bold to Helvetica to Zapf Chancery, produced by NEC. Comes with screen and printer fonts, kerning information, and a 100 page typeface catalog. Customers can register to purchase three typeface families. For IBM PCs and compatibles, requires 640K RAM, DOS 3.1 or later, one floppy disk drive - hard disk recommended, one empty expansion slot, and an IBM compatible CD - ROM drive.
Industrial and Technical Education
Dist - BEP

Necessary Capabilities for Swine Production 13 MIN
U-matic / VHS
Color
Covers the personal capabilities that are needed for feeder to finish swine production. Examines the attitude, skills and time allocations that contribute to a successful swine operation.
Agriculture
Dist - HOBAR **Prod** - HOBAR

Necessary Parties 110MIN
VHS
WonderWorks Series
Color (P)
$29.95 purchase _ #766 - 9009
Tells the story of a fifteen - year - old boy who launches an unprecedented lawsuit to stop his parents' divorce. Stars Alan Arkin, Julie Hagerty. Based on the book by Barbara Dana. Part of the WonderWorks Series which centers on themes involving rites of passage that occur during the growing - up years from seven to sixteen. Features young people as protagonists and portrays strong adult role models.
Fine Arts; Literature and Drama; Psychology; Sociology
Dist - FI **Prod** - PBS 1990

Neck and back strengthening and stretching
VHS / U-matic
Physical therapy series
Color (PRO C G)
$195.00 purchase _ #C890 - VI - 010
Informs patient educators and patients about the benefits of neck and back strengthening and stretching. Teaches effective techniques for minimizing pain and fatigue while enhancing the ability to perform daily activities. Part of a series by the physical therapy staff, St Luke's Hospital, Fargo, North Dakota.
Health and Safety; Physical Education and Recreation; Science - Natural
Dist - HSCIC

Neck Flex 10 MIN
Videoreel / VT2
Janaki Series
Color
Physical Education and Recreation
Dist - PBS **Prod** - WGBHTV

Neck, head and facial injuries
VHS
Athletic clinic series
Color (C A PRO)
$29.95 purchase _ #SVS1609V
Considers the causes and cures of injuries to the spinal and head areas. Looks at protective equipment and preventive exercises.
Health and Safety; Physical Education and Recreation; Science - Natural
Dist - CAMV

Neck Injuries 16 MIN
U-matic / VHS
Emergency Management - the First 30 Minutes, Vol I Series
Color
Discusses the symptoms, diagnosis and treatment of neck injuries.
Health and Safety; Science - Natural
Dist - VTRI **Prod** - VTRI

Neck Pain 18 MIN
U-matic / VHS / 16mm
Color (A PRO) (SPANISH)
Discusses causes, treatment and prevention of neck pain.
Health and Safety; Science - Natural
Dist - PRORE **Prod** - PRORE

Neck Pain
U-matic / VHS
Color
Presents a carefully detailed anatomical and biomechanical basis for neck/shoulder/arm pain syndromes with the underlying assumption that an understanding of the mechanism of pain will lead to more accurate diagnosis and management.
Science - Natural
Dist - AMEDA **Prod** - AMEDA

Neck, Pt 1 - Orientation, Fascia Superficial Structures 15 MIN
16mm / U-matic / VHS
Cine - Prosector Series
Color (PRO)
Introduces the anatomy of the neck.
Science - Natural
Dist - TEF **Prod** - AVCORP

Neck, Pt 3 - Root and Thoracic Inlet 18 MIN
U-matic / VHS / 16mm
Cine - Prosector Series
Color (PRO)
LC 75-701993
Locates the boundaries of the root of the neck and the thoracic inlet using several anatomical models.
Science - Natural
Dist - TEF **Prod** - AVCORP 1968

Neck, Pt 2 - Visceral and Neurovascular Units 17 MIN
16mm / U-matic / VHS
Cine - Prosector Series
Color (PRO)
LC 75-701992
Identifies the structures of the visceral unit, starting with the skeletal elements.
Science - Natural
Dist - TEF **Prod** - AVCORP 1968

Neck - Related Pain
U-matic / VHS
Color (ARABIC SPANISH)
Deals with the causes of most neck and upper back pain. Explains how proper diagnosis and treatment can lead to relief and long term recovery. Suggests how to avoid future neck problems.
Foreign Language; Science - Natural
Dist - MIFE **Prod** - MIFE

Neck Shaping and Hems 29 MIN
Videoreel / VT2
Busy Knitter I Series
B&W
Home Economics
Dist - PBS **Prod** - WMVSTV

The Necklace 20 MIN
16mm / U-matic / VHS
Humanities - Short Story Classics Series
Color (J H)
LC 80-701813
Tells the story of a woman who borrows a diamond necklace to wear for a formal occasion and describes the consequences to her and her husband when she loses it. Based on the short story The Necklace by Guy de Maupassant.
Fine Arts; Literature and Drama
Dist - EBEC **Prod** - EBEC 1980

The Necklace 23 MIN
U-matic / VHS / 16mm
Color (J)
LC 79-700516
Tells how a borrowed necklace brings sorrow to a young married couple. Adapted from the story The Diamond Necklace by Guy de Maupassant.
Literature and Drama
Dist - ALTSUL **Prod** - MDBMOK 1979

The Necklace 21 MIN
16mm / U-matic / VHS
Color (J)
LC 81-700062
Tells the story of a 19th century Frenchwoman who loses a borrowed necklace and is reduced to menial work to replace it. Based on the short story The Necklace by Guy de Maupassant.
Literature and Drama
Dist - BARR **Prod** - WILETS 1981

The Necklace 23 MIN
U-matic / VHS / 16mm
Captioned; Color (J)
LC 79-700516
Tells how a borrowed necklace brings sorrow to a young married couple. Adapted from the story The Diamond Necklace by Guy de Maupassant.
Literature and Drama
Dist - ALTSUL **Prod** - MDBMOK 1979

Necklace of death 26 MIN
VHS
Challenge of the seas series
Color (I J H)
$225.00 purchase
Looks at drift nets and the unintended fatalities resulting from their use - especially seals. Part of a 26 - part series on the oceans.
Industrial and Technical Education; Science - Natural; Science - Physical
Dist - LANDMK **Prod** - LANDMK 1991

Neckline Cut - with Curling Iron Technique
U-matic / VHS
Lessons on a Mannequin Series, Lesson VI
Color
Involves only hair at the back of the head and nape. Selects hair from the crown as a guideline. Starts behind the ear and using vertical partings, hair is cut so that it becomes progressively shorter towards the nape, ending with approximately 1 inch of hair. Presents a short, finished style at the end. Emphasizes techniques for iron use.
Education; Home Economics
Dist - MPCEDP **Prod** - MPCEDP 1984

Necrology 12 MIN
16mm
B&W (C)
$207.00
Experimental film by Standish D Lawder.
Fine Arts
Dist - AFA **Prod** - AFA 1970

Necromancy 5 MIN
16mm
Color (G)
$13.00 rental
Presents puppet animation, video and time - lapse cinematography. Looks at images as mirrors and windows. Produced by Steven Dye.
Fine Arts
Dist - CANCIN

Nectar of the cyclops 12 MIN
16mm
Color (G)
$45.00 rental
Presents a production by Rock Ross which is a reaction to the political 'bafflegab' surrounding society.
Civics and Political Systems; Fine Arts
Dist - CANCIN

Ned Williams Dance Theatre 14 MIN
16mm / U-matic / VHS
Color (I)
LC 76-701936
Features Ned Williams and students from the Ned Williams School of Theatre Dance performing African and Haitian dances at Gateway National Recreation Area, Brooklyn, New York.
Fine Arts
Dist - PHENIX **Prod** - PHENIX 1976

Need a Paycheck
VHS
Come Alive Series
$180.00 purchase _ #013 - 611
Documents several people's experiences in changing careers.
Guidance and Counseling
Dist - CAREER **Prod** - CAREER

Need a Paycheck 30 MIN
VHS / 16mm
Come Alive Series
Color (H)
$150.00 purchase _ #PAGP2V
Interviews people who are changing careers or looking for jobs. Features co - hosts of the television show PM Magazine.
Guidance and Counseling; Psychology
Dist - JISTW

Need a Paycheck? 30 MIN
U-matic / VHS
Come Alive Series
(H C A)
$180 _ #JWGP2V
Gives an account of several people's career experiences with interviews and personal narration.
Business and Economics
Dist - JISTW **Prod** - UAK

Need a Paycheck 30 MIN
U-matic / VHS
Come Alive Series no 2; No 2
Color (H C A)
LC 82-706310
Present TV hosts Cathy Brugett and Jim Finerty looking at career options and the changing job market as they introduce some real - life examples of people trying to deal with the situation of finding jobs and changing careers.
Guidance and Counseling
Dist - GPN **Prod** - UAKRON 1981

The Need for Christian peacemaking 28 MIN
VHS
Color (J H C G T A)
$19.95 purchase
Interviews Father George Zabelka, who outlines his journey from being the chaplain of the men who dropped the bomb on Hiroshima to his current advocacy of peace. Produced by Alan Nelson.
History - World; Sociology
Dist - EFVP

The Need for Economic Education 16 MIN
16mm
Building Economic Understanding Series
B&W (H A)
LC FI67-371
Explains the role of economic systems in world affairs and relates this role to U S national, state and local affairs and to the conflict between East and West. Explains the necessity for profits and the role of economics in personal affairs.
Business and Economics; Civics and Political Systems; Fine Arts
Dist - MLA **Prod** - RSC 1963

The Need for Pre - Supervisory Training 61 FRS
U-matic / VHS
Pre - Supervisory Training Series Module 1
Color
Points out the many reasons why an employee should be trained in supervision before actually becoming a supervisor.
Business and Economics; Psychology
Dist - RESEM **Prod** - RESEM

The Need for subroutines and stacks 50 MIN
U-matic / VHS
Computer languages series; Pt 1
Color
Discusses Backus - Naur Form (BNF) as a recursive structure definition and use of a stack for implementing recursive programs.
Industrial and Technical Education; Mathematics; Sociology
Dist - MIOT **Prod** - MIOT

Need it, make it 10 MIN
VHS / U-matic
Book, Look and Listen Series
Color (K P)
Focuses on the ability to create useful items from a wide range of materials.
English Language; Literature and Drama
Dist - AITECH **Prod** - MDDE 1977

The Need to Achieve - Motivation and Personality 29 MIN
16mm / U-matic / VHS
Focus on Behavior Series
B&W (H C A)
LC FIA65-1444
Dr David McClelland of Harvard University explains his psychological theory - - that the economic growth or decline of nations is dependent to a large extent upon the entrepreneurs of these nations. He seeks to substantiate his theory through motivational tests.
Business and Economics; Psychology
Dist - IU **Prod** - NET 1963

The Need to Explore 30 MIN
U-matic
Visions - Artists and the Creative Process Series
Color (H C A)
Two Canadian artists discuss their sources of inspiration and particular aspects of their work.
Fine Arts; History - World
Dist - TVOTAR **Prod** - TVOTAR 1983

A Need to know 25 MIN
VHS
Color (A)
$525.00 purchase
Brings out principles for complying with securities laws regarding insider information through dramatizations and discussion. Meets the Securities and Exchange Commission's requirement for compliance education for officers, directors, managers and financial personnel of banks, other financial institutions, and companies.
Business and Economics; Civics and Political Systems; Education
Dist - COMFLM **Prod** - COMFLM

The Need to know 25 MIN
VHS
Supervisors series
Color (A)
PdS50 purchase
Emphasizes the importance of communication at all staff levels. Examines some of the methods that have been successful in achieving this goal. Part of an eight-part series designed to help supervisors - particularly newly-appointed ones - to understand the demands of their individual roles through the experience of established supervisors who offer personal insights and strategies from within a framework of good practice.
Business and Economics; Social Science
Dist - BBCENE

The Need to Know 27 MIN
16mm
Color
LC 82-700775
Illustrates several of the safe waste disposal methods being employed by the chemical industry. Emphasizes that the chemical industry is hard at work to correct past mistakes and prevent future ones.
Health and Safety; Sociology
Dist - MTP **Prod** - CHEMMA 1982

Need to know 25 MIN
VHS
Color (G)
$190.00 purchase, $50.00 rental
Follows the quest of Jann Turner who returned to South Africa in search of the assassin of her father, a leading opponent of apartheid, murdered 15 years earlier in their home. Reveals much about the political climate in the new South Africa. Interviews Nelson Mandela, ANC leader Joe Slovo, and the family of Chris Hani, slain the week Turner arrived back. Produced by Jann Turner.
Fine Arts; History - World; Sociology
Dist - FIRS

The Need to Touch 28 MIN
VHS / 16mm
Sonrisas Series
Color (T P) (SPANISH)
$46.00 rental _ #SRSS - 124
Shows the importance of nurturing. In Spanish and English.
Sociology
Dist - PBS

Needle Injections - Equipment and Medications 20 MIN
16mm
B&W
LC 74-706504
Shows the uses of needle injections and the fully - equipped needle tray. Describes the aseptic procedure for preparation of syringes. Shows how to prepare medications for use when supplied as liquids or as powder in sealed vials in ampules or in tablet form.
Health and Safety; Science
Dist - USNAC **Prod** - USN 1957

Needle Injections - Intradermal, Subcutaneous and Intramuscular Injection Techniques 9 MIN
16mm
B&W
LC 74-706505
Explains the uses of intradermal, subcutaneous and intramuscular needle injections. Discusses precautions, aseptic procedure and appropriate needle size. Shows angle of penetration and location of tissue for injections.
Health and Safety
Dist - USNAC **Prod** - USN 1957

Needle Injections - Intravenous Injection 5 MIN
16mm
B&W
LC 74-706506
Describes aseptic procedures to be followed in intravenous injections. Shows injections and chart entries after injection and discusses precautions.
Health and Safety
Dist - USNAC **Prod** - USN 1957

Needle Play
U-matic
Staff Development Series
Color (PRO)
Concludes a presentation on teaching a child about anesthesia. Deals with giving injections to a dummy, clarifying reasons for an injection and play techniques demonstrating injection.
Guidance and Counseling; Health and Safety; Home Economics
Dist - CFDC **Prod** - CFDC

Needlepoint 53 MIN
VHS
Erica Wilson needle works series
Color (G)
$29.95 purchase
Presents basic needlepoint techniques, and teaches viewers how to create such items as a Roses rug, a William Morris pillow, a needlepoint cat, and more. Taught by Erica Wilson.
Home Economics
Dist - PBS **Prod** - WNETTV

Needlepoint and Crochet - Reader's Digest 120 MIN
VHS
(H A)
$39.95 purchase _ #CK200V
Explains the basics of needlepoint, including the fundamental stitches and techniques needed for any project. Includes a discussion of crochet, needlepoint, tapestry work, and more. Discusses different threads and buying tips.
Fine Arts; Home Economics
Dist - CAMV **Prod** - READER

Needlepoint - unusual - unique techniques 102 MIN
VHS
Color (G A)
$49.95 purchase _ #VVP008V
Teaches various needlepoint techniques, including transferring a design to needlepoint canvas, more than 20 diffferent stitches, and how to use various fibers and objects.
Home Economics; Physical Education and Recreation
Dist - CAMV

Needlepoint with Erica Wilson 50 MIN
VHS
Erica Wilson's Craft Series
(H A)
$34.95 purchase _ #3M300V
Presents techniques and tips for many needlpoint designs.
Fine Arts; Home Economics
Dist - CAMV **Prod** - CAMV

Needles and Bread 15 MIN
VHS / U-matic
Stories of America Series
Color (P)
Presents two stories based on Revolutionary War incidents that show how sewing and baking helped the war effort.
History - United States
Dist - AITECH **Prod** - OHSDE 1976

The Needle's Eye 27 MIN
U-matic / VHS / 16mm
Insight Series
Color (H C A)
Deals with the journey of two medical students who travel to Africa and encounter a clinic run by a woman physician. Explains that one of the students has an urge to stay even though it means giving up a lucrative practice. Stars Ron Howard and Jerry Hauser.

Psychology; Religion and Philosophy
Dist - PAULST **Prod** - PAULST

Needle's Eye 27 MIN
VHS / U-matic
Color (J A)
Dramatizes the story of a medical intern on a summer trip to Africa who must decide between service to the poor and a lucrative practice.
Fine Arts; Health and Safety; Sociology
Dist - SUTHRB **Prod** - SUTHRB

Needs and Wants 9 MIN
U-matic / VHS / 16mm
Color (J)
LC 76-700292
Presents a reproduction of a television game show in which Jose and Marcia battle for the big prize. Depicts each contestant describing his or her values, goals and lifestyle which are posted on the 'lifestyle board' behind them. Explains that they then see a parade of consumer products and must decide if each product represents a real need or merely a want in relation to their stated lifestyle.
Guidance and Counseling; Home Economics; Social Science
Dist - ALTSUL **Prod** - CSDE 1976

Needs of young children 30 MIN
VHS
Calico pie series
Color (C A T)
$69.95 purchase
Presents part 14 of a 16 - part telecourse for teachers who work with children ages three to five. Discusses the needs of young children in the classroom. Hosted by Dr Carolyn Dorrell, an early childhood specialist.
Education; Psychology
Dist - SCETV **Prod** - SCETV 1983

NEFA, Pt 1 15 MIN
16mm
Color (I)
Presents the North Eastern Frontier Agency as a fabulous mosaic consisting of over 30 tribes, of whom the Nagas, Abors, Daflas and Mishmis are the better known ones. Studies the pattern of their lives, which has remained unchanged for centuries but is now slowly changing after independence.
History - World
Dist - NEDINF **Prod** - INDIA

NEFA - Pt 2 15 MIN
16mm
Color (I)
Presents the North Eastern Frontier Agency as a fabulous mosaic consisting of over 30 tribes, of whom the Nagas, Abors, Daflas and Mishmis are the better known ones. Studies the pattern of their lives, which has remained unchanged for centuries but is now slowly changing after independence.
History - World
Dist - NEDINF **Prod** - INDIA

Negative Aspects in Teaching African History 58 MIN
U-matic / VHS
Blacks, Blues, Black Series
Color
Education; History - United States; Sociology
Dist - PBS **Prod** - KQEDTV

Negative behavior - positive discipline 25 MIN
VHS
Color (A T)
$79.95 purchase _ #CCP0227V-H
Shows parents and educators how to positively disciple children in a manner that makes the child more self-confident instead of less self-reliant by putting the responsibility of positive behavior on the child as well as the parent. Uses interviews with child psychologists, parents, teachers and children, interspersed with short vignettes that show how to implement the various steps and principles discussed.
Psychology; Sociology
Dist - CAMV

Negative Cultural Carryover 54 MIN
U-matic / VHS
Blacks, Blues, Black Series
Color
Education; History - United States; Sociology
Dist - PBS **Prod** - KQEDTV

The Negative kid 7 MIN
16mm / VHS
B&W (G)
$20.00 rental
Dives into an exploration of the child's archetype, the mythical objects and icons which are inanimate, yet have a life of their own. Journeys into the past and the intimate space where myths are formed and primordial images emerge. A Larry Kless production.
Fine Arts; Psychology; Religion and Philosophy
Dist - CANCIN

Negative of Simple Past Tense - 23 30 MIN
VHS
English 101 - Ingles 101 Series
Color (H)
$125.00 purchase
Presents a series of thirty 30 - minute programs in basic English for native speakers of Spanish. Focuses on a specific topic in order to emphasize a particular grammatical point or set of idioms. English is used from the beginning as the primary language of instruction but Spanish translations are included to ensure understanding. Part 23 considers negative sentences, the auxiliary 'did,' formation of the negative, word order, contractions.
English Language; Foreign Language
Dist - AITECH **Prod** - UPRICO 1988

Negative Rational Numbers 30 MIN
16mm
Mathematics for Elementary School Teachers Series no 29
Color (T)
Discusses positive and negative numbers. Describes the law of signs. To be used following 'MEASUREMENT OF SOLIDS.'.
Mathematics
Dist - MLA **Prod** - SMSG 1963

Negative Reinforcement 5 MIN
U-matic / VHS
Protocol Materials in Teacher Education - the Process of Teaching, 'Pt 2 Series
Color (T)
Education; Psychology
Dist - MSU **Prod** - MSU

Negative space 3 MIN
16mm
B&W (G)
$10.00 rental
Deals with spatial concerns which include the physical components of a Pennsylvania farm. Shows space undullating fluidly between two and three dimensions with the camera movement guiding and shaping the form of the image. A Caroline Savage - Lee production.
Fine Arts; Science - Physical
Dist - CANCIN

Negatives - Unit 2 50 MIN
VHS
French language file series
Color; PAL (I J H)
PdS29.50 purchase
Covers negative case. Supports the process of foreign language learning by developing pupils' awareness of how the language is structured and how it functions. Part two of a three - part series on French language.
Foreign Language
Dist - EMFVL

The Neglected 30 MIN
16mm / U-matic / VHS
B&W (C A S)
LC FIA66-501
A portrayal of children from hardcore families who are under the protection of community authorities. Considers techniques of child protective services and the problems of the war on poverty.
Psychology; Sociology
Dist - IFB **Prod** - MHFB 1965

Negligence and Error 30 MIN
U-matic
Medical - Legal Issues Series
(A)
Outlines the complexity of medical and legal regulatory systems which cover medical science.
Civics and Political Systems; Health and Safety; Sociology
Dist - ACCESS **Prod** - ACCESS 1983

Negligent Operation of Motor Vehicles 24 MIN
16mm / U-matic / VHS
Police Civil Liability Series Part 1
Color
LC 78-701781
Presents situations which demonstrate to police officers proper and improper use of their motor vehicles. Emphasizes the importance of determining whether or not an emergency situation exists before driving at high speeds, and points out the equipment that must be used during both emergency and nonemergency runs.
Civics and Political Systems
Dist - CORF **Prod** - HAR 1978

Negligent Use of Firearms 24 MIN
U-matic / VHS / 16mm
Police Civil Liability Series Part 2
Color
LC 78-701782
Presents situations which demonstrate to police officers proper and improper use of their firearms. Outlines the types of actions that courts across the United States have held to be reasonable and unreasonable uses of firearms.
Civics and Political Systems
Dist - CORF **Prod** - HAR 1978

The Negligent Use of Motor Vehicles 13 MIN
16mm / U-matic / VHS
Law Enforcement - Civil Liability Series
Color (PRO)
Discusses claims and lawsuits brought against police officers for vehicular negligence. Looks at vehicles in emergency situations, showing how to exercise due care for the safety of others and provide adequate warning to pedestrians and other motorists.
Civics and Political Systems; Social Science
Dist - AIMS **Prod** - AIMS 1978

Negocios, Comportamiento Y Resultados 23 MIN
16mm / U-matic / VHS
Color (H C A) (SPANISH)
A Spanish language version of Business, Behaviorism And The Bottom Line. Interprets the theories of B F Skinner and shows how they are applied in an industrial setting in order to modify behavior and increase productivity.
Business and Economics; Foreign Language; Psychology
Dist - MGHT **Prod** - MGHT 1977

Negotiate Like the Pros - Get Better Deals, Vol I 90 MIN
VHS
Negotiate Like The Pros Series
Color (G)
$99.95 purchase _ #20170
Features John Patrick Dolan. Discusses what one should know before making a deal and how to avoid fights and find solutions. Looks at the three crucial steps of pre - negotiation and 'wince' and 'nibbling' tactics. Part one of two parts.
Business and Economics; Psychology
Dist - CARTRP **Prod** - CARTRP

Negotiate Like the Pros - Get Better Deals, Vol II 90 MIN
VHS
Negotiate Like The Pros Series
Color (G)
$99.95 purchase _ #20172
Features John Patrick Dolan. Shows how to determine the bottom line and why one should listen first, then talk. Looks at how to break an impasse and why questions are the best tools of negotiating, as well as the use of silence. Part two of two parts.
Business and Economics; Psychology
Dist - CARTRP **Prod** - CARTRP

Negotiate Like The Pros Series
Negotiate Like the Pros - Get Better Deals, Vol I 90 MIN
Negotiate Like the Pros - Get Better Deals, Vol II 90 MIN
Dist - CARTRP

Negotiate Like the Pros, Vol I and II 180 MIN
VHS
Color (G)
$149.95 purchase _ #20170, #20172
Features John Patrick Dolan. Shows how to sharpen negotiating skills in order to accomplish what one wants - and to help others achieve what they want. Teaches deal making as a 'win - win' proposition, as well as presenting tips and strategies for scoring personal wins more often.
Business and Economics; Psychology
Dist - CARTRP **Prod** - CARTRP

Negotiating a major commercial lease in a difficult real estate market 210 MIN
VHS
Color (C PRO A)
$140.00, $200.00 purchase _ #M777, #P263
Features a course designed for the active real estate practitioner who engages in lease negotiations and is interested in seeing how a major transaction is negotiated by a panel of experts.
Business and Economics; Civics and Political Systems
Dist - ALIABA **Prod** - ALIABA 1990

Negotiating a settlement 51 MIN
VHS
Training the advocate - The Pretrial stage series
Color (C PRO)
$95.00 purchase, $71.25 rental _ #PTA11
Presents lectures and demonstrations of the steps of the pretrial stage. Outlines procedures for negotiating pretrial settlements.
Civics and Political Systems
Dist - NITA **Prod** - NITA 1985

Negotiating Civil Settlements 120 MIN
VHS / U-matic / Cassette
Color; Mono (PRO)
Discusses preparations for negotiation, types of negotiation, tactics and countermeasures, communications, court involvement, documentation and other alternatives to litigation.
Civics and Political Systems
Dist - CCEB **Prod** - CCEB

Negotiating conceptual framework, experience and process 26 MIN
U-matic / VHS
Art of negotiating series
Color
Business and Economics; Psychology
Dist - DELTAK **Prod** - DELTAK

Negotiating for whatever you want 50 MIN
VHS
Color (H C G)
$39.95 purchase _ #CCPCN200V
Offers an intense, informative discussion of the most successful negotiating techniques for use in personal life. Explains how to identify the issues in personal negotiations and offers insights on how to test assumptions about self and others. Uses expert commentary and dramatized examples to help establish effective strategies and emphasizes the importance of recognizing goals.
Guidance and Counseling; Psychology; Social Science
Dist - CAMV

Negotiating in today's world - successful 115 MMIN
deal making at home and abroad
VHS
Color (A)
$695.00 purchase
Presents a seminar program based on two videos focusing on effective negotiation principles useful both at home and across the globe. Stresses the importance of understanding the culture, ideological foundation, and governmental regulations applicable to negotiating partners from another country. Features Tufts University professor of law and diplomacy Jeswald W Salacuse. Includes two videos, one leader - viewer guide and one copy of the text Making Global Deals.
Business and Economics
Dist - COMFLM

Negotiating labor agreements in corporate mergers 50 MIN
VHS
Color (C PRO A)
$95.00 _ #P235
Examines the myriad labor law and employment issues that arise during a corporate merger or acquisition.
Civics and Political Systems; Social Science
Dist - ALIABA **Prod** - CLETV 1988

Negotiating - Parts I and II - 3 68 MIN
VHS
Working with Japan series
Color (C PRO G)
$395.00 purchase, $175.00 rental _ #822
Presents two parts on negotiating across cultures. Discusses what to expect in Part I, comparative negotiating styles, typical Japanese negotiating behaviors. Part II offers strategies and tactics - how to prepare, how to present with effective openings, key communicating strategies, required materials and visual aids, techniques for clarifying, persuading and the importance of saving face, reaching agreement. Part three of a six - part series on business relations with Japan. Produced by Intercultural Training Resources, Inc.
Business and Economics; Civics and Political Systems; Geography - World; Home Economics; Psychology
Dist - INCUL

Negotiating philosophies
16mm / U-matic
Art of negotiating series; Module 12
Color (A)
Shows how to appraise negotiating philosophy, explains why it should be a cooperative process, not a game, plus different philosophies.
Business and Economics; Psychology
Dist - BNA **Prod** - BNA 1983

Negotiating philosophies 15 MIN
VHS / U-matic
Art of negotiating series
Color
Business and Economics; Psychology
Dist - DELTAK **Prod** - DELTAK

Negotiating Profitable Sales 22 MIN
VHS / U-matic
Color (A)
Demonstrates how a salesperson can put theory into practice. Shows a seller at briefing time prior to the first major negotiation. Then presents him following through and actually making the sale.
Business and Economics; Psychology
Dist - XICOM **Prod** - XICOM

Negotiating profitable sales - Part II 22 MIN
VHS
Color (A PRO IND)
$695.00 purchase, $205.00 rental
Presents guidelines for sales negotiations. Covers subjects including how to absorb flak from customers, how to give customers choices to make them feel in control, and maintaining neutrality when appropriate.
Business and Economics; Psychology; Social Science
Dist - VLEARN **Prod** - VIDART

Negotiating profitable sales series
The Negotiation - Part 2 22 MIN
The Preparation - Part 1 23 MIN
Dist - VIDART

Negotiating Sales Series Pt II
The Negotiation 23 MIN
Dist - VISUCP

Negotiating sales series
The Preparation 21 MIN
Dist - VISUCP

Negotiating series
Complete negotiations - comparative techniques 45 MIN
Dist - ABACPE

Negotiating Settlements in Personal Injury Cases 120 MIN
VHS / U-matic / Cassette
Color; Mono (PRO)
Focuses on the procedures and techniques that can be used to negotiate the best settlement for clients. Covers such topics as evaluating the case for settlement, court settlement conferences and negotiating settlements in multiple party cases.
Civics and Political Systems
Dist - CCEB **Prod** - CCEB

Negotiating Skills for Managers 30 MIN
U-matic / VHS
Color
Teaches managers how to sway others with timing and association techniques, identify the other side's real but often hidden needs, use questions to control the thrust of a discussion, make concessions without losing, communicate their position clearly and precisely.
Business and Economics; Psychology
Dist - EFM **Prod** - EFM

Negotiating - strategies and tactics 24 MIN
U-matic / 16mm / VHS
Color (C A G H)
$540.00, $410.00, $380.00 purchase _ #A387
Reveals that good negotiators are skillful tacticians who apply the right strategies at the right moments. Shows how a successful negotiator has the right attitude, makes a careful study of the pros and cons, anticipates the other side, learns from experience - including mistakes, and always remembers that negotiation is a collaborative effort.
Business and Economics; Psychology; Social Science
Dist - BARR **Prod** - SANCIN 1985

Negotiating strategies and tactics 60 MIN
VHS
Effective manager seminar series
Color (H C A)
$95.00 purchase _ #NGC751V
Presents a multimedia seminar on negotiation strategies and tactics. Consists of a videocassette, a 60 - minute audiocassette, and a study guide.
Business and Economics; Psychology
Dist - CAMV

Negotiating Strategies and Tactics 60 MIN
Cassette / VHS
Effective Manager Series
Color (G)
$95.00 purchase _ #6421
Features Brian Tracy who shows how to negotiate successfully and leave the 'other guy' feeling good. Includes a 60 - minute video, two audiocassettes and two workbooks. Part of a fourteen - part series.
Business and Economics; Civics and Political Systems; Guidance and Counseling; Psychology
Dist - SYBVIS

Negotiating Successfully Series Part 1
What Makes a Good Negotiation 25 MIN
Dist - TIMLIF

Negotiating Successfully Series Part 2
Dangers in Negotiations 25 MIN
Dist - TIMLIF

Negotiating Successfully Series Part 3
You have more Power than You Think 25 MIN
Dist - TIMLIF

Negotiating Successfully Series Part 4
Tactics of Pressure 25 MIN
Dist - TIMLIF

Negotiating Successfully Series Part 6
How to Avoid a Deadlock 25 MIN
Dist - TIMLIF

Negotiating successfully series
A Better deal for both sides 25 MIN
Dist - TIMLIF

Negotiating Techniques, Arnold Ruskin
U-matic / VHS
Management Skills Series
Color (PRO)
Business and Economics; Psychology
Dist - AMCEE **Prod** - AMCEE

Negotiating the job offer
VHS
Job search series
Color (H C G)
$69.95 purchase _ #CCPTU130V
Teaches job seekers to be detectives when negotiating an offer. Shows how to set a salary range, negotiate a compensation package, fine out long - term earning and advancement potential and decide if an organization is right. Part of a three - part series which guides viewers through three stages of a successful job search.
Business and Economics; Guidance and Counseling
Dist - CAMV **Prod** - CAMV 1991

Negotiating - the win - win process 23 MIN
VHS
Color (A PRO IND)
$585.00 purchase, $140.00 rental
Presents a nine - step process by which all participants in negotiations can be 'winners.' Stresses cooperation and understanding over hostility.
Business and Economics; Psychology; Social Science
Dist - VLEARN **Prod** - BARR

Negotiating - the win - win process 24 MIN
VHS / U-matic / 16mm
Color (C A G H)
$565.00, $425.00, $395.00 purchase _ #A359
Shows how to make negotiating a win - win process. Demonstrates negotiation without hostility to achieve what is wanted. Illustrates a practical, problem - solving approach which promotes cooperation and understanding.
Business and Economics; Psychology; Social Science
Dist - BARR **Prod** - UNDERR 1984

Negotiating with the Government 72 MIN
VHS / U-matic
Preventive Antitrust - Corporate Compliance Program Series
Color (PRO)
Discusses practices of Justice Department's antitrust division regarding negotiation of consent decrees and civil investigative demands. Provides a set of rules to follow when negotiating with the antitrust division. Debates questions of the division leniency program.
Civics and Political Systems
Dist - ABACPE **Prod** - ABACPE

Negotiating within the family - you and your child can both get what you want 15 MIN
VHS
Boy's town parenting series
Color (G)
$29.95 purchase _ #FFB211V
Teaches parents to use a simple written agreement to help their children identify and achieve realistic, personal goals. Reveals research showing the success of children when they have specific goals. Part of an 11 - part series.
Guidance and Counseling; Health and Safety; Psychology; Sociology
Dist - CAMV **Prod** - FFBH

The Negotiation 23 MIN
VHS / U-matic
Negotiating Sales Series Pt II
Color
Shows a contest which calls for clear thinking and quick footwork as a salesman starts his negotiations with a buyer, who is also a skilled negotiator.
Business and Economics
Dist - VISUCP **Prod** - VISUCP

Negotiation 15 MIN
16mm / U-matic / VHS
Korean War Series
Color (H C A J)
$375 purchase - 16 mm, $250 purchase - video _ #5243C ; $375, $250 purchase _ #5243C
Shows the Chinese offensive, America's role in the war, and the end of the war.
History - United States
Dist - CORF

Negotiation 60 MIN
BETA / VHS
Manufacturing Series
(IND)
Focuses on principles and techniques of successful negotiations.
Business and Economics
Dist - COMSRV **Prod** - COMSRV 1986

Negotiation
VHS / U-matic
Asset Series
Color
Psychology; Sociology
Dist - RESPRC **Prod** - RESPRC

Negotiation 35 MIN
U-matic / VHS
Legal Ethics - Applying the Model Rules Series
Color (PRO)
Portrays an attorney attempting to settle a wrongful death case. Discusses competence, diligence, fairness, misrepresentation and disclosure.
Civics and Political Systems
Dist - ABACPE **Prod** - ABACPE

Negotiation 60 MIN
U-matic / VHS
Dilemmas in Legal Ethics Series
Color (PRO)
Raises several issues concerning attorney preparation, misrepresentation, attorney - client privilege, attorneys' duty to disclose criminal conduct, extortion, settlement tactics and obligation to represent client diligently.
Civics and Political Systems
Dist - ABACPE **Prod** - ABACPE

Negotiation 8 MIN
U-matic / VHS
ASSET - a social skills program for adolescents series; Session 6
Color (J H)
LC 81-706054
Presents skills involving negotiation which adolescents can use in their dealings with parents, teachers, peers and others.
Guidance and Counseling; Psychology
Dist - RESPRC **Prod** - HAZLJS 1981

Negotiation Lectures Series
Preparing for negotiations 50 MIN
Psychological Factors and Ethical Considerations in Negotiations 50 MIN
Strategy and Tactics in Negotiations 50 MIN
Dist - ABACPE

The Negotiation - Part 2 22 MIN
U-matic / VHS
Negotiating profitable sales series
Color (C A PRO)
$695.00 purchase, $205.00 rental
Shows that knowledge of negotiation can be more profitable than any other sales skill. Portrays a negotiation and includes tips on timing, control and neutrality. Part two of a two - part series on negotiating profitable sales.
Business and Economics
Dist - VIDART **Prod** - VIDART

Negotiation Preparations, Strategies, Tactics and Problems 55 MIN
U-matic / VHS
Negotiation Series
Color (PRO)
Civics and Political Systems; Psychology; Social Science
Dist - ABACPE **Prod** - ABACPE

Negotiation series
Basic negotiation approaches 28 MIN
Negotiation Preparations, Strategies, Tactics and Problems 55 MIN
Dist - ABACPE

Negotiation Settlements in Personal Injury Cases 120 MIN
U-matic / VHS
Color (PRO)
Discusses procedures and techniques used to negotiate the best settlement for a client.
Civics and Political Systems; Social Science
Dist - ABACPE **Prod** - CCEB

Negotiation Skills 25 MIN
VHS / 16mm
Color (J)
$180.00 purchase
Provides young people with step - by - step negotiating skills they can use to improve relations at home, in school or on the job. Includes leader's guide.
Psychology; Sociology
Dist - CHEF **Prod** - CHEF

Negotiation - strategies and tactics 24 MIN
VHS
Color (A PRO IND)
$595.00 purchase, $140.00 rental
Surveys negotiating strategies and how they can be used. Includes such strategies as blanket proposals, bracketing, intimidation, surprise, salami, and others. Suggests that a well - prepared negotiator should be able to understand the other side's positions so well that he or she could argue for them.
Business and Economics; Psychology; Social Science
Dist - VLEARN **Prod** - BARR

The Negro and the American Promise 60 MIN
16mm
B&W (C A)
Presents Dr Kenneth Clark interviewing James Baldwin, Martin Luther King Jr and Malcolm X.
Civics and Political Systems; History - United States; Psychology; Sociology
Dist - IU **Prod** - NET

The Negro and the American Promise - Pt 1 30 MIN
16mm
B&W (C A)
Presents Dr Kenneth Clark interviewing James Baldwin, Martin Luther King, Jr and Malcolm X.
History - United States
Dist - IU **Prod** - NET

The Negro and the American Promise - Pt 2 30 MIN
16mm
B&W (C A)
Presents Dr Kenneth Clark interviewing James Baldwin, Martin Luther King, Jr and Malcolm X.
History - United States
Dist - IU **Prod** - NET

The Negro and the South 30 MIN
16mm
History of the Negro People Series
B&W (H C A)
LC FIA68-1284
Explores the meaning of 'the Southern way of life.' Includes interviews with black and white citizens and shows scenes of segregated schools.
Geography - United States; History - United States; Psychology; Sociology
Dist - IU **Prod** - NET 1965

The Negro Ensemble Company 58 MIN
U-matic / VHS
Color (C)
$229.00, $179.00 purchase _ #AD - 1487
Documents the Negro Ensemble Company which was founded in 1967 by actor - playwright Douglas Ward, actor Robert Hooks and theater manager Gerald Drone. Features scenes from outstanding plays produced by the ensemble.
Fine Arts; Literature and Drama
Dist - FOTH **Prod** - FOTH

The Negro Ensemble Company 58 MIN
VHS / 16mm
Color (H)
$15.50 rental _ #60836
Traces the history of the Negro Ensemble Company (NEC) from its establishment in 1967 by actor Robert Hooks, playwright Douglas Turner Ward, and white producer Gerald Krone, through its production of the Pulitzer Prize - winning drama of 1982, A Soldier's Play. Features such alumni as Rosalind Cash, Phylicia Rashad, and Denzel Washington. Narrated by Ossie Davis.
Fine Arts; Literature and Drama
Dist - PSU

Negro Heroes from American History 11 MIN
16mm
Color (P I J)
LC FIA67-1509
Relates the biographies of several Black American heroes. Demonstrates the richness of Black contributions to the United States.
Biography; History - United States
Dist - ATLAP **Prod** - ATLAP 1967

Negro Kingdoms of Africa's Golden Age 17 MIN
16mm
Color (I J H)
LC 71-700472
Shows the changing climate of Africa. Discusses the trans - Saharan transportation and the growth of Islam as a prelude to the emergence of several prosperous and mighty empires in topical Africa. Presents the story of medieval Senegal, Mali and Ghana. Describes the initiation of slave trading and the emergence of new African states.
History - United States; History - World
Dist - ATLAP **Prod** - ATLAP 1968

Negro Slavery 25 MIN
16mm / U-matic / VHS
American History Series
Color (J H)
LC FIA68-2286
Discusses the beginning and development of slavery in the United States and shows the life of the slave. Describes the gradual division of American society over the slavery issue and explains how the division culminated in the Civil War.
History - United States
Dist - MGHT **Prod** - MGHT 1969

The Negro Soldier 42 MIN
16mm
B&W
LC 75-700799
Traces the role of the Negro soldier in American history from 1776 to 1944. Shows the accomplishments of Negro troops.
Civics and Political Systems; History - United States
Dist - USNAC **Prod** - USWD 1944

The Negro soldier 49 MIN
VHS
B&W (G)
$19.95 purchase _ #S00346
Provides insights into the important role of African - Americans in US history. Intended as a morale booster for black servicemen in World War II. Directed by Frank Capra.
History - United States; History - World
Dist - UILL **Prod** - IHF
IHF

Nehemiah 30 MIN
16mm
Color (R)
Portrays the leadership qualities exemplified by Nehemiah. Explains that Nehemiah went to Jerusalem to unite the people and helped them rebuild the walls around the city.
Literature and Drama
Dist - BROADM **Prod** - BROADM 1964

Nehemiah - the rebirth of a community 30 MIN
VHS
Color (G R)
$15.00 purchase _ #S10172
Depicts the Nehemiah Plan, a program designed to rebuild the community of East Brooklyn, NY, by constructing inexpensive single - family homes. Originally telecast by CBS.
Guidance and Counseling; Literature and Drama; Religion and Philosophy
Dist - CPH **Prod** - LUMIS

Nehemiah - Walls of Jericho and patience of Job - Volume 10 45 MIN
VHS
Superbook series
Color (K P I R)
$11.99 purchase _ #35 - 86615 - 979
Uses an animated format to tell the story of Chris and Joy and their time travels through Biblical places and events. 'Nehemiah - Walls of Jericho' tells the story of Nehemiah and Jericho, while 'Patience of Job' tells the story of Job and his trials.
Literature and Drama; Religion and Philosophy
Dist - APH **Prod** - TYHP

Nehi Cheii Toad Counts His Corn 9 MIN
VHS / 16mm
Color (P I J) (ENGLISH AND NAVAJO)
$168.00 purchase, $10.00 rental
Teaches the math concept of place value using the Coyote and Toad characters.
Mathematics
Dist - BIECC **Prod** - BIECC

Nehiyow
16mm
Color (G)
#3X52 I
Documents aspects of the life of Sioux, Chipewan, and Cree people. Depicts the annual 22 mile race by dogsled, tanning of hides, and porcupine quill work.
Social Science
Dist - CDIAND **Prod** - AINC 1976

Nehru 54 MIN
16mm
B&W (C A)
Presents Nehru at age 73, the political leader of 400 million people and president of the world's largest democracy, India. Describes how he is still wrestling with more problems than ever before in the history of his young democracy.
Biography; History - World
Dist - DIRECT **Prod** - DREW 1967

Nehru's India 29 MIN
Videoreel / VT2
Course of Our Times II Series
Color
History - World
Dist - PBS **Prod** - WGBHTV

The Neighbor 30 MIN
VHS
Color (I J H C G A R)
$24.95 purchase, $10.00 rental _ #35 - 824 - 8579
Presents a modern - day version of the parable of the Good Samaritan. Shows how a black man stops to help racist lawyer Graham Reid, who was beaten up and robbed in a city park.
Religion and Philosophy; Sociology
Dist - APH **Prod** - CPH

The Neighbor 15 MIN
16mm / U-matic / VHS
Color (H A)
Details the causes of drinking water contamination and illustrates solutions.
Science - Natural; Science - Physical; Sociology
Dist - KLEINW **Prod** - KLEINW

The Neighbor Islands 30 MIN
16mm
Color (J H C)
Covers in detail the islands of Kauai, Maui and Hawaii, and shows all the landmarks important in Hawaii's historical past which have become famous in legend.
Geography - United States; Geography - World; History - United States; Literature and Drama
Dist - CINEPC **Prod** - CINEPC

The Neighborhood 25 MIN
VHS
Dragon's tongue series
Color (C G) (CHINESE)
$195.00 purchase
Looks at life in the neighborhood in the People's Republic of China, using Putonghua - the, official language of China based on the dialect of Beijing. Part of a 10 - part series hosted by Prof Colin Mackerras, Co - Director of the Key Center for Asian Languages and Studies at Griffith University.
Foreign Language; Geography - World; Sociology
Dist - LANDMK **Prod** - LANDMK 1990

The Neighborhood 18 MIN
16mm
B&W
LC 75-701718
Presents an entertaining situation as a misunderstanding between a police officer and a slightly unorthodox citizen sets off a chase in the classic silent - move style.
Fine Arts; Psychology; Sociology
Dist - FMCOOP **Prod** - FMCOOP 1966

Neighborhood 28 MIN
VHS
Elephant show series
Color (P I)
$95.00 purchase, $45.00 rental
Presents program 11 in the Sharon, Lois and Bram's Elephant Show series. Teaches reading readiness and social skills while engaging children in making music. Each program explores a new theme through adventure, fantasy, mystery and song with recording artists Sharon, Lois and Bram. Uses traditional materials which stress participation - action songs, sing - along songs, story songs, clapping songs, singing games, playground chants and folk songs from many different traditions. Includes teacher's guide co - authored by a music education specialist.
Fine Arts; Sociology
Dist - BULFRG **Prod** - CAMBFP 1988

Neighborhood Drums 30 MIN
VHS / U-matic
Y E S Inc Series
Color (J H)
Shows that it's tough to resist the old gang and familiar neighborhood ways, but that succeeding at a job means sticking with it, in spite of divided loyalties.
Guidance and Counseling; Psychology
Dist - GPN **Prod** - KCET 1983

The Neighborhood of Coehlos 28 MIN
VHS
Color; PAL (I J H A)
$39.95 purchase _ #30920
Portrays the slums of Recife, Brazil, where residents work with an urban development program to create jobs, reclaim swampland, provide education and establish land tenure. Includes teaching notes.
Business and Economics; Geography - World; Social Science; Sociology
Dist - WB **Prod** - WB

Neighborhood Watch 20 MIN
8mm cartridge / 16mm
Color (J)
LC 75-701608
Discusses techniques designed to protect residences from burglaries. Describes alarm systems, lighting fixtures, locking hardware and other devices.
Guidance and Counseling; Health and Safety; Home Economics
Dist - MCCRNE **Prod** - MCCRNE 1974

Neighborhood Watch - Partners Against Crime 18 MIN
VHS / 16mm
(G A)
$365.00 purchase _ #AG - 5287M
Documents how one suburban town developed an effective partnership with local police by building and implementing a neighborhood watch program. Emphasizes the crime prevention benefits of such a program and gives specific information on the formation and handling of the group.
Civics and Political Systems; Social Science; Sociology
Dist - CORF

The Neighborhood Works Together 15 MIN
U-matic
We Live Next Door Series
Color (K)
Continues the story of Nutdale after the old store has been saved. The flashy Telephone Booth had expected a job in the city and resents the old store until he is saved from a neighborhood menace.
Psychology; Social Science
Dist - TVOTAR **Prod** - TVOTAR 1981

The Neighborhood Youth Corps 26 MIN
U-matic / VHS / 16mm
Career Job Opportunity Series
Color
Demonstrates how youths can stay in school and continue their education while earning needed money under the U S Department of Labor's Neighborhood Youth Corps program.
Civics and Political Systems; Guidance and Counseling
Dist - USNAC **Prod** - USDLMA 1968

Neighborhoods; 2nd ed 18 MIN
VHS / U-matic
Community series
Color (K P)
$415.00, $385.00 purchase _ #V238
Explores the changing communities where families live and work. Focuses on neighborhoods, the sorts of housing available, the sorts of people who live in them, how neighborhoods and communities are always changing. Part of a three - part series on the community.
Guidance and Counseling; Social Science; Sociology
Dist - BARR **Prod** - CEPRO 1991

Neighborhoods Series LINCOLN, NB 68501
Ethnic neighborhoods - city 15 MIN
Dist - GPN

Neighborhoods Series
City neighborhood - a beautiful place 15 MIN
City neighborhood - a general description I 15 MIN
City neighborhood - a general description II 15 MIN
City neighborhood - good neighbors help each other 15 MIN
Communication in neighborhoods 15 MIN
Ethnic Neighborhoods - Rural 15 MIN
Ethnic Neighborhoods - Town 15 MIN
My Neighbor and Me 15 MIN
Neighbors and Neighborhoods 15 MIN
Older and Newer Neighborhoods 15 MIN
Protection in Neighborhoods 15 MIN
Religious neighborhoods - city 15 MIN
Religious neighborhoods - rural 15 MIN
Religious neighborhoods - town 15 MIN
Rural Neighborhood - a Beautiful Place 15 MIN
Rural Neighborhood - a General Description 15 MIN
Rural Neighborhood - Good Neighbors Help each Other 15 MIN
Tale of Two Neighbors 15 MIN
Town Neighborhood - a General Description 15 MIN
Town Neighborhood - Good Neighbors Help each Other 15 MIN
Transportation in Neighborhoods 15 MIN
Welcoming New Neighbors 15 MIN
Dist - GPN

Neighboring - the Old West End, Toledo, Ohio 30 MIN
16mm
Color
Looks at a renovated neighborhood in Toledo, Ohio. Discusses the loss of neighborhoods in modern society and the pros and cons of urban neighborhoods.
History - United States; Sociology
Dist - HRC **Prod** - OHC

Neighbors 29 MIN
VHS / 16mm
Villa Alegre Series
Color (P T)
$46.00 rental _ #VILA - 111
Presents educational material in both Spanish and English.
Education; Social Science
Dist - PBS

Neighbors 9 MIN
U-matic / VHS / 16mm
Color (J H C A)
Employs the principles of frame by frame animation with live actors and without dialogue in a shorter, less violent version for less mature audiences of a parable about two neighbors who, after living side by side in friendliness and respect, come to blows over the possession of a flower growing on their property line.
Guidance and Counseling; Religion and Philosophy
Dist - IFB **Prod** - NFBC 1953

Neighbors 114 MIN
VHS
Color (G) (MANDARIN CHINESE (ENGLISH SUBTITLES))
$45.00 purchase _ #1022B
Presents a Mandarin Chinese language movie produced in the People's Republic of China.
Fine Arts; Geography - World; Literature and Drama
Dist - CHTSUI **Prod** - CHTSUI

Neighbors 28 MIN
16mm
No Place Like Home Series
Color
LC 74-706157
Shows how neighbors have traditionally offered help in times of trouble, but in modern society, more than neighborly help is needed. Tells how community services offer help to disadvantaged children and adults.
Social Science; Sociology
Dist - USNAC **Prod** - USSRS 1973

Neighbors 17 MIN
16mm
B&W (J)
Stars Buster Keaton.
Fine Arts
Dist - TWYMAN **Prod** - MGM 1920

Neighbors 33 MIN
VHS
Tales of the unknown South series
Color (J H C G T A)
Presents a dramatization of "Neighbors," a short story by Diane Oliver. Tells how a black student finds turmoil when he begins attending a previously all - white school. Hosted by author James Dickey. Available only to public television stations.
Geography - United States; Literature and Drama
Dist - SCETV **Prod** - SCETV 1987

Neighbors and Neighborhoods 15 MIN
VHS / U-matic
Neighborhoods Series
Color (P)
Discusses neighbors and neighborhoods.
Sociology
Dist - GPN **Prod** - NEITV 1981

Neighbors series film 3
At school 21 MIN
Dist - LUF

Neighbors series
Family lives 22 MIN
Four families in Europe - Film 1 21 MIN
Living together 22 MIN
Dist - LUF

Neighbors - the United States and Mexico 60 MIN
U-matic / VHS
Color (H C A)
$395 purchase, $90 rental
Focusses on the economic relationships between the U.S. and Mexico. Also talks about labor intensive factories owned by U.S. companies but located in Mexico. Features interviews with immigration specialists and economic and border authorities from the U S and Mexico. Directed by Jesus Salvador Trevino and Jose Luix Ruiz.
Business and Economics; History - World
Dist - CNEMAG

Neighbors to Nicaragua 30 MIN
VHS
Color (J H C G T A)
$35.00 purchase, $25.00 rental
Tells the story of a church - organized, "sister state" program between Minnesota and the state of Leon in Nicaragua. Produced by Gregory Rutchik and Robert Vaaler for PML.
Geography - World; History - World
Dist - EFVP

Neighbors to Nicaragua - the Story of the Project Minnesota - Leon 30 MIN
Videoreel / U-matic / VT3
(G)
$95.00 purchase, $45.00 rental
Looks at the story of the Project Minnesota - Leon, a sister - state program between Minnesota and the Department of Leon in Nicaragua.
Sociology
Dist - EFVP **Prod** - EFVP 1986

Neighbours - a Training Program for Community Volunteers Series
ESL Literacy 12 MIN
In the Neighbourhood 12 MIN
Intercultural Communications 14 MIN
Making Contact 20 MIN
Portraits 22 MIN
Dist - ACCESS

Neihardt - a Journey Home 60 MIN
VHS / U-matic
Color
Presents Dr. John G. Neihardt, Nebraska Poet Laureate, author of Black Elk Speaks, as he returns to Bancroft, his home town, and talks about his poetry and prose and the symbolism of the Sioux Prayer Garden. With performances of four poems - `Poet's Town', `Black Elk's Prayer,' `April Theology' and `L'Envoi.'.
History - United States; Literature and Drama; Social Science; Sociology
Dist - NETCHE **Prod** - NETCHE 1962

Neihardt - a Journey Home 60 MIN
U-matic / VHS
B&W (G)
Portrays the late John G Neihardt, Nebraska poet and author of Black Elk Speaks, at his home in Bancroft, Nebraska. Shows Neihardt's study and garden, follows his explication of his use of symbolism. Reads four of his poems, including Black Elk's Prayer.
Biography; Literature and Drama; Religion and Philosophy; Social Science
Dist - GPN **Prod** - NETV

Neihardt on Creative Writing 29 MIN
16mm
B&W (J)
LC 74-700172
Explains that great works of literature have endured for the reason that they deal in some measure with characteristic moods which occur in all races and times and relate man in an unbroken descent.
English Language; Literature and Drama; Sociology
Dist - UNEBR **Prod** - UNL 1968

Neil Wellever - Painting in Maine 25 MIN
16mm
Color (H A)
$65.00 rental
Features Neil Wellever painting a series of nudes in his sunlit barn, as well as at a gallery opening of his paintings. Produced by Rudy Burckhardt.
Fine Arts; Industrial and Technical Education
Dist - AFA

Neither damned nor doomed series
Presents a three - part series on children prenatally exposed to drugs and alcohol produced by the Elementary School Center - ESC. Focuses on the perspectives of drug abusing mothers, teachers who must confront the challenges of children prenatally exposed to drugs and other professionals who work with women in treatment and recovery programs.
Is Mommy alright - Video 3
Mothers' perspectives - Video 1
Teachers' perspectives - Video 2
Dist - SELMED

Neither Laggard Nor Wearied 29 MIN
U-matic
Future Without Shock Series
Color
Looks at the history of the computer.
Industrial and Technical Education; Mathematics; Sociology
Dist - UMITV **Prod** - UMITV 1976

Neither more nor less 12 MIN
16mm
Color (G)
$18.00 rental
Watches a little girl's fantasy day in San Francisco in which people are amusements and a strange friendship develops and ends. Presents a Paul Ryan production with music by Gene Turitz.
Fine Arts; Psychology; Sociology
Dist - CANCIN

Nekton - Swimmers 30 MIN
U-matic / VHS
Oceanus - the Marine Environment Series
Color
Focuses on the nektonic life - style. Lists the four principal categories of swimming organisms.
Science - Natural; Science - Physical
Dist - CDTEL **Prod** - SCCON
SCCON

Nell and Fred 28 MIN
16mm
B&W (H C)
LC 75-714355
Relates the difficulty of elderly people in remaining independent by focusing on a couple who must decide whether to move into a residence for senior citizens or to maintain their own familiar home.
Guidance and Counseling; Psychology; Sociology
Dist - NFBC **Prod** - NFBC 1971

Nellie Bly - daredevil, reporter, feminist 30 MIN
VHS
Author's night at the Freedom Forum series
Color (G)
$15.00 purchase _ #V94 - 07
Focuses on Brooke Kroeger, author of the book of the same title, in part of a series on freedom of the press, free speech and free spirit.
History - World; Social Science; Sociology
Dist - FREEDM **Prod** - FREEDM 1994

Nellie's Playhouse 14 MIN
U-matic / VHS
Color
Provides an overview of the folk art of Nellie Mae Rowe, black artist who uses found objects to create objects in her yard.
Fine Arts
Dist - SOFOLK **Prod** - SOFOLK

Nelson Mandela - February 7 - 12, 1990
VHS
Nightline news library series
Color (J H C)
$19.98 purchase _ #MH6177V - S
Overviews freedom and amnesty for Nelson Mandela in South Africa in a news story by the ABC News Team. Part of a series from the news program, Nightline.
Sociology
Dist - CAMV **Prod** - ABCNEW 1989

Nelson Mandela - the long walk to freedom 28 MIN
VHS
Color (J H C G)
$250.00 purchase
Marks the release of Nelson Mandela on February 11, 1990, after 27 years of imprisonment in South Africa. Uses archival footage to portray the birth of Apartheid and the African National Congress - ANC. Examines the effects of Apartheid and gives an account of Mandela's struggle for equality.
Geography - World; History - World; Sociology
Dist - LANDMK **Prod** - LANDMK 1990

Nelson Mandela - the long walk to freedom and The Last mile - Mandela, Africa and democracy 58 MIN
VHS
Color (H C)
$425.00 purchase
Presents two programs focusing on Nelson Mandela. Covers the turbulent events before, during and after the incarceration of Mandela by South Africa in The Long Walk to Freedom. Travels with Mandela through West Africa and discusses African problems in The Last Mile.
Civics and Political Systems; Geography - World; History - World; Sociology
Dist - LANDMK **Prod** - LANDMK 1990

Nemesis 9 MIN
16mm
B&W; Color (G)
$15.00 rental
Expresses Carl Jung's view that 'our intellect has created a new world that dominates nature, and has populated it with monstrous machines.' Points out that the machines are so useful that humans are blinded by their subservience to them and cannot possibly live without them. Humanity is still the victims of nature because it hasn't learned to control its own nature. Produced by Warren Haack.
Fine Arts; Psychology
Dist - CANCIN

Nemesis - Germany, February - May 1945 52 MIN
U-matic / VHS / 16mm
World at War Series
Color (H C A)
Describes the period from February to May 1945 which brought Germany's defeat and Russia's capture of Berlin. The end of the Third Reich was announced at Hitler's secret headquarters where he ended his own life.
History - World
Dist - MEDIAG **Prod** - THAMES 1973

Nemesis - Germany, February to May, 1945 60 MIN
16mm
World at War Series
Color (H C A)
LC 76-701778
History - World; Sociology
Dist - USCAN **Prod** - THAMES 1975

Neo - classism and romanticism 20 MIN
VHS
ARTV series
Color (J)
$44.95 purchase _ #E323; LC 90-708449
Offers two music videos which feature the art works of Eugene Delacroix in 'Action' and of Jacques - Louis David in 'A Call to Arms.' Includes Goya and Turner. Part of a ten - part ARTV series which uses TV format, including 'commercials' which sell one aspect of an artist's style and a gossip columnist who gives little known facts about the artists.
Fine Arts
Dist - GPN **Prod** - HETV 1989

Neon 5 MIN
16mm / U-matic / VHS
How It's made Series
Color (K)
Business and Economics
Dist - LUF **Prod** - HOLIA

Neon - an electric memoir 26 MIN
VHS
Color (G)
$250.00 purchase, $55.00 rental
Chronicles the history of neon. Shows how neon is utilized today by designers, photographers, artists, sculptors and architects.
Fine Arts
Dist - CNEMAG

Neonatal death 46 MIN
VHS
Understanding maternal grief series
Color (C G)
$195.00 purchase, $50.00 rental _ #38182
Explores the effects of the death of a baby on a mother's mental and physical health. Views the grief process within the context of the many problems experienced by a woman and her family during such a crisis - the impact of a premature birth; the stresses associated with having a seriously ill baby in neonatal intensive care; the difficulties in making decisions regarding medical interventions; and the consideration of siblings and their inclusion in the bonding and grief process. Part of a five - part series produced by Margaret Nicol, an Australian clinical psycologist specializing in the effects of reproductive loss on women's physical and mental health.
Guidance and Counseling; Health and Safety; Sociology
Dist - UCEMC

Neonatal mock codes 23 MIN
VHS / U-matic
Color (PRO C)
$395.00 purchase, $80.00 rental _ #C891 - VI - 082
Presents simulations of both proper and improper neonatal 'code' - cardiac arrest - performances. Stresses the vital points of familiarity with newborns, knowing professional role, knowing the equipment and knowledge of IV access and the administration of appropriate drugs. Presented by Julie Wade, RN.
Health and Safety
Dist - HSCIC

The Neonatal setting 20 MIN
U-matic / VHS
Ethical issues in nursing series
Color (PRO C)
$395.00 purchase, $80.00 rental _ #C920 - VI - 005
Looks at the values and principles that guide ethical decisionmaking regarding neonatal care and stresses that there are no easy answers. Reveals that clinical decisions in the nursery often involve multiple conflicting objectives and engage multiple values. Nurses have a vital role in contributing information, identifying issues and in clarifying their own values. Provides an overview of general principles as they apply to infant care. Part of a series on ethical issues in nursing presented by Dr Mary C Corley and Deborah A Raines, RN, Virginia Hospital Television Network, Office of Medical Education, Medical College of Virginia, Virginia Commonwealth University.
Health and Safety
Dist - HSCIC

Neonatal Surgery 27 MIN
16mm
Color (JAPANESE (ENGLISH SUBTITLES))
A Japanese language film with English subtitles. Describes neonatal surgery, which has developed as a new field in Japanese medicine.
Foreign Language; Health and Safety; Science
Dist - UNIJAP **Prod** - UNIJAP 1964

Neoplasia - Benign and Malignant 55 MIN
VHS / 16mm
Gross Pathology made Easy, Pt III; Pt III
(C)
$385.00 purchase _ #870VI054
Helps viewers differentiate between the gross morphologic features of benign and malignant neoplasia. Classifies neoplasias by origin and etiology.
Health and Safety
Dist - HSCIC **Prod** - HSCIC 1987

Neoplastic Disease 22 MIN
16mm
Color (PRO)
Explains that radical neck dissection is a safe and many times curative procedure for the removal of metastatic cancer arising from the head and neck. Demonstrates the anesthesia and positioning of the patient, the lymph nodes and anatomical structures involved.
Health and Safety; Science
Dist - ACY **Prod** - ACYDGD 1957

Neoromuscular Training for Golf with Pattyt Sheehan
VHS
(H C A)
$69.95 purchase _ #DG014V
Discusses neuromuscular training for women golf players.
Physical Education and Recreation
Dist - CAMV **Prod** - CAMV

Neosho - April 24 14 MIN
16mm
Color
LC 76-702699
Presents the story of the devastating tornado of April 24, 1975, which struck the small Missouri city of Neosho. Documents the disaster preparedness planning of the community, which was responsible for the survival of those who were caught in the path of the tornado.
Geography - United States; History - World
Dist - USNAC **Prod** - NOAA 1976

Nepal 21 MIN
VHS / 16mm
Paradise Steamship Co Series
Color (I H C A)
$300.00, $225.00
Looks at the contrasting kingdom of Nepal and observes the daily struggle of its 15 million people to survive. Also focuses on the unique craftwork of the Nepalese.
Geography - World
Dist - CAROUF **Prod** - KCBS 1989

Nepal - Land of the Gods 17 MIN
16mm
Color (P)
LC 71-701201
Explains the nature of the people of Nepal and describes their religions, their way of life, and their country's geography.
Geography - World; Sociology
Dist - AVED **Prod** - BAILYL 1968

Nepal - on top of the world - Pt 8 30 MIN
VHS / U-matic
Profiles in progress series
Color (H C)
$325.00, $295.00 purchase _ #V553
Looks at the mounting problem of deforestation in the Himalayan kingdom of Nepal. Reveals that vast mountainsides have been denuded of trees for fire wood, adversely affecting Nepal's wildlife. Prabhakar Rana, an industrialist, is balancing Nepal's need for industrialization with concerns for preserving the environment. Part of a 13 - part series on people who are moving their tradition - bound countries into modern times.
Business and Economics; Geography - World; Science - Natural; Social Science
Dist - BARR **Prod** - CEPRO 1991

Nepal - People of the Mountains 14 MIN
16mm
Color (P)
LC 75-701202
Describes the Sherpas tribe of the Himalaya Mountains of Nepal.
Geography - World; Sociology
Dist - AVED **Prod** - BAILYL 1968

Nepal - the People and the Culture 28 MIN
U-matic / VHS
Color (H C A)
Presents the people, culture and history of Nepal, a small, landlocked country which has a rich heritage. Explores the problems that face the people and their government.
Geography - World
Dist - JOU **Prod** - JOU

Nepalese Tea Worker of the Himalayas 14 MIN
16mm
Human Family, Pt 1 - South and Southeast Asia Series
Color (I)
Tells the story of the family of Dorji Lama, whose father and mother were among the Nepal poor farmers who were indentured and brought to work on the tea estates of India. Explains that Dorji has since lived and worked all of his life on the Phuguri Tea Estate and supports his wife, four sons, three daughters and a grandmother.
Geography - World; Social Science; Sociology
Dist - AVED **Prod** - AVED 1972

Nephro - Ureterectomy - Modified Single - Incision Approach 20 MIN
16mm
Color
LC 75-702281
Uses medical art and animation along with photography to illustrate an operative technique in a patient with a transitional cell tumor involving the renal pelvis and upper calyces. Employs diagnostic procedures and post - operative follow - up to emphasize the advantages of this modified approach.
Science
Dist - EATONL **Prod** - EATONL 1965

Nephrosis in Children 18 MIN
16mm
Color (PRO)
Describes the onset of nephrosis in children and some of the complications such as hernias, and shows the typical facies. Points out that progressive kidney failure is a major cause of death in childhood nephrosis.
Health and Safety
Dist - PFI **Prod** - PFI 1954

Neptune's cold fury 58 MIN
VHS / U-matic
Nova series
Color (H C A)
$250.00 purchase _ #HP - 6373C
Looks at the first close - up images of the planet Neptune transmitted by Voyager II on August 25, 1989. Reveals fascinating new facts about the planet's rings, moons and unexpected geologic activity, and why the Neptune flyby was one of the most complicated engineering and navigational tasks ever undertaken. Part of the Nova series.
History - World; Industrial and Technical Education; Science; Science - Physical
Dist - CORF **Prod** - WGBHTV 1990

Neptune's Nonsense 8 MIN
16mm
Color
Presents a Felix the Cat cartoon.
Fine Arts
Dist - RMIBHF **Prod** - VANBRN 1936

Neptunian space angel 9 MIN
16mm
B&W (G)
$35.00 rental
Deals with the alteration of human scaling within the 16mm frame. Creates an unusual and bizarre sense of timelessness and distance by having the character walk from one edge of the screen, passing the center, but never reaching the opposite edge.
Fine Arts; Mathematics; Psychology
Dist - CANCIN **Prod** - ANGERA 1977
FLMKCO

Nerine Barrett - Pianist 29 MIN
Videoreel / VT2
Young Musical Artists Series
Color
Presents the music of pianist Nerine Barrett.
Fine Arts
Dist - PBS **Prod** - WKARTV

A Nermish gothic 7 MIN
16mm
B&W (G)
$20.00 rental
Presents a haunting art - horror film in which a young woman is chased around by a giant glowing cone, a Nermish. Ends with her retaliation with the aid of a giant hair net. Filmed in stop - motion. Produced by Janice Findley.
Fine Arts
Dist - CANCIN

Nero Versteht Etwas Von Kunst 15 MIN
U-matic / VHS / 16mm
Guten Tag Wie Geht's Series
Color (H C) (GERMAN)
A German language film. Features Frau Schafer and her nephew Wolfgang searching for a painting to cover a spot on the wallpaper. Pictures Nero, her dog, making the final decision.
Foreign Language
Dist - IFB **Prod** - BAYER 1973

Nerve Deafness 17 MIN
VHS / 16mm / U-matic
Color (A) (SPANISH)
Reviews tinnitus, hearing aids, speech reading and learning to cope with hearing loss. Describes the function of the ear and causes of nerve deafness.
Health and Safety; Science - Natural
Dist - PRORE **Prod** - PRORE

Nerve Hearing Loss
U-matic / VHS
Color (ARABIC)
Film utilizes animation to show normal hearing and how hearing is affected through conductive blockage or nerve hearing loss. Subtitled version available.
Foreign Language; Guidance and Counseling
Dist - MIFE **Prod** - MIFE

The Nerve Impulse 21 MIN
U-matic / VHS / 16mm
Color (J H) (SPANISH)
A Spanish language version of the film and videorecording The Nerve Impulse.
Foreign Language; Science - Natural
Dist - EBEC **Prod** - EBEC 1971

Nerve muscle preparation 11 MIN
VHS
Color; PAL (H)
Performs the dissection of a frog so that the Gastrocnemius muscle, with the cut end of the sciatic nerve attached, can be removed. Uses a cathode ray oscilloscope to show that the nature of the impulse received when the nerve is stimulated is independent of the method of stimulation.
Science - Natural
Dist - VIEWTH

The Nerves 17 MIN
U-matic / VHS / 16mm
Anatomy of the Human Eye Series
Color (PRO)
LC 74-702441
Presents an explanation of the motor and sensory nerve supply for the globe, extraocular muscles and the anterior adnexa, including the light reflex pathways.
Science - Natural
Dist - TEF **Prod** - BAYCMO 1972

Nerves and nerve cells 28 MIN
VHS
Human body - the nervous system - series
Color (J H G)
$89.95 purchase _ #UW4173
Shows the structure and functioning of nerve cells. Explains what happens during local anesthesia and what can be done when a nerve has been destroyed in an accident. Part of a 39 - part series featuring computer animation, medical photography, electron micrography, full - color drawings and diagrams and three - dimensional working models to cover the workings of the human body from head to toe and inside out.
Science - Natural
Dist - FOTH

Nervous Breakdown 19 MIN
U-matic / VHS
Color (G)
$249.00, $149.00 purchase _ #AD - 1325
Focuses on the nature, identifying signs, symptoms and causes of nervous breakdown. Profiles a father who discusses his depression and guilt after learning that his teenage son is schizophrenic. His wife recounts the feelings that led to her near - breakdown. Discusses schizophrenia and visits the psychiatric clinic where the son is a patient.
Health and Safety; Psychology; Sociology
Dist - FOTH **Prod** - FOTH

Nervous Dogs 30 MIN
VHS / U-matic
Training Dogs the Woodhouse Way
Color (H C A)
Shows Barbara Woodhouse's method of handling nervous dogs.
Home Economics; Science - Natural
Dist - FI **Prod** - BBCTV 1982

Nervous, muscular and skeletal systems - Volume 2
Videodisc
STV - human body series
Color; CAV (J H)
$325.00 purchase _ #T81520; $225.00 purchase _ #T81562
Studies the nervous, muscular and skeletal sytems. Offers medical photography by Lennart Nilsson. Part of a three - part series. Includes videodisc, software diskettes with NGS magazine and book excerpts, glossary and presenter tool, user's guide with directions for interactive hook - up, barcode directory and activities and library catalog cards. Designed for Macintosh system. Contact distributor for hardware configuration. Basic kit available at lower price.
Science - Natural
Dist - NGS **Prod** - NGS 1992

Nervous Organs 15 MIN
U-matic
Microanatomy Laboratory Orientation Series
Color (C)
Demonstrates the anatomical organization of portions of the nervous system with emphasis on the cyoarchitectural detail of the spinal cord, cerebullum, cerebrum, dorsal root gangilon, para - sympathetic anglion, sympathetic ganglion, and choroid plexus.

Health and Safety; Science - Natural
Dist - UOKLAH **Prod** - UOKLAH 1986

Nervous System 20 MIN
VHS / U-matic
Human Body Series
Color (J H C A G)
$216.00 purchase _ #51308
Looks at the human nervous system and how the brain and spinal cord receive sensory information.
Science - Natural
Dist - NGS

Nervous System 23 MIN
U-matic / VHS / 16mm
Human Body Series
Color (J H C)
$560, $250 purchase _ #3963
Demonstrates how neurons' structure enables them to transmit electrochemical impulse and talks about the right and left hemispheres of the brain.
Science - Natural
Dist - CORF

The Nervous System 17 MIN
U-matic / VHS / 16mm
Color (J H) (SPANISH)
A Spanish language version of the film and videorecording The Nervous System.
Foreign Language; Science - Natural
Dist - EBEC **Prod** - EBEC 1981

The Nervous system 17 MIN
VHS
Color (J H)
$99.00 purchase _ #3667 - 026
Uses animation and micrographs to visualize how the nervous system controls and integrates specific bodily activities. Describes the effects of alcohol, drugs and caffeine. Includes teacher's guide.
Education; Science - Natural
Dist - GA **Prod** - EBEC

The Nervous system 29 MIN
U-matic
Introducing biology series; Program 19
Color (C A)
Explains how nervous system controls and coordinates the movements and functions of an organism. Uses animation to supplement discussion of electro - chemical nature of an impulse.
Science - Natural
Dist - CDTEL **Prod** - COAST

Nervous system 20 MIN
VHS
Your body series
Color (I)
$80.00 purchase _ #A51613
Makes use of animation and photography to explore the human nervous system internally, beginning with the brain. Includes discussion of the senses and reflexes. Includes a teacher's guide.
Science - Natural
Dist - NGS **Prod** - NGS 1994

The Nervous system 48 MIN
VHS
Color (J H)
$99.00 purchase _ #30931 - 026
Shows the structure and function of the components of the nervous system. Demonstrates how neurons link stimuli taken in by the senses with the responses of muscles and glands. Traces the series of electrical and chemical events that occur as a nerve impulse travels. Roles of the spinal cord, nerves and brain are described in detail. Includes teacher's guide.
Education; Science - Natural
Dist - GA

Nervous system anatomical chart
VHS
(J H C G A)
$36.50 purchase _ #AH70204
Portrays the anatomy of the nervous system from a variety of angles. Available with mounting rods or framed.
Health and Safety; Science - Natural
Dist - HTHED **Prod** - HTHED

The Nervous System - Decision 26 MIN
U-matic / VHS / 16mm
Living Body - an Introduction to Human Biology Series
Color
Shows how the brain organizes input and output to make a simple but life - saving decision. Looks at the cortex, which assesses incoming information and sends outgoing messages to the muscles and stores maps of the world and of the body. Disucsses how circuits of nerve cells operate in the brain and how individual nerve cells function.
Science - Natural
Dist - FOTH **Prod** - FOTH 1985

Nervous System in Animals 17 MIN
16mm
Color (J H C G)
Discusses the nervous system of animals such as, a euglena, amoeba, hydra, planaria, earthworm, grasshopper, pig, frog and cat. Shows the basic elements of the neuron and the pathway of the nerve impulse during a reflex arc.
Science - Natural
Dist - VIEWTH **Prod** - GATEEF

The Nervous System in Man 18 MIN
U-matic / VHS / 16mm
Human Physiology Series
Color (H C A)
LC FIA65-1662
Demonstrates how the human nervous system, with the endocrine system, provides coordination of body movement, integration of body functions and regulation of involuntary body systems. An animated film.
Psychology; Science - Natural
Dist - IU **Prod** - IU 1965

The Nervous System in Man 18 MIN
16mm
Color (J H C G)
Shows the interlocking of the effects of the endocrine and nervous systems. Illustrates the types of nerve cells and impulse transmission and discusses the functions of the cortex, cerebellum, hypothalamic area and medula. Describes the reflex arc and the peripheral, central and automatic divisions. Discusses diseases of the nervous system.
Science - Natural
Dist - VIEWTH **Prod** - GATEEF

The Nervous System - Nerves at Work 26 MIN
U-matic / VHS / 16mm
Living Body - an Introduction to Human Biology Series
Color
Looks at nerve signals and how they are transmitted. Discusses the part played by nerve messages in reflex activities and examines the chemical and electrical activities of networks of nerve cells in contact.
Science - Natural
Dist - FOTH **Prod** - FOTH 1985

The Nervous system - our information network 8 MIN
35mm strip / VHS
Color (I J)
LC 90-705187
Examines the nervous system. Includes teacher's guide with suggested activities and bibliography.
Education; Science - Natural
Dist - MARSH **Prod** - MARSH 1989

The Nervous System - Our Talented Brain 26 MIN
16mm / U-matic / VHS
Living Body - an Introduction to Human Biology Series
Color
Explores human culture, including man's physiological brain capacity, his use of memory, and his use of symbols. Discusses its relationship to the neural structure of the brain.
Science - Natural
Dist - FOTH **Prod** - FOTH 1985

The Nervous system - Pt 1 60 MIN
U-matic / VHS
Biology of Cognition and Language Series Program 9; Program 9
Color (A)
Presents biologist Humberto Maturana discussing the human nervous system.
Science - Natural
Dist - UCEMC **Prod** - UCEMC

The Nervous System Pt 2 60 MIN
VHS / U-matic
Biology of Cognition and Language Series Program 10; Program 10
Color (A)
Presents biologist Humberto Maturana discussing the human nervous system.
Science - Natural
Dist - UCEMC **Prod** - INTPC

Nervous System - Pt 1 - Central Nervous System 45 MIN
U-matic / VHS
Histology review series
Color (PRO)
Presents the major characteristics of the nervous system in general as well as the specific histological features of the central nervous system.
Health and Safety; Science - Natural
Dist - HSCIC **Prod** - HSCIC

Nervous System - Pt 2 - Peripheral Nervous System 39 MIN
U-matic / VHS
Histology review series
Color (PRO)
Discusses the peripheral nerve and examines the components of the reflex arc, includes collection of information in the periphery and transmission of that information to the CNS. Presents the route of the motor response to the peripheral effector organ and describes the components of the reflex arc of the autonomic nervous system.
Health and Safety; Science - Natural
Dist - HSCIC **Prod** - HSCIC

Nervous System, the, Pt 2 60 MIN
U-matic / VHS
Biology of Cognition and Language Series Program 10; Program 10
Color (A)
Presents biologist Humberto Maturana discussing the human nervous system.
Science - Natural
Dist - UCEMC **Prod** - UCEMC

Nervous Systems in Animals 17 MIN
16mm / U-matic / VHS
Animal Systems Series
Color (H C A)
LC 75-701110
Shows the response of different animals to stimuli shows the structure of the nervous systems in a variety of animals.
Science - Natural
Dist - IU **Prod** - IU 1971

Nervous Tissue I 18 MIN
U-matic
Microanatomy Laboratory Orientation Series
Color (C)
Demonstrates the neuron in its various forms, multipolar, bipolar and unipolar, with both aniline dye stained and metallic impregnation preparations.
Health and Safety; Science - Natural
Dist - UOKLAH **Prod** - UOKLAH 1986

Nervous Tissue II 12 MIN
U-matic
Microanatomy Laboratory Orientation Series
Color (C)
Covers the peripheral processes of the neuron. The supporting cells of the peripheral units are discussed with emphasis on the Schwann cell.
Health and Safety; Science - Natural
Dist - UOKLAH **Prod** - UOKLAH 1986

Nervous Tissue III 9 MIN
U-matic
Microanatomy Laboratory Orientation Series
Color (C)
Demonstrates the principle end organs including Meissner's, Golgi - Mazzone, Pacinian, and genital corpuscles and the muscle spindle.
Health and Safety; Science - Natural
Dist - UOKLAH **Prod** - UOKLAH 1986

Nervous Tissue - Stains 16 MIN
U-matic
Microanatomy Laboratory Orientation Series
Color (C)
Introduces the various special staining techniques required to demonstrate the cells and fibers of the nervous system.
Health and Safety; Science - Natural
Dist - UOKLAH **Prod** - UOKLAH 1986

Nesika - a Specialized Group Home 15 MIN
U-matic
Color
Relates the transfer of eight severely/profoundly handicapped adults to a specialized group home. Cautions that transfer should be based on decisions made by the client, family and professionals.
Psychology
Dist - UWASHP **Prod** - UWASHP

Nested for - NEXT Loops 60 MIN
U-matic / VHS
Introduction to BASIC Series Lecture 10; Lecture 10
Color
Industrial and Technical Education; Mathematics
Dist - UIDEEO **Prod** - UIDEEO

Nested loops and more about program design 30 MIN
VHS / U-matic
Programming for microcomputers series; Units 16 and 17
Color (J)
LC 83-707134
Examines programs which illustrate nested loops, crossed loops and three - level nesting. Displays programs with loops correctly and incorrectly nested. Demonstrates a program with three - level nesting and a final program which shows nested loops used with strings. Defines and analyzes a problem, then develops a solution and a

solution algorithm. Presents criteria against which these steps are checked. Designs program output using grid sheets and storyboarding techniques and shows the criteria to be considered.
Mathematics
Dist - IU **Prod** - IU 1983

Nesting of Patterns 10 MIN
BETA / VHS
Color (IND)
Explains the application of nesting patterns or parts together to eliminate wasteful cutting or shearing of sheet material.
Industrial and Technical Education; Psychology
Dist - RMIBHF **Prod** - RMIBHF

Nesting Redwinged Blackbirds 8 MIN
16mm
Color (I)
LC FIA66-500
Depicts the mating, nesting and migratory habits of the nesting redwinged blackbird. Shows alfalfa fields as nesting sites and explains a new census technique.
Science - Natural
Dist - OSUMPD **Prod** - OSUMPD 1965

Nesting - the relationship between nest site and survival 12 MIN
U-matic / VHS / BETA
Color (P I)
$29.95, $130.00 purchase _ #LSTF86
Explains the important relationship between a bird's nesting site and its survival and reproduction. Looks at the nests and nesting habits of the Bald Eagle, Eastern Bluebird and American Robin. Produced by Nature Episodes. Includes teachers' guide.
Science - Natural
Dist - FEDU

Nestle's Quick with Jimmy Nelson and Danny O'Day and Farfel 1 MIN
U-matic / VHS
Color
Shows a classic television commercial with great nostalgia and the Nestle's jingle.
Business and Economics; Psychology; Sociology
Dist - BROOKC **Prod** - BROOKC

Nestorians and Syrians - 4 30 MIN
U-matic / VHS / BETA
Abraham's posterity series
Color; PAL (G H C)
PdS50, PdS58 purchase
Follows the journeys which Abraham made some 4000 years ago. Offers a dramatic interpretation at the events which are today tearing the region apart. Part of a thirteen - part series. A Cine & Tele Production, Brussels, Belgium.
Fine Arts; History - World; Religion and Philosophy
Dist - EDPAT

Nestorians and Syrians, Primitive Christian Churches 27 MIN
VHS / U-matic
In the Footsteps of Abraham Series
Color (J H C A)
MV=$375.00
Evangelized by St Thomas, the Christians of Mesopotamia and Persia spread as far as India and China. Cut off from the West, these churches developed separately in seclusion.
Religion and Philosophy
Dist - LANDMK **Prod** - LANDMK 1984

Net Festival Series
The Chicago Picasso 60 MIN
Dist - IU

NET journal series
Justice and the Poor 60 MIN
The Poor pay more 60 MIN
The Poor pay more - Pt 1 30 MIN
The Poor pay more - Pt 2 30 MIN
Right of privacy 59 MIN
The Smoking Spiral 60 MIN
The Welfare Revolt 60 MIN
What Harvest for the Reaper 59 MIN
Dist - IU

NET Outtake series
Allen Ginsberg - 7 - 18 - 65 55 MIN
Anne Sexton - 3 - 1 - 66 90 MIN
Charles Olson - 7 - 1 - 65 26 MIN
Charles Olson - 3 - 12 - 66 120 MIN
Ed Sanders - 3 - 18 - 66 26 MIN
Frank O'Hara - 2 - 27 - 69 35 MIN
Gary Snyder - 7 - 1 - 65 37 MIN
John Ashbery - 3 - 4 - 66 46 MIN
John Wieners - 7 - 1 - 65 60 MIN
Kenneth Koch - 3 - 3 - 66 60 MIN
Lawrence Ferlinghetti - 2 - 13 - 65 37 MIN
Louis Zukofsky - 3 - 16 - 66 30 MIN
Michael McClure - 1 - 22 - 66 47 MIN
Philip Whalen - 11 - 10 - 65 37 MIN
Richard Wilbur - 3 - 8 - 66 38 MIN
Robert Creeley - 7 - 15 - 65 45 MIN
Robert Duncan - 11 - 2 - 65 42 MIN
William Everson - Brother Antoninus - 1 - 25 - 61 55 MIN
Dist - POETRY

Net Play 21 MIN
VHS / 16mm / U-matic
Tennis Series
Color (J)
LC 76-701218
Features a clinic approach to teaching group tennis. Shows how to teach net play.
Physical Education and Recreation
Dist - ATHI **Prod** - ATHI 1976

The Net Result is Survival 13 MIN
16mm / U-matic / VHS
Color (IND)
Shows how construction safety nets are manufactured, tested and installed, and how essential it is to use one on the site not only to prevent injury but to instill worker confidence.
Health and Safety; Industrial and Technical Education; Psychology
Dist - IFB **Prod** - CSAO

Net Worth
VHS
Financial Planning and Management Series
(C G)
$59.00_CA277
Covers personal net worth.
Business and Economics
Dist - AAVIM **Prod** - AAVIM 1989

The NETA comprehensive preparatory video course 240 MIN
VHS
Color (H)
$197.00 purchase _ #00368 - 126
Helps students improve their SAT scores. Offers drill and practice, a complete course of unit - by - unit instruction. Uses visual illustrations and explanations, over 20 hours of coordinated workbook exercises, diagnostic practice tests and teaches test strategies. Produced by National Educational Test Aids, Inc.
Education; Psychology
Dist - GA

Netherlands 30 MIN
VHS
Essential history of Europe
Color; PAL (H C A)
PdS65 purchase; Not available in Denmark
Presents the culture and history of the Netherlands from an insider's perspective. Fifth in a series of 12 programs featuring the history of European Community member countries.
Geography - World; History - World
Dist - BBCENE

The Netherlands 16 MIN
VHS
Color (J H G)
$59.00 purchase _ #MF - 4677C
Captures the beauty of the Netherlands in a nonverbal program. Views the countryside, waterways, castles in a production by the Netherlands Government Information Service.
Geography - World
Dist - INSTRU **Prod** - CORF

The Netherlands ; 1988 19 MIN
16mm
Modern Europe series
Color (I J H)
LC 88-712594; 88-712596
Illustrates the culture, history, geography, art economics, sports and government of the Netherlands.
History - World
Dist - JOU **Prod** - INTERF 1987

The Netherlands - a Traditional Menu 28 MIN
U-matic / VHS / 16mm
World of Cooking Series
Color (J)
Shows chef Hans Clemens preparing a traditional Dutch meal.
Geography - World; Home Economics
Dist - CORF **Prod** - SCRESC

The Netherlands - Blueprint for an Urban Society 16 MIN
U-matic / VHS / 16mm
Color (I J H)
Explains how the Netherlands is handling its development into an urban society. Shows the reclamation of land from the sea, the mechanized agriculture, and the large housing projects.
Agriculture; Geography - World; Industrial and Technical Education; Social Science; Sociology
Dist - EBEC **Prod** - EBEC 1971

The Netherlands - people against the sea 17 MIN
VHS
Color; PAL (P I J H)
Reveals that one - fourth of the land surface in the Netherlands is below sea level, that there are a thousand lakes and five thousand miles of waterways in the country. Looks at the population and their pursuit of agricultural and industrial vocations and leisure activities which characterize their traditions and outlook for the future.
Geography - World; History - World; Science - Natural
Dist - VIEWTH **Prod** - VIEWTH

The Netherlands - People Against the Sea 16 MIN
16mm / U-matic / VHS
Color (H)
LC 72-700526
Shows Dutch people engaged in a variety of agricultural, industrial and leisurely activities which characterize their traditions and outlook for the future.
Geography - World; Social Science; Sociology
Dist - CORF **Prod** - CORF 1972

Netscape - the easiet way to surf the Internet - your guide to downloading, searching, and browsing
VHS
Color (C PRO G)
$89.00 purchase _ #503
Shows how to navigate the Internet. Gives a brief history of Netscape, an explanation of the World Wide Web and its language and explains how to obtain your free copy of the Netscape for IBM or Macintosh platforms. Gives lessons on using major tools and icons and an overview of Home Pages. Features Chuck Drake as instructor.
Computer Science; Social Science
Dist - EDREGR **Prod** - EDREGR 1995

The Netsilik Eskimo Today 18 MIN
16mm
Color
LC 73-702043
Shows the settled community life of the Netsilik Eskimos, which was established since 1965 under the auspices of the Canadian government, replacing their traditional migrational pattern of life.
Geography - World; Social Science
Dist - EDC **Prod** - EDC 1973

Network 121 MIN
16mm
Color
Tells how a TV newsman with low ratings and suicidal tendencies becomes a folk hero and a media star. Stars Faye Dunaway, William Holden, Peter Finch and Robert Duvall. Directed by Sidney Lumet.
Fine Arts
Dist - UAE **Prod** - UAA 1977

Network analysis with muliple voltage sources 15 MIN
U-matic / VHS
Basic electricity and D C circuits - laboratory series
Color
Industrial and Technical Education; Science - Physical; Social Science
Dist - TXINLC **Prod** - TXINLC

Network analysis with multiple voltage sources
U-matic / VHS
Basic D C circuits series
Color
Industrial and Technical Education; Science - Physical
Dist - VTRI **Prod** - VTRI

Network Architecture 48 MIN
VHS / U-matic
Telecommunications and the Computer Series
Color
Describes network architecture.
Industrial and Technical Education; Mathematics
Dist - MIOT **Prod** - MIOT

Network Architectures - a Communications Revolution Series
Public Data Networks 45 MIN
Systems Network Architecture 45 MIN
Trends 45 MIN
Dist - DELTAK

Network Concepts for Users 20 MIN
U-matic / VHS
User - Directed Information Systems Series
Color
Develops the concepts of computer networks and communications alternatives and discusses the effects of these techniques on the business environment. Illustrates the user's role in planning and implementing these technologies.
Business and Economics; Industrial and Technical Education; Psychology
Dist - DELTAK **Prod** - DELTAK

Network Control for Operators 45 MIN
U-matic / VHS
Color
Discusses the functions involved in network control and the role of the network control operator. Presents the network control operator's responsibilities in monitoring and controlling the network, problem determination and resolution, and recording and reporting network information.
Industrial and Technical Education; Psychology
Dist - DELTAK **Prod** - DELTAK

Network News - That's the Way it is 29 MIN
VHS / U-matic
Inside Story Series
Color
Looks at the changing shape and direction of television's network news. Explores the topics of the stakes involved in the highly competitive race for ratings, the proposed hour - long evening news format and the question of whether the increasing use of high - tech video tools and the anchorman 'star' system put a higher premium on the image than on the essence of the story.
Fine Arts; Sociology
Dist - PBS **Prod** - PBS 1981

Network Structures for Finite Impulse Response - FIR - Digital Filters 51 MIN
VHS / U-matic
Digital Signal Processing Series
Color (PRO)
Covers network structures for finite impulse response (FIR)digital filters and parameter - quantification effects in digital filter structures.
Industrial and Technical Education; Mathematics
Dist - GPCV **Prod** - GPCV

Network Structures for Infinite Impulse - IIR - Digital Filters 40 MIN
U-matic / VHS
Digital Signal Processing - an Introduction Series
Color
Industrial and Technical Education; Mathematics
Dist - MIOT **Prod** - MIOT

Network Structures for Infinite Impulse Response - IIR - Digital Filters 40 MIN
U-matic / VHS
Digital Signal Processing Series
Color (PRO)
Industrial and Technical Education; Mathematics
Dist - GPCV **Prod** - GPCV

Networking 30 MIN
VHS / U-matic
Programmable Controllers Series
Color
Deals with networking. Covers topologies and access.
Industrial and Technical Education; Sociology
Dist - ITCORP **Prod** - ITCORP

Networking - connections to employment 12 MIN
VHS
From pink slip to paycheck series
Color (A G)
$69.00 purchase _ #4186
Shows older workers experiencing unemployment how to use networking in a seach for employment. Features Richard Bolles, author of What Color Is Your Parachute; William Morin - Drake Beam Morin; and others who offer practical, upbeat advice on developing a job search strategy, feeling positive about oneself, communicating clearly and learning to present oneself as an asset and a resource to potential employees. Part of a five - part series.
Business and Economics; Guidance and Counseling
Dist - NEWCAR

Networking Topologies and Routing, Pt 1 40 MIN
U-matic / VHS
Packet Switching Series
Color
Industrial and Technical Education; Mathematics; Sociology
Dist - MIOT **Prod** - MIOT

Networking Topologies and Routing, Pt 2 43 MIN
U-matic / VHS
Packet Switching Series
Color
Industrial and Technical Education; Mathematics; Sociology
Dist - MIOT **Prod** - MIOT

Networking your way to success 30 MIN
VHS
FYI video series
Color (H C G)
$79.95 purchase _ #AMA84010V
Shows how to create personal support systems, enhance professional development and take advantage of opportunities by building and using informal networks.
Business and Economics; Guidance and Counseling; Social Science
Dist - CAMV **Prod** - AMA 1991

Networking your way to success 30 MIN
VHS
Color (G PRO)
$79.95 purchase _ #739 - 67
Gives networking insights, guidelines and techniques - from breaking the ice in social situations to improving on - the - job performance. Shows how to build and use informal networks, take advantage of unexpected opportunities, create personal support systems and enhance professional development.
Business and Economics; Psychology; Social Science
Dist - MEMIND **Prod** - AMA

Networks and Distributed Data Processing 30 MIN
VHS / U-matic
Making it Count Series
Color (H C A)
LC 80-707583
Describes data communication techniques, network switching systems and network configurations. Discusses the different types of terminals and compares the advantages of centralized versus distributed systems.
Business and Economics; Mathematics
Dist - BCSC **Prod** - BCSC 1980

Networks and Matrices 14 MIN
16mm / U-matic / VHS
Color
Shows how a 'flow' in a network can be represented by a matrix.
Mathematics
Dist - MEDIAG **Prod** - OPENU 1979

Networks of Adaptation 28 MIN
U-matic / VHS
Life of Plants Series
Color (C)
$249.00, $149.00 purchase _ #AD - 1682
Considers the intricacies of adaptation. Looks at the consequences of changing the ecological balance, global consequences of the continual extinction of species, the ecological effect of international trade and travel which constantly transposes species from their natural to new habitats. Part of a series on plants.
Science - Natural
Dist - FOTH **Prod** - FOTH

Networks of Knowledge 26 MIN
16mm
Color (H C A)
LC 81-700066
Depicts work being done in various countries by the United Nations University.
Civics and Political Systems
Dist - UNUNIV **Prod** - UNUNIV 1979

Networks, paths and knots
VHS
Math vantage videos series
Color (I J H)
$39.00 purchase _ #654203 - HH
Looks at mathematical networks, paths and knots. Part of a five - part series using interactive learning, interdisciplinary approaches, mathematical connections, student involvement and exploration to enable students to use patterns to explain, create and predict situations.
Mathematics
Dist - SUNCOM **Prod** - NEBMSI 1994

Neues Leben Bluht Aus Den Ruinen 107 MIN
16mm
B&W (GERMAN (ENGLISH SUBTITLES))
A German language film with English subtitles. Combines a documentary and newsfilm from the German post - war era on the Ruhr.
Fine Arts; Foreign Language
Dist - WSTGLC **Prod** - WSTGLC 1980

Neues Vom Raeuber Hotzenplotz 98 MIN
16mm
Color (GERMAN (ENGLISH SUBTITLES))
A German language motion picture available with or without English subtitles. Features a robber's kidnapping of a grandmother and Sergeant Dimpfelmoser's attempt to free her.
Foreign Language; Sociology
Dist - WSTGLC **Prod** - WSTGLC 1978

Neun Leben Hat Die Katze 91 MIN
16mm
Color (GERMAN (ENGLISH SUBTITLES))
A German language film with English subtitles. Presents a collage about five women in the Federal Republic of Germany during a week's time. Portrays the five women, who are in pursuit of happiness, and who have, in reality, adjusted to the circumstances in which they live.
Fine Arts; Foreign Language
Dist - WSTGLC **Prod** - WSTGLC 1968

Neuro - Developmental Assessment 15 MIN
U-matic
Nursing Assessment of the Infant Series
(PRO)
Exhibits a regular clinic examination, during which the nurse tests for age appropriate reflexes of oral, eye, neck, grasp, gross and fine motor development in an infant.
Health and Safety
Dist - ACCESS **Prod** - ACCESS 1984

Neuro - Otologic Evaluation 58 MIN
U-matic / VHS
Color (PRO)
Reviews the auditory, vestibular and radiographic tests used to evaluate patients suspected of having a tumor when these internal audiometry canal and cerebellopontine angle lesions are producing minimal symptoms, particularly when small.
Guidance and Counseling; Health and Safety; Science - Natural
Dist - HOUSEI **Prod** - HOUSEI

Neuroanatomy Demonstrations, Pt 01 57 MIN
U-matic / VHS
Neuroanatomy Demonstrations Series
Color (PRO)
Includes topography - brain and spinal cord in situ, major divisions of the brain and their relation to the embryonic brain, and detailed topography of the major divisions of the brain.
Science - Natural
Dist - USNAC **Prod** - USHHS

Neuroanatomy Demonstrations - Pt 02 51 MIN
VHS / U-matic
Neuroanatomy Demonstrations Series
Color (PRO)
Includes topography - cranial nerves, cerebral blood vessels, ventricles and cerebrospinal fluid.
Science - Natural
Dist - USNAC **Prod** - USHHS

Neuroanatomy Demonstrations - Pt 03 58 MIN
VHS / U-matic
Neuroanatomy Demonstrations Series
Color (PRO)
Includes dissection of the brain stem - middle cerebellar peduncle and auditory nerve, inferior and superior cerebellar peduncles and dissection of the hemispheres - long association bundles, and extreme and external capsules and related structures.
Science - Natural
Dist - USNAC **Prod** - USHHS

Neuroanatomy Demonstrations - Pt 04 41 MIN
VHS / U-matic
Neuroanatomy Demonstrations Series
Color (PRO)
Includes dissection of the hemispheres - basal ganglia, anterior commissure and internal capsule, olfactory system and limbic system.
Science - Natural
Dist - USNAC **Prod** - USHHS

Neuroanatomy Demonstrations - Pt 05 55 MIN
U-matic / VHS
Neuroanatomy Demonstrations Series
Color (PRO)
Includes proprioception, vibratory, tactile, pain and temperature pathways and trigeminal pathways.
Science - Natural
Dist - USNAC **Prod** - USHHS

Neuroanatomy Demonstrations - Pt 06 56 MIN
U-matic / VHS
Neuroanatomy Demonstrations Series
Color (PRO)
Includes visceral afferents, vestibular and cochlear systems and visual system.
Science - Natural
Dist - USNAC **Prod** - USHHS

Neuroanatomy Demonstrations - Pt 07 36 MIN
U-matic / VHS
Neuroanatomy Demonstrations Series
Color (PRO)
Includes dorsal thalamus and pyradial system.
Science - Natural
Dist - USNAC **Prod** - USHHS

Neuroanatomy Demonstrations - Pt 08 53 MIN
VHS / U-matic
Neuroanatomy Demonstrations Series
Color (PRO)
Includes cerebellar connections and extrapyramidal system.
Science - Natural
Dist - USNAC **Prod** - USHHS

Neuroanatomy Demonstrations - Pt 09 53 MIN
VHS / U-matic
Neuroanatomy Demonstrations Series
Color (PRO)
Includes the autonomic nervous system and olfactory and limbic systems.
Science - Natural
Dist - USNAC **Prod** - USHHS

Neuroanatomy Demonstrations - Pt 10 12 MIN
U-matic / VHS
Neuroanatomy Demonstrations Series
Color (PRO)
Includes a video synopsis.
Science - Natural
Dist - USNAC **Prod** - USHHS

Neuroanatomy Demonstrations Series

Neuroanatomy Demonstrations - Pt 02	51 MIN
Neuroanatomy Demonstrations - Pt 03	58 MIN
Neuroanatomy Demonstrations - Pt 04	41 MIN
Neuroanatomy Demonstrations - Pt 05	55 MIN
Neuroanatomy Demonstrations - Pt 06	56 MIN
Neuroanatomy Demonstrations - Pt 07	36 MIN
Neuroanatomy Demonstrations - Pt 08	53 MIN
Neuroanatomy Demonstrations - Pt 09	53 MIN
Neuroanatomy Demonstrations - Pt 10	12 MIN
Neuroanatomy Demonstrations, Pt 01	57 MIN

Dist - USNAC

Neuroanatomy Series

Human Brain in Dissection, Pt I - Embryology and Introduction to the Dissection of the Brain	19 MIN
Human Brain in Dissection, Pt II - General Structure of the Brain	15 MIN
Human Brain in Dissection, Pt III - the Meninges and Dural Venous Sinuses	25 MIN
Human Brain in Dissection, Pt III - the Meninges and Dural Venous Sinuses - a	24 MIN
Human Brain in Dissection, Pt IV, the Blood Supply of the Brain	28 MIN
Human Brain in Dissection, Pt IV, the Blood Supply of the Brain - a Self - Evaluation	24 MIN
Human Brain in Dissection, Pt V - Topography of the Cerebral Hemispheres	20 MIN
Human Brain in Dissection, Pt V - Topography of the Cerebral Hemispheres - a	25 MIN
Human Brain in Dissection, Pt V (a) - Cerebral Localisation of Function - a	25 MIN
Human Brain in Dissection, Pt V (a) - Cerebral Localization of Function	36 MIN
Human Brain in Dissection, Pt VI - the White Matter of the Cerebral Hemispheres and the	39 MIN
Human Brain in Dissection, Pt VII (a) - the Rhinencephalon	18 MIN
Human Brain in Dissection, Pt VII (a) - the Rhinencephalon - a Self - Evaluation Exercise	19 MIN
Human Brain in Dissection, Pt X - the Brain Stem - External Features	37 MIN
Human Brain in Dissection, Pt X - the Brain Stem - External Features - a Self - Evaluation	25 MIN
Human Brain in Dissection, Pt X (a) - the Cranial Nerve Nuclei	40 MIN
Human Brain in Dissection, Pt XI - the Spinal Cord	51 MIN
Human Brain in Dissection, Pt XI - the Spinal Cord - a Self - Evaluation Exercise	28 MIN
The Human Brain in Section	57 MIN
Introduction to the examination of the brain in section	51 MIN
Lateral Cerebral Ventricle and the Fornix - a Self - Evaluation Exercise	18 MIN
Lateral Cerebral Ventricles and the Fornix	20 MIN
Practical examination in neuroanatomy - Pt I	56 MIN
Practical examination in neuroanatomy - Pt II	34 MIN

Dist - TEF

Neurobiology Series

The Basal ganglia and related nuclei	15 MIN
The Brainstem and the Cranial Nerves	13 MIN
The Cerebellum	15 MIN
The Diencephalon	20 MIN
The External circulation of the brain	15 MIN
The Internal Structure of the Brain	15 MIN
Major Divisions and Areas of Function	19 MIN
The Medulla Oblongata	15 MIN
The Mesencephalon	15 MIN
The Pons	15 MIN
The Ventricular System	15 MIN

Dist - HSCIC

Neurodevelopment 30 MIN
VHS
Beginnings - handicapped children birth to age 5 series
Color (G)
$75.00 purchase _ #BHCH - 102
Features Dr Philippa Campbell, who outlines the concepts of neurodevelopment in children. Focuses on problems which are common in handicapped children. Part of a series on child development focusing on handicapped children.
Health and Safety; Psychology; Science - Natural
Dist - PBS **Prod** - MDDE 1985

Neuroleptic Drugs and Adjunctive Medications 29 MIN
U-matic
Psychotropic Drugs and the Health Care Professional Series
Color
Illustrates and discusses neuroleptic or antipsychotic medications. Reviews major mental illnesses.
Health and Safety; Psychology
Dist - UWASHP **Prod** - UWASHP

Neurologic - Cranial Nerves and Sensory System; 2nd ed 22 MIN
16mm
Visual Guide to Physical Examination
Color (PRO)
LC 81-701523
Demonstrates the physical examination of the cranial nerves and sensory system, showing necessary procedures, manipulation, pacing, positions and patient - examiner interaction.
Health and Safety
Dist - LIP **Prod** - LIP 1981

Neurologic Examination, Pt 1 20 MIN
16mm
Pediatric Examination - Art and Process Series
Color (PRO)
LC 78-700681
Demonstrates techniques and processes involved in a thorough pediatric neurologic examination.
Health and Safety
Dist - LIP **Prod** - TUNNEW 1978

Neurologic Examination, Pt 2 20 MIN
16mm
Pediatric Examination - Art and Process Series
Color (PRO)
LC 78-700681
Demonstrates techniques and processes involved in a thorough pediatric neurologic examination.
Health and Safety
Dist - LIP **Prod** - TUNNEW 1978

Neurologic - Motor System and Reflexes; 2nd ed 18 MIN
16mm
Visual Guide to Physical Examination
Color (PRO)
LC 81-701524
Demonstrates the physical examination of the motor system and reflexes, showing necessary procedures, manipulations, pacing, positions and patient - examiner interaction.
Health and Safety
Dist - LIP **Prod** - LIP 1981

Neurological assessment 30 MIN
VHS
Physical assessment series
Color (PRO C)
$150.00 purchase, $70.00 rental _ #4411
Gives detailed information on how to conduct a systematic examination of the neurological system, including mental status, functions of the cranial nerves, motor ability, sensory perception and deep tendon reflexes. Includes information on how to use the reflex hammer and tuning forks. Part of a seven - part series providing step - by - step guides to physical assessment of various body systems for nursing students and professionals.
Health and Safety; Psychology
Dist - AJN **Prod** - ANSELM 1995

Neurological Assessment - Cerebellar Function, Motor Function, Reflexes and 20 MIN
U-matic / VHS
Physical Assessment Series
Color
Explains how to test for balance and coordination, motor function, reflex arcs and sensory perception of lights, touch, superficial and deep pain, temperature, position and vibration. Emphasizes those tests which are most commonly used.
Health and Safety; Science; Science - Natural
Dist - AJN **Prod** - SUNHSC

Neurological Assessment - Cranial Nerves 17 MIN
VHS / U-matic
Physical Assessment Series
Color
Shows how to perform a systematic examination of the cranial nerves. Demonstrates what equipment to use, how to perform each test and how to interpret the findings.
Health and Safety; Science; Science - Natural
Dist - AJN **Prod** - SUNHSC

Neurological assessment of the pediatric patient 28 MIN
U-matic / VHS
Color (PRO)
$285.00 purchase, $70.00 rental _ #7001S, 7001V
Describes the basic neurological examination for infants, toddlers, and children. Illustrates proper procedures in physical assessment and communication skills to obtain a reliable neurological assessment. Covers the components of assessment, including level of consciousness, the Glasgow Coma Scale, pupillary responses, motor function, vital signs, head measurements, and reflexes. Demonstrates the best techniques for examining the combative child or a child who is comatose, and variations in assessment for infants and older children. Approved for continuing education credit. Includes study guide.
Health and Safety; Psychology
Dist - AJN **Prod** - HOSSN 1990

Neurological exam, Part A 26 MIN
VHS / U-matic / BETA
Techniques of physical diagnosis - a visual approach series
Color (PRO)
$395.00 purchase _ #106 - A
Reviews the techniques for evaluating mental status, cranial nerves and the motor system. Part of a series by Dr Donald W Novey teaching the basic skills of physical examinations as seen through the eyes of the examiner.
Health and Safety
Dist - MEDMDS

Neurological exam, Part B 22 MIN
VHS / U-matic / BETA
Techniques of physical diagnosis - a visual approach series
Color (PRO)
$395.00 purchase _ #106 - B
Reviews the evaluation of deep tendon and superficial reflexes, sensory functions and additional tests. Part of a series by Dr Donald W Novey teaching the basic skills of physical examination as seen through the eyes of the examiner.
Health and Safety
Dist - MEDMDS

The Neurological Examination
U-matic / VHS
Color
Health and Safety; Psychology
Dist - MEDMDS **Prod** - MEDMDS

Neurological Examination
VHS / U-matic
Color
Reviews the appropriate techniques used to challenge or evaluate problems, or suspected problems in the nervous system. Reviews the neurological examination and demonstrates procedures at the patient's bedside.
Psychology; Science - Natural
Dist - AMEDA **Prod** - AMEDA

Neurological Examination of Children 41 MIN
VHS / U-matic
Color (PRO)
Demonstrates neurological examinations of young children. Includes general appearance, head, cranial nerves, motor system and primitive reflexes in newborn, at six, twelve and eighteen months.
Health and Safety
Dist - UARIZ **Prod** - UARIZ

Neurological Examination of the Newborn Infant 30 MIN
U-matic / VHS
Color (PRO)
Establishes standards in neonatal examination. Shows normal and abnormal responses to a series of neurological tests.
Health and Safety; Science - Natural
Dist - WFP **Prod** - WFP

Neurological Examination of the One Year Old 29 MIN
VHS / U-matic
Color (PRO)
Establishes standards for examination of infants at one year of age. Shows normal and abnormal responses to neurological tests.
Health and Safety; Science - Natural
Dist - WFP **Prod** - WFP

Neurological Health Assessment - Cerebellum 28 MIN
U-matic / VHS

Health Assessment Series
Color (PRO)
Views a physical assessment by a nurse practitioner of the cerebellum spinal nerves of a live patient.
Health and Safety; Science - Natural
Dist - BRA **Prod** - BRA

Neurological Health Assessment - Cerebellum 35 MIN
VHS / U-matic
Health Assessment Series Module 11; Module 11
Color (PRO)
Health and Safety; Science - Natural
Dist - MDCC **Prod** - MDCC

Neurological Health Assessment - Cerebellum Spinal Nerves 35 MIN
VHS / U-matic
Health Assessment Series
Color (PRO)
Views a physical assessment by a nurse practitioner of the cerebellum cranial nerves of a live patient.
Health and Safety; Science - Natural
Dist - BRA **Prod** - BRA

Neurological Instruments 12 MIN
U-matic
Instruments of Physical Assessment Series
Color (PRO)
LC 80-707629
Demonstrates various types of hammers and tuning forks used in neurological examinations. Discusses the use of common objects, such as safety pins, keys, and coins, during these examinations.
Health and Safety
Dist - LIP **Prod** - SUNYSB 1980

Neurological Test Film 30 MIN
16mm
Color (PRO)
Consists of a film designed for testing neurology students. Presents five patient examinations - - miltiple sclerosis, Parkinsonism, amyotropic lateral sclerosis, muscular dystrophy (child) and myasthenia gravis.
Health and Safety; Science - Natural
Dist - UCLA **Prod** - UCLA 1970

Neurologically disabled patient, pt 2 - nursing during the rehabilitative series
Activities of daily living - skin and joint intergrity 30 MIN
Dist - AJN

Neurology 46 MIN
U-matic / VHS
Attorneys' Guide to Medicine Series
Color (PRO)
Includes a review of basic terminology and anatomy of the nervous system, a description of typical neurological injuries and an explanation of how neurological problems are diagnosed for the benefit of attorneys.
Civics and Political Systems; Health and Safety
Dist - ABACPE **Prod** - PBI

Neuromotor Assessment of Cerebral Palsy, Athetosis 46 MIN
VHS / U-matic
Pediatric Assessment Series
Color
Health and Safety; Psychology
Dist - UMDSM **Prod** - UMDSM

Neuromotor Assessment of Cerebral Palsy, Pre - Post Test 23 MIN
VHS / U-matic
Pediatric Assessment Series
Color
Health and Safety; Psychology
Dist - UMDSM **Prod** - UMDSM

Neuromotor Assessment of Cerebral Palsy, Spastic Hemiplegia 52 MIN
U-matic / VHS
Pediatric Assessment Series
Color
Health and Safety; Psychology
Dist - UMDSM **Prod** - UMDSM

Neuromotor Assessment of Cerebral Palsy Spastic Quadriplegia 50 MIN
U-matic / VHS
Pediatric Assessment Series
Color
Health and Safety; Psychology
Dist - UMDSM **Prod** - UMDSM

Neuromuscular and Skeletal Systems Involvement 26 MIN
U-matic / VHS
Individuals with Dysfunction Series
Color
Discusses how to assess the effects of renal failure on the nervous system prior to dialysis when changes in the patient's neuromuscular and skeletal systems are most apparent.
Health and Safety; Psychology
Dist - AJN **Prod** - AJN

Neuromuscular Disorders in Systemic Diseases 49 MIN
U-matic
Intensive Course in Neuromuscular Diseases Series
Color (PRO)
LC 76-706059
Presents Dr Bernard M Pattern discussing neuromuscular disorders in systemic diseases.
Health and Safety; Science - Natural
Dist - USNAC **Prod** - NINDIS 1974

Neuromuscular Disorders of Infancy 43 MIN
U-matic
Intensive Course in Neuromuscular Diseases Series
Color (PRO)
LC 76-706060
Presents Dr Hans U Zellweger giving a lecture on neuromuscular disorders of infancy.
Health and Safety; Science - Natural
Dist - USNAC **Prod** - NINDIS 1974

Neuromuscular Junction Electron Microscopy 29 MIN
U-matic
Intensive Course in Neuromuscular Diseases Series
Color (PRO)
LC 76-706061
Presents Dr Michael Fardeau illustrating neuromuscular junction electron microscopy.
Health and Safety; Science; Science - Natural
Dist - USNAC **Prod** - NINDIS 1974

Neuromuscular Training for Golf with Al Geiberger
VHS
(H C A)
$69.95 purchase _ #DG013V
Demonstrates neuromuscular training for golf players.
Physical Education and Recreation
Dist - CAMV

The Neuron 60 MIN
U-matic
Nonbehavioral Sciences and Rehabilitation Series Part II
Color (PRO)
Describes the structural and functional unit of the nervous system. Discusses the supporting cells in relation to the neuron, types of neurons and differences of myelination in the central nervous system versus the parasympathetic nervous system, growth and development of neurons, and the importance of synapses.
Psychology; Science - Natural
Dist - AOTA **Prod** - AOTA 1980

The Neuron Suite 58 MIN
U-matic / VHS
Color
LC 83-706164
Presents host James Burke exploring research in brain chemistry, using a luxury hotel as a vast analog for the operation of the brain as an information transmitter.
Science - Natural
Dist - PBS **Prod** - PBS 1982

The Neuropathies 42 MIN
U-matic
Intensive Course in Neuromuscular Diseases Series
Color (PRO)
LC 76-706062
Presents Dr David E Pleasure lecturing on the neuropathies.
Health and Safety; Science - Natural
Dist - USNAC **Prod** - NINDIS 1974

Neuropathology laboratory sessions series
Basic changes in neuropathology 22 MIN
Cerebrovascular Diseases and Traumas of the Central Nervous System 26 MIN
Children at risk - alcohol and pregnancy 16 MIN
Congenital Anomalies and Metabolic Diseases of the Central Nervous System 25 MIN
Demyelinating and degenerative diseases of the central nervous system 22 MIN
Diagnosis and management of dysfunctional uterine bleeding 53 MIN
Diagnostic Amniocentesis - Indications and Technique 35 MIN
Infectious Diseases of the Central Nervous System 20 MIN
Toxic and Deficiency Diseases of the Central Nervous System and Neuromuscular Diseases. 20 MIN
Tumors of the Central Nervous System 21 MIN
Dist - HSCIC

Neurophysiology of Pain 24 MIN
U-matic
Management of Pain Series Module 1
Color (PRO)
LC 80-707393
Health and Safety
Dist - BRA **Prod** - BRA 1980

The Neuropsychology of self - discipline and 'the fire that burns within' 30 MIN
Cassette / VHS
Color (G)
$89.95 purchase _ #3017
Helps develop self - mastery for career advancement. Offers an interactive multimedia kit which includes the video 'The Fire That Burns Within,' eight audiocassettes, study guide and planner.
Psychology; Sociology
Dist - SYBVIS **Prod** - SYBVIS

The Neuropsychology of Staying Young 30 MIN
Cassette / VHS
Color (G)
$69.95, $49.95 purchase _ #2027, 2026
Shows how to slow the aging process. Offers either an interactive multimedia program which includes video, eight audiocassettes and study guide or eight audiocassettes with study guide.
Health and Safety; Physical Education and Recreation; Psychology
Dist - SYBVIS **Prod** - SYBVIS

Neurosciences citation index
CD-ROM
(PRO)
Presents a CD - ROM database with searchable, English language, author abstracts, as well as Related Records which link articles sharing one or more common bibliographic reference. Spans all aspects of study involving the brain and nervous system and covers more than 200 journals directly related to the neurosciences. Covers an estimated 40,000 - 50,000 articles a year. Contact distributor for equipment requirements.
Health and Safety; Psychology; Science; Science - Natural
Dist - ISINFO **Prod** - ISINFO 1991

Neurospora Techniques 8 MIN
U-matic / VHS / 16mm
BSCS Biological Techniques Series
Color (H C T)
Shows how to culture and handle neurospora to demonstrate genetic principles. Crosses albine and arginine - deficient types with normal to demonstrate the principle of genetic segregation.
Science; Science - Natural
Dist - IFB **Prod** - THORNE 1962

Neurosurgery
U-matic / VHS
Color (PRO)
Discusses the relief of intracranial pressure, anatomy of the intracranial space, intracranial hemorrhage, cerebral abscesses, skull fractures, spinal cord compression, evaluation of the patient, therapy for intracranial mass lesions and increased cranial pressure, the role of the neurosurgical nurse, herniated discs, hydrocephalus and meningomyelocele, tumors, aneurysm and subarachnoid hemorrhage.
Health and Safety; Psychology
Dist - UMICHM **Prod** - UMICHM 1978

Neurosurgery - Facial Neuralgia 13 MIN
16mm
Color (PRO)
LC FIE52-1175
Demonstrates the surgical treatment of trigeminal and glossopharyngeal neuralgia.
Health and Safety
Dist - USNAC **Prod** - USN 1946

Neurotic Behavior - a Psychodynamic View 19 MIN
U-matic / VHS / 16mm
Abnormal Psychology Series
Color (C A)
LC 73-702813
Shows the basic dilemma of the neurotic and how mental defenses serve to reduce the anxiety. Takes a psychodynamic approach to neurotic behavior as it follows an episode in the life of Peter, a troubled college student who attempts to cope with reality.
Psychology; Sociology
Dist - CRMP **Prod** - CRMP 1973

The Neurotic Child 28 MIN
16mm
B&W (C A)
LC FIA68-2697
Describes a psychoneurotic seven - year - old boy in a clinical interview. Discusses the defensive mechaisms he has aquired in relating to the world. Illustrates his reactions to reality testing, his attitude toward his father and his inhibited aggressions.
Psychology
Dist - PSU **Prod** - PSUPCR 1968

Neurotransmitters
VHS
Brain Triggers - Biochemistry and Human Behavior Series
Color
Deals with neurotransnmitter substances in the brain and their function. Explains the process of electrochemical communication between cells.
Science - Natural
Dist - IBIS **Prod** - IBIS

The Neutral Zone in Complete Dentures - Pt 1 - Clinical Procedures 19 MIN
16mm
Color (PRO)
LC 78-701355
Describes and demonstrates the clinical procedures involved in recording the neutral zone for positioning denture teeth and defining the contours of the polished surface for dentures.
Health and Safety
Dist - USNAC **Prod** - VADTC 1978

The Neutral Zone in Complete Dentures - Pt 2 - Laboratory Procedures 11 MIN
16mm
Color (PRO)
LC 78-701356
Demonstrates the technical procedures for developing matrices of the neutral zone record and using them in establishing an occlusal plane and in anterior, posterior and medial lateral positioning of the supplied tooth.
Health and Safety
Dist - USNAC **Prod** - VADTC 1978

The Neutrocentric occlusal concept - arranging zero - degree nonanatomic posterior teeth 12 MIN
VHS / U-matic
Color (C PRO)
$395.00 purchase, $80.00 rental _ #D881 - VI - 012
Demonstrates the preparation for and setting of maxillary and mandibular posterior teeth according to the Neutrocentric Occlusal Concept. Presents the procedure as performed on a Class I angle jaw relation. Describes teeth - setting procedures of other anatomical conditions. Presented by Drs Darunee Nabadalung and Dale H Andrews.
Health and Safety
Dist - HSCIC

Neutron Activation 8 MIN
16mm
Color
LC FIE64-135
Describes the analytic techniques that are involved in measuring the presence of radioactive elements from a substance irradiated with neutrons.
Mathematics; Science
Dist - USNAC **Prod** - USNRC 1964

Neutron Activation Analysis 40 MIN
16mm
Color (C A)
Presents analysis by neutron activation. Covers types of source used counting techniques and applications.
Science; Science - Physical
Dist - USERD **Prod** - USNRC 1964

Neutron Diffraction 9 MIN
16mm
Color
LC FIE64-137
Describes the principles of neutron diffraction and the new fields of investigation involving diffraction effects. Compares wavelengths of thermal neutrons to X - rays used in the study of crystal structures and contrasts their different scattering processes. Discusses the usefulness of neutron diffraction studies in determining the positions of light atoms in the crystal structure and in providing a technique for the study of magnetic orientation.
Science
Dist - USNAC **Prod** - USNRC 1964

Neutrons at Work 29 MIN
Videoreel / VT2
Interface Series
Color
Business and Economics; Science - Physical
Dist - PBS **Prod** - KCET

Nevada
VHS / U-matic
Portrait of America Series
Color
Presents five segments about the state of Nevada, where the landscape is beautiful but the life can be harsh.
Geography - United States; History - United States
Dist - TBSESI **Prod** - TBSESI

Nevada 60 MIN
VHS
Portrait of America series
Color (J H C G)
$99.95 purchase _ #AMB28V
Visits Nevada. Offers extensive research into the state's history. Films key locations and presents segments on history, government, education, folklore, science, journalism, sociology, industry, agriculture and business. Shows what is unique about Nevada and distinctive about its regional culture and how it got to be that way. Includes study guide. Part of a 50 - part series.
Geography - United States; History - United States
Dist - CAMV

Nevelson - a life's work 27 MIN
35mm strip / VHS
Color (J H C T A)
$93.00 purchase _ #MB - 540615 - 2, #MB - 540616 - 0
Profiles sculptor Louise Nevelson, whose sculptural collages did not receive critical recognition until she was 60 years old. Features her major works.
Fine Arts
Dist - SRA **Prod** - SRA 1988

Nevelson in Process 30 MIN
16mm / U-matic / VHS
Originals - Women in Art Series
Color (H C A)
LC 80-700047
Contrasts sculptor Louise Nevelson's public and private lives. Demonstrates her technique of creating pieces out of discarded wood and offers her thoughts on her work.
Fine Arts
Dist - FI **Prod** - WNETTV 1977

Nevelson - women in art 30 MIN
VHS
Color (J H C G)
$39.95 purchase _ #HVS10V
Features Russian sculptor Louise Nevelson who narrates a program centering around her life, her responsibility for her family, the influences on her work and her determination to get to where she is today. Shows how she overcame a lack of financial support for supplies by digging through the trash of New York City to construct her environmental art. Reveals that she was in her 70s before art critics recognized her contribution to sculpture in America.
Fine Arts
Dist - CAMV

Never Alone 18 MIN
16mm
Color (PRO)
Portrays some of the ways in which chaplains in institutions for the mentally retarded work with other disciplines to meet the needs of the patients.
Guidance and Counseling; Psychology; Sociology
Dist - NMAC **Prod** - NMAC

Never among Strangers 14 MIN
16mm
Color
LC 74-705198
Shows the training, job opportunities and liberty available for prospective women Marine Corps recruits.
Civics and Political Systems; Education; Guidance and Counseling; Sociology
Dist - USNAC **Prod** - USMC 1968

Never Ask what Country 30 MIN
16mm
B&W (R)
Dramatizes the life of William Green, the son of a coal miner, who went into the mines at the age of 15, and had to give up his hopes of becoming a Baptist minister. Tells how from 1924 until his death he was president of the American Federation of Labor. (Kinescope).
Religion and Philosophy
Dist - NAAJS **Prod** - JTS 1962

Never Cry Rape
VHS / BETA
Color (J H C)
Shows how to defend oneself against an attacker and how to protect oneself from rape. Demonstrates physical and psychological strategies for self - defense, and what common reactions should be avoided.
Physical Education and Recreation; Sociology
Dist - GA **Prod** - GA

Never Cry Wolf 30 MIN
16mm / U-matic / VHS
Film as Literature, Series 5 Series; Series 5
Color (I J H)
Tells of a young government biologist who travels to the Arctic to gather information about wolves. Shows how he finds them to be tender, courageous animals who live in total harmony with their environment. From the book Never Cry Wolf by Farley Mowat.
Literature and Drama
Dist - CORF **Prod** - DISNEY 1983

Never Give a Sucker an Even Break 63 MIN
16mm
B&W
Stars W C Fields as a man who somehow becomes the guardian of a young girl.
Fine Arts
Dist - SWANK **Prod** - UPCI

Never Give Up 30 MIN
U-matic / VHS
Developing Discipline Series
Color (T)
Presents illustration of behaviors and motivations for irresponsible actions, and examples of success under extreme conditions.
Education; Guidance and Counseling; Psychology; Sociology
Dist - GPN **Prod** - SDPT 1983

Never Give Up - Imogen Cunningham 28 MIN
U-matic / VHS / 16mm
Color (J A)
LC 75-702963
Pictures a visit with portrait photographer Imogen Cunningham.
Fine Arts; Industrial and Technical Education
Dist - PHENIX **Prod** - HERSHA 1975

Never listen to a bottle 10 MIN
VHS
Dr Cooper and his friends series
Color (P) (FRENCH)
$50.00 purchase _ #PVK11, #PVK26
Presents a research scientist who, with his puppet lab assistants, conduct experiments on various substances. Explores alcohol. Includes a teacher's guide and a poster.
Guidance and Counseling; Health and Safety
Dist - ARFO **Prod** - ARFO 1985

Never rest 23 MIN
VHS
Color; PAL; NTSC (T G A)
PdS69, PdS80.50 purchase
Investigates the hazards to children from farming and agricultural activities. Shows how to recognize and reduce the risks to children in a rural environment while allowing them to enjoy the environment safely.
Health and Safety
Dist - CFLVIS

Never Say Back Pain Again 13.5 MIN
VHS / 16mm
Taking Care FOCUS Series
(PRO G)
$270.00 purchase
Gives strategies and suggestions to help employees adopt healthier lifestyles. Focuses on the back and relieving back pain.
Business and Economics; Health and Safety
Dist - CNTRHP **Prod** - CNTRHP

Never Say Die
16mm
Color (IND)
Tells the story of Frank Russo, a rig hand who is on trial for his life due to attitudes toward job safety. Reveals as the trial progresses that skills, safety drills and training courses are valuable, but that nothing can substitute for a healthy attitude.
Health and Safety
Dist - FLMWST **Prod** - FLMWST 1982

Never say yes to a stranger 20 MIN
Videodisc / 16mm / U-matic / VHS
Color (I J)
$425.00, $325.00 purchase _ #JR - 4898M
Adapts the book 'Never Say Yes to a Stranger' by Susan Newman. Provides children and young teens with safety tips and preventive tactics which give them the confidence to recognize and protect themselves from potential dangers.
Health and Safety; Sociology
Dist - CORF **Prod** - CORF 1985

Never Say You Can't Until You Try 11 MIN
16mm / U-matic / VHS
Color (I J)
LC 75-703986
Explains the universality of trying, failing and finally succeeding. Exphasizes the importance of making a start and of asking for help when needed.
Guidance and Counseling; Sociology
Dist - GA **Prod** - GA 1975

Never the Easy Way, Version 1 14 MIN
16mm
Color (I)
LC 76-701747
Tells the story of a life or death race to save a trapped woman in a forest fire. Emphasizes water conservation and other fire prevention measures for rural residents.
Agriculture; Health and Safety; Social Science
Dist - FILCOM **Prod** - PUBSF 1966

Never the Easy Way, Version 2 13 MIN
16mm
Color
Presents the story of a life - or - death race to save a trapped woman in a forest fire caused by the negligence of her husband and son. Deals with fire prevention methods for both rural residents and city dwellers. Stresses child education on fire dangers.
Health and Safety
Dist - FILCOM **Prod** - PUBSF

Never to be forgotten 112 MIN
VHS
Color (G) (CHINESE)
$45.00 purchase _ #1011C
Presents a film from the People's Republic of China.
Geography - World; Literature and Drama
Dist - CHTSUI

Never too thin 57 MIN
VHS
Color (J H G)
$250.00 purchase
Looks at women's ideas about their bodies and at society's obsession with thinness and weight loss. Uses computer imaging to show how standards for a female form have changed throughout history. Offers suggestions for a healthier, wiser acceptance of one's characteristics.
Health and Safety; Psychology; Sociology
Dist - LANDMK

Never Too Young 30 MIN
U-matic
Fitness and You Series
Color (H A)
Stresses that more attention should be paid to developing fitness activities among the very young.
Physical Education and Recreation
Dist - TVOTAR **Prod** - TVOTAR 1985

Never Trust Anyone Under 60 60 MIN
16mm
Color
LC 74-705199
Describes graphically problems of aging, such as those discussed at the White House Conference on Aging - isolation, abandonment, housing and other problems.
Health and Safety; Psychology; Sociology
Dist - USNAC **Prod** - USSRS 1971

Never Turn Back - the Life of Fannie Lou Hamer 60 MIN
16mm
Color
Presents Fannie Lou Hamer, the great heroine of the bitter struggle for justice in Mississippi, speaking of non - violence and black power. Features a chronicle of a movement and a people in the songs and the words of the Southern Black.
History - United States
Dist - REPRO **Prod** - REPRO

Never Weaken - Why Worry 78 MIN
U-matic / VHS / 16mm
Harold Lloyd Series
B&W
LC 77-701699
Presents Harold Lloyd in a comedy in which he hustles customers for his girlfriend who works for an osteopath. Shows how he winds up trying to commit suicide and being lifted out of his office on a girder. Includes a reissue of the 1923 silent Harold Lloyd comedy Why Worry. Tells the story of a rich hypochondriac who visits Latin America to cure his ills and becomes embroiled in a revolution without realizing it.
Fine Arts
Dist - TIMLIF **Prod** - ROACH 1976

Neville Chamberlain
16mm / VHS
Archive series
B&W; PAL (G)
PdS280, PdS55 purchase
Presents eight newsreel stories featuring Chamberlain, including the special post - Munich newsreel speech to the Foreign Press Assn, December, 1938, and the Mansion House speech of January, 1940. Includes a substantial accompanying booklet. Uses material compiled by Alan Beattie, David Dilks and Nicholas Pronay.
History - World
Dist - BUFVC **Prod** - BUFVC

Neville Mariner Conducts the Academy of St Martin in the Fields 55 MIN
VHS
B&W (G)
$29.95 purchase _ #1128
Presents the music of Bach, Handel, Mozart, Grieg, Pachelbel, Borodin, Gluck and Rossini performed by the Academy of St Martin in the Fields. Features Neville Mariner as conductor in the historic, stately setting of Longleat House.
Fine Arts; Geography - World
Dist - KULTUR

The New 400B Ethylene Oxide Sterilizer 18 MIN
VHS / U-matic
Color (PRO)
Describes how ethylene oxide kills pathogens. Shows sterilization of a typical group of medical instruments as they are processed in the 3M - 400B ethylene oxide sterilizer, a machine which incorporates a unique electronic logic which automatically controls the entire sterilization cycle.
Health and Safety
Dist - WFP **Prod** - WFP

The New accreditation video guide 35 MIN
VHS
Color (C PRO)
$275.00 purchase, $75.00 rental _ #42 - 2457, #42 - 2457R
Demystifies the accreditation process for nursing educators. Gives a step - by - step guide to the entire procedure, including the current focus on outcomes. Includes the self - study, site visit and the Board of Review decision - making process.
Health and Safety
Dist - NLFN **Prod** - NLFN

New Actors for the Classics 60 MIN
16mm
B&W (J)
LC 74-701904
Presents a documentary on acting styles. Features the Juillard - trained City Center Acting Company.
Fine Arts
Dist - CANTOR **Prod** - WNETTV 1973

New Aetna Drivotrainer Film Series no 1
You and the Drivotrainer System 20 MIN
Dist - AETNA

New Age communities 40 MIN
VHS
Color (G)
$29.95 purchase
Visits five communities, from Findhorn to the Farm, searching for practical ways to live together harmoniously, despite their different economic and spiritual beliefs.
Fine Arts; Psychology; Social Science; Sociology
Dist - HP

New Age Communities 40 MIN
16mm
Color (J)
LC 77-700137
Examines contemporary efforts, both secular and spiritual, at establishing a utopian way of life.
Civics and Political Systems
Dist - HP **Prod** - HP 1977

New Age Communities - the Search for Utopia 40 MIN
U-matic / VHS
Color
Shows functioning, practical attempts at the utopian life, both secular and spiritual.
Religion and Philosophy
Dist - HP **Prod** - HP

A New Age for the Old 27 MIN
16mm
Color (J)
LC 80-700135
Presents an historical survey of the status of the elderly and examines attitudes toward them from classical times to the 1970's.
Psychology; Sociology
Dist - ALTANA **Prod** - KLUGDP 1979

New Age miracles - fact or fiction 45 MIN
VHS
Color (J H C G A R)
$49.95 purchase, $10.00 rental _ #35 - 95 - 2065
Features former psychic John Anderson in an expose of New Age 'miracles' such as walking on hot coals, stopping one's pulse and psychic surgery.
Religion and Philosophy
Dist - APH

The New Age of Diversity 30 MIN
VHS / U-matic
Third Wave Series
Color
Business and Economics; Sociology
Dist - DELTAK **Prod** - TRIWVE

New Age of the Train 14 MIN
VHS / U-matic
Color
Features the supertrains of Europe and Japan, which are filled to capacity and running 'in the black.' Shows new trains, future designs and some superflops.
Social Science
Dist - JOU **Prod** - JOU

New alchemists 50 MIN
VHS
Horizon series
Color; PAL (C PRO A H)
PdS99 purchase
Describes a quiet revolution which is changing material technology - the emerging science of smart materials. Explains a smart material as one that changes properties in response to changes in environment.
Business and Economics; Science; Sociology
Dist - BBCENE

The New Alchemists 29 MIN
16mm
Color (I A)
LC 75-704279
Shows how a group of scientists and their families are successfully working an experimental plant and fish farm near Falmouth, Massachusetts. Explains how they use only organic fertilizers and use solar heat and a windmill for energy.
Agriculture; Social Science
Dist - BNCHMK **Prod** - NFBC 1975

The New Alchemy 27 MIN
U-matic / VHS / 16mm
Perspective Series
Color (J)
Discusses the many beneficial uses, including industrial uses, of bacteria and fungi.
Business and Economics; Science - Natural
Dist - STNFLD **Prod** - LONTVS

New Alchemy - a Rediscovery of Promise 29 MIN
U-matic / 16mm / VHS
Color (J)
Looks at the accomplishments of the New Alchemy Institute which has conducted sophisticated and recognized research in the areas of solar aquaculture, bioshelters, wind power and organic agriculture.
Agriculture; Social Science; Sociology
Dist - BULFRG **Prod** - FLCK 1984

The New American home - a house of ideas 35 MIN
VHS
Color (H C G)
$29.95 purchase _ #WK1117V
Offers a wealth of ideas and information about interior decoration, home design, innovative building projects. Explains the development of a floor plan and interior scheme. Provides clues on how to customize a home within a planned community. Illustrates cutting edge solutions for home building and styling. Discusses the collection of interior design ideas on color, character and charm, space planning tips, the newest in architecture and home - building products, how to personalize design ideas.
Home Economics; Sociology
Dist - CAMV

The New American Neighborhood Road Show 60 MIN
U-matic / VHS
Color
Travels through six of Baltimore's ethnic communities including Highlandtown, Little Italy, Park Heights, Old West Baltimore, Hampden and South Baltimore through a stage production in which the six - member Voices Company portrays longtime residents of the neighborhoods.
History - United States
Dist - MDCPB **Prod** - MDCPB

The New Americans 49 MIN
VHS / U-matic
Color (J H)
$425.00, $395.00 purchase _ #V696
Interviews recent immigrants to the Los Angeles area who discuss why they left their homelands, what it's like to start a new life in the United States and how they're doing. Makes personal the immigration crisis and illustrates the similarities and differences in the experience of recent immigrants.
Geography - United States; History - United States; Sociology
Dist - BARR **Prod** - CEPRO 1991

New Amsterdam 15 MIN
U-matic / VHS
Stories of America Series
Color (P)
Relates some of the problems encountered by Peter Stuyvesant and the Indians on the island of Manhattan.
History - United States
Dist - AITECH **Prod** - OHSDE 1976

New and Improved 28 MIN
U-matic / VHS
Please Stand by - a History of Radio Series
(C A)
Fine Arts; History - United States; Psychology; Sociology
Dist - SCCON **Prod** - SCCON 1986

New and improved kids 47 MIN
VHS
Raising good kids in bad times series
Color (H C A)
$95.00 purchase
Illustrates problems among people and possible solutions, focusing on child - rearing methods. Provides material for educators and community leaders as well as young people. Written, produced and directed by Carol Fleisher.
Guidance and Counseling; Health and Safety; Sociology
Dist - PFP **Prod** - ASHAP

New and Novel - the Development of the Novel in England 45 MIN
U-matic / VHS
Survey of English Literature I Series
Color
Recounts the development of the novel in England.
Literature and Drama
Dist - MDCPB **Prod** - MDCPB

New and Renewable Sources of Energy 28 MIN
Videoreel / VHS
International Byline Series
Color
Presents a United Nations conference on new and renewable sources of energy. Includes interviews and film clips on energy sources. Hosted by Marilyn Perry.
Civics and Political Systems; Geography - World; Social Science
Dist - PERRYM **Prod** - PERRYM

The New and the Old 29 MIN
U-matic
Visions - the Critical Eye Series
Color (H C)
Explores modernist art and related subjects such as methods of marketing, drawbacks involved in adopting theories of mainstream art, the role of the critic and the ways in which art can express religious experience.
Fine Arts
Dist - TVOTAR **Prod** - TVOTAR 1985

New and used Cars 29 MIN
Videoreel / VT2
Way it is Series
Color
Business and Economics; Home Economics
Dist - PBS **Prod** - KUHTTV

The New Approach - the Aerospace Officer of the Future 14 MIN
16mm
Color
LC 74-706158
Shows how the ROTC program develops young men physically and mentally and prepares them to be officers.
Civics and Political Systems
Dist - USNAC **Prod** - USAF 1966

A New Approach to a Great Old Game 10 MIN
U-matic / VHS / 16mm
Four Steps to Better Bowling Series
Color (J)
Introduces the game of bowling, featuring the importance of shoe and ball selection and explaining how to keep score. Concludes with an introduction to the approach and delivery recommended for the beginning bowler.
Physical Education and Recreation
Dist - ATHI **Prod** - ATHI 1983

New Approaches to Big Problems 29 MIN
U-matic / VHS / 16mm
Dealing with Classroom Problems Series
Color (T)
Presents authorities who offer their ideas on a variety of problem areas including discipline, human relationships, authority, self - concept, truancy and violence. Visits a school where counseling is being used to solve campus violence problems.
Education
Dist - FI **Prod** - MFFD 1976

New Approaches to Childhood Lymphocytic Leukemia 50 MIN
U-matic
Color
Summarizes pediatric lymphocytic leukemia treatment as it is currently practiced. Describes the principles used in diagnosis and the rationale for treatment selection.
Health and Safety
Dist - UTEXSC **Prod** - UTEXSC

The New arms merchants 30 MIN
U-matic
Adam Smith's money world 1985 - 1986 season series; 239
Color (A)
Attempts to demystify the world of money and break it down so that small as well as large businesses and it's people understand and adjust to new social and economic trends. Reports on the major economic stories and discoveries of 1985 and 1986.
Business and Economics
Dist - PBS **Prod** - WNETTV 1986

New Art in the American West 22 MIN
16mm
Color
LC 80-700177
Looks at the lives and work of five artists of the American West.
Fine Arts
Dist - PHILMO **Prod** - PHILMO 1979

New Arts 16 MIN
16mm
Color (H C A)
LC 71-713590
Introduces technological art and artists. Includes interpretations by Andy Warhol, Roy Lichtenstein, Claes Oldenburg, Boyd Hefferd, Tony Smith, Newton Harrison and Rockne Krebs.
Fine Arts
Dist - VIEWFI **Prod** - SAARCH 1971

A New Attitude 64 FRS
U-matic / VHS
New Supervisor Series Module 1
Color
Examines the need for developing a new attitude based on the change in relationships that occurs on assuming the new job as supervisor.
Business and Economics; Psychology
Dist - RESEM **Prod** - RESEM

The New awareness 24 MIN
U-matic / VHS
Caring community - alcoholism and drug abuse series
Color
Helps develop an understanding of chemical dependency (including alcholism) as a treatable illness.
Psychology; Sociology
Dist - VTRI **Prod** - VTRI

A New Baby 30 MIN
U-matic
Magic Ring I Series
(K P)
Helps children understand the early care and attention needed by both animal and human babies.
Education; Literature and Drama
Dist - ACCESS **Prod** - ACCESS 1984

The New Baby 20 MIN
16mm
Family Life Education and Human Growth Series
Color; B&W (J)
Pictures a family preparing for the arrival of a new baby, with emphasis on the mother's prenatal medical supervision. Discusses the new baby's emotional needs and his daily care. Shows how parents can cope with the reactions of older children to the new arrival.
Guidance and Counseling; Home Economics; Psychology; Sociology
Dist - SF **Prod** - NFBC 1963

New baby care 23 MIN
VHS
Color (PRO G)
$250.00 purchase _ #OB - 100
Answers questions about the newborn's appearance, how to take care of the baby and how to interpret and respond to the baby's cries and signals. Reviews bathing and temperature taking, cord and genital care and even newborn finger nail care. Helps parents learn how to comfort a crying baby plus how to read a baby's moods and behaviors. Touches on ways of improving parent - infant interactions.
Health and Safety; Sociology
Dist - MIFE **Prod** - POLYMR

New backs for old 28 MIN
VHS
Color (H C G)
$295.00 purchase, $55.00 rental
Shows how the human back works, why problems arise and how they can be treated. Looks at treatments such as electric stimulation, gravity inversion therapy, spinal manipulation, acupuncture, exercise and posture training.
Physical Education and Recreation; Science - Natural
Dist - FLMLIB **Prod** - CANBC 1985

A New Beginning 15 MIN
16mm
Color
LC 74-706378
Surveys the new bulk mail system. Discusses the identification and philosophy of the system and shows the New York installation.
Business and Economics; Social Science
Dist - USNAC **Prod** - USPS 1974

A New Beginning 15 MIN
U-matic
Color (I)
Teaches writing skills while telling the story of Chris and his friends who give Samantha a memento of her work on their newspaper.
Education; English Language; Literature and Drama
Dist - TVOTAR **Prod** - TVOTAR 1982

New beginnings - Part 2 46 MIN
VHS
Pieces to peace series
Color (H C G A R)
$39.95 purchase, $10.00 rental _ #35 - 86 - 597
Provides advice and encouragement for people recovering from divorce. Suggests ideas for dating, sexuality, loneliness and other concerns of life after divorce.
Guidance and Counseling; Psychology; Sociology
Dist - APH **Prod** - NEWLIB

New Beginnings Video Program - Skills for Single Parents and Stepfamily Parents 30 MIN
VHS / 16mm
Color (A)
$285.00 purchase, $55.00 rental _ #2875VHS
Shows in eight sessions - stepfamily parenting, relationships, communication skills, decision making, discipline, and personal and family challenges.
Sociology
Dist - RESPRC **Prod** - RESPRC 1987

New Beginnings - Women, Alcohol and Recovery 20 MIN
U-matic / VHS / 16mm
Color (J)
LC 78-700644
Presents case studies of three women who have successfully overcome alcoholism. Emphasizes the importance of a total commitment to healing aimed at earlier awareness, identification and effective treatment for women.
Health and Safety; Psychology; Sociology
Dist - AIMS **Prod** - PMASS 1977
CMPCAR

New Blood for a Baby 15 MIN
16mm
Doctors at Work Series
B&W (H C A)
LC FIA65-1353
Explains to expectant mothers for whom the Rh - factor may present complications, the safety factors at childbirth. Shows an exchange transfusion performed for a baby soon after birth.
Health and Safety; Psychology; Science - Natural; Sociology
Dist - LAWREN **Prod** - CMA 1962

New blues 29 MIN
VHS / 16mm
Watch your mouth series
Color (H)
$46.00 rental _ #WAYM - 118
Emphasizes language and communication skills for high school students. Notes the difference between formal and informal word usage.
Education; English Language; Psychology; Social Science
Dist - PBS

The New boater's video
VHS
Color (G A)
$39.80 purchase _ #0051
Teaches the basics needed to run and dock a boat. Explains single or dual motor handling, the rules of the way, buoys and safety.
Health and Safety; Physical Education and Recreation
Dist - SEVVID

The New Boys 27 MIN
16mm / U-matic / VHS
West Series
Color (J)
LC 75-701477
Profiles St John's Cathedral Boy's School at Selkirk, Manitoba, Canada. Describes the initiation to the school as a 350 - mile canoe trip and shows that the boys learn outdoor lore as well as cooperation and confidence.
Education; Physical Education and Recreation
Dist - WOMBAT **Prod** - NFBC 1974

The New Boys 26 MIN
U-matic / VHS / 16mm
Color (J)
Describes a Canadian school where adolescent boys are sent on arduous canoe - and - portage trips in the belief that the experience will turn them into men.
Education; Physical Education and Recreation
Dist - WOMBAT **Prod** - NFBC

New Breath of Life 24 MIN
16mm / U-matic / VHS
Color (J) (DUTCH)
A Dutch language version of the revised edition of the film and video, New Breath Of Life. Demonstrates two of the ABC's of basic life support, A - Airway Opened and B - Breathing restored. Teaches how to open the airway of an unconscious victim, how to administer mouth to mouth breathing, and how to save a choking victim with back blows and abdominal thrusts. Narrated by Nanette Fabray.

Health and Safety
Dist - PFP Prod - PFP

A New Breed 26 MIN
U-matic / VHS
Color (C)
$249.00, $149.00 purchase _ #AD - 1982
Explores the applications of human medical breakthroughs to veterinary medicine, showing how new breeding techniques are resulting in stronger, healthier animals which are better suited to serve man.
Business and Economics; Health and Safety; Psychology; Science - Natural
Dist - FOTH Prod - FOTH

The New Breed of Rocket Power 14 MIN
16mm
Color
Recounts the basic design philosophy and method of manufacture that produced the Bullpup rocket. Pictures the acceptance test as well as several live firings of the Bullpup and describes the Navy's use of air - to - ground missiles utilizing packaged liquid fuel as an engine propellant.
Business and Economics; Industrial and Technical Education; Science
Dist - THIOKL Prod - THIOKL 1964

New Bronchodilators 16 MIN
VHS / U-matic
Color (PRO)
Reviews the mechanism of relaxation and dilation of bronchial smooth muscle as it reacts to drug preparations. Details the use, mode of action, duration, onset, dosages, side effects and preparation of the bronchodilators, isoproterenol, metaproterenol and terhutaline.
Health and Safety; Science - Natural
Dist - UMICHM Prod - UMICHM 1976

New Building Under the Water 12 MIN
U-matic / VHS
Color
Offers the sensation of perspective. Involves a dream of Beirut, and of China invoking the Western economy, causing a crash in Washington, D C.
Fine Arts
Dist - KITCHN Prod - KITCHN

New Building Under the Water 14 MIN
U-matic
Color (C)
$200.00
Experimental film by Ken Feingold.
Fine Arts
Dist - AFA Prod - AFA 1982

New Building Under the Water - Ken Feingold 14 MIN
U-matic
Color (A)
Fine Arts
Dist - AFA Prod - AFA 1982

New Caledonia - a Land in Search of Itself - Pt 4 28 MIN
VHS
Human Face of the Pacific Series, the
Color (S)
$79.00 purchase _ #118 - 9004
Looks behind the romance and mystery of the islands of the South Seas to reveal the islands as they really are - a heterogeneous group of countries and colonies struggling to meet the challenges of the modern world while trying to preserve their cultural identities. Part 4 of six parts examines the conflict between the Kanaks, who want to retain their tribal society, and the Caledonian French, who are more concerned with economic progress, in New Caledonia.
Foreign Language; Geography - World; History - World; Religion and Philosophy
Dist - FI Prod - FLMAUS 1987

The New Camp 15 MIN
VHS / U-matic
Encounter in the Desert Series
Color (I)
Shows a Bedouin doctor treating a patient.
Geography - World; Social Science; Sociology
Dist - CTI Prod - CTI

New Candian City Series
Quebec - the Citadel City 14 MIN
Dist - MORLAT

The New Car 8 MIN
16mm
B&W
Tells how Flip the Frog buys a new car, collides with a trolley, and is swallowed by a tunnel.
Fine Arts
Dist - RMIBHF Prod - UNKNWN 1930

The New Cell 41 MIN
35mm strip / VHS
Color (J)
$168.00 purchase _ #PE - 540791 - 4, #PE - 512799 - 7
Explores facts and theories of the living cell's structure, function, reproduction and components, including DNA and RNA. Video version is in two volumes. Filmstrip version has four filmstrips, four cassettes and teacher's guide.
Science - Natural
Dist - SRA Prod - SRA

New Channels for Sockeye 20 MIN
16mm
Color (G)
_ #106C 0173 502
Illustrates what can be done to improve on nature by establishing salmon stocks where none were found before. Shows the annual phenomenon along the Skeena River as silver hordes return to their parent streams to spawn and die.
Geography - World; Science - Natural
Dist - CFLMDC Prod - NFBC 1973

The New Cinema 100 MIN
VHS / U-matic
Color (A)
Presents many of the world's foremost filmmakers who attended the llth Annual Montreal International Festival of New Cinema. Includes interviews with the filmmakers, who discuss their views on art and life.
Fine Arts
Dist - CNEMAG Prod - CNEMAG 1983

New cinema II series
Act without words 10 MIN
Actua tilt 12 MIN
Dist - JANUS

New Cinema of Latin America, Pt 1, Pt 2 83 MIN
U-matic / VHS
Color (H C A)
$350 purchase (each), $85 rental (each)
Examines the social and artistic roots of the new national cinemas of Latin America. Part 1 examines the movement's origins, and focuses on the development of cinema in Cuba and the recent appearance of the new cinema in Nicaragua. Part 2 examines the development of new forms of representation, repression against filmmakers and the recent emergence of a new women's cinema. Directed by Michael Chanan.
Fine Arts
Dist - CNEMAG

New Cities of Macarthur 15 MIN
16mm
Color
LC 81-700710
Describes various aspects of the Macarthur Growth Centre, from industrial development and employment opportunities to education, community activities and housing.
Geography - World
Dist - TASCOR Prod - NSWF 1980

A New Coat for Anna
VHS / 35mm strip
ALA Notable Children's Filmstrips Series
Color (K)
$33.00 purchase
Presents a children's story. Part of the American Library Association series.
English Language; Literature and Drama
Dist - PELLER

New Concept in Urinary Infections 28 MIN
VHS / U-matic
Color (PRO)
Describes the pathogenesis of urinary infections and new concepts in the prophylactic control of recurrent infections.
Health and Safety
Dist - WFP Prod - WFP

New Concepts in Housing for Older Adults Series Program 3
Financing 21 MIN
Dist - UMICH

New Concepts in Housing for Older Adults Series Program 4
The Art of Managing 22 MIN
Dist - UMICH

New concepts in housing for older adults series
Assisted residential living - a form of congregate housing 14 MIN
The Design must be human 18 MIN
Dist - UMICH

New concepts in housing for older adults series
An Architect's vision 20 MIN
Dist - UMICH
UMITV

New Concepts in Marriage 30 MIN
U-matic / VHS
Moral Values in Contemporary Society Series
Color (J)
Presents Robert Rimmer, author of The Harrad Experiment, and Della Roy of Penn State University discussing new concepts in marriage.
Sociology
Dist - AMHUMA Prod - AMHUMA

New Concepts in Sludge Management 5 MIN
U-matic / VHS / 16mm
Color
Shows the progress being made in using sludges from municipal wastewater treatment plants to enrich agricultural land.
Agriculture; Science - Natural; Sociology
Dist - USNAC Prod - NSF

New conflicts - Pt 5 60 MIN
VHS / U-matic
Africans series
Color (G)
$45.00, $29.95 purchase
Examines the problems of post - colonial Africa. Considers urbanization, warrior traditions, national boundaries created by Europe, the Islamic jihad tradition and nationalist movements. Part of a nine - part series hosted by Dr Ali Mazrui, Cornell University and University of Michigan.
History - United States; History - World
Dist - ANNCPB Prod - WETATV 1988
BBCENE

New Convent Garden - Europe's Super Market 20 MIN
16mm / U-matic / VHS
Color (I J A)
Looks at Britain's largest wholesale market which receives fruit, vegetables and flowers from more than 70 countries and has an annual turnover of $200 million.
Agriculture; Business and Economics; Geography - World; Social Science
Dist - LUF Prod - LUF 1979

The New Country Doctors - Changing Concepts in Rural Medicine 22 MIN
16mm
Color
LC 76 - 702858
Examines advantages and disadvantages of solo and group medical practice and the attitudes of young family physicians. Offers guidelines to attract health professionals to rural areas.
Health and Safety; Sociology
Dist - UIOWA Prod - UIOWA 1976

New CPR Standards 15 MIN
U-matic / VHS
Color (C)
$249.00, $149.00 purchase _ #AD - 1472
Presents new standards for CPR which make the technique more effective.
Health and Safety; Science - Natural
Dist - FOTH Prod - FOTH

The New Cults as a Social Phenomenon 30 MIN
VHS / U-matic
Moral Values in Contemporary Society Series
Color (J)
Shows Ernest Van den Haag of the New School for Social Research and Rabbi Sherwin Wine of the Society for Humanistic Judaism discussing the new cults as a social phenomenon.
Religion and Philosophy; Sociology
Dist - AMHUMA Prod - AMHUMA

The New cutting edge 60 MIN
VHS
Man on the rim - the peopling of the Pacific series
Color (H C)
$295.00 purchase
Reveals that recent findings reinforce the relatively new concept of an Asian 'Bronze Age,' thousands of years earlier than suspected. Looks at sites in Thailand, Vietnam and other sites in Southeast Asia to reveal an ancient knowledge of metal - working. Part of an 11 - part series on the people of the Pacific rim.
History - World; Sociology
Dist - LANDMK Prod - LANDMK 1989

New Dance 30 MIN
16mm
Color (J)
LC 78-701821
Presents Doris Humphrey's 1935 dance of affirmation entitled New Dance, as reconstructed in 1972 by the Repertory Company of the American Dance Festival at Connecticut College.
Fine Arts
Dist - UR Prod - ADFEST 1978

A New Dawn 20 MIN
U-matic / VHS / 16mm
History Book Series
Color
Uses paintings, graphics, animation and historical footage to discuss the independence of small nations in the 1970's. Questions the future of these nations.
Civics and Political Systems; History - World; Social Science
Dist - CNEMAG **Prod** - TRIFC 1974

A New Day 14 MIN
VHS / U-matic
Strawberry Square Series
Color (P)
Fine Arts
Dist - AITECH **Prod** - NEITV 1982

A New Day Dawning 20 MIN
16mm
Color
Features the innovative growing and packing processes of the Florida tomato.
Agriculture; Geography - United States
Dist - FLADC **Prod** - FLADC

New Days New Horizons - Horizons Nouveaux 28 MIN
16mm
Color (H C A) (FRENCH)
#3X123
Deals with prejudice and cultural changes surrounding the Indians of Canada. Follows the attempts of one Indian to work as an equal in the lumbering bush.
Social Science; Sociology
Dist - CDIAND **Prod** - HOWARD 1982

New Deal 5 MIN
16mm / U-matic / VHS
Bitter Vintage Series
Color (H C A)
LC 73-703137
Presents a non - narrative vignette of old folks eating alone in cafeterias and coffee shops.
Sociology
Dist - CAROUF **Prod** - WNETTV 1973

The New Deal 30 MIN
VHS / U-matic
America - the second century series
Color (H C)
$34.95 purchase
Illustrates the New Deal, during which governmental programs took on an unprecedented scope and permanency. Part of a 30-part series covering social, political, and economic issues in the United States after 1875.
History - United States
Dist - DALCCD **Prod** - DALCCD
GPN

The New Deal 28 MIN
U-matic / VHS / 16mm
American History Series
Color (J)
LC 70-713126
Explains that the New Deal marked a fundamental change in government in the United States and brought an end to the laissez - faire philosophy. Analyzes the New Deal as a response to the problem of the Depression and shows that while it was a basic change, it was not a revolution.
Business and Economics; History - United States
Dist - MGHT **Prod** - MGHT 1971

The New Deal 25 MIN
U-matic / VHS / 16mm
American History Series
Color (J)
Analyzes the New Deal as a response to the massive problems of the Depression.
History - United States
Dist - CRMP **Prod** - CRMP 1972

The New Deal 30 MIN
VHS
America in perspective - US history since 1877 series
Color (H C G)
$99.00 purchase _ #AIP - 14
Discusses how President Franklin Delano Roosevelt and his administration responded to the crisis of the Depression. Assesses the short - term consequences of those responses. Part of a 26 - part series.
History - United States
Dist - INSTRU **Prod** - DALCCD 1991

The New Deal 15 MIN
VHS
Witness to history II series
Color (J H)
$49.00 purchase _ #60102 - 026
Takes a look at the role of Franklin Delano Roosevelt - FDR - in bringing America out of the Depression. Views the Civilian Conservation Corps, the WPA and the TVA build airports, parks and power plants. Witnesses dust storms devastating crops, families abandon their farms and the confrontation between striking steel workers and the Chicago police. Part of a four - part series. Includes teacher's guide and library kit.
Biography; Education; Fine Arts; History - United States
Dist - GA

The New Deal 15 MIN
VHS
Color (I J H)
$49.00 purchase _ #60102 - 026
Examines the role of Franklin Delano Roosevelt in bringing the United States out of the Depression. Observes the Civilian Conservation Corps, the WPA and TVA building airports, parks and power plants. Witnesses dust storms devastating crops, families abandoning their farms and the confrontation between striking steel workers and the Chicago Police. Includes a teachers' guide and a library kit.
Biography; History - United States
Dist - INSTRU

New Deal for the Dust Bowl - 1931 - 1945 - 9 20 MIN
VHS
Geography in US History Series
Color (H)
Centers on the geographic concept of human - environmental interaction. Features farm families on the Great Plains during the Depression. The depletion of soil, government intervention and policies, and the use of science to cope with economic and environmental problems are also presented. Part 9 of a ten - part series which emphasizes the study of American geography within the context of American history courses using geographic concepts.
Agriculture; Geography - United States; History - United States; Science - Natural
Dist - AITECH **Prod** - AITECH 1991

A 'New Deal' in divorce taxation - Negotiating a tax - wise divorce settlement in light of the 1984 and 1986 tax acts 210 MIN
VHS
Color (C PRO A)
$67.20, $160.00 purchase _ #M709, #P218
Covers tax planning issues that arise in the divorce context. Emphasizes the major changes in this area that have occurred since 1984. Program designed for family law and tax lawyers.
Civics and Political Systems; Sociology
Dist - ALIABA **Prod** - ALIABA 1988

New Delhi 10 MIN
U-matic / VHS / 16mm
Color (I J H)
Shows that New Delhi, the capital of India, is a city of stark contrasts reflecting the diversity of social and economic conditions in the country. Visits the crowded streets of Old Delhi and the offices and growing middle class of New Delhi.
Geography - World; History - World; Sociology
Dist - LUF **Prod** - LUF 1978

A New Design for Education 28 MIN
16mm
Color
Discusses innovations in flexible scheduling, staff utilization and curriculum. Explains how educational requirements can be formulated more flexibly.
Education
Dist - EDUC **Prod** - STNFRD 1964

New developments in nursing management of pain 28 MIN
U-matic / VHS
Pain management - Margo McCaffery discusses new concepts series
Color (PRO)
$275.00 purchase, $60.00 rental _ #7340S, #7340V
Explores the role of the health care team in a Pain Management Center. Discusses the physiological basis of the phenomenon of pain relief and the role of placebos in stimulating the patient's own endorphins. Discusses non - invasive forms of pain relief - acupuncture and transcutaneous electrical nerve stimulation - TENS. Part of a four - part series on pain management featuring Margo McCaffery.
Health and Safety
Dist - AJN **Prod** - HOSSN 1984

New Developments in Operational Amplifiers 30 MIN
VHS / U-matic
Linear and Interface Integrated Circuits, Part I - Linear Integrated Circuits Series
Color (PRO)
Covers design, characteristics and applications of chopper stabilized operational amplifiers that contain both bipolar and MOS integrated circuitry. Compares standard op - amps and emphasizes advantage of new type op - amp.
Industrial and Technical Education
Dist - TXINLC **Prod** - TXINLC

New Developments in the Clinical Application of Hyperalimentation 60 MIN
U-matic
Color
Discusses developments relating nutrition to immunology and cancer management.
Health and Safety
Dist - UTEXSC **Prod** - UTEXSC

New developments in the theory of geometric partial differential equations 60 MIN
VHS
ICM Plenary addresses series
Color (PRO G)
$49.00 purchase _ #VIDSCHOEN - VB2
Presents Richeard M Schoen who discusses new developments in the theory of geometric partial differential equations.
Mathematics
Dist - AMSOC **Prod** - AMSOC

New Diagnostic Procedures in the Diagnosis of Pituitary Disease 35 MIN
16mm
Clinical Pathology Series
B&W (PRO)
LC 74-705201
Summarizes new developments which have resulted in sensitive and specific methods of radioimmunoassay for the measurement in peripheral plasma of all pituitary hormones except prolactine.
Health and Safety; Science - Natural
Dist - USNAC **Prod** - NMAC 1969

The New digital imaging 20 MIN
VHS
Color (G C PRO)
$149.00 purchase
Examines new photographic technologies, including computer manipulation, digital cameras, scanners and disc - based storage of photos. Looks at the transmission of photographs via satellite and phone lines, ethical considerations of computer enhancement and the future of film cameras and existing photo libraries.
Industrial and Technical Education
Dist - FIRLIT **Prod** - FIRLIT 1994

New Dimensions 19 MIN
16mm
Color
LC 75-711361
Follows a manager through a typical day showing the advantages of playing the role of host.
Business and Economics; Sociology
Dist - MCDONS **Prod** - MCDONS 1971

New dimensions in concrete - through the 60's 16 MIN
16mm
Twelve decades of concrete in American architecture series
Color
Industrial and Technical Education
Dist - PRTLND **Prod** - PRTLND 1970

New Dimensions in School Building Flexibility 28 MIN
16mm
Color (T)
Presents a functional definition of space needed in a new school design.
Education
Dist - EDUC **Prod** - EDUC

New direction 50 MIN
VHS
Triumph of the West series
Color; PAL (H C A)
PdS99 purchase; Not available in the United States
Presents the history of Western civilization and documents the influence it continues to have on the rest of the world. Features an investigation of religious beliefs in secular ages. Second in a series of 13 programs written and presented by J M Roberts.
History - World; Sociology
Dist - BBCENE

A New Direction in Dance 58 MIN
16mm
Color
Presents the Barbara Mettler Dance Company of 17 men and women improvising collectively for an hour. Demonstrates dance as the language of movement and as expression of group feeling.
Fine Arts
Dist - METT **Prod** - METT 1978

New Direction in Dance, a, Pt 1 29 MIN
16mm
Color
Presents the Barbara Mettler Dance Company of 17 men and women improvising collectively for an hour. Demonstrates dance as the language of movement and as expression of group feeling.

Fine Arts
Dist - METT **Prod** - METT 1978

New Direction in Dance, a, Pt 2 29 MIN
16mm
Color
Presents the Barbara Mettler Dance Company of 17 men and women improvising collectively for an hour. Demonstrates dance as the language of movement and as expression of group feeling.
Fine Arts
Dist - METT **Prod** - METT 1978

New Directions
U-matic / VHS
Write Course - an Introduction to College Composition Series
Color (C)
Emphasizes future uses of the newly acquired writing skills and their application and development later in many areas.
Education; English Language
Dist - DALCCD **Prod** - DALCCD

New Directions 30 MIN
U-matic / VHS
Write Course - an Introduction to College Composition Series
Color (C A)
Discusses future uses of newly acquired writing skills.
English Language
Dist - FI **Prod** - FI 1984

New Directions 30 MIN
U-matic
Challenge of Time Series
(A)
Examines societal and individual attitudes toward aging.
Health and Safety; Sociology
Dist - ACCESS **Prod** - UALB 1984

New directions for harmonica - expanding your technique 90 MIN
VHS
Color (G)
$49.95 purchase _ #VD - LVY - HA01
Features harmonica viruoso Howard Levy, formerly of Bela Fleck and the Flecktones, with special guest Warren Bernhardt - piano. Shows how Levy has mastered the technique of playing chromatically on a basic ten - hole harmonica through the use of bends, overblows, overdraws and other techniques. Demonstrates the principle modes through arrangements of folk, classical and jazz standards, including Scarborough Fair, Rhythm Changes, Autumn Leaves, Sweet Georgia Brown and a disply of blues improvisations in all 12 keys. Includes music and diagrams.
Fine Arts
Dist - HOMETA **Prod** - HOMETA

New directions in differentiating and positioning - Part II 70 MIN
VHS / U-matic / BETA
Philip Kotler on competitive marketing series
Color; CC (C A G)
$995.00 purchase
Discusses new strategies in marketing - differentiating and positioning in areas such as speed, reliability, service, design, relationships, features, personality and technology. Features Philip Kotler who discusses Bank One and the San Jose Sharks, a young NHL franchise which is number one in merchandise sales. Interviews Kevin Clancy and Al Ries. Part two of two parts.
Business and Economics; Psychology
Dist - VIDART **Prod** - VIDART 1993

New Directions in Science Fiction 25 MIN
16mm
Literature of Science Fiction Series
Color (H C T)
LC 72-700536
Presents a seminar conducted by Harlan Ellison on the new direction of science fiction.
Literature and Drama
Dist - UKANS **Prod** - UKANS 1971

New directions in segmenting and targeting - Part I 50 MIN
VHS / U-matic / BETA
Philip Kotler on competitive marketing series
Color; CC (C A G)
$995.00 purchase
Discusses new strategies in marketing - segmenting, targeting, niches, customization and product proliferation. Features Philip Kotler who discusses Bank One, Toyota, Dell Computer, Nike and Forster Manufacturing. Interviews Kevin Clancy and Al Ries. Part one of two parts.
Business and Economics; Psychology
Dist - VIDART **Prod** - VIDART 1993

New Directions Series

Gefilte Fish	14 MIN
Howard Finster - Man of Visions	20 MIN
Joey Joey	12 MIN
Juggling Magic	3 MIN
No more Disguises	6 MIN
Semper Fi	13 MIN
Tater Tomator	15 MIN
Taylor Slough	5 MIN

Dist - FIRS

A New Double Helical Model for DNA 55 MIN
U-matic
Color
Proposes a new model for DNA and discusses its structure in detail.
Health and Safety; Science - Natural
Dist - UTEXSC **Prod** - UTEXSC

New Drugs in Gastroenterology 30 MIN
U-matic / VHS
Color
Discusses the organization and the various divisions of the Food and Drug Administration and the process of approval for new gastrointestinal drugs.
Health and Safety
Dist - ROWLAB **Prod** - ROWLAB

New Ear Drums by Surgery 50 MIN
16mm
B&W (PRO)
Details a surgical procedure in which a new ear drum is constructed using a section of vein from the patient's hand.
Health and Safety
Dist - LAWREN **Prod** - CMA

A New Earth 30 MIN
16mm
B&W
Portrays the life of Philip Murray, who was President of the United Steelworkers of America and of the Congress of Industrial Organizations. Concludes with a message from the honorable Arthur J Goldberg, associate justice of the Supreme Court. (Kinescope).
Business and Economics; Religion and Philosophy
Dist - NAAJS **Prod** - JTS 1963

The New Earth 22 MIN
16mm
B&W (J H C)
Documents the reclaiming of the Zuider Zee in Holland, a process which took ten thousand men ten years to perform.
History - World
Dist - CFS **Prod** - IVEFER

The New Eating on the Run Film 19 MIN
16mm / VHS
Color (I A)
$415.00, $375.00 purchase, $60.00 rental
Emphasizes need to be concerned about proper nourishment, even when eating in a hurry. Demonstrates that even a quick morning meal can provide good nourishment and that snacking can be a source of good nutrition if one pays attention to salt and sugar content, fats, and fiber in making fast food selections.
Health and Safety; Home Economics; Social Science
Dist - HIGGIN **Prod** - HIGGIN 1986

The New economic age - Vol I 33 MIN
VHS
Deming library series
Color (S)
Provides a plan of action for taking organizations into the future with confidence. Features business strategist and statistician Dr W Edwards Deming, journalist Lloyd Dobyn, producer Clare Crawford - Mason, Harvard Professor Robert B Reich and Ford Motor Company CEO Donald Peterson. Volume I features Deming and Reich who explain the new global economy and reveal their mandate for changing managerial thinking in America.
Business and Economics; Psychology; Religion and Philosophy
Dist - FI **Prod** - CCMPR 1989
VLEARN
EXTR

The New Economic Order 30 MIN
U-matic
North of Sixty Degrees - Destiny Uncertain Series
Color (H C)
Shows that the northern people must consider all the economic options and the quandaries each presents.
Geography - United States; Geography - World; History - World
Dist - TVOTAR **Prod** - TVOTAR 1985

The New Eldorado - invaders and exiles 98 MIN
VHS
Amazon series
Color; CC (G)
$19.95 purchase _ #3075
Examines the inhabitants of the Amazon River Region and their struggle with the invasion of the modern world. Part of a three - part series on the Amazon River by Jacques Cousteau with narration by actors and actresses who speak American English.
Geography - World; Science - Natural
Dist - APRESS

The New Elizabethan Era 29 MIN
Videoreel / VT2
Course of Our Times II Series
Color
History - World
Dist - PBS **Prod** - WGBHTV

New employee orientation - WSSC's program 20 MIN
VHS
Color (G A PRO)
$59.99 purchase _ #V3400GA
Presents the safety management team of the Washington Suburban Sanitation Commission reviewing their program for worker safety, including its policies and specific procedures. Looks at plans for equipment and vehicle maintenance.
Health and Safety; Psychology
Dist - WAENFE

New employee safety orientation 20 MIN
VHS
Color (G A PRO)
$59.99 purchase _ #V3200GA
Focuses on safety considerations necessary in each part of a wastewater plant. Considers proper care in chlorine storage, solids handling, blower maintenance, laboratory, vehicle maintenance and pump station maintenance operations. Outlines a safety management program with emphasis on each element of safety procedures.
Health and Safety
Dist - WAENFE

The New engineers 27 MIN
VHS
Color (J H)
$60.00 purchase _ #A5VH 1428
Looks at the special contributions made by engineers to energy, medicine and computer science. Interviews 13 engineers and includes footage on the wide variety of engineering disciplines.
Guidance and Counseling; Industrial and Technical Education; Science
Dist - CLRVUE **Prod** - CLRVUE

The New engineers 26 MIN
VHS / U-matic / 16mm
Color (H C G)
$395.00, $150.00 purchase, $25.00 rental _ #NC182216, #NC1822VU, #NC1822VH
Examines ground - breaking research in the areas of architecture, biomedical engineering, alternative energy source production and computer technology. Shows practical applications ranging from constructing earthquake resistant buildings and creating computer generated three - dimensional models to designing devices for monitoring bloodflow in premature infants and enabling paraplegics to walk. Hosted by Dick Cavett.
Business and Economics; Fine Arts; Industrial and Technical Education; Social Science
Dist - IU **Prod** - NSF 1987

New England 25 MIN
U-matic / VHS / 16mm
Untamed World Series
Color; Mono (J H C A)
$400.00 film, $250.00 video, $50.00 rental
Explores the wildlife and climate conditions of New England.
Geography - United States; Science - Natural
Dist - CTV **Prod** - CTV 1973

New England
VHS
Frugal gourmet - taste of America series
Color (G)
$19.95 purchase _ #CCP818
Shows how to prepare American food from New England. Features Jeff Smith, the Frugal Gourmet. Part of a ten - part series on American cooking.
Geography - United States; History - United States; Home Economics; Physical Education and Recreation
Dist - CADESF **Prod** - CADESF

New England 60 MIN
VHS
AAA travel series
Color (G)
$24.95 purchase _ #NA01
Explores New England.
Geography - United States; Geography - World
Dist - SVIP

New England 30 MIN
U-matic / VHS / 16mm
Color (I J H C)
Edited from the motion picture These States. Discusses the roles played by New Hampshire, Rhode Island, Massachusetts and Connecticut during the American Revolution. Focuses on the Boston Tea Party, the early battles at Concord and Lexington, and the monuments of Mystic and Saybrook.
Geography - United States; History - United States
Dist - FI **Prod** - BCTOS 1975

New England 15 MIN
U-matic / VHS / 16mm
U S Geography Series
Color (J)
LC 76-701773
Examines the people, industry, economy and landscape of the New England region of the United States.
Geography - United States; Geography - World; Social Science
Dist - MGHT **Prod** - MGHT 1976

New England 23 MIN
U-matic / VHS / 16mm
United States Geography Series
Color (I J)
Explores the New England states including Maine, New Hampshire, Vermont, Massachusetts, Connecticut and Rhode Island. Visits historic sites like Plymouth, where the Pilgrims first landed and Slater Mill, where the American textile industry was born.
Geography - United States
Dist - NGS **Prod** - NGS 1983

New England, an Independence of Spirit 30 MIN
16mm / U-matic / VHS
See America Series
Color (H A)
Records a traditional Rhode Island Independence Day parade, a Vermont oxen - pulling contest, a fog - enshrouded Maine island, and a cog railway on New Hampshire's highest mountain.
Geography - United States
Dist - MTOLP **Prod** - MTOLP 1985

A New England Christmas 29 MIN
VHS / 16mm
Color (G)
$55.00 rental _ #ANEC - 000
Follows John Emery back to his childhood home to spend the holiday with his father. Portrays what Christmas past might have been like for a New England family.
Geography - United States; Religion and Philosophy; Social Science
Dist - PBS **Prod** - ETVMAI

New England colonies 15 MIN
VHS / U-matic
America past series
(J H)
$125 purchase
Talks on the settlement and the culture of the New England colonies.
History - United States; History - World
Dist - AITECH **Prod** - KRMATV 1987

New England cooking 20 MIN
16mm
Cooking film series
Color
Examines early American recipes still in use today, such as Boston brown bread and brick oven beans, sea foods and clambakes, Anadama bread, corn pudding and fried apple pies.
Geography - United States; Home Economics
Dist - BUGAS **Prod** - BUGAS

New England Cooking 20 MIN
16mm
Color (J H A)
Explains the preparation of six authentic early American recipes. Also depicts the scenery of the New England countryside and maple syrup parties in Vermont. Adapted from the Time Life cookbook New England Cooking.
Home Economics
Dist - BUGAS **Prod** - BUGAS

A New England Fall Folio 27 MIN
VHS
Color (A)
Illustrates the scenic beauty of New England towns and countryside during the fall. Shows historic landmarks and present - day people.
Geography - United States
Dist - MTP **Prod** - MAUPIN

New England Fiddles 30 MIN
U-matic / VHS / 16mm
Color (G)
Describes playing the fiddle as both intensely personal and expression of cultural aesthetics. Presents seven of the finest traditional musicians in the Northeast.
Fine Arts; Geography - United States
Dist - DOCEDR **Prod** - DOCEDR 1983

New England Fishermen 11 MIN
U-matic / VHS
Color (I J)
$49.00 purchase, _ #2578
Considers the problems facing the industry of fishing by showing the fishing methods of one skipper and his crew and the possible further decline through the working conditions and slim wages.
Geography - United States; Physical Education and Recreation
Dist - EBEC

New England Sea Community 17 MIN
U-matic / VHS / 16mm
Pioneer Life Series
Color; B&W (I J)
Depicts daily life in a seacoast town in 1845, as it is seen by a 13 - year - old boy. Pictures the work of the town tradesmen. Describes seafaring life aboard a fishing boat, coastal trading ship and whaling vessel, as well as the home life of the young boy.
Geography - United States; History - United States; Social Science
Dist - IU **Prod** - IU 1963

The New Equality - How Much and for Whom 60 MIN
U-matic / VHS
Bill Moyers' Journal Series
Color
Explores the evolving concept of equality through interviews with three scholars.
Sociology
Dist - PBS **Prod** - WNETTV

The New Equation - Annexation and Reciprocity (1840 - 1860) 58 MIN
16mm
Struggle for a Border
B&W (G H C)
_ #106B 0168 081
Depicts the history of the border between Canada and the United States. Shows economic forces were in conflict with the concept of one nation, one continent. Illumines the alternatives for Canada - annexation, continentalism, free trade, economic nationalism.
History - United States; History - World
Dist - CFLMDC **Prod** - NFBC 1968

New Era in Control of Hypertension 30 MIN
U-matic
Color (PRO)
Reports on impact of beta - adrenergic blockade in treatment of hypertension. Discusses hemodynamic characteristics of essential hypertension, radionuclide imaging, and patient acceptance of beta - blockade therapy.
Health and Safety; Science - Natural
Dist - AYERST **Prod** - AYERST

New Era of a Champion 15 MIN
16mm
Color
Presents the birth of a new era in thoroughbred racing history at Gulfstream Park, Florida.
Geography - United States; Physical Education and Recreation
Dist - FLADC **Prod** - FLADC

The New Era of Biotechnology
VHS
Genetic Engineering - Prospects of the Future Series
Color
Focuses on the importance of DNA. Examines the functioning of genes, chromosomes, cucleotide bases, ribosomes and RNA. Describes how gene splicing creates hybrid forms of life.
Science; Science - Natural
Dist - IBIS **Prod** - IBIS

The New Europe - a Certain Amount of Violence 52 MIN
16mm / VHS
Europe, the Mighty Continent - no 12 Series; No 12
Color (G)
LC 77-701568
Analyzes the major historical developments in Europe in the mid - 1950's. Discusses the Soviet suppression of the Polish and Hungarian revolts, British and French involvement in the Suez and the formation of the European Economic Community.
Business and Economics; History - World
Dist - TIMLIF **Prod** - BBCTV 1976

The New Europe - a Certain Amount of Violence, Pt 1 26 MIN
U-matic
Europe, the Mighty Continent - no 12 Series; No 12
Color (G)
LC 79-707428
Analyzes the major historical developments in Europe in the mid - 1950's. Discusses the Soviet suppression of the Polish and Hungarian revolts, British and French involvement in the Suez and the formation of the European Economic Community.
History - World
Dist - TIMLIF **Prod** - BBCTV 1976

The New Europe - a Certain Amount of Violence, Pt 2 26 MIN
U-matic
Europe, the Mighty Continent - no 12 Series; No 12
Color (G)
LC 79-707428
Analyzes the major historical developments in Europe in the mid - 1950's. Discusses the Soviet suppression of the Polish and Hungarian revolts, British and French involvement in the Suez and the formation of the European Economic Community.
History - World
Dist - TIMLIF **Prod** - BBCTV 1976

The New Europeans 50 MIN
VHS / U-matic / 16mm
Window on the World Series
Color; Mono (J H C A)
MV $350.00 _ MP $600.00 purchase, $50.00 rental
Presents the stories of three different men from three different European countries and focuses on their struggles with the common difficulties of the new European industrial society.
Business and Economics
Dist - CTV **Prod** - CTV 1974

New Expectations 13 MIN
16mm
Color
LC 75-703112
Tells of the hope which exists for the mentally retarded, showing that there are more similarities than dissimilarities between normal and retarded people. Suggests what can be done to help the retarded.
Education; Health and Safety; Psychology
Dist - FMSP **Prod** - HRCA 1975

New Experiences for Mentally Retarded Children 31 MIN
16mm
B&W (C A)
Shows a camp experience for severely retarded children. Explains good procedures to use in working with those who are retarded.
Education; Psychology
Dist - VADE **Prod** - VADE 1958

New Expressions of Female Identity in Dance 30 MIN
VHS / U-matic
Changing Images of Men and Women Dancing Series
Color
Fine Arts; Industrial and Technical Education
Dist - ARCVID **Prod** - ARCVID

New Eyes and New Ears 20 MIN
16mm
B&W
LC FIE52-1940
Explains the use of audio - visual materials in Japan and shows how Civilian Information and Educational (CIE) Films of the Supreme Commander, Allied Powers were produced for and utilized in Japan.
Civics and Political Systems; Education; Geography - World; History - World; Sociology
Dist - USNAC **Prod** - USA 1951

The New Face of Racism - 110 30 MIN
U-matic
Currents - 1984 - 85 Season Series
Color (A)
Looks at the resurgence of racism in America.
Social Science; Sociology
Dist - PBS **Prod** - WNETTV 1985

New faces on make - up series 210 MIN
VHS
New faces on make - up series
Color (G A)
$159.95 purchase _ #PRO300SV
Presents a seven - part series covering the use of make - up and related subjects. Considers topics including hair styles, make - up tools, color, eyeglasses, and skin care.
Home Economics
Dist - CAMV

The New Family Homecoming 29 MIN
U-matic / VHS
Tomorrow's Families Series
Color (H C A)
LC 81-706907
Explains that when a couple brings their baby home from the hospital, there are always adjustments to make and problems to solve.
Home Economics; Sociology
Dist - AITECH **Prod** - MDDE 1980

A New - Fashioned Halloween 21 MIN
16mm
Color (P)
LC FIA66-499
Shows the people of Leoniz, N J, preparing for the show, 'TRICK - OR - TREAT FOR UNICEF' with Danny Kaye. Includes examples of UNICEF at work in many lands.
Sociology
Dist - UNICEF **Prod** - AFP 1965

New Fathers 28 MIN
U-matic / VHS
Color (G)
$249.00, $149.00 purchase _ #AD - 1590
Reveals that in the USA parenting is no longer an exclusively female job. Features four hundred fathers and their infants who get together with Phil Donahue to swap advice on parenting. Urges fathers - to - be to prepare for their new roles and responsibilities and discloses that fathers who share in the upbringing of their children are giving them a head start toward psychological success.
Health and Safety; Psychology; Sociology
Dist - FOTH **Prod** - FOTH

New fathers, new lives 23 MIN
VHS
Color (G)
$59.95 purchase _ #LCP300V-K
Offers instruction to men making the transition to fatherhood. Features four new fathers and a studio audience of 40 men with children under a year old.Includes discussion of father's role, paternal instinct, jealousy of the mother - baby relationship, coping with loss of privacy and intimacy, and juggling work and family time. Profiles various fathers, including a teen father and a remarried grandfather with a three-month-old baby.
Sociology
Dist - CAMV

New Fatima, Hope of the World 30 MIN
VHS / BETA
Color (SPANISH)
A Spanish Language Film explains the vision of Our Lady of Fatima in 1917.
Geography - World; Religion and Philosophy
Dist - DSP **Prod** - DSP

The New food guide pyramid 26 MIN
VHS
Color (H G IND)
$89.00 purchase _ #60494-027
Discusses government - endorsed dietary guidelines. Explains the five new food groups in detains and evaluates the role of calories, fat, cholesterol, vitamins, minerals, salt and sugar. Includes teacher's guide.
Education; Health and Safety; Social Science
Dist - VOCMA

The New Food Plant Employee - the Right Start 46 FRS
12 MIN
VHS / U-matic
Color
Emphasizes personal responsibility in handling and production of clean, safe food. Presents the common sense requirements of food plant employment.
Health and Safety; Industrial and Technical Education; Social Science
Dist - PLAID **Prod** - PLAID

The New found land 52 MIN
VHS / 16mm / U-matic
America - a personal history of the United States series; No 1
Color (J) (SPANISH)
LC 74-701570
Presents Alistair Cooke who explains how the white man got to North America and what he was seeking. Shows the arrival of the continent's two 'GREAT LOSERS,' the Spanish and the French, with the conquistadores, trappers, traders and missionaries.
Foreign Language; History - United States
Dist - TIMLIF **Prod** - BBCTV 1972

The New found Land 52 MIN
16mm / VHS
America Series
(J H C)
$99.95 each, $595.00 series
See series title for descriptive statement.
Geography - United States; History - United States
Dist - AMBROS **Prod** - AMBROS 1973

The New found land - Pt 1 26 MIN
U-matic / 16mm
America - a personal history of the United States series; No 1
Color (J)
LC 74-701570
Presents Alistair Cooke who explains how the white man got to North America and what he was seeking. Shows the arrival of the continent's two 'GREAT LOSERS,' the Spanish and the French, with their conquistadores, trappers, traders and missionaries.
History - World
Dist - TIMLIF **Prod** - BBCTV 1972

The New found land - Pt 2 26 MIN
16mm / U-matic
America - a personal history of the United States series; No 1
Color (J)
LC 74-701570
Presents Alistair Cooke who explains how the white man got to North America and what he was seeking. Shows the arrival of the continent's two 'GREAT LOSERS,' the Spanish and the French, with their conquistadores, trappers, traders and missionaries.
History - World
Dist - TIMLIF **Prod** - BBCTV 1972

A New Framework for Federal Personnel Management 30 MIN
U-matic
Launching Civil Service Reform Series
Color
LC 79-706270
Highlights the main features of the Civil Service Reform Bill, outlining the functions of various agencies with personnel management responsibilities.
Civics and Political Systems
Dist - USNAC **Prod** - USOPMA 1978

New France 15 MIN
U-matic / VHS
America past series
(J H)
$125 purchase
Features the French settlement and cultural influence in territories that became parts of the United States.
History - United States
Dist - AITECH **Prod** - KRMATV 1987

The New Friend
U-matic / 16mm
Color (P I)
Tells the story of a girl whose best friend becomes friends with another girl. Deals with her feeling betrayed and angry, but eventually realizing that change can mean new beginnings. Based on the book by Charlotte Zolotow.
Guidance and Counseling
Dist - PHENIX **Prod** - PHENIX 1984

The New Friend 14 MIN
16mm / U-matic / VHS
Color (I J)
LC 84-706800
Tells how a 'new friend' threatens the relationship of two little girls, until sorrow and resentment give way to the recognition of new beginnings and the happy possibilities that come with change.
Guidance and Counseling; Literature and Drama
Dist - PHENIX **Prod** - CHIESR 1983

New Friends 11 MIN
U-matic / VHS / 16mm
Color (K P I)
Tells the adventures of Howard, a mallard duck who misses his south bound flock and is forced to winter in the city. Shows how a fast - talking New York City rat helps the mallard muddle through good times, adversity and sometimes culturally enriching adventures. Based on the book Howard by James Stevenson.
Literature and Drama
Dist - MTOLP **Prod** - MTOLP 1983

New Friends 15 MIN
U-matic / VHS
La Bonne Aventure Series
Color (K P)
Deals with French - American children. Focuses on the theme of making friends.
Foreign Language; Sociology
Dist - GPN **Prod** - MPBN

The New frontier 15 MIN
VHS / U-matic
Discovering series; Unit 5 - Space
Color (I)
Science - Physical
Dist - AITECH **Prod** - WDCNTV 1978

New GED Examination Series
English and Reading Comprehension, Tape 2
English and Reading Comprehension, Tape 3
English and Reading Comprehension, Tape 4
English and Reading Comprehension, Tape 5
English and Reading Comprehension, Tape 6
Mathematics, Tape 2
Mathematics, Tape 4
Mathematics, tape 5
Dist - COMEX

New GED Examinations Series
English and Reading Comprehension, Tape 1
Mathematics, Tape 1
Dist - COMEX

The New Generation 25 MIN
16mm / U-matic / VHS
Untamed World Series
Color; Mono (J H C A)
$400.00 film, $250.00 video, $50.00 rental
Examines the wonders of birth and reproductive systems in the animal kingdom.
Science - Natural
Dist - CTV **Prod** - CTV 1969

The New Generation
VHS
Marriage, Family Living and Counseling Series
(C G)
$59.00_CA225
Talks about the new generation.
Guidance and Counseling
Dist - AAVIM **Prod** - AAVIM 1989

New Generation Intensive Care Incubators 10 MIN
16mm
Color (PRO) (FRENCH CHINESE SPANISH)
LC 82-700202
Integrates live action and state - of - the - art computer animation to explore the innovative design concepts behind the new generation infant life support system.
Foreign Language; Health and Safety; Sociology
Dist - OHMED **Prod** - OHMED 1981

New Generations - 118 30 MIN
U-matic
Currents - 1984 - 85 Season Series
Color (A)
Reviews the social and technological changes that are taking place in the ancient art of parenting.
Social Science; Sociology
Dist - PBS **Prod** - WNETTV 1985

New genes for old 30 MIN
VHS
Antenna series
Color (A PRO C)
PdS65 purchase
Explains that gene therapy has potential for revolutionizing medicine. Describes how Bob Williamson and his team at St. Mary's Hospital in London are trying to develop a method to incorporate a gene into a human cell. This would allow cystic fibrosis victims to make protein their bodies lack.
Science - Natural
Dist - BBCENE

A New Germany - 1933 - 1939 52 MIN
U-matic / VHS / 16mm
World at War Series
Color (H C A) (GERMAN)
Describes the social and political conditions in Germany from 1933 to 1939 which favored the rise of Adolph Hitler through the public's mystical enthusiasm for a New Germany which often took the form of a mass hysteria.
History - World
Dist - MEDIAG **Prod** - THAMES 1973
USCAN

The New girl 6 MIN
VHS / U-matic / 16mm
What should I do series
Color (P)
$195.00, $120.00 purchase _ #JC - 67810
Uses animation to portray Susie and Joanie who reject Mary, the new girl, until they learn the need for acceptance of new friends. Part of a series which dramatizes real life situations, gives possible options, alternatives and consequences, then leaves the final solution to students - for a learning situation which lasts.
Psychology; Sociology
Dist - CORF **Prod** - DISNEY 1970

New global markets - Part 1 25 MIN
VHS
Competing to win series
Color (PRO IND A)
Features H Ross Perot, T Boone Pickens, Rand Araskog, Roger Milliken and Prof Michael Porter of Harvard Business School. Part of a series on international business.
Business and Economics
Dist - CORF **Prod** - CORF 1990

New gods 55 MIN
VHS
Africans series
Color (A)

PdS99 purchase _ Unavailable in USA or Canada
Features Ali Mazuri examining the history and peoples of Africa. Explores Christianity and colonialism in Africa. Part of an eight-part series.
History - World; Religion and Philosophy
Dist - BBCENE

New Gold for Old Glory 24 MIN
VHS / U-matic
Color (A)
Documents the victories of the US Olympic hockey team in the 1980 winter games. Features Coach Herb Brooks. Narrated by Jack Whitaker.
Physical Education and Recreation; Psychology
Dist - SFTI **Prod** - SFTI

New Ground 9 MIN
16mm
Color
LC 75-703419
Presents an introduction to the IBM Canada components plant at Bromont, Quebec and its role in IBM Canada's manufacturing and development organization.
Business and Economics
Dist - IBM **Prod** - IBM 1972

New Guinea 25 MIN
16mm / U-matic / VHS
Untamed World Series Series
Color; Mono (J H C A)
$400.00 film, $250.00 video, $50.00 rental
Explores the jungles and swamps on the island of New Guinea looking at the people and environment they have created for themselves.
Geography - World; Sociology
Dist - CTV **Prod** - CTV 1972

New Guinea Coffee and Cocoa 22 MIN
16mm
Color (J)
Presents the thriving coffee and cocoa industry of Papua and New Guinea.
Business and Economics; Geography - World; Home Economics; Social Science
Dist - AUIS **Prod** - ANAIB 1971

New Guinea Patrol, and, Excerpts from Yumi Yet - Vol I 42 MIN
VHS
People in Change Series
Color (S)
$129.00 purchase _ #188 - 9057
Diverges into two directions through 'New Guinea Patrol,' filmed in 1958, which follows James Sinclair, an Australian patrol officer, through the Western Highlands of Papua New Guinea. Provides a vivid record from the period of colonial administration. In dramatic contrast, 'Yumi Yet' documents Papua New Guinea's independence celebrations. Volume I of a two - part series which deals with traditional culture and how and why these cultures change. This series clearly demonstrates the impact of other cultures on the tradional way of life in Papua New Guinea.
Civics and Political Systems; Geography - World; History - World; Social Science; Sociology
Dist - FI **Prod** - FLMAUS 1988

New Hampshire 60 MIN
VHS
Portrait of America series
Color (J H C G)
$99.95 purchase _ #AMB29V
Visits New Hampshire. Offers extensive research into the state's history. Films key locations and presents segments on history, government, education, folklore, science, journalism, sociology, industry, agriculture and business. Shows what is unique about New Hampshire and distinctive about its regional culture and how it got to be that way. Includes study guide. Part of a 50 - part series.
Geography - United States; History - United States
Dist - CAMV

New Hampshire Writers and the Small Town 18 MIN
16mm
Color (H C A)
Explores the attitudes of New hampshire authors toward the small town as revealed in their literary works. Covers three centuries and reveals significant changes in attitudes toward the land, the people and their communities.
History - United States; Literature and Drama
Dist - UNH **Prod** - UNH 1980

New Harmony - an Example and a Beacon 29 MIN
U-matic / VHS / 16mm
Color (J)
LC 74-714825
Traces the history and significance of New Harmony, Indiana, from its communal origins to its contemporary renaissance as a historic landmark.
Geography - United States; History - United States
Dist - IU **Prod** - IU 1971

New harvest old shame 60 MIN
VHS
Frontline series
Color; Captioned (G)
$300.00 purchase, $95.00 rental _ #FRON - 810K
Documents the poor working and living conditions for migrant farm workers in Florida. Focuses on the Silva family, who must travel from Indiana to Florida, in hopes of finding work for the winter but having no guarantees. Based in part on the 1960 Edward R Murrow broadcast 'Harvest of Shame.'
Business and Economics; Sociology
Dist - PBS **Prod** - DOCCON 1990

New heaven, new Earth 50 MIN
VHS
Spirit of the age series
Color (A)
PdS99 purchase
Examines the evolution of architecture in Britain since the Middle Ages. Part two of an eight-part series.
Fine Arts; Industrial and Technical Education
Dist - BBCENE

The New hip generation - total hip replacement 28 MIN
U-matic / VHS
Color (PRO)
$275.00 purchase, $60.00 rental _ #7611S, #7611V
Illustrates critical postoperative care following total hip replacement surgery. Traces the normal course of postoperative events, required nursing care, progressive movement, exercise and postoperative restrictions - prevention of abduction and acute internal rotation. Provides a full understanding of the problems that lead to this surgery, the types of prostheses and and complications. Shows the kinds of comprehensive nursing which facilitate timely discharge of patients.
Health and Safety
Dist - AJN **Prod** - HOSSN 1986

A New Hip - Nursing Care of the Patient with the Total Hip Arthroplasty 17 MIN
VHS / U-matic
Color (PRO)
Describes nursing care measures important in preoperative, postoperative and discharge planning care of the total hip arthroplasty patient. Includes prevention of dislocation, occupied bedmaking, patient transfer, positioning and exercises.
Health and Safety
Dist - USNAC **Prod** - VAMCCI

The New Hired Hand 27 MIN
16mm
Color
Shows how a computer can be used in the management of a farm.
Agriculture; Mathematics
Dist - IDEALF **Prod** - ALLISC

A New home 28 MIN
VHS
Color (G C)
$150.00 purchase, $45.00 rental
Presents four families who discuss choosing a long - term care facility for a family member indicating the decision - making process followed, adjustments required and day - to - day problems encountered.
Health and Safety; Sociology
Dist - TNF

A New Home for the London Bridge 14 MIN
VHS / U-matic
Color
Documents the sale, disassembly and reconstruction of the London Bridge, which was moved to Lake Havasu City, Arizona.
Geography - United States
Dist - JOU **Prod** - UPI

The New Hooked on Books
U-matic / VHS
Increasing Children's Motivation to Read and Write Series
Color (T)
Addresses teachers' concern for reading and writing competencies of students. Illustrates methods for cooperative student efforts to increase literacy.
Education; English Language
Dist - EDCORP **Prod** - EPCO

New Hope for the Handicapped 14 MIN
16mm
Color
LC 81-701085
Documents changes in attitudes about the handicapped and shows the latest technology designed to free the disabled as never before.
Education; Psychology
Dist - KLEINW **Prod** - KLEINW 1981

New hope in Central America 27 MIN
VHS
Color (J H C G A R)
$24.95 purchase, $10.00 rental _ #35 - 858345 - 93
Examines conditions in five Central American nations. Shows that poverty, injustice and war are no strangers to the people in these countries.
Geography - World; History - World; Sociology
Dist - APH **Prod** - FRPR

A New horizon 16 MIN
VHS
Color (G)
$19.95 purchase _ #BOR - 1
Explains the boundaries of the Great Plains Region, one of the five regions that make up the Bureau of Reclamation.
Geography - United States
Dist - INSTRU **Prod** - USBR

The New Horizons 29 MIN
U-matic
Maps - Horizons to Knowledge Series
Color (SPANISH)
Focuses on the use of remote sensing, the relaying of cartographic information from aircraft or satellite to the ground in map making.
Geography - United States; Geography - World; Social Science
Dist - UMITV **Prod** - UMITV 1980

New Horizons 12 MIN
VHS / U-matic
Color
Shows commentary by Howard K. Smith produced in the news format of TV magazine style. Tells how it can be used in its entirety or in three segments? including research, rehabilitation, and a laryngectomee who, through advances in cancer research, learned to speak again.
Health and Safety
Dist - AMCS **Prod** - AMCS 1980

New Horizons - Brazil 22 MIN
16mm
Color
Presents a general view of modern Brazil, including its geography, natural resources, topography and people.
Geography - World
Dist - PANWA **Prod** - PANWA

New Horizons - Fiji, New Caledonia 9 MIN
16mm
Color
Depicts the beauty and serenity of the Fiji and New Caledonia Islands.
Geography - World
Dist - PANWA **Prod** - PANWA

New Horizons - Hawaiian Islands 13 MIN
16mm
Color
Views the people and places of Hawaii.
Geography - United States
Dist - PANWA **Prod** - PANWA

New Horizons in Materials Handling 16 MIN
16mm
Color
Surveys the engineering and manufacturing of materials handling systems by the Barrett Cravens Company with emphasis on automated machines. Discusses the application of the automated, Guide - O - Matic tractor to traffic and work flows.
Business and Economics; Industrial and Technical Education
Dist - CCNY **Prod** - RAY

New Horizons - New Zealand 13 MIN
16mm
Color
Views the people and places of New Zealand.
Geography - World
Dist - PANWA **Prod** - PANWA

New Horizons - Portugal 13 MIN
16mm
Color
Views the people and places of Portugal.
Geography - World
Dist - PANWA **Prod** - PANWA

New Horizons - Samoa, Tahiti 9 MIN
16mm
Color
Presents a brief but pleasant visit to the historic islands of Samoa and Tahiti.
Geography - World
Dist - PANWA **Prod** - PANWA

New Horizons Series
Creating your own software
Evaluating and Selecting Software
Keeping in Touch
Matching the Computer to Your

Curriculum
Meeting Your Micro and the World of Computing
Methods for Managing the Computer in the Classroom
What the Computer Can do for You - Part I
What the Computer Can do for You - Part II
Dist - AITECH

New Horizons Series

Hawaiian Islands	14 MIN
India	12 MIN
Ireland	12 MIN
Japan	13 MIN
Thailand	13 MIN
Turkey	13 MIN

Dist - PANWA

New Horizons - the Low Countries 30 MIN
16mm
Color
Presents a tour of Belgium, Holland and Luxembourg.
Geography - World
Dist - PANWA Prod - PANWA

New house wiring 92 MIN
VHS
Color (H A T)
$49.95 purchase _ #AV100
Presents a complete step - by - step house wiring guide. Discusses switches, receptacles, GFIs, circuits, wire sizes and types, floor plans, service panels, fixtures and tools. Includes reference guide book.
Industrial and Technical Education
Dist - AAVIM Prod - AAVIM 1992

A New Human Life 10 MIN
16mm
Family Life and Sex Education Series
Color (K P I)
Details the stages of growth of a human baby inside the mother during the final five months of pregnancy. Describes the maternity hospital routine. Shows how a new baby is welcomed into a family. Discusses male and female differences at birth.
Science - Natural; Sociology
Dist - SF Prod - SF 1968

New Ideas in Psychology 29 MIN
U-matic
Color
Discusses why intelligence tests report higher scores for older children in a family rather than younger children. Covers treatment of migraine headaches and decision making.
Psychology
Dist - UMITV Prod - UMITV 1977

New Image Teen Theater 30 MIN
U-matic
Color (J C)
Features sketches written and performed by San Diego's New Image Teen Theatre, a project of Planned Parenthood. The skits deal frankly and humorously with such issues as handling peer pressure, communicating honestly, and making responsible choices about sex. The purpose of this program was to present teens as intelligent, talented and capable of making responsible choices.
Health and Safety; Psychology
Dist - SDSC Prod - SDSC 1985

The New immigrants 25 MIN
VHS
American foundations - wilderness to world power series
Color (J H C G)
$59.95 purchase _ #BU906V
Explores the newest of the immigrants to the United States of the 20th century. Part of a seven - part series on American history.
History - United States; Sociology
Dist - CAMV

New Immigrants - Russian Jews in Philadelphia 23 MIN
16mm
B&W
LC 79-700450
Documents the experiences of recent Jewish immigrants from the Soviet Union as they struggle to learn English and find new jobs in Philadelphia. Explores their reasons for immigrating and their reactions to urban America.
Sociology
Dist - TEMPLU Prod - JELPEP 1979

New Improved Institutional Quality 10 MIN
16mm
Color (C)
$448.00
Experimental film by George Owen (aka Owen Land).
Fine Arts
Dist - AFA Prod - AFA 1978

New improved institutional quality - in the environment of liquids and nasals a parasitic vowel sometimes develops 10 MIN
16mm
Color (G)
$20.00 rental
Reworks an earlier film, Institutional Quality. Concerns itself with the effects of a test on the test taker. An attmept is made to escape from the oppressive environment of the test, which is meaningless and impossible to follow, by entering into the imagination. An Owen Land production.
Fine Arts
Dist - CANCIN

The New Industrial Revolution 12 MIN
16mm
Color
LC 80-700941
Demonstrates techniques that are making assembly lines more efficient. Shows systems developed to speed up assembly processes and eliminate routine jobs.
Business and Economics
Dist - USNAC Prod - NSF 1979

New Insulins - Implications for Clinical Practice 21 MIN
VHS / U-matic
Color (PRO)
Explains the benefits, limitations, and appropriate clinical uses of new forms of purified and highly purified insulins, including biosynthetic and semisynthetic forms of manufactured human insulin. Provides a brief historical overview of the development and purification of insulin. Describes the structure of new insulins, relates this to their relative levels of immunogenicity, and describes the kinds of patients most likely to benefit from their use. Outlines some possible future developments in insulin research and applications.
Health and Safety
Dist - UMICHM Prod - UMICHM 1983

New Jane Fonda Workout 60 MIN
VHS
(C A)
$39.95
Features Jane Fonda, fitness expert and movie star, as she demonstrates her new workout.
Physical Education and Recreation
Dist - CAMV Prod - CAMV

New Jersey 60 MIN
VHS
Portrait of America series
Color (J H C G)
$99.95 purchase _ #AMB30V
Visits New Jersey. Offers extensive research into the state's history. Films key locations and presents segments on history, government, education, folklore, science, journalism, sociology, industry, agriculture and business. Shows what is unique about New Jersey and distinctive about its regional culture and how it got to be that way. Includes study guide. Part of a 50 - part series.
Geography - United States; History - United States
Dist - CAMV
TBSESI

New Jersey Prison System 22 MIN
16mm / U-matic
CTV Reports Series
Color; Mono (J H C A)
$400.00 film, $250.00 video, $50.00 rental
Presents a unique program in which inmates serving a life sentence may talk with young juvenile delinquents and show them the horrors of prison life.
Sociology
Dist - CTV Prod - CTV 1978

A New Job for U Thant 5 MIN
16mm
Screen news digest series; Vol 4; Issue 5
B&W
Reviews the election and installation of U Thant of Burma as acting Secretary - General of the United Nations.
Civics and Political Systems; Geography - World
Dist - HEARST Prod - HEARST 1961

New Joints for Old 50 MIN
16mm
B&W (PRO)
Depicts arthroplasty, a surgical procedure which enables elderly patients to regain use of their joints. Shows a stainless steel joint replacing the defective joint of a patient.
Health and Safety
Dist - LAWREN Prod - CMA

New Journal Series
Russia - the Unfinished Revolution 60 MIN
Dist - IU

A New key 29 MIN
U-matic
Beginning piano - an adult approach series; Lesson 9
Color (H A)
Reviews earlier pieces, scale forms and progression. Demonstrates and explains syncopated pedaling to produce legato connections between chords. Introduces the G - major scale.
Fine Arts
Dist - CDTEL Prod - COAST

The New Kid 11 MIN
U-matic / VHS / 16mm
Color (P I J)
Presents insights into the experience of children who have to endure new, unfamiliar worlds when their families move. Shows how, alone, the new kid has to meet the other kids on the block and make some kind of initial approach to them.
Guidance and Counseling; Social Science
Dist - PHENIX Prod - PHENIX 1972

New kid in town - 43 8 MIN
U-matic / VHS
Life's little lessons - self - esteem 4 - 6 series
Color (I)
$129.00, $99.00 purchase _ #V672
Looks at the difficulties of moving, of being the new kid, leaving old friends, making new ones. Shows how to make things easier for someone in that position. Part of a 65 - part series on self - esteem.
Guidance and Counseling; Home Economics; Psychology
Dist - BARR Prod - CEPRO 1992

New Kid on the Block 30 MIN
16mm
Footsteps Series
Color
LC 79-701551
Explains what social skills are, shows how young children acquire them, and suggests ways in which parents can facilitate this learning process.
Psychology; Sociology
Dist - USNAC Prod - USOE 1978

A New Kind of Joy 20 MIN
16mm
Color
Presents scenes from the many events of the Special Olympics.
Education
Dist - SPEOLY Prod - SPEOLY

New knowledge for old 50 MIN
U-matic / VHS
Arabs - a living history series
Color (H C A)
MV=$495.00
Reveals that oil - generated wealth has transformed Kuwait from a community of traders and fishermen into a place of new technological opportunities.
Geography - World; History - World
Dist - LANDMK Prod - LANDMK 1986

New Leader - Henry Winkler of U C 29 MIN
U-matic
Decision Makers Series
Color
Presents Henry Winkler, President of the University of Cincinnati. Describes his vision for higher education. Discusses who is responsible for a child's education.
Biography; Education
Dist - HRC Prod - OHC

New Leadership Styles - Towards Human and Economic Development 26 MIN
16mm / U-matic / VHS
Human Resources and Organizational Behavior Series
Color
Presents Dr Michael Maccoby, author of The Gamesmanship. Uses Maccoby's gamesmanship concept as a point of departure in scrutinizing the innovative leadership styles of two successful executives who have humanized their companies' work environments by giving more power to the people.
Business and Economics; Psychology
Dist - CNEMAG Prod - DOCUA

New Lease on Learning 22 MIN
16mm
Color
Describes the conversion of a former synagogue into a public school for children aged three to five.
Education
Dist - NYU Prod - NYU

New left note 26 MIN
16mm
Color (G)
$52.00 rental
Features rapid cutting of shots made between 1968 to 1982 of the anti - war, anti - racist and women's liberation movements. Represents a synthesis of ideas that are injected into a much - divided movement. Levine was editor of New Left Notes, the national SDS newspaper.

Fine Arts; Sociology
Dist - CANCIN **Prod** - LEVINE 1982

New - Liberal View of the US 30 MIN
U-matic
Realities
Color (A)
Delves into the political, social, economic and cultural trends of the 1980s. Probes a wide range of contemporary concerns. Each segment includes a guest speaker who is an expert in the field under discussion.
Business and Economics; Civics and Political Systems; Social Science; Sociology
Dist - TVOTAR **Prod** - TVOTAR 1985

New life 15 MIN
VHS / U-matic / 16mm
Color (G)
$275.00, $325.00, $350.00 purchase, $50.00 rental
Encourages the cardiac rehabilitation patient to take advantage of the benefits of an organized hospital recovery program. Provides frank information about lifestyle expectations. An upbeat production by Partners Against Substance Abuse.
Health and Safety
Dist - NDIM

A New Life 29 MIN
Videoreel / VT2
That's Life Series
Color
Psychology
Dist - PBS **Prod** - KOAPTV

New Life for a Spanish Farmer 18 MIN
U-matic / VHS / 16mm
Man and His World Series
Color (P I J H C)
LC 70-705484
Shows attempts of the Spanish government to improve farming and the life of the farmer.
Agriculture; Geography - World
Dist - FI **Prod** - FI 1969

New Life for Old Hands 23 MIN
16mm
Color
Deals with the implantation of manmade joints to replace diseased ones. Features an elderly patient who is examined and interviewed before and after joint replacement surgery on hands severely diseased by rheumatoid arthritis. Describes the actual surgical procedure, with a running commentary by the physician.
Health and Safety
Dist - WSTGLC **Prod** - WSTGLC

A New Life for Rose 25 MIN
U-matic / VHS / 16mm
Color (H C A)
Presents the planning program of a senior housing project.
Health and Safety; Sociology
Dist - FEIL **Prod** - FEIL 1976

New Life for Ruined Land 14 MIN
U-matic / VHS / 16mm
Color
Documents a two - year project by the Department of Energy's Land Reclamation Program at Argonne National Laboratory to rehabilitate an abandoned coal mining site in Southern Illinois, turning it into a wildlife refuge and recreation facility.
Civics and Political Systems; Geography - United States; History - United States; Science - Natural
Dist - USNAC **Prod** - USDOE 1983

New Life for the Great Plains 12 MIN
16mm
Color
LC 74-705204
Promotes the Great Plains soil conservation program by showing the progress made in soil and water conservation in Baca County, Colorado.
Geography - United States; Science - Natural
Dist - USNAC **Prod** - USDA 1965

New Life in Christ 21 MIN
16mm
Color
LC 79-701336
Features people of all ages discussing their new life in Christ, telling who he was and is. Sheds light on these issues from a Biblical standpoint, presenting Gospel messages.
Religion and Philosophy
Dist - FAMF **Prod** - FAMF 1979

New Life New Ways 16 MIN
16mm
Color
LC 80-701571
Focuses on the special problems of migrant women in adapting to Australian society.
Geography - World; Sociology
Dist - TASCOR **Prod** - TASCOR 1979

The New Life of Sandra Blain 27 MIN
16mm
Color
LC 77-700176
Tells the story of a fictional character, Sandra Blain, who has no job, no job skills, no husband, no family and no home. Shows how she puts her life together as a recovering alcoholic.
Health and Safety; Psychology; Sociology
Dist - SUTHRB **Prod** - SUTHRB 1977

A New Line of Sight 16 MIN
16mm
Color
LC 74-706159
Reviews the USAF research and development achievements since 1954 in missiles, satellites, re - entry projects, aerospace medicine activities and other vital space efforts.
Civics and Political Systems
Dist - USNAC **Prod** - USAF 1962

The New Literacy 26 MIN
U-matic / VHS
Color (G)
$249.00, $149.00 purchase _ #AD - 1808
Asks if the future definition of literacy will include the ability to operate a computer. Looks at how computers are changing the face of the American educational system and at the practical applications of computer technology in the classroom.
Computer Science; Mathematics; Sociology
Dist - FOTH **Prod** - FOTH

The New Literacy - an Introduction to Computers 900 MIN
U-matic / VHS
Color (C A)
Surveys electronic data processing, computer hardware and software systems, and developments that will provide the basis for further advancements in information processing.
Computer Science; Education; Guidance and Counseling; Mathematics
Dist - SCCON **Prod** - SCCON 1984

The New literacy - an introduction to computers series 780 MIN
U-matic / VHS
The New literacy - an introduction to computers series
Color (G)
$500.00, $350.00 purchase
Presents a 26 - part series on computing machines. Offers a comprehensive overview of the computer, data processing terminology, computer applications and typical computer environments. Includes interviews with Isaac Asimov, Michael Crichton and US Navy Commodore Grace N Hopper.
Computer Science; Mathematics
Dist - ANNCPB **Prod** - SCCON 1988

The New literacy - an introduction to computers series
The New literacy - an introduction to computers series 780 MIN
Dist - ANNCPB

New literacy - an introduction to computers
Computer operations - personal computing - Parts 11 and 12 60 MIN
Computer security - issues and trends in computing - Parts 25 and 26 60 MIN
The computing machine II - communicating with a computer - Parts 3 and 4 60 MIN
Computing services - computing, organizations and the individual - Parts 23 and 24 60 MIN
Data communications - office automation - Parts 21 and 22 60 MIN
Data representation - putting data in - Parts 5 and 6 60 MIN
From micros to monsters - system analysis and design - Parts 13 and 14 60 MIN
Getting information out - storing data - Parts 7 and 8 60 MIN
A Literate society - the computing machine I - Parts 1 and 2 60 MIN
Problem solving and program design - programming languages - Parts 15 and 16 60 MIN
The Programming environment - operating systems - Parts 17 and 18 60 MIN
Secondary storage - processors - Parts 9 and 10 60 MIN
Systems options - computer files and databases - Parts 19 and 20 60 MIN
Dist - ANNCPB

The New look 28 MIN
16mm
Government story series; No 20
Color
LC 74-707175
Stephen Horn discusses the need for congressional reforms with a panel of congressmen including Senator Karl E Mundt, Senator William Proxmire, Representative Jack Brooks and Representative James C Cleveland.
Civics and Political Systems
Dist - WBCPRO **Prod** - WBCPRO 1968

New Look 13 MIN
16mm
Family Relations Series
Color (K P)
LC 76-700140
Provides an explanation of family relations.
Sociology
Dist - MORLAT **Prod** - MORLAT 1974

A New look at algae 15 MIN
VHS / 16mm
Inhabitants of the planet Earth series
Color (H C)
$256.00, $180.00 purchase, $25.00 rental _ #194 W 2075, #193 W 2015, #140 W 2075
Illustrates striking examples of adaptation in freshwater and marine algae. Looks at diatoms with elongated spiny cases which reduce the rate of sinking, others which produce oil droplets in order to regulate their buoyancy, algae which live symbiotically within a host animal, multicellular algae which grow to 30 meters and support their elongated forms by means of gas - filled floats. Part of a series on microorganisms.
Science - Natural
Dist - WARDS **Prod** - WARDS

A New Look at an Old Planet 26 MIN
16mm
Color (I)
LC 79-701238
Shows the practical benefits of weather, communication, navigational, and earth resources satellites, through experiences in the lives of a Texas coastal family. Illustrates future potential uses of satellites in agricultural, oceanographic and natural resources studies.
Psychology; Science - Physical; Social Science
Dist - NASA **Prod** - NASA 1969

A New look at bacteria 16 MIN
16mm / VHS
Inhabitants of the planet Earth series
Color (H C)
$256.00, $192.00 purchase, $25.00 rental _ #194 W 2060, #193 W 2012, #140 W 2060
Uses live action sequences to show an unsuspected variety of locomotion patterns and behavior responses in bacteria. Examines gliding forms, spirochetes and bacilli. Part of a series on microorganisms.
Science - Natural
Dist - WARDS **Prod** - WARDS

A New Look at Jack be Nimble 30 MIN
Videoreel / VT2
Solutions in Communications Series
Color (T)
Education; English Language
Dist - SCCOE **Prod** - SCCOE

A New look at Leeuwenhoek's 'wee beasties' 12 MIN
VHS / 16mm
Inhabitants of the planet Earth series
Color; Captioned (H C) (FRENCH)
$192.00, $99.00 purchase, $25.00 rental _ #194 W 2000, #193 W 2001, #140 W 2000
Overviews the microscopic life of protists. Shows external structure and motion of cilia, cirri and flagella. Includes Paramecium, Euglena and Amoeba. Part of a series on microorganisms.
Science - Natural
Dist - WARDS **Prod** - WARDS

A New Look at Leeuwenhoek's Wee Beasties 12 MIN
16mm
Inhabitants of the Planet Earth Series
Color (J H C)
LC 75-701959
Examines free - living protists as viewed in natural time by differential interference cinemicrography. Discusses the classification and general characteristics of flagellates, amoebas and ciliates.
Science - Natural
Dist - MLA **Prod** - RUSB 1975

A New Look at Motivation 32 MIN
16mm / U-matic / VHS
Color (C A)
LC 80-700470
Examines the basic psychological principles of motivation and shows their application to worker behavior and managerial styles.
Business and Economics; Psychology
Dist - CRMP **Prod** - CRMP 1980
MGHT

A New Look at the Surgery of the Biliary Tree 34 MIN
16mm
Color (PRO)
Presents three cases to support the procedure of providing a by - pass for bile into the bowel in the event of further obstruction occuring at the lower end of the common duct.
Health and Safety; Science
Dist - ACY **Prod** - ACYDGD 1962

A New look at war 30 MIN
VHS
Blessed are the peacemakers series
Color (H C G A R)
$39.95 purchase, $10.00 rental _ #35 - 847 - 2076
Features Bishop Lowell Erdahl in an examination of Christian perspectives on warfare and the arms race. Produced by Seraphim.
Psychology; Sociology
Dist - APH

New Lost City Ramblers 52 MIN
U-matic / VHS
Rainbow quest series
Color
Features the New Lost City Ramblers performing on fiddle, guitar, banjo, mandolin and autoharp. Shows films of a Japanese Fiddle Band.
Fine Arts
Dist - NORROS **Prod** - SEEGER

The New Maid 34 MIN
16mm / U-matic / VHS
Color (J H C)
LC 81-700434
Tells the story of a Guatemalan woman who comes to work for an upper middle - class family when the mother returns to her job. Relates that the youngest son develops a deep affection for the maid and serious problems ensue.
Guidance and Counseling; Sociology
Dist - LCOA **Prod** - FCLPTF 1980

New Man at Millersville 20 MIN
U-matic / VHS
Color
Shows new food service employees in correctional facilities some of the problems they might encounter and how to solve them.
Industrial and Technical Education; Sociology
Dist - USNAC **Prod** - USDJ

New Man in the Forest 26 MIN
U-matic / VHS / 16mm
Color (J)
LC 70-712267
Presents suggestions and techniques for deriving maximum benefits from small or large plots of forested land by showing a new owner of a small forest and his young son exploring their land and talking with professional advisers. Discusses the basic concepts of forest land management.
Agriculture; Science - Natural
Dist - IFB **Prod** - SUCF 1971

The New manufacturing challenge - techniques for continuous improvement 193 MIN
VHS
Color (PRO A G)
$1895.00 purchase _ #YSUZ - 622
Presents four videocassettes which show how to involve an organization in the techniques and philosophies of continuous improvement. Includes case studies from Borg - Warner, Hewlett - Packard, Toyota, Apple Computer. Features Tom Peters and the teachings of Kiyoshi Suzaki. Includes a facilitator's guide, 10 workbooks and three copies of The New Manufacturing Challenge.
Business and Economics; Psychology
Dist - PRODUC
SME

The New manufacturing environment 30 MIN
VHS / U-matic
Manufacturing automation - a key to productivity series
Color
Discusses causes and effects behind the creation of the new manufacturing environment. 63 - 010.
Business and Economics; Industrial and Technical Education
Dist - DELTAK **Prod** - DELTAK

New Market - field of honor 59 MIN
VHS
Color (J H C G)
$24.95 purchase _ #PE782V
Follows the newly formed armies of John C Breckenridge and Franz Sigel as the move on a collision course resulting in the Battle of New Market. Presents a large scale Living History Commemoration reenactment staged on portions of the existing New Market Battlefield, Stonewall Jackson's gravesite, Lexington and the Virginia Military Institute. Uses historic narrative, stereo sound and graphic maps.
History - United States
Dist - CAMV

The New market places 40 MIN
VHS
Architecture at the crossroads series
Color (A)
PdS99 purchase _ Unavailable in Europe
Examines the main themes running through the world of architecture. Investigates how village squares are being replaced by shopping malls. The third program in a ten-part series.
Fine Arts; Industrial and Technical Education
Dist - BBCENE

New Maximilian Kolbe 21 MIN
VHS / BETA
Color (POLISH)
A Polish Language film covers the life and death of Maximilian Kilbe, a Franciscan monk who died in the Nazi concentration camp of Auschwitz and was later canonized.
Biography; Civics and Political Systems; History - World; Religion and Philosophy
Dist - DSP **Prod** - DSP

The New Me - Accepting Body Changes
VHS / U-matic
Color (I J)
Helps cope with puberty through matter - of - fact, supportive explanations of male and female body changes. Points out that though timetables vary, every boy and girl undergoes physical change. Promotes self - acceptance. Contains separate sections on male and female physiology.
Guidance and Counseling; Health and Safety; Psychology; Science - Natural
Dist - SUNCOM **Prod** - SUNCOM

The New media 26 MIN
U-matic / VHS / 16mm
Computer programme series; Episode 5
Color (J)
LC 82-701105
Discusses the beneficial potential of electronic communication through personal access to data bases, by means of computer networking and as seen in the office of the future.
Business and Economics; Mathematics
Dist - FI **Prod** - BBCTV 1982

The New Media Bible - Genesis 4 - Joseph 93 MIN
BETA / VHS
Color
LC 84-706669
Retells the Genesis, of Joseph's enslavement to the Egyptian pharoah in a series of four programs.
Religion and Philosophy
Dist - GNPROJ **Prod** - GNPROJ 1984

The New Media Bible - Luke I - Nativity to the Baptism 51 MIN
BETA / VHS
Color
LC 84-706670
Gives the story of Jesus' birth and early life as told in the book of Luke.
Religion and Philosophy
Dist - GNPROJ **Prod** - GNPROJ 1984

The New media Bible series
Presents a video account of the events in the books of Genesis and Luke. Based on the Revised Standard Version of the Bible, but the King James Version is available for special order purchase. Consists of eight tapes, four for each of the two books, along with a study guide.
Abraham - Tape 2
The Beginning - Tape 1
Book of Genesis series
Book of Luke series
Christmas - Tape 1
Early ministry - Tape 2
Easter - Tape 4
Isaac, Esau and Jacob - Tape 3
Joseph - Tape 4
Parables - Tape 3
Dist - APH **Prod** - VISVID 1984

The New media - what you must know
VHS
Marketing electronic information series
Color (G C PRO)
$195.00 purchase
Offers a checklist of new media tools with no - nonsense tips about when, how and where to use them. Part of an eight - part series on marketing electronic information.
Business and Economics
Dist - DEJAVI **Prod** - DEJAVI

New medical and allied health series
Presents a four - part series looking at medical and allied health careers. Includes the titles Physicians and Health Practitioners, Health Service Careers, Careers in Allied Health I and II.
Careers in allied health I 60 MIN
Careers in allied health II 60 MIN
Health services careers 48 MIN
Physicians and health practitioners 60 MIN
Dist - NEWCAR

New Methods of Hospital Reimbursement 32 MIN
U-matic / VHS
Future of Nursing Series
Color (PRO)
Explains the newest system for hospital payment, the Diagnostic Related Groupings (DRG) system. Discusses the system's pros and cons, long range, and its effects on nursing.
Health and Safety
Dist - HSCIC **Prod** - HSCIC 1985

New Mexico 60 MIN
VHS / U-matic
Portrait of America series
Color (J H C G)
$99.95 purchase _ #AMB31V
Visits New Mexico. Offers extensive research into the state's history. Films key locations and presents segments on history, government, education, folklore, science, journalism, sociology, industry, agriculture and business. Shows what is unique about New Mexico and distinctive about its regional culture and how it got to be that way. Includes study guide. Part of a 50 - part series.
Geography - United States; History - United States
Dist - CAMV
TBSESI

New Mexico Passive Solar Buildings 14 MIN
16mm
Color
LC 79-700464
Describes the major types of passive solar heating systems and explains how they work. Shows examples of buildings in New Mexico which are equipped with innovative solar energy systems.
Geography - United States; Social Science
Dist - USNAC **Prod** - USOE 1978

The New Miracle Worker 15 MIN
16mm
Color
LC 80-701525
Describes the activities of Helen Keller International in the prevention of blindness as well as the rehabilitation of the blind.
Psychology; Sociology
Dist - MTP **Prod** - HKELNT 1980

The New Miracle Workers 15 MIN
U-matic
Color
Explains work being done around the world to teach survival skills to the blind. Shows how vitamin therapy and education about nutrition can prevent blindness. Narrated by Alexander Scourby.
Education; Health and Safety; Psychology; Social Science
Dist - MTP **Prod** - HKELNT

The New Misadventures of Ichabod Crane 25 MIN
U-matic / VHS / 16mm
Color (P I J H C A)
$550, $250 purchase _ #4195
Tells the story of a horseman who frightens village folk and an attempt by Ichabod Crane and his friends to steal a book of magic spells. Animated.
Literature and Drama; Social Science
Dist - CORF

A New Missionary to Walker's Garage 30 MIN
16mm
Color
Features Andy Malloy whose aging car breaks down, and takes a job at Walker's garage. Pictures owner, Ted Hunter, sharing his Christian faith with Andy. Depicts Andy's uninterest. Portrays Andy as a loner except for occasional dates with Jill Dennis whose aunt runs the nearby coffee shop. Shows that, on the same night Andy and Jill mysteriously leave town, the garage and coffee shop are burglarized. Advocates that man can only do so much and must trust God to do the rest.
Guidance and Counseling; Religion and Philosophy
Dist - FAMF **Prod** - FAMF

The New Mobility 19 MIN
16mm
Color
LC 78-701319
Describes a fleet of 200 buses designed to serve all of the people of the Southern California Rapid Transit District, particularly the physically handicapped.
Social Science
Dist - MASCOT **Prod** - SCRTD 1978

New Mood 30 MIN
16mm
History of the Negro People Series
B&W (H C A)
LC FIA68-1282
Reviews highlights of the civil rights struggle from 1954 - 64. Examines the impact of Negro militancy on Negro and white Americans. Shows film coverage showing Martin Luther King, Malcolm X, Medgar Evers and Presidents Kennedy and Johnson. Features Ossie Davis.
Civics and Political Systems; History - United States; Psychology; Sociology
Dist - IU **Prod** - NET 1965

New moon 11 MIN
16mm
Paper film series
Color (G)
$35.00 rental
Defines film as an object or motion picture 'soft sculpture' constructed of 16mm strips of color Xerography in which the paper - or emulsion - is a kind of skin complete with hair and pores, half - tone dots and paper fiber. Second in a series of paper films by Donna Cameron.
Fine Arts
Dist - CANCIN

New Moon Prone 10 MIN
Videoreel / VT2
Janaki Series
Color
Physical Education and Recreation
Dist - PBS **Prod** - WGBHTV

New mother care 23 MIN
VHS
Color (G)
$395.00, $295.00 purchase, $40.00 rental
Discusses the physical aspects of postpartum recovery - how to insure getting enough rest, perineal care and vaginal flow as an indicator of fatigue, and helpful exercises, including some for cesarean mothers. Focuses on the emotional aspects of becoming a new parent - improving couple communication, resuming sexual relations and dealing with postpartum mood swings. Addresses issues new parents may not yet have had the courage or opportunity to discuss, offers suggestions for strengthening the new relationship between mother and father, parent and newborn. Includes a study guide.
Health and Safety; Social Science; Sociology
Dist - POLYMR **Prod** - FIE

New Mothers and Infant Care Series

Common problems	15 MIN
Everyday Care	18 MIN
Feeding	12 MIN
Illness, Immunization and Safety	20 MIN
Living with Baby	17 MIN

Dist - AIMS

A New mother's feelings 30 MIN
VHS
Color (G)
Helps new mothers cope with the many new emotions associated with the birth of a first child. Addresses what feelings can be expected and how to prepare for them. Discusses the crying baby, postpartum blues, the mother's role as a protector, feelings of the father, bonding and how a new baby looks immediately after birth.
Health and Safety; Sociology
Dist - CAMV
PRI

New Music 30 MIN
VHS / 16mm
Say Brother National Edition Series
Color (G)
$55.00 rental _ #SBRO - 111
Sociology
Dist - PBS **Prod** - WGBHTV

The New Music 53 MIN
U-matic / VHS
Man and Music Series
Color (C)
$279.00, $179.00 purchase _ #AD - 2065
Focuses on Vienna during the closing days of the Austrian empire. Looks at Arnold Schoenberg who in 1909 broke with the tonal system that had been the standard language of classical Western music. Schoenberg and his two students, Alban Berg and Anton Webern, comprised the so - called Second Viennese School. Part of a 22 - part series that sets Western music into the historial and cultural context of its time.
Fine Arts; Geography - World; History - World; Psychology
Dist - FOTH **Prod** - FOTH

The New Music 29 MIN
16mm / VHS
Color
Features two duets by cornetist Bobby Bradford and clarinetist John Carter. Shows two musicians who were associated with Ornette Coleman in the 1960's.
Fine Arts
Dist - RHPSDY **Prod** - RHPSDY 1980

New Music America #1 27 MIN
U-matic / VHS
Documentaries on Art Series
Color (G)
$120.00, $80.00 purchase, $45.00, $30.00 rental
Documents first annual New Music America festival in Minneapolis, 1980. Features tho string quartet of David Byrne and an excerpt from 'United States of America' by Laurie Anderson. Includes Liz Philips, Richard Lerman, Charlie Morrow, Chris Janney, Alvin Curran and the Love of Life Orchestra. Produced by Skip Blumberg.
Fine Arts; Psychology
Dist - IAFC

A New Nation - the Struggle to Survive, 1789 - 1815 25 MIN
16mm
Color (I J H)
Looks at the personalities and problems which shaped America during the first 26 years after it gained independence. Contrasts the views of such people as George Washington, Alexander Hamilton and Thomas Jefferson. Recounts how the country survived two attempts at secession and the War of 1812.
Biography; History - United States
Dist - BNCHMK **Prod** - BNCHMK

New Navy 3 MIN
16mm
Color
LC 75-704047
Tells an ancient sea legend which provides an introduction to life at sea in the U S Navy of today.
Civics and Political Systems; Guidance and Counseling
Dist - USNAC **Prod** - USN 1974

The New Negro I - Harlem Renaissance 29 MIN
Videoreel / VT2
Black Experience Series
Color
History - United States; Sociology
Dist - PBS **Prod** - WTTWTV

The New Negro II - Nationalism and Garveyism 29 MIN
Videoreel / VT2
Black Experience Series
Color
Civics and Political Systems; History - United States
Dist - PBS **Prod** - WTTWTV

The New Neuropsychology of Weight Control 30 MIN
Cassette / VHS
Color (G)
$99.95, $79.95 purchase _ #2115, 2113
Features the work of obesity experts Drs Dennis Remington and Garth Fisher. Focuses on foods that 'burn up fuel,' changing eating patterns, non - strenuous physical activity for the retention of lean muscle tissue and emotional motivation. Offers an interactive multimedia kit which includes video, eight audiocassettes, study guide and progress journal or eight audiocassettes with study guide and progress journal.
Health and Safety; Physical Education and Recreation; Psychology
Dist - SYBVIS **Prod** - SYBVIS

The New North Africa 16 MIN
U-matic / VHS / 16mm
Color; B&W (I J H)
LC FIA65-1822
Shows the new and old sections of the principal cities of North Africa, concentrating on Tunisia, the most progressive area. Discusses North Africa's geography, history, agriculture, mining and its current problems.
Geography - World; History - United States; Social Science
Dist - STANF **Prod** - STANF 1964

The New North CBC PROG 1 27 MIN
16mm
New North Series
B&W (G)
#3X53N
Explores the three northern districts of Mackenzie, Keewatin, and Franklin and the diverse cultures these lands harbor.
Geography - World
Dist - CDIAND **Prod** - CANBC

The New North CBC PROG 5 - Where Fur is King 27 MIN
16mm
B&W (G)
#3X57N
Investigates the economic structure of Spence Bay and other small communities in Canada where fur and family allowance are mainstays of the economy.
Geography - World; Physical Education and Recreation
Dist - CDIAND **Prod** - CANBC

The New North CBC PROG 2 - Land of Tomorrow 27 MIN
16mm
New North Series
B&W (G)
#3X54N
Discusses how the resources needed for the future must be investigated today.
Social Science
Dist - CDIAND **Prod** - CANBC

The New North CBC PROGRAM 3 27 MIN
16mm
B&W (G)
#3X55N
Exlpores Inuvik, located in th4e Mackenzie Delta, which is the communications, education and trading center of the north. Discusses its establishment.
Geography - World
Dist - CDIAND **Prod** - CANBC

The New North CBC PROGRAM 4 - the Searchers 27 MIN
16mm
B&W (G)
#3X56N
Discusses the foundation in the 1950's of the Arctic Institute, which was inspired by the realization that the North was a vast laboratory for all scientific professions.
Science - Natural
Dist - CDIAND **Prod** - CANBC

New North Series

The New North CBC PROG 1	27 MIN
The New North CBC PROG 2 - Land of Tomorrow	27 MIN

Dist - CDIAND

New Nursery School Series

Intellectual Development	18 MIN
Introduction to the New Nursery School	25 MIN
Learning Booths	17 MIN

Dist - USNAC

The New Nutrition - what it Means to Teenagers
VHS / 35mm strip
$165.00 purchase _ #014 - 866 filmstrip, $165.00 purchase _ #014 -
Examines the relationship of diet to health and links illness to diet and lifestyle. Emphasizes quick action on following diet guidelines. Provides basic guidelines of the new nutrition and lists foods to avoid and those to include.
Health and Safety; Home Economics; Industrial and Technical Education; Social Science
Dist - CAREER **Prod** - CAREER

New options - presenting nontraditional career options 30 MIN
VHS
Color (IND PRO C G)
$50.00 purchase _ #013
Trains service providers and Private Industry Council - PIC - staff who work directly with clients. Teaches from two role plays between an employment counselor and a female client - one demonstrating the right way to present nontraditional career options to women, the other demonstrating the wrong way.
Business and Economics; Guidance and Counseling; Sociology
Dist - WOWINC

New or Innovative Areas 10 MIN
U-matic / VHS
Practical M B O Series
Color
Business and Economics; Education; Psychology
Dist - DELTAK **Prod** - DELTAK

The New Order 27 MIN
U-matic / VHS / 16mm
Five Billion People Series
Color
Offers a historical perspective on the world trend toward neo - colonialism, using the example of current political affairs in Africa to show that the continuing attempt to impose neo - colonialism has become increasingly difficult and discredited.
Business and Economics
Dist - CNEMAG **Prod** - LEFSP

New Orleans 3 MIN
16mm
Of all Things Series
Color (P I)
Discusses the city of New Orleans, Louisiana.
Geography - United States
Dist - AVED **Prod** - BAILYL

New Orleans 30 MIN
VHS
Color (G)
Presents the sights and sounds of New Orleans, Louisiana's largest city. Includes a visit to the city's historic French Quarter.
Fine Arts; Geography - United States
Dist - UILL
RMIBHF

New Orleans
VHS
Frugal gourmet - taste of America series
Color (G)
$19.95 purchase _ #CCP826
Shows how to prepare American food New Orleans style. Features Jeff Smith, the Frugal Gourmet. Part of a ten - part series on American cooking.
Geography - United States; History - United States; Home Economics; Physical Education and Recreation
Dist - CADESF **Prod** - CADESF

New Orleans' Black Indians - a Case Study in the Arts 30 MIN
U-matic
Faces of Culture - Studies in Cultural Anthropology Series Lesson 22; Lesson 22
Color (C A)
Focuses on the annual Mardi Gras Carnival in New Orleans. Examines the origins of the ceremony in the black 'Indian' tribes and African heritage of the participants.
Sociology
Dist - CDTEL **Prod** - COAST

New Orleans dishes
VHS
Frugal gourmet international cooking I series
Color (G)
$19.95 purchase _ #CCP802
Shows how to prepare food New Orleans style. Features Jeff Smith, the Frugal Gourmet. Part of a ten - part series on international cooking.
Geography - United States; History - United States; Home Economics; Physical Education and Recreation
Dist - CADESF **Prod** - CADESF

New Orleans Dishes 30 MIN
BETA / VHS
Frugal Gourmet Series
Color
Presents New Orleans dishes including barbeque shrimp, file gumbo and jambalaya.
Health and Safety; Home Economics; Psychology
Dist - CORF **Prod** - WTTWTV

New Orleans, Mardi Gras 3 MIN
16mm
Of all Things Series
Color (P I)
Discusses the Mardi Gras held in the city of New Orleans, Louisiana.
Geography - United States
Dist - AVED **Prod** - BAILYL

New Orleans Profile 13 MIN
16mm
Color (J)
Depicts the industry, history, traditions and economic importance of New Orleans, the South's largest city.
Geography - United States; Social Science
Dist - WSUM **Prod** - WSUM 1959

New Orleans, the Big Easy 27 MIN
16mm / U-matic / VHS
See America Series
Color (H A)
Features map drawings and comments from local residents. Takes a scenic trip to New Orleans.
Geography - United States
Dist - MTOLP **Prod** - MTOLP 1985

New Orleans, the Crescent City 20 MIN
U-matic / VHS
Color (J)
LC 82-706782
Takes viewers to New Orleans. Discusses the city's historic events and visits the French Quarter and the Mardi Gras. Shows such architectural highlights as the lace balconies and the cornstalk fence.
Geography - United States; History - United States; Sociology
Dist - AWSS **Prod** - AWSS 1980

New Orleans - 'til the butcher cuts him down 53 MIN
VHS
Color (G)
$29.95 purchase
Puts forth a little New Orleans jazz with Kid Punch Miller.
Fine Arts
Dist - KINOIC **Prod** - RHPSDY

New Orleans Tribune 9 MIN
U-matic / VHS
Color
Tells the story of a newspaper published by free blacks in New Orleans in the 1860's. Combines dramatic scenes in period costumes with connecting graphics and narration.
Social Science; Sociology
Dist - NOVID **Prod** - NOVID

New Pacific Series, the
Jugs to be Filled or Candles to be Lit - Pt 7 50 MIN
Over Rich, Over Sexed and Over Here - Pt 4 50 MIN
The Pacific Age - Pt 1 50 MIN
Return to Paradise - Pt 3 50 MIN
Shadow of the Rising Sun - Pt 8 50 MIN
Dist - FI

New Pacific series
Echoes of war - Pt 2 50 MIN
Fifty ways to get enlightened - Pt 5 50 MIN
For Richer for poorer - Pt 6 50 MIN
Dist - FI

New Pajamas 27 MIN
16mm / U-matic / VHS
Ramona Series
Color (P I)
$3795 purchase - 16 mm (entire set), $435 purchase - 16 mm (per
Tells how Ramona decides to run away from home when Beezus makes fun of her for wearing pajamas under her clothes at school. From Ramona and Her Mother. A production of Atlantis Films, Ltd. in association wiath Lancit Media Productions, Ltd. and Revcom Television.
Literature and Drama
Dist - CF

New pajamas 30 MIN
VHS
Beverly Cleary's Ramona series
Color; CC (K P I)
$16.95 purchase _ #132585
Presents a Ramona story by Beverly Cleary.
Literature and Drama
Dist - KNOWUN

New Parents and Teacher Guide to Drug Abuse 55 MIN
VHS
Color (I J H C A)
Presents a comprehensive guide about drug abuse.
Guidance and Counseling; Psychology; Sociology
Dist - BENNUP **Prod** - BENNUP 1987

The New partnership 38 MIN
VHS
Color (PRO A G)
$695.00 purchase, $225.00 rental
Reveals the business strategies that bring customers and suppliers together for greater success. Presents Tom Melohn as he visits several companies and talks with workers. Includes a video workbook, video case study and a workbook.
Business and Economics; Psychology
Dist - EXTR **Prod** - ENMED

The New Partnership - Managing for Excellence with Tom Melohn 30 MIN
VHS
Color (G)
Suggests methods for improving productivity and profits while also lowering worker absenteeism and turnover. Shows how these methods can also be applied to customer relations. Includes video case study and video workbook.
Business and Economics
Dist - PBS **Prod** - ENMED 1989
PRODUC

New Partnerships Series
Almost home 27 MIN
Your Move 25 MIN
Dist - UCEMC

New Parts for Old 26 MIN
U-matic / VHS
Breakthroughs Series
Color
Demonstrates the fascinating beginning of a new generation of biochemical substances which interact with the natural living processes of the body.
Science - Natural
Dist - LANDMK **Prod** - NOMDFI

New party, old problems - Part four 58 MIN
VHS / U-matic / 16mm
Imperfect union - Canadian labour and the left series
Color (H C G)
$775.00, $180.00 purchase, $40.00 rental _ #CC440516, #CC4405VU, #CC4405VH
Traces the history of the New Democrat Party - NDP - from 1962 to 1988 in Canada. Reveals the frequent fallings out between the NDP and the Canadian Labor Congress - CLC. Part four of a four - part series on Canadian labor and politics.
Business and Economics; Civics and Political Systems; History - World
Dist - IU **Prod** - NFBC 1989

New Pastures 92 MIN
U-matic / VHS
B&W (CZECH (ENGLISH SUBTITLES))
Presents a comedy about three prisoners released from jail and their experiences returning to a small village. Directed by Vladimir Cech. With English subtitles.
Fine Arts; Foreign Language; Sociology
Dist - IHF **Prod** - IHF

New pathways in science quartet 120 MIN
BETA / VHS
Color (G)
$69.95 purchase _ #Q134
Presents a four - part series on new pathways in science. Includes 'The Universal Organism' with Dr Rupert Sheldrake, 'The Holographic Brain' with Dr Karl Pribram, 'Time and Destiny' with Dr Charles Muses and 'Evolution - the Great Chain of Being' with Arthur M Young.
History - World; Mathematics; Religion and Philosophy; Science - Natural
Dist - THINKA **Prod** - THINKA

New pathways in science series
Evolution - the great chain of being 30 MIN
The Holographic brain 30 MIN
Time and destiny 30 MIN
The Universal organism 30 MIN
Dist - THINKA

The New Patriotism 26 MIN
U-matic / VHS
Color (G)
$249.00, $149.00 purchase _ #AD - 1913
Examines the nature of patriotism in America. Considers the different beliefs about patriotism by different segments of society, including working people, intellectuals, writers, career military people and young enlistees.
Civics and Political Systems; History - United States; Social Science
Dist - FOTH **Prod** - FOTH

The New Patriotism - 126 30 MIN
U-matic
Currents - 1984 - 85 Season Series
Color (A)
Examines the growth of patriotism and nationalism during the Reagan administration.
Civics and Political Systems; Social Science
Dist - PBS **Prod** - WNETTV 1985

New Patterns on the Land 13 MIN
16mm
Color
LC 74-705207
Tells the story of modern conservation farming and how it has brought new patterns on the land to the American rural landscape.
Agriculture; Science - Natural
Dist - USNAC **Prod** - USDA 1967

New People for Old 50 MIN
16mm / BETA / U-matic / VHS
Color; Mono (J H C A)
$50.00 Rental
Reveals the importance of DNA experiments and interveiws various authorities who discuss the advantages and dangers of man's ability to use this substance. Includes interveiws with Linus Pauling, Dr. Vasken Oposian and Dr. Jose Delgado.
Health and Safety
Dist - CTV **Prod** - CTV 1972

A new people - the American mosaic
VHS
CC; Color (J H)
$249 purchase_#10420VL
Explores the cultural roots of U S society from the Native Americans to new immigrants. Presents a three - part series on the various ethnic groups that make up the United States and their influences on the culture.
Geography - United States; History - United States; Sociology
Dist - UNL

The New Pequot - a tribal portrait 60 MIN
U-matic / VT1 / VHS
Color (G)
$59.95 purchase, $35.00 rental
Explores the history and future of the Mashantucket Pequot Indians of Connecticut. Reveals that 15 years ago the Pequots were on the brink of extinction but the final command of Elizabeth George, one of the last surviving members of the tribe was, 'don't ever give up the land.' This was used as a rallying cry for the comeback of the

tribe in the 1970s and 1980s. Profiles the work of George's grandson Richard 'Skip' Hayward, member of the Pequot Tribal Council, in making her last words come true, and efforts of the tribe to regain tribal land and to find ways to achieve self - sufficiency.
History - United States; Social Science
Dist - NAMPBC **Prod** - CPT

New Perspectives 30 MIN
U-matic
Fast Forward Series
Color (H C)
Demonstrates what can be seen when machines supplement eyesight. Shows weather satellites and electronic microscopes opening new vistas.
Computer Science; Industrial and Technical Education; Science
Dist - TVOTAR **Prod** - TVOTAR 1979

New Perspectives in Normal and Neoplastic Lymphoid Cell Proliferation 60 MIN
U-matic
Color
Presents experiments in human cell proliferation.
Health and Safety; Science - Natural
Dist - UTEXSC **Prod** - UTEXSC

New physics and beyond quartet 120 MIN
BETA / VHS
Color (G)
$69.95 purchase _ #Q124
Presents a four - part series on new physics and beyond. Includes 'Physics and Consciousness' with Dr Fred Alan Wolf, 'A New Science of Life' with Dr Rupert Sheldrake, 'Consciousness and Hyperspace' with Saul - Paul Sirag and 'Consciousness and Quantum Reality' with Dr Nick Herbert.
Psychology; Religion and Philosophy; Science - Natural; Science - Physical
Dist - THINKA **Prod** - THINKA

New physics and beyond
Consciousness and hyperspace 30 MIN
Consciousness and quantum reality 30 MIN
A New science of life 30 MIN
Physics and consciousness 30 MIN
Dist - THINKA

The New physics - Newton revised - Program 9 52 MIN
VHS
Day the universe changed series
Color (H C G)
$695.00, $300.00 purchase, $75.00 rental
Reveals that a new era of scientific inquiry began around 1800 with the study of the properties of electricity. Reviews the advances in the study of magnetism, electricity, light and its proerties, sub - atomic particles and other phenomena. Explains how Einstein and others sorted out the scientific puzzle and how the process led to Heisenberg's Principle of Uncertainty. Shows how the public has continuously confused technology for science. Part of a ten - part series on Western thought hosted by James Burke.
Business and Economics; Civics and Political Systems; Science; Science - Physical; Sociology
Dist - CF **Prod** - BBCTV 1986

The New Pilgrims 25 MIN
VHS / U-matic
Color (J)
Examines the nationality and origins of the latest U S immigrants. Features interviews with new families from Central America, Mexico, Vietnam, Korea and the Phillipines talking about their adjustment to life in the U S. Examines their effect on the labor force caused by cheap wages and their desire to succeed.
Sociology
Dist - FI **Prod** - NBCNEW

New Pioneers 20 MIN
U-matic / VHS
Color
$335.00 purchase
Sociology
Dist - ABCLR **Prod** - ABCLR 1983

New places to look for jobs - technology and the 21st century
VHS
Color (J H G)
$98.00 purchase _ #4420
Shows high school students how they can expect the major economic, technological and work trends to impact their job prospects and their future. Emphasizes the importance of being willing to continuously learn and update technology - oriented skills. Covers very specific twists and turns the American economy has taken and shows what students must do to become and remain competitive in the workplace. Examines five major areas - business - management; production - technology; human - social services; family - consumer studies; and the planning - job search process.
Business and Economics; Guidance and Counseling; Sociology
Dist - NEWCAR

The New Position 5 MIN
Videoreel / VT2
How to Improve Managerial Performance - the AMA Performance 'Standards Program Series
Color (A)
LC 75-704236
Uses a case study in order to show what happens when a manager creates a new position in a department and violates certain organizational principles.
Business and Economics; Psychology
Dist - AMA **Prod** - AMA 1974

New Prescription for Life 48 MIN
16mm 27 MIN
Color (PRO)
LC 75-703876; 75-703878
Presents detailed instructions in cardiopulmonary, resuscitation, including artificial respiration, artificial circulation, and airway obstruction.
Health and Safety; Science; Science - Natural
Dist - BANDEL **Prod** - BANDEL 1975

The New Principal 5 MIN
Videoreel / VT2
How to Improve Managerial Performance - the AMA Performance 'Standards Program Series
Color (A)
LC 75-704242
Presents a case study which dramatizes a manager's attempt to upgrade performance for a key result area.
Business and Economics; Psychology
Dist - AMA **Prod** - AMA 1974

The New principal 50 MIN
VHS
Inside story series
Color (A)
PdS99 purchase
Reveals that Battersea Technology College in South London has one of the highest truancy rates and some of the worst exam results in the United Kingdom. Follows Michael Clark, who was appointed by the local council with a brief to turn the school into a success, over the period of a year to see how he - and the school - fare.
Education
Dist - BBCENE

New Principles of Training and Supervision I
U-matic / VHS
Deming Videotapes - Quality, Productivity, and Competitive Series
Color
Discusses the aim of supervision in industry.
Business and Economics
Dist - MIOT **Prod** - MIOT
SME

New Principles of Training and Supervision, II - Quality and the Consumer
VHS / U-matic
Deming Videotapes - Quality, Productivity, and Competitive Series
Color
Business and Economics
Dist - MIOT **Prod** - MIOT

A New Private Eye 30 MIN
U-matic
Realities
Color (A)
Delves into the political, social, economic and cultural trends of the 1980s. Probes a wide range of contemporary concerns. Each segment includes a guest speaker who is an expert in the field under discussion.
Business and Economics; Civics and Political Systems; Social Science; Sociology
Dist - TVOTAR **Prod** - TVOTAR 1985

The New Professionals 38 MIN
16mm 20 MIN
Color (C A)
A shorter version of the film The New Professionals. Demonstrates to professionals, consumers and providers the range of abilities of Gerontological Nurse Practitioners in the various levels of long term care. Introduces students to the common acute and chronic problems of the aged, showing the individuality of each person's needs. Focuses on institutional settings.
Health and Safety
Dist - UNKNWN **Prod** - MTSHC

A New public - fin de siecle - Parts 45 and 46 60 MIN
U-matic / VHS
Western tradition - part II series
Color (G)
$45.00, $29.95 purchase
Presents two thirty - minute programs tracing the history of ideas, events and institutions which have shaped modern societies hosted by Eugen Weber. Looks at public education and mass communications which created a new political life and leisure time in part 45. Part 46 examines how the everyday life of the working class was transformed by leisure, prompting the birth of an elite avant - garde movement. Parts 45 and 46 of a 52 - part series on the Western tradition.
Civics and Political Systems; Geography - World; Social Science; Sociology
Dist - ANNCPB **Prod** - WGBH 1989

New Pulse of Life 28 MIN
16mm / U-matic / VHS
Color (J) (SPANISH)
Presents the principles and techniques of C P R. Includes live subjects, manikins, colorful visuals, and dramatic re - enactments, which are used to demonstrate current standards and guidelines for A - Airway Opened, B - Breathing Restored, and C - Circulation Restored. Narrated by John Houseman.
Foreign Language; Health and Safety
Dist - PFP **Prod** - PFP

The New puritans - the Sikhs of Yuba City 27 MIN
VHS / U-matic
Color (G)
$150.00 purchase, $50.00 rental
Reveals that the Sikh religion is the result of an attempt to combine Hindu and Islamic faiths in 15th - century India. Discloses that Sikhs economically forced off their farms in the state of Punjab first came to California in the early 1900s, creating a rural life that mirrored their native India. Today, some 8,000 Sikhs live in the Yuba City area of California. Portrays the cultural and generational conflicts, assimilation and arranged marriages. Produced and directedby Ritu Sarin and Tenzing Sonam.
History - United States; History - World; Religion and Philosophy; Sociology
Dist - CROCUR

The New RCRA 180 MIN
VHS / U-matic
Color (A)
Disusses a teleconference which explains the major provisions of the New Resources Conservation and Recovery Act which became effective November 8, 1984.
Civics and Political Systems; Science - Natural
Dist - USNAC **Prod** - USEPA 1984

New RCRA, the Condensed Version 56 MIN
VHS / U-matic
Color (A)
Presents a condensed version of the teleconference examining the major provisions of the new Resource Conservation and Recovery Act which became effective November 8, 1984.
Civics and Political Systems; Science - Natural
Dist - USNAC **Prod** - USEPA 1984

New Realities 20 MIN
VHS
Color (H C G)
Examines recent changes which affect highway transportation.
Health and Safety; Psychology; Social Science
Dist - HUF **Prod** - HUF 1984

New realities - techniques of photo collage 20 MIN
VHS
Color (J H)
$149.00 purchase _ #87 - 002829
Introduces students to the history and technique of photo collage, an art form combining disassociative photography. Explores the evolution of the art form with a summary of its invention and development in the works of Picasso, Braque, Kurt Schwitters and Man Ray in part one, showing how three - dimensional works by Duchamp and Cornell expanded the concept. Discusses the story - telling element of art by David Hockney. Part two features artist Tom Mezzanotte who demonstrates how a photo collage is created, and an art student who shoots black and white photos, then arranges them into a finished piece.
Fine Arts
Dist - SRA **Prod** - SRA 1991

A New Reality 51 MIN
U-matic / VHS / 16mm
Color (H C A)
LC FIA67-5540
Traces the discovery of the structure of the atom, emphasizing the work of Niels Bohr.
Science; Science - Physical
Dist - IFB **Prod** - OECD 1965

New Reality, a, Pt 1 27 MIN
U-matic / VHS / 16mm
Color (H C A)
LC FIA67-5540
Traces the discovery of the structure of the atom, emphasizing the work of Niels Bohr.
Science - Physical
Dist - IFB **Prod** - OECD 1965

New Reality, a, Pt 2 24 MIN
U-matic / VHS / 16mm
Color (H C A)
LC FIA67-5540
Traces the discovery of the structure of the atom, emphasizing the work of Niels Bohr.
Science - Physical
Dist - IFB **Prod** - OECD 1965

New Relations 34 MIN
16mm / VHS
Color (G)
$265.00 purchase
Looks at the filmaker's decision to become a father and the responsibilities and changes that decision brought into his life.
Sociology
Dist - FANPRO **Prod** - FANPRO 1989

New relations - a film about fathers and sons 34 MIN
VHS
Color (G)
$99.00 purchase _ #CE - 015
Explores the costs and rewards of becoming a father and of a father choosing to share childcare equally with the mother of his children. Features interaction with filmmaker Achtenberg's own father to reflect on changes in fathering styles between the two generations.
Psychology; Sociology
Dist - FANPRO **Prod** - ACMISH

The New Reno - Tahoe - Two Worlds in One 28 MIN
16mm
Color
LC 79-701180
Points out various places of interest in and around Reno, Nevada, and Lake Tahoe in order to encourage travel to this vacation area.
Geography - United States
Dist - MTP **Prod** - UAL 1978

New Reserves Role 2 13 MIN
16mm
Color
LC 77-702993
Outlines the activities of Canadian Armed Forces reservists.
Civics and Political Systems; Geography - World
Dist - CDND **Prod** - CDND

The New Resource Conservation and Recovery Act - RCRA - Hazardous and Solid Waste Amendment of 1984 56 MIN
VHS / Slide
Color (G IND)
$155.00, $70.00 purchase _ #SHA12847, #SHA12851
Gives a general RCRA overview by covering the costs involved, details of the statutory provisions, permit requirements, recordkeeping, technological requirements, 'hammer provisions,' inspections, implementation and enforcement, adherence schedules, citizen rights, exposure information and health assessments. Reveals that the law is designed to regulate more closely those businesses and industries that are prime producers of hazardous waste. Slide version includes 161 color slides and a 21 - page script.
Health and Safety; Sociology
Dist - USNAC **Prod** - EPA 1984

New retail supervisor 32 MIN
VHS
Color (A PRO IND)
$550.00 purchase, $125.00 rental
Trains retail supervisors in five areas - time management, delegation, motivation, communication, and coaching or discipline. Includes leader's guide and participant workbooks.
Business and Economics; Guidance and Counseling; Psychology
Dist - VLEARN

The New revolution - Part 4 21 MIN
VHS
Cutting edge series
Color (G)
$150.00 purchase _ #8026
Examines research in genetic engineering and life sciences - embryo manipulation in cattle and transplantation to surrogate hosts, genetic manipulation of conifers to produce more hardy and disease - resistant trees, genetic manipulation of canola to make it a wax - bearing plant, drug testing and studies of the air environment. Part of a five - part series on the latest research and technology developments in Western Canada.
Agriculture; Geography - World; Science; Science - Natural
Dist - UCALG **Prod** - UCALG 1989

The New Russian revolution 47 MIN
VHS
Color (J H C G)
$29.95 purchase _ #TUR3065V
Uses original news footage to trace the historic events of the six days of the 'new' Russian revolution. Covers the hard - line coup that imprisoned President Mikhail Gorbachev and tried to drag the Soviet people back to the days of Stalin; the show of defiance outside the Russian White House by forces loyal to Boris Yeltsin; the return of Gorbachev and the collapse of communist rule. Features CNN Special Reports Senior Correspondent Mark Walton, who was in Moscow and Kiev during the crisis.
Civics and Political Systems; History - World
Dist - CAMV **Prod** - TBSESI 1991

New School, the 88 MIN
16mm / U-matic / VHS
Captioned; Color (A) (SPANISH (ENGLISH SUBTITLES))
Discusses the work - study program initiated during Cuba's 1961 literacy campaign in which students combine academic and agricultural work.
Fine Arts; History - World
Dist - CNEMAG **Prod** - CUBAFI 1973

A New science of life 30 MIN
VHS / BETA
New physics and beyond
Color (G)
$29.95 purchase _ #S495
Challenges mechanistic thinking in the life sciences. Proposes a bold alternative to the idea that genetic programming is solely responsible for diversity of form and development of behavior and mind in living creatures. Features Dr Rupert Sheldrake, biologist and author of 'A New Science of Life' and 'The Presence of the Past.' Part of a four - part series on new physics and beyond.
Psychology; Science - Natural; Science - Physical
Dist - THINKA **Prod** - THINKA

New secret adventure no 4
VHS
Color (R P I J)
$19.99 purchase
Portrays Drea Thomas who didn't win the science scholarship she had hoped for, her mother's been fired, and her rival Arlene Blake got free tickets to a sold - out concert. Reveals that, in order to recharge her sagging self - esteem, Drea shares an animated Secret Adventure with baby - sitting charges Matt and Rebecca Long. Includes a parents' guide for building the self - esteem of children.
Health and Safety; Psychology
Dist - PROVID **Prod** - BROADM

The new selling with service 56 MIN
VHS
Speaking of success series
Color (H C G)
$39.95 purchase _ #PD06
Features consultant Phil Weller. Part of a series.
Business and Economics
Dist - SVIP **Prod** - AUVICA 1993

The New Sexual Revolution 30 MIN
VHS / U-matic
Moral Values in Contemporary Society Series
Color (J)
Shows Albert Ellis of the Institute for Advanced Study in Rational Psychotherapy and Lester Kirkendall, Professor Emeritus of Oregon State University, talking about the new sexual revolution.
Psychology; Sociology
Dist - AMHUMA **Prod** - AMHUMA

New Skills for Managing the Work Force 240 MIN
U-matic / VHS
Color
Presents a seminar for direct people managers.
Business and Economics; Psychology
Dist - GOODMI **Prod** - GOODMI

New Slick and Old Lace 49 MIN
BETA / VHS / 16mm
Inquiry Series
Color; Mono (H C A)
MV $350.00 _ MP $600.00 purchase, $50.00 rental; LC 77-702835
Looks at the state of the fashion industry in Canada, the designs of clothes, and the quality of the merchandise sold. Suggests that the quality of clothes is not always good and that quality standards are not effective.
Home Economics
Dist - CTV **Prod** - CTV 1976

New Slick and Old Lace, Pt 1 25 MIN
16mm / VHS / BETA
Inquiry Series
Color
LC 77-702835
Explores what people wear, where they buy it and how much they pay.
Home Economics
Dist - CTV **Prod** - CTV 1976

New Slick and Old Lace, Pt 2 25 MIN
16mm / VHS / BETA
Inquiry Series
Color
LC 77-702835
Explores what people wear, where they buy it and how much they pay.
Home Economics
Dist - CTV **Prod** - CTV 1976

The New Society 30 MIN
VHS / U-matic
Focus on Society Series
Color (C)
Examines what the future may be and addresses the intellectual and value decisions facing U S society. Identifies trends in areas such as urbanism, family, work and leisure.
Sociology
Dist - DALCCD **Prod** - DALCCD

A New society 30 MIN
VHS
American adventure series
Color (G)
$150.00 purchase _ #TAMA - 106
Considers the awakening of freedom in the American colonies. Portrays the colonies' changing systems of government. Shows the growth of seaports and their impact on political and economic affairs.
History - United States
Dist - PBS

The New Solar Dawn 26 MIN
VHS / U-matic
Breakthroughs Series
Color
Shows how an Israeli scientist captures the imagination of scientists and industrialists with a remarkable method of harnessing the sun's energy which he claims will revolutionize solar energy systems.
Science - Physical
Dist - LANDMK **Prod** - NOMDFI

The New Solar System 15 MIN
16mm
Science in Action Series
Color (C)
Deals with the results of the automated spacecraft which have enabled scientists to probe the planets from close - up. Explains the result has been a virtually new portrait of the planets of the solar system, and their interactions with the sun and space. Examines several of these bodies including Mercury, Venus, Comet Kohoutek, Mars, Jupiter and Saturn.
Science - Physical
Dist - COUNFI **Prod** - ALLFP

New Sound in the Education of the Deaf, a 26 MIN
16mm
Captioned; Color (A)
Explains the community education and continuing education concept as it applies to schools for the deaf.
Education; Guidance and Counseling; Psychology
Dist - GALCO **Prod** - GALCO 1975

New South Wales Images 17 MIN
16mm
Color
LC 80-700827
Offers an overview of the sights and way of life in New South Wales.
Geography - World
Dist - TASCOR **Prod** - NSWF 1979

The New Space Race 30 MIN
VHS / U-matic
Enterprise II Series
Color (C A)
Looks at how the exploration of space is causing entrepeneurs to seek contracts to launch satellites and compete for their share of their lucrative market.
Business and Economics; Science - Physical
Dist - LCOA **Prod** - WGBHTV 1983

New Spain 15 MIN
U-matic / VHS
America past series
(J H)
$125 purchase
Discusses the Spanish settlement and cultural influence in territories that eventually became parts of the United States.

History - United States
Dist - AITECH **Prod** - KRMATV 1987

A New Spirit in Painting - Six Painters of the 1980s
U-matic / VHS
Color
Explores international developments in painting with portraits of Georg Baselitz, Marku Lupertz, Sandro Chia, Francesco Clemente, David Salle, and Julian Schnabel.
Fine Arts
Dist - BLACKW **Prod** - BLACKW

New stages for dance 30 MIN
U-matic / VHS
Dance on television and film series
Color
Fine Arts; Industrial and Technical Education
Dist - ARCVID **Prod** - ARCVID

A New Start 29 MIN
16mm
To Live Again Series
Color
LC 74-705210
Describes the life of an ex - prisoner before and after his rehabilitation. Shows his counselor talking about his success in working with public offenders.
Health and Safety; Psychology; Sociology
Dist - USNAC **Prod** - USSRS 1969

New Strategies for the Cure of Large Bowel Cancer 39 MIN
U-matic
Color
Discusses new strategies for treating large bowel cancer, the most important of which is early detection and diagnosis.
Health and Safety
Dist - UTEXSC **Prod** - UTEXSC

The New Superfund - emergency preparedness and community right to know - Part 5 48 MIN
BETA / U-matic / VHS
The New Superfund series
Color (G PRO)
$46.00, $155.00 purchase _ #LSTF29
Continues a 1987 EPA teleconference explaining the new Superfund hazardous waste cleanup law. Discusses emergency planning, emergency notification and inventories and data sheets on hazardous substances. Part 5 of 7 parts.
Civics and Political Systems; Sociology
Dist - FEDU **Prod** - USEPA 1990

The New Superfund - enforcement and federal facilities - Part 4 52 MIN
U-matic / VHS / BETA
The New Superfund series
Color (G PRO)
$46.00, $155.00 purchase _ #LSTF28
Continues a 1987 EPA teleconference explaining the new Superfund hazardous waste cleanup law. Discusses settlement options, judicial review and federal facilities. Part 4 of 7 parts.
Civics and Political Systems; Health and Safety; Sociology
Dist - FEDU **Prod** - USEPA 1990

The New Superfund - research and development - closing remarks - Part 7 33 MIN
U-matic / VHS / BETA
The New Superfund series
Color (G PRO)
$29.95, $130.00 purchase _ #LSTF31
Concludes a 1987 EPA teleconference explaining the new Superfund hazardous waste cleanup law. Discusses site program, university hazardous substances research centers, hazardous substance health research and training, research and development for Department of Defense wastes and closing remarks. Part 7 of 7 parts.
Civics and Political Systems; Sociology
Dist - FEDU **Prod** - USEPA 1990

The New Superfund series
The New Superfund - emergency preparedness and community right to know - Part 5 48 MIN
The New Superfund - enforcement and federal facilities - Part 4 52 MIN
The New Superfund - research and development - closing remarks - Part 7 33 MIN
The New Superfund - the changes in the remedial process - cleanup standards and state involvement requirements - Part 2 62 MIN
The New Superfund - the changes in the removal process - removal and additional program requirements - Part 3 48 MIN
The New Superfund - underground storage tank trust fund and response program - Part 6 21 MIN
The New Superfund - what is it, how does it work - Part 1 30 MIN
Dist - FEDU

The New Superfund - the changes in the remedial process - cleanup standards and state involvement requirements -Part 2 62 MIN
U-matic / VHS / BETA
The New Superfund series
Color (G PRO)
$46.00, $155.00 purchase _ #LSTF26
Continues a 1987 EPA teleconference explaining the new Superfund hazardous waste cleanup law. Discusses an overview, implementation, preliminary assessment, hazard ranking revisions, cleanup standards, off - site policy, permanent remedy, mandatory cleanup schedules and state involvement regulations. Part 2 of 7 parts.
Civics and Political Systems; Health and Safety; Sociology
Dist - FEDU **Prod** - USEPA 1990

The New Superfund - the changes in the removal process - removal and additional program requirements - Part 3 48 MIN
U-matic / VHS / BETA
The New Superfund series
Color (G PRO)
$46.00, $155.00 purchase _ #LSTF27
Continues a 1987 EPA teleconference explaining the new Superfund hazardous waste cleanup law. Discusses expanded removal authority, reportable quantities and public participation and technical assistance. Part 3 of 7 parts.
Civics and Political Systems; Health and Safety; Sociology
Dist - FEDU **Prod** - USEPA 1990

The New Superfund - underground storage tank trust fund and response program - Part 6 21 MIN
U-matic / VHS / BETA
The New Superfund series
Color (G PRO)
$29.95, $130.00 purchase _ #LSTF30
Continues a 1987 EPA teleconference explaining the new Superfund hazardous waste cleanup law. Discusses UST trust fund and delegation to states distribution program. Part 6 of 7 parts.
Civics and Political Systems; Sociology
Dist - FEDU **Prod** - USEPA 1990

The New Superfund - what is it, how does it work - Part 1 30 MIN
U-matic / VHS / BETA
The New Superfund series
Color (G PRO)
$29.95, $130.00 purchase _ #LSTF32
Introduces a 1987 EPA teleconference explaining the new Superfund hazardous waste cleanup law. Part 1 of 7 parts.
Civics and Political Systems; Health and Safety; Sociology
Dist - FEDU **Prod** - USEPA 1990

The New supervisor
VHS
Color (A PRO IND)
$965.00 purchase, $375.00 rental
Teaches new supervisors the skills that will make them more effective managers. Covers topics including motivation, interviewing, delegating, communicating, and leading.
Business and Economics; Guidance and Counseling; Psychology
Dist - VLEARN **Prod** - EFM

The New supervisor 25 MIN
VHS
Color (PRO IND A)
$495.00 purchase, $150.00 rental _ #CRI20
Covers areas of attitude, delegating, standards for production, and coaching, counseling and leadership skills. Gives supervisors a refresher course in doing their job - including the handling of difficult employees and avoiding specific on - the - job mistakes. Based on the book by Elwood N Chapman. Includes leader's guide and workbook.
Business and Economics
Dist - EXTR **Prod** - CRISP
DHB

The New supervisor - making the transition 24 MIN
U-matic / 16mm / VHS
Color (C A G)
$540.00, $410.00, $380.00 purchase _ #A978
Presents three experienced supervisors who explore the difference between being an individual worker and a supervisor. Uses a series of on - the - job vignettes to discuss the importance of thinking like a manager - not a worker, delegating versus doing the work oneself, employee training and development, communicating expectations, using feedback and employee ideas, handling behavior problems and the need to admit and learn from mistakes.
Business and Economics; Psychology
Dist - BARR **Prod** - SAIF 1984
VLEARN

New Supervisor Series Module 1
A New Attitude 64 FRS
Dist - RESEM

New Supervisor Series Module 2
The Message is Yours - Don't Lose it 55 FRS
Dist - RESEM

New Supervisor Series Module 5
Self - Development - the Key to Success 11 MIN
Dist - RESEM

New Supervisor Series
Presents five modules on supervision. Includes the titles A New Attitude, The Message is Yours - Don't Lose It, Getting the Job Done Through Others, Training - a Major Responsibility, Self - Development - the Key to Success.
Getting the job done through others 61 FRS
New supervisor series 53 MIN
Training - a Major Responsibility 64 FRS
Dist - RESEM **Prod** - RESEM 1984

A New Supervisor Takes a Look at His Job 13 MIN
16mm
Problems in Supervision Series
B&W
LC FIE52-138
A plant superintendent uses dramatized illustrations to explain to a machine tool operator who has been made a group leader the meaning of working with people instead of machines.
Business and Economics
Dist - USNAC **Prod** - USOE 1944

A New Surgical Absorbable Hemostat 21 MIN
U-matic / VHS
Color (PRO)
Demonstrates the properties of an absorbable hemostat derived from organic cellulose in the laboratory and some of its numerous clinical applications in humans.
Health and Safety
Dist - WFP **Prod** - WFP

A New Surgical Procedure for the Treatment of Gastro - Esophageal Reflux 8 MIN
VHS / U-matic
Color (PRO)
Shows placement around the esophagus below the diaphragm and above the stomach of a ring - like prothetic device made of a silicone gel. No recurrences of hiatal hernia or symptoms have occurred in any of the patients treated with this device.
Health and Safety
Dist - WFP **Prod** - WFP

The New Swedish Cinema 40 MIN
16mm
B&W
Presents a survey of the Swedish movie scene featuring lesser known Swedish film from the sixties and seventies.
Fine Arts; Geography - World
Dist - SIS **Prod** - SIS

The New tax plan - love it or loathe it 30 MIN
U-matic
Adam Smith's money world series; 116
Color (A)
Attempts to demystify the world of money and break it down so that small as well as large businesses and it's people understand and adjust to new social and economic trends. Reports on the major economic stories and discoveries of the day.
Business and Economics
Dist - PBS **Prod** - WNETTV 1985

New teacher training videos series
How to change kids' lives
How to discipline children
How to get new teachers started
How to lead a child to Christ
How to recruit teachers
How to talk with a young child
How to teach kids using guided conversation
How to teach young children about God
Dist - GOSPEL

New teams - Part 9 12 MIN
VHS
Total quality management - Ten elements for implementation series
Color (PRO IND A)
$300.00 purchase _ #GO02I
Presents part nine of a ten - part series which outlines a course of continuous improvement. Helps organizations, such as, educational institutions, manufacturing operations, hospitals and service industries. Includes extensive workshop materials. By Goal - QPC.
Business and Economics; Psychology
Dist - EXTR

New Technologies / Problems and Possibilities 26 MIN
VHS / U-matic
Focus on Change Series
Color
Sociology
Dist - DELTAK **Prod** - TVOTAR

New Technology in Education Series
Computer Gaming as an Integrated Learning Experience 32 MIN
Computer Literacy - a New Subject in the Curriculum 30 MIN
Implementing Technology in the Schools - Issues 42 MIN
Logo - the Computer as an Intellectual Tool 27 MIN
Research and Development - Interactive Computer Graphics for Intuitional Problem 41 MIN
School District Experiences in Implementing Technology 65 MIN
Software Development - Key Issues and Considerations 30 MIN
A Statewide Educational Computing Network - the Minnesota Educational Computing 23 MIN
Teacher Training Experiences and Issues 47 MIN
Using Computer Simulations in Social Science, Science and Math 21 MIN
Using the Computer to Develop Writing Abilities 27 MIN
Dist - USNAC

New Technology - Whose Progress 35 MIN
16mm
Color (A)
Evaluates new technology and speculates on its impact on workers. Comments on its implications are made by trade unionists, journalists and politicians in this British documentary.
Business and Economics; Sociology
Dist - AFLCIO **Prod** - EDM 1981

The New Tenant 31 MIN
U-matic / VHS / 16mm
Humanities - Short Play Showcase Series
Color (H C A)
LC 76-700875
Presents The New Tenant by Eugene Ionesco, a play from the Theater of the Absurd which expresses our sense of the ambiguity and incoherence of much of modern life.
Fine Arts; Literature and Drama
Dist - EBEC **Prod** - EBEC 1976

New Testament 40 MIN
VHS
Bible story time series
Color (K P I R)
$14.95 purchase _ #35 - 81001 - 19
Uses an animation format to tell four stories from the New Testament. 'The Small Town Boy Who Made Good' follows Jesus as he begins his ministry with miracles and parables. 'The Twelve Fishermen' tells how the twelve disciples were selected by Jesus. 'The Thank You People' presents stories of grateful and ungrateful people, while 'The Bread and Water Man' talks about the 'many faces of Jesus' described in the Gospel of John.
Literature and Drama; Religion and Philosophy
Dist - APH **Prod** - FAMF

New Thunder for the USAF - the a - 10, the AV10A Bronco, and the Huey Cobra 40 MIN
U-matic / VHS
Color
Shows three types of aircraft and awesome scenes of firepower, including historical footage of jet planes from the early '40's and '50's.
Civics and Political Systems
Dist - IHF **Prod** - IHF

The New Tijuana 58 MIN
VHS
Color (H C G A)
$295.00 purchase, $50.00 rental _ #38067
Profiles booming Tijuana, Mexico, the West Coast's second largest city after Los Angeles. Shows its struggles between its heritage as a Third World border town with a sordid past and its promise as a modern center of international finance and high technology. Divided into segments that explore the city's past, its future, and the challenges facing it today. Provides understanding of contemporary Mexico and the issues underlying the proposed Free Trade Agreement between it and the US. Produced by Paul Espinosa for KPBS - TV, San Diego.
Business and Economics; Geography - World; History - World
Dist - UCEMC

New Times 59 MIN
16mm
Best of Families Series
Color (H C A)
LC 82-700610
Presents the stories of three fictional families living in New York City in the 1880's and the 1890's. Shows how, on New Years Eve, 1899, the families look back on their lives and unrealized dreams and confront the approaching new century with speculation and renewed hope.
History - United States; Sociology
Dist - IU **Prod** - CTELWO 1977

New tribes mission 12 MIN
VHS / 16mm
Yanomamo series
Color (G)
$250.00, $130.00 purchase, $25.00 rental
Visits the mission in Bisaasi - teri which has existed since the 1950s. Interviews the missionary - teacher who explains that her goal is to bring the message of Jesus and salvation to the Yanomamo, to teach them to reject their false gods, demons and drugs. She leads schoolboys in a Spanish song and states that she speaks Yanomamo, not because she is interested in their culture but because it facilitates conversion of the people. Part of a series on the Yanomamo Indians of Venezuela by Timothy Asch and Napoleon Chagnon.
Geography - World; Religion and Philosophy; Social Science; Sociology
Dist - DOCEDR **Prod** - DOCEDR 1975

The New Underground Railroad 30 MIN
U-matic / VHS
Color (J)
LC 84-700388
Presents the story of a group of church people in Madison, Wisconsin, struggling to decide whether or not to defy U S law by giving sanctuary to Salvadorans fleeing the horrors of military persecution in their country. Looks at the story of a young Salvadoran family and their clandestine journey to the United States.
History - World; Sociology
Dist - IU **Prod** - CLOPRO 1984
CWS

The New understanding 27 MIN
U-matic / VHS
Caring community - alcoholism and drug abuse series
Color
Explains the typical psychological consequences of breaking down the denial system, as well as methods and modes by which the chemically dependent person can be helped to move from a state of demoralization to an understanding and acceptance of his or her illness.
Psychology; Sociology
Dist - VTRI **Prod** - VTRI

New Vehicle Technology Series Pt 2
Electric and Hybrid Vehicles, Lead - Acid Battery Systems - Range, Speed, and Cycle 120 MIN
Dist - UAZMIC

New vehicle technology series
Aerodynamics, rolling resistance, roll down tests, fifth wheel design and microprocessor 120 MIN
Comparison of computer simulation using data for each component of the vehicle with the 60 MIN
Dist - UAZMIC

New view - new eyes 50 MIN
16mm / VHS
Color (G)
$75.00, $125.00 rental, $250.00 purchase
Reflects on home, migration and the function of art - making. Travels with the filmmaker as she takes her aunt and uncle on a trip to Honest Ed's Department Store in Toronto, and herself on a trip to India to meet her father's family. She finds that India is in no simple way 'home,' and yet she cannot hide behind the tourist's camera. Challenges western representations of India through her resonant weave of location imagery, music, poetry, conversation and journal entries.
Geography - World; Sociology
Dist - WMEN **Prod** - SAXENA 1993

A New View of Mars 10 MIN
16mm
Color (I J H)
LC 75-703698
Delves into scientific thought concerning the planet Mars and discusses the possibility of life existing there.
History - World; Science - Physical
Dist - USNAC **Prod** - NASA 1975

A New View of Space 28 MIN
16mm
Color (J)
LC 73-701277
Presents a look at the space program through the use of the photographic medium. Emphasizes how the visual image of photography has contributed toward many achievements in research and engineering, in space science and exploration and in space benefits to mankind.
Industrial and Technical Education; Science
Dist - NASA **Prod** - NASA 1972

New views on Alzheimer's 28 MIN
VHS
Color; CC (G)
$89.95 purchase _ #UW5401
Shows that research has uncovered new facts about Alzheimer's disease and a test has been developed that may predict who will be afflicted. Reveals that 550 elderly Catholic nuns have been the focus of this research for six years. A Phil Donahue show focuses on four of these nuns and on Dr David Snowden who oversees the study. Meets David Masur who developed an Alzheimer's test.
Health and Safety
Dist - FOTH

A New vision - Michael Naranjo 30 MIN
VHS / U-matic
Color (G)
$49.95 purchase, $35.00 rental
Profiles Michael Naranjo of Santa Clara Pueblo, New Mexico, a Native American sculptor who was blinded during the Vietnam War. Follows him as he creates beautiful sculptures of bronze and stone, pieces based on his childhood memories of life at the pueblo.
Fine Arts; Guidance and Counseling; Social Science
Dist - NAMPBC

New Voice Series
Group Dynamics 30 MIN
Life Science 30 MIN
Marguerite 30 MIN
Series Wrap 30 MIN
Suicide 30 MIN
Dist - GPN

New Voices for Man 57 MIN
U-matic / VHS / 16mm
Music of Man Series
Color (H C A)
Explains how the opera was born during the Renaissance with a presentation by Monteverdi for the Court of Mantua. Probes how Corelli created the sonata form and introduced the concerto, with Venice becoming the musical capital of Europe. Looks at the musical contributions of Stradivari and Handel.
Fine Arts; History - World
Dist - TIMLIF **Prod** - CANBC 1981

A New Way of Gravure 13 MIN
16mm
B&W (C)
American artist Stanley William Hayter describes his technique of engraving on copper, from his first rough sketches on paper through pulling the final print.
Fine Arts
Dist - RADIM **Prod** - PALEY 1951

New Way of Gravure 13 MIN
16mm
B&W
Presents Stanley William Hayter, a modern artist who describes the technique for engraving on copper from his first sketches on paper through the final print of his series of Anglels Wrestling.
Fine Arts
Dist - RADIM **Prod** - FILIM

The New way of life 17 MIN
VHS
HSN series
Color (PRO A G)
$150.00 purchase _ #SN - 312
Provides asthmatic patients and their families comprehensive information to deal positively with asthma. Part of a four - part Hospital Satellite Network series that explains what asthma is, treatment options, the prevalence of quackery in asthma treatment, appropriate physical activities and lifestyle changes for young asthmatics.
Health and Safety; Science - Natural
Dist - MIFE **Prod** - HOSSN

A New Way of Life 16 MIN
VHS / 16mm
Learning about Diabetes Series
Color (H A PRO)
$195.00 purchase, $75.00 rental _ #8063
Considers the changes in lifestyle necessary for those who have just discovered that they are diabetic.
Health and Safety
Dist - AIMS **Prod** - HOSSN 1988

A New way of thinking for healthcare - part 1 27 MIN
VHS
New way of thinking for healthcare series
Color (IND PRO)
$595.00 purchase, $150.00 rental _ #FIL26A
Helps healthcare providers today deal with the revolutionary changes facing their industry. Explores how healthcare leaders must respond to those changes to ensure the survival of their organization. Features Dr Deming and Paul Batalden, MD, Chairman of the Institute for Healthcare Improvement, as they discuss Virginia's Reston Hospital Center's 14 Guiding Principles and their relationship to Dr Demings 14 points. Part of a two - part series. Includes a discussion guide.
Health and Safety
Dist - EXTR **Prod** - FI

A New way of thinking for healthcare - part 2 27 MIN
VHS
New way of thinking for healthcare series
Color (IND PRO)
$595.00 purchase, $150.00 rental _ #FIL26B
Helps healthcare providers today deal with the revolutionary changes facing their industry. Explores how healthcare leaders must respond to those changes to ensure the survival of their organization. Features Dr Deming and Paul Batalden, MD, Chairman of the Institute for Healthcare Improvement, as they discuss Virginia's Reston Hospital Center's 14 Guiding Principles and their relationship to Dr Demings 14 points. Part of a two - part series. Includes discussion guide.
Health and Safety
Dist - EXTR **Prod** - FI

New way of thinking for healthcare series
Explores how healthcare leaders must respond to the revolutionary changes occurring today in their industry. Joins Dr Deming and Paul Batalden, MD, chairman of the Institute for Healthcare Improvement, as they discuss the 14 Guiding Principles of Virginia's Reston Hospital Center and their relationship to Dr Deming's 14 points. A two - part series including two videos and a discussion guide.
A New way of thinking for healthcare - part 1 27 MIN
A New way of thinking for healthcare - part 2 27 MIN
Dist - EXTR **Prod** - FI

New Way to Get more Eggs 11 MIN
16mm
Color (J)
Shows the part antibiotics play in mixed feeds for laying flock and points out how to insure high productivity from the birds in and out of the hen house.
Agriculture; Science - Natural
Dist - PFI **Prod** - STARIF 1954

A New Way to Lift 10 MIN
U-matic / VHS / 16mm
Color (J H C)
LC 79-715424
Demonstrates the technique for safe lifting developed by B T Davies and shows the palmar grip, the proper position of back, chin, arms, feet and the correct distribution of body weight.
Health and Safety; Physical Education and Recreation
Dist - JOU **Prod** - NSC 1971

New Ways for Old Morocco 23 MIN
16mm
B&W
Details the customs, traditions and culture of the Berbers. Gives an explanation of their experiment in living. Shows the collaboration of the Seghouchen tribe of Mount Tichoukt and the tribe of Sidi Sais, a community of farmers.
Geography - World; History - World; Sociology
Dist - RADIM **Prod** - LEEN

New Ways of Knowing 30 MIN
U-matic
North of Sixty Degrees - Destiny Uncertain Series
Color (H C)
Explores the clash between the traditional technologies of the north and the modern scientific tools imported from the south.
Geography - United States; Geography - World; History - World
Dist - TVOTAR **Prod** - TVOTAR 1985

New ways of seeing - Picasso, Braque and the Cubist revolution 58 MIN
VHS
Color (G)
$39.95 purchase _ #HVS07V-F
Describes the roles played by Picasso and Braque in bringing about and shaping the Cubism movement in painting. Notes that by using extreme and unusual images the two transformed the Cubist movement into what is now commonly called modern art. Tracks the lives of each palnter as they evolved from very differnt backgrounds until their convergence within the Cubist movement.
Fine Arts
Dist - CAMV **Prod** - PHILMO
HOMVIS

New Ways to Disseminate Scientific Knowledge 15 MIN
16mm
Science in Action Series
Color (C)
Explains that to keep researchers around the world informed about new relevant scientific discoveries, organizations such as the Smithsonian Institution's Center for Short - Lived Phenomena and the Institute for Scientific Information have been founded.
History - World; Science
Dist - COUNFI **Prod** - ALLFP

New Ways with Chicken 12 MIN
16mm
Eat Right to Your Heart's Delight Series
Color (J H)
Presents a low - fat, low cholesterol approach to chicken, one of America's favorite foods, giving a simple, easy - to - follow approach to saturated fat reduction. Examines steps for the economical use of chicken, including detailed treatment of deboning, cutting up chicken and removing skin.
Health and Safety; Home Economics; Psychology
Dist - IPS **Prod** - IPS 1976

The New Willamette 26 MIN
16mm
Color
LC 75-700152
Shows how the Willamette River in Oregon was cleaned up through the cooperative efforts of citizens, industry and government.
Geography - United States; Science - Natural
Dist - MTP **Prod** - USAE 1974

The New Woman Athlete 9 MIN
VHS / U-matic
Sports Medicine for Coaches Series
Color
Reviews many of the traditional myths about women involved in active sports. Emphasizes the unique advantages for and athletic potential of the woman athlete, and addresses some of the medical and health - related concerns encountered by a woman's coach.
Health and Safety; Physical Education and Recreation
Dist - UWASH **Prod** - UWASH

The New Womb 30 MIN
U-matic / VHS
Innovation Series
Color
Points out that with the development of 'in vitro' fertilization it is now possible to begin monitoring life from the moment of conception. Shows that a new medical specialty, prenatal medicine, has begun to develop.
Health and Safety
Dist - PBS **Prod** - WNETTV 1983

The New Womb 24 MIN
VHS / 16mm
Color (G)
$149.00, $249.00, purchase _ #AD - 2036
Focuses on the development of in vitro fertilization. Shows how the life of a fetus can be monitored literally from the moment of conception. Examines the range, scope, procedures, purposes, and possible benefits of a new medical speciality, prenatal medicine.
Health and Safety
Dist - FOTH **Prod** - FOTH 1990

New Work for Greenville 8 MIN
16mm
Color
LC 74-705211
Shows job training for industrial survival in Greenville, Mississippi. Emphasizes the role of private industry in the rehabilitation process.
Business and Economics; Psychology
Dist - USNAC **Prod** - USSRS 1969

The new workplace 42 MIN
VHS
New workplace series
Color (PRO IND A)
$525.00 purchase, $150.00 rental _ #QMR06A & B
Draws upon the expertise of several CEOs, managers, line workers and consultants as they discuss changes in the workplace and how they affect managers and employees. Promotes an understanding of the nature of change for organizations undergoing transitions. By Quality Media Resources.
Business and Economics
Dist - EXTR

New workplace series
Leading the change - Part 2 - manager version 21 MIN
Making the change - Part 1 - employee version 21 MIN
The new workplace 42 MIN
Dist - EXTR

The New World 27 MIN
16mm
Color
Shows how the 35 Salesian agricultural schools are dedicated to improving farming among the small farmers and to producing dedicated men who can professionally advise and help others. Features the Salesian Agricultural School of La Vega in Santo Domingo.
Agriculture; History - World; Religion and Philosophy; Sociology
Dist - MTP **Prod** - SCC

The New World 59 MIN
16mm
Masters of Modern Sculpture Series no 3
Color
LC 78-701409
Surveys sculpture in America, beginning with David Smith and the abstract expressionists in the 1940's. Examines pop and minimal art in the works of Segal, Oldenburg, Andre, Serra, Morris, Judd, Christo and Kienholz. Shows the large - scale earthworks of Heizer and Smithson.
Fine Arts
Dist - BLACKW **Prod** - BLACKW 1978

A New world 50 MIN
VHS
Discoveries underwater series
Color; PAL (G)
PdS99 purchase
Portrays the reconstruction of exploit of early divers and marine archaeologists. Looks at the growing science of underwater archaeology and modern methodology. Part two of an eight - part series.
History - World; Physical Education and Recreation; Social Science
Dist - BBCENE

New World Ballet 60 MIN
VHS / U-matic
Color
Fine Arts
Dist - ABCLR **Prod** - ABCLR

New World / Day Without Incident 29 MIN
U-matic
As We See it Series
Color
Presents Asian - American students in San Francisco showing the changes achieved by bilingual - bicultural education in Bay area schools. Depicts students in Pontiac, Michigan, recommending that the restrictive school rules adopted after 1971 rioting be changed.
Education
Dist - PBS **Prod** - WTTWTV

A New World is Born 13 MIN
U-matic / VHS
Spain in the New World Series
Color (C)
$199.00, $99.00 purchase _ #AD - 952
Examines the Spanish contribution to American culture, including a hierarchical social order based on color. Reveals that American natives are at the bottom of this hierarchy, still unassimilated and most still speaking non - European languages.
Foreign Language; History - World; Social Science
Dist - FOTH **Prod** - FOTH

New World, more New Math 29 MIN
Videoreel / VT2
Color
Familiarizes parents and teachers with some of the ideas behind the teaching of new math.
Education; Mathematics
Dist - PBS **Prod** - WNETTV

A New world of television - 11 51 MIN
VHS
Eastern Europe - breaking with the past series
Color (H C G)
$50.00 purchase
Looks at Eastern European television as a reflection of values, interests, lifestyles and opinions. Includes commercials, sports, news features, soap operas, variety and game shows, documentaries, comedies, investigative reports and made - for - TV movies. Part 11 of 13 parts.

Civics and Political Systems; Fine Arts; History - World
Dist - GVIEW **Prod** - GVIEW 1990

The New World of Work
VHS
$129 purchase _ #ED344V
Provides an overview of the computer workplace. Discusses how computers work, what the various job opportunities are, and the skills necessary to enter into the computer industry.
Computer Science; Guidance and Counseling
Dist - CAREER **Prod** - CAREER

New world order 9 MIN
VHS
Color (G)
$20.00 purchase
Employs the soundbites, slogans and images from the Persian Gulf War that describe the spectacle of commodity associated with commercial television. Combines live - action protest footage and video banned from national broadcast. Questions the validity of media authority and the ideological characteristics of society by looking at how broadcast television underlined the moral and just cause for the mass destruction of Iraq. Made with Larry Kless.
Fine Arts; Guidance and Counseling; Sociology
Dist - CANCIN **Prod** - ALVARE 1991

New World, the, Pt 1 30 MIN
16mm
Masters of Modern Sculpture Series no 3
Color
LC 78-701409
Surveys sculpture in America, beginning with David Smith and the abstract expressionists in the 1940's. Examines pop and minimal art in the works of Segal, Oldenburg, Andre, Serra, Morris, Judd, Christo and Kienholz. Shows the large - scale earthworks of Heizer and Smithson.
Fine Arts
Dist - BLACKW **Prod** - BLACKW 1978

New World, the, Pt 2 29 MIN
16mm
Masters of Modern Sculpture Series no 3
Color
LC 78-701409
Surveys sculpture in America, beginning with David Smith and the abstract expressionists in the 1940's. Examines pop and minimal art in the works of Segal, Oldenburg, Andre, Serra, Morris, Judd, Christo and Kienholz. Shows the large - scale earthworks of Heizer and Smithson.
Fine Arts
Dist - BLACKW **Prod** - BLACKW 1978

New World Visions 120 MIN
VHS / U-matic
Color (H C A)
Examines and analyzes the first 250 years of concurrently developing styles of American art, architecture and design and how these forms reflected the emerging American consciousness. Begins with the dawn of American colonization and ends before World War I. Uses natural settings and New York's Metropolitan Museum of Art to illustrate various styles of art by well - known and little - known painters and craftsmen.
Fine Arts; History - United States
Dist - FI **Prod** - WNETTV

New World Visions - American Art and the Metropolitan Museum - 1650 - 1820 - Pt 1 59 MIN
VHS
Color (S)
$39.95 purchase _ #412 - 9008
Interweaves painting, sculpture, decorative arts and architecture in an exploration of uniquely American art forms. Uses the collection of the Metropolitan Museum as a starting point and moves to footage shot on location in New York, Pennsylvania, Washington DC, and New England. Part 1 covers the period 1650 to 1820.
Fine Arts; History - United States
Dist - FI **Prod** - MMOA 1986

New World Visions - American Art and the Metropolitan Museum - 1820 - 1914 - Pt 2 58 MIN
VHS
Color (S)
$39.95 purchase _ #412 - 9009
Interweaves painting, sculpture, decorative arts and architecture in an exploration of uniquely American art forms. Uses the collection of the Metropolitan Museum as a starting point and moves to footage shot on location in New York, Pennsylvania, Washington DC, and New England. Part 2 covers the period 1820 to 1914.
Fine Arts; History - United States
Dist - FI **Prod** - MMOA 1986

New Worlds 55 MIN
U-matic / VHS / 16mm
Living Planet Series Pt 12
Color (H C A)
Reveals how various species have adapted to manmade changes in their environment. Considers the fortunes of man himself and his impact through his time on the earth.
Science - Natural
Dist - TIMLIF **Prod** - BBCTV 1984

New Worlds 50 MIN
VHS
Triumph of the West
Color; PAL (H C A)
PdS99 purchase; Not available in the United States
Documents the rise of Western civilization and its continuing impact on the rest of the world. Focuses on the exploration and domination of the New World and features the conquistadors in the South and Protestants in the North. Seventh in a series of 13 programs.
History - World; Sociology
Dist - BBCENE

New Worlds 55 MIN
16mm / VHS
Living Planet Series
(J H C)
$99.95 each, $595.00 series
Sums up the Living Planet Series and looks at the future from a point of view of survival and adaptability. Hosted by David Attenborough.
Science; Science - Natural; Science - Physical
Dist - AMBROS **Prod** - AMBROS 1984

New Year 20 MIN
VHS / U-matic
Color; B&W (G)
$250.00, $200.00 purchase, $50.00 rental
Features fourth generation Chinese American Valerie Soe. Reveals that she hated getting Valentine cards which featured bucktooth Chinamen inscribed 'Ah So.' Uses coloring book characters and clips from TV programs, Hollywood movies and comic books to confront the images which fostered the prejudice Soe experienced as a child.
Sociology
Dist - WMEN **Prod** - VALSOE 1987

New Year promise 30 MIN
VHS
Davey and Goliath series
Color (P I R)
$19.95 purchase, $10.00 rental _ #4 - 8823
Illustrates how Davey hurt his sister Sally's feelings, but reconciled things in time for the New Year. Exemplifies the themes of love, forgiveness and new beginnings. Produced by the Evangelical Lutheran Church in America.
Literature and Drama; Religion and Philosophy
Dist - APH

New Year Sacrifice 100 MIN
VHS
Color (G) (MANDARIN CHINESE (ENGLISH SUBTITLES))
$45.00 purchase _ #1001A
Presents a Mandarin Chinese language movie produced in the People's Republic of China.
Fine Arts; Geography - World; Literature and Drama
Dist - CHTSUI **Prod** - CHTSUI

New Year's 15 MIN
U-matic
Celebrate Series
Color (P)
Social Science
Dist - GPN **Prod** - KUONTV 1978

New Year's Day(s) 15 MIN
VHS
America's special days series
Color (K P) (SPANISH)
$23.95 purchase
Shows groups of people celebrating New Year's Day in different ways, with a look at how the calendar was established. Includes a look at the Times Square celebration, Chinese New Year , and writing a new year's resolution. Part of a ten-part series on holidays celebrated in America.
Civics and Political Systems; Social Science
Dist - GPN **Prod** - GPN 1993

New Year's eve 3 MIN
16mm
Color (G)
$18.00 rental
Celebrates brotherhood and the creative spirit. Conveys youthful illusions passing into the night. Produced by Bruce Cooper.
Fine Arts
Dist - CANCIN

New Year's leave - Rosh Hashanah 30 MIN
VHS
Jewish holiday video series
Color (G)
$24.95 purchase _ #822
Follows an American Jewish sailor from the Sixth Fleet who spends an unexpected holiday in Israel when his ship is delayed because of engine trouble. Reveals that the High Holidays are about to be ushered in and the sailor is introduced to the meaning of Rosh Hashanah, its symbols and customs.
Geography - World; Religion and Philosophy; Sociology
Dist - ERGOM **Prod** - ERGOM

New York 60 MIN
VHS
Portrait of America series
Color (J H C G)
$99.95 purchase _ #AMB32V
Visits New York. Offers extensive research into the state's history. Films key locations and presents segments on its history, government, education, folklore, science, journalism, sociology, industry, agriculture and business. Shows what is unique about New York and what is distinctive about its regional culture and how it got to be that way. Includes teacher study guides. Part of a 50 - part series.
Geography - United States; History - United States
Dist - CAMV

The New York 36 nationals
VHS
Color (G)
$39.80 purchase _ #0224
Records the gathering of the 14 top boats from the United States at the 1982 Nationals on Long Island Sound.
Physical Education and Recreation
Dist - SEVVID **Prod** - OFFSHR

New York - a really great city 30 MIN
VHS
Color; CC (G)
$26.95 purchase _ #WW10
Visits the Big Apple.
Geography - United States
Dist - SVIP

New York and New Jersey 60 MIN
VHS
AAA travel series
Color (G)
$24.95 purchase _ #NA07
Explores New York and New Jersey.
Geography - United States; Geography - World
Dist - SVIP

The New York Central odyssey
VHS
Color (G)
$79.95 purchase _ #GFP008
Follows the New York Central trains through the midwest.
Geography - United States; Social Science
Dist - SIV

New York City 3 MIN
16mm
Of all Things Series
Color (P I)
Discusses New York City in the state of New York.
Geography - United States
Dist - AVED **Prod** - BAILYL

New York City 30 MIN
VHS
Color (G)
$29.95 purchase _ #S00643
Presents the sights and sounds of New York City. Includes tours of Broadway, Fifth Avenue, Central Park, Greenwich Village, and more.
Geography - United States; Sociology
Dist - UILL

New York City 60 MIN
VHS
Color (G)
$29.95 purchase _ #S01480
Features Tony Randall in a tour of New York City. Takes viewers to Broadway, Central Park, the United Nations building, Greenwich Village, and many of the city's major museums and department stores.
Geography - United States; History - United States
Dist - UILL **Prod** - RMNC

New York City - center of megalopolis 15 MIN
U-matic / VHS / 16mm
American legacy series
Color (I)
Shows that New York City from 1624 to the 1980's has always been a landing point for immigrants as well as a world center for commerce and culture.
Geography - United States; History - United States
Dist - AITECH **Prod** - KRMATV 1983

New York - city of cities 45 MIN
VHS
Color (G)

$29.95 purchase _ #S01976
Tours the major attractions of New York City. Provides historical background, as well as advice on where to go and what to do there.
Geography - United States; History - United States; Sociology
Dist - UILL

New York - city of cities 60 MIN
VHS
North American collection series
Color (J H C G)
$29.95 purchase _ #IVN604V-S
Tours New York City. Includes visits to Wall Street, Lincoln Center, Times Square, Little Italy, Greenwich Village, and more. Part of a five-part series on discovering North America. Also part of a larger series entitled Video Visits that travels to six continents.
Geography - United States
Dist - CAMV **Prod** - WNETTV

New York City, Too Far from Tampa Blues 47 MIN
U-matic / VHS / 16mm
Teenage Years Series
Color
LC 79-701008
Presents a musical comedy - drama focusing on the problems encountered by a Puerto Rican youngster and his family when they move from Tampa, Florida, to New York City. Originally shown on the television series ABC Afterschool Specials. Based on the book New York City, Too Far From Tampa Blues by T Ernesto Bethancourt.
Fine Arts; Literature and Drama
Dist - TIMLIF **Prod** - WILSND 1979

New York City's Waterfront Legacy 27 MIN
16mm
Color (H C A)
LC 81-700683
Takes a look at New York City's 578 miles of shoreline, including decaying docks, magnificent beaches and marinas, and riverfront expressways. Points out the conflicting demands of industry, commerce, shipping and recreation.
Geography - United States; Sociology
Dist - CORNRS **Prod** - CORNRS 1977

New York day and night 56 MIN
VHS
Color (G)
$50.00 purchase
Looks at New York through MA, a unique Japanese concept for time and space, in which the word MA was originally used to to define the distance between two points or spaces, with importance attributed to the emptiness or silence of the space in between. Consists of two parts - Day, where the sky over buildings is seen from near and far capturing the negative space - MA; and Night, darkness is seen through the streets and parks where light and shadow speak and negative space - MA - turns to the positive. Produced by Takahiko Iimura, with music by Takehisa Kosugi.
Fine Arts; Religion and Philosophy
Dist - CANCIN

New York Deafness Commission 7 MIN
16mm
Color (J) (AMERICAN SIGN)
LC 76-701698
Presents a reading in American sign language of a speech by John Schrodel of the New York Civic Association of the Deaf regarding undereducation, underemployment and discrimination of the deaf. Talks about the establishment of the New York Deafness Commission to act as watchdog and promoter of legislation for the deaf. Signed for the deaf by Lyle Hinks.
Guidance and Counseling; Psychology; Sociology
Dist - JOYCE **Prod** - JOYCE 1975

New York Eye and Ear Control (a Walking Woman Work) 34 MIN
16mm
B&W (C)
$820.00
Experimental film by Michael Snow.
Fine Arts
Dist - AFA **Prod** - AFA 1964

New York Faces the Sea 13 MIN
U-matic / VHS / 16mm
Color (J H A)
Considers the problems of commercial fishing, recreational uses of inland and coastal waters, power plant development, shipping and manipulation of wetlands. Introduces New York State's Sea Grant Program and shows how it assists in the development and use of the coastal areas of Long Island, the Great Lakes and the St Lawrence Seaway.
Geography - United States; Science - Natural; Social Science
Dist - CORNRS **Prod** - CUETV 1972

New York, Holland, Spain 27 MIN
16mm
Big Blue Marble - Children Around the World Series Program U; Program U
Color (P I)
LC 76-700633
Examines the lifestyles of children in New York, Holland and Spain. Presents a Dutch folk tale about a selfish widow who wants a sea captain to find her the most precious item in the world.
Geography - United States; Geography - World; Literature and Drama; Social Science
Dist - VITT **Prod** - ALVEN 1975

New York illustrated series
The Bairds of Barrow Street 24 MIN
Dist - NBCTV

New York loft 9 MIN
16mm
B&W; Color (G)
$35.00 rental
Makes 'something' out of interiors, specifically domestic spaces. Gives evidence of arranging things, moving, adjusting, and re - placing them. First are poles and sticks, then sheets and pillows and finally round things, such as machine parts and film cans. Filmed into a round mirror.
Fine Arts; Sociology
Dist - CANCIN **Prod** - BARHAM 1983

New York long distance 9 MIN
16mm
Color (H C A)
$25.00 rental
Looks at the relationship between Yann Beauvais and New York since 1962. Deals with the distance between a memory and the image of this memory. Produced by Yann Beauvais.
Geography - United States; Sociology
Dist - CANCIN

New York Mets' guide to baseball basics series
Basics of hitting
Basics of pitching
Dist - CAMV

New York - Miami Beach 6 MIN
16mm
B&W (G)
$12.00 rental
Documents a trip to New York and Miami Beach, filmmaker Virginia Giritlian's hometown, and shows its beauty and vulgarity.
Fine Arts; Geography - United States
Dist - CANCIN

New York near sleep for Saskia 10 MIN
16mm
B&W (G)
$10.00 rental
Examines suble changes of light and landscape in New York. Imposes the aesthetics of still photography and juxtapositions of shade and movement.
Fine Arts; Geography - United States
Dist - CANCIN **Prod** - HUTTON 1972

New York Philharmonic, Zubin Mehta, Leontyne Price 125 MIN
VHS
Color (S)
$29.95 purchase _ #384 - 9705
Joins two musical giants for the opening of the New York Philharmonic's 141st season. Opens with the Philharmonic's performance of the 'Jupiter' symphony by Mozart conducted by Zubin Mehta. Soprano Leontyne Price sings a concert of Mozart, Verdi and Strauss.
Fine Arts
Dist - FI **Prod** - PAR 1989

New York portrait - chapter one 16 MIN
16mm
B&W (G)
$30.00 rental
Delves into a search for the natural elements retaining their grace despite the city's artificial environments. Looks at clouds, flocks of birds and simple objects in an apartment to convey the producer's moods.
Fine Arts
Dist - CANCIN **Prod** - HUTTON 1979

New York portrait - chapter two 16 MIN
16mm
B&W (G)
$30.00 rental
Represents a continuation of daily observations from Manhattan compiled in 1980 and 1981. Offers the second part of an extended life's portrait of New York.
Fine Arts
Dist - CANCIN **Prod** - HUTTON 1981

New York portrait - part III 15 MIN
16mm
B&W (G)
$40.00 rental
Carries on the theme of exploring urban landscapes.
Fine Arts
Dist - CANCIN **Prod** - HUTTON 1990

New York Portrait, Pt II 35 MIN
16mm
B&W
Presents Peter Hutton's film entry selected from the 1985 Whitney Biennial Film and Video Exhibition.
Fine Arts
Dist - AFA **Prod** - AFA 1986

The New York School 55 MIN
U-matic / VHS
Color
Shows how New York City in the 1940s and 50s became the art center. Tells how artists who came to be called Abstract Expressionists started a group they called 'The New York School.' Features artists Arshile Gorky, Adolph Gottlieb, Philip Guston, Al Held, Hans Hofmann, Franz Kline, William de Kooning, Lee Krasner, Joan Mitchell, Robert Motherwell, Barnett Newman, Jackson Pollock, Mark Rothko and critics Clement Greenberg and Harold Rosenberg.
Fine Arts
Dist - BLACKW **Prod** - BLACKW

New York State College of Agriculture and Life Sciences 28 MIN
VHS
Color (C A)
$60.00 purchase, $20.00 rental
Documents the story of agriculture in New York state including the role Cornell University plays.
Agriculture
Dist - CORNRS **Prod** - CORNRS 1985

New York Times - Arno Press Films on Black Americans Series
Oh Freedom 26 MIN
Dist - SF

The New York Times Index 6 MIN
VHS / U-matic
Library Skills Tapes Series
Color
Demonstrates how to find a news item on a given subject published in the New York Times.
Education; English Language
Dist - MDCC **Prod** - MDCC

New York Trio Da Camera 29 MIN
Videoreel / VT2
Young Musical Artists Series
Color
Presents the music of the New York Trio da Camera.
Fine Arts
Dist - PBS **Prod** - WKARTV

New York University
VHS
Campus clips series
Color (H C A)
$29.95 purchase _ #CC0075V
Takes a video visit to the campus of New York University in New York City. Shows many of the distinctive features of the campus, and interviews students about their experiences. Provides information on the composition of the student body, professors, academics, social life, housing, and other subjects.
Education
Dist - CAMV

New York University Educational Film Institute series
The Children must learn 17 MIN
Dist - NYU

The New York World's Fair - Peace through Understanding 9 MIN
16mm
Screen news digest series; Vol 7; Issue 10
B&W (J)
LC FIA68-2096
Describes the New York World's Fair of 1964.
Business and Economics
Dist - HEARST **Prod** - HEARST 1965

New York Yankee Broadcast 34 MIN
U-matic / VHS
Color
Deals with the 1980 Yankee American League championship. Analyzes the history of the baseball broadcast.
Fine Arts; Physical Education and Recreation
Dist - KITCHN **Prod** - KITCHN

New Yorks Final Frontier 15 MIN
VHS / 16mm
Forever Wild Series
Color (I)

$125.00 purchase, $25.00 rental
Traces the development of the New York State Forest Preserve in the 1800s and stresses the differences between parks and a forest preserve, and between public and private land.
Agriculture; Geography - United States; Science - Natural
Dist - AITECH **Prod** - WCFETV 1985

New York's My Town 14 MIN
U-matic / VHS
Under the Blue Umbrella Series
Color (P)
Shows Sarah conducting a tour of her family's apartment and her city's buildings, parks, transportation, and other attractions.
Geography - United States
Dist - AITECH **Prod** - SCETV 1977

New Youth Connections 19 MIN
VHS
Color (J)
$225.00 purchase, $30.00 rental _ #D - 523; LC 87708350
Portrays students producing a newspaper for teenagers, focusing on the topics chosen and the young people who report them. Produced by Joe Windish.
English Language; Guidance and Counseling; Literature and Drama; Social Science; Sociology
Dist - ALTSUL

New Zealand 21 MIN
16mm / U-matic / VHS
Color (I J A)
Offers an overview of New Zealand, a productive land of friendly people who are justly proud of the high quality of life they have produced by imagination, hard work and a belief in the importance of the individual.
Geography - World
Dist - LUF **Prod** - LUF 1978

New Zealand 9 MIN
VHS / 16mm
Paradise Steamship Co Series
Color (I H C A)
$175.00, $125.00
Introduces the people and the scenery of this island neighbor of Australia in the South Pacific. A visit to a sheep ranch underscores New Zealand's standing as one of the foremost lamb and wool producing nations in the world.
Geography - World
Dist - CAROUF **Prod** - KCBS 1989

New Zealand - coast to coast 30 MIN
VHS
Color (G)
$29.95 purchase _ #S01977
Tours the coastal areas of New Zealand, including the cities of Auckland, Wellington, and Queenstown, as well as the various natural sites.
Geography - World; History - World; Sociology
Dist - UILL

New Zealand - island of adventure 60 MIN
VHS
South Pacific collection series
Color (J H C G)
$29.95 purchase _ #IVN404V-S
Teaches about the people, culture and history of New Zealand. Visits historic buildings, monuments and landmarks. Examines the physical topography of the country. Part of a two-part series on discovering the South Pacific. Also part of a larger series entitled Video Visits that travels to six continents.
Geography - World
Dist - CAMV **Prod** - WNETTV

New Zealand Lamb Promotional Shorts 29 MIN
16mm
Color
LC 77-702995
Presents short discussions of a variety of subjects, including sheep shearing, geysers, dogs, cattle, the Centerbury Plains and meat cuts.
Agriculture; Geography - World
Dist - CHET **Prod** - NZLC 1976

New Zealand - the Land and the People 16 MIN
VHS / 16mm
Color (P) (SWEDISH)
$325.00, $295.00 purchase, $35.00 rental _ #C - 49y; LC 86705014
Follows the people of New Zeland at work and at play. Portrays the geography, history, culture and dreams for the future of the country. Produced by Ken Nelson.
Geography - World
Dist - ALTSUL

New Zealand's Day with LBJ 15 MIN
16mm
Pictorial Parade Series
B&W
LC FI67-272
Follows President and Mrs Johnson on their round of activities during a day spent in Wellington, New Zealand, in the third week of October 1966, prior to the Manila Conference.
Biography; Civics and Political Systems; Geography - World
Dist - NZNFU **Prod** - NZNFU 1966

New Zebra in Town (Acceptance) 12 MIN
U-matic / VHS / 16mm
Forest Town Fables Series
Color (K P)
LC 74-700396
Uses a puppet story to examine the idea of discrimination in the subtle form of an individual's characteristics and to trace the change from suspicion of the individual to acceptance. Shows how Oni, Coslo and Butch learn a lesson in acceptance after they refuse to let a fellow - puppet, Zaybar Zebra, help them on their school project because he's so different.
Guidance and Counseling; Literature and Drama
Dist - CORF **Prod** - CORF 1974

The New Zimbabwe 28 MIN
U-matic / VHS
Color (H A)
Looks at the progress made in the new nation of Zimbabwe, showing how a policy of reconciliation was pursued so that its minority white population and its native Black people could live together peacefully. Covers the role of new educational, agricultural and vocational programs as well as the role of the church in helping Zimbabwe reach its goal of socialism. Features Prime Minister Mugabe and President Banana.
History - United States; History - World; Sociology
Dist - MAR **Prod** - FRMA 1983

Newbery Award - Winners Series
Across five Aprils
After the rain
Amos Fortune, free man
Annie and the Old One
The Black Pearl
Bridge to Terabithia
Caddie Woodlawn
Call it courage
The Courage of Sara Nobel
Dogsong
The Door in the wall
A Fine White Dust
The Fledgling
Ginger Pye
The Great Gilly Hopkins
Hatchet
The Hundred Dresses
The Hundred Penny Box
It's Like this, Cat
Jacob have I loved
Julie of the Wolves
King of the Wind
Like Jake and Me
Lincoln - a Photobiography
M C Higgins, the Great
The Matchlock Gun
Misty of Chincoteague
Mr Popper's Penguins
Mrs Frisbee and the Rats of NIMH
On My Honor
Philip Hall Likes Me
The Planet of Junior Brown
Sarah, Plain and Tall
Scorpions
The Sign of the Beaver
Sing Down the Moon
Strawberry Girl
The Upstairs Room
The Wish Giver
Dist - PELLER

Newbery Video Collection Series
Joyful Noise
Dist - PELLER

The Newborn
VHS
First 365 days in the life of a child series
Color (H C G)
$149.00 purchase, $75.00 rental _ #UW4197
Shows the normal development of an average healthy infant at birth. Part of a 13 - part series, each part 18 to 24 minutes long, that follows the normal development of a child during the first year of life at monthly intervals.
Health and Safety
Dist - FOTH **Prod** - SPCMUM

The Newborn 29 MIN
VHS / U-matic
Tomorrow's Families Series
Color (H C A)
LC 81-706905
Describes the medical procedures that assess and support the reflexes and capabilities of the infant. Points out that a newborn may appear strange to new parents.
Home Economics; Sociology
Dist - AITECH **Prod** - MDDE 1980

The Newborn 30 MIN
U-matic
Growing Years Series
Color
Shows the birth of a baby and discusses what reflexes and sensory capacities the normal infant possesses.
Psychology
Dist - CDTEL **Prod** - COAST

Newborn 29 MIN
16mm
Color
LC 72-702413
Shows to expectant parents the experiences of a young couple and their child during the first three months after the baby is born. Emphasizes how an infant reacts to, and is influenced by his environment, and describes the roles both parents play in providing comfort and affection, as well as the stimulus for early learning experiences.
Guidance and Counseling; Psychology; Science - Natural; Sociology
Dist - MTP **Prod** - JAJ 1972

Newborn 28 MIN
16mm
Color (H C A)
LC 78-701088
Shows the abilities, reflexes and degree of sensitivity in a newborn infant.
Psychology
Dist - FLMLIB **Prod** - CANBC 1978

The Newborn baby 24 MIN
VHS
Baby video library series
Color (G)
$29.95 purchase _ #MMI007V-K
Uses scenarios to show prospective parents what to expect with their newborn. Explains the advantages of careful early childhood care. Part of a 12-part series on giving birth and a child's first 18 months.
Health and Safety; Sociology
Dist - CAMV

Newborn basics 72 MIN
VHS
Color (G)
$39.95 purchase _ #CCP0073V
Guides new and expectant parents through the trying first months of infant care.
Health and Safety; Sociology
Dist - CAMV

Newborn Care 29 MIN
16mm
Nine to Get Ready Series no 8
B&W (C A)
LC 79-704213
Explains about care of the newborn, discussing the immediate care, infant examination, infant feeding, infant bathing and child development. Features Dr J Robert Bragonier and Leta Power Drake.
Home Economics; Psychology
Dist - UNEBR **Prod** - KUONTV 1965

Newborn care - step - by - step 30 MIN
VHS
Color (H A)
$29.95 purchase _ #PSS600V
Takes a comprehensive look at caring for newborns. Covers subjects including feeding, giving medication, cardiopulmonary resuscitation, and more. Includes a 34 - page pamphlet.
Health and Safety
Dist - CAMV

Newborn care - through the eyes of love
VHS
Color (H A)
$39.95 purchase _ #CTR100V
Covers the basics of caring for an infant. Considers subjects including the pros and cons of breastfeeding, bathing, crying, and common infant diseases. Includes a pamphlet which expands on the information covered in the video.
Health and Safety
Dist - CAMV

Newborn sensory development - Part Two 20 MIN
16mm / VHS
Sensational baby series
Color (H G)

$350.00, $275.00 purchase, $40.00 rental
Examines a newborn infant's sensory skills and ways parents and caregivers can tailor their behavior to an infant's level of readiness. Considers what infants can see, at what distance their eyes focus, whether they can discriminate between colors, see shapes, benefit from massage and gentle stroking. Presents the benefits of carrying a baby in a sling, reasons for varying a baby's position and how to rock a baby. Includes a sequence on hearing that explains how they respond to the tone of a voice and enjoy listening, particularly their mother's voices. Looks at the effects of different sounds on a baby's behavior. Part two of a two - part series.
Health and Safety; Sociology
Dist - POLYMR **Prod** - POLYMR

The Newborn, the Family, and the Dance 56 MIN
VHS / 16mm
Awakening and Growth of the Human - Studies in Infant Mental Health 'Series
Color (C A)
$150.00, $170.00 purchase _ #85852
Examines some of the factors that help children to become integrated, trusting adults, such as traits and expectations of primary caregivers, stress - free intra - uterine experience, and the "match" between the child and the parents. Asserts that only a complex social, biological, and psychological model can account for the interplay of these factors.
Psychology; Sociology
Dist - UILL **Prod** - IPIN 1986

Newborn - with Dr Berry Brazelton 28 MIN
16mm / VHS
Color (H C G)
$295.00 purchase, $55.00 rental
Documents the extraordinary capabilities of the newborn baby. Demonstrates the infant's readiness to face challenges, perceive its environment and establish its individuality. Having begun to learn in the womb, the baby is particularly alert in the first few hours after birth and far from helpless. Neonatal researchers Drs Berry Brazelton, Lewis Lipsitt and Louis Sanders demonstrate the components of normal infant development and how these are measured.
Health and Safety; Psychology
Dist - FLMLIB **Prod** - CANBC 1978

Newburyport - a Measure of Change 28 MIN
16mm
Color
Deals with urban renewal and historic preservation, focusing on a ten - year effort to rehabilitate the 19th - century commercial district of Newburyport, Massachusetts.
Geography - United States; History - United States; Sociology
Dist - URBNIM **Prod** - URBNIM 1975

The Newcomer 14 MIN
16mm / U-matic / VHS
Color (I)
LC 75-708045
Dramatizes two situations about a new student in the class. First shows David, the newcomer, unsure of himself and lonely in his interaction with his classmates. Stops the action and replays the scenes to allow students to see what might have been done instead to make David feel welcome.
Guidance and Counseling; Psychology; Sociology
Dist - PHENIX **Prod** - MUR 1969

Newcomer in School - Adventure or Agony 30 MIN
VHS
Color (C A)
$75.00 purchase, $35.00 rental
Explores the many concerns that families experience when they move from one location to another. Students share their fears and their feelings of loneliness.
Guidance and Counseling; Psychology; Sociology
Dist - CORNRS **Prod** - EDCC 1986

Newcomer in School - Adventure or Agony
U-matic / VHS
Vital Link Series
Color (A)
Familiarizes parents and teachers with the resources that can be made available to help children adjust to a new school.
Guidance and Counseling; Social Science; Sociology
Dist - EDCC **Prod** - EDCC

The Newcomers - Les Arrivants - Prologue (Gitksan) 55 MIN
16mm
Color (FRENCH)
LC 77-702996
Uses the songs, dances and rituals of the native peoples of Canada to tell a story about the conflicts faced by a young prospective chief, torn between his love and the call of the spirit.
Foreign Language; Geography - World; Social Science
Dist - IMO **Prod** - IMO 1977

The Newcomers - Les Arrivants - Prologue, Pt 1 (Gitksan) 28 MIN
16mm
Color (FRENCH)
LC 77-702996
Uses the songs, dances and rituals of the native peoples of Canada to tell a story about the conflicts faced by a young prospective chief, torn between his love and the call of the spirit.
Social Science
Dist - IMO **Prod** - IMO 1977

The Newcomers - Les Arrivants - Prologue, Pt 2 (Gitksan) 27 MIN
16mm
Color (FRENCH)
LC 77-702996
Uses the songs, dances and rituals of the native peoples of Canada to tell a story about the conflicts faced by a young prospective chief, torn between his love and the call of the spirit.
Social Science
Dist - IMO **Prod** - IMO 1977

The Newcomers - safety motivation 20 MIN
BETA / VHS / U-matic
Safety - live action video series
Color (IND G)
$495.00 purchase _ #805 - 15
Provides a good foundation in safe work practices for trainees and new hires. Asks viewers to identify 20 unsafe acts related to fire, machinery and guards, electricity, falls and falling objects, lifting and materials handling. Produced by Monitor Training Ltd. Part of a series on safety.
Health and Safety; Industrial and Technical Education; Psychology
Dist - ITSC

Newcomers to the City Series
Johnny from Fort Apache 15 MIN
Linda and Billy Ray from Appalachia 14 MIN
Dist - EBEC

Newfoundland - You Can't Buy Freedom 29 MIN
U-matic
Like no Other Place Series
Color (J H)
Visits a family that has lived in western Newfoundland since 1912 and examines the changes that occured when the areas's people gave up fishing and farming in favor of wage labor at a US Air Force base and at a linerboard factory.
Geography - World; History - World
Dist - TVOTAR **Prod** - TVOTAR 1985

Newfoundlanders - the Voices from the Sea 55 MIN
16mm
Color (G)
_ #106C 0178 373
Shows Newfoundland roots, culture and present day position in Canada as a significant sea community and as an important but little known part of Canadian history.
Geography - World; Social Science
Dist - CFLMDC **Prod** - NFBC 1978

The Newly diagnosed family 30 MIN
U-matic / VHS
Issues of cystic fibrosis series
Color (PRO C)
$395.00 purchase, $80.00 rental _ #C891 - VI - 041
Discusses cystic fibrosis and the newly diagnosed family. Features family members who talk about the impact on them as an individual and as a family. Discusses interactions with health professionals and how the information was conveyed. Part of a 13 - part series on cystic fibrosis presented by Drs Ivan Harwood and Cyril Worby.
Health and Safety; Science - Natural; Sociology
Dist - HSCIC

Newly Fathers 29 MIN
VHS / U-matic
Focus on Children Series
Color (C A)
LC 81-707443
Presents a specialist in early childhood education discussing the role of fathers in children's development, emphasizing the effects of fathers on educational motivation and achievement.
Psychology; Sociology
Dist - IU **Prod** - IU 1981

Newman's Magnetic Motor
BETA
Color (IND)
Consists of an assembly of nine United States telecasts on the controversial device of Joe Newman.
History - World; Social Science
Dist - PLACE **Prod** - PLACE

Newport '90 52 MIN
VHS
Fifty - foot world cup circuit series
Color (G)
$39.95 purchase _ #0938
Presents footage of racing action and interviews of sailing personnel in the 1990 Newport portion of the 50 foot World Cup Circuit.
Physical Education and Recreation
Dist - SEVVID

Newport mansions 30 MIN
VHS
VideoTours history series
Color (G I J H)
$19.95 purchase _ #HC06
Visits Newport, Rhode Island.
Geography - United States; Geography - World; History - United States
Dist - SVIP

News 15 MIN
U-matic / VHS
Watch Your Language Series
Color (J H)
$125.00 purchase
Describes the various forms of language use likely to be used in news broadcasting.
English Language; Social Science
Dist - AITECH **Prod** - KYTV 1984

News - 1901 - 1965
VHS
Hearst News library series
Color (G)
$29.95 purchase _ #TK041
Witnesses 87 historical events which changed the world during the years 1901 - 1965, from the Wright brothers' first flight to the Cuban missile crisis. Part of a series excerpted from 350 newsreels from the Hearst News Library.
History - United States; History - World; Literature and Drama
Dist - SIV

News - a Closer Look 15 MIN
16mm / U-matic / VHS
News Series
Color
LC 79-701812
Examines some of the constraints and potential pitfalls of news gathering, discussing such issues as honest news reporting, the objectivity of the news and the limits of television news. Emphasizes the need for quickly identifying important emerging public issues and for detailed, in - depth reporting.
Literature and Drama; Social Science
Dist - IU **Prod** - IITC 1979

News - a Free Press 15 MIN
16mm / U-matic / VHS
News Series
Color (J H)
LC 79-701816;
Examines some factors affecting freedom and objectivity in journalism. Considers such issues as whether the press is truly free, whether a reporter can bias a story and how freedom of the press affects other declared rights.
Civics and Political Systems; Literature and Drama; Social Science
Dist - IU **Prod** - IITC 1977

News - Careers 15 MIN
U-matic / VHS / 16mm
News Series
Color (J H)
LC 79-701815;
Examines some of the personal rewards and sacrifices of news work, addressing issues such as necessary qualifications, getting started in the business, the glamour of reporting and the demands of the profession.
Guidance and Counseling; Literature and Drama; Social Science
Dist - IU **Prod** - IITC 1977

News - Communication 15 MIN
U-matic / VHS / 16mm
News Series
Color
LC 79-701813;
Examines the uses of language and visual materials in journalism, emphasizing the need for precision, accuracy and selectivity appropriate to the medium used. Discusses the role of the intended audience and the influence of news topics in determining the way news is preseted.
Literature and Drama; Psychology; Social Science
Dist - IU **Prod** - IITC 1979

The News Connection - Effective Public Relations 39 MIN
U-matic
Color
Discusses the particular needs of television, radio, newspapers and magazines in regards to public relations stories.

Business and Economics; Fine Arts; Literature and Drama
Dist - MEDIAW **Prod** - MEDIAW 1979

News Diary '64 30 MIN
16mm
B&W
Shows presidential elections, beatles, Warren Report, Vietnam, Cyprus and space.
Civics and Political Systems; Fine Arts; History - World
Dist - SFI **Prod** - SFI

News Magazine of the Screen Series Vol 3, Issue 2
Wildlife in the Rockies - Animal Census in Alberta 7 MIN
Dist - HEARST

News Magazine of the Screen Series
Life of Elizabeth 10 MIN
Dist - HEARST

News of the Day 10 MIN
16mm
B&W
Shows Lee Harvey Oswald shooting and JFK's funeral.
Fine Arts
Dist - FCE **Prod** - FCE

News Parade '65 30 MIN
16mm
B&W
Shows space walk, Dominican revolt, Churchill, Watts riot and the Pope visiting the United States.
History - World
Dist - SFI **Prod** - SFI

News parade of 1939
16mm
News parade series
B&W (G)
$15.00 rental
Covers worldwide events with commentary by ace radio voices. Features part of a series edited from Universal newsreels and released in December of the year which is capsulized as a companion to feature films. 7 - 9 minutes in length. Contact distributor for detailed description of that year's events.
Civics and Political Systems; Fine Arts; History - World; Literature and Drama
Dist - KITPAR **Prod** - UNEWSR 1939

News parade of 1941
16mm
News parade series
B&W (G)
$15.00 rental
Covers worldwide events with commentary by ace radio voices. Features part of a series edited from Universal newsreels and released in December of the year which is capsulized as a companion to feature films. 7 - 9 minutes in length. Contact distributor for detailed description of that year's events.
Civics and Political Systems; Fine Arts; History - World; Literature and Drama
Dist - KITPAR **Prod** - UNEWSR 1941

News parade of 1942
16mm
News parade series
B&W (G)
$15.00 rental
Covers worldwide events with commentary by ace radio voices. Features part of a series edited from Universal newsreels and released in December of the year which is capsulized as a companion to feature films. 7 - 9 minutes in length. Contact distributor for detailed description of that year's events.
Civics and Political Systems; Fine Arts; History - World; Literature and Drama
Dist - KITPAR **Prod** - UNEWSR 1942

News parade of 1943
16mm
News parade series
B&W (G)
$15.00 rental
Covers worldwide events with commentary by ace radio voices. Features part of a series edited from Universal newsreels and released in December of the year which is capsulized as a companion to feature films. 7 - 9 minutes in length. Contact distributor for detailed description of that year's events.
Civics and Political Systems; Fine Arts; History - World; Literature and Drama
Dist - KITPAR **Prod** - UNEWSR 1943

News parade of 1945
16mm
News parade series
B&W (G)
$15.00 rental
Covers worldwide events with commentary by ace radio voices. Features part of a series edited from Universal newsreels and released in December of the year which is capsulized as a companion to feature films. 7 - 9 minutes in length. Contact distributor for detailed description of that year's events.
Civics and Political Systems; Fine Arts; History - World; Literature and Drama
Dist - KITPAR **Prod** - UNEWSR 1945

News parade of 1947
16mm
News parade series
B&W (G)
$15.00 rental
Covers worldwide events with commentary by ace radio voices. Features part of a series edited from Universal newsreels and released in December of the year which is capsulized as a companion to feature films. 7 - 9 minutes in length. Contact distributor for detailed description of that year's events.
Civics and Political Systems; Fine Arts; History - World; Literature and Drama
Dist - KITPAR **Prod** - UNEWSR 1947

News parade of 1948
16mm
News parade series
B&W (G)
$15.00 rental
Covers worldwide events with commentary by ace radio voices. Features part of a series edited from Universal newsreels and released in December of the year which is capsulized as a companion to feature films. 7 - 9 minutes in length. Contact distributor for detailed description of that year's events.
Biography; Civics and Political Systems; Fine Arts; History - World; Literature and Drama
Dist - KITPAR **Prod** - UNEWSR 1948

News parade of 1949
16mm
News parade series
B&W (G)
$15.00 rental
Covers worldwide events with commentary by ace radio voices. Features part of a series edited from Universal newsreels and released in December of the year which is capsulized as a companion to feature films. 7 - 9 minutes in length. Contact distributor for detailed description of that year's events.
Civics and Political Systems; Fine Arts; History - World; Literature and Drama
Dist - KITPAR **Prod** - UNEWSR 1949

News parade of 1951
16mm
News parade series
B&W (G)
$15.00 rental
Covers worldwide events with commentary by ace radio voices. Features part of a series edited from Universal newsreels and released in December of the year which is capsulized as a companion to feature films. 7 - 9 minutes in length. Contact distributor for detailed description of that year's events.
Civics and Political Systems; Fine Arts; History - World; Literature and Drama
Dist - KITPAR **Prod** - UNEWSR 1951

News parade of 1952
16mm
News parade series
B&W (G)
$15.00 rental
Covers worldwide events with commentary by ace radio voices. Features part of a series edited from Universal newsreels and released in December of the year which is capsulized as a companion to feature films. 7 - 9 minutes in length. Contact distributor for detailed description of that year's events.
Biography; Civics and Political Systems; Fine Arts; History - World; Literature and Drama
Dist - KITPAR **Prod** - UNEWSR 1952

News parade of 1953
16mm
News parade series
B&W (G)
$15.00 rental
Covers worldwide events with commentary by ace radio voices. Features part of a series edited from Universal newsreels and released in December of the year which is capsulized as a companion to feature films. 7 - 9 minutes in length. Contact distributor for detailed description of that year's events.
Biography; Civics and Political Systems; Fine Arts; History - United States; History - World; Literature and Drama
Dist - KITPAR **Prod** - UNEWSR 1953

News parade of 1954
16mm
News parade series
B&W (G)
$15.00 rental
Covers worldwide events with commentary by ace radio voices. Features part of a series edited from Universal newsreels and released in December of the year which is capsulized as a companion to feature films. 7 - 9 minutes in length. Contact distributor for detailed description of that year's events.
Civics and Political Systems; Fine Arts; History - World; Literature and Drama
Dist - KITPAR **Prod** - UNEWSR 1954

News parade of 1955
16mm
News parade series
B&W (G)
$15.00 rental
Covers worldwide events with commentary by ace radio voices. Features part of a series edited from Universal newsreels and released in December of the year which is capsulized as a companion to feature films. 7 - 9 minutes in length. Contact distributor for detailed description of that year's events.
Civics and Political Systems; Fine Arts; Health and Safety; History - World; Literature and Drama
Dist - KITPAR **Prod** - UNEWSR 1955

News parade of 1956
16mm
News parade series
B&W (G)
$15.00 rental
Covers worldwide events with commentary by ace radio voices. Features part of a series edited from Universal newsreels and released in December of the year which is capsulized as a companion to feature films. 7 - 9 minutes in length. Contact distributor for detailed description of that year's events.
Civics and Political Systems; Fine Arts; History - World; Literature and Drama
Dist - KITPAR **Prod** - UNEWSR 1956

News parade of 1957
16mm
News parade series
B&W (G)
$15.00 rental
Covers worldwide events with commentary by ace radio voices. Features part of a series edited from Universal newsreels and released in December of the year which is capsulized as a companion to feature films. 7 - 9 minutes in length. Contact distributor for detailed description of that year's events.
Biography; Civics and Political Systems; Fine Arts; History - World; Literature and Drama
Dist - KITPAR **Prod** - UNEWSR 1957

News parade of 1960
16mm
News parade series
B&W (G)
$15.00 rental
Covers worldwide events with commentary by ace radio voices. Features part of a series edited from Universal newsreels and released in December of the year which is capsulized as a companion to feature films. 7 - 9 minutes in length. Contact distributor for detailed description of that year's events.
Biography; Civics and Political Systems; Fine Arts; History - World; Literature and Drama
Dist - KITPAR **Prod** - UNEWSR 1960

News parade of 1961
16mm
News parade series
B&W (G)
$15.00 rental
Covers worldwide events with commentary by ace radio voices. Features part of a series edited from Universal newsreels and released in December of the year which is capsulized as a companion to feature films. 7 - 9 minutes in length. Contact distributor for detailed description of that year's events.
Biography; Civics and Political Systems; Fine Arts; History - United States; History - World; Literature and Drama
Dist - KITPAR **Prod** - UNEWSR 1961

News parade of 1964
16mm
News parade series
B&W (G)
$15.00 rental
Covers worldwide events with commentary by ace radio voices. Features part of a series edited from Universal newsreels and released in December of the year which is capsulized as a companion to feature films. 7 - 9 minutes in length. Contact distributor for detailed description of that year's events.
Civics and Political Systems; Fine Arts; History - United States; History - World; Literature and Drama
Dist - KITPAR **Prod** - UNEWSR 1964

News parade of 1966
16mm
News parade series
B&W (G)
$15.00 rental
Covers worldwide events with commentary by ace radio voices. Features part of a series edited from Universal newsreels and released in December of the year which is capsulized as a companion to feature films. 7 - 9 minutes in length. Contact distributor for detailed description of that year's events.
Civics and Political Systems; Fine Arts; History - United States; History - World; Literature and Drama
Dist - KITPAR **Prod** - UNEWSR 1966

News parade of 1967
16mm
News parade series
B&W (G)
$15.00 rental
Covers worldwide events with commentary by ace radio voices. Features part of a series edited from Universal newsreels and released in December of the year which is capsulized as a companion to feature films. 7 - 9 minutes in length. Contact distributor for detailed description of that year's events.
Civics and Political Systems; Fine Arts; History - United States; History - World; Literature and Drama
Dist - KITPAR **Prod** - UNEWSR 1967

News parade of 1968
16mm
News parade series
B&W (G)
$15.00 rental
Covers worldwide events with commentary by ace radio voices. Features part of a series edited from Universal newsreels and released in December of the year which is capsulized as a companion to feature films. 7 - 9 minutes in length. Contact distributor for detailed description of that year's events.
Biography; Civics and Political Systems; Fine Arts; History - World; Literature and Drama
Dist - KITPAR **Prod** - UNEWSR 1968

News parade of 1969
16mm
News parade series
B&W (G)
$15.00 rental
Covers worldwide events with commentary by ace radio voices. Features part of a series edited from Universal newsreels and released in December of the year which is capsulized as a companion to feature films. 7 - 9 minutes in length. Contact distributor for detailed description of that year's events.
Biography; Civics and Political Systems; Fine Arts; History - World; Literature and Drama
Dist - KITPAR **Prod** - UNEWSR 1969

News parade of 1970
16mm
News parade series
B&W (G)
$15.00 rental
Covers worldwide events with commentary by ace radio voices. Features part of a series edited from Universal newsreels and released in December of the year which is capsulized as a companion to feature films. 7 - 9 minutes in length. Contact distributor for detailed description of that year's events.
Civics and Political Systems; Fine Arts; History - World; Home Economics; Literature and Drama
Dist - KITPAR **Prod** - UNEWSR 1970

News parade of 1971
16mm
News parade series
B&W (G)
$15.00 rental
Covers worldwide events with commentary by ace radio voices. Features part of a series edited from Universal newsreels and released in December of the year which is capsulized as a companion to feature films. 7 - 9 minutes in length. Contact distributor for detailed description of that year's events.
Civics and Political Systems; Fine Arts; History - United States; History - World; Literature and Drama
Dist - KITPAR **Prod** - UNEWSR 1971

News parade of 1972
16mm
News parade series
B&W (G)
$15.00 rental
Covers worldwide events with commentary by ace radio voices. Features part of a series edited from Universal newsreels and released in December of the year which is capsulized as a companion to feature films. 7 - 9 minutes in length. Contact distributor for detailed description of that year's events.
Biography; Civics and Political Systems; Fine Arts; History - World; Literature and Drama; Physical Education and Recreation
Dist - KITPAR **Prod** - UNEWSR 1972

News parade of 1973
16mm
News parade series
B&W (G)
$15.00 rental
Covers worldwide events with commentary by ace radio voices. Features part of a series edited from Universal newsreels and released in December of the year which is capsulized as a companion to feature films. 7 - 9 minutes in length. Contact distributor for detailed description of that year's events.
Biography; Civics and Political Systems; Fine Arts; History - United States; History - World; Literature and Drama
Dist - KITPAR **Prod** - UNEWSR 1973

News parade of 1974
16mm
News parade series
B&W (G)
$15.00 rental
Covers worldwide events with commentary by ace radio voices. Features part of a series edited from Universal newsreels and released in December of the year which is capsulized as a companion to feature films. 7 - 9 minutes in length. Contact distributor for detailed description of that year's events.
Biography; Civics and Political Systems; Fine Arts; History - World; Literature and Drama
Dist - KITPAR **Prod** - UNEWSR 1974

News parade of 1975
16mm
News parade series
B&W (G)
$15.00 rental
Covers worldwide events with commentary by ace radio voices. Features part of a series edited from Universal newsreels and released in December of the year which is capsulized as a companion to feature films. 7 - 9 minutes in length. Contact distributor for detailed description of that year's events.
Biography; Civics and Political Systems; Fine Arts; History - United States; History - World; Literature and Drama
Dist - KITPAR **Prod** - UNEWSR 1975

News parade series
News parade of 1939
News parade of 1941
News parade of 1942
News parade of 1943
News parade of 1945
News parade of 1947
News parade of 1948
News parade of 1949
News parade of 1951
News parade of 1952
News parade of 1953
News parade of 1954
News parade of 1955
News parade of 1956
News parade of 1957
News parade of 1960
News parade of 1961
News parade of 1964
News parade of 1966
News parade of 1967
News parade of 1968
News parade of 1969
News parade of 1970
News parade of 1971
News parade of 1972
News parade of 1973
News parade of 1974
News parade of 1975
Dist - KITPAR

News Series
News - a Closer Look 15 MIN
News - a Free Press 15 MIN
News - Careers 15 MIN
News - Communication 15 MIN
News - the Business 15 MIN
News - what is it 15 MIN
Dist - IU

News Stories 15 MIN
VHS / U-matic
Word Shop Series
Color (P)
Literature and Drama
Dist - WETATV **Prod** - WETATV

News - the Business 15 MIN
16mm / U-matic / VHS
News Series
Color (J H)
LC 78-700295
Presents Walter Cronkite, Bill Moyers and others discussing keeping news reporting honest and objective while operating within a commercial, profitmaking structure.
Literature and Drama; Social Science
Dist - IU **Prod** - IITC 1979

News - the War Years 28 MIN
U-matic / VHS
Please Stand by - a History of Radio Series
(C A)
Fine Arts; History - United States; Psychology; Sociology
Dist - SCCON **Prod** - SCCON 1986

News travels fast - all about TV newscasting 18 MIN
VHS
Color (P I)
$89.00 purchase _ #RB810
Examines what happens behind the scenes of a 30 minute news show. Discusses the multitude of news stories available, the editing and checking for accuracy, and the number of staff involved. Shows that news comes from many sources - interviews, newspapers and global satellites.
Fine Arts; Literature and Drama
Dist - REVID **Prod** - REVID

The News Wars - 117 30 MIN
U-matic
Currents - 1984 - 85 Season Series
Color (A)
Focuses on the increased competition of daily newspapers in the face of rising costs and inroads into readership made by television.
Social Science
Dist - PBS **Prod** - WNETTV 1985

News - what is it 15 MIN
U-matic / VHS / 16mm
News Series
Color (J H)
LC 79-701811
Examines the roles of news writers, editors, columnists, and producers, and discusses topics such as the definition of news, who decides what is news, and the news needs of the public. Compares print and electronic media in terms of the demands which time and space impose on the selection, organization and treatment of news items.
Literature and Drama; Social Science
Dist - IU **Prod** - IITC 1977

Newscast from the Past Series
April 18, 1521 14 MIN
July 22, 1148 14 MIN
June 15, 1215 14 MIN
May 30, 1431 14 MIN
October 23, 1642 14 MIN
September 19, 1356 14 MIN
Dist - SSSSV

Newsfront 110 MIN
16mm
Color; B&W
Focuses on a group of newsreel - makers in the crucial years from 1948 to 1956. Directed by Phillip Noyce.
Fine Arts
Dist - NYFLMS **Prod** - UNKNWN 1978

Newspaper 15 MIN
16mm / U-matic / VHS
Color (J H A)
Deals with the role of the newspaper in a democratic society and discusses the kinds of information gathered to keep readers accurately informed. Explains the role of advertising and the economics that support a free press.
Business and Economics; Literature and Drama; Social Science; Sociology
Dist - LUF **Prod** - LUF 1979

Newspaper - a business 15 MIN
VHS
Newspaper - behind the lines series
Color (H C)
#E370; LC 90-713072
Demonstrates that a newspaper can best meet people's needs by operating as a business. Part of a series teaching about newspapers.
Business and Economics; Guidance and Counseling; Literature and Drama; Psychology; Social Science; Sociology
Dist - GPN **Prod** - CTI 1977
CTI

Newspaper - a closer look 15 MIN
VHS
Newspaper - behind the lines series
Color (H C)
#E370; LC 90-713070
Shows students how any newspaper meets people's needs by making special efforts to provide different kinds of useful information. Part of a series teaching about newspapers.

Guidance and Counseling; Literature and Drama; Social Science; Sociology
Dist - GPN **Prod** - CTI 1977
CTI

Newspaper - a free press 15 MIN
VHS
Newspaper - behind the lines series
Color (H C)
#E370; LC 90-713074
Shows students that freedom of the press impacts upon their individual freedoms, that it is important to people that newspapers be free to print the information that newspapers want to print. Part of a series teaching about newspapers.
Guidance and Counseling; Literature and Drama; Social Science; Sociology
Dist - GPN **Prod** - CTI 1977
CTI

Newspaper - behind the lines series 90 MIN
VHS
Newspaper - behind the lines series
Color (H C)
$135.00 purchase _ #E370; LC 90-713069
Presents six 15 - minute programs on three videocassettes about the newspaper industry.
Guidance and Counseling; Literature and Drama; Social Science; Sociology
Dist - GPN **Prod** - CTI 1977

Newspaper - Behind the Lines Series
Why a Newspaper 15 MIN
Dist - CTI

Newspaper - behind the lines series
Newspaper - a business 15 MIN
Newspaper - a closer look 15 MIN
Newspaper - a free press 15 MIN
Newspaper - careers 15 MIN
Newspaper - communication 15 MIN
Dist - CTI
GPN

Newspaper - behind the lines series
Newspaper - behind the lines series 90 MIN
Newspaper - why a newspaper 15 MIN
Dist - GPN

Newspaper - careers 15 MIN
VHS
Newspaper - behind the lines series
Color (H C)
#E370; LC 90-713073
Portrays how newspaper publishing requires a wide variety of skills and people. Part of a series teaching about newspapers.
Guidance and Counseling; Literature and Drama; Social Science; Sociology
Dist - GPN **Prod** - CTI 1977
CTI

Newspaper - communication 15 MIN
VHS
Newspaper - behind the lines series
Color (H C)
#E370; LC 90-713071
Illustrates how newspapers react to needs and interests, according to how they perceive their audience. Part of a series teaching about newspapers.
English Language; Guidance and Counseling; Literature and Drama; Social Science; Sociology
Dist - GPN **Prod** - CTI 1977
CTI

Newspaper in the Classroom Series
A Modern Newspaper Plant 20 MIN
Dist - GPN

Newspaper - its Role in a Democratic Society 15 MIN
16mm
Color (I)
LC 72-703000
Presents hard news, background stories, analysis and prediction by columnists, opinions of both editors and general public. Explains and illustrates each of these elements. Deals with the role advertising plays in promoting free press.
Civics and Political Systems; Literature and Drama; Social Science
Dist - ASPTEF **Prod** - ASPTEF 1969

Newspaper Layout 13 MIN
16mm / U-matic / VHS
Color (H C A)
LC FIA53-183
Presents the fundamental principles of newspaper layout, including balance, effective use of white space, accenting of hot spots and elimination of ornamentation. Compares selected pages of daily newspapers and applies principles of layout and redesign.
Industrial and Technical Education; Social Science
Dist - AIMS **Prod** - COP 1972

Newspaper Production using Space Age Technology 16 MIN
U-matic / VHS / 16mm
Color (J H)
LC 76-703737
Shows modern systems of newspaper production. Gives an overview of various newspaper functions and how they have been affected by technology.
Literature and Drama; Social Science; Sociology
Dist - AIMS **Prod** - WHICAF 1976

The Newspaper Reporter 15 MIN
VHS / 16mm
Harriet's Magic Hats IV Series
Color (P)
$175.00 purchase _ #207142
Presents thirteen new programs to familiarize children with more workers and their role in community life. Features Aunt Harriet's bottomless trunks of magic hats where Carrie has only to put on a particular hat to be whisked off to investigate the person and the role represented by the hat. 'The Newspaper Reporter' shows Carrie wondering whether reporting is difficult. She visits Judith, a newspaper reporter. Together they interview two students who write their own comic books. Judith illustrates the process involved in writing, editing and printing an article in a newspaper.
Business and Economics; Guidance and Counseling; Literature and Drama; Psychology
Dist - ACCESS **Prod** - ACCESS 1986

A Newspaper Serves its Community 14 MIN
16mm / U-matic / VHS
Color (I J H)
Shows process of printing a newspaper from reporting an event to final distribution of the paper. Includes views of the city room, the library, linotype machines and printing presses.
Literature and Drama; Psychology; Social Science
Dist - PHENIX **Prod** - GOLD 1959

Newspaper Wars 26 MIN
U-matic / VHS
Color (C)
$249.00, $149.00 purchase _ #AD - 1922
Examines the changing role of newspapers in society. Shows how newspapers have modified their style to accommodate the competition of television.
Business and Economics; Computer Science; Fine Arts; Psychology; Social Science; Sociology
Dist - FOTH **Prod** - FOTH

Newspaper - What's in it for Me Series
A Modern Newspaper Plant 15 MIN
Dist - GPN

Newspaper - why a newspaper 15 MIN
VHS
Newspaper - behind the lines series
Color (H C)
#E370; LC 90-713069
Demonstrates that newspapers meet people's needs by showing how information found in newspapers helps people deal with life. Part of a series teaching about newspapers.
Guidance and Counseling; Literature and Drama; Social Science; Sociology
Dist - GPN **Prod** - CTI 1977

Newspaper Writing 15 MIN
VHS / U-matic
Zebra Wings Series
Color (I)
Illustrates various forms of newspaper writing and stresses the skills a newswriter must use to deal accurately with the facts.
English Language; Literature and Drama
Dist - AITECH **Prod** - NITC 1975

Newspapers 30 MIN
U-matic
Today's Special Series
Color (K P)
Develops language arts skills in children. Programs are thematically designed around subjects of interest to youngsters. Action takes place in a department store where people, mannequins, puppets, comic characters and special guests present a light hearted approach to language arts.
Literature and Drama; Psychology
Dist - TVOTAR **Prod** - TVOTAR 1985

Newspapers 10 MIN
VHS
Stop, look, listen series
Color; PAL (P I J)
Chronicles the life of newspapers after a van delivers newspapers in bundles to shops and newspaper delivery people. Watches the delivery of papers, people buying papers in shops. Looks at the weather news, TV programming and sports items in the paper. Finally, children in a class are shown using old newspapers to make scrapbooks, paper figures, patterns and hats. Part of a series of films which start from some everyday observation and show more of what is happening, how and why. Builds vocabulary and encourages children to be more observant.
English Language; Literature and Drama; Social Science
Dist - VIEWTH

Newspapers - a Reading Adventure 19 MIN
16mm / U-matic / VHS
Color (I)
LC 82-700875
Uses animation and live action sequences to show how a young boy learns about newspapers. Explains how news articles are selected, researched, and written and how they are then organized and indexed for printing.
Literature and Drama; Social Science; Sociology
Dist - HIGGIN **Prod** - HIGGIN 1983

Newsprint, Newspaper and Trees 11 MIN
16mm
Color
Shows how trees are bred and grown for harvest as pulpwood. Traces the steps by which logs are converted into paper.
Agriculture; Social Science
Dist - GPN **Prod** - REGIS

Newsreel of Dreams, Part 2 8 MIN
16mm
Color
Presents dream matrix, history written in lighting image, memory and the TV syntax and images flowing and fused to other images.
Fine Arts; Industrial and Technical Education; Psychology
Dist - VANBKS **Prod** - VANBKS

Newsreel of Dreams, Part 3 9 MIN
16mm
Color
Presents dream matrix, history written in lighting image, memory and the TV syntax and images flowing and fused to other images.
Fine Arts; Industrial and Technical Education; Psychology
Dist - VANBKS **Prod** - VANBKS

Newsreel of Dreams (Parts I and II) 16 MIN
16mm
Color (C)
$448.00
Experimental film by Stan Vanderbeek.
Fine Arts
Dist - AFA **Prod** - AFA 1971

Newsreel of Dreams, Pt 1 8 MIN
16mm
Color
Presents dream matrix, history written in lighting image, memory and the TV syntax and images flowing and fused to other images.
Fine Arts; Industrial and Technical Education; Psychology
Dist - VANBKS **Prod** - VANBKS

Newsroom decision makers - the assignment editor 40 MIN
VHS
Color (J H C)
$29.95 purchase _ #IVMC41
Reveals that the assignment editor in a typical television newsroom is like an air traffic controller in a major airport. Shows that the assignment editor sends out news crews, keeps a close eye on what is happening in the market and is constantly making decisions. Features assignment editors from various sized markets who explain their everyday duties as well as their philosophy of news.
Fine Arts; Guidance and Counseling
Dist - INSTRU

Newsroom decision makers - the news director 40 MIN
VHS
Color (J H C)
$29.95 purchase _ #IVMC42
Discusses some of the more important duties of the news director in a television newsroom - setting up departmental budgets, hiring and firing news personnel, working on lawsuits filed against the station and working with management of a station to maintain station image in the community. Shares the views of a number of different news directors from various sized markets in the United States, as well as their different styles and news philosophies.
Fine Arts; Guidance and Counseling
Dist - INSTRU

Newsroom decision makers - the producer 40 MIN
VHS
Color (J H C)
$29.95 purchase _ #IVMC40
Takes a close look at a number of television news producers from small, medium and large markets as they explain their jobs. Shows how the news producer pulls together the news program, doing the lineup, determining the look

and feel of a show and must know how to pace a program for interest and dramatic effect. Numerous new producers discuss their jobs in the newsroom and how they manage people.
Fine Arts; Guidance and Counseling
Dist - INSTRU

Newsw
16mm
Paper film series
Color (G)
$20.00 rental
Depicts the news as nonsense and organic fibers rolling out toward the audience with increasing speed, thrown out of focus and off the screen. Uses the January 1, 1979 issue of Newsweek magazine and handmade papers and fibers such as cotton, linen and rice to create the film which is like the flipping of pages. First in a series of two. Produced by Donna Cameron.
Fine Arts; Social Science; Sociology
Dist - CANCIN

Newswomen 28 MIN
U-matic / VHS
Color (G)
$249.00, $149.00 purchase _ #AD - 1166
Features Jane Pauley, Maria Shriver, Leslie Stahl, Connie Chung, Joan Lunden, Rita Flynn and Mary Alice Williams, who join Phil Donahue. Discusses the politics of being women and having careers as professional journalists.
Literature and Drama; Sociology
Dist - FOTH **Prod** - FOTH

Newton in space 14 MIN
VHS
Color (J H C)
$14.95 purchase _ #NA203
Shows the principles of weightlessness in space and Newton's three principles of motion and how they apply to Earth and space. Uses animation to illustrate physics concepts such as weight, gravity, mass, force, acceleration and motion.
Science - Physical
Dist - INSTRU **Prod** - NASA

Newton Mini - Films 15 MIN
16mm
Color (K P I J H)
LC FIA67-5630
A demonstration of the creativity and skill of children, ages 11 to 17, as observed in their work in the planning and production of eight short animated films which they created using cutouts, drawing on film and flip cards.
Fine Arts
Dist - YELLOW **Prod** - NCAC 1967

Newton - the Mind that found the Future 27 MIN
16mm / VHS / U-matic
Color (J) (SPANISH)
LC 75-710041
Dramatizes the life of Sir Isaac Newton as told by his friend Edmund Halley. Takes viewers from Newton's study to the moon launching pad.
Biography; History - World; Science; Science - Physical
Dist - LCOA **Prod** - INCC 1971

Newtonian I 4 MIN
16mm
Color
Offers a musical composition by Jean Claude Risset accompanied by graphics which achieve a harmonious interleaving of changing shapes and patterns that move either asynchronously with the music or in counterpoint.
Fine Arts
Dist - LILYAN **Prod** - LILYAN

Newtonian II 6 MIN
16mm
Color
LC 78-701690
Uses computer techniques to blend music and imagery.
Fine Arts
Dist - LILYAN **Prod** - LILYAN 1978

Newton's 1st law - 5 45 MIN
VHS
Conceptual physics alive series
Color (H C)
$45.00 purchase
Introduces the law of inertia and the concept of mass. Supports these concepts with a variety of examples and demonstrations, such as the tablecloth and dishes stunt. Illustrates the concepts of net force and statics. Part 5 of a 35 - part series adapted from the college and high school textbook Conceptual Physics by Professor Paul Hewitt.
Science - Physical
Dist - MMENTE **Prod** - HEWITP 1992

Newton's 2nd law - 6 42 MIN
VHS
Conceptual physics alive series
Color (H C)
$45.00 purchase
Illustrates the relation of force, acceleration and mass with a variety of examples. Introduces friction and applies the concept to sliding and falling objects. Part 6 of a 35 - part series adapted from the college and high school textbook Conceptual Physics by Professor Paul Hewitt.
Science - Physical
Dist - MMENTE **Prod** - HEWITP 1992

Newton's 3rd law - 7 43 MIN
VHS
Conceptual physics alive series
Color (H C)
$45.00 purchase
Develops the notion that force is more than a push or pull; it is an interaction that involves at least two objects. Uses numerous examples, such as the tug of war, to illustrate the law, 'You cannot touch without being touched.' Part 7 of a 35 - part series adapted from the college and high school textbook Conceptual Physics by Professor Paul Hewitt.
Science - Physical
Dist - MMENTE **Prod** - HEWITP 1992

Newton's apple series
Kit / Videodisc
Color (I J H) (ENGLISH AND SPANISH)
$405.00 purchase _ #T81295; $585.00 purchase _ #T81298
Teaches scientific techniques and principles through lessons in the areas of physical sciences and life sciences. Includes teacher's guides and other supplementary materials. In two parts, with each part available in basic and more inclusive kit.
Science - Natural; Science - Physical
Dist - NGS

Newton's apple series
Life sciences
Physical sciences
Dist - NGS

Newton's Equal Areas 8 MIN
U-matic / VHS / 16mm
Color (H C)
LC FIA68-2898
Illustrates Newton's proof that if forces act toward a fixed point, the line connecting the moving body and that point sweeps out equal areas in equal times.
Science - Physical
Dist - IFB **Prod** - CORNW 1968

Newton's Law of Motion 31 MIN
VHS / U-matic
Mathematics and Physics Series
Color (IND)
Uses simple, practical examples to illustrate three laws of motion, with animation and graphics for illustrative purposes. Includes study of inertia, gravity, acceleration and action - reaction.
Science - Physical
Dist - AVIMA **Prod** - AVIMA 1980

Newton's Laws 240 MIN
VHS / U-matic
Mechanical Universe - High School Adaptation Series
Color (H)
Science - Physical
Dist - SCCON **Prod** - SCCON 1986

Newton's Laws 30 MIN
U-matic / VHS / 16mm
Mechanical Universe Series
Color (C A)
Presents Isaac Newton's laws explaining all the phenomena of the Mechanical Universe.
Science - Physical
Dist - FI **Prod** - ANNCPB

Newton's Laws of Motion - Demonstrations of Mass, Force, and Momentum 16 MIN
16mm / U-matic / VHS
Color (J H)
$50 rental _ #9777
Demonstrates Newton's three laws of motion and their relationship to each other.
Science; Science - Physical
Dist - AIMS **Prod** - SAIF 1984

Newton's Method 83 MIN
U-matic / VHS
Modern Control Theory - Deterministic Optimal Control Series
Color (PRO)
Discusses general philosophy of the Newton or quasilinearization method.
Industrial and Technical Education; Mathematics
Dist - MIOT **Prod** - MIOT

Newton's Method 3 MIN
16mm / U-matic / VHS
Color (H C A)
Uses animation to explain Newton's method.
Mathematics; Science
Dist - PFP **Prod** - EAMES 1974

Newton's Method 20 MIN
VHS
Calculus Series
Color (H)
LC 90712920
Discusses Newton's method. The 19th of 57 installments in the Calculus Series.
Mathematics
Dist - GPN

Newton's Method 10 MIN
16mm
MAA Calculus Series
Color (H C)
LC FIA68-1460
Considers the notion of an iterative procedure. Presents Newton's method as such and illustrates it. An animated film narrated by Herbert Wilf.
Mathematics
Dist - MLA **Prod** - MAA 1966

Newtown high 45 MIN
VHS
Becoming bilingual series
Color (C G)
$195.00 purchase, $40.00 rental _ #37878
Profiles students at a large high school, Newtown, with remarkable cultural diversity - speakers of nearly 50 languages, a quarter of whom have limited command of English. Offers first - hand accounts of students from China, Cuba, Korea, Afghanistan. Many students arrive with strong educational backgrounds but, without Newtown's extensive bilingual classes - Korean, Spanish, Mandarin and Cantonese, their participation at appropriate levels would be impossible. Newtown's 'transitional' bilingual program aims to guide students into mainstream English classes as soon as possible. Part of a two - part series on successful bilingual education programs in New York City Schools, produced by Lauren Goodsmith.
Education
Dist - UCEMC

NEWtrition 7 81 FRS
VHS / U-matic
Color (J H A)
LC 81-730181
Characterizes the seven Dietary Guidelines for Americans recently released by the United States Departments of Agriculture, and Health and Human Services. Explains with a 'computer type' voice why following these guidelines is beneficial to the body and enumerates the hazards of not heeding this advice.
Health and Safety; Social Science
Dist - POAPLE **Prod** - POAPLE

Newts and how they live 11 MIN
VHS
Animals and how they live series
Color (I J)
$220.00 purchase, $50.00 rental _ #8270
Illustrates the amphibian life cycle of the flat - tailed salamanders called newts. Part of a series on animal life cycles.
Science - Natural
Dist - AIMS **Prod** - IFFB 1991

The Next crisis - death in the mines 29 MIN
Videoreel / VT2
Turning points series
Color
Examines the circumstances surrounding mining disasters of the past decade and the proposals for improving mining safety. Describes Farmington, West Virginia, the site of five major mining disasters.
Geography - United States; Health and Safety
Dist - PBS **Prod** - WMULTV

Next Door 24 MIN
16mm / U-matic / VHS
Color (I)
LC 76-700191
Presents an adaptation of a short story from Welcome To The Monkey House by Kurt Vonnegut which tells what happens to an eight - year - old boy when his parents leave him at home alone for the first time.
Guidance and Counseling; Literature and Drama
Dist - PHENIX **Prod** - SILVEA 1975

The Next Frontier 26 MIN
VHS / 16mm
Computer Revolution Series
Color (J)
$149.00 purchase, $75.00 rental _ #OD - 2302
Describes changes brought by computers and how those changes have altered human environment. Examines how computers have made the work place more efficient while dehumanizing it. Reports the many advances in computer technology made by the military. The fifth of six installments in The Computer Revolution Series.
Computer Science
Dist - FOTH

The Next generation 18 MIN
VHS
Color (I J H)
$295.00 purchase
Portrays a boy spending the day at the beach who is transported on his surfboard to a dreamlike encounter with a playful sea lion. Ends sadly when a fishing trawler sets out its nylon - filament gill net. Teaches youngsters about marine life and the importance of wildlife conservation. Introduces the study of biology, marine life, the environment and wildlife preservation. Produced by Adam Ravetch Productions.
Science; Science - Natural
Dist - PFP

The Next Minority - White Americans 28 MIN
U-matic / VHS
Color (G)
$249.00, $149.00 purchase _ #AD - 2121
Considers the possible sociological and political consequences of whites becoming a minority in the US. Features Samuel Bentances and Ben Wattenberg on a Phil Donahue program.
Sociology
Dist - FOTH **Prod** - FOTH

The Next step 22 MIN
VHS
Color (G A)
$20.00 purchase
Examines the moral and legal implications of state - sanctioned killing on modern society. Places the death penalty in the international human rights context and presents compelling arguments for its abolition. Includes some graphic footage. Narrated by Glenda Jackson.
Civics and Political Systems
Dist - AMNSTY **Prod** - AMNSTY 1989

The Next Step 13 MIN
16mm
Color
LC 74-706507
Presents male and female Navy nurses discussing Navy nursing careers during a student nurse conference at the U S Naval Hospital in San Diego, California. Describes on - and off - duty activities in the Navy Nurse Corps.
Civics and Political Systems; Guidance and Counseling; Health and Safety
Dist - USNAC **Prod** - USN 1972

The Next Step 30 MIN
16mm
B&W
LC FIA67-29
Shows a polio campaign in Harrisburg, Pennsylvania. Gives a brief history of polio vaccine research, production of the live virus vaccine, the large scale clinical trials with live vaccine and laboratory techniques of production of vaccine.
Health and Safety
Dist - PFI **Prod** - PFI

Next Steps with Computers in the Classroom Series
Alternative futures 28 MIN
Creating Courseware 28 MIN
The Creative arts 28 MIN
Electronic tools 28 MIN
The Information Age 28 MIN
Interfacing 28 MIN
Learning Management 28 MIN
Programming Perspectives 28 MIN
Software Evaluation 28 MIN
Software Selection 28 MIN
Telecommunications 28 MIN
The Writing Process 28 MIN
Dist - PBS

Next Steps with Computers in the Classroom Series
Software Selection 360 MIN
Dist - PBS
UEUWIS

Next steps with computers in the classroom series
Presents a training telecourse for teachers and school administrators. This series ranges in topic from software selection to learning management and creating courseware. Companion print materials include a faculty manual, book of readings and study guide.
Alternate futures 360 MIN
Creating Courseware 360 MIN
The Creative arts 360 MIN
Electronic tools 360 MIN
The Information Age 360 MIN
Instructional Management 360 MIN
Interfacing 360 MIN
Programming Perspectives 360 MIN
Telecommunications 360 MIN
The Writing Process 360 MIN
Dist - UEUWIS **Prod** - UEUWIS

Next Stop - London, Paris, Rome 20 MIN
U-matic / VHS
Color (J)
LC 82-706781
Gives an overview of the cities of London, Paris, and Rome. Visits Buckingham Palace and Trafalgar Square in London, the cafes and artists along the Seine River and near the Eiffel Tower in Paris, and the Borghese gardens, Appian Way and other scenic highlights in Rome.
Geography - World; History - World
Dist - AWSS **Prod** - AWSS 1980

The Next ten lessons - Video Two 45 MIN
VHS
Ukelele for kids series
Color (K P I J)
$24.95 purchase _ #VD - MAX - UK02
Features instructor Marcy Marxer and Ginger - a dog puppet - who present five new chords and a variety of strumming techniques. Uses on - screen chord charts, graphics and lyrics to make understanding the chords and learning to sing and play easy and fun. Includes the songs Shortenin' Bread; Buffalo Gals; When the Saints Go Marching In; Twinkle, Twinkle, Little Star; Hukilau; I've Been Working on the Railroad; Muffin Man; Hush Little Baby; There's a Hole in the Bottom of the Sea. Book and progress chart included. Part two of a two part series.
Fine Arts
Dist - HOMETA **Prod** - HOMETA

Next Thing to a Miracle 20 MIN
U-matic / VHS
Color
$335.00 purchase
Health and Safety
Dist - ABCLR **Prod** - ABCLR 1984

Next Time 12 MIN
16mm
VD - Self - Awareness Project Series Module 2
Color
LC 75-702843
Stimulates discussion of feelings, values and the stigma of venereal disease.
Guidance and Counseling; Health and Safety
Dist - FMD **Prod** - AAHPER 1974

Next Time You Go Camping 25 MIN
U-matic / VHS
Color
Shows forestry rangers and search - and - rescue experts telling Mario Machado how to camp, bike and survive in the wilderness. Adds Dan Row and L.A. Dodgers pitching star Jim Brewer to contribute camping health facts.
Physical Education and Recreation
Dist - MEDCOM **Prod** - MEDCOM

Next Year's Model 47 MIN
VHS
Color (S)
$79.00 purchase _ #386 - 9029
Looks at the marriage of two of the most powerful technologies ever invented - the automobile and the computer. Addresses the implication of the partnership which has computers designing and producing automobiles.
Computer Science; Industrial and Technical Education
Dist - FI **Prod** - CANBC 1988

Next year's words - The Empire strikes back 60 MIN
VHS / 16mm
Story of English Series
Color (C)
PdS99 purchase
Makes the point that Latin, once a truly universal language, is now broken into French, Spanish, Italian, and others. Poses the question whether the same fate awaits the English language. Part 9 of the series.
English Language
Dist - BBCENE **Prod** - BBCTV 1986
FI
PSU

Nez Perce - Bring Us the Black Book 10 MIN
16mm
Color (I J H)
LC 74-703253
Presents the story of four Nez Perce Indians who travelled to St Louis in 1831 to ask for missionaries.
Social Science
Dist - NWFLMP **Prod** - NWFLMP 1974

Nez Perce - Portrait of a People 23 MIN
16mm / U-matic / VHS
Color (J A)
Discusses the history of the Nez Perce Indians who lived throughout Washington, Oregon and Idaho. Includes traditional chants and music, vintage photos, mini - dramatizations and scenes of contemporary tribal life.
Geography - United States; Social Science
Dist - USNAC **Prod** - USNPS 1984

Nezha conquers the dragon king 100 MIN
VHS
Color (G) (CHINESE)
$45.00 purchase _ #2009C
Presents a film from the People's Republic of China.
Geography - World; Literature and Drama
Dist - CHTSUI

NFL '87
VHS
NFL series
Color (G)
$24.95 purchase _ #NFL2020V
Presents highlights from the 1987 National Football League season. Produced by NFL Films.
Literature and Drama; Physical Education and Recreation
Dist - CAMV

NFL Action Series
This is a Football 28 MIN
Dist - NFL

NFL Championship Games - New York Vs Chicago Bears - 1956 30 MIN
16mm
Color
Presents highlights of the year.
Physical Education and Recreation
Dist - NBCTV **Prod** - NBCTV

NFL crunch course
VHS
NFL series
Color (G)
$24.95 purchase _ #NFL1020V
Takes a look at 'crunch' situations in the National Football League. Produced by NFL Films.
Literature and Drama; Physical Education and Recreation
Dist - CAMV

NFL head coach - a self portrait
VHS
NFL series
Color (G)
$29.95 purchase _ #NFL1018V
Profiles and interviews several of the National Football League's most successful head coaches. Produced by NFL Films.
Literature and Drama; Physical Education and Recreation
Dist - CAMV

NFL Pro Football 30 MIN
16mm
B&W
Shows the Chicago Bears and the New York City Giants in four half hour segments.
Physical Education and Recreation
Dist - SFI **Prod** - SFI

NFL quarterback 52 MIN
VHS
Color (G)
$19.95 purchase _ #NFL2023V
Examines the critical role of the quarterback in professional football. Covers the pressures, challenges, and aspirations NFL quarterbacks face. Interviews John Elway, Jim Kelly, Dan Fouts, and Boomer Esaison, all successful all - star quarterbacks.
Physical Education and Recreation
Dist - CAMV

NFL series
Presents a 32 - part collection of films produced by NFL Films. Includes 'bloopers,' game highlights, player and coach profiles, and historical reviews of the best of the National Football League.
All the best
Big game America
Boom, bang, whap, doink - Madden on football
The Fabulous fifties - Volume 1
The Fabulous fifties - Volume 2
Festival of funnies
The Great ones
History of pro football
History of the Super Bowl
In the crunch
Legendary lineman
Lombardi
Mavericks and misfits
N F L follies go Hollywood
NFL '87
NFL crunch course
NFL head coach - a self portrait
NFL's best ever - pros
NFL's best ever coaches
NFL's best ever runners
NFL's best ever teams
NFL's best quarterbacks
NFL's greatest games
NFL's greatest games 2
Sensational 60's
Son of football follies

Strange but true body shapes
Strange but true football stories
Dist - CAMV

NFL's best ever coaches
VHS
NFL series
Color (G)
$29.95 purchase _ #NFL1108V
Profiles several of the best coaches in National Football League history. Produced by NFL Films.
Literature and Drama; Physical Education and Recreation
Dist - CAMV

NFL's best ever - pros
VHS
NFL series
Color (G)
$29.95 purchase _ #NFL1109V
Presents highlights of the best of the National Football League. Produced by NFL Films.
Literature and Drama; Physical Education and Recreation
Dist - CAMV

NFL's best ever runners
VHS
NFL series
Color (G)
$29.95 purchase _ #NFL1106V
Profiles several of the best running backs in National Football League history. Produced by NFL Films.
Literature and Drama; Physical Education and Recreation
Dist - CAMV

NFL's best ever teams
VHS
NFL series
Color (G)
$29.95 purchase _ #NFL1107V
Presents highlights of the best teams in National Football League history. Produced by NFL Films.
Literature and Drama; Physical Education and Recreation
Dist - CAMV

NFL's best quarterbacks
VHS
NFL series
Color (G)
$29.95 purchase _ #NFL1105V
Profiles several of the best quarterbacks in National Football League history. Produced by NFL Films.
Literature and Drama; Physical Education and Recreation
Dist - CAMV

NFL's greatest games
VHS
NFL series
Color (G)
$24.95 purchase _ #NFL1038V
Presents highlights from some of the greatest games in National Football League history. Produced by NFL Films.
Literature and Drama; Physical Education and Recreation
Dist - CAMV

NFL's greatest games 2
VHS
NFL series
Color (G)
$24.95 purchase _ #NFL2002V
Presents highlights from more of the greatest games in National Football League history. Produced by NFL Films.
Literature and Drama; Physical Education and Recreation
Dist - CAMV

Ngorongoro Crater 25 MIN
16mm / U-matic / VHS
Untamed World Series
Color; Mono (J H C A)
$400.00 film, $250.00 video, $50.00 rental
Presents the Ngorongoro Crater in Tanzania from its origin as a volcano to the vast green bowl where Masai tribesmen and their animals live today.
Geography - World; Science - Physical; Sociology
Dist - CTV Prod - CTV 1972

Ngung Lai 26 MIN
16mm
Color
LC 74-705212
Presents the story of vessel preparation, special personnel training, deployment and patrol operations of the 26 82 - foot cutters and their crews assigned to operation market time in South Vietnam.
Civics and Political Systems; Geography - World
Dist - USNAC Prod - USGEOS 1967

Ngunglai 26 MIN
VHS / U-matic
Color
Depicts Operation Market Time, the special assignment of the U S Coast Guard to stop the Viet Cong bringing in supplies from the north. Shows vessel preparation, crew training and patrol operations of the 26 82 - foot Coast Guard cutters involved.
Civics and Political Systems; History - United States
Dist - IHF Prod - IHF

Nguzo Saba - Folklore for Children Series

Imani - Beegie and the Egg	8 MIN
Kujichagulia	6 MIN
Nia	5 MIN
Noel's Lemonade Stand (Ujamaa)	9 MIN
Ujima - Modupe and the flood	5 MIN
Umoja - tiger and the big wind	8 MIN

Dist - BCNFL

Nguzo Saba - Folklore for Children Series

Kuumba - Simon's New Sound	8 MIN

Dist - BCNFL
NGUZO

Nia 5 MIN
16mm / U-matic / VHS
Nguzo Saba - Folklore for Children Series
Color (K P I)
Tells the story of the young girl who saps the strength of her rural community by lack of cooperation. Shows how, when she asked for help, she learns to help others.
Psychology
Dist - BCNFL Prod - NGUZO 1982

The Niagara Escarpment - a Rock Video 52 MIN
VHS
Color (S)
$149.00 purchase _ #386 - 9030
Reveals that the Niagara Escarpment is an ancient vein of limestone that runs north from Niagara Falls through southern Ontario beyond Maintoulin Island. Shows that it dominates the landscape in one of Canada's most populous areas. The porous limestone that allows toxic wastes to poison the Niagara River also nurtures rich communities of plants and animals. Presents the two faces of the escarpment - the beautiful, and the dangerously poisonous.
Business and Economics; Geography - World; Science - Natural; Science - Physical; Social Science; Sociology
Dist - FI Prod - CANBC 1988

Niagara Falls Parkland 12 MIN
16mm
Color
LC FIA68-1566
Explores the parks, gardens, flowers beds and other landscaping projects that beautify the approaches to Niagara Falls in Ontario.
Geography - United States; Geography - World
Dist - MORLAT Prod - MORLAT 1967

Niagara Falls - the Changing Nature of a New World Symbol 28 MIN
16mm / U-matic / VHS
Color (I A G)
Tackles the fundamental question of what a nation does with its symbols. Chronicles the changing outlook on Niagra Falls, from the quintessential wilderness symbol of wilderness in the 17th century, to a representation of the moral and national strength of the new world in the 18th and 19th centuries.
Sociology
Dist - DIRECT Prod - FLRNTN 1985

Niambi - Sweet Melody 25 MIN
U-matic / VHS / 16mm
Color (P I)
Tells the story of Niambi Robinson, a little black girl who, at the age of five, broke the world's record for her age in the 100 meter dash. Explores the values and constant nurturing of her loving family and shows Niambi at school, at ballet class, on the track and at home.
History - United States; Physical Education and Recreation; Sociology
Dist - FI Prod - FI 1979

Nibbles Series

Module A - Introduction to the Computer	41 MIN
Module B - Programming	41 MIN
Module C - Impact on Society	73 MIN
Module D - Electronics and Technology	13 MIN
Module E - Information Processing	31 MIN

Dist - TVOTAR

Nibbling Away at Nutrition Myths 14 MIN
16mm
Color
Discusses the history of potato chips, how they are made, some misconceptions associated with them and how nutrition experts see the impact of snacks on the American diet.
Health and Safety; Psychology
Dist - MTP Prod - PCIB

Nibelungen 62 MIN
16mm
B&W ((ENGLISH SUBTITLES))
An expressionistic silent motion picture with music and English subtitles. Relates the Nibelungen Saga, showing Siegfried's wooing of Kriemhild and Siegfried's death in flashbacks, and continuing with the descent of the Burgunder at the court of the Huns.
Fine Arts
Dist - WSTGLC Prod - WSTGLC

Nibelungen Saga, Die - 'Kriemheld's Revenge' 100 MIN
VHS / U-matic
B&W
Presents the saga of the Nibelung in its complete second part.
Fine Arts; Foreign Language
Dist - IHF Prod - IHF

Nicaragua 1983
U-matic / VHS
Color
Covers a five day battle between the Sandinista Army and the counter - revolutionaries trained by the United States Central Intelligence Agency. Explores also the conditions of the Miskito Indians both in jail and in the countryside. Looks at daily life of Nicaraguans and the struggle for land reform.
Business and Economics; Civics and Political Systems; Geography - World; History - World; Sociology
Dist - DCTVC Prod - DCTVC

Nicaragua 79 - in the Beginning 30 MIN
VHS / U-matic
Color
Documents the battle against the Samoza regime, the Sandinista victory and the first days of the revolution. Presents a personal view of a people in the process of making a revolution, who they are and why they revolted.
Business and Economics; Civics and Political Systems; Geography - World; History - World; Sociology
Dist - DCTVC Prod - DCTVC

Nicaragua - a Failed Revolution 30 MIN
U-matic
Realities
Color (A)
Delves into the political, social, economic and cultural trends of the 1980s. Probes a wide range of contemporary concerns. Each segment includes a guest speaker who is an expert in the field under discussion.
Business and Economics; Civics and Political Systems; Social Science; Sociology
Dist - TVOTAR Prod - TVOTAR 1985

Nicaragua - After the Revolution 15 MIN
VHS / U-matic
Color (J H)
Examines the results of the revolution in Nicaragua. Points out that the Sandinista government has developed new alliances and a different political system, but it must still deal with many problems of the past.
Geography - World; History - World
Dist - JOU Prod - JOU

Nicaragua - Campaign '84 30 MIN
VHS
Inside Story Series
Color (G)
$50.00 purchase _ #INST - 412
Examines the Nicaraguan election of 1984. Focuses on the state of press coverage in Nicaragua, which included censorship of opposition candidates in the newspapers and only limited radio and television time. Hosted by Hodding Carter.
History - World
Dist - PBS

Nicaragua for the First Time 58 MIN
Videoreel / U-matic / VT3
(G)
$125.00 purchase, $50.00 rental
Documents the controversial Nicaraguan election of 1984. Interviews the international observers who were invited to witness the election, the party candidates, and the people themselves. Contradicts the assumption that the election was not a free and democratic one.
Civics and Political Systems; Geography - World
Dist - EFVP Prod - EFVP 1985

Nicaragua - Healing the Wounds of War 18 MIN
16mm
Color (SPANISH)
Shows how the Catholic Relief Services brought the first food to the embattled victims of Nicaragua's civil war. Looks at individual people whose stories are relived daily in Central America.
History - World; Religion and Philosophy; Sociology
Dist - MTP Prod - CATHRS

Nicaragua - hear - say - see - here 64 MIN
16mm
B&W (G)
$65.00 rental
Attempts to understand why America - the government and the media - have mystified and depersonalized Nicaragua by reducing their representations of that country to a war zone rather than as a place where people live their lives. Conveys filmmaker Jeffrey Skoller's personal response to the reality of daily life in Nicaragua. Asks the question - as a North American, what is my relationship to Nicaragua.

Fine Arts; Sociology
Dist - CANCIN

Nicaragua - Our Own Country 19 MIN
16mm / U-matic / VHS
Color (J)
Portrays Nicaragua today, including its history, its people and its hopes for the future.
Geography - World; History - World
Dist - CF **Prod** - FCP

Nicaragua - Planting the Seeds of Change 27 MIN
16mm
Color (H) (FRENCH SPANISH)
LC 77-700643
Depicts problems faced by small farmers in Nicaragua. Explains how the rural development program Invierno, which was designed by the Nicaraguan government and Supported by the United States, helps farmers by offering farm credit, technical agricultural assistance and social services. Tells the story of one small farmer and his family and how their prospects are brighter as a result of the program.
Agriculture; Civics and Political Systems; History - World; Sociology
Dist - USNAC **Prod** - USAID 1977

Nicaragua - Report from the Front 32 MIN
16mm
Color (G)
Presents an independent production by Deborah Shaffer, T Siegal and P Yates. Examines US foreign policy in Nicaragua.
Civics and Political Systems; Fine Arts; Geography - World; History - World; Sociology
Dist - FIRS

Nicaragua - Scenes from the Revolution 30 MIN
U-matic / VHS / 16mm
Captioned; Color (A) (SPANISH (ENGLISH SUBTITLES))
Portrays the forces that shaped the Nicaraguan Revolution, from the inception of Sandinismo in the 1930's to the general strike called by the Sandinistas in June of 1979. Discusses the first 100 days after the Sandinista victory and the problems facing the country.
Civics and Political Systems; Fine Arts; History - World
Dist - CNEMAG **Prod** - CNEMAG 1979

Nicaragua September 1978 41 MIN
U-matic / VHS / 16mm
Color
Documents the 1978 revolt against the Somoza dictatorship in Nicaragua.
Civics and Political Systems; History - World; Sociology
Dist - NEWTIM **Prod** - NEWTIM

Nicaragua - the Dirty War 68 MIN
U-matic / VHS / 16mm
Color (H C A)
$895 purchase - 16 mm, $595 purchase - video, $100 rental
Shows the contra army's war against the civilian population in Nicaragua. Directed by Daniele Lacourse and Yvan Patry.
History - World; Sociology
Dist - CNEMAG

Nicaragua - the Other Invasion 29 MIN
16mm / U-matic
Presente Series
Color (SPANISH (ENGLISH SUBTITLES))
Presents a documentary on the changes in health care in Nicaragua since the revolution. Documents the effects of the CIA - directed 'contra' attacks on health care, including the destruction of clinics and the killings of medical personnel.
Civics and Political Systems; Geography - World; History - World; Sociology
Dist - KCET **Prod** - KCET

Nicaragua was Our Home 56 MIN
U-matic / VHS / 16mm
Color (A)
Looks at the Miskito Indians of Nicaragua as they were terrorized by the Sandinista regime and as they fought for survival and freedom to preserve their way of life. Shows their ravaged villages, refugee camps and secret guerrilla bases and their mass exodus from their homeland.
History - World; Social Science
Dist - FI **Prod** - FI

Nicaraguan Countryside 15 MIN
U-matic / VHS
Other families, other friends series; Brown module; Nicaragua
Color (P)
Pictures lava fields, an indian settlement and a coffee plantation in Nicaragua.
Geography - World; Social Science
Dist - AITECH **Prod** - WVIZTV 1971

Nicaraguan women - contra war 28 MIN
VHS / U-matic
Color (H C A)
$425.00, $395.00 purchase _ #V443
Examines the role of women in war - torn Nicaragua. Reveals that the women, most of them with several children, work to keep the battle - torn economy going while their men are defending Nicaragua against the United States backed Contras. Focuses on the lives of three of these women.
Civics and Political Systems; Geography - World; Sociology
Dist - BARR **Prod** - CEPRO 1988

Nice and easy powerwalking 60 MIN
VHS
Color (G)
$29.95 purchase _ #P57
Features Gary Null, PhD who takes the viewer on a journey to learn the essential skills of powerwalking, from beginner to marathon runner. Includes right eating and selecting the right nutrients for optimal health.
Physical Education and Recreation; Social Science
Dist - HP

Nice Colored Girls 16 MIN
16mm / VHS
Color (G)
$275.00 purchase, $55.00 rental
Explores the relationships between Aboriginal women and white men in Australia over the past two hundred years. Juxtaposes the first encounters between native women and white male colonizers with the attempts of modern urban Aboriginal women to reverse their fortunes with what their foremothers called 'captains' - sugar daddies. Considers the situation from an Aboriginal point of view.
Geography - World; Guidance and Counseling; History - World; Psychology; Sociology
Dist - WMEN **Prod** - TRAMO 1987

Nice Coloured Girls 18 MIN
16mm
Color (G)
$600.00 purchase, $75.00, $55.00 rental
Examines the Australian urban ritual of Aboriginal women taking white men for a ride. Created by Tracey Moffatt.
Geography - World; Sociology
Dist - WMENIF **Prod** - WMENIF 1987

A Nice Flying Machine 9 MIN
U-matic / VHS / 16mm
Color (I)
Documents the Manned Maneuvering Unit, the jet pack that astronauts use to travel in space untethered from the space ship.
History - World; Science - Physical; Social Science
Dist - PHENIX **Prod** - PHENIX

The Nice Guy 4 MIN
16mm / U-matic / VHS
This Matter of Motivation Series
Color (PRO)
LC 75-703852
Asks what to do with the old company employee whose lack of performance affects the whole department.
Business and Economics; Psychology; Sociology
Dist - DARTNL **Prod** - CTRACT 1968

Nice guys finish first 50 MIN
VHS
Horizon series
Color (A PRO C)
PdS99 purchase
Presents Richard Dawkins who authored The Selfish Gene, which explains how natural selection can favor cooperation in nature - as long as it benefits the selfish gene. Describes his search for stable cooperative stratagies, involving a game known as The Prisoners' Dilemma. Player must wrestle with dilemma of whether to follow their natural cooperative instincts or their reasoning to behave selfishly.
Science - Natural; Sociology
Dist - BBCENE

Nice, Rain, Fish 10 MIN
U-matic
Readalong One Series
Color (K P)
Introduces reading and spelling for preschoolers and children in grades 1 to 3 with animation, puppets, humor and music. Comes with teacher's guide and kit.
Education; English Language; Literature and Drama
Dist - TVOTAR **Prod** - TVOTAR 1975

Nice shot 60 MIN
VHS
Color (G)
Explains that the problem with most golf games isn't physical but mental - and it can be controlled. Discusses - using the power of imagination; how to organize golfing information in a systematic way; how to habituate a golf swing; self - target awareness; relaxation and focus; pre - swing drills; five concepts of the swing; accurate observation; and more.
Physical Education and Recreation
Dist - SVIP
CAMV

Nice things kids can do 16 MIN
VHS
Let's get along - conflict skills training series
Color (P I)
$69.95 purchase _ #10381VG
Presents skills for solving conflicts and differences. Features Gary Wick, ventriloquist and comedian, as he shows kids how to communicate to solve conflict. Includes a reproducible teacher's guide. Part of a four - part series.
Psychology; Social Science
Dist - UNL

Nicholas and Alexandra 103 MIN
VHS
Color (H C)
Portrays the last days of the Russian monarchy. Stars Michael Redgrave and Laurence Olivier.
Civics and Political Systems; History - World
Dist - GA **Prod** - GA
ASPRSS
UILL

Nicholas and Alexandra - Prelude to Revolution, 1904 - 1905 29 MIN
16mm / U-matic / VHS
Color (H C A) (SPANISH)
LC 76-700111
Focuses on the years 1904 to 1905. Shows some of the causes of the Russian Revolution that were clearly visible more than a decade before Lenin arrived at the Finland Station. Reveals the extreme contrasts of Russia, the Czar's autocratic power set against the workers' seething powerless misery, the liberal leanings of some of the Czar's advisors versus the radical demands of the revolutionaries and the peasants mystical faith in their Czar contrasted to the remoteness of Nicholas himself.
Civics and Political Systems; History - World
Dist - LCOA **Prod** - LCOA 1976

Nicholas and Alexandra - the Bolshevik Victory, 1917 26 MIN
U-matic / VHS / 16mm
Color (H C A) (SPANISH)
LC 76-700113
Covers the second stage of the Russian Revolution, the October Revolution. Shows the phase that is common to many revolutions, growing radicalization, counterrevolution and civil war. Explains that Lenin returned to Russia promising peace, a new socialist order and all power to the Soviets. Tells how Kerensky and his party wanted to win the war, but became increasingly powerless. Concludes with the execution of the Czar and his entire family, which began a new era.
Civics and Political Systems; History - World
Dist - LCOA **Prod** - LCOA 1976

Nicholas and Alexandria - War and the Fall of the Tsar - 1914 - 1917 27 MIN
16mm / U-matic / VHS
Color (H C A)
Dramatizes the effect Russia's involvement in the war with Germany had on Nicholas and his abdication.
Biography; Civics and Political Systems; History - World
Dist - LCOA **Prod** - LCOA 1976

Nicholas and the Baby 23 MIN
16mm
Color
LC 81-700541
Presents the story of a four - year - old boy who is expecting a birth in his family. Follows the family through the stages of pregnancy, labor, birth and bringing the newborn home.
Guidance and Counseling; Health and Safety; Sociology
Dist - CEPRO **Prod** - NALNDA 1981

Nicholas Nickleby 103 MIN
VHS
B&W (J H)
$79.00 purchase _ #05915 - 126
Presents a 1947 screen adaptation of Nicholas Nickleby by Charles Dickens. Stars Sir Cedric Hardwick, Stanley Holloway.
Literature and Drama
Dist - GA **Prod** - GA

Nicholas Nickleby 108 MIN
16mm
B&W
Presents the story of the hard and hilarious times of a young man beset by the machinations of his unscrupulous uncle and the irrationality of Victorian society.
Fine Arts; Literature and Drama
Dist - LCOA **Prod** - UPCI 1947

Nicholas Roeg 34 MIN
VHS
Filmmakers on their craft series
Color (PRO G C)
$79.00 purchase, $29.00 _ #728
Features Nicholas Roeg, director of Performance, Walkabout, The Man Who Fell to Earth and Witches. Focuses on the 1985 Insignificance to discuss Roeg's preoccupation with fame as a theme and his sometimes edgy exploration of the borderline between tragedy and

farce. Features Peter Thompson as interviewer. Part of a six - part series on world famous filmmakers produced by the Australian Film, Television and Radio School.
Fine Arts; Industrial and Technical Education
Dist - FIRLIT

Nicholas Roerich - messenger of beauty 43 MIN
VHS
Color (G)
$21.95 purchase _ #TPNR
Portrays artist Nicholas Roerich, born in Russia, painter of 6,000 canvases. Remembers Roerich as a Tibetan explorer and philosopher.
Fine Arts; Religion and Philosophy
Dist - SNOWLI **Prod** - SNOWLI

Nichols and Dimes 25 MIN
16mm
Color (I)
LC 83-700151
Looks at the beautiful Arabian horses raised by director Mike Nichols. Views the first minutes of life of a horse worth 50 thousand dollars at birth.
Agriculture; Physical Education and Recreation
Dist - DIRECT **Prod** - MIDMAR 1982

Nicht Fur Geld Und Gute Worte 15 MIN
16mm / U-matic / VHS
Guten Tag Wie Geht's Series
Color (H C) (GERMAN)
A German language film. Features Gunther who encounters problems because Herr Hansen is not willing to abandon his house which is in the middle of the construction site.
Foreign Language
Dist - IFB **Prod** - BAYER 1973

Nick and Jon 20 MIN
VHS / U-matic
Color (C A)
Discusses male sexuality and homosexuality through the relationship of two college age men.
Health and Safety; Psychology; Sociology
Dist - MMRC **Prod** - MMRC

Nick Mazzuco 22 MIN
16mm
Color (G)
Presents an independent production by R Schmiechen and M Uhl. Offers a biography of an 'atomic' veteran.
Biography; Fine Arts; History - United States; Science - Physical
Dist - FIRS

A Nickel for the Movies 21 MIN
16mm / U-matic / VHS
Color (H C A)
Presents an introduction to motion picture study which tries to touch briefly on most of the issues of contemporary film making.
Fine Arts
Dist - IU **Prod** - IU 1984

Nickelodeon 121 MIN
16mm
Color
Stars Ryan O'Neal as a movie writer/director, Burt Reynolds as his leading man, and Tatum O'Neal as a 12 - year - old truck driver who rents anything to the pioneer movie makers.
Fine Arts
Dist - SWANK **Prod** - CPC

Nicky and Geoffrey in Japan 26 MIN
16mm
B&W
Recounts the summer's adventure in Japan of two American children, Geoffrey and his sister, Nicky. Captures the historic grace, life styles and monuments of today's Japan.
Geography - World; History - World
Dist - RADIM **Prod** - GBFP

Nicky and the Nerd 24 MIN
U-matic / 16mm / VHS
Color (K)
$495.00, $349.00, $249.00 purchase _ #AD - 1120
Portrays Nicky, a brash kid about to drop out of school, who meets Franklin, the 'nerd' with brains. Reveals that they form an unlikely partnership.
Literature and Drama; Psychology; Sociology
Dist - FOTH **Prod** - FOTH

Nicky - One of My Best Friends 15 MIN
U-matic / VHS / 16mm
Color (I)
LC 76-700710
Provides a sympathetic portrait of a multiply handicapped 12 - year - old boy and his successful integration into a suburban public school. Reveals his needs, as seen by his friends, and his similarity to them.
Education; Guidance and Counseling; Psychology; Social Science
Dist - MGHT **Prod** - TOGGFI 1976

Nicodemus 20 MIN
16mm
Living Bible Series
Color (I)
Joseph of Arimathea and Nicodemus agree to make arrangements for the burial of Jesus. They remove the body of Jesus and take it to Joseph's tomb. Nicodemus reflects on his experience with Jesus the night he questioned him about being born again.
Religion and Philosophy
Dist - FAMF **Prod** - FAMF

Nicolai Neilsen - Guitarist 29 MIN
Videoreel / VT2
Young Musical Artists Series
Color
Presents the music of guitarist Nicolai Neilsen.
Fine Arts
Dist - PBS **Prod** - WKARTV

Nicolas a Montmartre 13 MIN
16mm
En France Avec Nicolas Series Set I, Lesson 12; Set I; Lesson 12
B&W (J H)
LC 75-704480
Foreign Language
Dist - CHLTN **Prod** - PEREN 1968

Nicolas a Montmartre, Student Exercises 8 MIN
16mm
En France Avec Nicolas Series Set II, Lesson 12; Set II; Lesson 12
Color (J H)
LC 79-704481
Foreign Language
Dist - CHLTN **Prod** - PEREN 1968

Nicolas a Orly 13 MIN
16mm
En France Avec Nicolas Series Set I, Lesson 9; Set I; Lesson 9
B&W (J H)
LC 72-704482
Foreign Language
Dist - CHLTN **Prod** - PEREN 1968

Nicolas a Orly, Student Exercises 8 MIN
16mm
En France Avec Nicolas Series Set II, Lesson 9; Set II; Lesson 9
B&W (J H)
LC 76-704483
Foreign Language
Dist - CHLTN **Prod** - PEREN 1968

Nicolas Au Theatre 13 MIN
16mm
En France Avec Nicolas Series Set I, Lesson 5; Set I; Lesson 5
B&W (J H)
LC 70-704484
Foreign Language
Dist - CHLTN **Prod** - PEREN 1968

Nicolas Au Theatre, Student Exercises 8 MIN
16mm
En France Avec Nicolas Series Set II, Lesson 5; Set II; Lesson 5
B&W (J H)
LC 73-704485
Foreign Language
Dist - CHLTN **Prod** - PEREN 1968

Nicolas Chez Sa Tante 13 MIN
16mm
En France Avec Nicolas Series Set I, Lesson 7; Set I; Lesson 7
B&W (J H)
LC 77-704486
Foreign Language
Dist - CHLTN **Prod** - PEREN 1968

Nicolas Chez Sa Tante, Student Exercises 8 MIN
16mm
En France Avec Nicolas Series Set II, Lesson 7; Set II; Lesson 7
B&W (J H)
LC 70-704487
Foreign Language
Dist - CHLTN **Prod** - PEREN 1968

Nicolas Et La Libraire 13 MIN
16mm
En France Avec Nicolas Series Set I, Lesson 1; Set I; Lesson 1
B&W (J H)
LC 74-704488
Foreign Language
Dist - CHLTN **Prod** - PEREN 1968

Nicolas Et La Libraire, Student Exercises 8 MIN
16mm
En France Avec Nicolas Series Set II, Lesson 1; Set II; Lesson 1
B&W (J H)
LC 78-704489
Foreign Language
Dist - CHLTN **Prod** - PEREN 1968

Nicolas Prendra - T - Il Son Train 13 MIN
16mm
En France Avec Nicolas Series Set I, Lesson 11; Set I; Lesson 11
B&W (J H)
LC 72-704490
Foreign Language
Dist - CHLTN **Prod** - PEREN 1968

Nicolas Prendra - T - Il Son Train, Student Exercises 8 MIN
16mm
En France Avec Nicolas Series Set II, Lesson 11; Set II; Lesson 11
B&W (J H)
LC 76-704491
Foreign Language
Dist - CHLTN **Prod** - PEREN 1968

Nicolas Protege Les Amoureux 13 MIN
16mm
En France Avec Nicolas Series Set I, Lesson 4; Set I; Lesson 4
B&W (J H)
LC 70-704492
Foreign Language
Dist - CHLTN **Prod** - PEREN 1968

Nicolas Protege Les Amoureux, Student Exercises 8 MIN
16mm
En France Avec Nicolas Series Set II, Lesson 4; Set II; Lesson 4
B&W (J H)
LC 73-704493
Foreign Language
Dist - CHLTN **Prod** - PEREN 1968

Nicolas S'Ennuie Le Dimanche 13 MIN
16mm
En France Avec Nicolas Series Set I, Lesson 10; Set I; Lesson 10
B&W (J H)
LC 77-704494
Foreign Language
Dist - CHLTN **Prod** - PEREN 1968

Nicolas S'Ennuie Le Dimanche, Student Exercises 8 MIN
16mm
En France Avec Nicolas Series Set II, Lesson 10; Set II; Lesson 10
B&W (J H)
LC 70-704495
Foreign Language
Dist - CHLTN **Prod** - PEREN 1968

Nicolas Sur Les Quais 13 MIN
16mm
En France Avec Nicolas Series Set I, Lesson 13; Set I; Lesson 13
B&W (J H)
LC 74-704496
Foreign Language
Dist - CHLTN **Prod** - PEREN 1968

Nicolas Sur Les Quais, Student Exercises 8 MIN
16mm
En France Avec Nicolas Series Set II, Lesson 13; Set II; Lesson 13
B&W (J H)
LC 78-704497
Foreign Language
Dist - CHLTN **Prod** - PEREN 1968

Nicolas Telephone 13 MIN
16mm
En France Avec Nicolas Series Set I, Lesson 6; Set I; Lesson 6
B&W (J H)
LC 71-704498
Foreign Language
Dist - CHLTN **Prod** - PEREN 1968

Nicolas Telephone, Student Exercises 8 MIN
16mm
En France Avec Nicolas Series Set II, Lesson 6; Set II; Lesson 6
B&W (J H)
LC 75-704499
Foreign Language
Dist - CHLTN **Prod** - PEREN 1968

Nicolas VA a La Peche 13 MIN
16mm
En France Avec Nicolas Series Set I, Lesson 2; Set I; Lesson 2
B&W (J H)
LC 75-704500
Foreign Language
Dist - CHLTN **Prod** - PEREN 1968

Nicolas VA a La Peche, Student Exercises 8 MIN
16mm
En France Avec Nicolas Series Set II, Lesson 2; Set II; Lesson 2
B&W (J H)
LC 79-704501
Foreign Language
Dist - CHLTN **Prod** - PEREN 1968

Nicole Brossard - 10 - 23 - 86 72 MIN
VHS / Cassette
Poetry Center reading series
Color (G)
$15.00, $45.00 purchase _ #719 - 578
Features the writer at the Poetry Center, San Francisco State University, reading her books Fran Quebec; L'Amer - These Our Mothers; Screen Skin; and Typical, with an introduction by Frances Phillips. Includes a question and answer session.
Literature and Drama
Dist - POETRY **Prod** - POETRY 1986

Nicotine 30 MIN
VHS
Video encyclopedia of psychoactive drugs series
Color (J H G)
$44.95 purchase _ #LVP6618V
Presents the most up - to - date research in clinical and laboratory studies on nicotine. Discusses the effects of nicotine on the mind and body, addiction and abuse, recovery and rehabilitation, medical uses, importation and distribution facts, user methodology and current trends. Part of a series.
Guidance and Counseling; Health and Safety; Psychology
Dist - CAMV

NICU video series
Presents a seven - part series on development intervention for hospitalized infants in the neonatal intensive care unit. Includes five staff development programs and two programs for parents of hospitalized premies.

The Growing premie - staff development	12 MIN
Helping families in the special care nursery - staff development	14 MIN
NICU video series	110 MIN
Parenting the acutely ill infant - parent tape	14 MIN
Parenting the growing premie - parent tape	9 MIN
Positioning and handling the high risk infant - staff development	15 MIN
The Premie and the NICU environment - staff development	16 MIN
Premie development - an overview - staff development	14 MIN

Dist - POLYMR **Prod** - POKORJ 1991

Niels Stensen Liv Og Dod (Life and Death of Niels Stensen) 29 MIN
16mm
B&W (DANISH)
Draws a picture of the famous Danish medical scientist Niels Stensen as a pioneer in the anatomic science and as the founder of geology as a science with his work De Solido.
Biography; Foreign Language; Science - Natural; Science - Physical
Dist - STATNS **Prod** - STATNS 1970

Nierenberg's need theory of negotiation
U-matic / 16mm
Art of negotiating series; Module 3
Color (A)
Deals with satisfaction of needs, basic needs, recognizing needs, changing win - lose stands, finding common interest and varieties of applications in negotiations.
Business and Economics; Psychology
Dist - BNA **Prod** - BNA 1983

Nietzche and the post - modern condition
VHS / Cassette
Color (C A)
$149.95, $89.95 purchase _ #AI - B417
Presents eight lectures on the controversial, unsettling and provocative ideas of 19th century German philosopher, F W Nietzche. Features Asst Prof Rick Roderick of Duke University as lecturer.
History - World; Religion and Philosophy
Dist - TTCO **Prod** - TTCO

Nietzsche 45 MIN
VHS
Great philosophers series
Color; PAL (H C A)
PdS99 purchase
Introduces the concepts of Western philosophy and one of its greatest thinkers. Features a contemporary philosopher who, in conversation with Bryan Magee, discusses Nietzsche and his ideas. Part eleven of a fifteen part series.
Literature and Drama; Religion and Philosophy
Dist - BBCENE

Nigel Rolfe - Dance Slap for Africa 23 MIN
U-matic / VHS
Color
Provides two channels which juxtapose modern day experience with a more primitive and ethnic source.
Fine Arts; History - World
Dist - ARTINC **Prod** - ARTINC

Nigel Rolfe - the Rope that Binds Us Makes Them Free 15 MIN
VHS / U-matic
Color
Focuses on Leitrim, a northwestern county in Ireland where cottages deserted long ago remain mysteriously intact today.
Fine Arts; History - World
Dist - ARTINC **Prod** - ARTINC

Nigeria 5 MIN
16mm
Color (G)
$20.00 rental
Utilizes found footage about Nigeria. Alternates between images such as witch - doctor masks, failed rocket launchings, white big - game hunters and tropical fish.
Fine Arts; Geography - World
Dist - CANCIN **Prod** - HUDINA 1989

Nigeria - a Squandering of Riches 50 MIN
VHS / U-matic
Color (H C G T A)
Shows the New Year's Eve 1983 military coup that took place in Nigeria. Narrated by Nigerian singer and journalist Onyeka Onwenu. Shows her travels across the country to talk to various social groups, from the bankers and industrialists to the street traders and farmers. Captures the mood of the people in the weeks before the coup actually took place.
Civics and Political Systems; Geography - World; History - World
Dist - PSU **Prod** - PSU 1984

Nigeria - Africa in Miniature 16 MIN
U-matic / VHS / 16mm
Color (I J H) (AFRIKAANS)
LC FIA67-1727
Uses maps and photographs to describe the location, provinces, topography and rivers of Nigeria. Portrays major ethnic groups and discusses progress in economics, education, politics, religion, transportation and other important areas.
Geography - World
Dist - AIMS **Prod** - ASSOCF 1966

Nigeria and Biafra - the Story Behind the Struggle 14 MIN
16mm
Screen news digest series; Vol 11; Issue 2
B&W (J H)
LC 72-703469
Portrays the underlying and immediate causes of the Civil War between Nigeria and the breakaway province of Biafra.
History - United States; History - World
Dist - HEARST **Prod** - HEARST 1968

Nigeria - Problems of Nation Building 22 MIN
16mm
Color (I)
LC FIA68-772
Revised edition of 'AFRICA AWAKENS - MODERN NIGERIA.' Presents an insight into Africa through a study of Nigeria, the most populated country of the continent. Stresses the influences of climate and geography on the economy, urbanization and education.
Geography - World; History - United States; History - World
Dist - ATLAP **Prod** - ATLAP 1968

Nigerian Art - Kindred Spirits 60 MIN
VHS
Smithsonian World Series
Color; Captioned (G)
$49.95 purchase _ #SMIW - 504
Focuses on the artwork of several Nigerian artists. Shows that modern African art is fast gaining popularity. Narrated by actress Ruby Dee.
Sociology
Dist - PBS **Prod** - WETATV

Night 9 MIN
VHS / 16mm
Look again series
Color (P I J)
$150.00, $195.00 purchase, $25.00 rental
Presents a film in the Look Again series, without dialogue. Builds upon and develops children's natural interest in their surroundings. A girl views the city at night from her balcony, wondering about the sights and sounds of her familiar world after dark. Several viewings allow students to look again and experience the magic of night from different perspectives.
Psychology
Dist - BULFRG **Prod** - NFBC 1990

Night 30 MIN
U-matic
Today's Special Series
Color (K P)
Develops language arts skills in children. Programs are thematically designed around subjects of interest to youngsters. Action takes place in a department store where people, mannequins, puppets, comic characters and special guests present a light hearted approach to language arts.
Literature and Drama; Psychology
Dist - TVOTAR **Prod** - TVOTAR 1985

Night 7.19 MIN
U-matic / VHS
Photo Tips Series
Color (J H A)
Demonstrates and teaches the techniques of night photography using diverse lenses and filtering aparatus.
Fine Arts; Industrial and Technical Education
Dist - AITECH **Prod** - TURR 1986

Night and Day 30 MIN
U-matic
Polka Dot Door Series
Color (K)
Presents a variety show for pre - school children. Includes songs, mime, stories, film sequences, talk, dance and fantasy figures. Each show emphasizes a particular theme such as numbers, feelings, exploring, music or time. Comes with parent teacher guide.
Fine Arts; Literature and Drama
Dist - TVOTAR **Prod** - TVOTAR 1985

Night and Day 12 MIN
16mm
Color
LC 75-700153
Discusses day and night, the rising and setting of the Sun, the lengthening of days and nights at different latitudes, and the origin of the Arctic and Antarctic Circles.
Geography - World; Science - Natural; Science - Physical
Dist - SHAPEC **Prod** - SHAPEC 1974

Night and Fog 30 MIN
U-matic / VHS
B&W
Documents the Nazi concentrations camps and the Nazi atrocities. Creates the feeling of history's nightmare.
History - World
Dist - IHF **Prod** - IHF

Night and Fog 31 MIN
16mm / U-matic
Color (H C A S) (FRENCH (ENGLISH SUBTITLES))
LC 77-701530
Presents Director Alain Resnais' profoundly disturbing rumination on the atrocities of the Holocaust. Uses elegiac counterpoint between sound and image, stills and motion pictures, the past and the present, the living and the dead, to make a timeless and universal depiction of absolute evil.
Fine Arts; Foreign Language; Geography - World; History - World
Dist - FI **Prod** - ARGOS 1955
UILL

A Night at Asti's 44 MIN
VHS / U-matic
Color
Fine Arts
Dist - ABCLR **Prod** - ABCLR

A Night at the Peking Opera 20 MIN
16mm
Color (I J H C)
Presents four vignettes using authentic traditional music and costumes. Includes 'A FAIRY TALE,' 'LEGEND OF THE MONKEY KING AND THE JADE EMPEROR,' 'A COMEDY BALLET OF ERRORS' and 'A BEAUTEOUS LADY.' An American adaptation, originally produced in France.
Fine Arts
Dist - RADIM **Prod** - FILIM

A Night at the Show 19 MIN
16mm
B&W
Shows a vaudeville show and its effect on a drunken gallery spectator and a rowdy in the orchestra. Stars Charlie Chaplin.

Fine Arts
Dist - TWYMAN Prod - ENY 1915

A Night at the Show 25 MIN
16mm
Charlie Chaplin Comedy Theater Series
B&W (I)
Highlights Chaplin's dual role as a drunken playboy in the orchestra and as an obnoxious workman on a night - out in the balcony.
Fine Arts
Dist - TWYMAN Prod - MUFLM 1915

A Night at the Show 15 MIN
16mm
B&W
Presents a rare print of the early Chaplin classic A Night At The Show in which Chaplin plays a dual role. Explains that the plot is an adaptation of his original Karno music act.
Fine Arts
Dist - CFS Prod - CHAC

The Night Before 5 MIN
U-matic / VHS
Write on, Set 2 Series
Color (J H)
Demonstrates effective subordination in writing.
English Language
Dist - CTI Prod - CTI

The Night before Christmas 30 MIN
VHS
Rabbit Ears series
Color (K P)
$9.95 purchase _ #NIG - 01
Combines the famous poem by Clement Moore with a selection of holiday music that depicts a tradional family Christmas celebration. Narrated by Meryl Streep, music by George Winston.
Literature and Drama
Dist - ARTSAM Prod - RABBIT 1992

The Night Before Christmas 27 MIN
U-matic / VHS / 16mm
Color (P I) (SPANISH)
Re - enacts Clement Moore's poem A Visit From St Nicholas.
Foreign Language; Literature and Drama; Social Science
Dist - EBEC Prod - EBEC

Night Before Christmas 7 MIN
16mm
Color (K P)
Presents the traditional Christmas poem, The Night Before Christmas, set to music with live action and animation.
Fine Arts; Literature and Drama; Religion and Philosophy
Dist - SHUGA Prod - SHUGA 1970

The Night Before Christmas 10 MIN
16mm / U-matic / VHS
Color (K P A) (SPANISH)
LC 79-700178
An imaginative three - dimensional animation of the famous Christmas poem by Clement C Moore.
Literature and Drama; Religion and Philosophy
Dist - AIMS Prod - CAHILL 1968

Night call 27 MIN
VHS
Color; PAL; NTSC (G)
PdS85, PdS94.50 purchase
Tells of a motoring correspondent's search for the 'perfect driver.' Illustrates the hard facts of highway driving technique, especially at night or in bad weather. Discusses moving with the flow of traffic, avoiding excessive lane switching, following at safe distances and signalling properly while on the highway. Produced for the British Department of Transport.
Health and Safety
Dist - CFLVIS Prod - BRCOI 1977

Night Creatures 60 MIN
U-matic / 16mm / VHS
Last Frontier Series
Color; Mono (G)
MV $225.00 _ MP $550.00
Unveils the magical and astonishingly beautiful world of the night sea.
Science - Natural
Dist - CTV Prod - MAKOF 1985

Night cries - a rural tragedy 19 MIN
16mm / VHS / 35mm / U-matic
Color (G)
$225.00 purchase, $75.00, $60.00 rental
Examines the assimilation policies of Australia which forced the taking of Aboriginal children from their homes to be raised in white families in the 1950s. Portrays a middle - aged Aboriginal woman who nurses her dying adopted white mother - with mixed feelings.
History - World; Sociology
Dist - WMEN Prod - TRAMO 1990

Night Driving 20 MIN
U-matic / 35mm strip
Color (J H)
Highlights one of the most neglected areas of driver education, night driving. Focuses on headlight glare, highbeam and lowbeam problems and other areas of concern. 15 minutes long.
Health and Safety; Industrial and Technical Education
Dist - BUMPA Prod - BUMPA

Night Driving and Seeing 28 MIN
16mm
Sportsmanlike Driving Series no 18
Color (H A)
LC FIA68-918
Illustrates and tells how to deal with factors affecting night driving, such as glare blindness, slow glare recovery, shadows, night blindness, and overdriving headlights.
Health and Safety; Science - Natural
Dist - GPN Prod - AAA 1967

Night Driving Tactics 13 MIN
16mm / U-matic / VHS
Color (J H A)
Shows how the physiology of vision and reaction time make fast nighttime driving dangerous. Presents emergency procedures.
Health and Safety
Dist - AIMS Prod - AIMS 1984

Night - Eating 7 MIN
16mm
Color
Shows animated drawings that invoke the illusion of endless space, etchings in light and the perfect harmony of geometry and color.
Fine Arts; Industrial and Technical Education
Dist - VANBKS Prod - VANBKS

Night Ferry 55 MIN
16mm
Color (P I)
Tells the story of three boys who discover a plot to steal an Egyptian mummy and attempt to foil the thieves.
Fine Arts; Literature and Drama
Dist - LUF Prod - CHILDF 1979

Night Flight 23 MIN
U-matic / 16mm / VHS
Color; Captioned (H C A J) (FRENCH)
LC 79-700483
Tells of a young pilot lost in a storm. Raises questions about the sacrifice of one's life for a greater good. Based on the novel by Antoine de Saint Exupery.
Industrial and Technical Education; Literature and Drama; Social Science
Dist - LCOA Prod - SINGER 1979

Night Flight 5 MIN
16mm
Song of the Ages Series
B&W (C A)
LC 70-702131
Presents a modern interpretation of Psalm 62 using scenes of a man and what he sees of the desert at night from his plane.
Religion and Philosophy
Dist - FAMLYT Prod - FAMLYT 1964

A Night in the Art Gallery 18 MIN
16mm
Color
Presents an allegorical tale about censorship during China's cultural revolution. Depicts symbols representing the Gang of Four touring an art gallery, finding something offensive in each work and defacing it. Shows the figures in the artworks banding together to repair the damage and finally turning on the villains to chase them away.
History - World; Sociology
Dist - FLMLIB Prod - CHFE 1980

A Night in the Show 25 MIN
16mm
B&W
Features Charlie Chaplin.
Fine Arts
Dist - FCE Prod - FCE 1916

The Night is sinister
16mm / U-matic / VHS
History book series
Color (G)
$195.00, $350.00 purchase, $45.00 rental
Explores colonialism, foreign aid and multinational corporations and neo - colonialism. Shows history as it has been lived and experienced by common people. Part of a nine - part series of animated episodes surveying the development of society from the Middle Ages to the present time from a grassroots perspective. Each title is 15 - 20 minutes in length.
Business and Economics; Civics and Political Systems; Fine Arts; History - World; Sociology
Dist - CNEMAG

Night Journey 29 MIN
U-matic / VHS / 16mm
B&W
A presentation of Martha Graham's interpretation in dance of the Oedipus legend, depicting the moment of Jocasta's death.
Fine Arts
Dist - PHENIX Prod - KROLL 1960

Night, Mother 96 MIN
VHS
Color (G C H)
$99.00 purchase _ #DL102
Stars Anne Bancroft.
Fine Arts
Dist - INSIM

Night music, Rage net, Glaze of cathexis 4 MIN
16mm
Three hand - painted films series
Color (G)
$30.00 rental
Presents three hand - painted films by Stan Brakhage.
Fine Arts
Dist - CANCIN Prod - BRAKS 1990

Night 'N Gales 14 MIN
16mm
B&W
Tells how a storm forces the Little Rascals to spend the night at Darla's.
Fine Arts
Dist - RMIBHF Prod - UNKNWN

Night of a Million Years 30 MIN
16mm
Eye on New York Series
B&W
LC FIA67-523
Traces the history of man's development as seen through the eyes of two ten - year - old boys who tour the American Museum of Natural History in New York City. Shows exhibits which range from models of dinosaurs and savage jungles to forecasts of the future.
History - World; Science; Science - Natural; Sociology
Dist - CBSTV Prod - WCBSTV 1966

The Night of Counting the Years 100 MIN
16mm
Color (ARABIC (ENGLISH SUBTITLES))
Re - creates the discovery of a Royal Tomb near Thebes in 1881, and the resulting clash between tribal heritage and art preservation. Directed by Shadi Abdelsalam. With English subtitles.
Fine Arts; Foreign Language
Dist - NYFLMS Prod - UNKNWN 1969

A Night of Terror 30 MIN
16mm
Color (R)
Documents the 1972 earthquake that struck Managua, Nicaragua and the efforts of churches to clear the rubble, feed and house the homeless and minister to their spiritual needs.
Guidance and Counseling; History - World; Religion and Philosophy; Sociology
Dist - GF Prod - GF

Night of the Generals 148 MIN
16mm
Color (H C A)
Stars Peter O'Toole and Omar Sharif. Presents a strange manhunt for a psychopathic killer, with evidence pointing to one of three Nazi generals, against the background of the Nazi occupation in Warsaw and Paris in World War II.
Fine Arts
Dist - TWYMAN Prod - CPC 1967

Night of the Hummingbird 60 MIN
U-matic / VHS / 16mm
Color (H C A)
Uses eyewitness reports to detail how Adolf Hitler seized power on June 30, 1934 by killing his old comrade Roehm and other leaders of the brown shirt movement.
History - World
Dist - FI Prod - BBCTV 1983

The Night of the hunter 94 MIN
VHS
B&W (G)
$24.95 purchase _ #S01817
Tells the story of a psychopathic preacher in pursuit of two children who hold their dead father's fortune. Stars Robert Mitchum, Shelley Winters, Lillian Gish and others. Directed by Charles Laughton in his only directing role. From the novel by Davis Grubb.
Fine Arts; Literature and Drama
Dist - UILL

The Night of the iguana 125 MIN
VHS
Color (H C)

$89.00 purchase _ #05697 - 126
Stars Richard Burton in a drama of self - destruction by Tennessee Williams.
Fine Arts; Literature and Drama
Dist - GA **Prod** - GA

The Night of the Iguana
VHS / U-matic
American Literature Series
Color (G C J)
$89 purchase _ #05697 - 85
Re - enacts Tennessee Williams story about self - destruction. Stars Richard Burton and Ava Gardner.
Fine Arts; Literature and Drama
Dist - CHUMAN

Night of the Intruder, Pt 1 29 MIN
Videoreel / VT2
Our Street Series
Color
Sociology
Dist - PBS **Prod** - MDCPB

Night of the Intruder, Pt 2 29 MIN
Videoreel / VT2
Our Street Series
Color
Sociology
Dist - PBS **Prod** - MDCPB

Night of the spadefoot 9 MIN
VHS
Aspects of animal behavior series
Color (J H C G)
$99.00 purchase, $35.00 rental _ #37731
Shows the life cycle and behavior of a frog, the spadefoot, which has adapted to the Arizona desert. Part of a series on animal behavior produced by Robert Dickson and Prof George Bartholomew for the Office of Instructional Development, UCLA.
Geography - United States; Science - Natural
Dist - UCEMC

The night of the squid 22 MIN
16mm / U-matic / VHS
Undersea world of Jacques Cousteau series
Color (G)
$49.95 purchase _ #Q10608; LC 70-710108
A shortened version of The Night Of The Squid. Traces the life cycle of the squid from its wanderings in the deep to mating and spawning. Features Jacques Cousteau's underwater photography.
Science - Natural
Dist - CF **Prod** - METROM 1970

Night of the Sun 20 MIN
16mm
Color
LC 81-701663
Views various sites within the Wisconsin Ice Age National Scientific Reserve which show the causes, effects, and terrain features left by the last great ice sheet.
Geography - United States; Science - Physical
Dist - USNAC **Prod** - USNPS 1981

Night on Bald Mountain 15.16 MIN
VHS / U-matic
E a V Music Appreciation Series
Color (I J)
LC 88-700018
Instills an appreciation for the music of Mussorgsky in students in junior high and high school.
Fine Arts
Dist - EAV **Prod** - EAV 1988

A Night Out 9 MIN
16mm
Color (J)
LC 81-701201
Tells how Julie finally gets upperclassman Tom to ask her out. Explains how Tom is goaded into proving his manhood and shows what happens when mixed expectations and crossed communication set the stage for a violent attack of rape. A dramatization in sign language.
Health and Safety; Psychology; Sociology
Dist - ODNP **Prod** - ODNP 1981

A Night Out 10 MIN
VHS / U-matic
Setting Limits Series
Color (J)
LC 81-707274
A dramatization in sign language involving a girl looking for romance and a boy looking for sex, which sets the stage for a violent attack of rape.
Education; Sociology
Dist - ODNP **Prod** - ODNP 1981

Night Over China 55 MIN
U-matic / VHS
B&W
Offers a Soviet documentary which claims to expose Maoism including historical footage.
Fine Arts
Dist - IHF **Prod** - IHF

Night Owls 22 MIN
16mm
B&W
Tells the story of two tramps who try to help a policeman catch some burglars. Stars Stan Laurel and Oliver Hardy.
Fine Arts
Dist - RMIBHF **Prod** - ROACH 1930

Night People's Day 11 MIN
16mm / U-matic / VHS
Captioned; Color
LC 71-712664
Explores the city at night with special emphasis on the people and their occupations. Re - creates with human voices all of the sounds of the city and its activities.
Social Science
Dist - ALTSUL **Prod** - ALTSUL 1971

Night Piloting, Surface 18 MIN
16mm
B&W
LC FIE52-983
Studies a night piloting problem and shows the procedure of bringing the USS Savannah into a harbor at night.
Industrial and Technical Education; Science - Physical
Dist - USNAC **Prod** - USN 1959

Night Sailing
U-matic / VHS
$24.95 purchase
Physical Education and Recreation
Dist - BEEKMN **Prod** - BEEKMN 1988

Night Shift 7 MIN
16mm
Color
LC 75-703211
Shows a gas station attendant alone in the quiet hours of the night who is increasingly unnerved by seemingly sourceless sounds and visual distortions.
Fine Arts
Dist - USC **Prod** - USC 1967

The Night the Animals Talked 27 MIN
U-matic / VHS / 16mm
Color (P I)
LC 78-713888
An animated film about the Nativity as seen through the eyes of the animals in the stable. Music by Jule Styne and lyrics by Sammy Cahn.
Fine Arts; Literature and Drama; Religion and Philosophy
Dist - MGHT **Prod** - ABC 1971

A Night to remember
VHS
Color (G)
$24.95 purchase _ #0714
Recreates the drama of the sinking of the Titanic.
History - World; Physical Education and Recreation
Dist - SEVVID

Night Visions 11 MIN
U-matic
Color
Portrays a woman confronting past experiences in a dream journey. Explores aspects of the woman's personality through the use of masks.
Fine Arts; Sociology
Dist - WMENIF **Prod** - WMENIF

Night visions 55 MIN
VHS / U-matic / 16mm
Color (G)
$350.00 purchase, $125.00, $90.00 rental
Tells the overlapping stories of two women, Nea, a Native single mother in danger of losing custody of her daughter, and Morgan, a lesbian artist involved in an anti - censorship struggle who has had her erotic photographs seized by the police. Produced by Marusia Bociurkiw of Canada.
Sociology
Dist - WMEN

A Night with Gilda Peck 10 MIN
16mm
Color (G)
$20.00 rental
Provides a vehicle for Mrs Kathleen Hohalek, as the tenant of the Pyramid Penthouse, with George Kuchar and Bob Hohalek as the burglars, 'Slug' and 'Boom Boom,' John Thomas as 'the Cooper,' and Ainslie Pryor as 'the maid.'
Fine Arts
Dist - CANCIN **Prod** - MCDOWE 1973

Night Without Fear 38 MIN
16mm
Color (C)
$55.00, $70.00 rental
Explores the social and psychological causes underlying women's fears about being out alone at night. Discusses the danger of battering, sexual assault, and rape which are real dangers to women. Investigates stereotypical images of women held by men which contribute to violence against women. Includes clips from TV commercials and pornographic tapes. Produced by Laurie Meeker.
Home Economics; Sociology
Dist - WMENIF

Nightcats 8 MIN
16mm
Color (G)
$22.00 rental, $339 purchase
Uses living animals, unconscious of their roles, as abstract counters in a tone poem of color and chiaroscuro.
Fine Arts
Dist - CANCIN **Prod** - BRAKS 1956

Nightclub dance 60 MIN
VHS
Kathy Blake dance studios - let's learn how to dance series
Color (G A)
$39.95 purchase
Features dance instructors Kathy Blake and Gene Russo, who instruct viewers on the basics of nightclub dancing.
Fine Arts
Dist - PBS **Prod** - WNETTV

Nightclub - disco
VHS
Arthur Murray dance lessons series
Color (G)
$19.95 purchase _ #MC047
Offers lessons in classic ballroom dancing from instructors in Arthur Murray studios, focusing on nightclub and disco dancing. Part of a 12 - part series on various ballroom dancing styles.
Fine Arts; Physical Education and Recreation; Sociology
Dist - SIV

Nightclub, memories of Havana in Queens 6 MIN
VHS
Color (G)
$15.00 rental, $35.00 purchase
Highlights three Latin dancers in a nightclub in Queens performing the samba, a merengue and an Afro - Cuban dance. Satirizes the kitsch aspects while seriously presenting a tribute to this ancient sensuality. Produced by Silvianna Goldsmith.
Fine Arts; Sociology
Dist - CANCIN

Nightfighters 52 MIN
VHS
Color (J H G)
$250.00 purchase
Relates the history of the 332nd Fighter Group in World War II, also called the Tuskegee Airmen. Focuses on the all - black personnel and their experiences in the face of prejudiced ideas in the 1930s about the abilities of black Americans. Highlights their success in combat.
History - United States
Dist - LANDMK

The Nightgown of the Sullen Moon
VHS / 35mm strip
ALA Notable Children's Filmstrips Series
Color (K)
$33.00 purchase
Presents a children's story. Part of the American Library Association series.
English Language; Literature and Drama
Dist - PELLER

The Nightingale 35 MIN
16mm / U-matic / VHS
Color (I J H C)
Presents an adaptation of the story The Nightingale by Hans Christian Anderson about a Chinese kitchen girl and her relationship with a beautiful bird.
Literature and Drama
Dist - WOMBAT **Prod** - SANDSA

The Nightingale 16 MIN
16mm / U-matic / VHS
Color (K P I)
Features animated puppets who realistically unfold the classic Hans Christian Andersen story of the Emperor who finds a treasure living in his own garden - the nightingale.
Fine Arts; Literature and Drama
Dist - CORF **Prod** - CORF 1984

Nightlife 11 MIN
U-matic / VHS / 16mm
Color
LC 76-700391
Pictures the fantastic variety of color and forms of life found beneath the Irish Sea.
Geography - World; Science - Natural
Dist - PHENIX **Prod** - OPUS 1976

Nightlife 30 MIN
U-matic
Magic Ring II Series
(K P)
Continues the aim of the first series to bring added freshness to the commonplace and assist children to discover more about the many things in their world. Each program starts with the familiar, goes to the less familiar, then the new, and ends by blending new and old information.
Education; Literature and Drama
Dist - ACCESS **Prod** - ACCESS 1986

Nightline news library series
Assassination of Egyptian President Anwar Sadat - October 6, 1981
Challenger disaster - January 28, 1986
Chernobyl nuclear disaster - April 28, 1986
East Germany opens its borders - November 9, 1989
Jackie Robinson - April 6 - 8, 1987
Ku Klux Klan - November 13, 1980
Louis Farrakhan - April 5, 1984
Marcos - Aquino - February 5, 1986
Nelson Mandela - February 7 - 12, 1990
Oliver North - July 10, 1987
South Africa debate - September 4, 1985
Student protest in China - May 5, 1989
The Titanic - July 18, 1986
Dist - CAMV

Nightline series
Achille Lauro hijacked - Monday, October 7, 1985 30 MIN
AIDS - Friday, December 17, 1982 30 MIN
Akio Morita - Tuesday, April 24, 1990 30 MIN
Artificial heart - Thursday, December 2, 1982 30 MIN
Assassination attempt against Pope John Paul II - Wednesday, May 13, 1981 and Thursday, May 14, 1981 85 MIN
Assassination attempt against President Reagan - Monday, March 30, 1981 and Wednesday, April 1, 1981 60 MIN
Assassination of Indira Gandhi - Tuesday, October 30, 1984 30 MIN
Austrian President Kurt Waldheim - Monday, February 15, 1988 30 MIN
Baby Fae - Friday, November 16, 1984 30 MIN
Colonel Muammar Qaddafi - Tuesday, November 27, 1984 30 MIN
First Nightline - Monday, March 24, 1980 30 MIN
Flight 487 hijacked - Friday, June 14, 1985 and Friday, June 28, 1985 60 MIN
Freeing of the hostages 150 MIN
General Manuel Noriega indicted - Thursday, February 4, 1988 30 MIN
Geraldine Ferraro - Wednesday, October 17, 1984 30 MIN
Iranian jetliner shot down by the US - Monday, June 4, 1988 30 MIN
Jim and Tammy Faye Bakker - Wednesday, May 27, 1987 80 MIN
Jimmy Swaggart - Friday, February 19, 1988 and Monday, February 22, 1988 55 MIN
John Belushi's career - Friday, March 5, 1982 30 MIN
John Lennon murdered - Tuesday, December 9, 1980 30 MIN
Judge O'Connor nominated for Supreme Court - Tuesday, July 7, 1981 30 MIN
Klaus Barbie and his connections - Friday, April 22, 1983 30 MIN
Lucille Ball dies - Wednesday, April 26, 1989 30 MIN
Massacre of marines in Beirut - Monday, October 24, 1983 30 MIN
President Ronald Reagan's farewell address - Wednesday, January 11, 1989 30 MIN
Qaddafi's warning - Monday, January 13, 1986 30 MIN
Rock Hudson suffers from AIDS - Thursday, July 15, 1985 30 MIN
Ronald Reagan elected President - Wednesday, November 5, 1980 120 MIN
Ryan White - Wednesday, March 2, 1988 and Wednesday, April 11, 1990 60 MIN
Sir Laurence Olivier dies - Tuesday, July 11, 1989 30 MIN
The State of Israel is recognized by Palestine - Monday, November 14, 1988 30 MIN
Town meeting - Holy Land - Tuesday, April 26, 1988 30 MIN
TV evangelists - Monday, March 23, 1987 and Tuesday, March 24, 1987 75 MIN
US invades Panama - Tuesday, December 19, 1989 60 MIN
Yasir Arafat - Friday, January 8, 1988 80 MIN
Dist - INSTRU

Nightmare 10 MIN
U-matic / VHS / 16mm
Color (H C A)
LC 80-700669
Uses animation to tell a story about a man who climbs into bed, eager for repose, and experiences a series of nightmares that leave him unable to distinguish between dream and reality.
Fine Arts
Dist - IFB **Prod** - ZAGREB 1977

The Nightmare 5 MIN
16mm
Color; B&W
Combines humor with deadly serious subject matter, genocide in America. Erupts into rhythmic, fast paced photographic collage animation set to a pop music background.
Fine Arts; Sociology
Dist - BLKFMF **Prod** - BLKFMF

Nightmare at San Pedro 30 MIN
VHS / 16mm
World War II - G I Diary Series
(J H C)
$99.95 each, $995.00 series _ #22
Depicts the action and emotion that soldiers experienced during World War II, through their eyes and in their words. Narrated by Lloyd Bridges.
History - United States; History - World
Dist - AMBROS **Prod** - AMBROS 1980

Nightmare at San Pietro 30 MIN
U-matic / VHS
World War II - GI Diary Series
Color (H C A)
History - United States; History - World
Dist - TIMLIF **Prod** - TIMLIF 1980

Nightmare - Facing fear 30 MIN
VHS
Color (K P I G R)
$14.95 purchase _ #414VSV
Shows Eddie as he wakes from a nightmare. Using a song and Bible verses, his owner Ben comforts him and teaches him how to face fear.
Literature and Drama; Religion and Philosophy
Dist - GF

Nightmare for the Bold
16mm
B&W
LC FIE60-41
Presents the story of a young man who thought he could drive better than most people even when he had had a drink or two. Shows how one careless act on the part of the driver can effect the lives of many others. Depicts civil as well as criminal trials that can result. Emphasizes the importance of auto insurance, sober driving and responsibility behind the wheel.
Civics and Political Systems; Health and Safety
Dist - USNAC **Prod** - USAF 1959

Nightmare in Red 55 MIN
16mm / U-matic / VHS
Project 20 Series
B&W (J)
Discusses the growth of communism inside Russia, covering the old czarist order, the revolutions of 1905 and 1917, the provisional government, the early days of the communist era, the purge trials, World War II and postwar conditions.
Civics and Political Systems; History - World
Dist - MGHT **Prod** - NBCTV 1958

Nightmare in Red, Pt 1 27 MIN
U-matic / VHS / 16mm
Project 20 Series
B&W (J H C)
Discusses the growth of communism inside Russia, covering the old czarist order, the revolutions of 1905 and 1917, the provisional government, the early days of the communist era, the purge trials, World War II and postwar conditions.
History - World
Dist - MGHT **Prod** - NBCTV 1958

Nightmare in Red, Pt 2 27 MIN
U-matic / VHS / 16mm
Project 20 Series
B&W (J H C)
Discusses the growth of communism inside Russia, covering the old czarist order, the revolutions of 1905 and 1917, the provisional government, the early days of the communist era, the purge trials, World War II and postwar conditions.
History - World
Dist - MGHT **Prod** - NBCTV 1958

Nightmare on drug street 40 MIN
VHS
Color (H J T)
Delivers a message from teens to teens about the dangerous effects of alcohol and other drugs. Contains three vignettes narrated by three young people who share their experiences on alcohol and other drugs and state that they were under peer pressure when they used drugs. Suggests video for use in drug education classes.
Guidance and Counseling; Psychology; Sociology
Dist - CAMV
BRODAT
TWINTO

Nightmare on Drug Street 35 MIN
VHS
Color (I J H)
$19.98 purchase
Presents a Twilight Zone take - off of a story of three teens who died as result of drug abuse.
Guidance and Counseling; Literature and Drama; Psychology; Sociology
Dist - BRODAT **Prod** - TWINTO 1988

The Nightmare - Part I 23 MIN
U-matic / VHS / BETA
Jack Cade's nightmare - a supervisor's guide to laws affecting the 'workplace series
Color; CC; PAL (IND PRO G)
$595.00 purchase
Meets Jack Cade, an experience line worker who has just been promoted to supervisor. Reveals that, when offered a management training course, Cade declines, saying, 'I've watched other managers and the one thing they could all use is more common sense.' Watches as Cade's use of common sense gets him - and the organization - into trouble, causing a cumulative total of millions of dollars of liability for the organization. Drives home the message about the hazards of employment laws and regulations to save organizations from needless lawsuits, fines and other legal and regulatory troubles. Part one of two parts on workplace law.
Business and Economics; Guidance and Counseling
Dist - BNA **Prod** - BNA 1994

Nightmare series
Experimental film by Stan Brakhage.
Nightmare series 20 MIN
Dist - AFA **Prod** - AFA 1994

Nightmare - the immigration of Joachim and Rachael 24 MIN
VHS / U-matic
Young people's specials series
Color
Focuses on two Jewish children's escape from the Nazi - occupied Warsaw ghetto.
Fine Arts; History - World; Sociology
Dist - MULTPP **Prod** - MULTPP

Nightmare - the immigration of Joachim and Rachael 24 MIN
16mm / U-matic / VHS
Young people's specials series
Color (K)
$495.00, $349.00, $249.00 purchase _ #AD - 1501
Recalls the Nazi persecution of Jews. Thrusts two small children - Joachim and Rachael - into a frightening battle to survive the Warsaw ghetto alone after their parents have been taken away by Nazi soldiers. They scrounge for food, escape the ghetto and hide in the countryside until the end of the war. Part of the Young People's Specials series.
History - United States; Literature and Drama; Sociology
Dist - FOTH **Prod** - FOTH

Nightmare - the immigration of Joachim and Rachael 23 MIN
16mm
Color & B&W (G)
$360.00 purchase, $40.00 rental _ #HPF - 697, #HRF - 697
Dramatizes the harrowing experiences of two young orphans, a brother and a sister, who escape from the Warsaw Ghetto and from a train carrying passengers to a death camp. Uses black and white sequences to recall their nightmare while color scenes describe their trip to freedom in the United States where they are welcomed by an uncle.
History - World; Sociology
Dist - ADL **Prod** - ADL

The Nightmare years 210 MIN
VHS
Color (G A)
$79.95 purchase _ #TNO103OE
Tells the story of William Shirer, a journalist and author of the book 'The Rise And Fall Of The Third Reich,' and how he was a first - hand observer of events in Nazi Germany. Stars Sam Waterston and Marthe Keller. Originally broadcast on the TNT cable network.
History - World; Literature and Drama
Dist - TMM **Prod** - TMM

Nightmusic 1 MIN
16mm
Color (G)
$138.00 purchase
Presents a hand - painted film by Stan Brakhage. Attempts to capture the beauty of sadness.
Fine Arts; Guidance and Counseling
Dist - CANCIN **Prod** - BRAKS 1986

Nightrider 60 MIN
VHS
Inside story series
Color; PAL (H C A)
PdS99 purchase
Documents the attempts by the wife of slain civil rights leader, Medgar Evers, to bring her husband's murderer to justice in the southern state of Mississippi where racism and the Klu Klux Klan still flourish. Part of the Inside Story series.
History - United States; Sociology
Dist - BBCENE

Night's Nice 10 MIN
16mm
Color (K P I)
Explains that enchanting sounds and images make night a special time for discovery. Shows the stars, yellowed - eyed cats, city lights and sleeping, all elements that make up night's rich tapestry of wonderful things.
Fine Arts
Dist - SF **Prod** - SF 1970

NihongoWare 1
CD-ROM
Color (G A) (JAPANESE)
$623.00 purchase _ #1623
Offers an interactive program for studying business Japanese with sound and graphics. Contains ten self - contained lessons to enable users to study at their own pace and direction. Provides background information on the customs and culture of Japan. For Macintosh Plus, SE and II computers. Requires at least one M of RAM, one floppy disk drive, and an Apple compatible CD - ROM drive.
Business and Economics; Foreign Language
Dist - BEP

NihongoWare 1
CD-ROM
(C A PRO) (JAPANESE)
$629.00 purchase
Teaches Japanese the way it is used in actual business situations. Consists of ten lessons covering business situations with target expressions, dialogue, hits, vocabulary and exercises. Optional headphones available to allow students to compare their speaking with native speakers. Requires MacPlus or above, 2 MB RAM and compatible CD - ROM drive. Produced by Aradne Language Link, Japan.
Business and Economics; Foreign Language; Geography - World
Dist - CHTSUI

Niki Lauda Explains Formula One Racing 30 MIN
VHS
Color; Stereo (G)
$19.98 purchase _ #TT8028
Gives the viewer the experience of turbo - speed Formula One Racing through the eyes of three time world champion Niki Lauda.
Industrial and Technical Education; Literature and Drama; Physical Education and Recreation
Dist - TWINTO **Prod** - TWINTO 1990

Niki Lauda - Lauda Air, Vienna, Austria 47 MIN
VHS
Tycoons series
Color (J H G)
$225.00 purchase
Tells how Niki Lauda, Formula 1 race driver, later applied his determination to win to developing a highly efficient airline that is among the world's best.
Business and Economics; Industrial and Technical Education
Dist - LANDMK

Nikita Khrushchev 10 MIN
VHS / U-matic
B&W
Presents an in - depth examination of the rise and fall of Nikita Khrushchev providing an insight into his personality and career, including his historic visit to the United States in 1959.
Biography; History - World
Dist - KINGFT **Prod** - KINGFT

Nikita Khrushchev 26 MIN
16mm / U-matic / VHS
Biography Series
B&W (J)
LC FIA67-1391
Presents the career of Nikita Khrushchev, showing how he rose from a minor worker in the Communist Party of the USSR to the highest position in the party and to premiership. Discusses his de - Stalinization program, his Hungarian policy and his disputes with Red China.
Biography; Civics and Political Systems; History - World
Dist - MGHT **Prod** - WOLPER 1963

Nikki Giovanni - 12 - 4 - 84 61 MIN
VHS / Cassette
Poetry Center reading series
Color (G)
$15.00, $45.00 purchase, $15.00 rental _ #609 - 516
Features the African American poet reading from her works at the Poetry Center, San Francisco State University.
Literature and Drama
Dist - POETRY **Prod** - POETRY 1984

Nikko National Park 26 MIN
16mm
Color (JAPANESE)
A Japanese language film. Introduces Nikko National Park as one of the famous sight - seeing places in Japan and describes the geological history of the Nikko volcanic zone. Coves Kegon Fall, Mt Nantai, Lake Chuzenji and other places in the Nikko National Park. Depicts the gorgeous Toshogu Shrine and Daiyuin as well as remains of natural formation originating one million years ago.
Foreign Language; Geography - World; Science - Physical
Dist - UNIJAP **Prod** - UNIJAP 1967

Nikkolina 28 MIN
16mm / U-matic / VHS
Color (J P) (SPANISH)
Tells the story of a young Greek girl who does not share her father's traditional values.
Guidance and Counseling; Literature and Drama; Sociology
Dist - LCOA **Prod** - LCOA 1978

Niko - Boy of Greece 21 MIN
16mm / U-matic / VHS
Color (P I J)
LC FIA68-1143
Portrays the pride, hardships and pleasures of a traditional island community and one boy's preparation for manhood.
Geography - World
Dist - AIMS **Prod** - ACI 1968

Nikolaas Tinbergen's Discussion with Richard Evans - Ethology and Genetic Programming Versus Learning 30 MIN
16mm / U-matic / VHS
Notable Contributors to the Psychology of Personality Series
Color (C G T A)
Traces the evolution of ethology and his involvement in the field over four decades of observation, study, and research. Discusses naturalistic observations, genetic programming, learning, aggression, and sex roles.
Biography; Psychology
Dist - PSUPCR **Prod** - PSUPCR 1975

Nikolaas Tinbergen's Discussion with Richard Evans - Unique Contributions , Reflections, and Reactions 29 MIN
16mm / U-matic / VHS
Notable Contributors to the Psychology of Personality Series
Color (C G T A)
Discusses innate releasing mechanisms, nonverbal communication, and observation techniques in studies of autistic children. He reflects on his contributions, reacts to criticism of his work, and speculates on several contemporary social problems.
Biography; Psychology
Dist - PSUPCR **Prod** - PSUPCR 1975

Nikolai 30 MIN
VHS
Color (J H R)
$29.95 purchase, $10.00 rental _ #35 - 814 - 8516
Profiles Nikolai, a Soviet Christian who must maintain his faith in the face of the state's religious persecution.
Geography - World; Religion and Philosophy
Dist - APH **Prod** - GAFILM

Nikorima 27 MIN
16mm / U-matic / VHS
Storybook International Series
Color
Relates the New Zealand tale of an eccentric warrior who is left behind to guard his village. Shows that when a hostile band arrives, he convinces the invaders of their superiority and they retreat, thus making him a hero.
Guidance and Counseling; Literature and Drama
Dist - JOU **Prod** - JOU 1982

Nikos Kazantzakis - Selected Works 29 MIN
Videoreel / VT2
One to One Series
Color
Presents readings from selected works of Nikos Kazantzakis.
Literature and Drama
Dist - PBS **Prod** - WETATV

The Nile 25 MIN
16mm / U-matic
Untamed World Series
Color; Mono (J H C A)
$400.00 film, $250.00 video, $50.00 rental
Features a voyage down the Nile from the springs at its source 4,125 miles to the waters of the Mediterranean Sea.
Geography - World
Dist - CTV **Prod** - CTV 1972

The Nile 57 MIN
VHS / U-matic
River Journeys
Color (H C A)
$1225 purchase (entire series), $285 purchase (each)
Discusses Brian Thompson's journey down the Nile. Shows views of Khartoum, the Aswan Dam, Luxor, Cairo, and the Delta. Produced by BBC - TV and RKO Pictures for public television.
Geography - World
Dist - CF

The Nile Crocodile 30 MIN
U-matic / VHS / 16mm
Color (J H C)
Reveals that the crocodile is well - adapted for survival but is now threatened by man, who is hunting it relentlessly.
Science - Natural
Dist - EBEC **Prod** - EBEC 1982

The Nile in Egypt 13 MIN
16mm
Color (J H C G)
Illustrates Egypt's dependence on the River Nile for crop irrigation methods, and the Asuran Dam and its uses.
Agriculture; Geography - World; Science - Physical
Dist - VIEWTH **Prod** - GATEEF

Nile River Basin and the People of the Upper River - Uganda and Sudan 17 MIN
16mm
Color (J H C)
Follows the river northward from Lake Victoria to central Sudan. Living conditions, occupations, transportation and other habits of the people who are dependent upon the Nile and its tributaries are shown.
Geography - World
Dist - ACA **Prod** - ACA 1951

Nile River Valley and the People of the Lower River - Sudan and Egypt 17 MIN
16mm
Color (J H C)
LC FIA53-189
Explains the importance of the Nile to the people of Egypt and Sudan, by showing scenes of the Aswan Dam, the annual Nile flood which deposits fertile silt, the irrigated fields and the traffic on the river. Also contrasts the archeological ruins along the Nile with the modern city of Cairo.
Geography - World
Dist - ACA **Prod** - ACA 1951

Nim and Other Oriented Graph Games 63 MIN
16mm
MAA Individual Lecturers Series
B&W (H C T)
Professor Andrew M Gleason describes nim and related games and constructs an algebraic theory which gives information about games more complicated than nim.
Mathematics
Dist - MLA **Prod** - MAA 1966

Nimbus 5 MIN
16mm
Color (G)
$15.00 rental
Owes much to the poetry of Robert Creeley and the paintings of Edward Hopper.
Fine Arts
Dist - CANCIN **Prod** - DOBERG 1978

NIMBY - Not in my backyard 15 MIN
VHS
Color; PAL (I J H)
PdS15 purchase _ #1007
Discusses the main types of nuclear waste and its disposal and storage. Includes footage of storage sites in Sweden. Contains teacher's handbook with exercises and information and student worksheets on the ethics of nuclear waste disposal for classroom debate.

Social Science
Dist - UKAEA

Nimmo in Bangkok 25 MIN
16mm
Color
LC 80-700880
Takes a look around Bangkok through the eyes of English comedian Derek Nimmo. Probes the mystery of the American Thai silk millionaire Jim Thompson who vanished without a trace during an Asian holiday.
Geography - World
Dist - TASCOR **Prod** - VISMED 1973

Nimrod Workman - to Fit My Own Category 35 MIN
16mm
Color (H A)
LC 79-700618
Presents the reminiscences of Nimrod Workman, a 78 - year - old retired coal miner and ballad singer, about early union organizing and his life as a miner.
Biography; Business and Economics; Sociology
Dist - APPAL **Prod** - APPAL 1975

Nina and her diabetes 25 MIN
VHS / U-matic
Color (C PRO G)
$195.00 purchase _ #N921 - VI - 032
Looks at the life of 13 - year - old Nina who has been diabetic since she was seven. Demonstrates that with careful planning, diabetics can lead normal lives. Shows how diabetes affects the body, provides guidelines for the diabetic diet and demonstrates the procedures for blood sugar checks and insulin injections. Produced by Francie Lora, East Wind Productions.
Health and Safety
Dist - HSCIC

Nina Bawden 35 MIN
VHS
Color (H C G)
$79.00 purchase
Features the British writer with Edward Blishen discussing writing for both adults and children, creating characters and an effective setting. Talks about her works including Carrie's War; The Secret Passage; Squib; Circles of Deceit; and A Woman of My Age.
Literature and Drama
Dist - ROLAND **Prod** - INCART

Nina Cassian - 5 - 10 - 82 36 MIN
VHS / Cassette
Poetry Center reading series
Color (G)
$15.00 purchase, rental _ #494 - 417
Features the Romanian writer reading her works at the Poetry Center, San Francisco State University, with Laura Schiff translating.
Literature and Drama
Dist - POETRY **Prod** - POETRY 1982

Nina Sobel - Chicken on Foot 8 MIN
VHS / U-matic
B&W
Shows Nina Sobel smashing eggs on her knee while rocking a chicken on her foot.
Fine Arts
Dist - ARTINC **Prod** - LBMAV

Nina Sobel - Electro - Encephalographic Video Drawings 6 MIN
VHS / U-matic
Color
Combines absurdity and physicality.
Fine Arts
Dist - ARTINC **Prod** - LBMAV

Nina Sobel - Hey Baby Chickey 10 MIN
U-matic / VHS
B&W
Combines absurdity and physicality.
Fine Arts
Dist - ARTINC **Prod** - LBMAV

Nina Sobel - Hobby Horses in Paradise 14 MIN
U-matic / VHS
Color
Combines absurdity and physicality. Pokes fun at the housewife model.
Fine Arts
Dist - ARTINC **Prod** - LBMAV

Nina Sobel - Selected Works 1972 - 74 45 MIN
VHS / U-matic
B&W
Combines absurdity and physicality.
Fine Arts
Dist - ARTINC **Prod** - LBMAV

Nina Sobel - Six Moving Cameras, Six Converging Views 6 MIN
VHS / U-matic
B&W
Combines absurdity and physicality.
Fine Arts
Dist - ARTINC **Prod** - LBMAV

Nina's Strange Adventure 14 MIN
16mm / VHS
Wild World Series
Color (K P I)
$245.00, $295.00 purchase, $30.00 rental _ #9996
Tells the story of a young river otter named Nina who appreciates her muddy stream in the Amazon jungle after a harrowing experience in the city.
Literature and Drama; Psychology
Dist - AIMS **Prod** - AIMS 1989

9 - 64 - O Tannenbaum - Materialaktion - Otto Muehl - O Christmas tree - an Otto Muehl happening 3 MIN
16mm
Color (G)
$10.00 rental
Offers a visually descriptive development of a Muehl 'action.'
Fine Arts
Dist - CANCIN **Prod** - KRENKU 1964

Nine Artists of Puerto Rico 16 MIN
16mm
Color (J H C)
LC 75-700287
Visits the studios of Puerto Rico's most important artists.
Fine Arts; Geography - World
Dist - MOMALA **Prod** - OOAS 1970

Nine Artists of Puerto Rico 16 MIN
U-matic / VHS
Color (SPANISH)
LC 82-707018
Visits the studios of Puerto Rico's most important artists.
Fine Arts; Foreign Language
Dist - MOMALA **Prod** - MOMALA

Nine cows and an ox - Pt 5 50 MIN
VHS
Diary of a Maasai village series
Color (G)
$350.00 purchase, $50.00 rental
Depicts the ceremony called the 'ox of ilbaa,' from which Miisia emerges, acknowledged as a man. Part of a five-part series by Melissa Llelewyn - Davis, her diary of a 7-week visit to a single village in Kenya - Tanzania. Examines a village life centered around the senior man - the most important prophet and magician - the Laibon, who has 13 wives living in the village, a large number of children, 20 daughters-in-law and 30 grandchildren.
Geography - World; History - World; Sociology
Dist - DOCEDR **Prod** - BBCTV 1994
BBCENE

Nine days of hell - Japan's toughest school 18 MIN
VHS
Color (H C G)
$195.00 purchase, $50.00 rental
Reveals that Japan's most ambitious parents pack off their promising children at holiday time to an academic boot camp that will either make them or break them. Shows that successful completion of this ordeal enables them to stand up to the tremendous pressure of the Japanese school system. Up before dawn, drilled before eating, constantly quizzed, prodded and harrassed to learn by rote, these kids are on constant alert except for a few hours sleep at night. While many Japanese approve of this privately run program, there are some who question whether it stifles creativity and independent thought. Produced by the Norwegian Broadcasting Corporation.
Education; Geography - World; Health and Safety
Dist - FLMLIB

Nine Dollars Plus One Dollar Equals 20 Dollars Shortchanged 27 MIN
16mm / U-matic
Loss Prevention Series
Color (IND)
Explains that large cash losses are highly possible at every market, bank, department store, hotel, restaurant or filling station without any awareness of the cause. Tells how even the experienced clerk or cashier is likely to lose large sums of money to the smooth - talking, quick - acting, aggressive money manipulator.
Business and Economics
Dist - BNA **Prod** - BNA 1970

9 - 5 survival guide 21 MIN
VHS
Color (H A T G)
Offers students and others the opportunity to learn basic appropriate work habits before they offend customers and co-workers while learning by trial and error. Outlines wardrobe and work habits for entry level or support level employees. Comes with teacher's guide.
Business and Economics; Guidance and Counseling
Dist - CAMV
CFKRCM

9 - 5 survival guide
VHS
Color (H C G)
$99.00 purchase _ #M3603A
Provides success secrets for the newly employed or about - to - be employed such as work habits, wardrobe, grooming, communication, telephone etiquette, and courteous treatment of customers and co - workers.
Business and Economics; Guidance and Counseling
Dist - CFKRCM **Prod** - CFKRCM 1993

Nine Hundred - Thousandths Fine 28 MIN
16mm
Color
LC 74-706508
Combines 19th - century lithographs with live - action sequences to tell the story of the silver bonanza days, particularly the growth of Carson City, Nevada, where the famous dollars were minted. Narrated by Burgess Meredith.
History - United States
Dist - USNAC **Prod** - USGSA 1972

Nine in a Row 10 MIN
16mm
Color
Presents a documentary record of a college rowing team in action, showing the hallucinatory experiences the team encounters during the race through psychedelic visual images.
Physical Education and Recreation
Dist - CFS **Prod** - CFS

Nine Lives of Fritz the Cat 77 MIN
16mm
Color (C A)
Presents Ralph Bakaki's sequel to Fritz The Cat. Animated.
Fine Arts
Dist - TIMLIF **Prod** - AIP 1972

Nine Months 93 MIN
16mm
Color (HUNGARIAN (ENGLISH SUBTITLES))
Describes the love affair between a strong - willed young woman and an impulsive, often arbitrary fellow - worker in a chilly industrial city. Directed by Marta Meszaros. With English subtitles.
Fine Arts; Foreign Language
Dist - NYFLMS **Prod** - UNKNWN 1977

Nine months 25 MIN
VHS
Color (J H C G)
$195.00 purchase, $40.00 rental _ #37353
Portrays a pregnant Hispanic teenager who is torn between her mother's cultural beliefs and the advice of her prenatal teen clinic. Reveals that when the conflict becomes too great, she becomes depressed, stops going to the clinic and fails to take proper care of herself. Thanks to timely intervention from the clinic, all turns out well. Produced by Berkeley Productions for the School of Public Health, University of California, Berkeley.
Health and Safety; Sociology
Dist - UCEMC

Nine Months in Motion 19 MIN
U-matic / VHS / 16mm
Color
Illustrates exercises for expectant mothers which can strengthen and keep flexible certain muscles during pregnancy.
Health and Safety; Physical Education and Recreation
Dist - PEREN **Prod** - PEREN 1977

The Nine nations of North America 60 MIN
VHS
Color (G)
$200.00 purchase _ #NNNA - 000
Offers an alternative view of North America, one in which the three nations are divided into nine nations. Focuses on a region encompassing parts of Mexico and the Southwest U S. Interviews several residents of this area, including a San Antonio Mexican - American woman who is the first family member to attend college, a Chinese - American man whose family founded a bank in the U S, and controversial developer Charles Keating.
Geography - United States; Geography - World; Sociology
Dist - PBS

Nine O'Clock News 2 MIN
16mm
Color (H C A)
Presents a spoof on the communications media and its irrational comments.
Psychology; Social Science
Dist - SLFP **Prod** - MCLAOG

9 1 1 12 MIN
VHS / U-matic
(PRO A)
$195 Purchase, $95 Rental 5 days, $30 Preview 3 days
Follows George Kennedy as he instructs viewers in the usage of the emergency communication system.

Business and Economics; Health and Safety
Dist - ADVANM **Prod** - ADVANM

Nine - one - one plus adult lifesaving kit 40 MIN
VHS
Color (G PRO IND)
$24.95 purchase _ #AH45294
Presents the most current cardiopulmonary resuscitation and rescue breathing techniques for lifesaving of adults. Includes handbook, a compression point locator, CPR/rescue breathing simulator, and 911 emergency procedure guides.
Health and Safety
Dist - HTHED **Prod** - HTHED

Nine - one - one plus child lifesaving kit 40 MIN
VHS
Color (G PRO IND)
$24.95 purchase _ #AH45295
Presents the most current cardiopulmonary resuscitation and rescue breathing techniques for lifesaving of children. Includes handbook, a compression point locator, CPR/rescue breathing simulator, and 911 emergency procedure guides.
Health and Safety
Dist - HTHED **Prod** - HTHED

Nine - one - one plus infant lifesaving kit 40 MIN
VHS
Color (G PRO IND)
$24.95 purchase _ #AH45296
Presents the most current cardiopulmonary resuscitation and rescue breathing techniques for lifesaving of infants. Includes handbook, a compression point locator, CPR/rescue breathing simulator, and 911 emergency procedure guides.
Health and Safety
Dist - HTHED **Prod** - HTHED

Nine Out of Ten 31 MIN
16mm
Color
LC 74-705214
Features service - wide fire prevention problems of debris burning, industrial fires and recreation fires. Presents ten essentials for improving fire prevention and how to apply them.
Health and Safety
Dist - USNAC **Prod** - USDA 1971

Nine - Step Writing Process in Class 37 MIN
VHS / U-matic
Process - Centered Composition Series
Color (T)
LC 79-706297
Presents a step - by - step writing process and discusses the way it can be used.
English Language
Dist - IU **Prod** - IU 1977

Nine to Eleven Months 11 MIN
U-matic / VHS
Teaching Infants and Toddlers Series Pt 4
Color (H C A)
Shows how infants between the ages of nine to eleven months learn by seeing, hearing, feeling, general imitation, spatial relationships, self - awareness and cause - effect.
Home Economics; Psychology
Dist - GPN **Prod** - BGSU 1978

Nine - to - Eleven Year Olds 17 MIN
VHS / U-matic
Child Sexual Abuse - an Ounce of Prevention Series
Color (I)
Illustrates prevention of sexual abuse with examples of children using the safety rules of assertion, trusting their feelings and telling of their experiences. Teaches that sexual assault may involve tricks instead of violence and may happen at home or in familiar places. Encourages children to walk assertively, answer the phone when alone and make a scene.
Health and Safety; Home Economics; Sociology
Dist - AITECH **Prod** - PPCIN

Nine to Five 28 MIN
16mm
Color (A)
Discusses the role of women secretaries and clerical workers. Produced by WNET - TV, this documentary allows women to talk about their economic and social status, and their resentment at being categorized as coffee makers, housekeepers and errand runners.
Business and Economics; Sociology
Dist - AFLCIO **Prod** - WNETTV 1976

Nine to get ready - No 1 series
Preconception care and diagnosis of pregnancy 29 MIN
Dist - UNEBR

Nine to Get Ready Series no 10
Facilities in Counties and States 29 MIN
Dist - UNEBR

Nine to Get Ready Series no 2
Physiology of Conception 29 MIN
Dist - UNEBR

Nine to Get Ready Series no 5
Physiology of Pregnancy and Labor 29 MIN
Dist - UNEBR

Nine to Get Ready Series no 6
Hospital Care and Labor 29 MIN
Dist - UNEBR

Nine to Get Ready Series no 7
Obstetric Delivery 29 MIN
Dist - UNEBR

Nine to Get Ready Series no 8
Newborn Care 29 MIN
Dist - UNEBR

Nine to Get Ready Series - no 9a
Cesarean Section - Pt 2 29 MIN
Dist - UNEBR

Nine to Get Ready Series - no 9
Cesaerean Section 29 MIN
Cesaerean Section - Summary 29 MIN
Cesarean Section, Pt 1 29 MIN
Dist - UNEBR

Nine to get ready series
Caesarian section 29 MIN
Dist - PBS

Nine to get ready series
Family planning 29 MIN
Growth of the fetus 29 MIN
Twelve Recent Advances in Reproductive Physiology 29 MIN
Dist - UNEBR

Nine to get ready series
Prenatal care 29 MIN
Recent Advances in Reproductive Physiology 29 MIN
Dist - UNL

Nine Variations on a Dance Theme 13 MIN
16mm
B&W
Shows a dance theme repeated and interpreted in a surprising number of ways using the basic elements of film craft.
Fine Arts
Dist - RADIM **Prod** - RADIM 1966

Nine - Year - Olds Talk about Death 15 MIN
U-matic / VHS / 16mm
B&W (C A)
LC 80-700466
Shows fourth grade students relating their feelings about death.
Psychology; Sociology
Dist - IFB **Prod** - MHFB 1978

9 years behind the wheel 44 MIN
VHS
Color (G)
$75.00 rental, $75.00 purchase
Zooms around San Francisco in a taxi at night and shot with one hand on the wheel and the other on the camera. Features music by Jones, Dick Peddicord and Johnny and the Potato Chips.
Fine Arts
Dist - CANCIN **Prod** - JONESE 1986

1910 - 1919 60 MIN
VHS
History of the twentieth century series
Color; B&W (I J H)
$19.95 purchase _ #084646
Uses historic footage and other sources to cover William Howard Taft, women's suffrage and the Last Great Indian Council. Part of a nine - part series on 20th - century history of the United States.
Biography; History - United States; Social Science
Dist - KNOWUN

1912 to 1920 12 MIN
U-matic / VHS / 16mm
United States in the 20th century series
Color (J H C)
$215, $155 purchase _ #3675
Discusses the domestic and foreign policies of the Wilson administration, and the rejection of the League of Nations. Part of a series on twentieth century history in the United States.
Biography; Civics and Political Systems; History - United States
Dist - CORF

1914 - 1918 - World War I 25 MIN
BETA / VHS / U-matic
B&W (H G)
$110.00 purchase _ #C51518
Examines World War I as the dividing line between the 19th and 20th centuries. Uses archival footage to reveal the significance of the military and prominence of royalty prior to the war. Includes combat footage from the eastern and western fronts, Africa and Turkey. Shows how the global interests of Euope brought most of the world into the war. Maintans that the Versailles Treaty and the nationalism engendered by the war virtually ensured that World War I was not the war to end all wars.
History - World; Sociology
Dist - NGS **Prod** - NGS 1990

1914 - 1929 - Warring and roaring 30 MIN
VHS
American history series
Color (I J H)
$64.95 purchase _ #V - 18059X
Examines events leading up to World War I. Follows post - war America from the Age of Normalcy through the Roaring Twenties to the Crash of '29. Part of a nine - part series which reviews American history from Colonial times to World War II.
History - United States
Dist - KNOWUN

1920 - 1929 60 MIN
VHS
History of the twentieth century series
Color; B&W (I J H)
$19.95 purchase _ #085670
Uses historic footage and other sources to cover the Teapot Dome Affair, Sacco and Vanzetti, Al Capone, Herbert Hoover, boxer Jack Dempsey, aviator Charles Lindbergh and Black Tuesday. Part of a nine - part series on 20th - century history of the United States.
Biography; History - United States; Literature and Drama
Dist - KNOWUN

1920 to 1932 18 MIN
U-matic / VHS / 16mm
United States in the 20th century series
B&W (J H C)
$295.00, $210.00 purchase _ #1221
Shows how the United States became prosperous under Harding, Coolidge, and Hoover and how the Great Depression began. Part of a series on twentieth century history in the United States.
Biography; History - United States
Dist - CORF

The 1923 surveying expedition of the Colorado River in Arizona 24 MIN
VHS
Color (J H)
$19.95 purchase _ #IV183
Documents the 1923 survey of the Colorado River in the Grand Canyon in Arizona. Uses film taken by a member of the party and another member's voice as part of the sound track.
Geography - United States; History - United States
Dist - INSTRU **Prod** - USGEOS

1929 - 1941 - the Great Depression 25 MIN
U-matic / BETA / VHS
B&W (H G)
$110.00 purchase _ #C51450
Examines the worldwide economic collapse of the Great Depression which lasted for over a decade and ended only with the military production of World War II. Uses archival footage and photographs to portray life in the 1920s, the stock market crash, the banking collapse, unemployment, the farm depression, the New Deal, the rise of the labor movement, natural disasters and the expanded role of the United States government.
Business and Economics; History - United States
Dist - NGS **Prod** - NGS 1990

1930 - 1939 60 MIN
VHS
History of the twentieth century series
Color; B&W (I J H)
$19.95 purchase _ #087256
Uses historic footage and other sources to cover the Great Depression, the New Deal, Jesse Owens, John Dillinger, aviator Amelia Earhart and the 'War of the Worlds.' Part of a nine - part series on 20th - century history of the United States.
Business and Economics; History - United States; Literature and Drama; Physical Education and Recreation
Dist - KNOWUN

1932 8 MIN
U-matic
Color (G)
$275.00 purchase, $50.00, $40.00 rental
Shows a woman moving through a series of institutional spaces - home, church, school, acting out a series of tasks and chores. Created by Susan Rynard.
Religion and Philosophy; Social Science; Sociology
Dist - WMENIF **Prod** - WMENIF 1988

1932 to 1940 21 MIN
U-matic / VHS / 16mm
United States in the 20th century series
Color (J H C)
$315.00, $220.00 purchase _ #1638
Discusses the Great Depression, New Deal legislation, the Social Security Act, and the growing power of the Federal Government. Part of a series on twentieth century history in the United States.
Civics and Political Systems; History - United States
Dist - CORF

1933 4 MIN
16mm
Color (G)
$6.00 rental
Repeats images in a mechanical rhythmic structure. Evokes a sense of sadness within memories.
Fine Arts
Dist - CANCIN **Prod** - WIELNJ 1967

1935 - 1945 - Two great crusades 30 MIN
VHS
American history series
Color (I J H)
$64.95 purchase _ #V - 630 - 519
Looks at the Great Depression, the New Deal program and World War II. Reviews worldwide events that led up to World War II. Part of a nine - part series which reviews American history from Colonial times to World War II.
History - United States
Dist - KNOWUN

The 1937 flood of the Ohio River 9 MIN
VHS
Always a river video collection series
Color (G)
Contact distributor about rental cost #N92 - 033
Provides documentary footage showing the impact of flooding on people who live and work downriver.
Fine Arts; Geography - United States; History - United States
Dist - INDI

1940 - 1949 60 MIN
VHS
History of the twentieth century series
Color; B&W (I J H)
$19.95 purchase _ #090296
Uses historic footage and other sources to cover Winston Churchill, the Normandy invasion, V - E Day, the atom bomb and the House Un - American Activities Committee. Part of a nine - part series on 20th - century history of the United States.
Civics and Political Systems; History - United States
Dist - KNOWUN

1945 - 1989 - the Cold War 25 MIN
BETA / VHS / U-matic
Color (H G)
$110.00 purchase _ #C51469
Traces the origins and history of the Cold War, a struggle between the United States and the Soviet Union that dominated international politics for over 40 years. Examines Yalta, Potsdam, the Berlin airlift, the Korean War, the Cuban missile crisis, the building and dismantling of the Berlin Wall. Explores how the ideological conflict between capitalism and communism shaped these events.
Business and Economics; Civics and Political Systems; History - United States; History - World; Sociology
Dist - NGS **Prod** - NGS 1991

1945 - 52 - Volume 1 60 MIN
VHS
America and the world since World War II series
Color (I J H)
$29.98 purchase _ #VE51044
Covers the years from the Iron Curtain speech by Winston Churchill to civil war in Asia. Features part of a four - part series narrated by Peter Jennings and Ted Koppel.
History - United States; History - World; Sociology
Dist - KNOWUN **Prod** - ABCNEW

1950 - 1959 60 MIN
VHS
History of the twentieth century series
Color; B&W (I J H)
$19.95 purchase _ #093472
Uses historic footage and other sources to cover the dispute in Korea over the 38th Parallel; bomb shelters; suburbia; installment buying; and the presidency of Dwight D Eisenhower. Part of a nine - part series on 20th - century history of the United States.
Biography; History - United States
Dist - KNOWUN

1953 - 1960 - Volume 2 60 MIN
VHS
America and the world since World War II series
Color (I J H)
$29.98 purchase _ #VE51045
Covers the period that produced television, the Civil Rights Movement and polio vaccine. Features part of a four - part series narrated by Peter Jennings and Ted Koppel.
Civics and Political Systems; Fine Arts; Health and Safety; History - United States
Dist - KNOWUN **Prod** - ABCNEW

1955 eruption of Kilauea Volcano, Hawaiian Islands 20 MIN
VHS
Color (J H C)
$24.95 purchase _ #IV121
Portrays the 1955 eruption of Kilauea Volcano, Hawaii, from the first appearance of fissures that formed along the riff zone through the appearance of lava, the formation of cones and flows, the spectacular pyrotechnical displays of lava fountains and the great pillars of rising steam generated as the lava river plunges into the sea.
Geography - World; History - United States
Dist - INSTRU

1857 - fool's gold 25 MIN
16mm
Color (G)
$50.00 rental
Reflects an odyssey and the wounds of returning.
Fine Arts
Dist - CANCIN **Prod** - ELDERB 1981

1960 45 MIN
VHS
Fabulous Sixties series
Color & B&W (G)
$250.00 purchase, $60.00 rental
Covers the year 1960. Features Presidential election - Kennedy vs Nixon; U - 2 spy plane incident; African independence and the Congo; Sharpeville massacre; Caryl Chessman executed; Ban the Bomb demonstrations; Payola; Elvis is drafted; and more. Part of a ten - part series documenting the Sixties, a decade of change and upheaval. Narrated by Peter Jennings.
Civics and Political Systems; Fine Arts; History - United States; Sociology
Dist - CNEMAG **Prod** - HOBELP 1993

1960 - 1964 60 MIN
VHS
History of the twentieth century series
Color; B&W (I J H)
$19.95 purchase _ #096366
Uses historic footage and other sources to cover the Bay of Pigs incident in Cuba, Fidel Castro, the Berlin Wall, the Cuban Missile Crisis, the Civil Rights movement and the Peace Corps. Part of a nine - part series on 20th - century history of the United States.
Civics and Political Systems; History - United States; History - World
Dist - KNOWUN

1960 - Volume 1 60 MIN
VHS
Fabulous 60s - the decade that changed us all series
Color (G I J H)
$19.95 purchase _ #MP1331
Focuses on events in the year 1960 with footage from the archives of ABC News. Part of a ten - part series that examines the major political, cultural, and social issues from 1960 to 1969.
Biography; Civics and Political Systems; Fine Arts; History - United States
Dist - KNOWUN **Prod** - ABCNEW

1961 - 1975 - Volume 3 60 MIN
VHS
America and the world since World War II series
Color (I J H)
$29.98 purchase _ #VE51046
Covers the election and assassination of John F Kennedy, the gasoline shortage and the resignation of Richard M Nixon. Features part of a four - part series narrated by Peter Jennings and Ted Koppel.
Biography; History - United States
Dist - KNOWUN **Prod** - ABCNEW

1961 - Volume 2 60 MIN
VHS
Fabulous 60s - the decade that changed us all series
Color (G J H)
$19.95 purchase _ #MP1332
Focuses on events in the year 1961 with footage from the archives of ABC News. Part of a ten - part series that examines the major political, cultural, and social issues from 1960 to 1969.
Biography; Civics and Political Systems; History - United States
Dist - KNOWUN **Prod** - ABCNEW

1961 45 MIN
VHS
Fabulous Sixties series
Color & B&W (G)
$250.00 purchase, $60.00 rental
Covers the year 1961. Features JFK inauguration; first man in space; Kennedy meets Khrushchev; East Germany builds the wall; Bay of Pigs invasion; trial of Adolf Eichmann; Civil Rights Freedom Riders; the pill; Chubby Checker and the Twist; and more. Part of a ten - part series documenting the Sixties, a decade of change and upheaval. Narrated by Peter Jennings.
Civics and Political Systems; Fine Arts; History - United States; Sociology
Dist - CNEMAG **Prod** - HOBELP 1993

1962 45 MIN
VHS
Fabulous Sixties series
Color & B&W (G)
$250.00 purchase, $60.00 rental
Covers the year 1962. Features Malcolm X; bomb shelters; Cuban missile crisis and threat of nuclear confrontation; JFK vs the steel companies; James Meredith goes to school; Thalidomide tragedy; Seattle World's Fair; Marilyn Monroe dies; and more. Part of a ten - part series documenting the Sixties, a decade of change and upheaval. Narrated by Peter Jennings.
Civics and Political Systems; Fine Arts; History - United States; Sociology
Dist - CNEMAG **Prod** - HOBELP 1993

1962 - Volume 3 60 MIN
VHS
Fabulous 60s - the decade that changed us all series
Color (G I J H)
$19.95 purchase _ #MP1333
Focuses on events in the year 1962 with footage from the archives of ABC News. Part of a ten - part series that examines the major political, cultural, and social issues from 1960 to 1969.
Biography; Civics and Political Systems; History - United States
Dist - KNOWUN **Prod** - ABCNEW

1963 45 MIN
VHS
Fabulous Sixties series
Color & B&W (G)
$250.00 purchase, $60.00 rental
Covers the year 1963. Features racial tensions in the South; Martin Luther King, Jr; Kennedy forms Peace Corps; Vietnam under Diem; Surgeon General's report on smoking; Hugh Hefner; nuclear test ban treaty signed with Moscow; JFK assassinated; and more. Part of a ten - part series documenting the Sixties, a decade of change and upheaval. Narrated by Peter Jennings.
Civics and Political Systems; Fine Arts; History - United States; Sociology
Dist - CNEMAG **Prod** - HOBELP 1993

1963 - Volume 4 60 MIN
VHS
Fabulous 60s - the decade that changed us all series
Color (G I J H)
$19.95 purchase _ #MP1334
Focuses on events in the year 1963 with footage from the archives of ABC News. Part of a ten - part series that examines the major political, cultural, and social issues from 1960 to 1969.
Biography; Civics and Political Systems; History - United States
Dist - KNOWUN **Prod** - ABCNEW

1964 45 MIN
VHS
Fabulous Sixties series
Color & B&W (G)
$250.00 purchase, $60.00 rental
Covers the year 1964. Features The Beatles invading the US; Khrushchev overthrown; LBJ in the White House; Martin Luther King, Jr receives Nobel Prize; Cassius Clay; Marshall McLuhan; China becomes nuclear power; Civil Rights workers killed in Mississippi; and more. Part of a ten - part series documenting the Sixties, a decade of change and upheaval. Narrated by Peter Jennings.
Civics and Political Systems; Fine Arts; History - United States; Sociology
Dist - CNEMAG **Prod** - HOBELP 1993

1964 - Volume 5 60 MIN
VHS
Fabulous 60s - the decade that changed us all series
Color (G I J H)
$19.95 purchase _ #MP1335
Focuses on events in the year 1964 with footage from the archives of ABC News. Part of a ten - part series that examines the major political, cultural, and social issues from 1960 to 1969.
Biography; Civics and Political Systems; History - United States
Dist - KNOWUN **Prod** - ABCNEW

1965 45 MIN
VHS
Fabulous Sixties series

Color & B&W (G)
$250.00 purchase, $60.00 rental
Covers the year 1965. Features walks in space; Vietnam War; Timothy Leary and drug culture; assassination of Malcolm X; Salvador Dali and happenings; Watts riot; deaths of Albert Schweitzer and Winston Churchill; Pope Paul VI at UN; and more. Part of a ten - part series documenting the Sixties, a decade of change and upheaval. Narrated by Peter Jennings.
Civics and Political Systems; Fine Arts; History - United States; Sociology
Dist - CNEMAG **Prod** - HOBELP 1993

1965 - 1969 60 MIN
VHS
History of the twentieth century series
Color; B&W (I J H)
$19.95 purchase _ #097639
Uses historic footage and other sources to cover Vietnam, the presidency of Lyndon Baines Johnson, urban riots, Robert F Kennedy, the moon landing and the EPA - Environmental Protection Act. Part of a nine - part series on 20th - century history of the United States.
Biography; History - United States; History - World; Science - Natural
Dist - KNOWUN

1965 - Volume 6 60 MIN
VHS
Fabulous 60s - the decade that changed us all series
Color (G I J H)
$19.95 purchase _ #MP1336
Focuses on events in the year 1965 with footage from the archives of ABC News. Part of a ten - part series that examines the major political, cultural, and social issues from 1960 to 1969.
Biography; Civics and Political Systems; History - United States
Dist - KNOWUN **Prod** - ABCNEW

1966 45 MIN
VHS
Fabulous Sixties series
Color & B&W (G)
$250.00 purchase, $60.00 rental
Covers the year 1966. Features mass murderers Richard Speck and the Boston Strangler; Ralph Nader and auto safety; grape boycott in California; Cultural Revolution in China; credit card boom; Beatles banned in the South; George Wallace; and more. Part of a ten - part series documenting the Sixties, a decade of change and upheaval. Narrated by Peter Jennings.
Civics and Political Systems; Fine Arts; History - United States; History - World; Sociology
Dist - CNEMAG **Prod** - HOBELP 1993

1966 - Volume 7 60 MIN
VHS
Fabulous 60s - the decade that changed us all series
Color (G J H)
$19.95 purchase _ #MP1337
Focuses on events in the year 1966 with footage from the archives of ABC News. Part of a ten - part series that examines the major political, cultural, and social issues from 1960 to 1969.
Biography; Civics and Political Systems; History - United States
Dist - KNOWUN **Prod** - ABCNEW

1967 45 MIN
VHS
Fabulous Sixties series
Color & B&W (G)
$250.00 purchase, $60.00 rental
Covers the year 1967. Features Haight - Ashbury in San Francisco; three US astronauts die; March on the Pentagon; Six Day War in Mideast; Greek junta seizes power; LBJ and Kosygin meet; Pan American Games; urban revolt in Detroit; Che killed in Bolivia; and more. Part of a ten - part series documenting the Sixties, a decade of change and upheaval. Narrated by Peter Jennings.
Civics and Political Systems; Fine Arts; History - United States; Sociology
Dist - CNEMAG **Prod** - HOBELP 1993

1967 - Volume 8 60 MIN
VHS
Fabulous 60s - the decade that changed us all series
Color (G I J H)
$19.95 purchase _ #MP1338
Focuses on events in the year 1967 with footage from the archives of ABC News. Part of a ten - part series that examines the major political, cultural, and social issues from 1960 to 1969.
Biography; Civics and Political Systems; History - United States
Dist - KNOWUN **Prod** - ABCNEW

1968 45 MIN
VHS
Fabulous Sixties series
Color & B&W (G)
$250.00 purchase, $60.00 rental
Covers the year 1968. Features worldwide student protest; assassination of Martin Luther King, Jr; Abbie Hoffman and the Yippies; Eugene McCarthy's anti - war campaign; LBJ out of race; Tet Offensive; assassination of Robert Kennedy; Nixon elected president; and more. Part of a ten - part series documenting the Sixties, a decade of change and upheaval. Narrated by Peter Jennings.
Civics and Political Systems; Fine Arts; History - United States; History - World; Sociology
Dist - CNEMAG **Prod** - HOBELP 1993

1968 - Volume 9 60 MIN
VHS
Fabulous 60s - the decade that changed us all series
Color (G I J H)
$19.95 purchase _ #MP1339
Focuses on events in the year 1968 with footage from the archives of ABC News. Part of a ten - part series that examines the major political, cultural, and social issues from 1960 to 1969.
Civics and Political Systems; History - United States
Dist - KNOWUN **Prod** - ABCNEW

1969 45 MIN
VHS
Fabulous Sixties series
Color & B&W (G)
$250.00 purchase, $60.00 rental
Covers the year 1969. Features US POWs in Vietnam; John Lennon and Yoko Ono; Stokely Carmichael; Woodstock; Chinese Red Guards; Apollo 11 and first man on the moon; birth control pills; 'Easy Rider'; Vietnam Moratorium; Nixon's world tour; and more. Part of a ten - part series documenting the Sixties, a decade of change and upheaval. Narrated by Peter Jennings.
Civics and Political Systems; Fine Arts; History - United States; Sociology
Dist - CNEMAG **Prod** - HOBELP 1993

1969 13 MIN
16mm
Color (A)
$35.00 rental
Shares a personal recollection of a time past, when gay identity was a source of joy rather than of mourning. Explores the fiction of personal history, and the unreliability of memory.
Fine Arts; History - United States; Literature and Drama; Psychology; Sociology
Dist - CANCIN **Prod** - TARTAG 1991

1969 - Volume 10 60 MIN
VHS
Fabulous 60s - the decade that changed us all series
Color (G I J H)
$19.95 purchase _ #MP1340
Focuses on events in the year 1969 with footage from the archives of ABC News. Part of a ten - part series that examines the major political, cultural, and social issues from 1960 to 1969.
Biography; Civics and Political Systems; History - United States
Dist - KNOWUN **Prod** - ABCNEW

1970 30 MIN
16mm
Color (G)
$50.00 rental
Explains filmmaker Bartlett, '...so thorough a summation of Bartlett's personal work that it rendered him harmless for years to come.'
Fine Arts; Literature and Drama
Dist - CANCIN **Prod** - BARTLS 1972

1970 48 MIN
VHS
Sensational Seventies series
Color & B&W (G)
$250.00 purchase, $60.00 rental
Covers the year 1970. Features Kent State killings; Chicago 7 trial; ERA; Cambodia invasion; mercury pollution; Muhammad Ali; water beds; hot pants; Solzhenitzyn; Bernadette Devlin; tragedy at Chappaquiddick; 'Sesame Street'; civil war in Biafra; and more. Part of a ten - part series examining the major political, cultural and social issues of the years 1970 - 1979. Narrated by Peter Jennings.
Civics and Political Systems; Fine Arts; History - United States; Sociology
Dist - CNEMAG **Prod** - HOBELP 1993

1970 - 1979 60 MIN
VHS
History of the twentieth century series
Color; B&W (I J H)
$19.95 purchase _ #099540
Uses historic footage and other sources to cover Kent State, the fall of Saigon, Watergate, the presidency of Gerald Ford, school busing, the presidency of Jimmy Carter, the oil embargo and the Iran hostage crisis. Part of a nine - part series on 20th - century history of the United States.
Biography; Civics and Political Systems; History - United States
Dist - KNOWUN

1970 - Year of protest 48 MIN
VHS
Sensational 70s series
Color (G I J H)
$19.95 purchase _ #MP6400
Focuses on events in the year 1970 with footage from the archives of ABC News. Part of a ten - part series that examines the major political, cultural, and social issues from 1970 to 1979.
Biography; Civics and Political Systems; History - United States
Dist - KNOWUN **Prod** - ABCNEW

1971 48 MIN
VHS
Sensational Seventies series
Color & B&W (G)
$250.00 purchase, $60.00 rental
Covers the year 1971. Features Pentagon Papers; Attica prison revolt; Lt Calley and the My Lai massacre; Bangladesh; unisex hair and clothes; deaths of Khrushchev and Louis Armstrong; DNA; Apollo missions; DB Cooper; and more. Part of a ten - part series examining the major political, cultural and social issues of the years 1970 - 1979. Narrated by Peter Jennings.
Civics and Political Systems; Fine Arts; History - United States; Sociology
Dist - CNEMAG **Prod** - HOBELP 1993

1971 - Year of disillusionment 48 MIN
VHS
Sensational 70s series
Color (G I J H)
$19.95 purchase _ #MP6401
Focuses on events in the year 1971 with footage from the archives of ABC News. Part of a ten - part series that examines the major political, cultural, and social issues from 1970 to 1979.
Biography; Civics and Political Systems; History - United States
Dist - KNOWUN **Prod** - ABCNEW

1972 48 MIN
VHS
Sensational Seventies series
Color & B&W (G)
$250.00 purchase, $60.00 rental
Covers the year 1972. Features Nixon winning in landslide; Olympic terror; SALT talks; George Wallace shot; skyjackings; Betty Friedan; Howard Hughes biography hoax; Bobby Fischer and chess as spectator sport; Angela Davis; J Edgar Hoover dies; and more. Part of a ten - part series examining the major political, cultural and social issues of the years 1970 - 1979. Narrated by Peter Jennings.
Civics and Political Systems; Fine Arts; History - United States; Sociology
Dist - CNEMAG **Prod** - HOBELP 1993

1972 - Year of summits 48 MIN
VHS
Sensational 70s series
Color (G I J H)
$19.95 purchase _ #MP6402
Focuses on events in the year 1972 with footage from the archives of ABC News. Part of a ten - part series that examines the major political, cultural, and social issues from 1970 to 1979.
Biography; Civics and Political Systems; History - United States
Dist - KNOWUN **Prod** - ABCNEW

1973 48 MIN
VHS
Sensational Seventies series
Color & B&W (G)
$250.00 purchase, $60.00 rental
Covers the year 1973. Features Watergate grand jury proceedings; Agnew resigns; Wounded Knee; military coup in Chile; US out of Vietnam; Yom Kippur War; gas crisis; the Partridge Family; hang gliding; mass murders; LBJ dies; and more. Part of a ten - part series examining the major political, cultural and social issues of the years 1970 - 1979. Narrated by Peter Jennings.
Civics and Political Systems; Fine Arts; History - United States; Sociology
Dist - CNEMAG **Prod** - HOBELP 1993

1973 - Year of Watergate 48 MIN
VHS
Sensational 70s series
Color (G I J H)
$19.95 purchase _ #MP6403
Focuses on events in the year 1973 with footage from the archives of ABC News. Part of a ten - part series that examines the major political, cultural, and social issues from 1970 to 1979.
Biography; Civics and Political Systems; History - United States
Dist - KNOWUN **Prod** - ABCNEW

1974 48 MIN
VHS
Sensational Seventies series
Color & B&W (G)
$250.00 purchase, $60.00 rental
Covers the year 1974. Features Nixon resigning; gay rights demonstration in NYC; Boston anti - busing demonstrations; sex discrimination; Arctic pipeline; truckers' strike; streaking; Ford pardons Nixon; Fanne Fox scandal; and more. Part of a ten - part series examining the major political, cultural and social issues of the years 1970 - 1979. Narrated by Peter Jennings.
Civics and Political Systems; Fine Arts; History - United States; Sociology
Dist - CNEMAG **Prod** - HOBELP 1993

1974 - Year of resignation 48 MIN
VHS
Sensationsal 70s series
Color (G I J H)
$19.95 purchase _ #MP6404
Focuses on events in the year 1974 with footage from the archives of ABC News. Part of a ten - part series that examines the major political, cultural, and social issues from 1970 to 1979.
Biography; Civics and Political Systems; History - United States
Dist - KNOWUN **Prod** - ABCNEW

1975 48 MIN
VHS
Sensational Seventies series
Color & B&W (G)
$250.00 purchase, $60.00 rental
Covers the year 1975. Features the fall of Saigon; Margaret Thatcher elected; Ford assassination attempts; 'Saturday Night Live'; Patty Hearst arrested; UN equate Zionism with racism; Jimmy Hoffa disappears; primal scream therapy; Franco dies; and more. Part of a ten - part series examining the major political, cultural and social issues of the years 1970 - 1979. Narrated by Peter Jennings.
Civics and Political Systems; Fine Arts; History - United States; Sociology
Dist - CNEMAG **Prod** - HOBELP 1993

1975 - Year after the fall 48 MIN
VHS
Sensationsal 70s series
Color (G I J H)
$19.95 purchase _ #MP6405
Focuses on events in the year 1975 with footage from the archives of ABC News. Part of a ten - part series that examines the major political, cultural, and social issues from 1970 to 1979.
Biography; Civics and Political Systems; History - United States
Dist - KNOWUN **Prod** - ABCNEW

1976 48 MIN
VHS
Sensational Seventies series
Color & B&W (G)
$250.00 purchase, $60.00 rental
Covers the year 1976. Features American Bicentennial; Jimmy Carter elected; Viking spacecraft lands on Mars; mud wrestling; Israeli raid on Entebbe; post - Mao Party purge in China; Idi Amin; Legionnaire's disease; Howard Hughes dies; and more. Part of a ten - part series examining the major political, cultural and social issues of the years 1970 - 1979. Narrated by Peter Jennings.
Civics and Political Systems; Fine Arts; History - United States; Sociology
Dist - CNEMAG **Prod** - HOBELP 1993

1976 - 1985 - Volume 4 60 MIN
VHS
America and the world since World War II series
Color (I J H)
$29.98 purchase _ #VE51047
Covers events from the United States bicentennial to the Geneva Summit. Presents part of a four - part series narrated by Peter Jennings and Ted Koppel.
Civics and Political Systems; History - United States
Dist - KNOWUN **Prod** - ABCNEW

1976 - Year of the Bicentennial 48 MIN
VHS
Sensationsal 70s series
Color (G I J H)
$19.95 purchase _ #MP6406
Focuses on events in the year 1976 with footage from the archives of ABC News. Part of a ten - part series that examines the major political, cultural, and social issues from 1970 to 1979.
Civics and Political Systems; History - United States
Dist - KNOWUN **Prod** - ABCNEW

1977 48 MIN
VHS
Sensational Seventies series
Color & B&W (G)
$250.00 purchase, $60.00 rental
Covers the year 1977. Features Sadat and Begin peace talks; Carter inauguration; solar energy; Gary Gilmore execution; punk rock; Son of Sam murders; Elvis dies; NYC blackout; Sylvester Stallone in 'Rocky'; Bert Lance resigns; and more. Part of a ten - part series examining the major political, cultural and social issues of the years 1970 - 1979. Narrated by Peter Jennings.
Civics and Political Systems; Fine Arts; History - United States; Sociology
Dist - CNEMAG **Prod** - HOBELP 1993

1977 - Year of the Southern President 48 MIN
VHS
Sensationsal 70s series
Color (G I J H)
$19.95 purchase _ #MP6407
Focuses on events in the year 1977 with footage from the archives of ABC News. Part of a ten - part series that examines the major political, cultural, and social issues from 1970 to 1979.
Biography; Civics and Political Systems; History - United States
Dist - KNOWUN **Prod** - ABCNEW

1978 48 MIN
VHS
Sensational Seventies series
Color & B&W (G)
$250.00 purchase, $60.00 rental
Covers the year 1978. Features Proposition 12; Nazis march in Skopkie; Aldo Moro kidnapping; Vietnamese boat people; Jonestown suicides; Rev Sun Myung Moon; hot tubs; Panama Canal; Bakke case; disco music; Camp David; and more. Part of a ten - part series examining the major political, cultural and social issues of the years 1970 - 1979. Narrated by Peter Jennings.
Civics and Political Systems; Fine Arts; History - United States; Sociology
Dist - CNEMAG **Prod** - HOBELP 1993

1978 - Year of moral dilemma 48 MIN
VHS
Sensationsal 70s series
Color (G I J H)
$19.95 purchase _ #MP6408
Focuses on events in the year 1978 with footage from the archives of ABC News. Part of a ten - part series that examines the major political, cultural, and social issues from 1970 to 1979.
Civics and Political Systems; History - United States
Dist - KNOWUN **Prod** - ABCNEW

1979 48 MIN
VHS
Sensational Seventies series
Color & B&W (G)
$250.00 purchase, $60.00 rental
Covers the year 1979. Features Sandinistas oust Somoza in Nicaragua; Thatcher elected Prime Minister; Three Mile Island; the Shah flees and Khomeini returns to Iran; palimony; Idi Amin overthrown; Skylab falls; Chinese invasion of Vietnam; and more. Part of a ten - part series examining the major political, cultural and social issues of the years 1970 - 1979. Narrated by Peter Jennings.
Civics and Political Systems; Fine Arts; History - United States; Sociology
Dist - CNEMAG **Prod** - HOBELP 1993

1979 - Year of overthrow 48 MIN
VHS
Sensationsal 70s series
Color (G I J H)
$19.95 purchase _ #MP6409
Focuses on events in the year 1979 with footage from the archives of ABC News. Part of a ten - part series that examines the major political, cultural, and social issues from 1970 to 1979.
Civics and Political Systems; History - United States
Dist - KNOWUN **Prod** - ABCNEW

1980 - Volume 1 60 MIN
VHS
History of the 80s series
Color (G I J H)
$19.95 purchase _ #MP1900
Focuses on events in the year 1980 with footage from the archives of ABC News. Part of a ten - part series that examines the major political, cultural, and social issues from 1980 to 1989.
Civics and Political Systems; History - United States
Dist - KNOWUN **Prod** - ABCNEW

1981 - Volume 2 60 MIN
VHS
History of the 80s series
Color (G I J H)
$19.95 purchase _ #MP1901
Focuses on events in the year 1981 with footage from the archives of ABC News. Part of a ten - part series that examines the major political, cultural, and social issues from 1980 to 1989.
Civics and Political Systems; History - United States
Dist - KNOWUN **Prod** - ABCNEW

1982 - Volume 3 60 MIN
VHS
History of the 80s series
Color (G I J H)
$19.95 purchase _ #MP1902
Focuses on events in the year 1982 with footage from the archives of ABC News. Part of a ten - part series that examines the major political, cultural, and social issues from 1980 to 1989.
Civics and Political Systems; History - United States
Dist - KNOWUN **Prod** - ABCNEW

1983 - Volume 4 60 MIN
VHS
History of the 80s series
Color (G I J H)
$19.95 purchase _ #MP1903
Focuses on events in the year 1983 with footage from the archives of ABC News. Part of a ten - part series that examines the major political, cultural, and social issues from 1980 to 1989.
Civics and Political Systems; History - United States
Dist - KNOWUN **Prod** - ABCNEW

1983 world T and T championships, Helsinki 360 MIN
U-matic / VHS
IAAF videocassettes series
Color (H C A)
Features highlights of the 1983 world track and field championships.
Physical Education and Recreation
Dist - TRACKN **Prod** - TRACKN 1984

1984 110 MIN
VHS
Color (A H C)
$29.00 purchase _ #05940 - 126
Stars John Hurt and Richard Burton in the film version of 1984 by George Orwell. Rated R.
Literature and Drama
Dist - GA

1984 2 MIN
16mm
Color (G)
$10.00 rental
Fine Arts
Dist - CANCIN **Prod** - KRENKU 1984

1984 revisited 30 MIN
U-matic
Realities
Color (A)
Delves into the political, social, economic and cultural trends of the 1980s. Probes a wide range of contemporary concerns. Each segment includes a guest speaker who is an expert in the field under discussion. Part of a series.
Business and Economics; Civics and Political Systems; Social Science; Sociology
Dist - TVOTAR **Prod** - TVOTAR 1985

1984 - the future and beyond - the crystal ball network 30 MIN
U-matic
Adam Smith's money world series; 117
Color (A)
Attempts to demystify the world of money and break it down so that small as well as large businesses and it's people understand and adjust to new social and economic trends. Reports on the major economic stories and discoveries of the day.
Business and Economics
Dist - PBS **Prod** - WNETTV 1985

1984 - Volume 5 60 MIN
VHS
History of the 80s series
Color (G I J H)
$19.95 purchase _ #MP1904
Focuses on events in the year 1984 with footage from the archives of ABC News. Part of a ten - part series that examines the major political, cultural, and social issues from 1980 to 1989.
Civics and Political Systems; History - United States
Dist - KNOWUN **Prod** - ABCNEW

1985 - Volume 6 60 MIN
VHS
History of the 80s series
Color (G I J H)
$19.95 purchase _ #MP1905
Focuses on events in the year 1985 with footage from the archives of ABC News. Part of a ten - part series that examines the major political, cultural, and social issues from 1980 to 1989.
Civics and Political Systems; History - United States
Dist - KNOWUN **Prod** - ABCNEW

1986 - Volume 7 60 MIN
VHS

History of the 80s series
Color (G I J H)
$19.95 purchase _ #MP1906
Focuses on events in the year 1986 with footage from the archives of ABC News. Part of a ten - part series that examines the major political, cultural, and social issues from 1980 to 1989.
Civics and Political Systems; History - United States
Dist - KNOWUN **Prod** - ABCNEW

1987 - Volume 8 60 MIN
VHS
History of the 80s series
Color (G I J H)
$19.95 purchase _ #MP1907
Focuses on events in the year 1987 with footage from the archives of ABC News. Part of a ten - part series that examines the major political, cultural, and social issues from 1980 to 1989.
Civics and Political Systems; History - United States
Dist - KNOWUN **Prod** - ABCNEW

The 1988 Insider Trading Act - employers beware 50 MIN
VHS
Color (C PRO A COR)
$95.00 rental _ #Y105
Provides instruction for attorneys on the basic components of The Insider Trading and Securites Fraud Enforcement Act of 1988. Outlines the practices and procedures which broker - dealers, investment advisors and other firms must implement pursuant to these rules.
Business and Economics; Civics and Political Systems
Dist - ALIABA **Prod** - CLETV 1989

1988 - Volume 9 60 MIN
VHS
History of the 80s series
Color (G I J H)
$19.95 purchase _ #MP1908
Focuses on events in the year 1988 with footage from the archives of ABC News. Part of a ten - part series that examines the major political, cultural, and social issues from 1980 to 1989.
Civics and Political Systems; History - United States
Dist - KNOWUN **Prod** - ABCNEW

1989 All Taijiquan championships - San Francisco 120 MIN
VHS
Color (G)
$39.95 purchase _ #1113
Contains highlights of the tournament. Includes training tips and demonstrations by past winners.
Physical Education and Recreation
Dist - WAYF

1989 ATOC US all Taijiquan championships 120 MIN
VHS
Color (G)
$39.95 purchase _ #1112
Documents tournament push hands competition at the 1989 A Taste of China Championships. Includes demonstrations by winners and invited masters, plus interviews with other key competitors.
Physical Education and Recreation
Dist - WAYF

The 1989 San Francisco Bay area earthquake 53 MIN
VHS
Color (J H C)
$29.95 purchase _ #UGS04
Shows the cause and devastation of the 1989 earthquake in Loma Prieta - epicenter area. Collects narrations by seismologists.
History - United States
Dist - INSTRU

1989 - Volume 10 60 MIN
VHS
History of the 80s series
Color (G I J H)
$19.95 purchase _ #MP1909
Focuses on events in the year 1989 with footage from the archives of ABC News. Part of a ten - part series that examines the major political, cultural, and social issues from 1980 to 1989.
Civics and Political Systems; History - United States
Dist - KNOWUN **Prod** - ABCNEW

1990 ATOC and SF championships 120 MIN
VHS
Color (G)
$49.95 purchase _ #1111
Documents tournament push hands competition at the 1990 A Taste of China Championships and the San Francisco American Championships. Interlaces this coverage with instruction by Lenzie Williams, winner of both tournaments. Offers the opportunity to see two slightly different sets of tournament rules.
Physical Education and Recreation
Dist - WAYF

1992 conference collection series
Presents a three - part series from the 1992 Systems Thinking in Action Conference. Features Peter M Senge, Russell L Ackoff and Sue Miller Hurst in A Crisis of Perception, Organizational Learning and Beyond, and Come to the Edge.

1992 conference collection series	300 MIN
Peter M Senge - A Crisis of perception	100 MIN
Russell L Ackoff - Organizational learning and beyond	100 MIN
Sue Miller Hurst - Come to the edge	100 MIN

Dist - PEGASU **Prod** - PEGASU

Nineteen Eighteen
BETA / VHS
Color
Tells the story by Horton Foote of the effects of an epidemic on a Texas town during World War I, starring Matthew Broderick.
Geography - United States; Health and Safety; History - United States
Dist - GA **Prod** - GA

Nineteen Eighty - a New Taste Odyssey 41 MIN
16mm
Color (A)
LC 80-701326
Uses a space fantasy with multiple special effects to announce a food product created by the Coca - Cola company. Describes the sales incentive program.
Business and Economics
Dist - COCA **Prod** - COCA 1980

Nineteen eighty - eight presidential election 18 MIN
35mm strip / VHS
Color (J H C T A)
$57.00, $48.00 purchase _ #MB - 509193 - 3, #MB - 510004 - 5
Reviews the personalities and issues of the 1988 Presidential campaign. Stresses the importance of the electoral process.
Civics and Political Systems; History - United States
Dist - SRA **Prod** - NYT 1989

Nineteen Eighty - Five 18 MIN
16mm
Color
Examines the construction and functions of the Space Shuttle and Space Station by means of computer animation and space - earth photography.
Industrial and Technical Education; Science - Physical
Dist - NASA **Prod** - NASA

Nineteen Eighty - Four in 1984 60 MIN
U-matic / VHS
Color
Presents a two - channel installation of the tapes resulting from the 1984 New Year's Day transmission of Good Morning Mr Orwell in New York and in Paris.
Fine Arts
Dist - KITCHN **Prod** - KITCHN

Nineteen Eighty - Four Revisited 40 MIN
U-matic / VHS / 16mm
Color (J)
Reviews aspects of modern society to show how close it is to the Orwellian world of Big Brother. Discusses how networks of computers keep track of people's travels through the passport office, census bureau, credit card companies, banks, supermarkets, department stores, the Social Security system and the Internal Revenue Service.
Sociology
Dist - CORF **Prod** - CBSTV 1983

Nineteen eighty - nine through 1991 mission projects video
VHS
Color (G R)
$20.00 purchase _ #6889
Describes the mission projects conducted by the International Lutheran Laymen's League from 1989 through 1991.
Guidance and Counseling; Literature and Drama; Religion and Philosophy
Dist - CPH **Prod** - LUMIS

The Nineteen Eighty - One Annual Clinical Training Research Project Competition 60 MIN
U-matic
Color
Presents essays regarding milk protein synthesis in breast carcinoma, tumor - associated gastroparesis correction metoclopramide, computer optimization combining electron and proton beams and the effects of gastro on colon neoplasms in rats.
Health and Safety
Dist - UTEXSC **Prod** - UTEXSC

The Nineteen Eighty - One Kemper Open 28 MIN
16mm
Color
Depicts the excitement and frustration of the preliminaries and finals of the 1981 Kemper Open Golf Tournament. Shows Craig Stadler emerging victorious on the last day.
Physical Education and Recreation
Dist - MTP **Prod** - MTP

Nineteen Eighty - One PGA - Laws Principles and Preferences 58 MIN
VHS / U-matic
Color
Explains the five basic laws and twelve principles which are involved in a golfer's swing and demonstrates how to mold the multitude of individual preferences into a perfect swing.
Physical Education and Recreation
Dist - FILAUD **Prod** - FILAUD

Nineteen Eighty - One - Year in Review 50 MIN
U-matic / VHS
Color (J H)
Reviews the events that comprised international headline news in 1981.
History - World
Dist - JOU **Prod** - JOU

Nineteen Eighty Physician's Recognition Award 60 MIN
U-matic
Color
Presents case studies that have won recognition from the American Medical Association.
Health and Safety
Dist - UTEXSC **Prod** - UTEXSC

Nineteen eighty - seven America's Cup, the official film
VHS
Color (G)
$29.90 purchase _ #0296
Joins skipper Dennis Conner and the crew of the Stars and Stripes in their triumph over Kookaburra III of Australia in the 1987 America's Cup Race.
Physical Education and Recreation
Dist - SEVVID

Nineteen Eighty - Seven Versus the Constitution 60 MIN
VHS
Moyers - In Search Of The Constitution Series
Color (G)
$59.95 purchase _ #MOYR - 110
Examines a variety of legal issues dealing with privacy. Considers mandatory drug testing, computer technology and information gathering about individuals. Hosted by Bill Moyers.
Civics and Political Systems; Psychology
Dist - PBS

Nineteen eighty - six off - shore speed - boats season, sea beasts
VHS
Color (G)
$39.80 purchase _ #0395
Documents the 1986 World Offshore Powerboat Championship. Includes footage shot from helicopters.
Physical Education and Recreation
Dist - SEVVID

The Nineteen Eighty - Two Hall of Fame Regatta 60 MIN
BETA / VHS
Color
Shows world class sailors racing in the 1982 Hall Of Fame Regatta.
Geography - World; Physical Education and Recreation
Dist - OFFSHR **Prod** - NORVID

The Nineteen Eighty - Two J - 24 Worlds 50 MIN
BETA / VHS
Color
Shows the 1982 J - 24 Worlds sailing races.
Geography - World; Physical Education and Recreation
Dist - OFFSHR **Prod** - OFFSHR
SEVVID

Nineteen Eighty - Two Masters Tournament 30 MIN
16mm
Color
Presents the 46th Masters Tournament at the Augusta National Golf Club in Georgia. Follows the leading players to the final showdown, a sudden death playoff with Craig Stadler emerging as the winner.
Physical Education and Recreation
Dist - MTP **Prod** - OWENSI

The Nineteen Eighty - Two New York 36 Nationals 40 MIN
VHS / BETA
Color
Shows the 1982 regatta consisting of the 14 top boats from around the U S.
Geography - World; Physical Education and Recreation
Dist - OFFSHR **Prod** - OFFSHR

Nineteen Eighty - Year in Review 28 MIN
16mm / U-matic / VHS
Color (H C A)
Looks at the key events of 1980.
History - United States
Dist - JOU **Prod** - UPI

The Nineteen Fifties 60 MIN
VHS
Music, Memories and Milestones Series
Color (G)
$19.95 purchase _ #1603
Recollects the symbols of the fifties - Elvis, the four - minute mile, Sputnik. Reviews the fashions of the day - shorter skirts, bikinis. Combines Rock 'n' Roll, the Korean War, Suez and the Hungarian Revolution.
Fine Arts; Geography - World; History - United States; History - World; Home Economics
Dist - KULTUR

The Nineteen Fifty - Five Eruption of Kilauea 11 MIN
16mm
Color (P)
LC FIE58-367
Follows the 1955 eruption of Kilauea, Hawaii, from the first opening of fissures in the ground, to the APpearance of lava. Shows the formation of cone, flows, and fountains. Views clouds of steam caused by lava flowing into the ocean.
Geography - United States; Science - Physical
Dist - USNAC **Prod** - USGEOS 1958

Nineteen Fifty - Nine Chevy 2 MIN
VHS / U-matic
Color
Shows a classic television commercial with Pat Boone and Dinah Shore singing.
Business and Economics; Psychology; Sociology
Dist - BROOKC **Prod** - BROOKC

Nineteen Fifty - Seven Chevy Trucks 4 MIN
U-matic / VHS
Color
Shows a classic television commercial that demonstrates Chevy trucks conquering the Alcan run.
Business and Economics; Psychology; Sociology
Dist - BROOKC **Prod** - BROOKC

The Nineteen Forties 60 MIN
VHS
Music, Memories and Milestones Series
Color (G)
$19.95 purchase _ #1602
Records the days of World War II. Gives an account of Churchill, Hitler, Roosevelt and Stalin and the independence of India and creation of the state of Israel. Includes the music of Bing Crosby, the Andrew Sisters and Flanagan and Allan.
Fine Arts; History - United States; History - World
Dist - KULTUR

Nineteen Forty - Five to 1960
U-matic / VHS
Modern U S History - from Cold War to Hostage Crisis Series
Color (H)
Covers the Truman - Eisenhower years, including the Cold War, McCarthyism, Korea, Baby Boomers, Sputnik and Russia's first atomic bomb.
History - United States
Dist - GA **Prod** - GA

Nineteen Forty - Five - Year of Victory 20 MIN
U-matic / VHS
B&W (G)
$249.00, $149.00 purchase _ #AD - 1607
Contains newsreels shown to American and British movie audiences at year's end - important not only for the events shown, but for the emphases and biases of the participants in those events - the Russian attacks against Berlin, the Yalta Conference, air attacks on Germany, the death of Roosevelt and other major events in both the Pacific and European theaters of World War II.
History - United States; History - World; Sociology
Dist - FOTH **Prod** - FOTH

Nineteen Forty - One 120 MIN
16mm
Color
Tells what happens when a community becomes convinced that the Japanese are about to attack. Directed by Steven Spielberg.
Fine Arts
Dist - SWANK **Prod** - UPCI

Nineteen Fourteen - Nineteen Eighteen 56 MIN
U-matic / VHS
B&W (G)
$249.00, $439.00 purchase _ #AD - 1482
Portrays World War I - the war that was supposed to end wars. Documents it from its vainglorious beginning to its bitter end from the film archives of all the combatants.
History - United States; History - World; Sociology
Dist - FOTH **Prod** - FOTH

Nineteen Hundred 243 MIN
16mm / U-matic / VHS
Color
Presents an epic story of 20th century Italy, focusing on the conflicts between a peasant and a landowner. Stars Robert De Niro, Dominique Sanda and Burt Lancaster. Directed by Bernardo Bertolucci.
Fine Arts
Dist - FI **Prod** - PAR 1977

1900 - 1909 60 MIN
VHS
History of the twentieth century series
Color; B&W (I J H)
$19.95 purchase _ #083968
Uses historic footage and other sources to cover the Philippine insurrection, trustbusting, McKinley's assassination, Kitty Hawk, child labor and Teddy Roosevelt. Part of a nine - part series on 20th - century history of the United States.
Biography; History - United States
Dist - KNOWUN

Nineteen Hundred - Passing of an Age 25 MIN
16mm
American Challenge Series
Color
Describes how the coming of the automobile brought vast changes to small - town America and how quiet towns were replaced finally by smog - filled cities and crowded freeways. Based on Booth Tarkington's novel THE MAGNIFICENT AMBERSONS.
Literature and Drama; Sociology
Dist - FI **Prod** - RKOP 1975

Nineteen Hundred - Seventy U S Open 27 MIN
16mm
Color
Focuses on Tony Jacklin, the first Englishman in 50 years to win the United States open golf championship.
Physical Education and Recreation
Dist - GM **Prod** - CMD

Nineteen Hundred Sixty - Nine U S Open 28 MIN
16mm
Color
Shows winner, Orville Moody, as he leads top golfers on a charge across Firestone Country Club in Houston, Texas.
Physical Education and Recreation
Dist - GM **Prod** - CMD

1900 to 1912 12 MIN
16mm / U-matic / VHS
United States in the 20th century series
B&W (J H C G)
$215.00, $155.00 purchase _ #3674
Shows historical and newsreel footage from the Roosevelt and Taft administrations. Part of a series on history of the twentieth century in the United States.
Biography; History - United States
Dist - CORF

Nineteen Minutes to Earth 15 MIN
16mm
Color (A)
LC 77-703502
Examines scientific findings from the Viking missions to Mars and some difficulties in interpreting this data. Includes information on the soil, atmosphere and geology of Mars, as well as photographs of the planet.
Industrial and Technical Education; Science; Science - Physical
Dist - USNAC **Prod** - NASA 1977

Nineteen Ninety - Nine a D 26 MIN
U-matic / VHS / 16mm
Color
Looks to the future and how people relate to the computer - controlled environment of 1999 A D.
Industrial and Technical Education; Psychology; Sociology
Dist - FORDFL **Prod** - FORDFL

Nineteen ninety - two 30 MIN
VHS
Adam Smith's money world series
Color (H C A)
$79.95 purchase
Considers how the 1992 unification of the European Common Market will impact the United States. Features host Jerry Goodman, also known as 'Adam Smith,' and his guests Lord Young, Sir Roy Denman, Jurgen Rufus, Robert Hormats and Franklin Vargo.
Business and Economics
Dist - PBS **Prod** - WNETTV

Nineteen Seventeen - Revolution in Russia 27 MIN
VHS / U-matic
B&W (H C A G)
$235.00 purchase _ #51317
Explores prerevolutionary Russia and the events that led up to the revolution. Examines archival materials and introduces the key figures in this critical period of history.
Geography - World; History - World; Social Science
Dist - NGS

Nineteen Seventy all Star (Baseball) Game 26 MIN
16mm
Color (I)
LC 74-714273
Highlights the 1970 all star baseball game, showing baseball's unique qualities where every man stands alone, and his heroics and errors are seen by everyone.
Physical Education and Recreation
Dist - SFI **Prod** - MLBPC 1971

Nineteen Seventy - Eight 7up Marketing Plans 12 MIN
16mm
Color
LC 78-700397
Establishes the 1978 marketing plans for 7up, Sugar Free 7up and Fountain 7up. Outlines the markets for each brand and then shows the importance of the local bottler's efforts in making 1978 a successful sales year.
Business and Economics
Dist - SEVUP **Prod** - SEVUP 1977

Nineteen Seventy Low Speed Car Crash Costs 35 MIN
16mm
Color (J)
LC 72-700542
Demonstrates the high cost of low speed crashes by showing crash tests on 1970 model sedans, pony cars and small cars traveling at 5, 10 and 15 miles per hour.
Business and Economics; Health and Safety; Industrial and Technical Education
Dist - HF **Prod** - IIHS 1970

Nineteen Seventy National League Highlights 26 MIN
16mm
Color
Presents highlights of the 1970 National League Championship Series between the Cincinnati Reds and the Pittsburgh Pirates.
Physical Education and Recreation
Dist - SFI **Prod** - SFI 1971

Nineteen Seventy - Nine 7up and Sugar Free 7up Marketing Plans Film (Developer's Version) 19 MIN
16mm
Color
LC 79-700251
Shows the strategy, media plans and promotional activities the Seven - Up Company is employing to position and support their products nationally.
Business and Economics
Dist - FILMA **Prod** - SEVUP 1978

Nineteen Seventy One Rose Parade Film (through the Eyes of a Child) 30 MIN
16mm
Color (K)
LC 73-700799
Reproduces the Rose Parade of the year 1971.
Physical Education and Recreation; Sociology
Dist - TRA **Prod** - TRA 1971

The Nineteen Seventy Press on Regardless 11 MIN
16mm
Color
LC 72-700186
Uses a combination documentary/cinema verite style to show highlights of the 1970 press on regardless sports car rally from opening registration and car inspection through the two days of the rally and to the finish.
Industrial and Technical Education; Physical Education and Recreation
Dist - CIASP **Prod** - CIASP 1971

Nineteen Seventy Rose Parade Film (Holidays Around the World) 30 MIN
16mm
Color (K)
LC 73-700798
Reproduces the Rose Parade of the year 1970.
Physical Education and Recreation; Sociology
Dist - TRA **Prod** - TRA 1970

Nineteen Seventy - Six - no Goyakusoku 21 MIN
16mm
Color (JAPANESE)
LC 77-700396
Enumerates the Chessie System's various technological improvements which have resulted in better export facilities and greater customer services. Concentrates on the active railroad system.
Foreign Language; Social Science; Sociology
Dist - CSCTD **Prod** - CSCTD 1976

The Nineteen Seventy - Three Mgodo Wa Mbanguzi 53 MIN
16mm
Color (C A)
LC 75-700198
Documents a performance of the music and dance known as mgodo, composed for a Chopi village in southern Mozambique. Depicts dancers who are accompanied by large xylophone orchestras. Contains history and current affairs in the texts of the suites, along with preoccupations of tribe members about local events. Includes subtitles of songs in Chopi and English.
Fine Arts; Geography - World; History - World; Sociology
Dist - PSUPCR **Prod** - PSUPCR 1974

The Nineteen Seventy - Three Mgodo Wa Mkandeni 48 MIN
16mm
Color (C A)
LC 75-700197
Presents a traditional music and dance performance known as mgodo, composed by members of a Chopi village in southern Mozambique during the winter of 1973. Features dancers and a xylophone orchestra who present their village's suite. Depicts a large number of instruments tuned in several pitches, highly - developed xylophones and distinctive musical structure.
Fine Arts; Geography - World; History - World; Sociology
Dist - PSUPCR **Prod** - PSUPCR 1974

Nineteen Seventy Three Rose Parade Film (Movie Memories) 30 MIN
16mm
Color (K)
LC 73-700801
Reproduces the Rose Parade of the year 1973.
Physical Education and Recreation; Sociology
Dist - TRA **Prod** - TRA 1973

Nineteen Seventy - Two AAU Junior Olympics 28 MIN
16mm
Color
LC 73-701276
Follows the preparation of two athletes for the 1972 Junior Olympics and their participation in the events. Includes action highlights of all the major competitions.
Physical Education and Recreation
Dist - GM **Prod** - GM 1972

Nineteen Seventy Two Rose Parade Film (the Joy of Music) 30 MIN
16mm
Color (K)
LC 73-700800
Reproduces the Rose Parade of the year 1972.
Physical Education and Recreation; Sociology
Dist - TRA **Prod** - TRA 1972

Nineteen seventy world series 40 MIN
16mm
Color
Presents highlights of the 1970 World Series between the Baltimore Orioles and the Cincinnati Reds.
Physical Education and Recreation
Dist - SFI **Prod** - SFI 1970

The Nineteen Sixties 60 MIN
VHS
Music, Memories and Milestones Series
Color (G)
$19.95 purchase _ #1604
Recalls the Sixties, the era of sexual liberation, flower power, the threat of superpower confrontation. Remembers the Cuban missile crisis, the erection of the Berlin Wall, the war in Vietnam and the six - day war in the Middle East. Against the unrest blossom Beatlemania and demonstrations for a peaceful world, and Yuri Gagarin conquers space just eight years before Neil Armstrong becomes the first man on the moon.
Fine Arts; Geography - World; History - United States; History - World
Dist - KULTUR

Nineteen Sixty - Eight - a Look for New Meaning 110 MIN
U-matic / 16mm / VHS
Color (G)
$1185.00, $399.00, $249.00 purchase _ #AD - 146
Looks in detail at a pivotal year in American history - 1968. Covers the Tet Offensive, TV's role in bringing the Vietnam war home, Robert Kennedy and Nixon, the assassination of Martin Luther King and the ensuing riots. Includes the issues which sparked student unrest and the widening generation gap, the Democratic National Convention and the revolt of the Silent Majority.
Civics and Political Systems; History - United States; History - World; Sociology
Dist - FOTH **Prod** - FOTH

Nineteen Sixty - Eight - a Look for New Meanings 110 MIN
U-matic / VHS / 16mm
Color (J)
LC 79-700635
Reviews major political, cultural and social events of the year 1968. Covers the Vietnam War, the Living Room War, student dissent, the Civil Rights movement, the assassinations of Martin Luther King, Jr and Robert Kennedy, the Democratic National Convention and the election of Richard Nixon.
Civics and Political Systems; History - United States; Sociology
Dist - FOTH **Prod** - CBSTV 1978

Nineteen Sixty - Eight - a Look for New Meanings, Pt 1 27 MIN
16mm / U-matic / VHS
Color (J)
LC 79-700635
Reviews major political, cultural and social events of the year 1968. Covers the Vietnam War, the Living Room War, student dissent, the Civil Rights movement, the assassinations of Martin Luther King, Jr and Robert Kennedy, the Democratic National Convention and the election of Richard Nixon.
History - United States
Dist - FOTH **Prod** - CBSTV 1978

Nineteen Sixty - Eight - a Look for New Meanings, Pt 2 27 MIN
U-matic / VHS / 16mm
Color (J)
LC 79-700635
Reviews major political, cultural and social events of the year 1968. Covers the Vietnam War, the Living Room War, student dissent, the Civil Rights movement, the assassinations of Martin Luther King, Jr and Robert Kennedy, the Democratic National Convention and the election of Richard Nixon.
History - United States
Dist - FOTH **Prod** - CBSTV 1978

Nineteen Sixty - Eight - a Look for New Meanings, Pt 3 28 MIN
U-matic / VHS / 16mm
Color (J)
LC 79-700635
Reviews major political, cultural and social events of the year 1968. Covers the Vietnam War, the Living Room War, student dissent, the Civil Rights movement, the assassinations of Martin Luther King, Jr and Robert Kennedy, the Democratic National Convention and the election of Richard Nixon.
History - United States
Dist - FOTH **Prod** - CBSTV 1978

Nineteen Sixty - Eight - a Look for New Meanings, Pt 4 28 MIN
16mm / U-matic / VHS
Color (J)
LC 79-700635
Reviews major political, cultural and social events of the year 1968. Covers the Vietnam War, the Living Room War, student dissent, the Civil Rights movement, the assassinations of Martin Luther King, Jr and Robert Kennedy, the Demoncratic National Convention and the election of Richard Nixon.
History - United States
Dist - FOTH **Prod** - CBSTV 1978

Nineteen Sixty Eight Buick Open 28 MIN
Videoreel / VT1
Color
Recaps the $125,000 golf tournament with Tom Weiskopf winning by one stroke. Features Julius Boros, Lee Trevino and Johnny Pott.
Physical Education and Recreation
Dist - MTP **Prod** - MGM

Nineteen Sixty - Eight Rose Parade, 'Wonderful World of Adventure' 32 MIN
16mm
Color (K)
LC FIA68-627
Pictures the floats, bands and horses of the floral festival and parade held in Pasadena, California, on New Years Day, 1968.
Geography - United States; Physical Education and Recreation
Dist - TRA **Prod** - TRA 1968

The Nineteen Sixty - Five Green Bay Packers Highlights 27 MIN
16mm
Color (J)
LC FIA68-1407
Highlights the 1965 professional football season, featuring team and individual performances of the Green Bay Packers.
Physical Education and Recreation
Dist - NFL **Prod** - NFL 1966

The Nineteen Sixty - Five St Louis Cardinals Highlights 27 MIN
16mm
Color (J)
LC FIA68-1406
Highlights the 1965 playing season featuring the St Louis Cardinals professional football team.
Physical Education and Recreation
Dist - NFL **Prod** - NFL 1966

Nineteen Sixty - Four 54 MIN
16mm / U-matic / VHS
Saga of Western Man Series
Color (H C A)
LC FIA65-534
Explores the great power and the complex problems of the United States. Includes discussion on poverty in the midst of affluence, automation, old age, leisure time, unemployment and equal opportunity.
History - United States; Psychology; Sociology
Dist - MGHT **Prod** - ABCTV 1964

The Nineteen Sixty - Four Conventions - Goldwater, Johnson Nominated 20 MIN
16mm
Screen news digest series; Vol 7; Issue 2
B&W
Shows democracy in action at the 1964 Democratic and Republican National Conventions, where Goldwater and Johnson and their running mates were nominated.
Civics and Political Systems; History - United States
Dist - HEARST **Prod** - HEARST 1964

Nineteen Sixty - Four Presidential Election - Death of Herbert Hoover - Downfall of Krushchev 20 MIN
16mm
Screen news digest series; Vol 7; Issue 4
B&W
Pictures activities in the 50 states on election day, 1964. Reviews the life of the late President Herbert Hoover, and shows a nation in mourning. Examines the rise and fall of Nikita Krushchev, emphasizing the shake up in the kremlin where he was succeeded by Leonid Brezhnev and Aleksei Kosygin.
Civics and Political Systems; History - United States; History - World
Dist - HEARST **Prod** - HEARST 1964

Nineteen Sixty - Four, Pt 1 27 MIN
U-matic / VHS / 16mm
Saga of Western Man Series
Color (H C A)
Explores the great power and the complex problems of the United States. Includes discussion on poverty in the midst of affluence, automation, old age, leisure time, unemployment and equal opportunity.
History - United States
Dist - MGHT **Prod** - ABCTV 1965

Nineteen Sixty - Four, Pt 2 27 MIN
U-matic / VHS / 16mm
Saga of Western Man Series
Color (H C A)
Explores the great power and the complex problems of the United States. Includes discussion on poverty in the midst of affluence, automation, old age, leisure time, unemployment and equal opportunity.
History - United States
Dist - MGHT **Prod** - ABCTV 1965

Nineteen Sixty Nine Rose Parade Film (a Time to Remember) 30 MIN
16mm
Color (K)
LC 73-700797
Reproduces the Rose Parade of the year 1969.
Physical Education and Recreation; Sociology
Dist - TRA **Prod** - TRA 1969

Nineteen Sixty - Nine - Seventy Coaches all - American Basketball Team 25 MIN
16mm
Color (H C)
Features members of the 1969 - 70 coaches all - American basketball team. Includes Pete Maravich of LSU, Charlie Scott of North Carolina, Bob Lanier of St Bonaventure, Dan Issel of Kentucky and Rick Mount of Purdue.
Physical Education and Recreation
Dist - NINEFC **Prod** - GEMILL

Nineteen Sixty - Nine to 1981
U-matic / VHS
Modern U S History - from Cold War to Hostage Crisis Series
Color (H)
Examines the Nixon, Ford and Carter years, including withdrawal from Vietnam, reopening relations with China, Watergate, the rise of OPEC and the Iranian hostage crisis.
History - United States
Dist - GA **Prod** - GA

Nineteen Sixty - Nine Westchester Classic 27 MIN
16mm
Color (I)
LC 79-713001
Golf champion Jack Nicklaus demonstrates in competition how to handle uphill, sidehill and downhill unplayable lies. Provides split screen and slow motion analysis of the short iron, sand trap and putting techniques. Original theme music and narration by Jack Nicklaus.
Physical Education and Recreation
Dist - SFI **Prod** - TWA 1970

Nineteen Sixty - One to 1968
VHS / U-matic
Modern U S History - from Cold War to Hostage Crisis Series
Color (H)
Focuses on the Kennedy - Johnson years, including black civil rights, the Cuban missile crisis, Kennedy's assassination and Vietnam.
History - United States
Dist - GA **Prod** - GA

The Nineteen Thirties 60 MIN
VHS
Music, Memories and Milestones Series
Color (G)
$19.95 purchase _ #1601
Chronicles the era of the Big Band, the rise of Fascism in Europe and terrible worldwide depression. Focuses on the dalliance of Edward and Mrs. Simpson, athlete Jesse Owens, Amelia Earhart, Adolf Hitler, and musician Woody Herman.
Civics and Political Systems; Fine Arts; History - World; Industrial and Technical Education; Physical Education and Recreation
Dist - KULTUR

Nineteenth - century American art 25 MIN
35mm strip / VHS
Color (J H C T A)
$93.00 purchase _ #MB - 909738 - 3, #MB - 909716 - 2
Covers the development of 19th - century American art. Profiles artists including Cole, Bierstadt, Sargent, Cassatt, Sloane, Eakins, and Winslow Homer. Shows that American artists tried to emulate European styles, but found more success through their own creative impulses.
Fine Arts
Dist - SRA **Prod** - SRA 1990

Nineteenth - century nationalism 37 MIN
VHS
Color (H C)
LC 89-700170
Examines the development of nationalism from its early history in Europe before the French Revolution through World War I.
Civics and Political Systems; History - World
Dist - EAV **Prod** - EAV 1989

Nineteenth Century Nationalism / Liberalism 30 MIN
VHS / U-matic
Historically Speaking Series Part 13; Pt 13
Color (H)
Discusses the Congress of Vienna and the liberalism and nationalism in France, England, Italy and Germany.
History - World
Dist - AITECH **Prod** - KRMATV 1983

90s communications series
Constructive communications - talking your way to success 30 MIN
Effective listening skills - listening to what you hear 30 MIN
90s communications series 90 MIN
Writing for results - the winning written report 30 MIN
Dist - CAMV

90s communications series
Presents a three - part series on communication. Includes Constructive Communications, Writing for Results and Effective Listening Skills.
Constructive communications - talking your way to success 30 MIN
Effective listening skills - listening to what you hear 30 MIN
90s communications series 90 MIN
Writing for results - the winning written report 30 MIN
Dist - CAMV **Prod** - CAMV 1983

90s communications series
Constructive communications - talking your way to success 30 MIN
Effective listening skills - listening to what you hear 30 MIN
90s communications series 90 MIN
Writing for results - the winning written report 30 MIN
Dist - CAMV

Ninety days to a smoke - free workplace
VHS
Color (G A PRO IND)
$495.00 purchase _ #AH45274
Presents a plan for creating a corporate smoking policy. Consists of four videocassettes and a workbook.
Health and Safety; Psychology
Dist - HTHED **Prod** - HTHED

Ninety Degree Machine Cutting 4 MIN
BETA / VHS
Welding Training Comprehensive - - - Oxy - Acetylene Welding Series
Color (IND)
Industrial and Technical Education; Psychology
Dist - RMIBHF **Prod** - RMIBHF

Ninety Degree Round Elbow using Rise Method 10 MIN
BETA / VHS
Metal Fabrication - Parallel Line Development Series
Color (IND)
Industrial and Technical Education; Psychology
Dist - RMIBHF **Prod** - RMIBHF

Ninety Degrees South 15 MIN
U-matic / VHS / 16mm
Odyssey Series
Color
Describes life at South Pole Station in Antarctica.
Geography - World
Dist - GPN **Prod** - KRMATV

98.3 KHZ - Bridge at electrical storm 12 MIN
16mm
Color (G)
$25.00 rental
Features a Super 8 film shot at 60 mph on a San Francisco bridge then processed through a video synthesizer to produce imagery inherently different from film in terms of texture, dynamics and color.
Fine Arts
Dist - CANCIN **Prod** - RAZUTI 1973

94 3 MIN
16mm
Color (A)
$25.00 rental
Explores sex and male and female identities. Conveys intercourse between two people who never appear on the screen at the same time. Produced by Bette Gordon and James Benning.
Fine Arts; Psychology; Sociology
Dist - CANCIN

99 bottles of beer 23 MIN
VHS / 16mm
Color (J H C) (ENGLISH, SPANISH)
$199.00 purchase; PdS130, PdS138, purchase
Portrays alcohol abuse by young people. Makes no judgements and allows viewers to make their own decisions about alcohol.
Guidance and Counseling; Health and Safety; Psychology; Sociology
Dist - FMSP EDPAT **Prod** - FMSP

Ninety - Nine Bottles of Beer 23 MIN
16mm / U-matic / VHS
Color (J H C) (SPANISH)
LC 73-700604
Presents young alcoholics who share their experiences with drinking, with school problems, and with their family and friends.
Health and Safety; Psychology; Sociology
Dist - AIMS **Prod** - LAC 1974

Ninety telemarketing selling skills for the 90's 480 MIN
VHS
Color (A PRO IND)
$495.00 purchase, $195.00 rental
Features Stan Billue in a four - part look at 90 different telemarketing sales tips. Also considers subjects such as preparation, sales personality, closing, dealing with customer reluctance, and more.
Business and Economics; Psychology; Social Science
Dist - VLEARN

90 telemarketing skills 120 MIN
VHS / U-matic / BETA
Color (A G)
$495.00 purchase, $195.00 rental
Presents four separate video programs featuring telemarketing speaker Stan Billue. Serves up 90 techniques and ideas to raise the effectiveness and productivity of telephone sales. Produced by Double Five.
Business and Economics; Industrial and Technical Education; Psychology
Dist - TELDOC

Ninety Telemarketing Skills in 90 Minutes 90 MIN
VHS
(PRO)
$695.00 purchase, $195.00 rental
Presents the telemarketing techniques of Stan Billue, a successful telephone salesman.
Business and Economics
Dist - CREMED **Prod** - CREMED 1987

The 93rd Congress - restoring the balance 60 MIN
VHS / 16mm
Color (G)
$70.00 rental _ #NCON - 000
Examines the 93rd Congress, the Congress that challenged a President. Highlights the Congress' accomplishments and looks at the gradual erosion of its power and responsibility.
Civics and Political Systems
Dist - PBS **Prod** - NPACT

Nippon series
Being Japanese 60 MIN
Learning machine 60 MIN
Nippon series
Dist - BBCENE

Nirmal Verma 40 MIN
VHS
Color (H C G)
$79.00 purchase
Features the writer talking with Gita Sahgal about using the theme of human deprivation and how history affects an individual. Discusses his writings including his short story anthology The World Elsewhere.
Literature and Drama
Dist - ROLAND **Prod** - INCART

NIRS Forage Analysis - a New Idea 13 MIN
U-matic
Color; Mono (H C)
Discusses near infrared reflectance spectroscopy for forage analysis; how it works, why it is important, how it can save the farmer money and where testing can be done briefly explains how to apply NIRS results to be a feed management program.
Agriculture; Science - Physical
Dist - UWISCA **Prod** - UWISCA 1986

Nishnawbe - Aski - the People and the Land 28 MIN
16mm
Color (H C A)
#3X59 I
Visits the Cree and Ojibway Indians living in the remote Treaty No 9 area of northern Ontario, Canada. Discusses their way of life and current social and economic issues. Deals with increasing industrial pressures from the south and questions how industrialism should be regulated to protect the interests of these people.
Social Science; Sociology
Dist - CDIAND **Prod** - NFBC 1977

Nissan Ariana Window 21 MIN
16mm
Color (C)
$560.00
Experimental film by Ken Jacobs.
Fine Arts
Dist - AFA **Prod** - AFA 1969

Nitrate kisses 67 MIN
VHS / 16mm
B&W (G)
$200.00 rental, $250.00 purchase institutions only
Explores eroded emulsions and images for lost vestiges of lesbian and gay culture. Views the struggle for these two cultures to survive in the complex interaction of power and domination of a dominant heterosexist ideology.
Fine Arts; Sociology
Dist - CANCIN **Prod** - BARHAM 1992

Nitric Acid 18 MIN
16mm
Color (H C)
Presents the fundamentals of nitric acid, applying in descriptive chemistry. Describes how nitric acid may act as an acid, a base and as an oxidizing agent. Provides molecular models, activation energy curves and potential energy diagrams, as graphic illustrations of concepts.

Science - Physical
Dist - MLA **Prod** - MCA

Nitric acid 18 MIN
VHS / 16mm
Chem study video - film series
Color (H C)
$288.00, $99.00 purchase, $27.00 rental _ #192 W 0840, #193 W 2039, #140 W 4136
Shows how nitric acid may act as an acid base and as an oxidizing agent. Uses molecular models, activation energy curves and potential energy diagrams to provide graphic illustrations of the concepts. Part of a series for teaching chemistry to high school and college students.
Science - Physical
Dist - WARDS **Prod** - WARDS 1990

The Nitrogen Cycle 17 MIN
16mm
B&W (J H C G)
Demonstrates the route followed by nitrogen in its circulation between the atmosphere and compounds making up the protoplasm of living organisms. Shows the usual agricultural and industrial processes involved in maintaining the nitrogen content of the land.
Agriculture; Science - Natural
Dist - VIEWTH **Prod** - GBI

The Nitrogen cycle 16 MIN
VHS
Color (J H)
$79.95 purchase _ #10208VG
Looks at the role of nitrogen in the natural world and the need for a nitrogen cycle. Introduces some of the problems with too much or too little nitrogen in an ecosystem. Comes with an interactive video quiz; teacher's guide; activities; discussion questions; and 10 blackline masters.
Science - Natural
Dist - UNL

The Nitrogen Fix 29 MIN
VHS / 16mm
Color (G)
$55.00 rental _ #NTRO - 000
Examines the fixed nitrogen shortage and its impact on the world food supply. Looks at research being conducted by the Charles F Kettering Foundation. Includes guest speakers.
Agriculture
Dist - PBS **Prod** - KWSU

Nix v Whiteside - So your client wants to commit perjury 60 MIN
VHS
Color (C PRO A)
$17.40, $75.00 purchase _ #M658, #P186
Looks at the impact of the Supreme Court's decision regarding a client who threatens to commit perjury. Features a trial judge, criminal defense attorney and a civil litigator who examine and apply provisions of the Model Code of Professional Responsibility and the Model Rules of Professional Conduct.
Civics and Political Systems
Dist - ALIABA

Nixon 162 MIN
VHS
Color; PAL (H)
PdS55 purchase
Presents three 54 - minute programs looking at the life of Richard Nixon, the poor boy who became President of the United States. Reveals that his career was marked by a series of paradoxes - he entered politics promising to clean up Washington and left behind him one of the greatest scandals ever to hit American political life. Contact distributor about availability outside the United Kingdom.
Biography
Dist - ACADEM

Nixon - Checkers to Watergate 20 MIN
16mm / U-matic / VHS
Color
LC 77-700717
Looks at the political life of Richard Milhouse Nixon from the Eisenhower years to his resignation from office. Illustrates the intricacies of the executive branch of our government and the extraordinary demands of responsibility upon the office of President.
Biography; Civics and Political Systems; History - United States
Dist - PFP **Prod** - BRAMAN 1976

Nixon - 'Toughing it Out' 26 MIN
U-matic / VHS
Color (H C A)
Studies the attitudes of President Nixon as he fought to maintain office during the Watergate scandal. Chronicles both the legal and emotional defenses put forward, as well as the continuing list of defections from his camp during the affair.
Biography; History - United States
Dist - JOU **Prod** - UPI

Nixon's Checkers Speech 25 MIN
16mm
B&W (J)
LC 75-702529
Presents the famous 'Checkers' speech made by Richard Nixon when he was the 1952 vice presidential nominee. Explains how Nixon's defense in this speech against accusations that he financed his campaign through a slush fund kept him on the ticket.
Civics and Political Systems
Dist - NYFLMS **Prod** - NYFLMS 1952

Njangaan 80 MIN
16mm
Color (WOLOF (ENGLISH SUBTITLES))
A Wolof language film with English subtitles. Tells the story of a boy enslaved by marabouts purportedly teaching him the Koran. Directed by Mahama Johnson Traore.
Fine Arts; Foreign Language
Dist - NYFLMS **Prod** - UNKNWN 1974

Nkuleleko Means Freedom 28 MIN
16mm / VHS
Color (C)
$500.00, $280.00 purchase, $55.00 rental
Presents a film by Ron and Ophera Hallis. Portrays Zimbabwe's educational system, the roots of which were in the refugee camps of the liberation war.
Education; Geography - World; History - United States
Dist - ICARUS

NLP home study guide 109 MIN
VHS
Color; PAL; SECAM (G)
$99.00 purchase
Features Leslie Cameron - Bandler and Michael Lebeau. Presents a number of NLP concepts and techniques - The Outcome Frame, Calibration Skills, Representational System Cues, Anchoring, A Resource Strategy, A New Behavior Generator, Reframing. Introductory level of neuro - linguistic programming.
Psychology
Dist - NLPCOM **Prod** - NLPCOM

NLP in action - success strategies for rapid change 60 MIN
VHS
Color; PAL; SECAM (G)
$39.95 purchase
Features Charles Faulkner and Lucy Freedman. Shows how to make present actions a resource for positive results in the future, persuade others to see and accept one's point of view, create and utilize natural states of execellence, match mindsets with others to create common ground for communication, use the technique of Path Building towards goals and learn to be drawn naturally to goals. All levels of NLP, neuro - linguistic programming.
Psychology
Dist - NLPCOM **Prod** - NLPCOM 1993

No 5 MIN
U-matic / 16mm / VHS
Color; Mono (G)
MV $85.00 _ MP $170.00 purchase, $50.00 rental
Draws a comparison between the natural beauty and balance of the oceans and that of man's. Film stresses the need for the preservation of the marine environment and offers a warning as to the fate of this planet abused planet.
Science - Natural
Dist - CTV **Prod** - MAKOF 1982

No 11 - the Comedians - Pt 3 30 MIN
U-matic / BETA / VHS
American Movies - the First 30 Years Series
Color; B&W; Mono (C A)
Analyzes the artistry and style of Buster Keaton, the Great Stone Face, as the funny man who never smiled. Follows his career from the silent era into sound motion pictures.
Fine Arts
Dist - UIOWA **Prod** - UIOWA 1984

No 12 - Films of the Twenties 30 MIN
U-matic / BETA / VHS
American Movies - the First 30 Years Series
Color; B&W; Mono (C A)
Examines the Motion Picture Producers and Distributors of America, a solemn group that responded to public outcry about scandals in Hollywood with regulation and promotion of the industry in the 1920's.
Fine Arts
Dist - UIOWA **Prod** - UIOWA 1984

No Act of God 28 MIN
16mm / U-matic / VHS
Color (H C A)
LC 79-700269
Examines the topic of nuclear power, focusing on the problems of disposing of nuclear waste and the increasingly tight security that must be maintained to prevent plutonium from falling into the hands of terrorist groups.
Social Science; Sociology
Dist - BULFRG **Prod** - NFBC 1978

No action 5 MIN
16mm
Color (G)
$15.00 rental
Combines live action with animation to confuse the viewer with what is real or manipulated. Transforms natural settings with time - lapse animation. Sound and imagery are contrasted and uses lots of baseball images. Produced by Brady Lewis, who advises that this shows well with The Suicide Squeeze and should be played first in the program.
Fine Arts; Physical Education and Recreation
Dist - CANCIN

No and ambition 11 MIN
16mm
Family series
Color (G)
$30.00 rental
Presents the fourth in a series of four short films that deal with an idiosyncratic, personal and conceptual view of aspects of familial relationships. Combines movie footage and photographs of Maliga's father with sync - sound performances by Maliga and her daughter. Addresses two specific 'lessons' from Maliga's father. A Sandy Maliga production.
Fine Arts; Sociology
Dist - CANCIN

No Arriesgue Vidas 14 MIN
U-matic / VHS / 16mm
Color (A) (SPANISH)
A Spanish - language version of the motion picture Don't Take Chances. Shows common factory accidents. Illustrates efforts made by management to prevent accidents, but warns they will still occur if workers are thoughtless.
Business and Economics; Foreign Language; Health and Safety
Dist - IFB **Prod** - IAPA 1964

No baby now - family planning choices 24 MIN
VHS
Sex ed series
Color (J H G)
$295.00 purchase, $40.00 rental
Presents family planning information for a diverse population ranging from teens who are not yet sexually active to older women who have already experienced one or more pregnancies. Offers up - to - date information on birth control options in an open and comfortable manner, using style and language appropriate to a wide range of clinic audiences. Informs women and helps them to make responsible birth control decisions. Part of four parts on reproductive health.
Health and Safety
Dist - POLYMR **Prod** - VIDDIA

No barriers 60 MIN
VHS
Color (G)
$29.95 purchase
Follows paraplegic Mark Wellman and a small crew of disabled friends who climb El Capitan in Yosemite, as well as Half Dome, sea kayak with whales, alpine ski the steeps and deeps, whitewater kayak off waterfalls, cross - country ski across the high Sierra on arm power - and more.
Health and Safety; Physical Education and Recreation
Dist - NOLIMI **Prod** - NOLIMI 1995

No Better Gift 22 MIN
U-matic / VHS
Color
Provides guidelines for developing good eating habits and quality nutrition for young children.
Health and Safety; Home Economics
Dist - SNUTRE **Prod** - SIMONJ

No Big Money 15 MIN
16mm / U-matic / VHS
Color
LC 78-700151
Tells the story of a family which, with few modern conveniences, tries to wrest a living from a tract of land in British Columbia.
Sociology
Dist - WOMBAT **Prod** - NFBC 1978

No body's perfect 11 MIN
VHS / U-matic
Color (C PRO G)

$195.00 purchase _ #N921 - VI - 034
Teaches about the impact of perceptions, attitudes and behaviors on a child's physical appearance. Helps children to recognize the impact of the mass media on people's attitudes and behaviors regarding their physical appearance, identify healthy approaches to eating and exercise, discuss how peer groups and family members influence an individual's eating habits and body self - image, develop health attitudes about physical maturation, and identify behaviors and actions that enhance self - esteem in self and others. Produced by Connie Weed, Sue Heinze, Nancy Frosaker - Johnson, Debra Nelson, Susan Cordes - Green, St Luke's Hospital, Fargo, North Dakota.
Health and Safety; Physical Education and Recreation; Psychology; Sociology
Dist - HSCIC

No Brief Candle 27 MIN
VHS / 16mm
Color (G)
$245.00 purchase, $100.00, $50.00 rental
Looks at John and Marcie, who were an active couple when doctors found advanced cancer in Marcie and gave her three weeks to live. Follows two days in the lives of this couple a year after Marcie's cancer was found and raises compelling questions about the quality of our relationships and lives.
Sociology
Dist - FANPRO **Prod** - FANPRO 1989

No brushes today 15 MIN
Videoreel / VT2
Art corner series
B&W (P)
Explores ways of working with finger paints.
Fine Arts
Dist - GPN **Prod** - CVETVC

No Budget, Home Movies, Titles Film 8 MIN
16mm
B&W
LC 77-703003
Presents a pseudonarrative documentary comedy made without a budget.
Fine Arts; Industrial and Technical Education; Literature and Drama
Dist - CANFDC **Prod** - LIVNGN 1975

No Bull Sales Management - by Hank Trislek 60 MIN
VHS / U-matic
Stereo (C G T A S R PRO IND)
Shows how to have an effective sales team.
Business and Economics
Dist - BANTAP **Prod** - BANTAP 1986

No Bull Selling 60 MIN
U-matic / VHS
Stereo (C)
Shows how a salesperson can sell to an account.
Business and Economics
Dist - BANTAP **Prod** - BANTAP 1986

No, but I Saw the Movie 12 MIN
16mm
Color
LC FIA65-419
Provides a humorous approach to the history of recorded communication from cave paintings and the clay tablet to modern art and microfilm. Explores the resources of the modern library.
Education; Guidance and Counseling; History - United States; Psychology; Social Science
Dist - SIUFP **Prod** - SILLU 1961

No City or Community Without Risk 22 MIN
VHS
Color (G PRO)
$25.00 purchase _ #35376
Details the application of fire fighting foams and the use of related equipment. Includes types of foam, types of eductors and possible causes of malfunction, the venturi principle, operation of form equipment, application rates for different types of foam and maintenance of foam equipment.
Agriculture; Health and Safety; Industrial and Technical Education; Psychology; Science - Physical; Social Science
Dist - OKSU

The No Code 10 MIN
U-matic
Medical - Legal Issues - Observations Series
(A)
Deals with pertinent medical and legal issues in today's complex world of medicine. Co - produced by the Alberta Law Foundation.
Health and Safety; Sociology
Dist - ACCESS **Prod** - ACCESS 1984

No Comparison 30 MIN
16mm
Footsteps Series
Color
LC 79-701425
Explains that human differences are a fact of life and are not only natural, but desirable, and that society needs a range of talents and personalities to function well. Shows some of the ways in which children differ and tells parents how different responses can help or hinder a child's growth and development.
Home Economics; Psychology; Sociology
Dist - USNAC **Prod** - USOE 1978

No complaints? 50 MIN
VHS
No complaints series
Color (PRO IND COR A)
$1740.00 purchase, $500.00 rental, $50.00 preview
Presents customer care and quality management information. This two-part series are about complaints and the customer, and complaints and quality management. The key messages presented in both parts include, listen, sympathize, ask the right questions, agree on a course of action, check to see it is carried out, investigate and don't accuse, let staff find the solution, get departments to communicate, and agree on goals and monitor progress. This series targets customer care face-to-face, internal customer care, orientation, and all managers and team leaders on problem solving and quality process.
Business and Economics; Psychology
Dist - VIDART

No complaints series
Complaints and quality management - Pt 2 25 MIN
Complaints and the customer - Pt 1 25 MIN
No complaints? 50 MIN
Dist - VIDART

No Cooperation 6 MIN
16mm
Color
LC 79-706068
A dramatization in which a maintenance supervisor relives several situations in which his orders are countermanded by superiors, a subordinate goes over his head in asking for advancement and his subordinates object to working overtime.
Business and Economics
Dist - PSUPCR **Prod** - EPPI 1969

No Cop's a Hero - Until You Need One 24 MIN
U-matic / VHS / 16mm
Color (H A)
LC 75-700960
Dramatizes a number of everyday situations that are potentially troublesome in police - community relations. Shows the problems from both the police and the civilian point of view.
Social Science
Dist - AIMS **Prod** - CAHILL 1974

No Dam Good 28 MIN
U-matic / VHS / 16mm
Turning the Tide Series
Color (J)
$275.00, $250.00 purchase, $50.00 rental
Sets forth David Bellamy's belief that big dams symbolize humanity's assault on nature and the notion that size and expensive technology can solve economic and social problems.
Business and Economics; History - World; Industrial and Technical Education; Social Science
Dist - BULFRG **Prod** - TYNT 1988

No Easy Answers 14 MIN
16mm / U-matic / VHS
Science - New Frontiers Series
Color (J)
LC 74-702351
Draws examples from agriculture, genetic control, meteorology, computer technology and bio - feedback to illustrate the roles of science in the progress of man and to show how everything in the universe is interrelated.
History - World; Industrial and Technical Education; Science; Sociology
Dist - PHENIX **Prod** - CREEDM 1974

No easy answers 14 MIN
VHS
Color; PAL (I J H)
PdS15 purchase _ #1005
Tackles the conflict between the human need for energy and the need to protect the environment. Looks at leaded and unleaded gas, the greenhouse effect, acid rain and ozone depletion. Presents facts but leaves the issues open for discussion. Includes teacher's notes and student worksheets.
Science - Natural; Social Science
Dist - UKAEA

No easy answers 32 MIN
VHS
Color (I J H)
$95.00 purchase _ #429 - V8
Offers a sexual abuse prevention guide for junior and senior high students. Emphasizes awareness of the differences between nurturing and exploitative touch. Covers talking about sex; sexual decision making; incest, rape and acquaintance rape; and helping a victim.
Guidance and Counseling; Health and Safety
Dist - ETRASS **Prod** - ETRASS

No Easy Road 43 MIN
VHS
Color (S)
$129.00 purchase _ #825 - 9577
Features Michael Buerk who reported for four years on South Africa for BBC Television News. Uses footage from his reports on South Africa - some of it never shown before - to recall the emotions and experiences - including being shot at, gassed, beaten, locked up, censored and permanently expelled from South Africa - of living and working on the edge of a racial battleground.
Geography - World; History - United States; Sociology
Dist - FI **Prod** - BBCTV 1988

No Easy Walk - 1962 - 1966 60 MIN
VHS / 16mm
Eyes on the Prize Series
Color; Captioned (G)
$59.95 purchase _ #EYPZ - 104
Places the civil rights movement into a broad historical context, describing the growing commitment of activists to nonviolent tactics. Reveals that three cities were indelibly linked with the movement - Albany in Georgia, Birmingham in Alabama, and Washington, DC. School children filled Birmingham jails after marching against fire hoses, cattle prods and Bull Connor. Part of a six - part series on the civil rights struggle in America between 1954 and 1965.
Civics and Political Systems; Geography - United States; History - United States; Sociology
Dist - PBS **Prod** - BSIDE 1987

No Easy Walk, Pt 1, Pt 2, Pt 3 60 MIN
VHS / U-matic
Color
$395 purchase (each), $90 rental (each)
Chronicles the history of colonialism and the struggle for independence in three African countries - Ethiopia, Kenya, and Zimbabwe. Includes interviews with both European and African eyewitness survivors. Directed by Bernard Odjidja.
History - World
Dist - CNEMAG

No Easy Walk Series
Ethiopia 60 MIN
Kenya 60 MIN
Zimbabwe 60 MIN
Dist - CNEMAG

No Easy Walk to Freedom 60 MIN
U-matic / VHS
Bill Moyers' Journal Series
Color
LC 79-706946
Uses the speeches, writings and trial transcripts of Black South African leader Nelson Mandela to show his political odyssey from protest to violence in opposing apartheid.
Biography; Geography - World; History - United States; History - World
Dist - PBS **Prod** - WNETTV 1979

No easy way 30 MIN
16mm
Color (G IND)
$5.00 rental
Portrays a worker who is seriously burned while working in a foundry. Shows the activities of the union safety committee, a plant safety inspection, union and management discussion of safety hazards and how to correct them. Looks what can be done through collective bargaining and how a refusal to work can be handled.
Health and Safety; Social Science; Sociology
Dist - AFLCIO **Prod** - UWISC 1981

No 8 - the Stars Appear - Pt 2 30 MIN
U-matic / BETA / VHS
American Movies - the First 30 Years Series
Color; B&W; Mono (C A)
Continues the study of the careers of silent film stars in the 1920's such as Clara Bow, Gloria Swanson and Rudolph Valentino.
Fine Arts
Dist - UIOWA **Prod** - UIOWA 1984

No Entry 15 MIN
16mm
B&W
LC 76-701346
Shows an experimental film which places events in the mundane world against events in a fantasy world.

Fine Arts; Industrial and Technical Education
Dist - SFRASU **Prod** - SFRASU 1975

No escape from Christmas 30 MIN
VHS
Color (P I J H C G A R)
Tells the story of Margo, who lost her faith when her son died just before the previous Christmas. Reveals that an encounter with a small lost boy restores her faith.
Religion and Philosophy
Dist - APH **Prod** - CPH
CPH

No Exceptions (a Film about Rape) 24 MIN
U-matic / VHS / 16mm
Color (J)
LC 77-703084
Deals with three aspects of rape, including how to prevent it from happening, what to do if it happens and what to do afterward.
Sociology
Dist - ALTSUL **Prod** - ALTSUL 1977

No Excuse Sir 53 MIN
16mm
Color
LC 80-701481
Examines the role that the U S Military Academy at West Point plays in America's defense. Traces its history and explores it goals and expectations. Includes interviews with cadets, professors, officers trained at West Point, and critics of the academy.
Civics and Political Systems; Education
Dist - HUDRIV **Prod** - HUDRIV 1980

No Excuse Sir, Pt 1 27 MIN
16mm
Color
LC 80-701481
Examines the role that the U S Military Academy at West Point plays in America's defense. Traces its history and explores it goals and expectations. Includes interviews with cadets, professors, officers trained at West Point, and critics of the academy.
Civics and Political Systems
Dist - HUDRIV **Prod** - HUDRIV 1980

No Excuse Sir, Pt 2 26 MIN
16mm
Color
LC 80-701481
Examines the role that the U S Military Academy at West Point plays in America's defense. Traces its history and explores it goals and expectations. Includes interviews with cadets, professors, officers trained at West Point, and critics of the academy.
Civics and Political Systems
Dist - HUDRIV **Prod** - HUDRIV 1980

No Fair 15 MIN
VHS
Color (K P)
$95 purchase No. 2481-YZ
Presents stories and songs teaching illustrating for children grades K-2 about rules, compromise and fairness in dealing with others. Includes 15-minute video, eight student worksheets, and teacher's guide.
Education; Psychology
Dist - SUNCOM **Prod** - SUNCOM

No family pictures 22 MIN
16mm
Color (G)
$30.00 rental
Addresses film education and its effect on the relationship between women and the media. Questions why small format media are not used more often as a tool in education or as a weapon for women to make their mark in media.
Education; Fine Arts; Sociology
Dist - CANCIN **Prod** - IRWINJ 1983

No - fat cooking series
VHS
No - fat cooking series
Color (J H G)
$109.95 purchase _ #VB540SV
Presents a four - part series on no - fat cooking featuring Dr Jean Rosenbaum. Includes Guilt - Free Brownies; Noodle Making - Cheap and Easy; Fitness Muffins; Crusty Peasant Bread.
Health and Safety; Home Economics; Social Science
Dist - CAMV

No - Fault Insurance / Panty Hose / Homebuying
U-matic / VHS
Consumer Survival Series
Color
Discusses various aspects of no - fault insurance, panty hose and homebuying.
Business and Economics; Home Economics
Dist - MDCPB **Prod** - MDCPB

No Fault Kids
VHS
$89.95 purchase _ #UL163V
Points out the problem of divorce through candid interviews with teens. Tells how children of divorced parents first reacted to the situation and how they learned to cope with it. Suggests alternatives and positive approaches kids can take in dealing with their own situations.
Psychology; Sociology
Dist - CAREER **Prod** - CAREER

No Fault Kids 23 MIN
VHS
(I J H)
$89.95 purchase _ #UL163V
Discusses the problems facing the children of divorced parents. Investigates the anger, guilt, and embarassment associated with the issue. Discusses the availability of support groups and the need to develop a good support system and coping skills in adjusting to family changes.
Guidance and Counseling; Psychology; Sociology
Dist - CAMV **Prod** - CAMV

No Fault Kids
VHS
Is Anyone Listening - a Documentary Series
$89.95 purchase _ #ULNFK
Interviews teenagers who offer suggestions and positive approaches for dealing with the having divorced parents.
Psychology; Sociology
Dist - CAREER **Prod** - CAREER

No fault kids - a focus on kids with divorced parents 27 MIN
VHS
Color (J H C)
$95.00 purchase _ #163VG
Focuses on the problems facing kids with divorced parents. Features young people who are now dealing with divorce and feelings such as isolation, loneliness, sadness, anger, and guilt. They offer advice on how to deal with these emotions. Presents five ways to help oneself and outside help available. Include a leader's guide.
Sociology
Dist - UNL

No film 1 MIN
16mm
Color (G)
$10.00 rental
Presents a one - second production.
Fine Arts
Dist - CANCIN **Prod** - KRENKU 1983

No First Use - Preventing Nuclear War 30 MIN
16mm / U-matic / VHS
Color
Asks and answeres some of the most crucial questions in the debate over US and NATO defense policy.
Civics and Political Systems; Sociology
Dist - UCEMC **Prod** - UCS 1983

No Fishing this Year - Care and Handling of Drill Pipe, Drill Collars and Tool Joints 25 MIN
U-matic / VHS / 16mm
Color (IND)
Tells what the rig crew can do to increase the life of the drill stem. Shows unloading the pipe at the rig, running it into and out of the hole and laying it down after the hole is finished.
Industrial and Technical Education; Social Science
Dist - UTEXPE **Prod** - UTEXPE 1980

No 5 - the First Film Makers - Pt 2 30 MIN
BETA / VHS / U-matic
American Movies - the First 30 Years Series
Color; B&W; Mono (C A)
Continues the examination of D W Griffith's work and his influence on other directors. Gives an interpretation of his style.
Fine Arts
Dist - UIOWA **Prod** - UIOWA 1984

No flab workout
VHS
Rotation and motivation exercise series
Color (H C A)
$19.95 purchase _ #BW602V
Presents the second of a three - part series of exercise programs. Focuses on flattening the stomach, shaping and firming the midsection. Includes standing exercises for the waistline and floor exercises for flattening the waistline.
Physical Education and Recreation; Science - Natural
Dist - CAMV

No 4 - the First Film Makers - Pt 1 30 MIN
BETA / VHS / U-matic
American Movies - the First 30 Years Series
Color; B&W; Mono (C A)
Surveys the life of D W Griffith - his childhood, career as an actor and playwright, his experiments with editing, the kinds of stories he chose to film, and his development and contributions to the cinematic art.
Fine Arts
Dist - UIOWA **Prod** - UIOWA 1984

No Frames, no Boundaries 21 MIN
U-matic / VHS / 16mm
Color (J H C A)
LC 82-701179;
Traces human civilization from the earliest examples of nomadic people to the point where city states, their defense and weapons developed. Notes the fact that the world's major religions share a belief in the interdependence of people and urges the earth's inhabitants to admit their interdependence and to unite against the threat of nuclear annihilation.
Civics and Political Systems; Religion and Philosophy; Sociology
Dist - CREATI **Prod** - CREATI 1982

No Frames, no Boundaries 21 MIN
16mm
(G)
$175.00 purchase
Draws its theme from the perspective of astronaut Russell Schweickart as he stepped into space during the Apollo 9 flight. Looks at the man - made boundaries between nations and the threat of nuclear war.
Civics and Political Systems; Sociology
Dist - EFVP **Prod** - EFVP 1984

No Fuelin' - We're Poolin' 8 MIN
16mm
Color (H C A)
LC 77-700461
Describes the role of the employer in vanpool programs, including carpool matching, driver selection and determining fares.
Business and Economics; Science - Natural; Social Science
Dist - USNAC **Prod** - USDT 1976

No Game 17 MIN
16mm
B&W
An essay on the October 21st, 1967 Pentagon demonstration to end the war in Vietnam.
Civics and Political Systems; Psychology; Sociology
Dist - CANWRL **Prod** - CANWRL 1967

No Greater Challenge 14 MIN
16mm
Color
LC 78-702835
Studies the challenge to man to provide sufficient food and water for the future, and the contribution to be made when nuclear - powered agro - industrial desalting complexes are able to convert arid coastal regions into fertile productive communities.
Psychology; Science - Physical; Social Science
Dist - USNAC **Prod** - USNRC 1969

No Greater Love 74 MIN
VHS / U-matic
B&W
Tells the World War II story of a Russian who turns her villagers into partisans for revenge against the Germans, who have killed her husband and infant son. Directed by Frederic Emler and starring Vera Maretskaya.
Fine Arts; History - World
Dist - IHF **Prod** - IHF

No Greater Power 24 MIN
16mm
B&W (P)
Dramatizes the story of Zacheus as recorded by Luke. Shows him as an impoverished potter who takes advantages of circumstances to eventually gain the exalted position of tax collector of Jericho.
Religion and Philosophy
Dist - CAFM **Prod** - CAFM

No Gun Towers, no Fences 59 MIN
Videoreel / VT2
Syngerism - Troubled Humanity Series
Color
Sociology
Dist - PBS **Prod** - WMVU

No Guts - no Glory with Don Schula 11 MIN
16mm / VHS
Color (PRO)
$250.00 purchase, $150.00 rental, $75.00 preview
Presents famed football coach Don Schula who illustrates how to overcome adversity and describes the fortitude it takes to be a winner. Features film footage that motivates employees to greater success.
Business and Economics; Education; Physical Education and Recreation; Psychology
Dist - UTM **Prod** - UTM

No Handouts for Mrs Hedgepeth 27 MIN
16mm / U-matic / VHS
Color; B&W (H C A)
LC FIA68-362
Shows the situation of a domestic worker in Durham, North Carolina, to illustrate why, in the world's richest country, a woman can work all her life and still be trapped in poverty.
Civics and Political Systems; Guidance and Counseling; History - United States; Psychology; Sociology
Dist - PHENIX **Prod** - NCFUND 1968
PBS

No Harm in Logging 18 MIN
16mm
Color (IND)
LC 77-709257
Demonstrates safety precautions in felling and handling timber, showing mechanzied handling methods in timber producing areas of Australia.
Agriculture; Geography - World; Health and Safety
Dist - AUIS **Prod** - ANAIB 1970

No Heroic Measures 23 MIN
VHS / U-matic
Color (PRO)
Examines some of the issues raised concerning withdrawal of life support from the terminally ill.
Health and Safety; Sociology
Dist - BAXMED **Prod** - BAXMED 1986

No Hold Bard - a Video Introduction to Shakespeare 38 MIN
U-matic / VHS
Color
Offers a varied taste of Shakespeare's works by showing actors briskly changing costumes and characters as they quote the famous poet - dramatist. Presented in the manner of a television variety show.
Fine Arts; Literature and Drama
Dist - WALCHJ **Prod** - WALCHJ

No hunger in my home 26 MIN
VHS / 16mm
Color (H C G)
$595.00, $295.00 purchase, $100.00, $55.00 rental
Reveals that 20 million people in America are hungry, many for the first time. Profiles the experience of hunger in a California suburb through three women's stories - Nevida Butler, director of the Eucmenical Hunger Program; Donna Laurreano, her client, and a former community worker; and Dr Maxine Hayes of the Physician Task Force on Hunger in America. Produced by Nancy Brink.
Geography - United States; Social Science; Sociology
Dist - FLMLIB

No I won't and you can't make me 15 MIN
VHS
Boy's town parenting series
Color (G)
$29.95 purchase _ #FFB209V
Offers a method for handling children's and teens's defiance and temper flare - ups. Shows parents how to improve relationships with children, control their own anger and help an angry child to calm down. Part of an 11 - part series.
Guidance and Counseling; Health and Safety; Psychology; Social Science; Sociology
Dist - CAMV **Prod** - FFBH

No impact workout with Donna deVorona 50 MIN
VHS
Color (G)
$29.95 purchase _ #CH800V
Takes a comprehensive look at swimming. Explains and demonstrates the various swimming strokes, stretching exercises, competitive techniques, and drills for practice. Hosted by Donna deVorona.
Physical Education and Recreation
Dist - CAMV **Prod** - CAMV 1987

No Japs at My Funeral 56 MIN
VHS / U-matic
Color
Relates the views of an ex - IRA bomber about war in Northern Ireland, politics and experiences. Intercuts contrasting views.
Fine Arts; Sociology
Dist - KITCHN **Prod** - KITCHN

No Kid of Mine 30 MIN
VHS / 16mm
Color (A PRO)
$195.00 purchase, $50.00 rental _ #9900
Features parents of alcohol and drug addicted children who talk about their experiences, their mistakes, their feelings and the lessons they've learned.
Psychology; Sociology
Dist - AIMS **Prod** - AIMS 1987

No Kid of Mine 30 MIN
VHS / U-matic
Color (H C A)
Helps parents of addicted children discuss their experiences truthfully with the hope of alerting other individuals to the realities of adolescent drug and alcohol abuse.
Guidance and Counseling; Health and Safety; Psychology; Sociology
Dist - UEUWIS **Prod** - UEUWIS 1982

No Known Cure 31 MIN
VHS
Color (S)
$129.00 purchase _ #386 - 9049
Looks at new research techniques that may help find a cure for Alzheimer's disease which now takes a tragic toll on victims and their families.
Business and Economics; Health and Safety; Psychology; Sociology
Dist - FI **Prod** - CANBC 1988

No Laws Today 12 MIN
16mm / U-matic / VHS
Color (I J)
Tells the story of the chaos which ensues when a day without laws is declared. Shows the importance of laws and rules for traffic, consumer affairs and even sports.
Civics and Political Systems; Guidance and Counseling; Health and Safety; Home Economics
Dist - JOU **Prod** - JOU 1982

No Less a Woman 23 MIN
U-matic / VHS
Color (C A)
Takes a long look at the problems of single and married women who are attempting to recover from the far - reaching effects of mastectomy.
Health and Safety; Sociology
Dist - MMRC **Prod** - MMRC

No Lies 16 MIN
16mm
Color (H C A)
LC 73-702197
Explores the problems of rape through the story of a girl who has been raped but feels increasingly guilty about having dropped the whole affair at the police station. Explains that a detective took an unnatural interest in the details of the rape, paralleling it to his wife's own sexual problems. Features Alec Hirschfeld and Shelby Leverington.
Psychology; Sociology
Dist - DIRECT **Prod** - BLOCK 1973

No longer colonies - Hong Kong 1997, Macau 1999 30 MIN
VHS
Maryknoll video magazine presents series
Color (G)
$14.95 purchase
Considers the colonial and economic history of Hong Kong and Macau in relation to their coming unification with communist China.
History - World
Dist - MARYFA

No Longer Silent 56 MIN
16mm / U-matic / VHS
Color
$199 video purchase, $975 film purchase or $75 rental
Discusses the changing attitudes of women in India. Highlights the changing social, cultural, and political alienation of Indian women. Focuses on health care issues, abortion, nutrition, bride burning for dowry and activism.
History - World; Sociology
Dist - IFB

No Longer Vanishing - Renouveau Indian 25 MIN
16mm
Color (H C A) (FRENCH)
#3X103 ADMIN
Examines the occupations of native Indian people seen from the perspective of a young Indian. Focuses on the issue of racism.
Social Science; Sociology
Dist - CDIAND **Prod** - NFBC 1956

No Man is an Island 28 MIN
16mm
Color
LC 74-700625
Examines the work of the Salvation Army in helping solve the physical and spiritual problems of troubled people.
Religion and Philosophy; Sociology
Dist - SALVA **Prod** - SALVA 1973

No Man is an Island 11 MIN
16mm
Color (J)
LC 73-702198
Presents Orson Welles reciting John Donne's poem, 'NO MAN IS AN ISLAND.' Conveys the message 'BECAUSE I AM INVOLVED IN MANKIND' through scenes showing teenagers shaving bedridden patients and teachers feeding the retarded and handicapped.
Literature and Drama; Psychology; Sociology
Dist - DANA **Prod** - DANA 1973

No Man's Land 26 MIN
VHS / U-matic
Color
Records the plight of a quarter - million Kampucheans who are trapped between their homeland and Thailand. Reveals that they cannot return because the Khmer Rouge regime which slaughtered three million of their countrymen is now part of the government.
History - World
Dist - FLMLIB **Prod** - GRATV 1984

No Maps on My Taps 59 MIN
16mm
Color (H C A)
LC 80-700723
Features veteran jazz tap dancing stars, including Bunny Briggs, Chuck Green and Sandman Sims, as they reminisce about their art and careers. Includes scenes of street corner challenge dancing and stills from the 1930's of legendary figures from tap dancing's heyday.
Fine Arts
Dist - DIRECT **Prod** - NIERNG 1979

No Maps on My Taps, Pt 1 29 MIN
16mm
Color (H C A)
LC 80-700723
Features veteran jazz tap dancing stars, including Bunny Briggs, Chuck Green and Sandman Sims, as they reminisce about their art and careers. Includes scenes of street corner challenge dancing and stills from the 1930's of legendary figures from tap dancing's heyday.
Fine Arts
Dist - DIRECT **Prod** - NIERNG 1979

No Maps on My Taps, Pt 2 30 MIN
16mm
Color (H C A)
LC 80-700723
Features veteran jazz tap dancing stars, including Bunny Briggs, Chuck Green and Sandman Sims, as they reminisce about their art and careers. Includes scenes of street corner challenge dancing and stills from the 1930's of legendary figures from tap dancing's heyday.
Fine Arts
Dist - DIRECT **Prod** - NIERNG 1979

No Margin for Error 25 MIN
16mm
Color
LC FIA60-617
Describes the courses for training aviation safety officers taught at the University of Southern California. Includes scenes of classes in aeronautical engineering, accident investigation, aviation physiology and aviation psychology.
Education; Health and Safety; Industrial and Technical Education; Science - Physical
Dist - USC **Prod** - USC

No means no 13 MIN
VHS
Color (H G)
$40.00 rental, $195.00 purchase
Discusses date rape and helps to raise consciousness for both men and women about how misunderstandings can lead date rape to occur. Combines evocative images and text and personal testimonies. Recommended as resource for gender studies.
Fine Arts; Sociology
Dist - WMEN **Prod** - WOOSTE 1993

No means no 48 MIN
VHS
Color (J H C G)
$225.00 purchase
Takes a realistic look at teens dealing with emerging sexuality. Shows the consequences of behavior around sexual decision making. Demonstrates effective ways to negotiate personal relationships. Portrays Megan, a freshman, asked out by Doug, a popular senior. Illustrates the unequality between the two - Doug's refusal to believe that Megan doesn't want to have sex results in date rape. Michael and Sally, however, are working through their differing views of sexuality and what it means to be a 'girlfriend' or a 'boyfriend,' and arriving at a relationship between them which is comfortable and equitable to both of them.
Guidance and Counseling; Health and Safety; Psychology; Social Science; Sociology
Dist - MEDIAI **Prod** - MEDIAI 1990

No means no - understanding acquaintance rape 33 MIN
VHS
Color (I J H)
$189.00 purchase _ #CG - 931 - VS
Focuses on the phenomenon of rape in America - one occurs every 6 minutes. Points out that sixty to eighty percent of all rapes are committed by acquaintances or dates. Portrays an acquaintance rape mock trial in Baton Rouge, Louisiana. Victims describe their experiences, how they dealt with the rape and their interaction with health and law officials. Male college students discuss

their ambiguous feelings in dating and trying to understand when no means no.
Guidance and Counseling; Health and Safety; Sociology
Dist - HRMC **Prod** - HRMC

No Middle Road to Freedom 40 MIN
16mm
Color
Documents a terrorist attack in South Africa in the early 1980s. Discusses the massacre of hundreds of men, women, and children. Produced by Kevin Harris Productions.
History - World; Sociology
Dist - CCNCC

No money, no choice - a shameful standard 10 MIN
VHS
Color (G)
$10.00 suggested donation
Details the harmful effects of federal and state bans on abortion coverage for low - income women. Illustrates the way in which funding bans effectively deny Medicaid - eligible women the ability to make decisions about reproductive health and childbirth. Includes statistics and interviews with attorneys and health professionals and statements by low - income women who have experienced the discriminatory effects of singling out abortion as the only medically necessary procedure denied coverage under Medicaid.
Civics and Political Systems; Sociology
Dist - CREPLP

No more Aching Back - How to be Pain Free - Without Surgery 60 MIN
VHS
Color (G)
$29.95 purchase _ #XVMAB
Features Dr Leon Root, orthopedic surgeon, and comedian Chevy Chase. Introduces with humor an easy - to - follow ten - step, 15 - minutes - a - day program of exercises for reducing or eliminating most back pain.
Health and Safety; Physical Education and Recreation; Psychology; Science - Natural
Dist - GAINST

No more bullies
VHS
Good kids - karate kids series
Color (G)
$29.95 purchase _ #PNT014
Presents the third of three videos that teach self - defense, self - confidence, home safety, awareness, fitness, respect for elders, controls, manners and more. Stars 12 - year - old karate phenomenon Kim Murray, Jr.
Physical Education and Recreation; Psychology
Dist - SIV

No more crying - reducing distress during venipuncture 14 MIN
VHS / U-matic
Color (G)
$325.00 purchase, $100.00 rental
Reveals that children with catastrophic illnesses must routinely undergo highly invasive and often painful diagnostic and treatment procedures - and often develop severe aversion reactions. Shows some highly effective yet simple behavioral interventions to reduce the distress. Demonstrates the use of distraction, limit setting and postive reinforcement in winning the cooperation of both child and parent, reducing their anxiety and giving them some measure of control over these very difficult situations. Explains how to carry out a proper clinical assessment and how to implement behavior treatments.
Health and Safety; Psychology
Dist - BAXMED **Prod** - BAXMED

No more disguises 6 MIN
VHS
Color (G)
$75.00 purchase, $25.00 rental
Travels to China where Cui Jian, the country's answer to John Lennon, sings prophetically of the confusion and dissatisfaction of his nation's youth. Features footage shot entirely in Tiananmen Square before and during the 1989 student uprising. Produced by Boryana Varbanov, Tom Sigel and Pam Yates.
Fine Arts; Geography - World; Sociology
Dist - FIRS

No more Disguises 6 MIN
U-matic / VHS
New Directions Series
Color (G)
Presents an independent production by Boryana Varbanov, Tom Sigel and Pam Yates. Part of a comic series of first film shorts. Available also in 35mm film format.
Fine Arts; Literature and Drama
Dist - FIRS

No more headaches 37 MIN
VHS
Color (G)
$24.95 purchase
Educates consumers on causes and triggers of headache, as well as effective diagnostic procedures. Provides solutions to relieve pain and nausea and discusses new treatments and how to change daily habits to prevent or abort headache.
Health and Safety; Psychology
Dist - NHEADF

No more Hibakusha 55 MIN
16mm / U-matic / VHS
Color
Looks at the experiences of the Hibakusha, survivors of the atomic bomb blast at Hiroshima and Nagasaki who now dedicate their lives to warning humanity about the dangers of nuclear war.
Civics and Political Systems; History - World; Sociology
Dist - ICARUS **Prod** - NFBC 1983

No more Hiroshima 26 MIN
16mm
Color (G)
$470.00, $260.00 purchase, $55.00 rental
Introduces the audience to 'hibakusha,' anguished survivors of the nuclear attack on Hiroshima, who fear that their warnings will go unheeded and others will suffer the horrors of nuclear war. Presents a Martin Duckworth film. A 55 - minute version of the film is available.
Fine Arts; History - World
Dist - FIRS **Prod** - NFBC 1984

No more Kings 3 MIN
U-matic / 35mm strip
America Rock Series
Color (P I)
LC 76-730447
Traces the Pilgrims' flight to the New World. Shows the American Colonists' break from King George III and the fight for independence.
Civics and Political Systems; History - United States
Dist - GA **Prod** - ABCTV 1976

No more Mananas 28 MIN
U-matic / VHS / 16mm
Insight Series
B&W (J H A)
LC 73-713920
A dramatization in which the director of a barrio self - help agency tries to convince a recently paroled addict to return a sum of stolen money.
Fine Arts; Psychology; Sociology
Dist - PAULST **Prod** - PAULST 1971

No more Nice Girls 44 MIN
VHS / U-matic
Joan Braderman Series
Color (G)
$250.00, $200.00 purchase, $50.00 rental
Shows a generation of seasoned feminist veterans - black, white, lesbian, heterosexual - facing off the political backlash of the 1980s.
Civics and Political Systems; History - World; Sociology
Dist - WMEN **Prod** - JBRAD 1989

No more Secrets 13 MIN
16mm
Color (P I)
LC 82-701185
Advises children who have been sexually abused on actions they can take and warns of the guises of sexual abuse. Uses animated sequences to depict the abusive acts described by four youngsters as they frolic together in the woods.
Guidance and Counseling; Sociology
Dist - ODNP **Prod** - ODNP 1982

No more secrets - safety skills for children 13 MIN
VHS / 16mm
Color; Captioned (P I) (SPANISH)
$340.00, $295.00 purchase
Teaches children the skills and information they need to avoid abusive situations. Uses animated characters in real settings to provide straightforward and non - threatening demonstrations of assertiveness. Shows children how to say 'no,' how to tell a trusted adult about uncomfortable situations and how to talk about their problems.
Health and Safety; Social Science; Sociology
Dist - SELMED

No more teasing 16 MIN
VHS
Color (P I)
$95 purchase No. 2490-YZ
Used to show students grades 2-4 how changing their own behavior can help them protect themselves against teasing or bullying. Used to promote development of empathy and sensitivity to others' feelings.
Education; Psychology
Dist - SUNCOM **Prod** - SUNCOM

No mountain too high 14 MIN
VHS
Color (A PRO)
$400.00 purchase, $125.00 rental
Uses the example of a man and woman climbing a mountain to stress the need to overcome obstacles and fears in life. Suggests that all people should focus only on those elements that are truly within their control.
Psychology
Dist - VLEARN

The No Name Show 30 MIN
U-matic / VHS
Cookin' Cheap Series
Color
Presents basically crazy cooks Larry Bly and Laban Johnson who offer recipes, cooking and shopping tips.
Home Economics
Dist - MDCPB **Prod** - WBRATV

No Need to Hide 55 MIN
16mm
Color (R)
Traces the background of former gang leader, Nicky Cruz from his unhappy childhood to his discovery of Christ.
Guidance and Counseling; Religion and Philosophy; Sociology
Dist - GF **Prod** - GF

No need to repent - the ballad of Rev Jan Griesinger 27 MIN
VHS / U-matic / 16mm
Color (G)
$500.00, $225.00 purchase, $75.00 rental
Depicts Rev Jan Griesinger, ordained minister in the United Church of Christ who came out as a lesbian at age 35. Shows how she integrates her ministry, her politics and her personal life. Offers a glimpse of life at her farm in rural Appalachia, the 'Susan B Anthony Memorial UnRest Home.' Produced by Ann Alter.
Religion and Philosophy; Sociology
Dist - WMEN

No Neutral Ground - Cambodia and Laos 60 MIN
U-matic / VHS / 16mm
Vietnam - a television history series; Episode 9
Color (H C A)
Reveals that the U S extension of the Vietnam War into Laos and Cambodia to stop attacks and supplies from across those borders hurt those countries more than it hurt the object of the attack. Shows that Prince Sihanouk of Cambodia was overthrown and he joined the Khmers Rouges.
History - United States; History - World
Dist - FI **Prod** - WGBHTV 1983

No neutral ground - Cambodia and Laos and peace is at hand - Volume 5 120 MIN
VHS
Vietnam - a television history series
Color (H C A)
$14.95 purchase
Presents the ninth and tenth episodes of a 13 - part series covering the history of the Vietnam War. Includes the episodes 'No Neutral Ground - Cambodia And Laos' and 'Peace Is At Hand.'
History - United States
Dist - PBS **Prod** - WNETTV

No neutral ground - Volume 5 120 MIN
VHS
Vietnam - a television history series
Color (G)
$29.95 purchase _ #S01531
Consists of two 60 - minute episodes examining the US involvement in Vietnam - 'No Neutral Ground' and 'Peace is at Hand.' Covers the year 1973.
History - United States
Dist - UILL **Prod** - PBS

No News is Bad News 14 MIN
16mm
Color
LC 79-700252
Shows the key selling points of a newspaper and portrays what life might be like without the newspapers.
Literature and Drama; Social Science; Sociology
Dist - CZC **Prod** - CZC 1979

No 9 - the Comedians - Pt 1 30 MIN
BETA / VHS / U-matic
American Movies - the First 30 Years Series
Color; B&W; Mono (C A)
Examines the performances of comedians in the early years of film and the reasons for their success. Includes Buster Keaton, John Bunny, Mack Sennett and his Keystone Cops, Mabel Normand, Fatty Arbuckle and Charlie Chaplin.
Fine Arts
Dist - UIOWA **Prod** - UIOWA 1984

No no nooky TV 12 MIN
VHS
Color (A)
$30 rental, $35.00 purchase
Posits sexuality as a social construct in a 'sex - text' of satiric graphic representation of 'dirty pictures.' Confronts the feminist controversy around sexuality by way of using an Amiga computer with electronic language, pixels and interface to make the film. Pokes fun at romance, sex and love in the post - industrial age.
Fine Arts
Dist - CANCIN **Prod** - BARHAM 1987

The no - nonsense cholesterol guide
VHS
Color (G)
$19.95 purchase _ #XJN015
Explains methods to lower levels of cholesterol and explains the difference between 'good fat' and 'bad fat.'
Health and Safety; Psychology
Dist - SIV

The No - nonsense cholesterol guide - good fat - bad fat 35 MIN
VHS
Color (G)
$29.95 purchase _ #XJXEN66V
Defines a healthy cholesterol level. Shows how to reverse a cholesterol build - up, prepare healthy meals and decode misleading food labels. Discusses frequently used cholesterol - lowering drugs and medications which may affect cholesterol levels.
Health and Safety; Home Economics; Social Science
Dist - CAMV

No Nos Moveran 25 MIN
U-matic / VHS
Color
Examines the Mexican - American population in the Twin Cities, an urban sub - culture which is the largest minority in Minnesota. Reveals where they have come from and why they have chosen to live in Minnesota.
Geography - United States; Sociology
Dist - WCCOTV **Prod** - WCCOTV 1976

No nukes is good nukes 17 MIN
VHS
Nukes or no nukes series
Color (I J H C)
$59.00 purchase _ #505
Features energy expert Amory Lovins who explains why nuclear plants should be dismantled. Discusses why energy must be produced and used more efficiently and why safe, new, alternative energy sources must be found for the future.
Business and Economics; Science - Natural; Social Science
Dist - HAWHIL **Prod** - HAWHIL

No 1 - Introduction 30 MIN
BETA / VHS / U-matic
American Movies - the First 30 Years Series
Color; B&W; Mono (C A)
Introduces early motion picture productions with D W Griffith, Charlie Chaplin, Zukor, Lasky, Pickford, Fairbanks, Stroheim, Swanson and Valentino and others. Describes the silent era, the beginning of the star system, the role of the director, the development of comedy as genre, and the characteristic business practices of the American Film industry. Richard MacCann narrates.
Fine Arts
Dist - UIOWA **Prod** - UIOWA 1984

No One Saved Dennis 14 MIN
U-matic / VHS
Color (G)
$249.00, $149.00 purchase _ #AD - 1984
Traces the history of Dennis, adopted by a child abuser and her acquiescent husband, in a community of family members, social workers and health professionals, many of whom saw suspicious parts of the truth but were unwilling to take the risk of making the first accusation. Reveals that Dennis' death was treated as accidental and it was 20 years before his natural mother discovered information leading to a reopening of the case and the trial and conviction of the adoptive mother.
Guidance and Counseling; Health and Safety; Sociology
Dist - FOTH **Prod** - FOTH

No One Says Hello Anymore 45 MIN
VHS
(H C A)
$495.00 purchase _ #81976
Presents the story of an individual's struggle with alcoholism. Illustrates the alcoholic process of compulsion, craving, loss of control, and continuation of alcoholic behavior. Discusses finally his triumph in admitting to himself his alcoholic problem.
Guidance and Counseling; Health and Safety; Psychology; Sociology
Dist - CMPCAR

No One Stays a Child 14 MIN
16mm
Color
LC 76-700393
Pictures a day at Camp Highfields in Onondaga, Michigan, following some of the boys through a variety of everyday activities. Includes comments by the camp director on the philosophy of the institution.
Education; Geography - United States; Physical Education and Recreation
Dist - CIASP **Prod** - JRLL 1975

No One Told Me 8 MIN
16mm
Professional Selling Practices Series 2 Series
Color (H C A)
LC 77-702355
Points out some of the advantages of suggestion selling as a service which contributes to customer satisfaction. Illustrates opportunities for multiple sales.
Business and Economics
Dist - SAUM **Prod** - SAUM 1968

No ordinary genius 100 MIN
VHS
Horizon series
Color (C PRO H A)
PdS99; Not available in USA
Tells about the American genius - adventurer, bongo drummer, physicist and teacher - Richard Feynman, whose life was characterized by simplicity, irreverence and honesty. Gives insight into the how the mind of this creative scientist works, while painting a portrait of an unusual man. In two parts of 50 minutes each.
Biography; Science - Physical
Dist - BBCENE

No Other Choice 60 MIN
16mm
Color
Shows how three men sabotage a weapons' research center and are forced to hide out in the home of a professor, an old friend. Reveals distances between them and questions the real terms of the revolutionary consciousness.
Sociology
Dist - CANWRL **Prod** - MACHR

No other generation - 12 voices from the nuclear age - Program 7 56 MIN
VHS
How then shall we live series
Color (H C A)
$49.95 purchase
Features Dr Helen Caldicott, Ram Dass, Daniel Ellsberg, Patricia Ellsberg, and eight others in a discussion of how to create a positive future in the nuclear age.
Sociology
Dist - PBS **Prod** - WNETTV

No Other Generation - Twelve Voices from the Thirty - Seventh Year of the Nuclear Age 35 MIN
U-matic / VHS
How Then Shall We Live? Series
Color
Presents the personal and political thinking of twelve speakers who call upon us to protect life itself from 'threatened planetary extinction.' Features Ram Dass and Daniel Ellsberg.
Social Science; Sociology
Dist - ORGNLF **Prod** - ORGNLF

No Other Love 58 MIN
U-matic / VHS / 16mm
Teenage Years Series
Color (I)
LC 81-701134
Presents the story of two marginally retarded young adults who fall in love and plan to get married, only to have to overcome the objections of their families and friends. Shows that the mentally retarded have emotional needs and a right to achieve their potential and independence. Stars Richard Thomas and Julie Kavner.
Education; Psychology
Dist - TIMLIF **Prod** - TISAVN 1979

No outlet 7 MIN
16mm
Color & B&W (G)
$18.50 rental
Interprets the Sartre play No Exit. Delves into the meaning of violence against the intellect of both men and women in society and examines these extremes. Displaces scenes of violence from their original setting to show how absurd and oppressive cinematic violence can be.
Fine Arts; Sociology
Dist - CANCIN **Prod** - ALVARE 1990

No Picnic 88 MIN
16mm
B&W (G)
Presents an affectionate tribute to the eccentric and fragile Lower East Side of New York City. Focuses on Macabee Cohn, whose girlfriend left to join the Air Force, real estate sharks who are eating up his beloved Lower East Side, and on his brother who has embarked on a sexual tour of all 50 states, briefing Mac by postcard.
Fine Arts; Geography - United States; Sociology
Dist - FIRS

No place like home
VHS
Bippity boppity bunch series
Color (K P I R)
$14.95 purchase _ #35 - 815 - 8579
Deals with the subject of running away from home. Shows that many believe that doing so can help avoid having to deal with problems. Reveals that such an idea is mistaken, however.
Literature and Drama; Religion and Philosophy
Dist - APH **Prod** - FAMF

No Place Like Home 58 MIN
U-matic / VHS
Color (H C A)
LC 82-706432
Reports on nursing homes and on a range of alternative approaches to long - term care for the aged, including home care, day care and congregate living. Hosted by Helen Hayes.
Health and Safety; Sociology
Dist - FI **Prod** - WNETTV 1981

No place like home - long term care for the elderly 55 MIN
VHS
Color (H C G)
$445.00 purchase, $75.00 rental
Reveals that often providing home care is less costly to the public than institutionalized care for the elderly, and is more desirable for the older person. Estimates that one - third of the population now living in nursing homes would not need to be there if alternative services were more widely available. Shows several alternatives to institutionalizing the elderly in New York City's Greenwich Village, in rural Appalachia and in San Francisco. Features Helen Hayes. Produced for Public Policy Productions.
Health and Safety
Dist - FLMLIB **Prod** - RWEIS 1982

No place like home series

Bars on windows	28 MIN
From the attic	28 MIN
Front Porch	28 MIN
The Homebound	28 MIN
Homewrecker	28 MIN
House of cards	28 MIN
Neighbors	28 MIN
Nursing Home	28 MIN
The Open Door	28 MIN
Silent Walls	28 MIN

Dist - USNAC

No Place to be Me 15 MIN
16mm / U-matic / VHS
Just One Child Series
Color (I J) (SOMALI)
Depicts a day in the life of a 12 - year old boy who is a son of war refugees living in the Somalian desert. Shows how his day begins with Moslem prayers to Allah, includes two hours of rote learning at school, and the rest of his day consists of helping his mother search for fuel, visiting the market and playing briefly with friends.
Geography - World; Psychology; Sociology
Dist - BCNFL **Prod** - REYEXP 1983

No Place to Go 14 MIN
U-matic
A Matter of Time Series
(A)
Tells the story of a retired widower who reminds himself of missed opportunities to plan a retirement that could be meaningful.
Sociology
Dist - ACCESS **Prod** - ACCESS 1980

No Place to Hide 30 MIN
16mm
Color (H C A)
LC 82-700161
Contrasts actual civil defense films of the 1950s with film clips of the atomic devastation of Japan to show how naive the American of the 1950s were in believing the United States government's claims that protection against an atomic attack was as simple as hiding beneath a school desk. Presents actor Martin Sheen re - creating the feelings of a cold - war child and berates the government for minimizing the American people's awareness of the horrors of atomic warfare.
Civics and Political Systems; Health and Safety; Sociology
Dist - DIRECT **Prod** - MEDSTD 1982

No Place to Hide 58 MIN
U-matic
Color (H C A)
$150.00
Examines situations where women have been abused physically, sexually and emotionally. Surveys the legal and social options available to victims.
Sociology
Dist - LANDMK **Prod** - LANDMK 1986

No Place to Hide 58 MIN
BETA / VHS / U-matic
(H C A G)
$75.00
Investigates issues dealing with battered wives. Examines situations where women have been abused physically, sexually, or emotionally. Interveiws husbands who batter their wives and children who are exposed to these violent conflicts. Doctors and other professionals explain treatments and social remedies that are available to batterers and their victims.
Sociology
Dist - CTV **Prod** - GLNWAR 1985

No Place to Live 50 MIN
U-matic / 16mm
Assignment Maclear Series
Color; Mono (J H C A)
$500.00 film, $350.00 video, $50.00 rental
Describes the cities of Venice, New York, and Elliot Lake as different types of urban decay. Discusses the problem and possible solutions relating to the individual cases involved.
Sociology
Dist - CTV **Prod** - CTV 1977

No Place to Live 18 MIN
U-matic / BETA / VHS
(A G)
$100.00
Documents that over a million Canadians cannot find or afford a decent place to live. The government has established a new housing policy that will increase the number of homes available. The program depends on provincial funding and the provincial governments are slow to sign up for this project.
Sociology
Dist - CTV **Prod** - CTV 1986

No Points for Second Place 28 MIN
U-matic / 16mm
Color
Explores the history of fighter aircraft from World War I to the F - 14.
Civics and Political Systems; History - United States
Dist - WSTGLC **Prod** - WSTGLC

No Prenez Pas De Risques 14 MIN
U-matic / VHS / 16mm
Color (A) (FRENCH)
A French - language version of the motion picture Don't Take Chances. Shows common factory accidents. Illustrates efforts made by management to prevent accidents, but warns they will still occur if workers are thoughtless.
Business and Economics; Foreign Language; Health and Safety
Dist - IFB **Prod** - IAPA 1964

No problem 13 MIN
16mm / VHS
Color (H C G)
$300.00, $99.00 purchase, $50.00 rental
Offers a sophisticated tale of an anxious bachelor looking for a meaningful relationship aimed at mature audiences. Reveals that the hero vacillates between two inner selves - the naked, free spirit and the censorious cautious self - and has a tough time approaching the woman of his dreams. But, balding, paunchy, tired of living alone in his small apartment with his scruffy dog, he makes the leap. Produced by Craig Welch. Animated.
Guidance and Counseling; Sociology
Dist - FLMLIB **Prod** - NFBC 1993

No punching Judy 30 MIN
VHS
Color (K P I)
$325.00 purchase _ #2995
Teaches children nonviolent ways of resolving conflict. Discusses domestic violence and gender - role stereotyping which may reinforce the acceptance of domestic violence. Offers ways of handling violence in the home. Shows how to express negative as well as positive feelings without resorting to violence. Stresses the unique value of each human being and the right of each human being to live violence - free.
Guidance and Counseling; Psychology; Social Science; Sociology
Dist - ATRISK **Prod** - COMADV 1994

No Questions Asked 19 MIN
U-matic / VHS / 16mm
Color
Deals with unsafe trenches in the building industry. Concentrates on one accident and the events leading up to it. Shows procedures for accident investigations.
Health and Safety; Industrial and Technical Education
Dist - IFB **Prod** - NFBTE

No Real Pathology 21 MIN
16mm
B&W (PRO)
Describes the techniques in differential diagnosis to determine whether underlying cause is depression or anxiety in patients without symptom - related pathology.
Health and Safety; Psychology
Dist - UPJOHN **Prod** - UPJOHN 1962

No regrets for our youth 110 MIN
Videodisc / VHS
B&W (G) (JAPANESE WITH ENGLISH SUBTITLES)
$35.95, $49.95 purchase _ #CVC1035, #ID6897CS
Presents a feminist saga by Akira Kurosawa.
Fine Arts; Sociology
Dist - CHTSUI

No Respecter of Persons 17 MIN
16mm
Book of Acts Series
Color; B&W (J H T R)
Presents the story of Peter who preaches Christ to the house of Cornelius. Shows the universality of the Gospel and its application to all people regardless of race and nationality.
History - World; Religion and Philosophy
Dist - FAMF **Prod** - BROADM 1957

No rewind 23 MIN
VHS
Color (J H)
$150.00 purchase, $85.00 rental
Teaches safe sex attitudes and practices to teenagers to protect them from HIV infection. Uses a multicultural group of teenagers, original music and graphics to discuss abstinence, peer education, condom use, support groups, the connection of drinking and sex, apprehension about being tested and parental support.
Health and Safety; Psychology; Sociology
Dist - NXPRO **Prod** - NXPRO 1992

No rewind - teenagers speak out on HIV and AIDS awareness 22 MIN
VHS
Color (J H C)
$150.00 purchase _ #BO71 - V8
The HIV positive teenagers who speak out in No Rewind inform their peers that teens are the fastest growing group at risk for HIV and AIDS. Provides, through storytelling, role plays, and condom demonstrations, essential information on HIV transmission; the influence of drugs and alcohol on sexual behavior; abstinence; condoms; and HIV testing. Provides peer educators as role models to break through the denial myth - 'it can't happen to me' - and communicate about responsible attitudes.
Guidance and Counseling; Health and Safety; Sociology
Dist - ETRASS **Prod** - ETRASS

No Room at the Inn 13 MIN
16mm / U-matic / VHS
Simple Gifts Series
Color (I)
Presents R O Blechman's animated retelling of the traditional Nativity story.
Literature and Drama; Religion and Philosophy; Social Science
Dist - TIMLIF **Prod** - WNETTV

No Room at the Table 29 MIN
VHS / 16mm
Color (G)
$55.00 rental _ #NRAT - 000
Looks at the environmental fall - out of the good life in California. Shows how the American Dream has turned into a nightmare of consumption, waste and destruction of its natural resources.
Business and Economics; Geography - United States; Sociology
Dist - PBS **Prod** - KOCETV

No Room for Error 18 MIN
16mm / U-matic / VHS
Color (I J H)
Stresses safety awareness for students in school chemistry lab. Former teacher who became a human torch urges proper care.
Health and Safety; Science
Dist - BCNFL **Prod** - BORTF 1983

No room for wilderness 26 MIN
VHS
Color (G)
$350.00 purchase, $15.00 rental
Features Prof Robert C Stebbins who uses examples from Africa to demonstrate the workings of a natural ecology and the devastating impacts of technology and exploding population on that environment. Includes a soundtrack of indigenous African music and bird and animal sounds.
Geography - World; Science - Natural; Social Science; Sociology
Dist - CMSMS **Prod** - SIERRA 1968

No room in the marketplace - the healthcare of the poor 20 MIN
U-matic / VHS
Color (R G)
$75.00 purchase, $50.00 rental _ #435, #436, #434
Examines the issue of providing healthcare to the poor. Focuses on recommendations proposed by the Catholic Health Assocation Task Force on Healthcare of the Poor.
Health and Safety; Religion and Philosophy; Sociology
Dist - CATHHA **Prod** - CATHHA 1987

No room to roam 24 MIN
16mm / VHS
Color (J H C G)
$495.00, $250.00 purchase, $50.00 rental
Documents the buffalo hunt near Yellowstone National Park in Montana in which buffalo herds straying outside the park's boundaries are allowed to be hunted, despite protest and obstruction by animal rights activists. Uses the buffalo as a metaphor to illustrate how land available for wildlife is rapidly disappearing as human expansion increases into their habitat, destroyed by developers. Produced by Stuart Perkin.
Fine Arts; Geography - United States; Physical Education and Recreation; Science - Natural; Sociology
Dist - CANCIN

No Rouz 20 MIN
16mm
Color
Depicts the most important of Iranian festivals, No Rouz, the Iranian New Year, which derives from the ancient Persian festival of spring. Explains the significance of each ritual of the two week festival. Illustrates the preparation of special foods and portrays the fire jumping of Scharharshanbe Suri.
Religion and Philosophy
Dist - FRAF **Prod** - FRAF

No Sad Songs 10 MIN
16mm
Color
LC 80-701450
Depicts four people whose lives were improved as a result of the Cummins Engine Company charity fund.
Sociology
Dist - RICHMA **Prod** - RICHMA 1979

No Sad Songs for Me 88 MIN
16mm
B&W
Stars Margaret Sullivan as a dying woman who cheerfully carries on with her everyday routines, as well as choosing her husband's next wife,.
Fine Arts
Dist - KITPAR **Prod** - CPC 1950

No Sale 20 MIN
U-matic
Calling Captain Consumer Series
Color (P I J)
Shows a child from a well to do family who misuses his parent's charge account.
Business and Economics; Home Economics
Dist - TVOTAR **Prod** - TVOTAR 1985

No second chance 14 MIN
U-matic / BETA / 16mm / VHS
Color (J H G)
$325.00, $260.00 purchase _ #JR - 4952M
Dramatizes the tragic story of a popular 17 - year - old who now faces life as a paraplegic because he insisted that he could drive after drinking too much at a party. Produced by Gordon Kerckoff Productions, Inc.
Guidance and Counseling; Health and Safety; Industrial and Technical Education; Psychology; Sociology
Dist - CORF

No second chance 30 MIN
VHS
Color (J H)
$29.95 purchase _ #JF4004V
Meets AIDS patients and their families who describe the terrible consequences of AIDS to themselves and their loved ones. Interviews medical experts and health educators. Explains what AIDS is and how it is contracted, the difficulties in recognizing an AIDS carrier and the risks associated with sexual behavior.
Health and Safety
Dist - CAMV

No 7 - the Stars Appear - Pt 1 30 MIN
BETA / VHS / U-matic
American Movies - the First 30 Years Series
Color; B&W; Mono (C A)
Discusses the careers and performances of early film stars such as Mary Miles Minter, Florence Lawrence, Sarah Bernhardt, Geraldine Farrar, Theda Bara , Lillian Gish, and Mary Pickford.
Fine Arts
Dist - UIOWA **Prod** - UIOWA 1984

No Signature, no Shot - is Immunization Important 15 MIN
U-matic
(A)
Conveys the importance of immunization for selected communicable diseases. Co - produced by Alberta Social Services and Community Health and the Sturgeon Health Unit.
Health and Safety
Dist - ACCESS **Prod** - ACCESS 1983

No Simple Road 18 MIN
U-matic
Color (P)
LC 84-706147
Shows handicapped children participating in outdoor sports and activities. Helps youngsters to accept their disabilities, gain self confidence and react positively to their able - bodied peers.
Physical Education and Recreation; Psychology
Dist - CRYSP **Prod** - LENATK

No, Sir, Orison 3 MIN
16mm
Color (C)
$370.00
Experimental film by George Owen (aka Owen Land).
Fine Arts
Dist - AFA **Prod** - AFA 1975

No 6 - the First Film Makers - Pt 3 30 MIN
BETA / VHS / U-matic
American Movies - the First 30 Years Series
Color; B&W; Mono (C A)
Explores the work and influence of famous film directors from 1910 to 1930 such as Thomas Ince, William S Hart, Erich Von Stroheim, Cecil B DeMille and King Vidor.
Fine Arts
Dist - UIOWA **Prod** - UIOWA 1984

No Small Change - the Story of the Eaton's Strike 50 MIN
VHS
Color (C)
$350.00 purchase, $65.00, $80.00 rental
Documents the 1984 Toronto Eaton's Strike. Examines organizing a strike and issues of exploiting women in the workplace. Captures the emotions and the transformation of those who went through the strike. Produced by Emma Productions.
Business and Economics; Civics and Political Systems; Fine Arts; Sociology
Dist - WMENIF

No Smoking, Please
VHS / U-matic
Color
Uses humor to announce that no smoking is allowed. Presents a boss forbidding smoking in an extreme and explosive manner.
Business and Economics; Fine Arts; Health and Safety; Literature and Drama; Psychology
Dist - MEETS **Prod** - BBB

No Snow 14 MIN
16mm
B&W
LC 79-700253
Tells how a young man returns from college to his hometown, reunites with an old buddy, and is forced to confront the values he grew up with.
Fine Arts
Dist - JEFRES **Prod** - JEFRES 1978

No spare parts 25 MIN
VHS / 16mm
Nature of things series
Color (G)
Discusses technology appropriate for the African nation of Ghana. Part of the CBC series The Nature of Things.
Geography - World; Social Science; Sociology
Dist - ASTRSK **Prod** - ASTRSK 1990

No strain, no pain - seniors 27 MIN
VHS
Color (G)
$49.95 purchase
Explains the Mensendieck system developed in Europe nearly 100 years ago for correcting poor posture and faulty body mechanics. Features Karen Perlroth, graduate of the Mensendieck Institute of Amsterdam, who explains the anatomy of the lower back and describes correct posture and breathing techniques.
Health and Safety; Physical Education and Recreation; Science - Natural
Dist - BAXMED

No Strings on You 15 MIN
VHS / U-matic
All about You Series
Color (P)
Uses a dancing marionette clown to show the muscles of the human body. Considers muscles as bands that hold the framework of the body together and make movement possible. Explains why exercise is important.
Physical Education and Recreation; Science - Natural
Dist - AITECH **Prod** - NITC 1975

No Substitute for Experience - Pt 1 30 MIN
VHS
Natural History in the Classroom Series
Color (I)
$149.00 series purchase _ #899 - 9001
Shows how to use locally collected materials to pique students' curiosity and enliven the classroom experience. Presents collecting insects, building terrariums, using attractants and reassembling skeletons and other creative activities for teacher training and classroom use. Features instructor Rudy Mancke. Part 1 of three parts explains how to find appropriate objects for classroom use, incorporate them into lessons and encourage student participation. Available only as part of the series.
Agriculture; Education; Mathematics; Science; Science - Natural; Science - Physical
Dist - FI **Prod** - SCETV 1989

No Sugar Coating 17 MIN
16mm
Color
LC 79-701181
Follows a medical social worker, who is diabetic, as he helps young people understand and accept the illness of diabetes.
Health and Safety; Psychology
Dist - ADAS **Prod** - ADAS 1979

No surrender 100 MIN
35mm / 16mm
Color (G)
$250.00, $300.00 rental
Portrays the defiant act of an exiting nightclub manager who schedules a group of aging IRA Catholics as well as an organization of elderly Protestants to attend the club's New Year's Eve celebration. Offers a night of hilarious pandemonium which ends on a chilling note of reality. Features a cameo by Elvis Costello. Directed by Peter Smith.
Fine Arts; Religion and Philosophy; Sociology
Dist - KINOIC

No Sweat 25 MIN
U-matic
Not Another Science Show Series
Color (H C)
Explains how the human body works and how to take care of it. Shows the basics of fitness, the importance of pacing exercise routines and the target heart rate.
Physical Education and Recreation; Science
Dist - TVOTAR **Prod** - TVOTAR 1986

No sweat sewing projects series
Demonstrates with easy-to-understand instructions how to make a child's garment from a recycled adult's sweat shirt.
Banana peel 20 MIN
Kitten and mittens 16 MIN
No sweat sewing projects series
Pocket sweat suit 16 MIN
Dist - CAMV

No Swimming 16 MIN
16mm
B&W
Explores 'FREEDOM,' made at a beach resort in the dead of winter. Examines freedom from meaningless rules, and freedom to explore and to play.
Physical Education and Recreation; Sociology
Dist - UPENN **Prod** - UPENN 1965

No Talking 6 MIN
U-matic / VHS / 16mm
Golden Book Storytime Series
Color (P)
Introduces Lester, who can't talk but still manages to buy a birthday present for his mother.
Literature and Drama
Dist - CORF **Prod** - CORF 1977

No Tears for Kelsey 28 MIN
U-matic / VHS / 16mm
Color (H C A)
LC 73-705431
A dramatization about a hardened but successful man and his confrontations with his hippie daughter who ran away from home and rejected her father's materialistic values.
Fine Arts; Guidance and Counseling; Psychology; Sociology
Dist - MEDIAG **Prod** - PAULST 1969

No Tears for Kelsey 28 MIN
U-matic / VHS / 16mm
Insight Series
Color (H C A) (SPANISH)
LC 73-705431
A dramatization about a hardened but successful man and his confrontations with his hippie daughter who ran away from home and rejected her father's materialistic values.
Foreign Language; Guidance and Counseling; Psychology; Religion and Philosophy; Sociology
Dist - PAULST **Prod** - PAULST 1969

No Tears for Rachel 27 MIN
U-matic / VHS / 16mm
Color (J)
LC 74-702593
Explains and illustrates how the law functions and how friends and family react when a woman has been raped. Portrays one victim who discusses the difficulties she experienced when she told her friends that she had been raped and her psychiatrist who explains the importance of their reactions and the stigma associated with being raped.
Guidance and Counseling; Psychology; Sociology
Dist - IU **Prod** - EDUCBC 1974

No 10 - the Comedians - Pt 2 30 MIN
BETA / VHS / U-matic
American Movies - the First 30 Years Series
Color; B&W; Mono (C A)
Studies the life and career of Charlie Chaplin, total film author, from his impoverished childhood in London and his arrival in America, to his meteoric rise as a film star, writer, director and finally owner of United Artists.
Fine Arts
Dist - UIOWA **Prod** - UIOWA 1984

No Tenia Por Que Suceder 13 MIN
U-matic / VHS / 16mm
B&W (H A) (SPANISH)
A Spanish - language version of the motion picture It Didn't Have To Happen. Illustrates how the careless worker who scorns safety devices on modern machinery endangers not only his life but also the lives of fellow workers.
Business and Economics; Foreign Language; Health and Safety
Dist - IFB **Prod** - CRAF 1954

No thanks, I'm driving 16 MIN
16mm / VHS / BETA / U-matic
Color; PAL (G)
PdS125, PdS133 purchase
Features pilots and racers explaining their guidelines for the use of alcohol. Uses animated sequences that follow the path of alcohol in the bloodstream. Accident shots reinforce the fatal statistics for intoxicated drivers.
Health and Safety; Sociology
Dist - EDPAT

No thanks, just looking 24 MIN
VHS
Color (A PRO)
$550.00 purchase, $125.00 rental
Provides sales training through a series of retail vignettes, including clothing, shoes, jewelry, and more.
Business and Economics; Psychology; Social Science
Dist - VLEARN
CREMED

No Thanksgiving for Red 12 MIN
16mm
B&W (G)
$30.00 rental
Expresses a dark, brutally comic story of a woman who wanders the streets, trying to remember her mother's face. Employs jagged cutting and imagery. Music by Mike Land and Bryan Simmons.
Fine Arts
Dist - CANCIN **Prod** - EDEM 1982

No thanks...just looking 20 MIN
U-matic / 35mm strip / 16mm / BETA
Color (A)
#FC44
Presents an extensively researched program for the prevention of shoplifting. Encourages employees to practice courteous customer service, while meeting the demanding challenge of discouraging and preventing theft.
Sociology
Dist - CONPRO **Prod** - CONPRO

No - the positive answer 60 MIN
VHS
Color (J H R)
$79.99 purchase, $20.00 rental _ #35 - 89300 - 533
Features Christian author Josh McDowell in four - part discussion of teenage sexuality. Considers reasons for waiting until marriage, value influences and choices, as well as how to establish dating standards. Includes leader's guide and cassette with contemporary Christian music.
Health and Safety; Religion and Philosophy
Dist - APH **Prod** - WORD

No 3 - the First Tycoons - Pt 2 30 MIN
U-matic / BETA / VHS
American Movies - the First 30 Years Series
Color; B&W; Mono (C A)
Examines the careers of Adolph Zukor and Jesse Lasky, partners in the silent film production company Famous Players and Lasky which later became Paramount Pictures. Includes the fire in Zukor's New York studio, his first star, Mary Pickford, Lasky's theatrical background and first film, and the battle to buy and build movie theaters in the nation.

Fine Arts
Dist - UIOWA **Prod** - UIOWA 1984

No time soon - increasing male responsibility 16 MIN
16mm / VHS
Color (I J H)
$330.00, $275.00 purchase
Introduces positive, responsible male role models who have found alternatives to the pressures of teenage fatherhood. Discusses sex, condoms, relationships and school. Offers strategies for avoiding unplanned fatherhood. Stresses the importance of taking responsibility for birth control.
Guidance and Counseling; Health and Safety; Psychology; Sociology
Dist - SELMED

No time to stop - Women immigrants 29 MIN
VHS
Color (G)
$60.00 rental, $250.00 purchase
Looks at three women of color from Hong Kong, Ghana and Jamaica who have immigrated to Canada and are struggling to make a dignified life for themselves, despite the odds against them. Illuminates the obstacles they face including racial and sexual discrimination; lack of recognition for their skills and qualifications; and inadequate access to social services. Also reveals their wit and vision that inspires them to continue moving forward in pursuit of their dreams. Produced by Helene Klodawsky.
Fine Arts; Sociology
Dist - WMEN

No time to waste 30 MIN
VHS
Color (G)
$19.95 purchase
Looks at the strength and diversity of the grassroots movement against toxic waste. Examines the effects of toxic waste sites on communities throughout the American West, including the Navajo reservation in Dilcon, Arizona. Reflects upon the anger and frustration of citizens throughout the country who are plagued with toxics - related health problems and are unable to obtain adequate state or federal assistance.
Geography - United States; Health and Safety; History - United States; Science - Natural; Sociology
Dist - GRNPCE **Prod** - GRNPCE 1989

No Time to Waste 28 MIN
VHS / 16mm
Color (C PRO)
$275.00 purchase, $60.00 rental _ #8659S, #8659V
Discusses threat to patients and employees of hazardous waste, describing components of a waste management system that complies with government regulations and accreditation standards. Emphasizes open communication, commitment, and compliance. Includes study guide.
Health and Safety
Dist - AJN **Prod** - HOSSN 1990

No Trump Bidding and Play 30 MIN
VHS / U-matic
Play Bridge Series
Color (A)
Physical Education and Recreation
Dist - KYTV **Prod** - KYTV 1983

No Trump Bids and Responses 30 MIN
U-matic / VHS
Bridge Basics Series
Color (A)
Physical Education and Recreation
Dist - KYTV **Prod** - KYTV 1982

No Two Alike 19 MIN
U-matic / VHS / 16mm
Color (C A)
LC 83-700381
Examines how to meet the educational needs of visually handicapped students.
Education; Guidance and Counseling; Psychology
Dist - PHENIX **Prod** - AFB 1981

No Two Alike 15 MIN
U-matic / VHS
All about You Series
Color (P)
Explains that each person is a unique individual.
Guidance and Counseling
Dist - AITECH **Prod** - WGBHTV 1975

No two alike 19 MIN
VHS
Color (G S T)
$79.95 purchase
Explains how classroom teachers use a variety of support services and special or adaptive equipment to create learning environments for mainstreamed visually impaired students. Focuses on a team approach to individualized educational programs involving parents, teachers, blindness and low vision professionals, and the students themselves.
Education; Guidance and Counseling
Dist - AFB **Prod** - AFB

No Two Alike - Individual Differences and Psychological Testing 29 MIN
16mm / U-matic / VHS
Focus on Behavior Series
B&W (H C A)
Explores some of the ways in which psychologists are developing new testing methods for measuring and increasing human capabilities. Demonstrates the development of tests for choosing pilots in World War II.
Psychology
Dist - IU **Prod** - NET 1963

No Two of these Kids are Alike 28 MIN
16mm
League School for Seriously Disturbed Children Series
Color
LC 75-702412
Observes the day - to - day routine of the League School for seriously disturbed children. Shows how teachers in special education, supported by a staff of full - time clinicians, seek to provide as normal a schooling as possible for these withdrawn and often unmanageable children.
Education; Psychology
Dist - USNAC **Prod** - USBEH 1973

No 2 - the First Tycoons - Pt 1 30 MIN
BETA / VHS / U-matic
American Movies - the First 30 Years Series
Color; B&W; Mono (C A)
Discusses the careers of the first Americans to produce movies for entertainment - Thomas Edison, who tried to create a monopoly through his companies, Biograph, Essanay, Vitagraph, Carl Laemmle, who campaigned against the trust, and Adolph Zukor who circumvented it.
Fine Arts
Dist - UIOWA **Prod** - UIOWA 1984

No Vietnamese Ever Called Me Nigger 68 MIN
U-matic / VHS / 16mm
Color
Interviews Harlem residents and Black Vietnam veterans as they speak out against the war in Vietnam, linking it to domestic racial crisis.
History - United States; Sociology
Dist - CNEMAG **Prod** - AMDOC

No - Wax Floors 30 MIN
BETA / VHS
This Old House, Pt 2 - Suburban '50s Series
Color
Gives pointers on laying a no - wax floor.
Industrial and Technical Education; Sociology
Dist - CORF **Prod** - WGBHTV

No Way to Give it Away 10 MIN
U-matic
Calling Captain Consumer Series
Color (P I J)
Shows ten year olds who take part in an ad agency's test to choose which cereal box giveaway they prefer.
Business and Economics; Home Economics
Dist - TVOTAR **Prod** - TVOTAR 1985

No Wreath and no Trumpet 30 MIN
16mm
B&W
Tells the story of Emma Lazarus, the American Jewish poetess, whose verses are inscribed on the base of the Statue of Liberty. (Kinescope).
Civics and Political Systems; Literature and Drama; Religion and Philosophy
Dist - NAAJS **Prod** - JTS 1961

No5 reversal 10 MIN
16mm
B&W (G)
$20.00 rental
Begins with a scene of two women in bed talking to set up strong expectations of a narrative structure. Disrupts chronological sequence to employ 'horizontal montage' technique. Produced by Josephine Massarella.
Fine Arts
Dist - CANCIN

Noa at seventeen 86 MIN
VHS
Color (G) (HEBREW WITH ENGLISH SUBTITLES)
$79.95 purchase _ #535
Portrays a 17 - year - old, Noa, in 1951, who must decide whether she should finish high school or follow her youth movment friends to kibbutz. Stars Dalia Shimko, Idit Zur and Shmuel Shilo. Directed by Isaac Yeshurun.
Fine Arts; History - World; Literature and Drama; Sociology
Dist - ERGOM **Prod** - ERGOM 1982

Noah 20 MIN
16mm
Fant Anthology of AMESLAN Literature Series
Color (S R) (AMERICAN SIGN)
LC 74-701458
Shows the Noah story from Genesis told by Mr Louie J Fant in AMESLAN (American Sign Language.).
Guidance and Counseling; Literature and Drama
Dist - JOYCE **Prod** - JOYCE 1973

Noah of the North 29 MIN
16mm
Al Oeming - Man of the North Series
Color
LC 77-702871
Traces Al Oeming's interest in wildlife since the age of six and recaptures the mood and locations of his boyhood.
Biography; Geography - World; Science - Natural
Dist - NIELSE **Prod** - NIELSE 1977

Noah's Animals 27 MIN
U-matic / VHS / 16mm
Color (P)
Presents the story of Noah and the flood from the animal's viewpoint.
Literature and Drama; Religion and Philosophy
Dist - LUF **Prod** - LUF 1979

Noah's animals 25 MIN
VHS
Color (K P I R)
$10.00 rental _ #36 - 81 - 2506
Presents an account of the animals in Noah's ark. Includes such animal characters as the mutinous crocodile and the carefree polar bear.
Literature and Drama; Religion and Philosophy
Dist - APH **Prod** - FAMOS

Noah's Ark 24 MIN
16mm / U-matic / VHS
Famous Adventures of Mr Magoo Series
Color (P I J)
LC 79-701781
Presents an animated adaptation of the story of Noah and his ark with cartoon character Mr Magoo in the role of Noah.
Fine Arts
Dist - MCFI **Prod** - UPAPOA 1969

Noah's Ark
VHS / 16mm
Color (K)
$14.44 purchase _ #22446
Presents James Earl Jones narrating an animated version of Noah's Ark.
Fine Arts; Literature and Drama
Dist - EDUCRT **Prod** - HITOP

Noah's ark 30 MIN
VHS
Great Bible stories series
Color (P I R)
$15.95 purchase, $10.00 rental _ #35 - 8280 - 8936
Tells the Old Testament story of Noah and the ark.
Literature and Drama; Religion and Philosophy
Dist - APH

Noah's ark 30 MIN
VHS
Greatest adventure series
Color (P I R)
$14.95 purchase _ #35 - 830003 - 1518
Uses animation format to present the Biblical story of Noah's ark. Features the voice of Lorne Greene as Noah.
Literature and Drama; Religion and Philosophy
Dist - APH **Prod** - HANBAR

Noah's Ark - Multiplying with Fractions 9 MIN
U-matic
Color (P)
Tells how Noah's animals figure out how to diagram an area which is 1/4 mile wide and 1/2 mile long.
Mathematics
Dist - GA **Prod** - DAVFMS

Noah's big adventure 25 MIN
VHS
Greatest stories ever told series
Color (K P I R)
$19.95 purchase, $10.00 rental _ #35 - 84 - 2020
Uses an animated format to present the Biblical account of Noah and the great flood.
Literature and Drama; Religion and Philosophy
Dist - APH **Prod** - ANDERK

Noah's Park 27 MIN
U-matic / VHS / 16mm
Color (I)
LC 76-702511
Presents an adventure film about Israel's efforts to save and proliferate the Biblical animals that lived before the flood in Noah's time.
Geography - World; Science - Natural
Dist - PHENIX **Prod** - PHENIX 1976

Noam Chomsky - Parts I and II 30 MIN
VHS
World Of Ideas With Bill Moyers - Seaon I - series
Color (G)
$39.95 purchase _ #BMWI - 139D
Interviews Noam Chomsky, a political critic who was one of the first to speak out against the Vietnam War. Describes Chomsky's beliefs that democracy is in decline and his admiration for the common man. Hosted by Bill Moyers.
Civics and Political Systems; History - United States
Dist - PBS

Nobel jubilee concert - Kiri Te Kanawa and Sir Georg Solti 86 MIN
VHS
Color (G)
$24.95 purchase_#1340
Presents a concert including works by Mozart and Brahms' First Symphony. Features vocalist Dame Kiri Te Kanawa singing five Mozart concert arias, with George Solti conducting the Royal Stockholm Philharmonic Orchestra.
Fine Arts
Dist - KULTUR

Nobel prize series - biology
Barbara McClintock - pioneer of modern genetics 17 MIN
Michael Brown and Joseph Goldstein - unlocking the secrets of cholesterol 15 MIN
Susumu Tonegawa - the key to the immune system 17 MIN
Dist - SUNCOM

Nobel prize series - chemistry and physics
Dudley Herschbach - chemical reactions atom by atom 14 MIN
Georg Bednorz - exploring superconductivity 15 MIN
Dist - SUNCOM

Nobel prize series - literature
Joseph Brodsky - poet between empires 20 MIN
William Golding - the man and his myths 17 MIN
Wole Soyinka - a voice of Africa 16 MIN
Dist - SUNCOM

Nobel prize series - social studies
Desmond Tutu - apartheid in South Africa 21 MIN
Elie Wiesel - witness to the Holocaust 21 MIN
International physicians for the prevention of nuclear war 21 MIN
Dist - SUNCOM

Nobel prize series
Sheldon Glashow - unifying forces 16 MIN
Dist - SUNCOM

Nobel Prizewinners Series
Ernest Hemingway - Rough Diamond 30 MIN
Martin Luther King Jr - the Assassin Years 26 MIN
Dist - CORF

A Noble Venture 28 MIN
16mm
Color
Describes the vital area of conservation work, the protection and propagation of exotic game. Shows that as exotic game conservation programs spread throughout the United States, brood stock can then be provided for many such endangered species all over the world.
Science - Natural
Dist - GM **Prod** - CMD

Noblesse Oblige 25 MIN
16mm
Color; Silent (C)
$850.00
Experimental film by Warren Sonbert.
Fine Arts
Dist - AFA **Prod** - AFA 1981

Nobody but yourself series
Do not staple, bend or fold 20 MIN
Dist - GPN

Nobody Coddled Bobby 14 MIN
16mm / U-matic / VHS
Color (H C A)
LC 79-700562
Presents the story of the suicide of a teenage delinquent sentenced to a state correctional institute in order to focus on prison life and prison's rehabilitative value. Originally shown on the CBS television program 60 Minutes.
Sociology
Dist - CORF **Prod** - CBSTV 1979

Nobody Ever Died of Old Age 61 MIN
16mm
Color (H C A)
LC 76-700394
Uses both serious and humorous character studies to show what it is like to grow old in the United States in the 1970s. Dramatizes the lives of a number of resourcefully independent senior citizens who are struggling to survive in a youth - oriented society.
Psychology; Sociology
Dist - FI **Prod** - HSSETT 1977

Nobody Ever Died of Old Age, Pt 1 30 MIN
16mm
Color (H C A)
LC 76-700394
Uses both serious and humorous character studies to show what it is like to grow old in the United States. Dramatizes the lives of a number of resourcefully independent senior citizens who are struggling to survive in a youth - oriented society.
Sociology
Dist - FI **Prod** - HSSETT 1977

Nobody Ever Died of Old Age, Pt 2 31 MIN
16mm
Color (H C A)
LC 76-700394
Uses both serious and humorous character studies to show what it is like to grow old in the United States. Dramatizes the lives of a number of resourcefully independent senior citizens who are struggling to survive in a youth - oriented society.
Sociology
Dist - FI **Prod** - HSSETT 1977

Nobody Listens - Drop - Out Prevention 48 MIN
VHS
Color (I)
$189.00 purchase
Presents a true portrayal of one teen's struggle with life after dropping out of school. Shows the pain and frustration Jimmy endures after leaving school, the dead - end jobs, too much free time and no real purpose in life. Stars Marva Hicks and Nick Sadler.
Business and Economics; Guidance and Counseling; Psychology; Sociology
Dist - MEDIAI **Prod** - MEDIAI

Nobody Lives Here 27 MIN
U-matic / VHS
Color
Presents interviews with inmates at Washington State Penitentiary. Emphasizes the sense of confinement and the desire to escape mentally or physically.
Psychology; Sociology
Dist - MEDIPR **Prod** - MEDIPR 1979

Nobody Loves a Rich Uncle 27 MIN
U-matic / VHS / 16mm
Insight Series
B&W (J)
LC 72-702004
Shows that affluent nations are obligated to assist underdeveloped countries.
Business and Economics; Civics and Political Systems; Social Science
Dist - PAULST **Prod** - PAULST 1972

Nobody picks on me
VHS
Good kids - karate kids series
Color (G)
$29.95 purchase _ #PNT012
Presents the first of three videos that teach self - defense, self - confidence, home safety, awareness, fitness, respect for elders, controls, manners and more. Stars 12 - year - old karate phenomenon Kim Murray, Jr.
Physical Education and Recreation; Psychology
Dist - SIV

Nobody Saw it Coming 60 MIN
VHS / U-matic
Sixty Minutes on Business Series
Color (G)
Business and Economics
Dist - VPHI **Prod** - VPHI 1984

Nobody Saw it Coming (Douglas Fraser, UAW)
VHS / U-matic
Sixty Minutes on Business Series
Color
Part of a series of ten segments selected from the realities of the business world and chosen from key '60 Minutes' telecasts to provide insight into vital issues affecting business today. Includes sourcebook.
Business and Economics; Psychology
Dist - CBSFOX **Prod** - CBSFOX

Nobody tells me what to do - 2 24 MIN
U-matic / 16mm / VHS
Peer pressure series
Color (J H)
$530.00, $400.00, $370.00 _ #A975
Portrays Gary who is on the varsity baseball team and plays saxophone with the school band. Reveals that he can't understand why girls hang all over tough guys like Zack Thornton. Gary decides to hang out with Zack and his gang, but when their fun turns to theft and vandalism, Gary sees Zack for the loser he is. Even the girls he admired shoplift for kicks. Gary decides that nobody is going to tell him what to do, especially Zack. Part of a two - part series on peer pressure.
Guidance and Counseling; Psychology; Sociology
Dist - BARR **Prod** - SAIF 1984

Nobody told me 22 MIN
16mm / VHS / BETA / U-matic
Color; PAL (G)
PdS130, PdS138 purchase
Deals with general safety in the home including fires and falls. Shows how accidents happen and how to avoid them. Includes problems unique to families with young children or old people. Narrated by a doctor.
Health and Safety
Dist - EDPAT

Nobody Took the Time 26 MIN
U-matic / VHS / 16mm
B&W (T)
LC 73-701157
Depicts ghetto children handicapped with learning disabilities and most often labeled mentally retarded. Demonstrates that basic trust in himself and others is their first need. Shows how highly structured classroom and playground techniques result in an understanding of order and development of language.
Education; Psychology; Sociology
Dist - AIMS **Prod** - AIMS 1973

Nobody Treats Me Different 8 MIN
16mm / U-matic / VHS
Zoom Series
Color (I J H C)
LC 78-700143
Presents a young man with cerebral palsy discussing his life, his handicap, his prospects and what he feels people should know about those with disabilities.
Psychology
Dist - FI **Prod** - WGBH 1977

Nobody Waved Good - by 80MIN
16mm / U-matic / VHS
B&W (J H C)
LC FIA65-1851
Tells the story of a delinquent boy who rejects the middle class conventions, and shows his gradual deterioration through conflicts at school, and with his parents and girl friend. Stars Peter Kastner.
Guidance and Counseling; Psychology; Sociology
Dist - FI **Prod** - NFBC 1964

Nobody Waved Good - by, Pt 1 26 MIN
U-matic / VHS / 16mm
B&W (J H C)
LC FIA65-1851
Tells the story of a delinquent boy who rejects the middle class conventions, and shows his gradual deterioration through conflicts at school and with his parents and girl friend. Stars Peter Kastner.
Psychology
Dist - FI **Prod** - NFBC 1964

Nobody Waved Good - by, Pt 2 27 MIN
U-matic / VHS / 16mm
B&W (J H C)
LC FIA65-1851
Tells the story of a delinquent boy who rejects the middle class conventions, and shows his gradual deterioration through conflicts at school and with his parents and girl friend. Stars Peter Kastner.
Psychology
Dist - FI **Prod** - NFBC 1964

Nobody Waved Good - by, Pt 3 27 MIN
U-matic / VHS / 16mm
B&W (J H C)
LC FIA65-1851
Tells the story of a delinquent boy who rejects the middle class conventions, and shows his gradual deterioration through conflicts at school and with his parents and girl friend. Stars Peter Kastner.
Psychology
Dist - FI **Prod** - NFBC 1964

Nobody's Children - Foster Care in America 48 MIN
VHS / U-matic
Color
$455.00 purchase
Sociology
Dist - ABCLR **Prod** - ABCLR 1979

Nobody's Fault 30 MIN
U-matic
Color (I J)
Shows that insensitivity and anger are not the way to deal with problems.
Psychology; Sociology
Dist - TVOTAR **Prod** - TVOTAR 1986

Nobody's Fault 19 MIN
16mm / U-matic / VHS
Color
Shows a succession of seemingly minor incidents in a manufacturing plant which add up to a major accident and fire.
Business and Economics; Health and Safety
Dist - IFB **Prod** - MILLBK

Nobody's Home 20 MIN
VHS / 16mm
Color (I)
LC 90713245
Demonstrates how physical and emotional neglect can be forms of child abuse.
Health and Safety; Sociology
Dist - ALTSUL

Nobody's immune 29 MIN
U-matic / 16mm / VHS
Color (G A)
$305.00, $110.00, $75.00 purchase _ #TCA16421, #TCA16422, #TCA16423
Presents dramatic vignettes in which individual people with AIDS describe how they contracted the disease and its effect on themselves and their families. Covers the ways in which HIV transmission can be prevented. Includes leader's guide.
Health and Safety
Dist - USNAC **Prod** - WRAMC 1986

Nobody's Perfect
16mm
Color
LC 80-701604
Shows a scientist whose careless actions in the laboratory continually jeopardize the work and safety of his colleagues and himself in order to reinforce conscientious attitudes towards safety.
Health and Safety; Science
Dist - USNAC **Prod** - USNIH 1980

Nobody's Perfect 29 MIN
VHS / 16mm
Color (A PRO)
$790.00 purchase, $220.00 rental
Shows how to identify people in terms of their team role. Discusses how to compose a team with the correct mix of personnel. Management training.
Psychology
Dist - VIDART **Prod** - VIDART 1991

Nobody's Perfect 24 MIN
VHS / U-matic
Color
LC 80-707333
Shows a scientist whose careless actions in the laboratory continually jeopardize the work and safety of his colleagues and himself. Stresses conscientious attitudes towards safety.
Health and Safety
Dist - USNAC **Prod** - USNIH 1980

Nobody's perfect 4 MIN
U-matic / VHS
Meeting breaks series
Color (C A PRO)
$295.00 purchase
Looks at managers who make well - intentioned blunders and need support from their superiors. Features Mel Smith and Griff Rhys Jones who show the right way to learn from mistakes. Produced by Playback.
Business and Economics; Guidance and Counseling; Psychology
Dist - VIDART

Nobody's Useless 29 MIN
16mm / U-matic / VHS
Color (I J)
LC 80-701305
Shows how Tom convinces a young amputee that the challenge of overcoming a handicap can be met with humor and courage. Adapted from a portion of the children's book The Great Brain by John D Fitzgerald.
Guidance and Counseling; Literature and Drama
Dist - EBEC **Prod** - OSCP 1980

Nobody's Victim 20 MIN
U-matic / VHS / 16mm
Color (J)
LC 72-702098
Shows specifically and practically how to turn off agressive strangers in public or at your door, how to thwart purse snatchers, what to do when walking alone or when your car is stalled in a deserted area, protection against prowlers and basic precautions for the woman who lives alone. Shows how to deal with trouble when it comes and demonstrates physical defense skills that women can use against would - be attackers.
Health and Safety; Sociology
Dist - ALTSUL **Prod** - RAMFLM 1972

Nobody's Victim 2 24 MIN
16mm
Color (H C A)
LC 79-700117
A revised edition of Nobody's Victim. Uses dramatized vignettes, personal testimony and commentary to show women how to avoid danger, confrontations and rape. Stresses the statistical realities concerning violence as opposed to common beliefs. Points out the importance of women accepting responsibility for their own safety.
Health and Safety; Sociology
Dist - SUTHRB **Prod** - RAMFLM 1978

Nobu Fukui - Contemporary Artist 29 MIN
U-matic
Color
Interviews a leading contemporary artist who refuses to discuss what his paintings mean and explains why.
Fine Arts
Dist - UMITV **Prod** - UMITV 1974

Noche Cubana 29 MIN
VHS / 16mm
Que Pasa, U S a Series
Color (G)
46.00 rental _ #QUEP - 107
Social Science; Sociology
Dist - PBS **Prod** - WPBTTV

Nocon on photography 156 MIN
VHS
Color; PAL (J H)
PdS45 purchase
Features royal photographer Prince Andrew as moderator in a six - part series of 26 minute programs about photography and photographers. Focuses on top photographic printer Gene Nocon who looks at different photographic styles and techniques and talks to well - known people in the photography world. Contact distributor about availability outside the United Kingdom.
Industrial and Technical Education
Dist - ACADEM

Nocturna arficialia 30 MIN
16mm / VHS
Color (G)
$530.00, $290.00 purchase, $55.00 rental
Follows a mysterious figure who is walking through a dark city. Features the filmmakers' first venture into the terrain of East European style three - dimensional animation.
Fine Arts; Literature and Drama
Dist - FIRS **Prod** - QUAY 1979

The Nocturnal immaculation 27 MIN
16mm / VHS
B&W (G)
$30.00 rental, $40.00 purchase
Incorporates two men, two women, one God and many devils.
Fine Arts; Psychology; Religion and Philosophy
Dist - CANCIN **Prod** - KUCHAR 1980

Nocturnal omission 10 MIN
16mm
B&W (G)
$20.00 rental
Presents a surrealist view of a teenage boy's fascination with womanhood as he confuses his feeling between his grandmother, his sisters, and a beautiful young woman. By Beth Block.
Fine Arts; Psychology
Dist - CANCIN

Nocturne 10 MIN
16mm
B&W (G)
$35.00 rental
Takes place in a suburban neighborhood populated by kids at play and ominous parental figures. Rehearses a young boy's nighttime game of wielding a flashlight in a darkened room to produce effects of aerial combat and bombardment. Found footage is subtly worked into a war of dimly suppressed emotions raging beneath a veneer of household calm. Produced in 1980 and revised in 1989.
Fine Arts; Psychology; Sociology
Dist - CANCIN **Prod** - SOLOMO 1989

The Nodder 30 MIN
U-matic / VHS
Wodehouse Playhouse Series
Color (C A)
Presents an adaptation of the short story The Nodder by P G Wodehouse.
Literature and Drama
Dist - TIMLIF **Prod** - BBCTV 1980

Nodes 3 MIN
16mm
Color (G)
$155.00 purchase, $10.00 rental
Presents a handpainted film evoking the cathexis concepts given by Freud - in his Interpretation of Dreams.
Fine Arts; Psychology
Dist - CANCIN **Prod** - BRAKS 1981

Noel a Paris 25 MIN
VHS
Color (I J H) (FRENCH)
$39.95 purchase _ #W3441, #W3446
Spotlights French traditional celebrations from Reveillon through Epiphany. Shows light displays and Paris decorations of the season as well as family traditions.
Foreign Language
Dist - GPC

Noel Nutels 30 MIN
16mm / U-matic / VHS
Color
Presents an account of the life and work of Noel Nutels, a Jewish immigrant who dedicated himself to the problems of health and preventive medicine in the Brazilian jungles, particularly in the areas occupied by the Indians. Deals with the history of the government agency for Indian Affairs, the political processes affecting the Indian territories and the harm created by contact with the whites.
Biography; Health and Safety; History - World; Science; Social Science
Dist - CNEMAG **Prod** - ALTBEM

Noel's Lemonade Stand (Ujamaa) 9 MIN
16mm / U-matic / VHS
Nguzo Saba - Folklore for Children Series
Color (K P I)
Shows how a young sidewalk entrepreneur, having slow sales, was helped by a neighbor suggesting he offer homemade cookies with the lemonade. Concludes by relating how he bought bulked goods from many neighbors, thus all benefited from the combined effort.
Business and Economics
Dist - BCNFL **Prod** - NGUZO 1983

Noguchi - a Sculptor's World 28 MIN
16mm
Color (H C A)
LC 73-700556
Presents sculptor Isamu Noguchi talking about his life and work as he is shown in different countries working on different projects. Shows examples of his work as exhibited in various museums and presents photographs of his ballet set designs and fountains at the Osaka World Exposition.
Dist - MUSLAR **Prod** - EAGLE 1972

Noh - classical theater of Japan 28 MIN
VHS
Color (G C H)
$159.00 purchase _ #DL271
Presents master teacher Akira Matsui performing excerpts from 'Benkei on the Bridge' and 'The Lady Han' to illustrate masks, physical movements, and other aspects of Noh theater.
Fine Arts; History - World
Dist - INSIM

The Noh Drama - Hagoromo 43 MIN
16mm
Color
Presents a transcendent drama about a fisherman and an angel.
Literature and Drama
Dist - UNIJAP **Prod** - KAJIMA 1968

Noh tiger 4 MIN
16mm
B&W (G)
$10.00 rental
Depicts a tiger, once in motion, now still and fragmented, a noh mask offering a history of ritual. By Wendy Blair.
Fine Arts
Dist - CANCIN

Noise 20 MIN
16mm / U-matic / VHS
Color
Explains sound and recommends methods of reducing noise levels. Uses animated diagrams to show the components of the ear and demonstrate how sound waves are transmitted through the ear. Illustrates how sound waves are measured.
Health and Safety; Sociology
Dist - IFB **Prod** - NCAS

Noise 9 MIN
VHS / U-matic
Color
Encourages employees to wear hearing protection devices where necessary to prevent premature deafness.
Health and Safety; Sociology
Dist - FILCOM **Prod** - FLMAUS

Noise 10 MIN
U-matic / VHS / 16mm
Color (I)
LC 73-705624
Describes various types of noise familiar to young children and raises the questions, what is the difference between sound and noise, how much does noise affect the quality of our lives and how much noise can we tolerate.

Science - Physical; Sociology
Dist - PHENIX **Prod** - DICD 1970

Noise Abatement 45 MIN
U-matic / VHS
Color
Presents a step - by - step noise control program that includes planning, measurement, surveys, engineering, implementation and follow up. Includes a description of the program General Motors Corporation has developed in conforming to the noise exposure limits set by the federal government.
Business and Economics; Industrial and Technical Education; Sociology
Dist - SME **Prod** - SME

Noise and its Effects on Health 20 MIN
16mm / U-matic / VHS
Color (J)
LC 73-701222
Describes the adverse effects of noise on the human system, including slow and permanent hearing loss and increased incidence of stress - induced physical and mental illness.
Health and Safety; Psychology; Science - Natural; Sociology
Dist - ALTSUL **Prod** - VOBERN 1973

Noise destroys 17 MIN
16mm / VHS / BETA / U-matic
Color; PAL (G T)
PdS160, PdS168 purchase
Introduces a factory worker who learns his hearing is irrepairably damaged after years of working in a noisy environment and becomes determined that those who follow him will fare better.
Guidance and Counseling; Health and Safety
Dist - EDPAT **Prod** - TASCOR

Noise destroys 13 MIN
U-matic / BETA / VHS
Color (IND G)
$395.00 purchase _ #600 - 14
Demonstrates graphically the many problems which may accompany hearing loss. Reminds employees that hearing loss is preventable through the use of proper protective equipment. Satisfies annual training requirements.
Health and Safety; Industrial and Technical Education; Psychology; Science - Natural; Sociology
Dist - ITSC **Prod** - ITSC

Noise, Elephant, Forget 10 MIN
U-matic
Readalong One Series
Color (K P)
Introduces reading and spelling for preschoolers and children in grades 1 to 3 with animation, puppets, humor and music. Comes with teacher's guide and kit.
Education; English Language; Literature and Drama
Dist - TVOTAR **Prod** - TVOTAR 1975

Noise is Pollution Too 15 MIN
U-matic / VHS / 16mm
Color (I J H) (SPANISH)
LC 72-715425;
Points out that man - made noise seriously endangers hearing and psychological health. Demonstrates the types of dangerous noise that people are exposed to and illustrates ways in which people can protect themselves against this noise.
Health and Safety; Science - Natural
Dist - JOU **Prod** - WER 1971

Noise Kene Series
The Early years 12 MIN
Our Children Our Future 14 MIN
Dist - CDIAND

Noise not Sound 11 MIN
16mm
Color
LC 73-702045
Distinguishes between natural sounds of the environment and excessive, harmful sounds made by man.
Science - Natural
Dist - ATLAP **Prod** - ATLAP 1973

Noise - Polluting the Environment 14 MIN
U-matic / VHS / 16mm
Environmental Studies Series
Color; B&W (J H C) (SPANISH)
Considers some of the ways of alleviating the noise polluters. Shows researchers working to lower the noise level because of its possible psychological effects.
Science - Natural
Dist - EBEC **Prod** - OMEGA 1971

Noise Pollution 18 MIN
U-matic / VHS / 16mm
Captioned; Color (J)
Combines physics, biology and meteorology to study the effects of noise on the human ear and mind. Shows how noise pollution is responsible for changing physical structures and creating ecological imbalances.
Psychology; Science - Natural; Sociology
Dist - LCOA **Prod** - LCOA 1972

Noise Pollution 26 MIN
U-matic / VHS
Color (C)
$249.00, $149.00 purchase _ #AD - 1875
Looks at the latest research into the impact of noise on health. Considers efforts by aircraft manufacturers, airports and residents who live in the paths of low - flying planes to minimize noise or cancel it out through generation of anti - noise at selected frequencies.
Science - Natural; Science - Physical
Dist - FOTH **Prod** - FOTH

Noise Pollution 18 MIN
16mm / U-matic / VHS
Environmental Sciences Series
Color (J H)
LC 76-710052
Demonstrates the nature of sound and noise and the difference between them. Sees the effects of noise pollution as damaging to the ear, psychologically damaging to the individual and physically damaging to structures and changes in the ecology. Shows how the atmosphere affects the propagation of sound, including effects of wind velocity and temperature reflection, refraction and absorption.
Science - Natural; Sociology
Dist - LCOA **Prod** - LCOA 1972

Noise Presentation 10 MIN
16mm
Color
LC 75-701719
Presents various sources of noise pollution, showing how the noise levels range from quiet sounds to some which are extremely loud.
Science - Natural
Dist - USNAC **Prod** - USNBOS 1972

Noise - the New Pollutant 30 MIN
16mm
Spectrum Series
B&W (H C A)
Presents several research projects into the harmful effect of noise on human beings. Dr Vern O Knudsen demonstrates the nature of sound and explains the sensation of hearing.
Health and Safety; Science - Natural; Sociology
Dist - IU **Prod** - NET 1967

The Noise was Deafening 21 MIN
16mm / U-matic / VHS
Color
Emphasizes the irreversible effects of excessive noise on hearing, shows how noise surveys can be conducted and points out some methods for noise reduction.
Health and Safety; Sociology
Dist - IFB **Prod** - MILLBK

NOISE - You're in Control 15 MIN
U-matic
Color (IND)
Provides an introduction to the 1982 OSHA Noise Standard. Educates workers on the effects of noise on hearing, the types of hearing protection available and the effects of not wearing adequate protection.
Health and Safety; Science - Physical
Dist - BNA **Prod** - ERESI 1982

Noise - you're in control 14.15 MIN
VHS / U-matic
Industrial safety series
(H A)
$125.00 purchase
Demonstrates effective types of noise control and ear protection on the job.
Health and Safety; Science - Natural
Dist - AITECH **Prod** - ERESI 1986

Noises in the Night 9 MIN
16mm / U-matic / VHS
Color (P I)
LC 76-708659
Presents the story of Sherri who feared noises she heard in the dark and her parents who try to help her understand that night noises are made by familiar things.
Guidance and Counseling; Literature and Drama; Psychology
Dist - PHENIX **Prod** - BOSUST 1969

The Noisy Underwater World of the Weddell Seal 11 MIN
16mm
Color (P I J H)
LC FIA66-1178
Shows the weddell seal under Antarctic ice. Reports the strange sounds of the seal as picked up on hydrophones by a team of biologists and bio - acousticians.
Geography - World; Science; Science - Natural
Dist - SF **Prod** - NYZS 1966

Nolan Ryan's fastball 30 MIN
VHS
Color (H C G)
$29.95 purchase _ #WIC100V
Eavesdrops on candid conversations between pitching legend Nolan Ryan and 1992 American League strikeout champion Randy Johnson. Includes instruction for throwing a better fastball, tips designed specifically for pitchers and coaches at the youth league, high school and college level, biokinetic computer figures that present detailed, slow - motion techniques for throwing perfect pitches.
Physical Education and Recreation
Dist - CAMV

Noli Me Tangere 6 MIN
VHS / U-matic
Color
Combines sexual and technological anxieties in a single obsessive image.
Fine Arts
Dist - KITCHN **Prod** - KITCHN

Nomads of Africa 25 MIN
16mm / U-matic / VHS
Untamed World Series Series
Color; Mono (J H C A)
$400.00 film, $250.00 video, $50.00 rental
Looks at three different African tribes as they exist today and gives an historical view of their traditional behaviour.
Geography - World; Sociology
Dist - CTV **Prod** - CTV 1971

Nomads of Iran 13 MIN
U-matic / VHS / 16mm
Middle East Series
Color (I J)
Reveals the self - reliant, isolated existance of the Quashagai, a united and colorful tribe of the Zagros Mountains in Iran.
Geography - World
Dist - AIMS **Prod** - WULFFR 1976

Nomads of the rainforest 59 MIN
VHS
Color (J H C G)
$295.00 purchase, $45.00 rental _ #37559
Records a multidisciplinary expedition to research the Waorani, a fierce and isolated Indian tribe inhabiting the Amazon rainforest. Contains scenes of skilled Waorani blowgun hunters in their jungle environment. Examines the daily life and rituals of the egalitarian Waorani whose members have no concept of competition or rank and who are completely free of Western diseases such as cancer, strokes and heart disease. Produced by Grant Behrman.
Geography - World; Social Science; Sociology
Dist - UCEMC

Nomads of the wind series
Combines wildlife footage with drama and documentary in exploring the fundamental relationship between humans and nature across the world's largest ocean - the Pacific.
Burning their boats 50 MIN
Crossroads of the Pacific 50 MIN
Distand horizons 50 MIN
The Faraway heaven 50 MIN
The Pierced sky 50 MIN
Dist - BBCENE

Nomads on the Move 15 MIN
U-matic / VHS
Encounter in the Desert Series
Color (I)
Shows nomadic Bedouins moving to a new home.
Geography - World; Social Science; Sociology
Dist - CTI **Prod** - CTI

Nomenclature and placement of liners, cements and varnishes in operative dentistry 9 MIN
U-matic / VHS
Color (C PRO)
$395.00 purchase, $80.00 rental _ #D860 - VI - 093
Teaches dental students the correct nomenclature and placement of liners, cements and varnishes used in posterior and anterior tooth restorations. Lists the benefits of using the various types of liners, bases and varnishes. Presented by Dr William von de Lehr.
Health and Safety
Dist - HSCIC

Nominating a President 30 MIN
VHS / 16mm
Government by Consent - a National Perspective Series
Color (I J H C A)
Examines the presidential nominating process for both major parties and explains how recent changes have allowed for greater citizen participation.
Civics and Political Systems
Dist - DALCCD **Prod** - DALCCD 1990

The Nominating Process 30 MIN
U-matic / VHS
American Government Series; 1
Color (C)
Stresses the tremendous amount of organization required to nominate candidates for political office. Includes an overview of the evolution of our election process over the last 200 years, with several specific examples of political elections.
Civics and Political Systems
Dist - DALCCD **Prod** - DALCCD

Nomination, Election and Succession of the President 60 MIN
U-matic / VHS
Constitution - that Delicate Balance Series
Color
Explores the role of political parties in nominating a president, the flexibility of the Electoral College when no candidate is clearly electable and the governmental mechanisms set into motion when a president becomes disabled.
Civics and Political Systems
Dist - FI **Prod** - WTTWTV 1984
ANNCPB

The Nomination of Abraham Lincoln 22 MIN
16mm / U-matic / VHS
You are There Series
Color (I J)
LC 72-700112
Reveals the men, attitudes and machinery of a historic convention and shows the American political system at work.
Civics and Political Systems; History - United States
Dist - PHENIX **Prod** - CBSTV 1972

Non - arthropod invertebrates 15 MIN
U-matic / VHS
Discovering series; Unit 2 - Invertebrate animals
Color (I)
Science - Natural
Dist - AITECH **Prod** - WDCNTV 1978

Non Catholicam 10 MIN
16mm
B&W (C)
$213.00
Experimental film by Will Hindle.
Fine Arts
Dist - AFA **Prod** - AFA 1963

Non - Compliance - the Hidden Health Hazard 26 MIN
16mm
Color
LC 80-701572
Outlines the extent of patient non - compliance in various therapeutic settings.
Health and Safety
Dist - TASCOR **Prod** - SYDUN 1978

Non - Decimal Numeration Systems 30 MIN
16mm
Introduction to Mathematics Series no 2
B&W
LC FI67-417
Illustrates, explains and presents problems dealing with non - decimal numeration systems.
Mathematics
Dist - SCETV **Prod** - HRAW 1964

Non - demand pleasuring 23 MIN
VHS
Center for Marital and Sexual Studies film series
Color (C A)
$99.00 purchase, $50.00 rental
Depicts three coital positions useful in treating premature ejaculators, imotent males and pre - orgasmic females. The final position demonstrates the vaginal caress which is valuable in treating pre - orgasmic females. Graphic. Produced by Hartman and Marilyn Fithian for professional use in treating sexual dysfunction and - or training professional personnel.
Health and Safety; Sociology
Dist - FCSINT

Non - destructive test technician 5 MIN
VHS / 16mm
Good works 4 series
Color (A PRO)
$40.00 purchase _ #BPN225810
Presents the occupation of a non - destructive test technician. Gives a profile of a young person who is either undergoing an apprenticeship or has recently completed training in this field. Takes the viewer on a tour of this person's workplace and explains the practical skills and training offered by employers and schools. Gives a better understanding of the demand for skilled workers today and the potential for personal growth.
Guidance and Counseling
Dist - RMIBHF **Prod** - RMIBHF

Non - destructive test technician 5 MIN
U-matic
Good work series
Color (H)
Provides useful, up to date information on various occupations to aid high school students in career selection. Available in five series of ten jobs each.
Education; Guidance and Counseling; Industrial and Technical Education
Dist - TVOTAR **Prod** - TVOTAR 1981

Non - Destructive Testing 16 MIN
U-matic / VHS
Manufacturing Materials and Processes Series
Color
Shows types of non - destructive testing, advantages and disadvantages.
Industrial and Technical Education
Dist - WFVTAE **Prod** - GE

Non - Dismembering Procedures 20 MIN
16mm
Surgical Correction of Hydronephrosis, Pt 1 - Non - Dismembering 'Procedures Series
Color
LC 75-702261
Reviews the indications, contraindications and advantages of the non - dismembering surgical procedures for the surgical correction of hydronephrosis. Includes the classical Foley Y - Plasty, the modified Davis intubated ureterotomy and the vertical flap (Scardono technique) non - splinted.
Science
Dist - EATONL **Prod** - EATONL 1968

Non - Electric hot work 11 MIN
VHS / U-matic / BETA
Hazard management safety series
Color (IND G A)
$589.00 purchase, $125.00 rental _ #NON006
Looks at non - electric hot work, extremely hazardous work involving welding or hot tapping of equipment or piping containing hazardous materials. Discusses and illustrates six key requirements to follow before beginning hot work. Part of a four - part series on hazard management safety.
Health and Safety; Industrial and Technical Education; Psychology
Dist - ITF **Prod** - GPCV

Non - Equilibrium Thermodynamics Applied to Elecro - Osmosis and Streaming Potential 38 MIN
VHS / U-matic
Colloids and Surface Chemistry Electrokinetics and Membrane - - 'Series
B&W
Science - Physical
Dist - MIOT **Prod** - MIOT

Non - Equilibrium Thermodynamics Applied to Electro - Osmosis and Streaming Potential 38 MIN
U-matic / VHS
Colloid and Surface Chemistry - Electrokinetics and Membrane Series
Color
Science; Science - Physical
Dist - KALMIA **Prod** - KALMIA

Non - Euclidean Geometries 20 MIN
U-matic / VHS
Shapes of Geometry Series Pt 6
Color (H)
LC 82-707392
Presents teachers Beth McKenna and David Edmonds exploring two different geometries, Lobatchevskian and Riemannian, and differentiating them from Euclidean geometry. Uses spherical and hyperbolic models to investigate the properties of lines and figures.
Mathematics
Dist - GPN **Prod** - WVIZTV 1982

Non - Evaluative Feedback 28 MIN
Videoreel / VT2
Interpersonal Competence, Unit 02 - Communication Series; Unit 2 - Communication
Color (C A)
Features a humanistic psychologist who, by analysis and examples, discusses non - evaluative feedback.
Psychology
Dist - TELSTR **Prod** - MVNE 1973

Non - ferrous metals and alloys 25 MIN
VHS
Technical studies series
Color (A PRO IND)
PdS50 purchase
Shows how non - ferrous metals and alloys are engineered for use in manufacturing. Part of a series designed to take students out of the classroom setting and into the world of engineering.
Business and Economics; Industrial and Technical Education; Science - Physical
Dist - BBCENE

Non Fiction 30 MIN
U-matic
Communicating with a Purpose Series
(H C A)
Introduces the world of facts as revealed by non - fiction writings. Uses examples from Canadian writers to illustrate different forms of the essay.
Education; Literature and Drama
Dist - ACCESS **Prod** - ACCESS 1982

Non - Hodgkin's Lymphomas, Pt 1 - Systmes of Classification and Principles of Staging 20 MIN
U-matic / VHS
Color (PRO)
Presents a patient with early findings of lymphoma. Describes the Rappaport method of classification.
Health and Safety
Dist - UMICHM **Prod** - UMICHM 1979

Non - Hodgkin's Lymphomas, Pt 2 - Prognosis and Therapy 17 MIN
VHS / U-matic
Color (PRO)
Focuses on the results of a lymphoma staging and treatment program. Describes favorable prognoses for given lymphomas and subsequent treatment.
Health and Safety
Dist - UMICHM **Prod** - UMICHM 1979

Non - impact fitness with Margaret Richards 60 MIN
VHS
Color (H C A)
$29.95 purchase _ #BW625V
Features Margaret Richards, host of the PBS television show 'Body Electric,' with a series of low - impact exercise routines. Focuses on shaping and toning of various body parts.
Physical Education and Recreation; Science - Natural
Dist - CAMV

Non - invasive respiratory monitoring 28 MIN
VHS / U-matic
Color (PRO)
$275.00 purchase, $60.00 rental _ #8315S, #8315V
Discusses equipment for monitoring arterial oxygen saturation and exhaled CO2 levels. Identifies three types of noninvasive respiratory monitoring techniques for clinical use - the oximeter, capnography and transcutaneous monitoring. Explains the basic principles of operating equipment used in monitoring, the procedures and specific clinical situations in which noninvasive respiratory monitoring is applicable.
Health and Safety
Dist - AJN **Prod** - HOSSN 1984

Non - Linear Systems 30 MIN
U-matic
Introduction to Mathematics Series
Color (C)
Mathematics
Dist - MDCPB **Prod** - MDCPB

Non - mechanical Disorders of the Lumbar Spine 23 MIN
U-matic
Evaluation of Low Back Pain Series
Color (C)
Discusses the metabolic and soft tissue lesions and possible referral of pain to the low back.
Health and Safety; Science - Natural
Dist - UOKLAH **Prod** - UOKLAH 1978

Non Metals - Share and Share Alike 9 MIN
U-matic
Chemistry 101 Series
Color (C)
Discusses distribution of metallic and non - metallic elements in and on earth, showing the biosphere to be almost entirely non - metallic. Explains the basis for Lewis' bonding theory.
Science; Science - Physical
Dist - UILL **Prod** - UILL 1973

Non - Metric Geometry, Pt 1 30 MIN
16mm
Introduction to Mathematics Series no 5
B&W
LC FI67-413
Illustrates, explains and presents problems dealing with the fundamentals of non - metric geometry. Includes a brief discussion of geometry and of geometric symbols.
Mathematics
Dist - SCETV **Prod** - HRAW 1964

Non - Metric Geometry, Pt 2 30 MIN
16mm
Introduction to Mathematics Series no 6
B&W

LC FI67-414
Illustrates, explains and presents problems dealing with the fundamentals of non - metric geometry. Includes a disussion of curves, angles, polygons and the intersection and union of sets.
Mathematics
Dist - SCETV **Prod** - HRAW 1964

Non - Negotiable 20 MIN
16mm
Color (H C A)
Shows what happens in labor - management negotiations.
Business and Economics
Dist - WORLDR **Prod** - WORLDR 1982

Non - Objective Art 8 MIN
U-matic / VHS / 16mm
Understanding Modern Art Series
Color (J H C)
LC FIA57-193
Defines non - objective art and shows how it differs from other types of painting. Attention is directed to non - objective things in nature.
Fine Arts
Dist - PHENIX **Prod** - THIEB 1957

Non - Parametric Tests 30 MIN
U-matic / VHS
Engineering Statistics Series
Color (IND)
Covers non - parametric tests (the sign, Mann - Whitney U and Kolmogorov Smirnov tests) which prove extremely useful where assumptions for specific distributions may not be met, such as with ranked data.
Industrial and Technical Education; Mathematics; Psychology
Dist - COLOSU **Prod** - COLOSU

Non - Renewable Resources 20 MIN
VHS / U-matic
Terra - Our World Series
Color (I J)
Focuses on non - renewable resources, specifically those used in the manufacture and operation of automobiles. Presents a demonstration of recycling and considers the implications of diminishing resources for individual life - styles.
Science - Natural; Social Science
Dist - AITECH **Prod** - MDDE 1980

Non - Root Feeding of Plants 21 MIN
16mm
Color (SPANISH)
LC 80-700533
Describes the techniques of applying nutrients to the visible, above - ground portion of plants. Discusses the method of tracing the nutrients through the plant's system by means of radioisotopes.
Agriculture; Foreign Language; Science - Natural
Dist - USNAC **Prod** - MSU 1958

Non - Sexist Early Education Films Series
The Sooner the Better 27 MIN
The Time has Come 22 MIN
Dist - THIRD

The Non - Skid Surface is a Myth 7 MIN
VHS / U-matic
Color
Describes the coefficient of friction, explains acceptable levels of friction for skid - resistant surfaces and illustrates the use of simple, practical precautions to make the workplace safer.
Health and Safety
Dist - FILCOM **Prod** - FILCOM

NON - SLIP 25 MIN
16mm
Color (C T)
LC 78-701603
Demonstrates procedures used in the Non - Speech Language Initiation Program training, in which nonverbal mentally retarded persons learn communication skills through the use of plastic symbols representing words.
Education; Psychology
Dist - UKANS **Prod** - UKANS 1976

Non - Standard Analysis, Pt 1 67 MIN
16mm
Maa General Mathematics Series
B&W
Discusses the non - standard real numbers and the form which the calculus takes when based on this enlarged number system which includes infinitesimals.
Mathematics
Dist - MLA **Prod** - MAA

Non - Standard Analysis, Pt 2 67 MIN
16mm
Maa General Mathematics Series
B&W
Discusses the non - standard real numbers and the form which the calculus takes when based on this enlarged number system which includes infinitesimals.
Mathematics
Dist - MLA **Prod** - MAA

Non - steriodal anti - inflammatory drugs - 2 10 MIN
VHS
Focus on pharmacy series
Color (C PRO)
$200.00 purchase, $60.00 rental _ #4311S, #4311V
Presents basic information on non - steriodal anti - inflammatory drugs for nurses. Uses a talk - show format between a nurse and a pharmacist who discuss key points of safe administration of the drug. Covers how the drugs are used, how to observe target symptoms for positive therapeutic outcomes and what side effects to anticipate. Emphasizes the importance of nursing documentation and its contribution to therapy success. Includes supporting materials. Part of a six - part series on commonly used drugs in long - term care produced by the American Society of Consultant Pharmacists.
Health and Safety
Dist - AJN

Non - Structured Interaction 8 MIN
VHS / 16mm
English as a Second Language Series
Color (A PRO)
$165.00 purchase _ #290305
Demonstrates key teaching methods for English as a Second Language - ESL teachers. Features a teacher - presenter who introduces and provides a brief commentary on the techniques, then demonstrates the application of the technique to the students. 'Non - Structured Interaction' illustrates how informal and unplanned language situations can provide an effective stimulus for language learning.
Education; English Language; Mathematics; Psychology
Dist - ACCESS **Prod** - ACCESS 1989

Non - surgical breast biopsy 6 MIN
VHS
Color (G)
$250.00 purchase
Presents information on fine needle and core biopsy. Covers stereotactic procedures. Uses tasteful visuals and graphics.
Health and Safety
Dist - LPRO **Prod** - LPRO

Non - Swimming Rescues 7 MIN
16mm
Color (J)
Demonstrates a variety of extension, throwing and wading assists in pointing out that swimming rescues should be used only as a last resort.
Health and Safety
Dist - AMRC **Prod** - AMRC 1975

Non - Verbal Communication 14 MIN
U-matic / VHS / 16mm
Color (H C A)
LC 80-700117
Presents psychologist Dr Albert Mehrabian explaining non - verbal communication and how it works. Points out that an awareness of one's own non - verbal messages and those of others enhances the ability to communicate.
Psychology
Dist - SALENG **Prod** - SALENG 1980

Non - Verbal Communication 27 MIN
16mm
Psychotherapeutic Interviewing Series
B&W (S)
LC FIE53-98
Discusses the recognition of the clues of non - verbal communication and the manner in which these clues can be used in an interview situation to obtain information and to further therapy. Illustrates the various points through picture, with subtitles, of actual unrehearsed interview situations.
Education; English Language; Psychology; Social Science
Dist - USNAC **Prod** - USVA 1952

Non - verbal communication in the trial 50 MIN
VHS
Effective communication in the courtroom series
Color (C PRO)
$100.00 purchase _ #ZCX02
Features University of Nevada professor Gordon Zimmerman in a discussion of courtroom non - verbal communication.
Civics and Political Systems
Dist - NITA **Prod** - NITA 1982

Non - Verbal, Inc 17 MIN
16mm / VHS
Color (J)
$400.00, $360.00 purchase, $40.00 rental _ #C - 517; LC 87708644
Uses dramatization of a representative of Non - Verbal Inc, a shadowy organization, to make people aware of the importance of non - verbal communication. Shows how decisions are made on the basis of physical cues. Produced by Kuxtal, Inc.
Psychology; Social Science; Sociology
Dist - ALTSUL

Non - Violence - Mahatma Gandhi and Martin Luther King, the Teacher and the Pupil 15 MIN
16mm
Color
Interviews Mahatma Gandhi and presents his philosophy on non - violent protest and the necessity for his imprisonment in behalf of his cause. Shows how Martin Luther King Jr carries out Gandhis principle of non - violent protest.
Biography; Civics and Political Systems; History - United States; Religion and Philosophy
Dist - REAF **Prod** - INTEXT

Non - Violent Protest 15 MIN
16mm
B&W
Encourages students to inquire into the concept of protest by examining specific issues in the black protest movement.
Civics and Political Systems
Dist - REAF **Prod** - STEVA

Nonbehavioral Sciences and Rehabilitation Series Part I
General Review of the Nervous System 60 MIN
Dist - AOTA

Nonbehavioral Sciences and Rehabilitation Series Part II
The Neuron 60 MIN
Dist - AOTA

Nonbehavioral Sciences and Rehabilitation Series Part III
Myelination of the Central Nervous System or Myelogenesis 60 MIN
Dist - AOTA

Nonbehavioral Sciences and Rehabilitation Series Part IV
Behavioral Patterns in Relation to Genetic and Environmental Endowments 60 MIN
Dist - AOTA

Nonbehavioral Sciences and Rehabilitation Series Part V
Nature's Laws 60 MIN
Dist - AOTA

Nonbehavioral Sciences and Rehabilitation Series Part VI
CNS Vulnerability 60 MIN
Dist - AOTA

Nonbehavioral Sciences and Rehabilitation Series Part VII
Limbic System, the, Pt I 60 MIN
Limbic System, the, Pt II 60 MIN
Dist - AOTA

Nonbehavioral sciences and rehabilitation series
Diagnosing cns lesions 60 MIN
The Extrapyramidal system - Pt I 60 MIN
The Extrapyramidal system - Pt II 60 MIN
The Extrapyramidal system - Pt III 60 MIN
Dist - AOTA

Noncommunicable diseases 14 MIN
16mm / VHS
Color (J H)
$350.00, $265.00 purchase
Uses simple animation and interviews with disabled young people to show what causes noncommunicable diseases such as cerebral palsy, diabetes, cancer, juvenile arthritis, allergies and heart disease. Indicates that the risk of some diseases can be reduced through exercise, not smoking. The young people interviewed stress that, although there are some things they can't do, in other ways they are every bit as normal as other children.
Health and Safety
Dist - CF **Prod** - CF 1990

Nondestruct Testing 60 MIN
VHS
Equipment Alignment and Testing Series
Color (PRO)
$600.00, $1500.00 purchase _ #GMNDT
Explains the functions of four types of nondestructive tests - magnetic particle, ultrasonic, radiographic and dye - penetrant tests. Stresses applicable safety precautions and proper preparation. Part of a four - part series on equipment alignment and testing, part of a larger set on general and mechanical maintenance. Includes 10 textbooks and an instructor guide which provide four hours of instruction.
Education; Industrial and Technical Education; Psychology
Dist - NUSTC **Prod** - NUSTC

Nondestructive Inspection - a Dollar Saving Diagnostic Tool 20 MIN
16mm
Color
LC 75-700565
Reviews the cost of tearing down various aircraft components in order to ascertain the malfunctioning parts. Examines a number of nondestructive methods which can be used to meet the same end and which produce large cost savings.
Business and Economics; Industrial and Technical Education
Dist - USNAC **Prod** - USAF 1974

None for the Road 12 MIN
U-matic / VHS / 16mm
Color (H C A) (SPANISH)
Considers what happens to an ordinary social drinker when he climbs behind the wheel. Tells the story of one man who found himself facing a year in jail because his blood was found to contain .15 percent alcohol after an accident.
Health and Safety
Dist - AIMS **Prod** - CAHILL 1962

None so blind 66 MIN
16mm
B&W (G)
$50.00 rental
Tells the story of Aaron Abram's daughter Rachel, who marries Russell Mortimer, a gentile socialite. Deals with the themes of interfaith marriage, a rare occurence then, and the inflexibility of families who refuse to believe that love breaks all barriers. A film by Arrow Pictures, produced and directed by Burton King.
Fine Arts; Religion and Philosophy; Sociology
Dist - NCJEWF

Nonequivalent Sets - Inequalities 15 MIN
U-matic
Math Factory, Module I - Sets Series
Color (P)
Develops understanding of inequality and equality of numbers and presents the symbols for 'equal,' 'is greater than' and 'is less than.'.
Mathematics
Dist - GPN **Prod** - MAETEL 1973

Nonfat Dry Milk 14 MIN
Videoreel / VT2
Living Better I Series
Color
Home Economics; Social Science
Dist - PBS **Prod** - MAETEL

Nonferrous and Nonmetallic Materials 60 MIN
BETA / VHS / U-matic
Color
$400 purchase
Shows properties, corrosion behavior and prevention and applications of nonferrous metals and alloys and nonmetallic materials.
Science; Science - Physical
Dist - ASM **Prod** - ASM

Nonferrous Metals - Industrial Applications and Properties 54 MIN
U-matic / BETA / VHS
Color
$400 purchase
Shows how nonferrous metals such as aluminium, berylium, magnesium, titanium, copper, lead, tin, and zinc are extracted and made into a usable form.
Science; Science - Physical
Dist - ASM **Prod** - ASM

Nonlinear Centrifugal Pendulum 24 MIN
U-matic / VHS
Nonlinear Vibrations Series
B&W
Mathematics
Dist - MIOT **Prod** - MIOT

Nonlinear inequalities and applications 30 MIN
VHS
Intermediate algebra series
Color (H)
$125.00 purchase _ #M52
Explains nonlinear inequalities and applications. Features Elayn Gay. Part of a 27 - part series on intermediate algebra.
Mathematics
Dist - LANDMK **Prod** - MGHT

Nonlinear Vibrations Series

Aircraft jet rotor with ball bearings with clearances	32 MIN
Application of the phase - plane method	30 MIN
Applications	34 MIN
Exact solutions - 1	37 MIN
Exact solutions - 2	35 MIN
Forced undamped vibrator with nonlinear spring	33 MIN
Forced Vibrator with Nonlinear Damping	31 MIN
Method of Galerkin	34 MIN
Method of Krylov - Bogliubov	24 MIN
Modified Martienssen Method Subharmonic Resonance	32 MIN
Nonlinear Centrifugal Pendulum	24 MIN
Pendulum in a Rotating Plane	32 MIN
Periodic Reversal of Rotation of a DC Motor	34 MIN
The Phase - Plane Method	37 MIN
Physical Interpretation of the K and B Formulas	29 MIN
Piece - Wise Linear Systems	33 MIN
Relaxation Oscillations	30 MIN
Solution and Interpretation	33 MIN
The Sommerfeld Effect	32 MIN
Tuned Centrifugal Pendulum	24 MIN
The Van Der Pol Equation	31 MIN
Volterra's Fishes	37 MIN

Dist - MIOT

Nonna 20 MIN
16mm
Color (G)
$25.00 rental
Takes a loving look at filmmaker's grandmother, in her 90s, as she shops, eats and talks about her life, family and the deaths of her husband and son.
Fine Arts; Health and Safety; Sociology
Dist - CANCIN **Prod** - PALAZT 1979

Nonorganic Failure to Thrive 20 MIN
VHS / U-matic
Child Abuse Series
Color (PRO)
Teaches the diagnosis of failure to thrive and explains the hospital therapy recommended when no organic reasons for it are apparent.
Health and Safety; Sociology
Dist - HSCIC **Prod** - HSCIC 1978

Nonrecurrent Wavefronts W - 3 3 MIN
16mm
Single - Concept Films in Physics Series
B&W (J H C)
Considers tidal waves, shock waves from nuclear bombs, the spreading pulse of light from a nova reflected by a nearby cloud of interstellar gas and a disturbance spreading through a crowd of people.
Science - Physical
Dist - OSUMPD **Prod** - OSUMPD 1963

Nonsense and made - Up Words in Poetry 15 MIN
U-matic / VHS
Word Shop Series
Color (P)
Literature and Drama
Dist - WETATV **Prod** - WETATV

Nonspecific Defense Mechanisms 15 MIN
U-matic / VHS
Mechanisms of Disease - Host Defenses Series
Color (PRO)
Provides general description of nonspecific and specific defense mechanisms, compares physical versus physiologic defenses, explores cellular biotransformation, and the role of inflammation.
Health and Safety
Dist - BRA **Prod** - BRA

Nonspeech Communication - Augmentative Systems 330 MIN
U-matic / VHS
Meeting the Communication Needs of the Severely/Profoundly 'Handicapped 1981 Series
Color
Presents information concerning the use of manual signs and gestures and graphic representations.
Psychology; Social Science
Dist - PUAVC **Prod** - PUAVC

Nonspeech Communication - Augmentative Systems 314 MIN
U-matic / VHS
Meeting the Communications Needs of the Severely/Profoundly 'Handicapped 1980 Series
Color
Presents information concerning the use of manual signs and gestures and graphic representations.
Psychology; Social Science
Dist - PUAVC **Prod** - PUAVC

Nonsurgical Biliary Drainage and Lithocenosis 30 MIN
VHS / U-matic
Color
Outlines methods for the correct differential diagnosis of obstructive jaundice.
Health and Safety
Dist - ROWLAB **Prod** - ROWLAB

Nonswimming Rescues 7 MIN
16mm
Lifesaving and Water Safety Series
Color (I) (SPANISH)
LC 76-701569
Demonstrates a variety of extension, throwing and wading assists for rescuing swimmers in trouble, which may be used by those unable to swim themselves.
Health and Safety
Dist - AMRC **Prod** - AMRC 1975

Nonsyphiltic Venereal Diseases 30 MIN
16mm
Color (PRO)
Discusses the etiology, pathology, diagnosis and treatment of the four most common venereal diseases which are not of syphilitic origin.
Health and Safety; Science
Dist - SQUIBB **Prod** - SQUIBB 1955

Nonverbal amplification - 5 91 MIN
VHS
Creating therapeutic change series
Color; PAL; SECAM (G)
$95.00 purchase
Features Richard Bandler in the fifth part of a seven - part series on creating therapeutic change using advanced NLP, neuro - linguistic programming. Reveals that just solving problems often isn't enough and that time distinctions can be used to interlace beliefs, feeling states and 'chains' into complexes that generatively reorganize fundamental attitudes throughout a person's life. Recommended that tapes be viewed in order. Bandler sometimes uses profanity for emphasis, which may offend some people.
Health and Safety; Psychology
Dist - NLPCOM **Prod** - NLPCOM

Nonverbal Communication 23 MIN
U-matic / VHS / 16mm
Social Psychology Series
Color
Covers the numerous scientific findings on how people communicate on a nonverbal level. Defines what behavior falls into the category of nonverbal communication, what the functions are of nonverbal communication and the origins of nonverbal communication. Features laboratory experiments on proximity and facial expression.
Psychology
Dist - CORF **Prod** - CORF

Nonverbal communication - eye contact and kinesics 28 MIN
U-matic / BETA / VHS
Communication skills 1 - basic series
Color (H C G)
$101.95, $89.95 purchase _ #CA - 39
Examines two more nonverbal message systems - eye contact and kinesics. Shows how both concepts relate to communication and their use in public speaking. Part of a series on communication.
English Language; Social Science
Dist - INSTRU

Nonverbal Communication in the Trial 50 MIN
VHS / U-matic
Effective Communication in the Courtroom Series
Color (PRO)
Covers such topics as lawyer's body language, eye contact, gestures, voice inflection and silence. Explores some of the special programs that face the female advocate and explains how courtroom layout and the exchange of questions and answers affect presentation.
Civics and Political Systems; Psychology; Social Science
Dist - ABACPE **Prod** - ABACPE

Nonverbal communication - paralanguage and proxemics 28 MIN
U-matic / BETA / VHS
Communication skills 1 - basic series
Color (H C G)
$101.95, $89.95 purchase _ #CA - 38
Reveals that when an individual speaks, more of the message has to do with the appearance, actions and movements of the speaker than with the words used. Discloses that nonverbal communication includes all of the things that support, enhance and affect the verbal message. Nonverbal communication is by far a bigger component of the message than the words used. Discusses two nonverbal systems, paralanguage and proxemics. Part of a series on communication.
English Language; Social Science
Dist - INSTRU

Nonverbal communication through drama - Unit F 49 MIN
VHS
Drama forum series
Color; PAL (T)
PdS35.00 purchase
Features Pennie Fairbairn with students on an FE Access course in unit six of a ten - unit series of observational material on the work of drama teachers.

Education; Fine Arts; Social Science
Dist - EMFVL

Nonverbal elicitation and change - 2 78 MIN
VHS
Submodalities and hypnosis series
Color; PAL; SECAM (G)
$75.00 purchase
Features Richard Bandler in the second part of a five - part series on submodalities and hypnosis, from a seminar, March, 1987. Uses advanced NLP, neuro - linguistic programming. Recommended that tapes be viewed in order. Bandler sometimes uses profanity for emphasis, which may offend some people.
Health and Safety; Psychology
Dist - NLPCOM **Prod** - NLPCOM

Nonviolence - the building blocks of character 10 MIN
VHS
Color (K P I)
$45.00 purchase
Communicates the philosophy of nonviolence of Dr Martin Luther King, Jr. Features Yolanda King, the oldest child of Dr and Mrs King, as narrator. Considers the concepts of honesty, humility, courage and cooperation.
Civics and Political Systems; Psychology; Religion and Philosophy; Social Science; Sociology
Dist - KINGML **Prod** - KINGML

Nonviolent Crisis Intervention Series
Therapeutic Physical Intervention - Vol II 26 MIN
Dist - NCPI

Nonwovens and Carpets
U-matic / VHS
ITMA 1983 Review Series
Color
Industrial and Technical Education
Dist - NCSU **Prod** - NCSU

Noodle making - cheap and easy
VHS
No - fat cooking series
Color (J H G)
$29.95 purchase _ #VB500V
Demonstrates the making of a low - fat noodle using flour, yogurt and eggs. Explains how to use necessary tools and the difference between fresh and dried noodles. Part of a four - part series on no - fat cooking featuring Dr Jean Rosenbaum.
Health and Safety; Home Economics; Social Science
Dist - CAMV

Noodles 29 MIN
Videoreel / VT2
Joyce Chen Cooks Series
Color
Features Joyce Chen showing how to adapt Chinese recipes so they can be prepared in the American kitchen and still retain the authentic flavor. Demonstrates how to prepare noodles.
Geography - World; Home Economics
Dist - PBS **Prod** - WGBHTV

Noodles, dumplings, biscuits and scones
VHS
Frugal gourmet - American classics series
Color (G)
$19.95 purchase _ #CCP832
Shows how to prepare American style noodles, dumplings, biscuits and scones. Features Jeff Smith, the Frugal Gourmet. Part of the nine - part series, American Classics.
History - United States; Home Economics
Dist - CADESF **Prod** - CADESF

Nooks and Crannies 59 MIN
VHS / 16mm
Color (G)
$70.00 rental _ #NKAC - 000
Combines blues, ragtime, country and country - western in an informal musical performance. Features Gary Cooper as host.
Fine Arts
Dist - PBS

Nooks and crannies 30 MIN
Videoreel / VT2
Designing home interiors series; Unit 25
Color (C A)
Suggests ways to customize a home to meet individual storage needs. Show examples of how to organize a kitchen work area.
Home Economics
Dist - CDTEL **Prod** - COAST

Noon wine 81 MIN
VHS
American short story collection series
Color (J H)
$49.00 purchase _ #04031 - 126
Presents a short story by Katherine Anne Porter. Tells about murder and revenge in a small Texas town.
Literature and Drama; Sociology
Dist - GA **Prod** - GA

Noontime Nonsense 13 MIN
16mm
Secondary School Safety Series
Color; B&W
Shows an open campus and wild noontime driving by a small group of students. Illustrates how the student council solved this problem.
Guidance and Counseling; Health and Safety
Dist - NSC **Prod** - NSC 1955

Nora Ephron 15 MIN
VHS
Writer's workshop series
Color (C A T)
$69.95 purchase, $45.00 rental
Features Nora Ephron in a lecture and discussion of her work, held as part of a writing workshop series at the University of South Carolina. Hosted by author William Price Fox and introduced by George Plimpton. Part two of a 15 - part telecourse.
English Language; Literature and Drama
Dist - SCETV **Prod** - SCETV 1982

Nora Ephron 30 MIN
VHS
Writer's workshop series
Color (G)
$59.95 purchase _ #WRWO - 102
Features writer Nora Ephron in a lecture and discussion at the University of South Carolina. Discusses her experience as a journalist for the New York Post and how she feels it helped her writing. Presents secrets for good interviewing.
Literature and Drama
Dist - PBS **Prod** - SCETVM 1987

Nora Ephron on Everything 29 MIN
U-matic
Woman Series
Color
Features author Nora Ephron commenting on a number of issues surrounding the women's movement.
Sociology
Dist - PBS **Prod** - WNEDTV

Norbert, Snorebert 15 MIN
U-matic / VHS
Return to the magic library series
Color (P I)
#362407; LC 91-706820
Features a shepherd who tells puppet characters a strange story, 'The Cave of Snores' by Dennis Haseley, which discloses that snoring is very valuable. Part of a series that uses puppet mice and live storytellers to encourage students to read the featured story and respond with comments and questions. Includes teacher's guide and five readers.
Literature and Drama; Social Science
Dist - TVOTAR **Prod** - TVOTAR 1990

Nordens Arkaeologi (the Archaeology of Scandinavia) 31 MIN
16mm
B&W (DANISH)
A Danish language film. Describes the conditions of life of the Scandinavian people in the Stone Age, the Bronze Age and the Iron Age, based on archaeological find.
Foreign Language; History - World; Sociology
Dist - STATNS **Prod** - STATNS 1958

Nordicross 88 MIN
VHS
Color (H A G)
$69.95 purchase _ #CV904
Takes a look at traditional Nordic techniques which form the basis for cross - country, free - style skiing and ski skating. Features Dan Clausen who demonstrates some changes in cross - country skiing.
Physical Education and Recreation
Dist - AAVIM **Prod** - AAVIM

Nordjamb 58 MIN
16mm
Color
LC 76-700395
Presents a behind - the - scenes report of the 1975 World Boy Scout Jamboree in Lillehammer, Norway. Follows the activities of one south Florida scout during the week - long event.
Geography - World; Guidance and Counseling; Psychology; Social Science
Dist - WPBTTV **Prod** - WPBTTV 1976

Nordsee 1st Mordsee 90 MIN
16mm
Color (GERMAN (ENGLISH SUBTITLES))
A German language motion picture with English subtitles. Tells the story of two young boys who steal a sailboat, encounter numerous adventures after leaving home, and eventually head for the North Sea.
Foreign Language; Social Science
Dist - WSTGLC **Prod** - WSTGLC 1976

Norfolk - Fernandina - Volume 1
VHS
Way south series
Color (G)
$39.80 purchase _ #0362
Travels from Norfolk, Virginia to Fernandina Beach, Florida via the Intercoastal Waterway. Part one of a two - part series on the Intercoastal Waterway featuring Peter Smyth.
Geography - United States; Physical Education and Recreation
Dist - SEVVID

Norfolk Western 1218
VHS
Color (G)
$19.95 purchase _ #PX023
Travels through Virginia and St Louis on a huge 2 - 6 - 6 - 4 steam locomotive, one of the last of its kind.
Geography - United States; Social Science
Dist - SIV

Norge, Norge 15 MIN
VHS
Color (G)
Free loan
Offers a photographic portrait of Norway.
Geography - World
Dist - NIS

Norie Sato - After Image, TTLS 5 MIN
VHS / U-matic
Color
Presents the inner workings of the television as a metaphor for outer space.
Fine Arts
Dist - ARTINC **Prod** - ARTINC

Norie Sato - Farewell to Triangle 1 7 MIN
VHS / U-matic
Color
Explores the electronic properties of video. Points to the relationship between inner and outer realities.
Fine Arts
Dist - ARTINC **Prod** - ARTINC

Norie Sato - in Plus, Pulse 3 MIN
U-matic / VHS
Color
Compares the world of electrons to the 'real' world through seeing the output of the cross - pulse signal.
Fine Arts
Dist - ARTINC **Prod** - ARTINC

Norie Sato - on Edge 4 MIN
U-matic / VHS
Color
Explores the electronic properties of video. Makes a statement about inner and outer realities.
Fine Arts
Dist - ARTINC **Prod** - ARTINC

Norie Sato - Phosphor Read Out 4 MIN
U-matic / VHS
Color
Presents an image which exists somewhere between 'snow' and 'dropout'.
Fine Arts
Dist - ARTINC **Prod** - ARTINC

Norie Sato - Read Only Phosphor Memory 7 MIN
VHS / U-matic
Color
Presents an ephemeral image.
Fine Arts
Dist - ARTINC **Prod** - ARTINC

The Noriega Connection 60 MIN
VHS
Frontline Series
Color; Captioned (G)
$300.00 purchase, $95.00 rental _ #FRON - 803K
Describes the long - term working relationship between Panamanian dictator Manuel Noriega and the U S government. Shows that the U S government viewed Noriega as a valuable intelligence source, ignoring Noriega's questionable activities over the years. Interviews Panamanians and Americans who knew Noriega, and examines pertinent U S government documents.
Civics and Political Systems; History - World
Dist - PBS **Prod** - DOCCON 1990

Norien Ten 10 MIN
16mm
Color
Deals with broadening attitudes toward eroticism, and illustrates a different way of seeing.
Guidance and Counseling; Psychology; Sociology
Dist - MMRC **Prod** - MMRC

Norma Cole - 9 - 22 - 88
VHS / Cassette
Poetry Center reading series
Color (G)
$15.00, $45.00 purchase, $15.00 rental _ #823 - 647
Features the writer at the Poetry Center of San Francisco State University, reading selections from Metamorphopsia; Letters of Discipline; The Provinces; and from My Bird Book, with an introduction by Robert Gluck and Frances Phillips.
Literature and Drama
Dist - POETRY **Prod** - POETRY 1988

Norma Rae 113 MIN
VHS
Color (G)
$69.98 purchase _ #S00262
Tells the story of a young couple who try to organize North Carolina textile workers into a union. Based on a true story. Stars Sally Field, Ron Liebman, Beau Bridges, and Pat Hingle. Directed by Martin Ritt.
Business and Economics; Fine Arts; History - United States; Social Science; Sociology
Dist - UILL

Norma Rae
BETA / VHS
Color
Presents Sally Field's Oscar - winning performance as a Southern textile worker struggling to organize a union.
Business and Economics; Social Science
Dist - GA **Prod** - GA

Normal and abnormal neurologic function in infancy - Pt I 29 MIN
VHS / 16mm
Developmental neurologic approach to assessment in infancy and early childhood - Unit IV series
(C)
$330.00 purchase _ #821VI115
Presents the important gross and fine motor patterns of healthy 40 - week - old infants. Looks at the continuing normal development over the following year, noting salient adaptive behavior. Features three infants with normal intellectual potential but increasing degrees of neuromotor diabilities.
Health and Safety
Dist - HSCIC **Prod** - HSCIC 1982

Normal and abnormal neurologic function in infancy - Pt II 43 MIN
VHS / 16mm
Developmental neurologic approach to assessment in infancy and early childhood - Unit IV series
(C)
$330.00 purchase _ #821VI116
Presents cases of severe disabilities such as mental deficiency, borderline development, and cerebral palsy.
Health and Safety
Dist - HSCIC **Prod** - HSCIC 1982

Normal and abnormal neurologic function in infancy (updated) - Pt 1 29 MIN
U-matic / VHS
Developmental - neurologic approach to assessment in infancy and early childhood series
Color (PRO)
Presents the important gross and fine motor patterns of healthy forty - week - olds and the continuing normal development over the following year, noting salient adaptive behavior.
Health and Safety; Psychology
Dist - HSCIC **Prod** - HSCIC 1982

Normal and abnormal neurologic function in infancy (updated) - Pt 2 43 MIN
VHS / U-matic
Developmental - neurologic approach to assessment in infancy and early childhood series
Color (PRO)
Illustrates more severe disabilities than in Part 1 - mental deficiency, borderline development, cerebral palsy with unknown intellectual potential, and cerebral palsy with normal intelligence.
Health and Safety; Psychology
Dist - HSCIC **Prod** - HSCIC 1982

Normal and Abnormal Neurologic Functions in Infancy 28 MIN
16mm
B&W
Depicts the neuromotor patterns observed in infants with disabilities ranging from minimal to severe.
Psychology
Dist - OSUMPD **Prod** - OHIOSU 1964

Normal and Abnormal Peripheral Blood - Red Cell Morphology 19 MIN
VHS / 16mm
(C)
$385.00 purchase _ #860VI072
Presents red cell morphology. Examines Wright stained smears of blood under the oil immersion objective. Compares normal and abnormal peripheral blood samples.
Health and Safety
Dist - HSCIC **Prod** - HSCIC 1986

Normal and Abnormal Peripheral Blood - White Cell Morphology 19 MIN
VHS / 16mm
(C)
$385.00 purchase _ #851VI030
Shows examples of segmented neutrophils, eosinophils, basophils, monocytes and limphocytes. Describes diseases involving Dohle bodies and presents microscopic studies of Pelger - Huet anomaly, May - Hegglin syndrome, atypical limphocytes and infectious mononucleosis.
Health and Safety
Dist - HSCIC **Prod** - HSCIC 1986

Normal and Abnormal Platelets 20 MIN
16mm
B&W (PRO)
Shows the activity of platelets through the phase - contrast microscope. Examines hereditary thrombopathy in children, immunologic thrombopathy, lysis of platelets in antiserum, giant platelets in myeloid leukemia, giant platelets in platelet leukemia and autolysis.
Health and Safety; Science - Natural
Dist - SQUIBB **Prod** - SQUIBB

Normal and Abnormal Swallowing - Pt 4 - Treatment and Management 22 MIN
U-matic / VHS
Color (PRO)
Discusses diagnostic evaluation techniques for the types of dysphagia and the treatment and management of dysphagia patients.
Health and Safety; Science - Natural
Dist - USNAC **Prod** - VAMSLC 1984

Normal and Abnormal Swallowing - Pt 1 - Normal Anatomy 21 MIN
U-matic / VHS
Color (PRO)
Discusses normal anatomy of swallowing and the basic musculoskeletal structures involved in deglutition. Intended for students and medical clinicians.
Health and Safety; Science - Natural
Dist - USNAC **Prod** - VAMSLC 1984

Normal and Abnormal Swallowing - Pt 3 - Evaluation 13 MIN
VHS / U-matic
Color (PRO)
Discusses the types of dysphagia and how to evaluate suspected cases. Intended for the clinician familiar with anatomy and physiology of swallowing.
Health and Safety; Science - Natural
Dist - USNAC **Prod** - VAMSLC 1984

Normal and Abnormal Swallowing - Pt 2 - Physiology 7 MIN
U-matic / VHS
Color (PRO)
Discusses physiology involved in swallowing and deglutition.
Health and Safety; Science - Natural
Dist - USNAC **Prod** - VAMSLC 1984

Normal and emergency operation
U-matic / VHS
Distribution system operation series; Topic 11
Color (IND)
Discusses the effects of normal and abnormal conditions. Focuses on emergency operation and necessary actions for system protection.
Industrial and Technical Education
Dist - LEIKID **Prod** - LEIKID

Normal approximation to binomial
VHS
Probability and statistics series
Color (H C)
$125.00 purchase _ #8027
Provides resource material about normal approximations to binomials for help in the study of probability and statistics. Presents a 60 - video series, each part 25 to 30 minutes long, that explains and reinforces concepts using definitions, theorems, examples and step - by - step solutions to tutor the student. Videos are also available in a set.
Mathematics
Dist - LANDMK

A Normal Baby 40 MIN
Videoreel / VHS
Color (PRO)
Traces the growth of a normal baby from birth to one year. Covers gross and fine motor development, stages in development of hand function and eye - hand coordination.
Health and Safety; Psychology
Dist - VALHAL **Prod** - VALHAL

Normal Bone Marrow 30 MIN
VHS / 16mm
(C)
$385.00 purchase _ #851VI031
Introduces medical students to the cell sturcture within normal bone marrow. The phases of cell maturation of the granulocytic series are examined as well as those of the red cell series.
Health and Safety
Dist - HSCIC **Prod** - HSCIC 1986

Normal calculations - time series - Parts 5 and 6 60 MIN
U-matic / VHS
Against all odds - inside statistics series
Color (C)
$45.00, $29.95 purchase
Presents parts 5 and 6 of 26 thirty - minute programs on statistics hosted by Dr Teresa Amabile of Brandeis University. Provides real - world examples of normal calculations at work. Shows how statistical analysis can identify patterns that emerge in data sets over a period of time. Produced by the Consortium for Mathematics and Its Applications - COMAP - and the American Statistical Association and American Society of Quality Control.
Mathematics; Psychology
Dist - ANNCPB

Normal Child 25 MIN
16mm
B&W (C T)
LC FIA68-2698
Shows Karl, a six - year - old boy, interacting normally and positively with his environment. Shows how he handles affection. Illustrates his capacity for imagination and play and his constructive use of relationship with the examiner. Showings restricted.
Education; Psychology; Sociology
Dist - PSUPCR **Prod** - EPPI 1967

The Normal Cystourethrogram 14 MIN
16mm
Color (PRO)
LC 70-711368
Uses animation and plastic models, combined with Roentgen spotfilms taken during voiding cystourethrograms, to show how the Roentgen anatomy of the bladder, baseplate and urethra will change radically during the voiding cycle and to show normal anatomical landmarks and dynamic patterns which, in the past, have been mistakenly identified as pathological conditions.
Psychology; Science; Science - Natural
Dist - WINLAB **Prod** - WINLAB 1971

Normal Distribution
U-matic / VHS
Statistics for Managers Series
Color (IND)
Shows commonly occurring distributions which can describe sales distributions as well as lifetimes of products subject to mechanical wear. Discusses calculations of areas under the normal curve. Covers central limit theorem, and demonstrates setting of means and variances to meet specific goals.
Business and Economics; Mathematics; Psychology
Dist - COLOSU **Prod** - COLOSU

The Normal Distribution and Central Limit Theorem 30 MIN
U-matic / VHS
Engineering Statistics Series
Color (IND)
Describes use of normal distribution used for modelling many practical situations. Includes how to determine value of a particular mean or standard deviation to meet goals.
Industrial and Technical Education; Mathematics; Psychology
Dist - COLOSU **Prod** - COLOSU

Normal distribution and distribution and standardization
VHS
Probability and statistics series
Color (H C)
$125.00 purchase _ #8025
Provides resource material about normal distributions and standardization for help in the study of probability and statistics. Presents a 60 - video series, each part 25 to 30 minutes long, that explains and reinforces concepts using definitions, theorems, examples and step - by - step solutions to tutor the student. Videos are also available in a set.
Mathematics
Dist - LANDMK

Normal Eye 81 MIN
VHS / U-matic
Color
Presents the normal eye anatomy. Discusses vision and focusing. Explains myopia and hyperopia.

Science - Natural
Dist - MEDFAC Prod - MEDFAC 1974

A Normal Face - the Wonders of Plastic Surgery 57 MIN
16mm / U-matic / VHS
Nova Series
Color (H C A)
Looks at the history, heroes and miracles of plastic surgery in mending the accidents of war and birth.
Health and Safety
Dist - TIMLIF Prod - WGBHTV 1982

A Normal Face - the Wonders of Plastic Surgery 57 MIN
16mm / VHS
Nova Series
(J H C)
$99.95 each
Deals with the emotional triumph of patient's saved from hideous disfigurement through plastic surgery.
Science; Sociology
Dist - AMBROS Prod - AMBROS 1985

Normal Forms
16mm
B&W
Demonstrates the different normal forms to which a matrix can be reduced by changing the bases relative to which it is defined. Includes the canonical form, Hermite normal form, diagonal form, and Jordan normal form.
Mathematics
Dist - OPENU Prod - OPENU

The Normal gait pattern viewed laterally - Part I 24 MIN
VHS / U-matic
Observation of human gait series
Color (PRO C)
$395.00 purchase, $80.00 rental _ #C851 - VI - 020
Defines normal human gait patterns and illustrates and describes the best procedure for observing gait. Outlines the components of the gait cycle and teaches the viewer to observe joint motions in the saggital plane. Part one of a three - part series on observing human gait presented by physical therapist Ilse Koerner.
Health and Safety; Science - Natural
Dist - HSCIC

Normal Heart Sound and Innocent Heart Murmurs 41 MIN
16mm / VHS / U-matic
Color (PRO)
LC 79-706508
Provides a foundation for the use of the stethescope in the analysis of heart sounds and murmurs. Discusses normal cardiac auscultation and interprets cardiac events. Issued in 1964 as a motion picture.
Health and Safety
Dist - USNAC Prod - USPHS 1979

The Normal human gait pattern viewed anteriorly and posteriorly - Part II 38 MIN
VHS / U-matic
Observation of human gait series
Color (PRO C)
$395.00 purchase, $80.00 rental _ #C851 - VI - 021
Evaluates motions that occur in both transverse and coronal planes. Explores the mechanics and function of the foot and teaches the viewer about the role of gravity during the gait cycle. Part two of a three - part series on observing human gait presented by physical therapist Ilse Koerner.
Health and Safety; Science - Natural
Dist - HSCIC

Normal Human Locomotion 180 MIN
16mm
B&W (PRO)
Presents a lecture by Dr Cameron B Hall of the UCLA Surgery - Orthotics Department on normal human locomotion. Traces the evolutionary development of bipedal gait from the fish to the human and discusses the role of skeletal, muscular and neurological elements of the human anatomy.
Health and Safety; Science - Natural
Dist - UCLA Prod - UCLA

The Normal Neonate 22 MIN
16mm
Color
LC 80-701573
Shows a pediatrician examining a normal human infant.
Health and Safety
Dist - TASCOR Prod - SYDUN 1977

Normal Nutrition - Body Composition 38 MIN
VHS / U-matic / 16mm
Nutrition and Health Series
Color (PRO C)
$866.25 purchase _ #840VI024A - B - C
Defines normal body composition and examines the methods used to assess it, and nutritional status. Consists of three videocassettes covering caloric composition, fluid composition and mineral composition, and anthropometric measurements.
Health and Safety; Psychology; Social Science
Dist - HSCIC Prod - HSCIC 1984

Normal operating hazards and safety, tape 17a
VHS / U-matic
Electric power system operation series
Color (IND)
Covers generation, synchronism, transmission, transformers, surge arrestors, switching operations, supervisory control, protection of personnel and clearance procedures.
Health and Safety; Industrial and Technical Education
Dist - LEIKID Prod - LEIKID

Normal operating hazards and safety, tape 17b
VHS / U-matic
Electric power system operation series
Color (IND)
Covers generation, synchronism, transmission, transformers, surge arrestors, switching operations, supervisory control, protection of personnel and clearance procedures.
Health and Safety; Industrial and Technical Education
Dist - LEIKID Prod - LEIKID

Normal Patterns of Development 12 MIN
U-matic / VHS
Color (SPANISH)
LC 81-730128
Describes the intertwining tracks of a baby's physical, mental and social development and the effect that achievement in one area has on the others. Includes development of thumb and finger opposition, learning to sit unsupported, stranger anxiety and object permanence, plus discussing the development of attachment.
Foreign Language; Guidance and Counseling; Health and Safety; Home Economics
Dist - MEDCOM Prod - MEDCOM

Normal Physical Assessment - a Tool for the Beginning Practitioner 25 MIN
U-matic / VHS
Color
LC 81-707280
Demonstrates how a nurse carries out a physical assessment, including inspection, palpation, and auscultation of the heart and abdominal areas.
Health and Safety
Dist - USNAC Prod - USA 1977

Normal physiologic changes 23 MIN
BETA / VHS / U-matic
Assessing the elderly series
Color (C PRO)
$280.00 purchase _ #617.1
Explores the major physiologic changes that impact health assessment in the elderly. Discusses special considerations that may affect or require adjustments in health assessment techniques. Part of a five - part series on assessing the elderly produced by the School of Nursing, State University of New York at Stony Brook.
Health and Safety
Dist - CONMED

Normal Radiographic Anatomy of the Chest 30 MIN
U-matic
Radiology of the Respiratory System - a Basic Review
Color (C)
Presents normal and congenital variants of the respiratory system.
Health and Safety; Industrial and Technical Education; Science - Natural
Dist - UOKLAH Prod - UOKLAH 1978

Normal Roentgen Anatomy Series

Roentgen Anatomy of the Normal Alimentary Canal	27 MIN
Roentgen Anatomy of the Normal Bones and Joints	19 MIN
Roentgen Anatomy of the Normal Heart	27 MIN

Dist - AMEDA

Normal sinus rhythm and sinus dysrhythmias - Part 1 28 MIN
VHS / U-matic
Basic dysrhythmia interpretation
Color (PRO)
$275.00 purchase, $60.00 rental _ #7516S, #7516V
Covers normal conduction, normal sinus rhythm, sinus dysrhythmias and their clinical signs and ECG patterns. Instructs in the use of the ECG monitor and covers the circulatory consequences of dysrhythmias and their treatment. Part of three - parts on basic dysrhythmia interpretation.
Health and Safety
Dist - AJN Prod - HOSSN 1986

Normal Speech Articulation 25 MIN
16mm
Physiological Aspects of Speech Series
Color
LC FIA65-1901
Demonstrates through extensive use of X - ray motion pictures, some of the characteristics of speech sound articulation in normal speakers.
English Language; Science - Natural
Dist - UIOWA Prod - UIOWA 1965

Normal Vision - Malcolm Le Grice 26 MIN
16mm
Color (H A)
$650.00 purchase, $50.00 rental
Features Malcolm Le Grice, a theorist of the avant - garde and early member of the London Film Makers Coop.
Fine Arts
Dist - AFA Prod - ACGB 1984

Normality test
VHS
Probability and statistics series
Color (H C)
$125.00 purchase _ #8050
Provides resource material about normality tests for help in the study of probability and statistics. Presents a 60 - video series, each part 25 to 30 minutes long, that explains and reinforces concepts using definitions, theorems, examples and step - by - step solutions to tutor the student. Videos are also available in a set.
Mathematics
Dist - LANDMK

Norman 24 MIN
VHS / U-matic
Color (H C G)
$355.00, $325.00 purchase _ #V587
Interviews Norman, born with Downs Symdrome, who has become a spokesperson for handicapped people worldwide. Shares Norman's ideas on being mentally disabled and shows some of the people who have been inspired by him.
Health and Safety; Psychology
Dist - BARR Prod - CEPRO 1991

Norman and the Killer 27 MIN
16mm / U-matic / VHS
B&W
Relates the story of a young man who recognizes the mugger who killed his brother 16 years after the mugging took place. Reveals what happens when he confronts the killer. Based on a short story by Joyce Carol Oates.
Fine Arts; Literature and Drama
Dist - CORF Prod - QUKIGR 1981

Norman Blake's guitar techniques 90 MIN
VHS
Color (G)
$49.95 purchase _ #VD - BLA - GT01
Features country guitarist Norman Blake on flatpicking fundamentals such as alternating strokes, rolls, crosspicking, single string - rhythm chord combinations and other aspects of Blake's right - hand style. Combines these techniques with slides, pull - offs, hammer - ons, chord positions and melody notes. Includes the songs Whiskey Before Breakfast, Gray Coat Soldiers, Prettiest Little Girl in the County, The Wreck of the Old '97, Ginseng Sullivan and Bonaparte Crossing the Rhine. Wife and musical partner, Nancy Blake, joins him on second - guitar as Blake discusses her back - up technique, as well as providing tips on the use of the capo, getting the most from open strings, special tuning techniques and more. Includes tablature.
Fine Arts
Dist - HOMETA Prod - HOMETA

Norman Checks in 10 MIN
U-matic / VHS / 16mm
Color (C A)
Features a comedy about Norman, a silently suffering, slow burning man. Pictures him battling with a shower, noisy neighbors and a relaxing machine.
Literature and Drama
Dist - CORF Prod - CORF

The Norman Conquest of England 20 MIN
16mm
Color
Depicts the historic conquest of England by William I, Duke of Normandy. Includes the narration of the Battle of Hastings during which King Harold of England was killed.
History - World
Dist - RADIM Prod - RADIM 1971

The Norman Conquest of England - 1066 20 MIN
16mm
Color
Presents the famous Bayeux tapestry embroidered by the conquerors' Queen Mathilde, which depicts the historic events of William I, Duke of Normandy.
Biography; Fine Arts; Geography - World; History - World
Dist - RADIM Prod - LEEN

Norman Cousins, Education, Public Service 29 MIN
VHS / U-matic
Quest for Peace Series
Color (A)
Education; Social Science
Dist - AACD **Prod** - AACD 1984

Norman Fischer - 9 - 30 - 82 30 MIN
VHS / Cassette
Poetry Center reading series
Color (G)
$15.00, $45.00 purchase, $15.00 rental _ #500 - 423
Features the writer reading his works at the Poetry Center, San Francisco State University.
Literature and Drama
Dist - POETRY **Prod** - POETRY 1982

Norman Geske 28 MIN
Videoreel / VT2
Art Profile Series
Color
Fine Arts
Dist - PBS **Prod** - KUONTV

Norman Jacobson 59 MIN
16mm
Men who Teach Series
B&W (H C T)
LC FIA68-2616
Presents a study of Norman Jacobson, professor of political science, University of California, Berkeley. Features interviews with him, scenes of him with his students in seminars, and scenes of student involvement in current events.
Education
Dist - IU **Prod** - NET 1968

Norman Kennedy - a Man and His Songs 146 MIN
U-matic
B&W (J)
LC 80-706066
Presents a portrait of Norman Kennedy, singer of Scottish ballads and folksongs and master weaver at Colonial Williamsburg. Includes an interview with Kennedy in which he talks about weaving, the history of song, the nature of the oral tradition and the Scottish antecedents of American culture.
Fine Arts; History - United States
Dist - HERTZ **Prod** - HERTZ 1979

Norman Kennedy - a Man and His Songs, Pt 1 73 MIN
U-matic
B&W (J)
LC 80-706066
Presents a portrait of Norman Kennedy, singer of Scottish ballads and folksongs and master weaver at Colonial Williamsburg. Includes an interview with Kennedy in which he talks about weaving, the history of song, the nature of the oral tradition and the Scottish antecedents of American culture.
Fine Arts
Dist - HERTZ **Prod** - HERTZ 1979

Norman Kennedy - a Man and His Songs, Pt 2 73 MIN
U-matic
B&W (J)
LC 80-706066
Presents a portrait of Norman Kennedy, singer of Scottish ballads and folksongs and master weaver at Colonial Williamsburg. Includes an interview with Kennedy in which he talks about weaving, the history of song, the nature of the oral tradition and the Scottish antecedents of American culture.
Fine Arts
Dist - HERTZ **Prod** - HERTZ 1979

Norman Mailer 60 MIN
VHS
Color (S)
Features a self - portrait of Norman Mailer which includes interviews with Mailer's articulate family and clips from film adaptations of his works. Gives Mailer a chance to talk about his generation - drugs, power and boxing, his favorite sport. Also discusses Mailer's view of immortality in light of 'The Executioner's Song,' his book about mass murderer Gary Gilmore.
Literature and Drama
Dist - FI **Prod** - RMPR 1986
UILL

Norman McLaren's Opening Speech 8 MIN
U-matic / VHS / 16mm
B&W (H C A)
Portrays Norman McLaren and his struggle with an animated microscope.
Fine Arts
Dist - IFB **Prod** - IFB 1963

Norman Normal 6 MIN
16mm
Color
A modern morality play, arrayed in wit. Deals with the central dilemma of the time - how does one ethical man handle himself so as to save his private dignity within the seething arenas of today's life.
Guidance and Counseling
Dist - VIEWFI **Prod** - PFP

Norman Paul, MD, Associate Professor of Psychiatry, Boston Universtiy Medical School 60 MIN
U-matic / VHS
Perceptions, Pt B - Dialogues with Family Therapists Series Vol VII, Pt B14
Color (PRO)
Focuses on intergenerational family therapy and the effects of incompleted grief.
Guidance and Counseling; Health and Safety; Psychology; Sociology
Dist - BOSFAM **Prod** - BOSFAM

Norman Rockwell 58 MIN
VHS
Color (I)
$39.95 purchase _ #HV - 666
Documents the life and work of Norman Rockwell. Features Rockwell himself as narrator. Includes dramatic reenactments, archival film footage and the artist's own works.
Fine Arts; History - World
Dist - CRYSP **Prod** - CRYSP

Norman Rockwell - an American portrait 60 MIN
VHS
Color (G)
$39.95 purchase _ #VU1004V - F
Celebrates the commonplace yet insightful view of human nature seen in Norman Rockwell's art. Includes commentary by the artist, by his friends and by art historians on his unique place in American art.
Fine Arts
Dist - CAMV

Norman Rockwell's world - an American dream 30 MIN
VHS
Color (H C G T A)
Presents the words and artwork of American painter Norman Rockwell. Interviews Rockwell at home in New England and in his studio, offering his artistic vision of the world. Features film footage of the times depicted in Rockwell's paintings.
Fine Arts
Dist - UILL **Prod** - UILL
KNOWUN

Norman Rockwell's World - an American Dream 25 MIN
16mm
Color
LC 73-700605
Presents a tribute to America's best known and most popular artist, Norman Rockwell. Explains that Norman Rockwell has been sensitive to the movement of American history.
Fine Arts; History - United States
Dist - FI **Prod** - ARROW 1972

Norman Studer and Grant Rogers 52 MIN
U-matic / VHS
Rainbow quest series
Color
Presents Norman Studer talking about the folklore of upstate New York and introduces composer - fiddler - guitarist - quarry - worker Grant Rogers.
Fine Arts
Dist - NORROS **Prod** - SEEGER

Norman the Doorman 35 MIN
VHS / 16mm
Children's Circle Video Series
Color (K)
$18.88 purchase _ #CCV020
Also includes other stories - Brave Irene, Lentil.
Literature and Drama
Dist - EDUCRT

Norman the Doorman 14 MIN
16mm / U-matic / VHS
Color
LC 70-711944
Uses the original pictures and text from the children's book of the same title, written and illustrated by Don Freeman. Tells the story of a mouse who is a doorman at an art museum where he wins a prize and many friends with the tiny mobiles that he fashions from mousetraps.
Literature and Drama
Dist - WWS **Prod** - WWS 1971

Norman Vincent Peale - the power of positive thinking 60 MIN
VHS
Color (G)
$29.95 purchase
Features Dr Norman Vincent Peale in an exposition of his philosophy of positive thinking. Encourages viewers to 'take charge' of their thoughts, stop worrying, adopt a more positive attitude, stay energized, and accomplish their goals.
Psychology
Dist - PBS **Prod** - WNETTV

Normandy Invasion 19 MIN
U-matic / VHS / 16mm
Why We Fight Series
B&W (H C A)
LC FIE52-866
Presents on the spot coverage by U S Coast Guard combat photographers of the initial assault on Fortress Europe. Shows the tremendous invasion preparations and American troops storming French shores and establishing the beach - head.
Civics and Political Systems; History - United States; History - World
Dist - USNAC **Prod** - USCG 1944

Normandy to the Rhine - Western Front 1944 - 45 52 MIN
VHS
Century of warfare series
Color (G)
$19.99 purchase _ #0 - 7835 - 8412 - 1NK
Takes a frontline look at World War II, 1944 - 1945. Covers strategy, tactics, weapons, personalities, battles and campaigns, victories and defeats. Part of a 20 - part series on 20th - century warfare.
Civics and Political Systems; History - World; Sociology
Dist - TILIED

Norman's New Garden 13 MIN
U-matic / VHS / 16mm
Color
LC 81-700064
Tells how Norman decides to pay some attention to his yard and starts planting trees.
Agriculture; Fine Arts
Dist - WOMBAT **Prod** - GFILM 1981

NORPLANT insertion and removal procedures 20 MIN
VHS
Color (G)
#NRP - 004
Presents a free - loan program which introduces healthcare professionals to the insertion and removal techniques of the NORPLANT system, a subdermal contraceptive system that provides five years of continuous birth control, yet is completely reversible.
Health and Safety; Psychology
Dist - WYAYLA **Prod** - WYAYLA

NORPLANT system patient video 14 MIN
VHS
Color (G)
#NRP - 027
Presents a free - loan program which educates patients about the NORPLANT system, a subdermal contraceptive system that provides five years of continuous birth control but is completely reversible. Interviews women who have used the system. Explains side effects and general precautions.
Health and Safety
Dist - WYAYLA **Prod** - WYAYLA

Norrkoping - the Spiral 16 MIN
16mm
Color
Presents a picture of modern Norrkoping with its industries and recreational areas.
Geography - World; Social Science; Sociology
Dist - AUDPLN **Prod** - ASI

North Africa - Southwest Asia - Managing Basic Resources 15 MIN
VHS / U-matic
Global Geography Series
Color (I J)
$125.00 purchase
Discusses the problems facing North Africa and Southwest Asia in organizing and handling their natural resources.
Geography - World
Dist - AITECH **Prod** - AITECH 1987

North Africa, the desert war - Volume 2 35 MIN
VHS
War chronicles series
B&W (G)
$14.95 purchase _ #S01093
Presents the second segment of an eight - part series on World War II. Covers the desert battles in North Africa. Suggests that the battle at Kasserine Pass, an Allied victory, was the beginning of the end for the Axis.

History - United States
Dist - UILL

North Africa - the great Sahara 15 MIN
VHS
Great deserts of the world series
Color; PAL (H)
Reveals that moving sand dunes, rocky plains, rugged plateaus and mountains comprise the patchwork of deserts in the vast Sahara. Traces the history of the nomadic Touregs, the Romans, the Arabs, Berbers, and European scientists, explorers and priests, to the present nations of North Africa. Part of a six - part series on deserts of the world.
Geography - World; History - World; Science - Natural
Dist - VIEWTH **Prod** - VIEWTH
CORF

North Africa - the Great Sahara 15 MIN
U-matic / VHS / 16mm
Great Deserts of the World Series
Color (I J H)
$400 purchase - 16 mm, $250 purchase - video _ #5292C
Talks about the Sahara desert and the many people, such as nomads, Romans, Arabs, explorers, and priests, which have been a part of its history.
Geography - World
Dist - CORF

North America '90 52 MIN
VHS
Fifty - foot world cup circuit series
Color (G)
$39.95 purchase _ #0939
Presents footage of racing action and interviews of sailing personnel in the 1990 North American portion of the 50 foot World Cup Circuit.
Physical Education and Recreation
Dist - SEVVID

North America - Cenozoic 28 MIN
U-matic / VHS
Basic and Petroleum Geology for Non - Geologists - Historical - - 'Series; Historical
Color (IND)
Industrial and Technical Education; Science - Physical
Dist - GPCV **Prod** - PHILLP

North America - Early Paleozoic 43 MIN
VHS / U-matic
Basic and Petroleum Geology for Non - Geologists - Historical - - 'Series; Historical
Color (IND)
Industrial and Technical Education; Science - Physical
Dist - GPCV **Prod** - PHILLP

North America - Growth of a Continent Series
Delivering the goods 15 MIN
The Fossil storehouse 15 MIN
From the beginning 15 MIN
From the ground up 15 MIN
Harvesting the seas 15 MIN
Logging the Land 15 MIN
The Man made World 15 MIN
Mapping the Land 15 MIN
Patterns of Climate 15 MIN
The Search for Power 15 MIN
Then Came Man 15 MIN
Tilling the Land 15 MIN
Vegetation and Soil 15 MIN
Dist - TVOTAR

North America - its Coastlines 14 MIN
U-matic / VHS / 16mm
North America Series
Color (I J)
LC 79-714991
Traces the historic and economic roles of coastlines, and shows the different coastlines, how they form and how they slowly change.
Geography - United States; Geography - World; Science - Physical; Social Science
Dist - CORF **Prod** - CORF 1971

North America - its Mountains 14 MIN
U-matic / VHS / 16mm
North America Series
Color (I J)
LC 77-714988
Describes the mountain ranges of North America, showing how they vary in structure, climate, plant and animal life. Discusses ways in which they have affected man.
Geography - United States; Geography - World; Science - Natural; Science - Physical; Social Science
Dist - CORF **Prod** - CORF 1971

North America - its Plains and Plateaus 16 MIN
U-matic / VHS / 16mm
North America Series
Color (I J)
LC 70-714989
Shows the characteristics and location of major plains and plateaus of North America, and discusses some of the ways in which they have affected man's use of the land.
Geography - World; Science - Natural; Science - Physical; Social Science
Dist - CORF **Prod** - CORF 1971

North America - its Rivers 14 MIN
U-matic / VHS / 16mm
North America Series
Color (I J)
LC 75-714990
Explores the distinctive features of the major rivers of the continent, and discusses their contributions to the farming, recreation, transportation and hydroelectric power of North America.
Geography - United States; Geography - World; Science - Physical; Social Science
Dist - CORF **Prod** - CORF 1971

North America - Late Paleozoic 37 MIN
VHS / U-matic
Basic and Petroleum Geology for Non - Geologists - Historical - - 'Series; Historical
Color (IND)
Industrial and Technical Education; Science - Physical
Dist - GPCV **Prod** - PHILLP

North America - Mesozoic 32 MIN
U-matic / VHS
Basic and Petroleum Geology for Non - Geologists - Historical - - 'Series; Historical
Color (IND)
Industrial and Technical Education; Science - Physical
Dist - GPCV **Prod** - PHILLP

North America Series
North America - its Coastlines 14 MIN
North America - its Mountains 14 MIN
North America - its Plains and Plateaus 16 MIN
North America - its Rivers 14 MIN
North America - the Continent 17 MIN
Dist - CORF

North America - the Continent 17 MIN
U-matic / VHS / 16mm
North America Series
Color (I J)
LC FIA66-35
Shows the basic land forms and climates of the major regions of North America, including the coastal highlands, Western Cordillera and Appalachian highlands. Indicates the relationship of geography and human use.
Geography - United States; Geography - World; Social Science
Dist - CORF **Prod** - CORF 1966

North America - Vol I 85 MIN
VHS
Masters of Animation Series
Color (S)
$29.95 purchase _ #401 - 9006
Represents the peak achievements of 7000 artists from 13 countries. Provides an opportunity to experience the exciting diversity of the world's leading animation artists and state - of - the - art animation technology. Volume I showcases the best animation from the USA, the National Film Board of Canada and the CBC - Radio Canada - Canadian Independent Animators and interviews Chuck Jones, Barrie Nelson, Leo Salkin, master animator Norman McLaren, Caroline Leaf and Don Arioli. Artists represented by their works include Walt Disney, the Hubleys, Joanna Priestley, Derek Lamb, Ishu Patel, Frederick Back and Andre Theroux.
Fine Arts; Industrial and Technical Education
Dist - FI **Prod** - ITOONS 1988

North American Big Game 30 MIN
VHS
Sportsmans Workshop Video Library Series
Color (K IND)
Features ten North American big game animals in natural habitat and their specific areas for those interested in their natural surroundings and living. No killing scenes.
Physical Education and Recreation
Dist - WRBPRO **Prod** - WRBPRO 1985

North American collection series
Presents a five-part series on North America. Teaches about the people, culture and history of North American states, provinces and cities. Visits historic buildings, monuments and landmarks. Examines the physical topography of locations. Travels to Alaska, New York City, British Columbia, America's national parks.
Alaska experience 60 MIN
British Columbia - the Rockies to the Pacific 60 MIN
New York - city of cities 60 MIN
Dist - CAMV **Prod** - WNETTV 1985

North American Elk - the Wapiti 10 MIN
16mm / U-matic / VHS
Color (I J H)
LC FIA55-658
Tells the story of the reduction of the herds of elk in this country by the heavy winters of 1886 - 87 and the fencing of the open range which kept the elk from the food on which they had depended.
History - United States; Science - Natural
Dist - IFB **Prod** - WLF 1948

North American facsimile book - Mac
CD-ROM
Color (G A)
$489.00 purchase _ #2851m
Includes over 150,000 fax numbers, along with complete addresses for easy mailing list generation. Lists most major corporations in the US, Canada and Mexico. For Macintosh Plus, SE and II computers. Requires at least one M of RAM, one floppy disk drive, and an Apple compatible CD - ROM drive.
Computer Science; Literature and Drama
Dist - BEP

North American facsimile book - PC
CD-ROM
Color (G A)
$489.00 purchase _ #2851p
Includes over 150,000 fax numbers, along with complete addresses for easy mailing list generation. Lists most major corporations in the US, Canada and Mexico. For IBM PCs and compatibles. Requires 640K RAM, DOS Version 3.1 or greater, one floppy disk drive - a hard drive is recommended, one empty expansion slot, and an IBM compatible CD - ROM drive.
Computer Science; Literature and Drama
Dist - BEP

North American Framework 51 MIN
VHS / U-matic
Basic Geology Series
Color (IND)
Industrial and Technical Education; Science - Physical
Dist - GPCV **Prod** - GPCV

North American Indian Legends 21 MIN
U-matic / VHS / 16mm
Color (I J)
LC 73-701430
Describes tribal traditions, explains natural events and expresses the values of the North American Indian people. Features legends which represent the original stories of Indians in three different geographical regions of North America.
Literature and Drama; Social Science
Dist - PHENIX **Prod** - PHENIX 1973

North American Indian Series Part 1
Treaties made, Treaties Broken 18 MIN
Dist - MGHT

North American Indian Series Part 2
How the West was Won and Honor Lost 25 MIN
Dist - MGHT

North American Indian Series Part 3
Lament of the Reservation 24 MIN
Dist - MGHT

North American Indians - Mac
CD-ROM
(G A)
$129.00 purchase _ #2859m
Compiles from public and private information and images. Encompasses the lives and trying times of indigenous North Americans. Covers leadership, tribal heritage, religion, family life, customs, wars, art, artifacts, reservations and resettlement. For Macintosh Plus, SE and II computers. Requires at least one M of RAM, one floppy disk drive, and an Apple compatible CD - ROM drive.
History - United States; Social Science
Dist - BEP

North American Indians - PC
CD-ROM
(G A)
$129.00 purchase _ #2859p
Compiles from public and private information and images. Encompasses the lives and trying times of indigenous North Americans. Covers leadership, tribal heritage, religion, family life, customs, wars, art, artifacts, reservations and resettlement. For IBM and compatibles. Requires 640K RAM, DOS version 3.1 or greater, one floppy disk drive - hard disk drive recommended, one empty expansion slot, and and IBM compatible CD - Rom dirve.
History - United States; Social Science
Dist - BEP

North American Indians Today 25 MIN
U-matic / VHS / 16mm
Color (H C A)
LC 78-700739
Deals with the efforts of North American Indians to learn about their cultural heritage and to protect their lands.

Social Science; Sociology
Dist - NGS **Prod** - NGS 1977

North American Neighbors 24 MIN
16mm
Color (H A)
Presents the hopes, despairs and conflicts of life in the North American continent from Alaska to the islands of the Caribbean. Discusses the Christian responsibility of Protestantism to work cooperatively toward their solution.
Geography - United States; Geography - World; Guidance and Counseling; Religion and Philosophy; Sociology
Dist - YALEDV **Prod** - YALEDV

North American Species Series

Arctic oasis	16 MIN
Autumn with grizzlies	15 MIN
Bighorns of Beauty Creek	25 MIN
The Double Life of the Whooping Crane	15 MIN
The Magnificent Moose	16 MIN
The Majestic Wapiti	16 MIN
On Silent Wings	16 MIN
Sharp Eyes, Sharp Talons	16 MIN
Wolves and Coyotes of the Rockies	15 MIN

Dist - BCNFL

The North Atlantic - cradle of the continent 55 MIN
VHS
On the waterways series
Color (G H)
$29.95 purchase _ #OW01
Travels with the crew of the Driftwood down the St Lawrence River to chronicle Acadians, boat builders, lobstermen, environmentalists, and a Pasamaquoddy fisherman keeping his tribe's language and heritage alive. Narrated by Jason Robards. Part of a 13 - part series on the history, geography, culture and ecology of North American waterways.
Social Science
Dist - SVIP

North Beach 12 MIN
16mm
Color (G)
$25.00 rental
Documents filmmaker Henry Hills' neighborhood of three years.
Fine Arts; Geography - United States
Dist - CANCIN

North Beach 2 12 MIN
16mm
Color (G)
$25.00 rental
Edits the film, North Beach, to represent more of an 1980s style which the filmmaker, Henry Hills, states is more frenetic.
Fine Arts; Geography - United States
Dist - CANCIN

North Brazil 18 MIN
16mm
Latin American Series - a Focus on People Series
Color (I)
Explores Brazil, a land of extraordinary geography and Indian culture.
Geography - World; Social Science
Dist - SF **Prod** - CLAIB 1973

North California 60 MIN
VHS
Portrait of America series
Color (J H C G)
$99.95 purchase _ #AMB05V-S
Visits California. Offers extensive research into the state's history. Films key locations and presents segments on history, government, education, folklore, science, journalism, sociology, industry, agriculture and business. Shows what is unique about California and distinctive about its regional culture and how it got to be that way. Includes study guide. Part of a 50 - part series.
Geography - United States; History - United States
Dist - CAMV

North Carolina 60 MIN
VHS
Portrait of America series
Color (J H C G)
$99.95 purchase _ #AMB33V
Visits North Carolina. Offers extensive research into the state's history. Films key locations and presents segments on its history, government, education, folklore, science, journalism, sociology, industry, agriculture and business. Shows what is unique about North Carolina and what is distinctive about its regional culture and how it got to be that way. Includes teacher study guides. Part of a 50 - part series.
Geography - United States; History - United States
Dist - CAMV

North Carolina - Golf State, USA 15 MIN
16mm
Color (J)
LC 80-701043
Portrays North Carolina, the richest golf state, with its 500,000 dollar World Open, World Golf Hall of Fame and many other great attractions. Views public and private Alpine, Piedmont and Sandhill courses of the Tar Heel state.
Geography - United States; Physical Education and Recreation
Dist - KLEINW **Prod** - KLEINW 1975

North Carolina State
VHS
Campus clips series
Color (H C A)
$29.95 purchase _ #CC0081V
Takes a video visit to the campus of North Carolina State University. Shows many of the distinctive features of the campus, and interviews students about their experiences. Provides information on the composition of the student body, professors, academics, social life, housing, and other subjects.
Education
Dist - CAMV

North Central 60 MIN
VHS
AAA travel series
Color (G)
$24.95 purchase _ #NA15
Explores the North Central states.
Geography - United States; Geography - World
Dist - SVIP

The North Central United States - 2 30 MIN
VHS
50 States, 50 capitals - geography of the USA series
Color (H)
$89.00 purchase _ #60315 - 025
Discusses in detail the states included in the north cental region of the United States. Includes locations, industries, agriculture, capitals, populations, sizes and areas, climates and points of interest. Part one of four parts on US geography.
Geography - United States
Dist - GA **Prod** - GA 1992

The North central US - Volume 2c 35 MIN
VHS
Visions of adventure series
Color (P)
$24.95 purchase _ #GE04
Focuses on the north central United States. Part of an eight - part series on geography.
Geography - United States
Dist - SVIP

North China Commune 80 MIN
16mm
Color (H C A)
Looks at harvesting in a North China commune. Shows that intensive cropping methods and the orchestrated effort at harvest time of all commune members make it possible to support a population of 14,500 on only 3,000 acres of land.
Agriculture; Geography - World
Dist - NFBC **Prod** - NFBC 1979

North China Factory 57 MIN
16mm
Color (H C A)
Shows a factory community in China where over 6,000 workers process, spin and weave raw cotton into eighty million meters of high - quality cloth per year. Visits the workers' residential, social, recreational and educational facilities, all of which are located on factory property. Highlights retirement and wedding ceremonies in which factory management plays a major part.
Business and Economics; Geography - World; Social Science; Sociology
Dist - NFBC **Prod** - NFBC 1980

North Dakota 60 MIN
VHS
Portrait of America series
Color (J H C G)
$99.95 purchase _ #AMB34V
Visits North Dakota. Offers extensive research into the state's history. Films key locations and presents segments on its history, government, education, folklore, science, journalism, sociology, industry, agriculture and business. Shows what is unique about North Dakota and what is distinctive about its regional culture and how it got to be that way. Includes teacher study guides. Part of a 50 - part series.
Geography - United States; History - United States
Dist - CAMV

North Dakota Agriculture - Green and Gold 30 MIN
16mm
Color
LC 77-701821
Comments briefly on the world food problem and illustrates various facets of the agricultural industry in North Dakota. Shows the role of North Dakota State University in agricultural research.
Agriculture; Geography - United States; Health and Safety
Dist - NDSFL **Prod** - NDASU 1977

North Dakota - Flickertail Flashbacks 22 MIN
16mm
B&W
LC 75-702974
Uses still and moving pictures taken from 1915 to 1920 in order to show the life and times of that period in North Dakota.
History - United States; Industrial and Technical Education
Dist - SNYDBF **Prod** - SNYDBF 1974

North Hatley Antique Sale 14 MIN
16mm
Journal Series
Color
LC 74-701981
Highlights an antique sale in a small Quebec town.
Geography - World
Dist - FIARTS **Prod** - FIARTS 1973

North Indian Village 32 MIN
U-matic / VHS / 16mm
Color (H C A)
LC FIA64-1374
A study of the village of Khalapur between 1953 and 1955, emphasizing work on the land, the hereditary occupations of castes, the relationships between men and women and the forms of worship.
History - World; Sociology
Dist - IFB **Prod** - CORNRS 1959

North - Nord 16 MIN
16mm
Color (G)
#2X33 N
Presents the sights and sounds of the Northwest Territories of Canada. Not narrated.
Geography - World
Dist - CDIAND **Prod** - NFBC 1978

North of Capricorn 60 MIN
VHS
Australian ark series
Color (G)
$19.95 purchase _ #S02059
Portrays Australia in regions north of the Tropic of Capricorn.
Geography - World; History - World; Science - Natural
Dist - UILL

North of Hudson Bay 55 MIN
16mm
B&W
LC 75-708944
Presents a melodrama in which a man goes to Canada to investigate the murder of his brother, whose partner is wrongfully being charged with the crime.
Fine Arts
Dist - TWCF **Prod** - TWCF 1923

North of Sixty Degrees - Destiny Uncertain Series

The Alaska experience	30 MIN
Beautiful adversity	30 MIN
Canada's last colonies	30 MIN
Going south	30 MIN
Mending Bodies and Souls	30 MIN
The New Economic Order	30 MIN
New Ways of Knowing	30 MIN
Reading the rocks	30 MIN
Tell Me who I Am	30 MIN
Terms and Conditions	30 MIN
They Came to Stay	30 MIN
The True North	30 MIN
Yukon - the invisible history	30 MIN

Dist - TVOTAR

North of Slavery 29 MIN
Videoreel / VT2
Black Experience Series
Color
History - United States; Sociology
Dist - PBS **Prod** - WTTWTV

North of the Yukon 103 MIN
VHS / U-matic
Color (K A)
Features Lorne Greene narrating a story of an Eskimo's courage in a raw domain.
Geography - United States; Social Science
Dist - SUTHRB **Prod** - SUTHRB

North Sea Islanders 19 MIN
16mm / U-matic / VHS
Man and His World Series
Color (P I J H C)
LC 74-705485
Contrasts living on an island and living on a continental land mass, showing man against the elements and how he survives.
Geography - World; Social Science; Sociology
Dist - FI **Prod** - FI 1969

North Sea 1 - the Tectonic Framework 58 MIN
VHS / 16mm
Sedimentary Processes and Basin Analysis Series
Color (C)
$150.00, $185.00 purchase _ #269515
Illustrates the key concepts, economic relevance and influence of measurement technology advances in palaeoenvironmental and basin analysis. Observes how large parts of the earth's crust subside and accumulate thick deposits of sediments, possible reservoirs for oil, gas and coal. Divides into four themes - Sedimentary Petrology, Sedimentary Environments, Basin Analysis and North Sea - Western Canada Case Studies. 'North Sea 1' presents two models of sedimentary basin formation and development - McKenzie and Wernicke models - and demonstrates how the case for each has been argued and interpreted in terms of petroleum geology.
Geography - World; Industrial and Technical Education; Science - Physical; Social Science
Dist - ACCESS **Prod** - BBCTV 1987

North Sea 3 - Reservoirs 59 MIN
VHS / 16mm
Sedimentary Processes and Basin Analysis Series
Color (C)
$150.00, $185.00 purchase _ #269517
Illustrates the key concepts, economic relevance and influence of measurement technology advances in palaeoenvironmental and basin analysis. Observes how large parts of the earth's crust subside and accumulate thick deposits of sediments, possible reservoirs for oil, gas and coal. Divides into four themes - Sedimentary Petrology, Sedimentary Environments, Basin Analysis and North Sea - Western Canada Case Studies. 'North Sea 3' analyzes four of the North Sea's major hydrocarbon reservoirs - the Rotliegend, whose source rock is Westphalian coal, The Brent, located within an extensive mid - Jurassic sedimentation, the Brae, which taps upper - Jurassic sedimentation, and the Chalk, a geological phenomenon whose formative factors are investigated.
Geography - World; Industrial and Technical Education; Science - Physical; Social Science
Dist - ACCESS **Prod** - BBCTV 1987

North Sea 2 - the Origin and Migration of Hydrocarbons 58 MIN
VHS / 16mm
Sedimentary Processes and Basin Analysis Series
Color (C)
$150.00, $185.00 purchase _ #269516
Illustrates the key concepts, economic relevance and influence of measurement technology advances in palaeoenvironmental and basin analysis. Observes how large parts of the earth's crust subside and accumulate thick deposits of sediments, possible reservoirs for oil, gas and coal. Divides into four themes - Sedimentary Petrology, Sedimentary Environments, Basin Analysis and North Sea - Western Canada Case Studies. 'North Sea 2' focuses on the origin and nature of source rocks, how petroleum is generated, and how the timing of generation, migration and reservoir formation is evaluated. The main example used is the Brent field.
Geography - World; Industrial and Technical Education; Science - Physical; Social Science
Dist - ACCESS **Prod** - BBCTV 1987

North Shore Maui 30 MIN
VHS
Color (G)
$29.95 purchase _ #0808
Combines slow motion photography with on - board camera angles to capture surfing on the monster surf of Maui. Covers the Aloha Classic competition.
Physical Education and Recreation
Dist - SEVVID

A North - South Monologue 58
16mm / VHS
International Development Collection Series
Color (A)
$200.00 purchase, $50.00 rental _ #CC4126
Investigates multinational investment policies in Haiti with an indication that the profit motive underpins much foreign 'aid' and that the exploitation of developing nations by mining, tourism and manufacturing companies from industrialized nations serve to maintain a monologue in which only the powerful donor nations have a voice.
Business and Economics; Geography - World; History - World; Industrial and Technical Education; Social Science
Dist - IU **Prod** - NFBC 1990

North Star 800 and 800X
VHS
Loran operation guide series
Color (G A)
$29.90 purchase _ #0790
Teaches Loran C programming for the North Star 800 and 800X in nautical navigation. Shows how to enter the correct Loran chain for specific positions, how to program positions, determine the accuracy of a Loran C 'fix' and how to deal with the intricacies of specific machines.
Physical Education and Recreation; Social Science
Dist - SEVVID

North - the Land and the Man - Le Territoire Et L'Homme 21 MIN
16mm
Color (H C A) (FRENCH INUKTITUT)
#2X34 N
Glamorizes the exploitation of northern resources.
Social Science; Sociology
Dist - CDIAND **Prod** - AKOP 1971

North to Adventure 30 MIN
16mm
Color
Shows some of the most magnificent scenery on our continent while exploring a great variety of game as it is seen and hunted.
Geography - United States; Physical Education and Recreation
Dist - SFI **Prod** - SFI

North to Freedom 15 MIN
U-matic / VHS / 16mm
American Scrapbook Series
Color (I)
Describes the establishment and maintenance of the Underground Railroad, which helped freedom - seeking slaves on the journey north.
History - United States
Dist - GPN **Prod** - WVIZTV 1977

North Vs South in the Founding of the United States - 1787 - 1796 - 1 20 MIN
VHS
Geography in US History Series
Color (H)
Centers on the geographic theme of 'regions.' Examines how regional differences between Northern and Southern states complicated efforts to establish a workable constitutional government. Highlights the nature and effect of the compromises made and the roles of Madison and Washington. Part 1 of a ten - part series which emphasizes the study of American geography within the context of American history courses using geographic concepts.
Biography; Geography - United States; History - United States
Dist - AITECH **Prod** - AITECH 1991

The North Wind and the Sun 9 MIN
16mm / U-matic / VHS
Classic Tales Retold Series
Color (P I)
LC 77-700691
Presents the Greek and African legend of The North Wind And The Sun about a contest between these two powerful forces of nature to see which one is the stronger.
Fine Arts; Literature and Drama
Dist - PHENIX **Prod** - PHENIX 1977

The North Wind and the Sun 7 MIN
U-matic / VHS / 16mm
Color (P)
$190, $125 purchase _ #1472
Tells the story of a contest between the wind and the sun, and shows that gentleness is often more effective than force.
Literature and Drama
Dist - CORF

The North Wind and the Sun - a Fable by Aesop 3 MIN
16mm
Color (I)
Presents an animated version of the Aesop fable about the duel between the North Wind and the Sun to see which was a better force when it comes to making a man take off his coat.
Fine Arts; Literature and Drama
Dist - NFBC **Prod** - NFBC 1972

The North Wind and the Sun - an Aesop Fable 7 MIN
U-matic / VHS / 16mm
Color (P)
Animated story of a contest between the North Wind and the Sun. Teaches the lesson that you can sometimes do more by being gentle than you can by using force.
Literature and Drama
Dist - CORF **Prod** - GAKKEN 1962

North with the Spring 52 MIN
U-matic / VHS / 16mm
Four Seasons Series
Color (H C)
Focuses on the world's favorite season, Spring. Follows Spring on a 17,000 mile journey from the Florida Everglades to the Canadian Arctic.
Science - Natural
Dist - CNEMAG **Prod** - HOBLEI 1970

North with the Spring, Pt 1 30 MIN
16mm / U-matic / VHS
Color (H C)
Focuses on the world's favorite season, Spring. Follows Spring on a 17,000 mile journey from the Florida Everglades to the Canadian Arctic.
Science - Natural
Dist - CNEMAG **Prod** - HOBLEI 1970

North with the Spring, Pt 2 22 MIN
16mm / U-matic / VHS
Color (H C)
Focuses on the world's favorite season, Spring. Follows Spring on a 17,000 mile journey from the Florida everglades to the Canadian Arctic.
Science - Natural
Dist - CNEMAG **Prod** - HOBLEI 1970

Northeast Farm Community 15 MIN
U-matic / VHS / 16mm
Pioneer Life Series
Color; B&W (I J)
Portrays the life of a typical northeastern family in the early 1800's. Illustrates the farmer's increasing reliance on community services such as grist mill, blacksmith shop, general store, church and school.
Geography - United States; History - United States; Social Science
Dist - IU **Prod** - IU 1960

The Northeast United States - 1 30 MIN
VHS
50 States, 50 capitals - geography of the USA series
Color (H)
$89.00 purchase _ #60313 - 025
Discusses in detail the states included in the northeast region of the United States. Includes locations, industries, agriculture, capitals, populations, sizes and areas, climates and points of interest. Part one of four parts on US geography.
Geography - United States
Dist - GA **Prod** - GA 1992

Northeastern
VHS
Campus clips series
Color (H C A)
$29.95 purchase _ #CC0056V
Takes a video visit to the campus of Northeastern University in Massachusetts. Shows many of the distinctive features of the campus, and interviews students about their experiences. Provides information on the composition of the student body, professors, academics, social life, housing, and other subjects.
Education
Dist - CAMV

The Northeastern US - Volume 2a 35 MIN
VHS
Visions of adventure series
Color (P)
$24.95 purchase _ #GE02
Focuses on the Northeastern United States. Part of an eight - part series on geography.
Geography - United States
Dist - SVIP

Northern Arizona
VHS
Campus clips series
Color (H C A)
$29.95 purchase _ #CC0004V
Takes a video visit to the campus of Northern Arizona University. Shows many of the distinctive features of the campus, and interviews students about their experiences. Provides information on the composition of the student body, professors, academics, social life, housing, and other subjects.
Education
Dist - CAMV

Northern Australian Regional Survey, Pt 2 - the Barkly Region 28 MIN
16mm
Color (H A)
LC FIA65-1067
Deals with the Barkly region of the Northern Territory and Queensland, which was surveyed during 1948 - 49 by the CSIRO division of Land Research and Regional Survey. Describes the four main areas into which the region is divided, and discusses their topography, soils, vegetation, industries and potentialities.

Agriculture; Geography - World; Science - Natural
Dist - CSIROA **Prod** - CSIROA 1950

Northern Campus 14 MIN
16mm
B&W (H C A)
#2X75 I
Documents the problems encountered by native Indian children in schools which have poor curricula. Discusses steps taken by educators to rectify the situation.
Education; Sociology
Dist - CDIAND **Prod** - NFBC 1961

A Northern Challenge 22 MIN
16mm
Color (G)
_ #106C 0173 615
Gives a view at ground level of how new airfields built by the Canadian Armed Forces are helping to make the Canadian Arctic the crossroads of the north and flyway of the northern hemisphere. Shows what the introduction of air transport routes will mean to northern communities.
History - World; Social Science
Dist - CFLMDC **Prod** - NFBC 1973

Northern Coastal Lowlands, the, Pt 1 25 MIN
16mm
Color (H C A)
Discusses each German region's lifestyles, economy, problems, and opportunities for the future. Provides some unusual helicopter views of Germany's geography.
Geography - World; History - World; Sociology
Dist - WSTGLC **Prod** - WSTGLC

Northern Composition - Airs Du Nord 28 MIN
16mm
(G)
_ #106 0379 640
Combines image and music, moods and activities, far ranging landscapes and industrial complexes into a visual composition that suggests the many ingredients that have built a nation - Canada.
Geography - World; History - World
Dist - CFLMDC **Prod** - NFBC 1979

The Northern elephant seal - Living on the edge of extinction 14 MIN
16mm
Color (I J H C G)
$245.00, $315.00 purchase, $30.00 rental
Introduces students to the increasingly important subject of genetic diversity. Tells the story of the dramatic recovery of a formerly endangered species, the Northern elephant seal, which now breeds in impressive numbers. However, the seal and many other recovering species, are still on the edge of extinction due to the species' lack of genetic diversity. With study guide.
Science - Natural
Dist - BULFRG **Prod** - ZATZ 1987

The Northern Forests 55 MIN
16mm / VHS
Living Planet Series
(J H C)
$99.95 each, $595.00 series
Travels to forests in northern parts of the world to examine the survival capabliities of plants and animals there.
Science; Science - Natural; Science - Physical
Dist - AMBROS **Prod** - AMBROS 1984

The Northern Forests 55 MIN
U-matic / VHS / 16mm
Living Planet Series
Color (H C A)
Shows that trees of the coniferous forests have special adaptations that enable them to survive long cold winters. Reveals that many animals that inhabit these vast forests are dependent on the trees for leaves, cones or bark. Demonstrates that in the deciduous woodland, bears, skunks, raccoons, squirrels and opossums put on fat for the winter.
Science - Natural
Dist - TIMLIF **Prod** - BBCTV 1984

Northern Games 26 MIN
16mm
Color (G) (INUKTITUT)
#3X27
Documents the Northen Games, held every other summer in a selected Canadian community, in which Inuit and Dene Indians meet to play ancient Indian games.
Social Science
Dist - CDIAND **Prod** - FNL 1982

Northern Giant 29 MIN
16mm
B&W (H C A)
#3X60N
Investigates gold and mineral production in Canada. Presents Alvin Hamilton whe speculates on opening up the North with roads and rail.
History - World; Social Science
Dist - CDIAND **Prod** - CKCKTV 1958

Northern Ireland - a Decade of Civil Strife 26 MIN
U-matic / VHS
Color (H C A)
Focuses on the violent events in Northern Ireland between 1969 and 1979.
History - World
Dist - JOU **Prod** - UPI

Northern Ireland - mirror, mirror 50 MIN
VHS
Blood and belonging series
Color (A)
PdS99 purchase _ Available in UK only
Features host Michael Ignatieff taking a dramatic journey of discovery to examine nationalism in Northern Ireland. Examines the Loyalists, whose values hold up a distorted mirror to Britishness and who feel abandoned by the rest of the United Kingdom.
Civics and Political Systems; History - World
Dist - BBCENE

Northern Ireland - the Hunger Strikers 15 MIN
VHS / U-matic
Color (J H)
Discusses the death of IRA hunger strikers at Maze Prison in Belfast, Northern Ireland. Examines the history of the hostilities and the implications of growing world support for the IRA.
Geography - World; History - World
Dist - JOU **Prod** - JOU

Northern Ireland - the Troubles Continue 27 MIN
VHS / U-matic
Color (H C A)
Looks at elections in Northern Ireland which were held in hopes that a new Northern Ireland Assembly would aid in a political solution to the violence that has plagued Northern Ireland since 1967. Explores the conflicts, the factions and the government of this divided nation.
Geography - World; History - World
Dist - JOU **Prod** - JOU

Northern Irish People's Peace Movement, Pt 1 29 MIN
U-matic
Woman Series
Color
Explains the purpose of the nonsectarian and nonpartisan People's Peace Movement of Northern Ireland, founded after three Belfast children were killed during a gun battle. Tells how the violence affects the everyday lives of people on both sides of the political question.
Geography - World
Dist - PBS **Prod** - WNEDTV

Northern Irish People's Peace Movement, Pt 2 29 MIN
U-matic
Woman Series
Color
Presents the founders of the People's Peace Movement of Northern Ireland discussing their goals for peace.
Geography - World
Dist - PBS **Prod** - WNEDTV

The Northern Irish Question - Another View 29 MIN
U-matic
Woman Series
Color
Describes the Irish Republican movement's political plans for peace. Explains how funds contributed by Americans to the people of Northern Ireland are being used and assesses President Carter's human rights stand.
Geography - World
Dist - PBS **Prod** - WNEDTV

The Northern lakes 14 MIN
VHS
Color (G)
$29.95 purchase _ #S01841
Examines the ecosystems of the various lakes in north central America. Notes the fact that the top two feet of a lake is teeming with life. Presents forest footage of deer, bears, ducks, marmots, beavers, and many other animals.
Geography - World; Science - Natural
Dist - UILL

The Northern Lakes 14 MIN
U-matic / VHS / 16mm
Natural Environment Series
Color (I)
LC 79-700308
Surveys the lake region of the upper midwestern states and central provinces of Canada. Explores the ecosystem, the interrelationship of the water habitat and the forest and the relationship of the animal life to each habitat.
Geography - World; Science - Natural
Dist - JOU **Prod** - WILFGP 1978

Northern lifestyles series
A Fisherman's day 13 MIN
Dist - CDIAND

Northern Lights 90 MIN
U-matic / VHS
Color (H C A)
Focuses on the hardships encountered by first and second generation Scandinavians who emigrated to the U S and scattered over the plains, onto homesteads and into sod shanties. Reveals that poor families were victims of price fixing and foreclosure schemes which gave rise to a farmers' movement called the Nonpartisan League.
History - World; Sociology
Dist - FI **Prod** - FI 1979

The Northern Plains 30 MIN
U-matic
Silent Heritage - the American Indian Series
B&W
Examines the history of legendary plains warriors, the Sioux and Crow tribes, who fought tenaciously against the United States for their land and means of survival. Looks at the present status of their descendents.
Social Science; Sociology
Dist - UMITV **Prod** - UMITV 1966

Northern Spring 8 MIN
U-matic / VHS / 16mm
Color (P I)
LC 81-700681
Explores the effects of warmer weather on the flora of the forest.
Science - Natural
Dist - JOU **Prod** - JOU 1980

Northern Yukon Research Program 10 MIN
16mm
Discovery Series
Color
Describes a major archaeological research project in the northern Yukon which is producing evidence which suggests the presence of man in that region much earlier than was previously suspected.
History - World; Science - Physical; Sociology
Dist - UTORMC **Prod** - UTORMC

The Northlands 20 MIN
BETA / VHS / U-matic / 16mm
Physical geography of North America series
Color (P I J H)
$315.00, $90.00 purchase _ #C50483, #C51362
Examines the Northlands which stretch from the Atlantic to the Pacific across the northernmost reaches of North America. Explores the permanent ice caps of the high Arctic, the frozen tundra and the deep forests of the taiga. Observes how climate, plants and animals interact in a harsh environment. Part of a five - part series on the physical geography of North America.
Geography - United States; Geography - World; Science - Natural
Dist - NGS **Prod** - NGS 1989

Northrop Frye 30 MIN
VHS
World of ideas with Bill Moyers - Season I - series
Color (G)
$39.95 purchase _ #BMWI - 135
Interviews Canadian author, teacher and literary critic Northrop Frye. Considers cultural difference between the U S and Canada, focusing on Canada's search for a separate identity. Hosted by Bill Moyers.
History - World; Social Science; Sociology
Dist - PBS

Northstar 9000 60 MIN
VHS
Using Loran series
Color (G A)
$29.90 purchase _ #0943
Shows how to operate the Northstar 9000 Loran model. Includes installation tips, initialization, calibration, chain selection, notch filters, signal - to - noise ratio, time differentials, Lat - Lon functions, selecting and programming waypoints, setting anchor and waypoint alarm, cross - track error, determining course to steer and distance to go. Part of a series on the most popular Loran models.
Physical Education and Recreation; Social Science
Dist - SEVVID

The Northwest 15 MIN
U-matic / VHS / 16mm
American legacy series
Color (I)
Presents John Rugg reviewing the exploration and settlement of the American Northwest, including the Columbia River, the Lewis and Clark expedition and the Oregon Trail. Emphasizes the region's major industries, namely lumber products and aircraft manufacturing.
Geography - United States; History - United States
Dist - AITECH **Prod** - KRMATV 1983

Northwest Coast Indians 26 MIN
VHS / U-matic

Color
Reconstructs an abandoned village site on the basis of material evidence excavated from the artifacts from the Ozette Indian Village at Cape Alava, Washington.
History - United States; Social Science; Sociology
Dist - UWASHP **Prod** - UWASHP

Northwest Coast Indians - a Search for the Past 26 MIN
16mm
Color
Depicts the reconstruction of the abandoned village site of the Ozette Indians at Cape Alava, Washington by archaeologists and their students from Washington State University. Features material evidence they have excavated a rich variety of artifacts, such as pieces of baskets, bone and stone tools, combs, traces of houses and fire hearths.
Geography - United States; Social Science; Sociology
Dist - UWASHP **Prod** - KIRL

Northwest England 19 MIN
U-matic / VHS / 16mm
Regional Geography - British Isles Series
Color (I)
LC FIA68-2897
Shows the varied physical landscapes, types of land, use of the lake district of England and surrounding lowlands. Illustrates the importance of Carlisle as a trade route and market center and emphasizes the coal, iron, steel and shipbuilding industries of the region.
Geography - World
Dist - IFB **Prod** - BHA 1967

Northwest history - geography series
The Great river of the West - the Columbia 22 MIN
Dist - MMP

Northwest Medley 7 MIN
16mm
Color
LC 78-702492
Presents scences of the waters, woods and mountains of the American Northwest coordinated with a musical accompaniment to convey the moods of this region.
Geography - United States
Dist - LOH **Prod** - LOH 1968

Northwest Michigan - Prime Forestlands Identification Project 15 MIN
U-matic / VHS / 16mm
Color (H C A)
Explains how public groups, state agencies and the federal government all worked together to create 'The Prime Forestlands Identification Project.' Presents a lesson in resource management, as well as how cooperation among various groups can achieve common goals.
Science - Natural; Social Science; Sociology
Dist - BRAURP **Prod** - NWMRCD

The Northwest - Mountains to the Sea 23 MIN
U-matic / VHS / 16mm
Natural Environment Series
Color (I)
LC 77-703485
Surveys the natural habitats and plant and animal life in the seas, marshlands, rain forests and mountains of Northwest Canada.
Geography - World; Science - Natural
Dist - JOU **Prod** - WILFGP 1977
UILL

Northwest Passage 27 MIN
16mm
Color (G)
_ #106c 0170 005
Shows how a U S super tanker and a Canadian icebreaker realize a dream - the navigation of a commercial sea lane through the Arctic channels. Includes comments by ships' navigators and observers, and shipside sounds of sea ice breaking.
Geography - World; History - World; Social Science
Dist - CFLMDC **Prod** - NFBC 1970

Northwest passage - the story of Grand Portage 14 MIN
VHS
Color (G)
$24.95 purchase _ #R - 35C
Depicts the history of fur trade. Filmed in 1979.
History - United States
Dist - MINHS **Prod** - MINHS

The Northwest territory 20 MIN
U-matic / 16mm / VHS
United States expansion series
Color (J H C)
$420.00, $250.00 purchase _ #HP - 5767C
Dramatizes the history of the Northwest Territory from Indian days through the arrival of French missionary priests, from the French and Indian War through the growth of Chicago as an important transfer point. Part of a seven - part series on the post - Revolutionary settlement of the lands west and south of the original thirteen states.
Geography - United States; History - United States
Dist - CORF **Prod** - KLUCLA 1989

Northwest to Alaska 26 MIN
16mm
Audubon wildlife theatre series
Color (I)
Presents Alaska, always a bountiful land for man, enriching him with gold and now oil, but also reserving for wildlife some of the last primeval havens left in today's world. Shows the great reaches of the Alaskan wilderness, from the nameless mountains and the unpeopled valleys of Robert Service, to the Eskimo villages of Alaska's Northwest Coast, to the Pribiloff Islands in the Pacific.
Geography - United States; Geography - World; Social Science
Dist - AVEXP **Prod** - AVEXP

Northwest USA 22 MIN
U-matic
American scene series; No 10
B&W
LC 79-706696
Reviews the resources, industries and people of Oregon and Washington. Issued in 1949 as a motion picture.
Geography - United States
Dist - USNAC **Prod** - USOWI 1979

Northwest Visionaries 58 MIN
VHS / U-matic
Color
Documents the work of the Northwest American artists Mark Tobey, Kenneth Callahan, Morris Graves, Margaret Tomkins, Guy Anderson, Paul Horiuchi, Helmi Junoven and George Tsutakawa. Features the influence of nature and Indian culture.
Biography; Fine Arts; Sociology
Dist - MEDIPR **Prod** - LEVINK 1979

Northwest wild series
Covers the topics of ecology, social studies and environmental issues in a series of seven programs. Features the land and animals of diverse ecological systems, stresses the interdependence of species, and focuses on the conservation and preservation of ecosystems and wildlife. Highlights birds, the grizzly, the red wolf, forests, deserts, and coasts.
Creatures of the ancient forest 23 MIN
Creatures of the dry side 23 MIN
Edge of the continent 25 MIN
Gifts from the watershed 25 MIN
Northwest wild series 159 MIN
A passion for birds 23 MIN
Red wolf 13 MIN
Tracks of the grizzly 27 MIN
Dist - CF

Northwestern
VHS
Campus clips series
Color (H C A)
$29.95 purchase _ #CC0028V
Takes a video visit to the campus of Northwestern University in Illinois. Shows many of the distinctive features of the campus, and interviews students about their experiences. Provides information on the composition of the student body, professors, academics, social life, housing, and other subjects.
Education
Dist - CAMV

Northwestern American Indian War Dance Contest 12 MIN
16mm
Ethnic Music and Dance Series
Color (J)
LC 72-700244
Describes the Northwestern American Indian War Dance Contest, which is held annually in Seattle. Explains how groups and individuals from the western United States compete in various styles of dancing.
Fine Arts; Geography - United States; Social Science
Dist - UWASHP **Prod** - UWASH 1971

The Northwestern Hawaiian Islands 27 MIN
16mm
Color (J H G)
Studies the resources and ecology of some of the Hawaiian islands and the surrounding waters.
Geography - United States; Science - Natural
Dist - CINEPC **Prod** - TAHARA 1985

Norumbega - Maine in the age of exploration and settlement 14 MIN
VHS
Color (G)
$19.95 purchase
Uses slides to introduce the early history of Maine.
Fine Arts; History - United States
Dist - NEFILM

Norway 60 MIN
VHS
Traveloguer collection series
Color (I J H A)
$29.95 purchase _ #QC116V-S
Presents information about the historic past and the current status of Norway, including information about the cities and the countryside. Shows famous landmarks, out - of - the way sites, struggles and hardships, victories and championships, and the legends of the region. Uses live - action footage and historical clips to show the geography, history, and culture. Includes 16 60 - minute programs on northern, western, eastern, and southern Europe.
Geography - World
Dist - CAMV

Norway 17 MIN
U-matic / VHS / 16mm
Modern Europe Series
Color (J H)
Shows the land, people and industry of Norway.
Geography - World; History - World
Dist - JOU **Prod** - JOU

Norway 60 MIN
VHS
Traveloguer Northern Europe series
Color (J H C G)
$29.95 purchase _ #QC116V
Visits Norway and its cities. Illustrates notable landmarks, special events in history and the legends that are part of Norwegian culture. Part of a four part series on Northern Europe.
Geography - World
Dist - CAMV

Norway 29 MIN
Videoreel / VT2
International Cookbook Series
Color
Features home economist Joan Hood presenting a culinary tour of specialty dishes from around the world. Shows the preparation of Norwegian dishes ranging from peasant cookery to continental cuisine.
Geography - World; Home Economics
Dist - PBS **Prod** - WMVSTV

Norway - an oil and gas nation 17 MIN
VHS
Color (G)
Free loan
Examines the petroleum industry in Norway. Visits futuristic sea platforms, views the wild waves of northern seas and uses animated graphics to explain present conditions and future prospects of the industry.
Geography - World; Industrial and Technical Education
Dist - NIS
AUDPLN

Norway - nature's triumph 53 MIN
VHS
Color (G)
$29.95 purchase _ #ST - IV1804
Travels from fjords to rugged mountains to the medieval Akershus Fortress in Oslo. Attends a performance of A Doll's House by Ibsen in the Nation Theater and views sculpture by Vigeland. Visits the waterfront of Bergen, Nidaros Cathedral in Trondheim and Geiranger Fjord.
Geography - World
Dist - INSTRU

The Norway of Edvard Grieg 17 MIN
16mm
Idyllwild Youth Symphony in Scandinavia Series
Color (J)
LC FIA66-494
Shows composer Edvard Grieg's home and the Norwegian countryside as seen through the eyes of the Idyllwild Youth Symphony and interpreted through their performance of a Grieg concerto.
Biography; Fine Arts; Geography - World
Dist - AVED **Prod** - IDYLWD 1970

A Norwegian Fjord 13 MIN
U-matic / VHS / 16mm
Man and His World Series
Color (P I J H C)
LC 78-705486
Shows fishing, dairy farming, fruit farming and manufacturing of aluminum as well as the lakes and rivers that supply the water for an electric power plant along the fjord.
Agriculture; Geography - World; Social Science
Dist - FI **Prod** - FI 1969

Norwegian landscapes 27 MIN
VHS / 16mm
Color (G)
Free loan
Portrays the Norwegian landscape and its people during all seasons. Includes music by Norwegian composers.
Geography - World
Dist - NIS
AUDPLN

Norwegian notes 24 MIN
VHS / 16mm
Color (G)
Free loan
Meets Norwegians in various parts of Norway and from various walks of life. Informs about Norwegian culture, society and living conditions.
Geography - World
Dist - NIS

Norwegian Oil 25 MIN
16mm / U-matic / VHS
Update Europe Series
Color (J H)
$495 purchase - 16 mm, $250 purchase - video _ #5175C
Talks about the development of oil and gas in Norway. Produced by the BBC.
History - World
Dist - CORF

The Nose 38 MIN
16mm
Color (G)
$40.00 rental
Deals with the adventures of a man who loses his nose and searches for it in modern Los Angeles until the nose's recovery in a nightclub for monsters. Creates a comedy described as 'an adult dream fairy tale.'
Fine Arts; Literature and Drama
Dist - CANCIN **Prod** - LEHE 1972

The Nose 20 MIN
16mm
Color
LC 74-705215
Demonstrates physical examination of the nose. Includes normal and abnormal views of the exterior, vestibule, septum, mucosa and lateral wall. Shows conditions of rhinophyma, congenital syphilitic saddle nose, atrophy due to leprosy, tuberculin lupus vulgaris and disfigurement due to trauma. Considers nasal discharges as to cause and meaning.
Health and Safety; Science - Natural
Dist - USNAC **Prod** - USGSA 1969

The Nose 11 MIN
16mm
B&W
Presents Gogol's celebrated short story, The Nose, animated and without words, in fantastic moving pictures that capture the scene and spirit of 19th - century Russia. Produced by Alexander Alexeieff and Claire Parker.
Fine Arts; History - World
Dist - STARRC **Prod** - STARRC 1963

Nose and Tina 28 MIN
16mm
Color (C A)
Describes the love between Nose and Tina, a brakeman and a hooker. Captures the domestic details of their life together, and their hassles with the law, work and money.
Psychology; Sociology
Dist - NFBC **Prod** - NFBC 1980

A Nose for News 30 MIN
VHS / U-matic
High Feather Series
Color (I J)
LC 83-706050
Stresses that comparative shopping for fresh food is the economical way to good eating.
Health and Safety; Social Science
Dist - GPN **Prod** - NYSED 1982

Nose Job 11 MIN
16mm
Color
Studies the role of physical appearance in self - esteem. Follows a teenager before, during and after surgery, and interviews her, her parents and her surgeon.
Guidance and Counseling; Health and Safety; Psychology
Dist - MOKIN **Prod** - CBSTV

The Nose - Structure and Function 11 MIN
U-matic / VHS / 16mm
Color; B&W (J H C)
Uses animation and microphotography to illustrate the breathing and smelling functions of the nose. Explains the ingenious protective system of the breathing organs and shows the reasons for breakdowns in the nasal passages.
Science - Natural
Dist - EBEC **Prod** - EBEC 1954

Nosegays, One - Sided and Centerpiece Designs 60 MIN
BETA / VHS
Color (G)
$49.00 purchase _ #FA1001
Provides a step - by - step program on how to make nosegays, one - sided and centerpiece designs. Discusses basic design theory, and gives an overview of all the materials used in flower arranging.
Fine Arts; Physical Education and Recreation
Dist - RMIBHF **Prod** - RMIBHF

Noses 30 MIN
U-matic
Today's Special Series
Color (K P)
Develops language arts skills in children. Programs are thematically designed around subjects of interest to youngsters. Action takes place in a department store where people, mannequins, puppets, comic characters and special guests present a light hearted approach to language arts.
Fine Arts; Literature and Drama; Psychology
Dist - TVOTAR **Prod** - TVOTAR 1985

Nosey Dobson 55 MIN
16mm
Color (P I)
Tells the story of Nosey Dobson, a compulsive snooper whose attempts at being a detective irritate everyone, including the town constable. Reveals that when he stumbles onto a genuine plot to steal priceless silver, no one will believe him.
Fine Arts
Dist - LUF **Prod** - CHILDF 1979

Nosferatu 63 MIN
U-matic / 16mm
B&W (GERMAN (GERMAN SUBTITLES))
A silent motion picture with German subtitles. Tells the story of the Bremer secretary Hutter, who travels to Count Orlock, known as Nosferatu, in order to sign a bill of sale, and discovers that Nosferatu is a vampire. Continues as Nosferatu follows Hutter to Bremen where the plague breaks out, and ends with Hutter's young wife saving her husband and the city from the monster. Based on the book DRACULA by Bram Stoker.
Fine Arts
Dist - WSTGLC **Prod** - WSTGLC 1921

Nosferatu 84 MIN
VHS
B&W (G)
$29.95 purchase
Presents an Expressionist telling of Bram Stoker's novel of vampirism released nine years before Dracula. Directed by F W Murnau.
Fine Arts; Literature and Drama
Dist - KINOIC

Nosocomial infection and medical devices - reducing the risk 28 MIN
VHS / U-matic
Color (PRO)
$275.00 purchase, $60.00 rental _ #9924S, #9924V
Features two consultants to the Centers for Disease Control, Marguerite Jackson and Patricia Lynch. Differentiates nonpreventable nosocomial infections due to the patient's own flora - endogenous - from those which are preventable - exogenous. Reveals that these are often caused by indwelling medical devices such as catheters and by caregiver's dirty hands. Illustrates specific procedures to reduce such infections.
Health and Safety
Dist - AJN **Prod** - HOSSN 1986

Nosocomial infection control - body substance isolation 28 MIN
VHS / U-matic
Color (PRO)
$275.00 purchase, $60.00 rental _ #9923S, #9923V
Features two consultants to the Centers for Disease Control, Marguerite Jackson and Patricia Lynch. Presents a new technique developed to prevent nosocomial infection through body substance isolation incorporating CDC recommended universal precautions to protect staff from patients with HIV and HBV infections.
Health and Safety
Dist - AJN **Prod** - HOSSN 1986

Nosocomial pneumonia 16 MIN
VHS / U-matic
Breaking the chain of nosocomial infections series
Color (C PRO)
$395.00 purchase, $80.00 rental _ #C930 - VI - 004
Helps medical students, nurses, doctors and other hospital and nursing home staff to reduce the risk factors that cause nosocomial pneumonia. Demonstrates techiques and suggests types of drug therapy to lessen the chances of infection. Part of a five - part series on nosocomial infections presented by Crescent Counties Foundation for Medical Care.
Health and Safety; Science - Natural
Dist - HSCIC

Nosotros Venceremos (We Shall Overcome) 11 MIN
16mm
B&W
LC 72-700360
An organizing tool for United Farm Workers organizing committee members and their supporters. Presents still photographs of the Delano grape strike. Shows the march to Sacramento, the fast of Casear Chavez and the first victory, all combined with songs and speeches of the movement.
Agriculture; Business and Economics; Sociology
Dist - UFWA **Prod** - UFWOC 1971

Nossa Terra 40 MIN
16mm
B&W
Discusses how black people can take control of their destiny after 400 years of colonial oppression. Explains why the people of Portuguese Guinea have chosen armed struggle. Shows that conditions of life are constantly improved in the liberated areas while the struggle continues. Narrated by Julius Lester.
Civics and Political Systems; Geography - World; History - United States
Dist - CANWRL **Prod** - UNKNWN 1967

Nostalghia 120 MIN
16mm / 35mm
Color (G) (RUSSIAN AND ITALIAN)
$300.00 rental
Follows a young Soviet writer to Italy where he is researching the life of an expatriate Russian novelist. Reveals that, experiencing 'nostalghia,' a melancholy homesickness, he must come to terms with his own life and his new environment. Directed by Andrei Tarkovsky. With English subtitles.
Fine Arts; Guidance and Counseling
Dist - KINOIC

Nostalgia - 1926 - 1965
VHS
Hearst News library series
Color (G)
$29.95 purchase _ #TK040
Meets glamorous personalities, looks at bizarre fads and witnesses amazing feats documented in the period 1926 - 1965. Part of a series excerpted from 350 newsreels from the Hearst News Library.
History - United States; History - World; Literature and Drama
Dist - SIV

Not a Jealous Bone 11 MIN
VHS / U-matic
Cecilia Condit Series
Color (G)
$250.00, $200.00 purchase, $50.00 rental
Focuses on a remarkably spry 82 - year - old woman who finds a magic bone and goes off in search of her mother, cast as a much younger actress. Creates simultaneously absurd and quasi - epic commentary on death and aging.
Fine Arts; Health and Safety; Psychology; Sociology
Dist - WMEN **Prod** - CECON 1987

Not a Love Story - a Film about Pornography 69 MIN
16mm
Color (C A)
Documents the journey of two women who set off to explore the world of peep shows, strip joints and sex supermarkets. Offers insights and perspectives from men and women who earn their living in the porn trade, and with some of pornography's most outspoken critics.
Sociology
Dist - NFBC **Prod** - NFBC 1981

Not a music video 7 MIN
16mm
B&W (G)
$15.00 rental
Entertains with a very playful, spontaneous film made with and for people for whom the filmmaker has a high regard.
Fine Arts; Psychology
Dist - CANCIN **Prod** - MERRIT 1987

Not a Place 28 MIN
16mm
Dynamics of Change Series
Color
LC 73-700895
Documents the teacher - training program at Appalachian State University in Boone, North Carolina, designed to open lines of communication between the university, the public schools and the community.
Education; Social Science
Dist - EDSD **Prod** - EDSD 1973

Not a Pretty Picture 82 MIN
U-matic / VHS / 16mm
Color
LC 77-700001
Explores events surrounding the filmmaker's rape while in boarding school and its subsequent effects upon her. Touches on adolescent attitudes about sex, male and female roles, and relationships in our society.
Psychology; Sociology
Dist - FI **Prod** - FI 1976

Not a Pretty Picture, Pt 1 27 MIN
U-matic / VHS / 16mm
Color
LC 77-700001
Explores events surrounding the filmmaker's rape while in boarding school and its subsequent effects upon her. Touches on adolescent attitudes about sex, male and female roles, and relationships in our society.
Psychology; Sociology
Dist - FI **Prod** - FI 1976

Not a Pretty Picture, Pt 2 27 MIN
16mm / U-matic / VHS
Color
LC 77-700001
Explores events surrounding the filmmaker's rape while in boarding school and its subsequent effects upon her. Touches on adolescent attitudes about sex, male and female roles, and relationships in our society.
Psychology; Sociology
Dist - FI **Prod** - FI 1976

Not a Pretty Picture, Pt 3 28 MIN
16mm / U-matic / VHS
Color
LC 77-700001
Explores events surrounding the filmmaker's rape while in boarding school and its subsequent effects upon her. Touches on adolescent attitudes about sex, male and female roles, and relationships in our society.
Psychology; Sociology
Dist - FI **Prod** - FI 1976

Not a Sparrow Falls 28 MIN
16mm
Color
LC 74-702496
Designed to promote understanding and support for the alcoholics program of the Salvation Army's Harbor Light Center in Chicago.
Health and Safety; Psychology; Sociology
Dist - SALVA **Prod** - SALVA 1974

Not a Weapon or a Star 29 MIN
U-matic / VHS / 16mm
Color
Examines successful crime prevention programs in urban, suburban and rural communities. Emphasizes the need for communication and interaction between the community and the police.
Social Science; Sociology
Dist - CORF **Prod** - OLINC 1977

Not all Parents are Straight 58 MIN
16mm / U-matic / VHS
Color (H C A)
$895 purchase - 16 mm, $595 purchase - video, $95 rental
Examines the problems faced by the five million gay and lesbian parents in America. Includes interviews with the children and their parents, explores emotional conflicts in the family, legal custody problems, and the social discrimination faced by these families. Produced by Kevin White and Annamarie Faro.
Sociology
Dist - CNEMAG

Not alone anymore - caring for someone with Alzheimer's disease 22 MIN
VHS
Color (G C)
$135.00 purchase, $45.00 rental
Focuses on the family of an Alzheimer's patient as they care for the family member and for themselves. Gives practical advice on meeting needs without stressing anyone unduly.
Health and Safety; Sociology
Dist - TNF

Not Alone in the World - Caring for Someone with Alzheimer's Disease 22 MIN
VHS / 16mm
(C)
$385.00 purchase _ #870VI026
Presents several explanations of the aspects of Alzheimer's disease and how to minister to someone with it.
Health and Safety
Dist - HSCIC **Prod** - HSCIC 1987

Not Another Hero 27 MIN
16mm / VHS
Color (IND)
$595.00, $495.00 purchase
Uses the characters of Death and The Gas to relate the dangers of hydrogen sulfide and the risks in its production. Included is instruction for the use of breathing apparatuses.
Health and Safety; Industrial and Technical Education; Psychology
Dist - FLMWST

Not Another Science Show Series

Blue genes	25 MIN
Button up your overcoat	25 MIN
Chips ahoy	25 MIN
From rags to britches	25 MIN
Hair - the Untold Story	25 MIN
Heads I Win, Tails You Lose	25 MIN
Heavy Metal	25 MIN
How does your garden grow	25 MIN
If a Tree Falls in the Forest, who Cares	25 MIN
Is it Soup Yet	25 MIN
No Sweat	25 MIN
Play Ball	25 MIN
Please do not Adjust Your Set	25 MIN
Power to the People	25 MIN
Say Cheese	25 MIN
The Science Show	25 MIN
Something Wonderful is a Foot	25 MIN
Spoiled rotten	25 MIN
Testing 1 - 2 - 3	25 MIN
Tick tock	25 MIN
Twinkle, Twinkle, Little Star	25 MIN
Up, Up, and Away	25 MIN
Vroom	25 MIN
Waste not, Want not	25 MIN
What's the Sense	25 MIN
You are what You Eat	25 MIN

Dist - TVOTAR

Not Another Science Show
A Room with a view 15 MIN
Dist - AECT

Not as a Black Person, as a Person 25 MIN
16mm
Color
LC 79-711370
Describes a program initiated by Ford to acquaint Black students and faculty with the workings of the Ford Motor Company. Shows executives from the company as they hold talks and conduct seminars concerning business and education.
Business and Economics; Education; Guidance and Counseling; Sociology
Dist - FORDFL **Prod** - FMCMP 1970

Not by Bread Alone 25 MIN
16mm
B&W
Discusses the problems of feeding and nutrition of the aged and the nurses aide's key role in geriatric care.
Health and Safety; Psychology; Sociology
Dist - HF **Prod** - UHOSF 1966

Not by Jeans Alone 30 MIN
16mm / U-matic / VHS
Enterprise Series
Color (C A)
Tells how the Levi Strauss company sought to move beyond jeans to Levi Tailored Classics, a market - opening attempt that encountered problems in a fast - changing marketplace.
Business and Economics; Home Economics; Psychology
Dist - LCOA **Prod** - WGBHTV 1981

Not by Magic 14 MIN
16mm
B&W
LC 74-705216
Explains the function of the General Services Administration's federal supply service.
Civics and Political Systems; Sociology
Dist - USNAC **Prod** - USGSA

Not Crazy Like You Think - a Film Exploring Our Definitions of Mental Illness 60 MIN
U-matic / VHS
Studies the Solidarite Psychiatrie, a mutual support group for past and present mental patients. Depicts a meeting in a country house in which scenes fron patients lives are dramatized. Made by Jaqueline Levitin.
Health and Safety; Psychology
Dist - FANPRO **Prod** - FANPRO 1986

Not death by water baptism by fire 17 MIN
16mm
Color; B&W (G)
$35.00 rental
Brings together a danseuse and a detective who dance their way through the labyrinthine stage set of contemporary existence. Tells a love story where the object of desire is constantly inaccessible to everyone except the viewer.
Fine Arts; Psychology; Religion and Philosophy
Dist - CANCIN **Prod** - RAYHER 1989

Not Enough 30 MIN
16mm
Color (J H)
Questions whether the rich countries are doing enough to help the large and growing populations of Africa, Asia and Latin America, and what are the less developed countries doing themselves to improve their standard of living. Illustrates what is being done to solve these problems.
Civics and Political Systems; Geography - World; History - United States; Social Science
Dist - MLA **Prod** - OECD 1967

Not Even One Chance 10 MIN
16mm
Safety Wise Series
B&W
Shows man who takes chances because he's 'IN A HURRY' and for other 'GOOD' reasons. Suggests that taking chances is always a gamble, and that the wrong attitudes that cause chance taking need changing.
Guidance and Counseling; Health and Safety; Psychology
Dist - NSC **Prod** - DUNN 1960

Not Far from Home 30 MIN
16mm
Color
LC 75-704327
Presents a film journal of living in the country.
Sociology
Dist - CANFDC **Prod** - CANFDC 1974

Not for Everyone 11 MIN
VHS / U-matic
Color
Uses contemporary film techniques creating a montage of image and sound as a recruitment film for radiation technology aimed at high school students. Shows cancer research advantages with inner as well as material rewards.
Guidance and Counseling; Health and Safety; Science - Physical
Dist - AMCS **Prod** - AMCS 1984

Not for Ourselves Alone 29 MIN
U-matic / VHS / 16mm
Color
LC 76-700482
Emphasizes the contribution of the Armed Forces of the United States in upholding the ideals of the Founding Fathers. Offers an overview of four major crisis periods and conflicts in American history, including the Revolutionary War, the Civil War, the War of 1812 and the two World Wars.
Civics and Political Systems; History - United States
Dist - PHENIX **Prod** - USOIAF 1975

Not - for - Profit, not for Nothing 29 MIN
VHS / 16mm
Color (C)
$250.00 purchase _ #269401
Investigates the voluntary sector. Asks who volunteers their time and why, where should funding for not - for - profit organizations come from, will the demand for volunteer organizatons continue to grow. Examines successful volunteer endeavors, including the 'Man in Motion World Tour' by Rick Hansen, food banks and a suicide prevention center.
Business and Economics; Education; Psychology; Social Science; Sociology
Dist - ACCESS **Prod** - ACCESS 1987

Not for sale: Ethics in the American workplace 105 MIN
VHS
Color (J H)
$199 purchase No. 2420-YZ
Teaches students grades 7 - 12 ethical values and reinforcement of their existing ethical values. Presents scenarios about ethical dilemmas students may one day face on the job. Includes 105 minute video, 158 page leader's guide.
Business and Economics; Education
Dist - ETHICS **Prod** - SUNCOM

Not for sale - ethics in the American workplace
VHS
Color (G)
Dramatizes the importance of honesty, dependability, responsibility and respect in the workplace. Includes leader's guide.
Guidance and Counseling
Dist - ETHICS **Prod** - ETHICS 1992

Not if - but How 20 MIN
16mm
Color (S)
LC 82-700464
Focuses on a regular elementary classroom teacher with a new student who has cerebral palsy. Traces her progress from the student's initial seizure and fall, through her search for advice, to her consultation with the principal, the student's mother, a doctor and a physical therapist.
Education; Psychology
Dist - HUBDSC **Prod** - NMMCHP 1981

Not in my backyard 30 MIN
VHS
CNN special reports series
Color (G A)
$19.95 purchase _ #TCO115OE
Examines the potential environmental problems that could result if the growing problem with waste disposal is not solved. Hosted by CNN correspondent Mark Walton.

Health and Safety; Science - Physical; Sociology
Dist - TMM **Prod** - TMM

Not in My Family - Mothers Speak Out on Sexual Abuse of Children 33 MIN
16mm
Color (C A)
Presents mothers who tell how they learned their husbands were molesting their daughters, their reactions and what they wished they had done to protect their children.
Sociology
Dist - LAWREN **Prod** - BAKRSR 1983

Not in My Neighborhood - 223 30 MIN
U-matic
Currents - 1985 - 86 Season Series
Color (A)
Reveals the community resistance often encountered over the location of group homes for the retarded, handicapped, or problem people. Everyone agrees that such facilities are needed but they want them somewhere else.
Social Science; Sociology
Dist - PBS **Prod** - WNETTV 1985

Not just a cancer patient 23 MIN
VHS
Color (G)
$195.00 purchase, $100.00 rental _ #CN - 086
Focuses on several articulate teenagers who are undergoing cancer treatment. Helps nurses, physicians, social workers and psychologists to understand the needs and feelings of these patients, in order to improve communication, increase patients' involvement in their own treatment and give them a greater sense of control. Created by Jana Levenson and Tom Hill for Dana - Farber Cancer Institute.
Health and Safety
Dist - FANPRO

Not just a job - career planning for women 35 MIN
BETA / VHS / U-matic
Color (G A)
LC 90-714837
Documents a diverse group of women participating in a workshop to explore their interests, values and skills and how to apply this knowledge to the world of work. Features Radcliffe Career Services as the designer of the workshop.
Business and Economics; Guidance and Counseling; Psychology; Sociology
Dist - CMBRD **Prod** - CMBRD 1990

Not Just a Spectator 35 MIN
16mm
Color
Depicts sports and recreational activities open to the handicapped person if proper facilities are provided.
Education; Psychology
Dist - IREFL **Prod** - IREFL 1974

The Not - just - anybody family 15 MIN
VHS
More books from cover to cover series
Color (I G)
$25.00 purchase _ #MBCC - 111
Tells how Maggie and Vern try to solve family problems by themselves, as their brother is in the hospital, their grandfather is in jail and their mother on the road with a rodeo. Based on the book 'The Not - Just - Anybody Family' by Betsy Cromer Byars. Hosted by John Robbins.
Literature and Drama
Dist - PBS **Prod** - WETATV 1987

Not just passing through 54 MIN
VHS
Color (G)
$75.00 rental, $225.00 purchase
Juxtaposes four sites of lesbian courage and creativity in the past and present to convey hope and posssibility for the future. Memorializes African - American lesbian Mabel Hampton, Marge McDonald, and June Chan. Takes the viewer backstage of New York's WOW Cafe where The Five Lesbian Brothers and others show how theater and comedy can explode oppressive images.
Fine Arts; History - World; Sociology
Dist - WMEN **Prod** - CPSATH 1994

Not like sheep to the slaughter - the story of the Bialystok Ghetto 150 MIN
VHS
B&W (G)
$79.95 purchase _ #615
Reveals that in the summer of 1943, 24 - year - old Mordecai Tenenbaum led a small group of resistance fighters in an attempt to stop the Nazi eradication of the Bialystok Ghetto. Offers testimony from survivors and witnesses.
Civics and Political Systems; History - World; Sociology
Dist - ERGOM **Prod** - ERGOM

Not Me Alone 31 MIN
U-matic / VHS
Color (A)
Shows one couple's labor and delivery, presenting an unromanticized picture which will make childbirth more real and manageable and provide men a better understanding of the role they can play during pregnancy.
Health and Safety
Dist - POLYMR **Prod** - POLYMR

Not Me Alone - Preparation for Childbirth 31 MIN
16mm
Color (H C A)
LC 76-703278
Follows a couple at natural childbirth training classes, practicing breathing exercises at home, sharing labor and delivery and caring for the baby in the hospital.
Home Economics; Science - Natural; Sociology
Dist - POLYMR **Prod** - POLYMR 1970

Not me - innocence in the time of AIDS 53 MIN
VHS
Color (J H C)
$295.00 purchase
Presents HIV - positive young people in frank talk with high schoolers about HIV and AIDS and safe sex. Addresses the issues of sexuality, abstinence and condom availability and use. Delivers tough, explicit, culturally appropriate materials to teens through the eyes of their peers. A 38 - minute edited version is also available.
Health and Safety; Sociology
Dist - PFP

Not much time 8 MIN
16mm
Color (G)
$15.00 rental
Repeats a bank robbery several times, each time within a different context and from a different point of view. Asks if there is a double - cross and why the passersby are so calm. The audience must reconstruct the event and assume role of detective in this mystery of narrative space.
Fine Arts
Dist - CANCIN **Prod** - PIERCE 1982

Not My Kid 97 MIN
VHS / BETA
Color (G)
Tells the story of a family shattered by their teenage daughter's drug problem. Stars George Segal and Stockard Channing. From the book Not My Kid - A Parent's Guide To Kids And Drugs by Beth Polson and Dr Martin Newton.
Fine Arts; Psychology; Sociology
Dist - SONY
GA

Not One of the Crowd Series

David Lincoln	30 MIN
J S - Judy Snow	30 MIN
Liz	30 MIN
W H Bill McGovern	30 MIN
Wade Hampton	30 MIN

Dist - TVOTAR

Not Only Spectators 15 MIN
16mm
B&W
Presents a Swedish view of responsible journalism.
Geography - World; Social Science
Dist - AUDPLN **Prod** - ASI

Not Only Strangers 23 MIN
16mm / U-matic / VHS
Color (H C A)
$515, $250 purchase _ #80512; LC 80-700780
Explores the problems and emotional crises of the sexual assault victim, presenting the situation of a college girl attacked by a male acquaintance. Illustrates the circumstances under which rape commonly occurs and outlines some of the misconceptions surrounding rape and sexual assault.
Sociology
Dist - CORF

Not quite right 10 MIN
16mm
B&W (G)
$20.00 rental
Paints a stark and haunting psychological portrait of a man struggling with his demons and the need for change.
Fine Arts; Psychology
Dist - CANCIN **Prod** - MICHAL 1987

Not Ready to Die of AIDS 52 MIN
VHS / 16mm
Color (PRO G)
$149.00, $249.00, purchase _ #AD - 1272
Examines how one man who was told he is dying is living with AIDS. Follows him in his fight for acceptance by his family, for the right to continue in his job, and to come to grips with his illness and its inevitable outcome. Explains how he faces the same struggle as any terminal patient, including denial, acceptance of death, and the challenge to lead a worthwhile life in the time remaining. Shows how AIDS threatens not only his life, but his reason for living.
Health and Safety; Sociology
Dist - FOTH **Prod** - FOTH 1990

Not Reconciled 51 MIN
16mm
B&W (GERMAN)
Features the explanations offered by one German generation to another of the losses it suffered and mistakes it committed over a period of 70 years. Based on a novel by Heinrich Boll. Directed by Jean Marie Straub.
Civics and Political Systems; Fine Arts; Foreign Language; History - World
Dist - NYFLMS **Prod** - NYFLMS 1965

Not Sick Enough 11 MIN
16mm
Color
LC 74-705218
Depicts the special problem of mental illness in the unnoticed neurotic.
Health and Safety; Psychology
Dist - USNAC **Prod** - USSRS 1969

Not Since the Pyramids 29 MIN
16mm
Color
LC 75-700801
Shows the characteristics of the construction projects managed by the U S Naval Facilities Engineering Command in Vietnam.
Civics and Political Systems; Geography - World; Industrial and Technical Education
Dist - USNAC **Prod** - USN

Not So Easy 15 MIN
16mm / U-matic / VHS
Color (J)
Demonstrates the essential safety rules of motorcycle riding. Features Evil Knievel, with narration by Peter Fonda.
Health and Safety; Physical Education and Recreation; Psychology
Dist - ALTSUL **Prod** - VAUGHS 1973

Not So Easy - Motorcycle Safety 17 MIN
16mm / U-matic / VHS
Color (J)
Demonstrates the essential safety rules of motorcycle riding. Emphasizes that if done properly, motorcycle riding is above average in safety and pleasure. Narrated by Peter Fonda.
Health and Safety
Dist - ALTSUL **Prod** - ALTSUL

The Not - so - great escape
VHS
McGee and me series
Color (P I R)
$19.95 purchase, $10.00 rental _ #35 - 84154 - 979
Features Nick and his animated friend McGee. Shows that Nick sneaked out to see a horror movie. Emphasizes the importance of obeying parents.
Literature and Drama; Religion and Philosophy
Dist - APH **Prod** - TYHP

The Not - so great moments in sports 54 MIN
VHS
Color (G)
$19.99 purchase _ #HBO0024V
Presents a variety of sports moments that the persons involved might prefer to forget - the 'not - so great' moments. Includes footage of the famous wrong - way run in the 1929 Rose Bowl, the Boston Marathon victory of Rosy Ruiz, and temper tantrums by Bobby Knight, Woody Hayes, John McEnroe, and more.
Literature and Drama; Physical Education and Recreation
Dist - CAMV

Not So Long Ago - 1945 - 1950 54 MIN
U-matic / VHS / 16mm
Project 20 Series
B&W (H C A)
Looks at aspects of American life in the 1940's. Highlights the advent of rockets and television and discusses developments on the political and social scene.
History - United States
Dist - CRMP **Prod** - NBCTV 1965
MGHT

Not So Long Ago - 1945 - 1950, Pt 1 27 MIN
U-matic / VHS / 16mm
Project 20 Series
B&W (H C A)
Looks at aspects of American life in the 1940's. Highlights the advent of rockets and television and discusses developments on the political and social scene.
Geography - World; History - United States
Dist - CRMP **Prod** - NBCTV 1965
MGHT

Not So Long Ago - 1945 - 1950, Pt 2 27 MIN
16mm / U-matic / VHS
Project 20 Series
B&W (H C A)
Looks at aspects of American life in the 1940's. Highlights the advent of rockets and television and discusses developments on the political and social scene.
Geography - World; History - United States
Dist - CRMP **Prod** - NBCTV 1965
MGHT

Not so much a desert... more a way of life 30 MIN
VHS
Up a gum tree with David Bellamy series
Color; PAL (H C A)
PdS65 purchase
Travels around Australia and looks at the flora and fauna of the continent. Describes the life forms that exist in Australia's deserts. Employs David Bellamy as a tour guide. Part one of a five part series.
Geography - World; History - World
Dist - BBCENE

The Not - So - Private Eyes 26 MIN
U-matic / VHS / 16mm
Backstreet Six Series
Color (P I J)
LC 81-701255
Reveals that a young boy decides to play private detective when he becomes convinced that an elderly man is a foreign spy. Tells of the hilarious situations that ensue when the whole gang joins in.
Guidance and Counseling; Literature and Drama
Dist - PHENIX **Prod** - LPROP 1980

The Not - So - Solid Earth 30 MIN
U-matic / VHS / 16mm
Life Around Us Series
Color (J) (SPANISH)
LC 72-702452
Traces the discovery of powerful forces deep within the earth that move continents and shift oceans. Shows how geologists, oceanographers, paleontologists and mineralogists gather and analyze supporting data for the theory of continental drift. Illustrates erupting volcanoes and earthquake destruction.
Science - Physical
Dist - TIMLIF **Prod** - TIMLIF 1971

Not So Wild a Dream 58 MIN
VHS
American Experience Series
Color (H)
$9.50 rental _ #60940, VH
Documents journalist Eric Sevareid's change from a pacifist and isolationist in the 30's to an interventionist journalist covering the ascent of fascism in Europe. Compares Sevareid's change of heart with that of many other Americans at the time. Adapted from Sevareid's best - selling book. First of five parts in the American Experience Series.
Civics and Political Systems; History - United States; Literature and Drama; Religion and Philosophy
Dist - PSU **Prod** - PBS

Not So Young as Then 60 MIN
U-matic / VHS
Color
Looks at the life of teenagers today through profiles of five young people of different ages and backgrounds. Examines their views on adults, peers, sexuality, school, drugs, work, values, social concerns and rights.
Sociology
Dist - WCCOTV **Prod** - WCCOTV 1979

Not So Young Now as Then 18 MIN
16mm
Color
LC 74-701398
Uses the occasion of a fifteenth anniversary high school reunion in order to explore the feelings of the participants and to reveal the reunion's importance as a cultural event.
Guidance and Counseling; Social Science; Sociology
Dist - NEWDAY **Prod** - BRNDNL 1974

Not the same Old Story 58 MIN
U-matic / VHS / 16mm
Color (H C A)
Offers a positive look at aging in America. Uncovers some extraordinary ways that older people are not only adding years to their lives, but also life to their years. Shatters many of the stereotypes commonly associated with the aged.
Health and Safety; Sociology
Dist - FI **Prod** - DBA 1983

Not the Triumph, but the Struggle 28 MIN
16mm
Color
LC 78-701341
Focuses on athletes participating in Junior Olympic sports. Highlights the feelings of participants and offers a glimpse of potential athletic greats.
Physical Education and Recreation
Dist - MTP **Prod** - SEARS 1978

Not Together Now 25 MIN
VHS / U-matic
Color
Shows a separated couple and a discussion of why they were first attracted to each other, why they chose to marry and what happened during the course of their lives together.
Sociology
Dist - POLYMR **Prod** - POLYMR

Not Together Now - End of a Marriage 25 MIN
16mm
Color (H C A)
LC 75-700652
Features Sheldon and Barbara Renan in separate, informal interviews talking about the breakup of their marriage. Emphasizes one woman's experience of marriage and divorce.
Sociology
Dist - POLYMR **Prod** - POLYMR 1975

Not waving but drowning - debt 52 MIN
VHS
Color; PAL (H C G)
PdS30 purchase
Recreates the true story of a young family's struggle against multiple debts. Explores the practical problems of being in debt and shows the personal stresses and strains within the family. Contact distributor about availability outside the United Kingdom.
Business and Economics; History - World; Sociology
Dist - ACADEM

Not with a Bang but with Multiplication - Multiplication, Two Digits Times Two Digits 15 MIN
VHS / U-matic
Figure Out Series
Color (I)
Tells how Mac is saved from a kidnapping by Alice's ability to estimate and find the answer to multiplication problems in which regrouping is required.
Mathematics
Dist - AITECH **Prod** - MAETEL 1982

Not with an Empty Quiver 29 MIN
16mm
Color (H C A)
LC 73-700002
Features four young Indian men who have either succeeded or failed by society's standards. Combines in - depth interviews and the story of a young Indian boy fighting to overcome obstacles. Stresses the importance of making preparations to adjust to a modern world rather than going forth with 'AN EMPTY QUIVER.'.
Guidance and Counseling; Social Science; Sociology
Dist - BYU **Prod** - BYU 1971

Not with My Wife, You Don't 119 MIN
16mm / U-matic / VHS
Color (H C A)
Stars Tony Curtis, Virna Lisi and George C Scott in a comic love triangle.
Literature and Drama; Sociology
Dist - FI **Prod** - WB 1966

Not without sight 20 MIN
16mm / U-matic / VHS
Color (G S T)
$89.95 purchase
Reveals that most people regarded as blind do, in fact, have some usable vision. Describes the major types of visual impairment, their causes and effects on vision. Uses camera simulations to approximate what people with each type of impairment actually see. Demonstrates how people with low vision make the best use of the vision they have.
Guidance and Counseling; Health and Safety
Dist - AFB **Prod** - AFB
PHENIX

Not Worth a Continental 25 MIN
U-matic / VHS / 16mm
Decades of Decision - the American Revolution Series
Color
LC 80-706344
Presents a fictionalized account of the experiences of a colonial American family faced with the conflict between a desire to help the revolutionary forces and a need to keep food for themselves for the winter.
History - United States
Dist - NGS **Prod** - NGS 1975

Not Worth the Risk 27 MIN
VHS / 16mm
Color (J)
$180.00 purchase
Shows pre - teens and young teens how to handle peer pressure and act responsibly. Demonstrates refusal skills for dealing with friends who ask them to act in a way that risks contracting AIDS. Includes leader's guide.
Guidance and Counseling; Health and Safety; Psychology; Sociology
Dist - CHEF **Prod** - CHEF

Not yet 25 MIN
16mm
B&W; Color (G)
$25.00 rental
Strings together a montage of images and ideas in collusion with one another such as people and ecology, tearing down the Alhambra Theatre in Sacramento and Spike Jones' music. Presents a film by Darrell Forney.
Fine Arts
Dist - CANCIN

Not Yours to Give 15 MIN
16mm
Color (I)
Debate's the government's role as an issuer of charity using an account of an incident from the life of Congressman Davy Crockett.
Civics and Political Systems; History - United States; Sociology
Dist - WORLDR **Prod** - WORLDR 1982

Notable black American series
Presents four biographical sketches of famous black Americans - Jesse Jackson, Madame C J Walker, Jackie Robinson, and Paul Robeson. Uses archival photographs and original illustrations.
Notable black American series 74 MIN
Dist - SRA

Notable black Americans series
Jackie Robinson 19 MIN
Jesse Jackson 19 MIN
Madame C J Walker 17 MIN
Paul Robeson 19 MIN
Dist - SRA

Notable Contributors to the Psychology and Personality Series
Professor Erik Erikson - Pt 2 50 MIN
Dist - PSUPCR

Notable Contributors to the Psychology of Personality
U-matic / VHS / 16mm
Color; B&W (C G T A)
Psychology
Dist - PSU **Prod** - PSU

Notable contributors to the psychology of personality series
Albert Bandura - Pt 1 29 MIN
Albert Bandura - Pt 2 28 MIN
Conversation with Viktor Frankl 43 MIN
Discussion with Dr Carl Jung - introversion - extroversion and other contributions 36 MIN
Dr B F Skinner - Part 1 50 MIN
Dr B F Skinner - Part 2 50 MIN
Dr Ernest Hilgard - Part 1 27 MIN
Dr Ernest Hilgard - Part 2 30 MIN
Dr Gardner Murphy - Part 1 50 MIN
Dr Gardner Murphy - Part 2 50 MIN
Dr Hans Eysenck 32 MIN
Dr Henry Murray - Part 1 50 MIN
Dr Henry Murray - Part 2 27 MIN
Dr J B Rhine - Part 1 45 MIN
Dr J B Rhine - Part 2 45 MIN
Dr Jean Piaget with Dr Barbel Inhelder - Part 1 40 MIN
Dr Jean Piaget with Dr Barbel Inhelder - Part 2 40 MIN
Dr Nevitt Sanford - Part 1 31 MIN
Dr Nevitt Sanford - Part 2 26 MIN
Dr Raymond Cattell - Part 1 50 MIN
Dr Raymond Cattell - Part 2 50 MIN
A Psychology of creativity 31 MIN
Rollo May's Discussion with Richard Evans - Anxiety, Love, will and Dying 28 MIN
Rollo May's Discussion with Richard Evans - Maturity and Creativity 29 MIN
Dist - PSU

Notable contributors to the psychology of personality series
Carl Rogers, Pt 1 50 MIN
Carl Rogers, Pt 2 50 MIN
Erich fromm - part 1 50 MIN
Erich Fromm - Part 2 50 MIN
Gordon allport - Pt 1 50 MIN
Gordon allport - Pt 2 50 MIN
Konrad Lorenz's Discussion with Richard Evans - Aggression 31 MIN
Konrad Lorenz's Discussion with Richard Evans - Ethology and Imprinting 31 MIN
Konrad Lorenz's Discussion with Richard Evans - Motivation 30 MIN
Konrad Lorenz's Discussion with Richard Evans - Reactions and Reflections 29 MIN
Nikolaas Tinbergen's Discussion with 30 MIN

Richard Evans - Ethology and Genetic Programming Versus Learning
Nikolaas Tinbergen's Discussion with Richard Evans - Unique Contributions, Reflections, and Reactions 29 MIN
Professor Erik Erikson - Pt 1 50 MIN
Psychological Dialogue with Playwright Arthur Miller - Pt 1 50 MIN
Psychological Dialogue with Playwright Arthur Miller - Pt 2 51 MIN
R D Laing's discussion with Richard Evans - dilemma of mental illness 30 MIN
Rollo Mays Discussion with Richard Evans - Reactions to Psychoanalytic Concepts 29 MIN
Dist - PSUPCR

Notable people and events 10 MIN
VHS
Coburn collection series
Color (G)
Contact distributor about rental cost _ #N92 - 002
Portrays notable people and events between 1915 - 1925. Includes James Whitcomb Riley's Fairbanks notification, October 1916 visit of President Woodrow Wilson to Indianapolis, and the street car's beginnings at the G.S.R. National Encampment in 1921.
History - United States
Dist - INDI

Notating pitch 29 MIN
U-matic
Beginning piano - an adult approach series; Lesson 3
Color (H A)
Reviews materials from earlier programs. Introduces one - octave parallel motion scale. Identifies treble and bass clefs, clef signs, leger lines and other symbols.
Fine Arts
Dist - CDTEL **Prod** - COAST

A Note from Above 2 MIN
16mm
Color (J)
LC 72-700415
Tells the story of an incorrect issuance of one of the Ten Commandments as 'THOU SHALT KILL.' Shows how people, often too eager to accept and obey laws, followed the commandment before the error could be corrected.
Guidance and Counseling; Psychology; Sociology
Dist - MMA **Prod** - PHID 1970

The Note Machine 14 MIN
U-matic / VHS
Stepping into Rhythm Series
Color (P)
Invites students to make up their own quarter and half note sounds and to 'play' them with the note machine.
Fine Arts
Dist - AITECH **Prod** - WVIZTV

A Note of Uncertainty - the Universe Tomorrow 28 MIN
U-matic / VHS / 16mm
Understanding Space and Time Series
Color
Discusses the expansion of the universe and whether it will stop someday and contract upon itself.
Science - Physical
Dist - UCEMC **Prod** - BBCTV 1980

Note Value 15 MIN
U-matic / VHS
Music and Me Series
Color (P I)
Discusses note value in music.
Fine Arts
Dist - AITECH **Prod** - WDCNTV 1979

Notebook 6 MIN
16mm
B&W (C)
$336.00
Experimental film by Marie Menken.
Fine Arts
Dist - AFA **Prod** - AFA 1962

Notes 13 MIN
U-matic / VHS / 16mm
Study Strategies Series
Color (J H C)
$325, $235 purchase _ #3556
Shows different study methods, such as diagramming, outlining, and underlining.
Education
Dist - CORF

Notes 2 MIN
16mm
B&W (G)
$5.00 rental
Presents a series of sketches.
Fine Arts
Dist - CANCIN **Prod** - MERRIT 1979

Notes for an African Orestes 75 MIN
U-matic / VHS / 16mm
B&W (A)
Documents Pier Paolo Pasolini's plans to make a modern day version of Aeschylus' 'Orestes' in Africa. English language version.
Fine Arts; Literature and Drama
Dist - CNEMAG **Prod** - CNEMAG 1970

Notes for Jerome 45 MIN
16mm
Color (C)
Experimental film by Jonas Mekas.
Fine Arts
Dist - AFA **Prod** - AFA 1978

Notes from a Journey 24 MIN
VHS / 16mm
Color (G)
$190.00 purchase
Records the words of Cambodian refugee Ana Khong. Reflects on Khong's past and her adjustments to her new life in Switzerland.
Geography - World; History - World; Literature and Drama; Sociology
Dist - ICARUS

Notes from a lady at a dinner party 25 MIN
VHS / U-matic
Color (H C A)
$425.00, $395.00 purchase _ #V149; LC 90-705194
Dramatizes a Bernard Malamud story about Max, a prize winning architecture student who attends a small dinner party hosted by his former college mentor. Explores love, happiness, female - male relationships, marriage and power.
Literature and Drama; Sociology
Dist - BARR **Prod** - MTOLP 1989

Notes in origin 12 MIN
16mm
Color (G)
$25.00 rental
Employs the power of quietude through subtle long - rhythms and spartan visual means to evoke simplicity of technique.
Fine Arts
Dist - CANCIN **Prod** - EPPEL 1987

Notes of a Biology Watcher - a Film with Lewis Thomas 57 MIN
U-matic / VHS / 16mm
Nova Series
Color (H C A)
LC 82-701175
Introduces award - winning biologist Lewis Thomas, who explains that all human cells are inhabited by remnants of ancient organisms that took up residence millions of years ago. Offers an intimate portrait of individuality and interconnectedness in nature, examining the courtship of blue crabs, ferocious fights between sea anemones and tiny worms with even tinier plants thriving inside them.
Science; Science - Natural
Dist - TIMLIF **Prod** - WGBHTV 1982

Notes of the Fifth Position 29 MIN
Videoreel / VT2
Playing the Guitar II Series
Color
Fine Arts
Dist - PBS **Prod** - KCET

Notes on a Community Hospital, Pt 1 29 MIN
16mm
B&W
LC 76-703300
Presents an overview of hospital life as experienced by people involved in the daily operation of a Pennsylvania hospital.
Health and Safety
Dist - PSU **Prod** - WPSXTV 1976

Notes on a Community Hospital, Pt 2 29 MIN
16mm
B&W
LC 76-703300
Presents an overview of hospital life as experienced by people involved in the daily operation of a Pennsylvania hospital.
Health and Safety
Dist - PSU **Prod** - WPSXTV 1976

Notes on a Community Hospital - the Administrator 29 MIN
16mm
B&W (H C A)
LC 76-703209
Shows the administrator's role as the manager of a formal link between the community and the hospital. Reviews administrative problems and management methods and the hospital board's role and activities.
Health and Safety
Dist - PSU **Prod** - WPSXTV 1976

Notes on a Community Hospital - the Doctor 28 MIN
16mm
Color (H C A)
LC 76-703210
Follows an orthopedic surgeon who is vice - president of a hospital's medical staff on his daily routine at the hospital. Includes operating room, emergency room rounds and office scenes and meetings with staff.
Guidance and Counseling; Health and Safety; Sociology
Dist - PSU **Prod** - WPSXTV 1974

Notes on a Community Hospital - the Home - Care Coordinator 28 MIN
16mm
Color (H C A)
LC 76-703211
Shows the role of the community hospital home care coordinator, a member of the nursing team who arranges transfer of a patient to a nursing home, deals with a family reluctant to approve transfer and deals with a patient anxious about leaving the hospital.
Health and Safety; Sociology
Dist - PSU **Prod** - WPSXTV 1974

Notes on a Community Hospital - the Patient 29 MIN
16mm
Color (H C A)
LC 76-703212
Follows a young woman admitted to a hospital for surgery as she goes through admission, surgical preparation, surgery and recovery.
Health and Safety; Sociology
Dist - PSU **Prod** - WPSXTV 1974

Notes on a Community Hospital - the Patient Care Team 28 MIN
16mm
Color (H C A)
LC 76-703213
Shows the daily routine of patient care in a hospital focusing on individuals who do the work, primarily the nursing staff, but including medical technologists, dietary and housekeeping staffs.
Health and Safety; Sociology
Dist - PSU **Prod** - WPSXTV 1974

Notes on a Triangle 5 MIN
U-matic / VHS / 16mm
Color (J H C)
LC FIA67-2270
Uses animation to study the various characteristics of the equilateral triangle.
Mathematics
Dist - IFB **Prod** - NFBC 1968

Notes on an Appalachia County - Visiting with Darlene 45 MIN
16mm
B&W (C A)
LC 76-703214
Presents a documentary about a 28 - year - old married woman with four children who is living on welfare in a 14 - dollar - a - month house in Central Pennsylvania. Records her comments and observations as she goes about her household routine.
Geography - United States; Guidance and Counseling; Sociology
Dist - PSU **Prod** - WPSXTV 1974

Notes on Community Hospital 58 MIN
16mm
B&W
LC 76-703300
Presents an overview of hospital life as experienced by people involved in the daily operation of a Pennsylvania hospital.
Geography - United States; Health and Safety; Sociology
Dist - PSU **Prod** - WPSXTV 1976

Notes on Nuclear War 60 MIN
U-matic / VHS / 16mm
War Series
Color (C A)
Follows the development of the arms race and attempts to unravel some of the political doctrines and military strategies devised by the superpowers to 'govern' their nuclear weapons systems. Looks at the concepts of 'deterrence', 'mutual assured destruction' and 'limited nuclear war.'.
Civics and Political Systems; History - World; Sociology
Dist - FI **Prod** - NFBC

Notes on Seeing - a Film with Dorothy Medhurst 30 MIN
16mm
Color
Presents Canadian art teacher Dorothy Medhurst who has taught children to perceive the excitement and beauty of life around them. Shows how, at the Art Gallery of Ontario, she involves the children in both art and nature and reinforces their explorations in both areas. Explains why she is a critic of early reading, which she feels inhibits creativity in the child.

Education; Fine Arts
Dist - FLMLIB **Prod** - FLMLIB 1982

Notes on the Circus 12 MIN
16mm
Color (C)
$95.00
Experimental film by Jonas Mekas.
Fine Arts
Dist - AFA **Prod** - AFA 1966

Notes on the Fifth String 29 MIN
Videoreel / VT2
Playing the Guitar I Series
Color
Fine Arts
Dist - PBS **Prod** - KCET

Notes on the Fifth String, the Eighth Note 20 MIN
VHS / U-matic
Guitar, Guitar Series
Color (J H)
Fine Arts
Dist - GPN **Prod** - SCITV 1981

Notes on the First Two Strings 29 MIN
Videoreel / VT2
Playing the Guitar I Series
Color
Fine Arts
Dist - PBS **Prod** - KCET

Notes on the Fourth String 29 MIN
Videoreel / VT2
Playing the Guitar I Series
Color
Fine Arts
Dist - PBS **Prod** - KCET

Notes on the Fourth String, Tom Dooley 20 MIN
U-matic / VHS
Guitar, Guitar Series
Color (J H)
Fine Arts
Dist - GPN **Prod** - SCITV 1981

Notes on the Popular Arts 20 MIN
U-matic / VHS / 16mm
Color (J)
LC 78-700366
Uses live action, animation and special effects to show how popular arts in America serve as a means of self - projection and fantasy fulfillment.
Fine Arts; Sociology
Dist - PFP **Prod** - BASSS 1978

Notes on the Port of St Francis 22 MIN
16mm
B&W (H C)
A cinematic poem designed to portray the atmosphere of the city of San Francisco. Narration by Vincent Price is based on a descriptive essay by Robert L Stevenson.
Fine Arts; Geography - United States; Social Science
Dist - RADIM **Prod** - STAHER 1952

Notes on the Second String, using the Left Hand, Playing a Duet 20 MIN
VHS / U-matic
Guitar, Guitar Series
Color (J H)
Fine Arts
Dist - GPN **Prod** - SCITV 1981

Notes on the Sixth String 29 MIN
Videoreel / VT2
Playing the Guitar I Series
Color
Fine Arts
Dist - PBS **Prod** - KCET

Notes on the Sixth String, Octaves, the C Scale, the G Scale, on the Bridge to Avignon 20 MIN
U-matic / VHS
Guitar, Guitar Series
Color (J H)
Fine Arts
Dist - GPN **Prod** - SCITV 1981

Notes on the Third String 29 MIN
Videoreel / VT2
Playing the Guitar I Series
Color
Fine Arts
Dist - PBS **Prod** - KCET

Notes on the Third String, Playing a Trio 20 MIN
VHS / U-matic
Guitar, Guitar Series
Color (J H)
Fine Arts
Dist - GPN **Prod** - SCITV 1981

Notes, Reports, and Communications 14 MIN
U-matic / VHS
Professional Security Training Series Module 3
Color
Stresses careful observation and accurate, detailed note - taking as the critical factors in preparing good reports. Shows how to organize information to answer the who, what, where, why, when and how of a situation.
Health and Safety; Sociology
Dist - CORF **Prod** - CORF

Nothin' 14 MIN
16mm
Color (P I)
LC 71-713322
Follows a boy and a girl through the environment of San Francisco. Designed to develop and sharpen art, language and social studies skills through observation and awareness of the environment. Based on curriculum developed by Marion Roth.
Education; English Language; Fine Arts; Geography - United States; Social Science; Sociology
Dist - FILMSM **Prod** - FILMSM 1971

Nothin' but a Winner 30 MIN
VHS / U-matic
Color (A)
Presents University of Alabama football coach Bear Bryant illustrating and explaining his techniques for motivating his players toward athletic excellence. Interviewed by behavioral scientist Dr John Geier.
Physical Education and Recreation; Psychology
Dist - SFTI **Prod** - SFTI

Nothing 3 MIN
16mm
B&W
Images of Chicago and sad young love in summer, set to Petula Clark's recording of 'I WHO HAVE NOTHING.'.
Geography - United States
Dist - NWUFLM **Prod** - ACDRBR 1966

Nothing but Lookers 8 MIN
16mm
People Sell People Series
Color (H A)
Explores the first condition of a successful sale - - the customer buys. Emphasizes the positive effects of a co - operative person - to - person relationship with the customer and shows how to satisfy customer requests with available stock.
Business and Economics
Dist - MLA **Prod** - SAUM 1965

Nothing but Sing 15 MIN
U-matic / VHS
Stepping into Rhythm Series
Color (P)
Features a classical guitar and an electric guitar as solo instruments and as accompanying instruments.
Fine Arts
Dist - AITECH **Prod** - WVIZTV

Nothing but the Best 37 MIN
16mm
Color (LATIN)
Deals with the origins of the Jewish community in Latin America and traces the immigration of Jews to that continent. Gives a picture of Jewish life in South America and describes the operations of ORT in many Latin American countries.
Geography - World; Sociology
Dist - WAORT **Prod** - WAORT 1982

Nothing but the Truth 25 MIN
16mm
Color (IND)
Illustrates how union representatives prepare for a hearing before the Occupational Safety and Health Review Commission. Based on an actual case in a plant where a worker was killed.
Business and Economics; Health and Safety; Psychology
Dist - AFLCIO **Prod** - OHIOSU 1978

Nothing Ever Seems to Work Out for Me 4 MIN
U-matic / VHS / 16mm
Most Important Person - Attitudes Series
Color (K P I) (SPANISH)
Introduces Hairy, who feels that nothing ever works out for him. Features his friends telling him that everyone is disappointed at some time, but there may be ways to make the best of things.
Guidance and Counseling; Psychology
Dist - EBEC **Prod** - EBEC 1972

Nothing for Granted 14 MIN
16mm
Color
LC 74-705219
Describes the Navy Operational Test and Evaluation Force and procedures for testing and evaluating systems and equipment programmed for future Navy use.
Civics and Political Systems
Dist - USNAC **Prod** - USN 1970

Nothing happened this morning 21 MIN
16mm
Color (G)
$25.00 rental
Depicts a morning where nothing happens, yet everything happens when the wonder and magic of the universe is allowed to filter in. By David Bienstock.
Fine Arts
Dist - CANCIN

Nothing real can be threatened - a four part videotape workshop on a Course in Miracles 240 MIN
VHS
Color (G R)
$100.00 purchase _ #C055
Addresses the fundamental issue of fear which is at the root of most of the problems of humanity. Considers insecurity, anger, depression, blame, ambition and unfulfillment. Features spiritual teacher Tara Singh in a four - part workshop series on 'A Course in Miracles' by Dr Helen Shucman.
Health and Safety; Psychology; Religion and Philosophy
Dist - LIFEAP **Prod** - LIFEAP

Nothing real can be threatened series
Awakening to self - knowledge, pt IV 60 MIN
The Deception of learning - Pt II 60 MIN
The Question and the holy instant - Pt 1 60 MIN
Transcending the body senses, pt III 60 MIN
Dist - LIFEAP

Nothing to be Sorry about 29 MIN
VHS / 16mm
A Different Understanding Series
Color (G)
$90.00 purchase _ #BPN178013
Profiles four handicapped children, two deaf, one with cerebral palsy, and one mentally retarded. Shows how they enjoy the love and acceptance of their family and neighbors. Stresses that, in spite of their handicaps, the children are happy, well - adjusted members of society.
Education; Psychology
Dist - RMIBHF **Prod** - RMIBHF

Nothing to be Sorry about 29 MIN
U-matic
A Different Understanding Series
Color (PRO)
Profiles four handicapped children who enjoy the love and acceptance of their neighbors and families.
Psychology
Dist - TVOTAR **Prod** - TVOTAR 1985

Nothing to do - Four Summertime Episodes 10 MIN
U-matic / VHS / 16mm
Color (P I)
Suggests ways children can enjoy leisure time. Includes activities at home, nature and outdoor fun, day camp and visits to the library, park and zoo.
Guidance and Counseling; Psychology; Sociology
Dist - JOU **Prod** - JOU 1961

Nothing to Fear - the Legacy of FDR 52 MIN
16mm / U-matic / VHS
Color (H C A)
LC 83-701015
Explores the legacy of Franklin Delano Roosevelt by combining interviews from the 1980s with extensive historical material. Examines his response to the Great Depression and the radical changes in the role of the Federal government under his leadership. Lists the Roosevelt legacy including Social Security, collective bargaining, unemployment compensation and control of financial institutions.
Biography; History - United States
Dist - FI **Prod** - NBCNEW 1982

Nothing to lose 8 MIN
U-matic / VHS / BETA
Color; NTSC; PAL; SECAM (H C G)
PdS83
Offers guidelines to those who are called upon to give advice about dieting. Discusses the monitoring of daily food intake and recommends an all - around healthy eating regime.
Health and Safety; Social Science
Dist - VIEWTH

Nothing to sniff at - inhalants and their dangers 10 MIN
VHS
Dr Cooper and his friends series
Color (P T) (FRENCH)
$50.00 purchase _ #PVK32, #PVK35
Presents a video package for teachers about some commonly available substances with drug-like effects. Includes a teacher's guide and a poster.
Guidance and Counseling; Health and Safety
Dist - ARFO **Prod** - ARFO

Nothing's Stopping You 7 MIN
U-matic
Color
Presents an adventure guide who also happens to be a diabetic teaching mountain climbing skills to teenage diabetics. Explains how chemstrip, a new method of monitoring blood sugar levels, helps diabetics overcome many of the limitations imposed by their condition.
Health and Safety; Physical Education and Recreation; Sociology
Dist - MTP **Prod** - BIODYN

Notice to the public 15 MIN
U-matic / VHS
En Francais series
Color (H C A)
Discusses the celebration which occurs on Bastille Day.
Foreign Language; Geography - World
Dist - AITECH **Prod** - MOFAFR 1970

Notorious 103 MIN
16mm / U-matic / VHS
B&W (J)
Stars Cary Grant and Ingrid Bergman in a tale of suspense in which the daughter of a convicted treasonous German is paid as an American agent to spy on a German industrial cartel's head, whom she marries. Describes what happens when she learns that the cartel is secretly at work developing the atom bomb, passes the information on and is discovered by her husband who decides to slowly poison her.
Fine Arts
Dist - FI **Prod** - RKOP 1946

The Notorious Landlady 123 MIN
U-matic / VHS / 16mm
B&W (H C A)
Stars Kim Novak, Jack Lemmon and Fred Astaire. Presents a comedy about a young American diplomat in London who rents an apartment in the fashionable private home of a beautiful young woman, suspected by Scotland Yard of having murdered her husband.
Literature and Drama
Dist - FI **Prod** - CPC 1962

Notorious (the key) 13 MIN
16mm
Film study extracts series
B&W (J)
Presents an excerpt from the 1946 motion picture Notorious. Tells how Alicia steals the key to her Nazi husband's wine cellar and how she and an American agent search it to discover the husband's plot. Directed by Alfred Hitchcock.
Fine Arts
Dist - FI **Prod** - UNKNWN

Notre Dame
VHS
Campus clips series
Color (H C A)
$29.95 purchase _ #CC0029V
Takes a video visit to the campus of the University of Notre Dame in Indiana. Shows many of the distinctive features of the campus, and interviews students about their experiences. Provides information on the composition of the student body, professors, academics, social life, housing, and other subjects.
Education
Dist - CAMV

Nottingham - Fairfax County, Virginia - Vol 19, No 4 15 MIN
VHS
Project reference file - PRF - series
Color (G A PRO)
$60.00 purchase _ #N20
Studies land use plans and house designs employed on the outskirts of Washington DC where land is scarce and costs are high. Shows an innovative form, the angled Z-lot. Feature Spencer Stouffer, a principle of Miller and Smith Homes, and architect Walt Richardson of Richardson, Nagy, Martin.
Business and Economics; Geography - United States; Sociology
Dist - ULI **Prod** - ULI

The Noun 14.28 MIN
U-matic / VHS
Grammar Mechanic
(I J)
Designed to help the intermediate student apply the rules of grammar. Focuses on the four classes of nouns and their functions. Fourth in a 16 part series.
English Language
Dist - GPN **Prod** - WDCNTV

A Noun is a Person, Place or Thing 3 MIN
U-matic / VHS
Grammar Rock Series
Color (P)
Follows a little girl through a series of adventures that teach her all the things nouns can be.
English Language
Dist - GA **Prod** - ABCTV 1974

Nouns 15 MIN
VHS
Planet Pylon Series
Color (I)
LC 90712897
Uses character Commander Wordstalker from the Space Station Readstar to develop language arts skills. Studies nouns. Includes a worksheet to be completed by student with the help on series characters. Intended for third grade students.
Education; English Language
Dist - GPN

Nouns 8 MIN
16mm / U-matic / VHS
Basic Grammar Series
Color (I)
LC 81-700754
Examines the functions of nouns within simple English sentences.
English Language
Dist - AIMS **Prod** - LEVYL 1981

Nouns and Adjectives 9 MIN
16mm / U-matic / VHS
Wizard of Words Series
Color (P I)
Discusses the grammar elements of nouns and adjectives and their relationship to one another.
English Language
Dist - MGHT **Prod** - MGHT 1976

Nouns - Building blocks 18 MIN
VHS
Language construction company series
Color (H C G)
$50.00 purchase _ #LCC - 3
Assists students in improving their written and spoken English grammar skills. Bases all programs on a 'construction theme.' Includes review tests as an integral part of each lesson. Students may stop, start and repeat any part of the lesson. Visual cues are given for review purposes. Part of a 15 - part series.
English Language
Dist - INSTRU

Nouns in Sentences 14 MIN
U-matic / VHS / 16mm
Grammar Skills Series
Color (P I)
LC 81-701117
Defines a noun and shows how to identify nouns in sentences.
English Language
Dist - JOU **Prod** - GLDWER 1981

Nouns, Pronouns, Adjectives / Root Words 20 MIN
BETA / VHS
Color
Teaches basic vocabulary skills. Uses simple visuals and a story about a visitor from another planet trying to figure out English.
English Language
Dist - PHENIX **Prod** - PHENIX

Nouns, Pronouns and Adjectives 8 MIN
U-matic / VHS / 16mm
Color (I)
LC FIA62-1255
Defines the noun and the difference between common and proper nouns. Explains how the pronoun takes the place of a noun and how adjectives describe a noun. An animated film.
English Language
Dist - PHENIX **Prod** - ROE 1961

Nous avons faim 13 MIN
16mm
Les Francais chez vous series
B&W (I J H)
LC 72-704474
Foreign Language
Dist - CHLTN **Prod** - PEREN 1967

Nous irons peut - etre en Chine 13 MIN
16mm
Les Francais chez vous series
B&W (I J H)
LC 76-704475
Foreign Language
Dist - CHLTN **Prod** - PEREN 1967

Nous Jouons 10 MIN
VHS / U-matic
Salut - French Language Lessons Series
Color
Focuses on pastimes, the verb etre, and review of the 'Er' verbs - ie, tu, il, elle.
Foreign Language
Dist - BCNFL **Prod** - BCNFL 1984

A Nous les bijoux 13 MIN
16mm
Les Francais chez vous series
B&W (I J H)
Foreign Language
Dist - CHLTN **Prod** - PEREN 1967

Nous sommes seuls 13 MIN
16mm
Les Francais chez vous series
B&W (I J H)
LC 70-704476
Foreign Language
Dist - CHLTN **Prod** - PEREN 1967

Nova series

Artificial Heart	57 MIN
Bird brain	27 MIN
The case of ESP	57 MIN
The Case of the UFOs	57 MIN
Down on the farm	57 MIN
Eyes over China	57 MIN
Farmers of the sea	57 MIN
Fat chance in a thin world	57 MIN
Finding a Voice	57 MIN
Fountain of paradise	57 MIN
Frontiers of Plastic Surgery	57 MIN
Global village	57 MIN
The Great violin mystery	57 MIN
Jaws - the True Story	57 MIN
Lassa Fever	57 MIN
Make My People Live	57 MIN
Making of a Natural History Film	52 MIN
Mathematical Mystery Tour	57 MIN
Miracle of Life	57 MIN
A Normal Face - the Wonders of Plastic Surgery	57 MIN
Salmon on the Run	57 MIN
Shapes of Things	57 MIN
60 minutes to meltdown	84 MIN

Dist - AMBROS

Nova Series

Anthropology on trial	57 MIN
Asbestos - a lethal legacy	57 MIN
City of coral	57 MIN
The Lost World of the Maya	36 MIN
Nuclear Strategy for Beginners	57 MIN
The Pleasure of finding things out	57 MIN
Salmon on the run	57 MIN

Dist - AMBROS
TIMLIF

Nova Series

In the Land of Polar Bears	57 MIN

Dist - AMBROS
WNETTV

Nova series

Adrift on the Gulf Stream	58 MIN
Are you swimming in a sewer	58 MIN
Battles in the war on cancer - a wonder drug on trial	58 MIN
Battles in the war on cancer - breast cancer - turning the tide	58 MIN
The Big spill	58 MIN
The Bomb's lethal legacy	58 MIN
Buried in ice	58 MIN
Can AIDS be stopped?	58 MIN
Can we make a better doctor	58 MIN
Can you still get polio	58 MIN
Child survival - the silent emergency	58 MIN
The Children of Eve	58 MIN
Confronting the killer gene	58 MIN
The Controversial Dr Koop	58 MIN
The Countdown to the Invisible Universe	58 MIN
Death of a star	58 MIN
Decoding the book of life	58 MIN
The Desert doesn't bloom here anymore	58 MIN
Design wars	58 MIN
Freud under analysis	58 MIN
The Genius that was China series	232 MIN
God, Darwin and the dinosaurs	58 MIN
The Hidden city	58 MIN
High Tech Babies	58 MIN
The Hole in the Sky	58 MIN
Hot enough for you	58 MIN
How Babies Get made	58 MIN
How good is Soviet science?	59 MIN
How to Create a Junk Food	60 MIN
Hurricane	58 MIN
In the land of the llama	58 MIN
Is Anybody Out There?	58 MIN
Japan's American Genius	58 MIN
The KGB, the computer and me	58 MIN
Killing machines	58 MIN
The Last journey of a genius	58 MIN
Legends of Easter Island	58 MIN
Leprosy Can be Cured	58 MIN
The Light stuff	58 MIN

A Man, a Plan, a Canal, Panama 58 MIN
The Man who Loved Numbers 58 MIN
The Mystery of the Animal Pathfinders 58 MIN
The Mystery of the Master Builders 58 MIN
Neptune's cold fury 58 MIN
The Planet that Got Knocked on its Side 58 MIN
Poisoned winds of war 58 MIN
Race for the Superconductor 58 MIN
Race for top quark 58 MIN
Riddle of the Joints 58 MIN
The Robot Revolution 58 MIN
The Rocky Road to Jupiter 58 MIN
Sail wars 58 MIN
The Schoolboys who cracked the Soviet secret 58 MIN
The Search for the Disappeared 58 MIN
Secrets of Easter Island 58 MIN
Seeds of Tomorrow 58 MIN
Spy Machines 58 MIN
The Strange new science of chaos 58 MIN
To boldly go 58 MIN
Top gun and beyond 58 MIN
Volcano 58 MIN
We know where you live 58 MIN
Whale Rescue 58 MIN
What is music 58 MIN
What's killing the children 58 MIN
Who shot President Kennedy 58 MIN
Why Planes Burn 58 MIN
Will the World Starve? 58 MIN
The World is full of oil 58 MIN
Dist - CORF

Nova series
Design wars 58 MIN
The Hidden city 58 MIN
Dist - CORF
FOTH

Nova Series
The Williamsburg File 45 MIN
Dist - CWMS

Nova series
Are you doing this for me, doctor, or am I doing it for you 52 MIN
The Big if - interferon 50 MIN
Einstein - Pt 1 29 MIN
Einstein - Pt 2 29 MIN
Dist - FI

Nova Series
Life on a Silken Thread 58 MIN
The Safety Factor 60 MIN
Dist - KINGFT

Nova Series
Acid rain 57 MIN
AIDS - chapter one 57 MIN
Alcoholism - life under the influence 57 MIN
Animal imposters 57 MIN
Cashing in on the ocean 59 MIN
In the Event of Catastrophe 59 MIN
India - machinery of hope 58 MIN
A Mediterranean Prospect 58 MIN
What Price Coal 60 MIN
Dist - PBS

Nova Series
Across the silence barrier 57 MIN
Adventures of teenage scientists 57 MIN
Aging - the Methuselah Syndrome 57 MIN
Alcoholism - life under the influence 57 MIN
Anatomy of a volcano 57 MIN
Animal imposters 57 MIN
Antarctica - earth's last frontier 57 MIN
Artificial Heart 57 MIN
Artists in the Lab 57 MIN
The Asteroid and the dinosaur 57 MIN
Beyond the Milky Way 57 MIN
Bird brain - the mystery of bird navigation 27 MIN
Black Tide 58 MIN
Blindness - Five Points of View 57 MIN
Blueprints in the bloodstream 57 MIN
The Cancer detectives of Lin Xian 57 MIN
The case of ESP 57 MIN
The Case of the ancient astronauts 57 MIN
The Case of the UFOs 57 MIN
Cobalt Blues 57 MIN
Computers, Spies, and Private Lives 57 MIN
Dawn of the solar age - solar energy 29 MIN
Dawn of the solar age - wind and water energy 25 MIN
Dawn with no tomorrow 57 MIN
The Dead Sea Lives 57 MIN
Death of a disease 58 MIN
A Desert place 30 MIN
Did Darwin get it wrong 57 MIN
Do We Really Need the Rockies 57 MIN
The Doctors of Nigeria 57 MIN
The Elusive Illness 57 MIN
Eyes over China 57 MIN
Fat chance in a thin world 57 MIN
The Final Frontier 57 MIN
Finding a Voice 57 MIN
The First signs of Washoe 59 MIN
Fusion - the energy promise 56 MIN
The Gene Engineers 57 MIN
Goodbye Louisiana 57 MIN
The Great violin mystery 57 MIN
The Great wine revolution 57 MIN
The Green Machine 49 MIN
Hawaii - Crucible of Life 57 MIN
Here's Looking at You, Kid 57 MIN
Hot - Blooded Dinosaurs 52 MIN
The Hunt for the Legion Killer 57 MIN
Hunters of the Seal 30 MIN
Incident at Brown's Ferry 58 MIN
The Insect Alternative 57 MIN
Inside the Golden Gate 59 MIN
Inside the Shark 50 MIN
The Invisible Flame 57 MIN
The Keys of Paradise 57 MIN
Lassa Fever 57 MIN
Life - Patent Pending 57 MIN
Light of the 21st Century 57 MIN
Locusts - War Without End 57 MIN
The Making of a Natural History Film 52 MIN
Memories from Eden 57 MIN
Message in the Rocks 57 MIN
The Mind Machines 59 MIN
The Miracle of Life 57 MIN
Moving Still 57 MIN
The Mystery of the Anasazi 59 MIN
A Normal Face - the Wonders of Plastic Surgery 57 MIN
Notes of a Biology Watcher - a Film with Lewis Thomas 57 MIN
One Small Step 57 MIN
Palace of Delights 58 MIN
The Pinks and the Blues 57 MIN
A Plague on Our Children - Pt 1 - Dioxins 57 MIN
A Plague on Our Children - Pt 2 - PCBs 57 MIN
The Plutonium Connection 59 MIN
A Predictable Disaster 32 MIN
Race for Gold 57 MIN
The Renewable Tree 59 MIN
Resolution on Saturn 57 MIN
The Science of Murder 57 MIN
The Sea Behind the Dunes 57 MIN
The Search for Life 30 MIN
Secrets of Sleep 52 MIN
Sixty Minutes to Meltdown 84 MIN
Sociobiology - the Human Animal 57 MIN
Still Waters 59 MIN
Strange Sleep 59 MIN
The Sunspot Mystery - Sun - Weather Connection 30 MIN
The Sunspot Mystery - Sunspots Explained 31 MIN
Talking Turtle 57 MIN
The Television Explosion 57 MIN
Test - Tube Babies - a Daughter for Judy 57 MIN
To Live Until You Die 57 MIN
Tracking the Supertrains 57 MIN
The Transplant Experience 50 MIN
The Tsetse Trap 59 MIN
The Water Crisis 57 MIN
Whale Watch 57 MIN
Where Did the Colorado Go 59 MIN
A Whisper from Space 58 MIN
Why America Burns 57 MIN
Why do Birds Sing 27 MIN
Will the Fishing have to Stop 31 MIN
The Wizard who Spat on the Floor - Thomas Alva Edison 41 MIN
A World of Difference - B F Skinner and the Good Life 58 MIN
Dist - TIMLIF

Nova - the genius that was China series
Empires in collision 58 MIN
Rise of the dragon 58 MIN
The Threat from Japan 58 MIN
Will the dragon rise again 58 MIN
Dist - CORF

Nova video library series
Fat chance in a thin world 60 MIN
Dist - PBS

Nova video library series
Signs of the apes, songs of the whales 60 MIN
Dist - PBS
TIMLIF

Nova video library series
UFOs - are we alone 60 MIN
Dist - PBS
UILL

Nova video library
Animal olympians 60 MIN
Bermuda triangle 60 MIN
Einstein 60 MIN
Hitler's secret weapon 60 MIN
Saving the Sistine Chapel 60 MIN
Science of murder 60 MIN
Secret of the sexes 60 MIN
Shape of things 60 MIN
Visions of the deep 60 MIN
Whale watch 60 MIN
Wonders of plastic surgery 60 MIN
Dist - PBS

The Novel 28 MIN
U-matic / BETA / VHS
Communication skills 2 - advanced series
Color (H C G)
101.95, $89.95 purchase _ #CA - 24
Covers the role of storytelling in communications. Focuses on the novel and distinguishes it from an anecdote or a short story. Lists the five main elements of the novel and explains each element. Part of a 26 - part series.
Literature and Drama; Social Science
Dist - INSTRU

The Novel - 1914 - 1942 - the Loss of Innocence 30 MIN
U-matic / VHS / 16mm
USA Series
B&W (J)
LC 79-702108
Discusses the themes of the major works of prominent American authors - - Hemingway, Dos Passos, Anderson, Steinbeck, Wolfe, Fitzgerald, Farrell, faulkner and West - - and the relationship of each theme to certain geographical parts of America.
Literature and Drama
Dist - IU **Prod** - NET 1966

The Novel - Ralph Ellison on Work in Progress 30 MIN
16mm
USA Series
B&W (J)
Ralph Ellison explains the genesis of his first novel, 'THE INVISIBLE MAN,' and discusses his philosophy as to writers, American novels and the unity of the American spirit.
Literature and Drama
Dist - IU **Prod** - NET 1966

The Novel - Saul Bellow - the World of the Dangling Man 29 MIN
16mm / U-matic / VHS
USA Series
B&W (J)
LC 73-702109
Norman Podhoretz of 'CONTEMPORARY' magazine discusses the works of Saul Bellow. Quotations and annotations from Bellow's novels are included.
Literature and Drama
Dist - IU **Prod** - NET 1966

Novel Series
The Awakening - a novel by Kate Chopin 15 MIN
Maggie, a Girl of the Streets - a Novel by Stephen Crane 15 MIN
The Time Machine - a Novel by H G Wells 15 MIN
Dist - IU

The Novel - the Nonfiction Novel - a Visit with Truman Capote 30 MIN
16mm
USA Series
B&W (J)
Truman Capote describes his latest book 'IN COLD BLOOD' as a new art form, and explains how and why he wrote it.
Literature and Drama
Dist - IU **Prod** - NET 1966

The Novel - Vladimir Nabokov 30 MIN
16mm
USA Series
B&W (H C A)
Interviews Vladimir Nabokov about his life and work, illustrating his discussion of his past with scenes of that era. Nabokov demonstrates how he jots notes on index cards for later combination to form a novel.
Literature and Drama
Dist - IU **Prod** - NET 1966

The Novel - what it is, what It's about, what it Does 35 MIN
16mm / U-matic / VHS
Humanities - Narrative Series
Color (H C)
Presents Clifton Fadiman explaining motivation, characterization, style and the establishment of mood through description. Features the actors from the Old Vic Company.

Literature and Drama
Dist - EBEC **Prod** - EBEC 1962

November 10 MIN
U-matic / VHS
Emma and Grandpa series
(K P)
$180 VC purchase, $30 VC five day rental, $110 self dub
Uses simple rhyming couplets to help kindergartners and first graders understand nature and seasonal changes. Highlights the importance of conservation. Focuses on the signs of new growth visible despite the autumn die back of most plants. Eleventh in a series of 12.
Science - Natural
Dist - GPN

November 3 24 MIN
16mm
Color
LC 76-703791
Presents a drama about four escapees from a penitentiary who terrorize a young couple.
Fine Arts
Dist - CONCRU **Prod** - CONCRU 1975

November sketches 4 MIN
16mm
Color (G)
$10.00 rental
Notes a series of experiments with movement inspired by the cliffs and surf of Mendocino, California and 'psilly little mushrooms.' Features music by Richard Moffitt.
Fine Arts
Dist - CANCIN **Prod** - FERGCO 1978

Novi 30 MIN
16mm
B&W
A race fans's love affair.
Physical Education and Recreation
Dist - SFI **Prod** - SFI

Novice Dog Obedience 15 MIN
16mm
Dog Obedience Training Series
Color
LC 80-701007
Illustrates some basic techniques of novice dog training.
Science - Natural
Dist - KLEINW **Prod** - KLEINW 1973

Noviciat 19 MIN
16mm
B&W (H C)
Presents a Freudian psychodrama about a masochistic voyeur.
Psychology
Dist - CFS **Prod** - CFS 1960

The Now 17 MIN
16mm
Color (A)
$25.00 rental
Explains filmmaker Coni Beeson, 'These are my past lives when my lovers were black and my lovers were white, when I was male and when I was female.'
Fine Arts; Religion and Philosophy
Dist - CANCIN

Now 5 MIN
16mm
B&W
Presents a montage which captures the spirit and tempo of the civil rights movements, assembled from news footage and stills. Lena Horne sings the song 'NOW.'.
Civics and Political Systems; Fine Arts; History - United States
Dist - CANWRL **Prod** - ICAIC 1964

Now 14 MIN
16mm
Color
Examines the heritage of Marion County, Florida.
Geography - United States; History - United States
Dist - FLADC **Prod** - FLADC

Now about Lamb 14 MIN
16mm
Color (J H A)
LC 75-701972
Includes basic lamb cookery showing easy, versatile lamb dishes as prepared in the family kitchen and on the outdoor grill.
Home Economics
Dist - AUDPLN **Prod** - ASPC 1965

Now - After all these Years 60 MIN
16mm
Color (J)
LC 83-700627
Analyzes life in the Prussian village of Rhina where, before 1939, Christians and Jews lived in close harmony until a wave of anti - semitism swept the village. Interviews both Jews who left the village and residents who blame the Jews' troubles on the Nazis.
History - World; Religion and Philosophy
Dist - CANTOR **Prod** - CANTOR 1982

Now Age Reading Programs
Cassette / 16mm
Sound Filmstrip, Set 1 Series
Color (I J)
$275.00 purchase _ #8F - PN640003
Includes the classic tales Black Beauty, The Call of the Wild, Dr Jekyll & Mr Hyde, Dracula, Frankenstein, Huckleberry Finn, Moby Dick, The Red Badge of Courage, The Time Machine, Tom Sawyer, Treasure Island and 20,000 Leagues Under the Sea. Sets include filmstrips, cassettes, classroom exercise materials, books and posters.
English Language; Literature and Drama
Dist - MAFEX

Now Age Reading Programs
Cassette / 16mm
Sound Filmstrip, Set 2 Series
Color (I J)
$275.00 purchase _ #8F - PN640006
Brings classic tales to young readers. Filmstrip set includes filmstrip, cassette, corresponding book, classroom exercise materials and a poster. Books include The Great Adventures of Sherlock Holmes, Gulliver's Travels, The Invisible Man, Journey to the Center of the Earth, Kidnapped, The Mysterious Island, The Scarlet Letter, The Story of My Life, A Tale of Two Cities, The Three Musketeers, The War of the Worlds, and The Hunchback of Notre Dame.
English Language; Literature and Drama
Dist - MAFEX

Now age reading programs series
The Call of the wild
Tom Sawyer
Dist - MAFEX

Now Age Reading Programs, Set 1 Series
Black Beauty
Dr Jekyll and Mr Hyde
Dracula
Frankenstein
Moby Dick
The Red Badge of Courage
The Time Machine
Treasure Island
Twenty Thousand Leagues Under the Sea
Dist - MAFEX

Now Age Reading Programs, Set 3 Series
Around the World in Eighty Days
The Best of O Henry
The Best of Poe
Captains Courageous
A Connecticut Yankee in King Arthur's Court
The Hound of the Baskervilles
The House of Seven Gables
Jane Eyre
The Last of the Mohicans
Two Years Before the Mast
White Fang
Wuthering Heights
Dist - MAFEX

Now Age Reading Programs, Set 2 Series
The Great adventures of Sherlock Holmes
Gulliver's Travels
The Hunchback of Notre Dame
The Invisible Man
Journey to the Center of the Earth
Kidnapped
The Mysterious Island
The Scarlet Letter
The Story of My Life
A Tale of Two Cities
The Three Musketeers
The War of the Worlds
Dist - MAFEX

Now and Forever 77 MIN
16mm
Color (J)
LC 79-700543
Presents an historical survey of life in Oregon during the first half of the 20th century.
History - United States
Dist - OREGHS **Prod** - OREGHS 1979

Now and here my hand - a genesis of Christian unity 27 MIN
VHS / U-matic
Color (A)
Uses an historical docu - drama to retell the story of the first grass - root ecumenical initiative in the United States, one which led to the founding of the Christian Church (Disciples of Christ). Notes some reasons for the success of the unlikely unity venture. Concludes with an affirmation of the Disciples' ecumenical heritage and a plea for continued unity of all Christians.
History - United States; Religion and Philosophy
Dist - ECUFLM **Prod** - DCCMS 1982

Now Can I Tell You My Secret 15 MIN
16mm / U-matic / VHS
Color (P)
Shows that children have the right to protect themselves against sexual advances by any adults. Tells the story of a young boy who is keeping the secret that he was molested by a neighbor. Points out the difference between a 'good touch' and a 'bad touch' and shows children how to say no to situations that are uncomfortable to them.
Sociology
Dist - CORF **Prod** - DISNEY

The Now Crowd 30 MIN
16mm
Color (H A)
LC 77-715496
Dramatizes the pressures placed on a college student and his girl friend to conform to the sexual attitudes of their peers. Shows that Christian principles should be able to withstand the pressure of conformity.
Guidance and Counseling; Psychology; Religion and Philosophy; Sociology
Dist - CPH **Prod** - CPH 1968

Now for a change 15 MIN
U-matic / VHS
Dragons, wagons and wax - Set 2 series
Color (K P)
Discusses natural changes that can affect an ecosystem.
Science; Science - Natural
Dist - CTI **Prod** - CTI

Now Hear this 15 MIN
16mm
Color
Presents the Sanford Naval Academy in Florida, a boys' preparatory school which offers a liberal arts education for 350 students.
Education; Geography - United States
Dist - FLADC **Prod** - FLADC

Now Hear this 23 MIN
VHS / U-matic
Color (H C A)
Presents a quiz on hearing.
Science - Natural
Dist - CAROUF **Prod** - WNBCTV

Now I Can Speak 20 MIN
U-matic
Color
Illustrates the usage of pictographic language by the disabled.
Psychology
Dist - LAURON **Prod** - LAURON

Now I Can Talk - a Fluency - Shaping Program for Stutterers 21 MIN
16mm / U-matic / VHS
Color (H C A)
LC 76-700243
Takes a look at a three - week speech reconstruction program being carried out at Hollins College. Considers various aspects of the program, including its administration, its use of computer aids and the ways in which speech fluency is maintained after the program.
Education; English Language; Psychology
Dist - CORF **Prod** - HANOVC 1975

Now I can tell you my secret 15 MIN
U-matic / 16mm / VHS
Color (P)
$390.00, $295.00 purchase _ #JC - 67653
Teaches youngsters that they have the right to protect themselves from sexual advances by anyone. Tells the story of a young boy who is keeping the secret that he was molested by a neighbor. Stresses the fundamentals of child abuse prevention - understanding the difference between 'good touch' and 'bad touch,' saying 'no' to uncomfortable situations, getting away to a safe place, and telling an adult who will help.
Health and Safety; Sociology
Dist - CORF **Prod** - DISNEY 1985

Now I Know Library
U-matic / VHS
Now I Know Series
Color (K P)
$89.85 purchase _ #MN027
Presents an adaptation of the book Now I Know Library. Contains a 32 page hardcover book and a video.
English Language; Literature and Drama; Science - Natural; Science - Physical
Dist - TROLA

Now I Know Series
More about Dinosaurs 8 MIN
Now I Know Library
Stars 8 MIN
Dist - TROLA

Now I see it geometry video series
Angles
Area of circles
Area of common geometric figures
Geometric constructions
Perimeter, circumference and pi
Prisms and cones
Rectangular solids
Spheres
Triangles
Dist - GA

Now I'm five 20 MIN
VHS
Training for child care providers series
Color (H A)
$89.95 purchase _ #CEVK20365V
Discusses how to provide care for five - year olds. Provides examples of activities that can be used to reinforce positive self - esteem, such as learning to listen, handling negative events, personal hygiene, and more. Includes a leader's guide and reproducible study materials.
Health and Safety; Psychology
Dist - CAMV

Now I'm five 20 MIN
VHS
Color (H A T G)
$59.95 purchase _ #CV969
Presents over 40 examples of activities which reinforce positive self - talk statements. Illustrates learning listening skills, handling negative events, personal hygiene, the importance of friendship and how to like oneself. Guide available separately.
Fine Arts; Health and Safety; Home Economics; Psychology; Social Science
Dist - AAVIM **Prod** - AAVIM

Now I've Said My ABC's 30 MIN
U-matic
Family and the Law Series
(H C A)
Describes the legal and social services available to the abused child and parents of the abused.
Civics and Political Systems; History - World
Dist - ACCESS **Prod** - ACCESS 1980

Now One Foot, Now the Other 24 MIN
16mm / VHS
Color; Captioned (P)
$470.00, $420.00 purchase, $50.00 rental _ #C - 496; LC 86705016
Tells a story about family relationships and strength of love. Based on the book by Tomie dePaola. Available in captioned version. Produced by Don MacDonald.
Literature and Drama; Psychology; Sociology
Dist - ALTSUL

The Now Scene 14 MIN
16mm
Color
LC 74-705221
Shows U S Air Force facilities and demonstrations, such as the building of the North American Air Defense Command (NORAD,) suspended on coils inside mountains. Features the Thunderbirds and their spectacular F4 E Phantom demonstrations and life at Oxnard Air Force Base where fighter - interceptor squadrons are trained.
Civics and Political Systems; Industrial and Technical Education
Dist - USNAC **Prod** - USAF 1969

Now serving ... every customer 25 MIN
VHS
Color (J H T G)
Demonstrates methods of providing quality customer service to people with disabilities. Uses scenarios to spark conversation among participants as to how scenes relate to their own business or environment. Helps employers and teachers equip workers and students with skills to succeed in implementing the Americans with Disabilities Act.
Business and Economics; Health and Safety
Dist - CAMV
AMEDIA

Now that My World is Small 27 MIN
U-matic
Color
Shows a nursing home resident as she compares her past and present life and shares her feelings regarding the lack of understanding of perceptual problems that have led to her being labeled 'confused.'.
Health and Safety; Sociology
Dist - SUCBUF **Prod** - SUCBUF

Now that the Buffalo's Gone 7 MIN
16mm
Color (I J)
LC 74-709232
Uses group and individual still - photograph portraits of American Indians, combined with footage from old films treated in psychedelic techniques, to point up the silent dignity of the Indian in the face of his oppressors.
Psychology; Social Science; Sociology
Dist - CFS **Prod** - GERSHB 1969

Now that the Buffalo's Gone 75 MIN
U-matic / VHS / 16mm
Color (H C A)
Examines the fact that American Indians have endured a terrible past and suffer a hopeless present. Their history is one of massacres, broken promises, worthless treaties and land - grabbing. Most of the Indians in the United States live in barren reservations and infant mortality, suicide and alcoholism are common problems.
Social Science
Dist - MEDIAG **Prod** - THAMES 1969

Now that the Dinosaurs are Gone 25 MIN
16mm
Color (FRENCH)
LC 74-703228
Examines the current state of nuclear energy development in the United States and shows the role it will play in the future energy requirements of America.
Foreign Language; Social Science
Dist - AIF **Prod** - AIF 1974

Now that the Dinosaurs are Gone 25 MIN
16mm
Energy - an Overview Series
Color (J H)
Probes the reasons for the accelerated development of nuclear power plants. Discusses the issues surrounding the use of nuclear fission in power production.
Home Economics; Industrial and Technical Education; Science - Physical; Social Science
Dist - CONPOW **Prod** - CENTRO

Now that You have a New Baby 12 MIN
VHS / U-matic
Color
Helps new parents recognize the importance of childhood immunization and encourages them to complete their babies' vaccinations at an early age.
Health and Safety
Dist - AHOA **Prod** - AHOA

Now that you know - living healthy with HIV 134 MIN
VHS / U-matic / BETA
Color (G)
$50.00 purchase _ #703
Presents three parts on living with HIV - Coping with the News; Understanding HIV; Lifestyle Choices and Changes. Takes the viewer from receiving notice of a positive HIV status to developing a support system in Coping with the News. Illustrates how the HIV virus works and how to monitor the health of HIV positive patients in Understanding HIV. Shows how to maintain good health mentally and physically by examining one's lifestyle and making changes.
Health and Safety
Dist - CONMED **Prod** - KAISP

Now that You're Postpartum 21 MIN
16mm
Color (A)
LC 81-700240
Addresses the physical and emotional changes of new mothers, observing a postpartum class and a group of postpartum mothers.
Health and Safety; Psychology
Dist - POLYMR **Prod** - POLYMR 1980

Now, That's a Report 28 MIN
U-matic / VHS / 16mm
Color (C A)
Presents the four steps of report writing through the story of a young executive who is asked to write a report on report preparation. Discusses investigation, planning, writing and revision and points out that a report has to be clear, concise, complete and correct.
English Language
Dist - RTBL **Prod** - RANKAV 1977

Now that's service 23 MIN
VHS
Color (A PRO IND)
$660.00 purchase, $155.00 rental
Portrays effective customer service skills and attitudes in a variety of settings, such as banks, airline reservations, telephone customer service, and more.
Business and Economics; Guidance and Counseling; Psychology
Dist - VLEARN **Prod** - RTBL

Now the Chips are Down 50 MIN
U-matic / VHS / 16mm
Silicon Factor Series
Color (C A)
Shows the tasks being made possible by computer microprocessors such as a machine that can read aloud, move a driverless tractor and run a warehouse without any human staff.
Mathematics
Dist - FI **Prod** - BBCTV 1979

Now, Voyager 117 MIN
16mm
B&W
Stars Bette Davis as an obsessively aloof spinster who is transformed into a vibrant young woman. Tells how she falls in love with a married man. Stars Paul Heinreid and Claude Rains.
Fine Arts
Dist - UAE **Prod** - UNKNWN 1942

Now We are Free 26 MIN
16mm
B&W
LC FIE57-147
Follows a Hungarian family from Budapest, first to Austria, then to Camp Kilmer in New Jersey and finally to resettlement in a midwest city in the United States.
Guidance and Counseling; Psychology; Social Science; Sociology
Dist - USOE **Prod** - USIA 1957

Now We are Parents 30 MIN
16mm
Color; B&W (J H T R)
Presents a story about a young couple whose first baby suddenly becomes a third personality in the home. Shows how the solutions to their problems include spiritual insights into the meaning of the new life God has given them, their responsibilities to each other and the implications of Christian faith for their home.
Religion and Philosophy
Dist - FAMF **Prod** - FAMF

Now - West Africa 17 MIN
16mm
Color
LC 73-702047
Promotes interest in West Africa as a market for business and as a center for industrial development.
Business and Economics; Geography - World
Dist - MCDO **Prod** - MCDO 1973

Now You See Me, Now You Don't 20 MIN
16mm
Color (J)
LC 78-700336
Examines the various defense mechanisms employed by insects to avoid predators.
Science - Natural
Dist - MOKIN **Prod** - MANTIS 1977

Now You're an Artist 29 MIN
Videoreel / VT2
Tin Lady Series
Color
Fine Arts
Dist - PBS **Prod** - NJPBA

Nowhere to Hide 26 MIN
VHS / U-matic
Color
Reveals startling statistics that show that radiation can't be avoided.
Health and Safety; Science - Physical
Dist - WCCOTV **Prod** - WCCOTV 1980

Nowhere to Run 20 MIN
16mm / U-matic / VHS
Color
LC 76-702209
Uses the capture of wild horses of the western range as an example of the problem of preserving the natural heritage of the West.
Geography - United States; Science - Natural; Sociology
Dist - PHENIX **Prod** - JMAX 1976

Nowogrodek 26 MIN
VHS
Silent; Color; B&W (G) (ENGLISH AND YIDDISH INTERTITLES)
$54.00 purchase
Portrays people, institutions and activities in Nowogrodek, a lively Lithuanian - Jewish community, in a silent film, circa 1930.
Fine Arts; Religion and Philosophy; Sociology
Dist - NCJEWF

Noyes 3 MIN
16mm
Color (G)
$25.00 rental
Confronts the relativity of simultaneous multiple perspectives. Views a single action from alternative left and right perspectives, accentuating reversals. The sound is fragmented and focuses attention on the impossibility of a resolution in the film's dichotomy. Produced by Bette Gordon.
Fine Arts
Dist - CANCIN

The Nozzleman 25 MIN
16mm
Color (PRO)
Demonstrates the application of water on fire, using straight stream and fog nozzle.

Health and Safety; Social Science
Dist - LAFIRE **Prod** - LAFIRE

The Nozzleman 11 MIN
16mm
Color (H C A)
LC FIA63-668
Uses animation, an isolated situation and a complex situation to show the use of the direct, indirect and combination approach to fire situations in wooden structures. Explains thermal balance, nozzle operation, effects of steam and final overhaul.
Health and Safety
Dist - FILCOM **Prod** - ABMC 1961

The Nozzleman 20 MIN
VHS
Color (IND PRO)
$225.00 purchase, $95.00 rental
Looks at techniques important to the nozzleman as a vital part of the total firefighting operation. Teaches techniques through animation and actual live - action firefighting scenes. The program defines direct, indirect and combination attacks, thermal balance and other basic principles.
Fine Arts; Science - Physical
Dist - JEWELR

NPI Video CLE Series Vol 2
The Art of Legal Negotiations with Professor Gerald Williams, Pt 1 70 MIN
The art of legal negotiations with professor Gerald Williams, Pt 2 70 MIN
The Art of Legal Negotiations with Professor Gerald Williams, Pt 3 70 MIN
The Art of Legal Negotiations with Professor Gerald Williams, Pt 4 70 MIN
The Art of Legal Negotiations with Professor Gerald Williams, Pt 5 70 MIN
The Art of Legal Negotiations with Professor Gerald Williams, Pt 6 70 MIN
The Art of Legal Negotiations with Professor Gerald Williams, Pt 7 70 MIN
The Art of Legal Negotiations with Professor Gerald Williams, Pt 8 70 MIN
Dist - NPRI

NPI Video CLE Series Vol 4
Trial Techniques with Professor Irving Younger, Pt 1 52 MIN
Trial Techniques with Professor Irving Younger, Pt 2 52 MIN
Trial Techniques with Professor Irving Younger, Pt 3 52 MIN
Trial Techniques with Professor Irving Younger, Pt 4 52 MIN
Trial Techniques with Professor Irving Younger, Pt 5 53 MIN
Trial Techniques with Professor Irving Younger, Pt 6 53 MIN
Trial Techniques with Professor Irving Younger, Pt 7 53 MIN
Trial Techniques with Professor Irving Younger, Pt 8 53 MIN
Dist - NPRI

NPI video CLE series vol 5
Acquisitions, mergers, and business purchases with professor Wm D Kilbourn, pt 1 60 MIN
Dist - NPRI

NPI video CLE series Vol 6
Tax aspects of divorce with professor Frank E A Aander - Pt 1 52 MIN
Tax aspects of divorce with Professor Frank E A Sander - Pt 2 52 MIN
Tax aspects of divorce with Professor Frank E A Sander - Pt 3 53 MIN
Tax aspects of divorce with Professor Frank E A Sander - Pt 4 53 MIN
Dist - NPRI

NPI Video CLE Series
Buying and Selling the Small Business with Professor John E Moye, Pt 1 72 MIN
Dist - NPRI

NRC respiratory protection series
Acceptable practices for fitting respirator users 20 MIN
Acceptable practices for the use of air - purifying respirators 14 MIN
Acceptable practices for the use of atmosphere - supplying respirators 15 MIN
Dist - USNAC

NRL - the Naval Research Laboratory 29 MIN
16mm
Color
LC 75-701309
Describes the variety of research conducted at the U S Naval Research Laboratory.
Civics and Political Systems
Dist - USNAC **Prod** - USN 1974

An NSAID for adults of all ages
VHS
Color (PRO)
#LDN - 13
Presents a free - loan program which trains medical professionals. Contact distributor for details.
Health and Safety
Dist - WYAYLA **Prod** - WYAYLA

NSBA Reports - the Global Connection 30 MIN
16mm
Color
Using the format of a television news reporter, with Thomas A Shannon, Executive Director of the National School Boards Association, acting as host, the film features actor Joseph Campanella in the role of a tough network reporter who visits three classrooms of different educational levels, to see how teachers are teaching their students to develop global perspectives on political and economic events that affect their daily lives.
Education
Dist - SWRLFF **Prod** - NSBA

NSBA Reports - the Partnership in Career Education 34 MIN
16mm
Color
Using the format of a television news reporter, with Thomas A Shannon, Executive Director of the National School Boards Association, acting as host, the film features actor Joseph Campanella in the role of a tough network reporter who visits a community in which the school board has entered into a partnership relation with the local businesses and organizations in order to provide their students with opportunities to learn about the world of work.
Education
Dist - SWRLFF **Prod** - NSBA

Nuba 25 MIN
U-matic / VHS / 16mm
Untamed World Series Series
Color; Mono (J H C A)
$400.00 film, $250.00 video, $50.00 rental
Profiles the primitive Nuba people of Sudan and how they are adapting to the intrusion of modern society.
Geography - World; Sociology
Dist - CTV **Prod** - CTV 1973

Nubia 64 - Saving the Temples of Ancient Egypt (3500 BC - 1000 a D) 40 MIN
16mm
Color
Discusses saving the temples of Ancient Egypt dating from 3500 BC to 1000 A D.
Fine Arts; History - World; Science - Physical
Dist - ROLAND **Prod** - ROLAND

Nuclear Beach Party 15 MIN
16mm
B&W
LC 81-700424
Offers a beach movie satire in which a group of teenagers enact the boy - meets - girl, boy - loses - girl, boy - gets - girl plot in a bomb shelter after World War III.
Fine Arts
Dist - HOWTAL **Prod** - HOWTAL 1980

Nuclear by - products 10 MIN
U-matic
Nuclear Physics Series
Color (H C)
Discusses the fission process in the core of a nuclear reactor. Discusses the long life of nuclear waste and the difficulty of disposal.
Science; Science - Physical
Dist - TVOTAR **Prod** - TVOTAR 1986

Nuclear Conversation
VHS / U-matic
(J H C A)
$69.00 purchase _ #04467 94
Presents a conversation with famed nuclear scientist Amory Lovins as he discusses the technological and policy relationships between nuclear energy and war capability.
Civics and Political Systems; Fine Arts; Social Science; Sociology
Dist - ASPRSS

Nuclear Countdown 28 MIN
16mm / U-matic / VHS
Disarmament Series
Color
LC 78-701371
Focuses on the threat to human survival posed by nuclear weaponry and stresses that a lasting world peace cannot be achieved without disarmament.
Civics and Political Systems; Social Science; Sociology
Dist - JOU **Prod** - UN 1978

Nuclear cover - up - Chernousenko on Chernobyle 30 MIN
VHS
Color (G)
$29.95 purchase _ #P8
Presents Russian scientist Chernousenko who reveals what really happened at Chernobyl. Warns of the inescapable dangers of nuclear power and calls on the scientific community to save our planet. Narrated by Kevin Sanders.
Fine Arts; Health and Safety; History - World; Social Science
Dist - HP

Nuclear Defense at Sea 45 MIN
U-matic / VHS
Color
Illustrates evasive and survival techniques that US surface ships would have to employ in order to survive a nuclear war.
Civics and Political Systems
Dist - IHF **Prod** - IHF

The Nuclear Dilemma 50 MIN
U-matic / VHS / 16mm
Energy Crunch Series
Color
LC 77-702018
Discusses the advantages and disadvantages of using nuclear fission reactors as a major energy source.
Science - Physical; Social Science
Dist - FI **Prod** - BBCTV 1974

Nuclear Energy - a Perspective 28 MIN
16mm / U-matic
Color
Presents the many steps in the uranium fuel process, from the search for ore - bearing uranium to the shipping containers carrying the final fuel assemblies to the reactors. Highlights the future of the breeder reactor.
Science - Physical; Social Science
Dist - MTP **Prod** - EXXON

Nuclear energy and nuclear waste 30 MIN
VHS
Earth at risk environmental video series
Color (J H C G)
$49.95 purchase _ #LVPN6627V
Introduces and defines environmental terms and global ecological dilemmas in terms of nuclear energy and waste. Presents current statistical information. Part of a ten - part series on environmental issues based on a series of books by Chelsea House Publishers and featuring former MTV host Kevin Seal.
Science - Natural; Social Science
Dist - CAMV

Nuclear Energy Fundamentals and Issues 50 MIN
VHS / U-matic
Energy Issues and Alternatives Series
Color
Examines the fundamental principles of conventional nuclear fission along with breeder technology and fusion energy. Explains the operation of both pressurized and boiling water reactors.
Social Science
Dist - UIDEEO **Prod** - UIDEEO

Nuclear Energy / Home Filing Systems / Supermarket Alternatives
VHS / U-matic
Consumer Survival Series
Color
Discusses aspects of nuclear energy, home filing systems and supermarket alternatives.
Home Economics; Social Science
Dist - MDCPB **Prod** - MDCPB

Nuclear Energy - Peril or Promise
U-matic / VHS / 35mm strip
(J H C)
Describes how atomic power works and explains its potential for producing low cost electricity. Provides background information and interviews for making a criticial judgement about the benefits and hazards of nuclear energy. In 4 parts.
Social Science
Dist - ASPRSS GA **Prod** - SCIMAN

Nuclear Energy - the Great Controversy 29 MIN
16mm
Energy Sources - a New Beginning Series
Color
Questions the possibility of changing the image of nuclear power from weapon to energy producer. Discusses fission processes versus fusion technology and reactors and their possible dangers.
Science - Natural; Social Science
Dist - UCOLO **Prod** - UCOLO

Nuclear Energy - the Question Before Us 25 MIN
16mm / U-matic / VHS
Color (J)
LC 82-700343
Concentrates on the decisions about nuclear energy made and being made in the state of Wisconsin. Polls several professors, an engineer and a state representative about the short - and long - term effects of this controversial fuel.
Social Science; Sociology
Dist - NGS **Prod** - NGS 1981

Nuclear Fallout - Fiction and Fact 10 MIN
16mm
Screen news digest series; Vol 5; Issue 2
B&W (J H)
Discusses the hazards and shows the basic difference between local and world - wide nuclear fallout. Based on research by the Defense Atomic Support Agency.
Health and Safety; Science - Physical
Dist - HEARST **Prod** - HEARST 1962

The Nuclear Fudge 15.30 MIN
U-matic / BETA / VHS
(G)
$100.00
Suggests that Canadian uranium is being exported to the United States for use in nuclear weapons. A treaty between Canada and the United States prohibits the use of Canadian uranium in nuclear arms.
Civics and Political Systems
Dist - CTV **Prod** - CTV 1985

Nuclear Fuel Waste Research - the Canadian Program 24 MIN
16mm
Color (G)
_ #106C 0179 607
Explains the Canadian nuclear fuel waste management program through interviews with people working inside and outside the nuclear industry and by a visit to the Whiteshell Nuclear Research Establishment.
History - World; Social Science; Sociology
Dist - CFLMDC **Prod** - NFBC 1979

Nuclear Gas Stimulation - Tapping Our National Heritage 29 MIN
16mm
Energy Sources - a New Beginning Series
Color
Traces the historical use of natural gas. Explains that some reserves are only accessible through nuclear fracturing. Considers the potential dangers of this process to society and the environment.
Science - Natural; Social Science
Dist - UCOLO **Prod** - UCOLO

Nuclear Innovations in Process Control 17 MIN
16mm
Color (PRO)
LC 72-714172
Depicts the versatility and sophistication of nuclear methods that are now available for control of industrial processes and for nondestructive testing.
Business and Economics; Industrial and Technical Education; Science - Physical
Dist - USERD **Prod** - BATELL 1971

Nuclear Know - How 26 MIN
16mm
Color
Presents an up - to - date report on United Kingdom Atomic Energy Authority experimental facilities and services for reactor and fuel development.
Geography - World; Industrial and Technical Education; Science - Physical
Dist - UKAEA **Prod** - UKAEA 1971

Nuclear Magnetic Resonance 28 MIN
U-matic / VHS / 16mm
Color
LC 71-707710
Uses animation, sound, and color to demonstrate the basic working principles of nuclear magnetic resonance, the operation of the analytical instrument, and the interpretation of the data obtained.
Science - Physical
Dist - MEDIAG **Prod** - UCLA 1968

Nuclear Medicine 62 MIN
U-matic
Color (PRO)
LC 76-706064
Reviews the basic physics involved in the use of isotopes for medical applications. Discusses brain scanning, the diagnosis of pulmonary emboli through lung scanning and the diagnostic application of liver and spleen scanning. Describes the diagnosis and management of hyperthyroidism and hypothyroidism and the mechanism and diagnostic use of bone scanning.
Health and Safety; Science - Physical
Dist - USNAC **Prod** - WARMP 1971

Nuclear Medicine 26 MIN
VHS / U-matic
X - Ray Procedures in Layman's Terms Series
Color
Describes the six most widely used tests, the brain scan, bone scan, thyroid scan, liver scan, lung scan and cardiac imaging. Illustrates how these scans provide information that assists in diagnosis.
Health and Safety; Science
Dist - FAIRGH **Prod** - FAIRGH

Nuclear medicine - Lola's most excellent adventure 10 MIN
VHS
Color (C PRO G)
$250.00 purchase
Takes a lighthearted look at what nuclear medicine is - and isn't. Follows Lola as she meanders through a hospital and learns that nuclear medicine isn't something to run away from.
Health and Safety
Dist - LPRO **Prod** - LPRO

Nuclear Medicine, Pt 1 20 MIN
U-matic
Color (PRO)
LC 76-706064
Focuses on brain scanning.
Health and Safety
Dist - USNAC **Prod** - WARMP 1971

Nuclear Medicine, Pt 2 21 MIN
U-matic
Color (PRO)
LC 76-706064
Discusses the diagnosis of pulmonary emboli through lung scanning and the diagnostic application of liver and spleen scanning.
Health and Safety
Dist - USNAC **Prod** - WARMP 1971

Nuclear Medicine, Pt 3 21 MIN
U-matic
Color (PRO)
LC 76-706064
Describes the diagnosis and management of hyperthyroidism and hypothyroidism and the mechanism and diagnostic use of bone scanning.
Health and Safety
Dist - USNAC **Prod** - WARMP 1971

The Nuclear Navy 28 MIN
16mm
Color
Frank Blair narrates the story of the Navy's development of nuclear power and its application in longrange submarines and the growing nuclear surface force.
Civics and Political Systems; Industrial and Technical Education; Science - Physical
Dist - USNAC **Prod** - USN 1967

Nuclear neighbors 60 MIN
VHS
Color (J H C G)
$69.95 purchase _ #TIP100V
Takes a close look at how the controversial issue of nuclear power has divided a community in central California and raised questions about society's responsibility to the environment, as well as to the economy. Reveals that in 1968 contruction began on a nuclear power plant in Diablo Canyon, near San Luis Obispo, that in 1976 an earthquake faultline was discovered near the site. This intensified the local debate and polarized the citizenry.
Social Science
Dist - CAMV

Nuclear Newsreel - Reports on International Protest 28 MIN
VHS / U-matic
Color
Presents both sides of the nuclear debate with footage of the International Day of Nuclear Disarmment.
Civics and Political Systems; Sociology
Dist - FINLIN **Prod** - FINLIN

The Nuclear Nightmare
VHS
Is Anyone Listening - a Documentary Series
$89.95 purchase _ #ULNN
Presents a forum for teenagers to talk about the threat of nuclear war and how it affects their lives.
Psychology; Sociology
Dist - CAREER **Prod** - CAREER

The Nuclear Nightmare 50 MIN
16mm / U-matic / VHS
B&W
Portrays how a nuclear bomb dropped on New York City would affect a family living 50 miles away. A dramatization.
Civics and Political Systems; Social Science
Dist - USNAC **Prod** - USOCD 1950

Nuclear Nightmare Next Door 52 MIN
U-matic / VHS
Color (G)
$279.00, $179.00 purchase _ #AD - 1985
Reports on the controversy surrounding the use and disposal of radioactive materials. Considers the health effects on workers and nearby residents. Looks at some ordinary citizens organizing against the dangers nuclear power and weapons plants are creating for their families and their communities. A CBS '48 Hours' program.
Health and Safety; Industrial and Technical Education; Science - Physical; Social Science; Sociology
Dist - FOTH **Prod** - FOTH

Nuclear physics 60 MIN
VHS
Concepts in science - physics series
Color; PAL (J H)
PdS29.50 purchase
Shows how an interest in cathode rays led scientists to discover X - rays, then alpha, beta, gamma radiation and ultimately the conversion of matter into energy. Contains six ten - minute concepts - The Discovery of Radioactivity; Properties of Becqueral Rays; Natural Transmutations; Energy from the Nucleus; Electrical Energy from Fission; and Nuclear Byproducts. Part of a five - part series.
Health and Safety; Science; Science - Physical
Dist - EMFVL **Prod** - TVOTAR

Nuclear physics series

The Discovery of Radiation	0 MIN
Electrical Energy from Fission	10 MIN
Energy from the nucleus	10 MIN
Natural Transmutations	10 MIN
Nuclear by - products	10 MIN
Properties of Becquerel Rays	10 MIN

Dist - TVOTAR

Nuclear power 37 MIN
VHS
Color; CC (H C)
$129.00 purchase _ #113
Provides perspective on nuclear power. Contains footage from Los Alamos, Three Mile Island, Oak Ridge and other centers of nuclear research. Reveals how nuclear power was developed during World War II and how it has become such an important issue in science and society today in The History of Nuclear Power. Helps students to understand the basic scientific concepts involved in nuclear reactions and technology in Nuclear Power Today and Tomorrow. Defines the terminology of nuclear physics. Includes a book of the same title from the Learning Power series.
Science - Physical; Social Science
Dist - HAWHIL **Prod** - HAWHIL 1994

Nuclear Power 28 MIN
16mm
Color (H C A)
Examines the positive and negative aspects of replacing older methods of energy production with nuclear energy. Considers the dangers inherent in the disposal of nuclear waste and safety precautions taken to ensure the security of neighboring communities.
Social Science
Dist - FI **Prod** - CANBC

Nuclear power 37 MIN
VHS
Color (J H)
$130.00 purchase _ #A5VH 1251
Begins with the development of nuclear power during World War II. Explains radioactivity, fission vs fusion, the difference between controlled vs explosive nuclear reactions. Summarizes the pros and cons of nuclear power. Includes supplemental book.
Social Science
Dist - CLRVUE **Prod** - CLRVUE

Nuclear power and the press 30 MIN
VHS
Inside story series
Color (G)
$50.00 purchase _ #INST - 407
Examines press coverage of the construction of Arizona's Palo Verde nuclear plant. Questions whether local journalists were influenced by the Arizona Public Service Company in their coverage of Palo Verde, as well as whether most reporters would have the technological knowledge to cover nuclear and other technological issues. Hosted by Hodding Carter.
Industrial and Technical Education; Literature and Drama; Social Science
Dist - PBS

Nuclear Power and You Series

Radioactivity	29 MIN

Dist - UMAVEC

Nuclear power and you series

The Fear and the fact	29 MIN
The Future	29 MIN
The Reactor	29 MIN

Risk 29 MIN
Dist - UMITV

Nuclear power - dangerous energy 17 MIN
VHS
Color (G)
$19.95 purchase
Examines the failed promise of nuclear power. Explains why - contrary to what is said by the nuclear industry - nuclear power is not the solution to the energy crisis or to global warming. Provides an international perspective on the issue and documents the Chernobyl disaster. Offers positive solutions for a nuclear - free future. Produced by Greenpeace UK.
Science - Natural; Social Science
Dist - GRNPCE **Prod** - GRNPCE 1991

Nuclear power - energy for the future 33 MIN
VHS
Nukes or no nukes series
Color (I J H C)
$59.00 purchase _ #502
Features University of Pittsburgh physicist Bernard Cohen who explains his view that nuclear power is the best choice both economically and environmentally for the future.
Business and Economics; Science - Natural; Social Science
Dist - HAWHIL **Prod** - HAWHIL

Nuclear Power for Space - Snap - 9A 12 MIN
U-matic
Color
Shows the launching of a new satellite powered by a nuclear generator. Uses animation to explain the use of an isotopic generator to create power in operating electronic equipment, recording equipment and transmitting data back to earth for analysis. Discusses the advantages of nuclear energy over the use of chemical or solar energy.
Industrial and Technical Education; Science - Physical
Dist - USNAC **Prod** - USNAC 1972

Nuclear power - future quest 33 MIN
VHS
Future quest series
Color (J H C)
$79.00 purchase _ #313
Presents the conflicting views of nuclear power experts. Includes a guide. Part of ten parts.
Social Science
Dist - HAWHIL **Prod** - HAWHIL

Nuclear Power in Air Defense Command 7 MIN
16mm
Color
LC FIE64-96
Tells the story of the first nuclear power plant for remote radar sites. Reviews component shipment, assembly and radiological monitoring of the reactor. Explains safety features, economy and self - sufficiency of nuclear power.
Civics and Political Systems
Dist - USNAC **Prod** - USAF 1963

Nuclear Power Plant Fire Fighting 30 MIN
U-matic
Fire Protection Training Series Tape 3; Tape 3
Color (IND)
Examines fire safety procedures for nuclear power plants, covering topics such as fixed extinguisher systems, personnel and housekeeping safety, fire strategies, foam selection and fire suppression.
Health and Safety
Dist - ITCORP **Prod** - ITCORP

Nuclear Power Plant Fire Fighting 60 MIN
VHS / U-matic
Fire Fighting Training Series
Color (IND)
Includes a regulatory guide and information on coordinating with outside agencies, contamination and radiation.
Health and Safety; Industrial and Technical Education; Social Science
Dist - LEIKID **Prod** - LEIKID

Nuclear Power - Pro and Con 50 MIN
U-matic / VHS / 16mm
Color (H C A)
LC 77-701414
Investigates the advantages and disadvantages of utilizing nuclear energy power sources.
Science - Physical; Social Science
Dist - MGHT **Prod** - ABCF 1977

Nuclear Power - Pro and Con, Pt 1 - Against 25 MIN
U-matic / VHS / 16mm
Color (H C A)
Presents arguments against nuclear power.
Science - Physical; Social Science
Dist - MGHT **Prod** - ABCF 1977

Nuclear Power - Pro and Con, Pt 2 - for 25 MIN
16mm / U-matic / VHS
Color (H C A)
Presents arguments in favor of nuclear power.
Science - Physical; Social Science
Dist - MGHT **Prod** - ABCF 1977

Nuclear power production 25 MIN
VHS / U-matic / 16mm
Color (H C A)
$525.00 purchase
Describes the differences between nuclear powered plants and those using fossil fuels for energy. Examines the ecological impact of coal and oil burning plants and considers the future availability of such fuels. Looks at radiation from nuclear power plants, the Chernobyl type of reactor and the future design of nuclear power plants.
Industrial and Technical Education; Science - Physical; Social Science; Sociology
Dist - HANDEL **Prod** - HANDEL 1989

Nuclear power - the beginning of the end 28 MIN
35mm strip / VHS
Color (J H C A)
$93.00, $93.00 purchase _ #MB - 481129 - 0, #MB - 512762 - 8
Takes an objective look at the facts about nuclear power, using both scientific and historical knowledge.
Industrial and Technical Education; Social Science
Dist - SRA **Prod** - SRA

Nuclear power - the hot debate 47 MIN
VHS
Color (H C G)
$395.00 purchase, $65.00 rental
Looks at the pros and cons of nuclear power and at possible energy alternatives. Asks about the safety of nuclear power and if there is a secure and lasting way to dispose of radioactive wastes, the dangers to uranium miners and reactor personnel. Shows in detail how a nuclear reactor works and how its safe operation depends on interaction between complex technology and human operators.
Health and Safety; Social Science
Dist - FLMLIB **Prod** - CANBC 1991

Nuclear Power - Time, Space, and Spirit - 12 Keys to Scientific Literacy Series
The History of Nuclear Power 16 MIN
Nuclear Power - Today and Tomorrow 17 MIN
Dist - HAWHIL

Nuclear power today 21 MIN
VHS
Color; CC (H C)
$79.00 purchase _ #913
Explains how nuclear reactions work in producing electrical power. Outlines the pros and cons of future use of nuclear power. Part 2 of the program Nuclear Power. Includes a book of the same title from the Learning Power series.
Science - Physical; Social Science
Dist - HAWHIL **Prod** - HAWHIL 1994

Nuclear Power - Today and Tomorrow 17 MIN
U-matic / VHS
Nuclear Power - Time, Space, and Spirit - 12 Keys to Scientific 'Literacy Series
Color (J H)
LC 84-730272
Industrial and Technical Education; Science - Physical; Social Science
Dist - HAWHIL **Prod** - HAWHIL 1984

Nuclear Power - Today and Tomorrow 80 MIN
16mm
Color
Presents the 88th Faraday lecture of the Institution of Electrical Engineers, which was delivered by Mr R V Moore, managing director, reactor group of the United Kingdom Atomic Energy Authority. Explains how the UKAEA demonstrated that nuclear power was practicable, how they made it economic and how they plan to make it abundant for centuries.
Geography - United States; Geography - World; Industrial and Technical Education; Science - Natural; Science - Physical; Social Science
Dist - UKAEA **Prod** - UKAEA 1967

Nuclear Power - Today and Tomorrow, Pt 1 40 MIN
16mm
Color
Presents the 88th Faraday lecture of the Institution of Electrical Engineers, which was delivered by Mr R V Moore, managing director, reactor group of the United Kingdom Atomic Energy Authority. Explains how the UKAEA demonstrated that nuclear power was practicable, how they made it economic and how they plan to make it abundant for centuries.
Geography - United States; Geography - World; Industrial and Technical Education; Science - Natural; Science - Physical; Social Science
Dist - UKAEA **Prod** - UKAEA 1967

Nuclear Power - Today and Tomorrow, Pt 2 40 MIN
16mm
Color
Presents the 88th Faraday lecture of the Institution of Electrical Engineers, which was delivered by Mr R V Moore, managing director, reactor group of the United Kingdom Atomic Energy Authority. Explains how the UKAEA demonstrated that nuclear power was practicable, how they made it economic and how they plan to make it abundant for centuries.
Geography - United States; Geography - World; Industrial and Technical Education; Science - Natural; Science - Physical; Social Science
Dist - UKAEA **Prod** - UKAEA 1967

Nuclear Propulsion in Space 24 MIN
16mm
Color (J)
LC FIE68-92
Describes principles of nuclear rocket propulsion, indicating the possible use of such a system as the third stage of the Saturn Five rocket. Compares nuclear propulsion to chemical propulsion and electrical propulsion and describes a rocket which would use all three systems in future space travel.
Industrial and Technical Education; Science - Physical; Social Science
Dist - NASA **Prod** - NASA 1968

Nuclear reactions 28 MIN
Videoreel / VT2
Turning points series
Color
Looks at a Michigan community's debates over the construction of a nuclear reactor in their town.
Geography - United States; Industrial and Technical Education
Dist - PBS **Prod** - WUCM

Nuclear reactions 30 MIN
U-matic
Understanding the atom - 1980s - series; 06
B&W
LC 80-706620
Presents a lecture - demonstration by Dr Ralph T Overman discussing some of the basic concepts of nuclear reaction, neutron capture processes, nuclear fission, examples of calculations used in nuclear reactions and the technique of activation analysis.
Science; Science - Physical
Dist - USNAC **Prod** - USNRC 1980

Nuclear Reactor Space Power Systems 8 MIN
16mm
Color
LC FIE64-133
Summarizes the program aimed at developing nuclear reactor power supplies for large space vehicles. Reviews the reliability, high power levels, long unattended operating life and safety characteristics of space nuclear power systems.
Industrial and Technical Education; Science - Physical
Dist - USNAC **Prod** - USNRC 1964

Nuclear Reactors for Space 18 MIN
16mm
Color
LC 74-705224
Tells of the construction, testing and use of compact, low - powered nuclear reactors developed for use in the systems for nuclear auxiliary power program.
Science - Physical
Dist - USNAC **Prod** - USNRC 1961

Nuclear Safety Debate 26 MIN
U-matic / VHS
Color (H C A)
Documents the debates between pro - and anti - nuclear spokespeople.
Social Science
Dist - JOU **Prod** - UPI

Nuclear Ship 'Savannah,' the 29 MIN
16mm
Color
LC 74-705226
Discusses the basic principle of steam generation by nuclear reactor. Shows the world's first nuclear merchant ship Savannah, the design and construction of its pressurized water reactor and associated machinery.
Industrial and Technical Education; Social Science
Dist - USNAC **Prod** - USIA 1960

Nuclear Spectrum 28 MIN
16mm
Color
LC 74-700710
Documents some of the current research underway in the fields of physics, biology, radiation and anthropology conducted under the aegis of the Atomic Energy Commission and other organizations.
Science
Dist - USNAC **Prod** - ANL 1973

Nuclear Strategy for Beginners 57 MIN
U-matic / VHS / 16mm
Nova Series
Color (H C A)
Looks back over the four decades of the atomic age to try to understand how the modern world has acquired an arsenal of over 50,000 nuclear weapons ready to be fired at a moment's notice. Explores whether nuclear weapons deter such a war or only make it more likely.
Civics and Political Systems; Sociology
Dist - TIMLIF **Prod** - WGBHTV 1982
AMBROS

Nuclear Sunset 25 MIN
VHS / U-matic
Color
Examines nuclear energy as a source of electrical power. Considers the questions of plant safety, waste, storage and costs.
Science - Physical; Social Science
Dist - WCCOTV **Prod** - WCCOTV 1978

Nuclear tango 45 MIN
VHS
Color; PAL (G)
PdS100 purchase
Interviews veterans who participated in Soviet Union nuclear tests in the 1950s. Presents a Viktor Buturlin for C.I.M.R., Russia, production.
Fine Arts; History - World
Dist - BALFOR

Nuclear Theory and Energy 24 MIN
16mm / U-matic / VHS
Color (T)
Discusses basic nuclear theory relating to fission and fusion. Shows applications of both and points out the potential dangers of both.
Science - Physical; Social Science
Dist - EBEC **Prod** - EBEC 1985

Nuclear Transplantation 12 MIN
U-matic / VHS / 16mm
Color (H C A)
LC 76-703526
Uses photomicrography and time - lapse sequences to reveal the research technique of nuclear transplantation. Shows how nuclei are transplanted from donor body cells into activated eggs.
Science; Science - Natural
Dist - IU **Prod** - IU 1976

Nuclear War - a Guide to Armageddon 25 MIN
U-matic / VHS / 16mm
Color
Dramatizes the projected outcome of a one - megaton nuclear bomb exploding a mile above the dome of St Paul's Cathedral in the heart of London. Assesses the effectiveness of measures governments have proposed to protect their populations.
Civics and Political Systems; Sociology
Dist - FI **Prod** - BBCTV 1983

Nuclear War - the Incurable Disease 60 MIN
VHS / U-matic
Color (J)
Presents three American and three Soviet physicians who meet to discuss the medical consequences of nuclear war. Considers subjects including the effects of a one megaton bomb on a city, medical care for nuclear victims, long - term effects and the insanity of civil defense systems.
Civics and Political Systems; Health and Safety; Sociology
Dist - FI **Prod** - FI 1982

Nuclear Warning 23 MIN
U-matic / VHS
Color
Examines the nuclear debate. Discusses nuclear strategy, the civil defense system and the growing grassroots movement trying to end the arms race.
Civics and Political Systems; Sociology
Dist - WCCOTV **Prod** - WCCOTV 1982

Nuclear Waste Isolation - a Progress Report 25 MIN
16mm
Color
Reports on what has been accomplished and what is being done to find a safe disposal system for highly radioactive waste. Emphasizes the concept of totally isolating high - level nuclear waste from the environment.
Social Science; Sociology
Dist - MTP **Prod** - USDOE

Nuclear Waste - Political and Social Decisions 17 MIN
16mm
Battelle Science Education Series
Color (H C A)
LC 83-706570
Looks at the social and political issues inherent in the debate over what to do with nuclear waste.
Sociology
Dist - CIASP **Prod** - CIASP 1982

Nuclear Waste, Political and Social Decisions 17 MIN
U-matic
Color (H A)
LC 83-706570
Points out that it is the political process and public opinion that ultimately will choose between the viewpoints of engineers and environmentalists and will shape the future of the nuclear industry.
Social Science; Sociology
Dist - CINAS **Prod** - CINAS 1982

Nuclear Waste, what is it 26 MIN
U-matic
Color (H G)
LC 83-706568
Introduces the concepts and concerns of nuclear waste disposal. Defines terms using diagrams, animation and visual analogies to illustrate the elements of nuclear structure, fission and radiation.
Social Science; Sociology
Dist - CINAS **Prod** - CINAS 1982

Nuclear Waste - what is it 26 MIN
16mm
Battelle Science Education Series
Color (H C A)
LC 83-706568
Defines the terms which apply to the problem of nuclear waste disposal using diagrams, animation and visual analogies to illustrate the elements of nuclear structure, fission and radiation.
Sociology
Dist - CIASP **Prod** - CIASP 1982

Nuclear Waste, what to do with it 22 MIN
U-matic
Color (H G)
LC 83-706569
Discusses what can be done with nuclear waste, focusing on the technology and looking at the debate between reprocessing and permanent disposal. Surveys proprosed methods and visits a trial burial site.
Social Science; Sociology
Dist - CINAS **Prod** - CINAS 1982

Nuclear Waste - what to do with it 22 MIN
16mm
Battelle Science Education Series
Color (H C A)
LC 83-706569
Emphasizes the technology available to cope with the problem of nuclear waste. Shows nuclear fuel in temporary storage and debates the merits of reprocessing versus permanent disposal.
Sociology
Dist - CIASP **Prod** - CIASP 1982

Nuclear wasteland 53 MIN
VHS
First Tuesday series
Color; PAL (H C G)
PdS30 purchase
Reveals that in Great Britain millions of gallons of low - level nuclear waste are pumped each day into the sea. Discloses that in certain areas around nuclear plants, child leukemia cases are ten times the national average. Shows that nuclear warheads are carried by truck on some of the nation's busiest roads to factories where they are secretly assembled. Raises questions as to whether Great Britain is risking a nuclear wasteland. Contact distributor about availability outside the United Kingdom.
History - World; Sociology
Dist - ACADEM **Prod** - YORKTV

The Nuclear Watchdogs 13 MIN
16mm / U-matic / VHS
Color (H C A)
LC 80-701969
Describes safety inspections at the South Texas Nuclear Project. Points out that the Nuclear Regulatory Commission relies on written reports from employees of the project's construction company. Originally shown on the CBS television series Magazine.
Health and Safety; Social Science
Dist - CAROUF **Prod** - CBSTV 1980

Nuclear Weapons - Concepts and Controversies 30 MIN
VHS
Color (J H)
Traces the origin of nuclear weapons and explores how the discovery and use of the atom bomb has changed military strategies, foreign policies, and international relations.
Civics and Political Systems; Social Science
Dist - HRMC **Prod** - HRMC 1985

Nuclear winter - a growing global concern 20 MIN
Videoreel / U-matic / VT3
(G)
$95.00 purchase, $45.00 rental
Uses computer graphics and scientific information to portray the consequences of nuclear war.
Civics and Political Systems; Sociology
Dist - EFVP **Prod** - EFVP 1985

Nuclear Winter - Changing Our Way of Thinking 58 MIN
U-matic / VT3
(G)
$125.00 purchase, $45.00 rental
Features Dr Carl Sagan presenting the results of research into the effects of nuclear winter.
Civics and Political Systems; Sociology
Dist - EFVP **Prod** - EFVP 1985

The Nucleus 15 MIN
U-matic / VHS / 16mm
Cell Biology Series
Color (H C)
$420, $250 purchase _ #5224C
Discusses the many functions of a cell's nucleus, such as shielding chromosomes, and sending instructions for building enzymes. Talks about mitosis and cell division. Produced by Bill Walker Productions, Inc.
Science - Natural
Dist - CORF

The Nucleus and its Parts 17 MIN
16mm
Color (H C)
LC FIA66-1169
Focuses attention on atomic nuclei. Discusses transformation, anti - matter, fission, fusion and cosmic ray informational concepts as they are related to nuclear structure. Explains particle accelerators and detection devices.
Science - Physical
Dist - CLI **Prod** - CLI 1966

Nucleus I 13 MIN
U-matic
Chemistry 101 Series
Color (C)
Introduces nuclear composition, nuclear structure, defines and presents characteristics of nuclides, isotopes, isobars, nuclear build up, radioactivity and transmutation.
Science; Science - Physical
Dist - UILL **Prod** - UILL 1973

Nucleus II 19 MIN
U-matic
Chemistry 101 Series
Color (C)
Deals with pracitcal uses of nuclear energy. Radioactive tracers and their uses are reviewed with examples. Nuclear fusion is distinguished from fission.
Science; Science - Physical
Dist - UILL **Prod** - UILL 1973

The Nude 29 MIN
U-matic
Creation of Art Series
Color
Discusses the human form as a source of interest and inspiration to artists throughout the ages.
Fine Arts
Dist - UMITV **Prod** - UMITV 1975

Nude study 2 MIN
16mm
B&W (G)
$5.00 rental
Uses various tonalities of a male nude. Explores light, texture and graphic composition. Produced by Jack Walsh.
Fine Arts
Dist - CANCIN

Nudes - A Sketchbook 30 MIN
16mm
B&W (A)
$45.00 rental
Presents a series of portraits based on stylized, often graphically sexual interpretations of his or her personality. Ranges from compulsively erotic to light - hearted and self - debunking.
Fine Arts
Dist - CANCIN **Prod** - MCDOWE 1975

The Nuer 75 MIN
16mm / U-matic / VHS
Color (C A)
LC 70-711172
Presents the important relationships and events in the lives of the nuer, nilotic people in Sudan and on the Ethiopian border.
Geography - World; Sociology
Dist - MGHT **Prod** - GARDNR 1971

Nuer, the, Pt 1 39 MIN
16mm / U-matic / VHS
Color (C A)
Presents the important relationships and events in the lives of of the Nuer, nilotic people in Sudan and on the Ethiopian border.
Geography - World; Sociology
Dist - MGHT **Prod** - GARDNR 1971

Nuer, the, Pt 2 36 MIN
U-matic / VHS / 16mm
Color (C A)
Presents the important relationships and events in the lives of of the Nuer, nilotic people in Sudan and on the Ethiopian border.
Geography - World; Sociology
Dist - MGHT **Prod** - GARDNR 1971

Nuestro Milwaukee - Breakin' 28 MIN
16mm / U-matic
Color
Presents a musical adventure into the world of break dancing, developed in part by the Latino population of New York's South Bronx. Shows clips from videos by Gladys Knight and Chaka Khan inter - cut with scenes of sidewalk jam sessions which include Milwaukee's Lady Breakers. Includes interviews with instructors who explain the dance, gymnastic and martial art aspects of break dancing.
Fine Arts; Geography - United States; Physical Education and Recreation; Sociology
Dist - KCET **Prod** - WMVSTV

Nueva Artistas De Puerto Rico 16 MIN
16mm
Color (J H C)
LC 75-700622
Visits the studios of Puerto Rico's most important artists.
Fine Arts; Foreign Language; Geography - World
Dist - PAN **Prod** - OOAS 1970

Nueva vida 14 MIN
VHS
Color (H C G) (SPANISH)
$150.00 purchase, $35.00 rental _ #37497
Depicts the positive experiences - as well as the fears and concerns - of two Latino fathers who participate actively in the birth process. Includes an English discussion guide and script translation. Produced by Terry Looper and Claris Barahona - O'Connor, University of California, San Francisco.
Health and Safety; Sociology
Dist - UCEMC

Nuguria 25 MIN
16mm / U-matic / VHS
Untamed World Series Series
Color; Mono (J H C A)
$400.00 film, $250.00 video, $50.00 rental
Talks on the Nuguria island in the South Pacific and its various inhabitants.
Geography - World; Sociology
Dist - CTV **Prod** - CTV 1973

Nukes or no nukes series
Presents two progrms debating nuclear energy. Interviews University of Pittsburgh physicist Bernard Cohen in Nuclear Power - Energy for the Future, who explains why nuclear power is the best choice both environmentally and economically. No Nukes is Good Nukes features energy expert Amory Lovins who explains why nuclear plants should be dismantled. Discusses why energy must be produced and used more efficiently and why safe, new alternative energy sources must be found for the future.
No nukes is good nukes 17 MIN
Nuclear power - energy for the future 33 MIN
Dist - HAWHIL **Prod** - HAWHIL 1973

Nukumanu - En Atoll I Stillehavet (Nukumanu - an Atoll in the Pacific 28 MIN
16mm
Color (DANISH)
A Danish language film. Presents Nukumanu Atoll, an island in a coral reef inhabited by a small community whose culture is still undisturbed by the white man. Points out that living conditions in general are extremely bad.
Foreign Language; Geography - World; Sociology
Dist - STATNS **Prod** - STATNS 1967

N/um Tchai - the Ceremonial Dance of the)kung Bushmen 20 MIN
16mm
B&W
LC 75-702857
Features the dance of the Bushman medicine man, showing it to be both religiously significant in its purpose of warding off death and culturally significant in the music and dancing employed.
Religion and Philosophy; Sociology
Dist - DOCEDR **Prod** - DOCEDR 1968

Num - Ti - Jah Lodge 32 MIN
16mm
Journal Series
Color
LC 74-701637
Presents a study of nature and geography.
Geography - World
Dist - CANFDC **Prod** - FIARTS 1973

The Numbat 14 MIN
16mm
Color (J)
LC 71-709549
Uses close - up photography, including feeding scenes and shots of young numbats, to show this little - known Australian animal in its natural habitat.
Geography - World; Science - Natural
Dist - AUIS **Prod** - ANAIB 1970

Number 23 10 MIN
16mm
VD - Self - Awareness Project Series Module 3
Color
LC 75-702844
Shows the experiences involved in treatment of venereal disease at a typical public health facility.
Health and Safety
Dist - FMD **Prod** - AAHPER 1974

Number and meaning 30 MIN
BETA / VHS
Number, form and life series
Color (G)
$29.95 purchase _ #S462
Looks at numbers as more than abstract representatives of quantity. Features philosopher Arthur M Young, author of 'Geometry of Meaning,' who discusses a 'theory of process' which integrates science with ancient teachings. Includes a discussion of numerical correspondences such as point - line - plane - solid, fire - water - air - earth. Part of a four - part series on number, form and life.
Mathematics; Religion and Philosophy
Dist - THINKA **Prod** - THINKA

Number families
VHS
Lola May's fundamental math series
Color (P)
$45.00 purchase _ #10267VG
Presents number sentences and numbers that are related in both addition and subtraction. Shows number relationships and provides practice in the basic facts. Comes with a teacher's guide and blackline masters. Part 17 of a 30 - part series.
Mathematics
Dist - UNL

Number, form and life quartet 120 MIN
BETA / VHS
Color (G)
$69.95 purchase _ #Q394
Presents a four - part series on number, form and life. Includes 'The Presence of the Past' with Dr Rupert Sheldrake, 'Pattern and Transformation' with Jill Purce, 'Number and Meaning' with Arthur M Young and 'The Mystery of Incarnation' with Dr Richard Grossinger.
Fine Arts; Mathematics; Religion and Philosophy; Science - Natural; Science - Physical; Sociology
Dist - THINKA **Prod** - THINKA

Number, form and life series
The Mystery of incarnation 30 MIN
Number and meaning 30 MIN
Pattern and transformation 30 MIN
The Presence of the past 30 MIN
Dist - THINKA

Number line graphs of solution sets 22 MIN
16mm
Teaching high school mathematics - first course series; No 38
B&W (T)
Mathematics
Dist - MLA **Prod** - UICSM 1967

The Number of My Days 57 MIN
VHS / 16mm
Color (H C A)
$180.00 purchase, $35.00 rental _ #HC1338
Follows the progress of four organ transplant patients through interviews with the patients, their families and doctors.
Health and Safety; Social Science
Dist - IU **Prod** - WCCOTV 1987

Number One 30 MIN
16mm
Color
Shows an egocentric author who finds out how to know true life.
Religion and Philosophy
Dist - CAFM **Prod** - CAFM

Number one sun 15 MIN
VHS / U-matic
Dragons, wagons and wax - Set 2 series
Color (K P)
Shows how the earth is affected by the sun.
Science; Science - Physical
Dist - CTI **Prod** - CTI

Number Our Days 29 MIN
16mm
Color
LC 79-700437
Documents the lives of Jewish senior citizens who make the Israel Levin Senior Adult Center in Venice, California, the focal point of their existence. Offers views of the center, which serves to bring the spirited citizens together in a common bond of unity. Based on field research from the book Number Our Days by Barbara Myerhoff.
Health and Safety; Psychology; Sociology
Dist - LITMAN **Prod** - LITMAN 1978

Number Patterns 20 MIN
U-matic
Mainly Math Series
Color (H C)
Studies three areas involving numerical patterns, focusing on factoring, number divisibility and numerical sequences.
Mathematics
Dist - GPN **Prod** - WCVETV 1977

Number Patterns 15 MIN
U-matic
Mathematical Relationship Series
Color (I)
Shows the strange relationships to be found among even the most ordinary numbers.
Education; Mathematics
Dist - TVOTAR **Prod** - TVOTAR 1982

Number Properties 15 MIN
U-matic
Math Makers Two Series
Color (I)
Presents the math concepts of properties of addition and multiplication, logical challenges and the properties of zero as they relate to both addition and multiplication.
Education; Mathematics
Dist - TVOTAR **Prod** - TVOTAR 1980

Number Sentences, Dr Ernest Duncan 20 MIN
16mm
Teaching Modern School Mathematics - Struc - Ture and Use Series
Color; B&W (K)
Mathematics
Dist - HMC **Prod** - HMC 1971

Number Systems 24 MIN
VHS / 16mm
Programmable Controllers (PLC's) Series
Color (H A)
$465.00 purchase, $110.00 rental
Demonstrates digital devices which process information. Explains decimal, BCD, OCTAL and hexadecimal systems.
Computer Science; Industrial and Technical Education
Dist - TAT **Prod** - TAT 1984

Number Systems and Codes
U-matic / VHS
Microprocessor Series
Color
Industrial and Technical Education; Mathematics
Dist - HTHZEN **Prod** - HTHZEN

Number Systems and Digital Codes 60 TO 90 MIN
VHS
Fundamentals of Digital Electronics Module Series
Color (PRO)
$600.00 - $1500.00 purchase _ #DENSD
Introduces number and numerical codes, the language of digital computers, specifically bases 2, 8, 10 and 16. Demonstrates how number systems are used to construct digital codes which encode the information processed by computers. Part of a twelve - part series on fundamentals of digital electronics. Includes five student guides, five workbooks and an instructor guide.
Computer Science; Industrial and Technical Education; Psychology
Dist - NUSTC **Prod** - NUSTC

Number 10 Downing Street 108 MIN
VHS
Color (S)
$29.95 purchase _ #781 - 9009
Marks the first time that cameras were permitted to roam freely through Number 10, one of the world's most famous addresses. Includes a meeting in the cabinet room, a visit to the magnificent state rooms and interaviews with former Prime Ministers of England, their families and their staffs. Prime Minister Margaret Thatcher also speaks frankly about the problems and pleasures of living 'above the shop.'.

Civics and Political Systems; Geography - World; History - World
Dist - FI Prod - BBCTV 1987
UILL

Numbering Systems, Numbering Codes, and Logic Concepts 30 MIN
VHS / U-matic
Programmable Controllers Series
Color
Discusses numbering systems and codes including decimal, binary Octal and hexadecimal. Explores logic concepts.
Industrial and Technical Education; Sociology
Dist - ITCORP Prod - ITCORP

Numbers 30 MIN
U-matic / VHS
Say it with sign series; Pt 14
Color (H C A) (AMERICAN SIGN)
Presents Lawrence Solow and Sharon Neumann Solow introducing American Sign Language used by the hearing - impaired. Emphasizes signs that have to do with numbers.
Education
Dist - FI Prod - KNBCTV 1982

Numbers 15 MIN
U-matic / VHS
Cursive writing series
Color (P)
Presents techniques of handwriting, focusing on numbers.
English Language
Dist - GPN Prod - WHROTV 1984

Numbers
16mm
B&W
Discusses the peculiar flavor of infinite processes intimately associated with this branch of mathematics. Examines an approximation to the irrational number root 2 by rational numbers.
Mathematics
Dist - OPENU Prod - OPENU

Numbers 30 MIN
VHS
Bill Cosby picture pages series
Color (K P)
$9.95 purchase _ #FRV16002V - K
Helps prepare children for the skills required to recognize and understand numbers. Features Bill Cosby and builds on the fact that children enjoy learning. Includes two activity books. Part of a six - part series of building skills in reading and counting and in color, animal, words and letter recognition.
English Language; Mathematics; Psychology
Dist - CAMV

Numbers 30 MIN
U-matic
Polka Dot Door Series
Color (K)
Presents a variety show for pre - school children. Includes songs, mime, stories, film sequences, talk, dance and fantasy figures. Each show emphasizes a particular theme such as numbers, feelings, exploring, music or time. Comes with parent teacher guide.
Fine Arts; Literature and Drama
Dist - TVOTAR Prod - TVOTAR 1985

Numbers 30 MIN
VHS / 16mm
Growing a Business Series
(H C)
$99.95 each, $1,295.00 series
Expresses the necessity of understanding figures and what they mean in relation to business.
Business and Economics
Dist - AMBROS Prod - AMBROS 1988

Numbers all Around Us 13 MIN
U-matic / VHS / 16mm
Beginning Mathematics Series
Color (P)
Shows how numbers help people in different ways. Discusses zip codes, telephone numbers, room numbers, and measurements.
Mathematics
Dist - JOU Prod - JOU

Numbers all Around Us 11 MIN
16mm / U-matic / VHS
Beginning Mathematics Series
Color (P I) (SPANISH)
LC 74-701760;
Points out the uses of numbers in identifying and coding such things as room numbers, addresses, telephone numbers and zip codes.
Mathematics
Dist - JOU Prod - GLDWER 1974

Numbers and numerals - Pt 1 26 MIN
16mm
Teaching high school mathematics - first course series; No 1
B&W (T)
Mathematics
Dist - MLA Prod - UICSM 1967

Numbers and numerals - Pt 2 25 MIN
16mm
Teaching high school mathematics - first course series; No 2
B&W (T)
Mathematics
Dist - MLA Prod - UICSM 1967

Numbers and Order 9 MIN
U-matic / VHS / 16mm
Basic Math Series
Color (P)
LC 79-701670
Reviews vocabulary associated with comparison, such as same, different, more and less. Shows that arranging numbers in the order of a number line helps solve problems involving how many or how much.
Mathematics
Dist - PHENIX Prod - PHENIX 1979

Numbers at work 260 MIN
VHS
Color; PAL (H C G)
PdS55 purchase
Presents ten 26 - minute programs to help people who have problems with numbers deal with simple problems encountered in everyday life. Uses authentic situations to illustrate mathematical principles, such as a soccer pitch demonstrating the use of right angles. Contact distributor about availability outside the United Kingdom.
Education; Mathematics; Psychology
Dist - ACADEM

Numbers for Beginners 11 MIN
16mm
Color; B&W (P)
Through animation of familiar objects, visualizes the numbers from one through six to assist in separating the idea of number from the counting of objects. Emphasizes group recognition and number relationships.
Mathematics
Dist - MLA Prod - JHP 1954

Numbers in Our Lives 9 MIN
16mm / U-matic / VHS
Color (K P)
LC 76-708868
Focuses attention on some of the ways in which numbers and number names are used by almost everyone from the children to people working in the community. Shows that we use numbers to count, to measure and to play games.
Mathematics
Dist - PHENIX Prod - BOUNDY 1970

Numbers in Sign Language 15 MIN
16mm
Quick Flicks Series
Color (I) (AMERICAN SIGN)
LC 75-700657
Shows the American sign language numbering system. Includes practice sentences which demonstrate how to form the numbers with the hands and how to read the numbers from another person's hands.
Guidance and Counseling; Psychology; Social Science
Dist - JOYCE Prod - JOYCE 1975

The Numbers Racket 29 MIN
Videoreel / VT2
Koltanowski on Chess Series
Color
Physical Education and Recreation
Dist - PBS Prod - KQEDTV

The Numbers Start with the River 15 MIN
16mm
Color (A)
LC 76-704005
Depicts the quality of life in a small U S town in Iowa, which is representative of some 16,000 such towns across the United States. Illustrates an old farm couple's memories of play, work, family life, courtship and marriage.
Geography - United States; Health and Safety; History - United States; Sociology
Dist - USNAC Prod - USIA 1971

Numbers Systems and Codes
U-matic / VHS
Microprocessor Video Training Course Series
Color
Industrial and Technical Education
Dist - VTRI Prod - VTRI

Numbers to 20
VHS
Lola May's fundamental math series
Color (P)
$45.00 purchase _ #10255VG
Presents the numbers 11 through 20. Uses models of tens and ones to teach the value of each number and prepare for teaching place value. Comes with a teacher's guide and blackline masters. Part five of a 30 - part series.
Mathematics
Dist - UNL

Numbers to 9
VHS
Lola May's fundamental math series
Color (P)
$45.00 purchase _ #10254VG
Presents the numbers zero through nine. Teaches the value of the first nine numbers. Comes with a teacher's guide and blackline masters. Part four of a 30 - part series.
Mathematics
Dist - UNL

Numeration, addition and subtraction - Part 1 52 MIN
VHS
Mathematics learning activities series
Color (T)
$175.00 purchase _ #6806 - 1
Demonstrates structured mathematics learning activities developed by professor Richard Skemp. Shows Skemp and teacher Marilyn Harrison interacting with small groups of elementary children in Missing Stairs, Doubles and Halves Rummy, Number Targets, Stepping Stones, Crossing, Slippery Slope, The Handkerchief Game and Capture. Part of a two - part series. Additional sets of learning activities will be available in early 1991.
Education; Mathematics
Dist - UCALG Prod - UCALG 1990

Numeration - ones and tens
VHS
Lola May's fundamental math series
Color (P)
$45.00 purchase _ #10268VG
Teaches numeration and the modeling of numbers based on ones and tens. Includes practice in writing two - digit numbers using expanded notation. Comes with a teacher's guide and blackline masters. Part 18 of a 30 - part series.
Mathematics
Dist - UNL

Numeration to 999 15 MIN
U-matic
Studio M Series
Color (P)
Explains how to read and write the numbers 1 through 999.
Mathematics
Dist - GPN Prod - WCETTV 1979

Numeric display applications 30 MIN
VHS / U-matic
Optoelectronics series; Pt II - Optoelectronic displays
Color (PRO)
Illustrates use of visible light - emitting diodes in numeric display applications with specific circuit examples and device operation.
Industrial and Technical Education
Dist - TXINLC Prod - TXINLC

Numerical Abnormalities of Human Chromosomes 28 MIN
16mm
Clinical Pathology Series
B&W (PRO)
Points out that errors in cell division can result in embryos and occasionally live - born individuals with an abnormal number of chromosomes (aneuploidy.) Gives a brief description of monomy (45,X) trisomy 13, trisomy 18, trisomy 21 and polysomy for the X and Y sex chromosomes.
Health and Safety; Science - Natural
Dist - USNAC Prod - NMAC 1969

Numerical Control 30 MIN
U-matic / VHS
Color
Deals with the conversion to and setup of a numerically controlled machine shop. Points out problem areas.
Business and Economics; Industrial and Technical Education
Dist - SME Prod - CONNTV

Numerical control - computerized numerical control - advanced programming series module 2
Special cycles 17 MIN
Dist - LEIKID

Numerical control - computerized numerical control - advanced programming series
Cutter radius compensation 18 MIN
Dist - LEIKID

Numerical control - computerized numerical control, module 1 - fundamentals series
Basic drilling 16 MIN
Completed milling programs 16 MIN
Coordinate measurement systems 17 MIN
One - and Two - Axis Linear Milling 18 MIN
Dist - LEIKID

Numerical Control no 1 - Introduction to a Two Axis Vertical Mill 8 MIN
BETA / VHS
Machine Shop - C N C Machine Operations Series
Color (IND)
Provides an overview of a two axis vertical mill for the operation of both drilling and straightline milling through the point - to - point control system.
Industrial and Technical Education; Psychology
Dist - RMIBHF **Prod** - RMIBHF

Numerical Control no 3 - Tape Controlled Drilling Operations 5 MIN
VHS / BETA
Machine Shop - C N C Machine Operations Series
Color (IND)
Demonstrates a drilling setup, incorporating Numerical Control No. 1 and Numerical Control No. 2 as prerequisites.
Industrial and Technical Education; Psychology
Dist - RMIBHF **Prod** - RMIBHF

Numerical Control no 2 - Setup of Machine and Indexed Controls 19 MIN
BETA / VHS
Machine Shop - C N C Machine Operations Series
Color (IND)
Continues Numerical Control No. 1. Demonstrates the adjustment of spindle stops, insertion of tape in the Slo - Syn indexer and the settling of machine controls.
Industrial and Technical Education; Psychology
Dist - RMIBHF **Prod** - RMIBHF

Numerical Control/Computerized Numerical Control - Advanced Programming Series Module 2
Loopings 16 MIN
Polar Coordinate Program 19 MIN
Rotation 18 MIN
Scaling 16 MIN
Dist - LEIKID

Numerical control/computerized numerical control - advanced programming series
Sub - routines 18 MIN
Translations 18 MIN
Dist - LEIKID

Numerical Control/Computerized Numerical Control - Fundamentals series
Punching and Editing 16 MIN
Dist - LEIKID

Numerical Control/Computerized Numerical Control, Module 1 - Fundamentals Series
Circular milling 19 MIN
Drilling, Boring, and Spot Facing 19 MIN
Introduction to NC and CNC 15 MIN
Machine Setup and Safety 14 MIN
Manual Data Input 17 MIN
Program Preparation 16 MIN
Three - Axis Linear Milling 18 MIN
Dist - LEIKID

Numerical Eigenvalues
16mm
B&W
Explains the significance of the eigenvalue problem and discusses how the problem could be solved using determinants.
Mathematics
Dist - OPENU **Prod** - OPENU

Numerical Example - Estimation of Position, Velocity, and Ballistic Parameter for a 47 MIN
VHS / U-matic
Modern Control Theory - Stochastic Estimation Series
Color (PRO)
Gives numerical example illustrating how bias estimation errors associated with the use of an extended Kalman filter can he removed through the use of a second - order filter.
Industrial and Technical Education; Mathematics
Dist - MIOT **Prod** - MIOT

Numerical Example - Estimation of Positions Velocities, and Accelerations 32 MIN
VHS / U-matic
Modern Control Theory - Stochastic Estimation Series
Color (PRO)
Industrial and Technical Education; Mathematics
Dist - MIOT **Prod** - MIOT

Numerical Example of LQG Design for a Third - Order Continuous Time System 27 MIN
VHS / U-matic
Modern Control Theory - Stochastic Control Series
Color (PRO)
Industrial and Technical Education; Mathematics
Dist - MIOT **Prod** - MIOT

Numerical Example - Sensor Trade - Offs 47 MIN
U-matic / VHS
Modern Control Theory - Stochastic Estimation Series
Color (PRO)
Industrial and Technical Education; Mathematics
Dist - MIOT **Prod** - MIOT

Numerical Example - Solution of a Minimum Fuel Problem in the Apollo Project 21 MIN
U-matic / VHS
Modern Control Theory - Deterministic Optimal Control Series
Color (PRO)
Industrial and Technical Education; Mathematics
Dist - MIOT **Prod** - MIOT

Numerical Integrations 46 MIN
VHS / U-matic
Finite Element Methods in Engineering Mechanics Series
Color
Industrial and Technical Education; Mathematics
Dist - MIOT **Prod** - MIOT

Numerical Mathematics
16mm
B&W
Shows an example of a simple problem for which a numerical method is useful. Points out the increasing importance of numerical mathematics and digital computers in engineering.
Mathematics
Dist - OPENU **Prod** - OPENU

Numerical Solutions of Differential Equations
16mm
B&W
Discusses three numerical methods of solutions of a first - order differential equation.
Mathematics
Dist - OPENU **Prod** - OPENU

Numerical variables - developing the concept, 1 31 MIN
16mm
Teaching high school mathematics - first course series; No 22
B&W (T)
Mathematics
Dist - MLA **Prod** - UICSM 1967

Numerical variables - developing the concept, 2 30 MIN
16mm
Teaching high school mathematics - first course series; No 23
B&W (T)
Mathematics
Dist - MLA **Prod** - UICSM 1967

Nun and Deviant 20 MIN
VHS / U-matic
B&W
Explores identity issues of both woman and artist. Dispels stereotypes. Presented by Nancy Angelo and Candace Compton.
Fine Arts
Dist - ARTINC **Prod** - ARTINC

Nunatsiaq - the Good Land 14 MIN
16mm
Color (H C A)
#2X32 N
Tells the history of the Inuit Indians. Discusses their relationship with the land, their culture and its reaction to assimilation, and their determination to control their own destiny.
Social Science
Dist - CDIAND **Prod** - CRAF 1978

Nunavit - Our Land 11 MIN
16mm
Color (H C A)
#1X27N
Discusses how the great Inuit Indian people of Canada are slowly being destroyed by southern white civilization. Explains how Indians must now fight to retain land that was never surrendered by treaty.
Social Science; Sociology
Dist - CDIAND **Prod** - MONDUM 1977

The Nun's Priest's Tale and the Manciple's Tale 30 MIN
Videoreel / VT1
Canterbury Tales Series
B&W (A)
History - World; Literature and Drama
Dist - UMITV **Prod** - UMITV 1967

The Nun's Story 151 MIN
U-matic / VHS / 16mm
Color (J)
Stars Audrey Hepburn and Peter Finch. Develops the drama of Sister Luke's notable struggle to sublimate her own strong personality to the strict demands of her calling. Portrays her difficult postulancy, her period of work and service and her decision to be released from her vows.
Fine Arts; Religion and Philosophy
Dist - FI **Prod** - CPC 1959

Nunu and the Zebra 27 MIN
U-matic / VHS / 16mm
Color (P I)
LC 74-702140
Tells a story about a boy in East Africa who goes on an expedition with his father. Tells how they encounter a lion and how the boy becomes lost, makes friends with a zebra who protects him from a leopard and is found by his father and a park ranger.
Geography - World
Dist - AIMS **Prod** - ROBROL 1973

Nuptiae 15 MIN
16mm
Color (C)
$392.00
Experimental film by James Broughton.
Fine Arts
Dist - AFA **Prod** - AFA 1969

Nuremberg 76 MIN
16mm / U-matic
B&W (G)
$40.00 rental
Summarizes the Nuremberg war crimes trial of 1945 - 1946. Includes excerpts from the prosecutors' charges; the cross - examination of the Nazi defendants; their final statements; the summations; and the verdicts and sentences. Produced by the Civil Affairs Division of the US War Department.
Fine Arts; History - World
Dist - NCJEWF
USNAC

The Nuremberg Chronicle 22 MIN
16mm
B&W (H C)
Explores the woodcuts of the book The Nuremberg Chronicle, published in 1943, recounting world history as it was conceived in that period of turmoil and change.
History - World; Literature and Drama
Dist - CONNF **Prod** - CONNF

Nuremberg, Pt 1 38 MIN
U-matic
B&W
LC 79-706509
Records the trials of the Nazi leaders at Nuremberg, Germany. Includes scenes from films made by the Nazis which were presented as documentary evidence of the atrocities committed at concentration camps. Issued in 1949 as a motion picture.
History - World; Sociology
Dist - USNAC **Prod** - USDD 1976

Nuremberg, Pt 2 38 MIN
U-matic
B&W
LC 79-706509
Records the trials of the Nazi leaders at Nuremberg, Germany. Includes scenes from films made by the Nazis which were presented as documentary evidence of the atrocities committed at concentration camps. Issued in 1949 as a motion picture.
History - World; Sociology
Dist - USNAC **Prod** - USDD 1976

Nuremberg Trial 31 MIN
U-matic / VHS / 16mm
B&W (H C)
Tells that on October 18, 1945, the most sweeping indictment in history was filed against 24 Nazi leaders. Evaluates the evidence which showed the involvement of the defendents and gives the verdict of the special international tribunal. Concludes that some legalists continue to debate the validity of the trials.
Civics and Political Systems; History - World
Dist - FI **Prod** - METROM 1974

The Nuremberg Trials 76 MIN
16mm
B&W
Presents a film record of the trials of the Nazi leaders at Nuremberg, Germany. Includes scenes from films made by the Nazis, which were presented as the documentary evidence of the atrocities committed at concentration camps.

Geography - World; History - World
Dist - USNAC **Prod** - USDD 1949

Nuremberg trials - Part IV 30 MIN
16mm
Rise and fall of the Third Reich series
B&W (G)
$40.00 rental _ #HRF - 725
Chronicles the Nuremberg Trials. Attempts to establish that those who conspire to wage war stand guilty of crimes against humanity. Part four of a four - part series on Hitler.
Civics and Political Systems; History - World; Sociology
Dist - ADL **Prod** - ADL

Nurse 15 MIN
VHS
Color (P I J)
Teaches children about what happens when one is admitted into a hospital. Looks at how the work of nurses contributes to community health.
Health and Safety
Dist - VIEWTH **Prod** - VIEWTH

Nurse 30 MIN
BETA / VHS
American Professionals Series
Color
Describes the life of Barbara Subczyk, head emergency nurse at the Jersey City Medical Center, who suggests that her job is a test of the idea of 'survival of the fittest'.
Guidance and Counseling; Health and Safety; Social Science
Dist - RMIBHF **Prod** - WTBS

Nurse 10 MIN
U-matic
Readalong One Series
Color (K P)
Introduces reading and spelling for preschoolers and children in grades 1 to 3 with animation, puppets, humor and music. Comes with teacher's guide and kit.
Education; English Language; Literature and Drama
Dist - TVOTAR **Prod** - TVOTAR 1975

The Nurse and the Critically Ill - a Personal Approach to Helping, Pt I 14 MIN
U-matic / VHS
Color (C A)
Deals with the emotional needs of the patient and the common feelings of the nurse.
Guidance and Counseling; Health and Safety; Psychology; Sociology
Dist - TEF **Prod** - RALPRO

The Nurse as Client Advocate 18 MIN
U-matic / VHS
Color (C G T A)
Focuses on the realities and ethics involved in client advocacy as a nurse provides emotional support and medical information to a hospitalized patient and his family. The program consists of four vignettes. The tape may be halted after each segment for class discussion.
Health and Safety
Dist - PSU **Prod** - PSU 1984

The Nurse Combats Disease 12 MIN
16mm
Color
LC FIE63-112
Shows how nurses safeguard the public by understanding the transmission of disease and the measures necessary to prevent disease and promote recovery from illness.
Health and Safety
Dist - USNAC **Prod** - USPHS 1962

Nurse Edith Cavell 108 MIN
16mm
B&W
Tells how Nurse Cavell and two other women hide and nurse injured soldiers in Brussels after the Kaiser has seized Belgium. Describes their trial after they are caught. Stars Anna Neagle, Edna May Oliver and George Sanders.
Biography; Fine Arts; Health and Safety
Dist - KITPAR **Prod** - RKOP 1939

Nurse Maid 7 MIN
16mm
B&W
Explains how Flip the Frog, who is short of pocket money, agrees to watch an innocent - looking baby carriage for a mother.
Fine Arts
Dist - RMIBHF **Prod** - UNKNWN 1930

Nurse - Patient Communication 19 MIN
16mm
Developing Skills in Communications Series
Color
LC 78-712978
Defines communication, lists some of the problems in nurse - patient communication and provides methods which lead to effective communication between nurse and patient.
Health and Safety; Psychology; Sociology
Dist - TRNAID **Prod** - TRNAID 1969

Nurse patient interaction series
Blocks to therapeutic communication - 606.2 17 MIN
Interactions for study - 606.3 13 MIN
Techniques of therapeutic communication - 606.1 20 MIN
Dist - CONMED

The Nurse - Patient Relationship 240 MIN
VHS / U-matic
Color (C PRO)
$1,980.00 purchase _ #810VJ071
Shows eight scenes from an eleven - week relationship between a psychiatric nurse and her psychiatric patient. Contains eight videocassettes, a student work book of exercises, and instructor's guide.
Health and Safety
Dist - HSCIC **Prod** - HSCIC 1981

Nurse - Patient Relationships 17 MIN
16mm
Care of the Dying Patient Series
Color
LC 71-712979
Explains how terminally ill patients cope with death and shows the nurse how to care for the dying patient.
Health and Safety; Sociology
Dist - TRNAID **Prod** - TRNAID 1970

Nurse - physician relationship 20 MIN
VHS / U-matic / BETA
Ethics, values and health care series
Color (C PRO)
$150.00 purchase _ #132.6
Presents a video transfer from slide program which discusses the traditional nurse - physician relationship and shows how it influences the behavior of health professionals. Addresses the specific ethical problems of the nurse dealing with a physician who has made an error. Concludes with observations on how the establishment of good interpersonal communications helps resolve ethical conflicts of this nature. Part of a series on ethics, values and health care.
Guidance and Counseling; Health and Safety; Religion and Philosophy
Dist - CONMED **Prod** - CONMED

The Nurse Practitioner 14 MIN
16mm
Color (J)
LC 79-700696
Explores the role of the nurse practitioner within the health field. Discusses the education and training necessary to achieve certification.
Health and Safety
Dist - IA **Prod** - LAC 1978

Nurse Practitioner 14 MIN
U-matic / VHS
Color (J A)
Depicts how many patients are now being treated by nurse practitioners.
Health and Safety
Dist - SUTHRB **Prod** - SUTHRB

Nurse safety with Tubex
VHS
Color (PRO)
#TU - 301
Presents a free - loan program which trains medical professionals. Contact distributor for details.
Health and Safety
Dist - WYAYLA **Prod** - WYAYLA

The Nurse, the Physician, the Hospital and the Law 31 MIN
16mm
B&W
Illustrates the responsibility of the hospital for negligence or malpractice on the part of its employees by enacting a preliminary meeting between the attorney and the participants in a suit.
Civics and Political Systems; Health and Safety
Dist - AMEDA **Prod** - HOFLAR

Nurse Vera explains it all - chemical hazards 15 MIN
BETA / VHS / U-matic
Working in the hazard zone series
Color; PAL (IND G) (SPANISH)
$175.00 rental _ #OSH - 600
Highlights the various effects of chemical exposure on the human body and how to avoid them. Shows how chemicals are classified, illustrates the route of entry, outlines potential health hazards and demonstrates what to do if chemical exposure occurs. Includes leader's guide and 10 workbooks. Part of an eight - part series which teaches safety awareness to hazardous waste workers in compliance with OSHA and EPA - RCRA training regulations. Available also in NTSC.
Business and Economics; Health and Safety; Physical Education and Recreation; Psychology; Sociology
Dist - BNA **Prod** - BNA

Nurse, Where are You 49 MIN
U-matic / VHS
Color (H C A)
Documents the critical shortage of hospital nurses, explaining that they are overworked, underpaid and disillusioned. Shows an effort to unionize nurses.
Health and Safety; Sociology
Dist - CAROUF **Prod** - CBSTV

Nurse/Physician Interaction 10 MIN
U-matic
Color (PRO)
LC 79-707732
Presents three approaches to nurse/physician interactions, including the nurse who fails to communicate important patient information to the attending physician, the nurse who communicates ineffectively, and the nurse who communicates effectively.
Health and Safety
Dist - UMMCML **Prod** - UMICHM 1977

The Nursery 5 MIN
VHS
Seahouse series
Color (K P)
$29.95 purchase _ #RB8151
Studies the sea nursery at the edge of the sea where water meets the land. Shows that this is a place where small sea creatures can be safe, find places to hide and have plenty to eat. Part of a series of ten parts on marine animals.
Science - Natural
Dist - REVID **Prod** - REVID 1990

Nursery Rhymes in Song Volume 1 30 MIN
VHS / 16mm
Music Stories Series
Color (P)
$39.95 purchase _ #CL6902
Presents musical versions of nursery rhymes.
Fine Arts; Literature and Drama
Dist - EDUCRT

Nursery Rhymes in Song Volume 2 30 MIN
VHS / 16mm
Music Stories Series
Color (P)
$39.95 purchase _ #CL6904
Presents children's songs.
Fine Arts; Literature and Drama
Dist - EDUCRT

Nursery School Child - Mother Interaction - Three Head Start Children and their Mothers 41 MIN
16mm
Color
Depicts three Black mothers alone with their four - year - old boys, two of the children being 'difficult' and the third well - adjusted. Emphasizes the mother's influence and child's attachment to her. Shows the three children in their Head Start school, emphasizing social attitudes with scenes of mealtime behavior, preferred activities and goal pursuit. Points out differences in interaction patterns and maternal attitudes.
Education; Guidance and Counseling; Psychology; Sociology
Dist - NYU **Prod** - VASSAR

The Nursery school experience - Unit A 56 MIN
VHS
Looking at size and shape series
Color; PAL (H C T)
PdS35.00 purchase
Shows children experiencing and developing notions of size and shape and documents how the development of children's perception of space is a continuous process. Presents part of a six - part series of observation material.
Psychology
Dist - EMFVL

Nursery School for the Blind 20 MIN
16mm
Color
Explains that because the problems of the blind child are usually greater than parents can cope with unaided, they are often sent away from home into residential nurseries. Depicts a nursery school that enables blind children to stay at home by supplementing the care given by their parents - by helping to make up for missed stages of development, by encouraging curiosity and by keeping up continual verbal communication to facilitate orientation and compensate for missing visual contact.
Education; Guidance and Counseling; Psychology; Sociology
Dist - NYU **Prod** - VASSAR

Nursery Sepsis 28 MIN
16mm
Color (PRO) (FRENCH SPANISH PORTUGUESE)
Presents a review of problems of newborn infections in hospitals covering mothers, babies, personnel and environment in sepsis control.
Health and Safety; Home Economics; Science
Dist - WFP **Prod** - WFP 1961

Nursery Worker 15 MIN
U-matic / 16mm / VHS
Career Awareness
(I)
$130 VC purchase, $240 film purchase, $25 VC rental, $30 film rental
Presents an empathetic approach to career planning, showing the personal as well as professional qualities of nursery workers. Highlights the importance of career education.
Guidance and Counseling; Home Economics
Dist - GPN

Nurse's Aid, Orderly and Attendant Series
Making the Surgical (Postoperative) Bed 19 MIN
Making the Unoccupied (Closed) Bed 19 MIN
Wheelchair Transport 20 MIN
Dist - COPI

Nurse's Aide, Orderly and Attendant Series
Ambulating a patient to a chair or wheelchair 18 MIN
Answering the patient's call signal 16 MIN
The Bedbath - preparation and emotional support 13 MIN
The Bedbath - procedure 19 MIN
Care and prevention of decubiti 18 MIN
First time ambulation of the patient 20 MIN
Hospital Beds - Variable Heights 22 MIN
Making the unoccupied - closed - bed 13 MIN
Moving a Patient in Bed 16 MIN
Observation of Feces and Urine 19 MIN
Prevention and Care of Decubiti 17 MIN
The Skin - its Function and Care 16 MIN
Stretcher Transport 16 MIN
Use of Side Rails 22 MIN
Vital Signs - Blood Pressure 20 MIN
Vital Signs - Temperature 20 MIN
Dist - COPI

Nurse's aide, orderly and attendant series
Giving a bedpan or urinal 18 MIN
Dist - COPI
SUTHLA

Nurse's aides - making a difference 30 MIN
VHS
Color (G C PRO)
$95.00 purchase, $40.00 rental
Notes ways health care aides can effectively deal with behavioral problems commonly encountered among Alzheimer's or other dementia patients. For staff training.
Health and Safety
Dist - TNF

Nurse's Assistant
U-matic / VHS
Work - a - Day America
$59.95 purchase _ #VV116V
Helps students achieve career vocational preparation. Stresses the four main points of career awareness and exploration, specific skills intended, employability skills needed, and real people sharing on the job experiences.
Guidance and Counseling
Dist - CAREER **Prod** - CAREER

Nurse's Day with the Mentally Ill 22 MIN
16mm
Color; B&W (C T)
Shows the activities of a student nurse in a psychiatric hospital. Explains and demonstrates reassuring and supporting roles and illustrates nursing care in connection with shock therapies and a lobotomy operation. Includes many examples of the behavior of the mentally ill.
Health and Safety; Psychology
Dist - PSUPCR **Prod** - PSUPCR 1954

A Nurse's guide to the Hickman catheter - 3 25 MIN
VHS
Cancer education - for nurses - series
Color (PRO C G)
$395.00 purchase _ #R850 - VI - 004
Provides information about catheter insertion, assessment of a patient's general condition, blood drawing through the catheter, changing the injection cap, irrigating the catheter, cleansing the catheter insertion and exit sites, teaching patients how to care for the catheter and answering questions about the catheter. Part of a four - part series on cancer education for nurses.
Health and Safety
Dist - HSCIC **Prod** - LASU 1985

The Nurse's Role in Acute Psychiatric Emergencies 120 MIN
U-matic / VHS
Color (PRO)
LC 81-706296
Discusses several types of psychiatric patients and presents examples of aggressive behavior and problem - solving techniques.
Health and Safety
Dist - USNAC **Prod** - USVA 1980

Nurses Talk about Epilepsy 13 MIN
16mm
Color
LC 76-700533
Covers drug therapy for epilepsy, the nurse's role in observing and reporting seizure patterns, fears and concerns of epileptics and the nurse's role in handling these concerns.
Health and Safety; Psychology
Dist - GEIGY **Prod** - EFA 1975

Nurses - the web of denial 33 MIN
VHS
Color (C PRO)
$195.00 purchase, $100.00 rental _ #CJ - 112
Profiles several nurses who are recovering from addiction. Celebrates their strength and tenacity in turning around their lives and careers and emphasizes the need for effective substance abuse programs and support for recovery within nursing as well as in the entire health care field. Examines situations in which supportive peers and employers have helped addicted nurses to confront their dependency and to regain control of their professional and personal lives. Produced by Barbara Barde and Anne Pick.
Guidance and Counseling; Health and Safety; Psychology
Dist - FANPRO

Nursing 25 MIN
VHS
Career encounters series
Color (J H C A)
$95.00 purchase _ #MG3405V-J
Presents a documentary-style program that explores a career in nursing. Features professionals at work, explaining what they do and how they got where they are. Emphasizes diversity of occupational opportunities and of men and women in the field. Offers information about new developments and technologies and about educational and certification requirements for entering the profession. One of a series of videos about professions available individually or as a set.
Business and Economics; Guidance and Counseling; Health and Safety
Dist - CAMV

Nursing 20 TO 30 MIN
U-matic
Opportunity Profile Series
(H C A)
$99.95 _ #AI206
Illustrates the daily activities involved in a career in nursing. Working professionals in related occupations describe the negative and positive aspects of such jobs.
Guidance and Counseling; Health and Safety
Dist - CAMV **Prod** - CAMV

Nursing
U-matic / VHS
Career Builders Video Series
$95.00 purchase _ #ED110V
Uses actual professionals to talk about the job's demands, rewards, and frustrations. Shows the working environment of the career field.
Guidance and Counseling
Dist - CAREER **Prod** - CAREER

Nursing
VHS
Day in a career series
Color (J H T G)
$89.00 purchase _ #VOC05V-J
Presents information about the occupation of nurse, one of the careers that the United States Department of Labor projects as potentially successful by the year 2000. Profiles in detail the work day of a real person, with candid interviews and work situations and information about the educational requirements, credentials, job outlook, salaries, important associations, and contacts in the field. One of a series of ten videos, lasting 15 to 22 minutes, available individually or as a set.
Business and Economics; Guidance and Counseling; Health and Safety
Dist - CAMV

Nursing
VHS / U-matic
Opportunity Profile Series
$99.95 purchase _ #AJ105V
Provides advice on the skills and educational background desired by companies, the day to day activities of various careers, and the positive and negative aspects of various careers from corporate vice presidents, managers, and other working professionals.
Guidance and Counseling
Dist - CAREER **Prod** - CAREER

Nursing 20 MIN
VHS
Get a life - a day in the career series
Color (H C A)
$89.00 purchase _ #886696-06-3
Follows nursing professionals in a community hospital setting to learn how and why they became nurses. Lets the viewer discover the vast opportunities in this dynamic, humanitarian career. Looks at educational requirements, which vary greatly, along with salaries. Part of a ten-part series.
Business and Economics; Guidance and Counseling; Health and Safety
Dist - VOCAVD **Prod** - VOCAVD 1995

Nursing 24 MIN
VHS / 16mm
Career Builders Video Series
Color
$85.00 purchase _ #V110
Examines a potential career choice by taking the viewer into the working environment and interviewing professionals on the demands, rewards and frustrations on the job.
Business and Economics; Health and Safety; Sociology
Dist - EDUCDE **Prod** - EDUCDE 1987

Nursing - a Career for all Reasons 20 MIN
VHS / 16mm
(C)
$385.00 purchase _ #850VJ046
Explores the roles of nurses in a neonatal intensive care unit, a community health setting, and a pediatric dialysis unit.
Health and Safety
Dist - HSCIC **Prod** - HSCIC 1985

Nursing - a choice for life 12 MIN
U-matic / VHS
Color (H C G)
$195.00 purchase _ #C891 - VI - 013
Presents a program for use by recruiting teams at institutions offering nursing programs as well as for guidance and career counselors at high schools. Challenges the stereotypical concept of the nursing field as menial, unsophisticated 'women's work.' Follows a young man with an assignment to learn about the field of nursing through a variety of hospital settings where he learns how complex nursing is. Presented by Nursing Recruitment, University of California - Davis.
Guidance and Counseling; Health and Safety
Dist - HSCIC

Nursing - a Family Affair 28 MIN
U-matic / VHS / 16mm
Color
Covers complete information about breastfeeding information for new mothers. Demonstrates techniques which will make breastfeeding more comfortable and successful. Includes information on how breastfeeding works, prenatal preparation of nipples, preventing cracking and sore nipples, breast engorgement, when and how to begin nursing, inverted nipples and frequency of feedings.
Health and Safety; Home Economics
Dist - PEREN **Prod** - CWRU 1983

Nursing - a Medical Emergency 19 MIN
U-matic / VHS
Color (C)
$249.00, $149.00 purchase _ #AD - 2051
Focuses on the role of nurses in the monitoring and treatment of patients. Details the skills necessary for a successful career in nursing. Compares current requirements with the skills required several decades ago when nurses were restricted to a more conservative role in medical care. Examines the current nursing shortage and the role that low pay, difficult working conditions and low prestige have played.
Business and Economics; Guidance and Counseling; Health and Safety; Psychology; Sociology
Dist - FOTH **Prod** - FOTH

Nursing - a Professional Career 15 MIN
16mm
B&W (H C A)
Explains the advantages of a nursing career. Stresses the need for both a cultural and technical education.
Guidance and Counseling; Health and Safety; Psychology
Dist - WSUM **Prod** - WSUM 1958

Nursing actions prior to cancer chemotherapy administration - 10 30 MIN
VHS / U-matic
Chemotherapy series
Color (PRO)
$275.00 purchase, $60.00 rental _ #7123S, #7123V
Presents a program on nursing actions prior to cancer chemotherapy administration. Includes a 50 - question post - test. Part of a twelve - part series on chemotherapy.

Health and Safety
Dist - AJN **Prod** - HOSSN 1988

Nursing aids for normal elimination 29 MIN
16mm
Directions for education in nursing via technology series; Lesson 14
B&W (PRO)
LC 74-701788
Discusses the functions of the bowel and bladder. Discusses and demonstrates selected nursing measures that may be used to assist the process of elimination.
Health and Safety; Science - Natural
Dist - WSUM **Prod** - DENT 1974

Nursing and Allied Health - CINAHL
CD-ROM
(G PRO C)
$950.00 purchase _ #1485
Includes literature relevant to nursing and allied health issues. Includes thesaurus and backfiles to 1983. Monthly updates. IBM PCs and compatibles require at least 640k RAM, DOS 3.1 or later, one floppy disk drive - hard disk recommended, one empty expansion slot, and an IBM compatible CD - ROM drive.
Health and Safety; Literature and Drama
Dist - BEP

Nursing and Paramedics 15 MIN
VHS / 16mm
(H C A)
$24.95 purchase _ #CS311
Describes the skills required for a career in nursing and paramedics. Features interviews with people working in these areas.
Guidance and Counseling
Dist - RMIBHF **Prod** - RMIBHF

Nursing and the Law Series
Malpractice 44 MIN
Medical - Moral - Legal Issues 44 MIN
Wills, Insurance, Witness 44 MIN
Dist - AJN

Nursing as a Profession 30 MIN
U-matic / VHS
Lifelines Series
Color
Discusses nursing as a profession.
Guidance and Counseling; Health and Safety
Dist - MDCPB **Prod** - UGATV

Nursing assessment and management of the patient with acute pain 28 MIN
U-matic / VHS
Pain management - Margo McCaffery discusses new concepts series
Color (PRO)
$275.00 purchase, $60.00 rental _ #7317S, #7317V
Explores misconceptions which hamper accurate assessment of patients with acute pain. Presents pain assessment tools including a flow chart for documenting and evaluating the effectiveness of medication. Reviews common causes of undertreating acute pain such as fears of causing respiratory depression or addiction. Part of a four - part series on pain management featuring Margo McCaffery.
Health and Safety
Dist - AJN **Prod** - HOSSN 1984

Nursing Assessment of the Infant Series
Baby's first visit 15 MIN
Examination of the Head and Neck 17 MIN
Examination of the torso and extremities 16 MIN
Neuro - Developmental Assessment 15 MIN
Dist - ACCESS

Nursing assessment of the lower extremities - Part II 23 MIN
VHS
Foot care for the older adult series
Color (C PRO G)
$395.00 purchase _ #R921 - VI - 011
Focuses on the techniques used in a nursing assessment of normal and abnormal variations of gait and balance, range of motion and muscle strength, circulation, sensation, proprioception and the skin and toenails. Reviews pathological conditions such as venostasis, decreased circulation and diseases of the toenails in relation to assessment and documentation. Demonstrates a 'hands - on' approach to physical assessment as well as providing guidelines for observation and history taking with the older adult. Part of a four - part series on foot care for the elderly.
Health and Safety; Sociology
Dist - HSCIC **Prod** - CESTAG 1993

Nursing assessment of the postpartum patient 22 MIN
BETA / VHS / U-matic
Nursing care of the new family series
Color (C PRO)
$280.00 purchase _ #611.1
Prepares nursing students and inexperienced nurses to complete a thorough, systematic physical assessment of the postpartum patient, as well as a psychosocial assessment of the child - bearing family. Places emphasis on the demonstration of all components of the assessment so that the learner will be able to function in the maternity unit as soon as clinical experience begins. Part of a three - part series on nursing care of the new family produced by Tru - Health Films.
Health and Safety; Sociology
Dist - CONMED

The Nursing Audit 12 MIN
VHS / U-matic
Color (PRO)
Provides a step - by - step approach to the nursing audit. Discusses the use of the audit process in evaluating the quality of health services, selection of criteria measurements numerical rating scales and recording sheets.
Health and Safety
Dist - UMICHM **Prod** - UMICHM 1977

Nursing care and documentation - Part 2 28 MIN
U-matic / VHS
Nursing care of patients with casts series
Color (PRO)
$275.00 purchase, $60.00 rental _ #7643S, #7643V
Identifies nursing priorities in care of patients with casts - preventing complications, reducing pain, increasing mobility and providing information. Presents the most common nursing diagnoses and describes the nursing process for each one. Emphasizes the value of documentation. Part of a two - part series.
Health and Safety
Dist - AJN **Prod** - HOSSN 1986

Nursing care for the immunocompromised patient 28 MIN
VHS / U-matic
Color (PRO)
$275.00 purchase, $60.00 rental _ #7802S, #7802V
Provides a thorough understanding of the normal immune system and the mechanisms of common immune disorders, both primary and secondary. Recognizes the characteristic signs and symptoms of each of the common immune disorders and the role of the nurse in assessment and care. Gives special emphasis to nursing diagnoses common to these patients and appropriate nursing interventions for each.
Health and Safety
Dist - AJN **Prod** - HOSSN 1988

Nursing Care for the Patient in Traction 30 MIN
U-matic / VHS
Traction Series
Color
Points out common complications of traction. Discusses potential nursing care problems related to the various types of traction and suggests specific nursing measures to solve these problems.
Health and Safety
Dist - FAIRGH **Prod** - FAIRGH

Nursing care - labor and delivery 15 MIN
VHS
Clinical nursing skills - nursing fundamentals - series
Color (C PRO G)
$395.00 purchase _ #R890 - VI - 060
Instructs on the procedures and techniques for the care and assessment of mother and fetus during labor and delivery. Describes and demonstrates procedures for checking vital signs, performing Leopold's maneuvers, palpating for fetal position and assessing the progression of labor. Outlines criteria for the evaluation of contractions. Describes the characteristics of each stage of labor and methods for determining fetal position. Part of a 23 - part series on clinical nursing skills.
Health and Safety
Dist - HSCIC **Prod** - CUYAHO 1989

Nursing Care of Burn Patients - the Acute Phase 45 MIN
U-matic
Color (PRO)
LC 79-706231
Presents an overview of care required by major burn patients during the first 72 hours following injury. Discusses crucial problems in maintaining adequate oxygenation and fluid and electrolyte balance. Includes demonstrations of the care of the burn site and a review of major, life - threatening complications.
Health and Safety
Dist - AJN **Prod** - AJN 1978

Nursing Care of Burn Patients - the Intermediate Phase 45 MIN
U-matic
Critical Care Nursing - Patients with Burns Series
Color (PRO)
LC 79-706232
Shows continued wound care, including hydrotherapy, debridement, and selection and application of topical medications. Stresses the importance of active patient participation and the vital role of nutrition in patient recovery. Discusses skin grafting and the psychological problems of the patient.
Health and Safety
Dist - AJN **Prod** - AJN 1978

Nursing Care of Children with Cardiovascular Problems 36 MIN
U-matic
Color (PRO)
Teaches the elements of Pediatric Cardiovascular Assessment and its application.
Health and Safety; Science - Natural
Dist - UMITV **Prod** - UMITV 1981

Nursing Care of Children with Respiratory Problems 30 MIN
U-matic
Color (PRO)
Teaches the elements of Pediatric Respiratory Physical Assessment and its application.
Health and Safety; Science - Natural
Dist - UMITV **Prod** - UMITV 1980

Nursing Care of Patients in Acute Ventilatory Failure 30 MIN
U-matic
Critical Care Nursing - Patients in Acute Respiratory Distress 'Series
Color (PRO)
LC 79-706230
Deals with the care of a young patient who develops pulmonary edema as a result of an overdose of heroin. Evaluates assessment parameters and demonstrates the implementation of findings.
Health and Safety
Dist - USNAC **Prod** - AJN 1977

Nursing Care of Patients in Chronic Ventilatory Failure 30 MIN
U-matic
Critical Care Nursing - Patients in Acute Respiratory Distress 'Series
Color (PRO)
LC 79-706229
Deals with the care of a patient with chronic obstructive pulmonary disease who develops acute respiratory distress due to an infection. Explores case history, arterial blood gas studies, chest X - rays, respiratory pattern, ausculation and spirometry.
Health and Safety
Dist - USNAC **Prod** - AJN 1977

Nursing care of patients with casts series
Presents a two - part series on the nursing care of patients with casts. Informs on the purpose of, common types and materials used for casts, application and removal. Identifies nursing priorities in care of patients with casts and emphasizes the importance of documentation.
Nursing care and documentation - Part 2 28 MIN
Nursing care of patients with casts series 56 MIN
Purpose, types, application and removal - Part 1 28 MIN
Dist - AJN **Prod** - HOSSN 1977

Nursing Care of the Adult with Coronary Artery Surgery 21 MIN
16mm
Color (PRO)
Comments on the nature of coronary artery surgery, mortality rates and advancements in techniques. Covers the course of treatment of a patient, beginning with admission to the hospital.
Health and Safety; Science - Natural
Dist - NMAC **Prod** - UKY 1972

Nursing care of the cancer patient with compromised immunity - concepts and care
Videodisc
Color (PRO C G)
$1300.00 purchase _ #R901 - IV - 061
Offers an interactive tutorial module on the components of the immune system and how they work, the cause of immunocompromise in cancer patients, the clinical manifestations of immunocompromise and the diagnostic strategies necessary for the care of immunocompromised patients. Uses animated graphics and other visuals to provide clinical examples and illustrations of complex concepts. Requires IPI, consult distributor for other hardware and software requirements. Produced at the Univ of Texas, M D Anderson Cancer Center, Houston.
Health and Safety
Dist - HSCIC

Nursing care of the cancer patient with compromised immunity - the nursing process
Videodisc
Color (PRO C G)
$1300.00 purchase _ #R891 - IV - 023
Simulates interactively the five steps in the nursing process - assessment, diagnosis, planning, implementation and evaluation. Portrays a patient and wife as the patient checks into a clinic because he feels tired and run down. The patient is 60 years old, suffers from lymphoma and has been through chemotherapy. Allows student selection from the program index to determine how to deal with the patient. Alternative subindexes exist which allow active involvement in data collection and to work with the patient until he is admitted to the hospital for a suspected infection due to immunosuppression. Requires IPI, consult distributor for other hardware and software requirements. Produced at the Univ of Texas, M D Anderson Cancer Center, Houston.
Health and Safety
Dist - HSCIC

Nursing Care of the Confused Patient - an Update 30 MIN
U-matic / VHS
Color (C PRO)
$330.00 purchase _ #840VJ018
Helps viewers recognize, evaluate and use the behavioral skills necessary to care successfully for the confused patient.
Health and Safety
Dist - HSCIC **Prod** - HSCIC 1984

Nursing care of the kidney transplant patient 28 MIN
VHS / U-matic
Color (PRO)
$275.00 purchase, $60.00 rental _ #7715S, #7715V
Educates on the nurse's role in caring for the physical and psychosocial needs of kidney transplant patients. Interviews patients to indicate the range of emotions such patients encounter - preoperative fear and excitement, postoperative relief, and depression during rejection episodes. Encourages detailed discharge planning.
Health and Safety
Dist - AJN **Prod** - HOSSN 1987

Nursing care of the new family series
Presents a three - part series on nursing care of the new family by Tru - Health Films. Includes the titles Nursing Assessment of the Postpartum Patient; Ineffective Breastfeeding; Knowledge Deficit - Infant Care.

Ineffective breastfeeding	23 MIN
Knowledge deficit - infant care	23 MIN
Nursing assessment of the postpartum patient	22 MIN
Nursing care of the new family series	68 MIN

Dist - CONMED

Nursing Care of the Oral Surgery Patient 17 MIN
8mm cartridge / 16mm
Color (PRO)
LC 75-702475; 75-702474
Presents a demonstration by Harold Neibel of the special nursing care required for oral surgery patients. Reviews the anatomy of the mouth and face, preoperative workup and pre - and postoperative oral hygiene, immediate postoperative consideration and special supplies required for normal postoperative nursing.
Health and Safety
Dist - USNAC **Prod** - USVA 1974

Nursing Care of the Sick and Injured 28 MIN
16mm
Medical Self - Help Series
Color (SPANISH)
LC 74-705227
Discusses general care of illness and long - term care of injuries. Stresses the treatment of symptoms using medications found in the public shelter medical kit and the type kit usually found in the home. To be used with the course Medical Self - Help Training.
Health and Safety
Dist - USNAC **Prod** - USHHS 1965

Nursing care plans 27 MIN
16mm
Directions for education in nursing via technology series; Lesson 93
B&W (PRO)
LC 74-701872
Uses dramatization to identify the purposes of nursing care plans. Discusses types and steps involved in the development of plans and the role of the nurse in these processes.
Health and Safety
Dist - WSUM **Prod** - DENT 1974

Nursing Care - the Diabetic Patient 29 MIN
16mm
Color
LC 75-700802
Illustrates five points in the care of the diabetic patient, such as urine tests, insulin administration, proper diet, regulated physical activity and proper personal hygiene.
Health and Safety; Science
Dist - USNAC **Prod** - USVA 1966

Nursing Career Development Series Pt 2

Nursing Career Strategies and a Program Model	33 MIN

Dist - USNAC

Nursing Career Development Series Pt 3

Leadership Roles - First Line to Executive	45 MIN

Dist - USNAC

Nursing career development series

Career entry transition and early years of practice	23 MIN

Dist - USNAC

Nursing career encounters 28 MIN
VHS
Career encounters video series
Color (J H)
$89.00 purchase _ #4252
Offers a documentary on careers in the field of nursing. Visits workplaces and hears professionals explain what they do, how they got where they are and why they find the work so rewarding. Emphasizes human diversity in the professions. Dispels myths, misconceptions and stereotypes and offers practical information about the requirements for entering the field. Part of a 13 part series.
Business and Economics; Guidance and Counseling; Health and Safety
Dist - NEWCAR

Nursing Career Strategies and a Program Model 33 MIN
VHS / U-matic
Nursing Career Development Series Pt 2
Color (PRO)
LC 81-707108
Focuses on the options open to those in nursing to deal with a locked in feeling problematic to many staff members on long - term assignments, fear of change, or lack of information channeled to those able to facilitate lateral moves. Discusses the rationale for career planning and career revitalization.
Health and Safety; Psychology
Dist - USNAC **Prod** - USVA 1981

The Nursing challenge 18 MIN
VHS / U-matic / BETA
Pediatrics - psychosocial implications series
Color (C PRO)
$150.00 purchase _ #136.1
Presents a video transfer from slide program which emphasizes observation skills for monitoring the child's physical and emotional condition. Stresses the nurse's relationship with the family as a means of incorporating parents into the child's care. Discusses the importance of knowledge of human development in communicating with the child and evaluating developmental status. Part of a series on the psychosocial implications of pediatric nursing.
Health and Safety
Dist - CONMED **Prod** - CONMED

Nursing Crisis - Level Three 28 MIN
VHS / 16mm
Color (G)
Observes the health care workers of Newton - Wellesley, a community hospital in a Boston suburb. Presents a picture of the severe nursing shortage facing hospitals today.
Health and Safety
Dist - FANPRO **Prod** - FANPRO 1989

Nursing - cues behavior consequences series

A Behavioral approach to nursing care	30 MIN
Pinpointing and recording patient behavior	30 MIN
Using reinforcement techniques to manage patient behavior	30 MIN

Dist - UNEBR

Nursing diagnosis and care planning series

The Diagnostic statement and implementation	14 MIN
Practical applications - Pt 1	19 MIN
Practical applications - Pt 2	19 MIN
The What and why of nursing diagnosis	14 MIN
The Workup and NANDA nomenclature	14 MIN

Dist - CONMED

Nursing Diagnosis - Concepts and Practice 28 MIN
VHS / 16mm
Color (C PRO)
$275.00 purchase, $60.00 rental _ #7627S, #7627V
Explains nursing diagnosis as distinguished from medical diagnosis and identifies 11 functional health patterns, including food and fluid consumption and activity patterns. Uses actual patient examples to emphasize that appropriate use of nursing diagnosis gives clear direction to nursing activities, improves patient care, and strengthens professional identity. Approved for CE credit. Includes study guide.
Health and Safety
Dist - AJN **Prod** - HOSSN 1990

Nursing diagnosis in the acute care hospital - arriving at a diagnosis - Part II series 90 MIN
VHS
Nursing diagnosis in the acute care hospital - arriving at a 'diagnosis - Part II series
Color (C PRO)
$600.00 purchase _ #4303S
Presents a six - part series on common problems in nursing diagnosis, acute care situations. Discusses impaired physical mobility, obesity and alterations in nutrition, impairment of skin integrity, self - care deficit, knowledge deficit and acute pain.
Health and Safety; Physical Education and Recreation
Dist - AJN **Prod** - BELHAN

Nursing diagnosis in the acute care hospitals series - Part I

Arriving at a diagnosis	22 MIN

Dist - AJN

Nursing education series

Cardiac arrest - code call	16 MIN
Infection control - special report	31 MIN
Work practice guidelines for handling antineoplastic agents	11 MIN

Dist - CONMED

Nursing - Effective Evaluation Series

Analyzing classroom tests	28 MIN
Analyzing the clinical lab experience	28 MIN
Classroom tools of evaluation	28 MIN
Clinical Tools of Evaluation	28 MIN
Evaluation - a Form of Communication	28 MIN
Evaluation - its Meaning	28 MIN
Grades - nemesis or recompense	28 MIN
Individual Differences	28 MIN
Planning Classroom Tests	28 MIN
Principles of Evaluation	28 MIN

Dist - NTCN

Nursing, ethics and the law 31 MIN
VHS
Educational horizons videos series
Color (C PRO)
$250.00 purchase, $100.00 rental _ #42 - 2500, #42 - 2500R
Features educators, ethicists and clinicians who suggest effective ways to address ethical and legal issues in the classroom and at the bedside. Explores state nurse practice acts, patient's rights, informed consent, advanced directives, nurses as patient advocates and the ethics of the American health care system. Includes a study guide with discussion questions, related articles, bibliography and definitions of key terms. Offers .3 CEUs - certification education units - per program. Part of a series overviewing contemporary nursing issues.
Health and Safety; Religion and Philosophy
Dist - NLFN **Prod** - NLFN

Nursing - expanding the quality of caring 27 MIN
U-matic / VHS
Color (PRO)
$250.00 purchase, $60.00 rental _ #4268S, #4268V
Promotes the nursing profession. Demonstrates how the role of nursing staff has changed and expanded since the 1960s.
Health and Safety; Science
Dist - AJN **Prod** - UTEXMB 1985

Nursing History Interview with a Recently Sober Alcoholic Man 59 MIN
U-matic
Color
Demonstrates a nurse's assessment by interview with a recently sober alcoholic man for the purpose of obtaining a history and screening physical examination.
Health and Safety; Psychology
Dist - UWASHP **Prod** - UWASHP

Nursing History Interview with a Recently Sober Alcoholic Woman 50 MIN
U-matic
Color
Demonstrates a nurse's assessment by interview with a recently sober alcoholic woman for the purpose of obtaining a history and screening physical examination.
Health and Safety; Psychology
Dist - UWASHP **Prod** - UWASHP

Nursing Home 28 MIN
16mm
No Place Like Home Series
Color
LC 74-706161
Shows a nursing home in Connecticut, pointing out the expert care a good nursing home can provide and explaining what to look for in a nursing home.
Health and Safety; Sociology
Dist - USNAC **Prod** - USSRS 1973

The Nursing Home Volunteer 15 MIN
VHS / U-matic
Color (C A)
Presents cancer specialist Dr Ernest H Rosenbaum along with numerous volunteers, sharing experiences in working with critically ill and geriatric patients.
Health and Safety
Dist - TEF **Prod** - RALPRO

Nursing homes 30 MIN
U-matic / VHS
Consumer survival series; Health
Color
Presents tips on picking a nursing home.
Health and Safety; Home Economics; Sociology
Dist - MDCPB **Prod** - MDCPB

Nursing homes, environmental health and safety series
Accident prevention in nursing homes 14 MIN
Dist - USNAC

Nursing implementation of infection control principles - admission assessment 15 MIN
VHS
Color (C PRO G)
$395.00 purchase _ #R940 - VI - 006
Emphasizes the integration of infection control into the basic nursing admission assessment of the hospitalized patient as an automatic rather than a conditioned response. Stresses throughout the program when it is appropriate and - or required to wear gloves. Discusses temperature taking, blood pressure cuff, stethoscope and percussion hammer, wound care and respiratory infections. Produced by Echoes Seminars and Long Beach City College.
Health and Safety
Dist - HSCIC

Nursing implementation of infection control principles - bath and personal care 18 MIN
VHS
Color (C PRO G)
$395.00 purchase _ #R940 - VI - 007
Trains nursing students in the application of proper infection control principles in the bathing and personal care of hospitalized patients. Stresses throughout the program when it is appropriate and - or required to wear gloves. Discusses toothbrushing and oral hygiene, bed bathing - with detailed information on catheter, ostomy and wound care, and bed soiling and linen removal. Produced by Echoes Seminars and Long Beach City College.
Health and Safety
Dist - HSCIC

Nursing Implications in the Administration of Chemotherapy 47 MIN
U-matic
Color
Discusses several aspects of chemotherapy, including side effects, management, patient education and administration.
Health and Safety
Dist - UTEXSC **Prod** - UTEXSC

Nursing in a Multi - Cultural Society 30 MIN
16mm
Psychiatric - Mental Health Nursing Series
Color (PRO)
LC 76-701621
Discusses how socio - cultural differences between nurse and patient influence mutual expectations and participation in care. showing the need for a health care system designed to accommodate diverse groups which form a pluralistic society. Examines particular needs and problems of racial and ethnic minorities.
Health and Safety
Dist - AJN **Prod** - AJN 1976

Nursing in America - a history of social reform 30 MIN
VHS
Color (C PRO)
$275.00 purchase, $75.00 rental _ #42 - 2313, #42 - 2313R
Presents nursing historians, nurse educators and nursing leaders who relate the history of the American nurse as a leader in social reform. Includes archival photographs, period music, historic film footage and oral histories.
Health and Safety; History - World
Dist - NLFN **Prod** - NLFN

Nursing in America - through a feminist lens 28 MIN
VHS
Color (C PRO)
$275.00 purchase, $75.00 rental _ #42 - 2435, #42 - 2435R
Focuses on issues of autonomy and control through the comparison of nurses' historic struggle for independence with the feminist battle to empower women. Explores how the health care establishment undermined the autonomy of nursing in the early 20th century and gives nurses the concepts and approaches they need to become leaders in health care.
Health and Safety; History - World; Sociology
Dist - NLFN **Prod** - NLFN

Nursing Intervention - One Facet of Dementia 20 MIN
U-matic
Communicating with the Psychiatric Patient Series
Color (PRO)
LC 79-707283
Features a simulated interview between a patient and a nurse which illustrates various senile reactions. Shows appropriate nursing intervention skills.
Health and Safety; Psychology
Dist - USNAC **Prod** - VAHSL 1977

Nursing Intervention - the Admission Interview, the Depressed Patient 29 MIN
U-matic
Communicating with the Psychiatric Patient Series
Color (PRO)
LC 79-707280
Demonstrates nursing personnel's verbal and nonverbal communication skills with a newly admitted depressed patient.
Health and Safety; Psychology
Dist - USNAC **Prod** - VAHSL 1976

Nursing Intervention - the Delusional Patient 23 MIN
U-matic
Communicating with the Psychiatric Patient Series
Color (PRO)
LC 79-707281
Offers a simulated interview depicting nursing intervention involving a patient who is delusional. Highlights various aspects of the patient's reactions.
Health and Safety; Psychology
Dist - USNAC **Prod** - VAHSL 1975

Nursing Intervention - the Patient who is Experiencing Hallucinations 23 MIN
U-matic
Communicating with the Psychiatric Patient Series
Color (PRO)
LC 79-707284
Shows a simulated interview between a nurse and a hallucinating patient. Demonstrates the hallucinating process and appropriate nursing intervention skills.
Health and Safety; Psychology
Dist - USNAC **Prod** - VAHSL 1975

Nursing Intervention - the Patient with Aggressive Behavior 21 MIN
U-matic
Communicating with the Psychiatric Patient Series
Color (PRO)
LC 79-707285
Presents a simulated interview between a patient and a nurse, demonstrating the dynamics of anger and the value of prompt and appropriate nursing intervention.
Health and Safety; Psychology
Dist - USNAC **Prod** - VAHSL

Nursing Intervention - the Patient with Manipulative Behavior 21 MIN
U-matic
Communicating with the Psychiatric Patient Series
Color (PRO)
LC 79-707286
Presents a simulated interview between a nurse and a manipulative patient.
Health and Safety; Psychology
Dist - USNAC **Prod** - VAHSL 1975

Nursing Intervention - the Patient with Suspicious Behavior 37 MIN
U-matic
Communicating with the Psychiatric Patient Series
Color (PRO)
LC 79-707287
Presents a simulated interview between a nurse and a patient which demonstrates the dynamics of suspicious behavior and the appropriate intervention skills.
Health and Safety; Psychology
Dist - USNAC **Prod** - VAHSL 1976

Nursing is there 7 MIN
U-matic / VHS
Color (PRO)
$150.00 purchase, $40.00 rental _ #4280S, #4280V
Shows the many roles nursing staff may fill, including caregivers, teachers, managers and patient advocates. Interviews staff in a wide variety of settings who share the aspects of their work that bring them the greatest satisfaction - meeting vital human needs, making a positive difference in people's lives, being on the forefront of the rapidly advancing health sciences and being a respected professional.
Health and Safety; Science
Dist - AJN **Prod** - TULHC 1988

Nursing issues in arthritis - 3 11 MIN
VHS
Living well with arthritis series
Color (C PRO G)
$395.00 purchase _ #R911 - VI - 004
Reveals that there are more than 100 forms of arthritis affecting different people in different ways, with no one correct medication or treatment for all patients. Discusses medication, dietary intervention, quackery and sexuality. Part of a five - part series on arthritis.
Health and Safety
Dist - HSCIC **Prod** - BRMARH 1991

Nursing Issues in Bulimia 22 MIN
U-matic / VHS
Color (PRO)
Focuses on social cognitive developmental aspects of eating disorders, particularly bulimia.
Health and Safety
Dist - BAXMED **Prod** - BAXMED 1986

Nursing management in neurogenic bladder series
Assessment and management after stroke, Pt 3 17 MIN
Mechanism of Impairment in Spinal Cord Injury, Part 1 15 MIN
Urologic Nursing Care of Patients with Spinal Cord Lesions, Pt 2 24 MIN
Dist - RICHGO

Nursing management - interviewing for hire - 2 37 MIN
VHS
Nursing management series
Color (C PRO G)
$395.00 purchase _ #R871 - VI - 043
Introduces the interviewing for hire process. Provides basic knowledge, demonstrations of interviewing techniques and techniques on managing controversial issues during the interview. Includes two study guides for both student and instructor. Part of two parts on nursing managment.
Business and Economics; Guidance and Counseling; Health and Safety
Dist - HSCIC **Prod** - KENNYH 1988

Nursing Management Issues in Right and Left Stroke 80 MIN
VHS / 16mm
Color (PRO)
$120.00, $200.00 purchase, $50.00 rental _ 79 - 2
Discusses nursing management issues in right and left stroke victims. Presents the work of W Griggs, MSN, RN. Includes two 40 minute videos and instructor's guide for complete 80 minute program.
Health and Safety; Science - Natural
Dist - RICHGO **Prod** - RICHGO 1979

Nursing management of acute head injuries 28 MIN
U-matic / VHS
Color (PRO)
$275.00 purchase, $60.00 rental _ #7608S, #7608V
Illustrates the various types of head injuries and the nursing diagnoses for each. Features neuroscience nursing expert Connie Walleck. Shows a thorough neurological assessment, including Glasgow coma score, pupil size and reaction, and monitoring for increased intracranial pressure. Demonstrates methods of treatment and the nurse's role in each, nursing interventions to prevent or control increased intracranial pressure and common nursing diagnoses.
Health and Safety
Dist - AJN **Prod** - HOSSN 1986

Nursing management of dermal ulcers 28 MIN
VHS / U-matic
Color (PRO)
$275.00 purchase, $60.00 rental _ #7602S, #7602V
Illustrates measures to prevent dermal ulcers. Features Peggy Felice who explains and demonstrates skin risk factors, causes, steps in prevention, treatment methods and the various stages of dermal ulcers. Highlights treatment skills - cleansing, debridement, absorption techniques, protection and treatment combinations.
Health and Safety
Dist - AJN **Prod** - HOSSN 1986

Nursing management of diabetes in adults 28 MIN
VHS / U-matic
Color (PRO)
$275.00 purchase, $60.00 rental _ #7815S, #7815V
Shows how to differentiate between Type I and Type II diabetes by age onset, symptoms and management. Describes the complications of diabetes as macrovascular and microvascular. Defines the major goals of management - normalizing blood glucose levels and preventing acute and long - term care complications through diet, medication, exercise and blood glucose monitoring.
Health and Safety; Physical Education and Recreation
Dist - AJN **Prod** - HOSSN 1989

Nursing management of hypertension of pregnancy 28 MIN
U-matic / VHS
Color (PRO)
$275.00 purchase, $60.00 rental _ #7726S, #7726V
Looks at the second leading cause of maternal deaths in the United States - hypertension of pregnancy. Explains the possible causes of hypertension, how to screen patients at risk and how to recognize the condition at the outset. Emphasizes the importance of patient and family education, emotional support, rest and therapy. Stresses steps to prevent and treat seizures, indications for immediate delivery and possible complications in the child.
Health and Safety; Sociology
Dist - AJN **Prod** - HOSSN 1988

Nursing management of increased intracranial pressure 28 MIN
VHS / U-matic
Color (PRO)
$275.00 purchase, $60.00 rental _ #7609S, #7609V
Illustrates a neurological nursing assessment. Explains increased intracranial pressure with graphics. Explains the significance of intracranial pressure monitoring, differentiation of A, B, and C waves, prevention of infection, medical and nursing management, and how to care for patients in a barbiturate coma. Details the effects of nursing care on a patient's intracranial pressure level, activities which raise intracranial pressure and techniques for reducing it. Features Connie Walleck, neuroscience nursing expert.
Health and Safety
Dist - AJN **Prod** - HOSSN 1986

Nursing management of patients with diabetes 28 MIN
VHS
Color (C PRO)
$285.00 purchase, $70.00 rental _ #6017S, #6017V
Reviews the triad of modern diabetes treatment - diet, exercise and medications. Describes type I and type II diabetes, as well as the related genetic and physiological factors. Covers blood glucose monitoring and offers guidelines for the management of hospitalized diabietics who are experiencing acute complications - hypoglycemia, diabetic ketoacidosis, nonketotic hypersmolar hyperglycemic coma - or chronic complications - retinopathy, nephropathy, neuropathy, macrovascular changes. Produced by Health and Sciences Network.
Health and Safety; Physical Education and Recreation
Dist - AJN

Nursing Management of the Patient Receiving Radiation Therapy 22 MIN
16mm
Color (PRO)
Depicts the role of the nurse with patients being treated by radiation for cancer. Shows the nurse and physician explaining procedures to patients and giving them instructions in matters of diet, rest and skin care as well as providing emotional support.
Health and Safety; Sociology
Dist - AMCS **Prod** - AMCS 1973

Nursing Management of the Patient with Cancer 29 MIN
16mm
Color (PRO)
LC FI68-87
Illustrates in detail nursing procedures used after laryngectomy, tracheotomy, colostomy, or cystectomy.
Health and Safety
Dist - AMCS **Prod** - AMCS 1966

Nursing Management of the Patient with Head and Neck Cancer 31 MIN
16mm
Color (PRO)
Discusses special nursing procedures for patients who have had an orbital exenteration or combined jaw resection and radial neck dissection. Shows tracheostomy care and nasal feeding tube techniques.
Health and Safety; Science
Dist - AMCS **Prod** - AMCS 1970

Nursing management of wounds 28 MIN
VHS / U-matic
Color (PRO)
$275.00 purchase, $60.00 rental _ #7650S, #7650V
Gives the basics of proper wound care in an easy to follow and remember format. Shows the three phases of the healing process. Describes the difference between a normal and impaired healing by investigating the possible factors - malnutrition, diabetes and infection - which hinder a patient's healing. Demonstrates dressing techniques for packing a wound. Discusses the types of dressing available and documentation of wound status.
Health and Safety
Dist - AJN **Prod** - HOSSN 1988

Nursing management series
Presents two parts on nursing management. Discusses the fundamentals of nursing management for nurses in middle management and introduces the interviewing process for hiring.
Nursing management - interviewing for hire - 2 37 MIN
Nursing management - the basics - 1 37 MIN
Dist - HSCIC **Prod** - KENNYH 1988

Nursing management - the basics - 1 37 MIN
VHS
Nursing management series
Color (C PRO G)
$395.00 purchase _ #R871 - VI - 042
Provides fundamental information for nurses in middle management to help them do their jobs better. Defines management, teaches the three elements of managing, describes three theories of human relatons and identifies leadership styles. Part of two parts on nursing managment.
Business and Economics; Health and Safety
Dist - HSCIC **Prod** - KENNYH 1988

Nursing - No 5 28 MIN
VHS / U-matic
Career encounters series
Color (H C)
$110.00, $95.00 purchase
Looks at the field of nursing. Outlines educational requirements and discusses salaries. Sponsored by the National League for Nursing and the US Department of Veterans Affairs.
Business and Economics; Guidance and Counseling; Health and Safety; Psychology
Dist - PLEXPU **Prod** - PLEXPU 1990

Nursing obligations 17 MIN
BETA / VHS / U-matic
Ethics, values and health care series
Color (C PRO)
$150.00 purchase _ #132.7
Presents a video transfer from slide program which discusses the ethical issues of secret - keeping, confidentiality and professionalism. Addresses the responsibilities of nurses when they are and when they are not working in the role of a nurse. Part of a series on ethics, values and health care.
Guidance and Counseling; Health and Safety; Religion and Philosophy
Dist - CONMED **Prod** - CONMED

Nursing - Paramedic 15 MIN
VHS / U-matic / BETA
Career Success Series
(H C A)
$29.95 _ #MX311
Portrays the occupations of nursing and paramedics by reviewing their required abilities and interviewing people employed in these fields. Shows anxieties and rewards involved in pursuing careers in nursing and paramedics.
Education; Guidance and Counseling; Health and Safety; Science
Dist - CAMV **Prod** - CAMV

Nursing - patient teaching series
Implementing patient teaching 30 MIN
Philosophy of patient teaching 30 MIN
Planning patient teaching 30 MIN
Principles of learning 30 MIN
Readiness for learning 30 MIN
Dist - NTCN

A Nursing perspective - Part 1 28 MIN
U-matic / VHS
AIDS series
Color (PRO)
$275.00 purchase, $60.00 rental _ #7314S, #7314V
Introduces and defines AIDS - Acquired Immune Deficiency Syndrome - and the latest research developments. Examines the epidemiology and pathophysiology of AIDS, risk populations, and the problems of opportunistic infections such as pneumocystis carinii pneumonia, tuberculosis, enteric infections and herpes simplex. Presents the latest recommendations from the Centers for Disease Control for proper precautions without imposing social isolation. Emphasizes the importance of handwashing and differentiates precautions for AIDS and the opportunistic infections associated with it. Part of a two - part series.
Health and Safety
Dist - AJN **Prod** - HOSSN 1987

Nursing Preceptorship - an Introduction 10 MIN
U-matic
Nursing Preceptorship Series
(PRO)
Identifies the roles and responsibilities of the participants and describes the resulting benefits.
Health and Safety
Dist - ACCESS **Prod** - ACCESS 1983

Nursing Preceptorship Series
Nursing Preceptorship - an Introduction 10 MIN
Reality Shock 21 MIN
Scenarios for Discussion 16 MIN
Dist - ACCESS

Nursing Problems in the Implanting of the Internal Cardiac Pacemaker 18 MIN
16mm
Color (PRO)
Demonstrates a technique in repairing and implanting the internal cardiac pacemaker, and stresses the need for nursing and medical cooperation in preventing possible foreign body reaction.
Health and Safety; Science
Dist - ACY **Prod** - ACYDGD 1965

Nursing Procedures for Cytotoxic Agents 28 MIN
VHS / 16mm
Color (C PRO)
$275.00 purchase, $60.00 rental _ #7801S, #7801V
Teaches procedures for correct handling and proper administration of cytotoxic agents, using several different types of equipment. Details potentially harmful effects, highlights basic safety precautions. Study guide included, CE credit approved.
Health and Safety
Dist - AJN **Prod** - HOSSN 1990

The Nursing Process 55 MIN
U-matic / VHS
Color
Presents the implementation and evaluation phases of the nursing process. Emphasizes the barriers to implementation that can exist when the patient, nurse, family and the health care team are not working together.
Health and Safety
Dist - FAIRGH **Prod** - FAIRGH

Nursing process 17 MIN
VHS / U-matic / BETA
Critical thinking in nursing series
Color (C PRO)
$150.00 purchase _ #146.4
Presents a video transfer of a slide program which relates current topics of diagnostic reasoning and critical thinking to the nursing process. Discusses in depth each step of the nursing process and ties each to the nursing care plan. Part of a series on critical thinking in nursing.
Health and Safety
Dist - CONMED **Prod** - CONMED

The Nursing Process 8 MIN
U-matic / VHS / 16mm
Nursing Process in Action Series
Color (PRO)
Explains the four phases of the nursing process and the nursing care plan which helps nurses and staff members to function more effectively and give patients better care.
Health and Safety
Dist - USNAC **Prod** - WRAIR

Nursing Process Applied 27 MIN
VHS / 16mm
Color (PRO)
$295.00 purchase, $60.00 rental
Demonstrates use of the five step process - assessment, analysis and nursing diagnosis, planning, implementation, evaluation - through the eyes of a nurse who is caring for a client.
Health and Safety
Dist - FAIRGH **Prod** - FAIRGH 1986

Nursing Process in Action Series
The Nursing Process 8 MIN
Nursing Process in Action, the, Pt 1, the Use of Nursing Process to Plan, Implement, 32 MIN
Nursing Process in Action, the, Pt 2, Discharge Planning - the Key to Continuing Care 23 MIN
Dist - USNAC

Nursing Process in Action, the, Pt 1, the Use of Nursing Process to Plan, Implement, 32 MIN
U-matic / VHS / 16mm
Nursing Process in Action Series

Color (PRO)
Complete title is Nursing Process In Action, The, Pt 1, The Use Of Nursing Process To Plan, Implement, Evaluate Nursing Care. Reviews four phases of the nursing process as it applies to a diabetic patient and explains the nursing care plan and clinical nursing record.
Health and Safety
Dist - USNAC **Prod** - WRAIR

Nursing Process in Action, the, Pt 2, Discharge Planning - the Key to Continuing Care 23 MIN
U-matic / VHS / 16mm
Nursing Process in Action Series
Color (PRO)
Covers nursing care by emergency room, ward and recovery room nurses as they assess, plan, implement and evaluate the patient's nursing care.
Health and Safety
Dist - USNAC **Prod** - WRAIR

Nursing process - Pt 1 - assessment 25 MIN
16mm
Directions for education in nursing via technology series; Lesson 23
B&W (PRO)
LC 74-701796
Describes assessment, the first step in the nursing process. Demonstrates assessment in a patient situation.
Health and Safety
Dist - WSUM **Prod** - DENT 1974

Nursing process - Pt 3 - evaluating effectiveness of implementation 24 MIN
16mm
Directions for education in nursing via technology series; Lesson 25
B&W (PRO)
LC 74-701798
Deals with evaluating effectiveness of implementation.
Health and Safety
Dist - WSUM **Prod** - DENT 1974

Nursing process - Pt 2 - planning and implementation of plan 28 MIN
16mm
Directions for education in nursing via technology series; Lesson 24
B&W (PRO)
LC 74-701797
Uses a dramatization to show planning and implementation in patient care.
Health and Safety
Dist - WSUM **Prod** - DENT 1974

The Nursing process series
Presents a four - part series introducing first year nursing students to concepts of the nursing process. Breaks down the nursing process in to five steps - assessment, identification, planning, implementation and evaluation. Explains all aspects of the five steps and how they fit into the process as a whole.
The Nursing process series 67 MIN
Dist - HSCIC **Prod** - MUSC 1974

Nursing process test subseries - 2
VHS
Clinical simulations for teaching the nursing process series
Color (C PRO G)
$875.00 purchase _ #R880 - VI - 013
Presents five videocassettes which evaluate how well students understand the concepts of nursing.
Health and Safety
Dist - HSCIC **Prod** - UWISN 1988

Nursing quality assurance - defining quality patient care 28 MIN
U-matic / VHS
Color (PRO)
$275.00 purchase, $60.00 rental _ #9920S, #9920V
Shows nursing staff how to evaluate nursing care. Defines the key components of the quality assurance process, including written standards, monitoring systems and corrective actions. Demonstrates each step in the process within the context of a typical hospital unit. Identifies continuing education needs for health care professionals.
Business and Economics; Health and Safety
Dist - AJN **Prod** - HOSSN 1986

Nursing - R Plus M Equals C, Relationship Plus Meaning Equals Communication Series
Barriers to communication 30 MIN
Basic principles of communication 30 MIN
Interviews and Process Recordings 30 MIN
The Meaning of Communication 30 MIN
Team Conferences 30 MIN
Utilizing Effective Communication 30 MIN
Dist - NTCN

Nursing - R plus M equals C, relationship plus meaning equals communication series
Communicating with colleagues 30 MIN
Communication processes in nursing 30 MIN
Communication skills 30 MIN
Giving instructions, charting, reporting 30 MIN
Dist - NTCN

Nursing research - the state of the art
VHS
Practice of nursing series
Color (C PRO)
$275.00 purchase, $100.00 rental _ #42 - 2657, #42 - 2657R
Addresses the questions of what comprises nursing research, whether scholarship is separate from research and how nurse researchers can promote the use of research in clinical practice. Considers how nurse researchers document outcomes differently from the medical model. Looks at the contemporary area of study, health promotion in women's health, and how quantitative and qualitative methodologies are used to establish the outcomes of nursing interventions.
Health and Safety
Dist - NLFN **Prod** - NLFN

Nursing responsibilities in care of patient having gastric or intestinal decompression 30 MIN
16mm
Directions for education in nursing via technology series; Lesson 42
B&W (PRO)
LC 74-701816
Demonstrates appropriate nursing action for discomforts of patients having gastric or intestinal decompression therapy. Demonstrates procedures to be followed prior to, during and following ambulation of a patient.
Health and Safety
Dist - WSUM **Prod** - DENT 1974

Nursing responsibilities in care of patients receiving various methods of gavage 33 MIN
16mm
Directions for education in nursing via technology series; Lesson 43
B&W (PRO)
LC 74-701817
Identifies indications for gavage feeding and discusses types of feedings. Demonstrates methods, gravity and nursing responsibilities.
Health and Safety
Dist - WSUM **Prod** - DENT 1974

Nursing responsibilities in radiotherapy - Pt 1 31 MIN
16mm
Directions for education in nursing via technology series; Lesson 72
B&W (PRO)
LC 74-701849
Identifies sources of radiation. Compares and contrasts alpha, beta and gamma emanations. Discusses biologic effects of radiation on the cell and the concepts of time, distance and shielding.
Science - Natural; Science - Physical
Dist - WSUM **Prod** - DENT 1974

Nursing responsibilities in radiotherapy - Pt 2 30 MIN
16mm
Directions for education in nursing via technology series; Lesson 73
B&W (PRO)
LC 74-701850
Compares external and internal radiotherapy and sealed and unsealed therapy. Describes nursing responsibilities for patients receiving each type of therapy.
Health and Safety; Science - Physical
Dist - WSUM **Prod** - DENT 1974

Nursing Responsibilities in Screening and Detection of Breast Cancer, 15 MIN
VHS / 16mm
(C)
$385.00 purchase _ #840VJ034A
Demonstrates the correct technique for performing a breast examination, the essential elements in teaching breast self - examination, and the information to relate to a client regarding the use of mammography, xerography, thermography and ultrasound in breast cancer detection. Tape one of a set of two.
Health and Safety
Dist - HSCIC **Prod** - HSCIC 1984

Nursing Responsibilities in Screening and Detection of Breast Cancer 33 MIN
U-matic / VHS
Color (PRO)
Teaches nurses, in a four - module package, the current information on screening and detection of breast cancer. On two tapes.
Health and Safety
Dist - HSCIC **Prod** - HSCIC 1984

Nursing responsibilities in the care of patients with arterial peripheral vascular 31 MIN
16mm
Directions for education in nursing via technology series; Lesson 44
B&W (PRO)
LC 74-701818
Reviews anatomy, pathophysiology and the scientific basis for nursing care for patients with arterial peripheral vascular diseases.
Health and Safety; Science - Natural
Dist - WSUM **Prod** - DENT 1974

Nursing responsibilities in the care of the patient in a cast - Pt 1 30 MIN
16mm
Directions for education in nursing via technology series; Lesson 48
B&W (PRO)
LC 74-701822
Identifies reasons for a cast and discusses materials used. Demonstrates application of a cast and care of a patient in a new cast.
Health and Safety; Science; Science - Natural
Dist - WSUM **Prod** - DENT 1974

Nursing responsibilities in the care of the patient in a cast - Pt 2 29 MIN
16mm
Directions for education in nursing via technology series; Lesson 49
B&W (PRO)
LC 74-701823
Demonstrates the nurse's responsibility in the care of the patient in a cast.
Health and Safety; Science; Science - Natural
Dist - WSUM **Prod** - DENT 1974

Nursing responsibilities in the care of the patient in traction - Pt 1 35 MIN
16mm
Directions for education in nursing via technology series; Lesson 50
B&W (PRO)
LC 74-701824
Lists major methods used to provide traction. Demonstrates parts, types and operational principles of equipment used in straight, suspension and fixed traction.
Health and Safety; Science
Dist - WSUM **Prod** - DENT 1974

Nursing responsibilities in the care of the patient in traction - Pt 2 29 MIN
16mm
Directions for education in nursing via technology series; Lesson 51
B&W (PRO)
LC 74-701825
Demonstrates the nurse's responsibility in the care of the patient in traction.
Health and Safety; Science
Dist - WSUM **Prod** - DENT 1974

Nursing responsibilities in the care of the patient on a circ - olectric bed 27 MIN
16mm
Directions for education in nursing via technology series; Lesson 52
B&W (PRO)
LC 74-701826
Identifies the parts and operational principles of the Circ - Olectric bed. Demonstrates the use of the bed, turning patient and meeting the needs for intake and elimination.
Health and Safety
Dist - WSUM **Prod** - DENT 1974

Nursing responsibilities in the evaluation of central venous pressure 29 MIN
16mm
Directions for education in nursing via technology series; Lesson 63
B&W (PRO)
LC 74-701839
Identifies indications for measuring central venous pressure and displays equipment that is used. Demonstrates the nurse's responsibilities when taking central venous pressure.
Health and Safety; Science; Science - Natural
Dist - WSUM **Prod** - DENT 1974

Nursing responsibilities in the use of a mechanical device in the transfer of patients 29 MIN
16mm

Directions for education in nursing via technology series; Lesson 53
B&W (PRO)
LC 74-701827
Identifies and demonstrates parts and operational principles of the Hoyer lift. Demonstrates transfer of the patient from bed to chair and return to bed, and the use of scale attachment for weighing the patient.
Health and Safety
Dist - WSUM Prod - DENT 1974

Nursing responsibilities in the use of rotating tourniquets 28 MIN
16mm
Directions for education in nursing via technology series; Lesson 62
B&W (PRO)
LC 74-701838
Identifies the physiologic basis for the use of rotating tourniquets. Demonstrates the use of manual - and machine - type rotating tourniquets.
Health and Safety; Science
Dist - WSUM Prod - DENT 1974

Nursing responsibilities - nasal suctioning, oral suctioning and mouth care 29 MIN
16mm
Directions for education in nursing via technology series; Lesson 67
B&W (PRO)
LC 74-701843
Identifies the need for, and demonstrates the process of nasal and oral suctioning. Discusses and demonstrates means of providing mouth care for helpless patients.
Health and Safety
Dist - WSUM Prod - DENT 1974

Nursing responsibilities - sterile dressings 31 MIN
16mm
Directions for education in nursing via technology series; Lesson 69
B&W (PRO)
LC 74-701846
Identifies various types of dressings and demonstrates application of a simple dressing, dressing to a wound with drainage and a pressure dressing.
Health and Safety
Dist - WSUM Prod - DENT 1974

The Nursing Scene 12 MIN
16mm
Color
LC 74-705228
Describes the nursing profession, what nurses do, their specialties, the kind of training they need and the courses they should take in high school.
Guidance and Counseling; Health and Safety
Dist - USNAC Prod - NIMH 1972

Nursing series
Eye and vision 26 MIN
Dist - UMICHM

Nursing Series
Bathing the patient - home care 24 MIN
Care of the Patient with Diabetes Mellitus - Complicated 23 MIN
Care of the Patient with Diabetes Mellitus - Uncomplicated 29 MIN
Fundamentals of massage 12 MIN
Hydrotherapy 22 MIN
Radiotherapy - High Dosage Treatment 17 MIN
Therapeutic uses of heat and cold - Pt 1 - administering hot applications 21 MIN
Vital Signs and their Interrelation - Body Temperature, Pulse, Respiration, Blood Pressure 32 MIN
Dist - USNAC

Nursing Service Orientation - Beyond Medicine 28 MIN
16mm
Color
LC 79-701516
Describes the role of the naval chaplain and discusses spiritual beliefs as they relate to illness. Examines the nurse officer's role in identifying the patient who needs spiritual support in dealing with illness.
Guidance and Counseling; Health and Safety; Psychology
Dist - USNAC Prod - USN 1977

Nursing shortage level three - reports from the frontlines 28 MIN
VHS / U-matic
Color (C PRO)
$275.00 purchase, $100.00, $50.00 rental _ #049; LC 91-705300
Focuses on health care workers at Newton - Wellesley Hospital in a Boston suburb as they respond to the challenge of providing quality care despite staffing shortages. Considers the nationwide problem caused by the AIDS epidemic, an aging population, health care cost - cutting and other factors.
Health and Safety; Sociology
Dist - FANPRO Prod - ACMISH

Nursing Situations 31 MIN
U-matic
Color (PRO)
LC 76-706162
Presents nine commonly encountered nurse - patient situations to analyze verbal and nonverbal communication and to evaluate the effectiveness of various interventive techniques in dealing with patients.
Health and Safety; Psychology
Dist - USNAC Prod - NHWSN 1975

Nursing Skills - Intra - Arterial Balloon Pump - an Introduction to Counterpulsation 17 MIN
U-matic / VHS
Color (PRO)
LC 80-730879
Introduces the counterpulsation and the intra - aortic balloon pump. Illustrates the therapeutic effects of counterpulsation in the presence of myocardial depression. Shows a balloon pump system and control console.
Health and Safety
Dist - MEDCOM Prod - MEDCOM

Nursing Skills - Intra - Arterial Balloon Pump - Elements in Nursing Care 14 MIN
VHS / U-matic
Color (PRO)
LC 80-730880
Introduces important elements in the nursing care of patients receiving intra - aortic balloon pump therapy. Reviews counterpulsation and discusses implications to nursing care. Demonstrates techniques for changing the dressing over the catheter insertion site.
Health and Safety
Dist - MEDCOM Prod - MEDCOM

Nursing Skills - Intra - Arterial Pressure Monitoring - System Operation 14 MIN
VHS / U-matic
Color (PRO)
LC 80-730877
Explains the major components of systems used for intra - arterial pressure monitoring. Explains the specific criteria for evaluating the operation of the system.
Health and Safety
Dist - MEDCOM Prod - MEDCOM

Nursing skills series
Presents a three - part series on nursing skills produced by Lander Univ Nursing Education, Greenwood, South Carolina. Includes the titles Port - A - Cath - An Intravenous Access System; Buck's Traction; and Respiratory Therapy - An Introduction for Nurses.
Buck's traction - 2 12 MIN
Port - A - Cath - an intravenous access system - 1 6 MIN
Respiratory therapy - an introduction for nurses - 3 11 MIN
Dist - HSCIC

Nursing Skills - the 12 - Lead Electrocardiogram 21 MIN
VHS / U-matic
Color (PRO)
LC 80-730881
Demonstrates nursing skills in 12 - lead electrocardiography. Illustrates the formation of 12 leads using five electrodes and the difference in the way bipolar and unipolar leads monitor the heart's electrical activity.
Health and Safety; Science - Natural
Dist - MEDCOM Prod - MEDCOM

Nursing Skills - Transfusion Therapy, Platelets, Plasma, Cryoprecipitate 18 MIN
U-matic / 35mm strip
Color (PRO)
LC 80-730883;
Reviews the composition of whole blood and methods for obtaining specific blood components. Demonstrates transfusions of platelets, plasma and cryoprecipitate in clinical setting and explains specific precautions in the transfusion of these products.
Health and Safety; Science - Natural
Dist - MEDCOM Prod - MEDCOM

Nursing Skills - Transfusion Therapy - Red Blood Cells 23 MIN
U-matic / 35mm strip
Color (PRO)
LC 80-730882;
Demonstrates the transfusion of red blood cells. Reviews the function of red cells and the use of this blood component in transfusion therapy. Gives a step - by - step procedure used for the transfusion of red blood cells.
Health and Safety; Science - Natural
Dist - MEDCOM Prod - MEDCOM

Nursing small hopes
VHS
Frontiers series
Color; PAL (G)
PdS20 purchase
Looks at the problems and dilemmas involved in treating and allocating scarce hospital resources to very premature babies. Includes support material. Part of a series examining how developments at the frontiers of science, technology and psychology have had a major impact on a range of health and medical issues. Contact distributor about availability outside the United Kindgom.
Health and Safety; Religion and Philosophy
Dist - ACADEM

Nursing Support during Dialysis Therapy 12 MIN
VHS / U-matic
Color (PRO)
LC 80-730457
Illustrates the nurse's role in long - term dialysis therapy. Emphasizes interventions when explaining the nurse's role as a member of the dialysis team.
Health and Safety; Science - Natural
Dist - MEDCOM Prod - MEDCOM

A Nursing support group - dealing with death and dying 31 MIN
VHS / U-matic
Color (PRO C)
$200.00 purchase, $60.00 rental _ #5265S, #5265V; $285.00 purchase, $70.00 rental _ #5265S, 5265V
Witnesses an actual support group meeting of oncology nurses as they discuss the details of their work with terminal cancer patients and their families. Suggests the use of humor, peer support, and time off as ways for caregivers to deal with death and dying.
Health and Safety; Sociology
Dist - AJN Prod - MSKCC 1984

Nursing Techniques for the Care of Patients with Impaired Vision Series
Removal of Corneal and Scleral Contact Lenses 9 MIN
Dist - OSUMPD

Nursing the Cancer Patient - Diagnosis - Cancer of the Rectum 20 MIN
16mm
B&W (PRO)
Increases the understanding of the total impact of cancer to the patient and the family. Depicts problems of a patient undergoing surgery and the role of the nurse in comforting and assisting him and his family through the ordeal.
Health and Safety; Sociology
Dist - AMCS Prod - AMCS 1962

Nursing - the challenge of a lifetime 15 MIN
VHS
Color (C PRO)
$131.25 purchase, $60.00 rental _ #42 - 2225, #42 - 2225R
Presents a nurse recruitment program.
Health and Safety
Dist - NLFN Prod - NLFN

Nursing - the Politics of Caring 22 MIN
16mm / VHS
Color (G)
$220.00 purchase
Looks at the evolution of nurses' attitudes toward their work and their efforts to take an active role in shaping health care in the U.S.
Health and Safety; Science
Dist - FANPRO Prod - FANPRO 1989

Nursing the Psychiatric Patient 28 MIN
16mm
Color
LC 74-706509
Trains corpsmen as technicians in the care of disturbed patients. Tells how to observe and report behavior patterns and emphasizes the importance of paramedical personnel in psychiatric service.
Health and Safety; Psychology
Dist - USNAC Prod - USN 1972

Nursing theory - a circle of knowledge 52 MIN
U-matic / VHS
Color (C PRO)
%I $350.00 purchase, $100.00 rental _ #42 - 2206, #42 - 2207, #42 - 2206R, #42 - 2207R
Presents two parts featuring six of the foremost thinkers in nursing as they explore how theory and practice are interrelated in a never - ending circle of knowledge. Separates the introduction and in - depth discussion into Part I which examines the relevance of nursing theory to modern practice through excerpts of interviews with theorists, and Part II which explores the emerging world view of science, the difference between medical and nursing models and emerging changes in theory and practice. Includes two videos.
Health and Safety
Dist - NLFN Prod - NLFN

Nursing - Where are You Going, How will You Get There Series

The Care Plan 30 MIN
Combining teaching strategies 30 MIN
Developing behavioral objectives 30 MIN
Evaluation as a Teaching Strategy 30 MIN
The Lecture and Role - Playing Strategy 30 MIN
A Perspective on Teaching 30 MIN
Planning Clinical Experiences 30 MIN
Pre and Post Conferences 30 MIN
The Seminar and Role - Playing Strategy 30 MIN
Dist - NTCN

Nursing Worldwide 17 MIN
16mm
Color (H C A)
LC FIA65-126
Nursing leaders, who are educators, executives and world travelers, discuss their work and their ambitions. They show nursing to be a career offering opportunity for more than bedside care.
Guidance and Counseling; Health and Safety; Psychology
Dist - WSUM **Prod** - WSUM 1960

Nurturing 17 MIN
VHS / U-matic
Infant Development Series
Color
Offers practical suggestions of what caregivers can do to optimize infant development.
Psychology
Dist - DAVFMS **Prod** - DAVFMS

Nurturing 20 MIN
16mm
Color (J)
LC 78-701259
Explains the importance of a stimulating environment and the availability and encouragement of caregivers in fostering early childhood development. Provides examples of nurturing experiences in various daily activities of the infant and mother.
Education; Home Economics; Psychology; Sociology
Dist - DAVFMS **Prod** - DAVFMS 1978

Nurturing Creativity 10 MIN
U-matic / VHS
You (Parents are Special Series
Color
Explains the importance of nurturing creativity in children, with Fred Rogers.
Fine Arts; Psychology; Sociology
Dist - FAMCOM **Prod** - FAMCOM

Nurturing Emotional Development through Physical Routines 29 MIN
VHS / 16mm
Daycare - Caregiver Training Series
Color (C)
$250.00 purchase _ #293003
Assists in the educating of university and college students learning to care professionally for young children and professional caregivers employed in preschool centers. Documents the role and impact of caregivers on children, parents and families. 'Nurturing Emotional Development' discloses that daily routines such as toileting, eating and resting are interwoven with young children's discovery of how their bodies work and their development of a sense of self.
Guidance and Counseling; Home Economics; Psychology; Sociology
Dist - ACCESS **Prod** - ACCESS 1990

The Nutcracker 120 MIN
VHS
Color (S)
$39.95 purchase _ #623 - 9384
Recreates the ever - popular 'Nutcracker' starring Lesley Collier and Anthony Dowell. Features the Royal Ballet Company.
Fine Arts; Geography - World; Physical Education and Recreation
Dist - FI **Prod** - NVIDC 1986

The Nutcracker
VHS / BETA
Color
Presents The Nutcracker, performed by Mikhail Baryshnikov and the American Ballet Theater.
Fine Arts
Dist - GA **Prod** - GA

The Nutcracker 100 MIN
VHS
Color (K)
$16.95 purchase _ #0062
Stars Yekaterina Maximova and Vladimir Vasiliev in the Bolshoi Ballet production of 'The Nutcracker.'.
Fine Arts; Foreign Language; Geography - World; Physical Education and Recreation
Dist - KULTUR

The Nutcracker 26 MIN
U-matic / 16mm / VHS
Color (G)
$550.00, $415.00, $385.00 purchase _ #C261
Uses the music of Tchaikovsky and animation to portray the Christmas tale of a poor little serving girl whose kiss brings to life a wooden nutcracker prince. Features Hans Conried as narrator of the story by E T A Hoffman.
Fine Arts; Literature and Drama
Dist - BARR **Prod** - SYZMT 1978

The Nutcracker 79 MIN
VHS
Color (G)
$19.95 purchase _ #S01262
Features Mikhail Baryshnikov and Gelsey Kirkland in a performance of Tchaikovsky's 'Nutcracker Suite.'
Fine Arts
Dist - UILL

The Nutcracker - Live from the Bolshoi 87 MIN
VHS
Color (G)
$19.95 purchase _ #1201
Presents four of Russia's outstanding soloists, two husband and wife teams, in a glittering performance of the entire Bolshoi Ballet. Stars Vladimir Vasiliev and Yekaterina Maximova, and Vyacheslav Gordeyev and Nadia Pavlova.
Fine Arts; Foreign Language; Geography - World; Physical Education and Recreation
Dist - KULTUR

The Nutcracker - the Royal Ballet 102 MIN
VHS
Color (G)
$19.95 purchase_#1429
Brings to life Tchaikovsky's holiday masterpiece, The Nutcracker, in a Royal Ballet Covent Garden performance starring Lesley Collier and Anthony Dowell. Combines modern stage effects with original Ivanov/Sergueyev staging.
Fine Arts
Dist - KULTUR

Nutmeg - Nature's Perfect Package 26 MIN
U-matic / VHS
Spice of Life Series
Color (J A)
Describes the uses of nutmeg and mace.
Home Economics
Dist - BCNFL **Prod** - BLCKRD 1985

The Nutrient Express 11 MIN
VHS / U-matic
Nutrition for Children Series Pt II
Color (K P)
Tells the story of a little girl who ate the most improper foods, and how she changed after a train trip to the Land of Nutrients.
Health and Safety; Social Science
Dist - POAPLE **Prod** - POAPLE

Nutrient Needs - Basic Methabolic Process 38 MIN
VHS / 16mm
Nutrition and Health Series
(C)
$577.50 purchases _ #840VI025A - B
Explains the method for determining the nutritional adequacy of a meal, how digestion works, and intermediary metabolism of nutrients. Consists of two videocassettes and an instructional guide.
Health and Safety
Dist - HSCIC **Prod** - HSCIC 1984

Nutrient Needs - Fatty Acids and Vitamins 64 MIN
VHS / U-matic / 16mm
Nutrition and Health Series
Color (PRO C)
$866.25 purchase _ #840VI028A - B - C
Presents the concepts of recommended allowances and minimum requirements for nutrients. Examines human essential fatty acid requirements. Defines vitamins and provides an overview of their metabolic roles. Consists of three videocassettes.
Health and Safety; Psychology; Science - Physical; Social Science
Dist - HSCIC **Prod** - HSCIC 1984

Nutrient Needs - Protein and Calories 17 MIN
U-matic / VHS / 16mm
Nutrition and Health Series
Color (PRO C)
$577.50 purchase _ #840IVI026A - B
Identifies the body's normal nutritional needs for protein and calories and the methods used to assess those needs. Consists of two videocassettes and an instructional guide.
Health and Safety; Psychology; Social Science
Dist - HSCIC **Prod** - HSCIC 1984

Nutrient Needs - Water and Minerals 50 MIN
VHS / U-matic / 16mm
Nutrition and Health Series
Color (PRO C)
$577.50 purchase _ #840VI027A - B
Presents the concepts of recommended allowances and minimum requirements for nutrients - discusses water as a nutrient. Consists of two videocassettes and an instructional guide.
Health and Safety; Psychology; Social Science
Dist - HSCIC **Prod** - HSCIC 1984

Nutrients in tissues - 1 41 MIN
VHS
Introductory principles of nutrition series
Color (C PRO G)
$70.00 purchase, $16.00 rental _ #40402
Discusses synthesis and maintenance of the body's structural components with emphasis on soft connective and hard skeletal tissues. Part of a 20 - part series on basic principles of nutrition, evaluation of dietary intake, nutritional status, nutrition through the life cycle and world food supplies.
Health and Safety; Science - Natural; Social Science
Dist - PSU **Prod** - WPSXTV 1977

Nutrients in tissues - 2 33 MIN
VHS
Introductory principles of nutrition series
Color (C PRO G)
$70.00 purchase, $16.00 rental _ #34095
Discusses epithelial tissues and the highly coordinated neuromuscular system with emphasis on nerve transmission and muscle contraction. Part of a 20 - part series on basic principles of nutrition, evaluation of dietary intake, nutritional status, nutrition through the life cycle and world food supplies.
Health and Safety; Science - Natural; Social Science
Dist - PSU **Prod** - WPSXTV 1978

Nutrition 23 MIN
16mm
Color (H C A)
#3X105 ADMIN
Demonstrates the correlation between degeneration of health and the use of refined sugar and bleached flours. Documents cases of mass health degeneration among Eskimos, Indians and other isolated groups with the advent of white civilization and refined foods.
Social Science
Dist - CDIAND **Prod** - PPNF 1979

Nutrition 28 MIN
VHS
Dairy Production And Management Series
Color (G)
$95.00 purchase _ #6 - 096 - 303P
Looks at common feeds for dairy cattle, nutrition related problems and storage and handling of fodder. Part of a five - part series on dairy management.
Agriculture; Business and Economics
Dist - VEP **Prod** - VEP

Nutrition 25 MIN
VHS
Home care training videos - HCTV - series
Color (C PRO)
$125.00 purchase, $60.00 rental _ #42 - 2416, #42 - 2416R
Covers nutrition and the importance of a balanced diet. Shows how to encourage eating when a patient has appetite loss. Discusses special needs diets for patients with diabetes, cancer and other illnesses. Features consultation provided by the American Dietetic Assn. Includes instructional guide for review and testing and meets OBRA federal regulations. Part of a five - part series training home health aides in essential skills and teaching basic skills to nursing students.
Health and Safety; Social Science
Dist - NLFN **Prod** - NLFN

Nutrition 26 MIN
U-matic / VHS / 16mm
Color (H C A)
$425 purchase - 16 mm, $295 purchase - video, $55 rental
Provides nutritional information for teenagers.
Health and Safety
Dist - CNEMAG **Prod** - DOCUA 1988

Nutrition 30 MIN
U-matic
Growing Years Series
Color
Discusses the importance of nutrition for the three - to six - year - old child.
Social Science
Dist - CDTEL **Prod** - COAST

Nutrition - a Lifetime of Good Eating 8 MIN
U-matic / VHS
Color
Stresses the importance of good eating habits as people age. Presents basic information on nutrition with suggestions for maintaining interest in buying and preparing nutritious meals for people living alone.

Health and Safety; Social Science
Dist - UMICHM **Prod** - UMICHM 1976

Nutrition and Behavior - Basic Concepts and Principles 28 MIN
U-matic
Nutrition and Behavior Series
Color (J C)
Deals with psychohgenic versus biogenic theories of causation related to behavior. Dr Bernard Rimland explored the role of counseling and psychotherapy, the idea of the brain a 'soggy computer', metabolic dysperception and behavioral and mental disorders which are nutritionally treatable. The role of the professional and safety considerations in vitamin therapy are also discussed.
Health and Safety; Psychology; Social Science; Sociology
Dist - SDSC **Prod** - SDSC 1984

Nutrition and Behavior - Brain Allergies and Behavior
U-matic
Nutrition and Behavior Series
Color (J C)
Discusses the range of allergy - caused disorders particularly related to the brain and their treatment with vitamins. He deals with how to detect these allergies and provides sources for additional information.
Health and Safety; Psychology; Social Science; Sociology
Dist - SDSC **Prod** - SDSC 1984

Nutrition and Behavior - Delinquency, Criminality, Alcohol, Drugs 28 MIN
U-matic
Nutrition and Behavior Series
Color (J C)
Deals with The Cambridge and other studies - diet and malbehavior and learning disabilities and their relationship to delinquency. Dr Rimland talks about the dyslogic syndrome, impulse control, alcohol and heroin and the impact of nutrition on the treatment of substances abuse. The future of treatment for addiction is also discussed.
Health and Safety; Psychology; Social Science; Sociology
Dist - SDSC **Prod** - SDSC 1984

Nutrition and Behavior - Marital Problems , Fatigue, Depression 30 MIN
U-matic
Nutrition and Behavior Series
Color (J C)
Explains that faulty nutrition is at the root of many problems. He discusses irritability, impatience in relation to blood sugar levels, suicide, insomnia and sexual inadequacies. Dr. Rimland offers suggestions for correcting deficiencies, imbalances and intolerances. Sources for additional information are also presented.
Health and Safety; Psychology; Social Science; Sociology
Dist - SDSC **Prod** - SDSC 1984

Nutrition and Behavior - Megavitamin Treatment of Autistic Children 29 MIN
U-matic
Nutrition and Behavior Series
Color (J C)
Discusses studies with autistic children - the unexpected origins and the outcome. Dr Rimland presents information on other studies, one in conjunction with the University of California, one in France, and reports from other countries. The role of minerals is discussed and the current status of this approach to the treatment of autism is presented.
Health and Safety; Psychology; Social Science; Sociology
Dist - SDSC **Prod** - SDSC 1984

Nutrition and Behavior - Nutritional and Traditional Approaches Compared 30 MIN
U-matic
Nutritional and Behavior Series
Color (J C)
Compares the conventional practices of drug prescription in psychotherapy, counseling and psychoanalysis with the orthomolecular concept for treatment of mental and behavioral disorders. Dr Rimland presents the toximolecular concept and compares drugs versus nutrients and deficiencies versus dependencies. The future of these types of treatments is also covered.
Health and Safety; Psychology; Social Science; Sociology
Dist - SDSC **Prod** - SDSC 1984

Nutrition and Behavior - Nutritional Treatment of Retarded, Learning Disabled, and Hyperactive Children 30 MIN
U-matic
Nutrition and Behavior Series
Color (J C)
Provides new research on the reversibility of retardation - the safety of vitamins for children - learning disabilities reversed and rereversed - and diet and hyperactivity. Dr Rimland stresses encouraging no 'junk food' diets for children.
Health and Safety; Psychology; Social Science; Sociology
Dist - SDSC **Prod** - SDSC 1984

Nutrition and Behavior Series
Nutrition and Behavior - Basic Concepts and Principles 28 MIN
Nutrition and Behavior - Brain Allergies and Behavior
Nutrition and Behavior - Delinquency, Criminality, Alcohol, Drugs 28 MIN
Nutrition and Behavior - Marital Problems, Fatigue, Depression 30 MIN
Nutrition and Behavior - Megavitamin Treatment of Autistic Children 29 MIN
Nutrition and Behavior - Nutritional Treatment of Retarded, Learning Disabled, and Hyperactive Children 30 MIN
Nutrition and Behavior - Vitamins in the Treatment of Schizophrenia 29 MIN
Dist - SDSC

Nutrition and Behavior - Vitamins in the Treatment of Schizophrenia 29 MIN
U-matic
Nutrition and Behavior Series
Color (J C)
Introduces the particulars of the controversy with the psychiatric establishment over megavitamin therapy, and the alternative approaches to conventional treatment. He also discusses tardive dyskinesia and suggest methods beyond megavitamin therapy. Source for supplemental information are provided.
Health and Safety; Psychology; Social Science; Sociology
Dist - SDSC **Prod** - SDSC 1984

Nutrition and Body Composition 30 MIN
U-matic / VHS
Bodyworks Series
Color
Discusses nutrition and body composition as it pertains to physical fitness.
Health and Safety; Physical Education and Recreation
Dist - MDCPB **Prod** - KTXTTV

Nutrition and cancer 11 MIN
VHS
Color (C PRO G)
$250.00 purchase
Shows patients how to make good nutrition an effective component of any successful cancer treatment.
Health and Safety; Social Science
Dist - LPRO **Prod** - LPRO

Nutrition and Cancer - a Guide for the Nurse 16 MIN
VHS / 16mm
Cancer Education Series - for Nurses
(C)
$385.00 purchase _ #850VJ003
Teaches nurses to correctly perform a nutritional assessment of a cancer patient. Explains methods of administering nutritional supplements.
Health and Safety
Dist - HSCIC **Prod** - HSCIC 1985

Nutrition and Dental Health 12 MIN
16mm / U-matic / VHS
Color (J)
LC 81-701106
Shows how proper dental care and good nutrition aids in preventing the formation of plaque which attacks teeth and causes cavities.
Health and Safety
Dist - PRORE **Prod** - PRORE 1981

Nutrition and dietetics laboratory series
Anthropometry - body measurement - height, weight, circumference - Pt 1 14 MIN
Anthropometry - skinfold measurement - Pt 2 10 MIN
Bomb calorimetry 25 MIN
Resting Metabolic Heart Rate 17 MIN
Dist - IOWA

Nutrition and exercise 50 MIN
VHS
Healing arts series
Color; PAL (G F)
PdS99 purchase
Explains the need for a healthy diet to combat illness. Presents ideas and methods of nutrition and exercise to maintain a healthy lifestyle. Part nine of a nine - part series.
Physical Education and Recreation; Social Science
Dist - BBCENE

Nutrition and exercise for the '90s 36 MIN
VHS
Color (J H C)
$199.00 purchase _ #2276 - SK
Covers nutrition and exercise as key building blocks for good health. Discusses the various nutrients and their importance in health, differentiating among the various types of proteins and fats. Relates food choices to physical activity. Includes teacher's guide.
Health and Safety; Physical Education and Recreation; Psychology; Social Science
Dist - SUNCOM **Prod** - SUNCOM

Nutrition and Fitness in Pregnancy
U-matic / VHS
Color (ARABIC SPANISH FRENCH)
Stresses the necessity of good nutrition for mother and baby alike. Discusses the need for sensible, physical activity.
Foreign Language; Health and Safety; Home Economics; Physical Education and Recreation
Dist - MIFE **Prod** - MIFE

Nutrition and Fitness - Interfacing for Health Throughout the Lifecycle 120 MIN
U-matic / VHS
Color
Explores the integration of nutrition and fitness in childhood, pregnancy, young adulthood, middle age and the vintage years. Addresses application of sound nutrition principles. Focuses on the natural interrelationships of nutrition and exercise in promoting health.
Health and Safety; Social Science
Dist - ADA **Prod** - ADA

Nutrition and Fitness - Intervening in Risk Factor Determination and Disease 120 MIN
U-matic / VHS
Color
Discusses the combined impact of nutrition and exercise on hypertension, obesity, diabetes and coronary heart disease. Demonstrates health evaluation through body fat determination, laboratory analysis, exercise tolerance and stress testing.
Health and Safety; Psychology; Social Science
Dist - ADA **Prod** - ADA

Nutrition and Health 145 MIN
U-matic
University of the Air Series
Color (J H C A)
$750.00 purchase, $250.00 rental
Introduces guidelines for healthful eating at different ages and different stages in life. Program contains a series of five cassettes 29 minutes each.
Health and Safety; Social Science; Sociology
Dist - CTV **Prod** - CTV 1977

Nutrition and Health Series
Introduction to Nutritional Assessment 19 MIN
Malnutrition - Diagnosis and Therapeutic Alternatives 40 MIN
Normal Nutrition - Body Composition 38 MIN
Nutrient Needs - Basic Methabolic Process 38 MIN
Nutrient Needs - Fatty Acids and Vitamins 64 MIN
Nutrient Needs - Protein and Calories 17 MIN
Nutrient Needs - Water and Minerals 50 MIN
Dist - HSCIC

Nutrition and HIV 20 MIN
VHS
Color (H C A)
$145.00 purchase
Promotes attention to diet for people who are HIV - positive. Explains how better nutrition fights infection and what nutrients are needed in the diet. Provides recipes and shopping ideas as well as counseling. For health care staff and for patient education. Created by North South films.
Health and Safety; Social Science
Dist - PFP

Nutrition and hydration - complex decisions 51 MIN
VHS / U-matic
Color (R C PRO)
$125.00 purchase, $25.00 rental _ #451, #450
Presents the real - life stories of three patients and their parents who are faced with the decision of whether to maintain or remove artificially administered nutrition and hydration from their children. Features four experts on Catholic theology who discuss the ethical, clinical and legal issues involved.
Health and Safety; Religion and Philosophy
Dist - CATHHA **Prod** - CATHHA 1990

Nutrition and its Place in the Wellness Program 29 MIN
VHS / U-matic
Color
Health and Safety; Psychology; Social Science
Dist - SYLWAT **Prod** - RCOMTV 1982

Nutrition and Metabolism 14 MIN
U-matic / VHS / 16mm
Human Body Series
Color (J H C)
$340, $250 purchase _ #1289
Shows the differences between basal and active metabolism and discusses the five classes of chemical substances in all natural foods.

Science - Natural
Dist - CORF

Nutrition - Comment Savez - Vous Quels Aliments Sont Bons 11 MIN
16mm
Health (French Series
Color (FRENCH)
LC 76-700142
A French language version of the motion picture Nutrition - How Do You Know What Foods Are Good. Explains that both the human body and a car need a source of energy to run, but that the human body needs nourishment even when at rest.
Foreign Language; Health and Safety; Social Science
Dist - MORLAT **Prod** - MORLAT 1974

Nutrition - diet therapy 30 MIN
16mm
Directions for education in nursing via technology series; Lesson
B&W (PRO)
LC 74-701856
Discusses modification of the normal diet in relation to consistency, caloric value and nutrients. Deals with variations of the bland diet.
Health and Safety; Social Science
Dist - WSUM **Prod** - DENT 1974

Nutrition - eat and be healthy 18 MIN
VHS
Color; CC (G C PRO)
$175.00 purchase _ #GN - 14
Uses the latest USDA food guide pyramid to explain the concepts of healthy eating. Offers practical advice and presents examples of how to add more grains, vegetables and fruits into the diet. Contact distributor for special purchase price on multiple orders.
Health and Safety; Home Economics; Social Science
Dist - MIFE **Prod** - MIFE 1995

Nutrition - Eating to Live or Living to Eat 29 MIN
VHS
Here's To Your Health Series
Color (G)
$59.95 purchase _ #HEAW - 514
Focuses on the role of nutrition in maintaining good health. Gives advice on making good food choices.
Health and Safety
Dist - PBS **Prod** - KERA

Nutrition - eating to live or living to eat 29 MIN
VHS
Color (J H C G T A PRO)
$59.95 purchase _ #AH45203
Shows how diet affects a person's health. Gives guidelines for making good food choices.
Health and Safety; Science - Natural
Dist - HTHED **Prod** - HTHED

Nutrition - Eating Well 25 MIN
U-matic / VHS
Color (I)
Shows a group of students trying to digest the latest information on a subject of importance to everyone, nutrition. Teaches that there is more than one path to good nutrition.
Health and Safety
Dist - NGS **Prod** - NGS

Nutrition education series

The Big dinner table	11 MIN
Food, energy and you	18 MIN
Food for a modern world	22 MIN
Food for life	22 MIN
How a hamburger turns into you	20 MIN
Vitamins from Food	20 MIN

Dist - PEREN

Nutrition - energy, carbohydrates, fats and proteins - Pt 1 29 MIN
16mm
Directions for education in nursing via technology series; Lesson 75
B&W (PRO)
LC 74-701852
Discusses the purposes of energy and factors which determine caloric content of food. Identifies factors affecting weight maintenance, gain or loss. Shows the merits of various types of reduction diets.
Health and Safety; Social Science
Dist - WSUM **Prod** - DENT 1974

Nutrition - energy, carbohydrates, fats and proteins - Pt 2 26 MIN
16mm
Directions for education in nursing via technology series; Lesson 76
B&W (PRO)
LC 74-701854
Identifies the three energy - producing nutrients. Discusses the function of each nutrient in detail and identifies major food sources for each nutrient.
Health and Safety; Social Science
Dist - WSUM **Prod** - DENT 1974

Nutrition, Fitness and Stress 30 MIN
U-matic / VHS
Zoolab Series
Color (J H)
$180.00 purchase
Presents the current ideas and techniques of nutrition and exercise for captive animals.
Science - Natural
Dist - AITECH **Prod** - WCETTV 1985

Nutrition, Food, Growth, and Development 29 MIN
U-matic / VHS
Focus on Children Series
Color (C A)
LC 81-707444
Presents a consultant to a state board of health discussing and illustrating the variable nutritional needs of children from the prenatal period to the teenage years.
Health and Safety; Home Economics; Psychology
Dist - IU **Prod** - IU 1981

Nutrition food labels - the inside story on what's inside 40 MIN
VHS
Color (A G H J)
$79.95 purchase
Educates viewers on reading nutritional labels. Outlines briefly the evolution of food labels and leads up to a detailed discussion of the Nutrition Labeling and Education Act. Explains what is meant by light, less fat, and more. Provides information on the Dietary Guidelines for Americans and the Food Guide Pyramid, and how they relate to food labels. Includes a workbook for students.
Home Economics; Social Science
Dist - CAMV

Nutrition - Foods, Fads, Frauds, Facts 36 MIN
U-matic / VHS
Color (I J H C)
$165.00 purchase _ #06740 - 161
Describes the physiology of hunger and appetite. Explains how eating habits develop early in life and are affected by stress. Discusses nutrition and gives guidelines for an intelligently planned diet.
Health and Safety; Psychology
Dist - GA **Prod** - GA

Nutrition for better health 14 MIN
VHS
Color (PRO A)
Helps patients understand some of the problems caused by the bad nutritional habits characteristic of many people's diets such as the use of too much salt, sugar, saturated fat and alcohol. Cautions patients against fad diets and excesses of vitamin and mineral supplements. Provides background information about the key nutritional elements - calories, proteins, vitamins and minerals. Emphasizes that the best way to get vitamins and minerals is through eating a balanced diet.
Social Science
Dist - MIFE **Prod** - MIFE
EBEC

Nutrition for building better babies 10 MIN
VHS
Color (J H C G)
$95.00 purchase _ #CG - 972 - VS
Uses a more traditional approach for providing information about proper nutrition during pregnancy. Emphasizes the rule of four - gaining four pounds per month, eating from the four basic food groups, choosing four servings from the food groups except for protein because three servings are enough. Includes a pamphlet and separate sheets detailing meal plans, helpful hints and precautions.
Health and Safety
Dist - HRMC **Prod** - HRMC 1993

Nutrition for Children Series Pt III

George Gorge and Nicky Persnicky	12 MIN

Dist - POAPLE

Nutrition for Children Series Pt II

The Nutrient Express	11 MIN

Dist - POAPLE

Nutrition for Children Series Pt I

Break the Fast	7 MIN

Dist - POAPLE

Nutrition for infants and children under 6 30 MIN
VHS
Color (J H C G)
$79.95 purchase _ #CCP0159V - P
Focuses on the nutritional needs of infants and children under six as defined by The Food Guide Pyramid for three stages of development - birth to 12 months; toddlers - 1 - 3 years; and preschool - age children.
Health and Safety; Home Economics; Social Science; Sociology
Dist - CAMV **Prod** - CAMV 1994

Nutrition for living 59 MIN
VHS / Videodisc
Color (G)
$159.00, $149.00 purchase, $75.00 rental _ #UW4653V, #4653
Covers a wide range of topics in the area of nutrition through the use of live - action video sequences and over 50 color charts and medical illustrations. Includes - how societies shape food habits; the food guide pyramid; the anatomy of the digestive tract; the movement of food through the stomach; the roles of the liver, pancreas and gall bladder; blood salts, water volume and thirst; childhood and adult obesity; eating disorders.
Home Economics; Science - Natural; Social Science
Dist - FOTH

Nutrition for persons with HIV infection 20 MIN
U-matic / VHS
Color (PRO C G)
$145.00 purchase _ #C911 - VI - 037
Provides information for the home healthcare worker who assists persons with HIV infection. Explains the importance of good nutrition, when concern for good nutrition should start and how good nutrition allows HIV - positive persons to exert some control over their health. Provides information for helping patients to cope with problems that interfere with eating and digestion. Outlines procedures for preventing food - borne infections and provides suggestions for the nutritional care of lactose - intolerant patients. Includes study and nutritional guide. Presented by Tanya Bridges and Joyce Church, University of Michigan.
Health and Safety; Social Science
Dist - HSCIC

Nutrition for Sports - Facts and Fallacies 20 MIN
16mm / U-matic / VHS
Color (J)
LC 81-700860
Offers a nutritional program for athletes, discussing protein, fats, carbohydrates and calories.
Health and Safety; Physical Education and Recreation; Social Science
Dist - HIGGIN **Prod** - HIGGIN 1982

Nutrition for the Low Birth Weight Infant 13 MIN
U-matic / VHS
Color (PRO)
Discusses nutritional considerations for non - stressed infants of more than 30 weeks' gestation weighing 1500 to 2500 grams at birth. Considers fluid, caloric, electrolyte and vitamin requirements as well as feeding schedules.
Health and Safety
Dist - UMICHM **Prod** - UMICHM 1983

Nutrition for the Newborn Series Pt II

Formula Feeding	15 MIN

Dist - POAPLE

Nutrition for the newborn series

Breast feeding	75 FRS
Supplemental foods	74 FRS

Dist - POAPLE

Nutrition for the Overweight
U-matic / VHS
Color (SPANISH)
Cautions the overweight dieter to be nutrition conscious in adapting a reducing diet. Stresses maximum nutrition with minimum calories.
Health and Safety
Dist - MIFE **Prod** - MIFE

Nutrition for Today's Woman 15 MIN
VHS / U-matic / 16mm
Color (G)
Outlines the basics of good nutrition with special attention to women's needs and concerns. Discussed are weight control, disease prevention, and the importance of calcium, iron and other nutrients, while practical ideas and suggestions for living healthier are provided.
Health and Safety
Dist - PRI **Prod** - PRI 1986

Nutrition for wellness 11 MIN
VHS / 16mm
Lifestyles for wellness series
Color (C A PRO)
Discusses the importance of good nutrition. Tells how to choose food in the four food groups in the proper quantities. Features a clinical nutritionist who give tips on food quality and developing new habits for wellness. Part two of a five-part series.
Health and Safety; Home Economics; Psychology; Social Science
Dist - AIMS **Prod** - SANDE 1987
AJN

Nutrition for Young People - You are what You Eat 85 MIN
U-matic / 35mm strip
Color (J H I C)

$229.00 purchase _ #06778 - 161
Answers questions about nutrition and diet. Provides a basic understanding of the relationship between health and diet. Emphasizes the need for good eating habits and a varied diet. Filmstrip is in six parts.
Health and Safety; Home Economics; Science - Natural; Social Science
Dist - GA **Prod** - GA

Nutrition - Fueling the Human Machine 18 MIN
U-matic / VHS / 16mm
Color (J H C)
LC 78-700914
Demonstrates how nutrition affects the condition of the human body. Emphasizes the importance of nutritional balance and variety and the need for exercise, and points out the possible dangers of food additives and sugar.
Health and Safety; Home Economics; Physical Education and Recreation; Social Science
Dist - PHENIX **Prod** - WINTNC 1978

The Nutrition gap 30 MIN
VHS / U-matic
Contemporary health issues series; Lesson 12
Color (C A)
Focuses on the food we eat. Depicts a 'typical' family eating 'typical' foods throughout the day. Examines the impact of these poor nutritional habits on one's health.
Health and Safety; Home Economics; Social Science
Dist - CDTEL **Prod** - SCCON

Nutrition - How do You Know what Foods are Good 11 MIN
16mm
Health Series
Color
LC 76-700142
Explains that both the human body and a car need a source of energy to run, but that the human body needs nourishment even when at rest.
Health and Safety; Social Science
Dist - MORLAT **Prod** - MORLAT 1974

Nutrition in action series
Presents a ten - part series preparing K - 6 educators to teach nutrition, each program covering a specific nutritional topic and demonstrating creative classroom activities for teaching the concepts. Includes self - help manual.

The Challenge of making food choices	30 MIN
Composition and safety of foods	30 MIN
Extending the nutrient environment	30 MIN
Food for fuel	30 MIN
Food habits	30 MIN
Guidelines for food selection	30 MIN
Minerals	30 MIN
Nutrition information and misinformation	30 MIN
Nutritional needs in childhood	30 MIN
Vitamins	30 MIN

Dist - PSU **Prod** - WPSXTV 1974

Nutrition in aging 50 MIN
VHS
Introductory principles of nutrition series
Color (C PRO G)
$70.00 purchase, $16.00 rental _ #40397
Discusses the physical and physiological factors influencing food choices and nutrient utilization by the elderly. Part of a 20 - part series on basic principles of nutrition, evaluation of dietary intake, nutritional status, nutrition through the life cycle and world food supplies.
Health and Safety; Social Science
Dist - PSU **Prod** - WPSXTV 1978

Nutrition in Black Americans 28 MIN
16mm
Color (P)
LC 74-702348
Points out the necessity of a well - balanced diet for Black Americans.
Health and Safety; History - United States; Social Science
Dist - LEECC **Prod** - LEECC 1974

Nutrition in infancy 50 MIN
VHS
Introductory principles of nutrition series
Color (C PRO G)
$70.00 purchase, $16.00 rental _ #50695
Compares human and cow milk. Discusses the introduction of solid foods, nutritional considerations during childhood, food likes and dislikes, and establishment of food habits. Part of a 20 - part series on basic principles of nutrition, evaluation of dietary intake, nutritional status, nutrition through the life cycle and world food supplies.
Health and Safety; Social Science
Dist - PSU **Prod** - WPSXTV 1977

Nutrition in pregnancy 60 MIN
VHS
Introductory principles of nutrition series
Color (C PRO G)
$70.00 purchase, $16.00 rental _ #60350
Discusses the physiological adjustments, stages of fetal growth, pergnancy during adolescence, physiological and psychological aspects of lactation and interviews with nutrition experts. Part of a 20 - part series on basic principles of nutrition, evaluation of dietary intake, nutritional status, nutrition through the life cycle and world food supplies.
Health and Safety; Social Science
Dist - PSU **Prod** - WPSXTV 1977

Nutrition in Pregnancy
U-matic / VHS
Care of the Pregnant Patient Series
Color (PRO)
Health and Safety; Science - Natural; Social Science
Dist - OMNIED **Prod** - OMNIED

Nutrition in Sports - Fueling a Winner 55 MIN
VHS
Color (G)
$69.95 purchase _ #CCP0008
Examines how body composition, the right diet and weight control play a major role in an athlete's performance. Includes a weight management program. Also available in Beta or 3/4".
Physical Education and Recreation
Dist - CADESF **Prod** - CADESF

Nutrition in the Injured Patient 15 MIN
16mm
Color
Discusses nutrition in the injured and post - operative patient. Compares the nutritional status of the starved individual and that of the post - operative patient. Shows that the surgical patient loses more protein than in simple starvation and that this protein loss cannot be prevented by calories alone.
Health and Safety; Social Science
Dist - EATONL **Prod** - EATONL 1973

Nutrition in the Later Years 24 MIN
U-matic / VHS / 16mm
Color (C A)
$450 purchase - 16 mm, $315 purchase - video
Talks about the nutritional requirements of older people. Directed by John McDonald.
Health and Safety; Psychology
Dist - CF

Nutrition in the Later Years 24 MIN
16mm / U-matic / VHS
Be Well - the Later Years Series
Color (C A)
LC 83-700398
Discusses the special nutritional requirements of older people, as well as the dangers and discomforts of too much or too little. Presents tips on how to change.
Health and Safety; Social Science; Sociology
Dist - CF **Prod** - CF 1983

Nutrition information and misinformation 30 MIN
VHS
Nutrition in action series
Color (C T)
$200.00 purchase, $20.50 rental _ #34735
Helps children to evaluate nutritional claims and become more discriminating shoppers. Part of a ten - part series preparing K - 6 educators to teach nutrition, each program covering a specific nutritional topic and demonstrating creative classroom activities for teaching the concepts. Includes self - help manual.
Education; Health and Safety; Home Economics; Social Science
Dist - PSU **Prod** - WPSXTV 1987

Nutrition is 26 MIN
16mm
Color
LC 76-702861
Summarizes the basic principles of nutrition and their relationship to good health.
Health and Safety; Social Science
Dist - WSTGLC **Prod** - SUGARI 1976

Nutrition - keep your balance 19 MIN
VHS
Color (P I)
$59.95 purchase _ #10190VG
Focuses on proper eating habits, nutrition, and the role food plays as a fuel for the human body. Presents a puppet play of Ralphie's class as they put together a presentation on balance in diet and the food pyramid. Includes a teacher's guide, discussion questions, student activities, and blackline masters.
Health and Safety; Home Economics; Social Science
Dist - UNL

Nutrition kit - eating sensibly in the 1990s
VHS / 35mm strip
Color (G A)
$79.00, $69.00 purchase _ #LS35V, #LS35F
Portrays the efforts of O D, a junk food junkie trying to adopt better nutrition habits. Explains various nutrition concepts, including density, calories, saturated fats, cholesterol, and the revised dietary guidelines for Americans. Includes six reproducible booklets covering the 'commandments' of good nutrition.
Health and Safety; Home Economics; Social Science
Dist - CAMV

Nutrition Labeling - Marilyn Stephenson, RD, MS 27 MIN
U-matic
Food and Nutrition Seminars for Health Professionals Series
Color (PRO)
LC 78-706163
Explores the background of nutrition labeling and its use on food products. Discusses how to use the labels of products to save money and provide a good diet.
Home Economics; Social Science
Dist - USNAC **Prod** - USFDA 1976

Nutrition labels - our guides to healthy eating 18 MIN
VHS
CC; Color (I J H G A)
$95 purchase _ #10334VG
Explains how to read food labels and interpret nutrition facts. Defines terms such as cholesterol, calories, sodium, carbohydrates, and dietary fiber. Relates U S Food and Drug Administration's Nutrition Facts label with the food pyramid. Includes a teacher's guide, activities, discussion questions, and blackline masters.
Health and Safety; Home Economics; Social Science
Dist - UNL

Nutrition - minerals and vitamins 31 MIN
16mm
Directions for education in nursing via technology series; Lesson 77
B&W (PRO)
LC 74-701855
Discusses major minerals and vitamins, their functions and food sources. Identifies recommended daily allowance for selected minerals and vitamins.
Health and Safety; Social Science
Dist - WSUM **Prod** - DENT 1974

Nutrition News 30 MIN
U-matic / VHS
CNN Special Reports Series
(G C J)
$129 purchase _ #31384 - 851
Informative vignettes cover how to shop smart and how to eat healthy.
Health and Safety
Dist - CHUMAN

Nutrition News 29 MIN
U-matic
Color
Shows nutrition editor Carol Williams and nutrition educator Ronald Deutsch commenting on current nutritional information. Explains how food consumers can be better informed. Demonstrates techniques used at Kroger stores to put nutritional knowledge to work.
Health and Safety; Social Science
Dist - MTP **Prod** - KROGER

Nutrition news 36 MIN
VHS
Color (H)
$139.00 purchase _ #31384 - 126
Discusses the relationship between calcium and high blood pressure. Looks at what's good to eat, what's not, sources of protein.
Health and Safety; Psychology; Social Science
Dist - GA **Prod** - TURNED

Nutrition - psychosocial and physiologic basis 30 MIN
16mm
Directions for education in nursing via technology series; Lesson 74
B&W (PRO)
LC 74-701851
Discusses psychosocial factors which influence an individual's pattern of eating. Identifies nutrients of an adequate diet and food sources of the essential nutrients.
Health and Safety; Social Science
Dist - WSUM **Prod** - DENT 1974

Nutrition Puppets 10 MIN
U-matic
Color (P I)
LC 81-707091
Presents nineteen thirty - second public service announcements concerning food, nutrition and eating habits. Features Grandma and Puddles, Super Broccoli and Junk Food Monster.
Health and Safety; Home Economics; Social Science
Dist - CORNRS **Prod** - CUETV 1979

Nutrition Related Problems 15 MIN
U-matic / VHS
Color
Discusses the characteristics and preventive feeding practices of nutrient related early postpartum problems of the cow. Identifies feeding practices in preventing certain diseases in calves and cows.
Agriculture
Dist - HOBAR **Prod** - HOBAR

Nutrition, Relaxation and Information - Your Keys to Successful Breastfeeding 19 MIN
U-matic / VHS
Color (SPANISH)
Reviews the nutrients important to breastfeeding, food sources and substitutes that provide protein and calcium. Includes the importance of fluid intake and the baby's sucking action.
Health and Safety; Home Economics; Social Science; Sociology
Dist - UARIZ **Prod** - UARIZ

Nutrition Resource Centers - the Information Connection
U-matic
Color
Examines the operations of five nutrition resource centers, comparing their similarities and differences while emphasizing the need for reliable sources of information.
Health and Safety; Social Science
Dist - RYERI **Prod** - RYERI

Nutrition Resources 30 MIN
VHS / U-matic
Food for Life Series
Color
Home Economics; Social Science
Dist - MSU **Prod** - MSU

Nutrition Series
Nutrition - the all American Meal 11 MIN
Nutrition - You are what You Eat 10 MIN
Dist - BARR

Nutrition Series
Basic nutrition - let's make a meal 17 MIN
Food preparation 15 MIN
Options for Life 12 MIN
Weight Control 13 MIN
Dist - JOU

Nutrition - some Food for Thought 16 MIN
16mm / U-matic / VHS
Color (I J)
LC 81-701473
Deals with proper nutrition by examining the various categories of nutrients, offering examples of types of food which supply them and explaining the importance of each. Stresses the need for a balanced diet.
Health and Safety; Science - Natural; Social Science
Dist - CORF **Prod** - CENTRO 1981

Nutrition Survey - Kingdom of Thailand 36 MIN
16mm
Color
LC FIE65-65
Depicts the work of scientists in a nutritional survey of Thailand and relates their findings. Represents the daily activities of clinicians, dentists, biochemists, nutritionists and food technologists. Presents important findings about anemia, endemic goiter, riboflavin and thiamaine malnutrition, and dental disease.
Geography - World; Health and Safety
Dist - USNAC **Prod** - WRAIR 1962

Nutrition Survey - Republic of Lebanon 15 MIN
16mm
Color
Presents a nationwide survey of nutrition conducted in Lebanon. Shows exactly how the survey was conducted. Explains that goiter and mouth lesions were widely prevalent due to lack of iodine and B vitamins.
Geography - World; Social Science
Dist - NMAC **Prod** - USPHS 1963

Nutrition - Teen Pregnancy
VHS / Slide
$160.00 purchase _ #LC10 slides, $160.00 purchase _ #LC10V VHS
Emphasizes the need for proper care and nutrition for the pregnant teenager and her child. Points out the four basic food groups, the amount of food required to fulfill daily requirements, and the important functions of nutrients.
Health and Safety; Psychology; Social Science
Dist - CAREER **Prod** - CAREER

Nutrition - the all American Meal 11 MIN
VHS / U-matic / 16mm
Nutrition Series
Color (I J H C G)
$240, $170, $200 purchase _ #B198; LC 76-701632
Points out that there is more to food than just eating. Combines interviews on the street and sequences at a fast food emporium with an analysis of the nutritional and sociological implications of the hamburger, fries and soft drink American diet. Offers suggestions for improving the nutritional value of meals.
Health and Safety; Social Science
Dist - BARR **Prod** - BARR 1976

Nutrition - the First Years 16 MIN
16mm / U-matic / VHS
Color (A)
Discusses basic information for mothers on child care and nutrition.
Health and Safety; Home Economics; Psychology; Social Science
Dist - USNAC **Prod** - USNAC 1980

Nutrition - the Inner Environment 15 MIN
U-matic / VHS / 16mm
Color (P I J) (SPANISH)
LC 73-700969
Explores from the earliest time to the present what men have eaten, why and what it has done to their bodies. Shows what we must eat and how we can improve our health by eating properly.
Health and Safety; Social Science
Dist - AMEDFL **Prod** - AMEDFL 1972

Nutrition - the Spice of Life 8 MIN
16mm
Discovery Series
Color
Offers an overview of nutritional research studies in a university environment. Discusses the effect of diet on human behavior, improving intravenous feeding and the development of new foods from existing Canadian crops.
Health and Safety; Social Science
Dist - UTORMC **Prod** - UTORMC

Nutrition to Grow on 28 MIN
VHS / 16mm
Color (I)
$475.00, $185.00 purchase, $50.00 rental _ #8142; LC 90705074
Convinces preteens and teens that snacking, skipped meals and dangerous dieting are serious matters. Encourages regular balanced meals.
Psychology; Social Science; Sociology
Dist - AIMS **Prod** - HRMC 1989

Nutrition Trio's Fantastic Voyage through Your Body 30 MIN
VHS / 16mm
Science, Health and Math Series
Color (P)
$39.95 purchase _ #CL7907
Introduces basic concepts concerning the digestive system.
Health and Safety; Psychology; Social Science
Dist - EDUCRT

Nutrition - Try it, You Might Like it 30 MIN
U-matic
Dimensions of Child Development Series
Color (PRO)
Reinforces the interrelationship of nutrition with other areas of child development and provides a variety of teaching strategies for integrating the topic.
Education
Dist - ACCESS **Prod** - ACCESS 1983

Nutrition - Try it, You'll Like it 11 MIN
U-matic / VHS / 16mm
Color (P I) (SPANISH)
Points out that there really is a difference between good, nutritious food and junk food. Introduces the concept of the four food groups.
Health and Safety; Social Science
Dist - AIMS **Prod** - AIMS 1981

Nutrition - Two Differing Perspectives 30 MIN
U-matic / VHS
Dancer's Health Series
Color
Fine Arts; Social Science
Dist - ARCVID **Prod** - ARCVID

Nutrition - Vitamin Wise 19 MIN
16mm / U-matic / VHS
Color (H C A)
Explains what vitamins are, how the body uses them, and which foods have which vitamins. Provides tips on choosing a balanced diet and preserving the vitamins in preparing and cooking food. Emphasizes the importance of vitamins and points out that supplements probably aren't necessary for people who follow the guidelines presented.
Health and Safety; Social Science
Dist - AIMS **Prod** - AIMS 1981

Nutrition - What's in it for Me 26 MIN
16mm / U-matic / VHS
Color (J)
LC 76-701189
Follows high school students through their day, recording their eating habits and feelings about food. Discusses with doctors and nutritionists the factors that affect our physical and emotional well - being when we eat.
Guidance and Counseling; Health and Safety; Psychology; Social Science
Dist - CNEMAG **Prod** - HOBLEI 1976

Nutrition - you and baby too 6 MIN
VHS
Color (J H C G)
$89.00 purchase _ #CG - 971 - VS
Uses rap music to present vital information pregnant women need to know about proper nutrition during pregnancy, recommended weight gain and the importance of avoiding drugs, alcohol and tobacco.
Health and Safety
Dist - HRMC **Prod** - HRMC 1993

Nutrition - You are what You Eat 10 MIN
VHS / U-matic / 16mm
Nutrition Series
Color (P I K)
$220, $155, $185 purchase _ #B199; LC 76-701634;
Uses animated sequences to explain the importance of choosing foods from all of the basic food groups. Provides information on how proteins, carbohydrates, fats, vitamins, and minerals are used in our bodies. Discusses how digestion changes the food we eat so our bodies can use the nutrients and how exercise and rest are needed to help us grow strong and healthy.
Health and Safety; Physical Education and Recreation; Science - Natural; Social Science
Dist - BARR **Prod** - BARR 1976

The Nutritional Advocate 28 MIN
U-matic / VHS
Color (C)
$249.00, $149.00 purchase _ #AD - 1510
Discusses the relationship between diet and health. Features consumer advocate Ellen Hass and biochemist Paul Stitt. Examines their efforts to get the government, farmers, food manufacturers and grocers to promote and support nutrition. Adapts a Phil Donahue show.
Health and Safety; Psychology; Social Science
Dist - FOTH **Prod** - FOTH

Nutritional and Behavior Series
Nutrition and Behavior - Nutritional and Traditional Approaches Compared 30 MIN
Dist - SDSC

Nutritional Anemia, Pt 2 - Megaloblastic Anemia 32 MIN
16mm
Color (PRO)
Uses clinical samples and case studies in order to show the effects of anemia due to vitamin B12 and folic acid deficiencies. Presented by Dr William B Castle.
Science - Natural; Social Science
Dist - WSUM **Prod** - FLEMRP 1975

Nutritional Aspects of Breastfeeding 15 MIN
VHS
Color (G PRO)
$195.00 purchase _ #N900VI044
Serves as a guide to infant nutrition for the breastfeeding mother. Describes the stages of breast milk production and the benefits of breastfeeding to both mother and child. Outlines the caloric needs of and selection of foods for the breastfeeding mother, as well as common factors affecting milk production, and techniques for storing and freezing breast milk.
Health and Safety; Home Economics; Psychology; Social Science; Sociology
Dist - HSCIC

Nutritional Assessment and Therapy in Cancer 30 MIN
U-matic / VHS
Color
Brings out the recent developments in nutritional assessment and the role of nutrition in the cancer patient.
Health and Safety
Dist - ROWLAB **Prod** - ROWLAB

Nutritional assessment in primary care 28 MIN
VHS / U-matic
Color (PRO C)
$395.00 purchase, $80.00 rental _ #C850 - VI - 124
Introduces procedures to use during the routine physical examination to assess the patient's nutritional status. Uses three simulated patient interviews to demonstrate how nutritional care should vary according to the patient's needs. Shows how the physician counsels the patient with a normal diet, the patient with an elevated cholesterol level and the obese patient. Presented by Dale Rasman and Drs David Sheridan and Jane Barclay Mandel.

Health and Safety; Social Science
Dist - HSCIC

Nutritional assessment of the elderly 28 MIN
VHS
Color (C PRO)
$285.00 purchase, $70.00 rental _ #8661S, #8661V
Discusses the effects of human aging as it relates to standard measurement of nutritional assessment. Enables early identification of the need for nutritional intervention by the health care provider. Stresses the importance of a thorough history and consistent evaluation. Discusses normal physiological aging, socioeconomic status, acute and chronic illness, genetics, accessibility of care, climate and individual nutrition habits. Describes major changes in aging and demonstrates evaluation measures such as anthropometric methods, biochemical measures, hematologic measures, immune function evaluation, oral examination, polypharmacy evaluation, psychosocial factors and functional status related to activities of daily living.
Health and Safety; Social Science
Dist - AJN **Prod** - HOSSN

Nutritional Management of High - Risk Pregnancy 22 MIN
VHS / U-matic
Color
Demonstrates the effectiveness of a team approach to counseling in which doctor, nurse, nutritionist, and the pregnant patient herself are all actively involved.
Health and Safety
Dist - SNUTRE **Prod** - SNUTRE

Nutritional Misinformation and Food Faddism 120 MIN
VHS / U-matic
Color
Examines the increasing prevalence of nutrition cults, fads and fallacies commonly promoted in the popular media and health marketplace. Discusses terms such as `health foods,' `natural,' `organic,' `megavitamins,' hair analysis and fad diets.
Health and Safety; Psychology; Social Science
Dist - ADA **Prod** - ADA

Nutritional needs in childhood 30 MIN
VHS
Nutrition in action series
Color (C T)
$200.00 purchase, $20.50 rental _ #34728
Overviews six essential nutritients. Discusses their relationship to nutritional needs during childhood. Part of a ten - part series preparing K - 6 educators to teach nutrition, each program covering a specific nutritional topic and demonstrating creative classroom activities for teaching the concepts. Includes self - help manual.
Education; Health and Safety; Social Science
Dist - PSU **Prod** - WPSXTV 1987

Nutritional Needs in Growing Up 30 MIN
U-matic / VHS
Food for Life Series
Color
Home Economics; Social Science
Dist - MSU **Prod** - MSU

Nutritional Needs of Older Folks 30 MIN
U-matic / VHS
Food for Life Series
Color
Health and Safety; Home Economics; Social Science
Dist - MSU **Prod** - MSU

Nutritional Quackery 20 MIN
16mm / U-matic / VHS
Color (H C A)
LC 74-713040
Counteracts the conflicting claims of food faddists and emphasizes a balanced or varied diet as the key to health. Exposes false food fads, explodes the false facts, or myths, on which they thrive and explains sound, simple principles of nutrition.
Health and Safety; Home Economics
Dist - AIMS **Prod** - ASSOCF 1967

Nutritional Therapy of the Lung Cancer Patient 24 MIN
U-matic
Color
Describes how to recognize nutritional depletion in patients with lung cancer and suggests ways of improving nutrition.
Health and Safety
Dist - UTEXSC **Prod** - UTEXSC

Nutritional Therapy - some New Perspectives 43 MIN
16mm
Color (PRO)
LC 72-707713
Reports on current aspects in four different areas of nutritional therapy - - malnutrition due to chronic illness, obesity, conditions requiring surgical treatment and alcoholism. Follows patients through therapy and shows the results of diets geared to their nutritional needs.
Health and Safety
Dist - SQUIBB **Prod** - SQUIBB 1967

Nutritious Snacks and Fast Foods 15 MIN
16mm / U-matic / VHS
Color (P I)
LC 81-700079
Shows that snacks don't have to be junk food. Demonstrates how to create healthy snacks that fulfill all the nutritional needs of the four food groups.
Health and Safety; Social Science
Dist - PHENIX **Prod** - PHENIX 1981

The Nuts and Bolts of Nutrition - Basic Nutrition
VHS
$79.00 purchase _ #FY600V
Uses animated characters to teach basic nutrition. Describes the five primary nutrients.
Health and Safety; Home Economics; Social Science
Dist - CAREER **Prod** - CAREER

The Nuts and Bolts of Performance Appraisal 32 MIN
U-matic / VHS
Color (SPANISH)
Focuses on increased productivity through the use of employee evaluations. Emphasizes step - by - step procedure for effective performance appraisal.
Business and Economics; Foreign Language; Psychology
Dist - CREMED **Prod** - CREMED

Nuts to You 8 MIN
16mm
Mathematics for Elementary School Students - Whole Numbers Series
Color (P)
LC 73-701846
Mathematics
Dist - DAVFMS **Prod** - DAVFMS 1974

NY law 52 MIN
VHS
Color (H C G)
$445.00 purchase, $75.00 rental
Overviews the judicial system of the United States by following a group of idealistic minority law students from England who spend a summer as interns in New York City. Shows prosecutors, defense attorneys and judges, many black, in an everyday struggle for justice. Features Judge Bruce Wright who makes biting pronouncements on white justice. Produced by Dick Fontaine.
Civics and Political Systems; History - United States; Sociology
Dist - FLMLIB

NY - NJ USA 17 MIN
U-matic
Color (A)
Presents the wide variety of unusual tourist attractions in New York and New Jersey. Narrated by actor Eli Wallach.
Geography - United States
Dist - MTP **Prod** - PANYNJ 1983

Nyamakuta - the one who receives - an African midwife 32 MIN
VHS
Color (H C G)
$295.00 purchase, $55.00 rental
Focuses on Mai Mafuta, a nyamakuta - traditional midwife - in Zimbabwe. Reveals that half the births in the world are attended by women like her without the help of modern medicine. People seek out Mai Mafuta because she is skillful, compassionate, and because her grandmother was a midwife. However, five years ago Mafuta's skills were inadequate to save her own daughter's life and the daughter died in childbirth. In order to prevent such deaths over 80 countries are training traditional midwives in modern medical methods and Mafuta has enrolled in one such program. Observes Mafuta delivering a baby on the dirt floor of a hut. Produced by Chris Sheppard. Mai Mafuta narrates.
Geography - World; Health and Safety
Dist - FLMLIB

Nyaya Panchayat 16 MIN
16mm
B&W (I)
Shows how under the new dispensation of the Panchayati Raj, people in the rural areas of India are able to get justice at a quicker pace and lower cost. Explains that judicial wings attached to village panchayats are welcome substitutes to law courts in remote areas.
Civics and Political Systems
Dist - NEDINF **Prod** - INDIA

NYC, nightfall, framed, PPII, Turner
16mm
Color; B&W (G A)
$40.00 rental
Presents the work of filmmaker M M Serra. Offers a set of five 1 - 2 minute films created over a five - year period. 'NYC' features shots of New York at night set to pop music. 'Nightfall' watches a flashlight flicker across a fence and grass while text in French from Sartre's 'The Words' is narrated.
Fine Arts; Industrial and Technical Education
Dist - PARART **Prod** - FMCOOP 1988

Nyiregyhazi - Return of the Prodigy 33 MIN
U-matic / 16mm
Prime Time Series
Color; Mono (J H C A)
$400.00 film, $350.00 video, $50.00 rental
Relates the history of Erwin Nyiregyhazi who was considered by many to be the only contemporary composer and pianist of the stature of the long dead giants such as Mozart. It traces his life in detail up until his 'rediscovery' at the age of 70.
Fine Arts
Dist - CTV **Prod** - CTV 1978

Nymphing with Gary Borger 30 MIN
VHS / BETA
From the Sportsman's Video Collection Series
Color
Shows the best techniques for catching trout subsurface where they do 90 percent of their feeding.
Physical Education and Recreation
Dist - CBSC **Prod** - CBSC

Nyoka and the tigerman - perils of Nyoka 270 MIN
35mm
Republic cliffhanger serials series
B&W (G)
Features the heroine up against the exotic ruler Vultura and her gorilla, Satan. Offers 15 episodes, 18 minutes each. Contact distributor for rental price.
Fine Arts; Sociology
Dist - KITPAR **Prod** - REP 1942

Nzinga Asele - 2 - 18 - 84 33 MIN
VHS / Cassette
Poetry Center reading series
Color (G)
$15.00 purchase, rental _ #576 - 486
Features African - American Asele Nzinga - Gwen Campbell - reading her works at the Poetry Center, San Francisco State University.
Literature and Drama
Dist - POETRY **Prod** - POETRY 1984

Nzuri - East Africa 32 MIN
U-matic / VHS / 16mm
Color (J H C)
LC 70-706071
Visualizes the Biblical creation of the earth and follows man from ancient times to the modern city of Nairobi, Kenya. Shows the people, animals, rivers and cities to convey the mood of East Africa.
Geography - World; History - United States; History - World
Dist - PFP **Prod** - TWA 1970

O

O 12 MIN
16mm
Color (G)
$15.00 rental
Refers to the center point in the picture frame around which people and objects revolve. Divides into two parts - figure dominates ground and ground dominates figure. Much of the film is improvised and double exposed in the camera.
Fine Arts
Dist - CANCIN **Prod** - PALAZT

O Brave new world - science in the Renaissance 19 MIN
VHS
Soul of science series
Color; CC (H C)
$79.00 purchase _ #184
Meets giants of science such as Copernicus and Galileo - persecuted by the Church for their scientific inquiry - and Newton. Shows how scientists in the Arab world saved the science of ancient Greece during the Dark Ages of religious persecution of scientific inquiry, passing it on to the Europe of the Middle Ages and helped to bring about the European Renaissance and the scientific revolution of today. Part two of a four - part series on the history of science. Includes a book of the same title from the Learning Power series.
History - World; Science
Dist - HAWHIL **Prod** - HAWHIL 1994

O Canada 4 MIN
16mm
Color
LC 72-712458
Presents a kinestatic history of Canada from the arrival of the French to the present. Without narration.
Geography - World; History - World
Dist - VIEWFI **Prod** - SWGMNM 1971

O Canada - an introduction to Canadian government and politics 30 MIN
VHS
Remaking of Canada - Canadian government and politics in the 1990s 'series
Color (H C G)
$89.95 purchase _ #WLU - 501
Discusses what is unique to government and politics in Canada and why the failure of the Meech Lake Accord in June, 1990, was a significant turning point for Canadian government and politics. Considers the reformation of government and politics after the Meech Lake failure. Part of a 12 - part series incorporating interviews with Canadian politicians and hosted by Dr John Redekop.
Civics and Political Systems; History - World
Dist - INSTRU **Prod** - TELCOL 1992

O Captain, My Captain 12 MIN
U-matic / VHS / 16mm
Reading Poetry Series
Color (I J H)
LC 70-713280
Presents a reading of Walt Whitman's poem O Captain, My Captain in three sections that lend mood, feeling and tempo to the work. Shows a sailing ship in the first section, the words of the poem superimposed over visuals of Lincoln and Civil War scenes in the second section and scenes superimposed over pictures of national heroes in the third section.
Literature and Drama
Dist - AIMS **Prod** - EVANSA 1971

O - Circle - 2 20 MIN
16mm
Color (G)
$20.00 rental
Experiments with a two - dimensional square figure. Adds color and time using the sun directly for light and 16mm film on a core to form the image. The projected result is a fiery pulsing light that enters the screen from opposing sides. A Mark McGowan film.
Fine Arts
Dist - CANCIN

O Dear - a History of Woman Suffrage in Ohio 39 MIN
U-matic / 16mm
Color
Describes the personalities, places and politics of women's suffrage in Ohio.
Civics and Political Systems; History - United States; Sociology
Dist - HRC **Prod** - OHC

O Dreamland 14 MIN
16mm
B&W (H C A)
Lindsay Anderson comments on modern popular culture as seen at a British amusement park.
Physical Education and Recreation; Social Science; Sociology
Dist - GROVE **Prod** - GROVE

O Henry's Jimmy Valentine 55 MIN
16mm / VHS / U-matic
Color (J)
Features story of a former safecracker turned straight, who must reveal his background as a result of rescuing a young boy locked in a vault. Edited version.
Fine Arts; Guidance and Counseling; Health and Safety; Sociology
Dist - LCOA **Prod** - LCOA 1985

O is for Old People 6 MIN
VHS / U-matic
ABC's of Canadian Family Life Series
Color (H C)
Asks why so many Canadian old people are confined to institutions, why mental disorders are the main reason for their hospital stays, why two out of three widows live in poverty and how the younger population can be more responsive to the needs of old people.
History - World; Sociology
Dist - UTORMC **Prod** - UTORMC 1978

O is for Our Old People 6 MIN
16mm
ABC's of Canadian Life Series
Color
Asks why so many elderly Canadians are confined to institutions, why mental disorders are the main reason for their hospital stays, why two out of three widows live in poverty and how Canadians can be more responsive to the needs of their elderly.
Geography - World; Sociology
Dist - UTORMC **Prod** - UTORMC

O J Simpson - Juice on the Loose 47 MIN
16mm
Color
Offers insight into the career of football player O J Simpson. Includes interviews with Howard Cosell, Lou Saban and John McKay.
Biography; Physical Education and Recreation
Dist - COUNFI **Prod** - COUNFI 1974

O M Ungers 58 MIN
16mm / VHS
Color (H C)
$875.00, $290.00 purchase, $110.00 rental
Features the German architect, O M Ungers.
Biography; Fine Arts
Dist - BLACKW **Prod** - BLACKW 1986

O no Coronado 40 MIN
VHS / 16mm
Color (G)
$80.00 rental, $30.00 purchase
Reconstructs the 1540 Spanish invasion of the Pueblo Indian lands now known as the American Southwest. Uses a multifarious, mixed - tense montage. Live - action vignettes are densely woven into wildly diverse found footage, video - to - film FX, and a time - warped musical mix. Produced by Craig Baldwin.
Fine Arts; History - United States
Dist - CANCIN

O Panama 28 MIN
16mm
Color (G)
Presents an independent production by James Benning. Offers Willem Defoe as a sick man dealing with the world around him.
Fine Arts
Dist - FIRS

O Say Can You Sing 60 MIN
Videoreel / VT2
Synergism - Command Performance Series
Color
Explores the allegations that the Star Spangled Banner is unsingable. Offers suggested substitutes played by the Marine Corps Band, contrasted with anthems from other countries.
Fine Arts
Dist - PBS **Prod** - WETATV

O T O - a Classroom Community 29 MIN
16mm / U-matic / VHS
Dealing with Classroom Problems Series
Color (T)
Introduces the Opportunities To Teach Ourselves program, which is an integrated learning experience at Andrew Warde High School in Fairchild, Connecticut. Visits with OTO teachers and students, whose real - life experiences are an integral part of their learning climate.
Education
Dist - FI **Prod** - MFFD 1976

O that We were There 26 MIN
U-matic / VHS / 16mm
Color (J)
LC 81-700921
Shows the Madrigal Singers of Saint Louis and their unusual performances of Renaissance music which include songs in English, Italian, Spanish and French. Offers an integrated study of the fine arts during the Renaissance through performances featuring authentic songs, dances, musical instruments and period costumes.
Fine Arts; History - World
Dist - PHENIX **Prod** - PHENIX 1979

O Youth and Beauty 59 MIN
16mm / U-matic / VHS
Cheever Short Stories Series
Color (A)
LC 81-701549
Dramatizes the story of a man whose obsession to stay young eventually leads to his untimely death. Based on the story O Youth And Beauty by John Cheever.
Fine Arts; Literature and Drama
Dist - FI **Prod** - WNETTV 1981

Oahu, Hawaii
VHS
Color (G)
$29.95 purchase _ #0844
Visits the island of Oahu in Hawaii. Drives in a rainforest of fragrant eucalyptus trees to the Upside - Down Falls. Tours from Makai to Mauka.
Geography - United States; Geography - World; Science - Natural
Dist - SEVVID

The Oak 12 MIN
16mm / U-matic / VHS
Many Worlds of Nature Series
Color (I)
Studies the characteristics of the oak, which provides shelter and food for more wild animals than any other wild plant in North America.
Science - Natural
Dist - CORF **Prod** - SCRESC

Oak Ridge National Laboratory and its Scientific Activities 17 MIN
16mm
Color
LC FIE67-92
Surveys the numerous and varied activities and facilities at the Atomic Energy Commission's Oak Ridge National Laboratory, including activities involving nuclear research, fundamental and applied research in all fields of science and research on the central technical problems of society.
Science; Science - Physical
Dist - USNAC **Prod** - ORNLAB 1967

Oak Ridge Research Reactor 20 MIN
16mm
Color
LC FIE63-172
Describes the components, facilities, uses and operation of the Oak Ridge research reactor, a tank - type, heterogenous reactor, immersed in a pool, designed to operate at 20 to 30 MW.
Science; Science - Physical
Dist - USNAC **Prod** - USNRC 1958

Oak Street chronicles and the good news series
The Beginning, the wrong choice, the telescope, going home - Tape 1
The Birthday, the race, the spooky story - Tape 2
Mr Wolenski, the treasure, the rescue - Tape 3
Dist - APH

Oak Valley, USA 16 MIN
U-matic / VHS / 16mm
Color (H)
LC 73-701737
Explores a typical native plant and animal community both before and after the arrival of man, showing how self - maintaining patterns of life have been changed with his arrival. Develops the theme that man's actions alter his environment, and emphasizes the importance of conservation. Reinforces interest in current efforts being made to improve environmental conditions.
Science - Natural
Dist - STANF **Prod** - STANF 1970

Oakleaf Project 28 MIN
16mm
B&W (C T S)
LC FIA68-2315
Documents individual - centered instruction at Baldwin school district's Oakleaf Elementary School. Follows one child in the project.
Education
Dist - MATHWW **Prod** - UPITTS 1968

Oaksie 22 MIN
16mm
Color (H A)
LC 80-700305
Shows Oaksie Caudill playing the fiddle and making anooak baskets while he talks about his family and life on Cowan Creek in Letcher County, Kentucky.
Biography
Dist - APPAL **Prod** - APPAL 1980

Oasis 15 MIN
16mm
B&W
Presents a humorous look at student life, showing a 'TYPICAL' student reviewing his experiences. Portrays a 'SURE FIRE' study system that was more system than study, how a friend helped him register for classes, and how he fell in love when his car broke down in a snowstorm.
Education; Guidance and Counseling; Sociology
Dist - UPENN **Prod** - UPENN 1963

Oasis in the Desert 5 MIN
16mm
B&W
LC 76-701347
Takes a look at the work of Sister Malinda Thorne and her efforts to relieve some of the loneliness and despair experienced by those living in Vancouver's Skid Row.
Health and Safety; Sociology
Dist - SFRASU **Prod** - SFRASU 1973

Oasis in the Sahara 16 MIN
U-matic / VHS / 16mm
Man and His World Series
Color (P I J H C)
LC 71-705487
Shows the variety of geography and the varying natural forces in the Sahara which produce the Saharan climate and weather. Describes the way of life of the inhabitants of this region.
Geography - World; Social Science
Dist - FI **Prod** - FI 1969

Oasis of the Sahara 8 MIN
16mm / U-matic / VHS
Color (I J)

LC FIA66-1285
Describes the way of life of the people of the Sahara. Considers the importance of water in the hot, dry lands of the desert.
Geography - World; Social Science; Sociology
Dist - MGHT **Prod** - MGHT 1965

The Oath is Taken 8 MIN
16mm
Screen news digest series; Vol 7; Issue 7
B&W
Follows the events of President Johnson's inauguration day in 1965, emphasizing the inauguration's significance as a symbol of continuing U S democracy. Shows the actual ceremony, the inaugural address, the parade and the ball.
Civics and Political Systems; History - United States
Dist - HEARST **Prod** - HEARST 1965

OAU 28 MIN
Videoreel / VHS
International Byline Series
Color
Interviews Ambassador Omarou Youssoufou of the Organization of African United on the goals and main objectives of the international organization. Includes a film clip. Hosted by Marilyn Perry.
Business and Economics; Civics and Political Systems; Geography - World
Dist - PERRYM **Prod** - PERRYM

Oaxaca
VHS
Color (J H G) (SPANISH)
$44.95 purchase _ #MCV5007, #MCV5008
Presents a program on the history of Mexico.
History - World
Dist - MADERA **Prod** - MADERA

OB emergencies - babies at risk 20 MIN
VHS
Color (PRO C)
$285.00 purchase, $70.00 rental _ #4417
Offers the information obstetrical nurses need to spot the first signs of fetal distress, assess the situation, make a diagnosis and initiate the proper life - saving emergency response. Shows how continuous fetal heart rate monitoring, often used during labor, can differentiate between normal fetal heart rates and fetal stress and distress. Demonstrates fetal heart rates and their possible causes. Covers other biochemical and biophysical techniques that can help diagnose fetal distress. Prepares OB nurses to recognize a crisis and make on - the - spot decisions that can save the life of the baby.
Health and Safety
Dist - AJN **Prod** - AJN 1995

Obedience 45 MIN
16mm
B&W (C T)
LC 71-702990
Presents an experiment conducted during 1962 at Yale University on obedience to authority. Describes both obedient and defiant reactions of subjects who are instructed to administer electric shock of increasing severity to another person.
Psychology
Dist - NYU **Prod** - MILS 1965

Obedience 45 MIN
U-matic / VHS / 16mm
B&W (H C G T A)
Documents Stanley Milgram's classic research on obedience to authority, based on candid material filmed at Yale University. Subjects are told to administer electric shocks of increasing severity to others. Both obedient and defiant reactions are shown, and subjects explain their actions after the experiment.
Psychology; Science
Dist - PSU **Prod** - PSU 1969

Obelisks of ancient Egypt 50 MIN
VHS
Secrets of lost empires series
Color; PAL (G)
PdS99 purchase; Not available in the United States or Canada
Traces the efforts of engineers and historians as they test theories of the methods used by ancient Egyptians to erect 100 foot granite obelisks. Intermingles practical demonstrations and debates with location sequences from Egypt and explorations of the ancient Egyptian culture. Part four of a four - part series.
History - United States; History - World; Industrial and Technical Education
Dist - BBCENE

Oberbayern 15 MIN
U-matic / VHS / 16mm
Color (H C A) (GERMAN)
LC 70-700225
A German language film. Depicts life in northern Bavaria, showing views of the village church and the people of the town who take part in the passion play in Oberammergau. Includes scenes of other Bavarian towns, artisans at work, an Alpine lake and Linderhof.
Foreign Language
Dist - IFB **Prod** - IFB 1961

Obesity 29 MIN
VHS
Life Matters Series
Color (G)
$59.95 purchase _ #LIFM - 110
Describes the efforts of Joseph Benintende, a San Diego man who lost 170 pounds and saved his life as a result. Identifies useful strategies for weight loss. Explains the medical hazards of obesity.
Health and Safety
Dist - PBS **Prod** - KERA 1988

Obesity 58 MIN
U-matic
Color
Features Dr Lester B Salans, Associate Director of the National Institute of Arthritis, Metabolism and Digestive Disease, explaining energy metabolism. Discusses the effects of too much food and too little exercise on waistline and health.
Health and Safety
Dist - MTP **Prod** - NIH

Obesity 40 MIN
16mm
Boston Medical Reports Series
B&W (PRO)
LC 74-705229
Compares the function of caloric input and expenditures in normal man and in obesity.
Health and Safety; Science - Natural
Dist - NMAC **Prod** - NMAC 1966

Obesity and Energy Metabolism 60 MIN
VHS / U-matic
Medicine for the Layman Series
Color
LC 81-707589
Present Dr Lester Salans defining obesity from a biochemical point of view. Explains how the human body uses food as fuel and suggests that good eating habits from birth may prevent obesity.
Health and Safety
Dist - USNAC **Prod** - NIH 1980

Obesity and Overweight
U-matic / VHS
Color
Follows the progress of actual patients who have undertaken weight reduction programs. Examines the multiple causes of excess weight. Distinguishes between overweight and obesity. Describes fat metabolism and evaluates methods of quantitative measurement.
Health and Safety
Dist - AMEDA **Prod** - AMEDA

Obesity and the Slimming of America 29 MIN
VHS
Here's To Your Health Series
Color (G)
$59.95 purchase _ #HEAW - 515
Reveals statistics that show that one out of every four Americans are clinically obese. Discusses the relationship between obesity and disease. Suggests ways to reduce caloric intake.
Health and Safety; Physical Education and Recreation
Dist - PBS **Prod** - KERA

Obesity and the slimming of America 29 MIN
VHS
Color (J H C G T A PRO)
$59.95 purchase _ #AH45206
Describes the relationship between obesity and disease. Suggests methods for reducing caloric intake.
Health and Safety
Dist - HTHED **Prod** - HTHED

Obesity - Effective Management 27 MIN
VHS / U-matic
University of Michigan Media Library - Clinical Commentary Series
Color (PRO)
LC 81-707080
Provides an overview of how a multidisciplinary approach can be used to effectively manage the obese patient. Discusses caloric restriction, physical exercise and training, psychosocial support and vocational rehabilitation.
Health and Safety
Dist - UMICH **Prod** - UMICH 1981

Object conversation 10 MIN
16mm
Color (G)
$25.00 rental
Plays with language, the viewer's memory, assumptions about familiar objects, puns and processes of thinking. Conjures up a series of objects such as scissors, a barbell, piano, hourglass and ladders which are then progressively re - invented. Produced by Paul Glabicki.
Fine Arts
Dist - CANCIN

An Object Lesson in Fire Prevention 21 MIN
16mm
B&W
LC FIE52-1283
Explains the fire hazards in aviation overhaul and repair shops and the importance of protective measures.
Health and Safety; Industrial and Technical Education
Dist - USNAC **Prod** - USN 1950

Object permanence 23 MIN
16mm
Aecom scales of motorsensory development series
Color
Depicts stages in early cognitive development in accordance with Piaget's definition. Shows the developmental sequences involved, beginning when infants behave as though an object has ceased to exist when it disappears from view to the point when behavior indicates the presence of an internalized 'MENTAL REPRESENTATION.'.
Psychology
Dist - NYU **Prod** - VASSAR

Object Permanence 40 MIN
16mm
Ordinal Scales of Infant Psychological Development Series
Color (C A)
LC 73-703095
Presents a demonstration of a scale on the development of visual pursuit and the permanence of objects. Shows 12 different infants ranging in age from three weeks to two years as their psychological development is tested.
Psychology
Dist - UILL **Prod** - UILL 1968

Object Relations in Space 28 MIN
16mm
Ordinal Scales of Infant Psychological Development Series
Color (C A)
LC 73-703095
Presents a demonstration of the scale for the construction of object relations in space. Shows evidences of perceiving and of anticipating the loci of concrete things with 12 infants ranging in age from three to 23 months.
Psychology
Dist - UILL **Prod** - UILL 1968

Objection 28 MIN
16mm
Color (G)
$40.00 rental
Catalogues the contents of a house with ever - increasing horror, originally begun as a document for insurance purposes. Features the voices and sounds of the family unseen.
Fine Arts
Dist - CANCIN **Prod** - KELLEM 1974

Objection overruled 29 MIN
VHS
America's drug forum series
Color (G)
$19.95 purchase _ #109
Features a team of prosecutors and a team of defense lawyers who discuss the legal aspects of the War on Drugs. Asks if the law should be bent in order to aid anti - drug efforts or would the United States criminal justice system be overturned. Guests include Robert Merkle, former prosecutor who returned the indictment on Manuel Noriega, William Moffitt, public defender, Victoria Toensing, former Deputy Assistant Attorney General, Kevin Zeese, General Counsel of the Drug Policy Foundation.
Civics and Political Systems; Psychology
Dist - DRUGPF **Prod** - DRUGPF 1991

Objective - Acculturation 30 MIN
Videoreel / VT2
Unconscious Cultural Clashes Series
Color
Psychology; Sociology
Dist - SCCOE **Prod** - SCCOE

Objective - Energy 25 MIN
16mm
Color (G)
_ #106C 0178 436
Describes how and when oil and gas were formed, how petroleum is found and produced. Explains the need for frontier exploration and problems in the Arctic and Atlantic frontiers. Demonstrates solutions to problems caused by harsh environment at an isolated drilling island in the Beaufort Sea.
Geography - World; Social Science
Dist - CFLMDC **Prod** - NFBC 1978

Objective - Healthy Babies 25 MIN
VHS / U-matic
Color
Illustrates a few of the new techniques developed by March of Dime research scientists to combat birth defects, along with health tips for prospective mothers.
Health and Safety; Sociology
Dist - MEDCOM **Prod** - MEDCOM

Objective Hemodynamic Measurement of the Impact of Lifestyle, Behavior and Stress 52 MIN
U-matic / VHS
Color (PRO)
Relates the investigation into the alarming rate of sudden death among aerospace workers during the 1960s at Kennedy Space Center and shows that the classical risk factors of smoking, hypertension, and other behaviors could not account for the high incidence of sudden death. Places coronary artery disease, myocardial disease, and electrical instability against a biobehavioral background.
Health and Safety
Dist - AMCARD **Prod** - AMCARD

Objective Slip Preparation 11 MIN
16mm
Color (J)
LC 76-700569
Demonstrates a new method of woolclassing.
Agriculture; Business and Economics
Dist - AUIS **Prod** - FLMAUS 1975

Objectives in the Affective Domain 30 MIN
16mm
Making Behavioral Objectives Meaningful Series
B&W (T)
Presents Dr Madeline Hunter teaching the Krathwohl Taxonomy Of Educational Objectives, Handbrook II - Affective Domain. Discusses levels of internalization of feelings, attitudes and appreciations in classroom terms. Develops examples of behavioral objectives for each level of this domain using the taxonomy to teach appreciation of poetry and to develop desirable self - concept. Shows how values and attitudes can become teachable objectives.
Education; Psychology
Dist - SPF **Prod** - SPF

Objectives in the Cognitive Domain 30 MIN
16mm
Making Behavioral Objectives Meaningful Series
B&W (T)
Presents Dr Madeline Hunter teaching the six levels of Bloom's Taxonomy Of Educational Objectives, Handbook I - Cognitive Domain. Cites classroom examples for each level in several subject areas. Describes the relationship of behavioral objectives to problem solving, critical thinking and the higher cognitive processes. Demonstrates the importance of the taxonomy to individualization of instruction with examples of use in daily teaching.
Education; Psychology
Dist - SPF **Prod** - SPF

Objectives, Strategy, Behaviors 30 MIN
U-matic / VHS
Eager to Learn Series
Color (T)
Education; Psychology
Dist - KTEHTV **Prod** - KTEHTV

Obligations of Muslims in North America
VHS
Color (G)
$15.00 purchase _ #110 - 043
Features Dr Mohammad Yunus who delivers an important lecture about the responsibility of dawa. Includes two other lectures on the topic of community building.
Religion and Philosophy
Dist - SOUVIS **Prod** - SOUVIS

Oblomov 145 MIN
16mm
Color (H C A) (RUSSIAN)
LC 82-700457
Presents a comedic drama about a landowner in 19th - century Russia whose indolence destroys his life. Based on the novel Oblomov by Ivan Goncharov.
Fine Arts; Foreign Language; Literature and Drama
Dist - IFEX **Prod** - MOSFLM 1981

Oblomov - Pt 1 37 MIN
16mm
Color (H C A) (RUSSIAN)
LC 82-700457
Presents a comedic drama about a landowner in 19th - century Russia whose indolence destroys his life. Based on the novel Oblomov by Ivan Goncharov.
History - World; Literature and Drama
Dist - IFEX **Prod** - MOSFLM 1981

Oblomov - Pt 2 36 MIN
16mm
Color (H C A) (RUSSIAN)
LC 82-700457
Presents a comedic drama about a landowner in 19th - century Russia whose indolence destroys his life. Based on the novel Oblomov by Ivan Goncharov.
History - World; Literature and Drama
Dist - IFEX **Prod** - MOSFLM 1981

Oblomov - Pt 3 36 MIN
16mm
Color (H C A) (RUSSIAN)
LC 82-700457
Presents a comedic drama about a landowner in 19th - century Russia whose indolence destroys his life. Based on the novel Oblomov by Ivan Goncharov.
History - World; Literature and Drama
Dist - IFEX **Prod** - MOSFLM 1981

Oblomov - Pt 4 36 MIN
16mm
Color (H C A) (RUSSIAN)
LC 82-700457
Presents a comedic drama about a landowner in 19th - century Russia whose indolence destroys his life. Based on the novel Oblomov by Ivan Goncharov.
History - World; Literature and Drama
Dist - IFEX **Prod** - MOSFLM 1981

Obmaru 4 MIN
16mm
Color (H C)
Captures the moods of stylized voodoo ritual music.
Religion and Philosophy; Sociology
Dist - CFS **Prod** - MARX

Oboe 29 MIN
VHS / 16mm
Junior High Music - Instrumental Series
Color (I)
$175.00, $200.00 purchase _ #288105
Features a host who introduces each program and offers a brief history of the instrument to be studied. Presents a master teacher, a professional musician with a symphony philharmonic, who demonstrates proper assembly, breathing and tone production, hand position, embouchure and articulation. A performance rounds out the program. 'Oboe' presents the soprano voice of the family of double reed woodwinds. Successful playing includes special attention to breathing and breath control, avoiding producing too much air and accumulation of moisture under the keys. The instructor explains how to deal with these problems.
Fine Arts
Dist - ACCESS **Prod** - ACCESS 1988

The Oboe 18 MIN
16mm
Color
Studies the oboe using a combination of live performances, examinations of related instruments and verbal explanations. Explores the history of the instrument and its musical characteristics.
Fine Arts
Dist - UTORMC **Prod** - UTORMC

The Oboe - Advanced Seminar 62 MIN
VHS / BETA
Color
Demonstrates techniques for the advanced oboe player. Features John Mack, principal oboist of the Cleveland Orchestra.
Fine Arts
Dist - MOHOMV **Prod** - MOHOMV

The Oboe - Beginning 59 MIN
BETA / VHS
Color
Provides instruction in learning to play the oboe.
Fine Arts
Dist - MOHOMV **Prod** - MOHOMV

The Oboe Reed 21 MIN
16mm
Color
LC 74-701982
Shows the process of making an oboe reed.
Fine Arts
Dist - UTORMC **Prod** - UTORMC 1973

Observation 15 MIN
Videoreel / VT2
AMA Assessment Center Program for Identifying Supervisory Potential 'Series
Color (PRO)
LC 75-704222
Explains to management assessors the pitfalls of objective observation in evaluating management potential.
Business and Economics; Psychology
Dist - AMA **Prod** - AMA 1974

Observation and Memory 13 MIN
16mm
Color (I)
Presents a series of flash tests to improve observation and memory. Includes 'BALLOONS ARE FLYING,' 'JACK - O - LANTERN HAS LOST HIS HAT,' 'BIRTHDAY FLASH,' 'FUN THINGS FLASH, PART 1,' 'FUN THINGS FLASH, PART 2' AND 'LOLLIPOP GARDEN.'.
Education; Psychology
Dist - SF **Prod** - SF 1968

Observation and Perception 22 MIN
16mm / U-matic / VHS
Law Enforcement - Patrol Procedures Series
Color (PRO)
Explains how police officers can improve their powers of observation, perception and decision - making.
Civics and Political Systems
Dist - CORF **Prod** - MTROLA 1973

Observation of Behavior 30 MIN
VHS / U-matic
Teaching Children with Special Needs Series
Color (T)
Deals with the observation of behavior when dealing with children with special needs.
Education
Dist - MDCPB **Prod** - MDDE

Observation of Centipede 20 MIN
16mm
Color
Shows the relation between mode of life and environment of the centipede and the difference from other arthropods.
Science - Natural
Dist - UNIJAP **Prod** - TOEI 1971

Observation of Feces and Urine 19 MIN
U-matic
Nurse's Aide, Orderly and Attendant Series
Color (IND H C A)
LC 73-701055
Illustrates the observation of the characteristics of normal and abnormal urine and feces as an indicator of the patient's condition.
Health and Safety
Dist - COPI **Prod** - COPI 1971

Observation of Ferns 14 MIN
16mm
Color (JAPANESE)
A Japanese language film. Shows in detail the native environment and life - history of the fern, the representative of the sporophyte generation. Depicts various types of ferns and their respective habitats, their structure, bearing of spores and fertilization and formation of a new fern plant. Points out important areas of differences from other plants.
Foreign Language; Science - Natural
Dist - UNIJAP **Prod** - GAKKEN 1969

Observation of human gait series
Presents a three - part series on observing human gait presented by physical therapist Ilse Koerner. Includes the titles The Normal Gait Pattern Viewed Laterally, The Normal Human Gait Pattern Viewed Anteriorly and Posteriorly, Kinematic and Kinetic Analyses of the Gait.
Kinematic and kinetic analyses of the gait - Part III 38 MIN
The Normal gait pattern viewed laterally - Part I 24 MIN
The Normal human gait pattern viewed anteriorly and posteriorly - Part II 38 MIN
Dist - HSCIC

Observation of Mushrooms 21 MIN
16mm
Color
Points out that there are several thousand kinds of mushrooms in Japan and that therefore sunshine is not requisite for the living and growth of mushrooms. Stresses this unique feature of the mushroom. Uses microscopic and slow - motion photography. Explains its interrelation with other plants in the natural world.
Geography - World; Science - Natural
Dist - UNIJAP **Prod** - TOEI 1970

Observational Learning 23 MIN
U-matic / VHS / 16mm
Color (C)
LC 78-701672
Gives a detailed overview of the workings of observational learning, the role of the model and the role of the observer. Uses experiments, findings of research and practical applications of the observational learning model to demonstrate that observational learning is a complex and powerful method of learning in both children and adults.
Psychology
Dist - CORF **Prod** - HAR 1978

Observations of Living Primordial Germ Cells in the Mouse 10 MIN
16mm
B&W (A)
LC 70-703518
Shows the appearance of the living primordial germ cells in the mouse embryo, and demonstrates the ability of the germ cells to undergo ameboid movement at a number of different stages of development.
Science - Natural
Dist - UWASHP **Prod** - BLDHAY 1967

The Observatories 27 MIN
16mm
Color
Visits six new astronomy centers in North and South America. Describes the functions of different telescopes, newly - developed equipment and explains many space phenomena.
Science; Science - Physical
Dist - USNAC **Prod** - NSF 1982

Observeillance 3 MIN
VHS / 16mm
Six interviews series
B&W (G)
$10.00 rental
Takes the viewer on a trip down the Wakulla River in north Florida. Focuses on the lyrical guide as his vivid descriptions of nature give a better view than total visual mobility of the camera. Part two of a six - part series of 'interviews' from 1973 - 1981. Although not serial in content, the films should be shown in chronological order when viewed as a group. Produced by Tyler Turkle.
Fine Arts; Geography - United States; Guidance and Counseling
Dist - CANCIN
FLMKCO

Observing 15 MIN
U-matic / VHS
Out and about Series
Color (P)
Shows that while in the grocery store and in the library, Molly and her friends learn to use all their senses to observe the characteristics of an object.
Guidance and Counseling
Dist - AITECH **Prod** - STSU 1984

Observing and Classifying 15 MIN
VHS / U-matic
Hands on, Grade One Series Unit 1 - Observing; Unit 1 - Observing
Color (P)
Science; Science - Natural; Science - Physical
Dist - AITECH **Prod** - VAOG 1975

Observing and Describing 10 MIN
16mm / U-matic / VHS
Science Processes Series
Color (I)
LC 77-703316
Discusses the importance of observing and describing to the scientist, and shows that people use their senses to collect information and need only to describe their observations in a clear and accurate way.
Science
Dist - MGHT **Prod** - MGHT 1969

Observing and Documenting in a Mental Health Setting, Pt I 60 MIN
VHS / U-matic
Color
Discusses the important principles of observation and documentation of clients in a mental health setting. Shows a number of principles to be essential, such as objectivity in observation and documentation, being descriptive and precise and meeting the needs of the facility.
Health and Safety; Psychology; Sociology
Dist - UWISC **Prod** - MORVMC 1979

Observing and Documenting in a Mental Health Setting, Pt III 27 MIN
U-matic / VHS
Color
Continues a presentation concerning observing and documenting in a mental health setting. Emphasizes the documentation of the familiar as well as the unusual actions of the patient.
Health and Safety; Sociology
Dist - UWISC **Prod** - SCDMH 1979

Observing and Recording Behavior 17 MIN
16mm
Behavioral Counseling - a Package of Eight Films Series
Color (C G)
Presents a counselor helping a teacher learn how to observe and record so that she can tell if a student is changing his behavior in response to her efforts.
Guidance and Counseling; Psychology
Dist - AACD **Prod** - AACD 1975

Observing Animal Camouflage 15 MIN
U-matic / VHS
Hands on, Grade 4 - Cars, Cartoons, Etc Series Unit 1 - Observing; Unit 1 - Observing
Color (I)
Gives experience in observing animal camouflage.
Science
Dist - AITECH **Prod** - WHROTV 1975

Observing Animal Feeding Behavior 14 MIN
U-matic / VHS
Hands on, Grade 4 - Cars, Cartoons, Etc Series Unit 1 - Observing; Unit 1 - Observing
Color (I)
Gives experience in observing animal feeding behavior.
Science
Dist - AITECH **Prod** - WHROTV 1975

Observing Behavior 15 MIN
U-matic / VHS / 16mm
BSCS Behavior Film Series
Color
LC 74-701942
Follows two high school students as they observe the nesting behavior of some geese.
Science - Natural
Dist - PHENIX **Prod** - BSCS 1974

Observing Change 15 MIN
U-matic / VHS
Hands on, Grade 3 Series Unit 1 - Observing; Unit 1 - Observing
Color (P)
Science; Science - Physical
Dist - AITECH **Prod** - VAOG 1975

Observing Drips and Drops 14 MIN
U-matic / VHS
Hands on, Grade 4 - Cars, Cartoons, Etc Series Unit 1 - Observing; Unit 1 - Observing
Color (I)
Gives experience in observing drips and drops.
Science
Dist - AITECH **Prod** - WHROTV 1975

Observing eye series

The American Lobster	29 MIN
Animal tails	29 MIN
Animal weapons	29 MIN
Animals from A to Z	29 MIN
Animals that lay eggs	29 MIN
Chisel Tooth tribe	29 MIN
Dangerous to Man	29 MIN
Eight - legged pets	29 MIN
The Eye and sight	29 MIN
Fossils are Fun	29 MIN
How do animals eat	29 MIN
Insects	29 MIN
The Laws of Motion	29 MIN
Mineral Curiosities	29 MIN
Nature's Superlatives	29 MIN
The Old Flame	29 MIN
Our Ocean of Air	29 MIN
Physics of Diving	29 MIN
Records in the Rocks	29 MIN
Reptiles	29 MIN
Science on the light	29 MIN
Seashore life	29 MIN
Seeing is Deceiving	29 MIN
Sense of Balance	29 MIN
Sound Around	29 MIN
Sound of Music	29 MIN
The Swing of Things	29 MIN
Unfried Clams	29 MIN
Up in the Air	29 MIN
Wild Pets	29 MIN

Dist - PBS

Observing for Safety 20 MIN
U-matic / VHS
Foreman's Accident Prevention Series
Color (IND)
Deals with the psychology of observation and perception as they relate to the supervisors' accident prevention responsibilities.
Health and Safety
Dist - GPCV **Prod** - GPCV

Observing in Science 14 MIN
U-matic / VHS
Whatabout Series
Color (J)
Shows a biologist using special night - vision equipment to observe how bats pollinate tropical plants.
Science
Dist - AITECH **Prod** - AITECH 1983

Observing Living Chicken Embryos 56 MIN
VHS
Color (C A)
$125.00 purchase, $18.00 rental
Shows new techniques for both in vitrio and in vivo observation.
Science - Natural
Dist - CORNRS **Prod** - CORNRS 1984

Observing Motion 15 MIN
U-matic / VHS
Hands on, Grade 3 Series Unit 1 - Observing; Unit 1 - Observing
Color (P)
Science; Science - Physical
Dist - AITECH **Prod** - VAOG 1975

Observing Ourselves 29 MIN
16mm
Real Revolution - Talks by Krishnamurti Series
B&W
LC 73-703038
Features Indian spiritual leader Krishnamurti who discusses man's need to change himself and his society by removing the network of escapes that prevent him from knowing himself and his problems. Teaches that man must free his mind of all beliefs and experiences in gaining the truth.
Guidance and Counseling; Religion and Philosophy
Dist - IU **Prod** - KQEDTV 1968

Observing Role Play 15 MIN
U-matic / VHS
B&W (PRO)
Illustrates role play experiences teachers can recognize and encourage in children, such as pretending to be someone else, sharing a 'pretend' situation with another person and imitating actions or sounds.
Education; Psychology
Dist - HSERF **Prod** - HSERF

Observing Sounds 15 MIN
VHS / U-matic
Hands on, Grade 3 Series Unit 1 - Observing; Unit 1 - Observing
Color (P)
Science; Science - Physical
Dist - AITECH **Prod** - VAOG 1975

Observing Spatial Arrangements 14 MIN
VHS / U-matic
Hands on, Grade 2 - Lollipops, Loops, Etc Series Unit 1 - Observing; Unit 1 - Observing
Color (P)
Gives experience in observing spatial arrangements.
Science
Dist - AITECH **Prod** - WHROTV 1975

Observing Teaching 50 MIN
U-matic / VHS
Strategies in College Teaching Series
Color (T)
LC 79-706290
Shows how to conduct a preobservation interview, what to look for in observing a class and how to conduct a followup session with the instructor.
Education
Dist - IU **Prod** - IU 1977

Obsession 28 MIN
U-matic / VHS
Color (G)
$249.00, $149.00 purchase _ #AD - 1152
Considers what happens when the object of passion becomes the victim of an obsession that threatens the safety and possibly even the life of the loved one. Features Phil Donahue, Theresa Saldana, author of 'Beyond Survival,' and Dr Michael Liebowitz.
Health and Safety; Psychology; Sociology
Dist - FOTH **Prod** - FOTH

Obsessive - Compulsive Disorder 24 MIN
U-matic / VHS
Color (G)
$249.00, $149.00 purchase _ #AD - 2031
Reveals that obsessive - compulsive behavior appears to be rooted in the chemistry of the brain, although it was once thought to be a psychological problem. Reports that drug treatment now offers hope to many whose lives have been dominated and sometimes ruined by uncontrollable urges and needs to perform and repeat actions needlessly.
Health and Safety; Psychology; Sociology
Dist - FOTH **Prod** - FOTH

Obsessive - Compulsive Disorder - the Boy who Couldn't Stop Washing 28 MIN
U-matic / VHS
Color (G)
$249.00, $149.00 purchase _ #AD - 2035
Reveals that for some daily rituals have taken over and rule their lives. Features Dr Judith L Rapaport and Phil Donahue who examine compulsive behavior - fearing that something terrible will happen if an individual does not repeat an act a certain number of times or in a certain way regardless of whether it needs to be done or the person really wants to do it. Looks at the symptoms, the diagnosis and what is known about cures.
Health and Safety; Psychology; Sociology
Dist - FOTH **Prod** - FOTH

Obsolescence and Burnout 30 MIN
VHS / U-matic
Business of Managing Professionals Series
Color
Discusses obsolescence and burnout as it pertains to managing professionals.
Business and Economics
Dist - KYTV **Prod** - KYTV 1983

The Obsolete Menopause 18 MIN
16mm
Upjohn Vanguard of Medicine Series
Color
LC FIA67-530
Six medical authorities explain why and how millions of suffering women can be spared physical and mental deterioration through the easy and inexpensive replacement of their former levels of female sex hormones.
Health and Safety; Sociology
Dist - UPJOHN **Prod** - UPJOHN 1966

Obstacles to Success 50 MIN
VHS / U-matic
Deming Video Tapes - Quality, Productivity and the Competitive 'Series
Color
Business and Economics
Dist - SME **Prod** - MIOT

Obstacles to Success, II
VHS / U-matic
Deming Videotapes - Quality, Productivity, and Competitive Series
Color
Business and Economics
Dist - MIOT **Prod** - MIOT

Obstetric Delivery 29 MIN
16mm
Nine to Get Ready Series no 7
B&W (C A)
LC 72-704214
Explains about obstetric delivery, discussing labor, hospital versus home delivery, analgesia and anesthesia and normal delivery. Includes views of the delivery room. Features Dr J Robert Bragonier and Leta Powell Drake.
Health and Safety
Dist - UNEBR **Prod** - KUONTV 1965

Obstetric Hemorrhage 27 MIN
16mm
Color
Points out that obstetric hemorrhage is one of the chief causes of maternal death in many countries. Shows the mechanism of the obstetric hemorrhage, mainly cases of hypofibrinogenemia, the methods of hematrogic and blood chemical examinations, the emergency treatments at delivery and after parturition and periodic management and guidance for the pregnant. Emphasizes that in Japan today, an acute shortage of blood for transfusion is posing a grave social problem.
Geography - World; Health and Safety; Science; Science - Natural
Dist - UNIJAP **Prod** - UNIJAP 1970

Obstetrical Anesthesia and Analgesia
VHS / U-matic
Color
Presents various types of anesthesia and analgesia available to obstetrical patients and explains the risks and benefits of using each as they relate to the patient and her unborn child.
Health and Safety
Dist - MIFE **Prod** - MIFE

Obstetrical Anesthesia - Cesarean Section 27 MIN
U-matic / VHS
Anesthesiology Clerkship Series
Color (PRO)
Describes the preparation for cesarean section and the choice of anesthesia. Indicates regional block as a preferred method. Discusses technical aspects of the administration of spinal or epidural anesthesia in this group of patients. Considers the use of general anesthesia for cesarian section.
Health and Safety
Dist - UMICHM **Prod** - UMICHM 1982

Obstetrical Anesthesia - Evaluation and Preparation 20 MIN
U-matic / VHS
Anesthesiology Clerkship Series
Color (PRO)
Discusses the preoperative evaluation of the patient requiring obstetrical anesthesia. Emphasizes potentially serious problems such as dehydration, the full stomach and caval compression. Describes patient education in the goals of obstetrical anesthesia. Considers analgesia and sedation during labor.
Health and Safety
Dist - UMICHM **Prod** - UMICHM 1982

Obstetrical Anesthesia - Normal Vaginal Delivery 20 MIN
VHS / U-matic
Anesthesiology Clerkship Series
Color (PRO)
Discusses the provision of anesthesia and analgesia for normal vaginal delivery. Reviews parturition pain pathways which must be understood for the use of regional anesthesia, and discusses commonly used regional blocks. Considers inhalation analgesia for spontaneous delivery. Covers management of problems which may arise during and after labor and delivery.
Health and Safety
Dist - UMICHM **Prod** - UMICHM

Obstetrical anesthesia series
Presents a two - part series on obstetrical anesthesia presented by Dr Ezzat Abouleish. Includes epidural and spinal anesthesia and discusses procedures and complications.

Epidural - Part I	46 MIN
Obstetrical anesthesia series	88 MIN
Spinal - Part II	42 MIN

Dist - HSCIC

Obstetrical Ultrasound
U-matic / VHS
Color (SPANISH)
Describes how an ultrasound examination provides important information about the well being of the fetus without the risk of x - rays.
Health and Safety
Dist - MIFE **Prod** - MIFE

Obstetrics and gynecology
CD-ROM
Color (PRO)
$395.00 purchase _ #1960
Contains the full text of the Journal of the American College of Obstetrics and Gynecology, 1985 - 89. Includes images. For IBM PCs and compatibles. Requires 640K RAM, DOS Version 3.1 or greater, one floppy disk drive - a hard drive is recommended, one empty expansion slot, and an IBM compatible CD - ROM drive.
Health and Safety; Literature and Drama
Dist - BEP

Obstetrics and Gynecology in a West African Community 40 MIN
16mm
Color (PRO)
Deals with the problems of gynecology and obstetrics in West African cultures.
Health and Safety; Social Science; Sociology
Dist - UCLA **Prod** - UCLA

Obstetrics and gynecology series

Birth	10 MIN
Breast self - examination	10 MIN
Caesarean birth	10 MIN
Contraceptive methods, pt 1	10 MIN
Contraceptive methods, Pt 2	10 MIN
The Diaphragm	10 MIN
Genetic Counseling I - Heredity and Birth Defects	10 MIN
Genetic Counseling II - Amniocentesis	10 MIN
Genetic Counseling III - the Rh Negative Mother	10 MIN
Natural Childbirth	10 MIN
The Pill	10 MIN

Dist - MIFE

Obstructed Airway Management 17 MIN
VHS / U-matic
Basic Life Support Series Module 3; Module 3
Color (PRO)
Shows how to manage obstructed airways for adult or infant victims who are conscious, become unconscious or are found unconscious.
Health and Safety
Dist - IU **Prod** - NICEPR

Obstructing Carcinoma of the Transverse Colon 25 MIN
VHS / U-matic
Gastrointestinal Series
Color
Health and Safety; Science - Natural
Dist - SVL **Prod** - SVL

Obstructive Jaundice Complicated by Diaphragmatic Hiatal Hernia 27 MIN
16mm
Color (PRO)
Presents Harry H Mc Carthy, MD, who points out that it is often necessary to make the operative procedure flexible enough to fit the individual problem, and instead use compromising techniques. Stresses a method of approach to a complicated problem, whereas, the technique of the operation assumes a relatively minor role.
Health and Safety; Science
Dist - ACY **Prod** - ACYDGD 1955

Obtaining Agreement on Objectives 10 MIN
U-matic / VHS
Practical M B O Series
Color
Business and Economics; Education; Psychology
Dist - DELTAK **Prod** - DELTAK

Obtaining and preserving foods series
Science corner I, Unit VII - obtaining and preserving foods - a series
Dist - GPN

Obtaining Needed Financing 25 MIN
U-matic / VHS
Financing, Starting and Marketing a Flock Series
Color
Focuses on information needed to prepare to secure a business loan for sheep production.
Agriculture; Business and Economics
Dist - HOBAR **Prod** - HOBAR

Obtaining what You Need - Ari Masu Ka 28 MIN
U-matic / VHS
Japanese for Beginners Series
Color (C) (JAPANESE)
$249.00, $149.00 purchase _ #AD - 2097
Shows how to get specific items in a store, as well as how to get to the person one wishes to see when encountering a receptionist. Part of the Japanese for Beginners Series.
Foreign Language; Geography - World
Dist - FOTH **Prod** - FOTH

Obturation of the root canal 11 MIN
U-matic / VHS
Color (C PRO)
$395.00 purchase, $80.00 rental _ #D881 - VI - 013
Demonstrates the instrumentation, preparation of materials and procedures for the obturation of the root canal system. Describes master cone, spreader and accessory cone selection. Presents in detail the obturation procedure using the lateral condensation technique. Presented by Drs Jeffrey Hoover, Ming M Wang and Richard M Madden.
Health and Safety
Dist - HSCIC

Obturator Construction for a Surgical Soft Palate Defect, Pt 1 - Impression 14 MIN
16mm
Color (PRO)
LC 79-701823
Describes an impression procedure for construction of an obturator in an edentulous patient. Shows how the patient's existing maxillary - complete denture isused as a carrier for the compound and fluid wax impression. Describes insertion of the completed hollow obturator.
Health and Safety
Dist - USNAC **Prod** - VADTC 1979

Obturator Construction for a Surgical Soft Palate Defect, Pt 2 - Laboratory 9 MIN
16mm
Color (PRO)
LC 79-701724
Describes laboratory procedures for developing a hollow acrylic resin obturator which is attached to an existing maxillary complete denture.
Health and Safety
Dist - USNAC **Prod** - VADTC 1979

Ocamo is my town 23 MIN
VHS / 16mm
Yanomamo series
Color (G)
Describes the work of Salesian priest, Padre Cocco, head of the Ocamo River mission since 1957. Explains the mission goal as softening the impact of 'civilization' on the Yanomamo of the area. Baptism and monogamy are considered as less important than treating the Yanomamo as human beings and respecting their culture. Hallucinogenic drugs are intrinsic to spirit communication and spirit medicine and should neither be forbidden nor discouraged, according to the priest. Part of a series on the Yanomamo Indians of Venezuela by Timothy Asch and Napoleon Chagnon.
Geography - World; History - World; Religion and Philosophy; Social Science; Sociology
Dist - DOCEDR PSUPCR **Prod** - DOCEDR 1974

OCAPT's basic SPC training program
VHS
Color (A PRO IND)
$1,795.00 purchase _ #SPCAV - 721
Presents a comprehensive, 10 - part course in Statistical Process Control. Includes 10 videocassettes, instructor's manual, trainer's notes, overhead transparency masters, a course manual, and related forms.
Business and Economics; Computer Science
Dist - PRODUC **Prod** - PRODUC

Occidental
VHS
Campus clips series
Color (H C A)
$29.95 purchase _ #CC0007V
Takes a video visit to the campus of Occidental College in California. Shows many of the distinctive features of the campus, and interviews students about their experiences. Provides information on the composition of the student body, professors, academics, social life, housing, and other subjects.
Education
Dist - CAMV

Occlusal Adjustment, Pt I 17 MIN
VHS / U-matic
Color
Entails indications, principles and methods for adjustment of occlusion to optimal freedom and stability, both in centric relation and centric occlusion.
Health and Safety; Science
Dist - AMDA **Prod** - VADTC 1970

Occlusal Adjustment, Pt 1 - Centric 17 MIN
8mm cartridge / 16mm
Color
LC 75-702029; 74-705231
Shows indications, principles and methods for adjustment of occlusion to optimal freedom and stability, both in centric relation and centric occlusion.
Health and Safety; Science
Dist - USNAC **Prod** - USVA 1970

Occlusal Adjustment, Pt 2 - Lateral and Protrusive Excursions 12 MIN
8mm cartridge / 16mm
Color
LC 75-702030; 74-705232
Illustrates adjustment of occlusal interferences in various eccentric contact relations by means of mounted casts and intra - oral recording. Explains to what extent eccentric movement patterns should be adjusted.
Health and Safety; Science; Science - Natural
Dist - USNAC **Prod** - USVA 1970

Occlusal Radiography, Pt 1 - Introduction and Maxillary Projections 13 MIN
8mm cartridge / 16mm
Color
LC 75-701660; 75-700803
Presents five specific types of occlusal radiographic examination of the maxilla. Explains common errors in positioning and demonstrates their correction.
Health and Safety; Science; Science - Natural
Dist - USNAC **Prod** - USVA 1972

Occlusal Reconstruction and Restoration with Fixed Prosthesis, Pt 4 - Bridge Completion, 14 MIN
16mm
Color
LC 75-701313
Demonstrates bridge assembly and methods for maintaining proper oral hygiene after bridge cementation.
Health and Safety
Dist - USNAC **Prod** - USVA 1974

Occlusal Reconstruction and Restoration with Fixed Prosthesis, Pt I - Occlusal 8 MIN
U-matic / VHS
Color
Demonstrates the restoration of the occlusal curve by tooth reduction and tooth preparation for fixed prosthesis.
Health and Safety; Science
Dist - AMDA **Prod** - VADTC 1974

Occlusal Reconstruction and Restoration with Fixed Prosthesis, Pt II - Construction and 9 MIN
VHS / U-matic
Color
Demonstrates the construction of a temporary bridge using a hand - formed rectangular block of activated acrylic placed directly on the prepared teeth.
Health and Safety; Science
Dist - AMDA **Prod** - VADTC 1974

Occlusal Reconstruction and Restoration with Fixed Prosthesis, Pt III - Waxing of Dies 12 MIN
U-matic / VHS
Color
Shows the waxing procedure for the full crowns, demonstrating the investing, casting and methodology for evaluation of the finished castings.
Health and Safety; Science
Dist - AMDA **Prod** - VADTC 1974

Occlusal Reconstruction and Restoration with Fixed Prosthesis, Pt IV - Bridge Completion 14 MIN
U-matic / VHS
Color
Uses autopolymerizing acrylic to demonstrate a bridge assembly to join the units prior to investing for soldering. Shows soldering operation.
Health and Safety; Science
Dist - AMDA **Prod** - VADTC 1974

Occlusal Reconstruction and Restoration with Fixed Prosthesis, Pt 1 - Occlusal 14 MIN
16mm
Color
LC 75-701310
Demonstrates the restoration of the occlusal curve by tooth reduction and tooth preparation for fixed prosthesis.
Health and Safety; Science; Science - Natural
Dist - USNAC **Prod** - USVA 1974

Occlusal Reconstruction and Restoration with Fixed Prosthesis, Pt 3 - Waxing of Dies and 12 MIN
16mm
Color
LC 75-701312
Shows the waxing procedure for full dental crowns. Emphasizes the proper anatomical considerations in the formation of contact areas, marginal ridges and alignment of the central grooves, and buccal and lingual cusps.
Health and Safety; Science; Science - Natural
Dist - USNAC **Prod** - USVA 1974

Occlusal Reconstruction and Restoration with Fixed Prosthesis, Pt 2 - Construction and 9 MIN
16mm
Color
LC 75-701311
Shows construction of a temporary bridge using a hand - formed rectangular block of activated acrylic placed directly on the prepared teeth.
Health and Safety; Science; Science - Natural
Dist - USNAC **Prod** - USVA 1974

Occult Blood 5 MIN
U-matic / BETA / VHS
Basic Clinical Laboratory Procedure Series
Color; Mono (C A)
Demonstrates the proper equipment, procedures, attention to critical details and efficient, accurate methods for proper collection of specimens.
Health and Safety; Science
Dist - UIOWA **Prod** - UIOWA 1985

The Occult Experience 95 MIN
16mm / VHS
Color (H C G)
Examines alternate belief systems in the Western World. Covers shamanism, witchcraft, demon exorcism and occult practices by people in the US, Switzerland, Ireland, England and Australia. Film version 95 minutes. Available in 56 minute version in video.
Religion and Philosophy; Sociology
Dist - CINETF **Prod** - CINETF 1985

The Occult - Mysteries of the Supernatural 24 MIN
U-matic / VHS
Color (J C)
$89.00 purchase _ #3541
Uses three techniques to explore the world of the occult. Includes interviews, an animated sequence providing a background for the history and development of astrology, and films showing the dramatic power of supernatural subjects.
Sociology
Dist - EBEC

The Occult - Mysteries of the Supernatural 24 MIN
16mm / U-matic / VHS
Wide World of Adventure Series
Color (J H)
Explores the occult through interviews with a witch, an astrologer and an ESP expert.
Religion and Philosophy
Dist - EBEC **Prod** - AVATLI 1977

The Occult - X Factor or Fraud? 20 MIN
16mm
Color (H C A)
$365 purchase, $45 rental
Examines current interest in the occult and colleges that are offering courses in the occult. Includes views against occultism.
Religion and Philosophy; Sociology
Dist - CNEMAG **Prod** - DOCUA 1988

Occupant Restraint 8 MIN
U-matic / VHS / 16mm
Color (H C A)
Portrays the importance of wearing seat belts and shoulder harnesses.
Education; Health and Safety; Industrial and Technical Education; Psychology
Dist - USNAC **Prod** - NHTSA 1981

Occupation - 1939 - 1945 60 MIN
VHS
Struggles For Poland Series
Color; Captioned (G)
$59.95 purchase _ #STFP - 104
Reviews the history of Poland under German and Soviet occupation. Shows that the Soviets nationalized land and industry, as well as jailing opponents, while the Germans deported many Poles and imposed a government. Focuses on the activities of the Polish resistance movement.
History - World
Dist - PBS **Prod** - WNETTV 1988

Occupation - Holland, 1940 - 1944 52 MIN
16mm / U-matic / VHS
World at War Series
Color (H C A)
Describes how the Gestapo, the German secret police commanded by Himmler, carried out Germany's crimes and atrocities during its occupation of Holland from 1940 to 1944, creating a nightmare for its citizens. Jews were victims of genocide and 105,000 of Holland's 140,000 Jews were killed during the Nazi occupation.
History - World
Dist - MEDIAG USCAN **Prod** - THAMES 1973

Occupation - Mother 29 MIN
U-matic
Woman Series
Color
Explores the conflict between women's needs for individual fulfillment and the demands made on them as mothers of young children.
Sociology
Dist - PBS **Prod** - WNEDTV

Occupation - Volume 4 60 MIN
VHS
Struggles for Poland series
Color (H C A)
$59.95 purchase
Covers the history of Poland from 1939 to 1945. Focuses on the occupation of Poland during World War II, and the suffering the Polish people endured. Reveals that half of all Polish children experienced atrocities during the war. Hosted and narrated by Roger Mudd.
History - World
Dist - PBS **Prod** - WNETTV

Occupational Behavior - Application and Justification 24 MIN
U-matic
Biofeedback Strategies Series Pt VI; Pt 6
Color (PRO)
Shows transfer of training skills used by a former drug addict to apply cultivated relaxation to stress in order to maintain a drug - free lifestyle. Discusses how these stress - control principles can be applied to numerous physical or psychological stress - related dysfunctions.
Health and Safety; Psychology; Sociology
Dist - AOTA **Prod** - AOTA 1981

Occupational Behavior Expectations 15 MIN
U-matic
Color (PRO)
Presents a view of the future of the occupational therapy profession and suggests steps to prevent failure. Narrated by Mary Reilly.
Education; Guidance and Counseling; Health and Safety
Dist - AOTA **Prod** - AOTA 1977

Occupational Health 30 MIN
U-matic
Health Care Today Series
Color (H A)
Discusses the role of the health professional in industry in the maintenance of a high health standard.
Health and Safety
Dist - TVOTAR **Prod** - TVOTAR 1985

Occupational Health 29 MIN
VHS / 16mm
Health Care Today series
Color (H C G)
$90.00 purchase _ #BPN109809
Discusses the role of the health professional in industry. Interviews two health professionals in industry. Outlines the responsibilities of industry and individual workers in the maintenance of a high health standard.
Health and Safety
Dist - RMIBHF **Prod** - RMIBHF

Occupational Health 29 MIN
VHS / 16mm
Washington Connection Series
Color (G)
$55.00 rental _ #WACO - 111
Civics and Political Systems; Health and Safety; Social Science
Dist - PBS **Prod** - NPACT

Occupational heat stress 15 MIN
BETA / VHS / U-matic
Color (IND G)
$395.00 purchase _ #600 - 26, #600 - 34
Alerts employees to the potential hazards of occupational heat stress. Explains important first aid procedures. Offered in two versions - one discussing the use of an ice vest, the other not mentioning the vest.
Health and Safety; Industrial and Technical Education; Psychology
Dist - ITSC **Prod** - ITSC

Occupational medical surveillance 13 MIN
U-matic / BETA / VHS
Color (IND G)
$395.00 purchase _ #600 - 22
Defines clearly how and why medical information is collected. Emphasizes the potential health benefits of a comprehensive medical surveillance program.
Health and Safety; Industrial and Technical Education; Psychology
Dist - ITSC **Prod** - ITSC

Occupational Preparation 30 MIN
U-matic / VHS
Career Choices Series
(H C)
$125 _ #CC9V
Depicts a school counselor preparing students for their occupations. Illustrates options in military training, programs for apprenticeship, and professional programs.
Business and Economics; Education
Dist - JISTW **Prod** - JISTW

Occupational preparation 30 MIN
VHS
Choices today - for career satisfaction tomorrow series
Color (I J H)
$98.00 purchase _ #CTV102
Focuses on developing and implementing an effective, realistic educational and training program. Explains the importance of high school course and program selection. Covers post - secondary educational and training opportunities. Discusses military education, apprenticeship and professional programs. Part of a three - part series on making career choices.
Business and Economics; Education; Guidance and Counseling; Psychology
Dist - CADESF **Prod** - CADESF

Occupational Preparation 30 MIN
BETA / VHS / U-matic
Choices Today for Career Satisfaction Tomorrow
(H C PRO)
$98.00 _ #CCP5300V
Features live action, while depicting the necessity of following useful, informative courses in high school to have success in the world of work. Deals with establishing a feasable career plan and preparing oneself for entering the job market.
Business and Economics; Education
Dist - CAMV **Prod** - CAMV

Occupational Preparation 30 MIN
VHS
Color (H)
$98.00 purchase _ #CCP5300, #CCP5300V-J
Focuses on how to develop an effective, realistic educational training program. Teaches that high school course selection is a means of expanding upon interests. Comes with a student - teacher manual.
Guidance and Counseling
Dist - CADESF **Prod** - CADESF 1988
CAMV

Occupational Profiles - Careers in Computer Services 30 MIN
16mm / U-matic / VHS
Color (J A)
Introduces the full range of computer service occupations, from programmers and analysts to technicians and sales personnel. Examines training requirements.
Business and Economics; Education; Industrial and Technical Education; Mathematics; Sociology
Dist - EBEC **Prod** - EDUDYN 1983

Occupational Profiles - Careers in Food Services 30 MIN
16mm / U-matic / VHS
Color (H C)
Looks at careers in food services, emphasizing the job requirements and duties of waiters and waitresses, cooks, restaurant managers, cocktail waitresses, bartenders and executive chefs.
Guidance and Counseling; Industrial and Technical Education; Psychology
Dist - EBEC **Prod** - EDUDYN 1983

Occupational Profiles - Careers in Food Services - Bartender 5 MIN
U-matic / VHS / 16mm
Color (J)
Relates the duties and qualifications of a bartender.
Guidance and Counseling; Industrial and Technical Education
Dist - EBEC **Prod** - EBEC 1983

Occupational Profiles - Careers in Food Services - Cocktail Waitress 5 MIN
U-matic / VHS / 16mm
Color (J)
Relates the duties and qualifications of a cocktail waitress.
Guidance and Counseling; Industrial and Technical Education
Dist - EBEC **Prod** - EBEC 1983

Occupational Profiles - Careers in Food Services - Cook 5 MIN
U-matic / VHS / 16mm
Color (J)
Relates the duties and qualifications of a cook.
Guidance and Counseling; Industrial and Technical Education
Dist - EBEC **Prod** - EBEC 1983

Occupational Profiles - Careers in Food Services - Executive Chef 5 MIN
U-matic / VHS / 16mm
Color (J)
Relates the duties and qualifications of an executive chef.
Guidance and Counseling; Industrial and Technical Education
Dist - EBEC **Prod** - EBEC 1983

Occupational Profiles - Careers in Food Services - Restaurant Manager 5 MIN
16mm / U-matic / VHS
Color (J)
Relates the duties and qualifications of a restaurant manager.
Guidance and Counseling; Industrial and Technical Education
Dist - EBEC **Prod** - EBEC 1983

Occupational Profiles - Careers in Food Services - Waiter/Waitress 5 MIN
U-matic / VHS / 16mm
Color (J)
Relates the duties and qualifications of a waiter or waitress.
Guidance and Counseling; Industrial and Technical Education
Dist - EBEC **Prod** - EBEC 1983

Occupational Profiles - Careers in Health 37 MIN
U-matic / VHS / 16mm
Color (J)
Delineates the kinds of training, responsibilities, physical and mental traits and qualifying examinations required to launch a career in health care. Gives information about salaries and opportunities for advancement as it explores the demanding daily routines of paramedics, physical therapists, respiratory therapists, lab technicians, nursing aids and orderlies, medical secretaries and accredited record technicians.
Guidance and Counseling; Health and Safety
Dist - EBEC **Prod** - EDUDYN 1983

Occupational Profiles - Careers in Health - Accredited Records Technician 5 MIN
U-matic / VHS / 16mm
Color (J)
Relates the duties and qualifications of an accredited records technician.
Guidance and Counseling; Science
Dist - EBEC **Prod** - EBEC 1982

Occupational Profiles - Careers in Health - Lab Technician 5 MIN
16mm / U-matic / VHS
Color (J)
Relates the duties and qualifications of a lab technician.
Guidance and Counseling; Science
Dist - EBEC **Prod** - EBEC 1982

Occupational Profiles - Careers in Health - Medical Secretary 5 MIN
U-matic / VHS / 16mm
Color (J)
Relates the duties and qualifications of a medical secretary.
Guidance and Counseling; Science
Dist - EBEC **Prod** - EBEC 1982

Occupational Profiles - Careers in Health - Nursing Aide/Orderly 5 MIN
U-matic / VHS / 16mm
Color (J)
Relates the duties and qualifications of a nursing aide or orderly.
Guidance and Counseling; Science
Dist - EBEC **Prod** - EBEC 1982

Occupational Profiles - Careers in Health - Paramedic 5 MIN
U-matic / VHS / 16mm
Color (J)
Relates the duties and qualifications of a paramedic.
Guidance and Counseling; Science
Dist - EBEC **Prod** - EBEC 1982

Occupational Profiles - Careers in Health - Physical Therapist 5 MIN
16mm / U-matic / VHS
Color (J)
Relates the duties and qualifications of a physical therapist.
Guidance and Counseling; Health and Safety; Science
Dist - EBEC **Prod** - EBEC 1982

Occupational Profiles - Careers in Health - Respiratory Therapist 5 MIN
16mm / U-matic / VHS
Color (J)
Relates the duties and qualifications of a respiratory therapist.
Guidance and Counseling; Science
Dist - EBEC **Prod** - EBEC 1982

Occupational Profiles Series
Careers in Computer Services 30 MIN
Careers in Food Services 31 MIN
Careers in Health 27 MIN
Dist - EBEC

Occupational Research 30 MIN
U-matic / VHS
Making a Living Work Series Program 107
Color (C A)
Centers around the 'What, Where, How' approach to job hunting. Emphasizes the need for high self esteem and relaxation during the job hunt. Gives tips on maintaining self esteem.
Guidance and Counseling; Psychology
Dist - OHUTC **Prod** - OHUTC

Occupational Research - the Job Search 30 MIN
VHS
Making a Living Work Series
Discusses Richard Bolles' - what, where, and how - approach to defining a job objective and getting it.
Business and Economics; Guidance and Counseling
Dist - CAREER **Prod** - CAREER
CAMV
JISTW

Occupational research - what can you do 29 MIN
VHS / 16mm
Career Planning for Special Needs Series
Color (J)
$200.00 purchase _ #277804
Addresses the concerns of individuals with special needs - the physically disabled, deaf, educable and trainable mentally handicapped, gifted and talented, Native Americans, and gender stereotyped. Suggests positively how they can achieve career satisfaction and success. 'Occupational Research' emphasizes the value of completing occupational and educational research in career planning. Offers practical suggestions on how to do occupational research by considering the nature of the work, future outlook, advancement opportunities, places of employment, earnings, work conditions and necessary qualifications.
Business and Economics; Guidance and Counseling; Psychology
Dist - ACCESS **Prod** - ACCESS 1989

Occupational therapist 16 MIN
VHS
Get a life - a day in the career guidance series
Color (H C A)
$89.00 purchase _ #886696-08-X
Takes viewers through a day in the life of Cara, an occupational therapist. Looks at how OTs are part of the allied health professions offering patients rehabilitative therapies that are critical to recovery from accidents or illness. Includes Cara's patients to give the viewer an idea of how this profession affects and enhances lives. Outlines educational requirements, salaries, credentials and professional associations. Part of a ten-part series.
Business and Economics; Guidance and Counseling; Health and Safety
Dist - VOCAVD **Prod** - VOCAVD 1995

Occupational therapist
VHS
Day in a career series
Color (J H T G C A)
$89.00 purchase _ #VOC06V-J ; $89.00 purchase _ #VOC06V-G
Presents one of a ten-part series of videocassettes featuring various careers with the highest potential for success in the years before 2000. Profiles the detailed workday of a real person, with interviews and work situations. Includes

information about educational requirements, credentials, job outlook, salaries, and important associations and contacts. Each program 15 to 22 minutes in length.
Business and Economics; Guidance and Counseling; Health and Safety
Dist - CAMV

An Occupational Therapist Evaluating Functional Living Skills in Psychiatry
VHS / U-matic
Color
Presents the philosophy of assessing basic living skills, as well as the utilization of results in treatment planning. Discusses the Kohlman Evaluation of Living Skills, an assessment tool developed by an occupational therapist working in a University of Washington affiliated hospital, which evaluates a person's ability to function in the areas of self - care, safety and health, money management, transportation and telephone, and work and leisure.
Health and Safety
Dist - UWASH **Prod** - UWASH

An Occupational Therapist using a Screening Test
VHS / U-matic
Color
Reviews the utilization and guidelines for administration of the Denver Developmental Screening Tests. Illustrates actual scenes with therapists giving the test to two four - year - old children. Discusses test scores and interpretations.
Health and Safety; Psychology
Dist - UWASH **Prod** - UWASH

Occupational therapy and stroke rehabilitation 20 MIN
VHS / U-matic
Color (PRO C)
$395.00 purchase, $80.00 rental _ #C900 - VI - 052
Presents techniques of occupational therapy for effective rehabilitation of stroke patients. Offers treatment techniques for maximum functional return of patient's involved extremities, encouraging and developing independence in activities of daily living and problems of perception. Presented by Sarah Brickley, OTR, L Self Memorial Hospital, Upper Savannah AHEC.
Health and Safety
Dist - HSCIC

Occupational Therapy Evaluation - Klein - Bell Activities 29 MIN
U-matic / VHS
Color
Describes and presents guidelines for utilizing the Klein - Bell ADL scale. Illustrates the administration of this scale with a woman who has left hemiplegia. Shows procedure for marking the form as well as transferring this information to the score sheet. Reviews advantages of this scale.
Health and Safety; Psychology; Science - Natural
Dist - UWASH **Prod** - UWASH

Occupational Therapy Evaluation of the Hemiplegic Patient 11 MIN
16mm
Color
LC 75-702031; 74-705234
Demonstrates techniques and methods for the occupational evaluation of hemiplegic patients prior to initiating therapy.
Health and Safety; Psychology; Science - Natural
Dist - USNAC **Prod** - USPHS 1966

Occupational therapy - intervention in the rehabilitation of a client with basilar artery occlusion 45 MIN
VHS
Color (C PRO G)
$395.00 purchase _ #R851 - VI - 005
Presents a 34 - year - old male who suffers from bailar artery occlusion. Presents highlights of the rehabilitation process, an interview of the patient by the occupational therapist and an interdisciplinary team conference discussing the case. Considers psychosocial ramifications of the patient's condition along with occupational therapy intervention to remediate his physical limitations.
Health and Safety
Dist - HSCIC **Prod** - MCVA 1985

The Occupational Therapy Patient on the Nursing Unit 14 MIN
16mm / U-matic / VHS
Color
Points out how important it is for nursing unit personnel to let occupational therapy patients help themselves with dressing, personal hygiene and meals.
Health and Safety
Dist - USNAC **Prod** - USA

Occupational Therapy Skills Handicrafts Series

Art Series - Block Printing	13 MIN
Art Series - Silk Screening	27 MIN
Art Series - Stenciling	9 MIN

Dist - HSCIC

Occupational Therapy using a Screening - Sensory - Motor Evaluation of Hemiplegia 3 MIN
VHS / U-matic
Color
Illustrates portions of a sensory motor evaluation with a 30 - year - old man who has left hemiplegia. Includes a study guide that provides an extensive list of references and reviews the major theoretical bases for evaluation and treatment of hemiplegia.
Psychology; Science - Natural
Dist - UWASH **Prod** - UWASH

Occupations 15 MIN
16mm
Off to Adventure Series
Color (P I J)
Geography - World
Dist - YALEDV **Prod** - YALEDV

Occupations - Parts 15 and 16 60 MIN
VHS / U-matic
French in action - part I series
Color (C) (FRENCH)
$45.00, $29.95 purchase
Illustrates talking about work, degrees of assent, days and months of the year, buying and spending, approximating, 'aller' versus 'venir,' prepositions, contractions, adverbial pronouns 'y' and 'en,' 'voloir,' 'pouvoir,' formation of adverbs in Parts 15 and 16. Parts of a 52 - part series teaching the French language, all in French, written by Pierre Capretz, Director of the Language Laboratory at Yale.
Foreign Language; History - World
Dist - ANNCPB **Prod** - YALEU 1987

Occupations - Parts 17 and 18 60 MIN
VHS / U-matic
French in action - part I series
Color (C) (FRENCH)
$45.00, $29.95 purchase
Illustrates talking about work, degrees of assent, days and months of the year, buying and spending, approximating, 'aller' versus 'venir,' prepositions, contractions, adverbial pronouns 'y' and 'en,' 'voloir,' 'pouvoir,' formation of adverbs in Parts 17 and 18. Parts of a 52 - part series teaching the French language, all in French, written by Pierre Capretz, Director of the Language Laboratory at Yale.
Foreign Language; History - World
Dist - ANNCPB **Prod** - YALEU 1987

Occupations Series

Baking - the flour people	19 MIN
Behind the Scenes	24 MIN
Building maintenance	19 MIN
Child Care	24 MIN
Hairdressing	19 MIN
Helping hand	19 MIN
How do you feel about art	20 MIN
In for Servicing	24 MIN
Power Sewing	19 MIN
Preparing the food	24 MIN
Pump Island Serviceman	24 MIN
Selling to the Customer	24 MIN
Serving the customer	24 MIN
Small engines	19 MIN
That's the Flower Business	20 MIN
Welding	19 MIN
Woods Guiding - Fishing	19 MIN
Woods Guiding - Hunting	19 MIN

Dist - TVOTAR

Occupied Bed Making 15 MIN
16mm
Color (J)
Describes the various articles of bedding, their purpose and preferred type of material for hospital use. Demonstrates the changing of linen when the bed is occupied by a patient and shows the techniques of stripping and making the bed.
Education; Health and Safety
Dist - SF **Prod** - SF 1968

An Occurrence at Owl Creek Bridge 30 MIN
VHS
Classic short stories
Color (H)
#E362; LC 90-708394
Presents 'An Occurrence at Owl Creek Bridge' by Ambrose Bierce. Part of a series which combines Hollywood stars with short story masterpieces of the world to encourage appreciation of the short story.
Literature and Drama
Dist - GPN **Prod** - CTI 1988

An Occurrence at Owl Creek Bridge 17 MIN
16mm
Color
LC FIA60-618
A dramatic adaptation of Ambrose Bierce's famous Civil War story, told in flash back during the hanging of a Southern planter being executed for sabotage. (A USC Cinema Graduate Workshop Production.).
History - United States; Literature and Drama
Dist - USC **Prod** - USC 1956

An Occurrence at Owl Creek Bridge 27 MIN
16mm / U-matic / VHS
B&W (J)
LC FIA66-963
Presents an adaptation of Ambrose Bierce's Civil War story An Occurrence At Owl Creek Bridge, about a young man caught in an act of sabotage and hanged. Tells how in his last seconds of life he escapes and, in a dream - like sequence, races to join his beloved wife.
Fine Arts; Literature and Drama
Dist - FI **Prod** - ICHAC 1964

The Ocean 14 MIN
Videoreel / VT2
Images and Memories Series
Color
Features nature photographer Jim Bones celebrating the beauty of the ocean.
Fine Arts; Industrial and Technical Education
Dist - PBS **Prod** - KERA

Ocean 10 MIN
16mm / U-matic / VHS
Color (I J H C)
LC 71-709810
Presents a poetic interpretation of the sea in all its moods. Includes The Sea by John Keats and selections from Byron's Childe Harolde. Features specially composed music.
Fine Arts; Literature and Drama
Dist - PHENIX **Prod** - PFP 1969

The Ocean - a First Film 11 MIN
U-matic / VHS / 16mm
Color (P I) (SPANISH)
Discusses the marine life in the ocean, shows the ocean as a source of food and a great influence on all living things, including man. Explains that without the waters of the ocean, life as we know it could not exist.
Science - Natural
Dist - PHENIX **Prod** - BAILEY 1968

The Ocean - a First Film 11 MIN
U-matic / VHS / 16mm
Color (P I)
LC FIA68-2847
Explains that the ocean, which is the home of most of the world's life, influences all living things, including man.
Science - Natural; Science - Physical
Dist - PHENIX **Prod** - FA 1968

Ocean action
VHS
Color (G)
$24.50 purchase _ #0345
Overviews ocean sports. Includes boogie boarding, surfing, skateboarding, jet skis, parasailing, windsurfing.
Physical Education and Recreation
Dist - SEVVID

Ocean Adventure no 2 70 MIN
VHS
Ocean Adventure video magazine series
Color (G)
$100.00 rental _ #0502
Covers America's Cup '88, a powerboat which takes records in the Atlantic, the Kenwood Cup, water - skiing's Indy, the Carlsberg TransAtlantic Singlehanded Race, and new production multihulled catamarans. Presents the premiere issue of Ocean Adventure which follows the international racing scene, explores new cruising and chartering destinations, and teaches about new equipment and sailing techniques.
Physical Education and Recreation
Dist - SEVVID

Ocean Adventure no 1 - premiere issue 70 MIN
VHS
Ocean Adventure video magazine series
Color (G)
$100.00 rental _ #0501
Covers the America's Cup formula, recreational submarines, singlehanded sailing to Hawaii, trouble - shooting marine diesel engines, orientation at sea, a guide to cruising in Micronesia, wind weapon. Presents the premiere issue of Ocean Adventure which follows the international racing scene, explores new cruising and chartering destinations, and teaches about new equipment and sailing techniques.
Physical Education and Recreation
Dist - SEVVID

Ocean Adventure video magazine series
Ocean Adventure no 2 70 MIN
Ocean Adventure no 1 - premiere issue 70 MIN
Dist - SEVVID

The Ocean - always the weak and the strong; 2nd ed. 15 MIN
U-matic
Search for science series; Unit IV - Life in the ocean
Color (I)
Establishes the relationship between symbiosis and predation.
Geography - World; Science - Natural; Science - Physical
Dist - GPN **Prod** - WVIZTV

The Ocean - animal relationships; 2nd ed. 15 MIN
U-matic
Search for science series; Unit IV - Life in the ocean
Color (I)
Shows that unique relationships occur among and between the simplest animals.
Geography - World; Science - Natural; Science - Physical
Dist - GPN **Prod** - WVIZTV

Ocean animals 15 MIN
U-matic / VHS
Animals and such series; Module blue - habitats
Color (I J)
Considers characteristics of a host of marine creatures, including starfish, sea slugs and octopi.
Science - Natural
Dist - AITECH **Prod** - WHROTV 1972

The Ocean - animals of a different kind; 2nd ed. 15 MIN
U-matic
Search for science series; Unit IV - Life in the ocean
Color (I)
Looks at the unusual animals which live in the tidepools and shows their unique adaptive qualities.
Geography - World; Science - Natural; Science - Physical
Dist - GPN **Prod** - WVIZTV

Ocean Apart Series
An Ocean Apart - Vol I 121 MIN
An Ocean Apart - Vol II 122 MIN
An Ocean Apart - Vol III 121 MIN
An Ocean Apart - Vol IV 61 MIN
Dist - FI

An Ocean Apart - Vol I 121 MIN
VHS
Ocean Apart Series
Color (S)
$99.00 purchase _ #825 - 9510, 825 - 9511
Scrutinizes the 'special relationship' which has existed between the United States and Great Britain since the US gained its independence from the latter. Examines the people and the ideas that have shaped the mutual history of these two world powers through harmony and hostility. Volume I features two parts, 'Part 1 - Hats Off To Mr Wilson,' which explores the relationship between the two countries during World War I and features interviews with commanders and commoners who recall the war years, and, 'Part 2 - Home In Pasadena,' which uncovers the subterfuge some American companies used to challege British supremacy over world trade in the 1920s. The social impact of American cinema is also highlighted.
Civics and Political Systems; Fine Arts; Geography - World; History - United States
Dist - FI **Prod** - BBCTV 1988

An Ocean Apart - Vol II 122 MIN
VHS
Ocean Apart Series
Color (S)
$99.00 purchase _ #825 - 9512, 825 - 9543
Scrutinizes the 'special relationship' which has existed between the United States and Great Britain since the US gained its independence from the latter. Examines the people and the ideas that have shaped the mutual history of these two world powers through harmony and hostility. Volume II features two parts, 'Part 3 - Here Come The British, Bang! Bang!,' features Winston Churchill who did all in his power to woo the US into World War II. Shows how America's entry into the war did not save Britain's place in the world. 'Part 4 - Trust Me To The Bitter End' reveals the tensions and disagreement which divided the two countries during the war.
Civics and Political Systems; Geography - World; History - United States
Dist - FI **Prod** - BBCTV 1988

An Ocean Apart - Vol III 121 MIN
VHS
Ocean Apart Series
Color (S)
$99.00 purchase _ #825 - 9514, 825 - 9515
Scrutinizes the 'special relationship' which has existed between the United States and Great Britain since the US gained its independence from the latter. Examines the people and the ideas that have shaped the mutual history of these two world powers through harmony and hostility. Volume III features two parts, 'Part 5 - If You Don't Like Our Peaches, Quit Shaking The Tree,' features President Truman announcing an end to aid for Britain, and 'Part 6 - Under The Eagle's Wing' shows the 'special relationship' in tatters in 1957, until the USSR prompts a new partnership. In the 1960s American pop music is changed by the 'British invasion.'.
Fine Arts; Geography - World; History - United States
Dist - FI **Prod** - BBCTV 1988

An Ocean Apart - Vol IV 61 MIN
VHS
Ocean Apart Series
Color (S)
$99.00 purchase _ #825 - 9516
Scrutinizes the 'special relationship' which has existed between the United States and Great Britain since the US gained its independence from the latter. Examines the people and the ideas that have shaped the mutual history of these two world powers through harmony and hostility. Volume IV, 'Part 7 - Turning Up The Volume,' examines the people and events of recent years which may have stretched the 'special relationship' to the breaking point.
Geography - World; History - United States
Dist - FI **Prod** - BBCTV 1988

The Ocean at night - The Sea of Cortez 30 MIN
VHS
Return to the sea series
Color (I J H G)
$24.95 purchase _ #RTS104
Discloses that the drama of life in the sea goes on 24 hours a day. Visits a coral reef at night to meet a whole new cast of characters. Shows 'sleeping' fish, squid on the prowl for food and behaviors never before captured on film. Travels to the Sea of Cortez to observe giant Pacific manta rays, huge schools of hammerhead sharks and enormous pods of dolphin. Part of a 13 - part series on marine life produced by Marine Grafics and University of North Carolina Public TV.
Science - Natural; Science - Physical
Dist - ENVIMC

Ocean beat 60 MIN
16mm
Color (G)
$150.00 rental
Invites the viewer on a personal exploration of the oceanic realm, of the music and philosophy that arise from the protagonism of ocean and coast, ocean and living organisms - plants, animals and man. Travels back to the boundless reaches of the inner world. Filmed from 1980 - 1990 on California's Northern and Central coasts, in Alaska's Glacier Bay and on Hawaii's Volcanoes National Park.
Fine Arts; Geography - United States; Geography - World
Dist - CANCIN **Prod** - ZDRAVI 1990

Ocean Biologics electrophoresis techniques - DNA and proteins 40 MIN
VHS
Electrophoresis made easy series
Color (J H)
$85.00 purchase _ #A5VH 1089
Demonstrates for students the differences between horizontal and vertical systems of electrophoresis, focusing on Ocean Biologics equipment. Answers questions such as 'Which system is recommended for DNA analysis' and 'Why is agarose used with the horizontal system.' Covers the role of the power supply, function of the electrophoresis chambers, use of the buffer solution, pipetting methods, completion of the electrophoresis experiment and proper staining techniques. Uses time lapse photography to show electrophoresis of both an unknown DNA and an unknown protein. Concludes by analyzing the molecular weight of these unknown samples. Part of a series on electrophoresis.
Science - Physical
Dist - CLRVUE **Prod** - CLRVUE 1992

Ocean circulation - depth
VHS
Oceanography series
Color (J H)
$34.95 purchase _ #193 W 0062
Examines three main causes of water movement deep beneath the surface of the ocean. Part of a six - part single concept video series on basic principles of oceanography which include original demonstrations and photographic studies at the Woods Hole Oceanographic Institute.
Science - Physical
Dist - WARDS **Prod** - WARDS

Ocean circulation - surface
VHS
Oceanography series
Color (J H)
$34.95 purchase _ #193 W 0063
Depicts the currents found on the ocean's surface - caused primarily by the Earth's wind systems and modified by the Earth's rotation. Part of a six - part single concept video series on basic principles of oceanography which include original demonstrations and photographic studies at the Woods Hole Oceanographic Institute.
Science - Physical
Dist - WARDS **Prod** - WARDS

Ocean Corridors to World Trade 15 MIN
16mm
Color (I J H)
LC 79-700033
Shows how maritime trade has made people interdependent and has encouraged the growth of large population centers and harbors. Features harbor operations and various modes of cargo handling.
Business and Economics; Geography - World; Social Science
Dist - INMATI **Prod** - INMATI 1979

Ocean Currents 30 MIN
U-matic / VHS
Oceanus - the Marine Environment Series Lesson 12
Color
Lists the physical factors that cause ocean currents. Explains some of the effects of currents on surface productivity and localized weather conditions.
Science - Physical
Dist - CDTEL **Prod** - SCCON
SCCON

Ocean currents and winds 15 MIN
VHS
Color (I J H)
$69.00 purchase _ #GW - 5059 - VS
Examines the general oceanic circulation ranging from barely discernible drifts to surging warm currents, cold upswellings and bottom currents that spread icy waters from pole to pole. Shows how winds are a driving force behind most currents and how both systems are responsible for the global distribution of solar energy. Includes an account of how the El Nino event affects worldwide weather.
Science - Physical
Dist - HRMC **Prod** - EMECOR

Ocean, Desert and Thin Air 60 MIN
U-matic / VHS
Flight of the Condor Series
Color (H C A)
Shows a condor flying over the Pacific Coast of South America where the cold waters are among the richest in the world while the shore is the driest desert in the world. Views the condor searching the beach for carrion while vampire bats feed on the blood of sleeping sea lions.
Geography - World
Dist - FI **Prod** - BBCTV 1982

Ocean desert - the Sargasso Sea 10 MIN
VHS
Natural history series
Color (I J H)
$60.00 purchase _ #A5VH 1103
Visits the Sargasso Sea. Uses underwater photography to show an ocean desert lacking in nutrients but containing a variety of animal species. Shows how members of this unique ecosystem have adapted to life among the sargassum weed. Part of a series on natural history.
Science - Natural
Dist - CLRVUE **Prod** - CLRVUE

Ocean Dream 5 MIN
U-matic / 16mm / VHS
Color; Mono (G)
MV $85.00 _ MP $170.00
Explores the mysterious draw that the ocean seems to have over each of us. A beautiful young woman guides us through this film.
Geography - World
Dist - CTV **Prod** - MAKOF 1982

Ocean Dynamics - the Work of the Sea 23 MIN
U-matic / VHS / 16mm
Color (J H)
LC 82-700085
Presents an investigation of ocean movement. Describes the movement and direction of waves and longshore currents, the appearance and formation of the sea floor, the creation of surface currents, and the tracking of deep - sea storm systems.
Science - Physical
Dist - EBEC **Prod** - BORKBV 1981

The Ocean Ecosystem 15 MIN
VHS / 16mm
Ecosystems of the Great Land Series
Color (I H)
$125.00 purchase, $25.00 rental
Shows the journey Pacific salmon make to spawn and illustrates their role in the food chain.
Geography - United States; Science - Natural
Dist - AITECH **Prod** - ALASDE 1985

Ocean floor 25 MIN
U-matic / VHS
Oceanography series
Color (H C)
$250.00 purchase _ #HP - 5737C
Includes archival footage of William Beebe and his pioneering bathysphere. Visits Project FAMOUS and Robert Ballard to observe ocean crust formation from the submersible Alvin. Shows hydrothermal plumes, undersea volcanoes and evidence of massive rivers of sand flowing

down from the land in turbidity currents. Ends with a glimpse of the unique marine organisms which live in the cold, dark depths of the ocean. Part of a series on oceanography.
Science - Natural; Science - Physical
Dist - CORF **Prod** - BBCTV 1989

Ocean Instruments for Deep Submergence Vehicles 29 MIN
16mm
Color
LC 74-706546
Describes the special instrumentation requirements for deep submergence vehicles and highlights developments in this field.
Science; Science - Physical
Dist - USNAC **Prod** - USN 1969

Ocean Life 30 MIN
U-matic / VHS
Earth, Sea and Sky Series
Color (C)
Explores the phenomena of upwelling and its influence on ocean life. Demonstrates methods of studying the ocean. Explains the requirements, joys and dangers of scuba and snorkel diving.
Science - Physical
Dist - DALCCD **Prod** - DALCCD

An Ocean of air 10 MIN
VHS / U-matic
Weather wise series
Color (P I J)
$120.00, $170.00 purchase, $50.00 rental
Covers high and low air pressure, weather fronts, how air is affected by air pressure, temperature, direction of wind speed and relative humidity.
Science - Physical
Dist - NDIM **Prod** - LAWRN 1990

Ocean of Light - Pt 2 58 MIN
VHS
Atlantic Realm Series
Color (S)
$149.00 purchase _ #568 - 9023
Takes a 10,000 - mile odyssey of discovery to reveal the geology and natural history of the world's second largest ocean. Captures for the first time many of the mysterious life forms that inhabit the ocean's depths. Includes unique footage of a lemon shark giving birth, colonies of transparent fish, modern sea life previously seen only as fossils and the inside of an active volcano vent. Part 2 of three parts captures the wildlife that makes its home in the photic zone - the area where light penetrates the ocean waters. Examines the effects of winds and currents upon these creatures.
Geography - World; Science - Natural; Science - Physical
Dist - FI **Prod** - BBCTV 1989

Ocean of Wisdom
VHS / 16mm
Color (G)
$49.95 purchase _ #OCOW - N903
Profiles the Dalai Lama, winner of the 1990 Nobel Peace Prize. Reveals that he describes himself as 'a simple Buddhist monk, no more, no less.' The Dalai Lama heads a non - violent campaign to free his homeland Tibet from China. China was found guilty of Tibetan genocide in 1960 by the United Nations International Commission of Jurists. Produced by Mediart Films and KTEH, San Jose CA.
Biography; History - World; Religion and Philosophy
Dist - PBS

Ocean of wisdom - video presentation of the life and teaching of His Holiness the Fourteenth Dalai Lama 35 MIN
VHS
Color (G)
$49.95 purchase _ #POOW
Offers an intimate portrait of the Dalai Lama as a monk and as a spiritual leader. Follows him during his private religious practice, his daily routine and his infrequent recreation.
Biography; Religion and Philosophy
Dist - SNOWLI **Prod** - SNOWLI

Ocean Phenomenon - the Deep Scattering Layer 29 MIN
16mm
Color
LC 73-701404
Describes the search for the cause of sound reflecting layers of marine life living in the oceans of the world and how new information has helped in solving this mystery.
Science - Natural; Science - Physical
Dist - USNAC **Prod** - USN 1970

The Ocean Planet - the Death of the Mississippi 23 MIN
VHS / 16mm
Blue Revolution Series
Color (J)
$149.00 purchase, $75.00 rental _ #OD - 2295
Documents the decline of the Mississippi as a result of pollution. The 15th of 16 installments of the Blue Revolution Series.
Geography - United States; Sociology
Dist - FOTH

Ocean Racing 100 MIN
VHS / BETA
Color
Features ocean racing. Combines the short films 'Maximum Effort,' 'Kialoa To Jamaica,' 'Reckon With The Wind' And 'Rapid Transit.' Includes footage of the 1979 Transpac, the 1976 Victoria to Maui race and the voyage of Kialola III from Miami to Montego Bay.
Geography - World; Physical Education and Recreation
Dist - OFFSHR **Prod** - OFFSHR

Ocean racing combination
VHS
Color (G)
$49.95 purchase _ #0225
Presents four sequences on racing and cruising. Travels on the Kialoa III, Rapid Transit, Impossible.
Physical Education and Recreation
Dist - SEVVID

The Ocean realm - saltwater ecology 20 MIN
VHS
Biology of water series
Color (J H)
$90.00 purchase _ #A5VH 1336; $89.00 purchase _ #1973VG
Examines the intricate webs of food production and consumption existing in the sea. Presents food producers and photosynthesis. Looks at the primary food consumers - filter feeders, scavengers and the role of decomposers. Uses many phyla of sea creatures as examples and underwater photography to enhance material. Part of a four - part series on the role of water.
Science - Natural; Science - Physical
Dist - CLRVUE **Prod** - CLRVUE
UNL

The Ocean - Resource for the World 15 MIN
16mm / U-matic / VHS
Color; Captioned (I)
Examines the nature and diversity of the ocean's resources and emphasizes the need for conservation.
Science - Natural
Dist - HANDEL **Prod** - HANDEL 1980

Ocean salinity
VHS
Oceanography series
Color (J H)
$34.95 purchase _ #193 W 0064
Studies the basics of ocean salinity and explains why the amount of salt in proportion to water varies in different locations. Part of a six - part single concept video series on basic principles of oceanography which include original demonstrations and photographic studies at the Woods Hole Oceanographic Institute.
Science - Physical
Dist - WARDS **Prod** - WARDS

The Ocean Shore 18 MIN
16mm
Color (I J H)
LC 74-703484
Examines some of the different kinds of ocean shorelines and shows the variety of plants and animals that live in a shoreline environment.
Science - Natural; Science - Physical
Dist - MLA **Prod** - JHP 1974

The Ocean Sink 29 MIN
VHS / 16mm
Blue Revolution Series
Color (J)
$149.00 purchase, $75.00 rental _ #OD - 2296
Shows how governments are unwilling to act on environmental problems without proof of some damage. Studies polluted sites and explores the difficulty of waste disposal. The final of 16 installments of the Blue Revolution Series.
Science - Natural; Science - Physical; Sociology
Dist - FOTH

Ocean Studies Series
Life Under the Sea 17 MIN
World Beneath the Sea 23 MIN
Dist - AIMS

Ocean symphony 47 MIN
VHS
Color (G)
$29.90 purchase _ #0720
Presents an 11 part underwater adventure film with an original music score. Discusses killer whales, great white sharks, sea lions, octopus, humpback whales.
Fine Arts; Science - Natural; Science - Physical
Dist - SEVVID

Ocean temperatures
VHS
Oceanography series
Color (J H)
$34.95 purchase _ #193 W 0065
Explores reasons for distinct temperature differences in oceans and how these differences create currents. Part of a six - part single concept video series on basic principles of oceanography which include original demonstrations and photographic studies at the Woods Hole Oceanographic Institute.
Science - Physical
Dist - WARDS **Prod** - WARDS

Ocean tides
VHS
Oceanography series
Color (J H)
$34.95 purchase _ #193 W 0067
Presents the causes of ocean tides and the changes they produce in the landscapes and seascapes along the world's coasts. Part of a six - part single concept video series on basic principles of oceanography which include original demonstrations and photographic studies at the Woods Hole Oceanographic Institute.
Science - Physical
Dist - WARDS **Prod** - WARDS

Ocean Tides - Bay of Fundy 14 MIN
U-matic / VHS / 16mm
Color; B&W (I J H)
Explains that the constant rhythmic motion of ocean tides is caused by the gravitational pull of the moon and the sun, how the tidal range varies in different localities, and how the tides affect the activities of people who live near the ocean.
Science - Natural; Science - Physical
Dist - EBEC **Prod** - EBEC 1957

Ocean waves
VHS
Oceanography series
Color (J H)
$34.95 purchase _ #193 W 0066
Studies the motion of water in waves and delineates wave characteristics. Part of a six - part single concept video series on basic principles of oceanography which include original demonstrations and photographic studies at the Woods Hole Oceanographic Institute.
Science - Physical
Dist - WARDS **Prod** - WARDS

Ocean World 29 MIN
U-matic / VHS / 16mm
Color
Highlights resources of the sea and coastal zone, shows commercial fishery management, aquaculture research, seafloor mineral mining, and scientific measurements along the sea - air boundary to improve weather forecasting.
Geography - World; Industrial and Technical Education; Science - Natural; Science - Physical; Social Science
Dist - USNAC **Prod** - USNOAA

Oceania - the promise of tomorrow 48 MIN
VHS
Color (G)
$39.95 purchase
Features Estella Myers who spent eight years gathering material for this production showing our connections with dolphins. Includes scenes of tiny babies swimming underwater like dolphins.
Fine Arts; Science - Natural
Dist - HP

Oceanic Environment 22 MIN
VHS / U-matic
Basic Geology Series
Color (IND)
Industrial and Technical Education; Science - Physical
Dist - GPCV **Prod** - GPCV

Oceanic Processes 46 MIN
VHS / U-matic
Basic and Petroleum Geology for Non - Geologists - Landforms II 'Series; Landforms II
Color (IND)
Industrial and Technical Education; Science - Physical
Dist - GPCV **Prod** - PHILLP

Oceanic Topography 38 MIN
VHS / U-matic
Basic and Petroleum Geology for Non - Geologists - Landforms II 'Series; Landforms II
Color (IND)
Industrial and Technical Education; Science - Physical
Dist - GPCV **Prod** - PHILLP

Oceanographer in the Polar Regions 29 MIN
16mm
Color
LC 77-705625
Explains how oceanographers study the polar regions.

Science - Natural; Science - Physical
Dist - USNPC **Prod** - USNO 1969

Oceanographic Prediction System 30 MIN
16mm
Color
LC 73-701248
Discusses oceanographic prediction systems and programs and their relationship to defense and economic needs. Tells how predictions increase the use of oceanographic data for a fuller understanding and exploration of the seas.
Business and Economics; Civics and Political Systems; Science - Physical
Dist - USNAC **Prod** - USN 1966

Oceanographic Research with the Cousteau Diving Saucer 27 MIN
16mm
Color
LC 74-705236
Describes how U S Naval Electronics Laborabory scientists made use of the souscoupe and sous - marine of Jacques Cousteau over a period of six months.
Industrial and Technical Education; Science; Science - Physical
Dist - USNAC **Prod** - USN 1966

Oceanography 30 MIN
U-matic / VHS
Earth, Sea and Sky Series
Color (C)
Explores the Gulf Stream.
Science - Physical
Dist - DALCCD **Prod** - DALCCD

Oceanography in the Polar Regions 29 MIN
16mm
Color
LC 74-706511
Discusses oceanographic research in the Arctic and the Antarctic. Shows how men master the oceans for defense and for the economic betterment of the world.
Geography - World; Science - Physical
Dist - USNAC **Prod** - USN 1969

Oceanography - Science for Survival 27 MIN
16mm
Color
LC 74-705237
Shows the role of the navy within the framework of the inter - agency committee on numerous projects in oceanography.
Civics and Political Systems; Science - Natural; Science - Physical
Dist - USNAC **Prod** - USN 1964

Oceanography - Science of the Sea 11 MIN
16mm / U-matic / VHS
Color; B&W (I J H)
Describes how oceanographers explore the ocean waters, the sea floor and the earth's interior beneath the floor. Explains how sediments from the ocean floor provide clues to past history. Discusses the moho - the boundary between the earth's crust and mantle.
Science; Science - Natural; Science - Physical
Dist - PHENIX **Prod** - FA 1962

Oceanography series
Currents 25 MIN
Global sea level 25 MIN
Introduction to oceanography 50 MIN
Jamaica and the sea 25 MIN
Ocean floor 25 MIN
Oceans and climate 25 MIN
Polar oceans 25 MIN
Rockall 25 MIN
Waves 25 MIN
Dist - CORF

Oceanography series
Ocean circulation - depth
Ocean circulation - surface
Ocean salinity
Ocean temperatures
Ocean tides
Ocean waves
Dist - WARDS

Oceanography - the Role of People in Ocean Sciences 19 MIN
16mm / U-matic / VHS
Color (I J H)
LC 76-701301
Demonstrates the importance of personal investigation in the science of oceanography using simple tools, such as a snorkle, metric square and bags of dye.
Science; Science - Physical
Dist - PHENIX **Prod** - LIVDC 1966

Oceanography - the Study of Oceans 15 MIN
16mm / U-matic / VHS
Captioned; Color
LC 78-713644
Describes the scientific disciples involved in oceanography, including meteorology, physics, chemistry, biology and geology.
Science - Natural; Science - Physical
Dist - JOU **Prod** - WER 1970

Oceanography videos
VHS
Color (J H)
$175.00 purchase _ #193 W 0070
Presents a six - part series of single concept videos on basic principles of oceanography which include original demonstrations and photographic studies at the Woods Hole Oceanographic Institute. Covers ocean depth and surface circulation, salinity, temperatures, waves and tides.
Science - Physical
Dist - WARDS **Prod** - WARDS

Oceans 29 MIN
VHS / 16mm
Villa Alegre Series
Color (P T)
$46.00 rental _ #VILA - 122
Presents educational material in both Spanish and English.
Education; Science - Natural
Dist - PBS

The Oceans 145 MIN
U-matic
University of the Air Series
Color (J H C A)
$750.00 purchase, $250.00 rental
Considers the early knowledge of the oceans, ocean circulation, inlets, estuaries, waves and tides. Program contains a series of five cassettes 29 minutes each.
Geography - World
Dist - CTV **Prod** - CTV 1977

Oceans 55 MIN
16mm / VHS
Living Planet Series
(J H C)
$99.95 each, $595.00 series
Studies the vastness of water bodies and the minuteness of life forms therein. Hosted by David Attenborough.
Science; Science - Natural; Science - Physical
Dist - AMBROS **Prod** - AMBROS 1984

Oceans 55 MIN
U-matic / VHS / 16mm
Living Planet Series Pt 11
Color (H C A)
Looks at oceans in their broadest aspects, from drowned plants and hidden mountains to minute drifting plankton and forests of kelp. Features the food webs of the oceans and the evolution of fish and mammals that live there.
Science - Natural
Dist - TIMLIF **Prod** - BBCTV 1984

Oceans 16 MIN
U-matic / VHS
Color
Employs irony in an investigation of the conflicts between the personal and the political, the meditative and the active in a political mystery. An experimental film.
Fine Arts; Literature and Drama
Dist - MEDIPR **Prod** - MEDIPR 1980

Ocean's 11 127 MIN
U-matic / VHS / 16mm
Color (H C A)
Stars Frank Sinatra, Dean Martin, Sammy Davis Jr, Peter Lawford and Akim Tamiroff. Describes the comedy that ensues when a big - time racketeer plans a caper involving five top Las Vegas casinos and arranges with Danny Ocean, a former World War II sargeant, to round up ten of his buddies, each a specialist in the field of military sabotage, to carry it out.
Fine Arts
Dist - FI **Prod** - WB 1960

Oceans alive - Oceanos vivos series
Oceans alive - Part 1 - Oceanos vivos - Part I 50 MIN
Oceans alive - Part 2 - Oceanos vivos - Part II 50 MIN
Dist - ENVIMC

Oceans alive - Part 1 - Oceanos vivos - Part I 50 MIN
VHS
Oceans alive - Oceanos vivos series
Color (I J H G) (SPANISH)
$49.95 purchase _ #OA101, #OA105
Presents 10 five - minute programs illustrating the interrelationship of marine life and supporting instruction in life sciences. Discusses marine predators, cnidaria, coral, coral reefs, interdependence in marine animals, clownfish and anemone, camouflage behavior, marine animal weaponry. Coproduced with Marine Grafics.
Science - Natural; Science - Physical
Dist - ENVIMC **Prod** - ENVIMC

Oceans alive - Part 2 - Oceanos vivos - Part II 50 MIN
VHS
Oceans alive - Oceanos vivos series
Color (I J H G) (SPANISH)
$49.95 purchase _ #OA102, #OA106
Presents 10 five - minute programs illustrating the interrelationship of marine life and supporting instruction in life sciences. Discusses sponges, crustaceans, echinoderms, fish and their sensory apparatus, sharks and rays, how marine animals breath, what color the sea looks to be and the variety of ways that marine animals use to reproduce. Coproduced with Marine Grafics.
Science - Natural; Science - Physical
Dist - ENVIMC **Prod** - ENVIMC

Oceans alive - Part 3 50 MIN
VHS
Oceans alive series
Color (I J H G)
$49.95 purchase _ #OA103
Presents 10 five - minute programs illustrating the interrelationship of marine life and supporting instruction in life sciences. Discusses water cycles, marine mammals, dolphins, sea birds, salt marshes, the marine food web, plankton, mollusks, ocean sand, marine habitats. Coproduced with Marine Grafics.
Science - Natural; Science - Physical
Dist - ENVIMC **Prod** - ENVIMC

Oceans alive - Part 4 50 MIN
VHS
Oceans alive series
Color (I J H G)
$49.95 purchase _ #OA107
Presents 10 five - minute programs illustrating the interrelationship of marine life and supporting instruction in life sciences. Discusses how old, wrecked ships under the sea become islands of life, sea slugs, tunicates, rays, specialized reef fish, the ocean depths, the colors and patterns on sea animals, tides, humans and the sea. Coproduced with Marine Grafics.
Geography - World; Science - Natural; Science - Physical
Dist - ENVIMC **Prod** - ENVIMC

Oceans alive series
Presents a four - part series, each part containing 10 five - minute programs illustrating the interrelationship of marine life and supporting instruction in life sciences. Coproduced with Marine Grafics.
Oceans alive - Part 3 50 MIN
Oceans alive - Part 4 50 MIN
Dist - ENVIMC **Prod** - ENVIMC

Oceans and climate 25 MIN
U-matic / VHS
Oceanography series
Color (H C)
$250.00 purchase _ #HP - 5740C
Presents the experiences of oceanographers and other scientists as they develop ways to better predict global weather changes. Illustrates the key role that oceanic temperatures play in determining climate, the effect of polar regions in regulating ocean temperature and of carbon dioxide gain and loss in ocean waters. Part of a series on oceanography.
Geography - World; Science - Physical
Dist - CORF **Prod** - BBCTV 1989

Ocean's Edge 30 MIN
VHS / U-matic
Oceanus - the Marine Environment Series Lesson 5
Color
Discusses the seashore as a changing, dynamic environment. Looks at the various kinds of coastlines of the world. Explores the minerals found in both continental and island beach sands.
Science - Natural; Science - Physical
Dist - CDTEL **Prod** - SCCON
SCCON

The Oceans - going under in the Bahamas 24 MIN
VHS
Wild refuge series
Color (G)
$39.95 purchase
Uses a mini - submarine on an underwater expedition to a luxuriant Atlantic reef. Encounters tiger sharks, sea turtles and dolphins. Presents part of a thirteen - part series on the North American wilderness. Each episode documents a different area and shows how animal species cope with their surroundings to survive.
Geography - World; Science - Natural
Dist - CNEMAG **Prod** - HOBELP 1976

The Oceans - Living in Liquid Air 22 MIN
U-matic / VHS / 16mm
Color
Suggests that the vast, uncharted depths of the oceans will not stay that way for much longer. Shows that so far man can live under water for more than 60 days. Interivews marine experts and scientists who speak of artificial lungs and gills.

Science - Natural; Science - Physical
Dist - CNEMAG **Prod** - DOCUA 1971

Oceans of Science 27 MIN
16mm
Color (G)
_ *#106C 0174 544*
Shows what fisheries science is doing to ensure that life survivies in the seas and inland waters. Views projects on Canada's coasts and waters which illustrate the research directed toward restoring and protecting marine life.
Geography - World; Science - Natural
Dist - CFLMDC **Prod** - NFBC 1974

Oceans of Water, but - None to Spare 22 MIN
U-matic / VHS / 16mm
Color (I) (SPANISH)
LC 79-713190
Shows what is happening to the sea and its life, and explores the problems involved in conserving its resources. Features C Leroy French.
Science - Natural
Dist - AIMS **Prod** - TFW 1971

Oceans of Water, but None to Spare 22 MIN
16mm / U-matic / VHS
Color (I)
Features C Leroy French, Underwater Photographer of the Year.
Science - Natural; Science - Physical
Dist - AIMS **Prod** - AIMS 1971

Oceans Surround Us 20 MIN
U-matic
Understanding Our World, Unit II - Geography We Should Know Series
Color (I)
Shows hidden plant and animal worlds in the depths of the oceans.
Geography - World; Science - Physical
Dist - GPN **Prod** - KRMATV

Oceans - the cradle of life 15 MIN
VHS
Our wondrous oceans series
CC; Color (I J)
$69.95 purchase _ #10400VG
Examines the change in oceans and how they support life. Explores plate tectonics, topography, marine life and evolution. Comes with a video interactive quiz, teacher's guide and blackline masters. Part one of a two - part series.
Geography - World; Science - Natural; Science - Physical
Dist - UNL

Oceans, weather and climate 14 MIN
VHS
Junior oceanographer series
CC; Color (P I)
$69.95 purchase_#10367VG
Outlines the important link between the world's oceans and its weather and climate. Addresses issues such as the water cycle; the effect of the ocean on weather; and ocean currents. Comes with an interactive video quiz, a teacher's guide and six blackline masters. Part three of a four - part series.
Geography - World; Science - Physical
Dist - UNL

Oceanus - the Marine Environment 900 MIN
U-matic / VHS
Color (C A)
Introduces oceanography, its concepts, theories, and predictions, featuring America's leading oceanographers.
Science - Natural; Science - Physical; Social Science
Dist - SCCON **Prod** - SCCON 1980

Oceanus - the Marine Environment - Epilogue 30 MIN
U-matic / VHS
Oceanus - the Marine Environment Series Lesson 30
Color
Comprises final lecture in series. Focuses on future aspects of the world's oceans.
Science - Natural; Science - Physical
Dist - CDTEL **Prod** - SCCON

Oceanus - the Marine Environment Series Lesson 1
The Water Planet 30 MIN
Dist - CDTEL
SCCON

Oceanus - the Marine Environment Series Lesson 3
Historical Perspectives 30 MIN
Dist - CDTEL

Oceanus - the Marine Environment Series Lesson 4
The Waters of the Earth 30 MIN
Dist - CDTEL
SCCON

Oceanus - the Marine Environment Series Lesson 5
Ocean's Edge 30 MIN
Dist - CDTEL
SCCON

Oceanus - the Marine Environment Series Lesson 7
Continental Margins 30 MIN
Dist - CDTEL
SCCON

Oceanus - the Marine Environment Series Lesson 11
Marine Meteorology 30 MIN
Dist - CDTEL
SCCON

Oceanus - the Marine Environment Series Lesson 12
Ocean Currents 30 MIN
Dist - CDTEL
SCCON

Oceanus - the Marine Environment Series Lesson 15
Plankton - Floaters and Drifters 30 MIN
Dist - CDTEL

Oceanus - the marine environment series lesson 17
Reptiles and birds 30 MIN
Dist - CDTEL
SCCON

Oceanus - the Marine Environment Series Lesson 18
Mammals - Seals and Otters 30 MIN
Dist - CDTEL

Oceanus - the Marine Environment Series Lesson 19
Mammals - Whales 30 MIN
Dist - CDTEL

Oceanus - the Marine Environment Series Lesson 21
Light in the Sea 30 MIN
Dist - CDTEL

Oceanus - the Marine Environment Series Lesson 23
Life Under Pressure 30 MIN
Dist - CDTEL

Oceanus - the Marine Environment Series Lesson 26
Mineral Resources 30 MIN
Dist - CDTEL
SCCON

Oceanus - the marine environment series lesson 27
Biological resources 30 MIN
Dist - CDTEL
SCCON

Oceanus - the Marine Environment Series Lesson 28
Marine Pollution 30 MIN
Dist - CDTEL
SCCON

Oceanus - the Marine Environment Series Lesson 30
Oceanus - the Marine Environment - Epilogue 30 MIN
Dist - CDTEL

Oceanus - the marine environment series
Living together 30 MIN
The Polar seas 30 MIN
Dist - CDTEL

Oceanus - the marine environment series
Beyond land's end 30 MIN
Cosmic Origins 28 MIN
The Ebb and flow 30 MIN
Hawaii - a case study 30 MIN
Intertidal zone 30 MIN
Nekton - Swimmers 30 MIN
Sound in the Sea 30 MIN
The Tropic seas 30 MIN
Wind, Waves, and Water Dynamics 28 MIN
Dist - CDTEL
SCCON

Oceanus - the Marine Environment Series
Epilogue 28 MIN
Historical Perspectives 28 MIN
Islands 28 MIN
Life Under Pressure 28 MIN
Mammals - Seals and Otters 28 MIN
Mammals - Whales 28 MIN
Plankton - Floaters and Drifters 28 MIN
Plate Tectonics 28 MIN
The Tropic Seas 28 MIN
Dist - SCCON

OCS - Officer Candidate School 28 MIN
16mm
Color
LC 74-705238
Shows a dynamic and intimate personal profile of men enrolled in the training program of the U S Naval Officer Candidate School, which prepares them to be naval officers.
Civics and Political Systems; Education
Dist - USNAC **Prod** - USN 1972

The OCS Story 29 MIN
16mm
Big Picture Series
Color
LC 74-706162
Describes the special training which officer candidates receive in the U S Army Officer Candidate Schools.
Civics and Political Systems
Dist - USNAC **Prod** - USA 1967

Octavio Paz - an Uncommon Poet 29 MIN
16mm / U-matic / VHS
Color (H C A)
LC 79-700650
Presents Mexican poet Octavio Paz talking about his childhood, his activities as a political activist and his views on poets, poetry and language.
Biography; Literature and Drama
Dist - FOTH **Prod** - WNETTV 1979

October 10 MIN
VHS / U-matic
Emma and Grandpa series
Color (K P)
$180.00 purchase, $30.00 rental, $110.00 self dub
Focuses on Grandpa showing Emma greenhouse plants and cultivation. Tells of how outdoor cultivation is becoming more rare, and how greenhouses are necessary. Intermixed are humorous scenarios with Emma.
Geography - World; Science - Natural; Sociology
Dist - GPN **Prod** - GRIFN 1983

October
VHS
Silent; B&W (G)
$29.95 purchase _ #1621
Presents the classic silent chronicle of the Russian Revolution by Sergei Eisenstein. Includes rare footage of the Czar's Winter Palace in Leningrad. Based on John Reed's book, 'Ten Days That Shook The World,' musical background score by Dimitri Shostakovich.
Fine Arts; Foreign Language; Geography - World; Industrial and Technical Education
Dist - KULTUR

October 1917 52 MIN
U-matic / VHS
B&W (G)
$249.00, $149.00 purchase _ #AD - 1483
Follows the events of the October Revolution in 1917, from the defeat of the Czarist army and famine in Russia, to the overthrow of Czar Nicholas and the assumption of power by the Communists. Draws from newsreel footage and Soviet propaganda films. Shows the effects of the Revolution in Western Europe - innocents and idealists cynically goaded and provoked to marches, protests and strikes that were met with brutal repression.
Civics and Political Systems; History - United States; History - World; Sociology
Dist - FOTH **Prod** - FOTH

October 23, 1642 14 MIN
VHS / 16mm
Newscast from the Past Series
Color (I J H)
$58.00 purchase _ #ZF226V
Uses TV news format to portray October 23, 1642 - civil war in England, Catholic uprising in Ulster, Galileo recants cosmic theory, completion of Taj Mahal, Pocahontas dies, ads feature cocoa and mechanical clocks. Six different historical dates in series.
History - World; Social Science
Dist - SSSSV **Prod** - ZENGER 1984

October Harvest - Pt 5 58 MIN
VHS
Comrades Series
Color (S)
$79.00 purchase _ #351 - 9026
Follows twelve Soviet citizens from different backgrounds to reveal what Soviet life is like for a cross section of the 270 million inhabitants in the vast country of fifteen republics. Features Frontline anchor Judy Woodruff who also

interviews prominent experts on Soviet affairs. Part 5 of the twelve - part series considers the Kulinich family which lives and works on a collective farm in Southern Russia. The Kulinichs, like many other peasants, have formed their own version of the communist way of life - Leninism with loopholes.
Agriculture; Civics and Political Systems; Geography - World; Social Science; Sociology
Dist - FI **Prod** - WGBHTV 1988

October - Ten Days that Shook the World 106 MIN
16mm / U-matic / VHS
B&W (H C A)
LC 81-701031
Depicts events of the Russian Revolution of October, 1917. Describes the Kerensky regime and the European War, and discusses the conflicting plans and ambitions of various participants.
History - World
Dist - PHENIX **Prod** - SOVKNO 1981

October - Ten Days that Shook the World , Pt 1 36 MIN
U-matic / VHS / 16mm
B&W (H C A)
LC 81-701031
Depicts events of the Russian Revolution of October, 1917. Describes the Kerensky regime and the European War, and discusses the conflicting plans and ambitions of various participants.
History - World; Sociology
Dist - PHENIX **Prod** - SOVKNO 1981

October - Ten Days that Shook the World , Pt 2 35 MIN
U-matic / VHS / 16mm
B&W (H C A)
LC 81-701031
Depicts events of the Russian Revolution of October, 1917. Describes the Kerensky regime and the European War, and discusses the conflicting plans and ambitions of various participants.
History - World; Literature and Drama
Dist - PHENIX **Prod** - SOVKNO 1981

October - Ten Days that Shook the World , Pt 3 35 MIN
U-matic / VHS / 16mm
B&W (H C A)
LC 81-701031
Depicts events of the Russian Revolution of October, 1917. Describes the Kerensky regime and the European War, and discusses the conflicting plans and ambitions of various participants.
History - World; Literature and Drama
Dist - PHENIX **Prod** - SOVKNO 1981

Octopuff in Kumquat 9 MIN
16mm
Color (P I)
Presents an anti - smoking message in the form of a cartoon adventure story.
Fine Arts; Health and Safety; Psychology
Dist - AMLUNG **Prod** - NTBA 1975

Octopus 25 MIN
VHS
Nature watch series
Color (P I J H C)
$49.00 purchase _ #320202; LC 89-715846
Shows that the octopus is one of the sea's most sophisticated animals and is expert at ambush and camouflage. Part of a series that explores the curious and uncommon characteristics of a variety of mammals, insects, birds and sea creatures.
Science - Natural
Dist - TVOTAR **Prod** - TVOTAR 1988

The Octopus 12 MIN
U-matic / VHS / 16mm
Wild, Wild World of Animals Series
Color
LC 77-701752
Studies the eating habits, survival techniques and mating behavior of the octopus. Edited from the television program Wild, Wild World Of Animals.
Science - Natural
Dist - TIMLIF **Prod** - TIMLIF 1976

The Octopus 11 MIN
U-matic / VHS / 16mm
Animal Families Series
Color (K P I)
$275, $195, $225 purchase _ #B425
Explains the anatomy, eating habits, and general life cycle of the octopus using narration.
Science - Natural
Dist - BARR **Prod** - BARR 1986

Octopus, octopus 22 MIN
U-matic / VHS / 16mm
Undersea world of Jacques Cousteau series
Color (G)
$49.95 purchase; LC 78-70046
A shortened version of the 1971 motion picture Octopus, Octopus. Features the undersea photography of Jacques Cousteau and his team to reveal little - known facts about the life of the octopus.
Science - Natural
Dist - CF **Prod** - METROM 1977

Octopus, the Unique Mollusk 14 MIN
16mm
Color
Studies the octopus and it's characteristics such as very good eyesight and a brain larger than that of any other invertebrate animal. Views its method of reproduction.
Science - Natural
Dist - RARIG **Prod** - RARIG

Ocular Examination, Pt 1 14 MIN
U-matic / VHS
Color (PRO)
Discusses such topics as taking a pertinent history for ocular patients, evaluating visual acuity and visual fields, giving an external examination and the appropriate methods for examination.
Health and Safety; Science - Natural
Dist - UMICHM **Prod** - UMICHM 1976

Ocular Examination, Pt 2 14 MIN
VHS / U-matic
Color (PRO)
Presents a detailed evaluation of the external eye and intraocular structures. Provides a comprehensive description of the examination procedures, and discussion of an opthalmic examination.
Health and Safety; Science - Natural
Dist - UMICHM **Prod** - UMICHM 1976

Ocular Injuries, Pt 1 16 MIN
U-matic / VHS
Color (PRO)
Discusses the evaluation process for ocular injuries commonly seen by primary care physicians, including how to avert the eyelids. Describes treatment of foreign bodies, corneal abrasions, chemical burns and radiant burns.
Health and Safety; Science - Natural
Dist - UMICHM **Prod** - UMICHM 1976

Ocular Injuries, Pt 2 16 MIN
U-matic / VHS
Color (PRO)
Discusses initial evaluation and treatment of ocular trauma and indications for referral to an opthalmologist.
Health and Safety; Science - Natural
Dist - UMICHM **Prod** - UMICHM 1976

The Oculomotor Disorders 30 MIN
16mm
Color
Shows the recent advance of electrophysiology in the field of neuro - ophthalmology. Points out that the extraocular muscle is one of the most important parts for diagnosing the diseases occurring in the brain if we employ modern electronics for analysis. Explains clinical and basic problems of neuro - ophthalmology in the past several years, including possible sympathetic innervation and parasympathetic innervation onto the extrocaular muscle.
Health and Safety; Psychology; Science; Science - Natural
Dist - UNIJAP **Prod** - UNIJAP 1967

Odd and Even 15 MIN
U-matic
Studio M Series
Color (P)
Tells how to distinguish between odd and even digits.
Mathematics
Dist - GPN **Prod** - WCETTV 1979

Odd and even numbers
VHS
Lola May's fundamental math series
Color (P)
$45.00 purchase _ #10256VG
Introduces the concepts of odd and even. Uses models of squares to illustrate odd and even number sequences. Comes with a teacher's guide and blackline masters. Part six of a 30 - part series.
Mathematics
Dist - UNL

Odd obsession 96 MIN
VHS
Color (G) (JAPANESE WITH ENGLISH SUBTITLES)
$22.95 purchase _ #NEL6060
Offers a complex morality tale of an older man's perversions and the destruction they bring upon his family. Directed by Kon Ichikawa.
Fine Arts
Dist - CHTSUI

The Oddball 30 MIN
16mm
Color (R)
Shows the importance of maintaining keenly felt Christian convictions in the face of any pressure. Points out that the oddball in this story is Christian young person who is on trial for being a misfit in his peer group.
Guidance and Counseling; Religion and Philosophy; Sociology
Dist - BROADM **Prod** - BROADM 1971

Odds and Ends 5 MIN
16mm
Color (H C)
Presents a collage film comedy.
Industrial and Technical Education; Literature and Drama
Dist - CFS **Prod** - CFS 1959

Odds and Ends 15 MIN
U-matic / VHS
Primary Art Series
Color (P)
Shows how old scraps of wood, plastic, cardboard and other materials can be used to make art. Examines the assemblage works of Pablo Picasso, Kurt Schwitter and Abe Vigil.
Fine Arts
Dist - AITECH **Prod** - WETATV

The Odds and Ends Playground 6 MIN
16mm / U-matic / VHS
Golden Book Storytime Series
Color (P)
Shows how Danny and his neighbors turn a littered vacant lot into a playground.
Literature and Drama
Dist - CORF **Prod** - CORF 1977

Ode to Nature 5 MIN
16mm
Color (I)
LC 74-700075
Presents a series of short vignettes on recycling and anti - litter scenes relevant to today's environmental problems.
Science - Natural
Dist - MARALF **Prod** - MARALF 1973

Odeon Cavalcade 35
16mm / VHS
Color (H A)
$720.00 purchase, $65.00 rental
Explores the art deco movie palaces built by Odeon, one of the first movie chains, whose theaters took distinctive architectural forms. Reflects the design aesthetics of entrepreneur Oscar Deutsch and architect Harry Weldon.
Fine Arts
Dist - AFA **Prod** - ACGB 1974

The Odessa Steps 15 MIN
16mm
B&W
Features excerpts from Sergi Eisensteins's classic 'POTEMKIN'.
Fine Arts
Dist - FCE **Prod** - FCE 1925

Odessa Steps Sequence 10 MIN
16mm
B&W
Features the Odessa Steps sequence from Sergei Eisenstein's film Potemkin.
Fine Arts
Dist - REELIM **Prod** - ESNSTN 1925

OdilonOdilon 21 MIN
16mm
B&W (G)
$35.00 rental
Portrays an adolescent boy discovering his own indentity and his place within his family society. Uses historic sound, such as Edward R Murrow's Christmas Eve broadcast during World War II to the parents of the young children of London's families, urging them to send their youngest to the country to save their lives as a protection against the nightly bombing raids.
Fine Arts; History - World; Psychology; Sociology
Dist - CANCIN **Prod** - COUZS 1984

Odontogenesis - Early 11 MIN
U-matic
Microanatomy Laboratory Orientation Series
Color (C)
Covers the development of the enamel organ following the cellular patterns through the bud, cup and bell stages.
Health and Safety; Science - Natural
Dist - UOKLAH **Prod** - UOKLAH 1986

Odontogenesis - Late 12 MIN
U-matic
Microanatomy Laboratory Orientation Series
Color (C)
Covers the development of the tooth from the period of apposition and calcification through the period of eruption, both before and after emergence, and finally considers attrition to the deciduous tooth and the changes involved during its replacement by the permanent tooth.

Health and Safety; Science - Natural
Dist - UOKLAH **Prod** - UOKLAH 1986

Odyceka 10 MIN
16mm
Color (G)
$20.00 rental
Records an odyssey of kayacking during a summer in Prince William Sound, Alaska. Features music by Stephan Ruppenthal and Richard Moffitt.
Fine Arts; Geography - United States
Dist - CANCIN **Prod** - FERGCO 1980

Odysseus and Ithaca 12 MIN
VHS / 16mm
Greek and Roman Mythology in Ancient Art Series
Color (I)
LC 90708205
Gives an account of the adventures of Odysseus. Shows their relationship to Ithaca.
Fine Arts; History - World; Religion and Philosophy
Dist - BARR

Odyssey 15 MIN
VHS
Color (G)
$25.00 rental
Aims to heighten viewer's spiritual awareness by evoking a visual poem. Portrays the odyssey of a woman - goddess born from the sand. Filmed in the Anza - Borrego Desert, California, with floor temperatures reaching 140 degrees. Produced by Barry J Hershey.
Fine Arts; Geography - United States
Dist - CANCIN

Odyssey 4 MIN
16mm
Color
Presents a graphic journey through a world of apparent horrors where the main character strives to return to its womb, but learns that one can never return to the past.
Fine Arts
Dist - USC **Prod** - USC 1980

Odyssey - a Quest for Energy 28 MIN
16mm
Color
Utilizes colorful animation and cinematography in taking an exploration of oil and petroleum, coal, nuclear and solar power, synthetic fuels and geothermal energy.
Social Science
Dist - MTP **Prod** - API

The Odyssey of Dr Pap 30 MIN
16mm
Color (C A)
LC 72-700665
Traces the career of Dr Papanicolaou from the early days in Greece to his emergence as one of the world's outstanding scientists. Points out that Dr Pap's discovery of cancer cells in the vaginal discharges of women, before there were symptoms of the disease, was a landmark in medicine.
Biography; Health and Safety; Science; Science - Natural
Dist - AMCS **Prod** - OLSKRH 1969

Odyssey of Rita Hayworth 26 MIN
16mm
Hollywood and the Stars Series
B&W
LC 74-701940
Presents a study of the career of Rita Hayworth, using clips from her films. Includes scenes of her personal life and her comments on her life and career.
Biography; Fine Arts
Dist - WOLPER **Prod** - WOLPER 1964

The Odyssey, Pt 1 - the Structure of the Epic 27 MIN
16mm / U-matic / VHS
Humanities - Narrative Series
Color (H C)
LC FIA66-1152
Presents Gilbert Highet discussing the basic framework of the Odyssey and tracing the background of the Trojan War and events in Odysseus' home while he was away. Dramatizes highlights of Odysseus' travels.
Literature and Drama
Dist - EBEC **Prod** - EBEC 1966

The Odyssey, Pt 3 - the Central Themes 28 MIN
U-matic / VHS / 16mm
Humanities - Narrative Series
Color (H C)
Presents Gilbert Highet discussing the central themes of the Odyssey, including Odysseus' wanderings among giants and monsters, Odysseus' return home and Telemachus' growing to manhood.
Literature and Drama
Dist - EBEC **Prod** - EBEC 1965

The Odyssey, Pt 2 - the Return of Odysseus 26 MIN
U-matic / VHS / 16mm
Humanities - Narrative Series
Color (H C)
Focuses upon Odysseus' activities after his return to Ithaca and the manner in which these actions slowly reveal his true character.
Literature and Drama
Dist - EBEC **Prod** - EBEC 1965

The Odyssey Reading Center 16 MIN
U-matic / VHS
Odyssey Reading Center Series
(I J)
Contains 7 paperbacks, 7 read along cassettes, and 30 spirit masters.
Literature and Drama; Religion and Philosophy
Dist - TROLA **Prod** - TROLA 1986

Odyssey Reading Center Series
The Odyssey Reading Center 16 MIN
Dist - TROLA

Odyssey Series
Ben's mill 59 MIN
The Chaco Legacy 59 MIN
Dadi's family 59 MIN
The Incas 59 MIN
Little Injustices - Laura Nader Looks at the Law 59 MIN
Maya Lords of the Jungle 59 MIN
Myths and Moundbuilders 59 MIN
On the Cowboy Trail 59 MIN
Dist - DOCEDR

Odyssey Series
Franz Boas, 1858 - 1942 60 MIN
Margaret Mead - Taking Note 59 MIN
Other people's garbage 60 MIN
Seeking the first Americans 60 MIN
Dist - DOCEDR
PBS

Odyssey Series
The Arctic conquest 15 MIN
The Arctic ice 15 MIN
The Arctic people 15 MIN
The Arctic resources 15 MIN
The Arctic tundra 15 MIN
Creatures of the continent 15 MIN
Equatorial conquest 15 MIN
Equatorial jungle 15 MIN
Equatorial products 15 MIN
Equatorial young people 15 MIN
Ice Over Land 15 MIN
Men of Courage 15 MIN
Ninety Degrees South 15 MIN
Operation Deep Freeze 15 MIN
Dist - GPN

Odyssey series
The Ancient mariners 58 MIN
Ben's mill 58 MIN
The Chaco Legacy 59 MIN
Dadi's Family 58 MIN
Franz Boas - 1852 - 1942 60 MIN
The Incas 58 MIN
Little Injustices - Laura Nader Looks at the Law 58 MIN
Maya Lords of the Jungle 58 MIN
Myths and Moundbuilders 58 MIN
On the Cowboy Trail 58 MIN
The Three Worlds of Bali 60 MIN
Dist - PBS

The Odyssey Tape 30 MIN
VHS / U-matic
Color
Presents spoken form of Homer's ancient poem The Odyssey by concert artist Richard Dyer - Bennet.
Fine Arts; Literature and Drama
Dist - MOMA **Prod** - MOMA

The Odyssey Tapes 30 MIN
VHS / U-matic
Color
Presents spoken form of Homer's ancient poem The Odyssey by concert artist Richard Dyer - Bennet.
Fine Arts; Literature and Drama
Dist - SULANI **Prod** - SULANI

The Odyssey - the central themes 29 MIN
VHS
Color (J H)
$99.00 purchase _ #47593 - 026
Features Gilbert Highet explaining that the diverging themes in The Odyssey are based on a moral truth - heroism demands both bravery and intelligence. Includes teacher's guide.
Education; Literature and Drama; Religion and Philosophy
Dist - GA **Prod** - EBEC

Odyssey
Other People's Garbage 59 MIN
Dist - DOCEDR

Oedipus at Colonus 120 MIN
U-matic / VHS
Theban Plays Series
Color (C)
$349.00, $199.00 purchase _ #AD - 1319
Presents the second part of the Oedipus saga with Oedipus an old man, blind and outcast. Features Anthony Quayle, Juliet Stevenson and Kenneth Haigh in the cast.
History - World; Literature and Drama
Dist - FOTH **Prod** - FOTH

Oedipus at Colonus 120 MIN
VHS / 16mm
Theban Plays Series
Color (C)
$16.50 rental _ #90413
Portrays the later years of Oedipus. Now old, blind and outcast, Oedipus wanders through Greece, guided by his daughter Antigone to Colonus, where he knows he will die. Protected by Thebes against the pursing armies of Creon, Oedipus curses his son Polynices for indifference and ingratitude. Stars Anthony Quayle, Juliet Stevenson, and Kenneth Haigh. Part 2 of the series.
Literature and Drama
Dist - PSU **Prod** - BBC 1987

Oedipus at Colonus, Pt 2 120 MIN
VHS
Theban Plays Series
Color (C)
$16.50 rental _ #90413
Tells the story of Oedipus, now old, blind and outcast, wandering through Greece and guided to Colonus, where he knows he will die, by his daughter Antigone. One of the three Theban Plays, which tell the entire story of Oedipus and his family. Features Anthony Quayle, Juliet Stevenson and Kenneth Haigh.
Literature and Drama
Dist - PSU

Oedipus Rex 90 MIN
VHS
Color (G C H)
$119.00 purchase _ #DL36
Recreates the play by Sophocles. Uses the W B Yeats translation and authentic period masks.
Fine Arts; History - World
Dist - INSIM

Oedipus rex 110 MIN
35mm
Color (G) (ITALIAN WITH ENGLISH SUBTITLES)
$300.00 rental
Begins with the autobiographical prologue of director Pier Paolo Pasolini set in Lombardy, Italy, in the 1920s. Presents a ferocious, astounding vision of humankind and its unchanging nature.
Fine Arts; Literature and Drama
Dist - KINOIC

Oedipus Rex 30 MIN
VHS / 16mm
Play Series
Color (H)
Presents Sophocles' Oedipus Rexs. The seventh of eight installments of CTI's The Play Series, which attempts to give students an appreciation of the unique elements of the play through detailed examination of classic and trendsetting productions.
Fine Arts; Literature and Drama
Dist - GPN **Prod** - CTI 1990

Oedipus Rex and the Flood 83 MIN
VHS
Color (S)
$49.95 purchase _ #833 - 9288
Features Bernard Haitink conducting the Concertgebouw Orchestra performance of 'Oedipus Rex,' music by Igor Stravinsky, libretto by Jean Cocteau. Recreates also 'The Flood,' a musical play developed by Stravinksy and George Balanchine for CBS Television and first broadcast in 1962. Jaap Drupsteen uses modern video effects to present the play as originally envisioned by Stravinsky and Balanchine.
Fine Arts
Dist - FI **Prod** - RMART 1987

Oedipus Rex - man and God 30 MIN
VHS
Color (G C H)
$129.00 purchase _ #DL386
Analyzes the theme of subordination of man to God, as developed in Oedipus Rex. Uses excerpts from the play to examine the results of Oedipus' initial rejection of religion, as represented by the oracle Tiresius, and his subsequent realization that man is not the measure of all things.
Fine Arts; Literature and Drama; Religion and Philosophy
Dist - INSIM

Oedipus Rex - Oedipus the King 20 MIN
U-matic / VHS
Color (S)

Presents the classic Greek Play Oedipus Rex. Signed.
Fine Arts; Guidance and Counseling; Literature and Drama; Psychology
Dist - GALCO **Prod** - GALCO 1957

Oedipus Rex, Pt 4 - the Recovery of Oedipus 30 MIN
16mm / U-matic / VHS
Humanities - the Drama Series
Color (H C) (SPANISH)
Considers how the Greek tragedy shows man as somewhere between God and beast, always looking for his rightful place.
Literature and Drama
Dist - EBEC **Prod** - EBEC 1959

Oedipus Rex, Pt 3 - Man and God 30 MIN
U-matic / VHS / 16mm
Humanities - the Drama Series
Color (H C) (SPANISH)
Explains that one philosophical message of Oedipus is that man, no matter how great his ability, is subordinate to God. Shows how this theme is reinforced when Oedipus, representing the worldly liberal thought infusing Greek civilization, is beaten by the gods.
Literature and Drama
Dist - EBEC **Prod** - EBEC 1959

Oedipus the King 58 MIN
Videoreel / VT2
Dialogue of the Western World Series
Color
Features Dean Robert A Goldwin of St John's College of Annapolis and three of his students discussing Oedipus the King with a special guest.
History - World; Literature and Drama
Dist - PBS **Prod** - MDCPB

Oedipus the King 30 MIN
U-matic / VHS
Communicating through Literature Series
Color (C)
Literature and Drama
Dist - DALCCD **Prod** - DALCCD

Oedipus the King 120 MIN
U-matic / VHS
Theban Plays Series
Color (C)
$349.00, $199.00 purchase _ #AD - 1318
Begins the Oedipus saga. Features Michael Pennington, John Gielgud and Claire Bloom in the cast.
History - World; Literature and Drama
Dist - FOTH **Prod** - FOTH

Oedipus the King 120 MIN
VHS / 16mm
Theban Plays Series
Color (C)
$16.50 rental _ #90412
Presents Sophocles' most famous tragedy, Oedipus the King. This sets the stage and creates the characters to be followed through the Oedipus saga in the other two plays in this series. Stars Michael Pennington, Sir John Gieglud, and Claire Bloom. Part 1 of the series.
Literature and Drama
Dist - PSU **Prod** - BBC 1987

Oedipus the King, Pt 1 120 MIN
VHS
Theban Plays Series
Color (C)
$16.50 rental _ #90412
Begins the story of Oedipus and his family. Stars Michael Pennington, Sir John Gielgud and Claire Bloom. One of the three Theban Plays, which tell the entire story of Oedipus and his family.
Literature and Drama
Dist - PSU

Oedipus Tyrannus 60 MIN
U-matic / VHS
Drama - play, performance, perception series; Dramatis personae
Color (H C A)
Explores methods of character development. Uses the play Oedipus Tyrannus as an example.
Literature and Drama
Dist - FI **Prod** - BBCTV 1978

Oedipus Tyrannus 60 MIN
VHS
Color (G C H)
$129.00 purchase _ #DL393
Combines an excerpted version of Sophocles' play with scenes of Greek theaters and an examination of Aristotle's definition of tragedy
Fine Arts; History - World; Literature and Drama
Dist - INSIM

O'er Upland and Lowland 29 MIN
U-matic
Edible Wild Plants Series
Color
Demonstrates how to identify plant foliage in the spring for use in autumn harvesting.
Health and Safety; Science - Natural
Dist - UMITV **Prod** - UMITV 1978

Of all Places to Meet a Monster 14 MIN
16mm
Color
LC 79-701112
Shows Busch Gardens' Old Country at Williamsburg, Virginia, a family entertainment complex featuring European designs of the 17th and 18th centuries.
Business and Economics; Geography - United States; History - United States; Sociology
Dist - MTP **Prod** - ANHBUS 1979

Of all Things Series

Acapulco - water sports	3 MIN
Alaska fur seals	3 MIN
Alaskan salmon industry	3 MIN
An Amusement park	3 MIN
Animals of Africa	3 MIN
Animals under the sea	3 MIN
Argentina	3 MIN
Avocets	3 MIN
Banana industry - Ecuador	3 MIN
Birds of prey	3 MIN
The Black - Crowned Night Heron	3 MIN
Boats of the Mississippi	3 MIN
Brazil	3 MIN
Brussels' World's Fair	3 MIN
Bullfight	3 MIN
Butterflies - life cycle	3 MIN
Capri	3 MIN
Carlsbad caverns	3 MIN
Castles on the Rhine	3 MIN
Cedar waxwing	3 MIN
Chile	3 MIN
The Circus	3 MIN
Commercial fishing - tuna	3 MIN
Copenhagen	3 MIN
County Fair	3 MIN
Cypress Gardens	3 MIN
Dairy Industry	3 MIN
Dog show	3 MIN
Dogs - field trials	3 MIN
Down the Mississippi	3 MIN
Duck Families	3 MIN
Ducks of North America	3 MIN
Ecuador	3 MIN
The Egret	3 MIN
Egypt	3 MIN
Endless Caverns of Virginia	3 MIN
Face of the land	3 MIN
The Finches	3 MIN
Fireworks - Mexico	3 MIN
Flamingoes	3 MIN
Food processing	3 MIN
Frankfurt	3 MIN
Fruit Harvest	3 MIN
Grape industry	3 MIN
The Great blue heron	3 MIN
The Grosbeak	3 MIN
Hamlet's Castle	3 MIN
Handicrafts (Mexico)	3 MIN
Harness Horses	3 MIN
Helpful insects	3 MIN
Historic Virginia	3 MIN
Honeybees	3 MIN
Horse Farm	3 MIN
Horse Show	3 MIN
The Hummingbird	3 MIN
Indians of New Mexico	3 MIN
Insect enemies	3 MIN
Irrigation	3 MIN
London	3 MIN
Los Angeles	3 MIN
Mammals	3 MIN
Mexico - Land of Contrast	3 MIN
Mexico City	3 MIN
Morocco	3 MIN
Motor Boat Racing	3 MIN
New Orleans	3 MIN
New Orleans, Mardi Gras	3 MIN
New York City	3 MIN
Orange Industry	3 MIN
Panama Canal	3 MIN
Panama Hats (Ecuador)	3 MIN
Paris, Left Bank	3 MIN
Paris, Tourist Town	3 MIN
Peru	3 MIN
Petroleum Industry	3 MIN
Phalaropes	3 MIN
Polo	3 MIN
Pompeii	3 MIN
Quarter Horses	3 MIN
Red - Winged Blackbirds	3 MIN
Rio De Janeiro	3 MIN
River Logging	3 MIN
Rocks and Gems	3 MIN
Rodeo	3 MIN
Rome	3 MIN
Rome, City of Fountains	3 MIN
Rose parade - Pasadena	3 MIN
Sailing	3 MIN
Salmon - Life Cycle	3 MIN
San Francisco - City of Bridges	3 MIN
San Francisco - City of Hills	3 MIN
Sandpipers, Pt 1	3 MIN
Sandpipers, Pt 2	3 MIN
Sea Gulls	3 MIN
The Sea Otter	3 MIN
Skiing	3 MIN
Snakes	3 MIN
The Sparrow Family	3 MIN
Sports Car Racing	3 MIN
Sports Fishing	3 MIN
St Peters, Rome	3 MIN
Steel Industry	3 MIN
Story of Power	3 MIN
Summer sports - summer fun	3 MIN
Swallows	3 MIN
Textile Industry	3 MIN
Tobacco	3 MIN
University of Mexico	3 MIN
Vegetable Industry	3 MIN
Vintage Cars	3 MIN
Warsaw, Poland	3 MIN
Washington, DC	3 MIN
Water Skiing, Acapulco	3 MIN
Winter Fun	3 MIN
Wonders of Florida	3 MIN
Woodpeckers	3 MIN
The Work of Rivers	3 MIN
Yellow - Headed Blackbird	3 MIN
Yellowstone	3 MIN
Yosemite	3 MIN
Zurich	3 MIN

Dist - AVED

Of Artificial Reefs 60 MIN
VHS / U-matic / 16mm
Last Frontier Series
Color; Mono (G)
MV $225.00 _ MP $550.00
Examines the practice of placing old ships in the sea to act as artificial barrier refs. Various countries are using the ships to attract coral and fishes to help repopulate areas that have been depleted by overfishing.
Science - Natural
Dist - CTV **Prod** - MAKOF 1985

Of big bangs, stickmen and galactic holes 50 MIN
VHS
Horizon series
Color; PAL (H C A)
PdS99 purchase
Investigates the questions surrounding the Big Bang theory, which attempts to explain the origins of the earth. Discusses other inexplicable phenomena of space, including clusters of galaxies and voids.
History - World; Science - Physical
Dist - BBCENE

Of Birds, Beaks and Behavior 11 MIN
U-matic / VHS / 16mm
Many Worlds of Nature Series
Color
LC 77-700178
Shows the wide variety of physical features, nesting habits, songs and displays of birds. Tells how these relate to a bird's food and habitat preferences.
Science - Natural
Dist - CORF **Prod** - MORALL 1975

Of Black America series

Black History - Lost, Stolen or Strayed	54 MIN
Black History - Lost, Stolen or Strayed, Pt 1	27 MIN
Black History - Lost, Stolen or Strayed, Pt 2	27 MIN
The Black Soldier	26 MIN
Body and soul - Pt 1 - body	24 MIN
Body and soul - Pt 2 - soul	28 MIN
The Heritage of Slavery	53 MIN
The Heritage of slavery - Pt 1	26 MIN
The Heritage of slavery - Pt 2	27 MIN

Dist - PHENIX

Of Broccoli and Pelicans and Celery and Seals 30 MIN
16mm / U-matic / VHS
Our Vanishing Wilderness Series no 1
Color (H C A)
LC 72-710654
Traces the deterioration of environment in California. Points out how pesticides sprayed on the Oxnard Plain are being washed to sea where they are contaminating fishes which are in turn, eaten by birds, seals and man. Stresses the dangers of DDT to man and nature.

Science - Natural
Dist - IU **Prod** - IU 1971

Of Broccoli and Pelicans and Celery and Seals 29 MIN
16mm
Color (J H C G)
Discusses man's use of pesticides and the resulting environmental disruption. Focuses on DDT as an example of the havoc pesticides can wreak on the environment.
Agriculture; Science - Natural; Social Science; Sociology
Dist - VIEWTH **Prod** - GATEEF

Of Business and Ethics 24 MIN
VHS / U-matic
Color
$335.00 purchase
Business and Economics
Dist - ABCLR **Prod** - ABCLR 1983

Of Business and friendship - 7 44 MIN
VHS / U-matic
Glendon programs - a series
Color (C A)
$305.00, $275.00 purchase _ #V594
Looks at a group of people who have combined friendship, a unique understanding of psychology and ingenious business skills to create highly successful business ventures. Shows how this unusual combination entails an open and direct style of communication which is used to explore creative ideas, solve problems and deal with personal issues. Part of a 12 - part series featuring Dr Robert W Firestone, who is noted for his concept of the 'inner voice' and Voice Therapy.
Business and Economics; Fine Arts; Guidance and Counseling; Psychology; Social Science
Dist - BARR **Prod** - CEPRO 1991

Of Camouflage and Defence 60 MIN
VHS / U-matic / 16mm
Last Frontier Series
Color; Mono (G)
MV $225.00 _ MP $550.00
Considers the methods used by marine animals to protect themselves in the sometimes hostile world that exists beneath the surface.
Science - Natural
Dist - CTV **Prod** - MAKOF 1985

Of Course You Can 19 MIN
16mm
Color
LC 79-701443
Watches a mother teach her teenage son and daughter how to can fresh fruits and vegetables safely and then follows the teenagers as they attempt to handle the task themselves.
Home Economics
Dist - MTP **Prod** - BALCOR 1979

Of Critical Importance - AIDS Precautions in Radiology 13 MIN
VHS / 16mm
(PRO)
$65/3 Day VHS/3/4
Helps radiologists and radiology department staff to minimize the risks in dealing with patients with AIDS. Highlights the effective use of gowns, masks, gloves and goggles during angiograms, insertion of contrast during uro - radiology, insertion of barium enema catheters, percutaneous biopsy during CAT scans, and ultrasound guided thoracentesis. Also discusses precautions necessary to aviod needlesticks and cuts, and demonstrates proper instrument cleaning techniques.
Health and Safety
Dist - BAXMED **Prod** - ENVIC 1989

Of Dice and Men 11 MIN
16mm / VHS
Color (H)
LC 90707573
Uses animation to explain theories of probability and statistics. Shows how probability is used to predict the outcome of uncertain situations.
Mathematics
Dist - BARR

Of Energy, Minerals, and Man Series
The Cutting edge 27 MIN
Energy 27 MIN
Our Mineral Heritage 27 MIN
Responsibility for the Future 27 MIN
Dist - JOU

Of Epidemic Proportions 20 MIN
U-matic / VHS
Color
$335.00 purchase
Health and Safety
Dist - ABCLR **Prod** - ABCLR 1982

Of Forest Soil 10 MIN
16mm
Color
LC 81-701220
Describes the Weyerhaeuser Company's soil survey process. Explains the benefits that Weyerhaeuser has received from its own surveys and other possible benefits to forest management.
Science - Natural
Dist - AMMPCO **Prod** - WEYCO 1981

Of grace and steel 20 MIN
VHS
Color (G C)
$120.00 purchase, $16.00 rental _ #24019
Explores a summer training camp for women who practice the unique spiritual discipline of American Sikhs, a tradition originating in India 500 years ago. Reveals that the purpose of the camp is to enable women to achieve dignity, divinity and grace, thought by the Sikhs to be the proper foundation for society. Raises questions about preparation for violence as part of a commitment to peace, about women as 'superwomen,' and about the choice to live one's life in a highly defined religious community. Produced by Phyllis Jeroslow.
Religion and Philosophy; Sociology
Dist - PSU

Of Greeks and Gods Series
Adventurers 30 MIN
Myth as History 29 MIN
Dist - UMITV

Of heroes and helicopters 60 MIN
VHS
Color & B&W (G)
$29.99 purchase
Focuses on the Vietnam War experiences of a helicopter pilot.
History - United States; Industrial and Technical Education
Dist - DANEHA **Prod** - DANEHA 1994

Of Holes and Corks 10 MIN
U-matic / VHS / 16mm
Color (J)
LC 76-707564
An animated allegory which explores man's problems with reality, illusion and self - deception.
Fine Arts
Dist - IFB **Prod** - ZAGREB 1970

Of Human Bondage 83 MIN
16mm
B&W
Presents Somerset Maugham's study of a club - foot young doctor and the Cockney prostitute who obsesses and almost destroys him. Stars Bette Davis and Leslie Howard.
Fine Arts
Dist - NYFLMS **Prod** - NYFLMS 1934

Of Lives Uprooted 10 MIN
16mm / VHS
Color (C A)
$295.00, $95.00 purchase, $25.00 rental _ #CC4131
Examines how war devastates home, family and community as seen by children. Features the artwork of children from El Salvador and Nicaragua.
Fine Arts; Geography - World; Health and Safety; Sociology
Dist - IU **Prod** - NFBC 1990

Of lobbyists and lawmakers - the Greek American presence in Washington 28 MIN
VHS
Illuminations series
Color (G R)
#V - 1047
Focuses on the Greek American lobbying groups that work in Washington, D C. Identifies their agenda, which includes Cyprus, arms sales to Turkey, oil drilling rights in the Aegean Sea, and others. Takes the perspective that lobbying need not be a 'special interests' concern.
Civics and Political Systems
Dist - GOTEL **Prod** - GOTEL 1990

Of Masks and Men 30 MIN
U-matic / VHS
In Our Own Image Series
Color (C)
Fine Arts
Dist - DALCCD **Prod** - DALCCD

Of Men and Machines - Engineering Psychology 29 MIN
U-matic / VHS / 16mm
Focus on Behavior Series
B&W (H C A)
Studies the man - machine relationship by examining the ways in which man handles and processes information, the dynamics of information feedback between man and machines, the human being's behavior in complex man - machine systems and the redesigning of machines.
Psychology; Sociology
Dist - IU **Prod** - NET 1963

Of Men and Trees 30 MIN
16mm
Color (J H)
Offers a comprehensive and explanatory documentary of the daily operations of Alaska's logging industry.
Agriculture; Geography - United States
Dist - AKLOGA **Prod** - AKLOGA 1977

Of Men and Women 1 MIN
16mm
Color
LC 73-702344
Presents a prolog for a series of Warner Brothers specials for television showing the volatile and humorous relations between men and women.
Psychology; Sociology
Dist - WB **Prod** - WB 1972

Of Monkeys and Men 30 MIN
16mm
B&W (H C A)
LC FIA68-1776
Reports on the issues surrounding the repeal by the Tennessee Legislature of the so - called 'MONKEY LAW' which prohibited teaching of the principle of evolution in the state. Presents speeches by legislators and interviews John T Scopes and citizens of Tennessee.
Civics and Political Systems; History - United States
Dist - IU **Prod** - NET 1968

Of Monuments and Myths 30 MIN
VHS
Color (G)
$39.95 purchase _ #OFMM - 000
Tells the stories behind many of Washington, D.C.'s monuments. Shows that the history of these monuments often included humorous sides. Hosted by Bryson Rash.
History - United States
Dist - PBS **Prod** - WETATV 1988

Of Mouse and Ben 10 MIN
U-matic / VHS / 16mm
Meet Professor Balthazar Series
Color (I J H C K P)
Uses animation to show how Professor Balthazar helps his friends who have problems with solutions that are ostensibly magical but actually use the spiritual resources the friends already have.
Guidance and Counseling; Religion and Philosophy
Dist - IFB **Prod** - ZAGREB 1986

Of Mules and Men 51 MIN
VHS / 16mm
Color (G)
$70.00 rental _ #OMAM - 000
Looks at the life and times of Pennsylvania's canal era. Includes vintage film and sketches. Interviews take place with three surviving boatmen who worked the canal.
History - United States; Industrial and Technical Education; Social Science
Dist - PBS **Prod** - WITFTV

Of Muppets and Men 52 MIN
VHS
Muppets Series
Color (K)
$49.00 purchase _ #064 - 9004
Goes behind the scenes to meet the men and women who make Muppet magic happen. Offers this program as part of 'The Muppets' series.
Fine Arts; Health and Safety; Literature and Drama; Sociology
Dist - FI **Prod** - HENASS 1988

Of Pawns and Powers 29 MIN
U-matic
Conversations with Allen Whiting Series
Color
Looks at power politics in Southeast Asia. Reflects on small countries caught up in big events and dominated by big powers.
Civics and Political Systems
Dist - UMITV **Prod** - UMITV 1979

Of Preemies and Pills 25 MIN
VHS / U-matic
Color
Tells of the latest progress in reducing infant mortality. Shows how infants, born prematurely, are nurtured until their fragile little bodies can support life. Discusses, in second portion of program, a new distribution system that helps prevent drug accidents, and the role of the pharmacist as part of the health team.
Health and Safety; Sociology
Dist - MEDCOM **Prod** - MEDCOM

Of pure blood 75 MIN
VHS
Color (G)
$39.95 purchase _ #S00991
Presents an expose of the Nazi intentions to create a 'super race' of ideal Germans.
Civics and Political Systems; History - World
Dist - UILL

Of Race and Blood 89 MIN
VHS / U-matic / 16mm
Color (G)
$95.00 rental _ #ORAB - 000
Looks at the art and artists of the Third Reich. Reveals Hitler's plan for art as an important part of the Nazi machine. Recreates the artistic climate of Nazi Germany.
Fine Arts; History - World
Dist - PBS **Prod** - KRMATV

Of Rockets, Ships and Sealing Wax 17 MIN
16mm
Color
Relates the growth of the Thiokol Chemical Corporation and the expansion of the locale around the Wasatch Division, Brigham City, Utah.
Business and Economics; Geography - United States; Industrial and Technical Education
Dist - THIOKL **Prod** - THIOKL 1959

Of Sharks and men
VHS
Color (G)
$19.90 purchase _ #0133
Travels from the Red Sea to the Yucatan, from Tahiti to Australia to follow different breeds of sharks.
Geography - World; Science - Natural
Dist - SEVVID

Of sound mind and body 70 MIN
VHS
Color (G)
$50.00 purchase
Explores the healing nature of sound with leading experts in the field. Features Don Campbell, Barbara Crowe, Jonathan Goldman, Jill Purce, John Beauliet, Deforia Lane, Rupert Sheldrake, Bernie Siegel, MD and Deepak Chopra, MD. Includes composers and performers who view music as a healing tool.
Fine Arts; Health and Safety
Dist - HP

Of sound mind and body - music and vibrational healing 60 MIN
VHS
Color (G)
$50.00 _ #VAS - H001
Presents Jeff Volk surveying ancient and modern traditions and techniques that use music, rhythm and resonance, key elements for a healthy relationship with our world. Features Bernie Siegel, Deepak Chopra, Jill Purce, and more. By Lumina Productions.
Fine Arts; Health and Safety; Psychology
Dist - NOETIC

Of Stars and Men (2nd Ed Series
Matter and Energy 11 MIN
Dist - RADIM

Of Stars and Men Series
A Journey through Space 8 MIN
A Journey through Time 9 MIN
Prologue - the Lion and the Crown 7 MIN
Dist - RADIM

Of Stars and Men
Life on Other Planets 18 MIN
Dist - RADIM

Of Sugar Cane and Syrup 15 MIN
16mm / U-matic / VHS
Color
LC 77-702117
Documents the traditional techniques of making syrup from sugar cane. Centers on a Southern man and his wife who have been making syrup since the days when this was a necessary part of rural life.
Agriculture; Geography - United States; Home Economics
Dist - CORF **Prod** - KSPRO 1977

Of that Time 17 MIN
16mm
Color
LC 81-701142
Tells the story of a young girl whose family moves to a new neighborhood. Shows how she gives up a special doll because of peer and family pressures, and makes friends with the boy next door.
Fine Arts
Dist - USC **Prod** - USC 1981

Of the Earth - Agriculture and the new biology 28 MIN
VHS / U-matic / 16mm
Color (H C G)
$250.00, $300.00, $585.00 purchase, $40.00 rental
Views biotechnology and its applications to agricultural research and crop development. Includes discussions with the top academic scientists in this area.
Agriculture
Dist - NDIM **Prod** - IBA 1986

Of the people 28 MIN
16mm
Government story series; No 1
Color
LC 71-707177
A profile of the United States Congress, its history and present functions. Includes interviews with Carl Albert, Melvin Laird, Bourke B Hickenlooper, Charles Vanik and James H Scheuer.
Civics and Political Systems
Dist - WBCPRO **Prod** - WBCPRO 1968

Of the People 30 MIN
U-matic / VHS
Japan - the Changing Tradition Series
Color (H C A)
History - World
Dist - GPN **Prod** - UMA 1978

Of Thee I Sing 15 MIN
VHS / U-matic
Stepping into Rhythm Series
Color (P)
Teaches patriotic songs and introduces a brass ensemble.
Fine Arts
Dist - AITECH **Prod** - WVIZTV

Of Time and a River 27 MIN
U-matic / VHS / 16mm
Color
Tells the story of the Columbia River and the Grand Coulee Dam, covering the geological forces that formed the river basin.
Geography - United States; Science - Physical
Dist - USNAC **Prod** - USBR 1982

Of Time and Consequence 29 MIN
U-matic
Future Without Shock Series
Color
Illustrates the role and milieu of the engineer from ancient to modern times. Analyzes the changing environment in which the engineer works today.
Industrial and Technical Education; Sociology
Dist - UMITV **Prod** - UMITV 1976

Of Time and the Artist 29 MIN
Videoreel / VT2
Museum Open House Series
Color
Fine Arts; Sociology
Dist - PBS **Prod** - WGBHTV

Of Time, Tombs and Treasure - the treasures of Tutankhamun 27 MIN
U-matic
Color
Presents a journey through the resplendent 3000 - year - old tomb of King Tutankhamen. Examines the treasures found in the tomb. Tells the story of the tomb's discovery.
Geography - World; History - World
Dist - MTP **Prod** - EXXON
USNGA

Of wheels and wings - Video 12 47 MIN
VHS
Physical science - secrets of science series
Color (I J H C)
$49.95 purchase
Presents two parts in two segments each, examining the evolution of land and water transportation, offering a brief history of air transportation and showing how airplanes fly. Includes Rolling on Land and Sailing on Water in Part I, Flying Through the Air and The Magic of Flight in Part II. Hosted by Discover Magazine Editor in Chief Paul Hoffman. Third of four parts on physical science.
Industrial and Technical Education; Social Science
Dist - EFVP **Prod** - DSCOVM 1994

Of Wings and Women 15 MIN
16mm
Color
LC 74-705240
Portrays the history, contributions and traditions of the Women's Air Force. Points out the career opportunities available to eligible women and depicts educational, occupational and social aspects of life as a WAF.
Civics and Political Systems; Sociology
Dist - USNAC **Prod** - USAF 1966

Of Wits and Dimwits 30 MIN
U-matic
Ukrainian Folktales Series
(P) (UKRAINIAN)
Includes the Ukrainian folktales Two Billy Goats And Two Nanny Goats, The Gingerbread Boy, The Hedgehog And The Rabbit and The Wren And the Bear. In the Ukrainian language.
Foreign Language; History - World; Literature and Drama
Dist - ACCESS **Prod** - ACCESS 1985

Off and Running 30 MIN
VHS / 16mm
Marketing Series
Color (C A)
$130.00, $120.00 purchase _ 15 - 19
Features sales promotion at the Santa Anita Race Track.
Business and Economics
Dist - CDTEL **Prod** - COAST 1989

Off duty - an analysis of officers killed 17 MIN
VHS
Analysis of officers killed series
Color (PRO)
$295.00 purchase, $100.00 rental _ #8418
Discourages off - duty investigations without benefit of back up or weapons and acts of heroism. Suggests that the best role of an off - duty officer is that of a good witness. Part of a series utilizing information provided by the Uniform Crime Reporting Section of the Federal Bureau of Investigation.
Civics and Political Systems; Social Science; Sociology
Dist - AIMS **Prod** - AIMS 1992

Off guard 11 MIN
VHS
Color; PAL; NTSC (G)
PdS57, PdS67 purchase
Reveals that in the past five years the HSE has investigated ten fatal accidents and 35 serious injuries involving power take off - PTO - shafts on farm machinery. Discloses that PTO shafts with broken, damaged or badly fitted guards can kill. Contrasts the absence of adequate safety procedures on the farm of Peter Stiles with his son's learning the correct safety procedures at agricultural college.
Health and Safety
Dist - CFLVIS

The Off - handed jape 9 MIN
16mm
Color (G)
$25.00 rental
Studies everyday behavior. Suggests a vaudeville of daily life. Similar to Andy Warhol's films of 1963 - 4.
Fine Arts; Sociology
Dist - CANCIN **Prod** - NELSOR 1967

Off limits 52 MIN
VHS
Color (G PRO)
$295.00 purchase, $90.00 rental
Offers insights into the experience of torture. Features interviews with three torture victims who recount their personal stories and reveal the permanent physical and psychic scars left by such a trauma. Discusses the inhumane behavior of the torturers, responses aimed at self - preservation and the sometimes bizarre relationship between torturer and victim. Directed by Isabelle Benkemoun and Francis Allegret. In French with English subtitles.
Sociology
Dist - CNEMAG

Off - line editing - An Introduction 45 MIN
VHS
Off - line editing series
Color (G C PRO)
$149.00 purchase
Covers the mechanics and strategies of the off - line session, from raw footage to the final cut. Includes the topics of linear and non - linear editing, control track and time code, blacking, window dubs, logging, assemble and insert editing, straight cuts, split edits and multi - generational editing technique. Part of a two - volume series.
Fine Arts
Dist - FIRLIT **Prod** - FIRLIT 1994

Off - line editing series 72 MIN
VHS
Off - line editing series
Color (G C PRO)
$249.00 purchase
Presents two parts on off - line editing. Includes an introduction covering the mechanics and strategies of an off - line session from raw footage to the final cut and 'Working with Edit Decision Lists,' which guides the viewer through the list management process.
Fine Arts
Dist - FIRLIT **Prod** - FIRLIT 1994

Off - line editing - Working with edit decision lists 27 MIN
VHS
Off - line editing series
Color (G C PRO)
$149.00 purchase
Guides the viewer through the list management process. Includes the topics of how to read an EDL, linear and non - linear formats, editing tips to improve list accuracy, cleaning, tracing and final preparation for the on - line. Part of a two - volume series.
Fine Arts
Dist - FIRLIT **Prod** - FIRLIT 1994

Off - road controversy 27 MIN
VHS

Color (G)
$350.00 purchase, $15.00 rental
Discusses the use of off - road vehicles in wilderness areas, deserts, mountains, beaches and forests. Examines individual rights to property and privacy, varying tastes in recreation and leisure activities, and ecological damage to fragile environments. Shows that the land belongs to everyone and to future generations, and that certain characteristics of open spaces should be preserved and protected.
Physical Education and Recreation; Science - Natural
Dist - CMSMS **Prod** - SIERRA 1973

Off soundings 1986 57 MIN
VHS
Color (G)
$19.95 purchase _ #0830
Covers the sailing race organized by the Off Soundings Club in 1986.
Physical Education and Recreation
Dist - SEVVID

Off soundings 1987 60 MIN
VHS
Color (G)
$19.95 purchase _ #0831
Covers the sailing race organized by the Off Soundings Club in 1987. Features Bill Ames as narrator.
Physical Education and Recreation
Dist - SEVVID

Off soundings 1988 50 MIN
VHS
Color (G)
$19.95 purchase _ #0832
Covers the sailing race organized by the Off Soundings Club in 1988. Features Bill Ames as narrator.
Physical Education and Recreation
Dist - SEVVID

Off stage series
Alternative theatre 29 MIN
Artist in Residence 29 MIN
Body language and the art of mime 30 MIN
Bread and Roses - a New Play 29 MIN
Dance Theatre 29 MIN
Experimental Theatre Festival 29 MIN
Marionette Theatre 29 MIN
Theatre - Why Criticize? 29 MIN
Theatre of China 29 MIN
Dist - UMITV

The Off - Target Interview 15 MIN
U-matic
Job Seeking Series
Color (H C A)
Explains what not to do during a job interview.
Guidance and Counseling; Psychology
Dist - GPN **Prod** - WCETTV 1979

Off the Edge 53 MIN
VHS
Color; Stereo (G)
$19.98 purchase _ #TT8040
Takes the viewer up to 10,000 feet for a look at high altitude skiing and hang gliding.
Literature and Drama; Physical Education and Recreation
Dist - TWINTO **Prod** - TWINTO 1990

Off the edge 53 MIN
VHS
Color (G)
$29.95 purchase _ #S01427
Takes an in - flight view of high altitude skiing and hang gliding.
Industrial and Technical Education; Physical Education and Recreation
Dist - UILL

Off the Pig 15 MIN
16mm
B&W
Presents a dialogue between Black Panthers Huey P Newton and Eldridge Cleaver. Includes illustrative pictures of Panthers.
Biography; History - United States; Psychology; Sociology
Dist - CANWRL **Prod** - CANWRL 1968

Off the pig 20 MIN
16mm
B&W (G)
$20.00 rental
Documents leaders of the Black Panther Party discussing their revolutionary views on the Panthers, Vietnam, armed struggle, opposition to the system's oppression and more. Captures a sense of what they were about then, their strengths as well as their shortcomings. Represents revolutionary filmmakers in the 1960s whose work provides a window to that period.
Civics and Political Systems; Fine Arts; History - United States; Sociology
Dist - CANCIN **Prod** - SINGLE 1968

Off the Wall 56 MIN
16mm
Color (G)
Fine Arts; Geography - World
Dist - CFLMDC **Prod** - NFBC 1981

Off the Wall 15 MIN
U-matic / VHS / 16mm
Color
LC 80-700171
Uses live action footage to capture the game of racquetball as it is played by professionals and amateurs.
Physical Education and Recreation
Dist - PFP **Prod** - PFP 1979

Off to adventure series
Arts 15 MIN
Buddhism 15 MIN
City life of a small boy 15 MIN
Farm life 15 MIN
Going to church 15 MIN
Home life 15 MIN
Occupations 15 MIN
School 15 MIN
Shintoism 15 MIN
Dist - YALEDV

Off Your Duff 30 MIN
U-matic / VHS / 16mm
Color (H C A)
LC 79-701416
Presents experts, amateurs and beginners engaged in various physical activities. Offers advice and suggestions for finding the right kind of exercise.
Guidance and Counseling; Health and Safety; Physical Education and Recreation
Dist - LCOA **Prod** - WGBHTV 1979

Offense 30 MIN
U-matic / VHS
Basketball Fundamentals Series
Color
Discusses offense, which requires patience while the team works the ball around the floor and finds the defensive mistake. Illustrates methods of drilling the team to learn the multiple possibilities of the offense.
Physical Education and Recreation
Dist - NETCHE **Prod** - NETCHE 1972

Offense 57 MIN
VHS
Coach of the year - Bob Hurley championship basketball series
Color (H C G)
$29.95 purchase _ #BSA110V
Discusses ball handling, setting screens, moving without the ball, shooting techiques and winning strategy as taught by high school basketball coach Bob Hurley.
Physical Education and Recreation
Dist - CAMV

Offense - Volume 1 25 MIN
VHS
Rick Pitino basketball series
Color (H C G)
$29.95 purchase _ #DRP101V
Covers ball handling, one on one, shooting, ball fake and eliminating travel turnovers in Volume 1 of 2 on offense. Part of a four - part series on basketball featuring head coach Rick Pitino, U of Kentucky.
Physical Education and Recreation
Dist - CAMV

Offense - Volume 2 25 MIN
VHS
Rick Pitino basketball series
Color (H C G)
$29.95 purchase _ #DRP102V
Examines the three - point shot, how to use screens, low post - game, fast break and five plus five in Volume 2 of 2 on offense. Part of a four - part series on basketball featuring head coach Rick Pitino, U of Kentucky.
Physical Education and Recreation
Dist - CAMV

The Offensive Backfield 15 MIN
16mm
Color (J H C)
LC FIA68-630
Football players and coaches discuss the offensive backfield. Illustrates the center exchange, hand - off, stance, cutting, guarding against fumbles, play - calling, passing and receiving. Joe Namath and Mike Taliaferro demonstrate quarterback moves in the passing and running game.
Physical Education and Recreation
Dist - MOKIN **Prod** - MOKIN 1967

Offensive Backs 60 MIN
VHS
One on One Coaching Series
(J H C)
$39.95 _ #CVN1040V
Features football coach Axman of U C L A who demonstrates skills for offensive backs, including stance, take off, hand off, ball security, breaking the block, endrun, option drills, pitches, dive squeeze, counter option, and more.
Physical Education and Recreation
Dist - CAMV **Prod** - CAMV

Offensive baseball series
VHS
N C A A instructional video series
Color (H C A)
$64.95 purchase _ #KAR1108V
Presents a three - part series on offensive baseball. Focuses on hitting, baserunning and catching skills.
Physical Education and Recreation
Dist - CAMV **Prod** - NCAAF

Offensive Basketball 11 MIN
16mm
Color (J)
LC 78-701961
Presents the fundamentals of offensive basketball, including both individual and team skills.
Physical Education and Recreation
Dist - BKBA **Prod** - BKBA 1973

Offensive Drills
VHS / U-matic
Basketball Basics Series/Mens Series
Color
Features instruction in basketball for men.
Physical Education and Recreation
Dist - ATHI **Prod** - ATHI

Offensive ice hockey series
VHS
N C A A instructional video series
Color (H C A)
$64.95 purchase _ #KAR1507V
Presents a three - part series on offensive ice hockey. Focuses on stickhandling, passing and receiving, and shooting skills.
Physical Education and Recreation
Dist - CAMV **Prod** - NCAAF

Offensive Line 60 MIN
VHS
One on One Coaching Series
(J H C)
$39.95 _ #CVN1080V
Presents football coach Johnson who explains how to beat the defense with dominant offensive line play. Discusses proper stance, the pass set, pulling right and left, using body, target points and more.
Physical Education and Recreation
Dist - CAMV **Prod** - CAMV

Offensive Line 60 MIN
VHS
Tom Landry Football Series
(J H C)
$39.95 _ #MXS120V
Presents center Pete Brock and Coach Tom Landry who discuss the basics of interior line play and its importance in football.
Physical Education and Recreation
Dist - CAMV **Prod** - CAMV

The Offensive Line 15 MIN
16mm
Color (J H C)
LC FIA68-627
Football players and coaches discuss the offensive line. Pictures the option trap, cut - off, and pass protection blocks and shows the function of the center in the kicking game.
Physical Education and Recreation
Dist - MOKIN **Prod** - MOKIN 1967

Offensive line techniques
VHS
NCAA football instructional videos series
Color (H C A)
$39.95 purchase _ #KAR1304V
Features college football coach Mervin Johnson teaching various skills and drills for pass receivers. Produced by the National Collegiate Athletic Association.
Physical Education and Recreation
Dist - CAMV **Prod** - NCAAF

Offensive line techniques
VHS
NCAA football videos - offensive series
Color (A G T)
$39.95 purchase _ #KAR1304V-P
Presents instruction on skills and drills given by NCAA coaches. Features Mervin Johnson explaining offensive line techniques. One of a series of videos that provide coaching tips to offensive and defensive players and coaches. Series is available as a set of offensive series, defensive series, or both combined.

Physical Education and Recreation
Dist - CAMV

Offensive Play 61 MIN
BETA / VHS
Fundamentals of Women's Basketball Series
Color
Demonstrates and discusses offensive play in women's basketball.
Physical Education and Recreation
Dist - MOHOMV **Prod** - MOHOMV

Offensive post play
VHS
NCAA basketball instructional video series
Color (G)
$39.95 purchase _ #KAR1207V
Features former Minnesota basketball coach Jim Dutcher in an instructional video on offensive post play in basketball.
Physical Education and Recreation
Dist - CAMV **Prod** - NCAAF

Offensive scoring workout - Volume 1
VHS
Converse basketball series
Color (G)
$29.95 purchase _ #AN000
Demonstrates 8 offensive moves used by pros.
Physical Education and Recreation
Dist - SIV

Offensive series
VHS
NCAA basketball videos series
Color (H C G)
$89.95 purchase _ #KAR1209V
Features Ray Meyer, Tom Davis, Jim Valvano and Jim Dutcher teaching offensive skills in basketball. Includes the titles Ball Handling and Dribbling, Passing Techniques, Shooting and Offensive Post Play on one videocassette.
Physical Education and Recreation
Dist - CAMV **Prod** - NCAA

Offensive tactics
VHS
Team tactics and team drills - coaching boys' volleyball II series
Color (J H C G)
$49.95 purchase _ #TRS579V
Features Bill Neville, USA National Team coach. Teaches offensive tactics in volleyball. Part of a three - part series on team tactics and team drills in volleyball and an eight - part series on boys' volleyball.
Physical Education and Recreation
Dist - CAMV

Offensive Team Play 11 MIN
16mm / U-matic / VHS
How to Play Hockey Series no 7; No 7
B&W (J H C)
Illustrates methods of hockey by which a team can clear the puck out of its own end, by - pass defensemen, get into scoring position and beat the goal tender.
Physical Education and Recreation
Dist - IFB **Prod** - CRAF 1956

Offerings 54 MIN
VHS
Color (PRO)
$39.95 purchase
Documents the process of finding and interpreting the story of African - Americans and bringing it into the mainstream of history. Demonstrates the importance of community involvement in preservation of culture. Features exhibits at the Afro - American Historical and Cultural Museum, the African American Family History Association and Herndon Home. Produced by the Center for Museum Studies at the Smithsonian for use in museum training.
History - United States; Psychology
Dist - SMITHS

Office assessment of physical fitness and the exercise prescription 30 MIN
VHS
Color (A PRO)
$275.00 purchase, $50.00 rental
Describes how to determine a patient's level of physical fitness and how to develop an appropriate exercise program for that patient. Targeted to family care physicians, but appropriate for other health care personnel. Includes instructional guide, patient handouts, and other forms.
Business and Economics; Health and Safety; Physical Education and Recreation
Dist - UARIZ **Prod** - UARIZ

Office automation concepts series
Clerical and administrative services 30 MIN
Communications services 30 MIN
Decision support services 30 MIN
Dist - DELTAK

Office Automation Game Plan 45 MIN
VHS / U-matic
Management Strategies for Office Automation Series
Color
Outlines a generic blueprint for managing office automation evolution. Covers such topics as managing expectations, states of office automation growth, staffing, management awareness, user involvement and continuing evolution.
Business and Economics; Industrial and Technical Education; Psychology
Dist - DELTAK **Prod** - DELTAK

Office Automation - Technology and Management 480 MIN
VHS / U-matic
(PRO A)
$4,320.00
Provides introduction to topics covering types of equipment used to automate a business office.
Business and Economics; Computer Science
Dist - VIDEOT **Prod** - VIDEOT 1988

Office diagnosis and management of anxiety disorders 60 MIN
VHS / U-matic
Color (PRO C)
$395.00 purchase, $80.00 rental _ #C850 - VI - 030
Introduces the epidemiology, diagnosis and management of anxiety disorders. Estimates that 15 percent of cardiology patients and 30 percent of family practice patients shows signs and symptoms of major anxiety disorders. Presented by Drs Earl A Burch and William M Patterson.
Health and Safety
Dist - HSCIC

Office ergonomics 12 MIN
VHS
Blueprints for safety
Color (IND)
$249.00 purchase _ #CLM50
Presents a guideline for safety and compliance requirements, created by certified safety professionals. Includes an instructor's guide, training tips, a learning exercise, five employee handbooks, glossary of terms and template for transparencies.
Health and Safety
Dist - EXTR **Prod** - CLMI

Office ergonomics - everybody's different - Part 2
VHS
Office ergonomics series
Color (IND)
$395.00 purchase, $95.00 rental _ #840 - 20
Shows management how to help employees design the best workstation for the person, not just the job. Part two of a two - part series on office ergonomics.
Business and Economics; Health and Safety
Dist - ITSC **Prod** - ITSC 1992

Office ergonomics - make yourself comfortable - Part 1
VHS
Office ergonomics series
Color (IND)
$395.00 purchase, $95.00 rental _ #840 - 19
Motivates employees to set up their workstations to meet their own needs. Part one of a two - part series on office ergonomics.
Health and Safety
Dist - ITSC **Prod** - ITSC 1992

Office ergonomics series
Presents a two - part series on office ergonomics which takes the perspectives of both employees and management. Motivates employees to set up their workstations to meet their own needs in Part 1. Part 2 shows management how to help employees design the best workstation for the person, not just the job.
Office ergonomics - everybody's different - Part 2
Office ergonomics - make yourself comfortable - Part 1
Dist - ITSC **Prod** - ITSC 1992

Office ergonomics - video display terminals 11 MIN
8mm cartridge / VHS / BETA / U-matic
Color; PAL (IND G)
$395.00 purchase, $175.00 rental _ #SOU - 104
Shows the best ways to work at video display terminals to reduce stress and possible injury without sacrificing productivity. Provides a step - by - step examination of the components of the VDT workstation, including the height and distance of the monitor, the keyboard, the chair and an explanation of the science of ergonomics and its benefits. Presents five stress - relieving exercises employees can do at their workstations and includes a quiz on workstation ergonomics. Includes a leader's guide and ten participant workbooks.
Health and Safety; Science - Natural
Dist - BNA

Office Evaluation of Urinary Incontinence 18 MIN
U-matic / VHS
Color (PRO)
Discusses office evaluation of urinary incontinence.
Health and Safety
Dist - WFP **Prod** - WFP

Office fire safety - getting out alive 5 MIN
VHS
Color (G)
$99.00 purchase _ #9865 - HDLQ
Stresses individual responsibility in an office emergency. Teaches evacuation procedures and explains why it's vital to know the locations of alarms, exits and fire extinguishers. Includes a training kit emphasizing how to hold an effective training session.
Health and Safety
Dist - KRAMES **Prod** - KRAMES

Office Machines - Amount and Percent of Increase or Decrease 10 MIN
BETA / VHS
Office Machines - Calculations Series
Color
Discusses percentage problems.
Business and Economics; Mathematics
Dist - RMIBHF **Prod** - RMIBHF

Office Machines - Bank Reconciliation 11 MIN
VHS / BETA
Office Machines - Calculations Series
Color
Business and Economics; Mathematics
Dist - RMIBHF **Prod** - RMIBHF

Office Machines - Calculations Series
Office Machines - Amount and Percent of Increase or Decrease 10 MIN
Office Machines - Bank Reconciliation 11 MIN
Office Machines - Cash Discount and Net Amount 8 MIN
Office Machines - Compound Annual Interest 14 MIN
Office Machines - Compound Semi - Annual Interest 14 MIN
Office Machines - Determining the Real Estate Tax Rate 6 MIN
Office Machines - Discounting Notes 6 MIN
Office Machines - Markup Based on Cost and on Selling Price 13 MIN
Office Machines - Payroll, Gross Earnings 9 MIN
Office Machines - Payroll, Net Earnings 12 MIN
Office Machines - Percent of Markup Based on Cost or on Selling Price 9 MIN
Office Machines - Proration, Direct Method 8 MIN
Office Machines - Proration, Indirect Method 12 MIN
Office Machines - Simple Interest, 360 Day Method 12 MIN
Office Machines - Simple Interest, Exact Days and Exact Interest 12 MIN
Office Machines - Simple Interest, Finding the Principal 12 MIN
Office Machines - Simple Interest, Finding the Rate 12 MIN
Office Machines - Simple Interest, Finding the Time 13 MIN
Office Machines - Taxes, Determining Amount of Real Estate Taxes 10 MIN
Office Machines - Taxes, Determining Total Assessed Valuation 6 MIN
Office Machines - Trade Discount, Single and Chain 13 MIN
Dist - RMIBHF

Office Machines - Cash Discount and Net Amount 8 MIN
BETA / VHS
Office Machines - Calculations Series
Color
Business and Economics; Mathematics
Dist - RMIBHF **Prod** - RMIBHF

Office Machines - Compound Annual Interest 14 MIN
BETA / VHS
Office Machines - Calculations Series
Color
Business and Economics; Mathematics
Dist - RMIBHF **Prod** - RMIBHF

Office Machines - Compound Semi - Annual Interest 14 MIN
VHS / BETA
Office Machines - Calculations Series
Color
Business and Economics; Mathematics
Dist - RMIBHF **Prod** - RMIBHF

Office Machines - Determining the Real Estate Tax Rate 6 MIN
VHS / BETA
Office Machines - Calculations Series
Color
Business and Economics; Mathematics
Dist - RMIBHF **Prod** - RMIBHF

Office Machines - Discounting Notes 6 MIN
BETA / VHS
Office Machines - Calculations Series
Color
Business and Economics; Mathematics
Dist - RMIBHF **Prod** - RMIBHF

Office Machines - Markup Based on Cost and on Selling Price 13 MIN
BETA / VHS
Office Machines - Calculations Series
Color
Business and Economics; Mathematics
Dist - RMIBHF **Prod** - RMIBHF

Office Machines - Payroll, Gross Earnings 9 MIN
BETA / VHS
Office Machines - Calculations Series
Color
Business and Economics; Mathematics
Dist - RMIBHF **Prod** - RMIBHF

Office Machines - Payroll, Net Earnings 12 MIN
BETA / VHS
Office Machines - Calculations Series
Color
Business and Economics; Mathematics
Dist - RMIBHF **Prod** - RMIBHF

Office Machines - Percent of Markup Based on Cost or on Selling Price 9 MIN
VHS / BETA
Office Machines - Calculations Series
Color
Business and Economics; Mathematics
Dist - RMIBHF **Prod** - RMIBHF

Office Machines - Proration, Direct Method 8 MIN
BETA / VHS
Office Machines - Calculations Series
Color
Business and Economics; Mathematics
Dist - RMIBHF **Prod** - RMIBHF

Office Machines - Proration, Indirect Method 12 MIN
BETA / VHS
Office Machines - Calculations Series
Color
Business and Economics; Mathematics
Dist - RMIBHF **Prod** - RMIBHF

Office Machines - Simple Interest, 360 Day Method 12 MIN
VHS / BETA
Office Machines - Calculations Series
Color
Business and Economics; Mathematics
Dist - RMIBHF **Prod** - RMIBHF

Office Machines - Simple Interest, Exact Days and Exact Interest 12 MIN
VHS / BETA
Office Machines - Calculations Series
Color
Business and Economics; Mathematics
Dist - RMIBHF **Prod** - RMIBHF

Office Machines - Simple Interest, Finding the Principal 12 MIN
VHS / BETA
Office Machines - Calculations Series
Color
Business and Economics; Mathematics
Dist - RMIBHF **Prod** - RMIBHF

Office Machines - Simple Interest, Finding the Rate 12 MIN
VHS / BETA
Office Machines - Calculations Series
Color
Business and Economics; Mathematics
Dist - RMIBHF **Prod** - RMIBHF

Office Machines - Simple Interest, Finding the Time 13 MIN
BETA / VHS
Office Machines - Calculations Series
Color
Business and Economics; Mathematics
Dist - RMIBHF **Prod** - RMIBHF

Office Machines - Taxes, Determining Amount of Real Estate Taxes 10 MIN
VHS / BETA
Office Machines - Calculations Series
Color
Business and Economics; Mathematics
Dist - RMIBHF **Prod** - RMIBHF

Office Machines - Taxes, Determining Total Assessed Valuation 6 MIN
VHS / BETA
Office Machines - Calculations Series
Color
Business and Economics; Mathematics
Dist - RMIBHF **Prod** - RMIBHF

Office Machines - Trade Discount, Single and Chain 13 MIN
VHS / BETA
Office Machines - Calculations Series
Color
Business and Economics; Mathematics
Dist - RMIBHF **Prod** - RMIBHF

Office Management of Chronic Emphysema 22 MIN
U-matic
Color (PRO)
LC 76-706065
Discusses office treatment of chronic emphysema. Describes prophylactic treatment, methods of monitoring treatment progress, and tests and equipment useful in office treatment.
Health and Safety
Dist - USNAC **Prod** - WARMP 1970

Office Management of Vascular Tension Headache 23 MIN
U-matic
Color (PRO)
LC 76-706066
Discusses approaches to the treatment of vascular tension headache. Emphasizes the establishment of rapport and confidence with the patient. Explains drug therapy.
Health and Safety
Dist - USNAC **Prod** - WARMP 1970

Office Occupations
VHS
Career Profiles - Business and Office Series
$75.00 purchase _ #KW - 109
Discusses the pros and cons of this occupational field plus the necessary aptitudes and training.
Guidance and Counseling
Dist - CAREER **Prod** - CAREER

Office of the future 28 MIN
16mm / VHS
Color (G IND)
$5.00 rental
Considers the impact of new technology on office workers. Traces the evolution of information processing from the beginning of the century. Interviews union representatives, clerical workers and managers to reveal that today's problems are similar to those that workers have always faced - monitoring, stress, contracting out, insufficient training, health and safety concerns and deskilling of jobs.
Business and Economics; Mathematics; Social Science; Sociology
Dist - AFLCIO **Prod** - LIPA 1988

Office of the Future 12 MIN
BETA / VHS / U-matic
(G)
$100.00
Presents a veiw of the office of the future, complete with robots and computers and lacking secretaries, typewriters, and filing clerks.
Business and Economics
Dist - CTV **Prod** - CTV 1983

Office of the future 30 MIN
VHS
Perspectives - industrial design - series
Color; PAL; NTSC (G)
PdS90, PdS105 purchase
Discloses that individuals are now able to communicate as though they were face to face, even though they are thousands of miles apart. Shows how work life is being transformed by advances in telecommunications and information technology, such as video conferencing.
Business and Economics; Social Science
Dist - CFLVIS **Prod** - LONTVS

Office on the Move 25 MIN
U-matic / VHS
Electronic Office Series
Color (H C A)
Examines the broad principles of what technology can do to make the tasks of those who work in offices easier. Shows how a typical chain of administrative tasks can be tackled on a computer system and explores the extent which text, voice, image and data can be handled by office systems. Includes a look at a mature system in use in an American company.
Business and Economics; Industrial and Technical Education
Dist - FI **Prod** - BBCTV 1984

Office Practice - Manners and Customs 14 MIN
U-matic / VHS / 16mm
Office Practice Series
Color (H C A)
LC 72-702151
Provides an introduction to the manners and customs of office work, including reception of visitors, telephone courtesy and forms of address for co - workers.
Business and Economics; Guidance and Counseling
Dist - CORF **Prod** - CORF 1972

Office Practice Series
Office Practice - Manners and Customs 14 MIN
Office Practice - Working with Others 14 MIN
Office Practice - Your Attitude 11 MIN
Dist - CORF

Office Practice - Working with Others 14 MIN
16mm / U-matic / VHS
Office Practice Series
Color (H C A)
LC 72-702152
Fosters an awareness of the importance of human relations in office work through use of appropriate behavior and language.
Business and Economics; Guidance and Counseling; Sociology
Dist - CORF **Prod** - CORF 1972

Office Practice - Your Attitude 11 MIN
U-matic / VHS / 16mm
Office Practice Series
Color (H C A)
LC 72-702150
Shows how personal attitudes are reflected by the way in which people talk and listen and through their grooming, posture and dress.
Business and Economics; Guidance and Counseling; Psychology
Dist - CORF **Prod** - CORF 1972

Office Safety 19 MIN
16mm / VHS
Color (A)
LC 90708924
Identifies preventive measures to avoid accidents and other safety problems in the office setting.
Business and Economics; Health and Safety; Psychology
Dist - BARR

Office safety 12 MIN
VHS
Color (H)
$79.00 purchase _ #05218 - 126
Uses humor to teach that it takes just a little bit of caution and common sense to avoid most office accidents. Produced by William Poll Producers.
Business and Economics; Health and Safety
Dist - GA

Office safety 13 MIN
VHS
Color (G) (SPANISH)
$395.00 purchase, $100.00 rental _ #8410
Shows employees the hazards that can exist in any office environment. Includes presenter's guide.
Business and Economics; Health and Safety
Dist - AIMS **Prod** - MARCOM 1991

Office Safety 12 MIN
16mm
Color (A)
Points out that it takes just a bit of caution and common sense to avoid most office accidents.
Health and Safety
Dist - GA **Prod** - XEROXF 1978

Office Safety 17 MIN
U-matic / VHS
Color (A)
Shows how seemingly innocent actions can result in serious accidents involving open file drawers and swinging doors.
Business and Economics; Health and Safety
Dist - CORF **Prod** - OLINC 1980

Office safety - Friday the 13th 11 MIN
VHS / U-matic / BETA
Color; PAL (IND G A)
Uses humor to overcome complacency about the potential for accidents in the office. Portrays incidents involving a paper cutter, copying machine, electric stapler, moving supplies, falls and file drawers. Includes leader's guide and 10 workbooks.
Business and Economics; Health and Safety; Psychology
Dist - BNA **Prod** - BNA
ITF

Office safety - it's a jungle in there 20 MIN
VHS
Color (IND)
$495.00 purchase, $95.00 rental _ #805 - 10; $495.00 purchase, $150.00 rental, $35.00 preview _ #IAJ/ITS
Shows big game hunter Foster Safewell taking viewers on a tour of a jungle - the office. Explains hazards - slips and falls, safe lifting, electrical hazards and fire safety. Includes leader's guide.
Business and Economics; Health and Safety
Dist - ITSC **Prod** - ITSC
ADVANM

Office safety - it's serious business 14 MIN
VHS / U-matic / 16mm
Hot safety programs series
Color (G IND A)
$365.00, $355.00, $325.00 purchase, $85.00 rental
Explains and illustrates the potential dangers of loose cords, open drawers, crowded aisle spaces, office chemicals, lifting, cigarettes, stairs, ladders and a host of other hazards which may be present in the office workplace. Stresses the importance of proper lifting techniques, good housekeeping, proper training on the use of equipment, fire safety, evacuation and emergency action plans, ergonomics, exercise and other aspects of safety actions.
Business and Economics; Health and Safety
Dist - JEWELR **Prod** - JEWELR 1991

Office safety saves 15 MIN
VHS / U-matic / BETA
Color (IND G A)
$667.00 purchase, $125.00 rental _ #OFF031
Discusses the prevention of accidents, illness and injuries in the office environment. Emphasizes safe working practices with office machines and supplies, the necessity for good housekeeping and response to emergency situations. Considers posture, correct lifting and participation in a health and wellness program.
Business and Economics; Health and Safety; Physical Education and Recreation; Psychology
Dist - ITF **Prod** - ERF 1991

Office Safety - the Thrill Seekers 12 MIN
U-matic / VHS / 16mm
Color (A)
Points out safety hazards that seem to attract a breed of office workers termed 'thrill seekers.' Shows how they consider themselves too adventurous to heed prudent safety rules. Discusses the remedy for this situation.
Health and Safety
Dist - CENTEF **Prod** - CENTRO 1983
CORF

Office services 10 MIN
VHS
Skills - occupational programs series
Color (H A)
$49.00 purchase, $15.00 rental _ #316607; LC 91-709328
Features office workers - from entry level to supervisory positions - employed in a variety of offices, small and large. Part of a series featuring occupations in the skilled trades, in service industries and in business leading to careers in areas of demand and future growth. Includes teacher's guide with reproducible wooksheets.
Guidance and Counseling; Psychology
Dist - TVOTAR **Prod** - TVOTAR 1990

Office skills series
Describes a videotape series designed to help people improve their office and customer skills. Deals with issues such as how to answer a telephone, how to help customers, and learning basic clerical skills. Each videotape in the series is 30 minutes in length and includes a workbook and - or teacher's manual.
May I help you - commendable customer service 30 MIN
Dist - CAMV

Office Surgery 58 MIN
16mm
Color (PRO)
Demonstrates many of the minor diagnostic and therapeutic surgical procedures that could be done in the office by general practitioners and industrial physicians.
Health and Safety; Science
Dist - ACY **Prod** - ACYDGD 1961

Office Visit - Sexual Review of Systems 30 MIN
VHS / U-matic
Color (PRO)
Provides examples of how the primary care physician can incorporate questions about sexual functioning and sex - related concerns of patients into the office visit.
Health and Safety
Dist - HSCIC **Prod** - HSCIC

Officer as a Source of Change
16mm
View and do Series
B&W (PRO)
LC 73-700191
Explores the officer's role in inmate security and rehabilitation.
Sociology
Dist - SCETV **Prod** - SCETV 1971

Officer Down, Code 3 25 MIN
U-matic / VHS / 16mm
Police Training Films Series
Color
LC 75-702977
Explains and explores ten errors that are often the cause of the deaths of policemen.
Civics and Political Systems
Dist - CORF **Prod** - MTROLA 1975

Officer - Inmate Relationship
16mm
View and do Series
B&W (PRO)
LC 73-700190
Explores the background and reasons behind the importance of the correctional officer.
Sociology
Dist - SCETV **Prod** - SCETV 1971

Officer safety 18 MIN
VHS
Tactical training series
Color (PRO)
$360.00 purchase, $75.00 rental _ #9907
Shows that following safety procedures at all times is a matter of life and death. Asks officers to test themselves as they watch the video to see if they have developed bad habits or carelessness in their daily encounters with the public. Dramatizes the consequences of not following proper safety procedures.
Civics and Political Systems; Education; Health and Safety
Dist - AIMS **Prod** - AIMS 1988

Officer Stress 29 MIN
VHS
Crime to Court Procedural Specials Series
Color (PRO)
$99.00 purchase
Dramatizes hidden signs of police officer stress, how it affects work loads and schedules, attitude, home life and relations with co - workers. Presents recommendations for coping with pressure in law enforcement. Trains law enforcement personnel. Part of an ongoing series which looks in depth at topics presented in 'Crime To Court.' Produced in conjunction with the South Carolina Criminal Justice Academy and the National Sheriff's Association.
Civics and Political Systems; Psychology; Social Science; Sociology
Dist - SCETV **Prod** - SCETV

Officer Stress Awareness 20 MIN
16mm / U-matic / VHS
Color (PRO)
LC 76-702270
Uses a number of different physical, emotional and interpersonal stresses encountered by patrol officers in surveying the mental and physical stress of law enforcement.
Civics and Political Systems; Guidance and Counseling; Health and Safety; Psychology
Dist - CORF **Prod** - HAR 1976

Officer Stress Awareness - Externalizing Problems 20 MIN
16mm / U-matic / VHS
Color (PRO)
LC 76-702272
Examines conditions of physical, emotional and interpersonal stress presented by the aggressive, tough policeman. Shows how he may become careless, callous and create bad will toward the entire police force by his actions.
Civics and Political Systems; Guidance and Counseling; Health and Safety; Psychology; Sociology
Dist - CORF **Prod** - HAR 1976

Officer Stress Awareness - Internalizing Problems 20 MIN
16mm / U-matic / VHS
Color (PRO)
LC 76-702271
Examines conditions of physical, emotional and interpersonal stress presented by the police officer who internalized problems. Shows how to recognize these internalizations of stress before they affect the officer, his partner or the department.
Civics and Political Systems; Guidance and Counseling; Health and Safety; Psychology
Dist - CORF **Prod** - HAR 1976

Officer survival - an approach to conflict management series
Approaching potentially explosive conflicts 22 MIN
Conflict Resolution - Mediating Disputes 22 MIN
Conflict Resolution - Utilizing Community Resources 22 MIN
The Day everything went wrong 22 MIN
Defusing hostile individuals 22 MIN
Dist - CORF

Officer survival - an approach to conflict management series
Problem identification - determining the underlying issues of a conflict 22 MIN
Dist - CORF
HAR

Officer Survival III 10 MIN
16mm
Color
LC 77-701822
Presents a re - enactment of a shooting incident resulting in the death of four California Highway Patrol officers. Shows the correct procedures to be followed in similar situations.
Civics and Political Systems; Sociology
Dist - LACSD **Prod** - LACSD 1977

Officer Survival - Night Vs Day Patrol 20 MIN
U-matic / VHS / 16mm
Color
LC 79-701704
Presents reenactments of various situations which may occur during day and night patrols and discusses issues and questions which may arise as a result.
Civics and Political Systems
Dist - CORF **Prod** - HAR 1979

Officer survival series
Armed suspect 6 MIN
Barricaded suspect 6 MIN
Felony stop 12 MIN
Dist - CORF

Officer's bookcase
CD-ROM
(G)
$149.00 purchase
Presents a full - text database - dictionary of military terms and acronyms. Includes the Joint Chiefs of Staff 'Military Terms Dictionary' and the Defense Systems Mangement College 'Defense Acquisition Acronyms and Terms,' as well as the 'Soviet Terms Dictionary' from the Soviet Military Thought Series in a separate data area. Covers terms from the 1960s to the present day. Uses a customized version of LIST software for quick search and retrieval. Available in MS - DOS and MAC format.
Civics and Political Systems; History - United States; History - World; Sociology
Dist - QUANTA **Prod** - QUANTA

Officer's bookcase - Mac
CD-ROM
Color (PRO)
$129.00 purchase _ #1939m
Offers the equivalent to a dictionary of military oriented terms and acronyms. Includes Military Terms Dictionary, Defense Acquisition Acronyms and Terms, and Soviet terms Dictionary. For Macintosh Plus, SE and II computers. Requires at least one M of RAM, one floppy disk drive, and an Apple compatible CD - ROM drive.
Civics and Political Systems; English Language; Literature and Drama
Dist - BEP

Officer's bookcase - PC
CD-ROM
Color (PRO)
$129.00 purchase _ #1939p
Gives the equivalent to a dictionary of military oriented terms and acronyms. Includes Military Terms Dictionary, Defense Acquisition Acronyms and Terms, and Soviet Terms Dictionary. For IBM PCs and compatibles. Requires 640K RAM, DOS Version 3.1 or greater, one floppy disk drive - hard disk drive recommended, one empty expansion slot, and an IBM compatible CD - ROM drive.
Civics and Political Systems; English Language; Literature and Drama
Dist - BEP

The Official RBBS - PC - RBBS - in - a - box
CD-ROM
(G)
$149.00 purchase
Presents almost 9,000 DOS based programs. Includes full running shareware, freeware and public domain computer programs in the .ZIP (PKware) compressed format. Contains the CDACCESS program which features indexed, instant access to any program on the disc.
Computer Science; Mathematics
Dist - QUANTA **Prod** - QUANTA

The Official Rules of Golf Explained 35 MIN
VHS / BETA
Color
Explains the rules of golf, including unplayable lies, water hazards, lifting and dropping and movable and immovable obstructions. Gives tips on golf etiquette and shows highlights from championship events. With Tom Watson and Peter Alliss.
Physical Education and Recreation
Dist - CARAVT **Prod** - CARAVT

Official War Films 30 MIN
U-matic / VHS
B&W
Offers official War Films from the U S, 1934 - 44 including U S Marines at New Britain and Advance on Burma.
History - United States; History - World
Dist - IHF **Prod** - IHF

Offon 10 MIN
16mm
Color (C)
$280.00
Presents an experimental film by Scott Bartlett.
Fine Arts
Dist - AFA **Prod** - AFA 1968

Offset Taper - Side View Method, Openings not Parallel 35 MIN
VHS / BETA
Metal Fabrication - Round Tapers Series
Color (IND)
Industrial and Technical Education; Psychology
Dist - RMIBHF **Prod** - RMIBHF

Offset Taper - Side View Rotational Subtraction Method, Openings not Parallel 32 MIN
BETA / VHS
Metal Fabrication - Round Tapers Series
Color (IND)
Industrial and Technical Education; Psychology
Dist - RMIBHF **Prod** - RMIBHF

Offset Taper - Triangulation Plan View Method, Openings Parallel 31 MIN
BETA / VHS
Metal Fabrication - Round Tapers Series
Color (IND)
Industrial and Technical Education; Psychology
Dist - RMIBHF **Prod** - RMIBHF

Offshore 18 MIN
U-matic
Color
Narrates the story of the extensive search for offshore petroleum, which will become increasingly important to the world's energy supply. Describes the efforts being taken to preserve the environment while the search goes on.
Industrial and Technical Education; Science - Natural; Social Science
Dist - MTP **Prod** - EXXON

Offshore 20 MIN
16mm
Color (G)
_ *#106C 0173 530*
Views marine oil exploration. Shows the round the clock activities and precautions taken against pollution aboard an oil drilling rig off the Nova Scotia coast.
Geography - World; History - World; Social Science
Dist - CFLMDC **Prod** - NFBC 1973

Offshore Crane Operation, Pt 1 34 MIN
VHS / U-matic
Color (IND)
Describes how offshore pedestal cranes work, how the operator determines load capacity and how the crane must be checked out prior to use. Comprises the first of a two - part section on offshore crane operation.
Industrial and Technical Education
Dist - UTEXPE **Prod** - UTEXPE 1972

Offshore Crane Operation, Pt 2 21 MIN
U-matic / VHS
Color (IND)
Covers hoisting techniques, safety devices, rough - water techniques and proper handling of personnel nets. Comprises the second of a two - part section on offshore crane operation.
Industrial and Technical Education
Dist - UTEXPE **Prod** - UTEXPE 1972

Offshore cruising guide
VHS
Color (G A)
$49.80 purchase _ #0265
Shows how to prepare a boat for an extended offshore cruise, for a weekend or for months at a time.
Physical Education and Recreation
Dist - SEVVID

Offshore Fire Prevention 30 MIN
VHS / 16mm
Color (A IND)
$175.00 purchase _ #40.1400
Reveals often overlooked fire hazards in offshore oil rigs. Suggests preventive measures for dealing with such hazards.
Health and Safety; Industrial and Technical Education
Dist - UTEXPE

Offshore Oil - are We Ready 37 MIN
16mm
Color (H C A)
Explores the impact that offshore oil discoveries have had on Stavanger, Norway and on Aberdeen and the Shetland Islands in Scotland, especially on fisheries.
Geography - World; History - World; Social Science
Dist - NFBC **Prod** - NFBC 1981

Offshore Operations Series
Drill Floor Terms and Equipment
Going offshore for the first time
Offshore Terms and Equipment
Whittaker 50 - Man Escape Capsule
Working with Offshore Cranes
Dist - GPCV

Offshore Rescue 23 MIN
VHS / U-matic
Offshore Safety Series
Color
Follows the abandonment of an offshore oil installation by enclosed lifeboat and the successful evacuation of the lifeboat. Emphasizes how to get out of an enclosed lifeboat safely.
Health and Safety
Dist - FLMWST **Prod** - FLMWST

Offshore Rig Abandonment 25 MIN
U-matic / VHS
Color (IND)
Provides an overview of the safety procedures, equipment and possible hazards involved in a rig abandonment.
Industrial and Technical Education
Dist - UTEXPE **Prod** - UTEXPE 1970

Offshore safety series
Helicopter operations 21 MIN
Offshore Rescue 23 MIN
Safe Diving 22 MIN
Dist - FLMWST

Offshore Terms and Equipment
U-matic / VHS
Offshore Operations Series
Color (IND)
Presents a visual glossary of terms for offshore tasks and equipment. Details major rig work areas, job titles and general duties, basic drilling activities and equipment, basic crane activities, mud mixing and circulation terms and equipment, personal safety gear and basic hand tools in use offshore.
Business and Economics; Industrial and Technical Education; Social Science
Dist - GPCV **Prod** - GPCV

Offshore - the Search for Oil and Gas 18 MIN
16mm
Color
Describes the intensive search for petroleum supplies from the ocean. Describes the big equipment, big investment and big risks involved and discusses the efforts to preserve the ocean environment.
Business and Economics; Industrial and Technical Education; Science - Natural; Social Science
Dist - MTP **Prod** - EXXON

Offsoundings Races
VHS
Color (G)
$19.95 purchase
Presents a short video from the Mystic Seaport Museum selections on museum exhibits, races taped by the media division or compilations from museum archives. Features races on 'Offsoundings Races.' Please inquire by year of race for availability.
Literature and Drama; Physical Education and Recreation
Dist - MYSTIC **Prod** - MYSTIC

Ofra Haza - from sunset till dawn 42 MIN
VHS
Color (G)
$34.95 purchase _ #778
Presents Israeli vocalist Ofra Haza. Offers Yemenite folklore and dance.
Geography - World; Sociology
Dist - ERGOM **Prod** - ERGOM

Oglethorpe
VHS
Campus clips series
Color (H C A)
$29.95 purchase _ #CC0025V
Takes a video visit to the campus of Oglethorpe University in Georgia. Shows many of the distinctive features of the campus, and interviews students about their experiences. Provides information on the composition of the student body, professors, academics, social life, housing, and other subjects.
Education
Dist - CAMV

The Ogre 10 MIN
16mm
B&W (G)
$20.00 rental
Explains filmmaker Barnett, 'The first episode of a series in which every episode is identical.
Fine Arts
Dist - CANCIN **Prod** - BARND 1970

Oh 12 MIN
16mm
Color
Presents a haunting view of man through animation and graphics. Depicts mankind as falling down.
Fine Arts; Industrial and Technical Education; Religion and Philosophy; Sociology
Dist - VANBKS **Prod** - VANBKS

Oh Brother, My Brother 14 MIN
16mm / U-matic / VHS
Color
LC 79-701074
Focuses on the love and affection of two young brothers, following the boys through a day of ordinary activity.
Guidance and Counseling
Dist - PFP **Prod** - LOWCAR 1979

Oh Dem Watermelons 11 MIN
16mm
Color (C)
$504.00
Experimental film by Robert Nelson.
Fine Arts
Dist - AFA **Prod** - AFA 1965

Oh, for a Life of Sensations 22 MIN
U-matic / VHS / 16mm
Color (C A)
Shows educators using innovative techniques to involve students. Highlights a visiting poet and construction of a dome by students under an architect's supervision.
Education; Psychology
Dist - KANLEW **Prod** - KANLEW 1981

Oh Freedom 26 MIN
16mm
New York Times - Arno Press Films on Black Americans Series
Color
LC 76-710620
Traces the Black Civil Rights Movement from 1955 when a Black woman refused to give up her seat on a bus to a White man, to the cry for Black Power nearly a decade later. Explores the movement and its impact through the words of the people involved and through examination of the concept of Black Power.
Civics and Political Systems; History - United States
Dist - SF **Prod** - NYT 1970

Oh, Freedom - the Story of the Civil Rights Movement 28 MIN
16mm
Color (J H)
LC 76-701620
Traces the Black Civil Rights Movement from 1955 when a Black woman refused to give up her seat on a bus to a White man, to the cry for Black Power nearly a decade later. Explores the movement and its impact through the words of the people involved, and through examination of the concept of Black Power.
History - United States
Dist - REPRO **Prod** - REPRO

Oh Happy Day 23 MIN
16mm
Color
Features Ray Hildebrand and John Westbrook of the Fellowship of Christian Athletes displaying their comedy and musical repertoire in a high school assembly. John sings 'I BELIEVE' and Ray adds songs he has written, including the national pop hit 'MR BALLOON MAN.'.
Fine Arts; Religion and Philosophy
Dist - FELLCA **Prod** - FELLCA

Oh, I Saw a Fox 14 MIN
VHS / U-matic
Stepping into Rhythm Series
Color (P)
Demonstrates playing tone bells and singing with various accompaniments.
Fine Arts
Dist - AITECH **Prod** - WVIZTV

Oh Kojo - How Could You
VHS / 35mm strip
ALA Notable Children's Filmstrips Series
Color (K)
$33.00 purchase
Presents a children's story. Part of the American Library Association series.
English Language; Literature and Drama
Dist - PELLER

Oh life - A woe story - The A test news 5 MIN
16mm
B&W (G)
$10.00 rental, $219.00 purchase
Says filmmaker Brakhage, 'Three TV 'concretes'.'
Fine Arts
Dist - CANCIN **Prod** - BRAKS 1963

Oh my aching back 30 MIN
VHS
Color (G A)
$39.95 purchase _ #WES1901V
Presents a comprehensive guide to understanding back problems and injuries. Features interviews with orthopedic surgeons and back specialists, who explain the facts in laymen's language. Covers rehabilitation, but stresses the importance of prevention through exercises.
Physical Education and Recreation; Science - Natural
Dist - CAMV

Oh, My Aching Back 25 MIN
U-matic / VHS
B&W
Discusses low back pain caused by faulty posture, arthritis and stress. Demonstrates body mechanics to relieve low back pain.
Health and Safety
Dist - BUSARG **Prod** - BUSARG

Oh My Aching Back 21 MIN
16mm
Color
LC 74-705242
Shows workmen the correct method of lifting, including good posture, position and smooth application of lifting power. Illustrates how strains occur and how discs are pinched. Emphasizes the need for proper lifting and handling of working tools and materials.
Health and Safety; Science - Natural
Dist - USNAC **Prod** - USBM 1965

Oh My Aching Back 30 MIN
U-matic / VHS
Here's to Your Health Series
Color
Presents orthopedic specialist Dr Vert Mooney explaining ways to prevent back pains, and demonstrates exercises to strengthen the back. Offers tips on good posture.
Health and Safety; Physical Education and Recreation
Dist - PBS **Prod** - KERA 1979

Oh, my aching back 20 MIN
VHS
Color (I J H G)
$19.95 purchase _ #K45255
Covers the complete spectrum of back problems, also the prevention and rehabilitation of back injuries.
Health and Safety; Science - Natural
Dist - HTHED **Prod** - HTHED

Oh, My Aching Back 30 MIN
U-matic / VHS
Here's to Your Health Series
Color
Health and Safety; Psychology
Dist - DELTAK **Prod** - PBS

Oh, My Aching Head 24 MIN
U-matic / VHS
Color (C)
$279.00, $179.00 purchase _ #AD - 2205
Examines the causes, costs and possible cures of chronic, recurrent headaches. Differentiates between different types of headaches and demonstrates how continued consumption of analgesics can lead to drug dependency while prolonging and worsening pain. Visits headache treatment centers and shows a variety of self - management techniques.
Health and Safety; Psychology; Science - Natural
Dist - FOTH **Prod** - FOTH

Oh My Darling 8 MIN
U-matic / VHS / 16mm
Color (H C A)
Tells the story of a girl growing up to womanhood and of the growing her family has to do to keep up with her. Animation and no narration.
Fine Arts; Guidance and Counseling; Sociology
Dist - MOKIN **Prod** - CRAMAN 1980

Oh no not Another Lab Test 25 MIN
U-matic / VHS
Color (A)
LC 81-706191
Describes the reasons for and the processes involved in conducting hospital lab tests. Shows how blood tests are performed and analyzed, and observes medical technologists doing various tests to analyze body chemistry.
Health and Safety; Science
Dist - CONTED **Prod** - CONTED 1980

Oh Shoelaces 7 MIN
16mm
Color (K P)
LC 72-701244
Provides the stimulus for learning the basic skill of typing shoelaces. Shows many and various types of shoes in the process of being tied by children and adults.
Psychology
Dist - FILMSM **Prod** - FILMSM 1971

Oh Theatre, Pt 1 29 MIN
Videoreel / VT2
University of Chicago Round Table Series
Color
Fine Arts
Dist - PBS **Prod** - WTTWTV

Oh Theatre, Pt 2 29 MIN
Videoreel / VT2
University of Chicago Round Table Series
Color
Fine Arts
Dist - PBS **Prod** - WTTWTV

Oh what a Beautiful Morning 7 MIN
16mm
B&W
LC 75-703212
Contrasts the fantasies of luxury dreamed of by three wandering youths with the realities of unemployment and hunger which they face.
Fine Arts
Dist - USC **Prod** - USC 1967

Oh, what a Knight 4 MIN
U-matic / VHS / 16mm
Color (A)
Features the drawings of Dutch animator Paul Driessen.
Fine Arts; Literature and Drama
Dist - MTOLP **Prod** - CRAMAN 1984

Oh, what a Zany Zoo 10 MIN
U-matic / VHS
Book, Look and Listen Series
Color (K P)
Presents a collection of fanciful animals.
English Language; Literature and Drama
Dist - AITECH **Prod** - MDDE 1977

Oh what the Hell - Pt 1 18 MIN
VHS / 16mm
Oh what the Hell Series
Color (A PRO)
$435.00 purchase, $160.00 rental
Features Rowan Atkinson as the Devil in a dramatization about safety in offices, factories, warehouses and building sites. Part 1 of a two - part series on safety in the workplace. Management training.
Business and Economics; Health and Safety; Psychology
Dist - VIDART **Prod** - VIDART 1990

Oh what the Hell - Pt 2 15 MIN
VHS / 16mm
Oh what the Hell Series
Color (A PRO)
$435.00 purchase, $160.00 rental
Features Rowan Atkinson as the Devil in a dramatization about safety in offices, factories, warehouses and building sites. Part 2 of a two - part series on safety in the workplace. Management training.
Business and Economics; Health and Safety; Psychology
Dist - VIDART **Prod** - VIDART 1990

Oh what the Hell Series
Oh what the Hell - Pt 1 18 MIN
Oh what the Hell - Pt 2 15 MIN
Dist - VIDART

Oh Yes, these are Very Special Children 20 MIN
16mm
Color (J)
LC 72-702321
Uses an example of retarded children and their dancing teacher to show how much retarded children can learn if given the chance.
Education; Psychology
Dist - CMPBL **Prod** - CMPBL 1971

Ohana 25 MIN
16mm
Color (J H C G)
Reveals the family structure of the Hawaiian people both in the past and as it has evolved today.
Geography - United States; History - United States; Sociology
Dist - CINEPC **Prod** - TAHARA 1978

Ohio 60 MIN
VHS
Portrait of America series
Color (J H C G)
$99.95 purchase _ #AMB35V
Visits Ohio. Offers extensive research into the state's history. Films key locations and presents segments on its history, government, education, folklore, science, journalism, sociology, industry, agriculture and business. Shows what is unique about Ohio and what is distinctive about its regional culture and how it got to be that way. Includes teacher study guides. Part of a 50 - part series.
Geography - United States; History - United States
Dist - CAMV

Ohio River - Industry and Transportation 16 MIN
U-matic / VHS / 16mm
Color (J)
Follows the Ohio River from Pittsburgh to Cairo, Illinois, showing the locks and dams that make the river navigable. Shows the many factories that have been built along the Ohio and discusses how they have contributed to the pollution of the river.
Geography - United States; Science - Natural
Dist - PHENIX **Prod** - EVANSA 1970

Ohio River odyssey 37 MIN
VHS
Always a river video collection series
Color (G)
Contact distributor about rental cost _ #N92 - 034
Takes a walking tour through Huntington Museum of Art's display along the Ohio River. Goes from town to town on the river.
Geography - United States
Dist - INDI

Ohio State
VHS
Campus clips series
Color (H C A)
$29.95 purchase _ #CC0087V
Takes a video visit to the campus of Ohio State University. Shows many of the distinctive features of the campus, and interviews students about their experiences. Provides information on the composition of the student body, professors, academics, social life, housing, and other subjects.
Education
Dist - CAMV

The Ohio - the big blue collar river 55 MIN
VHS
On the waterways series
Color (G H)
$29.95 purchase _ #OW08
Travels with the crew of the Driftwood to explore the Ohio River through the words of its bridgebuilders, barge handlers and songsters. Narrated by Jason Robards. Part of a 13 - part series on the history, geography, culture and ecology of North American waterways.
Social Science
Dist - SVIP

Ohio University
VHS
Campus clips series
Color (H C A)
$29.95 purchase _ #CC0088V
Takes a video visit to the campus of Ohio University. Shows many of the distinctive features of the campus, and interviews students about their experiences. Provides information on the composition of the student body, professors, academics, social life, housing, and other subjects.
Education
Dist - CAMV

The Ohmeter and its use 15 MIN
U-matic / VHS
Basic electricity and D C circuits - laboratory series
Color
Industrial and Technical Education; Science - Physical; Social Science
Dist - TXINLC **Prod** - TXINLC

Ohm's Law 9 MIN
16mm / U-matic / VHS
Basic Electricity Series
Color (H C A)
Discusses amperes, volts, ohms, the effect of resistance and resistors in a circuit.
Science - Physical
Dist - IFB **Prod** - STFD 1979

Ohm's Law 6 MIN
VHS / 16mm
Electrical Theory Series
Color (S)
$50.00 purchase _ #241302
Illustrates 22 concepts fundamental to the training of second year electrical apprentices using graphic animation. Demonstrates the relationship between current, voltage and resistance in 'Ohm's Law.'.

Education; Industrial and Technical Education; Psychology
Dist - ACCESS **Prod** - ACCESS 1983

Ohm's Law 21 MIN
16mm
B&W (H C A)
LC 74-705243
Lists the elements of electricity. Notes the source, transmission and use of electrical energy. Explains how Ohm's law functions by describing resistance in electrical circuits.
Science - Physical
Dist - USNAC **Prod** - USA 1943

Ohm's law and power 30 MIN
VHS / U-matic
Basic electricity and D C circuits series
Color
Applies Ohm's law to predict voltage, current and resistance behavior in simple circuits. Allows calculation of resistive power loss through concept of power dissipation, plus mathematics of squares and square roots.
Industrial and Technical Education; Science - Physical; Social Science
Dist - TXINLC **Prod** - TXINLC

Ohm's law and series circuits - including building circuits from schematic diagrams 15 MIN
U-matic / VHS
Basic electricity and D C circuits - laboratory series
Color
Industrial and Technical Education; Science - Physical; Social Science
Dist - TXINLC **Prod** - TXINLC

Ohm's Law - no 4 60 MIN
U-matic
AC/DC Electronics Series
Color (PRO)
One of a series of electronic and electrical training sessions for electronics workers on direct and alternating current and how to work with each.
Industrial and Technical Education
Dist - VTRI **Prod** - VTRI 1986

Ohoyo - Indian Women Speak 33 MIN
VHS / U-matic
Color
Features a panel of Indian women speaking to an assembly on the issue of sovereignty and the struggles to maintain and retain Indian life and traditions. Discusses such topics as equality, the non - Indian court system, adoption and activism.
Social Science; Sociology
Dist - UWISC **Prod** - VRL 1983

Oil 30 MIN
U-matic
Adam Smith's money world series; 105
Color (A)
Attempts to demystify the world of money and break it down so that small as well as large businesses and it's people understand and adjust to new social and economic trends. Reports on the major economic stories and discoveries of the day.
Business and Economics
Dist - PBS **Prod** - WNETTV 1985

The Oil Age 26 MIN
16mm / U-matic / VHS
Today's History Series
Color (H C)
Tells how later twentieth century history is inextricably entwined with the history of oil. Examines oil, and its parallels with coal, from Kuwait in the 1920's through the crisis of 1974 to oil's shaky future.
Civics and Political Systems; History - United States; History - World; Social Science
Dist - JOU **Prod** - JOU 1984

Oil and American Power Series

Egypt	16 MIN
Iran	22 MIN
Israel	13 MIN
Pressure Points - Oman, South Yemen, North Yemen	21 MIN
Saudi Arabia	18 MIN

Dist - FI

Oil and gas operations offshore - an introduction 20 MIN
VHS
Color (IND PRO)
$400.00 purchase _ #40.3301
Tells about offshore exploration, drilling, production and transportation in the oil and gas industries.
Industrial and Technical Education
Dist - UTEXPE **Prod** - UTEXPE 1993

Oil and Gas Production 24 MIN
U-matic / VHS
Color (IND)
Covers the nature of oil and gas reservoirs and gives the sequence of events involved in producing and processing oil, gas and water from the reservoir to the pipeline.
Business and Economics; Social Science
Dist - UTEXPE **Prod** - UTEXPE 1974

Oil and Gas Production 30 MIN
Slide / VHS / 16mm
(A PRO)
$200.00 purchase _ #14.1260, $210.00 purchase _ #54.1260
Covers the basic asects of reservoirs and discusses natural flow, artificial lift, separation, treating, and water disposal.
Health and Safety; Industrial and Technical Education; Social Science
Dist - UTEXPE **Prod** - UTEXPE 1985

Oil and its Products 14 MIN
16mm / U-matic / VHS
Color (I) (SWEDISH)
LC 79-700505
Tells how oil is formed, located, mined and refined into fuels and made into petrochemicals. Surveys the impact of petroleum in the 20th century and probes into the possible effects it may have on the future.
Industrial and Technical Education; Social Science
Dist - PHENIX **Prod** - BAYERW 1979

Oil and Water 60 MIN
VHS
Oil Series
Color (G)
$59.95 purchase _ #OILO - 107
Highlights the exploration, drilling and oil production of the North Sea area by both the United Kingdom and Norway. Discusses the impact of technological advances, territorial disagreements, and falling oil prices.
History - World
Dist - PBS

Oil, arms and the Gulf 30 MIN
VHS
America's defense monitor series; War with Iraq
Color (J H C G)
$29.95 purchase _ #ADM412V
Examines the role of oil and arms sales in events in the Middle East. Part of a six - part series examining the United States war with Iraq, 1990 - 1991.
Business and Economics; Civics and Political Systems; History - World
Dist - CAMV

Oil but for One Day 30 MIN
16mm
B&W (R)
Theodore Bikel celebrates Hanukkah with drama and songs. (Kinescope).
Religion and Philosophy
Dist - NAAJS **Prod** - JTS 1959

Oil Change, Filter and Lube 20 MIN
VHS
Tune Up America - Home Video Car Repair Series
(A)
$24.95
Provides the viewer with a methodical demonstration of an oil change so that he can perform one himself.
Industrial and Technical Education
Dist - CAMV **Prod** - CAMV

Oil Change, Filters, and Lube 21 MIN
VHS
Color (G)
$19.95 _ TA103
Presents the benefits of frequent oil and filter change as well as lubrication for automobiles.
Industrial and Technical Education
Dist - AAVIM **Prod** - AAVIM 1989

Oil Country Tubular Goods - an Introduction 25 MIN
U-matic / VHS / 16mm
Color (IND)
Explains in basic terms the need for casing and tubing in oil and gas wells. Discusses some of the factors necessary for the planning of good tubular strings.
Industrial and Technical Education; Social Science
Dist - UTEXPE **Prod** - HYDRIL 1980

Oil Country Tubular Goods - an Introduction 25 MIN
16mm / VHS
(A PRO)
$350.00 purchase _ #30.0113, $325.00 purchase _ #50.0113
Exlains in basic terms the need for casing and tubing in oil and gas wells and discusses some of the factors necessary for the planning of good tubular strings.
Health and Safety; Industrial and Technical Education; Social Science
Dist - UTEXPE **Prod** - UTEXPE 1980

Oil Crisis 20 MIN
U-matic / VHS
B&W (G)
$249.00, $149.00 purchase _ #AD - 1625
Traces Japan's history from Perry's landing in 1853, Japan's subsequent efforts to achieve technological parity with the West. Considers the effect of the economic crash of 1929 on Japan's economy and the Japanese decision to find solutions through military expansion. Looks at the American occupation after World War II which provided a base for Japan's post - war economic resurgence until the 1973 oil crisis forced new recognition of Japan's total economic dependence on foreign trade.
Business and Economics; Geography - World; History - World
Dist - FOTH **Prod** - FOTH

Oil Driller 30 MIN
VHS / BETA
American Professionals Series
Color
Describes the life of Steve Joiner, an oil driller who works on an oil rig 15 miles off the coast of Louisiana, in the Gulf of Mexico. Discusses the effects his work has on family relationships, as he works two weeks of every month, from noon to midnight.
Geography - United States; Guidance and Counseling; Social Science
Dist - RMIBHF **Prod** - WTBS

Oil Equipment 30 MIN
U-matic
Media and Methods of the Artist Series
Color (H C A)
Looks at various types of equipment used by an artist in the execution of an oil painting.
Fine Arts
Dist - TVOTAR **Prod** - TVOTAR 1971

Oil Field Corrosion
Slide / VHS / 16mm
(A PRO)
$550.00 purchase _ #15.9998, $590.00 purchase _ #55.9998
Provides help to field operators and junior engineers in understanding the principles of corrosion and its control.
Health and Safety; Industrial and Technical Education; Social Science
Dist - UTEXPE **Prod** - UTEXPE 1981

Oil Field Corrosion Series

Consequences of Change	25 MIN
Corrosion Measuring and Monitoring	25 MIN
Inspection Techniques	25 MIN
What is Corrosion	25 MIN

Dist - UTEXPE

Oil Field Electricity, Pt 1 22 MIN
U-matic / VHS
Color (IND)
Outlines the basic principles of electricity. Points out safe procedures that should be followed when working with electrical components on the lease.
Health and Safety; Industrial and Technical Education; Social Science
Dist - UTEXPE **Prod** - UTEXPE 1983

Oil Films in Action 18 MIN
16mm
Color (H C T)
Shows how oil film pressures vary at different points around the circumference of a journal and proportionally with the load. Demonstrates that viscosity and journal speeds have no effect on oil film pressures. Illustrates the action of converging oil films.
Industrial and Technical Education
Dist - GM **Prod** - GM 1951

Oil Filter Story 26 MIN
16mm
Color
Shows how oil filters are made and tested. Illustrates their significance to the operation of an automobile engine.
Business and Economics; Industrial and Technical Education
Dist - GM **Prod** - GM

Oil - Finds for the Future 25 MIN
VHS / 16mm
Earth's Physical Resources Series
Color (S)
$200.00 purchase _ #236215
Presents a global view of the earth's resource potential. Features footage filmed in Britain, Europe and North America. 'Oil - Finds For The Future' examines methods for projecting existing, extractable hydrocarbon reserves - Hubbands Curve - and describes alternate methods for finding new conventional reserves, as well as for developing synthetic fuels from a variety of resources.
Science - Physical; Social Science
Dist - ACCESS MEDIAG **Prod** - BBCTV 1984

Oil - from Fossil to Flame 13 MIN
U-matic / VHS / 16mm
Captioned; Color (I J)
$325.00, $235.00 purchase _ #74508; LC 76-701825
Provides a general description of the oil industry, including its geographic distribution, production and drilling, transportation, uses and economic importance.
Business and Economics; Geography - World; Industrial and Technical Education; Science - Physical; Social Science
Dist - CORF **Prod** - CENTEF 1976

The Oil Game 48 MIN
U-matic / VHS
Color
$455.00 purchase
Presents a program on the U.S. involvement in the oil industry. From the ABC TV Program, Close Up.
Business and Economics; Social Science
Dist - ABCLR **Prod** - ABCLR 1982

The Oil Gear Hydraulic Traversing Mechanism, Principles of Operation 22 MIN
16mm
B&W
LC FIE52-1336
Shows how the oil gear traverse mechanism operates and the path and functioning of oil through an elevated mechanism.
Industrial and Technical Education
Dist - USNAC **Prod** - USA 1944

Oil in Libya 15 MIN
U-matic / VHS / 16mm
Man and His World Series
Color (P I J H C)
LC 75-705488
A study of the oil industry and market in Tripoli, Libya. Includes the process of oil - drilling to the final loading of oil on tankers for transportation to foriegn markets.
Business and Economics; Geography - World; History - United States
Dist - FI **Prod** - FI 1969

Oil - in - Water Emulsions - Formation and Stability, Pt 2 3 MIN
16mm
Food and Nutrition Series
Color (J)
LC 70-710175
Illustrates factors which influence structures in food. Demonstrates the preparation of typical temporary, semi - permanent and permanent emulsions and compares the stability of each type at specified intervals after emulsification.
Science - Physical
Dist - IOWA **Prod** - IOWA 1971

Oil in your engine
VHS
Color (G)
$39.95 purchase _ #6 - 046 - 103A
Discusses the crucial role of oil in keeping an engine running. Discusses the properties, functions, selection, engine wear, viscosity improvers - multigrade, and other additives.
Industrial and Technical Education
Dist - VEP **Prod** - BPCO

The Oil kingdoms series
Kings and Pirates - Pt 1 59 MIN
The Petrodollar coast - Pt 2 59 MIN
Sea of conflict - Pt 3 59 MIN
Dist - FI

Oil, Money and Politics - Pt 3 59 MIN
VHS
Saudi Arabia Series
Color (S)
$49.00 purchase _ #315 - 9003
Interweaves historical information with current footage of Arabian life, from the nomadic Bedouins to modern cities in this in - depth political, economic and cultural look at Saudi Arabia. Part 3 of three parts investigates the power of oil in the world, as well as in Saudi Arabia's domestic affairs.
Foreign Language; Geography - World; History - World; Religion and Philosophy; Social Science; Sociology
Dist - FI **Prod** - PP 1986

Oil muds 24 MIN
VHS / U-matic / Slide
Rotary drilling fluids series; 03
Color (IND)
Discusses uses, composition and precautions to exercise when using oil - base and inverted muds.
Business and Economics; Industrial and Technical Education; Social Science
Dist - UTEXPE **Prod** - UTEXPE 1976

Oil on the River 23 MIN
16mm
Color (P I J H)
Documents problems of oil pollution on the Ohio River from 1865 to the present, describing various examples of pollution, their causes, and ways to prevent future occurrences. Explains that most manufacturers and oil handlers are assuming their responsibilities and that the careless general public is becoming the largest contributor to pollution.
Business and Economics; Geography - United States; Science - Natural
Dist - FINLYS **Prod** - ORVWSC 1961

Oil Over the Andes 27 MIN
16mm
Color
LC 80-701250
Focuses on oil exploration and discovery in the rain forests of Peru.
Geography - World; Social Science
Dist - MTP **Prod** - OCCPC 1980

Oil Painting Basics 60 MIN
BETA / VHS
Color (G)
$34.95 purchase _ #500108
Presents the fundamentals of painting. Discusses supplies, use of color, commposition, perspective and layouts.
Fine Arts
Dist - HOMEAF **Prod** - HOMEAF
UILL

Oil Painting 1 - Landscape 60 MIN
BETA / VHS
Color
Shows how to create a serene forest by following easy instructions.
Fine Arts
Dist - HOMEAF **Prod** - HOMEAF

Oil painting - Part 1 - misty forest landscape 60 MIN
VHS
Color (G)
$34.95 purchase _ #S00109
Presents a step - by - step lesson on painting a misty forest landscape, using oil paints. Provides useful hints for beginners and experienced artists alike. From the Learn - By - Video Painting Series.
Fine Arts
Dist - UILL

Oil painting - Part 3 - mountain lake and pines 60 MIN
VHS
Color (G)
$34.95 purchase _ #S00111
Presents a step - by - step lesson on painting a traditional mountain scene, using oil paints. Provides useful hints for beginners and experienced artists alike. From the Learn - By - Video Painting Series.
Fine Arts
Dist - UILL

Oil Painting 3 - Mountain Lakes 60 MIN
BETA / VHS
Color
Reveals how to capture and experience three dimensional painting through the use of colors, layout techniques and perspective in developing this mountain scene.
Fine Arts
Dist - HOMEAF **Prod** - HOMEAF

Oil Painting 2 - Seascape 60 MIN
BETA / VHS
Color (G)
$34.95 purchase _ #500110
Shows how the intricacy of a wave in motion is captured and made simple in painting seascapes.
Fine Arts
Dist - HOMEAF **Prod** - HOMEAF
UILL

Oil Pigments 30 MIN
U-matic
Media and Methods of the Artist Series
Color (H C A)
Demonstrates techniques involved in executing an oil painting, concentrating on the qualities of the paint itself.
Fine Arts
Dist - TVOTAR **Prod** - TVOTAR 1971

Oil Pollution Prevention Regulations 18 MIN
U-matic / VHS
Color (IND)
Gives a general orientation to the scope of the Federal Water Pollution Control Act of 1972 and the Spill Prevention Control and Countermeasure (SPCC) plans required to comply with the act.
Business and Economics; Industrial and Technical Education; Social Science
Dist - UTEXPE **Prod** - UTEXPE 1975

The Oil price crash - how low will it go 30 MIN
U-matic
Adam Smith's money world 1985 - 1986 season series; 222
Color (A)
Attempts to demystify the world of money and break it down so that small as well as large businesses and it's people understand and adjust to new social and economic trends. Reports on the major economic stories and discoveries of 1985 and 1986.
Business and Economics
Dist - PBS **Prod** - WNETTV 1986

Oil series
Reviews the history of oil. Focuses on the development of the petroleum industry, the beginning of OPEC, and the influence oil has had on industry, politics and societies. Interviews a wide variety of experts. Eight - part series was produced by Grampian Television and NRK, the Norwegian National Radio and Television Corporation.
The Devil gave us oil 60 MIN
Floating to victory 60 MIN
The Global gamble 60 MIN
God bless standard oil 60 MIN
The Independents 60 MIN
Oil and Water 60 MIN
The Rise of OPEC 60 MIN
Sisters Under Siege 60 MIN
Dist - PBS

Oil Shale - the Rock that Burns 29 MIN
16mm
Energy Sources - a New Beginning Series
Color
Asks if today's technology and pre - planning can prevent the feared consequences of strip mining. Considers the economic and environmental problems which would remain unsolved.
Science - Natural; Social Science
Dist - UCOLO **Prod** - UCOLO

Oil Shales and Tar Sands 36 MIN
VHS / U-matic
Basic and Petroleum Geology for Non - Geologists - Hydrocarbons and '- - Series; Hydrocarbons
Color (IND)
Industrial and Technical Education; Science - Physical
Dist - GPCV **Prod** - PHILLP

Oil spill - patterns in pollution 17 MIN
VHS
Color (G)
$275.00 purchase, $12.50 rental
Reveals that the demands of industialized society for oil, gas and coal have resulted in rash exploitation of natural resources and in terrible environmental disasters. Discusses the energy problems of the United States.
Science - Natural; Social Science; Sociology
Dist - CMSMS **Prod** - SIERRA 1972

Oil Strike 15 MIN
16mm
B&W
Presents oil workers in Northern California who strike Standard and Shell Oil Companies. Shows the companies response with goon squads. Includes scenes of students at San Francisco State College and U C Berkeley coming out and supporting the strike.
Business and Economics; Sociology
Dist - CANWRL **Prod** - CANWRL

Oil Techniques 1 30 MIN
U-matic
Media and Methods of the Artist Series
Color (H C A)
Demonstrates techniques involved in executing an oil painting.
Fine Arts
Dist - TVOTAR **Prod** - TVOTAR 1971

Oil Techniques 2 30 MIN
U-matic
Media and Methods of the Artist Series
Color (H C A)
Demonstrates techniques involved in executing an oil painting.
Fine Arts
Dist - TVOTAR **Prod** - TVOTAR 1971

Oil Techniques 3 30 MIN
U-matic
Media and Methods of the Artist Series
Color (H C A)
Demonstrates techniques involved in executing an oil painting.
Fine Arts
Dist - TVOTAR **Prod** - TVOTAR 1971

Oil the Hard Way - an Introduction to Enhanced Recovery 25 MIN
U-matic / VHS / 16mm
Color (IND)
Provides a nontechnical description of the reasons for and the basic mechanics of various secondary and tertiary recovery techniques.

Industrial and Technical Education; Social Science
Dist - UTEXPE **Prod** - UTEXPE 1979

Oil - the OPEC Case 17 MIN
U-matic / VHS
Color (H C A)
Focuses on the pledge of oil - consuming nations to reduce their oil imports, as well as the changes and modernization occurring within the exporting countries.
Social Science
Dist - JOU **Prod** - UPI

The Oil tycoon 30 MIN
VHS
Money makers series
Color (A)
PdS30 purchase
Takes a look at Robert Orville Anderson, America's top private landowner and the head of the seventh largest oil company in the country. Examines the background history and vicissitudes of his business empire and uses interviews to determine the practicality and fallibility of his commercial philosophy. Part of a series featuring six of the world's leading entrepreneurs.
Business and Economics
Dist - BBCENE

The Oil Weapon 50 MIN
VHS / U-matic / 16mm
Window on the World Series
Color; Mono (J H C A)
MV $350.00 _ MP $600.00 purchase, $50.00 rental
Presents a comprehensive veiw of the oil trade situation, the people of the Arab nations, their way of life and their goals.
Business and Economics; Civics and Political Systems
Dist - CTV **Prod** - CTV 1975

Oil Well Drilling
U-matic / VHS
Field Trips in Environmental Geology - Technical and Mechanical 'Concerns Series
Color
Visits a number of oil well drill sites showing the sequence of events from land acquisition and drilling to site reclamation and product transportation. Stresses the geologic aspects of a producing well and the uncertainty of exploration and production.
Industrial and Technical Education; Science - Natural; Science - Physical; Social Science
Dist - KENTSU **Prod** - KENTSU

Oilwell 11 MIN
16mm
Color
LC 75-703213
Presents a timely satire about man's self - destructive urge, using oilwells to portray pollution, mechanization and self - interest.
Fine Arts
Dist - USC **Prod** - USC 1960

Oilwell Blowouts - an Introduction 20 MIN
16mm / VHS
(A PRO)
$375.00 purchase _ #30.0108, $350.00 purchase _ #50.0108
Covers the principles of kick detection and well control techniques in a basic, understandable manner.
Health and Safety; Industrial and Technical Education; Social Science
Dist - UTEXPE **Prod** - UTEXPE 1976

Oilwell Blowouts - an Introduction 25 MIN
16mm / U-matic / VHS
Color (IND)
Covers the principles of kick detection and well control techniques in a basic manner.
Industrial and Technical Education; Social Science
Dist - UTEXPE **Prod** - HYDRIL 1976

Oisin 17 MIN
U-matic / VHS / 16mm
Color (I)
LC 73-702924
Records the images of trees, mountains, lakes, flowers and animals of Ireland.
Geography - United States; Geography - World
Dist - IFB **Prod** - AENGUS 1973

Ojiisan 9 MIN
16mm
B&W (H C A)
LC 79-700125
Shows how a young man comes to grips with his feelings as he stands a vigil over his grandfather who is dying in a hospital.
Fine Arts; Sociology
Dist - USC **Prod** - USC 1979

Ojo Alerta 15 MIN
16mm / U-matic / VHS
Color (K P) (SPANISH)
A Spanish - language version of the motion picture One Little Indian. Portrays Magic Bow, a young boy on his first visit to the city who is mystified by the whirl of traffic until he learns some basic safety precautions.
Foreign Language; Health and Safety
Dist - IFB **Prod** - NFBC 1973

The OK Classroom 29 MIN
16mm / U-matic / VHS
Human Relations and School Discipline Series
Color (C)
Introduces the techniques and terminology of transactional (TA) analysis explicated by Dr Thomas Harris, author of 'I'M OK, YOU'RE OK.' Discusses ta concepts with teachers and explains the special meaning of the terms 'PARENT,' 'CHILD,' 'ADULT,' 'TRANSACTION,' 'STROKES,' 'LIFE POSITIONS' and 'GAMES.'.
Education; Psychology; Sociology
Dist - FI **Prod** - MFFD

OK to be me - building self - esteem 24 MIN
VHS
Color (I J)
$169.00 purchase _ #2308 - SK
Uses the story of six children and their reactions to their new school pictures to present messages about self - esteem. Traces the origins of self - esteem to the messages received from parents and others. Suggests that people with low self - esteem reinforce their feelings by giving themselves negative messages. Stresses the concept that self - esteem can be developed, but must be worked at. Includes teacher's guide.
Education; Psychology; Sociology
Dist - SUNCOM **Prod** - SUNCOM

OK to Say no - the Case for Waiting
VHS / 35mm strip
$165.00 purchase _ #015 - 097 filmstrip, $165.00 purchase _ #015 -
Points out the case for abstaining from sex as an option. Emphasizes the role of personal choice, emotional readiness, and the need for assertiveness in dealing with peer pressures.
Health and Safety; Psychology
Dist - CAREER **Prod** - CAREER

O'Keeffe 60 MIN
VHS
Women in art series
Color (G)
$39.95 purchase _ #X006
Visits with artist George O'Keeffe and traces the history of her career from Wisconsin to New York City to Abiqiui, New Mexico. Shows O'Keeffe painting and telling about her life odyssey.
Biography; Fine Arts
Dist - STRUE **Prod** - PMI 1993

The Okies - Uprooted Farmers 24 MIN
16mm
American Challenge Series
B&W (J A)
LC 75-703356
Examines the plight of American farmers who were forced off their farms by drought and foreclosure during the 1930's. Based on the motion picture entitled The Grapes Of Wrath.
History - United States; Social Science; Sociology
Dist - FI **Prod** - TWCF 1975

Okinawa 22 MIN
16mm
Color
No descriptive material available.
History - United States
Dist - NAMP **Prod** - NAMP 1972

Okinawa - at the Emperor's Doorstep 30 MIN
VHS / U-matic
World War II - GI Diary Series
Color (H C A)
History - United States; History - World
Dist - TIMLIF **Prod** - TIMLIF 1980

Oklahoma 60 MIN
VHS
Portrait of America series
Color (J H C G)
$99.95 purchase _ #AMB36V
Visits Oklahoma. Offers extensive research into the state's history. Films key locations and presents segments on its history, government, education, folklore, science, journalism, sociology, industry, agriculture and business. Shows what is unique about Oklahoma and what is distinctive about its regional culture and how it got to be that way. Includes teacher study guides. Part of a 50 - part series.
Geography - United States; History - United States
Dist - CAMV

Oklahoma 145 MIN
VHS
Color (C H G A)
$39.00 purchase _ #DL148
Presents the 1955 film production of Oklahoma starring Shirley Jones and Gordon McRae and choreography by Agnes de Mille.
Fine Arts
Dist - INSIM
TWYMAN

Oklahoma Oasis 15 MIN
16mm
Color
LC 77-703155
Presents Chief Dan George lecturing on the natural beauty and the history of Platt National Park in Oklahoma.
Geography - United States
Dist - USNAC **Prod** - USNPS 1974

Oktoberfest in Munich 30 MIN
VHS
Color (G) (GERMAN)
$65.00 purchase _ #W7233, #W7234
Shows Germans celebrating the harvesttime Oktoberfest to highlight their culture. Includes a tapescript, audiocassette and teacher's guide with test material along with the video.
Foreign Language
Dist - GPC

Oktoberfest in Munich 30 MIN
VHS
World of festivals series
Color (J H C G)
$195.00 purchase
Looks at the 16 days of Oktoberfest in Munich, Germany, which features carnival rides, sideshows, food stalls and seven enormous, brightly decorated and very noisy marquees holding 6,000 drinkers. Part of a 12 - part series on European festivals.
Geography - World; Social Science
Dist - LANDMK **Prod** - LANDMK 1988

Oku no Hosomichi - a Haiku Poet's Pilgrimage 27 MIN
16mm
Color (H)
$6.50 rental _ #33788
Examines the life and work of Japanese poet Matsu Basho and depicts his five - month, 2400 - kilometer journey through Japan, at the age of 46. Makes extensive use of passages from 'Oku No Hosomichi.' Translated by Dorothy Britton.
Geography - World; Literature and Drama
Dist - PSU

Ol' Man River and the 20th century 25 MIN
VHS
Mississippi River series
Color (I J)
$89.00 purchase _ #RB832
Traces the history of the Mississippi River during the 20th century. Visits major cities from St Paul in Minnesota to New Orleans, Louisiana. Part of a series on the Mississippi River.
Geography - United States; History - United States
Dist - REVID **Prod** - REVID

Old Acquaintance 110 MIN
16mm
B&W
Stars Bette Davis and Miriam Hopkins as competing novelists who are also old friends.
Fine Arts
Dist - UAE **Prod** - UNKNWN 1943

The Old African Blasphemer 55 MIN
16mm / U-matic / VHS
Fight Against Slavery Series no 1; No 1
Color
LC 78-700500
Depicts the horrors of a typical slave ship's Atlantic voyage during the late 18th century.
History - United States; Sociology
Dist - TIMLIF **Prod** - BBCTV 1977

Old Age - do not Go Gentle, Pt 1 - Problems of the Aged 52 MIN
U-matic / VHS / 16mm
Color (H C)
LC 80-707523
Looks at the daily lives of American senior citizens. Explores the effects of poverty, isolation, violent crime, and discrimination.
Psychology; Sociology
Dist - CORF **Prod** - KGOTV 1978

Old Age, do not Go Gentle, Pt 2 - Alternative Solutions 52 MIN
16mm / U-matic / VHS
Color (H C A)

LC 81-701534
Describes existing social programs in Europe which successfully provide housing, nutritional aid and medical care for the elderly. Contrasts these programs with similar welfare programs in the United States, pointing out the failure of American programs to meet the needs of the elderly.
Health and Safety; Sociology
Dist - CORF **Prod** - KGOTV 1980

Old age - out of sight out of mind 60 MIN
16mm / U-matic / VHS
America's crises series
B&W (C A)
LC 79-709122
Provides a documentary on the institutions and rehabilitation programs for the aged. Includes segments of the U S Senate subcommittee investigation of nursing homes. Shows Goldwater and Middletown hospitals in New York and an 'OLD - FOLKS' farm in Kentucky.
Health and Safety; Psychology; Sociology
Dist - IU **Prod** - NET 1968

Old age - the wasted years 60 MIN
16mm
America's crises series
B&W (C A)
LC 72-709123
Discusses the problem of reduced income for the aged caused by retirement or unemployment. Contrasts living in the slums with that of luxury retirement. Provides interviews with senior citizens, government officials and social workers.
Psychology; Sociology
Dist - IU **Prod** - NET 1966

Old and New Investments 25 MIN
VHS / U-matic
Your Money Matters Series
Color
Teaches how and why municipal bonds are good tax shelters.
Business and Economics
Dist - FILMID **Prod** - FILMID

The Old and the New in Modern China 7 MIN
VHS / 35mm strip / U-matic
Modern China Series
Color; Sound
$25 each color sound filmstrip, $115 filmstrip series, $115 five
Explores the changes taking place in China. Highlights traditions, technology and philosophy. Focuses on the art of transition. Photographed in China.
Geography - World; History - World; Social Science
Dist - IFB

Old argument on MacDougal Street 3 MIN
16mm
Color (G)
$10.00 rental
Delineates the many types of arguments, such as those that become the turning points of relationships and ones that stay in memory no matter what the outcome.
Fine Arts
Dist - CANCIN **Prod** - IRWINJ 1985

Old Art for a New Science 28 MIN
16mm
Color
LC 76-702455
Demonstrates the process of designing and building a glass dewar or cryostat for Raman studies of crystals.
Science
Dist - UTORMC **Prod** - UTORMC 1974

The Old Astronomical Clock 13 MIN
16mm / U-matic / VHS
Color (J)
LC 79-700438
Uses animation of the wood carvings of Jan Tippmann to dramatize the legendary creation of the astronomical clock on Prague's old town hall. Tells how upon completion of the clock, the town and its council were consumed with pride and selfish greed and set out to make certain that there would never be another clock like theirs.
Fine Arts; Literature and Drama
Dist - PHENIX **Prod** - KRATKY 1978

The Old Banjo
VHS / 35mm strip
ALA Notable Children's Filmstrips Series
Color (K)
$33.00 purchase
Presents a children's story. Part of the American Library Association series.
English Language; Literature and Drama
Dist - PELLER

Old Before My Time 18 MIN
VHS / 16mm
Color (H)
$95.00 purchase
Describes the experience of a 33 - year - old sociologist who used makeup and a wig to become an 80 - year - old man and gain a new understanding of the elderly.
Social Science; Sociology
Dist - FLMWST

Old believers 29 MIN
VHS / 16mm
Color (J H C G)
$580.00, $195.00 purchase, $45.00 rental _ #11297, #37344
Portrays the Old Believers of Oregon who are descended from religious dissenters who rebelled against reforms in traditional Orthodox Christian rituals in 17th - century Russia. Shows how the language, dress and social life of the Old Believers stand as a strong testament to the value of cultural diversity in the United States. Produced by Margaret Hixon.
Geography - United States; History - United States; History - World; Religion and Philosophy
Dist - UCEMC

Old Believers 28 MIN
U-matic / VHS
Color
Explores the traditions and beliefs of 5000 members of an Old Believer community in Woodburn, Oregon. Focuses on the preparations for a wedding ceremony, the roles of men and women, the richness of the rituals and traditions and the beautiful costumes.
Geography - United States; Religion and Philosophy; Sociology
Dist - MEDIPR **Prod** - MEDIPR 1981

Old, Black and Alive 30 MIN
VHS / 16mm
Say Brother National Edition Series
Color (G)
$55.00 rental _ #SBRO - 101
Sociology
Dist - PBS **Prod** - WGBHTV

Old, Black and Alive - some Contrasts in Aging 27 MIN
16mm
Color (J)
LC 74-702146
Uses a variety of interviews with aging blacks in order to show the different ways in which blacks adapt to the aging process.
Health and Safety; Psychology; Sociology
Dist - NEWFLM **Prod** - NEWFLM 1974

An Old Box 9 MIN
16mm
Color (J)
Uses experimental animation to tell how an elderly man finds an old box in the trash. Reveals that when he paints it and pretends it is a music box, the box becomes a rainbow of colors and Christmas scenes.
Fine Arts
Dist - NFBC **Prod** - NFBC 1976

Old Campsites at Tika Tika 11 MIN
16mm / U-matic / VHS
People of the Australian Western Desert Series
B&W (H C G T A)
Remnants of old campsites surround a family encamped at ancient Tika Tika well. A woman mends a cracked wooden dish and prepares a headache lotion made from the seeds of the quandong tree.
Geography - World; Social Science; Sociology
Dist - PSU **Prod** - PSU 1965

Old Capitol - Restoration of a Landmark 25 MIN
VHS / U-matic / 16mm
Color; Mono (J H C A)
Introduces the process of historical restoration along with a condensed history of the territory and state of Iowa. Introduces the people connected with Old Capitol from the founding fathers and the architect of Iowa's first capitol building to the school children who contributed money earned in class projects for its restoration.
Fine Arts; History - United States; Industrial and Technical Education
Dist - UIOWA **Prod** - UIOWA 1976

Old Clothing and Textiles 30 MIN
U-matic / VHS
Antique Shop Series
Color
Presents guests who are experts in their respective fields who share tips on collecting and caring for old clothing and textiles.
Fine Arts
Dist - MDCPB **Prod** - WVPTTV

Old Confederacy - New Direction 28 MIN
U-matic
Interface Series
Color
Looks at the 1973 elections in Atlanta, Georgia.
Civics and Political Systems; Geography - United States
Dist - PBS **Prod** - WETATV

The Old Corner Store will be Knocked Down by the Wreckers 22 MIN
16mm
B&W
LC 74-703605
Shows the destruction of a neighborhood area in Montreal, including a 70 - year - old corner store, in order to make way for a new high rise complex.
Science - Natural; Sociology
Dist - CFDEVC **Prod** - BRUCKJ

Old Delhi - New Delhi 16 MIN
U-matic / VHS / 16mm
Color (J H C)
LC 79-701792
Contrasts the twin cities of Old Delhi, an ancient city, and New Delhi, a modern city constructed by the British.
Geography - World; History - World
Dist - MCFI **Prod** - COLSON 1975

Old digs 20 MIN
16mm
Color (G)
$35.00 rental
Travels to the small Swedish city of Kristinehamn focusing on its central river.
Fine Arts; Geography - World; Sociology
Dist - CANCIN **Prod** - NELSOG 1992

Old, dirty and late 50 MIN
VHS
Inside story series
Color (A)
PdS99 purchase
Reveals that half a million commuters pour into London on British Rail trains every day, and every day something goes wrong. Spends a week behind the scenes with Network South East points out what lies behind the commuter's misery. Follows the attempts of staff who are trying to improve efficiency and customer service in the busiest railway in the world.
Social Science
Dist - BBCENE

Old Dog - New Tricks - the Coyote 23 MIN
VHS / U-matic
Color (K)
Focuses on the coyote, the one animal in North America which can adapt to anything man throws at him. Celebrates the wily coyote, an old dog who knows all the new tricks.
Science - Natural
Dist - NWLDPR **Prod** - NWLDPR 1982

Old Economy Kunstfest 57 MIN
Videoreel / VT2
Festivals of Pennsylvania Series
Color
Presents a visit to the annual festival of the Harmony Society, a two - day crafts festival which goes through the village of Old Economy, Pennsylvania, for a review of history.
Fine Arts; Geography - United States; Sociology
Dist - PBS **Prod** - WQED

Old English 8 MIN
16mm
Color
LC 74-702754
Depicts the period of the Viking raids on Anglo - Saxon England. Shows a peasant, whose house has been destroyed by Vikings, being interviewed by the captain of a troop of Anglo - Saxon militiamen who have come to the rescue.
History - World
Dist - QFB **Prod** - QFB 1973

Old English - Beowulf 28 MIN
VHS
Color (H C G)
$295.00 purchase, $55.00 rental
Overviews historically the evolution of the English language. Features Dr Joe Gallagher who travels to locations significant in the development of the language - Sutton Hoo, the site of Britain's oldest Viking burial grounds, Canterbury, the destination of Chaucer's pilgrims, the Globe Theatre, home of Shakespeare. Gallagher gives a dramatic recitation of a portion of Beowulf. Produced by Caritas Productions.
English Language, History - World; Literature and Drama
Dist - FLMLIB **Prod** - SFRASU 1993

Old English Poetry 27 MIN
VHS
Color (H)
$14.00 rental _ #35254
Presents translations of Old English poems 'The Seafarer,' 'The Dream Of Rood' and 'Beowulf.' Interweaves old and contemporary English to enhance understanding and retain elements of the original.

Literature and Drama
Dist - PSU

Old English Poetry 28 MIN
U-matic / VHS
Survey of English Verse Series
Color (C)
$249.00, $149.00 purchase _ #AD - 1294
Presents readings of modern translations of three riddle poems - 'The Seafarer,' 'The Dream Of The Rood' and 'Beowulf.' Interweaves the original Old English with contemporary English to convey the power of the poetic language of the original.
Literature and Drama
Dist - FOTH **Prod** - FOTH

Old enough to care series
Alterations 15 MIN
Dist - AITECH

Old Enough to do Time 60 MIN
U-matic / VHS
Color
Examines the impact of 'get tough' juvenile justice policies across America. Explores the methods that different states employ to crack down on juvenile crime and looks at four alternative correctional programs.
Civics and Political Systems; Sociology
Dist - PBS **Prod** - WNETTV

Old enough to do time - juvenile justice policies 55 MIN
VHS
Color (H C G)
$445.00 purchase, $75.00 rental
Examines punitive juvenile justice measures and alternative rehabilitation techniques. Looks at juveniles as young as 13 tried as adults and incarcerated with adult criminals. Shows four alternative programs - one referring juveniles to community boards instead of courts, a wilderness 'outward bound' program, a residential model and a 'tracking program' which keeps close tabs on youthful offenders. Produced for Public Policy Productions.
Civics and Political Systems; Sociology
Dist - FLMLIB **Prod** - RWEIS 1984

Old Fashioned Bread Baking in Rural Pennsylvania 13 MIN
16mm
B&W (J)
LC 76-703215
Mrs Yoder of Mifflin County, Pennsylvania, demonstrates essential steps and equipment in old - fashioned bread baking.
Geography - United States; Home Economics; Social Science
Dist - PSUPCR **Prod** - PSU 1966

Old Fashioned Deer Camp 15 MIN
16mm
Color
Shows deer hunting in Michigan's Upper Peninsula, when hunters thought nothing of camping out among the hemlocks in zero weather.
Geography - United States; Physical Education and Recreation
Dist - SFI **Prod** - SFI

Old - Fashioned Woman 49 MIN
16mm / U-matic / VHS
Color (J H C)
Portrays a strong - willed eighty - six - year - old Yankee woman as she reminisces and airs her views on birth control, abortion and death.
Health and Safety; Religion and Philosophy; Sociology
Dist - FI **Prod** - COOLM 1975

The Old Flame 29 MIN
Videoreel / VT2
Observing Eye Series
Color
Sociology
Dist - PBS **Prod** - WGBHTV

Old Friends - New Friends 510 MIN
VHS / U-matic
Old Friends - New Friends Series
Color
Introduces the series of 17 half hour videocassette programs featuring Fred Rogers as host. Titles profile the lives of people who make a difference in the lives of others, including Lee Strasberg, Dr Jerry Jampolsky, Lorin Hollander, and Willie Stargell.
Biography; Sociology
Dist - FAMCOM **Prod** - FAMCOM

Old Friends - New Friends Series
Old Friends - New Friends 510 MIN
Dist - FAMCOM

Old Friends - New Friends Series
The Carradines 28 MIN
Edgar Tolson 28 MIN
Gerald Jampolsky 28 MIN
Henry John Heinz III 28 MIN
The Interviewers 58 MIN
Melody 28 MIN
Nancy Acosta 28 MIN
Padre 28 MIN
Welcome 28 MIN
Dist - PBS

Old Glory 28 MIN
16mm
Big Picture Series
B&W
LC 74-706163
Presents a tribute to the American flag, explaining how it has been an inspiration to the American fighting man since it carried its 13 original stars.
Civics and Political Systems
Dist - USNAC **Prod** - USA 1965

Old Gold with Dennis James 1 MIN
U-matic / VHS
Color
Shows a classic television commercial with a dancing cigarette pack.
Business and Economics; Psychology; Sociology
Dist - BROOKC **Prod** - BROOKC

Old - growth forest - an ecosystem 25 MIN
VHS
Color; CC (J H A)
$110.00 purchase - #A51635
Teaches fundamental ecological concepts through a study of interrelationships between plants and animals of the Pacific Northwest. Explores such principles as adaptation, succession, and symbiosis. Includes a teacher's guide.
Science - Natural
Dist - NGS **Prod** - NGS 1994

Old - growth forest management 15 MIN
VHS / U-matic / Slide
Color (I J H G)
$90.00 purchase, $25.00 rental _ #914
Defines old - growth forests. Describes the benefits and values derived from them, their role in the natural system and why their management is so controversial. Available as an Adult Briefing Package or as a Teacher's Package for elementary through high school. Reviewed in 1992 and determined to contain appropriate and timely material.
Agriculture; Science - Natural; Social Science
Dist - OSUSF **Prod** - OSUSF 1988

Old habits die hard 32 MIN
VHS
Color; PAL; NTSC (G IND)
PdS96, PdS112 purchase
Examines worker safety problems in the foundry - dust, fumes, molten metal, machinery - and looks at safety techniques and the consequences if safety procedures are not followed.
Health and Safety; Psychology
Dist - CFLVIS

Old hard rocks 15 MIN
VHS
Color; PAL (P I J)
PdS29
Shows the nature of granite and slate rocks and their associated landscapes. Visits the granite upland of Dartmoor, granite coastline at Land's End, extractive industries associated with granite - road metal, china clay and tin ore - and the metamorphic rocks of North Wales and slate mining.
Geography - World; Science - Physical
Dist - BHA

An Old hound 46 MIN
VHS / U-matic / Cassette
Florida through the decades as seen by High - Sheriff Jim Turner 'series
Color; PAL (G)
$79.95, $24.95, $9.95 purchase _ #1100
Portrays the life of a former High - Sheriff of Levy County, Florida, Jim Turner. Depicts the early 1970s, when Turner tracks down some marijuana smugglers, direct descendants of Big Charlie Watson. Part ten of an eleven - part historical docudrama.
Civics and Political Systems; Fine Arts; History - United States; Sociology
Dist - NORDS **Prod** - NORDS 1991

Old House, New House 27 MIN
16mm
Color (H C A)
LC 82-700694
Documents the renovation of Canada's Ecology House, a Victorian - era mansion, which now houses literature on energy conservation and natural resources and where lectures and tours are held. Includes animated sequences of various retrofitting procedures.
Science - Natural; Social Science
Dist - FLMLIB **Prod** - OMENGY 1981

The Old house, passing 45 MIN
16mm
B&W (G)
$50.00 rental
Spooks with a ghost - film and evokes the dark forces in our lives. Uses unconventional, not typical, narrative means to tell the story.
Fine Arts; Literature and Drama
Dist - CANCIN **Prod** - JORDAL 1967

Old Ironsides 102 MIN
VHS
B&W (G)
$29.95 purchase _ #0896
Presents a story based on the 1830 poem 'Constitution' by Oliver Wendell Holmes. Tells about conquering the Tripolitan pirates of 1804 in the Mediterranean Sea. Produced in 1926.
Geography - World; History - United States; Literature and Drama
Dist - SEVVID

Old is 13 MIN
16mm
Aging in Our Times Series
Color
LC 79-700243
Reveals the challenges, frustrations, pleasures and satisfactions of aging through the portraits of four vigorously active women and men in their seventies, eighties and nineties.
Health and Safety; Psychology; Sociology
Dist - SF **Prod** - SF 1978

Old Isaac - The Pawnbroker 10 MIN
VHS
(G) (ENGLISH INTERTITLES)
$50.00 purchase
Tells the story of a small girl in an urban slum desparately seeking aid for her sick and starving mother. Depicts the pawnbroker who hears about her and sets out to help her family. Inaugurated a series of films portraying compassionate Jewish images. A silent production directed by Wallace McCutcheon.
Religion and Philosophy; Social Science; Sociology
Dist - NCJEWF

Old King Cole 28 MIN
U-matic / VHS / 16mm
Insight Series
Color; B&W (H C A)
LC 70-708581
Uses a dramatization in which a bartender lures a band of down - and - outers to abdicate their dignity and do his bidding to portray the importance of freedom over security.
Fine Arts; Psychology
Dist - PAULST **Prod** - PAULST 1970

Old King Log 60 MIN
16mm / U-matic / VHS
I, Claudius Series Number 13; No 13
Color (C A)
Tells how Claudius dies knowing that Nero will end family rule violently, but certain that his epic history will make him immortal.
History - World
Dist - FI **Prod** - BBCTV 1977

Old Ladies Lost 29 MIN
Videoreel / VT2
Our Street Series
Color
Sociology
Dist - PBS **Prod** - MDCPB

Old Lady's Camping Trip 10 MIN
U-matic / VHS
Color (H C A)
Features an animated cartoon which stresses fire prevention and safety on camping trips, barbeques and simple outings.
Fine Arts; Health and Safety; Physical Education and Recreation
Dist - FILCOM **Prod** - NFBC

Old like me 28 MIN
VHS / 16mm
Color (H C G)
$525.00, $295.00 purchase, $55.00 rental
Follows young reporter Pat Moore who disguised herself as a helpless 85 - year - old woman and ventured out into the streets of more than a hundred cities. Reveals how she experienced the terror that society can inflict on the weak and the old. She was rendered helpless by the speed and noise of a youth - oriented culture, ignored when seeking assistance and even attacked by a gang of 13 - year - olds. She discovered that even the simplest products can frustrate the elderly and make their lives miserable - arthritic hands cannot easily open jars or hold pens, labels are hard to read, survival in a world designed for the young is difficult.

Guidance and Counseling; Health and Safety
Dist - FLMLIB **Prod** - CANBC 1987

Old Man 8 MIN
16mm
Color
LC 76-703144
Portrays the last moments of an old man's life as he remembers his most beautiful dream, which is only to be fulfilled in his death.
Sociology
Dist - JANOWJ **Prod** - JANOWJ 1976

Old Man and Outdoor Cooking 15 MIN
16mm
Color (J)
LC 80-701045
Uses a humorous story to tell viewers about outdoor cooking grills and outdoor cookery.
Home Economics
Dist - KLEINW **Prod** - KLEINW 1978

The Old Man and the Gun 58 MIN
VHS / BETA
Frontline Series
Color
Examines the conflict in Ireland through the eyes of Irish - Americans who support the Irish Republican Army and its strategy of violence. Follows Michael Flannery through his day as the Grand Marshal of New York City's Saint Patrick's Day Parade, then travels back to Ireland to the spot where Flannery participated in an ambush on British troops some 50 years ago.
History - World; Sociology
Dist - PBS **Prod** - DOCCON

The Old Man and the Lake 19 MIN
16mm
Color
LC 79-701444
Tells how an old man takes his grandson fishing at a lake on Ottawa Silica Company property and explains how, many years ago, he actually mined silica sand at the bottom of the lake.
Social Science
Dist - IPHC **Prod** - OTTASC 1979

Old man and the mouse 9 MIN
35mm
Eastern European animation series
Color (G)
Features a timid old man using cats and dogs to rid him of a mouse. Presents a Czech non - narrative production. Part of a four - part series. Contact distributor for rental price.
Fine Arts
Dist - KITPAR

The Old Man and the Paragraph 5 MIN
U-matic / VHS
Write on, Set 2 Series
Color (J H)
Shows how to develop paragraphs through the use of comparison.
English Language
Dist - CTI **Prod** - CTI

The Old Man and the Rose 5 MIN
16mm
Color (J)
LC 73-702555
Portrays an old man's admiration for a rose, based on Donald Bisset's poem 'THE ROSE AND THE MAN.'.
Guidance and Counseling; Literature and Drama
Dist - MMA **Prod** - LONWTV 1973

The Old Man and the Sea 86 MIN
U-matic / VHS / 16mm
Color
Stars Spencer Tracy as a poor Cuban fisherman waging an epic struggle with a giant marlin. Based on the novella The Old Man And The Sea by Ernest Hemingway.
Fine Arts; Literature and Drama
Dist - FI **Prod** - WB 1958

Old Man in a Hurry 25 MIN
BETA / VHS
B&W
Tells the life story of Bion Shively, the oldest man to win the Hambletonian Trotting Classic.
Physical Education and Recreation
Dist - EQVDL **Prod** - USTROT

Old Man Stone 30 MIN
16mm
B&W
Tells the story of old man stone, an immigrant druggist in a Detroit slum, who fought juvenile delinquency by having faith in individual boys and girls. (Kinescope).
Religion and Philosophy
Dist - NAAJS **Prod** - JTS 1956

The Old Man's Story - Junior Version 25 MIN
16mm / U-matic / VHS
Color (P I)
LC 80-701759
A young boy's attraction to a 13 - year - old orphan girl starts a chain of events that ends in tragedy and awakens him to the harsh realities of adult life.
Fine Arts
Dist - CORF **Prod** - GFILM 1979

The Old Man's Story - Senior Version 25 MIN
U-matic / VHS / 16mm
Color (J)
LC 80-701759
A young boy's attraction to a 13 - year - old orphan girl starts a chain of events that ends in tragedy and awakens him to the harsh realities of adult life.
Fine Arts
Dist - CORF **Prod** - GFILM 1979

The Old masters 45 MIN
VHS
Color; PAL (J H)
PdS30 purchase
Presents a companion series to The Old Testament in Art. Features Oliver Hunkin who examines the life of Christ as seen by the world's great painters. Covers the Birth of Christ, Madonna and Child and Faces of Christ in three 15 - minute parts. Includes works by Leonardo da Vinci, Michelangelo, Raphael, Rembrandt and Botticelli with a background of music by Bach, Monteverdi and Palestrina. Includes teacher's notes compiled by the Farmington Institute for Christian Studies. Contact distributor about availability outside the United Kingdom.
Fine Arts; Religion and Philosophy
Dist - ACADEM

Old oaks - episode 1 25 MIN
VHS
Spirit of trees series
Color (G)
$195.00 purchase, $50.00 rental
Visits England's Windsor Great Park, celebrated site for ancient oaks. Reveals the importance of trees in the ecosystem's complex process of renewal and regeneration. Monks of Ireland explain a spiritual and commercial interest in trees. Part of an eight - part series on trees and their relationship with the world around them. Hosted by environmentalist Dick Warner, who meets with conservationists, scientists, folklorists, woodsmen, seed collectors, forest rangers, wood turners and more.
Agriculture; Science - Natural; Social Science
Dist - CNEMAG

Old or New 10 MIN
U-matic
Calling Captain Consumer Series
Color (P I J)
Explores antique stores and an auction sale.
Business and Economics; Home Economics
Dist - TVOTAR **Prod** - TVOTAR 1985

The Old Order Amish 32 MIN
VHS
Color (J H C)
$35.00 purchase
Portrays the Amish of Pennsylvania. Examines farmlife, a barn - raising, farmers' markets, Amish women in their homes, the one - room school and an Amish church - meeting. Uses a musical score based on traditional Amish hymn themes.
History - United States; Religion and Philosophy; Sociology
Dist - APPLAS **Prod** - APPLAS

The Old Oregon Trail - 1928 Classic 39 MIN
16mm
B&W (I A)
Offers a 'classic Western' made in the John Day River country in 1928. Shown only at a preview and never circulated, a print was discovered in 1978 and given to the Oregon Historical Society. Stars Art Mix, brother of Tom Mix, and assorted local folks.
Fine Arts; Geography - United States; History - United States
Dist - OREGHS **Prod** - OREGHS

Old People 32 MIN
16mm
B&W
Presents a debate on the problems of senior citizens in Denmark.
Health and Safety; History - World; Sociology
Dist - AUDPLN **Prod** - RDCG

Old People and the New Politics 30 MIN
U-matic
Growing Old in Modern America Series
Color
Health and Safety; Sociology
Dist - UWASHP **Prod** - UWASHP

Old Peoples, New Consciousness 30 MIN
VHS / 16mm
World of the 30s Series
Color (J)
$149.00 purchase, $75.00 rental _ #OD - 2267
Examines Colonialism in the Middle East and Latin America and explains how problems of today are rooted in the 1930s. The tenth of 13 installments of The World Of The 30s Series.
Geography - World; History - World
Dist - FOTH

The Old person's friend 13 MIN
VHS
Discussions in bioethics series
Color (H C A)
$95.00 purchase
Focuses on an institution's dilemma when a chronically ill patient comes down with pneumonia - should she be treated, or left without treatment, as she seems to wish. Provokes discussion. Includes discussion guide.
Health and Safety; Religion and Philosophy
Dist - PFP **Prod** - NFBC

Old Quabbin Valley - Politics and Conflict in Water Distribution 28 MIN
16mm / U-matic / VHS
Color (J A G)
Traces the history of Boston's water supply, the construction of the Quabbin Reservoir and the nationwide debate over the urban use of rural water supplies.
History - United States; Social Science; Sociology
Dist - DIRECT **Prod** - FLRNTN 1983

Old Salem 30 MIN
VHS
VideoTours history series
Color (G I J H)
$19.95 purchase _ #HC05
Visits Old Salem, Massachussetts.
Geography - United States; Geography - World; History - United States
Dist - SVIP

Old Salem - North Carolina 30 MIN
VHS
Color (I J)
$19.95 purchase _ #ST - VT1015
Visits Old Salem in the state of North Carolina to show how early Moravians lived a simple life that gave birth to many principles that became part of the historical foundation of the United States.
History - United States; Religion and Philosophy
Dist - INSTRU

Old San Francisco 26 MIN
16mm
History of the Motion Picture Series
B&W (I T)
Presents Delores Costello and Warner Oland in the motion picture production Old San Francisco. Tells the story of the boss of San Francisco's Chinatown underworld plots whose dastardly efforts are foiled by the 1906 earthquake.
Geography - United States; Sociology
Dist - KILLIS **Prod** - SF 1970

The Old Sheepdog 10 MIN
U-matic / VHS / 16mm
Color (P I)
LC 73-736581
Tells the story of an old sheepdog who is supplanted by a new, young dog in his duties of guarding his master's sheep, but who proves his worth and trust when the wolf comes.
Literature and Drama
Dist - AIMS **Prod** - UILL 1973

Old Skills Alive 17 MIN
VHS / U-matic
Color
Reports on the many ancient skills and crafts kept alive by a handful of skilled artisans. Includes demonstrations of lacemaking, hand bookbinding, glass blowing and silversmithing.
Fine Arts
Dist - JOU **Prod** - UPI

The Old Soldier - a Biography of Douglas Mac Arthur 15 MIN
16mm
Screen news digest series; Vol 6; Issue 10
B&W
LC FIA68-2084
Presents the life and times of Douglas Mac Arthur.
Biography; History - United States
Dist - HEARST **Prod** - HEARST 1964

Old Sturbridge Village 30 MIN
VHS
VideoTours history series
Color (G I J H)
$19.95 purchase _ #HC01
Visits Old Sturbridge Village in Massachussetts.
Geography - United States; Geography - World; History - United States
Dist - SVIP

Old Surbridge Village - growing up in New England 30 MIN
VHS
VideoTours history series
Color (G I J H)
$19.95 purchase _ #HC07
Visits Old Sturbridge Village, Massachussetts.
Geography - United States; Geography - World; History - United States
Dist - SVIP

Old Testament 40 MIN
VHS
Bible story time series
Color (K P I R)
$14.95 purchase _ #35 - 81002 - 19
Uses an animation format to tell four stories from the Old Testament. 'It's Time To Begin' is based on the Genesis story of the creation of the earth, while 'Hello There, Mr Adam and Mrs Eve' focuses on the story of the creation of Adam and Eve. 'The Everything Boat' tells the story of Noah and his ark. Concludes with 'The Fire That Didn't Burn,' which is based on the story of Moses and the burning bush.
Literature and Drama; Religion and Philosophy
Dist - APH **Prod** - FAMF

The Old Testament in art 90 MIN
VHS
Color; PAL (J H)
PdS40 purchase
Presents six 15 - minute programs on art inspired by the Old Testament, including Michelangelo's masterpieces in the Sistine Chapel and works at the Walker Art Gallery in Liverpool. Shows how these works illustrate the Creation, the crossing of the Red Sea and Daniel in the Lion's Den. Examines the Old Testament as the shared history of Judaism, Christianity and Islam. Encourages viewers to read the original stories. Includes teacher's notes compiled by the Farmington Institute for Christian Studies. Contact distributor about availability outside the United Kingdom.
Fine Arts; Religion and Philosophy
Dist - ACADEM

Old Testament Scriptures Series
Joshua, the Conqueror 17 MIN
Dist - CPH

Old Testament series - Tape 1 80 MIN
VHS
Old Testament series
Color (I J H C G A R)
$14.95 purchase _ #35 - 87581 - 2086
Profiles several of the prominent personalities of the Old Testament. Includes four episodes - 'Abraham, Man of Faith,' 'Jacob, Bearer of the Promise,' 'Joseph, the Young Man,' and 'Joseph, Ruler of Egypt.'
Literature and Drama; Religion and Philosophy
Dist - APH **Prod** - VANGU

Old Testament series - Tape 2 60 MIN
VHS
Old Testament series
Color (I J H C G A R)
$14.95 purchase _ #35 - 87582 - 2086
Profiles several of the prominent personalities of the Old Testament. Includes three episodes - 'Moses, Called by God,' 'Moses, Leader of God's People,' and 'Joshua, the Conquerer.'
Literature and Drama; Religion and Philosophy
Dist - APH **Prod** - VANGU

Old Testament series - Tape 3 60 MIN
VHS
Old Testament series
Color (I J H C G A R)
$14.95 purchase _ #35 - 87583 - 2086
Profiles several of the prominent personalities of the Old Testament. Includes three episodes - 'Gideon, the Liberator,' 'Ruth, A Faithful Woman,' and 'Samuel, A Dedicated Man.'
Literature and Drama; Religion and Philosophy
Dist - APH **Prod** - VANGU

Old Testament series - Tape 4 80 MIN
VHS
Old Testament series
Color (I J H C G A R)
$14.95 purchase _ #35 - 87584 - 2086
Profiles several of the prominent personalities of the Old Testament. Includes four episodes - 'David, A Young Hero,' 'David, King of Israel,' 'Solomon, Man of Wisdom,' and 'Elijah, A Fearless Prophet.'
Literature and Drama; Religion and Philosophy
Dist - APH **Prod** - VANGU

Old Testament series
Old Testament series - Tape 1 80 MIN
Old Testament series - Tape 2 60 MIN
Old Testament series - Tape 3 60 MIN
Old Testament series - Tape 4 80 MIN
Dist - APH

The Old Testament Unveiled 26 MIN
U-matic / VHS
Every Window Tells a Story Series
Color (H C A)
$300.00
Shows the beauty and purpose of the stained glass windows in the churches built in the Middle Ages. Narrated by Malcom Miller.
Fine Arts; History - World
Dist - LANDMK **Prod** - LANDMK 1986

Old - time banjo styles 90 MIN
VHS
Color (G)
$49.95 purchase _ #VD - SEE - BJ01
Features Mike Seeger and guests Doc Watson, Kirk Sutphin, Greg Hooven, Etta Baker, Joe and Odell Thompson and Backstep. Teaches old - time picking techniques - clawhammer, two - finger, three - finger, up - picking in several tunings and styles. Offers the banjo styles of Doc Watson - North Carolina; Kirk Sutphin and Greg Hooven - Mount Airy and Galax; Etta Baker and Joe and Odell Thompson - African - American, as well as Mike Seeger's renditions of classic old - time tunes. Includes the tunes - Molly Dear, Snowdrop, French Waltz, Reuben's Train; Tom Dooley; Willie Moore; Frosty Morn; Old Joe Clark; John Brown's Dream; Backstop Cindy; Old Corn Likker; Marching Jaybird; Soldier's Joy; Needle Case; Baptist Shout; White House Blues; and tablature.
Fine Arts
Dist - HOMETA **Prod** - HOMETA

The Old Warrior 11 MIN
16mm
Color (J G)
Tells one of the legends of Hawaii explaining that the wild morning glory grows on desolate shores because of the good deeds of an old warrior left to die on a barren island.
Geography - United States; History - United States; Literature and Drama; Religion and Philosophy; Sociology
Dist - CINEPC **Prod** - TAHARA 1986

Old ways, new game - 1 50 MIN
VHS
Challenge to America series
Color (PRO IND A)
$295 purchase, $125.00 rental _ #FFH24A
Presents Hedrick Smith who discloses business strategies used by German and Japanese industries to gain competitive advantage. Challenges American industry through views of foreign technical and automotive companies.
Business and Economics; Psychology
Dist - EXTR **Prod** - FOTH

Old Well 130 MIN
VHS
Color (G) (MANDARIN CHINESE (ENGLISH SUBTITLES) (CHINESE SUBTITLES))
$45.00 purchase _ #1114A
Presents a Mandarin Chinese language movie produced in the People's Republic of China.
Fine Arts; Geography - World; Literature and Drama
Dist - CHTSUI **Prod** - CHTSUI

Old West Trail Country 30 MIN
VHS / 16mm
Color (H C G)
$29.95 purchase _ #TVC104
Features the best of what America has to offer in outdoor recreation and family fun and education. Takes a video visit to the nation's mountains, prairies, badlands, waterfalls and presents some western history.
Geography - United States
Dist - RMIBHF **Prod** - RMIBHF

The Old Woman 2 MIN
U-matic / VHS / 16mm
Color (J)
LC 76-702241
Presents a confrontation between an old woman and Death, in the form of a skeleton. Shows, in animated style, how the unwelcome visitor leaves when he sees how much work the woman still has to do.
Fine Arts; Health and Safety; Sociology
Dist - AIMS **Prod** - ACI 1973

Old Woman in a Shoe - Beginning Number Concepts 9 MIN
U-matic / VHS / 16mm
Color (K P)
$245.00, $170.00 purchase _ #4037
Uses the nursery rhyme about the old lady in the shoe to introduce primary number concepts.
Mathematics
Dist - CORF **Prod** - CORF 1980

Old World, New World 52 MIN
U-matic / VHS / 16mm
Destination America Series
Color (J)
Describes how sixteen million immigrants arrived through Ellis Island after enduring the incredible hardships of transatlantic voyages and meeting the conditions necessary to leave their countries and enter America. Historical film footage and interviews describe the promise of freedom and opportunity in a new world.
History - United States; Sociology
Dist - MEDIAG **Prod** - THAMES 1976

Old Yeller 28 MIN
U-matic / VHS / 16mm
Film as Literature, Series 2 Series; Series 2
Color (P I J)
LC 79-701255
Edited from the Disney film Old Yeller, based on the book of the same title by Fred Gipson. Tells the story of two young brothers and a stray dog, Old Yeller, who risks his life to save the boys.
Fine Arts; Literature and Drama
Dist - CORF **Prod** - DISNEY 1979

Old Yeller 84 MIN
VHS
Color; CC (I J H)
$22.95 purchase _ #474608
Stars Fess Parker in a story about a poor 1860s Texas family and the dog who befriends them. Adapts the story by Fred Gipson.
Literature and Drama
Dist - KNOWUN

The Olden Days Coat 30 MIN
U-matic / VHS / 16mm
Color (I J A)
LC 81-701021
Tells the story of Sal who anticipates being bored when she must spend Christmas with her grandmother. Shows her discovering an old blue coat in a trunk which magically transports her back in time. Based on the book The Olden Days Coat by Margaret Laurence.
Literature and Drama; Social Science
Dist - LCOA **Prod** - ATLAP

Older adult series
Presents a four - part series about older adults. Includes the titles In Sickness and Health; The Loss of a Spouse; The Last Home; and Looking Back.
Older adults - in sickness and health - 1 16 MIN
Older adults - looking back - 4 10 MIN
Older adults - the last home - 3 10 MIN
Older adults - the loss of a spouse - 2 21 MIN
Dist - HSCIC **Prod** - SMEUNC

Older adults - in sickness and health - 1 16 MIN
VHS
Older adult series
Color (C PRO G)
$395.00 purchase _ #R840 - VI - 041
Examines the attitudes of adults towards their own health or sickness and towards healthcare expenditures. Interviews individuals who relate their problems, optimism or pessimism concerning their condition and their feelings about their extensive medication schedules. Helps viewers to gain an understanding of health and health care needs in the elderly. Part of a four - part series.
Health and Safety; Sociology
Dist - HSCIC **Prod** - SMEUNC 1984

Older adults - looking back - 4 10 MIN
VHS
Older adult series
Color (C PRO G)
$395.00 purchase _ #R851 - VI - 023
Focuses on an elderly couple before the husband's death, and his wife following the death. Listens to the husband talk about their optimistic attitude about aging, their health problems and their reflections on what life will be like when one of them dies. Contrasts this with the wife's actual feelings following the death of her husband and her thoughts about surviving alone. Part of a four - part series.
Health and Safety; Sociology
Dist - HSCIC **Prod** - SMEUNC 1984

Older Adults Series
In Sickness and Health 16 MIN
The Last Home 10 MIN
Looking Back 10 MIN
The Loss of a Spouse 21 MIN
Dist - HSCIC

Older adults - the last home - 3 10 MIN
VHS
Older adult series
Color (C PRO G)
$395.00 purchase _ #R840 - VI - 043
Gives older adults' opinions and attitudes about the complex issue of institutionalization. Encourages healthcare professionals to deal with the elderly as individuals and to help them maintain a sense of independence in a dependent situation. Part of a four - part series.
Health and Safety; Sociology
Dist - HSCIC **Prod** - SMEUNC 1984

Older adults - the loss of a spouse - 2 21 MIN
VHS
Older adult series
Color (C PRO G)
$395.00 purchase _ #R840 - VI - 042
Illustrates how a spouse's death affects each individual differently. Stresses the importance of recognizing these differences, as well as recognizing symptoms of bereavement. Presents contrasting portraits of two women's lives after the death of a spouse. Part of a four - part series.
Health and Safety; Sociology
Dist - HSCIC **Prod** - SMEUNC 1984

Older Americans 14 MIN
VHS / U-matic
Tax tips on tape series
Color (A PRO IND) (SPANISH)
$20.00, $40.00 purchase _ #TCA17621, #TCA17620
Discusses tax laws for older Americans. Reveals how and why some older Americans with incomes below a certain level may not have to file an income tax return. Explains the higher standard deductions for taxpayers who are blind or age 65 or over. Also available in a Spanish - language version.
Business and Economics; Civics and Political Systems; Social Science; Sociology
Dist - USNAC **Prod** - USIRS 1988

Older and better 29 MIN
VHS
Color (H C G A R)
$24.95 purchase, $10.00 rental _ #35 - 87362 - 460
Profiles senior citizens who are active in caring for the needy around them. Includes a photo meditation, 'Elderly Beatitudes,' which honors senior citizens.
Religion and Philosophy; Sociology
Dist - APH **Prod** - FRACOC

Older and Bolder 14 MIN
U-matic
Color
Examines the experience of aging. Shows a group of older women who meet weekly to talk, laugh and share problems.
Health and Safety; Sociology
Dist - EDC **Prod** - WGBHTV

Older and Newer Neighborhoods 15 MIN
U-matic / VHS
Neighborhoods Series
Color (P)
Compares older and newer neighborhoods.
Sociology
Dist - GPN **Prod** - NEITV 1981

The Older baby 15 MIN
VHS
Feeding with love and good sense series
Color (G)
$59.95 purchase _ #BUL002V
Discusses how during the second six months of life an infant learns to eat solid food. Part of a four - part series featuring real parents, child care providers and children who show what works and doesn't work in feeding, as well as helping children to eat well, staying out of eating struggles with children, understanding feeding from the child's perspective and knowing when to hold the line.
Health and Safety; Sociology
Dist - CAMV

Older but Wiser - the Case of the Disputed Promotion 23 MIN
U-matic / VHS / 16mm
Color
Tells the story of an employee at a tire manufacturing plant who lost out on a promotion to a junior employee. Asks whether a company can use different standards in evaluating the qualifications of job applicants and whether a company will be subject to criticism when it allows a supervisor to provide informal training to an ambitious worker.
Business and Economics
Dist - AARA **Prod** - AARA 1982

Older people 28 MIN
U-matic
Are you listening series
Color (J)
LC 80-707148
Presents a group of senior citizens talking about ways to keep on living and growing in a country that worships youth. Discusses the need to be in contact with younger people, social security problems, senior citizen centers as political power bases, and mandatory retirement.
Sociology
Dist - STURTM **Prod** - STURTM 1976

The Older Person in the Family 30 MIN
U-matic
Growing Old in Modern America Series
Color
Health and Safety; Sociology
Dist - UWASHP **Prod** - UWASHP

Older, Stronger, Wiser 28 MIN
VHS / 16mm
Color (H)
$550.00, $160.00 purchase, $30.00 rental _ #CC4225
Tells the story of five black Canadian women whose community activity and perseverance are credited with providing role models and preserving black culture.
Geography - World; History - United States; Sociology
Dist - IU **Prod** - NFBC 1990

Older Women and Love 26 MIN
VHS / 16mm
Color (G)
$450.00 purchase, $65.00 rental
Looks at older women and their relationships with younger men. Interviews a multiracial group of housewives, artists, singers, writers - and their younger partners who offer an unapologetic look at their relationships.
Guidance and Counseling; Psychology; Sociology
Dist - WMEN **Prod** - CBJH 1987

The Oldest Game 28 MIN
16mm
Color
Concerns the pursuit of America's most common and most sought after big game animal - the whitetail deer.
Physical Education and Recreation
Dist - SFI **Prod** - SFI

The Oldest Game 45 MIN
VHS / BETA
Color
Presents a bowhunting classic with beautiful fall colors in the Allegheny Mountains of Pennsylvania. Shows hunting whitetail deer from blinds and stalking.
Physical Education and Recreation; Science - Natural
Dist - HOMEAF **Prod** - HOMEAF

The Oldest shipwrecks in the world 50 MIN
VHS
Discoveries underwater series
PAL; Color (G)
PdS99 purchase
Looks at ancient shipwrecks and their cargoes. Presents the growing science of underwater archaeology, its methods and history. Part four of an eight - part series.
History - World; Physical Education and Recreation
Dist - BBCENE

Oldies - 1962
16mm
Color
Presents the 1962 America's Cup races.
Geography - World; Physical Education and Recreation
Dist - OFFSHR **Prod** - OFFSHR

Oldies - 1964
16mm
Color
Consists of footage of the 1964 America's Cup races.
Geography - World; Physical Education and Recreation
Dist - OFFSHR **Prod** - OFFSHR

Oldies - 1967
16mm
Color
Consists of footage of the 1967 America's Cup races.
Geography - World; Physical Education and Recreation
Dist - OFFSHR **Prod** - OFFSHR

Oldies - 1970
16mm
Color
Consists of footage from the 1970 America's Cup races.
Geography - World; Physical Education and Recreation
Dist - OFFSHR **Prod** - OFFSHR

Ole Eyemo Sees the Truth 13 MIN
U-matic / VHS / 16mm
Color (K P I J) (SPANISH)
LC 76-703559
Explores the real world that lies behind outward appearances, telling the story of a boy with a painted third eye which comes magically alive and allows him unsual insights into himself and others.
Guidance and Counseling
Dist - BARR **Prod** - CALLFM 1976

The Oleander Years 28 MIN
16mm / U-matic / VHS
Insight Series
B&W (H C A)
LC 77-705432
Depicts an apparently happy couple on vacation who find that their marriage has become an empty shell.
Guidance and Counseling; Psychology
Dist - PAULST **Prod** - PAULST 1966

Oleo Strut Servicing - ITP Practical Project Series 15 MIN
U-matic / VHS
Aviation Technician Training Program Series
Color (IND)
Gives complete rundown of servicing procedures for oleo struts. Includes complete breakdown of strut components and a description of general operating theory of the air - oil shock strut.
Industrial and Technical Education
Dist - AVIMA **Prod** - AVIMA 1980

Olga Broumas - 4 - 12 - 85 25 MIN
VHS / Cassette
Poetry Center reading series
Color (G)
$15.00, $45.00 purchase, $15.00 rental _ #631 - 531
Features the writer at the Poetry Center at San Francisco State University reading Landscape with Leaves and Figure; Little Red Ridinghood; and No Harm Shall Come, with an introduction by Frances Phillips.
Literature and Drama
Dist - POETRY **Prod** - POETRY 1985

Oligopolies - Whatever Happened to Price Competition 30 MIN
U-matic / VHS
Economics USA Series
Color (C)
Business and Economics
Dist - ANNCPB **Prod** - WEFA

Oliver 146 MIN
VHS
Color (J H)
$29.00 purchase _ #04469 - 126
Presents the musical adaptation of Oliver Twist by Charles Dickens.
Fine Arts; Literature and Drama
Dist - GA **Prod** - GA

Oliver 145 MIN
16mm
Color
Presents a musical adaptation of Charles Dickens' novel OLIVER TWIST.
Fine Arts
Dist - TIMLIF **Prod** - CPC 1968

Oliver Cromwell 30 MIN
VHS
Late great britons
Color; PAL (C H)
PdS65 purchase
Covers the life of Oliver Cromwell. Describes his transition from an unknown Englishman to a renowned soldier and statesman. Sixth in the six - part series Late Great Britons, which covers the lives of six important figures in British history.
Civics and Political Systems; History - World
Dist - BBCENE

Oliver Hardy - Bela Lugosi Interviews 10 MIN
16mm
B&W
Features interviews with Bela Lugosi and Oliver Hardy.
Fine Arts; Guidance and Counseling
Dist - FCE **Prod** - FCE

Oliver Jones 10 MIN
VHS / U-matic / BETA / 16mm
Color (P I)
$290.00, $250.00 purchase _ #JR - 5877M
Adapts the story 'Oliver Jones' by Jack Korshak. Tells about seven - year - old Oliver Jones who is the overly proud owner of the bluest skin in the world. When his skin color mysteriously changes, Oliver learns that the true measure of a person isn't color, shape or size but what's inside.
Psychology; Sociology
Dist - CORF **Prod** - CORF 1989

Oliver North and the moderate Iranians 6 MIN
U-matic / VHS
Color (G)
$25.00, $50.00 purchase
Compares the environment of testimony between the witch hunt trials of the 1950s and the Iran - Contra scandal of the 1980s. Uses footage from the army hearings against Senator McCarthy and the Iran - Contra hearings to expose the hysteria of anti - communism. Produced by Niccolo Caldararo.
Civics and Political Systems; Fine Arts
Dist - CANCIN

Oliver North - July 10, 1987
VHS
Nightline news library series
Color (J H C)
$19.98 purchase _ #MH6160V - S
Examines Oliver North and his role in secret arms deals with Iran in a news story by the ABC News Team. Part of a series from the news program, Nightline.
Civics and Political Systems; History - United States
Dist - CAMV **Prod** - ABCNEW 1987

Oliver North - memo to history 90 MIN
VHS
Color (G)
$19.95 purchase _ #S01568
Documents the Congressional testimony of Marine Lt Col Oliver North in the Iran - Contra investigation. Includes excerpts from the testimony of other witnesses, as well as background information on the key persons and events of Iran - Contra.
Civics and Political Systems; History - United States
Dist - UILL

Oliver Twist 77 MIN
16mm
B&W
Presents the story of Oliver Twist and the nefarious Fagin. Based on the novel OLIVER TWIST by Charles Dickens. Stars Jackie Coogan and Lon Chaney.
Fine Arts
Dist - RMIBHF **Prod** - COOGAN 1922

Oliver Twist
U-matic / VHS
Color (J C I)
Presents the film version of Charles Dicken's story about a London orphan.
Fine Arts; Literature and Drama
Dist - GA **Prod** - GA

Oliver Twist 109 MIN
16mm
B&W (G)
Adapts the Dickens classic of a loveable urchin who falls in with pickpockets in the lower depths of London before being rescued by a wealthy benefactor. Features Alec Guinness, who brings a touch of humor to his portrayal of mean old Fagin. Also stars John Howard Davies. Directed by David Lean.
Fine Arts; Religion and Philosophy; Sociology
Dist - NCJEWF **Prod** - FOTH 1947
FOTH
UILL

Oliver's 30 MIN
U-matic
Frontrunners Series
Color (H C A)
Explains how a small bakery has grown into a highly profitable complex of restaurants.
Business and Economics
Dist - TVOTAR **Prod** - TVOTAR 1985

Olives 3 MIN
16mm
B&W (G)
$5.00 rental
Purports to answer the question 'why' if Richard Nixon ever stages a comeback. Presents a film by Darrell Forney.
Fine Arts
Dist - CANCIN

Ollero Yucateco - Yucatan Potter 25 MIN
16mm
Color
LC FIA66-503
Demonstrates the technique of Mayan pottery making, traces the evolution of this ceramic tradition and illustrates an experimental design by which archeologists and ethnographers hope to increase their knowledge.
Fine Arts; Science - Physical; Sociology
Dist - UILL **Prod** - UILL 1965

Olly Olly Oxen Free 89 MIN
VHS / U-matic
Color
Describes how Miss Pudd, an eccentric junkyard owner helps young Alby celebrate his late grandfather's birthday by flying the circus balloon his grandfather used to fly. Stars Katherine Hepburn and Dennis Dimster.
Fine Arts
Dist - TIMLIF **Prod** - TIMLIF 1982

Olmsted and Central Park 25 MIN
VHS / BETA
Color (G)
$29.95 purchase
Examines the work of landscape designer Frederick Law Olmsted in New York's Central Park. Shows the designer's urban creativity, using the Metropolitan Museum exhibition Art of the Olmsted Landscape as a starting point and viewing the park. Features Dr Charles Beveridge, Olmsted's writings, historic photographs and engravings.
Agriculture; Fine Arts
Dist - ARTSAM **Prod** - MMOA

Olympia - Diving Sequence 4 MIN
U-matic / VHS / 16mm
B&W (H C A)
Features the diving sequence in the classic film documentary, Olympia by Leni Riefenstahl of the 1936 Olympic Games in Berlin.
Physical Education and Recreation
Dist - PHENIX **Prod** - RIEFSL

Olympia I and II 212 MIN
U-matic / VHS / 16mm
B&W (H C A)
Presents the classic film documentary by Leni Riefenstahl of the 1936 Olympic Games in Berlin.
Physical Education and Recreation
Dist - PHENIX **Prod** - RIEFSL

Olympia - Marathon Sequence 13 MIN
U-matic / VHS / 16mm
B&W (H C A)
Features the marathon sequence in the classic film documentary, Olympia by Leni Riefenstahl of the 1936 Olympic Games in Berlin.
Physical Education and Recreation
Dist - PHENIX **Prod** - RIEFSL

Olympia, Part 1 - Festival of the People 112 MIN
U-matic / VHS
B&W
Presents the 1936 Olympics held in the capital of the third Reich, Berlin. Directed by Leni Riefenstahl, with music by Herbert Windt.
Civics and Political Systems; History - World; Physical Education and Recreation; Social Science
Dist - IHF **Prod** - IHF

Olympia, Part 2 - Festival of Beauty 91 MIN
U-matic / VHS
B&W
Presents the 1936 Olympics held in Berlin, the capital of the third Reich. Directed by Leni Riefenstahl, with music by Herbert Windt.
Civics and Political Systems; History - World; Physical Education and Recreation; Social Science
Dist - IHF **Prod** - IHF

Olympia, Pt 1 115 MIN
16mm / U-matic / VHS
B&W (H C A)
LC 73-702743
Presents part one of Leni Riefenstahl's original filming of the 1936 Olympic Games in Berlin.
Fine Arts; Physical Education and Recreation
Dist - PHENIX **Prod** - RIEFSL

Olympia, Pt 2 97 MIN
16mm / U-matic / VHS
B&W (H C A)
LC 73-702745
Presents part two of Leni Riefenstahl's original filming of the 1936 Olympic Games in Berlin.
Fine Arts; Physical Education and Recreation
Dist - PHENIX **Prod** - RIEFSL

Olympiad 3 MIN
16mm
Color
Presents figures of computer - stylized athletes in brilliant hues chasing each other across the screen.
Fine Arts; Mathematics
Dist - LILYAN **Prod** - LILYAN

Olympiad Series
The Africans are coming 50 MIN
The Australians 50 MIN
The Big ones that got away 50 MIN
The Canadians 50 MIN
The Decathalon 50 MIN
The Incredible five 50 MIN
Jesse Owens Returns to Berlin 50 MIN
The Marathon 50 MIN
The Persistent Ones 50 MIN
The Russian Athlete 50 MIN
Women Gold Medalists 50 MIN
Dist - CTV

Olympic Champ 8 MIN
U-matic / VHS / 16mm
Color
Presents an animated cartoon in which Goofy leads a comical history of the Olympics.
Fine Arts
Dist - CORF **Prod** - DISNEY 1979

Olympic Coins 8 MIN
16mm
Color
LC 76-702457
Presents Canada's designers and makers of coins as they practice the skills that produce valuable and lasting mementos of events in history.
Business and Economics; Industrial and Technical Education; Physical Education and Recreation
Dist - CEAEAO **Prod** - CEAEAO 1975

Olympic combination
VHS
Color (G)
$54.90 purchase _ #0226
Overviews the sailing events of the 1972 and 1976 Olympics. Photographs the parade of tall ships into Kiel harbor. Focuses on the American team, especially on the sailing. Features the 1976 Olympics in Canada in the second part.
Physical Education and Recreation
Dist - SEVVID

The Olympic Elk 26 MIN
U-matic / VHS / 16mm
Color (I J H) (SWEDISH SPANISH FRENCH)
Documents the Olympic elk's annual trek through Washington wilderness areas.
Foreign Language; Science - Natural
Dist - CORF **Prod** - DISNEY 1956

Olympic Fragments 12 MIN
VHS / U-matic
Color
Comments on the normal media appraisal of sport. Emphasizes the skill, beauty and joy of kineticism.
Fine Arts; Physical Education and Recreation
Dist - KITCHN **Prod** - KITCHN

Olympic National Park - wilderness heritage 30 MIN
VHS
Color (G)
$29.95 purchase _ #V112
Travels to Olympic National Park in Washington State. Visits glacier - carved mountains, the rugged Pacific Coast and lush rain forest. Offers close - up views of plant and animal life.
Geography - United States
Dist - INSTRU

Olympic Sailing 54 MIN
BETA / VHS
Color
Features Olympic sailing. Combines the shorter titles Kingston Olympiad and Kiel Olympiad.
Geography - United States; Physical Education and Recreation
Dist - OFFSHR **Prod** - OFFSHR

Olympic Sports 3 MIN
16mm
Color
LC 80-701251
Uses the kinestasis technique to present photographs of Olympic athletes.
Industrial and Technical Education; Physical Education and Recreation
Dist - GUSD **Prod** - GUSD 1980

Olympic Style Back Crawl, Breast Stroke, and Turns 60 MIN
VHS
Swimming with Dick Hannula Series
(H C A)
$39.95 purchase _ #MXS2000V
Shows proper arm and leg action, breathing and turns for olympic back crawl and breast stroke.
Physical Education and Recreation
Dist - CAMV

Olympic Style Crawl and Butterfly 60 MIN
VHS
Swimming with Dick Hannula Series
(H C A)
$39.95 purchase _ #MXS2100V
Demonstrates proper techniques for leg and arm action and breathing in olympic crawl and butterfly stokes.
Physical Education and Recreation
Dist - CAMV

Olympic style swimming with Dick Hannula series
Offers swimming instruction from coach Dick Hannula in two programs. Includes back crawl, breast stroke, turns, crawl, and butterfly. Concentrates on arm and leg action and breathing. Uses underwater photography and slow motion and provides drills to develop techniques. Videos available individually.
Olympic style swimming with Dick Hannula series
Dist - CAMV

Olympic Volleyball - Official Technical Film of the 1984 Olympics 30 MIN
U-matic / VHS
Color (H C A)
Breaks volleyball into six components and illustrates each using freeze frames and slow motion. Features 1984 Olympic games.
Physical Education and Recreation
Dist - CVA **Prod** - CVA 1985

Olympic Wilderness Encounters 23 MIN
16mm
Color
LC 81-700648
Presents comments by backpackers and area residents on their thoughts and feelings towards the Olympic National Park in northwestern Washington.
Geography - United States
Dist - USNAC **Prod** - USNPS 1981

The Olympics - Images of Gold 24 MIN
U-matic / VHS
Color
Focuses on track and field, swimming and gymnastics as well as the dedication young athletes exhibit necessary to compete in the most prestigious amateur sporting events.
Physical Education and Recreation
Dist - KAROL **Prod** - KAROL

The Olympics of Racing 14 MIN
16mm
Color
Presents thoroughbred racing at Gulfstream Park, Florida.
Geography - United States; Physical Education and Recreation
Dist - FLADC **Prod** - FLADC

Olympics of the Mind 30 MIN
U-matic / VHS
Creativity with Bill Moyers Series
Color
Fine Arts; Psychology
Dist - DELTAK **Prod** - PBS

Olympics of the Mind 29 MIN
U-matic / VHS
Creativity with Bill Moyers Series
Color (H C A)
LC 83-706165
Presents host Bill Moyers examining an extracurricular school program called Olympics of the mind. Shows how a competition of mental games can illustrate that creative thought can be taught in schools.
Education; Fine Arts; Psychology
Dist - PBS **Prod** - CORPEL 1982

Olympics - the Eternal Torch 27 MIN
16mm / U-matic / VHS
Color (H C A)
LC 74-702612
Traces the history of modern Olympic Games with footage dating back to their revival in 1896. Discusses the ideals of sportsmanship in the quadrennial Games.
Physical Education and Recreation
Dist - AIMS **Prod** - ASPRSS 1973

Omaha Nebraska 4 MIN
16mm
Color (G)
$5.00 rental
Consists of approximately 200 postcards. Features Groucho singing the title. Produced by Darrell Forney.
Fine Arts
Dist - CANCIN

Omai Fa'atasi - Samoa mo Samoa 30 MIN
VHS / U-matic
Color (G)
$125.00 purchase, $50.00 rental
Explores the challenges facing an Asian Pacific group, the Samoans, in a documentary about a Southern Californian community group, Omai Fa'atasi. Focuses on the youth of the community who feel alienated from the mainstream and detached from Samoan culture. Directed by Takashi Fuji.
History - United States; Sociology
Dist - CROCUR **Prod** - VISCOM 1974

Oman 28 MIN
Videoreel / VHS
International Byline Series
Color
Interviews Sheikh Farid Mbarak Ali Al - Hinai, Ambassador of Oman to the United States. Hosted by Marilyn Perry.
Business and Economics; Civics and Political Systems; Geography - World
Dist - PERRYM **Prod** - PERRYM

Omara 26 MIN
16mm
Cuba - a view from inside series
Color (G)
$400.00 purchase, $50.00 rental
Profiles one of Cuba's best known singers, Omara Portunondo, with interviews and film clips of her performances from the 1940s and '50s. Features part of a 17 - part series of shorts by and about Cuban women. Directed by Fernando Perez. Illustrated catalog available. Contact distributor for programming advice and discount package rental fees.
Fine Arts
Dist - CNEMAG

O'Mara's Chain Miracle 10 MIN
16mm
B&W
Deals with personal experiences in getting along with other people.
Guidance and Counseling; Psychology; Sociology
Dist - GM **Prod** - GM

Omega 13 MIN
16mm / U-matic / VHS
Color (P)
LC 79-709804
Deals with the end of mankind on earth, emphasizing rebirth rather than death. Uses special effects to prophesy man's liberation from his earthly bounds in order to roam the universe at will, implying man's faith and idealism. Renders into visual imagery the complex philosophical concept of the filmmaker. Stimulates thought and discussion.
English Language; Fine Arts; Religion and Philosophy
Dist - PFP **Prod** - FOXD 1970

The Omega Long - Range Navigation System 18 MIN
16mm
Color
LC 74-706512
Shows a worldwide long - range navigation system that is simple and dependable under all weather conditions. Shows how to use the AN/SRN - 2 receiver.
Social Science
Dist - USNAC **Prod** - USN 1970

Omega Long - Range Navigation System - AN/SRN - 12 Receiver Operation 17 MIN
16mm
Color
LC 74-706547
Shows the use of the AN/SRN - 12 receiver in the Omega long - range navigation program.
Social Science
Dist - USNAC **Prod** - USN 1970

Omelets 30 MIN
VHS / U-matic
Cooking Now Series
(C A)
$19.95 _ #CH260V
Features Franco Palumbo, former chef of Weight Watchers International, as he demonstrates simple, methodical recipes for preparing omelets.
Home Economics; Industrial and Technical Education
Dist - CAMV **Prod** - CAMV

The Omelette Show 29 MIN
Videoreel / VT2
French from the French Chef - French Series
Color
Features Julia Child of Haute Cuisine au Vin demonstrating how to prepare an omelette. With captions.
Foreign Language; Home Economics
Dist - PBS **Prod** - WGBHTV

Omelettes 33 MIN
VHS
Cookbook videos series
Color (G)
$19.95 purchase _ #ALW128
Shows how to prepare omelettes in short, easy - to - learn segments. Lists each ingredient as it is added in subtitles and visually reinforces spoken instructions. Gives recipe background and nutritional facts. Part of the Cookbook Videos series.
Home Economics; Social Science
Dist - CADESF **Prod** - CADESF

Omelettes 33 MIN
VHS
Cookbook videos series; Vol 15
Color (G)
$19.95 purchase
Shows how to cook omelettes. Includes printed abstract of recipes. Part of a series.
Home Economics; Social Science
Dist - ALWHIT **Prod** - ALWHIT

Omelettes - Seven Different Types - Lesson 21 30 MIN
VHS
International Cooking School with Chef Rene Series
Color (G)
$69.00 purchase
Presents classic methods of cooking that stress essential flavor. Introduces newer, lighter foods. Lesson 21 focuses on omelettes.
Fine Arts; Home Economics; Psychology; Social Science; Sociology
Dist - LUF **Prod** - LUF

The Omens of war and Tempest - Volume 2 120 MIN
VHS
Korean war series
Color; B&W (G)
$19.95 purchase _ #1646
Examines in two parts events immediately before the Korean War which were instrumental in its birth and the beginning of the war. Includes film footage from both North and South Korea and interviews with Korean, American and Russian military and political leaders who personally participated in the events. Part two of a five - part series on the Korean War. Produced by the Korean Broadcast System.
History - World
Dist - KULTUR

Omnibus series

John Sell Cotman	30 MIN
Lucie Rie	55 MIN
Stevenson's travels	100 MIN
Three Looms Waiting	50 MIN

Dist - BBCENE

Omnivac's Troubles Add Up - Addition of Hundreds 15 MIN
VHS / U-matic
Figure Out Series
Color (I)
Tells how Mac and Alice attempt to repair the world computer. Explains addition with and without regrouping of digits.
Mathematics
Dist - AITECH **Prod** - MAETEL 1982

Omowale - the Child Returns Home 30 MIN
16mm
History of the Negro People Series
B&W (H C A)
LC FIA66-825
Discusses negro novelist John William's trip to Africa to explore his ancestral roots. Studies the relationship of the American Negro to the African. Presents an interview with James Meredith. Discusses the 'BACK TO AFRICA' movement. Features Ossie Davis.
History - United States; Psychology; Sociology
Dist - IU **Prod** - NET 1965

On a Clear Day You Could See Boston 52 MIN
U-matic / VHS / 16mm
Destination America Series
Color (J)
Relates that by 1900 one - third of the population of Ireland, which lost more of its people to the United States than any other single country, had emigrated to America. They were fleeing the famine and became the first immigrant group who achieved a political foothold, especially in Boston.
Geography - United States; History - United States; History - World; Sociology
Dist - MEDIAG **Prod** - THAMES 1976

On a Perdu Nicolas 13 MIN
16mm
En France Avec Nicolas Series Set I, Lesson 3; Set I; Lesson 3
B&W (J H)
Foreign Language
Dist - CHLTN **Prod** - PEREN 1968

On a Perdu Nicolas, Student Exercises 8 MIN
16mm
En France Avec Nicolas Series Set II, Lesson 3; Set II; Lesson 3
Color (J H)
Foreign Language
Dist - CHLTN **Prod** - PEREN 1968

On a String 8 MIN
16mm / U-matic / VHS
Color (K P I)
LC 74-702584
Presents a story about a father, mother and son. Tells how the father and son get the idea of using a clothes line as a springboard for flying.
Geography - World; Guidance and Counseling; Physical Education and Recreation; Sociology
Dist - PHENIX **Prod** - CZECFM 1974

On American Soil 28 MIN
VHS / 16mm
Color (J H C G)
$250 purchase, $50 rental
Shows the nature and extent of the soil erosion problem in America today. Explains the economic bind in which farmers find themselves using interviews with farmers and soil conservation experts, and the use of old photographs and film clips. Discusses contradictory government policies and the effectiveness of soil conservation programs.
Agriculture; Social Science; Sociology
Dist - BULFRG **Prod** - BULFRG 1985

On and about instruction - microcomputers series

Database management	30 MIN
Electronic spreadsheets and graphing tools	30 MIN

Dist - GPN

On and about instruction - microcomputers

Programming and problem - solving - BASIC	30 MIN
Programming and problem - solving - LOGO	30 MIN

Dist - GPN

On and about Instruction Series
Buying hardware 30 MIN
Buying software 30 MIN
Classroom management skills 27 MIN
Microcomputers for Instruction 29 MIN
The Middle School 30 MIN
Role of Department Chairpersons 28 MIN
Shaping Curriculum 30 MIN
Shaping Instruction 30 MIN
Shaping the Classroom 30 MIN
Teacher stress - Pt 1 20 MIN
Teacher stress - Pt 2 29 MIN
Teaching and Testing for Results 30 MIN
Teaching Styles 29 MIN
Teaching to objectives - Pt 1 30 MIN
Teaching to objectives - Pt 2 30 MIN
Videotape - Disc - or 30 MIN
Volunteerism 29 MIN
Dist - GPN

On and about Instruction...Microcomputers
Ethical, Social and Economic Issues 30 MIN
Dist - GPN

On and on about Instruction - Microcomputers Series
Computer - assisted instruction - Pt 1 30 MIN
Computer - Assisted Instruction - Pt 2 30 MIN
Computer - Managed Instruction 30 MIN
Computer Components and Terminology 30 MIN
Computers and Teacher - Administrator Support 30 MIN
Electronic databases 30 MIN
Ethical, Social and Economic Issues 30 MIN
Running software and keyboarding skills 30 MIN
Skills for employment in the information society 30 MIN
Software Evaluation - Pt 1 30 MIN
Software Evaluation - Pt 2 30 MIN
Word Processing 30 MIN
Dist - GPN

On Any Street 30 MIN
U-matic / VHS / 16mm
Color (H C A)
Looks at the complex life of police work. Documents the fears, frustrations, pressures and rewards experienced by actual officers on the job while illustrating the difficulties in a constantly changing environment.
Social Science
Dist - CORF **Prod** - LAPD 1983

On assignment - the video guide for photography series 720 MIN
VHS
On assignment - the video guide for photography series
Color (J H C G)
$215.00 purchase _ #MED108SV VHS
Presents an eight - part series hosted by nationally known photographer Brian D Ratty. Includes Video Guide to Basic Photography, Photographic Design, Photographic Light, The Darkroom, Video Guide to Videography, Business of Photography, The Studio, Glamour Photography.
Fine Arts; Industrial and Technical Education
Dist - CAMV

On Becoming a Nurse - Psychotherapist 42 MIN
U-matic / VHS / 16mm
Color (J)
LC 71-712936
A dramatized case study of the experience of a young nursing student as she learns to assume the role of nurse - psychotherapist. Follows her first case and shows the development of two parallel relationships, nurse with patient and nurse with instructor.
Guidance and Counseling; Health and Safety; Psychology
Dist - UCEMC **Prod** - UCSNUR 1970

On Becoming a Woman 90 MIN
16mm / VHS
Color (G)
$950.00, $195.00 purchase, $150.00, $80.00 rental
Documents candid conversations between mothers and daughters about menstruation, sexuality, birth control, teenage pregnancy and relationships during National Black Women's Health Project workshop sessions. Empowers young women to take control of their lives. Provides a model to aid in communication between mothers and daughters. Produced by Cheryl Chisholm.
Health and Safety; Psychology; Sociology
Dist - WMEN **Prod** - CHEC 1987

On being 17, bright and unable to read 29 MIN
VHS / 16mm
Watch your mouth series
Color (H)
$46.00 rental _ #WAYM - 122
Emphasizes language and communication skills for high school students. Notes the difference between formal and informal word usage.
Education; English Language; Psychology; Social Science
Dist - PBS

On being a white African with Nadine Gordimer 30 MIN
U-matic / VHS
World of ideas with Bill Moyers, season 2 series
Color; Captioned (A G)
$39.95, $59.95 purchase _ #WIWM - 236
Confronts the turbulent political reality of South Africa as it engulfs the people who live there. Features author Nadine Gordimer who discusses growing up as a white South African under apartheid, the causes of the tensions and violence in black townships today and her views on the future of South Africa. Part of a series with Bill Moyers featuring some of the most important and inventive minds of the 20th century who explore the ideas and values shaping our future.
Geography - World; Sociology
Dist - PBS **Prod** - PATV 1990

On being gay - a conversation with Brian McNaught 80 MIN
VHS
Color (I J H)
$39.95 purchase _ #480 - V8
Catches the author, counselor, and lecturer Brian McNaught at home, at the lectern, and at peace with himself as he talks to young adults about the fallacies, facts, and feelings of being gay in a straight world. Encourages both gay and non - gay viewers to realize their own potential and replace self - doubt with self - esteem, self - knowledge, and self - confidence.
Health and Safety; Sociology
Dist - ETRASS **Prod** - ETRASS

On Being Human 30 MIN
VHS / U-matic
In Our Own Image Series
Color (C)
Fine Arts
Dist - DALCCD **Prod** - DALCCD

On Being Sexual 22 MIN
U-matic / VHS / 16mm
Color (C A)
LC 76-700461
Features a discussion between parents and professionals about sexuality and the mentally retarded. Emphasizes that the mentally retarded are sexual beings.
Education; Psychology
Dist - STNFLD **Prod** - SLARC 1975

On Black America 30 MIN
VHS / U-matic
Moral Values in Contemporary Society Series
Color (J)
Presents James Farmer, founder of the Congress of Racial Equality and Director of Public Policy Training Institute, talking about Black America.
Religion and Philosophy; Sociology
Dist - AMHUMA **Prod** - AMHUMA

On borrowed land 51 MIN
VHS
Color (G A) (FILIPINO AND ENGLISH)
$350.00 purchase, $90.00 rental
Traces the history of the People's Power Revolution in the Philippines, and the tensions between the wealthy developers, the Aquino government and the urban poor in Manila as each attempts to achieve their vision of future prosperity. Features Willem Dafoe as narrator.
Geography - World; History - World; Sociology
Dist - CNEMAG **Prod** - STONEO 1991

On Borrowed Time 48 MIN
VHS / U-matic
Color
$455.00 purchase
Presents a program on the international debt. From the ABC TV program Close Up.
Business and Economics
Dist - ABCLR **Prod** - ABCLR 1983

On Borrowed Time - Living with Heart Disease 50 MIN
U-matic / VHS / 16mm
Color (H C A)
LC 80-701781
Presents Ron Drimak describing how a heart attack almost ended his life and leading medical authorities explaining the causes, treatment and prevention of heart disease.
Health and Safety
Dist - CORF **Prod** - BBINC 1980

On Camera - Pt 5 - Appearing on Camera 44 MIN
VHS / 16mm
On Camera Series
Color (H)
$21.50 rental _ #50858
Provides information for anyone who is likely to be interviewed on broadcast television or on corporate or in - house videotape. Describes what may happen before, during, and after the interview, and distills the expertise of four individuals who often have been in front of the camera. Study guide included.
Fine Arts; Industrial and Technical Education
Dist - FI **Prod** - BBC 1984

On Camera - Pt 4 - Editing 58 MIN
VHS / 16mm
On Camera Series
Color (H)
$21.50 rental _ #60510
Explains the prinicples of film editing, using as an illustration a report about a factory that claims to have increased production by instituting an employee exercise program. Stresses the important of selecting which shots to use, what order to put them in, and how long to keep them on the screen. Includes raw footage for students use in editing practice. Study guide included.
Fine Arts; Industrial and Technical Education
Dist - FI **Prod** - BBC 1984

On Camera - Pt 1 - the Camera 35 MIN
VHS / 16mm
On Camera Series
Color (H)
$21.50 rental _ #40424
Demonstrates in four segments how to make video equipment reflect the mind's eye. Explores light movement, angle shots, and use of camera location in order to see as the camera sees. Looks at focal length, angle of view, focus, depth of field, aperture, and creative use of camera controls. Illustrates basic terminology for describing different shots, and shows how to maintain continuity of direction. Study guide included.
Fine Arts; Industrial and Technical Education
Dist - FI **Prod** - BBC 1984

On Camera - Pt 3 - Interviews 17 MIN
VHS / 16mm
On Camera Series
Color (H)
$21.50 rental _ #23643
Presents an extract from an imaginary interview that contains at least twenty mistakes, and then explains how interviews should be shot. Emphasizes the necessity of relating the positions of interviewer, guest, and camera to what is seen on screen and the importance of taking cutaways, choosing the proper shot sizes, and correctly positioning props. Study guide included.
Fine Arts; Industrial and Technical Education
Dist - FI **Prod** - BBC 1984

On Camera - Pt 2 - Planning a Programme 17 MIN
VHS / 16mm
On Camera Series
Color (H)
$21.50 rental _ #23642
Illustrates the importance of proper planning in successful video production by comparing the often comical results of an ill - prepared television crew's attempts to shoot a disorganized retirement ceremony with a demonstration of how the recording of the ceremony should have been handled. Employs cartoon graphics to show how to organize camera positions, lights, and participants for maximum effect. Study guide included.
Fine Arts; Industrial and Technical Education
Dist - FI **Prod** - BBC 1984

On Camera Series
The Camera 35 MIN
Editing 59 MIN
Interviews 22 MIN
On Camera - Pt 5 - Appearing on Camera 44 MIN
On Camera - Pt 4 - Editing 58 MIN
On Camera - Pt 1 - the Camera 35 MIN
On Camera - Pt 3 - Interviews 17 MIN
On Camera - Pt 2 - Planning a Programme 17 MIN
Planning a Program 18 MIN
Dist - FI

On camera series
Appearing on camera - Pt 5 44 MIN
The Camera - Pt 1 34 MIN
Editing - Pt 4 58 MIN
Interviews, Pt 3 20 MIN
Planning a Programme - Pt 2 17 MIN
Dist - PSU

On cannibalism 6 MIN
VHS
Color (G)
$50.00 rental, $200.00 purchase
Explores the West's insatiable appetite for native bodies in museums, world's fairs and early cinema. Intertwintes personal narrative about race and identity in the United States with layered footage, artifacts and video effects.
Fine Arts; History - United States; Sociology
Dist - WMEN **Prod** - RONYFT 1994

On Castro Street 10 MIN
16mm
B&W (G)
$9.00 rental
Depicts a walk down Castro St. with 'me and my dog Hugh.' By Victor Barbieri.
Fine Arts
Dist - CANCIN

On child care 14 MIN
U-matic / VHS / BETA
Erikson series
Color; PAL (T PRO)
PdS40, PdS48 purchase
Features part of a three - part series.
Psychology
Dist - EDPAT

On course for growth 12 MIN
VHS
Color; PAL; NTSC (G)
PdS57, PdS67 purchase
Details the investment, recruitment, training and overall strategy being adopted by the Civil Aviation Authority - CAA - to cope with projected increases in air travel. Highlights the magnitude of the responsibilities facing airports such as Heathrow and Gatwick. Produced by the British Civil Aviation Authority.
Industrial and Technical Education
Dist - CFLVIS

On Death and Dying 58 MIN
U-matic / VHS / 16mm
Color (H C)
Features Dr Elizabeth Kubler - Ross in a discussion about helping the terminally ill face death without fear. Stresses the importance of communication which recognizes the patient's feelings.
Psychology; Sociology
Dist - FI **Prod** - NBCNEW 1974

On developmental stages 21 MIN
U-matic / VHS / BETA
Erikson series
Color; PAL (T PRO)
PdS40, PdS48 purchase
Features part of a three - part series.
Psychology
Dist - EDPAT

On Display 4 MIN
16mm / U-matic
Color (G)
$75.00, $105.00 purchase, $50.00, $40.00 rental
Examines pervasive power of media images which inundate the public with images of women as sex objects, victims of sanctioned violence, and as subservient, empty - headed housewives. Considers rock music and television, as well as advertising. Presented by Kim Blain.
Business and Economics; History - United States; Sociology
Dist - WMENIF **Prod** - WMENIF 1988

On Dreams and dreaming 30 MIN
BETA / VHS
Working with the unconscious series
Color (G)
$29.95 purchase _ #S332
Considers that even negative dreams and nightmares can be a source of positive value and growth when one chooses to interact creatively with the dream imagery. Features Dr Patricia Garfield who offers various methods of working with dreams. Part of a four - part series about working with the unconscious.
Guidance and Counseling; Psychology; Religion and Philosophy
Dist - THINKA **Prod** - THINKA

On earth as it is in heaven 60 MIN
VHS
Moyers - God and politics series
Color; Captioned (G)
$59.95 purchase _ #MYGP - 103
Examines the Christian Reconstructionist movement. Shows that Christian Reconstructionists believe that the Bible should be the basis for not just church matters, but as a model for the government and the economy as well. Hosted by Bill Moyers.
Religion and Philosophy
Dist - PBS **Prod** - WNETTV 1987

On Equal terms - sex equity in the workplace 29 MIN
VHS / U-matic
Color (J H C G)
$340.00, $315.00 purchase _ #V368
Explores why young women need to understand and accept the fact that they will need self - supporting careers. Looks at language stereotyping, schools, so - called 'women's work' and 'men's work.'
Sociology
Dist - BARR **Prod** - CEPRO 1987
CEPRO

On Every Hand 10 MIN
U-matic / VHS / 16mm
Captioned; Color (J H)
LC 71-711379
Informs students how to escape serious hand injury from commonly used but potentially dangerous equipment such as shearing devices, fans, drills and presses. Concludes with a poignant reminder of the importance of our hands. Produced in conjunction with the National Safety Council.
Health and Safety
Dist - JOU **Prod** - NSC 1970

On Fire with faith 60 MIN
VHS
Color (R)
$29.95 purchase _ #422 - 8
Explores the history of Hispanic Catholics in North America from the arrival of the first missionaries to the Hispanic Catholic community of today. Includes study guide.
Religion and Philosophy; Sociology
Dist - USCC **Prod** - USCC 1991

On follow - up 17 MIN
BETA / VHS / U-matic
Main video series
Color (A G)
$495.00 purchase, $125.00 rental
Presents a sales training film that offers ideas and techniques for sales staff that will help increase profits. Shows how to follow - up on prospects already in the sold files. Leader's guide and additional support material provided.
Business and Economics; Industrial and Technical Education; Psychology
Dist - TELDOC **Prod** - TELDOC

On Giant's Shoulders 92 MIN
VHS / U-matic
Color (J)
Presents Terry Wiles, a thalidomide - damaged child who was adopted by Leonard and Hazel Wiles after they overcame their initial fears. Shows how Leonard's considerable talents at invention resulted in devices that made Terry's life much more pleasant and mobile while Hazel spent her time teaching Terry to fend for himself.
Education; Psychology
Dist - FI **Prod** - BBCTV 1982

On Golden Pond
VHS / BETA / U-matic
Color (J C I)
Depicts an older couple grappling with their own mortaililty and their family's emotional distance. Stars Henry Fonda and Katherine Hepburn.
Sociology
Dist - GA **Prod** - GA

On Guard 28 MIN
VHS / U-matic
Color (J A)
Illustrates schemes that are used to defraud the public.
Sociology
Dist - SUTHRB **Prod** - SUTHRB

On guard 51 MIN
VHS / 16mm
Color (G)
$90.00, $125.00 rental, $350.00 purchase
Features a 'heist' movie with a radical new twist. Depicts frankly the heroines' domestic and sexual lives.
Fine Arts; Sociology
Dist - WMEN **Prod** - DULA 1983

On Guard 14 MIN
16mm
Color
Outlines the benefits of Thiokol polysulfide base sealants and caulking materials.
Industrial and Technical Education
Dist - THIOKL **Prod** - THIOKL 1971

On guard 11 MIN
BETA / VHS / U-matic
Color (IND G A)
$622.00 purchase, $150.00 rental _ #ONG085; $175.00 rental _ ASF-147
Emphasizes that any moving part of a machine is a potential hazard. Demonstrates the various types of guards and procedures, proper use, removal or repair. Shows the barrier, interlock, two - hand switch, ram block and power transmission guards. Encourages workers to look at the way they use machinery and to make sure that guards are inspected and kept in place.
Health and Safety; Industrial and Technical Education; Psychology
Dist - ITF **Prod** - BNA 1991
BNA

On Guard 51 MIN
Videoreel / VHS
Color
Depicts four women conspiring to sabotage the research program of a multinational firm engaged in reproductive engineering. Raises the issue of the ethical debate over biotechnology as a potential threat to women and their rights to self - determination.
Sociology
Dist - WMEN **Prod** - REDHP

On Guard - Bunco 27 MIN
U-matic / VHS / 16mm
Color (H C A) (SPANISH)
LC 77-708895
Dramatizes schemes used to defraud the public, including confidence rackets and others.
Civics and Political Systems; Guidance and Counseling; Psychology; Sociology
Dist - AIMS **Prod** - CAHILL 1970

On Guard - Bunco 26 MIN
U-matic / VHS
Color
Alerts and informs the public about the various methods and the con games criminals use to prey upon the unwary.
Sociology
Dist - IA **Prod** - LACFU

On Guard for Thee, Pt 1 - Dangerous Spy 57 MIN
16mm
On Guard for Thee
Color
_ #106C 0181 067N
Geography - World
Dist - CFLMDC **Prod** - NFBC 1981

On Guard for Thee, Pt 3 - Shadows 57 MIN
16mm
Color
_ #106C 0181 069N
Geography - World
Dist - CFLMDC **Prod** - NFBC 1981

On Guard for Thee, Pt 2 - Blanket, Ice 57 MIN
16mm
On Guard for Thee
Color
_ #106C 0181 068N
Geography - World
Dist - CFLMDC **Prod** - NFBC 1981

On Guard for Thee
On Guard for Thee, Pt 1 - Dangerous Spy 57 MIN
On Guard for Thee, Pt 2 - Blanket, Ice 57 MIN
Dist - CFLMDC

On guard - infection control for safety and health care workers 30 MIN
VHS
Color (C A)
$325.00 purchase
Demonstrates correct procedures for first - response and emergency room caregivers to protect them from infection when performing their duties. Talks about AIDS, hepatitis and other contagious diseases. Explains barriers to infection, methods to avoid needle injuries, and universal precautions to take. Acts out a case study and shows interviews with infection control experts. Produced by Katherine West in cooperation with JEMS.
Health and Safety
Dist - PFP **Prod** - FOCPOI

On guard - protection is everybody's business 30 MIN
U-matic / VHS
Color (PRO)
$29.95 purchase
Takes an in - depth look at the wide variety of security measures performed by all museum staff. Highlights fire and safety hazards, thefts and vandalism and protection and damage prevention. Produced by the Center for Museum Studies at the Smithsonian for use in museum training.
Health and Safety; Psychology; Sociology
Dist - SMITHS

On her baldness 22 MIN
VHS
Color (G)
$60.00 rental, $250.00 purchase
Suprises with a powerful documentary about bald women. Interviews six women who have all become bald for different reasons, medical or political, but have in common the struggle to deal with their baldness, which acts as a catalyst towards further acceptance of the total self. Challenges viewers to question and confront their own ingrained prejudices regarding the true nature of beauty and femininity. Produced by Wendy Rowland.
Fine Arts; Sociology
Dist - WMEN

On Hinduism and Buddhism 35 MIN
VHS
Color (G T)

$29.95 purchase
Teaches about Hinduism and Buddhism religions by extracting sequences from the Hartley Foundation's library on the world's religions. Contains graphics with multiple answer questions after each sequence so the student can immediately discover how much he or she has learned.
Religion and Philosophy
Dist - HP

On incoming calls 17 MIN
VHS / U-matic / BETA
Main video series
Color (A G)
$495.00 purchase, $125.00 rental
Covers three topics - unnecessary transfers, the dreaded hold, and getting the caller's name every time. Recommended for new employee orientation or as a refresher course. Leader's guide and additional support material provided.
Business and Economics; Industrial and Technical Education; Psychology
Dist - TELDOC **Prod** - TELDOC

On land over water - six stories 60 MIN
16mm
Color (G)
$150.00 rental
Presents six stories. Indian Camp is a reading of Hemingway's story by the same title from the point of view of a boy who confronts the mysteries of death and his father's meanness; Shotgun Story depicts an Indian taxidermist in a shop full of stuffed animals with the camera hand - held verite style; Drive to Work is autobiographical; Spirit Astray relates the tale of a minor transgression by a young black girl; His Romantic Movement shows images of a trip to the Florida Keys where the dream of freedom turns sour; and At Her Cottage depicts a woman who recounts an episode of a young medical student refusing to perform an abortion. Produced by Richard Kerr.
Fine Arts; Literature and Drama
Dist - CANCIN

On Leadership - Part 1 23 MIN
VHS / 16mm
Profiles in Management Series
Color (C A)
$375.00 purchase, $150.00 rental _ #188
Includes Leader's Guide. Interviews three nationally known leaders and gets their point of view on leadership skills for successful managers. First part of two - part series.
Business and Economics; Guidance and Counseling; Psychology
Dist - SALENG **Prod** - SALENG 1987

On - Line Systems Concepts for Users Series
Communications facilities 20 MIN
Understanding on - Line Systems 20 MIN
Using on - Line Systems 20 MIN
Dist - DELTAK

On Loan 52 MIN
U-matic / VHS
Winners from Down Under Series
Color (K)
$349.00, $249.00 purchase _ #AD - 1353
Reveals that for ten years Lindy has been brought up in Australia believing that she is a Vietnamese war orphan. Shows that she is torn between her old and her new parents when she receives a letter from her natural father. Part of an eight - part series on children's winning over their circumstances produced by the Australian Children's Television Foundation.
Literature and Drama; Sociology
Dist - FOTH **Prod** - FOTH

On Loan from Russia - Forty - One French Masterpieces 30 MIN
16mm
Color (J)
LC 73-702241
Documents the exhibition entitled 'IMPRESSIONIST AND POST - IMPRESSIONIST PAINTING FROM THE USSR' which was held at the national gallery of art in 1973. Shows behind - the - scenes preparations for the exhibit and provides historical background on the paintings, which were selected from the Hermitage and Pushkin Museums.
Fine Arts; Geography - World
Dist - USNGA **Prod** - WNETTV 1973

On Location 30 MIN
U-matic / VHS
In Our Own Image Series
Color (C)
Fine Arts
Dist - DALCCD **Prod** - DALCCD

On Location - Night of the Iguana 26 MIN
16mm
Hollywood and the Stars Series
B&W
LC FI68-193
Features Director John Huston describing on - location filming of the motion picture 'NIGHT OF THE IGUANA,' near the Mexican village of Puerto Vallarta. Shows the building of the set and demonstrates how day and night scenes are shot.
Fine Arts
Dist - WOLPER **Prod** - WOLPER 1964

On Location with Rolf Harris 28 MIN
16mm
Color
LC 80-700914
Highlights the making of the film Rolf Harris In Tasmania.
Fine Arts
Dist - TASCOR **Prod** - TASCOR 1976

On location
Editing 7.12 MIN
Effects 6.53 MIN
Pre - production 5.17 MIN
Production - Shooting Tips 8.55 MIN
Scripting 9.24 MIN
Selecting and Researching a Production Topic 5.43 MIN
Set up and operation of small format video equipment 9 MIN
Speaking on Camera 6.57 MIN
Dist - GPN

On Ludlow in Blau 12 MIN
16mm
Color; B&W (G A)
$50.00 rental
Presents the work of filmmaker Christoph Janetzko. Does a slow pan across the window and walls of a room in an old tenement building on Ludlow Street in New York.
Fine Arts; Industrial and Technical Education
Dist - PARART **Prod** - CANCIN 1987

On Making a Thumb - One Hundred Years of Surgical Effort 45 MIN
U-matic / VHS
Color (PRO)
Discusses the principles and methods for providing a prime thumb - like digit.
Health and Safety
Dist - ASSH **Prod** - ASSH

On Merit 23 MIN
16mm / U-matic / VHS
Color (J)
LC 77-700497
Investigates the Federal Government's commitment to the merit system and its effect on the employment and promotion of women and minorities.
Business and Economics; Civics and Political Systems; Guidance and Counseling; Social Science; Sociology
Dist - GREAVW **Prod** - USCSC 1975

On mission 30 MIN
VHS
Faith completed by works series
Color (R G)
$39.95 purchase _ #FCBW4
Witnesses the work of lay missionaries in several mission fields in the United States and abroad. Starts from the premise that all Christians are challenged to become missionaries, to bring the good news of Jesus to the poor and marginalized of the world. Part of six parts on evangelization in the Roman Catholic Church.
Religion and Philosophy
Dist - CTNA **Prod** - CTNA 1994

On Motivation - Part 2 16 MIN
VHS / 16mm
Profiles in Management Series
Color (C A)
$375.00 purchase, $150.00 rental _ #189
Includes Leader's Guide. Captures motivational techniques of three nationally known CEO's. Second part of two - part series.
Business and Economics; Guidance and Counseling; Psychology
Dist - SALENG **Prod** - SALENG 1987

On My Honor 24 MIN
U-matic / 16mm / VHS
Color (K)
$495.00, $349.00, $249.00 purchase _ #AD - 1992
Portrays Joel, who is 'on his honor' to limit his activities. Shows what happens when he gives in to a dare and learns the consequences of his actions. His parents help him to face the music and to understand the importance of keeping one's word.
Literature and Drama; Psychology; Sociology
Dist - FOTH **Prod** - FOTH

On My Honor
35mm strip / VHS / Cassette
Newbery Award - Winners Series
Color (I)
$66.00, $14.00 purchase
English Language; Literature and Drama
Dist - PELLER

On My Own, Feeling Proud 15 MIN
16mm
Color
Shows the process of preparing handicapped people, especially young people, for vocations. Includes a three part process of appraisal, education and placement accompanied by a musical theme.
Guidance and Counseling; Psychology
Dist - MILPRO **Prod** - MILPRO

On my own - the traditions of Daisy Turner 28 MIN
VHS
Color (H C G)
$295.00 purchase, $55.00 rental
Traces the life of 102 - year - old Daisy Turner, daughter of Alex Turner who was born a slave in Virginia but moved to Grafton, Vermont in 1872 to work in a saw mill. Reveals that Daisy Turner was one of 13 children whose days were spent on farm chores and evenings in storytelling and singing.
Biography; History - United States
Dist - FLMLIB **Prod** - UVT 1987

On my way to father's land 98 MIN
VHS
Color & B&W (G)
Follows the filmmaker's struggle to discover his father's history. Journeys to Vienna where the father visits his childhood home to share stories of his youth during the Nazi occupation. A second journey sees the father as a young immigrant in Palestine where he hoped to create a better world after fleeing the antisemitism of Europe, and established the Hebrew Communist Party. Directed and produced by Aner Preminger who uses interviews and archival material to discover his father's part in politics and the ideology debated back then.
Civics and Political Systems; Fine Arts; Geography - World; History - World; Religion and Philosophy; Sociology
Dist - NCJEWF

On new ground 30 MIN
VHS / U-matic
With silk wings - Asian American women at work series
Color (G)
$160.00 purchase, $50.00 rental
Shows how ten Asian American women broke the barriers of such traditional male jobs as stockbroker, police officer and welder. Discusses what they've learned about the conflicts between traditional expectations and personal aspirations. Produced and directed by Loni Ding.
Sociology
Dist - CROCUR

On - Off 4 MIN
16mm
Mini Movies - Springboard for Learning - Unit 3, Why is it Series
Color (P I)
LC 76-703326
Presents an introduction to electricity during a day of a child.
Science - Physical
Dist - MORLAT **Prod** - MORLAT 1975

On our land 55 MIN
16mm / VHS
Color (G)
$875.00, $390.00 purchase, $100.00 rental
Tells the story of an ill - treated segment of Israel's population which has largely been ignored - Palestinians who choose to remain on their land after the creation of Israel in 1948. Centers on Umm el - Fahm, the largest Arab village in Israel. Looks at how much of their land has been lost to kibbutz and moshav settlements and at discrimination regarding housing, employment and education. Produced by Antonio Caccia.
Civics and Political Systems; Fine Arts; History - World; Sociology
Dist - FIRS

On Our Own 29 MIN
16mm / U-matic / VHS
Footsteps Series
Color (A)
LC 80-707200
Explores the development of responsibility in children through the dramatization of a situation in the fictional Tristan family in which young Paul learns that he must give as well receive. Includes a brief introduction and commentary by real - life families and child development experts.
Psychology; Sociology
Dist - USNAC **Prod** - USDED

On Our Own Land 29 MIN
VHS / 16mm
Color (G)

$100.00 purchase _ #ONOOLVH
Reviews the history of the broad form deed, which allowed mining companies to stripmine Kentucky land without the permission of landowners. Focuses on the confrontations between the various parties involved. Portrays the struggle to eliminate the broad form deed.
Business and Economics; Geography - United States; Industrial and Technical Education; Social Science; Sociology
Dist - APPAL

On Our Way 60 MIN
16mm
World at War Series
Color (H C A)
LC 76-701778
History - World; Sociology
Dist - USCAN **Prod** - THAMES 1975

On Our Way - U S A, 1939 - 1942 52 MIN
U-matic / VHS / 16mm
World at War Series
Color (H C A)
States that when Roosevelt declared war on Japan, Hitler declared war on the United States, relieving the President of many of the domestic political difficulties he faced, such as rationing, blackouts and the internment of Japanese - Americans as security risks.
History - United States; History - World
Dist - MEDIAG **Prod** - THAMES 1973

On outgoing calls 17 MIN
VHS / U-matic / BETA
Telephone doctor series
Color (A PRO)
Shows techniques to improve the telemarketing abilities of salespeople, telemarketers and busy administrators. Features 10 tips that will have an immediate impact on anyone who makes outgoing calls. Leader's guide and additional support material provided. Part seven of a 16-part series of programs for training in telephone skills with Nancy Friedman, customer service consultant.
Business and Economics; Industrial and Technical Education; Psychology
Dist - TELDOC **Prod** - TELDOC 1991
EXTR

On Parade 18 MIN
16mm
Color
LC 74-706164
Describes the reflections of a young WAC on her growth as a result of her military training and experiences since joining the Women's Army Corps.
Civics and Political Systems; Sociology
Dist - USNAC **Prod** - USA 1969

On Post Safety 22 MIN
16mm
B&W
LC FIE52-2200
Analyzes the causes of common accidents in the armed forces, re - creating typical accidents in which carelessness of the individual soldier was the cause.
Civics and Political Systems; Health and Safety
Dist - USNAC **Prod** - USA 1952

On Reversing the Arms Race 55 MIN
U-matic / VHS
Briefings on Peace and the Economy - Converting from a Military to a Civilian Economy Series
Color (C)
Talks about the problems of too much military spending and discusses disarmament. Produced by the Office for East Asia and the Pacific and the NCCC.
Civics and Political Systems; Sociology
Dist - CWS

On Seeing Film - Film and Literature 17 MIN
16mm
B&W
LC FIA60-619
Made from footage filmed behind the scenes in Ceylon during production of the academy - winning film, The Bridge on the River Kwai.
Fine Arts; Literature and Drama
Dist - USC **Prod** - USC 1957

On Seven Hills they Built a City - Rome 26 MIN
16mm / U-matic / VHS
Village Life Series
Color (H C A)
Presents the diversity of the people and places of Rome.
Geography - World; Sociology
Dist - JOU **Prod** - JOU 1978

On Silent Wings 16 MIN
U-matic / VHS / 16mm
North American Species Series
Color (P I J H)
Depicts the appearance, feeding habits and adaptability of the owl. Discloses the predatory skills of this commonly unobserved species.
Science - Natural
Dist - BCNFL **Prod** - KARVF 1984

On size and shape - IV 150 MIN
VHS / U-matic
For all practical purposes - introduction to contemporary 'mathematics series
Color (G)
$130.00, $85.00 purchase
Presents a five - part module on size and shape. Includes an overview and the titles 'How Big Is Too Big,' 'It Grows and Grows,' 'Stand Up Conic' and 'It Started in Greece.' Shows geometric and numerical concepts applied to a diverse spectrum of problems from structural design to population growth and mechanical invention. Part of a series on contemporary mathematics produced by the Consortium for Mathematics and Its Applications - COMAP. On three videocassettes. Hosted by Professor Solomon Garfunkel.
Mathematics
Dist - ANNCPB

On size and shape module - how big is too big - it grows and grows - Parts 17 and 18 60 MIN
VHS / U-matic
For all practical purposes - introduction to contemporary 'mathematics series
Color (G)
$45.00, $29.95 purchase
Shows that geometric similarity and scale help mathematically balance the tensile strength of materials with the maximum size of the structure in Part 17. Demonstrates the mathematical growth of population and the importance of calculating population growth in Part 18. Parts of a five - part On Size and Shape module and a 26 - part series on contemporary mathematics. Produced by the Consortium for Mathematics and Its Applications - COMAP. Hosted by Professor Solomon Garfunkel.
Mathematics
Dist - ANNCPB

On size and shape module - stand up conic - it started in Greece - Parts 19 and 20 60 MIN
U-matic / VHS
For all practical purposes - introduction to contemporary 'mathematics series
Color (G)
$45.00, $29.95 purchase
Looks closely at the use and importance of conic sections in the design of important 20th - century inventions in Part 19. Shows how Euclidean geometry explains the congruence of triangles, the Pythagorean theorem and similarity in Part 20. Parts of a five - part On Size and Shape module and a 26 - part series on contemporary mathematics. Produced by the Consortium for Mathematics and Its Applications - COMAP. Hosted by Professor Solomon Garfunkel.
Mathematics
Dist - ANNCPB

On Size and Shape, Pt 1 - Overview 30 MIN
VHS
For all Practical Purposes Series
Color (C)
$8.00 _ #35104
Examines geometry and its relationship to natural beauty and art. Uses da Vinci's window to record proper linear perspective in art and the symmetry - based classification systems of archaeology. Discusses the Fibonacci sequence fractals and their use by many professions. The use of fractals in computer graphics is also discussed. An installment of the For All Practical Purposes Series.
Computer Science; Fine Arts; History - World; Mathematics
Dist - PSU

On Size and Shape, 2 - How Big is Too Big 30 MIN
VHS
For all Practical Purposes Series
Color (C)
$8.00 _ #35105
Examines problems related to geometric similarity and scale. Explains the relation between tensile strength of building materials and the maximum size of a structure. Discusses changes in size and proportion. Tiling patterns, two - dimensional Penrose tilings and their importance to crystallography usage are also discussed. An installment of the For All Practical Purposes Series.
Fine Arts; Industrial and Technical Education; Mathematics
Dist - PSU

On Snow White 51 MIN
U-matic / VHS / 16mm
Featurettes for Children Series
Color (I J)
Presents the story of Katka, who spins girlish fantasies about being carried off by a prince on a white horse. Tells how she must drop out of a school play of Snow White when she falls and breaks her leg while riding with Jerry, a handsome horseman. Shows that, while she can no longer prepare for the play, she has finally caught Jerry's attention and enjoys a visit by the entire cast in costume.
Literature and Drama
Dist - FI **Prod** - AUDBRF

On Stage 15 MIN
U-matic / VHS
Strawberry Square Series
Color (P)
Fine Arts
Dist - AITECH **Prod** - NEITV 1982

On Stage and Screen 10 MIN
U-matic / VHS / 16mm
Zoom Series
Color
LC 78-700144
Presents two young people who talk about their involvement in the performing arts.
Fine Arts; Sociology
Dist - FI **Prod** - WGBHTV 1977

On Stage Tonight 22 MIN
U-matic / VHS / 16mm
B&W (H C A)
Outlines aspects of theater operation and the responsibilities of the production staff. Illustrates the contribution of amateur theater and its importance in the lives of those who participate in its productions.
Fine Arts; Literature and Drama
Dist - IFB **Prod** - MADDEN 1961

On strike 25 MIN
16mm
B&W (G)
$20.00 rental
Records teachers and students mobilizing themselves and literally fighting the police and administration at San Francisco State University to set up programs for ethnic studies. Represents revolutionary filmmakers in the 1960s whose work provides a window to that period.
Civics and Political Systems; Education; Fine Arts; History - United States; Sociology
Dist - CANCIN **Prod** - SINGLE 1969

On Strike 30 MIN
16mm
Color
Presents an in - depth study on the people and the issues behind the country's longest student strike and how it relates nationally.
Business and Economics; Sociology
Dist - CANWRL **Prod** - CANWRL

On Strike 56 MIN
U-matic / VHS
Color (G)
$279.00, $179.00 purchase _ #AD - 2161
Examines the 1989 United Mine Workers' strike against the Pittston Company. Considers both sides - the coal miners believe the existence of both their union and unionism itself is at stake, the company says that it cannot meet foreign competition if costs rise. A '48 Hours' program.
Business and Economics; Psychology; Social Science
Dist - FOTH **Prod** - FOTH

On strike - a winning strategy 24 MIN
16mm / VHS
Color (G IND)
$5.00 rental
Focuses on a successful AFSCME strike among county workers in Minnesota. Stresses the importance of advanced planning, building committees, strategies to keep up morale, reaching out to other groups in the community. Produced by the American Federation of State, County and Municipal Employees.
Business and Economics; Civics and Political Systems; Social Science
Dist - AFLCIO **Prod** - AFLCIO 1988

On Strike - San Francisco State 23 MIN
16mm
B&W
Studies the people and issues behind the nation's longest student strike. Examines the real nature of the BSU and Third World demands.
Education; History - United States; Sociology
Dist - CANWRL **Prod** - CANWRL

On Sundays 26 MIN
16mm
B&W (H C A)
$60.00 rental
Uses documentary and fantasy to portray a woman in San Franciso, California. Directed by Bruce Baillie.
Fine Arts
Dist - CANCIN

On Target 66 MIN
16mm
Color
Depicts Columbus aircraft division products and activities.
Business and Economics; Industrial and Technical Education
Dist - RCKWL **Prod** - NAA

On Target 22 MIN
16mm
B&W
LC FIE58-325
Portrays the exciting story of the Strategic Air Command's annual bombing, navigational and reconnaisance competition from the viewpoint of a B - 47 crew member.
Civics and Political Systems
Dist - USNAC **Prod** - USDD 1958

On Target 21 MIN
U-matic / VHS
Color
Documents the USMC F - 4s flying mission out of Danang, South Vietnam.
Civics and Political Systems; History - United States; History - World
Dist - IHF **Prod** - IHF

On target - in tree spraying
VHS
Color (G)
$210.00 purchase _ #6 - 208 - 001P
Presents a three - part series on hydraulic tree spraying to train tree workers. Looks at the operation and calibration of hydraulic tree sprayers and their use in pesticide application. Includes an eight - page calibration manual. Produced by the National Arborist Association.
Agriculture; Health and Safety; Psychology; Science - Natural
Dist - VEP

On target - in tree spraying series
Hydraulic sprayer calibration
Hydraulic sprayer operation
Pesticide application techniques
Dist - VEP

The On - Target Interview 15 MIN
U-matic
Job Seeking Series
Color (H C A)
LC 80-706573
Explains how to prepare for an interview, telling what to bring, discussing the most frequently asked questions, and emphasizing appearance and attitude. Demystifies the interview, encouraging the job seeker to have some control over the situation.
Guidance and Counseling; Psychology
Dist - GPN **Prod** - WCETTV 1979

On Television - how to stay cool in the hot seat 93 MIN
U-matic / VHS
Color (G)
$995.00, $895.00 purchase, $250.00 rental
Features Jack Hilton who gives tips on how to handle televisions appearances.
Business and Economics; English Language; Fine Arts
Dist - VPHI **Prod** - VPHI 1985

On Television - Public Trust or Private Property 50 MIN
VHS
Color (S)
$129.00 purchase _ #820 - 9002
Addresses concerns about management of the nation's airwaves. Features Edwin Newman as host who asks if television is 'just a business.' Questions rights of precedence, the broadcaster's right to make money, or the viewer's right to receive diverse programming, whether or not broadcasters should be required to cover all sides of controversial issues of public importance.
Business and Economics; Fine Arts; Sociology
Dist - FI **Prod** - OTVL 1988

On Television - the Violence Factor 58 MIN
VHS / U-matic
Color (H C A)
Examines television as a powerful tool of commerce, reviews the findings of numerous scientific studies and Congressional hearings from the last 30 years and compares gratuitous violence to violence used in appropriate context. Explores the possible relationship between TV violence and an increase in real - life crime and the influence of TV violence on children. Shows both positive and negative impacts of TV.
Fine Arts; Literature and Drama; Psychology; Sociology
Dist - FI **Prod** - SCETV

On the Air 22 MIN
16mm
B&W
Tells how radio DJ Barry Roberts tires of his 'on the air' persona and seeks to reveal his real self in a nightclub act. Shows how Barry and some of his most devoted fans find out who they are.
Fine Arts
Dist - USC **Prod** - USC 1980

On the air - creating a smoke - free workplace 15 MIN
VHS
Color (A)
$195.00 purchase
Uses a dramatized talk show format to present arguments for a company smoke - free policy. Shows managers and supervisors how to answer objections with information and reasoning. Includes a pamphlet by the American Lung Association on how to organize a smoke - free workplace.
Guidance and Counseling; Health and Safety; Psychology
Dist - PFP **Prod** - PFP

On the Beach
VHS / U-matic
B&W
Deals with the devastating effects of nuclear war. Stars Gregory Peck, Ava Gardner, Fred Astaire and Anthony Perkins.
Civics and Political Systems; Fine Arts; Science - Physical; Sociology
Dist - IHF **Prod** - IHF

On the Border 82 MIN
16mm
Color (G)
Presents an independent production by P Torbionsson. Examines poitical and economic refugees in Central America.
Civics and Political Systems; Fine Arts; Geography - World; Sociology
Dist - FIRS

On the Border of Life 20 MIN
16mm
B&W
Presents glimpses of French biological research on the embryonic cell. Reviews the structure and function of the cell, ovum, spermatozoon, chromosome and gene. Uses experiments in the use of sexual hormones to raise the question of whether man's dream for immortality will be realized.
Science; Science - Natural
Dist - RADIM **Prod** - VEDROS

On the Boulevard 28 MIN
U-matic / VHS / 16mm
Color (A)
Examines the relationship between romance and economics. Portrays a fictional couple seeking artistic success in Hollywood. Filmed in Hollywood by Gregory Andracke, with Lawrence Hilton - Jacobs and Gloria Charles in the title roles. Written by Pamela Douglas and Martin Yarbuongh, who adapted it from an article in a Los Angeles newspaper. Encourages an examination of male - female relationships in a success - oriented society.
Fine Arts; Guidance and Counseling; Sociology
Dist - CHAMBA **Prod** - BRNSTC

On the Brink 29 MIN
16mm
Footsteps Series
Color (A)
LC 80-701392
Examines child abuse through the dramatization of a situation in the fictional Tristero family, in which Ann Marie helps a friend who is an abusing parent. Points out that there are two victims in child abuse, the parent and child. Includes a brief introduction and commentary by real - life families and child development experts.
Sociology
Dist - USNAC **Prod** - USOE 1980

On the brink - an AIDS chronicle 38 MIN
U-matic / VHS
Color (C H G A)
$515.00, $485.00 purchase _ #V439
Examines the global impact and social implications of AIDS and the barriers to the development of a vaccine. Interview international experts, top researchers and AIDS victims.
Civics and Political Systems; Health and Safety; Sociology
Dist - BARR **Prod** - CEPRO 1988
CEPRO

On the Brink - Child Abuse 23 MIN
16mm / U-matic
Footsteps Series
Color
Tells about sources of help for abusing parents. Shows how abusing parents are usually reacting to stress in their own lives.
Guidance and Counseling; Psychology; Sociology
Dist - PEREN **Prod** - PEREN

On the brink of perfection 6 MIN
VHS
Color (PRO IND A)
$295.00 purchase, $150.00 rental _ #VCO04
Uses the tools of film footage, humor and clever narration to explore the results when a minor defect ends up in the final product. Helps managers start meetings or enrich their Total Quality program. Includes Leader's Guide.
Business and Economics
Dist - EXTR

On the bus 30 MIN
U-matic / VHS
Art of being human series; Module 14
Color (C)
History - World; Literature and Drama; Religion and Philosophy
Dist - MDCC **Prod** - MDCC

On the Comet
U-matic / VHS
$29.95 purchase
Takes you on a celestial journey into the world of Jules Verne.
Literature and Drama
Dist - BESTF **Prod** - BESTF

On the community 19 MIN
U-matic / VHS / BETA
Erikson series
Color; PAL (T PRO)
PdS40, PdS48 purchase
Features part of a three - part series.
Psychology; Social Science
Dist - EDPAT

On the corner 5 MIN
16mm
B&W (G)
$15.00 rental
Surveys an urban ballet performed by street children.
Fine Arts
Dist - CANCIN **Prod** - HUDINA 1983

On the Cowboy Trail 59 MIN
16mm
Odyssey Series
Color (G)
Shows cowboy culture in southeastern Montana. Explores three households and their cattle, and the imminent demise of what remains of cowboy culture.
Agriculture; Sociology
Dist - DOCEDR **Prod** - DOCEDR 1981

On the Cowboy Trail 58 MIN
VHS / U-matic
Odyssey Series
Color
Shows a visit to a ranch in Montana to examine how modern technology and ranching methods are changing the role of the American cowboy.
Social Science; Sociology
Dist - PBS **Prod** - PBA

On the Critical Path 23 MIN
16mm
Color (G)
_ #106C 0171 503
Explains how a nuclear power plant is put together. Shows nuclear power plants can be manufactured as an exportable commodity.
History - World; Industrial and Technical Education; Social Science
Dist - CFLMDC **Prod** - NFBC 1971

On the Downbeat 29 MIN
VHS / U-matic
Color (J)
LC 84-706389
Reviews the history of jazz in Indiana from the beginnings of ragtime at the turn of the century, through the big - band era of the thirties to the flourishing bebop following World War II and to current forms.
Fine Arts; History - United States
Dist - IU **Prod** - DERKDA 1983

On the Edge 90 MIN
U-matic / VHS
Color
Follows a foursome of black, inner - city teenagers who, after minor brushes with the law, are trying to make decisions about jobs, careers, school, family, street life and themselves.
Guidance and Counseling; Sociology
Dist - WCCOTV **Prod** - WCCOTV 1982

On the edge - nature's last stand for coast redwoods 33 MIN
VHS
Color (J H C G)
$250.00 purchase, $40.00 rental _ #37987
Illustrates the 65 - million year natural history of the coastal redwood, Earth's largest living thing. Explores the attitudes and relationships of California Indians to the redwoods and shows how the Gold Rush and the population growth in California and the West resulted in 95 percent of all redwood forest areas being cut down by 1989. Traces the history of conservationist efforts to protect and preserve the trees. Produced by James Daniels for the Sempervirens Fund and the California Dept of Parks and Recreation.
Geography - United States; History - United States; Science - Natural
Dist - UCEMC

On the edge of extinction - Panthers and cheetahs 60 MIN
VHS
National Audubon Society specials series
Color; Captioned (G)
$49.95 purchase _ #NTAS - 204
Focuses on the Florida panther and African cheetah, two of the world's most endangered feline species. Shows scientific efforts in biotechnology, being tried to preserve the rare cats. Visits East Africa's Masai Mara Game Reserve, where the clash between people and animals is frequent. Also produced by Turner Broadcasting and WETA - TV. Narrated by actress Loretta Swit.
Science - Natural
Dist - PBS **Prod** - NAS 1988

On the Edge of Paradise 60 MIN
VHS / U-matic
Color (H C A)
Looks at how the future of the Caribbean is being threatened by such factors as hurricanes and volcanoes, while man hacks out banana farms, denuding the jungles, mangrove swamps become marinas and coral reefs fall victim to pollution.
Geography - World; History - World
Dist - FI **Prod** - WNETTV 1982

On the Edge of the Forest 32 MIN
U-matic / VHS / 16mm
Color
LC 80-700585
Presents author, lecturer and economist E F Schumacher's views on forests, fuel, mankind and all of Earth's resources.
Science - Natural; Social Science
Dist - BULFRG **Prod** - OLDMB 1979

On the Eighth Day 60 MIN
VHS / U-matic
Color (J)
Considers the effects of global nuclear war beyond radioactivity. Shows how scientists tested a model of the earth's atmosphere to discover that the temperatures would fall to below freezing for months. Discusses the possible destruction caused by this nuclear winter.
Sociology
Dist - FI **Prod** - BBCTV

On the eighth day 102 MIN
VHS / 16mm
Color (G)
$125.00 rental, $350.00 purchase
Features a two - part series dealing with reproductive and genetic technologies. Explores the origins and applications of in vitro fertilization. Poses disturbing questions about why these technologies are being developed and how they may affect the lives of women and society as a whole by examining the social and economic pressures which influence the manufacture and application of these new procedures. Produced by Gwynne Basen.
Fine Arts; Science - Natural; Sociology
Dist - WMEN

On the Floor 10 MIN
Videoreel / VT2
Janaki Series
Color
Physical Education and Recreation
Dist - PBS **Prod** - WGBHTV

On the fragility of existence 5 MIN
16mm
B&W (G)
$25.00 rental
Features a short lyric and horrific abstract film - essay. Uses illustrations from a book on surgical techniques as a springboard to examine the ephemeral nature of the fleshy entanglements of humanity.
Fine Arts; Psychology
Dist - CANCIN **Prod** - SCHLEM 1992
FLMKCO

On the fringes of Indian society 52 MIN
16mm
Phantom India series; Part 6
Color
Views groups living in India for centuries, yet who are either excluded from Indian society or who refuse to become a part of it. Includes glimpses at the Bonda, an aboriginal tribe, the Ashran in Pondicherry, the Jews in Cochin, the Catholics and the Pharsees in Bombay.
Geography - World; Sociology
Dist - NYFLMS **Prod** - NYFLMS 1967

On the Fringes of Science 145 MIN
U-matic
University of the Air Series
Color (J H C A)
$750.00 purchase, $250.00 rental
Profiles the individuals who are researching and experimenting on the borderlands of science. Program contains a series of five cassettes 29 minutes each.
Science
Dist - CTV **Prod** - CTV 1977

On the Ground 15 MIN
16mm / U-matic / VHS
Place to Live Series
Color (I J H)
Looks at small invertebrates, such as slugs and woodlice, which live under stones, dead wood or litter. Includes other life forms which live at ground level, such as toadstools and ground beetles.
Science - Natural
Dist - JOU **Prod** - GRATV

On the homefront 114 MIN
VHS
March of time - America at war series
B&W (G)
$24.95 purchase _ #S02122
Presents the first installment of a six - part series of newsreel excerpts covering the American effort in World War II. Segments include 'Our America at War,' 'When Air Raids Strike,' 'The FBI Front.'
History - United States
Dist - UILL

On the House - Restoring a Victorian House 97 MIN
VHS
Color (S)
$29.95 purchase _ #781 - 9043
Goes through each detailed step of the restoration of Number 50, a once dirty and neglected Victorian house. Teaches how to restore a beautiful plaster ceiling hidden under years of paint and grime, how to replace a floor and everything in between.
Fine Arts; Geography - World; Home Economics; Sociology
Dist - FI **Prod** - BBCTV 1989

On the Island of Taveuni 17 MIN
16mm
South Pacific Series
Color (I J H C)
Provides a visit to a copra plantation, located on Taveuni, one of the Fiji Islands. Shows the production and processing of copra and coconuts. Depicts the life of the planters and native and East Indian workers on the prosperous plantation.
Geography - World; Social Science
Dist - MMP **Prod** - MMP 1958

On the Job 19 MIN
VHS / U-matic
Jobs - Seeking, Funding, Keeping Series
Color (H)
Tells how Sandy has a hard time at her first job on a dockyard welding crew and how another employee helps her out.
Guidance and Counseling
Dist - AITECH **Prod** - MDDE 1980

On the Job 30 MIN
VHS / 16mm
Color (H)
$189.00 purchase _ #MC111V
Tells new workers what to expect on their first job. Discloses how new workers are evaluated. Includes instructor's guide and word games with job related themes.
Guidance and Counseling; Psychology
Dist - JISTW

On the job 25 MIN
VHS
Color (H A)
$189.00 purchase _ #MC5000V
Presents a comprehensive look at what to expect and how to handle a first job. Stresses the importance of making good impressions from day one. Uses humorous scenarios to show what and what not to do. Includes a manual.
Psychology
Dist - CAMV

On the job 18 MIN
VHS / U-matic
Color (H C G)
$245.00, $295.00 purchase, $50.00 rental
Teaches students good job behavior, how to survive the critical first days on the job and appropriate grooming and dress for work.
Education; Guidance and Counseling
Dist - NDIM **Prod** - LAWRN 1989

On - the - Job Assessment 13 MIN
U-matic / 35mm strip
Assessing Employee Potential Series
Color
Shows how to consider all requirements of a job to be filled and make maximum use of on - the - job observations to determine suitability for promotion.
Business and Economics; Psychology
Dist - RESEM **Prod** - RESEM

On - the - job housekeeping procedures 7 MIN
U-matic / BETA / VHS
Color (IND G)
$295.00 purchase _ #800 - 16
Trains all personnel in good housekeeping procedures while dramatically highlighting the hazards of careless, disorganized work practices.
Health and Safety; Industrial and Technical Education; Psychology
Dist - ITSC **Prod** - ITSC

On - the - Job Survival Skills
VHS / 35mm strip
$119.00 purchase _ #SB428 for filmstrip, $139.00 purchase _ #013 -
Describes survival skills fundamental to success as an employee and points out regular stresses and challenges at work.
Business and Economics; Guidance and Counseling
Dist - CAREER **Prod** - CAREER

On - the - Job Training 30 MIN
U-matic / VHS
Training the Trainer Series
Color (T)
Points out the difference between classroom and on - the - job training, highlighting the use of job aids.
Education; Psychology
Dist - ITCORP **Prod** - ITCORP

On - the - Job Training 60 MIN
VHS
Systems Operations Series
Color (PRO)
$600.00 - $1500.00 purchase _ #OTOJT
Examines issues to consider when planning and implementing on - the - job training - OJT - in process plants. Explains the basic steps in planning effective OJT. Includes performing a task analysis and developing training objectives and checklists. Part of a seventeen - part series on systems operations. Includes ten textbooks and an instructor guide to support four hours of instruction.
Education; Industrial and Technical Education; Psychology
Dist - NUSTC **Prod** - NUSTC

On the level communication skills - Video I 15 MIN
BETA / U-matic / VHS
Communication series
Color (G)
$495.00 purchase, $110.00 rental
Focuses on receptive skills - getting information, observing, listening and empathizing - and expressive skills - giving information, questioning, describing, concluding - in communications. Part one of a three - part series on communication.
Business and Economics; English Language; Social Science
Dist - AMEDIA **Prod** - AMEDIA

On the Line 13 MIN
16mm
Color (A)
Tells the story of a factory worker who resists going for a health checkup because of a great fear that he might have cancer. Shows that his gradual turnabout is climaxed when a representative of the American Cancer Society speaks to the plant's employees urging them to have regular checkups. Features James Broderick and all - pro football star, Jack Pardee.
Health and Safety; Science; Sociology
Dist - AMCS **Prod** - AMCS

On the Line 50 MIN
16mm / U-matic / VHS
Color (A)
Examines contemporary problems of the American economy. Discusses how these problems affect the lives of people and their communities.
Business and Economics
Dist - CNEMAG **Prod** - CNEMAG 1977

On the margin 30 MIN
VHS
Perspective - agriculture - series
Color; PAL; NTSC (G)
PdS90, PdS105 purchase
Looks at how a 'wasteland' in northwest Scotland has been transformed to provide food and employment.
Geography - World; Science - Natural
Dist - CFLVIS **Prod** - LONTVS

On the Marriage Broker Joke as Cited by Sigmund Freud in Wit and its Relation to the Unconscious, or Can the Avant - garde Artist be Wholed 17.5 MIN
16mm
Color (C)
$532.00
Experimental film by George Owen (aka Owen Land).
Fine Arts
Dist - AFA **Prod** - AFA 1981

On the menu 30 MIN
VHS
Color (H)
$139.00 purchase _ #31385 - 126
Looks at Creole light cuisine. Discusses heritage vegetables, wholesome and quick breakfasts, how to buy and cook fish, what's new on the school lunch menu.
Health and Safety; Home Economics; Social Science
Dist - GA **Prod** - TURNED

On the Menu 30 MIN
VHS / U-matic
CNN Special Reports Series
(G J C)
$129 purchase _ #31385 - 851
Shows how to prepare healthy foods that are pleasing to the eye and the palate.
Health and Safety; Home Economics
Dist - CHUMAN

On the Mines 13 MIN
16mm
B&W (H C A)
LC 76-703920
Explores the world of the South African mines in order to bring an understanding and appreciation of what it means to labor in the mines of South Africa.
Business and Economics; Geography - World; Health and Safety; History - World; Industrial and Technical Education; Sociology
Dist - BFPS **Prod** - BFPS 1976

On the Money Series

All things beautiful	30 MIN
Baby makes three	30 MIN
Bills, bills, bills	30 MIN
Give and take	30 MIN
Home Sweet Home	30 MIN
Investments - They're Debatable	30 MIN
Just in Case	30 MIN
More Precious than Gold	30 MIN
On Your Own	30 MIN
Risky Business	30 MIN
Smart Money	30 MIN
Starting Small	30 MIN
Taking Stock	30 MIN

Dist - CORF

On the move 30 MIN
VHS
Nature by design series
Color (A PRO C)
PdS65 purchase _ Unavailable in USA and Canada
Aims to create understanding of what it means to be on the move in the area of design. Part of a series which utilizes a visual style blending natural history footage, graphics and video effects - moving back and forth between science and nature. Emphasizes that good design is essential for the success of any product, in the natural world and today's high-tech world.
Psychology
Dist - BBCENE

On the Move 19 MIN
16mm
Color
LC 79-701472
Presents a profile of the 4 - H movement, depicting various 4 - H projects, communications programs, camp and special activities, and support services.
Agriculture; Physical Education and Recreation
Dist - CENTWO **Prod** - ADAIB 1979

On the Move 28 MIN
16mm
Color
LC 74-703084
Explains many aspects of packaging and shipping radioactive materials, including the extreme concern for safety in normal and accident environments. Emphasizes the package testing program for highly radioactive materials and shows the accident environment that accident - resistant packages are designed to protect against.
Health and Safety; Industrial and Technical Education; Science - Physical
Dist - USNAC **Prod** - USNRC 1974

On the Move - Careers in Transportation 13 MIN
16mm
Working Worlds Series
Color (I J H)
LC 75-701537
Explores the variety of careers available in transportation.
Guidance and Counseling; Psychology
Dist - FFORIN **Prod** - OLYMPS 1974

On the Nature of Love
VHS / Cassette
(G)
$29.95, $9.95 purchase
Features Krishnamurti. Presents a psychological and spiritual examination of love, suffering and death.
Psychology; Religion and Philosophy; Sociology
Dist - BKPEOP **Prod** - MFV

On the Night Stage 100 MIN
16mm
B&W
Stars William S Hart as a soft - hearted bandit who is tamed by a dance - hall girl.
Fine Arts
Dist - KITPAR **Prod** - UNKNWN 1915

On the Nose 13 MIN
16mm / U-matic / VHS
Human Senses Series
Color (P I)
Employs animation to show how odor molecules released into the air enter the nose and are picked up by smell receptors that carry the information to the brain.
Science - Natural
Dist - NGS **Prod** - NGS 1982

On the Open Sea 30 MIN
BETA / VHS
Under Sail Series
Color
Explains how to use weight and balance to control boat direction and speed. Focuses upon navigation.
Physical Education and Recreation
Dist - CORF **Prod** - WGBHTV

On the problem of the autonomy of art in bourgeois society, or splice 23 MIN
16mm
Color (G)
Represents, reconstructs and reinterprets a panel presentation on the subject of 'Avant - Garde Film Practice,' by the Pacific Cine Centre as part of National Film Week in March 1986. Features the first five panelists offering views on individualism - Snow; new narrative - Gruben; eros and aestheticism - Rimmer; and anti - marxism - psychonanalysis - semiotics - audience - Wieland and McLaren. The second half is devoted to the performance - screening - direct action conducted by Razutis which is entitled 'Splice.' This re - creation contains traces of the original film, most of which was destroyed in the projector bleach bath.
Fine Arts
Dist - CANCIN **Prod** - RAZUTI 1986

On the Road 15 MIN
U-matic / VHS
It's Your Move Series
Color (P)
Depicts a young boy selecting a bicycle and practicing stops, signals and turns before he drives in street traffic.
Health and Safety
Dist - AITECH **Prod** - WETN 1977

On the road 30 MIN
VHS
Tales from the map room
Color; PAL (H C A)
PdS65 purchase; Not available in the United States
Presents actors who re - create significant events in the history of cartography. Features road atlases that first appeared in the nineteenth century. Third in a series of six programs.
Geography - World
Dist - BBCENE

On the road going through and You can drive the big rigs 30 MIN
VHS
Color (G)
$50.00 purchase
Offers two productions from 1987 - 1989. Provides a portrait of a fragment of rural life in Iowa with a composite of many small towns that implies a unified single town. Interweaves complex images and brief interviews with local people. You Can Drive The Big Rigs is an impressionistic documentary of small town cafes in the rural Midwest.
Fine Arts; Geography - United States; Geography - World; Sociology
Dist - CANCIN **Prod** - PIERCE

On the Road - in the City 25 MIN
16mm
Color (H A)
Shows city driving situations and discusses proper turning procedures, parking, route alterations, accidents, driver illness, and night driving.
Health and Safety
Dist - VISUCP **Prod** - VISUCP

On the Road - in the Country 26 MIN
16mm
Color (H A)
Discusses rural driving, focusing on blocked roads, passenger illness, bus breakdown, railroad hazards, convoy driving and freeway driving.
Health and Safety
Dist - VISUCP **Prod** - VISUCP

On the Road - Pt 2 50 MIN
VHS / 16mm
At the Wheel - Unedited Version - Series
Color (S)
$750.00, $79.00 purchase _ #101 - 9107
Investigates a matter of increasing public concern, death and destruction on our roads and highways. Examines four aspects of the problem of drunk driving. Part 2 of the four part series documents with dramatic immediacy death and destruction 'on the road.' Unedited version.
Health and Safety; Industrial and Technical Education; Psychology; Sociology
Dist - FI **Prod** - NFBC 1987

On the road - the light side of lifting 22 MIN
8mm cartridge / VHS / BETA / U-matic
Color; PAL (IND G)
$395.00 purchase _ #PPI - 001
Reveals that there is no 'single' right way to lift because most objects are different in size, shape and weight - but the basic procedures of lifting correctly do remain the same. Presents four easy - to - understand rules to help employees lighten a load and remove stress from the back and reduce the risk of back injury. Includes a leader's guide and test materials for duplication.
Health and Safety
Dist - BNA

On the Road to Find Out 70 MIN
16mm
Time of Youth Series
Color
LC 73-700898
Explores the day - to - day experiences of five Boston teenagers to help reveal their attitudes about their lives, their futures and the people around them.
Psychology
Dist - WCVBTV **Prod** - WCVBTV 1973

On the Road to Manufacturing Excellence 40 MIN
VHS / 16mm
Color (PRO)
$300.00 purchase, $150.00 rental
Looks at Motorola, Allan - Bradley, Xerox and Hewlett - Packard as manufacturing role models.
Business and Economics; Psychology
Dist - VICOM **Prod** - VICOM 1990

On the Road with Duke Ellington 55 MIN
16mm
Bell Telephone Hour Series
Color
LC FIA68-109
An informal study of American composer - conductormusician Duke Ellington. Follows him during a performance, on tour and in moments of relaxation as he reminisces about his family and background.
Biography; Fine Arts
Dist - DIRECT **Prod** - NBCTV 1967

On the rocks 30 MIN
VHS
Wall to wall series
Color (A)
PdS65 purchase
Examines stone as a building material in Kinver, Staffordshire, and Drum Castle, Scotland. Examines the vast range of dwelling places and buildings which can be found in the United Kingdom and abroad, and charts their history and evolution. Looks at the different building materials used through the centuries and compares and contrasts British buildings with similar structures found abroad.
Fine Arts; Industrial and Technical Education
Dist - BBCENE

On the Rocks 29 MIN
16mm / U-matic / VHS
Color (J)
Offers a lighthearted perspective on rock gymnastics, the sport which applies the natural grace and rhythm of gymnastics to the art of rock climbing. Reveals the motivation and climbing methods of some of the world's best climbers. Filmed during climbs in California, Colorado and Wyoming.
Physical Education and Recreation
Dist - PFP **Prod** - PFP

On the rocks 30 MIN
VHS
Tales from the map room
Color; PAL (H C A)
PdS65 purchase; Not available in the United States
Features actors who re - create significant events in the history of cartography. Presents early maps as valuable tools for avoiding disasters at sea. Second in a series of six programs.
Geography - World
Dist - BBCENE

On the roof 15 MIN
U-matic / VHS
En Francais series
Color (H C A)
Involves a chief electrician and a chimney repairman.
Foreign Language; Geography - World
Dist - AITECH **Prod** - MOFAFR 1970

On the Run 22 MIN
U-matic / VHS / 16mm
Color (J)
LC 80-700586
Presents running trainer Arthur Lydiard and the world competition runners who use his program as they comment about long - distance mountain running and its resulting increase in their stamina and the pleasures of roaming over the varied terrain. Features scenes of New Zealand.
Physical Education and Recreation
Dist - PFP **Prod** - EVRARD 1980

On the Run 60 MIN
U-matic / VHS
Color
Gives a first - hand account of the growing runaway problem from both a local and national perspective. Follows the stories of three runaways and interviews others face - to - face on the streets of New York, Los Angeles, Denver and Florida.
Sociology
Dist - WCCOTV **Prod** - WCCOTV

On the Run 55 MIN
U-matic / VHS
Color (H C A)
Looks at the issue of runaway children in our society. Features encounters with more than a dozen runaways, who are usually female, trying to escape an abusive home situation. From the Moore Report Series.
Home Economics; Sociology
Dist - IU **Prod** - WCCOTV 1983

On the Run 57 MIN
16mm / U-matic / VHS
Color (P I)
Tells the story of a holiday that becomes a series of highly charged narrow escapes when an attempt is made to kidnap the son of a visiting African potentate. Shows how the children pit their wits against the would - be kidnappers.
Literature and Drama
Dist - LUF **Prod** - SF 1972

On the Run 27 MIN
U-matic / VHS / 16mm
Color
Examines the reasons why kids run away. Presents actual runaways who provide insights into the situations that caused them to leave home and what they expected to find elsewhere. Shows youth facilities designed to help young people cope with life on the run.
Sociology
Dist - CORF **Prod** - MCBRID

On the Run - Growing Up with Alcohol 20 MIN
16mm / VHS
Color (H A)
$395.00, $495.00 purchase, $75.00 rental _ #8190
Focuses on Doug Smith, 51 - year - old adult child of an alcoholic and former alcoholic himself. Illuminates issues concerning children raised in alcoholic homes.
Guidance and Counseling; Psychology; Sociology
Dist - AIMS **Prod** - KENCOM 1990

On the Safe Side 20 MIN
16mm
Color
Outlines the necessary precautions and uses the message as an easily remembered word to cover the sequences that must be followed to make apparatus safe in a high voltage research environment.
Health and Safety; Industrial and Technical Education; Science; Science - Physical
Dist - UKAEA **Prod** - UKAEA 1967

On the Seven Seas 22 MIN
16mm
Color
Describes the world - wide exchange of goods which make shipping an all - important factor in international trade and commerce. Shows the importance of Danish shipping for the economy of the country.
Business and Economics; Geography - World; Social Science
Dist - AUDPLN **Prod** - RDCG

On the Seventh Day 20 MIN
16mm
B&W (I)
Shows a Jewish family preparing for and celebrating their Sabbath.
Religion and Philosophy
Dist - NYU **Prod** - NYU 1962

On the Seventh Day She Wore it 15 MIN
Videoreel / VT2
Umbrella Series
Color
Home Economics; Psychology; Social Science
Dist - PBS **Prod** - KETCTV

On the shady side of the street 30 MIN
VHS
America in World War II - The home front series
Color (G)
$49.95 purchase _ #AWWH - 105
Covers American troops' advances into New Guinea and Sicily, as well as the around - the - clock bombing of Germany. Reveals that American social mores, especially in sex, were changing during the war. Shows that black markets, hoarding and other social problems were becoming more common as the war went on. Narrated by Eric Sevareid.
History - United States
Dist - PBS

On the Shoulders of Giants 60 MIN
VHS / U-matic
Smithsonian World Series
Color (J)
Journeys to the Galapagos and Cook Islands with naturalist David Steadman. Shows exotic creatures and cultures. Sheds new light on the work of Charles Darwin and the mysteries of evolution.
History - World; Science; Science - Natural
Dist - WETATV **Prod** - WETATV

On the Shoulders of Giants 30 MIN
U-matic / VHS
(G)
Features two Nebraska research professors, Bernice Slote, English, and Norman Cromwell, chemistry, who discuss the importance of pure and applied research to Nebraska and Nebraskans. Covers medical and urban research as well as the two researchers' specialties.
Education; English Language; Science; Science - Physical
Dist - GPN **Prod** - NETV 1979

On the Side of Life 9 MIN
16mm
Color
Features a folk music background and fast - changing scenes of nursing activities that emphasize the challenge and involvement of the profession.
Health and Safety
Dist - JAJ **Prod** - JAJ 1970

On the stand - testifying in court 29 MIN
VHS
Color (A)
$525.00 purchase
Prepares managers or staff members to effectively testify in court or in hearings. Highlights the importance of telling the truth, being candid with the attorney, and listening to questions before attempting to answer them. Includes one sample user's reinforcement guide with purchase.
Business and Economics; Civics and Political Systems; Education
Dist - COMFLM **Prod** - COMFLM

On the Surface
16mm
B&W
Discusses the geometry of surfaces. Examines the problem of finding local maxima and minima of a function of two variables.
Mathematics
Dist - OPENU **Prod** - OPENU

On the Surface of Things 8 MIN
16mm
Discovery Series
Color
Explores a facet of chemical research being conducted to gain a better understanding of the way atoms and molecules act at the interface of two materials.
Science; Science - Natural
Dist - UTORMC **Prod** - UTORMC

On the Third Day 27 MIN
VHS
Color (G)
Shows many of the 18,000 native species of flowering plants of South Africa and explains how they are protected and propagated. Available for free loan from the distributor.
Geography - World; Science - Natural
Dist - AUDPLN

On the threshold of change 20 MIN
VHS
Diversity series
Color; CC (C PRO)
$425.00 purchase, $150.00 rental
Focuses on the fundamental diversity issues of conflict resolution, communication styles and respecting those who are different. Features diversity experts, human resources professionals, managers and employees who outline the main messages. Part one of a four- part series with segments specifically addressing gender, sexual orientation, race, ethnicity, language, religion, age and physical ability as workplace issues. Includes facilitator's guide and handouts. Produced by Quality Media Resources.
Business and Economics; Psychology; Social Science; Sociology
Dist - VTCENS
EXTR

On the threshold of change - Part 1 20 MIN
VHS
Diversity series
Color (PRO IND A)
$425.00 purchase, $150.00 rental _ QMR05A
Utilizes dramatization to teach management of fears and prejudice in the workplace. Discusses issues of gender and sexual orientation, and matters related to EEO and ADA. Part one of a four - part series.
Business and Economics; Sociology
Dist - EXTR

On the threshold of change - Pt 1 17 MIN
VHS
The diversity series
Color (PRO IND COR A)
$425.00 purchase, $150.00 rental, $50.00 preview
Focuses on conflict and communication as essential components of positive working relationships. Since each employee brings values, experiences and preconceived notions to the workplace, conflict resolution is dramatized in order to meet the needs of a diverse work force.
Sociology
Dist - VIDART

On the Threshold of the Future 30 MIN
U-matic
Changing Music Series
Color
Fine Arts
Dist - PBS **Prod** - WGBHTV

On the Tiles 16 MIN
16mm
Color (P I)
Details what occurs when Alice the chimp escapes from the children's grandmother's house and climbs on to the roof of the house next door. Reveals what happens when she climbs down the chimney.
Literature and Drama
Dist - LUF **Prod** - LUF 1977

On the Totem Trail 30 MIN
U-matic / VHS
Color (I J H)
Tells how a school assignment helps two students discover the rich heritage of the Pacific Northwest Indian tribes. Visits an Indian museum, a working artist, and an Indian village.
Social Science
Dist - JOU **Prod** - CANBC

On the Track of the Bog People 35 MIN
16mm
Color
Shows the method Danish archeologists employ in tracing the habits and patterns of daily life of the people of the Iron Age.
History - World; Science - Physical
Dist - AUDPLN **Prod** - RDCG

On the Track to the Midnight Sun 34 MIN
16mm
Color
LC FIA66-1392
Depicts a train ride through the northern part of Sweden where the summer sun shines twenty - four hours a day. Pictures the age - old customs and folk dances of the Lapps.
Geography - World; Social Science; Sociology
Dist - SWNTO **Prod** - SSRR 1955

On the tracks of the wild otter - The Mouse's tale 83 MIN
VHS
BBC wildlife specials series
Color (G)
$24.95 purchase _ #TRA05
Tells the story of wild otters in the Shetland Islands of Great Britain. Follows the adventures of four species of mice in and around a country cottage in Wiltshire, England.
Literature and Drama; Science - Natural
Dist - HOMVIS **Prod** - BBCTV 1990

On the trail of the bighorn 24 MIN
VHS
Wild refuge series
Color (G)
$39.95 purchase
Follows the elusive bighorn sheep into the remote outback of Utah, Nevada and the Rockies. Observes their habits successfully, even though they can spot a human up to five miles away. Part of a thirteen - part series on the North American wilderness. Each episode documents a different area and shows how animal species cope with their surroundings to survive.

Geography - United States; Geography - World; Science - Natural
Dist - CNEMAG **Prod** - HOBELP 1976

On the Twelfth Day 21 MIN
16mm
Color (J H)
LC FIA67-1871
Dramatizes the traditional English folksong 'The Twelve Days Of Christmas,' in which a lover brings his lady an unusual assortment of gifts.
Fine Arts; Religion and Philosophy
Dist - FI **Prod** - ARTHUR 1964

On the US nuclear highway 10 MIN
VHS
Magnum eye series
Color (G)
$125.00 purchase, $30.00 rental
Juxtaposes the surreal Southwest, with its Native American history and rituals, and the incongruous stretch of nuclear test sites that line Interstate 25, the 1000 mile highway that crosses Colorado, Wyoming and New Mexico. Interviews ranchers and farmers who disclose unexplained inconsistencies with crops and livestock. Records the Gathering of Nations Pow Wow, Trinity Site and White Sands missile base. Directed by Rene Burri. Part of a series by photographers from the Magnum Photo Agency.
Agriculture; Fine Arts; Geography - United States; Social Science
Dist - FIRS **Prod** - MIYAKE 1993

On the Wallaby Track 10 MIN
16mm
Australian Eye Series
Color
LC 80-700786
Presents a painting by Frederick Mc Cubbin. Illustrates the artist's adaptations of the French Impressionists' techniques of brushwork to make his figures meld naturally into their atmospheric space.
Fine Arts; Geography - World
Dist - TASCOR **Prod** - FLMAUS 1978

On the Waterfront 18 MIN
16mm
B&W
An abridged version of the motion picture On The Waterfront. Portrays what happens when a member of New York's longshoreman's union defies its leaders by testifying against them after his brother is killed. Stars Marlon Brando, Eva - Marie Saint and Karl Malden.
Fine Arts
Dist - TIMLIF **Prod** - CPC 1982

On the Waterfront 108 MIN
16mm
B&W
Portrays a broken - down ex - prizefighter who must decide whether to testify against his fellow longshoremen. Stars Marlon Brando, Rod Steiger, Eva Marie Saint, Karl Malden and Lee J Cobb.
Fine Arts
Dist - TIMLIF **Prod** - CPC 1957

On the waterways - Big Blue Collar River 54 MIN
VHS
Always a river video collection series
Color (G)
Contact distributor about rental cost _ #N92 - 035
Follows the Driftwood's trip down the Ohio River through the narration of Jason Robards.
Geography - United States
Dist - INDI

On the waterways series
Presents a 13 - part series on North American waterways. Includes the titles - The North Atlantic - Cradle of the Continent; The Western Gulf Coast - From the Border to the Bayou; Florida - Too Much, Too Fast; The Upper Mississippi - Mark Twain's River; The Lower Mississippi - The Working River; The South Atlantic - A Coast of Constrasts; Lake Superior - Hiawatha's Gitche Gumee; The Hudson River and the Erie Canal - America's Historic Waters; The Eastern Great Lakes - The Fragile Bond; The Mid - Atlantic - The Eastern Shore; Lake Michigan and the Illinois River - The Midwest River; The Ohio - The Big Blue Collar River; Tennessee - Tombigbee Waterway - Slicing Through the South.
On the waterways series 715 MIN
Dist - INSTRU

On the waterways series
The Eastern Great Lakes - the fragile bond 55 MIN
Florida - too much, too fast 55 MIN
The Hudson River and the Erie Canal - America's historic waters 55 MIN
Lake Michigan and the Illinois River - the Midwest Riviera 55 MIN
Lake Superior - Hiawatha's Gitche Gumee 55 MIN
The Lower Mississippi - the working river 55 MIN
The Mid - Atlantic - the eastern shore 55 MIN
The North Atlantic - cradle of the continent 55 MIN
The Ohio - the big blue collar river 55 MIN
The South Atlantic - a coast of contrasts 55 MIN
Tennessee - Tombigbee Waterway - slicing through the South 55 MIN
The Upper Mississippi - Mark Twain's river 55 MIN
The Western Gulf Coast - from the border to the bayou 55 MIN
Dist - SVIP

On the way 30 MIN
VHS
Gospel of Mark series
Color (R G)
$39.95 purchase _ #GMAR6
Examines the structures and the key messages of the Gospel of Mark, as well as examining the life and times of Mark, according to the teachings of the Roman Catholic Church. Features Biblical scholar Father Eugene LaVerdiere, SSS. Part six of ten parts.
Literature and Drama; Religion and Philosophy
Dist - CTNA **Prod** - CTNA

On the Way 31 MIN
16mm
Color
Documents development problems in general and transport facilities in particular in Malawi, Lebanon, Iran and Afghanistan.
Geography - World; Social Science
Dist - AUDPLN **Prod** - RDCG

On the wings of Hermes - Greek Americans and the media 28 MIN
VHS
Illuminations series
Color (G R)
#V - 1049
Explores the growing influence of Greek Americans in mass media. Shows that ethnically - oriented media are also becoming more common. Interviews Greek Americans in the media world, including TV correspondent Ike Pappas.
Biography; Fine Arts; Sociology
Dist - GOTEL **Prod** - GOTEL 1990

On the wire 85 MIN
16mm
Color; PAL (G)
Portrays a soldier in the South African Defence Force who has served eight years and is now traumatized by the atrocities he has seen and committed. Records his increasing inability to function and dangerous isolation in the rigidly Calvinist community where he and his wife live. Directed by Elaine Proctor. Contact distributor about price and availibility outside the United Kingdom.
Fine Arts; Psychology; Sociology
Dist - BALFOR **Prod** - NATLFM 1990

On their honor 30 MIN
16mm
Color; B&W (G)
$30.00 rental
Portrays prison life at the Hocking Honor prison camp. Takes an in - depth look at the neverending monotony of their days. Filmmaker Brian Patrick spent time living with the men and became so bored with the mundane life and shy inmates that he was compelled to be more aggressive, directing and setting up events for the camera and interviewing the prisoners about their past and hopes for the future.
Fine Arts; Sociology
Dist - CANCIN

On their Way - the Courage Story 18 MIN
16mm
Color
LC 81-700340
Shows how the rehabilitative services at the Courage Center in Golden Valley, Minnesota, affect the lives of people with disabilities, helping them on their way to more active and productive lives.
Education; Health and Safety; History - United States
Dist - COURGE **Prod** - COURGE 1980

On this Rock 15 MIN
BETA / VHS
Color (G)
Looks at the archaeological findings beneath Saint Peter's Basilica in Rome which have led researchers to the authentic tomb of Saint Peter.
Geography - World; Religion and Philosophy; Sociology
Dist - DSP **Prod** - DSP

On this rock - a look inside the Vatican 26 MIN
VHS
Color (G R)
$49.95 purchase _ #S02196
Visits Vatican City, focusing on the elements that make it an independent state - diplomats, post office, telephone system, police force, and more. Considers the dual spiritual and temporal roles of the pope in running the Vatican.
Civics and Political Systems; Religion and Philosophy
Dist - UILL

On to Jerusalem 30 MIN
VHS
Gospel of Mark series
Color (R G)
$39.95 purchase _ #GMAR7
Examines the structures and the key messages of the Gospel of Mark, as well as examining the life and times of Mark, according to the teachings of the Roman Catholic Church. Features Biblical scholar Father Eugene LaVerdiere, SSS. Part seven of ten parts.
Literature and Drama; Religion and Philosophy
Dist - CTNA **Prod** - CTNA

On to the Bay 25 MIN
16mm
Color (J H C)
Traces the development of the Hudson Bay Railway; features interviews with surveyor J. L. Charles, who revisits the line.
History - World; Social Science
Dist - QUEENU **Prod** - QUAF 1976

On to the Bay 25 MIN
16mm
Color
LC 77-702597
Presents the story of the building of the Hudson's Bay Railway across the northern Manitoba tundra of Canada.
History - World; Social Science
Dist - CANFDC **Prod** - CNR 1977

On to the Polar Sea - a Yukon Adventure 50 MIN
16mm
(G)
Shows a 15 day whitewater canoe expedition on the Bonnet Plume and Peel rivers in the Upper Yukon of Canada.
Geography - World; Physical Education and Recreation
Dist - CFLMDC **Prod** - NFBC

On to tomorrow series
Beyond Earth 29 MIN
Do no harm 29 MIN
Energy systems 30 MIN
In control or in fear 29 MIN
A Time to Live 29 MIN
A World Society 29 MIN
Dist - UMITV

On top of the whale 83 MIN
VHS
Color (G) (MULTILINGUAL WITH ENGLISH SUBTITLES)
$29.95 purchase
Offers a parody of imperialism, language and culture. Follows a pair of anthropologists who attempt to study two Indians from an undiscovered tribe. Directed by Raul Ruiz.
Fine Arts; History - World; Literature and Drama; Sociology
Dist - KINOIC

On top of the world series
Argentina 30 MIN
Barbados 37 MIN
Dominican Republic 24 MIN
Grenada 24 MIN
Isle of Man 24 MIN
Jamaica 24 MIN
Taiwan 30 MIN
Dist - SVIP

On track video 40 MIN
VHS
Color (H C G)
$118.75 purchase _ #458500 - X
Supports a course combining real conversational language with humor. Features comedy skits with humor to which students can relate and facilitates class discussion. Written by Susan Park, Gerald Bates, Anna Thibeault and Mary Lee Wholey.
Education; English Language; Literature and Drama
Dist - OUP

On Trial - Criminal Justice 75 MIN
16mm
Color (J H)
Depicts the Maryland workshop on crime and correction, convened with the goal of promoting needed reform in the penal system. Explains that the eight - day conference, designed to bring confrontation, communication and revelation, brought together more than 100 judges, prison officials, correctional officers, parole supervisors, policemen, lawyers, private citizens, ex - convicts and prison inmates.
Civics and Political Systems; Sociology
Dist - WBCPRO **Prod** - WBCPRO 1970

On trial - the William Kennedy Smith case 50 MIN
VHS
ABC News collection series
Color (G)
$29.98 purchase _ #6302461987
Shows how a charge of rape against a member of one of the United States' most prominent political family leads to a dramatic trial in a Palm Beach, Florida courtroom.
Civics and Political Systems
Dist - INSTRU **Prod** - ABCNEW 1992

On Two Wheels 29 MIN
VHS / 16mm
Color (G)
$55.00 rental _ #ONTW - 000
Helps the new motorcyclist identify potential hazards, predict possible points of conflict and decide how to avoid dangerous situations by executing the proper maneuvers.
Industrial and Technical Education
Dist - PBS

On We Go
U-matic / VHS / 16mm
Color
Demonstrates a selection of teaching points about English as a second language through scenes in the daily life of four young teenagers who are away from home for the first time.
English Language
Dist - NORTNJ **Prod** - NORTNJ

On Wings of Love 36 MIN
16mm
Color
LC 77-701449
Looks at the personal lives of a couple preparing for overseas service with Mission Aviation Fellowship.
Guidance and Counseling; Religion and Philosophy
Dist - ECRF **Prod** - ECRF 1977

On with Your Life 13 MIN
16mm
Color (C A)
Takes the viewer behind the scenes during the production of the television show 'MISSION - IMPOSSIBLE' where the cast discusses the importance of an annual health checkup, including the procto. Features Peter Graves, Greg Morris, Peter Lupus and others from the 'MISSION - IMPOSSIBLE' cast.
Health and Safety; Science; Sociology
Dist - AMCS **Prod** - AMCS

On Working 30 MIN
U-matic / VHS
Color
Documents the nature of work in America. Offers insight into the lives of working men and women and the emotional, psychological and social factors which influence career decisions and self image. Features commentary by Studs Terkel.
Business and Economics; Psychology; Sociology
Dist - OHUTC **Prod** - OHUTC

On your knees 30 MIN
VHS
Bodymatters series
Color (H C A)
PdS65 purchase
Discusses the knee joint and its relation to the rest of the body. Part of a series of 26 30-minute videos on various systems of the human body.
Health and Safety; Science - Natural
Dist - BBCENE

On Your Marks, Pt 1 7 MIN
16mm
Color (J H)
LC 70-714193
Examines punctuation marks and gives examples of their use. Identifies the eight most common punctuation marks - the period, comma, question mark, colon, quotation marks, apostrofphe, exclamation point and hyphen. Shows each punctuation mark taking on a persoality that shows its proper use.
English Language
Dist - CGWEST **Prod** - CGWEST 1971

On Your Marks, Pt 2 7 MIN
16mm
Color (J H)
LC 70-714193
Provides an imaginative look at punctuation marks. Identifies eight less common marks - the semicolon, underlining, parentheses, dash, asterisk, caret, brackets and ellipses.
English Language
Dist - CGWEST **Prod** - CGWEST 1971

On Your Own 23 MIN
U-matic / VHS / 16mm
Color (J)
Presents students describing what consumer and homemaking education means to them. Explores a wide range of instruction and offers an overview of consumer and homemaking education curriculum.
Education; Home Economics
Dist - ALTSUL **Prod** - ALTSUL

On Your Own 24 MIN
16mm / U-matic / VHS
Consumer Education Series
Color (J)
LC 72-703048
Introduces the surprising diversity of subjects covered in high school consumer education classes. Serves both to summarize the content possibilities of consumer education classes and to spur the interest in such training for both boys and girls.
Civics and Political Systems; Home Economics; Sociology
Dist - ALTSUL **Prod** - ALTSUL 1972

On Your Own 30 MIN
VHS / BETA
On the Money Series
Color
Discusses financing a college education. Gives advice on avoiding having a tax shelter roof fall in. Examines being self - employed.
Business and Economics; Home Economics
Dist - CORF **Prod** - WGBHTV

On your own 21 MIN
VHS / U-matic
Color (H C G A PRO)
$249.00 purchase _ #ES978A-H, #ES978I3-H, #ES978I5-H, #ES978W-H ; $249.00 purchase _ #ES978A, #ES978I5, #ES978I3, #ES978W ; $475_$129_$99; $250.00 purchase, $75.00 rental; LC 79-701469
Educates the viewer on the responsibilities involved in living alone, including selecting housing, cleaning, cooking and making a budget. Includes Skills for Living video, instructor's notes, a pad of competency requirements, Living Alone - Job World Life Skills software, a pad of student activity worksheets - Moving Into Your Apartment and Personal Budget Sheet, a pad of assessment checklists and an assessment checklist answer key. IBM - compatible versions available in 3.5 and 5.25 diskettes. Available in Windows version.
Business and Economics; Guidance and Counseling; Home Economics
Dist - VLEARN

On Your Own 14 MIN
16mm
Color (I)
Teaches young children safety measures and self care skills for times when they are home alone, and shows them how to confront their fears. Stresses the need for communication between parent and child, and encourages children to view being alone as a positive, rewarding experience.
Guidance and Counseling; Health and Safety
Dist - CORF **Prod** - DISNEY 1985

On Your Own at Home 12 MIN
U-matic / VHS / 16mm
Taking Responsibility Series
Color (P I)
$350, $250 purchase _ #4641C
Explains the things children need to know to stay home alone safely. Produced by Bill Walker Productions.
Health and Safety
Dist - CORF

On Your own at home 11 MIN
VHS
Taking responsibility series
Color (P)
Uses animation to portray a fairytale princess in her castle who learns to handle the kinds of problems that might arise when a child is home alone. Shows the Queen and King helping the princess to plan and practice what to say and do to keep safe, and when, where and how to get help. Part of a series teaching health, safety and responsibility to youngsters.
Health and Safety; Home Economics; Psychology; Sociology
Dist - VIEWTH **Prod** - VIEWTH

On Your Own - Being Your Own Best Motivator 7 MIN
U-matic / VHS / 16mm
Color
Deals with self - motivation, and contrasts the training a racehorse receives with educational opportunities provided throughout life. Narrated by Dennis Weaver.
Education; Psychology
Dist - CCCD **Prod** - CCCD 1984

On your own - living independently with cerebral palsy 28 MIN
VHS
Color (J H C G)
$125.00 purchase, $40.00 rental _ #38150
Features 12 adults with cerebral palsy and shows the rewards and challenges these individuals have experienced by living independently. Shares their stories and views on topics such as access to the community, education, attendant care and dealing with social stigmas. Produced by Worthwhile Films, Madison, Wisconsin.
Health and Safety
Dist - UCEMC

On Your Own - Preparing for a Standardized Test 26 MIN
U-matic / VHS / 16mm
Color (J)
$515.00, $250.00 purchase _ #4398; LC 83-700623
Covers basic concepts of test preparation. Develops such topics as use of test bulletins, types of tests, understanding content of the test and knowing item formats.
Education
Dist - CORF **Prod** - ETS 1983

On Your Own Series
Jennifer Muller and Marjorie Mussman 30 MIN
Dist - ARCVID

On Your Way to School 10 MIN
16mm / U-matic / VHS
Color (P I)
LC 78-714128
Follows two school children to school pointing out the safety rules.
Health and Safety
Dist - AIMS **Prod** - DAVP 1971

On Your Way to School 8 MIN
16mm / U-matic / VHS
Learning to Look Series
Color (P)
Shows a girl winding her way to school through a bright collage of images, colors and textures.
English Language; Guidance and Counseling; Psychology
Dist - MGHT **Prod** - MGHT 1973

The Ona people - life and death in Tierra del Fuego 55 MIN
16mm / VHS
Color (G)
$400.00 purchase, $80.00, $60.00 rental
Tells the history of the Ona people of the Tierrra del Fuego islands off the southern tip of South America, who numbered between 3500 and 4000 until their extermination began in the last twenty years of the 19th century. Records the shamanic chants and rituals and geneologies of Kiepja who died in 1966, and Angela Loij, the last surviving Ona who died in 1974. Produced by Anne Chapman and Ana Montes de Conzales.
History - World; Religion and Philosophy; Social Science
Dist - DOCEDR **Prod** - DOCEDR 1977

Onandarka Fire 18 MIN
16mm
Color
Presents footage of coverage of the fire at Newhall, Olive View Sanitarium and Gene Autry's Melody Ranch in August, 1962.
Health and Safety; Social Science
Dist - LAFIRE **Prod** - LAFIRE

Once a cesarean 35 MIN
VHS
Color (G)
$145.00 purchase _ #AJ - 132
Informs and encourages women to explore the option of a vaginal birth after a prior cesarean section. Follows one couple from their decision through the natural breech birth of their son. Intertwines scenes from a VBAC - vaginal birth after cesarean - workshop and commentary from obstetricians on the pros and cons of this alternative.
Health and Safety
Dist - FANPRO

Once a face 2 MIN
16mm
B&W (G)
$10.00 rental
Presents a pixilated film set to poetry with a beat. Swings from disheveled misfit to strangled yuppie.
Fine Arts; Literature and Drama
Dist - CANCIN **Prod** - MICHAL 1984

Once a Mouse
VHS / 35mm strip
Caldecotts on Filmstrip Series
Color (K)
$35.00 purchase
Presents a children's story. Part of the Caldecott series.
English Language; Literature and Drama
Dist - PELLER

Once again 4 MIN
16mm
Color (G)

$10.00 rental
Pays homage to Vermeer with humorous stop - animation. Consists of a surreal quality with stark settings, costumes and lighting. Produced by Dave Gearey.
Fine Arts
Dist - CANCIN

Once and future planet 23 MIN
VHS
Color (J H C G)
$250.00 purchase, $50.00 rental
Examines global warming and the effect that industries and human lifestyles have on the Earth's atmosphere. Embarks on a joint US - Soviet research voyage where scientists introduce the viewer, with the aid of animation, to natural and human - made gases accumulating in the atmosphere. Reveals that concrete steps can be taken to improve the atmosphere significantly and slow greenhouse gas emmissions to give the air time to clear up. Produced by John Stern for King Broadcasting Company.
Fine Arts; Science - Natural; Science - Physical
Dist - BULFRG

Once, at a Border - Aspects of Stravinsky 166 MIN
VHS
Color (G)
$29.95 purchase _ #1157
Chronicles the long journey in the life and works of Igor Stravinsky. Reveals that Stravinsky saw Tchaikovsky conduct and was still composing music after the Beatles broke up. Considers him the foremost Russian composer of our time.
Biography; Fine Arts; Geography - World
Dist - KULTUR

Once I had an operation 17 MIN
VHS
Color (P I)
$175.00 purchase
Informs and prepares children for hospitalization, surgery, and recovery by showing a group of healthy children sharing their experiences. Explains medical procedures and recovery in reassuring language appropriate for children. Film by Laurie Wagman Productions.
Health and Safety
Dist - CF

Once in a lifetime
VHS
Color (G)
$29.95 purchase _ #0836
Presents full coverage of the 1987 Chicago - Mackinac Race.
Physical Education and Recreation
Dist - SEVVID

Once in a Million Years 50 MIN
16mm / U-matic / VHS
Color (H C A)
Discusses the safety factors which engineers have been designing into nuclear reactors since 1950 in order to contain certain explosive reactions which could pump lethal quantities of radioactivity into the environment.
Social Science
Dist - FI **Prod** - BBCTV 1982

Once Insane, Twice Forgotten 25 MIN
VHS / U-matic
Color
Presents a report on the lack of help for the criminally insane who have been released from state mental hospitals. Traces experiences of a man who six years ago shot and killed another man, but has been released to a life with no job, few friends, and an income of welfare money.
Health and Safety; Psychology
Dist - MEDCOM **Prod** - MEDCOM

Once Kittyhawk 36 MIN
U-matic / VHS / 16mm
Color (H C)
LC 79-701876
Focuses on the Once Group, a performing company in Ann Arbor, Michigan, known for their work in experimental theater. Shows how the group gathers abstract ideas from diverse fields such as architecture, music, film, graphic arts, and mechanics, then formulates them into a theater statement. Includes excerpts from their space theater piece known as Kittyhawk.
Fine Arts
Dist - MCFI **Prod** - SITSON 1974

Once more with Meaning 28 MIN
VHS / 16mm
Adult Literacy Series
Color (PRO G A)
$90.00 purchase _ #BPN220601
Discusses individual and large group literacy classes. Outlines the features of an adult literacy program that is likely to succeed. Features reading expert, Dr Ken Goodman.
Education; English Language
Dist - RMIBHF **Prod** - RMIBHF

Once more with Meaning 30 MIN
U-matic
Adult Literacy Series
Color (PRO)
Outlines the features of a literacy program that is likely to succeed and visits literacy teachers and adult learners who are making a successful entry into the world of print.
English Language; Literature and Drama
Dist - TVOTAR **Prod** - TVOTAR 1985

Once on a Barren Hill 27 MIN
BETA / VHS
Color
Tells the story of the appearance of the Virgin of Guadalupe to Aztec Indian Juan Diego.
Geography - World; Religion and Philosophy
Dist - DSP **Prod** - DSP

Once the Ferns 9 MIN
16mm
Color (K P I J H C)
LC 72-703329
Presents a film - poem fantasy about the human condition as revealed in a fantasy acted out by ferns and ladybugs.
Guidance and Counseling; Sociology
Dist - MARALF **Prod** - ALBM 1973

Once the Fire is Out - what Next 16 MIN
U-matic / VHS / 16mm
Color
Describes the Forest Service role in managing and protecting National Forest watersheds in the aftermath of wildfire. Describes how vulnerable burned - over soil is to erosion.
Agriculture; Civics and Political Systems; Science - Natural; Social Science
Dist - USNAC **Prod** - USFS

Once There was a Last Call 8 MIN
16mm
Color
LC 77-702598
Looks at various forms of wildlife found in Ontario, Canada. Draws attention to the common loon and its status as an endangered species.
Geography - World; Science - Natural
Dist - VIK **Prod** - BOGNER 1976

Once There was a Strike in Levittown 60 MIN
VHS / U-matic
Bill Moyers' Journal Series
Color
Explores the underlying issues and consequences of a prolonged teachers' strike in Levittown, Long Island.
Business and Economics; Education
Dist - PBS **Prod** - WNETTV 1979

Once There were Bluebirds 5 MIN
U-matic / VHS / 16mm
Bill Martin's Freedom Series
Color (K P I J)
LC 72-701769
Uses animation and live action to acquaint children with the beauty of nature and the ecological problems caused by the encroachments of modern society.
Guidance and Counseling; Science - Natural; Social Science; Sociology
Dist - ALTSUL **Prod** - ALTSUL 1972

Once this land was ours 19 MIN
VHS
Color (G) (INDIAN WITH ENGLISH SUBTITLES)
$60.00 rental, $250.00 purchase
Documents women agricultural workers in India and their struggle to provide for their families. Illustrates, through moving testimonies and images of the women at work, the increasing difficulties feeding their own children while working to produce food for others. Explores the feminization of poverty in rural India. By Shikha Jhingan. Narration written in English.
Agriculture; Fine Arts; Geography - World; Sociology
Dist - WMEN

Once to Every Man 30 MIN
U-matic / VHS
Color
Offers a fictional account of an encounter between a typical colonial farmer and a foraging party of British soldiers.
History - United States
Dist - MDCPB **Prod** - MDCPB

Once to make Ready 8 MIN
16mm
Color
LC 75-700567; 75-700566
Explains to the average citizen what it can mean to him personally when his local government undertakes a Community Shelter Program (CSP) to provide the best available protection for all its citizens.
Civics and Political Systems; Health and Safety; Sociology
Dist - USNAC **Prod** - USOCD 1967

Once upon a Boa 28 MIN
16mm / U-matic / VHS
Color
LC 81-700867
Presents the story of a boa constrictor owner who is consulted by a neighbor who wants to buy a boa for his own son. Shows them discussing the boa as a pet.
Science - Natural
Dist - PHENIX **Prod** - BOAFLM 1978

Once upon a Climb 7 MIN
16mm
B&W
LC 76-702038
Illustrates old and new mountain climbing techniques.
Physical Education and Recreation
Dist - SFRASU **Prod** - SFRASU 1975

Once upon a Couch - Gretel 120 MIN
VHS / U-matic
Color (PRO)
Uses the fairy tale character Gretel to introduce the ten crucial steps in the psychotherapeutic session.
Health and Safety; Psychology
Dist - HSCIC **Prod** - HSCIC 1981

Once upon a Dime 11 MIN
16mm
Kids and Cash Series
Color (P I J)
Addresses the subject of savings. Encourages direct money savings by students and promotes the saving of money through conservation of resources, such as electric lights, water and fuel.
Home Economics; Social Science
Dist - COUNFI **Prod** - COUNFI

Once upon a dinosaur 15 MIN
U-matic / VHS
Dragons, wagons and wax - Set 1 series
Color (K P)
Explores evidence of life that existed in the past.
Science; Science - Natural
Dist - CTI **Prod** - CTI

Once upon a manta 26 MIN
VHS
Challenge of the seas series
Color (I J H)
$225.00 purchase
Studies manta rays in Mexico's Sea of Cortez. Reveals that they are harmless to humans and feed solely on plankton. Part of a 26 - part series on the oceans.
Science - Natural; Science - Physical
Dist - LANDMK **Prod** - LANDMK 1991

Once upon a Mouse 26 MIN
U-matic / VHS / 16mm
Color
Offers segments from various Walt Disney cartoons which show a variety of Disney themes including music, love, villains and happy endings.
Fine Arts
Dist - CORF **Prod** - DISNEY 1982

Once upon a time 30 MIN
VHS
Maryknoll video magazine presents series
Color (G)
$14.95 purchase
Highlights the place of storytelling and other traditional arts in Kenya's culture and how the Catholic Church is welcoming those who practice these arts into its fold.
Religion and Philosophy
Dist - MARYFA

Once upon a time 12 MIN
16mm
Color (G)
$15.00 rental
Introduces an animated cobweb castle, spirits on the screen and soundtrack and a female guide who escorts a young man into a series of antechambers.
Fine Arts
Dist - CANCIN **Prod** - JORDAL 1974

Once upon a Time 25 MIN
16mm
Color (J)
Emphasizes the importance of protecting economic and political freedom from excessive government controls.
Business and Economics; Civics and Political Systems
Dist - USCHOC **Prod** - USCHOC

Once upon a Time 5 MIN
16mm
Color
LC 79-700254
Shows how Dr Einstein's theory of relativity goes berserk when a college student takes an overdose of time - release tablets to calm his nerves.
Fine Arts; Literature and Drama
Dist - CINESO **Prod** - CINESO 1978

Once upon a Time 18 MIN
16mm
Color (G)
#2X711
Follows a commissionaire on his night rounds through the Historic Sights building of Ottowa. Glamorizes the colonial era in Canada.
History - World
Dist - CDIAND **Prod** - CNHS 1977

Once upon a Time - 1900 - 1923 60 MIN
VHS
Struggles For Poland Series
Color (G)
$59.95 purchase _ #STFP - 101
Shows that Poland began the 20th century not as an independent nation, but as parts of Prussia, Russia and Austria - Hungary. Tells how two Polish patriots, Jozef Pilsudski and Roman Dmowski, sought independence for their people. Describes how major events such as the Russo - Japanese War, World War I and the Bolshevik revolution paved the way for Poland's regaining its independence in 1918.
Civics and Political Systems; History - World
Dist - PBS **Prod** - WNETTV 1988

Once upon a time - Can ya ma Can 22 MIN
VHS
Color (K P) (ARABIC)
$25.00 purchase _ #VPR001
Contains three children's stories in Arabic. Includes a small coloring book and crayons.
Foreign Language; Literature and Drama
Dist - IBC

Once upon a Time - Man Series

The Age of Pericles	28 MIN
The Age of Reason	28 MIN
America	28 MIN
And the earth appeared	28 MIN
Awakening of the people	28 MIN
The Belle Epoque	28 MIN
The Carolingians	28 MIN
The Cathedral builders	28 MIN
The Crazy Years	28 MIN
Cro Magnon - the caveman	28 MIN
The Earth	28 MIN
Elizabethan England	28 MIN
The Fertile valley	28 MIN
The First empires	28 MIN
The French Revolution	28 MIN
The Golden ages of Spain	28 MIN
The Golden ages of the low countries	28 MIN
The Hundred Years War	28 MIN
Islamic Conquests	28 MIN
Leonardo	28 MIN
Louis XIV's Great Century	28 MIN
Marco Polo's Travels	28 MIN
The Neanderthal Man	28 MIN
Pax Romana	28 MIN
Peter the Great	28 MIN
The Vikings	28 MIN

Dist - LANDMK

Once upon a Time Series

A Matter of Time	20 MIN

Dist - AITECH

Once upon a Time There was a Point 8 MIN
U-matic / VHS / 16mm
Color
LC 80-700694
Shows a point that transforms itself into a myriad of different shapes and forms. Previously released as Once Upon A Time There Was A Dot.
Fine Arts
Dist - IFB **Prod** - ZAGREB 1977

Once upon a Town Series

All kinds of animals	20 MIN
Because I am different	20 MIN
Beyond words	20 MIN
Caring and sharing	20 MIN
Earth care	20 MIN
Hobbies Happening	20 MIN
How do I do it	20 MIN
Is My Way Better	20 MIN
It Makes Me Laugh	20 MIN
Me Alone, on My Own	20 MIN
Mind and Muscle Power	20 MIN
Scare Me	20 MIN
Where do I Live	20 MIN

Dist - AITECH

Once upon a Wilderness 19 MIN
U-matic / VHS / 16mm
Color
LC 74-711377
Uses passages from an early pioneer's journal, engravings, photographs and live action photography to dramatize the contrast between the American wilderness of a hundred years ago and the environment today, showing the destructive technological alterations wrought by highways and housing developments.
History - United States; Science - Natural
Dist - STANF **Prod** - STANF 1971

Once upon her time 34 MIN
VHS
Color (J H C G)
$285.00 purchase, $60.00 rental
Offers a kaleidoscope of images and thoughts by and about contemporary women. Features women of all ages and walks of life who talk about their joys and angers, goals, myths, treatment and life options. Includes a cook whose joy is singing the blues, a self - defense class for women, peace demonstrators, comedians, teen women making their first confusing approaches to the opposite sex. Features Lindsay Wagner as host.
Sociology
Dist - CF **Prod** - BELLDA 1989

Once When I was Scared
VHS / 35mm strip
Children's Sound Filmstrips Series
Color (K)
$33.00 purchase
Adapts a children's story by H C Pittman. Part of a series.
English Language; Literature and Drama
Dist - PELLER

Onchocerciasis in Ghana 31 MIN
16mm
Color (PRO)
LC 74-705247
Emphasizes the entomological and parasitological aspects of the African vector of onchocerciasis.
Geography - World; Health and Safety
Dist - USNAC **Prod** - USPHS 1967

Ondra and the Snow Dragon 7 MIN
U-matic / VHS / 16mm
Color (K P)
Presents Ondra, a lonely young boy who is transported to a faraway land by the Snow Dragon, a friendly winged creature. Shows how Ondra finds a ballroom full of dancers frozen by a strange spell, and a princess whose heart is frozen in sadness. Tells how Ondra, by his kindness, frees the dancers and the princess.
Literature and Drama
Dist - MOKIN **Prod** - KRATKY 1983

One 14 MIN
VHS / 16mm
Color (K P I)
LC 79-701050
Depicts an encounter between a little boy and a street mime. Describes the boy's adventures with an invisible balloon.
Fine Arts
Dist - LRF **Prod** - LRF 1980

One 10 MIN
16mm
B&W (J)
Presents a drama set at a railroad station where a young woman awaits the arrival of the man she loves.
Fine Arts
Dist - UWFKD **Prod** - UWFKD

1 - 57: Versuch mit synthetischem Ton - Test 2 MIN
16mm
B&W (H C A)
$10.00 rental
Presents an experiment in synthetic sound. Produced by Kurt Kren.
Fine Arts
Dist - CANCIN

One A M 14 MIN
16mm / U-matic / VHS
Charlie Chaplin Comedy Theater Series
B&W (I)
Features Charlie Chaplin in a solo appearance as a drunken playboy returning home from a night on the town. Shows him running an obstacle course with his front door, the stairs to his room and his bed.
Fine Arts
Dist - FI **Prod** - MUFLM

One - Alpha 13 MIN
U-matic / VHS
Color (PRO)
Simulates the crash of a 70 - passenger jet plane to describe to potential rescuers what they might expect to deal with in such an emergency.
Health and Safety; Social Science
Dist - FILCOM **Prod** - FILCOM

One AM 20 MIN
16mm
B&W
Shows Charlie Chaplin returning home drunk after a night on the town.
Fine Arts
Dist - FCE **Prod** - FCE 1916

One and more than One - Birthday on a Farm 8 MIN
16mm / U-matic / VHS
Read on Series
Color (P)
LC 76-702238
Describes ways of making plural words through a story about three children who go shopping for birthday presents for a friend. Gives examples of single and plural forms of words.
English Language
Dist - AIMS **Prod** - ACI 1971

The One and only 15 MIN
U-matic / VHS
Dragons, wagons and wax - Set 2 series
Color (K P)
Illustrates the characteristics which make humans different from other creatures.
Science; Science - Natural
Dist - CTI **Prod** - CTI

The One and only 30 MIN
VHS
Color (J H C G A R)
$10.00 rental _ #36 - 88 - 1521
Presents a unique vision of God as an ordinary - appearing person. In a monologue, 'God' speaks to viewers in a person - to - person manner. Uses humor, argument, drama and common sense.
Religion and Philosophy
Dist - APH **Prod** - MMM

The One and Only Bing 26 MIN
16mm
Hollywood and the Stars Series
B&W
LC 75-701943
Presents the biography of Bing Crosby, the nonchalant crooner who became a star in radio, recording, and television, as well as in films. Includes clips from his early pictures and scenes of his home life and children.
Biography; Fine Arts
Dist - WOLPER **Prod** - WOLPER 1963

One and only you 14 MIN
U-matic / 16mm / VHS
Think it through with Winnie the Pooh series
Color (P I)
$400.00, $280.00 purchase _ #JC - 67190
Promotes a positive self - image and getting along with others. Uses live action, Puppetronics characters to stress the importance of communication in developing interpersonal skills and respecting the feelings of others. Part of the Thinking It Through with Winnie the Pooh series.
Fine Arts; Psychology
Dist - CORF **Prod** - DISNEY 1989

One and the same 4 MIN
16mm
Color (G)
$10.00 rental
Presents a self - portrait by two women filmmakers in celebration of their friendship and filmmaking. Features co - maker Freude.
Fine Arts; Psychology
Dist - CANCIN **Prod** - NELSOG 1972

One - and Two - Axis Linear Milling 18 MIN
VHS / U-matic
Numerical Control - Computerized Numerical Control, Module 1 - Fundamentals Series
Color (IND)
Discusses climb and conventional milling, programming rapid position movement and several aspects of programming.
Business and Economics; Industrial and Technical Education
Dist - LEIKID **Prod** - LEIKID

One angry man 50 MIN
VHS
Trial series
Color; PAL (H C A)
PdS99 purchase
Presents Edinburgh criminal defense lawyer, George More, whose policy is to defeat the prosecution by any legal means possible. Follows his defense of a woman accused of shoplifting and his colleague's defense of a reckless driver facing a five year jail sentence. Third in a series of five programs filmed by the BBC in Scottish courts.
Civics and Political Systems; Sociology
Dist - BBCENE

The One Armed Man 27 MIN
16mm / U-matic / VHS
Insight Series
Color; B&W (J)
LC 75-700942
Tells a story about a one - armed traveling salesman who uses his affliction to gain sympathy. Shows how he learns to accept his limitations and to overcome his loneliness when he meets a woman who makes him aware of his self - pity.

Guidance and Counseling; Psychology; Sociology
Dist - PAULST **Prod** - KIESER 1974

One at a Time 20 MIN
16mm
Color
Shows the manufacturing of equipment at the Allis - Chalmers plant.
Agriculture
Dist - IDEALF **Prod** - ALLISC

One Banana, Two Banana 32 MIN
VHS / 16mm
Color (H)
LC 90712986
Documents experiences of Lynn Sternberg, a Michigan housewife suffering from multiple sclerosis.
Health and Safety; Science - Natural
Dist - COMMED

One Beautiful Experience 14 MIN
16mm
Color
LC 79-700396
Uses a comedy about a junior executive's first venture into cigar smoking to illustrate the qualities of a well - made cigar, different types of cigars and how to smoke a cigar.
Health and Safety
Dist - KLEINW **Prod** - AMCIG 1978

One Big Ocean 13 MIN
U-matic / VHS / 16mm
Captioned; Color (K P)
LC 77-708154
Illustrates basic concepts about the ocean, includes scenes of men at work on the ocean floor and of creatures that inhabit the ocean. Explains what causes the ocean waves, why the ocean tastes salty and the ways in which the ocean is important to man.
Science - Natural; Science - Physical
Dist - JOU **Prod** - WER 1970

One Bite at the Apple 38 MIN
16mm
Color
LC 74-705248
Stresses familiarization with procurement procedures relative to contracting by formal advertising. Shows a discussion between a disappointed bidder and a procurement agent setting the scene for procedural review, focusing on the role of the Federal Supply Service.
Business and Economics; Civics and Political Systems
Dist - USNAC **Prod** - USGSA 1970

One bowl muffins 60 MIN
VHS
Cookbook videos series
Color (G)
$19.95 purchase
Demonstrates nine easy muffin recipes. Provides brief, practical and easy-to-understand instructions for several recipes. Uses close-up photography and detailed on-screen ingredients, so even a novice can duplicate the dishes demonstrated. Includes a printed abstract of recipes. Part of a series.
Home Economics; Social Science
Dist - ALWHIT **Prod** - ALWHIT
CAMV

One by One 30 MIN
U-matic / VHS
Color (IND)
Presents the minority person as an individual. Defines and exposes unconscious prejudice and examines why it still exists. Focuses on the dangers of grouping people, of oversensitivity, of racial backlash and of special treatment of minorities.
Business and Economics; Guidance and Counseling; Sociology
Dist - JONEST **Prod** - DRUKRR

One child at a time 29 MIN
VHS / U-matic
Color (J H C G)
$425.00, $395.00 purchase _ #V442
Follows the work of Heal The Children, an organization which finances and arranges for children from all over the world to come to the United States for medical treatment. Meets three of these children and shows their culture, their foster families in the US and the founders of Heal The Children.
Health and Safety; History - World; Sociology
Dist - BARR **Prod** - CEPRO 1988

One day 17 MIN
16mm
Diaries no 1 - no 8 - 1979 - 1983
Color (G)
$25.00 rental
Features part three of an eight - part series by Andras Szirtes.
Fine Arts; Literature and Drama
Dist - CANCIN

One Day 18 MIN
16mm
B&W (I)
Gives an impressionistic view of an average Indian town, poona. Shows glimpses of the lives of people in different strata of society.
Social Science; Sociology
Dist - NEDINF **Prod** - INDIA

One day a week 33 MIN
VHS / 16mm
Documentaries for learning series
B&W (C G PRO)
$70.00 purchase, $39.00 rental _ #35703
Shows the workday of a community psychiatrist consulting to the staff of a Job Corps center. Illustrates the range of experiences involved in such work. Includes print material. Part of a series produced for use by health care professionals and educators.
Health and Safety; Psychology
Dist - PSU **Prod** - MASON 1967

One day at a time 30 MIN
VHS
Color; PAL (G)
PdS35 purchase
Presents personal experiences of faith and coping with terminal illness and chronic disability. Shows that these sufferers are often lonely, afraid and sometimes angry at the failure of medicine and the apparent absence of God. Contact distributor about availability outside the United Kingdom.
Guidance and Counseling
Dist - ACADEM **Prod** - YORKTV

One day at a time 30 MIN
Cassette
Color (G)
$350.00, $10.00 purchase
Discloses that one day at a time is the only way life can be lived.
Guidance and Counseling; Health and Safety; Psychology
Dist - KELLYP **Prod** - KELLYP

One Day at a Time
VHS
Daddy Doesn't Live Here Anymore - the Single - Parent Family Series
Color
Shows the day - to - day realities of running a single - parent household.
Guidance and Counseling; Sociology
Dist - IBIS **Prod** - IBIS

One Day at Teton Marsh 47 MIN
16mm / U-matic / VHS
Color (I)
LC FIA67-1286
Describes the wild life in a swamp where animals and birds are free and nature reigns supreme. Based on a book by Sally Carrighar.
Science - Natural
Dist - CORF **Prod** - DISNEY 1966

One Day at Teton Marsh, Pt 1 23 MIN
16mm / U-matic / VHS
Color (I)
LC FIA67-1286
Describes the wild life in a swamp where animals and birds are free and nature reigns supreme. Based on a book by Sally Carrighar.
Science - Natural
Dist - CORF **Prod** - DISNEY 1966

One Day at Teton Marsh, Pt 2 24 MIN
U-matic / VHS / 16mm
Color (I)
LC FIA67-1286
Describes the wild life in a swamp where animals and birds are free and nature reigns supreme. Based on a book by Sally Carrighar.
Science - Natural
Dist - CORF **Prod** - DISNEY 1966

One day in the life of Ivan Denisovich 105 MIN
VHS
Color (H G A)
$79.95 purchase _ #S02081
Presents the film version of Alexander Solzhenitsyn's novel 'One Day in the Life of Ivan Denisovich.' Portrays a single day in the life of Ivan Denisovich, a prisoner in a Siberian labor camp. Shows how, despite the hardships and oppression of the camp, Denisovich endures.
Fine Arts; Literature and Drama
Dist - UILL **Prod** - GROUPW 1971
TIMLIF

One day in the life of Tryon 40 MIN
16mm
Color (G)
$75.00 rental
Presents a story, which is never resolved, of characters on the run and an Edsel dealership. Operates through many devices, ranging from home movies to tourist photography and gangster narrative. A variety of filmstocks and camera techniques were used including seven different 16mm cameras. Commissioned by the Upstairs Gallery in Tyron, North Carolina.
Fine Arts
Dist - CANCIN **Prod** - SONDHE 1985

One day the heart opens - a concert of ethnic music 28 MIN
VHS
Jewish music heritage library series
Color (G)
$39.95 purchase _ #797
Records the gathering of eight musical ensembles from Bukhara, Ethiopia, Georgia - USSR, India, Iraq, Kurdistan, Persia and Tajkhistan at David's Tower in Jerusalem for a concert. Presents authentic instruments and melodies characteristic of their communities. Includes instruments such as the santour - a Persian dulcimer; the ou - an Arabic lute; the darabukka - an Arab drum; and the sorna - a Kurdish wind instrument. Includes a song composed by Israeli rock star Ehud Banai for the occasion. Part of a series on Jewish music from around the world, featuring Martin Bookspan as narrator.
Fine Arts; Sociology
Dist - ERGOM **Prod** - IMHP

One Day with Shiva 8 MIN
16mm
Color
LC 76-701348
Presents an impressionistic documentary of south India.
Geography - World
Dist - CONCRU **Prod** - CONCRU 1974

One designer - two designer 10 MIN
U-matic / VHS / BETA
Color; PAL (G H C)
PdS40, PdS48 purchase
Uses animation and humor to explore the importance of good design and pitfalls of impractical design. Emphasizes the need for consumers to check products before purchase.
Fine Arts; Home Economics
Dist - EDPAT

One Dimension, Two Dimension, Three Dimension Four 15 MIN
U-matic
B&W
Illustrates the plight of urban centers in the United States, the problems of pollution, transportation, education and housing. Describes how these problems affect its inhabitants and how some urban areas have tried to solve these problems. Stresses planning for the future as essential to the survival of the cities.
Science - Natural; Sociology
Dist - USNAC **Prod** - USNAC 1972

One Dish Meals
BETA / VHS
Video Cooking Library Series
Color
Demonstrates recipes for one - dish meals such as Veal au Gratin and Lemon Garlic Salmon.
Home Economics
Dist - KARTES **Prod** - KARTES

One door 28 MIN
16mm
Color (G A)
$5.00 rental
Shows four families receiving comprehensive, high quality medical care through prepaid group practice. Examines a Kaiser health center and United Mine Workers center. Emphasizes preventive care, team work and treating the whole patient.
Health and Safety
Dist - AFLCIO **Prod** - USHHS 1969

One Drink Too many 13 MIN
VHS / U-matic
Color (H C G)
Explains how alcohol affects the ability to drive and what people can do to prevent friends from driving drunk.
Health and Safety; Psychology; Social Science; Sociology
Dist - HUF **Prod** - HUF

One eye leads 10 MIN
16mm
Color (G)
$30.00 rental
Defines and destroys the ideals of what a woman should be with the illumination of the matyr Lucy, patron saint of the eyes. Shows how the thirteen virtues of a 'lady' as conceived by society are the weapons used against a renegade saint who was reinterpreted by the Catholic Church. A Jennifer Gentile production.
Fine Arts; Religion and Philosophy; Sociology
Dist - CANCIN

The One - Eyed Cyclops 15 MIN
U-matic / VHS
Homer's Odyssey Series
Color (C)
$239.00, $139.00 purchase _ #AD - 2042
Retells quickly of the fall of Troy, visiting the Land of the Lotus - Eaters. Follows Odysseus and his crew to the Land of the Cyclops where the murderous one - eyed giant Polyphemus disobeys the law of the gods to be hospitable to strangers. Only the cunning of Odysseus saves the Greeks from wholesale slaughter at the hands of Polyphemus. Part of a six - part series.
History - World; Literature and Drama
Dist - FOTH **Prod** - FOTH

One - Eyed Men are Kings 15 MIN
U-matic / VHS / 16mm
Color (J)
LC 74-701714
Tells the story of a man's quest for friendship, told with humor and pathos. Describes how he masquerades as a blind man, acquires new respect and becomes the center of attention. Depicts how his ruse is detected and he resumes his lonely existence.
Psychology; Sociology
Dist - MGHT **Prod** - CAPAC 1974

One false move 105 MIN
16mm / 35mm
Color (G)
Portrays three very different killers being tracked by three very different cops. Opens in Los Angeles with a drug - related massacre perpetrated by Pluto, a cool black sociopath, Ray, his redneck former cellmate and Fantasia, Ray's mysterious mulatto girlfriend. Follows the trio to Star City, Arkansas, where they are met by two world - weary and racially diverse LA cops, and Dale 'Hurricane' Dixon, the dim, but enthusiastic local police chief. Directed by Carl Franklin.
Fine Arts; History - United States; Literature and Drama; Sociology
Dist - KINOIC

One Film - Three Scripts 21 MIN
U-matic / VHS / 16mm
Color (H C)
Presents the same footage of Puerto Rico three times with different narratives to show how different communication techniques can be used in film.
Education; Fine Arts; Geography - World
Dist - FI **Prod** - IFFB 1974

One fine day 6 MIN
Cassette
Color (G H C)
$75.00, $50.00, $35.00, $10.00 purchase,$ 45.00 rental
Features a fast - paced overview of women's history. Begins with over 100 still portraits of early feminists, dissolves into live action suffrage parades then marches into contemporary footage. Shown on PBS and the USIA's Worldnet. Produced by Kay Weaver, who also wrote the musical anthem, and Martha Wheelock.
History - World; Sociology
Dist - ISHTAR **Prod** - ADL
ADL

One Five Six 19 MIN
16mm
Color
Touches briefly on the background of the 'big solids' (solid propellant rockets) now being considered for the space shuttle and progresses to the 156 - inch motor program. Concludes with a static test of the motor which generates more than 1.4 million pounds of thrust.
Industrial and Technical Education
Dist - THIOKL **Prod** - THIOKL 1965

One Flew Over the Cuckoo's Nest
VHS / U-matic
Color (J C I)
Tells about life in a mental hospital. Stars Jack Nicholson and Louise Fletcher in an adaptation of Ken Kesey's novel.
Fine Arts; Literature and Drama; Psychology
Dist - GA **Prod** - GA

One Flew Over the Cuckoo's Nest 129 MIN
16mm
Color
Focuses on a free - spirited man (Jack Nicholson) who tries to explain to the other mental hospital patients that the difference between sanity and insanity is just society's attempt to stifle individualism. Based on the novel One Flew Over The Cuckoo's Nest by Ken Kesey. Directed by Milos Forman.
Fine Arts
Dist - UAE **Prod** - UAA 1976

One Flew Over the Cuckoo's Nest
VHS / U-matic
Contemporary Literature Series
Color (G C J)
$59.00 purchase _ #05657 - 85
Documents the lives of patients in a mental ward. Stars Jack Nicholson and Louise Fletcher. Based on the novel by Ken Kesey.
Fine Arts; Literature and Drama
Dist - CHUMAN

One for My Baby 30 MIN
U-matic / VHS / 16mm
Color (H C A)
Points out the historical and cultural forces in society that perpetuate drinking and investigates both the medical and human aspects of fetal alcohol syndrom (FAS). Examined are research into prenatal drinking and the common characteristics of FAS in children. Parents of FAS children candidly share their experiences.
Health and Safety; Psychology; Sociology
Dist - UEUWIS **Prod** - UEUWIS 1981

One for My Baby 28 MIN
16mm / U-matic / VHS
Color (H C A)
Presents the potential dangers of alcohol use by pregnant women.
Health and Safety; Sociology
Dist - AIMS **Prod** - WHATV 1983

One for the Money 30 MIN
16mm
Color
LC FIA66-750
Shows the hard work, planning, preparation and teamwork involved in entering a car in the Indianapolis 500.
Industrial and Technical Education; Physical Education and Recreation
Dist - SFI **Prod** - TI 1966

One for the Road 29 MIN
U-matic / VHS / 16mm
Color (J H A)
Looks at what happens to a driver's vision and judgment while under the influence of alcohol. Shows volunteers at a party taking part in a series of games which require alertness, information processing and split attention, first while sober, then while drunk.
Health and Safety
Dist - CORF **Prod** - CTV 1981

One Force 20 MIN
16mm
B&W
LC 74-706165
Points out heroic deeds from 1776 to the Korean conflict, which provide evidence that Americans, although of many racial and national origins, join in one military force dedicated to peace and freedom.
Civics and Political Systems; History - United States
Dist - USNAC **Prod** - USDD 1964

One Fourth of Humanity 74 MIN
16mm
Color
Documents China in 1935 when Edgar Snow first met Mao - Tse Tung at the beginning of Mao's historic rise to power and contrasts that with what happened to China in the wake of the 'PROLETARIAN CULTURAL REVOLUTION.'.
Civics and Political Systems; History - World; Sociology
Dist - IMPACT **Prod** - IMPACT 1968

One frame duration 12 MIN
16mm
Color; B&W (G)
$40.00 rental
Asks the audience to concentrate completely on critical elements of the film experience too often ignored. A Takahiko Iimura production.
Fine Arts; Foreign Language
Dist - CANCIN

One Friday 10 MIN
16mm
Color
LC 73-702346
Follows a tiny boy who is unaware of the death and destruction around him as he chases his dog into the open and by his innocence wins over an armed combatant.
Guidance and Counseling; Sociology
Dist - COUNTR **Prod** - COUNTR 1973

One full moon 98 MIN
35mm
Color; PAL (G)
Follows the story of a man who, after a long prison sentence, returns to his village on the night of a full moon. Witnesses his reactions when he is forced to confront ghosts of his troubled past, namely ghosts of his poverty - stricken childhood; his past obsession with Christianity; and of the young girl for whose murder he was imprisoned. Directed by Endaf Emlyn for Ffilm Cymru Ltd. Contact distributor about price and availability outside the United Kingdom.
Fine Arts; Literature and Drama; Psychology; Religion and Philosophy; Sociology
Dist - BALFOR

One Generation is not Enough 24 MIN
U-matic / VHS
Color
Presents the art of violin - making as the family of Max Frirsz have practiced it for nearly 200 years.
Fine Arts
Dist - DENOPX **Prod** - DENONN

One Ghost Too many 15 MIN
U-matic
Color (I)
Teaches writing skills while telling the story of Chris and Lynne who try to send back the ghost of Mr Wetherby who was a school principal because of his strict supervision.
Education; English Language; Literature and Drama
Dist - TVOTAR **Prod** - TVOTAR 1982

One Giant Leap 60 MIN
U-matic / VHS
Spaceflight Series
Color
Explores the history of the Apollo program, including the death of three astronauts in a launch pad fire, Wally Schirra's manning of the successful flight of Apollo 7, powered by Wehrner Von Braun's Saturn 5 rockets, and the climatic flight of Apollo 11 and Neil Armstrong's walk on the moon. Discusses Soviet achievements and setbacks, the first space station and the last Apollo mission's historic handshake in space with the Soviets.
Science - Physical
Dist - PBS **Prod** - PBS

One Giant Step - the Integration of Children with Special Needs Series
Educable mentally handicapped 20 MIN
Gifted 20 MIN
Hearing Impaired 20 MIN
Overview 20 MIN
Physically Impaired 20 MIN
Trainable Mentally Handicapped 20 MIN
Visually Impaired 20 MIN
Dist - ACCESS

One giant step - the integration of children with special needs series
Behaviorally disordered 20 MIN
Dependent handicapped 20 MIN
Learning Disabled 20 MIN
Dist - ACCESS

One God 1 MIN
16mm
Color
LC 77-702501
Features a presentation of many things that have gained importance along side of God.
Religion and Philosophy
Dist - USC **Prod** - USC 1968

One, Going on Two 25 MIN
VHS / U-matic
Color
Shows how pediatricians chart the physical and psychological developments during a child's second year. Has a group of mothers with their children enjoying a picnic in the park and a chance to question the doctors about discipline, potty training, thumb sucking and other early childhood problems.
Health and Safety; Home Economics; Psychology
Dist - MEDCOM **Prod** - MEDCOM

One Good Turn 20 MIN
16mm
Color (J)
Examines the principles behind the Social Security program.
History - United States; Sociology
Dist - WORLDR **Prod** - WORLDR 1982

One Good Turn Deserves Another 10 MIN
U-matic
Calling Captain Consumer Series
Color (P I J)
Shows a man who wins an air conditioner. After reading the guarantee and consumer reports, interviewing former owners and a repairman, he decides he doesn't want it.
Business and Economics; Home Economics
Dist - TVOTAR **Prod** - TVOTAR 1985

One Good Turn - Social Security 20 MIN
U-matic / VHS
Color
Examines the principles behind Social Security. Promotes discussion on the philosophical and sociological implications of welfare systems.
Sociology
Dist - WORLDR **Prod** - WORLDR

One hand don't clap 92 MIN
VHS / 35mm
Color (G)
$300.00 rental
Takes a look at the modern wave of Calypso and Soca music, featuring Calypso Rose and Lord Kitchener. Directed by Kavery Dutta.

Fine Arts
Dist - KINOIC

One heart, many nations 30 MIN
VHS / U-matic
Color (G)
$49.95 purchase, $25.00 rental
Shows the historic 1992 White House Conference on Indian Education, the first time tribal and community leaders, educators and administrators gathered to set a national agenda for education reform. Explains five major themes in the 113 resolutions made by the delegates. Footage of dancing and celebrations in Alaska, Mississippi and North Carolina portrays the unique and holistic Indian experience.
Social Science
Dist - NAMPBC

One Hoe for Kalabo 27 MIN
16mm
Color (J)
The story of how machine tools have given dignity and power to human labor and world civilization.
Industrial and Technical Education; Psychology; Social Science; Sociology
Dist - MTP Prod - NATMTB

One Hour a Week 18 MIN
16mm
League School for Seriously Disturbed Children Series
Color
LC 75-702417
Describes the home training program of the League School for seriously disturbed children, showing how it helps parents cope with their child's emotional handicap by demonstrating techniques in behavior modification that they can practice at home.
Education; Psychology; Sociology
Dist - USNAC Prod - USBEH 1973

One Hour to Zero 56 MIN
16mm
Color (P I)
Portrays what happens when two children set off to find a runaway boy and return to their village, not knowing it has been abandoned because of the imminent danger of explosion at a nearby nuclear research station.
Literature and Drama
Dist - LUF Prod - LUF 1980

One Hundred and Fifteen Volts - Deadly Shipmate 19 MIN
U-matic
Color
LC 79-707973
Dramatizes actual incidents to point out the disastrous effects of low voltage electrical shock when the basic rules of electrical safety are violated or ignored.
Fine Arts; Industrial and Technical Education
Dist - USNAC Prod - USN 1979

One Hundred and Fifty Lbs of Fire Fighting Clout 5 MIN
VHS / U-matic
Color (IND)
Highlights the use of an Ansul brand wheeled fire extinguisher, model 150 - D. Shows the use of mobile equipment in fighting fuel spills and overhead flange pressure fires. Illustrates recharging extinguishers.
Health and Safety
Dist - ANSUL Prod - ANSUL 1980

One Hundred and One Critical Days 6 MIN
16mm
Color
LC 74-706166
Cites the interval from Memorial Day through Labor Day as a critical period for accidents, urging strict observance of safety rules by swimmers, boaters and motorists.
Health and Safety; Psychology
Dist - USNAC Prod - USAF 1968

One Hundred and One Dalmatians - a lesson in self - assertion 8 MIN
U-matic / VHS / 16mm
Disney's animated classics - lessons in living series
Color (K P I)
Uses a sequence from 101 Dalmatians to show two children and two dogs standing up to a villainess. Shows that it is important to defend one's own rights and the rights of others.
Guidance and Counseling; Literature and Drama
Dist - CORF Prod - DISNEY 1982

One Hundred and One Dalmations 79 MIN
16mm
Color
Shows how the hateful Cruella De Vil dognaps 15 dalmation puppies so that she can use their pelts for a fur coat.
Fine Arts
Dist - UAE Prod - DISNEY 1961

One hundred and one things for kids to do 60 MIN
VHS
Color (K P I T)
$19.95 purchase _ #S01351; $14.95 purchased _ #XV101
Features Shari Lewis and Lamb Chop, who demonstrate 101 tricks, games, puzzles, puns and 'dopey - dares' that children can perform with basic household materials.
Fine Arts; Physical Education and Recreation
Dist - UILL
GAINST

110 percent service - the edge that counts 21 MIN
VHS
Color (COR PRO)
$525.00 purchase, $245.00 rental _ #BTC11
Gives examples of extraordinary customer relations and its benefits. Includes a leader's guide. Produced by Banctraining.
Business and Economics
Dist - EXTR

120 over 80 - are you in control 30 MIN
VHS
Color (G)
$210.00 purchase, $19.50 rental _ #35236
Examines risk factors and nutrition concerns related to hypertension. Shows viewers how to examine and modify behaviors that increase susceptibility to high blood pressure. Uses a quiz format to answer questions about a wide variety of eating situations. Includes print material.
Health and Safety; Social Science
Dist - PSU Prod - WPSXTV 1988

102 Boulevard Haussmann 75 MIN
VHS
Color (A)
PdS99 purchase
Features Alan Bates as Marcel Proust venturing outside the Paris apartment where he is cared for by his devoted housekeeper Celeste - Janet McTeer, only occasionally. Reveals that, following a rare visit to a concert, Proust becomes fascinated by the tune that is to become a recurring motif of his celebrated work, A la Recherche du Temps Perdu. Written by Alan Bennett.
Biography; Fine Arts; Literature and Drama
Dist - BBCENE

One Hundred Children Waiting for a Train 57 MIN
16mm / VHS
Color (G)
$890.00, $590.00 purchase, $125.00 rental
Shows a group of Chilean children from one of Santiago's poorest slums in a filmmaking workshop conducted by Professor Alicia Vega. Reveals that most of the children in the workshop have never been to the movies, but quickly become versed in film history and filmmaking techniques.
Fine Arts; Geography - World; Health and Safety
Dist - FIRS Prod - FIRS 1988

One Hundred Entertainments 28 MIN
16mm / U-matic / VHS
Human Face of China Series
Color (H C A)
LC 79-701736
Focuses on the Shensi Provincial Acrobatic Troupe of China.
Geography - World; History - World; Physical Education and Recreation; Social Science; Sociology
Dist - LCOA Prod - FLMAUS 1979

The 115th edition of Ringling Brothers, Barnum and Bailey Circus 110 MIN
VHS
Color (G)
$89.95 purchase _ #S01352
Presents excerpts from the 115th Ringling Brothers, Barnum and Bailey Circus season. Includes such stars as the Living Unicorn, clowns, high - wire acts, and many animals.
Fine Arts; History - United States; Physical Education and Recreation
Dist - UILL

The 147 pound gobbler 46 MIN
VHS / U-matic / Cassette
Florida through the decades as seen by High - Sheriff Jim Turner 'series
Color; PAL (G)
$79.95, $24.95, $9.95 purchase _ #1070
Portrays the life of a former High - Sheriff of Levy County, Florida, Jim Turner. Brings cousin Chauncey up from Miami, supposedly to hunt turkey. Chauncey stays drunk for a week and Turner hires Tom Gilchrist to kill a gobbler for proof to Chauncey's wife that he's been hunting. Part seven of an eleven - part historical docudrama.
Civics and Political Systems; Fine Arts; Health and Safety; History - United States; Physical Education and Recreation; Psychology
Dist - NORDS Prod - NORDS 1991

100 metres free style 4 MIN
VHS
Color; PAL (G)
PdS25 purchase
Uses swimming as a metaphor for the victory of life over death. Presents an Annette Riisager for Buxton Films Limited, Denmark production.
Fine Arts; Literature and Drama; Physical Education and Recreation; Sociology
Dist - BALFOR

The 100 percent tax penalty - what employers need to know 50 MIN
VHS
Color (C PRO COR)
$95.00 purchase _ #Y137
Describes how the IRS is authorized to assess a 100 percent penalty against responsible officers of a business that fails to pay over trust fund taxes. Examines the workings of IRS section 6672 with a detailed look at the concept of responsibility and willfulness as proof of liability.
Civics and Political Systems
Dist - ALIABA Prod - CLETV 1991

One Hundred Sixty - Seven St, Bronx '83 29 MIN
U-matic / VHS
Color
Provides an impressionistic yiew of a street jam. Presented by Bob Harris and Rii Kanzaki.
Fine Arts
Dist - ARTINC Prod - ARTINC

One Hundred - Thirty - Nine 25 MIN
16mm
B&W
Shows the student take - over of Sproul and Moses Halls on the Berkeley campus to protest the regents' refusal to grant credit for Social Analysis 139x, a course for which Eldridge Cleaver was to be a guest lecturer.
Civics and Political Systems; Education; History - United States
Dist - CANWRL Prod - CANWRL 1968

One Hundred Thousand Piece Jigsaw Puzzle 26 MIN
16mm
Color
Describes the work and care involved in restoring and preserving the remnants of old Viking ships found in Roskilde Fjord in Denmark.
History - World; Social Science
Dist - AUDPLN Prod - RDCG

One Hundred Twenty - Five Rooms of Comfort 80 MIN
16mm
Color
LC 75-701906
Tells how the owner of a hotel in St Thomas, Ontario, returns from a mental hospital where he went to recover after the death of his father.
Fine Arts
Dist - CFDEVC Prod - CFDEVC 1974

One Hundred Twenty - Nine Close - Up 7 MIN
16mm
Color
LC 75-701907
Examines the manufacture of the IBM 129 Data Recorder at IBM Canada.
Business and Economics
Dist - IBM Prod - IBM 1972

100 years of Marxism - Leninism in Bohemia 4 MIN
16mm / VHS
Color (G C)
$150.00, $100.00 purchase, $25.00 rental
Encapsulates the emergence of Marxist thinking, its manifestation through Lenin and the ultimate rejection of an ideology which shaped 20th - century European history, all in a four - minute cartoon by Pavel Koutsky.
Civics and Political Systems; Fine Arts; History - World
Dist - FIRS

One Hundred Years to Live 30 MIN
VHS / 16mm
Color
Shows how a 99 - year - old mother and her daughter react to being placed in a nursing home. Looks at various attitudes toward old age.
Health and Safety; Sociology
Dist - HRC Prod - OHC

One Hundred Years Voyage 28 MIN
16mm
Color
Presents an historical overview of the 100 year old development of the oil tanker, from the days of the sailing schooners, when oil was loaded in barrels and cases, to the age of the supertanker.
Industrial and Technical Education; Social Science
Dist - MTP Prod - EXXON

One if by Land 12 MIN
U-matic / VHS / 16mm
Color (J H)
LC 79-701785
Takes a position on why the people of Middlesex County did something about independence while the rest of the American colonies talked about it and uncovers some unsung heroes in the process.
History - United States
Dist - MCFI **Prod** - USFL 1975

One in Eleven 14 MIN
U-matic / VHS / 16mm
Color
LC 82-700069
Informs women that there is a viable alternative to mastectomy. Presents evidence that early detection of breast cancer can make it possible to avoid surgical removal of a breast. Notes that this knowledge tends to produce more breast self - examination and early treatment.
Health and Safety; Sociology
Dist - PFP **Prod** - STANDC 1982

One in Five 17 MIN
U-matic / VHS / 16mm
Color (A)
LC 83-700666
Presents the basic facts of heart disease and explains that the manual laborer is just as susceptible as the executive.
Health and Safety
Dist - IFB **Prod** - MILLBK 1982

One in the Lord 30 MIN
U-matic / VHS / 16mm
Color (A)
Studies the people and ministry of the ethnic minority local Methodist churches. Focuses on a Black church, an Hispanic congregation, an Asian church and a Native American congregation. Looks at their cultural heritage and current needs and the challenges they face in the future.
Religion and Philosophy; Sociology
Dist - ECUFLM **Prod** - UMCOM 1978

One in the same - 'a special look at teenagers and diversity' with W Mitchell 30 MIN
VHS
Color (J H G)
$199.00 purchase
Joins a diverse group of teenagers who discuss gangs, violence, pregnancy, HIV, AIDS, prejudice, dreams, solutions, survival. Includes insights from W Mitchell, author of The Man Who Would Not Be Defeated.
Health and Safety; Sociology
Dist - CHERUB **Prod** - CHERUB

One in the Spirit 20 MIN
16mm
Color
LC 78-705628
Shows the activities of a group of teen - aged White boys and girls from a reformed church who participate in a work - camp project on a Black school campus in Brewton, Alabama, working with the Black students for one week.
Geography - United States; Psychology; Sociology
Dist - RECA **Prod** - RECA 1969

1 in 20 - cystic fibrosis 10 MIN
VHS
Color (G)
$59.95 purchase _ #UW5336
Uses animation to explain how cystic fibrosis affects the body, how it is treated and managed, and what those who have it and those who care for them can expect. Features a narrator who delivers a very personal account of her life with CF, talking openly about physiotherapy, enzymes and gastrostomy operations, as well as the social and psychological effects of the condition.
Health and Safety
Dist - FOTH

One is a whole number 160 MIN
16mm / VHS
Color (J H C G A R)
$129.95, $255.00 purchase _ #918VSV
Features Dr Harold Ivan Smith speaking on moral standards for single Christian adults. Considers topics such as singleness, marriage, divorce and sexuality, comparing Biblical standards with those of the secular world. Includes a comedy performance by the team of Hicks and Cohagan. Includes a study guide. Produced by Victory Films, Inc.
Guidance and Counseling; Literature and Drama; Religion and Philosophy; Sociology
Dist - GF

One is a whole number series
Features the comedy team of Hicks and Cohagan in dramatizations of situations Christian single adults often face. Covers topics related to being single, marriage, divorce and sexuality. Narrated by Dr Harold Ivan Smith. Consists of four 40 - minute episodes and includes study guide.
Divorce and sexuality - Tape 2 80 MIN
One is a whole number series 160 MIN
Singleness and marriage - Tape 1 80 MIN
Dist - APH **Prod** - SPAPRO

One Kitten for Kim 16 MIN
16mm / U-matic / VHS
Reading Short Stories Series
Color (P I)
LC 74-703746
Presents the story of a little boy who owns seven kittens and is told by his parents that he may only keep one and must give the other six away. Encourages discussion of Kim's adventures, the reactions of his parents and the students own experiences with finding homes for animals in the lower grades.
English Language; Literature and Drama
Dist - AIMS **Prod** - MORLAT 1973

One Lap Around the World 28 MIN
16mm
Color
LC 78-701563
Shows professional drivers travelling around the world in two cars owned by National Car Rental System.
Geography - World
Dist - MTP **Prod** - NCRENT 1977

One Last Shock 21 MIN
U-matic / VHS / 16mm
Color (IND)
LC 81-700774
Dramatizes the events leading to an electrical accident. Outlines the misuses of electrical equipment in the factory and office.
Health and Safety
Dist - IFB **Prod** - MILLBK 1980

One Length Bob - Cut
U-matic / VHS
Lessons on a Mannequin Series, Lesson I
Color
Shows how the mannequin is sectioned using a special technique, and how to establish length. Explains many haircutting terms as work progresses. Emphasizes scissor control. Demonstrates how hair is held low during cutting with special emphasis to the sectioning and cutting of the hang area.
Education; Home Economics
Dist - MPCEDP **Prod** - MPCEDP 1984

One Little Girl Alone 6 MIN
U-matic / VHS
Color
Portrays the successful efforts of a somewhat retarded child discovering pride and self - respect in learning to do interesting things within the scope of her learning power. Uses the story and illustrations from the book of the same title.
Psychology
Dist - PRIMED **Prod** - PRIMED

One Loaf of Bread 15 MIN
16mm
Color (H C)
Symbolizes man's age - old struggle against hunger and want in a never - ending search for a better life for all. Traces thousands of years of human history, highlighting the evolution of wheat growing, milling and baking from prehistoric times to the automated electronically controlled triumphs of the present.
Agriculture; Home Economics; Social Science; Sociology
Dist - NINEFC **Prod** - GEMILL

One Man 30 MIN
16mm
B&W
LC FIA64-1163
Reconstructs the mysterious case of Raoul Wallenberg, a Swedish diplomat, who disappeared behind the Iron Curtain in 1945, while attempting to save the Jewish community of Budapest.
History - World; Religion and Philosophy
Dist - NAAJS **Prod** - JTS 1958

One man alone
Videodisc
Laser learning set 1 series; Set 1
Color; CAV (P I)
$375.00 purchase _ #8L5405
Chronicles the experience of Admiral Richard E Byrd in 1934 when he was the sole proprietor of a weather station in the interior of Antarctica. Reveals that the experience nearly cost him his life. Considers character. Part of a series of six theme - based interactive videodisc lessons. Requires a Pioneer LD - V2000 or 2200, with barcode reader and adapter, or a Pioneer LD - V4200 or higher. Includes user's guide, two readers.
Biography; Geography - United States; History - United States
Dist - BARR **Prod** - BARR 1992

One - man show 48 MIN
16mm
Color; B&W (G)
$150.00 rental
Offers a special package price to encourage viewers to show all of Peter Kubelka's films together in one evening. Includes Mosaik im Vertrauen, Adebar, Schwechater, Arnulf Rainer, Unsere Afrikareise and Pause, all made between 1954 and 1966.
Fine Arts
Dist - CANCIN

One Man Show 14 MIN
16mm
B&W
Depicts the struggles of a contemporary sculptor in a satire aimed at pop art.
Fine Arts; Literature and Drama
Dist - NYU **Prod** - NYU

One Man's Alaska 27 MIN
U-matic / VHS / 16mm
Color
LC 78-700945
Profiles conservationist and wildlife cinematographer Dick Proenneke at his wilderness home in the Lake Clark area of Alaska. Includes scenes of area wildlife along with clips of Proenneke carving his log cabin home out of the wilderness.
Geography - United States; Science - Natural
Dist - USNAC **Prod** - USNPS 1977

One Man's Dream - to Someday Find a Cure for ALS 25 MIN
16mm
Color
Presents the story of the courageous fight of Les Turner, a young father of three, who died of Amyotrophic Lateral Sclerosis, a fatal nerve disorder commonly known as Lou Gehrig's disease.
Biography; Health and Safety
Dist - MTP **Prod** - TURNL

One Man's Family 27 MIN
16mm
Color
LC 76-703251
A shortened version of the motion picture Thirty - Nine Hundred Million And One. Takes a look at India's population problem with special emphasis on women's roles and problems.
History - World; Sociology
Dist - ASTRSK **Prod** - OXFAM 1975

One Man's Fight for Life 56 MIN
U-matic / VHS
Color (A)
LC 84-706265
Records Saif Ullah's lung cancer and its treatment. Looks at the emotional toll cancer takes on its victims and their families.
Health and Safety
Dist - FI **Prod** - BELLDA 1983

One man's history - Orwell's Animal Farm 30 MIN
VHS
Color (A)
PdS65 purchase
Explains the reason for George Orwell's decision to write the animal fantasyAnimal Farm. The author had wanted to write a history of Russia from 1917 - 1940 in simple terms. To do this he chose to use an allegory, using animals for the main protagonists. The program uses extracts from the animated film version of Animal Farm and archive footage and stills of the Russian Revolution and World War II to illustrate Orwell's analogies.
Literature and Drama
Dist - BBCENE

One Man's Multinational 30 MIN
16mm / U-matic / VHS
Enterprise Series
Color (C A)
Tells about Thomas Bata's shoe - manufacturing empire and how, as he moves into Third World countries, he willingly does business with democracies and dictatorships alike.
Business and Economics; Social Science
Dist - LCOA **Prod** - WGBHTV 1981

One Man's Property 56 MIN
U-matic / VHS / 16mm
Fight Against Slavery Series no 2; No 2
Color
LC 78-700501
Traces the events leading up to the Somerset Case in 1772, in which the judge declared that it was unlawful for one man to be the property of another on the soil of England.
History - United States; History - World; Sociology
Dist - TIMLIF **Prod** - BBCTV 1977

One Man's Revolution - Mao Tse - tung 20 MIN
16mm / U-matic / VHS
Twentieth Century History Series
Color (H C A)
Focuses on the life and career of Mao Tse - tung, who led the Chinese Communist Party for 42 years.
Biography; History - World
Dist - FI **Prod** - BBCTV 1981

One Man's Revolution - Mao Tse - Tung - Pt 11 20 MIN
16mm
Twentieth Century History Series - Vol III
Color (S)
$380.00 purchase _ #548 - 9228
Illuminates the events and issues which shaped our modern world. Uses archival footage, maps, drawings, feature film segments, paintings and posters to illustrate historic events. The first thirteen programs are available separately on 16mm. Part 11 of Volume III of thirteen programs, 'One Man's Revolution - Mao Tse - tung,' covers the career of Mao, including his rural beginnings, the legendary Long March, the Japanese invasion of China and the Cultural Revolution.
Civics and Political Systems; Geography - World; History - United States; History - World
Dist - FI **Prod** - BBCTV 1981

One Million Hiroshimas 28 MIN
16mm
Color
Captures the workings and the spirit of the Second Congress of the International Physicians for the Prevention of Nuclear War. Views the plenary session, workshops, informal discussions and banquet. Interviews such prominent participants as Jonas Salk, Helen Caldicott and Carl Sagan.
Civics and Political Systems; Sociology
Dist - ANDMIC **Prod** - ANDMIC 1982

One Million Hours 21 MIN
16mm / U-matic / VHS
Color
Deals with an accident investigation in an engineering plant in England where an employee has been struck and injured by a truck. Shows how the work force and management can work together in accident investigation in order to prevent recurring incidents and future accidents.
Health and Safety
Dist - IFB **Prod** - MILLBK

The One minute cook - microwave made easy 60 MIN
VHS
Color (H C G)
$39.95 purchase _ #MX501V
Shows how mastering a few simple techniques will enable making delicious meals in only a few minutes. Teaches about carry over cooking and why it's important, proper utensils to use, defrosting tips, foolproof ways to determine cooking and more. Offers tips on how to give meat a 'gourmet' look, techniques of microwaving and recipes.
Home Economics
Dist - CAMV

The One Minute Cook - Microwave made Easy with Best Selling Author, B Harris 61 MIN
BETA / VHS
Color
Provides instruction in microwave cooking. Features Barbara Harris, author of Let's Cook Microwave.
Home Economics
Dist - MOHOMV **Prod** - MOHOMV

One minute management system series

Building the one minute manager skills	48 MIN
Leadership and the one minute manager	80 MIN
The One minute manager	50 MIN
Putting the one minute manager to work	59 MIN

Dist - MAGVID

The One minute manager 50 MIN
U-matic / 16mm / VHS
One minute management system series
Color (G PRO A)
$1295.00, $995.00, $895.00 purchase, $350.00, $250.00 rental
Presents Dr Ken Blanchard who introduces his 'one minute manager' system.
Business and Economics; Psychology
Dist - MAGVID **Prod** - MAGVID 1982

The One Minute Manager 50 MIN
16mm / BETA
Color (A)
Presents Dr Ken Blanchard offering advice about how to manage one's time and one's employees more efficiently. Focuses on goals, praises and reprimands.
Business and Economics; Psychology
Dist - CBSFOX **Prod** - CBSFOX

One Minute Manager 50 MIN
Cassette / VHS / 16mm
Stereo (A C PRO)
$950.00 purchase, $200.00 rental
Contains information useful in both business and personal life by Kenneth Blanchard, PhD, and Spencer Johnson, MD. Gives simple system to increase productivity. Book and six cassettes included.
Business and Economics; Psychology
Dist - VLEARN

One minute manager - getting fit 55 MIN
VHS
Color (A PRO)
$69.00 purchase _ #S01125
Focuses on lifestyle choices as the key to feeling best. Emphasizes the importance of balance, stress management, and commitment to good choices. Hosted by Ken Blanchard.
Business and Economics; Physical Education and Recreation; Psychology
Dist - UILL

One minute meditator 60 MIN
VHS
Color (G)
$39.95 purchase _ #P40
Teaches meditation in a production by the Edgar Cayce Foundation.
Religion and Philosophy
Dist - HP

One minute movies 5 MIN
16mm
Color (G)
$10.00 rental
Features the Residents, an underground performance group,in four individual one minute movies. Employs cultural sabotage with humor. Directed by Graeme Whifler and the Residents. Produced by Cryptic Corporatioon aka Ralph Records.
Fine Arts
Dist - CANCIN

One Minute Please 8 MIN
16mm
Professional Selling Practices Series 1 Series
Color (H A)
LC 77-702358
Presents attitudes, behavior and techniques which enable the salesperson to give individual attention and service to more than one customer at a time, thus multiplying sales without sacrificing goodwill.
Business and Economics
Dist - SAUM **Prod** - SAUM 1967

The One Minute Safety Manager - Part 1
BETA / VHS
One Minute Safety Manager Series
Color (PRO)
Features Dr Kenneth Blanchard, co - author of THE ONE MINUTE MANAGER.
Health and Safety
Dist - NCONCO **Prod** - NCONCO

The One Minute Safety Manager - Part 2
VHS / BETA
One Minute Safety Manager Series
Color (PRO)
Features Dr Kenneth Blanchard, co - author of THE ONE MINUTE MANAGER.
Health and Safety
Dist - NCONCO **Prod** - NCONCO

The One Minute Safety Manager - Part 3
VHS / BETA
One Minute Safety Manager Series
Color (PRO)
Features Dr Kenneth Blanchard, co - author of THE ONE MINUTE MANAGER.
Health and Safety
Dist - NCONCO **Prod** - NCONCO

One Minute Safety Manager Series
The One Minute Safety Manager - Part 1
The One Minute Safety Manager - Part 2
The One Minute Safety Manager - Part 3
Dist - NCONCO

The One Minute Salesperson
VHS
$39.95 purchase _ #BZ100V
Demonstrates the secrets of how to prosper personally as well as financially with less stress.
Business and Economics
Dist - CAREER **Prod** - CAREER

One Monday Morning 10 MIN
U-matic / VHS / 16mm
Color (P)
LC 73-700796
Presents the children's story 'ONE MONDAY MORNING' by Ura Shulevitz.
Guidance and Counseling; Literature and Drama
Dist - WWS **Prod** - WWS 1972

One more among them 31 MIN
16mm
Cuba - a view from inside series
Color & B&W (G)
$400.00 purchase, $50.00 rental
Profiles Tania, the guerilla active in Che Guevara's Bolivian campaign who was killed in 1967, shortly before Che. Features part of a 17 - part series of shorts by and about Cuban women. Directed by Rebecca Chavez. Illustrated catalog available. Contact distributor for programming advice and discount package rental fees.
Civics and Political Systems; Fine Arts
Dist - CNEMAG

One more Hurdle 45 MIN
VHS
Color (J)
$495.00 purchase, $50.00 rental _ #D - 534; LC 89706223
Tells a true story of individual struggle to achieve and the strength of a family united in the fulfillment of a dream.
Physical Education and Recreation; Psychology; Sociology
Dist - ALTSUL **Prod** - BRKFLD 1989

One more season 60 MIN
VHS
Color (H C G A R)
$59.95 purchase, $10.00 rental _ #35 - 897 - 8936
Profiles All - American athlete and coach Charlie Wedemeyer and his battle with a mysterious, incurable disease.
Guidance and Counseling; Health and Safety
Dist - APH

One more Season - the Charlie Wedemeyer Story 52 MIN
U-matic / VHS
Color (C)
$249.00, $149.00 purchase _ #AD - 1435
Tells the story of high school football coach Charlie Wedemeyer and his ten - year battle with Lou Gehrig's disease. Shows that he is determined to continue coaching with the support and help of his family and that he has overcome the obstacles of nearly total disability and defied the odds of terminal illness.
Fine Arts; Health and Safety; Psychology
Dist - FOTH **Prod** - FOTH

One more Smoke
VHS / U-matic
Color (SPANISH)
Details the effect of nicotine on the lungs and heart as well as the lethal dangers of carbon monoxide.
Psychology; Science - Natural
Dist - MIFE **Prod** - MIFE

One more Winter 15 MIN
16mm
Color (H C)
Shows how an old couple's romance generates envy in a young man who is still untouched by love. Written and directed by Francoise Sagan.
Fine Arts; Guidance and Counseling
Dist - FI **Prod** - PROBEL 1976

One nation indivisible - 1845 - 1865 14 MIN
VHS / 16mm
Railroad series
Color (I J H G)
$280.00, $39.95 purchase
Reveals that by the 1850s, railroads were dramatically changing the American way of life - faster transportation, bigger loads and year - round operation. Shows that the rail system ran east and west, tying the big river systems together, deciding the locations of towns and cities and, during the Civil War, giving the North a distinct military advantage. Part of a series on American railroads.
Geography - United States; History - United States; Social Science
Dist - KAWVAL **Prod** - KAWVAL

One Nation Under God 60 MIN
U-matic / VHS
Color
Tours the so - called 'New Right' and 'Moral Majority.' Features interviews with James Robison, Rev Jerry Falwell and Sen George McGovern.
Religion and Philosophy; Sociology
Dist - WCCOTV **Prod** - WCCOTV 1981

One nation under God 83 MIN
VHS / 16mm
Color (G)
$490.00, $1350.00 purchase, $125.00 rental
Investigates the world of 'ex - gay' ministries and 'conversion' therapies. Reveals techniques to 'cure' homosexuals, such as makeovers for lesbians and tackle football for gay men. Focuses on two former leaders of Exodus, one of the ex - gay ministries. Produced by Teodoro Maniaci and Francine M. Rzeznick.
Fine Arts; Literature and Drama; Religion and Philosophy; Sociology
Dist - FIRS

One Nation Under Stress 52 MIN
U-matic / VHS
Color (G)
$279.00, $179.00 purchase _ #AD - 1687
Considers what causes stress. Explains the consequences of stress. Demonstrates ways in which stress can be turned into a positive force. Features Merlin Olsen as host.
Health and Safety; Psychology; Sociology
Dist - FOTH **Prod** - FOTH

One of a Kind 58 MIN
16mm / U-matic / VHS
Color
LC 81-700925
Deals with the love between a mother and daughter and the problem of child abuse.
Sociology
Dist - PHENIX **Prod** - BAKERD 1978

One of a Million 22 MIN
16mm
Doctors at Work Series
B&W (H C A)
LC FIA65-1354
A few startling events cause a young executive to recognize his impending state of alcholism and to seek rehabilitation.
Guidance and Counseling; Health and Safety
Dist - LAWREN **Prod** - CMA 1963

One of many - Dr Nhan 16 MIN
U-matic / VHS / 16mm
Color (J)
Highlights the problems faced by the displaced 'boat people' of Vietnam who emigrated to the West.
History - World; Sociology
Dist - LUF **Prod** - LUF

One of Our Own 55 MIN
16mm
Color (H C A)
LC 82-700421
Presents the story of the close - knit family of a mentally retarded boy that moves to a new community and must re - evaluate the wisdom of keeping him at home. Shows the retarded boy adjusting to his new home and learning skills that will help him become independent.
Psychology; Sociology
Dist - FLMLIB **Prod** - CANBC 1981

One of Our Own 30 MIN
VHS / 16mm
Color (PRO)
$565.00 purchase, $195.00 rental, $45.00 preview
Educates employees about AIDS in the workplace. Discusses the legal, social, and business repercussions of this disease. Works to dispel the fear among employees that the virus is contagious. Explains legal issues involved if an employee contracts the virus. Includes a management guide, leader's guide, questions and answers about AIDS, and a poster.
Business and Economics; Health and Safety; Psychology; Sociology
Dist - UTM **Prod** - UTM

One of Our Own - Dealing with AIDS in the Workplace 30 MIN
16mm / VHS
(G)
$140/3 Day 16mm/VHS/3/4
Educates workers and management on workplace - related aspects of the AIDS epidemic - how to deal with employees who have AIDS. Includes two study guides, a poster, and several brochures.
Business and Economics; Health and Safety
Dist - BAXMED **Prod** - DARTNL 1989

One of the Family 27 MIN
16mm
Color (A)
LC 79-700697
Shows the difficulties and mutual adjustments that must be made for the adoption of an older child. Explores efforts by the adoption agency in Los Angeles County to prepare the child for adoption.
Home Economics; Sociology
Dist - IA **Prod** - LAC 1974

One of the Family 29 MIN
U-matic
A Different Understanding Series
Color (PRO)
Interviews the parents of a son with cerebral palsy who describe the trials and joys of having a special child.
Psychology
Dist - TVOTAR **Prod** - TVOTAR 1985

One of the Family 28.5 MIN
VHS / 16mm
A Different Understanding Series
Color (G)
$90.00 purchase _ #BPN178012
Describes the adjustments that the parents of a child with cerebral palsy went through and the joy they found in the process.
Education; Psychology
Dist - RMIBHF **Prod** - RMIBHF

One of the family 15 MIN
VHS
Color (P I J)
Features Eammon, an eight year old boy who is disabled by spina bifida. Looks at his life with his family. Enables children to understand the needs of handicapped people.
Guidance and Counseling; Health and Safety; Psychology
Dist - VIEWTH **Prod** - VIEWTH

One of the Gang 30 MIN
U-matic / VHS / 16mm
Powerhouse Series
Color (I J)
Reveals that despite a physical handicap, Mike holds his own and prevents a diamond theft at the Powerhouse.
Psychology
Dist - GA **Prod** - EFCVA 1982

One of the Missing 6 MIN
16mm
B&W
LC 78-701621
Deals with the bizarre fate of a sharpshooter in the Civil War. Based on the story One Of The Missing by Ambrose Bierce.
Fine Arts; Literature and Drama
Dist - USC **Prod** - USC

One of Thirty - Five Million 18 MIN
VHS / U-matic
Color
Presents the story of one arthritic sufferer, George Brown, and a critical year in his life, the year in which his arthritis is diagnosed, treated and controlled, and the year when his sense of humor, determination, and medical regimen help him to learn how to live with his disease.
Health and Safety; Psychology
Dist - WSTGLC **Prod** - WSTGLC

One of those Days
U-matic / 16mm
Color (A)
Uses humor to motivate workers to analyze their materials handling procedures and make them safer.
Health and Safety
Dist - BNA **Prod** - BNA 1983

One of those People 29 MIN
16mm
Color (A)
Looks at corporate/industrial alcoholism and the possibilities for effectiveness of a well - developed Employee Assistance Program. Stresses on - the - job performance, personal interaction, intervention and company - union cooperation.
Business and Economics; Health and Safety; Psychology
Dist - FMSP **Prod** - UPR 1975

One on one 15 MIN
VHS
Color (C A PRO)
$295.00 purchase
Provides training for public safety personnel in handling people under the influence of PCP, emphasizing the physical effects of the drug on the user, warning signs to recognize and precautions for fire and police personnel to take. Includes booklet with the videocassette.
Civics and Political Systems; Guidance and Counseling; Health and Safety; Psychology
Dist - PFP

One on one canvassing program
VHS / 16mm
Color (G IND)
$5.00 rental
Teaches the basic principles of the one - on - one canvassing program which is being used by many unions to reach members on different issues. Emphasizes the three keys to successful canvassing - always be confident, controlled and considerate.
Business and Economics; Social Science
Dist - AFLCIO **Prod** - LIPA 1986

One on one coaching series

Defensive ends	60 MIN
Defensive middle guard	60 MIN
Defensive secondary	60 MIN
Linebackers	60 MIN
Mental Game	60 MIN
Offensive Backs	60 MIN
Offensive Line	60 MIN
Quarterbacks	60 MIN
Strength Training	60 MIN

Dist - CAMV

One - on - one training
VHS
Color (PRO A G)
$995.00 purchase, $165.00 rental
Presents a skit showing how not to conduct on - the - job training, explains six steps for effective training and illustrates them.
Business and Economics; Guidance and Counseling; Psychology
Dist - EXTR

One on One Training Skills 25 MIN
VHS / 16mm
ITC Supervisory Methods Series
(C PRO)
$995.00 purchase, $165.00 rental
Teaches a step - by - step approach to effective one - on - one training. Provides all materials to conduct a day - long session.
Education
Dist - VLEARN **Prod** - INTRFL

One - on - one with the master - Video One 90 MIN
VHS
Mandolin of Bill Monroe series
Color (G)
$49.95 purchase _ #VD - MON - MN01
Features Bill Monroe, 'Father of Bluegrass,' who demonstrates his mandolin techniques and repertoire. Plays over 25 tunes - some never heard before - including favorites such as Rawhide; Wheel Hoss; Pike Country Breakdown; Bluegrass Stomp and Get Up John. Includes footage of a special performance by Monroe for President Jimmy Carter at the White House, 1979. John Hartford hosts and The Blue Grass Boys are special guests. Part one of a two - part series.
Fine Arts
Dist - HOMETA **Prod** - HOMETA

One Out of Eleven 26 MIN
U-matic / VHS
Color (C)
$249.00, $149.00 purchase _ #AD - 1889
Examines the psychological trauma suffered by victims of breast cancer. Reveals that one out of eleven women in America will develop breast cancer. Explains the various treatment options available and the factors that put women at risk for this type of cancer.
Health and Safety; Psychology; Sociology
Dist - FOTH **Prod** - FOTH

One Out of Five 6 MIN
16mm
B&W
LC FIA66-1146
Describes a situation in which a new truck has arrived to replace one of the five used in a telephone company's installation and repair operation. Discusses how to select the driver to whom this new truck should be assigned, and how a formula can be worked out to settle this kind of problem.
Business and Economics
Dist - GCCED **Prod** - UGA 1959

One out of ten 29 MIN
VHS / 16mm
Color (H A)
$280.00, $450.00 purchase, $50.00 rental _ #9559
Examines the increasing problem of alcoholism, with emphasis on the less publicized needs of minority groups. Explores the physical, mental, and environmental causes of alcoholism and describes treatment programs by government agencies. Provides ten questions viewers should ask themselves to discover if they are now or on their way to becoming another 'one out of ten.'
Health and Safety; Psychology
Dist - AIMS **Prod** - AIMS 1978

One Out of Ten 28 MIN
U-matic / VHS
Color
Reveals that medical authorities agree that at least ten per cent of the people who drink are alcoholics. Presents the latest medical information and demonstrates therapy and treatment.
Psychology; Sociology
Dist - IA **Prod** - LACFU

One People 12 MIN
16mm
Color (I J H C A)
Shows how the United States was settled by groups of every nationality. Points out the various contributions of each group. An animated film, narrated by Ralph Bellamy.
Guidance and Counseling; History - United States; Psychology; Sociology
Dist - ADL **Prod** - ADL 1946

One Percent of Us 53 MIN
U-matic / VHS
Color (G)

$249.00, $149.00 purchase _ #AD - 1795
Presents the third segment about five mentally handicapped children. Looks at them at ages between 25 and 31, leading full and active lives and appearing to have fulfilled much of their potential. Part of three parts which document twenty years in the lives of five handicapped people.
Education; Health and Safety; Psychology
Dist - FOTH **Prod** - FOTH

One Person Too Late 28 MIN
U-matic
Color
Carries the Red Cross home safety message to the public.
Health and Safety
Dist - AMRC **Prod** - GALSD

One person's struggle with gender - biased language 35 MIN
VHS
Color (PRO A G)
$49.95 purchase _ #WBGU010V-B
Fosters an awareness of problems with gender - biased language. Presents, through the mind of a imaginary viewer, scenes where gender insensitive language is used. Discusses the scenes with experts on language and diversity. Includes discussions on such words as he, man, and Dear Sir; sport team names; Miss, Ms, and Mrs,; broad, dame, male hegemony; man and wife; diminutive job titles for women; and race and class concerns.
Psychology; Sociology
Dist - CAMV

One Plus One 25 MIN
16mm
Color (R)
Takes a humorous look at problems that plague the home, exposing conflicts that trouble marriages whether they be good or bad. Shows how God's plan for happy marriages is summed up in a simple equation.
Guidance and Counseling; Sociology
Dist - GF **Prod** - GF

One Plus One Equals New 15 MIN
U-matic / VHS
Magic Shop Series no 4
Color (P)
LC 83-706149
Employs a magician named Amazing Alexander and his assistants to explore compound words.
English Language
Dist - GPN **Prod** - CVETVC 1982

One Plus One Equals Three 10 MIN
16mm
Color (K P I)
LC 72-700414
A satire on the power struggle at every level of life, and the distortion of truth which ensues. Tells the story of a midget who fails in his attempt to persuade a giant that one plus one equals two.
English Language; Guidance and Counseling; Literature and Drama; Sociology
Dist - MMA **Prod** - VIBAF 1970

One PM 95 MIN
16mm
Color
Features Jean - Luc Godard's never completed One American Movie (One AM). With Rip Torn, Jefferson Airplane, Leroi Jones, Tom Hayden, and Eldridge Cleaver. By D A Pennebaker with Jean - Luc Godard and Richard Leacock.
Fine Arts
Dist - PENNAS **Prod** - PENNAS

One Pot Meals 28 MIN
VHS / 16mm
What's Cooking Series
Color (G)
$55.00 rental _ #WHAC - 105
Home Economics
Dist - PBS **Prod** - WHYY

One Rescuer CPR 15 MIN
16mm / U-matic / VHS
REACT - Review of Emergency Aid and CPR Training Series
Color (H C A)
Health and Safety
Dist - CORF **Prod** - CORF

One - Rescuer CPR 18 MIN
U-matic / VHS
Cardiopulmonary Resuscitation Series
Color (PRO)
Teaches how to tell whether a person is unconscious, how to administer rescue breathing and how to perform external chest compressions.
Health and Safety
Dist - HSCIC **Prod** - HSCIC 1984

One - Ring Circus 29 MIN
VHS / 16mm
Color (G)
$100.00 purchase _ #ORCRVHS
Follows one of the last traveling circuses as it moves through the mountain towns of Appalachia. Illustrates the life of the circus and its performers behind the scenes.
Geography - United States; Physical Education and Recreation; Sociology
Dist - APPAL

One River, One Country - the U S - Mexico Border 47 MIN
VHS / 16mm
Color (H C A)
$445.00, $330.00
The hybrid culture of the borderland between the U.S. and Mexico has produced economic and social problems. Citizens of the two nations exchange ideas on how an aggressive "good - neighbor" policy of American trade with Mexico might alleviate economic troubles and also benefit the U.S. With CBS News Correspondent Bill Moyers.
Business and Economics; Geography - United States; Geography - World; Sociology
Dist - CAROUF **Prod** - CBSTV 1986

The One romantic adventure of Edward 8 MIN
16mm
B&W (A)
$15.00 rental
Stars a young man, played by Stan Brakhage, who finds himself in a seriously funny mix - up by indulging in semi - sexual fantasies and allowing the fantasies to take over.
Fine Arts
Dist - CANCIN **Prod** - JORDAL 1956

One Room Schoolhouse
16mm
Color
Shows one teacher coping with fifteen children in eight grades in one room.
Education
Dist - DIRECT **Prod** - DREWAS 1979

One - Sample Testing - Product Evaluation
U-matic / VHS
Statistics for Managers Series
Color (IND)
Cites one - sample testing as a formal way to determine if goals are being met, as defined by mean and variance. Discusses hypothesis testing and confidence intervals in the one - sample case for the mean with variance known or unknown. Tells about testing for variance as well.
Business and Economics; Mathematics; Psychology
Dist - COLOSU **Prod** - COLOSU

One - Sample Tests for Qualitative Data 30 MIN
VHS / U-matic
Engineering Statistics Series
Color (IND)
Incorporates hypothesis testing and confidence intervals for the normal and student's distributions. Shows a useful and practical discussion for those with sample means. Reviews question, 'Do we have an unusual sample mean value or has our process shifted?'.
Industrial and Technical Education; Mathematics; Psychology
Dist - COLOSU **Prod** - COLOSU

One Second Before Sunrise - A Search for Solutions, Program 1 Series
Fish farming in Amazonia 13 MIN
Organic Farming in the South Bronx 15 MIN
Preserving Holland's Tidal Ecology 16 MIN
Wave - Powered Desalination 13 MIN
Wildflower Seed Bank
Dist - BULFRG

One second before sunrise - A Search for solutions - Program 2 series
Spiders help farmers grow safer crops 23 MIN
Dist - BULFRG

One second before sunrise - a search for solutions series
Cooperating for clean air 37 MIN
Cooperating for clean air, and Spiders help farmers grow safer crops 60
Dist - BULFRG

One second in Montreal 26 MIN
16mm
B&W (G)
$40.00 rental
Discloses odd bleak black and white photographs of snow scenes causing the viewer to analyze and concentrate on the images far more attentively than one normally would. Generates a sense of mystery. Made with Joyce Wieland.
Fine Arts
Dist - CANCIN **Prod** - SNOWM 1969

The One - Shot Stapler 9 MIN
U-matic
Color (PRO)
Illustrates use of skin stapling closure by a stapler dispensing a single staple. Shows Emergency Room (ER) and office treatment of minor wounds and lacerations.
Health and Safety
Dist - MMAMC **Prod** - MMAMC

One - sided limits 30 MIN
VHS
Calculus series
Color (C)
$125.00 purchase _ #6035
Explains one - sided limits. Part of a 56 - part series on calculus.
Mathematics
Dist - LANDMK **Prod** - LANDMK

One Sky 13 MIN
16mm
Color (A)
LC 77-702204
Describes the aviation training program for foreign nationals at the Federal Aviation Administration Academy in Oklahoma City, Oklahoma.
Geography - United States; Industrial and Technical Education
Dist - USNAC **Prod** - USFAA 1977

One Small Step 17 MIN
16mm
Screen news digest series; Vol 14; Issue 8
Color (I)
LC 72-702749
Captures the momentous events of President Nixon's visit to the people's Republic of China.
Biography; Civics and Political Systems; Geography - World; History - United States
Dist - HEARST **Prod** - HEARST 1972

One Small Step 28 MIN
U-matic / VHS / 16mm
Color
Advises people to think about the world in which they live, and to reevaluate the era of self and remember there are other selfs in the world. Points out the contagious quality of good and bad behavior and provides some ideas on how managers and employees can improve theirwork environments through cooperation. Features James Whitmore and Dr Roderic Gorney.
Psychology
Dist - CCCD **Prod** - CCCD 1980

One Small Step 57 MIN
VHS / U-matic / 16mm
Nova Series
Color (G)
LC 79-708144; 79-701904
Examines the history of space exploration up to July, 1975, when the Soviet Soyuz and the American Apollo met and docked in space. Explores the vistas that remain ahead.
History - World; Science - Physical
Dist - TIMLIF **Prod** - WGBHTV 1979

One Special Dog 17 MIN
16mm / VHS / U-matic
Color (P I)
LC 70-708660
Presents the story of a Southwest Indian family and their special dog. Portrays the universal qualities of family life, concern for another, warmth and understanding.
Social Science
Dist - PHENIX **Prod** - BOSUST 1968

One special dog and a boy and a boa 30 MIN
VHS
Color (K P I J)
$89.00 purchase _ #S01102
Presents two children's stories. 'One Special Dog' tells how a stray dog is accepted by a Native American family after saving a pet lamb, while 'A Boy and a Boa' finds Martin and his pet boa Nigel recalling some of the boa's adventures.
Literature and Drama; Sociology
Dist - UILL **Prod** - PHENIX
PHENIX

One spring day 9 MIN
U-matic / VHS / BETA
Color; PAL (P I J)
PdS30, PdS38 purchase
Explores insects and flowers in part of a series, Things that grow Wild, on the environment.
Education; Science - Natural
Dist - EDPAT

A One - Stage Hypospadias Repair - a Combined Urological and Plastic Procedure 20 MIN
16mm
Color

LC 75-702279
Points out that hypospadias, a congenital defect in which there is incomplete development of the urethra, occurs about three to four times in each 1000 live male births. Emphasizes the execution and technique of handling tissue in several types of hypospadias. Demonstrates a complete repair procedure and shows post - operative results in several cases.
Science
Dist - EATONL **Prod** - EATONL 1960

One Stage Pan - Colectomy for Ulcerative Colitis 21 MIN
16mm
Color (PRO)
Points out that one stage pan - colectomy and abdominal ileostomy is the procedure of choice in patients with irretrievable damage to the colon from chronic ulcerative colitis or in patients with fulminating attacks of ulcerative colitis or massive hemorrhage.
Health and Safety; Science
Dist - ACY **Prod** - ACYDGD 1969

One - Stage Total Colectomy for Ulcerative Colitis 22 MIN
16mm
Color (PRO)
Points out that experience has demonstrated that a one - stage total colectomy for ulcerative colitis has great advantages over the multistage procedures which include a permanent ileostomy, a right hemicolectomy and a left hemicolectomy.
Health and Safety; Science
Dist - ACY **Prod** - ACYDGD 1950

One step ahead 18 MIN
VHS / U-matic
Color (G)
$250.00 purchase, $100.00 rental
Teaches safety awareness - the need of parents to be constantly vigilant. Shares the experiences of parents whose children were injured or experienced 'near misses.' Interviews health professionals in pediatrics and poison control to point out potentially dangerous situations. Offers a 'child's eye' view of hazards in the home to show the dangers of household items - dish detergent, shampoo, aspirin, garden fertilizers and pesticides. Stresses the importance of keeping emergency phone numbers at hand and presenting objective information in times of crisis. Produced by Kristine Samuelson.
Health and Safety
Dist - BAXMED

One Step Ahead - a Guide to Better Football Officiating 17 MIN
16mm
National Federation Sports Films Series
Color (I)
LC 80-701096
Covers the complex strategies and formations of football. Shows the official's responsibility for controlling the game flow without dominating it.
Physical Education and Recreation
Dist - NFSHSA **Prod** - NFSHSA 1980

One Step Ahead I 28 MIN
16mm / U-matic / VHS
Color (H C A)
Explores the various types of emotional crisis situations and presents viable solutions based on the degree of violence involved. Presents three main goals of crisis control in mental health patient care facilities.
Health and Safety; Psychology
Dist - CORF **Prod** - AMERIM 1975

One Step Ahead II - the Seclusion Room 24 MIN
16mm / U-matic / VHS
Color
Provides in - depth information on the use of the seclusion room in hospital crisis control. Observes its therapeutic use for patients who are dangerous to themselves or others. Illustrates the requirements for the physical set - up of the room, as well as the procedures involved in entrance, exit, observation and patient transport.
Health and Safety
Dist - CORF **Prod** - CORF

One Step Ahead III - Verbal Techniques 20 MIN
16mm / U-matic / VHS
Color
Focuses on proper intervention techniques which can deescalate a volatile situation and calm a potentially aggressive patient. Shows several verbal techniques in action and stresses their use in responding to the patient's needs while avoiding physical confrontation.
Health and Safety
Dist - CORF **Prod** - CORF

One Step at a Time 25 MIN
U-matic / VHS / 16mm
Children Growing Up Series
Color (H C A)
Relates that children start off as bundles of reflexes but gradually gain control over their bodies as muscles and nerves develop. Demonstrates that doctors are able to assess the development of a child by studying the degree of voluntary control a child has.
Psychology
Dist - FI **Prod** - BBCTV 1980

One Step at a Time - an Introduction to Behavior Modification 32 MIN
U-matic / VHS / 16mm
Abnormal Psychology Series
Color (C)
LC 73-703357
Reveals that behavioral characteristics are much more effectively shaped by rewarding for desirable traits rather than by punishing for undesirable ones. Points out that positive reinforcement can take many forms.
Psychology; Sociology
Dist - CRMP **Prod** - CRMP 1973

One Step at a Time - Deinstitutionalizing the Mentally Retarded 28 MIN
16mm
Color
Discusses the deinstitutionalizing of the mentally retarded.
Education; Psychology
Dist - LAWREN **Prod** - UWISC 1983

One step away 15 MIN
VHS
Color; PAL; NTSC (G IND)
PdS57, PdS67 purchase
Highlights the golden rules that can help to make roof work safer. Reveals that every year about 20 roof workers fall to their deaths in the United Kingdom. Interviews three workers who have been in roofing accidents. Reconstructs each incident to illustrate what went wrong.
Health and Safety
Dist - CFLVIS

One Step Closer 13 MIN
U-matic
Color (PRO)
Presents the theory behind surgical skin asepsis and use of plastic surgical drapes.
Health and Safety
Dist - MMAMC **Prod** - MMAMC

One step forward - Part 7 60 MIN
U-matic / VHS
War and peace in the nuclear age series
Color (G)
$45.00, $29.95 purchase
Unfolds the Nixon - Kissinger era of military detente. Considers the factors which led to US - USSR pursuit of arms control talk - SALT I. Part seven of a thirteen - part series on war and peace in the nuclear age.
Civics and Political Systems; History - United States; History - World; Sociology
Dist - ANNCPB **Prod** - WGBHTV 1989

One step up 60 MIN
VHS
Color (G)
$29.95 purchase _ #BD200V
Teaches step aerobic exercise. Shows how to exercise correctly, how to avoid injury and how to recognize physiological changes that occur during exercize.
Physical Education and Recreation
Dist - CAMV

One Strong Link Series

Definition of the aide's job	30 MIN
Evaluation	26 MIN
The Home Visit - I	25 MIN
The Home Visit - II	29 MIN
Learning	29 MIN
Motivation	33 MIN
Values and Attitudes	27 MIN
Working with Groups	30 MIN

Dist - CORNRS

One Superlative Song 29 MIN
VHS / 16mm
Color (G)
$55.00 rental _ #OSLS - 000
Takes the viewer to Camp Holiday Trails in Virginia, where children have special health problems. Shows how activities help each child capitalize on his or her assets as well as develop empathy for others.
Health and Safety
Dist - PBS **Prod** - WCVETV

One thing after another 25 MIN
16mm / U-matic / VHS
Computer programme series; Episode 2
Color (J)
Defines a computer program as a series of instructions that a computer must follow.
Business and Economics; Mathematics
Dist - FI **Prod** - BBCTV 1982

One Third of a Nation 55 MIN
U-matic / VHS
Color (G)
$249.00, $149.00 purchase _ #AD - 1150
Presents a theater piece designed to provoke social change. Dramatizes the problem of housing during the Depression. Produced by the Federal Theatre Project's 'Living Newspaper.'.
Civics and Political Systems; Fine Arts; History - United States; Sociology
Dist - FOTH **Prod** - FOTH

One - Third of a Nation - the Depression in the South 60 MIN
VHS
Color (J)
$95.00 purchase, $55.00 rental
Documents the plight of the American South during the Great Depression. Uses archival photographs from the Library of Congress collection together with songs of the period and rare film footage to recreate the South during the 1930s.
Fine Arts; Geography - United States; History - United States; Industrial and Technical Education; Sociology
Dist - SCETV **Prod** - SCETV 1983

One Thousand and One Launches 26 MIN
16mm
Color
LC 74-702498
Traces the development of the American space program from early rocket experiments to the exploration of the Moon's surface by men in 1969.
History - United States; History - World; Science; Science - Physical
Dist - RCKWL **Prod** - RCKWL 1973

The One Thousand Dollar Bill 24 MIN
U-matic / VHS / 16mm
Color (I J)
LC 79-700086
Tells a story about a young man who tells off his employer, makes plans to marry his sweetheart and takes on the local establishment when a huge sum of money temporarily changes his life. Illustrates that what a person believes about himself can be worth more than any sum of money. Based on the story The One Thousand Dollar Bill by Manuel Komroff. An ABC Weekend Special.
Fine Arts; Guidance and Counseling; Literature and Drama
Dist - CORF **Prod** - ABCF 1979

The One Thousand Dozen 55 MIN
VHS / U-matic
Jack London's Tales of the Klondike Series
Color (C A)
$139.00 purchase _ #3741
Presents an obsessive man who believes he can sell eggs for five dollars a dozen in a golden city. Portrays the man and his trailmates as he refuses them any nourishment from his precious cache of eggs. Depicts the ending as the eggs are broken for a feast as the story takes a surprising turn. Narrated by Jack London.
Literature and Drama
Dist - EBEC **Prod** - NORWK 1982

One thousand kilmeters beyond Yellow River 60 MIN
VHS
Silk road series
Color (G)
$29.95 purchase _ #CPM1003
Presents a documentary focused on the Silk Road linking China and Europe and traveled by Marco Polo. Explores the art, culture and history of China. Includes a soundtrack by Kitaro. Part of a series of six. Produced by Central Park Media.
Fine Arts; Geography - World; History - World
Dist - CHTSUI

1000 years of Polish Cavalry - 1000 lat jazdy Polskie 51 MIN
VHS
Color (G A) (POLISH)
$29.95 purchase _ #V100
Follows the history of Polish cavalry from the Cedynia Battle in 972 until the last battles with German tanks in 1939.
Fine Arts; History - World
Dist - POLART

One to Grow on - Prologue 10 MIN
16mm
One to Grow on Series
Color (T)
LC 73-701935
Outlines the methods and goals aimed at in achieving an understanding of the mental health aspects of student - teacher relationships.

Guidance and Counseling; Psychology; Sociology
Dist - USNAC **Prod** - NIMH 1973

One to Grow on Series
Act II - lindsey 17 MIN
He Comes from Another Room 28 MIN
Learning Strategies 11 MIN
One to Grow on - Prologue 10 MIN
A Pretty Good Class for a Monday 25 MIN
Sarah 10 MIN
A Teacher in Reflection 11 MIN
Dist - USNAC

One - to - One 13 MIN
16mm
People Sell People Series
Color (IND)
LC 77-702362
Documents the importance of establishing a person - to - person relationship between customer and salesperson.
Business and Economics; Psychology
Dist - MLA **Prod** - SAUM 1975

One to one 24 MIN
VHS
Color (G C)
$189.00 purchase, $55.00 rental
Shows discussions among teenagers and older adults on such issues as death, self - worth, parenting and aging and on the roles of teens and elders in society.
Health and Safety; Psychology
Dist - TNF

One to one 30 MIN
VHS
How do you manage series
Color (A)
PdS65 purchase
Examines working one-to-one; the difference between negative criticism and positive feedback. Shows how to give and receive feedback; developing listening skills; motivating other people; making sure that one is understood; rewarding success, minimizing failure. Part of a six-part series featuring Dr John Nicholson, a business psychologist who specializes in helping people to develop new attitudes and ways of thinking to improve both job performance and satisfaction.
Business and Economics; Psychology; Social Science
Dist - BBCENE

One to One Correspondence 10 MIN
16mm
MAA Elementary Arithmetic Series
Color (P T)
Mathematics
Dist - MLA **Prod** - MAA 1967

One to one series
Adlai Stevenson - Campaign speeches 29 MIN
Children's books 29 MIN
Dramatic Literature - the Skin of Our Teeth 29 MIN
E B White - essays and a short story 29 MIN
Emily Dickinson - Selected Poems 28 MIN
F Scott Fitzgerald - the Great Gatsby 29 MIN
Graham Greene - the heart of the matter 29 MIN
Henry David Thoreau - Walden 29 MIN
Henry James - the beast in the jungle 29 MIN
James Agee - a Death in the Family 29 MIN
The Literature of Sports 29 MIN
Mark Twain - HUCKLEBERRY FINN 29 MIN
Mark Van Doren - Poems and Criticism 29 MIN
Nikos Kazantzakis - Selected Works 29 MIN
A Sampler of Selections from Favorite Authors 29 MIN
Short Stories by John Cheever and Eudora Welty 29 MIN
T H White - the once and future king 26 MIN
T S Eliot - Selected Poetry 29 MIN
Vladimir Nabokov - LOLITA 29 MIN
William Shakespeare - Antony and Cleopatra 29 MIN
Dist - PBS

One to Speak, One to Hear 15 MIN
U-matic / VHS / 16mm
Color
Portrays the life of a hearing impaired woman. Shows that many of the difficulties and obstacles confronting the impaired are self - imposed while others are presented by a verbally oriented society. Stresses communication between the hearing and the nonhearing.
Guidance and Counseling; Psychology
Dist - STNFLD **Prod** - BOURKR 1977

One to Three Months 9 MIN
U-matic / VHS
Teaching Infants and Toddlers Series Pt 1
Color (H C A)
Discusses seeing, hearing and feeling in infants from one to three months.
Home Economics; Psychology
Dist - GPN **Prod** - BGSU 1978

One Too many 30 MIN
16mm / VHS / U-matic
Color (J)
Centers around four high school students affected by drinking and driving. Full version.
Psychology; Sociology
Dist - LCOA **Prod** - ABCTV 1985

One Trillion Dollars for Defense 60 MIN
U-matic / VHS / 16mm
Color (J)
LC 83-706385
Shows why the United States requires such a large defense budget. Looks at sophisticated weapons as Bill Moyers talks with military personnel, representatives from weapons manufacturers, a government defense expert and others about the issue of where all the high technology will lead.
Civics and Political Systems
Dist - FI **Prod** - WNETTV 1982

One Turkey, Two Turkey 6 MIN
U-matic / VHS / 16mm
Starting to Read Series
Color (K P)
LC 76-702233
Introduces the youngest readers and pre - readers to words and concepts, including pictures and songs.
English Language
Dist - AIMS **Prod** - GME 1971

One, Two, Plop 11 MIN
U-matic / VHS / 16mm
Kingdom of Kite Series
Color (P I J)
Presents a schizophrenic witch who manages to make all the 3's in the kingdom disappear to point up the value of being able to regard matters from another person's unique point of view.
Guidance and Counseling
Dist - PHENIX **Prod** - KINGSP 1971

One, two, that's it 11 MIN
16mm
Cuba - a view from inside series
Color (G)
$150.00 purchase, $25.00 rental
Delves into boxing, as seen through the faces, gestures and shouted comments of the ringside trainers. Features part of a 17 - part series of shorts by and about Cuban women. Directed by Miriam Talavera. Illustrated catalog available. Contact distributor for programming advice and discount package rental fees.
Fine Arts; Physical Education and Recreation
Dist - CNEMAG

One - Two - Three - Advanced Features 30 MIN
U-matic / VHS
Color
Continues the presentation of Lotus 1 - 2 - 3. Fully describes various features such as consolidation, keyboard macros, graphic generation and data management. Includes written text.
Industrial and Technical Education
Dist - BERGL **Prod** - MICROV

One - Two - Three - Advanced Features
VHS / U-matic
Color (A)
Covers the use of keyboard macros, advanced graphics, multiple spreadsheet consolidation and data management for the experienced Lotus 1 - 2 - 3 user.
Mathematics
Dist - DSIM **Prod** - DSIM

One, Two, Three - Clean 13 MIN
16mm
Color (J)
Describes today's modern sewage treatment process and how a sewage treatment plant works.
Civics and Political Systems; Health and Safety
Dist - FINLYS **Prod** - FINLYS

One - Two - Three - Introduction to the Integrated Spreadsheet
VHS / U-matic
Color (A)
Shows how to create a Lotus 1 - 2 - 3 spreadsheet. Covers the basics including the Lotus 1 - 2 - 3 control panel, menu selection and entering labels, numbers and formulas. Moves to the command structures such as changing column widths, using the anchor cell and the free cell in range commands, moving and centering labels, and formatting the display. Explains naming, storing on disk, and printing the worksheet.
Business and Economics; Industrial and Technical Education; Mathematics; Psychology
Dist - DSIM **Prod** - DSIM

1 - 2 - 3 magic 120 MIN
VHS
Color (G)
$39.95 purchase _ #CMI100V
Provides parents with the tools to discipline children 2 - 12 without arguing, yelling or spanking. Shows how to stop children's unwanted behavior such as throwing tantrums, screaming, whining, pouting and fighting, and to start desired behaviors such as eating meals, cleaning rooms and going to bed. Illustrates how to avoid the Talk - Persuade - Argue - Yell - Hit Syndrome, how to handle misbehavior at home or in public, how to recognize the Six Types of Testing and Manipulation. Increases the self - esteem of both parent and child.
Guidance and Counseling; Health and Safety; Psychology; Social Science; Sociology
Dist - CAMV

One, Two, Three - Un, Deux, Trois 5 MIN
16mm / U-matic / VHS
Color (J H C)
LC 77-701532
Presents an animated story, without narration, about the life of an imaginary Mr X, for whom the slightest variations of daily routines create insoluble problems.
Fine Arts; Literature and Drama; Sociology
Dist - FI **Prod** - LESFG 1977

One, Two, Three, Zero - Infertility 28 MIN
16mm
Color (A)
LC 80-701693
Discusses infertility, focusing on several couples who have sought help for their inability to have children. Deals with the couples' feelings of failure, anxiety and hopelessness and shows one couple being questioned, tested and treated. Notes the common causes and methods for treating and circumventing the medical difficulties posed by these health problems.
Health and Safety; Sociology
Dist - FLMLIB **Prod** - CANBC 1980

One voice in the cosmic fugue 60 MIN
U-matic / VHS / 16mm
Cosmos series; Program 2
Color (J)
LC 81-701148
Addresses the topic of life and its origins. Speculates on life in other worlds and examines molecular biology, the Miller - Urey experiment, and DNA. Based on the book Cosmos by Carl Sagan. Narrated by Carl Sagan.
Science - Natural; Science - Physical
Dist - FI **Prod** - KCET 1980

One was Johnny 3 MIN
16mm / U-matic / VHS
Color (P)
Uses verses by Maurice Sendak to teach the fundamentals of counting.
Mathematics
Dist - WWS **Prod** - WWS 1978

One - way analysis of variance
VHS
Probability and statistics series
Color (H C)
$125.00 purchase _ #8053
Provides resource material about one - way variance analysis for help in the study of probability and statistics. Presents a 60 - video series, each part 25 to 30 minutes long, that explains and reinforces concepts using definitions, theorems, examples and step - by - step solutions to tutor the student. Videos are also available in a set.
Mathematics
Dist - LANDMK

One Way Boogie Woogie 60 MIN
16mm
Color (C)
$1680.00
Experimental film by James Benning.
Fine Arts
Dist - AFA **Prod** - AFA 1977

One Way Ticket 30 MIN
U-matic
(H C A)
Presents a drama of two young girls, one English and one Ukrainian, who meet in a colonist railcar travelling to Alberta, Canada in 1905.
History - World; Sociology
Dist - ACCESS **Prod** - ACCESS 1985

One Way to Better Cities 29 MIN
16mm
Color (C A)
Shows influence of property tax on urban decay, suburban sprawl and land speculation. Explains how private industry can be provided with better incentives to help meet renewal and development needs of the country.
Business and Economics; Science - Natural; Sociology
Dist - MTP **Prod** - SCHALK 1970

One Way to Build a Flat 15 MIN
16mm
B&W
Demonstrates a method of building a stage flat from reference to the blueprint through the covering of the flat with cloth.
Fine Arts
Dist - UCLA **Prod** - UCLA 1950

One Week
16mm
Color (J H)
LC 74-707447
Shows the working methods and psychological realities of a journalist's life.
Education; Psychology; Social Science
Dist - MLA **Prod** - NEWSWK 1969

One Week 20 MIN
16mm
B&W (J)
Stars Buster Keaton.
Fine Arts
Dist - TWYMAN **Prod** - MGM 1920

One Week in October 29 MIN
16mm
B&W
LC 74-705254
Tells the story of the cuban crisis, describing the civil and military buildup during this critical period.
Geography - World; History - United States; History - World
Dist - USNAC **Prod** - USOCD 1964

One who was there 36 MIN
VHS / 16mm / U-matic
Color (J A)
Dramatizes the journey home of sixty - year - old Mary Magdalene who is saddened by the lonely years of waiting for Jesus' return. Shows how the journey becomes spiritual as well as physical as she discovers that the strong faith of the disciples has been passed to a new generation of believers. Uses flashbacks to show the events of the Passion, Passover and the healing of Mary Magdalene.
Religion and Philosophy
Dist - ECUFLM **Prod** - UMCOM 1979

The One who Wasn't Afraid 15 MIN
VHS / 16mm
Stories and Poems from Long Ago Series
Color (I)
Uses character of retired sea captain to tell the Russian folk tale The One Who Wasn't Afraid. The fifth of 16 installments of the Stories And Poems From Long Ago Series, which is intended to encourage reading and writing by young viewers.
Literature and Drama
Dist - GPN **Prod** - CTI 1990

One Wish Too many 55 MIN
16mm / U-matic / VHS
B&W (K P I)
LC FIA65-1302
Tells the story of a young boy who finds a marble which makes his wishes come true when he rubs it. Shows how he is carried away by the power of his marble and gets into trouble, but realizes his folly in the end.
Literature and Drama
Dist - LUF **Prod** - CHILDF 1964

The One within 16 MIN
U-matic
Color (H C A)
Shows a young woman's quest for a satisfying philosophy, a sense of unity and participation in life. Tells how she explores T'ai Chi, Zen, Sufi dancing and the teachings of Pir Vilayat Khan.
Guidance and Counseling; Psychology; Religion and Philosophy
Dist - LAWREN **Prod** - LAWREN

The One within - a Journey of Self - Discovery 20 MIN
16mm
Color (H C A)
LC 75-701609
Shows how a young American working woman finds a greater sense of unity and participation through self - discipline and self - mastery. Offers an alternative to drug - induced experiences.
Guidance and Counseling; Psychology; Sociology
Dist - LAWREN **Prod** - PERLE 1975

One Woman Waiting 9 MIN
16mm
Color (C)
$300.00 purchase, $35.00, $45.00 rental
Raises questions about the relationship between women using symbolic images. Produced by Josephine Massarella.
Fine Arts; Science - Natural; Sociology
Dist - WMENIF

One world, many worlds - Hispanic diversity in the United States 22 MIN
VHS
Multicultural history series
Color (I J)
$89.00 purchase _ #RB878
Reveals that Hispanic Americans came from a diversity of countries and cultures. Shows how and why Hispanics migrated to the United States. Examines their present day struggle with discrimination and their contribution to American culture. Part of a series on multicultural history.
History - United States; Sociology
Dist - REVID **Prod** - REVID 1993

One World Series
From the Caribbean 20 MIN
Made in Barbados 20 MIN
People on the Move 20 MIN
Trading the Sun 20 MIN
Dist - FI

One year through toddlerhood 45 MIN
VHS
Touchpoints series
Color (G)
$34.95 purchase _ #COV203V-K
Offers advice from Dr T Berry Brazelton about managing touchpoints, predictable times in the first years of life when bursts of rapid growth and learning occur. Recommends videos for new parents, so they can anticipate and recognize the touchpoints. Part three of a three-part series.
Psychology; Sociology
Dist - CAMV

The One Your with 29 MIN
Videoreel / VT2
Our Street Series
Color
Sociology
Dist - PBS **Prod** - MDCPB

One Zillion Valentines
VHS
Children's Literature on Video Series
Color (K)
$33.00 purchase
Literature and Drama
Dist - PELLER

Onegin 96 MIN
VHS
Color (S)
$39.95 purchase _ #833 - 9298
Recreates prerevolutionary Russia with the National Ballet of Canada production of 'Onegin,' music by Stravinksy, story by Pushkin. Stars Sabine Allemann as Tatiana and Frank Augustyn as Onegin.
Fine Arts; Geography - World; Physical Education and Recreation
Dist - FI **Prod** - RMART 1987

Oneida 28 MIN
U-matic / VHS
Color
Takes a look at the past and present lives of the Oneida people in northern Wisconsin. Includes interviews with a few of the older members of the tribe who talk about their personal past experiences and their feelings about the younger generation.
History - United States; Social Science; Sociology
Dist - UWISC **Prod** - UWISC 1975

Oneiro - in the shadow of Isadora 14 MIN
VHS
Color (G)
$100.00 purchase
Features Lori Belilove, dancer and choreographer, performing five dances in the style of Isadora Duncan. Utilizes computer - generated and other experimental effects, to bring meaning to 'oneiro', which means 'dream' in Greek, and Jungian's shadow - self. Produced by Silvianna Goldsmith.
Fine Arts; Psychology
Dist - CANCIN

One's a Heifer 26 MIN
16mm / U-matic / VHS
Color (I J) (FRENCH)
Describes how conscientious Peter loses two calves and must travel to a remote area of his uncle's ranch to find them. Reveals what can happen when a situation is approached by a preconceived point of view. Based on the story by Sinclair Ross.
Agriculture; Foreign Language; Literature and Drama; Psychology; Sociology
Dist - BCNFL **Prod** - ATLAF 1985

Ongoing network optimization coordinates operations to improve service and reduce costs
VHS
Color (C PRO G)
$150.00 purchase _ #91.08
Reveals that, as one of the largest less - than - truckload operations in the US, Yellow Freight, with revenue of over $2 billion a year, provides direct service to more than 24,000 cities. Discloses that approximately 60,000 shipments are handled daily. This optimization model addresses service and cost implications of key network design decisions - establishing guidelines that allow situations to be analyuzed day by day, reflecting changing local business conditions. Yellow Freight System Inc. William W Graham, John W Braklow, Warren B Powell.
Business and Economics; Social Science
Dist - INMASC

The Ongoing Prenatal Assessment 18 MIN
U-matic / VHS / 16mm
Family - Oriented Maternity Care by the Nurse Clinician Series
Color
Guidance and Counseling; Sociology
Dist - USNAC **Prod** - EMORYU

Onie series
Theonie - Baklavas 15 MIN
Theonie - Dolmathes - Stuffed Grape Leaves 15 MIN
Theonie - Ghighes Me Arni (Giant Beans with Lamb) 14 MIN
Theonie - Hilopittas - noodles 15 MIN
Theonie - moussaka - eggplant 15 MIN
Theonie - ornitha kokkinisti - pot - roasted chicken 15 MIN
Theonie - phinikia - spiced bars in lemon syrup 14 MIN
Theonie - portokalli glyko - orange sweets 14 MIN
Theonie - psari plaki and horiatiki salata - baked fish and peasant salad 15 MIN
Theonie - psaria nissiotika - island fish soup 15 MIN
Theonie - ravanie - walnut cake 15 MIN
Theonie - salates kalorkerines - summer salads 14 MIN
Theonie - souppa avgolemono - egg lemon soup 14 MIN
Theonie - souppes hymoniatikes - winter soups 14 MIN
Theonie - spanikopitta - spinach pie 15 MIN
Theonie - stiffato - beef stew 14 MIN
Theonie - tiropittes - cheese triangles 15 MIN
Theonie - youvetsi - lamb with orzo 15 MIN
Dist - PBS

An Onion Celebration 30 MIN
BETA / VHS
Frugal Gourmet Series
Color
Demonstrates cooking stuffed onion leaves and onions sauteed with peppers Italian style. Discusses the Walla Walla Sweet and the Georgia Vandalia onions.
Health and Safety; Home Economics; Psychology
Dist - CORF **Prod** - WTTWTV

Onion farming 7 MIN
16mm
African village life - Mali series
Color (K P I J H C)
LC 73-707531
Shows the growing of onions and explains that it is a highly developed skill among the natives of the Dogon tribe who live along the Niger River.
Geography - World; History - United States; Social Science; Sociology
Dist - IFF **Prod** - BRYAN

Onion farming - Dogon people 7 MIN
VHS / U-matic
African village life - Mali series
Color
Agriculture; Geography - World; History - World; Sociology
Dist - IFF **Prod** - IFF

Onions - Rings, Halving, Slicing and Mincing 20 MIN
VHS / U-matic
Color (PRO)
Explains how to prepare green, Spanish and Bermuda onions, and tells what tools and techniques to use.
Home Economics; Industrial and Technical Education
Dist - CULINA **Prod** - CULINA

Online, or How do You Spell Relief 9 MIN
U-matic / VHS
Color
Describes some of the advantages of an automated library circulation system.

Education; Industrial and Technical Education; Mathematics; Social Science; Sociology
Dist - LVN **Prod** - LVN

Online Processing 30 MIN
U-matic / VHS
Making it Count Series
Color (H C A)
LC 80-707575
Introduces and compares online with batch processing. Studies characteristics of online systems such as I/O functions, data transmissions, file access and response time.
Business and Economics; Mathematics
Dist - BCSC **Prod** - BCSC 1980

Only a Film 12 MIN
U-matic / VHS / 16mm
Color (PRO)
Discusses correct procedures designed to minimize hazards in operating rooms.
Health and Safety
Dist - VIEWTH **Prod** - USAMP

Only about Woman 45 MIN
U-matic / VHS
B&W
Documents the different occupations open to women in the USSR.
History - World; Sociology
Dist - IHF **Prod** - IHF

Only Angels have Wings 121 MIN
16mm
B&W (H C A)
Describes the deterioration of the friendship of two South American cargo fliers who both fall for the same girl. Stars Cary Grant and Jean Arthur.
Fine Arts
Dist - TIMLIF **Prod** - CPC 1939

The Only Child 7 MIN
U-matic / VHS / 16mm
Color (J)
LC 81-701007
Presents an animated satirical statement about a father whose misguided love leads him to direct his son's life from pampering infancy through school, romance and finally medical school. Reveals that while he is unprepared for his role as a doctor, the son is shocked to discover that his first patient on the operating table is his father.
Fine Arts; Literature and Drama; Sociology
Dist - PHENIX **Prod** - SFTB 1981

Only Emptiness Remains 95 MIN
35mm strip / VHS / U-matic
Color (H C A) (SPANISH (ENGLISH SUBTITLES))
$175 rental
Examines political repression in Argentina in the late 1970s. Features testimonials from Marta, member of a wealthy Catholic family in Buenos Aires, Antonia and Maria, grandmothers of missing children, and Herbe Pastor de Fonafini, President of the Mothers' Movement. Directed by Rodolfo Kuhn.
History - World; Sociology
Dist - CNEMAG

Only for children - Volume 1 30 MIN
VHS
Color (P I R)
$19.99 purchase, $10.00 rental _ #35 - 83555 - 533
Presents three cartoons with messages teaching integrity. 'The Lost Bunny' and 'Ilya the Great' both teach the importance of friendship, while 'Marsha's Magic Shoes' emphasizes responsibility.
Literature and Drama; Religion and Philosophy
Dist - APH **Prod** - WORD

Only for children - Volume 2 30 MIN
VHS
Color (P I R)
$19.99 purchase, $10.00 rental _ #35 - 83556 - 533
Presents three cartoons with messages teaching integrity. 'The Difficult Donkey' reveals that no matter how hard a person tries, not everyone will like him or her. 'The Rainbow' stresses the importance of sharing, while caring is the message of 'The Little Ballerina.'
Literature and Drama; Religion and Philosophy
Dist - APH **Prod** - WORD

Only for children - Volume 3 30 MIN
VHS
Color (P I R)
$19.99 purchase, $10.00 rental _ #35 - 83557 - 533
Presents three cartoons with messages teaching integrity. 'Snout Nose' focuses on the importance of honesty. Being true to self is the theme of 'The Little Mouse,' while 'The Brave Little Bird' teaches that a person can make other people happy.
Literature and Drama; Religion and Philosophy
Dist - APH **Prod** - WORD

Only for children - Volume 4 10 MIN
VHS
Color (P I R)
$9.99 purchase _ #35 - 83558 - 533
Presents a cartoon, 'The Lion and the Turtle,' which teaches children creativity.
Literature and Drama; Religion and Philosophy
Dist - APH **Prod** - WORD

The only forgotten take of Casablanca 4 MIN
35mm
B&W (G)
Presents a short film directed by Charley Weller.
Fine Arts
Dist - KINOIC

The Only Good Indian 24 MIN
16mm
American Challenge Series
Color (J H)
Shatters myths regarding American Indians by recounting how unfairly they were treated by the white man. Tells how a cavalry scout named Tom Jeffords discovers the humanity of the Indian when he arranges a deal with the great chief Cochise to allow mail riders to pass through Indian land. Uses excerpts from the motion picture Blood Brother starring James Stewart and Jeff Chandler.
History - United States; Social Science
Dist - FI **Prod** - TWCF 1975

Only Hooked a Little 29 MIN
16mm
This is the Life Series
Color
Features a hospital chaplain discussing the helplessness felt by addicts in the drug rehabilitation program he runs. Describes how he speaks from first - hand knowledge because he was an addict himself.
Health and Safety; Psychology; Sociology
Dist - LUTTEL **Prod** - LUTTEL 1981

Only in America 20 MIN
16mm
Color (J H)
Underscores the importance of innovation, invention and enterprise in the growth of the United States. Presents the history of Michigan as well and explains how the state's natural resources helped produce an industrial economy.
Business and Economics; History - United States
Dist - CONPOW **Prod** - CENTRO

Only Losers Play 10 MIN
16mm
Color (P I J)
Shows the seriousness of the shoplifting crime and warns young people about the consequences, including guilt, embarrassment, the shame of disappointing one's parents, and a criminal record.
Guidance and Counseling; Sociology
Dist - KLEINW **Prod** - KLEINW

Only one earth series
Big fish, little fish - Pt 6 28 MIN
China's changing face - Pt 7 28 MIN
City in the sand - Pt 8 28 MIN
The Fate of the forest - pt 3 58 MIN
The Monk, the Village, and the Bo Tree - Pt 11 28 MIN
The Muck and the Mystery Men - Pt 10 28 MIN
People of the Desert - Pt 9 28 MIN
The Road to Ruin - Pt 1 58 MIN
The Sinking Ark - Pt 2 58 MIN
The Struggling people - Pt 4 28 MIN
Valley of Heart's Delight - Pt 5 28 MIN
Dist - FI

Only one road - the bike - car traffic mix 26 MIN
VHS
Color (H G)
$35.00 purchase _ #451
Stresses that greater understanding and cooperation are needed between bicyclists and motorists to safely share the roadways.
Health and Safety
Dist - AAAFTS **Prod** - AAAFTS 1975

Only One Road - Three Families Coping with Childhood Cancer 53 MIN
VHS / U-matic
Color (PRO)
Presents interviews of three children, ages 5 - 9, and their families who are past the initial stages of diagnosis and treatment of cancer. Reveals through interviews with and actual footage of these families interacting in the home, public school and hospital settings, concerns regarding remission of cancer, school problems, long - term side effects, survival of the marriage and handling 'left out' siblings.
Health and Safety; Psychology
Dist - UMICHM **Prod** - UMICHM 1983

The Only Rule is Win 60 MIN
VHS
Secret Intelligence Series
Color; Captioned (G)
$59.95 purchase _ #SEIN - 101
Charts the beginnings of the FBI and the Office of Strategic Services, later known as the CIA. Focuses on the successes and failures of intelligence during World War II.
Civics and Political Systems; History - United States
Dist - PBS **Prod** - KCET 1989

Only Subliminals Series
Stop Smoking 30 MIN
Dist - VSPU

The Only take 3 MIN
16mm
Color (A)
$12.00 rental
Presents the tale of a fool hired to shoot a 'snuff porn' movie. Reveals that he has been told by his director that petroleum jelly on the lens will give an 'artsy, Penthouse effect,' the fool piles on globs of it just before the director yells action, so the audience can hear but not see what is going on. Explains director Gorman Bechard, '...a very funny, very sick little film.'
Fine Arts
Dist - CANCIN

Only the ball was white 30 MIN
16mm / U-matic / VHS
Color (H C A)
LC 81-700325
Examines the isolation of black baseball talent from the major leagues until 1946. Presents the recollections of Satchel Paige, Don Newcombe and Roy Campanella.
History - United States; Physical Education and Recreation
Dist - FI **Prod** - WTTWTV 1980
CAMV

Only the Beginning 10 MIN
16mm
Color
Deals with the confrontation which took place in the streets of Paris in May 1968 between students and the police.
Geography - World; Sociology
Dist - CANWRL **Prod** - CANWRL

Only the beginning 20 MIN
16mm
Color (G)
$20.00 rental
Presents an account of rebellion in the troops against the war in Vietnam. Records vets tearing off their medals and decorations from their uniforms and tossing them into a trash heap on the White House lawn. Shows the gruesome genetic effects of Agent Orange on the land and on Vietnamese babies. United States soldiers talk about how GIs are killing their own officers. Represents new filmmakers in the 1960s whose work provides a window to that period.
Fine Arts; History - United States; Sociology
Dist - CANCIN **Prod** - SINGLE 1971

Only the Good Need Apply 15 MIN
VHS / 35mm strip
$43.50 purchase _ #XY861 for film, $84.95 purchase _ #XY811 for VHS
Gives tips on presenting a good impression when completing an application. Points out the importance of being neat, honest and accurate.
Business and Economics; Guidance and Counseling
Dist - CAREER **Prod** - CAREER

Only the Good Need Apply 9 MIN
VHS / U-matic
(H C)
$98 _ #EA6V
Introduces the basic expectations of employers and methods of completion when filling out a job application.
Business and Economics
Dist - JISTW **Prod** - JISTW

Only the good need apply
VHS
Career process series
Color (H A)
$84.95 purchase _ #ES1210V
Focuses on job application forms. Stresses the importance of neat writing, honesty, using correct grammar, taking along a resume, and clearly answering open - ended questions.
Psychology
Dist - CAMV

Only the News that Fits 30 MIN
VHS / 16mm
Color (G)
$190.00 purchase, $50.00 rental
Focuses on journalists covering Nicaragua during the Arias Peace Plan negotiations in November, 1987. Follows John Quinones of ABC in Managua, records the editorial decisions made by Peter Jennings and other senior editors in New York. Includes journalists Randolph Ryan,

Edith Coron, and photographer Bill Gentile. Reveals how the news business works and exposes the distortions that are inevitable. This is a shorter version of 'The World Is Watching.'.
Civics and Political Systems; Geography - World; Literature and Drama; Sociology
Dist - FIRS **Prod** - FIRS 1989

Only the Strong 27 MIN
16mm
Color
Documents and compares the various weapons systems of the United States and the Soviet Union. Includes portions filmed inside the USSR.
Civics and Political Systems
Dist - THIOKL **Prod** - THIOKL 1972

Only Then Regale My Eyes 59 MIN
VHS / 16mm
Color (G)
$70.00 rental _ #OTRE - 000
Examines the most chaotic period of French history through its art.
History - World
Dist - PBS **Prod** - WTVSTV

The Only Thing I Can't do is Hear 27 MIN
U-matic / VHS / 16mm
Color
LC 77-700565
Describes the pre - college programs available for deaf high school students at Gallaudet College. Presents classroom situations and comments by students and faculty. Uses sign language.
Education; Guidance and Counseling; Psychology
Dist - GALCO **Prod** - GALCO 1977

The Only Thing You Know 85 MIN
16mm
Color
LC 74-701211
Presents the story of an 18 - year - old girl from a middle class family who is searching for substance and meaning in her life.
Guidance and Counseling; Psychology
Dist - CANFDC **Prod** - CFDEVC 1971

Only yesterday 15 MIN
VHS
Color; PAL (P I J H)
Portrays 14 year old Ane who wants to know more about her long dead grandmother. Reveals that as she questions people and searches through the records that remain, she learns about life in the 1930s and during World War II. Introduces the concept of local history.
History - World; Sociology
Dist - VIEWTH

Only Yesterday - Award Series 1965 29 MIN
Videoreel / VT2
Synergism - Gallimaufry Series
B&W
Points out the ever - changing environment of man. Foscuses on the sights and sounds of yesterday's 'gaslight America.'.
History - United States; Social Science; Sociology
Dist - PBS **Prod** - WMVSTV

Only You Can Put Your Best Foot Forward 51 MIN
U-matic / VHS
Color
LC 80-706508
Discusses standard procedures for job announcements and interviews for civil service positions. Portrays interviews with not - so - typical applicants.
Guidance and Counseling; Psychology
Dist - USNAC **Prod** - VAHSL 1978

Onset of labor 14 MIN
VHS
Color (PRO G) (ARABIC SPANISH)
$250.00 purchase _ #OB - 102
Explains the proper time to contact the doctor and emphasizes the importance of accurate communication between the expectant couple and the physician. Deals with the concerns women have about labor. Discusses Braxton - Hicks contractions, cervical thinning, dilation, lightening, the 'show', false labor, breaking of water, contractions, going in for delivery, episiotomy and delivery - coach attending.
Health and Safety
Dist - MIFE **Prod** - MIFE 1991

Onstage at Quartz Mountains 20 MIN
16mm
Color
Focuses on high school students who attended the Oklahoma summer arts camp in 1978. Tells of their experiences studying ballet, modern dance, acting, mime, painting, printmaking, poetry and music.
Education; Fine Arts
Dist - MTP TULSAS **Prod** - OKSAI 1978

Onstage with Judith Somogi 29 MIN
16mm
Color
LC 80-701457
Focuses on Judith Somogi, a young conductor. Demonstrates the dedication and hard work needed to build a music career.
Fine Arts
Dist - MTP **Prod** - OKSAI 1980

Ontario 60 MIN
VHS
AAA travel series
Color (G)
$24.95 purchase _ #NA18
Explores Ontario.
Geography - World
Dist - SVIP

Ontario 1 15 MIN
U-matic
It's Your World Series
Color (I)
Introduces students to the world around them. Segment titles are; The Province, Northern Ontario, Southern Ontario, Wilderness.
Education; Geography - World
Dist - TVOTAR **Prod** - TVOTAR 1984

Ontario 2 15 MIN
U-matic
It's Your World Series
Color (I)
Introduces students to the world around them. Segment titles are; Mining, Forestry And Logging, Fishing And Fur Trapping.
Education; Geography - World
Dist - TVOTAR **Prod** - TVOTAR 1984

Ontario Land 7 MIN
16mm
B&W
LC 77-702599
Features experiments with color, time intervals and sound by painting and scratching clear film and black leader.
Fine Arts; Industrial and Technical Education
Dist - CANFDC **Prod** - CANFDC 1972

Onto the Page and into the World 13 MIN
16mm
Color
Follows the project of the production of a book of poems by mentally retarded students at the Dr Franklin Perkins School in Lancaster, Massachusetts. Shows the work on the book as the students compose the poems, carve woodcuts for illustrations, set the type, print, bind and mail copies to customers.
Education; Psychology
Dist - CMPBL **Prod** - CMPBL 1973

Ontogeny 60 MIN
U-matic / VHS
Biology of Cognition and Language Series Program 7; Program 7
Color (A)
Presents biologist Humberto Maturana discussing ontogeny.
Science - Natural
Dist - UCEMC **Prod** - UCEMC

The Ontological Argument 25 MIN
VHS / U-matic
Introduction to Philosophy Series
Color (C)
Psychology; Religion and Philosophy
Dist - UDEL **Prod** - UDEL

Onward Christian Soldiers 52 MIN
VHS / 16mm
Color (G) (LATIN)
$75.00 rental; $390.00 purchase
Surveys and analyzes the growing presence of U.S. - sponsored evangelical churches in Latin America. Looks at this new Protestant regime, which is often closely aligned with the military.
Geography - World; Religion and Philosophy
Dist - ICARUS FIRS **Prod** - FIRS 1989

Oobieland series
Explores the gateways of humankind in a repeated series of movements from the familiar and safe to the unknown and dangerous, where cycles are incomplete, chases never consummated and the day ends with no promise of rebirth. Touches on the oldest instincts of humanity, leaving the viewer saddened and scared by the knowledge of a world that will never know freedom through the completion of action. Contains five episodes - Introduction to Oobieland - part one; Ubi est terram Oobiae - part two; Solstice - part three; The Terrible Mother - part four; Epilogue to Oobieland - part five. Made between 1969 - 1974.
Introduction to Oobieland - part one 10 MIN
Solstice - part three 35 MIN
The Terrible mother - part four 25 MIN
Ubi est terram oobiae - Pt two 5 MIN
Dist - CANCIN **Prod** - UNGRW 1989

The Oompahs 8 MIN
16mm
Color
Presents an animated story about a family of musical instruments.
Fine Arts
Dist - TIMLIF **Prod** - TIMLIF 1982

Oopa 14 MIN
16mm
Color
Presents a day in the life of a cabaret belly dancer, filmed in the cinema verite style.
Fine Arts
Dist - NYU **Prod** - NYU

Oops 20 MIN
16mm
Color (C A)
LC 70-714052
Shows how careless actions within an industrial plant can result in stream pollution. Points out ways to guard against such situations, emphasizing the individual's control of potential pollution sources within a plant.
Business and Economics; Geography - United States; Science - Natural
Dist - FINLYS **Prod** - ORVWSC 1965

Oops, I made a Mistake 4 MIN
16mm / U-matic / VHS
Most Important Person - Attitudes Series
Color (K P I) (SPANISH)
Explains that a disappointing mistake can be solved by figuring out what went wrong and trying again.
Guidance and Counseling; Psychology
Dist - EBEC **Prod** - EBEC

Oops - time for service recovery 22 MIN
VHS
Color (PRO IND A)
Features Ron Zemke and Chip Bell who recommend six research - proven steps for rectifying mistakes in customer service.
Business and Economics
Dist - SALENG **Prod** - SALENG 1990

Oosplasmic segregation during Ascidian development 6 MIN
16mm
EDC Developmental biology series
Color (J H C)
$96.00 purchase, $21.00 rental _ #194 W 8290, #140 W 8290
Shows formation of the yellow crescent through cytoplasmic streaming and segregation of crescent materials during cleavage and development in Boltenia villosa and Styela partita. Part of a series featuring time - lapse photomicrography which depict events never seen clearly before to illustrate an important problem, process or principle.
Science - Natural
Dist - WARDS **Prod** - WARDS

Op Art 15 MIN
VHS / U-matic
Young at Art Series
Color (P I)
Discusses op art.
Fine Arts
Dist - AITECH **Prod** - WSKJTV 1980

Op Odyssey - Dance Ten 30 MIN
U-matic / VHS
Doris Chase Dance Series
Color
Presents dance performance based on Doris Chase Kinetic sculpture.
Fine Arts; Physical Education and Recreation
Dist - CHASED **Prod** - CHASED

Opal Palmer Adisa - 11 - 17 - 83 30 MIN
VHS / Cassette
Poetry Center reading series
Color (G)
$15.00, $45.00 purchase _ #570 - 481
Features the African - American poet reading at the Poetry Center, San Francisco State University.
Literature and Drama
Dist - POETRY **Prod** - POETRY 1983

Opaque Watercolor 12 MIN
16mm
Introduction to Commercial Art Series
Color (J)
LC 80-700518
Shows the basic techniques used to apply opaque watercolors.
Fine Arts
Dist - SF **Prod** - SF 1979

OPEC - End of an Era 12 MIN
U-matic / VHS
Color (H C A)
Describes OPEC, once a powerful, united group, forced to lower its prices in the face of an international oil surplus. Looks at the OPEC ministers, their countries and their policies.
Civics and Political Systems; Geography - World; Social Science
Dist - JOU **Prod** - JOU

The Open Alveolus 20 MIN
16mm
Color
LC 79-701051
Describes respiratory rehabilitation of postoperative patients.
Health and Safety
Dist - CHEPON **Prod** - CHEPON 1979

Open and closed wounds; Rev Ed 11 MIN
16mm / U-matic / VHS
First aid series
Color
Highlights practical application of first aid techniques showing different types of open and closed wounds, and the proper methods of first aid treatment. Demonstrates control of bleeding, application of sterile dressings, cravat and triangular cover bandages, and care of the injured for physical shock. Stresses the importance of obtaining competent medical assistance.
Health and Safety
Dist - USNAC **Prod** - USMESA 1981

Open and independent adoption - starting new families 30 MIN
VHS / U-matic
Adoption series
Color (G)
$149.00 purchase _ #7439
Asks if adoption should be kept closed with no information or contact with the birth family or if it should be an open process where birth families have a right to choose which home, environment and family their child is raised in. Presents two 'new' families who tried the open adoption process. Emphasizes the need to exchange information and knowledge between birth parents and adoptive parents when relinquishing a child. Part of a three - part series on adoption.
Sociology
Dist - VISIVI **Prod** - VISIVI 1991

Open and Shut 15 MIN
Videoreel / VT2
Umbrella Series
Color
Fine Arts
Dist - PBS **Prod** - KETCTV

Open and Shut Case 15 MIN
16mm
Color (J)
Discusses garage door openers, covering garage door cost, installation, power, security, fire protection, carbon monoxide protection and safety.
Health and Safety; Home Economics
Dist - KLEINW **Prod** - KLEINW

Open angle glaucoma 13 MIN
VHS
Color (G PRO C)
$250.00 purchase _ #EY - 24
Reveals that open angle glaucoma can cause permanent vision loss if left untreated. Describes how medications such as drops can lower eye pressure and prevent damage to the optic nerve. Reviews laser surgery and reinforces the importance of compliance with treatment plan and periodic checkups.
Health and Safety; Science - Natural
Dist - MIFE **Prod** - MIFE 1993

The Open Cathedral 13 MIN
16mm
Color (R)
LC 72-702194
Explains that when members in the congregation of a typical church are confronted by non - members they are made aware of the role of people in the church.
Guidance and Counseling; Religion and Philosophy; Sociology
Dist - FAMF **Prod** - FAMF 1972

Open city 103 MIN
VHS
B&W (H G) (ITALIAN)
$59.00 purchase _ #05830 - 126
Gives an account of life in Rome under German occupation as created by director Roberto Rosellini.
Fine Arts; Literature and Drama
Dist - GA **Prod** - GA

The Open Classroom 29 MIN
U-matic / VHS / 16mm
Human Relations and School Discipline Series
Color (C)
Studies the various forms of open education in operation in several public schools in New York, Washington and California, featuring Professor Lillian Weber, a leading proponent of the open - class - roon concept and director of ccny's workshop center for open education.
Education; Sociology
Dist - FI **Prod** - MFFD

Open Corner 16 - Gauge Steel Horizontal or Flat Demonstration 4 MIN
BETA / VHS
Color (IND)
Illustrates the proper technique for welding an open corner joint in 16 - gauge steel in the horizontal or flat position.
Industrial and Technical Education; Psychology
Dist - RMIBHF **Prod** - RMIBHF

Open Corner 16 - Gauge Steel Vertical Down Demonstration 3 MIN
BETA / VHS
Color (IND)
Points out the proper technique for welding an open corner joint in 16 - gauge steel in the vertical down position.
Industrial and Technical Education; Psychology
Dist - RMIBHF **Prod** - RMIBHF

Open Corner Joint 5 MIN
VHS / BETA
Welding Training Comprehensive Oxy - Acetylene Welding Series
Color (IND)
Industrial and Technical Education; Psychology
Dist - RMIBHF **Prod** - RMIBHF

Open Corner Ten - Gauge Weld Joint Demonstration 5 MIN
VHS / BETA
Color (IND)
Demonstrates the proper technique for applying the weld on an open corner join in ten - gauge steel.
Industrial and Technical Education; Psychology
Dist - RMIBHF **Prod** - RMIBHF

The Open Cuff Technique in Vaginal Hysterectomy 10 MIN
U-matic / VHS
Color (PRO)
Shows the Open Cuff Technique in which the patient required abdominal surgery for a hernia as well as for a vaginal hysterectomy. Includes drawings of the procedure.
Health and Safety
Dist - WFP **Prod** - WFP

Open Dog Obedience 15 MIN
16mm
Dog Obedience Training Series
Color
LC 75-700105
Illustrates a variety of techniques for developing open dog obedience.
Science - Natural
Dist - KLEINW **Prod** - KLEINW 1974

The Open Door 28 MIN
16mm
No Place Like Home Series
Color
LC 74-706167
Shows the activities and training of mentally restored patients in the friendly, supportive atmosphere of a halfway house.
Health and Safety; Psychology
Dist - USNAC **Prod** - USSRS 1973

Open doors 19 MIN
VHS
Color (G A R)
$24.95 purchase, $10.00 rental _ #4 - 85033
Presents strategies and resources for outreach efforts to Christian day schools, preschools and child care centers. Companion manual also available.
Religion and Philosophy
Dist - APH **Prod** - APH

Open Fender Straightening 31 MIN
VHS / BETA
Color (A PRO)
$113.50 purchase _ #KTI78
Deals with auto body repair. Provides a step - by - step description of the rough - out through metal finishing, using a Ford Pinto as an example.
Industrial and Technical Education
Dist - RMIBHF **Prod** - RMIBHF

Open Fractures 20 MIN
U-matic / VHS
Fracture Management Series
Color (PRO)
Health and Safety
Dist - WFP **Prod** - WFP

Open hand forms - Part 1 41 MIN
VHS
Color (G)
$49.95 purchase _ #1164
Shows men and women of Beijing and Shanghai demonstrating open hand forms such as Hsing I, Bagua, Praying Mantis, Don Bei, Lan Shou, Chi Jiao, Wu Shong Tu Kao, and others. Includes Shaolin temple monks demonstrating forms.
Physical Education and Recreation
Dist - WAYF

Open hand forms - Part 2 38 MIN
VHS
Color (G)
$49.95 purchase _ #1165
Shows men and women of Beijing and Shanghai demonstrating more open hand forms such as Hsing I, Yu family forms, dragon and snake Bagua, Praying Mantis, Lan Shou, Ba Ji, Cha fist, and others. Includes Shaolin temple monks demonstrating forms.
Physical Education and Recreation
Dist - WAYF

Open Hearing 51 MIN
VHS / U-matic
Color
Offers a response to the 'Fair Game Faggot' program about gays. Offers wide range of opinions on such issues as gay teachers, civil rights legislation for gays and the Bible's stand on homosexuality.
Psychology; Sociology
Dist - WCCOTV **Prod** - WCCOTV 1977

Open heart surgery 30 MIN
VHS
Doc Martin's casebook series
Color; PAL (G)
PdS40 purchase
Follows Colin, a heart disease sufferer, as he goes in for open heart surgery. Examines the role of the 16,000 patients who undergo heart bypass surgery every year in the United Kingdom. Dr. Martin Hughes narrates. Part six of an eight - part series.
Health and Safety
Dist - BBCENE

Open - Heart Surgery 17 MIN
VHS / U-matic
Color
LC 77-730600
Explains to the patient what will take place before and after open - heart surgery, equipment used and operation procedures. Describes recovery room, intensive care unit and discusses need for postoperative deep - breathing and coughing. Emphasizes caution and graduality in recovery.
Health and Safety; Science - Natural
Dist - MEDCOM **Prod** - MEDCOM

Open Heart Surgery 27 MIN
16mm
Color (PRO)
Portrays the physiologic hemodynamics related to defects in the interventricular septum and demonstrates methods of closure utilizing extracorporeal bypass with a pump - oxygenator.
Health and Safety; Science
Dist - ACY **Prod** - ACYDGD 1958

Open heart surgery 45 MIN
VHS
Surgical procedures series
Color (G)
$149.00 purchase, $75.00 rental _ #UW4568
Features Dr Gaudiani of Sequoia Hospital in Redwood City, California, explaining why and how heart valve defects occur and how they are repaired. Uses a head camera to look inside a human heart and examine in detail how a surgical team replaces malfunctioning heart valves. Part of a 17 - part series recording surgical procedures in detail, with specialists who explain the ailment, the anatomical function of the part of the body being operated on, and how successful surgery might improve the patient's quality of life, hosted by Dr Donna Willis.
Health and Safety
Dist - FOTH

Open heart surgery - a new beginning 25 MIN
VHS
Color (PRO A)
$250.00 purchase _ #HA - 31
Uses patient interviews to educate viewers about what to expect before, during and after surgery. Includes information about life - style changes and explores the emotional and sensory experiences of those undergoing open heart surgery. Meets the needs of a variety of patient educators, to be used in a one - on - one setting or in a group discussion. Produced by Presbyterian Hospital of Charlotte, NC.
Health and Safety
Dist - MIFE

Open Heart Surgery - an Overview - Parts 1 and 2 64 MIN
U-matic / VHS
Color (PRO)
Provides, on two tapes, information about all aspects of bypass surgery. Covers anatomy of chest and heart (tape 1), surgery preparation (tape 1), skin grafts (tape 1) and the operation itself (tape 2).
Science - Natural
Dist - HSCIC **Prod** - HSCIC 1984

Open heart surgery - home recovery 15 MIN
VHS
Color (G PRO C)
$200.00 purchase _ #HA - 32
Educates patients about what to expect after returning home from the hospital after open heart surgery. Discusses normal sensations and symptoms to report to the doctor. Reviews incision care, lifestyle changes and activity guidelines. Addresses the emotional impact of the surgery and explains participation in a cardiac rehabilitation program.
Health and Safety
Dist - MIFE **Prod** - MIFE 1993

Open - Heart Surgery using the Kay - Anderson Heart - Lung Machine 22 MIN
16mm
Color (PRO)
Presents Dr Jerome H Kay and his surgical team as they correct a narrowing at the origin of the pulmonary artery and also repair a ventricular septal defect, assisted by Dr Robert M Anderson and his heart - lung machine.
Health and Safety; Science; Science - Natural
Dist - UPJOHN **Prod** - UPJOHN 1958

The Open Hearth Furnace 7 MIN
16mm
Making, Shaping and Treating Steel Series
Color (J H)
Business and Economics; Science - Physical
Dist - USSC **Prod** - USSC

Open hearts 50 MINS.
VHS
Courage to fail
Color; PAL (C H PRO)
PdS99 purchase; not available in South Africa
Covers the developments in heart surgery since 1945. Focuses on the advancements achieved in open heart procedures. Second in the five - part series Courage to Fail, which presents the stories of pioneers in the field of modern surgery.
Health and Safety
Dist - BBCENE

Open house - shared living for the elderly with Maggie Kuhn 37 MIN
VHS / 16mm
Color (H C G)
$400.00, $295.00 purchase, $50.00 rental
Shows viable living alternatives for elderly persons who no longer want to live alone but are too independent to live in an institution. Shows how the 'shared housing' concept combines privacy and companionship in a supportive, friendly environment. Illustrates a variety of arrangments - roommates, communal living, extended families. Produced by Action for Boston Community Development Inc and the Boston University Film Unit.
Health and Safety
Dist - FLMLIB

The Open Laboratory 28 MIN
16mm
Innovations in Education Series
Color
Dr Dwight Allen, Professor of Education at Stanford University, describes laboratories which provide for individualization and an expanded range of instructional alternatives based on performance criteria.
Education; Psychology
Dist - EDUC **Prod** - STNFRD 1966

An Open letter 6 MIN
16mm
B&W (G)
$7.00 rental
Provides an open letter to the world and a detective story. Experiments in dramatic technique and inexpensive optical effects. Produced by Focus Pocus Film Squad.
Fine Arts
Dist - CANCIN

Open letter - grasp the bird's tail 15 MIN
VHS / 16mm
Body, soul and voice - new work by women series
Color (G)
Portrays a young woman who confronts her fears of being an Asian woman in a world distorted by misogynistic and anti - Asian hostilities in a letter to her lover. Reveals that she imagines herself as a woman contortionist in a magician's box, twisting her body to avoid the intrusion of knives. Contemplates race, gender and violence. Directed by Brenda Joy Lem, Canada.
Sociology
Dist - CROCUR

An Open Mind 20 MIN
U-matic / VHS
Rights and Responsibilities Series
Color (J H)
Contrasts student comments about police and law in general with the thoughts of three police officers as they act out their rights and responsibilities in daily routines.
Civics and Political Systems; Guidance and Counseling; Psychology; Social Science
Dist - AITECH **Prod** - VAOG 1975

The Open Mind - a Talk with Margaret Mead 29 MIN
U-matic
B&W
Features anthropologist Margaret Mead as she offers her views on a variety of topics, including women's liberation and the Vietnam War.
Sociology
Dist - UMITV **Prod** - UMITV 1972

Open - Pit Mining Hazards 17 MIN
16mm
Color
LC 74-705257
Re - enacts mining accidents involving dump trucks, power shovels, front - end loaders, rail haulage and highwall blasting to show what happens from workers' carelessness, when safety precautions are overlooked, or where unsafe machinery and mining methods are used. Explains why the accidents happened and then stresses the correct and safe way of performing various mining jobs to prevent future accidents.
Health and Safety; Industrial and Technical Education
Dist - USNAC **Prod** - USBM 1967

Open Plan Concept - Nongraded School 19 MIN
16mm
Individualizing Elementary Education Series
B&W (C T)
LC 72-701999
Describes the open plan concept and the nongraded school, and shows how these programs are used to individualize learning for elementary grade students.
Education
Dist - EDUC **Prod** - EDUC 1971

Open Reduction and Fixation, Fracture of Mandible at the Angle - the Submandibular 16 MIN
16mm
Color
LC 74-705255
Demonstrates the open reduction and fixation of a mandibular fracture at the angle by the submandibular approach.
Science; Science - Natural
Dist - USNAC **Prod** - USVA 1968

Open Reduction and Internal Fixation of Forearm Fractures 35 MIN
16mm
Color (PRO)
Deals with the technique for the two standard procedures for operative reduction and internal fixation of forearm fractures, namely, fixation by intramedullary device and by plates and screws.
Health and Safety; Science
Dist - ACY **Prod** - ACYDGD 1952

Open Reduction of 'T' and 'Y' Fractures of the Humerus 15 MIN
16mm
Color (PRO)
Shows the operative treatment of 'T' and 'Y' fractures of the lower end of the humerus. Uses the transolecranon approach and the fragments fixed with screws.
Health and Safety; Science
Dist - ACY **Prod** - ACYDGD 1962

Open road series
The Great smokies, mountains for millions 7 MIN
Dist - AUDPLN

Open Season 10 MIN
U-matic / VHS / 16mm
Color
LC 81-700946
Tells how a young boy tries unsuccessfully to make two deer hunters leave the woods on his family's land.
Fine Arts; Physical Education and Recreation
Dist - PHENIX **Prod** - SUGERA 1979

Open Season 30 MIN
16mm
B&W
LC FI67-107
Relates the true experiences of a Wisconsin game warden in 1928 who refused to be intimidated by a vacationing mobster and who risked his life to uphold the game laws.
Science - Natural
Dist - WB **Prod** - GE 1963

Open Secrets 25 MIN
U-matic / VHS / 16mm
Color (J)
Encourages communication within the family and between teenagers and their peers to avert the possibly tragic consequences of substance abuse.
Health and Safety; Psychology; Sociology
Dist - CORF **Prod** - CORF

Open Sesame 15 MIN
U-matic
Keys to the Office Series
Color (H)
Focuses on job search skills and how to acquire them. Consultants and business people give helpful advice.
Business and Economics
Dist - TVOTAR **Prod** - TVOTAR 1986

Open space series
Al Dawaah - the invitation 30 MIN
All those in favour 30 MIN
Champs or cheats 30 MIN
Dance of the pen 30 MIN
Dead centre 30 MIN
Dietbreakers 30 MIN
Disaster never 30 MIN
Kids aren't alright 30 MIN
Leave country sports alone 30 MIN
Let's kill nanny 30 MIN
License to kill 30 MIN
Look back in anger 30 MIN
Lunch is for wimps 30 MIN
Male rape 25 MIN
Scratching the surface 30 MIN
Shadow of suicide 35 MIN
Unspeakable acts 30 MIN
What am I doing here 30 MIN
Your furniture, their lives 40 MIN
Dist - BBCENE

Open space special series
Car sick 50 MIN
A Fate worse than debt 90 MIN
Dist - BBCENE

Open space
Adoption: whose needs come first? 30 MINS.
Dist - BBCENE

Open Surgical Prostatectomy Techniques 34 MIN
16mm
Color (PRO)
Explains that no single method of prostatectomy can be used for the relief of bladder neck and prostatic obstruction if best results are to be obtained. Depicts methods of open prostatectomy, perineal, suprapubic, retropubic and trans - vesico - capsular used at the Massachusetts General Hospital.
Health and Safety; Science
Dist - ACY **Prod** - ACYDGD 1963

Open Talk about Sex 20 MIN
Videoreel / VHS
Color (H) (AMERICAN SIGN)
Presented in American sign language with voice interpretation. Explains sexual anatomy by a deaf peer counselor using anatomical models and charts to teach male and female differences.
Education; Health and Safety; Psychology
Dist - PPASED **Prod** - PPASED

Open the Door 28 MIN
16mm / U-matic / VHS
Color
Features communications expert Bill Welp who presents his system OPEN Communication. Stars Ron Masak.
English Language; Psychology
Dist - CCCD **Prod** - CCCD 1980

Open the Door to Advanced Skiing 29 MIN
Videoreel / VT2
Skiing Series
Color
Physical Education and Recreation
Dist - PBS **Prod** - KTCATV

The Open Theatre Presents the Serpent 80 MIN
16mm
B&W
Features a performance of The Serpent, concerning the creation and fall of man as interpreted by playwright Jean - Claude Van Italie and as presented by the Open Theatre.
Fine Arts; Literature and Drama
Dist - CANTOR **Prod** - CANTOR

Open to our divine life call 60 MIN
VHS
Guidelines for growing spiritually mature series
Color (R G)
$49.95 purchase _ #GGSM2
Challenges Christians in today's world to hear anew and respond joyfully to the universal call to holiness. Focuses on one phase of the journey to maturity in the spiritual sense. Offers guidelines according to the teachings of the Roman Catholic Church. Features Dr Susan Muto and the Rev Adrian Van Kaam. Part two of six parts.
Religion and Philosophy
Dist - CTNA **Prod** - CTNA

Open Treatment of Aortic Stenosis with Pump Oxygenator 19 MIN
16mm
Color (PRO)
Shows the surgical relief of congenital valvular and subvalvular and acquired valvular aortic stenosis. Combines cardiopulmonary bypass with hypothermia to allow work on the aortic valve and adjacent heart.
Health and Safety; Science
Dist - ACY **Prod** - ACYDGD 1960

Open Up My Eyes 10 MIN
U-matic / VHS / 16mm
Color (I)
LC 72-701731
Examines the beauty of wildflowers intermingled with the excitement of quiet streams.
Science - Natural
Dist - ALTSUL **Prod** - BEZF 1971

Open Waters 20 MIN
16mm / U-matic / VHS
Color
Describes the role of the Army Corps of Engineers in the development, maintenance and operation of the nation's waterway system.
Civics and Political Systems; Geography - United States; Industrial and Technical Education
Dist - USNAC **Prod** - USAE

The Open Window 12 MIN
U-matic / VHS / 16mm
Color (J)
Presents an adaptation of Saki's classic ghost story.
Literature and Drama
Dist - PFP **Prod** - AMERFI 1972

The Open Window 18 MIN
16mm / U-matic / VHS
Color
Features 60 paintings, chosen to demonstrate the differences and the points of similarity between the works of artists from several Western European countries. Explores the mixture of light and color known as impressionism.
Fine Arts; History - World
Dist - IFB **Prod** - STORCH 1957

Open Window 18 MIN
U-matic / VHS / 16mm
Color (H C)
Covers various approaches to landscape painting from the 15th century to the French Impressionists.
Fine Arts
Dist - IFB **Prod** - IFB 1957

The Open window and Child's play 39 MIN
VHS
American short story collection series
Color (J H)
$49.00 purchase _ #60392 - 126
Presents two ghost stories by Saki.
Literature and Drama
Dist - GA **Prod** - GA

Open Wire Transposition Systems 17 MIN
16mm
B&W
LC FIE55-75
Illustrates and explains the need for transpositions, how they improve communication and the construction of various types of physical or single - point transpositions.
Civics and Political Systems; Industrial and Technical Education; Social Science
Dist - USNAC **Prod** - USA 1954

Open Your Eyes 29 MIN
16mm
Color (J)
LC FIA65-444
Describes the service Senior Girl Scouts can give to their communities in small towns and in big cities. Explains the projects with which these teen - age girls are related.
Physical Education and Recreation; Psychology; Sociology
Dist - GSUSA **Prod** - GSUSA 1965

The Opening 15 MIN
16mm
Journal Series
Color
LC 77-702862
Studies the life and work of Canadian artist Gerald Humen. Shows him working to meet a deadline for an exhibition of 70 of his paintings.
Fine Arts
Dist - CANFDC **Prod** - FIARTS 1976

Opening a Telemarketing Call 14 MIN
VHS / U-matic
Telemarketing for Better Business Results Series
Color
Business and Economics; Psychology
Dist - DELTAK **Prod** - COMTEL

Opening a telephone campaign 11 MIN
VHS / 16mm
Color (G IND)
$5.00 rental
Shows how to set up a telephone bank to work on a political campaign. Supporting materials available. Produced by the Labor Institute of Public Affairs for COPE.
Business and Economics; Civics and Political Systems; Social Science
Dist - AFLCIO **Prod** - LIPA 1986

Opening and closing pipe flanges 10 MIN
BETA / VHS / U-matic
Color (IND G)
$295.00 purchase _ #800 - 11
Instructs operating personnel in the correct procedures for opening and closing pipe flanges and replacing gaskets.
Health and Safety; Industrial and Technical Education; Psychology; Science - Physical
Dist - ITSC **Prod** - ITSC

Opening Day at the Fair 29 MIN
Videoreel / VT2
Children's Fair Series
B&W (K P)
Science; Science - Natural; Science - Physical
Dist - PBS **Prod** - WMVSTV

Opening Doors 13 MIN
U-matic / VHS
Making it Work Series
Color (H A)
Explains that job seeking is easier if the seeker is prepared with a job history, a letter of application, and references or recommendations. Shows how Pete learns from a personnel director how to gather these materials and send them.
Guidance and Counseling; Psychology
Dist - AITECH **Prod** - ERF 1983

Opening Doors - a Positive Approach to AIDS 55 MIN
VHS
Color (G)
$35.00 purchase _ #402
Documents the AIDS support group conducted by Louise L Hay since 1985. Includes interviews and Hay discussing curing herself of cancer.
Health and Safety
Dist - HAYHSE **Prod** - HAYHSE

Opening doors - an introduction to peer coaching 60 MIN
VHS
Color (T C A PRO)
$445.00 purchase, $75.00 rental _ #614 - 182X01
Shows how a peer coaching program can improve morale and motivation by building trust and reducing teacher isolation; promote better teaching in an environment where ideas are freely exchanged; ensure that training transfers from workshop to classroom practice. Explains how to set goals, observe efforts toward those goals and communicate ideas and suggestions. Describes a step - by - step approach to peer coaching and shows exactly what peer coaching is like. Includes two videos and a facilitator's manual.
Education
Dist - AFSCD **Prod** - AFSCD 1989

Opening Doors to Creative Expression 28 MIN
16mm
Color
Teaches how to heighten creative sensibility as an aid to problem solving. Shows how to increase productivity through awareness of personal decision style, promoting better interpersonal relations and building cooperative team skills.
Fine Arts; Psychology
Dist - HP **Prod** - HP

Opening Doors to the Future 25 MIN
U-matic / VHS
Color
Discussion and demonstration of career possibilities and educational requirements for fields of physical therapy, occupational therapy, special education, speech pathology, and psychology.
Education; Guidance and Counseling; Health and Safety
Dist - UNEBO **Prod** - UNEBO

Opening hearts 10 MIN
VHS
Magnum eye series
Color (G)
$125.00 purchase, $30.00 rental
Documents the effects of the Gulf War and UN sanctions against Iraq on the alarming deterioration of Iraq's medical facilities - with the children among the first to suffer. Travels to Iraq with Medicine for Peace where five children - from among hundreds - are chosen to have surgery in the US for their severe heart conditions. Reveals yet another tragedy overlooked by Western media. Directed by Susan Meiselas. Part of a series by photographers from the Magnum Photo Agency.
Fine Arts; Health and Safety; History - World; Sociology
Dist - FIRS **Prod** - MIYAKE 1993

Opening in Moscow 45 MIN
16mm
Color
Discloses impressions of Moscow and its citizens under the Krushchev regime. Centered around the opening of the 1959 American Exhibition. By D A Pennebaker.
Civics and Political Systems; History - World
Dist - PENNAS **Prod** - PENNAS

Opening Leads and Play of the Hand 30 MIN
VHS / U-matic
Bridge Basics Series
Color (A)
Physical Education and Recreation
Dist - KYTV **Prod** - KYTV 1982

Opening Night 30 MIN
U-matic / VHS
In Our Own Image Series
Color (C)
Fine Arts
Dist - DALCCD **Prod** - DALCCD

The Opening of the American West 36 MIN
VHS
Color (I J H)
$135.00 purchase _ #UL1903VA
Presents two parts which use artwork, diary entries and narrative to teach about the westward expansion in the United States after Lewis and Clark. Focuses on the expedition of Lewis and Clark, the disruption of native cultures and the role of the Hudson Bay Company in part one. Part two follows a five - month journey of a typical wagon train, including preparations, homesteading, disease and other hardships of the pioneer experience. Includes two videos, 15 duplicating masters and a teacher's guide.
Geography - United States; History - United States
Dist - KNOWUN

An Opening of the heart 46 MIN
VHS / BETA
Color; PAL (G)
PdS15 purchase
Introduces the Friends of the Western Buddhist Order, founded in 1964 by Sangharakshita who lived as a monk for 20 years in India. Explores why he returned to England and how members felt then and now about his form of Buddhism and its effect on their lives. Part 1 of 2 parts.
Fine Arts; Religion and Philosophy
Dist - MERIDT

An Opening of the heart - part 2 - Kindling the flame 39 MIN
VHS / BETA
Color; PAL (G)
Continues the story of the Friends of the Western Buddhist Order, founded in 1964 by Sangharakshita who lived as a monk for 20 years in India. Begins in 1971 and charts its growth and direction. Part 2 of 2 parts.
Fine Arts; Religion and Philosophy
Dist - MERIDT

Opening principles
VHS
Color (G)
$39.95 purchase
Teaches the opening principles of playing chess. Features Bruce Pandolfini.
Physical Education and Recreation
Dist - CHESSR **Prod** - CHESSR 1991

Opening principles, Understanding chess
VHS
Color (G)
$75.00 purchase
Presents two videos on chess - Opening Principles and Understanding Chess. Teaches chess strategies. Features Bruce Pandolfini.
Physical Education and Recreation
Dist - CHESSR **Prod** - CHESSR 1991

Opening process systems - Parts 1 and 2
VHS
Color (IND)
$695.00 purchase _ #800 - 65, #800 - 66
Shows how to plan every aspect of a line or vessel opening. Part 1 - Making a Plan - follows two operators as they plan to open a line, examine existing documentation, make a positive identification of the line and its content, plan the isolation, evaluate potential hazards, and review their plan using a 'what if' approach. Part 2 - Shutdown and Isolation - shows steps to isolate work area, replace a control valve and reopen the line. For anyone who will participate in or be impacted by a line or vessel opening.
Business and Economics; Health and Safety
Dist - ITSC **Prod** - ITSC

Opening Speech - Mc Laren 7 MIN
U-matic / VHS / 16mm
Mc Laren Films Series
B&W (I)
Presents an animated film in which Norman Mc Laren is caught by his own film tricks - - Mc Laren attempts to welcome the audience but is frustrated by a microphone which has a will of its own.
English Language
Dist - IFB **Prod** - NFBC 1963

Opening statement 42 MIN
VHS
Trial masters forum series
Color (C PRO)
$70.00 purchase _ #1V2-93
Describes achievement of three crucial objectives of the opening statement - establishment of credibility, explaination of the client's case, and assistance to the jury in understanding its role. Presented by Roxanne Barton Conlin.
Civics and Political Systems
Dist - ATLA

Opening statement - civil and criminal 28 MIN
VHS
Opening statement series
Color (C PRO)
$75.00 purchase, $30.00 rental _ #OPX01
Demonstrates techniques for preparing and presenting opening statements in civil and criminal trials.
Civics and Political Systems
Dist - NITA **Prod** - NITA

Opening statement - criminal and complex civil case 46 MIN
VHS
Opening statement series
Color (C PRO)
$75.00 purchase, $50.00 rental _ #OPX03
Demonstrates techniques for preparing and presenting opening statements in criminal and complex civil trials.
Civics and Political Systems
Dist - NITA **Prod** - NITA

Opening statement in a criminal case 27 MIN
VHS
Opening statement series
Color (C PRO)
$75.00 purchase, $30.00 rental _ #OPX02
Demonstrates techniques for preparing and presenting opening statements in criminal trials.
Civics and Political Systems
Dist - NITA **Prod** - NITA

Opening statement series
Opening statement - civil and criminal 28 MIN
Opening statement - criminal and complex civil case 46 MIN
Opening statement in a criminal case 27 MIN
Dist - NITA

Opening statements 58 MIN
VHS
Training the advocate series
Color (C PRO)
$115.00 purchase, $95.00 rental _ #TTA02
Uses a nuclear power plant accident case to teach basic trial advocacy skills. Gives guidelines for opening statements. Co - produced by the American Bar Association.
Civics and Political Systems
Dist - NITA **Prod** - NITA 1983

Opening Statements 59 MIN
U-matic / VHS
Training the Advocate Series
Color (PRO)
Gives opening statement demonstrations. Gives suggestions on what juries need to see and hear during opening statements.
Civics and Political Systems
Dist - ABACPE **Prod** - AMBAR

Opening statements 53 MIN
VHS
Business litigation series
Color (C PRO)
$95.00 purchase, $71.25 rental _ #LBC07
Gives guidelines for opening statements in business litigation cases.
Civics and Political Systems
Dist - NITA **Prod** - NITA 1987

Opening statements 53 MIN
Cassette
Medical malpractice litigation - new strategies for a new era series
Color (PRO)
$125.00, $30.00 purchase, $50.00 rental _ #MED2-005, #AME2-005
Discusses and demonstrates innovative litigation strategies and techniques developed in response to the rapidly changing climate in which medical malpractice cases are litigated. Details opening statements. Includes demonstrations by skilled trial lawyers, interviews of those conducting the demonstrations and panel discussions. Includes study guide.
Civics and Political Systems
Dist - AMBAR **Prod** - AMBAR 1987

Opening statements 56 MIN
Cassette
Winning the business jury trial series
Color (PRO)
$125.00, $30.00 purchase, $50.00 rental _ #BUS1-003, #ABUS-003
Provides sophisticated trial skills training for the business litigator. Demonstrates business cases including lender liability, securities fraud and antitrust. Explains how to present opening statements, giving the viewer an analytical framework in which to view subsequent demonstrations and discussions. Gives an insider's look at nationally recognized business litigators as they plan their strategies. Includes a psychologist who specializes in persuasive communication strategies and decision - making processes providing analysis based on empirical research and juror interviews. Includes study guide.
Business and Economics; Civics and Political Systems
Dist - AMBAR **Prod** - AMBAR 1992

Opening statements 58 MIN
VHS
Winning at trial series
Color (C PRO)
$115.00 purchase, $95.00 rental _ #WAT02
Uses a wrongful death case to teach the skills of trial advocacy. Teaches about opening statements. Includes excerpts from the trial, comments from the lawyers involved, and critiques.
Civics and Political Systems; Education
Dist - NITA **Prod** - NITA 1986

Opening Statements and Closing Arguments 24 MIN
U-matic / Cassette / VHS / 16mm
Color; Mono (PRO)
Focuses on preparation and presentation of opening statements and closing arguments in a trial. Covers such topics as selecting arguments, organizing the opening statement, psychology of the argument, stating facts and issues, using pleadings, scope of closing argument and strategies.
Civics and Political Systems
Dist - CCEB **Prod** - CCEB

Opening Statements and First Witness 43 MIN
U-matic / VHS
Remedies Phase of an EEO Case - Individual Determinations Series Pt '2
Color (PRO)
Shows opening statements that cover burdens of proof and the kinds of exhibits to be presented. Demonstrates the examination and cross - examination of the first claimant.
Civics and Political Systems
Dist - ABACPE **Prod** - ALIABA

Opening Statements - Civil and Criminal 28 MIN
VHS / U-matic
Color (PRO)
Demonstrates several techniques common to effective opening statements in a trial, including introductory remarks, presentation of the story, its theme, characters and evidence, use of exhibits and varied pace, voice and gestures.
Civics and Political Systems
Dist - ABACPE **Prod** - ABACPE

Opening Statements - Criminal and Complex Civil 50 MIN
U-matic / VHS
Color (PRO)
Presents model opening statements in two cases - State vs Diamond, a murder case, and Spotts vs General Construction Manufacturer, Inc, a tort action.
Civics and Political Systems
Dist - ABACPE **Prod** - ABACPE

Opening statements in a contract action 115 MIN
VHS
The Art of advocacy - opening statements and closing arguments series
Color (C PRO)
$390.00 purchase, $180.00 rental _ #OAC03, #OAC04
Features U S, British and Australian lawyers in a presentation of effective jury persuasion strategies. Focuses on opening statements in a contract action.
Civics and Political Systems
Dist - NITA **Prod** - NITA 1987

Opening Statements in a Federal Narcotics Case 27 MIN
U-matic / VHS
Trial of a Criminal - Federal Narcotics Case Series
Color (PRO)
Demonstrates techniques and styles for an effective opening statement in a federal narcotics case.
Civics and Political Systems; Health and Safety
Dist - ABACPE **Prod** - ABACPE

Opening statements in a products liability case 115 MIN
VHS
The Art of advocacy - opening statements and closing arguments series
Color (C PRO)
$390.00 purchase, $180.00 rental _ #OAC01, #OAC02
Features U S, British and Australian lawyers in a presentation of effective jury persuasion strategies. Focuses on opening statements in a products liability case.
Civics and Political Systems
Dist - NITA **Prod** - NITA 1987

Opening Statements in a Products Liability Case 60 MIN
U-matic / VHS
Trial Techniques - a Products Liability Case Series
Color (PRO)
Presents opening statements for plaintiff and defense in a products liability case. Offers critiques of the presentations by skilled litigators.
Civics and Political Systems; Home Economics
Dist - ABACPE **Prod** - ABACPE

Opening statements series
Demonstrates techniques for preparing and presenting opening statements in trials.
Opening statements series 101 MIN
Dist - NITA **Prod** - NITA

Opening Suit Bids of One and Responses 30 MIN
VHS / U-matic
Bridge Basics Series
Color (A)
Physical Education and Recreation
Dist - KYTV **Prod** - KYTV 1982

Opening the Door 19 MIN
U-matic / 35mm strip
Basic Sales Series
Color
Examines preparation and procedures for first sales calls and shows how to handle this crucial first step successfully.
Business and Economics; Psychology
Dist - RESEM **Prod** - RESEM

Opening the gates of Hell - American liberators of the Nazi concentration camps 45 MIN
VHS
Color; B&W (G)
$39.95 purchase _ #638
Discloses that many American soldiers who witnessed the liberation of Nazi concentration camps have chosen not to speak of the horrors they witnessed. Interviews American veterans who have chosen to remember and to share their terrible memories. Includes graphic archival footage.
History - United States; History - World; Sociology
Dist - ERGOM **Prod** - ERGOM 1993

Opening the right doors
VHS
The Respectful workplace - redefining workplace violence series
Color (IND)
$425.00 purchase, $150.00 rental _ #QMR08A
Helps businesses end hostility, intimidation, harassment and other damaging behaviors. Includes a facilitator guide, handouts and overhead transparencies. Part of a three - part series. Produced by Quality Media Resources.
Business and Economics; Guidance and Counseling; Health and Safety; Social Science; Sociology
Dist - EXTR

Opening the right doors - Pt 1 25 MIN
VHS
The respectful workplace - Redefining workplace violence series

Color (PRO IND COR A)
$425.00 purchase, $150.00 rental, $50.00 preview
Helps organizations put an end to the destructive conflicts that occur on a daily basis. It redefines workplace violence and shows the importance of a defined value system, how to defuse hostile situations and how to use alternative dispute resolution as a means of resolving conflict.
Sociology
Dist - VIDART

Opening the Sale 30 MIN
16mm / U-matic / VHS
B&W (PRO)
Explains that the way a salesman opens the sale determines the kind of an interview he will get, the resistance he will meet, and the callbacks he must make. Demonstrates tested skills a salesman can develop to ease his way to the order.
Business and Economics; Psychology; Social Science; Sociology
Dist - DARTNL **Prod** - DARTNL

Opening the West
U-matic / VHS
Color
History - United States
Dist - MSTVIS **Prod** - MSTVIS

Opening to acceptance
VHS
(G)
$16.00, $39.00 purchase _ #AG001, #AG002
Presents Jack Kornfield, monk, psychologist and teacher of vipassana meditation, and psychotherapist Robert Hall. Approaches places in oneself touched by violence, separation and fear with the intention of awakening nurturing and acceptance.
Health and Safety; Psychology; Religion and Philosophy
Dist - BIGSUR

Opening to angels 60 MIN
VHS
Color (G)
$29.95 purchase _ #V - OTA
Shows how angels intercede human affairs and how to invoke their presence.
Religion and Philosophy
Dist - PACSPI

Opening to grief - the task - purification by fire - the passage through pain 54 MIN
U-matic / VHS
How then shall we live series
Color
Examines the healing nature of grief and the process of coping with loss. Features author and thanatologist Stephen Levine.
Sociology
Dist - ORGNLF **Prod** - ORGNLF

Opening to grief - the threshold task 23 MIN
U-matic / VHS
Conscious living - conscious dying - the work of a lifetime series
Color
Reveals several participants deepest feelings about their own deaths and the deaths of those close to them. Observes that if confronting death is postponed, life is postponed.
Sociology
Dist - PELICN **Prod** - ORGNLF

Opening to intuition quartet 120 MIN
BETA / VHS
Color (G)
$69.95 purchase _ #Q334
Presents a four - part series on opening to intuition. Includes 'The Superconscious Mind' with Kevin Ryerson, 'Channeling and the Self' with Jon Klimo, 'The Intuitive Connection' with Dr William Kautz and 'Awakening Intuition' with Dr Frances E Vaughan.
Psychology; Religion and Philosophy
Dist - THINKA **Prod** - THINKA

Opening to intuition series
Awakening intuition 30 MIN
Channeling and the self 30 MIN
The Intuitive connection 30 MIN
The Superconscious mind 30 MIN
Dist - THINKA

Opening Up the Walls 26 MIN
U-matic / VHS
Every Window Tells a Story Series
Color (H C A)
$300.00
Shows the beauty and purpose of the stained glass windows in the churches built in the Middle Ages. Narrated by Malcom Miller.
Fine Arts; History - World
Dist - LANDMK **Prod** - LANDMK 1986

Opening Your House to Solar Energy 28 MIN
16mm / U-matic / VHS
Home Energy Conservation Series
Color (A)
LC 81-700074
Focuses on the retrofitting of passive solar devices, explaining how to add greenhouses, maximize roofs and southern exposures, and install special solar - heated water tanks and thermal chimneys.
Social Science
Dist - BULFRG **Prod** - RPFD 1980

Opera 30 MIN
U-matic
Today's Special Series
Color (K P)
Develops language arts skills in children. Programs are thematically designed around subjects of interest to youngsters. Action takes place in a department store where people, mannequins, puppets, comic characters and special guests present a light hearted approach to language arts.
Fine Arts; Literature and Drama; Psychology
Dist - TVOTAR **Prod** - TVOTAR 1985

Opera 11 MIN
U-matic / VHS / 16mm
Color (J)
Offers a satirical commentary on the problems of the technological age.
Fine Arts; Literature and Drama
Dist - TEXFLM **Prod** - BOZETO 1975

Opera 15 MIN
U-matic / VHS
Pass it on Series
Color (K P)
Focuses on plays, music and operas.
Education; Fine Arts
Dist - GPN **Prod** - WKNOTV 1983

Opera - Man, Music and Drama 18 MIN
U-matic / VHS / 16mm
Humanities Series
Color (H C)
LC 74-714100
Introduces the study of the opera.
Fine Arts
Dist - MGHT **Prod** - MGHT 1971

Opera - One Hundred Years of Bayreuth 17 MIN
VHS / U-matic
Color (H C A)
Discusses the Bayreuth Festival, which celebrates the musical genius of Richard Wagner.
Fine Arts
Dist - JOU **Prod** - UPI

Opera stars in concert series
Opera stars in concert - Vol 1 60 MIN
Opera stars in concert - Vol 2 60 MIN
Opera stars in concert - Vol 3 80 MIN
Dist - KULTUR

Opera stars in concert - Vol 1 60 MIN
VHS
Opera stars in concert series
Color (G)
$24.95 purchase_#1317
Presents Alfredo Kraus, Katia Ricciarelli and Ruggero Raimondi performing favorite arias and duets. Includes pieces from La Traviata, Tosca, Faust, Don Carlos, I Puritani, and The Tales of Hoffman. Also includes appearance of Lucia Valentini - Terrani and Paolo Coni.
Fine Arts
Dist - KULTUR

Opera stars in concert - Vol 2 60 MIN
VHS
Opera stars in concert series
Color (G)
$24.95 purchase_#1325
Features opera stars Alfredo Kraus, Katia Ricciarelli and Ruggero Reimondi in performance of pieces from the world's favorite operas. Includes Rigoletto, Elisir d'Amore and The Barber of Seville.
Fine Arts
Dist - KULTUR

Opera stars in concert - Vol 3 80 MIN
VHS
Opera stars in concert series
Color (G)
$24.95 purchase_#1330
Features Alfredo Kraus and Paolo Coni - joined by Renata Scotto, Mellanie Holiday, Ramon Vargas and Gail Gilmore - performing selections from favorite operas and songs. Presents a live concert from Barcelona.
Fine Arts
Dist - KULTUR

Opera two to six - great operatic ensembles - the Bell Telephone Hour 52 MIN
VHS
Bell Telephone Hour series
Color (G)
$19.95 purchase_#1346
Presents Joan Sutherland, Tito Gobbi, Nicolai Gedda, Jerome Hines, Mildred Miller and Charles Anthony in concert. Features performances of scenes and ensembles from Tosca, Rigoletto, Faust, Die Meistersinger and Lucia Di Lammermoor. Includes a range of groups from duet to sextette.
Fine Arts
Dist - KULTUR

Opera with Henry Butler 26 MIN
16mm / U-matic / VHS
Color (J H C A) (SPANISH)
LC 77-708189
Illuminates the nature of traditional and modern opera in top professional performances from Pagliacci and La Traviata. Henry Butler, stage director for the Metropolitan Opera Company, comments on the emotional inspiration for opera, famous opera houses and trends in opera today. Includes interviews with the performers.
Fine Arts; Foreign Language
Dist - LCOA **Prod** - IQFILM 1970

Operando Su Grua Con Confianza 17 MIN
U-matic / VHS / 16mm
Color (IND) (SPANISH)
A Spanish - language version of the motion picture Craning With Confidence. Explains how to ensure safe crane operation and reviews how to set up a crane for a job, how to read and use the load chart and how to tell when a crane might tip or break.
Foreign Language; Health and Safety; Industrial and Technical Education
Dist - IFB **Prod** - IFB 1975

Operant Audiometry with Severely Retarded Children 15 MIN
16mm
Color (PRO)
LC 72-702026
Demonstrates the use of positive reinforcement to test the hearing of a severely retarded subject. Traces the progress of a 13 - year - old retarded boy through several clinical sessions designed to detect and diagnose impairments. Demonstrates how the child is conditioned to wear a headset and how reinforcement techniques are employed to train the child to respond to auditory stimuli.
Psychology
Dist - UKANS **Prod** - UKANS 1968

Operant Conditioning 16 MIN
16mm
Basic Psychology Series
Color (H C A)
LC 76-702924
Considers various aspects of operant conditioning in psychology, including punishment, discrimination, escape and avoidance and schedules of reinforcement.
Psychology
Dist - EDMDC **Prod** - EDMDC 1973

Operant Conditioning 29 MIN
U-matic
Understanding Human Behavior - an Introduction to Psychology Series 'Lesson 16
Color (C A)
Examines B F Skinner's theory of operant conditioning. Discusses examples of the wide applications of operant conditioning in advertising, classrooms and therapy.
Psychology
Dist - CDTEL **Prod** - COAST

Operant Learning 10 MIN
U-matic / VHS
Protocol Materials in Teacher Education - the Process of Teaching, 'Pt 2 Series
Color (T)
Education; Psychology
Dist - MSU **Prod** - MSU

Operate the Foundry
VHS
Metalworking Industrial Arts Series
(C G)
$59.00 _ CA211
Shows the importance of metal castings in modern life.
Industrial and Technical Education
Dist - AAVIM **Prod** - AAVIM 1989

Operating a Calder Hall Reactor Series
Refuelling 32 MIN
Dist - UKAEA

Operating an Incubator or Radiant Warmer 14 MIN
U-matic / VHS

Color (PRO)
Describes the main features of both incubators and radiant warmer, operation of each in both manual and serva mode, monitoring infant and incubator temperatures and daily equipment maintenance.
Health and Safety
Dist - UMICHM **Prod** - UMICHM 1983

Operating Audiovisual Equipment - Pt 1 26 MIN
U-matic / BETA / VHS
Operating Audiovisual Equipment Series
Color; Mono (H C A)
Introduces general operating principles of the DuKane Sound Filmstrip Projector, 3M Overhead Projector, Beseler Opaque Projector and Panasonic Portable Audio Cassette Recorder.
Education; English Language; Fine Arts; Industrial and Technical Education
Dist - UIOWA **Prod** - UIOWA 1983

Operating Audiovisual Equipment - Pt 2 28 MIN
BETA / VHS / U-matic
Operating Audiovisual Equipment Series
Color; Mono (H C A)
Demonstrates operation of four types of audiovisual equipment, including the Kodak Ekta III 35mm Slide Projector, Sony Single Camera VCR System, Kodak Pageant 16mm Film Projector, and Draper Portable Tripod Screen.
Education; English Language; Fine Arts; Industrial and Technical Education
Dist - UIOWA **Prod** - UIOWA 1983

Operating Audiovisual Equipment - Pt 3 26 MIN
BETA / VHS / U-matic
Operating Audiovisual Equipment Series
Color; Mono (H C A)
Demonstrates the basic procedures for producing simple instructional materials for classroom use. Includes laminating audiovisual materials, dry mounting audiovisual materials, basic lettering for AV materials, 3M Thermofax for transparencies, spirit masters and paper copies, and using the A B Dick Spirit Duplicator.
Education; Fine Arts; Industrial and Technical Education
Dist - UIOWA **Prod** - UIOWA 1983

Operating Audiovisual Equipment Series
Operating Audiovisual Equipment - Pt 1 26 MIN
Operating Audiovisual Equipment - Pt 2 28 MIN
Operating Audiovisual Equipment - Pt 3 26 MIN
Dist - UIOWA

Operating drill presses 13 MIN
VHS / U-matic
Introduction to machine technology series
Color (IND)
1 Series. Gives basic safety procedures for operating drill presses. Discusses setup and operation of a sensitive drill and a radial drill.
Industrial and Technical Education
Dist - LEIKID **Prod** - LEIKID

Operating electrical switches for process equipment 8 MIN
BETA / VHS / U-matic
Color (IND G)
$295.00 purchase _ #800 - 14
Intructs operating personnel in techniques for safely disconnecting energy sources of electrically driven process equipment. Stresses the importance of following correct lockout and tagout procedures.
Health and Safety; Industrial and Technical Education; Psychology
Dist - ITSC **Prod** - ITSC

Operating Emergency Vehicles 30 MIN
VHS
Pumping Apparatus Video Series
Color (G PRO)
$125.00 purchase _ #35408
Discusses the safe operation of fire fighting apparatus. Presents safe driving techniques, how to correctly start and drive both automatics and diesels. Demonstrates driving exercises and performance evaluations of the driver - operator.
Agriculture; Health and Safety; Psychology; Social Science
Dist - OKSU **Prod** - OKSU

Operating Experience - Dresden 10 MIN
16mm
Color
LC FIE64-138
Reports on the routine - day operation of the Dresden Nuclear Power Station, reviewing the success of the operating experience of the boiling water nuclear electric power station in terms of dependability, safety and ease of operation and maintenance.
Health and Safety; Industrial and Technical Education; Science - Physical
Dist - USNAC **Prod** - USNRC 1964

Operating Experience - Hallam 10 MIN
16mm
Color
LC FIE64-139
Describes the operation of the 79 - megawatt electric Hallam Nuclear Power Station, which is powered by a 252 - megawatt sodium - graphite reactor. Demonstrates Hallam's heat transfer cycle and plant - operation features, including fuel transfer and sodium handling.
Industrial and Technical Education; Science - Physical
Dist - USNAC **Prod** - USNRC 1964

Operating Experience - Yankee 10 MIN
16mm
Color
LC FIE64-141
Examines the various plant features and performance data of the nuclear power station that is operated by the Yankee Atomic Electric Company.
Industrial and Technical Education
Dist - USNAC **Prod** - USNRC 1964

Operating Fire Pumps 30 MIN
VHS
Pumping Apparatus Video Series
Color (G PRO)
$125.00 purchase _ #35410
Instructs driver - operators in methods for operating pumps under a variety of circumstances. Explains how pump operates with different water supplies, how to operate the pump using the water in the pumper, from a hydrant and from draft. Trains firefighting personnel.
Agriculture; Health and Safety; Industrial and Technical Education; Psychology; Science - Physical; Social Science
Dist - OKSU **Prod** - OKSU

Operating Parameters of Robots
VHS / 35mm strip
Robotics Series
Color
$42.00 purchase _ #LX5403 filmstrip, $62.00 purchase _ #LX5403V VHS
Describes accuracy and repeatability, payload, end of arm tooling, efficiency, and the dependency of robots on humans.
Industrial and Technical Education; Mathematics; Psychology
Dist - CAREER **Prod** - CAREER

Operating Parameters of Robots
VHS / 16mm
(A PRO)
$89.00 purchase _ #RB03
Discusses accuracy and repeatability, payload, end - of - arm tooling, efficiency, and the robot's dependency on humans.
Computer Science; Education
Dist - RMIBHF **Prod** - RMIBHF

Operating procedures and safety - counterbalance version 15 MIN
BETA / VHS / U-matic
Forklift operator training series
Color (IND G)
$395.00 purchase _ #817 - 23
Trains forklift operators. Discusses basic operating procedures, working around pedestrians, types of loads and load handling and general in - plant safety practices. Focuses on counterbalance forklifts. Part of a series on skills in forklift operation.
Health and Safety; Industrial and Technical Education; Psychology
Dist - ITSC **Prod** - ITSC

Operating procedures and safety - narrow aisle version 14 MIN
U-matic / BETA / VHS
Forklift operator training series
Color (IND G)
$395.00 purchase _ #817 - 22
Trains forklift operators. Discusses basic operating procedures, working around pedestrians, types of loads and load handling and general in - plant safety practices. Focuses on narrow aisle forklifts. Part of a series on skills in forklift operation.
Health and Safety; Industrial and Technical Education; Psychology
Dist - ITSC **Prod** - ITSC

Operating Room 30 MIN
VHS / U-matic
Adult Math Series
Color (A)
Shows how to multiply and divide fractions and solve some of the real - life problems of adult math students.
Education; Mathematics
Dist - KYTV **Prod** - KYTV 1984

Operating room cleaning 15 MIN
VHS
Housekeeping series
Color (H A G T)
$225.00 purchase _ #BM112
Follows guidelines recommended by the Association of Operating Room Nurses for cleaning and disinfecting operating rooms. Part of a series on housekeeping.
Health and Safety; Home Economics; Industrial and Technical Education; Psychology
Dist - AAVIM **Prod** - AAVIM

Operating room cleaning 14 MIN
VHS / U-matic / BETA
Medical housekeeping series
(PRO A)
$225 _ #1012
Focuses on the proper procedures used in cleaning hospital operating rooms. Uses recommendations by the Association of Operating Room Nurses, and demonstrations to emphasize points.
Education; Guidance and Counseling; Health and Safety
Dist - CTT **Prod** - CTT

Operating Room Deaths 28 MIN
16mm
Clinical Pathology - Forensic Medicine Outlines Series
B&W
LC 74-705258
Discusses operating room deaths due to improperly controlled diagnostic or therapeutic procedures, such as perforation of the bowel with a barium enema, perforation of the trachea during an attempt to remove an obstruction, transfixation of the trachea during an attempt to remove an obstruction and traumatic death due to explosion of anesthetic gases. (Kinescope).
Health and Safety; Science; Sociology
Dist - USNAC **Prod** - NMAC 1970

Operating Room Kaleidoscope - Oral Endoscopy 20 MIN
16mm
Color (PRO)
Shows the nursing and surgical management of a pediatric patient having general anesthesia for a laryngoscopy and an adult patient having a local anesthetic for bronchoscopy. Shows the nurse teaching and assisting a patient in rehabilitation.
Health and Safety; Science
Dist - ACY **Prod** - ACYDGD 1968

Operating Room Nursing Care of the Burn Patient 26 MIN
16mm
Color (PRO)
Illustrates operating room nursing care of the severely burned patient. Emphasizes the importance of preplanning to save anesthesia time during the many procedures involved in cleansing, debridement, dressings and skin grafting.
Health and Safety; Science
Dist - ACY **Prod** - ACYDGD 1962

Operating Room Nursing Care Plan for the Separation of Conjoined Twins 29 MIN
VHS / U-matic
Color (PRO)
Acquaints nurses, anesthesiologists, pediatricians, and surgical residents with a complex nursing care plan for the separation of conjoined twins.
Health and Safety
Dist - HSCIC **Prod** - HSCIC 1984

Operating Room Orientation - Attire, Scrubbing, Gowning, and Gloving 25 MIN
VHS / U-matic
Color (PRO)
Reviews basic principles of asepsis to be observed while preparing to serve as a scrubbed surgical team member. Demonstrates step - by - step procedures to follow in donning proper attire, performing a timed scrub, and maintaining asepsis while gowning and gloving. Presents techniques for maintaining asepsis of both sterile areas of clothing and sterile fields in the operating room during surgery.
Health and Safety
Dist - UMICHM **Prod** - UMICHM 1982

Operating Room Table Set - Up 18 MIN
VHS / BETA
Color
Demonstrates the tasks and procedures an operating room technician follows to set up the operating room for surgery.
Health and Safety
Dist - RMIBHF **Prod** - RMIBHF

Operating Room Techniques 15 MIN
U-matic / VHS
Basic Clinical Skills Series
Color (PRO)
Illustrates proper techniques for opening and maintaining sterile fields, anesthesia induction, skin prepping, draping and instrument handling.
Health and Safety; Science
Dist - HSCIC **Prod** - HSCIC 1984

Operating Systems 30 MIN
U-matic / VHS
Micros for Managers - Software Series
Color (IND)
Describes general operating - system concepts, and discusses the popular UNIX operating system as an example. Pros and cons of using UNIX are explored.
Industrial and Technical Education; Mathematics; Sociology
Dist - COLOSU **Prod** - COLOSU

Operating telescoping and articulating equipment 20 MIN
VHS
Aerial apparatus series
Color (IND)
$135.00 purchase _ #35451
Presents one of a five - part series that is a teaching companion for IFSTA's Fire Department Aerial Apparatus. Demonstrates, in step - by - step methods, how to elevate, rotate, extend, and lower telescoping and articulating apparatus. Emphasizes safe operation of equipment. Shows steps for prolonging the life of the equipment. Based on chapters 6 and 7.
Health and Safety; Science - Physical; Social Science
Dist - OKSU **Prod** - ACCTRA

Operating the Commercial Meat Slicer 20 MIN
BETA / VHS
Color (G PRO)
$59.00 purchase _ #QF04
Explains the basic parts of the commercial meat slicer which must be operated with special care. Features Chef Paul, who explains how to set up, clean and operate a slicer.
Home Economics
Dist - RMIBHF **Prod** - RMIBHF

Operating the Food Grinder 20 MIN
BETA / VHS / 16mm
Color (G PRO)
$59.00 purchase _ #QF08
Shows the basic parts of the food grinder, how to assemble, operate, and clean it.
Home Economics; Industrial and Technical Education
Dist - RMIBHF **Prod** - RMIBHF

Operating the Pendant Crane 7 MIN
VHS / U-matic
Steel Making Series
Color (IND)
Discusses the accuracy and good judgement required of the person operating the pendant crane.
Business and Economics; Health and Safety; Industrial and Technical Education
Dist - LEIKID **Prod** - LEIKID

Operating Tractors and Equipment 21 MIN
VHS / U-matic
Agricultural Accidents and Rescue Series
Color
Focuses on safely starting and stopping tractors powered by different fuels. Explains the safe handling of the tractor's hydraulic system. Shows how to release hydraulic pressure in an emergency.
Agriculture; Health and Safety
Dist - PSU **Prod** - PSU

Operation Affirmative 14 MIN
16mm
Color
LC 74-705259
Emphasizes the importance of the Ready Reserve when a Naval Reserve destroyer crew is called to duty to track a Russian fishing trawler off the coast of Seattle, Washington.
Civics and Political Systems
Dist - USNAC **Prod** - USN 1970

Operation and Application - Ansul Dry Chemical Hand Portable Extinguishers 18 MIN
VHS
Color (IND)
Demonstrates the basic steps of proper operation and effective extinguishment of uncontained flammable liquid spill fires, contained flammable liquid - in - depth fires, three - dimensional flammable liquid pressure fires and flammable gas pressure fires using dry chemicals in a hand held extinguisher.
Health and Safety
Dist - ANSUL **Prod** - ANSUL

Operation and Application, Ansul Dry Chemical Wheeled Extinguishers 13 MIN
VHS
Color (IND)
Demonstrates the basic sequential steps of proper operation and effective extinguishment of uncontained flammable liquid spill fires, contained flammable liquid - in - depth fires, three - dimensional flammable liquid pressure fires and flammable gas pressure fires using dry chemical wheeled extinguishers.
Health and Safety
Dist - ANSUL **Prod** - ANSUL

Operation and Application, Ansul Large Dry Chemical Hand Hose Line Systems 12 MIN
VHS
Color (IND)
Demonstrates regular and alternate methods of actuating a large dry chemical hand hose line system and the most effective fire fighting techniques for combating uncontained flammable liquid - in - depth fires, gravity - fed flammable liquid pressure fires, and flammable gas pressure fires.
Health and Safety
Dist - ANSUL **Prod** - ANSUL

Operation and Care of the Bell and Howell Specialist Filmsound Projector 11 MIN
U-matic / VHS / 16mm
Color (J)
LC FIA65-404
Revised edition of 'OPERATION OF THE BELL AND HOWELL SOUND PROJECTOR.' Demonstrates the operation and proper maintenance of the filmsound projector, using specialist models 540 and 542.
Education
Dist - IFB **Prod** - IFB 1962

Operation and Care of the Kodak Pageant Projector 11 MIN
U-matic / VHS / 16mm
Color (J)
LC 71-700271
Shows how to operate and maintain the projector.
Education
Dist - IFB **Prod** - IFB 1963

Operation and Maintenance of a Video System 30 MIN
U-matic / VHS
Video - a Practical Guide and more Series
Color
Outlines a step - by - step procedure for setting up, checking and maintaining a video system.
Fine Arts; Industrial and Technical Education
Dist - VIPUB **Prod** - VIPUB

Operation and Maintenance of an Air - Drill or Air - Grinder 8 MIN
VHS / 16mm
Kirkwood Community College Auto Mechanics Series
(G PRO)
$56.00 purchase _ #KTI52
Instructs on the operation and maintenance of an air - drill or air - grinder.
Industrial and Technical Education
Dist - RMIBHF **Prod** - RMIBHF

Operation and maintenance of the high speed burnisher - Part 9 13 MIN
VHS
Floor care series
Color (IND)
$275.00 purchase _ #6894
Trains caretaking and housekeeping staff in the operation of a high - speed floor burnishing unit. Features the operation of the Kent 2000 - RPM burnisher. Covers minor maintenance and clean - up procedures.
Education; Home Economics; Psychology
Dist - UCALG **Prod** - UCALG 1989

Operation and Process Control
U-matic / VHS
Pulp and Paper Training - Thermo - Mechanical Pulping Series
Color (IND)
Reviews safety and operating parameters. Examines various control systems and protection devices.
Health and Safety; Industrial and Technical Education
Dist - LEIKID **Prod** - LEIKID

Operation at the Suction Side of a Pump 17 MIN
U-matic / VHS
Industrial Hydraulic Technology Series Chapter 3; Chapter 3
Color (IND)
Discusses pump location, measuring atmospheric pressure, cavitation, and terms and idioms associated with the suction side of a pump.
Education; Industrial and Technical Education; Science - Physical
Dist - TAT **Prod** - TAT

Operation Behavior Modification 40 MIN
16mm
B&W (PRO)
LC 72-702025
Traces the progress of an institutionalized retarded girl through a program of behavior modification designed to give her a better chance at integration with girls her own age and train her for employment as a nurse's aid.
Education; Psychology
Dist - NMAC **Prod** - UKANS 1967

Operation biberon 13 MIN
16mm
Les Francais chez vous series
B&W (I J H)
Foreign Language
Dist - CHLTN **Prod** - PEREN 1967

Operation Big Lift 6 MIN
16mm
Screen news digest series; Vol 6; Issue 4
B&W (J) (GERMAN)
LC FIA68-2073
Studies 'OPERATION BIG LIFT,' showing the military airlift from Bergstron Air Force Base in Texas to Rhein Main in Germany. Discusses the lift's implications throughout the world.
Civics and Political Systems
Dist - HEARST **Prod** - HEARST 1963

Operation Bluenose 27 MIN
16mm
Color
Discusses the mission over the North Pole by a B - 52.
Social Science
Dist - RCKWL **Prod** - NAA

Operation Breakthrough 28 MIN
16mm
Color
Describes the research and development program which resulted in the Navy's Polaris missle system. Explains how military and private industry worked together to develop the project.
Civics and Political Systems; Industrial and Technical Education
Dist - CCNY **Prod** - USN

Operation Cool - it 26 MIN
16mm
Color (G)
LC 79-706076
Shows scenes of a weekend of snowmobiling in northern Wisconsin, including views of trail rides, dances, games and competition.
Geography - United States; Physical Education and Recreation; Sociology
Dist - SS **Prod** - OMC 1970

The Operation - Coronary Artery Bypass, Pt 1 - the Surgery 60 MIN
VHS / U-matic
Color
Gives close - ups of the coronary artery bypass surgery, clear graphics and detailed explanations of the responsibilities procedures and equipment in the OR and ICU.
Health and Safety; Science - Natural
Dist - AJN **Prod** - ARIZHI

The Operation - Coronary Artery Bypass, Pt 2 - the Nursing Care 30 MIN
U-matic / VHS
Color
Shows the ICU nurse and physician planning and beginning immediate postoperative care and monitoring of the patient's cardiovascular, respiratory and neurological status following coronary artery bypass surgery.
Health and Safety; Science - Natural
Dist - AJN **Prod** - ARIZHI

Operation Crossroads 26 MIN
16mm
Color
LC FIE52-1346
Documents the Able Day and Baker Day blasts of the atomic bomb tests at Bikini Island in the Pacific.
Civics and Political Systems; History - United States; Science - Physical
Dist - USNAC **Prod** - USN 1949

Operation Cue 14 MIN
16mm
B&W
LC 74-705998
Points out the contrast between the Nevada test in 1955 and present nuclear devices, continues as a documentary report on the operation cue exercise of 1955 as told from the viewpoint of a newspaper woman who was invited as an observer.
Civics and Political Systems; Science - Physical
Dist - USNAC **Prod** - USOCD 1964

Operation Deep Freeze 15 MIN
U-matic / VHS / 16mm
Odyssey Series
Color
Describes Operation Deep Freeze, the U S Navy's scientific research program in Antarctica.
Civics and Political Systems; Geography - World; Science
Dist - GPN **Prod** - KRMATV

Operation Firestop 25 MIN
16mm
Color (PRO)
Documents fire research conducted at Camp Pendleton, pertaining mainly to watershed fires.
Health and Safety; Science; Social Science
Dist - LAFIRE **Prod** - LAFIRE

Operation for Vaginal Agenesis 20 MIN
16mm
Color
LC 75-702327
Presents the most up - to - date information on the development of the female genital tract. Illustrates the construction of an artificial vagina using the embryologic development of the vagina as the basis for the operative approach.
Health and Safety; Science
Dist - EATONL **Prod** - EATONL 1969

Operation Greenhouse 25 MIN
16mm
Color
LC FIE53-131
Describes the scientific and technical operations during the proof - testing of atomic weapons at Eniwetok in the spring of 1951. Illustrates the blast and thermal effects on structures, aircraft, and various other items.
Civics and Political Systems; Science - Physical
Dist - USNAC **Prod** - USNRC 1951

Operation Gwamba 25 MIN
U-matic / VHS / 16mm
Untamed World Series
Color; Mono (J H C A)
$400.00 film, $250.00 video, $50.00 rental
Highlights the rescue of over 10,000 animals from certain death when an artificial lake was produced in Sirinam forcing the native animals to seek higher ground or perish. Most of the animals were unable to accomplish this move without the help of this task force of liberators.
Geography - World; Science - Natural
Dist - CTV **Prod** - CTV 1969

Operation Head Start 27 MIN
16mm
B&W (G)
LC FIA66-131
Describes the objectives of Operation Head Start and shows how these objectives are carried into action in a pre - school classroom.
Education
Dist - GOLDES **Prod** - CHIBED 1965

Operation Ivy 28 MIN
16mm
Color; B&W
LC FIE54-454
Presents a documentary record of a thermonuclear test at the Atomic Energy Commission's Pacific proving grounds in 1952. Includes introductory remarks by President Dwight D Eisenhower and a closing statement by FCDA administrator Val Peterson.
History - United States; Science; Science - Physical
Dist - USNAC **Prod** - USAF 1954

Operation Last Patrol 54 MIN
16mm
Color
Examines the cross - country march to the Republican National Convention, staged by the Vietnam Veterans against the War in 1972.
Guidance and Counseling; Sociology
Dist - IMPACT **Prod** - IMPACT

Operation Long Shot 13 MIN
16mm
Color
LC FIE66-10
Reports on an underground nuclear test in the fall of 1965 in the Aleutian Islands that was part of the Vela uniform series of experiments to increase U S capability to detect, identify and locate underground nuclear detonations at intercontinental ranges. Follows the steps involved in Operation Long Shot to investigate the possible travel - time anomalies associated with seismic events occurring in island - arc structures.
Industrial and Technical Education; Science - Physical
Dist - USNAC **Prod** - USNRC 1966

Operation machines 24 MIN
16mm
Teaching high school mathematics - first course series; No 11
B&W (T)
Mathematics
Dist - MLA **Prod** - UICSM 1967

Operation Morning Light 18 MIN
16mm
Color (H C A)
#2X851
Covers the search and recovery of the satellite Cosmos 954, which crashed in the Northwest Territories. Explains how experts searched for radioactive clues that would indicate the location of debris.
Industrial and Technical Education
Dist - CDIAND **Prod** - NFBC 1978

Operation Moses 27 MIN
U-matic / 16mm / VHS
Color (G)
$250.00, $49.95, $29.95 purchase, $35.00 rental _ #ZPF - 781, #ZVC - 781, #ZHC - 781, #ZRP - 781
Looks at the 2500 year history of Ethiopian Jewry. Reveals that Operation Moses out of Israel is taking these ancient Jewish people 'home' to Israel.
Geography - World; Sociology
Dist - ADL **Prod** - ADL

Operation Nightwatch 30 MIN
16mm
Color (I J H)
Provides a you - are - there look at an inspiring ministry being carried on in the skidrow section of Seattle, Washington. Follows Bud, a suburban minister, as he walks the downtown streets from midnight until dawn, visiting the bars and cafes and bringing the presence of Christ to the lonely and dispossessed.
Guidance and Counseling; Religion and Philosophy
Dist - FAMF **Prod** - FAMF

Operation Noah 25 MIN
16mm / U-matic / VHS
Untamed World Series
Color; Mono (J H C A)
$400.00 film, $250.00 video, $50.00 rental
Documents the rescue operation of African wildlife when the construction of a dam creates a 200 square mile inland sea thus destroying the home of thousands of creatures.
Geography - World; Science - Natural
Dist - CTV **Prod** - CTV 1969

Operation of an Oxy - Fuel Gas Heating Torch 14 MIN
U-matic / VHS
Steel Making Series
Color (IND)
Looks at the operation and safety requirements of the heating torch.
Business and Economics; Health and Safety; Industrial and Technical Education
Dist - LEIKID **Prod** - LEIKID

Operation of Daniel Senior Orifice Fittings 13 MIN
VHS / 16mm
Color (A IND)
$100.00 purchase _ #40.0300
Reviews procedures for inspecting and changing the orifice plate in a Daniel senior orifice fitting. Stresses safety in all procedures.
Industrial and Technical Education; Mathematics; Social Science
Dist - UTEXPE

Operation of Jet Aircraft Engines 18 MIN
16mm
B&W
LC FIE58-290
Illustrates principles of jet propulsion by Newton's law of action and shows its application to a jet engine to produce horsepower and thrust power.
Industrial and Technical Education; Science - Physical
Dist - USNAC **Prod** - USN 1949

The Operation of the Fuel System 72 MIN
VHS / 35mm strip
(H A IND)
#407XV7
Provides a comprehensive overview of the operation of an automotive fuel system. Includes basic parts and operations, fuel lines, air cleaner and the carburetor, carburetor circuits (Pt 1 and 2), manifolds and heat control, and the origin of fuel (6 tapes). Prerequisite required. Includes a Study Guide.
Education; Industrial and Technical Education
Dist - BERGL

Operation of the GM Unit Injectors 4 MIN
16mm
B&W
LC 74-705261
Shows construction, function and operation of the GM unit injector, including functions, locations and operations of components, flow of fuel through unit to engine and importance of proper maintenance.
Industrial and Technical Education
Dist - USNAC **Prod** - USA 1958

Operation of the Hypodermic Jet Injection Apparatus 43 MIN
16mm
Color
LC 74-706168
Demonstrates the functioning and operation of the hypodermic jet injector, showing cocking, firing, dosage adjustment, disassembly, sterilization, assembly and safety precautions.
Health and Safety
Dist - USNAC **Prod** - USA 1972

Operation of the Laminar Flow Biological Safety Cabinet 23 MIN
U-matic
Color
LC 80-706596
Compares the various safety cabinets available to the clinical laboratory technician. Focuses on the safe, effective use of the class III laminar flow cabinet, stressing the role and responsibilities of the researcher.
Science
Dist - USNAC **Prod** - CFDISC 1979

Operation of the Motorcycle 14 MIN
16mm
American Honda Series
Color (H A)
Stresses the safe operation of the motorcycle with emphasis on defensive driving tactics.
Health and Safety; Social Science
Dist - AHONDA **Prod** - AHONDA

Operation of the Shredder - Grater Attachment 20 MIN
BETA / VHS / 16mm
Color (G PRO)
$59.00 purchase _ #QF09
Shows the correct method of assembling the grater and shredder attachment to the standard 20 - quart table mixer.
Home Economics; Industrial and Technical Education
Dist - RMIBHF **Prod** - RMIBHF

Operation of the Varian A60A NMR Spectrometer 28 MIN
VHS / U-matic
Chemistry - master - apprentice series; Program 500
Color (C A)
LC 82-706060
Demonstrates the operation of the Varian Associates A60A NMR spectrometer for ambient temperature work. Illustrates tuning the instrument, running a spectrum of a sample, integrating the peak, and expanding the scale.
Health and Safety; Science; Science - Physical
Dist - CORNRS **Prod** - CUETV 1981

Operation One Plus Two 15 MIN
16mm
Color
LC 75-702459
Shows the U S Marine Corps naval flight officer's program for college students.
Education; Guidance and Counseling; Industrial and Technical Education
Dist - USNAC **Prod** - USMC 1973

Operation Orchid 16 MIN
16mm
Color
Presents a tour of the Orchid Isle, the Big Island of Hawaii and features the sun, sand, surf and spectacular sights of Hawaii's largest island.
Geography - United States
Dist - MTP **Prod** - UAL

Operation Paradise 7 MIN
U-matic / VHS / 16mm
Color (I)
LC 81-700800
Presents an animated story about two enterprising Italian cats named Don Porfirio and Pepe who endeavor to bring together a young woman and her shy suitor.
Fine Arts
Dist - PHENIX **Prod** - ITCART 1980

The Operation - Part Two 15 MIN
VHS
Cardiac surgery - a new beginning series
Color (G PRO)
$195.00 purchase _ #E930 - VI - 030
Explains the various stages of the hospital stay and surgery, including the early stages of recovery. Part of a three - part of series on cardiac surgery.
Health and Safety
Dist - HSCIC

Operation Reentry 30 MIN
16mm
To Save Tomorrow Series
B&W (H C A)
Demonstrates successful rehabilitation of patients through first giving them tokens for rewards, then making a transition from token use to sheltered workshop training and finally to work outside of the hospital.
Psychology
Dist - IU **Prod** - NET

Operation responsible, safe refuse collection 20 MIN
U-matic

Color
LC 80-707128
Describes safety techniques in refuse collection. Shows how supervisors can train the men who collect solid waste. Issued in 1972 as a motion picture.
Health and Safety
Dist - USNAC **Prod** - USEPA 1980

Operation responsible, safe refuse collection 20 MIN
16mm
Color
LC 74-705262
Gives a safety training program, tailor - made for the solid waste collection industry, both public and private.
Business and Economics; Health and Safety
Dist - USNAC **Prod** - USEPA 1972

Operation responsible, safe refuse collection 20 MIN
16mm
Color (SPANISH)
LC 79-700539
Shows how supervisors in charge of solid waste collection can learn about their duties and train the men who work for them.
Foreign Language; Health and Safety
Dist - USNAC **Prod** - USEPA 1978

Operation San Francisco Smoke - Sprinkler Test Video 15 MIN
VHS
Color (G PRO)
$45.00 purchase _ #35232
Documents life safety fire testing for hotels, apartments, corridors and exhibit halls. Depicts the effectiveness of sprinkler and smoke detections systems by illustrating heat, smoke and toxic gas levels in fire test rooms. Summarizes Operation San Francisco findings. Promotes sprinkler and smoke detector ordinances and laws.
Health and Safety; Psychology; Social Science
Dist - OKSU

Operation Sandstone 21 MIN
16mm / U-matic / VHS
Color
Explains the extensive preparations for the first USAEC development and test at the Pacific proving grounds in spring 1948. Shows the three test detonations at Eniwetok Atoll.
Civics and Political Systems; Geography - World; History - United States; Science - Physical
Dist - USNAC **Prod** - USAF

Operation - Shark Attack 45 MIN
VHS
Color; Stereo (G)
$19.98 purchase _ #TT8038
Shows how shark experts use pieces of fish and a steel mesh suit to become the target of a dangerous shark attack.
Literature and Drama; Science - Natural
Dist - TWINTO **Prod** - TWINTO 1990

Operation Sting - Courtroom Cameras 18 MIN
16mm / U-matic
CTV Reports Series
Color; Mono (J H C A)
$200.00 film, $200.00 video, $50.00 rental
Examines the use of video cameras as a crime deterent and also looks at their use within the courtroom for a variety of purposes.
Civics and Political Systems; Industrial and Technical Education; Sociology
Dist - CTV **Prod** - CTV 1977

Operation thunderbolt 126 MIN
16mm
Color (G)
$200.00 rental
Dramatizes the Israeli army's rescue of 104 hostages at Uganda's Entebbe airport. Uses professional Israeli paratroopers, some of the actual hostages and officals playing themselves alongside a huge Israeli cast. Recreates not only the specific military operations but also explores the actions and responses of all participants. Not to be confused with the ABC and NBC made - for - TV movies about Entebbe. Produced by Menachem Golan and Yorum Globus.
History - World; Religion and Philosophy
Dist - NCJEWF

Operation Under Fallout 28 MIN
16mm
Color
LC 75-700568
Portrays the preplanning, organization, training and rehearsals required to insure proper performance of base personnel and their dependents in event of attack.
Civics and Political Systems; Health and Safety
Dist - USNAC **Prod** - USAF 1963

Operation Undersea 20 MIN
16mm
Color
Revised edition of 'WINFRITH PIPELINE.' Discusses the Winfrith Pipeline, showing underwater sequences.
Industrial and Technical Education
Dist - UKAEA **Prod** - UKAEA 1960

Operation Up - Lift 30 MIN
16mm
Color
Documents the success story of 'The Young Saints,' an Academy for the Performing Arts based in Los Angeles. Shows the group performing before Ed Sullivan, Jonathan Winters and in many television and community shows.
Fine Arts
Dist - MTP **Prod** - CARNA

Operation Urgent Fury 60 MIN
VHS
Frontline Series
Color; Captioned (G)
$59.95 purchase _ #FRON - 602K
Reviews 'Urgent Fury,' the U.S. military invasion of Grenada in 1984. Scrutinizes the performance of the American military forces, suggesting that they did not perform as well as expected. Questions whether the invasion was justified in the first place.
Civics and Political Systems
Dist - PBS **Prod** - DOCCON 1988

Operation Usak 20 MIN
16mm
B&W
Examines how a nation shows grief, and how a film can and should convey grief. Presents homage to the great, and a study of a nation's attitude toward greatness and mourning.
Fine Arts; Psychology; Sociology
Dist - UPENN **Prod** - UPENN 1964

Operation Van Pool 16 MIN
16mm
Color
Presents the story of corporate - sponsored commuter service programs. Shows how these programs provide the answer to reducing traffic congestion and conserving precious energy while cutting commuter costs by 25 percent.
Business and Economics; Science - Natural; Social Science; Sociology
Dist - MTP **Prod** - GM

Operation X - 70 10 MIN
U-matic / VHS / 16mm
Color (H C A)
LC 80-701508
Satirizes scientific warfare with a briefing on the experimental results of the latest weapon, a gas that leaves its victims in a lethargic and mystical state. Shows how the weapon affects the population by making them angelic, rather than lethargic. Features animation.
Civics and Political Systems; Fine Arts; Literature and Drama
Dist - IFB **Prod** - SERVA 1975

Operation You 15 MIN
16mm
Color
Provides information which suggests that patients might need to more fully participate in decisions about their surgical care.
Health and Safety
Dist - MTP **Prod** - AMCSUR

Operation Zero - Zero - Project Narrow Gauge 19 MIN
16mm
B&W
LC FIE60-44
Shows the extensive testing of an integrated visual approach and landing aids system (IVALA) to prove that this improvement can provide aviation with greater and safer aircraft landing capability.
Industrial and Technical Education
Dist - USNAC **Prod** - USDD 1959

Operational Amplifier Applications - I 30 MIN
U-matic / VHS
Linear and Interface Integrated Circuits, Part I - Linear Integrated'Circuits Series
Color (PRO)
Discusses general items important to the application of operational amplifiers, first, followed by specific examples and actual studio demonstration of a sample and hold circuit.
Industrial and Technical Education
Dist - TXINLC **Prod** - TXINLC

Operational Amplifier Applications - II 30 MIN
U-matic / VHS
Linear and Interface Integrated Circuits, Part I - Linear Integrated'Circuits Series
Color (PRO)
Covers more specific applications including design of active filters, differential amplifiers, servo motor devices, clamping circuits and a low - noise audio pre - amplifier.
Industrial and Technical Education
Dist - TXINLC **Prod** - TXINLC

Operational Amplifier Design - I 30 MIN
VHS / U-matic
Linear and Interface Integrated Circuits, Part I - Linear Integrated'Circuits Series
Color (PRO)
Deals with low frequency characteristics. Goes into past and present of linear integrated circuit design of operational amplifiers; from ideal characteristics to that of present day. Includes discussion of synthesized circuit components, active load devices, super beta transistors, split - collector fixed beta transistors and pinch resistors.
Industrial and Technical Education
Dist - TXINLC **Prod** - TXINLC

Operational Amplifier Design - II 30 MIN
U-matic / VHS
Linear and Interface Integrated Circuits, Part I - Linear Integrated'Circuits Series
Color (PRO)
Discusses operational amplifier frequency response and techniques used to compensate those amplifiers and assure stability. Discusses large signal operation as well to define terms such as sleu - rate settling time, and transient response.
Industrial and Technical Education
Dist - TXINLC **Prod** - TXINLC

Operational Amplifiers 40 MIN
VHS / U-matic
Operational Amplifiers Circuits Series
Color (IND)
Covers techniques of solving circuit problems using operational amplifiers. Examines many practical circuits with reagard to frquency response, bandwidth, step response, ouput impedance and other features. Discusses, in addition to frequency - dependent gain characteristics, other operational amplifier limitations such as offset, slewing, and dynamic range.
Industrial and Technical Education
Dist - COLOSU **Prod** - COLOSU

Operational amplifiers - 1 60 MIN
VHS
Electronic systems and equipment series
Color (PRO)
$600.00 - $1500.00 purchase _ #ICOA1
Enables trainees to use schematic diagrams to recognize voltage and inverted voltage followers, inverting and non - inverting amplifiers, differential and instrumentation amplifiers. Part of a nineteen - part series on electronic systems and equipment, which is part of a 49 - unit set on instrumentation and control. Includes five workbooks and an instructor guide to support four hours of instruction.
Education; Industrial and Technical Education; Psychology
Dist - NUSTC **Prod** - NUSTC

Operational amplifiers - 2 60 MIN
VHS
Electronic systems and equipment series
Color (PRO)
$600.00 - $1500.00 purchase _ #ICOA2
Shows how to use schematic diagrams to recognize basic op amp summing amplifier, comparator, integrator and differentiator circuits. Part of a nineteen - part series on electronic systems and equipment, which is part of a 49 - unit set on instrumentation and control. Includes five workbooks and an instructor guide to support four hours of instruction.
Education; Industrial and Technical Education; Psychology
Dist - NUSTC **Prod** - NUSTC

Operational Amplifiers Circuits Series
Operational Amplifiers 40 MIN
Dist - COLOSU

Operational Analysis Circuits Series
Active Filters 40 MIN
Part One - Frequency Domain 40 MIN
Dist - COLOSU

Operational Causality 21 MIN
16mm
Ordinal Scales of Infant Psychological Development Series
Color (C A)
LC 73-703095
Demonstrates the scale for the construction of operational causality. Includes concepts of causality, space and time. Shows infants ranging in age from 12 weeks to 23 months.
Psychology
Dist - UILL **Prod** - UILL 1968

Operational Definitions, Conformance, and Performance
VHS / U-matic

Deming Videotapes - Quality, Productivity, and Competitive Series
Color
Discusses the operational definitions of quality needed for understanding between vendor and purchaser.
Business and Economics
Dist - MIOT **Prod** - MIOT

Operational Definitions, Conformation, and Performance 50 MIN
VHS / U-matic
Deming Video Tapes - Quality, Productivity and the Competitive 'Series
Color
Business and Economics; Psychology
Dist - SME **Prod** - MIOT

Operational design for inbound call centers
VHS
Color (C PRO G)
$150.00 purchase _ #93.01
Reveals that since 1978 the Call Processing Simulator - CAPS - has become the pivotal tool for AT&T's 800 market, resulting in increased call completion and revenue, customer retention and winback, and greater market penetration. Discloses that in the last year over 400 CAPS studies increased 800 revenues in excess of $1 billion in a $5 billion market. One reorganization yielded an 8 percent increase in calls completed at annual savings over $24 million in AT&T revenues in 1992, $3 million in 1993 and a projected $7 million per year for each following year. Thomas Spencer III, Anthony J Brigandi, Dennis R Dargon, Michael J Sheehan.
Business and Economics
Dist - INMASC

Operational practices
VHS
Professional tree care safety series
Color (G) (SPANISH)
$75.00, $90.00 purchase _ #6 - 204 - 401P, #6 - 204 - 411P - Spanish Version
Teaches good habits of safety for tree workers. Demonstrates the safest way to carry out common tree care procedures. Part of a four - part series on tree worker safety. Produced by the National Arborist Association.
Agriculture; Health and Safety; Psychology; Science - Natural
Dist - VEP

Operational Readiness 19 MIN
16mm
Color
LC 74-706169
Explains logistics by following the logistic results of a battle in Vietnam and showing how aircraft engines are ordered and repaired. Describes various activities of the Air Force Logistics Command and its methods of supplying forces.
Civics and Political Systems; Sociology
Dist - USNAC **Prod** - USAF 1969

Operational tests - checking for short and grounds 60 MIN
VHS / U-matic
Electrical maintenance training series; Module 1 - Control equipment
Color (IND)
Industrial and Technical Education
Dist - LEIKID **Prod** - LEIKID

Operationalizing Frankl's logotherapy 60 MIN
VHS
Color (G C PRO)
$54.95 purchase
Features Dr Gary Reker addressing the 1989 annual meeting of the American Society on Aging.
Health and Safety
Dist - TNF

Operations - binary, singulary 24 MIN
16mm
Teaching high school mathematics - first course series; No 10
B&W (T)
Mathematics
Dist - MLA **Prod** - UICSM 1967

Operations for Correction of Congenital Biliary Atresia 30 MIN
16mm
Color (PRO)
Presents the operative treatment of biliary obstruction in infancy. Includes cases of congenital atresis and post hepatitis ductal obliseration.
Health and Safety; Science
Dist - ACY **Prod** - ACYDGD 1954

Operations Frequently Performed on the Drill Press
U-matic / VHS
Basic machine technology series
Color (SPANISH)
Foreign Language; Industrial and Technical Education
Dist - VTRI **Prod** - VTRI

Operations Frequently Performed on the Drill Press
VHS / U-matic
Basic machine technology series
Color (SPANISH)
Foreign Language; Industrial and Technical Education
Dist - VTRI **Prod** - VTRI

Operations Moses - a documentary 27 MIN
VHS
Jewish life around the world series
Color (G)
$34.95 purchase _ #108
Tells the epic story of the rescue, immigration and absorption of Ethiopian Jewry. Uses testimonials and rare footage to recall the efforts of the world Jewish community.
History - World; Sociology
Dist - ERGOM **Prod** - ERGOM

Operations of Distributed Control Systems 60 TO 90 MIN
VHS
Distributed Control Systems Module Series
Color (PRO)
$600.00 - $1500.00 purchase _ #DCODC
Addresses basic concepts of control system operation as a means for understanding how to repair it. Part of a fourteen - part series on distributed contol systems. Includes five student guides, five workbooks and an instructor guide.
Computer Science; Education; Industrial and Technical Education; Psychology
Dist - NUSTC **Prod** - NUSTC

Operations of polynomials
VHS
Beginning algebra series
Color (J H)
$125.00 purchase _ #2005
Teaches fundamental concepts of writing polynomials and adding, subtracting, multiplying and dividing them. Part of a series of 31 videos, each between 25 and 30 minutes long, that explain and reinforce basic concepts of algebra. Tutors the student through definitions, theorems, step - by - step solutions and examples. Videos are also available in a set.
Mathematics
Dist - LANDMK

Operations on fractions
VHS
Beginning algebra series
Color (J H)
$125.00 purchase _ #2016
Teaches fundamental concepts of adding, subtracting, multiplying, and dividing fractions. Part of a series of 31 videos, each between 25 and 30 minutes long, that explain and reinforce basic concepts of algebra. Tutors the student through definitions, theorems, step - by - step solutions and examples. Videos are also available in a set.
Mathematics
Dist - LANDMK

Operations on polynomials 30 MIN
VHS
Intermediate algebra series
Color (H)
$125.00 purchase _ #M41
Explains operations on polynomials. Features Elayn Gay. Part of a 27 - part series on intermediate algebra.
Mathematics
Dist - LANDMK **Prod** - MGHT

Operations on Polynomials 30 MIN
VHS
Mathematics Series
Color (J)
LC 90713155
Explores operations on polynomials. The 21st of 157 installments of the Mathematics Series.
Mathematics
Dist - GPN

Operations on polynomials 30 MIN
VHS
Beginning algebra series
Color (J H)
$125.00 purchase _ #M21
Teaches about operations on polynomials. Features Elayn Gay. Part of a 19 - part series on beginning algebra.
Mathematics
Dist - LANDMK **Prod** - MGHT

Operations on radical expressions 30 MIN
VHS
Intermediate algebra series
Color (H)
$125.00 purchase _ #M48
Explains operations on radical expressions. Features Elayn Gay. Part of a 27 - part series on intermediate algebra.
Mathematics
Dist - LANDMK **Prod** - MGHT

Operations on rational expressions 30 MIN
VHS
College algebra series
Color (C)
$125.00 purchase _ #4002
Explains operations on rational expressions. Part of a 31 - part series on college algebra.
Mathematics
Dist - LANDMK **Prod** - LANDMK

Operations on Rational Expressions 30 MIN
VHS
Mathematics Series
Color (J)
LC 90713155
Examines operations on rational expressions. The 64th of 157 installments in the Mathematics Series.
Mathematics
Dist - GPN

Operations on Real Numbers 30 MIN
VHS
Mathematics Series
Color (J)
LC 90713155
Explains operations on real numbers. The 17th of 157 installments in the mathematics series.
Mathematics
Dist - GPN

Operations on real numbers
VHS
Beginning algebra series
Color (J H)
$125.00 purchase _ #2001
Teaches fundamental concepts of adding, subtracting, multiplying, and dividing real numbers. Part of a series of 31 videos, each between 25 and 30 minutes long, that explain and reinforce basic concepts of algebra. Tutors the student through definitions, theorems, step - by - step solutions and examples. Videos are also available in a set.
Mathematics
Dist - LANDMK

Operations on real numbers 30 MIN
VHS
Intermediate algebra series
Color (H)
$125.00 purchase _ #M35
Explains operations on real numbers. Features Elayn Gay. Part of a 27 - part series on intermediate algebra.
Mathematics
Dist - LANDMK **Prod** - MGHT

Operations on Signed Numbers 30 MIN
VHS
Mathematics Series
Color (J)
LC 90713155
Explains operations on signed numbers. The 13th of 157 installments in the Mathematics Series.
Mathematics
Dist - GPN

Operations on signed numbers 30 MIN
VHS
Beginning algebra series
Color (J H)
$125.00 purchase _ #M17
Teaches about operations on signed numbers. Features Elayn Gay. Part of a 19 - part series on beginning algebra.
Mathematics
Dist - LANDMK **Prod** - MGHT

Operations on signed numbers
VHS
Basic mathematical skills series
Color (J H)
$125.00 purchase _ #1013
Teaches the concepts of signed numbers and operations. Presents part of a series that provides 27 videos, each between 25 and 30 minutes long, that explain and reinforce basic mathematical concepts. Tutors the student through definitions, theorems, step - by - step solutions and examples. Videos are also available in a set.
Mathematics
Dist - LANDMK

Operations on the horizontal boring mill - Setup for Face Milling with a Fixture - no 1 20 MIN
16mm
Machine Shop Work Series
B&W (IND)
Explains how the horizontal boring, drilling and milling machine operates. Shows how to install the fixture, set up the workpiece, and select and install an end mill and a face mill.

Industrial and Technical Education
Dist - USNAC **Prod** - USOE 1945

Operations Planning 60 MIN
VHS / BETA
Manufacturing Series
(IND)
Teaches how to plan the receiving, storing and shipping functions of a company and the physical managment of materials.
Business and Economics
Dist - COMSRV **Prod** - COMSRV 1986

Operations with polynomials
VHS
Algebra 1 series
Color (J H)
$125.00 purchase _ #A8
Teaches the concepts involved in operations using polynomial expressions and equations. Part of a series of 16 videos, each between 25 and 30 minutes long, that explain and reinforce 89 basic concepts of algebra. Includes a stated objective for each segment. Tutors the student through definitions, theorems, step - by - step solutions and examples. Videos are also available in a set.
Mathematics
Dist - LANDMK
GPN

Operations with real numbers
VHS
Algebra 1 series
Color (J H)
$125.00 purchase _ #A2
Teaches the concepts of real numbers and operations. Part of a series of 16 videos, each between 25 and 30 minutes long, that explain and reinforce 89 basic concepts of algebra. Includes a stated objective for each segment. Tutors the student through definitions, theorems, step - by - step solutions and examples. Videos are also available in a set.
Mathematics
Dist - LANDMK
GPN

Operations with Whole Numbers 22 MIN
16mm
Interpreting Machematics Education Research Series
Color
LC 74-705263
Explores procedures for interrelating addition and substraction. Shows materials, methods and strategies that are particularly effective. Focuses on the use of multiple techniques for misproving instruction in multiplication. Emphasizes algorithms, which have been found to be particularly effective.
Mathematics
Dist - USNAC **Prod** - USOE 1970

Operative Cholangiography and its Indications 18 MIN
16mm
Color (PRO)
Describes the advantages of operative cholangiography in locating stones that may be overlooked by palpation and inspection. Illustrates the technic of positioning the patient, and injecting the contrast medium.
Health and Safety; Science
Dist - ACY **Prod** - ACYDGD 1960

Operative Dentistry - Advanced Concepts 28 MIN
16mm
Color
LC 74-706548
Demonstrates how to introduce and prepare dental patients. Shows the preparation of cavity, matrix, removal of dam, checking of occulusion and reappointment. Describes the techniques of finishing and polishing.
Health and Safety; Science
Dist - USNAC **Prod** - USN 1966

Operative Drainage for Empyema 9 MIN
VHS / U-matic
Pediatric Series
Color
Health and Safety
Dist - SVL **Prod** - SVL

Operative hysteroscopy 12 MIN
VHS
Color (G PRO C)
$250.00 purchase _ #OB - 125
Describes procedures that may be performed with the technique of operative hysteroscopy, including endometrial ablation, removal of polyps and fibroids, separation of adhesions and removal of uterine septa. Gives an overview of what patients may expect before and after operative hysteroscopy. Mentions that laparscopy may be used concomitantly.
Health and Safety
Dist - MIFE **Prod** - MIFE 1993

Operative laparoscopy 10 MIN
VHS
Color (G PRO C)
$250.00 purchase _ #OB - 126
Discusses disorders that may benefit from operative laparoscopy, including endometriosis, pelvic adhesions, ectopic pregnancy and infertility. Describes laparscopic hysterectomy. Covers briefly preoperative events, the surgical process and risks. Stresses the importance of following recovery instructions carefully.
Health and Safety
Dist - MIFE **Prod** - MIFE 1993

Operative Laparoscopy - Tubal Sterilization 16 MIN
16mm
Color (PRO)
Demonstrates the techniques of electrocauterization and division of the uterine tubes on an extripated specimen.
Health and Safety; Science
Dist - SCITIF **Prod** - SCITIF 1969

Operative Procedures 17 MIN
U-matic / VHS / 16mm
Woman Talk Series
Color (H C A)
Considers a woman's fears when she is faced with surgery involving her reproductive system. Dismisses old wives' tales and the patient is given a better understanding of procedures and results so that she gains a positive attitude.
Health and Safety; Sociology
Dist - CORF **Prod** - CORF 1983

The Operative Repair of Single Cleft Lips 34 MIN
16mm
Color (PRO)
Includes simple standard design and marking to uniformly obtain the best possible result with the least sacrifice of tissue and the operation to repair a single cleft lip, step - by - step.
Health and Safety; Science
Dist - ACY **Prod** - ACYDGD 1957

The Operative Treatment of Chronic Stasis Ulcer 26 MIN
16mm
Color (PRO)
Demonstrates the technique of excision of chronic stasis ulcers and the covering of the cutaneous defect with grafts. Shows a method of delimiting the requisite area of excision by lymphatic injections.
Health and Safety; Science
Dist - ACY **Prod** - ACYDGD 1955

Operative Treatment of Clubfoot 24 MIN
U-matic
Color (C)
Shows the technique of operative release of resistant clubfoot in a sixteen month old girl.
Health and Safety; Science - Natural
Dist - UOKLAH **Prod** - UOKLAH 1980

Operative Treatment of Hirschsprung's Disease 16 MIN
16mm
Color (PRO)
Demonstrates Dr Swenson's technique for Hirschsprung's disease. Explains that he found that by removing a region in the upper rectum lacking proper nerve cells and then re - establishing the continuity of the colon, it was possible to cure this disease.
Health and Safety; Science
Dist - ACY **Prod** - ACYDGD 1950

The Operator and His Job 12 MIN
16mm
B&W
LC FIE52-331
Illustrates the three responsibilities of the bus operator - - safety and comfort of his passengers, maintenance of schedules and a courteous attitude toward passengers.
Social Science
Dist - USNAC **Prod** - USOE 1945

The Operator and His Passengers 18 MIN
16mm
B&W
LC FIE52-332
Discusses the importance of good customer relations and shows ways of handling such problems as expired transfers, people who miss their stops and persuading passengers to move to the rear of the bus.
Social Science
Dist - USNAC **Prod** - USOE 1945

Operator - Patient and Light Positions 9 MIN
U-matic
Scaling Techniques Series; No 2
Color (PRO)
LC 77-706008
Demonstrates operator, patient and light positioning for maximum vision and comfort while working on upper and lower arches.
Health and Safety; Science
Dist - USNAC **Prod** - UTENN 1976

Operator's adjustments D - 7 tractor, No 1 series
Adjusting the Le Tourneau power control unit 11 MIN
Dist - USNAC

The Operator's role
U-matic / VHS
Distribution system operation series; Topic 13
Color (IND)
Focuses on operator's role and how it fits into other associated areas such as maintenance and power system operation. Covers press and public communication.
Industrial and Technical Education
Dist - LEIKID **Prod** - LEIKID

Ophthalmic Optics - Refraction by the Eye 10 MIN
16mm / U-matic / VHS
Optics of the Human Eye Series
Color (H C A)
Health and Safety; Science - Natural
Dist - TEF **Prod** - BAYCMO

Ophthalmic Optics - Refractive Errors and Optical Aberrations 10 MIN
16mm / U-matic / VHS
Optics of the Human Eye Series
Color (H C A)
Health and Safety; Science - Natural
Dist - TEF **Prod** - BAYCMO

Ophthalmic Surgery System at the Jules Stein Eye Institute 13 MIN
16mm
Color (PRO)
Describes the unique features of the Jules Stein Eye Institute such as the operating room facilities, which includes a patient transport system, hydraulic columns, a remote control operating pedestal, closed circuit television, surgical microscopes, and facilities for filming and television recording.
Guidance and Counseling; Health and Safety; Science - Natural
Dist - UCLA **Prod** - UCLA

Ophthalmoscope 11 MIN
U-matic
Instruments of Physical Assessment Series
Color (PRO)
LC 80-707625
Demonstrates how to use and care for an ophthalmoscope. Describes the anatomical features the examiner should be able to see when the instrument is used correctly.
Health and Safety
Dist - LIP **Prod** - SUNYSB 1980

Opinion of the Publics 37 MIN
16mm
Color
Presents a composite of mini - case histories showing public relations programs in action. Features people meeting challenges with documented solutions.
Civics and Political Systems; Social Science
Dist - MTP **Prod** - PRSAIC 1973

The Opium Poppies Bloom Again - Turkey 13 MIN
VHS / U-matic
Color (H C A)
Describes the cultivation and distribution of opium in Turkey.
Geography - World; Sociology
Dist - JOU **Prod** - UPI

Opportunities 19 MIN
U-matic / VHS
Jobs - Seeking, Finding, Keeping Series
Color (H)
Shows Andy and Brenda learning about job - opportunity resources.
Guidance and Counseling
Dist - AITECH **Prod** - MDDE 1980

Opportunities for Growth 15 MIN
U-matic
Special Children - Responding to their Needs Series
Color (PRO)
Introduces the philosophy of ECS and states that all children, like those with special needs, are unique. Demonstrates that integration of special children into a general program, with the help of specialists, is of benefit to all.
Education; Psychology
Dist - ACCESS **Prod** - ACCESS 1985

Opportunities for Learning 27 MIN
VHS / U-matic
B&W (PRO)
Illustrates how most one - and two - year - olds learn the process of exploration and discovery through play situations. Suggests how parents can provide opportunites for learning in the home.
Education; Psychology; Sociology
Dist - HSERF **Prod** - HSERF

Opportunities for Productive Roles 30 MIN
U-matic
Growing Old in Modern America Series
Color
Health and Safety; Sociology
Dist - UWASHP **Prod** - UWASHP

Opportunities for the Disadvantaged 16 MIN
16mm / U-matic / VHS
Color (J H)
LC 73-700966
Discusses the development of special strategies for the minority group individual or economically deprived. Describes agencies and programs designed for the disadvantaged along with dramatic examples of success by people from minority backgrounds.
Guidance and Counseling; Sociology
Dist - AMEDFL **Prod** - AMEDFL 1972

Opportunities in Clerical Work 10 MIN
U-matic / VHS / 16mm
Career Job Opportunity Series
Color
LC 74-706549
Describes the variety of the more than 15 million clerical jobs existing today. Covers career entry jobs and company - sponsored training programs. Emphasizes opportunities in computer data processing areas and stresses the possibilities for steady advancement.
Business and Economics; Guidance and Counseling
Dist - USNAC **Prod** - USDLMA

Opportunities in Logging 28 MIN
16mm
Color
Shows the opportunities available to young men who like the outdoors and the challenge of physical work including the operation of heavy equipment. Covers the many facets of the logging industry.
Business and Economics; Guidance and Counseling
Dist - RARIG **Prod** - RARIG 1967

Opportunities in Sales and Merchandising 11 MIN
16mm
Color (J A)
Portrays the career opportunities in sales and merchandising occupations, including work settings, levels of occupations and information about preparatory work experience available through part - time work or a summer job in the retailing industry. Shows actual work settings and the occupational skills to be found in sales and merchandising.
Business and Economics
Dist - SF **Prod** - SF

Opportunities in the Machine Trades 7 MIN
16mm
Color (J A)
Presents many job opportunities for beginners in the machine trades. Stresses good pay for entry workers and points out avenues for career advancement, including shop ownership for those who have mastered their trade.
Guidance and Counseling; Industrial and Technical Education; Psychology
Dist - SF **Prod** - SF 1970

Opportunities in the Retail Automobile Business 20 MIN
16mm
Color
Presents the story of two high school seniors who visit an automotive dealership and learn about the opportunities in the retail automotive business.
Guidance and Counseling; Psychology
Dist - GM **Prod** - GM

Opportunities in Welding 7 MIN
16mm
Color (J A)
Describes job sites and opportunities in welding. Shows welding in shops, shipyards, airports and on a construction site 20 stories high.
Guidance and Counseling; Industrial and Technical Education; Psychology
Dist - SF **Prod** - SF 1970

The Opportunities Presented by Television 30 MIN
VHS / U-matic
Dance on Television - Ipiotis Series
Color
Fine Arts; Industrial and Technical Education
Dist - ARCVID **Prod** - ARCVID

Opportunities Unlimited 20 MIN
16mm
Color (J H A)
LC 72-700615
Describes the advantages for students in enrolling in a vocational education program.
Education
Dist - VADE **Prod** - VADE 1970

The Opportunity Class 22 MIN
16mm
Color
Documents the origin, development and activities of a special nursery class for both handicapped and normal children under seven years of age. Shows how the opportunity class plays a useful role in preparing the physically or mentally handicapped child for entrance into a formal classroom setting. Points out that mothers also benefit from social contact with other parents.
Education; Guidance and Counseling; Psychology; Sociology
Dist - NYU **Prod** - VASSAR

Opportunity Cost 15 MIN
VHS / 16mm
Econ and Me Series
Color (P)
$95.00 purchase, $25.00 rental
Shows that giving up alternatives occurs when people make a choice. Presents children making choices on what to keep when space is limited.
Business and Economics
Dist - AITECH **Prod** - AITECH 1989

Opportunity for all - Making a Go of EEO
U-matic / VHS / 16mm
Color (A)
Explains how managers and supervisors can avoid discrimination complaints when hiring. Discusses the Equal Employment Opportunity law and specific guidelines for performance, documentation, career development planning, defining minimum qualifications, recognizing and correcting equal pay problems and identifying nonprofessional behavior which results in discriminatory practices.
Business and Economics; Guidance and Counseling; Psychology
Dist - RTBL **Prod** - RTBL

The Opportunity for Leadership 30 MIN
U-matic / VHS
Organizational Transactions Series
Color
Establishes the achievements and satisfactions available to both the organization and individual at all levels. Focuses on a positive idea of leadership. Uses the idea of a three person personality of human behavior, the 'parent, adult and child.'.
Psychology
Dist - PRODEV **Prod** - PRODEV

Opportunity Profile Series

Accounting	20 TO 30 MIN
Computers	20 TO 30 MIN
Journalism	20 TO 30 MIN
Law	20 TO 30 MIN
Nursing	20 TO 30 MIN
Physician	20 TO 30 MIN
Sales	20 TO 30 MIN
Secretarial	20 TO 30 MIN
Teaching	20 TO 30 MIN

Dist - CAMV

Opportunity profile series
Advertising
Dist - CAMV
CAREER

Opportunity Profile Series
Provides advice on the skills and educational background desired by companies, the day to day activities of various careers, and the positive and negative aspects of various careers from corporate vice presidents, managers, and other working professionals.
Accounting
Computers
Journalism
Law
Nursing
Physicians
Sales
Secretarial
Teaching
Dist - CAREER **Prod** - CAREER

Opportunity - the land and its people 50 MIN
VHS
Entrepreneurs - an American adventure series
Color (H C A PRO)
$49.95 purchase _ #EMI102V-B
Shows the importance of natural resources in the development of the United States. Explores the central role of United States natural resources and food production in domestic and world economies. Part of a six-part series that looks at American entrepreneurial adventures in natural resources, food production, transportation systems, the manufacturing industry, marketing and promotion, and high technology.
Business and Economics; Geography - United States; History - United States
Dist - CAMV

An Opportunity to Become 20 MIN
16mm
Color
LC 79-700397
Documents the ten areas of athletics sponsored by the Department of Women's Intercollegiate Athletics at the University of Minnesota. Explores the emotions experienced by people involved in athletics and how these experiences help women in their lives after college.
Physical Education and Recreation
Dist - FILMA **Prod** - UMNAD 1978

Opportunity to influence 19 MIN
Cassette
Color (G)
$95.00, $10.00 purchase
Teaches about the dangers of chemical addiction.
Guidance and Counseling; Health and Safety; Psychology
Dist - KELLYP **Prod** - KELLYP

Opportunity to learn 30 MIN
VHS
Effective teacher telecourse series
Color (T)
$69.95 purchase, $50.00 rental
Discusses creation of learning opportunities within the classroom. Hosted by Dr Loren Anderson.
Education; Psychology
Dist - SCETV **Prod** - SCETV 1987

Opportunity Unlimited - Friendly Atoms in Industry 29 MIN
16mm
Color
Presents the nature and method of use of radioisotopes. Covers their application to thickness control, density measurement, quality control and industrial radiography and their use as tracers in chemical reactions.
Science - Physical
Dist - USERD **Prod** - USNRC 1962

The Opposite of Love 30 MIN
U-matic
Ounce of Prevention Series
Color
Guidance and Counseling; Health and Safety; Home Economics
Dist - CFDC **Prod** - CFDC

The Opposite - same Machine 15 MIN
U-matic / VHS
Magic Shop Series no 9
Color (P)
LC 83-706154
Employs a magician named Amazing Alexander and his assistants to explore word meanings.
English Language
Dist - GPN **Prod** - CVETVC 1982

Opposites 17 MIN
U-matic / BETA / VHS
Color (K P)
$79.00 purchase _ #C51470
Joins a girl and her magical helper Otto as they sort through an amazing variety of things in Otto's vast collection. Uses animation to introduce the concept of opposites - gigantic and tiny, loud and soft, and other ways concepts and objects can be grouped.
Literature and Drama; Psychology
Dist - NGS **Prod** - NGS 1991

Opposites in Harmony 17 MIN
16mm
Color (J H)
Recreates an early meeting between President Washington and his cabinet and charts the early development of the executive branch of the U S government.
Biography; Civics and Political Systems; History - United States
Dist - USNAC **Prod** - USNPS 1975

Opposition to Islam yesterday and today
VHS
Video lectures of Hamza Yusuf series
Color (G)
$12.00 purchase _ #110 - 081
Features Islamic lecturer Hamza Yusuf who focuses on how the Prophet faced the enmity of his people in Makkah. Includes Omar Ahmad who discusses current stereotypes of Muslims, and journalist Greg Noakes who asks, 'Is the West really afraid of Islam.'
Religion and Philosophy; Sociology
Dist - SOUVIS **Prod** - SOUVIS 1995

Opt - an illusionary tale - 76
VHS
Reading rainbow series
Color; CC (K P)
$39.95 purchase
Reveals that seeing isn't always believing in a book by Arline and Joseph Baum. Joins LeVar as he walks through a world of optical illusions. Shows how the eye can be fooled and meets an artist who specializes in art that tricks the eye. Part of a series offering a multicultural approach to generating reading enthusiasm with cross - curricular applications, hosted by LeVar Burton.
English Language; Literature and Drama; Psychology; Science
Dist - GPN **Prod** - LNMDP

Opt - an illusionary tale - A Three - hat day
VHS
Reading rainbow treasury series
Color (K P)
$12.95 purchase _ #PBS445
Presents two animated stories. Features Levar Burton as host. Part of a six - part series.
English Language; Fine Arts; Literature and Drama
Dist - KNOWUN **Prod** - PBS

Optic nerve 16 MIN
16mm / VHS
B&W; Color (G)
$50.00 rental, $30.00 purchase
Reflects filmmakers thoughts on family and aging. Employs filmed footage which, through optical printing and editing, is layered to create a striking meditation on her visit to her grandmother in a nursing home.
Fine Arts; Health and Safety; Sociology
Dist - CANCIN **Prod** - BARHAM 1985

Optical Alignment 34 MIN
16mm
Color (IND)
Shows the application of optical alignment equipment to production lines where straightness is of utmost importance.
Industrial and Technical Education
Dist - MOKIN **Prod** - MOKIN

Optical Character Reader 11 MIN
16mm
Color
Shows the use of control data's OCR page reader in a variety of applications for translation of ASA - font typewriting into digital terms recorded on magnetic tape.
Business and Economics; Mathematics
Dist - CONTR **Prod** - CONTR

Optical Craftsmanship Series Spherical Surfaces
Rough Grinding by Pin - Bar 19 MIN
Dist - USNAC

Optical fiber communications series
Comparison of fiber optics with conventional transmission technologies 50 MIN
Fiber testing techniques, mode transmission properties, concatenation properties 50 MIN
Dist - AMCEE

Optical Inspection Methods, Pt 1 26 MIN
16mm
B&W
Explains visual methods of inspection, the use of gages, the necessity for checking the gages and the theory and use of Newton's rings as an inspection method.
Psychology; Science - Physical
Dist - USNAC **Prod** - USN 1944

Optical Interferometry in Astronomy 30 MIN
U-matic / VHS
Color (C)
$249.00, $149.00 purchase _ #AD - 1141
Looks at new advances in radio telescopic measurement of celestial objects. Explains how such measurements are enlarging the scope of knowledge about the universe.
History - World; Industrial and Technical Education; Science - Physical
Dist - FOTH **Prod** - FOTH

Optical Motions and Transformations as Stimuli for Visual Perception 25 MIN
16mm
B&W (C T)
LC 76-703730
Describes the dimensions of movement of geometric forms in terms of simple mathematical transformations. Presents examples showing how such dimensions of movement arouse the perception of moving objects in tridimensional space. The film is an exposition of some of the recent research of J J Gibson.
Psychology; Science - Natural
Dist - PSUPCR **Prod** - GIBSOJ 1957

Optical Poem 7 MIN
16mm
Color (H C)
Sets Oskar Fischinger's abstractions to the music of The Hungarian Rhapsody.
Fine Arts
Dist - FI **Prod** - MGM 1939

Optical Spectroscopy for Diagnostics and Process Control
U-matic / VHS
Plasma Process Technology Fundamentals Series
Color (IND)
Covers uses of optical emission or absorption spectroscopy as well as mass spectroscopy in plasma etching and deposition reactors. Describes commercial optical monitors for end - point detection in a plasma - etch reactor.
Industrial and Technical Education; Science - Physical
Dist - COLOSU **Prod** - COLOSU

Optical Waveguide Modes 34 MIN
VHS / U-matic
Integrated Optics Series
Color (C)
Describes optical wave propagation in various types of waveguides illustrated with photographs and experimentally measured mode profiles.
Science - Physical
Dist - UDEL **Prod** - UDEL

Optics - making light work 19 MIN
VHS
Color (J H)
$14.95 purchase _ #NA205
Looks at the physics of light and shows how scientists are looking at new aspects of light. Defines and illustrates light and shows how visible light fits into the entire electromagnetic spectrum. Concentrates on visible light but looks at the many properties of light, including reflection, telescopes, lasers and holograms. Uses computer animation, graphics and live action to illustrate principles. Offers natural section breaks in the program to enable class discussion.
Industrial and Technical Education; Science - Physical
Dist - INSTRU **Prod** - NASA

Optics of the Human Eye Series
Ophthalmic Optics - Refraction by the Eye 10 MIN
Ophthalmic Optics - Refractive Errors and Optical Aberrations 10 MIN
Refraction of light by spherical lenses 10 MIN
Refraction of Light by Spherocylindrical Lenses 10 MIN
Dist - TEF

Optics series
Curved mirrors - Pt 1 22 MIN
Curved mirrors - Pt 2 22 MIN
Refraction, Pt 2 22 MIN
Dist - GPN

Optimal Control of a Macroeconomic Model of the US Economy 1957 - 1962 44 MIN
U-matic / VHS
Modern Control Theory - Deterministic Optimal Linear Feedback Series
Color (PRO)
Industrial and Technical Education; Mathematics
Dist - MIOT **Prod** - MIOT

Optimal performance quartet 120 MIN
BETA / VHS
Color (G)
$69.95 purchase _ #Q354
Presents a four - part discussion about optimal performance. Includes 'Stress Management' with Dr Janelle M Barlow, 'Qualities of High Performance' with Dr Lee Pulos, 'What Makes Work Meaningful' with Dr Dennis T Jaffe, and 'Mind Power' with Dr Bernie Zilbergeld.
Business and Economics; Health and Safety; Psychology; Religion and Philosophy
Dist - THINKA **Prod** - THINKA

Optimal performance series
Mind power 30 MIN
Qualities of high performance 30 MIN
Stress management 30 MIN
What makes work meaningful 30 MIN
Dist - THINKA

Optimist and Pessimist 8 MIN
U-matic / VHS / 16mm
Color (C A)
LC 80-701638
Features a confrontation between an optimist and a pessimist. Attempts to comment on the state of the film media and the social values that the media reflects. Satirizes sex, religion and politics as they are portrayed by the film industry.
Education; Fine Arts; Literature and Drama; Sociology
Dist - IFB **Prod** - ZAGREB 1975

An Optimization approach to analyzing price quotations under business volume discounts
VHS
Color (C PRO G)
$150.00 purchase _ #93.06
Discusses PDSS, a user - friendly, PC - based decision support program developed to assist Bellcore client companies in analyzing vendor price quotations under business volume discounts. Reveals that PDSS uses a 0 - 1 mixed integer programming model to minimize the total cost of all purchases, subject to several types of constraints. PDSS can save an organization 5 - 10 percent on purchase costs and has been applied successfully to contracts in excess of $100 million. Bellcore. Paul Katz, Amir Sadrian, Patrick Tendick.
Business and Economics; Computer Science
Dist - INMASC

Optimization using differentiation - critical points 30 MIN
VHS
Calculus series
Color (C)
$125.00 purchase _ #6011
Explains optimization using differentiation - critical points. Part of a 56 - part series on calculus.
Mathematics
Dist - LANDMK **Prod** - LANDMK

Optimization using Differentiation - Critical Points 30 MIN
VHS
Mathematics Series
Color (J)
LC 95713155
Demonstrates the critical points of optimization using differentiation. The 120th of 157 installments of the Mathematics Series.
Mathematics
Dist - GPN

Optimizer, a multi - echelon inventory system for service logistics management
VHS
Color (C PRO G)
$150.00 purchase _ #89.04
Focuses on research on multi - echelon inventory theory by IBM and the Wharton School which resulted in Optimizer, a system for the flexible and optimal control of service levels and inventory. Reveals that the inherent complexity of the problem required development of unusual data structures and memory management techniques. Optimizer operates with 20 percent less inventory while maintaining or improving service levels and is a highly flexible system for managerial control. IBM. Armen Tekerian, Pasumarti Kamesam, Morris Cohen, Paul Kleindorfer, Hau Lee.
Business and Economics
Dist - INMASC

Optimum Burn - in 30 MIN
U-matic / VHS
Reliability Engineering Series
Color (IND)
Uses plot of data on Weibull Probability Paper to locate transition from early to chance failure. Says transition point is maximum burn - in. Uses published Xerox data to illustrate procedures to define optimum burn - in less than maximum.
Industrial and Technical Education
Dist - COLOSU **Prod** - COLOSU

An Option 19 MIN
16mm
Color (A)
LC 77-703230
Documents inner - city neighborhood leaders' reactions to Washington D C's Summer in the Parks program.
Geography - United States; Physical Education and Recreation; Sociology
Dist - USNAC **Prod** - USNPS 1971

Option for the Future 16 MIN
16mm
Color
LC 80-700432
Justifies the Bell System's switch from flat - rate pricing to measured - rate pricing. Shows how telephone usage has evolved and how disparities in individual usage have led to inequities with flat - rate pricing and to measured service as a response to change.
Business and Economics; Industrial and Technical Education; Social Science
Dist - MTBAVC **Prod** - MTBAVC 1979

Optional dives - Pt 1 20 MIN
16mm / U-matic / VHS
Diving series
Color

LC 79-700786
Demonstrates the most commonly performed optional dives.
Physical Education and Recreation
Dist - ATHI **Prod** - ATHI 1977

Optional dives - Pt 2 20 MIN
16mm / U-matic / VHS
Diving series
Color
LC 79-700786
Demonstrates the most commonly performed optional dives.
Physical Education and Recreation
Dist - ATHI **Prod** - ATHI 1977

Options 19 MIN
16mm
Color (G) (FRENCH)
#2X35 I
Discusses the responsibility of Indian Affairs in economic development in Canada and the shifting control of land.
Social Science
Dist - CDIAND **Prod** - BOMI 1977

Options - Career, Education, Life 60 MIN
U-matic / VHS
(H C)
$165 _ #ED1V
Views the major decisions young people must make in choosing a career after school.
Business and Economics; Education
Dist - JISTW **Prod** - JISTW

Options - Dental Health in the Later Years 17 MIN
16mm
Color
Discusses the outcomes of dental neglect and focuses on prevention of periodontal disease through daily personal care, diet and proper nutrition.
Health and Safety
Dist - MTP **Prod** - AMDA
AMDA

Options for Infertility 19 MIN
VHS / 16mm
Color (G)
$149.00, $249.00, purchase _ #AD - 1377
Focuses on male and female infertility. Examines two non - traditional means of having children, in vitro fertilization and artificial insemination with donor sperm.
Health and Safety
Dist - FOTH **Prod** - FOTH 1990

Options for Life 12 MIN
16mm / U-matic / VHS
Nutrition Series
Color (J)
LC 80-700252
Shows how a person can facilitate the making of informed decisions regarding eating habits, exercise, smoking and drugs.
Health and Safety; Psychology
Dist - JOU **Prod** - ALTSUL 1979

Optiques - la vie quotidienne 60 MIN
VHS
VideoFrance series
Color (H C) (FRENCH)
$119.95 purchase _ #E1468 - X
Reveals issues of concern to French people through interviews filmed in varied locations. Includes teacher's manual.
Foreign Language
Dist - NTCPUB **Prod** - NTCPUB

Optische Glaser - Brillenglasfertigung 5 MIN
U-matic / VHS / 16mm
European Studies - Germany - German Series
Color (H C A) (GERMAN)
A German - language version of the motion picture Making Eye Glass Lenses. Describes the modern German eye glass manufacturing industry as well as the historical development of the process.
Business and Economics; Foreign Language; Geography - World
Dist - IFB **Prod** - MFAFRG 1973

Optoelectronic device reliability 30 MIN
VHS / U-matic
Optoelectronics series; Pt II - Optoelectronic displays
Color (PRO)
Repeats from Part I the comparison of optoelectronic devices compared to silicon. Completes working engineer's knowledge of displays in cases where section on emitters, sensors and couplers has not been viewed.
Industrial and Technical Education
Dist - TXINLC **Prod** - TXINLC

Optoelectronic device reliability 30 MIN
U-matic / VHS
Optoelectronics series; Pt I - optoelectronic emitters, sensors and couplers
Color (PRO)
Reviews basic fabrications to help establish similarities and differences of reliability of optoelectronic devices compared to silicon. Cites actual data to establish data base, and covers all types of optoelectronic devices.
Industrial and Technical Education
Dist - TXINLC **Prod** - TXINLC

Optoelectronics, Part II - optoelectronic displays series
Critical emitter parameters and their measurement 30 MIN
Dist - TXINLC

Optoelectronics series
Alphanumeric display applications 30 MIN
Applications of visible displays integrated with logic 30 MIN
The Emmiter and its characteristics 30 MIN
General emitter, sensor, coupler applications 30 MIN
Human factors associated with displays 30 MIN
Infrared emitter applications 30 MIN
Introduction to displays 30 MIN
Introduction to optoelectronics 30 MIN
Introduction to optoelectronics (optoelectronics, part i) 30 MIN
Numeric display applications 30 MIN
Optoelectronic device reliability 30 MIN
Photocoupler applications 30 MIN
Photocouplers and their characteristics 30 MIN
The Sensor and its characteristics 30 MIN
Sensor applications 30 MIN
VLED devices - process and fabrication 30 MIN
Dist - TXINLC

Optometry 15 MIN
BETA / VHS / U-matic
Career Success Series
(H C A)
$29.95 _ #MX212
Portrays the occupation of optometry by reviewing its required abilities and interviewing people employed in this field. Shows anxieties and rewards involved in pursuing a career as an optomotrist.
Education; Guidance and Counseling; Health and Safety; Science
Dist - CAMV **Prod** - CAMV

Optometry 15 MIN
VHS / 16mm
(H C A)
$24.95 purchase _ #CS212
Describes the skills necessary for a career in optometry. Features interviews with optometrists.
Guidance and Counseling
Dist - RMIBHF **Prod** - RMIBHF

Opus 1 4 MIN
16mm
Color
Explores the primary techniques of film painting.
Fine Arts
Dist - FMCOOP **Prod** - SPINLB 1967

Opus 44, Jerry West's Own Story 24 MIN
16mm
Color
LC 74-700360
Examines the private and public life of basketball player Jerry West.
Biography; Physical Education and Recreation
Dist - JANTZN **Prod** - JANTZN 1973

Opus I 5 MIN
16mm
Color
Presents a long - lost film by Walter Ruttmann, the first abstract film to be shown publicly anywhere in the world and which was recently discovered in a European film archive in its original hand - colored version.
Fine Arts
Dist - STARRC **Prod** - STARRC 1921

Opus II, III, IV 10 MIN
16mm
B&W
Presents 'a series of moving patterns' in a film by Walter Ruttman, one of the world's great abstract artists. Produced 1922 - 25.
Fine Arts
Dist - STARRC **Prod** - STARRC

Or - or - War 6 MIN
16mm
Color
Presents man's symmetrical hate - love, love - hate duel.
Industrial and Technical Education; Psychology; Sociology
Dist - VANBKS **Prod** - VANBKS

Oracle of the Branch 12 MIN
U-matic / VHS / 16mm
Color (A)
Presents a dance composed by Marks and performed by soloist James Croshaw.
Fine Arts
Dist - CNEMAG **Prod** - SFCT 1965

Oral Administration of Medications 14 MIN
16mm
B&W
LC FIE60-84
Presents the duties of hospital corpsmen in administering medications by mouth to patients in wards of naval hospitals. Demonstrates in detail the preparation of medication and treatment cards in accordance with the orders of medical officers.
Health and Safety
Dist - USNAC **Prod** - USN 1959

Oral Biopsy Procedure 15 MIN
16mm
Color (PRO)
LC 79-701665
Presents examples of some of the most common oral lesions and suggests biopsy procedures for each lesion, including excisional, incisional and aspirational techniques. Shows suturing techniques.
Health and Safety
Dist - USNAC **Prod** - VADTC 1978

Oral Cancer 22 MIN
16mm
Color
LC FI68-88
Demonstrates a five - minute visual and digital examination for oral cancer. Shows various oral lesions, discusses the necessity for a biopsy in diagnosis, and describes several successfully treated cases, stressing early detection as the key to cure.
Health and Safety
Dist - AMCS **Prod** - AMCS 1966

Oral Cancer - Intra - Oral Examination 6 MIN
16mm
Color
LC 75-702034
Demonstrates a methodical procedure for examining the intra - oral soft tissues. Presents six cases of early cancer in this area, pointing out their clinical signs.
Science
Dist - USNAC **Prod** - VADTC 1968

Oral Cancer Screening 24 MIN
U-matic / VHS / 16mm
Color (PRO C)
$330.00 purchase _ #840VI015
Teaches health professionals how to perform a thorough cancer screening of the mouth and the adjacent structures of the head and neck. Features a practice procedure.
Health and Safety; Science - Natural
Dist - HSCIC **Prod** - HSCIC 1984

Oral Cancer Self Exam Technique 60 MIN
U-matic
Color (C)
Illustrates the proper technique of self examination for detection of oral cancer.
Health and Safety; Science - Natural
Dist - UOKLAH **Prod** - UOKLAH 1986

Oral Care 7 MIN
U-matic / VHS
Basic Nursing Skills Series
Color (PRO)
Health and Safety
Dist - BRA **Prod** - BRA

Oral care 22 MIN
BETA / VHS / U-matic
Basic patient care - comfort and hygiene series
Color (C PRO)
$150.00 purchase _ #127.5
Presents a video transfer from slide program which discusses the effects of illness on oral health and emphasizes the importance of maintaining oral hygiene. Describes in detail the assessment of the mouth an illustrates conditions which require special care. Suggests methods for preparing both conscious and unconscious patients for oral care. Part of a series on basic patient care.
Health and Safety
Dist - CONMED **Prod** - CONMED

Oral Care 8 MIN
U-matic / VHS
Basic Nursing Skills Series Tape 4; Tape 4
Color (PRO)
Health and Safety
Dist - MDCC **Prod** - MDCC

The Oral Cavity 11 MIN
VHS / U-matic
Skull Anatomy Series
Color (C A)
Describes the boundaries, demonstrates the bones and identifies the bony regions of the oral cavity.

Health and Safety; Science - Natural
Dist - TEF **Prod** - UTXHSA

Oral Cavity 33 MIN
VHS / 16mm
Histology review series; Unit IX
(C)
$330.00 purchase _ 821VI045
Discusses the microscopic anatomy of the lips, tongue, and salivary glands. Part 1 of the Digestive system Unit.
Health and Safety
Dist - HSCIC **Prod** - HSCIC 1983

Oral communicating - content and confidence series 60 MIN
VHS
Oral communicating - content and confidence series
Color (I J H)
$136.00 purchase _ #GW - 5100 - VS; $136.00 purchase _ #983VG
Presents two parts on oral communication. Includes the titles How to Research and Organize an Oral Presentation; and Preparation and Delivery. Comes with teacher's guides and blackline masters.
English Language
Dist - HRMC **Prod** - UNL 1990
UNL

Oral communicating - content and confidence series
Oral communicating - content and confidence series 60 MIN
Preparation and delivery 30 MIN
Dist - HRMC
UNL

Oral Communication 28 MIN
16mm
You in Public Service Series
Color (A)
LC 77-700965
Defines what things are most important in oral communication and applies them to person - to - person communication, informal interviews and group discussions.
English Language; Sociology
Dist - USNAC **Prod** - USOE 1977

Oral Contaceptives - a New Look for Physicians and Patients 47 MIN
VHS / 16mm
(C)
$385.00 purchase _ #850VI110
Provides a complete overview of oral contraceptives, beginning with their introduction in the 1960s. Covers contradictions, recommended methods for prescribing, myths concerning pill use, and beneficial as well as deleterious side effects of oral contraceptives.
Health and Safety
Dist - HSCIC **Prod** - HSCIC 1985

Oral Contraception - the 21 Day Pill 15 MIN
U-matic / VHS
Color
Explains how to use the birth control pill. Focuses on the use of the 21 day package.
Health and Safety; Sociology
Dist - MEDFAC **Prod** - MEDFAC 1979

Oral Contraception - the 28 Day Pill 16 MIN
U-matic / VHS
Color
Explains how to use the birth control pill. Focuses on the use of the 28 day package.
Health and Safety; Sociology
Dist - MEDFAC **Prod** - MEDFAC 1979

The Oral Contraceptives 29 MIN
16mm
Concepts and Controversies in Modern Medicine Series
B&W (PRO)
LC 74-705265
Debates the efficacy of oral contraceptives versus their adverse consequences.
Health and Safety; Sociology
Dist - NMAC **Prod** - NMAC 1969

Oral Endoscopy 20 MIN
16mm
Color
LC 79-702507
Shows the nursing and surgical management of a pediatric patient having general anesthesia for a laryngoscopy and an adult patient having a local anesthetic for bronchoscopy. Includes scenes showing the care and handling of oral endoscopic instruments and equipment.
Health and Safety
Dist - ACY **Prod** - ACYDGD 1968

Oral Exam 10 MIN
U-matic / VHS
Color
Describes a three - part oral examination for the detection of cancer in dental patients. Consists of visual inspection, palpatory examination and lymph adenopathy examination.
Health and Safety; Science - Natural
Dist - UWASH **Prod** - UWASH

Oral Exfoliative Cytology 17 MIN
16mm
Color
LC 74-705266
Depicts how oral exfoliative cytology can disclose early and unsuspected cancer of the mouth. Demonstrates the technique for obtaining a cytology specimen and presents the variation of the microscopic appearance of normal cells and cancer cells.
Health and Safety; Science - Natural
Dist - NMAC **Prod** - USVA 1963

Oral Exfoliative Cytology - a Diagnostic Tool for Detection of Early Mouth Cancer 18 MIN
U-matic
Color
LC 78-706105
Describes how oral exfoliative cytology can disclose early and unsuspected cancer of the mouth. Shows several clinical examples of unsuspected mouth cancers andd illustrates the technique for obtaining a cytology specimen. Issued in 1963 as a motion picture.
Health and Safety
Dist - USNAC **Prod** - USVA 1978

Oral Expressive Language 30 MIN
VHS / U-matic
Teaching Children with Special Needs Series
Color (T)
Deals with oral expressive language in children with special needs.
Education
Dist - MDCPB **Prod** - MDDE

An Oral historian's work with Dr Edward Ives 30 MIN
VHS
Color (G)
$39.95 purchase
Demonstrates techniques used by oral historian Dr Edward Ives in his work.
Fine Arts; History - United States
Dist - NEFILM

Oral History 60 MIN
VHS / 16mm
Color
Relates how a black village chief learns that members of his village are hiding guerrilla infiltrators and takes that information to the police - with tragic results.
Fine Arts
Dist - TLECUL **Prod** - TLECUL

Oral History 20 MIN
U-matic
Access Series
Color (T)
LC 76-706249
Gives an overview of what is involved in undertaking an oral history project, including estimates of the staff, equipment and time necessary.
Education
Dist - USNAC **Prod** - UDEN 1976

Oral Hygiene 17 MIN
16mm
Color
LC FIE62-22
Shows how to brush the teeth. Gives care of brushes, tips on eating habits and effects of good care and neglect.
Health and Safety; Science - Natural
Dist - USNAC **Prod** - USN 1960

Oral Hygiene for Hospitalized Patients 14 MIN
16mm
Color
Presents a hygienist demonstrating how to clean teeth on a model, on herself, on a sitting patient and on a bed patient.
Health and Safety
Dist - USVA **Prod** - USVA 1957

Oral Hygiene for the Orthodontic Patient 8 MIN
U-matic / VHS / 16mm
Color
Demonstrates the importance of personal care of teeth and removing harmful bacteria from hard - to - reach places using the toothbrush and pick, dental floss, water irrigator and disclosing wafers.
Health and Safety
Dist - PRORE **Prod** - PRORE

Oral Hygiene for the Total Care Patient 16 MIN
VHS / 16mm
(C)
$385.00 purchase _ #870VJ012
Introduces nursing students to an extensive oral hygiene regimen for the total care patient. The techniques of the regimen are demonstrated for patients with natural dentition, complete dentures as well as removable partial dentures.
Health and Safety
Dist - HSCIC **Prod** - HSCIC 1987

Oral Hygiene for the Total - Care Patient 14 MIN
16mm
Color
LC 74-705267
Points out how oral hygiene is a problem of the hospitalized patient who is physically or mentally unable to care for himself. Shows value of ingestible tooth paste, completely stable stannous flouride jet and the electric tooth brush in the oral hygiene care of these patients.
Health and Safety; Science - Natural
Dist - USNAC **Prod** - USVA 1949

Oral Hygiene Procedures for the Bedridden Patient 15 MIN
VHS
Color (PRO)
$395.00 purchase _ #N900VI048
Provides a procedural guide for those giving basic oral care to bedridden patients. Focuses on toothbrushing and flossing techniques, as well as procedures for cleaning removable appliances. Demonstrates each procedure as well as how to adapt the procedure for unresponsive and comatose patients.
Health and Safety; Science
Dist - HSCIC

Oral Intubation in the Adult, using the MacIntosh Laryngoscope 19 MIN
VHS / U-matic
Color (PRO)
Demonstrates the proper technique for tracheal intubation using the MacIntosh blade. Reviews the rationale for intubation, the equipment needed for successful intubation, and the correct procedures for positioning and intubating the patient.
Health and Safety
Dist - HSCIC **Prod** - HSCIC

Oral Language 29 MIN
VHS / 16mm
Breaking the Unseen Barrier Series
Color (C)
$180.00, $240.00 purchase _ #269705
Demonstrates through dramatic vignettes effective teaching strategies to help students with learning disabilities reach their full potential. Offers insight into integrating learning disabled students into the classroom. 'Oral Language' shows that Sarah has difficulty with receptive language so she doesn't understand much of what is said to her. Tony's expressive language problems have resulted in an inability to retrieve and pronounce words he knows. Sources to help their grade four teacher meet the challenge of oral language learning disabilties are investigated.
Education; English Language; Mathematics; Psychology
Dist - AITECH **Prod** - ACCESS 1988

Oral Language 30 MIN
VHS / U-matic
Rainbow Road Series Pt 2
Color (A)
LC 82-707394
Shows how parents can help their children develop oral or spoken language through riddles, games and wordless books, and by talking with them and listening to their children.
Home Economics; Sociology
Dist - GPN **Prod** - KAIDTV 1982

Oral Language - a Breakthrough to Reading 24 MIN
16mm
Color
LC FIA68-782
Describes a six - week language development project conducted by the Columbus City School District. Shows how an art teacher, a music teacher, a physical education teacher and a language teacher cooperate to develop the language abilities of a group of inner - city children.
Education; English Language
Dist - OSUMPD **Prod** - COLPS 1967

The Oral Language Proficiency Test 23 MIN
U-matic
Color (T)
LC 77-706160
Illustrates a technique for testing foreign language speaking and comprehension skills. Describes the test, the interview techniques commonly employed, the government's civil service proficiency definitions, the rating standards and their general application.

Civics and Political Systems; Foreign Language
Dist - USNAC **Prod** - USILR 1977

Oral Language Teaching Techniques 20 MIN
16mm
Color (T)
LC 72-700184
Explores reasons why many urban youngsters are not totally familiar with standard English, and discusses the theory behind language materials prepared by the Michigan Department of Education. Covers special problem areas for teachers, including large classes, boredom, non - talkers and mixed ability groups.
Education; English Language
Dist - CIASP **Prod** - CIASP 1971

The Oral law - the Talmud and the scholar 58 MIN
VHS
Color (G)
$34.95 purchase _ #847
Focuses on Rabbi Adin Steinsaltz, a leading rabbinical scholar.
Religion and Philosophy; Sociology
Dist - ERGOM **Prod** - ERGOM

Oral Love 10 MIN
U-matic / VHS
Mutuality Series
Color
Provides a sustained look at fellatio and cunnilingus. Documents the emotional bond in which two adults responsively give of themselves to each other.
Health and Safety; Psychology
Dist - MMRC **Prod** - MMRC

Oral medication administration 23 MIN
VHS / U-matic / BETA
Medications administration and absorption series
Color (C PRO)
$280.00 purchase _ #613.1
Describes preparation, administration and documentation of oral medications using the 'Five Rights of Medicine Administration.' Stresses the legal and ethical responsibilities governing medication administration. Demonstrates step - by - step the procedure for safely and effectively administering medications. Emphasizes the importance of a knowledge base of each medication to be administered with assessment, implementation, evaluation and documentation. Produced by Golden West College. Part of a six - part series on medications administration and absorption including five video programs and supporting software simulation.
Health and Safety
Dist - CONMED

Oral medications 14 MIN
VHS
Clinical nursing skills - nursing fundamentals - series
Color (C PRO G)
$395.00 purchase _ #R890 - VI - 058
Reveals that the administration of oral medications is a simple procedure but requires special skills to ensure proper performance. Introduces nursing students to techniques appropriate for accurate administration of oral medications. Describes types of oral medications, as well as types of delivery and supply systems. Demonstrates procedures for administering all types, including periodic safety checks to ensure accuracy. Presents record keeping and patient assessment skills. Part of a 23 - part series on clinical nursing skills.
Health and Safety
Dist - HSCIC **Prod** - CUYAHO 1989

Oral medications for diabetes 12 MIN
VHS
AADE patient education video series
Color; CC (G C PRO)
$175.00 purchase _ #DB - 27
Explains the use of pills - oral hypoglycemics - to lower blood sugar. Covers signs of possible side effects and ways to avoid risks. Introduces the concept of pattern management. Part of an eight - part series produced in cooperation with the American Association of Diabetes Educators. Contact distributor for special purchase price on multiple orders.
Health and Safety; Science - Natural
Dist - MIFE

Oral Motor Problems 45 MIN
U-matic / VHS
Meeting the Communications Needs of the Severely - Profoundly Handicapped 1980 Series
Color
Discusses congenital pathologies of the central nervous system, primitive and pathological oral motor reflexes and the minimum motor prerequisites for speech.
Psychology; Social Science
Dist - PUAVC **Prod** - PUAVC

Oral Mucosa and Epithelial Attachment 19 MIN
U-matic
Microanatomy Laboratory Orientation Series
Color (C)
Reviews Orban's classification of the oral mucosa and the fundamental patterns of the various forms of moist stratified squamous found in the oral cavity.
Health and Safety; Science - Natural
Dist - UOKLAH **Prod** - UOKLAH 1986

Oral Pathology - an Overview
VHS
Color (PRO)
$395.00 purchase, $197.50 members _ #N901 - VI - 087
Provides increased understanding of the importance of the mouth as a source of diagnostic information, focusing on common pathologies of the mouth. Presented in an interactive videodisc program by William S Parker, DMD, PhD. Requires MS - DOS 3.2 or 3.3 and the InfoWindow Control Program and Presentation Interpreter (Level 50) software. Includes user's manual and study guide.
Health and Safety
Dist - HSCIC

Oral Reasons for Horse Judging 45 MIN
VHS
Horse Judging Set Z - 2 Series
Color (H C A PRO)
$79.95 purchase _ #CV304
Includes - what it takes to be competitive in the reasons room at a national level, discussion on orgranization, terminology and presentation, and sample sets of reasons critiqued by a panel of experts.
Agriculture; Physical Education and Recreation
Dist - AAVIM **Prod** - AAVIM 1990

Oral Reasons for Livestock Judging 34 MIN
VHS
Introduction and Reasons Series
(C)
$79.95 _ CV121
Examines what it takes to be successful at giving competitive reasons in national competitions plus basic requirements and important points of good reasons.
Agriculture; English Language
Dist - AAVIM **Prod** - AAVIM 1989

Oral Receptive Language 30 MIN
U-matic / VHS
Teaching Children with Special Needs Series
Color (T)
Deals with oral receptive language in children with special needs.
Education
Dist - MDCPB **Prod** - MDDE

Oral Rehabilitation 29 MIN
16mm
Color
Deals with the surgical treatment of gingival hyperplasia in a patient in whom the condition has developed as a result of the administration of diphenyl hydantoin sodium for the control of epilepsy. and demonstrates curettage, postoperative treatment, insertion of the acrylic splint and the instruction of the patient in oral hygiene.
Health and Safety
Dist - USVA **Prod** - USVA 1954

Oral Sex 11 MIN
VHS / U-matic
EDCOA Sexual Counseling Series
Color
Demonstrates a variety of oral sex techinques. A couple discusses their religiously - based concerns about engaging in this behavior.
Health and Safety; Psychology
Dist - MMRC **Prod** - MMRC

Oral Surgery Clinic Routine, Pt 1, Sterilizing Oral Surgery Instruments 9 MIN
U-matic / VHS
Color
Demonstrates the process of sterilizing oral surgery instruments and explains the importance of each step.
Health and Safety; Science
Dist - USNAC **Prod** - MUSC

Oral Surgery Clinic Routine, Pt 2, Patient Positioning and Preparation of the 7 MIN
U-matic / VHS
Color
Complete title is Oral Surgery Clinic Routine, Pt 2, Patient Positioning And Preparation of The Instrument Tray For Clinical Oral Surgery.
Health and Safety; Science
Dist - USNAC **Prod** - MUSC

Oral Surgery Clinic Routine, Pt 3, Hand Scrub and Basic Protocol for Clinical Oral Surgery 7 MIN
VHS / U-matic
Color
Demonstrates proper scrubbing and gloving techniques to be used in an oral surgery clinic.
Health and Safety; Science
Dist - USNAC **Prod** - MUSC

Oral Surgery Clinic Routine, Pt 4, Establishing an Uninterrupted Intraoral 7 MIN
VHS / U-matic
Color
Complete title is Oral Surgery Clinic Routine, Pt 4, Establishing An Uninterrupted Intraoral Surgical Field. Shows the step - by - step process with explanations of each step in establishing an uninterrupted intraoral surgical field.
Health and Safety; Science
Dist - USNAC **Prod** - MUSC

Oral Surgery Clinic Routine Series
Establishing an Uninterrupted Intra - Oral Surgical Field 7 MIN
Hand Scrub and Basic Protocol for Clinical Oral Surgery 7 MIN
Patient Positioning and Preparation of the Instrument Tray for Clinical Oral Surgery 7 MIN
Sterilizing Oral Surgery Instruments 9 MIN
Dist - USNAC

Orang-utan - out on a limb 30 MIN
VHS
Wildlife on one series
Color; PAL (H C A)
PdS65 purchase; Not available in the United States or Canada
Documents the activities of an orang-utan population in the wild. Describes the orang-utan as one of man's closest biological relatives. Follows the first three years of a new - born orang-utan named Yossa.
Science - Natural
Dist - BBCENE

Orang - utans 27 MIN
U-matic / VHS / BETA
Stationary ark series
Color; PAL (G H C)
PdS50, PdS58 purchase
Discusses the recreation of humankind, nature and wildlife in part of a 12 - part series. Features Gerald Durrell. Filmed on location in Jersey, England.
Science - Natural
Dist - EDPAT

Orange 26 MIN
16mm / VHS / BETA / U-matic
Color; PAL (G)
PdS140, PdS148 purchase
Witness nature's elements, including the movements of sun, clouds, light and shadows, as dawn arrives growing to a blinding red of boiling clouds into which man's machines intrudes until nature rebels with an explosive holocaust.
Industrial and Technical Education
Dist - EDPAT

Orange 3 MIN
U-matic / 16mm
Color (C A)
Presents a sensual macro - study of the hidden universe within a fruit taken for granted.
Health and Safety; Psychology
Dist - MMRC **Prod** - MMRC

Orange and Blue 15 MIN
U-matic / VHS / 16mm
Color (P A)
Provides a visual perspective of the world as seen by two child - like personalities, orange and blue. Juxtaposes visual images with a musical score.
Fine Arts
Dist - EBEC **Prod** - CHE 1962

Orange Bowl 1972 - 1973 28 MIN
16mm
Color
Highlights the King Orange Jamboree Parade in downtown Miami and the annual gridiron classic Orange Bowl 1972 - 1973.
Physical Education and Recreation
Dist - FLADC **Prod** - FLADC

Orange Bowl Festival 27 MIN
16mm
Color
Presents colorful Orange bowl Festival activities including the famed nighttime parade and football classic.
Geography - United States; Physical Education and Recreation
Dist - MIMET **Prod** - MIMET

Orange Free State 10 MIN
16mm / VHS

Color (G)
Explores the tourist attractions of South Africa's land - locked regions, including Vaal Dam, Golden Gate National Park and the Willem Pretorius Game Reserve. Includes visits to gold mines, farms and the Bloemfontein. Available for free loan from the distributor.
Geography - World
Dist - AUDPLN

The Orange Grower 16 MIN
U-matic / VHS / 16mm
Color (I) (SPANISH)
Depicts all phases of orange growing from planting to shipping and emphasizes the work and care required to produce quality fruit. Portrays a typical orange grower and his family at work, budding, pruning, planting, fertilizing, irrigating and controlling insects and frost.
Agriculture; Foreign Language; Social Science
Dist - EBEC **Prod** - EBEC 1967

Orange Industry 3 MIN
16mm
Of all Things Series
Color (P I)
Discusses the orange industry.
Business and Economics; Social Science
Dist - AVED **Prod** - BAILYL

Orange sherbet kisses 50 MIN
VHS
Horizon series
Color; PAL (G)
PdS99 purchase
Investigates the phenomenon of synaesthesia, a mixing of the senses in which hearing includes colors as well as words. Explores the occurrence as one method of studying the workings of the brain.
Psychology
Dist - BBCENE

Orange Souffle 6 MIN
U-matic / VHS
Cooking with Jack and Jill Series
Color (P I)
$95.00
Portrays the skills of twins Jack and Jill as they cook nutritious and delicious snacks that are easy to prepare. Kitchen safety is emphasized. Animated.
Home Economics
Dist - LANDMK **Prod** - LANDMK 1986

Orangutan 60 MIN
VHS
Color (G)
$24.95 purchase _ #S01998
Portrays the orangutans of Indonesia's rain forests. Shows that orangutans struggle to survive.
Science - Natural
Dist - UILL **Prod** - SIERRA

Orangutan - the Man of the Forest 22 MIN
VHS / 16mm
Let Them Live Series
Color (I)
$450.00, $205.00 purchase
Follows Dr John Mckinnon and others as they study orangutans in their threatened jungle habitat. Reveals that 4000 orangutans still live in the lush tropical rain forests of Borneo and Sumatra.
Geography - World; Science - Natural
Dist - LUF **Prod** - LUF

Orangutans 10 MIN
VHS
Animal profile series
Color (P I)
$59.95 purchase _ #RB8109
Studies orangutans, intelligent primates native to Southeast Asia. Discusses the mythology and mystery surrounding these apes because of their human - like size and features. Part of a series on animals which looks at examples from the mammal, snake and bird classes, filmed in their natural habitat.
Geography - World; Science - Natural
Dist - REVID **Prod** - REVID 1990

Orb 5 MIN
16mm
Color (C)
$196.00
Experimental film by Larry Jordan.
Fine Arts
Dist - AFA **Prod** - AFA 1973

Orb 5 MIN
16mm
Color (G)
$15.00 rental
Presents a cut - out animated orb - sun, moon or symbol of the self - bouncing a joyous course through scenes of celestial ephemera until it encases the lovers it has been following.
Fine Arts
Dist - CANCIN **Prod** - JORDAL 1973

The Orbit 13 MIN
16mm / U-matic / VHS
Anatomy of the Eye Series
Color (C A)
Health and Safety; Science - Natural
Dist - TEF **Prod** - BAYCMO

The Orbit 10 MIN
U-matic / VHS
Skull Anatomy Series
Color (C A)
Describes the boundaries, demonstrates the bones and identifies the bony regions of the orbit.
Health and Safety; Science - Natural
Dist - TEF **Prod** - UTXHSA

The Orbit from Above 11 MIN
U-matic / VHS / 16mm
Guides to Dissection Series
Color (C A)
Focuses on the head and neck. Demonstrates the orbit.
Health and Safety; Science - Natural
Dist - TEF **Prod** - UCLA

Orbital Recession Operation for Malignant Exophthalmos 37 MIN
16mm
Color (PRO)
Presents a number of patients suitable for operation for progressive exophthalmos. Demonstrates measurements of the degree of proptosis and shows the operative technique in detail.
Health and Safety; Science
Dist - ACY **Prod** - ACYDGD 1951

Orbital Repair with Methlethacrylate 11 MIN
16mm
Color (PRO)
Demonstrates the method of using methylmethacrylate in its rapidly polymerizing form for the repair of orbital floor fractures. Shows the skin approach, the method of elevating the periosteum and the use of retractors for inspection of the floor.
Health and Safety; Science
Dist - ACY **Prod** - ACYDGD 1971

Orbital Shapes and Paths 11 MIN
16mm / U-matic / VHS
Space Science Series
Color (I J H)
Illustrates how a stellite's shape, path and period may be modified. Demonstrates the establishing of weather and communications satellites.
Science - Physical
Dist - JOU

Orbitals and Bonding 16 MIN
VHS
Chem 101 - Beginning Chemistry Series
Color (C)
$50.00 purchase, $21.00 rental _ #00112
Describes the formation and characteristics of sigma and pi bonds and the mixing of atomic orbitals to form hybrid orbitals. Shows how electron arrangement around an atom can be used to predict the hybrid orbitals and atomic orbitals used in bonding. Uses models to show the lack of rotation around a pi bond and the difference between cis and trans isomers.
Science - Physical
Dist - UILL **Prod** - UILL 1987

Orbiter Thermal Protection System 6 MIN
U-matic / VHS / 16mm
Space Shuttle Profile Series
Color
Describes how the thermal protection system shields the space craft from high temperatures during re - entry and ascent, the types of insulation used on the orbiter and the advantages of silica fiber tiles.
Industrial and Technical Education; Science - Physical
Dist - USNAC **Prod** - NASA

Orbiting Solar Observatory 26 MIN
VHS / U-matic
Color
LC 81-706391
Discusses the functioning of the orbiting solar observatory in gathering data about the effects of the Sun on the Earth and its inhabitants, pointing out that the solar observatory was launched March 7, 1962, to study the Sun from above the Earth's atmosphere.
Science - Physical
Dist - USNAC **Prod** - USGSFC 1981

Orca - killer whale or gentle giant 26 MIN
VHS
Color (J H C G A)
$59.95 purchase, $25.00 rental
Explores the orcas, also known as "killer whales," in their natural habitat. Dispels the notion that they are dangerous creatures. Features underwater cinematography. Filmed by Hiroya Minakuchi.
Geography - World; Science - Natural
Dist - EFVP

The Orchestra 30 MIN
VHS / U-matic
Musical Encounter Series
Color (P I)
Presents the Cleveland Instiutue Of Music Youth Orchestra and its conductor Christopher Wilkins. Demonstrates the great variety of sounds capable of being produced by the orchestra, 'the world's largest musical instrument.'.
Fine Arts
Dist - GPN **Prod** - WVIZTV 1983

The Orchestra
CD / VHS / Cassette
(G)
$19.98, $15.98, $9.98 purchase _ #8328, #D326, #326
Tells about the orchestra, why there are more violins than any other instrument and other facts. Features Peter Ustinov as narrator.
Fine Arts
Dist - MULIPE **Prod** - MULIPE

Orchestra Rehearsal 72 MIN
16mm
Color (ITALIAN (ENGLISH SUBTITLES))
Uses the spectacle of the orchestra rehearsal as a metaphor for the chaos of 20th century Western civilization. Directed by Federico Fellini. With English subtitles.
Fine Arts; Foreign Language
Dist - NYFLMS **Prod** - UNKNWN 1979

Orchestre Opera de Paris - conductor, Georges Pretre 48 MIN
VHS
Color (G)
$14.95 purchase_#1433
Presents two great Mozart works, Concerto for Bassoon and Orchestra - K.191 - with Jean Claude Montac, and Concerto for Clarinet - K.622 - with Michael Arrignon. Utilizes the conducting skills of Georges Pretre with the Orchestre Opera de Paris.
Fine Arts
Dist - KULTUR

Orchid Fancier 29 MIN
U-matic
House Botanist Series
Color
Explores the world of exotic orchids. Includes simple and wild varieties.
Agriculture; Science - Natural
Dist - UMITV **Prod** - UMITV 1978

Orchid Flowers and Composition 30 MIN
VHS / 16mm
Chinese Brush Painting Series
Color (C A)
$85.00, $75.00 purchase _ 20 - 03
Describes painting the flower, effective composition.
Fine Arts
Dist - CDTEL **Prod** - COAST 1987

Orchid Leaves 30 MIN
VHS / 16mm
Chinese Brush Painting Series
Color (C A)
$85.00, $75.00 purchase _ 20 - 02
Describes positioning the body and hand, initial strokes.
Fine Arts
Dist - CDTEL **Prod** - COAST 1987

Orchids 30 MIN
VHS / 16mm
Art of decorating cakes series
(G)
$49.00 purchase _ #BCD24
Instructs in the art of decorating cakes. Shows how to make various orchids out of gum paste using cutters and molding. Taught by master cake decorator Leon Simmons.
Home Economics; Industrial and Technical Education
Dist - RMIBHF **Prod** - RMIBHF

Orchids - 49 2 MIN
VHS / U-matic
Plants Need Love Too Series
Color (G)
Agriculture
Dist - TVSS **Prod** - TVSS

Ordeal of a President 22 MIN
U-matic / VHS / 16mm
You are There Series
Color (I J)
LC 70-714891
Covers President Woodrow Wilson's decision to enter America into World War I and discusses the influence of the publication of the Zimmermann telegram on the opinion of the American people.
Biography; Civics and Political Systems; History - United States
Dist - PHENIX **Prod** - CBSTV 1971

The Ordeal of Greece and Cyprus 29 MIN
Videoreel / VT2
Course of Our Times II Series
Color
History - World
Dist - PBS **Prod** - WGBHTV

The Ordeal of Jacobo Timerman 60 MIN
U-matic / VHS
Bill Moyers' Journal Series
Color
Presents an interview with Argentine newspaper editor Jacobo Timerman, who discusses imprisonment and torture, resurgent Nazism and the politics of hate in Argentina.
Civics and Political Systems; History - World
Dist - PBS **Prod** - WNETTV 1981

Ordeal of Power - the President and the Presidency 56 MIN
VHS / U-matic
Color
LC 81-706674
Explains how the powers of the presidency are defined by the Constitution and shows how these powers have changed, grown and been curbed through history. Illustrates the decision - making process of the presidency through examples from recent history. Asks how a fictional president might solve a typical policy problem.
Civics and Political Systems
Dist - GA **Prod** - GA 1981

Ordeal of the American city series
Cities have no limits, pt 1 25 MIN
Cities have no limits, pt 2 25 MIN
Dist - NBCTV

Order 30 MIN
U-matic / VHS
Writing for a Reason Series
Color (C)
English Language
Dist - DALCCD **Prod** - DALCCD

Order Alterations, Reschedules and Returns 60 MIN
VHS / BETA
Manufacturing Series
(IND)
Examines the types of changes than may need to be made in a customer's order and the process to follow in handling those changes.
Business and Economics
Dist - COMSRV **Prod** - COMSRV 1986

Order Entry and Delivery Promising 60 MIN
BETA / VHS
Manufacturing Series
(IND)
Looks at the process and components of order entry and delivery promising.
Business and Economics
Dist - COMSRV **Prod** - COMSRV 1986

Order, Growth, Change 30 MIN
U-matic
Parent Puzzle Series
(A)
Notes that as a baby grows, parents tend to assume negative motivations in what is often exploratory behavior. By overcoming this thinking there can be behavior acceptable to both parent and child.
Psychology; Sociology
Dist - ACCESS **Prod** - ACCESS 1982

Order of fractions
VHS
Lola May's fundamental math series
Color (I)
$45.00 purchase _ #10280VG
Explains and practices all three cases of the order of fractions. Covers ordering when the denominators are the same; when the numerators are the same; and when both are different. Comes with a teacher's guide and blackline masters. Part 30 of a 30 - part series.
Mathematics
Dist - UNL

Order of Operations 15 MIN
VHS
Power of Algebra Series
Color (J)
LC 90712872
Uses computer animation and interviews with professionals who use algebra to explain order of operations. The second of 10 installments of The Power Of Algebra Series.
Mathematics
Dist - GPN

Order of operations
VHS
Basic mathematical skills series
Color (J H)
$125.00 purchase _ #1025
Teaches the concept of order of operations. Presents part of a series that provides 27 videos, each between 25 and 30 minutes long, that explain and reinforce basic mathematical concepts. Tutors the student through definitions, theorems, step - by - step solutions and examples. Videos are also available in a set.
Mathematics
Dist - LANDMK

Order of precedence 24.11 MIN
VHS / U-matic
Meeting will come to order series
(G)
Combines narration and dramatization to explain the basics of parliamentary procedure. Explains order of precedence. Written by the Members of the National Association of Parliamentarians. Follows the revised Robert's Rules of Order. Third in a six part series.
English Language
Dist - GPN **Prod** - NETV 1983

The Order of the Silver Platter 30 MIN
U-matic / VHS
Color (A) (PORTUGUESE SPANISH)
Teaches basic sales skills. Demonstrates how to turn seven sins of selling into strengths. Narrated by Ed McMahon.
Business and Economics; Foreign Language; Psychology
Dist - AMEDIA **Prod** - AMEDIA

Order order 50 MIN
VHS
The great palace - the story of parliament
Color; PAL (C H)
PdS99 purchase
Provides a view of the Speaker's residence. Hosted by Lord Tonypandy. Fifth in the eight - part series The Great Palace: The Story of Parliament, which documents the significance of the institution.
Civics and Political Systems; History - World
Dist - BBCENE

Ordered Pairs and the Cartesian Product 6 MIN
16mm
Maa Arithmetic Series
Color (T)
LC 73-703198
Introduces the concept of an ordered pair and defines the cartesian product using examples from navigation and rectangular grids.
Mathematics
Dist - MLA **Prod** - MLA 1966

Orderly Development of Removable Partial Denture Design, Pt 1 - the Mandibular Cast 15 MIN
U-matic
Color (PRO)
LC 78-706194
Describes requirements for partial denture design, including rigidity, support, retention, reciprocation, guidance and mesh for resin bases. Demonstrates the fulfillment of these requirements in designing a partial denture using a stone case mounted on a dental surveyor. Issued in 1970 as a motion picture.
Health and Safety; Science
Dist - USNAC **Prod** - USVA 1978

Orderly Development of Removable Partial Denture Design, Pt 2 - the Maxillary Cast 15 MIN
U-matic
Color (PRO)
LC 78-706196
Describes requirements for partial denture design, including rigidity, support, retention, reciprocation, guidance and mesh for resin bases. Demonstrates the fulfillment of these requirements in designing a partial denture using a stone case mounted on a dental surveyor. Issued in 1970 as a motion picture.
Health and Safety; Science
Dist - USNAC **Prod** - USVA 1978

Orderly Development of Removable Partial Design, Pt 1 - the Mandibular Cast 14 MIN
16mm
Color
LC 75-701352
Presents Dr J Demer stating that the requirements of partial denture design include rigidity, support, retention, reciprocation, guidance and mesh for resin bases. Demonstrates the fulfillment of these requirements in designing a manibular partial denture using a stone cast mounted on a dental surveyor.
Health and Safety; Science
Dist - USNAC **Prod** - USVA 1970

Orders 13 MIN
U-matic / VHS / 16mm
Discovering Insects Series
Color
LC 79-701322
Explains the various categories of common insects.
Science - Natural
Dist - CORF **Prod** - MORALL 1979

Ordinal scales of infant psychological development series
Development of means 34 MIN
Development of schemas 36 MIN
Imitation - Gestural and Vocal 35 MIN
Object Permanence 40 MIN
Object Relations in Space 28 MIN
Operational Causality 21 MIN
Dist - UILL

The Ordinary Can be Extraordinary 15 MIN
VHS / U-matic
Tyger, Tyger Burning Bright Series
Color (I)
Deals with developing new perceptions about ordinary situations.
English Language
Dist - CTI **Prod** - CTI

Ordinary Days 24 MIN
16mm
B&W
LC 74-702659
Depicts the struggles of a woman as she seeks to identify her needs in and apart from her situation with the man with whom she lives.
Psychology; Sociology
Dist - NLC **Prod** - HECKS 1974

Ordinary guy 70 MIN
VHS
Color (J H C G A R)
$35.00 rental _ #36 - 81 - 2022
Portrays how an ordinary guy is surprised at how his Christianity impacts on all areas of his life - his career, his free time, his romantic interests.
Religion and Philosophy
Dist - APH **Prod** - DAYSTR

An Ordinary Life 27 MIN
U-matic / VHS / 16mm
Color (C A)
Takes a look at some of the many advances which are helping the disabled to find a voice and a place in our society.
Psychology
Dist - STNFLD **Prod** - LONTVS

Ordinary People 28 MIN
16mm
Color (PRO)
LC 77-701823
Presents a dramatization about a family under stress. Tells the story of a woman living in a new town and finding it difficult to handle her problems. Shows how she looks for help when she begins abusing her child.
Guidance and Counseling; Psychology; Sociology
Dist - UPITTS **Prod** - UPITTS 1977
CORF

Ordinary People
BETA / U-matic / VHS
Color (J C I)
Presents a story of a middle - class family's emotional disintegration. Directed by Robert Redford.
Guidance and Counseling; Sociology
Dist - GA **Prod** - GA

Ordinary people series
Presents a series of eight programs in which each episode chronicles an event in South Africa through the eyes of three or four 'ordinary' people, chosen to represent diverse backgrounds or dissimilar points of view. Seeks to provide insight into the collective South African conscience. Features the first independently produced current affairs series aired by the South African Broadcasting Corporation's TV1, historically the mouthpiece of the white apartheid government. Titles, available for separate rental or purchase, include The Peacemaker; The Lawyer, the Farmer and the Clerk; The Tooth of the Times; City of Dreams; Sebokeng by Night; The Penalty Area; and Make Believe.
City of dreams 26 MIN
The Lawyer, the farmer and the clerk 26 MIN
Make Believe 26 MIN
The Peacemakers 26 MIN
The Penalty area 26 MIN
Sebokeng by night 26 MIN
The Tooth of the times 26 MIN
Dist - FIRS **Prod** - GAVSHO

An Ordinary rape 54 MIN
VHS
Color (G)
$390.00 purchase, $75.00 rental
Interviews high school and college students, journalists, criminologists, psychologists, lawyers, police and physicians to present many divergent attitudes on date rape. Examines the cultural misconceptions which

surround date rape in the United States. Focuses on a victim of rape who goes far beyond the abstract theoretical discussions and speaks frankly about the need to educate others about the violent crime committed against her. Produced by Isabelle Coulet. A 29 minute version is available.
Fine Arts; Guidance and Counseling; Sociology
Dist - FIRS

Ordinary Time
U-matic / VHS
Christian Year Series
Color (G)
Examines the place and purpose of the time outside the church's formal seasons.
Religion and Philosophy
Dist - CAFM **Prod** - CAFM

Ordinary work 19 MIN
16mm
Audio visual research briefs series
Color
LC 74-705269
Shows the successful rehabilitation of mentally retarded subjects in the field of agricultural work. Shows the detailed use of sports activities in teaching coordination, self - confidence, learning to work in a group and independence.
Agriculture; Psychology
Dist - USNAC **Prod** - USSRS 1972

Ore Genesis 25 MIN
VHS / 16mm
Earth's Physical Resources Series
Color (S)
$200.00 purchase _ #236205
Presents a global view of the earth's resource potential. Features footage filmed in Britain, Europe and North America. 'Ore Genesis' examines various classical types of ore deposits in Cornwall, England. Offers a variety of theoretical explanations for the genesis of the ore deposits in Cornwall.
Geography - World; History - World; Science - Physical; Social Science
Dist - ACCESS **Prod** - BBCTV 1984

Orefus and Julie 7 MIN
16mm
Color
Expresses feelings of danger and happiness through modern ballet and animation. Performed by Sorella Englund and Eske Holm of the Royal Danish Ballet.
Fine Arts
Dist - AUDPLN **Prod** - RDCG

Oregon 60 MIN
VHS
Portrait of America series
Color (J H C G)
$99.95 purchase _ #AMB37V
Visits Oregon and offers extensive research into the state's history. Films key locations and presents segments on its history, government, education, folklore, science, journalism, sociology, industry, agriculture and business. Shows what is unique about Oregon and what is distinctive about its regional culture and how it got to be that way. Includes teacher study guides. Part of a 50 - part series.
Geography - United States; History - United States
Dist - CAMV **Prod** - TBSESI 1993
TBSESI

Oregon History for New Oregonians 60 MIN
VHS / U-matic / BETA
Color (J H C G T A)
Shows pivotal themes and events in American and Pacific Northwest history shot at locations carefully chosen to correlate with historically significant places in Oregon, Washington, and Idaho. Includes precontact Indians, exploration by sea and land, the inland fur trade, the work of missionaries to the Pacific Northwest, the Oregon Trail, early pioneer settlement, and Oregon statehood.
History - United States
Dist - OREGHS **Prod** - OREGHS 1987

An Oregon Message 24 MIN
VHS / U-matic
Color
Features Oregon poet William Stafford. Uses actors, documentary footage, old historical stills, animation and a sound track of poetry music and interviews.
Fine Arts; Geography - United States; History - United States; Industrial and Technical Education; Literature and Drama
Dist - MEDIPR **Prod** - MEDIPR 1977

Oregon Scenics 13 MIN
16mm
Travelbug Series
Color
Shows the Columbia River Highway, trip up Mt Hood to Timberline Lodge and Crater Lake National Park.
Geography - United States
Dist - SFI **Prod** - SFI

Oregon Territory 15 MIN
16mm / U-matic / VHS
United States Expansion Series
Color (J H)
$420 purchase - 16 mm, $250 purchase - video _ #5723C
Discusses the debate over slavery, the exploration of Lewis and Clark, and the establishment of Catholic and Methodist missions. A Donald Klugman Communication production.
History - United States
Dist - CORF

The Oregon Trail 25 MIN
16mm / U-matic / VHS
B&W (I J H) (SPANISH)
Dramatizes the experiences of a family migrating to Oregon in a wagon train. Stresses the hardships of the journey, the long treks under the prairie sun, the dangerous river crossing, the threat of Indian attack and the punishing climb into the mountains.
History - United States
Dist - EBEC **Prod** - EBEC 1956

The Oregon Trail 31 MIN
U-matic / VHS / 16mm
Color (I A)
LC 76-700054
Recounts the period of migration westward on the Oregon Trail and the experiences of the pioneers who made the journey.
History - United States
Dist - PHENIX **Prod** - WHITEJ 1975

The Oregon Trail 32 MIN
16mm / U-matic / VHS
Color
Describes the travels of 19th century pioneers over the Oregon Trail.
Geography - United States; History - United States
Dist - KAWVAL **Prod** - KAWVAL

The Oregon Trail 32 MIN
VHS
Color (I J)
$89.00 purchase _ #RB839
Traces the history of the Oregon Trail.
Geography - United States; History - United States
Dist - REVID **Prod** - REVID

Oregon Trail 15 MIN
U-matic / VHS
Stories of America Series
Color (P)
Spins a couple of adventures of Moses the cat who traveled the Oregon Trail by wagon train.
History - United States
Dist - AITECH **Prod** - OHSDE 1976

Oregon Woodcarvers 24 MIN
U-matic / VHS
Color
Explores the works, lives and philosophies of four very different Oregon wood artists. Portrays Ed Quigley, Douglas MacGregor, Gary Hauser and Roy Setzoil.
Biography; Fine Arts; Geography - United States
Dist - MEDIPR **Prod** - MEDIPR 1980

Oregon Work 30 MIN
U-matic / VHS
Color
Features Dave Vincent, owner of a small mill in Philomath, Oregon, discussing how he made a profit while fulfilling his responsibility to the community. Examines the practice and attitudes of corporate responsibility in general.
Biography; Business and Economics; History - United States; Sociology
Dist - MEDIPR **Prod** - MEDIPR 1982

Oregon's ocean 28 MIN
VHS / U-matic
Color (J H)
$280.00, $330.00 purchase, $50.00 rental
Records the rugged coast of the United States Pacific Northwest with its own unique ecology and climate. Documents the various tidal and sub - tidal zones, the industries, the controversies and the concerns of this geographic niche.
Geography - United States; Science - Natural; Science - Physical
Dist - NDIM **Prod** - OSU 1991

Orel Hershiser on excellence 30 MIN
VHS
Color (J H A)
$29.95 purchase _ #HSV7259V
Features Los Angeles Dodgers pitcher Orel Hershiser speaking on excellence and how to achieve it. Suggests that setting realistic goals, establishing priorities, and practice are essential to achieving excellence. Discusses overcoming obstacles and failures through persistence, concentration, patience, and commitment to a cause.
Physical Education and Recreation; Science - Natural
Dist - CAMV

Orel Hershiser on excellence 25 MIN
VHS
Color (J H C G A R)
$14.99 purchase _ #35 - 83604 - 533
Features Los Angeles Dodgers pitcher Orel Hershiser in a discussion of excellence. Interviews Betsy King, Bobby Jones and others on achieving excellence in daily life.
Physical Education and Recreation; Religion and Philosophy
Dist - APH **Prod** - WORD

The Oresteia
U-matic / VHS
Color
Presents a performance of The Oresteia trilogy, classical Greek tragedy by Aeschylus.
Literature and Drama
Dist - FOTH **Prod** - FOTH

Orfeo Ed Euridice 127 MIN
VHS
Color (S)
$39.95 purchase _ #833 - 9278
Discloses that Dame Janet Baker chose Sir Peter Hall's staging of 'Orfeo Ed Euridice' by Gluck for her farewell to the operatic stage. Features also Elizabeth Gale and Elisabeth Speiser, with Raymond Leppard conducting the Royal Philharmonic Orchestra. A Glyndebourne production.
Fine Arts; Geography - World
Dist - FI **Prod** - NVIDC 1987

Orff - a music education program 58 MIN
VHS
Key changes - a seminar for music educators series
Color (T A PRO)
$69.95 purchase _ #1263 - 0005
Presents part four of a 13 - part telecourse for music educators seeking renewal of their certification. Combines lecture and discussion of Orff, a music education program.
Education; Fine Arts
Dist - SCETV **Prod** - SCETV 1990

The Organ Builders of Bethnal Green 25 MIN
16mm
Color (H A)
$400.00 purchase, $45.00 rental
Focuses on Noel Mander and Son in London's East End where craftsmen work in ways unchanged through the centuries to construct organs.
Fine Arts
Dist - AFA **Prod** - CCGB 1980

Organ Donation 19 MIN
U-matic / VHS
Color (C)
$249.00, $149.00 purchase _ #AD - 1460
Focuses on the network of organ donation through a transplant program. Shows the stages involved in organ transplantation. The computer room manager of a transplant program explains how donated organs are matched with suitable recipients and what difficulties are encountered in getting the organ to the recipient.
Health and Safety; Science - Natural
Dist - FOTH **Prod** - FOTH

Organ donation - a dilemma for black Americans 13 MIN
VHS / U-matic
Color (PRO C G)
$195.00 purchase _ #C911 - VI - 061
Reveals that the need for organs to be used for transplatation far outweighs the supply. Discloses that Afro - Americans in particular suffer a high incidence of kidney failure but seem reluctant to donate organs. Addresses fears and misinformation concerning organ donation. Interviews people who have received organs and those who are waiting. Presented by Transplantation Service, University Hospital, State University of New York at Stony Brook and Howard University Transplant Center, Washington, DC.
Health and Safety; History - United States
Dist - HSCIC

Organ Transplants 19 MIN
U-matic / VHS
Color (C)
$249.00, $149.00 purchase _ #AD - 1461
Focuses on the transplanting of organs and on the body's acceptance or rejection of the new organ. Explains the process of rejection. Shows a heart transplant, including the removal of the heart from the donor and its placement into the recipient.
Health and Safety; Science - Natural
Dist - FOTH **Prod** - FOTH

Organelles in Living Plant Cells 26 MIN
U-matic / VHS / 16mm
Color (H C)
LC FIA65-545
Shows the appearance and behavior of all organelles that can be resolved by the phase and dark - field microscope, such as nuclei, chloroplasts, golgi bodies and kinoplasm. Discloses the interactions between the organelles and cytoplasmic network.

Science - Natural
Dist - UCEMC **Prod** - KAHANA 1965

Organic Chemical Processes 60 MIN
VHS
Systems Operations Series
Color (PRO)
$600.00 - $1500.00 purchase _ #COOCP
Introduces some of the more common chemical processes used in the manufacture of organic chemicals. Examines alcohol manufacture, hydrogenation, alkylation, halogenation and polymerization. Includes ten textbooks and an instructor guide to support four hours of instruction.
Education; Industrial and Technical Education; Psychology; Science - Physical
Dist - NUSTC **Prod** - NUSTC

Organic chemistry laboratory techniques series
Presents three parts on organic chemistry lab techniques. Discusses distillation and infrared spectroscopy in Part I, recrystallization, melting point determination and extraction in Part II, and chromatography in Part III.
Organic chemistry laboratory techniques - Videotape I 45 MIN
Organic chemistry laboratory techniques - Videotape II 45 MIN
Organic chemistry laboratory techniques - Videotape III 45 MIN
Dist - AMCHEM

Organic Chemistry Laboratory Techniques Series
Presents a nine - part series which covers the essential theory and procedures for a particular technique, stressing safety and equipment care. Includes the titles Simple Distillation, Fractional Distillation, Recrystallization, Melting Point Determination, Extraction, Column Chromatography, Thin Layer Chromatography, Gas Chromatography and Infrared Spectroscopy. Produced by the UCLA Office of Instructional Development.
Column chromatography 15 MIN
Extraction 13 MIN
Fractional Distillation 20 MIN
Infrared Spectroscopy 16 MIN
Melting Point Determination 17 MIN
Recrystallization 21 MIN
Simple Distillation 12 MIN
Thin Layer Chromatography 13 MIN
Dist - UCEMC

Organic chemistry laboratory techniques - Videotape I 45 MIN
VHS
Organic chemistry laboratory techniques series
Color (C PRO)
$495.00 purchase _ #V - 3001 - 11981
Discusses simple distillation, fractional distillation and infrared spectroscopy. Part one of three parts on organic chemistry lab techniques.
Science; Science - Physical
Dist - AMCHEM

Organic chemistry laboratory techniques - Videotape II 45 MIN
VHS
Organic chemistry laboratory techniques series
Color (C PRO)
$495.00 purchase _ #V - 3002 - 1199X
Discusses recrystallization, melting point determination and extraction. Part two of three parts on organic chemistry lab techniques.
Science; Science - Physical
Dist - AMCHEM

Organic chemistry laboratory techniques - Videotape III 45 MIN
VHS
Organic chemistry laboratory techniques series
Color (C PRO)
$495.00 purchase _ #V - 3003 - 12007
Discusses column chromatography, thin layer chromatography and gas chromatography. Part three of three parts on organic chemistry lab techniques.
Science; Science - Physical
Dist - AMCHEM

Organic chemistry 1 - the carbon connection 60 MIN
VHS
Concepts in science - chemistry series
Color; PAL (J H)
PdS29.50 purchase
Begins with a look at the structure of carbon and investigates the properties of carbon and some of its uses in fuels, plastics, and industry. Uses computuer animation to illustrate bonding and reaction at a molecular level. Divided into six 10 - minute concepts - Carbon the Compromiser; The Shape of Carbon; Carbon Bonding; Fixing Fuels; Polyethylene; and Harvest of Enzymes. Part of a six - part series.
Industrial and Technical Education; Science; Science - Physical
Dist - EMFVL **Prod** - TVOTAR

Organic chemistry 2 - industrial applications 60 MIN
VHS
Concepts in science - chemistry series
Color; PAL (J H)
PdS29.50 purchase
Uses 3 dimensional animation to show how the molecules and properties of compounds lend themselves to a wide variety of industrial applications. Looks at a number of synthetic compounds. A sequel to Organic Chemistry 1. Divided into six 10 - minute concepts - Fibres; Soaps; Glues; ASA; Cosmetics; and Life after Chemistry. Part of a six - part series.
Industrial and Technical Education; Science; Science - Physical
Dist - EMFVL **Prod** - TVOTAR

An Organic Chemist's Introduction to Polymer Chemistry 180 MIN
VHS / U-matic
Color
Aimed at chemists who have not had polymer science but have had undergraduate organic and physical chemistry. It is a very broad introduction to polymer chemistry.
Industrial and Technical Education; Science - Physical
Dist - UNKNWN

Organic evolution 60 MIN
VHS
Concepts in science - biology series
Color; PAL (J H)
PdS29.50 purchase
Traces the development of various theories of evolution. Begins with the Biblical account of creation, then goes on to discuss Darwin, Mendel, the Hardy - Weinberg law and more. Divided into six ten - minute concepts - In the Beginning; Darwin, Naturally; Facturing in Mendel; The Meiotic Mix; The Population Picture; and Mutation and All That. Part of a six - part series.
Science; Science - Natural
Dist - EMFVL **Prod** - TVOTAR

Organic evolution series
Darwin naturally 10 MIN
Factoring in Mendel 10 MIN
In the Beginning 10 MIN
The Meiotic Mix 10 MIN
Mutation and all that 10 MIN
The Population picture 10 MIN
Dist - TVOTAR

Organic Farming 20 MIN
16mm
Color (H C A)
$400 purchase, $50 rental
Examines the development of organic farming in response to concerns about the effects of chemicals used to grow our food.
Agriculture
Dist - CNEMAG **Prod** - DOCUA 1988

Organic Farming - Can it Feed the Multitudes 20 MIN
U-matic / VHS / 16mm
Color
Describes the battle between those people who advocate the total use of organic farming and those that insist that only the use of chemicals can produce as much food as is needed.
Agriculture
Dist - CNEMAG **Prod** - DOCUA

Organic Farming in the South Bronx 15 MIN
U-matic / VHS / 16mm
One Second Before Sunrise - Search for Solutions, Program 1 Series
Color (J)
$110.00, $85.00 purchase, $25.00 rental
Describes efforts by South Bronx residents and other individuals to maintain a greenhouse and herb farm in the South Bronx.
Agriculture; Business and Economics; Civics and Political Systems; Psychology; Science - Natural; Social Science
Dist - BULFRG **Prod** - HCOM 1990

Organic Functional Groups 20 MIN
U-matic
Chemistry 102 - Chemistry for Engineers - Series
Color (C)
Introduces the structure, nomenclature and basic properties of the main organic functional groups, mentioning ways in which this knowledge is applicable in solving practical problems.
Industrial and Technical Education; Science - Physical
Dist - UILL **Prod** - UILL 1984

Organic Gardening - Composting 11 MIN
U-matic / VHS / 16mm
Color
LC 72-703391
Explains the role compost plays in natural life processes. Includes demonstrations of how to build a compost heap, samples of different types of composts piles and bins, what materials can go into the heap and how compost can be used as a natural fertilizer.
Agriculture
Dist - BULFRG **Prod** - RPFD 1972

Organic Mental Disorders 30 MIN
VHS / U-matic
Psychiatry Learning System, Pt 2 - Disorders Series
Color (PRO)
Deals with organic brain syndromes (section one). Covers all other organic mental disorders, related to aging and drug consumption.
Psychology
Dist - HSCIC **Prod** - HSCIC 1982

The Organic vampire 7 MIN
16mm
Color (G)
$20.00 rental
Examines Melvin the vampire who repents and becomes a vegetarian. Deals with his uncontrollable lust for blood.
Fine Arts
Dist - CANCIN **Prod** - DEGRAS 1973

Organism 20 MIN
U-matic / VHS / 16mm
Color (J A)
LC 75-704189
Studies urbanization, in which the structure of cities is compared to living tissus. Shows traffic arteries as the bloodstream circulating through the urban body and skyscrapers as the skeletal structure.
Sociology
Dist - PHENIX **Prod** - HARH 1975

Organiverse 8 MIN
16mm
Color
LC 76-703252
Presents a visual interpretation of the miracle called life, embracing art, science, religion and philosophy.
Fine Arts; Religion and Philosophy; Science - Natural
Dist - CANFDC **Prod** - CANFDC 1975

Organization 31 MIN
VHS / U-matic
Quality Planning Series
Color
Discusses typical organizational arrangements and responsibilities for a quality - control function.
Business and Economics; Industrial and Technical Education
Dist - MIOT **Prod** - MIOT

Organization and Mechanics of Writing 35 MIN
16mm
B&W
LC FIE60-115
Explains techniques used to develop good paragraphs and ideas. Shows how to organize a paper, arrange the words in proper order and punctuate.
English Language
Dist - USNAC **Prod** - USAF 1959

Organization and Planning 12 MIN
U-matic / VHS
Color
LC 84-706399
Shows how to plan a day's work by preparing a list of tasks to be done, establishing priorities, and keeping the work area neat.
Psychology
Dist - USNAC **Prod** - USSS 1983

Organization at the top 29 MIN
16mm
Government story series; No 24
Color
LC 79-707179
Traces the history of the changing roles of the Vice President and the President's Cabinet, and discusses the role of the Cabinet as an administrative tool. Examines the creation and growth in importance of the White House office.
Civics and Political Systems
Dist - WBCPRO **Prod** - WBCPRO 1968

Organization Development Series Module 1
The Well Being of the Organization 59 FRS
Dist - RESEM

Organization Development Series Module 3
What is Organization Development? 61 FRS
Dist - RESEM

Organization Development Series Module 4
Getting Started in OD 16 MIN
Dist - RESEM

Organization development series
Presents four modules on organizational development. Includes the titles The Well - Being of the Organization, Approaches to Organizational Development, What Is Organization Development, Getting Started in OD.
Approaches to organization development 62 FRS

Organization development series 61 MIN
Dist - RESEM **Prod** - RESEM 1968

Organization for hazmat emergencies 79 MIN
VHS
Color (A)
$645.00 purchase
Presents a three - step process for organizing a response to a hazardous materials crisis before one occurs and ensuring compliance with federal laws and national standards. Includes three videos, Hazards Analysis, The Emergency Plan and Exercises.
Business and Economics; Education; Sociology
Dist - COMFLM

The Organization in Transition 45 MIN
U-matic / VHS
Information Resource Management - Challenge for the 1980s Series
Color
Discusses the forces that are affecting organizations and the information explosion they must deal with. 60 - 010.
Industrial and Technical Education
Dist - DELTAK **Prod** - DELTAK

Organization is strategic - Volume II 30 MIN
VHS
What America does right series
Color (G C PRO)
$795.00 purchase, $225.00 rental
Presents the second part of two parts drawing from the book What America Does Right by Bob Waterman. Offers two corporate examples showing why organizational arrangement is a most powerful strategic tool.
Business and Economics; Industrial and Technical Education; Psychology
Dist - FI **Prod** - ENMED 1995

Organization - Key to Air Power 17 MIN
16mm
Color
LC FIE58-266
Shows the basic principles of organization and their application to various types of Air Force activities. Stresses the need for organizational methods that will insure a quick - striking air force.
Civics and Political Systems
Dist - USNAC **Prod** - USDD 1957

Organization of African Unity 28 MIN
Videoreel / VHS
International Byline Series
Color
Presents an up - date on the present situation in Africa. Includes an interview with Ambassador Dramane Ouattara, Executive Secretary of the Organization of African Unity.
Business and Economics; Civics and Political Systems; Geography - World
Dist - PERRYM **Prod** - PERRYM

The Organization of Language 33 MIN
16mm
Principles and Methods of Teaching a Second Language Series
B&W (H T) (ENGLISH, GERMAN)
Discusses pre - school children's use of form and arrangements of words. Explains that these forms and arrangements constitute the organization or grammar of language. Uses a German class for English speakers to show how to teach grammatical patterns and variations.
Education; English Language
Dist - IU **Prod** - MLAA 1961

Organization of the Body 15 MIN
16mm
B&W (J H C G)
Surveys the skeletal, muscular, vascular, respiratory, excretory, endocrine and nervous systems of the human body. Places emphasis on the interdependence of these systems and their collaboration in the life of the body as a whole.
Science - Natural
Dist - VIEWTH **Prod** - GBI

Organization of the logistics function 30 MIN
VHS
Business logistics series
Color (G C)
$200.00 purchase, $20.50 rental _ #34981
Discusses organization of the logistics function. Part of a 30 - part series on business logistics which deals with movement and storage of raw and finished products, and with managerial activities important for effective control of these operations. Interviews logistics managers of major US corporations and transportation companies. Uses on - site segments to demonstrate logistical carrier operations. Features program author Dr John Coyle.
Business and Economics
Dist - PSU **Prod** - WPSXTV 1987

Organization - Organizacion 29 MIN
VHS / 16mm
Sonrisas Series
Color (T P) (ENGLISH & SPANISH)
$46.00 rental _ #SRSS - 119
Shows why the children choose to organize the Carriage House into a Neighborhood Center. In Spanish and English.
Sociology
Dist - PBS

Organization - Stations, Everyone 30 MIN
U-matic / VHS
Reading is Power Series no 3
Color (T)
LC 81-707518
Uses interviews and candid classroom scenes to show how innovative teachers are designing and organizing their classrooms in order to enhance learning and reading comprehension.
English Language
Dist - GPN **Prod** - NYCBED 1981

Organizational Climate 27 MIN
16mm / VHS
#109066 - 5 3/4
Looks at the concept of organizational climate - the way employees percieve their workplace. Examines the environment - related factors that affect employee performance, and offers techniques that any manager can use to improve the climate within a work group or organization.
Business and Economics
Dist - MGHT

Organizational Communication 30 MIN
VHS / U-matic
Business of Management Series Lesson 12; Lesson 12
Color (C A)
Looks at the kinds of information passed through organization channels, and barriers that can occur along the way. Features leaders from various companies discussing techniques used by their organizations.
Business and Economics; Psychology
Dist - SCCON **Prod** - SCCON

Organizational Development 30 MIN
16mm / U-matic / VHS
Management Development Series
Color (C A)
LC FIA68-3170
Applies behavioral science to organizational aims. Demonstrates organizational development technology in the context of cultural change within an organization.
Business and Economics
Dist - UCEMC **Prod** - UCLA 1968

Organizational Goal - Planning 29 MIN
16mm
Management by Objectives Series
B&W (IND)
LC 70-703325
Business and Economics; Psychology
Dist - EDSD **Prod** - EDSD

Organizational learning series
Presents two parts on organizational learning. Features Peter M Senge in Transforming the Practice of Management and Jay W Forrester in Systems Thinking in Education - Remaining Competitive in the 21st Century.
Jay W Forrester - Systems thinking in education - remaining competitive in the 21st century 90 MIN
Peter M Senge - Transforming the practice of management 60 MIN
Dist - PEGASU **Prod** - PEGASU

Organizational patterns 30 MIN
VHS / U-matic
Effective listening series; Tape 6
Color
Shows how to recognize structure and organize while listening.
English Language
Dist - TELSTR **Prod** - TELSTR

Organizational Quality Improvement Series
Charting activities and processes
Comparing costs and benefits
Getting Started
Improving Processes
Introduction to Organizational Quality Improvement
Looking at Processes
Problem Solving
Putting it all Together
Quality Circles
Using Industrial Statistics
Dist - BNA

Organizational Transactions Series
Competition and conflict 30 MIN
Customer transactions 30 MIN
The Opportunity for Leadership 30 MIN
Planning and Control 30 MIN
Problem - solving and decision - making 30 MIN
Time, the most Precious Resource 30 MIN
Dist - PRODEV

Organizational vision, values and mission 21 MIN
VHS
Captioned; Color (A PRO)
$495.00 purchase, $150.00 rental
Promotes determining personal goals and values in the context of the workplace. Helps an organization's leaders articulate a motivating statement of vision for the company and then build dedication to the goal.
Business and Economics; Guidance and Counseling; Psychology
Dist - DHB EXTR **Prod** - CRISP 1994

The Organizations 27 MIN
16mm / U-matic / VHS
Five Billion People Series
Color
Examines the rules which govern the operation of all contemporary financial institutions, including local, national or international, and considers some of the implications of their growing power.
Business and Economics
Dist - CNEMAG **Prod** - LEFSP

Organize 15 MIN
16mm
B&W
Shows an organizing project in Appalachia that is helping the people fight the destructive effects of strip mining.
Business and Economics; Science - Natural; Sociology
Dist - CANWRL **Prod** - CANWRL

Organize your job search - adult version
VHS
Job search - adult version series
Color (A G)
$89.00 purchase _ #JW3015V
Shows how to cut job search time in half. Part of a five - part series on job searches for adults.
Business and Economics; Guidance and Counseling
Dist - CAMV **Prod** - JISTW 1991

Organized Brain 5 MIN
16mm
Color
LC FIA68-783
Accompanies a man on a journey through his mind as he describes the memories and images he has filed away there.
Psychology
Dist - HENASS **Prod** - HENASS 1968

Organized Mosquito Control 16 MIN
16mm
Color
LC FIE55-328
Shows a sampling to determine the species of mosquitoes, their relative abundance and types of breeding places. Demonstrates dipping for larvae to determine major problem areas. Discusses breeding sites as determinants of flight ranges. Shows three common methods of mosquito abatement and five big problem areas.
Health and Safety
Dist - USNAC **Prod** - USPHS 1955

The Organizers - Careers in Business Office 13 MIN
16mm
Working Worlds Series
Color (I J H)
LC 75-701548
Explores the variety of careers available in businesss and office services.
Guidance and Counseling; Psychology
Dist - FFORIN **Prod** - OLYMPS 1974

Organizing
VHS / U-matic
Essentials of Management Series Unit III; Unit III
Color
Concentrates on the vital technique of organizing through delegation. Teaches managers to use their own talents and the talents of others for maximum effectiveness.
Business and Economics; Psychology
Dist - AMA **Prod** - AMA

Organizing 12 MIN
U-matic / VHS
Management of Work Series Module 3
Color
Examines the structural and social aspects of organizing and some of the problems and decisions associated with them.
Business and Economics; Psychology
Dist - RESEM **Prod** - RESEM

Organizing 50 MIN
U-matic / VHS
Effective Writing Series
Color
English Language; Psychology
Dist - DELTAK **Prod** - TWAIN

Organizing a Group 15 MIN
VHS / U-matic
By the People Series
Color (H)
Discusses various individual roles which can help or hinder the group process.
Civics and Political Systems; Social Science
Dist - CTI **Prod** - CTI

Organizing a new society 28.40
U-matic / VHS
Meeting will come to order series
(G)
Combines narration and dramatization to explain the basics of parliamentary procedure. Follows the revised Robert's Rules of Order. Written by the Members of the National Association of Parliamentarians. Focuses on organization. Sixth in a six part series.
Civics and Political Systems; English Language
Dist - GPN **Prod** - NETV 1983

Organizing a Year's Program 29 MIN
VHS / U-matic
Teaching Writing - a Process Approach Series
Color
Presents guidelines to make a long - range plan and goals and identifies characteristics of a successful writing assignment.
Education; English Language
Dist - PBS **Prod** - MSITV 1982

Organizing America - the history of trade unions
VHS
Color (H C A IND PRO)
$89.95 purchase
Outlines the history of the labor union movement in the United States from the 18th Century until modern times. Looks at the issues behind labor strife and the struggle workers faces as technology changes the workplace. Useful for both workers and management in negotiating the challenges presented by a globalized, high-technology economy.
Business and Economics; Social Science
Dist - CAMV

Organizing and advising partnerships and joint ventures 165 MIN
Cassette
(PRO)
$70.00, $125.00 purchase, $55.00 rental - #BU - 54173, #BU - 64173
Instructs how to interview clients who want to form a business; protect the partnership name; identify responsibilities of partners; draft agreements; structure financing arrangements; allocate profits and losses; and more. Includes handbook.
Business and Economics; Civics and Political Systems
Dist - CCEB **Prod** - CCEB 1991

Organizing and counseling closely held corporations 330 MIIN
VHS
(PRO)
$97.00, $175.00 purchase, $69.00 rental _ #BU-53132, #BU-63132
Presents information about forming, running, and ending private corporations in California, with details on types of corporations and the financing, tax, management, and legal questions pertaining to them. Includes a 548-page handbook.
Civics and Political Systems
Dist - CCEB

Organizing and Planning for Results 64 FRS
VHS / U-matic
Improving Managerial Skills Series
Color
Offers some practical steps for organizing and planning and shows some examples for typical job situations. Examines difference between procrastination and simply deciding not to decide.
Business and Economics; Psychology
Dist - RESEM **Prod** - RESEM

Organizing Business Writing 67 FRS
U-matic / VHS
Business Writing Skills Series
Color
Presents seven basic rules of organization and offers examples of proper and improper application in organizing business writing.
English Language; Psychology
Dist - RESEM **Prod** - RESEM

Organizing classrooms 30 MIN
VHS
Effective teacher telecourse series
Color (T)
$69.95 purchase, $50.00 rental
Outlines classroom organization strategies. Hosted by Dr Loren Anderson.
Education; Psychology
Dist - SCETV **Prod** - SCETV 1987

Organizing Course Content 15 MIN
VHS / 16mm
Focus on Adult Learners Series
Color (C)
$150.00 purchase _ #270603
Combines dramatizations of teaching situations, interviews with exemplary adult instructors, footage of adult education classrooms and voice - over narration. Includes a print support manual which summarizes the key points of each program, recommends further reading and assigns exercises for both individual and group use. 'Organizing Course Content' reveals that a well - organized instructor enhances the learning process. Identifies the steps in getting organized - updating knowledge of subject area, completing a pre - class needs assessment and identifying course content. Covers a plan for setting lessons.
Education; Guidance and Counseling; Mathematics; Psychology
Dist - ACCESS **Prod** - ACCESS 1987

Organizing for Change 29 MIN
VHS / 16mm
About Women Series
Color (S)
$250.00 purchase _ #678605
Examines issues raised by the women's movement. Focuses on matters crucial to an understanding of the position of women in contemporary society. Four main topics are considered - the personal and domestic sphere, economic and work - related issues, women's health and well - being, and the politics and strategies of working for change. 'Organizing For Change' reveals that fundamental changes in attitude and law through the conventional political structure have been slow. As a result, women have moved out of the mainstream locally, nationally and internationally in order to achieve progress in the areas of world peace, and to eliminate racism and poverty and the other disadvantages of a patriarchal value system.
Civics and Political Systems; Guidance and Counseling; Sociology
Dist - ACCESS **Prod** - ACCESS 1986

Organizing for Power - the Alinsky Approach Series
Through Conflict to Negotiation 47 MIN
Dist - FI

Organizing for Successful Project Management 30 MIN
VHS / 16mm
Project Management Series
Color (PRO)
$400.00 purchase, $100.00 rental
Includes Project Characteristics, Process of Project Management, A Systems Approach, Project Life Cycle and Major Organizational Structures. Part of a six - part series on project management.
Business and Economics; Industrial and Technical Education; Psychology
Dist - ISA **Prod** - ISA

Organizing for Successful Project Management 30 MIN
U-matic / VHS
Project Management Series
Color
Describes the process of project management. Discusses a systems approach. Identifies major organizational structures.
Business and Economics; Psychology
Dist - ITCORP **Prod** - ITCORP

Organizing Free Play 20 MIN
16mm
Head Start Training Series
B&W (J)
LC FIE-101
Shows that free play in nursery school is neither helter - skelter chaos nor regimented uniformity, but a crucially important segment of the day when children may choose among a variety of carefully prepared activities. Presents scenes from a dozen Head Start and other pre - school centers to show how a teacher organizes and supervises such a program and what it means to children as a curriculum of discovery.
Education; Sociology
Dist - NYU **Prod** - VASSAR

Organizing Free Play 22 MIN
16mm
B&W (T S R)
LC FIE67-101
Focuses on the facet of early childhood education called free play.
Education
Dist - USNAC **Prod** - USOEO 1967

Organizing Ideas 30 MIN
U-matic / VHS
Writing for Work Series Pt 5
Color (A)
LC 81-706738
Presents basic writing skills for office workers, emphasizing the importance of organizing ideas. Describes various ways of organizing ideas, such as chronological, inductive and deductive. Hosted by Cicely Tyson.
Business and Economics; English Language
Dist - TIMLIF **Prod** - TIMLIF 1981

Organizing knowledge by deduction 47 MIN
16mm
Teaching high school mathematics - first course series; No 31
B&W (T)
Mathematics
Dist - MLA **Prod** - UICSM 1967

Organizing Lesson Content 15 MIN
VHS / 16mm
Focus on Adult Learners Series
Color (C)
$150.00 purchase _ #270604
Combines dramatizations of teaching situations, interviews with exemplary adult instructors, footage of adult education classrooms and voice - over narration. Includes a print support manual which summarizes the key points of each program, recommends further reading and assigns exercises for both individual and group use. 'Organizing Lesson Content' demonstrates organizing lesson plans according to learner needs. Plans should outline subtopics, time allotments for each topic and learning objectives. Identifies a method of accommodating different learning styles - TELL, SHOW and DO - and shows how to incorporate the methods into lesson plans. Introduces the ROPES - Review, Overview, Presentation, Exercise and Summary - model for lesson planning.
Education; Guidance and Counseling; Mathematics; Psychology
Dist - ACCESS **Prod** - ACCESS 1987

Organizing - Making it all Happen 28 MIN
VHS / U-matic
Management Skills for Nurses Series
Color
Examines the uses and misuses of authority, and emphasizes a clear chain of command.
Guidance and Counseling; Health and Safety
Dist - AJN **Prod** - INTGRP

Organizing, Operating, and Terminating Closely Held Corporations 240 MIN
VHS / U-matic / Cassette
Color; Mono (PRO)
Looks at changes in the tax and securities laws, conflicts of interest, relaxed requirements for corporations and planning for liquidity. Emphasizes both state and federal securities law issues.
Business and Economics; Civics and Political Systems
Dist - CCEB **Prod** - CCEB

Organizing Pointers 30 MIN
U-matic / VHS
Drafting - Piping Pointers Series
Color (IND)
Industrial and Technical Education
Dist - GPCV **Prod** - GPCV

Organizing - Structuring the Work of the Plan 20 MIN
U-matic / VHS
Supervisory Management Course, Pt 1 Series Unit 3
Color
Defines organization, reviews its purposes and outlines ways to organize subordinates for maximum productivity.
Business and Economics; Psychology
Dist - AMA **Prod** - AMA

Organizing Technical Activities 30 MIN
U-matic / VHS
Management for Engineers Series
Color
Business and Economics; Industrial and Technical Education; Psychology
Dist - SME **Prod** - UKY

Organizing the Reading Environment 29 MIN
U-matic / VHS / 16mm
Teaching Children to Read Series

Color
Examines the premise that experiences which encourage language growth can and should be so organized that they can happen any time a student wants or needs them, not only during a daily reading period. Includes numerous documentary tips for the teacher.
Education; English Language
Dist - FI **Prod** - MFFD 1975

Organizing - the Road to Dignity 40 MIN
U-matic
Color (H)
Describes the beginning of an organizing drive with union advocates trying to persuade other workers to join the union, followed by the signing of cards and the election, and finally bargaining for a contract.
Business and Economics; Sociology
Dist - AFLCIO **Prod** - UFOOD 1984

Organizing the speech 28 MIN
U-matic / BETA / VHS
Communication skills 1 - basic series
Color (H C G)
$101.95, $89.95 purchase _ #CA - 44
Addresses the four methods of delivery, identifies the major parts of a speech and suggests approaches to content, audience attention and speech conclusion. Part of a series on communication.
English Language; Social Science
Dist - INSTRU

Organizing - the Structuring Function
U-matic / VHS
Principles of Management Series
Color
$150.00 purchase _ #P5107
Differentiates between the various types of organizational structures. Describes the delegation process and the relationship of authority, responsibility and accountability.
Business and Economics; Psychology
Dist - RMIBHF **Prod** - RMIBHF

Organizing unions - the Catholic perspective 9 MIN
16mm / VHS
Color (G IND)
$5.00 rental
Quotes Pope John Paul II - 'Unions are good for working people,' to look at the tradition of support for labor within the Roman Catholic Church. Focuses primarily on the career of Monsignor George Higgins, a priest worker for the rights of labor and working people, who expresses his strong support for unions throughout his interview. Produced by the Department of Organizing and Field Services, AFL - CIO.
Business and Economics; Religion and Philosophy; Social Science
Dist - AFLCIO **Prod** - AFLCIO 1989

Organizing your job search - the key to getting a good job fast
VHS
JIST job search series
Color (H A T)
$89.00 purchase _ #JW3004
Covers five major points in organizing a job search - organizing time to schedule more interviews, developing a basic job search schedule, having written weekly and daily plans, documenting employer contacts and following up all prospects. Part of a five - part series.
Business and Economics; Guidance and Counseling; Psychology; Social Science
Dist - AAVIM **Prod** - JISTW 1992

Organizing Your Time 31 MIN
U-matic / VHS
Personal Time Management Series
Color
Business and Economics
Dist - DELTAK **Prod** - TELSTR

Organizing Your Work and Others' Work 30 MIN
U-matic / VHS
Personal Time Management Series
Color
Discusses short and long range details of time organization. Covers bi - weekly agenda and 12 month calendar.
Business and Economics; Psychology
Dist - TELSTR **Prod** - TELSTR

Organizing Your Writing Course 31 MIN
VHS / U-matic
Process - Centered Composition Series
Color (T)
LC 79-706296
Shows how to organize a composition course around a nine - step writing process, including the editing process, the use of journals and specifics on structuring a syllabus.
English Language
Dist - IU **Prod** - IU 1977

Organophosphate Pesticide Poisonings - Diagnosis and Treatment 20 MIN
16mm
Color
LC 74-705271
Shows that a correct diagnosis of organophosphate poisoning and proper treatment can save lives.
Health and Safety
Dist - USNAC **Prod** - NMAC 1969

Organs of Special Sense - Pt 1 - Eye 45 MIN
VHS / U-matic
Histology review series
Color (PRO)
Reviews the major histological and functional features of the eye, as well as its accessory structures (including eyelids, conjunctiva, and lacrimal, sebaceous, and Meibomian glands).
Health and Safety; Science - Natural
Dist - HSCIC **Prod** - HSCIC

Organs of Special Sense - Pt 2 - the Ear 25 MIN
U-matic / VHS
Histology review series
Color (PRO)
Covers the structure and histology of the external, middle, and inner ear.
Health and Safety; Science - Natural
Dist - HSCIC **Prod** - HSCIC

Orgasmic expulsions of fluid in the sexually stimulated female 9 MIN
16mm / VHS
Color (C A)
$190.00, $125.00 purchase, $50.00 rental
Examines the issue of whether or not women ejaculate during orgasm. Depicts the expulsion of fluid from the female urethra and describes its nature as 'semen without sperm' as opposed to urine. Describes the Grafenberg Spot within the vagina which seems to trigger orgasm when stimulated and shows how to locate it. Explicit. Produced by Beverly Whipple.
Health and Safety; Science - Natural; Sociology
Dist - FCSINT **Prod** - FCSINT 1981

Orgasmic Expulsions of Fluid in the Sexually Stimulated Female 9 MIN
U-matic / VHS
Color (C A)
Depicts the event of orgasmic expulsions of fluid in the sexually stimulated female. Examines examples of beginning evidence of the existence of a yet to be fully explained sexual function and/or anatomical feature.
Health and Safety; Psychology; Sociology
Dist - MMRC **Prod** - MMRC

The Orient
CD-ROM
(G A)
$249.00 purchase _ #2701m
Offers the first volume of the Interactive Travel Encyclopedia. Covers the region's 16 countries - Brunei, Cambodia, China, Hong Kong, Indonesia, Japan, Laos, Macau, Malaysia, North Korea, Philippines, Singapore, South Korea, Taiwan, Thailand and Vietnam, and 42 major cities. For Macintosh Plus, SE and II Computers. Requires at least one M of RAM, one floppy disk drive, and an Apple compatible CD - ROM drive.
Geography - World
Dist - BEP

Orient express 62 MIN
VHS
Chronicle travel library series
Color (G)
$29.95 purchase
Takes viewers on a ride on the Orient Express, the train that runs from Paris to Istanbul. Presents side tours to Reims, Salzburg, Vienna, and the Transylvanian countryside.
Geography - World
Dist - PBS **Prod** - WNETTV

Orient - Occident 30 MIN
VHS / U-matic
World of Islam Series
Color
Shows the influence that Islam has had on the Western world by causing the crusades, strongly influencing the cultures of Spain, Sicily and Southern France, and providing concepts of chivalry and courtly love.
Religion and Philosophy
Dist - FOTH **Prod** - FOTH 1984

Oriental Art 30 MIN
VHS / U-matic
Antique Shop Series
Color
Presents guests who are experts in their respective fields who share tips on collecting and caring for antique Oriental art.
Fine Arts
Dist - MDCPB **Prod** - WVPTTV

Oriental brush painting 30 MIN
VHS
Color (G)
PdS19.95 purchase _ #A4-ARG09
Demonstrates Oriental brush painting, including creating flowing lines and delicate strokes. Shows beginners how to manipulate the bruch and pigment. Features Kit Nicol.
Fine Arts
Dist - AVP **Prod** - ARGUS

An Oriental journey 50 MIN
VHS
Color (G)
$19.95 purchase _ #S01459
Takes viewers to various sites in Thailand and Burma, including Buddhist temples, rivers, floating markets, and more.
Geography - World; Religion and Philosophy
Dist - UILL

The Oriental mind and the modern world 45 MIN
35mm strip / VHS
Western man and the modern world series - Unit VIII
Color (J H C T A)
$102.00, $102.00 purchase _ #MB - 510374 - 5, #MB - 510303 - 6
Examines the Orient and its response to the modern world. Shows that in some ways, the region has resisted change even as it has led change in other areas. Focuses on China.
Geography - World; History - World
Dist - SRA

The Oriental Mind and the Modern World 45 MIN
U-matic / Kit / VHS
Western Man and the Modern World in Video
Color (J H)
$1378.12 the 25 part series _ #C676 - 27347 - 5, $89.95 the individual
Draws parallels between ancient and modern China to demonstrate inherent unity under apparent dissimilarities. Highlights the influence of religious belief on social custom, reaction to foreign invasion and commercial exploitation, and the widespread civil upheavals of the last two centuries.
History - World; Sociology
Dist - RH

Oriental Rugs 30 MIN
VHS / U-matic
Antique Shop Series
Color
Presents guests who are experts in their respective fields who share tips on collecting and caring for antique Oriental rugs.
Fine Arts
Dist - MDCPB **Prod** - WVPTTV

Oriental Vegetables 30 MIN
BETA / VHS
Victory Garden Series
Color
Explores the Protea Gardens in Hawaii. Features bok choy and chinese greens. Shows how to plant pumpkins, beans and lettuce.
Agriculture; Physical Education and Recreation
Dist - CORF **Prod** - WGBHTV

Orientation 29 MIN
Videoreel / VT2
Discover Flying - Just Like a Bird Series
Color
Industrial and Technical Education; Social Science
Dist - PBS **Prod** - WKYCTV

Orientation and Indoctrination of Safe Workmen 27 MIN
16mm
Color
LC 74-705272
Follows a group of new employees through pre - employment testing, hiring and actual working situations. Highlights job safety and the value of accident prevention training for all employees.
Health and Safety; Psychology
Dist - USNAC **Prod** - USBM 1961

Orientation and Training 30 MIN
VHS / U-matic
You - the Supervisor Series
Color (PRO)
Explores the task of orientating a new employee into the company and training him to do the job. Introduces the principles of learning, which must be observed in the industrial setting.
Business and Economics; Guidance and Counseling; Psychology
Dist - DELTAK **Prod** - PRODEV

The Orientation Express 14 MIN
16mm / VHS
Color (G)

$400.00, $175.00 purchase, $45.00 rental
Animates cut - out images spanning three decades of Life Magazine's version of the feminine mystique. Features the Quaker Oats man, Colonel Saunders and the Kool - Aid jug as hosts of a rocky ride through conservative morality and pompous patriarchy. Produced by Frances Leeming.
Business and Economics; Fine Arts; Industrial and Technical Education; Literature and Drama; Psychology; Social Science; Sociology
Dist - WMEN **Prod** - FL 1988

The Orientation Film
VHS
Color (A)
$34.95 purchase _ #6901
Explores issues of chemical dependency during treatment.
Education; Guidance and Counseling; Health and Safety; Psychology; Sociology
Dist - HAZELB

Orientation for the medical staff II 31 MIN
VHS
Color (C PRO G)
$500.00 purchase
Trains health care workers and medical staff in chemical dependency orientation. Features Dr David Ohlms who emphasizes the physiological and genetic aspects of addiction disease, common behaviors and histories, laboratory and history red flags, techniques of intervention, referral and successful case management.
Guidance and Counseling; Health and Safety; Psychology
Dist - FMSP

Orientation of New Workers, Pt I of Styles of Supervision 45 MIN
U-matic / VHS
B&W
Demonstrates two contrasting types of supervision in role plays depicting a new worker meeting with his/her super - visor for the first time. Deals with some of the employees' initial fears.
Business and Economics; Guidance and Counseling; Psychology
Dist - UWISC **Prod** - UWISC 1977

Orientation of the camera 11 MIN
VHS
Lessons in visual language series
Color (PRO G C)
$99.00 purchase, $39.00 rental _ #752
Shows how humans orient themselves in space through a combination of what they see and other physiological cues. Reveals that moving images lack these cues and that special effects must be made to provide the viewer with a sense of balance and equilibrium. Considers how moving images can be used to deliberately disturb and challenge the physiological equilibrium of the viewer. Features Peter Thompson as creator and narrator of a ten - part series on visual language. Produced by the Australian Film, Television and Radio School.
Industrial and Technical Education; Social Science
Dist - FIRLIT

Orientation - planning and anticipating - Parts 1 and 2 60 MIN
U-matic / VHS
French in action - part I series
Color (C) (ENGLISH AND FRENCH)
$45.00, $29.95 purchase
Introduces the French in Action series in Part 1, the only program in English. Covers salutations, health, expressing surprise, decisiveness and indecisiveness, planning, anticipating, subject pronouns, the gender of adjectives, articles, future tenses, gender and number agreement, 'aller,' 'etre,' present indicative of ' - er' verbs in Part 2. Parts of a 52 - part series teaching the French language, all in French, written by Pierre Capretz, Director of the Language Laboratory at Yale.
Foreign Language; History - World
Dist - ANNCPB **Prod** - YALEU 1987

Orientation to ABE 30 MIN
U-matic / VHS
Basic Education - Teaching the Adult Series
Color (T)
Gives an overview of adult basic education.
Education
Dist - MDCPB **Prod** - MDDE

Orientation to Civil Service Reform - a Discussion of the Highlights 31 MIN
U-matic
Launching Civil Service Reform Series
Color
LC 79-706275
Outlines the development of the Civil Service Reform Act and highlights its major provisions.
Civics and Political Systems
Dist - USNAC **Prod** - USOPMA 1978

Orientation to Communication Methods in the Metal Fabricating Industries 20 MIN
VHS / BETA
Color (IND)
Discusses the importance of proper communications in the various metal fabricating industries and the different methods used.
Industrial and Technical Education; Social Science
Dist - RMIBHF **Prod** - RMIBHF

Orientation to Communication Skills I 14 MIN
BETA / VHS
English and Speech Series
Color
English Language
Dist - RMIBHF **Prod** - RMIBHF

Orientation to Course - Misconceptions about Shakespeare - Elizabethan Life, no 1 45 MIN
Videoreel / VT2
Shakespeare Series
B&W (C)
Literature and Drama
Dist - GPN **Prod** - CHITVC

Orientation to multimedia 30 MIN
VHS
Multimedia series
Color (C T PRO)
$79.95 purchase
Provides an overview of a five - part series on multimedia technology as a new learning tool hosted by news anchor Joan Stafford. Covers different aspects of multimedia and the merger between video, print and the computer industries. Discusses what multimedia means and how to apply it to the learning environment. Examines the future direction and the growth of the medium.
Education
Dist - AECT

Orientation to Sexuality of the Physically Disabled 39 MIN
U-matic
Sexuality and Physical Disability Series
Color
Introduces the seven - part series. Discusses several assumptions and objectives basic to the sexuality and disability sex education and treatment program at the University of Michigan.
Health and Safety; Psychology
Dist - UMITV **Prod** - UMITV 1976

An Orientation to the Audit Process 29 MIN
U-matic
Color (PRO)
LC 79-707717
Suggests ways of formulating guidelines for setting up an audit committee and explains why an orientation is essential for all audit committee members. Emphasizes the importance of encouraging peer discussion during the audit process.
Health and Safety
Dist - UMMCML **Prod** - UMICHM 1977

Orientation to the Sexuality of Physical Disability 40 MIN
U-matic / VHS
Sexuality and Physical Diability Video Tape Series
Color (C A)
Discusses assumptions and objectives basic to disability sex education and treatment programs.
Health and Safety; Psychology
Dist - MMRC **Prod** - MMRC

Orientation to the Use of Crutches 6 MIN
8mm cartridge / 16mm
Color
LC 75-702037; FIE67-11
Shows the fitting of underarm crutches, the tripod principles, and crutch walking. Emphasizes the disadvantages of ill - fitting crutches and the manipulation of crutches on stairs.
Health and Safety; Science - Natural
Dist - USNAC **Prod** - USPHS 1965

Orientation to Volunteerism 27 MIN
U-matic / VHS
Color
Presents an overview of volunteerism. Includes the historical context of volunteers, the motivation for volunteering, society's need for volunteers, various types of volunteer activities and the management of volunteers. Shows the problems and potential of working with volunteers.
Psychology; Social Science
Dist - PSU **Prod** - PSU 1984

Orienteering 30 MIN
VHS / BETA
Great Outdoors Series
Color
Describes the Scandinavian sport of orienteering. Features the wilderness of Minnesota's Boundary Waters and the temples of Katmandu.
Physical Education and Recreation
Dist - CORF **Prod** - WGBHTV

Orienteering 10 MIN
16mm / U-matic / VHS
Color (J H A)
LC 77-700889
Explains the sport of orienteering in which contestants must travel a course as quckly as possible, choosing the routes by map and compass. Pictures scenes from the first Canadian orienteering championship in Guelph, Ontario.
Physical Education and Recreation
Dist - IFB **Prod** - CRAF 1969

Orienting students 30 MIN
VHS
Effective teacher telecourse series
Color (T)
$69.95 purchase, $50.00 rental
Discusses the most effective ways of orienting students to the classroom. Hosted by Dr Loren Anderson.
Education; Psychology
Dist - SCETV **Prod** - SCETV 1987

Orifice Plates and Orifice Fittings 24 MIN
U-matic / VHS
Color (IND)
Describes the types of plates and fittings most commonly used and gives instructions for proper installation.
Business and Economics; Industrial and Technical Education; Social Science
Dist - UTEXPE **Prod** - UTEXPE

Origami 9 MIN
16mm
Color (I J A)
LC 70-707940
Demonstrates the ancient art of paper folding. Suggests many shapes and figures that can be conjured out of colored paper.
Fine Arts
Dist - NFBC **Prod** - NFBC 1970

Origami for kids 60 MIN
VHS
Color (P I J G)
$24.95 purchase _ #MET211V - K
Teaches children how to fold paper into insects, pigeons, swans, cranes, frogs, Christmas tree ornaments, hats, coin purses, party favors, ornate refrigerator magnets, a super jet plane and more.
Fine Arts
Dist - CAMV

Origami - Free Form 12 MIN
16mm
Color (I J)
LC 74-702299
Describes the simple basics of free - form origami and demonstrates the variety of forms and animals which can be made using the diamond base and kite base.
Fine Arts; Geography - World
Dist - DANREE **Prod** - DANREE 1974

Origami - Geometrical Form 10 MIN
16mm
Color (J H)
LC 74-702300
Presents origami expert Wendy Mukai demonstrating the construction of a variety of three - dimensional figures, flowers and designs using the geometrical blintz base.
Fine Arts; Geography - World; Mathematics
Dist - DANREE **Prod** - DANREE 1974

Origami - the Folding Paper of Japan 16 MIN
16mm
Color
Looks at origami, the ancient art of Japanese paper folding.
Fine Arts; Geography - World; History - World
Dist - MTP **Prod** - MTP

Origin and Accumulation of Oil and Gas 15 MIN
VHS / U-matic
Color (A PRO IND)
$180.00 purchase _ #14.1360
Presents a comprehensive introductory lesson on the natural process of how oil and gas form and become trapped in rock layers.
Industrial and Technical Education; Science - Physical; Social Science
Dist - UTEXPE **Prod** - UTEXPE 1983

Origin and Development of NATO - 1945 - 1990 - 10 20 MIN
VHS
Geography in US History Series
Color (H)
Features the geographic concept of regions. Reviews the US world view and military and economic alliances that developed out of World War II. Foreign policy decisions of Presdient Truman and the role of George Kennan are considered, and the changing role of NATO in 1989 as new relations develop between the Superpowers. Part 10 of a ten - part series which emphasizes the study of American geography within the context of American history courses using geographic concepts.

Biography; Civics and Political Systems; Geography - United States; History - United States; History - World
Dist - AITECH **Prod** - AITECH 1991

The Origin and Evolution of Life 145 MIN
U-matic
University of the Air Series
Color (J H C A)
$750.00 purchase, $250.00 rental
Talks on the evolution and development of self replicating molecules through the invertebrates and faunas of Paleozoic seas. Program contains a series of five cassettes 29 minutes each.
Science - Physical
Dist - CTV **Prod** - CTV 1974

The Origin and History of Program Budgeting 25 MIN
16mm
B&W
LC 74-705273
Traces the history of planning - programming - budgeting (PPB) and describes the fundamentals of the system.
Business and Economics; Mathematics; Sociology
Dist - USNAC **Prod** - USCSC 1970

Origin and Synthesis of Plastics Materials 16 MIN
16mm
Plastics Series no 1
B&W
Explores the organic origin of plastics and the resemblance of synthetic compounds to natural substances. Shows how plastics are made and typical uses for them.
Industrial and Technical Education; Science - Physical
Dist - USNAC **Prod** - USOE 1945

Origin of Cellular Life 46 MIN
U-matic / VHS
Color (H C)
$43.95 purchase _ #52 1213A
Introduces the hypothesis regarding the steps in the origin of life. Discusses synthesis of various kinds of organic molecules, and presents hypotheses for the origin of prokaryotic and eukaryotic cells. Video version of 35mm filmstrip program, with live open and close.
Science - Natural
Dist - CBSC **Prod** - BMEDIA

Origin of Land Plants - Liverworts and Mosses 14 MIN
U-matic / VHS / 16mm
Biology Series Unit 6 - Plant Classification and Physiology; Unit 6 - Plant classification and physiology
Color (H) (SPANISH)
Traces the evolution of land plants and illustrates the structural characteristics, reproductive processes and adaptive mechanisms of liverworts and mosses. Photomicrography, macrophotography and animated drawings are used.
Science - Natural
Dist - EBEC **Prod** - EBEC 1963

The Origin of Life 28 MIN
16mm / VHS
Origins - How the World Came to be Series
Color (H)
LC 90712079
Relates a creationist viewpoint of the origins of human life. Explores questions of DNA and cell biology.
Education; Fine Arts; Religion and Philosophy; Sociology
Dist - EDENF

The Origin of life 21 MIN
U-matic / VHS / 16mm
Cosmos series; Edited version
Color (J H C)
Points out that the cells of people, trees, fish, or bacteria are all similar because they are all descended from ancestral molecules which arose from the oceanic soup during the earth's infancy. Presents Dr Carl Sagan who recreates the experiment of Miller and Urey in which the environment of the primitive earth is reproduced in a laboratory flask.
Science - Natural
Dist - FI **Prod** - SAGANC 1980

Origin of Life
VHS / U-matic
Color
Science - Natural
Dist - MSTVIS **Prod** - MSTVIS

Origin of Life 25 MIN
U-matic / VHS / 16mm
Color
LC 70-715060
Uses animated diagrams, cinemicrography and narration to illustrate the organization and development of the living cell. Examines the structure, atomic components and characteristics of the four major categories of organic compounds. Shows the growth of organic compounds from the primitive elements of methane, ammonia and water, and pictures the development of the more complex and efficient cell that utilized oxygen and evolved into more intricate and varied forms of life.
Science - Natural; Science - Physical
Dist - MEDIAG **Prod** - WILEYJ 1971

Origin of life 60 MIN
VHS
Color (J H)
$75.00 purchase _ #A5VH 1277
Provides an historical understanding of Darwinian theory. Illustrates the different stages of animal and human development from the beginnings of fossil history. Presents actual footage of the Scopes trial with Clarence Darrow and William Jennings Bryan.
Religion and Philosophy; Science - Natural; Science - Physical
Dist - CLRVUE **Prod** - CLRVUE

The Origin of Life - Chemical Evolution 12 MIN
16mm / U-matic / VHS
Biology Series Unit 10 - Evolution; Unit 10 - Evolution
Color; B&W (SPANISH)
LC 71-704175
Describes evidence supporting the evolution of life in the Primordial Sea and traces the evolution of life from the molecular level to the present.
Science - Natural
Dist - EBEC **Prod** - EBEC 1969

The Origin of Rocks and Mountains 13 MIN
U-matic / VHS / 16mm
Evolution of Life Series
Color (I)
LC FIA67-5875
Explains how various natural phenomena affect the formation of the earth's interior and surface structures.
Science - Physical
Dist - MGHT **Prod** - HALAS 1968

The Origin of species 13 MIN
VHS
Color (J H)
$39.95 purchase _ #49 - 8257 - V
Features Franciso J Ayala. Explains how species arise. Illustrates both geographic and quantum speciation. Still frame.
Science - Natural
Dist - INSTRU **Prod** - CBSC

Origin of the crown dance - an Apache narrative and Ba'ts'oosee - an Apache trickster 40 MIN
U-matic / VHS
Words and place series
Color (APACHE (ENGLISH SUBTITLES))
Apache with English subtitles. Shows an Apache elder telling a story of a boy who became a gaan, a supernatural being with curative powers.
Literature and Drama; Social Science
Dist - NORROS **Prod** - NORROS

The Origin of the drama and the theater 24 MIN
VHS
Color (G C H)
$129.00 purchase _ #DL477
Uses photographs and illustrations to trace the development of Greek drama from religious festivals honoring the gods. Explains how vulgar jests evolved into sophisticated comedies, and how hymns developed into tragedies. Discusses acting technique, costuming, and design of the early Greek theater. Examines the role of theater in ancient Greek society.
Fine Arts; History - World; Religion and Philosophy
Dist - INSIM

The Origin of the Elements 18 MIN
U-matic / VHS / 16mm
Physical Science Film Series
Color (C A)
LC 73-701094
Explores the five major processes instrumental in the formation of all the elements in the universe. Explains the evolution of the universe and the birth, life and death of stars.
Science - Physical
Dist - CRMP **Prod** - CRMP 1973

The Origin of the modern mind
VHS / Cassette
Color (C A)
$149.95, $89.95 purchase _ #AI - B453
Presents eight lectures which examine the philosophical foundations set down by great 17th century thinkers - Bacon, Descartes, Locke, Newton, Pascal. Features Prof Alan Charles Kors of the University of Pennsylvania as lecturer.
History - World; Religion and Philosophy
Dist - TTCO **Prod** - TTCO

Origin of the Moon 5 MIN
U-matic / VHS / 16mm
Color (I J)
LC 76-708048
Discusses the how the earth and its moon may have begun about five billion years ago in a cloud of cold gases.
Science - Physical
Dist - PHENIX **Prod** - CBSTV 1970

Origin of Weather 26 MIN
U-matic / VHS / 16mm
Conquest Series
B&W (J)
Explains the elemental forces behind weather and some new theories of its origin. Delves into the creation and effects of storms, calms and freak weather. Shows how cloud formations develop and demonstrates new electronic methods of determining weather.
Science - Physical
Dist - CAROUF **Prod** - CBSTV 1960

The Original Adventures of Betty Boop 30 MIN
16mm
B&W
Features three cartoon favorites, including Betty Boop, Henry and The Little King.
Fine Arts
Dist - FCE **Prod** - FCE 1986

Original cast album - Company 53 MIN
35mm / 16mm
Color (G)
Chronicles the eighteen and a half hour marathon recording session of the landmark Stephen Sondheim - George Furth - Harold Prince musical comedy entitled Company. Contact distributor for price.
Fine Arts
Dist - OCTOBF

Original cocaine babies series
Cocaine babies - the innocent victims 18 MIN
Training tape for caretakers of drug babies 20 MIN
Dist - VISIVI

The original dance instrument series - the dance instrument 27 MIN
16mm
Dance experience series
Color (A G)
$28.95 rental _ #243 - 28294
Explores the movement, range, and creative possibilities for the various body parts, and presents to teachers and students a usable technique and vocabulary for dance communication. Demonstrates the conceptual roots and motivations of modern dance. Produced by the Athletic Institute. Conceived and choreographed by Lynda Davis with Nancy Smith Fichter as a consultant.
Fine Arts; Physical Education and Recreation
Dist - AAHPER **Prod** - AAHPER 1975

The Original fairy tale - Cinderella
CD-ROM
Discis Books on CD - ROM
(P) (SPANISH)
$69.00 purchase _ #2557
Contains text and illustrations of the Cinderella tale. Enhances understanding with real voices, music, and sound effects. Every word in the text has an in - context explanation, pronunciation and syllables, available through a click of the mouse. Spanish - English version available for an extra $5 per disc. For Macintosh Classics, Plus, II and SE computers, requires 1MB of RAM, one floppy disk drive, and an Apple compatible CD - ROM drive.
English Language; Literature and Drama
Dist - BEP

Original issue newsreel series
International news no. 27 10 MIN
Mutual weekly no. 109 10 MIN
Selig Tribune no. 21 10 MIN
Dist - KITPAR

Original pain - 2 39 MIN
VHS / U-matic
Healing families - life's journey home series
Color (G)
$249.00 purchase _ #7476
Aids viewers in the recognition of lost childhood, abuse, neglect or trauma. Examines and discusses roles unconsciously acted out by members of dysfunctional families. Explores the five developmental stages of childhood, including personality growth, emotional well - being and the groundwork for healthy self - esteem. Part of a five - part series hosted by Art Linkletter.
Health and Safety; Psychology; Sociology
Dist - VISIVI **Prod** - VISIVI 1991

The Originals 15 MIN
16mm
Color
LC 77-702488
Presents the 1976 Dr Pepper radio advertising campaign. Shows six musicians singing and performing their own arrangements of the Dr Pepper song in recording sessions.

Business and Economics; Fine Arts; Psychology
Dist - COMCRP **Prod** - DRPEP 1976

Originals Series
Alice Walker - Pt 1 30 MIN
Beate Klarsfeld - Pt 5 30 MIN
Dr R Adams Cowley - Pt 4 30 MIN
George Melly 30 MIN
Gloria Steinem - Pt 2 30 MIN
Hoyt Axton - Pt 3 30 MIN
Dist - FI

Originals - women in art series
Alice Neel - collector of souls 30 MIN
Dist - AFA

Originals - women in art series
Anonymous was a woman 30 MIN
Dist - AFA
FI

Originals - women in art series
Mary Cassatt - Impressionist from Philadelphia 30 MIN
Dist - ARTSAM
CAMV
FI

Originals - Women in Art Series
Frankenthaler - toward a New Climate 30 MIN
Georgia O'Keeffe 60 MIN
Georgia O'Keeffe, Pt 1 30 MIN
Georgia O'Keeffe, Pt 2 30 MIN
Nevelson in Process 30 MIN
Spirit catcher - the art of Betye Saar 28 MIN
Dist - FI

Origins 7 MIN
16mm
Color (H C A)
LC 79-700126
Presents a tongue - in - cheek look at the origins of life on a distant planet.
Fine Arts
Dist - USC **Prod** - USC 1978

Origins - 1 20 MIN
U-matic / VHS / BETA
Religion and civilisation series
Color; PAL (G H C)
PdS40, PdS48 purchase
Conducts a search for clues of humankind's earliest religious feeling and the light this sheds on prehistoric life. Features part of a two - part series exploring religions within their individual traditions. Produced in Britain by Charles Harris.
Religion and Philosophy
Dist - EDPAT

The Origins and development of European Marxism 60 MIN
VHS
Europe and America in the modern age - 1776 to the present series
Color (H C PRO)
$95.00 purchase
Presents a lecture by James Sheehan. Focuses on a critical period in European and American history and on leaders of the time. Part of a 20 - part series that looks at the last two centuries in Europe and America. Series presents lectures by David M Kennedy and James Sheehan of Stanford University on such figures as Adam Smith, Marx, Lincoln, Washington, Jefferson, Freud, Margaret Sanger, Susan B Anthony and Jane Adams and their impact on the events of their day. For history resource material and continuing education courses.
Civics and Political Systems; History - United States; History - World
Dist - LANDMK

Origins and Evidence 58 MIN
U-matic / VHS / 16mm
Crossroads of Civilization Series
Color (A)
Discusses the sudden emergence of the Persian Empire under the leadership of Cyrus the Great. Portrays Darius's founding of the Achaemenian dynasty in which mankind moved from primitive to civilized society.
History - World
Dist - CNEMAG **Prod** - CNEMAG 1978

Origins and Influences of Ethnic Dance 30 MIN
U-matic / VHS
Third World Dance - Tracing Roots Series
Color
Fine Arts; Industrial and Technical Education; Sociology
Dist - ARCVID **Prod** - ARCVID

Origins - How the World Came to be Series
The Fossil record 30 MIN
The Origin of Life 28 MIN
The Origins of Mankind 29 MIN
Dist - EDENF

The Origins of Art in France - Neolithic 400 A D 40 MIN
16mm
B&W
Discusses the origins of art in France from the Neolothic period to 400 A D.
Fine Arts; History - World
Dist - ROLAND **Prod** - ROLAND

Origins of black theater 15 MIN
VHS
Panorama of African - American theater series
Color (G C H)
$99.00 purchase _ #DL482
Traces the development of African - American theater from the 1820s to the present. Part of a series.
Fine Arts; History - United States; Sociology
Dist - INSIM

The Origins of Change 20 MIN
VHS / U-matic
Evolution Series
Color
Discusses the functions of DNA and recapitulates the evidence for evolution.
Science - Natural; Science - Physical
Dist - FOTH **Prod** - FOTH 1984

Origins of liturgical drama 35 MIN
VHS
Color (C A)
$149.00 purchase _ #DF321
Uses a live performance of a 13th - century Easter play from the manuscript Visitatio Sepulchri to examine the genre of liturgical drama used to teach about events in the Bible. Offers photographs of medieval paintings amd recitations of liturgical texts of the period to trace the development of the drama from the 10th century through the mystery cycles of the 14th and 15th centuries.
Literature and Drama
Dist - INSIM

Origins of Man 30 MIN
16mm
B&W (H C A)
Dr William White Howells, Professor of Anthropology at Harvard University, presents the latest findings and theories on the origins of man. Visits Harvard's Peabody Museum, showing its large collection of fossils. Points out that many of the most important discoveries about the early forerunners of man have been made in the last twenty years.
History - World; Science - Natural; Sociology
Dist - IU **Prod** - NET 1967

Origins of man series
From homo erectus to neanderthal 18 MIN
Dist - FI

The Origins of Mankind 29 MIN
16mm / VHS
Origins - How the World Came to be Series
Color (H)
LC 90712083
Suggests that evolutionary theories of human evolution from ape - like creatures may not be valid. Casts doubt on missing link theories and discusses differences between humans and primates. Emphasizes a creationist viewpoint.
Education; Fine Arts; Religion and Philosophy; Sociology
Dist - EDENF

Origins of Mental Illness 27 MIN
VHS
Color (J H)
Reveals the major causes of mental illness in America. Explores genetic defects, poor personality development, environmental stress, and sociological and cultural influences.
Health and Safety; Psychology
Dist - HRMC **Prod** - HRMC 1978

Origins of the Cold War
16mm / VHS
Archive series
B&W; PAL (G)
PdS280, PdS55 purchase
Presents eight newsreel items including the Yalta Conference, February, 1945; Churchill's 'Iron Curtain' speech, March, 1946; Gen George Marshall testifying to Congress, November, 1947; the Berlin blockade and war in Korea. Includes a substantial accompanying booklet. Uses material compiled by Peter Boyle.
History - World; Sociology
Dist - BUFVC **Prod** - BUFVC

Origins of the Constitution
CD-ROM
Color (J H C G)
$50.00 purchase _ #CLE5019MCD - S, #CLE5019BCD - S
Allows students to see and hear how personalities, philosophies and political realities contributed to the making of the Constitution. Teaches about the American Revolution, the Articles of Confederation, the Constitution, the Declaration of Independence, the Federalist Papers and the Declaration of Rights. Includes optional quizzes on vocabulary and comprehension; scores can be printed or saved to a Class Manager system on the disk. Available for Macintosh or IBM - compatible computers. Consult with distributor for hardware requirements.
Civics and Political Systems; History - United States
Dist - CAMV

Origins of the Motion Picture 21 MIN
16mm
B&W (J)
LC FIE55-252
A historical record of the development of the machinery and arts of the motion picture, from the earliest suggestions of Leonardo da Vinci to the perfected sound motion picture of Edison.
Fine Arts; History - World
Dist - USNAC **Prod** - USN 1955

Origins of the motion picture 20 MIN
VHS
Color (J H C)
$39.95 purchase _ #IVMC23
Expands on the history and development of the motion picture, dating back to the 11th century. Shows how the concept of the motion picture developed through the steps of persistence of vision, designing the apparatus, transparent photography and motion. Discusses the earliest development of film - Leonardo da Vinci's 'camera obscura' and Leon Straford's zoopraxiscope. Includes old film clips dating back to the Cuban War and to the invention of kintographic theater by Edison.
Fine Arts; Industrial and Technical Education; Sociology
Dist - INSTRU

Origins of the Universe 28 MIN
U-matic / VHS
Video Encyclopedia of Space Series
Color (C)
$249.00, $149.00 purchase _ #AD - 2107
Introduces briefly the geocentric view of the universe and the contributions of Kepler and Galileo. Moves on to explain the Big Bang theory. Covers the concepts of galaxies, Hubble and the 'red - shift,' quasars, red giants, white dwarfs, supernovas and neutron stars. Part of an eleven - part series on space.
Industrial and Technical Education; Science - Physical
Dist - FOTH **Prod** - FOTH

Origins - Retracing Man's Steps 28 MIN
VHS / 16mm
Color (H)
$21.50 rental _ #34818
Surveys the records of man's past. Highlights the cave paintings at Lascaux that show the rise of symbolic thinking, the change in larynx placement that documents the development of speech, and the evidence that reveals the time when bones became digging tools and weapons. Hosted by Christopher Reeves, narrated by William Conrad.
English Language; Fine Arts; History - World
Dist - PSU **Prod** - BBC 1987

Origins Series
The Big bang and beyond 26 MIN
Can Man Survive 28 MIN
The Mutation Machine 26 MIN
Retracing Man's Steps 28 MIN
Dist - FOTH

Orion 15 MIN
U-matic / VHS
Strawberry Square II - Take Time Series
Color (P)
Fine Arts
Dist - AITECH **Prod** - NEITV 1984

The Orissa Dombs 25 MIN
16mm / U-matic / VHS
Untamed World Series Series
Color; Mono (J H C A)
$400.00 film, $250.00 video, $50.00 rental
Explains the Hindu religion and cultural effects seen in the Dombs of the Orissa province.
Religion and Philosophy; Sociology
Dist - CTV **Prod** - CTV 1973

Orissa - the Land and the People 19 MIN
16mm
B&W (I)
Shows the rich tradition in temple architecture which can be seen in Bhubaneshwar, Puri and Konarak. Explains how Orissa takes pride in its Rourkella steel complex and Hirakud Dam. Documents the old and new Orissa.
Geography - World; History - World
Dist - NEDINF **Prod** - INDIA

Orlando and Kissimmee - St Cloud, Florida 30 MIN
VHS / 16mm
Color (H C G)

$29.95 purchase _ #TVC102
Describes the vacation attractions of Florida, such as Walt Disney World, Epcot Center, Sea World, Circus World, Medieval Times and others. Includes Florida's lakes, wild life sanctuaries, and gator farms.
Geography - United States
Dist - RMIBHF **Prod** - RMIBHF

Orlando Furioso 206 MIN
VHS
Color (G)
$39.95 purchase _ #ORL01
Presents the San Francisco Opera production of Orlando Furioso by Vivaldi which was based on an epic poem by Ariosto. Stars American mezzo - soprano Marilyn Horne in the title role, Susan Patterson as Angelica and Kathleen Kuhlman as Alcina.
Fine Arts
Dist - HOMVIS **Prod** - RMART 1990

The Orlando Story 22 MIN
16mm
Color
LC 74-706550
Shows construction of the Navy's newest training facility, a campus - like school where recruits learn to become sailors.
Civics and Political Systems; Industrial and Technical Education
Dist - USNAC **Prod** - USN 1972

Ormosia Inn 100 MIN
VHS
Color (G) (MANDARIN CHINESE (ENGLISH SUBTITLES))
$45.00 purchase _ #6006A
Presents a Mandarin Chinese language movie produced in the People's Republic of China.
Fine Arts; Geography - World; Literature and Drama
Dist - CHTSUI **Prod** - CHTSUI

Ornamentals 10 MIN
16mm
Color (G)
$30.00 rental
Juxtaposes light and rhythm, dream and image, color and composition. Employs intentional overload of shots to enhance theme of rhythm of the body, nerve and mind.
Fine Arts
Dist - CANCIN **Prod** - CHILDA 1979

The Ornette Coleman trio 26 MIN
VHS
B&W (G)
$24.95 purchase
Showcases the talents of Ornette Coleman, David Izenon and Charles Moffett in Ornette's trio.
Fine Arts
Dist - KINOIC **Prod** - RHPSDY

Oroville Kaleidoscope 11 MIN
16mm
Color
Presents the Oroville Dam, keystone of the California State Water Project and one of the largest earthfill dams in the world. Shows the kaleidoscope of activities that built the dam and describes the benefits the facilities provide today.
Geography - United States; Industrial and Technical Education; Science - Natural; Social Science
Dist - CALDWR **Prod** - CSDWR 1973

An Orphan Boy of Vienna 85 MIN
U-matic / VHS
B&W (GERMAN (ENGLISH SUBTITLES))
Tells the story of an orphan boy who meets a street singer who gets him accepted by the Vienna Boys Choir. Features songs by the Vienna Boys Choir. Directed by Max Neufeld. With English subtitles.
Fine Arts; Foreign Language
Dist - IHF **Prod** - IHF

The Orphan Lions 18 MIN
U-matic / VHS / 16mm
Color (I)
LC 73-702214
Presents an edited version of the film Living Free, which documents the concern of Joy and George Adamson with the survival of the lion Elsa's cubs after her death.
Geography - World; Literature and Drama; Science - Natural
Dist - LCOA **Prod** - LCOA 1973

The Orphan trains 60 MIN
VHS
Color; CC (H C A)
$59.95 purchase _ AMEX-804-WC95; $69.95 purchase _ AMEI-804-WC95; $19.95 purchase _AMEX-904-WC95
Delves into the story of 10,000 homeless children who lived in New York City in 1853. Discusses the efforts of minister Charles Loring Brace to establish the Children's Aid Society, which sent more than 150,000 children to live in homes in 47 different states over the following 75 years.
Sociology
Dist - PBS **Prod** - GRAYE 1995

The Orphans 21 MIN
16mm / U-matic / VHS
Color (P I) (SPANISH)
LC 75-702384
Describes life on a farm for a man and four city orphans he takes in.
Guidance and Counseling; Literature and Drama; Social Science
Dist - LCOA **Prod** - SINCIN 1975

The Orphans 100 MIN
16mm
Color (H C A) (RUSSIAN (ENGLISH SUBTITLES))
LC 83-700201
Tells about a successful novelist who searches for his two brothers whom he hasn't seen since adulthood in an effort to reconstruct his own identity. Shows him discovering the value of human sympathy, passion, love and care.
Fine Arts; Foreign Language
Dist - IFEX **Prod** - MOSFLM 1980

Orphans of the Storm 126 MIN
16mm
B&W
Tells the story of two orphans, marooned in Paris, who become separated by the turbulent maelstrom that preceded the French Revolution. Reveals that one orphan is released from the Bastille and seeks to find her sister in the chaos that is the new Paris. Shows that after terrifying adventures, the orphans are finally reunited at the tribunal of Robespierre's Reign of Terror. Stars Lillian and Dorothy Gish. Directed by D W Griffith.
Fine Arts
Dist - KILLIS **Prod** - GFITH 1921

Orphans of the Storm, Pt 1 27 MIN
16mm
History of the Motion Picture Series
B&W
Presents D W Griffith's adventure of the French Revolution, the biggest film of 1921. Stars Lillian and Dorothy Gish, Monte Blue and Joseph Schildkraut.
History - World
Dist - KILLIS **Prod** - SF 1960

Orphans of the Storm, Pt 2 27 MIN
16mm
History of the Motion Picture Series
B&W
Presents D W Griffith's adventure of the French Revolution, the biggest film of 1921. Stars Lillian and Dorothy Gish, Monte Blue and Joseph Schildkraut.
History - World
Dist - KILLIS **Prod** - SF 1960

The Orphans, Pt 1 33 MIN
16mm
Color (H C A) (RUSSIAN (ENGLISH SUBTITLES))
LC 83-700201
A Russian - language film with English subtitles. Tells about a successful novelist who searches for his two brothers whom he hasn't seen since adulthood in an effort to reconstruct his own identity. Shows him discovering the value of human sympathy, passion, love and care.
Foreign Language
Dist - IFEX **Prod** - MOSFLM 1980

The Orphans, Pt 2 33 MIN
16mm
Color (H C A) (RUSSIAN (ENGLISH SUBTITLES))
LC 83-700201
A Russian - language film with English subtitles. Tells about a successful novelist who searches for his two brothers whom he hasn't seen since adulthood in an effort to reconstruct his own identity. Shows him discovering the value of human sympathy, passion, love and care.
Foreign Language
Dist - IFEX **Prod** - MOSFLM 1980

The Orphans, Pt 3 34 MIN
16mm
Color (H C A) (RUSSIAN (ENGLISH SUBTITLES))
LC 83-700201
A Russian - language film with English subtitles. Tells about a successful novelist who searches for his two brothers whom he hasn't seen since adulthood in an effort to reconstruct his own identity. Shows him discovering the value of human sympathy, passion, love and care.
Foreign Language
Dist - IFEX **Prod** - MOSFLM 1980

Orpheus 86 MIN
VHS
Orpheus trilogy series
B&W (G)
$29.95 _ #ORP010
Adapts the Orpheus and Eurydice legend. Depicts the love of the poet Orpheus for Princess Death, who travels constantly between this world and the next. The second in Cocteau's Orphic trilogy, which also includes Blood of a Poet and Testament of Orpheus.
Fine Arts; Literature and Drama; Religion and Philosophy; Sociology
Dist - HOMVIS **Prod** - JANUS 1949

Orpheus 96 MIN
16mm
B&W (FRENCH (ENGLISH SUBTITLES))
Retells the Greek legend of Orpheus, the poet whose wife Euridice was kidnapped and carried off to the underworld. Tells how he followed and rescued her, beguiling her guardians with his songs.
Fine Arts; Foreign Language; Literature and Drama; Religion and Philosophy
Dist - KITPAR

Orpheus and Eurydice 10 MIN
16mm
Color (P)
Puppet version of the classic Greek legend of the Minstrel Orpheus and his descent into Hades in quest of his lost bride, Eurydice.
Literature and Drama
Dist - SF **Prod** - VIKING 1963

Orpheus Taming the Furies 28 MIN
U-matic / VHS
Beethoven by Barenboim Series
Color (C)
$249.00, $149.00 purchase _ #AD - 1227
Views the Fourth Concerto which opens in gentle, angelic statements to explode in the second movement. Shows the piano subduing the aggressive orchestra, an effect that Franz Liszt compared to Orpheus taming the Furies. Part of a thirteen - part series placing Beethoven, his music and his life within the context of his time and the history of music, Beethoven by Barenboim.
Fine Arts; History - World
Dist - FOTH **Prod** - FOTH

Orpheus trilogy series
Blood of a poet 52 MIN
Orpheus 86 MIN
Testament of Orpheus 79 MIN
Dist - HOMVIS

Orpheus underground 40 MIN
16mm / VHS
Color (G)
$50.00 rental, $35.00 purchase
Follows an artist's interior voyage to the unknown. Depicts rape from a woman's angle of vision. Shot in New York City with Coney Island and the Lower East Side as the Underworld. Produced by Silvianna Goldsmith.
Fine Arts; Religion and Philosophy; Sociology
Dist - CANCIN

Orpheus Underground and The Transformation of Persephone 41 MIN
VHS
Color (G)
$50.00 purchase
Features two productions, 1973 - 1975, by Silvianna Goldsmith. See individual titles for description and availability for rental in 16mm format.
Fine Arts
Dist - CANCIN

Orson Welles Great Mysteries Series
Ice Storm 25 MIN
The Ingenious Reporter 25 MIN
The Inspiration of Mr Budd 25 MIN
La Grande Breteche 24 MIN
A Terribly Strange Bed 24 MIN
Dist - EBEC

Ortho video series
Basic electrical projects 60 MIN
Basic plumbing 60 MIN
Easy outdoor projects 60 MIN
Growing Beautiful Lawns 60 MIN
Growing Beautiful Roses 60 MIN
Dist - VEP

Orthodontics - a Special Kind of Dentistry 14 MIN
16mm
Color (SPANISH)
LC 73-702199
Emphasizes the importance of orthodontic treatment as a means of conserving dental health by showing the analogous relationship between ancient engineers and architects who built cities to last forever and the orthodontist who plans the functions of the teeth to last a liftime.
Health and Safety
Dist - MODVID

Orthodontics and You 25 MIN
16mm
Color (SPANISH)
LC 79-700398
Explores the orthodontic experience as seen by doctors, patients, parents and educators.
Health and Safety; Sociology
Dist - MTP **Prod** - AAORTH 1979

Orthodox Chinese Tai ji sword 108 MIN
VHS
Color (G)
$49.95 purchase _ #1153
Teaches the sword form, composed of 32 postures divided into four parts. Features Madam Wang Ji Yung. Comes with pamphlet.
Physical Education and Recreation
Dist - WAYF

Orthodox Christian Association of Medicine, Psychology and Religion 28 MIN
VHS
Illuminations series
Color (G R)
#V - 1038
Explores the possible relationship between medicine, psychology and religion in the healing process. Describes the work of the Orthodox Christian Association of Medicine, Psychology and Religion in this exploration. Considers the relationships between doctors, patients and priests.
Religion and Philosophy; Sociology
Dist - GOTEL **Prod** - GOTEL 1989

Orthodox Christianity - the Rumanian Solution 52 MIN
16mm / VHS
Long Search Series
(H C)
$99.95 each, $595.00 series
Deals with the intense beliefs of the one communist country that still actively practices religion, Rumania.
Religion and Philosophy
Dist - AMBROS **Prod** - AMBROS 1978

Orthodox Christianity - the Rumanian Solution 52 MIN
16mm / U-matic / VHS
Long Search Series no 6
Color (H C A)
LC 78-700476
Examines the relationship between the Eastern Orthodox Church and the Communist state in Rumania. Visits a number of Rumanian churches and shows how the Orthodox liturgy is conducted.
Geography - World; Religion and Philosophy; Sociology
Dist - TIMLIF **Prod** - BBCTV 1978

Orthodox Taijiquan 88 MIN
VHS
Color (G)
$49.95 purchase _ #1152
Teaches the standard 24 style simplified form in a series of 8 lessons. Designed as an introduction for beginners, it also shows some push hands and applications for intermediate and advanced practitioners. Taped in China.
Physical Education and Recreation
Dist - WAYF

Orthognathic Surgery 10 MIN
VHS / U-matic
Color
Explains what orthognathic surgery is and why it is recommended. Discusses relationship between patient, orthodontist and oral surgeon to make certain best results are obtained. Covers what to expect upon entering the hospital, surgery procedure and recovery.
Health and Safety; Science
Dist - MEDCOM **Prod** - MEDCOM

Orthogonal Functions 34 MIN
VHS / U-matic
Calculus of Linear Algebra Series
B&W
Mathematics
Dist - MIOT **Prod** - MIOT

Orthogonal Projection 12 MIN
U-matic / VHS / 16mm
College Geometry Series
Color
LC FIA66-506
Defines orthogonal projection, discusses its properties and introduces and solves a relevant geometric problem.
Industrial and Technical Education; Mathematics
Dist - IFB **Prod** - NSF 1965

Orthogonal Projection 13 MIN
U-matic / VHS / 16mm
Geometry Series
Color (H C)
Introduces an elementary transformation involving triangles transformed into a problem involving conics.
Mathematics
Dist - IFB **Prod** - UMINN 1971

Orthographic Projection - Three - View Working Drawings, Blueprints 7 MIN
VHS / BETA
Color (IND)
Explains the application of the positioning of a part for illustration on a blueprint by using a clear glass box visual aid.
Mathematics; Psychology
Dist - UNKNWN **Prod** - RMIBHF

Orthographic Projections
U-matic / VHS
Drafting - Process Piping Drafting Series
Color (IND)
Industrial and Technical Education
Dist - GPCV **Prod** - GPCV

Orthographic Projections - Drafting - Piping Familiarization
U-matic / VHS
Drafting - Piping Familiarization Series
Color (IND)
Industrial and Technical Education
Dist - GPCV **Prod** - GPCV

Orthopaedic Examination of the Lower Extremities, Pt 1 - Pelvis to Knee 16 MIN
VHS / BETA
Color (PRO)
Health and Safety; Science - Natural
Dist - UNKNWN **Prod** - RMIBHF

Orthopaedic Examination of the Lower Extremities, Pt 2 - Knee to Foot 22 MIN
VHS / BETA
Color (PRO)
Health and Safety; Science - Natural
Dist - UNKNWN **Prod** - RMIBHF

Orthopaedic nursing series
Presents a six - part series on orthopedic nursing. Includes A Look at Traction Therapy; Assessment and Care of the Patient with a Neck Immobilizer; HALO Immobilizer and Patient Care; A Look at Cast Therapy; Assessment and Care of the Patient with an External Fixator; Assessment and Care of the Patient in Continuous Passive Motion Therapy.

Assessment and care of the patient in continuous passive motion therapy - 6	60 MIN
Assessment and care of the patient with a neck immobilizer - 2	7 MIN
Assessment and care of the patient with an external fixator - 5	15 MIN
HALO immobilizer and patient care - 3	11 MIN
A Look at cast therapy - 4	9 MIN
A Look at traction therapy - 1	15 MIN

Dist - HSCIC **Prod** - UTXHSH

Orthopedic assessment 28 MIN
U-matic / VHS
Color (PRO)
$275.00 purchase, $60.00 rental _ #7509S, #7509V
Demonstrates up - to - date skills in orthopedic assessment. Illustrates how a nurse performs a thorough, well - organized assessment of a healthy adult. Shows how to examine a patient's musculoskeletal system for range of motion, muscle strength and reflexes. Techniques include inspection and palpation, measuring and grading. Includes special aspects of assessment.
Health and Safety
Dist - AJN **Prod** - HOSSN 1985

Orthopedic complications and how to handle them 30 MIN
VHS
Color (PRO C)
$285.00 purchase, $70.00 rental _ #6524
Focuses on two orthopedic complications, fat emboli and compartment syndrome. Explains the need for prompt recognition and treatment. Covers the etiology, or sequence of events in the development of each problem, the incidence of occurrence after traume and the signs and symtoms associated with each problem. Describes the diagnostic tests that can be performed to make an accurate diagnois. Stresses the need for continued awareness and prompt recognition of orthopedic complications to avoid dire results. Emphasizes accurate nursing assessment.
Health and Safety
Dist - AJN **Prod** - HESCTV

Orthopedic Procedures 15 MIN
U-matic / VHS
Color (PRO)
Presents various orthopedic procedures.
Health and Safety
Dist - WFP **Prod** - WFP

Orthopedics 50 MIN
U-matic / VHS
Attorneys' Guide to Medicine Series
Color (PRO)
Includes a brief review of basic terminology and anatomy of the skeletal system and an explanation of the considerations in selecting treatment for the benefit of attorneys.
Civics and Political Systems; Health and Safety
Dist - ABACPE **Prod** - PBI

Orthoplast Resting Splint 11 MIN
U-matic / VHS
Color (PRO)
Shows how to construct an orthoplast resting splint. Presents procedure for making a pattern, forming the splint, and adding support straps, includes tips on a preparatory procedure that makes the orthoplast easier to cut.
Health and Safety
Dist - HSCIC **Prod** - HSCIC

Ortho's Video Series

Electrical Projects and Repair	60 MIN
Lawns - Planting and Care	60 MIN
Outdoor Garden Projects	60 MIN
Roses - Planting and Care	60 MIN
Upgrading your kitchen	60 MIN

Dist - AAVIM

Os Fuzis 109 MIN
16mm
B&W (PORTUGUESE (ENGLISH SUBTITLES))
An English subtitle version of the Portuguese language film. Tells a story of suffering experienced by Brazilians during a drought. Considers the problems of maintaining law and order among starving, desperate people.
Fine Arts; Foreign Language; Social Science
Dist - NYFLMS **Prod** - NYFLMS 1963

OS - 2 for DOS users - introduction 46 MIN
VHS
Video professor operating systems series
Color (J H C G)
$29.95 purchase _ #VP138V
Introduces concepts in OS - 2 for DOS users. Allows viewer to see keyboard and monitor simultaneously so that students can see the result of every keystroke. Part of a seven - part series on operating systems.
Computer Science
Dist - CAMV

Osaka Elegy 75 MIN
VHS
Japan Film Collection from SVS Series
B&W (G) (JAPANESE (ENGLISH SUBTITLES))
$59.95 purchase _ #K0684
Presents a movie produced in Japan. Features Kenji Mizoguchi as director. Stars Isuzu Yamada.
Fine Arts; Geography - World
Dist - CHTSUI **Prod** - SONY

Osaka elegy 71 MIN
VHS
B&W (G)
$39.95 _ #OSA010
Features a candid and revealing look at discrimination against women in 1930s Japan. Chronicles the heartbreaking fall of a young telephone operator who consents to become her boss's mistress in order to support her alcoholic father and put her brother through school. Directed by Kenji Mizoguchi.
Fine Arts; Sociology
Dist - HOMVIS **Prod** - JANUS 1936

Oscar 8 MIN
VHS / U-matic
Color (J A)
Focuses on alcohol abuse problems in Black America. Filmed in the Bedford Stuyvesant area of New York City.
Health and Safety; Sociology
Dist - SUTHRB **Prod** - SUTHRB

Oscar at Home 10 MIN
16mm
Exploring Childhood Series
B&W (J)
LC 76-701892
Shows Oscar, a four - year - old, and his family at mealtime. Shows he is a member of a working - class Mexican - American family living in Texas.
Home Economics; Psychology; Sociology
Dist - EDC **Prod** - EDC 1975

Oscar at School 6 MIN
16mm
Exploring Childhood Series
B&W (J)
LC 76-701893
Shows Oscar on the playground and in class where his teacher takes a strong, directive role and alternates between speaking Spanish and English.
Education; Psychology
Dist - EDC **Prod** - EDC 1975

Oscar, Aunt Lorrie and the Top Hat 15 MIN
16mm / U-matic / VHS
Creative Writing Series
Color (I J)
LC 73-702566
Shows that many different stories may be written using the same basic ingredients. Helps develop critical skills and the ability to evaluate style and content.
English Language; Literature and Drama
Dist - AIMS **Prod** - MORLAT 1973

Oscar Howe, the Sioux painter 29 MIN
U-matic / VT1 / VHS
Color (G)
$49.95 purchase, $25.00 rental
Profiles the late Artist Laureate of South Dakota, Oscar Howe. Recalls the early childhood of Howe and discusses his Sioux heritage and its influence on every facet of his painting. Howe's creations derive their uniqueness from his geometric use of lines and aesthetic points. His bright colors and abstract shapes allowed him to paint contemporary humanity within a traditional context. Produced by KUSD - TV.
Fine Arts; History - United States; Social Science
Dist - NAMPBC

Oscar Micheaux, Film Pioneer 28 MIN
U-matic / VHS / 16mm
Were You There Series
Color (J)
LC 83-700395
Presents scenes from the works of black film entrepeneur Oscar Micheaux. Includes his recollections of Bee Freeman, dubbed the 'sepia Mae West' and Lorenzo Tucker, the 'Black Valentino.'
Fine Arts; History - United States
Dist - BCNFL **Prod** - NGUZO 1982

Oscar Peterson 15 MIN
BETA / VHS / U-matic
(G)
$100.00
Relates the story of Oscar Peterson, one of the world's greatest jazz musicians, who found fame and fortune interpreting American jazz.
Fine Arts
Dist - CTV **Prod** - CTV 1985

Oscar Remembered 90 MIN
VHS / U-matic
English Language; Literature and Drama
Dist - ABCLR **Prod** - ABCLR

Oscar W Underwood 51 MIN
U-matic / VHS
Profiles in Courage Series
B&W (I J H)
LC 83-706541
Dramatizes Alabama Senator Oscar Underwood's opposition to the Ku Klux Klan during his campaign for the 1924 Democratic presidential nomination. Based on book Profiles In Courage by John F Kennedy. Stars Sidney Blackmer and Victor Jory.
Biography; Civics and Political Systems; History - United States; Sociology
Dist - SSSSV **Prod** - SAUDEK 1964

Oscar Zariski and his work by David Mumford 60 MIN
VHS
AMS - MAA joint lecture series
Color (PRO G)
$59.00 purchase _ #VIDMUMFORD - VB2
Looks at mathematician Oscar Zariski. Sketches his life from his birth in Russia to his doctoral training in Italy to his move to the United States in 1927. Chronicles influences on Zariski's mathematical directions. Uses Zariski's work on the Riemann - Roch theorem to give a flavor of the field of mathematics as Zariski practiced it. Recorded in Atlanta.
Mathematics; Science
Dist - AMSOC **Prod** - AMSOC 1988

Oscar's birthday party
VHS
Jake's world series
Color (K P)
$89.95 purchase
Features Jake, the gnome, who helps Oscar the mouse plan a birthday party while demonstrating the value of meeting new friends.
Literature and Drama; Psychology
Dist - COLLIE **Prod** - COLLIE

The Oscars - Moments of Greatness, Pt 1 26 MIN
16mm
Hollywood and the Stars Series
B&W
LC FI68-198
Traces the history of the academy of Motion Picture Arts and Sciences. Includes excerpts of award - winning films and some presentations of Oscars.
Fine Arts
Dist - WOLPER **Prod** - WOLPER 1964

The Oscars - Moments of Greatness, Pt 2 26 MIN
16mm
Hollywood and the Stars Series
B&W
LC FI68-199
Discusses the activities behind the Oscar headlines, the scramble for nominations, and the top secret security of the ballot. Shows various ways in which movie stars accept awards.
Fine Arts
Dist - WOLPER **Prod** - WOLPER 1964

Oscillations Along a Heavy Spring
16mm
B&W
Analyzes oscillations along a spring.
Mathematics
Dist - OPENU **Prod** - OPENU

Oscillators 13 MIN
16mm / U-matic / VHS
Radio Technician Training Series
B&W
LC FIE52-913
Studies oscillation and variations in oscillations. Uses animation to explain the functioning of a common circuit and tank circuit.
Industrial and Technical Education
Dist - USNAC **Prod** - USN 1945

Oscillators, Modulators, Demodulators 17 MIN
U-matic / VHS
Introduction to Solid State Electronics Series Chapter 6
Color (IND) (SPANISH)
LC 80-707264
Discusses method by which oscillator develops an AC signal with only DC applied. Explains use of positive and negative feedback. Covers different types of circuits.
Education; Industrial and Technical Education
Dist - TAT **Prod** - TAT

Oscilliscope Synchronization and Measurement 32 MIN
VHS / 16mm
Electronics Series
(C A IND)
$99.00 purchase _ #VCI12
Gives the learner practice in advanced use of the oscilliscope. Displays and explains functions such as signal measurement, frequency and rise time measurement. Covers the delayed sweep function and how to identify and interpret lissajous figures. Utilizes an additional workbook.
Industrial and Technical Education
Dist - RMIBHF **Prod** - RMIBHF

Oscilloscope operation - soldering and troubleshooting solid - state devices 60 MIN
U-matic / VHS
Electrical maintenance training series; Module 7 - Solid - state devices
Color (IND)
Industrial and Technical Education
Dist - LEIKID **Prod** - LEIKID

Oscilloscope Synchronization and Measurement
VHS
Industrial Electronics Training Program Series
$99.00 purchase _ #RPVCI12
Industrial and Technical Education
Dist - CAREER **Prod** - CAREER

Oscilloscopes - Frequency and Measurement 21 MIN
16mm
B&W
LC 74-705889
Shows, on an oscilloscope screen, various waveshapes of different frequencies, amplitudes and phase relationships. Explains the general operation of the oscilloscope and shows how it is used to find frequency and voltage amplitude.
Industrial and Technical Education; Mathematics; Science - Physical
Dist - USNAC **Prod** - USAF

OSHA 25 MIN
16mm
Color (A)
Tells how the Occupational Safety and Health Administration (OSHA) was set up to stem the tide of disease, injury and death in the workplace. Explains how tests are conducted, standards are set and how OSHA inspectors investigate complaints. Discusses health hazards in textile mills and foundries.
Civics and Political Systems; Health and Safety
Dist - AFLCIO **Prod** - USDL 1981

OSHA and Us 17 MIN
U-matic
Color
Discusses the Occupational Safety And Health Act and the impact of the regulations. Filmed on location in research and teaching laboratories. Illustrates potentially dangerous health and safety situations.
Health and Safety
Dist - UMITV **Prod** - UMITV 1977

OSHA File - the Cases and Compliances 20 MIN
VHS / 16mm / U-matic
Color
Shows supervisors, through court cases drawn from actual OCcupational Safety and Health Administration (OSHA) files, the steps they must take to live up to the law.
Business and Economics; Health and Safety
Dist - BBP **Prod** - BBP

OSHA lab standard 15 MIN
BETA / VHS / U-matic
Hazard communication - live - action video series
Color (IND G)
$495.00 purchase _ #801 - 20
Recognizes the differences in scale and method between general industries and laboratories through the OSHA Lab Standard. Covers hazard identification, monitoring, the availability of medical services, employee training, use of protective equipment including Lab Hoods and facility - specific Chemical Hygiene Plan. Part of a series on hazard communication.
Business and Economics; Health and Safety; Industrial and Technical Education; Psychology
Dist - ITSC **Prod** - ITSC 1990

The OSHA laboratory standards - an overview 9 MIN
8mm cartridge / VHS / BETA / U-matic
Color; PAL (IND G)
$295.00 purchase, $175.00 rental _ #SOU - 001
Gives employees an overview of the OSHA Laboratory Chemical Standard. Looks at the regulations, equipment and proper procedures involved in handing hazardous chemicals in the laboratory. Describes contents of the standard and its meaning to employees, the role of the chemical hygiene plan, methods for hazard identification, safe lab practices and procedures, permissable exposure limits for OSHA - regulated chemicals. Illustrates the signs and symptoms of chemical exposure. Discusses monitoring, recordkeeping, the availability of medical consultation and more. Includes a leader's guide.
Health and Safety; Psychology; Science - Physical
Dist - BNA

OSHA - Life at Work II 15 MIN
16mm
Color (H C A)
LC 80-701046
Discusses occupational diseases, covering techniques of prevention. Deals with personal cleanliness, proper ventilation, reduction of noise pollution and job accidents. Examines the tenets of the government's occupational health and safety regulations.
Business and Economics; Civics and Political Systems; Health and Safety
Dist - KLEINW **Prod** - KLEINW 1977

O'Shea 20 MIN
VHS
Color (H C G A R)
$19.95 purchase, $10.00 rental _ #35 - 873 - 8516
Tells how O'Shea marries a woman of ill repute who proves to be unfaithful to him. Likens this story to the relationship between God and people.
Literature and Drama; Religion and Philosophy
Dist - APH **Prod** - VISVID

Oslo Live 26 MIN
VHS
Color (H)
Portrays Oslo as a rapidly growing and turbulent city. Available for free loan from the distributor.
Geography - World; History - World
Dist - AUDPLN

Oslo Philharmonic Orchestra 30 MIN
VHS
Color (G)
Free loan
Records selections from the 1988 summer concert of the Oslo Philharmonic Orchestra at the Holmenkollen Ski Jump. Includes performances from the Oslo concert hall, the permanent base of the Orchestra.
Fine Arts; Geography - World
Dist - NIS
AUDPLN

Osmoregulation 10 MIN
U-matic
Homeostasis Series
Color (H C)
Explores the process of osmoregulation, using as an example the complex filtering process that takes place in the kidneys.

Science; Science - Natural; Science - Physical
Dist - TVOTAR Prod - TVOTAR 1984

Osmosis and fluid compartments 31 MIN
16mm
Directions for education in nursing via technology series; Lesson 35
B&W (PRO)
LC 74-701808
Defines and demonstrates the concepts of diffusion, osmosis and osmotic pressure. Describes and demonstrates the effects of hypotonic, hypertonic and isotonic solutions on living cells. Identifies the major fluid compartments of the body, the major electrolytes and the factors involved in maintenance of a constant volume in each compartment.
Science - Natural; Science - Physical
Dist - WSUM Prod - DENT 1974

Osprey 35 MIN
U-matic / VHS / 16mm
RSPB Collection Series
Color (I)
Explores the breeding behavior and fishing adaptations of osprey, or sea eagle, in Scotland. Depicts how the osprey had been hunted to extinction in the early 1900s, but revived with the return to the lock of a single breeding pair. Shows complete breeding cycle, from pair formation, nest construction, incubation and feeding habits.
Science - Natural
Dist - BCNFL Prod - RSFPB 1980

Osprey's Domain 15 MIN
16mm / U-matic / VHS
Animals and Plants of North America Series
Color (J)
LC 80-701737
Examines the life cycle of the osprey, a fish - eating hawk.
Science - Natural
Dist - LCOA Prod - KARVF 1980

Oss, 'Oss, Wee 'Oss 17 MIN
16mm
Color
Shows spring - time rites in Padstow, Cornwall, featuring a dance which is a modern remnant of ancient practices celebrating the revived fertility of the land.
Fine Arts
Dist - CFI Prod - CRAF

Osseous Surgery in the Maxilla, Pt 2 11 MIN
16mm
Color
LC 74-705274
Describes techniques which permit suturing of the buccal flap, independently of the lingual or palatal flap, showing how it is performed with a continuous how it assures close adaptation of the tissue to the teeth and bone.
Health and Safety; Science; Science - Natural
Dist - NMAC Prod - USVA 1968

Ossicular Problems in Middle Ear Surgery 32 MIN
16mm
Color (PRO)
Illustrates the various types of ossicular discontinuity and demonstrates their surgical correction.
Health and Safety
Dist - EAR Prod - EAR

Osteoarthritis 20 MIN
VHS / 16mm
Learning about arthritis series
Color (H C A PRO)
$195.00 purchase, $75.00 rental _ #8085
Considers osteoarthritis.
Health and Safety; Science - Natural
Dist - AIMS Prod - HOSSN 1988

Osteology of the Skull - a Self - Evaluation Exercise 22 MIN
VHS / U-matic
Osteology of the Skull Series
Color (C A)
Health and Safety; Science - Natural
Dist - TEF Prod - UWO

Osteology of the Skull - an Introduction 26 MIN
VHS / U-matic
Osteology of the Skull Series
Color (C A)
Health and Safety; Science - Natural
Dist - TEF Prod - UWO

Osteology of the Skull - Inferior Surface of the Cranium 26 MIN
VHS / U-matic
Osteology of the Skull Series
Color (C A)
Health and Safety; Science - Natural
Dist - TEF Prod - UWO

Osteology of the Skull Series
Osteology of the Skull - a Self - Evaluation Exercise 22 MIN
Osteology of the Skull - an Introduction 26 MIN
Osteology of the Skull - Inferior Surface of the Cranium 26 MIN
Osteology of the Skull - the Cranial Cavity 28 MIN
Osteology of the Skull - the Mandible 23 MIN
Osteology of the Skull - the Mandible - a Self - Evaluation Exercise 16 MIN
Osteology of the Skull - the Temporal Bone 30 MIN
Osteology of the Skull - the Temporal Bone - a Self - Evaluation Exercise 25 MIN
Dist - TEF

Osteology of the Skull - the Cranial Cavity 28 MIN
VHS / U-matic
Osteology of the Skull Series
Color (C A)
Health and Safety; Science - Natural
Dist - TEF Prod - UWO

Osteology of the Skull - the Mandible 23 MIN
U-matic / VHS
Osteology of the Skull Series
Color (C A)
Health and Safety; Science - Natural
Dist - TEF Prod - UWO

Osteology of the Skull - the Mandible - a Self - Evaluation Exercise 16 MIN
U-matic / VHS
Osteology of the Skull Series
Color (C A)
Health and Safety; Science - Natural
Dist - TEF Prod - UWO

Osteology of the Skull - the Temporal Bone 30 MIN
VHS / U-matic
Osteology of the Skull Series
Color (C A)
Health and Safety; Science - Natural
Dist - TEF Prod - UWO

Osteology of the Skull - the Temporal Bone - a Self - Evaluation Exercise 25 MIN
VHS / U-matic
Osteology of the Skull Series
Color (C A)
Health and Safety; Science - Natural
Dist - TEF Prod - UWO

Osteology of the Upper Limb, Pt I - the Upper Limb Girdle 23 MIN
U-matic / VHS
Color (C A)
Presents the anatomy of the upper limb.
Health and Safety; Science - Natural
Dist - TEF Prod - UWO

Osteopathic Examination and Manipulation Series
Articulatory Procedures I 14 MIN
Cervical Region - Pt 1 13 MIN
Cervical Region - Pt 2 - Occipitaotlantal 15 MIN
Introduction to Soft Tissue Techniques, Pt 1 13 MIN
Lower Extremity, Pt 1
Lumbar Region, Pt 1 17 MIN
Lumbar Region, Pt 2 10 MIN
Manipulative Techniques to Assist Fluid Flow 14 MIN
Pelvic Region, Pt 1 - Iliosacral 17 MIN
Pelvic Region, Pt 2 - Sacroliac 13 MIN
Pelvis Region, Pt 3 - Alternative Direct Techniques 12 MIN
Structural Examination - Gross Motion Testing 14 MIN
Structural Examination - Initial Screen 14 MIN
Structural Examination - Local Scan 18 MIN
Structural Examination - Spinal Segmental Definition
Thoracic cage - Pt 1 - true ribs 14 MIN
Thoracic region - Pt 1 14 MIN
Thoracic region - Pt 2 12 MIN
Upper Extremity - Clavicle 20 MIN
Dist - MSU

Osteoporosis 15 MIN
VHS
Color; CC (G C PRO) (SPANISH)
$175.00 purchase _ #OB - 132 ; $200.00 purchase _ #OB - 62
Discusses how women in general and certain women in particular are susceptible to osteoporosis, a debiliating bone disease. Uses 3 generations of the same family to explain how and when bone loss takes place, and how it can be detected, and how a combination of diet, exercise, calcium and estrogen supplements can help prevent osteoporosis from ever developing.
Health and Safety; Science - Natural; Sociology
Dist - MIFE Prod - MIFE

Osteoporosis 30 MIN
VHS
At time of diagnosis series
Color (G)
$19.95 purchase _ #1 - 5757 - 7005 - 9NK
Provides patients who have just been diagnosed with osteoporosis and their families with thorough, comprehensive and understandable information. Examines what is going on in the body and what might have caused the condition. Explains the type of medical professionals a patient may encounter and how the condition is monitored. Explores treatment options, including medication, surgery and lifestyle changes. Looks at practical issues surrounding the illness and answers the most common questions. Part of an ongoing series to provide the in - depth medical information patients and their families need to know.
Health and Safety; Sociology
Dist - TILIED Prod - TILIED 1995

Osteoporosis - a preventable tragedy 15 MIN
VHS
Color (G)
#PRM - 242
Presents a free - loan program which educates women about some of the causes and treatments for osteoporosis. Discusses interventions in terms of diet remodification, calcium supplements, use of pharmacological intervention such as Estrogen Replacement Therapy and appropriate exercise. Examines risk factors such as nicotine, caffeine and alcohol. Interviews three women with osteoporosis.
Science - Natural
Dist - WYAYLA Prod - WYAYLA

Osteoporosis - a realistic guide to prevention, detection and treatment 12 MIN
VHS
Color; CC (G)
$24.95 purchase _ #OSTE
Discusses osteoporosis and its occurrence in older women. Produced by Apogee Communications.
Science - Natural; Sociology
Dist - APRESS

Osteoporosis - How to Prevent it 60 MIN
VHS / U-matic
Health Series
Stereo
Shows how to prevent osteoporosis.
Health and Safety
Dist - BANTAP Prod - BANTAP 1986

Osteoporosis - is it Preventable 13 MIN
U-matic
Color; Mono (H C)
Covers general information about osteoporosis and discusses how young women can protect themselves from developing the disease in their later years.
Health and Safety; Home Economics; Social Science; Sociology
Dist - UWISCA Prod - UWISCA 1987

Osteoporosis - the Calcium Connection 19 MIN
U-matic / VHS
Color (C)
$249.00, $149.00 purchase _ #AD - 1436
Focuses on current knowledge about osteoporosis, the loss of calcium from the skeletal structure of women after menopause. Profiles a woman athlete protecting herself from this crippling disease.
Health and Safety; Science - Natural; Sociology
Dist - FOTH Prod - FOTH

Osteoporosis the Silent Disease 18 MIN
U-matic
Color (A)
Introduces osteoporosis as health care professionals discuss the nature of the disease and demonstrate prevention and treatment through proper diet and exercise.
Health and Safety
Dist - VLEARN Prod - VLEARN 1986

Osterrich - Im Herzen Europas 20 MIN
16mm / U-matic / VHS
Color (H C A) (ENGLISH AND GERMAN)
$425.00 film, $35.00 rental, $325.00 video
Visits Austria, highlighting the history and culture. Includes Vienna, Salzburg, Graz and Innsbruck. Highlights the Tyrol, the Wienerwald and the wine producing areas along the Danube.
Foreign Language; Geography - World; History - World; Social Science
Dist - IFB Prod - POLNIS 1982

Ostomy - a New Beginning
VHS / U-matic
Color (SPANISH)
Deals primarily with the psychological aspects of having an Ostomy as experienced by actual Ostomates. Demonstrates how the normal digestive system works and how a colostomy or ileastomy changes things.
Foreign Language; Science - Natural
Dist - MIFE **Prod** - MIFE

Ostomy care 24 MIN
VHS
Color (PRO C)
$250.00 purchase, $70.00 rental _ #4374
Provides basic information on ostomies and ostomy care. Begins with a description of the anatomy and physiology of the GI tract. Continues with an explanation of the difference between a colostomy and ileostomy. Details why a patient may need to have a stoma, such as a megacolon, Crohn's disease, ulcerative colitis or cancer. Discusses the different types of ostomies, using diagrams for further clarification. Stresses the importance of patient education in both pre and post - op teaching, diet, signs and symptoms of problems that may require medical attention, and irrigation of the stoma.
Health and Safety
Dist - AJN **Prod** - MEDCOM

Ostomy care - 10 13 MIN
VHS
Basic clinical skills series
Color (C PRO G)
$330.00 purchase _ #R860 - VI - 062
Informs about the physical and psychological care necessary for ostomy patients. Reviews common types of ostomies and discusses postoperative preparation, assessment of the patient and post - operative needs. Part of a series produced by Southern Illinois Univ, School of Medicine.
Health and Safety
Dist - HSCIC

Ostomy care - 16 22 MIN
VHS
Clinical nursing skills - nursing fundamentals - series
Color (C PRO G)
$395.00 purchase _ #R890 - VI - 070
Presents types of ostomies and their clinical care. Conducts a nursing interview with a patient who has had a urinary diversion - ilial conduit - in the right lower quadrant, and a descending colostomy in the left lower quadrant. The patient provides information on ostomy care, pouching system preferences, diet, activities and emotional health. Observes the performance of clinical ostomy care on the patient. Part of a 23 - part series on clinical nursing skills.
Health and Safety
Dist - HSCIC **Prod** - CUYAHO 1989

Ostomy care at home 28 MIN
VHS
Home care video series
Color (G PRO C)
$100.00 purchase _ #GI - 20
Teaches practical self - care skills, including care of ileostomy and colostomy stoma, use of appropriate appliances and outlines warning symptoms that necessitate physician contact. Reviews diet and lifestyle changes and provides emotional support. Part of a series on home care for cancer patients.
Health and Safety
Dist - MIFE **Prod** - SMRMC 1993

Ostomy care - Part 1 15 MIN
U-matic / VHS
Ostomy care series
Color (PRO C)
$395.00 purchase, $80.00 rental _ #C911 - VI - 055
Describes three basic kinds of stoma surgery - colostomy, ileostomy and urostomy. Shows elements of proper skin and possible stoma complications. Illustrates different appliances available and their applications. Part of a four - part series presented by Ann Crippen, RN, Twelve Oaks Hospital and the University of Texas at Houston.
Health and Safety
Dist - HSCIC

Ostomy care - Part 4 19 MIN
VHS / U-matic
Ostomy care series
Color (PRO C)
$395.00 purchase, $80.00 rental _ #C911 - VI - 058
Describes the preparation, application and removal of both a one - piece and a two - piece ostomy appliance. Part of a four - part series presented by Ann Crippen, RN, Twelve Oaks Hospital and the University of Texas at Houston.
Health and Safety
Dist - HSCIC

Ostomy care - Part 3 - patient self - ostomy care 30 MIN
VHS / U-matic
Ostomy care series
Color (PRO C)
$395.00 purchase, $80.00 rental _ #C911 - VI - 057
Reveals that patient reaction to ostomy surgery may include depression, suicidal thinking, panic and severe loss of confidence. Interviews a woman who has had an ostomy as a result of Crohn's disease. Part of a four - part series presented by Ann Crippen, RN, Twelve Oaks Hospital and the University of Texas at Houston.
Health and Safety
Dist - HSCIC

Ostomy care - Part 2 - skin complications associated with ostomy 6 MIN
U-matic / VHS
Ostomy care series
Color (PRO C)
$395.00 purchase, $80.00 rental _ #C911 - VI - 056
Describes skin compliations associated with ostomy surgery. Reveals that it is imperative that meticulous care be given to the peristomal area to prevent excoriation and skin breakdown. Discusses how the attitudes and knowledge of healthcare professionals can greatly affect how well patients will manage before, during and after their surgery. Part of a four - part series presented by Ann Crippen, RN, Twelve Oaks Hospital and the University of Texas at Houston.
Health and Safety; Science - Natural
Dist - HSCIC

Ostomy care series
Presents a four - part series presented by Ann Crippen, RN, Twelve Oaks Hospital and the University of Texas at Houston. Discusses the three types of ostomy surgery - colostomy, ileostomy and urostomy, skin complications associated with the surgery, patient mental health and the use of ostomy appliances.
Ostomy care - Part 1 15 MIN
Ostomy care - Part 4 19 MIN
Ostomy care - Part 3 - patient self - ostomy care 30 MIN
Ostomy care - Part 2 - skin complications associated with ostomy 6 MIN
Dist - HSCIC

The Ostomy Visitor 12 MIN
16mm
Color (PRO)
LC 77-701316
Shows how rehabilitated ostomates can help newly operated ostomy patients by visiting the hospital and giving general facts about diet, appearance, day - to - day care and activity.
Health and Safety
Dist - AMCS **Prod** - AMCS 1974

Ostrich 10 MIN
U-matic / VHS
Eye on nature series
Color (I J)
$250.00 purchase _ #HP - 5852C
Looks at the ostrich species. Gives an understanding of the physical advantages and disadvantages of being the world's largest bird. Part of the Eye on Nature series.
Science - Natural
Dist - CORF **Prod** - BBCTV 1989

The Ostrich 7 MIN
16mm / U-matic / VHS
Color (P I)
Shows feeding and nesting habits of ostriches in their natural habitat in South Africa. Attention is given to their appearance, especially the structure of their legs, feet, neck and head.
Geography - World; Science - Natural
Dist - IFB **Prod** - BHA 1956

Ostrich - Part 10 8 MIN
VHS
Safari TV series
Color (P I)
$125.00 purchase
Studies the daily life of the ostrich. Part of a 13 - part series on African animals.
Geography - World; Science - Natural
Dist - LANDMK **Prod** - LANDMK 1993

Ostrich people - manic denial 11 MIN
16mm / VHS
Color (I J H G)
$475.00, $195.00 purchase, $60.00 rental
Presents an animated, hand - painted production by Hal Rucker. Depicts Dr Susan Gray, a psychiatrist, who is horrified to discover a nuclear weapon silo near her uncle's farm. Gray has a vision of herself as one of the 'ostrich people' who deal with potential disaster by denying it - the kind of behavior which allowed Hitler to carry out genocide. Inspired by her professional understanding of how denial relates to living in an age of nuclear weapons, she organizes a thought - provoking political action for which she is arrested. In her courtroom defense, she presents a picture of a complacent public sticking its head in the sand.
Guidance and Counseling; Sociology
Dist - CF

Ostriches 5 MIN
U-matic / VHS / 16mm
Zoo Animals in the Wild Series
Color (K P)
$135.00, $95.00 purchase _ #3991
Describes the lifestyle of the ostrich, the tallest, heaviest bird on the planet which can run as fast as a horse and lay eggs 20 times heavier than chicken eggs.
Science - Natural
Dist - CORF **Prod** - CORF 1981

Osu no Hosomichi - a Haiku Poet's Pilgrimage 27 MIN
16mm
Color (H)
$6.50 rental _ #33788
Introduces the life and work of the 17th century Japanese poet Matsu Basho and traces the five - month, 2,400 kilometer journey he made through Japan on foot at the age of forty - six. Draws extensively on passages from the Oku No Hosomichi (The Narrow Road to a Far Province), the diary of Basho's travels, and a number of haiku poems he composed en route.
Geography - World; Literature and Drama
Dist - USNAC

The OT Story 17 MIN
16mm
B&W (C A)
Describes a career of occupational therapy, work with the handicapped and information on preparation of an OT career.
Guidance and Counseling; Health and Safety; Psychology; Science
Dist - AOTA **Prod** - AOTA 1957

Otello 145 MIN
VHS
Color (G)
$39.95 purchase _ #S00581
Presents an open - air performance of Verdi's tragic opera 'Otello' in the Arena di Verona. Stars Vladimir Atlantov, Kiri Te Kanawa, and Piero Cappuccilli.
Fine Arts
Dist - UILL **Prod** - SRA
SRA

Otello - Placido Domingo 123 MIN
VHS
Color (G) (ITALIAN (ENGLISH SUBTITLES))
$39.95 purchase _ #1184
Presents 'Otello' by Giuseppe Verdi starring Placido Domingo, directed by Franco Zeffirelli. Features Justino Diaz as Iago, Katia Ricciarelli as Desdemona, the La Scala Orchestra and Chorus. Filmed on location throughout Italy and Crete.
Fine Arts; Geography - World
Dist - KULTUR

Othello 44 MIN
16mm
B&W
A condensed version of 'OTHELLO' presented by an English cast including John Slater, Sebastian Cabot and Luanne Shaw.
Literature and Drama
Dist - RMIBHF **Prod** - HALST 1947

Othello 29 MIN
U-matic
Plays of Shakespeare Series
B&W
Discusses the themes of faith and treachery and love and hatred. Tells the story of the fall of a man who is destroyed by jealousy.
Literature and Drama
Dist - UMITV **Prod** - UMITV 1961

Othello 93 MIN
VHS
Color (G C H)
$109.00 purchase _ #DL419
Presents a restoration of Orson Welles' version of the play. Includes an introduction by Welles' daughter.
Fine Arts
Dist - INSIM

Othello 208 MIN
VHS / 16mm
BBC's Shakespeare Series
(H A)
$249.95
Depicts Shakespeare's moving drama of deception and infidelity, Othello.
Literature and Drama
Dist - AMBROS **Prod** - AMBROS 1982

Othello 10 MIN
16mm / U-matic / VHS
Shakespeare Series

Color (H C A)
An excerpt from the play of the same title. Presents Iago's Soliloquy in Act II, Scene 1 as he reveals his method of revenge and Act V, Scene 2 as Othello kills Desdemona in her bed.
Fine Arts; Literature and Drama
Dist - IFB **Prod** - IFB 1974

Othello 90 MIN
VHS
Understanding Shakespeare - The Tragedies series
Color; CC (I J H C)
$49.95 purchase _ #US01
Features key scenes, along with commentary by Shakespearean scholars. Cuts through the 16th - century language barrier to provide a way for students to increase their comprehension of these classics. Includes a teacher's guide.
Literature and Drama
Dist - SVIP

Othello 208 MIN
VHS
BBC Shakespeare series
Color (G C H)
$109.00 purchase _ #DL461
Fine Arts
Dist - INSIM **Prod** - BBC

Othello 202 MIN
U-matic / VHS
Shakespeare Plays Series
Color (H C A)
LC 82-707355
Presents Othello, William Shakespeare's play about a man whose jealousy of his wife leads to tragic consequences.
Literature and Drama
Dist - TIMLIF **Prod** - BBCTV 1982

Othello - a Stage Production Series
Program I 40 MIN
Program II 43 MIN
Program III 39 MIN
Program IV 44 MIN
Dist - NETCHE

Other 3 MIN
16mm
Color; Silent (C)
$112.00
Experimental film by Stan Brakhage.
Fine Arts
Dist - AFA **Prod** - AFA 1980

The Other Bridge 27 MIN
U-matic / VHS
Color (J H C A)
Explores the San Francisco - Oakland Bay Bridge construction, design, operation and engineering points.
Geography - United States; Industrial and Technical Education
Dist - CEPRO **Prod** - CEPRO

Other Cats 25 mniutes
16mm / U-matic / VHS
Untamed World Series
Color; Mono (J H C A)
$400.00 film, $250.00 video, $50.00 rental
Examines the history, habits and behaviour of the cat. Looks at their first appearance some forty million years ago to the domesticated house pets of today.
Science - Natural
Dist - CTV **Prod** - CTV 1971

The Other Child - Burns in Children 50 MIN
VHS / U-matic
Color
Presents poignant and revealing conversations with several children with severe burns as well as informative interviews with nurses, physicians, psychiatrists and physio - therapists. Examines the physical and emotional suffering of the young victims, emphasizing the critical importance of helping parents deal with their child's injury.
Health and Safety; Science - Natural
Dist - AJN **Prod** - CANBC

The Other City 11 MIN
16mm
Color (H C A)
Explains that 75,000 Americans could be saved each year through health checkups and learning to recognize the Seven Danger Signals of cancer.
Health and Safety
Dist - AMCS **Prod** - AMCS

Other Clawed Animals 15 MIN
U-matic
Tell Me what You See Series
Color (P)
Explains how other animals, such as oppossums, raccoons and skunks are adapted for living in a wild state.
Science - Natural
Dist - GPN **Prod** - WVIZTV

Other countries, other views series
Russia - off the record 58 MIN
Dist - JOU

Other Data Structures 30 MIN
VHS / U-matic
Pascal, Pt 2 - Intermediate Pascal Series
Color (H C A)
LC 81-706049
Describes structure of variant RECORDS and shows examples. Introduces the stack data structure and an example of execution of a Pascal arithmetic expression using a stack.
Industrial and Technical Education; Mathematics; Sociology
Dist - COLOSU **Prod** - COLOSU 1980

The Other Diabetes 22 MIN
U-matic / VHS
Color
Explains risk factors which can lead to Type II diabetes and the lifestyle measures which can be taken to control it, such as exercise, nutrition and weight control.
Health and Safety
Dist - PELICN **Prod** - PELICN

The Other Diabetes 24 MIN
16mm
Color (P)
Addresses persons with Type II diabetes, covering all aspects of this disease from diagnosis and treatment to emotional issues.
Health and Safety
Dist - ADAS **Prod** - ADAS

Other faces of AIDS 60 MIN
VHS
Color (J H C G A PRO)
$59.95 purchase _ #AH45626
Describes the rapid growth of AIDS in the U S's minority communities. Interviews former Surgeon General C Everett Koop, the Reverend Jesse Jackson, and other people involved in the fight against AIDS.
Health and Safety; Sociology
Dist - HTHED **Prod** - PBS

Other Faces of AIDS 60 MIN
VHS
Color; Captioned (G)
$59.95 purchase _ #OTFA - 000C
Covers the rapid growth of AIDS in minority communities. Shows that the AIDS epidemic in minority communities hits heterosexuals, drug users and children hard. Interviews experts and minority community leaders and views several AIDS education programs targeted to minority populations. Hosted by ABC News correspondent George Strait. Also available in a Spanish - language version.
Health and Safety; Psychology
Dist - PBS **Prod** - MPTPB 1989

The Other Facts of Life 52 MIN
U-matic / VHS
Winners from Down Under Series
Color (K)
$349.00, $249.00 purchase _ #AD - 1354
Portrays Ben who cannot understand how people can live so happily with all the injustice and disaster in the world. Shows him trying to shock his family into caring, but a crisis closer to home causes Ben to refocus his energies. Part of an eight - part series on children's winning over their circumstances produced by the Australian Children's Television Foundation.
Literature and Drama; Psychology; Sociology
Dist - FOTH **Prod** - FOTH

Other families 49 MIN
VHS
Color (G)
$245.00 purchase, $100.00 rental _ #CJ - 117
Explores the perceptions and feelings of seven adults from ages 18 to 40 who were raised by lesbian mothers. Confronts the questions asked so frequently, '...but how are the kids going to turn out.' Three of those interviewed are themselves gay, four identify themselves as heterosexual, all are well - adjusted. All seven share problems arising from the need they or their parents felt to keep secrets from a society that did not accept their kind of identity. Produced by Doroth Chvatal.
Sociology
Dist - FANPRO

Other families, other friends series
Aloha 15 MIN
Amanda's adventures in London 15 MIN
At Home on San Blas Island 15 MIN
Bon Bini 15 MIN
City of 500 mosques 15 MIN
City of the smoky bay 15 MIN
Crossroads of the world 15 MIN
The Gift of the Nile 15 MIN
Island in the Sun 15 MIN
Jane and Suzanne 15 MIN
Jerusalem the Golden 15 MIN
Land of Frost and Fire 15 MIN
Land of the Kapriska Purara 15 MIN
Land of the Pineapple 15 MIN
A Little Bit of Paris 15 MIN
Little Dutch Island 15 MIN
Lobsterman 15 MIN
A Long Way from Home 15 MIN
Maria and the Coconuts 15 MIN
Monique of Amsterdam 15 MIN
Nicaraguan Countryside 15 MIN
Out of many, One People 15 MIN
Said the whiting to the snail 15 MIN
School days 15 MIN
Shalom Aleichem 15 MIN
Steve and Kathy and Al 15 MIN
Vasillis of Athens 15 MIN
Visit to Aruba 15 MIN
Watchia 15 MIN
Weather is Out 15 MIN
Windmills and Wooden Shoes 15 MIN
Dist - AITECH

Other Features, Pt 1 30 MIN
U-matic / VHS
Pascal, Pt 2 - Intermediate Pascal Series
Color (H C A)
LC 81-706049
Introduces the unconditional branch and the GOTO statement. Shows block, statement and type syntax diagrams completed for Pascal. Presents packed data structures as well.
Industrial and Technical Education; Mathematics; Sociology
Dist - COLOSU **Prod** - COLOSU 1980

Other Features, Pt 2 30 MIN
VHS / U-matic
Pascal, Pt 2 - Intermediate Pascal Series
Color (H C A)
LC 81-706049
Concludes discussion of Pascal programming features and describes commenting, forward references, function and procedure names as argument parameters and formatting within the WRITE and WRITELN output procedures.
Industrial and Technical Education; Mathematics; Sociology
Dist - COLOSU **Prod** - COLOSU 1980

Other Finger Weaves 29 MIN
Videoreel / VT2
Exploring the Crafts - Weaving Series
Color
Fine Arts; Home Economics
Dist - PBS **Prod** - NHN

Other Fish, Other Ways 30 MIN
U-matic
Sport Fishing Series
Color (G)
Looks at four unusual fishing excursions, a carp derby using bows and arrows, a search for muskellunge, a snowmobile trip to a remote northern lake and a family's lazy late afternoon outing to catch brown bullhead.
Physical Education and Recreation
Dist - TVOTAR **Prod** - TVOTAR 1985

The Other Guy 60 MIN
16mm
Color (J H C A)
LC 76 - 701822; 76-701822
Examines the problem of alcoholism from the perspective of several experts in the field and from the experiences of alcoholics themselves.
Health and Safety; Psychology; Sociology
Dist - NABSP **Prod** - NABSP 1971

The Other Guy, Pt 1 30 MIN
U-matic / VHS
Color (J A)
Focuses on the subject of troubled employees.
Business and Economics; Psychology
Dist - SUTHRB **Prod** - BCBSA

The Other Guy, Pt 2 30 MIN
U-matic / VHS
Color (J A)
Focuses on the subject of troubled employees.
Business and Economics; Psychology
Dist - SUTHRB **Prod** - BCBSA

The Other Guy - Pts 1 and 2 60 MIN
16mm
Color (J H C A)
LC 76-701822
Examines the problem of alcoholism from the perspective of several experts in the field and from the experiences of alcoholics themselves.
Health and Safety; Psychology; Sociology
Dist - BCBSA **Prod** - BCBSA 1971

Other Half of the Safety Team 12 MIN
U-matic / VHS
Color
Promotes a positive safety attitude. Emphasizes need for positive state of mind, cooperation with supervisors, awareness of safety hazards and importance of reporting even the slightest accident.

Business and Economics; Health and Safety
Dist - EDRF Prod - EDRF

The Other Half of the Safety Team 10 MIN
16mm / U-matic / VHS
Color
Points out that good safety attitudes can prevent most job - related accidents. Discusses OSHA, protective equipment and proper handling of materials.
Health and Safety
Dist - CORF Prod - ERF

The Other half of the safety team 11 MIN
U-matic / VHS
Industrial safety series
(H A)
$125.00 purchase
Introduces basic safety on the job and emphasizes the need for a positive attitude, cooperation and awareness of hazards.
Health and Safety
Dist - AITECH Prod - ERESI 1986

The Other Half of the Sky - a China Memoir 74 MIN
16mm
Color (J)
LC 77-700785
Depicts life in the People's Republic of China as seen by a delegation of eight American women who visited in 1973. Includes glimpses of a Peking family's apartment, visits to schools, nurseries and recreational centers and interviews with Chinese citizens who discuss their own and American lifestyles.
Geography - World; History - World; Sociology
Dist - NEWDAY Prod - SMLCW 1976

Other Implementations 30 MIN
U-matic / VHS
IEEE 488 Bus Series
Color (IND)
Covers problems created by new, low - cost, nonstandard devices and other ways to implement the IEEE 488 Bus but with their associated limitations.
Industrial and Technical Education; Mathematics; Sociology
Dist - COLOSU Prod - COLOSU

Other Investment Opportunities 30 MIN
VHS / U-matic
Personal Finance Series Lesson 19
Color (C A)
Focuses on speculative investments including the commodity market, the foreign exchange money market, precious and strategic metals, collectible items and equipment leasing. Discusses alternative opportunities such as investing in either an existing or a new business.
Business and Economics
Dist - CDTEL Prod - SCCON

Other Investment Opportunities 28 MIN
U-matic / VHS
Personal Finance and Money Management Series
Color (C A)
Business and Economics; Civics and Political Systems
Dist - SCCON Prod - SCCON 1987

Other lives, other selves 47 MIN
VHS
Color (G)
$29.95 purchase
Shows participants in a workshop with psychotherapists where Roger Woolger, a Jungian analyst, employs his past life regression techniques with several volunteers from the audience. Views dramatic results. Looks at the way the person relives this story in his or her own current life to make past life regression become present life therapy.
Fine Arts; Psychology; Religion and Philosophy
Dist - HP

The Other Networks 28 MIN
U-matic / VHS
Please Stand by - a History of Radio Series
(C A)
Fine Arts; History - United States; Psychology; Sociology
Dist - SCCON Prod - SCCON 1986

The Other New Yorkers - New York City 24 MIN
VHS / 16mm
Amateur naturalist series
Color (I J H C G)
$495.00, $195.00 purchase
Describes the dependency of mice upon humans in cities. Observes flocks of birds, a zebra jumping spider, earthworm, dogs and rats. Part of a 13 - part series featuring a naturalist and a zoologist, Gerald and Lee Durrell, on field trips to different habitats.
Geography - United States; Science - Natural
Dist - LANDMK Prod - LANDMK 1988

The Other ninety percent 25 MIN
VHS
Color (G)
$29.95 purchase
Features Apollo 14 astronaut Edgar Mitchell telling about his experience on the moon which opened the door to 'the other 90 percent' of his brain and changed his life. Looks at his dedication to keeping the earth beautiful by founding the Institute of Noetic Sciences.
Fine Arts; Psychology
Dist - HP Prod - NOETIC

Other number bases
VHS
Lola May's fundamental math series
Color (I)
$45.00 purchase _ #10276VG
Uses models to illustrate number bases other than ten. Teaches how to change a base ten number to another base and then back again. Comes with a teacher's guide and blackline masters. Part 26 of a 30 - part series.
Mathematics
Dist - UNL

The Other observers - women photographers from 1850 to the present day 72 MIN
VHS
Color; PAL (J H C G)
PdS29.50 purchase
Traces the history of women's extensive involvement in photography. Begins with the work of early amateurs and professionals in the nineteenth century and continues with the work of contemporary photographers.
Fine Arts; Industrial and Technical Education
Dist - EMFVL

Other People at School 7 MIN
16mm
Project Bilingual Series
Color
LC 75-703524
Introduces beginning school children to the mysterious grownups they meet at school, including the principal, the office and custodial staff and the cafeteria personnel.
Guidance and Counseling; Social Science
Dist - SUTHLA Prod - SANISD 1975

Other people's garbage 60 MIN
VHS
Odyssey series
Color; Captioned (G)
$59.95 purchase _ #ODYS - 107
Follows several historical anthropologists as they study the lives of black slaves, early city dwellers and other past cultures. Takes viewers to Georgia slave quarters, California mining towns and historic sites in Boston.
History - United States; History - World; Sociology
Dist - PBS Prod - PBA 1980
DOCEDR

Other People's Garbage 59 MIN
16mm
Odyssey
Color (J H A)
Explores the current work of historical archaeologists at three sites across the U.S. Details of peoples' lives are revealed in excavations at slave quarters on St. Simon Island, GA, slag heaps in northern California mining towns occupied from 1859 to 1902 had subway construction sites in Cambridge, MA.ch.
History - United States; Sociology
Dist - DOCEDR Prod - DOCEDR 1980

Other People's Money 60 MIN
VHS
Frontline Series
Color; Captioned (G)
$300.00 purchase, $95.00 rental _ #FRON - 811K
Considers the savings and loan scandal. Focuses on Charles Keating Jr, whose Lincoln Savings was the largest savings and loan to fail. Suggests that five US senators may have exercised undue influence on Keating's behalf.
Business and Economics
Dist - PBS Prod - DOCCON 1990

Other Pieces of the Puzzle 30 MIN
Videoreel / VT2
Solutions in Communications Series
Color (T)
Education; English Language
Dist - SCCOE Prod - SCCOE

Other Planets - no Place Like Earth 30 MIN
16mm / VHS
Life Around Us Series
(J H C)
$99.95 each, $695.00 series
Presents the knowledge we have about the planets and tours the solar system.
Science - Natural; Science - Physical; Sociology
Dist - AMBROS Prod - AMBROS 1971

Other Planets - no Place Like Earth 30 MIN
U-matic / VHS / 16mm
Life Around Us Series
Color (I) (SPANISH)
Summarizes the knowledge that scientists have gathered about the planets. Covers such subjects as the seasonal changes on Mars, the atmosphere of Venus, the motion of Jupiter, the rings of Saturn and the discoveries of Neptune and Pluto. Takes the viewer on a tour of the outer planets, simulating a trip actually planned for the late '70'S.
Science - Physical
Dist - TIMLIF Prod - TIMLIF 1971

The Other Poland 40 MIN
16mm / U-matic / VHS
Color (J)
Portrays the steam engines called 'chukchas', which are still the main means of transport in Poland from one village to another. Shows old soldiers on a train north of Warsaw and a wedding in a 500 year old church.
Geography - World; History - World; Social Science
Dist - FI Prod - BBCTV 1983

Other reckless things 20 MIN
16mm
Color (G)
$55.00 rental
Responds to a newspaper account of a self - inflicted Caesarian section. Alternates medical footage with clips of news resports bringing into question issues of invasion of privacy, voyeurism, control over one's body and the use of technology in situations that may not require it.
Fine Arts
Dist - CANCIN Prod - LIPZIN 1984

The other shore 79 MIN
VHS
Color; PAL (G)
PdS100 purchase
Examines the filmmaker's close relationship with a Peruvian family. Presents a Mikael Wistrom for Manharen Film & Television production.
Fine Arts; Geography - World; Sociology
Dist - BALFOR

The Other Side 30 MIN
U-matic / VHS
Color
Reports on some of the contrasts and complexities of the Soviet Union.
Civics and Political Systems; Geography - World; History - World
Dist - WCCOTV Prod - WCCOTV 1982

The Other Side 10 MIN
16mm
B&W (H)
LC 72-701714
Presents a commentary without words on the tragedy of conformity in which men and women ruled by a hidden fascist dictatorship are forced to sidestep down the sidewalk in a single, shoulder - to - shoulder line, bodies facing the buildings, hands sliding along the walls.
Civics and Political Systems; Guidance and Counseling; Psychology; Sociology
Dist - VIEWFI Prod - WUYTS 1972

The Other side of faith 27 MIN
16mm
Color (G)
Portrays 16 - year - old Stefania Podgorska, a Polish Catholic girl, and her six - year - old sister, Helena, who were left alone after their father died and their mother and brothers were forcibly taken by the Nazis to a German labor camp. Reveals that Stefania sheltered 13 Jewish people for nearly 2.5 years in the attic of her home.
History - World
Dist - ADL Prod - DOCINT 1991

The Other Side of Japan 30 MIN
U-matic / VHS
Journey into Japan Series
Color (J S C G)
MV=$195.00
Shows that the traditional village life of Japan can still be found in remote areas.
Geography - World; History - World
Dist - LANDMK Prod - LANDMK 1986

The Other Side of Rape 30 MIN
VHS / U-matic
Color (PRO)
Increases awareness of the many difficulties faced by the victims of rape.
Health and Safety; Social Science; Sociology
Dist - HSCIC Prod - HSCIC 1982

The Other side of the border 60 MIN
VHS
Color (G)
$100.00 purchase _ #OSOB - 000
Examines issues surrounding illegal immigration into the U S, particularly from Mexico and Central America. Reveals that although many blame the illegal immigrants for stealing jobs, the immigrants actually benefit the U S

economy. Discusses the possible effects of Congressional legislation passed in 1986 which imposes penalties on employers who hire illegal immigrants. Features two Mexican immigrant families.
Sociology
Dist - PBS **Prod** - KERA 1987

The Other Side of the Canvas 29 MIN
Videoreel / VT2
Museum Open House Series
Color
Fine Arts
Dist - PBS **Prod** - WGBHTV

The Other Side of the Desk 25 MIN
U-matic / VHS
Desk Set II Series
Color
Psychology
Dist - DELTAK **Prod** - ERF

The Other Side of the Desk 30 MIN
VHS / U-matic
Desk Set II Series
Color (H A)
Features a secretary promoted to supervisor, who knows her subordinates and communicates constructively with them, suggests to unsuccessful job applicants how to improve their prospects through promptness, organization and discretion and asks her staff for suggestions while delegating responsibilities appropriately. Emphasizes importance of clear communication.
Business and Economics; Guidance and Counseling
Dist - AITECH **Prod** - ERESI

The Other Side of the Fence 10 MIN
VHS / 16mm
Color (J H A)
$75.00 rental
Tries to make young people aware of the way veal calves are raised. Offers tangible steps young people can take to improve these animals' lives.
Agriculture
Dist - VARDIR

The Other Side of the Ledger 42 MIN
16mm
Color (H C A)
#4X6 I
Presents criticisms by the Canadian Indian and Metis people of the official celebrations of the Hudson Bay Company's 300th anniversary.
Social Science
Dist - CDIAND **Prod** - NFBC 1972

The Other Side of the Mountain 30 MIN
16mm
Glory Trail Series
B&W (I)
LC FIA66-1237
Relays the spirit of adventure in the exploration and conquest of the American West.
History - United States
Dist - IU **Prod** - NET 1965

The Other Side of the River 29 MIN
U-matic / VHS / 16mm
Color (J)
LC 79-701802
Discusses floods, showing the causes, the terrors of a flood in action, and the emotional, social and economic impact associated with such a disaster.
History - World; Science - Physical
Dist - MCFI **Prod** - COUKLA 1975

The Other Six Days 30 MIN
16mm
Color (J H T R)
LC FIA66-1140
Compares the values of the Church with the values of the business world, discussing whether or not a Christian can be both a good churchman and businessman wiouout conflict.
Business and Economics; Guidance and Counseling; Psychology; Religion and Philosophy; Sociology
Dist - FAMF **Prod** - FAMF 1965

The Other Thailand 29 MIN
VHS / U-matic
Journey into Thailand Series
Color (J S C A)
MV=$195.00
Shows the south of Thailand, an area of rubber plantations, tin mines and mangrove swamps. The majority of people are Muslim and mosques dominate the skyline.
Geography - World; History - World
Dist - LANDMK **Prod** - LANDMK 1986

Other Treatment Modalities 18 MIN
U-matic / VHS
Psychiatry Learning System, Pt 2 - Disorders Series
Color (PRO)
Explains somatic therapies and hypnotherapy.
Health and Safety; Psychology
Dist - HSCIC **Prod** - HSCIC 1982

Other Uses for Ceramics 28 MIN
Videoreel / VT2
Wheels, Kilns and Clay Series
Color
Features Mrs Peterson describing certain ceramic processes for her classroom at the University of Southern California. Demonstrates various uses for ceramics.
Fine Arts
Dist - PBS **Prod** - USC

The Other victim - coping and caring techniques for the caregivers of Alzheimer's patients 47 MIN
U-matic / VHS
Color (PRO C G)
$195.00 purchase _ #C870 - VI - 049
Demonstrates behavior modification techniques for caregivers to use with Alzheimer's victims. Presents ways to respond to questions and accusations without provoking the catastrophic reactions that often result when the caregiver reacts to an Alzheimer's victim normally. Uses a series of vignettes to demonstate the techniques. Presented by Dick Bakkerud and the Creighton School of Nursing.
Health and Safety; Psychology
Dist - HSCIC **Prod** - HSCIC 1987

Other Voices 90 MIN
16mm
B&W
Explores the lives of five young mental patients. Follows their lives together in a family setting in the homes of married staff therapists and as they undergo treatment called reality confrontation.
Psychology; Sociology
Dist - NATTAL **Prod** - NATTAL

Other voices, other songs - the Armenians 30 MIN
VHS
Color (H C G)
$195.00 purchase, $55.00 rental
Celebrates the survival of the Armenians despite repeated persecution. Features performances by folk music and dance companies, including the Sayat Nova Armenian Folk Dance Company. Produced by Sapphire Productions.
Fine Arts; History - United States
Dist - FLMLIB

Other voices, other songs - the Greeks 30 MIN
VHS
Color (H C G)
$195.00 purchase, $55.00 rental
Examines the roots of Hellenic music through films of both Europe and America. Looks at a country festival in Greece and authentic songs and dances by several Greek - American companies. Produced by Sapphire Productions.
Fine Arts; History - United States; History - World
Dist - FLMLIB

The Other Way 50 MIN
16mm / U-matic / VHS
Color (C A)
Presents E F Schumacher's contention that the idea that everything bigger is better is a 20th century myth. Argues that human needs must come first rather than adapting people to the needs of machines. Provides examples in favor of this argument.
Sociology
Dist - FI **Prod** - BBCTV 1975

The Other World 19 MIN
16mm
Captioned; Color (I)
LC 77-700232
Demonstrates that in a balanced ecology the materials of life and death are constantly recycled by showing the biological ladder from microscopic plants and animals to the otter.
Science - Natural
Dist - MOKIN **Prod** - NFBC 1976

The Other world of Winston Churchill 54 MIN
VHS
Color (G)
$29.95 purchase _ #1614
Portrays the 'second career' of Winston Churchill as a painter, in his own words. Features actor Paul Scofield as narrator.
Fine Arts; Literature and Drama
Dist - INSTRU **Prod** - KULTUR 1964

Other Worlds Series
Guatemala - Land of Looms 30 MIN
Dist - AVED

Others 14 MIN
U-matic / VHS / BETA
Color; PAL (J H)
PdS40, PdS48 purchase
Looks at the dilemma of youngsters when they act out revenge by vandalism. Reveals the psychological ramifications when he or she discovers that the person hated is a human being too.
Psychology; Sociology
Dist - EDPAT

Others 13 MIN
16mm / U-matic / VHS
Color (I J)
LC 72-702590
Presents Greg, a ten - year - old boy, who is caught up in a common childhood situation, being treated unfairly by his teachers. Shows children that there are other people with problems whom we must learn to understand and that they are not the center of the universe.
Education; Guidance and Counseling; Sociology
Dist - WOMBAT **Prod** - WOMBAT 1972

Others 30 MIN
VHS
Color (I J H R G A)
$24.95 purchase _ #87EE0121
Profiles a family struggling to make ends meet and how they learned that putting others first makes a big difference. Espouses the 'J - O - Y' philosophy - 'Jesus first, Others, then You.'
Guidance and Counseling; Literature and Drama; Religion and Philosophy
Dist - CPH **Prod** - CPH

Others 28 MIN
VHS
Color (I J H C G A R)
$24.95 purchase, $10.00 rental _ #35 - 8121 - 19
Tells how Jerry comes to see that joyfulness can be a part of ordinary life.
Literature and Drama; Religion and Philosophy
Dist - APH **Prod** - FAMF

The Others 59 MIN
VHS / 16mm
Color (G)
$70.00 rental _ #OTRS - 000
Documents the problems of the mentally retarded and severely handicapped. Compares the work of the public and private sectors in dealing with these problems and examines services in Minnesota as examples of good care.
Health and Safety
Dist - PBS

Otherwise Known as Sheila the Great 24 MIN
16mm / VHS / U-matic
Color; Captioned (K P I)
$565.00, $395.00, $425.00 purchase _ #A542
Adapts the Judy Blume story in which a young girl spends a summer vacation facing some of her fears - spiders, swimming, the dark and dogs. Examines her contradictory feelings about herself as adventures and a new friend help her overcome her fears. Directed by Lawrence Blume.
Literature and Drama; Psychology
Dist - BARR **Prod** - CFJB 1988

Othon 88 MIN
16mm
Color (GERMAN (ENGLISH SUBTITLES) GERMAN (FRENCH SUBTITLES))
A French subtitle version of the German language film. Bases its story on the drama by Corneille. Juxtaposes the requirements of a man's drive for power with those of his love affair with a woman. Takes place in ancient settings with modern noises in the background.
Fine Arts
Dist - NYFLMS **Prod** - NYFLMS 1969

Otis Brown - 10 - 30 - 75 30 MIN
VHS / Cassette
Poetry Center reading series
Color (G)
#152 - 118
Features the African - American writer reading from his works at the Poetry Center, San Francisco State University, with an introduction by Lewis MacAdams. Available for listening purposes only at the Center; not for purchase or rent.
Literature and Drama
Dist - POETRY **Prod** - POETRY 1975

Otitis media 8 MIN
VHS
Color (PRO G)
$250.00 purchase _ #OT - 09
Explains otitis media to parents whose children have this condition. Uses animation to illustrate the procedure and discusses risks as well as recovery. Teaches that myringotomy and placement of pressure equalizing tubes are often recommended and that adenoids may need to be removed. The importance of keeping ears dry after tube placement is stressed. Developed in cooperation with and endorsed by the American Academy of Otolaryngology - Head and Neck Surgery.

Health and Safety; Science - Natural
Dist - MIFE Prod - MIFE 1991

The Otoneurological Examination for Vestibular Cerebellar Function 25 MIN
U-matic / VHS
Color (PRO)
Illustrates various office procedures for establishing a patient's degree of vestibular - cerebellar function.
Health and Safety
Dist - WFP **Prod** - WFP

Otoplasty - a Tribute to Dr Becker 24 MIN
16mm
Color (PRO)
Illustrates the dissecting techniques used by Dr Oscar J Becker and outlines the mattress suture technique.
Health and Safety; Science
Dist - SCITIF **Prod** - SCITIF 1971

Otorhinolaryngological Hemorrhage 28 MIN
16mm
Color
Points out nosebleeding is a symptom very commonly encountered in daily clinical activities. Shows the capillary structures and function at the nasal area, the mechanism of nosebleeding, especially cases of epistaxis, the methods of the hematrogic and blook chemical examinations, the effects of local hemostatic agents by microscopy and treatment of bleeding in surgical operation.
Health and Safety; Science; Science - Natural
Dist - UNIJAP **Prod** - UNIJAP 1971

Otosclerosis Surgery 50 MIN
U-matic / VHS
Color (PRO)
Presents a review of all aspects of otosclerotic surgery, including the early history of stapes surgery, a step - by - step presentation of technique, various footplate problems, causes of sensorineural hearing impairment following stapes surgery, the incus replacement prosthesis procedure, fistula problems, and dizziness.
Guidance and Counseling; Health and Safety; Science - Natural
Dist - HOUSEI **Prod** - HOUSEI

Otosclerosis Surgery - the Early Years 55 MIN
U-matic / VHS
Color (PRO)
Presents the recollections of Drs House and Shambaugh about their early experience in otosclerosis surgery.
Guidance and Counseling; Health and Safety; Science - Natural
Dist - HOUSEI **Prod** - HOUSEI

Otosclerosis Surgery - the Stapes Era 79 MIN
U-matic / VHS
Color (PRO)
Presents recollections about the Lempert era and the early years of stapes surgery.
Guidance and Counseling; Health and Safety; Science - Natural
Dist - HOUSEI **Prod** - HOUSEI

Otosclerosis - the Fenestration and Stapes Eras 58 MIN
VHS / U-matic
Color (PRO)
Presents recollections of the historical aspects and early days of otosclerosis surgery.
Guidance and Counseling; Health and Safety; Science - Natural
Dist - HOUSEI **Prod** - HOUSEI

Otoscope 15 MIN
U-matic
Instruments of Physical Assessment Series
Color (PRO)
LC 80-707626
Discusses various types of otoscopes and tells how to use and maintain each piece of equipment.
Health and Safety
Dist - LIP **Prod** - SUNYSB 1980

Ottawa 76 5 MIN
16mm
Color
LC 77-700233
Presents computer animation of the owl logo of the first international animated film festival held in North America, Ottawa 76.
Fine Arts; Industrial and Technical Education
Dist - CFI **Prod** - CFI 1976

Ottawa - Canada's Capital 11 MIN
16mm
Color
LC FIA68-1222
Pictures different parts of Ottawa. Views the Parliament and describes ceremonies associated with the Parliament building.
Civics and Political Systems; Geography - World
Dist - MORLAT **Prod** - MORLAT 1967

Otter coast 26 MIN
VHS
Challenge of the seas series
Color (I J H)
$225.00 purchase
Reveals that once more than 100,000 sea otters lived on the coast of California. Discloses that fur traders decimated the population and made the sea otter almost extinct in California. When the population came back under protection, otters were in conflict with humans over resources such as abalone. Part of a 26 - part series on the oceans.
Science - Natural; Science - Physical
Dist - LANDMK **Prod** - LANDMK 1991

Otter, seal, and penguin 25 MIN
VHS
Nature watch series
Color (P I J H C)
$49.00 purchase _ #320213; LC 89-715857
Demonstrates the unique qualities of the otter, the penguin and the seal in captivity and in their natural habitats. Part of a series that explores the curious and uncommon characteristics of a variety of mammals, insects, birds and sea creatures.
Science - Natural
Dist - TVOTAR **Prod** - TVOTAR 1988

Otters 10 MIN
U-matic / VHS
Eye on Nature Series
Color (I J)
$250 purchase
Explains the behavior, male and female physiology, and mating rituals of otters. Produced by the BBC.
Science - Natural
Dist - CORF

Otters, Clowns of the Sea 14 MIN
U-matic / VHS / 16mm
Color (J H)
LC 74-702693
Presents the Southern sea otter in a variety of moods. Shows the mothers' devoted care and feeding of the pups and their playful antics as they are growing up and begin their own constant search for food. Explains that as a protected species, it is now flourishing in colonies along the California coast.
Science - Natural
Dist - AIMS **Prod** - CHANGW 1973

Otto - a Study in Abnormal Psychology 27 MIN
U-matic / VHS / 16mm
Otto Series
Color (C)
LC 76-701900
Presents Otto as a middle - aged man suffering from real and imagined pressures at home and at work. Shows how he feels overburdened and insecure in his job as senior book editor. Observes him struggling to relate calmly to his secretary, his assistant and his boss. Shows also how, at home, his wife complains that he never listens to her and never tells her about his feelings. Watches Otto suffering from insomnia and becoming increasingly withdrawn and anxious.
Psychology; Sociology
Dist - IU **Prod** - IU 1976

Otto asks a riddle 5 MIN
16mm
Otto the auto - pedestrian safety - B series
Color (K P)
$30.00 purchase _ #160
Features Otto the Auto who discusses the need for obeying and cooperating with school safety patrols and crossing guards. Part of a series on pedestrian safety. Complete series available on 0.5 inch VHS.
Health and Safety
Dist - AAAFTS **Prod** - AAAFTS 1958

Otto goes ice skating 4 MIN
16mm
Otto the auto - pedestrian safety - D series
Color (K P)
$30.00 purchase _ #200
Features Otto the Auto who points out why a driver might not see a child pedestrian even though that child seems to be in plain sight. Part of a series on pedestrian safety. Complete series available on 0.5 inch VHS.
Health and Safety
Dist - AAAFTS **Prod** - AAAFTS 1971

Otto meets a puppet 5 MIN
16mm
Otto the auto - pedestrian safety - B series
Color (K P)
$30.00 purchase _ #165
Features Otto the Auto who emphasizes the need for looking all ways before crossing a street. Part of a series on pedestrian safety. Complete series available on 0.5 inch VHS.
Health and Safety
Dist - AAAFTS **Prod** - AAAFTS 1958

Otto Messmer and Felix the Cat 25 MIN
U-matic / VHS / 16mm
Color (J)
LC 81-700885
Offers a tribute to Otto Messmer and his famous cartoon character, Felix the Cat. Features the cartoonist, who describes the evolution of Felix's personality, and includes excerpts from five vintage shorts starring Felix the Cat.
Fine Arts
Dist - PHENIX **Prod** - CANEJ 1978

Otto Series
Otto - a Study in Abnormal Psychology 27 MIN
Otto - the Behavioral Perspective 26 MIN
Otto - the Phenomenological Perspective 25 MIN
Otto - the Psychoanalytic Perspective 28 MIN
Otto - the Social Perspective 26 MIN
Dist - IU

Otto the auto - A series
Otto the auto - series A - pedestrian safety 13 MIN
Otto the auto, series A 14 MIN
Dist - AAAFTS

Otto the auto - B series
Otto the auto - series B - Pedestrian safety 13 MIN
Otto the auto, series B 14 MIN
Dist - AAAFTS

Otto the auto - bicycle safety - F series
Bicycle border patrol 4 MIN
Bikes go with the flow 4 MIN
Dream bike 4 MIN
Dist - AAAFTS

Otto the auto - C series
Otto the auto - series C - pedestrian safety 18 MIN
Dist - AAAFTS

Otto the auto, D series
Otto the auto - series D - pedestrian safety 16 MIN
Otto the auto, series D 22 MIN
Dist - AAAFTS

Otto the auto - E series
Otto the auto - series E - seatbelts and school bus safety 12 MIN
Dist - AAAFTS

Otto the auto - F series - bicycle safety 12 MIN
VHS
Otto the auto - F series
Color (K P)
$30.00 purchase _ #461
Contains three, four - minute bicycle safety films based on the recommendations of Dr Kenneth Cross about bicycle accidents, their causes and what safety lessons need to be stressed with primary grade children. Includes the titles 'Bicycle Border Patrol', 'Dream Bike', 'Bikes Go With the Flow'. Titles available separately on 16mm film.
Health and Safety
Dist - AAAFTS **Prod** - AAAFTS 1981

Otto the auto - F series
Otto the auto - F series - bicycle safety 12 MIN
Dist - AAAFTS

Otto the auto - pedestrian safety - A series
Inky and Blinky 5 MIN
The Little white line that cried 5 MIN
Dist - AAAFTS

Otto the auto - pedestrian safety - B series
The Bright yellow raincoat 5 MIN
Otto asks a riddle 5 MIN
Otto meets a puppet 5 MIN
Dist - AAAFTS

Otto the auto - pedestrian safety - C series
Billy's new tricycle 5 MIN
Peter the pigeon 5 MIN
Squeaky and his playmates 5 MIN
Timothy the turtle 5 MIN
Dist - AAAFTS

Otto the auto - pedestrian safety - D series
Horseplay 4 MIN
Otto goes ice skating 4 MIN
The Secret of pushbuttons 4 MIN
Dist - AAAFTS

Otto the auto - pedestrian safety series
Two sleeping lions 5 MIN
Dist - AAAFTS

Otto the auto - seatbelt and school bus safety - E series
Buckle up 4 MIN
Inside the school bus 4 MIN

Outside the school bus 4 MIN
Dist - AAAFTS

Otto the auto, series A 14 MIN
16mm
Otto the auto, A series
Color (K P)
LC 72-701492
Presents three films entitled Two Sleeping Lions, Inky And Blinky and The Little White Line That Cried. Uses animation to illustrate traffic safety rules for pedestrians, including crossing streets at the corner instead of between parked cars, and the importance of wearing white at night.
Health and Safety
Dist - AAAFTS **Prod** - AAAFTS 1957

Otto the auto - series A - pedestrian safety 13 MIN
VHS
Otto the auto - A series
Color (K P)
$30.00 purchase _ #456
Contains three, five - minute safety films for young children about pedestrian safety. Features Otto the Auto presenting safety education lessons in short, animated learning sequences. Includes the titles 'Two Sleeping Lions', 'The Little White Line That Cried', 'Inky and Blinky'. Titles available separately on 16mm film.
Health and Safety
Dist - AAAFTS **Prod** - AAAFTS 1957

Otto the auto, series B 14 MIN
16mm
Otto the auto, B series
Color (K P I)
LC 72-701493
Presents three films entitled The Bright Yellow Raincoat, Otto Meets A Puppet and Otto Asks A Riddle. Uses animation to illustrate pedestrian traffic safety rules for school areas, bad weather and crossing streets.
Health and Safety
Dist - AAAFTS **Prod** - AAAFTS 1958

Otto the auto - series B - Pedestrian safety 13 MIN
VHS
Otto the auto - B series
Color (K P)
$30.00 purchase _ #457
Contains three, five - minute safety films for young children about pedestrian safety. Features Otto the Auto presenting safety education lessons in short, animated learning sequences. Includes the titles 'Otto Asks a Riddle', 'Otto Meets a Puppet', 'The Bright Yellow Raincoat'. Titles available separately on 16mm film.
Health and Safety
Dist - AAAFTS **Prod** - AAAFTS 1958

Otto the auto, series C 18 MIN
16mm
Otto the auto series
Color (K P I)
LC 72-701494
Presents four films entitled Squeaky And His Playmates, Billy's New Tricycle, Peter The Pigeon and Timothy The Turtle. Uses animation to illustrate safety rules for walking, playing and bike riding near traffic.
Health and Safety
Dist - AAAFTS **Prod** - AAAFTS 1959

Otto the auto - series C - pedestrian safety 18 MIN
VHS
Otto the auto - C series
Color (K P)
$30.00 purchase _ #458
Contains four, five - minute safety films for young children about pedestrian safety. Features Otto the Auto presenting safety education lessons in short, animated learning sequences. Includes the titles 'Squeaky and His Playmates', 'Billy's New Tricycle', 'Peter the Pigeon', 'Timothy the Turtle'. Titles available separately on 16mm film.
Health and Safety
Dist - AAAFTS **Prod** - AAAFTS 1959

Otto the auto, series D 22 MIN
16mm
Otto the auto, D series
Color
LC 78-711386
Presents four films entitled A Surprise For Otto, Otto Goes Ice Skating, Horseplay and The Secret Of Push Buttons. Uses animation to illustrate traffic safety rules for pedestrians.
Health and Safety; Social Science
Dist - AAAFTS **Prod** - AAAFTS 1971

Otto the auto - series D - pedestrian safety 16 MIN
VHS
Otto the auto - D series
Color (K P)
$30.00 purchase _ #459
Contains four, four - minute safety films for young children about pedestrian safety. Features Otto the Auto presenting safety education lessons in short, animated learning sequences. Includes the titles 'A Surprise for Otto', 'Otto Goes Ice Skating', 'Horseplay', 'The Secret of Pushbuttons'. Titles available separately on 16mm film.
Health and Safety
Dist - AAAFTS **Prod** - AAAFTS 1971

Otto the auto - series E - seatbelts and school bus safety 12 MIN
VHS
Otto the auto - E series
Color (K P)
$30.00 purchase _ #460
Contains three, four - minute safety films for young children about seatbelts and school bus safety. Features Otto the Auto presenting safety education lessons in short, animated learning sequences. Includes the titles 'Buckle Up', 'Inside the School Bus', 'Outside the School Bus'. Titles available separately on 16mm film.
Health and Safety
Dist - AAAFTS **Prod** - AAAFTS 1976

Otto the Auto Series
Otto the auto, series C 18 MIN
A Surprise for Otto 4 MIN
Dist - AAAFTS

Otto - the Behavioral Perspective 26 MIN
16mm / U-matic / VHS
Otto Series
Color (C)
LC 76-701902
Presents Dr John Gottman of Indiana University interpreting the Otto case study film from the behavioral perspective. Tells how he sees Otto coping with catastrophic expectations by trying to be all things to all people and how he does not see people as resources to help him cope with stress. Discusses how, in terms of treatment, Dr Gottman would align himself with Otto's goals and Otto's perception of things and how he believes Otto would benefit from social skills training both in terms of his work and his marriage.
Psychology; Sociology
Dist - IU **Prod** - IU 1976

Otto - the Phenomenological Perspective 25 MIN
U-matic / VHS / 16mm
Otto Series
Color (C)
LC 76-701904
Presents Dr Gary Stollak of Michigan State University interpreting the Otto case study film from the phenomenological perspective. Tells how he does not believe that Otto necessarily has a problem and how he feels that Otto is very lonely because neither his wife nor his co - workers share his particular sense of values. Discusses how Dr Stollak would not consider Otto as a patient but rather as a fellow human being and how his encounters with Otto would not focus on producing changes but on giving him a sense of togetherness.
Psychology; Sociology
Dist - IU **Prod** - IU 1976

Otto - the Psychoanalytic Perspective 28 MIN
U-matic / VHS / 16mm
Otto Series
Color (C)
LC 76-701901
Presents Dr Bruce Denner of Governors State University, Illinois, interpreting the Otto case study film from the psychoanalytic perspective. Tells how he believes that Otto is not coping with getting old and how he sees Otto moving away from mature reactions, over - reacting and using defense mechanisms. Discusses how, according to Dr Denner, the reality principle has broken down for Otto and how, as Otto's analyst, Dr Denner would act as a transfer figure, taking on properties of early figures in Otto's life so Otto could work out his early conflicts.
Psychology; Sociology
Dist - IU **Prod** - IU 1976

Otto - the Social Perspective 26 MIN
U-matic / VHS / 16mm
Otto Series
Color (C)
LC 76-701905
Presents Dr Richard Price of the University of Michigan interpreting the Otto case study film from the social perspective. States that the world is making unreasonable demands on Otto and that he does not believe that anything inside of Otto is causing his breakdown. Tells that, according to Dr Price, Otto is being cast in the role of mental patient by the people around him. Discusses how Dr Price would try to help Otto by teaching him to appreciate the nature of the external events around him.
Psychology; Sociology
Dist - IU **Prod** - IU 1976

Otto, Zoo Gorilla 58 MIN
16mm / U-matic / VHS
Color (I)
LC 79-700168
Takes a behind - the - scenes look at the Lincoln Park Zoo in Chicago. Focuses on the transfer of the great apes to new quarters, a delicate and dangerous process which afforded scientists an opportunity to gather data on the apes.
Science - Natural
Dist - FI **Prod** - LINCPK 1978

Otto, Zoo Gorilla, Pt 1 29 MIN
U-matic / VHS / 16mm
Color (I)
LC 79-700168
Takes a behind - the - scenes look at the Lincoln Park Zoo in Chicago. Focuses on the transfer of the great apes to new quarters, a delicate and dangerous process which afforded scientists an opportunity to gather data on the apes.
Science - Natural
Dist - FI **Prod** - LINCPK 1978

Otto, Zoo Gorilla, Pt 2 29 MIN
U-matic / VHS / 16mm
Color (I)
LC 79-700168
Takes a behind - the - scenes look at the Lincoln Park Zoo in Chicago. Focuses on the transfer of the great apes to new quarters, a delicate and dangerous process which afforded scientists an opportunity to gather data on the apes.
Science - Natural
Dist - FI **Prod** - LINCPK 1978

The Ottoman empire - 1280 - 1683 30 MIN
VHS
World - A Television history series
Color (C A T)
$55.00 rental
Covers developments in the Ottoman Empire in the period from 1280 to 1683. Based on "The Times Atlas of World History." Serves as part 14 of a 26 - part telecourse. Available only to institutions of higher education.
History - World; Sociology
Dist - SCETV **Prod** - SCETV 1986

The Ottoman Empire - 1280 - 1683 26 MIN
VHS / 16mm / U-matic
World - a Television History Series
Color (J H C)
$400.00, $475.00 purchase
Describes the Turks emerging from their homeland in the steppes of Central Asia and expanding to capture the Byzantine city of Constantinople, which they establish as their capital, Istanbul.
History - World
Dist - LANDMK **Prod** - NETGOL 1985

Ottorino Respighi - a Dream of Italy 75 MIN
VHS / U-matic
Color
Presents the work of composer Ottorino Respighi. Examines the influence of Italy on his musical vision.
Fine Arts
Dist - FOTH **Prod** - FOTH

Ou Va - t - Il, D'ou Vient - Il 13 MIN
16mm
Les Francaise Chez Vous Series
B&W (I J H)
Foreign Language
Dist - CHLTN **Prod** - PEREN 1967

Ouch 30 MIN
VHS
Bodymatters series
Color (H C A)
PdS65 purchase
Discusses tolerance of pain and how the body deals with it. Part of a series of 26 30-minute videos on various systems of the human body.
Science - Natural
Dist - BBCENE

The Ouchless house - your baby safe home 30 MIN
VHS
Color (H C G)
$59.95 purchase _ #CCP0071V
Shows how to create a baby safe home, avoid unnecessary injuries and be prepared for quick action if accidents should occur. Includes The Perfectly Safe Home book and poster.
Health and Safety
Dist - CAMV **Prod** - CAMV 1992

The Ounce 29 MIN
VHS / 16mm
Watch your mouth series
Color (H)

$46.00 rental _ #WAYM - 112
Emphasizes language and communication skills for high school students. Notes the difference between formal and informal word usage.
Education; English Language; Psychology; Social Science
Dist - PBS

An Ounce of Cure 26 MIN
16mm / U-matic / VHS
Color (H C A)
Tells the story of a woman who looks back with humor and irony as she recalls her first experience with love and heartbreak in the 1950's. Her steadfast friend sees her through an impulsive experiment with alcohol from which she emerges with a new appreciation for life's absurdities. From the story by Alice Munro.
Health and Safety; Literature and Drama; Psychology; Sociology
Dist - BCNFL **Prod** - ATLAF 1984

An Ounce of different 15 MIN
VHS
Color (IND PRO G)
$595.00 purchase, $150.00 rental _ #WSB09
Introduces Emory Austin, businesswoman and professional speaker. Teaches the viewer how to appreciate diversity and committment in the workplace and in personal life. Produced by Washington Productions.
Business and Economics; Psychology
Dist - EXTR

An Ounce of Prevention 14 MIN
U-matic / VHS / 16mm
Learning Values with Fat Albert and the Cosby Kids, Set II Series
Color (P I)
Reports that alcoholism can be a problem with children and discusses how it is related to emotional stress.
Guidance and Counseling; Health and Safety
Dist - MGHT **Prod** - FLMTON 1977

An Ounce of Prevention 26 MIN
U-matic / VHS / 16mm
Color (J)
Sheds light on such problems as why people drink alcohol, what does excessive drinking do to the body and the cost of alcohol abuse to alcoholics, their families, industry and government.
Health and Safety; Sociology
Dist - CORF **Prod** - HARVP

Ounce of Prevention 30 MIN
U-matic / VHS
Dealing in Discipline Series
Color (T)
Education; Psychology
Dist - GPN **Prod** - UKY 1980

An Ounce of Prevention
U-matic / VHS
Color
Features Bugs Bunny and Daffy Duck who demonstrate practical ways to prevent burn injuries at home.
Health and Safety
Dist - NFPA **Prod** - NFPA

An Ounce of prevention 20 MIN
U-matic / VHS
Child sexual abuse - an ounce of prevention series
Color (A)
Features a pediatrician and social worker explaining to adults how to prevent child sexual abuse and how to deal with it if it happens. Explains that most abusers are persons the parents and children know and trust and that most assault is not violent and leaves no physical signs on children. Urges parents to listen to and believe children and encourage them not to keep secrets.
Health and Safety; Home Economics; Sociology
Dist - AITECH **Prod** - PPCIN

An Ounce of Prevention 27 MIN
16mm
Color
LC 77-702602
Presents interviews with authorities on alcoholism in order to highlight the problem. Details methods of rehabilitation tried in Saskatchewan in the mid - 1970's.
Health and Safety; Psychology; Sociology
Dist - SASKDH **Prod** - SASKDH 1976

An Ounce of Prevention 30 MIN
U-matic / VHS
Loosening the Grip Series
Color (C A)
Health and Safety
Dist - GPN **Prod** - UMA 1980

An Ounce of prevention - a product liability case study 20 MIN
VHS
Color (A)
$525.00 purchase
Illustrates the necessary provisions of an effective loss prevention program for any organization. Uses actual situations to emphasize important points concerning design, manufacturing, labeling, and marketing. Includes one sample leader's manual. Additional copies are available separately.
Business and Economics; Civics and Political Systems; Education
Dist - COMFLM **Prod** - COMFLM

Ounce of Prevention Series
Decisions decisions - before your baby is born 30 MIN
The Opposite of Love 30 MIN
Dist - CFDC

Our 49th state 15 MIN
16mm / U-matic / VHS
American legacy series
Color (I)
Presents John Rugg discussing Alaska, covering geographical features, wildlife and the Eskimo. Covers such topics as climate changes, the importance of the floatplane, comparisons between the modern Eskimo and their ancestors, and the significance of Prudhoe oil and the trans - Alaska pipeline to the American economy. Uses a dramatic vignette portraying William Seward's determination to purchase Alaska from Russia.
Geography - United States; History - United States; Social Science
Dist - AITECH **Prod** - KRMATV 1983

Our Aching Backs 26 MIN
U-matic / VHS
Color (C)
$249.00, $149.00 purchase _ #AD - 1888
Reveals that four out of five Americans experience severe back pain at some point in their lives. Looks at traditional and new methods of treating back problems and of preventing such problems.
Health and Safety; Psychology; Science - Natural
Dist - FOTH **Prod** - FOTH

Our Aching Backs 14 MIN
16mm
Color (H C A)
LC 76-706078
Combines limited animation, live action, artwork, and still photography to present information on back safety, with major emphasis on home hazards.
Health and Safety
Dist - SANDIA **Prod** - SANDIA 1969

Our Aching Backs 18 MIN
U-matic / VHS / 16mm
Color
Presents information on back safety in animation, with emphasis on home hazards. Includes humor, stylized sets and mod dress.
Health and Safety; Science - Natural
Dist - USNAC **Prod** - USNRC

Our amazing world series
Adventures at the zoo - Volume 6 30 MIN
Adventures in the desert - Volume 1 30 MIN
Adventures in the forest - Volume 4 30 MIN
Adventures in the sea - Volume 5 30 MIN
Adventures on the earth - Volume 2 30 MIN
Adventures on the farm - Volume 3 30 MIN
Dist - APH

Our American Crossroads 15 MIN
16mm
Color (J H A)
Shows what the typical little crossroads community was like back at the turn of the century and how it was changed by the increasing popularity of the automobile.
History - United States; Social Science; Sociology
Dist - GM **Prod** - GM 1968

Our American Flag 8 MIN
16mm / U-matic / VHS
American Values for Elementary Series
Color (P I)
LC 72-702674
John Forsythe narrates what the American flag represents and the role of each person as a citizen of his community and his country.
Civics and Political Systems; Social Science
Dist - AIMS **Prod** - EVANSA 1971

Our Ancestors the Bedouins 30 MIN
U-matic
Africa File Series
Color (J H)
Places the Maghreb area of north Africa in perspective, historically, geographically and politically.
Business and Economics; Geography - World; History - World; Religion and Philosophy
Dist - TVOTAR **Prod** - TVOTAR 1985

Our Angry Feelings 12 MIN
16mm / U-matic / VHS
Color (P)
LC FIA68-3267
Uses six dramatic episodes to provide insights into angry feelings people have. Illustrates why we become angry, shows the effects of anger and indicates how we may deal effectively and constructively with our angry feelings.
Geography - World; Psychology
Dist - PEREN **Prod** - PESHAK 1968

Our Animal Neighbors 11 MIN
16mm / U-matic / VHS
Color (P I)
$280 purchase - 16 mm, $195 purchase - video _ #3854
Shows diferent kinds of animals in different activities.
Science - Natural
Dist - CORF

Our Art Class Makes a Film 16 MIN
16mm / U-matic / VHS
Color (I J H C)
LC 73-701400
Traces the filmmaking activities of an art class. Shows preliminary research on the film topic, construction of scenery and papier - mache figures, special effects problems, handling of the camera, processing, photographic composition and the results of the completed project.
Fine Arts; Industrial and Technical Education
Dist - ALTSUL **Prod** - SIGMA 1971

Our Art Class Makes a Film - We Travel with Marco Polo 14 MIN
16mm / U-matic / VHS
Color
Follows each step in the production of a 16mm film on the travels of Marco Polo made by seventh graders. Shows the motion picture the students made.
Fine Arts; Industrial and Technical Education
Dist - ALTSUL **Prod** - SIGMA

Our baby is hearing - Part 1
VHS
Pathways for parenting - a program for deaf parents with hearing 'children series
Color (S R)
Advises deaf parents on dealing with hearing children. Available on a free - loan basis from the Lutheran Church - Missouri Synod's Deaf Ministry.
Guidance and Counseling; Literature and Drama; Religion and Philosophy
Dist - CPH **Prod** - LUMIS

Our Bible - How it Came to Us, Pt 1 - Formation of the Bible 25 MIN
16mm
B&W
Documents the background of the Bible, showing the Scriptures in use in Palestine in the time of Jesus and how the letters of Paul and the Gospels were written and used in the church.
Religion and Philosophy
Dist - ABS **Prod** - ABS

Our Bible - How it Came to Us, Pt 3 - Making of the English Bible 35 MIN
16mm
B&W
Opens with the invention of printing and the introduction of the Gutenberg Bible. Tells of the translation of the Bible into Latin and the spoken languages of Europe.
Religion and Philosophy
Dist - ABS **Prod** - ABS

Our Bible - How it Came to Us, Pt 2 - the Bible Crosses Europe 24 MIN
16mm
B&W
Tells of the translation of the Bible into the languages of the people.
Religion and Philosophy
Dist - ABS **Prod** - ABS

Our biosphere - the Earth in our hands 45 MIN
VHS
Smithsonian collection series
Color (J H C G)
$39.95 purchase _ #PMV001V
Reveals that, in an effort to unlock the mysteries of the fragile ecosystems of Earth, scientists at the Smithsonian's Museum of Natural History are creating living models of Earth's complex and diverse ecosystems. Features Robert Redford as narrator. Examines the controlled environment experiment of Biosphere II in the Arizona desert, an attempt to provide its inhabitants with fresh air, water and food in a self - sufficient complex. Part of a three - part series on Smithsonian collections.
Science - Natural
Dist - CAMV **Prod** - SMITHS 1991

Our biosphere - the Earth in our hands 48 MIN
VHS
Color (I J H)
$35.00 purchase _ #A5VH 1363
Visits Smithsonian's National Museum of Natural History to view living models of the Earth's delicate and diverse ecosystems. Features Robert Redford as host who leads a tour of ecological models of the Florida Everglades mangrove swamps and Chesapeake Bay blue crabs

swimming among clumps of marsh grasses in a museum basement. Travels to Biosphere II in the Arizona desert to study an experiment in which eight women and men are living together for two years in a sealed 2.5 acre glass dome.
Science - Natural
Dist - CLRVUE **Prod** - CLRVUE

Our Birth Film - Prepared Childbirth - the Human Drama of a Woman and Man in a Delivery 26 MIN
16mm
Color (H C A)
LC 75-700011
Shows the emotional interactions of a woman and a man sharing the experience of natural childbirth in the delivery room.
Guidance and Counseling; Sociology
Dist - MIFE **Prod** - MIFE 1973

Our Bodies, Ourselves 29 MIN
U-matic
Woman Series
Color
Interviews the authors of the women's health book Our Bodies, Ourselves.
Health and Safety; Sociology
Dist - PBS **Prod** - WNEDTV

Our Bones - a Delicate Matter 26 MIN
U-matic / VHS
Color (C)
$249.00, $149.00 purchase _ #AD - 1886
Focuses on current knowledge about osteoporosis, the loss of calcium from the skeletal structure of women after menopause. Examines the causes, diagnosis, treatment and prevention. Looks at stress fractures and spinal curvature and experimental treatment and proposed methods of prevention.
Health and Safety; Science - Natural; Sociology
Dist - FOTH **Prod** - FOTH

Our bread basket 15 MIN
16mm / U-matic / VHS
American legacy series
Color (I)
Provides an insight into modern - day wheat farming on both irrigated and dry land in the Great Plains. Shows cultivating the soil, planting seed, harvesting the kernels and marketing the crop. Highlights the history of the area by showing a sod house and shed, prairie grass, a one - room school, a windmill and other aspects of prairie life.
Agriculture; Geography - United States; History - United States
Dist - AITECH **Prod** - KRMATV 1983

Our Chance Series
Parents and Schools - St Louis, Missouri - 3 30 MIN
Partners - Burlington, Wisconsin - 1 30 MIN
Dist - AITECH

Our Changing Cities - Can they be Saved? 20 MIN
U-matic / VHS
Color (J C)
$79.00 purchase _ #3153
Concentrates on the crises of the city - its unemployment, social conflicts, poverty, and crime and ponders whether or not cities can survive the failure of dealing with technological changes.
Sociology
Dist - EBEC

Our changing continent 30 MIN
VHS
Color (J H)
$29.95 purchase _ #IV137
Explores concepts of paleontology - the study of ancient environments. Looks at the methods scientists use to determine what ancient environments once look like. Once this has been established, scientists can make predictions on what oil or mineral resources might be found associated with a particular environment. Allows scientists to predict what will happen to present areas such as lakes, river deltas and mountain chains. Investigates fossils as clues, rocks as clues, the Great Ice Age, the Age of Dinosaurs and geologic mapping.
Science - Physical
Dist - INSTRU

Our Changing Earth 14 MIN
16mm / U-matic / VHS
Color (I J H C) (SPANISH)
Points out changes in land masses through maps depicting different geologic periods. Shows geologists unearthing fossils and working in laboratories to determine the ages of rocks and fossils.
Foreign Language; Science - Physical
Dist - PHENIX **Prod** - FA 1961

Our changing earth 22 MIN
VHS
Color (P I J)
$89.00 purchase _ #RB856
Studies the earth. Considers the concepts of earth components - land, water, crust mantle and core, rotation of the earth on its axis, its revolution around the sun, its land buildup through volcanism and mountains, its erosion through weathering, erosion, glaciers and earthquakes.
Science - Physical
Dist - REVID **Prod** - REVID 1991

Our Changing Shores 21 MIN
16mm
Color (J H C)
Pictures how wind, water, ice and other natural phenomena affect the shore line of the Great Lakes area.
Geography - United States; Science - Natural; Science - Physical
Dist - OSUMPD **Prod** - OSUMPD 1958

Our Changing Way of Life - Cattleman - a Rancher's Story 22 MIN
U-matic / VHS / 16mm
Color (I J)
Shows activities on a cattle ranch during the four seasons, leading to the annual shipment of livestock to market. Compares old and new methods of operation, showing how technology is affecting cattle industries.
Agriculture; Social Science
Dist - EBEC **Prod** - EBEC 1964

Our Changing Way of Life - the Dairy Farmer 17 MIN
U-matic / VHS / 16mm
Color (I J)
Presents the contrasting views of two dairy farmers on problems associated with rising farm labor costs. Examines the changing way of life in the Midwest dairy region and discusses the role of automation in the modern dairy community.
Agriculture; Geography - United States; Social Science; Sociology
Dist - EBEC **Prod** - EBEC 1965

Our child goes to school - Part 2
VHS
Pathways for parenting - a program for deaf parents with hearing 'children series
Color (S R)
Advises deaf parents on dealing with hearing children. Available on a free - loan basis from the Lutheran Church - Missouri Synod's Deaf Ministry.
Guidance and Counseling; Literature and Drama; Religion and Philosophy
Dist - CPH **Prod** - LUMIS

Our child with Downs Syndrome 15 MIN
VHS / U-matic
Color
Portrays some of the experiences of new parents of a baby with Downs Syndrome. Emphasizes the importance of early intervention by integrating children with Downs Syndrome into family, school and society.
Psychology; Sociology
Dist - MIFE **Prod** - MIFE

Our children at risk 60 MIN
U-matic / VHS
Color (G C PRO)
$150.00 purchase _ #C920 - VI - 010; $395.00 purchase, $75.00 rental
Examines the crisis of child poverty and health care delivery. Examines ways to remove barriers to health development for disadvantaged children in the United States. Reveals that in the decade 1980 - 1990, the number of babies born to mothers who did not receive prenatal care, the number of children living in poverty, the number of children without health care and the number of children born to single mothers rose significantly. Hosted by Walter Cronkite.
Health and Safety; Sociology
Dist - HSCIC **Prod** - WNETTV 1992
FLMLIB

Our Children Our Future 14 MIN
16mm
Noise Kene Series
Color (H C A)
#2X114
Discusses the importance of the Indian child for the family, community, and for the future. Explains how values and traditional Indian ways can be communicated through examples set in storytelling.
Social Science
Dist - CDIAND **Prod** - CICH 1981

Our children series
A Bigger reward 15 MIN
A Clean house 15 MIN
First impressions 15 MIN
Flying straight 15 MIN
God's Christmas gift 15 MIN
Half Inch of Selfishness 15 MIN
I Don't Want to Win 15 MIN
King of the Block 15 MIN
Sharing is fun 15 MIN
Spending Money 15 MIN
Tokens of Love 15 MIN
Turn the Other Cheek 15 MIN
You Can't Buy Friendship 15 MIN
Dist - FAMF

Our children - Undzere kinder 80 MIN
35mm
Silent; B&W (G) (YIDDISH WITH ENGLISH SUBTITLES SPANISH AND YIDDISH INTERTITLES)
Depicts the poverty and political repression of Jews in Czarist Russia in the late 1920s where official policy opposed the prevailing antisemitism of the populace. Constructs a skeptical portrait, both negative and positive, of prerevolutionary shtetl life. Based on Sholem Aleichem's stories 'Motl peysi, the Cantor's Son.' Contact distributor for rental fee.
History - World; Religion and Philosophy; Social Science; Sociology
Dist - NCJEWF

Our Choice, Our Challenge 26 MIN
16mm
Color
LC 80-700515
Shows enlisted Navy women as they participate in some of the nontraditional jobs open to women.
Civics and Political Systems; Sociology
Dist - USNAC **Prod** - USN 1979

Our Cities - Our Right 26 MIN
16mm
Color (H C A)
LC 76-702149
Uses the example of Paris in order to show how high - rise buildings and other structures are making life and the urban environment unlivable for the average citizen.
Geography - World; Sociology
Dist - NYFLMS **Prod** - BERTUC 1975

Our City Government 10 MIN
U-matic / VHS / 16mm
Color; B&W (A)
LC FIA66-295
Views the urban community and its government. Considers how a city government provides services and makes and enforces laws. A city councilman cites the functions of a city council, mayor or city manager and courts, and he reviews the citizen's role.
Civics and Political Systems; Social Science
Dist - PHENIX **Prod** - WAT 1965

Our Clothes 17 MIN
16mm / U-matic / VHS
Captioned; Color (P I)
Examines the raw materials and the manufacturing process used to make clothes. Shows the sources of leather, wool, cotton, rubber and synthetic fiber.
Business and Economics; Home Economics; Social Science
Dist - IFB **Prod** - BHA 1978

Our Community Services 12 MIN
U-matic / VHS / 16mm
Color; B&W (P)
LC 70-704148
Uses a story about a boy who is hit by a motorcycle to demonstrate many public services, such as police and fire departments. Discusses how these services are paid for by everyone through taxes.
Health and Safety; Social Science; Sociology
Dist - EBEC **Prod** - EBEC 1969

Our community - USA 48 MIN
16mm
Color (G A)
$5.00 rental
Portrays many facets of the community service program developed in Arizona. Tells of an injured worker who becomes concerned about the community service program during his rehabilitation. Details the development of a recreational program for children, a Salk vaccine program, the building of a hospital for crippled children and other services which unions support. Produced by the Phoenix and Maricopa County AFL - CIO.
Business and Economics; Psychology; Social Science
Dist - AFLCIO **Prod** - AFLCIO 1960

Our Constitution 13 MIN
16mm
B&W (I)
Explains the Indian constitution and how liberty, equality and justice are ensured for all Indians.
Civics and Political Systems; History - World
Dist - NEDINF **Prod** - INDIA

Our constitution - the document that gave birth to a nation 25 MIN
VHS
Color (P I J)
$89.00 purchase _ #RB815
Explains the historical significance of the United States Constitution. Interviews Senators Robert Dole, Robert Byrd and Arlen Specter, and Congressmen Jim Wright and William Gray and others. Includes footage of actor James Earl Jones and Chief Justice of the United States

Supreme Court - 1966 - 1986 - Warren Burger explaining the principles behind 'We the People'.
Civics and Political Systems; History - United States
Dist - REVID **Prod** - REVID

Our Constitution - the document that gave birth to a nation 25 MIN
VHS
Color (I J)
$89.00 purchase _ #RB815
Explains the historical significance of the United States Constitution, its structures and functions and its present day meaning and importance. Includes a teacher's guide.
Civics and Political Systems
Dist - KNOWUN **Prod** - KNOWUN 1989

Our Country, Too 30 MIN
16mm
History of the Negro People Series
B&W (H C A)
LC FIA68-1584
Examines the values and attitudes of the American Negro. Shows such things as an African rite in Harlem, a Negro debutante ball, a Negro radio station, a Negro newspaper and the New York experimental social welfare group, Haryou - act. Features Ossie Davis.
Civics and Political Systems; History - United States; Psychology; Sociology
Dist - IU **Prod** - NET 1965

Our Country's Birthday 15 MIN
VHS / U-matic
Stories of America Series
Color (P)
Presents an overview of the events that preceded the signing of the Declaration of Independence.
Civics and Political Systems; History - United States
Dist - AITECH **Prod** - OHSDE 1976

Our country's flag 12 MIN
U-matic / 16mm / VHS
America's story series
Color (P I)
$350.00, $250.00 purchase _ #HP - 5755C
Stars all - American puppet US Eagle who tells the story of the American flag. Traces its history from the original thirteen colonies and its evolution to the modern US flag with thirteen stripes for the original colonies and one star for each state. Part of the America's Story series produced by William - Sherman Entertainment.
Civics and Political Systems; History - United States
Dist - CORF

Our Country's Flag 10 MIN
U-matic / VHS / 16mm
Color (P I J H)
LC 74-700456
Presents the story of the American flag, its origin and development. Illustrates this story by using prints, paintings, manuscripts and animated maps plus the actual flags themselves.
Civics and Political Systems; History - United States; Social Science
Dist - LUF **Prod** - WALLAL 1971

Our Country's Flag 11 MIN
U-matic / VHS / 16mm
Color (P I)
$280, $195 purchase _ #1304
Teaches the symbolism, significance, and history of the American flag.
Civics and Political Systems
Dist - CORF

Our Credo 15 MIN
16mm
Color
LC 76-702863
Shows how a large corporation re - evaluates its moral responsibilities towards its employees and the community at large through a series of top - level meetings.
Business and Economics
Dist - JAJ **Prod** - JAJ 1976

Our Crucial Deterrent 28 MIN
16mm
Color
LC 74-706513
Gives a historical review of the fleet ballistic missile weapon system.
Civics and Political Systems; History - United States
Dist - USNAC **Prod** - USN 1973

Our Cultural Heritage 10 MIN
16mm
Problems of World Order Series
Color (J H)
LC 73-703428
Raises essential questions about the value of national cultural heritages in relation to current problems of population growth and poverty. Looks at the international problems of preserving cultural monuments. Shows a variety of cultural landmarks and the threat to them from tourism, industrial pollution and other modern developments as they become more familiar and more accessible.
History - World
Dist - AGAPR **Prod** - VISNEW 1972

Our culture, our selves - 9 60 MIN
VHS
Land, location and culture - a geographical synthesis series
Color (J H C)
$89.95 purchase _ #WLU109
Explains that culture is essentially the story of a group of people - their collective traditional beliefs, ideas and lifestyle. Reveals that geographical considerations of culture focus not only on the content but the spatial distribution and impact of a particular culture on the landscape. Journeys through the farms, market places and families of a distinctive cultural group - the Old Order Mennonites. Assesses and discusses through a study of the origins and dispersals of agriculture, the role of independent invention versus diffusion as a contributor to cultural change. Discloses that diffusions also encounter obstacles to cultural change, obstacles which geographers refer to as barriers, concluding the program. Part of a 12 - part series.
Geography - World; Sociology
Dist - INSTRU

Our Daily Bread 71 MIN
16mm
B&W
Looks at life on a subsistence farm during the Depression. Tells how the men and women attempt to defeat the drought by digging a two - mile irrigation ditch. Directed by King Vidor.
Fine Arts
Dist - REELIM **Prod** - UNKNWN 1934

Our Disintegrating Public Schools 30 MIN
U-matic / VHS
Moral Values in Contemporary Society Series
Color (J)
Shows Albert Shanker, President of the American Federation of Teachers, and Maxine Greene of Columbia Teachers College discussing the plight of American public schools.
Education; Religion and Philosophy; Sociology
Dist - AMHUMA **Prod** - AMHUMA

Our Dog Show 15 MIN
16mm
Color (P)
A family attends a large dog show and the children decide to have a dog show of their own. Good sportsmanship and desirable social attitudes are illustrated.
Guidance and Counseling; Psychology
Dist - MLA **Prod** - JHP 1958

Our Drug Culture 48.53 MIN
VHS
Drug Abuse Series
Color (J H C)
LC 88-700282
Discusses the emotional, social, family and physical ramifications of the drug - oriented culture that lives in America.
Sociology
Dist - SRA **Prod** - SRA 1986

Our dwelling place series

The birth of Jesus	30 MIN
God keeps his promises	30 MIN
In the beginning	30 MIN
Jesus' concern for people	30 MIN
Jesus in my place	30 MIN
Jesus our friend	10 MIN
Journey to the promised land	30 MIN
Man after God's own heart	30 MIN
Man of vision	30 MIN

Dist - APH

Our Dynamic Earth 23 MIN
U-matic / VHS / 16mm
Color (H C A)
LC 80-700159
Examines information about continental drift gathered from deep sea research.
Science - Physical
Dist - NGS **Prod** - NGS 1979

Our Earth
CD-ROM
Wonders of learning CD-ROM library series
Color (K P) (ENGLISH, SPANISH)
$89.95 purchase _ #T05741
Teaches about planet Earth, what elements are necessary for life, about air, why it rains, the basics of using maps. Includes activity guide, user's guide, poster and booklets. Designed for use with Macintosh computer.
Science - Physical; Social Science
Dist - NGS

Our Earth 17 MIN
16mm / VHS
Color (P)
$380.00, $340.00 purchase, $60.00 rental
Presents three children and a world traveler learning about the different geographical features of the earth. Gives an overview of what makes up the surface of our planet, describing variations in altitude and surface features.
Geography - World; Science - Natural; Science - Physical; Social Science
Dist - HIGGIN **Prod** - HIGGIN 1987

Our economy - how it works series 107 MIN
35mm strip / VHS
Our economy - how it works series
Color (J H C A)
$189.00, $189.00 purchase _ #MB - 510658 - 2, #MB - 508852 - 5
Presents a six - part series on basic concepts of economics. Examines the production and distribution of commodities in the U S free enterprise system. Reviews the roles of money, banking, and government in the U S economic system.
Business and Economics
Dist - SRA **Prod** - SRA

Our Election Day Illusions - the Beat Majority Series Part 1
Representation and Gerrymandering 29 MIN
Dist - CAROUF

Our electrical world 10 MIN
VHS
Junior electrician series
CC; Color (P I)
$55.00 purchase _ #1353VG
Illustrates uses and production of electricity. Presents human dependence on electricity in everyday life. Comes with a teacher's guide and blackline masters. Part four of a four - part series.
Science - Physical
Dist - UNL

Our endangered Earth 18 MIN
VHS
Color (I J H)
$65.00 purchase _ #A5VH 1364
Examines the intertwined problems of poverty, population growth and pollution that underlie the environmental crisis on Earth. Introduces the issues.
Science - Natural; Sociology
Dist - CLRVUE **Prod** - CLRVUE

Our endangered Earth
VHS
Color (I J H)
$55.00 purchase _ #5870VD
Overviews the intertwined problems of poverty, population growth and pollution that underlie the global environmental crisis. Introduces major environmental problems and stresses what can be done to alleviate them.
Science - Natural; Sociology
Dist - KNOWUN **Prod** - KNOWUN 1990

Our Endangered Wildlife 51 MIN
U-matic / VHS / 16mm
Color (J A)
LC FIA68-1626
Describes those species of wildlife which are becoming extinct. Discusses the present - day conservation methods applied by various agencies in the United States.
Science - Natural
Dist - MGHT **Prod** - NBCTV 1968

Our Endangered Wildlife, Pt 1 25 MIN
U-matic / VHS / 16mm
Color (J A)
LC FIA68-1626
Describes those species of wildlife which are becoming extinct. Discusses the present - day conservation methods applied by various agencies in the United States.
Science - Natural
Dist - MGHT **Prod** - NBCTV 1968

Our Endangered Wildlife, Pt 2 26 MIN
U-matic / VHS / 16mm
Color (J A)
LC FIA68-1626
Describes those species of wildlife which are becoming extinct. Discusses the present - day conservation methods applied by various agencies in the United States.
Science - Natural
Dist - MGHT **Prod** - NBCTV 1968

Our environment
Videodisc
Color (I J H)
$400.00 purchase _ #A5LD 1356
Offers more than 11,000 images from around the world covering subjects ranging from acid rain to deforestation to oil spills to species extinction. Organizes maps, charts, photographs and film segments from leading world environment organizations by topic - sequence and

geographical area. Includes bar code user index. Teacher's manual and Macintosh, Apple II and IBM support software available separately.
Science - Natural
Dist - CLRVUE **Prod** - CLRVUE 1992

Our Environment - Everybody's Business 14 MIN
U-matic / VHS / 16mm
Color (J)
LC 72-703102
Shows how citizen concern about the environment has changed to citizen action.
Guidance and Counseling; Science - Natural; Sociology
Dist - CORNRS **Prod** - NYSCAG 1972

Our environment - the law and you 23 MIN
BETA / VHS / U-matic
Color (IND G)
$495.00 purchase _ #800 - 03
Overviews the RCRA, Superfund, Clean Air Act, Clean Water Act, Safe Drinking Water Act, NEPA, TSCA, Community Right - To - Know regulations. Looks at personal and business liabilities associated with failure to comply with these regulations.
Industrial and Technical Education; Psychology; Science - Natural; Sociology
Dist - ITSC **Prod** - ITSC 1990

Our Fair Lady 12 MIN
16mm
Color
Describes the different uses of a new home appliance, the kitchen center. Shows Judy making new friends and amazing her neighbors with her skill at preparing foods, the climax of the fun being a food contest.
Home Economics
Dist - MTP **Prod** - OSTER

Our Family Works Together 11 MIN
U-matic / VHS / 16mm
Color (P)
$280, $195 purchase _ #3759
Shows how chores can be done faster when people cooperate together to get them done.
Psychology; Sociology
Dist - CORF

Our Father 10 MIN
16mm
Color
LC 73-713273
Uses three vignettes to pose the fundamental question of having acknowledged God as our Father, do we have the right to choose our brothers.
Religion and Philosophy; Sociology
Dist - MARTC **Prod** - MARTC 1970

Our Federal Constitutional System 20 MIN
16mm
Government and Public Affairs Films Series
B&W (H A)
Dr Ivan Hinderaker, Professor of Political Science, UCLA, shows that the Federal government is the result of compromise and fear of centralized political power.
Civics and Political Systems
Dist - MLA **Prod** - RSC 1960

Our federal district 15 MIN
16mm / U-matic / VHS
American legacy series
Color (I)
Presents John E Rugg visiting significant locations in and around Washington, DC, to show its important role in the country's history and contemporary times. Uses archival photographs and a historical reenactment to help tell the story.
Geography - United States; History - United States
Dist - AITECH **Prod** - KRMATV 1983

Our federal government series
Electing a president - the process 22 MIN
Our federal government - the legislative branch 22 MIN
Our federal government - the Presidency 22 MIN
Our federal government - the Supreme Court 22 MIN
Dist - REVID

Our federal government - the legislative branch 22 MIN
VHS
Our federal government series
Color (I J)
$89.00 purchase _ #RB869
Uses live action, historical prints, graphics and documentary footage to tell the story of the creation and function of the Legislative Branch of federal government. Looks at the requirements for becoming a member of Congress, the process by which a bill becomes a law, the structure of the House of Representatives and the Senate, the role of committees, Speaker of the House, the Vice President, the powers of Congress and the interaction of the legislative branch with other branches of government. Part of a four - part series on the federal government.
Civics and Political Systems; History - United States
Dist - REVID **Prod** - REVID 1993

Our federal government - the Presidency 22 MIN
VHS
Our federal government series
Color (I J)
$89.00 purchase _ #RB867
Shows how the United States Constitution established the Executive Branch and provided for the separation of powers. Examines the relationship of the Executive Branch to the Legislative and Judicial branches of the federal government. Covers the powers granted to the Executive branch, the requirements for holding the office of President. Explains how the Presidency has evolved in terms of its influence and exercise of power since the Constitution was ratified. Part of a four - part series on the federal government.
Civics and Political Systems
Dist - REVID **Prod** - REVID 1993

Our federal government - the Supreme Court 22 MIN
VHS
Our federal government series
Color (I J)
$89.00 purchase _ #RB868
Addresses the origins of the Judicial Branch of federal government and the Supreme Court. Examines the power of the Court to influence American history and society in profound ways. Shows how the exercise of this power has often been controversial, that the philosophy of the Court can change as different justices are appointed and because of the political and social climates of the times. Looks at the influence of the Court on other branches of government. Part of a four - part series on the federal government.
Civics and Political Systems; History - United States
Dist - REVID **Prod** - REVID 1993

Our Feelings Affect each Other 13 MIN
16mm / U-matic / VHS
Color (P)
Shows how understanding our own feelings and how we show them helps us to understand and respect the feelings of others. Includes appropriate ways to show strong feelings, including anger, as well as suggestions for healthy expression of other feelings.
Guidance and Counseling
Dist - HIGGIN **Prod** - HIGGIN 1984

Our fighting Navy 90 MIN
VHS
Color (G)
$39.80 purchase _ #0919
Looks at air warfare as conducted by the United States Navy during World War II and the Korean conflict. Records Pearl Harbor and the first carrier attack in history. Covers the Battle of Midway, the Black Cats, aircraft carrier action and Korea.
Civics and Political Systems; History - United States; Industrial and Technical Education
Dist - SEVVID

Our flexible frame - the skeletal and muscular systems 22 MIN
VHS
Color (P I J)
$89.00 purchase _ #RB848
Uses graphics to illustrate the role of the skeleton in providing support and shape to the body. Examines the other functions of the skeleton - protecting internal organs, producing blood cells, providing attachment places for muscles. Muscles cover the skeleton and move the bones. Shows that any kind of bodily movement requires muscles, that muscles are required even to stand still.
Science - Natural
Dist - REVID **Prod** - REVID

Our Friend Angela 25 MIN
VHS / U-matic
B&W
Highlights the controversial visit to the USSR of Angela Davis with friends Kendra and Franklin Alexander.
History - World
Dist - IHF **Prod** - IHF

Our friend EDI - juvenile diabetes 11 MIN
VHS
Color (PRO K P G)
$150.00 purchase _ #DB - 01
Features an antimated pixie named Edi who helps patients and their parents understand what diabetes is and how exercise, diet and insulin will control it. Edi and his friends review the need for insulin and blood glucose monitoring.
Health and Safety
Dist - MIFE **Prod** - MIFE

Our Friend the Policeman 11 MIN
U-matic / VHS / 16mm
Color (P I)
LC 76-702239
Explains the daily work of a policeman, with emphasis on ways he helps people. Uses simple narration and a song superimposing words on appropriate scenes to build reading vocabulary.
English Language; Social Science
Dist - AIMS **Prod** - ACI 1972

Our Friends in Historic Cities - Philadelphia, Pennsylvania, Washington, DC 7 MIN
16mm / U-matic / VHS
Friends in the City Series
Color (P I)
LC 79-700509
Describes the life of two people who live in the historic cities of Philadelphia and Washington, DC.
Geography - United States; Social Science
Dist - EBEC **Prod** - BOBC

Our friends on Wooster Square series
Being spiteful is a no no, loving you is a promise - Volume 4 60 MIN
Don't be selfish - Volume 21 30 MIN
The Flower that cried 30 MIN
Friend, help, peace, faith - Vol 3 60 MIN
Gertie, the hungry goldfish - Volume 11 30 MIN
Grown - ups can be friends too, imagination - Volume 7 60 MIN
Hurt feelings - Volume 16 30 MIN
I forgive you - Volume 14 30 MIN
I think I'm dumb - Volume 12 30 MIN
Jealousy is no fun, finders keepers, losers weepers - Volume 9 60 MIN
The Kid inside of you - Volume 15 30 MIN
Like who you are, be you - Volume 13 30 MIN
The Love in my heart, it's okay to cry - Volume 8 60 MIN
Love of God, feelings, sharing, joy - Volume 1 60 MIN
Making fun of others isn't fun at all, love is a special gift - Volume 6 60 MIN
A Pat on the back - Volume 19 30 MIN
Please don't tease 30 MIN
A Present for Gramps - Volume 17 30 MIN
Rattle tattletail - Vol 18 30 MIN
Say you're sorry when you're wrong, the importance of saying thank you - Volume 5 60 MIN
Special, give, honest, love - Volume 2 60 MIN
Zip your lip to gossip - Volume 20 30 MIN
Dist - APH

Our Friends the Germans 50 MIN
U-matic / VHS
Color (H C A)
LC 83-707216
Presents correspondent Bill Moyers reporting on the people and government of West Germany. Focuses on topics that directly involve the United States, such as the rapidly growing German peace movement, relations with the Soviet bloc, the plight of Berlin and America's military presence in West Germany.
Civics and Political Systems; History - World
Dist - MOKIN **Prod** - CBSTV 1983

Our Gang Classics 75 MIN
U-matic / VHS
B&W
Features 3 original Our Gang Classics, including 'Champeen', 'Mary Queen Of Tots' and 'Uncle Tom's Uncle'.
Fine Arts
Dist - FCE **Prod** - FCE 1986

Our gang comedies series
Barnum and Ringling, inc 28 MIN
Dist - RMIBHF

Our Gang Follies of 1936 18 MIN
16mm
B&W
Shows that the neighborhood musical is going great until the boys are forced to don the girls' costumes for the finale. A Little Rascals film.
Fine Arts
Dist - RMIBHF **Prod** - ROACH 1936

Our Gang Follies of 1938 21 MIN
16mm
B&W
Features the Little Rascals in a take - off of the swing musicals of the 1930's.
Fine Arts
Dist - RMIBHF **Prod** - ROACH 1938

Our Goal is Giving Our Task is Asking 60 MIN
U-matic / VHS
Color
Discusses the financial dilemma of the American Red Cross. Puts forth a program which can be used to help provide staff and fund - raising teams with a realistic assessment of the problems they face and how they can succeed in their fund - raising efforts.
Social Science; Sociology
Dist - AMRC **Prod** - AMRC

Our god the condor 30 MIN
VHS / 16mm
Color (H C G)
$550.00, $295.00 purchase, $55.00 rental
Documents the 'Yawar Fiesta,' a yearly event representing Indian triumph over the Spanish. Reveals that the ceremony pits two animals with symbolic meaning against each other - a condor representing the mountain spirit of the Andes and a bull, symbol of Spain. The condor is tied to the back of the bull and the two are locked in ritual battle, the wildly flopping condor atop the lurching, spinning bull. Finally, the two are separated and the condor soars over the mountains, a symbol of freedom for the Andean people. The Roman Catholic Church has traditionally opposed this ritual as a 'savage custom,' but for the Indians it is 'a protest we want to continue.' Produced by Paul Yule and Andy Harries.
Geography - World; History - World; Religion and Philosophy; Social Science
Dist - FLMLIB

Our great ally France 1938 - 40
16mm / VHS
Archive series
B&W; PAL (G)
PdS280, PdS55 purchase
Looks at the portrayal of France at the height of the pre - war crisis. Emphasizes its strength and ties with Great Britain, following through the reaction to the defeat of France in 1940. Includes a substantial accompanying booklet. Uses material compiled by Philip Bell and Ralph White.
History - World
Dist - BUFVC **Prod** - BUFVC

Our heritage from ancient Greece
VHS
Color (J H C)
$109.00 purchase _ #06268 - 126
Overviews Greek history to illustrate the major Greek literary, artistic and philosophical contributions to western civilization. Dramatizes quotations from Pericles, Homer, Thucydides, Plato, Aeschylus and Croesus. Traces Greek civilization from early Minoan society and follows the achievements of the Achaean Greeks. Highlights the Golden Age of Athens. Includes teacher's guide and library kit. In two parts.
History - World; Religion and Philosophy; Sociology
Dist - GA **Prod** - GA

Our heritage from ancient Rome
VHS
Color (J H C)
$109.00 purchase _ #06207 - 126
Overviews the development of ancient Rome and Roman achievements in literature, philosophy, political organization, law and technology. Presents excerpts from translations of Virgil, Cicero, Suetonius, Julius Caesar, Horace, Juvenal, Augustus, Strabo, Pliny and historian Cassius Dio. Includes teacher's guide and library kit. In two parts.
History - World; Religion and Philosophy; Sociology
Dist - GA **Prod** - GA

Our Heritage from the Past 82 MIN
U-matic / VHS
Our Heritage from the Past Series
Color (I J)
Contains 1 videocassette.
Social Science; Sociology
Dist - TROLA **Prod** - TROLA 1987

Our Heritage from the Past Series
Our Heritage from the Past 82 MIN
Dist - TROLA

Our Hidden National Product 25 MIN
16mm / U-matic / VHS
Color
Shows hazardous waste facilities around the country where wastes are recycled, treated and disposed of in monitored landfills. Discusses regulations and the conflict between public demand for action vs public opposition to local sites.
Sociology
Dist - USNAC **Prod** - USEPA

Our Hidden Wealth 11 MIN
16mm
B&W (I)
Gives a detailed description of the discovery, examination and mining of minerals such as gold, bauxite, manganese, mica, coal and oil.
Industrial and Technical Education; Science - Physical
Dist - NEDINF **Prod** - INDIA

Our Hispanic friends 10 MIN
VHS
Mission videos series
Color (G R)
$12.50 purchase _ #S12349
Looks at Hispanic life and culture, with emphasis on encouraging Lutheran Church - Missouri Synod congregations to evangelize among Hispanics.
Guidance and Counseling; Literature and Drama; Religion and Philosophy
Dist - CPH **Prod** - LUMIS

Our Hispano - American Friends 10 MIN
U-matic / VHS / 16mm
Friends of many Cultures Series
Color (P I)
LC 79-700512
Profiles three children who have Hispano - American ethnic heritages. Describes their lives in Miami, Florida, East Los Angeles and New York City.
Social Science; Sociology
Dist - EBEC **Prod** - BOBC

Our Hospital Friends 30 MIN
U-matic
Magic Ring I Series
(K P)
Tells the story of a trip to the hospital for the robot Matilda.
Education; Literature and Drama
Dist - ACCESS **Prod** - ACCESS 1984

Our Hospitality 72 MIN
16mm
B&W (J)
Stars Buster Keaton in a satire on the famed Hatfield - Mc Coy feud ending with a chase sequence involving a rescue at a waterfall.
Fine Arts; Literature and Drama
Dist - TWYMAN **Prod** - MGM 1923

Our House is Safe 15 MIN
16mm / U-matic / VHS
Color (J)
LC 80-701047
Shows which common plants are fatal to children, how to avoid appliance shocks, how to make one's home safer with coded paint areas, and how to avoid slippery surfaces in making one's home safe.
Health and Safety
Dist - KLEINW **Prod** - KLEINW 1975

Our Immune System 25 MIN
16mm
Color (J H C A G)
$384.00 purchase _ #50412
Shows phagocytes, lymphocytes and T cells and how they anchor our immune system. Examines challenges to the immune system and how science is helping.
Science - Natural
Dist - NGS

Our Indian People 15 MIN
16mm / VHS
Color (H)
$350.00 purchase, $45.00 rental
Promotes an appreciation of the richness of Native American culture and reinforces traditional values. Teaches friendship, respect and sharing for all people.
Social Science; Sociology
Dist - SHENFP **Prod** - SHENFP 1990

Our invisible friend - electricity 17 MIN
VHS
Basic safety series
Color (IND G)
$395.00 purchase, $75.00 rental _ #8305
Provides information on common electrical equipment found in the workplace in compliance with OSHA regulations.
Health and Safety; Psychology; Science - Physical
Dist - AIMS **Prod** - MARCOM 1991

Our invisible neighbor 30 MIN
VHS
Color (H C G A R)
$19.95 purchase, $10.00 rental _ #4 - 85012
Focuses on how to include disabled individuals in the ministry. Provides suggestions from congregations and disabled ministers. Produced by the Lutheran Commission on Ministry with Disabled Persons.
Health and Safety; Religion and Philosophy
Dist - APH

Our Job in Japan 18 MIN
U-matic / VHS / 16mm
B&W
Focuses on the Japanese mind as perceived by the United States after World War II. Suggests there must be changes in the Japanese psyche before Japan can hope to rejoin the community of peaceful nations.
Civics and Political Systems; Geography - World; History - World
Dist - USNAC **Prod** - USAPS 1982

Our job's not done 17 MIN
VHS / 16mm
Color (G IND)
$5.00 rental
Reminds retired union members that they can still play an active part in achieving the goals that they struggled for during their working lives. Uses flashbacks to the Roosevelt era to show workers wages and working conditions during the Great Depression, and the victories achieved by workers through unions. Urges voluntary activity in the Committee on Political Education Retiree Program.
Business and Economics; Social Science; Sociology
Dist - AFLCIO

Our Kinda Talk - an Introduction to Margaret Laurence 23 MIN
16mm
Color (G)
_ #106C 0178 927
Portrays Margaret Laurence, one of the most celebrated Canadian novelists.
Biography; Literature and Drama
Dist - CFLMDC **Prod** - NFBC 1978

Our Knowledge, Our Beauty - the Expressive Culture of the Canelos Quichua of Ecuador 29 MIN
VHS
Color (C A)
$26.00 rental _ #85819
Records a Quichua song expressing the basic creation myth with voiceover translation and commentary. Shows how principal myths of the culture are expressed in ceramic and wooden artifacts. Describes the Quichua people who speak a dialect of Inca and who believe that music originates in the spirit world, conveying messages from that world. Comments on features of their daily life and the role of the Shaman in their society.
Geography - World; Social Science; Sociology
Dist - UILL **Prod** - UILL 1985

Our Korean Children 29 MIN
16mm
Color (A)
LC 74-702015
Discusses the different life - style and cultural background from which the Korean child comes. Shows and describes the various aspects of a Korean child's life in a family environment and in a children's center. Explains that the child's adjustment to his new environment can be eased by helping understand the cultural differences.
Geography - World; Sociology
Dist - VCI **Prod** - CHSM 1974

Our Lady of the Sphere 10 MIN
16mm
Color (C)
$375.00
Experimental film by Larry Jordan.
Fine Arts
Dist - AFA **Prod** - AFA 1969

Our lady of the sphere 10 MIN
16mm
Color (G)
$25.00 rental
Features animation of a mystical lady with orbital head moving through the carnival of life in a surreal adventure. Juxtaposes color collage of roccoco imagery with symbols of the space age.
Fine Arts
Dist - CANCIN **Prod** - JORDAL 1969

Our Land Australia 12 MIN
16mm
Color (J)
LC 73-702483
Presents a collage of Australian scenes, giving a brief overall view of the country and its people.
Geography - World
Dist - AUIS **Prod** - FLMAUS 1973

Our Land is Our Life 58 MIN
16mm
Color (H C A) (FRENCH)
#3X64 N
Documents the meeting of the Cree Indian people of the Mistassini area in Northern Quebec in which issues concerning the long term future of the Indian people were discussed. Explains how 'compensation' offered by the white government cannot make up for the loss of land. In 4 parts.

Social Science
Dist - CDIAND **Prod** - NFBC 1974

Our Land - It's many Faces 14 MIN
U-matic
Color
Illustrates the ways in which man has preserved the land as a source of food, fiber and water.
Science - Natural; Social Science
Dist - USDA **Prod** - USDA 1972

Our Land, its many Faces 14 MIN
16mm
Color
LC FIE63-212
Features the story of the conservation movement since the time of Jefferson. Shows many kinds of land we have in America and the conservation work of our farmers and ranchers.
Agriculture; Geography - United States; History - United States; Science - Natural
Dist - USNAC **Prod** - USSCS 1961

Our land too - the legacy of the Southern Tenant Farmers Union 57 MIN
VHS / 16mm
Color (G IND)
$5.00 rental
Traces the history of the Southern Tenant Farmers' Union, an interracial organization formed in July, 1934, in Arkansas. Tells how black and white leaders organized farmer laborers who earned 75 cents or less a day. Cotton pickers went on strike when farmers cut wages to 40 cents per 100 pounds of cotton. Produced by Kudzu Productions.
Agriculture; Business and Economics; History - United States; Social Science
Dist - AFLCIO

Our Largest Minority - the Disabled 60 MIN
16mm
Color
Looks at the wide variety of persons who are supposedly disabled including Roy Campanella, violinist Itzhak Perlman and Ray Charles. Demonstrates the creative approaches of such groups as the Quad Squad and the Center for Independent Living. Introduces disabled theologians Howard Rice and Harold Wilke who put the church's attitudes and efforts toward positive goals in perspective.
Education; Psychology
Dist - CCNCC **Prod** - NBCTV

Our Legal System 19 MIN
VHS / U-matic
Ways of the Law Series
Color (H)
Presents interviews with prominent attorneys from around the country.
Civics and Political Systems
Dist - GPN **Prod** - SCITV 1980

Our life - the journey 27 MIN
U-matic / VHS / 16mm
Color (A)
Focuses on the 1982 Assembly of United Methodist Women which was held in Philadelphia and attended by 10,000. Shows women discussing their journey of faith. Discusses the Christian response to issues such as nuclear disarmament, racism and sexism.
Religion and Philosophy; Sociology
Dist - ECUFLM **Prod** - WDBGM 1982

Our lives from Tibet to England 75 MIN
VHS / BETA
Color; PAL (G)
PdS27.50 purchase
Features three masters from the Gelug tradition who have been living and teaching in England for several years - the Venerable Geshes Kelsang, Wangchen and Konchok. Recounts the story of their early lives and their impressions of life in the West. A Geshe or Doctor of Buddhist Philosophy is a title given to an individual who has passed a rigorous series of exams and is the culmination of up to 20 years studying the classical Indian and Tibetan commentaries to the major branches of Buddhist philosophy and thought. Recorded in London and Cumbria, England. Translated by Tenzin P Phunrabpa.
Fine Arts; Religion and Philosophy
Dist - MERIDT

Our lives in our hands 49 MIN
VHS / 16mm
Color (G)
$600.00, $300.00 purchase, $60.00, $40.00 rental
Examines the traditional native American craft of split ash basketmaking as a means of economic and cultural survival for Aroostook Micmac Indians of northern Maine. Films basketmakers at work in their homes, at local potato fields and at business meetings of the Basket Bank, a cooperative formed by the Aroostook Micmac Council. Includes first person commentaries and 17th century Micmac music. Produced by Harald Prins and Karen Carter.
Geography - United States; Social Science
Dist - DOCEDR **Prod** - DOCEDR

Our Living Heritage 28 MIN
16mm
Color (J H)
LC 77-703231
Explores a wide selection of parks and national shrines. Features various figures and events in American history. Explains that much of America's natural and historic heritage is preserved in the National Park system.
Geography - United States; History - United States
Dist - USNAC **Prod** - USNPS 1966

Our Living Shield 21 MIN
U-matic / VHS
Phenomenal World Series
Color (J C)
$129.00 purchase _ #3967
Focuses on the skin, the largest single organ of the human body, that sweats, breathes, keeps body fluids in and other fluids out, that serves as a sensor for pleasure and pain, and many others.
Science - Natural
Dist - EBEC

Our Magic Land 17 MIN
16mm
Color
LC FIE58-158
Introduces a magician performing in a carnival setting to point up the magic of man and nature working together to maintain and improve land through conservation.
Agriculture; Science - Natural; Sociology
Dist - USNAC **Prod** - USSCS 1961

Our Man in China Series
The Culture Keepers 25 MIN
The Politburo Presents 25 MIN
The Waiting Generation 25 MIN
Dist - CTV

Our Man in China
Comrades of the River 25 MIN
Dist - CTV

Our March 21 MIN
U-matic / VHS
Color
Celebrates the Russian Revolution and the communistic doctrine it spawned, affecting the whole world. Features speeches by Lenin, the massacre of peasant marchers in city streets and the final storming of government buildings. Highlights other events of that period culminating in World War II and the victory that followed. Uses a wide - screen triptych technique and includes clips from Soviet feature films.
Civics and Political Systems; History - World
Dist - IHF **Prod** - IHF

Our Middle Life 30 MIN
VHS / U-matic
Color
Looks at the physiological and psychological changes that may occur in middle life. Covers the role of estrogens in the menopause and bone changes in this period. Discusses whether or not there is a male menopause. Examines the idea of the re - evaluation of one's life that can occur in middle life.
Health and Safety; Psychology
Dist - AL **Prod** - UILCCC

Our Mineral Heritage 27 MIN
U-matic / VHS / 16mm
Of Energy, Minerals, and Man Series
Color (J H A)
Surveys the Geological mechanisms that create minerals.
Science - Physical; Social Science
Dist - JOU **Prod** - GAZEL

Our Mineral World 28 MIN
U-matic / VHS
Color (H C A)
Surveys the world's mineral deposits and mankind's dependence on such resources. Shows world's outstanding natural features in North America, Africa, New Zealand, Europe and Britain, and gives clear explanation of continental drift and formation of minerals over millions of years.
Geography - United States; Geography - World; Science - Physical; Social Science
Dist - EDMI **Prod** - GAZEL 1978

Our mission, our goals - goal setting for individuals, committees, and the institution - Tape 2 60 MIN
VHS
Management skills for church leaders series
Color (G R PRO)
$10.00 rental _ #36 - 82 - 223
Focuses on goal setting at all levels of church organization.
Business and Economics; Religion and Philosophy
Dist - APH

Our Mr Sun 60 MIN
8mm cartridge / 16mm
Bell System Science Series
Color (P I J H)
Discusses the sun and its effect upon life on earth. Shows the sun in eclipse with its corona, sun spots and explosions on the sun's face. Discusses attempts to use the sun's energy to perform work now done by wood, coal, gas and oil. Animated sequences present information about the size, weight, heat, energy and and radiation of the sun.
Science - Physical; Social Science
Dist - WAVE **Prod** - ATAT 1956

Our Mr Sun 60 MIN
VHS
Color (G)
$19.95 purchase _ #341876
Reissues a Frank Capra production featuring Eddie Albert which explores the mysteries of the sun. Includes also a cranky Father Time, voice by Lionel Barrymore, and Old Sol himself who investigate the sun's history, power and potential.
Fine Arts; Science - Physical
Dist - INSTRU **Prod** - CAPRA

Our Mr Sun, Pt 1 30 MIN
16mm
Bell System Science Series
Color
Discusses the sun and its effect upon life on earth. Shows the sun in eclipse with its corona, sun spots and explosions on the sun's face. Discusses attempts to use the sun's energy to perform work now done by wood, coal, gas and oil. Animated sequences present information about the size, weight, heat, energy and and radiation of the sun.
Science - Physical
Dist - WAVE **Prod** - ATAT 1956

Our Mr Sun, Pt 2 30 MIN
16mm
Bell System Science Series
Color
Discusses the sun and its effect upon life on earth. Shows the sun in eclipse with its corona, sun spots and explosions on the sun's face. Discusses attempts to use the sun's energy to perform work now done by wood, coal, gas and oil. Animated sequences present information about the size, weight, heat, energy and and radiation of the sun.
Science - Physical
Dist - WAVE **Prod** - ATAT 1956

Our Mutual Friend 29 MIN
U-matic
Dickens World Series
Color
Examines Dickens' rebuke to the status quo and the shallow people it can create.
Literature and Drama
Dist - UMITV **Prod** - UMITV 1973

Our National Parks 43 MIN
U-matic / VHS
Our National Parks Series
Color (P I)
Contains 1 videocassette.
Geography - United States; Social Science
Dist - TROLA **Prod** - TROLA 1987

Our national parks 15 MIN
16mm / U-matic / VHS
American legacy series
Color (I)
Presents John Rugg introducing the national park system, focusing on Yellowstone, Grand Canyon and Mesa Verde. Shows historical reenactments portraying Theodore Roosevelt, John Burroughs and John Wesley Powell. Examines the Anasazi Indian culture.
Geography - United States; Social Science
Dist - AITECH **Prod** - KRMATV 1983

Our National Parks Series
Our National Parks 43 MIN
Dist - TROLA

Our nation's health...a question of choice 59 MIN
VHS / U-matic
Color (G)
$99.00 purchase
Takes a comprehensive look at lifestyle as the main determinant of good health. Argues that it's never too late to make positive lifestyle changes to ensure a healthier future. Discusses fat and cholesterol, dietary intake, exercise and wellness studies. Produced by CWI Productions, Inc.
Health and Safety; Physical Education and Recreation; Social Science
Dist - BAXMED

Our nation's homeless - who, where and why 22 MIN
35mm strip / VHS
Color (J H C T A)
$57.00, $48.00 purchase _ #MB - 909456 - 2, #MB - 909453 - 8
Considers the problem of homelessness in the US. Suggests that a growing shortage of affordable housing has helped to increase the number of homeless people. Examines possible strategies to combat the problem, including those by George Bush and Jack Kemp.
History - United States; Sociology
Dist - SRA **Prod** - NYT 1989

Our Natural Heritage Series
Environments 30 MIN
Living Together 30 MIN
The Mountains 30 MIN
The Plains 30 MIN
Pretty Insects 30 MIN
Seashores 30 MIN
Dist - EDUCRT

Our natural heritage series
Baby animals
Western birds and flowers
Dist - INSTRU

Our Nearest Star 12 MIN
16mm
Color
LC FIE63-174
Depicts the first application of nuclear power in space - - the snap isotopic power system used in transit4A navigation satellite. Gives a semi - technical explanation of development and testing of the radioisotope fuel capsule and thermoelectric generator.
Science - Physical
Dist - USERD **Prod** - USNRC 1961

Our new life begins today 27 MIN
VHS
Color (A R)
$15.00 purchase _ #S10170
Portrays a Nebraska farming family as they are forced to sell their farm. Shows how they reacted to the event, as well as how their church responded.
Guidance and Counseling; Literature and Drama; Religion and Philosophy
Dist - CPH **Prod** - LUMIS

Our next president 4 MIN
16mm
B&W (G)
$8.00 rental
Documents the 1980 Wisconsin presidential primary in which media kids from the 1960s take on the image - making professionals. Features candidates John Anderson, Jerry Brown, Ronald Reagan, George Bush and Ted Kennedy. Produced by Paul Heilemann.
Fine Arts
Dist - CANCIN

Our Normal Childhood 15 MIN
VHS / 16mm
Color (G)
$300.00 purchase, $50.00, $40.00 rental
Shows two women discussing their experience of sexual and disciplinary abuse suffered during childhood. Presented by Lorna Boschmann.
Sociology
Dist - WMENIF **Prod** - WMENIF 1988

Our Obligation 26 MIN
16mm
Color (H C A)
LC FIA61-1107
The story of a school fire, the panic that developed and the loss of life that occurred. Discusses the obligation of teachers, school administrators and parents to provide fireproof buildings and all other safety devices necessary to prevent fires.
Education; Health and Safety
Dist - FILCOM **Prod** - LACFD 1960

Our Ocean of Air 29 MIN
Videoreel / VT2
Observing Eye Series
Color
Science - Physical; Sociology
Dist - PBS **Prod** - WGBHTV

Our Original Inhabitants 10 MIN
16mm
B&W (I)
Discusses the tribal population of India. Explains that, numbering over 25 million, the tribals belong to 172 distinctive groups each with its own culture pattern, dress, decorations and dances. Highlights the lives of some of the tribes, such as the Gonds, Bhils, Santhals, Nagas and Todas.
Sociology
Dist - NEDINF **Prod** - INDIA

Our Own Newspaper 15 MIN
U-matic
Garage Gazette Series
(I J)
Explores the purpose of a newspaper, the role of an editor and what types of stories are considered newsworthy.
English Language; Literature and Drama
Dist - ACCESS **Prod** - ACCESS 1981

Our Pensions, Our Money, Our Jobs 25 MIN
16mm
Color (A)
Presents examples of how union pension funds can be invested to provide both jobs and a sound investment.
Business and Economics; Sociology
Dist - AFLCIO **Prod** - IUD 1982

Our Physical Selves - Well - being 60 MIN
U-matic
Perspectives on Women
Color (A)
Focuses on women in the economy, women and physical well being and how men and women are working to improve women's status in society.
Sociology
Dist - ACCESS **Prod** - ACCESS 1986

Our Place 15 MIN
U-matic / VHS
La Bonne Aventure Series
Color (K P)
Deals with French - American children. Focuses on the theme of needing to be alone sometimes.
Foreign Language; Sociology
Dist - GPN **Prod** - MPBN

Our planet - a closer look
Videodisc
A closer look series
Color (I J)
$189.00 purchase _ #Q11130
Illustrates environmental concepts by examining the earth from the vantage point of outer space. Explains concepts of ecology, how deforestation is affecting the earth, and the function of the ozone layer. Includes barcoded teacher's guide. Part of a series of five programs.
Science - Physical; Sociology
Dist - CF

Our planet Earth 23 MIN
VHS / 16mm
Color; Captioned; CC (J H C G)
$285.00 purchase, $45.00 rental, $470.00 purchase
Presents 17 astronauts and cosmonauts from 10 countries sharing their experiences and insights. Conveys the fragility of the Earth beyond political and geographical boundaries. Features a spectacular display of Earth's color and light. Produced by Mickey Lemle for the United Nations, with the cooperation of the Association of Space Explorers.
Fine Arts; Industrial and Technical Education; Science; Science - Natural; Science - Physical
Dist - BULFRG **Prod** - UN 1991

Our planet Earth
VHS
Junior geologist series
CC; Color (P I)
$55 purchase_#10026VL
Presents the geological aspects of Earth to elementary school students in correlation with curriculum. Covers areas of physical geology and erosion. Part one of a four - part series.
Science - Physical
Dist - UNL

Our Planet Earth 9 MIN
16mm
Basic Facts about the Earth, Sun, Moon and Stars Series
Color (K P I)
Discusses the concept of the earth as a planet, its physical properties and man's relationship to it.
Science - Physical
Dist - SF **Prod** - MORLAT 1967

Our Polluted Waters 15 MIN
VHS / U-matic
Matter and Motion Series Module Blue; Module blue
Color (I)
Introduces plants, plant - like organisms and sea animals that thrive in polluted water.
Science - Natural
Dist - AITECH **Prod** - WHROTV 1973

Our Priceless Gift 34 MIN
U-matic / VHS
Color; B&W (S)
Presents various selections from deaf culture and sign language from 1910 to 1980's. Signed.
Guidance and Counseling; Psychology
Dist - GALCO **Prod** - GALCO 1982

Our Priceless Heritage 15 MIN
16mm
Color
Depicts several before and after pollution scenes, including both air and water scenes, at eight company plant locations. Demonstrates the complexity of many pollution problems and shows that they can be solved by the same technology that created them.
Science - Natural; Sociology
Dist - HERC **Prod** - HERC

Our Relations 70 MIN
16mm / U-matic / VHS
B&W (I J H C)
Stars Laurel and Hardy in a tale of a pair of twin brothers, one good and one bad.
Fine Arts
Dist - FI **Prod** - MGM 1936

Our Responsibilities - Theresa Demus, MS 27 MIN
U-matic
Food and Nutrition Seminars for Health Professionals Series
Color (PRO)
LC 78-706165
Discusses the responsibility of the consumer in making the Food and Drug Administration (FDA) a responsible government agency. Focuses on the FDA'S function, how to communicate with the FDA and the limits of the FDA'S responsibilities.
Home Economics; Social Science
Dist - USNAC **Prod** - USFDA 1976

Our restless atmosphere 12 MIN
VHS
Color (I J)
$79.95 purchase _ #10038VG
Explains the atmosphere and its impact on all forms of life. Describes the composition, changes, and pollutants of the atmosphere. Comes with a teacher's guide, discussion questions and blackline masters.
Geography - World; Science - Natural; Science - Physical
Dist - UNL

Our Round Earth - How it Changes 11 MIN
16mm / U-matic / VHS
Our Round Earth Series
Color (P I)
LC 78-713120
Shows forces that change the land, and uses demonstrations with clay models to compare views of molten lava, earthquakes and giant cracks in the earth's surface.
Science - Physical
Dist - CORF **Prod** - CORF 1971

Our Round Earth - its Atmosphere 11 MIN
U-matic / VHS / 16mm
Our Round Earth Series
Color (P I)
LC 71-713121
Describes visible clues to the nature of the invisible atmosphere that protects the earth. Uses special breathing equipment to reveal the importance of the atmosphere for living things.
Science - Physical
Dist - CORF **Prod** - CORF 1971

Our Round Earth - its Land 11 MIN
U-matic / VHS / 16mm
Our Round Earth Series
Color (P I)
LC 75-713122
Views land masses and land forms from the air, states the importance of the land for farming and mining and emphasizes the problems of conservation.
Geography - World; Science - Natural; Science - Physical
Dist - CORF **Prod** - CORF 1971

Our Round Earth - its Waters 11 MIN
U-matic / VHS / 16mm
Our Round Earth Series
Color (P I)
LC 79-713123
Shows what the oceans are like from above, as well as below the water and gives sources of fresh water and ways in which it can be controlled.
Geography - World; Science - Natural; Science - Physical
Dist - CORF **Prod** - CORF 1971

Our Round Earth Series
Our Round Earth - How it Changes 11 MIN
Our Round Earth - its Atmosphere 11 MIN
Our Round Earth - its Land 11 MIN
Our Round Earth - its Waters 11 MIN
Our Round Earth - what It's Like 11 MIN
Dist - CORF

Our Round Earth - what It's Like 11 MIN
16mm / U-matic / VHS
Our Round Earth Series

Color (P I)
LC 72-713124
Views of the earth from the ground, from a plane and from a space ship show major features of the land, the oceans and the atmosphere.
Geography - World; Science - Physical
Dist - CORF **Prod** - CORF 1971

Our Russian Front 43 MIN
VHS / U-matic
B&W
Deals with the Russian people's determination and preparation for war against the advancing German Army. Includes many scenes of civilian life and abrupt changes incurred by war.
History - World
Dist - IHF **Prod** - IHF

Our Sacred Land 28 MIN
BETA / VHS / U-matic
Color; Stereo (S C A G)
Looks into the issues of American Indian religious freedom and treaty rights.
Social Science
Dist - UCV **Prod** - TCPT 1984

Our sea and sky - Video 7 47 MIN
VHS
Earth and space science - secrets of science series
Color (I J H C)
$49.95 purchase
Presents two parts in two segments each, looking at the primary characteristics of the Earth's oceans and the many forms of life inhabiting the seas, how weather - from rain to hurricanes - is created in the Earth's atomosphere and examining how much is known about comets. Includes An Ocean Overview and Life Beneath the Waves in Part I, Creating Our Climate and Comets - Spectacles in the Sky in Part II. Hosted by Discover Magazine Editor in Chief Paul Hoffman. Third of five parts on Earth and space science.
Science - Physical
Dist - EFVP **Prod** - DSCOVM 1994

Our Senior Years 30 MIN
16mm
B&W (J H T R)
Presents the story of a retired man who becomes bored and bewildered. Describes how he is helped by his wife, grandson and Christian friends to find a new adventure in living by serving God.
Religion and Philosophy
Dist - FAMF **Prod** - FAMF

Our Small World 6 MIN
16mm
Color
Discusses the involvement of people in the United States in helping people in the developing countries around the world work their way out of poverty and despair. Shows how CARE'S International Partnership Programs help bring a better life to needy people who are still without the basic necessities of life.
Guidance and Counseling; Social Science; Sociology
Dist - CARE **Prod** - CARE

Our Small World - Business and Industry Volunteers 9 MIN
16mm
Color
Provides suggestions from volunteers on how people from business and industry can participate in helping to improve the plight of needy people.
Social Science; Sociology
Dist - CARE **Prod** - CARE

Our Small World - Student Volunteers 10 MIN
16mm
Color
Presents suggestions from volunteers on how students can help to improve the plight of needy people.
Guidance and Counseling; Social Science; Sociology
Dist - CARE **Prod** - CARE

Our Small World - Women Volunteers 9 MIN
16mm
Color
Provides suggestions from volunteers on how women volunteers can participate in helping to improve the plight of needy people.
Social Science; Sociology
Dist - CARE **Prod** - CARE

Our solar system 9 MIN
VHS
Junior space scientist series
CC; Color (P I)
$55.00 purchase _ #10361VG
Introduces the planets of the solar system along with terms such as gravity, rotation, orbit, stars, and density. Uses animation, space footage and demonstration to show the structure of the solar system. Comes with a teacher's guide and blackline masters. Part one of a three - part series.
Science - Physical
Dist - UNL

Our Solar System 5 MIN
16mm
Color
LC 75-702555
Uses animation to teach the names, placement and characteristics of the planets in the solar system.
Science - Physical
Dist - USNAC **Prod** - NASA 1973

Our solar system series
Presents a series exploring the big bang theory of the origin of the universe, and looking at the Milky Way and Earth's solar system. Includes The History of Occidental Astronomy, The Inner Planets, The Outer Planets and Life on the Edge of the Milky Way. Set of four videos, also available separately.

The History of occidental astronomy	30 MIN
The Inner planets	30 MIN
Life on the edge of the Milky Way	30 MIN
The Outer planets	30 MIN

Dist - LANDMK

Our Son John 25 MIN
16mm
Color
LC 74-700106
Deals with the value systems in interpersonal relations. Shows the parents of a handicapped child, pointing out how they consider themselves fortunate.
Health and Safety; Sociology
Dist - CMHOSP **Prod** - SCHMNJ 1973

Our Songs will Never Die 35 MIN
16mm / U-matic / VHS
Color
Visits the Yurok, Karuk and Tolowa cultural sites which were established for the purpose of reconstructing early village dance sites. Shows young visitors working with tribal elders and experiencing surf - fishing, fish drying, sand - breadmaking, Indian card games, songs, stick - games, net making, and the history of their grandfathers and great - grandfathers.
Social Science
Dist - SHENFP **Prod** - SHENFP

Our Special Way of Life 22 MIN
16mm
Color
LC 79-700063
Shows the lifestyles of a farmer, a rancher and their families in the United States.
Agriculture; Sociology
Dist - FARMI **Prod** - FARMI 1978

Our Story in Stamps 12 MIN
16mm
Color
Shows how new Malaysian stamps are printed from designs drawn by Malaysian artists.
Geography - World; Social Science
Dist - PMFMUN **Prod** - FILEM 1957

Our Story - Part 1 30 MIN
U-matic
Today's Special Series
Color (K P)
Develops language arts skills in children. Programs are thematically designed around subjects of interest to youngsters. Action takes place in a department store where people, mannequins, puppets, comic characters and special guests present a light hearted approach to language arts.
Fine Arts; Literature and Drama; Psychology
Dist - TVOTAR **Prod** - TVOTAR 1985

Our Story - Part 2 30 MIN
U-matic
Today's Special Series
Color (K P)
Develops language arts skills in children. Programs are thematically designed around subjects of interest to youngsters. Action takes place in a department store where people, mannequins, puppets, comic characters and special guests present a light hearted approach to language arts.
Fine Arts; Literature and Drama; Psychology
Dist - TVOTAR **Prod** - TVOTAR 1985

Our Street Series

Audition	29 MIN
Before You Walk	29 MIN
Books and covers	29 MIN
Cathy's turn	29 MIN
Caught	29 MIN
Dark darkness	29 MIN
Departure	29 MIN
Doomsday	29 MIN
Family Affair	29 MIN
From Whence He Came	29 MIN
Fronts	29 MIN
The Glory bag	29 MIN
Happy Birthday, Brother	29 MIN
Have You Seen My Little Boy	29 MIN
Home Again, Home Again	29 MIN
I'm Staying	29 MIN
It's a Small World	29 MIN
Keep Track	29 MIN
Let Me Count the Ways, Baby	29 MIN
The Lineage	29 MIN
The Lost days of glory - Pt 1	29 MIN
The Lost days of glory - Pt 2	29 MIN
Love's Sweet Song	29 MIN
Making Friends	29 MIN
The Man of the House	29 MIN
Miss Clara Let Us be	29 MIN
Mrs Ryder has the Blues	29 MIN
Night of the Intruder, Pt 1	29 MIN
Night of the Intruder, Pt 2	29 MIN
Old Ladies Lost	29 MIN
The One Your with	29 MIN
The Political candidate	29 MIN
Pride	29 MIN
Reverence Day	29 MIN
Struck	29 MIN
There Goes the Bride	29 MIN
Too Proud to Beg	29 MIN
The Ultimates	29 MIN

Dist - PBS

Our Street was Paved with Gold 29 MIN
16mm
Color
_ *#106C 0173 086N*
Geography - World
Dist - CFLMDC **Prod** - NFBC 1973

Our sun and its planets 16 MIN
VHS / U-matic / 16mm
Color (P)
$420.00, $250.00 purchase _ #HP - 5883C
Draws from the archival film collection of NASA to help young astronomers define a planet, moon, sun and solar system. Uses computer simulation to visualize the characteristics of each of the nine planets and their moons or rings. Discusses the planets' positions relative to the sun and to each other, as well as the differences in their days, seasons and years because of orbital distance from the sun and the rate of rotation and revolution for each planet.
History - World; Science - Physical
Dist - CORF

Our Sun and its Planets 11 MIN
U-matic / VHS / 16mm
Color (P)
$280, $195 purchase _ #3002
Explains basic facts about the sun, planets, and solar system.
Science - Physical
Dist - CORF

Our sun and solar system - Video 9 47 MIN
VHS
Earth and space science - secrets of science series
Color (I J H C)
$49.95 purchase
Presents two parts in two segments each, looking at the forces governing the universe of the sun - from gravity to electromagnetism, exploring the solar system and how the sun works and its importance to humans, and studying the nature of light. Includes The Four Fundamental Forces and Our Solar System in Part I, The Sun - Source of Life and What is Light in Part II. Hosted by Discover Magazine Editor in Chief Paul Hoffman. Fifth of five parts on Earth and space science.
Science - Physical
Dist - EFVP **Prod** - DSCOVM 1994

Our Sweet Heritage 29 MIN
16mm
Color
Examines the love affair between Americans and the cookie. Presents a journey through history to explore the background behind some of the cookies that have served as tasty footnotes to America's past.
Home Economics
Dist - MTP **Prod** - ARCHCO

Our Sweet Way 27 MIN
16mm
Color
Takes a look at the charming and picturesque history of the cookie. Visits one of today's most modern bakeries.
Health and Safety; Home Economics
Dist - MTP **Prod** - ARCHCO

Our threatened heritage 19 MIN
VHS
Color (P I J H C G A)
$29.95 purchase
Documents the fact that more than 50 acres of rain forests are destroyed or heavily damaged every minute. Suggests that the consequences of continuing this destruction will be costly - global weather changes, increased hunger and poverty, and elimination of valuable

biological resources. Presents footage of the wildlife and vegetation of the rain forest. Considers the causes and solutions to this crisis.
Agriculture; Science - Natural; Social Science
Dist - EFVP **Prod** - NWF 1988

Our time in the garden 15 MIN
VHS
B&W (G)
$50.00 purchase
Tells the true story of a young Jewish woman growing up in Berlin at the time of Hitler's rise to power. Begins as a vividly detailed chronicle of her secure life centering around her family's walled garden. Antisemitism becomes a shattering force as Nazis take control and her family decides to abandon Germany forever. The home movies they escaped with are treated through special - effects photography and combined with overlapping soundtracks. Produced, written and directed by Ron Blau.
Fine Arts; History - World; Religion and Philosophy; Sociology
Dist - NCJEWF

Our Time is Our Time 13 MIN
U-matic / 35mm strip
Management of Time Series Module 4
Color
Shows how to save time by conducting efficient meetings and how to treat all meetings and contacts with others with a view toward saving time.
Business and Economics; Psychology
Dist - RESEM **Prod** - RESEM

Our Times 58 MIN
VHS / U-matic
Bill Moyers' Journal Series
Color (H C A)
LC 80-706744
Uses historic footage to recall the events of the 1960's and 1970's.
History - World
Dist - PBS **Prod** - WNETTV 1980

Our Totem is the Raven 21 MIN
16mm / U-matic / VHS
Color (I J H)
LC 77-712924
Dramatizes the ordeal of an Indian boy in his endurance and ritual ascent to manhood. Shows how Indians clash with twentieth - century values by giving some background into the Indian cultural heritage.
Social Science
Dist - PHENIX **Prod** - KINGSP 1972

Our Town 28 MIN
16mm
Color
LC 73-702347
Compares a contemporary industrial city to a mythical American turn - of - the - century city. Analyzes a contemporary city with respect to one of its most vicious problems - drugs.
Sociology
Dist - PATRSN **Prod** - PATRSN 1973

Our Town
U-matic / VHS
Color (J C I)
Presents the TV version of Thornton Wilder's play about turn - of - the - century life in a small New England town.
Fine Arts; Literature and Drama
Dist - GA **Prod** - GA 1977

Our Town 30 MIN
VHS / 16mm
Play Series
Color (H)
Presents Thornton Wilder's drama about life in a small New Hamshire town during the early 1900s. The fourth of eight installments of CTI's The Play Series, which attempts to give students an appreciation of the unique elements of the play through detailed examination of classic and trendsetting productions.
Fine Arts; Literature and Drama
Dist - GPN **Prod** - CTI 1990

Our Town 90 MIN
U-matic / VHS / 16mm
B&W
LC 81-701252
Presents an adaptation of Thornton Wilder's play Our Town.
Fine Arts; Literature and Drama
Dist - PHENIX **Prod** - UAE 1940

Our town and our universe 29 MIN
VHS
Color (H C G)
$129.00 purchase _ #DL413
Introduces the basic story of Our Town and analyzes the play's elements and unusual conventions. Features Clifton Fadiman who describes how Thornton Wilder dispensed with many of the realistic conventions of modern theater. Relates the use of both the past and present tense in the dialogue of the Stage Manager to the themes of the play and shows how Williams places life in a small town into a universal context.
Fine Arts; Literature and Drama
Dist - INSIM

Our town and ourselves 29 MIN
VHS
Color (H C G)
$129.00 purchase _ #DL414
Examines three devices Thornton Wilder used in Our Town. Features Clifton Fadiman who explains how the repetition of musical themes conveys the emotions of the characters and ties together various life events. Considers the use of the condensed sentence in the dialog and shows how Wilder developed the idea that the understanding of life only comes after death.
Fine Arts; Literature and Drama
Dist - INSIM

Our Town, Pt 1 30 MIN
U-matic / VHS / 16mm
B&W
LC 81-701252
Presents an adaptation of Thornton Wilder's play Our Town.
Literature and Drama
Dist - PHENIX **Prod** - UAE 1940

Our Town, Pt 1 14 MIN
16mm
Color
LC 73-402347
Compares an industrial city to a mythical american turn - of - the - century city. Analyzes the city of the 1970's with respect to one of its most vicious problems, drugs.
Sociology
Dist - PATRSN **Prod** - PATRSN 1973

Our Town, Pt 2 14 MIN
16mm
Color
LC 73-702347
Compares an industrial city to a mythical American turn - of - the - century city. Analyzes the city of the 1970's with respect to one of its most vicious problems, drugs.
Sociology
Dist - PATRSN **Prod** - PATRSN 1973

Our Town, Pt 2 30 MIN
16mm / U-matic / VHS
B&W
LC 81-701252
Presents an adaptation of Thornton Wilder's play Our Town.
Literature and Drama
Dist - PHENIX **Prod** - UAE 1940

Our Town, Pt 3 30 MIN
U-matic / VHS / 16mm
B&W
LC 81-701252
Presents an adaptation of Thornton Wilder's play Our Town.
Literature and Drama
Dist - PHENIX **Prod** - UAE 1940

Our Town, Pt 1 - Our Town and Our Universe 30 MIN
U-matic / VHS / 16mm
Humanities - the Drama Series
Color (H C)
Introduces the play Our Town. Presents an evaluation of the play by Clifton Fadiman who comments on the contrast between each tiny moment of our lives and the vast stretches of time and place in which each individual plays his role.
Literature and Drama
Dist - EBEC **Prod** - EBEC 1959

Our Town, Pt 2 - Our Town and Ourselves 30 MIN
U-matic / VHS / 16mm
Humanities - the Drama Series
Color (H C)
Discusses the conventions and techniques used in Our Town, such as the playwright's use of music, of light motif and variations, and of the condensed line or word. Considers the significance of the play for each member of the audience.
Fine Arts; Literature and Drama
Dist - EBEC **Prod** - EBEC 1959

Our trip 4 MIN
16mm
Color (G)
$15.00 rental
Showcases filmmaker's trip to Peru through a diaristic animation of photographs of landscapes and portraits. Reflects the rich folk art of the Incan people by framing and texturing with magic markers and tempera paint. Soundtrack features Incan music.
Fine Arts; Geography - World; Literature and Drama
Dist - CANCIN **Prod** - BARHAM 1980

Our vanishing forests - long version 58 MIN
VHS
Color (H C G)
$250.00 purchase, $80.00 rental
Delves into the waning survival of United States national forest and reserves from clearcutting which, at the current rate, will wipe out all of its remaining native national forests within 20 years. Urges Americans to consider their tax dollars that are subsidizing the destruction of their forests. Exposes the roles played by the US Forest Service which is selling at below market value to the powerful timber industry. Produced by Arlen Slobodowl - Public Interest Video Network.
Agriculture; Fine Arts; Science - Natural; Social Science
Dist - BULFRG **Prod** - PIVN 1993

Our vanishing forests - short version 27 MIN
VHS
Color (J H C G)
$195.00 purchase, $50.00 rental
Delves into the waning survival of United States national forest and reserves from clearcutting which, at the current rate, will wipe out all of its remaining native national forests within 20 years. Urges Americans to consider their tax dollars that are subsidizing the destruction of their forests. Exposes the roles played by the US Forest Service which is selling at below market value to the powerful timber industry. Produced by Arlen Slobodowl - Public Interest Video Network.
Agriculture; Fine Arts; Science - Natural; Social Science
Dist - BULFRG **Prod** - PIVN 1993

Our Vanishing Lands 24 MIN
16mm / U-matic / VHS
Smithsonian Series
Color (I J H)
LC FIA67-1694
Discusses the problem of conservation of America's resources, including its land, wildlife and natural beauty.
Agriculture; Psychology; Science - Natural; Sociology
Dist - MGHT **Prod** - NBCTV 1967

Our Vanishing Marshland 22 MIN
VHS / U-matic
Phenomenal World Series
Color (J C)
$129.00 purchase _ #3972
Probes the development of the destruction of the marshland, an ecological system that sustains billions of living things, including much plant life of potential value to humans, due to human greed.
Science - Natural
Dist - EBEC

Our Vanishing Wilderness, no 5 Series
Will the Gator Glades Survive 30 MIN
Dist - IU

Our Vanishing Wilderness Series no 1
Of Broccoli and Pelicans and Celery and Seals 30 MIN
Dist - IU

Our Vanishing Wilderness Series no 2
Prairie Killers 30 MIN
Dist - IU

Our Vanishing Wilderness Series no 4
Slow Death of the Desert Water 30 MIN
Dist - IU

Our Vanishing Wilderness Series no 6
Santa Barbara - Everybody's Mistake 30 MIN
Dist - IU

Our Vanishing Wilderness Series no 7
Water is So Clear that a Blind Man Could See 30 MIN
Dist - IU

Our Vanishing Wilderness Series
The Chain of Life 30 MIN
Prudhoe Bay - or Bust 30 MIN
Dist - IU

Our Violent Heritage 28 MIN
U-matic / VHS / 16mm
Color (H C A)
Looks at violence in America by reviewing the various political assassinations. Shows measures citizens are adopting to protect life and property, including buying guns and attending self - defense classes.
Sociology
Dist - CAROUF **Prod** - HOTRDS

Our water, our lives 30 MIN
VHS / U-matic / 16mm
Color (J H C)
$595.00, $445.00, $415.00 purchase _ #C539
Covers a variety of water and sanitation efforts in the developing and industrialized countries of Nepal, Indonesia, Mali, Sweden, Czechoslovakia and France. Discusses the success stories, as well as the barriers to safe drinking water and adequate sanitation.

Geography - World; Health and Safety; History - World; Science - Natural; Social Science
Dist - BARR Prod - UN 1988

Our way of loving 50 MIN
VHS
Under the sun series - Hamar trilogy
Color (A)
PdS99 purchase
Examines the Hamar, an isolated people living in the dry scrubland of south-western Ethiopia. Concentrates on the proud and outspoken Hamar women. Kuka and her husband talk about their life together and hopes for the future.
Psychology
Dist - BBCENE

Our Winning Season 92 MIN
16mm
Color
Follows a group of teenagers through their senior year in high school.
Fine Arts
Dist - SWANK Prod - AIP

Our Wonderful Body - How it Grows 11 MIN
U-matic / VHS / 16mm
Our Wonderful Body Series no 5
Color (P)
LC FIA68-2284
Illustrates that people grow at different rates and to different sizes. Explains that different parts of the body grow at different rates and shows the physical reasons for growth. Introduces the concepts of cell multiplication and growth. Explains that growth brings increased body control.
Science - Natural
Dist - CORF Prod - CORF 1968
VIEWTH

Our Wonderful Body - How it Moves 11 MIN
16mm / U-matic / VHS
Our Wonderful Body Series no 3
Color (P)
LC FIA68-2282
Uses a skeleton to demonstrate body movements. Illustrates the co - ordinated movement of muscles, bones and joints. Teaches ways of keeping the body healthy.
Health and Safety; Science - Natural
Dist - CORF Prod - CORF 1968
VIEWTH

Our Wonderful Body - How its Parts Work Together 11 MIN
U-matic / VHS / 16mm
Our Wonderful Body Series no 4
Color (P)
LC FIA68-2283
Uses life size models to demonstrate how parts of the body work together in different situations. Indicates that the brain signals muscles to move.
Science - Natural
Dist - CORF Prod - CORF 1968

Our Wonderful Body - How We Breathe 11 MIN
U-matic / VHS / 16mm
Our Wonderful Body Series no 2
Color (P)
LC FIA68-2281
Uses an operating model of a lung to illustrate breathing. Shows the movement of the diaphragm and carbon dioxide.
Science - Natural
Dist - CORF Prod - CORF 1968
VIEWTH

Our Wonderful Body - How We Keep Fit 10 MIN
U-matic / VHS / 16mm
Our Wonderful Body Series no 6
Color (P)
LC 73-702896
Shows how exercise, food and rest, dressing for the weather, proper treatment of injuries and sickness and getting regular check - ups are important in keeping fit.
Guidance and Counseling; Health and Safety; Physical Education and Recreation
Dist - CORF Prod - CORF 1973

Our Wonderful Body - Medicines, Drugs and Poisons 10 MIN
16mm / U-matic / VHS
Our Wonderful Body Series no 7
Color (P)
LC 73-702895
Offers such safety guidelines as the importance of reading labels, following a doctor's recommendation and the storage of drugs, medicines and household chemicals away from children.
Guidance and Counseling; Health and Safety; Home Economics
Dist - CORF Prod - CORF 1973

Our Wonderful Body Series no 1
Our Wonderful Body - the Heart and its Work 11 MIN
Dist - CORF
VIEWTH

Our Wonderful Body Series no 2
Our Wonderful Body - How We Breathe 11 MIN
Dist - CORF
VIEWTH

Our Wonderful Body Series no 3
Our Wonderful Body - How it Moves 11 MIN
Dist - CORF
VIEWTH

Our Wonderful Body Series no 4
Our Wonderful Body - How its Parts Work Together 11 MIN
Dist - CORF

Our Wonderful Body Series no 5
Our Wonderful Body - How it Grows 11 MIN
Dist - CORF
VIEWTH

Our Wonderful Body Series no 6
Our Wonderful Body - How We Keep Fit 10 MIN
Dist - CORF

Our Wonderful Body Series no 7
Our Wonderful Body - Medicines, Drugs and Poisons 10 MIN
Dist - CORF

Our wonderful body series
The Heart and its Work 11 MIN
How it grows 11 MIN
How it moves 11 MIN
How its parts work together 10 MIN
How We Breathe 11 MIN
How We Keep Fit 10 MIN
Medicines, Drugs and Poisons 10 MIN
Dist - CORF

Our Wonderful Body - the Heart and its Work 11 MIN
16mm / U-matic / VHS
Our Wonderful Body Series no 1
Color (P)
LC FIA68-2280
Constructs a model of the circulatory system which indicates functions of the heart, blood and blood vessels.
Science - Natural
Dist - CORF Prod - CORF 1968
VIEWTH

Our Wonderful Senses 13 MIN
U-matic / VHS / 16mm
Color (K P)
LC 80-700790
Describes the five senses, their functions, and how to take care of them.
Science - Natural
Dist - HIGGIN Prod - HIGGIN 1980

Our wonderful wetlands 11 MIN
VHS
Color (J H)
$79.95 purchase_#10210VL
Shows the wetland environment as a natural filtration system and home for a variety of plants and animals. Uses on - location footage of swamps, bogs and marshes to teach the preservation and uses of wetlands. Comes with a teacher's guide and lesson plans; student activities; discussion questions; and six blackline masters.
Science - Natural
Dist - UNL

Our wondrous oceans series
Explores the oceans' mysteries through narration, graphics, music and underwater footage. Examines marine life, currents, waves, change in oceans, and the water cycle. Consists of two videos; interactive video quizzes; teacher's guide; discussion questions; and a set of blackline masters.
Oceans - the cradle of life 15 MIN
Planet water 15 MIN
Dist - UNL

Our world 270 MIN
VHS
Color; PAL (K P)
PdS35 purchase
Presents an 18 - part series of 15 - minute programs to encourage young minds to explore the home, the classroom and the great outdoors. Examines everyday events such as food, dress, games and weddings in the first five programs. The next five introduce music from basic principles of rhythm and beat to the performance of a classroom opera. Programs 11 to 18 go on summer days out with the school and with the family from locations ranging from the local park and the seaside to a 17th - century role - playing museum. Includes background notes for teachers. Contact distributor about availability outside the United Kingdom and individual titles in the series.
Education; Geography - World; Home Economics; Social Science; Sociology
Dist - ACADEM

Our World 18 MIN
16mm / U-matic / VHS
Color (I J T)
Shows what children learn as they make a globe and how they continue to learn from the globe after it has been completed.
Social Science
Dist - IFB Prod - IFB 1957

Our World is an Island 17 MIN
16mm
Color (J H)
LC 76-700460
Interprets the relationship of life found on an island, focusing on the ecology of living things. Traces the history of the island as a land formation from its volcanic origins through the geo - physical changes that have occurred before and after the arrival of man.
Science - Natural; Science - Physical
Dist - INMATI Prod - INMATI 1976
INSTRU

Our world of minerals and rocks 38 MIN
35mm strip / VHS
Color (J H C A)
$93.00, $93.00 purchase _ #MB - 512998 - 1, #MB - 512760 - 1
Reveals how to distinguish minerals from rocks, and how to classify them. Describes the mechanical, chemical and organic actions required to form and transform rocks and minerals. Teaches scientific methods for positive identification.
Science - Physical
Dist - SRA Prod - SRA

Our world - topic and early learning support 270 MIN
VHS
Color; PAL (T)
PdS30
Presents a ten - part series of 15 - minute programs to help teachers working with very young children in putting the home, school and the outside world into perspective. Looks at a child's first experiences at school in the first five programs, including teacher's day, making friends and visitors to school, talking to others, questioning and understanding. Other topics include visits to the hospital and dentist, looking after pets and personal safety, helping children to face an increasingly difficult world. Contact distributor about availability outside the United Kingdom and individual titles in the series.
Education; Guidance and Counseling; Social Science
Dist - ACADEM

Our Youth Culture 30 MIN
16mm
Color (J H T R)
LC FIA67-5773
Investigates the struggle of youth for maturity and identity in an adult world. Points out that the church must make its message relevant to the needs of youth.
Guidance and Counseling; Psychology; Religion and Philosophy; Sociology
Dist - FAMF Prod - FAMF 1966

Ours to care for 6 MIN
VHS
Color (G)
$90.00 purchase, $25.00 rental
Emphasizes the importance of good nutrition and prenatal care for contemporary Native American women within the context of a rich cultural heritage.
Social Science; Sociology
Dist - SHENFP Prod - SHENFP

Ourselves 30 MIN
U-matic
Pearls Series
Color (H C A)
Presents five women sharing what it is like to grow up Asian and female in America.
Sociology
Dist - GPN Prod - EDFCEN 1979

Ourselves and that Promise 27 MIN
16mm
Color (H A)
LC 79-700619
Studies the relationship between an artist and his environment.
Fine Arts; Psychology; Sociology
Dist - APPAL Prod - APPAL 1977

Ourselves to Know - Alexander Pope's Essay on Man - what Oft was Thought but Ne'er So Well Expressed 45 MIN
VHS / U-matic
Survey of English Literature I Series
Color
Analyzes Alexander Pope's Essay On Man.
Literature and Drama
Dist - MDCPB **Prod** - MDCPB

Out and about 15 MIN
VHS
Color; PAL (P I J H)
Contrasts life in a city, Birmingham, England, with that in a village adjoining the city. Introduces concepts in geography.
Geography - World; Sociology
Dist - VIEWTH

Out and about Series

Describing	15 MIN
Detecting	15 MIN
Keeping Friends	15 MIN
Making Friends	15 MIN
Observing	15 MIN
Think Ahead	15 MIN
Ways to Solve a Problem	15 MIN
Why Did it Happen	15 MIN

Dist - AITECH

Out Art 29 MIN
U-matic / VHS
Creativity with Bill Moyers Series
Color (H C A)
Describes how artists break with tradition to shape new messages that are unique, outrageous, unconventional, delightful and even absurd.
Fine Arts; Psychology
Dist - PBS **Prod** - CORPEL 1982

Out in suburbia - the stories of eleven lesbians 28 MIN
VHS
Color (H C G)
$295.00 purchase, $55.00 rental
Features 11 lesbian women who discuss with frankness their lives in local neighborhoods, covering marriage, motherhood, discrimination, stereotypes and female roles. Shows that many lesbians have mainstream values and lead conventional lives. Produced by Pam Walton.
History - United States; Sociology
Dist - FLMLIB

Out in the open 26 MIN
VHS
Color (J H R)
$29.95 purchase, $10.00 rental _ #35 - 82 - 2549
Features young people discussing the joys and problems of their sexuality. Discusses how to build strong relationships and dealing with expectations. Produced by Inter - Varsity Christian Fellowship's 2100 Productions.
Health and Safety; Religion and Philosophy
Dist - APH

Out of Africa 50 MIN
VHS
Redemption song series
Color; PAL (H C A)
PdS99 purchase
Investigates slavery and voodooism in Haiti and Jamaica and features interviews with native inhabitants who discuss the history of these topics. Second in a series of seven programs focusing on the history of the Caribbean.
History - World; Sociology
Dist - BBCENE

Out of Body Travel 42 MIN
U-matic / VHS
B&W
Examines the fluctuating borders between opposites such as mind versus body and male versus female. Emphasizes the distance between things.
Fine Arts
Dist - KITCHN **Prod** - KITCHN

Out of Bondage 25 MIN
16mm
Color
Traces the roots of Russian Jewry and the events which led to the recent exodus to Israel.
History - World; Sociology
Dist - ALDEN **Prod** - UJA
NCJEWF

Out of breath 14 MIN
16mm / VHS / BETA / U-matic
Color; PAL (IND)
PdS130, PdS138 purchase
Defines occupational asthma, the causes and cures. Follows the activities of a man who works in a furniture factory, where exposure to dust from wood has caused chronic asthma, and the only cure for him is finding another job with a safer environment.
Fine Arts; Health and Safety
Dist - EDPAT **Prod** - TASCOR 1982

Out of Conflict - Accord Series

Dimensions of bargaining	29 MIN
The Harmonics of conflict	25 MIN
Waldenville I	38 MIN
Waldenville II	31 MIN
Waldenville III	36 MIN
Waldenville Jogger	39 MIN

Dist - USNAC

Out of control - hyperactive children 14 MIN
VHS
Color (H C G)
$275.00 purchase, $50.00 rental
Reveals that hyperactivity, now called Attention Deficit Disorder, affects five percent of American children, mostly boys. Discloses that it causes disruptive behavior in school and home and, if left untreated, can lead to criminal acts in later life. Traditionally, Attention Deficit Disorder has been treated with Ritalin which only masks the symptoms but does not cure. Features Dr James Satterfield, Director of the National Center for Hyperactive Children who discusses current therapy. Helps teachers to identify hyperactive children.
Health and Safety; Sociology
Dist - FLMLIB **Prod** - ABCNEW 1989

Out of darkness - an introduction to light 20 MIN
VHS
Color (P I J)
$89.00 purchase _ #RB813
Studies light. Examines reflection, refraction, the spectrum, the speed of light. Shows how light has energy and how the energy of sunlight is used by plants in photosynthesis. Explains how prisms and different types of lenses work.
Science - Physical
Dist - REVID **Prod** - REVID

Out of Harm's Way 25 MIN
VHS / 16mm
Color (H)
$95.00 purchase
Reviews dangers to children in the home and demonstrates safe storage of medicines, emergency intervention and prevention of accidents.
Health and Safety; Home Economics; Sociology
Dist - FLMWST

Out of Left Field 7 MIN
U-matic / VHS / 16mm
Color (J H)
Demonstrates how blind and visually impaired youths can be integrated with their sighted peers. Presents panel discussions by sighted, blind and visually impaired children and tells how they met the problems of integration. Shows blind and visually impaired children swimming, playing ball, wrestling, singing, dancing and playing many different games with sighted children.
Guidance and Counseling; Psychology
Dist - PHENIX **Prod** - AFB 1984
AFB

Out of many, One People 15 MIN
VHS / U-matic
Other families, other friends series; Brown module; Jamaica
Color (P)
Shows preparations for Christmas, a fair and a concert in Jamaica.
Geography - World; Religion and Philosophy; Social Science
Dist - AITECH **Prod** - WVIZTV 1971

Out of Michigan's Past 9 MIN
16mm
Color (P)
Visits Michigan's historical and geographical landmarks, such as Greenfield Village, Mackinaw Island and the Sleeping Bear Sand Dunes.
Geography - United States
Dist - WSUM **Prod** - WSUM 1958

Out of Order 89 MIN
16mm
Color (G)
Presents an independent production by D Christian and B Jackson. Reveals the female identity as seen by six former nuns.
Fine Arts; Religion and Philosophy; Sociology
Dist - FIRS

Out of Our Time 70 MIN
16mm / VHS
B&W (G)
$900.00 purchase, $135.00 rental
Examines the struggles of two circles of women, the first in the 1930s, the second in the academic - feminist community of contemporary Chicago. Shares the dreams of Jacquelyn Matthews, writer for a 1930s fashion magazine, and her granddaughter Valeri Ward, typesetter for a small feminist newspaper, who want to publish their own works. Valeri and lover Marilyn unearth her grandmother's correspondence with an aviatrix and discover the links and differences in friendship, feminism and personal fulfillment during those two eras. Produced by Casi Pacilio and L M Keys from Back Porch Productions.
Civics and Political Systems; Fine Arts; History - United States; Literature and Drama; Psychology; Social Science; Sociology
Dist - WMEN **Prod** - PAK 1988

Out of Rock 30 MIN
U-matic / VHS / 16mm
Color (H C A)
Focuses on the creative process and the forces embodied in the work of sculptor Boz Vaadia. Shows him creating from mountain rocks and discarded building materials. Juxtaposes his work, highlighting the interplay between nature and technology.
Fine Arts
Dist - FI **Prod** - FI 1980

Out of sight 60 MIN
VHS
Madness
Color; PAL (C PRO H)
PdS99 purchase; Not available in the United States
Covers the emergence of the asylum. Describes the function it served in the treatment of mental illness. Shows why asylums failed as a method of treatment. Second in the five - part series Madness, which covers the history of mental illness.
Psychology
Dist - BBCENE

Out of Sight, Out of Mind 25 MIN
16mm / VHS
Big Ice Series
Color (H)
$990.00, $390.00 purchase
Presents the history of Antarctic exploration and the necessity of careful, methodical planning for success there.
Geography - World; History - World; Science - Natural
Dist - FLMWST

Out of Step 30 MIN
16mm / VHS / U-matic
Color (J H)
Features story of a teenage girl who chooses dance as her life career. Presents excellent dance sequences. Full version.
Fine Arts; Guidance and Counseling; Psychology
Dist - LCOA **Prod** - HGATE 1985

Out of the Air - 1 20 MIN
U-matic / VHS
Chemistry in Action Series
Color (C)
$249.00, $149.00 purchase _ #AD - 1279
Shows the importance of air as an industrial raw material. Examines the separating of atmospheric air into its constituent gases. Part of a series, Chemistry in Action.
Industrial and Technical Education; Science - Physical
Dist - FOTH **Prod** - FOTH

Out of the Air - 2 20 MIN
U-matic / VHS
Chemistry in Action Series
Color (C)
$249.00, $149.00 purchase _ #AD - 1280
Looks at two importance products derived from air, ammonia and nitric acid.
Industrial and Technical Education; Science - Physical
Dist - FOTH **Prod** - FOTH

Out of the Ashes 24 MIN
16mm / U-matic / VHS
American Chronicles Series
Color (J H C G T A)
$75 rental _ #9819
Shows the trials at Nuremburg and the military tribunal in Tokyo condemn 'war criminals' to death.
History - World
Dist - AIMS **Prod** - AIMS 1986

Out of the Ashes - 1917 to 1945 - Pt 8 60 MIN
16mm / VHS
Heritage - Civilization and the Jews Series
Color (J)
$800.00, $49.00 purchase _ #405 - 9128
Explores more than 3000 years of the Jewish experience and its intimate connections with the civilizations of the world. Uses all available resources to weave an extraordinary tapestry of the Jewish history and people. Hosted by Abba Eban, Israel's former ambassador to the UN and the US. Part 8 presents the turmoil of the 1920s, the fury of Nazism and the Holocaust, the beginnings of reconstruction - and a glimmer of hope for the future.
Civics and Political Systems; History - World; Psychology; Religion and Philosophy; Sociology
Dist - FI **Prod** - WNETTV 1984

Out of the Blue 15 MIN
U-matic / VHS
TNRC Presents - Health and Self Series
Color (J H)
Presents members of the Twelfth Night Repertory Company using humor, satire, music, dance and drama to focus attention on attitudes regarding pollution. Recounts that when J J Biggley's Progress Products plans to build a factory on the last virgin forest in the state, Rodney Redwood organizes a boycott. Shows that Morganna Doomsday thinks it's hopeless until a close encounter with a spaceship captain and Mr Smock convinces her that she can make a difference in the fight against pollution.
Sociology
Dist - AITECH **Prod** - KLCSTV 1984

Out of the Darkness 53 MIN
U-matic / VHS
Man and Music Series
Color (C)
$279.00, $179.00 purchase _ #AD - 1767
Focuses on Rome in the 150 years following 1420 when the Popes returned. Views the resurgence of Rome as a cultural center, the changing of Church music from the Gregorian chant to Palestrina, Dufay, Josquin and Orlando di Lassus. Part of a 22 - part series that sets Western music into the historial and cultural context of its time.
Fine Arts; Geography - World; History - World
Dist - FOTH **Prod** - FOTH

Out of the Depths - the Miners' Story 55 MIN
VHS / U-matic
Walk through the 20th Century with Bill Moyers Series
Color
Deals with the struggle of miners and laborers in the American West, with miners recalling working conditions in the mines of the early 1900s. Describes the events which led to the famous 1913 United Mine Workers' strike and the 1914 Ludlow Massacre.
Business and Economics; Social Science; Sociology
Dist - PBS **Prod** - CORPEL

Out of the Dust 40 MIN
16mm
Color (J A) (LATIN)
Features an American engineer who has become a missionary in Latin America, telling his story to an amazed salesman.
Guidance and Counseling; Religion and Philosophy
Dist - YALEDV **Prod** - YALEDV

Out of the East 26 MIN
16mm
Winston Churchill - the Valiant Years Series no 10
B&W
LC FI67-2110
Uses documentary footage to describe a series of successful Japanese military victories in 1941 - 42, including the sinking of the British Navy's ships Prince of Wales and Repulse. Shows Churchill and Roosevelt meeting in a series of talks in Washington, and describes the American sea victory at Midway.
History - World
Dist - SG **Prod** - ABCTV 1961

Out of the fiery furnace series
Explains the role of metals and minerals in the building of civilization. Traces the use of metals and minerals from the Stone Age to the present day. Seven - part series is hosted by radio and BBC television commentator Michael Charlton.

The Age of metals - can it last	60 MIN
From alchemy to the atom	60 MIN
From stone to bronze	60 MIN
Into the Machine Age	60 MIN
Out of the fiery furnace series	420 MIN
The Revolution of necessity	60 MIN
Shining conquests	60 MIN
Swords and plough shares	60 MIN

Dist - PBS **Prod** - OPUS 1961

Out of the Limelight, Home in the Rain 52 MIN
16mm / U-matic / VHS
Magic of Dance Series
Color (J)
Explores the life of the dancer, including the rigors of ballet class, the rehearsals and preparation, and the moment of performance.
Fine Arts
Dist - TIMLIF **Prod** - BBCTV 1980

Out of the Mouth of Babes 24 MIN
VHS / U-matic
Sherry Millner Series
Color (G)
$250.00, $200.00 purchase, $50.00 rental
Juxtaposes US foreign policy in Central America with the process of a young child acquiring language to comment ironically on America.
Civics and Political Systems; Fine Arts; Psychology; Sociology
Dist - WMEN **Prod** - SHEMIL 1987

Out of the mouth of babes - the acquisition of language 28 MIN
16mm / VHS
Nature of things series
Color (H C G)
$295.00 purchase, $55.00 rental
Illustrates the chronology of language acquisition during the first six years of life. Shows active youngsters talking and notes the gradual progression that occurs from random babbling to jargon and one - word sentences, to the use of complicated structures and linguistic concepts. Emphasizes how children seem to learn language on their own, as part of their biological maturation, extracting the rules of language from the language they hear around them. Features Peter and Jill de Villiers of Harvard University who provide a clear and informative description of linguistic development.
Health and Safety; Psychology; Social Science
Dist - FLMLIB **Prod** - CANBC 1980

Out of the Mouths of Babes and Other People, Too 30 MIN
U-matic / VHS
Coping with Kids Series
Color
Provides an overview to conducting classroom meetings, what they are and how they can be helpful. Features Dr Brenda Dew as guest expert.
Guidance and Counseling; Sociology
Dist - OHUTC **Prod** - OHUTC

Out of the Mouths of Babes and Other People Too 29 MIN
U-matic / VHS
Coping with Kids Series
Color (T)
Education
Dist - FI **Prod** - MFFD

Out of the past, adult children of alcoholics 52 MIN
VHS
Color (H C G)
$445.00 purchase, $75.00 rental
Focuses on three 'adult children' who are struggling to come to terms with the profound effect of their parents' drinking. Shows that as they relive the memories and conflicting emotions of childhood they become aware of the danger of repeating the cycle of addiction in their own lives.
Guidance and Counseling; Health and Safety; Sociology
Dist - FLMLIB **Prod** - KENCOM 1990

Out of the Sea
16mm
Color (I J H C)
LC 72-701039
Records one of the many incidents that took place along the North Pacific coast during a violent October storm. Shows how a shipwrecked seaman managed to obtain his needs. Illustrates numerous survival techniques, including shelter construction, fire building, setting a fishing line and obtaining drinking water on the ocean beach.
Guidance and Counseling; Health and Safety; Social Science
Dist - LSTI **Prod** - LSTI

Out of the Shadows 28 MIN
VHS / 16mm
Adult Literacy Series
Color (PRO A G)
$90.00 purchase _ #BPN220601
Explores the problems encountered by those with limited literacy. Features actress Jackie Burroughs.
Education; English Language
Dist - RMIBHF **Prod** - RMIBHF

Out of the Shadows 30 MIN
U-matic
Adult Literacy Series
Color (PRO)
Explores the problems experienced by teenagers and adults with limited literacy, people who fell through the cracks of the educational system.
English Language; Literature and Drama
Dist - TVOTAR **Prod** - TVOTAR 1985

Out of the Shadows 17 MIN
16mm
Color (C A)
LC 72-702024
Demonstrates an intensive care program for severely retarded children instituted at Parsons State Hospital and Training Center at Parsons, Kansas.
Psychology; Sociology
Dist - UKANS **Prod** - UKANS 1969

Out of the Wilderness 28 MIN
16mm
Color
Features General Avraham Joffee speaking on ecology in Israel.
Geography - World; Science - Natural
Dist - ALDEN **Prod** - ALDEN

Out of the wilderness 60 MIN
VHS
Transformers series
Color (A T C)
PdS99 purchase _ Not available in Israel
Explains the teaching patterns devised by Prof Reuven Feuerstein for children in refugee camps. Tells how the methods are now being used in communities of black teenagers in New York. Part of a three-part series which looks at teaching children with learning difficulties.
Education
Dist - BBCENE

Out of the wood 30 MIN
VHS
Wall to wall series
Color (A)
PdS65 purchase
Reveals the new wooden structures that evolved in England from the 12th - 16th centuries, examining the construction techniques employed. Examines the vast range of dwelling places and buildings which can be found in the United Kingdom and abroad, and charts their history and evolution. Looks at the different building materials used through the centuries and compares and contrasts British buildings with similar structures found abroad.
Fine Arts; Industrial and Technical Education
Dist - BBCENE

Out of Thin Air 60 MIN
VHS / 16mm
Color (G)
$70.00 rental _ #OOTA - 000
Features Bert Houle and Sophie Wibaux demonstrating the art of mime.
Fine Arts
Dist - PBS **Prod** - NETCHE

Out of this World 13 MIN
16mm
Color
Examines five futuristic kitchens from the General Motors Futurama exhibit at the New York World's Fair.
Home Economics; Sociology
Dist - GM **Prod** - GM

Out of this World 21 MIN
16mm
Color
Shows the early stages of the Mercury program with particular emphasis on Minuteman and Polaris rocket motors.
History - World; Industrial and Technical Education
Dist - HERC **Prod** - HERC

Out of Tunes 15 MIN
U-matic
It's Mainly Music Series
Color (I)
Teaches children about how to write a melody that complements the theme of a song.
Fine Arts
Dist - TVOTAR **Prod** - TVOTAR 1983

Out on the Edge 25 MIN
U-matic
Color
Illustrates that the edge to a downhill racer is years of training, split - second decision and sometimes, the luck of the draw.
Physical Education and Recreation
Dist - LAURON **Prod** - LAURON

'Out' Side Word Processing 13 MIN
U-matic
Word Processing Series
(PRO)
$235.00 purchase
Reviews 'output' choices for word processing equipment. Explains basic types of equipment and capabilities.
Business and Economics
Dist - MONAD **Prod** - MONAD

Out there 55 MIN
VHS
Color (I J H C G A R)
$29.95 purchase, $10.00 rental _ #35 - 8524 - 1518
Shows how Glen McClain faces new realizations about God after his business is destroyed, his wife dies of cancer, and he suffers a heart attack. Set in the Alaska wilderness.
Religion and Philosophy; Sociology
Dist - APH **Prod** - SPAPRO

Out they Go 20 MIN
16mm
Color
LC 79-700527
Pays tribute to the people who are the heart and soul of the old fruit and vegetable markets in Sydney, Australia. Questions whether progress is always for the best.
Geography - World; Sociology
Dist - AUIS **Prod** - FLMAUS 1975

Out to Lunch 12 MIN
16mm / VHS
Color (G)
$300.00 purchase, $50.00, $40.00 rental
Shows through animation a series of incidents between women and men in a cafe setting. Men take up all the space and time they need while women apologize for getting in their way. Created by the Leeds Animation Workshop.
Sociology
Dist - WMENIF **Prod** - WMENIF 1989

Out with the Girls 5 MIN
U-matic / VHS
Color
Documents screaming women in the audience of male dancers. Deals with sexual politics. Presented by Carol Porter and Joan Merrill.
Fine Arts; Sociology
Dist - ARTINC **Prod** - ARTINC

Outback 24 MIN
16mm
Heading Out Series
Color
LC 76-703071
Presents an overview of the Peace River area of Canada.
Geography - World
Dist - CENTWO **Prod** - CENTWO 1975

The Outboard engine tuneup, Evinrude and Johnson
VHS
Outboard engine tuneup series
Color (G A)
$49.80 purchase _ #0439
Teaches outboard engine tuneup techniques for the Evinrude and Johnson outboards, all models and sizes built after 1972.
Industrial and Technical Education; Physical Education and Recreation
Dist - SEVVID

The Outboard engine tuneup, Mercruiser I - O
VHS
Outboard engine tuneup series
Color (G A)
$59.80 purchase _ #0428
Teaches outboard engine tuneup techniques for the Mercruiser I - O and inboard engines.
Industrial and Technical Education; Physical Education and Recreation
Dist - SEVVID

The Outboard engine tuneup, Mercury and Mariner
VHS
Outboard engine tuneup series
Color (G A)
$49.80 purchase _ #0429
Teaches outboard engine tuneup techniques for the Mercury and Mariner outboards, all models and sizes built after 1972.
Industrial and Technical Education; Physical Education and Recreation
Dist - SEVVID

Outboard engine tuneup series
The Outboard engine tuneup, Evinrude and Johnson
The Outboard engine tuneup, Mercruiser I - O
The Outboard engine tuneup, Mercury and Mariner
Dist - SEVVID

Outboard Fisherman USA 27 MIN
VHS / U-matic
Color
LC 80-707613
Shows how independent commercial fishermen, using outboard motors, contribute to the national economy. Issued as a motion picture in 1956.
Industrial and Technical Education
Dist - USNAC **Prod** - USBSFW 1980

An Outbreak of Salmonella Infection 14 MIN
16mm
Color (SPANISH)
LC 74-705280
Presents a stimulated typical outbreak of food - borne illness caused by organisms of the salmonella group. Discusses source and means of contamination, factors contributing to the survival and transfer of the organism, important conditions of environment and general good handling practices and effects of the outbreak.
Health and Safety; Home Economics; Science - Natural; Social Science
Dist - USNAC **Prod** - USPHCD 1954

An Outbreak of Salmonella Infection 14 MIN
16mm
Food Handling Series
Color
Studies a simulated outbreak of food - borne illness caused by organisms of the salmonella group. Examines source and means of contamination, factors aiding the survival and transfer of the organism, conditions of environment and general food handling practices, and effects of the outbreak.
Health and Safety
Dist - USNAC **Prod** - USPHS 1954

An Outbreak of Staphylococcus Intoxication 12 MIN
16mm
Food Handling Series
Color
LC FIE55-36
Studies a typical outbreak of food - borne illness due to staphylococcus organisms. Examines the symptoms of the victims and traces the source of the organisms to Staphylococcus aureus in pastry filling. Gives reasons for the incidence of the organisms in the food.
Health and Safety
Dist - USNAC **Prod** - USPHS 1954

An Outbreak of Staphylococcus Intoxication 12 MIN
16mm
Color (SPANISH)
LC 74-705281
Presents a case study of a typical outbreak of food - borne illness caused by staphylococcus organisms, including symptoms of the victims, tracing the source of the organisms as staphylococcus aureus in pastry filling and the reasons for the incidence of the organisms in the food.
Health and Safety; Home Economics; Science - Natural; Social Science
Dist - USNAC **Prod** - USPHCD 1954

Outcast 90 MIN
VHS
Color (G) (MANDARIN CHINESE (ENGLISH SUBTITLES))
$45.00 purchase _ #6005A
Presents a Mandarin Chinese language movie produced in the People's Republic of China.
Fine Arts; Geography - World; Literature and Drama
Dist - CHTSUI **Prod** - CHTSUI

The Outcast 29 MIN
VHS / 16mm
Watch your mouth series
Color (H)
$46.00 rental _ #WAYM - 119
Emphasizes language and communication skills for high school students. Notes the difference between formal and informal word usage.
Education; English Language; Psychology; Social Science
Dist - PBS

Outcome - based education series 100 MIN
VHS
Outcome - based education series
Color (T C PRO)
$880.00 purchase, $360.00 rental _ #614 - 244X01
Introduces the principles of outcome - based education and shows the dramatic impact OBE programs have had on schools in suburban Chicago and Phoenix. Explains how OBE helps ensure that all students understand the goals of learning, demonstrate their mastery of material and meet high expectations. Shows administrators how to implement and manage OBE throughout their districts. Illustrates to school board members and other community leaders an approach to schooling that helps students develop skills essential for the real world. Includes four videos - Four Guiding Principles of OBE; How OBE Changes Classroom Instruction; The District's Role in OBE; OBE - Executive Overview and a facilitator's guide. The first three videos are available separately.
Education
Dist - AFSCD **Prod** - AFSCD 1992

Outcome - based education series
The District's role in outcome - based education - Tape Three 30 MIN
Four guiding principles of outcome - based education - Tape One 40 MIN
Four guiding principles of outcome - based education - Tape One 40 MIN
How outcome - based education changes classroom instruction - Tape Two 20 MIN
How outcome - based education changes classroom instruction - Tape Two 20 MIN
Outcome - based education series 100 MIN
Dist - AFSCD

Outcomes of Child Abuse and Neglect 30 MIN
U-matic / VHS
Child Abuse and Neglect Series
Color (H C A)
Home Economics; Sociology
Dist - GPN **Prod** - UMINN 1983

Outdoor asbestos removal 25 MIN
BETA / VHS / U-matic
Color (IND G)
$495.00 purchase _ #820 - 35
Describes procedures employees should follow during outdoor asbestos abatement. Demonstrates both glove bag and bag techniques for removing asbestos.
Business and Economics; Health and Safety; Industrial and Technical Education; Psychology
Dist - ITSC **Prod** - ITSC

Outdoor cooking 15 MIN
16mm
Cooking film series
Color (J H A)
Presents tips on how to prepare various dishes with the outdoor gas grill, including veal chops, grilled scampi, spareribs, and barbecued chicken. Features famous sports figures.
Home Economics
Dist - BUGAS **Prod** - BUGAS

Outdoor Cooking 10 MIN
16mm
Outdoor Recreation - Winter Series
Color (I)
LC FIA68-1364
Describes how to prepare a kitchen area in a winter wilderness camp. Explains that subsistence diets are not an automatic part of roughing it outdoors. Shows ways of using nature's natural resources to aid in personal comfort.
Home Economics; Physical Education and Recreation
Dist - SF **Prod** - MORLAT 1967

Outdoor Cooking 30 MIN
U-matic / VHS
Roughing it Series
Color
Discusses outdoor cooking as part of 'roughing it' during camping.
Physical Education and Recreation
Dist - KYTV **Prod** - KYTV 1984

Outdoor Education 29 MIN
16mm
Color (T)
Shows how outdoor experiences may be provided for today's children through the use of the school site and other outdoor settings as learning laboratories, outdoor schools, outdoor interests, skills and teacher education.
Education
Dist - AAHPER **Prod** - AAHPER

Outdoor education mountaineering series
Basic rock climbing 14 MIN
Dist - MORLAT

Outdoor Education Mountaineering Series
Advanced rock climbing 17 MIN
Mountain Rescue 14 MIN
Solo Survival 11 MIN
Dist - SF

Outdoor Education White Water Paddling Series
Lake and River Kayaking 14 MIN
Dist - SF

Outdoor Fish Cookery 28 MIN
16mm
Color (P I J H C)
LC FIE67-201
Links the past with today by showing fishing and some methods of cooking fish outdoors. Includes mention of chowders, stews, fish fries and oyster and clam bakes.
Home Economics
Dist - USNOAA **Prod** - USBSFW 1959

Outdoor Furniture 30 MIN
VHS
Building Furniture Series
$39.95 purchase _ #DI - 404
Discusses the various information necessary to build outdoor furniture.
Industrial and Technical Education
Dist - CAREER **Prod** - CAREER

Outdoor Furniture - Hexagonal Picnic Table
VHS
Woodworking Series
(G)
$19.95 _ SH404
Covers choosing stock, tools and materials, design and plans, building center wheels, cutting angles, assembling top and seat, building and attaching legs, protecting wood.

Industrial and Technical Education
Dist - AAVIM **Prod** - AAVIM 1989

Outdoor Garden Projects 60 MIN
U-matic / VHS
Ortho's Video Series
Color (A)
$24.95 _ #OR100
Gives the viewer tips on designing and maintaining such outdoor garden projects as raised beds, gates, trellises, brick edgings, and more.
Agriculture; Science - Natural
Dist - AAVIM **Prod** - AAVIM

Outdoor Gear 30 MIN
VHS / U-matic
Roughing it Series
Color
Discusses outdoor gear needed for various outdoor activities when 'roughing it.'.
Physical Education and Recreation
Dist - KYTV **Prod** - KYTV 1984

Outdoor learning 30 MIN
VHS
Calico pie series
Color (C A T)
$69.95 purchase
Presents the final part of a 16 - part telecourse for teachers who work with children ages three to five. Discusses how outdoor environments can be used for teaching. Hosted by Dr Carolyn Dorrell, an early childhood specialist.
Education; Psychology
Dist - SCETV **Prod** - SCETV 1983

Outdoor Play - a Motivating Force for Learning 17 MIN
16mm
Color
Presents the unique physical and intellectual development provided by outdoor play activities and shows the extensive use of improvised materials. Highlights children's exploration of space, experimentation with balance, development of muscular coordination and body awareness. Illustrates developmental differences, self - determined activities and goals and the role of the teacher.
Education; Physical Education and Recreation; Psychology
Dist - CFDC **Prod** - QC 1973

Outdoor projects 40 MIN
VHS
Woodworking video series
Color (G)
$39.95 purchase _ #254
Explains building two outdoor woodworking projects - a hexagonal picnic table and a planter. Shows how to choose stock, tools, materials, design, assemble and finish both projects.
Home Economics; Industrial and Technical Education
Dist - DIYVC **Prod** - DIYVC

Outdoor Pursuits 26 MIN
U-matic
Alberta Elementary Physical Education Series
Color (PRO)
Describes skating, cross country skiing, orienteering and snow shoeing.
Geography - World; Physical Education and Recreation
Dist - ACCESS **Prod** - ACCESS 1983

Outdoor Recreation - Winter Series
Ice Fishing, Pt 1 12 MIN
Ice Fishing, Pt 2 12 MIN
Ice Safety 11 MIN
Outdoor Cooking 10 MIN
Proper Winter Clothing 13 MIN
Dist - SF

Outdoor safety series
Presents a five - part series concerned with different outdoor activities. Explains the necessary safety factors to assure well - being and survival in recreational sports. Includes Firearms Safety and the Hunter; Judgement on the Water - A Lesson in Small Boat Safety; Shoot - Don't Shoot; Survival; and Swept Away - A Guide to Water Rescue Operations. Titles available separately.
Firearms safety and the hunter 29 MIN
Judgment on the water - A Lesson in small boat safety 24 MIN
Survival 28 MIN
Swept away - A Guide to water rescue operations 30 MIN
Dist - NDIM **Prod** - MADISA 1983

Outdoor Sculpture and its Care 16 MIN
VHS / 16mm
Color (H A)
$150.00 purchase, $25.00 rental
Describes and illustrates preservation and restoration techniques used on stone and metal works in the outdoor sculpture garden at the Hirshhorn Museum in Washington, DC.
Fine Arts
Dist - AFA **Prod** - SMITHS 1986

Outdoor sculpture - preserving the Hirshhorn Museum's collection 15 MIN
BETA / VHS / U-matic
Color (PRO)
$19.95 purchase
Features conservators who demonstrate a variety of preventive care treatments for outdoor sculpture. Provides examples from the diverse collection exhibited in the Hirshhorn sculpture garden. Produced by the Center for Museum Studies at the Smithsonian for use in museum training.
Fine Arts; Psychology
Dist - SMITHS

Outdoor skills 30 MIN
VHS / U-matic
Sow seeds/trust the promise series
Color (J A)
Covers creative teaching activities for outdoor ministry. Includes movement and values education, communication games and the flow hike. Features Clifford Knapp and Joseph Cornell.
Religion and Philosophy
Dist - ECUFLM **Prod** - UMCOM

Outdoor survival series
Shoot - don't shoot 24 MIN
Dist - NDIM

Outdoor Toys 25 MIN
U-matic / VHS
Blizzard's Wonderful Wooden Toys Series
Color (H C A)
Shows how to build a see - saw and other yard toys like a wheelbarrow, stilts and rope ladders.
Fine Arts
Dist - FI **Prod** - BBCTV

Outdoorsman,The 25 MIN
U-matic
Human Foible Series
Color (H C A)
Shows Dr. Irvine Schiffer searching for that rugged outdoors look but quickly turning to leisure sports such as sailing.
Psychology
Dist - TVOTAR **Prod** - TVOTAR 1985

Outer Banks Fisherman 25 MIN
16mm
Color
Presents a pair of fisherman chasing trophy stripers from surf and boat.
Physical Education and Recreation
Dist - KAROL **Prod** - BRNSWK

The Outer circle 30 MIN
U-matic / VHS
Art of being human series; Module 6
Color (C)
History - World; Literature and Drama; Religion and Philosophy
Dist - MDCC **Prod** - MDCC

Outer Door Panel Replacement 46 MIN
VHS / BETA
Color (A PRO)
$136.00 purchase _ #AB132
Deals with auto body repair.
Industrial and Technical Education
Dist - RMIBHF **Prod** - RMIBHF

The Outer envelope 15 MIN
35mm strip / VHS
Inside the living cell series
Color (I J H)
$49.95 purchase _ #193 Y 6443, #70 Y 6443
Examines the plasma membrane and how materials are transported in and out of cells. Explains osmosis and the mechanisms of active transport, how cells ingest materials by phagocytosis, pinocytosis and receptor mediated endocytosis. Part of a six - part series on the living cell.
Science - Natural
Dist - WARDS **Prod** - WARDS 1990

The Outer planets 11 MIN
VHS
Color; PAL (P I)
PdS29.50 purchase
Explores the planets Jupiter and Saturn and their moons, as well as Uranus, Neptune and Pluto.
Science; Science - Physical
Dist - EMFVL **Prod** - STANF

The Outer planets 30 MIN
VHS
Our solar system series
Color (G)
$195.00 purchase
Looks at the outer planets. Covers primarily Jupiter and Saturn. Part of a four - part series.
Science - Physical
Dist - LANDMK

The Outer reaches of sailing
VHS
Color (G)
$29.80 purchase _ #0053
Experiences ice boating in Wisconsin and Maxiboating in San Francisco Bay. Visits the Aussie 18 World Championship in Australia and shows Hobie 33s in Arizona.
Physical Education and Recreation
Dist - SEVVID

Outer Space 15 MIN
VHS / U-matic
Draw Along Series
(K P)
$125.00 purchase
Discusses how to draw an imaginary scene on an unknown planet.
Fine Arts
Dist - AITECH **Prod** - AITECH 1986

Outfield play
VHS
NCAA instructional video series
Color (H C A)
$39.95 purchase _ #KAR1107V
Presents the fourth of a four - part series on defensive baseball. Focuses on outfield play.
Physical Education and Recreation
Dist - CAMV **Prod** - NCAAF

Outfitting a Welder with a Personal Sample Collector 8 MIN
VHS / BETA
Color
Discusses dust measurement, air filters and air sampling apparatus.
Health and Safety; Sociology
Dist - RMIBHF **Prod** - RMIBHF

Outfitting a Worker with a Personal Sample Collector 8 MIN
VHS / BETA
Color
Discusses dust measurement and environmental health.
Health and Safety; Sociology
Dist - RMIBHF **Prod** - RMIBHF

Outing in the Park, an / Trouble in the Bargain Basement / Paddington Takes the Stage 15 MIN
U-matic / VHS / 16mm
Paddington Bear, Series 2 Series
Color (K P I)
LC 80-700949
Describes Paddington Bear's adventures in a park, in a bargain basement and at a drama society show. Based on chapters two, six and seven of the book Paddington At Large by Michael Bond.
Literature and Drama
Dist - ALTSUL **Prod** - BONDM 1980

Outlasting the quakes 4 MIN
U-matic / VHS / 16mm
Search encounters in science series
Color (I J H)
LC 73-700901
Points out areas of the United States that are vulnerable to earthquakes. Describes the tragedies that earthquakes cause. Shows the largest earthquake simulator and the research efforts in earthquake engineering.
History - World; Science; Science - Physical
Dist - AMEDFL **Prod** - NSF 1974
EDPAT

Outlaw 26 MIN
VHS
Color (G)
$60.00 rental, $195.00 purchase
Presents Leslie Feinberg, a self - identified 'gender outlaw' who has spent much of her life passing as a man, speaking with passion and intelligence about her experiences. Asks the audience to examine their assumptions about the 'nature' of gender and calls for more sensitivity and awareness of human rights and the dignity of transgendered people. Raw and confrontational.
Civics and Political Systems; Fine Arts; Sociology
Dist - WMEN **Prod** - LEBOW 1994

The Outlaw and his wife 73 MN
VHS
Color tint (G)
$29.95 purchase
Presents a film by Swedish director Victor Sjostrom.
Fine Arts
Dist - KINOIC

Outlaw poverty, not prostitutes 21 MIN
VHS
Color (G)

$30.00 purchase
Features a documentary of the 1989 World Whores' Summit in San Francisco. Features prostitutes and activists from Thailand, Korea, Amsterdam and other countries who report on immigration, health care, and human rights as they affect prostitutes.
Civics and Political Systems; Fine Arts; Health and Safety; Sociology
Dist - CANCIN **Prod** - LEIGHC 1989

Outlaws of the marsh - or Water margin 1610 MIN
VHS
Color (G) (MANDARIN)
$695.00 purchase _ #5182
Presents television programming produced in the People's Republic of China. Includes 20 videocassettes.
Geography - World
Dist - CHTSUI

Outlet Boxes
VHS / 35mm strip
Wiring a House Series
$85.00 purchase _ #DXWAH020 filmstrips, $85.00 purchase _ #DXWAH020V
Teaches about switch boxes, receptacle boxes, and ceiling outlets.
Industrial and Technical Education
Dist - CAREER **Prod** - CAREER

Outline History of Europe Series
An age of revolutions 26 MIN
The Greeks 29 MIN
The Middle Ages 31 MIN
The Myth of Nationalism 30 MIN
Towards a Modern Europe 30 MIN
Dist - IFB

An Outline of vertebrate evolution 16 MIN
VHS
Color (J H)
$39.95 purchase _ #49 - 8260 - V
Features Edwin H Colbert. Reviews the fossil history of vertebrates. Explores how they have adapted to the extremely varied environments they now inhabit. Still frame.
Science - Natural
Dist - INSTRU **Prod** - CBSC

Outloading of Diesel Locomotives 13 MIN
16mm
B&W
LC FIE52-2051
Presents the problems and proper techniques for loading diesel locomotives aboard a cargo ship. Emphasizes the importance of teamwork and of stevedoring know - how.
Industrial and Technical Education; Social Science
Dist - USNAC **Prod** - USA 1952

Outlook 30 MIN
Videoreel / VT2
Unconscious Cultural Clashes Series
Color
Psychology; Sociology
Dist - SCCOE **Prod** - SCCOE

Outlook Southeast Asia 17 MIN
16mm
Color
LC 75-700569
Depicts the political, social and economic progress of Indonesia, Malaysia, Philippines, Singapore, Republic of Vietnam, Laos, Cambodia, Thailand and Burma. Describes the rich agricultural and industrial resources of Southeast Asia.
Geography - World; History - World
Dist - USNAC **Prod** - USDD 1968

Outpatient Chemotherapy - Patient - Teaching Session 25 MIN
U-matic
Color
Shows staff how to deal with patients involved in chemotherapy.
Health and Safety
Dist - UTEXSC **Prod** - UTEXSC

Outpatient evaluation and management of congestive heart failure 27 MIN
VHS / U-matic
Color (PRO C)
$395.00 purchase, $80.00 rental _ #C901 - VI - 036
Depicts the management and treatment of a patient presenting with classic symptoms of congestive heart failure. Focuses on current diagnostic technology and drug therapies, including the rationale for selection of drugs and management of patients on specific drugs. Presented by Drs Robert M Centor, Michael L Hess and Robert B Williams, Medical College of Virginia, Virginia Commonwealth University.
Health and Safety
Dist - HSCIC

Outpatient Hemorrhoidectomy - Ligation Technique 11 MIN
16mm
Color (PRO)
LC 73-701951
Demonstrates an effective painless treatment of internal hemorrhoids by the rubber - band ligation technique. Points out that the technique has been performed on over 700 patients within a period of five years and is a time - saving procedure performed in the clinic.
Health and Safety
Dist - SQUIBB **Prod** - KAISP 1969

Outpatient Treatment of Minor Burn Injuries 18 MIN
U-matic / VHS
Color (PRO)
LC 81-730384
Identifies the nurse's role in the care of the patient with a minor burn injury. Discusses the causes of minor burn injuries and gives a definition of a minor burn wound. Discusses promotion of patient comfort, wound care, infection control, patient teaching and follow - up care.
Health and Safety
Dist - MEDCOM **Prod** - MEDCOM

Outpatients 100 MIN
VHS
Understanding group psychotherapy series
Color (C G)
$225.00 purchase, $95.00 rental _ #38161
Uses four segments from 16 sessions to show how a group serves as a social microcosm. Features Dr Irvin D Yalom, Prof of Psychiatry, Stanford University School of Medicine, who illustrates how interactions within the group mirror important issues group members struggle with in their everyday lives. Demonstrates and discusses - selecting and preparing group members, establishing group norms, dealing with self - disclosure, ensuring a supportive environment, building a trust in confidentiality, dealing with an attack on the leaders, extra - group socializing, and combining 'here and now' experience with reflective analysis. Part of a three - part series on group psychotherapy produced by the Brooks Cole Publishing Co.
Psychology
Dist - UCEMC

Outpost Berlin 35 MIN
16mm
B&W
Shows Berlin from May 1945 to the September 1960 Billy Graham Crusade conducted before the Reichstag.
Geography - World; History - World; Religion and Philosophy
Dist - WWPI **Prod** - GRAHAM 1960

An Outpost of the kingdom - Part 5
VHS
Keith Miller - new wine series
Color (H C G A R)
$10.00 rental _ #36 - 87405 - 533
Proposes the theory that living one's faith can provide good opportunities for evangelism. Based on the Keith Miller book 'A Taste of New Wine.'
Religion and Philosophy
Dist - APH **Prod** - WORD

Outrage 60 MIN
VHS
Shoulder to shoulder series
Color (G)
$59.95 purchase _ #SHOU - 105
Tells how Emily Wilding Davidson became the first martyr for British women's suffrage when, in 1913, she threw herself under the hoofs of the king's horse. Reveals that there were other martyrs for this cause as well. Includes an account of the break betweeen sisters Sylvia and Christabel Pankhurst. Hosted by actress Jane Alexander.
Civics and Political Systems; History - World
Dist - PBS **Prod** - MKNZM 1988

Outside 28 MIN
VHS
Living with spinal cord injury series
Color (G)
$195.00 purchase, $100 rental _ #CE - 043
Looks at the lifelong process by which some injured people have created active and rewarding lives in part of a three - part series on spinal cord injuries.
Health and Safety
Dist - FANPRO **Prod** - CORBTB

Outside 28 MIN
16mm / VHS
Color (G)
$300.00 purchase, $100.00, $50.00 rental
Looks at people who are physically challenged and examines the way they deal with their challenges.
Health and Safety; Psychology
Dist - FANPRO **Prod** - FANPRO 1989

Outside 28 MIN
16mm
Color
Explores the lives of spinal cord injured Americans from all walds of life who have been successfully reintegrated into society. Provides hope and information on the wide variety of opportunities available to the disabled person.
Health and Safety; Psychology; Science - Natural
Dist - MTP **Prod** - NRAMRC

An Outside chance 156 MIN
VHS
Color; PAL (G)
PdS55 purchase
Presents six 26 - minute programs investigating cheaper and, arguably, more effective ways of dealing with offenders who are a nuisance to society, rather than a threat. Contact distributor about availability outside the United Kingdom.
Psychology; Sociology
Dist - ACADEM

Outside corner v groove 15 MIN
U-matic / VHS
Arc welding training series
Color (IND)
Industrial and Technical Education
Dist - AVIMA **Prod** - AVIMA

Outside in sight - the music of the United Front 30 MIN
VHS
Color (G)
$19.95 purchase
Offers the music of the United Front.
Fine Arts
Dist - KINOIC **Prod** - RHPSDY

Outside in ... skin 18 MIN
U-matic / VHS / BETA
Full of life series
Color; NTSC; PAL; SECAM (I J H)
PdS58
Introduces the variety of skin types, the structure and function of the skin, as well as ways of keeping it in good condition. Part of a series showing a group of youngsters, learning with the help of their older sister Sally how to combine diet, exercise, relaxation and skin care to create a balanced and healthy lifestyle.
Guidance and Counseling; Home Economics; Science - Natural
Dist - VIEWTH

Outside Leg Sweep (O - Soto - Gari) 4 MIN
16mm
Combative Measures - Judo Series
B&W
LC 75-700836
Demonstrates the outside leg sweep in judo and explains its effectiveness.
Civics and Political Systems; Physical Education and Recreation
Dist - USNAC **Prod** - USAF 1955

The Outside Micrometer 13 MIN
U-matic / VHS
Metalworking - Precision Measuring Series
Color (A)
Tells types of micrometers, their main parts, how to handle, read and care for them.
Industrial and Technical Education
Dist - VISIN **Prod** - VISIN

Outside Safety 15 MIN
VHS / U-matic
Well, Well, Well with Slim Goodbody Series
Color (P)
Demonstrates how to be safe on a bike, walking, swimming, on the playground and in a car. Teaches children safe places to play and how to deal with people who try to touch private parts of their bodies. Tells how to act around wild or stray animals.
Health and Safety
Dist - AITECH **Prod** - AITECH

Outside - Spinal Cord Injury and the Future 28 MIN
16mm
Color (J)
LC 83-700673
Presents people with spinal cord injuries who feel they are not deprived of choice because of a physically disabling accident and talk about the diverse and challenging opportunities that were open to them in their new life outside the rehabilitation center.
Education; Psychology
Dist - CRYSP **Prod** - NRAMRC 1983

The Outside tells us about the inside 30 MIN
VHS
New faces on make - up series
Color (G A)

$24.95 purchase _ #PRO216V
Interviews a dermatologist about the most common skin problems and how they can be corrected.
Home Economics
Dist - CAMV

Outside the Golden Ring 22 MIN
16mm
Color (H C A)
LC 75-702603
Examines various kinds of nontraditional marriages today. Shows the lifestyles of several different couples along with comments by psychologists and a marriage counselor.
Guidance and Counseling; Sociology
Dist - CRTVLC **Prod** - WRCTV 1975

Outside the Law 78 MIN
16mm
B&W
Tells a story of crime, Oriental philosophy, and social reform, set in San Francisco's Chinatown. Stars Lon Chaney in a duel role as a ruthless gangster and a soft - spoken servant.
Fine Arts
Dist - KITPAR **Prod** - UPCI 1921

Outside the school bus 4 MIN
16mm
Otto the auto - seatbelt and school bus safety - E series
Color (K P)
$30.00 purchase _ #225
Features Otto the Auto and Buster the Bus who tell children about the danger zone around buses that children must avoid. Part of a series on seatbelts and school bus safety. Complete series available on 0.5 inch VHS.
Health and Safety
Dist - AAAFTS **Prod** - AAAFTS 1976

Outside Your Door 15 MIN
VHS / U-matic
Up Close and Natural Series
Color (P I)
$125.00 purchase
Examines the study of insects and other creatures found close to home.
Agriculture; Science - Natural; Social Science
Dist - AITECH **Prod** - NHPTV 1986

The Outsiders
U-matic / VHS
Color (J C I)
Presents a dramatization of S E Hinton's story about the rivalry between poor and rich kids.
Fine Arts; Guidance and Counseling; Literature and Drama
Dist - GA **Prod** - GA

The Outsiders 20 MIN
U-matic / VHS
Matter of Fiction Series no 10
Color (J H)
Presents THE OUTSIDERS by Susan E H Hinton. Focuses on warring gangs in a Midwestern city whose conflicts result in the death of a boy. (Broadcast quality).
Literature and Drama; Psychology; Social Science
Dist - AITECH **Prod** - WETATV

The Outsiders
Videodisc
Laserdisc learning series
Color; CAV (J H)
$40.00 purchase _ #8L207
Depects the explosive conflict between rival gangs of poor and rich kids in the mid 1960s. Adapts a work by Sharon E Hinton. A teacher's guide is available separately.
History - United States; Literature and Drama; Sociology
Dist - BARR **Prod** - BARR 1992

The Outsiders
U-matic / VHS
Classic Films - on - Video Series
Color (G C J)
$89 purchase _ #05647 - 85
Re - tells S. E. Hinton's story of rivalry between poor and rich children. Stars Matt Dillon.
Fine Arts
Dist - CHUMAN

Outskirts of Hope 54 MIN
16mm
Color (A)
Examines the lives of different low - income groups to determine what impact the Reagan budget cuts have had.
Civics and Political Systems; Sociology
Dist - AFLCIO **Prod** - AFLCIO 1982

Outsmarting Crime - an Older Person's Guide to Safer Living 16 MIN
U-matic / VHS / 16mm
Color
Discusses the vulnerability of senior citizens to robbery, burglary and fraud. Demonstrates measures that can be taken by older citizens to avoid being victimized.
Health and Safety; Sociology
Dist - CORF **Prod** - HAR 1984

Outtakes 14 MIN
16mm / U-matic / VHS
Color (H C A)
LC 80-701667
Shows the outtakes of a low - budget crime drama. Depicts a cast that includes an incompetent actor, an overly calm director, and a bewildered character actor.
Fine Arts
Dist - WOMBAT **Prod** - HAIRY 1980

Outtakes - Paysage De Guerre 26 MIN
16mm
Color
LC 79-700258
Uses experimental techniques to reveal the horror and tragedy of war by creating a contrast between detachment and objective reality.
Fine Arts; Sociology
Dist - BREKEP **Prod** - BREKEP 1979
MEDIPR

Outward bound
VHS
Color (G)
$39.90 purchase _ #0801
Follows eight Outward Bound sailing school students in a small boat off the rocky coast of Maine. Shares their thoughts and feelings, the discomfort, the fun and the victories.
Physical Education and Recreation
Dist - SEVVID **Prod** - OUTB

Outward bound 30 MIN
VHS
Hidden assets series
Color (A)
PdS65 purchase _ Available in UK and Ireland only
Reveals that family responsibilities, limited access to training or unenlightened employers still prevent some women from advancing at work. Looks at case studies of some women who have been able to overcome their lack of confidence and to discover talents they never knew they had. Part of a two part series on women and employment.
Business and Economics; Sociology
Dist - BBCENE

Outward Bound 26 MIN
16mm / VHS
Space Experience Series
Color (G)
$425.00, $295.00 purchase, $55.00 rental; LC 89715679
Investigates how space exploration has had a profound impact on human consciousness. Shows that it is the first major exploration to be lived vicariously through television by vast numbers of people. Part of a six - part series on space hosted by astronaut Marc Garneau, veteran of the Challenger Space Shuttle.
History - World; Industrial and Technical Education; Religion and Philosophy; Science - Physical
Dist - CNEMAG **Prod** - REIDW 1988

Outward Bound 28 MIN
16mm
Color
LC 74-706080
Introduces the ideas and activities of America's five Outward Bound schools, designed to confront youth with meaningful challenges, including mountain climbing, sailing, canoeing, kayaking, hiking and a marathon. The highlight of the course is solo when each boy spends three days and nights alone with minimal shelter and no food.
Education; Physical Education and Recreation
Dist - CRYSP **Prod** - OUTB 1970

The Outward disciplines - Tape 3 50 MIN
VHS
Celebration of discipline series
Color (H C G A R)
$29.95 purchase, $10.00 rental _ #35 - 869 - 8516
Features Richard Foster in an exploration of the role spiritual disciplines can play in spiritual growth. Based on the book of the same title by Foster.
Religion and Philosophy
Dist - APH **Prod** - VISVID

Outwitting the Purse Snatcher 9 MIN
U-matic / VHS / 16mm
Color (A)
Opens with brief scenes of a purse snatcher at work and then reenacts each scene to show how the thief could have been outwitted.
Health and Safety; Sociology
Dist - RTBL **Prod** - RTBL

OV - 10A Multi - Mission 8 MIN
16mm
Color
Presents early development footage of the ov - 10a.
Industrial and Technical Education
Dist - RCKWL **Prod** - NAA

Ovals 15 MIN
VHS / U-matic
Let's Draw Series
Color (P)
Fine Arts
Dist - AITECH **Prod** - OCPS 1976

Ovals Unlimited 15 MIN
U-matic / VHS
Draw Along Series
(J H)
$125.00 purchase
Shows how to draw animals and other things using many ovals.
Fine Arts
Dist - AITECH **Prod** - AITECH 1986

Ovarian Cycle 32 MIN
VHS / 16mm
Histology review series; Unit XIII
(C)
$330.00 purchase _ #821VI056
Covers the menstrual cycle and related hormonal and histological changes during each of the four phases; menstrual, proliferative, secretory, and ischemic. Part 3 of the Female Reproductive System Unit.
Health and Safety
Dist - HSCIC **Prod** - HSCIC 1983

Ovarian Tumor Resection and Abdominal Hysterectomy 19 MIN
U-matic / VHS
Gynecologic Series
Color
Health and Safety
Dist - SVL **Prod** - SVL

Ovarian Tumors 24 MIN
16mm
Color (PRO)
Illustrates the gross diagnosis of ovarian tumors with a series of cases at the operating table ranging from the simple retention cysts through complicated carcinomas. Discusses implications for treatment.
Health and Safety; Science
Dist - ACY **Prod** - ACYDGD 1965

Ovary 24 MIN
VHS / 16mm
Histology review series; Unit XIII
(C)
$330.00 purchase _ #821VI054
Describes the basic structure of the internal organs of the female reproductive system. Covers special features and functions of the ovary including ovulation. Includes the development of primary oocytes, primordial follicles, and ovarian follicles. Part 1 of the Female Reproductive System Unit.
Health and Safety
Dist - HSCIC **Prod** - HSCIC 1983

Over a Barrel 15 MIN
U-matic
Color (H C A)
Examines the power of oil companies in controlling supply and setting prices. Explores the ramifications in terms of human suffering, especially as it affects the elderly and those on fixed incomes.
Social Science
Dist - USERI **Prod** - USERI 1979

Over a Barrel - Energy in the 80's 90 MIN
U-matic
Color (J)
Presents a panel discussion between a labor leader, a consumer advocate and an oil company spokesman on the power of oil companies.
Social Science
Dist - USERI **Prod** - USERI 1979

Over Hill, Over Dale 15 MIN
VHS / U-matic
Pass it on Series
Color (K P)
Looks at the things around us when traveling to a park or taking a hike.
Education
Dist - GPN **Prod** - WKNOTV 1983

Over in the Meadow 10 MIN
16mm / U-matic / VHS
Color (K P)
LC 77-702903
Features a sing - along film. Presents an old counting song for children.
Fine Arts; Literature and Drama
Dist - WWS **Prod** - WWS 1969

Over One Hundred 28 MIN
U-matic / VHS
Color (C)
$249.00, $149.00 purchase _ #AD - 1576
Interviews three women and three men who explain what life is like after 100. Reveals that all are active and all agree that the secret of longevity lies in both genetics and a positive attitude.

Health and Safety; Psychology; Sociology
Dist - FOTH **Prod** - FOTH

Over Rich, Over Sexed and Over Here - Pt 4 50 MIN
VHS
New Pacific Series, the
Color (S)
$79.00 purchase _ #833 - 9110
Explores the cultural, historical, economic and political facets of the Pacific Basin which supports a third of the world's population. No other region contains so great a diversity of race, language and culture. Part 4 of eight parts reveals the Pacific as an ideal example of traditional culture actually being strengthened by tourism.
Business and Economics; Civics and Political Systems; Geography - World; Guidance and Counseling; History - World
Dist - FI **Prod** - BBCTV 1987

Over the Andes in Ecuador 18 MIN
U-matic / VHS / 16mm
Man and His World Series
Color (P I J H C)
LC 79-705489
Presents transportation, industry, dress and customs of the people of Ecuador.
Geography - World; Social Science
Dist - FI **Prod** - FI 1969

Over the counter drugs - addiction within reach of the medicine cabinet 15 MIN
VHS / U-matic
Color (G)
$249.00 purchase _ #7494
Educates about the dangers of over the counter dug abuse. Discusses various remedies, including the effects of certain legal, but potentially lethal, ingredients. Warns about the risky practice of using compound cold medications to relieve symptoms.
Guidance and Counseling; Health and Safety; Psychology; Sociology
Dist - VISIVI **Prod** - VISIVI 1991

Over - the - counter drugs and human physiology 14 MIN
16mm / VHS
Human physiology series
Color (H C PRO)
$350.00, $275.00 purchase, $75.00 rental _ #8279
Explores the physiological effects and the potential dangers of the active ingredients in cold remedies, cough syrups, pain killers, stimulants and sleep and diet aids. Reveals that when these drugs are carelessly combined with coffee, alcohol or other OTC or prescription medicines, these drugs may have adverse or even dangerous side effects.
Guidance and Counseling; Health and Safety; Psychology
Dist - AIMS **Prod** - AIMS 1991

Over-the-counter drugs and valium
VHS
Surviving lifestyle drugs series
Color
Provides a framework for choosing and using cver - the - counter drugs, including aspirin. Deals with Valium.
Health and Safety
Dist - IBIS **Prod** - IBIS

Over - the - counter medicines 26 MIN
VHS
Color (G)
$149.00 purchase, $75.00 rental _ #UW2370
Takes a look at the thousands of over - the - counter medications for headaches, upset stomachs and allergies. Reveals that, when taken as directed, they present few risks. Explains some of the problems that can occur when over - the - counter drugs are taken carelessly.
Health and Safety
Dist - FOTH

Over - the - Counter Pills and Promises 17 MIN
16mm / U-matic / VHS
Color (J)
LC 77-700867
Describes how millions of dollars are spent each year on over - the - counter medication as a result of misleading advertising. Shows alternative remedies for many health problems.
Business and Economics; Health and Safety; Home Economics
Dist - HIGGIN **Prod** - HIGGIN 1977

Over the edge series
The Spark 30 MIN
The Wannabes 30 MIN
Dist - BBCENE

Over the Hill to the Moon 8 MIN
16mm / U-matic / VHS
Space Science Series
Color (I J H)
Explains how a spacecraft overcomes conflicting gravity pulls when traveling to the moon. Dramatizes an entire lunar flight, with animation and live footage. Clarifies the process of moving a spacecraft through the gravity fields of earth and moon.
Science - Physical
Dist - JOU

Over the influence series
Preventing our kids from using drugs and alcohol 46 MIN
Recovering our kids from drugs and alcohol 46 MIN
Dist - PFP

Over the moon with the cavalier 50 MIN
VHS
From A to B series
Color (A)
PdS99 purchase
Interviews male company car drivers as they cruise the motorways of Great Britain. Shows how the company car has contributed to the rise of a new form of snobbery. The drivers believe that the type of car provided by their company will affect the way other people view them and their work status.
Psychology; Sociology
Dist - BBCENE

Over the rim - the Grand Canyon story 29 MIN
U-matic / VHS / BETA
National park series
Color (G)
$29.95, $130.00 purchase _ #LSTF96
Looks at the Grand Canyon from all angles - both rims, on mule packs, from the air and from a river raft. Produced by KHR, Enterprises.
Geography - United States
Dist - FEDU

Over There 24 MIN
16mm
Color (J H)
Follows American expeditionary forces from 1914 until the day of armistice as seen in Paris, London, New York and the White House.
Civics and Political Systems; History - United States; History - World
Dist - REAF **Prod** - INTEXT

Over, under and through 10 MIN
VHS / U-matic
Tana Hoban's skill building adventures series
Color (P)
$250.00 purchase _ #HP - 6081C
Uses a treasure hunt as an exercise to teach children direction of movement and spatial relationships. Identifies vocabulary words for direction and movement and the concept of opposites. Part of a series based on the books by Tana Hoban, featuring music by Robin Frederick. Produced by Advanced American Communications.
English Language; Fine Arts; Physical Education and Recreation; Psychology
Dist - CORF

Overall Organization 30 MIN
U-matic / VHS
Better Business Letters Series Lesson 2; Lesson 2
Color
Focuses on the main idea in a letter. Shows where to put the main idea in a sales letter and a collection letter.
Business and Economics; English Language
Dist - TELSTR **Prod** - TELSTR
DELTAK

Overall Skiing 30 MIN
U-matic / VHS
Superstar Sports Tapes Series
Color
Covers several aspects of waterskiing. Includes competition, training, tournament strategy and the future. Stars Sammy Duvall.
Health and Safety; Physical Education and Recreation
Dist - TRASS **Prod** - TRASS

The Overanxious Patient and the Overactive Patient 19 MIN
U-matic / VHS
Basic Therapeutic Approaches to Abnormal Behaviors Series
Color
Presents issues concerned with the anxious patient and includes documentation, nursing care plans, associated hypochondria, preoccupation with his/her body, planned rest times and prescribed sedatives.
Health and Safety; Sociology
Dist - UWISC **Prod** - SCDMH 1979

Overarm Sweep and Shoulder Shrug / Trunk Stretcher / Forward and Backward Leg Lifts 15 MIN
VHS / U-matic
Roomnastics Series
Color (P)
Presents several exercises which can be performed in a classroom setting.
Physical Education and Recreation
Dist - GPN **Prod** - WVIZTV 1979

Overcalls 30 MIN
VHS / U-matic
Bridge Basics Series
Color (A)
Physical Education and Recreation
Dist - KYTV **Prod** - KYTV

Overcoming 30 MIN
16mm
Color
LC 79-700259
Documents different types of unique and unusual educational processes for deaf and blind children from preschool to secondary school. Concentrates on the adjustment and education of one such student, Donald Lenhartz.
Education; Guidance and Counseling; Psychology
Dist - DIETEL **Prod** - DIETEL 1978

Overcoming a painful childhood and the heritage - Tape 3 100 MIN
VHS
Turn your heart toward home series
Color (H C G A R)
$10.00 rental _ #36 - 89983 - 533
Features Dr James Dobson and his wife Shirley in two presentations on issues affecting the family. 'Overcoming a Painful Childhood' features Shirley Dobson in a reminiscence of her alcoholic father and how she came to faith in a loving God. 'The Heritage' outlines four traditional values which can be applied to family relationships.
Psychology; Sociology
Dist - APH **Prod** - WORD

Overcoming barriers in negotiations 24 MIN
U-matic / VHS
Art of negotiating series
Color
Business and Economics; Psychology
Dist - DELTAK **Prod** - DELTAK

Overcoming codependency - the path to wellness 30 MIN
VHS
Color (G)
$395.00 purchase, $125.00 rental _ #8377
Features Melodie Beattie, author of Codependent No More. Uses dramatizations to illustrate codependency. Shows how to identify and change patterns of codependent behavior.
Guidance and Counseling; Health and Safety; Psychology
Dist - AIMS **Prod** - AIMS 1991

Overcoming compulsive behavior 30 MIN
VHS / BETA
Working on oneself series
Color (G)
$29.95 purchase _ #S124
Reveals that Buddhist philosophy regards compulsive and addictive behavior as common to all 'normal' individuals. Features Shinzen Young, Buddhist monk and director of the Community Meditation Center of Los Angeles, who advocates the use of meditation to enable the recognition of the root cause of addiction as a lack of mindfulness. Part of a four - part series on working on the self.
Psychology; Religion and Philosophy
Dist - THINKA **Prod** - THINKA

Overcoming differences - an historic public address by the Dalai Lama 90 MIN
VHS
Color (G)
$29.95 purchase _ #OVDIVI
Records the March 26, 1991, address by the Dalai Lama at Cornell University to an audience of 12,000, inaugurating the 'Year of Tibet.' Discusses the relationship of world peace and inner peace. Reminds the audience that humans are social animals and must learn to live together in order to achieve happiness, as well as to survive.
Psychology; Religion and Philosophy
Dist - SNOWLI

Overcoming Direct Mail Pitfalls 30 MIN
U-matic / VHS
Business of Direct Mail Series
Color
Explains how to overcome direct mail pitfalls.
Business and Economics
Dist - KYTV **Prod** - KYTV 1983

Overcoming Erection Problems, Pt 1 11 MIN
U-matic / VHS
EDCOA Sexual Counseling Series
Color
Demonstrates interrupted stimulation exercises designed to reduce and extinguish anxieties related to the male's ability to attain an erection and/or regain a 'lost' erection.
Health and Safety; Psychology
Dist - MMRC **Prod** - MMRC

Overcoming Erection Problems, Pt 2 10 MIN
VHS / U-matic
EDCOA Sexual Counseling Series
Color
Shows how to combine interrupted penile stimulation with successive vaginal approximation until couple is assured of the male's erectile competence.
Health and Safety; Psychology
Dist - MMRC **Prod** - MMRC

Overcoming fear 30 MIN
VHS
Color (G)
$200.00 purchase _ #4028
Examines the structure of fear. Offers concrete ways to work through fear. Identifies the three common types of fear and how to manage them. Considers the impact of learned fears upon day to day life. Features Earnie Larsen.
Guidance and Counseling; Health and Safety; Psychology
Dist - HAZELB **Prod** - LARSE 1992

Overcoming fear - 20 13 MIN
VHS / U-matic
Life's little lessons - self - esteem K - 3 - series
Color (K P)
$129.00, $99.00 _ #V619
Reveals that the Swamperosa is about to be taken over by a band of outlaws who have captured Pa and the boys. Shows that Elmo, the timid fearful son, is left to rescue them and looks at how he overcomes his fears and becomes the hero of the day. Part of a 30 - part series on self - esteem.
Guidance and Counseling; Psychology
Dist - BARR **Prod** - CEPRO 1992

Overcoming fears, phobias, panic, and anxiety 50 MIN
VHS
Color (G)
$59.95 purchase _ #BPG453V-G
Presents a step-by-step guide to comprehending, coping with, and confronting fears. Uses personal success stories and offers the coping strategies that helped. Hosted by a psychologist, who founded the support network Power Over Panic.
Psychology
Dist - CAMV

Overcoming handicaps - 44 16 MIN
VHS / U-matic
Life's little lessons - self - esteem 4 - 6 series
Color (I)
$129.00, $99.00 purchase _ #V673
Looks at Karl Hilzinger who teaches children with amputations to overcome their handicaps and downhill ski. Reveals that Hilzinger was a pro football player who lost both his legs in an automobile accident. Part of a 65 - part series on self - esteem.
Guidance and Counseling; Health and Safety; Psychology
Dist - BARR **Prod** - CEPRO 1992

Overcoming Inferiority
VHS / 35mm strip
$98.00 purchase _ #HR630 filmstrip, $139.00 purchase _ #HR630V VHS
Tracks the origin of inferiority to childhood experiences. Points out why adolescents are particularly vulnerable to these feelings.
Guidance and Counseling; Psychology
Dist - CAREER **Prod** - CAREER

Overcoming Inferiority 23 MIN
VHS
Color
Provides your students with practical and proven techniques for overcoming their feelings of inferiority, through alteration of behavior patterns.
Guidance and Counseling; Health and Safety; Psychology
Dist - HRMC **Prod** - HRMC 1978

Overcoming Irrational Fear of AIDS 22 MIN
U-matic
Color (PRO)
Offers a candid appraisal of the feelings of the people who care for people with AIDS.
Health and Safety
Dist - BAXMED **Prod** - BAXMED 1986

Overcoming Objections 17 MIN
16mm / U-matic / VHS
Color (C A)
LC 82-701116
Explains and demonstrates how to anticipate customers' objections, listen for their expressed needs, define problem areas and then overcome specific objections.
Business and Economics
Dist - CRMP **Prod** - CRMP 1982

Overcoming Objections 30 MIN
U-matic / VHS / 16mm
B&W (PRO)
Demonstrates how salesmen, no matter what they sell or how they sell, can change stumbling blocks into stepping stones. Shows how American's sales champions make objections lose force without making a buyer lose face. Tells how to take the standard answers to common objections used by your salesmen, and make them doubly effective.
Business and Economics; Psychology; Social Science; Sociology
Dist - DARTNL **Prod** - DARTNL

Overcoming Objections in the Financial Marketplace 17 MIN
U-matic / VHS
(PRO A)
$195 Purchase, $100 Rental 5 days, $19.95 Preview 3 days
Teaches financial institution employees to handle client complaints effectively.
Business and Economics
Dist - ADVANM **Prod** - ADVANM

Overcoming Resistance 60 MIN
U-matic / VHS
Strategic Selling - a Thinking Person's Guide Series Pt 3
Color (A)
Shows how to make each of the buyer's objections in a selling situation the basis for a joint problem - solving situation that can lead to a close.
Business and Economics
Dist - TIMLIF **Prod** - TIMLIF 1984

Overcoming Resistance to Change 30 MIN
16mm / 8mm cartridge
Color; B&W (H C) (SWEDISH SPANISH DANISH DUTCH PORTUGUESE GERMAN)
LC fia66-1085; FIA66-1085
Shows supervisors how to recognize the emotional factors which breed resistance to change and how to prevent and overcome it.
Business and Economics; Foreign Language; Psychology
Dist - RTBL **Prod** - RTBL 1962

Overcoming sales objections 60 MIN
VHS
Color (A PRO)
$795.00 purchase, $250.00 rental
Demonstrates the selling cycle and successful techniques for field sales personnel.
Business and Economics; Psychology
Dist - VLEARN

Overcoming the fear of selling 30 MIN
VHS
Color (IND PRO)
$525.00 purchase, $245.00 rental _ #BTC07
Teaches sales skills including setting goals and behaviors for overcoming fear. Includes a leader's guide. Produced by Banctraining.
Business and Economics
Dist - EXTR

Overcoming the obstacles - Program 1 28 MIN
VHS
Saving a generation I and II series
Color (T PRO C)
$95.00 purchase
Profiles four teachers and their pioneering HIV education in their communities. Stresses the need for effective HIV - AIDS education for all young people and the role of administrative and comminity - wide support in helping teachers in this task. Part one of a two - part series offering strategies to teachers for teaching about HIV and AIDS prevention in grades 4 - 12.
Education; Health and Safety; Social Science
Dist - SELMED **Prod** - SACVP

Overdenture Technique - Diagnosis 9 MIN
16mm
Overdenture Technique Series
Color
LC 76-702731
Shows how the overdenture procedure provides a practical and simple alternative to conventional complete dentures. Emphasizes selection of roots to be retained and demonstrates the advantages of the overdenture technique.
Science
Dist - USNAC **Prod** - USVA 1975

Overdenture Technique - Laboratory Procedures, Denture Insertion and Oral Hygiene 7 MIN
16mm
Overdenture Technique Series
Color
LC 76-702733
Demonstrates technical variations which are utilized in adapting the usual laboratory procedures to the fabrication of an overdenture. Shows the use of pressure indicator paste to obtain equalized contacts at the time of delivery and explains oral hygiene procedures.
Science
Dist - USNAC **Prod** - USVA 1975

Overdenture Technique Series
Overdenture Technique - Diagnosis 9 MIN
Overdenture Technique - Laboratory Procedures, Denture Insertion and Oral Hygiene 7 MIN
Overdenture Technique - Treatment Procedures 10 MIN
Dist - USNAC

Overdenture Technique - Treatment Procedures 10 MIN
16mm
Overdenture Technique Series
Color
LC 76-702732
Shows how some teeth can frequently be selected to be retained beneath an overdenture. Shows how the retained teeth are modified by endodontics, periodontal treatment, crown reduction and an amalgam restoration. Shows how to make the final impression.
Science
Dist - USNAC **Prod** - USVA 1975

Overdose 17 MIN
VHS / U-matic
Emergency medical training series; Lesson 2
Color (IND)
Discusses not only what to do, but what not to do, for victims of chemical overdose.
Health and Safety; Industrial and Technical Education
Dist - LEIKID **Prod** - LEIKID

Overdose - the Crucial Minutes 28 MIN
U-matic / VHS
Color
LC 81-706268
Deals with the management of an acute poisoning victim involving medicinal drugs. Follows a victim from initial unconsciousness in his home to the emergency room at the hospital.
Health and Safety
Dist - USNAC **Prod** - USFDA 1979

Overeaters Anonymous - it Works 15 MIN
16mm / VHS
Color (G)
$325.00, $149.00 purchase, $60.00 rental _ #6225, 6226, 6227, 0435J
Explains the Overeaters Anonymous program through the dramatization of one woman's life struggle with compulsive eating. Produced by Overeaters Anonymous.
Health and Safety; Physical Education and Recreation; Psychology
Dist - HAZELB

Overeating - an American obsession 25 MIN
VHS / U-matic
Color (C A)
$295.00 purchase, $65.00 rental
Presents a documentary on the problem of overeating in America, where up to 25 per cent of the population is overweight and where five of the leading ten causes of death are linked to fatty diets and obesity. Interviews recovering overeaters discussing self - esteem and the use of food for emotional support. Discusses leading causes of obesity, genetic predisposition, environment and lifestyle factors, and decreased physical activity. Stresses the importance of comprehensive weight loss programs involving medical treatment, counseling and exercise education. Includes a section on childhood obesity.
Health and Safety
Dist - BAXMED

Overhand Throw and Ball Dodging 15 MIN
VHS / U-matic
Leaps and Bounds Series no 13
Color (T)
Explains how to teach primary students the overhand throw for the pattern, distance, force or accuracy, and how to dodge a rolled or thrown ball.
Physical Education and Recreation
Dist - AITECH

Overhaul Procedures 21 MIN
VHS / U-matic
Color (PRO)
Describes techniques for securing the fire scene and procedures for total extinguishment. Shows how the importance of fire cause is tied in to overhaul procedures.
Health and Safety; Social Science
Dist - FILCOM **Prod** - LACFD

Overhaul procedures 20 MIN
VHS
Firefighter II series
Color (IND)
$130.00 purchase _ #35657
Presents one part of a 14 - part series that is the teaching companion for IFSTA's Essentials of Fire Fighting manual. Identifies procedures and safety precautions to follow during overhaul. Describes several indicators of structural instability. Demonstrates procedures for restoring premises after fire. Based on Chapter 14.

Health and Safety; Science - Physical; Social Science
Dist - OKSU **Prod** - ACCTRA

Overhauling a mechanical petrol pump - Unit A 40 MIN
VHS
Motor vehicle engineering crafts - workshop practice series
Color; PAL (J H IND)
PdS29.50 purchase
Shows workshop practice lessons with a class of second year public service engineering apprentices. Consists of an introduction and demonstration of overhauling a mechanical petrol pump, followed by the students' own attempts. Part of a five - part series.
Industrial and Technical Education
Dist - EMFVL

Overhauling an S U carburettor - Unit B 31 MIN
VHS
Motor vehicle engineering crafts - workshop practice series
Color; PAL (J H IND)
PdS29.50 purchase
Shows workshop practice lessons with a class of second year public service engineering apprentices. Consists of an introduction and demonstration of overhauling an S U carburettor, followed by the students' own attempts. Part of a five - part series.
Industrial and Technical Education
Dist - EMFVL

Overhauling camshaft assembly and crankcase section 19 MIN
16mm
Aircraft work series; Power plant maintenance
B&W
LC FIE52-149
Explains how to inspect the camshaft and gear case cover assembly, inspect and recondition the crankcase section, measure crankcase bearings and inspect and recondition the remaining parts.
Industrial and Technical Education
Dist - USNAC **Prod** - USOE 1945

Overhauling crankshaft assembly 19 MIN
16mm
Aircraft work series; Power plant maintenance
B&W
LC FIE52-150
Explains how to clean the parts of a disassembled engine, inspect and recondition crankshaft assembly parts, determine clearances and check for out - ofround and inspect clearances against specifications.
Industrial and Technical Education
Dist - USNAC **Prod** - USOE 1945

Overhauling the carburetor 23 MIN
16mm
Aircraft work series; Power plant maintenance
B&W
LC FIE52-251
Shows how to remove the carburetor assembly from the engine, disassemble, clean, inspect and reassemble the carburetor, check the fuel level and reinstall the carburetor assembly.
Industrial and Technical Education
Dist - USNAC **Prod** - USOE 1945

Overhauling the small engine 43 MIN
VHS
Small engine - a video manual series
Color (H A)
$319.00 purchase _ #VMA31372V
Presents a comprehensive look at how to overhaul a small automobile engine. Portrays the complete sequence from disassembly to reassembly. Consists of three videocassettes and a program guide.
Industrial and Technical Education
Dist - CAMV

The Overhead 29 MIN
VHS / U-matic
Vic Braden's Tennis for the Future Series
Color
Physical Education and Recreation
Dist - PBS **Prod** - WGBHTV 1981

Overhead fillet weld 8 MIN
VHS / BETA
Welding training - comprehensive - advanced shielded metal arc welding series
Color (IND)
Industrial and Technical Education; Psychology
Dist - RMIBHF **Prod** - RMIBHF

Overhead passing and attack
VHS
Essential skills - coaching boys' volleyball I series
Color (J H C G)
$49.95 purchase _ #TRS576V
Features Bill Neville, USA National Team coach. Teaches the essential skills of overhead passing and attack. Part of a three - part series on essential skills in volleyball and an eight - part series on boys' volleyball.
Physical Education and Recreation
Dist - CAMV

The Overhead Router 37 MIN
U-matic / VHS
Furniture Manufacturing Series
Color (IND)
Reviews ordinal skills of shaping stock edge and routing vein lines or decorative designs into the face of the stock. Shows rabbit cuts, grooves and dovetail joints.
Industrial and Technical Education
Dist - LEIKID **Prod** - LEIKID

Overhead v - butt weld 9 MIN
BETA / VHS
Welding training - comprehensive - advanced shielded metal arc welding series
Color (IND)
Industrial and Technical Education; Psychology
Dist - RMIBHF **Prod** - RMIBHF

Overhead v butt weld technic 6 MIN
VHS / BETA
Arc welding and M I G welding series
Color (IND)
Industrial and Technical Education; Psychology
Dist - RMIBHF **Prod** - RMIBHF

Overload relays - controllers - coils 60 MIN
U-matic / VHS
Electrical maintenance training series; Module 1 - Control equipment
Color (IND)
Industrial and Technical Education
Dist - LEIKID **Prod** - LEIKID

The Overly Suspicious Patient 27 MIN
VHS / U-matic
Color
Presents an in - depth definition of the overly suspicious patient and methods used to effectively deal with this type of patient in a hospital setting. Illustrates identifying characteristics such as insecurity, delusions of persecution and grandeur, hypochondria and hallucinations.
Health and Safety; Sociology
Dist - UWISC **Prod** - SCDMH 1979

Overmanagement or How an Exciting Idea Can be Transferred into a Dull Project 13 MIN
U-matic / VHS / 16mm
Color (C A)
LC 76-700239
Illustrates the effect a complicated, bureaucratic, decisionmaking process has on a simple idea. Promotes discussion on overmanagement of corporations.
Business and Economics; Psychology
Dist - SALENG **Prod** - SYKES 1976

Overmedicating the Elderly 28 MIN
VHS / 16mm
Color (A)
$149.00 purchase, $75.00 rental _ #OD - 2228
Features Phil Donahue in a discussion about how the proliferation of drugs in combination with aggressive marketing has led to overmedication of the elderly. Often drugs are prescribed to control the reaction of drugs previously prescribed for the elderly patient.
Health and Safety; Sociology
Dist - FOTH

Overnight 28 MIN
VHS
Elephant show series
Color (P I)
$95.00 purchase, $45.00 rental
Presents program 29 in the Sharon, Lois and Bram's Elephant Show series. Teaches reading readiness and social skills while engaging children in making music. Each program explores a new theme through adventure, fantasy, mystery and song with recording artists Sharon, Lois and Bram. Uses traditional materials which stress participation - action songs, sing - along songs, story songs, clapping songs, singing games, playground chants and folk songs from many different traditions. Includes teacher's guide co - authored by a music education specialist.
Fine Arts; Sociology
Dist - BULFRG **Prod** - CAMBFP 1991

Overnight Camping 30 MIN
U-matic / VHS
Roughing it Series
Color
Discusses overnight camping as outdoor activity that requires 'roughing it.'.
Physical Education and Recreation
Dist - KYTV **Prod** - KYTV 1984

Overnight Sensation 30 MIN
16mm / U-matic / VHS
Color (H C A)
Presents a contemporary film adaptation of Somerset Maugham's short story, The Colonel's Lady. Focuses on a couple whose marriage is tested when the wife's first novel is an unexpected success, and the husband must deal with a new perspective on a traditional relationship. Features actors, Louise Fletcher, Robert Loggia, and Shari Belafonte.
Fine Arts; Literature and Drama
Dist - PFP **Prod** - PFP 1984

Overpriced, Overpackaged 10 MIN
U-matic
Calling Captain Consumer Series
Color (P I J)
Shows a boy who, after a shopping trip with his mother, notices the needless garbage from unnecessary wrappings.
Business and Economics; Home Economics
Dist - TVOTAR **Prod** - TVOTAR 1985

Overseas taxpayers 14 MIN
U-matic / VHS
Tax tips on tape series
Color; Captioned (A PRO IND)
$20.00, $40.00 purchase _ #TCA17591, #TCA17590
Covers tax laws for taxpayers who reside overseas. Discusses how to compute income, overseas housing expenses, and how much overseas income can be excluded.
Business and Economics; Civics and Political Systems; Social Science; Sociology
Dist - USNAC **Prod** - USIRS 1988

Overtaking at Night 15 MIN
16mm
Color
LC FIE52-947
Illustrates the correct use of whistle signals in overtaking situations on the ocean and in inland waters.
Civics and Political Systems; Health and Safety; Social Science
Dist - USNAC **Prod** - USN 1943

Overtaking Situation 15 MIN
16mm
B&W
LC FIE52-944
Gives whistle signals to be used when overtaking on the ocean, in inland waters and in narrow channels. Demonstrates examples of their use.
Civics and Political Systems; Health and Safety; Social Science
Dist - USNAC **Prod** - USN 1943

Overton - rifle company 30 MIN
VHS
Vietnam home movies series
Color (J H C G)
$29.95 purchase _ #BV153V
Features actual footage shot by soldiers during their tour of duty in Vietnam. Tells the story of one soldier in his own words, the combat missions, his friends, his joy after a successful rescue, the devastation after an enemy raid, the sounds of war. Offers footage aboard a UH1 Huey helicopter gunship, a pass dodging sniper fire from the Viet Cong, looking down the rocket sight on a search and destroy mission. Part of a four - part series.
History - United States; Sociology
Dist - CAMV

Overture 2012 6 MIN
U-matic / VHS / 16mm
Color (H C A)
LC 77-703138
Presents an animated interpretation of the future of man's discordant world.
Fine Arts; Sociology
Dist - IFB **Prod** - ZAGREB 1977

Overture - Linh from Vietnam 26 MIN
16mm / U-matic / VHS
Color (J)
LC 80-701630
Introduces Linh Tran, a Vietnamese girl who has settled with her family into the first real home they have had since immigrating from Vietnam to America. Shows the hardships they endure and the adjustments they must make in a country where they are neither accepted or wanted.
Guidance and Counseling; Social Science; Sociology
Dist - LCOA **Prod** - LCOA 1981

Overture to glory - Der Vilner shtot Khazn 85 MIN
VHS
Moyshe Oysher film classics series
B&W (G) (YIDDISH WITH ENGLISH SUBTITLES)
$79.95 purchase _ #730
Features Moyshe Oysher as Vilner Balbesi, the cantor who leaves his position as Vilna Cantor in order to seek fame and fortune as an opera star in Warsaw. Reveals that

Balbesi feels uncomfortable in his new environment and yearns to return to his wife, child and community. With Helen Beverly and Florence Weiss, Directed by Max Nosseck and produced by Ira Greene and Ludwig Landy.
Fine Arts; Literature and Drama; Religion and Philosophy; Sociology
Dist - ERGOM **Prod** - ERGOM 1940

Overturning tractors 17 MIN
VHS
Color; PAL; NTSC (G)
PdS57, PdS67 purchase
Shows eight different ways to overturn a tractor.
Health and Safety
Dist - CFLVIS

Overuse Injuries - Too Much, Too Fast, Too Soon 10 MIN
VHS / U-matic
Sports Medicine for Coaches Series
Color
Presents information on recognizing and managing overuse injuries. Presents definitions of the injury, how they develop and the mechanism of injury, particularly in the lower extremity. Describes treatment techniques as well as steps coaches and athletes can take to help prevent overuse injuries.
Health and Safety; Physical Education and Recreation
Dist - UWASH **Prod** - UWASH

Overuse Syndromes of the Lower Extremity 27 MIN
U-matic / VHS
Sports Medicine Series
Color (C A)
$69.00 purchase _ #1462
Discusses the disabilities caused by overuse syndromes, their symptoms, their diagnosis, their treatment and their effect on athletic performance. Includes information on shin splints, runner's knee, jumper's knee, Osgood Schlatter's disease, ankle pronation, Cavas' foot and Morton's foot.
Health and Safety; Physical Education and Recreation
Dist - EBEC

An overview 46 MIN
VHS
Art of advocacy - selecting and persuading the jury series
Color (C PRO)
$95.00 purchase, $71.25 rental _ #Z0301
Presents an overview of techniques used in jury selection and persuasion of the jury. Covers techniques applicable to both civil and criminal cases, and draws on social science insights.
Civics and Political Systems
Dist - NITA **Prod** - NITA 1988

Overview 14 MIN
Videoreel / VT2
AMA Assessment Center Program for Identifying Supervisory Potential 'Series
Color (PRO)
LC 75-704221
Explains the purpose of the AMA Assessment Center and the manner in which it functions.
Business and Economics; Psychology
Dist - AMA **Prod** - AMA 1974

Overview 150 MIN
U-matic
Electronics Manufacturing - Components, Assembly and Soldering 'Series
Color (IND)
Discusses the electronics manufacturing flow, including making printed circuit boards, and testing, quality, reliability, documentation and manufacturing control.
Business and Economics; Industrial and Technical Education
Dist - INTECS **Prod** - INTECS

Overview 11 MIN
U-matic / VHS / 16mm
Community Helpers Series
Color (P I)
$280, $195 purchase _ #79519
Discusses division of labor, municipal services, local government, and specialization.
Civics and Political Systems
Dist - CORF

Overview 20 MIN
U-matic
One Giant Step - the Integration of Children with Special Needs 'Series
Color (PRO)
Introduces the concept of integration as it relates to various handicaps and information on the difficulties inherent in the integration process.
Education
Dist - ACCESS **Prod** - ACCESS 1983

An Overview 46 MIN
VHS / U-matic
Patients with Rheumatic Disorders Series
Color
Defines the scope and nature of rheumatic diseases and related pathophysiologic changes. Presents patients with a variety of diagnoses, which are often complex and for which a wide range of treatments are available.
Health and Safety; Science; Science - Natural
Dist - AJN **Prod** - AJN

Overview 18 MIN
VHS / 16mm / U-matic
Information Security Briefing Series
Color (A)
Discusses Executive Order 12356, signed by President Reagan in April, 1982. Defines National Security Information, information security personnel and their responsibilities, and methods used in classification and declassification of materials.
Civics and Political Systems
Dist - USNAC **Prod** - USISOO 1982

Overview 29 MIN
VHS / 16mm
Junior High Ethics Resource Package Series
Color (J)
$200.00 - $250.00 purchase _ #278401
Presents a comprehensive series on ethics for educators, junior high students and concerned adults. Describes an ethics course introduced in Alberta, Canada, schools and suggests teaching strategies for educators. The last five programs are dramas for students to teach key ethical concepts. 'Overview' sets out the philosophy, rationale, goals and objects of the Grade 8 ethics course and shows how the course is organized into modules.
Business and Economics; Guidance and Counseling; Psychology; Religion and Philosophy; Sociology
Dist - AITECH **Prod** - ACCESS 1989

Overview 15 MIN
VHS / 16mm
Managing Spinal Injury in Sport Series
Color (C)
$150.00 purchase _ #292601
Presents a standardized, systematic and comprehensive approach to the management of spinal injuries in various sports settings. Reveals that sport and recreational activities are the second most common cause of spinal fractures resulting in paralysis. Improper management of this serious injury may increase the chance of lifetime paralysis or death. Trains sports and recreational professionals in the management of spinal injuries. 'Overview' introduces the topic of spinal injury in sport and recreational settings and includes statistics on injury from various sports and the anatomy of spinal injury.
Health and Safety; Physical Education and Recreation
Dist - ACCESS **Prod** - ACCESS 1989

Overview 29 MIN
VHS / 16mm
Junior High Health and Personal Life Skills in - Service Series
Color (C)
$175.00, $225.00 purchase _ #271801
Orients teachers to the revised 1986 Junior High Health and Personal Life Skills Curriculum. Introduces a change of emphasis in both content and teaching strategies. Knowledge of the human body is superseded by knowledge, attitudes, skills and lifelong behavior for healthy lifestyles. 'Overview' identifies the five themes of the 1986 curriculum and outlines the contents of each. Explains the decision - making model and its emphasis throughout the curriculum.
Education; Guidance and Counseling; Health and Safety; Psychology
Dist - ACCESS **Prod** - ACCESS 1986

An Overview 30 MIN
U-matic / VHS
Digital Sub - Systems Series
Color
Covers rationale of course and describes the current on - going revolution in digital design techniques. Gives insight of how digital systems are designed.
Industrial and Technical Education; Mathematics; Sociology
Dist - TXINLC **Prod** - TXINLC

Overview and background of America's involvement - Book 1 98 MIN
VHS
Vietnam - the 10,000 day war series
Color (H C A)
$24.95 purchase
Presents Book One of the 'Vietnam - The 10,000 Day War' series. Gives an overview and background information on America's involvement in the Vietnam War.
History - United States
Dist - PBS **Prod** - WNETTV

Overview and Disease - Specific Isolation
U-matic / VHS
Infection Control III Series
Color
Discusses the basic principles of disease transmission, the initiation of isolation precautions, the psychologic impact of isolation and the importance of patient teaching.
Health and Safety
Dist - CONMED **Prod** - CONMED

Overview and Natural History of Lung Cancer 32 MIN
U-matic
Color
Presents a statistical study of lung cancer and identifies the major predisposing factors, including environmental, personal habits, occupational and date of birth.
Health and Safety
Dist - UTEXSC **Prod** - UTEXSC

Overview - Disabilities Common in Elderly Persons, Tape 1 13 MIN
VHS
Increased Mobility for the Elderly Series
Color (PRO)
$50.00 purchase _ #876
Discusses aging changes influencing mobility and desired mobility outcomes in elderly patients with Hemiplegia, Parkinsons's Disease, and Arthritis. Intended to teach nurses and health professionals mobility skills in acute rehabilitation or for long term care settings. Presents the work of W Griggs and K S Black.
Health and Safety
Dist - RICHGO **Prod** - RICHGO 1985

Overview - Job Analysis and Manning Table 29 MIN
16mm
Job Instructor Training Series
B&W (IND)
LC 77-703324
Business and Economics; Psychology
Dist - EDSD **Prod** - EDSD

Overview module - Spanish language basics
VHS
Practical Spanish for health - care providers series
Color (A PRO) (SPANISH AND ENGLISH)
$350.00 purchase
Instructs in the basics of Spanish for health - care workers. Develops speaking ability for communication with Spanish - speaking patients. Recommended as prerequisite for the other modules of the series. Includes facilitator's guide, study guide and audiocassettes. Additional sets for students are available at a nominal charge.
Foreign Language; Health and Safety; Psychology
Dist - UARIZ **Prod** - UARIZ

Overview of Apparel Manufacturing 14 MIN
VHS / 16mm
Mass Production Procedures in Apparel Manufacturing Series
Color (H C A)
Features on site photography and a graphic presentation of the structure and organization of the apparel business. Defines and explains the functional divisions of an apparel firm.
Business and Economics
Dist - IOWA **Prod** - IOWA 1987

Overview of child development 30 MIN
VHS
Beginnings - handicapped children birth to age 5 series
Color (G)
$75.00 purchase _ #BHCH - 101
Discusses the steps of normal development in children from birth through five years. Uses these steps as an aid in diagnosis of children with special needs. Features psychologist and educator Dr Michael Guralnick. Part of a series on child development focusing on handicapped children.
Health and Safety; Psychology; Sociology
Dist - PBS **Prod** - MDDE 1985

An Overview of Decision Analysis 55 MIN
U-matic / VHS
Decision Analysis Series
Color
Discusses the objectives, structure and central issues of decision analysis.
Industrial and Technical Education
Dist - MIOT **Prod** - MIOT

Overview of dual diagnosis - Tape 1 60 MIN
VHS
Dual diagnosis - Haight - Ashbury training series
Color (C G PRO)
$250.00 purchase
Examines the historical basis for dual diagnosis, the differing approaches of the drug treatment community and the mental health community, the problems of treating these overlapping illnesses, and personal accounts from clients

in treatment. Part of a three - part series on dual diagnosis in drug abuse treatment.
Guidance and Counseling; Health and Safety; Psychology
Dist - FMSP

Overview of electronic instruments 30 MIN
VHS
Color (J H C G)
$59.95 purchase _ #VC - 1303
Features Don Muro, specialist in MIDI and electronic keyboards, who presents and demonstrates synthesizers, drum computers, samplers and digital processors.
Fine Arts
Dist - ECS **Prod** - ECS

Overview of Energy 15 MIN
VHS / 16mm
Exploring Technology Series
Color (I J)
$180.00 purchase, $25.00 rental
Defines energy and shows its sources, forms, technological advances, uses and impact on society and the environment.
Business and Economics; Psychology; Science - Physical
Dist - AITECH **Prod** - AITECH 1990

Overview of Energy - 1 16 MIN
VHS
Exploring Technology Education - Energy, Power and Transportation - 'Series
Color (I)
$180.00 purchase
Defines energy and shows its sources, forms, technological advances, uses and impact on society and the environment. Considers exhaustible, renewable and inexhaustable sources of energy. Builds the technological literacy vital for current and future careers. Part of the Exploring Technology Series.
Education; Industrial and Technical Education; Social Science
Dist - AITECH **Prod** - AITECH 1990

An Overview of Intrathoracic Neoplasia 24 MIN
U-matic
Radiology of the Respiratory System - a Basic Review
Color (C)
Presents a concept of the radiographic appearance and behavior of pulmonary neoplasia.
Health and Safety; Industrial and Technical Education; Science - Natural
Dist - UOKLAH **Prod** - UOKLAH 1978

Overview of Laryngectomy - Preop and Postop Care 9 MIN
VHS / 16mm
(C)
$385.00 purchase _ #840VI073
Describes the voicebox and surrounding structures, the laryncectomy procedure, and the postoperative period. Helps patients to deal with the fear of speech and communication impairment.
Health and Safety
Dist - HSCIC **Prod** - HSCIC 1984

An Overview of logotherapy and its application to aging 100 MIN
VHS
Color (G C PRO)
$59.95 purchase
Features Dr Melvin Kimble addressing the 1989 annual meeting of the American Society on Aging.
Health and Safety
Dist - TNF

Overview of Mainstreaming 29 MIN
VHS / U-matic
Mainstreaming the Exceptional Child Series
Color (T)
Provides an overview of mainstreaming.
Education; Psychology
Dist - FI **Prod** - MFFD

Overview of Management and Treatment Issues in Acute Intervention in Emergency Room 30 MIN
U-matic / VHS
Management and Treatment of the Violent Patient Series
Color
Discusses control of staff, patients and their families and dystonic and dysphoric qualities of violence as a symptom of the violent patient.
Health and Safety; Psychology
Dist - HEMUL **Prod** - HEMUL

An Overview of Master Production Scheduling 60 MIN
VHS / BETA
Manufacturing Series
(IND)
Describes the role of the master productions scheduler in the manufacturing organization.
Business and Economics
Dist - COMSRV **Prod** - COMSRV 1986

An Overview of MOS 30 MIN
U-matic / VHS
MOS Integrated Circuit Series
Color (PRO)
Looks at past, present and future of MOS, outlining history and citing motivations behind the rapid growth of MOS technology.
Industrial and Technical Education
Dist - TXINLC **Prod** - TXINLC

Overview of Preventive Antitrust Activities 89 MIN
VHS / U-matic
Preventive Antitrust - Corporate Compliance Program Series
Color (PRO)
Offers a panel discussion touching on major issues involved in antitrust compliance programs.
Civics and Political Systems
Dist - ABACPE **Prod** - ABACPE

Overview of Public Law 94 - 142 - the wrongs Congress required schools to right - Tape 1 49 MIN
VHS
Legal challenges in special education series
Color (G)
$90.00 purchase
Reveals that Congress has ordered substantial change in special education regarding exclusion of students with severe handicaps, appropriateness of programming, interruptions in service through discipline of summer vacation, individualization, least restrictive environment, related services, parental involvement, record access and impartial hearings. Features Reed Martin, JD. Includes resource materials. Part of a 12 - part series on Public Law 94 - 142.
Education
Dist - BAXMED

An Overview of School Mathematics in the 80's
U-matic / VHS
Third R - Teaching Basic Mathematics Skills Series
Color (T)
Provides an overview of the Third R - Teaching Basic Mathematics Skills series and of Ten Basic Skill areas. Suggests how skills can be imcorporated into total math curriculum. Includes a brief segment from five programs in the series.
Education; Mathematics
Dist - EDCORP **Prod** - EPCO

An Overview of service - Tape I 30 MIN
VHS
All about aging series
Color (A G)
$195.00 series purchase, $25.00 series rental
Describes services available to older adults and families. Explains financial resources such as Medicare and Medicaid. Part one of a four - part series not available separately. Includes workbook and provider's guide.
Civics and Political Systems; Sociology
Dist - AGEVI **Prod** - AGEVI 1990

Overview of small business 28 MIN
VHS
How to start your own business series
Color (H A T)
$69.95 purchase _ #NC115
Overviews aspects of small businesses. Part of a ten - part series on starting a business.
Business and Economics
Dist - AAVIM **Prod** - AAVIM 1992

Overview of Technology 15 MIN
VHS / 16mm
Exploring Technology Series
Color (I J)
$180.00 purchase, $25.00 rental
Shows how developments of the past lead to those of the future and how students use technology to solve problems.
Business and Economics; Computer Science; Education
Dist - AITECH **Prod** - AITECH 1990

Overview of the Christian Year
U-matic / VHS
Christian Year Series
Color (G)
Examines the history and development of the Christian year and gives a brief summary of the major seasons.
Religion and Philosophy
Dist - CAFM **Prod** - CAFM

An Overview of the human anatomy - the head and torso 40 MIN
VHS
Color (J H)
$180.00 purchase _ #A5VH 1087
Introduces human anatomy. Features Dr Tom Quinn of Creighton University School of Medicine who reviews human anatomy using a Denoyer - Geppart teaching torso model. Begins with the head and identifies the major organs and structures and continues through the torso. Discusses four regions and the organs in each region - the cranial region; the cervical region; the thoracic region and the abdominal region. Includes teacher's guide.
Science - Natural
Dist - CLRVUE **Prod** - CLRVUE

Overview of the period of the precatechumenate 60 MIN
VHS
Introduction and overview of RCIA series
Color (R G)
$49.95 purchase _ #RCIA1
Assists Roman Catholic individuals and parish teams involved in the implementation of the Order of Christian Initiation of Adults in further understanding the periods and stages of the initiation process. Gives particular emphasis to the varieties of implementations and adaptation for various parish settings. Produced in collaboration with the North American Forum on the Catechumenate. Part of three parts on Roman Catholic initiation of adults.
Religion and Philosophy
Dist - CTNA **Prod** - CTNA

Overview of the petroleum industry series

Completing a well	17 MIN
The Crust of the Earth	18 MIN
Drilling a Well	15 MIN
Exploration for Oil and Gas	12 MIN
Formation of oil and gas deposits	15 MIN
The Nature of Crude Oil and Natural Gas	11 MIN
Transporting and Refining	12 MIN

Dist - GPCV

Overview of the US Environmental Protection Agency 17 MIN
BETA / U-matic / VHS
Color (G PRO)
$29.95, $130.00 purchase _ #LSTF6
Explains how the United States Environmental Protection Agency works.
Civics and Political Systems; Science - Natural; Sociology
Dist - FEDU **Prod** - USEPA 1986

An Overview of Tibetan Buddhism with a commentary on Bodhicharyavatara 660 MIN
VHS / BETA
Color; PAL (G)
PdS90, $180.00 purchase
Features a program recorded from His Holiness The Dalai Lama of Tibet's 1988 visit to England. Divides the teachings into three sections - an overview of Tibetan Buddhism; a commentary on Bodhicharyavatara; and a question and answer session.
Fine Arts; Religion and Philosophy
Dist - MERIDT **Prod** - MERIDT 1988

Overview - Teaching Operations and Associated Strategies 29 MIN
VHS / U-matic
Strategies of Effective Teaching Series
Color (T)
Provides an introduction to the Strategies Of Effective Teaching series.
Education
Dist - AITECH **Prod** - PCSB 1980

Overview - what is successful aging - Part 1 28 MIN
VHS / U-matic / BETA
Human development - successful aging series
Color (C PRO)
$150.00 purchase _ #128.1
Presents a video transfer from slide program which examines the aging process in terms of its biological, psychological, social and chronological components. Delineates the changes that occur as people age and demonstrates that while some of those changes indicate decline, others reflect growth and development. Part one of two parts of an overview of a series on successful aging.
Health and Safety
Dist - CONMED **Prod** - CONMED

Overview - what is successful aging - Part 2 25 MIN
VHS / U-matic / BETA
Human development - successful aging series
Color (C PRO)
$150.00 purchase _ #128.2
Presents a video transfer from slide program which discusses and evaluates various social - psychological approaches such as disengagement theory, activity theory, adaptive tasks and personality theory, which attempt to explain how successful aging can be achieved. Explains a method of measuring life satisfaction and describes three different but equally successful patterns of aging. Part two of two parts of an overview of a series on successful aging.
Health and Safety
Dist - CONMED **Prod** - CONMED

Overwater Flying 25 MIN
16mm
Color (PRO)
LC 76-704008
Demonstrates equipment and procedures for aviation pilots flying over water in light aircraft. Shows emergency survival gear, optical illusions over water and navigational and radio equipment. Covers proper ditching procedures and water survival techniques.
Health and Safety; Industrial and Technical Education
Dist - USNAC **Prod** - USFAA 1976

Overweight 30 MIN
VHS / U-matic
Here's to Your Health Series
Color (C T)
Discusses poor eating habits and ways to break them. Describes the many health risks of being fat.
Health and Safety; Psychology
Dist - DALCCD **Prod** - DALCCD

Overweight - How Did I Get this Way?
U-matic / VHS
Color
Presents the psychological inputs that seduce one into eating more than one needs. Explains the signals that trigger improper eating and offers ways to combat their influence.
Health and Safety
Dist - MIFE **Prod** - MIFE

Overweight - obesity 30 MIN
VHS
At time of diagnosis series
Color (G)
$19.95 purchase _ #1 - 5757 - 7014 - 8NK
Provides patients who suffer from being overweight or obesity and their families with thorough, comprehensive and understandable information. Examines what is going on in the body and what might have caused the condition. Explains the type of medical professionals a patient may encounter and how the condition is monitored. Explores treatment options, including medication and lifestyle changes. Looks at practical issues surrounding the illness and answers the most common questions. Part of an ongoing series to provide the in - depth medical information patients and their families need to know.
Health and Safety
Dist - TILIED **Prod** - TILIED 1996

Overweight - what Can I do about it?
U-matic / VHS
Color (SPANISH ARABIC)
Gives the overweight person guidelines for losing weight and keeping it off. Covers setting a daily calorie limit and substituting low for high calorie foods.
Health and Safety
Dist - MIFE **Prod** - MIFE

Overweight - who's in control
VHS
Color (PRO A)
$250.00 purchase _ #WC - 05
Gives encouragement and guidelines to the patient struggling to lose weight. Emphasizes that 'weight control' is a lifestyle modification while 'diet' implies a temporary change. Explains how 'dieting' may make it more difficult to lose weight. Helps raise awareness of behavior patterns, emotional aspects of eating and pitfalls in maintaining a weight control plan. Exercise is also stressed.
Health and Safety; Physical Education and Recreation
Dist - MIFE **Prod** - MIFE 1991

An Ovicide Called Lannate 7 MIN
16mm
Color
LC 78-701321
Introduces an insecticide which controls cotton pests before they hatch.
Agriculture
Dist - DUPONT **Prod** - DUPONT 1978

Oviduct, Uterus, Cervix, Vagina, Mammary Gland 40 MIN
VHS / 16mm
Histology review series; Unit XIII
(C)
$330.00 purchase _ #821VI055
Gives a physical description and discusses the anatomy, function, and histological organization of the oviduct, uterus, cervix, vagina, and mammary gland. Part 2 of the Female Reproductive System Unit.
Health and Safety
Dist - HSCIC **Prod** - HSCIC 1983

Ovulation and Egg Transport in Mammals 14 MIN
16mm
Color (H C A)
LC 72-701495
Illustrates ovulation in the living mammal by showing the mechanism whereby the ovulated egg is transported from the surface of the ovary into the oviduct and then to the site of fertilization within the oviduct.
Science - Natural
Dist - UWASHP **Prod** - UWASHP 1972

The Owl 11 MIN
U-matic / VHS / 16mm
Color
LC 74-701702
Shows the savage violence which occurs when an owl is surprised by a flock of blackbirds as it attacks the blackbirds' young chicks in their nest.
Science - Natural
Dist - IFB **Prod** - DUNAV 1974

The Owl and the Lemming 6 MIN
16mm
Color (P I)
LC 76-702246
Presents an animated story in which two puppets act out an Eskimo legend in which an owl hunts a lemming because his family needs food. Shows how he is outsmarted by the lemming.
Literature and Drama
Dist - NFBC **Prod** - CDIAND 1971

The Owl and the Pussycat 3 MIN
U-matic / VHS / 16mm
Color
LC 78-715125
Uses the pictures and text of the poem by Edward Lear to tell the story about the owl and the pussycat who take an amorous voyage.
Literature and Drama
Dist - WWS **Prod** - WWS 1971

The Owl and the Pussycat 6 MIN
U-matic / VHS / 16mm
Color (P)
Uses animation to portray the children's poem, 'THE OWL AND THE PUSSYCAT,' by Edward Lear, in which the owl and the pussycat jump into their pea - green boat and sail out to sea.
Literature and Drama
Dist - MGHT **Prod** - NBCTV 1962

The Owl and the Pussycat 7 MIN
U-matic / VHS / 16mm
Color
LC 81-701268
Offers an animated version of the romance and marriage of an owl and a pussycat.
Fine Arts; Literature and Drama
Dist - PHENIX **Prod** - HALAS 1981

The Owl and the Pussycat 30 MIN
BETA / VHS
Color
Presents the classic children's story of The Owl And The Pussycat.
Fine Arts; Literature and Drama
Dist - HOMEAF **Prod** - HOMEAF

Owl and the Pussycat, the / Little Birds 8 MIN
U-matic / VHS / 16mm
Color
LC 81-700261
Offers an animated version of nonsense poems by Edward Lear and Lewis Carroll.
Literature and Drama
Dist - TEXFLM **Prod** - TEXFLM 1980

The Owl and the Raven 8 MIN
16mm
Color (P I)
LC 75-700381
Presents an Eskimo legend which explains why the raven is black.
Literature and Drama; Social Science
Dist - NFBC **Prod** - CDIAND 1974

OWL Animal Studies Series
Bats 8 MIN
Hibernating Ground Squirrels 8 MIN
Polar bear 11 MIN
Sleeping bears 8 MIN
Dist - BULFRG

Owl - Master Hunter of the Night 23 MIN
U-matic / VHS
Color (K)
Explores the true nature of the fabled night predator, the great horned owl. Shows a new breed of conservationist, one who intervenes on the owl's behalf.
Science - Natural
Dist - NWLDPR **Prod** - NWLDPR

Owl Moon 9 MIN
16mm / VHS
Color (K P I)
$100.00, $195.00 purchase, $20.00 rental _ #VC333V, #MP333
Presents the story adapted from the book Owl Moon by Jane Yolen and narrated by the author. A father and his young daughter trek through the snow in search of the Great Horned Owl.
Health and Safety; Literature and Drama; Psychology
Dist - WWS **Prod** - WWS 1989

Owl moon 35 MIN
VHS
Children's circle collection series
Color (K P I)
$14.95 purchase _ #WK1172
Contains title story along with The Caterpillar and the Polliwog; Hot Hippo; and The Time of Wonder.
Fine Arts; Literature and Drama
Dist - KNOWUN

OWL North American Indians Series
Inuit Kids 15 MIN
The Taos Pueblo 9 MIN
Dist - BULFRG

OWL special needs series
Blissymbolics 8 MIN
Free Dive 9 MIN
T R O T 7 MIN
Dist - BULFRG

Owl - TV #1 series
Owl - TV - Series 1 - Programs 1 - 10 290 MIN
Dist - BULFRG

Owl - TV #2 series
Owl - TV - Series 2 - Programs 11 - 20 290 MIN
Dist - BULFRG

Owl - TV #3 series
Owl - TV - Series 3 - Programs 21 - 30 290 MIN
Dist - BULFRG

Owl - TV #4 series
Owl - TV - Series 4 - Programs 31 - 40 290 MIN
Dist - BULFRG

Owl - TV #5 series
Owl - TV - Series 5 - Programs 41 - 50 290 MIN
Dist - BULFRG

Owl - TV #6 series
Owl - TV - Series 6 - Programs 51 - 60 290 MIN
Dist - BULFRG

Owl - TV - Individual programs 29 MIN
VHS
Owl - TV series
Color (P I J)
$100.00 purchase, $50.00 rental
Offers individual programs in the Owl - TV series - 60 videocassettes which are a series of 6 with 10 programs each. Introduces a nature and science series packed with answers to the questions kids have about the world and filled with the delight of discovery and the spirit of invention. Encourages learning through active involvement. Takes an imaginative approach to a wide range of subjects including animals, science, experiments, their bodies, the future and especially how they can have a beneficial impact on their own environment.
Psychology; Science; Science - Natural; Sociology
Dist - BULFRG **Prod** - YNF 1991

OWL TV - Programs 101 through 110 28 MIN
U-matic / VHS
OWL TV Series
Color (P I J)
A 10 part science and nature series designed to build on children's natural curiosity about the world around them and give them a solid grounding in basic science. Children ask questions dealing with animals, experiments, their bodies, the future, and especially how they can have a beneficial impact on their environment. Encourages learning through active involvement. Each part is 28 minutes.
Education; English Language; Guidance and Counseling; Health and Safety; Science; Science - Natural; Social Science
Dist - BULFRG **Prod** - OWLTV 1986

Owl - TV - Series 5 - Programs 41 - 50 290 MIN
VHS
Owl - TV #5 series
Color (P I J)
$780.00 purchase
Introduces a nature and science series packed with answers to the questions kids have about the world and filled with the delight of discovery and the spirit of invention. Encourages learning through active involvement. Takes an imaginative approach to a wide range of subjects including animals, science, experiments, their bodies, the future and especially how they can have a beneficial

impact on their own environment. Goes on location to Australia, Texas and Costa Rica to see primates, reptiles, migrating birds, the Great Barrier Reef and rainforests; greenhouse effect, acid rain; principles of flight; enjoy Halloween the environmental way.
Geography - United States; Geography - World; Psychology; Science; Science - Natural; Social Science; Sociology
Dist - BULFRG **Prod** - YNF 1994

Owl - TV - Series 4 - Programs 31 - 40 290 MIN
VHS
Owl - TV #4 series
Color (P I J)
$780.00 purchase
Introduces a nature and science series packed with answers to the questions kids have about the world and filled with the delight of discovery and the spirit of invention. Encourages learning through active involvement. Takes an imaginative approach to a wide range of subjects including animals, science, experiments, their bodies, the future and especially how they can have a beneficial impact on their own environment. Emphasizes the environment with the ecologies of Belize, Canada, England and the Seychelles; focus on environmental action such as recycling, composting, avoiding waste, rehabilitating lakes and saving endangered species.
Geography - World; Psychology; Science - Natural; Sociology
Dist - BULFRG **Prod** - YNF 1991

Owl TV - Series III 29 MIN
VHS / 16mm
Owl TV Series
(P)
$50.00 rental
Answers children's questions about nature and science. Features the Galapagos Islands and the Great Barrier Reef. Ten programs with teacher's guide.
Psychology; Science; Science - Natural; Social Science
Dist - BULFRG **Prod** - NAS 1988

Owl - TV - Series 1 - Programs 1 - 10 290 MIN
VHS
Owl - TV #1 series
Color (P I J)
$780.00 purchase
Introduces a nature and science series packed with answers to the questions kids have about the world and filled with the delight of discovery and the spirit of invention. Encourages learning through active involvement. Takes an imaginative approach to a wide range of subjects including animals, science, experiments, their bodies, the future and especially how they can have a beneficial impact on their own environment. Emphasizes engaging with animals and scientists who study them; learning about their bodies; kids with disabilities; exploring the insect world; and building things.
Health and Safety; Psychology; Science; Science - Natural; Sociology
Dist - BULFRG **Prod** - YNF 1986

Owl - TV - Series 6 - Programs 51 - 60 290 MIN
VHS
Owl - TV #6 series
Color (P I J)
$780.00 purchase
Introduces a nature and science series packed with answers to the questions kids have about the world and filled with the delight of discovery and the spirit of invention. Encourages learning through active involvement. Takes an imaginative approach to a wide range of subjects including animals, science, experiments, their bodies, the future and especially how they can have a beneficial impact on their own environment. Travels to Kenya, Newfoundland, Central America and the United Kingdom for rhinos, moose, jaguars, penguins and polar bears; Newton's laws of motion; ways to conserve water, riding bikes to save fuel; visit a fluvarium.
Geography - World; Psychology; Science; Science - Natural; Science - Physical; Sociology
Dist - BULFRG **Prod** - YNF 1994

Owl - TV - Series 3 - Programs 21 - 30 290 MIN
VHS
Owl - TV #3 series
Color (P I J)
$780.00 purchase
Introduces a nature and science series packed with answers to the questions kids have about the world and filled with the delight of discovery and the spirit of invention. Encourages learning through active involvement. Takes an imaginative approach to a wide range of subjects including animals, science, experiments, their bodies, the future and especially how they can have a beneficial impact on their own environment. Visits the Galapagos and Great Barrier Reef revealing unusual creatures; learning ancient crafts; questions of sleep and dreams; the brain, hiccups, fat and thin and hair; making musical instruments, shadow puppets and more.
Fine Arts; Psychology; Science; Science - Natural; Sociology
Dist - BULFRG **Prod** - YNF 1988

Owl - TV - Series 2 - Programs 11 - 20 290 MIN
VHS
Owl - TV #2 series
Color (P I J)
$780.00 purchase
Introduces a nature and science series packed with answers to the questions kids have about the world and filled with the delight of discovery and the spirit of invention. Encourages learning through active involvement. Takes an imaginative approach to a wide range of subjects including animals, science, experiments, their bodies, the future and especially how they can have a beneficial impact on their own environment. Looks at indigenous cultures in the Arctic and US Southwest; habitats and animal adaptions; hibernating squirrels and sleeping bears, lemurs; building ice castles, desert sculpture, mobiles, webs, sewing soft people.
Psychology; Science - Natural; Social Science; Sociology
Dist - BULFRG **Prod** - YNF 1987

OWL TV Series
Owl - TV - Individual programs 29 MIN
OWL TV - Programs 101 through 110 28 MIN
Owl TV - Series III 29 MIN
Dist - BULFRG

The Owl who Gave a Hoot 14 MIN
16mm
B&W; Color (SPANISH)
LC 74-705282; 74-705283
An animated cartoon film that tells it like it is - exploitation, connivance and fraud in the consumer world of the ghettos and what to do about it.
History - United States; Psychology; Sociology
Dist - USNAC **Prod** - USOEO 1967

Owls 16 MIN
U-matic / VHS / 16mm
Elementary Natural Science Series
Color (P I J)
$375, $250 purchase _ #75523
Shows different varieties of owls and their eating habits and behavior.
Science - Natural
Dist - CORF

Owls in the Family 15 MIN
U-matic / VHS
Best of Cover to Cover 1 Series
Color (P)
Literature and Drama
Dist - WETATV **Prod** - WETATV

Owls - Lords of Darkness 26 MIN
16mm
Color
Looks at the habits and characteristics of the major species of owl found in North America including the screech owl, the great horned owl and the barn owl.
Science - Natural
Dist - STOUFP **Prod** - STOUFP 1983

Owner Applied Numbers 7 MIN
16mm / U-matic / VHS
Color (A)
$25 rental _ #9870
Describes and demonstrates the ideal locations and various methods of applying OANs.
Sociology
Dist - AIMS **Prod** - AIMS 1986

Owning a Car 29 MIN
U-matic
You and the Law Series Lesson 21
Color (C A)
Examines rights and responsibilities of owning and operating a car. Focuses on buying a car, registration and driver's responsibilities.
Civics and Political Systems; Health and Safety; Industrial and Technical Education
Dist - CDTEL **Prod** - COAST

Owning your first horse
VHS
You and your horse series
Color (G)
$49.95 purchase _ #6 - 027 - 102A
Shows what to look for and how to make a wise decision when considering the purchase of a first horse. Part of a six - part series on training the western horse featuring B F Yeates, Extension Horse Specialist Emeritus of Texas A&M University.
Physical Education and Recreation
Dist - VEP **Prod** - VEP

Ox - cart man 8 MIN
VHS
Storybook library series
Color (P I)
$34.95 purchase
Presents a video version of the Donald Hall book 'Ox - Cart Man.' Uses verse and the illustrations of Barbara Cooney to depict the cycle of life from season to season in 19th century New England.
Literature and Drama; Science - Natural
Dist - LIVOAK **Prod** - LIVOAK PELLER

Ox - cart man - 18
VHS
Reading rainbow series
Color; CC (K P)
$39.95 purchase
Features Lorne Greene who relates a lyrical account of family life in 19th - century New England. Follows LeVar Burton to Old Sturbridge Village, Massachussettes, a hands - on museum of the 1800s. Part of a series offering a multicultural approach to generating reading enthusiasm with cross - curricular applications, hosted by LeVar Burton.
English Language; History - United States; Literature and Drama
Dist - GPN **Prod** - LNMDP

Ox Cell Hemolysin Test for Diagnosis of Infectious Mononucleosis 10 MIN
8mm cartridge / 16mm
Color
LC 75-702040; FI67-52
Demonstrates a rapid test based on the presence of a hemolysin in the sera in I M patients that will cause lysis of ox cells in the presence of complements.
Health and Safety; Science
Dist - USNAC **Prod** - USPHS 1965

Ox Tail Soup 7 MIN
16mm
Color (I) (AMERICAN SIGN)
LC 76-701699
Tells in American sign language a true life adventure of a large family growing up on a sharecrop farm in the depression years and what happened one day when they were making oxtail soup. Signed for the deaf by Herb Larson.
Fine Arts; Guidance and Counseling; Psychology
Dist - JOYCE **Prod** - JOYCE 1975

The Oxcart 20 MIN
16mm / U-matic / VHS
Color; Captioned (SPANISH (ENGLISH SUBTITLES))
Portrays the migration of a Puerto Rican family from the countryside, to a San Juan ghetto, to Spanish Harlem in New York City.
Fine Arts; Foreign Language; History - United States
Dist - CNEMAG **Prod** - CNEMAG

Oxford English dictionary
CD-ROM
(G)
$279.00, $895.00 purchase _ #1764, #1211
Contains the original 12 volume Oxford English Dictionary on CD - ROM. Includes eight indexes - definition, etymology, parts of speech, subjects, date, author, work and text. For IBM PCs and compatibles, requires 640K RAM, DOS 3.1 or later, one floppy disk drive - hard disk recommended, one empty expansion slot, and an IBM compatible CD - ROM drive.
English Language; Literature and Drama
Dist - BEP

Oxford Philosophy, Pt 5 - You Might Just as Well Say that I See what I Eat the same 60 MIN
16mm
Color
Focuses on linguistic philosophy and the work of one of its chief exponents, Gilbert Ryle. Questions whether linguistic philosophy has somehow missed certain issues which have always been believed to be central to traditional philosophy.
Education; English Language; Psychology; Religion and Philosophy
Dist - NYFLMS **Prod** - NYFLMS 1972

Oxford Philosophy, Pt 4 - Appearance and Reality 60 MIN
16mm
Color
Presents a conversation between Sir Alfred Ayer and Professor Bernard Williams of Cambridge University on science and its relation to philosophy.
Education; Religion and Philosophy; Science
Dist - NYFLMS **Prod** - NYFLMS 1972

Oxford Philosophy, Pt 1 - Logic Lane 60 MIN
16mm
Color
Presents a retrospective of philosophy at Oxford over the past 40 years as explained by Professor Sir Alfred Ayer. Discusses the social and historical background of the university and its importance in the training of British politicians.
Education; Religion and Philosophy
Dist - NYFLMS **Prod** - NYFLMS 1972

Oxford Philosophy, Pt 6 - Language and Creativity 60 MIN
16mm
Color
Discusses linguistic and semantic theory as viewed by P F Strawson and Gareth Evans. Asks if language is something organic and constantly changing.
Education; English Language; Psychology; Religion and Philosophy
Dist - NYFLMS **Prod** - NYFLMS 1972

Oxford Philosophy, Pt 3 - the Idea of Freedom 60 MIN
16mm
Color
Presents a conversation between Iris Murdoch, novelist and philosopher, and Oxford professor, David Pears on the subject of Murdoch's book, THE SOVEREIGNTY OF GOOD. Focuses on individual freedom, determinism and self - knowledge.
Education; Religion and Philosophy; Sociology
Dist - NYFLMS **Prod** - NYFLMS 1972

Oxford Philosophy, Pt 2 - I'm Going to Tamper with Your Beliefs a Little 60 MIN
16mm
Color
Discusses the philosophy of J L Austin, who lectured at Harvard before he died in 1960. Includes an excerpt from the only surviving recording of his lectures, made one year before his death and never before heard publicly.
Education; Religion and Philosophy
Dist - NYFLMS **Prod** - NYFLMS 1972

Oxford student 10 MIN
U-matic / VHS / BETA
Life in Britain in the forties series
Color; PAL (G H C)
PdS30, PdS38 purchase
Examines the historic past, traditions, colleges and life at the University of Oxford. Visits the small classes, tutorial supervision underscoring the reliance on individual initiative. Without narration. Part of a five - part series.
Education; Fine Arts; History - World
Dist - EDPAT **Prod** - IFF

Oxford textbook of medicine
CD-ROM
(C PRO)
$589.00 purchase _ #1212
Contains the second edition - 1987 - of the Oxford Textbook of Medicine on CD - ROM. Serves medical students and practicioners. Can be searched full text. For IBM PCs and compatibles, requires at least 640K RAM, DOS 3.1 or later, one floppy disk drive - hard disk recommended, one empty expansion slot, and an IBM compatible CD - ROM drive.
Health and Safety; Literature and Drama
Dist - BEP

Oxidation and Reduction 8 MIN
U-matic
Chemistry Videotape Series
Color
Demonstrates several redox reactions. Introduces electrochemical cell as a source of information about redox strengths.
Science; Science - Physical
Dist - UMITV **Prod** - UMITV

Oxidation and Reduction 45 MIN
BETA / VHS / U-matic
Color
$300 purchase
Shows extractive metallurgy and ore treatment.
Industrial and Technical Education; Psychology; Science - Physical
Dist - ASM **Prod** - ASM

Oxidation Reduction Equations 20 MIN
U-matic
Chemistry 101 Series
Color (C)
Analyzes oxidation reduction equations into their qualitative and quantitative aspects, gives simple rules for balancing them in the instance of ionic substances and in the more complex instances of covalent substances.
Science; Science - Physical
Dist - UILL **Prod** - UILL 1976

Oxidative Phosphorylation I 24 MIN
16mm / U-matic / VHS
Color
Introduces the concept of respiratory electron transport in the microenvironment of the mitochondrial membrane. Shows the structure of mitochondria, the general nature of oxidation reactions and the energy - requiring phosphorylation reactions. Considers the nature of the string which couples energy - releasing and energy - requiring processes in the pulley model.
Science - Natural
Dist - MEDIAG **Prod** - OPENU 1978

Oxidative Phosphorylation II 25 MIN
16mm / U-matic / VHS
Color
Demonstrates that proton pumping is produced by an oxidation reaction known as electron transport. Describes the four main tenets of Mitchell's chemiosmotic hypothesis and explores some of the current ideas about how ATP is synthesized by an enzyme.
Science - Natural
Dist - MEDIAG **Prod** - OPENU 1978

Oxidizers 53 MIN
VHS
Color (IND)
$52.00 purchase _ #35432
Discusses the physical forms and the hazards of oxidizers. Explains protection procedures. Reviews necessary precautions when dealing with these chemicals.
Health and Safety; Science - Physical; Social Science; Sociology
Dist - OKSU **Prod** - CHEMMA

Oxidizers - IV ; Rev. 7 MIN
8mm cartridge / VHS / BETA / U-matic
Chemsafe 2000 series
Color; CC; PAL (IND G)
$395.00 purchase, $175.00 rental _ #CS2 - 400
Reveals that highly - reactive oxidizers can be solids, liquids or gases and can enter the body by almost any route. Shows how to prevent fires and explosions caused by oxidizers. Offers guidance on the role protective gear and industrial hygiene play in keeping workers safe and healthy. Part of a nine - part series providing comprehensive training in chemical safety. Includes a trainer's manual and ten participant handouts.
Health and Safety; Psychology; Science - Physical
Dist - BNA **Prod** - BNA 1994

Oxidizers - Module 4 7 MIN
BETA / VHS / U-matic
Chemsafe series
Color; PAL (IND G) (SPANISH DUTCH ITALIAN)
$175.00 rental _ #CSF - 400; $546.00 purchase, $150.00 rental _ #OXI005
Looks at highly reactive oxidizers which can be solids, liquids or gases and can enter the body by almost any route. Shows how to prevent fires and explosions caused by oxidizers. Illustrates the value of protective gear and industrial hygiene. Part of a comprehensive nine - part series on chemical safety in the workplace. Includes leader's guide and 10 workbooks which are available in English only.
Business and Economics; Health and Safety; Psychology; Science - Physical
Dist - BNA **Prod** - BNA
ITF

Oxo - Omo - Ono 2 MIN
16mm
Color
LC 75-703217
Presents an animated pop - art battle between eye - creatures and Mickey Mouse.
Fine Arts
Dist - USC **Prod** - USC 1970

Oxy - Acetylene Equipment Set - Up and Safety 33 MIN
VHS / BETA
Welding Training (Comprehensive - - - Oxy - Acetylene Welding 'Series
Color (IND)
Industrial and Technical Education; Psychology
Dist - RMIBHF **Prod** - RMIBHF

Oxy - Acetylene Flame, the Master of Metals 19 MIN
16mm
Color
Shows how oxygen and acetylene are blended to form a flame to cut, weld, solder, braze and harden metal. Depicts uses, such as forming teeth on tractor gears, molding grey cast iron and hardening edges of plows.
Industrial and Technical Education; Science - Physical
Dist - USDIBM **Prod** - USDIBM 1950

Oxy - Acetylene Welding and Cutting - Braze Welding 13 MIN
U-matic / VHS / 16mm
Welding Series
Color
LC 74-701438
Demonstrates techniques for braze welding of sheet steel, plate and castings. Shows how to set up welding equipment, adjust oxygen and acetylene pressures, light the welding torch and adjust the flame for braze welding.
Industrial and Technical Education
Dist - FI **Prod** - UCC 1972

Oxy - Acetylene Welding - Light Metal 21 MIN
16mm
Welding Procedures Series Oxyacetylene Welding, no 1
B&W
LC FIE52-293
Shows how to assemble a gas welding outfit, adjust gas pressures, adjust the flame, and make a butt weld and a 'T' weld in light tubing.
Industrial and Technical Education
Dist - USNAC **Prod** - USOE 1944

Oxy - Acetylene Welding Series 120 MIN
VHS / U-matic
Aviation Technician Training Program Series
Color (IND)
Contains 12 separate programs encompassing two hours on Basic Oxy - Acetylene Welding. Includes equipment setup, flame adjustment, and chemistry, puddle control, edge welding, running beads with filler, butt - joint welding, lap - joint welding, beads on tubing, butt - joint on tubing, T - joint on tubing and cluster welding techniques.
Industrial and Technical Education
Dist - AVIMA **Prod** - AVIMA 1979

Oxy - Acetylyne Cutting 42 MIN
VHS
Oxy - Acetylyne Welding And Cutting Series
Color (G IND)
$89.95 purchase _ #6 - 040 - 129P
Examines safety involved in setting up and shutting down both oxy - acetylyne cutting machine and track torch, proper dress, safety and equipment, turning on and adjusting cylinders and gauges, assembly of torch and equipment needed for cutting. Demonstrates ten different cuts utilizing various types of metal with the torch and track torch. Part of a three - part series on oxy - acetylyne welding and cutting.
Health and Safety; Industrial and Technical Education; Psychology
Dist - VEP **Prod** - VEP

Oxy - Acetylyne Welding and Brazing 40 MIN
VHS
Oxy - Acetylyne Welding And Cutting Series
Color (G IND)
$89.95 purchase _ #6 - 040 - 128P
Discusses safety, clothing and operation. Provides step - by - step demonstrations of turning on cylinders, gauge setting and flame adjustment. Discusses rods and flux used in welding and brazing and metal preparation. Shows welding a puddle, running a bead with a filler rod, lap and T - weld and outside corner welds. Part of a three - part series on oxy - acetylyne welding and cutting.
Health and Safety; Industrial and Technical Education; Psychology
Dist - VEP **Prod** - VEP

Oxy - Acetylyne Welding And Cutting Series
Oxy - Acetylyne Cutting 42 MIN
Oxy - Acetylyne Welding - Safety and Introduction 27 MIN
Oxy - Acetylyne Welding and Brazing 40 MIN
Dist - VEP

Oxy - Acetylyne Welding - Safety and Introduction 27 MIN
VHS
Oxy - Acetylyne Welding And Cutting Series
Color (G IND)
$89.95 purchase _ #6 - 040 - 127P
Introduces oxy - acetylyne welding and the equipment and safety procedures necessary for successful welding. Includes setup and safety, proper care of equipment, name, purpose and installation of each piece of equipment, demonstration of safety procedures for hose hookups and gauge coupling and proper gauge adjustment. Part of a three - part series on oxy - acetylyne welding and cutting.
Health and Safety; Industrial and Technical Education; Psychology
Dist - VEP **Prod** - VEP

Oxyacetylene cutting 42 MIN
VHS
Oxyacetylene welding and cutting series
Color (H A T)
$89.95 purchase _ #CV989; $89.95 purchase _ #CEV30816V - T
Discusses safety procedures involved in setting up and shutting down the oxyacetylene hand torch and track torch. Looks at proper dress and safety equipment, turning on cylinders and adjusting regulators to attain correct working pressures, assembling the torch and equipment needed for cutting. Shows ten different cuts of metal of various thicknesses with the hand torch and track torch. Features Prof Billy Harrell of Sam Houston State University.
Health and Safety; Industrial and Technical Education; Psychology
Dist - AAVIM **Prod** - AAVIM 1992
CAMV

Oxyacetylene Cutting 12 MIN
16mm
Color (IND)
Demonstrates how to set up an oxyacetylene outfit in a safe fashion, how to pull it away, the proper safety practices and how to always make a clean cut with little practice.
Industrial and Technical Education
Dist - MOKIN **Prod** - MOKIN

Oxyacetylene Cutting Explained 25 MIN
VHS / 35mm strip
Color (H A IND)
#904XV7
Shows how to safely set up and operate oxyacetylene cutting equipment (2 tapes). Prerequisite required. Includes a Study Guide.
Education; Industrial and Technical Education
Dist - BERGL

Oxyacetylene hammerwelding applications 11 MIN
VHS
Color (H A T)
$62.95 purchase _ #SS604
Features California antique car and street rod restorer John Ecclesine who demonstrates hammerwelding in flat and vertical positions during restoration of a 1957 Chevrolet hardtop. Demonstrates the need for good penetration while tack welding, fusion welding and hammerwelding. Explains the similarities and differences between flat and vertical welding. Discusses heat control, shrinkage, metal integrity and safety. Includes quiz and answer sheet.
Health and Safety; Industrial and Technical Education
Dist - AAVIM **Prod** - AAVIM

Oxyacetylene hammerwelding techniques 11 MIN
VHS
Color (H A T)
$78.95 purchase _ #SS605A
Features California antique car and street rod restorer John Ecclesine who demonstrates tack welding, fusion welding and filler rod oxyacetylene welding in the process of hammerwelding. Discusses heat control, shrinkage, metal integrity and safety. Includes quiz and answer sheet.
Health and Safety; Industrial and Technical Education
Dist - AAVIM **Prod** - AAVIM

Oxyacetylene heating tip applications 11 MIN
VHS
Color (H A T)
$69.95 purchase _ #SS606A; $69.95 purchase _ #SWE253V
Covers some of the practical heat application processes using the 'rosebud' heating tip of the oxyacetylene welding outfit. Uses animated graphics to explain how metal reacts to heat. Discusses various shaft and collar applications, including shrinkage fitting, straight interference fitting and taper fitting. Stresses the importance of controlling heat while shrinking and expanding metal and safety procedures. Includes quiz and answer sheet.
Health and Safety; Industrial and Technical Education
Dist - AAVIM **Prod** - AAVIM
CAMV

Oxyacetylene Safety 24 MIN
U-matic / VHS
Color (IND)
LC 80-707267
Introduces safe practices in handling and using oxyacetylene welding and burning equipment.
Industrial and Technical Education
Dist - TAT **Prod** - TAT 1980

Oxyacetylene Safety and Setup
VHS / 35mm strip
Welding Series
Color
$42.00 purchase _ #LX75C filmstrip, $62.00 purchase _ #LX75V VHS
Discusses hookup and adjustment of cylinders, gauges and torches for fusion welding, flame cutting, soldering and brazing.
Health and Safety; Industrial and Technical Education
Dist - CAREER **Prod** - CAREER

Oxyacetylene Welding
VHS / 35mm strip
$379.00 purchase _ #PX964 filmstrips, $379.00 purchase _ #PX964V VHS
Provides training on various aspects of oxyacetylene welding including basic process and equipment, equipment assembly process, lighting and adjusting flame - shut down procedures, basic welding process, weld variations, brazing operation, and oxyacetylene cutting process.
Education; Industrial and Technical Education
Dist - CAREER **Prod** - CAREER

Oxyacetylene welding and brazing 40 MIN
VHS
Oxyacetylene welding and cutting series
Color (H A T)
$89.95 purchase _ #CV990; $89.95 purchase _ #CEV30815V - T
Discusses proper safety, dress and operation procedures for oxyacetylene welding and brazing. Demonstrates step - by - step the proper way to turn on cylinders, set working pressures and adjust flame for different uses. Considers rods and fluxes used in welding and brazing, as well as methods for metal preparation. Performs puddle welds, bead with a filler rod, butt weld, lap weld, T - weld and outside corner weld. Looks at tinning - brazing and multi - pass fillet - bronze welding. Features Prof Billy Harrell of Sam Houston State University.
Health and Safety; Industrial and Technical Education; Psychology
Dist - AAVIM **Prod** - AAVIM 1992
CAMV

Oxyacetylene welding and cutting series
Oxyacetylene cutting 42 MIN
Oxyacetylene welding - safety and introduction 27 MIN
Oxyacetylene welding and brazing 40 MIN
Dist - AAVIM
CAMV

Oxyacetylene welding and cutting series
Acetylene cylinder safety 20 MIN
Dist - CAMV

Oxyacetylene Welding - Equipment 16 MIN
16mm / U-matic / VHS
Industrial Education Series
Color (H A) (SPANISH)
LC 76-711084
Describes the equipment used in bench - type gas welding and brazing. Shows the correct procedures for assembling the equipment, lighting the torch and adjusting the flame.
Industrial and Technical Education
Dist - PHENIX **Prod** - BROSEB 1971

Oxyacetylene Welding - Joining Steel 14 MIN
U-matic / VHS / 16mm
Industrial Education Series
Color (H A) (SPANISH)
LC 73-711086
Shows advanced techniques of gas welding, including multiple pass (thick plate) joining, structural section fabrication and forming horizontal, vertical and overhead welds.
Industrial and Technical Education
Dist - PHENIX **Prod** - BROSEB 1971

Oxyacetylene welding multiple - curved and vertical surfaces 20 MIN
VHS
Color (H A T)
$84.95 purchase _ #SS603; $84.95 purchase _ #SWE256V
Covers the unusual techniques used to weld in unique surface positions. Uses the curved fender of a 1933 Ford to pose the problem of replacing a rusted section and retaining the original shape of the fender. Emphasizes safety. Includes quiz and answer sheet.
Health and Safety; Industrial and Technical Education
Dist - AAVIM **Prod** - AAVIM
CAMV

Oxyacetylene welding - safety and introduction 27 MIN
VHS
Oxyacetylene welding and cutting series
Color (H A T)
$89.95 purchase _ #CV988; $89.95 purchase _ #CEV30814V - T
Introduces oxyacetylene welding equipment for successful welding and cutting. Includes set up and safety, proper care of equipment, name, purpose and installation of each piece of equipment, demonstration of the correct and safe way to set up a station for operation including setting of working pressures. Features Prof Billy Harrell of Sam Houston State University.
Health and Safety; Industrial and Technical Education; Psychology
Dist - AAVIM **Prod** - AAVIM 1992
CAMV

Oxyacetylene welding - safety and operation 75 MIN
16mm / VHS / BETA / U-matic
Metal shop & woodshop series
Color; PAL (IND)
PdS125, PdS133 purchase
Features part of a six - part series.
Health and Safety; Industrial and Technical Education
Dist - EDPAT

Oxyacetylene welding - safety and operations 15 MIN
VHS
Color (J H A G)
$49.95 purchase _ #AM1425
Defines gas welding. Explains procedures for opening regulatory valves, adjusting pressure of oxy and gas, lighting the torch and adjusting the flame. Describes the uses of carburizing flame, neutral flame, oxydizing flame and shows procedures for puddling, fusion without a filler rod and rod welding.
Health and Safety; Industrial and Technical Education
Dist - AAVIM **Prod** - AAVIM 1992

Oxyacetylene welding - safety and operations 15 MIN
VHS
Color (G) (SPANISH)
$49.95 purchase _ #6 - 203 - 600A, #6 - 203 - 601A
Defines gas welding. Explains procedures for opening regulator valves, adjusting pressure of oxy and gas, lighting the torch and adjusting flame. Describes the uses of carburizing flame, neutral flame, oxidizing flame and shows procedures for puddling, fusion without a filler rod and rod welding.
Health and Safety; Industrial and Technical Education
Dist - VEP **Prod** - VEP

Oxyacetylene Welding - Safety and Operations 14 MIN
U-matic / VHS / 16mm
Metal Shop - Safety and Operations Series
Color (J) (ARABIC SPANISH)
LC 75-706477
Discusses the safety points and basic techniques in oxyacetylene welding.
Foreign Language; Industrial and Technical Education
Dist - AIMS **Prod** - EPRI 1970

Oxyacetylene Welding - Series
Puddling and Running Beads with Oxyacetylene
Dist - VTRI

Oxyacetylene Welding - Spanish Series
Automatic flame cutting with oxyacetylene
Brazing and Fusion Welding on Gray Cast Iron
Bronze Welding in Flat and Horizontal Positions
Cutting metal with the combination torch
Flat and horizontal butt welds with filler rod
Joint Design and Welding Terms
Oxyacetylene Welding T - Joints, Lap Joints, Corner Joints and Edge Joints
Piercing, Cutting Holes and Cutting 45 - Degree Bevels with the Cutting Torch
Set - up and shut down of oxyacetylene welding equipment
Silver Brazing and Soft Soldering
The Three Types of Oxyacetylene Flames - Neutral, Oxidizing, Carburizing
Vertical and Overhead Butt Welds with Filler Rod
Welding Equipment, Accessories and Shop Safety
Dist - VTRI

Oxyacetylene Welding T - Joints, Lap Joints, Corner Joints and Edge Joints
VHS / U-matic
Oxyacetylene Welding - Spanish Series
Color (SPANISH)
Foreign Language; Industrial and Technical Education
Dist - VTRI **Prod** - VTRI

Oxyacetylene welding techniques 13 MIN
VHS
Color (H A T)
$69.95 purchase _ #SS607A; $69.95 purchase _ #SWE252V
Covers some of the practical oxyacetylene welding techniques used in actual shop settings. Explains carbon content in mild carbon steel. Shows basic sheet metalworking tools as used with autobody panel repairs. Demonstrates tack welding, fusion welding and filler rod welding. Emphasizes safety procedures. Includes quiz and answer sheet.
Health and Safety; Industrial and Technical Education
Dist - AAVIM **Prod** - AAVIM
CAMV

Oxyacetylene Welding - Torch Techniques 19 MIN
U-matic / VHS / 16mm
Industrial Education Series
Color (H A) (SPANISH)
LC 72-711083
Explains the correct techniques for running a bead, welding without a rod, adding a rod to a butt weld and blazing.
Foreign Language; Industrial and Technical Education
Dist - PHENIX **Prod** - BROSEB 1971

Oxygen 11 MIN
VHS
Chemistry - from Theory to Application Series
Color (H)
$190.00 purchase
Considers the elementary substance oxygen which is found in the air, in the sea and in the earth. Examines the qualities of oxygen and separates liquid oxygen from nitrogen in a fractionating column.
Science; Science - Physical
Dist - LUF **Prod** - LUF 1989

Oxygen - an Introduction to Chemistry 15 MIN
U-matic / VHS / 16mm
Elementary Physical Science Series
Color (I J)
LC 79-700570
Explores the nature of oxygen. Explains the structure of atoms and molecules, oxidation and the production of oxygen through the process of photosynthesis.
Science - Physical
Dist - BARR **Prod** - HALDAR 1979

Oxygen - an Introduction to Chemistry 15 MIN
U-matic / VHS / 16mm
Elementary Physical Science Series
Color; Captioned (I J)
$340, $240, $270 purchase _ #A250
Explores the nature of oxygen. Teaches about atoms, molecules, and chemical reactions. Shows that oxygen like any atom has the three forms of solid, liquid and gas.
Science - Physical
Dist - BARR **Prod** - BARR 1979

Oxygen Equipment 27 MIN
16mm
Color (PRO)
LC 77-701152
Depicts various types of aircrew oxygen equipment, including constant flow, demand and pressure demand masks and emergency and seat kits. Demonstrates use of each type of equipment and defines advantages and limitations of each.
Industrial and Technical Education
Dist - USNAC **Prod** - USAF 1964

Oxygen - Fuel Gas Cutting 60 MIN
U-matic / VHS
Welding Training Series
Color (IND)
Covers safety, equipment setup and use and cutting procedures.
Education; Industrial and Technical Education
Dist - ITCORP **Prod** - ITCORP

Oxygen - Nitrogen Generating Plant Distillation Column Control 24 MIN
16mm
Color
LC FIE62-75
Shows the progressive flow and treatment of atmospheric air through a typical oxygen - nitrogen generating plant to produce either liquid or gaseous oxygen or nitrogen.
Civics and Political Systems; Science
Dist - USNAC **Prod** - USAF 1960

The Oxygen story 15 MIN
VHS
Color (J H)
$79.95 purchase _ #10323VG
Examines oxygen, the most common element on the planet, and the oxygen cycle. Looks at the structure of oxygen atoms; photosynthesis; and the dynamics of oxidation. Comes with a teacher's guide, discussion questions and seven blackline masters.
Science - Natural; Science - Physical
Dist - UNL

Oxygen Therapy 13 MIN
VHS / U-matic
Color (PRO)
Discusses guidelines for safe use of oxygen therapy in newborn infants. Stresses monitoring of arterial or arterialized capillary oxygen tension and inspired oxygen concentration. Outlines consequences of inadequate and excessive oxygenation.
Health and Safety; Science - Natural
Dist - UMICHM **Prod** - UMICHM 1983

Oxygen - what a gas 28 MIN
U-matic / 16mm / VHS
Color (J H C)
$700.00, $425.00, $395.00 purchase
Covers the composition of the earth's atmosphere, the history of the discovery of oxygen, the chemistry of oxidation - differentiating covalent and ionic bonding, human respiration and circulation, the effects of low oxygen at high and low altitudes due to heart and lung disease, human and animal adaptations to low oxygen conditions and the modern manufacture of oxygen. Uses four original music videos, animation, archival footage and sequences shot in the Canadian Rockies, the Himalayas, decompression chambers and McMaster University Hospital.
Science - Natural; Science - Physical
Dist - MEDCIN **Prod** - MEDCIN 1991

Oxygenation Assessment of the Critically Ill Patient 30 MIN
VHS / U-matic
University of Michigan Media Library - Clinical Commentary Series
Color (PRO)
LC 81-707081
Explains that the assessment of oxygenation in the critically ill patient requires more than the usual patient assessment and measurement of arterial blood gases. Discusses variables which must be considered and how they interrelate and stresses the importance of oxygen delivery. Covers the measurement of oxyhemoglobin - dissocation curves, wedge pressure cardiac output and the mixed venous pO2.
Health and Safety
Dist - UMICH **Prod** - UMICH 1981

Oyster bar 6 MIN
16mm
B&W (G) (ENGLISH AND FRENCH WITH SUBTITLES)
$15.00 rental
Presents the vision of filmmaker Tina Bastajian, of a speculated encounter where a woman ignores her man and explicitly describes her love for a crustacean.
Fine Arts; Guidance and Counseling
Dist - CANCIN

Oyster Development and Survival 26 MIN
16mm
Color
Looks at the life of oysters in the waters of the Pacific Northwest, from the fertilization of the egg to full growth.
Science - Natural
Dist - RARIG **Prod** - RARIG

Oysters are in Season 17 MIN
16mm
B&W
Features the improvised humor of Swede Sorenson, Dean Preece and Molly Parkin as they play out sharply satiric situations, in three skits.
Fine Arts; Literature and Drama
Dist - IMPACT **Prod** - IMPACT 1966

Ozawa 60 MIN
VHS
Color (G)
$19.95 purchase _ #1237
Profiles the director and conductor of the Boston Symphony Orchestra, Ozawa. Includes Rudolf Serkin, Yo - Yo Ma, Jessye Norman and Edith Weins.
Fine Arts
Dist - KULTUR

Ozawa 60 MIN
VHS
Color (G)
$19.95 purchase _ #S02082
Profiles Seiji Ozawa, the Japanese - born classical musician who is now conductor and director of the Boston Symphony. Includes musical excerpts such as Mahler's 'Symphony No 2,' Beethoven's 'Concerto No 2' and 'Symphony No 6,' and Dvorak's 'Concerto in B Minor.'
Fine Arts
Dist - UILL

The Ozone layer 30 MIN
VHS
Earth at risk environmental video series
Color (J H C G)
$49.95 purchase _ #LVPN6628V
Introduces and defines environmental terms and global ecological dilemmas in terms of the ozone layer. Presents current statistical information. Part of a ten - part series on environmental issues based on a series of books by Chelsea House Publishers and featuring former MTV host Kevin Seal.
Science - Natural; Science - Physical
Dist - CAMV

The Ozone Layer - How Important is it 23 MIN
35mm strip / VHS
Color (J)
$84.00 purchase _ #PE - 540606 - 3, #PE - 540607 - 1; $84.00 purchase _ #193Y1502
Discusses the ozone layer of the atmosphere and how it affects life on earth. Considers whether ozone depletion causes higher temperatures, droughts and rising seas. Encourages students to examine facts and draw their own conclusions. Filmstrip version includes two filmstrips, two cassettes and teacher's guide.
Science - Physical
Dist - SRA **Prod** - SRA
WARDS

Ozone - protecting the invisible shield 25 MIN
VHS
Color; CC (H A)
$110.00 purchase - #A51616
Teaches the history and chemistry of ozone in the Earth's atmosphere as background for a discussion of actions that can be taken to prevent further depletion of the ozone layer. Shows how governments and individuals are cooperating to tackle this and other environmental problems. Includes a teacher's guide.
Science - Natural; Science - Physical
Dist - NGS **Prod** - NGS 1994

O,ZOO - the making of a fiction film 23 MIN
16mm
B&W; Color (G)
$55.00 rental
Uses a diary format to skirt along the edge of someone else's filmed narrative and to delve into pre image - making. Meditates on the illusion of visual purity and wrestles with the dilemma of distance between the 'neutral' image and the value - laden narrative. Produced by Philip Hoffman.
Fine Arts
Dist - CANCIN

Ozzie Tollefson, Performance 15 MIN
U-matic / VHS
Pass it Along
(I)
$130 purchase, $25 rental, $75 self dub
Uses art and outstanding artists to teach upper elementary level students about environmental concerns. Highlights the plight of seals, turtles and whales using the puppeteering talents of Ozzie Tollefson. Fourth in an eight part series.
Fine Arts; Science - Natural; Social Science
Dist - GPN

P

The P - 38 pilot 15 MIN
VHS
Color (G)
$30.00 purchase
Looks at the fastest chair in the air. Parallels Dante's Purgatorio.
Fine Arts
Dist - CANCIN **Prod** - BAILB 1990

P-47 Thunderbolt High - Altitude Flight and Aerobatics 22 MIN
VHS / U-matic
B&W
Depicts the P - 47 aircraft in various power - driving and aerobatic maneuvers.
Civics and Political Systems; Industrial and Technical Education
Dist - IHF **Prod** - IHF

P A G E S - Case of the missing stock certificate 20 MIN
U-matic / VHS
Color
Pictures police officers trying to track down a stock certificate left in a book. Highlights all aspects of a library circulation assistant's job, including shelving, straightening shelves and possessing a courteous attitude.
Education; Social Science
Dist - LVN **Prod** - HRFDCL

P, B, M, F, V
U-matic / VHS
Educational Video Concepts for Early Childhood Language Development 'Series
Color
English Language
Dist - ECCOAZ **Prod** - ECCOAZ

P C T F 3 MIN
16mm
B&W (G)
$8.00 rental
Makes the statement thata trailers are an art form. Shows the official trailer of the Crucifiction Trinity. Credits the roof of the Reno Hotel and a cast of thousands. This film is available for rent free of charge when renting The Cop, The Lawyer or Christ of the Rooftops.
Fine Arts
Dist - CANCIN **Prod** - DEGRAS 1969

P D James 40 MIN
VHS
Color (H C G)
$79.00 purchase
Features the writer discussing with A S Byatt how to write several books involving a single character and using real - life homicides as material for detective novels. Talks about her works including A Shroud for a Nightingale; Innocent Blood; and A Taste for Death.
Literature and Drama
Dist - ROLAND **Prod** - INCART

P E I - the Million Acre Farm 29 MIN
U-matic
Like no Other Place Series
Color (J H)
Compares life in P E I to that in other areas of Canada and discusses the problems of farmers, what it means to live on an island and the role of fishing and tourism in the economy.
Geography - World; History - World
Dist - TVOTAR **Prod** - TVOTAR 1985

P E - Lever to Learning 20 MIN
16mm
Color (C T)
LC 70-702249
Discusses how specially organized physical education programs can be most productive both physically and mentally.
Physical Education and Recreation
Dist - FINLYS **Prod** - FINLYS 1969

P E M - Group Training Formula 19.5 MIN
BETA / VHS / U-matic
Supervisory Series
(PRO A)
$225 _ #1023
Provides steps and tips for formulating and presenting a training seminar in the custodial field.
Education; Guidance and Counseling
Dist - CTT **Prod** - CTT

P is for potato 14 MIN
VHS / U-matic / 16mm
Food from A to Z series
Color (P I)
$310.00 purchase
Looks at the history of the cultivation of potatoes and their role in the Western Hemisphere. Examines the economic value of potatoes as a human foodstuff, and in industry.
Agriculture; Home Economics; Social Science; Sociology
Dist - HANDEL **Prod** - HANDEL 1988

P, J 15 MIN
U-matic / VHS
Cursive writing series
Color (P)
Presents techniques of handwriting, focusing on the lower case letters p and j.
English Language
Dist - GPN **Prod** - WHROTV 1984

P J and the President's Son 47 MIN
U-matic / VHS / 16mm
Teenage Years Series
Color
LC 77-702489
Pictures two 15 - year - olds in Washington, DC, one an average middle class boy named P J, and the other the President's son. Portrays them looking enough alike to pass for identical twins, so they decide to change places for a few days.
Civics and Political Systems; Literature and Drama
Dist - TIMLIF **Prod** - WILSND 1977

P - N - P Transistor and Transistor Specifications 60 MIN
Videoreel / VT1
Understanding Semiconductors Course Outline Series no 08
Color (IND)
Describes how P - N - P transistors are used in circuits and how they work.
Industrial and Technical Education
Dist - TXINLC **Prod** - TXINLC

P S My Sister Sends Her Love 20 MIN
16mm
Color
LC 78-702843
Demonstrates the vital importance of overseas mail movement in keeping the postal link unbroken between servicemen and families. Includes quotations from letters and flashbacks which connect hometown scenes with overseas servicemen.
Psychology; Social Science
Dist - USPOST **Prod** - USPOST 1968

P Sound 14 MIN
VHS / U-matic
I - Land Treasure Series
Color (K)
English Language
Dist - AITECH **Prod** - UWISC 1980

P T Barnum 11 MIN
U-matic / VHS
Color (G)
$69.95 purchase _ #EX1863
Profiles P T Barnum, an entertainer who combined oddity, the exotic and the bizarre with the hoopla which characterized all his ventures. Credits Barnum for the saying, 'There's a sucker born every minute.'
Biography; Fine Arts; Physical Education and Recreation
Dist - FOTH **Prod** - FOTH

P4W - Prison for Women 81 MIN
16mm
Color
Looks at Canada's only federal penitentiary for women, focusing on five women who have been incarcerated for crimes ranging from drug possession and computer fraud to murder. Describes their stories, their relationships with the other inmates and family, and how they cope with their lives in prison.
Sociology
Dist - FIRS **Prod** - FIRS

Pa ch'ien li lu yun he yueh - volume 10
VHS
Color (G)
$45.00 _ #27899
Features travel descriptions of various parts of China in volume 10 of Eight Thousand Miles Clouds and Moon, a popular TV series in Taiwan, by Feng Ling. Focuses on Yunnan. Produced by Tai - pei.
Geography - World
Dist - PANASI

Pa ch'ien li lu yun he yueh - volume 11
VHS
Color (G)
$45.00 _ #278900
Features travel descriptions of various parts of China in volume 11 of Eight Thousand Miles Clouds and Moon, a popular TV series in Taiwan, by Feng Ling. Focuses on the southcoast province of Fujian. Produced by Tai - pei.
Geography - World
Dist - PANASI

Pa ch'ien li lu yun he yueh - volume 12
VHS
Color (G)
$45.00 _ #27901
Features travel descriptions of various parts of China in volume 11 of Eight Thousand Miles Clouds and Moon, a popular TV series in Taiwan, by Feng Ling. Focuses on Guangxi. Produced by Tai - pei.
Geography - World
Dist - PANASI

Pa ch'ien li lu yun he yueh - volume 13
VHS
Color (G)
$45.00 _ #27902
Features travel descriptions of various parts of China in volume 11 of Eight Thousand Miles Clouds and Moon, a popular TV series in Taiwan, by Feng Ling. Focuses on the province of Zhejiang. Produced by Tai - pei.
Geography - World
Dist - PANASI

Pa ch'ien li lu yun he yueh - volume 8
VHS
Color (G)
$45.00 _ #27897
Features travel descriptions of various parts of China in volume 8 of Eight Thousand Miles Clouds and Moon, a popular TV series in Taiwan, by Feng Ling. Focuses on Gansuint. Produced by Tai - pei.
Geography - World
Dist - PANASI

Pa ch'ien li lu yun he yueh - volume 9
VHS
Color (G)
$45.00 _ #27898
Features travel descriptions of various parts of China in volume 9 of Eight Thousand Miles Clouds and Moon, a popular TV series in Taiwan, by Feng Ling. Focuses on Xinjiang. Produced by Tai - pei.
Geography - World
Dist - PANASI

Pa - Hay - Okee - Grassy Waters 18 MIN
16mm
Color
LC 81-700649
Explores the natural features, wildlife and relationship between man and nature in the Everglades of south Florida.
Geography - United States; Science - Natural
Dist - USNAC **Prod** - USNPS 1981

Pablita Velarde - an Artist and Her People 20 MIN
16mm / U-matic / VHS
Color (J A)
Portrays the work of Pablita Velarde, a native American Indian and noted painter who paints to preserve Indian heritage and provide a bridge for Anglo and Indian culture.
Fine Arts; Social Science
Dist - USNAC **Prod** - USNPS 1984

Pablo Fernandez - 11 - 13 - 81 45 MIN
VHS / Cassette
Poetry Center reading series
Color (G)
$15.00, $45.00 purchase, $15.00 rental _ #458 - 389
Features the poet reading from The Book Of The Heroes, written soon after the Cuban Revolution, at the Poetry Center, San Francisco State University.
Literature and Drama
Dist - POETRY **Prod** - POETRY 1981

Pablo Neruda - Fulgor Y Muerte De Joaquin Murrieta 60 MIN
U-matic / VHS / 16mm
Color (SPANISH)
Offers an adaptation of Pablo Neruda's play Fulgor Y Muerte De Joaquin Murrieta which takes place during the California gold rush.
Foreign Language; Literature and Drama
Dist - FOTH **Prod** - FOTH 1984

Pablo Neruda - Poet 30 MIN
U-matic / VHS / 16mm
B&W (SPANISH)
Offers a testament to the life and work of Nobel Prize - winning poet Pablo Neruda. Presents the poet giving his views on love, hate, life and death, and explains his work methods. Intercuts the discussion with poems and commentary tracing the development of Neruda's poetic vision.
Literature and Drama
Dist - CNEMAG **Prod** - CNEMAG

Pablo Picasso 13 MIN
U-matic / VHS
Color (C)
$69.95 purchase _ #EX1859
Presents a portrayal of the life and works of Pablo Picasso, and examines his influence on the modern aesthetic vision.
Biography; Fine Arts; History - World
Dist - FOTH **Prod** - FOTH

Pablo Picasso - the Legacy of a Genius 44 MIN
VHS / U-matic
Color (J)
LC 82-701119
Traces the life and art of Pablo Picasso. Focuses on the content and style of representative pieces of his work, as well as showing the people and places that influenced his painting and sculpture.
Biography; Fine Arts
Dist - BLACKW **Prod** - BLACKW 1982

PACA - Parents as Change Agents 27 MIN
16mm
Color (C A)
LC 78-701604
Describes the function and purpose of PACA, a community base behavior management program in which paraprofessionals teach parents how to measure and change specific problem behaviors in children.
Psychology; Sociology
Dist - UKANS **Prod** - UKANS 1976

Pace 22 MIN
16mm
Color (H C A)
LC 79-700528
Takes a look at the sport of trotting in Australia, including a view behind the scenes.
Physical Education and Recreation
Dist - AUIS **Prod** - FLMAUS 1976

Pace of the Seasons 15 MIN
16mm
Color (A)
LC 78-700946
Views seasonal changes in the land lying north and west of Lake Superior. Focuses on Voyageurs National Park and the wilderness area of the peninsula between Lake Kabetogama and Rainy Lake where travel is still on foot or by canoe.
Geography - United States; Geography - World; Science - Natural; Science - Physical
Dist - USNAC **Prod** - USNPS 1977

The Pacemaker - Clinical Evaluation Elective Replacement 14 MIN
16mm
Color (PRO)
Explains that impending pacemaker failure can be detected by external electronic testing in a pacemaker clinic. Points out that the rate of change of various aspects of the amplified electrical stimulus is determined and the impulse, repetition rate, pulse width, amplitude and configuration are measured.
Health and Safety; Science
Dist - ACY **Prod** - ACYDGD 1969

Pacemakers 7 MIN
VHS
Color (G PRO C)

$250.00 purchase _ #HA - 30
Explains why an abnormal heart rate may require implantation of a pacemaker. Shows how a pacemaker works and what to expect during surgery and recovery. Reviews heart rate monitoring and symptoms that need to be reported to the doctor. Addresses incision care, physical activity, body image, electrical interference, battery replacement and long - term follow up care. Produced by the Mercy Heart Institute of Pittsburgh.
Health and Safety
Dist - MIFE

Pacemakers 15 MIN
16mm / U-matic / VHS
Color (A)
Explains what pacemakers are and how they benefit patients with heart problems. Reviews pathophysiology of the heart, pacemaker components, how they work and various procedures of implantation. Teaches postoperative monitoring techniques, warning signs and precautionary measures.
Health and Safety; Science - Natural
Dist - PRORE **Prod** - PRORE

Pacemakers - Pumping Gold 20 MIN
U-matic / VHS
Color
$335.00 purchase
Health and Safety
Dist - ABCLR **Prod** - ABCLR 1982

Pacemakers - Technology's Gift of Life 10 MIN
16mm
Color
Looks at the effect pacemakers have on heart patients' lives. Explains the workings of the heart's electrical system and how pacemakers can correct malfunctions in the system. Discusses the history and future technology of heart pacing.
Health and Safety; Science; Science - Natural
Dist - MTP **Prod** - MTP

Pacemakers - the Electric Heartbeat 19 MIN
VHS / 16mm
Color (A)
$149.00 purchase, $75.00 rental _ #OD - 2225
Discusses a pacemaker's function, advances in pacemaker technology and the purpose of the META M - V. Examines and discusses the automatic internal cardioverter defibrillator.
Health and Safety
Dist - FOTH

Pacer 22 MIN
16mm
Color
LC 76-703148
Presents a documentary on trotters, horses trained by men which represent man's exploitation of nature for his own selfish interests.
Physical Education and Recreation
Dist - TEMPLU **Prod** - KOSALB 1976

The Pacesetter 6 MIN
16mm / U-matic / VHS
This Matter of Motivation Series
Color (PRO)
LC 75-703854
Asks what to do with a good man of genuine promise who isn't giving his best effort to the job.
Business and Economics; Psychology; Sociology
Dist - DARTNL **Prod** - CTRACT 1968

The Pacesetter in Aisle Number Three 16 MIN
16mm
Color (H C)
Presents a training film for store clerks in food industry. Portrays a young man eagerly starting on the job in a supermarket. Shows the store manager training him in proper shelf stocking and product space allocation, highlighting the importance of this job.
Business and Economics; Home Economics; Industrial and Technical Education
Dist - NINEFC **Prod** - GEMILL

Pachango - Camp Out 29 MIN
VHS / 16mm
Sonrisas Series
Color (T P) (ENGLISH & SPANISH)
$46.00 rental _ #SRSS - 114
Shows how role model expectations can cause confrontations. In Spanish and English.
Sociology
Dist - PBS

Pachmayr's Shotgun Hunting School 60 MIN
VHS / BETA
Color
Reveals highlights of Pachmayr's famous two and one - half day Shotgun Hunting School. Includes practice of stance, weight distribution, mounting, swing and pointing.
Physical Education and Recreation
Dist - HOMEAF **Prod** - HOMEAF
SIV

Pachmayr's Skeetshooting 50 MIN
BETA / VHS
Color
Presents a demonstration video of proper skeetshooting techniques and strategy that shows students how to improve their skills.
Physical Education and Recreation
Dist - HOMEAF **Prod** - HOMEAF

Pachmayr's skeetshooting with Ken Robertson
VHS
Color (G)
$29.95 purchase _ #SZ005
Teaches and reviews stance, gun hold, eye hold, timing and leading in skeetshooting.
Physical Education and Recreation
Dist - SIV

Pachmayr's Trapshooting 50 MIN
VHS / BETA
Color
Shows how to enhance trapshooting skills, including fundamentals for beginners to experts.
Physical Education and Recreation
Dist - HOMEAF **Prod** - HOMEAF

Pachmayr's trapshooting with Ken Robertson
VHS
Color (G)
$29.95 purchase _ #SZ006
Explains stance, gun hold, eye hold, timing, and leading.
Physical Education and Recreation
Dist - SIV

Pachyderms 25 MIN
U-matic / VHS / 16mm
Untamed World Series
Color; Mono (J H C A)
$400.00 film, $250.00 video, $50.00 rental
Gives an account of the history, present status, and possible future of the pachyderm. Looks at elephants, hippopotami, and the rhinoceros with footage from the African plains.
Geography - World; Science - Natural
Dist - CTV **Prod** - CTV 1973

Pacific 60 MIN
16mm
World at War Series
Color (H C A)
LC 76-701778
History - World; Sociology
Dist - USCAN **Prod** - THAMES 1975

The Pacific Age - Pt 1 50 MIN
VHS
New Pacific Series, the
Color (S)
$79.00 purchase _ #833 - 9108
Explores the cultural, historical, economic and political facets of the Pacific Basin which supports a third of the world's population. No other region contains so great a diversity of race, language and culture. Part 1 of eight parts considers the dynamic economic growth of the countries on the Asian rim of the Pacific.
Business and Economics; Geography - World; History - World
Dist - FI **Prod** - BBCTV 1987

The Pacific Boils Over 27 MIN
U-matic / VHS / 16mm
Victory at Sea Series
B&W (J H)
Shows the background to the attack on Pearl Harbor on December 7, 1941.
Civics and Political Systems; History - United States; History - World
Dist - LUF **Prod** - NBCTV

Pacific bridges series

By our hands	30 MIN
Do our best	30 MIN
Stand tall	30 MIN
Staying here	30 MIN
Then and now	30 MIN
To a new land	30 MIN

Dist - GPN

Pacific Coast 25 MIN
16mm / U-matic
Untamed World Series
Color; Mono (J H C A)
$400.00 film, $250.00 video, $50.00 rental
Highlights the unusual plants and animals that make up the environment of the British Columbia Pacific coastline.
Geography - World
Dist - CTV **Prod** - CTV 1972

Pacific Coast of Mexico - Baja California 11 MIN
16mm
Color; B&W (I J)
Shows the people and their mode of living on the peninsula of Baja California. Scenes include Ensenada, Turtle Bay, Magdalena Bay, Cape San Lucal, vineyards at Santo Tomas, lobster fishing and abalone fishing.
Geography - World
Dist - MLA **Prod** - JHP 1949

Pacific Coast of Mexico - the Mainland 11 MIN
16mm
Color; B&W (I J)
Deals with the coast from Mazatlan to Acapulco. Shows the towns, the people and the modes of living.
Geography - World
Dist - MLA **Prod** - JHP 1949

The Pacific Coast States 25 MIN
16mm / U-matic / VHS
United States Geography Series
Color (I J)
Looks at the characteristics of California, Oregon and Washington where original tiny settlements have grown into major cities. Shows the effect of nature in the area such as the Mount St Helens volcano.
Geography - United States
Dist - NGS **Prod** - NGS 1983

The Pacific edge 20 MIN
VHS / U-matic / 16mm / BETA
Physical geography of North America series
Color (P I J H)
$315.00, $90.00 purchase _ #C50471, #C51358
Examines the most active geological region of North America, the Pacific coast, which is marked by volcanoes and fault lines. Examines the gradual climate change from the Baja Peninsula to Alaska, and the surprisingly sudden change in climate from west to east. Part of a five - part series on the physical geography of North America.
Geography - United States; Geography - World
Dist - NGS **Prod** - NGS 1989

Pacific far east lines 12 MIN
16mm
Color (G)
$30.00 rental
Depicts the urban landscape of downtown San Francisco and constructed from materials gathered over two years. Scrutinizes time redefining space - the erector and helicopter appear as toys.
Fine Arts
Dist - CANCIN **Prod** - CHILDA 1979

Pacific, February 1942 - 1945 52 MIN
16mm / U-matic / VHS
World at War Series
Color (H C A)
Describes an island - hopping strategy that captured islands one at a time across the Pacific, finally ending the war there, winning back the Philippines and bringing a striking force to Japan's doorstep at Iwo Jima and Okinawa.
History - World
Dist - MEDIAG **Prod** - THAMES 1973

Pacific Frontier 29 MIN
16mm
Color
LC 75-700871
Surveys the operations of the Pacific and Seventh Fleets of the U S Navy. Shows how they perform everything from antisubmarine warfare to goodwill activities ashore. Includes some of the Navy activities in Vietnam.
Civics and Political Systems; Geography - World
Dist - USNAC **Prod** - USN 1965

Pacific frontiers 60 MIN
VHS
Scenic wonders of America series
Color; CC (G)
$24.95 purchase _ #901
Begins in Death Valley and travels to Hawaii to see closeups of rare nene birds nesting in the crater of a dormant volcano. Visits a dense rain forest, crashing waves, icy glaciers and treasure troves. Views the Sequoias of California, the frozen landscapes of Alaska's Glacier Bay and Crater Lake in Oregon. Part of a series on the scenic regions of the United States.
Geography - United States
Dist - APRESS **Prod** - READ

Pacific high
VHS
Color (G)
$39.90 purchase _ #0757
Takes part in the Newport - Ensenada Yacht Race. Uses aerial photography. Includes on - board and on - land activities and interviews.
Physical Education and Recreation
Dist - SEVVID

Pacific in eruption - Volume 1
VHS
Crusade in the Pacific series
B&W (H C A)
$24.95 purchase
Covers the land and sea battles in the Pacific during World War II. Includes wartime footage and narration.
History - World
Dist - PBS **Prod** - WNETTV

Pacific in transition - Volume 3
VHS
Crusade in the Pacific series
B&W (H C A)
$24.95 purchase
Covers the land and sea battles in the Pacific during World War II. Includes wartime footage and narration.
History - World
Dist - PBS **Prod** - WNETTV

Pacific inferno
VHS
Color (G)
$100.00 rental _ #0944
Portrays a band of American divers who are captured by the Japanese in World War II and forced to dive for $16 million in silver dumped by the US Army in Manila Bay. Recalls the actual historical event by shooting in the location where General Wainwright dumped the silver during the war.
Fine Arts; History - United States; History - World; Literature and Drama
Dist - SEVVID

Pacific Island 18 MIN
16mm
B&W (P I)
Shows life on Likiep, one of the Marshall Islands - practicing navigation, building a boat, basket weaving, repairing thatched homes and village activities.
Geography - World; Sociology
Dist - IFF **Prod** - IFF 1949

Pacific Island life series
Food from the sea 13 MIN
Village life 15 MIN
Dist - EDPAT

Pacific Island life series
The Coconut tree 15 MIN
Family life 16 MIN
Fishing 13 MIN
Dist - EDPAT
IFF

Pacific Island Life Series
Food from the sea 13 MIN
Village Life 15 MIN
Dist - IFF

Pacific - islands of the south seas 25 MIN
VHS
Color (G)
$19.95 purchase _ #S01465
Portrays the people and customs of Papua New Guinea and its surrounding islands. Shows that some of the people remain largely uninfluenced by Western ways.
Geography - World; History - World
Dist - UILL

Pacific Islands Series
People of the Free Train 15 MIN
Dist - MMP

The Pacific Missile Range 15 MIN
16mm
Color
Shows the operation and mission of the navy - operated Pacific Missile Range at Point Mugu, California.
Civics and Political Systems; Geography - United States
Dist - USNAC **Prod** - USN 1960

The Pacific Northwest 18 MIN
U-matic / VHS / 16mm
U S Geography Series
Color (J)
LC 76-701774
Examines the people, industry, economy and landscape of the Pacific Northwest region of the United States.
Business and Economics; Geography - United States; Geography - World; Social Science
Dist - MGHT **Prod** - MGHT 1976

Pacific Northwest 60 MIN
VHS
AAA travel series
Color (G)
$24.95 purchase _ #NA08
Explores the Pacific Northwest.
Geography - United States; Geography - World
Dist - SVIP

Pacific Outpost - Pt 8 58 MIN
VHS
Comrades Series
Color (S)
$79.00 purchase _ #351 - 9029
Follows twelve Soviet citizens from different backgrounds to reveal what Soviet life is like for a cross section of the 270 million inhabitants in the vast country of fifteen republics. Features Frontline anchor Judy Woodruff who also interviews prominent experts on Soviet affairs. Part 8 of the twelve - part series considers Tatyana Naukmova, a member of the Communist Party, well - versed in Soviet ideals and zealously evangelical in promoting communism.
Civics and Political Systems; Geography - World; Religion and Philosophy
Dist - FI **Prod** - WGBHTV 1988

Pacific - Pacific 52 MIN
16mm
Color (J H C)
Follows a voyage into the Pacific by a mineralogical expedition as they make contact with people on several islands, Malekula, Fiji, Tonga and Malden Island.
Geography - World; History - World; Sociology
Dist - CINETF **Prod** - CINETF 1973

The Pacific - Paradise in Pain 60 MIN
VHS / 16mm
Color (G A)
$495.00 purchase, $75.00 rental
Reveals that many of the Pacific's residents are confronting either colonial domination by France, military domination by the U S, or economic dominmation by Japan and Southeast Asia. Looks at the origin of these problems and potential solutions.
Civics and Political Systems; Geography - World
Dist - CNEMAG **Prod** - CNEMAG

Pacific paradise - Philippines - Part 23 8 MIN
VHS
Natures kingdom series
Color (P I J)
$125.00 purchase
Reveals that the rare 18 - inch mouse deer shares its island home with camouflage spiders and the imperial pidgeon. Shows that the mangroves are home to mudhoppers, tiny fish which skip about on land. Part of a 26 - part series on animals showing the habitats and traits of various species.
Geography - World; Science - Natural
Dist - LANDMK **Prod** - LANDMK 1992

Pacific passage
VHS
Color (G)
$100.00 rental _ #0227
Covers the 1986 Kenwood Cup, one of the grand prix IOR sailing races.
Physical Education and Recreation
Dist - SEVVID

The Pacific Rim 50 MIN
U-matic / 16mm / VHS
Window on the World Series
Color; Mono (J H C A)
MV $350.00 _ MP $600.00 purchase, $50.00 rental
Provides new insights into the ways government ad business are working to improve trade contacts in the expanding Pacific market.
Business and Economics; History - World
Dist - CTV **Prod** - CTV 1974

Pacific time 45 MIN
16mm
Color (G)
$120.00 rental
Engages in an allegory of Plato's cave. Uses a technique whereby two reels of film are projected simultaneously side by side using non - synchronous projectors with the same image size. Produced by Louis Hock.
Fine Arts; Literature and Drama
Dist - CANCIN

Pacificanada Series
Whistling Smith 27 MIN
Dist - WOMBAT

The Pacing road 20 MIN
U-matic / VHS
Efficient reading - instructional tapes series; Tape 5
Color
Demonstrates how to develop reading skills that overcome bad reading habits by the pacing technique.
English Language
Dist - TELSTR **Prod** - TELSTR

Pack Up Your Troubles 75 MIN
16mm
B&W (H C A)
Stars Laurel and Hardy in a story about two misfit army privates who upset Uncle Sam's routine.
Fine Arts
Dist - KITPAR **Prod** - ROACH

Package Bees 30 MIN
VHS / U-matic
Bees and Honey Series
Color
Shows how to select an apiary site, dressing properly, installing and feeding, package building and the 21 - day cycle.
Agriculture; Science - Natural
Dist - MDCPB **Prod** - WGTV

Package Four 50 MIN
U-matic
See, Hear - Canada's North Series
Color (I J)
Contains segments titled Alaska, Dawson, Wild Yukon, Yukon The Eleventh Province, The Duality Of The Northwest Territories.
Geography - United States; Geography - World; History - World
Dist - TVOTAR **Prod** - TVOTAR 1985

Package One 50 MIN
U-matic
See, Hear - Canada's North Series
Color (I J)
Contains segments titled Gold, Economic Development, Oil and Gas, Transportation, Mining.
Geography - World; History - World
Dist - TVOTAR **Prod** - TVOTAR 1985

Package Three 50 MIN
U-matic
See, Hear - Canada's North Series
Color (I J)
Contains segments titled The Mackenzie Delta, The Mackenzie Valley, The Central Arctic, The Keewatin, Baffin.
Geography - World; History - World
Dist - TVOTAR **Prod** - TVOTAR 1985

Package Two 50 MIN
U-matic
See, Hear - Canada's North Series
Color (I J)
Contains segments titled Early History Of The Inuit, Inuit Art, Education, Health, Inuvik - Inuit In Transition.
Geography - World; History - World
Dist - TVOTAR **Prod** - TVOTAR 1985

Packaged to Sell 13 MIN
16mm
Color
LC 81-701363
Shows packaging line operations, demonstrating quality control steps throughout the packaging line.
Business and Economics
Dist - MBC **Prod** - MBC 1981

Packaging 10 MIN
16mm
B&W (C)
Presents old methods of packaging versus new ones.
Business and Economics
Dist - NYU **Prod** - NYUIME 1940

Packaging and Labeling 30 MIN
U-matic / VHS
Marketing Perspectives Series
Color
Covers the role of packaging in the marketing mix, role of shape and function in packaging design, use of packaging as a communications tool and types of labelling.
Business and Economics; Education
Dist - WFVTAE **Prod** - MATC

Packaging Food for You 17 MIN
16mm
Color
LC 74-705286
Tells that by improved packaging of foods, made possible through research by the USDA and private industry, there are improvements in economy, quality, freshness and convenience of packaged foods.
Business and Economics; Health and Safety; Social Science
Dist - USNAC **Prod** - USDA 1966

Packaging hazardous waste 18 MIN
VHS / U-matic / BETA
Handling hazardous waste series
Color; PAL (IND G) (SPANISH ITALIAN)
$175.00 rental _ #HWH - 200; $730.00 purchase, $175.00 rental #PAC001
Instructs hazardous waste workers who prepare hazardous waste for safe storage, transportation and disposal. Covers proper packaging, labeling and marking procedures and discusses common problems. Includes leader's guide and 10 participant handouts. Part of a seven - part series which trains hazardous waste management workers. .
Business and Economics; Health and Safety; Psychology; Sociology
Dist - BNA **Prod** - BNA
ITF

Packaging Operations 60 MIN
VHS
Systems Operations Series
Color (PRO)
$600.00 - $1500.00 purchase _ #RCPOP
Presents the concepts of a plant packaging operation. Discusses packaging operation components, container labeling and handling, and container loading, warehousing and shipping procedures. Includes ten textbooks and an instructor guide to support four hours of instruction.

Education; Industrial and Technical Education; Psychology
Dist - NUSTC Prod - NUSTC

Packaging Rocket Power 27 MIN
16mm
Color
Summarizes the liquid and solid fuel propellant rocket manufacturing capability of the Thiokol Chemical Corporation. Stresses systems used by the Armed Services and NASA.
Business and Economics; Industrial and Technical Education
Dist - THIOKL Prod - THIOKL 1960

Packaging the Product 15 MIN
U-matic
Job Seeking Series
Color (H C A)
LC 80-706689
Tells how to make the best appearance for an interview and emphasizes that dress is crucial in selling oneself on a job interview.
Guidance and Counseling; Psychology
Dist - GPN Prod - WCETTV 1979

Packer to Consumer 20 MIN
VHS
Conception to Consumer (Set K) Series
(C)
$69.95 _ CV145
Gives the basics in red meat production from packer to consumer, including slaughter, inspection, grading, fabrication, packaging, and marketing.
Agriculture; Business and Economics
Dist - AAVIM Prod - AAVIM 1989

The Packet of an Uncertain Gaussian 10 MIN
16mm / U-matic / VHS
Color (C)
LC 73-700853
Combines computer animation with conventional artwork to display properties of wave function in introductory quantum mechanics. Among the topics covered are plane waves, the Fourier composition of the Gaussian wave packet and its transform, Heisenberg's uncertainty principle, and the spreading of the time dependent Gaussian wave packet.
Science - Physical
Dist - IFB Prod - POLYIB 1968

Packet Switching Operation and Protocols, Pt 1 54 MIN
VHS / U-matic
Packet Switching Series
Color
Industrial and Technical Education; Mathematics; Sociology
Dist - MIOT Prod - MIOT

Packet Switching Operation and Protocols, Pt 2 49 MIN
U-matic / VHS
Packet Switching Series
Color
Industrial and Technical Education; Mathematics; Sociology
Dist - MIOT Prod - MIOT

Packet Switching Operation and Protocols, Pt 3 57 MIN
U-matic / VHS
Packet Switching Series
Color
Industrial and Technical Education; Mathematics; Sociology
Dist - MIOT Prod - MIOT

Packet Switching Operation and Protocols, Pt 4 53 MIN
U-matic / VHS
Packet Switching Series
Color
Industrial and Technical Education; Mathematics; Sociology
Dist - MIOT Prod - MIOT

Packet switching, Pt 1 29 MIN
U-matic / VHS
Distributed processor communication architecture series
Color
Introduces definitions applicable to packet - switched networks, traffic types, hierarchy of design concepts in a network and design issues in a network.
Industrial and Technical Education; Mathematics
Dist - MIOT Prod - MIOT

Packet switching, Pt 2 27 MIN
VHS / U-matic
Distributed processor communication architecture series
Color
Discusses protocols, layered structure of protocols, routing taxonomy and routing algorithms, distributed routing techniques and centralized routing techniques.
Industrial and Technical Education; Mathematics
Dist - MIOT Prod - MIOT

Packet switching series
Analysis and comparison of switched networks - Pt 1 56 MIN
Analysis and comparison of switched networks - Pt 2 51 MIN
Common carrier services - Pt 1 58 MIN
Common carrier services - Pt 2 54 MIN
Elements of packet data networks 55 MIN
Integrated Services Digital Networks, Pt 1 55 MIN
Integrated Services Digital Networks, Pt 2 52 MIN
Introduction to Packet Networks 55 MIN
Networking Topologies and Routing, Pt 1 40 MIN
Networking Topologies and Routing, Pt 2 43 MIN
Packet Switching Operation and Protocols, Pt 1 54 MIN
Packet Switching Operation and Protocols, Pt 2 49 MIN
Packet Switching Operation and Protocols, Pt 3 57 MIN
Packet Switching Operation and Protocols, Pt 4 53 MIN
Satellite applications and demand assignment for data - Pt 1 53 MIN
Satellite applications and demand assignment for data - Pt 2 55 MIN
Dist - MIOT

Packing and Seals 120 MIN
U-matic / VHS
Mechanical Equipment Maintenance Series
Color (IND) (SPANISH)
Discusses pump and valve packing. Examines mechanical seals.
Industrial and Technical Education
Dist - ITCORP Prod - ITCORP

Packing for dive travel
VHS
Color (G)
$19.95 purchase _ #0859
Presents a video checklist for traveling divers. Includes choosing a destination, choosing clothing, photography equipment, helpful hints, customs procedures, packing the dive bag, security measures.
Geography - World; Industrial and Technical Education; Physical Education and Recreation
Dist - SEVVID

Packing Front Wheel Bearings 4 MIN
16mm
Color
LC FI68-212
Illustrates how to remove a front wheel, remove the bearing from the wheel, inspect, clean and grease the bearing and replace the bearing and the wheel on the car.
Industrial and Technical Education; Social Science
Dist - RAYBAR Prod - RAYBAR 1966

Packing pumps and valves 11 MIN
U-matic / BETA / VHS
Color (IND G)
$295.00 purchase _ #800 - 13
Presents a step - by - step review of the techniques for repacking or adding packing to pumps and valves.
Health and Safety; Industrial and Technical Education; Psychology
Dist - ITSC Prod - ITSC

Packingtown, USA 32 MIN
16mm
Color (C A)
LC 73-703096
Presents the story of the meat strike of 1904. Includes the efforts of the Meatcutters Union, the Teamsters, Jane Addams and Mary Mc Dowell to help the immigrant workers in their fight for human liberties.
Business and Economics; History - United States; Sociology
Dist - UILL Prod - UILL 1968

Packy 25 MIN
U-matic / VHS / 16mm
Insight Series
Color (J)
Revolves around the encounter in heaven between God and a flamboyant theatrical agent, who has always thought of himself as a failure. Shows that God does not think of him as a failure because of his many acts of kindness. Stars Bob Newhart and Jack Klugman.
Guidance and Counseling; Psychology; Religion and Philosophy
Dist - PAULST Prod - PAULST

Pad drills - Number 1
VHS
Foundations of gymnastic excellence series
Color (H C A)
$39.95 purchase _ #WES1601V
Presents the first of a four - part series on gymnastics. Covers terminology, body positions, and the fundamental skills of the sport.
Physical Education and Recreation
Dist - CAMV

Paddington and the 'Cold Snap' / Paddington Makes a Clean Sweep / Mr Gruber's Mystery 22 MIN
16mm / U-matic / VHS
Paddington Bear, Series 1 Series
Color (K P I)
LC 80-707221
Discusses Paddington Bear's efforts as a plumber and a chimney sweep. Tells how he visits a wax museum and makes preparations to attend his aunt's birthday party. Based on chapters one, three, four and seven of the book Paddington Marches On by Michael Bond.
Literature and Drama
Dist - ALTSUL Prod - BONDM 1977

Paddington and the 'Finishing Touch' / Paddington and the Mystery Box 11 MIN
U-matic / VHS / 16mm
Paddington Bear, Series 2 Series
Color (K P I)
LC 80-700950
Tells how Paddington Bear tries to spruce up Mr Gruber's patio. Explains how he solves the mystery of a buried treasure. Based on the books Paddington Goes To Town and The Great Big Paddington Book by Michael Bond.
Literature and Drama
Dist - ALTSUL Prod - BONDM 1980

Paddington Bakes a Cake / Paddington Clears the Coach / Paddington Weighs in 16 MIN
U-matic / VHS / 16mm
Paddington Bear, Series 2 Series
Color (K P I)
LC 80-700951
Tells how Paddington Bear bakes a birthday cake and misinterprets a chef's instructions in a train dining car. Explains what happens when he steps onto a weighing machine. Based on chapters one, three and six of the book Paddington Takes To TV by Michael Bond.
Literature and Drama
Dist - ALTSUL Prod - BONDM 1980

Paddington Bear 1 series
A Shopping expedition - Paddington and the Old Master - A disappearing trick 17 MIN
Dist - ALTSUL

Paddington Bear Program Number Eight 23 MIN
VHS / U-matic
Paddington Bear Programs Series
Color (K P I)
Literature and Drama
Dist - ALTSUL Prod - BONDM

Paddington Bear Program Number Eleven 28 MIN
VHS / U-matic
Paddington Bear Programs Series
Color (K P I)
Literature and Drama
Dist - ALTSUL Prod - BONDM

Paddington Bear Program Number Five 24 MIN
VHS / U-matic
Paddington Bear Programs Series
Color (K P I)
Literature and Drama
Dist - ALTSUL Prod - BONDM

Paddington Bear Program Number Four 24 MIN
U-matic / VHS
Paddington Bear Programs Series
Color (K P I)
Literature and Drama
Dist - ALTSUL Prod - BONDM

Paddington Bear Program Number Nine 23 MIN
U-matic / VHS
Paddington Bear Programs Series
Color (K P I)
Literature and Drama
Dist - ALTSUL Prod - BONDM

Paddington Bear Program Number One 24 MIN
VHS / U-matic
Paddington Bear Programs Series
Color (K P I)
Literature and Drama
Dist - ALTSUL Prod - BONDM

Paddington Bear Program Number Seven 23 MIN
VHS / U-matic
Paddington Bear Programs Series
Color (K P I)
Literature and Drama
Dist - ALTSUL Prod - BONDM

Paddington Bear Program Number Six 24 MIN
U-matic / VHS
Paddington Bear Programs Series
Color (K P I)
Literature and Drama
Dist - ALTSUL **Prod** - BONDM

Paddington Bear Program Number Ten 23 MIN
U-matic / VHS
Paddington Bear Programs Series
Color (K P I)
Literature and Drama
Dist - ALTSUL **Prod** - BONDM

Paddington Bear Program Number Three 24 MIN
VHS / U-matic
Paddington Bear Programs Series
Color (K P I)
Literature and Drama
Dist - ALTSUL **Prod** - BONDM

Paddington Bear Program Number Two 24 MIN
VHS / U-matic
Paddington Bear Programs Series
Color (K P I)
Literature and Drama
Dist - ALTSUL **Prod** - BONDM

Paddington Bear Programs Series
Paddington Bear Program Number Eight 23 MIN
Paddington Bear Program Number Eleven 28 MIN
Paddington Bear Program Number Five 24 MIN
Paddington Bear Program Number Four 24 MIN
Paddington Bear Program Number Nine 23 MIN
Paddington Bear Program Number One 24 MIN
Paddington Bear Program Number Seven 23 MIN
Paddington Bear Program Number Six 24 MIN
Paddington Bear Program Number Ten 23 MIN
Paddington Bear Program Number Three 24 MIN
Paddington Bear Program Number Two 24 MIN
Dist - ALTSUL

Paddington Bear, Series 1 Series
A Family group - a spot of decorating - Paddington turns detective 17 MIN
Mr Curry Takes a Bath - Fortune Telling 11 MIN
Paddington and the 'Cold Snap' / Paddington Makes a Clean Sweep / Mr Gruber's Mystery 22 MIN
Paddington Cleans Up 6 MIN
Paddington Hits Out / a Visit to the Hospital 11 MIN
Paddington Hits the Jackpot / a Sticky Time 11 MIN
Paddington Makes a Bid / do - it - Yourself / Something Nasty in the Kitchen / Trouble 22 MIN
Dist - ALTSUL

Paddington Bear, Series 2 Series
Outing in the Park, an / Trouble in the Bargain Basement / Paddington Takes the Stage 15 MIN
Paddington and the 'Finishing Touch' / Paddington and the Mystery Box 11 MIN
Paddington Bakes a Cake / Paddington Clears the Coach / Paddington Weighs in 16 MIN
Paddington Buys a Share / Paddington in a Hole 11 MIN
Paddington Goes to the Movies 20 MIN
Paddington in Court / Keeping Fit / Paddington in Touch / Comings and Goings at 22 MIN
Paddington in the Hot Seat / Paddington's Puzzle / Paddington Takes a Snip 17 MIN
Dist - ALTSUL

Paddington Bear series
A Picnic on the River - Paddington Dines Out 11 MIN
Picture Trouble - Trouble on the Beach - A Visit to the Theatre 16 MIN
Please look after this bear - A bear in hot water - Paddington goes underground 17 MIN
Too much off the top 6 MIN
Trouble at number thirty - two - Paddington and the Christmas shopping - Christmas 17 MIN
Visit to the Bank - Paddington's Patch - in and Out of Trouble - Paddington at the Tower 22 MIN
Visit to the Dentist - Paddington Recommended 11 MIN
Dist - ALTSUL

Paddington Buys a Share / Paddington in a Hole 11 MIN
U-matic / VHS / 16mm
Paddington Bear, Series 2 Series
Color (K P I)
LC 80-700952
Tells how Paddington buys oil stocks from a shady character. Describes his foray into home construction. Based on chapters three and five of the book Paddington At Work by Michael Bond.
Literature and Drama
Dist - ALTSUL **Prod** - BONDM 1980

Paddington Cleans Up 6 MIN
16mm / U-matic / VHS
Paddington Bear, Series 1 Series
Color (K P I)
LC 77-700674
Presents an animated version of chapter 2 of the children's book Paddington On Top by Michael Bond. Features a small, dark bear named Paddington and his attempts to demonstrate a vacuum cleaner.
Fine Arts; Literature and Drama
Dist - ALTSUL **Prod** - BONDM 1977

Paddington Comes to Virginia Beach 28 MIN
U-matic / VHS / 16mm
Color (K P I)
Shows the creative teaching possibilities that exist for the utilization of the Paddington Bear films. Shows a wide variety of locally - made learning materials which were created for the project and which are circulated from the media center.
English Language; Literature and Drama
Dist - ALTSUL **Prod** - VBCSB 1982

Paddington Goes to the Movies 20 MIN
U-matic / VHS / 16mm
Paddington Bear, Series 2 Series
Color (K P I)
LC 83-700508
Tells what hilarious things happen when Paddington Bear is introduced to the world of motion pictures through a peek in a theater playing Singing In The Rain.
Fine Arts; Guidance and Counseling; Literature and Drama
Dist - ALTSUL **Prod** - ALTSUL 1983

Paddington Hits Out / a Visit to the Hospital 11 MIN
16mm / U-matic / VHS
Paddington Bear, Series 1 Series
Color (K P I)
LC 77-700672
Presents an animated adaptation of chapters 2 and 3 from the children's book Paddington Goes To Town by Michael Bond. Features Paddington the bear, and his adventures in a golf competition and at a hospital.
Fine Arts; Literature and Drama
Dist - ALTSUL **Prod** - BONDM 1977

Paddington Hits the Jackpot / a Sticky Time 11 MIN
16mm / U-matic / VHS
Paddington Bear, Series 1 Series
Color (K P I)
LC 77-700671
Presents an animated adaptation of chapters 4 and 5 from the children's book Paddington At Large by Michael Bond. Features Paddington, the bear whose experiences as a quiz contestant and a cook bring unexpected results.
Fine Arts; Literature and Drama
Dist - ALTSUL **Prod** - BONDM 1977

Paddington in Court / Keeping Fit / Paddington in Touch / Comings and Goings 22 MIN
U-matic / VHS / 16mm
Paddington Bear, Series 2 Series
Color (K P I)
LC 80-700953
Describes Paddington's adventures in court and in a rugby match. Tells how he builds a body building set and pulls part of the fence down. Based on chapters three, five, six and seven of the book Paddington On Top by Michael Bond.
Literature and Drama
Dist - ALTSUL **Prod** - BONDM 1980

Paddington in the Hot Seat / Paddington's Puzzle / Paddington Takes a Snip 17 MIN
U-matic / VHS / 16mm
Paddington Bear, Series 2 Series
Color (K P I)
LC 80-700954
Describes Paddington's adventures on a quiz show, tells how he tries to create a jigsaw puzzle and explains how he tries his hand at topiary.
Literature and Drama
Dist - ALTSUL **Prod** - BONDM 1980

Paddington Lace 24 MIN
16mm
Color (A)
LC 78-713557
Portrays the Bohemian life - style of the Australian artists' colony Paddington, a suburb of Sydney, by presenting a dramatization about two young people who live there.
Fine Arts; Geography - World; Sociology
Dist - AUIS **Prod** - ANAIB 1971

Paddington Makes a Bid / do - it - Yourself / Something Nasty in the Kitchen / Trouble 22 MIN
U-matic / VHS / 16mm
Paddington Bear, Series 1 Series
Color (K P I)
LC 77-700673
Features an animated adaptation of chapters 2 - 3 and 5 - 6 of the children's book Paddington Helps Out by Michael Bond. Presents Paddington, a small, dark bear, and his adventures at an auction, and as a carpenter and a cook. Includes Trouble At The Launderette.
Fine Arts; Literature and Drama
Dist - ALTSUL **Prod** - BONDM 1977

Paddle - to - the - Sea 28 MIN
16mm
Color (I)
LC FIA67-1617
Tells about the journey of a hand - carved toy canoeman from Canada's northern forest downstream to the sea. Adapted from story of same title by Holling C Holling.
Fine Arts; Geography - World; Literature and Drama
Dist - NFBC **Prod** - NFBC 1967

Paddy Chayefsky 29 MIN
Videoreel / VT2
Elliot Norton Reviews II Series
Color
Presents exchanges and arguments between the dean of American theatre critics, Elliot Norton, and Paddy Chayefsky.
Fine Arts
Dist - PBS **Prod** - WGBHTV

Paderewski's homecoming - Powrot Paderewskiego 40 MIN
VHS
Color (G A) (POLISH)
$29.95 purchase _ #V268, #V269
Reveals that the last wish of the great Polish pianist and Prime Minister, Ignacy Paderewski, was to be buried in free Poland. Describes how, years later, when Poland regained freedom, his coffin was moved from Arlington Cemetery in the US to St John's Cathedral in Warsaw. Includes President Bush's White House meeting with Polish Americans in June 1992, the last tribute in Poznan, and the meeting of Presidents Bush and Walesa with Poles at Castle Square in Warsaw in July 1992. Also available with Polish narration.
Fine Arts; History - World
Dist - POLART

Padlocks - standard and heavy security 21 MIN
VHS
Forcible entry video series
Color (IND)
$159.95 purchase _ #35610
Exhibits types and construction of padlocks - both US and foreign. Shows usual padlock locations, mounting devices and standard lock and heavy security opening techniques. Demonstrates use of the Halligan tool, bolt cutters, dent puller, and other special tools. One part of a five - part series that is a teaching companion for IFSTA's Forcible Entry manual.
Health and Safety; Science - Physical; Social Science
Dist - OKSU **Prod** - FIREEN

Padre 28 MIN
U-matic / VHS
Old Friends - New Friends Series
Color
Presents a portrait of American priest, William Wasson and some of the 4,000 Mexican children whom he has adopted in the past 25 years.
Religion and Philosophy
Dist - PBS **Prod** - FAMCOM 1981

Padre Nuestro 90 MIN
35mm
Color (G) (SPANISH WITH ENGLISH SUBTITLES)
$300.00 rental
Portrays a dying Cardinal who returns to his native Spain to straighten out his affairs with the family he never really knew. Directed by Francisco Regueiro.
Fine Arts; Literature and Drama; Religion and Philosophy; Sociology
Dist - KINOIC

Padre Pro 29 MIN
BETA / VHS
B&W
Covers the life of Jesuit Miguel Pro who was executed in Mexico in the 1920's.
Biography; Geography - World; Religion and Philosophy
Dist - DSP **Prod** - DSP

Paella Valenciana 23 MIN
U-matic / VHS
Color (PRO)
Demonstrates the preparation of Paella with chicken, clams, mussels, scallops, shrimp and chorizo.
Home Economics; Industrial and Technical Education
Dist - CULINA **Prod** - CULINA

Pagan rhapsody 24 MIN
16mm / VHS
Color (G)
$30.00 rental, $40.00 purchase
Features Jane Elford and Lloyd Williams in their first big acting roles.
Fine Arts
Dist - CANCIN **Prod** - KUCHAR 1970

Paganini, the Violin, and Desmond Bradley 26 MIN
U-matic / VHS / 16mm
Musical Triangles Series
Color (J)
Presents Italian violinist and composer Niccolo Paganini (1782 - 1840), who is considered a legendary virtuoso. Features professional violinist Desmond Bradley discussing Paganini's music and life and playing some of Paganini's music. Includes several of his 24 caprices for solo violin.
Fine Arts
Dist - MEDIAG **Prod** - THAMES 1975

Page 169 30 MIN
U-matic / VHS
Eager to Learn Series
Color (T)
Education; Psychology
Dist - KTEHTV **Prod** - KTEHTV

Page, Dr Joyce 29 MIN
U-matic
Like it is Series
Color
Describes the Children's Defense Fund. Discusses the needs of poor and minority children.
Sociology
Dist - HRC **Prod** - OHC

Page fright - inside the world of the learning disabled 28 MIN
VHS
Color (H C G)
$295.00 purchase, $55.00 rental
Reveals that a surprising number of people with learning disabilities have difficulty reading simple words. Tells about Patricia Hatt who took 15 years to complete her BA because her difficulty with reading denied her access to education. Discusses the problems of coping with everyday life - filling out deposit slips, reading price tags, following directions.
English Language; Psychology
Dist - FLMLIB **Prod** - CANBC 1992

A Pageant of grouse 52 MIN
VHS / U-matic
In Wildness series
Color (H C G)
$250.00 purchase _ #HH - 6357L
Reveals the habits, interrelationships and habitats of several species of North American grouse. Takes a close - up look at the flamboyant ruffed grouse, the trusting spruce grouse and the dancing sharptail. Examines differences between the species - distinctive calls, acrobatic gestures, plumage displays and camouflage colors.
Science - Natural
Dist - LCA **Prod** - LCA 1990

Pagemaker 360 MIN
VHS / U-matic
(A PRO)
$395.00 purchase, $495.00 purchase
Teaches how to create and place text, set defaults and typespace. Provides exercises on mouse use, graphics and laser printing. Includes printed guide and diskettes in addition to video.
Computer Science
Dist - VIDEOT **Prod** - VIDEOT 1988

Pagemaker 2.0a introduction
VHS
Video professor Macintosh series
Color (J H C G)
$29.95 purchase _ #VP301V
Makes the most complex operations of the Pagemaker 2.0a easy to understand. Uses advanced production techniques which allow viewer to see keyboard and monitor simultaneously. Allows students to learn at their own pace, rewinding or pausing for any section they don't fully understand. Part of six - part series on Macintosh graphics.
Computer Science; Industrial and Technical Education
Dist - CAMV

Pagemaker 2.0a level II
VHS
Video professor Macintosh series
Color (J H C G)
$29.95 purchase _ #VP304V
Makes the most complex operations of the Pagemaker 2.0a Level II easy to understand. Uses advanced production techniques which allow viewer to see keyboard and monitor simultaneously. Allows students to learn at their own pace, rewinding or pausing for any section they don't fully understand. Part of six - part series on Macintosh graphics.
Computer Science; Industrial and Technical Education
Dist - CAMV

PageMaker 2.0a level II 58 MIN
VHS
Macintosh series
Color (G)
$29.95 purchase _ #60027
Looks at PageMaker 2.0a Level II for the Macintosh computer. Examines creating a newsletter, picture boxes, creating irregular columns, flowing text around irregular shapes, creating graphics and special effects. Part of a series on Macintosh computers.
Computer Science; Mathematics
Dist - CARTRP **Prod** - CARTRP

PageMaker 4.0 series
Presents three videocassettes teaching PageMaker 4.0 desktop publishing. Includes Advanced, Secrets and Timesavers, and Learning for the PC.
Advanced
Learning for the PC
Secrets and timesavers
Dist - SIV

Pages from the Talmud 30 MIN
16mm
B&W
LC FIA64-1142
Presents readings and dramatizations from the Aggadic portions of Talmud, with many excerpts from the Ethics of the Fathers (pirke Avot.).
Religion and Philosophy
Dist - NAAJS **Prod** - JTS 1954

Paha Sapa - The Struggle for the Black Hills 59 MIN
VHS
Color; PAL (G)
$29.95 purchase
Chronicles the struggle by the Dakotas to regain their sacred Black Hills, their holy grounds, which have come to symbolize the misappropriation of Indian lands by the United States government. Features narration entirely by members of the Lakota and Cheyenne tribes and music by various Native American artists.
Fine Arts; History - United States; Social Science
Dist - SOAR

Paid to Care 30 MIN
VHS
Color (G)
$39.95 purchase _ #PAID - 000
Notes the growth of the day care industry and how it has become an important social and political force. Examines the role day care workers have in child development.
Health and Safety; Sociology
Dist - PBS **Prod** - WETATV 1988

Paige 10 MIN
16mm / U-matic / VHS
People You'd Like to Know Series
Color (I J H)
LC 78-701953
Focuses on an 11 - year - old girl with Down's syndrome, a form of mental retardation. Shows how she copes with her condition and adjusts to her surroundings.
Education; Psychology
Dist - EBEC **Prod** - WGBHTV 1978

Pain 30 MIN
U-matic / VHS / 16mm
Coping with serious illness series; No 1
Color (H C A)
LC 80-701660
Shows approaches to coping with both pain and the fear of pain. Explains the effects of suffering on the personality.
Health and Safety; Psychology
Dist - TIMLIF **Prod** - TIMLIF 1980

Pain 28 MIN
VHS
Human body - the senses - series
Color (J H G)
$89.95 purchase _ #UW4171
Shows and explains the nature of the sensation of pain. Examines its chemical and electrical components, how a message is conveyed from the tiniest receptor to the cerebrum and the effect of willpower on sensitivity to pain. Part of a 39 - part series featuring computer animation, medical photography, electron micrography, full - color drawings and diagrams and three - dimensional working models to cover the workings of the human body from head to toe and inside out.
Science - Natural
Dist - FOTH

Pain 17 MIN
16mm
Color (PRO)
LC FIA66-529
Traces the subjectivity and treatment of pain from its aboriginal beginnings to modern psychiatry.
Health and Safety; Psychology
Dist - AMEDA **Prod** - HOFLAR

Pain and Healing 60 MIN
VHS
Mind Series
Color; Captioned (G)
$59.95 purchase _ #MIND - 105
Scrutinizes the relationship between mind and body, focusing particularly on the role of the mind in controlling pain and healing the body. Reveals that the body can respond to hypnosis, placebos and particular mental attitudes. Suggests that the mind can be an essential factor in health.
Psychology
Dist - PBS **Prod** - WNETTV 1988

Pain and Healing 30 MIN
VHS
Mind/Brain Classroom Series
Color (H G)
$59.95 purchase _ #MDBR - 107
Analyzes the role the mind plays in controlling pain and healing diseases. Suggests that hypnosis, placebos and attitudes can all affect the healing process. Intended for high school students.
Psychology
Dist - PBS **Prod** - WNETTV

Pain and Hypnosis 29 MIN
U-matic
Understanding Human Behavior - an Introduction to Psychology Series 'Lesson 18
Color (C A)
Shows that many factors influence pain. Discusses pain - treating strategies. Compares differing interpretations of hypnosis.
Psychology
Dist - CDTEL **Prod** - COAST

Pain and Soft Tissue Injury Series
Approaches to treatment 57 MIN
Interplay of Psychology and Physiology 55 MIN
Pain - Examples of Frequent Types of Pain and How to Examine for Pain 58 MIN
Dist - ABACPE

The Pain and stress relief clinic, Boston U S A 50 MIN
VHS
Healing arts series
Color; PAL (G F)
PdS99 purchase
Shows the work of an unusual clinic in Boston that treats pain and stress in a multidisciplinary way. Explores the possible use of the clinic's ideas in other areas of medicine. Part six of a nine - part series.
Health and Safety; Psychology
Dist - BBCENE

Pain Control through Behavior Modification 23 MIN
U-matic
Management of Pain Series Module 5
Color (PRO)
LC 80-707393
Health and Safety
Dist - BRA **Prod** - BRA 1980

Pain - Examples of Frequent Types of Pain and How to Examine for Pain 58 MIN
U-matic / VHS
Pain and Soft Tissue Injury Series
Color (PRO)
Civics and Political Systems; Health and Safety
Dist - ABACPE **Prod** - PBI

The Pain killers 30 MIN
VHS
Perspectives - health and medicine - series
Color; PAL; NTSC (G)
PdS90, PdS105 purchase
Looks at new pain - relieving techniques demonstrated at the Walton Hospital, Liverpool, England.

Health and Safety
Dist - CFLVIS **Prod** - LONTVS

Pain Management 37 MIN
U-matic
Terminal Illness Series
B&W
Sociology
Dist - UWASHP **Prod** - UWASHP

Pain management - Margo McCaffery discusses new concepts series 112 MIN
VHS / U-matic
Pain management - Margo McCaffery discusses new concepts series
Color (PRO)
$900.00 purchase _ #7230S
Presents a four - part series on new approaches to pain management featuring Margo McCaffery. Discusses the role of health care teams in pain management centers. Teaches nursing staff how to communicate with patients to assess and manage pain, particularly pediatric and elderly patients. Shows how to document pain management to assess its effectiveness. Looks at the administration of analgesics to patients with special pain problems of an acute or chronic nature.
Health and Safety
Dist - AJN **Prod** - HOSSN 1984

Pain - Mechanisms and Management
U-matic / VHS
Color
Focuses on clinical applicability of major pain research developments. Reviews progress in the individualized management of chronic pain due to benign or malignant disease and considers patients' psychological experiences.
Health and Safety; Psychology
Dist - AMEDA **Prod** - AMEDA

Pain - Nursing Action, Pt 1 76 FRS
U-matic / VHS
Pain - Sleep Series
Color (PRO)
LC 74-739165
Psychology; Sociology
Dist - CONMED **Prod** - CONMED 1971

Pain - Nursing Action, Pt 2 86 FRS
VHS / U-matic
Pain - Sleep Series
Color (PRO)
LC 78-739166
Psychology; Sociology
Dist - CONMED **Prod** - CONMED 1971

Pain of shyness 17 MIN
VHS
Color (H C G)
$275.00 purchase, $45.00 rental
Features Dr Phillip Zimbardo, Stanford University, author of The Shy Child, who explains some techniques for overcoming shyness. Shows that role playing enables young children to try new situations. Dr Carlo Piccione shows desensitizing exercises for adults.
Health and Safety; Psychology
Dist - FLMLIB **Prod** - ABCNEW 1985

The Pain of Shyness 20 MIN
VHS / U-matic
Color
$335.00 purchase
From the ABC TV program, 20 20.
Health and Safety; Sociology
Dist - ABCLR **Prod** - ABCLR 1984

The Pain of Silence 13 MIN
16mm
Color (J)
Focuses on the personal concern of a teenage girl who suspects that she has contracted a venereal disease.
Guidance and Counseling; Health and Safety
Dist - MLA **Prod** - MLA 1971

Pain, passion and profit 49 MIN
VHS
Color (G)
$75.00 rental, $275.00 purchase
Visits women entrepreneurs in Africa who have successfully developed small - scale business enterprises in their own communities. Features Anita Roddick, founder of The Body Shop, who maintains a strong committment to the idea of 'profits with principles.' Roddick questions them about how the role and status of women affects their businesses and what benefits women in the community gain economically and socially. Gives an in - depth look at global feminism. A British production by Gurinder Chadha.
Business and Economics; Fine Arts; Geography - World; Sociology
Dist - WMEN

Pain - Sleep Series
Nature of Pain, Pt 1 17 MIN
Nature of Pain, Pt 2 19 MIN
The Nature of Sleep 89 FRS
Pain - Nursing Action, Pt 1 76 FRS
Pain - Nursing Action, Pt 2 86 FRS
Sleep - Nursing Action 89 FRS
Dist - CONMED

Painful Confession 30 MIN
16mm
Color (H C R)
LC 70-715497
A dramatization about a hit - and - run accident and the ensuing guilt of the person who committed it to show the importance of God's forgiveness.
Fine Arts; Guidance and Counseling; Religion and Philosophy; Sociology
Dist - CPH **Prod** - CPH 1968

Painful Reminder 69 MIN
16mm
Color (G)
Presents an independent production by S Morrison. Recalls the liberation of the Nazi concentration camps during World War II.
Civics and Political Systems; Fine Arts; History - World
Dist - FIRS

A Painful reminder 69 MIN
16mm / VHS
Color (G)
$995.00, $450.00 purchase, $110.00 rental
Features the actual moments in which Nazi concentration camp prisoners were liberated. Includes interviews with survivors. These Allied films were hidden from the public eye for 40 years and finally assembled with Alfred Hitchcock's help. Produced by Granada International.
Fine Arts; History - World
Dist - FIRS

The Painful Step 19 MIN
16mm
Doctors at Work Series
B&W (H C A)
LC FIA65-1356
Uses drawings of the foot's anatomy and X - rays to explain the cause of bunions. Shows the corrective surgery for a bunion condition. Demonstrates procedures for correction of the foot from the initial binding of the foot to the final excision of bone and closing sutures.
Health and Safety
Dist - LAWREN **Prod** - CMA 1961

Paint 101 MIN
VHS
Color (S)
$29.95 purchase _ #781 - 9046
Teaches how to see with a 'painter's eye.' Features painter and art historian John Fitzmaurice Mills who shows the basic techniques and materials used by artists, and explores the problems faced by a painter translating reality onto canvas.
Fine Arts
Dist - FI **Prod** - BBCTV 1989

Paint 15 MIN
U-matic / VHS
Primary Art Series
Color (P)
Demonstrates various painting techniques and the uses of a variety of painting tools. Shows a group of primary level children at a painting party.
Fine Arts
Dist - AITECH **Prod** - WETATV

Paint 14 MIN
U-matic / VHS / 16mm
Color
Deals with paint and painting, both artistic and commercial.
Fine Arts
Dist - KAWVAL **Prod** - KAWVAL

Paint 5 MIN
16mm
Color; B&W (G)
$15.00 rental
Presents a study of light, form and movement.
Fine Arts
Dist - CANCIN **Prod** - HUDINA 1971

Paint an Exciting Picture Without a Brush 59 MIN
VHS / BETA
Children's Crafts Series
Color (K P)
Shows how to paint with materials such as string, cotton swabs and rollers.
Fine Arts
Dist - MOHOMV **Prod** - MOHOMV

Paint Engravings 15 MIN
U-matic / VHS
Young at Art Series
Color (P I)
Discusses paint engravings.
Fine Arts
Dist - AITECH **Prod** - WSKJTV 1980

Paint Gun Operation 18 MIN
BETA / VHS / 16mm
Color (A PRO)
$81.00 purchase _ #KAB03
Covers common paint gun problems and adjustment.
Industrial and Technical Education
Dist - RMIBHF **Prod** - RMIBHF

Paint Like a Professional 30 MIN
VHS / 16mm
Build Your Own Series
Color (H C A PRO)
$15.00 purchase _ #TA220
Demonstrates interior and exterior painting.
Home Economics; Industrial and Technical Education
Dist - AAVIM **Prod** - AAVIM 1990

Paint Me a Mood 10 MIN
U-matic / VHS
Book, Look and Listen Series
Color (K P)
Points out that moods can be created or induced by external forces.
English Language; Literature and Drama
Dist - AITECH **Prod** - MDDE 1977

Paint Me a Story 15 MIN
VHS / 16mm
Native Imagery Series
Color (I)
$200.00 purchase _ #283503
Introduces the rich traditions as well as the new directions of Native North American imagery in contemporary visual art. Includes commentary from artists in the series. 'Paint Me A Story' reveals different aspects of telling a story with visual art. Shows how artists paint or draw pictures to illustrate legends and how symbols in paintings can tell stories. Uses the example of the traditional winter count as an example of how Native Americans used pictures to record events in the past.
Fine Arts; Social Science
Dist - ACCESS **Prod** - ACCESS 1988

Paint Prep 30 MIN
VHS
Color (H C A PRO)
$20.00 purchase _ #TP100
Shows how to use simple tools for a prepaint prep job on an automobile. Demonstrates how to remove chrome and door handles, repair dings, sand, prime and glaze, as well as tips for detailing after the paint job.
Industrial and Technical Education
Dist - AAVIM **Prod** - AAVIM 1990

Paint Safety 10 MIN
BETA / VHS
Color (A PRO)
$59.75 purchase _ #AB160
Deals with auto body repair. Explains the hazards involved in painting and what precautions should be practiced. Shows the proper use of paint respirators.
Industrial and Technical Education
Dist - RMIBHF **Prod** - RMIBHF

Paint series program 10
Abstract painting 25 MIN
Dist - FI

Paint Series Program 1
Beginning a Still Life 25 MIN
Dist - FI

Paint Series Program 4
Perspective and Painting with a Knife 25 MIN
Dist - FI

Paint Series Program 5
Painting Outdoors 25 MIN
Dist - FI

Paint Series Program 6
Wash Techniques of Painting 25 MIN
Dist - FI

Paint Series Program 7
Painting from Photographs 25 MIN
Dist - FI

Paint Series Program 8
How to Tackle an Interior View 25 MIN
Dist - FI

Paint series
Completing a still life 25 MIN
Completing an interior view 25 MIN
Flower painting 25 MIN
Dist - FI

Paint Stripping Hints 30 MIN
VHS / BETA
This Old House, Pt 1 - the Dorchester Series

Color
Shows work on the deck of an old house underway, and offers hints on paint stripping. Introduces an alternative to ceramic wall tile around a bathtub.
Industrial and Technical Education; Sociology
Dist - CORF **Prod** - WGBHTV

Paint the Rain 10 MIN
16mm
Color
LC 74-702880
Presents a dramatization about a young mental patient's brief escape from the bleakness of his surroundings. Shows how the palette and canvas of an old artist become the vehicles which carry him momentarily into a world of life and color.
Fine Arts; Health and Safety; Psychology
Dist - BROSEB **Prod** - PANHAL 1974

Paint to Music 15 MIN
U-matic / VHS
Primary Art Series
Color (P)
Compares art and music explaining that the rhythm, movement, mood and pattern of music can be expressed in art by line, color, shape and texture.
Fine Arts
Dist - AITECH **Prod** - WETATV

Painted Day - Glo Smile 4 MIN
16mm
Color (H C)
Presents a visual interpretation of the Chad and Jeremy recording 'PAINTED DAY - GLO SMILE.'.
Fine Arts
Dist - CFS **Prod** - CFS 1958

Painted Landscapes of the Times 30 MIN
16mm
Color (G)
Presents an independent production by H Klodawsky. Explores the passionate art of Sue Coe and the nature of her pesonal and artistic vision.
Fine Arts
Dist - FIRS

The Painted poor 26 MIN
U-matic / VHS / 16mm
Color
Tells the story of love, regret and death. Describes how the marriage of John and Anne disintegrates when their farm becomes the dominant factor in John's life and Anne's existence is only lightened by the friendship of their neighbor, Stephen. During a blizzard Anne betrays her husband with Stephen only to quickly realize the horrifying implications of her betrayal. From the Sinclair Ross story.
Literature and Drama; Psychology; Sociology
Dist - BCNFL **Prod** - BCNFL 1985

The Painted Truck 28 MIN
16mm
Color (J)
LC 73-702756
Features an Afghanistani, multi - colored truck loaded with rice, soap, wheat, wood, melons and seasoned truck travelers making a rugged journey across the 12,700 foot Hajigak Pass from Kabul to Bamian. Views the unusual twists modernity creates in Afghanistan's culture and the inequity of the master - servant relationship.
Geography - World; Sociology
Dist - RADIM **Prod** - RADIM 1973

Painted wall finishes made easy 50 MIN
VHS
Color (H C G)
$34.95 purchase _ #FAU100V
Demonstrates step - by - step how to create decorative wall finishes. Shows seven different techniques, including sponge painting, dragging, rag painting, marbleizing and more.
Home Economics
Dist - CAMV

The Painter 8 MIN
U-matic / VHS / 16mm
Art of silence, pantomimes with Marcel Marceau series
Color (J H C)
LC 75-703449
Presents an interpretation of The Painter In Central Park by Marcel Marceau.
Fine Arts
Dist - EBEC **Prod** - EBEC 1975

Painter of the American West 55 MIN
16mm
Color (H C A)
LC 79-700594
Focuses on Olaf Wieghorst, artist of the American West, as he talks about his life and work.
Biography; Fine Arts
Dist - NOSMER **Prod** - NOSMER 1978

Painters and Pioneers 29 MIN
Videoreel / VT2
Museum Open House Series
Color
Fine Arts
Dist - PBS **Prod** - WGBHTV

Painters in the Modern World 20 MIN
U-matic / VHS / 16mm
Color (H C)
LC 70-707277
Presents three part - time artists and the ways in which they deal with the problems of painting in the context of today's world. Points out that they are typical of the artists of today who are free to choose their own subject and style, and who stand alone economically.
Fine Arts
Dist - IFB **Prod** - WONASO 1970

Painters of History - the Great American West 243 MIN
U-matic / VHS / 16mm
Color (K P I J H C G T A S R PRO IND)
Contains a series of 9 films from the prestigious collection of the Gilcreue Museum of History and Art. Contains striking studios of art works and original footage of the locations as they appear tody. The narration provides an accurate summation of the artists own words with current evaluation of the subjects in historical terms.
Fine Arts; History - United States
Dist - SF **Prod** - SF 1984

Painters Painting 116 MIN
16mm
Color
LC 74-701038
Illustrates and examines the work and ideas of several modern, abstract, expressionist painters, including Willem De Kooning, Jasper Johns, Robert Motherwell and Andy Warhol.
Fine Arts
Dist - NYFLMS **Prod** - NYFLMS 1973

Painter's world series
Abstraction 28 MIN
The Arrested moment 28 MIN
The Artist and the nude 27 MIN
Painting and the public - patronage, museums and the art market 27 MIN
Portraits 28 MIN
The Training of painters 28 MIN
Dist - CORF

Painter/Sculptor/Welder, Gerald Scheck 29 MIN
U-matic / VHS
Creativity with Bill Moyers Series
Color (H C A)
Explores the painter's sense of purpose and his unconscious drives and feelings.
Fine Arts; Psychology
Dist - PBS **Prod** - CORPEL 1982

Painting 15 MIN
U-matic / VHS
Art cart series
Color (P I)
LC 79-708039
Shows how to use flat and round brushes and tempura paint. Demonstrates color mixing and shading.
Fine Arts
Dist - AITECH **Prod** - WBRATV 1979

Painting 15 MIN
U-matic / VHS
Expressions
(I J)
$130 purchase, $25 rental, $75 self dub
Designed to interest fifth through ninth graders in art. Emphasizes creativity and experimentation. Features painter Pegge Hopper explaining technique. Fifth in an 18 part series.
Fine Arts
Dist - GPN

Painting - 3 28 MIN
U-matic / VHS
Think new series
Color (C G)
$129.00, $99.00 purchase _ #V578
Gives theoretical motivation and practical ideas about painting. Draws content from mathematics, science, history, human feelings, every human endeavor. Part of an 11 - part series that treats art as an essential mode of learning.
Fine Arts
Dist - BARR **Prod** - CEPRO 1991

Painting a Panelled Door 14 MIN
U-matic / VHS
Color (H C A)
Shows dusting, cleaning and knotting, preparation of the primer, application of the primer, stopping and filling, the undercoat and the final coat.
Home Economics; Industrial and Technical Education
Dist - SF **Prod** - SF

Painting - a Visual Record 18 MIN
16mm / U-matic / VHS
Humanities Series
Color (J H C)
LC 73-714124
Presents an introduction to painting.
Fine Arts
Dist - MGHT **Prod** - MGHT 1971

Painting and decorating 10 MIN
VHS
Skills - occupational programs series
Color (H C)
$49.00 purchase, $15.00 rental _ #316618; LC 91-712442
Features an industrial painter, a sign painter, a decorator, a commercial painter and a custom finisher. Part of a series that features occupations in the skilled trades, in service industries, and in business leading to careers in areas of demand and future growth. Includes teacher's guide with reproducible worksheets.
Guidance and Counseling; Home Economics; Psychology
Dist - TVOTAR **Prod** - TVOTAR 1990

Painting and Decorating - Paperhanging Application 14 MIN
16mm
Color (H C A)
Shows paste preparation, commercial and individual mixes, paper fitting, pattern and paper matching, applying paste, pasting the wall, lapping and butt joints. Starting and finishing points in a room, plumb line and chalk marks. Fitting around doors and windows, smoothing out bubbles, achieving a professional finish.
Home Economics
Dist - SF **Prod** - SF

Painting and Decorating - Paperhanging Preparation 14 MIN
16mm
Color (H C A)
Shows the various methods of cutting wallpaper. Depicts the needed equipment, such as shears, rollers, smoothing utensils, and the various types of knives. Describes the paster process, preparation of the wall, filling cracks, removing old paint or calcimine, stripping old paper and wall sizing.
Home Economics
Dist - SF **Prod** - SF

Painting and Decorating - the Art of Painting a Door 14 MIN
16mm
Color (H C A)
Shows dusting, cleaning and knotting, preparation of the primer, application of the primer, stopping and filling, the undercoat and the final coat.
Home Economics; Industrial and Technical Education
Dist - SF **Prod** - SF

Painting and Possessions 25 MIN
U-matic / VHS / 16mm
Ways of Seeing Series
Color (H C A)
LC 77-701960
Presents art critic John Berger, who discusses paintings as material possessions and how paintings and advertising present objects in a way which makes people want to possess them.
Business and Economics; Fine Arts; Psychology
Dist - FI **Prod** - BBCTV 1974

Painting and Staining - Spray and Roller Painting, Staining Wood 30 MIN
BETA / VHS
Wally's Workshop Series
Color
Home Economics; Industrial and Technical Education
Dist - KARTES **Prod** - KARTES

Painting and the public - patronage, museums and the art market 27 MIN
U-matic / 16mm / VHS
Painter's world series
Color (H C A)
$595.00, $250.00 purchase _ #HP - 6098C
Examines the factors which affect the appreciation and value of art. Visits an art auction at Sotheby's. Traces the development of patronage, museums and the art market from the Renaissance to the present through interviews with painters, dealers, collectors and museum directors. Includes the Louvre, Metropolitan Museum, Dulwich Collection, Beaubourg, the de Menil Collection and Soho. Part of a series on painters.
Fine Arts
Dist - CORF **Prod** - WGBHTV 1989

Painting and Wood graining - Volume 5 89 MIN
VHS
Collector car restoration home video libary series
Color (G)

$24.95 purchase
Shows how to select the right equipment, tools and supplies for painting and wood graining collector cars. Demonstrates that many tools and equipment can be improvised at very little cost. Illustrates techniques. Part five of a six - part series on classic car restoration.
Industrial and Technical Education
Dist - COLLEC **Prod** - COLLEC 1993

Painting Barns in Watercolor 50 MIN
VHS
Design and Watercolor Series
Color (J)
$29.95 purchase _ #VC - - 737
Presents a detailed drawing of barn buildings on location. Shows the use of a value sketch and preparation of watercolor paper. Part of a three - part series on design and watercolor by Tony Couch.
Fine Arts
Dist - CRYSP **Prod** - CRYSP

Painting by Numbers 60 MIN
U-matic / VHS / 16mm
Color (H C A)
Introduces the world of computer graphics, demonstrating how computers can be programmed to produce sophisticated Disney - like animated images. Interviews the engineer who invented the very first video game and the inventor of the first coin - operated arcade games.
Mathematics
Dist - FI **Prod** - BBCTV 1982

Painting - Creating a Point of View 30 MIN
U-matic
Humanities through the Arts with Maya Angelou Series Lesson 19; Lesson 19
Color (C A)
Explores major elements of painting. Shows how color can have sensory impact. Illustrates specific points about elements of painting by looking at the work of such artists as Monet, Delacroix and El Greco.
Fine Arts
Dist - CDTEL **Prod** - COAST

Painting - Drawing - Stasack 11 MIN
16mm
Color (H C)
Features artist Stasack revealing his personal approach to art which brought him acclaim in his field.
Fine Arts
Dist - CINEPC **Prod** - CINEPC

Painting from Photographs 25 MIN
U-matic / VHS
Paint Series Program 7
Color (H C A)
Fine Arts
Dist - FI **Prod** - BBCTV

Painting in America - Copley to Audubon 21 MIN
16mm
Color (J)
A survey of 18th - century art in America from Copley to Audubon.
Fine Arts
Dist - RADIM **Prod** - DETRIA 1957

Painting in monochrome 30 MIN
VHS
Color (G)
PdS19.95 purchase _ #A4-ARG05
Introduces viewer to tone, shape, and contrast. Provides drawing that viewer traces and paints along with the artist Walter Roberts to learn about brush techniques, tone and texture, and light and shade. Notes that experienced artists can paint subjects of their choice.
Fine Arts
Dist - AVP **Prod** - ARGUS

Painting in the South - Artists and Regional Heritage 28 MIN
16mm
Color
Presents a program based on the exhibition organized by the Virginia Museum, comprised of paintings and drawings, along with interviews of artists represented in the exhibition.
Fine Arts
Dist - MTP **Prod** - PHILMO

Painting - Landscape into Landscape 145 MIN
U-matic
University of the Air Series
Color (J H C A)
$750.00 purchase, $250.00 rental
Looks at the artist's translation of landscape into painting. Program contains a series of five cassettes 29 minutes each.
Fine Arts
Dist - CTV **Prod** - CTV 1978

Painting Marge Ann 29 MIN
U-matic
Artist at Work Series
Color
Gives a lesson in the flexibility of oil paint.
Fine Arts
Dist - UMITV **Prod** - UMITV 1973

Painting Movement and Color with Chalk 11 MIN
U-matic / VHS / 16mm
Color (I J H)
Points out that by making abstractions of situations in life, in large forms, with chalk as the medium, the student need not have skill in representational drawing, but can easily reach an understanding of rhythm and color in art.
Fine Arts
Dist - IFB **Prod** - ISU 1958

Painting on Copper 5 MIN
16mm
Screen news digest series; Vol 4; Issue 10
B&W (J H)
Shows the thousand - year - old relics of the Maya civilization in the jungles of Honduras. Presents the works of artist Arturo Lopez - Rodezno, who finds the inspiration for his copper enamellings in the Mayan stone sculptures. Shows his copper enamelling technique.
Fine Arts; Geography - World; History - World
Dist - HEARST **Prod** - HEARST 1962

Painting operations 14 MIN
BETA / VHS / U-matic
Hazard communication series
Color (IND G)
$395.00 purchase _ #820 - 13
Informs employees of the potentially hazardous ingredients used in paints, the health hazards including routes of entry, physical hazards, appropriate work practices and emergency procedures. Emphasizes the importance of consulting the Material Safety Data Sheet - MSDS - for complete physical and health hazard information on the hazardous ingredients of paints. Part of a series on hazard communication.
Health and Safety; Industrial and Technical Education; Psychology
Dist - ITSC **Prod** - ITSC

Painting Outdoors 30 MIN
VHS / 16mm
Focus on Watercolor Series
Color (C A)
$85.00, $75.00 purchase _ 21 - 05
Demonstrates painting outdoors with creative spontaneity, pouring paint, sight - size drawing, setting up outdoors.
Fine Arts
Dist - CDTEL **Prod** - COAST 1987

Painting Outdoors 25 MIN
VHS / U-matic
Paint Series Program 5
Color (H C A)
Fine Arts
Dist - FI **Prod** - BBCTV

Painting People 28 MIN
16mm
Color (H C A)
LC FIA67-5960
Several contempory Australian portrait painters discuss their styles of painting and the problems involved in their work.
Fine Arts
Dist - AUIS **Prod** - ANAIB 1966

Painting Pictures about People 13 MIN
U-matic / VHS / 16mm
Color (J H)
Encourages experimentation and inventiveness in painting by using the activities of people in real life.
Fine Arts
Dist - IFB **Prod** - IFB 1957

Painting Potential 24 MIN
VHS / U-matic
Discovering Physics Series
Color (H C)
Introduces the physical science concepts of field and potential by demonstrating the relationships between those concepts as well as their application. Shows computer assisted mapping of gradiant and distance, relationships between force and energy, and electrostatic spray painting to explain how charged terminals form a pattern in chemical powder.
Science; Science - Physical
Dist - MEDIAG **Prod** - BBCTV 1983

Painting Rocks and Surf Action 60 MIN
U-matic
E John Robinson Fine Art Instruction Series
Color (A)
Teaches the process of painting rocks in an active surf using oils. Explains the structure, color and texture of rocks and how they relate to the surf action.
Fine Arts
Dist - CANSTU **Prod** - CANSTU

Painting - Rousseau - the Lovely Dream 30 MIN
U-matic
Humanities through the Arts with Maya Angelou Series Lesson 20; Lesson 20
Color (C A)
Examines what are known as the innocent and poetic works of Henri Rousseau. Offers a biography of Rousseau as a framework within which the artist and his works can be understood.
Fine Arts
Dist - CDTEL **Prod** - COAST

Painting Streams, Rocks, and Trees in Watercolor 55 MIN
VHS
Design and Watercolor Series
Color (J)
$29.95 purchase _ #VC - - 738
Shows step - by - step how to paint streams, rocks and trees in watercolor. Includes close - up views of brush strokes and palette. Part of a three - part series on design and watercolor by Tony Couch.
Fine Arts
Dist - CRYSP **Prod** - CRYSP

Painting Surf and Foam Patterns 60 MIN
U-matic
E John Robinson Fine Art Instruction Series
Color (A)
Demonstrates how to paint foam patterns over the surf in oils.
Fine Arts
Dist - CANSTU **Prod** - CANSTU

Painting that fools the eye - trompe l'oeil 32 MIN
35mm strip / VHS
Color (J H C T A)
$93.00 purchase _ #MB - 540800 - 7, #MB - 512526 - 9
Examines the trompe l'oeil painting genre, which uses highly realistic illusions. Reveals the secrets behind the genre.
Fine Arts
Dist - SRA **Prod** - SRA 1988

Painting - the Creative Process 15 MIN
16mm / U-matic / VHS
Color (J)
LC 79-700922
Features artist Reginald Pollack and shows a painting from conception to completion. Conveys the idea that a work of art comes from the artist's mastery of tools and materials, his factual and visual information, his emotions and moods, and his knowledge of all past art.
Fine Arts
Dist - PHENIX **Prod** - KAHANA 1967

Painting the English village 50 MIN
VHS
Color (G)
PdS19.95 purchase _ #A4-ARG07
Concentrates on buildings and street scenes to teach principles that can be applied to both rural and urban situations. Features Walter Roberts, who explains the theory of perspective and how to apply it in this kind of composition. Notes that the knowledge is handy for recording holiday, travel, and other memories.
Fine Arts
Dist - AVP **Prod** - ARGUS

Painting the Sea at Sunset 60 MIN
U-matic
E John Robinson Fine Art Instruction Series
Color (A)
Explains how to paint a sunset at sea in oils. Shows brush selection, color mixing and application.
Fine Arts
Dist - CANSTU **Prod** - CANSTU

Painting - Things We have Passed 30 MIN
U-matic
Humanities through the Arts with Maya Angelou Series Lesson 21; Lesson 21
Color (C A)
Discusses criticism in painting. Focuses on abstract painting and reactions to it. Includes painter Glen White and Maya Angelou.
Fine Arts
Dist - CDTEL **Prod** - COAST

Painting Time 8 MIN
16mm
Exploring Childhood Series
Color (J)
LC 76-701894
Shows a four - year - old using his already developed abilities in making lines and shapes. Provides strong data for exploring ways in which children continually teach themselves.
Psychology
Dist - EDC **Prod** - EDC 1974

Painting - Visions through the Ages 30 MIN
U-matic
Humanities through the Arts with Maya Angelou Series Lesson 18; Lesson 18

Color (C A)
Demonstrates how humans from diverse cultures and different times have expressed in two - dimensional forms their unique perceptions of the world around them. Shows several artists' work.
Fine Arts
Dist - CDTEL **Prod** - COAST

Painting with a limited palette 40 MIN
VHS
Color (G)
PdS19.95 purchase _ #A4-ARG06
Introduces viewer to advanced use of watercolor, including choosing the right colors for the palette, mixing them, and applying them to a landscape subject. Features Walter Roberts, who demonstrates and leads the exercise. Notes that experienced artists can paint subjects of their choice.
Fine Arts
Dist - AVP **Prod** - ARGUS

Painting with guitar - loops, delays, harmonizers and other sonic alternatives - Video One 60 MIN
VHS
Painting with guitar series
Color (G)
$49.95 purchase _ #VD - TOR - GT01
Features guitarist David Torn. Demonstrates basic equipment set - up for maximum sonic impact, using pick - ups, switches, tone controls and Torn's innovative 'TransTrem' whammy bar. Details the use of channel switching amplifiers for tone - shaping, use of foot - pedal devices and signal - processing gear. Part one of a two - part series.
Fine Arts
Dist - HOMETA **Prod** - HOMETA

Painting with guitar - loops, delays, harmonizers and other sonic alternatives - Video Two 70 MIN
VHS
Painting with guitar series
Color (G)
$49.95 purchase _ #VD - TOR - GT02
Features guitarist David Torn. Covers delay - based effects and looping components to build textures, colors, sound washes, orchestral effects and other 'sonic alternatives.' Includes time - delay devices, echo and reverb units, effects pedals, pitch and phase shifting and other electronic equipment for sound layering. Looks at the essentials for film scores, orchestration, record production sweetening and live performance. Part two of a two - part series.
Fine Arts
Dist - HOMETA **Prod** - HOMETA

Painting with guitar series
Presents a two - part series featuring guitarist David Torn. Looks at basic equipment for maximum sonic impact using pick - ups, switches tone controls and the 'whammy bar' in Video One. Covers delay - based effects and looping components to build textures, colors, sound washes, orchestral effects and other 'sonic alternatives,' time - delay devices, echo and reverb units, effects pedals, pitch and phase shifting and other electronic equipment for sound layering in Video Two.
Painting with guitar - loops, delays, harmonizers and other sonic alternatives - Video One 60 MIN
Painting with guitar - loops, delays, harmonizers and other sonic alternatives - Video Two 70 MIN
Dist - HOMETA **Prod** - HOMETA

Painting with Light 15 MIN
16mm
Color (G)
_ #106C 0178 497
Documents the processes involved in the making of stained glass art through the work of artist Robert Jekyll.
Fine Arts
Dist - CFLMDC **Prod** - NFBC 1978

Painting with light 80 MIN
VHS
Color (G)
$39.95 purchase _ #S02083
Presents artwork done using the Quantel Paint Box, a graphics machine. Shows how artists David Hockney, Howard Hodgkin, Jennifer Bartlett and Larry Rivers combined efforts on a major work using the Quantel Paint Box.
Fine Arts; Industrial and Technical Education
Dist - UILL

Painting with Words 10 MIN
U-matic / VHS / 16mm
Color (P I J) (SPANISH)
LC 79-706478
Illustrates the expansion of a 'kernel' sentence, with emphasis on the correct placing of added words in a sentence.
English Language; Foreign Language
Dist - AIMS **Prod** - ASSOCF 1970

Painting Without a Brush 59 MIN
VHS / 16mm
Children's Crafts Series
(K P)
$39.00 purchase _ #VT1126
Demonstrates different ways to paint pictures without a brush. Teaches how to mix certain colors to form new ones, using wet chalk and paints. Also teaches what symmetry means. Taught by Julie Abowitt, Multi - Arts Coordinator for the Seattle Public Schools.
Fine Arts
Dist - RMIBHF **Prod** - RMIBHF

Paintings and Plastics 12 MIN
16mm
Color
Presents James Davis, an American painter and sculptor in transparent plastics, opening new fields of art and design. Records his art in the collections of the Museum of Modern Art, other museums and private collections.
Fine Arts
Dist - RADIM **Prod** - DAVISJ

Paintings in the White House - a Close - Up 28 MIN
16mm
Color (J)
LC FIA68-1773
Surveys 47 paintings in the White House, picturing events of the last 150 years. Includes works by Stuart, Peale, Whistler and Sargent. Presents an introduction by Mrs Lyndon B Johnson.
Fine Arts; Geography - United States
Dist - MLA **Prod** - WEC 1965

Paintings of L S Lowry 60 MIN
VHS
Color (G)
PdS19.95 purchase _ #A4-MC4
Guides the viewer through the L S Lowry collection in Salford Art Gallery. Features narration by Harold Riley. Produced by Master Class.
Fine Arts
Dist - AVP

Paintings - Rx for Survival, Pt 1 20 MIN
16mm
Color (H)
Covers the conservation basics relative to the care and handling of oil paintings. Describes the delicate physical makeup of an oil painting, the harm that may come to a painting while hanging or being hung, how a layman can check for signs of deterioration and decay, how to physically carry a painting, how a professional conservator cleans the surface and describes first - aid procedures in case of major or minor damage.
Fine Arts
Dist - HAMPRO **Prod** - HAMPRO 1980

Paintings - Rx for Survival, Pt 2 20 MIN
16mm
Color (H)
Covers the conservation basics relative to the care and handling of oil paintings. Describes the delicate physical makeup of an oil painting, the harm that may come to a painting while hanging or being hung, how a layman can check for signs of deterioration and decay, how to physically carry a painting, how a professional conservator cleans the surface and describes first - aid procedures in case of major or minor damage.
Fine Arts
Dist - HAMPRO **Prod** - HAMPRO 1980

Paintings - the Permanent Collection of the Art Institute of Chicago 58 MIN
VHS / 16mm
Color (G)
$70.00 rental _ #PTPC - 000
Takes a comprehensive look at over 200 paintings in the Chicago Art Institute's permanent collection and overviews the founding and history of the Institute.
Fine Arts
Dist - PBS **Prod** - WTTWTV

A Pair of Mocassins - Une Paire De Mocassins by Mary Thomas 15 MIN
16mm
Color (G) (FRENCH)
#2X80 I
Details the many different types of Indian mocassins and how they are made.
Social Science
Dist - CDIAND **Prod** - NAIFL 1977

A Pair of Red Clogs 15 MIN
VHS / U-matic
Magic Pages Series
Color (P)
Literature and Drama
Dist - AITECH **Prod** - KLVXTV 1976

Pairs 1 MIN
16mm
B&W (A)
$7.00 rental
Appears to present many images of female flesh at very high cutting speeds. Explains its maker, Gorman Bechard, 'comic delight.'
Fine Arts
Dist - CANCIN

Pak Bueng on fire 25 MIN
VHS / U-matic
Color (G) (ENGLISH AND THAI)
$125.00 purchase, $50.00 rental
Presents a fresh look into the struggle of first generation Thai immigrants in Los Angeles. Focuses on two friends, a student who needs tuition money and another who supports himself by gambling and working in a small grocery store, playing cat - and - mouse with the INS. Directed and written by Supachai Surongsain. With English subtitles.
History - United States; Sociology
Dist - CROCUR **Prod** - VISCOM 1987

Pak Menggung - a Javanese Aristocrat 21 MIN
16mm
Asian Neighbors - Indonesia Series
Color (H C A)
LC 75-703585
Examines the life of a Javanese aristocrat who devotes his life to recording the disappearing traditions and ceremonies of his culture.
Geography - World; Social Science
Dist - AVIS **Prod** - FLMAUS 1975

Paka's 15 MIN
VHS / U-matic
Teletales Series
Color (P)
$125.00 purchase
Presents a children's fable from Hawaii.
Education; Literature and Drama
Dist - AITECH **Prod** - POSIMP 1984

Pakistan - Children of the Road 26 MIN
U-matic / VHS
Growing Up Young Series
Color
Documents the lives of children in Pakistan.
Geography - World; Sociology
Dist - FOTH **Prod** - FOTH

Pakistan - Land of Promise 15 MIN
16mm
Color
LC 76-703714
Surveys the relief effort of the U S government and other international sources in helping Pakistan increase food production and improve health conditions, emphasizing the role of the U S Agency for International Development. Recounts Pakistan's efforts to reduce its birthrate by at least 20 percent by 1978.
Geography - World; Health and Safety; History - World; Social Science; Sociology
Dist - USNAC **Prod** - USAID 1976

Pakistan - Mound of the Dead 27 MIN
U-matic / VHS / 16mm
People and Places of Antiquity Series
Color (J)
LC 77-703105
Presents a shortened version of the motion picture entitled Mound Of The Dead. Concentrates on the partially excavated site of Mohenjo - daro and its architectural brick remains which date from 2300 - 1700 BC.
Geography - World; History - World; Sociology
Dist - CORF **Prod** - CFDLD 1977

Pakistani Chapli Kebabs and Pearl Barley and Nuts 28 MIN
VHS / U-matic
Color (PRO)
Shows how to saute pine nuts and cook them with ground lamb and serve in pita bread with barley.
Home Economics; Industrial and Technical Education
Dist - CULINA **Prod** - CULINA

Pal Joey 109 MIN
16mm
Color (C A)
Stars Rita Hayworth, Frank Sinatra and Kim Novak in the story of a night - club entertainer, a heel with a heart of gold, and two women, a beautiful socialite who responds to his rowdy appeal and a beautiful chorine who teaches him that he has a heart after all. Presents a score by Rogers and Hart, including songs 'BEWITCHED, BOTHERED AND BEWILDERED,' 'I DIDN'T KNOW WHAT TIME IT WAS' and 'THE LADY IS A TRAMP.'.
Fine Arts
Dist - TIMLIF **Prod** - CPC 1957

Palace Cars and Paradise 28 MIN
16mm
Color
Presents the story of the Pullman model town, created in the 1880s by George Pullman as the ideal industrial community.
Sociology
Dist - ILHS **Prod** - ILHS

Palace of Delights 58 MIN
16mm / U-matic / VHS
Nova Series
Color
Visits San Francisco's Exploratorium, a hands - on science museum dedicated to the joys of curiosity and understanding.
Science; Science - Natural; Science - Physical
Dist - TIMLIF **Prod** - WGBHTV 1982

Palaces of pleasure 30 MIN
VHS
Hurray for today series
Color; PAL (G)
PdS25
Examines exotic buildings in the United Kingdom to illustrate changes in British architecture in recent years. Features Lucinda Lambton, an architectural photographer for over 20 years. Part of a six - part series studying architectural changes in Britain from the grim years of modernization, comprehensive redevelopment and concrete blocks to a new age of beautiful and exciting modern buildings.
Fine Arts; Geography - World; History - World
Dist - ACADEM

Palaces of Reason and Delight - Pt 2 58 MIN
VHS
Treasure Houses of Britain Series
Color (S)
$29.95 purchase _ #362 - 9017
Transports the viewer to some of Great Britain's most magnificent houses from the fifteenth century to the twentieth. Features John Julius Norwich as narrator who interviews current owners to reveal the privileges and the problems of living in an historic house. Part 2 of the three - part series features an unprecedented view of Blenheim Palace, Houghton Hall, Bowhill, Newark Castle, Drumlanrig Castle, Boughton House, West Wycombe Park, St Lawrence Church in West Wycombe and Syon House.
Fine Arts; Geography - World; History - World
Dist - FI **Prod** - NATLGL 1989

Palaeolithic Society 20 MIN
U-matic / VHS
Color (I J H C G)
Details the lives of people of the Lower, Middle and Upper Palaeolithic eras. Utilizes archaeological evidence, including cave paintings, students making flint artifacts, and the study of primitive ethnic groups in Africa and Australia from which possible parallels may be deduced.
History - World; Sociology
Dist - VIEWTH **Prod** - GATEEF

The Palaeontologist 15 MIN
VHS / 16mm
Harriet's Magic Hats IV Series
Color (P)
$175.00 purchase _ #207145
Presents thirteen new programs to familiarize children with more workers and their role in community life. Features Aunt Harriet's bottomless trunks of magic hats where Carrie has only to put on a particular hat to be whisked off to investigate the person and the role represented by the hat. 'The Palaeontologist' reveals that Ralph has dug up what looks like a dinosaur tooth. Ralph suggests that Carrie visit Darrell, the paleontologist. Carrie meets Darrell in the museum where he explains to her the steps involved in recovering, rebuilding and displaying dinosaur fossils.
Guidance and Counseling; Psychology; Science - Natural; Science - Physical
Dist - ACCESS **Prod** - ACCESS 1986

The Palatal Flap in Periodontics 13 MIN
16mm
Color
LC 74-705287
Demonstrates the surgical management of osseous deformities involving the palatal and proximal periodontal areas. Shows how a palatal flap is created using an internal beveled incision, thus preserving the remaining attached gingiva and permitting access to the underlying alveolar process.
Health and Safety; Science - Natural
Dist - USNAC **Prod** - USVA 1968

The Palate 19 MIN
U-matic
Microanatomy Laboratory Orientation Series
Color (C)
Demonstrates the development of the palate in human embryos showing the lateral palatine processes from formation to the fusion in midline with the nasal septum.
Health and Safety; Science - Natural
Dist - UOKLAH **Prod** - UOKLAH 1986

Palawan 15 MIN
16mm
Color (DANISH)
A Danish language film. Portrays daily life in a small community on the philippine Island Palawan. Shows housebuilding, primitive farming and preparation of a meal.
Foreign Language; Geography - World
Dist - STATNS **Prod** - STATNS 1963

Palazzo Giustiniani, Venice 26 MIN
U-matic / VHS / 16mm
Place in Europe Series
Color (H C A)
Describes how this last of the palazzos, which was originally financed by merchants of Venice, is now maintained by receipts from a section that has been turned into flats by the only living descendant of the family. Descendants of original merchant families meet weekly for coffee.
Geography - World
Dist - MEDIAG **Prod** - THAMES 1975

Palazzolo's Chicago 60 MIN
VHS
Color (G)
$50.00 purchase
Features four fun films on Chicago. Includes - Your Astronauts; Jerry's; The Tattooed Lady; Enjoy Yourself, It's Later Than You Think. The astronauts visit and America fantasizes about lift off. Visits Jerry the screaming deli owner and the local run - down amusement park where the tatooed lady tells her story. Joins an old - folks' picnic run by the Democratic Machine. See individual titles for more description and availability for rental in 16mm format.
Fine Arts
Dist - CANCIN **Prod** - PALAZT

Palazzolo's underground shorts from the '60s 75 MIN
VHS
Color (G)
$75.00 purchase
Includes - He; O; The Bride Stripped Bare; Love It - Leave It; Venus Adonis; and Campaign, produced between 1966 - 1973. See individual titles for description and availability for rental in 16mm format.
Fine Arts
Dist - CANCIN **Prod** - PALAZT

The Paleface 22 MIN
16mm
B&W (J)
Stars Buster Keaton.
Fine Arts
Dist - TWYMAN **Prod** - MGM 1921

Palenque - Mayan history
VHS
Color (J H G) (SPANISH)
$44.95 purchase _ #MCV5003, #MCV5004
Presents a program on the history of the Maya of Mexico.
History - World; Social Science
Dist - MADERA **Prod** - MADERA

The Paleolithic Society 21 MIN
U-matic / VHS / 16mm
Color (J)
Appraises the lives of the people of the lower, middle and upper Paleolithic eras by traditional archaeology, examination of artifacts and habitation sites, and the study of primitive societies in Africa and Australia from which possible parallels may be deduced.
History - World; Science - Physical
Dist - LUF **Prod** - LUF 1980

Palestine
VHS
About the United Nations series
Color (J H C G)
$29.95 purchase _ #UNE91129V - S
Covers the complex and emotional issue of Palestine. Offers a balanced insight into the plight of the Palestinian people and the multilateral effort to bring peace to this troubled region. Part of a seven - part series on the United Nations.
Civics and Political Systems
Dist - CAMV **Prod** - UN

Palestine - Abdication 86 MIN
16mm / U-matic / VHS
Palestine Series
Color (H C A)
Tells how the United Nations partitioned Palestine but could not enforce its policy. Shows how Jews and Arabs resorted to terrorism and massacre, resulting in the siege of Jerusalem.
History - World
Dist - MEDIAG **Prod** - THAMES 1978

Palestine Liberation Organization 28 MIN
Videoreel / VHS
International Byline Series
Color
Interviews Mr Zehdi Terzi, permanent observer to the United Nations, about the position and objectives of the Palestinians. Hosted by Marilyn Perry and John Law, former Middle East editor of U S News And World Report.
Business and Economics; Civics and Political Systems; Geography - World
Dist - PERRYM **Prod** - PERRYM

Palestine - Promises 72 MIN
U-matic / VHS / 16mm
Palestine Series
Color (H C A)
Points out that Palestine, primarily populated by Arabs and placed under British supervision in 1914, is the location of Jerusalem, Holy City of Christians, Jews and followers of Islam. Shows how the decades of the 1920s and 1930s brought violence and social upheaval because of resettlement and rebellion.
History - World
Dist - MEDIAG **Prod** - THAMES 1978

Palestine - Rebellion 86 MIN
U-matic / VHS / 16mm
Palestine Series
Color (H C A)
Shows that the 1940s era in Palestine witnessed political and employment discrimination against Arabs and the emergence of Zionist forces demanding a homeland for Jews fleeing Hitler and looking to America for support. Points out that the resulting violence depleted Britain's patience and resources, culminating in Britain's withdrawal.
History - World
Dist - MEDIAG **Prod** - THAMES 1978

Palestine Series
Palestine - Abdication 86 MIN
Palestine - Promises 72 MIN
Palestine - Rebellion 86 MIN
Dist - MEDIAG

The Palestinian People do have Rights 48 MIN
U-matic / VHS / 16mm
Color (H C A)
LC 80-700478
Traces events in Palestine from 1947, when the United Nations recommended a partition of the region. Includes archival footage, maps, shots of refugee camps, and interviews with Palestinians.
Geography - World; History - World
Dist - ICARUS **Prod** - UN 1979

Palestinian portraits 22 MIN
16mm / VHS
Color (G)
$410.00, $230.00 purchase, $45.00 rental
Introduces a diverse group of women and men who shatter the simplistic and negative stereotypes of Palestinians as terrorists or refugees. Interviews expatriate clergy, both Muslim and Christian, neurosurgeons, ballet dancers and university professors, among the hundreds of thousands of Palestinians now working and living in the United States. A Simone de Bagno film.
Fine Arts
Dist - FIRS **Prod** - UN 1987

Palestinians 29 MIN
VHS / U-matic
Are you listening series
Color (H C A)
LC 84-706134
Dwells upon a number of Palestinians dispersed throughout the world as refugees. Describes their anguish in trying to keep their culture alive, and how they say they want to resolve the Israeli problem without destroying the Jewish nation, but offer no concrete formulas to accomplish this.
Geography - World; History - World; Sociology
Dist - STURTM **Prod** - STURTM 1983

Palette Knife Painting 29 MIN
16mm
Color
LC 73-702049
Presents a step - by - step demonstration of all the conventional aspects of rendering a landscape, from preparation of the white ground to mixing the basic color wheel and filling the overlapping planes of depth.
Fine Arts
Dist - NILLU **Prod** - NILLU 1973

A Palette of Glass 25 MIN
U-matic / VHS / 16mm
Color (J)
LC 79-700867
Documents the creation of Marc Chagalls' American windows, located in the Chagall Gallery of Chicago's Art Institute. Shows how appropriate glass is chosen and blown into colored sheets and how Chagall applies the grisaille, the painted decorations that give unity and dimension to the glass fragments.

Fine Arts
Dist - PHENIX **Prod** - ARTINC 1978

Palette series

The Astronomer 30 MIN
The Cheat with the ace of diamonds 30 MIN
The Feast in the House of Levi 30 MIN
Japanese bridges 30 MIN
Krater of Heracles and Antaeus 30 MIN
Liberty leading the people 30 MIN
Madonna, child and Saint Anne 30 MIN
Madonna with Chancellor Rolin 30 MIN
The Polyptych of San Francesco at Sansepolcro 30 MIN
Seaport at sunset 30 MIN
Self portraits 30 MIN
A Sunday on La Grande Jatte 30 MIN
The Turkish bath 30 MIN
Dist - PSU

Palimpsest and Palimpsest II 4 MIN
16mm / 8mm cartridge
Color; B&W (G)
$16.00 rental
Presents a pure celluloid sculpture. Notes that this is a double projection piece; contact Canyon Cinema for details.
Fine Arts
Dist - CANCIN **Prod** - RAYHER 1979

Palimpsest III 3 MIN
16mm
B&W (G)
$10.00 rental
Describes itself as calligraphy and the silver screen. Allows viewer to run at silent or sound speed.
Fine Arts
Dist - CANCIN **Prod** - RAYHER 1980

Palimpset periplum 5 MIN
16mm
B&W (G)
$10.00 rental
Evokes the 'periplum' or voyage on which experience is encountered directly. Considers the hero who sees many cities and manners of humans and knows their minds. He also enters the world of myth. From Pound's Canto LIX. Produced by Walter Henry.
Fine Arts
Dist - CANCIN

Palio 29 MIN
U-matic / VHS / 16mm
Color (H C A)
LC 76-702510
Shows an 18th - century political horse race still held in Siena, Italy, between 17 city districts.
Geography - World; History - World; Sociology
Dist - PHENIX **Prod** - PHENIX 1976

Palladio - Venetian villas and palazzos 28 MIN
VHS
Color (G)
$29.95 purchase _ #ACE13V - F
Shows the development of the Neoclassical style of architecture through adaptations from Greek and Roman styles to Renaissance forms, focusing on the works of Andrea Palladio seen in such locations as Vicenza and Venice.
Fine Arts
Dist - CAMV

Palm Beach Arts Festival 12 MIN
16mm
Color (I J H C)
LC FIA66-511
Highlights the annual Creative Arts Pageant in Palm Beach, Florida. Features ballerina Claudi Cravi.
Fine Arts; Geography - United States
Dist - FDC **Prod** - FDC 1965

Palm play 30 MIN
VHS / 16mm
Movement style and culture series
Color (H C G)
$600.00, $195.00 purchase, $45.00 rental _ #10460, #37250
Shows why people in some parts of the world dance with their palms completely covered or turned in while others openly present their palms to their partners. Explains the symbolism and cultural determinants of a universal dance element - palm gestures. Part of a series on movement style and culture.
Fine Arts; Sociology
Dist - UCEMC **Prod** - CHORP 1980

Palm Sunday 15 MIN
U-matic / VHS
Color
Mixes documentary footage with extravagant subtitles to create an experimental film.
Fine Arts
Dist - MEDIPR **Prod** - KROGST 1980

Palm Sunday and crucifixion - Tape 4 30 MIN
VHS
Jesus Christ series
Color (J H C G A)
$39.95 purchase, $10.00 rental _ #35 - 860569 - 1
Focuses on the events of Palm Sunday and Jesus' crucifixion.
Literature and Drama; Religion and Philosophy
Dist - APH **Prod** - ABINGP

Palm Sunday with the Disciples of Christ 58 MIN
U-matic / VHS
Color (A)
Presents a Palm Sunday worship at National City Christian Church in Washington, D C as it is presided over by Dr William C Howard, minister. Looks at the Disciples' emphasis on communion as well as National City's music program and the architectural grandeur of the church in the nation's capital.
Religion and Philosophy
Dist - ECUFLM **Prod** - NBCNEW 1982

Palm trees and icebergs 24 MIN
U-matic / VHS
Young people's specials series
Color
Shows reports by the youth of Alaska and Hawaii.
Geography - United States; Sociology
Dist - MULTPP **Prod** - MULTPP

Palmar Hand, the, Pt 1 14 MIN
16mm / U-matic / VHS
Cine - Prosector Series
Color
LC FIA68-365
Presents a demonstration of the anatomy of the palmar hand, its muscles, blood supply and nerves.
Health and Safety; Science - Natural
Dist - TEF **Prod** - TEF 1968

Palmar Hand, the, Pt 2 Intrinsic Muscles 14 MIN
16mm / U-matic / VHS
Cine - Prosector Series
Color
LC FIA68-366
Presents a demonstration of the anatomy of the intrinsic muscles of the palmar hand and their function.
Health and Safety; Science - Natural
Dist - TEF **Prod** - TEF 1968

The Palmetto 14 MIN
Videoreel / VT2
Images and Memories Series
Color
Features nature photographer Jim Bones celebrating the beauty of the palmetto.
Fine Arts; Industrial and Technical Education
Dist - PBS **Prod** - KERA

The Palpable Osler 33 MIN
U-matic / VHS
Color
Reviews Sir William Osler's life and contributions to clinical medicine, medical literature and the practice of humanistic medicine.
Biography; Science
Dist - USNAC **Prod** - USHHS

Pals 29 MIN
U-matic / VHS / 16mm
Footsteps Series
Color (A)
Focuses on peer groups and pressures through the dramatization of a situation in the fictional Riley family, in which young Ned questions the price he must pay for friendship. Includes a brief introduction and commentary by real - life families and child development experts.
Psychology; Sociology
Dist - USNAC **Prod** - USDED 1980

Pals 60 MIN
U-matic / VHS
Rainbow Movie of the Week Series
Color (J A)
Tells of four high school friends of various backgrounds who produce a local teen program via a public access channel and struggle to keep the show afloat after one of the group suddenly becomes ego - maniacal.
Psychology; Sociology
Dist - GPN **Prod** - RAINTV 1981

Pals 15 MIN
16mm
Color
LC 79-701184
Offers a look at day care programs for preschool children. Discusses the advantages for working parents and suggests how to evaluate existing programs.
Education; Sociology
Dist - VICTFL **Prod** - VICTFL 1979

Pamela Edwards - 5 - 22 - 75 17 MIN
VHS / Cassette
Poetry Center reading series
Color (G)
#134 - 101
Features the Academy of American Poets Contest winner reading from her works at the Poetry Center, San Francisco State University. Available only for listening purposes at the Center; not for sale or rent.
Literature and Drama
Dist - POETRY

Pamela Wong's Birthday for Grandma 8 MIN
U-matic / VHS / 16mm
Color; Captioned (P I)
$49.00 purchase _ #3502; LC 77-703271
Depicts a special event in the life of a Chinese - American family while showing various aspects of life in Chicago's Chinatown.
Sociology
Dist - EBEC **Prod** - LIFSTY 1977

Pamela's Tree 14 MIN
16mm
Color
LC 74-705288
Tells what help both large and small timber owners can obtain from their state forester to save their trees, through the story of Pamela, a tree farmer's daughter. Shows how her favorite tree becomes infested with bark beetles and how it is saved.
Agriculture; Science - Natural
Dist - USNAC **Prod** - USDA 1965

Pampas wildlife - Argentina - Part 9 8 MIN
VHS
Natures kingdom series
Color (P I J)
$125.00 purchase
Observes sheep, Chilean plovers, tinamoo and Patagonian hare and their neighbors on the short grass plains of Argentina. Shows also the armadillo and burrowing owl. Part of a 26 - part series on animals showing the habitats and traits of various species.
Geography - World; Science - Natural
Dist - LANDMK **Prod** - LANDMK 1992

Pamplona - the Running of the Bulls 10 MIN
U-matic / VHS
Color
Documents the running of the bulls in Pamplona, Spain.
Geography - World
Dist - JOU **Prod** - UPI

Pam's Story 11 MIN
U-matic / 16mm
CTV Reports Series
Color; Mono (J H C A)
$200.00 film, $200.00 video, $50.00 rental
Profiles children with serious illnesses and shows how they cope and what their futures may hold. Focuses on Pam Zilio who has cancer of the nervous system and is fighting for her life.
Health and Safety; Sociology
Dist - CTV **Prod** - CTV 1978

Pan Am's World 24 MIN
16mm
Color
LC 72-702324
Tells how Pan American Airways travels to most of the places people want to go, and that their employees work to make the trip a success when they get there. Shows activities that make running an international airline a full - time job.
Geography - World; Industrial and Technical Education; Social Science
Dist - PANWA **Prod** - PANWA 1972

Pan Am's World - Czechoslovakia 14 MIN
16mm
Color
A travel documentary that includes glimpses of the culture and history of Czechoslovakia.
Geography - World
Dist - PANWA **Prod** - PANWA

Pan Am's World - Romania 14 MIN
16mm
Color
Shows the routes of Pan Am Airways and the activities of the airline on a trip to Romania.
Geography - World
Dist - PANWA **Prod** - PANWA

Pan Fish I
BETA / VHS
Color
Shows how to catch Blue Gills, Crappie and Perch through the ice, as well as fall and winter patterns.
Physical Education and Recreation; Science - Natural
Dist - HOMEAF **Prod** - HOMEAF

Pan Pacific 22 MIN
16mm
Color
LC 80-700217
Traces the history of the Pan Pacific Auditorium in Hollywood, an example of streamline modern architecture. Raises the issue of whether the auditorium should be preserved or demolished.
Fine Arts
Dist - PELICN **Prod** - ASLA 1979

Panama 11 MIN
16mm / U-matic / VHS
Color (K P)
LC 82-700603
Tells the story of Little Bear and Little Tiger, who leave their comfortable home to go in search of Panama, the land of their dreams and end up in the most beautiful place in the world.
Literature and Drama
Dist - WWS **Prod** - WWS 1982

Panama Canal 3 MIN
16mm
Of all Things Series
Color (P I)
Discusses the Panama Canal.
Geography - World
Dist - AVED **Prod** - BAILYL

Panama Canal 17 MIN
U-matic / VHS / 16mm
Color
LC FIA63-1162
Depicts ships from the Pacific entering the canal and being lifted 85 feet by the Miraflores and Pedro Miguel Locks to Galliard Cut and Gatun Lake. The vessels are returned to sea level by the three giant locks at Gatun.
Geography - World
Dist - MCFI **Prod** - HOE 1962

The Panama Canal 32 MIN
VHS
Color (I J)
$89.00 purchase _ #RB838
Uses location photography, old photographs and movies to recreate the history of the Panama Isthmus and the digging of the 51 - mile - long Panama Canal.
Geography - World; History - United States; History - World
Dist - REVID **Prod** - REVID

The Panama Canal 11 MIN
VHS
Color; PAL (H)
Traces the history of the Panama Canal from its construction to the 1978 Treaty. Explains how the canal operates and its significance to world transportation. Travels through the canal and views the life in nearby cities.
Geography - World; History - World; Social Science
Dist - VIEWTH **Prod** - VIEWTH

Panama Canal 16 MIN
VHS / U-matic
B&W
Covers the construction and history of the Panama Canal. Interspersed with rare footage from the early 1900's.
Geography - World; History - World
Dist - KINGFT **Prod** - KINGFT

Panama Canal
VHS
Color (G A)
$39.80 purchase _ #0278
Joins the crew of the 51 foot ketch Limey Limey for a 4,000 mile journey from California through the Panama Canal to the San Blas Islands. Films sights along the Central American coastline.
Geography - World; Physical Education and Recreation
Dist - SEVVID

The Panama Canal 32 MIN
16mm / U-matic / VHS
Color
Recounts the history of the Isthmus and the task of digging a canal through Panama.
History - World
Dist - KAWVAL **Prod** - KAWVAL

Panama Canal, the 11 MIN
16mm / U-matic / VHS
Color
Traces the history of the Panama Canal from its construction to the 1978 treaty. Explains how the canal operates and its significance to world tranportation.
Geography - World; History - World; Social Science
Dist - CORF **Prod** - CORF 1978

Panama Canal - the Longest Shortcut 28 MIN
16mm / U-matic / VHS
Color (I)
Employs archival photographs, color maps, live footage and animation to recall the digging of the Panama Canal, one of man's greatest engineering achievements.
Geography - World; History - World
Dist - MCFI **Prod** - SWAIN

Panama Hats (Ecuador) 3 MIN
16mm
Of all Things Series
Color (P I)
Discusses the industry for Panama hats in the country of Ecuador.
Business and Economics
Dist - AVED **Prod** - BAILYL

Panama - the Fifth Frontier 78 MIN
16mm / U-matic / VHS
Captioned; B&W (A) (SPANISH (ENGLISH SUBTITLES))
Discusses the Panama Canal, its construction, the role of the U S, its operation and its social, political and economic impact.
Fine Arts; History - World
Dist - CNEMAG **Prod** - CUBAFI 1975

The Panare - Scenes from the Frontier 60 MIN
U-matic / VHS / 16mm
Worlds Apart Series
Color (J)
Argues that unless the Panare tribe of Venezuela are protected by legal title to their traditional hunting and fishing grounds, one more group of America's original inhabitants will fall victim to the process of national development. Explains that roads are being driven through their land, a huge mine is planned, and there are more and more cattle.
History - World; Sociology
Dist - FI **Prod** - BBCTV 1982

Pancakes 28 MIN
VHS / 16mm
What's Cooking Series
Color (G)
$55.00 rental _ #WHAC - 102
Home Economics
Dist - PBS **Prod** - WHYY

Pancakes with Surprises 9 MIN
16mm / U-matic / VHS
Color (K P)
LC 77-703260
Shows how a little dog makes pancakes only to have them stolen by a lazy cat.
Literature and Drama
Dist - PHENIX **Prod** - ROMAF 1977

Pancho Villa 12 MIN
U-matic / VHS
Color (C)
$229.00, $129.00 purchase _ #AD - 1856
Follows the life of Pancho Villa who was born and raised in the poverty of the Mexican hills. Reveals that he began his career as a cattle thief and bandit, but ended his life as a champion of Mexico's peasants and a national hero.
Biography; Foreign Language; Geography - World; History - United States; History - World; Social Science
Dist - FOTH **Prod** - FOTH

Pancho Villa 27 MIN
16mm
B&W (H C A)
Recalls the life and career of the Mexican revolutionary, Pancho Villa, with period photographs and a narrative taken from his biography.
Biography; History - World
Dist - NYU **Prod** - NYU

Pancho Villa's Columbus Raid 26 MIN
16mm / U-matic / VHS
Color (J)
Discusses the raid of Columbus, New Mexico, by Pancho Villa in 1916 and the subsequent 11 month expedition led by General John Pershing into Northern Mexico to capture Villa and his men.
History - United States; History - World
Dist - CNEMAG **Prod** - NMNR 1983

PANCOM beginning total communication program for hearing parents, Level 1
Asking questions and making statements 16 MIN
Dist - JOYCE

PANCOM Beginning Total Communication Program for Hearing Parents of deaf children series
Playing in the Park 16 MIN
Dist - JOYCE

PANCOM Beginning Total Communication Program for Hearing Parents of Series Level 1
Action words 16 MIN
People Signs 16 MIN
Places Pattern 16 MIN
Signs for Time 15 MIN
Where Action Happens 16 MIN
Dist - JOYCE

PANCOM Beginning Total Communication Program for Hearing Parents of Series Level 2
Manual Alphabet 16 MIN
Morning 16 MIN
Preparing for Bed 16 MIN
Preparing for Dinner 16 MIN
Some Problems 15 MIN
Dist - JOYCE

PANCOM beginning total communication program for hearing parents of series
Being specific about people and objects 16 MIN
Descriptive language pattern 16 MIN
Dinner 16 MIN
Dist - JOYCE

PANCOM beginning total communication program for hearing parents of series
Leaving for School - Level 2 16 MIN
Relating facts 15 MIN
Dist - JOYCE

PANCOM beginning total communication program for hearing parents series
Backyard activity 16 MIN
Backyard discovery 15 MIN
Basic question pattern 16 MIN
Dist - JOYCE

PANCOM beginning total communication program for hearing parents series
Coming home from school 16 MIN
Dist - JOYCE

Pancreatic Cysts 28 MIN
16mm
Color (PRO)
Includes retention cysts and pseudocysts of the pancreas. Shows roentgenograms which aid in the diagnosis of pancreatic cysts. Demonstrates the various types of surgical therapy.
Health and Safety; Science
Dist - ACY **Prod** - ACYDGD 1953

Pancreatic Disease 30 MIN
U-matic / VHS
Color
Discusses and updates some of the newer modalities of diagnosis and certain aspects of treatment of diseases of the pancreas.
Health and Safety
Dist - ROWLAB **Prod** - ROWLAB

Pancreatitis Update 30 MIN
U-matic / VHS
Color
Reveals the conceptual changes which the treatment of pancreatitis has undergone in the past decade. Relates that toxic metabolic processes rather than mechanical factors induce pancreatic inflammation especially as regards the alcoholic variety.
Health and Safety
Dist - ROWLAB **Prod** - ROWLAB

Panda 47 MIN
VHS
Color (P I J H G)
$225.00 purchase
Uses newsreel, archival and contemporary footage to trace the history, biology and habitat of the Giant Panda. Reveals that possibly only 1000 Giant Pandas now live in China.
Geography - World; Science - Natural
Dist - LANDMK **Prod** - LANDMK 1991

Panda 30 MIN
VHS / 16mm
Chinese Brush Painting Series
Color (C A)
$85.00, $75.00 purchase _ 20 - 07
Describes habitat, habits, anatomy and proportions of the panda.
Fine Arts
Dist - CDTEL **Prod** - COAST 1987

Pandas - a Gift from China 14 MIN
U-matic / VHS / 16mm
Color (P I)
LC 74-702304
Portrays giant pandas whose natural home is in the bamboo forest of the high mountain country of southern China where today about 2,000 of these furry, rotund animals live.
Science - Natural
Dist - EBEC **Prod** - EBEC 1974

Pandas and Applesauce 10 MIN
U-matic / VHS
Book, Look and Listen Series
Color (K P)
Focuses on the ability to differentiate between fantasy and reality, and an appreciation of the need in life for fantasy and imagination.

English Language; Literature and Drama
Dist - AITECH Prod - MDDE 1977

The Panda's Boutique 17 MIN
VHS / 16mm
Color (P)
$360.00, $49.00 purchase _ #548 - 9749
Uses an unusual pastel watercolor technique. Tells the story of a little panda who uses all his resources to see that the customers of his clothing shop get what they want. From the People's Republic of China.
Fine Arts; Geography - World; Literature and Drama; Science - Natural
Dist - FI Prod - BBCTV 1983

Pandas of the sleeping dragon 50 MIN
VHS
Natural world series
Color; PAL (H C A)
PdS99 purchase; Not available in the United States or Canada
Documents the courtship of the giant panda. Records the activities of a mother and baby panda in a tree nest. Includes footage of the panda's relationships with other animals in the bamboo forest, including the red panda, the blue-faced monkey and the bamboo rat.
Science - Natural
Dist - BBCENE

The Panda's Thumb 480 MIN
U-matic / VHS
Color (G)
$16.50 rental _ #2142
Deepens and extends the viewer's examination of evolution, a centerpiece of modern science.
Science
Dist - BKSOTP Prod - BKSOTP 1988

Pandora's Bottle - the Drinking Woman 41 MIN
U-matic / VHS
Color
Explores the social background and behavior of the female alcoholic for causes, preventions and solutions. With Mariette Hartley.
Health and Safety; Psychology; Sociology
Dist - MTVTM
AVANT
HAZELB

Pandora's Box 12 MIN
U-matic / VHS / 16mm
Color (K P I)
Relates the ancient story first written by the Greek poet and story teller, Hesiod, and retold often by such as Milton, Voltaire, Goethe and Longfellow. Justifies the myth's perpetuation as an entertaining story because it portrays the human condition in a way that gives insights into important problems of our lives.
Fine Arts; Literature and Drama; Religion and Philosophy
Dist - BCNFL Prod - BROKEV 1983

Pandora's box 110 MIN
VHS
B&W; Silent (G) (GERMAN)
$24.95 _ #PAN010
Tells the story of Lulu, an effervescent chorus girl who destroys everyone she comes in contact with before she is murdered by Jack the Ripper. Adapts the plays Erdgeist and The Box of Pandora by Wedekind and brings out the erotic power of this singular beauty, who, lacking all moral sense and devoid of guile and malevolence, does evil unconsciously. Directed by G W Pabst.
Fine Arts; Sociology
Dist - HOMVIS Prod - JANUS 1928
KINOIC

Pandramic Impression of Old New York (1903 - 05) 14 MIN
16mm
B&W
LC 72-701847
Explains that as 1899 faded into the twentieth century, New York City was growing by leaps and bounds. Points out that all over the city the landscape was changing, old buildings were demolished to make way for the new and giant skyscrapers and the growing city was captured by early motion picture cameras erected from the top of the New York Times Building which overlooked Times Square.
Geography - United States; History - United States; Science - Natural; Social Science; Sociology
Dist - RMIBHF Prod - RMIBHF

The Panel 16 MIN
VHS
The Panel interview series
Color (IND)
$495.00 purchase, $150.00 rental _ #VCO12A
Discusses the selection process from the panel's perspective. Includes a leader's guide. Part of a two - part series. Produced by Video Communicators.
Business and Economics; Guidance and Counseling
Dist - EXTR

Panel Cartoons 15 MIN
Videoreel / VT2
Charlie's Pad Series
Color
Fine Arts
Dist - PBS Prod - WSIU

Panel Discussion 37 MIN
U-matic / VHS
Remedies Phase of an EEO Case - Individual Determinations Series Pt '2
Color (PRO)
Presents the trial attorneys and judge as they are joined in a panel discussion with law faculty. Focuses on the utility of case - by - case determinations rather than a formula approach in both liability and remedy phases.
Civics and Political Systems
Dist - ABACPE Prod - ALIABA

Panel Discussion on Loxapine Succinate Lederle - a Clinical Review of a New 25 MIN
16mm
Color (PRO)
Presents a panel discussion on Loxapine Succinate Lederle, a new chemical entity for the manifestations of schizophrenia. Features the participants reviewing their own experiences with the new drug in treating acute and chronic schizophrenia. Touches on symptoms of schizophrenia encountered, the dosages used, the side effects encountered and the relative effectiveness of the new entity.
Health and Safety; Psychology
Dist - LEDR Prod - ACYLLD 1975

Panel Discussion on Surgery of the Colon 46 MIN
16mm
Color (PRO)
Recreates the panel discussion on colon surgery held at the 1955 Cine Clinic Program of the A C S.
Health and Safety; Science
Dist - ACY Prod - ACYDGD 1956

A Panel Discussion on the Management of Incurable Breast Cancer 46 MIN
16mm
Color (PRO)
Presents a panel discussion on the management of incurable breast cancer with Dr Joseph H Farrow, Chief of the Breast Service at Memorial Hospital in New York, bringing eleven typical composite cases of breast cancer before the panelists. Features Dr H Gilbert discussing radiological treatment, Dr Samuel G Taylor III speaking on the use of hormonal therapy, Dr Jeanne C Batemen speaking for the use of chemical agents and Dr Henry T Randall reporting on the surgical approach.
Health and Safety
Dist - LEDR Prod - ACYLLD 1962

Panel Discussions 49 MIN
U-matic / VHS
Remedies Phase of an EEO Case - Class Back Pay and Proof of Claims 'Series Pt 1
Color (PRO)
Features a panel discussion concerning the back pay conference. Includes participants in the conference speaking candidly about their strategies and objectives.
Civics and Political Systems
Dist - ABACPE Prod - ALIABA

A Panel Feedback Session - Midway in Course 29 MIN
16mm
CHEM Study Teacher Training Series
B&W (T)
LC 76-701169
CHEM study staff members and high school teachers discuss questions raised by teachers using the CHEM study materials and participating in the in - service training program. The topics include difficulties in teaching certain concepts, teacher preparation and institutes, further applications of the concept of randomness, the use of models, specific laboratory techniques and evaluations.
Science
Dist - MLA Prod - CHEMS 1966

The Panel interview series
Discusses panel job interviewing preparation. Includes two videos featuring interviews from the panel's standpoint and from the applicant's, with leader's guide. Produced by Video Communicators.
The Applicant 19 MIN
The Panel 16 MIN
The Panel interview series 35 MIN
Dist - EXTR

Paneling 45 MIN
VHS
Color (A)
$19.95 purchase _ #S01167
Covers paneling home improvement projects. Includes plank boards, panels, trimming and erection of shelves.
Home Economics; Industrial and Technical Education
Dist - UILL

Paneling 30 MIN
VHS
Home improvement video series
Color (G)
$39.95 purchase _ #215
Discusses paneling. Shows how to install 4x8 panels over new or existing walls, trim techniques, how to install shelving and individual plank boards to walls.
Home Economics
Dist - DIYVC Prod - DIYVC

Paneling 30 MIN
VHS / 16mm
Woodworking Series
Color (H C A PRO)
$39.95 purchase _ #SH515
Shows how to install 4 x 6 panels over new or existing walls, trim techniques and shelving installation.
Home Economics; Industrial and Technical Education
Dist - AAVIM Prod - AAVIM 1990

Paneling and Shelving 33 MIN
VHS / 16mm
Do it Yourself Series
(G)
Shows how to install 4 by 8 panels over new or existing walls, and how to trim them. Includes how to install various types of shelving, and how to install individual plank board to walls and trim techniques.
Home Economics
Dist - RMIBHF Prod - RMIBHF
CAMV

Paneling - Wood Paneling, Wood Paneling Over Masonry 30 MIN
BETA / VHS
Wally's Workshop Series
Color
Home Economics; Industrial and Technical Education
Dist - KARTES Prod - KARTES

Panels for the Walls of the World 8 MIN
16mm
Color
Presents an experiment in video tape control, an electric collage that mixes the images by way of electronic mats, superimpositions and other electronic means of integration.
Fine Arts; Industrial and Technical Education; Social Science
Dist - VANBKS Prod - VANBKS 1966

Panic 28 MIN
U-matic / VHS
Please Stand by - a History of Radio Series
(C A)
Fine Arts; History - United States; Psychology; Sociology
Dist - SCCON Prod - SCCON 1986

Panic, anxiety and other stress disorders 30 MIN
VHS
At time of diagnosis series
Color (G)
$19.95 purchase _ #1 - 5757 - 7018 - 0NK
Provides patients who suffer from panic, anxiety and other stress disorders and their families with thorough, comprehensive and understandable information. Examines what is going on in the body and what might have caused the condition. Explains the type of medical professionals a patient may encounter and how the condition is monitored. Explores treatment options, including medication and lifestyle changes. Looks at practical issues surrounding the illness and answers the most common questions. Part of an ongoing series to provide the in - depth medical information patients and their families need to know.
Health and Safety; Psychology
Dist - TILIED Prod - TILIED 1996

Panic attack 30 MIN
VHS
QED series
Color; PAL (G)
PdS65 purchase
Examines the problem of panic attacks and anxiety disorders. Presents the research on these debilitating feelings which strike without warning and seemingly for no reason. Looks into possible aids for sufferers as the attacks can happen to anybody, anywhere.
Health and Safety; Psychology
Dist - BBCENE

The Pankhurst family 60 MIN
VHS
Shoulder to shoulder series
Color (G)
$59.95 purchase _ #SHOU - 101
Profiles the Pankhurst family and their efforts for women's suffrage and other reformist causes. Shows that the whole family - Richard, Emmeline and their daughters Christabel and Sylvia - participated in these efforts. Hosted by actress Jane Alexander.

Civics and Political Systems; History - World
Dist - PBS **Prod** - MKNZM 1988

Panna Maria - First Polish Colony in Texas 7 MIN
U-matic / VHS / Slide
Ethnic Studies Series
Color; Mono (J H)
Biography; History - United States; Sociology
Dist - UTXITC **Prod** - UTXITC 1971

Panographic Diagnostic Pathology Radiolucencies 30 MIN
U-matic
Color (PRO)
LC 78-706198
Deals with panographic diagnostic pathology radiolucencies, showing abnormal radiolucencies. Discusses etiology and treatment. Issued in 1968 as a motion picture.
Health and Safety; Science
Dist - USNAC **Prod** - USVA 1978

Panographic Diagnostic Pathology Radiolucencies, Pt 1 15 MIN
U-matic
Color (PRO)
LC 78-706198
Deals with panographic diagnostic pathology radiolucencies, showing abnormal radiolucencies. Discusses etiology and treatment. Issued in 1968 as a motion picture.
Health and Safety
Dist - USNAC **Prod** - USVA 1978

Panographic Diagnostic Pathology Radiolucencies, Pt 2 15 MIN
U-matic
Color (PRO)
LC 78-706198
Deals with panographic diagnostic pathology radiolucencies, showing abnormal radiolucencies. Discusses etiology and treatment. Issued in 1968 as a motion picture.
Health and Safety
Dist - USNAC **Prod** - USVA 1978

Panorama 30 MIN
VHS / U-matic
Color (H C A)
$250 purchase, $50 rental
Shows the diverse rhythms and dance forms that have evolved in Cuba. Examines the Afro Latin roots of Cuban music, and recreates the history of Cuban dance. Directed by Melchor Casals.
Fine Arts
Dist - CNEMAG

Panorama de la France 60 MIN
VHS
VideoFrance series
Color (H C) (FRENCH)
$119.95 purchase _ #E1485 - X
Presents visits to several villages and cities of France and interviews with residents to display French culture and customs. For beginning to intermediate - level students. Includes one videotape and teacher's manual.
Foreign Language
Dist - NTCPUB **Prod** - NTCPUB

Panorama of African - American theater series 60 MIN
VHS
Panorama of African - American theater series
Color (G C H)
$299.00 purchase _ #DL486 (4 videos)
Presents a four - part series that traces the development of African - American theater from the 1820s to the present. Includes Origins of Black Theater, Emergence of the Performing Arts, Power of the Playwright, and Future Direction.
Fine Arts; History - United States; Literature and Drama
Dist - INSIM

A Panorama of Smokers' Attitudes 6 MIN
16mm
Color (I J)
LC 74-703691
Presents a variety of opinions from ordinary people about smoking.
Health and Safety; Psychology
Dist - SUMHIL **Prod** - SUMHIL 1974

Panorama series
Alaska - oil on the rocks 40 MIN
Alcohol - more harm than heroin 40 MIN
Bhopal - a lingering tragedy 40 MIN
Piper Alpha - the human price of oil 40 MIN
Dist - BBCENE

Panoramic impressions of old New York 11 MIN
16mm
B&W (G)
$15.00 rental
Features a fascinating series of early sequences from 1903 - 1906.

Fine Arts; Geography - United States; Literature and Drama
Dist - KITPAR

The Pantheon of American Heroes 44 MIN
U-matic / VHS
Color (G)
$249.00, $149.00 purchase _ #AD - 2201
Asks what America's founders and great heroes might think of Martin Luther King, Jr. Presents a dramatization in which Dr King is denied admittance into the Pantheon of American heroes and then welcomed in by Patrick Henry, George Washington, Thomas Jefferson, Robert E Lee and Abraham Lincoln.
Civics and Political Systems; Fine Arts; Literature and Drama
Dist - FOTH **Prod** - FOTH

Panther girl of the Kongo 180 MIN
35mm
Republic cliffhanger serials series
B&W (G)
Features crawfish ingesting a chemical that causes them to grow into monsters that scare the natives. Offers 12 episodes, 15 minutes each. Contact distributor for rental price.
Fine Arts
Dist - KITPAR **Prod** - REP 1955

The Pantomime Dame 50 MIN
U-matic / VHS / 16mm
Color (J)
LC 84-706013
Explores the British Christmas custom of portraying in pantomime a mother caricature called the dame. Presents leading comedic actors who explain how the figure is portrayed by a man and give the reasons for the annual tradition. Includes archival stills and film footage.
Fine Arts; History - World
Dist - WOMBAT **Prod** - BCACGB 1983

Pantomime for the Actor 20 MIN
16mm
Color (J H C)
LC FIA65-1587
Earl Lewin, pantomime artist, demonstrates the importance of pantomime to the beginning actor. He shows how pantomime can be used to convey emotion, action, character, setting and plot.
Fine Arts
Dist - SLFP **Prod** - SLFP 1965

Pantomime - Large and Small Action 20 MIN
VHS / U-matic
Creative Dramatics Series
Color (I)
Shows some things that pantomime can do and presents beginning pantomime activities.
Fine Arts; Physical Education and Recreation
Dist - AITECH **Prod** - NEWITV 1977

Pantomime - large and small action - teacher 30 MIN
VHS / U-matic
Creative dramatics - teacher series
Color (T)
Demonstrates various pantomime areas and activities, some that would be useful in language arts and social studies.
Fine Arts
Dist - AITECH **Prod** - NEWITV 1977

Pantomime - the language of the heart 10 MIN
16mm / U-matic / VHS
Art of silence, pantomimes with Marcel Marceau series
Color (J H C)
Presents Marcel Marceau talking about mime and how body movement and gestures communicate attitudes and emotions. Includes brief clips from many pantomimes to illustrate his words.
Fine Arts
Dist - EBEC **Prod** - EBEC 1975

Pantomime - the language of the heart; Bip as a skater, the creation of the world - group 1 29 MIN
VHS / U-matic
Art of silence, pantomimes with Marcel Marceau series
Color (I J C)
$119.00 purchase _ #4125
Utilizes common ideas to explain and demonstrate the art of mime, the art of nonverbal communication. Performed by Marcel Marceau.
Fine Arts; Psychology
Dist - EBEC

Pantone - the Language of Color 17 MIN
U-matic
Color
Describes the workings of the Pantone Matching System, which is used for matching colors. Explains its use in all phases of graphic arts, from the creative end to production and printing.
Fine Arts; Science - Physical
Dist - MTP **Prod** - PANTN

Paolo Carbonara 5 MIN
U-matic / VHS
Write on, Set 1 Series
Color (J H)
Teaches subject - verb agreement.
English Language
Dist - CTI **Prod** - CTI

Paolo Uccello Nel Chiostro Verde 30 MIN
VHS
Treccani Italian Renaissance art series
Color (H C A)
$29.95 purchase
Examines the life and works of Paolo Uccello, a pioneer of Italian Renaissance art in forms ranging from public monuments to smaller commissioned works.
Fine Arts; History - World
Dist - ARTSAM

Pap smear and colposcopy 10 MIN
VHS
5 - part gynecological series
Color (G)
$100.00 purchase, $40.00 rental _ #5308S, #5308V
Gives up - to - date information on the diagnosis and treatment of cervical dysplasia. Uses dramatizations, detailed graphics, animation and actual clinic visits to demonstrate colposcopy, biopsy, cryosurgery, cone biopsy and laser therapy. Emphasizes the importance of early diagnosis through regular Pap smear testing. Part of a five - part series on gynecology.
Health and Safety
Dist - AJN **Prod** - VMED

PAP Test and Self - Breast Examination 9 MIN
U-matic / VHS
Color
Explains what a pelvic exam and PAP test are. Presents step - by - step method for self - breast examination.
Health and Safety; Science - Natural; Sociology
Dist - MEDFAC **Prod** - MEDFAC 1981

PAPA - Participant Action Plan Approach - or How do I Know Training is Worth all that Money 20 MIN
U-matic / VHS
Color
Describes a five - step process by which trainers - managers can assess the usefulness of their training programs. Tells how to use the Participant Action Plan Approach (PAPA) and how to adapt it to a particular organization's needs.
Business and Economics; Education; Industrial and Technical Education; Psychology
Dist - USNAC **Prod** - USOPMA

PAPA - Participant Action Plan Approach - the Follow - Up Interview 20 MIN
VHS / U-matic
Color
Tells how to conduct the follow - up interview and stresses the importance of gathering meaningful data on the impact of training from the participant.
Business and Economics; Education; Industrial and Technical Education; Psychology
Dist - USNAC **Prod** - USOPMA

Papa Penguin's Home Movies 8 MIN
16mm / U-matic / VHS
Color (P)
Presents Papa Penguin showing home movies of his penguin friends from the Falkland Islands nesting ground. Describes the penguins' daily activities, feeding habits, nesting process and life cycle.
Science - Natural
Dist - CORF **Prod** - CORF 1978

Papa What's it 13 MIN
16mm
Color (I)
Depicts the feeding habits, nesting area and hatching of the Great Blue Heron in its natural habitat. Uses macro and time lapse photography to show the development of the embryo.
Science - Natural
Dist - SHUGA **Prod** - SHUGA

Papanicolaou Stain - Materials and Methods 21 MIN
U-matic / VHS
Cytotechnology Techniques Series
Color (PRO)
Health and Safety
Dist - WFP **Prod** - WFP

Papanicolaou Stain - Principles 15 MIN
U-matic / VHS
Cytotechnology Techniques Series
Color (PRO)
Health and Safety
Dist - WFP **Prod** - WFP

Papa's pest 20 MIN
16mm
B&W (G)
$15.00 rental
Presents a humorous disaster when Izzie Cohen bribes his father for a motorcycle on his birthday. Records the father accidentally starting it without knowing how to steer or turn it off, thus creating a panic as it runs wildly through the house and streets out of control. Produced by the Weiss Brothers. Written and directed by Les Goodwins.
Fine Arts
Dist - NCJEWF

Paper 13 MIN
16mm / VHS
Color (P I J)
$260.00, $29.95 purchase
Explores the history of paper, how it is made and its variety of uses.
Industrial and Technical Education
Dist - KAWVAL **Prod** - KAWVAL

Paper 29 MIN
VHS / 16mm
Villa Alegre Series
Color (P T)
$46.00 rental _ #VILA - 108
Presents educational material in both Spanish and English.
Education
Dist - PBS

Paper - anaerobic pretreatment of combined domestic - industrial wastewater
VHS
Water Environment Federation Annual Conference Videotapes series
Color (G A PRO)
$39.00 purchase _ #9311
Describes a pretreatment system set up by the City of Tulare, California to prepare domestic and industrial wastewater for later processing because of increasingly heavy pollution. Discusses the design considerations, layout and operating results of the system. Presents a technical paper by R C Landine, M J McMullin, M Preszler and J Tindel. Part of a series.
Science - Natural
Dist - WAENFE

Paper and silk - the conservation of Asian works of art 26 MIN
U-matic / VHS
Color (G)
$100.00, $39.95 purchase
Begins with a brittle 18th - century Chinese scroll painting in hundreds of fragments. Features Asian curator Robert Jacobsen - Minneapolis Institute of Arts - and conservators David Dudley and Downey Rugtiv - Upper Midwest Conservation Association - who lead the viewer through the restoration process from the initial piecing together of the work to its rebacking and painting and remounting onto a paper panel. Explains the tools and techniques of Asian conservation, the rational for procedures - what objects deserve repairing and why.
Fine Arts; History - World
Dist - ARTSAM **Prod** - MIA

Paper Animals 29 MIN
U-matic
Drawing with Guy Palazzola Series
Color
Uses live animals to show how to paint animals on canvas.
Fine Arts
Dist - UMITV **Prod** - UMITV 1970

The Paper bag princess
CD-ROM
Discis Books on CD - ROM
(K P) (SPANISH)
$69.00 purchase _ #2556
Contains the original text and illustrations of The Paper Bag Princess by Robert Munsch. Enhances understanding with real voices, music, and sound effects. Every word in the text has an in - context explanation, pronunciation and syllables, available through a click of the mouse. Spanish - English version available for an extra $5 per disc. For Macintosh Classics, Plus, II and SE computers, requires 1MB of RAM, one floppy disk drive, and an Apple compatible CD - ROM drive.
English Language; Literature and Drama
Dist - BEP

Paper bag puppets 15 MIN
Videoreel / VT2
Art corner series
B&W (P)
Utilizes experimenting with paper bags and crayons and cut paper to create puppets resulting in individual, spontaneous creative dramatics.
Fine Arts
Dist - GPN **Prod** - CVETVC

Paper Bag Puppets, Paper Dolls, and Cut Paper 56 MIN
VHS / 16mm
Children's Crafts Series
(K P)
$39.00 purchase _ #VT1090
Shows how to make and use paper bag puppets, paper dolls, and cut paper snowflakes. Taught by Julie Abowitt, Multi - Arts Coordinator for the Seattle Public Schools.
Fine Arts
Dist - RMIBHF **Prod** - RMIBHF

Paper Bandits - Checks, Counterfeit, Credit Cards 14 MIN
U-matic / VHS / 16mm
Color (H C A)
$425, $295 purchase _ #83054
Explains how millions of dollars in cash and merchandise are stolen by people useing false credit cards and counterfeit money.
Sociology
Dist - CORF

Paper Blizzard 30 MIN
16mm
Color
LC 73-700515
Introduces the array of information sources within the federal government and identifies the use of these resources with professionalism. Surveys the range of services that may be expected from a representative information source from the viewpoint of the librarian.
Education
Dist - USNAC **Prod** - USOE 1970

The Paper Boy 52 MIN
U-matic / VHS
Winners from Down Under Series
Color (K)
$349.00, $249.00 purchase _ #AD - 1356
Portrays Christmas 1932. Shows that Joe's father is unemployed and Joe's newspaper sales are his family's sole means of support. After a row with his father, Joe moves out to the streets. When he returns for Christmas, things have changed. Part of an eight - part series on children's winning over their circumstances produced by the Australian Children's Television Foundation.
Literature and Drama; Religion and Philosophy; Sociology
Dist - FOTH **Prod** - FOTH

Paper camera 25 MIN
VHS / U-matic
Color (I J H G)
$295.00, $345.00 purchase, $60.00 rental
Tells the story of a ten - year - old Oriental immigrant student and his transition into an English - speaking school. Delves into the friendship between the boy and his schoolmates which transcends the verbal language barrier. Produced by PC & B Productions.
Psychology
Dist - NDIM

Paper Chromatography 15 MIN
U-matic / VHS / 16mm
Biological Techniques Series
Color (H C)
Shows the basic principles and techniques for analyzing dissolved substances by using paper chromatographic separations.
Science; Science - Natural
Dist - IFB **Prod** - THORNE 1961

Paper - considerations in the selection and design of high solids centrifuges
VHS
Water Environment Federation Annual Conference Videotapes series
Color (G A PRO)
$39.00 purchase _ #9313
Describes performance data for high solids waste devices that make use of various technologies. Discusses high - torque and diaphragm and recessed - chamber filter presses as well as specific results from two recently - installed systems in Virginia and Maryland. Presents a technical paper by James H Reynolds, Scott Murphy, Forrest Vaughan, Nicolay Voutchkov and V K Naidu. Part of a series.
Social Science
Dist - WAENFE

Paper construction 15 MIN
U-matic / VHS / 16mm
Rediscovery - art media film series
Color (I) (SPANISH FRENCH)
LC FIA67-1527
Introduces the use of paper as a sculptural medium. Shows how the techniques of cutting, scoring, bending and folding may be used to create three - dimensional forms which lend themselves to an unlimited range of variations and combinations.
Fine Arts
Dist - AIMS **Prod** - ACI 1967

Paper - control of deicing fluids at the new Denver - CO - international airport
VHS
Water Environment Federation Annual Conference Videotapes series
Color (G A PRO)
$39.00 purchase _ #9303
Describes the glycol monitoring system at the Denver International Airport that complies with stormwater discharge regulations to maintain the established load limits at the Denver wastewater treatment plant. Features D Backer, D Smith, and C Habben's technical paper. Part of a series.
Science - Natural
Dist - WAENFE

The Paper crane - 39
VHS
Reading rainbow series
Color; CC (K P)
$39.95 purchase
Shows how a generous restaurant owner receives a wonderful magical gift in the story by Molly Bang. Celebrates Japanese culture with LeVar when he visits Gasho of Japan in Central Valley, New York. Surrounded by lush gardens, LeVar dons a kimono and explores the ancient art of origami and the artistry of a Japanese vegetable carver. LeVar joins the Japanese dancers Soh Daiko as they perform the celebratory 'festival of the drums.' Part of a series offering a multicultural approach to generating reading enthusiasm with cross - curricular applications, hosted by LeVar Burton.
English Language; Literature and Drama; Sociology
Dist - GPN **Prod** - LNMDP

Paper - cycling for compliance
VHS
Water Environment Federation Annual Conference Videotapes series
Color (G A PRO)
$39.00 purchase _ #9302
Describes improvements achieved at the Washington - East Washington Joint Authority Wastewater Treatment Plant as a result of adding a tertiary biotower to its operating system, enhancing its effluent clarity. Features M C Mulbarger, M Nikiolich, J A Haines and R A Dami presenting a technical paper. Part of a series.
Social Science
Dist - WAENFE

Paper - field application of the Clarifier Research Technical Committee's protocol for evaluating secondary clarifier performance
VHS
Water Environment Federation Annual Conference Videotapes series
Color (G A PRO)
$39.00 purchase _ #9308
Discusses the results of studies of secondary clarifier performance made at the San Jose Creek Water Reclamation Plant in Los Angeles County. Focuses on stress tests of a rectangular unit that showed the relation between effluent suspended solids - ESS - and surface overflow rates - SOR. Presents a technical paper by Eric J Wahlberg, James F Stahl, Ching Lin Chen and Max Augustus. Part of a series.
Social Science
Dist - WAENFE

Paper film series
Fauve 10 MIN
New moon 11 MIN
Newsw
Dist - CANCIN

Paper girl 30 MIN
VHS
Color (P I R)
$19.95 purchase, $10.00 rental _ #35 - 820 - 2020
Portrays Sue as she tries to figure out why Mrs Waverly hasn't been picking up her papers. Suggests that by solving this mystery, Sue learns to trust God for direction.
Literature and Drama; Religion and Philosophy
Dist - APH **Prod** - ANDERK

Paper house 5 MIN
VHS
Color (G)
$69.00 purchase _ #CE - 073
Features a homeless woman who scrawls a child - like drawing on the wall of an urban pedestrian underpass. Shows that memories of her childhood play across the screen in colorfully animated crayon drawings which recall the warmth and security of home. As these images dissolve into the chaos of her current bleak existence, they illuminate her intense feelings of loss. Produced by Suvane Myers.
Sociology
Dist - FANPRO

Paper job search tools - adult version
VHS
Job search - adult version series
Color (A G)
$89.00 purchase _ #JW3013V
Provides tips on creating resumes and filling out applications that will get interviews. Part of a five - part series on job searches for adults.
Business and Economics; Guidance and Counseling
Dist - CAMV **Prod** - JISTW 1991

Paper job search tools - from resumes to applications
VHS
JIST job search series
Color (H A T)
$89.00 purchase _ #JW3003
Shows how to create and use chronological or 'skills' resumes, how to complete applications which will not be screened out. Presents examples of cover letters. Stresses the importance of sending thank you notes following interviews and other contacts. Part of a five - part series.
Business and Economics; Guidance and Counseling; Psychology; Social Science
Dist - AAVIM **Prod** - JISTW 1992

Paper - local pretreatment limits - implementation allocation strategies
VHS
Water Environment Federation Annual Conference Videotapes series
Color (G A PRO)
$39.00 purchase _ #9304
Discusses methods used to establish area - wide wastewater pretreatment limits for the Phoenix, Arizona valley and to develop tactics for implementing, allocating and regulating the limits among the various jurisdictions and plants of the area. Features a technical paper by P G Trahern, S L Mays and L Landrith. Part of a series.
Science - Natural
Dist - WAENFE

Paper losses - a modern epic of greed and betrayal at America's two largest newspaper companies 30 MIN
VHS
Author's night at the Freedom Forum series
Color (G)
$15.00 purchase _ #V94 - 01
Focuses on Bryan Gruley, author of the book of the same title, in part of a series on freedom of the press, free speech and free spirit.
Social Science; Sociology
Dist - FREEDM **Prod** - FREEDM 1994

The Paper Makers 22 MIN
16mm
Color
LC 80-700916
Shows the activities of the Australian newsprint mills in Southern Tasmania through the eyes of five men.
Geography - World; Social Science
Dist - TASCOR **Prod** - TASCOR 1980

The Paper of Analysis 30 MIN
U-matic / VHS
Writing for a Reason Series
Color (C)
English Language
Dist - DALCCD **Prod** - DALCCD

The Paper of Classification 30 MIN
VHS / U-matic
Writing for a Reason Series
Color (C)
English Language
Dist - DALCCD **Prod** - DALCCD

The Paper of Comparison 30 MIN
U-matic / VHS
Writing for a Reason Series
Color (C)
English Language
Dist - DALCCD **Prod** - DALCCD

The Paper of Definition 30 MIN
U-matic / VHS
Writing for a Reason Series
Color (C)
English Language
Dist - DALCCD **Prod** - DALCCD

The Paper Party 10 MIN
VHS
Color (P)
$79.00 purchase _ #235 - 9001
Inspires children's imaginations and encourages them to develop their own stories or to perform plays with puppets. Follows the adventures of a young boy named Joey. One day while Joey is watching his favorite TV program, its puppet characters suddenly come to life and invite him in for a party.
Fine Arts; Literature and Drama
Dist - FI

Paper plates to silver spoons - the complete guide to table manners
VHS
Color (J H C G)
$39.95 purchase _ #CCP0148V
Takes both a serious and a humourous look at the importance of learning table manners. Shows the benefits of learning proper techniques so that they become natural rather than using correct manners only on special occasions. Discusses different kinds of meal settings, utensils and the order in which they are used. Illustrates the importance of good posture, how to hold and use utensils and how to be prepared for conversation. Shows the correct way to eat common foods - salad, soup, pizza, bread, tricky situations such as when a drink is spilled or a utensil is dropped or when one is offered a food that one doesn't eat.
Home Economics
Dist - CAMV **Prod** - CAMV 1994

Paper Play 60 MIN
VHS / BETA
Children's Crafts Series
Color (K P)
Demonstrates paper crafts such as collage and greeting cards.
Fine Arts
Dist - MOHOMV **Prod** - MOHOMV

Paper Route 13 MIN
16mm
Color
LC 80-701369
Shows an 18 - year - old retarded boy's budding relationship with a woman he meets on his newspaper route.
Fine Arts; Psychology
Dist - RAINY **Prod** - RAINY 1980

Paper Sculpture 5 MIN
16mm / U-matic / VHS
Creative Hands Series
Color (P I J)
Illustrates the variety of three - dimensional objects that can be made out of paper and cardboard.
Fine Arts
Dist - IFB **Prod** - IFB 1949

Paper Sculpture 10 MIN
16mm
Color; B&W (I)
Techniques of paper sculpturing are demonstrated and varied uses of this medium from party favors to lifesize figures for drapery displays are illustrated.
Fine Arts; Home Economics
Dist - AVED **Prod** - ALLMOR 1958

Paper sculpture and masks 15 MIN
U-matic / VHS
Art cart series
Color (P I)
Explains how to make paper sculptures and paper monster masks.
Fine Arts
Dist - AITECH **Prod** - WBRATV 1979

Paper Sculpture Animals 14 MIN
U-matic / VHS
Young at Art Series
Color (P I)
Discusses paper sculpture animals.
Fine Arts
Dist - AITECH **Prod** - WSKJTV 1980

Paper - sewer rehabilitation using trenchless technology on mainlines and service laterals
VHS
Water Environment Federation Annual Conference Videotapes series
Color (G A PRO)
$39.00 purchase _ #9310
Discusses a pilot program used by the Unified Sewerage Agency of Washington County, Oregon to assess the costs and effectiveness of sewer line rehabilitation. Presents a technical paper by Nora M Curtis and Anthony H Krutsch. Part of a series.
Industrial and Technical Education; Social Science
Dist - WAENFE

Paper - sliplining large diameter sewers
VHS
Water Environment Federation Annual Conference Videotapes series
Color (G A PRO)
$39.00 purchase _ #9314
Presents problem situations encountered in Los Angeles County projects involving sliplining sewer pipes for rehabilitation. Shows solutions worked out for the problems and demonstrates results obtained. Presents a paper by Calvin Jin and Tommy Sung. Part of a series.
Industrial and Technical Education
Dist - WAENFE

Paper - state - of - the - art evaluation of high cake solids centrifuge technology for municipal ;wastewater solids dewatering
VHS
Water Environment Federation Annual Conference Videotapes series
Color (G A PRO)
$39.00 purchase _ #9312
Discusses a study of high cake solids centrifuge technology for solid waste processing and the current system with cost - benefit analysis of replacing it for St Paul, Minnesota's Wastewater Treatment Plant. Presents a technical paper by James H Reynolds, Scott Murphy, Forrest Vaughan, Nicolay Voutchkov and V K Naidu. Part of a series.
Social Science
Dist - WAENFE

Paper - status of on - site bioremediation for site restoration by the US Army Corps of Engineers
VHS
Water Environment Federation Annual Conference Videotapes series
Color (G A PRO)
$39.00 purchase _ #9309
Discusses hazardous waste sites that have been used for or are being considered for bioremediation by the US Army Corps of Engineers. Mentions various methods of site restoration and their cost and suitability for different locations. Presents a technical paper by Donna Kuroda. Part of a series.
Sociology
Dist - WAENFE

Paper Stencils 29 MIN
Videoreel / VT2
Exploring the Crafts - Silk Screen Printing Series
Color
Fine Arts; Industrial and Technical Education
Dist - PBS **Prod** - NHN

Paper - summary of water reuse regulations and guidelines in the US
VHS
Water Environment Federation Annual Conference Videotapes series
Color (G A PRO)
$39.00 purchase _ #9301
Summarizes state laws governing reuse of water for irrigating crops, providing recreation, and urban, environmental and industrial reuse. Covers water treatment regulations and quality requirements for the separate uses allowed. Features Jeffrey F Payne presenting a technical paper. Part of a series.
Social Science
Dist - WAENFE

Paper - the implementation of EPA's technical sludge regulations - 40 CFR part 503
VHS
Water Environment Federation Annual Conference Videotapes series
Color (G A PRO)
$39.00 purchase _ #9307
Discusses the consequences of the EPA rule for sludge disposal 40 CFR Part 503 and the Modifications to State Program Regulations 40 CFR Part 501 to future use of sludge. Evaluates technical details of the rule for pollutants, pathogens and reduction of vector attractions. Presents a technical paper by Robert G O'Dette. Part of a series.
Science - Natural; Social Science
Dist - WAENFE

Paper - vacuum wastewater collection - 10 years later - still a practical solution
VHS
Water Environment Federation Annual Conference Videotapes series
Color (G A PRO)
$39.00 purchase _ #9305
Discusses the reasons that Queen Anne's County, Maryland chose vacuum wastewater collection as its sewer service method in 1982 and again in 1992. Features a technical paper by Gary A Moore. Part of a series.
Social Science
Dist - WAENFE

Paper Wasp (Polistes Exclamans) 17 MIN
Behavior
16mm
Color (C A)
LC 80-701579
Documents the behavior of paper wasps, Polistes exclamans, at the wasp nest. Looks at feeding, cell construction, egg laying, defense and social grooming.
Science - Natural
Dist - PSUPCR **Prod** - MAHERG 1979

Paper Weaving 15 MIN
U-matic
Is the Sky Always Blue Series
Color (P)
Fine Arts
Dist - GPN **Prod** - WDCNTV 1979

Paper Week 30 MIN
U-matic
Polka Dot Door Series
Color (K)
Presents a variety show for pre - school children. Includes songs, mime, stories, film sequences, talk, dance and fantasy figures. Each show emphasizes a particular theme such as numbers, feelings, exploring, music or time. Comes with parent teacher guide.
Fine Arts; Literature and Drama
Dist - TVOTAR **Prod** - TVOTAR 1985

Paper Wheat 58 MIN
16mm
Color (G)
_ #106C 0179 497
Describes the lives of the early Saskatchewan settlers and the foundation of the Coop movement on the Prairies, largely through the determination of people like E A Partridge.
Fine Arts; History - World
Dist - CFLMDC **Prod** - NFBC 1979

Paper Wings 13 MIN
16mm / U-matic / VHS
Color (K P)
$49.95 purchase _ #L10926
Features a young girl and an older woman who share an interest in all things that fly. Emphasizes friendship as a relationship that has no boundaries based on age or background. No narration.
Psychology
Dist - CF **Prod** - CF 1985

The Paperback computer 50 MIN
VHS
Dream machine series
Color; PAL (G)
PdS99 purchase; Not available in the United States
Presents the advance of computer technology to the microchip and mass production. Traces the development of the computer, the machine that changed the world. Part three of a five - part series.
Computer Science
Dist - BBCENE

Paperhanging Application 14 MIN
U-matic / VHS
Color (H C A)
Shows paste preparation, commercial and individual mixes, paper fitting, pattern and paper matching, applying paste, pasting the wall, lapping and butt joints.
Home Economics
Dist - SF **Prod** - SF

Paperhanging Preparation 14 MIN
U-matic / VHS
Color (H C A)
Shows the various methods of cutting wallpaper. Depicts the needed equipment, such as shears, rollers, smoothing utensils, and the various types of knives. Describes the paster process, preparation of the wall, filling cracks, removing old paint or calcimine, stripping old paper and wall sizing.
Home Economics
Dist - SF **Prod** - SF

Papermaking - 1 60 MIN
VHS
Systems Operations Series
Color (PRO)
$600.00 - $1500.00 purchase _ #POPM1
Explains a typical stock preparation system in papermaking. Describes stock preparation equipment, refiners, cleaners and screens. Covers chemical additive operations, fiber recovery operations and water recovery operations. Includes ten textbooks and an instructor guide to support four hours of instruction.
Education; Industrial and Technical Education; Psychology
Dist - NUSTC **Prod** - NUSTC

Papermaking - 2 60 MIN
VHS
Systems Operations Series
Color (PRO)
$600.00 - $1500.00 purchase _ #POPM2
Outlines wet end operations in papermaking. Includes the functions of devices in approach systems, forming sections and press sections. Considers headboxes and Fourdrinier and twinwire formers as well as press section theory and equipment. Includes ten textbooks and an instructor guide to support four hours of instruction.
Education; Industrial and Technical Education; Psychology
Dist - NUSTC **Prod** - NUSTC

Papermaking - 3 60 MIN
VHS
Systems Operations Series
Color (PRO)
$600.00 - $1500.00 purchase _ #POPM3
Focuses on devices and equipment used in dry end and finishing operations in papermaking. Considers dryers, coaters and calenders. Discusses reel changes, finishing operations - winder and supercalender operations - and preparation of rolls and sheets for shipment. Includes ten textbooks and an instructor guide to support four hours of instruction.
Education; Industrial and Technical Education; Psychology
Dist - NUSTC **Prod** - NUSTC

Papermaking - 4 60 MIN
VHS
Systems Operations Series
Color (PRO)
$600.00 - $1500.00 purchase _ #POPM4
Describes a typical paper machine breakdown and the procedures for shutdown and startup. Shows a wire - felt change and a grade change in papermaking. Includes ten textbooks and an instructor guide to support four hours of instruction.
Education; Industrial and Technical Education; Psychology
Dist - NUSTC **Prod** - NUSTC

Papermaking, Pt 1
VHS / U-matic
Pulp and Paper Training, Module 3 - Papermaking Series
Color (IND)
Covers the basic process in papermaking and Fourdrinier and cylinder machines.
Business and Economics; Industrial and Technical Education; Social Science
Dist - LEIKID **Prod** - LEIKID

Papermaking, Pt 2
VHS / U-matic
Pulp and Paper Training, Module 3 - Papermaking Series
Color (IND)
Discusses grades, qualities and chemical additives used in papermaking. Covers definition of types.
Business and Economics; Industrial and Technical Education; Social Science
Dist - LEIKID **Prod** - LEIKID

Papermaking, Pt 3
VHS / U-matic
Pulp and Paper Training, Module 3 - Papermaking Series
Color (IND)
Includes several aspects of papermaking such as color, deposits, fibre structure and stock process.
Business and Economics; Industrial and Technical Education; Social Science
Dist - LEIKID **Prod** - LEIKID

Papermaking series
Stock preparation equipment
Dist - LEIKID

Papermill 15 MIN
U-matic / VHS
Explorers Unlimited Series
Color (P I)
Journeys to the Hammermill Company to learn how paper is made from pulpwood.
Social Science
Dist - AITECH **Prod** - WVIZTV 1971

Papers for printing 60 MIN
VHS
Color (H C)
$79.95 purchase _ #SE - 19
Provides a basic understanding of the manufacture of paper, paper properties, paper - related printing and bindery problems, ordering and specifying paper and proper paper storage. Covers bond paper, coated and uncoated book, text, cover, board and envelopes, as well as specialty papers such as carbonless and pressure sensitive. Includes a brief history of paper and how it is made. Teaches how to figure jobs, allowances for spoilage, how to write a paper specification, price, weight, color, finishes, grade and brightness. Offers solutions to piling, blanket contamination, curl, set off, sheet distortion, static, misregistration and more paper - related printing problems.
Industrial and Technical Education
Dist - INSTRU

Paperweights 30 MIN
U-matic
Antiques series
Color
Fine Arts
Dist - PBS **Prod** - NHMNET

Papier Mache 30 MIN
U-matic / VHS
Arts and Crafts Series
Color (H A)
LC 81-706996
Demonstrates techniques and materials used in making papier - mache objects.
Fine Arts
Dist - GPN **Prod** - GPN 1981

Papier Mache 15 MIN
U-matic / VHS / 16mm
Rediscovery - Art Media Series
Color (I) (SPANISH)
LC FIA67-1526
Demonstrates the wide expressive range achieved with this easily available material. Presents the basic processes in fashioning three - dimensional forms, from making the core to finishing and painting the surface.
Fine Arts
Dist - AIMS **Prod** - ACI 1967

Papier - Mache Birds 14 MIN
VHS / U-matic
Young at Art Series
Color (P I)
Discusses the construction of papier - mache birds.
Fine Arts
Dist - AITECH **Prod** - WSKJTV 1980

Papier - mache - more than a common craft 23 MIN
35mm strip / VHS
Color (J H C T A)
$93.00 purchase _ #MB - 909740 - 5, #MB - 909472 - 4
Surveys the history and techniques of papier - mache. Reveals that papier - mache originated in China and became popular in Europe during the 18th and 19th centuries. Shows the many types of projects that can be done with papier - mache.
Fine Arts
Dist - SRA **Prod** - SRA 1990

Papillon 150 MIN
16mm
Color
Recounts the attempts of one man to escape from Devil's Island. Stars Steve McQueen. Based on the novel PAPILLON by Henri Charriere.
Fine Arts; Literature and Drama
Dist - CINEWO **Prod** - AA 1973

Papo 20 MIN
16mm
Color
Chronicles a day in the life of a teenager who seeks revenge against a street gang as a test of his own code of honor.
Psychology; Sociology
Dist - BLKFMF **Prod** - BLKFMF

Pappa Piccolo - learning about freedom and responsibility
VHS
Key concepts in self - esteem
Color (K P)
$79.95 purchase _ #MF93RA
Presents one of an 11 - part series teaching key curriculum concepts such as independence, freedom and responsibility, and peer pressure. Includes video, storybook and teaching guide with activities and games. In this video, a cat named Piccolo teaches kids a lesson about sharing their strength with those who are smaller, younger, or weaker
Education; Psychology
Dist - CFKRCM **Prod** - CFKRCM

Papua and New Guinea Development 13 MIN
16mm
Color (H C A)
LC FIA68-3059
Describes the part to be played by private enterprise in the industrial and economic development of Papua and New Guinea.
Business and Economics; Geography - World
Dist - AUIS **Prod** - ANAIB 1968

Papua New Guinea Report 42 MIN
16mm
Color (H C A)
LC 72-701525
Examines a wide range of social and economic conditions in Papua New Guinea and reviews the changing political climate as the territory comes closer to self - government.

Business and Economics; Geography - World; Sociology
Dist - AUIS **Prod** - AUSCOF 1971

Papua New Guinea series
First contact 54 MIN
Joe Leahy's neighbours 90 MIN
Dist - DOCEDR

Papua New Guinea - the center of fire 60 MIN
VHS
Jacques Cousteau series
Color; CC (G)
$19.95 purchase _ #3044
Travels to Papua New Guinea with Jacques Cousteau where divers explore the remains of violent World War II battles - a 500 - foot Japanese freighter and a famous B - 17 Flying Fortress still surprisingly intact. Part of a series by Jacques Cousteau featuring narration by American English speaking actors and actresses.
Geography - World; History - World
Dist - APRESS

Paquita Y Su Conejo 11 MIN
U-matic / VHS / 16mm
Color (P) (SPANISH)
A Spanish language version of Frances And Her Rabbit. Tells how Frances and her pet rabbit draw a crayon picture.
Fine Arts
Dist - IFB **Prod** - IFB 1955

Para 1000 17 MIN
16mm
Color (I)
LC 78-708662
An art film which uses psychedelic lighting and colors, set against sounds of folk - rock and electronic music, to show pop culture and the mod generation.
Fine Arts; History - World; Psychology
Dist - GROVE **Prod** - BACONB 1970

Para El Hombre - Esterilizacion Como Un Metodo Anticonceptivo 27 MIN
16mm
Consentimiento Informado Por Modelos De Instruccion Series
Color (A) (SPANISH)
LC 77-702240
Provides basic information about surgical contraception for men.
Foreign Language; Sociology
Dist - USNAC **Prod** - USOFP 1977

Para La Mujer - La Esterilizacion Voluntaria 42 MIN
16mm
Consentimiento Informado Por Modelos De Instruccion Series
Color (A) (SPANISH)
LC 77-702241
Provides basic information about surgical contraception for women.
Sociology
Dist - USNAC **Prod** - USOFP 1977

Parable of the Sadhu 30 MIN
VHS / 16mm
Harvard Business Review Video Series
(A PRO)
$650.00 purchase _ #AG - 5190M
Define's critical organizational needs and demonstrates techniques for handling them with solid practical management strategies.
Business and Economics; Psychology
Dist - CORF **Prod** - WGBH 1987

Parable Series
The Stray 14 MIN
Dist - FRACOC

The Parables by Jay O'Callahna 30 MIN
VHS / BETA
Color
Shows Jay O'Callahan, a storyteller, as he retells the parables of Jesus.
Religion and Philosophy
Dist - DSP **Prod** - DSP

Parables from Nature, Pts 1 - 5 30 MIN
VHS / 16mm
Color (K P I J)
$39.95 purchase
Illustrates the parables of Jesus retold as animal stories in cartoon form. Five parts.
Religion and Philosophy
Dist - CAFM **Prod** - CAFM 1987

Parables from nature series - Tape 1 30 MIN
VHS
Parables from nature series
Color (K P I R)
$39.95 purchase, $10.00 rental _ #35 - 810 - 528
Uses a cartoon format to present three stories based on the parables of Jesus. 'The Wind and the Seeds' is based on the parable of the sower, while 'The Fairy Ring' is based on the parable of the wheat and the weeds. Concludes with 'The Pearl of Great Price,' based on the parable of the same name. Includes study guides.
Literature and Drama; Religion and Philosophy
Dist - APH **Prod** - CAFM

Parables from nature series - Tape 2 30 MIN
VHS
Parables from nature series
Color (K P I R)
$39.95 purchase, $10.00 rental _ #35 - 811 - 528
Uses a cartoon format to present three stories based on the parables of Jesus. 'Speedy the Snail' is based on the parable of the unforgiving debtor, while 'Bruso the Beaver' is based on the parable of the laborers. Concludes with 'Justus the Ant,' based on the parable of the vineyard. Includes study guides.
Literature and Drama; Religion and Philosophy
Dist - APH **Prod** - CAFM

Parables from nature series - Tape 3 30 MIN
VHS
Parables from nature series
Color (K P I R)
$39.95 purchase, $10.00 rental _ #35 - 812 - 528
Uses a cartoon format to present three stories based on the parables of Jesus. 'Corky the Crow' is based on the parable of the wedding garment, while 'Silly Excuses' is based on the parable of the wedding feast. Concludes with 'House of the Wren,' based on the parable of the two builders. Includes study guides.
Literature and Drama; Religion and Philosophy
Dist - APH **Prod** - CAFM

Parables from nature series - Tape 4 30 MIN
VHS
Parables from nature series
Color (K P I R)
$39.95 purchase, $10.00 rental _ #35 - 813 - 528
Uses a cartoon format to present three stories based on the parables of Jesus. 'The Busy Bee' is based on the parable of the wise and foolish virgins, while 'School Days in the Ocean' is based on the parable of the talents. Concludes with 'Dr Retriever's Surprise,' based on the parable of the sheep and the goats. Includes study guides.
Literature and Drama; Religion and Philosophy
Dist - APH **Prod** - CAFM

Parables from nature series - Tape 5 30 MIN
VHS
Parables from nature series
Color (K P I R)
$39.95 purchase, $10.00 rental _ #35 - 814 - 528
Uses a cartoon format to present three stories based on the parables of Jesus. 'Peppy the Pup' is based on the parable of the prodigal son, while 'Chuckie the Chipmunk' is based on the parable of the good Samaritan. Concludes with 'Bushy the Squirrel,' based on the parable of the foolish rich man. Includes study guides.
Literature and Drama; Religion and Philosophy
Dist - APH **Prod** - CAFM

Parables from nature series - tape 6 30 MIN
VHS
Parables from nature series
Color (K P I R)
$39.95 purchase, $10.00 rental _ #35 - 815 - 528
Uses a cartoon format to present three stories based on the parables of Jesus. 'Bootsie the Lamb' is based on the parable of the lost sheep, while 'The Feather That Was Lost' is based on the parable of the lost coin. Concludes with 'Commencement at the Obedience Academy,' based on the parable of the Pharisee and the publican. Includes study guides.
Literature and Drama; Religion and Philosophy
Dist - APH **Prod** - CAFM

Parables from nature series
Uses a cartoon format to present 18 stories based on the parables of Jesus. Includes study guides. Stories are presented three to a tape, with six tapes in the overall series.
Parables from nature series 180 MIN
Parables from nature series - Tape 1 30 MIN
Parables from nature series - Tape 2 30 MIN
Parables from nature series - Tape 3 30 MIN
Parables from nature series - Tape 4 30 MIN
Parables from nature series - Tape 5 30 MIN
Parables from nature series - tape 6 30 MIN
Dist - APH **Prod** - CAFM

Parables of power - Marlowe's Dr Faustus 26 MIN
VHS
Color (H C G)
$169.00 purchase _ #DL497
Examines the theme of power in Dr Faustus by Christopher Marlowe in scenes from the play. Shows how Faustus chose to sell his soul in order to achive power over nature.
Fine Arts; History - World; Literature and Drama
Dist - INSIM

Parables of power - Marlowe's Tamburlaine 22 MIN
VHS
Color (H C G)
$169.00 purchase _ #DL496
Presents the death scene from Tamburlaine by Christopher Marlowe to profile the main character's thirst for power and provide examples of Marlowe's blank verse style.
Fine Arts; History - World; Literature and Drama
Dist - INSIM

Parables Series
A Talent for Tony 13 MIN
Dist - FRACOC

Parables - Tape 3
VHS
The New media Bible series
Color (I J H C G A R)
$49.95 purchase, $10.00 rental _ #35 - 82 - 8516
Presents a video account of the events described in the New Testament book of Luke. Portrays the events of the entry into Jericho, Jesus' teachings, and relates the parables of the Mustard Seed and the Prodigal Son. Based on the Revised Standard Version of the Bible.
Literature and Drama; Religion and Philosophy
Dist - APH **Prod** - VISVID

Parables - Volume 1 40 MIN
VHS
Color (K P I R)
$12.97 purchase _ #35 - 86750 - 979
Uses an animated cartoon format to present some of the parables of Jesus. Includes the parables of the good neighbor, the talents, the unforgiving person, and others.
Literature and Drama; Religion and Philosophy
Dist - APH **Prod** - TYHP

Parables - Volume 2 40 MIN
VHS
Color (K P I R)
$12.97 purchase _ #35 - 86751 - 979
Uses an animated cartoon format to present some of the parables of Jesus.
Literature and Drama; Religion and Philosophy
Dist - APH **Prod** - TYHP

Paracelsus 105 MIN
16mm
B&W (C A) (GERMAN (ENGLISH SUBTITLES))
A German language motion picture which tells the story of the unconventional Swiss doctor and sometime professor whose life and personality are considered as a basis for the Faust legend. Shows Paracelsus' attempt to save the city from the plague, despite the suspicions and stubbornness of the people.
Foreign Language; Literature and Drama
Dist - TRANSW **Prod** - TRANSW 1943

Paracentesis (Abdominal) 9 MIN
U-matic / VHS
Medical Skills Films Series
Color (PRO)
Health and Safety
Dist - WFP **Prod** - WFP

Parachute Development at Sandia 11 MIN
16mm
Color (H C)
LC FIA67-546
Describes the special uses for parachutes being developed at the Sandia Corporation, New Mexico. Uses live action and animation to illustrate the problems of and solutions to the deployment of large parachutes at supersonic speeds. Includes test footage.
Business and Economics; Industrial and Technical Education
Dist - SANDIA **Prod** - SANDIA 1966

Parada wspomnien 51 MIN
VHS
(G A) (POLISH)
$19.95 purchase _ #V141
Offers a documentary about the most exciting years of the Solidarity movement which includes conspiracy, famous escapes from police traps and more.
Civics and Political Systems; Fine Arts; History - World; Social Science; Sociology
Dist - POLART

Parade 18 MIN
16mm
Color
LC 73-701618
Offers an overview of the goals and spirit of a school marching band program.
Fine Arts; Sociology
Dist - FAIRFX **Prod** - LEE 1973

Parade 85 MIN
VHS
Color (G)

$29.95 purchase _ #PAR040
Offers funny visual gags in a neverending flow from one act to another in this fantasy about the circus. Features director Jacques Tati as Monsieur Loyal with outstanding mime and visual humor reminiscent of Chaplin and Keaton. Digitally remastered with original hand - painted color inserts.
Fine Arts; Literature and Drama; Physical Education and Recreation
Dist - HOMVIS **Prod** - JANUS 1973

Parade 26 MIN
16mm
Color
LC 71-707553
Features industrial sites of Nova Scotia, interspersed with marching bands and rural and country scenes. Designed to promote industrial growth in Nova Scotia.
Geography - World
Dist - CRAF **Prod** - NOSIS 1970

Parade of the Tall Ships 20 MIN
16mm
Color
LC 77-701450
Presents sailboat crews and captains as they prepare for a transatlantic race. Follows the ships as they parade into New York Harbor on July 4, 1976.
Physical Education and Recreation; Social Science
Dist - MTP **Prod** - IBM 1977

A Parade of witnesses - Martin Luther jubilee 60 MIN
VHS
Color (J H C G A R)
$10.00 rental _ #36 - 81 - 999
Presents excerpts from the Martin Luther 500th Jubilee Festival held in Washington, D C. Features David Stone portraying Luther, and other actors portray Luther's family and friends. Reviews the events in Luther's life.
Literature and Drama; Religion and Philosophy
Dist - APH **Prod** - LUTHER

Parades and changes 40 MIN
16mm
B&W (G)
$45.00 rental
Illustrates a dance in which the dancers relate to space and objects in it, including trapdoors in the floor and ceiling, scaffolding and a weather balloon. Features a nude paper dance in part two in which dancers tear large rolls of paper creating a sculptured image of naked bodies. Performed in 1955 in Sweden. Filmed by Anne Arneborn and produced by Anna Halprin.
Fine Arts
Dist - CANCIN

Paradice 17 MIN
16mm
Color
LC 80-701217
Examines the history of Atlantic City as a background for the changes accompanying casino development there.
Geography - United States; History - United States; Sociology
Dist - ANNSC **Prod** - SMIRUS 1979

Paradigm - creating loops 65 MIN
VHS / Cassette
Beyond fragmentation - memory of the whole series
Color; PAL (G C PRO)
$150.00, $25.00 purchase _ #V9332, #T9332
Features Daniel H Kim who explores how the current worldview affects the way humans perceive and respond to problems. Offers a way of going beyond problem solving to fundamentally redefine the way the world is viewed. Part two of three parts on breaking down the myth that human relationships can be separated into their constituent parts and showing how this myth is slowly being replaced by an appreciation for interconnectedness and the integrity of the whole.
Business and Economics; Psychology
Dist - PEGASU

Paradigm pioneers 31 MIN
VHS
Discovering the future series
Color (PRO IND A)
$895.00 purchase, $200.00 rental _ #CHA10
Challenges thinking with a pioneering spirit through the concepts and patterns presented by Joel Barker. Encourages management to deal with the future, change and opportunity in practical ways. Includes leader's guide and extensive leader's guide.
Business and Economics; Psychology
Dist - EXTR **Prod** - CHARTH

Paradigm prism
VHS
Color (IND PRO)

Geography - World; Religion and Philosophy; Sociology
Dist - LANDMK **Prod** - LANDMK 1987

The Paradigms of performance 37 MIN
VHS
Color (G PRO)
$695.00 purchase, $195.00 rental
Defines paradigm. Recognizes that everyone has an individual system of beliefs or paradigms. Examines the difference between effective and ineffective paradigms. Shows how to avoid distorting reality with generalizations and selective perceptions and to apply the APE model for optimal performance - Abilities, Paradigms, Environment. In two parts. Includes leader guide and paradigm - shifter eyeglasses.
Business and Economics; Guidance and Counseling; Psychology; Sociology
Dist - AMEDIA **Prod** - AMEDIA

The Paradine Case 115 MIN
16mm / U-matic / VHS
B&W (J H C)
Stars Gregory Peck as an attorney who becomes infatuated with his client, a beautiful woman on trial for poisoning her husband. Shows how he begins to have doubts about her innocence as he searches into her mysterious background for evidence.
Fine Arts
Dist - FI **Prod** - UNKNWN 1947

Paradise postponed 55 MIN
VHS
Color (H C G)
$250.00 purchase
Charts the course of the Iranian Revolution and the rise of the Ayatollah Khomeini. Reveals that the Ayatollah promised eternal paradise for those who died. Interviews people who knew the Ayatollah.
Geography - World; Religion and Philosophy
Dist - LANDMK **Prod** - LANDMK 1989

The Paradise Principle 15 MIN
16mm
Color (J)
LC 77-701864
Portrays and assesses Washington State's coastal land and water resources. Examines the effects of management decisions on the preservation, conservation and restoration of natural resources.
Geography - United States; Science - Natural; Social Science
Dist - MARALF **Prod** - MARALF 1977

Paradise Steamship Co series

India	21 MIN
Nepal	21 MIN
New Zealand	9 MIN
Russia	21 MIN
Tokyo	21 MIN

Dist - CAROUF

Paradise Steamship Co

Australia	11 MIN
China	21 MIN
Egypt and Israel	21 MIN

Dist - CAROUF

Paradiso 3 MIN
16mm
B&W (G)
$10.00 rental
Satirizes Dante's conception of heaven, where the blessed sit around in concentric circles forever gazing on the beatific vision. Shows how individuals idolize and make themselves in the image of commercial deities - in this case the 'Cross - your - heart - bra woman.' A David E Simposon production.
Fine Arts; Literature and Drama; Religion and Philosophy
Dist - CANCIN

Paradox 10 MIN
16mm
Color
LC 78-701506
Shows three volunteers at a soup kitchen as they are arrested for salvaging food from a produce warehouse. Tells how they must decide if they will continue their actions with the hope of changing the law.
Guidance and Counseling; Sociology
Dist - FRACOC **Prod** - FRACOC 1977

Paradox 3.0 220 MIN
VHS
Color (G)
$149.95 purchase
Provides video PC software training in IBM Paradox 3.0. Includes training guide.
Computer Science
Dist - HALASI **Prod** - HALASI

Paradox 3.5
VHS
Color (G)

$1995.00 purchase _ #AUR12
Consists of a two - day workshop with Joel Barker and Wayne Burkan on building a quality program within an organization. Includes three facilitator training videos, workshop videos, a facilitator manual, five team workbooks, 21 participant guidebooks, 31 overhead transparencies, a facilitator reference notebook, facilitator presentation notes, 60 minutes telephone hotline service and one year electronic bulletin board service. Produced by Aurora.
Business and Economics
Dist - EXTR

Paradise 15 MIN
16mm / U-matic / VHS
Color (P A G)
Features detailed visuals and haunting music in the telling of this humorous moral tale.
Fine Arts
Dist - DIRECT **Prod** - NFBC 1985

Paradise camp 56 MIN
VHS
Color (G)
$350.00 purchase, $90.00 rental
Tells the story of the Theresienstadt concentration camp in Czechoslovakia which was used by the Nazis during WWII in an elaborate hoax to deceive world opinion about the Third Reich's extermination campaign against the Jews. Shows how the camp was transformed into a 'model Jewish community' prior to an inspection by the Red Cross. The deception was so successful that Hitler commissioned a film 'Hitler Gives a Town to the Jews.' Interviews survivors, uses archival footage and photos, paintings and drawings by camp inmates and excerpts from the propaganda film. Directed by Frank Heimans and Paul Rea.
Fine Arts; History - World
Dist - CNEMAG
CINETF

Paradise lies at the foot of the mother 50 MIN
VHS
Living Islam
Color; PAL (H C A)
PdS99 purchase; Not available in the United States or Puerto Rico
Examines significant events in Islamic history and how they relate to modern Islam. Provides information about the faith and many cultures of Islam with a particular emphasis on what it means to be a Muslim in today's world. Fourth in a series of six programs.
History - World; Religion and Philosophy
Dist - BBCENE

Paradise lost 50 MIN
VHS
Redemption song series
Color; PAL (H C A)
PdS99 purchase
Investigates Spanish influences in the Caribbean and focuses specifically on the city of Santo Domingo, the capital of the Dominican Republic. Features interviews with residents who discuss the history of their city. Third in a series of seven programs documenting the history of the Caribbean.
History - World
Dist - BBCENE

Paradise Lost 52 MIN
U-matic / VHS
Testament - the Bible and History Series
Color (G)
$279.00, $179.00 purchase _ #AD - 1731
Looks at the Bible in modern history. Considers scientific discoveries which add historical dimensions to the text. Part of a seven - part series on the Bible and history.
History - World; Literature and Drama; Religion and Philosophy
Dist - FOTH **Prod** - FOTH

Paradise now 10 MIN
16mm
B&W (G)
$15.00 rental
Takes the viewer on a magical trip. Considers the possibility of seeing New York City in a new and different light. A Fred Safran production.
Fine Arts; Geography - United States; Geography - World; Religion and Philosophy
Dist - CANCIN

Paradise of martyrs 55 MIN
VHS
Color (H C G)
$250.00 purchase
Portrays Iran, a country in the throes of rediscovering its meaning. Follows a young boy's journey to the war. Awaits the fate of Mostafa the butcher on trial for his life in a court of retaliation - the family of the man he murdered will decide if he hangs.

$149.95 purchase _ #PDOX
Provides video PC software training in Paradox 3.5. Includes training guide.
Computer Science
Dist - HALASI **Prod** - HALASI

Paradox 3.5 - advanced
VHS
Paradox 3.5 series
Color (G)
$49.95 purchase _ #VIA004
Teaches advanced Paradox 3.5 database management.
Computer Science
Dist - SIV

Paradox 3.5 - introduction
VHS
Paradox 3.5 series
Color (G)
$49.95 purchase _ #VIA030
Introduces Paradox 3.5 database management.
Computer Science
Dist - SIV

Paradox 3.5 - programming
VHS
Paradox 3.5 series
Color (G)
$49.95 purchase _ #VIA012
Teaches Paradox 3.5 database management programming.
Computer Science
Dist - SIV

Paradox 3.5 series
Presents three videocassettes on Paradox 3.5 database management. Includes an introduction, advanced, and programming information.
Paradox 3.5 - advanced
Paradox 3.5 - introduction
Paradox 3.5 - programming
Dist - SIV

The Paradox of Norval Morrisseau - Norvel Morisseau Un Paradoxe 28 MIN
16mm
Color (G) (FRENCH)
#3X65 I
Presents the life and works of Indian artist Norval Morrisseau, a man who emerged from a life of hardship in the Canadian bush to become one of Canada's most reknown painters. Shows how he continues to paint in the wild and cling to the vanishing Indian heritage as a source of inspiration.
Fine Arts; Social Science
Dist - CDIAND **Prod** - HENJAC 1974

The Paradox of Plenty 22 MIN
16mm
Color
LC 77-702120
Studies electricity and its role in the energy problem. Uses live action and animation to show where electricity comes from and possible choices for the future.
Social Science
Dist - DUQLC **Prod** - DUQLC 1977

Paradox on 72nd Street 60 MIN
16mm / U-matic / VHS
Color (H C A)
Looks at how the goings - on at the intersection of 72nd Street and Broadway in New York can reflect the larger society. Includes voiceovers by Philip Slater and Lewis Thomas who discuss the American conflict between individual freedom/expression and social harmony/equality.
Geography - United States; Sociology
Dist - FI **Prod** - WNETTV 1982

The Paradoxes of Tocqueville's Democracy in America 60 MIN
VHS
Europe and America in the modern age - 1776 to the present series
Color (H C PRO)
$95.00 purchase
Presents a lecture by David M Kennedy. Focuses on a critical period in European and American history and on leaders of the time. Part of a 20 - part series that looks at the last two centuries in Europe and America. Series presents lectures by David M Kennedy and James Sheehan of Stanford University on such figures as Adam Smith, Marx, Lincoln, Washington, Jefferson, Freud, Margaret Sanger, Susan B Anthony and Jane Adams and their impact on the events of their day. For history resource material and continuing education courses.
Civics and Political Systems; History - United States; History - World
Dist - LANDMK

Paradoxical Puzzle 3 MIN
U-matic
Color
Explains how an artist discovered more about herself through the experiences of other women documented in her work.
Fine Arts; Sociology
Dist - WMENIF **Prod** - WMENIF

Parafango 37 MIN
VHS
Color
Presents Charles Atlas' video entry selected from the 1985 Whitney Biennial Film and Video Exhibition.
Fine Arts
Dist - AFA **Prod** - AFA 1986

Paraffin bath home program
VHS / U-matic
Physical therapy series
Color (PRO C G)
$195.00 purchase _ #C890 - VI - 011
Informs patient educators and patients about a paraffin bath home program. Teaches effective techniques for minimizing pain and fatigue while enhancing the ability to perform daily activities. Part of a series by the physical therapy staff, St Luke's Hospital, Fargo, North Dakota.
Health and Safety; Physical Education and Recreation
Dist - HSCIC

The Paragraph 30 MIN
U-matic / VHS
Writing for a Reason Series
Color (C)
English Language
Dist - DALCCD **Prod** - DALCCD

The Paragraph 28 MIN
U-matic / BETA / VHS
Communication skills 1 - basic series
Color (H C G)
$101.95, $89.95 purchase _ #CA - 31
Identifies the topic sentence in a paragraph. Shows how to write a topic sentence and recognize types of paragraph organization and signal words associated with paragraph development. Part of a series on communication.
Social Science
Dist - INSTRU

The Paragraph Connection 14 MIN
16mm / U-matic / VHS
Effective Writing Series
Color (J H C)
$340, $240 purchase _ #3069
Talks about paragraph structure and topic sentences.
English Language
Dist - CORF

Paragraph organization and style - the designer touch 18 MIN
VHS
Language construction company series
Color (H C G)
$50.00 purchase _ #LCC - 13
Assists students in improving their written and spoken English grammar skills. Bases all programs on a 'construction theme.' Includes review tests as an integral part of each lesson. Students may stop, start and repeat any part of the lesson. Visual cues are given for review purposes. Part of a 15 - part series.
English Language
Dist - INSTRU

Paragraph Patterns
U-matic / VHS
Write Course - an Introduction to College Composition Series
Color (C)
Examines the paragraph's flexibility and realistic use in writing. Avoids traditional misconceptions about its role as a writing unit.
Education; English Language
Dist - DALCCD **Prod** - DALCCD

Paragraph Patterns 30 MIN
VHS / U-matic
Write Course - an Introduction to College Composition Series
Color (C A)
LC 85-700984
Discusses the flexibility of the paragraph and its use in expository writing. Avoids traditional misconceptions about its role as a unit.
English Language
Dist - FI **Prod** - FI 1984

Paragraph reading road 20 MIN
VHS / U-matic
Efficient reading - instructional tapes series; Tape 10
Color
Discusses reading paragraphs to structure the main idea and improve comprehension.
English Language
Dist - TELSTR **Prod** - TELSTR

Paragraph variety 28 MIN
U-matic / BETA / VHS
Communication skills 1 - basic series
Color (H C G)
$101.95, $89.95 purchase _ #CA - 32
Enables the viewer to write more stimulating paragraphs. Shows how this can be done through understanding methods of organization and development and by using creative, yet specific details. Part of a series on communication.
Social Science
Dist - INSTRU

Paragraphs - Like Scenes in a Film 15 MIN
U-matic / VHS / 16mm
Sentences and Paragraphs Series
Color (I J H)
LC 81-700052
Illustrates the usefulness of paragraphs by comparing them to scene changes in a motion picture. Demonstrates the value of a topic sentence and shows ways to create supporting sentences.
English Language
Dist - CORF **Prod** - CENTRO 1981

Paragraphs with Ralph and Stanley 14 MIN
U-matic / VHS / 16mm
Writing Skills Series
Color (P)
LC 79-700740
Tells how two boys learn the basic skills involved in organizing a paragraph when they embark upon an adventurous escapade.
English Language
Dist - PHENIX **Prod** - BEANMN 1979

Paraguay - the Forgotten Dictatorship 27 MIN
U-matic / VHS / 16mm
Color (H C A) (SPANISH (ENGLISH SUBTITLES))
$250 purchase, $50 rental
Looks at the dictatorship in Paraguay under General Alfredo Stroessner. Examines the development of opposition forces and human rights abuses. Includes interviews with government officials, religious and opposition leaders, and former political prisoners. Directed by Patricia Boero.
Civics and Political Systems; History - World
Dist - CNEMAG

Paralegal 20 MIN
VHS
Get a life - a day in the career guidance series
Color (H C A)
$89.00 purchase _ #886696-10-1
Takes viewers through a day in the life of a paralegal, with candid interviews and insights from top paralegal instuctors and attorneys. Describes educational and other professional requirements for the job, along with salary range and opportunities within the profession. Part of a ten-part series.
Business and Economics; Guidance and Counseling
Dist - VOCAVD **Prod** - VOCAVD 1995

Paralegal
VHS
Day in a career series
Color (C H A J T G)
$89.00 purchase _ #VOC01V-G ; $89.00 purchase _ #VOC01V-J
Presents information about the occupation of paralegal, one of the careers that the United States Department of Labor projects as potentially successful by the year 2000. Profiles in detail the work day of a real person, with candid interviews and work situations and information about the educational requirements, credentials, job outlook, salaries, important associations, and contacts in the field. One of a series of ten videos, lasting 15 to 22 minutes, available individually or as a set.
Business and Economics; Civics and Political Systems; Guidance and Counseling
Dist - CAMV

Paralegal
VHS
Vocational visions career series
Color (H A)
$39.95 purchase _ #CDS500
Interviews people in the paralegal profession. Answers questions about the educational requirements and necessary skills for the occupation, as well as its career opportunities, salary range and outlook for the future. Part of a series which examines the potential of various occupations.
Business and Economics; Civics and Political Systems; Guidance and Counseling; Psychology
Dist - CADESF **Prod** - CADESF 1989

The Parallel bars
VHS
N C A A instructional video series
Color (H C A)
$39.95 purchase _ #KAR2604V
Presents the fourth of a four - part series on gymnastics. Focuses on the parallel bars.

Physical Education and Recreation
Dist - CAMV **Prod** - NCAAF

Parallel Bars - Beginning Exercises 12 MIN
16mm / U-matic / VHS
Color (I)
LC FIA67-1728
Demonstrates proper width adjustment of the parallel bars. Shows mounts, support positions, basic swinging movements, straddle seat travels, upper arm stands and rolls, front and rear swing rises, simple turns and dismounts. Includes slow motion close - ups and performance of stunts of intermediate difficulty.
Physical Education and Recreation
Dist - AIMS **Prod** - ASSOCF 1965

Parallel circuits analysis 30 MIN
VHS / U-matic
Basic electricity and D C circuits series
Color
Outlines circuit analysis of parallel circuits including procedures for calculating unknown voltages, current and resistances in any part of a simple parallel circuit. Covers differences between series and parallel circuits for predicting circuit behavior.
Industrial and Technical Education; Science - Physical; Social Science
Dist - TXINLC **Prod** - TXINLC

Parallel circuits and their analysis 15 MIN
U-matic / VHS
Basic electricity and D C circuits - laboratory series
Color
Industrial and Technical Education; Science - Physical; Social Science
Dist - TXINLC **Prod** - TXINLC

Parallel Data Transfer Devices 60 TO 90 MIN
VHS
Microprocessors Module Series
Color (PRO)
$600.00 - $1500.00 purchase _ #MIPDT
Introduces parallel interfacing and the design and operation of a parallel data transfer device. Part of an eleven - part series on microprocessors. Includes five student guides, five workbooks and an instructor guide.
Computer Science; Education; Industrial and Technical Education; Psychology
Dist - NUSTC **Prod** - NUSTC

Parallel for Variety 29 MIN
Videoreel / VT2
Skiing Series
Color
Physical Education and Recreation
Dist - PBS **Prod** - KTCATV

Parallel Interfacing, Pt 1 42 MIN
U-matic / VHS
Microprocessor Interfacing Series
Color
Industrial and Technical Education; Mathematics
Dist - MIOT **Prod** - MIOT

Parallel Interfacing, Pt 2 44 MIN
U-matic / VHS
Microprocessor Interfacing Series
Color
Industrial and Technical Education; Mathematics
Dist - MIOT **Prod** - MIOT

Parallel Lines 10 MIN
16mm
Color; B&W (I J)
Explains the concept of parallel lines, illustrates the prevalence of parallel lines in industry and architecture and gives specific instances of the application of the laws of parallel lines.
Mathematics
Dist - MLA **Prod** - JHP 1951

Parallel Lines 30 MIN
VHS
Mathematics Series
Color (J)
LC 90713155
Discusses parallel lines. The 146th of 157 installments of the Mathematics Series.
Mathematics
Dist - GPN

Parallel lines 30 MIN
VHS
Geometry series
Color (H)
$125.00 purchase _ #7005
Explains parallel lines. Part of a 16 - part series on geometry.
Mathematics
Dist - LANDMK **Prod** - LANDMK

Parallel Needle Internal Jugular Catheterization Technique 4 MIN
U-matic / VHS
Color (PRO)
Illustrates the combination of a small gauge needle to locate the vein and a larger bore over - the - needle catheter to enter the vein.
Health and Safety; Science - Natural
Dist - UARIZ **Prod** - UARIZ

Parallel - Pin Retention for a Full Crown 14 MIN
16mm
Color (PRO)
LC 77-700861
Demonstrates the use of a parallel - pin technique to retain a full crown for a tooth with insufficient coronal tooth structure remaining for adequate retention by means of conventional preparation.
Health and Safety; Science
Dist - USNAC **Prod** - VADTC 1977

Parallel RC Circuits 20 MIN
U-matic / VHS / 16mm
B&W
Reviews the operation of parallel RC circuits and shows how to solve for branch currents and total impedance using Ohm's Law. Discusses vector representations and the approximation of total current and phase angle by vector measurement. Introduces trig functions and reviews power.
Industrial and Technical Education; Science - Physical
Dist - USNAC **Prod** - USAF 1983

Parallel RC, RL, and RCL Circuits - Graphic Solutions 32 MIN
U-matic
B&W
LC 79-707512
Shows how to solve for branch current, total current, total impedance, and phase angle in parallel RC, RL and RCL circuits using Ohm's law and vectors.
Industrial and Technical Education
Dist - USNAC **Prod** - USAF 1979

Parallel RC, RL, and RCL Circuits - Trigonometric Solutions 39 MIN
U-matic
B&W
LC 79-707513
Shows how parallel RC, RL and RCL circuit values are computed in trigonometric functions by first determining the phase angle and then computing theta. Presents the procedure for solving for total impedance by Ohm's law.
Industrial and Technical Education
Dist - USNAC **Prod** - USAF 1979

Parallel RCL Circuits 17 MIN
16mm / U-matic / VHS
B&W
Shows the formula for determining the resonant frequency of a parallel tank circuit. Compares the Z, live current and tank current below, above and at resonance. Compares series and parallel resonant circuits and discusses Q. Uses vectors to show phase angles.
Industrial and Technical Education; Science - Physical
Dist - USNAC **Prod** - USAF 1983

Parallel resistances 15 MIN
VHS / U-matic
Basic electricity and D C circuits - laboratory series
Color
Industrial and Technical Education; Science - Physical; Social Science
Dist - TXINLC **Prod** - TXINLC

Parallel Resistive Circuit - Power Troubleshooting 17 MIN
U-matic / VHS / 16mm
B&W
Tells what determines power in a parallel circuit. Uses a voltmeter, ammeter and ohmmeter to show symptoms of open and shorted components.
Industrial and Technical Education; Science - Physical
Dist - USNAC **Prod** - USAF 1983

Parallel Resistive Circuits 33 MIN
16mm
B&W
LC 74-705296
Explains the requirements for a parallel circuit, showing how to measure and compute the voltage across each branch, as well as the total voltage. Demonstrates how to measure current and resistance in a parallel circuit.
Industrial and Technical Education
Dist - USNAC **Prod** - USAF 1972

Parallel Resistive Circuits - Analysis 17 MIN
U-matic / VHS / 16mm
B&W
Discusses how current, voltage and resistance are related in a parallel circuit.
Industrial and Technical Education; Science - Physical
Dist - USNAC **Prod** - USAF 1983

Parallel Resistive Circuits - Bridges 14 MIN
U-matic / VHS / 16mm
B&W
Explains the principles of the Wheat Stone Bridge and demonstrates its use in measuring resistance and as part of a control system.
Industrial and Technical Education; Science - Physical
Dist - USNAC **Prod** - USAF 1983

Parallel Resistive Circuits - Circuit Analysis 22 MIN
16mm
B&W
LC 74-705297
Defines the principles of Ohm's and Kirchoff's laws as they apply to solving the problems related to branch currents, resistances and applied voltage. Uses actual problems as a means of proving the principles of parallel circuitry.
Industrial and Technical Education; Science - Physical
Dist - USNAC **Prod** - USAF 1972

Parallel Resistive Circuits - DC Power 14 MIN
16mm
B&W
LC 74-705299
Demonstrates the distribution of power in a parallel circuit. Shows how to determine the power dissipated in the individual branches as well as the total power.
Industrial and Technical Education; Science - Physical
Dist - USNAC **Prod** - USAF 1971

Parallel Resistive Circuits - Troubleshooting 21 MIN
16mm
B&W
LC 74-705300
Discusses symptoms produced by open and shorted parallel resistors. Shows how an ammeter and voltmeter are used to detect such troubles.
Industrial and Technical Education
Dist - USNAC **Prod** - USAF 1971

Parallel Resonant Circuits 53 MIN
U-matic
B&W (IND)
LC 79-707518
Shows how to calculate resonant frequency and compare the magnitude of current at and off resonance. Shows how to compare the impedance and current curves of parallel and series RCL circuits.
Industrial and Technical Education
Dist - USNAC **Prod** - USAF 1979

Parallel Resonant Circuits 24 MIN
16mm
B&W
LC 74-705302
Shows how to compare the impedance and current curves of parallel and series RCL circuits. Compares the line current of a parallel resonant circuit to that of a series resonant circuit.
Industrial and Technical Education; Science - Physical
Dist - USNAC **Prod** - USAF 1971

Parallel Resonant Circuits, Pt 1 27 MIN
U-matic
B&W (IND)
LC 79-707518
Shows how to calculate resonant frequency and compare the magnitude of current at and off resonance.
Industrial and Technical Education
Dist - USNAC **Prod** - USAF 1979

Parallel Resonant Circuits, Pt 2 26 MIN
U-matic
B&W (IND)
LC 79-707518
Shows how to compare the impedance and current curves of parallel and series RCL circuits.
Industrial and Technical Education
Dist - USNAC **Prod** - USAF 1979

Parallel RL Circuits 11 MIN
U-matic / VHS / 16mm
B&W
Reviews several methods of solving parallel RL circuits when frequency and applied voltage are known. Shows how to find total current and phase angle vectorially and trigonometrically and discusses true and apparent power.
Industrial and Technical Education; Science - Physical
Dist - USNAC **Prod** - USAF 1983

Parallel - series circuits 30 MIN
U-matic / VHS
Basic electricity and D C circuits series
Color
Reviews behavior rules for series and parallel circuits. Introduces series - parallel and parallel - series circuits with an in - depth parallel - series circuit analysis. Includes explanation of process of circuit reduction.
Industrial and Technical Education; Science - Physical; Social Science
Dist - TXINLC **Prod** - TXINLC

Parallel Structure 8 MIN
BETA / VHS
English and Speech Series
Color
English Language
Dist - RMIBHF **Prod** - RMIBHF

Parallels - the President and the Dictator, Pt 1 24 MIN
16mm
Color
Traces parallel developments in the United States and Germany in the years between world wars.
Civics and Political Systems; History - United States; History - World
Dist - REAF **Prod** - INTEXT

Parallels - the President and the Dictator, Pt 2 24 MIN
16mm
Color
Examines two wartime leaders - Franklin Delano Roosevelt and Adolf Hitler.
Biography; Civics and Political Systems; History - United States; History - World
Dist - REAF **Prod** - INTEXT

The Paralyzed Face 60 MIN
U-matic / VHS
Color (PRO)
LC 81-706297
Discusses various degrees of facial paralysis and includes a presentation of facial anatomy and neurology.
Health and Safety
Dist - USNAC **Prod** - USVA 1980

Paramagnetism of Liquid Oxygen E - 2 3 MIN
16mm
Single - Concept Films in Physics Series
Color (J H C)
Shows a comparison between liquid oxygen, which adheres to pole pieces of magnet, and liquid nitrogen, which is not paramagnetic.
Science - Physical
Dist - OSUMPD **Prod** - OSUMPD 1963

The Paramecium 30 MIN
VHS / U-matic
Color
Illustrates the complexities of the paramecium. Includes fourteen follow - up questions at end of program.
Science - Natural
Dist - EDMEC **Prod** - EDMEC

The Paramecium 12 MIN
16mm
Color (H C)
Describes the appearance, external structures and internal structures of paramecium. Relates that the macronucleus regulates all vital processes and that two contractile vacuoles are very efficient in pumping out excess water.
Science - Natural
Dist - BNCHMK **Prod** - BNCHMK 1983

The Paramecium 12 MIN
U-matic / VHS
Modern Biology Series
Color (H C)
Covers the biology of paramecium, showing both internal and external anatomy. Shows, through live photography cilia motion, shape change, egestion, food vacuole formation and defensive actions.
Science - Natural
Dist - BNCHMK **Prod** - INFB 1985

The Paramecium - are you my type 30 MIN
U-matic / VHS / BETA
Color (T)
$39.95 purchase _ #5103
Teaches teachers of junior high students and up how to teach concepts in biology. Shows paramecium, a one - celled protozoan belonging to phylum Ciliophora in long sequences to allow observations and note taking. Highlights types of reproduction, movement, nervous response, protection by trichocysts, food gathering, waste removal, dying and death and other general biological features by sequences which allow close observation and interpretation.
Science - Natural
Dist - INSTRU

The Paramedic 16 MIN
16mm / U-matic / VHS
Color (I)
LC 77-701100
Presents on - the - scene footage of various medical emergencies being handled by paramedics from the Santa Ana Fire Department. Provides narration by the men describing the function of their jobs. Describes the paramedics' training, duty hours and relations with other fire department employees, police, physicians and nurses.
Health and Safety; Psychology; Science; Social Science
Dist - PFP **Prod** - BRAVC 1977

Paramedic 30 MIN
BETA / VHS
American Professionals Series
Color
Presents Bill Olsen, who brings the emergency room to the patient, and who describes his work as a 'no second chance' profession.
Guidance and Counseling; Health and Safety
Dist - RMIBHF **Prod** - WTBS

Paramedic 15 MIN
U-matic / 16mm / VHS
Career Awareness
(I)
$130 VC purchase, $240 film purchase, $25 VC rental, $30 film rental
Presents an empathetic approach to career planning, showing the personal as well as the professional qualities of paramedics. Highlights the importance of career education.
Guidance and Counseling; Health and Safety
Dist - GPN

Paranoia corridore 3 MIN
16mm
Color; Silent (H C A)
$15.00 rental
Combines luminescent greens and blues in constantly shifting symmetrical shapes which suggest, rather than delineate, passage through a corridore. Evolves into an increasingly menacing pattern until interrupted by a series of static shapes which appear to be symbols of resolution. Produced by Stan Brakhage.
Fine Arts; Science - Physical
Dist - CANCIN

Paranoid schizophrenia - Part I 115 MIN
VHS
Client sessions series
Color; PAL; SECAM (G)
$95.00 purchase
Features Richard Bandler in the third part of a four - part series of client sessions, using NLP, neuro - linguistic programming. Demonstrates clinical applications of NLP methods. Bandler sometimes uses profanity for emphasis, which may offend some people. All levels.
Health and Safety; Psychology
Dist - NLPCOM **Prod** - NLPCOM

Paranoid schizophrenia - Part II 116 MIN
VHS
Client sessions series
Color; PAL; SECAM (G)
$95.00 purchase
Features Richard Bandler in the fourth part of a four - part series of client sessions, using NLP, neuro - linguistic programming. Demonstrates clinical applications of NLP methods. Bandler sometimes uses profanity for emphasis, which may offend some people. All levels.
Health and Safety; Psychology
Dist - NLPCOM **Prod** - NLPCOM

Paranoid State and Deterioration Following Head Injury 11 MIN
16mm
B&W (C)
Paranoid delusions, violent rages and serious neglect of person led to the commitment of a patient two years after a skull fracture. The film illustrates the rambling, circumstantial flow of talk which conveys disjointed, inconsistent, but dominant notions of persecution.
Psychology
Dist - PSUPCR **Prod** - PSUPCR 1939

Paranormal Phenomena - Reality or Illusion 30 MIN
U-matic / VHS
Moral Values in Contemporary Society Series
Color (J)
Features Lawrence LeShan, author of the Medium, The Mystic And The Physicist, and Khoren Arisian, Leader of the New York Society for Ethical Culture, discussing paranormal phenomena.
Psychology; Sociology
Dist - AMHUMA **Prod** - AMHUMA

The Paranormal - Science or Pseudoscience 30 MIN
U-matic / VHS
Ethics in America Series
Color (H C A)
Presents professional conjurer James Randi, professor of psychology Ray Hayman, author Ethel Grodzins and psycho - physicist Wilbur Franklin discussing the mushrooming interest in the paranormal and psychic phenomena.
Psychology; Religion and Philosophy; Sociology
Dist - AMHUMA **Prod** - AMHUMA

Paraplegic Ambulation, Initial Parallel Bar Exercises 8 MIN
16mm
Color
LC 74-705305
Describes how the ambulation of the paraplegic patient wearing bilateral long leg braces with a pelvic band is preceded by exercises in the parallel bars to develop initial balance during stance and trunk movements, and initial weight shifting with accompanying anterior pelvic tilt and head positon. Outlines the therapists spotting carefully and portrays push - ups in the bars and jacknifing which are the last of the initial parallel bar exercises taught.
Health and Safety; Psychology
Dist - USNAC **Prod** - USPHS

Paraplegic Patient Education - Activities in Your New Life 7 MIN
16mm
Color
LC 74-705306
Examines some of the problems of adjusting to a new life following a crippling disease or accident. Suggests ways to solve these problems, build self - confidence and achieve physical and financial independence.
Guidance and Counseling; Health and Safety; Psychology
Dist - USNAC **Prod** - NMAC 1969

Paraplegic Patient Education - an Active Future 5 MIN
16mm
Color
LC 74-705307
Stresses the importance of setting realistic goals during the rehabilitation program of a paraplegic in order to achieve success later. Emphasizes the necessity of maintaining good health, activity and interest.
Education; Health and Safety; Psychology
Dist - USNAC **Prod** - NMAC 1969

Paraplegic Patient Education - Joint Motion 5 MIN
16mm
Color
LC 74-705308
Explains methods of maintaining joint motion for the paraplegic including range of motion exercises, positioning and activity.
Education; Health and Safety; Psychology
Dist - USNAC **Prod** - NMAC 1969

Paraplegic Patient Education - Moving in and Out of Your Wheelchair 5 MIN
16mm
Color
LC 74-705309
Explains the steps involved in the independent transfer of a paraplegic to and from a wheelchair.
Guidance and Counseling; Health and Safety; Psychology
Dist - USNAC **Prod** - NMAC 1969

Paraplegic Patient Education - Planning Your Bowel Program 5 MIN
U-matic
Color
LC 80-706284
Stresses the importance of a paraplegic establishing a well - planned bowel program based on scheduling, diet and stimulation. Issued in 1969 as a motion picture.
Health and Safety
Dist - USNAC **Prod** - AMRF 1980

Paraplegic Patient Education - Prevention of Bladder Problems 8 MIN
16mm
Color
LC 74-705313
Explains bladder dysfunction related to spinal cord injury. Stresses the importance of catheter irrigation, good drainage and fluid intake in the prevention of calcium deposits in the bladder or kidneys.
Guidance and Counseling; Health and Safety; Psychology
Dist - USNAC **Prod** - NMAC 1970

Paraplegic Patient Education - Prevention of Skin Problems 8 MIN
16mm
Color
LC 74-705311
Cites causes of decubitus ulcers resulting from pressure sores. Warns of the dangers involved and outlines a simple deterring program.
Guidance and Counseling; Health and Safety; Psychology
Dist - USNAC **Prod** - NMAC 1970

Paraplegic Patient Education - the Effects of Spinal Cord Injury 8 MIN
16mm
Color
LC 74-705314
Cites causes of spinal injuries, discusses the effect these injuries may have on the individual and points out how best to become as independent as possible.

Guidance and Counseling; Health and Safety; Psychology
Dist - USNAC **Prod** - NMAC 1970

The Paraplegic Patient - in and Out of Car - Patient using Crutches and Wearing Braces 5 MIN
16mm
Color
LC 74-705316
Demonstrates the use of crutches and braces in moving in and out of a car.
Guidance and Counseling; Health and Safety; Psychology
Dist - USNAC **Prod** - NMAC 1970

The Paraplegic Patient - Putting on a Full Body Brace in Wheelchair 11 MIN
16mm
Color
LC 74-705317
Depicts the most effective methods for the paraplegic patient to put on full body braces in a wheelchair.
Health and Safety
Dist - USNAC **Prod** - USPHS 1968

The Paraplegic Patient - Taking Off a Full Body Brace in Bed 8 MIN
16mm
Color
LC 74-705318
Depicts the method used by a paraplegic to remove a full body brace in bed.
Health and Safety
Dist - USNAC **Prod** - USPHS 1968

The Paraplegic Patient - Transfer from Wheelchair to Car and Reverse 4 MIN
16mm
Color
LC 74-705319
Demonstrates the transfer between wheel chair and car.
Guidance and Counseling; Health and Safety; Psychology
Dist - USNAC **Prod** - NMAC 1970

Paraprofessionals and Volunteers 30 MIN
U-matic / VHS
Basic Education - Teaching the Adult Series
Color (T)
Discusses the uses of paraprofessionals and volunteers when teaching adult basic education students.
Education
Dist - MDCPB **Prod** - MDDE

Pararescue - its Role in the Space Age 24 MIN
16mm
Color
LC 76-700483
Portrays the role of the air rescue service pararescue teams. Presents rigorous physical and mental training that prepares airmen for pararescue service in any environment.
Health and Safety; Social Science
Dist - USNAC **Prod** - USAF 1976

Parasacral Approach to Lesions of the Rectum 18 MIN
VHS / U-matic
Color (PRO)
Illustrates parasacral approach to removal of lesions of the rectum.
Health and Safety; Science - Natural
Dist - HSCIC **Prod** - HSCIC 1984

Parasites 11 MIN
16mm / U-matic / VHS
Color (J H) (FRENCH SWEDISH)
LC 72-708753
Describes the relationships between some common parasites and their hosts, and shows that both plants and animals may be parasites.
Science - Natural
Dist - PHENIX **Prod** - PHENIX 1970

Parasitism - Parasitic Flatworms 17 MIN
U-matic / VHS / 16mm
Biology (Spanish Series Unit 7 - Animal Classification and 'Physiology; Unit 7 - Animal classification and physiology
Color (H) (SPANISH)
Traces the development of parasitic flatworms. Illustrates predation, mutualism, and internal and external parasitism.
Foreign Language; Science - Natural
Dist - EBEC **Prod** - EBEC

Parasitology Series
Infective Larvae of Wuchereria Bancrofti 4 MIN
Microfilariae of Wuchereria Bancrofti 4 MIN
Movements of Endamoeba Histolytica 2 MIN
Dist - USNAC

Parasympathomimetic Blocking Agents, Anticholinergics and Antispasmodics 30 MIN
16mm
Pharmacology Series
B&W (C)
LC 73-703342
Shows the effect produced by parasympathetic blocking agents and describes their clinical uses and side effects.
Health and Safety; Psychology
Dist - TELSTR **Prod** - MVNE 1971

Parasympathomimetics 30 MIN
16mm
Pharmacology Series
B&W (C)
LC 73-703341
Health and Safety; Psychology
Dist - TELSTR **Prod** - MVNE 1971

Parataxis 3 MIN
16mm
Color; Sound (C)
$112.00
Experimental film by Skip Battaglia.
Fine Arts
Dist - AFA **Prod** - AFA 1980

Parathyroidectomy 12 MIN
VHS / U-matic 40 MIN
Head and Neck Series
Color
Health and Safety; Science - Natural
Dist - SVL **Prod** - SVL

Paratransits 6 MIN
16mm
Color (A)
LC 78-700813
Demonstrates two prototype taxicabs operating in both city and suburban settings. Highlights innovations, such as ramps for the elderly and handicapped, increased luggage space and protection for the driver.
Social Science; Sociology
Dist - USNAC **Prod** - USDT 1977

Paratroopers 95 MIN
16mm
Color
Calls for a reassessment of life in contemporary Israel. Tells the story of a misfit in an army boot camp, who commits suicide during training maneuvers. Portrays the army as a microcosm of Israeli society, regimented and disciplined, with little leeway for dissidence.
Geography - World; Sociology
Dist - ICARUS **Prod** - ICARUS

Parcelle 3 MIN
16mm
Color (G)
$10.00 rental
Composes frame by frame in the camera. Depicts the alternate appearance and variable duration of tiny colored squares and circles on a black background. Title is a French word for a fragment, particle or bit.
Fine Arts
Dist - CANCIN **Prod** - LOWDER 1979

The Parching Winds of Somalia 30 MIN
VHS / 16mm
Color (H C A)
$150.00 purchase, $25.00 rental _ #CC3286
Traces the history of Somalia from its battles for independence under the Muslim leader Sayyid Muhammad Abdille Hasan up to the present and considers several contemporary concerns such as the challenge of Muslim patriarchal customs by Somali women.
Civics and Political Systems; Geography - World; History - World; Sociology
Dist - IU **Prod** - NENDOW 1984

Pardon Me for Living 30 MIN
U-matic / VHS / 16mm
LCA Short Story Library Series
Color (I J H)
LC 82-700408
Deals with the value of true friendship when a girl named Emily is tricked into presenting a petition against geography homework to her stern teacher Miss Holderness. Based on the short story The Scarlet Letter by Jean Stafford.
Guidance and Counseling; Literature and Drama
Dist - LCOA **Prod** - LCOA 1982

Pardon Us 56 MIN
16mm
B&W
Tells the story of two men who decide to market their own home brew during Prohibition. Shows what happens when they make their first sale to a policeman and land in jail. Stars Stan Laurel and Oliver Hardy.
Fine Arts
Dist - RMIBHF **Prod** - ROACH 1931

Pardoner's Secret 45 MIN
U-matic / VHS
Survey of English Literature I Series
Color (C)
Features a close reading of the crucial passages of Pardoner's Secret, as part of a sophomore literature course.
Education; Literature and Drama
Dist - MDCPB **Prod** - MDCPB

Parent - Adult - Child 27 MIN
Videoreel / VT2
Interpersonal Competence, Unit 04 - Helping Series; Unit 4 - Helping
Color (C A)
Features a humanistic psychologist who, by analysis and examples, discusses that helping relationships are an important aspect of interpersonal relationships. Describes the helping relationships involved between parents and their children.
Psychology; Sociology
Dist - TELSTR **Prod** - MVNE 1973

Parent and Child Relationships - It's My Decision, as Long as It's what You Want 14 MIN
U-matic / VHS / 16mm
Conflict and Awareness Series
Color (I J H)
LC 74-701920
Dramatizes a discussion between a mother and daughter to promote conversation on the problems of communication and the various ways parents and children communicate with each other.
Guidance and Counseling; Psychology; Sociology
Dist - CRMP **Prod** - CRMP 1974

Parent - Child Relations in the Early Years Series
Getting Ready for the Dentist 11 MIN
Let Your Child Help You 11 MIN
Dist - NYU

Parent - Child Value Conflicts about Drugs 7 MIN
U-matic
Color
Dramatized situations of parent - child conflicts about drugs. Shows typical situations in our modern world regarding drug use.
Psychology
Dist - UWASHP **Prod** - UWASHP

Parent Conferencing 30 MIN
VHS / U-matic
Teaching Students with Special Needs Series
Color
Features consultants who discuss parent and teacher attitudes reflected in conferencing. Recommendations are made for productive parent - professional interactions that provide support, while avoiding adversarial situations.
Sociology
Dist - PBS **Prod** - MSITV 1981

Parent Consumers Speak Out 40 MIN
U-matic / VHS
B&W
Presents three different conceptual models of looking at family stress within families who have developmentally disabled children.
Health and Safety; Psychology; Sociology
Dist - UWISC **Prod** - VRL 1983

Parent Counseling 30 MIN
U-matic / VHS
Stretch Strategies for Teaching Handicapped Children Series
Color (T)
Presents methods for effective counseling of parents of handicapped children.
Education; Sociology
Dist - HUBDSC **Prod** - HUBDSC

Parent Education 24 MIN
16mm
International Education of the Hearing Impaired Child Series
Color
LC 74-705321
Shows home and clinic instruction in Sweden, Germany, England and the Netherlands.
Guidance and Counseling; Sociology
Dist - USNAC **Prod** - USBEH 1970

Parent Education at Heidelberg, Germany 11 MIN
U-matic / VHS
International Education of the Hearing Impaired Child Series
Color (GERMAN)

LC 80-707443
Presents Arman Lowe's home teaching and parent education program at the Paedo - audiological Guidance Center in Germany.
Education; Psychology
Dist - USNAC **Prod** - USBEH 1980

Parent Education - Attitude Films Series
Anger and fear 10 MIN
Creative play 10 MIN
Discipline 10 MIN
Feelings 10 MIN
Learning 10 MIN
Learning to Live Together 10 MIN
Parental Aspirations 10 MIN
Problem Solving 10 MIN
Dist - TC

Parent education film series information series
Getting the idea 8 MIN
Dist - TC

Parent Education Film Series Parent Attitude Series, no 1
Fundamental Needs of People 10 MIN
Dist - TC

Parent education - information films series
The Beginnings of speech 10 MIN
Check and double check 10 MIN
Eyes, ears and hands 10 MIN
Getting the Idea 10 MIN
Hearing and not Hearing 10 MIN
Holding the Reins 10 MIN
Making a Choice 10 MIN
Stepping Stones 10 MIN
Talk, Talk, Talk 10 MIN
Dist - TC

Parent for Tonight 15 MIN
16mm
Color (I)
LC 80-701048
Tells the story of today's baby - sitter. Demonstrates safe and proper baby - sitting conduct.
Home Economics; Sociology
Dist - KLEINW **Prod** - KLEINW 1975

Parent Involvement 29 MIN
U-matic / VHS
Mainstreaming the Exceptional Child Series
Color (T)
Discusses the role of the parents in helping their handicapped child be successfully mainstreamed into a regular school.
Education; Psychology
Dist - FI **Prod** - MFFD

A Parent Perspective - Mental Retardation, Pt 1, Karma 23 MIN
U-matic
Impact of a Handicap on the Family Structure
Color (H C A)
Interviews the mother of an 11 year old girl with Down's Syndrome who describes her grief and adjustment. Original diagnosis, hospital events and the child's early years are described, along with attitudes of her husband and other family members, advice received and interactions with other children.
Psychology; Sociology
Dist - UILL **Prod** - UILL 1982

A Parent Perspective - Mental Retardation, Pt 2, Karma 18 MIN
U-matic
Impact of a Handicap on the Family Structure
Color (H C A)
Continues talking with the mother of a Down's Syndrome child focusing on experiences with parent groups and feelings of siblings. Describes the child's abilities and concerns felt regarding her adolescence and future.
Psychology; Sociology
Dist - UILL **Prod** - UILL 1982

A Parent Perspective - Mental Retardation, Pt 3, Tom 27 MIN
U-matic
Impact of a Handicap on the Family Structure
Color (H C A)
Interview with the father of a 13 year old girl with Down's syndrome. He describes his experiences and attitudes relating to the birth, genetic counseling, medical treatment, early development, role of religion and the effect having a handicapped child had on their marriage.
Psychology; Sociology
Dist - UILL **Prod** - UILL 1982

A Parent Perspective - Mental Retardation, Pt 4, Tom 27 MIN
U-matic
Impact of a Handicap on the Family Structure
Color (H C A)
Continues an interview with the father of a Down's Syndrome girl. He discusses feelings about other children, abortion, grief, impact of a handicapped child on the family, sibling attitudes and the future of the handicapped child.
Psychology; Sociology
Dist - UILL **Prod** - UILL 1982

Parent Puzzle Series
Contracting 30 MIN
Create a Climate 30 MIN
Individual Differences 30 MIN
Order, Growth, Change 30 MIN
Parenting as a Process 30 MIN
The Pre - natal crisis 30 MIN
Self Discipline 30 MIN
The Six Months Blues 30 MIN
Taking Time for Ourselves 30 MIN
What is Discipline 30 MIN
Dist - ACCESS

Parent talk - the art of parenting 52 MIN
VHS
Color (G)
$19.95 purchase
Presents a practical guide to raising children two to five years of age. Covers subjects including bedtime, toilet training, tattling, hyperactivity, mealtime hassles, thumb sucking, stuttering, whining, and more. Hosted by child development expert and columnist Evelyn Petersen.
Guidance and Counseling
Dist - PBS **Prod** - WNETTV

Parent - Teacher Conference
VHS / U-matic
Vital Link Series
Color (A)
Demonstrates the way an informative working relationship can be established in a parent - teacher conference.
Social Science; Sociology
Dist - EDCC **Prod** - EDCC

Parent - Teenager Communications 20 MIN
16mm / U-matic / VHS
Color (A)
Presents 13 vignettes explaining how a parent can handle discussions with a teenager dealing with independence and responsibility, drugs and alcohol, honesty and openness, interpersonal relationships, sex, schoolwork and sibling rivalry.
Psychology; Sociology
Dist - CORF **Prod** - CORF

Parent to Child about Sex 31 MIN
16mm / U-matic / VHS
Color (J H A)
LC FIA67-2007
Shows parents how to teach their children important facts and wholesome attitudes about sex. Concerns itself with when and how facts are taught and the method of their teaching. Stresses a comfortable relationship and free communication between parent and child for building a foundation of responsible, healthy, mature attitudes.
Psychology; Sociology
Dist - PEREN **Prod** - MARFLE 1967

Parent Training 150 MIN
U-matic / VHS
Meeting the Communications Needs of the Severely/Profoundly 'Handicapped 1980 Series
Color
Focuses on training parents to take an active role in intervention. Discusses traditional roles for parents, approaches to parent training, as well as critical issues in implementing a program.
Psychology; Social Science
Dist - PUAVC **Prod** - PUAVC

Parent Training Group - a Behavioral Perspective 14 MIN
U-matic / VHS
B&W
Features a discussion by a parents group talking about what has occurred in the week since the last meeting. Focuses on one couple whose daughter dallies at bedtime.
Sociology
Dist - UWISC **Prod** - VRL

Parental ambivalence - 8 34 MIN
VHS / U-matic
Glendon programs - a series
Color (C A)
$305.00, $275.00 purchase _ #V595
Considers that parents have both positive and negative feelings about themselves which can translate into both tender feelings and covertly aggressive feelings toward their children. Shows parents recalling painful events in their childhood to understand the sources of their ambivalent feelings toward their own children and to develop a more positive approach to child - rearing. Part of a 12 - part series featuring Dr Robert W Firestone, who is noted for his concept of the 'inner voice' and Voice Therapy.
Guidance and Counseling; Psychology; Sociology
Dist - BARR **Prod** - CEPRO 1991

Parental Aspirations 10 MIN
16mm
Parent Education - Attitude Films Series
B&W
Education; Guidance and Counseling; Psychology; Sociology
Dist - TC **Prod** - TC

The Parental Imperative 29 MIN
U-matic
Country of Old Men Series
Color
Details results of an aging study in Kansas City.
Sociology
Dist - UMITV **Prod** - UMITV 1974

Parental Scripts 16 MIN
16mm
Giving Birth and Independence Series
Color (H C A)
LC 81-701610
Enacts five scripts, showing the roles parents may assume and how they affect the child.
Education; Home Economics; Sociology
Dist - LAWREN **Prod** - JRLLL 1981

Parental timeline reimprinting 43 MIN
VHS
Color; PAL; SECAM (G)
$60.00 purchase
Features Connirae Andreas. Presents a method developed by Andreas which generates a foundation of inner resourcefulness. Enables the transformation of 'sense of self' usually emerging out of cumulative past history. Creates the experience of resources lacking in parents to shift the overall sense of self. Demonstrates the pattern with a woman whose father was an alcoholic and includes a follow - up interview. Intermediate level of NLP, neuro - linguistic programming.
Psychology; Sociology
Dist - NLPCOM **Prod** - NLPCOM

Parenteral medication administration series
Presents a four - part series on parenteral medication administration produced by Healthcare Media. Includes the titles Equipment Preparation; Preparing Medication from an Ampule; Preparing Medication from a Vial; Site Selection and Injection Techniques.
Equipment preparation 19 MIN
Preparing medication from a vial 16 MIN
Preparing medication from an ampule 13 MIN
Site selection and injection techniques 27 MIN
Dist - CONMED

Parenteral Therapy - Blood Drawing Procedures 9.5 MIN
VHS / 16mm
Parenteral Therapy Pt 1 Series
(C)
$330.00 purchase _ #811VJ057
Demonstrates the proper procedures for drawing blood specimens. Discusses basic blood drawing equipment and a method for identifying and verifying patients prior to the procedure.
Health and Safety
Dist - HSCIC **Prod** - HSCIC

Parenteral Therapy Pt II Series
Parenteral Therapy - Starting Intravenous Infusions 17 MIN
Dist - HSCIC

Parenteral Therapy, Pt III, Series
Parenteral Therapy - Special Procedures in IV Therapy 18.5 MIN
Dist - HSCIC

Parenteral Therapy Pt 1 Series
Parenteral Therapy - Blood Drawing Procedures 9.5 MIN
Dist - HSCIC

Parenteral therapy series
Blood drawing procedures - Part 1 10 MIN
Special Procedures in IV Therapy - Part 3 19 MIN
Starting Intravenous Infusions - Part 2 17 MIN
Dist - HSCIC

Parenteral Therapy - Special Procedures in IV Therapy 18.5 MIN
VHS / 16mm
Parenteral Therapy, Pt III, Series
(C)
$330.00 purchase _ #811VI059
Illustrates two special procedures in IV therapy, the heparin lock and the teflon stylet.
Health and Safety
Dist - HSCIC **Prod** - HSCIC 1982

Parenteral Therapy - Starting Intravenous Infusions 17 MIN
VHS / 16mm

Parenteral Therapy Pt II Series
(C)
$330.00 purchase _ #811VJ058
Demonstrates the proper procedure for starting an intravenous, or IV, infusion. Discusses the basic IV materials, equipment, and the importance of obtaining positive identification of patients.
Health and Safety
Dist - HSCIC **Prod** - HSCIC

Parenthood - bringing new life into the world series
Birth
Pregnancy
Preparing for parenthood
Preparing to give birth
Dist - GA

Parenthood - Program 4 29 MIN
VHS
Sex education series
Color (I J H)
$189.00 purchase _ #CG - 832 - VS
Presents two parts which look at responsible and desired parenthood. Examines what it means to be 'ready' to have a baby. Part two visits a couple from part one several months after their baby's birth and finds their lifestyle greatly changed. Part four of a five - part series on sex education.
Guidance and Counseling; Health and Safety; Psychology
Dist - HRMC **Prod** - HRMC

Parenthood - Training Before Trouble 20 MIN
16mm
Color (J)
LC 76-700264
Dramatizes everyday conflicts between parents and children, showing how these problems can be solved through better understanding and effective communication techniques.
Guidance and Counseling; Home Economics; Sociology
Dist - TECKLA **Prod** - TECKLA 1976

Parenting 50 MIN
VHS
God's blueprint for the Christian family series
Color (R G)
$29.95 purchase _ #6140 - 9
Features Dr Tony Evans. Discusses parenting from a conservative Christian viewpoint. Part of six parts on marriage, parenting and families.
Guidance and Counseling; Literature and Drama; Religion and Philosophy; Sociology
Dist - MOODY **Prod** - MOODY

Parenting 30 MIN
U-matic
Transitions - Caught at Midlife Series
Color
Explores the parental problems that can occur during mid - life.
Psychology; Sociology
Dist - UMITV **Prod** - UMITV 1980

Parenting and human development video series
Presents a five - part series which captures the healthy interactions of toddlers, preschoolers, children, teens and teen parents, as well as unhealthy interactions in reactions to the anger, frustration and abuse of others. Developmental psychologists provide a conceptual framework for viewers. Includes discussion guide and reproducible worksheets.
Living the life - child 25 MIN
Living the life - pre - schooler 25 MIN
Living the life - teen 25 MIN
Living the life - teen parent 25 MIN
Living the life - toddler 25 MIN
Dist - CAMV

Parenting and the Home 60 MIN
U-matic
Perspectives on Women
Color (A)
Focuses on women in the economy, women and physical well being and how men and women are working to improve women's status in society.
Sociology
Dist - ACCESS **Prod** - ACCESS 1986

Parenting as a Process 30 MIN
U-matic
Parent Puzzle Series
(A)
Shows that the repetition of certain manners and customs is the essence of culture. As a process, parenting is a way of transmitting culture from one generation to the next.
Psychology; Sociology
Dist - ACCESS **Prod** - ACCESS 1982

Parenting - bringing new life into the world series
Active parenting
Dist - GA

Parenting children with special needs ; 2nd Ed. 30 MIN
VHS
Parenting special children series
Color (H C G)
$99.00 purchase _ #UL296V - K _ #296VL
Deals exclusively with the subject of parenting children with physical or mental disabilities. Emphasizes the care of children from infancy through early childhood. Discusses the birth and diagnosis of a child with disabilities, the impact of such a birth on the family system; the psychological stages that most parents of children with disabilities experience; the importance of early intervention. Reviews federal laws for developing appropriate and effective educational programs. Features candid interviews with parents of children with disabilities who share their concerns and experiences. Part of two parts on parenting special children.
Sociology
Dist - CAMV **Prod** - UNL 1995
UNL

Parenting Concerns - Preparing for Kindergarten 21 MIN
U-matic / VHS / 16mm
Color (A)
Shows methods of handling the various normal problems that arise during a child's second to fifth years of age. Deals with such problems as possessiveness, aggression, interaction with others, self - control, self - esteem, sex roles and independence.
Home Economics; Psychology; Sociology
Dist - PEREN **Prod** - CINIMA

Parenting Concerns - the First Two Years 21 MIN
16mm / U-matic / VHS
Color (H C A)
Explores common child - rearing problems encountered during the child's first two years. Includes information on discipline, a child's independence, toilet training and sibling rivalry.
Home Economics; Psychology; Sociology
Dist - PEREN **Prod** - PEREN 1978

Parenting Experience Series
The Teenage Pregnancy Experience 26 MIN
Dist - COURTR

Parenting experience series
The Breastfeeding experience 24 MIN
Dist - PARPIC

Parenting - Growing with Children 22 MIN
16mm / U-matic / VHS
Color (J)
LC 76-700062
Describes the realities, responsibilities, and rewards of being a parent in today's society.
Sociology
Dist - ALTSUL **Prod** - SCHNZP 1976

Parenting Heart - to - Heart
VHS / 35mm strip
Color
$55.00 purchase _ #VMPH filmstrip, $65.00 purchase _ #VMPV VHS
Discusses unconditional love as the foundation for relationships between parents or caregivers and children. Points out four methods for conveying this love.
Sociology
Dist - CAREER **Prod** - CAREER

Parenting in today's society 30 MIN
VHS / U-matic
Contemporary health issues series; Lesson 9
Color (C A)
Examines the many aspects of parenting, beginning with the decision to have or not to have children. Discusses advantages and disadvantages of having children. Emphasizes the parent's role in the child's emotional, social and intellectual development.
Sociology
Dist - CDTEL **Prod** - SCCON

Parenting Our Parents 26 MIN
U-matic / VHS
Color (C)
$249.00, $149.00 purchase _ #AD - 1934
Reveals that as the population of senior citizens grows, more middle - aged couples find themselves staggering under the double burden of growing kids and chronically ill or disabled parents. Examines various ways of coping with the stress of caring for aging parents. Suggests personal and political remedies.
Health and Safety; Sociology
Dist - FOTH **Prod** - FOTH

Parenting preschoolers 55 MIN
VHS
Color (H A)
$39.95 purchase _ #HPG600V
Takes a comprehensive look at parenting of preschool - age children. Covers 12 different subjects including sibling rivalries, temper tantrums, meal time, public behavior, and more.
Health and Safety
Dist - CAMV

Parenting special children series
Presents two parts on parenting special children. Includes the titles Parenting Children with Special Needs and Parents' Views of Living with a Child with Disabilities.
Parenting children with special needs 30 MIN
Dist - CAMV **Prod** - UNL
UNL

Parenting special children series
Parents' views of living with a child with disabilities 27 MIN
Dist - UNL

Parenting the acutely ill infant - parent tape 14 MIN
VHS / U-matic
NICU video series
Color (PRO G)
$175.00 purchase
Presents a film for showing to parents whose infants have recently been admitted to NICU, as a way of facilitating their adjustment to a new and frightening environment. Explains what happens in the NICU and shares the common feelings of other parents to help parents to understand and care for their infant's needs and become more actively involved in care. Part of a seven - part series on developmental intervention for hospitalized infants in the neonatal intensive care unit.
Health and Safety; Sociology
Dist - POLYMR **Prod** - POKORJ

Parenting the child who is handicapped series
Early intervention - 2 30 MIN
A Matter of expectations - 1 30 MIN
What was I supposed to do - 3 30 MIN
Winning 21 MIN
Dist - EDPAT

Parenting the growing premie - parent tape 9 MIN
U-matic
NICU video series
Color (PRO G)
$175.00 purchase
Reveals that after parents have adjusted to the environment of care in the NICU, they need to be prepared for playing a more active role in preparation for taking their infant home. Gives parents an overview of premie development and encourages them to handle and interact with their hospitalized infant,to better prepare them for discharge. Part of a seven - part series on developmental intervention for hospitalized infants in the neonatal intensive care unit.
Health and Safety; Sociology
Dist - POLYMR **Prod** - POKORJ

Parenting the infant with prolonged hospitalization - parent tape 12 MIN
VHS / U-matic
Pediatric video series
Color (PRO G)
$175.00 purchase
Presents a program for showing to parents whose infants will be hospitalized for a prolonged period, to help them to adjust and play a more positive role. Helps parents to cope with the stress of having an infant in the pediatric unit, explains how they can become more actively involved with their hospitalized child and offers them advice for helping siblings, grandparents and other close relatives deal with their own feelings. Part of a three - part series on infants with prolonged hospitalization.
Health and Safety; Sociology
Dist - POLYMR **Prod** - POKORJ

Parenting the Special Needs Child 25 MIN
U-matic / VHS / 16mm
Color (A)
Presents 16 vignettes showing situations which the parent of a special needs child is likely to encounter including teachers and coaches who stereotype children and exaggerate their vulnerabilities, relatives who offer well - meaning but unacceptable advice, babysitters and neighbors who are afraid to accept any responsibility for the child and parents themselves whose relationship is strained by guilt and anger.
Education; Psychology; Sociology
Dist - CORF **Prod** - CORF

Parenting video - a day in the life series
A Day in the life - pre - schooler 25 MIN
A Day in the life - teen 25 MIN
A Day in the life - teen parent 25 MIN
A Day in the life - toddler 25 MIN
Dist - CADESF
CAMV

Parenting video - a day in the life series
A Day in the life - child 25 MIN
Dist - CAMV

Parenting video series - a day in the life 125 MIN
VHS
Parenting video series
Color (H C A)
$449.00 purchase _ #CDIL200V
Presents a five - part series on parenting, from the perspective of the child. Portrays the daily business of children, teenagers, and teen parents, showing both healthy and unhealthy interactions. Consists of five videocassettes, discussion guides, and reproducible worksheets.
Health and Safety; Sociology
Dist - CAMV

Parenting video series
Parenting video series - a day in the life 125 MIN
Dist - CAMV

Parenting your teen 23 MIN
VHS / U-matic
Teen - family life series
Color (J H G)
$179.00, $229.00 purchase, $60.00 rental
Presents a method of parental discipline that focuses on the objective of gradually increased individual responsibility for the teen. Looks at setting limits that are age - appropriate, understanding the rationale of what works with teens, clarifying many conflicts in the parent - teen relationship and more.
Sociology
Dist - NDIM Prod - FAMLIF 1993

Parenting/Adolescence 15 MIN
VHS / U-matic
Health, Safety and Well - Being Series
Color
Health and Safety; Sociology
Dist - CAMB Prod - MAETEL

The Parents 60 MIN
16mm
America's crises series
B&W (H C A)
LC FIA65-551
A documentary report of today's American parents and their attempts to find identity, meaning and purpose in their lives.
Psychology; Sociology
Dist - IU Prod - NET 1965

The Parents 17 MIN
VHS
Let's talk about it series
Color; PAL (I J)
PdS29.50 purchase
Features the parents of the children participating in this project, discussing their reactions and concerns regarding filmed sex education through the school. Part of a five - part series on sex education.
Health and Safety; Sociology
Dist - EMFVL

Parents 14 MIN
16mm / U-matic / VHS
BSCS Behavior Film Series
Color
LC 74-702532
Discusses the need for parents. Shows dogs, cats and monkeys nurturing, protecting and teaching their young. Includes human parent - child interactions.
Guidance and Counseling; Psychology; Sociology
Dist - PHENIX Prod - BSCS 1974

Parents and Children 24 MIN
16mm
Color
Examines the parent - child relationship and shows how behavioral methods can be used to teach children. Explains how to use rewards effectively and how to strengthen and maintain good behavior.
Home Economics; Psychology; Sociology
Dist - RESPRC Prod - RESPRC 1979

Parents and Children 30 MIN
U-matic
Explorations in Shaw Series
Color (H)
Tells of George Bernard Shaw's childhood with a drunken father and an indifferent mother. Shows how these circumstances affected the young Shaw and reappeared in his plays.
Literature and Drama
Dist - TVOTAR Prod - TVOTAR 1974

Parents and Children - a Positive Approach to Child Management 24 MIN
16mm
Color
LC 80-701254
Discusses the teaching of children by parents using behavioral techniques. Features an overview of reinforcement principles in nontechnical language and offers common examples of this approach.
Home Economics; Psychology; Sociology
Dist - RESPRC Prod - RESPRC 1979

Parents and children series
Effective limit setting subseries 70 MIN
Handling misbehavior subseries 48 MIN
Praise and rewards subseries 40 MIN
Dist - HSCIC

Parents and children who have adopted each other 29 MIN
VHS / U-matic
Are you listening series
Color (H C A)
LC 82-706878
Shows adoptive parents discusssing the risks, fears, and rewards they have encountered, and some of the children describe their early relationships with their parents and tell why they asked to be adopted. Shows some parents telling of obstacles they faced, such as in the adoption of of a child of a different race.
Psychology; Sociology
Dist - STURTM Prod - STURTM 1982

Parents and School - Community Program 30 MIN
VHS / 16mm
Your Choice - Our Chance Series
Color (I A)
$295.00 purchase, $35.00 rental
Considers drug abuse and features `Parents as Teachers', a program that emphasizes training inner - city parents to be the first and best prevention teachers and builds links between families and schools.
Health and Safety; Psychology
Dist - AITECH Prod - AITECH 1990

Parents and Schools-St Louis, Missouri -3 30 MIN
VHS
Our Chance Series
Color (A)
$395.00 purchase
Focuses on knowledge, attitudes and behaviors that influence drug free and drug use life styles. Emphasizes that effective drug abuse prevention education must begin before children are established users of tobacco, alcohol or other addictive drugs. Targets children in the vulnerable preteen years. Program 3 emphasizes the family and the family - school partnership as the bedrock of drug abuse prevention. Parents as Teachers is one of several programs develped by the Missouri Department of Elementary and Secondary Education.
Guidance and Counseling; Health and Safety; Psychology; Social Science; Sociology
Dist - AITECH Prod - AITECH 1990

Parents and Staff in a Children's Ward 45 MIN
16mm
B&W (PRO)
LC 72-700824
Deals with the sick child's need for emotional support when in the hospital. Gives both parents' and staff's views of the other's roles, difficulties and concerns with the ideas of improving mutual relations.
Health and Safety; Psychology; Social Science; Sociology
Dist - PSUPCR Prod - PSUPCR 1972

Parents and Teenagers 30 MIN
VHS
Soapbox With Tom Cottle Series
Color (G)
$59.95 purchase _ #SBOX - 202
Reviews relationships between teenagers and their parents. Conveys the teenagers' views that parents should show support and interest. Shows what can happen when communication breaks down. Hosted by psychologist Tom Cottle.
Psychology; Sociology
Dist - PBS Prod - WGBYTV 1985

Parents and the Young Teen - a Delicate Balance
VHS / U-matic
Vital Link Series
Color (A)
Explores areas in which teenagers and parents can work towards a better understanding of each other.
Guidance and Counseling; Sociology
Dist - EDCC Prod - EDCC

Parents and the Young Teen - a Delicate Balance 27 MIN
VHS
Color (C A)
$75.00 purchase, $35.00 rental
Examines the challanges presented to parents by the complex nature of their changing young teens.
Psychology; Sociology
Dist - CORNRS Prod - EDCC 1986

Parents are Human Too 28 MIN
VHS / 16mm
Color (A)
$89.95 purchase _ RMI 206
Assists parents in assessing their needs so they can develop as human beings.
Psychology; Sociology
Dist - CADESF Prod - CADESF

Parents are human too 28 MIN
VHS
Prime time for parents video series
Color (G)
$89.95 purchase _ #RMI206
Stresses that only parents who understand and accept their own basic human needs can fulfill their children's needs. Identifies the skills and knowledge for changes in life - style which promote human development. Part of a series on parenting. Study guide available separately.
Health and Safety; Home Economics; Psychology; Sociology
Dist - CADESF Prod - CADESF

Parents are Special, Too 15 MIN
U-matic
Special Children - Responding to their Needs Series
Color (PRO)
Examines the role of parents in establishing a meaningful program to meet the needs of the handicapped child and outlines support services available to parents.
Education; Psychology
Dist - ACCESS Prod - ACCESS 1985

Parents are Teachers, Too 18 MIN
U-matic
B&W
Stresses the role of parents as the child's first and continuing teachers. Shows how learning comes easier with a flow of understanding between school and home.
Education; Guidance and Counseling; Psychology; Social Science; Sociology
Dist - USNAC Prod - USNAC 1972

Parents are Teachers Too 22 MIN
16mm
Head Start Starts at Home Series
B&W
LC FIE67-137
Discusses the role of parents as the child's first and continuing teachers. Points out that learning comes easier with a flow of understanding between school and home.
Education; Guidance and Counseling; Psychology; Social Science; Sociology
Dist - USNAC Prod - USOEO 1967

Parents as role models 50 MIN
VHS
Creating family series
Color (H C G A R)
$10.00 rental _ #36 - 871505 - 460
Features marriage counselor and therapist Clayton Barbeau in an exploration of the importance of parents being role models for their children.
Guidance and Counseling; Psychology; Religion and Philosophy; Sociology
Dist - APH Prod - FRACOC

Parents discuss kids, cars and alcohol 20 MIN
VHS / U-matic
Color (H G)
$55.00, $35.00 purchase _ #583, #452
Encourages parental discussion of young drivers and alcohol.
Health and Safety; Sociology
Dist - AAAFTS Prod - AAAFTS 1990

Parents - do You Know what Your Kids are Doing 23 MIN
16mm
Color (J H A)
Follows a group of teens into the drug culture to show parents their actions. Includes group sessions at a Florida drug rehabilitation center.
Sociology
Dist - BECKLY Prod - BECKLY 1983

Parents Education Programs 30 MIN
16mm
Color
LC 74-705323
Illustrates both formal and informal programs for parents of young hearing impaired children. Presents issues in family dynamics and parent - child communication and language development.
Guidance and Counseling; Psychology; Social Science; Sociology
Dist - USNAC Prod - USHHS

The Parents' Group 19 MIN
VHS / U-matic

Color
Discusses the common frustrations and victories experienced when integrating an older child into an adoptive family.
Sociology
Dist - IA **Prod** - LACFU

The Parent's Group 19 MIN
U-matic / VHS
Color (J A)
Explores the unique challenges of integrating an older child into an adoptive family.
Sociology
Dist - SUTHRB **Prod** - SUTHRB

The Parents' Group - Working with the Adoptive Family 19 MIN
16mm
Color (PRO)
LC 79-700699
Shows how a parents' group can be a useful device for dealing with some of the frustrations experienced when integrating a child into an adoptive family.
Home Economics; Sociology
Dist - IA **Prod** - LAC 1975

The Parents' Hospital Experience 29 MIN
U-matic / VHS
Tomorrow's Families Series
Color (H C A)
LC 81-706906
Discusses the experiences of the parents during the period after the birth of their child. Tells how the mother begins her physical recovery and both parents begin their emotional adjustment to parenting.
Health and Safety; Sociology
Dist - AITECH **Prod** - MDDE 1980

Parents in the special education process 136 MIN
VHS
Color (G)
$37.50 purchase
Features Reed Martin, attorney, in 3 parts on parents in the special education process. Explains what parents have a right to expect from their school districts in regard to the evaluation and education of their child in Tape One, The Role Congress Expected Parents to Play. Tape Two, The Parent in the IEP Process, coaches parents on the steps to take to insure that their child has an appropriate IEP and that the IEP is reviewed on a regular basis. Tape Three, Seeking Services in the Least Restrictive Environment, points out that the goal of all programs has to be integration into as normal a life as possible.
Civics and Political Systems; Education
Dist - BAXMED

Parents / Learning Disabilities 30 MIN
VHS / U-matic
Characteristics of Learning Disabilities Series
Color (C A)
Discusses the parent's role in caring for and educating the learning disabled child.
Education; Psychology
Dist - FI **Prod** - WCVETV 1976

The Parent's license 15 MIN
VHS
Color (J H C A)
$195.00 purchase
Proposes that at some future day those wanting to become parents will have to prove their maturity, readiness and fitness in order to be licensed to have children. Dramatizes adults facing the question as a challenge to viewers. Produced in association with USAA.
Sociology
Dist - PFP **Prod** - ASHAP

Parents Look at Genetic Counseling 27 MIN
U-matic / VHS
Color (PRO)
Presents comments from parents of handicapped or impaired children who are involved in genetic counseling at The University of Michigan Medical Center. Discusses topics such as how they were informed of the condition, their reactions, positive and negative aspects, their opinion of genetic couseling and their plans for future children.
Health and Safety; Psychology; Science - Natural
Dist - UMICHM **Prod** - UMICHM 1981

Parents of Disturbed Children 28 MIN
16mm
Color
Presents a discussion by parents of emotionally disturbed children about their experiences in learning to cope with their child's disturbance.
Psychology
Dist - STURTM **Prod** - STURTM 1975

Parents' point of view series
Presents advice on caring for children under five years old. Targeted to both parents and care givers. Considers topics including child care, play, health care and nutrition, toys, safety, and more. Hosted by Nancy Thurmond, ex - wife of Senator Strom Thurmond. Consists of 15 programs.

Changing families	30 MIN
Child health care and nutrition	30 MIN
Children and television	30 MIN
Children's fears	30 MIN
Child's toys and violence	30 MIN
Choosing child care	30 MIN
Early language	30 MIN
Exploring nature with your child	30 MIN
Family literacy - Pt I	30 MIN
Family literacy - Pt II	30 MIN
For new parents	30 MIN
Learning through play	30 MIN
Making everyday events special	30 MIN
Safety tips	30 MIN
Your child's school experiences	30 MIN

Dist - SCETV **Prod** - SCETV 1975

Parent's Responses to their Children's Illnesses 27 MIN
VHS / U-matic
Color (PRO)
Presents a discussion between a hospital social worker and four parents of cronically ill children. Illustrates parent's responses to their children's illnesses which parallel those of dying patients outlined by Elisabeth Kubler - Ross. Shows denial, anger, bargaining, depression and acceptance.
Health and Safety; Psychology
Dist - UMICHM **Prod** - UMICHM 1977

Parents shape - up - total fitness for the new mother 35 MIN
VHS
Color (H A)
$19.95 purchase _ #GJ1012V
Presents a fitness program targeted to new mothers. Focuses on the muscles stressed during pregnancy.
Health and Safety; Physical Education and Recreation
Dist - CAMV

Parents - silence condones
VHS / Cassette
(G)
$95.00, $10.00 purchase
Advocates parental confidence in confronting children.
Guidance and Counseling; Health and Safety; Psychology; Sociology
Dist - KELLYP **Prod** - KELLYP

The Parents speak I 29 MIN
VHS / U-matic
Mind and body series
Color (PRO C)
$395.00 purchase, $80.00 rental _ #C850 - VI - 042
Features parents of the mentally ill. Explains that only by facing the problem of mental illness in the family, learning coping skills, seeking expert medical advice and, in many cases, leaving the ill member completely on his own, can the family deal with this type of illness. Presented by Dr Jonathan A Freedman. Part of a series.
Health and Safety; Psychology; Sociology
Dist - HSCIC

The Parents speak II 18 MIN
U-matic / VHS
Mind and body series
Color (PRO C)
$395.00 purchase, $80.00 rental _ #C850 - VI - 109
Presents the viewpoints and feelings of two mothers of sons who are mentally ill. Presented by Dr Jonathan A Freedman. Part of a series.
Health and Safety; Psychology; Sociology
Dist - HSCIC

Parents, Teachers, and the Community - Building Partnerships for the Child 14 MIN
VHS
Color (C A)
$38.00 purchase, $16.00 rental
Encourages parent involvement in their child's education and closer interaction between teachers and parents.
Education; Psychology; Sociology
Dist - CORNRS **Prod** - CORNRS 1988

Parents - to - be series 73 MIN
VHS
Parents - to - be series
Color (J H C)
$698.00 purchase _ #CG - 951 - VS
Presents a six - part series answering many of the questions and concerns of parents - to - be and new parents regarding the safety and care of their children - before and after birth. Includes the titles Pregnancy and Nutrition, Prenatal Care, Birth, First Days of Parenthood, When Your Baby Is Sick and Early Childhood Safety.
Health and Safety; Sociology
Dist - HRMC **Prod** - HRMC

A Parent's Underground Guide to Understanding Teenagers 25 MIN
16mm / U-matic / VHS
Color (J)
Provides answers, direction and hope for parents who find themselves confronting the problem of teenage drug and alcohol abuse. Offers specific approaches, attitudes and actions that open lines of communication between parents and teenagers.
Psychology; Sociology
Dist - CORF **Prod** - WQED

Parents' views of living with a child with disabilities; 2nd Ed. 27 MIN
VHS
Parenting special children series
CC; Color (G F H)
$99 purchase _ #297VL
Features interviews with parents of children with disabilities. Examines the difficulties and daily life conflicts voiced by parents of disabled children. Comes with a leader's guide.
Health and Safety; Sociology
Dist - UNL

Parents' visit 12 MIN
16mm
Color (G)
$22.00 rental
Documents interaction between filmmaker Hudina's parents, the equipment and himself when his parents arrive for a weekend visit.
Fine Arts; Sociology
Dist - CANCIN **Prod** - HUDINA 1974

Parents' Voices 12 MIN
VHS / 16mm
Sex, Feelings and Values Series
Color
LC 77-700399
Features two young people who enact their reactions to sexual intercourse, while others act as parents' voices. Shows how parental influence affects sexual behavior. Challenges parents' use of drugs and alcohol.
Psychology; Sociology
Dist - LRF **Prod** - DF 1976

Parents Weekend 1978 60 MIN
VHS / U-matic
Color
Shows Sri Gurudev speaking on the purpose of life and spiritual meaning of Mother and Father.
Religion and Philosophy
Dist - IYOGA **Prod** - IYOGA

Parents who have Lost Children 29 MIN
U-matic / VHS
Color (PRO)
Presents a couple talking about their efforts to cope with the loss of their thirteen - month - old daughter. Illustrates the importance of a local support group. Discusses their feelings of grief, depression, isolation and panic.
Health and Safety; Sociology
Dist - UARIZ **Prod** - UARIZ

Parents with Alcoholism
VHS
$139.00 purchase _ #HR648V
Uses case studies to portray situations experienced by children of alcoholics. Talks about constructive methods of handling these situations. Discusses the effects of alcoholism on different members of a family.
Health and Safety; Sociology
Dist - CAREER **Prod** - CAREER

Parents with Alcoholism - Kids with Hope 30 MIN
VHS
Color (I H)
Examines the many ways that a parent's drinking affects the rest of the family. Drawing from actual case studies, the program presents various situations often experienced by children of alcoholics, and discusses constructive methods of dealing with these situations.
Guidance and Counseling; Health and Safety; Psychology; Sociology
Dist - HRMC **Prod** - HRMC

Parents with careers - practical ways to balance career mnd family 32 MIN
VHS
Color (G PRO)
$149.00 purchase _ #AG6031V
Addresses the issues of working parents and offers sensible options. Presents six sessions for two - career families, especially those with small children. Includes guide, parent's action plan, leader's guide, promotional guide and brochures.
Guidance and Counseling; Health and Safety; Sociology
Dist - CAMV

Parergastic Reaction (Schizophrenia) in a Person of Low Intelligence 15 MIN
16mm
B&W (C T)
Shows stereotypic grimaces and speech, vagueness, concrete use of abstract expressions and neologism in a schizophrenic with probable mental retardation.
Psychology
Dist - PSUPCR **Prod** - PSUPCR 1939

Pareto analysis 25 MIN
VHS
Tools for continual improvement - two series
Color (IND PRO)
$395.00 purchase _ #ELI02
Provides skills to enhance employee performance. Includes trainer's notes, wall charts and reference cards. Available in healthcare and general business versions. Produced by Executive Learning, Inc.
Business and Economics
Dist - EXTR

Pareto Diagram
U-matic / VHS
Implementing Quality Circles Series
Color
Introduces the Pareto diagram, a graph used to help set priorities.
Business and Economics; Psychology
Dist - BNA **Prod** - BNA

Paricutin 23 MIN
16mm
B&W
A documentary of the 1946 research expedition to Paricutin Volcano in Mexico.
History - World; Science - Physical
Dist - USNAC **Prod** - USAF 1949

Paris 30 MIN
VHS
Color (G)
$29.95 purchase _ #S02028
Tours Paris. Features Notre Dame, the Eiffel Tower, the Louvre, the Folies Bergere, and more.
Geography - World
Dist - UILL

Paris 30 MIN
BETA / VHS / U-matic
Color; Stereo (S C A G)
Demonstrates a composition for two dancers, a puppet face and a pianist. A personal evocation of a Parisian bohemia composed by Meredith Monk.
Fine Arts
Dist - UCV **Prod** - TCPT 1982

Paris 50 MIN
VHS
Color (G) (FRENCH)
$39.95 purchase _ #W5475, #W5476
Presents the people, history and culture of the capital city of France. Shows a panorama of the city and its well - known sites. Includes a visit to Versailles.
Foreign Language; Geography - World
Dist - GPC

Paris 26 MIN
16mm
Scenes de la vie Francaise series
Color (G)
$50.00 rental
Presents one in a series of French cities and scenes in which the material is woven together on an ordinary printer according to a certain pattern. Shows several Parisian landmarks by means of a composition of frames recorded at various times from a similar viewpoint.
Fine Arts; Geography - World
Dist - CANCIN **Prod** - LOWDER 1986

Paris 25 MIN
16mm
Color (J H)
LC 75-703871
Shows how the fashion industry operates in Paris, Describing the changing nature of the industry and discussing designing and marketing.
Business and Economics; Fine Arts; Home Economics
Dist - BASIST **Prod** - BASIST 1975

Paris a Mon Coeur 10 MIN
16mm
Aspects De France Series
Color (H C) (FRENCH)
Describes famous landmarks of Paris and gives their historical significance.
Geography - World
Dist - MLA **Prod** - WSUM 1955

Paris, Aujourd' Hui 19 MIN
U-matic / VHS / 16mm
La France Telle Qu'Elle Est Series
Color (H C)
Highlights buying tickets and requesting information in Paris, a modern city with a new airport and cultural center. Shows La Defense, a new suburb and a new deep - level suburban metro system.
Foreign Language; Geography - World
Dist - MEDIAG **Prod** - THAMES 1977

Paris Commune 20 MIN
16mm
B&W (C A)
Jan pere documents the struggle of Paris against the Prussians during the Franco - German War of 1870 - 1871. Emphasizes the conditions of the poor and working class and draws an analogy to oppression in the U S.
History - World; Sociology
Dist - GROVE **Prod** - GROVE

The Paris Commune 30 MIN
U-matic
Color
Talks about the worker's revolution of Paris, 1871, and women's contributions to the revolution. Raises questions about women's strategies within other social movements.
Civics and Political Systems; Sociology
Dist - WMENIF **Prod** - WMENIF

Paris Hier 19 MIN
U-matic / VHS / 16mm
La France Telle Qu'Elle Est Series
Color (H C)
Features ordering food and something to drink in a Paris cafe, visiting traditional Parisian sights such as the Seine, the Madeleine, Sacre - Coeur, Notre - Dame, the Eiffel Tower, the Metro and the boulevards.
Foreign Language; Geography - World
Dist - MEDIAG **Prod** - THAMES 1977

Paris - Imperial City 24 MIN
U-matic / VHS / 16mm
Color
Delineates conditions and policies encouraged by Napoleon in the beginning of the 19th century to sustain and control societal instability and to encourage the urban growth of Paris as an administrative and cultural center.
History - World
Dist - MEDIAG **Prod** - OPENU 1981

Paris in the Month of may 35 MIN
16mm
Color
Outlines the demands of French students as they take to the streets to breathe the air of revolution and almost succeed in toppling the De Gaulle government. Shows workers and students united behind the closed doors of the factories fighting pitched battles with the police.
Geography - World; Sociology
Dist - CANWRL **Prod** - CANWRL

Paris in the Time of Balzac 26 MIN
U-matic / VHS
Color (C)
$249.00, $149.00 purchase _ #AD - 967
Chronicles the history of Paris during the time of Balzac. Covers the period of the Consulate, the Empire, the Restoration and the July Monarchy.
Civics and Political Systems; Foreign Language; Geography - World; History - World; Literature and Drama
Dist - FOTH **Prod** - FOTH

Paris in the Time of Proust 26 MIN
U-matic / VHS
Color (C)
$249.00, $149.00 purchase _ #AD - 969
Documents Paris and Proust of the Belle Epoque. Shows modernity creeping in, automobiles and the foreboding of the Great War which will bring Proust's world to an end.
Foreign Language; Geography - World; History - World; Literature and Drama
Dist - FOTH **Prod** - FOTH

Paris in the Time of Zola 26 MIN
U-matic / VHS
Color (C)
$249.00, $149.00 purchase _ #AD - 968
Uses rare period film footage of Paris and Parisian life during the time of Zola to provide documentary background for his work.
Foreign Language; Geography - World; History - World; Literature and Drama
Dist - FOTH **Prod** - FOTH

Paris - La Belle Epoque 24 MIN
16mm / U-matic / VHS
Rise of Modernism in Music Series
Color (A)
LC 82-700863
Looks at Paris at the beginning of the 20th century and the milieu in which Claude Debussy and his contemporaries composed their revolutionary music. Provides examples of the cultural influences that shaped his music and includes performances of some of his works and those of his contemporaries.
Fine Arts
Dist - MEDIAG **Prod** - BBCTV 1982

Paris, Left Bank 3 MIN
16mm
Of all Things Series
Color (P I)
Discusses the Left Bank of the city of Paris in France.
Geography - World
Dist - AVED **Prod** - BAILYL

Paris - Living Space 27 MIN
16mm / U-matic / VHS
Understanding Cities Series
Color (H C A)
Traces the history of Paris' design through the work of five individuals whose efforts shaped the city. Shows that their work set in motion a self - perpetuating system of linked thoroughfares, boulevards and axes that created a vision of life of its own which transcended individual projects to form the modern city.
Geography - World; Sociology
Dist - FI **Prod** - FI 1983

Paris Mai 68 9 MIN
16mm
B&W (H C A) (FRENCH (ENGLISH SUBTITLES))
Documents the student revolution which seized the Sorbonne and rocked the French government.
Civics and Political Systems; Sociology
Dist - UWFKD **Prod** - UWFKD

The Paris of Robert Doisneau 20 MIN
16mm
Color (H C A)
LC 76-702384
Presents photographer Robert Doisneau's famous black - and - white photographs taken over a period of 30 years juxtaposed with filmed color sequences from similar vantage points in the city of Paris.
Geography - World; Industrial and Technical Education; Sociology
Dist - RADIM **Prod** - PORCIL 1976

Paris on the Seine 20 MIN
16mm
Color
Presents a camera study of Paris. Photographed by Jack Cardiff.
Geography - World; Social Science
Dist - REMBRT **Prod** - REMBRT 1955

Paris, Tourist Town 3 MIN
16mm
Of all Things Series
Color (P I)
Discusses the city of Paris in France.
Geography - World
Dist - AVED **Prod** - BAILYL

Paris Uprising - may 1968 30 MIN
16mm
B&W (A) (FRENCH)
Focuses on the violent reaction against the Paris police during the social protests of May, 1968. Sketches the upheaval taking place in French society at that time.
Civics and Political Systems; Geography - World; Sociology
Dist - NYFLMS **Prod** - NYFLMS

Paris X 2 26 MIN
16mm / VHS
Color (G)
$50.00 rental, $50.00 purchase
Tells a story about love and looks at love stories - the static and the electricity, the pain of letting go and the attempt to re - capture. Views an American man who is obsessed with a French woman who is obsessed with films. A Jay Rosenblatt production.
Fine Arts; Literature and Drama; Psychology; Religion and Philosophy
Dist - CANCIN

The Parish nurse - a ministry to older adults 20 MIN
VHS
Color (G C)
$79.00 purchase, $35.00 rental
Views the functions of a parish nurse through the eyes of the older adults served. Looks at personal health counseling, health teaching, support group development and community work done by the nurse.
Health and Safety; Religion and Philosophy
Dist - TNF

Parish pastoral councils 240 MIN
VHS
Color (G R)
$69.95 purchase _ #380
Contains four one - hour sessions for training Catholic parish pastoral councils. Includes principles of organization, understanding of church and meaning of parish, purpose and functions of parish pastoral councils, and skills for a collaborative model of decision - making.

Joseph Cardinal Bernardin introduces the tape which features Sister Mary Benet McKinney and the Revs Robert Heidenreich, Gerard Broccolo, Michael Place and Sister Dorothy Monikowski as trainers. Includes a study guide.
Business and Economics; Psychology; Religion and Philosophy; Sociology
Dist - ACTAF **Prod** - ACTAF

Parisian blinds 6 MIN
16mm
B&W; Color (G)
$25.00 rental
Investigates the nature of spectator perception in an unfamiliar environment. Questions the perceptual experience of mass tourism as the Bateau Mouche endlessly circles the Ile de la Cite.
Fine Arts; Geography - World
Dist - CANCIN **Prod** - BARHAM 1984

Parisian Sights and Shops 20 MIN
U-matic / VHS / 16mm
Touring Paris Series
Color (H C A)
Presents a visit to Sacre Coeur, a boatride on the Seine, buying souvenirs and exploring the stores in a modern shopping complex. Shows how to ask questions of sales people.
Foreign Language
Dist - MEDIAG **Prod** - THAMES 1985

The Park 28 MIN
16mm
Color (J)
LC 76-702700
Analyzes the effect of the nuclear materials industry on the National Environmental Research Park in South Carolina. Explores the effects of nuclear industry on natural resources and the living species around it.
Science; Science - Natural; Social Science; Sociology
Dist - USNAC **Prod** - USERD 1975

The Park 11 MIN
16mm / U-matic / VHS
Color (K P)
LC 72-706479
Uses the discoveries of a little boy as he walks through a park to stress the technique of observation.
English Language; Fine Arts; Science; Social Science
Dist - AIMS **Prod** - ASSOCF 1970

The Park 10 MIN
VHS
Stop, look, listen series
Color; PAL (P I J)
Visits a park where children and adults play and enjoy themselves. Part of a series of films which start from some everyday observation and show more of what is happening, how and why. Builds vocabulary and encourages children to be more observant.
English Language; Physical Education and Recreation; Social Science; Sociology
Dist - VIEWTH

Park 15 MIN
16mm
Color (G)
$20.00 rental
Looks at the Cleveland metropolitan parks. Uses a variety of techniques such as pixilation, jump - cuts and time sequencing to view the people enjoying the park as an escape from the city. A Kon Petrochuk production.
Fine Arts; Social Science
Dist - CANCIN

The Park 7 MIN
U-matic / VHS / 16mm
Color (P I)
LC 75-709495
Uses mood music, a narration which includes Thoreau's 'WALDEN,' and color photography to portray a park as it blends one season into the next.
Literature and Drama; Science - Natural
Dist - AIMS **Prod** - COMICO 1970

A Park Community 10 MIN
16mm / U-matic / VHS
Color (I J)
LC 74-703503
Shows how a community park forms an ecosystem of plants and animals which are mutually dependent on one another. Examines the interrelationships of these different forms of life.
Science - Natural
Dist - BARR **Prod** - BARR 1974

Park Interpreter 15 MIN
U-matic
Harriet's Magic Hats I Series
(P I J)
Follows the characters of the series to a national park where they learn that the park interpreters teach enjoyment and preservation of nature in its wildlife state.
Guidance and Counseling
Dist - ACCESS **Prod** - ACCESS 1980

Park Police Driver Training 22 MIN
16mm
Color (A)
LC 77-703232
Examines methods of handling automobiles in skid and sharp turn situations, as well as when operating at high speed. Explains how the National Park Service trains its uniformed patrol officers.
Civics and Political Systems; Geography - United States; Health and Safety
Dist - USNAC **Prod** - USNPS 1970

The park that kids built 19 MIN
U-matic / VHS / 16mm
Color (I J)
$49.95 purchase _ #P10310; LC 82-700571
Follows a group of children who, in their efforts to get a neighborhood park, learn how to work with each other and within their community. Shows how the children circulate petitions, lobby, and, with the help of some business people, succeed in raising enough money to purchase some vacant lots and turn them into a park.
Social Science; Sociology
Dist - CF **Prod** - CF 1982

The Park that Went to Sea 14 MIN
16mm
Color
LC 75-702514
A view of Pennekamp, an underwater state park in the Florida Keys, the only living coral reef in the United States. Uses underwater photography to reveal the beauty of the coral formations, the richness of the marine life, and the pleasures of skin diving.
Geography - United States; Science - Natural; Science - Physical
Dist - FDC **Prod** - FDC 1968

Parker Adderson, Philosopher 39 MIN
U-matic / VHS / 16mm
American Short Story Series
Color (J H C A)
Tells of the violence that occurs when Parker Adderson is captured by the enemy and has to face his impending execution. Teleplay written and directed by Arthur Barron. Based on the story by Ambrose Bierce.
Literature and Drama
Dist - CORF
CDTEL
GA

Parking 24 MIN
U-matic / VHS
Right Way Series
Color
Tells how to make parking, often a stressful situation, easier.
Health and Safety
Dist - PBS **Prod** - SCETV 1982

Parking on Hills 8 MIN
16mm
Color (H)
Presents two methods of parking on hills, with the use of the foot brake or the parking brake. Covers the method of parking up and down hills and how to leave the curb when parked on a hill.
Health and Safety
Dist - SF **Prod** - SF 1974

Parking Tactics 16 MIN
U-matic / VHS / 16mm
Color (H A) (SPANISH)
LC 77-700180
Presents the importance of parking skills to overall driving ability, and techniques for parallel parking, diagonal parking, hill parking, backing and parking in parking lots.
Health and Safety
Dist - AIMS **Prod** - CAHILL 1968

Parkinsonism and Convulsive Disorders 30 MIN
16mm
Pharmacology Series
Color (C)
LC 73-703338
Health and Safety; Psychology
Dist - TELSTR **Prod** - MVNE 1971

Parkinson's Disease 19 MIN
U-matic / VHS
Color (C)
$249.00, $149.00 purchase _ #AD - 1437
Examines the pharmaceutical and surgical treatments of Parkinson's Disease. Profiles 61 - year - old author and educator who has struggled for 25 years to control his symptoms. Explores the relationship between 'designer drugs' and the sudden onset of Parkinson's symptoms in young drug abusers.
Fine Arts; Health and Safety
Dist - FOTH **Prod** - FOTH

Parkinson's Disease - Natural and Drug - Induced Causes 59 MIN
VHS / U-matic
Color (A)
Describes the symptoms of Parkinson's disease that have developed in young people as a result of experimentation with an illicit drug contaminated with a toxic substance. Discusses the parts of the brain affected, the chemical abnormalities that occur, the successes and limitations of current treatments and the search for better therapies.
Health and Safety; Science - Natural
Dist - USNAC **Prod** - USPHS 1985

Parkinson's Law 7 MIN
16mm
B&W (H A)
LC 72-700413
Tells a story about a man at a lathe making metal parts who fades out of the picture completely as the machinery of organization becomes both the end and the means of production. Uses miniaturization, multiple image and other special effects to show how bureaucracy often defeats its purpose.
Business and Economics; Psychology; Sociology
Dist - MMA **Prod** - ZAGREB 1970

Parklands 25 MIN
U-matic / VHS / 16mm
Untamed World Series
Color; Mono (J H C A)
$400.00 film, $250.00 video, $50.00 rental
Features some of the Canadian parklands and photographically observes the wide variety of wildlife residing there.
Geography - World; Science - Natural
Dist - CTV **Prod** - CTV 1971

Parks and Plazas 25 MIN
Videoreel / VHS
Color (A)
LC 80-707697
Discusses typology of urban parks based on source, size and demographics with examples drawn from New York City. Shows utility of parks, variety of users and their contribution to the urban environment.
Social Science; Sociology
Dist - SLDTRS **Prod** - SLDTRS 1980

Parks or people 39 MIN
VHS
Color; PAL (J H G)
PdS29.50 purchase
Looks at two approaches to rainforest conservation in Korup National Park and at the Kilum Mountain Forest Project. Explores Korup's solution to move people out of the forest while Kilum encourages people to return in order to develop sustainable forest industries. Produced by Forest in the United Kingdom.
Science - Natural
Dist - EMFVL

Parks, Pleasant Occasions and Happiness 17 MIN
16mm
Color (P I J H C)
LC 77-700993
Dramatizes, without narrations, occasions of pleasure and happiness that city parks provide throughout the seasonal calendar. Depicts the companionship that an elderly man finds with an elderly woman in the course of visiting a city's various parks in different seasons over a two - year period. Emphasizes the importance of public parks for leisure and recreation.
Health and Safety; Physical Education and Recreation; Social Science; Sociology
Dist - MARALF **Prod** - MARALF 1977

Parkside - a Neighborhood Comes Back 28 MIN
U-matic / VHS / 16mm
Color (H C A)
Demonstrates how Parkside, a Chicago neighborhood of deteriorated and abandoned buildings with a high tenant turnover, is transformed to a place where the buildings have been dramatically improved and the residents really care about their neighborhood.
Sociology
Dist - CORF **Prod** - OLINC 1983

Parlez - moi 1 Series

Sol and the Artist	10 MIN
Sol and the Burgler	10 MIN
Sol and the Cinema Ticket	10 MIN
Sol and the Clockmaker	10 MIN
Sol and the Fisherman	10 MIN
Sol and the Flea Market	10 MIN
Sol and the Fortune Teller	10 MIN
Sol and the Gambler	10 MIN
Sol and the Game Show	10 MIN
Sol and the Garage Mechanic	10 MIN
Sol and the Lumberjack	10 MIN
Sol and the Mailman	10 MIN
Sol and the Photographer	10 MIN

Sol and the Pizza 10 MIN
Sol and the Policeman 10 MIN
Sol and the Sailboat 10 MIN
Sol and the Scout Tent 10 MIN
Sol and the Tomatoes 10 MIN
Sol and the TV Commercial 10 MIN
Sol and the Vacuum Cleaner 10 MIN
Sol and the Washing Machine 10 MIN
Sol at the Airport 10 MIN
Sol at the Candy Store 10 MIN
Sol at the Doctor's 10 MIN
Sol at the Drug Store 10 MIN
Sol at the Grocer's 10 MIN
Sol at the Hairdresser's 10 MIN
Sol at the Hardware Store 10 MIN
Sol at the Hotel 10 MIN
Sol at the Record Store 10 MIN
Sol at the Shoe Store 10 MIN
Sol at the Tailor 10 MIN
Sol at the Travel Agency 10 MIN
Sol Buys a House 10 MIN
Sol Goes through Customs 10 MIN
Sol Goes to Court 10 MIN
Sol Goes to Jail 10 MIN
Sol Goes to the Bank 10 MIN
Sol Goes to the Beach 10 MIN
Sol Goes to the Dentist 10 MIN
Sol in the Garden 10 MIN
Sol in the Haunted House 10 MIN
Sol in the Hospital 10 MIN
Sol in the Jewelry Store 10 MIN
Sol in the Library 10 MIN
Sol in the Restaurant 10 MIN
Sol Joins the Army 10 MIN
Sol Minds the Fruit Store 10 MIN
Sol on the Telephone 10 MIN
Sol Plays Golf 10 MIN
Sol the Babysitter 10 MIN
Sol the Dishwasher 10 MIN
Sol the Painter 10 MIN
Sol's Birthday Cake 10 MIN
Sol's Dancing Lesson 10 MIN
Sol's Job Interview 10 MIN
Sol's Physical Training 10 MIN
Sol's Singing Lesson 10 MIN
Sol's Weather Report 10 MIN
Dist - TVOTAR

Parlez - moi 2 Series
Sol and Journalist 15 MIN
Sol and the Assembly Line 15 MIN
Sol and the Balloon Race 15 MIN
Sol and the Carpenter 15 MIN
Sol and the Disk Jockey 15 MIN
Sol and the Great Detective 15 MIN
Sol and the Lovers 15 MIN
Sol and the Optician 15 MIN
Sol and the Pirates 15 MIN
Sol and the Spies 15 MIN
Sol and the used Car 15 MIN
Sol at the Baker's 15 MIN
Sol at the Butcher's 15 MIN
Sol at the Fashion Botique 15 MIN
Sol at the Train Station 15 MIN
Sol Goes West 15 MIN
Sol in the Elevator 15 MIN
Sol in the Laundry 15 MIN
Sol in the Park 15 MIN
Sol in the Post Office 15 MIN
Sol in the Sports Shop 15 MIN
Sol Learns Good Manners 15 MIN
Sol on the Bus 15 MIN
Sol on the Stage 15 MIN
Sol Plays Hockey 15 MIN
Sol Rents a Room 15 MIN
Sol Rides a Horse 15 MIN
Sol Sets the Table 15 MIN
Sol the Office Boy 15 MIN
Sol's First Aid Lesson 15 MIN
Dist - TVOTAR

Parliament at work 30 MIN
VHS
Inside Britain 1 series
Color; PAL; NTSC (G) (BULGARIAN CZECH HUNGARIAN SPANISH POLISH ROMANIAN RUSSIAN SLOVAK UKRAINIAN ENGLISH WITH ARABIC SUBTITLES)
PdS65 purchase
Visits Westminster, 'the Mother of Parliaments,' which includes the House of Lords and the democratically elected House of Commons. Accompanies an MP on his daily routine in his constituency and in the House.
Civics and Political Systems
Dist - CFLVIS **Prod** - OWNUNI 1991

Parliamentary in Review
VHS
FFA Training Series
Color (P I J H G)
$79.00 purchase _ #6 - 001 - 300P
Assists in teaching parliamentary procedure at any grade level or type of organization. Contains eight lessons covering 28 parliamentary abilities. Includes an instruction booklet.
Business and Economics; Psychology; Sociology
Dist - VEP **Prod** - FFA

Parliamentary Procedure 18 MIN
16mm
Color (A)
Explains the workings of parliamentary procedure. Discusses the function of the chairman, the purpose and correct manner of presenting a motion, an amendment, a point of order, or appealing the decision of the chair.
Business and Economics; Sociology
Dist - AFLCIO **Prod** - NFBC 1955

Parliamentary Procedure 22 MIN
16mm
B&W
_ #106B 0155 027N
Geography - World
Dist - CFLMDC **Prod** - NFBC 1955

Parliamentary Procedure - I 35 MIN
VHS
Parliamentary Procedure (Set V) Series
(J C G A)
$49.95 _ CV188
Introduces parliamentary procedure and is recommended for training parliamentary procedure teams.
Business and Economics; Civics and Political Systems; Education
Dist - AAVIM **Prod** - AAVIM 1989

Parliamentary procedure I 32 MIN
VHS
FFA parliamentary procedures series
Color (G)
$69.95 purchase _ #6 - 040 - 130A
Includes explanations and examples of the main motion, lay on the table, previous question, refer to committee, amend, point of order and appeal from the decision of the chair. Provides the purpose, pertinent facts and an example of each motion, and questions for study and discussion. Part of a series on parliamentary procedure.
Business and Economics; Sociology
Dist - VEP **Prod** - VEP 1990

Parliamentary Procedure - II 28 MIN
VHS
Parliamentary Procedure (Set V) Series
(J C G A)
$49.95 _ CV198
Gives fundamentals of parliamentary procedure.
Business and Economics; Civics and Political Systems; Education
Dist - AAVIM **Prod** - AAVIM 1989

Parliamentary procedure II 30 MIN
VHS
FFA parliamentary procedures series
Color (G)
$69.95 purchase _ #6 - 040 - 131A
Includes explanations and examples of the suspend standing rules, division of the assembly, nominations and elections, parliamentary inquiry, leave to withdraw a motion, adjourn, take from the table, reconsider, rescind, and opening and closing ceremonies. Discusses the purpose, pertinent facts and an example of each motion, along with questions for study and discussion. Part of a series on parliamentary procedure.
Business and Economics; Sociology
Dist - VEP **Prod** - VEP 1990

Parliamentary Procedure III 32 MIN
VHS
FFA Training Series
Color (I J H G)
$69.95 purchase _ #6 - 040 - 130P
Explains and gives examples of the following parliamentary motions - main motion, lay on the table, previous question, refer to committee, amend, point of order and appeal from the decision of the chair. Provides the purpose, pertinent facts and questions for study and discussion of each motion. Trains parliamentary procedure teams.
Business and Economics; Psychology; Sociology
Dist - VEP **Prod** - FFA 1990

Parliamentary Procedure IV 30 MIN
VHS
FFA Training Series
Color (I J H G)
$69.95 purchase _ #6 - 040 - 131P
Explains and gives examples of the following parliamentary motions - suspend standing rules, division of the assembly, nominations and elections, parliamentary inquiry, leave to withdraw a motion, adjourn, take from the table, reconsider, rescind, and opening and closing ceremonies. Provides the purpose, pertinent facts and questions for study and discussion of each motion. Trains parliamentary procedure teams.
Business and Economics; Psychology; Sociology
Dist - VEP **Prod** - FFA 1990

Parliamentary Procedure (Set V) Series
Parliamentary Procedure - I 35 MIN
Parliamentary Procedure - II 28 MIN
Dist - AAVIM

Parole 59 MIN
VHS / 16mm
Color (G)
$70.00 rental _ #PAR - 000
Studies the nation's parole system. Goes behind the walls of Washington State Penitentiary to look at the feelings of inmates slated for parole hearings. Raises questions about the rationale of the parole system.
Civics and Political Systems; Sociology
Dist - PBS **Prod** - NPACT

Parole Agent 30 MIN
BETA / VHS
American Professionals Series
Color
Describes the life of G A Patrick, who has been a parole agent for the California Department of Corrections for 26 years, and who began his career as a correctional officer at San Quentin.
Guidance and Counseling; Social Science; Sociology
Dist - RMIBHF **Prod** - WTBS

The Parole Game 48 MIN
16mm / U-matic / VHS
Color (H C A)
LC 83-700674
Looks at the parole system in America. Traces the course of the parole process, beginning with the convict's initial parole board hearing through his/her attempts at adjusting to life on the outside with the aid of the parole officer.
Civics and Political Systems; Sociology
Dist - CORF **Prod** - CBSTV 1983

Parole, Probation and the Police 28 MIN
U-matic / VHS / 16mm
Legal Information for Law Enforcement Series
Color (PRO)
LC 76-701665
Deals with search and seizure in relation to parolees, probationers and narcotics outpatients. Points out that the parole agent and probation officer generally have broader powers of search over such persons than do police officers.
Civics and Political Systems; Sociology
Dist - AIMS **Prod** - CAGO 1974

Paroles d'echanges 1 series
Bon anniversaire 25 MIN
Double faute 25 MIN
Le Choix d'un ete 25 MIN
Quelle blague 25 MIN
Dist - TVOTAR

Paroles d'echanges 2 series
Drole de coincidence 30 MIN
La Bonne aventure 30 MIN
La Tete en fete 30 MIN
L'Amour a la quebecoise 30 MIN
Dist - TVOTAR

The Parotid and Submandibular Regions 14 MIN
U-matic / VHS / 16mm
Guides to Dissection Series
Color (C A)
Focuses on the head and neck. Demonstrates the dissection of the parotid and submandibular regions.
Health and Safety; Science - Natural
Dist - TEF **Prod** - UCLA

Parotidectomy 18 MIN
16mm
Color
LC 73-700745
Demonstrates an effective technique of parotidectomy, showing how to successfully remove the tumor mass and to preserve the facial nerve that runs through the gland.
Health and Safety
Dist - EATONL **Prod** - EATONL 1972

Parotidectomy 25 MIN
16mm
Color (PRO)
Presents surgical removal of the superficial lobe of the parotid gland. Shows the method of identifying the facial nerve prior to its entrance and demonstrates the use of a nerve stimulator to aid in the identification.
Health and Safety; Science
Dist - ACY **Prod** - ACYDGD 1951

Parquet and Tile Floors 30 MIN
BETA / VHS
This Old House, Pt 1 - the Dorchester Series
Color
Demonstrates how to lay a parquet kitchen floor. Considers a home security system. Shows how to install a tile floor in the bathroom.

Industrial and Technical Education; Sociology
Dist - CORF **Prod** - WGBHTV

Parquet Floors and Carpet Installations 30 MIN
BETA / VHS
Wally's Workshop Series
Color
Home Economics; Industrial and Technical Education
Dist - KARTES **Prod** - KARTES

Parrish Blue 26 MIN
U-matic / VHS / 16mm
Color (H C)
LC 72-702124
Explores the life and work of the American artist - illustrator, Maxfield Parrish, whose imaginative book illustrations, advertisements, magazine covers and prints are a landmark in American history. Interviews Norman Rockwell, who evaluates the role and status of the commercial artist. Explains the stylistic qualities which may have accounted for Parrish's popularity, and shows a wide sampling of Parrish's work.
Biography; Fine Arts
Dist - IFB **Prod** - IFB 1971

Parrot 30 MIN
VHS / 16mm
Art of decorating cakes series
(G)
$49.00 purchase _ #BCD5
Instructs in the art of cake decorating. Shows how to figure pipe a parrot directly on top of a cake, using buttercream icing. Taught by master cake decorator Leon Simmons.
Home Economics; Industrial and Technical Education
Dist - RMIBHF **Prod** - RMIBHF

Parrot Jungle 29 MIN
16mm
Color
Tours Miami's parrot jungle with a look at its birds and plant life and features a segment on performing birds.
Geography - United States; Science - Natural
Dist - MIMET **Prod** - MIMET

Parrying and Striking 8 MIN
16mm
Combative Measures - Judo Series
B&W
LC 75-700843
Demonstrates parries, blocks and counters in judo. Shows fist, hand and elbow blows, finger thrusts, knuckle blows and kicking.
Civics and Political Systems; Physical Education and Recreation
Dist - USNAC **Prod** - USAF 1955

Parsifal 255 MIN
VHS
Color (G) (GERMAN (ENGLISH SUBTITLES))
$59.95 purchase _ #1195
Presents 'Parsifal' by Wagner directed by Hans - Jurgen Syberberg. Features Armin Jordan who conducts and stars as King Amfortas, and the Prague Philharmonic Choir with the Monte Carlo Philharmonic Orchestra.
Fine Arts; Foreign Language
Dist - KULTUR

Part Four - Factors Affecting Chemical Reactions 50 MIN
VHS
Basic Chemistry Series
Color (J H C)
LC 88-700288
Investigates various realms of chemistry and its applications to the everyday world.
Science - Physical
Dist - SRA **Prod** - SRA 1986

Part Four - Finding the Way Home 48.53 MIN
VHS
Drug Abuse Series
Color (J H C)
LC 88-700282
Discusses the various outlets that a drug addict can seek when he has realized that he needs help.
Sociology
Dist - SRA **Prod** - SRA 1986

Part 4 - Mixed - Gas Saturation Diving 19 MIN
VHS / U-matic
Diving Orientation for Offshore Personnel Series
Color (IND)
Discusses the theory of saturation, equipment used and a hyperbaric welding job in 500 feet of water.
Industrial and Technical Education
Dist - UTEXPE **Prod** - UTEXPE 1980

Part Four - Photosynthesis and Plant Activities 56.58 MIN
VHS
Plants Series
Color (J H C)
LC 88-700285
Aids students in the study of the anatomy of plants to understand plant functions, use of photosynthesis and reproduction.
Science - Natural
Dist - SRA **Prod** - SRA 1986

Part Four - the Tragic Theme 58.18 MIN
VHS
Understanding Shakespeare Series
Color (J H C)
LC 88-700287
Provides students with an understanding of William Shakespeare and his works in relation to the world today.
Literature and Drama
Dist - SRA **Prod** - SRA 1986

Part Handling Equipment 54 MIN
U-matic / BETA / VHS
Color
$400 purchase
Gives factors affecting the design of induction heating systems.
Industrial and Technical Education; Science; Science - Physical
Dist - ASM **Prod** - ASM

Part I - Introductory Comments 17 MIN
U-matic
Holistic Medicine in Primary Care Series
Color (C)
Gives a brief look at past and present interpretations of holistic medicine. Discusses how the use of religion, magic and nature has changed in the current philosophy of medicine.
Health and Safety; Science - Natural
Dist - UOKLAH **Prod** - UOKLAH 1986

Part I - preparing for downsizing 18 MIN
VHS
Change in the workplace - a 3 - part series
Color (COR)
$695.00 purchase _ #EPD/ETC
Provides managers and supervisors with practical tools with which to communicate the details of anticipated changes in the workplace. Includes information on transitional resources available to employees as well as security procedures. Also available in a 27 - minute Employee's version. Part one of a three - part series.
Business and Economics; Guidance and Counseling
Dist - ADVANM

Part II - life after downsizing 18 MIN
VHS
Change in the workplace - a 3 - part series
Color (COR)
$695.00 purchase _ #ELA:ETC
Presents information to help managers prevent drastic losses in morale and productivity in the aftermath of corporate downsizing. Also available in a 27 - minute Employee's version.
Business and Economics; Guidance and Counseling
Dist - ADVANM

Part II - Palpitation 35 MIN
U-matic
Holistic Medicine in Primary Care Series
Color (C)
Discusses the case of a patient suffering from palpitations in the context of psychosomatic, cultural and situational variables.
Health and Safety; Science - Natural
Dist - UOKLAH **Prod** - UOKLAH 1986

Part III - Epigastric Pain 43 MIN
U-matic
Holistic Medicine in Primary Care Series
Color (C)
Discusses the case of a patient suffering from epigastric pain in the context of psychosomatic cultural, and situational variables.
Health and Safety; Science - Natural
Dist - UOKLAH **Prod** - UOKLAH 1986

Part III - facility closing 18 MIN
VHS
Change in the workplace - a 3 - part series
Color (COR)
$695.00 purchase _ #EFC/ETC
Presents information to help managers minimize the low morale, absenteeism, potential sabotage, and other disruptions that may be caused by the news of an impending business facility closing. Also available in a 27 - minute Employee's version.
Business and Economics; Guidance and Counseling
Dist - ADVANM

Part IV - Headache 46 MIN
U-matic
Holistic Medicine in Primary Care Series
Color (C)
Discusses the case of a patient suffering from headaches in the context of psychosomatic cultural, and situational variables.
Health and Safety; Science - Natural
Dist - UOKLAH **Prod** - UOKLAH 1986

Part of Something 15 MIN
VHS / U-matic
Math Mission 2 Series
Color (P)
LC 82-706331
Shows how a space robot helps two second - graders divide up their purchase of candy equitably and then brings them back to his spaceship for a lesson on fractions. By dividing candy bars in different ways, the children find out that all parts of a fraction must be the same size.
Mathematics
Dist - GPN **Prod** - WCVETV 1980

Part of the Flip track instructional series
Audiotapes
Dist - FLIPLS

Part of the Harriet's magic hats II series
Auctioneer 15 MIN
Dist - ACCESS

Part of the How people age 50 and up can plan for a more successful retirement series
Attitude and role adjustments 29 MIN
Dist - SYLWAT

Part of the Interactions series
Attitudes and beliefs 30 MIN
Dist - AITECH

Part of the International education of the hearing impaired child series
Auditory assessment 26 MIN
Dist - USNAC

Part of the Psychology of human relations series
Attitudes and actions 30 MIN
Dist - WFVTAE

Part of the Quality control series
Attribute sampling (MIL - STD - 105D) 30 MIN
Dist - MIOT

Part of the Remedies phase of an EEO case - contested settlement and attorneys' fees trial series
Attorneys' fees trial 55 MIN
Dist - ABACPE

Part of the write course - an introduction to college composition series
The Audience 30 MIN
Dist - FI

Part of this World 28 MIN
U-matic
Color
Portrays how 2 parents learn to cope with, understand, and ultimately accept their child's deafness.
Guidance and Counseling; Health and Safety
Dist - BELLAG **Prod** - BELLAG 1981

Part of Your Loving 10 MIN
VHS / U-matic
Color
Focuses on baker Ben Togati, who brings the breadmaking process to life.
Home Economics
Dist - DENOPX **Prod** - DENONN

Part One - a Life in the Theater 58.18 MIN
VHS
Understanding Shakespeare Series
Color (J H C)
LC 88-700287
Provides an understanding of William Shakespeare and his works in relation to the world today.
Literature and Drama
Dist - SRA **Prod** - SRA 1986

Part 1 - Career Planning and Goal Setting
U-matic / VHS
Administrative Woman Series
Color (A)
Looks at how the a Administrative woman of the eighties must learn new skills and accept new responsibilities and how the computer can enhance work life. Tells how to put together a clear cut path for planning and implementing career goals.
Business and Economics; Psychology
Dist - GPCV **Prod** - GPCV

Part One - Chemistry in Everyday Life 50 MIN
VHS
Basic Chemistry Series
Color (J H C)
LC 88-700288
Investigates various realms of chemistry in relation to the everyday world and the lives of the students.

Science - Physical
Dist - SRA **Prod** - SRA 1986

Part One - Dada and the Surrealist Revolution 18 MIN
VHS
Understanding Surrealism - Painters of the Dream Series
Color (J H C)
LC 88-700277
Discusses the absence of stylistic unity among surrealist artists, and their use of unlike and improbable images.
Fine Arts
Dist - SRA **Prod** - SRA 1986

Part One - Everywhere on Earth 56.58 MIN
VHS
Plants Series
Color (J H C)
LC 88-700285
Aids students in the study of the anatomy of plants to learn how they function, use photosynthesis, and reproduce.
Science - Natural
Dist - SRA **Prod** - SRA 1986

Part One - Frequency Domain 40 MIN
U-matic / VHS
Operational Analysis Circuits Series
Color (IND)
Covers techniques of circuit theory which are widely used in solution of practical problems. Shows how to apply theory to practice in order to calculate and interpret the step and sinusoidal steady - state response of networks and relate changes in frequency response to circuit elements.
Industrial and Technical Education
Dist - COLOSU **Prod** - COLOSU

Part 1 - Introduction 26 MIN
U-matic / VHS
Diving Orientation for Offshore Personnel Series
Color (IND)
Explains the uses of diving, diving terms, responsibilities and the physiological and psychological changes that occur to the underwater diver.
Industrial and Technical Education
Dist - UTEXPE **Prod** - UTEXPE 1980

Part One - Manners at Home, in School and Public Places 14.16 MIN
VHS
Good Manners Series
Color (J H C)
LC 88-700281
Helps students to understand and establish for themselves the basic guidelines of today's etiquette in various situations.
Home Economics
Dist - SRA **Prod** - SRA 1986

Part One - Reavealing the Hidden Self 23.46 MIN
VHS
Addictive Personality Series
Color (J H C)
LC 88-700283
Helps students to assess their vulnerability to addictive behavior, and offers advice to prevent them from falling into the trap of addiction.
Guidance and Counseling; Psychology
Dist - SRA **Prod** - SRA 1986

Part One - Redesigning Our Modern World 11.17 MIN
VHS
Memphis - the New Design Series
Color (J H C)
LC 88-700278
Looks at Memphis art in relation to its style, sense of contradiction, and its heirs in Scandanavian design.
Fine Arts
Dist - SRA **Prod** - SRA 1986

Part 1 - Road to Freedom (1770 - 1900) 20 MIN
U-matic / VHS / 16mm
From the Black American Odyssey
Color; Captioned (J H)
Shows a history of Black Americans in the United Stated from 1770 - 1900.
History - United States; Social Science; Sociology
Dist - HANDEL **Prod** - HANDEL 1987

Part One - Taking Charge 30 MIN
U-matic / VHS
Sky's the Limit Series
Color
Business and Economics; Psychology
Dist - DELTAK **Prod** - LCOA

Part One - the Candy Coated Hell - Cocaine 48.53 MIN
VHS
Drug Abuse Series
Color (J H C)
LC 88-700282
Discusses the emotional, social, family and physical ramifications of using cocaine.
Sociology
Dist - SRA **Prod** - SRA 1986

Part One - the Facts and Phobias 36.24 MIN
VHS
Truth about AIDS Series
Color (J H C)
LC 88-700284
Gives students important information about Acquired Immune Deficiency Syndrome (AIDS). Tells how AIDS can be treated, transmitted, prevented, and much more.
Health and Safety
Dist - SRA **Prod** - SRA 1986

Part One - the Key! 22.35 MIN
VHS
Unlocking the Creative Self Series
Color (J H C)
LC 88-700274
Teaches students how to use thier creativity, and how to respond to visual and verbal clues to release their imaginations.
Fine Arts
Dist - SRA **Prod** - SRA 1986

Part One - using Logic in Everyday Life 28.34 MIN
VHS
Logic Series
Color (J H C)
LC 88-700275
Discusses the connection between thinking soundly and using common sense. Examines ways of reaching conclusions about reality through logic.
Religion and Philosophy
Dist - SRA **Prod** - SRA 1986

Part Positioning for Shear Layout using Architect's Scale 14 MIN
BETA / VHS
Color (IND)
Shows the common sense approach to planning the arrangement of parts for economical shearing, eliminating as much waste as possible. Demonstrates use of an architect's scale to position parts 'to scale' on a simulated shear layout.
Industrial and Technical Education; Mathematics; Psychology
Dist - RMIBHF **Prod** - RMIBHF

Partial Dentures - Biomechanics 15 MIN
16mm
Color
LC FIE52-1488
Demonstrates the influence of forces of mastication on the design of partial dentures by dividing parts of partial dentures into bracing, supporting and retaining elements. Emphasizes important construction details.
Health and Safety; Science - Physical
Dist - USNAC **Prod** - USN 1951

Partial fractions 30 MIN
VHS
Calculus series
Color (C)
$125.00 purchase _ #6041
Explains partial fractions. Part of a 56 - part series on calculus.
Mathematics
Dist - LANDMK **Prod** - LANDMK

Partial Glossectomy and Osteotomy to Improve Function 24 MIN
16mm
Color
LC 72-700356
Presents the case history of a teenage girl who has an osteotomy and a partial glossectomy. Follows her from the preoperative interview, through surgery, to one - week and one - year postoperative interviews.
Health and Safety
Dist - OSUMPD **Prod** - OSUMPD 1972

Partial Ileal by - Pass Operation for Hypercholesterolemia 34 MIN
16mm
Color (PRO)
Explains that the partial ileal bypass operation is a direct surgical approach to treatment of the hyperlipidemias and atherosclerosis. Reviews patient data and shows the operative procedure.
Health and Safety; Science
Dist - ACY **Prod** - ACYDGD 1969

Partial Nephrectomy 22 MIN
16mm
Color
LC 75-702297
Illustrates a technique for the conservation of renal tissue. Stresses the principles of partial nephrectomy, including accurate diagnosis of focal disease, good exposure of vessels, ligate vessels of the diseased segment, saving capsule for closure, suturing small vessels and calyx drain.
Health and Safety; Science
Dist - EATONL **Prod** - EATONL 1966

The Partially Hearing 15 MIN
16mm
International Education of the Hearing Impaired Child Series
Color
LC 74-705326
Shows classes at the newly constructed school for people with partial hearing in Stockholm, in the Alviksskolan.
Education; Guidance and Counseling; Psychology
Dist - USNAC **Prod** - USBEH 1971

Participant's Overview 5 MIN
Videoreel / VT2
AMA Assessment Center Program for Identifying Supervisory Potential 'Series
Color (PRO)
LC 75-704228
Familiarizes management assessors with the training course objectives and management simulation workshop activities.
Business and Economics; Psychology
Dist - AMA **Prod** - AMA 1974

Participating in Implementation 45 MIN
U-matic / VHS
User Responsibilities in Information Management Series
Color
Illustrates the challenges which the information system user will face in the implementation process and presents feasible alternatives for project management.
Business and Economics; Industrial and Technical Education; Psychology
Dist - DELTAK **Prod** - DELTAK

Participation 30 MIN
16mm
Success in Supervision Series
B&W
LC 74-706171
Shows how a supervisor can get his people to work with him to solve problems, set goals and get results.
Business and Economics; Guidance and Counseling
Dist - USNAC **Prod** - WETATV 1965

Participation in Tomorrow 15 MIN
16mm
Color (H C A)
#1X31 I
Discusses the economic development of Indian people across Canada. Shows hoe they have overcome much suppression to create industries of their own including scrap metal slavage, clothing manufacture, fish packing, bicycle manufacture, amd more.
Social Science
Dist - CDIAND **Prod** - AINC 1976

Participative Management 30 MIN
U-matic / VHS
Management for Engineers Series
Color
Business and Economics; Industrial and Technical Education; Psychology
Dist - SME **Prod** - UKY

Participative Management Skills
VHS / U-matic
Color
Teaches the skills needed to implement participative decision making, and allows participants to examine the characteristics of a participative environment, explore ways to enhance power through participation, improve team communication and achieve consensus decisions. Includes a student text and a set of diskettes.
Business and Economics; Psychology
Dist - DELTAK **Prod** - CONCO

Participative Management - We Learn from the Japanese 28 MIN
U-matic / VHS / 16mm
Color (C A)
Presents a case study of participative management at Nissan's Smyrna plant. Examines some of the key ideas from Japanese business philosophy and how these ideas help improve productivity and employee relations. Includes comments from leaders in business, industry, unions and education.
Business and Economics
Dist - EBEC **Prod** - EBEC 1984

Particle, flake, and filled composites 22 MIN
BETA / VHS / U-matic
Composites I the basics series
Color
$400 purchase
Industrial and Technical Education; Science - Physical
Dist - ASM **Prod** - ASM

The Particle Model 10 MIN
U-matic
Wave Particle Duality Series
Color (H C)
Looks at the early explanations of the source and behaviour of light, from the Greeks to Isaac Newton's particle model which explained geometric reflection, refraction and dispersion.
Science; Science - Physical
Dist - TVOTAR **Prod** - TVOTAR 1984

The Particle Model of Matter 60 MIN
U-matic / VHS
Chemistry Training Series
Color (IND)
Covers states of aggregation and energy content, states of aggregation and thermal motion, density of matter in the three states of aggregation, diffusion, osmosis, attractive forces between particles and the nature of the atttractive forces between particles.
Science; Science - Physical
Dist - ITCORP **Prod** - ITCORP

Particle Size Determination, Optics 56 MIN
VHS / U-matic
Colloid and Surface Chemistry - Lyophobic Colloids Series
Color
Science; Science - Physical
Dist - KALMIA **Prod** - KALMIA

Particles in Space 4 MIN
16mm
B&W (A)
Presents an experimental film by Lyn Lye which uses drums and sound effects and kinetic sculptures.
Fine Arts
Dist - STARRC **Prod** - STARRC 1957

Particles in Space 4 MIN
16mm
B&W
Deals with the energy of movement, of shaping light in darkness, by scratching on the film surface. By Len Lye.
Fine Arts
Dist - STARRC **Prod** - STARRC 1979

Particles in space and Tal Farlow 6 MIN
16mm
B&W (G)
$22.00 rental
Reveals virtually unknown underground films by the pioneer kinetic artist, sculptor and filmmaker, Len Lye. Concerns itself with the energy of movement and of shaping light in darkness by scratching on the film surface. The musical counterpoint is provided with African drums. Tal Farlow is his last scratch film which features a jazz guitar solo by Farlow. Particles in Space and Tal Farlow are on one reel.
Fine Arts
Dist - CANCIN **Prod** - LYEL 1980

Particular Solutions
16mm
B&W
Illustrates the algebraic ideas of vector spaces and linear transformations behind the method of 'undetermined coefficients.' Shows how this method works for a simple case study equation.
Mathematics
Dist - OPENU **Prod** - OPENU

Particularly Poor Albert 17 MIN
U-matic / VHS / 16mm
Color
Presents the various events which culminate in a fatal accident while operating a forklift. Reviews loading, driving and parking procedures.
Health and Safety
Dist - IFB **Prod** - WALGRV

The Parting 52 MIN
VHS
Color (H C G) (DUTCH WITH ENGLISH SUBTITLES)
$295.00 purchase, $75.00 rental
Follows the last two months of 29 - year - old Aleida Hartstra, leukemia patient, as she prepares to meet death. Observes her taking leave of her family, friends and life.
Guidance and Counseling; Sociology
Dist - FLMLIB **Prod** - KALAHR 1989

The Parting 16 MIN
U-matic / VHS / 16mm
Color (H C A)
LC 73-702076
Portrays a man's death and burial in a rural Yugoslavian village as the community gathers to wash and anoint his body, burn his old clothes, dress him in finery, celebrate the resurrection of the soul and then sing, pray and weep at the graveside.
Social Science; Sociology
Dist - WOMBAT **Prod** - DUNAV

Parting glances 94 MIN
35mm / 16mm
Color (G)
Concerns two men who have been lovers for years. Robert is being transferred out of the country and Michael is staying behind; Robert says their affair has become too predictable and Michael seems to care more for Nick, who has AIDS. Deals with caring, friendships and working at relationships. Looks at the impact of AIDS on the attitudes of several generation of gays and the interaction between gays and straights. Executive producer Paul A Kaplan; produced by Yoram Mandel and Arthur Silverman; written, directed and edited by Bill Sherwood. Contact distributor for price.
Fine Arts; Health and Safety; Psychology; Sociology
Dist - OCTOBF

The Parting of the Ways 57 MIN
16mm / U-matic / VHS
Music of Man Series
Color
Points out that in America, the synthesis of cultures and musical forms created new music, such as the songs of Stephen Foster, the rags of Scott Joplin and the marches of John Philip Sousa. Shows how the Victorian Age ushered in concert hall melodramas and parlor pianos. Discusses how in Europe the old conventions were fragmented under the impact of the impressionism of Debussy, and the splendors of Strauss and Mahler. Tells how Stravinsky advanced the revolution with The Rite Of Spring.
Fine Arts
Dist - TIMLIF **Prod** - CANBC 1981

The Partisan Leaders of the Backcountry - Pt 9 30 MIN
VHS
And Then There were Thirteen Series
Color (H)
$69.95 purchase
Focuses on the backcountry partisan leaders. Uses footage shot on battleground locations. Describes command personalities, weapons and uniforms. Part 9 of a twenty - part series on Southern theaters of war during the American Revolution.
Biography; Civics and Political Systems; Guidance and Counseling; History - United States
Dist - SCETV **Prod** - SCETV 1982

Partisans of Vilna 130 MIN
VHS
Color; B&W (G) (ENGLISH HEBREW YIDDISH)
$70.00 purchase
Explores Jewish resistance during World War II. Recounts the untold tale of the moral dilemma facing the Jewish youth who organized an underground resistance in the Vilna ghetto, and fought in the woods as partisans against the Nazis. Features 40 interviews with the former partisans in Hebrew, Yiddish and English interspersed with archival footage. Directed by Josh Waletzky. Produced by Aviva Kempner.
Civics and Political Systems; Fine Arts; History - World; Religion and Philosophy
Dist - NCJEWF

Partly Sunny or Partly Cloudy 19 MIN
VHS
Active Atmosphere Series
Color (J)
$79.00 purchase _ #2240V
Discusses solar and terrestrial radiation and their interaction with the atmosphere. Considers the Greenhouse effect, cloud formation and the effects of cloud - radiation interaction. Part of an eight - part series on the atmosphere and the weather it creates. Includes a comprehensive study guide.
Science - Physical
Dist - SCTRES **Prod** - SCTRES

Partner 112 MIN
16mm
Color (ITALIAN (ENGLISH SUBTITLES))
Presents a Dostoyevksy - inspired story of a man who meets his own double. Directed by Bernardo Bertolucci. With English subtitles.
Fine Arts; Foreign Language
Dist - NYFLMS **Prod** - UNKNWN 1968

Partner Stunts for Cheerleading 25 MIN
VHS / U-matic
Video for Cheerleading Series
Color
Physical Education and Recreation
Dist - ATHI **Prod** - ATHI

Partner Video Sequences - German - Advanced German 100 MIN
VHS / U-matic
Color (H C A) (GERMAN)
Provides conversational practice for advanced German classes and for those who plan to travel abroad. Follows a family through their daily life and a trip to Austria. Increases gradually in sophistication and complexity.
Foreign Language
Dist - MEDIAG **Prod** - THAMES 1985

Partnering - the heart of selling today 24 MIN
BETA / U-matic / VHS
Color (G)
$475.00 purchase, $125.00 rental
Features Jerry Manning and Berry Reece who teach personnel how to build customer relationships. Shows how to establish and maintain a relationship and improve sales.
Business and Economics; Psychology
Dist - AMEDIA **Prod** - AMEDIA

Partners 13 MIN
U-matic / VHS / 16mm
Many Worlds of Nature Series
Color (I J)
Examines a number of interrelationships occurring within nature. Looks at such host specific insects as the monarch, viceroy and Baltimore butterflies contrasted with the more mutually beneficial partnerships occurring among fungus and algae, aphids and ants, yucca and the yucca moth, and bees and flowers.
Science - Natural
Dist - CORF **Prod** - MORALL 1984

Partners 5 MIN
VHS
Seahouse series
Color (K P)
$29.95 purchase _ #RB8156
Shows how animals in the sea have ways of living together which is mutually helpful. Studies the clownfish and the anemone which live together - the clownfish keeps the anemone clean while hiding in the stinging tentacles of the anemone. Part of a series of ten parts on marine animals.
Science - Natural
Dist - REVID **Prod** - REVID 1990

Partners - Burlington, Wisconsin - 1 30 MIN
VHS
Our Chance Series
Color (A)
$395.00 purchase
Focuses on knowledge, attitudes and behaviors that influence drug free and drug use life styles. Emphasizes that effective drug abuse prevention education must begin before children are established users of tobacco, alcohol or other addictive drugs. Targets children in the vulnerable preteen years. Program 1 examines how a small rural community involved a broad cross - section of people in the prevention of drug abuse. Burlington's prevention effort - called PARTNERS - began with the arrival of a new school superintendent in 1986 and has been guided by a committee comprised of leaders from all parts of the community.
Guidance and Counseling; Health and Safety; Psychology; Social Science; Sociology
Dist - AITECH **Prod** - AITECH 1990

Partners - Community Program 30 MIN
VHS / 16mm
Your Choice - Our Chance Series
Color (I A)
$295.00 purchase, $35.00 rental
Shows how a community can work through the schools and outside them to get students and families expert help in drug prevention.
Health and Safety; Psychology
Dist - AITECH **Prod** - AITECH 1990

Partners for life 30 MIN
VHS
Lifesense series
Color; PAL (H C A)
PdS65 purchase; Not available in the United States
Examines the history of human development from the point of view of other species. Describes humans and domestic animals as 'partners for life.' Part of the Lifesense series.
Science - Natural
Dist - BBCENE

Partners for Life - the Human Heart and Lungs 30 MIN
VHS
Color
Examines the human heart and lungs and suggests habits that are necessary to maintain good health and a normal lifespan.
Health and Safety
Dist - IBIS **Prod** - IBIS 1985
HRMC

Partners in change 17 MIN
VHS
Color (G)
$22.00 purchase
Educates employers about hiring displaced homemakers and mature women. Documents situations in which employers overcame their reluctance to hire mature women. Discusses the impressive skills, dependability, positive attitudes and rich and varied work experience that mature women bring to the workplace.

Business and Economics; Sociology
Dist - WOMEN **Prod** - AARP

Partners in Health 22 MIN
16mm
Color
LC 79-700002
Uses an animated cartoon character to inform Department of the Army employees about the scope of on - the - job health protection services offered by the Army's occupational health clinics. Emphasizes worker responsibility in following safety procedures, wearing safety equipment and reporting injuries.
Health and Safety
Dist - USNAC **Prod** - USAEHA 1977

Partners in Mission 16 MIN
16mm
Color (H C T) (LATIN)
LC FIA67-5571
Mortimer Arias, a Bolivian pastor, and Dick Chartier, a missionary to Argentina, speak on the social revolution now occurring in Latin America and how the church and the American people participate in this liberating change.
Geography - World; Psychology; Religion and Philosophy; Sociology
Dist - UMCBM **Prod** - UMCBM 1967

Partners in Safety 13 MIN
16mm
Color
LC 76-700474
Demonstrates the use of signs, barricades and flagmen in controlling traffic that has been disrupted because of construction or maintenance activities. Shows traffic from the driver's perspective and presents the workman's point of view.
Industrial and Technical Education
Dist - USNAC **Prod** - USDTFH 1975

Partners - Program 3 25 MIN
VHS
Sex education series
Color (I J H)
$169.00 purchase _ #CG - 831 - VS
Presents two parts which help students to evaluate what kinds of sexual behavior are appropriate in the teen years and encourages them to make responsible, mutual decisions. Explores the issues of sexual abstinence vs activity in part one. Part two visits a couple from part one a year later. Reveals that each is struggling to decide if they are 'ready' for a sexual relationship. Part three of a five - part series on sex education.
Guidance and Counseling; Health and Safety; Psychology
Dist - HRMC **Prod** - HRMC

Partners with Industry 13 MIN
16mm
Color (J H A)
LC 76-701538
Tells how America's industry can benefit from NASA technology now and in the future. Touches almost every branch of science in almost every discipline of technology.
Health and Safety; Industrial and Technical Education; Science
Dist - USNAC **Prod** - NASA 1975

Partners with your doctor I 8 MIN
VHS
Color (H C A PRO)
$72.50 purchase _ #AH44101
Features a female physician, who shows how she cares for her own breasts via breast self - examination techniques. Justifies the need for mammography as an additional diagnostic tool.
Health and Safety; Science; Science - Natural; Sociology
Dist - HTHED **Prod** - HTHED

Partners with your doctor II 7 MIN
VHS
Color (H C A PRO)
$72.50 purchase _ #AH44105
Covers the subject of mammography. Explains how mammography is done, why it is important, and stresses the low amount of radiation involved in the procedure.
Health and Safety; Science; Science - Natural; Sociology
Dist - HTHED **Prod** - HTHED

Partners with your doctor - men
VHS
Color (J H C G T A PRO)
$72.50 purchase _ #AH45210
Discusses testicular cancer and the importance of discovering it as soon as possible. Teaches techniques for performing self - examinations, but also encourages men to get regular physician exams. Reveals that testicular cancer is the leading form of cancer for men under 30.
Health and Safety; Science; Science - Natural
Dist - HTHED **Prod** - HTHED

Partners with your doctor series
Discusses breast self - examination and mammography. Gives an overview of BSE techniques. Explains why and how mammography is done, stressing the safety of the procedure.
Partners with your doctor series 15 MIN
Dist - HTHED **Prod** - HTHED

The Partnership 103 MIN
VHS
Color (G)
$39.95 purchase _ #0809
Joins the crew of the Entracte for a seven - year saga. Watches the crew build the 27 foot sloop in three years. Voyages with the Entracte for four years across the Atlantic to the French Canals, through the Mediterranean and following the tradewind path of Columbus to the West Indies.
Physical Education and Recreation
Dist - SEVVID

Partnership for Progress
16mm
B&W (C A)
Traces federal involvement in the control of infectious diseases, the origins of the national institutes of health and the work of the vaccine development program of the National Institute of Allergy and Infectious Diseases.
Health and Safety; Sociology
Dist - NMAC **Prod** - CAPFL 1967

Partnership into Space - Mission Helios 27 MIN
16mm
Color (H C A)
Deals with the spaceship Helios, the product of an American - German partnership, with an orbit closer to the sun than any other spacecraft.
Geography - World; History - World; Science - Physical
Dist - WSTGLC **Prod** - WSTGLC

A Partnership - textile - apparel and the arbitration process 31 MIN
BETA / VHS / U-matic
Color (PRO)
$90.00 purchase
Addresses 12 procedural issues which might arise prior to or at an arbitration hearing involving textile and apparel disputes. Includes prehearing fabric inspection, prehearing settlement, opening statements, claims, arbitrator disclosure, acceptance of written testimony, unidentified evidence and oral summation versus written briefs. Includes a discussion guide.
Industrial and Technical Education; Psychology
Dist - AARA **Prod** - AARA

Partnership - the Heart of Selling Today 24 MIN
VHS / 16mm
Color (PRO)
$475.00 purchase, $125.00 rental
Trains sales personnel in building client rapport.
Business and Economics; Psychology
Dist - VICOM **Prod** - VICOM 1990

Partnerships 30 MIN
U-matic / VHS
Tax Reform Act of 1984 Series
Color (PRO)
Presents questions on partnerships as affected by the Tax Reform Act of 1984 with answers by the individuals from government who developed the legislation.
Business and Economics; Civics and Political Systems; Social Science
Dist - ALIABA **Prod** - ALIABA

Parto por Cesarea 11 MIN
VHS
Color (H C G) (SPANISH)
$150.00 purchase, $30.00 rental _ #37498
Shares the experiences of a Latino couple of a caesarean birth with the father present during the surgery. Explains caesarean section, its common medical indications and depicts the emotional concerns of both the mother and father. Includes an English discussion guide and script translation. Produced by Terry Looper and Claris Barahona - O'Connor, University of California, San Francisco.
Health and Safety; Sociology
Dist - UCEMC

Partons En Vacances 6 MIN
16mm
Voix Et Images De France Series
Color (I) (FRENCH)
LC 70-710640
A French language film. Provides a tour of French scenic and historic landmarks. Pictures several winter and summer sports.
Foreign Language
Dist - CHLTN **Prod** - PEREN 1962

Parts and Materials 30 MIN
VHS / U-matic
Maintenance Management Series
Color
Describes the parts and materials control process. Illustrates inventory control. Stresses making procurement decisions.
Business and Economics; Psychology
Dist - ITCORP **Prod** - ITCORP

Parts and Wholes 16 MIN
VHS / U-matic
Math Cycle Series
Color (P)
Discusses parts and wholes in arithmetic.
Mathematics
Dist - GPN **Prod** - WDCNTV 1983

Parts of a Book 15 MIN
VHS
Planet Pylon Series
Color (I)
LC 90712897
Uses character Commander Wordstalker of the Space Station Readstar to improve language arts skills. Examines the parts of a book. Includes a worksheet to be competed by student with the aid of series characters.
Education; English Language
Dist - GPN

The Parts of speech 90 MIN
VHS
Color (I J H)
$194.00 purchase _ #TK120
Presents six separate programs that clearly define rules of usage for nouns, verbs, pronouns, adjectives, adverbs, conjunctions, prepositions and interjections. Uses lively cartoon art. Video transfer from filmstrips.
English Language
Dist - KNOWUN

Parts of speech - taking inventory 18 MIN
VHS
Language construction company series
Color (H C G)
$50.00 purchase _ #LCC - 1
Assists students in improving their written and spoken English grammar skills. Bases all programs on a 'construction theme.' Includes review tests as an integral part of each lesson. Students may stop, start and repeat any part of the lesson. Visual cues are given for review purposes. Part of a 15 - part series.
English Language
Dist - INSTRU

Parts of the Guitar, Types of Guitars Holding the Guitar, Striking the String, 20 MIN
VHS / U-matic
Guitar, Guitar Series LINCOLN, NB 68501
Color (J H)
Provides instruction on how to play the guitar, discussing parts of the guitar, types of guitars, holding the guitar, striking the string and notes on the first string.
Fine Arts
Dist - GPN **Prod** - SCITV 1981

Parturition in the Cow
16mm
Color (PRO)
LC 73-703090
Documents the labor, birth and afterbirth of two cows. Discusses some of the dangers, the veterinary procedures and the progressive stages of parturition.
Agriculture; Health and Safety
Dist - UILL **Prod** - UILLCA 1973

The Party 28 MIN
16mm / U-matic / VHS
Color (J) (SPANISH)
LC 79-713919
A dramatization about a teenage girl who is torn by peer group pressure, the demands of her boyfriend and her own feelings toward love and sexual commitment.
Guidance and Counseling; Psychology; Religion and Philosophy; Sociology
Dist - MEDIAG **Prod** - PAULST 1971

Party 28 MIN
VHS
Elephant show series
Color (P I)
$95.00 purchase, $45.00 rental
Presents program 12 in the Sharon, Lois and Bram's Elephant Show series. Teaches reading readiness and social skills while engaging children in making music. Each program explores a new theme through adventure, fantasy, mystery and song with recording artists Sharon, Lois and Bram. Uses traditional materials which stress participation - action songs, sing - along songs, story songs, clapping songs, singing games, playground chants and folk songs from many different traditions. Includes teacher's guide co - authored by a music education specialist.

Fine Arts; Sociology
Dist - BULFRG **Prod** - CAMBFP 1988

Party, Dress, Game 10 MIN
U-matic
Readalong One Series
Color (K P)
Introduces reading and spelling for preschoolers and children in grades 1 to 3 with animation, puppets, humor and music. Comes with teacher's guide and kit.
Education; English Language; Literature and Drama
Dist - TVOTAR **Prod** - TVOTAR 1975

Party Fare 3 MIN
Videoreel / VT2
Beatrice Trum Hunter's Natural Foods Series
Color
Shows how to make a crustless cheese and onion pie, assembling most of the ingredients in a blender. Demonstrates how to make a pizza using a whole wheat dough layered with cheese and tomatoes and sprinkled with spices.
Home Economics; Social Science
Dist - PBS **Prod** - WGBH

The Party Game 30 MIN
U-matic / VHS
Acquaintance Rape Prevention Series
Color (H)
Focuses on an interview with a young woman who tells what it is like to be the victim of an acquaintance rape.
Guidance and Counseling; Health and Safety; Sociology
Dist - GPN **Prod** - GPN

The Party Game 8 MIN
16mm
Acquaintance Rape Prevention Series
Color (H C A)
LC 79-701269
Presents the story of a teenage girl whose dancing partner sexually assaults her. Emphasizes the need for young people to understand their own sexual values and those of others.
Health and Safety; Psychology; Sociology
Dist - ODNP **Prod** - NCPCR 1978

Party Leader 15 MIN
U-matic / VHS
Modern President Series
Color (H C)
$250 purchase
Shows how modern presidents have needed to be effective in their own political parties. Produced by Focus Enterprises.
Biography; Civics and Political Systems
Dist - CORF

Party Line 25 MIN
VHS / U-matic
Color
Tells a story about an outlandish conflict between two telephone companies. Uses black humor in an experimental film.
Fine Arts; Literature and Drama
Dist - MEDIPR **Prod** - KROGST 1977

Party Pajamas and Evening Skirts 29 MIN
Videoreel / VT2
Designing Women Series
Color
Home Economics
Dist - PBS **Prod** - WKYCTV

Party safe - with Diana and Bambi 25 MIN
VHS
Color (G)
$50.00 rental, $175.00 purchase
Presents DiAna and her partner Dr Bambi Sumpter, who travel to New York, Chicago, Los Angeles and Toronto, to hold safe sex informational parties. Includes explicit and frank discussions about sex and carries a message about human relationships that surpass even its clearly articulated perspective on AIDS. A sequel to DiAna's Hair Ego by Ellen Spiro.
Fine Arts; Health and Safety; Sociology
Dist - WMEN

Party time 15 MIN
VHS
Color; PAL (P I J H)
Introduces the concepts of anthropology through the comparison of a Bar Mitzvah with an ordinary birthday party for a 13 year old. Features commentary by an anthropologist on what can be learned from the two examples.
Religion and Philosophy; Sociology
Dist - VIEWTH

Party Time Songs that Tickle Your Funny Bone
VHS / 16mm
Color (K)
$9.88 purchase _ #PPI25282
Presents Ruth Roberts singing children's songs.
Fine Arts
Dist - EDUCRT **Prod** - PIONR

The Party's Over 15 MIN
16mm
Jackson Junior High Series
Color (J)
LC 76-704031
Introduces problems of alcohol and peer pressure. Depicts a girl's quiet slumber party, which becomes raucous when a group of high school boys arrive with liquor. Shows how the girl's parents step in and control the situation.
Guidance and Counseling; Health and Safety; Psychology; Sociology
Dist - USNAC **Prod** - USOLLR 1976

The Party's Over 18 MIN
VHS / U-matic
Color
Offers a new approach to the drinking driver problem.
Health and Safety; Sociology
Dist - PARPRO **Prod** - PARPRO

The Party's over 47 MIN
VHS
Color (C A)
$325.00 purchase
Dramatizes the technique of crisis intervention to encourage an alcoholic or substance abuser to recognize his or her problem and seek help. Shows with several skits demonstrating various problems and various motives for action how family members and friends can use the technique to help someone they care about. Produced by Niemack - Hassett Productions Inc.
Guidance and Counseling; Health and Safety; Psychology
Dist - PFP

Pas De Deux 14 MIN
16mm / U-matic / VHS
B&W (K)
LC 78-703710
Illuminates the grace and movement of classical ballet form through the use of strobe - like or multi - image patterns. Features Margaret Mercier and Vincent Warren of Les Grands Ballets Canadiens.
Fine Arts; Industrial and Technical Education
Dist - LCOA **Prod** - NFBC 1969

Pas De Moutarde 10 MIN
U-matic / VHS
Salut - French Language Lessons Series
Color
Focuses on food and expressions of equality.
Foreign Language
Dist - BCNFL **Prod** - BCNFL 1984

Pasadena Freeway Stills 6 MIN
16mm
Color; Silent (C)
$196.00
Gary Beydler.
Fine Arts
Dist - AFA **Prod** - AFA 1974

The Pasadena Tournament of Roses Story - Tradition on Parade 31 MIN
16mm
Color
LC 76-702207
Takes a look at the history and traditions of the Tournament of Roses Parade in Pasadena, California.
Geography - United States; Physical Education and Recreation
Dist - INMATI **Prod** - TRA 1976

PASCAL - a modern programming language - - a series
Decision making
Dist - EDUACT

PASCAL - a Modern Programming Language Series
Introduction to PASCAL
Loops
Procedures
Variables and Keyboard Input
Dist - EDUACT

Pascal - beginning pascal series, Pt 1
Control structures - loops 30 MIN
Control structures - selectors 30 MIN
Dist - COLOSU

Pascal - Pt 1 - beginning Pascal series
Array - Structured Data Types 30 MIN
Example program 30 MIN
Expressions 30 MIN
Functions 30 MIN
Procedures 30 MIN
User - Defined Data Types 30 MIN
Dist - COLOSU

Pascal, Pt 3 - Advanced Pascal Series
Beyond pascal 30 MIN
The Compiler 30 MIN
Microcomputer Example 30 MIN
More I/O 30 MIN
Recursion 30 MIN
Writing Compilers 30 MIN
Dist - COLOSU

Pascal, Pt 2 - Intermediate Pascal Series
File structures 30 MIN
Limitations 30 MIN
Other Data Structures 30 MIN
Other Features, Pt 1 30 MIN
Other Features, Pt 2 30 MIN
Pointers 30 MIN
Record structures 30 MIN
Dist - COLOSU

The Pasciak family 52 MIN
16mm
Six American families series
Color (A)
Features the daily routine of a second - generation Polish - American family who speak their native tongue and belong to ethnic organizations and generally cling to the 'old ways'. Shows how the younger children seem to be moving away. Looks at a traditional Christmas celebration where the family is reunited, perhaps for the last time.
Psychology; Sociology
Dist - ECUFLM **Prod** - GROUPW 1976

Pasht 5 MIN
16mm
Color (G)
$12.00 rental, $247.00 purchase
Says Brakhage, 'In honor of the cat, so named, and the goddess of all cats which she was named after.'
Fine Arts
Dist - CANCIN **Prod** - BRAKS 1965

Pass, Dribble, Shoot 10 MIN
16mm
Color (H)
Shows three ways of moving the ball in soccer, passing with the side of the foot, dribbling with the inside and outside of the foot and kicking with the instep. Isolates the techniques and shows them in practice sessions and in actual game situations.
Physical Education and Recreation
Dist - SOCCER **Prod** - SOCCER 1970

Pass it Along Series
Ansel adams - photography 15 MIN
Friedensreich hundertwasser - painting 15 MIN
Introduction 15 MIN
Martita Goshen - Dance 15 MIN
Paul Winter - Music 15 MIN
Peter Bohlin - architecture 15 MIN
Dist - GPN

Pass it along
Introduction 15 MIN
Jean George, Writing 15 MIN
Ozzie Tollefson, Performance 15 MIN
Dist - GPN

Pass it on 11 MIN
16mm / U-matic / VHS
Color
Points out that unclear or misunderstood messages or instructions or meanings are costly in loss of time and energy and in frustration. Presents the verify and clariy technique to prevent communication problems.
Business and Economics; English Language; Psychology
Dist - CCCD **Prod** - CCCD 1982

Pass it on series
Acting is pretending 15 MIN
Architecture 15 MIN
Ballet 15 MIN
Black History and Art 15 MIN
Body parts 15 MIN
Communicating 15 MIN
Computer Magic 15 MIN
Fire, Fire 15 MIN
Hobbies 15 MIN
Holiday - Halloween 15 MIN
Holiday B - an International Holiday Feast 15 MIN
Holiday C - an International Holiday Season 15 MIN
Holiday D - be My Valentine 15 MIN
A Junior Art Exhibit 15 MIN
Listening and Singing 15 MIN
Literature 15 MIN
Man's Best Friend 15 MIN
Me, Myself and I 15 MIN
Names 15 MIN
Opera 15 MIN
Over Hill, Over Dale 15 MIN
Recycling 15 MIN
Ring, ring 15 MIN

A River Museum	15 MIN
Round Shapes	15 MIN
Safe summer fun	15 MIN
Spring is Here	15 MIN
A Trip to the Hospital	15 MIN
TV is for Learning	15 MIN
Winter - a Museum Experience	15 MIN

Dist - GPN

Pass receiving
VHS
NCAA football videos - offensive series
Color (A G T)
$39.95 purchase _ #KAR1303V-P
Presents instruction on skills and drills given by NCAA coaches. Features Bobby Bowden explaining pass receiving techniques. One of a series of videos that provide coaching tips to offensive and defensive players and coaches. Series is available as a set of offensive series, defensive series, or both combined.
Physical Education and Recreation
Dist - CAMV

Pass Transistor Networks for Gating 55 MIN
U-matic / VHS
Introduction to VLSI Design Series
Color (PRO)
Discusses pull - down structures of inverters. Gates and good or bad forms are reviewed, plus the selector as a network of pass transistors. Includes use of enhancement and depletion mode transistors in networks, and switches, counting circuits and gate comparisons.
Industrial and Technical Education
Dist - MIOT **Prod** - MIOT

Passage 23 MIN
16mm
B&W (G)
$50.00 rental
Consists of images of friends and strangers. Moves freely between locations in Turkey, Poland and the US. The shooting and editing process combines formal composition and improvisation. A Robert Fenz production.
Fine Arts; Geography - United States; Geography - World
Dist - CANCIN

Passage 4 MIN
16mm
Color
LC 73-702349
Presents a mood piece which uses stills to reveal the lonely aspects of the airport and its transitory inhabitants.
Fine Arts; Social Science
Dist - SUTHLA **Prod** - ROCOM 1973

Passage a l'acte 12 MIN
16mm
B&W (G)
$40.00 rental
Deconstructs a typical American scenario of a family at the breakfast table by destroying its original continuity. Catches on the tinny sounds and bizarre body movements of the subjects, which, in reaction, become snagged on the continuity. An underlying message of war lies deep under the surface of the family idyll. Produced by Martin Arnold.
Fine Arts; Sociology
Dist - CANCIN

Passage of food through the digestive tract 6 MIN
VHS
Systems of the human body series
Color (I J)
$24.95 purchase _ #L9622
Shows how food passes through each stage of digestion. Uses X - ray images to augment a 'working' model of the human digestive system. Part of a seven - part series on the human body, using the single - concept format.
Science - Natural
Dist - HUBDSC **Prod** - HUBDSC
WARDS

The Passage of the bride 6 MIN
16mm
B&W (G)
$20.00 rental
Features a production composed entirely from a 100 - foot roll of wedding footage and what appears to be the honeymoon. Repeats recognizable images until they hypnotically melt away.
Fine Arts
Dist - CANCIN **Prod** - SOLOMO 1980

The Passage of Time 26 MIN
16mm
B&W (C A)
Illustrates superposition and the process of transfer. Explains that transfer is composed of the elements of erosion, which removes rock - - transportation, which moves rock and deposition, which produces rock. Points out that faults, intrusions and fossils are other indications of the passage of time. Discusses the principle that like fossil assemblages at two points indicate like geologic ages of the rocks sur rounding them.
Science - Physical
Dist - UTEX **Prod** - UTEX 1960

Passage through - a ritual 33 MIN
16mm
Color (G)
$1604.00 purchase, $80.00 rental
Evolves from Philip Corner's Through the Mysterious Barricade, Lumen 1 - after F Couperin - which evolved from the Stan Brakhage film, The Riddle of Lumen.
Fine Arts
Dist - CANCIN **Prod** - BRAKS 1990

Passages - A National course of healing and hope for teens, their parents, friends and caregivers series

Experiencing your feelings	60 MIN
Understanding our losses	60 MIN
Your recovery and growth	60 MIN

Dist - CTNA

Passages from Finnegans Wake 97 MIN
U-matic / VHS / 16mm
B&W
Recreates James Joyce's novel, FINNEGANS WAKE, in a film based on a play by Mary Manning. Produced and directed by Mary Ellen Bute.
Fine Arts
Dist - STARRC **Prod** - STARRC

Passages in Fathering - Sharing My Work and Myself 28 MIN
U-matic / VHS
B&W
Features five panelists discussing their childhood experiences and the relationships they had with their fathers. Presents ideas on bettering the father/child relationship.
Sociology
Dist - UWISC **Prod** - SWWGFP 1981

Passed 3 MIN
16mm
Color (G)
$6.00 rental
Features a syncopated chronicle of a trip to New York. Varies shot duration while traveling in trains, cars or on foot which creates rhythms. Edited in camera. A Caroline Savage - Lee production.
Fine Arts; Geography - World
Dist - CANCIN

Passenger locomotive road operation
VHS
Color (G)
$34.95 purchase _ #HDS001
Presents the second of a 3 - part series covering the ins and outs of running a steam locomotive. Takes a close look at three locomotives spanning the 20th century.
Social Science
Dist - SIV

Passengers - Driving Hazards, Safety 14 MIN
16mm
B&W
LC FIE52-330
Points out the driver's responsibility for the safety of child passengers. Discusses safe driving habits and safety in handling children getting on and off the bus.
Health and Safety
Dist - USNAC **Prod** - USOE 1945

Passengers in the same Boat - 102 30 MIN
U-matic
Currents - 1984 - 85 Season Series
Color (A)
Focuses on the self help groups widely available.
Psychology; Social Science
Dist - PBS **Prod** - WNETTV 1985

The Passer 11 MIN
16mm
B&W
Illustrates with slow - motion photography, the correct techniques of grip, position, and balance in passing a football. Narrated by Eddie Erdalatz of Annapolis.
Physical Education and Recreation
Dist - COCA **Prod** - BORDEN

Passin' it on 57 MIN
16mm / VHS
Color (G)
$895.00, $390.00 purchase, $125.00 rental
Examines the 1971 troubling case of Black Panther leader Dhoruba Bin Wahad - then Richard Moore - convicted of shooting two New York City police officers. Utilizes archival footage and personal accounts. After serving 19 years of a 25 year to life sentence, Dhoruba was released in 1990 on the basis of prosecutorial misconduct. Offers insights into the Civil Rights Movement while recounting the personal history of one Panther's ordeals. Produced by John Valadez and Peter Miller.
Civics and Political Systems; History - United States; Sociology
Dist - FIRS

Passing 6 MIN
U-matic / VHS / 16mm
How to Play Hockey Series no 3; No 3
B&W (J H C)
Demonstrates the techniques of passing the hockey puck between both stationary and on the move players.
Physical Education and Recreation
Dist - IFB **Prod** - CRAF 1956

Passing and receiving
VHS
N C A A instructional video series
Color (H C A)
$39.95 purchase _ #KAR1502V
Presents the second of a three - part series on offensive ice hockey. Focuses on passing and receiving skills.
Physical Education and Recreation
Dist - CAMV **Prod** - NCAAF

Passing by 2 MIN
16mm
B&W
Presents Alexander Alexeieff and Claire Parker's film set to a French - Canadian folk song, En Passant. Made for the National Film Board of Canada during Alexeieff and Parker's stay in the U S during World War II.
Fine Arts
Dist - STARRC **Prod** - STARRC 1942

Passing clouds - smoking 52 MIN
VHS
Color; PAL (G)
PdS30 purchase
Examines the history of smoking. Explores the halycon days of smoking from the 1890s to the 1960s when it was almost a universal habit, and the last 25 years when, in the light of medical reports, millions of British people kicked the habit. Contact distributor about availability outside the United Kingdom.
Guidance and Counseling; Health and Safety; Psychology
Dist - ACADEM

The Passing Hours 13 MIN
16mm
B&W
Explains the history of clocks from the days of the Egyptians and shows how their style always reflected fashion. Depicts how life is governed by clocks and the difficulties encountered in keeping up with various timepieces.
Mathematics
Dist - RADIM **Prod** - RAYMIL

Passing Lane 15 MIN
16mm
Color
LC 75-703218
Presents a satire on urbanization which has created many problems for society, not the least of which is the impersonal nature of the megalopolis.
Fine Arts; Sociology
Dist - USC **Prod** - USC 1969

Passing of Peron - the End of an Era 24 MIN
U-matic / VHS
Color (H C A)
Examines the life of Juan Peron, the best - known leader of Argentina. Studies his personal and political life, his career, his famous wives and Argentinian culture.
Biography; History - World
Dist - JOU **Prod** - JOU

Passing of remoteness 50 MIN
VHS
Dream machine series
Color; PAL (G)
PdS99 purchase; Not available in the United States
Shows the spread of computer networks and their influences on society. Traces the development of the computer, the machine that changed the world. Part five of a five - part series.
Computer Science
Dist - BBCENE

Passing on dance series

Carrying on tradition in a company dedicated to the work of its founding choreographer	30 MIN
Doris Humphrey Dance Reconstruction	30 MIN
Reconstruction of Early Ballet Repertory	30 MIN
Recreating the Earliest Modern Dance	30 MIN

Dist - ARCVID

Passing on Tradition 15 MIN
U-matic / VHS
Across Cultures Series
Color (I)
Explains that when a group passes on traditions, it provides for cultural continuity and identity. Recounts how the Indians of West Africa pass on woodcarving, weaving and ceramics, the Japanese pass on gardening, flower arranging and the tea ceremony and the Tarahumara pass on musical instrument making, costumes and dance.

Geography - World; Social Science; Sociology
Dist - AITECH **Prod** - POSIMP 1983

A Passing Phase 7 MIN
16mm
Color (J A)
LC 72-700412
Shows how the evolution of man is related to the evolution of war weaponry and human power struggles.
Guidance and Counseling; Psychology; Science - Natural; Sociology
Dist - MMA **Prod** - PHID 1970

Passing Quietly through 28 MIN
16mm
B&W
LC 77-711391
Presents a story about an old man, dying, alone and bereft, who tries to understand his dying and to establish his eternity through a relationship with his only contact, a practical nurse assigned to him by the city.
Health and Safety; Psychology; Sociology
Dist - GROVE **Prod** - NYU 1970

Passing, setting and spiking
VHS
N C A A volleyball instructional video series
Color (H C A)
$39.95 purchase _ #KAR1602V
Features Dr Marv Dunphy instructing in basic volleyball skills. Covers the skills of passing, setting, and spiking.
Physical Education and Recreation
Dist - CAMV **Prod** - NCAAF

Passing Shadows 15 MIN
16mm / VHS
Color (H)
$310.00, $135.00 purchase
Documents the creative process as experienced by poet Andrew Suknaski, who finds images for a poem about ancestry in gypsy culture.
Fine Arts; Literature and Drama
Dist - FLMWST

Passing techniques
VHS
NCAA basketball instructional video series
Color (G)
$39.95 purchase _ #KAR1205V
Features Iowa basketball coach Tom Davis in an instructional video on passing techniques in basketball.
Physical Education and Recreation
Dist - CAMV **Prod** - NCAAF

Passing the cup of faith - Part 6
VHS
Keith Miller - new wine series
Color (H C G A R)
$10.00 rental _ #36 - 87406 - 533
Proposes the theory that living one's faith can provide good opportunities for evangelism. Based on the Keith Miller book 'A Taste of New Wine.'
Religion and Philosophy
Dist - APH **Prod** - WORD

Passing the Message 47 MIN
U-matic / VHS / 16mm
Color
Views the struggle to organize trade unions for the black majority in South Africa in the face of a vast entanglement of repressive government policies.
Civics and Political Systems; History - World; Sociology
Dist - ICARUS **Prod** - BSTGAV 1983

Passing the Word 24 MIN
16mm
B&W (I J)
Portrays the development of communication lines in California. Includes pony express, stage coach operations, telegraph, railroad and mail systems.
Psychology; Social Science
Dist - MLA **Prod** - ABCTV 1963

passing through - torn formations 43 MIN
16mm
B&W; Color (G)
$90.00 rental
Deals with the life and history of filmmaker Philip Hoffman's Czech - born mother and her family. Unravels a tapestry of family relations.
Fine Arts; Sociology
Dist - CANCIN

Passion 8 MIN
16mm
Color
Tells Jozsef Nepp's amusing tale about a compulsive smoker who is ordered by his doctor to cut it out. Shows how the passion for the weed obsesses him and nearly makes him a murderer. Concludes with his death by a falling flowerpot on his head instead of smoking.
Health and Safety
Dist - FI **Prod** - PANNOF 1961

Passion and Coolness 52 MIN
U-matic / VHS
Royal Shakespeare Company Series
Color
Explains that Shakespearean drama demands a balancing of heightened language, naturalistic performance, emotion and intellect. Reveals how Hamlet's advice to the players expresses Shakespeare's direction that actors be natural and not false or grotesque. Shows how Shakespeare's language can be made to work on the audience. Uses examples from King Lear, Hamlet, Julius Caesar and King John.
Literature and Drama
Dist - FOTH **Prod** - FOTH 1984

A passion for birds 23 MIN
VHS
Northwest wild series
Color (J H C A)
$89.95 purchase _ #P11094
Investigates the migration of shorebirds up the Pacific coast from northwest wetlands to Alaska. Describes the wetlands environment and the life habits of shorebirds. Part of a series of seven programs.
Science - Natural
Dist - CF

A Passion for customers 67 MIN
VHS / U-matic
Color (G PRO A)
$895.00, $795.00 purchase, $200.00 rental
Visits five organizations with Tom Peters which provide superior customer services.
Business and Economics; Psychology
Dist - MAGVID **Prod** - MAGVID 1987
VPHI

Passion for Excellence
VHS / 16mm
(C PRO)
Explores how to grab the lion's share of the market by taking exceptional care of customers via superior service, superior quality, and constant innovation.
Education
Dist - VLEARN

Passion for Excellence 60 MIN
16mm / U-matic / VHS
Color (G)
Targets areas of competition that determine long term excellence.
Business and Economics; Education
Dist - VPHI **Prod** - VPHI 1985

The Passion of Christ 28 MIN
U-matic / VHS / 16mm
Color (J)
LC 83-706717
Presents an interpretation of the Easter story from the Gospel according to St. Matthew, chapters 26 - 27, as depicted through a series of 160 paintings by the late artist, William Kurelek.
Religion and Philosophy
Dist - BCNFL **Prod** - BCNFL 1982

The Passion of Christ According to St Matthew 28 MIN
U-matic / VHS / 16mm
Color (I)
LC 83-700567
Blends 160 of William Kurelek's paintings with the words of the biblical book of Matthew to convey Jesus Christ's final days and crucifixion.
Religion and Philosophy
Dist - BCNFL **Prod** - EARNSP 1982

The Passion of goose egg tuffy 11 MIN
16mm
B&W (G)
$25.00 rental
Explores the complex subtext of marriage and relationship dynamics. Contains two acts in a stylized home movie style.
Fine Arts; Psychology; Sociology
Dist - CANCIN **Prod** - WHITED 1989

The Passion of Jesus Christ, Son of God 30 MIN
VHS
Gospel of Mark series
Color (R G)
$39.95 purchase _ #GMAR9
Examines the structures and the key messages of the Gospel of Mark, as well as examining the life and times of Mark, according to the teachings of the Roman Catholic Church. Features Biblical scholar Father Eugene LaVerdiere, SSS. Part nine of ten parts.
Literature and Drama; Religion and Philosophy
Dist - CTNA **Prod** - CTNA

The Passion of Joan of Arc 82 MIN
16mm
B&W (H C A)
LC 73-701738
Presents the story of the trial of Joan of Arc.
Biography; Fine Arts; Religion and Philosophy
Dist - KITPAR **Prod** - UNKNWN 1929

The Passion of remembrance 80 MIN
VHS
Color (G)
$85.00 rental, $375.00 purchase
Presents a drama of a man and woman meeting in an anonymous landscape and talking of how each other's past has shaped the present in terms of race, sex and gender and the complexities of sharing destinies. Intertwines this encounter with a video document of images of England through the decades. Gives a mosaic impression of the different dimensions of Black experience lived and imagined by a generation of filmmakers in the UK. By Maureen Blackwood and Isacc Julien; produced by Sankofa Film and Video.
Fine Arts; Sociology
Dist - WMEN

The Passion of Spain 25 MIN
16mm
Eye of the Beholder Series
Color
LC 75-701910
Examines the sport of bullfighting in Spain, pointing out that the viewing audience participates in the sport.
Geography - World; Physical Education and Recreation; Sociology
Dist - VIACOM **Prod** - RCPDF 1972

Passion play videos 15 MIN
VHS
Color (J H R)
$34.95 purchase, $10.00 rental _ #35 - 87437 - 460
Presents three themes based on the Passion story of Jesus - 'There's a Man,' 'Let Your Light Shine Before Men,' and 'Jesus, My Son.' Uses a popular music video format, akin to that of MTV, with dance, mime and contemporary music. Based on performances held at the Park Theater.
Literature and Drama; Religion and Philosophy
Dist - APH **Prod** - FRACOC

Passion Vine Butterfly - Gulf Fritillary 10 MIN
U-matic / VHS / 16mm
Color; Captioned (I) (SPANISH)
LC 73-701064
Presents the life cycle of the butterfly. Covers the larva to fully developed caterpillar to chrysalis, through metamorphosis to butterfly.
Science - Natural
Dist - AIMS **Prod** - AIMS 1973

A Passionate Harmony 30 MIN
U-matic
Visions - Artists and the Creative Process Series
Color (H C A)
Three Canadian artists show how they expand on the harmonies they find in nature.
Fine Arts; History - World
Dist - TVOTAR **Prod** - TVOTAR 1983

Passione D'Amore 117 MIN
U-matic / VHS / 16mm
Captioned; Color (A) (ITALIAN (ENGLISH SUBTITLES))
Portrays an unusual love affair in 19th century Italy, during the period of the Risorgimento and at the height of the Romantic movement.
Fine Arts
Dist - CNEMAG **Prod** - CNEMAG 1981

Passionless Moments 13 MIN
16mm
Films by Jane Campion Series
Color (G)
Considers existence in one's neighborhood moment by moment with an ironic Australian subtext.
Fine Arts; Geography - World
Dist - FIRS
WMEN

Passivation 60 MIN
U-matic / VHS
Corrosion Engineering Series
Color (PRO)
Industrial and Technical Education; Science - Physical
Dist - GPCV **Prod** - GPCV

Passive loss regulations - A Guide to the new 'activity' rules 210 MIN
VHS
Color (C PRO A)
$67.20, $200.00 purchase _ #M763, #P256
Offers a practical analysis of the second set of regulations issued by the IRS under the passive loss rules. Presents a course for tax and non - tax practitioners as well as CPAs.
Civics and Political Systems
Dist - ALIABA **Prod** - ALIABA 1989

Passive Range of Motion Exercises 16 MIN
16mm
Color (H C A)
LC 75-704185
Demonstrates proper range of motion procedures to be used on a patient. Shows both upper and lower extremities in supine as well as prone positions.
Health and Safety
Dist - KRI **Prod** - KRI 1974

Passive range of motion exercises for the lower extremity
U-matic / VHS
Physical therapy series
Color (PRO C G)
$195.00 purchase _ #C890 - VI - 012
Informs patient educators and patients about passive range of motion exercises for the lower extremity. Teaches effective techniques for minimizing pain and fatigue while enhancing the ability to perform daily activities. Part of a series by the physical therapy staff, St Luke's Hospital, Fargo, North Dakota.
Health and Safety; Physical Education and Recreation; Science - Natural
Dist - HSCIC

Passive range of motion exercises for the upper extremity
U-matic / VHS
Physical therapy series
Color (PRO C G)
$195.00 purchase _ #C890 - VI - 013
Informs patient educators and patients about passive range of motion exercises for the upper extremity. Teaches effective techniques for minimizing pain and fatigue while enhancing the ability to perform daily activities. Part of a series by the physical therapy staff, St Luke's Hospital, Fargo, North Dakota.
Health and Safety; Physical Education and Recreation; Science - Natural
Dist - HSCIC

Passive Solar Heating and Insulation Series
Choosing and modifying a house site 11 MIN
Home insulation 27 MIN
How to Control Air Leaks 16 MIN
Passive Solar Space Heating 24 MIN
Dist - MOKIN

Passive Solar Space Heating 24 MIN
VHS / U-matic
Passive Solar Heating and Insulation Series
Color (H C A)
Explains the theory and advantages of passive solar space heating and shows various methods, including double - glazed, south - facing windows, moveable nighttime insulation and thermal mass.
Home Economics; Industrial and Technical Education; Social Science
Dist - MOKIN **Prod** - NCDCC

Passives - Video 1
VHS
Video - cued structural drills series
Color (G) (JAPANESE)
$79.95 purchase _ #VJ - 01
Uses short, often humorous sketches portraying contemporary life in real Japanese schools, offices, restaurants and homes to illustrate the use of passives in Japanese. Incorporates oral drills, grammar patterns and reviews and shows gestures and expressions unique to the Japanese. Part one of a seven - part series by Professor Ken'ichi Ujie, produced by Tokyo Shoseki Co.
Foreign Language
Dist - CHTSUI

The Passover 30 MIN
16mm
Color (R)
Introduces Christians to the festival meal of the first night of the Jewish Passover. Presents three generations of one family gathered together in a Dallas, Texas home.
Guidance and Counseling; Religion and Philosophy
Dist - GF **Prod** - GF

Passover 15 MIN
16mm
Color
Shows how the Festival of Passover is celebrated in Israel.
Geography - World; Religion and Philosophy; Social Science
Dist - ALDEN **Prod** - ALDEN

Passover 30 MIN
U-matic / VHS / 16mm
Color (J)
LC 83-706399
Describes the history, practice and significance of Passover, one of the oldest religious customs in existence. Narrated by Ed Asner.
Religion and Philosophy; Sociology
Dist - FI **Prod** - FI 1981

Passover 29 MIN
VHS
Eenie's kitchen series
Color (G)
$19.95 purchase _ #361
Shows how to prepare haroset, matzah kugel, Latvian beet relish and jam nut filled cookies for Passover. Features Chef Eenie Frost. Part of a two - part series.
History - United States; Home Economics; Religion and Philosophy; Sociology
Dist - ERGOM **Prod** - ERGOM

Passover adventure 28 MIN
VHS
Jewish holiday video series
Color (G)
$24.95 purchase _ #821
Features an Israeli guide who explains the history and traditins of Passover. Teaches about the Children of Israel's exodus from Egypt and observes traditional matzah baking. Celebrates the seder with a kibbutz of American immigrants.
Geography - World; Religion and Philosophy; Sociology
Dist - ERGOM **Prod** - ERGOM

The Passover of Rembrandt Van Rijn 30 MIN
16mm
B&W
Relates the story of Rembrandt's search for a model of Moses in the streets of Amsterdam. Tells how the face of a poor bread - seller inspires him and he becomes imbued with the spirit of Judaism while taking part in a Passover Seder.
Religion and Philosophy
Dist - NAAJS **Prod** - JTS 1953

Passover - Traditions of freedom 57 MIN
VHS
Color (G)
$29.95 purchase
Documents the festival of Passover, which commemorates the Jews' journey of freedom from the bonds of Egyptian slavery and is celebrated around the world by Jews. Explores the many facets of this holiday from the preparatory cleaning to visits to a matzah factory, a Passover winery, and four seders, or ritual Passover meals, with Ashkenazic and Sephardic families. Looks at the cultural diversity within the unity of Jewish tradition.
Fine Arts; Religion and Philosophy; Sociology
Dist - NCJEWF

Passover with Jan Pierce 30 MIN
16mm
Eternal Light Series
B&W (H C A)
LC 76-700973
Jan Pierce, Metropolitan Opera Star, sings traditional and modern melodies associated with the Passover holiday and the seder service. He explains some of the Passover customs and comments on the answers to the traditional four questions. (Kinescope).
Fine Arts; Religion and Philosophy; Science
Dist - NAAJS **Prod** - JTS 1968

Passport to freedom 24 MIN
VHS
Color (G)
$19.95 purchase
Journeys beyond borders with world citizen Garry Davis through the New Europe and back through his life. Interviews refugees who explain why they want to reclaim their sovereignty by becoming world citizens. Davis details how to use the World Passport and other documents. Includes commentary by Philip Agee and footage of the Berlin Wall being torn down. Directed by Robin Lloyd, written by Greg Guma.
Civics and Political Systems; History - World
Dist - GREVAL

Passport to treasure 126 MIN
VHS
Color; PAL (I J)
PdS30 purchase
Presents six 21 - minute programs introducing youngsters to the work of the National Trust. Explains the purpose of preserving the past for the future. Visits six properties, including a Tudor manor house in the Cotswolds, a bird sanctuary in the Farne Islands and the first house in England to install electric lights. Uses dramatized ghost stories to evoke the atmosphere of the properties and the spirit of their first inhabitants. Contact distributor about availability outside the United Kingdom.
History - World
Dist - ACADEM

The Past 15 MIN
U-matic / VHS
Arts Express Series
Color (K P I J)
Fine Arts
Dist - KYTV **Prod** - KYTV 1983

Past and Future 10 MIN
16mm
Drugs and Medicine Series
Color
LC 76-702553
Uses live action and graphics in showing how the Earth's natural resources and synthetic laboratory chemicals are researched and developed to produce a variety of drugs and medicines.
Health and Safety; Social Science
Dist - MORLAT **Prod** - MORLAT 1975

The Past in Our Words 30 MIN
VHS / U-matic
Language and Meaning Series
Color (C)
English Language; Psychology
Dist - GPN **Prod** - WUSFTV 1983

The Past is Prologue 30 MIN
U-matic / VHS
Career Alternatives Series
Color
Discusses the factors that may influence high school graduates in their career choices.
Guidance and Counseling; Psychology
Dist - NETCHE **Prod** - NETCHE 1974

Past life regression and spirit depossession 30 MIN
BETA / VHS
Spiritual psychology quartet series
Color (G)
$29.95 purchase _ #S410
Features Dr Edith Fiore, author of 'You Have Been Here Before' and 'The Unquiet Dead,' who discusses her transformation from a conventional behavior therapist to a specialist in the application of spiritualist principles of reincarnation and spirit possession to psychotherapy. Discusses 'past - life regression' as a therapeutic technique. Part of a series on spiritual psychology.
Psychology; Religion and Philosophy; Sociology
Dist - THINKA **Prod** - THINKA

Past plus present equals future - or does it 60 MIN
VHS
Color (A)
$199.00 purchase _ #S01057
Features Morris Massey and his perspectives on American society. Focuses on both the past and the future, particularly the massive changes Massey predicts for the 1993 - 1995 period.
Business and Economics; History - United States; Psychology
Dist - UILL

Past, present, and promise - understanding research - Parts 1 and 2 60 MIN
U-matic / VHS
Discovering psychology series
Color (C)
$45.00, $29.95 purchase
Presents parts 1 and 2 of the 26 - part Discovering Psychology series. Provides an introduction to the science of psychology and its origins. Studies the scientific method within the context of psychological research, and highlights the value of critical thinking in interpreting research findings. Two thirty - minute programs hosted by Professor Philip Zimbardo of Stanford University.
Psychology
Dist - ANNCPB **Prod** - WGBHTV 1989

Past, Present, Future - Marie Sandoz 30 MIN
U-matic / VHS
(G)
Interviews Nebraska author Marie Sandoz. Traces the writing of her stories from the initial impulse through research and writing technique.
Literature and Drama; Social Science
Dist - GPN **Prod** - NETV

Past - Present Tense 15 MIN
VHS
Planet Pylon Series
Color (I)
LC 90712897
Uses character Commander Wordstalker from the Space Station Readstar to develop language arts skills. Studies the past and present tense. Includes a worksheet to be done by the student with help from series characters.
Education; English Language
Dist - GPN

Past Tense of Irregular Verbs - 22 30 MIN
VHS
English 101 - Ingles 101 Series
Color (H)
$125.00 purchase
Presents a series of thirty 30 - minute programs in basic English for native speakers of Spanish. Focuses on a specific topic in order to emphasize a particular grammatical point or set of idioms. English is used from the beginning as the primary language of instruction but

Patent pending 60 MIN
VHS
Color (G)
$30.95 purchase _ #S00853
Tells the history of the US Patent Office. Reveals that during the first century of the Office's existence, inventors had to submit a working model of the product they wanted patented. Shows many examples of these models, mostly spread between the Smithsonian Institute and private collectors.
Civics and Political Systems; Fine Arts; History - United States
Dist - UILL

Patently offensive - porn under siege 58 MIN
VHS
Color (H C G)
$350.00 purchase, $125.00 rental
Discloses that video cassette recorders, computers and other new technologies have catapulted pornography into a $10 billion industry, that porn profits soar despite sustained attacks by feminists and traditional groups concerned with a moral environment. Examines pornography in its social and historical context. Debates the conflict between freedom of expression and preservation of values defining a society. Produced by Harriet Koskoff.
Civics and Political Systems; Guidance and Counseling; Sociology
Dist - FLMLIB

The Patents video 40 MIN
VHS
Color (G)
$279.00 purchase
Covers the basics of patents to help viewers make business decisions. Shows how to maintain United States' and foreign filing rights. Discusses the circumstances under which an idea can be patented. Describes different ways to protect intellectual property. Includes The Patents Primer booklet.
History - World
Dist - IPVIDE **Prod** - IPVIDE 1994

The Path 21 MIN
16mm
Color
Describes the Buddhist religion, with shots of Rangoon.
Religion and Philosophy
Dist - STATNS **Prod** - STATNS 1969

The Path 34 MIN
16mm / VHS
Color (G)
$345.00, $35.00 purchase
Examines the tea ceremony, a traditional art form of Japan. Records the chronology of an usucha - thin tea - service. Includes the book, Japanese Tea.
History - World; Religion and Philosophy
Dist - SUMAI **Prod** - SUMAI 1974

The Path 20 MIN
16mm
B&W (G)
$20.00 rental
Journeys mysteriously by a recreation of a dream. Directs the viewer visually toward forms and substances rather than to the protagonists.
Fine Arts; Psychology
Dist - CANCIN **Prod** - MYERSR 1960

Path of cessation 15 MIN
16mm
B&W; Color (G)
$10.00 rental
Integrates Tibetan culture with a collage of dynamic rhythms. Communicates a mystifying image and, instead of analyzing Tibetan life, succumbs to it.
Fine Arts
Dist - CANCIN **Prod** - FULTON 1974

A Path of His Own 53 MIN
16mm
(G)
Follows the path of painter Milne. Broadens the context for a better understanding and enjoyment of the artist's paintings.
Biography; Fine Arts
Dist - CFLMDC **Prod** - NFBC

The Path of least resistance 15.23 MIN
VHS / U-matic
Industrial safety series
(H A)
$125.00 purchase
Emphasises the prevention of electrical accidents caused by common mistakes on the job.
Health and Safety; Industrial and Technical Education
Dist - AITECH **Prod** - ERESI 1986
BNA

The Path of Life 26 MIN
U-matic / VHS / 16mm
Color
Dramatizes the third part of an Ojibway Indian legend telling of a man's journey to the spirit world to find his dead wife. Begins in The Path Of Souls and The World Between.
Literature and Drama; Social Science
Dist - FOTH **Prod** - FOTH

The Path of nonviolence 90 MIN
VHS / BETA
Color; PAL (G)
PdS31, $62.00 purchase
Travels with His Holiness the Dalai Lama to Stockholm, Sweden in October 1988 where he speaks of the value of nonviolence as a path to world harmony and of how developing altruism makes for a happier person. Features a production by Amaryllis Data, Sweden.
Fine Arts; Religion and Philosophy
Dist - MERIDT **Prod** - MERIDT 1988

The Path of Our Elders 20 MIN
U-matic
Color (I J H)
Shows in the Pomo culture much of the past survives through the songs, the dances, the games, the ageless art of basketry, and above all the language, by which so much has been passed on. Several elders portray a way of life that has been handed down throughout the generations.
Social Science
Dist - SHENFP **Prod** - SHENFP 1986

The Path of Souls 26 MIN
U-matic / VHS / 16mm
Color
Dramatizes the first part of an Ojibway Indian legend telling how a young man entered on the Path of Souls to find his dead wife. Continues in The World Between and The Path Of Life.
Literature and Drama; Social Science
Dist - FOTH **Prod** - FOTH

Path of the mindful heart
VHS
(G)
$16.00, $39.00 purchase _ #AG003, #AG004
Presents Jack Kornfield, monk, psychologist and teacher of vipassana meditation, and psychotherapist Robert Hall. Explores meditation and psychotherapy as useful tools for entering and working with the places within oneself that need to be touched with forgivenness and acceptance.
Health and Safety; Psychology; Religion and Philosophy
Dist - BIGSUR

Path of the Paddle Series
Solo Basic 28 MIN
Dist - NFBC

Path to Fulfillment 38 MIN
16mm
Color
Presents an overview of the facilities and techniques of the care of the mentally retarded in Europe. Features Scandinavian and English facilities in particular.
Geography - World; Psychology; Sociology
Dist - USOE **Prod** - GWASHU

The Path to Prosperity 10 MIN
16mm / U-matic / VHS
Foundations of Wealth Series
Color
Compares primitive subsistence economies and complicated modern industrial economies. Summarizes the stages of the change from subsistence to surplus.
Business and Economics; Social Science
Dist - FOTH **Prod** - FOTH

The Path to recovery 20 MIN
VHS / U-matic / BETA
Co - dependency series
Color (G)
$280.00 purchase _ #801.3
Discusses common concerns of co - dependents entering treatment - effects of treatment on significant others, spiritual issues and the misuse of will - power and analytic thinking in overcoming co - dependency. Examines common treatment modalities, the importance of groups, letter writing to parents, a personal 'bill of rights' to establish boundaries and personal affirmations. Part of a five - part series on co - dependency.
Guidance and Counseling; Health and Safety; Psychology; Sociology
Dist - CONMED

The Path to Rome 54 MIN
16mm
Color
LC 73-700489
Retraces the path taken in 1902 by Hilaire Belloc on a pilgrimage from Toul to Rome. Compares the path as it is today to the path of the 1902 journey.
Geography - World; History - World
Dist - MEYERF **Prod** - MEYERF 1972

Path to Safety 20 MIN
16mm
Color
LC FIE67-104
Points out that more accidents are caused by human eRror than by any other factor. Stars Cliff Robertson as a flight instructor briefing a class of student pilots on dramatic incidents occurring as a result of misjudgment.
Industrial and Technical Education; Psychology
Dist - USFAA **Prod** - FAAFL 1967

Path to Success in Changing Times 15 MIN
U-matic / VHS
Color (IND)
Provides a comprehensive list of pork cuts that can help in matching the pork product mix with the customer mix. Covers importance of packaging, piece and demand.
Business and Economics
Dist - NLSAMB **Prod** - NLSAMB

A Path to Wings - the Air Force ROTC Flight Instruction Program 15 MIN
16mm
Color
LC 74-705328
Encourages Air Force ROTC cadets to pursue a career as Air Force pilots through the flight instruction program. Shows how the program determines the cadet's potential for formal Air Force training. Cites the benefits of learning to fly and of possessing a pilot's license regardless of future plans.
Civics and Political Systems; Education; Industrial and Technical Education
Dist - USNAC **Prod** - USAF 1968

The Pathans 45 MIN
VHS
Disappearing world series
Color (G C)
$99.00 purchase, $19.00 rental _ #51250
Focuses on the Pathans, bound by a common language, a common heritage and the unifying force of Islam. Reveals that they do not acknowledge the geographical boundary between Afghanistan and Pakistan which divides their people. Their code of honor is based on personal honor and revenge, and they accept no imposed leadership - as the Soviet invaders of Afghanistan discovered. Features anthropologist Akbar Ahmed. Part of a series working closely with anthropologists who lived for a year or more in societies whose social structures, beliefs and practices are threatened by the expansion of technocratic civilization.
Religion and Philosophy; Sociology
Dist - PSU **Prod** - GRANDA 1980

Patheways to Reading Series
Was it Worth Reading 14 MIN
Dist - AVED

Pathfinder 88 MIN
VHS / 35mm
Color (G) (NORWEGIAN WITH ENGLISH SUBTITLES)
$300.00 rental
Travels back a thousand years to portray a boy in Lapland who struggles to avenge the deaths of his family killed by a band of marauders. Directed by Nils Gaup.
Fine Arts; Literature and Drama
Dist - KINOIC **Prod** - IFEX 1990

Pathfinders from the Stars 48 MIN
16mm
Color
LC FIA68-543
Traces the history of man's ability to determine his position on the surface of the earth using the stars. Illustrates the possibilities of precise positional control across vast distances, in remote areas and at the surface or bottom of the sea.
Science - Physical; Social Science
Dist - USNAC **Prod** - USNOAA 1967

Pathfinders to Progress 25 MIN
16mm
Color
LC 74-706172
Tells the story of the 1370th Photo - Mapping Wing and its worldwide photographic and charting responsibilities. Shows the Wing's contributions to the global geodetic puzzle and the tools and techniques used to carry out this mission.
Civics and Political Systems; Geography - World; History - United States; Industrial and Technical Education
Dist - USNAC **Prod** - USAF 1963

Pathnames
U-matic / VHS
UNIX Fundamentals Series
Color
Describes how the UNIX file system is organized as a hierarchical inverted tree and identifies the levels of a

UNIX file system. Describes the common administrative directories and full pathname and how to reference a file by a full pathname.
Industrial and Technical Education; Mathematics; Sociology
Dist - COMTEG **Prod** - COMTEG

Pathogenesis of Anemia 31 MIN
16mm
Clinical Pathology Series
B&W (PRO)
LC 74-705330
Discusses the major types of anemias, their differentiation, tests to establish specific types, and basis for therapy.
Health and Safety; Science; Science - Natural
Dist - USNAC **Prod** - NMAC 1969

Pathogenesis of Burn Trauma, Part 1 22 MIN
U-matic / 35mm strip
Burn Trauma Series
Color (PRO)
Presents specific responses of three key organ systems of burn trauma, discusses normal functions of skin and its vulnerability. Describes each class of burn trauma as they relate to destruction of skin layers and functions. Highlights major cardiovascular and hemodynamic responses to burn trauma.
Health and Safety; Psychology
Dist - BRA **Prod** - BRA

Pathogenesis of Burn Trauma, Part 2 23 MIN
U-matic / 35mm strip
Burn Trauma Series
Color (PRO)
Covers more specific responses of major organ systems to burn trauma. Emphasizes multi - system assault of burn trauma. Describes pulmonary system with causes of inhalation injury/pulmonary edema in burn trauma highlighted. Features renal, cerebral, gastro - intestinal and metabolic responses.
Health and Safety; Psychology
Dist - BRA **Prod** - BRA

The Pathogenesis of Spinal Cord Damage in Decompression Sickness 33 MIN
16mm
Color
LC 79-701853
Documents research conducted at the Naval Medical Research Institute in Bethesda, Maryland, showing that the fundamental pathogenetic underlying spinal cord damage in decompression sickness is not arterial embolization of bubbles, but rather venous obstruction at the level of the epidural vertebral venous system.
Health and Safety
Dist - USNAC **Prod** - USN 1977

Pathologic Conference Case Presentation 60 MIN
U-matic
Color
Presents the case study of a 59 - year - old woman with epigastric pain.
Health and Safety
Dist - UTEXSC **Prod** - UTEXSC

The Pathology of congenital heart disease 75 MIN
VHS / U-matic
Color (C PRO)
$395.00 purchase, $80.00 rental _ #C921 - VI - 021A,B
Introduces the anatomical changes and pathophysiological conditions associated with congenital heart diseases. Begins with an examination of the normal heart following the course of blood through the chambers, valves and conduits. Uses prepared slides and gross specimens to examine the anatomical changes that accompany acyanotic heart disease, atrial septal defects, patent ductus arteriosus, coartations of the aorta, aortic valve stenosis, cyanotic heart disease, tetralogy of Fallot, hypoplastic left ventricle complexes and truncus arteriosus. Discusses the pathology of each disease along with possible pharmacological and surgical interventions. Presented by Dr Robert P Bolande.
Health and Safety
Dist - HSCIC

Pathology of Intramuscular Nerve Endings and the Neuromuscular Junction 48 MIN
U-matic
Intensive Course in Neuromuscular Diseases Series
Color (PRO)
LC 76-706070
Presents Dr Christian Coers lecturing on the pathology of intramuscular nerve endings and the neuromuscular junction.
Health and Safety; Science - Natural
Dist - USNAC **Prod** - NINDIS 1974

Pathology of Screening and Detection of Breast Cancer
U-matic
Color
Discusses breast cancer, including incidence, prognostic factors, screening methods, and pathological and psychological factors. Includes multimedia kit.
Health and Safety
Dist - USNAC **Prod** - OHIOSU

Pathophysiological Approach to Calcium Stones 21 MIN
U-matic / VHS
Color (PRO)
LC 81-707082
Provides a review of the etiological bases for hypercalcemia, hypercalciuria, hyperoxaluria, hyperuricosuria and decreased inhibitors which are considered to be metabolic risk factors for calcium nephrolithiasis. Cites examples showing how the identification of these disorders would allow specific and more rational therapy.
Health and Safety
Dist - UMICH **Prod** - UMICH 1981

Pathophysiology 20 MIN
U-matic
Acute myocardial infarction series; Unit 1
Color (PRO)
LC 77-706059
Describes and explains underlying pathophysiological changes occuring in patients with acute myocardial infarction in terms of changes in ventricular force generation and compliance.
Health and Safety; Science - Natural
Dist - USNAC **Prod** - NMAC 1977

Pathophysiology and Surgical Management of Achalasia of the Esophagus 27 MIN
16mm
Color (PRO)
Presents a classification of achalasia of the esophagus, followed by a description of the physiological derangement demonstrated by motility and cineroentgenographic studies. Discusses the indications for surgical treatment and preoperative preparation.
Health and Safety; Science
Dist - ACY **Prod** - ACYDGD 1961

Pathophysiology of alcohol abuse, alcohol - a critical illness series 24 MIN
U-matic / VHS
Alcohol - a critical illness series
Color
Health and Safety; Psychology; Sociology
Dist - BRA **Prod** - BRA

Pathophysiology of Diarrhea 18 MIN
16mm
Color
LC 73-701619
Describes the three pathophysiology diarrheal conditions - celiac sprue, cholera and lactase deficiency.
Health and Safety; Science - Natural
Dist - EATONL **Prod** - EATONL 1973

Pathophysiology of Opthalmology
U-matic / VHS
Color (PRO)
Reviews anatomy and normal physiology, trauma, inflammation, degenerations of the eye and systemic diseases of the eye.
Health and Safety; Science - Natural
Dist - UMICHM **Prod** - UMICHM 1977

Pathophysiology of Otorhinolaryngology
U-matic / VHS
Color (PRO)
Reviews ear anatomy, hearing loss and hearing tests, diseases of the external, middle and inner ear, anatomy of the nose and throat, conditions of the nose and conditions of the mouth and throat.
Health and Safety; Science - Natural
Dist - UMICHM **Prod** - UMICHM 1977

Paths in the Wilderness 28 MIN
16mm
Color
LC 76-702662
Portrays the humanistic and explorative achievements of Padre Eusebio Kino, a Jesuit who helped settle the Southwest. Features the Sonora Desert of Northern Mexico and Southern Arizona.
Biography; History - World; Religion and Philosophy
Dist - UARIZ **Prod** - UARIZ 1976

Paths of Development Series

Behind the Image	30 MIN
Bread and Blue Jeans	30 MIN
Days of Future Past	30 MIN
Justice for all	30 MIN
The Monster Machine	30 MIN
Striking a Balance	30 MIN

Dist - ACCESS

Paths of memory 30 MIN
VHS
Color; PAL (H C G)
Follows Schmuel Gogol, internationally - acclaimed virtuoso and founder of the world's only harmonica orchestra, a Holocaust survivor who returns to his native Poland nearly 50 years later. Searches the scenes of his childhood, from the orphanage of Dr Janush Korczak to the Jewish ghetto of Warsaw and the Polish countryside, to the Nazi Auschwitz - Birkeneu Death Camp. Produced by Moshe Golan Productions Ltd.
History - World; Sociology
Dist - VIEWTH

Paths of Steel 26 MIN
16mm
Color (J)
A description of the engineering and technical aspects of men and machines illustrating the use of various scientific instruments.
Industrial and Technical Education; Science - Physical
Dist - USSC **Prod** - USSC

Paths of survival 70 MIN
VHS
Animals of Africa series
Color (I J H)
$25.00 purchase _ #A5VH 1128
Observes highly socialized African relatives of the mongoose in 'Suricats.' Focuses on lions and the members of a pride in 'Lions as Family Patriarch.' Presents the desert and its many facets, ranging from sandstorms to oases in 'Anvil of the Sun.' Part of a nine - part series on African animals hosted by Joan Embery of the San Diego Zoo.
Geography - World; Science - Natural
Dist - CLRVUE

A Pathway from within 18 MIN
U-matic / VHS / 16mm
Color (H C A)
LC 76-702040
Discusses the works and philosophy of Elizabeth Fraser Williamson, a prominent Canadian sculptor.
Biography; Fine Arts
Dist - JOU **Prod** - HAMILB 1975

Pathway to a Winning Season 8 MIN
VHS / U-matic
Sports Medicine for Coaches Series
Color
Addresses the many problems encountered in the weight control program of the high school wrestler, such as the common dehydration problem and starvation practices. Provides information on how to determine the best competitive weight for each athlete and then how to maintain that weight through a sensible diet and exercise program.
Physical Education and Recreation; Psychology; Social Science
Dist - UWASH **Prod** - UWASH

Pathway to the Stars 20 MIN
16mm
Color
Presents a typical flight of the X - 15 research airplane from pre - flight arrangements to touch - down.
Industrial and Technical Education; Science
Dist - THIOKL **Prod** - THIOKL 1961

Pathways 60 MIN
VHS
Color (P I)
$89.00 purchase _ #ACE15A
Brings career information to grades 3 through 6. Informs students about several jobs as they watch people at work, describing their job duties, why they chose that occupation, explaining the equipment used and mentioning education required. Includes curriculum guide.
Business and Economics; Guidance and Counseling
Dist - CFKRCM **Prod** - CFKRCM

Pathways - exercise video for people with limited mobility 48 MIN
VHS
Color (G)
$29.95 purchase _ #MOB010V-P
Presents an exercise video for seniors, people who are overweight, people who have multiple sclerosis or arthritis, and others with limited mobility. Demonstrates moves that can be done individually or in a group setting and includes assisted versions of each position for those who need help. Combines stretches, strengthening, range of motions exercises, and a relaxation segment.
Physical Education and Recreation
Dist - CAMV

Pathways for parenting - a program for deaf parents with hearing children series
From teenager to adult - Part 3
Our baby is hearing - Part 1
Our child goes to school - Part 2
Dist - CPH

Pathways of Modern Painting Series
The Prophets - Pont - Aven, the Nabis, and Toulouse - Lautrec 18 MIN
Dist - IFB

Pathways through Nursery School 25 MIN
16mm / U-matic / VHS
Color (C A)
Depicts a typical day in a laboratory nursery school for two - , three - and four - year - olds. Shows that the qualities of a good nursery school are a wholesome environment, good equipment and mutual effort of qualified teachers and interested parents.
Education; Psychology; Sociology
Dist - IFB Prod - STECOL 1962

Pathways to modern math series
Relating sets to numbers 11 MIN
Thinking in Sets 11 MIN
Dist - GE

Pathways to Parenthood 35 MIN
VHS
Color (G)
$24.95 purchase _ #6318
Reveals that fifteen percent of all American couples have trouble conceiving a child. Discusses options such as drug therapies, surgery, in vitro fertilization and donor programs and when to see a specialist.
Health and Safety; Sociology
Dist - SYBVIS Prod - SYBVIS

Pathways to Reading Series
How to Read 13 MIN
What did you read - from the pathways to reading series 15 MIN
What's in a Book 9 MIN
Why Read 15 MIN
Dist - AVED

Pathways to Success 30 MIN
U-matic / VHS
Developing Discipline Series
Color (T)
Discusses the importance of people taking control of their lives and building personal strengths.
Education; Guidance and Counseling; Psychology; Sociology
Dist - GPN Prod - SDPT 1983

Pathways toward Personal Progress 60 MIN
Cassette / VHS
Effective Manager Series
Color (G)
$95.00 purchase _ #6427
Features Brian Tracy who shows how to get into the 'fast track' and save years in moving ahead. Includes a 60 - minute video, two audiocassettes and two workbooks. Part of a fourteen - part series.
Business and Economics; Civics and Political Systems; Guidance and Counseling; Psychology
Dist - SYBVIS
CAMV

Patience 27 MIN
VHS
Sunshine factory series
Color (P I R)
$14.99 purchase _ #35 - 83589 - 533
Features P J the repairman and kids in his neighborhood as they travel to the Sunshine Factory, a land populated by puppets, a computer and caring adults. Teaches a Biblically - based lesson on patience.
Religion and Philosophy
Dist - APH Prod - WORD

The Patient 30 MIN
VHS
Beverly Cleary's Ramona series
Color; CC (K P I)
$16.95 purchase _ #132785
Presents a Ramona story by Beverly Cleary.
Literature and Drama
Dist - KNOWUN

Patient admission to and discharge from a hospital 34 MIN
16mm
Directions for education in nursing via technology series; Lesson 27
B&W (PRO)
LC 74-701799
Dramatizes a patient's reaction to admission and discharge from a hospital. Demonstrates the nurse's responsibility to patients and emergency admission procedures.
Health and Safety
Dist - WSUM Prod - DENT 1974

Patient Advocacy in Nursing Practice 83 FRS
Slide / U-matic
Bioethics in Nursing Practice Series Module 2; Module 2
Color (PRO)
LC 81-720076; 81-707063
Health and Safety; Religion and Philosophy
Dist - BRA Prod - BRA 1981

Patient and caregiver education in the home - teaching techniques for home health nurses 25 MIN
VHS
Color (C PRO)
$195.00 purchase, $70.00 rental _ #4347S, #4347V
Reveals that home health nursing, more than any other field, requires accountability for patient teaching. Shows a variety of teaching techniques. Discusses cognitive, affective and psychomotor learning. Includes demonstration - return demonstration, family interaction, use of printed instruction sheets and contracting. Stresses the importance of communication between health team members about the patient's learning progress, requirements for teaching plans and reimbursement.
Health and Safety
Dist - AJN Prod - BELHAN 1993

Patient as a Person Series
Physiological and Emotional Aspects of Pain 17 MIN
Dist - TRNAID

Patient as Teacher 25 MIN
VHS / 16mm
Color (PRO)
LC 89716220
Helps health professionals in hospitals deal more effectively with patients.
Health and Safety
Dist - AIMS Prod - HP 1988

Patient autonomy 21 MIN
VHS / U-matic / BETA
Ethics, values and health care series
Color (C PRO)
$150.00 purchase _ #132.5
Presents a video transfer from slide program which discusses ways in which health care personnel erode patient autonomy. Addresses issues of paternalism, coercion versus informed consent and truth - telling. Part of a series on ethics, values and health care.
Guidance and Counseling; Health and Safety; Religion and Philosophy
Dist - CONMED Prod - CONMED

Patient Care Appraisal 30 MIN
U-matic
Color (PRO)
LC 76-706071
Discusses methods of appraising patient care in hospitals, clinics or offices.
Health and Safety
Dist - USNAC Prod - WARMP 1972

Patient Care Appraisal - Establishing Criteria, Setting Standards 26 MIN
U-matic
Color (PRO)
LC 76-706072
Discusses how to establish criteria and standards for patient care.
Health and Safety
Dist - USNAC Prod - WARMP 1972

Patient care strategies - reflex or research 45 MIN
U-matic / VHS
Color (PRO)
$300.00 purchase, $60.00 rental _ #4271S, #4271V
Presents three parts on nursing research in clinical setting. Deals with identifying the problem in Part 1. Part 2 frames the research question and its theoretical structure. Part 3 covers methodologies and utilization of results. Includes study guide.
Health and Safety
Dist - AJN Prod - UTEXSC 1986

Patient - Centered Approach to Improving Compliance 10 MIN
VHS
Color (PRO)
$395.00 purchase _ #N900VI057
Recognizes behaviors that alienate patients from their care takers, and teaches behaviors that enhance the relationship between patient and doctor. Considers that good communication between patient and doctor is more likely to promote patient compliance.
Health and Safety; Science
Dist - HSCIC

Patient Classification Systems - Components and Benefits 28 MIN
VHS / 16mm
Color (C PRO)
$275.00 purchase, $60.00 rental _ #7617S, #7617V
Presents an actual case study to illustrate benefits of patient classification and how such a system helps hospitals use nursing staff more effectively. Study guide includes examples of classification recording systems from several institutions. Approved for CE credit.
Health and Safety
Dist - AJN Prod - HOSSN 1990

Patient consent for colonoscopy and polypectomy
Videodisc
Color (C PRO)
$1600.00 purchase _ #N921 - IV - 039
Presents a Level III interactive videodisc which describes in detail diagnostic colonoscopy and polypectomy procedures with both graphic and live action sequences. Lists and describes both the benefits and risks and asks patient if the presentation of the procedure was understood and if further discussion is required with the physician. After the patient has gone through each module, a form may be printed out listing benefits and risks of the procedure and the level of understanding the patient has of these elements. Presented by Drs Lee Bairnsfather, Dennis Pernott and William Sodeman, Louisiana State University Medical Center at Shrevesport. Check with distributor on hardware and software requirements.
Health and Safety
Dist - HSCIC

Patient consent for endoscopy
Videodisc
Color (C PRO)
$1600.00 purchase _ #N921 - IV - 040
Presents a Level III interactive videodisc for use by patients undgergoing endoscopy. Serves four basic functions - fully informs patients about procecure so they can grant informed consent, ensures that all candidates for the procedure receive a consistent presentation of the facts, provides the doctor with a means of quickly pinpointing those areas the patient does not fully comprehend or has questions about, and provides a printout of patient responses for the patient file and a consent form for the patient's signature. Presented by Drs Lee Bairnsfather, Dennis Pernott and William Sodeman, Louisiana State University Medical Center at Shrevesport. Check with distributor on hardware and software requirements.
Health and Safety
Dist - HSCIC

Patient Considerations and Packaging Techniques 40 MIN
VHS
Extrication Video from Carbusters Series
Color (G PRO)
$149.95 purchase _ #35344
Prepares rescuer for handling the patient involved in a vehicle accident. Includes the physical and psychological considerations, rapid treatment, assessment, spinal immobiliation, mechanisms of injury, hospital communications, long board techniques, case studies and critiques of actual rescues.
Health and Safety; Psychology; Social Science
Dist - OKSU

Patient - controlled analgesia 11 MIN
VHS / U-matic
Special issues in pain control series
Color (PRO C)
$395.00 purchase, $80.00 rental _ #C901 - VI - 041
Introduces the benefits of patient - controlled analgesia. Outlines health risks associated with ineffectively - treated pain. Compares PRN - as needed - pain control and patient - controlled analgesia. Cites benefits and risks, labor considerations, serum drug concentration and patient comfort. Presented by Bethany Geldmaker, RN, Mark Lehman, PharmD, Brenda Jackson, PT, and Janet Kues, PT, Medical College of Virginia, Virginia Commonwealth University.
Health and Safety
Dist - HSCIC

Patient - controlled analgesia - a nursing perspective 15 MIN
VHS / U-matic / BETA
High tech skills in nursing series
Color (C PRO)
$280.00 purchase _ #608.2
Illustrates the difference between PCA and traditional IM medication for pain management. Describes advantages of PCA for the patient and the nurse. Discusses principles of PCA including concepts such as loading dose, intermittent dose and lockout time. Discusses nursing assessment and patient teaching. Produced by New England Baptist Hospital. Part of a five - part series.
Health and Safety; Science - Natural
Dist - CONMED

Patient - controlled analgesia - a patient's perspective 8 MIN
BETA / VHS / U-matic
High tech skills in nursing series
Color (C PRO)
$75.00 purchase _ #608.4
Explains briefly to patients the procedure for PCA. Demonstrates patient role in delivery of pain medication through a computerized pump attached to the IV line.

Stresses safety mechanisms built into the systems. Produced by New England Baptist Hospital. Part of a five - part series.
Health and Safety; Science - Natural
Dist - CONMED

Patient controlled analgesia - a patient's perspective 8 MIN
VHS
Color (PRO A)
$200.00 purchase _ #GS - 08
Demonstrates the patient's role in delivery of his or her own pain medication. Stresses the safety mechanisms that are built into the system to keep patients from administering too much. Produced by the New England Baptist Hospital, Boston, MA.
Health and Safety
Dist - MIFE

Patient counseling films series
Diabetes in adults
Ear surgery
Dist - WFP

Patient counseling library series
Controlling heartburn 10 MIN
Controlling high blood pressure 10 MIN
Dist - SUTHLA

Patient education and support - Part III 30 MIN
VHS
Caring for the transplant patient series
Color (PRO C)
$225.00 purchase, $70.00 rental _ #6532
Shows how nursing professionals can provide necessary information for the transplant patient to avoid complications. Stresses the importance of thorough patient information and understanding. Covers the topics of vital signs and daily weight measurements as indicators of complications, medications, diet, daily activities - including work, sex and sports - finances and changes in lifestyle that may be necessary. Focuses on the hospital support group which includes nurses, patients who are waiting for organs and postoperative patients and their families. Part three of three parts on transplant patient care.
Health and Safety
Dist - AJN **Prod** - HESCTV

Patient education and technology - health on - line 28 MIN
VHS
Color (G)
$149.00 purchase, $75.00 rental _ #UW5113
Shows what happens when patients are given responsibility for making decisions about their health care. Looks at the ways in which this is happening, from interactive computer dialogs to CD - ROM family health compendia to consultations with physicians via television. Reveals that different areas of the country have different rates of surgery based on patterns of practice rather than on the patient's condition. Discusses the value of high technology in remote areas and how patients are willing to give computers more information than they give their doctor. Explains the workings of a computer on - line service for patients.
Health and Safety
Dist - FOTH

Patient Education Programs - Clinical Diet Series
Your Cancer Diet 13 MIN
Your Coronary Care Diet 11 MIN
Your Renal Diet 9 MIN
Your ulcer diet 63 FRS
Your Weight Reduction Diet 74 FRS
Dist - POAPLE

Patient Feeding and Mouth Care 12 MIN
16mm
Patients are People Series
B&W (H A)
LC 75-707789
A training film for nurses' aids describing care of the mouth and dentures. Explains the importance of nutrition and demonstrates how to assist the patient in eating.
Science
Dist - MLA **Prod** - CALVIN 1967

Patient in Isolation Series
Sensory Deprivation 15 MIN
Dist - TRNAID

The Patient in Prerenal Failure 19 MIN
VHS / 16mm
(C)
$385.00 purchase _ #870VI064
Outlines the indications of prerenal failure, including urine output, urine and blood composition, and the body's mechanisms for restoring kidney function.
Health and Safety
Dist - HSCIC **Prod** - HSCIC 1987

Patient Interview - Right and Wrong 8 MIN
U-matic
Color (C)
Illustrates the initial interview between dentist and prospective patient through role playing techniques. Both correct and incorrect questioning techniques are presented and the resulting patient responses noted.
Health and Safety; Science - Natural
Dist - UOKLAH **Prod** - UOKLAH 1986

Patient Interview - Science or Art Series
The Medical Interview 13 MIN
The Surgical Interview 13 MIN
Dist - PRIMED

Patient lifting techniques 22 MIN
VHS
Color (C PRO G)
$395.00 purchase _ #R900 - VI - 013
Instructs viewers on how to move or assist in moving a patient safely, efficiently and comfortably. Reviews and demonstrates normal body movement and outlines the basic principles of lifting. Describes and performs techniques for the following lifts and transfers - moving a patient up in bed; rolling a patient onto her - his side; moving a patient from a lying to a sitting position, then into a wheelchair; repositioning a patient in a wheelchair or cardiac chair, three - person lifting from bed to stetcher; and transferring from floor to a chair. Produced at the Calgary General Hospital, Calgary, Alberta, Canada.
Health and Safety; Science - Natural
Dist - HSCIC

Patient module - Tape 3 26 MIN
VHS
Dual diagnosis - Haight - Ashbury training series
Color (C G PRO)
$250.00 purchase
Shows clients that recovery is possible. Describes the environmental and biological basis for mental illness and how psychoactive drugs, legal and illegal - including those used to treat mental illness, affect the individual both positively and negatively. Part of a three - part series on dual diagnosis in drug abuse treatment.
Guidance and Counseling; Health and Safety; Psychology
Dist - FMSP

Patient module - Tape 3 45 MIN
VHS
Methamphetamines - Haight - Ashbury training series
Color (G)
$250.00 purchase
Condenses information from the first two tapes for clients and the lay public. Includes history, pharmacology, effects, detoxification, initial abstinence, sobriety, recovery and personal narrative. Part three of a three - part series on methamphetamines.
Guidance and Counseling; Psychology
Dist - FMSP

Patient Monitoring by Clinical Pharmacists 15 MIN
U-matic
Color (C)
Provides information about the role of inpatient monitoring by clinical pharmacists.
Health and Safety; Science - Natural
Dist - UOKLAH **Prod** - UOKLAH 1978

The Patient not in Acute Distress - Admission, Care and Discharge 25 MIN
16mm
Intensive Coronary Care Multimedia Learning System (ICC/MMLS Series
Color (PRO)
LC 73-701770
Discusses the team approach to coronary care. Compares treatment of the patient not in acute distress and the patient suffering acute distress.
Health and Safety
Dist - SUTHLA **Prod** - SUTHLA 1969

Patient - Operator Positioning in Dental Hygiene 9 MIN
U-matic
Color
LC 79-706752
Demonstrates positioning for the dental hygienist and patient during dental hygiene procedures.
Health and Safety
Dist - USNAC **Prod** - MUSC 1978

Patient Positioning and Preparation of the Instrument Tray for Clinical Oral Surgery 7 MIN
U-matic
Oral Surgery Clinic Routine Series
Color
LC 79-706763
Depicts proper positioning of a patient during oral surgery and demonstrates the handling of sterile forceps in arranging surgical instruments on a tray.
Health and Safety
Dist - USNAC **Prod** - MUSC

The Patient - Preanesthetic Evaluation 25 MIN
VHS / U-matic
Anesthesiology Clerkship Series
Color (PRO)
Explains the medical and legal importance of conducting a preanesthetic evaluation. Outlines steps for evaluating the patient's preanesthetic condition. Shows how to elicit both individual and family anesthetic history, reviews current medications (especially cardiovascular, corticosteroid and neurologic drugs) for expected interaction with various anesthetic agents and altered physiologic responses. Assesses the patient's physical status (especially cardiovascular, respiratory, airway airway and renal systems). Determines patient's ASA risk classification.
Health and Safety
Dist - UMICHM **Prod** - UMICHM 1982

The Patient - Preoperative Preparation Choice of Anesthesia and Premedication 22 MIN
U-matic / VHS
Anesthesiology Clerkship Series
Color (PRO)
Discusses the preoperative cardiovascular and respiratory preparation of the patient for anesthesia. Indentifies factors to be considered in choosing the anesthetic agent and technique. Describes rationale for premedication selection.
Health and Safety
Dist - UMICHM **Prod** - UMICHM 1982

The Patient presentation 25 MIN
VHS
Color (A PRO)
$225.00 purchase, $50.00 rental
Covers the general principles of patient presentation for medical students in clinical training. Provides step - by - step analysis of one student's presentation at the bedside of a seriously ill patient. Includes instructional guide and a suggested presentation format.
Health and Safety
Dist - UARIZ **Prod** - UARIZ

Patient Problems in Emergency Psychiatry 60 MIN
U-matic / VHS
Color (PRO)
Illustrates common psychiatric disorders seen in emergency settings. Features patients who are - inaccessible, violent, anxious, depressed, and or psychotic. Identifies important symptoms.
Health and Safety
Dist - UARIZ **Prod** - UARIZ

Patient rights 30 MIN
VHS / U-matic
Consumer survival series; Health
Color
Presents tips on how a medical patient can protect his rights.
Health and Safety; Home Economics
Dist - MDCPB **Prod** - MDCPB

Patient Rights / Air Fare / OTC Drugs
VHS / U-matic
Consumer Survival Series
Color
Presents tips on patient rights, air fare and over - the - counter drugs.
Health and Safety; Home Economics; Social Science
Dist - MDCPB **Prod** - MDCPB

Patient Room Cleaning 17 MIN
16mm 14 MIN
Housekeeping Personnel Series
Color (IND)
LC 73-701691
Presents the proper procedures and equipment used in cleaning the patient's room. Stresses consideration of the patient while working in the room.
Health and Safety
Dist - COPI **Prod** - COPI 1973

Patient Room Cleaning 13.5
BETA / VHS / U-matic
Medical Housekeeping Series
(PRO A)
$225 _ #1010
Gives the acceptable method for cleaning non - isolation hospital rooms.
Education; Guidance and Counseling; Health and Safety
Dist - CTT **Prod** - CTT

Patient room cleaning 14 MIN
VHS
Housekeeping series
Color (H A G T)
$225.00 purchase _ #BM110
Covers correct procedures for cleaning occupied as well as terminal non - isolation patient rooms. Part of a series on housekeeping.
Health and Safety; Home Economics; Industrial and Technical Education; Psychology
Dist - AAVIM **Prod** - AAVIM

Patient Safety I 22 MIN
VHS / U-matic
Color
Points out hazards and illustrates how to prevent accidental injuries to patients in and around patients' rooms.
Health and Safety
Dist - FPF **Prod** - FPF

Patient Safety II 14 MIN
VHS / U-matic
Color
Teaches nursing staff orderlies and others how to prevent accidental injuries to patients while they are ambulatory, on crutches, using walker and other situations.
Health and Safety
Dist - FPF **Prod** - FPF

Patient Transfer and Positioning - Part 1 28 MIN
VHS / 16mm
Basic Techniques for Transferring Patients Safely
Color (C PRO)
$275.00 purchase, $60.00 rental _ #7638S, #7638V
Part one of two - part series, defines key principles for nurses, aidesand paraprofessionals in safe and caring transfer of patients. Includes need to know patient, teamwork, control of environment, and application of proper body mechanics. Uses actual patients in real - life health care settings. Approved for CE credit. Study guide included.
Health and Safety
Dist - AJN **Prod** - HOSSN 1990

Patient Transfer and Positioning - Part 2 28 MIN
VHS / 16mm
Principles for Positioning Immobilized Patients
Color (C PRO)
$275.00 purchase, $60.00 rental _ #7640S, #7640V
Second part of two - part series demonstrates four basic patient positions and correct methods for moving patients from one to the other. Stresses prevention of pressure sores, loss of muscle tone, and decreased circulation. Approved for CE credit. Includes study guide.
Health and Safety
Dist - AJN **Prod** - HOSSN 1990

Patient transfer and positioning series
Presents a two - part series on patient transfer and positioning. Defines the key principles of safe transfer. Demonstrates four basic positions for immobilized patients. Provides guidelines for documentation.
Basic techniques for transferring patients safely - Part 1 28 MIN
Principles for positioning immobilized patients - Part 2 28 MIN
Dist - AJN **Prod** - HOSSN 1990

Patient with Malignancy and Hypercalcemia 60 MIN
U-matic
Color
Presents case studies of patients with malignant tumors and hypercalcemia. Discusses diagnosis and treatment of both problems.
Health and Safety
Dist - UTEXSC **Prod** - UTEXSC

The Patient with Rheumatoid Arthritis 23 MIN
U-matic / VHS
Color (PRO)
Describes a comprehensive management plan for the patient with rheumatoid arthiritis which includes differential diagnosis and patient education.
Health and Safety
Dist - UMICHM **Prod** - UMICHM 1975

Patients are People Series
Bathing the patient 18 MIN
The Bed and the Bedside Unit 18 MIN
Patient Feeding and Mouth Care 12 MIN
The Patient's Excretory Needs 18 MIN
To Care Enough 18 MIN
TPR - Temperature, Pulse and Respiration 18 MIN
Dist - MLA

Patients ... are people, too - patient care 14 MIN
VHS
Color (C PRO G)
$395.00 purchase _ #R861 - VI - 008
Offers a discussion - trigger videotape designed to increase awareness among healthcare personnel that thoughtlessness, discourtesy and inappropriate advice can adversely affect patient care. Presents four dramatized vignettes to illustrate the effects of incorrect information and callous or indiscreet remarks. Produced by Dr E M Colvin, South Carolina Medical Assn.
Health and Safety; Psychology; Social Science
Dist - HSCIC

Patients at Risk of Delivering Low Birth Weight Infants 10 MIN
VHS / U-matic
Color (PRO)
Describes how socioeconomic deprivation, obstetric history, maternal age and medical conditions affect the risk of delivering a low birth weight infant. Presents the management measures which minimize this risk.
Health and Safety
Dist - UMICHM **Prod** - UMICHM 1983

A Patient's bill of rights 25 MIN
BETA / VHS / U-matic
Ethics, values and health care series
Color (C PRO)
$150.00 purchase _ #132.3
Presents a video transfer from slide program which presents the 12 provisions of the American Hospital Association's statement on patient's rights. Features Elsie Bandman, RN, an authority on patient's rights, who gives her interpretation of each provision, along with some problems inherent in implementing them and the role of the nurse as patient advocate in insuring that these rights are not violated. Part of a series on ethics, values and health care.
Guidance and Counseling; Health and Safety; Religion and Philosophy
Dist - CONMED **Prod** - CONMED

The Patient's Excretory Needs 18 MIN
16mm
Patients are People Series
Color (H A)
Science
Dist - MLA **Prod** - CALVIN 1967

A Patient's Guide to CT Scanning
U-matic / VHS
Color
Addresses the fears of patients facing their first CT scan and explains the value of this complex technology in lay terms.
Health and Safety
Dist - GRANVW **Prod** - GRANVW

A Patient's Guide to Home Care of the Hickman Catheter 18 MIN
VHS / 16mm
Cancer Education - for Patients - Series
(C G)
$385.00 purchase _ #850VLI005
Demostrates how the Hickman catheter is inserted, and describes the procedure for its use and maintenance.
Health and Safety
Dist - HSCIC **Prod** - HSCIC 1985

A Patient's Guide to Radiotherapy 7 MIN
VHS / 16mm
Cancer Education - for Patients - Series
(C G)
$385.00 purchase _ #850VI002
Explains to patients the process of radiotherapy, how long treatment lasts, and its side effects and how long they can be expected to last. Teaches the importance of diet and skin care during treatment.
Health and Safety
Dist - HSCIC **Prod** - HSCIC 1984

The Patient's Right to Know the Truth 59 MIN
U-matic
Ethics and Medicine Series
Color
Deals with the consent to therapy and access to records of hospitalized competent adult patients.
Health and Safety; Religion and Philosophy
Dist - HRC **Prod** - OHC

Patients' Rights and Physician Accountability - Problems with PSRO's 59 MIN
U-matic
Ethics and Medicine Series
Color
Dicusses professional standards review organizations.
Health and Safety; Religion and Philosophy; Sociology
Dist - HRC **Prod** - OHC

The Patients' Story 46 MIN
VHS / U-matic
Understanding Cancer Series
Color (G)
$150.00
Addresses the social isolation of many cancer patients and portrays the stories of a number of such people.
Health and Safety
Dist - LANDMK **Prod** - LANDMK 1985

Patients with Rheumatic Disorders Series
Common patient problems - alterations in mobility and self - care activities 30 MIN
An Overview 46 MIN
Dist - AJN

Patients with rheumatic disordes series
Common patient problems - alterations in comfort 45 MIN
Dist - AJN

Patients without doctors 29 MIN
Videoreel / VT2
Turning points series
Color
Examines the grass - roots beginning of a revolution in health care delivery. Includes the townspeople throughout Tennessee banding together to create a new form of medical care for themselves.
Health and Safety; Social Science; Sociology
Dist - PBS **Prod** - WDCNTV

Patients...are people too 14 MIN
VHS / U-matic
Color (PRO C)
$395.00 purchase, $80.00 rental _ #C861 - VI - 008
Presents four vignettes which illustrate the effects of incorrect information and callous or indiscreet remarks from health care personnel. Presented by Dr Euta M Colvin.
Health and Safety; Psychology
Dist - HSCIC

Patio Gardening 30 MIN
BETA / VHS
Victory Garden Series
Color
Gives pointers on starting a deck or brick walkway garden in containers.
Agriculture; Physical Education and Recreation
Dist - CORF **Prod** - WGBHTV

Patricia Goedicke - 10 - 8 - 81 30 MIN
VHS / Cassette
Poetry Center reading series
Color (G)
$15.00 purchase, rental _ #446 - 380
Features Patricia Goedicke reading selections from her works at the Poetry Center, San Francisco State University.
Literature and Drama
Dist - POETRY **Prod** - POETRY 1981

Patricia Hampl - 2 - 6 - 80 30 MIN
VHS / Cassette
Poetry Center reading series
Color (G)
$15.00, $45.00 purchase, $15.00 rental _ #374 - 311
Features Patricia Hampl reading her works at the Poetry Center, San Francisco State University, with an introduction by Tom Mandel.
Literature and Drama
Dist - POETRY **Prod** - POETRY 1980

Patricia Highsmith 50 MIN
VHS
Color (S)
$39.95 purchase _ #833 - 9160
Presents America's first lady of crime Patricia Highsmith who is best known for her creation of Tom Ripley, amoral crook and killer. Combines conversations with author Highsmith with dramatizations showing Ripley in a chilling tale of fraud, impersonation, murder, the stuff of which mysteries are made.
Fine Arts; Literature and Drama; Sociology
Dist - FI **Prod** - RMART 1986

Patricia's Moving Picture 26 MIN
U-matic / VHS / 16mm
Color (A)
LC 80-701694
Focuses on a woman who experienced deep depression when her children began to grow up and her duties as a wife and mother began to shrink. Explains how her husband, her psychiatrist, and a woman's center helped her come to grips with her new life role.
Psychology; Sociology
Dist - MEDIAG **Prod** - NFBC 1980

Patrick 32 FRS
U-matic / VHS / 16mm
Color (K P I)
LC 73-736520; 73-701582
Presents an animated feature in which Patrick sets out for the town marketplace, searching for a fiddle which he buys from a junkman.
Literature and Drama
Dist - WWS **Prod** - WWS 1973

Patrick Henry - Give Me Liberty or Give Me Death 29 MIN
VHS / 16mm
Color (G)
$55.00 rental _ #PHEN - 000
Dramatizes Patrick Henry's speech. Re - enacted by Virginia's Barksdale Theatre. Highlights the personal drama behind the speech as well as its historical significance.
History - United States
Dist - PBS **Prod** - WCVETV

Patrick Henry of Virginia 16 MIN
16mm
Color; B&W (I)
Depicts the life of Patrick Henry from his early struggles, through Williamsburg and the 'GIVE ME LIBERTY OR DEATH' speech, to his days at Red Hill. Narrated in first person.
Biography; History - United States
Dist - VADE **Prod** - VADE 1948

Patrick Henry's Liberty or Death 15 MIN
U-matic / VHS / 16mm
Great American Patriotic Speeches Series
Color (J H C)
LC 73-701830
Features Barry Sullivan.
Biography; English Language
Dist - AIMS **Prod** - EVANSA 1973

The Patriot 20 MIN
VHS / U-matic
French Revolution - revolutionary witness series
Color (H C)
$250.00 purchase _ #HP - 5956C
Dramatizes the life of Palloy, patriot and astute businessman in the French Revolution, portrayed by Simon Callow. Explains that Palloy was contracted to demolish the Bastille - and he sold every inch of it as a souvenir. Part of a four - part series on the French Revolution written by playwright Peter Barnes.
History - World
Dist - CORF **Prod** - BBCTV 1989

The Patriot game 93 MIN
16mm / VHS
B&W (G)
$1295.00 purchase, $125.00 rental
Tells the story of the long and bitter battle for Northern Ireland. Covers Ireland's history from British colonization to the territory's division in 1922 then details the events that began in 1968. Shows the IRA at work, much of it filmed clandestinely, through portraits of rebellion and eye witness accounts of killings and massacres like Bloody Sunday. Produced by Arthur MacCaig.
Fine Arts; History - World
Dist - FIRS

Patriotic Music - its Influence on United States History, 1775 - 1900 21 MIN
16mm
Color (I)
Tells the story behind the seven most popular patriotic anthems and how they affected the history of the United States.
Fine Arts; History - United States; Social Science
Dist - DANA **Prod** - DANA 1974

Patriotism 10 MIN
U-matic / VHS / 16mm
American Values for Elementary Series
Color (P I)
LC 72-703124
Illustrates the meaning of the word patriotism. Features actor Bob Crane, who narrates an exploration of the place of a person in relation to the community.
Civics and Political Systems; Guidance and Counseling; Social Science
Dist - AIMS **Prod** - EVANSA 1972

The Patriots 82 MIN
VHS / U-matic
B&W (GERMAN AND RUSSIAN (ENGLISH SUBTITLES))
Tells the story of a German prisoner of war who gets a job as a shoemaker in a Russian provincial town in World War I. Directed by B Barnett. Stars Elena Kuzmina and Hans Klering. With English subtitles.
Civics and Political Systems; Foreign Language; History - World; Sociology
Dist - IHF **Prod** - IHF

Patriots 54 MIN
VHS
Red empire series
Color (J H C G)
$19.98 purchase _ #FFO9609V
Discloses that there is confusion in the Soviet Union over whom to support in World War II, but Hitler brings about a decision by invading in 1941. Reveals that the Soviets are no match for the Nazis, who destroy everything on the way to Moscow. Eventually the harsh Soviet winter defeats the Germans, leaving Stalin a hero and unlikely ally of the United States and Great Britain. Part of a seven - part series tracing Russian history from the fall of the Tsar and rise of Lenin, through World War I, the internal war for communism, the emergence of Stalin, World War II, Krushchev, Brezhnev and Gorbachev.
Civics and Political Systems; History - World
Dist - CAMV

Patrol officer scheduling with an optimization based decision support system
VHS
Color (C PRO G)
$150.00 purchase _ #88.01
Focuses on an optimization based decision support system for patrol officer deployment which provides analysis of strategic and tactical police options, evaluates schedule changes and deployment scenarios, forecasts hourly officer needs and automatically schedules to fulfill needs, allowing for 'fine tuning' of optimal schedule. Reveals that the intelligent primal dual integer search procedure produced a 25 percent increase in patrol units available when needed - equivalent to adding 200 officers or a cost saving of $11 million annually. Response times declined 29 percent, traffic citations increased 62 percent - adding another $3 million per year to the city treasury. City of San Francisco Police Dept. Philip E Taylor, Stephen J Huxley.
Business and Economics; Civics and Political Systems
Dist - INMASC

Patrolling Your Health Care Facility 15 MIN
U-matic / VHS
Health Care Security Training Series
Color
Teaches essential patrol skills and stresses communicating with other hospital employees.
Civics and Political Systems; Health and Safety; Sociology
Dist - CORF **Prod** - GREESM

Patron - Piaget in New Perspective 18 MIN
16mm
Color
LC 78-700207
Presents a personal view of child psychologist and educator, Jean Piaget, as seen by friends and colleagues. Shows Piaget lecturing and in private moments.
Biography; Psychology
Dist - PARENT **Prod** - PARENT 1977

Pat's Birthday 13 MIN
16mm
B&W (C)
$258.00
Experimental film by Robert Breer.
Fine Arts
Dist - AFA **Prod** - AFA 1962

Pat's difficult day 14 MIN
VHS
Postman Pat series
Color (P I)
$175.00 purchase
Reveals that Postman Pat wakes up late, gets tangled up in sticky tape, drops metal objects in the grass and hurts his hand but Sam Waldron helps him. Part of a 13 - part animated puppet series which teaches values.
Guidance and Counseling; Literature and Drama
Dist - LANDMK **Prod** - LANDMK 1991

Pat's foggy day 14 MIN
VHS
Postman Pat series
Color (P I)
$175.00 purchase
Reveals that Postman Pat gets lost because of the fog but the Reverend Timms rings the church bells so Pat can follow the sound and find his way home. Part of a 13 - part animated puppet series which teaches values.
Guidance and Counseling; Literature and Drama
Dist - LANDMK **Prod** - LANDMK 1991

Pat's rainy day 14 MIN
VHS
Postman Pat series
Color (P I)
$175.00 purchase
Reveals that heavy rain is causing problems for Postman Pat and the citizens of Greendale. Shows how Peter Fogg saves the day with his bulldozer. Part of a 13 - part animated puppet series which teaches values.
Guidance and Counseling; Literature and Drama
Dist - LANDMK **Prod** - LANDMK 1991

Pat's thirsty day 14 MIN
VHS
Postman Pat series
Color (P I)
$175.00 purchase
Reveals that during a hot day a water shortage occurs because the old village pump is broken. Shows that Postman Pat calls on Ted Glenn who fixes the pump and everyone is able to get water. Part of a 13 - part animated puppet series which teaches values.
Guidance and Counseling; Literature and Drama
Dist - LANDMK **Prod** - LANDMK 1991

Pat's tractor express 14 MIN
VHS
Postman Pat series
Color (P I)
$175.00 purchase
Reveals that Postman Pat borrows a tractor in order to deliver a registered letter to a camper who is visiting a hard - to - get - to waterfall. Part of a 13 - part animated puppet series which teaches values.
Guidance and Counseling; Literature and Drama
Dist - LANDMK **Prod** - LANDMK 1991

Pat's windy day 14 MIN
VHS
Postman Pat series
Color (P I)
$175.00 purchase
Reveals that heavy winds have caused havoc - trees and telegraph poles have blown down and block Postman Pat's route. Shows that after the mess is cleared Pat loses his hat but finally finds it. Part of a 13 - part animated puppet series which teaches values.
Guidance and Counseling; Literature and Drama
Dist - LANDMK **Prod** - LANDMK 1991

Pattern Alteration 29 MIN
Videoreel / VT2
Sewing Skills - Tailoring Series
Color
Features Mrs Ruth Hickman demonstrating how to alter a pattern.
Home Economics
Dist - PBS **Prod** - KRMATV

Pattern and transformation 30 MIN
VHS / BETA
Number, form and life series
Color (G)
$29.95 purchase _ #S342
Considers patterning in nature. Emphasizes understanding sound vibrations. Demonstrates an ancient Mongolian 'polyphonic' chanting technique. Features former biophysics researcher Jill Purce, author of 'The Mystic Spiral.' Part of a four - part series on number, form and life.
Fine Arts; Religion and Philosophy; Science - Natural; Science - Physical
Dist - THINKA **Prod** - THINKA

The Pattern development video 75 MIN
VHS
Color (PRO C G)
$149.00 purchase _ #611
Illustrates pattern development for stage costumes. Features Rosemary Ingham, author of The Costume Designer's Handbook, who measures an actor, analyzes the costume sketch, develops a paper pattern, makes and fits a design mock - up. Includes the 100 page Pattern Development Handbook. Produced by the Theater Arts Video Library.
Fine Arts; Home Economics
Dist - FIRLIT

Pattern for Change 32 MIN
16mm
Color
LC 74-705332
Illustrates how the instiitution provides for its permanent members today and how it acts as a catalytic agent to involve community services for the more able retarded.
Psychology
Dist - USNAC **Prod** - USBEH

Pattern for Change 33 MIN
16mm
Color
Presents an overview of the care of the mentally retarded in the United States. Emphasizes historical and institutional out reach programs.
Psychology; Sociology
Dist - USOE **Prod** - GWASHU

Pattern for Instruction 21 MIN
16mm / U-matic / VHS
Color (IND) (PORTUGUESE SWEDISH SPANISH NORWEGIAN DUTCH DANISH FRENCH)
Uses actual basketball sequences to illustrate each step of proper job instruction. Shows how a four - step method can be used to teach anything.
Business and Economics; Foreign Language; Psychology
Dist - RTBL **Prod** - RTBL 1982

Pattern Layouts for Plaids 29 MIN
Videoreel / VT2
Sewing Skills - Tailoring Series
Color
Features Mrs Ruth Hickman demonstrating how to layout a pattern for plaids.
Home Economics
Dist - PBS **Prod** - KRMATV

Pattern Measurements and Alterations 20 MIN
U-matic / VHS
Clothing Construction Techniques Series
Color (C A)
Covers taking body measurements, altering bust size, altering pattern hip size, altering pattern sleeve length and circumference, and fitting pants patterns.

Home Economics
Dist - IOWASP Prod - IOWASP

Pattern patrol 15 MIN
VHS
Art's place series
Color (K P)
$49.00 purchase, $15.00 rental _ #295809
Shows how Kim and Leo play a pattern - spotting game and then learn to design their own patterns. Reveals that Mirror tells a story about a hunter trying to capture a beautifully patterned creature to please his maharajah. Part of a series combining songs, stories, animation, puppets and live actors to convey the pleasure of artistic expression. Includes an illustrated teacher's guide.
Fine Arts
Dist - TVOTAR Prod - TVOTAR 1989

Pattern - Program 4 15 MIN
U-matic
Artscape Series
Color (I)
Shows children running away from a magic castle and finding themselves in a pattern of trees where they learn that everything around them has patterns.
Fine Arts
Dist - TVOTAR Prod - TVOTAR 1983

Patterned Films - Dry - Plasma Etching, I 35 MIN
U-matic / VHS
Plasma Etching and Pattern - for VLSI Fabrication Series
Color (IND)
Outlines dry - plasma etching mechanisms in terms of physical and chemical mechanisms that occur at the surface. Notes how this process allows for tailored etch profiles from the vertical to gently sloped. Includes overview of wet versus dry processes.
Industrial and Technical Education; Science
Dist - COLOSU Prod - COLOSU

Patterned Films - Dry - Plasma Etching, II 35 MIN
U-matic / VHS
Plasma Etching and Pattern - for VLSI Fabrication Series
Color (IND)
Describes some commercial plasma equipment used for dry etching, from gas - phased chemical etch of photoresist and parts of a living cell, which are in constant motion as compared silicon nitride in barrel reactors, to the physical etching of silicon dioxide in rare - gas ion beams, and to the chemical plus ion - assisted etching of polysilicon in plasma diode reactors.
Industrial and Technical Education; Science
Dist - COLOSU Prod - COLOSU

Patterned Films - Wet Chemical Etching, I 35 MIN
VHS / U-matic
Plasma Etching and Pattern Transfer - for VSLI Fabrication Series
Color (IND)
Discusses patterned microelectronic films produced by wet chemical etching and photoresist masking. Talks in terms of selectivity to contiguous films, device damage, etch profiles and minimum feature size.
Industrial and Technical Education
Dist - COLOSU Prod - COLOSU

Patterned Films - Wet Chemical Etching , II 35 MIN
VHS / U-matic
Plasma Etching and Pattern - for VLSI Fabrication Series
Color (IND)
Discusses wet chemical etching in five conceptual stages, including parent reactants in liquid phase, absorption of reactants on the surface, chemical breakdown of reactants at the surface, formation of new soluble products, and the desorption and release of products from the surface into solution.
Industrial and Technical Education; Science
Dist - COLOSU Prod - COLOSU

Patterns 12 MIN
U-matic / VHS / 16mm
Many Worlds of Nature Series
Color
LC 79-701323
Illustrates the premise that the infinite variety of forms in nature are based on only a few basic patterns.
Science - Natural
Dist - CORF Prod - MORALL 1979

Patterns 18 MIN
16mm
Search for Solutions Series
Color (J)
LC 79-701461
Demonstrates how identifying patterns helps to facilitate the problem solving process in scientific investigation.Narrated by Stacy Keach.
Science
Dist - KAROL Prod - PLYBCK 1979

Patterns 15 MIN
U-matic
Math Makers Two Series
Color (I)
Presents the math concepts of tessellations involving rectangles, squares and triangles.
Education; Mathematics
Dist - TVOTAR Prod - TVOTAR 1980

Patterns
VHS
Lola May's fundamental math series
Color (K)
$45.00 purchase _ #10253VG
Shows how to recognize simple to relatively complex patterns. Presents young children with exercises to teach differentiation. Comes with a teacher's guide and blackline masters. Part three of a 30 - part series.
Mathematics
Dist - UNL

Patterns - Aids in Generalization 20 MIN
U-matic
Let's Figure it Out Series
B&W (P)
Mathematics
Dist - NYSED Prod - WNYE 1968

Patterns and Fabrics 29 MIN
Videoreel / VT2
Sewing Skills - Tailoring Series
Color
Features Mrs Ruth Hickman demonstrating various patterns and fabrics.
Home Economics
Dist - PBS Prod - KRMATV

Patterns for Health 14 MIN
16mm
B&W
LC FIE68-138
Discusses the establishment of early health habits for the pre - school child, and shows how this early training develops patterns found in the well - adjusted adult. Covers general as well as specific health needs of the four - to - five - year - old child.
Health and Safety
Dist - USNAC Prod - USOEO 1967

Patterns for Survival - a Study of Mimicry and Protective Coloration in Tropical Insects 27 MIN
16mm
Color (I)
LC 77-709100
Presents an over - all view of protective coloration in insects. Interprets how the various adaptations have evolved in the context of predators' feeding behavior.
Science - Natural
Dist - AMHRST Prod - AMHRST 1968

Patterns in Development 24 MIN
U-matic / VHS / 16mm
Color
Presents three systems of pattern specification by which cells receive differential spatial signals during development. Shows three different methods for studying the development of pattern specification - direct observation, genetic tricks and surgical transplantations.
Science - Natural
Dist - MEDIAG Prod - OPENU 1982

Patterns in Development - Cell Movement 24 MIN
U-matic / VHS / 16mm
Color
Describes two aspects of cell movements during morphogenesis - one where cells cooperate to organize themselves to rebuild an organ and another where cells interact during cellular reaggregation. Demonstrates such characteristics of cell development as contact guidance, the recognition of and alignment of cells along underlying patterns of collagen bundles.
Science - Natural
Dist - MEDIAG Prod - OPENU 1982

Patterns in green 25 MIN
U-matic / VHS
Developmental biology series
Color (H C)
$250.00 purchase _ #HP - 5980C
Introduces the three repeating geometric patterns to which virtually all plant leaves and flowers conform - spiral, zig - zag, and whorled. Teaches that plant phyllotaxy is related to evolution. Discovers the 'ulterior motives' lurking behind leaf and petal phyllotaxy and what causes plants to group parts in one of three common patterns. Part of a four - part series on biology which addresses regeneration, internal and external structures, cellular communication, gender influences, growth and stability of form.
Science; Science - Natural
Dist - CORF Prod - BBCTV 1990

Patterns in Language 20 MIN
U-matic / VHS / 16mm
Literacy Instructor Training Series
Color (T)
LC 78-700887
Focuses on literacy instruction techniques as well as the backgrounds and motivations of adult students.
Education; English Language
Dist - IU Prod - NEWPAR 1978

Patterns in Teacher - Pupil Interaction - Bacteria 11 MIN
U-matic / VHS / 16mm
Concepts and Patterns in Teacher - Pupil Interaction Series
Color (T)
LC 75-703651
Shows a high school science class reviewing the forms and uses of bacteria and applying this information to a demonstration of bacterial action.
Education; Psychology
Dist - IU Prod - IU 1975

Patterns in Teacher - Pupil Interaction - Ecology 11 MIN
U-matic / VHS / 16mm
Concepts and Patterns in Teacher - Pupil Interaction Series
Color (T)
LC 75-703652
Shows a field trip in which a seventh - grade teacher analyzes the problem of environmental pollution with her students. Exemplifies the conceptss of probing and informing and approving and disapproving.
Education; Psychology
Dist - IU Prod - IU 1975

Patterns in Teacher - Pupil Interaction - Esentials for Life 10 MIN
16mm / U-matic / VHS
Concepts and Patterns in Teacher - Pupil Interaction Series
Color (T)
LC 75-703653
Shows a seventh - grade class recitation on the basic essentials of life and the discussion that follows. Shows the teacher's behavior in this situation and emphasizes the concepts of reproductive and productive questioning and approving and disapproving.
Education; Psychology
Dist - IU Prod - IU 1975

Patterns in Teacher - Pupil Interaction - People who Help Us 11 MIN
U-matic / VHS / 16mm
Concepts and Patterns in Teacher - Pupil Interaction Series
Color (T)
LC 75-703654
Presents a second - grade teacher and her class exploring the topic of community helpers. Shows the teacher's behavior in this situation.
Education; Psychology
Dist - IU Prod - IU 1975

Patterns in Teacher - Pupil Interaction - Population Control 10 MIN
U-matic / VHS / 16mm
Concepts and Patterns in Teacher - Pupil Interaction Series
Color (T)
LC 75-703655
Shows a high school social studies class as they discuss the problem of population growth and control. Shows the teacher's behavior in this situation and exemplifies probing and informing techniques.
Education; Psychology
Dist - IU Prod - IU 1975

Patterns in Teacher - Pupil Interaction - the Five Senses 12 MIN
U-matic / VHS / 16mm
Concepts and Patterns in Teacher - Pupil Interaction Series
Color (T)
LC 75-703656
Shows a second - grade teacher as she explores with her class the concept of the five senses. Shows the teacher's behavior in this situation and exemplifies learning concepts.
Education; Psychology
Dist - IU Prod - IU 1975

Patterns in the air 60 MIN
VHS
Miracle planet - the life story of Earth series
Color (I J H)
$100.00 purchase _ #A5VH 1323
Follows continents from their barren beginnings, unprotected from the sun, to the eventual development of the ozone layer and the emergence of plant life. Shows that alterations in today's atomosphere will eventually

affect every inhabitant of Earth. Part of a six - part series examining the intricate balance of systems known as planet Earth.
Science - Natural; Science - Physical
Dist - CLRVUE

Patterns of Change 14 MIN
16mm
Color
LC 75-700469
Offers an impressionistic view of the interaction between man and his environment. Depicts seasonal change, elemental forces, growth of life forms and man's modification of the land.
Science - Natural; Sociology
Dist - NYSM **Prod** - NYSM 1975

Patterns of Climate 15 MIN
U-matic
North America - Growth of a Continent Series
Color (J H)
Explains how latitude, earth rotation, water currents, altitude and wind currents affect climate.
Geography - United States; Geography - World
Dist - TVOTAR **Prod** - TVOTAR 1980

Patterns of Development 25 MIN
16mm / U-matic / VHS
Genetics Series
Color (H C)
$550 purchase - 16 mm, $250 purchase - video _ #5042C
Shows how genes help build the forms of living creatures. Produced by the BBC for the Open University.
Science - Natural
Dist - CORF

Patterns of Development in Art 7 MIN
U-matic
Take Time Series
(A)
Demonstrates the influence of parents and others caring for pre - schoolers on the physical and emotional development of the child.
Health and Safety; Psychology; Sociology
Dist - ACCESS **Prod** - ACCESS 1976

Patterns of Diversity 25 MIN
U-matic / VHS / 16mm
Genetics Series
Color (H C)
$550 purchase - 16 mm, $250 purchase - video _ #5043C
Discusses how animals adapt to their surroundings over geological time. Produced by the BBC for the Open University.
Science - Natural
Dist - CORF

Patterns of Eating Behavior in Infants 80 MIN
16mm
Color (PRO)
Directs attention to the postural adjustments in healthy infants that adapt the mouth for sucking, chewing and biting, and the arms and hands for grasping and lifting. Demonstrates mother - infant interaction showing examples of reinforcement of sensitivity and consistency in social behavior.
Home Economics; Science - Natural
Dist - UCLA **Prod** - UCLA

Patterns of Electromagnetic Fields 13 MIN
U-matic / VHS
Introductory Concepts in Physics - Electricity Series
Color (C)
$229.00, $129.00 purchase _ #AD - 1179
Demonstrates the formation of magnetic fields around straight wires and coils using iron filings and wire with current flowing through it.
Science - Physical
Dist - FOTH **Prod** - FOTH

Patterns of Evolution 25 MIN
U-matic / VHS / 16mm
Genetics Series
Color (H C)
$550 purchase - 16 mm, $250 purchase - video _ #5044C
Portrays evolutionary biology, looking at relationships between organisms and their environment. Produced by the BBC for the Open University.
Science - Natural
Dist - CORF

Patterns of Immigration 30 MIN
U-matic
Challenge Series
Color (PRO)
Deals with innovative approaches to life with changes in the areas of creativity, medicine, men in transition and multiculturalism.
History - World; Psychology; Sociology
Dist - TVOTAR **Prod** - TVOTAR 1985

Patterns of Inheritance 33 MIN
VHS
Color (J H C)
$189.00 purchase _ #FG - 110 - VS
Helps students sort out the complexities of Mendelian genetics. Traces the processes and logic of Mendel's experiments with peas to demonstrate the principles of dominance, segregation and independent assortment. Shows students how to make Punnett squares to determine the probability that particular traits will show up in successive generations in hybrid, dihybrid and trihybrid crosses. Part Two explores ways in which later findings have modified some of Mendel's orginal theories. Looks at the principles of codominance and linkage. Shows examples in which a single gene affects many traits and in which a single trait is affected by many genes and how the environment interacts with the genotype to produce the phenotype.
Science - Natural
Dist - HRMC **Prod** - HRMC 1994

Patterns of Inheritance 25 MIN
U-matic / VHS / 16mm
Genetics Series
Color (H C)
$550 purchase - 16 mm, $250 purchase - video _ #5041C
Shows how surprisingly few genetic changes are needed to produce the different colors and patterns on the wings of butterflies. Produced by the BBC for the Open University.
Science - Natural
Dist - CORF

Patterns of Intrathoracic Disease 23 MIN
U-matic
Radiology of the Respiratory System - a Basic Review
Color (C)
Reviews abnormal radiographic patterns rather than individual disease processes.
Health and Safety; Industrial and Technical Education; Science - Natural
Dist - UOKLAH **Prod** - UOKLAH 1978

Patterns of living 13 MIN
VHS
Color; PAL (H)
Shows how the distribution and internal structure of settlements were linked to social and economic issues. Examines shopping facilities in the area of Bordeaux, France, to develop the theory of settlement hierarchy, and follows with other complementary European samples. Studies Rotterdam, Holland, to demonstrate the internal structure of a city in terms of major land use zones. Introduces related themes such as employment, communications and the relationship with the environment.
Geography - World; Guidance and Counseling; Science - Natural; Social Science; Sociology
Dist - VIEWTH

Patterns of Pain 28 MIN
16mm
Color
Presents a professor of psychology, a zoologist and a doctor discussing the perception of pain in the nervous system. Deals with such phenomena as the absence of pain perception by the wounded in battle, pain control through hypnosis, acupuncture and yoga, thresholds of pain, the body's ability to produce its own analgesic, and surgical techniques for implanting electrodes in the brain to block the perception of chronic pain.
Psychology; Science - Natural
Dist - FLMLIB **Prod** - CANBC

Patterns of Play 14 MIN
16mm
Color
Describes the history of tennis, squash, table tennis and badminton.
Physical Education and Recreation
Dist - MTP **Prod** - GNRLPO

Patterns of Slave Resistance 29 MIN
Videoreel / VT2
Black Experience Series
Color
History - United States; Sociology
Dist - PBS **Prod** - WTTWTV

Patterns of Sound 13 MIN
16mm
Color (H)
Points out that Shakespeare used not only the meaning of words, but also their sounds to express ideas.
Literature and Drama
Dist - SVE **Prod** - SINGER 1969

Patterns of Subcultures 20 MIN
U-matic
Exploring Our Nation Series
Color (I)
Discusses the different groups of people practicing various cultural traditions in the United States.
Sociology
Dist - GPN **Prod** - KRMATV 1975

Patterns of Subsistence - Food - Producers and the Rise of Civilization 30 MIN
U-matic
Faces of Culture - Studies in Cultural Anthropology Series Lesson 5; Lesson 5
Color (C A)
Covers transition from a hunting - gathering way of life to a food - producing way of life. Suggests some of the factors which lead to this change. Shows examples of cultures following subsistence patterns.
Sociology
Dist - CDTEL **Prod** - COAST

Patterns of Subsistence - Hunter - Gatherers and Pastoralists 30 MIN
U-matic
Faces of Culture - Studies in Cultural Anthropology Series Lesson 4; Lesson 4
Color (C A)
Reviews the characteristics and environmental setting for two types of subsistence. Presents concepts of adaptation, cultural ecology and culture area.
Sociology
Dist - CDTEL **Prod** - COAST

Patterns of the Wild 26 MIN
U-matic / VHS / 16mm
Color
Shows, through the eyes of a wild fox, that the wildlife of a forest is a part of its structure. Shows what proper wildlife management is doing to make the National Forests more livable for animals and more enjoyable for people.
Civics and Political Systems; Science - Natural; Social Science
Dist - USNAC **Prod** - USDA

Patterns of Time and Distance 19 MIN
16mm
Color (J)
LC 73-702484
Shows how time has changed the southern continent of Australia as it sets out the overall pattern of Australia's development from primitive isolation to modern urbanized society. Explains that although once isolated by distance, Australia is today linked by communications and transport into the global society.
Geography - World; Social Science; Sociology
Dist - AUIS **Prod** - FLMAUS 1973

Patterns Series
The Hunters 20 MIN
The Loser 20 MIN
A Woman's Touch 20 MIN
Dist - SF

Patterns with ten
VHS
Math vantage videos series
Color (I J H)
$39.00 purchase _ #653003 - HH
Looks at the mathematical patterns in tens. Part of a five - part series using interactive learning, interdisciplinary approaches, mathematical connections, student involvement and exploration to enable students to use patterns to explain, create and predict situations.
Mathematics; Sociology
Dist - SUNCOM **Prod** - NEBMSI 1994

The Patti Page Video Songbook 60 MIN
BETA / VHS
B&W
Features songs by vocalist Patti Page. How Much Is That Doggie In The Window; I Don't Care If The Sun Don't Shine; I Went To Your Wedding; Melody Of Love; Oklahoma Blues; A Blossom Fell; Smiles; Tennessee Waltz; Mr And Mississippi; When Your Lover Has Gone; Everyday I Fall In Love; You Call Everybody Darling; This Is My Song; In The Blue Of The Evening; Way Down Yonder In New Orleans; Sunny Side Of The Street; Father, Father; Would I Love You.
Fine Arts
Dist - KARTES **Prod** - KARTES

Patton
VHS / U-matic
Color (J C I)
Portrays the life of brillant but controversial World War II General George Patton. Stars George C Scott.
Biography; Fine Arts; History - United States
Dist - GA **Prod** - GA

Patton series
The Goal setters 6 MIN
Morale and the Team Effort 4 MIN
Dist - UTM

Patty Goes to Washington 30 MIN
16mm
Color
Shows how Patty and her classmates organize a study of the amount of energy used by home appliances and how energy can be used more efficiently.

Social Science
Dist - SUNCO **Prod** - GRAVAR

Patty's Dark Christmas 40 MIN
16mm
Color
Relates how a power failure on Christmas Eve forces Santa Claus to make an unexpected personal visit to a family, explain why the lights went out and show the family how to avoid blackouts in the future.
Social Science
Dist - SUNCO **Prod** - GRAVAR

Patty's Magic Formula for Dealing with Boys - Never Fails, Vol 6 22 MIN
VHS / 16mm
Friend Like Patty Series
Color (G)
$95.00 purchase
Focuses upon positive messages to teenage girls. Looks at boys and dating. Part of an eight - part series, 'A Friend Like Patty,' featuring Patty Ellis.
Guidance and Counseling; Health and Safety; Psychology; Sociology
Dist - PROSOR

The Patuxent Wildlife Research Center 20 MIN
16mm
Color
LC 81-701444
Explains the research being conducted at the Patuxent Wildlife Research Center near Laurel, Md, into modern society's impact on wildlife. Reviews their studies on the effects of organic phosphates and the DDT - derivative DDE on life cycles and environment, breeding patterns of endangered species and birds' migratory behavior.
Science; Science - Natural
Dist - USNAC **Prod** - USBSFW 1981

Patzcuaro 11 MIN
16mm
Color; B&W (J)
Displays architectural highlights of Patzcuaro. Shows the House of the Giant, the Cross of Humility and other famous landmarks. The Dance of Old Men is presented with a background of native music.
Fine Arts; Geography - World
Dist - AVED **Prod** - BARONA 1957

Patzcuaro
VHS
Color (J H G) (SPANISH)
$44.95 purchase _ #MCV5045, #MCV5046
Presents a program on the culture of Mexico.
Geography - World
Dist - MADERA **Prod** - MADERA

Pauce Droit, Pouce Gauche 9 MIN
16mm
Color (FRENCH)
LC 74-703751
Tells the story of a young boy who is sent to the store on his own for the first time. Shows how he learns the value of being attentive and following directions. Based on the book Right Thumb - Left Thumb by Osmond Molarsky.
Foreign Language; Guidance and Counseling; Literature and Drama
Dist - MORLAT **Prod** - MORLAT 1973

Paul Adams - in the Trenches 31 MIN
16mm
Color (H C)
Uses some actual newsreel footage to tell the story of the life of Paul Adams, who was killed on Armistice Day, while leading his company in a raid on a German stronghold, unaware of the truce, during World War I.
Biography; History - United States
Dist - FI **Prod** - WOLPER 1974

Paul Adams - Soldier for Democracy 22 MIN
16mm
Color (H C)
Tells of a world plunging from peace into catastrophic war and of the political and military leaders who forged the events that would become the destiny of millions including Paul Adams during World War I.
Biography; History - United States
Dist - FI **Prod** - WOLPER 1974

Paul and the Christian churches 30 MIN
VHS
Introduction to St Paul series
Color (R G)
$39.95 purchase _ #INSP4
Examines the role of St Paul in the formation of the early Church. Features Father Eugene LaVerdiere, SSS, as instructor. Part four of four parts.
Literature and Drama; Religion and Philosophy
Dist - CTNA **Prod** - CTNA 1994

Paul - apostle to the nations series
Athens, Corinth, Rome - tape 3 30 MIN
Ephesus, Philippi, Thessaloniki - Tape 2 30 MIN
Tarsus, Jerusalem, Antioch - Tape 1 30 MIN
Dist - APH

Paul Auster - 3 - 16 - 89 60 MIN
VHS / Cassette
Poetry Center reading series
Color (G)
$15.00, $45.00 purchase _ #848 - 660
Features the experimental writer, Paul Auster, reading from his novel Moon Palace at the Poetry Center, San Francisco State University, with an introduction by Robert Gluck. Includes an interview by Geoffrey Green.
Literature and Drama
Dist - POETRY **Prod** - POETRY 1989

Paul Bailey 35 MIN
VHS
Color (H C G)
$79.00 purchase
Features the British writer, Paul Bailey, with Margaret Walters discussing development of characters, particularly old people. Talks about his works including At the Jerusalem; A Distant Likeness; Gabriel's Lament and others.
Literature and Drama
Dist - ROLAND **Prod** - INCART

Paul Bowles - The Complete outsider 57 MIN
16mm / VHS
Color (G)
$895.00, $390.00 purchase, $125.00 rental
Presents a documentary about the masterful writer and composer, Paul Bowles. Looks at his career as author of 20 books and gifted composer. Interviews the reclusive Bowles, now in his 80s, from his Tangier, Morocco home of 40 years. Also includes interviews with Allen Ginsberg and Ned Rorem. Produced by Catherine Warnow and Regina Weinreich.
Fine Arts; Literature and Drama
Dist - FIRS

Paul Bunyan 11 MIN
U-matic / VHS / 16mm
American Folklore Series
Color (I J)
LC 75-709811
Tells the legend of Paul Bunyan through the use of artwork and music.
Literature and Drama
Dist - PHENIX **Prod** - HRAW 1970

Paul Bunyan 17 MIN
U-matic / VHS / 16mm
Color (I J)
LC 76-714977
Presents the legend of larger - than - life Paul Bunyan and his partner, Babe, an ox, as they cut a wide swath through the woods from Maine to the West.
Literature and Drama
Dist - CORF **Prod** - DISNEY 1970

Paul Bunyan 15 MIN
VHS / 16mm
Stories and Poems from Long Ago Series
Color (I)
Uses character of retired sea captain to tell the story of Paul Bunyan. The first of 16 installments of the Stories And Poems From Long Ago Series, which is intended to encourage reading and writing by young viewers.
Literature and Drama
Dist - GPN **Prod** - CTI 1990

Paul Bunyan 30 MIN
U-matic / VHS
Reading Rainbow Series
Color (P)
Tells of how legendary Paul Bunyan dug the Great Lakes, created the Grand Canyon and was the greatest logger who ever lived. Narrated by Buddy Ebsen and illustrated by Steven Kellogg, host LeVar Burton joins Smokey the Bear for a trip to Maine, legendary home of Paul Bunyan.
Agriculture; English Language; Literature and Drama
Dist - GPN **Prod** - WNEDTV

Paul Bunyan 30 MIN
VHS
Rabbit ears collection series
Color; CC (K P I J)
$12.95 purchase _ #199640
Features comedian Jonathan Winters as narrator of a story about Paul Bunyan and his blue ox, Babe.
Literature and Drama
Dist - KNOWUN **Prod** - RABBIT

Paul Bunyan and the Blue Ox 6 MIN
U-matic / VHS / 16mm
Color (P)
$170.00, $125.00 purchase _ #713
Tells the story of how Paul Bunyan found the Blue Ox and put him to work.
English Language; Literature and Drama
Dist - CORF **Prod** - CORF 1952

Paul Bunyan - Lumber Camp Tales 11 MIN
U-matic / VHS / 16mm
Color (P I)
$270.00, $190.00 purchase _ #1398
Recounts some of the most famous tall tales of the American folk - hero, Paul Bunyan, such as the bunkhouse beds stacked 137 feet high, the gigantic flapjack riddle, the popcorn blizzard and the straightening of the Big Onion River.
Literature and Drama
Dist - CORF **Prod** - CORF 1962

Paul Cadmus - Enfant Terrible 64 MIN
16mm / VHS / U-matic
Color (A)
Presents a film portrait of WPA painter Paul Cadmus, in which the artist is both host and subject and in which Cadmus, now eighty, draws from the nude, demonstrates his mastery of ancient painting techniques and recounts his past as a prominent American scene painter and controversial social satirist. Produced by David Sutherland.
Fine Arts
Dist - STHLND **Prod** - STHLND

Paul Cadwell, Mississippi John Hurt 52 MIN
U-matic / VHS
Rainbow quest series
Color
Presents Paul Cadwell playing several banjo solos including a cakewalk. Features Mississippi John Hurt, a singer who faded from public view and was rediscovered in his eighties and began a whole new career.
Fine Arts
Dist - NORROS **Prod** - SEEGER

The Paul Carlson Story 53 MIN
16mm
Color
LC FIA66-515
Tells the story of Paul Carlson, a missionary who was slain in the Congo, November 24, 1964.
Religion and Philosophy
Dist - GF **Prod** - ECCA

Paul Cezanne 29 MIN
U-matic
Meet the Masters Series
B&W
Illustrates Cezanne's geometric techniques that led to analytical cubism and earned him the title Father of Modern Art.
Fine Arts
Dist - UMITV **Prod** - UMITV 1966

Paul Cezanne - the man and the mountain 58 MIN
VHS
Color (H C A)
$39.95 purchase _ #CEZ-01
Focuses on the use of a single image - Mont St Victoire in Provence - by artist Paul Cezanne to define form, color and light. Focuses on the artist at the age of 67, when he was at odds with both peers and critics, and traces his career to his final recognition as the 'father of modern painting.'.
Fine Arts
Dist - ARTSAM **Prod** - RMART 1986
FI
UILL

Paul Delvaux Dans Son Atelier 8 MIN
16mm / U-matic / VHS
Color (FRENCH)
A French language videocassette. Features the painter Paul Delvaux explaining his view of sketches as related to a painting. Comments on the objects he uses in his paintings and tells how these objects are related to his own childhood and memories.
Fine Arts; Foreign Language
Dist - IFB **Prod** - STORCH 1978

Paul Delvaux in His Studio 8 MIN
U-matic / VHS / 16mm
Color (FRENCH)
LC 80-700663
Shows surrealist painter Paul Delvaux at work while he explains his views on art.
Fine Arts
Dist - IFB **Prod** - STORCH 1978

Paul Draper 52 MIN
U-matic / VHS
Rainbow quest series
Color
Features dancer Paul Draper improvising to music played by accompanist Coleridge Perkinson and to several songs and rhythms played by Pete Seeger.
Fine Arts
Dist - NORROS **Prod** - SEEGER

Paul Ehrlich's Earth watch 18 MIN
VHS
Color (I J H C)
$149.00 purchase _ #CG - 899 - VS
Features Paul Ehrlich who takes students on a tour of planet Earth and surveys three of its biggest environmental problems - the exploding population bomb, the extinction of tens of thousands of species and global warming. Discusses possible solution - cutting consumption of fossil

fuels by 50 percent, cessation of tropical forest burning, massive tree planting and getting the nations of the world to quickly work together and act immediately to save the environment.
Science - Natural; Science - Physical; Sociology
Dist - HRMC **Prod** - HRMC

Paul Ehrlich's Earth watch 18 MIN
VHS
Color (I J H)
$150.00 purchase _ #A5VH 1365
Features author and Stanford University biology professor Paul Ehrlich who hosts a tour of planet Earth. Examines three of the biggest environmental challenges - species extinction, the human population boom and global warming. Discusses solutions.
Science - Natural; Sociology
Dist - CLRVUE **Prod** - CLRVUE

Paul Ehrlich's energy watch 18 MIN
VHS
Color (I J H)
$150.00 purchase _ #A5VH 1387
Takes a look at the enormous problem of burning fossil fuels and the resulting damage to the Earth's ecosytem and atmosphere. Features biologist Paul Ehrlich who examines current plans to reverse the problem, including higher energy efficiency, alternative fuels, higher energy prices and other innovations.
Science - Natural
Dist - CLRVUE **Prod** - CLRVUE 1992

Paul Ehrlich's energy watch 18 MIN
VHS
Color (I J H C)
$149.00 purchase _ #CG - 929 - VS
Features Paul Ehrlich, who takes a look at the enormous problem of the burning of fossil fuels and the resulting damage to the Earth's ecosystems and atmosphere. Points out that the world is now using 50 times more fossil fuels - oil, gas and coal - than it did 120 years ago. Look at current plans to reverse the problem, including higher energy efficiency, alternative fuels, higher energy prices - especially for oil and gas - and new innovations.
Science - Natural; Science - Physical; Social Science
Dist - HRMC **Prod** - HRMC

Paul Emile Borduas 21 MIN
16mm
Color (G)
_ #106C 0163 010
Follows the life of the Canadian painter Borduas. Shows his progression from religious to surrealism, cubism and automatism.
Biography; Fine Arts
Dist - CFLMDC **Prod** - NFBC 1973

Paul Galdone's illustrated spooky stories series
Presents a four - part series featuring spooky stories by Paul Galdone on a single videocassette. Includes The Tailypo; The Monster and the Tailor; The Teeny - Tiny Woman; and The Greedy Old Fat Man.
The Greedy old fat man
The Monster and the tailor 11 MIN
The Tailypo 12 MIN
The Teeny - tiny woman
Dist - KNOWUN

Paul Gauguin - the savage dream 45 MIN
VHS / U-matic
Color (H C A)
$39.95 purchase _ #GAU-01
Examines the search by Paul Gauguin for a primitive, 'savage' alternative to his own culture in which to paint, which led him to one of the most remote islands in the world. Focuses on the artist's final years and his paintings of that period, with views of Tahiti and the Marquesas.
Fine Arts
Dist - ARTSAM FI **Prod** - NATLGL

Paul Hodge 30 MIN
U-matic / VHS
Play Bridge with the Experts Series
Color (A)
Presents bridge master Paul Hodge discussing bidding, dummy play and defensive problems.
Physical Education and Recreation
Dist - GPN **Prod** - KUHTTV 1980

Paul Hornung 20 MIN
16mm
Sports Legends Series
Color (I J)
Interviews Paul Hornung. Presents some action - filled segments of Paul's career at Notre Dame and with the champion Green Bay Packers. Discusses the difficulties and pleasures of being a recognizable athlete and sports commentator.
Biography; Physical Education and Recreation
Dist - COUNFI **Prod** - COUNFI

Paul J Flory 40 MIN
VHS / U-matic
Eminent Chemists - the Interviews Series
Color
Reviews the experiences of Dr Paul J Flory in polymer research and his perspectives on research gained from his industrial experiences.
Science; Science - Physical
Dist - AMCHEM **Prod** - AMCHEM 1982

Paul Jacobs and the Nuclear Gang 58 MIN
U-matic / VHS / 16mm
Color (GERMAN)
LC 80-700438
Tells how reporter Paul Jacobs began investigating the health effects of exposure to low - level radiation on soldiers and civilians present at the atomic bomb tests in Nevada.
Health and Safety; Social Science; Sociology
Dist - NEWTIM **Prod** - CNDOC 1979

Paul Jacobs and the Nuclear Gang, Pt 1 29 MIN
U-matic / VHS / 16mm
Color (GERMAN)
LC 80-700438
Tells how reporter Paul Jacobs began investigating the health effects of exposure to low - level radiation on soldiers and civilians present at the atomic bomb tests in Nevada.
Sociology
Dist - NEWTIM **Prod** - CNDOC 1979

Paul Jacobs and the Nuclear Gang, Pt 2 29 MIN
16mm / U-matic / VHS
Color (GERMAN)
LC 80-700438
Tells how reporter Paul Jacobs began investigating the health effects of exposure to low - level radiation on soldiers and civilians present at the atomic bomb tests in Nevada.
Sociology
Dist - NEWTIM **Prod** - CNDOC 1979

Paul Kane Goes West 16 MIN
U-matic / VHS / 16mm
Color (I J H)
LC 74-701891
Follows 19th century Canadian artist Paul Kane as he creates visual impressions of the Indian life and customs of the North American continent.
Biography; Fine Arts; Social Science
Dist - EBEC **Prod** - NFBC 1974

Paul Klee 29 MIN
U-matic
Meet the Masters Series
B&W
Shows how Paul Klee's ideas have been copied by commercial artists and discusses his unique use of line, light and humor. Explores his contribution to the modern art world.
Fine Arts
Dist - UMITV **Prod** - UMITV 1966

Paul Klee - Child of Creation 8 MIN
16mm / U-matic / VHS
Color (P I J H)
LC 70-712930
Presents an introduction to Paul Klee. Points out the message which Paul Klee conveys to the student of the arts of any age - - having the courage to be simple. Includes quotations of Paul Klee, candid commentary by children and contrasts the works of the artist with those of the children.
Fine Arts
Dist - PHENIX **Prod** - KINGSP 1970

Paul Klee or the Act of Creation 1879 - 1940 25 MIN
16mm
Color
Examines the representative works of the artist Paul Klee which illustrate the general theme of creation of forms.
Fine Arts
Dist - RADIM **Prod** - FILIM

Paul Kos - Battle Mountain 24 MIN
U-matic / VHS
B&W
Blurs fact and fiction.
Fine Arts
Dist - ARTINC **Prod** - ARTINC

Paul Kos - Deposit 6 MIN
U-matic / VHS
Color
Features Marlene Kos.
Fine Arts
Dist - ARTINC **Prod** - ARTINC

Paul Kos - Search Olga - Gold 19 MIN
VHS / U-matic
B&W
Transforms `Olga' into `gold,' repeating the fact - fiction of Olga's disappearance.
Fine Arts
Dist - ARTINC **Prod** - ARTINC

Paul Laurence Dunbar 22 MIN
16mm / U-matic / VHS
Color (J)
LC 73-702351
Presents a visit to the home of America's first black poet, Paul Laurence Dunbar. Portrays his childhood as one of the first generation of blacks to be born free in the U S. Includes close - ups of first editions, a pen, spectacles and a ride in the elevator in which he first worked.
Biography; History - United States; Literature and Drama
Dist - PFP **Prod** - PFP 1973

Paul Laurence Dunbar - American Poet 14 MIN
U-matic / VHS / 16mm
Color (A)
LC FIA66-1330
Portrays the life of American poet Paul Dunbar, a Negro whose poems reflect pride in his race and heritage. Relates his struggles from age 13, when his father, an escaped slave who fought in the Civil War, died, to his time of world - wide fame.
Biography; History - United States; Literature and Drama
Dist - PHENIX **Prod** - VIGNET 1966

Paul MacCready - Doing more with Less 26 MIN
U-matic / VHS
Color (C)
$249.00, $149.00 purchase _ #AD - 2138
Shows the flip side of razzle - dazzle technological glitz. Portrays Paul MacCready, inventor, engineer, entrepreneur and philosopher, who shows that one alternative to money in research is thinking.
Business and Economics; Psychology; Science
Dist - FOTH **Prod** - FOTH

Paul Masson 12 MIN
16mm
Color
LC 76-703151
Shows the winemaking process at the Paul Masson vineyards in California. Touches on the life of Paul Masson, who brought the winemaking tradition to America over 100 years ago.
Agriculture
Dist - FURMAN **Prod** - FURMAN 1976

Paul Newman - Actor in a Hurry 26 MIN
16mm
Hollywood and the Stars Series
B&W
LC FI68-216
Describes the personality and the acting career of Paul Newman. Includes scenes from some of his films.
Fine Arts
Dist - WOLPER **Prod** - WOLPER 1964

Paul R Ehrlich, Biology 29 MIN
U-matic / VHS
Quest for Peace Series
Color (A)
Science
Dist - AACD **Prod** - AACD 1984

Paul Revere 30 MIN
16mm / U-matic / VHS
Mr Magoo in Great World Classic Series
Color
Magoo as the renowned silversmith who gained eternal fame by his midnight ride at the start of the American Revolution, to warn Lexington of the arrival of British troops.
Biography; History - United States; Literature and Drama
Dist - FI **Prod** - FLEET 1965

Paul Revere 24 MIN
U-matic / VHS / 16mm
Famous Adventures of Mr Magoo Series
Color (P I J)
LC 79-701871
Presents an animated reconstruction of the life of Paul Revere with Mr Magoo in the role of the American patriot.
Fine Arts
Dist - MCFI **Prod** - UPAPOA 1976

Paul Revere - the messenger of liberty 24 MIN
VHS
American lifestyle series; The Singular American
Color (I J H C A)
$70.00 purchase, $50.00 rental _ #9894
Profiles Paul Revere, famous for his ride to alert American colonists of advancing British troops. Shows that Revere did more for the cause of American independence. Hosted and narrated by Cliff Robertson.
Biography
Dist - AIMS **Prod** - COMCO 1986

Paul Revere's Ride 11 MIN
16mm
B&W (I)
The story of Paul Revere's famous ride is told with sketches by Bernard Garbutt, and narration which includes the vocabulary of colonial New England.
History - United States
Dist - MLA **Prod** - JHP 1955

Paul Revere's Ride 15 MIN
16mm / U-matic / VHS
Magic Carpet Series
Color (P)
Describes the ride of Paul Revere.
Literature and Drama
Dist - GPN **Prod** - SDCSS

Paul Revere's Ride 22 MIN
U-matic / VHS / 16mm
You are There Series
Color (I J H)
LC 71-714894
Simulates on - the - spot interviews by CBS correspondents with Patriot and Tory leaders that reveal the conflicts and immediate events leading to the American Revolution. Discusses the role of Paul Revere and his ride to warn the Patriots of the arrival of the British soldiers.
Biography; History - United States
Dist - PHENIX **Prod** - CBSTV 1971

Paul Robeson 19 MIN
35mm strip / VHS
Notable black Americans series
Color (J H C T A)
$45.00 purchase _ #MB - 909838 - X, #MB - 539735 - 8
Presents a biographical sketch of Paul Robeson, the black singer and actor who was controversial for his political beliefs. Includes archival photographs and original illustrations.
Biography; Fine Arts; History - United States
Dist - SRA

Paul Robeson 29 MIN
VHS
Color (J H G)
$195.00 purchase
Relates events in the singer and actor's life as he used his world - wide recognition to focus attention on racial injustices in America of the 1930s, '40s and '50s. Shows footage of him and his career, with an analysis of his impact on the times.
Civics and Political Systems; History - United States
Dist - LANDMK

Paul Robeson - the Tallest Tree in Our Forest 90 MIN
U-matic / VHS / 16mm
Color (H C A)
Features the contributions of Paul Robeson, scholar, actor, singer and humanitarian. Includes footage on Mr Robeson's career gathered from the Paul Robeson archives and other sources throughout the world.
Fine Arts; Sociology
Dist - PHENIX **Prod** - NOBLEG

Paul Robeson - tribute to an artist 101 MIN
VHS
Color; B&W (G)
$49.95 purchase _ #S02171
Presents a biographical sketch of African - American actor Paul Robeson. Notes Robeson's accomplishments not just as an actor, but as an athlete, scholar, attorney, and human rights activist as well. Includes the complete text of Robeson's film 'The Emperor.'
Biography; Fine Arts
Dist - UILL

Paul Robeson - Tribute to an Artist 29 MIN
U-matic / VHS / 16mm
Color
LC 80-701452
Presents a biography of black singer Paul Robeson.
Biography; History - United States
Dist - FI **Prod** - JANUS 1979

Paul Runyan's - Short Way to Lower Scoring, Volume 1
VHS
(J H C A)
$29.95 purchase _ #DG002V
Discusses ways to improve scoring in golf.
Physical Education and Recreation
Dist - CAMV

Paul Runyan's Short Way to Lowering Scoring, Volume 2
VHS
(J H C A)
$29.95 purchase _ #DG003V
Discusses ways to improve scoring in golf.
Physical Education and Recreation
Dist - CAMV

Paul Sherman - 11 - 1 - 78
VHS / Cassette
Poetry Center reading series
Color (G)
$15.00, $45.00 purchase, $15.00 rental _ #372 - 309
Features the poet Paul Sherman at the Charles Olson Conference at the University of Iowa. Includes readings, talks and lectures. Co - readers are George Butterick, Edward Dorn, Robert Creeley and Robert Duncan. Available for listening purposes only at the Center; not for sale or rent.
Literature and Drama
Dist - POETRY **Prod** - POETRY 1978

Paul Signac and Saint - Tropez 1892 - 1913 26 MIN
VHS
Color; PAL (G)
PdS50 purchase
Traces impressionist painter Paul Seurat's passions for boating and art during his years on the Riviera. Features a Charles de l'Artique, France, production.
Fine Arts
Dist - BALFOR

Paul Simon's concert in the park
CD / VHS / Cassette
Color (G)
$9.98, $16.98, $8.98 purchase _ #8211, #D2324, #2324
Records the August 15, 1991, Central Park concert of Paul Simon. Offers nineties arrangements of older songs with backup by African and Brazilian musicians.
Fine Arts
Dist - MULIPE **Prod** - MULIPE

Paul Taylor 60 MIN
U-matic / VHS
Dance in America Series
Color (H C A)
Presents the Paul Taylor Dance Company performing Esplanade, set to the music of Bach's E Major and D Minor Violin Concertos and Runes, a Druidic - inspired dance of mystery and imagination.
Fine Arts
Dist - FI **Prod** - WNETTV

Paul Taylor and Company - an Artist and His Work 32 MIN
U-matic / VHS / 16mm
Color
LC 75-700816
Documents the Paul Taylor modern dance company.
Fine Arts
Dist - PFP **Prod** - HARCOM 1968

Paul, the Christian missionary 30 MIN
VHS
Introduction to St Paul series
Color (R G)
$39.95 purchase _ #INSP2
Examines the role of St Paul in the formation of the early Church. Features Father Eugene LaVerdiere, SSS, as instructor. Part two of four parts.
Literature and Drama; Religion and Philosophy
Dist - CTNA **Prod** - CTNA 1994

Paul Tillich 30 MIN
16mm
Sum and Substance Series
B&W (H C A)
LC FIA67-5104
Presents Paul Tillich, Protestant theologian and authority on religious philosophy, explaining his concept of Ultimate Concern, or concern about the meaning of one's life. Develops his distinction between faith and belief.
Religion and Philosophy
Dist - MLA **Prod** - USC 1964

Paul Tomkowicz, Street - Railway Switchman 10 MIN
16mm
B&W (H C A)
LC FIA54-258
Presents a Polish - born Canadian in the streets of Winnipeg as he sweeps the tracks of mud and snow. Talks about his work and the retirement he is looking forward to after 23 years on the job.
Social Science
Dist - NFBC **Prod** - NFBC 1953

Paul Winter - Music 15 MIN
VHS / U-matic
Pass it Along Series
Color (I)
$130.00 purchase, $25.00 rental, $75.00 self dub
Visits Paul Winter in Mineapolis and St. Paul as the contemporary composer and performer shares his interest in animals and music inspired by animals with young people at museum and zoo. Shows students his understanding of how all animals including man make joyful sounds.
Fine Arts; Science - Natural
Dist - GPN **Prod** - SCITV

Paula Gunn Allen - 3 - 21 - 85 28 MIN
VHS / Cassette
Poetry Center reading series
Color (G)
$15.00, $45.00 purchase _ #626 - 528
Features the Native American poet, Paula Gunn Allen reading selections from Shadow Country; Skins and Bones; and A Cannon Between My Knees at the Poetry Center, San Francisco State University, with an introduction by Frances Phillips.
Literature and Drama; Social Science
Dist - POETRY **Prod** - POETRY 1985

Paula Gunn Allen - 2 - 26 - 87 67 MIN
VHS / Cassette
Poetry Center reading series
Color (G)
$15.00, $45.00 purchase _ #738 - 591
Features an interview by Mark Linenthal with Native American poet Paula Gunn Allen and the poet reading her works, including a series of short poems, Runes, at the Poetry Center, San Francisco State University, with an introduction by Frances Phillips.
Guidance and Counseling; Literature and Drama; Social Science
Dist - POETRY **Prod** - POETRY 1987

Paula Modersohn - Becker (1876 - 1907) 15 MIN
16mm
Color
Presents the work of Paula Modersohn - Becker who spent much of her life painting the black canals, brown fields and crisp fir trees of her native North Germany.
Fine Arts
Dist - ROLAND **Prod** - ROLAND

Paule Paulaender 100 MIN
16mm
Color (GERMAN (ENGLISH SUBTITLES))
Tells the story of a 15 - year - old who, through his friendship with a girl from a reform school in the nearby city, becomes more and more aware of the injustice imposed upon him by his authoritarian father.
Foreign Language; Sociology
Dist - WSTGLC **Prod** - WSTGLC 1976

Pauline 22 MIN
16mm
B&W (G)
$40.00 rental
Explores the friendship of two artists, obliquely, through the exploration of a house, a garden and a painting. Uses the qualities of light and time to heighten the properties simple acts and objects may take on when mediated by these two elements. Delves into an artist's process and her relation to the world.
Fine Arts; Psychology
Dist - CANCIN **Prod** - COUZS 1985

Pauline Kael 30 MIN
VHS
Writer's workshop series
Color (G)
$59.95 purchase _ #WRWO - 104
Features film critic Pauline Kael in a lecture and discussion at the University of South Carolina. Discusses her views on criticism, trends in American movies, screenwriting and the importance of reading for all writers.
Literature and Drama
Dist - PBS **Prod** - SCETVM 1987

Pauline Kael 15 MIN
VHS
Writer's workshop series
Color (C A T)
$69.95 purchase, $45.00 rental
Features film critic Pauline Kael in a lecture and discussion of her work, held as part of a writing workshop series at the University of South Carolina. Hosted by author William Price Fox and introduced by George Plimpton. Part four of a 15 - part telecourse.
English Language; Literature and Drama
Dist - SCETV **Prod** - SCETV 1982

Pauline - Water - Cracker 5 MIN
16mm
Color
LC 77-702605
Uses experimental techniques to show a phone ringing, a woman standing naked in a hallway and a whistling kettle on a stove.
Fine Arts
Dist - CANFDC **Prod** - LOCKK 1976

Paul's adventures 25 MIN
VHS
Greatest stories ever told series
Color (K P I R)
$19.95 purchase, $10.00 rental _ #35 - 81 - 2020
Uses an animated format to present the life of the Apostle Paul.

Literature and Drama; Religion and Philosophy
Dist - APH **Prod** - ANDERK

Paul's Case 55 MIN
16mm / U-matic / VHS
American Short Story Series
Color (J H C)
LC 80-700091
Presents an adaptation of Willa Cather's short story Paul's Case about a romantic young man who drops out of high school in turn - of - the - century Pittsburgh and journeys to New York City.
Fine Arts; Literature and Drama
Dist - CORF **Prod** - LEARIF 1980
CDTEL

Paul's case 55 MIN
VHS
American short story collection series
Color (J H)
$49.00 purchase _ #05957 - 126
Tells of a sensitive young man's desire for a sophisticated and glamorous life which leads to a tragic ending. Written by Willa Cather.
History - United States; Literature and Drama
Dist - GA **Prod** - GA

Paul's ministry and trials - Program 13 20 MIN
VHS
Children's heroes of the Bible series
Color (K P I R)
$14.95 purchase _ #35 - 864 - 8516
Uses an animated format to tell the story of the Apostle Paul's ministry and the trials he faced in attempting to spread the Christian message.
Literature and Drama; Religion and Philosophy
Dist - APH **Prod** - VISVID

Pauper's dream - a tribute to the Montana hard rock miner 58 MIN
VHS
Color (G)
$18.00 purchase _ #1903
Traces the history of immigrant miners in the hard rock state of Montana.
History - United States; Social Science
Dist - MTHISO

Pause 7 MIN
16mm
B&W
LC 76-703851
Presents a fable - documentary on street people.
Fine Arts
Dist - SFRASU **Prod** - SFRASU 1976

Pause 12 MIN
16mm
Color (G)
$40.00 rental
Presents a Peter Kubelka production.
Fine Arts
Dist - CANCIN

Pavarotti at Juilliard 168 MIN
U-matic / VHS / 16mm
Color (J)
Presents famed master of operatic repertory, Luciano Pavarotti as he shares his expertise with a group of talented young singers at the Juilliard School in New York.
Fine Arts
Dist - PHENIX **Prod** - KROLL 1980

Pavarotti at Juilliard 28 MIN
16mm
Color
LC 80-700439
Shows operatic tenor Luciano Pavarotti working in a class at Juilliard School with a group of gifted young singers, sharing his musical expertise in a critique and demonstration of Italian operatic arias.
Fine Arts
Dist - KROLL **Prod** - KROLL 1980

Pavarotti at Juilliard - opera master class 60 MIN
VHS
Color; Dolby stereo (G)
$29.95 purchase _ #1265
Features Luciano Pavarotti who coaches young singers at the Juilliard School of Music. Uses arias by Mozart, Puccini and Verdi. Includes Pavarotti singing the aria, 'Per la gloria' from Griselda by Buononcini.
Fine Arts
Dist - KULTUR **Prod** - KULTUR 1990

Pavarotti at Juilliard, Pt 1 30 MIN
16mm / U-matic / VHS
Color
LC 80-700439
Shows Luciano Pavarotti, the world's leading operatic tenor, working in a class situation at the Juilliard School with a group of gifted young singers, sharing his musical expertise in a critique and demonstration of Italian operatic arias and responding to questions from the audience.
Fine Arts
Dist - PHENIX **Prod** - KROLL 1980

Pavarotti at Juilliard, Pt 2 30 MIN
16mm / U-matic / VHS
Color
LC 80-700439
Shows Luciano Pavarotti, the world's leading operatic tenor, working in a class situation at the Juilliard School with a group of gifted young singers, sharing his musical expertise in a critique and demonstration of Italian operatic arias and responding to questions from the audience.
Fine Arts
Dist - PHENIX **Prod** - KROLL 1980

Pavarotti at Juilliard, Pt 3 30 MIN
U-matic / VHS / 16mm
Color
LC 80-700439
Shows Luciano Pavarotti, the world's leading operatic tenor, working in a class situation at the Juilliard School with a group of gifted young singers, sharing his musical expertise in a critique and demonstration of Italian operatic arias and responding to questions from the audience.
Fine Arts
Dist - PHENIX **Prod** - KROLL 1980

Pavarotti at Juilliard, Pt 4 30 MIN
U-matic / VHS / 16mm
Color
LC 80-700439
Shows Luciano Pavarotti, the world's leading operatic tenor, working in a class situation at the Juilliard School with a group of gifted young singers, sharing his musical expertise in a critique and demonstration of Italian operatic arias and responding to questions from the audience.
Fine Arts
Dist - PHENIX **Prod** - KROLL 1980

Pavarotti at Juilliard, Pt 5 30 MIN
16mm / U-matic / VHS
Color
LC 80-700439
Shows Luciano Pavarotti, the world's leading operatic tenor, working in a class situation at the Juilliard School with a group of gifted young singers, sharing his musical expertise in a critique and demonstration of Italian operatic arias and responding to questions from the audience.
Fine Arts
Dist - PHENIX **Prod** - KROLL 1980

Pavarotti at Juilliard, Pt 6 30 MIN
16mm / U-matic / VHS
Color
LC 80-700439
Shows Luciano Pavarotti, the world's leading operatic tenor, working in a class situation at the Juilliard School with a group of gifted young singers, sharing his musical expertise in a critique and demonstration of Italian operatic arias and responding to questions from the audience.
Fine Arts
Dist - PHENIX **Prod** - KROLL 1980

Pavarotti in Concert in China
VHS
Color (G)
$29.95 purchase _ #1262
Presents Luciano Pavarotti in recital in Beijing, China, during his 1986 tour. Features areas from Verdi and Puccini.
Fine Arts; Foreign Language; Geography - World; History - World
Dist - KULTUR

Pavarotti in confidence - with Peter Ustinov 50 MIN
VHS
Color (G)
$19.95 purchase_#1406
Explores the ideas, feelings, opinions and memories of Pavarotti in a warm encounter with Peter Ustinov. Centers around music, including excerpts from Pavarotti's diverse repertoire - from folk songs to the greatest romantic arias.
Fine Arts
Dist - KULTUR

Pavement 9 MIN
U-matic / VHS / 16mm
Color (A)
LC 72-700795
Describes, without narration, the characteristics, textures, patterns and use of pavement. Includes scenes of rain glistening on pavement, children rollerskating on it, pennies stuck in it and flowers growing through it.
Industrial and Technical Education; Science - Natural; Social Science
Dist - PHENIX **Prod** - GOLLIN 1972

Pavlov 6 MIN
16mm
B&W (G)
$25.00 rental
No description provided.
Fine Arts
Dist - CANCIN **Prod** - SCHLEM 1991
FLMKCO

Pavlov - the Conditioned Reflex 25 MIN
U-matic / VHS / 16mm
B&W (H C A)
LC 75-700101
English version of the Russian film Academician Pavlov. Depicts Ivan Pavlov in his Leningrad research center. Uses documentary footage to recreate the salivating dog experiment which led the physiologist to the concept of the conditioned reflex. Features Pavlov who speaks about the need for objectivity in scientific experimentation and the application of conditioned reflex methods to the problems of neurology and psychiatry.
Psychology; Science
Dist - FOTH **Prod** - MANTLH 1975

Pavlova - a Tribute to the Legendary Dancer 81 MIN
VHS
Color (G)
$29.95 purchase _ #1234
Documents a tribute to the prima ballerina Pavlova. Includes Bissell and Tcherkassky.
Biography; Fine Arts; Geography - World; Physical Education and Recreation
Dist - KULTUR

Pawkedee of the mighty 5 MIN
16mm
B&W (G)
$10.00 rental
Tells the story of a mysterious child prodigy and his piano teacher who simultaneously become infatuated and annoyed with each other.
Fine Arts; Psychology
Dist - CANCIN **Prod** - WHITED 1984

The Pawnbroker
VHS / U-matic
Contemporary Literature Series
(G C J)
$79 purchase _ #05920 - 85
Documents the life of a concentration camp survivor who runs a ghetto pawnshop. Stars Rod Steiger.
Fine Arts; Literature and Drama
Dist - CHUMAN

The Pawnbroker 100 MIN
VHS
B&W (H C)
$39.00 purchase _ #05920 - 126
Stars Rod Steiger in a story of a concentration camp survivor who runs a ghetto pawnshop.
Fine Arts; Literature and Drama
Dist - GA **Prod** - GA

Pawnee - Men of Men 30 MIN
16mm
Great Plains Trilogy, 2 Series Nomad and Indians - Early Man on the 'Plains; Nomad and Indians - early man on the plains
B&W (H C A)
Tells the story of the oldest of Nebraska tribes, the Pawnee, friend of the white man and his scout against hostile Indians. Describes how the Pawnees lived, hunted and farmed.
Social Science; Sociology
Dist - UNEBR **Prod** - UNL 1954

Pawnee Pronghorn 15 MIN
16mm
Color
LC 74-702682
Discusses the research conducted on pronghorn antelope as a component of the grassland ecosystem studies. Shows how the pronghorn were captured and studied and discusses various aspects of the study and some of the findings.
Geography - United States; Science; Science - Natural
Dist - OPCOMM **Prod** - NREL 1974

The Pawnshop 30 MIN
16mm / U-matic / VHS
Charlie Chaplin Comedy Theater Series
B&W (I)
LC 75-711885
Features Charlie Chaplin as a combination janitor and clerk in a pawnshop. Shows how Charlie becomes involved in a comic rivalry with another clerk over his girl friend, the daughter of the shop owner. Describes how, in the resulting confusion, Charlie becomes the hero in an attempted robbery.
Fine Arts
Dist - FI **Prod** - MUFLM 1916

Paws, claws, feathers and fins
VHS
Color (K P I PRO A)
$14.95 purchase
Helps families decide which pet to get and presents the joys and responsibilities of living with an animal day to day, including facing the death of a pet. Emphasizes the lasting influence pets have on children. Developed in consultation with experts from the American Veterinary Medical Association, ASPCA and the American Humane Association. Includes activity guides for follow - up to viewing. Designed for home use as well as for use by professionals working with children and families.
Science - Natural
Dist - KVIDZ **Prod** - KVIDZ 1993

Pax Romana 28 MIN
U-matic / VHS
Once upon a Time - Man Series
Color (P I)
MV=$99.00
Portrays daily life in the time of the transformation of the Roman Republic to Empire under Julius Caesar.
History - World
Dist - LANDMK **Prod** - LANDMK 1981

Pay as You Go - Social Security 20 MIN
U-matic
Dollar Data Series
Color (J H)
LC 81-707385
Gives a brief history of the Social Security Act to show why social security is compulsory.
Business and Economics; Sociology
Dist - GPN **Prod** - WHROTV 1974

Pay Attention - Problems of Hard of Hearing Children 29 MIN
16mm
Studies of Normal Personality Development Series
B&W (C T)
Shows the problems of the child who is hard of hearing but not deaf and tells how parents and teachers help. Stresses understanding the problem, early treatment, and use of 'CONTEXT' methods of speech reading.
Education; Psychology; Sociology
Dist - NYU **Prod** - NYU 1949

Pay attention to details 29 MIN
VHS
Fitness for life series
Color (G)
$170.00 purchase, $17.50 rental _ #35450
Stresses that fitness programs are often curtailed because of exercise - related injuries. Presents methods for prevention, first aid and rehabilitation. Part of a six - part series.
Health and Safety; Physical Education and Recreation
Dist - PSU **Prod** - WPSXTV 1988

Pay Day 30 MIN
VHS
Soapbox With Tom Cottle Series
Color (G)
$59.95 purchase _ #SBOX - 512
Interviews teenagers who have after - school jobs. Discusses whether jobs can interfere with academic pursuits. Hosted by psychologist Tom Cottle.
Business and Economics; Guidance and Counseling; Mathematics; Psychology
Dist - PBS **Prod** - WGBYTV 1985

Pay Equity 28 MIN
U-matic
Color (A)
Highlights the fight of a University of Maryland librarian who leads a group of clerical workers in equalizing their salaries with those of male workers in comparable jobs. Followed by a discussion.
Business and Economics; Sociology
Dist - AFLCIO **Prod** - LIPA 1984

Pay for the Home Team - 108 30 MIN
U-matic
Currents - 1984 - 85 Season Series
Color (A)
Takes a look at the whole field of professional sports and the effect on society and the individual.
Physical Education and Recreation; Social Science
Dist - PBS **Prod** - WNETTV 1985

The Pay - Off 27 MIN
U-matic / VHS
Speed Learning Series
Color (J H)
Reveals a reading pattern which can be applied to any type of reading.
English Language
Dist - AITECH **Prod** - LEARNI 1982

The Pay - Off 30 MIN
VHS / U-matic
Speed Learning Video Series Show 9
Color
Demonstrates the combination of all seven skills needed in reading. Presents a complete review of reading skills presented in the eight preceding programs.
Education; English Language; Literature and Drama; Psychology
Dist - LEARNI **Prod** - LEARNI

Pay or Die 111 MIN
16mm
B&W (C A)
Presents a drama based on the chilling, factual incidents in the life of a New York detective who has uncovered the roots of the Mafia of 1908. Shows that he risks everything he holds dear in his relentless pursuit of the vicious brotherhood who prey on their fellow Italians.
Fine Arts; Sociology
Dist - CINEWO **Prod** - CINEWO 1960

Paycheck Power 16 MIN
16mm / U-matic / VHS
Color (J)
Defines Paycheck Power as the ability to control your money in a precise, controlled manner, thus establishing the basis for a successful and secure life. Details a step - by - step approach to building paycheck power from an understanding of the use of money, to constructing budgets, to avoiding credit traps, to preparing for the future, as well as providing a whole new series of tips on how to spend wisely and enhance income.
Home Economics
Dist - JOU **Prod** - JOU 1981

The Paycheck Puzzle
VHS / 35mm strip
$119.00 purchase _ #IE6673 filmstrip, $159.00 purchase _ #IE6673V
Discusses the most common paycheck deductions and some types of employee benefits.
Business and Economics
Dist - CAREER **Prod** - CAREER

The Paycheck puzzle 20 MIN
VHS
Color (H)
$159.00 purchase _ #06673 - 126
Uses humor to explain the most common paycheck deductions, as well as some typical employee benefits. Looks at the difference between voluntary and involuntary deductions such as disability insurance and FICA - Social Security. Covers voluntary deductions for group health and life insurance. Discusses how federal withholding tax is related to the number of dependents an employee has. Shows the kind of benefits young workers can expect to receive, paid vacation time, workman's compensation, state employment insurance and company pensions.
Business and Economics; Guidance and Counseling
Dist - GA **Prod** - GA

Payday 19 MIN
16mm
Color
LC 80-701482
Describes the computerized payroll system. Follows payroll through Chemical Bank's processing cycles, showing typical clients at critical points for testimonials.
Business and Economics; Mathematics
Dist - CHMBNK **Prod** - CHMBNK 1979

Payday 18 MIN
VHS / U-matic / 16mm
Color (I J H)
$295.00, $345.00, $395.00 purchase, $45.00 rental
Dramatizes the importance of school bus safety. Builds in intensity, with a surprise ending that reinforces the need to observe safety rules and respect the school bus driver.
Education; Health and Safety
Dist - NDIM **Prod** - HOWET 1985

Paying attention - 45 9 MIN
U-matic / VHS
Life's little lessons - self - esteem 4 - 6 series
Color (I)
$129.00, $99.00 purchase _ #V674
Portrays Ludwick Wilmsey, a very absent - minded hairdresser. Reveals that many of his unfortunate customers came in with full heads of hair and left bald because of Wilmsey's mind was never on his work. Shows how Wilmsey learned to pay attention to the present. Part of a 65 - part series on self - esteem.
Guidance and Counseling; Psychology
Dist - BARR **Prod** - CEPRO 1992

Paying for college - myths and mistakes of financial aid 25 MIN
VHS
Color (J H)
$98.00 purchase _ #CD6100V
Identifies the major traps students fall into when pursuing financial aid. Explores the eight most common problems students encounter when securing a financial aid package. Includes reproducible exercises.
Education
Dist - CAMV

Paying for College Series
Myths and Mistakes of Financial Aid
Types of Financial Aid
Dist - CADESF

Paying for college - types of financial aid 25 MIN
VHS
Color (J H)
$98.00 purchase _ #CD6200V
Covers the basics of financial aid. Looks at grants, scholarships, part - time employment, military assistance, loans, personal and family funds.
Education
Dist - CAMV

Paying for Programs 15 MIN
VHS / U-matic
Broadcasting Series
Color (J H)
Examines some of the decisions advertisers make when scheduling an advertisement on a broadcast station.
Business and Economics; Fine Arts; Industrial and Technical Education; Social Science; Sociology
Dist - CTI **Prod** - CTI

Paying the freight 60 MIN
VHS
Learning in America series
Color (G)
$49.95 purchase _ #LEIA - 105
Shows that while Americans generally agree that their schools need reform, there is little agreement on what should be done. Interviews President George Bush on the future of American learning. Hosted by Roger Mudd.
Education
Dist - PBS **Prod** - WETATV 1989

The Payment of Teresa Videla 11 MIN
16mm
Color; B&W (A)
$15.00 rental
Portrays an Argentine army officer who discovers the secret police use of political prisoners for sex exploitation film purposes and protests after the murder of a young girl. Utilizes a documentary film style. Produced by Niccolo Caldararo.
Fine Arts
Dist - CANCIN

The Payoff 26 MIN
U-matic / VHS
Art of Reading - Speed Learning Series
Color
English Language
Dist - DELTAK **Prod** - LEARNI

Payoff in the Pacific, Pt 1 30 MIN
16mm
Big Pictures Series
B&W
LC 74-705334
Surveys World War II from Pearl Harbor and the loss of the Philippines to the early victories in the South Pacific. Describes the B - 29 bases constructed on Saipan.
History - United States
Dist - USNAC **Prod** - USA 1960

Payoff in the Pacific, Pt 2 29 MIN
16mm
Big Pictures Series
B&W
LC 74-705335
Documents the war in the Pacific. Covers the island hopping victories of the Allies to the Japanese surrender aboard the battleship Missouri.
History - United States
Dist - USNAC **Prod** - USA 1960

PBL 2 1 MIN
16mm
Color (C)
Experimental film by Robert Breer.
Fine Arts
Dist - AFA **Prod** - AFA 1968

PC blue
CD-ROM
(G)
$99.00 purchase _ #1504
Contains 440 volumes of shareware from the New York Amateur Computer Club. Includes communications, DOS utilities, bulletin boards, math, science, education, and more. To search and retrieve programs, a text lister or word processor is needed. IBM and compatibles require at least 640K of RAM, DOS 3.1 or greater, one floppy disk drive - hard disk recommended, one empty expansion slot, and an IBM compatible CD - ROM drive.
Computer Science
Dist - BEP

PC - DOS for hard disks
Videodisc
(H A)
$2195.00
Explains the background of PC - DOS, loading DOS programs, accessing DOS with commands, and more advanced concepts to increase a user's ability to work with the computer. Requires basic knowledge of computer operation. Four to six hours.
Computer Science; Education
Dist - CMSL **Prod** - CMSL

PC DOS Hard Disks 240 - 360 MIN
Videodisc
(A PRO)
$1995.00
Introduces self paced course for IBM personal computer users. Orients to hard disk use. Covers fundamentals of PC DOS systems.
Computer Science
Dist - VIDEOT **Prod** - VIDEOT 1988

PC Hardware and Ladder Logic 23 MIN
VHS / 16mm
Programmable Controllers - PLC's Series
Color (H A)
$465.00 purchase, $110.00 rental
Demonstrates sorting operations transferred to PC management, input/output and OPC functions.
Computer Science; Industrial and Technical Education
Dist - TAT **Prod** - TAT 1984

PC Mentor 240 - 360 MIN
Videodisc
(A PRO)
$990.00 purchase
Introduces user to personal computers through guided video tour of PC and DOS.
Computer Science
Dist - VIDEOT **Prod** - VIDEOT 1988

PC - SIG library
CD-ROM
(G)
$295.00 purchase _ #1521
Contains the equivalent of 2485 floppy disks of PC software on one CD - ROM. Includes a variety of shareware and public domain software - word processors, spreadsheets, databases, educational, business and financial, telecommunications, programming languages, utilities, graphics, games, home applications, Windows, desktop publishing and networks. For IBM PCs and compatibles, requires 640K RAM, DOS 3.1 or later, one floppy disk drive - hard disk recommended, one empty expansion slot, and an IBM compatible CD - ROM drive.
Computer Science
Dist - BEP

PC video training for DOS series
Presents a four - part series which teaches students how to use DOS - Disk Operating System - without the confusion and frustration of a software training manual. Uses an interactive system which allows students to watch the video and practice at the same time at their computers. Shows how to upgrade to DOS 5. Includes DOS Introduction and Basics; DOS Intermediate; DOS Advanced and Upgrading to DOS 5.
DOS advanced 60 MIN
DOS intermediate 60 MIN
DOS introduction and basics 60 MIN
Upgrading to DOS 5 60 MIN
Dist - CAMV

PCA - patient controlled analgesia and the management of pain 20 MIN
VHS
Color (C PRO)
$285.00 purchase, $70.00 rental _ #4343S, #4343V
Discusses the safe, efficient use of PCA - patient controlled analgesia, components of the system, its benefits and contraindications. Shows how, using information from the PCA system, the nurse can analyze the adequacy of the prescribed medication regimen. Covers common drugs used for PCA and describes their benefits and side effects. Explores the nursing role in patient education, pain assessment, handling of drug side effects and contraindications for PAC usage. Outlines AHCPR guidelines.
Health and Safety
Dist - AJN **Prod** - AJN 1993

PCB Fabrication 150 MIN
U-matic
Electronics Manufacturing - Components, Assembly and Soldering Series
Color (IND)
Discusses printed circuit board (PCB) fabrication processes, single, double and multilayer boards, and quality control.
Business and Economics; Industrial and Technical Education
Dist - INTECS **Prod** - INTECS

PCBs in the Food Chain 18 MIN
VHS / 16mm
Fragile Planet Series
Color (J)
$139.00 purchase, $75.00 rental _ #OD - 2324
Documents how marine pollutants like PCBs moves through the food chain and tend to concentrate themselves in increasing amounts. The fifth of six installments of The Fragile Planet Series.
Science - Natural; Sociology
Dist - FOTH

PCP 20 MIN
U-matic / VHS / 16mm
Color (J)
LC 81-700026
Explains the chemical makeup of PCP and follows the activities of a PCP pusher.
Health and Safety; Psychology; Sociology
Dist - PHENIX **Prod** - NEWDON 1981

PCP Labs, FS - 64 60 MIN
U-matic / VHS
Color (PRO)
Shows how to recognize a PCP lab and become alert to chemical hazards of ethers and other noxious chemicals. Includes a look at victims of chemical explosions.
Health and Safety; Social Science; Sociology
Dist - FILCOM **Prod** - LACFD

The PCP Story 25 MIN
16mm
Color
Presents an overview of the physiological and psychological effects of the drug phencylcidine and its dangers.
Health and Safety
Dist - ARTCOP **Prod** - ARTCOP 1976

PCP - You Never Know 15 MIN
U-matic / VHS / 16mm
Color (I J H C)
LC 79-700300
Presents information on PCP, known as 'angel dust', 'Sherman' and 'crystal' and reveals the unique dangers of this drug.
Health and Safety; Psychology; Sociology
Dist - CF **Prod** - CF 1979

PC's - Specialized Computers 24 MIN
VHS / 16mm
Programmable Controllers - PLC's Series
Color (H A)
$465.00 purchase, $110.00 rental
Demonstrates the internal operation of PC's and operation of CPU, scan cycles and memory registers.
Computer Science; Industrial and Technical Education
Dist - TAT **Prod** - TAT 1984

PDQ Bach - the Abduction of Figaro 144 MIN
VHS
Color (S)
$59.95 purchase _ #055 - 9012
Presents the comedic operatic company PDQ Bach in its production of 'The Abduction of Figaro.' Features Professor Peter Schickele as leader, the Minnesota Opera, a stellar cast, chorus and 'corpse' de ballet.
Fine Arts; Literature and Drama
Dist - FI **Prod** - VAI 1988

Peabody 60 MIN
VHS
Kathy Blake dance studios - let's learn how to dance series
Color (G A)
$39.95 purchase
Features dance instructors Kathy Blake and Gene Russo, who instruct viewers on the basics of the Peabody.
Fine Arts
Dist - PBS **Prod** - WNETTV

Peace 2 MIN
16mm
Meditation Series
Color (I)
LC 80-700745
Creates a mood for discussion, thought, prayer or meditation on the subject of peace.
Religion and Philosophy
Dist - IKONOG **Prod** - IKONOG 1975

Peace - a Conscious Choice 4 MIN
U-matic / VHS / 16mm
Color (I)
LC 82-700879
Presents a Russian and an American verbalizing their fear of war between their two nations.
Civics and Political Systems; Sociology
Dist - BULFRG **Prod** - FADMND 1982

Peace - a goal of all religions 60 MIN
VHS / BETA
Color; PAL (G)
PdS25 purchase
Follows His Holiness the Dalai Lama's tour of Britain in 1984 to his first stop at the ancient Catholic Abbey and seminary at Ampleforth. Records his talk to the students and monks stressing his main theme of the tour - that peace must be achieved on the individual level if peace is to prevail in the world at large. Includes a brief meditational instruction on developing compassion. The talk concludes with a series of questions and answers. Translated by Prof Jeffrey Hopkins.
Fine Arts; Religion and Philosophy
Dist - MERIDT

Peace and discipline for mental illnesses according to Tibetan medicine 120 MIN
VHS / BETA
Color; PAL (G)
PdS35, $70.00 purchase
Features the Venerable Dr Trogawa Rinpoche discussing the effects of mental stress, how it can create physical disease, how one can develop an attitude of patience to bear with the discord of life and how to relate to others in this world with happiness.
Fine Arts; Psychology; Religion and Philosophy
Dist - MERIDT **Prod** - MERIDT

Peace begins here 29 MIN
VHS
Color (J H C G T A)
$39.95 purchase, $25.00 rental
Profiles U S citizens who have been activists on Central American issues. Features a former Air Force captain, a Presbyterian minister, a retired social worker and teacher, and a single parent. Produced by Liz Walker and Bliss Bruen.
Civics and Political Systems; Geography - World; History - World
Dist - EFVP

Peace Child 30 MIN
16mm
Color (R)
Documents the reaction of today's Stone Age people to the message of the Gospel.
Guidance and Counseling; Religion and Philosophy
Dist - GF **Prod** - GF

The Peace Conference 30 MIN
U-matic / VHS
How Wars End Series
Color (G)
$249.00, $149.00 purchase _ #AD - 913
Reports that the aims of the peace conference following World War I were both vengeful and idealistic, but its precautions to prevent Germany from starting another war failed. Reveals that the conference failed to resolve the issue of Poland - which nearly led to a new war in 1920 and sparked World War II. Part of a six - part series on how wars end, hosted by historian A J P Taylor.
History - United States; History - World; Sociology
Dist - FOTH **Prod** - FOTH

Peace Corps Partnership Program 18 MIN
16mm
Color
Demonstrates how the Peace Corp combines financial assistance and cultural exchange to enable people in foreign countries to meet basic needs with limited resources.
Civics and Political Systems; Social Science
Dist - MTP **Prod** - ACTON

Peace Corps to Go 68 MIN
16mm
Color
LC 75-700872
Depicts different situations which involve Peace Corps staff and volunteers, including a staff meeting, individual staff - volunteer confrontations, staff site visits, volunteers on the job, meetings with host country officials and the wedding ceremony of a Peace Corps couple.
Civics and Political Systems; Psychology; Sociology
Dist - USNAC **Prod** - USPC 1968

The Peace Dividend with Seymour Melman 30 MIN
VHS
World Of Ideas With Bill Moyers - Season II - series
Color; Captioned (G)
$39.95 purchase _ #WIWM - 214
Interviews Dr Seymour Melman, chairman of the National Commission for Economic Conversion and Disarmament. Shares Melman's views that military spending has been a drain on the American economy. Suggests that the resources used in the defense - related industries could be used for technological advances. Hosted by Bill Moyers.
Business and Economics; Civics and Political Systems
Dist - PBS

Peace Fund 30 MIN
VHS / U-matic
B&W
Documents Soviet workers contributing to the fund which helps victims of earthquakes, floods and U S bombing raids in North Vietnam.

History - World
Dist - IHF **Prod** - IHF

The Peace Game 26 MIN
VHS
Color (G)
Documents the wildlife and natural settings of the Game Parks of South Africa. Available for free loan from the distributor.
Geography - World; Science - Natural
Dist - AUDPLN

Peace is at Hand 60 MIN
U-matic / VHS / 16mm
Vietnam - a television history series; Episode 10
Color (H C A)
Recalls that from 1968 to 1973, Richard Nixon and Henry Kissinger worked to end the war, preferably with a victory through increased bombing, but end it any way necessary. Shows that Vietnamization continued, prisoners of war exchanged and the spirit of detente with Russia and China helped lead to a sort of peace.
History - United States; History - World
Dist - FI **Prod** - WGBHTV 1983

Peace is Our Profession 20 MIN
U-matic / VHS / 16mm
Color (J H A)
LC 70-713552
Presents the daily life of Officer Bryan - - his home, his family, his involvement in different cases and situations.
Psychology; Social Science; Sociology
Dist - AIMS **Prod** - DAVP

Peace - keeping
VHS
About the United Nations series
Color (J H C G)
$29.95 purchase _ #UNE91126V - S
Captures the drama of the United Nations' role in promoting peace. Helps students to assess the value of the international body's presence in local disputes and teaches about those who sacrifice their own safety to keep the peace. Part of a seven - part series on the United Nations.
Civics and Political Systems
Dist - CAMV **Prod** - UN

Peace march 13 MIN
16mm
Color (G)
$15.00 rental
Features a historical documentary. Captures the American Peace Movement march on New York in 1967. Produced by Anthony Reveaux.
Fine Arts; Sociology
Dist - CANCIN

Peace o' mind 10 MIN
16mm / VHS
B&W (G)
$20.00 rental
Describes personal and political isolation, trying to stay 'safe at home,' but being trapped there. Presents footage from educational films of the 1950s. Produced by Mary Filippo.
Fine Arts
Dist - CANCIN

Peace of Mind a Green Place Gives Me 28 MIN
16mm
Color (H C A)
LC 76-703302
Presents Mike Ondik, deer pen supervisor at a whitetail deer research farm at the Pennsylvania State University, explaining the facets of deer research.
Science; Science - Natural
Dist - PSU **Prod** - WPSXTV 1976

Peace of mind - peace in action 60 MIN
VHS / BETA
Color; PAL (G)
PdS25 purchase
Follows His Holiness the Dalai Lama's tour of Britain in 1984. Records his talk to an audience of 5500 people in Royal Albert Hall, London. Reiterates his message of peace in the world being achieved by through the development of peace within each person's heart. Speaks of the global concerns and personal frustrations facing everyone in this age of materialism and economic inequality, and how the basic good human qualities of kindness, tolerance and concern for others can overcome even apparently insurmountable problems. His Holiness is introduced by the Very Reverend, the Dean of Westminster. Translated by Prof Jeffrey Hopkins.
Fine Arts; Religion and Philosophy
Dist - MERIDT

Peace, order and good government - the Canadian Constitution and Canadian federalism 30 MIN
VHS
Remaking of Canada - Canadian government and politics in the 1990s 'series
Color (H C G)
$89.95 purchase _ #WLU - 502
Discusses the part that executive federalism played in the failure of the Meech Lake Accord, the division of powers between the federal government and the provinces in the Consitution Act of 1867, and Canada's evolution from a highly - centralized to a highly - decentralized federal state. Part of a 12 - part series incorporating interviews with Canadian politicians and hosted by Dr John Redekop.
Civics and Political Systems; History - World
Dist - INSTRU **Prod** - TELCOL 1992

Peace pickets arrested for disturbing the peace 7 MIN
16mm
Color (G)
$10.00 rental
Depicts the preparations for and development of the October 1967 non - violent, anti - draft demonstration at the Oakland Induction Center that led to the arrest of Joan Baez and twenty pacifists. Features singing and speaking by Joan Baez and songtext by Bob Dylan. Produced by Leonard Henny.
Fine Arts; Sociology
Dist - CANCIN

Peace, surrender, home with honor - Book 6 147 MIN
VHS
Vietnam - the 10,000 day war series
Color (H C A)
$24.95 purchase
Presents Book Six of the 'Vietnam - The 10,000 Day War' series. Documents the end of American involvement in Vietnam, and the final fall of South Vietnam to the Communists.
History - United States
Dist - PBS **Prod** - WNETTV

Peace through human understanding 60 MIN
VHS / BETA
Color; PAL (G)
PdS25 purchase
Follows His Holiness the Dalai Lama's tour of Britain in 1984 to his first public talk of the tour speaking of the need to develop a kind heart and awareness of the oneness of humankind. Continues with his thoughts on the opportunities even our enemies can provide for us to test the extent of our tolerance and love for everyone. In conclusion, he offers a short meditation and answers questions from the audience. Introduced by the Vice - Convener of the Lothian Region. Recorded in Edinburgh, Scotland. Translated by Prof Jeffrey Hopkins.
Fine Arts; Religion and Philosophy
Dist - MERIDT

Peace through Strength 26 MIN
U-matic / VHS
Color (A)
Shows the strategic nuclear balance between the US and USSR.
Civics and Political Systems; Social Science
Dist - ASCEF **Prod** - ASCEF 1984

Peace - Volume 11 48 MIN
VHS
Vietnam - the ten thousand day war series
Color (G)
$34.95 purchase _ #S00679
Reviews American attitudes and expectations about their involvement in Vietnam. Interviews South Vietnam President Thieu, Alexander Haig and US Secretary of Defense Melvin Laird. Narrated by Richard Basehart.
History - United States
Dist - UILL

Peace Women 16 MIN
U-matic / VHS / 16mm
Color (H C A)
LC 77-702446
Documents the origins and growth of the Peace People movement in Northern Ireland. Includes interviews with Betty Williams, founder of the movement, who discusses her abhorrence of violence, the present dangers to her children, her desire for Northern Ireland's independence and her decision to someday leave Ireland if peace is not achieved.
Civics and Political Systems; Geography - World; History - World; Sociology
Dist - CAROUF **Prod** - CBSTV 1977

The Peaceable Kingdom 8 MIN
16mm
Color; Silent (C)
$246.00
Experimental film by Stan Brakhage.
Fine Arts
Dist - AFA **Prod** - AFA 1972

Peaceful Ones 12 MIN
16mm
Color (I J)
Shows life and customs of the Hopi in the Painted Desert. Includes cultivating the land, harvesting crops, weaving, kachinas and snake dance.
Social Science; Sociology
Dist - MLA **Prod** - DAGP 1953

Peaceful warrior workout video 30 MIN
VHS
Color (G)
$29.00 purchase _ #V - PWWV
Shows how to release old patterns, restore flexibility and increase inner strength, confidence and energy. Features Dan Millman, author of 'Way of the Peaceful Warrior.' Combines yoga, martial arts, dance and fitness training.
Physical Education and Recreation
Dist - PACSPI

Peacemaker 7 MIN
16mm
Color
LC 75-703526
Presents the subject of fear and mistrust of peace and nonviolence with an allegory about a medieval knight who spares the life of a young challenger, an act of peace the young man cannot understand.
Guidance and Counseling; Sociology
Dist - FRACOC **Prod** - FRACOC 1974

The Peacemakers 26 MIN
VHS
Ordinary people series
Color (G)
$190.00 purchase, $50.00 rental
Records the annual commemoration of the Sharpeville massacre of 1961. Visits Vosloorus township with four people, a policeman and three political activists. The rallies, historically a day for demonstrations of unity and resistance to apartheid, became in 1993 more dramatic when separate and opposing assemblies were convened by both the Inkatha Freedom Party and the African National Congress. Part of a series which chronicles an event in South Africa through the eyes of three or four 'ordinary' people, chosen to represent diverse backgrounds or dissimilar points of view. This current affairs series seeks to provide insight into the collective South African conscience.
Fine Arts; History - World; Sociology
Dist - FIRS **Prod** - GAVSHO 1993

The Peacemakers - featuring Amos Oz and Rabbi David Hartman 57 MIN
VHS
Color (H C G)
$295.00 purchase, $75.00 rental
Visits Israel to reveal voices for peace seldom heard by the outside world. Focuses on novelist Amos Oz, leader in the Peace Now movement, and Rabbi David Hartman, a voice of enlightened orthodoxy who believes that pluralism - the free expression of a wide variety of religious and political beliefs - should be the Israeli ideal. At Ulpan Akiva, Ali Ahir teaches his native Arabic to Israeli soldiers so that they can talk to Palestinians in their own language, and observes an enclave of Christians who live in Israel without proselytizing, seeking to overcome the historical anti - Semitism of Christianity. Produced by the Mockingbird Company.
Geography - World; Religion and Philosophy
Dist - FLMLIB

Peacemakers series
Explores the facets of conflict management, anger and mediation. Uses a mix of live - action, graphics and music to teach children how to cope with temper and negotiation. Includes three videos, teacher's guides and blackline masters.
Anger
Let's make a deal 11 MIN
Pros in conflict 13 MIN
Dist - UNL

Peacetime Deaths in the Military 20 MIN
VHS / U-matic
Color
$335.00 purchase
Civics and Political Systems; Sociology
Dist - ABCLR **Prod** - ABCLR 1983

Peach Flan 6 MIN
U-matic / VHS
Cooking with Jack and Jill Series
Color (P I)
Portrays the skills of twins Jack and Jill as they cook nutritious and delicious snacks that are easy to prepare. Kitchen safety is emphasized. Animated.
Home Economics
Dist - LANDMK **Prod** - LANDMK 1986

Peachboy
CD / VHS / Cassette
Color (K P G)
$9.98, $16.98, $8.98 purchase _ #8511, #D2455, #2455
Tells the story of an elderly Japanese couple who rejoice when a child emerges from a giant peach. Follows the Peachboy, Momotaro as he grows to manhood and sets off to rescue his long - lost brothers and sisters. Features Sigourney Weaver as narrator with music by Ryuichi Sakamoto.
Fine Arts; Geography - World; Literature and Drama
Dist - MULIPE **Prod** - MULIPE

Peaches and cream 6 MIN
16mm
Color (G)
$20.00 rental
Supplies visual movement by eliminating the audience's distance from the collage paintings of Stanley Fisher. Features music by Louis Niciagna.
Fine Arts
Dist - CANCIN **Prod** - LEVCHI 1964

The Peacock - a Sculpture in Watermelon 7 MIN
U-matic / VHS
Color (PRO)
Shows how to make a peacock from a watermelon and how to prepare the strawberries, melon balls and pineapple fans which decorate the body of the centerpiece.
Home Economics; Industrial and Technical Education
Dist - CULINA **Prod** - CULINA

The Peacock Princess 120 MIN
VHS
Color (G) (MANDARIN CHINESE (ENGLISH SUBTITLES))
$45.00 purchase _ #1012B
Presents a Mandarin Chinese language movie produced in the People's Republic of China.
Fine Arts; Geography - World; Literature and Drama
Dist - CHTSUI **Prod** - CHTSUI

Peacock's War 60 MIN
16mm / VHS
(P A)
$895.00, $475.00 purchase, $90.00 rental
Tells the story of a Vietnam vet's determination to resist the destructive forces which threaten the physical world and the survival of the wild creatures who live in it by retreating to the last islands of uninhabited wilderness in the American West.
Science - Natural
Dist - BULFRG **Prod** - EARTH 1989

Peak Harvest 30 MIN
BETA / VHS
Victory Garden Series
Color
Introduces two semi - finalists in The Fifth Annual Victory Garden Contest. Presents a Greek tomato salad. Features a vegetable harvest at its peak.
Agriculture; Physical Education and Recreation
Dist - CORF **Prod** - WGBHTV

Peak performance
VHS
(G PRO)
$99.95 purchase _ #V237L2
Presents skills used by top performers to succeed as examples of ways the individual can improve performance.
Psychology
Dist - BARR

Peak performance 60 MIN
VHS
Color (G)
$19.95 purchase _ #S00057
Discusses research findings that high achievers share certain qualities. Outlines these qualities and shows how they can be developed. Hosted by Dr Charles Garfield.
Business and Economics; Guidance and Counseling; Psychology
Dist - UILL **Prod** - KARTES
KARTES

Peak 10 to fitness - upper and lower body set 140 MIN
VHS
Color (G)
$39.95 purchase _ #P58
Features Chris Imbo, fitness trainer. Teaches the exercises that he uses with celebrities around the world called Total Fitness in 10 weeks. Set of two tapes, 70 minutes each, includes upper body and lower body. Supermodel Frederique shares her workout and diet program.
Physical Education and Recreation; Social Science
Dist - HP

Peaked roof collapse 19 MIN
VHS
Collapse of burning buildings video series
Color (IND)
$140.00 purchase _ #35604
Presents one part of a five - part series that is a teaching companion for the Collapse of Burning Buildings book, as well as to the IFSTA Building Construction manual. Presents roof types and construction and the three ways they can collapse. Depicts firefighter protection and firefighter falls. Shows the most dangerous surfaces and safety procedures. Produced by Fire Engineering Books & Videos.
Health and Safety; Science - Physical; Social Science
Dist - OKSU

Peanut Butter 5 MIN
U-matic / VHS / 16mm
How It's made Series
Color (K)
Business and Economics
Dist - LUF **Prod** - HOLIA

Peanut News and Views 15 MIN
16mm
Color
Shows where and how peanuts are grown and harvested, lists their varied uses and discusses their nutritional value.
Agriculture; Home Economics; Social Science
Dist - MTP **Prod** - ELANCO

Peanut the Pinto Horse 15 MIN
U-matic / VHS / 16mm
Color (P I J)
Documents the first five months of the life of a show horse and shows her emerging victorious in her first competition.
Literature and Drama; Physical Education and Recreation
Dist - IFB **Prod** - BERLET 1983

Peanuts to the Presidency 75 MIN
U-matic / 16mm / VHS
Color (J)
LC 78-701046; 78-701045
A shortened version of the motion picture Peanuts To The Presidency. Follows Jimmy Carter's campaign for the Presidency from its inception through the cross - country campaigning, the primaries, the Democratic Convention and the election itself.
Biography; Civics and Political Systems; History - United States
Dist - PFP **Prod** - BRAMAN 1978

The Pearl
VHS
Color
Adapts the story by John Steinbeck of a fisherman who finds a valuable pearl, only to have it bring him bad luck.
Fine Arts; Literature and Drama
Dist - GA **Prod** - GA

The Pearl
U-matic / VHS
Films - on - Video Series
B&W (G C J)
$89 purchase _ #05648 - 85
Screens the film version of Steinbeck's tale that examines the bittersweet effects of jealousy and greed.
Fine Arts; Literature and Drama
Dist - CHUMAN

The Pearl 77 MIN
VHS
B&W (G)
$69.95 purchase _ #S01813
Presents the 1948 film version of John Steinbeck's tale 'The Pearl,' in which a Mexican fisherman finds a valuable pearl and finds his life being ruined as a result. Stars Pedro Armendariz as the fisherman.
Fine Arts; Literature and Drama
Dist - UILL

The Pearl 77 MIN
16mm / U-matic / VHS
B&W (I J H)
An enactment of John Steinbeck's short novel about unexpected wealth of a poor Mexican pearl diver and his family.
Literature and Drama
Dist - FI **Prod** - DNCGRS 1947

Pearl and puppet 14 MIN
16mm
B&W (G)
$30.00 rental
Presents the filmmaker's sister showing a hand - puppet to her two young children. Features hand - processing and music from Bizet's opera, The Pearl Fishers.
Fine Arts; Industrial and Technical Education
Dist - CANCIN **Prod** - JACBYR 1975

Pearl Buck - the Woman, the Word and Two Good Earths 25 MIN
16mm
American lifestyle series; Cultural leaders
Color
LC 78-700208
Discusses the life and works of novelist Pearl Buck. Features a tour of her farm in Bucks County, Pennsylvania.
Biography; Literature and Drama
Dist - COMCO **Prod** - COMCO
AIMS

Pearl Buck - the woman, the world, and two good earths 24 MIN
VHS
Color (H C T A)
$69.95 purchase _ #S01329; $50.00 rental _ #9747
Profiles the life and work of author Pearl Buck. Reveals that Buck is also a sculptor, pianist, organist, philanthropist, and mother of nine adopted children. Tours her Pennsylvania home, Green Hills, which contains many artworks and furniture from her years in China.
Biography; History - World; Literature and Drama
Dist - UILL **Prod** - AIMS
AIMS

Pearl diver 5 MIN
16mm
Color (G)
$20.00 rental
Elucidates the frustration between two women who try to tell each other 'I love you' underwater. Emphasizes the quality of light underwater by filming in Super - 8 then rephotographed in 16mm. Filmed in Baja, California. The dual nature of living in both air and water reflects the female experience of living in a man's world.
Fine Arts
Dist - CANCIN **Prod** - BARHAM 1984

Pearl Diving in the Persian Gulf 5 MIN
U-matic
See, Hear - the Middle East Series
Color (J)
Recounts the history of pearl diving and shows the divers at work, plunging to depths of 100 feet.
Geography - World; History - World
Dist - TVOTAR **Prod** - TVOTAR 1980

Pearl Fisher 28 MIN
U-matic / VHS / 16mm
Color (J H G)
Documents Barnett Bass as he fishes for fresh water mollusks in the White River in southern Indiana, seeking gem quality pearls and the 'mother of pearl' lining of shells.
Fine Arts; Geography - United States; Science - Natural
Dist - DOCEDR **Prod** - DOCEDR 1985

Pearl Harbor - 50 years after 60 MIN
VHS
Color (J H C G)
$29.95 purchase _ #TUR3101V
Examines United States' involvement in the biggest war the world has ever known. Chronicles events leading to the conflict, battles of the war and lessons learned. Features Bob Cain as host and interweaves live action footage and graphics.
History - United States; History - World; Sociology
Dist - CAMV **Prod** - TBSESI 1991

Pearl Harbor to Hiroshima 20 MIN
U-matic / VHS / 16mm
Twentieth Century History Series
Color (H C A)
$380.00 purchase _ #548-9223
Portrays the economic, political and military background that led Japan into World War II and discusses the war period and the reasons the United States dropped the Atomic bombs on Hiroshima and Nagasaki. Shows Japan as it emerges from feudal isolation, becomes a great aggressive power and, upon losing the war, redirects itself into industrial technology.
History - World
Dist - FI **Prod** - BBCTV 1981

Pearl Harbor to Midway 45 MIN
VHS
V for victory series
B&W (J H G)
$14.95 purchase _ #ATL325
Examines activities in the Pacific Theater during World War II. Presents part of a six - part series featuring select newsreels that depict the leaders, soldiers and battles of World War II. Narrated by Eric Sevareid and Edwin Newman.
History - United States; Sociology
Dist - KNOWUN

Pearl Harbor - two hours that changed the world 100 MIN
VHS
ABC News collection series
B&W/Color (G)

$29.98 purchase _ #6302316561
Features David Brinkley who anchors the history of and discussion about the attack on Pearl Harbor. Includes rare archival still photos, film footage and interviews with American survivors and Japanese participants of the attack.
History - United States
Dist - INSTRU **Prod** - ABCNEW 1991

Pearl of the Orient 20 MIN
16mm
Color
Presents Penang as home to a medley of cultures primarily based on Asia's three great civilizations, Chinese, Indian and Malay. Shows the unique Snake Temple, the third largest statue in the world of a reclining Buddha, the Kek Lok Si Pagoda, the rice fields and rubber estates and how batik making is done.
Geography - World; History - World
Dist - PMFMUN **Prod** - FILEM 1973

Pearlfishers and peopleteachers 18 MIN
16mm
Diaries no 1 - no 8 - 1979 - 1983
Color (G)
$25.00 rental
Features part six of an eight - part series by Andras Szirtes.
Fine Arts; Literature and Drama
Dist - CANCIN

Pearls in the Alphabet Soup 29 MIN
VHS / 16mm
A Different Understanding Series
Color (G)
$90.00 purchase _ #BPN183503
Explores alternative education programs for gifted shildren such as special provisions in a regular classroom, enrichment classes, and `withdrawal' programs. Discusses the need for such programs and their benefits from the viewpoints of teachers, education experts, and children.
Education; Psychology; Sociology
Dist - RMIBHF **Prod** - RMIBHF

Pearls in the Alphabet Soup 30 MIN
U-matic / VHS / 16mm
Color (C A)
Presents a variety of program models which can be adapted to the educational needs of gifted students at primary and secondary levels. Shows alternatives such as gifted students in a congregated class, or in the framework of the regular classroom, or partial - withdrawal classes, and at high school level, enriched classes and mentor programs.
Education
Dist - BCNFL **Prod** - PLAYTM

Pearls in the North 14 MIN
16mm
Color (J)
LC 73-702258
Shows the revival of the pearling industry and the operation of a cultured pearl farm on Australia's north - west coast.
Business and Economics; Geography - World
Dist - AUIS **Prod** - ANAIB 1972

Pearls of the Mediterranean 60 MIN
VHS
Mediterranean and African collection series
Color (J H C G)
$29.95 purchase _ #IVN283V-S
Introduces the islands of the Mediterranean Sea. Looks at the people and rich history while exploring these lands, along with historic buildings, monuments, landmarks and hidden treasures. Part of a 16-part series on European countries. Also part of a larger series entitled Video Visits that travels to six continents.
Geography - World
Dist - CAMV

Pearls Series

Emi	30 MIN
Fujikawa	30 MIN
Gin and Don	30 MIN
Mako	30 MIN
Ourselves	30 MIN
Pinoy	30 MIN

Dist - GPN

Peary's Race for the North Pole 53 MIN
16mm
Color (J)
Describes Commander Robert Peary's discovery of the North Pole. Narrated by Lorne Greene.
History - World
Dist - FI **Prod** - WOLPER 1974

Peasant Ecology in the Rural Phillippines 26 MIN
16mm
Color (C)
LC 74-702799
Illustrates the complexity of relationships between culture patterns, physical environment and limited technology in the rural Philippines.
Geography - World; Science - Natural; Sociology
Dist - PSUPCR **Prod** - PSUPCR 1971

Peasant Painter - Pintor Campesino 18 MIN
U-matic / VHS / 16mm
Inhabitants in the Land of Grace Series
Color (H A)
Shows Cleto Rojas, a peasant who paints memories of his journey to Caracas, his fantastic visions, scenes inspired by mythology or the local cinema, and the rural life around him.
Fine Arts; Geography - World
Dist - DOCEDR **Prod** - DOCEDR 1984

The Peasant's Pea Patch 8 MIN
U-matic
Desire to Read Series
Color (P)
Tells of the misadventures of a Russian peasant trying in vain to protect his pea patch from a flock of hungry cranes.
Literature and Drama
Dist - GA **Prod** - BOSUST

The Peasants' Revolt - Pt 1 20 MIN
VHS
Middle Ages Series
Color (I)
$79.00 purchase _ #825 - 9433
Incorporates source and historic material to recreate medieval life. Depicts accurately the main social groups and captures the political climate of the time. Visits castles, cathedrals and battlegrounds, dramatizes pilgrimages and uprisings, uses close - up views of historical artifacts and architecture to bring the Middle Ages to life. Part 1 of five parts depicts the living and working conditions of peasants in the 14th century through a dramatization based on real people.
Geography - World; History - United States; History - World; Social Science; Sociology
Dist - FI **Prod** - BBCTV 1987

Pebbles, Rocks and Bigger Chunks 29 MIN
VHS / 16mm
Villa Alegre Series
Color (P T)
$46.00 rental _ #VILA - 147
Presents educational material in both Spanish and English.
Education
Dist - PBS

Peck's Bad Boy 51 MIN
16mm
B&W
Introduces a young boy who is the nemesis of grocers, parsons, dogcatchers and, most especially, his own parents. Stars Jackie Coogan and Raymond Hatton. Directed by Sam Wood.
Fine Arts
Dist - KILLIS

Pecos 12 MIN
U-matic / VHS / 16mm
Color (J A) (SPANISH)
Portrays the history of the Pecos National Monument in New Mexico from the first nomadic peoples to the building of Indian pueblos and the coming of the Spanish Conquistadors. Includes vintage photos, original illustrations and costumed reenactments. Available in Spanish language version narrated by Ricardo Montalb.
Geography - United States; History - United States
Dist - USNAC **Prod** - USNPS 1984

Pecos Bill 15 MIN
VHS / U-matic
Stories of America Series
Color (P)
Spins a few yarns about Pecos Bill and early cowpunching days in the Southwest.
Literature and Drama
Dist - AITECH **Prod** - OHSDE 1976

Pecos Bill 11 MIN
U-matic / VHS / 16mm
American Folklore Series
Color (I J)
LC 79-709812
Tells the story of Pecos Bill, an American folk character, through the use of artwork and original music.
Literature and Drama
Dist - PHENIX **Prod** - HRAW 1970

Pecos Bill 17 MIN
16mm
Walt Disney Archives Series
Color (P I)
Captures the larger than life quality of folk hero Pecos Bill, who embodies the essence of the American cowboy in the days of the Lone Prairie.
History - United States; Literature and Drama
Dist - CORF **Prod** - DISNEY 1986

Pecos Bill
CD / VHS / Cassette
Color (K P G)
$9.98, $16.98, $8.98 purchase _ #8116, #D328, #328
Retells the story of Pecos Bill created by J C Bowman. Features Robin Williams as narrator with music by Ry Cooder.
Fine Arts; Literature and Drama
Dist - MULIPE **Prod** - MULIPE

Pecos - Una Promesa 16 MIN
16mm
Color (A)
LC 77-703233
Explains how an annual festival mass has been held for 350 years at the ruin of a Spanish mission church at Pecos National Monument. Tells how Indians, Spanish - Americans and visitors to the Southwest United States still meet in celebration of this special Catholic mass.
Geography - United States; History - United States; Religion and Philosophy
Dist - USNAC **Prod** - USNPS 1973

The Pectoral Region 9 MIN
16mm / U-matic / VHS
Guides to Dissection Series
Color (C A)
Demonstrates the dissection of the pectoral region.
Health and Safety; Science - Natural
Dist - TEF **Prod** - UCLA

Pectoral Region and Axilla - Unit 10 20 MIN
U-matic / VHS
Gross Anatomy Prosection Demonstration Series
Color (PRO)
Discusses the muscles and thoracoacromial trunk of the pectoral region, locates the boundaries of the axilla and describes the brachial plexus and the axillary artery.
Health and Safety; Science - Natural
Dist - HSCIC **Prod** - HSCIC

Pectoralis Major Transplant for Serratus Anterior Paralysis 14 MIN
16mm
Color (PRO)
Shows the manner in which the pectoralis major transplant was performed to alleviate serratus anterior paralysis.
Guidance and Counseling; Health and Safety; Science - Natural
Dist - UCLA **Prod** - UCLA

Pectus Excavatum 29 MIN
VHS / U-matic
Thoracic Series
Color
Health and Safety; Science - Natural
Dist - SVL **Prod** - SVL

Pectus Excavatum - Indications for Surgery and Operative Management 23 MIN
16mm
Cine Clinic Series
Color (PRO)
Explains that severe pectus excavatum (funnel chest) is a serious cosmetic and postural deformity which can be corrected with a modified ravitch - type repair. Shows the indications, technique and management.
Health and Safety; Science
Dist - NMAC **Prod** - ACYDGD 1970

A Peculiar People 39 MIN
U-matic / VHS / 16mm
Christians Series Episode 1; Episode 1
Color (H C A)
LC 78-701649
Traces the growth of Christianity from its beginnings to the time the Christians ceased to be a secret, persecuted sect.
History - World; Religion and Philosophy
Dist - MGHT **Prod** - GRATV 1978

Pedal Power 19 MIN
16mm / U-matic / VHS
Color (I J H C)
LC 78-701234
Uses animated still photographs, drawings and early motion picture footage to trace the history of pedal - powered machines from Leonardo da Vinci to the 1970's. Based on the book Pedal Power In Work, Leisure And Transportation by James C Mc Cullagh.
History - United States; Physical Education and Recreation; Social Science
Dist - BULFRG **Prod** - RPFD 1978

Pedal smarts 18 MIN
VHS
Bicycle safety video series
Color (I J H)
$22.00 purchase
Presents a news - style, flashy show to demonstrate safe cycling and safe motoring skills. Uses colorful graphics, animation and offbeat segments to teach these skills. Includes study guide.

Fine Arts; Health and Safety; Physical Education and Recreation; Sociology
Dist - ROLAND **Prod** - LEPAGE 1994

Pedal steel guitar 60 MIN
VHS
Video music lesson series
Color (J H C G)
$29.95 purchase _ #TMV15V
Offers step - by - step pedal steel guitar instruction. Features studio musicians, composers, arrangers and educators who lend hands - on instruction about tuning the instrument, chord progressions, smooth and fluent style, timing and finger exercises, common note combinations, instrument set - up, special sound techniques. Includes examples of chord and scale theory, examples for technical improvement and songs to teach the principles of the instrument. Includes booklet. Part of a 16 - part series on musical instruction.
Fine Arts
Dist - CAMV

Peddlin' Safety 14 MIN
16mm
Color (P I J)
Discusses bicycle safety practices, including hand signals, observance of traffic laws and riding defensively.
Health and Safety
Dist - VADE **Prod** - VADE 1975

Peddling paradise 26 MIN
VHS
Challenge of the seas series
Color (I J H)
$225.00 purchase
Shows that Hawaii has always been thought as a paradise and is changing constantly. Offers footage of volcanic activity in the area and explores the effect of increasing population on the islands. Part of a 26 - part series on the oceans.
Geography - United States; Geography - World; Science - Natural; Sociology
Dist - LANDMK **Prod** - LANDMK 1991

The Pedestal Grinder
U-matic / VHS
Basic Machine Technology Series
Color (SPANISH)
Industrial and Technical Education
Dist - VTRI **Prod** - VTRI

Pedestrian Safety 15 MIN
VHS / U-matic
Safer You Series
Color (P I)
Demonstrates the proper attire to wear when walking at night. Explains the meanings of stop and yield signs, walk/don't walk signals, traffic lights and the proper ways to cross at each.
Health and Safety
Dist - GPN **Prod** - WCVETV 1984

Pedestrian Signs and Signals 11 MIN
U-matic / VHS / 16mm
Color (P I) (SPANISH)
LC 73-700954
Point out that streets are made for cars, not pedestrians. Describes the variety of signs, signals and markings to help people cross streets safely. Features the new international signs.
Health and Safety
Dist - AIMS **Prod** - AIMS 1972

Pedestrians - Watch Out 10 MIN
U-matic / VHS / 16mm
Color (K P I) (SPANISH)
LC 79-700880
Shows various traffic situations and how pedestrians should deal with them. Uses animation to emphasize situations which could be dangerous for the pedestrian.
Health and Safety
Dist - AIMS **Prod** - GOLDCF 1978

Pediatric Anesthesia 27 MIN
VHS / U-matic
Anesthesiology Clerkship Series
Color (PRO)
Describes the differences in anatomy and physiology of the pediatric patient, with special attention to the child's airway. Identifies specific problems of pediatric gas exchange. Discusses cardiovascular monitoring, pediatric fluid/blood replacement and problems related to thermal regulation. Covers unique problems of drug administration in children.
Health and Safety
Dist - UMICHM **Prod** - UMICHM 1982

Pediatric Assessment Series
Neuromotor Assessment of Cerebral Palsy, Athetosis 46 MIN
Neuromotor Assessment of Cerebral Palsy, Pre - Post Test 23 MIN
Neuromotor Assessment of Cerebral Palsy, Spastic Hemiplegia 52 MIN
Neuromotor Assessment of Cerebral Palsy Spastic Quadriplegia 50 MIN
Principles of Neuromotor Assessment 19 MIN
Dist - UMDSM

The Pediatric code 24 MIN
VHS
Color (PRO C)
$285.00 purchase, $70.00 rental _ #4309
Teaches nursing professionals how to function effectively in a code situation. Addresses the population at risk and the causes of pediatric cardiac arrest. Discusses the signs of decompensation, outlines the steps commonly taken in a code situation, describes the roles and responsibilities of pediatric code members, provides a comprehensive review of common drugs and stresses the need to prevent the occurence of pediatric cardiac arrests. Demonstrates one - handed CPR on a young child and its conformation to 1992 Pediatric Basic Life Support Guidelines published by JAMA, October 28, 1992, to provide a complete step - by - step review of a pediatric code.
Health and Safety
Dist - AJN **Prod** - AJN

Pediatric diabetes 28 MIN
VHS
Color (G)
$149.00 purchase, $75.00 rental _ #UW5332
Looks at how children learn to analyze their blood sugar levels and manage their care. Shows children aged 9 to 15 who have diabetes and their parents who illustrate how they handle daily injections of insulin, numerous blood checks every day and a complex balancing of food and exercise.
Health and Safety
Dist - FOTH

Pediatric emergencies 60 MIN
VHS
Color (J H C G)
$29.95 purchase _ #CVP100V - K
Presents real - life situations that threaten the safety of children to instruct parents or caregivers of children. Features paramedics and physicians who cover use of the 911 system, how to talk to injured children to keep them calm, and how to respond to choking, burns, head injuries and much more. Urges parents to attend CPR or first aid classes.
Health and Safety
Dist - CAMV

Pediatric emergency management series
Accidental ingestions in children 20 MIN
Cardiopulmonary resuscitation 28 MIN
Foreign bodies 25 MIN
Head Trauma 22 MIN
Status Epilepticus 20 MIN
Upper Airway Infections 19 MIN
Dist - VTRI

Pediatric Examination - Art and Process Series
Examination of the infant - Pt 1 25 MIN
Examination of the infant - Pt 2 25 MIN
Examination of the pre - school age child - Pt 1 22 MIN
Examination of the pre - school age child - Pt 2 23 MIN
Examination of the school age child 45 MIN
Neurologic Examination, Pt 1 20 MIN
Neurologic Examination, Pt 2 20 MIN
Pediatric Neurologic Examination 40 MIN
Dist - LIP

Pediatric Growth Measurements - Height, Weight, and Head Circumference 6 MIN
VHS / U-matic
Color (PRO)
Illustrates basic procedures involved in measuring and charting a child's height, weight and head circumference.
Health and Safety
Dist - HSCIC **Prod** - HSCIC 1982

A Pediatric History and Physical Examination 37 MIN
U-matic
Color (C)
Demonstrates a screening pediatric history and physical examination.
Health and Safety; Science - Natural
Dist - UOKLAH **Prod** - UOKLAH 1980

Pediatric IV therapy 40 MIN
U-matic / VHS
Color (PRO)
$300.00 purchase, $60.00 rental _ #4270S, #4270V
Shows the assembly of intravenous - IV - flow devices and electronic infusion monitors. Explores compassionately children's needs, with appropriate explanations for each developmental stage. Discusses physiological aspects such as the size of the child, metabolic rate, fluid and electrolyte balance, elimination and acid - base balance. Considers cognitive factors of age, experience, education and family background in teaching patients about the process, and the importance of monitoring their developmental progress.
Health and Safety; Psychology; Sociology
Dist - AJN **Prod** - UNCN 1986

Pediatric Mist Tent 20 MIN
VHS / U-matic
Color
Designed to identify nursing responsibilities related to the care of a child in a mist tent. Discusses potential problems and solutions.
Health and Safety
Dist - FAIRGH **Prod** - FAIRGH

Pediatric mock code 18 MIN
U-matic / VHS
Color (C PRO)
$285.00 purchase, $70.00 rental _ #4309S, 4309V
Outlines the roles and responsibilities of each member of a pediatric code team in the time period before, during, and after a pediatric code, when a child goes into cardiopulmonary arrest. Addresses recognition of signs of decompensation, IVs and intubation, and commonly used first - line drugs. Approved for continuing education credit.
Health and Safety
Dist - AJN **Prod** - AJN 1991

Pediatric mock codes 28 MIN
U-matic / VHS
Color (PRO C)
$395.00 purchase, $80.00 rental _ #C881 - VI - 042
Demonstrates two simulated codes - cardiac arrests. Uses the first simulation to show everything that can go wrong when personnel are not prepared or do not follow procedures properly - anxious and excited behavior, unfamiliarity with the crash cart, improper CPR and intubation, unclear roles for the people helping with the code and incomplete knowledge of drugs and drug dosage. The second simulation gives a clear picture of how to respond to a pediatric 'code' and demonstrates how smoothly an arrest can be handled when the proper steps are taken. Presented by Judy Grisell, RN, and Lisa Blissard, RN.
Health and Safety
Dist - HSCIC

Pediatric Neurologic Examination 40 MIN
U-matic
Pediatric Examination - Art and Process Series
Color (PRO)
Demonstrates techniques and processes of a neurologic examination of normal children from infancy through school age.
Health and Safety
Dist - LIP **Prod** - TUNNEW 1977

Pediatric Nursing Series
The Child with a Heart Defect 44 MIN
Kidney Transplants and Hemodialysis 44 MIN
Dist - AJN

Pediatric Office Bacteriology - Obtaining and Culturing Urine 14 MIN
U-matic / VHS
Color (PRO)
Details three means of obtaining urine - clean catch, catheterization, and superpubic bladder aspiration.
Health and Safety; Science - Natural
Dist - HSCIC **Prod** - HSCIC 1981

Pediatric pain 19 MIN
U-matic / VHS
Special issues in pain control series
Color (PRO C)
$395.00 purchase, $80.00 rental _ #C901 - VI - 040
Trains nurses, pharmacists, allied health professionals, medical ethicists and students. Provides up - to - date information on pediatric pain management. Outlines the physiology of the pain response and techniques for response assessment. Discusses pain intervention options. Presents ethical and legal parameters. Presented by Bethany Geldmaker, RN, Mark Lehman, PharmD, Brenda Jackson, PT, and Janet Kues, PT, Medical College of Virginia, Virginia Commonwealth University.
Health and Safety
Dist - HSCIC

Pediatric Physiotherapy 14 MIN
16mm / U-matic / VHS
Physical Respiratory Therapy Series
Color (C A)
Discusses the application of respiratory physiotherapy to neonates and children, including patient psychology, proper techniques and infant physiology.
Health and Safety; Science; Science - Natural
Dist - TEF **Prod** - VISCI

Pediatric procedures - Module I
Videodisc
Color (PRO C)

$1300.00 purchase _ #C901 - IV - 033
Presents hospital pediatric nursing procedures through interactive technology. Demonstrates the procedures of lumbar puncture, bone marrow aspiration and central line placement. Produced by Drs Cynthia Tinsley and Geoffrey C Ashton and Holger - Axel G Mason, Health Instructional Resources Unit, University of Hawaii, John A Burns School of Medicine. Includes Level III interactive videodisc, 3.5 or 5.25 inch floppy disks, user's manual and study guide. Requires IBM compatible 30 MB hard disk and videodisc player. Ask distributor about other requirements.
Health and Safety
Dist - HSCIC

Pediatric procedures - Module II
Videodisc
(PRO C)
$1300.00 purchase _ #C911 - IV - 049
Invites the viewer to walk with Dr Cynthia Tinsley to see a newborn circumcision, an endotracheal intubation, a thoracentesis and a thorastomy being performed on pediatric patients at a major medical center. Includes a quiz at the end of each procedure. Presented by Drs Cynthia Tinsley and Geoffrey C Ashton, Holger Axel G Mason, Drs Melinda J Ashton, Alan G Britten and Dr Larry R Tinsley. Contact distributor for technical requirements.
Health and Safety
Dist - HSCIC

Pediatric Series

Abdomino - perineal pull through for imperforate anus	29 MIN
Ambulatory surgery clinic and myringotomy	12 MIN
Circumcision by dissection /circumcision with plastic ring	10 MIN
Excision of thyroglossal duct cyst	28 MIN
Gastroschsis	27 MIN
Hepato - enterostomy for biliary atresia	18 MIN
Indirect Hernia	20 MIN
Operative Drainage for Empyema	9 MIN
Pyloric Stenosis	9 MIN
Resection of an Adrenal Tumor	10 MIN
Scrotal Hydrocele	15 MIN
Three Appendectomies	30 MIN
Undescended Testis	15 MIN

Dist - SVL

Pediatric Ultrasonography 21 MIN
U-matic
Ultrasound in Diagnostic Medicine Series
Color
LC 79-707579
Discusses areas in which ultrasound is being used as a diagnosis tool in pediatric medicine. Describes the use of ultrasound in determining midline shifts in the head, congenital and acquired abnormalities in the heart and in outlining effusions on the chest.
Health and Safety; Science
Dist - USNAC **Prod** - NSF 1976

Pediatric venipuncture 14 MIN
VHS
Color (PRO C)
$250.00 purchase, $70.00 rental _ #4405
Reviews all the information needed to perform venipuncture on a pediatric patient. Outlines the entire procedure, including items to check before the procedure is started, the equipment needed and the correct labeling and handling of tubes to guarantee accurate results. Discusses safety precautions. Stresses the two main goals of venipuncture - to do the procedure with the lease amount of injury and discomfort and to get a specimen that will yield the most accurate results. Offers tips on how to avoid problems and trouble - shooting. Produced by Vanderbilt University Medical Center.
Health and Safety
Dist - AJN

Pediatric video series
Presents a three - part series on infants with prolonged hospitalization. Includes two staff development programs for helping families of hospitalized infants adjust to the experience and a program for showing to parents whose infants will be hospitalized for a prolonged period, to help them to adjust and play a more positive role.

Helping families of infants with prolonged hospitalization - staff development	11 MIN
Parenting the infant with prolonged hospitalization - parent tape	12 MIN
Pediatric video series	36 MIN
Promoting the development of infants with prolonged hospitalization - staff development	13 MIN

Dist - POLYMR **Prod** - POKORJ 1995

Pediatrics in review - Redbook - 1985 - 1990
CD-ROM
(PRO)
$150.00 purchase _ #1950pm
Includes complete full - text articles and graphics from Pediatrics in Review, as well as the latest edition of Redbook, which provides current information on children's communicable diseases. Produced by CMC. For Macintosh Plus, SE, and II computers. Requires 1MB RAM, floppy disk drive, Apple compatible CD - ROM drive. IBM PCs and compatibles require 640K RAM, DOS 3.1 or later, one floppy disk drive - hard disk recommended, one empty expansion slot, and an IBM compatible CD - ROM drive. Updated annually.
Health and Safety; Literature and Drama
Dist - BEP

Pediatrics infectious disease - 1985 - 1990
CD-ROM
(PRO)
$395.00 purchase _ #1957pm
Features articles and original studies from the Pediatrics Infectious Disease Journal, published by Williams & Wilkins. Produced by CMC. For Macintosh Plus, SE, and II computers. Requires 1MB RAM, floppy disk drive, Apple compatible CD - ROM drive. IBM PCs and compatibles require 640K RAM, DOS 3.1 or later, one floppy disk drive - hard disk recommended, one empty expansion slot, and an IBM compatible CD - ROM drive. Updated annually.
Health and Safety; Literature and Drama
Dist - BEP

Pediatrics on disk - 1983 - 1990
CD-ROM
(PRO)
$395.00 purchase _ #1952pm
Contains the complete original full - text of all articles and supplements from Pediatrics, including graphics. Produced by CMC. For Macintosh Plus, SE, and II computers. Requires 1MB RAM, floppy disk drive, an Apple compatible CD - ROM drive. IBM PCs and compatibles require 640K RAM, DOS 3.1 or later, floppy disk drive - hard disk recommended, one empty expansion slot, and an IBM compatible CD - ROM drive. Updated annually.
Health and Safety; Literature and Drama
Dist - BEP

Pediatrics - physical care series

Administering oral and IM medications	18 MIN
Evaluating children	20 MIN
Fluid balance and IV therapy	16 MIN
Physical differences	20 MIN
Safety	13 MIN
Using an otoscope	18 MIN

Dist - CONMED

Pediatrics - psychosocial implications series

Alleviating fear and pain	21 MIN
Alterations in body image	18 MIN
Behavioral responses to illness	21 MIN
Deprivations resulting from illness	17 MIN
The Dying child - focus on the child	20 MIN
The Dying child - focus on the family	17 MIN
I went to the hospital	13 MIN
The Nursing challenge	18 MIN
Working with the troubled family	20 MIN

Dist - CONMED

Pediatrics series

Feeding	9 MIN

Dist - JOU

Pedicle Flaps for Wound Closure 23 MIN
16mm
Color (PRO)
Explains that when important muscle structures, nerves, tendons, bones, joints or major blood vessels are exposed in a wound, they must be covered and protected with skin and its attached subcutaneous fat. Points out that if this covering is not available because of the magnitude of the defect, one may use some type of pedicle to supply this deficiency.
Health and Safety; Science
Dist - ACY **Prod** - ACYDGD 1960

Pediculosis and Scabies - Questions of Concern 24 MIN
16mm
Color
Summarizes current data on the human louse insect and scabies mite and samples common patient concerns. Provides information on the accepted diagnostic procedures and preferred course of therapy for each of these frequentyly encountered infestations.
Health and Safety; Sociology
Dist - MTP **Prod** - REDCRN

The Pedlar's Dream 27 MIN
U-matic / VHS / 16mm
Storybook International Series
Color
Relates the English tale of a pedlar who dreams of finding his fortune in a faraway market. Reveals that once he gets there, he finds that his fortune is really back at his own house and that his generousity to his friends is appreciated.
Guidance and Counseling; Literature and Drama
Dist - JOU **Prod** - JOU 1982

Pedophile - Child Molester 20 MIN
16mm / U-matic / VHS
Color (H C A)
LC 76-702172
Presents an in - depth study of the child molester, showing the many different types of child molesters, the tricks of how they operate and the underlying causes of their deviation.
Psychology; Sociology
Dist - AIMS **Prod** - DAVP 1972

Pedro Zero Percent 20 MIN
VHS / 35mm strip / U-matic
Color (SPANISH (ENGLISH SUBTITLES))
$195 purchase, $40 rental
Portrays Cuban dairy farmer Pedro Acosta who has never lost a cow from illness. Directed by Luis Felipe Bernaza.
Agriculture
Dist - CNEMAG

Pee Wee Reese for Gillete 1 MIN
U-matic / VHS
Color
Shows a classic television commercial with a Brooklyn Dodgers ball player.
Business and Economics; Psychology; Sociology
Dist - BROOKC **Prod** - BROOKC

Peed into the wind 60 MIN
16mm
B&W (G)
$80.00 rental
Presents McDowell's life story. Features a saga of Mick Terrific, rock 'n' roll star and the cast of 50 he encounters during his search for Mr Wonderful.
Fine Arts; Literature and Drama
Dist - CANCIN **Prod** - MCDOWE

Peege 28 MIN
16mm / U-matic / VHS
Color
$525 rental - 16 mm, $315 rental - video
Portrays a family making a Christmas Day visit to see the father's mother in a nursing home. Discusses the relationship of youth to senior citizens.
Health and Safety; Sociology
Dist - CCNCC **Prod** - CCNCC 1985

Peege 28 MIN
16mm / U-matic / VHS
Color; Captioned
LC 73-702352
Shows how a young man who comes home from college for the Christmas holidays is able to break through communication barriers and reach his grandmother who has become isolated by age and failing mental and physical capacities.
Fine Arts; Guidance and Counseling; Literature and Drama; Sociology
Dist - PHENIX **Prod** - KLEKNP 1973

Peege 30 MIN
U-matic / VHS
Color
Shows how a fairly typical middle class family deals with an aging mother and grandmother during the annual Christmas visit to the nursing home where the grandmother resides.
Health and Safety; Sociology
Dist - AJN **Prod** - PHENIX

Peel 9 MIN
16mm
Films of Jane Campion Series
Color (G)
$40.00 rental
Focuses on a recalcitrant, freckled, red - headed family of three who go on a picnic on a hot Australian summer day. Reveals that their outing results in an intrigue of belligerance.
Geography - World; Literature and Drama; Psychology; Sociology
Dist - WMEN FIRS **Prod** - JACAM 1986

Peelings 7 MIN
16mm / U-matic / VHS
Color (H C A)
LC 77-702331
Introduces the viewer to latex sculpture by following the process required to produce this type of art.
Fine Arts
Dist - PHENIX **Prod** - FEINSP 1976

Peel's Beer with Bert and Harry Peel 1 MIN
U-matic / VHS
Color
Shows a classic television commercial with live and animated action.
Business and Economics; Psychology; Sociology
Dist - BROOKC **Prod** - BROOKC

The Peep show 30 MIN
U-matic
Antiques series
Color
Fine Arts
Dist - PBS **Prod** - NHMNET

Peephole art - Beckett for television 58 MIN
VHS
Color (H C G)
Contains four full - length performances of the work of Samuel Beckett. Features Irish actor Chris O'Neill introducing each piece. Includes Not I - 1989, which fills the screen with the image of a large mouth spewing forth a haunting monolog about a woman who has been speechless most of her life; Film - 1964, starring Buster Keaton and directed by Alan Schneider in the only screenplay that Beckett wrote; Quad I & II - 1988, comprising poetry, dance, mathematics, geometry, 'a ballet for four people' said Beckett, in which the cameras view the dancers from above; and What Where - 1988, his first American production and his last published play.
Fine Arts; Literature and Drama
Dist - GLOBAL **Prod** - GLOBAL

Peeping Tom 101 MIN
VHS
Color (G)
$39.95 _ #PEE030; $250.00, $300.00 rental
Features a psychological thriller where stark terror meets art in a deadly game of cat and mouse. Follows Mark Lewis, son of a famous scientist who devoted his life to studying the psychology of fear with young Mark as a guinea pig. Mark has grown into a psychopathic killer obsessed with capturing his victims' fear on film. Directed by Michael Powell. Digitally remastered.
Fine Arts; Psychology; Sociology
Dist - HOMVIS KINOIC **Prod** - JANUS 1960

Peer Conducted Behavior Modification 24 MIN
U-matic / VHS / 16mm
Color (C A)
Illustrates the way in which a child's schoolmates and their parents are mobilized in a neighborhood to modify some behavior problems.
Psychology
Dist - MEDIAG **Prod** - MEDIAG 1976

Peer Facilitators - Youth Helping Youth 27 MIN
16mm
Color (J)
LC 76-703659
Presents a model for training high school students in helping skills. Features counselor Tom Erney in a demonstration of the peer facilitator program that he developed for high school students in Gainesville, Florida.
Education; Sociology
Dist - EDMDC **Prod** - EDMDC 1976

Peer Group Interactions 30 MIN
U-matic / VHS
Interaction - Human Concerns in the Schools Series
Color (T)
Looks at peer group interactions in an educational setting.
Education
Dist - MDCPB **Prod** - MDDE

Peer Gynt 60 MIN
U-matic / VHS
Drama - play, performance, perception series; Introduction to critical appreciation
Color (H C A)
Provides a framework for understanding drama and the basic skills needed to view a play critically. Uses the play Peer Gynt as an example.
Literature and Drama
Dist - FI **Prod** - BBCTV 1978

Peer intervention - drug abuse 17 MIN
16mm / VHS
Color (J H A PRO)
$425.00, $345.00 purchase, $75.00 rental _ #8209
Outlines high risk factors which may contribute to drug use as well as the signs of chemical dependency. Discusses five steps to take in order to stop enabling drug dependent persons. Enacts helping skills for those who will be intervening. Shows how to recognize the difference between a problem and a crisis and to know how to get immediate help.
Guidance and Counseling; Psychology; Social Science; Sociology
Dist - AIMS **Prod** - AIMS 1990

Peer power 8 MIN
VHS
Color; Captioned (G)
$25.00 purchase
Features high school students who discuss their fears, experiences and the positive of peer tutoring with students with disabilties.
Health and Safety
Dist - UATP **Prod** - UATP 1994

Peer Pressure 15 MIN
VHS / U-matic
Watch Your Language Series
Color (J H)
$125.00 purchase
Diagrams the use of proper language within peer groups and discusses the pressures involved to conform.
English Language; Social Science
Dist - AITECH **Prod** - KYTV 1984

Peer pressure 15 MIN
U-matic / VHS
Drug wise series; Module 3
Color (J)
Explores peer pressure as an influence in making decisions and demonstrates six techniques of saying No.
Health and Safety; Psychology
Dist - GPN **Prod** - WDCNTV

Peer Pressure 25 MIN
VHS / U-matic
Color (J H C A)
Looks at groups of teens from three high schools in the Boston area to reveal their differences in dress, speech and attitudes.
Psychology; Sociology
Dist - GERBER **Prod** - SIRS

Peer pressure 30 MIN
VHS
Club connect series
Color (J H G)
$59.95 purchase _ #CCNC-511-WC95
Describes a good method teenagers can use to determine their real friends. Explains to teens the meaning of friendship and offers methods to help them decide who their friends are. Includes an interview with race car driver Willy T. Ribbs.
Dist - PBS **Prod** - WTVSTV 1992

Peer pressure 15 MIN
U-matic / VHS
Drug wise series
(J)
$40 purchase, $25 rental, $75 self dub
Examines the effects of peer pressure in making decisions and highlights six ways of saying no.
Sociology
Dist - GPN **Prod** - NCGE 1984 - 1985

Peer pressure - 46 6 MIN
VHS / U-matic
Life's little lessons - self - esteem 4 - 6 series
Color (I)
$129.00, $99.00 purchase _ #V675
Discusses the social pressures everyone is subjected to. Urges youngsters to ask if they live for what everyone else thinks or if they have the courage to stand alone. Part of a 65 - part series on self - esteem.
Guidance and Counseling; Psychology
Dist - BARR **Prod** - CEPRO 1992

Peer pressure and drugs 20 MIN
VHS / U-matic / BETA
Color (J H)
$395.00 purchase _ #JR - 6018M
Discusses low self - esteem, the need to belong to a group, home and school problems as common reasons why young adults start using drugs. Uses a series of discussions and dramatizations to illustrate typical problems teens face today, and offers positive methods to avoid drug use.
Guidance and Counseling; Psychology; Sociology
Dist - CORF **Prod** - CORF 1989

Peer pressure and excellence - Tape 1 60 MIN
VHS
Champions series
Color (J H R)
$10.00 rental _ #36 - 896001 - 533
Features former Phoenix Cardinals quarterback Neil Lomax discussing peer pressure and Los Angeles Dodger pitcher Orel Hershiser discussing excellence. Includes musical segments from contemporary Christian musicians Amy Grant, Mylon LaFevre, Petra and Michael W Smith.
Religion and Philosophy
Dist - APH **Prod** - WORD

Peer pressure cooker - developing self discipline
VHS
School solutions video series
Color (I J H)
$98.00 purchase _ #CDSCH106V
Describes and illustrates the many forms of peer pressure through color footage and student interviews. Shows how to detect and deal with negative peer pressure. Reveals that peer pressure can also be positive as a function of learning the signs and limits and consequences of behavior. Offers a section on time management and how to deal with the many conflicting demands of a teen schedule. Includes reproducible worksheets. Part of a ten - part series to build student success.
Education; Psychology; Sociology
Dist - CAMV

Peer pressure, drugs - and you 32 MIN
VHS
Color (J H)
$189.00 purchase _ #2338 - SK
Discusses peer pressure among teenagers. Teaches assertiveness strategies for resisting peer pressure to use drugs. Explores the dynamics of group behavior that create peer pressure. Includes teacher's guide.
Guidance and Counseling; Psychology; Sociology
Dist - SUNCOM **Prod** - SUNCOM

Peer pressure series
Presents a two - part series on peer pressure. Includes the titles 'Learning to Be Yourself' and 'Nobody Tells Me What to Do.'
Learning to be yourself - 1 21 MIN
Nobody tells me what to do - 2 24 MIN
Dist - BARR **Prod** - SAIF

Peer Pressure - Single Parenting Parents are People Too - Handicapped Children 60 MIN
U-matic / VHS
From the Successful Parenting Series
Color (G)
Guidance and Counseling; Religion and Philosophy; Sociology
Dist - DSP **Prod** - DSP

The Peer pressure squeeze
VHS
Personality games for Macintosh series
Color (H C)
$79 purchase - #CDPVS106M-D
Looks at how students tend to respond differently to peer pressure. Explains where peer pressure comes from and what to do about it. Teaches students response skills as they interact with the tutorials and games in the program.
Business and Economics; Guidance and Counseling; Psychology
Dist - CAMV

Peer pressure - when the heat's on 30 MIN
VHS
Teen - aiders video series
Color (I J H G)
$149.95 purchase _ #NIMBS2V
Helps teens to become away of the problems of peer pressure in order to cope with everyday situations. Dramatizes teenagers who reveal real life pressures and how they cope. Discusses how to say NO when everyone else is saying YES. Includes a workbook. Part of a four - part series on teen issues.
Psychology; Sociology
Dist - CAMV

Peer pressure - when the heat's on 28 MIN
VHS
Color (I J H)
$149.00 purchase _ #NC109
Interviews teens who reveal real life pressures and explain how they cope. Uses dramatizations with young actors. Features discussions with Christopher Ewing, professional actor. Includes workbook.
Psychology; Sociology
Dist - AAVIM **Prod** - AAVIM

Peer pressure - why are all my friends staring at me 15 MIN
VHS
Understanding who you are - the personality video series
Color (J H)
$79.00 purchase _ #PVS514
Asks why pressure is so hard on a teen and if its effects are stronger on some personality types than others. Explores the interaction of peer pressure and personality type. Part of a ten - part series on personality.
Guidance and Counseling; Psychology; Sociology
Dist - CADESF **Prod** - CADESF 1990

Peer support ADHD - ADD teens SPEAKOUT 80 MIN
VHS
Color (I J H)
$49.95 purchase
Offers a support system for teens with attention deficit disorders or attention deficit hyperactive disorder. Shows teens how to cope with day - to - day life and addresses the issues of medication, school and communication in a workshop for ADHD - ADD teens.
Health and Safety; Psychology
Dist - STARBS **Prod** - STARBS 1994

Peer tutoring 30 MIN
U-matic / VHS
Project STRETCH - Strategies to Train Regular Educators to Teach Children with Handicaps Series; Module 8

Color (T S)
LC 80-706644
Shows a teacher interacting with a group of high school students as they implement a peer tutoring program for elementary level children.
Education; Psychology
Dist - HUBDSC **Prod** - METCO 1980

Peermanship 10 MIN
U-matic / VHS
Leadership Link - Fundamentals of Effective Supervision Series
Color
Business and Economics; Psychology
Dist - DELTAK **Prod** - CHSH

Peers in Middle Childhood 24 MIN
U-matic / VHS / 16mm
Color (T)
LC 80-701639
Shows the importance of the peer group to the nine - year - old child. Enters the classroom to examine the child's growing social identity, his desire to master learning skills and his methods of building self - esteem.
Education; Psychology
Dist - IFB **Prod** - MHFB 1975

Peewee Had a Little Ape 20 MIN
16mm
Magnificent 6 and 1/2 Series
Color (K P I)
Tells how the Magnificent Six And 1/2 mistake one of their members for an ape after he dons a gorilla suit. Concludes with a chase involving the police, a clown and a keeper from the circus.
Literature and Drama
Dist - LUF **Prod** - CHILDF 1970

Peewee's Pianola 16 MIN
16mm
Magnificent 6 and 1/2 Series
Color (K P I)
Shows how the Magnificent Six And 1/2 gang stumbles upon a player piano in the country and attempts to get it back to the city.
Fine Arts; Literature and Drama
Dist - LUF **Prod** - SF 1970

Pegasus 9 MIN
16mm / U-matic / VHS
Color (H C A)
LC 75-701623
Presents the mythological tale of a blacksmith who creates a sheet - metal horse as a protest against the advancement of technology over nature. Points out the relationship between modern man and his technology.
Literature and Drama; Social Science; Sociology
Dist - IFB **Prod** - PENFIL 1975

Peggy and Fred in Hell Series
Peggy and Fred in Kansas 11 MIN
The Prologue 21 MIN
Dist - WMEN

Peggy and Fred in Hell, the prologue 21 MIN
16mm
B&W (G A)
$50.00 rental
Presents the work of filmmaker Leslie Thornton. Involves two children, Peggy and Fred, in a post - apocalyptic, ersatz science fiction, arbitrary universe.
Fine Arts; Industrial and Technical Education; Literature and Drama
Dist - PARART **Prod** - WMEN 1988

Peggy and Fred in Kansas 11 MIN
VHS / U-matic
Peggy and Fred in Hell Series
Color (G)
$250.00, $200.00 purchase, $50.00 rental
Returns to the Peggy and Fred saga. Shows the girl and boy heroes a few years older and mumbling their way through mid America's wasteland. By Leslie Thornton.
Fine Arts; Psychology; Sociology
Dist - WMEN **Prod** - LETH

Peggy and Pierre 13 MIN
16mm
B&W (K)
A light - hearted vignette about a small girl and a large dog.
Literature and Drama
Dist - NYU **Prod** - NYU 1962

Peggy Collins 9 MIN
U-matic / VHS / 16mm
American Family - an Endangered Species Series
Color (H C A)
Presents a divorced mother who is raising her children alone.
Sociology
Dist - FI **Prod** - NBCNEW 1979

Peggy's Final Victory 28 MIN
16mm
Color (H C A)
LC 83-700620
Features the husband of a world class runner who died of cancer at age 28. Shows how they dealt with each other, family, friends and health care professionals during the illness and his thoughts at the time of her death.
Psychology; Sociology
Dist - IOWA **Prod** - IOWA 1983

Peinture Votive Au Quebec 27 MIN
16mm
Color (FRENCH)
_ *#106C 0282 005*
Geography - World
Dist - CFLMDC **Prod** - NFBC 1982

Peiping Family 21 MIN
16mm
B&W (P I)
Protrays middle - class Chinese family life prior to the communist rule. Depicts games and amusements, ritual respect for elders, and the parents' struggles for health and security in war - ravaged Peiping.
Geography - World; History - World; Psychology; Sociology
Dist - IFF **Prod** - IFF 1948

Peking dates 14 MIN
16mm
B&W (G)
$10.00 rental
Expresses the relationships between camera and subjects. Looks at how the balance between those watching and those being watched shifts frequently and with unusual power. A Rob Savage production.
Fine Arts; Psychology
Dist - CANCIN

Peking Duck, Pt 1 29 MIN
Videoreel / VT2
Joyce Chen Cooks Series
Color
Features Joyce Chen showing how to adapt Chinese recipes so they can be prepared in the American kitchen and still retain the authentic flavor. Demonstrates how to prepare Peking duck.
Geography - World; Home Economics
Dist - PBS **Prod** - WGBHTV

Peking Duck, Pt 2 29 MIN
Videoreel / VT2
Joyce Chen Cooks Series
Color
Features Joyce Chen showing how to adapt Chinese recipes so they can be prepared in the American kitchen and still retain the authentic flavor. Demonstrates how to prepare Peking duck.
Geography - World; Home Economics
Dist - PBS **Prod** - WGBHTV

Peking Ravioli 29 MIN
Videoreel / VT2
Joyce Chen Cooks Series
Color
Features Joyce Chen showing how to adapt Chinese recipes so they can be prepared in the American kitchen and still retain the authentic flavor. Demonstrates how to prepare Peking ravioli.
Geography - World; Home Economics
Dist - PBS **Prod** - WGBHTV

Peldanos del crecimiento - el video 10 MIN
VHS
Color (G) (SPANISH)
$19.95 purchase
Presents the essential components of a successful preschool program for blind and visually impaired children, featuring interviews with parents. Discussion guide included. Produced by Betty and Joe Dominguez.
Education; Guidance and Counseling
Dist - AFB **Prod** - AFB

Pele 12 MIN
U-matic / VHS
Color (G)
$229.00, $129.00 purchase _ #AD - 1851
Profiles Pele, universally acclaimed soccer player of South America. Reveals that he led his team to three World Cup championships and by entering the American sports arena generated unprecedented American interest in the sport of soccer.
Health and Safety; History - United States; Physical Education and Recreation
Dist - FOTH **Prod** - FOTH

Pele, the Master and His Method 60 MIN
VHS
(J H C)
$29.95 _ #BPG400V
Presents soccer star Pele who discusses ball control, passing, dribbling, kicking, trapping, and heading, as well as goal tending and physical training.
Physical Education and Recreation
Dist - CAMV

Pele - the Master and His Method 32 MIN
16mm
Color (GERMAN DUTCH FRENCH PORTUGUESE SPANISH)
LC 73-701865
Presents Argentine soccer player, Edson Arantes Do Nascimento, known as Pele, demonstrating his techniques.
Physical Education and Recreation
Dist - PEPSI **Prod** - PEPSI 1973

Peleliu - the Killing Ground 30 MIN
VHS / U-matic
World War II - GI Diary Series
Color (H C A)
History - United States; History - World
Dist - TIMLIF **Prod** - TIMLIF 1980

Peleliu - the Killing Ground 30 MIN
VHS / 16mm
World War II - G I Diary Series
(J H C)
$99.95 each, $995.00 series _ #19
Depicts the action and emotion that soldiers experienced during World War II, through their eyes and in their words. Narrated by Lloyd Bridges.
History - United States; History - World
Dist - AMBROS **Prod** - AMBROS 1980

Pelican 22 MIN
16mm / U-matic / VHS
Animals, Animals, Animals Series
Color (P I)
Presents Edward Lear's tale The Pelican Chorus told through animation and takes a whimsical at the pelican's sociable nature. Describes how an ornithologist studies this bird's life style, migration and feeding, and shows how a Floridian couple care for wounded birds at their sanctuary. Hosted by Hal Linden.
Science - Natural
Dist - MEDIAG **Prod** - ABCNEW 1977

Pelican Island 28 MIN
16mm
Nature Guide Film Series
Color (H A)
Presents the fascinating story of the white pelican, member of the species pelecanus erthrorhynchos, who, year after year, travel thousands of miles to a small island in the Great Salt Lake of Utah to build nests and hatch their eggs.
Geography - United States; Geography - World; Science - Natural
Dist - AVEXP **Prod** - AVEXP

Pelicans 6 MIN
U-matic / VHS / 16mm
Zoo Animals in the Wild Series
Color (K P I)
$135.00. $95.00 purchase _ #4000
Depicts the habits of pelicans as they gracefully fly, build nests, catch fish and feed their young.
Science - Natural
Dist - CORF **Prod** - CORF 1981

Pelicans - Ostriches - Rhinos and hippos - Cassette 3
VHS
Zoo animals in the wild series
Color; PAL (P)
Presents three short films on pelicans, ostriches and rhinos, and hippos in their natural habitat. Shows how they hunt for food, feed and care for their young. Points out attributes and behavior particular to each species and their environment. Part of a series on zoo animals in the wild.
Science - Natural
Dist - VIEWTH **Prod** - VIEWTH

Pelicula a Las Once, Sandinista TV News 28 MIN
VHS / U-matic
Color
Attacks the ideology and economics of mass media. Presented by Paper Tiger Television.
Fine Arts; Social Science
Dist - ARTINC **Prod** - ARTINC

Pelleas et Melisande 145 MIN
VHS
Color (G)
$29.95 purchase_#1409
Presents Pelleas et Melisande - Debussy's only opera. Features opera stars Francois Le Roux and Collette Alliot-Lugaz in the roles of Pelleas and Melisande. An imaginative and sensitive love story portraying jealousy and remorse.
Fine Arts
Dist - KULTUR

Pelts - Politics of the fur trade 56 MIN
VHS

Color (H C G)
$850.00, $350.00 purchase, $85.00 rental
Gives viewers an inside look at the hotly debated animal rights issues. Takes an objective look at the ethical, environmental and economic issues raised by the debate. Tours the largest fur auction house in North America. Visits witn native peoples whose livelihood depends on the fur trade. Watches the craftsmanship involved in making a fur coat. Goes behind the scenes of the public relations campaigns waged by both animal rights activists and the fur industry. A film by Nigel Markham.
Fine Arts; Physical Education and Recreation; Social Science; Sociology
Dist - CANCIN **Prod** - NFBC 1990

Pelvic and Balanced Suspension Traction 13 MIN
VHS / BETA
Color
Demonstrates how to apply and adjust pelvic and balanced suspension traction.
Health and Safety
Dist - RMIBHF **Prod** - RMIBHF

Pelvic Area - Female 30 MIN
VHS / U-matic
Health Assessment Series
Color (PRO)
Views a physical assessment by a nurse practitioner of the pelvic area of a live female patient.
Health and Safety; Science - Natural
Dist - BRA **Prod** - BRA

Pelvic Area - Male 25 MIN
VHS / U-matic
Health Assessment Series
Color (PRO)
Views a physical assessment by a nurse practitioner of the pelvic area of a live male patient.
Health and Safety; Science - Natural
Dist - BRA **Prod** - BRA

The Pelvic exam - Part II 45 MIN
VHS
Gynecological teaching associate instructional program on breast and pelvic examination series
Color (C PRO G)
$395.00 purchase _ #R910 - VI - 038
Teaches the pelvic portion of the gynecological exam. Shows how gynecological teaching assistants - GTAs - work with students, portraying the patient and guiding the student through the exam. The GTA gives the student instruction and feedback about appropriate diagnostic techniques while creating the psychological dynamics of the examination procedure. Shows the external genital exam, the speculum exam - without the pap smear, and bimanual and rectovaginal exams. During the external exam, the patient is given detailed information about each external genital structure and what its function is. Stresses appropriate interpersonal communication throughout. Produced at Univ of Medicine and Dentistry of New Jersey.
Health and Safety
Dist - HSCIC

The Pelvic examination 26 MIN
VHS / U-matic
Color (C PRO)
$395.00 purchase, $80.00 rental _ #C920 - VI - 032
Instructs medical students on how to achieve rapport with a patient when performing a pelvic examination. Demonstrates step - by - step procedures for conducting the vaginal pelvic, bimanual and rectovaginal exams. Contains procedures for obtaining specimens for the Pap test, gonorrhea and chlamydia and saline wet mount. Presented by Dr Ronald Brimberry.
Health and Safety
Dist - HSCIC

Pelvic examination 17 MIN
VHS / U-matic / BETA
Techniques of physical diagnosis - a visual approach series
Color (PRO)
$395.00 purchase
Reviews the techniques for patient preparation, external genital examination, speculum use and internal palpation. Part of a series by Dr Donald W Novey teaching the basic skills of physical examination as seen through the eyes of the examiner.
Health and Safety
Dist - MEDMDS

The Pelvic examination and pap smear 28 MIN
U-matic / VHS
Color (PRO C)
$385.00 purchase, $80.00 rental _ #C881 - VI - 057
Introduces medical students to the procedures and techniques of the pelvic examination and the pap smear. Performs the entire examination in a step - by - step manner, including speculum examination, bi - manual examination and the pap smear. Provides charts, illustrations and anatomical models for understanding pelvic anatomy, cervical characteristics and ovarian anomalies. Describes and demonstrates equipment used. Emphasizes proper patient communication, especially psychological preparation of the patient prior to examination. Presented by Dr Jaroslaw Hulka.
Health and Safety
Dist - HSCIC

Pelvic Examination for Contraception 25 MIN
16mm
Color (BENGALI PORTUGUESE SPANISH)
Uses animation to demonstrate the key elements of pelvic anatomy and shows bimanual examination through both live and animated footage. Teaches proper techniques for insertion of intrauterine devices (both push - in and withdrawal methods) and diaphragm fitting.
Health and Safety
Dist - PATHFU **Prod** - PATHFU 1981

Pelvic examination for contraception 23 MIN
VHS / U-matic
Color (PRO) (BENGALI SPANISH PORTUGUESE)
Discusses how to do a thorough pelvic examination in preparation for IUD insertion or fitting a diaphragm.
Health and Safety; Sociology
Dist - WFP **Prod** - WFP

Pelvic Examination Series
Anatomy for abdominal and pelvic examination
Exam Findings - Description and Classification
Examination Procedures
Dist - OMNIED

Pelvic Exenteration for Cervical Cancer 31 MIN
16mm
Color (PRO)
LC FIA68-788
Illustrates the technique employed in total excision of the pelvic organs for cancer of the uterine cervix. Shows excision of pelvic viscera, pelvic lymphadenectomy, terminal sigmoid colostomy and ileal conduit procedures.
Health and Safety; Science - Natural
Dist - EATONL **Prod** - UMIAMI 1968

Pelvic floor muscle re - education 24 MIN
VHS / U-matic
Understanding and treating incontinence series
Color (PRO C)
$395.00 purchase, $80.00 rental _ #C891 - VI - 006
Discusses the anatomy of female and male pelvic girdles. Makes the point that pelvic floor exercises can be used to cure incontinence where pelvic floor laxity has caused or aggravated the condition. Stresses the importance of pelvic floor exercises as part of the lifelong routine of women who have delivered children. Presents two case histories - one illustrating the use of exercise following multiple pregnancies to treat stress incontinence, the other demonstrating the use of exercise in a male patient suffering from post - prostatectomy incontinence. Part of a seven - part series on incontinence presented by J C Brocklehurst and Bernadette M Ryan - Wooley.
Health and Safety; Physical Education and Recreation; Science - Natural
Dist - HSCIC

Pelvic inflammatory disease 9 MIN
VHS
Color (G PRO C) (SPANISH)
$100.00 purchase _ #OB - 53
Explains how PID - pelvic inflammatory disease - is an infection caused in most cases by contracting a sexually transmitted disease. Describes the symptoms, treatment and what the long term effects may be if allowed to go untreated.
Health and Safety; Sociology
Dist - MIFE **Prod** - MIFE

Pelvic Inflammatory Disease 47 MIN
VHS / 16mm
(C)
$385.00 purchase _ #850VI029
Explains all aspects of pelvic inflammatory disease - PID - , its diagnosis, and its treatment.
Health and Safety
Dist - HSCIC **Prod** - HSCIC 1985

Pelvic Lymph Node Dissection and I - 125 Implantation for Prostatic Cancer 20 MIN
16mm
Color (PRO)
LC 79-700260
Demonstrates the procedure for implanting needles into the prostate for application of I - 125 therapy. Describes how to calculate correct dosage and shows how to administer the medication.
Health and Safety
Dist - EATONL **Prod** - EATONL 1978

Pelvic Mass in an Amenorrheic Woman 45 MIN
U-matic
Color
Presents a case study of a 27 - year - old amenorrheic woman who has secondary symptoms of ovarian neoplasm.
Health and Safety
Dist - UTEXSC **Prod** - UTEXSC

Pelvic Region, Pt 1 - Iliosacral 17 MIN
VHS / U-matic
Osteopathic Examination and Manipulation Series
Color (PRO)
Focuses on diagnostic and manipulative procedures for iliosacral aspects of pelvic motion. Shows a test for pelvic mobility by introduction of motion from below. Demonstrates direct manipulative techniques for iliosacral dysfunction.
Health and Safety; Science - Natural
Dist - MSU **Prod** - MSU

Pelvic Region, Pt 2 - Sacroiliac 13 MIN
U-matic / VHS
Osteopathic Examination and Manipulation Series
Color (PRO)
Presents examples of postural stresses in the sagittal plane and gives manipulative techniques to relieve such stress. Identifies more complex minor motion properties. Applies the principles of both direct and indirect manipulation for sacroiliac dysfunction in the seated position.
Health and Safety; Science - Natural
Dist - MSU **Prod** - MSU

Pelvic Ultrasound
U-matic / VHS
X - Ray Procedures in Layman's Terms Series
Color
Health and Safety; Science
Dist - FAIRGH **Prod** - FAIRGH

The Pelvis - Part II 45 MIN
U-matic / VHS
Gynecological teaching associate instructional program on breast and pelvic examination series
Color (PRO C)
$395.00 purchase, $80.00 rental _ #C910 - VI - 038
Instructs medical students in the pelvic portion of the gynecologic examination. Features a gynecological teaching associate - GTA - who takes the place of the patient and guides the student through the exam. Gives instruction and feedback about appropriate diagnostic techniques. Part one of a two - part series presented by Josie Hasle and Lisa Quackenbush, University of Medicine and Dentistry of New Jersey.
Health and Safety
Dist - HSCIC

Pelvis Region, Pt 3 - Alternative Direct Techniques 12 MIN
VHS / U-matic
Osteopathic Examination and Manipulation Series
Color (PRO)
Continues discussion of the development of concepts of sacroiliac dysfunction. Demonstrates direct sacroiliac manipulative procedures in sidelying and supine positions.
Health and Safety; Science - Natural
Dist - MSU **Prod** - MSU

Pen and Ink 12 MIN
16mm
Introduction to Commercial Art Series
Color (J)
LC 80-700519
Shows common tools used to produce black and white illustrations and techniques to create texture and shading in the rendering of an animal.
Fine Arts
Dist - SF **Prod** - SF 1979

The Pen is Mightier than the Sword 30 MIN
U-matic / VHS
Alphabet - the Story of Writing Series
Color
Deals with Celtic scripts in the Dark Ages, the Carolingian script, the impact of the new quill pen and the medieval scribes and illuminators.
English Language; History - World
Dist - WSTGLC **Prod** - WSTGLC

The Pen is Mightier than the Sword 28 MIN
16mm
Alphabet - the Story of Writing Series
Color
Discusses the language of the Western World, the fall of the Roman empire, Celtic scripts in the Dark Ages, the Carolingian script, the making of a quill pen and the techniques of illumination.
English Language; History - World
Dist - FILAUD **Prod** - CFDLD 1982

Pen Point Percussion with Loops 10 MIN
U-matic / VHS / 16mm
Color (C A)
Presents an explanation of the principles and production of synthetic sound, showing Norman Mc Laren's experimentation with hand - drawn sounds on film. Closes with 'LOOPS,' an example of this technique.
Fine Arts
Dist - IFB **Prod** - NFBC 1951

The Pen Register 14 MIN
U-matic
Color (J H C)
LC 82-707073
Describes the Texas wiretap law, including the legal rulings on use of the pen register and civil liberties concerns.
Civics and Political Systems; History - United States
Dist - SWINS **Prod** - SWINS 1982

The Penalty area 26 MIN
VHS
Ordinary people series
Color (G)
$190.00 purchase, $50.00 rental
Presents an unprecedented sporting event and the first filming inside a South African prison. Covers a soccer game between South Africa's most popular team - symbol of Soweto and heroes to the inmates - and the home prison team at a maximum security prison, once notorious for its inhumane conditions until soccer was introduced. Looks at the match through a warrant officer, who runs the recreation progam; a bank robber - soccer coach; and the goalkeeper of the opposing team. Part of a series which chronicles an event in South Africa through the eyes of three or four 'ordinary' people, chosen to represent diverse backgrounds or dissimilar points of view.
Fine Arts; History - World; Physical Education and Recreation; Sociology
Dist - FIRS **Prod** - GAVSHO 1993

Penalty Kick - Risk Factors 15 MIN
VHS / 16mm
Your Choice - Our Chance Series
Color (I A)
$180.00 purchase, $25.00 rental
Suggests that understanding factors that put them at risk and learning how to handle them can help students avoid early use of tobacco, alcohol and drugs.
Health and Safety; Psychology
Dist - AITECH **Prod** - AITECH 1990

Penance - Part 7 30 MIN
VHS
Sacraments - Signs of faith and grace series
Color (R G)
$39.95 purchase _ #SACR7
Explores the sacrament of penance to bring about a better understanding of the meaning of the rite through examination of the actions, symbols and words. Features Bruce Baumgarten. Part seven of an eight - part series on the sacraments.
Religion and Philosophy
Dist - CTNA **Prod** - CTNA

Penance - Sacrament of Peace 11 MIN
16mm
Sacrament Series
Color (J)
LC 72-700509
Uses a dramatization about the emotional response of a young architect who seriously injures a ten - year - old girl while driving home from a cocktail party to suggest various aspects and effects of the Sacrament of Penance.
Guidance and Counseling; Religion and Philosophy
Dist - FRACOC **Prod** - FRACOC 1969

The Pencil 5 MIN
U-matic / VHS / 16mm
How It's made Series
Color (K)
Business and Economics
Dist - LUF **Prod** - HOLIA

The Pencil 8 MIN
U-matic / VHS / 16mm
Color (P I)
LC 77-703372
Presents a visual description without narration to show how pencils are made and the variety of ordinary and unusual ways in which they can be used.
English Language; Fine Arts; Social Science
Dist - JOU **Prod** - INCC 1977

Pencil booklings 14 MIN
16mm
Color (G)
$200.00 purchase, $40.00 rental
Presents simple, line - drawn characters who come to life and begin to direct themselves in a quirky tale of the creative process of animation.
Fine Arts; Literature and Drama
Dist - WMEN **Prod** - ROSEK

Pencil drawing 20 MIN
VHS
Color (J H C G)
$29.95 purchase _ #CPC880V
Demonstrates the drawing of individual objects such as fruit, vegetables, plants, animals, birds, cars, balls and saddles to show accent line, contour line, values, form, gradation, textures, as well as crosshatch, pointillism and scumble. Discusses types of pencils, papers and other materials. Features artist and teacher Gail Price.
Fine Arts
Dist - CAMV

Pencil of nature 25 MIN
VHS
Pioneers of photography series
Color (A)
PdS65 purchase
Examines the work of W Henry Fox Talbot, the first person to fix a negative photographic image onto paper permanently. Part of an eight-part series that examines the contributions made by pioneers in photography.
Fine Arts; Industrial and Technical Education
Dist - BBCENE

Pencils and Paper 30 MIN
U-matic
Media and Methods of the Artist Series
Color (H C A)
Demonstrates a variety of pencils and papers for art work.
Fine Arts
Dist - TVOTAR **Prod** - TVOTAR 1971

Pendant cranes 20 MIN
8mm cartridge / VHS / BETA / U-matic
Color; PAL (IND G)
$295.00 purchase, $175.00 rental _ #BTH - 100
Provides step - by - step training in basic rigging and handling procedures for overhead pendant cranes. Shows the proper procedures for rigging and handling loads, outlines each element of the inspection checklist, illustrates special procedures for radio - controlled and magnetic cranes and highlights speical precautions to take when handling loads and more. Includes a leader's guide and ten workbooks.
Health and Safety; Psychology
Dist - BNA

Pendulum in a Rotating Plane 32 MIN
U-matic / VHS
Nonlinear Vibrations Series
B&W
Discusses application of phase - plane method to a simple pendulum rotating about a vertical center line in a vertical plane. Teaches effect of centrifugal force on the oscillation.
Mathematics
Dist - MIOT **Prod** - MIOT

Pendulums 15 MIN
U-matic / VHS
Let Me See Series no 1
Color (P)
Uses clocks and swings to introduce the concept of a pendulum. Presents Hocus and Myrtle investigating pendulums at home and a magician demonstrating how they work.
Science - Physical
Dist - AITECH **Prod** - WETN 1982

The Penelope gang 35 MIN
VHS
Color (P I R)
$39.00 rental _ #36 - 80 - 2028
Portrays the adventures some kids went through after discovering an old circus calliope. Teaches lessons about growing up. Produced by Kuntz Brothers.
Literature and Drama; Religion and Philosophy
Dist - APH

Penelope Gilliatt 40 MIN
VHS
Color (H C G)
$79.00 purchase
Features the writer discussing with Penelope Lively how to use childhood experiences in writing and to develop characters and plots. Talks about her works that include The New Statesman and The Guardian.
Literature and Drama; Sociology
Dist - ROLAND **Prod** - INCART

Penelope Lively 42 MIN
VHS
Color (H C G)
$79.00 purchase
Features the writer discussing with Nicholas Bagnall her explorations of people and situations through her writing. Looks at creating certain unfamiliar character types in one's work. Talks about her stories for children and her adult novels Treasure of Time and Moon Tiger.
Literature and Drama
Dist - ROLAND **Prod** - INCART

Penetrating Wounds of the Abdomen 14 MIN
16mm
Color
LC FIE54-448
Demonstrates five steps for handling penetrating wounds of the abdomen, including make a speedy and accurate diagnosis, keep the patient on his back, apply a sterile dressing, treat for shock and prepare for speedy evacuation.
Health and Safety; Science
Dist - USNAC **Prod** - USN 1953

Penetrating Wounds of the Large Intestine 21 MIN
16mm
Color (PRO)
Points out that mortality and morbidity from penetrating wounds of the colon have been reduced progressively during the twentieth century through aggressive surgery. Presents various types of colon wounds to illustrate these principles in two cases.
Health and Safety; Science
Dist - ACY **Prod** - ACYDGD 1962

Penguins 8 MIN
U-matic / VHS / 16mm
Color (P I J H C A)
$215, $155 purchase _ #3953
Shows lots of penguin in funny situations accompanied by piano music. A Perspective film.
Fine Arts; Science - Natural
Dist - CORF

Penguins 15 MIN
VHS
Animal profile series
Color (P I)
$59.95 purchase _ #RB8111
Studies penguins. Includes rare footage of Humboldt penguins 'braying'. Part of a series on animals which looks at examples from the mammal, snake and bird classes, filmed in their natural habitat.
Science - Natural
Dist - REVID **Prod** - REVID 1990

Penguins 25 mniutes
U-matic / VHS / 16mm
Untamed World Series
Color; Mono (J H C A)
$400.00 film, $250.00 video, $50.00 rental
Features the evolutionary story of the penguin with emphasis on the Adelie and its habits and behaviors.
Science - Natural
Dist - CTV **Prod** - CTV 1971

Penguins of the Antarctic 13 MIN
U-matic / VHS / 16mm
Color; Captioned (I)
LC 73-702553
Presents emperor and adelie penguins exhibiting their eccentric habits in the comfort of their Antarctic homeland. Supplies information emphasizing man's positive role in assisting the penguin in its formidable environment.
Geography - World; Science - Natural
Dist - AIMS **Prod** - BOSMS 1972

Penile Curvature - Lateral and Ventral 20 MIN
U-matic / VHS
Color (PRO)
Describes a unique surgical procedure to correct penile curvature.
Health and Safety
Dist - WFP **Prod** - WFP

Penile Implant 9 MIN
VHS / U-matic
Color
Provides a basic review of anatomy and physiology of the penis and discusses the two most commonly used prosthetic devices, the rod - shaped silicone and the inflatable version.
Health and Safety; Science - Natural
Dist - MEDCOM **Prod** - MEDCOM

Penitentiaries personnel training series
Control of inmates 27 MIN
Dist - IFB

Penitentiary Staff Training Series
The Correctional Process 53 MIN
Custodial procedures 25 MIN
Inmate Training, Pt 1 29 MIN
Inmate Training, Pt 2 30 MIN
The Prison Community 29 MIN
Reception 28 MIN
Square Johns 28 MIN
Types of Inmates 31 MIN
Dist - IFB

Penman, Printer and Engraver 30 MIN
U-matic / VHS
Alphabet - the Story of Writing Series

Color
Deals with the making of books, the Gothic and Italic scripts, the development of printing and metal engraving, and the steel nib pen that made everyone a writer.
English Language; History - World
Dist - WSTGLC **Prod** - WSTGLC

Penman, Printer and Engraver 28 MIN
16mm
Alphabet - the Story of Writing Series
Color
Deals with the making of books and the chair libraries, how the scribe corrected his errors, the Gothic and Italic script, the development of printing, copperplate engraving, copperplate handwriting and the birth of the steel nib.
English Language; History - World
Dist - FILAUD **Prod** - CFDLD 1982

Pennies from Heaven 81 MIN
16mm
B&W (H C A)
Relates the story of a drifter who befriends an orphaned girl and her grandfather. Stars Bing Crosby, Edith Fellows and Madge Evans.
Fine Arts
Dist - TIMLIF **Prod** - CPC 1936

Pennies from heaven 11 MIN
VHS
Color; PAL; Silent (K P)
PdS20 purchase
Adapts a story from the fairy tales collected by the Grimm Brothers. Uses animation to illustrate the plot and turn abstract ideas into clear and understandable images. Encourages classroom discussion. Contact distributor about availability outside the United Kingdom.
Literature and Drama
Dist - ACADEM

The Pennines 17 MIN
16mm / U-matic / VHS
Color (J H)
LC FIA68-2894
Examines the Pennine landscape, emphasizing similarities and differences between the southern, central and northern parts of the mountain chain. Illustrates each section's detail, describing natural routes to the east and west, using aerial photography.
Geography - World
Dist - IFB **Prod** - BHA 1967

Penn's Dream 29 MIN
U-matic / VHS / 16mm
Color (J H C G T A)
Shows how Penn defined a form of government based on the fundamental ideas of tolerance, liberty, and human rights. Features a reenactment of the famous Penn/Mead trial of 1670, which demonstrates the principles on which Penn sought to base the new colony. Other segments recall the threats to freedom which the Commonwealth has faced in its history - the 'Walking Purchase,' the burning of Pennsylvania Hall, and the Kensington riots. The Penn/Mead trial was filmed on location at the Cambria County courthouse in Ebensburg, Pennsylvania, with Bob Leonard portraying William Penn.
Biography; Geography - United States; History - United States
Dist - PSU **Prod** - PSU 1981

Pennsylvania 60 MIN
VHS
Portrait of America series
Color (J H C G)
$99.95 purchase _ #AMB38V
Visits Pennsylvania. Offers extensive research into the state's history. Films key locations and presents segments on its history, government, education, folklore, science, journalism, sociology, industry, agriculture and business. Shows what is unique about Pennsylvania and what is distinctive about its regional culture and how it got to be that way. Includes teacher study guides. Part of a 50 - part series.
Geography - United States; History - United States
Dist - CAMV

Pennsylvania Country Cooking 20 MIN
16mm
Color
Presents five recipes which are representative of the everyday foods served on the tables of the Pennsylvania Dutch. Adapted from the American Heritage Cookbook.
History - United States; Home Economics
Dist - BUGAS **Prod** - BUGAS

Pennsylvania Dutch
VHS
Frugal gourmet - taste of America series
Color (G)
$19.95 purchase _ #CCP824
Shows how to prepare American food in Pennsylvania Dutch style. Features Jeff Smith, the Frugal Gourmet. Part of a ten - part series on American cooking.
Geography - United States; History - United States; Home Economics; Physical Education and Recreation
Dist - CADESF **Prod** - CADESF

Pennsylvania Journey 27 MIN
U-matic / VHS
Color
Focuses on the geographic space and history of Pennsylvania. Features professor of geography, Peirce Lewis, as he travels through the state. Includes historical sites, farm country, mining areas, mountains, business and industry and the major city of Pittsburgh.
Geography - United States; History - United States
Dist - PSU **Prod** - PSU 1984

The Pennsylvania Railroad
VHS
Color (G)
$49.95 purchase _ #GFP010
Captures the end of the steam locomotive era and the transition to the first generation diesels.
Geography - United States; Social Science
Dist - SIV

Penny and Sonya Cohen 52 MIN
U-matic / VHS
Rainbow quest series
Color
Covers work songs and lullabyes. Shows men singing as they work. Pete Seeger welcomes his sister Penny and her infant daughter Sonya Cohen to the show.
Fine Arts
Dist - NORROS **Prod** - SEEGER

Penny Serenade 125 MIN
16mm
B&W
Features Irene Dunne as a woman about to break up with her husband, played by Cary Grant. Directed by George Stevens.
Fine Arts
Dist - REELIM

Penny serenade 30 MIN
VHS
Classic short stories
Color (H)
#E362; LC 90-708403
Presents 'Penny Serenade' by Martha Cheavens. Part of a series which combines Hollywood stars with short story masterpieces of the world to encourage appreciation of the short story.
Literature and Drama
Dist - GPN **Prod** - CTI 1988

A Penny Suite 5 MIN
16mm / U-matic / VHS
Color
LC 77-700400
Presents an animated story about a carousel whose animals come to life and play like children.
Fine Arts
Dist - PHENIX **Prod** - AFI 1977

Penny wise 30 MIN
Videoreel / VT2
Designing home interiors series; Unit 29
Color (C A)
Discusses how to create interesting effects in interior design with a limited budget. Demonstrates one room with three different designs and three budgets.
Home Economics
Dist - CDTEL **Prod** - COAST

Pennywise - Review 15 MIN
VHS / U-matic
Pennywise Series no 12
Color (P)
LC 82-706014
Uses the format of a television program to review the economic concepts presented in the first 11 recordings of the Pennywise Series. Summarizes how wants and needs, consumption of goods and services, production, income, money and credit are important to understanding how the American economy works.
Business and Economics
Dist - GPN **Prod** - MAETEL 1980

Pennywise Series no 12
Pennywise - Review 15 MIN
Dist - GPN

Pennywise Series no 1
Wants and Needs 15 MIN
Dist - GPN

Pennywise Series no 3
Consumption 15 MIN
Dist - GPN

Pennywise Series no 5
Production 15 MIN
Dist - GPN

Pennywise Series no 6
Specialization 15 MIN
Dist - GPN

Pennywise Series no 7
Interdependence 15 MIN
Dist - GPN

Pennywise series
Credit 15 MIN
Income 15 MIN
Dist - GPN

A Pennzoil Day 34 MIN
16mm
Color
LC 75-703527
Describes the scope of the Pennzoil Company with views of its employees making the most of natural resources in different parts of the United States.
Business and Economics; Industrial and Technical Education; Social Science
Dist - PENNZ **Prod** - PENNZ 1975

Penology - the Keepers of the Keys 22 MIN
U-matic / VHS / 16mm
Color (J)
Predicts that the future may use everything from electronic controls to rehabilitative group therapy to handle the criminal problem.
Sociology
Dist - CNEMAG **Prod** - DOCUA

Pens and Inks 30 MIN
U-matic
Media and Methods of the Artist Series
Color (H C A)
Demonstrates a variety of pens and inks for art work and looks at relevant techniques for their use.
Fine Arts
Dist - TVOTAR **Prod** - TVOTAR 1971

Pensacola Panorama 15 MIN
16mm
Color
Presents Pensacola, one of Florida's oldest cities and the home of the Naval Air Training Command.
Geography - United States; History - United States
Dist - FLADC **Prod** - FLADC

Pense a Ton Desir 28 MIN
U-matic
Color (C) (FRENCH (ENGLISH SUBTITLED))
$350.00 purchase, $45.00, $65.00 rental
Presents a French language film - Make A Wish - with subtitles in English. Takes a look at aging women. Tells how a woman is changed by menopause, her children leaving home, and her husband's retirement. Looks at the plight of older women in a society sees only young and beautiful women. Produced by Diane Poitras and Les Productions Contre - Jour.
Psychology; Sociology
Dist - WMENIF

The Pension cookie jar 30 MIN
VHS / 16mm
Color (G IND)
$5.00 rental, $49.00 purchase _ #322-9305
Examines cases of companies which terminated pensions to skim surplus funds and leave workers with reduced pensions. Looks at the history of pension funds which built up a surplus during the 1980s because of high interest rates. Reveals that financial consultants discovered a loophole in the pension law which allowed corporations to skim off the surplus funds. Since 1980, 1400 companies have skimmed off $18 billion from the 'pension cookie jar.'
Business and Economics; Sociology
Dist - AFLCIO **Prod** - NBCNEW 1988
FI

The Pentagon 60 MIN
VHS
Power Game Series
Color; Captioned (G)
$59.95 purchase _ #TPGE - 102
Questions whether the high military spending of the Reagan years made America more secure. Suggests that rivalries between the different service branches have hurt fighting effectiveness. Shows that political and economic interests can be more important in determining Pentagon policy than security reasons.
Civics and Political Systems; Computer Science; History - United States
Dist - PBS **Prod** - MPTPB 1988

The Pentagon Papers 30 MIN
16mm
B&W
Examines our government's record of public deception, the right of the public to receive full information on government policy, the rights of free speech and the need to support a government which is truly responsible to the

people. Depicts the change in Ellsberg's social conscience, from that of a dedicated defense department worker to a public citizen understanding that our first trust must be in the Constitution and in the Bill of Rights.
Biography; Civics and Political Systems; Sociology
Dist - IMPACT **Prod** - STOLLJ 1973

The Pentagon Papers 14 MIN
VHS / U-matic
Color (H C A)
Tells how the secret history of America's conduct in Vietnam was revealed through the nation's press. Documents the controversy between the government's need for secrecy and the people's right to know.
History - United States; Literature and Drama
Dist - JOU **Prod** - UPI

Pentode Crystal Oscillator 30 MIN
16mm
B&W
LC 74-705337
Explains the importance of stability in the pentode crystal oscillator and discusses the importance of each component. Tells how the correct amount and phase of feedback voltage is obtained and demonstrates the correct tuning procedure for the most stable operation.
Industrial and Technical Education; Science - Physical
Dist - USNAC **Prod** - USAF 1970

Pentodes and Pentagrids 28 MIN
16mm
B&W
LC 74-705338
Illustrates the schematic of a pentode tube and identifies the elements. Explains the purpose of the suppressor grid. Shows the schematic of a pentagrid grid and the additional screen grid. Discusses multiknit tubes, explaining what they are and how they work. (Kinescope).
Industrial and Technical Education; Science - Physical
Dist - USNAC **Prod** - USAF 1972

Penumbra 14 MIN
16mm
Color (H C A)
$35.00 rental
Presents a poetic exploration of the nature of dreams; the way they slip in and out of our waking lives, offering glimpses into our unconscious and beyond. Suggests links between dreams and our ancestral past or our future. Produced by Hillary Morgan.
Psychology
Dist - CANCIN

Peony Composition 30 MIN
VHS / 16mm
Chinese Brush Painting Series
Color (C A)
$85.00, $75.00 purchase _ 20 - 15
Illustrates pink and red peonies, yellow poppy, and blue iris.
Fine Arts
Dist - CDTEL **Prod** - COAST 1987

Peony Elements 30 MIN
VHS / 16mm
Chinese Brush Painting Series
Color (C A)
$85.00, $75.00 purchase _ 20 - 14
Shows the bud and surrounding elements, leaves and veins.
Fine Arts
Dist - CDTEL **Prod** - COAST 1987

Peony Flowers 30 MIN
VHS / 16mm
Chinese Brush Painting Series
Color (C A)
$85.00, $75.00 purchase _ 20 - 13
Describes the legends, symbolic meaning and subtle shadings of the peony flower.
Fine Arts
Dist - CDTEL **Prod** - COAST 1987

People 15 MIN
VHS / U-matic
Let's Draw Series
Color (P)
Fine Arts
Dist - AITECH **Prod** - OCPS 1976

People 22 MIN
16mm
Color
Looks at the men and women of the U S Army Corps of Engineers who perform a variety of jobs in the U S and overseas. Describes the wide range of Corps missions that support the Army and the nation, and portrays the spectrum of surprising jobs performed.
Civics and Political Systems; Guidance and Counseling; Industrial and Technical Education
Dist - MTP **Prod** - USAE

People 3 MIN
16mm
Color (G)
$5.00 rental
Features the Red Mountain Tribe hanging out in the filmmaker's backyard.
Fine Arts; Sociology
Dist - CANCIN **Prod** - LIPTNL 1969

The People 28 MIN
U-matic / VHS
Color
Documents the struggle of the Siletz Indian tribe in Oregon to regain federal recognition of their tribe. Interweaves a history of federal Indian policies with personal remembrances from tribal members.
Social Science; Sociology
Dist - MEDIPR **Prod** - DAWSH 1976

People 11 MIN
U-matic / VHS / 16mm
Color (K)
LC 78-704202
Shows scenes of people of all ages and races as they rest, work and play to demonstrate that people are different yet alike.
Psychology; Social Science; Sociology
Dist - ALTSUL **Prod** - FILMSW 1969

The People and Apollo 19 MIN
16mm
Color
LC 74-705340
Tells a unique story of civil preparedness at the local level in connection with the Apollo 16 moon shot from Cape Kennedy. Shows how the Civil Defense Office organized a task force for traffic control, crowd handling and a variety of emergency services.
Psychology; Social Science
Dist - USNAC **Prod** - USDCPA 1973

People and cultures series
Culture, what is it 13 MIN
Cultures - why are they different 13 MIN
World cultures - similarities and differences 50 MIN
Dist - KNOWUN

People and Environment 29 MIN
VHS / 16mm
Villa Alegre Series
Color (P T)
$46.00 rental _ #VILA - 1
Presents educational material in both Spanish and English.
Education; Social Science
Dist - PBS

People and Particles 28 MIN
16mm
B&W
LC FIA68-544
Follows physicists at the Cambridge electron accelerator as they design, construct and assemble equipment for an experiment in high energy physics.
Science - Physical
Dist - MLA **Prod** - HPP 1967

People and Places of Antiquity Series
Egypt - gift of the Nile 29 MIN
Iran - Landmarks in the Desert 27 MIN
Iraq - Stairway to the Gods 27 MIN
Pakistan - Mound of the Dead 27 MIN
Peru - People of the Sun 25 MIN
Dist - CORF

People and Problems 28 MIN
16mm
Water Supply and Sanitation in Development Series
Color (H C A)
$550.00, $150.00 purchase, $25.00 rental _ #NC1824
Considers the world - wide problem of inadequate clean water suppies and the sanitary disposal of human waste, documenting the relationship between these factors and enteric disease. Discusses solutions.
Health and Safety; Science - Natural
Dist - IU **Prod** - NFBC 1985

People and Productivity - We Learn from the Japanese 28 MIN
U-matic / VHS / 16mm
Color (H C A)
LC 82-700549
Presents a former U S ambassador to Japan and a professor from the Harvard business school who analyze the values of the respectful and industrious Japanese people that have made them world leaders in manufacturing. Includes views of assembly lines in Japan and the Honda plant in Ohio which applies proven Japanese practices to its U S operation.
Business and Economics; Geography - World
Dist - EBEC **Prod** - OLINC 1982

The People and their Guns 97 MIN
16mm
B&W
Provides an understanding of the way in which the Laotian people relate to each other and their struggle to develop the new patterns of socialist life which are being forged in the very process of struggle.
Civics and Political Systems; Geography - World; Sociology
Dist - IMPACT **Prod** - IMPACT 1970

People and Things - Careers in Manufacturing 13 MIN
16mm
Working Worlds Series
Color (I J H)
LC 75-701543
Deals with the broad range of career opportunities within the manufacturing industry. Looks at these careers in terms of the design function, capital goods manufacturing and consumer goods manufacturing. Examines assembly line occupations as both a source of career opportunity and as an area of the working world which has been a source of worker dissatisfaction.
Guidance and Counseling; Psychology
Dist - FFORIN **Prod** - OLYMPS 1974

People and Values
VHS
Personal Development Series
Color (H)
$98.00 purchase _ #ABV 103
Features four students discussing values, motivations and life priorities. Features the students playing values auction, where they must choose what values they are willing to pay for. Also available in Beta or 3/4".
Psychology
Dist - CADESF **Prod** - CADESF 1988

People are all Alike 10 MIN
16mm
Human Factors in Safety Series
Color
LC FIA66-518
Uses case histories of five completely different workers to demonstrate to supervisors that people all have the same basic motivations and needs, which must be recognized in an efficiently run operation.
Business and Economics; Guidance and Counseling; Psychology; Sociology
Dist - NSC **Prod** - NSC 1965

People are different and alike 11 MIN
VHS / U-matic / 16mm
Color (P I)
$320.00, $250.00 purchase _ #HP - 5963C
Presents a parade to show the differences that make people special. Demonstrates the humanness and needs for food, shelter, love, friendship and care that are common to everyone. Shows that being a member of a group is a way to find friends who satisfy different needs and that people who are different can learn to appreciate each other when working in cooperation toward a common goal.
Psychology
Dist - CORF **Prod** - TAKTEN 1989

People are Different and Alike 11 MIN
U-matic / VHS / 16mm
Color (P I)
LC FIA67-721
Points out that it is easy to see differences in people but that people are more alike in the important ways. Shows that all people need friendship and love, food and a place to live and that they want an education, fun and happiness.
Guidance and Counseling; History - United States; Psychology; Social Science; Sociology
Dist - CORF **Prod** - CORF 1967

People are Just People 18 MIN
16mm
Color (H C)
LC 74-700471
Discusses human frailties and the costly effects of the frailties when they are allowed to affect one's performance on the job. Shows human weaknesses, indifference, laziness, carelessness, forgetfulness and temptation.
Business and Economics; Guidance and Counseling; Psychology
Dist - NCR **Prod** - NCR 1966

People are many, Fields are Small 32 MIN
16mm
Faces of Change - Taiwan Series
Color
Presents three farm families who are engaged in Taiwan's long two - crop summer rice cycle and compares their lives to those of industrial laborers. Shows them expressing both pride and anger concerning conditions of farm life.
Geography - World
Dist - WHEELK **Prod** - AUFS

People are People 8 MIN
U-matic / VHS / 16mm
Zoom Series
Color
Introduces Ginny, who is an 11 - year - old dwarf. Shows her daily activities such as helping her mother, riding her bike, and playing with her brother and other children. Reveals some of the problems with which she is faced.

Education; Psychology
Dist - FI **Prod** - WGBHTV 1978

People are the Puzzle 10 MIN
16mm
Key Man Series
Color
Shows that the relation of the foreman to his men is a key ingredient in safety.
Business and Economics; Health and Safety
Dist - NSC **Prod** - NSC

People Ask about Cancer 25 MIN
VHS / U-matic
Color
Presents five top cancer researchers who take questions on cancer from an in - studio audience. Includes topics on current theories on the diagnosis and cure of cancer, cancer quacks and promising areas of research that may lead to a cure of this dreaded disease.
Health and Safety
Dist - MEDCOM **Prod** - MEDCOM

People Ask about Heart Disease 25 MIN
VHS / U-matic
Color
Shows a heart surgeon, cardiologists and heart attack victims answering questions from a studio audience. Includes as topics the effects of smoking and cholesterol on the circulatory system, the vein - graft bypass operation and what life is like after a heart attack.
Health and Safety; Science - Natural
Dist - MEDCOM **Prod** - MEDCOM

The People Ask James Cardwell - Commissioner of Social Security 29 MIN
VHS / 16mm
Washington Connection Series
Color (G)
$55.00 rental _ #WACO - 117
Civics and Political Systems; Social Science
Dist - PBS **Prod** - NPACT

The People Ask William Simon 29 MIN
VHS / 16mm
Washington Connection Series
Color (G)
$55.00 rental _ #WACO - 112
Civics and Political Systems; Social Science
Dist - PBS **Prod** - NPACT

People at Work 15 MIN
VHS / 16mm
(C PRO)
$500.00 purchase, $135.00 rental
Shows what happened to a company and a group of its workers as a result of a significant change in their workplace. Presents tension, bickering, lack of communication, poor product quality, diminished teamwork, and loss of employee pride.
Education
Dist - VLEARN

People at Work 20 MIN
U-matic
Exploring Our Nation Series
Color (I)
Shows people who make goods and provide services. Tells how they get to work and discusses labor and management.
Sociology
Dist - GPN **Prod** - KRMATV 1975

People at Work - a Right to Refuse 13 MIN
16mm / U-matic
(C H A)
Presents a situation where a floor supervisor has a deadline to meet but his employees walk out because they feel conditions are unsafe. Examines what mistakes can be made in such situations, and how to avoid them.
Business and Economics; Health and Safety
Dist - MGHT **Prod** - NFBC 1982
CRMP

The People bomb 90 MIN
VHS
Color (J H G)
$24.95 purchase _ #TUR3105V
Discloses that nine babies are born into the world every two seconds; 270 babies every minute; 338,000 babies each day. Predicts that in the next century three times as many people will inhabit planet Earth - nearly 15 billion people vying for food, shelter and jobs. Examines the potential stress on an increasingly fragile environment. Travels to 13 countries for a look at personal, national and global efforts to contain the population explosion.
Sociology
Dist - CAMV **Prod** - TBSESI 1992

People - Bringing Life to the City 13 MIN
U-matic / VHS / 16mm
Color
LC 75-712874
Examines the ethnic neighborhood and earlier immigrant neighborhoods and shows a variety of activities in which people act out parts of their own particular traditions. Includes scenes of the Chinese New Year celebration, an ice hockey game, the smashing of the pinata at a Mexican party and a Black choir singing gospel music.
Social Science; Sociology
Dist - JOU **Prod** - JOU 1971

People Business 17 MIN
16mm
Color
LC 74-702501
Traces the history of the London Life Insurance Company in celebration of its 100th anniversary.
Business and Economics
Dist - LONLIF **Prod** - LONLIF 1974

The People called Methodist 28 MIN
VHS / U-matic / 16mm
Color (SPANISH)
LC 76-700401
Shows the variety of ministries among Methodists in five representative locations, including Australia, Singapore, Bolivia, Sierra Leone and Jerusalem.
Foreign Language; Religion and Philosophy
Dist - ECUFLM **Prod** - UMCOM 1975

A People Chosen - who is a Jew 57 MIN
16mm / U-matic / VHS
Color (J)
LC 76-702512
Centers on the intensive, continuing debate by governments and their private sectors, inside and outside of Israel, over the role that religion plays in identity. Questions Jews from different walks of life about their identity.
Religion and Philosophy; Sociology
Dist - PHENIX **Prod** - KROSNY 1976

People, Communication and Negotiation 13 MIN
VHS / U-matic
Thinking in Action Series Module 3
Color (A)
Reveals that instead of the traditional clash method of negotiation, an exploratory process called exlectics can be used in which the 'logic bubbles' of other people are looked at and all sides of a situation can be examined.
Business and Economics; Psychology
Dist - FI **Prod** - BBCTV 1983

People count 31 MIN
VHS / U-matic
Battle for the planet series
Color (H C G)
$160.00 purchase, $30.00 rental _ #CC4252VU, #CC4252VH
Focuses on Kenya, a nation with the highest population growth rate in the world. Examines how traditional values influence family size even in the midst of modernization and urbanization. Provides examples of successful programs which encourage family planning through providing economic independence and incentives to women. Emphasizes the need to empower women. Part of a series.
Geography - World; Sociology
Dist - IU **Prod** - NFBC 1987

People - Different but Alike 10 MIN
16mm / U-matic / VHS
Color (P I) (SPANISH)
LC 76-703540
Uses pantomime, music and rhyme to show the effects of making fun of people who are superficially different. Emphasizes that it is what is inside a person that counts. Formerly entitled Little Bigots.
Guidance and Counseling; Sociology
Dist - AIMS **Prod** - CAHILL 1975

People Don't Dance to Jazz 30 MIN
16mm
Color (J)
Deals with the day in a teenager's life when he must decide about his life's ambitions despite changes in his family and pressures from his friends.
Guidance and Counseling; Psychology
Dist - MOKIN **Prod** - PREMI 1979

People Don't Resist Change 24 MIN
U-matic / 16mm
Color (IND)
Examines the different approaches to motivating people to accept change.
Business and Economics; Psychology
Dist - BNA **Prod** - BNA 1967

The People Factor in Our Productivity Improvement 35 MIN
U-matic / VHS
Color
Explains why the people factor in productivity improvement for one company focuses on specific projects instead of psychological generalities, enabling employees to make substantial productivity improvements.
Business and Economics; Psychology
Dist - SME **Prod** - SME

The People Factor - the Hawthorne Studies for Today's Managers 11 MIN
16mm / U-matic / VHS
Color (C A)
LC 76-700241
Considers research associated with the Hawthorne studies and its implications in personnel management. Shows that informal social organizations among employees can have important effects on employee morale and productivity.
Business and Economics; Psychology
Dist - SALENG **Prod** - ROBINH 1976

People - Figures in Action 15 MIN
VHS / U-matic
Let's Draw Series
Color (P)
Fine Arts
Dist - AITECH **Prod** - OCPS 1976

People first 34 MIN
16mm / VHS / BETA / U-matic
Color; PAL (J H C G PRO T)
PdS175, PdS183 purchase
Features an ambitious and startling project in which over 25,000 feet of film was shot to document the private lives and political activities of People First, the first Self - Advocacy Group of Developmentally Disabled Citizens. Records the disabled speaking openly about their problems and their rights in a production made by themselves.
Health and Safety; Sociology
Dist - EDPAT

People Helping People - Nursing Home 9 MIN
16mm
Color
LC 75-700806
Depicts the modern facilities of well - built, well - managed and well - equipped nursing homes.
Health and Safety
Dist - USNAC **Prod** - USDHUD 1970

People in Action 15 MIN
U-matic / VHS
Draw Along Series
(K P)
$125.00 purchase
Focuses on how to draw figures walking, running or sitting.
Fine Arts
Dist - AITECH **Prod** - AITECH 1986

People in Change Series

New Guinea Patrol, and, Excerpts from Yumi Yet - Vol I	42 MIN
Towards Baruya Manhood - Vol II	143 MIN

Dist - FI

People in Crisis 30 MIN
U-matic / VHS
Color
Deals with the importance of coordinating a hospital's efforts to assure timely and efficient patient discharges. Illustrates hospital and patient benefits through interaction among medical, nursing, social work and community services.
Health and Safety; Psychology
Dist - AHOA **Prod** - AHOA

People in Jazz Series

Dorothy Ashby	29 MIN
George Benson	29 MIN
H P Barnum	30 MIN
Joe Williams	28 MIN
Lou Rawls	28 MIN
Michigan State University Jazz Ensemble	29 MIN
Misty Wizards	30 MIN
Roland Kirk	30 MIN
Ron Brooks and Group	29 MIN
Trudy Pitts	30 MIN
Wes Montgomery	30 MIN

Dist - PBS

People in Management 18 MIN
U-matic / VHS / 16mm
Color (J)
LC 76-701295
Takes a look at jobs in the management field through the experiences of several people with jobs covering all levels of management experience, from management trainee to company president.
Business and Economics; Guidance and Counseling; Psychology
Dist - PHENIX **Prod** - PHENIX 1976

People in motion - changing ideas about physical disability series 180 MIN
VHS
People in motion - changing ideas about physical disability series
Color; CC (G)

$249.00 purchase _ #UW5676
Presents three parts on how society is changing its beliefs about physical disability. Includes the titles The Shortest Distance; Ready to Live; Redesigning the Human Machine.
Computer Science; Health and Safety
Dist - FOTH

People in motion - changing ideas about physical disability series

People in motion - changing ideas about physical disability series	180 MIN
Ready to live	60 MIN
Redesigning the human machine	60 MIN
The Shortest distance	60 MIN

Dist - FOTH

A People in Progress - Ecuador 28 MIN
16mm
Color
Explains how the Salesian Missions are helping small farmers in Ecuador achieve independence and a measure of prosperity through cooperatives and low interest loans. Shows how poverty can be overcome by personal effort, organization and cooperation.
Agriculture; History - World; Religion and Philosophy; Sociology
Dist - MTP **Prod** - SCC

People in trouble - Beirut 52 MIN
VHS
Color (H C G)
$445.00 purchase, $75.00 rental
Brings the chaos of daily life in war - torn Lebanon to the screen. Reveals that Beirut, once the Paris of the Middle East, has for the past 15 years been a battle zone. Emphasizes the severe emotional stress endured by the people, most particularly the children who have known only war. Shows that ordinary citizens yearn for peace and feel victimized by leaders who protract the conflict for their own gain. Produced by Jean - Pierre Dauzun and Gerard Rivoalan - Little Big One - Brussels.
History - World; Sociology
Dist - FLMLIB

People in trouble - South Africa - the Mozambican trap 55 MIN
VHS
Color (H C G)
$445.00 purchase, $75.00 rental
Examines the border situation between South Africa and Mozambique. Reveals that South Africa has built a deadly electrically - fortified border of 50 miles to prevent the entrance of refugees fleeing civil war in Mozambique. Over 100,000 have managed to enter South Africa but they end up in impoverished black homelands subject to the harshness of South African rule. Coproduced by Jean - Pierre Dauzun - Little Big One, Brussels, and Job - Briade.
Geography - World; Sociology
Dist - FLMLIB

The People Inside Me 20 MIN
VHS / U-matic
Color
$335.00 purchase
Health and Safety
Dist - ABCLR **Prod** - ABCLR 1983

People into Politics 45 MIN
U-matic
Urban Change and Conflict Series
Color (H C A)
Considers the extent and motive of citizens' involvement in political activity within the urban context.
Sociology
Dist - ACCESS **Prod** - BBCTV 1983

A People is Born - 3500 BCE to 6th Century BCE - Pt 1 60 MIN
VHS / 16mm
Heritage - Civilization and the Jews Series
Color (J)
$800.00, $49.00 purchase _ #405 - 9121
Explores more than 3000 years of the Jewish experience and its intimate connections with the civilizations of the world. Uses all available resources to weave an extraordinary tapestry of the Jewish history and people. Hosted by Abba Eban, Israel's former ambassador to the UN and the US. Part 1 examines the origins of Judaism among the ancient civilizations of Egypt and Mesopotamia.
History - World; Religion and Philosophy; Sociology
Dist - FI **Prod** - WNETTV 1984

The People Left Behind 31 MIN
16mm
Public Broadcast Laboratory Series
B&W (H C A)
LC FIA68-1503
Depicts the plight of Mississippi's ex - plantation laborers whose jobs have been eliminated by the cotton picking machine, minimum - wage laws and legislation, which pays farmers for not cultivating land. Former plantation workers describe their situation and show scenes of their impoverished environment.
Agriculture; Business and Economics; Geography - United States; History - United States; Psychology; Sociology
Dist - IU **Prod** - NET 1968

A People like any other 30 MIN
16mm
Color (G)
$30.00 rental
No desciption provided for this Israeli documentary.
Dist - NCJEWF

People like my mum don't get AIDS 40 MIN
VHS
Everyman series
Color; PAL (G A)
PdS65 purchase
Discusses the issues of having a child with women who are infected with the HIV virus. Examines the dilemma of the 25 per cent chance of passing the virus to the unborn child and whether or not the infected mother is entitled to take the risk.
Health and Safety; Sociology
Dist - BBCENE

People living in other lands

Alaska	10 MIN
Borneo	10 MIN
Egypt	10 MIN
Greenland	10 MIN
Iran	10 MIN
Java	10 MIN
Kenya	10 MIN
Thailand	10 MIN

Dist - VIEWTH

People make it Happen 23 MIN
16mm
Color
LC 76-703437
Emphasizes the importance of consumer behavior in product safety. Shows how selection, use, maintenance, storage and disposal of consumer products affects the safety of those products.
Health and Safety; Home Economics
Dist - USNAC **Prod** - USCPSD 1976

People make it Happen 24 MIN
16mm
Further Education Series
Color (T)
LC 77-702845
Discusses the need for creating effective adult education courses.
Education
Dist - CENTWO **Prod** - ADEAV 1976

People make programs 12 MIN
VHS / U-matic
Getting the most out of TV series
Color (P I J)
$195.00, $245.00 purchase, $50.00 rental
Introduces the television team members who plan and produce shows. Looks at the different kinds of programs and their time slots. Part of a seven - part series.
Fine Arts; Industrial and Technical Education
Dist - NDIM **Prod** - YALEU 1981

People make Programs 12 MIN
U-matic / VHS / 16mm
Getting the most Out of TV Series
Color (I J)
LC 81-700099
Uses narration, dramatizations and tours of a TV studio to help show how television programs are developed from the original idea to the finished show.
Fine Arts; Sociology
Dist - CORF **Prod** - TAPPRO 1981

People matter series
Presents a six - part series on human rights around the globe. Includes the titles 'Bolivia - Union Rights,' 'Chile - Torture as a Political Instrument,' 'India - Women's Rights,' 'Peru - Children's Rights,' 'Southern Africa - the Right to Development' and 'Unganda - the Right to Life.'

Bolivia - union rights - 1	28 MIN
Chile - torture as a political instrument - 2	28 MIN
India - women's rights - 3	28 MIN
Peru - children's rights - 4	28 MIN
Southern Africa - the right to development - 5	28 MIN
Uganda - the right to life	28 MIN

Dist - BARR **Prod** - CEPRO 1981

The People Movers 10 MIN
16mm
Color
LC 80-700917
Describes a twin hull ferry designed and built by a Hobart, Australia firm.
Industrial and Technical Education; Social Science
Dist - TASCOR **Prod** - TASCOR 1977

People near here 12 MIN
16mm
B&W; Color (G)
$25.00 rental
Arranges found footage without internal editing. Pays homage to the Americanlove affair with home movies beginning in the late 1920s. Records people across all stages of life, such as in the backyard or at a graduation picnic, revealing their emotions. Produced by Ron Finne.
Fine Arts
Dist - CANCIN

The People next door 10 MIN
VHS
Magnum eye series
Color (G)
$125.00 purchase, $30.00 rental
Explores Belleville, Paris, historically a melting pot for immigrants of all races; home to Chinese, Arabs, Jews, Algerians, Tunisians, Africans and French. Discovers that the district is facing gentrification, high unemployment and the rise of right wing extremism. Explores this small diverse universe and captures the nuances of racism, spoken and not, in a community that exists not by choice, but by circumstance. Directed by Patrick Zachmann. Part of a series by photographers from the Magnum Photo Agency.
Fine Arts; History - World; Social Science; Sociology
Dist - FIRS **Prod** - MIYAKE 1993

People, not Paper 18 MIN
16mm
Color (A)
LC 77-703363
Documents the problem caused by bureaucratic paperwork. Includes illustrations and examples drawn from the work of the two - year Commission on Federal Paperwork. Demonstrates steps which can be taken to alleviate the situation.
Business and Economics; Civics and Political Systems
Dist - USNAC **Prod** - USCFP 1977

People of Africa 25 MIN
U-matic / VHS / 16mm
Untamed World Series Series
Color; Mono (J H C A)
$400.00 film, $250.00 video, $50.00 rental
Examines the African peoples and the effects of modern technology and urbanization on their traditional values and customs.
Geography - World; Sociology
Dist - CTV **Prod** - CTV 1969

The People of Brazil 23 MIN
16mm
Color
LC 74-702660
Looks at the life of Brazilians in the cities, on the waterways and the plantations, in the marketplaces, including views of the people at work, at prayer and at play.
Geography - World; Social Science; Sociology
Dist - MMAMC **Prod** - MMAMC 1974

People of Chile 22 MIN
U-matic / VHS / 16mm
Color (I J H)
Depicts a land of contrasts and mixed races. Shows habits, customs, social and economic problems and agriculture of Chile.
Geography - World; Sociology
Dist - IFB **Prod** - GRUBBS 1947

People of faith and the arms race 105 MIN
VHS
Color (H C G T A)
$39.00 purchase, $25.00 rental
Presents a six - module series on the nuclear arms race and possible church responses to it. Produced by the Presbyterian Peacemaking Program.
Civics and Political Systems; History - World; Religion and Philosophy; Sociology
Dist - EFVP

The People of Hungary 18 MIN
16mm
Color (I)
Portrays an eastern European country under the dominance of Russian communism. The land, people and culture are depicted through a variety of scenes emphasizing the history and the current political implications faced by the people of Hungary.
Civics and Political Systems; Geography - World
Dist - AVED **Prod** - WIANCK 1962

People of Influence 30 MIN
U-matic / VHS / 16mm
Russians Series
Color (H C A)

LC 79-701741
Examines the human 'troika' which governs the lives of all Russians at the local level and which includes the Director, the Trade Union Chairman and the Communist Party Secretary.
Business and Economics; Civics and Political Systems; Geography - World; History - World
Dist - LCOA **Prod** - FLMAUS 1979

The People of Israel 30 MIN
VHS
Shalom Sesame series
Color (K P)
$19.95 purchase _ #243
Features Mandy Patinkin who meets the colorful mix of folk making up Israel's population. Part of an eight - part series on Israel with the Sesame Street Muppets.
Geography - World; Sociology
Dist - ERGOM **Prod** - ERGOM

People of Kolevu 27 MIN
16mm
Color (G)
#3X90 N
Discusses how people in a small community on the Fiji Islands solved many of their economic problems by starting their own credit union.
Business and Economics; Social Science
Dist - CDIAND **Prod** - MCHUGH 1964

People of many Lands - Eskimos 20 MIN
16mm
Color (H C A)
#2X38 N
Documents the winter months at Carol Island for a small community of Eskimos. Discusses the chores and machines that are necessary to survive. Shows how these people spend their time.
Social Science
Dist - CDIAND **Prod** - BBCTV 1972

The People of Nes Ammin 60 MIN
16mm
Bill Moyers' Journal Series
Color (A)
LC 79-700651
Focuses on a farming community of ecumenical Christians in northern Israel, whose inhabitants seek to build a bridge of understanding and mutual respect between Jews and Christians.
Geography - World; Religion and Philosophy; Social Science; Sociology
Dist - PBS **Prod** - WNETTV 1979

People of no Interest 28 MIN
16mm
(H C A)
Shows internationally financed megaprojects in Northern Brazil. Shows the prestige the world's financial centers gain while also showing the farmers who have been forced off the land and into slums in the cities as a result of the projects. Illustrates the peasants' struggle for human and land rights.
Business and Economics; Civics and Political Systems; Geography - World
Dist - RTVA **Prod** - RTVA 1984

The People of People's China 52 MIN
U-matic
Color (H C)
Probes the myths and realities of life in China. Discusses the lifestyles and values of typical working people and focuses on the struggle between educational traditionalists and revolutionaries since the Cultural Revolution.
Geography - World; Sociology
Dist - GA **Prod** - ABCTV

People of Peru 11 MIN
16mm / U-matic / VHS
Color (I J H)
Shows the prosperous society folk, primitive plateau Indians and jungle dwellers of Peru. Illustrates the effects of geography on the manner of living.
Geography - World; Sociology
Dist - IFB **Prod** - GRUBBS 1947

People of refuge 60 MIN
VHS
Color (H C G A R)
$49.99 purchase, $10.00 rental _ #35 - 82800 - 533
Shows Christians how to practice a non - scolding, healing compassion for others. Hosted by Charles Swindoll.
Religion and Philosophy
Dist - APH **Prod** - WORD

People of the Australian Western Desert
U-matic / VHS / 16mm
B&W (H C G T A)
Consists of Sociology, Anthropology, Social Science/Society, and Primitive.
Geography - World; Social Science; Sociology
Dist - PSU **Prod** - PSU

People of the Australian Western Desert Series

Cooking kangaroo	17 MIN
Fire Making	7 MIN
Gum Preparation, Stone Flaking - Djagamara Leaves	19 MIN
Old Campsites at Tika Tika	11 MIN
Seed Cake Making and General Camp Activity	21 MIN
Spear making - boy's spear fight	9 MIN
Spear Thrower Making, Including Stone Flaking and Gum Preparation	33 MIN
Spinning hair string - getting water from well, binding girl's hair	12 MIN

Dist - PSU

People of the beatitudes - Tape 9 30 MIN
VHS
Acts of the Apostles series
Color (I J H C G A R)
$29.95 purchase, $10.00 rental _ #35 - 8370 - 1502
Presents stories of the early Christian church as described in the New Testament book of Acts. Covers the events of Paul and Silas' ministry in Philippi, the healing of the possessed girl, Paul at Corinth with Aquila and Priscilla, and Paul's arrest.
Literature and Drama; Religion and Philosophy
Dist - APH **Prod** - BOSCO

The People of the Book 41 MIN
16mm / U-matic / VHS
Christians Series
Color (H A)
Discusses the effects which Christian, Islamic and Jewish people have had on each other throughout the centuries. Describes the Crusades, the Inquisition and the expulsion of Jews from Spain.
History - World; Religion and Philosophy
Dist - MGHT **Prod** - GRATV 1978

The People of the Book 30 MIN
16mm
B&W (JEWISH)
LC FIA64-1122
Portrays the diversity of Israel's inhabitants. Includes scenes of Premier David Ben - gurion, engineers and technicians at Israel's Institute of Technology at Haifa, Druse children taught by a Christain Arab woman, Jewish orphans studying and learning trades at a children's village as well as scribes, soldiers, clerics, curators, archeologists, farmers, shepherds, stone - masons and merchants.
Biography; History - World
Dist - NAAJS **Prod** - JTS 1962

People of the Buffalo 15 MIN
U-matic / VHS / 16mm
Color (I J H)
Portrays the relationship between Indians and buffalo through contemporary painting of life on the Western Plains. Explains the westward advance of the white settlers and Plains Indians for possession of the Western Plains.
History - United States; Social Science; Sociology
Dist - EBEC **Prod** - NFBC 1969

People of the Caribbean 25 MIN
VHS
Hispanic culture video series
Color (J H)
$49.95 purchase _ #VK45353
Explores the heritage of minority groups that trace their origins to the islands of Caribbean. Presents part of a six - part series that examines the background and history of Spanish influences on the history, culture and society of different parts of the world.
History - United States; Sociology
Dist - KNOWUN

People of the Chad 13 MIN
16mm
B&W
Records native life in the interior of French Equatorial Africa. Shows how the inhabitants work the natural resources of the region in the most primitive ways.
Geography - World; Science - Natural; Sociology
Dist - RADIM **Prod** - VICASV 1945

People of the Cities 30 MIN
16mm / U-matic / VHS
Russians Series
Color (H C A)
LC 79-701744
Shows a bus driver, a dockworker and a doctor in Russia. Examines the urban structure of Russian cities.
Geography - World; History - World; Social Science; Sociology
Dist - LCOA **Prod** - FLMAUS 1979

People of the Country 30 MIN
16mm / U-matic / VHS
Russians Series
Color (H C A)
LC 79-701742
Explores the collective farms of Russia.
Agriculture; Civics and Political Systems; Geography - World; History - World; Social Science; Sociology
Dist - LCOA **Prod** - FLMAUS 1979

People of the Dawn 30 MIN
U-matic / VHS
Color
$250 rental
Presents conversations with elders of the Passanaquoddy, Penobscot, and Maliceet Indian tribes of Maine, who are receiving aid from the U. S. government.
Social Science
Dist - CCNCC **Prod** - CCNCC 1985

People of the Desert - Pt 9 28 MIN
VHS
Only One Earth Series
Color (S)
$79.00 purchase _ #227 - 9009
Explores and demystifies the links between environment and development and illustrates the detrimental clashes between economics and ecology in the first three programs. Presents positive examples of how development can be achieved without harming the environment in the last eight half - hour programs. Part 9 of eleven considers that human - induced ecological changes are causing once life - supporting deserts to become uninhabitable, because of overuse and overpopulation. New policies to reduce population pressure and livestock overgrazing are renewing desert life.
Agriculture; Geography - World; Science - Natural
Dist - FI **Prod** - BBCTV 1987

People of the First Light - a Series
VHS / U-matic
People of the First Light Series
Color (G)
Shows how Native American people in southern New England have maintained their cultural identity through various means such as dance, art, and a strong sense of family and community. Tribal history and tradition are integrated into the daily activities of present day Native American children and adults.
Social Science; Sociology
Dist - NAMPBC **Prod** - NAMPBC 1979

People of the First Light Series

The Boston Indian community	30 MIN
The Indian experience	30 MIN
The Indians of Connecticut	30 MIN
Indians of Southern New England	30 MIN
The Mashpee Wamponogs	30 MIN
The Narragansetts	30 MIN
The Wampanoags of Gay Head	30 MIN

Dist - GPN

People of the First Light Series

The Boston Indian community - change and identity	29 MIN
The Indian experience, urban and rural - survival	29 MIN
Indian in Southern New England - the Survivors	29 MIN
Indians of Connecticut - the Importance of Land	29 MIN
The Mashpee Wampanoags - Tribal Identity	29 MIN
The Narragansetts - Tradition	29 MIN
People of the First Light - a Series	
The Wampanoags of Gay Head - Community Spirit and Island Life	29 MIN

Dist - NAMPBC

People of the forest 100 MIN
VHS
Color (G)
$24.95 purchase _ #FOR100
Follows a chimpanzee family in Africa.
Science - Natural
Dist - INSTRU **Prod** - DISCOV 1991

People of the Free Train 15 MIN
16mm
Pacific Islands Series
Color (I J)
Depicts the life of the East Indian farmers of Fiji who work for the sugar company and use the free train ride to visit friends or the market. Shows sugar cane planting, rice harvesting, villages and the market.
Geography - World; Social Science; Sociology
Dist - MMP **Prod** - MMP 1961

People of the Macon Plateau 10 MIN
VHS / U-matic / VT1
Color (G)
$39.95 purchase, $20.00 rental
Offers a brief portrayal of the eastern United States Indian tribes. Blends scenery, archival photographs and modern day technology to present the contrast between the power of technology and the power of Mother Earth. Produced by Thomas Radford.

Geography - United States; Social Science; Sociology
Dist - NAMPBC

People of the Northeast
VHS
Indians of North America Video Series
Color (P)
$39.95 purchase
Combines original artwork and photographs from the Museum of the American Indian to examine the contributions of the native peoples who once populated the Northeast region of the United States.
History - United States; Literature and Drama; Social Science; Sociology
Dist - PELLER

People of the palace 50 MIN
VHS
The great palace - the story of Parliament
Color; PAL (C H)
PdS99 purchase
Presents a view of the 200 people who staff the Royal Palace. Provides insight on their contribution to the smooth operation of Parliament. Eighth in the eight - part series The Great Palace: The Story of Parliament.
Civics and Political Systems; History - World
Dist - BBCENE

People of the People's Temple 24 MIN
16mm / U-matic / VHS
Color (H C A)
LC 80-701818
Analyzes the 1978 massacre of over 900 members of the People's Temple in Jonestown, Guyana.
History - United States; Religion and Philosophy; Sociology
Dist - FI **Prod** - NBCTV 1980

People of the Plains
VHS
Indians of North America Video Series
Color (P)
$39.95 purchase
Combines original artwork and photographs from the Museum of the American Indian to examine the contributions of the native peoples who once populated the Plains region of the United States.
History - United States; Literature and Drama; Social Science; Sociology
Dist - PELLER

People of the Seal, Pt 1 52 MIN
16mm
Color (J)
LC 73-700245
Presents an examination of the lives of the Netsilik Eskimos of the Canadian Arctic, their work and play and the ways in which they cope with the frigid climate of the North.
Geography - World; Social Science; Sociology
Dist - EDC **Prod** - BBCL 1971

People of the Seal, Pt 2 52 MIN
16mm
Color (J)
LC 73-700245
Presents an examination of the lives of the Netsilik Eskimos of the Canadian Arctic, their work and play and the ways in which they cope with the frigid climate of the North.
Geography - World; Social Science; Sociology
Dist - EDC **Prod** - BBCL 1971

People of the Seal Series
Eskimo Summer 52 MIN
Eskimo Winter 52 MIN
Dist - EDC

People of the Southeast
VHS
Indians of North America Video Series
Color (P)
$39.95 purchase
Combines original artwork and photographs from the Museum of the American Indian to examine the contributions of the native peoples who once populated the Southeast region of the United States.
History - United States; Literature and Drama; Social Science; Sociology
Dist - PELLER

People of the Waters 25 MIN
U-matic / VHS / 16mm
Untamed World Series Series
Color; Mono (J H C A)
$400.00 film, $250.00 video, $50.00 rental
Examines societies that have built their civilizations on the shores and waterways of the world.
Geography - World; Sociology
Dist - CTV **Prod** - CTV 1969

People of Venice 15 MIN
VHS
Color; PAL (P I J H)
Interviews the family of a Venetian working man against the background of Venice's past. Displays the Doge's Palace, the Piazzetta, the Rialto Bridge and the Grand Canal of Venice and meets Toni Biasi who repairs diesel boats, his gondolier cousin, Biasi's wife and children.
Geography - World; History - World
Dist - VIEWTH **Prod** - VIEWTH

People on market street series
Cost 19 MIN
Demand 21 MIN
Market Clearing Price 23 MIN
Property Rights and Pollution 19 MIN
Scarcity and planning 16 MIN
Supply 19 MIN
Wages and Production 18 MIN
Dist - CORF

People on the Macon Plateau 12 MIN
16mm
Color
LC 81-701095
Introduces the history of Indian cultures of the Macon Plateau in Georgia and the area around the Ocmulgee National Monument. Emphasizes the Mississippian Indian culture.
History - United States; Social Science
Dist - USNAC **Prod** - USNPS 1981

People on the Move 20 MIN
U-matic / VHS / 16mm
One World Series
Color (J H)
Portrays a Jamaican family whose roots are in a relatively poor rural mountain part of the island. Reveals that part of the family still lives in the country while the rest have migrated to Kingston and beyond.
Geography - World; History - World; Sociology
Dist - FI **Prod** - BBCTV 1982

The 'People' People in Social Service 13 MIN
U-matic / VHS / 16mm
Color (H C G T A)
$25 rental _ #4599
Shows the variety of unskilled, skilled, semiprofessional, and professional occupations.
Education; Guidance and Counseling
Dist - AIMS **Prod** - AIMS 1975

People People in Social Services 13 MIN
U-matic / VHS / 16mm
Color (H)
LC 75-703672
Introduces the various aspects of the social service field to students.
Guidance and Counseling; Social Science; Sociology
Dist - AIMS **Prod** - SCLARA 1975

People, People, People 5 MIN
16mm / U-matic / VHS
Color (I)
LC 77-701101
Gives an animated overview of America's many - peopled heritage. Shows the peopling of America from the first Mongolian crossing the Bering land bridge on through the many explorers, settlers and immigrants.
History - United States; Sociology
Dist - PFP **Prod** - HUBLEY 1976

The People Places 22 MIN
VHS / U-matic
Phenomenal World Series
Color (J C)
$129.00 purchase _ #3975
Takes a look at American cities and shows that their growth is determined by the health and diversity of the commerce and transportation. Tells how the automobile has significantly changed the look and form of American cities.
Industrial and Technical Education; Sociology
Dist - EBEC

People power 53 MIN
VHS
Color (G)
$390.00 purchase, $75.00 rental
Presents a comprehensive exploration of non - violent means to achieve social reform. Focuses primarily on the fall of Pinochet in Chile, the Palestinian intifada and Cory Aquino's 'People Power' revolution in the Philippines. Demonstrates how Filipinos jogged to gain political momentum, or how a small concession by Pinochet became the vehicle to rally a nation around a simple slogan: the word 'no.' Features Gene Sharp, a leading expert on non - violent struggles.
Fine Arts; History - World; Sociology
Dist - FIRS **Prod** - ZIVILN 1989

People power 40 MIN
VHS
Town hall
Color; PAL (C H)
PdS65 purchase
Follows the Lewisham council as it deals with housing problems wihtin the borough. Highlights the ways grievances are presented to the council. Third in the eight - part series Town Hall, which documents the operation of local government in Great Britain.
Civics and Political Systems
Dist - BBCENE

People, Product and Performance 29 MIN
16mm
Color
LC 78-700209
Shows 23 different General Motors Corporation plants in different countries as well as the people, customs and lifestyles in these nations.
Business and Economics; Industrial and Technical Education; Sociology
Dist - GM **Prod** - GM 1978

People, Products and Prices 26 MIN
16mm
Color
Discusses both hedging and speculating in the futures market from the vantage point of a farmer, exporter, processor, the brokerage house and traders on the floor. Explains the complexities of the futures market in operation and how it can benefit all levels of the marketing chain as well as public speculators.
Business and Economics
Dist - MTP **Prod** - CBT

The People Project 13 MIN
16mm
Color
LC 79-700399
Presents an overview of the Salt River Project in Arizona.
Geography - United States; Social Science
Dist - SARIV **Prod** - SARIV 1978

A People Sampler 29 MIN
U-matic
Conversations with Allen Whiting Series
Color
Looks at the ordinary citizens of China, Russia and the United States.
Civics and Political Systems; Geography - United States; History - World
Dist - UMITV **Prod** - UMITV 1979

People sell people series
Goodwill ambassadors 7 MIN
Nothing but Lookers 8 MIN
One - to - One 13 MIN
The Sales Building Role 7 MIN
You've Sold Me, Mrs Marlowe 9 MIN
Dist - MLA

The People Shop - the Hospital in Your Community 18 MIN
U-matic / VHS / 16mm
Color (K P I)
LC 72-702554
Presents a typical community hospital and the services it offers. Surveys the job of the hospital in the community. Confronts a child's concern when he has to enter.
Health and Safety; Social Science; Sociology
Dist - LUF **Prod** - ASPTEF 1972

The People Side of Cancer 14 MIN
16mm
Color (PRO)
LC 73-700746
Acquaints doctors and medical personnel and others with the human anguish of those experiencing cancer. Probes aspects including cancer in children, the effects of cancer on the family and the acceptance of death and the realities of terminal cancer.
Health and Safety; Psychology
Dist - AMCS **Prod** - AMCS 1972

People Signs 16 MIN
16mm
PANCOM Beginning Total Communication Program for Hearing Parents of 'Series Level 1
Color (K)
LC 77-700504
Education; Guidance and Counseling; Psychology; Social Science; Sociology
Dist - JOYCE **Prod** - CSDE 1977

People sketching techniques series
Presents five programs on sketching people. Includes Sketching Eyes with Expression, Heads and Faces, Hands in Action, Wrinkles and Caricatures.
People sketching techniques series 150 MIN
Dist - CAMV

People Soup 13 MIN
16mm / U-matic / VHS
Color (K)
LC 72-708134
Tells of the knack two brothers have for mixing magic potions from household ingredients. Enhances the inter - relationship of the two boys by one turning into a chicken and the other becoming a sheepdog. Produced by Alan Arkin and features his two sons.
English Language; Fine Arts; Literature and Drama
Dist - LCOA **Prod** - PNGLOS 1970

People, Technology and the Environment 15 MIN
VHS / 16mm
Exploring Technology Series
Color (I J)
$180.00 purchase, $25.00 rental
Considers the benefits and complex social and environmental problems technology brings.
Business and Economics; Computer Science; Sociology
Dist - AITECH **Prod** - AITECH 1990

People, Technology and the Environment - 2 14 MIN
VHS
Exploring Technology Education - Introduction - Series
Color (I)
$180.00 purchase
Considers that choices we make about technology have both benefits and risks and involve complex social and environmental problems. Uses atomic power and the car as examples of technology have profound effects. Builds the technological literacy vital for current and future careers. Part of the Exploring Technology Series.
Education; Social Science
Dist - AITECH **Prod** - AITECH 1990

People that Time Forgot 90 MIN
16mm
Color (I A)
Describes the rescue by major McBride of his old friend from a prehistoric island. Sequel to Land That Time Forgot. Stars Patrick Wayne and Doug McClure.
Fine Arts
Dist - TIMLIF **Prod** - AIP 1977

People to People - Careers in Communications and Media 13 MIN
16mm
Working Worlds Series
Color (I J H)
LC 75-701542
Explores the variety of careers available in communications and media.
Guidance and Counseling; Psychology
Dist - FFORIN **Prod** - OLYMPS 1974

The People Vs Inez Garcia 88 MIN
VHS / 16mm
Color (G)
$95.00 rental _ #PVIG - 000
Dramatizes the rape and murder trial of Inez Garcia. Shows how Garcia was found guilty of second degree murder for the shooting death of the accomplice of the man she accused of rape. Raises questions about the criminal justice system and a woman's right to defend herself in the context of an alleged rape.
Civics and Political Systems
Dist - PBS **Prod** - KQEDTV

The People Vs Job Shattuck 31 MIN
U-matic / VHS / 16mm
Decades of Decision - the American Revolution Series
Color (H C A)
Presents a recreation of the dilemma faced by many veterans at the close of the Revolutionary War when they found themselves deeply in debt and their creditors foreclosing. Explains that Job Shattuck lead a group of debt - ridden farmers to the courthouse in Concord, Massachusetts to prevent the court from sitting and thereby forestalling additional foreclosures.
Civics and Political Systems; History - United States
Dist - NGS **Prod** - NGS 1975

People who are fighting blindness 29 MIN
U-matic / VHS
Are you listening series
Color (H C A)
LC 83-706226
Victims of genetic diseases which cause blindness and, in some cases, loss of hearing talk about the adjustments that they and their family members have made.
Education; Guidance and Counseling
Dist - STURTM **Prod** - STURTM 1982

People who have epilepsy 28 MIN
16mm
Are you listening series
Color (I)
LC 80-701145
Designed to enlighten the public about epilepsy by introducing several epileptics who discuss such topics as recognition of a seizure, the importance of feeling independent and ways of copinng with marriage, jobs and travel.
Health and Safety; Psychology
Dist - STURTM **Prod** - STURTM 1979

People who Help - Careers in Aviation 16 MIN
16mm / U-matic / VHS
Color (J)
LC 75-704006
Discusses commercial aviation, general aviation and aerospace, focusing on career opportunities in these areas.
Guidance and Counseling; Industrial and Technical Education; Science; Science - Physical
Dist - PHENIX **Prod** - LIEBJH 1975

People who Help - Health Careers 18 MIN
U-matic / VHS / 16mm
Color (H C A)
LC 75-702539
Examines some of the career opportunities available in the field of health.
Guidance and Counseling; Psychology
Dist - PHENIX **Prod** - SMITG 1975

People who Help You 30 MIN
VHS / 16mm
Science, Health and Math Series
Color (P)
$39.95 purchase _ #CL7912
Informs children about helping adults.
Psychology; Sociology
Dist - EDUCRT

People who make a difference 30 MIN
VHS
Return to the sea series
Color (I J H G)
$24.95 purchase _ #RTS106
Focuses on unique and dedicated people who are drawn to diving. Includes Norine Rouse who began her diving career at age 50 and at age 65 became a spokesperson for marine environment. Meets disabled divers Jill Robinson and Ted Bridis to discover the freedom and special challenges of diving. Part of a 13 - part series on marine life produced by Marine Grafics and University of North Carolina Public TV.
Physical Education and Recreation; Science - Natural; Science - Physical
Dist - ENVIMC

People who move 14 MIN
U-matic / VHS
Tax tips on tape series
Color; Captioned (A PRO IND)
$20.00, $40.00 purchase _ #TCA17600, #TCA17599
Discusses how to determine if a move can be tax - deductible. Shows what moving expenses can be deducted completely, and which ones have dollar limits.
Business and Economics; Civics and Political Systems; Social Science
Dist - USNAC **Prod** - USIRS 1988

People who Sell Things 18 MIN
16mm / U-matic / VHS
Color (H A)
LC 76-700055
Describes the different kinds of sales careers and the kinds of people suited to them with examples of the daily activities of an insurance agent, a real estate broker, a telephone systems salesman and an automobile salesman.
Education; Guidance and Counseling; Psychology
Dist - PHENIX **Prod** - SMITG 1975

People who Work in Manufacturing 17 MIN
U-matic / VHS / 16mm
Color (H C A)
LC 75-703883
Presents a vocational education film which shows key personnel in an electronics factory as they work, give their reasons for entering electronics and tell of the rewards and problems they meet each day.
Business and Economics; Guidance and Counseling; Industrial and Technical Education; Psychology; Social Science
Dist - PHENIX **Prod** - SMITG 1975

People who Work with People 14 MIN
U-matic / VHS / 16mm
Color (J)
LC 76-703586
Explores the importance and rewards of working to help others. Follows the daily routine of several service workers as they discuss why they chose service work, what they get out of their jobs and what they offer in return.
Guidance and Counseling; Social Science; Sociology
Dist - BARR **Prod** - BARR 1976

People will Talk 4 MIN
16mm / U-matic / VHS
This Matter of Motivation Series
Color (IND)
LC 73-702804
Shows the effect which rumors and gossip can have on both the employees and employer.
Business and Economics; Guidance and Counseling; Psychology; Sociology
Dist - DARTNL **Prod** - CTRACT 1966

People with Herpes Speak to Ann Landers 28 MIN
16mm
Color (H)
Conveys the message that herpes is manageable in discussions between victims with Ann Landers and Dr Sam Nixon.
Health and Safety
Dist - MTP **Prod** - ICHD

People Working - Behavior Modification as a Management Tool 30 MIN
U-matic
Color (C A)
LC 79-706003
Presents the key concepts of behavior modification and their application to industry. Gives examples of how behavior modification was used to motivate employees in three organizational situations.
Business and Economics; Psychology
Dist - CSUF **Prod** - CSUF 1978

People Working - George Allen on Motivation and Leadership 20 MIN
U-matic
Color (C)
LC 80-706790
Presents football coach George Allen giving his views on motivation and leadership.
Guidance and Counseling
Dist - CSUF **Prod** - CSUF 1979

People Working - Management Behavior, what Does a Manager do all Day 20 MIN
U-matic
Color (C)
LC 80-706788
Presents Robert Clifford, president of Air California, discussing his activities as an executive, the roles he performs, and his views on being a manager.
Business and Economics; Psychology
Dist - CSUF **Prod** - CSUF 1980

People Working - Pat Haden on Career and Life Planning 20 MIN
U-matic
Color (C)
LC 80-706789
Presents professional football player Pat Haden discussing his views on career and life planning.
Guidance and Counseling
Dist - CSUF **Prod** - CSUF 1979

People Working with Data 7 MIN
U-matic / VHS / 16mm
Career Awareness Series
Color (P I)
LC 75-702741
Introduces people whose work is collecting, organizing and communicating data. Uses songs to describe a wide range of data - oriented occupations, including news reporter, astronomer and postal clerk.
Guidance and Counseling; Social Science
Dist - MGHT **Prod** - MGHT 1975

People Working with People 7 MIN
16mm / U-matic / VHS
Career Awareness Series
Color (P I)
LC 75-702740
Introduces people whose work is teaching, serving and caring for other people. Uses songs to describe a wide range of people - oriented occupations, including math teacher, store clerk and rescue squad attendant.
Guidance and Counseling; Social Science
Dist - MGHT **Prod** - MGHT 1975

People Working with Things 7 MIN
16mm / U-matic / VHS
Career Awareness Series
Color (P I)
LC 75-702739
Introduces people whose work is creating, operating and fixing things. Uses songs to describe a wide range of occupations, including chef, TV cameraman and bicycle repairman.
Guidance and Counseling; Social Science
Dist - MGHT **Prod** - MGHT 1975

People You Meet
U-matic / VHS / 16mm
Color
Presents different episodes to demonstrate an important language item in English, at the intermediate level.
English Language
Dist - NORTNJ **Prod** - NORTNJ

The People You Never See 28 MIN
16mm
Color
Depicts a 12 - year - old girl with severe cerebral palsy eagerly participating in class activities through the use of Bliss symbols and a typewriter. Shows six handicapped

adults who have left the protection of institutions and live as an extended family despite the architectural barriers they encounter.
Education; Psychology
Dist - FLMLIB **Prod** - CANBC

People You'd Like to Know Series
C J 10 MIN
Dee 10 MIN
Diana 10 MIN
Elizabeth 10 MIN
Harold 10 MIN
John 10 MIN
Kai 10 MIN
Mark 10 MIN
Paige 10 MIN
Dist - EBEC

The People's army
VHS
The Great wall of iron series
Color (J H G)
$225.00 purchase
Presents part 2 of a four - part series that tells of the Chinese People's Liberation Army, known to the Chinese as the Great Wall of Iron. Looks at its development through struggles with the Nationalists and with the Japanese. Also available in a set of four videos.
Geography - World; History - World
Dist - LANDMK

People's Court 28 MIN
VHS / U-matic
Color (PRO)
Describes the operation of the People's Court in Chicago. Explains the purpose and procedures. Offers suggestions for out - of - court settlements and preparations for court appearances.
Civics and Political Systems
Dist - ABACPE **Prod** - ABACPE

Peoples Like Us 15 MIN
U-matic / VHS / 16mm
Color (I)
Shows how diversity is reflected in the equally vast variety of social structures that different people have developed over many hundreds of years.
Sociology
Dist - LUF **Prod** - LUF 1982

A People's Music - Soviet Style 23 MIN
U-matic / VHS / 16mm
Soviet Style Series
Color (J)
Examines Soviet culture, from highly regarded professional troupes to the work of amateurs who've achieved remarkably high standards. Shows how traditional songs and dances are kept alive by all the people.
Fine Arts; Geography - World; History - World; Sociology
Dist - JOU **Prod** - JOU 1982

Peoples of China 21 MIN
16mm
Color (J H C G)
Surveys China today. Covers country life, city life and industry.
Business and Economics; Geography - World; Social Science; Sociology
Dist - VIEWTH **Prod** - GATEEF

Peoples of the Island World 17 MIN
16mm / U-matic / VHS
Cultures of Southern Seas Series
Color (I J)
LC FIA67-5555
Describes how the islands of the South and Central Pacific were originally populated by three major groups of native people - - the Melanesians, the Micronesians and the Polynesians. Shows their movement to Australia from Asia, then migrating by fragile canoes to the islands to the north, east and south.
Geography - United States; Geography - World; Sociology
Dist - MCFI **Prod** - HOE 1967

Peoples of the Soviet Union 33 MIN
16mm
B&W (I J H C)
Surveys the different nationalities that make up the people of the USSR, from the city dwellers of Moscow and Leningrad to the primitive tribes of the Caucasus and Siberia. Photographed in the 30's.
Geography - World
Dist - IFF **Prod** - IFF 1952

People's park 25 MIN
16mm
B&W (G)
$20.00 rental
Documents a bloody and protracted battle over a mere city block of land. Follows students and radical youth of Berkeley declaring in manifesto and deed that the corporation's and the university's 'property rights' cannot be held above the interests of the people. This vision holds up against vicious maimings by government troops and an airstrike against United States civilians. Represents revolutionary filmmakers in the 1960s whose work provides a window to that period.
Civics and Political Systems; Education; Fine Arts; History - United States; Sociology
Dist - CANCIN **Prod** - SINGLE 1969

People's Park 20 MIN
16mm
B&W
Shows the giant university using brutal repression as the students and community of Berkeley transform a vacant university - owned lot into a people's park. Explains that private property is valued over human life and that the police and National Guard will protect the interests of the giant corporations while new weapons of counter - insurgency are tested on the citizens.
Business and Economics; Civics and Political Systems; Education; Social Science; Sociology
Dist - CANWRL **Prod** - CANWRL

People's Temple 24 MIN
16mm
Color
LC 73-702353
Documents the origins of the People's Temple Community in California. Includes interviews with Pastor Jim Jones, providing insight into his charismatic character, and presents case histories.
Religion and Philosophy; Sociology
Dist - USC **Prod** - USC 1973

The Peoples Theatre 30 MIN
U-matic / VHS
Kaleidoscope Series
Color
Fine Arts
Dist - SCCOE **Prod** - KTEHTV

People's Wall 25 MIN
16mm
Color (J)
LC 81-701583
Shows the progress of a 200 - foot - long mural in San Francisco which depicts the unofficial labor history of the city. Includes footage of the events shown on the mural.
Fine Arts; Geography - United States
Dist - CANCIN **Prod** - FINLIN 1978

People's War 45 MIN
16mm
B&W
Presents the trip to North Vietnam in the summer of 1969 and shows the daily struggle of the Vietnamese people.
Civics and Political Systems; Sociology
Dist - CANWRL **Prod** - CANWRL

PEP subseries 109 MIN
U-matic / VHS
PEP subseries - Autism series
Color (C PRO)
$948.00 purchase _ #C850 - VI - 135S
Presents a three - part subseries on PEP - PsychoEducational Profile - presented by Dr Eric Schopler, which is part of a series on autism. Shows how to convert PEP results into an individualized teaching program, how to score PEP and how to score PEP correctly.
Health and Safety; Psychology
Dist - HSCIC

PEP subseries - Autism series
An Individualized education program - conversion of a Psychoeducational Profile - PEP - into an individualized teaching program 21 MIN
PEP subseries 109 MIN
The Psychoeducational Profile - introduction to scoring the PEP 33 MIN
The Psychoeducational Profile test tape - scoring the PEP 55 MIN
Dist - HSCIC

Pepe 157 MIN
16mm
Color (I J H C)
Stars Cantinflas as Pepe, a simple - hearted peon ranch hand, who, through his devotion to a horse he has raised from a colt, finds himself flung into the never - never land of the entertainment world to have amusing encounters with many famous stars.
Guidance and Counseling; Sociology
Dist - TWYMAN **Prod** - CPC 1960

Pepe's family 41 MIN
VHS / 16mm
Films from Andalusia, Spain series
B&W (G)
$600.00, $250.00 purchase, $65.00, $40.00 rental
Portrays the concerns of a migrant laborer who works in Germany. Examines his holiday visit, his social networks, foreign experiences, plans for the future of his family. When his father insists upon remaining in the rural area, he must decide whether to move his large family to a factory town. Part of a series.
Geography - World; History - World; Sociology
Dist - DOCEDR **Prod** - MINTZJ 1978

Pepe's Family 45 MIN
U-matic / VHS / 16mm
B&W (H C A) (GERMAN)
LC 79-700097
Concerns the rural exodus from Andalusia, Spain, and its effect on the family life of a migrant laborer who works in Germany. Depicts the family relationships while the father is absent and focuses on his concerns during holiday visits.
History - World; Sociology
Dist - IU **Prod** - MINTZJ 1978

Pepita's Surprise 16 MIN
16mm / U-matic / VHS
Color (I J H)
Depicts a girl's birthday celebration which includes an excursion with her father and a family fiesta.
Literature and Drama
Dist - IFB **Prod** - IFB 1957

Pepper - the Master Spice 26 MIN
U-matic / VHS
Spice of Life Series
Color (J A)
Documents the importance of pepper in medieval times and how it motivated the voyages of early European explorers. Describes the various uses of pepper today.
Health and Safety; Home Economics
Dist - BCNFL **Prod** - BLCKRD 1985

Peppercorns - Fresh Ground Flavor 26 MIN
U-matic / VHS
Spice of Life Series
Color (J A)
Describes the uses of peppercorn around the world.
Health and Safety; Home Economics
Dist - BCNFL **Prod** - BLCKRD 1985

The peppered moth - a population study
VHS
BSCS Classic Inquiries Series
Color (H C)
$59.95 purchase _ #193 W 2211
Poses questions, raises problems and presents experimental data on the peppered moth population and its adaptation to changing environmental factors. Part of a series on the life sciences.
Science - Natural
Dist - WARDS **Prod** - WARDS

Peppermint Soda 97 MIN
16mm
Color (FRENCH (ENGLISH SUBTITLES))
Centers on the friends, family, classes, vacations, sulks, sexual misconceptions, pop records, bad grades, adventures, and misadventures of a French - Jewish schoolgirl in 1963. Directed by Diane Kurys. With English subtitles.
Fine Arts; Foreign Language
Dist - NYFLMS **Prod** - UNKNWN 1978

Peppermint Stick Selection Series
The Dancing Princess 15 MIN
Delicious inventions 15 MIN
Milo's Journey 15 MIN
Pushmi - Pullyu 11 MIN
Runt of the Litter 13 MIN
The Singing Bone 13 MIN
Talk to the Animals 10 MIN
Wilbur's Story 15 MIN
Dist - FI

Pepsodent Commercial 1 MIN
VHS / U-matic
Color
Shows a classic television commercial with the line 'You'll wonder where the yellow went.'.
Business and Economics; Psychology; Sociology
Dist - BROOKC **Prod** - BROOKC

Peptic Ulcer
VHS / U-matic
Color (SPANISH)
Covers the classic symptoms of peptic ulcer happening to ordinary people. Stresses the importance of accurate diagnosis and explains appropriate therapy to relieve pain, promote healing, prevent recurrence and avoid complications.
Foreign Language; Science - Natural
Dist - MIFE **Prod** - MIFE

Peptic Ulcer
U-matic / VHS
Color
Examines the inter - relationships of anatomical and physiologic factors in the genesis of peptic ulcer. Assesses indications, advantages and limitation of modern methods of diagnosis. Summarizes the role of H - 2 blocking agents.

Health and Safety
Dist - AMEDA **Prod** - AMEDA

Peptic Ulcer 60 MIN
VHS / U-matic
Medicine for the Layman Series
Color
LC 81-707590
Presents Dr Denis McCarthy explaining the difference between gastric and peptic ulcers. Discusses warning signals indicating the onset of ulcers, types of jobs associated with increased risk of ulcers and factors that aggravate ulcers.
Health and Safety
Dist - USNAC **Prod** - NIH 1980

Peptic Ulcer 16 MIN
U-matic / 8mm cartridge / VHS / 16mm
Color (PRO) (SPANISH)
Discusses peptic ulcer disease and the patient's role in therapy.
Health and Safety; Science - Natural
Dist - PRORE **Prod** - PRORE

Peptic Ulcer Disease 30 MIN
U-matic / VHS
Color
Discusses the latest aspects of the diagnosis, treatment and Pathophysiology of peptic ulcer, a disorder in which advances have been startling.
Health and Safety
Dist - ROWLAB **Prod** - ROWLAB

Peptic Ulcers 58 MIN
U-matic
Color
Shows Dr Denis McCarthy, senior investigator for the National Institute of Arthritis, Metabolism and Digestive Diseases, talking about kinds of ulcers, who gets them, why and various treatments.
Health and Safety; Psychology
Dist - MTP **Prod** - NIH

Pequis 15 MIN
16mm
Color (G)
#2X12I
Depicts the people of Pequis as they earn their living and as they spend their leisure time. Shows farmers, berry pickers, fisherman at work. Presents a traditional Indian dinner of Moose and an evening Pow Wow.
Social Science
Dist - CDIAND **Prod** - BORTF 1977

Per Cent Problems 12 MIN
U-matic
Basic Math Skills Series Converting to Per Cent; Converting to per cent
Color
Mathematics
Dist - TELSTR **Prod** - TELSTR

Perc, Pop, Sprinkle 11 MIN
16mm
Color (K P I)
LC 76-702954
Presents a series of visual experiences for children after which they are asked to interpret the experience physically.
Education; Physical Education and Recreation
Dist - MMP **Prod** - MMP 1969

Perceiving and Believing 28 MIN
U-matic / VHS
Color
Develops the essential ground work for effective Affirmative Action. Shows that the act of pre - judging others based on stereotyped preconceptions is an act of prejudice. With Ed Asner.
Sociology
Dist - MTVTM **Prod** - MTVTM

Percent 14 MIN
VHS / U-matic
Math Matters Series Green Module
Color (I J)
Illustrates the meaning of percent in the context of commercials, newscasts, a quiz show and a consumer tips feature.
Mathematics
Dist - AITECH **Prod** - KRLNTV 1975

Percent 30 MIN
VHS
Basic mathematical skills series
Color (J H)
$125.00 purchase _ #M11
Teaches about percent. Features Elayn Gay. Part of a 15 - part series on basic math.
Mathematics
Dist - LANDMK **Prod** - MGHT

Percent and Applications 30 MIN
VHS
Mathematics Series
Color (J)
LC 90713155
Explains the applications of percent. The 10th of 157 installments in the Mathematics Series.
Mathematics
Dist - GPN

Percent and applications
VHS
Basic mathematical skills series
Color (I J H)
$125.00 purchase _ #1010
Teaches the concept of percentage and how it is applied to practical problems. Presents part of a series that provides 27 videos, each between 25 and 30 minutes long, that explain and reinforce basic mathematical concepts. Tutors the student through definitions, theorems, step - by - step solutions and examples. Videos are also available in a set.
Mathematics
Dist - LANDMK

Percent and Applications, Pt 2 30 MIN
VHS
Mathematics Series
Color (J)
LC 90713155
The second of two tapes explaining percents and their applications. The 11th of 157 installments in the Mathematics Series.
Mathematics
Dist - GPN

Percent applications II
VHS
Basic mathematical skills series
Color (I J H)
$125.00 purchase _ #1011
Expands the concept of percentage and how it is applied to practical problems. Presents part of a series that provides 27 videos, each between 25 and 30 minutes long, that explain and reinforce basic mathematical concepts. Tutors the student through definitions, theorems, step - by - step solutions and examples. Videos are also available in a set.
Mathematics
Dist - LANDMK

Percent Defectives for Small Samples 20 MIN
U-matic / VHS
Statistics for Technicians Series
Color (IND)
Presents necessary distributions for acceptance sampling. Shows where sample sizes are small the Poisson and binomial distributions are often appropriate. Discusses when and how to use these distributions for calculating the probabilities of occurrence of a number of defectives.
Business and Economics; Mathematics; Psychology
Dist - COLOSU **Prod** - COLOSU

Percent - Why and How 11 MIN
16mm / U-matic / VHS
Color (I J)
$270.00, $190.00 purchase _ #1675
Shows the different types of problems percentages are used to solve, such as test scores, the interest on savings accounts, and others.
Mathematics
Dist - CORF **Prod** - CORF 1966

Percentage 10 MIN
16mm
Color; B&W (I)
LC 77-701208
Gives in animation the definition of percentage. Treats percentage as a special form of fractions and emphasizes its relationship to decimal fractions. Gives examples of two different types of problems.
Mathematics
Dist - MLA **Prod** - JHP 1968

Percentage of Modulation 29 MIN
16mm
B&W
LC 74-705341
Deals with percentage of modulation. Explains over, under and complete modulation and gives the advantages and disadvantages of each. Explains how to determine the percentage of modulation. (Kinescope).
Industrial and Technical Education; Social Science
Dist - USNAC **Prod** - USAF 1972

The Percentage Revolution 30 MIN
VHS / U-matic
Adult Math Series
Color (A)
Shows adult math students the importance of percentages when paying property tax, borrowing money and checking prices on marked - down sale items in stores.
Education; Mathematics
Dist - KYTV **Prod** - KYTV 1984

Percentages 20 MIN
U-matic
Mainly Math Series
Color (H C)
Discusses the use of percentages, focusing on practical math problems dealing with discounts, sales taxes and interest.
Mathematics
Dist - GPN **Prod** - WCVETV 1977

Percents
VHS
Color (P I)
$39.95 purchase _ #VAD017
Features Dr Peter Lanzer of The Learning Channel. Teaches percent.
Mathematics
Dist - SIV

Percents 98 MIN
VHS
Video tutor basic math series
Color (I J H)
$29.95 purchase _ #VIT101V
Teaches what percent is and how it is used. Uses computer graphics and an electronic chalkboard to illustrate the concepts. Includes a workbook. Part of a seven - part series on basic mathematics.
Mathematics
Dist - CAMV

Percents 91 MIN
VHS
Color (I J)
$29.95 purchase _ #S01790
Covers mathematical operations related to percents. Includes workbook, with additional workbooks available at an extra charge.
Mathematics
Dist - UILL

Percents 120 MIN
VHS
Math for life series
Color (H C A)
$39.95 purchase _ #VA332V
Presents the third of a four - part series which reviews basic mathematics skills. Focuses on the daily application of these skills. Reviews various percent concepts, including finding percentages, determining the percent of increase or decrease, and more. Includes a study guide.
Mathematics
Dist - CAMV

Perception 30 MIN
U-matic / VHS
Psychology of Human Relations Series
Color
Examines the effects of perceptual processes on sensory information, the effects of expectation of perception, the figure - ground principle of perception and other aspects of perception.
Psychology
Dist - WFVTAE **Prod** - MATC

Perception 15 MIN
16mm
Color (PRO)
Provides insight into how man perceives the world around him, which influences how he behaves. Includes demonstrations of figure - ground relationships, Bruner's experiment, phi phenomenon, color satiation and others.
Psychology; Sociology
Dist - PHM **Prod** - APPLE 1970

Perception 27 MIN
U-matic / VHS / 16mm
Color (H C A)
LC 79-700853
Explores the physiological, psychological and cultural forces that influence human perception. Explains the necessity of a balance between subjective perceptions and objective truths.
Psychology; Science - Natural
Dist - MGHT **Prod** - CRMP 1979

Perception 16 MIN
16mm
Basic Psychology Series
Color (H C A)
LC 76-702925
Considers concepts associated with perception in psychology, including Gestalt psychology, figure - ground relationship, perceptual satiation and depth perception.
Psychology
Dist - EDMDC **Prod** - EDMDC 1973

Perception and Communication 32 MIN
16mm
Communication Theory and the New Educational Media Series
B&W (P I J H C)

LC 74-705342
Gives concrete examples of how human perceptions affect the communication process and the individual's concept of reality, introduces two major theories of perception - - the cognitive and the transactional.
Education; Psychology; Social Science
Dist - USNAC **Prod** - USOE 1967

Perception and self - awareness 28 MIN
U-matic / BETA / VHS
Communication skills 1 - basic series
Color (H C G)
$101.95, $89.95 purchase _ #CA - 37
Begins the exploration of oral communication by examining the role of perception and self - awareness as basic conepts in the process of speaking to others. An effective speaker must be aware of individual uniqueness and what the speaker brings to communication, requiring skill in self - analysis and perception. Part of a series on communication.
Psychology; Social Science
Dist - INSTRU

Perception - Key to Effective Management Communication 52 MIN
16mm / U-matic / VHS
Color (C A)
LC 81-700786
Presents a training program on perception designed to help correct communication problems in management. Makes participants aware of their unconscious misperceptions about themselves, their co - workers and their work environment.
Business and Economics; Psychology
Dist - CRMP **Prod** - MGHT 1981

Perception of Danger 20 MIN
16mm
Color
LC 75-700471
Presents a police training film which explains normal behavioral responses to danger. Discusses relative and distorted perceptions and encourages police personnel to discuss fear openly and to assist each other in overcoming it.
Civics and Political Systems; Guidance and Counseling; Psychology; Social Science
Dist - UNCMID **Prod** - UNCMID 1974

Perception of Words 12 MIN
16mm
B&W (C T)
LC 70-713859
Presents a test to demonstrate influence of word usage frequency on perception. Uses group data computed to show whether frequency of usage influences perceptual accuracy.
English Language; Psychology
Dist - PSUPCR **Prod** - SF 1971

Perception - the Effect of Past Experience on what We See 29 MIN
16mm
Developing Communication Skills Series
B&W (IND)
LC 70-703322
Guidance and Counseling; Psychology; Social Science
Dist - EDSD **Prod** - EDSD

Perception - Tragedy of the Friendly Breakfast 6 MIN
U-matic / VHS / 16mm
Color (H C A)
LC 79-701493
Edited from the motion picture Communication Roadblocks by Robert Allen Johnson. Tells how a fatal shot ruins a friendly breakfast. Features three eyewitnesses who offer three different views of the tragedy. Emphasizes the importance of keeping an open mind.
Psychology; Social Science
Dist - SALENG **Prod** - JONSRA 1977

Perceptions - dialogues with family therapists Series
Alberto Serrano, MD, Professor of psychiatry, University of Texas Medical School 60 MIN
Carl Whitaker, MD - professor of psychiatry, University of Wisconsin 60 MIN
Carolyn Attneave, PhD - professor of Indian studies and psychology 60 MIN
Charles Kramer, MD, Director, Jan Kramer, RN, Instructor, Family Institute of Chicago 60 MIN
Dist - BOSFAM

Perceptions - interventions in family therapy series
Alberto Serrano, MD - a nice family 60 MIN
Carl Whitaker, MD - an isolated father in the family 60 MIN
Charles Kramer, MD, Jan Kramer, RN Co - therapy with a family 60 MIN
Dist - BOSFAM

Perceptions, Pt a - Interventions in Family Therapy Series Vol I, Pt A2
James Framo, PhD - a Couples Group Demonstration 60 MIN
Dist - BOSFAM

Perceptions, Pt a - Interventions in Family Therapy Series Vol IV, Pt A7
Robert MacGregor, PhD, Mary MacGregor, MPsych - Single Parent Struggle 60 MIN
Dist - BOSFAM

Perceptions, Pt a - Interventions in Family Therapy Series Vol IV, Pt A8
Lois Jaffe, MSW - a Need to Know - a Family Faces Death 60 MIN
Dist - BOSFAM

Perceptions, Pt a - Interventions in Family Therapy Series Vol VI, Pt A12
Yetta Bernhard, MA - Conflict Resolution with a Couple 60 MIN
Dist - BOSFAM

Perceptions, Pt A- Interventions in Family Therapy Series
David Rubenstein, MD - the past in your eyes a couple's search 60 MIN
John Howells, MD - Assessment of the Family 60 MIN
Vincent Sweeney, MD and Jane Donner, PhD - How Far Can We Go a Family's Question 60 MIN
Virginia Satir, MSW - Sisters and Parents - a Family Finds Options 60 MIN
Dist - BOSFAM

Perceptions, Pt B - Dialogues with Family Therapists Series Vol I, Pt B2
James Framo, PhD - Professor of Psychology at Temple University 60 MIN
Dist - BOSFAM

Perceptions, Pt B - Dialogues with Family Therapists Series Vol II, Pt B4
Leonard Unterberger, MA - Director, Family Workshop, Chicago 60 MIN
Dist - BOSFAM

Perceptions, Pt B - Dialogues with Family Therapists Series Vol IV, Pt B7
Robert MacGregor, PhD, Mary MacGregor, 1 MPsych - Private Practice, Chicago 60 MIN
Dist - BOSFAM

Perceptions, Pt B - Dialogues with Family Therapists Series Vol IV, Pt B8
Lois Jaffe, MSW - Associate Professor, University of Pittsburgh School of Social Work 60 MIN
Dist - BOSFAM

Perceptions, Pt B - Dialogues with Family Therapists Series Vol VI, Pt B12
Yetta Bernhard, MA, Private Practice , Los Angeles, California 60 MIN
Dist - BOSFAM

Perceptions, Pt B - Dialogues with Family Therapists Series Vol VII, Pt B14
Norman Paul, MD, Associate Professor of Psychiatry, Boston Universtiy Medical School 60 MIN
Dist - BOSFAM

Perceptions, Pt B - dialogues with family therapists series Vol VIII, Pt B16
Salvador Minuchin, MD, Director, Philadelphia Child Guidance Clinic 60 MIN
Dist - BOSFAM

Perceptions, Pt B - dialogues with family therapists series
David Rubenstein, MD, professor of psychiatry at temple university medical school 60 MIN
Edgar Auerswald, MD - interview with Frederick J Duhl, MD 60 MIN
John Howells, MD, Director, Institute of Family Psychiatry, Ipswich, England 60 MIN
Vincent Sweeney, MD, Jane Donner, PhD, Center for the Study of Human Systems, Chevy Chase, MD 60 MIN
Dist - BOSFAM

Perceptions, Pt B - Interventions in Family Therapists Series Vol II Pt A4
Leonard Unterberger, MA - Just Making it - on Being White and Poor 60 MIN
Dist - BOSFAM

Perceptrons and hill climbing 45 MIN
U-matic / VHS
Artificial intelligence series; Fundamental concepts, Pt 1
Color (PRO)
Features such topics as seduction of neural imitations, perceptrons, the limits of learning, and a search alternative - hill climbing.
Mathematics
Dist - MIOT **Prod** - MIOT

Perceptual Disabilities 30 MIN
U-matic / VHS
Characteristics of Learning Disabilities Series
Color (C A)
Defines perception in terms of learning disabilities and describes types of perceptual disorders.
Education; Psychology
Dist - FI **Prod** - WCVETV 1976

Perceptual grids - 4 86 MIN
VHS
Creating therapeutic change series
Color; PAL; SECAM (G)
$95.00 purchase
Features Richard Bandler in the fourth part of a seven - part series on creating therapeutic change using advanced NLP, neuro - linguistic programming. Reveals that just solving problems often isn't enough and that time distinctions can be used to interlace beliefs, feeling states and 'chains' into complexes that generatively reorganize fundamental attitudes throughout a person's life. Recommended that tapes be viewed in order. Bandler sometimes uses profanity for emphasis, which may offend some people.
Health and Safety; Psychology
Dist - NLPCOM **Prod** - NLPCOM

Perceptual Motor Evaluation of a Child with Dysfunction 33 MIN
16mm
B&W (PRO)
Uses standard and non - standard tests in evaluating the degree and type of perceptual - motor dysfunction in a seven - year - old girl with a neurological deficit. Assesses visual, tactile, and kinesthetic perception and motor planning.
Health and Safety; Science - Natural
Dist - UCLA **Prod** - UCLA

Perceptual Motor Evaluation of a Perceptually Normal Child 33 MIN
16mm
B&W (PRO)
Presents a method of assessing visual, tactile, and kinesthetic perception and related motor functions using standardized tests and some non - standardized procedures.
Education; Health and Safety; Psychology; Science - Natural
Dist - UCLA **Prod** - UCLA

Perceptual - Motor Skills - System Approach to Instruction
VHS / U-matic
Learning System Design Series Unit 6
Color (T)
Education; Psychology
Dist - MSU **Prod** - MSU

The Perceptual - Motor Specialist in the Arlington School System 26 MIN
U-matic / VHS
B&W
Shows how the perceptual - motor specialist assesses learning disabilities in five - year - old students and plans remediation in conjunction with a tutor, physical education specialist and classroom teacher.
Education; Health and Safety
Dist - BUSARG **Prod** - BUSARG

Perceval 140 MIN
16mm
Color (FRENCH (ENGLISH SUBTITLES))
Presents a 12th century courtly romance spoken in verse. Directed by Eric Rohmer.
Fine Arts; Foreign Language
Dist - NYFLMS

Perch
VHS
Pieper - zoology prelab dissections - series
Color (J H C)
$95.00 purchase _ #CG - 895 - VS
Presents dissection instruction and an anatomy review of the perch. Includes a brief post test to gauge student retention. Part of a 15 - part series on zoological lab dissection, including a lab safety review, produced by Bill Pieper.
Science; Science - Natural
Dist - HRMC

Perch Anatomy 17 MIN
U-matic / VHS / 16mm
Anatomy Series
Color (H C A)
Shows dissection techniques and internal structures of a perch. Examines the circulatory, respiratory, digestive, excretory and reproductive systems, the olfactory tract and the brain.
Science - Natural
Dist - IU **Prod** - IU 1963

Perch dissection 12 MIN
VHS
Dissection videos series
Color (H C)
$129.95 purchase _ #193 Y 0026
Covers dissection and anatomy of the perch. Includes dissection manual. Part of a series on dissection.
Science; Science - Natural
Dist - WARDS **Prod** - WARDS 1990

Perch dissection 13 MIN
VHS
Dissection video II series
Color (J H)
$100.00 purchase _ #A5VH 1222
Shows the dissection of a perch, start - to - finish. Provides clear and detailed presentations of the external anatomy, the correct procedures used for dissection and a review of the internal anatomy and physiological systems. Includes a dissection manual and a written examination. Part of a series on dissection.
Science - Natural
Dist - CLRVUE **Prod** - CLRVUE

Perchance to Dream 30 MIN
U-matic / VHS
Innovation Series
Color
Explores sleep, pointing out that people spend a third of their lives sleeping and yet for some this is not a peaceful sleep.
Psychology
Dist - PBS **Prod** - WNETTV 1983

Perchance to dream 27 MIN
U-matic / VHS
Color (H C G)
$129.00, $99.00 purchase _ #V544
Focuses on the Jimmy Carter Work Project for Habitat for Humanity. Shows how homeowners and volunteers develop new homes and neighborhoods where families can flourish.
Guidance and Counseling; Sociology
Dist - BARR **Prod** - CEPRO 1991

Perchance to Dream 5 MIN
U-matic / VHS
Write on, Set 2 Series
Color (J H)
Reviews lessons in the Write On, Set 1 Series. See also the title The Dreamer.
English Language
Dist - CTI **Prod** - CTI

Percussion 25 MIN
U-matic
Instruments of the Orchestra and their Techniques Series
Color
Fine Arts
Dist - UWASHP **Prod** - UWASHP

Percussion and Auscultation of the Lungs and Thorax, Pt 1 20 MIN
U-matic
Physical Assessment - Heart and Lungs Series Program 2; Program 2
Color (PRO)
Presents the nature and characteristics of sound as they relate to percussion and auscultation. Discusses various percussion tones and where they might be encountered, demonstrates techniques of indirect percussion and delineates the procedure for percussion of the thorax.
Health and Safety
Dist - CONMED **Prod** - CONMED 1976

Percussion and Auscultation of the Lungs and Thorax, Pt 2 30 MIN
U-matic
Physical Assessment - Heart and Lungs Series Program 3; Program 3
Color (PRO)
Focuses on aspects of auscultation of lungs, covering breath, adventitious, voice and whispered sounds and the procedure for auscultation.
Health and Safety
Dist - CONMED **Prod** - CONMED 1976

Percussion and Vibration Techniques 37 MIN
U-matic / VHS
B&W
Demonstrates techniques of postural drainage, and twelve positions for patient to assume during treatment.
Health and Safety
Dist - BUSARG **Prod** - BUSARG

The Percussion family 15 MIN
U-matic / VHS
Music machine series
Color (P)
Teaches recognition of percussion musical instruments.
Fine Arts
Dist - GPN **Prod** - GPN

The Percussion Family - 6 15 MIN
VHS
Music and Me Series
Color (P)
$125.00 purchase
Looks at musical instruments in the percussion family. Encourages student participation to develop skills in singing, listening, rhythmic expression and playing simple instruments. Part of the Music And Me Series.
Fine Arts
Dist - AITECH **Prod** - WDCNTV 1979

Percussion Instruments 13 MIN
16mm
Listening to Music Series
Color (P I J)
Covers several types of drums, the cymbals, the triangle, the tambourine and the castanets.
Fine Arts
Dist - VIEWTH **Prod** - GATEEF

Percussion Noel 29 MIN
VHS / 16mm
Color (G)
$55.00 rental _ #PERN - 000
Features Christmas music perfomed by the West Virginia University Percussion Ensemble under the direction of Phil Faini.
Fine Arts
Dist - PBS **Prod** - WWVUTV

Percussion Part I 50 MIN
VHS / 16mm
Junior High Music - Instrumental Series
Color (I)
$175.00, $200.00 purchase _ #288110
Features a host who introduces each program and offers a brief history of the instrument to be studied. Presents a master teacher, a professional musician with a symphony philharmonic, who demonstrates proper assembly, breathing and tone production, hand position, embouchure and articulation. A performance rounds out the program. 'Percussion Part I' demonstrates a variety of percussion instruments. Part I includes the snare drum, bass drum, tympani, Glockenspiel and xylophone.
Fine Arts
Dist - ACCESS **Prod** - ACCESS 1988

Percussion Part II 15 MIN
VHS / 16mm
Junior High Music - Instrumental Series
Color (I)
$175.00, $200.00 purchase _ #288111
Features a host who introduces each program and offers a brief history of the instrument to be studied. Presents a master teacher, a professional musician with a symphony philharmonic, who demonstrates proper assembly, breathing and tone production, hand position, embouchure and articulation. A performance rounds out the program. 'Percussion Part II' introduces a selection of small percussion instruments - cymbals, triangles, maracas, claves and the tambourine. Demonstrates the special techniques used in playing these instruments.
Fine Arts
Dist - ACCESS **Prod** - ACCESS 1988

Percutaneous Nephrostomy 15 MIN
16mm
Color
Discusses the rationale and advantages of percutaneous nephrostomy. Shows required armamentarium and demonstrates the procedure on a patient who required emergency nephrostomy drainage.
Science
Dist - EATONL **Prod** - EATONL 1971

Percutaneous Nephrostomy with Needle and Guide Wire 12 MIN
16mm
Color
LC 72-700183
Shows to members of the medical profession the procedures followed in performing a nephrostomy with the use of a needle and guide wire rather than a trocar needle.
Health and Safety; Science
Dist - EATONL **Prod** - EATONL 1971

Percutaneous Transluminal Coronary Angioplasty 7 MIN
U-matic / VHS
Color (PRO)
Introduces techniques involved in percutaneous transluminal coronary angioplasty.
Health and Safety; Science - Natural
Dist - HSCIC **Prod** - HSCIC 1984

Percutaneous transluminal coronary angioplasty - PTCA 28 MIN
U-matic / VHS
Color (PRO)
$275.00 purchase, $60.00 rental _ #7502S, #7502V
Follows a patient through the procedure of percutaneous transluminal coronary angioplasty - PTCA - and shows the role of nursing staff before, during and after the procedure. Details the characteristics of ideal candidates for the procedure and the major advantages and risk factors. Reviews staff role in patient education and post - procedural care.
Health and Safety
Dist - AJN **Prod** - HOSSN 1985

Percy Bysshe Shelley 30 MIN
VHS
Famous Authors Series
Color (H)
$11.50 rental _ #35508
Examines Percy Shelley's interest in the supernatural, considers the influence of the French Revolution, and studies his friendships with Lord Byron and Leigh Hunt. An installment of the Famous Authors Series, which examines important English writers in the context of their times.
English Language; History - World; Literature and Drama
Dist - PSU **Prod** - EBEC 1987
EBEC

Percy Mayfield - poet laureate of the blues 30 MIN
VHS
Color (G)
$19.95 purchase
Blues the blues with Percy Mayfield.
Fine Arts
Dist - KINOIC **Prod** - RHPSDY

The Peregrine falcon 20 MIN
U-matic / VHS / BETA
Color; PAL (G H C)
PdS50, PdS58 purchase
Covers the history of the relationship between humankind and falcon. Shows their natural life cycle and the efforts to reintroduce captive - bred falcons to the wild.
Science - Natural
Dist - EDPAT

Perennial gardening 60 MIN
VHS
Color (G)
$19.95 purchase _ #HT17
Looks at design and planning; combining different plants by size, shape, color and texture; dividing and transplanting to control size and rejuvenate old plants; and protecting perennials from pests. Shows closeups of leaf and root cuttings. Includes Planting Guidebook.
Agriculture
Dist - SVIP

The Perennial patriot 9 MIN
VHS
Color (G)
$25.00 purchase
Covers United States cotton history from its planting by the first settlers in Virginia to the present. Serves as a teaching aid and fits into the curriculum of any American history class.
Agriculture; Fine Arts
Dist - NCCA **Prod** - NCCA

Peres - the road to peace 57 MIN
VHS
Color (H C G)
$295.00 purchase, $75.00 rental
Portrays Shimon Peres, 'a hawk turned diplomatic dove,' who has spent his life trying to make Israel strong enough to accept peace. Chronicles his efforts to navigate the labyrinth of Middle East politics, his part in the events leading to the Palestinian uprising, political wins and losses and thoughtful reflections. Traces his history from his childhood as a Polish immigrant through his early adulthood as the architect of Israel's defense. Reveals that Peres converted from unconciliatory hawk to a proponent of negotiated peace as a result of the historic visit of Egyptian president Anwar Sadat to Jerusalem. Produced by Julie Gal for the Galex Foundation.
Geography - World; History - World; Religion and Philosophy
Dist - FLMLIB

Perestrioka from below 52 MIN
VHS
Color (G)
$390.00 purchase, $75.00 rental
Chronicles a 1989 trip made by a group of labor historians to Donetsk, Ukraine after the first mass strike in the USSR since the 1920s. Interviews coal miners who had just concluded their historic strike and provides sharp contrast to the propaganda films edited into the production. Produced by Daniel J Walkowitz and Barbara Abrash.
Fine Arts; History - World; Sociology
Dist - FIRS

Perestroika papers 49 MIN
VHS
Color (C G)
$70.00 purchase, $12.50 rental _ #50994
Features participants in the 1988 Dartmouth Conference of Soviet and American intellectuals held at the Lyndon B Johnson Library and Museum in Austin, Texas. Discusses the concept of perestroika within the contexts of economics, politics, democratization in the Soviet Union and a new relationship between the two nations. Experts from both nations offer details from each of the four papers presented at the end of the conference.
Civics and Political Systems
Dist - PSU **Prod** - KF 1988

Perestroika - profits or perils 30 MIN
VHS
Adam Smith's money world series
Color (H C A)
$79.95 purchase
Examines the business relationships several American companies have with the Soviet Union. Questions whether perestroika will ultimately help or hurt U S business interests. Features host Jerry Goodman, also known as 'Adam Smith,' and his guests Toby Gati, John Edwin Mroz, and Michael Murphy.
Business and Economics
Dist - PBS **Prod** - WNETTV

The Perfect Balance 8 MIN
VHS / U-matic
Winner's Circle Series
Color (A)
Presents Olympic standout basketball player Ann Meyers telling of the challenges she faced as a woman athlete. Shows the heights reached by her and her team.
Physical Education and Recreation; Psychology
Dist - SFTI **Prod** - SFTI

Perfect balance workout 61 MIN
VHS
Color (G H A)
$24.98 purchase _ #VTI9734V-P
Combines a variety of disciplines to lead user through warm-up, breathing, meditation, cardiovascular exercise, self-defense techniques, dance, aerobics, strengthening, toning, and relaxation. Includes Tai Chi, karate, salsa, ballet, and yoga. Notes that segments are led by experts in each discipline.
Physical Education and Recreation
Dist - CAMV

Perfect Competition and Inelastic Demand - Can the Farmer make a Profit 30 MIN
U-matic / VHS
Economics USA Series
Color (C)
Business and Economics
Dist - ANNCPB **Prod** - WEFA

Perfect Day 19 MIN
U-matic / VHS / 16mm
B&W (J)
Stars Laurel and Hardy. Describes their preparations for a picnic that ends in total disaster.
Fine Arts
Dist - FI **Prod** - ROACH 1929

The Perfect Day 27 MIN
U-matic / VHS / 16mm
Ramona Series
Color (P I)
$3795 purchase (entire set) - 16 mm, $435 purchase - 16 mm (per
Tells how Ramona helps out when things start to go wrong in a wedding ceremony between her aunt and Howie's Uncle Hobart. From Ramona Forever. A production of Atlantis Films, Ltd. in association with Lancit Media Productions, Ltd. and Revcom Television.
Literature and Drama
Dist - CF

Perfect day - Bad day 60 MIN
VHS
Beverly Cleary's Ramona series
Color; CC (K P I)
$29.95 purchase _ #KA435
Presents two Ramona stories by Beverly Cleary.
Color
Shows how society pressures women to have children and to meet impossibly high standards in raising them.
Home Economics; Sociology
Dist - PBS **Prod** - WNEDTV

Perfect peace 30 MIN
VHS
Color (G R)
$19.95 purchase, $10.00 rental _ #35 - 88122 - 87
Combines footage of nature scenes with hymns to create a vision of the world God made. Includes such hymns as 'My Faith Looks Up to Thee,' 'It Is Well With My Soul,' and 'Rock of Ages.' Produced by Zondervan.
Fine Arts; Religion and Philosophy
Dist - APH

Perfect picture 14 MIN
VHS
Color (G)
$39.95 purchase _ #S01393
Provides professional tests and instructions for home picture and audio adjustment for video cassette recorders. Includes user's guide.
Industrial and Technical Education
Dist - UILL

The Perfect President - a Man for His Time 52 MIN
U-matic / VHS / 16mm
Presidency Series
Color (J)
Discusses the 12 successive presidents from Teddy Roosevelt to Gerald Ford in order to examine presidential personalities.
Biography; Civics and Political Systems
Dist - LUF **Prod** - CORPEL 1976

The Perfect sale 20 MIN
U-matic / 16mm / VHS
Color (C A G H)
$495.00, $375.00, $345.00 purchase _ #A360
Demonstrates the steps for closing a sale successfully. Shows how to present an appropriate business image, why salespeople should approach customers in a courteous, helpful manner and why knowing the product and the market are essential for successful sales.
Business and Economics; Psychology
Dist - BARR **Prod** - HALBH 1984

The Perfect stargazer 57 MIN
VHS
Color (J H C G A)
Portrays the design and creation of the Automatic Photoelectric Telescope. Interviews people involved in the process on their hopes for the APT. Suggests that continuous observation of the skies, now possible only by space telescopes, will become a possibility from earth because of the APT.
Computer Science; Industrial and Technical Education; Religion and Philosophy; Science - Physical
Dist - SCETV **Prod** - SCETV 1990

Perfect Teacher 180 - 420 MIN
U-matic / VHS
(A PRO)
$495.00
Introduces basic concepts and advanced functions of WordPerfect.
Computer Science
Dist - VIDEOT **Prod** - VIDEOT 1988

Perfect the Pig 30 MIN
U-matic / VHS
Reading Rainbow Series
Color (P)
Presents the high flying adventures of a special pig with wings in Susan Jeschke's Perfect The Pig, narrated by James Coco. Follows with host LeVar Burton's own adventure in the library, shown in a lively discussion with Kermit the Frog about life, happiness and pursuit of 'Miss Piggy.' Also visits a hog farm in rural Oahu, in Hawaii.
English Language; Literature and Drama
Dist - GPN **Prod** - WNEDTV

Perfecting the art of criticism 48 MIN
VHS
Speaking of success series
Color (H C G)
$39.95 purchase _ #PD14
Features Francine Bergen explaining how to reduce office tension and increase productivity by criticizing problems rather than people, and by learning to take criticism constructively. Part of a series.
Business and Economics; Social Science
Dist - SVIP **Prod** - AUVICA 1993

Perfecting the family 44 MIN
VHS
Building the family of God series
Color (R G)
$29.95 purchase _ #6112 - 3
Shows how ordinary Christians can change their world and perfect their family relationships. Features Dr John MacArthur.
Literature and Drama
Dist - KNOWUN

The Perfect Drug Film 32 MIN
16mm
Color (J)
LC 72-701573
Presents a historical examination of mankind's quest for relaxation and enjoyment through narcotics. Concludes that drugs are not needed for these purposes.
Health and Safety; Psychology; Sociology
Dist - FI **Prod** - AVANTI 1971

The Perfect Gift 22 MIN
16mm
Color
LC 80-701256
Illustrates how infant car safety seats work and points out that they are the infant's only protection while in a car.
Health and Safety; Home Economics
Dist - VISUCP **Prod** - VISUCP 1980

Perfect harmony 50 MIN
VHS
Color (G)
$19.95 purchase_#1440
Celebrates Tanglewood's 50 years of music with live performances and personal stories shared by Tanglewood fellows. Includes Leon Fleisher, Seiji Ozawa, John Williams and the Boston Symphony Orchestra. Hosted by Marvin Hamlisch.
Fine Arts
Dist - KULTUR

Perfect Harmony - the Whiffenpoofs in China 28 MIN
U-matic / VHS / 16mm
Color (H A G)
Documents the Whiffenpoofs tour of the People's Republic of China.
Fine Arts; Geography - World; Sociology
Dist - DIRECT **Prod** - NIERNG 1986

Perfect image 30 MIN
VHS
Color (G)
$65.00 rental, $225.00 purchase
Features two actresses who constantly change their personae while the film poses questions about how Black women see themselves and each other and the pitfalls that await those who internalize the search for the 'perfect image.' Exposes stereotypical images of Black women and delves into their own ideas of self - worth. By Maureen Blackwood; produced by Sankofa Film and Video. Recommended as a companion piece to Hairpiece or The Body Beautiful.
Fine Arts; Sociology
Dist - WMEN

The Perfect Job for Jim 4 MIN
U-matic / VHS / 16mm
This Matter of Motivation Series
Color (PRO)
LC 75-703848
Asks how to handle the situation with an employee who is very capable in his present job, but is unhappy and would rather resign, if he is unable to attain a transfer with the company.
Business and Economics; Psychology; Sociology
Dist - DARTNL **Prod** - CTRACT

Perfect Leader 4 MIN
VHS / U-matic
Color
Features a satire about an omnipotent computer.
Fine Arts
Dist - KITCHN **Prod** - KITCHN

Perfect Lives 182 MIN
U-matic / VHS
Color
Features the keyboard inventions of 'Blue' Gene Tyranny and the singing of Jill Kroesen and David Van Tieghem. Produced for Channel Four Television, Great Britain.
Fine Arts
Dist - KITCHN **Prod** - KITCHN

The Perfect Moment 11 MIN
U-matic / VHS / 16mm
Color
LC 79-701213
Focuses on that moment in sports when technique, opportunity, training, drive and environmental conditions produce a super - charged moment of excitement. Shows a hang - glider, a skier and a surfer experiencing this moment of perfection.
Physical Education and Recreation
Dist - PFP **Prod** - MCGIF 1979

The Perfect Mother - Paradox or Possibility 29 MIN
U-matic
Woman Series

Literature and Drama; Religion and Philosophy; Sociology
Dist - MOODY **Prod** - MOODY

A Perfectly Normal Day 27 MIN
16mm / U-matic / VHS
Color (C A)
Shows how to reduce and manage crises and interruptions, presenting a typical day as a jigsaw puzzle.
Guidance and Counseling; Psychology; Sociology
Dist - CCCD **Prod** - CCCD 1978

Performance 20 MIN
U-matic / VHS / 16mm
Art of film series
Color
LC 75-703764
Uses selections from the motion pictures Richard III, Summertime, The Gold Rush, and La Strada to illustrate the nature of acting for films.
Fine Arts
Dist - CORF **Prod** - JANUS 1975

Performance 41 MIN
U-matic / VHS
Systems Engineering and Systems Management Series
Color
Provides a general systematic approach for analyzing system performance. Illustrates the procedure for performing a system error analysis.
Industrial and Technical Education
Dist - MIOT **Prod** - MIOT

Performance and Dance Theatre 30 MIN
VHS / U-matic
Political and Social Comment in Dance Series
Color
Fine Arts
Dist - ARCVID **Prod** - ARCVID

Performance and Evaluation 30 MIN
U-matic / VHS
Business of Managing Professionals Series
Color
Discusses performance and evaluation as part of managing professionals.
Business and Economics
Dist - KYTV **Prod** - KYTV 1983

Performance Appraisal 20 MIN
VHS / 16mm / U-matic
Color (H C G A PRO)
$520.00, $365.00, $395.00
Discusses the importance of performance reviews of employees. Highlights critical steps in the performance appraisal process. Dramatizes both good and bad practices when conducting performance reviews.
Business and Economics; Psychology; Social Science
Dist - BARR **Prod** - BARR 1986

Performance Appraisal 120 MIN
VHS / U-matic
AMA's Program for Performance Appraisal Series
Color
Explains how the appraisal process relates to the overall management function and presents a concise four - step process for effectively planning and conducting a performance appraisal within an organization.
Business and Economics; Psychology
Dist - AMA **Prod** - AMA

Performance Appraisal 18 MIN
VHS / 16mm
ITC Supervisory Methods, Module 9, Series
(C PRO)
$924.00 purchase, $165.00 rental
Provides all materials needed to conduct an eight - hour performance appraisal training session. Explores ethics, potential problems, purpose preparation, conducting the appraisal and skills development.
Education
Dist - VLEARN **Prod** - INTRFL

Performance Appraisal
U-matic / VHS
Management Training Series
Color
Business and Economics; Psychology
Dist - DELTAK **Prod** - THGHT

Performance appraisal 22 MIN
VHS
Color (PRO A G)
$695.00 purchase, $175.00 rental
Explores the process involved in appraising someone's performance, including the pitfalls of bias and subjectivity. Helps evaluators avoid problems that might otherwise arise through lack of awareness. Includes a leader's guide.
Business and Economics; Psychology
Dist - EXTR **Prod** - CRMP

Performance Appraisal and Workforce Discipline 22 MIN
U-matic
Launching Civil Service Reform Series
Color
LC 79-706271
Outlines the major changes brought about by the Civil Service Reform Bill affecting actions involving unacceptable performance and conduct problems.
Civics and Political Systems
Dist - USNAC **Prod** - USOPMA 1978

Performance appraisal - Balance of work - family issues - Tape 3 20 MIN
VHS
Diversity - creating success for business series
Color (PRO IND A)
$495.00 purchase _ #ENT21C
Uses real - life vignettes to deal with all aspects of diversity. Teaches recognition of how biases influence objective decision - making, judgment calls and assessment of others; and aids in distinguishing between diversity and organizational, managerial and personal issues. Parts five and six of an eight - part series. Extensive workshop materials available.
Business and Economics
Dist - EXTR **Prod** - ENMED

Performance Appraisal Series Module 1
Why Appraise? 8 MIN
Dist - RESEM

Performance Appraisal Series Module 2
What to Appraise 53 FRS
Dist - RESEM

Performance Appraisal Series Module 3
How and When to Appraise 10 MIN
Dist - RESEM

Performance appraisal series
Presents three modules on performance appraisal. Includes the titles Why Appraise, What to Appraise, How and When to Appraise.
Performance appraisal series 26 MIN
Dist - RESEM **Prod** - RESEM

Performance Appraisal - the Human Dynamics 25 MIN
16mm / U-matic / VHS
Behavior in Business Series
Color (C A) (SPANISH)
LC 78-701014
Explains a different approach to performance appraisal, emphasizing the open exchange of ideas to motivate employees to work with more enthusiasm toward organizational goals.
Business and Economics; Psychology
Dist - MGHT **Prod** - MGHT 1978

Performance appraisal training series
Communicating the performance appraisal 33 MIN
Doing the performance appraisal 25 MIN
Giving negative feedback - a model 20 MIN
Planning for improvement - a model 20 MIN
Dist - DELTAK

Performance Appraisals 28 MIN
Videoreel / VT2
How to Improve Managerial Performance - the AMA Performance 'Standards Program Series
Color (A)
LC 75-704235
Features James L Hayes, president of the American Management Associations, explaining how the performance appraisal process relates to the overall management function and presents a four - step process for planning and conducting a performance appraisal.
Business and Economics; Psychology
Dist - AMA **Prod** - AMA 1974

Performance assessment - Tape 3 34 MIN
VHS
Redesigning assessment series
Color (A C PRO)
$350.00 purchase, $120.00 rental _ #614 - 227X01
Emphasizes performance - based assessment with a variety of test strategies. Shows teachers and administrators who use performance - based techniques in the classroom, with film of student performances for examples. Includes leader's guide. Part of a series.
Education
Dist - AFSCD

Performance Bounds - the Cramer Rao Inequality 28 MIN
U-matic / VHS
Probability and Random Processes - Limit Theorems and Statistics 'Series
B&W (PRO)
Mathematics
Dist - MIOT **Prod** - MIOT

Performance Counseling 21 MIN
16mm
B&W
LC FIE64-19
Presents guidelines for effective performance and non - directive methods of counseling.
Education; Guidance and Counseling; Psychology
Dist - USNAC **Prod** - USA 1963

Performance Curriculum I - Issues in Innovation 28 MIN
16mm
Innovations in Education Series
Color
Dr Dwight Allen, Professor of Education at Stanford University, discusses the problems and issues of innovation, emphasizing curriculum and educational change.
Education
Dist - EDUC **Prod** - STNFRD 1966

Performance Curriculum II - Issues in Organization 28 MIN
16mm
Innovations in Education Series
Color
Dr Dwight Allen, Professor of Education at Stanford University, considers a flexible model for organizational innovation.
Education
Dist - EDUC **Prod** - STNFRD 1966

Performance Evaluation 10 MIN
16mm
Supervison and Management Series
Color
LC 74-712977
Presents a review of the philosophy, objectives and techniques of performance evaluations. Emphasizes the need for accurate and objective record - keeping and portrays the value of anecdotal records and self - evaluation.
Business and Economics; Guidance and Counseling; Psychology
Dist - TRNAID **Prod** - TRNAID 1969

Performance Evaluation 26 MIN
16mm
B&W
LC 74-705343
Explains to Air Force supervisors the importance of discussing frequently with their employees their performance of duties.
Civics and Political Systems
Dist - USNAC **Prod** - USDD 1960

Performance Feeding for Your Horse 61 MIN
VHS / BETA
Horse Care and Training Series
Color
Deals with proper feeding of horses, from colts to mature adults.
Agriculture; Physical Education and Recreation
Dist - MOHOMV **Prod** - MOHOMV

Performance Feeding Your Horse 61 MIN
VHS
Horse Care and Training Series
Color (H C A PRO)
$30.00 purchase _ #TA237
Shows how to feed a horse from foal through maturity.
Agriculture; Physical Education and Recreation
Dist - AAVIM **Prod** - AAVIM 1990

Performance Improvement Program Series
Developing job accountabilities and writing performance standards 35 MIN
Identifying Developmental Needs and Actions to Improve Performance 45 MIN
Introducing the Performance Appraisal Process 45 MIN
Preparing for and Conducting Effective Performance Reviews 40 MIN
Dist - PRODEV

Performance in depth - the many roles of Alec Guinness 28 MIN
U-matic / VHS / 16mm
Art of film series
Color
Focuses on the art of actor Alec Guinness. Includes segments from Oliver Twist, Great Expectations, The Horse's Mouth, Tunes Of Glory, Kind Hearts And Coronets and other films. Narrated by Douglas Fairbanks, Jr.
Fine Arts
Dist - CORF **Prod** - JANUS 1979

A Performance - Mamoko 30 MIN
VHS / 16mm
First International Mime Clinic and Festival
Color (G)
$55.00 rental _ #FMFI - 002
Fine Arts
Dist - PBS **Prod** - KTCATV

Performance management 25 MIN
VHS
Color (COR)
$495.00 purchase, $125.00 five - day rental _ #APE/AIM
Offers step - by - step techniques for conducting employee performance appraisals. Provides tips to help the manager to broaden the role to include not only supervision but also coaching for the employee. Available with closed captioning. Includes a Leader's Guide.
Business and Economics; Guidance and Counseling; Psychology
Dist - ADVANM

Performance Manager 65 MIN
Transp / VHS / 16mm
Color (PRO)
$995.00 purchase, $350.00 rental, $35.00 preview
Instructs managers and supervisors on the skills needed to make performance appraisals of employees more productive. Explains how good managers communicate their expectations, provide regular feedback, and offer a constructive evaluation of the employee's performance. Includes four videotapes, eight workbooks, leader's guide, transparencies and sample questionnaires.
Business and Economics; Guidance and Counseling; Psychology
Dist - UTM **Prod** - UTM

Performance measurement 63 MIN
VHS
Color (PRO IND A) (DUTCH FRENCH)
$695.00 purchase _ #VIM17
Deals with performance measures - which measures are being used and which should be. Helps directors and line managers through performance issues addressed by Prof Tony Hope.
Business and Economics
Dist - EXTR

Performance Measurements 60 MIN
BETA / VHS
Manufacturing Series
(IND)
Describes properly designed performance measurements to provide the master scheduler with the control to implement the planned schedule. Describes the need for and the methods used in installing performance measurments.
Business and Economics
Dist - COMSRV **Prod** - COMSRV 1986

Performance of an EKG 21 MIN
VHS / U-matic
Procedures for the family physician series
Color (PRO C)
$395.00 purchase, $80.00 rental _ #C850 - VI - 012
Illustrates the performance of an EKG. Part of a six - part series on procedures for the family physician presented by Dr Peter Coggan.
Health and Safety
Dist - HSCIC

Performance of Skills - the Pyramidal System 18 MIN
U-matic / VHS / 16mm
Anatomical Basis of Brain Function Series
Color (PRO)
Science - Natural
Dist - TEF **Prod** - AVCORP

Performance of the Minuet 30 MIN
U-matic / VHS
Glances at the Past Series
Color
Fine Arts; Industrial and Technical Education
Dist - ARCVID **Prod** - ARCVID

Performance review 11 MIN
VHS / U-matic
Applied management series
Color
Business and Economics
Dist - DELTAK **Prod** - ORGDYN

Performance Reviews that Build Commitment Series
The Critical role of performance review 30 MIN
Developing performance standards 30 MIN
The Review that Builds Commitment 30 MIN
Supportive coaching 30 MIN
Why the Traditional Approach Fails 30 MIN
Writing Challenging Specific Objectives 30 MIN
Dist - DELTAK

Performance Reviews that Get Results 30 MIN
U-matic / VHS
You - the Supervisor Series
Color (PRO)
Deals with the concept of performance reviews and introduces an approach to performance standards that can be useful to the new supervisor.
Business and Economics; Guidance and Counseling; Psychology
Dist - DELTAK **Prod** - PRODEV

Performance series
Features well-known and established actors performing in contemporary dramas for presentation on the BBC.
The Changeling 90 MIN
A Doll's house 135 MIN
Hedda Gabler 125 MIN
Roots 105 MIN
Dist - BBCENE

Performance Standards and Objectives 22 MIN
VHS / 16mm / U-matic
Color (H C G)
$505.00, $355.00, $385.00 _ #A441; $585.00 purchase, $140.00 rental
Demonstrates how the standards and objectives process allows managers to monitor an employee's daily or weekly progress toward meeting expectations. Discusses the skill of developing standards and objectives and using them for performance appraisals.
Business and Economics; Social Science
Dist - BARR **Prod** - BARR 1987
VLEARN

Performance theater series
Outlines a six-part videotape series - plus one handbook - designed to help aspiring a actors, directors and others select, organize and direct a play. Notes series especially useful for classroom or group settings. Covers Building a Character, The Directing Process, Creative Drama and Improvisation, Mime Over Matter, Combat for the Stage, and Audition Techniques. Notes tapes may be purchased separately or as a whole. Each videotape comes with a teacher's guide.
Audition techniques 70 MIN
Building a character 86 MIN
Creative drama and improvisation 90 MIN
The Directing process 90 MIN
Dist - CAMV

Performance theatre series
Audition techniques 70 MIN
Combat for the stage 96 MIN
Creative drama and improvisation 90 MIN
Dist - CAMV

Performance theatre series
Mime over matter 101 MIN
Dist - CAMV
INSIM

Performance tuning
VHS
Color (G A)
$30.00 purchase _ #0916
Shows how to tune fixed and movable rigging on J - 24 sailboats. Explains sail trim supported by Nort Sail. Uses graphics.
Physical Education and Recreation
Dist - SEVVID

Performance Under Pressure 17 MIN
16mm
Color (G)
Explains the role of compressed air and gas in today's world. Discusses how compressed gasses are essential to the operation of items suchs as stoves and automobiles as well as the production of everything from interstate highways to clothing. Describes the principles of compressed air and gas, the major types of compressors, how they operate, and some of their modern day applications.
Industrial and Technical Education
Dist - CAAGI **Prod** - CAAGI

Performance - Walsh 60 MIN
U-matic
(H C A)
Records the relationship between Sitting Bull and Major James Morrow Walsh of the North West Mounted Police, the man responsibe for dealing with the Sioux who had escaped from the United States.
History - World; Social Science
Dist - ACCESS **Prod** - ACCESS 1985

The Performed Word 58 MIN
VHS / U-matic
Color
Views black religion in its cultural context. Examines a variety of performance situations. Captures the power of the performed word and the congregation's strong response to it.
Religion and Philosophy; Sociology
Dist - SOFOLK **Prod** - SOFOLK

The Performer 30 MIN
U-matic / VHS
Grant Johannesen - Pianist Series
Color
Presents Grant Johannesen, who performs Faure's Ballade and Prokofieff's Seventh Sonata, and comments that performers shouldn't 'rely on someone else's success with a selection, but go into a recital and play what you feel with the greatest naturalness'.
Fine Arts
Dist - NETCHE **Prod** - NETCHE 1973

Performers on Teaching 28 MIN
VHS / 16mm
Color (C A)
$75.00 purchase, $25.00 rental _ #EC2355
Presents three Indiana University artist - teachers - master cellist Janos Starker, actor Howard Jensen and ballet master Jean Pierre - Bonnefoux discussing a variety of pedagogical issues.
Education; Fine Arts
Dist - IU **Prod** - IU 1988

The Performers - the Asian republic of Uzbekistan 52 MIN
VHS
Icebreaker - family life in the Soviet Union series
Color (I J H)
$295.00 purchase
Visits the Fazildjanova family of four in Uzbekistan, central Asians who live in the Moslem heartland of the USSR famous for the ancient cities of Tashkent and Sarmarkand on the old Silk Route. Reveals that today Tashkent is a city of modern avenues, home to some of the USSR's most highly regarded universitys and of one of its three top ballet schools. Part of a six - part series on ethnically different families in the Soviet Union.
Geography - World; Religion and Philosophy; Sociology
Dist - LANDMK **Prod** - LANDMK 1989

Performing 15 MIN
BETA / VHS / U-matic
Job Catch Series
Color; Stereo (H)
Performing means putting yourself forward positively, with what you say and how you say it. This program covers interview hints to help the applicant stand out as someone with a bit of initiative.
Guidance and Counseling
Dist - SEVDIM **Prod** - SEVDIM 1985

Performing After a Serious Injury 30 MIN
VHS / U-matic
Dancers' Bodies Series
Color
Fine Arts; Health and Safety
Dist - ARCVID **Prod** - ARCVID

The Performing Arts 19 MIN
U-matic / VHS / 16mm
Humanities Series
Color (H C A)
LC 71-713373
Illustrates how man expresses his attitudes toward himself and his world through the performing arts. Shows performing artists in the process of mastering techniques in order to convey them to the audience. Includes scenes of Phillip Burton directing student actors in Shakespeare's 'AS YOU LIKE IT.'.
Fine Arts; Literature and Drama; Psychology
Dist - MGHT **Prod** - MGHT 1971

Performing Arts 15 MIN
BETA / VHS / U-matic
Career Success Series
(H C A)
$29.95 _ #MX161
Portrays occupation in the performing arts by reviewing their required abilities and interviewing people employed in this field. Shows anxieties and rewards involved in pursuing a career as a performing artist.
Fine Arts
Dist - CAMV **Prod** - CAMV

Performing Arts
U-matic / VHS
Career Builders Video Series
$95.00 purchase _ #ED106V
Uses actual professionals to talk about the job's demands, rewards, and frustrations. Shows the working environment of the career field.
Guidance and Counseling
Dist - CAREER **Prod** - CAREER

Performing Arts 24 MIN
VHS / 16mm
Career Builders Video Series
Color
$85.00 purchase _ #V106
Examines a potential career choice by taking the viewer into the working environment and interviewing professionals on the demands, rewards and frustrations on the job.
Business and Economics; Fine Arts; Sociology
Dist - EDUCDE **Prod** - EDUCDE 1987

The Performing arts in China 15 MIN
VHS
Color (G C H)
$119.00 purchase _ #DL379
Examines the tradition of the performing arts in China. Shows actors rehearsing at the Lu Opera, visits a training school for acrobats, and looks at instruction in the martial arts.

History - World
Dist - INSIM

The Performing Arts, Pt 1 30 MIN
U-matic / VHS
Japan - the Living Tradition Series
Color (H C A)
Examines the performing arts in Japan.
Fine Arts; History - World
Dist - GPN **Prod** - UMA 1976

The Performing Arts, Pt 2 30 MIN
U-matic / VHS
Japan - the Living Tradition Series
Color (H C A)
Examines the performing arts in Japan.
Fine Arts; History - World
Dist - GPN **Prod** - UMA 1976

Performing arts technician 15 MIN
VHS
Career success series
Color (H C A)
$29.95 purchase _ #MX161
Presents an introduction to performing arts technician careers. Covers the necessary skills, and interviews people in these careers on the rewards and stresses involved.
Education
Dist - CAMV

Performing Arts Technology 15 MIN
VHS / 16mm
(H C A)
$24.95 purchase _ #CS161
Describes the requisite skills for a career in performing arts technology. Features interviews with people working in this field.
Guidance and Counseling
Dist - RMIBHF **Prod** - RMIBHF

Performing Shakespeare 75 MIN
VHS
Color (PRO G)
$149.00 purchase, $49.00 rental _ #618
Presents a unique and highly physical series of exerciese that move from exploration of specific words and phrases through the development of complete Shakespearean scenes. Enables actors to merge visceral, physical, vocal and imaginative work with the demands of complex text. Features Kathleen Conlin, director of the Ohio University School of Theater. Produced by the Theater Arts Video Library.
Fine Arts; Literature and Drama
Dist - FIRLIT

Performing the SMAW 2G, 3G, and 4G weld test - plate - E-6010 35 MIN
VHS
Color (G H VOC IND)
$89.95 purchase _ #CEV00854V-T
Demonstrates the proper method to perform welding upon a three-eighths inch plate using the 2G, 3G, and 4G positions using a E-6010 electrode. Explains running the root pass, hot pass, filler pass and cap pass and includes short reviews after each explanation. Discusses the proper procedure of each weld that will help students attatin a welding certification.
Education; Industrial and Technical Education
Dist - CAMV

Performing the SMAW 5G weld test - pipe - E-6010 and E-7018 24 MIN
VHS
Color (G H VOC IND)
$89.95 purchase _ #CEV00855V-T
Demonstrates the proper method to perform welding in the 5G position. Allows students to view the weld as they would see it through the lens of a welding helmet. Explains the correct procedure for welding a three-eighths inch wall pipe using different rods, running the root pass, hot pass, filler pass, and cap weld. Includes a review of each type of weld.
Education; Industrial and Technical Education
Dist - CAMV

Performing the SMAW 6G weld test - pipe - E-6010 20 MIN
VHS
Color (G H VOC IND)
$89.95 purchase _ #CEV00856V-T
Demonstrates the proper method to perform welding in the 6G position. Allows students to view the weld as they would see it through the lens of a welding helmet. Explains the correct procedure for welding an eight-inch .375 diameter pipe using different rods, running the root pass, hot pass, filler pass, and cap weld. Includes a review of each type of weld.
Education; Industrial and Technical Education
Dist - CAMV

Perfume 27 MIN
VHS
Color (H C G)
$195.00 purchase
Examines the process of creating a new fragrance. Meets flower pickers, chemists, extractors, distillers, perfumers, packaging designers and tycoons of the industry such as Robert Ricci, Pierre Vigne and George Vindry.
Business and Economics; Science - Natural
Dist - LANDMK **Prod** - LANDMK 1990

The Perfumed Handkerchief 70 MIN
VHS
Color (G)
$39.95 purchase _ #1149
Presents 'The Perfumed Handkerchief' filmed on location at the Imperial Summer Palace of Peking. Features stars from the Peking Opera Theatre.
Fine Arts; Geography - World
Dist - KULTUR

The Perfumed handkerchief 102 MIN
VHS
Color (G) (CHINESE (ENGLISH SUBTITLES))
$39.95 purchase _ #KLT11149 - 3
Offers a classic Chinese opera of manners.
Fine Arts
Dist - CHTSUI

Perfumed nightmare 91 MIN
16mm / U-matic / VHS
Color (G)
$1200.00, $600.00, $350.00 purchase
Presents a semi - autobiographical fable by a young Philippino named Kidlat Tahimak about his awakening to and reaction against American cultural colonialism. Reveals that Tahimak, born in 1942 during the Occupation, spent 'the next 33 typhoon seasons in a cocoon of American dreams,' a perfumed nightmare, the lotus - land of American technological promise. In his primitive village he worships the heroism of the Machine, the sleek beauty of rockets, the efficiency of industrialism. He's the president of the Werner von Braun fan club, he longs to visit Cape Canaveral and he has produced a bizarre, hallucinatory movie full of dazzling immages and outlandish ideas.
History - World; Social Science
Dist - FLOWER

Perfumes 14 MIN
VHS / U-matic
En Francais series
Color (H C A)
Leads a young couple to the altar and provides an anniversary present.
Foreign Language; Geography - World
Dist - AITECH **Prod** - MOFAFR 1970

Perfusion Failure 94 FRS 19 MIN
U-matic
Shock Series Module 2
Color (PRO)
LC 80-720331; 80-707733
Explains the basic defect underlying shock, describing clinical and physiologic signs, hemodynamic effects, and the different classifications of shock.
Health and Safety
Dist - BRA **Prod** - BRA 1980

The Periaortic Approach to the Renal Pedicle 22 MIN
16mm
Color
LC FIA66-57
Shows two procedures illustrating the periaortic approach to the renal pedicle in patients with renal neoplasm or renal trauma. Explains that the occlusion of the renal artery and vein early in the operation is made possible, thus preventing tumor embolization or hemorrhage while dissecting the kidney.
Health and Safety
Dist - EATONL **Prod** - EATONL 1965

Periapical Surgery of an Actinomycosis Lesion 35 MIN
U-matic
Color (C)
Demonstrates a surgical access in the region of the maxillary sinus of a lesion involving actinomycosis organism.
Health and Safety; Science - Natural
Dist - UOKLAH **Prod** - UOKLAH 1986

Periapical Surgery of an Open Apex 55 MIN
U-matic
Color (C)
Contains the complete surgical treatment of a maxillary incisor from incision to closure.
Health and Safety; Science - Natural
Dist - UOKLAH **Prod** - UOKLAH 1986

Pericardiectomy 25 MIN
16mm
Color (PRO)
Illustrates the operative technique for the cure of chronic constrictive pericarditis. Emphasizes completeness of the resection.
Health and Safety; Science
Dist - ACY **Prod** - ACYDGD 1958

Pericles 177 MIN
VHS
BBC Shakespeare series
Color (G C H)
$109.00 purchase _ #DL462
Fine Arts
Dist - INSIM **Prod** - BBC

Pericles 275 MIN
VHS
Shakespeare series
Color (A)
PdS25 purchase
Stars Juliet Stevenson, Patrick Allen and Mike Gwilym. Part of a series of plays by Shakespeare performed by leading stage and screen actors and interpreted by directors and producers such as Jonathan Miller, Elijah Mohinsky and Jack Gold.
Literature and Drama
Dist - BBCENE

Pericles 177 MIN
VHS / 16mm
BBC's Shakespeare Series
(H A)
$249.95
Recounts Shakespeare's play, Pericles, the story of the Prince of Tyre.
Literature and Drama
Dist - AMBROS **Prod** - AMBROS 1983

Pericles 177 MIN
U-matic / VHS
Shakespeare Plays Series
Color (H C A)
Presents William Shakespeare's play Pericles which tells the story of the Prince of Tyre, who is pursued by the vengeance of the King Antiochus because he discovered the monarch's incestuous relationship with his daughter. Reveals the adventures which befall Pericles and his family as he tries to elude the king.
Literature and Drama
Dist - TIMLIF **Prod** - BBCTV 1984

Pericles in America 70 MIN
VHS / 16mm
Color (G)
$490.00 purchase
Portrays immigrant clarinetist Pericles Halkias and the Greek community of Astoria, New York.
Fine Arts; Sociology
Dist - ICARUS

Perico the bowlmaker 45 MIN
VHS / 16mm
Films from Andalusia, Spain series
B&W (G)
$650.00, $250.00 purchase, $65.00, $40.00 rental
Considers the changing role of a traditional Andalusian craftsman and the social and personal factors which shape his occupation. Depicts techniques of carving and the problems of marketing the wares and off - season tasks of harvesting cork. Part of a series.
Fine Arts; Geography - World; History - World
Dist - DOCEDR **Prod** - MINTZJ 1987

Perilous journey 30 MIN
VHS
Perspectives - health and medicine - series
Color; PAL; NTSC (G)
PdS90, PdS105 purchase
Looks at early diagnosis of disorders such as Down's syndrome in the unborn fetus.
Health and Safety
Dist - CFLVIS **Prod** - LONTVS

Perilous voyage 90 MIN
VHS
Color; PAL (J)
PdS30 purchase
Presents a series of six 15 - minute programs, an animated version of the Odyssey by Homer adapted for children, and a companion piece to Pilgrim's Progress. Features Sir Michael Horden as narrator. Includes background notes for teachers. Contact distributor about availability outside the United Kingdom.
Literature and Drama; Religion and Philosophy
Dist - ACADEM

The Perilous Voyage 23 MIN
VHS / U-matic
Color (K)
Shows a young seal, vulnerable and stranded on the California beach, rescued by a man.

Science - Natural
Dist - NWLDPR **Prod** - NWLDPR

Perils - Mayhem 30 MIN
VHS
Is this what you were born for series
B&W (G)
$75.00 purchase
Features two films, produced between 1985 - 1987, from the ongoing series Is This What You Were Born For. Investigates aggressions of the twentieth century. See separate titles for description and availability for rental in 16mm format.
Fine Arts; Sociology
Dist - CANCIN **Prod** - CHILDA

Perils, mayhem and mercy 35 MIN
VHS / 16mm
Color; B&W (G)
$130.00 rental, $295.00 purchase
Features three productions which are part of Child's series titled Is This What You Were Born For, which investigates power and gender relations. Pays homage to silent pictures in Perils. Focuses on sexuality and the erotic, specifically a Japanese lesbian scene, in Mayhem. Mercy dissects the game mass media plays in private perceptions.
Fine Arts; Sociology
Dist - WMEN **Prod** - CHILDA 1989

Perils of plastic - handling credit
VHS
Color (H C G)
$79.95 purchase _ #CCP0082V
Shows how credit fuels the economy of the United States and how advertisers entice consumers to go into debt to supposedly improve their social status. Describes what credit is and why it is needed, the advantages and disadvantages of using credit, how credit is obtained and how credit ratings work. Shows how to establish credit, how to use it wisely, the importance of good credit and how it affects the futures of individuals.
Business and Economics; Home Economics
Dist - CAMV **Prod** - CAMV 1993

The Perils of Priscilla 17 MIN
U-matic / VHS / 16mm
Color (P I J)
LC 75-703956
Shows that through the eyes of a cat, an ordinary household and neighborhood looks quiet different. Follows Priscilla the cat as she meets such needs as food, warmth and a place to rest.
Guidance and Counseling; Literature and Drama
Dist - CF **Prod** - DF 1969

Perils of Priscilla 17 MIN
VHS
Color (P)
Presents a view of the world as seen by a cat. Stimulates discussion of pet owner responsibilities and obligations.
Psychology; Science - Natural
Dist - VIEWTH **Prod** - VIEWTH

The Perils of Priscilla 14 MIN
U-matic / VHS / 16mm
Color (P)
LC 80-700534
A shortened version of the film The Perils Of Priscilla. Points out the needs of a pet cat by presenting the adventures of a cat who endures the indignation of a busy family and the dangers of being lost in a big city.
Fine Arts; Science - Natural
Dist - CF **Prod** - DF 1980

Perils - Part 5 5 MIN
16mm / VHS
Is this what you were born for series
B&W (G)
$25.00 rental
Pays homage to silent films where ambiguous inocence clashes with unsophisticated villainy. Pictures seduction, revenge, jealousy and combat. Illustrates the isolation and dramatization of emotions through the isolating technique of the camera and editing of gesture.
Fine Arts
Dist - CANCIN **Prod** - CHILDA 1986

Perimeter 15 MIN
U-matic
Math Makers Two Series
Color (I)
Presents the math concepts of grids and perimeters and the formulas for the perimeter of rectangles, equilateral triangles and squares.
Education; Mathematics
Dist - TVOTAR **Prod** - TVOTAR 1980

Perimeter 15 MIN
VHS / U-matic
Math Cycle Series
Color (P)
Introduces the concept of perimeter, along with a method for finding the perimeter of a rectangle and a triangle.
Mathematics
Dist - GPN **Prod** - WDCNTV

Perimeter and area
VHS
Basic mathematical skills series
Color (I J H)
$125.00 purchase _ #1012
Teaches the concepts of perimeter and area. Presents part of a series that provides 27 videos, each between 25 and 30 minutes long, that explain and reinforce basic mathematical concepts. Tutors the student through definitions, theorems, step - by - step solutions and examples. Videos are also available in a set.
Mathematics
Dist - LANDMK

Perimeter and Area 30 MIN
VHS
Mathematics Series
Color (J)
LC 90713155
Explains perimeter and area. The 12th of 157 installments in the Mathematics Series.
Mathematics
Dist - GPN

Perimeter, circumference and pi
VHS
Now I see it geometry video series
Color (J H)
$79.00 _ #60249 - 026
Connects with students' lives and interests by linking lessons to everyday objects ranging from automobiles to ice cream cones, stereos to honeycombs. Includes reproducible worksheet book and answer key. Part of a nine - part series.
Education; Mathematics
Dist - GA

Perinatal AIDS - infection control for hospital personnel 17 MIN
VHS
Color (PRO)
$295.00 purchase, $75.00 rental
Shows health professionals how the AIDS virus can be transmitted in the workplace, particularly in perinatal settings where blood and body fluids are so much a part of routine care of both mother and newborn infant. Describes which body fluids are most infectious, ways of identifying patients at higher risk and appropriate infection control measures specific to prenatal, labor and delivery, postpartum and nursery settings. Acknowledges nurses' fears, presenting interviews nurses who tell of their first encounter with HIV positive women and babies. Interviews a young mother who was told she was HIV positive on the day she was due to deliver. Includes a handout which may be photocopied.
Health and Safety; Psychology
Dist - POLYMR

Perinatal and Child Development 30 MIN
U-matic / VHS
Endocrine Gland Function Series
Color
Describes the process through which the child first identifies its gender. Reviews some of the major findings concerning the extent to which this process is influenced by heredity (in the form of the endocrine system) and the environment (both social and physical).
Psychology; Science - Natural; Sociology
Dist - NETCHE **Prod** - NETCHE 1975

Perinatal Assessment of Maturity 20 MIN
VHS / 16mm
(C)
$385.00 purchase _ #870VI035
Presents the three steps nurses go through to assess a newborn's maturity. Demonstrates these steps with an average gestational age infant and a premature infant.
Health and Safety
Dist - HSCIC **Prod** - HSCIC 1987

Perineal External Urethrotomy 10 MIN
16mm
Color
LC 75-702311
Explains that perineal external urethrotomy is of value to the transurethral resectionist in cases of anterior urethral strictures and large prostate glands. Demonstrates Dr Michael K O'Heeron's technique and discusses its advantages.
Health and Safety; Science
Dist - EATONL **Prod** - EATONL 1965

Perineal Prostatectomy 15 MIN
16mm
Color
LC 75-702247
Demonstrates a modified Huson - belt (simple) perineal prostatectomy, stressing surgical detail. Emphasizes the technique and importance of post - prostatectomy perineal exercises and their relationship to urinary continence.
Health and Safety; Science; Science - Natural
Dist - EATONL **Prod** - EATONL 1972

Perineal Repair of Urethral Strictures with Skin Graft Patch 14 MIN
16mm
Color (PRO)
LC 75-702236
Demonstrates the surgical repair of a urethral stricture by approaching the stricture through a perineal incision, incising the strictured area and replacing the deficient tissue with a patch graft of full thickness skin removed from the penis.
Health and Safety; Science; Science - Natural
Dist - EATONL **Prod** - EATONL 1975

Perineal Rib Graft for Male Incontinence 15 MIN
16mm
Color
LC 75-702291
Illustrates an operation devised to correct post - prostatectomy incontinence using a segment of the seventh rib, which is screwed to permanently bridge the ischial tuberosities and raise the urogenital diaphragm into the "nonvoiding" position.
Health and Safety; Science
Dist - EATONL **Prod** - EATONL 1969

A Period piece 4 MIN
VHS
Color (G)
$175.00 purchase, $35.00 rental
Comments on menstruation and 'feminine protection' using animation, printed text and two dreadlocked rap performers who tell the story of April, May and June, women who spot up their clothese at the most inopportune moments.
Literature and Drama; Psychology; Sociology
Dist - WMEN **Prod** - ZDAVIS 1991

The Periodic check - up 18 MIN
16mm
Automotive operation and maintenance - preventive maintenance series; No 4
B&W
LC FIE52-343
Shows how to tune up the engine, check and adjust the brake system and inspect the steering system, chassis and body.
Industrial and Technical Education
Dist - USNAC **Prod** - USOE 1945

Periodic Classification of the Elements 16 MIN
U-matic
Chemistry 101 Series
Color (C)
Introduces the concept of the periodic table, the nature of its structure and the history of its organization.
Science; Science - Physical
Dist - UILL **Prod** - UILL 1980

Periodic Functions 17 MIN
U-matic / VHS / 16mm
Radio Technician Training Series
Color
LC FIE52-914
Explains that a sine wave or function is periodic and that the voltage of an alternating current is a sine function. Shows how A C generators may differ in voltage, frequency and phase.
Industrial and Technical Education
Dist - USNAC **Prod** - USN 1945

Periodic Inputs and Fourier Series 28 MIN
VHS / U-matic
Probability and Random Processes - Linear Systems Series
B&W (PRO)
Continues the frequency domain analysis of LTI systems by developing the Fourier series representation for periodic signals and considering the response of such systems to periodic inputs.
Mathematics
Dist - MIOT **Prod** - MIOT

Periodic Inspection - Engine 22 MIN
16mm
B&W
LC FIE52-257
Shows how to inspect the general condition of an engine, examine internal parts, check ignition and fuel system, examine the propeller and prepare an engine for run - up.
Industrial and Technical Education
Dist - USNAC **Prod** - USOE 1945

Periodic Motion 33 MIN
16mm
PSSC Physics Films Series
B&W (H C)
Uses a simple harmonic motion as an example of periodic motion. Shows how a pen moving in SHM plots its own displacement time graph and how graphs of velocity and acceleration versus time are derived from it.

Science - Physical
Dist - MLA **Prod** - PSSC 1961

The Periodic Paralysis 48 MIN
U-matic
Intensive Course in Neuromuscular Diseases Series
Color (PRO)
LC 76-706073
Presents Dr Robert C Griggs lecturing on periodic paralysis.
Health and Safety; Science - Natural
Dist - USNAC **Prod** - NINDIS 1974

Periodic Preventive Medical Examinations, Pt 1, Principles and Plan 16 MIN
VHS / U-matic
Color (PRO)
Presents a plan for doing preventive medical exams. Identifies desirable characteristics of screening tests. Presents the principles of screening and follow - up.
Health and Safety
Dist - UMICHM **Prod** - UMICHM 1979

Periodic Properties of the Elements 18 MIN
U-matic
Chemistry 101 Series
Color (C)
Introduces the periodic properties of elements. The chemical behavior of families of elements in the periodic table is directly related to the electronic structure of their atoms.
Science; Science - Physical
Dist - UILL **Prod** - UILL 1977

Periodic Reversal of Rotation of a DC Motor 34 MIN
U-matic / VHS
Nonlinear Vibrations Series
B&W
Mathematics
Dist - MIOT **Prod** - MIOT

Periodic table 20 MIN
VHS
Science topics series
Color; PAL (H C A)
PdS50 purchase
Discusses the elements of the periodic table as arranged in order of their atomic number. Describes the substances that make up the earth as comprised of these elements.
Science - Physical
Dist - BBCENE

The Periodic Table and Periodicity 23 MIN
16mm / U-matic / VHS
Chemistry Series
Color (J H C)
$480, $250 purchase _ #4362
Shows the different physical and chemical properties of the elements and the patterns of these properties in the periodic table.
Science - Physical
Dist - CORF

The Periodic table - chemical bonds - Parts 7 and 8 60 MIN
U-matic / VHS
World of chemistry series
Color (C)
$45.00, $29.95 purchase
Presents parts 7 and 8 of the 26 - part World of Chemistry series. Examines the development of the Periodic Table of Elements by Mendeleev. Considers how elements form compounds by giving, taking or sharing electrons. Explains the differences between ionic and covalent bonds. Two thirty - minute programs hosted by Nobel laureate Roald Hoffmann.
Science - Physical
Dist - ANNCPB **Prod** - UMD 1990

Periodic vibrations in an elastic medium 16 MIN
16mm
Color (G)
$40.00 rental
Eliminates the narrative sequence to obtain the concept of simultaneity which is usually associated with painting and is demonstrated by the poetry of William Carlos Williams. Pictures pale blue passages dividing film into three sections, composed from several thousand feet of film exposed between 1975 and 1976 at various geographical sites. The title alludes to Newton's corpuscular theory of light.
Fine Arts
Dist - CANCIN **Prod** - LIPZIN 1976

Periodicals and Anthologies, Indexes and Abstracts
U-matic / VHS
College Library Series
Color
Education
Dist - NETCHE **Prod** - NETCHE 1973

Periodicity - the Logical and Systematic Arrangement of Symbols 30 MIN
VHS / U-matic
HTM - Hazardous Toxic Materials Series Unit I; Unit I
Color (PRO)
Health and Safety; Social Science
Dist - FILCOM **Prod** - FILCOM

Periodontal
VHS
Color (K P)
$85.00 purchase _ #K45191
Describes causes of and contributing factors to periodontal disease, its degenerative process from gingivitis through periodontitis. Explains treatment procedures including scaling, root planting and curettage.
Health and Safety
Dist - HTHED **Prod** - HTHED

Periodontal Disease 8 MIN
VHS / 16mm / U-matic
Color (PRO) (SPANISH)
Describes the nature of periodontal disease, its causes, progression and prevention.
Health and Safety
Dist - PRORE **Prod** - PRORE

Periodontal disease 58 MIN
U-matic / VHS
Color (A PRO)
$155.00 purchase _ #TCA15007, #TCA15006
Features Dr William Wright, who discusses how periodontal disease is caused, the various forms of periodontal disease, preventive measures, and more.
Health and Safety
Dist - USNAC **Prod** - USDHHS 1986

Periodontal Disease - Prevention and Early Treatment 22 MIN
U-matic
Color (PRO)
LC 79-707566
Stresses the importance of early diagnosis and treatment of periodontal disease. Issued in 1963 as a motion picture.
Health and Safety
Dist - USNAC **Prod** - USN 1979

Periodontal Examination, Pt 1 - Examination Procedures 17 MIN
16mm
Color (PRO)
LC 75-701255; 75-701354
Illustrates clinical examination of the periodontium, emphasizing gingival color, density, relation of the gingival margin to the cemento - enamel junction, pocket depth and bleeding tendency. Includes roentgenological examination. Presented by Drs Sigurd P Ramfjord and Edward Green.
Health and Safety; Science
Dist - USNAC **Prod** - USVA 1970

Periodontal Packs 11 MIN
U-matic
Color
LC 79-706753
Demonstrates procedures for mixing and applying two types of periodontal packs and discusses the advantages and disadvantages of each.
Health and Safety
Dist - USNAC **Prod** - MUSC 1978

Periodontal probing 15 MIN
U-matic / VHS
Color (C PRO)
$395.00 purchase, $80.00 rental _ #D880 - VI - 005
Demonstrates proper probing techniques with the periodontal probe and the furcation probe. Shows viewers how to recognize common probing errors, identify important anatomical landmarks used in probing and locate and classify the types of furcation involvements in multi - rooted teeth. Presented by Dr A E Plotzke.
Health and Safety
Dist - HSCIC

Periodontal Surgery 180 MIN
VHS / U-matic
Color (PRO)
Shows a maxillary quadrant of surgery which involves five mm and six mm deep pockets in premolar and molar areas. Diagrams the differences between buccal and palatal internal bevelled incisions, discusses tuberosity management and presents a new technique.
Health and Safety
Dist - USNAC **Prod** - USHHS

Periodontal Suturing 15 MIN
16mm
Color (PRO)
LC 80-700767
Demonstrates four methods of periodontal suturing, using patients and a typodont. Shows techniques for making an interrupted suture, a sling ligation, a continuous ligation and an anchor suture.
Health and Safety
Dist - USNAC **Prod** - VADTC 1979

Periodontal Suturing 10 MIN
U-matic
Color
LC 79-706754
Describes the instruments and materials used in suturing and presents procedures for placing interrupted and sling sutures.
Health and Safety
Dist - USNAC **Prod** - MUSC 1978

Periodontics 6 MIN
U-matic / VHS / 16mm
Color (A)
Presents the course of professional care and treatment. Includes the anatomy of teeth and gums, cementum ligaments, bone opposing teeth, effects of periodontal disease, gingivitis, plaque, calculus, periodontitis, systemic disorders, home care and professional care.
Health and Safety
Dist - PRORE **Prod** - PRORE

Periodontium 25 MIN
U-matic
Microanatomy Laboratory Orientation Series
Color (C)
Covers the three divisions of the periodontium, the cementum, the periodontal ligament and the alveolar bone.
Health and Safety; Science - Natural
Dist - UOKLAH **Prod** - UOKLAH 1986

Perioperative nursing 16 MIN
U-matic / VHS
Color (PRO)
$275.00 purchase, $60.00 rental _ #4255S, #4255V
Surveys the role of the contemporary operating room nurse. Shows circulating and scrub nurses at work and OR tasks - scrubbing, counting equipment, gowning and gloving, nonverbal signals, collecting and documenting specimens and cleanup and restocking after surgery.
Health and Safety
Dist - AJN **Prod** - UABMT 1984

Peripheral administration of IV chemotherapeutic agents 10 MIN
VHS
Color (C PRO)
$250.00 purchase, $70.00 rental _ #4333S, #4333V
Covers the essentials of chemotherapy administration. Stresses that professionals administering these drugs must be aware of proper safety precautions during compounding and adminsistration and what to do in the case of an accidental spill. Describes proper evaluation of the patient prior to the administration of intravenous chemotherapy and the steps involved. Demonstrates preparation under a vertical flow hood and the administration to a patient. Describes care of gloves, gowns and equipment. Produced by Perivascular Nurse Consultants.
Health and Safety; Science - Natural
Dist - AJN

Peripheral Blood 15 MIN
VHS / 16mm
Histology review series; Unit III
(C)
$330.00 purchase _ #821VI035
Illustrates the important histological features of peripheral blood. Identifies the major structural and functional characteristics of the cellular elements of blood. Part 4 of the Connective Tissue Unit.
Health and Safety
Dist - HSCIC **Prod** - HSCIC 1983

Peripheral Blood Smear 6 MIN
BETA / VHS / U-matic
Basic Clinical Laboratory Procedure Series
Color; Mono (C A)
Demonstrates the proper equipment, procedures, attention to critical details and efficient, accurate methods for proper collection of specimens.
Health and Safety; Science
Dist - UIOWA **Prod** - UIOWA 1985

Peripheral intravenous therapy - Part 1 28 MIN
U-matic / VHS
Intravascular therapy series
Color (PRO)
$275.00 purchase, $60.00 rental _ #7631S, #7631V
Depicts the basic procedures and nursing responsibilities for peripheral intravenous - IV - therapy. Illustrates vascular anatomy through graphics. Demonstrates needle insertion technique and the indications for IV therapy. Presents the Centers for Disease Control guidelines for nursing care. Discusses potential complications and appropriate intervention, discontinuation procedures and IV pumps. Part of two - parts on IV therapy.
Health and Safety
Dist - AJN **Prod** - HOSSN 1987

Peripheral Nerve Grafting and Results 60 MIN
VHS / U-matic
Color (PRO)
Demonstrates various points in peripheral nerve grafting and its results. Narrated by Dr Hanno Millesi. Accompanies film 'Peripheral Nerve Grafting - Demonstration of Technique.'.
Health and Safety
Dist - ASSH **Prod** - ASSH

Peripheral Nerve Grafting - Demonstration of Technique 60 MIN
U-matic / VHS
Color (PRO)
Demonstrates Dr Hanno Millesi's technique of nerve grafting as done under the microscope. Accompanies film 'Peripheral Nerve Grafting And Results.'.
Health and Safety
Dist - ASSH **Prod** - ASSH

Peripheral Nerve Surgery - Repair of the Radial Nerve in the Distal One - Third of the Arm 12 MIN
16mm
Color
Demonstrates a complete lesion of the radial nerve in the lower one - third of the arm, the surgical exploration and suture and the clinical resuet.
Health and Safety; Science - Natural
Dist - USVA **Prod** - USVA 1962

Peripheral Nerve Surgery - Result Following Repair of the Radial Nerve in Mid - Third Arm 6 MIN
16mm
Color
Demonstrates complete lesion of radial nerve in the mid - one - third of the arm, the surgical exploration and suture and the result following suture two and one - half years postoperatively.
Health and Safety; Science - Natural
Dist - USVA **Prod** - USVA 1961

Peripheral Nervous System 39 MIN
VHS / 16mm
Histology review series; Unit V
(C)
$330.00 purchase _ #821VI039
Discusses the peripheral nerve and examines the components of the reflex arc; includes collection of information in the periphery and transmission of that information to the CNS Part 2 of the Nervous System Unit.
Health and Safety
Dist - HSCIC **Prod** - HSCIC 1983

The Peripheral Nervous System 19 MIN
16mm / U-matic / VHS
Color
LC 80-700689
Deals with reflex action and the components of the spinal reflex arc. Covers the nature of the nerve impulse in terms of the action potential and the movement of ions across the axonal membrane. Examines the transmission of the nerve impulse from neuron to neuron and shows how a determination can be made of the velocity of transmission of nerve impulses.
Psychology; Science - Natural
Dist - IFB **Prod** - BFL 1977

Peripheral Neuropathies - Clinical and Investigative Aspects 51 MIN
U-matic
Color (PRO)
LC 79-707688
Reviews the pathology of peripheral nerve disease, enumerates the mechanisms producing pathology and outlines a clinical approach to diagnosis.
Health and Safety
Dist - USNAC **Prod** - NINDIS 1976

Peripheral phlebotomy - three techniques for drawing blood 14 MIN
VHS
Color (C PRO)
250.00 purchase, $70.00 rental _ #4321S, #4321V
Presents clear demonstrations of three methods of phlebotomy - vacutainer, needle and syringe, and butterfly. Covers criteria and advantages in selecting each method, how to match vein to technique, and what supplies are needed. Describes procedure from set - up through insertion, disposal of equipment and care of specimen. Produced by Perivascular Nurse Consultants.
Health and Safety; Science - Natural
Dist - AJN

Peripheral Vascular 20 MIN
U-matic / VHS
Health Assessment Series
Color (PRO)
Views a physical assessment by a nurse practitioner of the peripheral vascular of a live patient.
Health and Safety; Science - Natural
Dist - BRA **Prod** - BRA

Peripheral venipuncture - site placement and management 28 MIN
VHS
Color (C PRO)
$285.00 purchase, $70.00 rental _ #6016S, #6016V
Presents current information from Intravenous Nurses Society Standards and the Centers for Disease Control. Trains nurses in improved venipuncture techniques to achieve more successful first starts. Illustrates clearly all procedures on real patients. Describes the purposes of a peripheral IV and demonstrates the entire procedure, including vein selection, site disinfection, device insertion, securing the device and dressing application. Shows and describes the devices and presents guidelines on choosing the correct device. Emphasizes three major areas of concern for health care providers - proper use of aseptic technique, familiarity with CDC Universal Precautions and proper site selection. Produced by Health and Sciences Network.
Health and Safety; Science - Natural
Dist - AJN

Periphery 29 MIN
U-matic
Color (G)
$350.00 purchase, $75.00, $60.00 rental
Depicts a group of refugees from World War II in Berlin who decide not to return to society after the war. They live in abandoned attics and cellars and begin to communicate through telepathy. The film, by Penelope Buitenhuis, focuses on the group's eventual confrontation with society and authority.
History - United States; History - World; Psychology; Sociology
Dist - WMENIF **Prod** - WMENIF 1986

Periquin 9 MIN
16mm / U-matic / VHS
Color (SPANISH)
LC 73-702769
A Spanish version of 'LENTIL.' Tells of a boy whose harmonica playing contributes to the success of his town's homecoming celebration for its leading citizen.
Foreign Language
Dist - WWS **Prod** - WWS 1960

Perishable Goods 60 MIN
VHS / U-matic
Body in Question Series Program 13; Program 13
Color (H C A)
LC 81-706956
Shows how the detective work of the post mortem reveals the secrets of bodily function. Confronts the inevitability of death and celebrates the renewal of life by presenting an extract from a production of Monteverdi's Orfeo. Based on the book The Body In Question by Jonathan Miller. Narrated by Jonathan Miller.
Health and Safety; Sociology
Dist - FI **Prod** - BBCTV 1979

Perisphere 14 MIN
16mm
B&W (G)
$25.00 rental
Sweeps the viewer along with the camera which is horizontally tracking in varying arcs of a circle within a suburban setting. Intensifies the optical tension by intercutting fast, close - up, telephoto swishes with more placid and comprehensive pans.
Fine Arts
Dist - CANCIN **Prod** - SINGJO 1975

Peritoneal Dialysis 8 MIN
16mm
Color (PRO)
LC 72-706452
Demonstrates the use of peritoneal dialysis in cases of acute or chronic renal failure, severe electrolyte imbalance, refractory heart failure or poisoning.
Science - Natural; Science - Physical
Dist - UWISC **Prod** - UWISC 1969

Peritoneal Dialysis 18 MIN
U-matic / VHS
Color (PRO)
LC 80-730456
Demonstrates the nurse's role in the delivery of peritoneal dialysis. Gives a brief review of selected highlights of principles and techniques of peritoneal dialysis and presents and explains step - by - step procedures for manual peritoneal dialysis. Demonstrates nurse's responsiblities.
Health and Safety; Science - Natural
Dist - MEDCOM **Prod** - MEDCOM

Peritoneal Dialysis - a Bedside Procedure 24 MIN
VHS / U-matic
Color (PRO)
Shows use of peritoneal dialysis in great detail on several patients with renal failure. Animated drawings develop the theoretical aspects of the procedure.
Health and Safety
Dist - WFP **Prod** - WFP

Peritoneal Lavage 10 MIN
VHS / U-matic
Color (PRO)
Outlines the diagnostic value of peritoneal lavage in blunt abdominal trauma, reviews essential equipment and provides an illustrated step - by - step analysis of demonstration of the procedure as carried out on two trauma victims.
Health and Safety; Psychology; Science - Natural
Dist - UWASH **Prod** - UWASH

Peritoneal Lavage in Blunt Abdominal Trauma 25 MIN
U-matic / VHS
Color (PRO)
Gives clinical examples which determine when peritoneal lavage should be performed and the proper technique to be used. Discusses the advantages of lavage versus paracentesis. Presents methods of evaluating the results.
Health and Safety
Dist - UMICHM **Prod** - UMICHM 1972

Peritonitis - some Causes and Management 22 MIN
16mm
Color (PRO)
Presents three pathologic conditions which illustrate common mechanisms by which peritonitis and its complications are produced - - perforated peptic ulcer, small bowel obstruction and the mechanism by which left colon obstruction results in perforation of the cecum.
Health and Safety; Science
Dist - ACY **Prod** - ACYDGD 1960

The Periyar 13 MIN
16mm
B&W
LC FI67-2303
Shows dams, hydroelectric stations, irrigation systems industries and the life of the people along the 140 mile length of the Periyar River, Kerala, India.
Geography - World; Industrial and Technical Education
Dist - NEDINF **Prod** - INDIA 1959

Perk Up 8 MIN
VHS / 16mm
Muppet Meeting Films Series
Color (PRO)
$550.00 purchase, $300.00 rental, $30.00 preview
Presents Jim Henson's muppets who introduce and humorously comment on business meetings and breaks. Consists of three to four segments each approximately two and a half minutes.
Business and Economics; Psychology; Sociology
Dist - UTM

Perk Up the Salad 3 MIN
Videoreel / VT2
Beatrice Trum Hunter's Natural Foods Series
Color
Suggests perking up the salad bowl by adding such ingredients as grated raw turnip, onion rings soaked in beet juice, sunflower or pumpkin seeds and bits of onions that have begun to sprout, as well as a modification of the basic oil and vinegar dressing with the additions of herbs, yogurt or a favorite cheese.
Home Economics; Social Science
Dist - PBS **Prod** - WGBH

The Perkins Story 40 MIN
16mm
Color (I)
Presents a documentary film about the Perkins School for the Blind, located in Watertown, Massachusetts. Deals primarily with the children and their daily life at the school - - their classes, sports and fun, including roller skating, a square dance party and other activities which the average person would think impossible for a blind child.
Health and Safety; Psychology; Science - Natural
Dist - CMPBL **Prod** - CMPBL 1959

Permafrost 40 MIN
16mm
(H C A)
Investigates the properties of permafrost, when temperature is permanently below zero. Discusses the origin and distribution of this condition, ground ice, offshore permafrost and climate changes.
Science - Physical
Dist - CDIAND **Prod** - EWING 1971

The Permafrost Frontier 28 MIN
16mm
Color
LC 77-702121
Illustrates the properties of permafrost and explains the engineering methods used to design and build the trans - Alaskan pipeline.
Geography - United States; Industrial and Technical Education; Science - Natural
Dist - MTP **Prod** - ALYSKA 1977

Permanency Planning at Intake 40 MIN
U-matic / VHS
Color
Carries out a non - emergency child welfare investigation of neglect in which potential danger exists though actual harm does not warrant removal of the foster child.
Sociology
Dist - UWISC **Prod** - UWISC 1981

Permanency Planning - Use of the Task - Centered Model with an Adolescent Pt I 43 MIN
U-matic / VHS
Color
Presents scenes from a task - centered contracting session between an actual social practitioner and her teenage client, showing the practitioner helping an involuntary client target a problem which she wishes to reduce voluntarily.
Psychology; Sociology
Dist - UWISC **Prod** - UWISC 1981

Permanency Planning - Use of the Task - Centered Model with an Adolescent Pt II 46 MIN
VHS / U-matic
Color
Includes scenes from a task - centered review session in which obstacles are identified and new tasks are mutually developed. Provides guidance for the middle phase of task - centered casework.
Psychology; Sociology
Dist - UWISC **Prod** - UWISC 1981

Permanency Planning with Natural Parents 60 MIN
VHS / U-matic
B&W
Presents a role play between a social worker and a parent of a child presently in foster care. Illustrates stable relationships for foster children.
Sociology
Dist - UWISC **Prod** - UWISC 1979

Permanency Planning - Work with the Child 40 MIN
VHS / U-matic
Color
Explains the causes of child placement in a foster home, explores expectations and develops plans with a nine - year - old client.
Sociology
Dist - UWISC **Prod** - UWISC 1981

Permanency Planning - Work with the Family of an Adolescent 50 MIN
VHS / U-matic
Color
Shows a session contract in which target problems have included return home of a teenager and compliance with curfew and chores. Reveals problems which can arise between parents and social practitioner.
Sociology
Dist - UWISC **Prod** - UWISC 1981

Permanent Planning Casework - the Initial Interview 18 MIN
U-matic / VHS
B&W
Features the initial interview between a young mother with a child in foster care and a permanency planning caseworker for the purpose of developing a permanent plan. Demonstrates the skills and techniques necessary to obtain the three goals of this first contact.
Guidance and Counseling; Sociology
Dist - UWISC **Prod** - PSC

Permanent Teeth 14 MIN
VHS / U-matic
Conrad Series
Color (I)
Discusses dental health.
Health and Safety
Dist - AITECH **Prod** - SCETV 1977

The Permanent War Economy 55 MIN
VHS / U-matic
Briefings on Peace and the Economy - Converting from a Military to a'Civilian Economy Series
Color (C)
Tells how the arms industry takes resources from cilivian production. Produced by the Office for East Asia and the Pacific and the NCCC.
Civics and Political Systems; Social Science
Dist - CWS

Permanent Wave Blocking Patterns
U-matic / VHS
Color
Illustrates and demonstrates the single halo, double halo and the straight back wrap. Demonstrates special wraps for bangs, drop crown and piggyback for long hair. Includes body waves and permanent waving for men, the partial perm and the stack perm techniques.
Education; Home Economics
Dist - MPCEDP **Prod** - MPCEDP 1984

Permeability 8 MIN
VHS
Hydrology concept series
Color (H C)
$24.95 purchase _ #S9020
Observes how water passes through material in a single - concept format. Part of an 8 - part series covering water and soil topics.
Science - Physical
Dist - HUBDSC **Prod** - HUBDSC

The Permeability of Plant Cell Membranes 2 MIN
16mm
Food and Nutrition Series
Color
LC 79-710172
Shows the rehydration of dried apple sections with water and the cooking of hydrated dried and fresh apples in a sugar solution to demonstrate applications of osmosis and dialysis. Compares the cellular structure of prepared apples with fresh samples.
Home Economics; Science - Natural
Dist - IOWA **Prod** - IOWA 1971

Permian strata 4 MIN
16mm
B&W (G)
$10.00 rental
Uses found footage to encourage the 'hero' to respond light as the truth. Interjects clear frames or flash frames.
Fine Arts
Dist - CANCIN **Prod** - CONNER 1969

Permiso Para Trabajar - Permit to Work 23 MIN
U-matic / VHS / 16mm
Color (IND)
Dramatizes an accident in a chemical storage tank. Emphasizes the importance of individual alertness and responsibility in addition to safety check systems.
Health and Safety
Dist - IFB **Prod** - MILLBK

Permissible Dreams 30 MIN
16mm / VHS
As Women See it - Global Feminism Series
Color (G)
$500.00, $250.00 purchase, $60.00 rental
Tells the story of Om Said, a traditional and typical Egyptian woman. Reveals that she married at the age of fifteen, has eight children and does not read or write, yet she is the economist, the physician, the planner of her family's future. Part of a series of films by and about women in Third World countries which include English voice over.
Fine Arts; History - World; Religion and Philosophy; Sociology
Dist - WMEN **Prod** - FAUST

Permission to be healed 30 MIN
VHS
Developing our wholeness under God series
Color (H C G A R)
$39.95 purchase, $10.00 rental _ #35 - 831 - 2076
Features pastoral counselor Dr William Hulme in a discussion of the differences between physical illness and psychological illness. Produced by Seraphim.
Health and Safety; Religion and Philosophy
Dist - APH

Permit to Work 23 MIN
16mm / U-matic / VHS
Color
Dramatizes an accident in the confined space of a chemical storage tank and shows safety procedures for those who work in potentially hazardous, confined spaces.
Health and Safety
Dist - IFB **Prod** - MILLBK

The Permutation Group
16mm
B&W
Demonstrates the general principle that permutations are compounded of cycles. Develops a relationship between permutations and group cards.
Mathematics
Dist - OPENU **Prod** - OPENU

Permutations 27 MIN
U-matic / VHS / 16mm
Color
Demonstrates the newest computer production in the field of 'motion graphics' and an explanation of how it was done.
Fine Arts; Industrial and Technical Education
Dist - PFP **Prod** - WHIT 1968

Permutations 8 MIN
16mm
Color
LC 72-702516
A computer - made art film which demonstrates the graphic art potential of the computer. Presents a set of permutations of an equation in geometry.
Fine Arts; Mathematics
Dist - MOMA **Prod** - IBM 1968

Permutations and Combinations 31 MIN
16mm
Advanced Algebra Series
B&W (H)
States the fundamental principle of permutations and combinations and uses it to solve several problems. Uses three formulas to solve the problem of designing license plates under various restrictive conditions.
Mathematics
Dist - MLA **Prod** - CALVIN 1960

Permutations and combinations 8 MIN
16mm
Color (G)
$10.00 rental
Creates movements at the points of fusion of still images resulting in completely reversible movements. Forms into a loop. All vestiges of drama are eliminated from the film. A companion piece to She Is Away.
Fine Arts
Dist - CANCIN **Prod** - ELDERB 1976

Permutations and Combinations 8 MIN
16mm
Color
LC 77-702609
Creates movements by using experimental techniques coupled with still images.
Fine Arts
Dist - CANFDC **Prod** - LITWKS 1976

Permutations and factorials
VHS
Probability and statistics series
Color (H C)
$125.00 purchase _ #8015
Provides resource material about using permutations and factorials in probability problems for help in the study of probability and statistics. Presents a 60 - video series, each part 25 to 30 minutes long, that explains and reinforces concepts using definitions, theorems, examples and step - by - step solutions to tutor the student. Videos are also available in a set.
Mathematics
Dist - LANDMK

Perpeteia 1 9 MIN
16mm
Color (G)
$25.00 rental
Offers an exploration of the movement of forest and body. Features the fall season in the Oregon coastal rain forest.
Fine Arts; Science - Natural
Dist - CANCIN **Prod** - CHILDA 1977

Perpeteia 2 12 MIN
16mm
Color (G)
$30.00 rental
Extends from Peripeteia 1, a navigation of light, by contrasting the camera's fixed sight with 'in site' movement. Depicts a sculpture of glass, mirrors and film competing with dense shelter, rain and red emulsion. Filmed in June in the Oregon coastal forest.
Fine Arts
Dist - CANCIN **Prod** - CHILDA 1978

Perpetual Motion 11 MIN
U-matic / VHS / 16mm
Color (I J H)
LC 75-705638
Uses several models of man's attempts to create a perpetual motion machine to explore the laws of thermodynamics. Points out that energy must be continually added to any system to maintain orderly operation.
Science - Physical
Dist - PHENIX **Prod** - PHENIX 1969

Perpetum and Mobile 5 MIN
16mm
Color (J)
LC 72-700411
Portrays the technological crisis and the power of industrialism over man by telling the story of a man who runs an assembly - line machine which makes metal bolts. Shows how he is magnetized by the beeping call of the machine, fed into a cylinder and shaped into a metal nut to be mated to a bolt.
Guidance and Counseling; Social Science; Sociology
Dist - MMA **Prod** - ZAGREB 1971

Perro Pepe - 1 15 MIN
VHS
Amigos Series

Color (K) (SPANISH)
$125.00 purchase
Enables teachers with no knowledge of Spanish to introduce basic words to children in kindergarten through second grade. Uses simple concepts and music and features Perro Pepe, a six - foot orange dog, and Senorita Fernandez as instructors. Promotes awareness of and appreciation for Hispanic culture and sparks interest in the geography of Spanish - speaking countries. Part 1, 'Perro Pepe,' introduces the series of thirty 15 - minute programs.
Foreign Language; Geography - World
Dist - AITECH

Perro Pepe En La Television - 26 15 MIN
VHS
Amigos Series
Color (K) (SPANISH)
$125.00 purchase
Enables teachers with no knowledge of Spanish to introduce basic words to children in kindergarten through second grade. Uses simple concepts and music and features Perro Pepe, a six - foot orange dog, and Senorita Fernandez as instructors. Promotes awareness of and appreciation for Hispanic culture and sparks interest in the geography of Spanish - speaking countries. Part 26 is entitled 'Perro Pepe En La Television.'.
Foreign Language; Geography - World
Dist - AITECH

Perro Pepe Es Un Perro - 3 15 MIN
VHS
Amigos Series
Color (K) (SPANISH)
$125.00 purchase
Enables teachers with no knowledge of Spanish to introduce basic words to children in kindergarten through second grade. Uses simple concepts and music and features Perro Pepe, a six - foot orange dog, and Senorita Fernandez as instructors. Promotes awareness of and appreciation for Hispanic culture and sparks interest in the geography of Spanish - speaking countries. Part 3 talks about the dog named Pepe.
Foreign Language; Geography - World
Dist - AITECH

A Perro Pepe Le Duele Un Diente - 27 15 MIN
VHS
Amigos Series
Color (K) (SPANISH)
$125.00 purchase
Enables teachers with no knowledge of Spanish to introduce basic words to children in kindergarten through second grade. Uses simple concepts and music and features Perro Pepe, a six - foot orange dog, and Senorita Fernandez as instructors. Promotes awareness of and appreciation for Hispanic culture and sparks interest in the geography of Spanish - speaking countries. Part 27 is entitled 'A Perro Pepe Le Duele Un Diente.'.
Foreign Language; Geography - World
Dist - AITECH

Perro Pepe Tiene Seis Anos - 2 15 MIN
VHS
Amigos Series
Color (K) (SPANISH)
$125.00 purchase
Enables teachers with no knowledge of Spanish to introduce basic words to children in kindergarten through second grade. Uses simple concepts and music and features Perro Pepe, a six - foot orange dog, and Senorita Fernandez as instructors. Promotes awareness of and appreciation for Hispanic culture and sparks interest in the geography of Spanish - speaking countries. Part 2 deals with numbers and age.
Foreign Language; Geography - World
Dist - AITECH

Persephone
VHS / 35mm strip
Timeless Tales - Myths of Ancient Greece - Set I
Color (I)
$39.95, $28.00 purchase
Recreates the myth of Persephone. Part of a five - part series on Greek mythology.
English Language; History - World; Literature and Drama; Religion and Philosophy
Dist - PELLER

Persephone 5 MIN
16mm
Color (G)
$10.00 rental
Looks at a girl, a dog and other animals.
Fine Arts
Dist - CANCIN **Prod** - OSBONS 1975

Perseus 20 MIN
U-matic / VHS / 16mm
Mythology of Greece Series
Color (I J H)
LC 88-713601
Tells the story of Perseus who kills Medusa, a creature who turns to stone all who look at her.
History - World; Literature and Drama
Dist - BARR **Prod** - BRIANJ 1987

Perseus 20 MIN
VHS / 16mm / U-matic
Mythology of Greece Series
Color (I J H)
$470, $330, $360 _ #A504
Deals with Greek mythology and the virtues of purity and innocence using animated film.
Religion and Philosophy
Dist - BARR **Prod** - BARR 1987

Perseus and Medusa
VHS / 35mm strip
Timeless Tales - Myths of Ancient Greece - Set II
Color (I)
$39.95, $28.00 purchase
Recreates the myth of Perseus and the Medusa. Part of a five - part series on Greek mythology.
English Language; History - World; Literature and Drama; Religion and Philosophy
Dist - PELLER

The Pershing Story - The American Siberian Expeditionary Force 58 MIN
U-matic / VHS
B&W
Offers a biography of General John Pershing which emphasizes his exploits during World War I.
History - United States; History - World
Dist - IHF **Prod** - IHF

Persia 29 MIN
Videoreel / VT2
International Cookbook Series
Color
Features home economist Joan Hood presenting a culinary tour of specialty dishes from around the world. Shows the preparation of Persian dishes ranging from peasant cookery to continental cuisine.
Geography - World; Home Economics
Dist - PBS **Prod** - WMVSTV

Persian gulf tensions 18 MIN
35mm strip / VHS
Color (J H C T A)
$57.00, $57.00 purchase _ #MB - 540337 - 4, #MB - 540023 - 5
Examines the continuing tensions in the Middle East, focusing on the Lebanese civil war and the disputes between Iran and Iraq. Suggests that petroleum will keep the Persian Gulf region a vital interest to the world.
Civics and Political Systems; History - World; Sociology
Dist - SRA **Prod** - NYT 1989

Persian miniatures from the Shahnameh 30 MIN
VHS / 16mm / U-matic
Color (C)
$89.95 purchase _ #EX148
Traces the history of the Shahnameh of Iran, the national epic written by the poet Firdausi in the early eleventh century. Draws parallels between minature paintings and other art forms of the time and the cultural setting in which this art flourished. Produced with the assistance of the Fogg Art Museum.
Fine Arts; History - World
Dist - FOTH **Prod** - FOTH

Persimmon - a Nuclear Physics Experiment 16 MIN
16mm
Color
LC FIE68-26
Explains that for several years the Los Alamos Scientific Laboratory has used intense bursts of neutrons produced by underground detonations of nuclear explosives to perform a variety of nuclear physics experiments. Discusses the experiments and describes the nuclear detonations and the collapse and cratering of the ground above it.
Science - Physical
Dist - LASL **Prod** - LASL 1968

The Persistence of memory 60 MIN
16mm / U-matic / VHS
Cosmos series; Program 11
Color (J)
LC 81-701152
Explores the study of genetic information, the functions of the human brain, the relationship of brain and environment, and the physiologic synaptic response. Based on the book Cosmos by Carl Sagan. Narrated by Carl Sagan.
Psychology; Science - Natural
Dist - FI **Prod** - KCET 1980

The Persistent Ones 50 MIN
U-matic / 16mm
Olympiad Series
Color; Mono (J H C A)
$650.00 film, $350.00 video, $50.00 rental
Focuses on Olympic athletes that have overcome physical or emotional handicaps to become gold medal winners.
Physical Education and Recreation
Dist - CTV **Prod** - CTV 1976

The Persistent Ones - Pt 1 25 MIN
BETA / 16mm / VHS
Color
LC 77-702542
Presents a television special from the CTV program Olympiad, which focuses on athletes who have overcome physical or emotional handicaps to become Olympic gold medal winners.
Physical Education and Recreation
Dist - CTV **Prod** - CTV 1976

The Persistent Ones - Pt 2 25 MIN
16mm / VHS / BETA
Color
LC 77-702542
Presents a television special from the CTV program Olympiad, which focuses on athletes who have overcome physical or emotional handicaps to become Olympic gold medal winners.
Physical Education and Recreation
Dist - CTV **Prod** - CTV 1976

Persistent Stapedial Artery 7 MIN
16mm
Color (PRO)
Shows two cases of persistent stapedial artery accidentally found during stapes surgery. Explains that the stapedial artery in man normally disappears early in embryonic development and very rarely persists into adult life.
Health and Safety
Dist - EAR **Prod** - EAR

The Person in crisis 16 MIN
VHS / U-matic / BETA
Communicating and interacting effectively series
Color (C PRO)
$150.00 purchase _ #137.8
Presents a video transfer from slide program which utilizes interviews with health professionals. Illustrates behaviors of clients that often confuse and upset health professionals. Discusses specific helping measures that can be taken with a client who sustains an unexpected traumatic event. Part of a series on communicating and interacting effectively.
Guidance and Counseling; Health and Safety; Social Science
Dist - CONMED **Prod** - CONMED

The Person of the Counselor, a Very Personal Perspective 30 MIN
16mm
Color (C G)
Presents Gilbert Wrenn discussing his views that a counselor should have a positive self image, have positive views about others and about life, and demonstrate concern and caring for others.
Guidance and Counseling; Psychology
Dist - AACD **Prod** - AACD 1981

Person to person 52 MIN
VHS
Color (G)
$195.00 purchase, $100.00 rental _ #CE - 120
Discusses sex education for persons with developmental disabilities. Shows students, parents and staff tackling a variety of issues in an honest and open manner - menstrual hygiene, sexually transmitted diseases, personal space and safety, appropriate behavior on the job and in public places, and marriage. Produced by Mary Ann Carmody, Jon Lieberman and Brian Pascale.
Health and Safety; Psychology
Dist - FANPRO

Person to Person Communication 14 MIN
U-matic / 8mm cartridge / VHS / 16mm
Color; B&W (H C) (SWEDISH DANISH GERMAN DUTCH NORWEGIAN JAPANESE)
Emphasizes listening with understanding. Shows that false assumptions, preconceived viewpoints and exaggerated personal feelings can lead to misunderstandings in normal conversation.
Business and Economics; English Language; Foreign Language; Guidance and Counseling; Psychology
Dist - RTBL **Prod** - MCMGP 1956

Person to Person in Infancy 22 MIN
16mm
Color

LC 73-700106
Stresses the importance of the human relationships between infant and adult, and shows that in group care as well as at home there can be a considerable range of warmth and adequacy of relationship. Suggests the impact of this relationship of the infant's readiness and eagerness for new experience.
Guidance and Counseling; Psychology; Sociology
Dist - USNAC **Prod** - USHHS 1970

Person to Person - Learning to Communicate
35mm strip / VHS
(G)
$155.00, $165.00 purchase _ #SB2089 filmstrip, #SB2089V VHS
Teaches the interpersonal skills required for effective communication. Tells why communication breakdowns occur and provides techniques for preventing them.
Social Science; Sociology
Dist - CAREER **Prod** - CAREER

Person to Person - Learning to Communicate
U-matic / VHS
Color (J H C)
Teaches interpersonal communication skills. Examines typical problems in speaking and listening. Includes teacher's guide.
Guidance and Counseling; Psychology; Sociology
Dist - SUNCOM **Prod** - SUNCOM

Person to Person - Making Communications Work for You 10 MIN
16mm / U-matic / VHS
Color (H C A)
LC 73-702613
Explores four areas of office communication, including facial expression, body language, eye contact and vocal enthusiasm. Presents examples of both positive and negative communication in each area.
Business and Economics; Guidance and Counseling; Psychology
Dist - BARR **Prod** - SAIF 1973

Person - to - Person Relationships 28 MIN
16mm
You in Public Service Series
Color (A)
LC 77-700966
Explores skills and attitudes that aid people in public service in getting along well with others in one - to - one situations.
Civics and Political Systems; Guidance and Counseling; Sociology
Dist - USNAC **Prod** - USOE 1977

Person to person series
Creating respectful workplaces 28 MIN
Dist - VIDART

Personal action for better health series
Alcohol and drugs package
Back strength and fitness package
Cholesterol control package
Fitness - the high performance lifestyle package
High blood pressure package
Smoking - the road to a smoke - free life package
Stress management package
Weight management package
Dist - HTHED

Personal action system series
Presents a 13 - part video series to educate employees on the importance of health. Discusses fitness, blood pressure, weight management, time management, back fitness, alcohol and drugs, stress management, smoking, preventing burnout, men and self - care, diet and cancer, wellness, cholesterol, and women and self - care.
Alcohol and drugs
Back fitness
Cholesterol control
Diet and cancer
Fitness
Preventing burnout
Smoking
Stress management
Time management
Weight management
Wellness
Dist - GPERFO

Personal and Family Security 22 MIN
U-matic / VHS / 16mm
Color (SPANISH)
Covers protection for executives and their families. Deals with maintaining a low profile, driving tips, office security and communications procedures.
Business and Economics; Foreign Language
Dist - MCI **Prod** - WORON

Personal and Family Security 25 MIN
16mm / U-matic / VHS
Color
Provides security information which can be followed by executives and their families to counteract the threat of terrorist violence. Covers security procedures for the home, the office and while driving.
Business and Economics; Psychology; Sociology
Dist - CORF **Prod** - WORON

Personal and social change quartet 120 MIN
BETA / VHS
Color (G)
$69.95 purchase _ #Q384
Presents a four - part series on personal and social change. Includes 'Brain, Mind and Society' with Marilyn Ferguson, 'The Art of Communicating' with Dr Jacob Needleman, 'Transforming Human Nature' with George Leonard and 'Biological and Spiritual Growth' with Joseph Chilton Pearce.
Guidance and Counseling; Psychology; Religion and Philosophy; Science - Natural; Social Science; Sociology
Dist - THINKA **Prod** - THINKA

Personal and social change series
The Art of communicating 30 MIN
Biological and spiritual growth 30 MIN
Brain, mind and society 30 MIN
Transforming human nature 30 MIN
Dist - THINKA

Personal and social development - 10
VHS
Teaching for tomorrow series
Color; PAL (C T)
PdS20 purchase
Uses real teachers and schools to evaluate ideas and support professional development for secondary teachers in the area of the personal and social development of students. Stimulates discussion on classroom management, handling curriculum changes and developing new teaching techniques. Contact distributor about availability outside the United Kingdom.
Education; Psychology
Dist - ACADEM

Personal and social development - 11
VHS
Teaching for tomorrow series
Color; PAL (C T)
PdS20 purchase
Uses real teachers and schools to evaluate ideas and support professional development for primary teachers in the area of the personal and social development of students. Stimulates discussion on classroom management, handling curriculum changes and developing new teaching techniques. Contact distributor about availability outside the United Kingdom.
Education; Psychology
Dist - ACADEM

Personal and spiritual development quartet 120 MIN
BETA / VHS
Color (G)
$69.95 purchase _ #Q184
Presents a four - part discussion on personal and spiritual development. Includes 'Waking Up' with Dr Charles Tart, 'The Practice of Meditation' with Dr Jack Kornfield, 'Personality Development and the Psyche' with Dr Helan Palmer and 'Spiritual Training' with Irina Tweedie.
Psychology; Religion and Philosophy
Dist - THINKA **Prod** - THINKA

Personal and spiritual development series
Personality development and the psyche 30 MIN
The Practice of meditation 30 MIN
Spiritual training 30 MIN
Waking up 30 MIN
Dist - THINKA

Personal banking 30 MIN
VHS
Business concepts series
Color (H C)
LC 89-715834
Presents seven five - minute programs that explore bank services and various accounts available, and show how to reconcile those accounts. Includes teachers' guide.
Business and Economics; Education
Dist - TVOTAR **Prod** - TVOTAR 1989

Personal budgeting 31 MIN
VHS
Color (J H)
$99.00 purchase _ #06717 - 026
Uses dramatization to help students identify their spending patterns, material needs and financial resources. Provides budgeting techniques such as how to do an expense analysis, a yearly budget and a cash flow chart.
Business and Economics; Education
Dist - GA

Personal Capabilities of Feeder Pig Producers 9 MIN
VHS / U-matic
Color
Discusses what personal capabilities are needed for feeder pig production.
Agriculture
Dist - HOBAR **Prod** - HOBAR 1985

Personal care and hygiene 25 MIN
VHS
Home care training videos - HCTV - series
Color (C PRO)
$125.00 purchase, $60.00 rental _ #42 - 2379, #42 - 2379R
Covers bathing and toilet techniques for different types of patients, as well as dressing and grooming. Discusses skin care basics, including moisturizing and bathing and the importance of personal care to patient self - image. Includes instructional guide for review and testing and meets OBRA federal regulations. Part of a five - part series training home health aides in essential skills and teaching basic skills to nursing students.
Health and Safety; Home Economics
Dist - NLFN **Prod** - NLFN

Personal Care Considerations of the Diabetic 22 MIN
U-matic / VHS
Understanding Diabetes Series
Color
Outlines daily care routines and the diabetic's personal responsibility. Explains techniques, evaluation and equipment for self - administered urine tests, recognizing an insulin reaction and what to do about it, importance of personal hygiene and precautions during non - diabetic illness.
Health and Safety
Dist - FAIRGH **Prod** - FAIRGH

Personal Computer Applications in Business 30 MIN
VHS / U-matic
Personal Computers in Business Series
Color
Defines the nature of personal computers and explores the impact they are having on the business community.
Industrial and Technical Education; Psychology
Dist - DELTAK **Prod** - DELTAK

Personal Computer Hardware 30 MIN
U-matic / VHS
Personal Computers in Business Series
Color
Examines the terminology and functions of different hardware components and discusses some of the purchasing and service issues involved in using a personal computer.
Industrial and Technical Education; Psychology
Dist - DELTAK **Prod** - DELTAK

Personal Computer Instructional Videocassette - Split Screen 120 MIN
U-matic / VHS
Flip Track Instructional Series
#89529
Instructs the viewer on the use of the Effective Split Screen Video Techniques For IBM PC.
Computer Science
Dist - FLIPLS **Prod** - KENPUB

Personal Computer Instructional Videocassettes - Split Screen 120 MIN
VHS / U-matic
Flip Track Instructional Series
#89528
Instructs the viewer on the use of the Effective Split Screen Video Techniques For Apple IIe.
Computer Science
Dist - FLIPLS **Prod** - KENPUB

Personal Computer Software 30 MIN
U-matic / VHS
Personal Computers in Business Series
Color
Examines the 'buy vs create' software question and looks at some of the advantages and disadvantages on both sides. Discusses the various programming languages and operating systems available for personal computers and what they mean to the user.
Industrial and Technical Education; Psychology
Dist - DELTAK **Prod** - DELTAK

Personal Computers - Basic Concepts
U-matic / VHS
Computer Concepts Series
Color
Presents an overview of home computers, describing how they operate. Defines basic computer terminology.
Industrial and Technical Education; Mathematics
Dist - LIBFSC **Prod** - LIBFSC

Personal Computers in Business Series
Determining your needs 30 MIN
Personal Computer Applications in Business 30 MIN
Personal Computer Hardware 30 MIN
Personal Computer Software 30 MIN
Dist - DELTAK

Personal computers in manufacturing 28 MIN
VHS / 16mm
Manufacturing Insights series
Color (A IND)
$200.00, $190.00 purchase _ #VT250, #VT250U
Demonstrates the flexibility and compatibility of today's PC systems, making various applications possible without costly add - ons.
Business and Economics; Computer Science; Industrial and Technical Education
Dist - SME **Prod** - SME 1986

Personal Computing 30 MIN
U-matic
Fast Forward Series
Color (H C)
Reveals that the computer has come into the home as instructor, entertainer, accountant and ubiquitious conmmunications tool.
Computer Science; Science
Dist - TVOTAR **Prod** - TVOTAR 1979

Personal Construct Psychology Series
Clinical applications - pt 4 52 MIN
Constructive Metatheory and Models of Human Change - Pt 5 52 MIN
Current Applications and Future Trends - Pt 11 52 MIN
Dialogue on development, the self as theorist - pt 9 52 MIN
Dialogue on interpersonal communication and relationships - pt 8 52 MIN
Dialogue on Methods - Pt 10 52 MIN
Dialogue on Philosophy - Pt 7 52 MIN
Dialogue on psychotherapy - pt 6 52 MIN
Human Change Processes - Pt 12 255 MIN
An Introduction to Non - Grid Methods of Assessment - Pt 3 52 MIN
The Psychology of Personal Constructs, an Introduction - Pt 1 52 MIN
Repertory Grid Technique - Research and Assessment - Pt 2 52 MIN
Dist - SCETV

Personal Construct Theory as Applied to Nutrition Education 42 MIN
U-matic
Color
Reveals how psychologists use personal construct theory to predict behavior. Reveals that this theory makes it possible to understand and change eating patterns by recording and analyzing a person's beliefs about food.
Health and Safety
Dist - SNUTRE **Prod** - SNUTRE

Personal Decisions 30 MIN
VHS / 16mm
Color (G A)
$295.00 purchase, $50.00 rental
Covers the important issues of women's rights and particularly the right of women to control their own reproductive lives. Also looks at the complex considerations a woman faces in deciding whether or not to have an abortion.
Sociology
Dist - CNEMAG **Prod** - CNEMAG 1988

Personal Development and Professional Growth - Mike McCaffrey's Focus Seminar Series
Conclusions 30 MIN
Conditioning 30 MIN
How to Communicate - Receiving 30 MIN
How to Communicate - Sending 30 MIN
How to Use Affirmations 30 MIN
Image Impressions 30 MIN
Responsibility - the Key to Freedom 30 MIN
Thought Processes - Conscious and Subconscious 30 MIN
Your Self - Images 30 MIN
Dist - DELTAK

Personal development and professional growth - Mike McCaffrey's focus seminar series
Affirmations 30 MIN
Building your self - esteem 30 MIN
Dealing with pressure 30 MIN
Goal achievement 30 MIN
Dist - DELTAK

Personal Development Objectives - Appraisal by Results 12 MIN
U-matic / VHS
Practical M B O Series
Color
Business and Economics; Education; Psychology
Dist - DELTAK **Prod** - DELTAK

Personal Development Series
Getting Along with Others
People and Values
Self Esteem
Shyness and Assertiveness
Stress
Dist - CADESF

Personal development video series
Presents a five - part series dealing with issues critical to adolescents. Includes the titles Self Esteem, Getting Along With Others, People and Values, Shyness and Assertiveness, and Stress.
Personal development video series
Dist - CADESF **Prod** - CADESF

Personal Development Video Series
Getting along with others 30 MIN
Self - Esteem 30 MIN
Shyness and assertiveness 30 MIN
Stress 30 MIN
Dist - CAMV

Personal development video series
Presents a five - part series for dealing with common adolescent problems. Covers the subjects of stress, values, self - esteem, shyness and assertiveness, and getting along with others. Consists of five videocassettes.
Values 30 MIN
Dist - CAMV
NEWCAR

A Personal discovery of Islam
VHS
Color (G)
$12.00 purchase _ #110 - 082
Tells the stories of Abdur Rehman Tennat and Abd al Hayy Moore and their coming to Islam. Reveals two Americans who found peace in Islam.
Religion and Philosophy
Dist - SOUVIS **Prod** - SOUVIS 1995

Personal Finance and Management Series
Financing a Home 28 MIN
Dist - SCCON

Personal Finance and Money Management Series
Work, Income, and Your Career 28 MIN
Dist - CDTEL
SCCON

Personal Finance and Money Management Series
Buying a home 28 MIN
Credit and borrowing 28 MIN
The Economy 28 MIN
Estate Planning - the Tools You'll Use 28 MIN
Financial Institutions 28 MIN
Financial Planning for Later Years 28 MIN
Frauds and Swindles 28 MIN
Health and Income Insurance 28 MIN
Housing Costs and Regulations 28 MIN
How income taxes work 28 MIN
Leisure and Recreation 28 MIN
Life Insurance 28 MIN
Making Your Money Grow 28 MIN
The Money Market 28 MIN
Other Investment Opportunities 28 MIN
Real Estate Investments 28 MIN
Renting 28 MIN
Selling Your Home 28 MIN
The Stock Market 28 MIN
Tax Saving Strategies 28 MIN
Transportation 28 MIN
Dist - SCCON

Personal Finance and Money Mangement 900 MIN
U-matic / VHS
Color (C A)
Provides individuals with a means of keeping up with the increasingly complex financial world. Includes resources to cope with the changes affecting taxes, credit, consumer laws and investment opportunities. The course has just been revised to reflect the recent changes in income tax laws.
Business and Economics; Civics and Political Systems
Dist - SCCON **Prod** - SCCON 1987

Personal finance and money mangement series
Creating a workable financial plan 28 MIN
Estate Planning - Achieving Your Objectives 28 MIN
Dist - SCCON

Personal Finance Series Lesson 11
Renting 30 MIN
Dist - CDTEL

Personal Finance Series Lesson 5
Frauds and Swindles 30 MIN
Dist - CDTEL

Personal Finance Series Lesson 7
Leisure and Recreation 30 MIN
Dist - CDTEL

Personal Finance Series Lesson 9
Financing a Home 30 MIN
Dist - CDTEL

Personal Finance Series Lesson 10
Housing Costs and Regulations 30 MIN
Dist - CDTEL

Personal Finance Series Lesson 12
Selling Your Home 30 MIN
Dist - CDTEL

Personal Finance Series Lesson 16
The Money Market 30 MIN
Dist - CDTEL

Personal Finance Series Lesson 19
Other Investment Opportunities 30 MIN
Dist - CDTEL

Personal Finance Series Lesson 20
Life Insurance 30 MIN
Dist - CDTEL

Personal Finance Series Lesson 22
Financial Planning for Later Years 30 MIN
Dist - CDTEL

Personal Finance Series Lesson 23
Estate Planning - the Tools You'll Use 30 MIN
Dist - CDTEL

Personal finance series lesson 26
Tax - saving strategies 30 MIN
Dist - CDTEL

Personal Finance Series
Buying a home 30 MIN
Creating a workable financial plan - lesson 3 30 MIN
Credit and borrowing 30 MIN
The Economy 30 MIN
Estate Planning - Achieving Your Objectives - Lesson 24 30 MIN
Health and Income Insurance 30 MIN
How income taxes work 30 MIN
Making your money grow 30 MIN
Real Estate Investments 30 MIN
The Smart Shopper 30 MIN
The Stock market 30 MIN
Dist - CDTEL

Personal finances 35 MIN
VHS
Color (R G)
$19.95 purchase _ #9324 - 6
Features Christian financial expert Larry Burkett who discusses budgeting and debt reduction.
Religion and Philosophy
Dist - MOODY **Prod** - MOODY 1994

Personal Finances 19 MIN
U-matic / VHS
Jobs - Seeking, Finding, Keeping Series
Color (H)
Describes a stock boy who finally learns to budget his income realistically.
Business and Economics
Dist - AITECH **Prod** - MDDE 1980

Personal Financial Planning 11 MIN
16mm
Color; B&W (J H)
LC FIA62-1677
Discusses the relationship between financial planning and the attainment of goals, showing how to handle personal income wisely to guarantee personal security and to perpetuate our free economic system.
Business and Economics; Guidance and Counseling; Psychology
Dist - SUTHLA **Prod** - SUTHLA 1960

Personal Flotation Devices - Your Friends for Life 7 MIN
U-matic / VHS
Color (A)
Discusses personal flotation devices and care requirements, types, and activities relating to them. Comments on drowning as the second leading cause of accidental death below age 75.
Health and Safety; Physical Education and Recreation
Dist - USNAC **Prod** - USCG 1983

Personal grooming and hygiene 11 MIN
U-matic / VHS / 16mm
Communications and selling program series
Color (A)
Illustrates the importance of proper personal hygiene in a business environment. Offers detailed information on bathing, care of teeth, and use of deodorants, perfumes and cosmetics. Stresses the role played by well - groomed hair, beard and fingernails in non - verbal communication.

Business and Economics; Health and Safety; Home Economics
Dist - NEM **Prod** - NEM

Personal grooming and hygiene 11 MIN
U-matic / VHS / 16mm
Customer service, courtesy and selling programs - Spanish series
Color (SPANISH)
Shows the importance of personal grooming and hygiene in business.
Business and Economics; Foreign Language; Home Economics
Dist - NEM **Prod** - NEM

Personal Growth 30 MIN
VHS / U-matic
Interaction - Human Concerns in the Schools Series
Color (T)
Discusses personal growth in a school setting.
Education
Dist - MDCPB **Prod** - MDDE

Personal Growth for the Supervisor 30 MIN
Videoreel / VT2
You - the Supervisor Series
Color (PRO)
Deals with some of the steps that a supervisor can take to continue to grow on his job.
Business and Economics; Guidance and Counseling
Dist - PRODEV **Prod** - PRODEV

Personal Health 16 MIN
16mm
Color
LC 78-701744
Outlines the basics of preventive medicine for promoting physical health. Illustrates personal hygiene techniques which should be used to prevent the spread of germs and infection.
Health and Safety
Dist - USNAC **Prod** - USA 1976

Personal Health for Girls 14 MIN
U-matic / VHS / 16mm
Color (J H)
LC 72-700496
Presents principles of hygiene for girls and shows the importance of observing good habits of eating and cleanliness for health and social reasons.
Health and Safety; Home Economics
Dist - CORF **Prod** - CORF 1972

Personal Hygiene 18 MIN
VHS / 16mm
Catering with Care Series
Color (H)
$205.00 purchase
Demonstrates personal hygiene practices for food service workers. Considers hair cleanliness, makeup, cuts, abrasions and illness. Includes support materials.
Health and Safety; Home Economics; Industrial and Technical Education
Dist - FLMWST

Personal hygiene 13 MIN
VHS / U-matic / BETA
Color; PAL (IND G)
$175.00 rental _ #AEB - 114
Focuses on the importance of protection from the more subtle hazards in the workplace. Explains the long - term benefits of established safety procedures for dealing with various sources of stress on the job, including invisible chemicals, mechanical hazards, excessive noise and unsafe extremes of temperature and radiation. Includes leader's guide and 10 workbooks.
Health and Safety; Psychology
Dist - BNA **Prod** - BNA

Personal Hygiene for Boys 11 MIN
U-matic / VHS / 16mm
Color (I J)
Shows five boys, Bill, Steve, Jeff, Larry and Rick, who all have special problems regarding personal hygiene and the changes taking place in their maturing bodies. Offers guidance on the common standards of of good body care including shaving, showering and skin and hair care.
Guidance and Counseling; Health and Safety; Home Economics; Psychology
Dist - CORF **Prod** - CORF 1971

Personal hygiene in foodservice 14 MIN
VHS
Color (IND VOC)
$395.00 purchase, $100.00 five - day rental, $30.00 three - day preview _ #SA3
Emphasizes the need for food handlers to maintain high standards of personal hygiene. Discusses the importance of proper hygiene and grooming habits to ensure cleanliness and prevent illness. Demonstrates key hygiene habits, proper hand - washing, importance of hair - nets, fingernail - grooming, and use of testing utensils. Includes facilitator's guide, materials for 25 trainees, and other materials.
Health and Safety; Industrial and Technical Education
Dist - ADVANM

Personal Information Form 25 MIN
VHS / 16mm
Job Search - How to Find and Keep a Job Series
(H)
$69.00 _ #PA103V
Presents a basic form that will help in filling out job applications, resume writing and interviewing. Summarizes personal data, education, experience and other details.
Guidance and Counseling
Dist - JISTW

Personal Information Form - Program 3 19 MIN
VHS / 16mm
Job Search - How to Find and Keep a Job series
Color (H C A PRO)
$720.00 purchase _ #SD100
Presents a basic personal information form to develop before filling out job applications. Available only as part of the complete series. Part 3 of 12 parts.
Business and Economics; Guidance and Counseling
Dist - AAVIM **Prod** - AAVIM 1990

Personal inventory 25 MIN
U-matic / VHS
Caring community - alcoholism and drug abuse series
Color
Discusses the nature of an important component of effective recovery from drug dependency, such as systematic self - assessment.
Psychology; Sociology
Dist - VTRI **Prod** - VTRI

A Personal matter - Gordon Hirabayashi v the United States 30 MIN
VHS / U-matic
Color (G)
$125.00 purchase, $50.00 rental
Profiles Gordon Hirabayashi who in 1944 defied Executive Order 9066, refusing to be interned on the grounds that the order violated his constitutional rights. Chronicles Hirabayashi's 42 year struggle to get his conviction overturned. Discusses the basic protections of the American Constitution - due process of law and individual rights. Produced and directed by John de Graaf with the Constitution Project.
History - United States; Sociology
Dist - CROCUR

Personal Needs - 5 29 MIN
VHS
Interactions in Science and Society - Teacher Programs - Series
Color (T PRO)
$150.00 purchase
Reveals that when the most basic needs - food, water, clean air and shelter - have been met, new lifestyles are developed with new needs and rising expectations. Considers that meeting these needs and expectations gives rise to new technologies reinforced by marketing and advertising which create new needs and put a severe strain on the world's resources.
Business and Economics; Education; History - United States; Psychology; Social Science; Sociology
Dist - AITECH **Prod** - WHATV 1990

A Personal Perspective - Cerebral Palsy Pt 1, Joyce 26 MIN
U-matic
Impact of a Handicap on the Family Structure
Color (H C A)
Interview with a woman with athetoid cerebral palsy who talks about growing up disabled, early misdiagnoses of severe retardation, special education, mainstreaming, professionals, independence and problems faced by parents.
Psychology
Dist - UILL **Prod** - UILL 1982

A Personal Perspective - Cerebral Palsy Pt 2, Joyce 24 MIN
U-matic
Impact of a Handicap on the Family Structure
Color (H C A)
Describes devastating incidents Joyce had in high school and discusses speech therapy, dating, sexuality and association among the disabled. Gives advice to able bodied individuals and professionals on interacting with the handicapped and their families.
Psychology
Dist - UILL **Prod** - UILL 1982

A Personal Perspective - Cleft Lip and Palate, Pt 1, Cindy 23 MIN
U-matic
Impact of a Handicap on the Family Structure
Color (H C A)
Describes the experiences and feelings of a woman with repaired bilateral cleft lip and palate. Reports the feelings of others towards her and her own coping mechanisms and reactions to surgery and speech therapy.
English Language; Health and Safety; Psychology; Sociology
Dist - UILL **Prod** - UILL 1982

A Personal Perspective - Cleft Lip and Palate, Pt 1, Earlene 28 MIN
U-matic
Impact of a Handicap on the Family Structure
Color (H C A)
Discusses feelings and attitudes of withdrawal, anger and grief in the mother of a child with bilateral cleft lip and palate. Conflicting information regarding speech therapy, genetic counseling, discipline, surgery and parental feelings are presented. She describes professional behavior which she felt was supportive and helpful.
English Language; Health and Safety; Psychology; Sociology
Dist - UILL **Prod** - UILL 1982

A Personal Perspective - Cleft Lip and Palate, Pt 2, Cindy 20 MIN
U-matic
Impact of a Handicap on the Family Structure
Color (H C A)
Continues the discussion with a repaired bilateral cleft lip and palate patient. Focuses on her feelings regarding dating, marriage and children. Presents suggestions to professionals involved in treating such individuals.
English Language; Health and Safety; Psychology; Sociology
Dist - UILL **Prod** - UILL 1982

A Personal Perspective - Hearing Impairment Pt 1, Peter 26 MIN
U-matic
Impact of a Handicap on the Family Structure
Color (H C A)
Presents a hearing impaired man discussing feelings, family reactions, misdiagnoses, medical treatment, amplification, peer and teacher attitudes.
Psychology
Dist - UILL **Prod** - UILL 1982

A Personal Perspective - Hearing Impairment, Pt 2, Joe and Alice 20 MIN
U-matic
Impact of a Handicap on the Family Structure
Color (H C A)
Continues interviewing parents of a 19 year old hearing impaired daughter. Focuses on adolescent problems and social development. Reviews decisions about busing, social activity, siblings, parental needs and which world, deaf or hearing, their child will be involved in most.
Health and Safety; Psychology; Sociology
Dist - UILL **Prod** - UILL 1982

A Personal Perspective - Hearing Impairment, Pt 2, Joe and Alice 25 MIN
U-matic
Impact of a Handicap on the Family Structure
Color (H C A)
Discusses feelings and attitudes of the parents of a 19 years old hearing impaired daughter starting with the rubella pregnancy and question of abortion. Parental conflicts regarding varying approaches to treating the hearing imparied are also presented.
Health and Safety; Psychology; Sociology
Dist - UILL **Prod** - UILL 1982

A Personal perspective - hearing impairment Pt 2 - Peter 27 MIN
U-matic
Impact of a handicap on the family structure series
Color (H C A)
Presents a hearing impaired man discussing feelings, family reactions, misdiagnoses, medical treatment, amplification, peer and teacher attitudes.
Psychology
Dist - UILL **Prod** - UILL 1982

Personal Perspectives 53 MIN
VHS / U-matic
Shared Realities Series
Color (A)
Presents a selection of videotapes produced at LBMA Video.
Fine Arts
Dist - LBMART **Prod** - LBMART 1983

A Personal Plan for Wellness 30 MIN
16mm / U-matic / VHS
Planning for Wellness System Series
Color
Introduces a system designed to initiate and maintain healthy lifestyle changes. Shows how bad habits are replaced by a series of steps and goals.
Health and Safety
Dist - CORF **Prod** - CORF

Personal power 15 MIN
VHS / U-matic
Drug wise series; Module 1

Color (I)
Informs viewers that they have the power to decide what goes into the body and that they can learn to use that power wisely.
Health and Safety
Dist - GPN **Prod** - WDCNTV

Personal Power 60 MIN
Cassette / VHS
Color (G)
$49.95, $179.95 purchase _ #XVPP, XAPP
Presents a 30 - day program for Unlimited Success by Anthony Robbins. Available as a video or in an audiocassette kit containing 24 audiocassettes, journal and summary cards.
Psychology
Dist - GAINST

Personal power 15 MIN
U-matic / VHS
Drug wise series
(I)
$40 purchase, $25 rental, $75 self dub
Explains to viewers their power over what they put in their bodies. Emphasizes that they can learn to use this power wisely.
Health and Safety
Dist - GPN **Prod** - NCGE 1984 - 1985

Personal Productivity, the Key to Success 25 MIN
16mm
Color (C A)
Portrays major causes, consequences, and approaches for dealing with both the job related and environmental stresses in today's society.
Psychology
Dist - UTEX **Prod** - MANDEC 1982

Personal pronouns - sub material 18 MIN
VHS
Language construction company series
Color (H C G)
$50.00 purchase _ #LCC - 4
Assists students in improving their written and spoken English grammar skills. Bases all programs on a 'construction theme.' Includes review tests as an integral part of each lesson. Students may stop, start and repeat any part of the lesson. Visual cues are given for review purposes. Part of a 15 - part series.
English Language
Dist - INSTRU

Personal protection 13 MIN
BETA / VHS / U-matic
Color; PAL (IND G)
$175.00 rental _ #AEB - 110
Demonstrates equipment for protecting the head, eyes, ears, respiratory system, hands, feet and the entire body. Emphasizes the correct use of protective equipment and shows the hazards of neglect in its use. Includes leader's guide and 10 workbooks.
Health and Safety; Psychology
Dist - BNA **Prod** - BNA

Personal protection
VHS
Professional tree care safety series
Color (G) (SPANISH)
$75.00, $90.00 purchase _ #6 - 204 - 201P, #6 - 204 - 211P - Spanish Version
Shows tree workers how to protect themselves while working around trees. Includes protective wear and proper positioning around equipment. Part of a four - part series on tree worker safety. Produced by the National Arborist Association.
Agriculture; Health and Safety; Psychology; Science - Natural
Dist - VEP

Personal protective clothing 18 MIN
VHS
Firefighter I series
Color (IND)
$130.00 purchase _ #35635
Presents one part of a 19 - part series that is the teaching companion for IFSTA's Essentials of Fire Fighting manual. Identifies types of protective clothing. Demonstrates correct methods for the use and care of protective clothing. Explains the limits of protection. Based on Chapter 3.
Health and Safety; Science - Physical; Social Science
Dist - OKSU **Prod** - ACCTRA

Personal protective equipment 10 MIN
VHS
Supervisors' development program series
Color (IND)
$280.00 purchase _ #15488 - 2222
Instructs on personal protective equipment and employee motivation to use such equipment. Features William Shatner as host. Part of a 13 - part series on employee safety which stresses the four - step SAFE model - Search for hazards, Assess risks, Find solutions, Enforce solutions.
Business and Economics; Health and Safety; Industrial and Technical Education; Psychology
Dist - NSC **Prod** - NSC

Personal protective equipment 17 MIN
VHS
Personal protective equipment series
Color; PAL (IND G)
PdS95 purchase
Outlines for management the main legislative requirements of EC. Advises on implementation and highlights the duties of employers. Shows how to carry out risk assessments. Explains training regulations, storage facilities and gives clear, concise explanations of changes to existing legislation. Part of a two - part series to assist businesses in conforming with new EC directives. Includes a booklet and checklist.
Business and Economics; Health and Safety; Psychology
Dist - CFLVIS **Prod** - SCHWOP 1992

Personal Protective Equipment
U-matic / VHS
Safety Action for Employees Series
Color (IND)
Details various personal protective equipment available to workers in industry and visually demonstrates how each is used.
Health and Safety
Dist - GPCV **Prod** - GPCV

Personal protective equipment - a refresher session - IV 16 MIN
8mm cartridge / VHS / BETA / U-matic
Refresher course in chemical safety series
Color; PAL (IND G)
$495.00 purchase, $175.00 rental _ #REF - 104
Offers an across - the - board review of personal protective equipment required when working with chemicals. Starts with gloves and ends with fully encapsulating suits. Helps workers to understand why and when PPE is required. Presents a total review of the respirator classes, along with selection criteria nd fit testing. Demonstrates the EPA and OSHA system of A - B - C - D ensemble classification is demonstrated and explained. Part of a four - part series on chemical safety. Includes a trainer's manual and ten employee manuals.
Health and Safety; Psychology; Science - Physical
Dist - BNA **Prod** - BNA

Personal protective equipment series
It won't happen to me 10 MIN
Personal protective equipment 17 MIN
Dist - CFLVIS

Personal Requirements - Personal Rewards 21 MIN
VHS / U-matic
Financing, Starting and Marketing a Flock Series
Color
Introduces an eastern Montana family that raises sheep. Shows how they share some of their personal joys and frustrations during the busy lambing season.
Agriculture; Social Science
Dist - HOBAR **Prod** - HOBAR

Personal Safety 3 MIN
16mm
Safety in the Laboratory Series
Color (H C A)
LC 72-702620
Discusses safety rules including wearing eye protection, tieing back long hair, wearing loose, inexpensive clothing, wearing a lab coat or apron and wearing protective shoes. Shows techniques for smothering a clothing fire with a fire blanket and a lab apron.
Guidance and Counseling; Health and Safety
Dist - KALMIA **Prod** - KALMIA 1972

Personal Safety 12 MIN
U-matic / VHS / 16mm
Color (A)
Shows that although personal assault is on the rise, prevention and defense techniques can be employed by the average person to minimize loss and injury. Emphasizes the psychological posture of being prepared.
Health and Safety; Physical Education and Recreation; Sociology
Dist - RTBL **Prod** - RTBL

Personal Safety 60 MIN
VHS
Plant Safety Series
Color (PRO)
$600.00, $1500.00 purchase _ #GMPSA
Describes plant hazards - electricity, machinery - and personal safety equipmet - hard hats, safety shoes, eye gear. Part of a four - part series on plant safety, which is part of a set on general and mechanical maintenance. Includes 10 textbooks and an instructor guide which provide four hours of instruction.
Education; Health and Safety; Industrial and Technical Education; Psychology; Sociology
Dist - NUSTC **Prod** - NUSTC

Personal Safety and Awareness 29 MIN
VHS / 16mm
Color (G)
$150.00 purchase, $75.00 rental; $295.00 purchase, $100.00 rental
Presents techniques for personal safety and prevention of rape. Features Nancy Hightshoe as trainer.
Business and Economics; Physical Education and Recreation; Psychology; Sociology
Dist - PROSOR

Personal safety - I'm lost 15 MIN
VHS / U-matic
It's a rainbow world series
(P)
Designed to teach social studies to primary grade students. Explains concepts in terms of everyday situations. Focuses on advisable actions to take when lost.
Psychology; Sociology
Dist - GPN

Personal Safety in Tanker Truck Loading and Offloading 16 MIN
VHS / 16mm
Color (A IND)
LC 91705373
Trains drivers of tanker trucks in a complex set of safety procedures for carrying cargo ranging from liquid or compressed gases to chemical wastes.
Health and Safety; Industrial and Technical Education; Social Science; Sociology
Dist - IFB

Personal safety - Pt 1 15 MIN
VHS / U-matic
Industrial safety series
Color (IND)
Discusses the importance of safety for personal protection. Covers the role of OSHA, use of safety clothes, eye protection and safe lifting practices.
Health and Safety; Industrial and Technical Education
Dist - LEIKID **Prod** - LEIKID

Personal safety - Pt 2 20 MIN
U-matic / VHS
Industrial safety series
Color (IND)
Discusses the need for and types of hearing protection, skin protection, protection of lungs from dangerous particles and types of respirators and which to use.
Health and Safety; Industrial and Technical Education
Dist - LEIKID **Prod** - LEIKID

Personal safety - the voices of victims 19 MIN
16mm / U-matic / VHS
Color (J H C A)
$435.00, $250.00 purchase _ #76557
Shows how ordinary citizens can avoid becoming victims of burglary, robbery, vandalism or personal assault.
Health and Safety; Sociology
Dist - CORF **Prod** - CENTRO 1980

Personal Safety - what Should You do? 15 MIN
U-matic / VHS
It's a Rainbow World
(P)
Designed to teach social studies to primary grade students. Explains concepts in terms of everyday situations. Focuses on safety awareness.
Psychology; Sociology
Dist - GPN

Personal Security 30 MIN
U-matic
Challenge of Time Series
(A)
Gives valuable suggestions to elderly people who may be concerned about questions of security and safety.
Health and Safety; Sociology
Dist - ACCESS **Prod** - UALB 1984

Personal Service 6 MIN
U-matic / VHS / 16mm
Kingdom of Could be You Series
Color (K P I)
Guidance and Counseling
Dist - EBEC **Prod** - EBEC 1974

Personal Service Cluster 20 MIN
VHS / U-matic
Vocational Visions Series
Color
Discusses the requirements and duties for such jobs as cosmetologists, food service worker, educational assistant and law enforcement worker.
Guidance and Counseling; Psychology
Dist - GA **Prod** - GA

Personal Services 10 MIN
U-matic
Color (P)
Profiles self - employed people in the business of service. Explains how they arrange and maintain the daily undertakings of other people.
Guidance and Counseling
Dist - GA **Prod** - MINIP

The personal side - 12 30 MIN
VHS
Venturing - the entrepreneurial challenge series
Color (G)
$14.95 purchase
Discusses the challenges involved in balancing work and family, functioning effectively with a partner and working with parents or siblings in a family business. Part 12 of a 13 - part series on the steps involved in starting and developing an entrepreneurial company. Viewers' guide available separately. Sponsored under a grant from the Farmers Home Administration to help small and rural businesses.
Business and Economics; Psychology; Sociology
Dist - VTETV **Prod** - VTETV 1992

Personal side of safety series
Decide to be safe 10 MIN
Get a Grip on Yourself 13 MIN
Let Habit Help 10 MIN
Safety Record 10 MIN
Two Steps to Safety 10 MIN
Dist - NSC

The Personal stamp 30 MIN
Videoreel / VT2
Designing home interior series; Unit 27
Color (C A)
Explores the special qualities imparted by room accessories. Demonstrates how to construct a picture wall.
Home Economics
Dist - CDTEL **Prod** - COAST 1987

Personal Stress Management
VHS / BETA
R M I Stress Management Series Series
Color
Health and Safety; Physical Education and Recreation; Psychology
Dist - RMIBHF **Prod** - RMIBHF

Personal Stress Management
VHS / 16mm
RMI Stress Management Series
(PRO)
$80.00 purchase _ #RSM1004
Looks at personal stress management.
Business and Economics; Psychology
Dist - RMIBHF **Prod** - RMIBHF

Personal Tax and Financial Planning for Professionals 160 MIN
VHS / U-matic
Color (PRO)
Discusses the options to be considered in structuring a professional business and minimizing taxes on earned and unearned income for a law practice and its professional clients.
Business and Economics; Civics and Political Systems
Dist - ABACPE **Prod** - CCEB

Personal Time Management Series
Filing systems that work for you 25 MIN
How good is your time management 25 MIN
Organizing Your Time 31 MIN
Scheduling Your Time 29 MIN
Staff Meetings that Work for You 19 MIN
Dist - DELTAK

Personal time management series
Doing the distasteful and difficult 22 MIN
Dist - DELTAK
TELSTR

Personal Time Management Series
Filing for your own needs 30 MIN
Getting Staff Meetings to Work for You 30 MIN
How to distribute your time effectively 30 MIN
Organizing Your Work and Others' Work 30 MIN
Scheduling Your Time and Others' Time 30 MIN
Dist - TELSTR

Personal Touch 30 MIN
U-matic / VHS
Better Business Letters Series Lesson 6; Lesson 6
Color
Covers how to convey a personal touch in business letters. Includes methods of persuasion and how to get results.
Business and Economics; English Language
Dist - TELSTR **Prod** - TELSTR

Personal Touch 31 MIN
U-matic / VHS
Better Business Letters Series
Color
Business and Economics; English Language
Dist - DELTAK **Prod** - TELSTR

The Personal Touch 15 MIN
U-matic / VHS / 16mm
Adventure of the Mind Series
Color (H C A)
LC 80-701719;
Aims to dispel the idea that computers are impersonal robots or functionaries useful only in business and industry. Looks at the many ways computers can serve personal interests by expanding the individual's mental capabilities.
Mathematics
Dist - IU **Prod** - IITC 1980

Personal trainer I - the start
VHS
Gold's Gym personal trainer series
Color (G H A)
$29.95 purchase _ #MCA62745V-P
Features professional trainers demonstrating exercises and weight training routines for beginners. Includes tips from diet and nutrition experts and appearances by celebrities. One of a series of two videos. Length varies from 46 to 55 minutes. Available separately or as a set.
Physical Education and Recreation
Dist - CAMV

Personal trainer II - intermediate
VHS
Gold's Gym personal trainer series
Color (G H A)
$29.95 purchase _ #MCA68898V-P
Features professional trainers demonstrating exercises and weight training routines for intermediate level exercisers. Includes tips from diet and nutrition experts and appearances by celebrities. One of a series of two videos. Length varies from 46 to 55 minutes. Available separately or as a set.
Physical Education and Recreation
Dist - CAMV

Personal Transformation - the Way through 44 MIN
U-matic / VHS
Color
Presents transformer therapy as a direction - finding experience for those recovering from chemical dependency.
Health and Safety; Psychology; Sociology
Dist - WHITEG **Prod** - WHITEG

Personal Values 11 MIN
16mm
Family Life Education and Human Growth Series
Color (J H A)
Questions whether the honesty taught in school is better forgotten if it helps one to get ahead in the outside world.
Guidance and Counseling; Psychology
Dist - SF **Prod** - SF 1970

Personality 30 MIN
VHS / 16mm
Psychology - the Study of Human Behavior Series
Color (C A)
$99.95, $89.95 purchase _ 24 - 14
Explores current research into theories of personality.
Psychology
Dist - CDTEL **Prod** - COAST 1990

Personality - Adolescence 21 MIN
16mm / U-matic / VHS
Color (C T)
LC 78-701008
Discusses personality development during adolescence, emphasizing the importance of independence, self - esteem and sexuality in a search for identity.
Guidance and Counseling; Psychology
Dist - MGHT **Prod** - UCSD 1978

Personality and love - is the opposite sex strange or am I from a different planet 15 MIN
VHS
Understanding who you are - the personality video series
Color (J H)
$79.00 purchase _ #PVS510
Shows how socialized and neurological and biological differences between women and men can lead to interesting communication problems. Part of a ten - part series on personality.
Guidance and Counseling; Psychology; Social Science; Sociology
Dist - CADESF **Prod** - CADESF 1990

Personality and values - what is important to you 15 MIN
VHS
Understanding who you are - the personality video series
Color (J H)
$79.00 purchase _ #PVS518
Looks at what values are and how individuals develop their own value system. Shows how each of the major personality themes tends to cluster around core value systems and how understanding those core values can increase tolerance and acceptance. Part of a ten - part series on personality.
Guidance and Counseling; Psychology; Sociology
Dist - CADESF **Prod** - CADESF 1990

Personality at school - school is great - it's the teachers I can't stand 15 MIN
VHS
Understanding who you are - the personality video series
Color (J H)
$79.00 purchase _ #PVS506
Examines the effect of personality upon success in school. Shows how different personalities can be successful in school and addresses the issues of 'teacher style' as it relates to students' learning styles. Part of a ten - part series on personality.
Education; Psychology; Social Science; Sociology
Dist - CADESF **Prod** - CADESF 1990

Personality development and the psyche 30 MIN
BETA / VHS
Personal and spiritual development series
Color (G)
$29.95 purchase _ #S065
Suggests that certain paranoid and neurotic states can open the mind to a range of intuitive and psychic experiences. Features Dr Helen Palmer, psychologist and author of 'The Enneagram.' Part of a four - part series on personal and spiritual development.
Psychology; Religion and Philosophy
Dist - THINKA **Prod** - THINKA

Personality disorders 25 MIN
VHS / U-matic / BETA
Psychopathologies - descriptions and interventions series
Color (C PRO)
$150.00 purchase _ #134.5
Presents a video transfer from slide program which explains the broad category of personality disorder. Describes two major disorders in depth - the antisocial and the borderline. Gives case examples and suggestions for effective interaction and communication with these patients. Part of a series on psychopathologies.
Health and Safety; Psychology
Dist - CONMED **Prod** - CONMED

Personality Disorders 66 MIN
VHS / U-matic
Psychiatry Learning System, Pt 2 - Disorders Series
Color (PRO)
Identifies theories of the etiology of personality disorders. Discusses paranoia, schizophrenia, narcissism, compulsive and passive aggressivity.
Guidance and Counseling; Health and Safety; Psychology
Dist - HSCIC **Prod** - HSCIC 1982

Personality disorders - antisocial, histrionic, schizotypal behaviors - Part IV 31 MIN
U-matic / VHS
Simulated psychiatric profiles series
Color (PRO C)
$250.00 purchase _ #C871 - VI - 005
Examines cases of personality disorders - antisocial, histrionic, schizotypal behaviors - to illustrate theories about those illnesses. Demonstrates therapeutic techniques such as clarification, confrontation and interpretation. Part four of a five - part series progressing from adjustment disorders to major psychoses presented by Dr Donald C Fidler.
Health and Safety; Psychology
Dist - HSCIC

Personality Disorders - Failures of Adjustment 57 MIN
VHS
Color (J)
LC 85-703979
Dramatizes sociopathic, paranoid, schizoid, avoidant, narcissistic, histrionic, passive - aggressive and compulsive disorder types. Shows causes of these disorders and recent breakthroughs in treatment.
Psychology
Dist - HRMC **Prod** - HRMC

Personality Disorders - Failures of Adjustment 45 MIN
VHS
Color (H)
Uses dramatizations to illustrate a wide variety of personality disorder types. Teaches some of the psychological causes of these disorders and recent breakthroughs in their treatment.
Psychology
Dist - IBIS **Prod** - IBIS 1981

Personality disorders simulated 56 MIN
VHS / U-matic
Color (PRO C)
$250.00 purchase _ #C881 - VI - 030
Introduces medical students to characteristics of behavior associated with common personality disorders. Uses the dramatizations of 11 actors to portray paranoid, schizoid, schizotypal, antisocial, borderline, histrionic, narcissistic, avoidant, dependent, obsessive - compulsive and passive - aggressive disorders. Focuses on the dynamics of interaction among these 'patients.' Presented by Drs Donald C Fidler and Timothy C Isley.
Health and Safety; Psychology
Dist - HSCIC

Personality - Early Childhood 20 MIN
U-matic / VHS / 16mm
Color (H C A)
LC 78-700468
Explores various personality traits that develop during the preschool years, including dependence, identification, aggression, fear and anxiety. Explains the special significance of each in the child's development.
Psychology
Dist - MGHT **Prod** - COAST 1978

Personality games for Macintosh series
The Peer pressure squeeze
Personality in conflict
Six self-esteem styles
Why people work
Dist - CAMV

Personality in conflict
VHS
Personality games for Macintosh series
Color (H C)
$79 purchase - #CDPVS108M-D
Describes the six major personality orientations and looks at how each of them tends to deal with conflict. Teaches students the many responses available when frustration sets in.
Business and Economics; Guidance and Counseling; Psychology
Dist - CAMV

Personality in conflict with others - why does this person drive me nuts 15 MIN
VHS
Understanding who you are - the personality video series
Color (J H)
$79.00 purchase _ #PVS512
Shows that conflict resolution is a skill that can be learned once an individual understands what is important to the parties involved. Looks at how each personality theme tends to solve problems and resolve conflict. Part of a ten - part series on personality.
Psychology; Social Science; Sociology
Dist - CADESF **Prod** - CADESF 1990

Personality in the family - who's the boss 15 MIN
VHS
Understanding who you are - the personality video series
Color (J H)
$79.00 purchase _ #PVS508
Looks at the family as a mixture of several personality themes. Explores how people 'get along' and can even be happy in a sometimes difficult family environment. Recreates familiar family scenarios. Part of a ten - part series on personality.
Guidance and Counseling; Psychology; Sociology
Dist - CADESF **Prod** - CADESF 1990

Personality (Interviews Series

Dr Bernard Siegan	26 MIN
Dr Dom Armentano and Dr Randy Haydon	28 MIN
Dr Walter Williams	26 MIN
Edwin Meese III	26 MIN
John Pugsley	22 MIN

Dist - WORLDR

Personality - Middle Childhood 19 MIN
U-matic / VHS / 16mm
Color (C T)
LC 78-701013
Describes the middle years of childhood as a time of increasing independence for children which includes finding a place among peers, arriving at new concepts of self and mastering new skills. Explains how all of these contribute to the child's growing sense of independence.
Psychology
Dist - MGHT **Prod** - UCSD 1978

Personality, Normality, and Adjustment 45 MIN
BETA / VHS
Psychological Growth and Spiritual Development Series
Color (G)
Psychology; Religion and Philosophy
Dist - DSP **Prod** - DSP

Personality of a Market 16 MIN
16mm
Color
LC 70-712180
Portrays the Houston, Texas, radio market in order to encourage business concerns to purchase commercial time on the radio.
Business and Economics; Geography - United States; Social Science
Dist - KXYZ **Prod** - KXYZ 1970

Personality of the West 145 MIN
U-matic
University of the Air Series
Color (J H C A)
$750.00 purchase, $250.00 rental
Looks at the geography of the four western provinces of Canada. Program contains a series of five cassettes 29 minutes each.
Geography - World
Dist - CTV **Prod** - CTV 1977

Personality on the job - why people work 15 MIN
VHS
Understanding who you are - the personality video series
Color (J H)
$79.00 purchase _ #PVS504
Looks at how personality effects work habits. Shows how to motivate different personality themes in the work environment and examines why some jobs are more suited to certain personalities. Part of a ten - part series on personality.
Guidance and Counseling; Psychology; Sociology
Dist - CADESF **Prod** - CADESF 1990

Personality Styles Series

Describing nine classic personality styles	36 MIN
Interpreting Your Own Self - Perception Profile	24 MIN
Motivating the Conservative and the Cautious Personality, Case Examples - Personalities	35 MIN
Motivating the Dominant and the 'People - Oriented' Personality	25 MIN
Practical Approach to Understanding	20 MIN

Dist - AMA

Personality Tests 29 MIN
U-matic
Understanding Human Behavior - an Introduction to Psychology Series 'Lesson 23
Color (C A)
Discusses great number and variety of psychological tests in current use. Makes distinction between IQ and intelligence. Emphasizes many factors that influence intelligence scores.
Psychology
Dist - CDTEL **Prod** - COAST

Personality Theory 29 MIN
U-matic
Understanding Human Behavior - an Introduction to Psychology Series 'Lesson 22
Color (C A)
Surveys and compares approaches and contributions of the major theories of personality. Defines personality and theory. Looks at work of Freud, Erikson, Rogers and Maslow.
Psychology
Dist - CDTEL **Prod** - COAST

Personality Types 45 MIN
BETA / VHS
Psychological Growth and Spiritual Development Series
Color (G)
Psychology; Religion and Philosophy
Dist - DSP **Prod** - DSP

Personalize Your Presentation 9 MIN
16mm
Professional Selling Practices Series 1 Series
Color (H A)
LC 77-702360
Business and Economics
Dist - SAUM **Prod** - SAUM 1967

Personalized Academic Services 30 MIN
16mm
Color (C A) (NAVAJO)
LC 75-702926
Uses Navajo Indian children in order to show the techniques and methods used in special education for second language acquisition, for teching language arts, reading and for the development of prescriptive learning.
Education; Foreign Language
Dist - AVED **Prod** - USBIA 1975

Personnel 31 MIN
U-matic / VHS
How to be more Successful in Your Own Business Series
Color (G)
$279.00, $179.00 purchase _ #AD - 2009
Addresses the issues of finding, training, motivating, compensating and retaining good employees. Features Mitchell Fromstein, president, Manpower, Inc. Part of an eight - part series on successful business management moderated by David Susskind.
Business and Economics; Guidance and Counseling; Psychology
Dist - FOTH **Prod** - FOTH

Personnel Basket Safety 7 MIN
VHS / U-matic
Color (IND)
Shows how to ride the personnel basket when getting on or off offshore rigs and platforms. Gives safety tips and common sense advice for experienced personnel and visitors.
Business and Economics; Industrial and Technical Education; Social Science
Dist - UTEXPE **Prod** - UTEXPE

Personnel Loading Capabilities of the C - 130 Aircraft 11 MIN
16mm
B&W
LC FIE56-172
Demonstrates the conversion of the C - 130 from cargo to personnel carrier. Depicts its capabilities to carry paratroops, personnel and medical station equipment.
Civics and Political Systems; Social Science
Dist - USNAC **Prod** - USDD 1954

Personnel Parachute Malfunctions and Activation of Reserve Parachute 14 MIN
16mm
B&W
LC 80-701838
Discusses the causes, prevention and appropriate responses to partial or complete parachute malfunction. Stresses timely use of the reserve parachute.
Civics and Political Systems
Dist - USNAC **Prod** - USA 1980

Perspective 15 MIN
U-matic / VHS
Expressions
(I J)
$130 purchase, $25 rental, $75 self dub
Designed to interest fifth through ninth graders in art. Emphasizes creativity and experimentation. Features author and artist Duane Preble explaining perspective. Fourth in an 18 part series.
Fine Arts
Dist - GPN

Perspective 30 MIN
VHS
Learning to paint with Carolyn Berry series
Color (H G)
$49.95 purchase
Offers an easy to follow, step - by - step method for creating a finished painting or drawing from a blank canvas. Features part of an eight - part series covering everything from arranging or selecting your subjects to an explanation of the material needed and the specific techniques to be applied. Professional art instructor Carolyn Berry designed this series for students, hobbyists, amateur painters and professionals seeking new tips. Produced by Artists Video and directed by Christian Surette; 1991 - 1994. Video jackets available.
Fine Arts
Dist - CNEMAG

Perspective - agriculture - series

Blooming science	30 MIN
Flatworms	30 MIN
Food for thought	30 MIN
Insect war	30 MIN
On the margin	30 MIN
A Question of balance	30 MIN

Dist - CFLVIS

Perspective and Painting with a Knife 25 MIN
U-matic / VHS
Paint Series Program 4
Color (H C A)
Fine Arts
Dist - FI **Prod** - BBCTV

Perspective - biotechnology - series
Biosensors 30 MIN
The Molecule mine 30 MIN
Natural factory 30 MIN
Dist - CFLVIS

Perspective - computers and electronics - series
Computers in medicine 30 MIN
Making the connection 30 MIN
Dist - CFLVIS

Perspective Drawing 8 MIN
16mm / U-matic / VHS
B&W (J)
Presents an introduction to mechanical perspective. Useful in teaching free hand sketching.
Fine Arts
Dist - UCEMC **Prod** - UCLAT 1952

Perspective drawing - how to do it 31 MIN
35mm strip / VHS
Color (J H C T A)
$93.00 purchase _ #MB - 540799 - X, #MB - 512520 - X
Covers principles of perspective drawing. Provides step - by - step instruction through the use of drawings and diagrams. Considers both one - point and two - point perspectives.
Fine Arts
Dist - SRA **Prod** - SRA

Perspective - energy resources - series
Cash from trash 30 MIN
Eco - engines 30 MIN
Guarding the atom 30 MIN
Natural force 30 MIN
Wind energy 30 MIN
Dist - CFLVIS

Perspective - health and medicine - series
A Chance to live 30 MIN
Dist - CFLVIS

Perspective II series
Includes 13 videos on various science and technology topics, including Light as Information; A Chip Off the Old Block; Car and D; Robotics; Amazing Laser; Technology Starts Here; Satellites; Fiber Optics; Gift of Life; Medicine in Sport; Information Technology - General Introduction; Information Technology - In the Office; and Information Technology - In Work. Videos are also available separately.
Amazing laser 30 MIN
Car and D 30 MIN
A Chip off the old block 30 MIN
Fiber optics 30 MIN
Gift of Life 30 MIN
Information Technology - General Introduction 30 MIN
Information Technology - in the Office 30 MIN
Information Technology - in Work 30 MIN
Light as Information 30 MIN
Medicine in Sport 30 MIN
Robotics 30 MIN
Satellites 30 MIN
Technology Starts Here 30 MIN
Dist - LANDMK

Perspective in drawing - 5 15 MIN
VHS
Drawing with Paul Ringler series
Color (I)
$125.00 purchase; $25.00 rental
Shows how to set up and use one - and two - point perspective to indicate distance and depth. Focuses on the drawing process, for older students, rather than drawing specific objects. Part of a thirty - part series.
Fine Arts
Dist - AITECH **Prod** - OETVA 1988

Perspective, Measuring and Two - Point 60 MIN
VHS
Color, Perspective and Composition - Hal Reed Series
Color (J)
$29.95 purchase _ #HV - 689
Presents two 30 - minute lessons on perspective measuring and two - point perspective. Part of a six - part series on color, perspective and composition by Hal Reed.
Fine Arts
Dist - CRYSP **Prod** - CRYSP

A Perspective of Hope 28 MIN
16mm / VHS
Color (C A PRO)
$240.00 purchase
Looks at the impact of the Robert Wood Johnson Foundation's Teaching Nursing Home Program. Looks at nursing students, faculty, staff members, patients and their families.
Health and Safety; Science; Sociology
Dist - FANPRO **Prod** - FANPRO 1989

Perspective on new organizations series
Presents a five - part series on IBM, Gore - Tex and Motorola and how each organization achieved excellence, the indicators that led to success or downfall and how they valued and utilized human resources. Features Drs J Clayton Lafferty and Delmar 'Dutch' Landen as co - hosts and contributors, as well as other corporate visionaries. Includes the titles - Beyond TQM - The Democratization of the Workplace; Insights into Achievement and Leadership; Ideas for Fashioning New Labor - Management Relationships; Strategic Thinking - Creating Cultures that Work; Blueprint for Tomorrow - Planning the Learning Organization.
Beyond TQM - the democratization of the workplace - Part I
Blueprint for tomorrow - planning the learning organization - Part V
Ideas for fashioning new labor - mangement relationships - Part III
Insights into achievement and leadership - Part II
Strategic thinking - Creating cultures that work - Part IV
Dist - HUMSYN **Prod** - HUMSYN 1989

Perspective on Pesticides 15 MIN
16mm
Color
LC 74-705348
Describes the various pesticides, their benefits to mankind, the hazards associated with their use - in the home and on the farm and the proper method of application and storage.
Agriculture; Science - Natural; Science - Physical
Dist - USNAC **Prod** - USPHS 1967

A Perspective on Teaching 30 MIN
16mm
Nursing - Where are You Going, How will You Get There Series
B&W (C A)
LC 74-700177
Defines teaching, analyzes elements in a philosophy of education and examines related implications.
Education; Health and Safety
Dist - NTCN **Prod** - NTCN 1971

Perspective - Program 7 15 MIN
U-matic
Artscape Series
Color (I)
Shows children entering a magic perspective highway where they learn about overlapping, shadows and diminution.
Fine Arts
Dist - TVOTAR **Prod** - TVOTAR 1983

Perspective Series
Computer Aided Design 27 MIN
Consulting Cambridge 27 MIN
Electronic music 27 MIN
Fifth generation computers 27 MIN
Forensic science 27 MIN
The Magic Bullet 27 MIN
Microsurgery 27 MIN
The New Alchemy 27 MIN
Pictures in a Patient 27 MIN
Rampaging Carbons 27 MIN
Science at Kew Gardens 27 MIN
Science in Museums 27 MIN
Uses of Blood 27 MIN
Dist - STNFLD

Perspective Series
A Community priest 26 MIN
Families on the Road - to Somewhere 58 MIN
The Gospel singers 14 MIN
Let no Man Put Asunder 25 MIN
The Lonely Crime 48 MIN
A Sylvan Sewer 25 MIN
Dist - WRCTV

Perspective 10 series
AIDS 30 MIN
Bridges 30 MIN
The Burrowers 30 MIN
Crowds on the move 30 MIN
Gene therapy 30 MIN
In the pipeline 30 MIN
The Inner game 30 MIN
Medical joinery 30 MIN
Medical robots 30 MIN
Mother of invention 30 MIN
Potatoes 30 MIN
Repairing the damage 30 MIN
Wetlands 30 MIN
Dist - CFLVIS

Perspective - the environment - series
Acid rain 30 MIN
Decade of water 30 MIN
The Dirty sea 30 MIN
Environmental architecture 30 MIN
Figures in a landscape 30 MIN
The Fragile forest 30 MIN
From a howl to a whisper 30 MIN
Small is beautiful 30 MIN
Valley 30 MIN
Washing of a river 30 MIN
Dist - CFLVIS

Perspective, Theory and One - Point 60 MIN
VHS
Color, Perspective and Composition - Hal Reed Series
Color (J)
$29.95 purchase _ #HV - 688
Presents two 30 - minute lessons on perspective theory and one - point perspective. Part of a six - part series on color, perspective and composition by Hal Reed.
Fine Arts
Dist - CRYSP **Prod** - CRYSP

Perspectives - A Dance portrait 5 MIN
16mm
Color (G)
$15.00 rental
Explores a dancer in motion, seen from fifteen perspectives simultaneously. Combines partial views of the dancer into a grid format to reveal a harmonious and dynamic composite image. Features Katie Nelson of the Oberlin Dance Collective in San Francisco. Produced by Robert Schiappacasse.
Fine Arts
Dist - CANCIN

Perspectives - health and medicine - series
AIDS - completing the jigsaw 30 MIN
Blindness 30 MIN
Cholera 30 MIN
Eye into the heart 30 MIN
Heart - lung transplants 30 MIN
Laser surgery 30 MIN
The Mummy's blessing 30 MIN
Nature's cure 30 MIN
The Pain killers 30 MIN
Perilous journey 30 MIN
Physiology of muscles 30 MIN
Posture and pain 30 MIN
Premature babies 30 MIN
Prostheses 30 MIN
Rehabilitation 30 MIN
Science in the saddle 30 MIN
To have and to hold 30 MIN
Unruly cells 30 MIN
The Vital force 30 MIN
Dist - CFLVIS

Perspectives - Historical, Anthropological , Political, Economic and Social 30 MIN
U-matic / VHS
Interaction - Human Concerns in the Schools Series
Color (T)
Discusses historical, anthropological, political, economic and social perspectives in the field of education.
Education
Dist - MDCPB **Prod** - MDDE

Perspectives in Science Series
Stimulates student interest in science. Tackles three environmental subjects - Toxic Waste, Biotechnology and Water from a science, technology and society - STS - perspective. Begins with a short drama that highlights a real - life situation. Shows the relevance of topics to student lives and investigates scientific concepts, latest technological solutions to the problem and responses of citizens to specific dilemmas. Each program divides into chapters; each chapter has science, technology and society sections. Information on the CLV discs is organized into short sub - chapters embedded in each disk to give teacher more flexibility in using the huge amount of information each program contains.
Biotechnology 60 MIN
The Program in action 22 MIN
Toxic Waste 60 MIN
Water 60 MIN
Dist - BULFRG **Prod** - NFBC

Perspectives - industrial design - series
Boots, boots, boots 30 MIN
Brainwave 30 MIN
Fire 30 MIN
Formula one 30 MIN
Glass - a material with a future 30 MIN
Hampton Court - a palace preserved 30 MIN
Materials revolution 30 MIN
Moving a mountain 30 MIN
Office of the future 30 MIN
Sporting science 30 MIN
Dist - CFLVIS

Perspectives lectures series
Dr Arnold Weissberger - Perspectives and recollections
Dist - AMCHEM

Perspectives - natural science - series
Animal psychology 30 MIN
Astronomy 30 MIN
Copycat 30 MIN
Crystal world 30 MIN
Land - locked ark 30 MIN
Limitations 30 MIN
Rhythms of light 30 MIN
Dist - CFLVIS

Perspectives of Space 30 MIN
U-matic / VHS
What a Picture - the Complete Photography Course by John Hedgecoe ˚Series Program 6
Color (H C A)
Demonstrates architectural photography at chateaux in Normandy and the canyons of New York City. Explains the problems of perspective and scale and ways to introduce comment and humor into a photograph. Looks at the relationship of people and their environments, fashion designer Zandra Rhodes, the Pearly King and Queen of Westminster and sculptor Henry Moore.
Industrial and Technical Education
Dist - FI

Perspectives on ecosystem management - Tapes 1 and 2 145 MIN
VHS
Color (C PRO A)
$130.00 purchase, $25.00 rental _ #941.1, #941.2
Focuses on the long - term productivity of ecosystems as conducted at H J Andrews Experimental Forest in western Oregon for over 25 years. Introduces the program and gives a brief history of research at H J Andrews in Part One. Part Two discusses the composition, structure and function of old - growth forest systems as they change through time. Part Three explains the need for managing forest ecosystems on a landscape scale rather than on a stand basis. Part Four describes the balance between soil, small mammals and dead wood. Part Five looks closely at riparian zones. Part Six summarizes the entire series.
Agriculture; Business and Economics; Industrial and Technical Education; Science - Natural; Social Science
Dist - OSUSF **Prod** - OSUSF 1988

Perspectives on healing quartet 120 MIN
VHS / BETA
Color (G)
$69.95 purchase _ #Q284
Presents a four - part discussion on alternative perspectives on healing. Includes 'Psychic and Spiritual Healing' with Dr Stanley Krippner, 'Communication as Healing' with Patricia Sun, 'Sound and Hearing' with Jill Purce and 'The Inner Mechanisms of Healing' with Brendan O'Regan.
Fine Arts; Health and Safety; Psychology; Science - Natural; Science - Physical
Dist - THINKA **Prod** - THINKA

Perspectives on healing series
Communication as healing 30 MIN
The Inner mechanics of healing 30 MIN
Psychic and spiritual healing 30 MIN
Sound and healing 30 MIN
Dist - THINKA

Perspectives on Insulin Pump Therapy 29 MIN
VHS / U-matic
Color (PRO)
Examines the principles involved in the use of continuous subcutaneous insulin infusion (CSII) for patients with Type 1 diabetes. Covers the basis for the use of the insulin pump, the principles of how it works, the identification of patients suitable for pump therapy, hazards of CSII therapy, and the patient and professional responsibilities involved in this therapy. Discusses patient training and education program for pump patients on the MDRTC's inpatient unit at The University of Michigan Hospitals.
Health and Safety
Dist - UMICHM **Prod** - UMICHM 1984

Perspectives on Language Training 30 MIN
16mm
Color (PRO)
LC 78-701605
Discusses and demonstrates four general perspectives concerning language training, including the assessment of the language - delayed child, the structure of a language training session, procedures utilized in a language training session and the extension of training from the clinical to the natural environment.
Education; English Language; Psychology
Dist - UKANS **Prod** - UKANS 1975

Perspectives on the family 17 MIN
BETA / VHS / U-matic
Family theories and assessment series
Color (C PRO)
$150.00 purchase _ #149.1
Presents a video transfer of a slide program which describes the many diverse forms of the family. Discusses five family social science theories, including family development theory and systems theory. Describes the traits of a healthy family. Provides commentary by Dr Marilyn Friedman, RN, California State University. Part of a series on family theories and assessment.
Guidance and Counseling; Health and Safety; Sociology
Dist - CONMED **Prod** - CONMED

Perspectives on Women
Change through Political Action - Alternative Approaches 60 MIN
Change through Political Action Traditional Structures 60 MIN
Changing Women's Work - Paid Employment 60 MIN
The Economics of aging 60 MIN
The Future of women's work - in the light of microtechnology in the work place 60 MIN
Health Issues - Our Physical Selves 60 MIN
Images of Women in Popular Culture 60 MIN
The Issue of Poverty 60 MIN
Looking at Gender Roles 60 MIN
Our Physical Selves - Well - being 60 MIN
Parenting and the Home 60 MIN
Violence Against Women 60 MIN
Women and Work - Paid and Unpaid 60 MIN
Dist - ACCESS

Perspectives - science in action - series
Art restoration 30 MIN
Flies, stones and fishes 30 MIN
Magazine I 30 MIN
Magazine II 30 MIN
Measurement 30 MIN
Sensing the future 30 MIN
Dist - CFLVIS

Perspectives - transport and communication - series
Archaeology under the microscope 30 MIN
Communications 30 MIN
Docklands renewed 30 MIN
Downbursts 30 MIN
Dustbins in the sky 30 MIN
Mayday - Mayday 30 MIN
Microlights 30 MIN
The Picture programme 30 MIN
Remote sensing 30 MIN
Wheels 30 MIN
Wings on the water 30 MIN
Dist - CFLVIS

Perspectre 7 MIN
16mm / U-matic / VHS
Color (H C) (FRENCH)
LC 77-700203
A French language film. Presents an animated film in which a simple geometric form is duplicated, arranged and rearranged into a flow of patterns and perspectives.
Fine Arts
Dist - IFB **Prod** - NFBC 1976

The Persuaders 11 MIN
VHS / 16mm
History of Advertising Series
Color (J)
$155.00 purchase
Focuses on 20th century advertising and asks if people are pressured into buying things they do not need. Presents some successful and unsuccessful ad campaigns.
Business and Economics; Fine Arts; Literature and Drama
Dist - FLMWST

Persuading the Jury 35 MIN
U-matic
Picking and Persuading a Jury Series Program 6
Color (PRO)
LC 81-706171
Explains some techniques used to persuade a jury. Describes four fundamental principles of advocacy.
Civics and Political Systems
Dist - ABACPE **Prod** - ABACPE 1980

Persuading the jury in a civil case - opening statements for the defendants 59 MIN
VHS
Art of advocacy - selecting and persuading the jury series
Color (C PRO)
$95.00 purchase, $71.25 rental _ #Z0304
Presents lectures and demonstrations of techniques used in jury persuasion in civil cases. Focuses on opening statements for the defendants. Draws on social science insights.
Civics and Political Systems
Dist - NITA **Prod** - NITA 1988

Persuading the jury in a civil case - opening statements for the plaintiff 55 MIN
VHS
Art of advocacy - selecting and persuading the jury series
Color (C PRO)
$95.00 purchase, $71.25 rental _ #Z0303
Presents lectures and demonstrations of techniques used in jury persuasion in civil cases. Focuses on opening statements for the plaintiff. Draws on social science insights.
Civics and Political Systems
Dist - NITA **Prod** - NITA 1988

Persuading the jury in a criminal case - opening statements for the defendant 49 MIN
VHS
Art of advocacy - selecting and persuading the jury series
Color (C PRO)
$95.00 purchase, $71.25 rental _ #Z0307
Presents lectures and demonstrations of techniques used in persuasion of the jury in criminal cases. Focuses on opening statements for the defendant. Draws on social science insights.
Civics and Political Systems
Dist - NITA **Prod** - NITA 1988

Persuading the jury in a criminal case - opening statements for the prosecution 54 MIN
VHS
Art of advocacy - selecting and persuading the jury series
Color (C PRO)
$95.00 purchase, $71.25 rental _ #Z0306
Presents lectures and demonstrations of techniques used in persuasion of the jury in criminal cases. Focuses on opening statements for the prosecution. Draws on social science insights.
Civics and Political Systems
Dist - NITA **Prod** - NITA 1988

Persuading the Public 14 MIN
16mm / U-matic / VHS
Color (J)
LC 78-700915
Dramatizes humorous episodes illustrating the persuasion techniques of intensifying the positive attributes and downplaying the negative qualities of an idea or product that is to be sold to the public.
Business and Economics; Psychology
Dist - PHENIX **Prod** - JOHR 1978

Persuasion 29 MIN
U-matic
Understanding Human Behavior - an Introduction to Psychology Series ˚Lesson 29
Color (C A)
Discusses power and limits of persuasion in spreading ideas and changing attitudes. Uses examples from advertising and political campaigns.
Psychology
Dist - CDTEL **Prod** - COAST

Persuasion gone awry 28 MIN
U-matic / BETA / VHS
Communication skills 2 - advanced series
Color (H C G)
$101.95, $89.95 purchase _ #CA - 12
Presents several types of persuasion fallacies and gives examples of each. Shows how to apply the tests of validity to each fallacy. Distinguishes faulty persuasion from legitimate appeal. Gives fallacies from each classification of persuasive appeal - ethical, emotional and logical. Part of a 26 - part series.
Social Science
Dist - INSTRU

Persuasion - or, the Spoken Heart 13 MIN
16mm
Color
LC 80-700273
Presents a monolog spoken by a girl who is trying to understand her own difficulties in loving.
Fine Arts
Dist - GIANVJ **Prod** - GIANVJ 1978

Persuasive appeals 28 MIN
U-matic / BETA / VHS
Communication skills 2 - advanced series
Color (H C G)
$101.95, $89.95 purchase _ #CA - 11
Distinguishes among a belief, an attitude and a value. Identifies the four functions that attitudes perform, as well as the three basic persuasive appeals - ethical, emotional and logical. Compares the forms of appeals and identifies the advantages and disadvantages of each. Part of a 26 - part series.
Social Science
Dist - INSTRU

The Persuasive Essay 30 MIN
U-matic
Communicating with a Purpose Series
(H C A)
Examines the technique employed when composing a persuasive essay. Explores techniques used when specifying either fact or opinion and the concept of propaganda.
Education; Literature and Drama
Dist - ACCESS **Prod** - ACCESS 1982

Persuasive expert testimony 60 MIN
VHS
Color (C PRO)
$195.00 purchase _ #FVZ050S
Features trial attorney David M Malone in a presentation on effective use of expert testimony. Covers topics including creating rapport between the witness and the jury, use of repetition, visual aids, defusing cross - examination, and others. Consists of two videocassettes and a support manual.
Civics and Political Systems
Dist - NITA **Prod** - NITA 1990

Persuasive Negotiating 60 MIN
BETA / 16mm
Color
Shows Herb Cohen, professional negotiator, demonstrating a collaborative or win - win approach to negotiation. A sequel to Everyone's A Negotiator.
Business and Economics; Psychology
Dist - CBSFOX **Prod** - CBSFOX

The Persuasive Paper 30 MIN
VHS / U-matic
Writing for a Reason Series
Color (C)
English Language
Dist - DALCCD **Prod** - DALCCD

Persuasive Presentations 120 MIN
VHS / 16mm
(C PRO)
$995.00 purchase, $350.00 rental
Covers organizing techniques, creating visuals, staging, delivery skills, promoting questions and large group presentations.
Education
Dist - VLEARN **Prod** - TWAIN

Persuasive presentations guaranteed 41 MIN
VHS
Color (G)
$495.00 purchase, $150.00 rental _ #V1073 - 06
Shows how to prepare a talk and speak effectively before a group, with attention to dealing with nervousness, organizing notes, and using visual aids for confidence before listeners. Includes video and leader's guide.
Business and Economics; English Language; Psychology
Dist - BARR

Persuasive Speaking 60 MIN
U-matic / VHS
(H C A PRO)
$39.95_#EQ400V
Introduces viewers to skills in communication necessary to a successful career. Emphasizes styles in public speaking, while applying techniques used in mass audience speeches to intimate conversations. Covers vital elements of effective communication, such as body language and eye contact.
Business and Economics; Social Science
Dist - CAMV **Prod** - CAMV

Persuasive Speaking
VHS / BETA
Color
Gives pointers from communications experts and shows clips of master speakers in action to explain the keys to speech and presentation - making.
English Language
Dist - GA **Prod** - GA

Persuasive Speaking
VHS
$39.95 purchase - #013 - 258
Assists people develop good speech communication skills which are necessary for success on the job.
English Language; Social Science
Dist - CAREER **Prod** - CAREER

Persuasive speaking 60 MIN
VHS
Color (H C A)
$29.95 purchase _ #S00058
Features public speaking experts Dorothy Sarnoff, Roger Ailes, Aram Dashian, Jr, and Michael Kahn on the subject of persuasive speaking. Tells how to assess an audience, eliminate nervous speech habits, use eye contact and body language, and come across effectively on camera. Produced by Esquire magazine.
English Language
Dist - PBS **Prod** - WNETTV
UILL

Persuasive Speaking - Making Effective Speeches and Presentations 60 MIN
VHS / U-matic
JIST Conference Presentations
(C A P)
$69.95 _ #PC4V
Unveils tips and tactics for preparing and delivering effective speeches. Features such personalities as Ronald Reagan, Dick Cavett, and Michael Kahn.
Business and Economics; English Language
Dist - JISTW **Prod** - JISTW

Persuasive techniques for opening statements 150 MIN
VHS
Color (PRO)
$64.00, $149.00 purchase, $49.00 rental _ #CP-53210, #CP-63210
Provides examples illustrating establishing a theme, holding jurors' interest, introducing issues, and neutralizing jurors' biases. Shows how to use description and humor in opening statements. Tape program materials are included.
Civics and Political Systems
Dist - CCEB

Persuasive Writing 40 MIN
VHS / U-matic
Effective Writing Series
Color
English Language; Psychology
Dist - DELTAK **Prod** - TWAIN

Persuasive Writing 15 MIN
VHS / U-matic
Zebra Wings Series
Color (I)
Considers persuasion and defines propaganda. Analyzes letters to the editor, public service announcements and political persuasive writing.
English Language; Literature and Drama
Dist - AITECH **Prod** - NITC 1975

PERT - Milestone System - PERT Introduction 27 MIN
16mm
Color
LC 74-705349
Brings management and operating levels together for the planning and execution of complex research and development projects.
Business and Economics
Dist - USNAC **Prod** - USN 1962

Pertaining to Chicago 15 MIN
16mm
Color (J H C)
LC FIA58-931
Presents a series of personal impressions of certain aspects of Chicago, featuring architectural masterpieces of Sullivan, Frank Lloyd Wright and Mies Van der Rohe. Includes the fire escapes of the Loop and the electrical signs which express the American obsession with motion.
Fine Arts; Geography - United States; Psychology; Sociology
Dist - RADIM **Prod** - DAVISJ 1958

Pertaining to Marin 10 MIN
16mm
Color
Presents the water - colorist John Marin and studies his oils and water - colors.
Fine Arts
Dist - RADIM **Prod** - FILIM

Peru 3 MIN
16mm
Of all Things Series
Color (P I)
Discusses the country of Peru.
Geography - World
Dist - AVED **Prod** - BAILYL

Peru 50 MIN
VHS
Secrets of lost empires series
Color; PAL (G)
PdS99 purchase; Not available in the United States or Canada
Observes the efforts of rigging expert Philip Petit as he attempts to recreate one of the woven grass suspension bridges of the ancient Incas. Intersperses practical demonstrations and debate with location sequences in Peru and explorations of the Incan culture. Part two of a four - part series.
History - World; Industrial and Technical Education
Dist - BBCENE

Peru - a golden treasure 53 MIN
VHS
Color (G)
$29.95 purchase _ #ST - IV1556
Explores the legacy of the Incas in Lima. Travels to Cuzo, City of Kings. Discovers the oceanside resort of Las Dunas. Views the Nazca Lines.
Geography - World
Dist - INSTRU

Peru - children's rights - 4 28 MIN
VHS / U-matic
People matter series
Color (H C G)
$385.00, $355.00 purchase _ #V474
Examines how the civil war in Peru has resulted in blatant violations of children's rights. Shows that the war between the guerrilla movement and the Peruvian military has left many orphans, while other children develop physical and mental scars growing up in the midst of violence. Part four of a six - part series on human rights around the globe.
Civics and Political Systems; Geography - World; Health and Safety; Sociology
Dist - BARR **Prod** - CEPRO 1989

Peru - Inca Heritage 17 MIN
U-matic / VHS / 16mm
Color (J)
LC 76-701557
Compares the culture of the Indians of Peru with that of their ancestors, the Incas. Discusses such points as the similarities between religious festivals of the two groups. Concludes with an exploration of the Inca citadel of Machu Pichu, which remains a fitting monument to the stone architecture of the Incas.
Geography - World; Sociology
Dist - AIMS **Prod** - HP 1970

Peru - People of the Sun 25 MIN
U-matic / VHS / 16mm
People and Places of Antiquity Series
Color (J)
LC 77-703106
Presents a shortened version of the motion picture entitled People Of The Sun. Establishes the geographical setting and traces the migrations of prehistoric peoples into Peru.
Geography - World; History - World; Sociology
Dist - CORF **Prod** - CFDLD 1977

Peru - politics and the Drug War 29 MIN
VHS
America's drug forum second season series
Color (G)
$19.95 purchase _ #221
Considers the case of Peru and the fact that more and more United States tax dollars are on their way to Latin America, ostensibly to curtail the flow of drugs to the United States. Asks whether exported US policy is helping or hurting human rights in Andean countries. Features Roberto MacLean, Peruvian ambassador to the US, Holly Burkhalter, America's Watch, Peter Andreas, research associate, Institute for Policy Studies.
Civics and Political Systems; History - United States; Psychology
Dist - DRUGPF **Prod** - DRUGPF 1992

Peru - the Revolution that Never was 27 MIN
U-matic / VHS / 16mm
South America - a Trilogy Series
Color (J H)
Tells how creating cooperatives from farms formerly run by 15,000 rich landowners forced Peruvian peasants into poverty, even though they now own the land. States that lack of both capitol for financing and cash for provisions produce the irony of revolution that brought a decade of despair.
Geography - World
Dist - MEDIAG **Prod** - THAMES 1979

Peru - the Vanishing Animals 27 MIN
16mm
Color (P)
As a result of the irresponsible slaughter of wildlife, Felipe Benavide attempts to instill an awareness that the extinction of any species is an irreparable tragedy.
Geography - World; Science - Natural
Dist - AVED **Prod** - FISC

A Peruvian equation 10 MIN
VHS
Magnum eye series
Color (G)
$125.00 purchase, $30.00 rental
Documents the Quecha Indian community in Lima, Peru, who descended from the mountains in search of work and consequently were forced to set up shantytowns just outside the city. Features the film director living with one family for a week where life includes a daily struggle for food and water; everpresent military brutality; and the unpredictable and ultraviolent Shining Path. This portrait is enhanced by subtitles which provide a stream of statistics that place the family's life in the broader context of Peruvian poverty. Directed by Gilles Peress. Part of a series by photographers from the Magnum Photo Agency.
Fine Arts; Geography - World; Social Science; Sociology
Dist - FIRS **Prod** - MIYAKE 1993

The Peruvian Paso - a borrowed treasure 28 MIN
VHS
Color (A)
Presents the Peruvian Paso horse, unique for its 'termino' flowing movement of the front legs, which allows it to be a fine riding horse. Reveals that the Paso is descended from horses introduced in Peru by Spanish conquistadors. Includes footage from two horse farms, a horse show in

Reno, Nevada, and an illustration of the traditional Peruvian riding implements. Available only to public television stations.
Agriculture; Physical Education and Recreation
Dist - SCETV **Prod** - SCETV 1990

The Peruvian Paso - for those with Champagne Taste 25 MIN
BETA / VHS
Color
Gives a history of the Peruvian Paso horse. Demonstrates the smoothness of the gait. Talks about buying and showing.
Physical Education and Recreation
Dist - EQVDL **Prod** - MHRSMP

Peruvian Plateau 10 MIN
16mm / U-matic / VHS
Color; B&W (I J H)
Illustrates how the plateau and its climate served as barriers to progress. Contrasts primitive methods of weaving, mining, smelting and transportation with mass production and other benefits of modern technology.
Geography - World
Dist - IFB **Prod** - GRUBBS 1947

Peruvian Weaving - a Continuous Warp for 5,000 Years 25 MIN
16mm / U-matic / VHS
Color (A)
Discusses warp pattern weaving in Peru, an Andean Indian tradition. Interviews Dr Junius Bird of the American Museum of Natural History, who traced this weaving tradition in Peru back to a pre - ceramic period. Includes archival footage of his 1946 archaeological excavation in Huaca Prieta.
Fine Arts; Science - Physical; Social Science
Dist - CNEMAG **Prod** - CNEMAG 1980

PES - safety and computer control 23 MIN
VHS
Color; PAL; NTSC (G IND)
PdS69, PdS85.50 purchase
Shows that Programmable Electronic Systems - PES - enable production facilities to be very efficient, but withdrawing human control means that safety has to be thoroughly planned from the beginning.
Health and Safety; Industrial and Technical Education; Psychology
Dist - CFLVIS

Pesah - the Jewish festival of Passover 24 MIN
VHS
Color; PAL (I J H)
PdS29.50 purchase
Introduces members of the Jewish faith talking about their religion in their own way and in their chosen setting. Provides teachers with an authentic means of helping pupils to understand what Judaism is all about.
Religion and Philosophy
Dist - EMFVL

Pest Control 18 MIN
VHS / 16mm
Catering with Care Series
Color (H)
$205.00 purchase
Shows a dirty, pest - infested kitchen to illustrate the importance of cleanliness and maintenance in keeping pests away. Includes support materials.
Agriculture; Health and Safety; Home Economics; Industrial and Technical Education
Dist - FLMWST

Pest Control - Fumigating with Aluminum Phosphide 25 MIN
16mm
Color
LC 78-701081
Presents step - by - step procedures for fumigating stock and a railroad car of foodstuff. Shows how to handle aluminum phosphide safely and gives defumigation instructions.
Agriculture; Health and Safety; Social Science
Dist - USNAC **Prod** - USA 1977

Pest control integrated pest management - a chance for the future 20 MIN
U-matic / VHS
Color (IND)
$45.00, $95.00 purchase _ #TCA16737, #TCA16736
Defines Integrated Pest Management and its environmental and economic advantages for growers. Suggests that the boll weevil eradication program was a perfect example of IPM. Shows that there are a variety of alternatives to pesticide use.
Agriculture
Dist - USNAC **Prod** - USDA 1987

Pest control series
Presents a two - part series on pest control. Includes the titles Herbicide Use and Safety in the Landscape, Pesticide Safety in the Landscape.
Pest control series 78 MIN
Dist - VEP **Prod** - VEP 1987

Pest Management 30 MIN
U-matic / VHS
Corn - Planning to Harvest Series
Color
Discusses a concept called integrated pest management, a program that integrates the control techniques for weeds, diseases, insects and mites into the total cropping program which is a business approach to protecting the crop against economic loss. Discusses four basic pest management tools, choosing a hybrid variety of seed that has a resistance to disease and a tolerance to insects, planting crops on a planned rotation basis, early planting to give the corn a head start on pests, and pesticides. Shows many of the common pests and ways to determine their presence.
Agriculture
Dist - NETCHE **Prod** - NETCHE 1981

Pest Management and Programs 14 MIN
U-matic / VHS
Supervisor's Role in Food Distribution Series
Color
Discusses rodents and their control in the food distribution center, including control measures and recommended practices either for an in - house or contracted control program.
Agriculture; Health and Safety; Social Science
Dist - PLAID **Prod** - PLAID

Pest wars 50 MIN
VHS
Horizon series
Color; PAL (H A C)
PdS99 purchase; Not available in the United States or Canada
Examines the use of chemical pesticides in the 20th century and mentions that scientists have begun to question their efficiency. Proposes that natural solutions are becoming more mainstream in global agriculture. Part of the Horizon series.
Agriculture; Fine Arts
Dist - BBCENE

Pesta Pilau Pinang 25 MIN
16mm
Color
Shows a festival on the island of Penang, Malaysia.
Geography - World
Dist - PMFMUN **Prod** - FILEM 1968

Pesticide and Herbicide Kit
VHS
Color (G)
$200.00 purchase _ #6 - 100 - 000P
Teaches the terms and concepts needed to make safe decisions about landscape herbides in part one. Looks at the proper ways to reduce the hazards of pesticides.. Includes pest identification, toxicity, labels, pesticide formulation, application equipment, mixing and application techniques, disposal and storage in part two.
Agriculture; Health and Safety
Dist - VEP **Prod** - VEP

Pesticide And Herbicide Kit Series
Herbicide use and safety in the landscape
Pesticide Safety in the Landscape 27 MIN
Dist - VEP

Pesticide and Wildlife 27 MIN
16mm
Color
LC 74-706514
Explains why military and civilian pesticide operators should exercise caution in the use of pesticides. Gives specific recommendations for protecting wildlife from the hazards of pesticide use.
Agriculture; Science - Natural
Dist - USNAC **Prod** - USN 1973

Pesticide application techniques
VHS
On target - in tree spraying series
Color (G)
$75.00 purchase _ #6 - 208 - 301P
Trains tree workers. Discusses hydraulic tree sprayers and their use in dispersing pesticides. Looks at environmental considerations. Demonstrates movement and positioning of spray guns, spraying patterns and distance from targets, reducing spray drift and wind considerations. Includes an eight - page calibration manual. Produced by the National Arborist Association.
Agriculture; Health and Safety; Psychology; Science - Natural
Dist - VEP

Pesticide applicator safety 18 MIN
U-matic / VHS
Integrated pest management series
Color (IND)
$45.00, $95.00 purchase _ #TCA17370, #TCA17369
Describes the clothing and equipment required for different types and applications of pesticides.
Agriculture
Dist - USNAC **Prod** - USNPS 1987

Pesticide Politics 23 MIN
U-matic / VHS
B&W (J)
Focuses on the residents of Pritt, Minnesota, who took legal action against the spraying of '245 T,' the chemical brush - killer used in Vietnam that created health problems for animals, people and vegetation overseas and at home.
History - United States; Science - Natural
Dist - UCV **Prod** - UCV

Pesticide Safety in the Greenhouse
VHS
Color (G) (SPANISH)
$89.95 purchase _ #6 - 064 - 104P, #6 - 064 - 204P - Spanish Version
Takes a greenhouse managerial look at pesticide safety. Emphasizes employee supervision around pesticides. Looks at greenhouse spray scheduling, application techniques, storage and handling.
Agriculture; Health and Safety; Psychology
Dist - VEP **Prod** - VEP

Pesticide Safety in the Landscape 27 MIN
VHS
Pesticide And Herbicide Kit Series
Color (G)
$89.95 purchase _ #6 - 100 - 100P
Looks at the proper ways to reduce the hazards of pesticides. Includes pest identification, toxicity, labels, pesticide formulation, application equipment, mixing and application techniques, disposal and storage. Part two of a two - part series on herbicides and pesticides.
Agriculture; Health and Safety
Dist - VEP **Prod** - VEP

Pesticides and other environmental risks 22 MIN
VHS
Color (H C)
$59.00 purchase _ #510
Interviews Bruce Ames, one of the world's leading biochemists. Explains why Ames thinks pesticide residues are not as serious a problem as once thought. Discusses why nature's chemicals may be more serious.
Sociology
Dist - HAWHIL **Prod** - HAWHIL

Pesticides and Pest Management 26 MIN
U-matic / VHS
Supervisor's Role in Food Distribution Series
Color
Presents pest management problems, pesticides and regulations controlling their use as applicable to supervisory monitoring of in - house pest activity and control.
Agriculture; Health and Safety; Industrial and Technical Education; Social Science
Dist - PLAID **Prod** - PLAID

Pesticides in Agriculture 30 MIN
VHS
Color (G)
$89.95 purchase _ #6 - 105 - 100P
Examines the issues of pesticide use in agriculture.
Agriculture; Health and Safety
Dist - VEP **Prod** - VEP

Pesticides in forestry - risk analysis 46 MIN
U-matic / VHS
Pesticides in forestry series
Color (G A PRO)
$130.00 purchase, $25.00 rental _ #911.4
Combines the concepts of environmental behavior of chemicals and toxicology to discuss risk analysis. Discusses margins of safety, probabilities of reversible and irreversible effects, potency and ecosystem recovery. Conducts two sample calculations to illustrate the quantitative basis of risk analysis - one for reversible effects and one for cancer. Includes a instructor's guide and viewer's summary. Part of a four - part series providing a comprehensive look at the behavior of pesticides in the forest environment, toxicology and risk analysis.
Agriculture; Science - Natural
Dist - OSUSF **Prod** - OSUSF 1991

Pesticides in forestry - series introduction 6 MIN
VHS / U-matic
Pesticides in forestry series

Color (G)
Available only with purchase or rental of other programs in series. No additional charge _ #911.1
Outlines the content of the entire series and describes the relationship between the various components. Part of a four - part series providing a comprehensive look at the behavior of pesticides in the forest environment, toxicology and risk analysis.
Agriculture; Science - Natural
Dist - OSUSF **Prod** - OSUSF 1987

Pesticides in forestry series
Pesticides in forestry - risk analysis 46 MIN
Pesticides in forestry - series introduction 6 MIN
Pesticides in forestry - the behavior of pesticides in the forest environment 29 MIN
Pesticides in forestry - toxicology 32 MIN
Dist - OSUSF

Pesticides in forestry - the behavior of pesticides in the forest environment 29 MIN
VHS / U-matic
Pesticides in forestry series
Color (G)
$130.00 purchase, $25.00 rental _ #911.2
Describes the movement, persistence and fate of pesticides in forest environments. Discusses interactions that occur between pesticides and environment and the role of these two factors in determining the fate of pesticides following application. Includes a instructor's guide and viewer's summary. Part of a four - part series providing a comprehensive look at the behavior of pesticides in the forest environment, toxicology and risk analysis.
Agriculture; Science - Natural
Dist - OSUSF **Prod** - OSUSF 1987

Pesticides in forestry - toxicology 32 MIN
U-matic / VHS
Pesticides in forestry series
Color (G A PRO)
$130.00 purchase, $25.00 rental _ #911.3
Introduces the basic concepts of forest pesticide toxicology. Discusses the dose - response relationship. Gives examples of the interaction between pesticides and biological systems and how these interactions affect toxicity. Defines key terms and concepts. Includes a instructor's guide and viewer's summary. Part of a four - part series providing a comprehensive look at the behavior of pesticides in the forest environment, toxicology and risk analysis.
Agriculture; Science - Natural
Dist - OSUSF **Prod** - OSUSF 1990

Pestilence and punishment 40 MIN
VHS
Dreaded lurgi series
Color (H C A)
PdS65 purchase _ Not available in the United States
Highlights the moral issues surrounding the plague, with discussion of its physical consequences. Part of a four-part series.
Health and Safety
Dist - BBCENE

Pests 30 MIN
VHS / 16mm
Home Gardener Series
Color (C A)
$85.00, $75.00 purchase _ 7 - 20
Discusses insects that hurt or help in the home garden.
Science - Natural
Dist - CDTEL **Prod** - COAST 1980

Pet Care 10 MIN
16mm
Color (P I)
LC 75-701529
Emphasizes the 'why' of pet care. Explains the basics of 'how' to care for the family pet. Discusses the elements of food, water, sleep, exercise and general care.
Science - Natural
Dist - FFORIN **Prod** - FFORIN 1974

Pet Evaporated Milk 2 MIN
U-matic / VHS
Color
Shows a classic television commercial featuring a lullaby with mother and baby.
Business and Economics; Psychology; Sociology
Dist - BROOKC **Prod** - BROOKC

Pet or pest 30 MIN
VHS
Cats series
Color; PAL (H C A)
PdS65 purchase
Describes the history of the domestic cat. Delves into the myths and legends about the feline, and discusses the varieties of cat. Part three of a five part series.
Science - Natural
Dist - BBCENE

The Pet Shop 15 MIN
U-matic / VHS
Strawberry Square Series
Color (P)
Fine Arts
Dist - AITECH **Prod** - NEITV 1982

Pete Rose - Reach for the Sky
VHS
(H C A)
$39.95 purchase _ #MXS151V
Presents athlete Pete Rose who discusses how to develop a winning attitude and how to apply this attitude to personal life. Focuses on bringing out natural talents and building confidence.
Physical Education and Recreation; Psychology
Dist - CAMV

Pete Rose - Winning Baseball 55 MIN
VHS
(SPANISH)
$29.95 _ #CIN200V
Presents baseball star Pete Rose who explains proper stance, step and weight distribution, bat control, switch hitting and bunting, as well as plate coverage. Focuses on mental motivation.
Physical Education and Recreation
Dist - CAMV

Pete Seeger - solo 52 MIN
VHS / U-matic
Rainbow quest series
Color
Features Pete Seeger, tracing the history of political satire from the early days of the U S.
Fine Arts; Literature and Drama
Dist - NORROS **Prod** - SEEGER

Pete Takes a Chance 26 MIN
U-matic / VHS / 16mm
Color (I J)
Deals with a youngster who borrows money from a girl for joke and novelty items then buys raffle tickets instead. Shows that when one of the boy's dissatisfied customers threatens violence for a refund, the lad sells off his tickets, repays his disgruntled customer and creditor, and surprieses all with the raffle's outcome.
Business and Economics; Religion and Philosophy; Sociology
Dist - BCNFL **Prod** - PLAYTM 1983

Peter and Elba - Travel Training of a Retardate 15 MIN
16mm
Color
LC 76-700403
Features Elba Becknam, a travel training instructor, teaching Peter Panos, a retardate, how to travel through the streets of New York.
Education; Physical Education and Recreation; Psychology
Dist - HF **Prod** - NYCDT 1976

Peter and the magic egg 24 MIN
VHS
Color (P)
Presents an animated version of 'Peter and the Magic Egg.' Tells about Mama and Papa Doppler whose farm is threatened by the villain Tobias Tinwhistle. When baby Peter arrives, he grows as big as a 12 year old in just one year and solves all the Dopplers' problems - until Tinwhistle gets the best of him, too. Only a miracle, a magic egg, negates Tinwhistle's evil.
Fine Arts; Literature and Drama
Dist - VIEWTH **Prod** - VIEWTH

Peter and the Magic Egg 24 MIN
U-matic / 16mm
Color (K P I)
$540.00, $250.00 purchase _ #4448
Presents an animated film, narrated by Ray Bolger, about Mama and Papa Doppler who needed a miracle to save their farm from arch - villain Tobias Tinwhistle. The miracle arrives in the form of Peter, a baby who grew to be as big as a twelve - year - old in one year.
Fine Arts; Literature and Drama
Dist - PERSPF **Prod** - PERSPF 1984
CORF

Peter and the magic seeds 25 MIN
VHS
Color (P I R)
$14.95 purchase _ #35 - 8106 - 8936
Portrays a young boy who learns that self - worth comes from giving yourself to others.
Literature and Drama; Religion and Philosophy
Dist - APH **Prod** - WORD

Peter and the Wolf 28 MIN
16mm / U-matic / VHS
Color (P I) (SWEDISH)
A Swedish language version of the film of Peter And The Wolf, Prokofiev's musical introduction to the orchestra. Features real people and real animals in a turn - of - the - century American setting. Narrated by Ray Bolger, with music performed by the Santa Cruz Chamber Orchestra.
Fine Arts; Foreign Language
Dist - PFP **Prod** - SHIRE

Peter and the Wolf 14 MIN
U-matic / VHS / 16mm
Color (P)
An excerpt from the feature length film 'MAKE MINE MUSIC,' which is an adaptation of Serge Prokofieff's famous composition in which the characters in the tale are represented by different musical instruments.
Fine Arts
Dist - CORF **Prod** - DISNEY 1964

Peter and the Wolf 12 MIN
16mm
Animatoons Series
Color
LC FIA67-5507
Tells the story of Peter, a little boy who wanders into the forest after his grandfather warned him not to leave the yard. Shows how Peter meets a wolf in the forest and captures him.
Literature and Drama
Dist - RADTV **Prod** - ANTONS 1968

Peter Berger 30 MIN
VHS
World Of Ideas With Bill Moyers - Season I - series
Color (G)
$39.95 purchase _ #BMWI - 124
Interviews Peter Berger, a teacher of religion and sociology. Discusses the strong economic growth of East Asia, focusing on Japan. Suggests that while the Japanese style of capitalism is successful, it may not work in other nations. Hosted by Bill Moyers.
Business and Economics; Civics and Political Systems; Geography - World
Dist - PBS

Peter Berton 5 MIN
U-matic / VHS
Write on, Set 1 Series
Color (J H)
Teaches the use of commas with dates and addresses.
English Language
Dist - CTI **Prod** - CTI

Peter Block on consulting 30 MIN
VHS
(PRO)
$39.95 one half inch video purchase _ #C451 - AJ; #451-BE
Discusses the profession of consulting. Topics covered include authenticity, risk, roles, deroling, power, integrity, destiny, pressure and fads. J William Pfeiffer interviews Peter Block.
Business and Economics; Religion and Philosophy
Dist - UNIVAS **Prod** - UNIVAS 1987
UNIASS

Peter Bohlin - architecture 15 MIN
U-matic / VHS
Pass it along series
Color (I)
$30.00 purchase, $25.00 rental, $75.00 self dub
Takes viewers to a special place, Shelley Ridge Girl Scout Camp near Philadelphia, Pennsylvania, where Peter Bohlin, architect, explains to a group of young people there that Shelley Ridge is designed to fit the surrounding environment. Focuses on important architectural details and stresses to students how architecture should be planned around the environment.
Fine Arts; Science - Natural
Dist - GPN **Prod** - SCITV 1987

Peter Brook's La Tragedie De Carmen 82 MIN
VHS
Color (S)
$39.95 purchase _ #833 - 9280
Presents the film adaptation of the Peter Brook's stage production of 'La Tragedie De Carmen' by Bizet. Stars Helene Delavault, Howard Hensel, Agnes Host and Jake Gardner.
Fine Arts; Geography - World
Dist - FI **Prod** - NVIDC 1987

Peter Caranicas and Bobby Mariano 30 MIN
VHS / U-matic
Eye on Dance - Dance on Television Series
Color
Discusses narrowcasting dance for cable television.
Fine Arts
Dist - ARCVID **Prod** - ARCVID

Peter Carey 45 MIN
VHS

Color (H C G)
$79.00 purchase
Features the Australian writer with Margaret Walters discussing the role of Australian culture in its art and literature, including Aboriginal culture. Talks about his work including the short stories of The Fat Man in History, and Oscar and Lucinda.
Geography - World; History - World; Literature and Drama; Religion and Philosophy
Dist - ROLAND **Prod** - INCART

Peter, Donald, Willie, Pat 28 MIN
VHS
Color (G)
$195.00 purchase, $100.00 rental _ #CE - 118
Follows four homeless men through their routines over a period of six months. Documents their techniques for survival on the streets. Peter is an ex - hippie who collects trash to sell at flea markets. Donald served ten years at Leavenworth on a bank robbery charge. Willie came to the shelter to recover after he lost six fingers to frostbite after a night in a snowbank. Pat was sexually abused as a child and has been in and out of foster homes for 13 years. Produced by Jim Kaufman and Mike Majoros.
Sociology
Dist - FANPRO

Peter Drucker 30 MIN
VHS
World Of Ideas With Bill Moyers - Season I - series
Color (G)
$39.95 purchase _ #BMWI - 148
Interviews management expert Peter Drucker, who discusses changes in the American working class and challenges for the US in the 21st century.
Business and Economics; Fine Arts; History - World; Sociology
Dist - PBS

Peter Everwine - 5 - 10 - 73 25 MIN
VHS / Cassette
Poetry Center reading series
B&W (G)
#8 - 5B
Features the writer reading his works at the Poetry Center, San Francisco State University. Available only for listening purposes at the Center; not for sale or rent.
Literature and Drama
Dist - POETRY **Prod** - POETRY 1973

Peter Grimes 160 MIN
VHS
Color (S)
$39.95 purchase _ #623 - 9562
Stars Jon Vickers in the title role of 'Peter Grimes' by Benjamin Britten. Includes Heather Harper and Norman Bailey as other cast members in the Royal Opera production.
Fine Arts; Geography - World
Dist - FI **Prod** - NVIDC 1986

The Peter Hill Puzzle 31 MIN
16mm / VHS / U-matic
Professional Management Program Series
Color (J) (SPANISH)
LC 75-702992
Tells a story about an organization with serious low - cost problems that threaten its existence and the search for the reasons why. Identifies the causes of mismanagement to be lack of communication, poor leadership, isolation and strong - willed, uncontrollable subordinates.
Business and Economics; Foreign Language; Psychology
Dist - NEM **Prod** - NEM 1975

Peter Jennings reporting - man, sex and rape 75 MIN
VHS
ABC News collection series
Color (G)
$29.98 purchase _ #630246188X
Features broadcast journalist Peter Jennings who reports from Palm Beach, Florida, site of the highly publicized trial of William Kennedy Smith for rape. Raises questions about the volatile subject of rape.
Civics and Political Systems
Dist - INSTRU **Prod** - ABCNEW 1992

Peter Keenan - Why Me 5 MIN
VHS / U-matic
B&W
Pokes fun at everything.
Fine Arts; Literature and Drama
Dist - ARTINC **Prod** - ARTINC

Peter M Senge - A Crisis of perception 100 MIN
Cassette
1992 conference collection series
Color; PAL (C G PRO)
$150.00, $25.00 purchase _ #V9201, #T9201
Features the author of The Fifth Discipline and The Art and Practice of the Learning Organization. Identifies a crisis in perception as a challenge to creating learning organizations and a learning society. Speculates that the individual and collective ability to perceive into the future will be required for success in classrooms and boardrooms. Part of a three - part series on the 1992 Systems Thinking in Action Conference.
Business and Economics; Education; Psychology; Sociology
Dist - PEGASU **Prod** - PEGASU 1992

Peter M Senge - Transforming the practice of management 60 MIN
Cassette
Organizational learning series
Color (C G PRO)
$60.00, $20.00 purchase _ #V9101, #T9109
Features the author of The Fifth Discipline and The Art and Practice of the Learning Organization. Discusses a new management paradigm that is emerging and how it will change the role of the leader to that of designer, teacher and steward. Part of two parts on organizational learning.
Business and Economics; Guidance and Counseling; Psychology; Sociology
Dist - PEGASU **Prod** - PEGASU 1991

Peter Martins - a Dancer 54 MIN
VHS
Color (G)
$39.95 purchase _ #1118
Presents the dancing and choreography of Peter Martins. Features three full - length pas de deux - Suzanne Farrell and Martins in the first pas de deux from 'Chaconne' and the pas de deux from 'Agon' choreographed by Balachine, and Heather Watts and Daniel Duell performing the last duet from Martins' 'Calcium Light Night.'.
Fine Arts; Physical Education and Recreation
Dist - KULTUR

Peter Pan
VHS / 16mm
Color (P)
$22.22 purchase _ #COL59233
Re - issues the original Mary Martin classic.
Fine Arts; Literature and Drama
Dist - EDUCRT

Peter Parker on Life and Death of King John 25 MIN
VHS
Shakespeare in perspective series
Color (A)
PdS45 purchase _ Unavailable in USA
Films Peter Parker and his commentary on location and includes extracts of the Shakespeare play The Life and Death of King John. Challenges many of the more traditional interpretations of Shakespeare's works. Part of a series produced between 1978 and 1985.
Literature and Drama
Dist - BBCENE

The Peter Principle 25 MIN
16mm / U-matic / VHS
Color
LC 77-702223
Features Dr Laurence J Peter as he discusses the Peter principle and its implications for individual employees and the organizations in which they work.
Business and Economics; Psychology
Dist - FI **Prod** - BBCTV 1975

Peter Principle 10 MIN
BETA / VHS / U-matic
(G)
$100.00
Reports on the principle "In the heirarchy indivuals tend to rise to their level of incompetence." Dr. Laurence Peter caught the world's attention with his book.
Psychology
Dist - CTV **Prod** - CTV 1985

The Peter Principle - Why Things Go Wrong 31 MIN
U-matic / VHS / 16mm
Color (H C A)
LC 75-701565
Presents Dr Laurence Peter explaining in a satire of management theory, why things always go wrong.
Business and Economics; Guidance and Counseling; Psychology
Dist - SALENG **Prod** - SALENG 1975

Peter Rabbit and Friends from the Picture Book Parade
U-matic / VHS
Mono (K P I)
Includes the following titles - THE TALE OF PETER RABBIT, THE TALE OF MR JEREMY FISHER, THE TALE OF TOM KITTEN, THE TALE OF BENJAMIN BUNNY and THE TALE OF TWO BAD MICE.
English Language; Literature and Drama
Dist - WWS **Prod** - WWS 1986

Peter Sichel's Complete Guide to Wine 92 MIN
16mm
Color
Features Peter Sichel of the French and German wine - producing family, as he discusses domestic and imported vintages. Explains every aspect of wine - making, blending, tasting and storing.
Home Economics; Physical Education and Recreation
Dist - NYFLMS **Prod** - NYFLMS 1973

The Peter Tchaikovsky Story 30 MIN
U-matic / VHS / 16mm
Color (I)
LC FIA65-1027
Tells the story of the struggles, loves, failures and successes of Peter Tchaikovsky.
Biography; Fine Arts
Dist - CORF **Prod** - DISNEY 1964

Peter the First - Pt 1
VHS
Color (G)
$29.95 purchase _ #1619
Presents a two - part epic by Soviet director Vladimir Petrov, 'Peter The Firest.' Tells the story of Peter the Great who made Russia a world power. Part 1 portrays the founding of St Petersburg and the creation of the Russian navy.
Civics and Political Systems; Foreign Language; Geography - World; History - World
Dist - KULTUR

Peter the First - Pt 2
VHS
Color (G)
$29.95 purchase _ #1620
Presents a two - part epic by Soviet director Vladimir Petrov, 'Peter The Firest.' Tells the story of Peter the Great who made Russia a world power. Part 2 recreates Peter's battle with the King of Sweden, the Russian nobility, and his own son Alexei, whom Peter sentenced to death for treason.
Civics and Political Systems; Foreign Language; Geography - World; History - World; Sociology
Dist - KULTUR

Peter the Great 28 MIN
U-matic / VHS
Once upon a Time - Man Series
Color (P I)
$99.00
Traces the evolution of Russian history in the 17th century. Shows the transformation of Russia to a European power under Peter the Great. Animated.
Civics and Political Systems; History - World
Dist - LANDMK **Prod** - LANDMK 1981

Peter the pigeon 5 MIN
16mm
Otto the auto - pedestrian safety - C series
Color (K P)
$30.00 purchase _ #185
Features Otto the Auto and his animal friends who teach the importance of walking on the left side facing traffic. Part of a series on pedestrian safety. Complete series available on 0.5 inch VHS.
Health and Safety
Dist - AAAFTS **Prod** - AAAFTS 1959

Peter Ustinov Presents the Orchestra
VHS / 16mm
Color (G)
$18.88 purchase _ #MRPV107
Introduces the symphonic orchestra and classical music.
Fine Arts
Dist - EDUCRT

Peter Ustinov's Leningrad 25 MIN
U-matic / VHS / 16mm
Cities Series
Color (H C A)
LC 80-701295
A shortened version of the motion picture Peter Ustinov's Leningrad. Presents actor Peter Ustinov on a tour of the city of Leningrad.
Geography - World; Sociology
Dist - LCOA **Prod** - NIELSE 1980

Peter Ustinov's Leningrad 51 MIN
U-matic / VHS / 16mm
Cities series
Color (I H C A) (SPANISH)
LC 78-701703
Presents actor Peter Ustinov as he tours the Russian city of Leningrad.
Geography - World; Sociology
Dist - LCOA **Prod** - NIELSE 1978

Peter Ustinov's Leningrad 25 MIN
16mm / U-matic / VHS
Color (H C A) (SPANISH)
Investigates the culture and history of Leningrad, the birthplace of the Russian Revolution. Edited version.

Foreign Language; Geography - World
Dist - LCOA **Prod** - NIELSE 1980

Peter Weir 45 MIN
VHS
Filmmakers on their craft series
Color (PRO G C)
$79.00 purchase, $29.00 _ #729
Features Peter Weir, director of Green Card. Interviews Weir in 1982, shortly after the production of The Year of Living Dangerously. Discusses his working methods and the dark elements of his films. Considers the components of good education - experience, excitement and risk - versus Weir's overcoming his own bad education to show the roots of Dead Poets Society, the films Weir would make in 1988. Features Peter Thompson as interviewer. Part of a six - part series on world famous filmmakers produced by the Australian Film, Television and Radio School.
Fine Arts; Industrial and Technical Education
Dist - FIRLIT

Peter's Chair 6 MIN
16mm / U-matic / VHS
Color (K P T)
LC 76-713614
Illustrates the skill of Ezra Jack Keats in capturing the small but important events that fill a youngster's life.
Fine Arts; Literature and Drama
Dist - WWS **Prod** - WWS 1971

Peters series
Beyond close to the customer
Dist - VLEARN

Petersburg - Cannon Firing 6 MIN
16mm
Color (A)
LC 77-703128
Demonstrates, through the use of historically accurate horse - drawn limbers, uniforms and guns, how a mounted artillery unit moved, set up and fired its artillery piece.
History - United States
Dist - USNAC **Prod** - USNPS 1973

Petey and Johnny
U-matic / VHS
Color
Describes the experiences of a former teen gang leader who returns as a social worker.
Sociology
Dist - DIRECT **Prod** - DREWAS

Petey the Pelican 10 MIN
U-matic / VHS / 16mm
Color (P) (DANISH)
LC 80-700598;
Introduces Petey the Pelican, who tells about the growth of his new feathers, his fear of gulls, his eating habits, his parents' fishing tactics and his struggle to learn how to fly.
Science - Natural
Dist - IFB **Prod** - BERLET 1978

Petit mal 18 MIN
16mm
Color (G)
$40.00 rental
Offers 'The abstracted voice of one and many women searching,' according to filmmaker Betzy Bromberg.
Fine Arts; Sociology
Dist - CANCIN

Petra 5 MIN
U-matic
See, Hear - the Middle East Series
Color (J)
Shows Petra, once a prosperous city at the crossroads of trade routes, now home to a handful of Bedouin who occupy crumbling ruins.
Geography - World; History - World; Religion and Philosophy
Dist - TVOTAR **Prod** - TVOTAR 1980

Petra - on fire video event
VHS
Color (J H R)
$59.95 purchase _ #35 - 85090 - 533
Utilizes songs by the Christian rock group Petra to present the message that a person can live an 'on fire' life for God. Includes leader's guide with games, skits and life simulations.
Fine Arts; Religion and Philosophy
Dist - APH **Prod** - WORD

The Petrified dog 18 MIN
16mm
B&W (G)
$45.00 rental
Introduces Sidney Peterson, one of the originators of the American avant - garde cinema, and his classic films made in San Francisco between 1947 and 1950. Features a metaphorical film dealing with the search for meaning in life by way of portraying chases within chases. A mother runs after her child, a man seems to be pursuing himself and the pursuit of art is represented by painter daubing at a landscape in an empty frame.
Fine Arts; Literature and Drama; Psychology; Religion and Philosophy
Dist - CANCIN

The Petrified Forest 83 MIN
16mm
B&W
Presents an adaptation of Robert Sherwood's play about a group of travelers trapped by a fleeing gangster.
Fine Arts; Literature and Drama
Dist - UAE **Prod** - UAA 1936

The Petrodollar coast - Pt 2 59 MIN
VHS
The Oil kingdoms series
Color (S)
$49.00 purchase _ #315 - 9006
Offers a fascinating look at the history of five small countries - Kuwait, Qatar, Bahrain, the United Arab Emirates and Oman - and their transfoarmation from Biblical times to today's extremely wealthy socities. Reveals that the discovery of oil is merly the latest chapter in the colorful story of the Persian Gulf. Part 2 of three parts shows how immense wealth has changed the desert society near the Persian Gulf. The contrast between traditional and modern is clear in the existence of camel races and luxury cars, women newscasters and veiled wives.
Foreign Language; Geography - World; History - World; Religion and Philosophy; Social Science; Sociology
Dist - FI **Prod** - PP 1986

Petroleum Exploration 31 MIN
U-matic / VHS
Petroleum Geology Series
Color (IND)
Industrial and Technical Education; Science - Physical
Dist - GPCV **Prod** - GPCV

Petroleum Exploration Methods 53 MIN
U-matic / VHS
Basic and Petroleum Geology for Non - Geologists - Reservoirs and - '- Series; Reservoirs
Color (IND)
Industrial and Technical Education; Science - Physical
Dist - GPCV **Prod** - PHILLP

Petroleum Geology Case Histories 58 MIN
U-matic / VHS
Petroleum Geology Series
Color (IND)
Industrial and Technical Education; Science - Physical
Dist - GPCV **Prod** - GPCV

Petroleum Geology - Eastern United States 49 MIN
U-matic / VHS
Basic and Petroleum Geology for Non - Geologists - Petroleum Geology'Series; Petroleum geology
Color (IND)
Industrial and Technical Education; Science - Physical
Dist - GPCV **Prod** - PHILLP

Petroleum Geology Series

Drilling and Completing a Well	45 MIN
Hydrocarbons	33 MIN
Petroleum Exploration	31 MIN
Petroleum Geology Case Histories	58 MIN
Reservoir Mechanics and Secondary and Tertiary Recovery	27 MIN
Reservoir Rocks	37 MIN
Source Rocks, Generation, Migration, and Accumulation	33 MIN
Traps	43 MIN
Well Logging	40 MIN

Dist - GPCV

Petroleum Geology - Western United States 56 MIN
VHS / U-matic
Basic and Petroleum Geology for Non - Geologists - Petroleum Geology'Series; Petroleum geology
Color (IND)
Industrial and Technical Education; Science - Physical
Dist - GPCV **Prod** - PHILLP

Petroleum Geology - World 39 MIN
VHS / U-matic
Basic and Petroleum Geology for Non - Geologists - Petroleum Geology'Series; Petroleum geology
Color (IND)
Industrial and Technical Education; Science - Physical
Dist - GPCV **Prod** - PHILLP

Petroleum Geology - World Exploration 27 MIN
U-matic / VHS
Basic and Petroleum Geology for Non - Geologists - Petroleum Geology'Series; Petroleum geology
Color (IND)
Industrial and Technical Education; Science - Physical
Dist - GPCV **Prod** - PHILLP

Petroleum Industry 3 MIN
16mm
Of all Things Series
Color (P I)
Discusses the petroleum industry.
Business and Economics; Social Science
Dist - AVED **Prod** - BAILYL

Petroleum - River of Energy 59 MIN
VHS / 16mm
Color (S)
$350.00 purchase _ #284301
Follows the journey of petroleum from raw to finished product. Explains in simple terms the stages of exploration, acquisition of rights, drilling, production and marketing, natural gas processing, oil refining, petrochemicals and transportation. Investigates specialized recovery techniques used for heavy oil, tar sands and offshore drilling. Reviews the highlights of oil history, the creation of Canada's first oil company, the first oil well in North America - Williams #1 - drilled in 1858, and the building of pipelines beginning in 1889 under the Detroit River, to the construction of the Inter - Provincial, Trans - Mountain and Trans - Canada pipelines years later.
Geography - World; History - World; Industrial and Technical Education; Social Science
Dist - ACCESS **Prod** - ACCESS 1988

Petroleum Safety Hazard Precautions at Unit and Organizational Level 26 MIN
U-matic / VHS / 16mm
B&W (A)
Illustrates safe handling practices at military field fuel supply points, explains the health hazards posed by fuel and shows how fire may occur.
Civics and Political Systems; Health and Safety; Social Science
Dist - USNAC **Prod** - USA 1984

Petroleum Stock Footage 12 MIN
16mm
Color (IND)
Presents footage from PETEX movies cut together and printed as a B - wind roll. Also available as a CRI, can be used in movie or video productions without copyright infringement.
Business and Economics; Industrial and Technical Education; Social Science
Dist - UTEXPE **Prod** - UTEXPE

Petronella 12 MIN
U-matic / VHS / 16mm
Captioned; Color (P I) (SWEDISH)
LC 77-703085
Presents an animated fairytale about a princess who, because she is an only child, must perform the traditionally princely duty of rescuing a princess. Shows how she rescues a prince instead. Based on the book Petronella by Jay Williams.
Fine Arts; Literature and Drama
Dist - ALTSUL **Prod** - ALTSUL 1977

Pets 10 MIN
VHS
Stop, look, listen series
Color; PAL (P I J)
Shows the teacher with his dog and parrot, also with various pets from school needing homes during the holidays - the rabbit, budgie and tortoise. Reveals that his neighbor keeps pigeons, a cat and a dog as pets. Part of a series of films which start from some everyday observation and show more of what is happening, how and why. Builds vocabulary and encourages children to be more observant.
English Language; Science - Natural; Social Science
Dist - VIEWTH

Pets 30 MIN
U-matic
Today's Special Series
Color (K P)
Develops language arts skills in children. Programs are thematically designed around subjects of interest to youngsters. Action takes place in a department store where people, mannequins, puppets, comic characters and special guests present a light hearted approach to language arts.
Fine Arts; Literature and Drama; Psychology
Dist - TVOTAR **Prod** - TVOTAR 1985

Pets 25 MIN
16mm / U-matic / VHS
Untamed World Series
Color; Mono (J H C A)
$400.00 film, $250.00 video, $50.00 rental
Presents a detailed look at pets, caring for them, different types, history of domestication, and individual profiles.
Science - Natural
Dist - CTV **Prod** - CTV 1971

Pets - a Boy and His Dog 11 MIN
16mm / U-matic / VHS
Color (K P I)
LC 79-705639
Shows the companionship and affection between a boy in the inner city and his pet. No narration.
Guidance and Counseling; Psychology; Science - Natural; Sociology
Dist - PHENIX **Prod** - GABOR 1969

Pets - a First Film 14 MIN
16mm / U-matic / VHS
Color (K P I)
LC 79-700487
Presents the story of a little boy who searches for the owner of a beautiful dog and in the process learns about animal shelters, veterinarians, pet stores and the responsibilities that accompany the fun of having a pet.
Science - Natural
Dist - PHENIX **Prod** - BEANMN 1979

Pets - a Girl and Her Lamb 11 MIN
U-matic / VHS / 16mm
Color (P I)
LC 70-706592
Presents the story of Linda, who learns that even though she loves her pet lamb and tries to take good care of him, he is just not the right kind of pet for her home setting.
Social Science
Dist - PHENIX **Prod** - GABOR 1969

Pets and People 14 MIN
16mm
Color
Presents a primer for pet owners, including choosing the right pet for the owner's lifestyle and rules for the proper care and feeding of a dog or cat. Hosted by Ed Asner.
Guidance and Counseling; Science - Natural
Dist - MTP **Prod** - PURINA 1982

Pets and their Care 15 MIN
U-matic / VHS / 16mm
Color (P)
$35 rental _ #9802
Teaches children that fresh food, clean water, love and affection, a clean home, exercise, baths, grooming, and regular medical care are important to their pets.
Science; Science - Natural
Dist - AIMS **Prod** - SAIF 1985

Pets and their wild relatives 15 MIN
VHS / U-matic / 16mm / BETA
Exploring the animal kingdom series
Color (K P)
$245.00, $68.00 purchase _ #C50521, #C51369
Compares pets with their wild relatives and notes similar characteristics. Part of a five - part series on the animal kingdom.
Science - Natural
Dist - NGS **Prod** - NGS 1989

Petunia 30 MIN
VHS / 16mm
Art of decorating cakes series
(G)
$49.00 purchase _ #BCD25
Instructs in the art of decorating cakes. Shows how to hand - mold petunias out of gum paste. Illustrates the technique of making the flower in the palm of the hand with the aid of small rolling sticks. Taught by Leon Simmons, master cake decorator.
Home Economics; Industrial and Technical Education
Dist - RMIBHF **Prod** - RMIBHF

Petunia 10 MIN
16mm / U-matic / VHS
Color (K P)
LC 74-715124
Features Petunia, the silly goose, who goes about giving advice to all the farm animals with a book under her wing which she can't read. Concludes with naive Petunia learning a bit of philosophy and the definition of wisdom.
English Language; Literature and Drama
Dist - WWS **Prod** - AVANZ 1971

Peutz - Jeghers Syndrome 30 MIN
16mm
Color (PRO)
Presents two interesting patients with Peutz - Jeghers syndrome and illustrates the essential diagnostic components, complications and surgical treatment of this disease.
Health and Safety; Science
Dist - ACY **Prod** - ACYDGD 1964

Pewter 15 MIN
Videoreel / VT2
Making Things Work Series
Color
Home Economics
Dist - PBS **Prod** - WGBHTV

Peyote queen 8 MIN
16mm
Color (G)
$15.00 rental
Pursues the color of ritual and thought with abstractions drawn directly on the film. Journeys through the underworld of sensory derangement. Produced by Storm De Hirsch.
Fine Arts
Dist - CANCIN

Peyronie's Disease 11 MIN
U-matic / VHS
Color (PRO)
Describes a surgical technique to correct the effects of Peyronie's disease.
Health and Safety
Dist - WFP **Prod** - WFP

Pfingstausflug 88 MIN
16mm
Color (GERMAN)
A German language motion picture. Presents an elderly couple who feel hampered in their activities and bored with everyday life, and who make their escape from a nursing home.
Foreign Language; Sociology
Dist - WSTGLC **Prod** - WSTGLC 1978

PFR 27 MIN
16mm
Color (IND)
Records the construction of the Prototype Fast Reactor.
Science - Physical
Dist - UKAEA **Prod** - UKAEA 1975

PFS - database and spreadsheet level II 50 MIN
VHS
Spreadsheet series
Color (J H C G)
$29.95 purchase _ #VP135V
Offers intermediate concepts in PFS dataabase and spreadsheet. Allows viewer to see keyboard and monitor simultaneously so that students can see the result of every keystroke. Part of a nine - part series on spreadsheets.
Business and Economics; Computer Science
Dist - CAMV

PFS - First Choice level II - database and spreadsheet 50 MIN
VHS
PFS series
Color (G)
$29.95 purchase _ #60023
Introduces PFS database. Looks at planning, creating and building a database, exiting and retrieving, searching, using wild cards. Examines the spreadsheet and entering formulas. Part of a series on PFS software training.
Computer Science; Mathematics
Dist - CARTRP **Prod** - CARTRP

PFS - First Choice level III - putting it all together 40 MIN
VHS
PFS series
Color (G)
$29.95 purchase _ #60083
Looks at creating a report from a PFS database. Examines editing a report, creating graphs, pulling graphs from a spreadsheet, creating slides on the wordprocessor and using a modem with PFS First Choice. Part of a series on PFS software training.
Computer Science; Mathematics
Dist - CARTRP **Prod** - CARTRP

PFS - first choice - word processor introduction 54 MIN
VHS
Word processing series
Color (J H C G)
$29.95 purchase _ #VP130V
Introduces concepts in PFS - First Choice - word processing. Allows viewer to see keyboard and monitor simultaneously so that students can see the result of every keystroke. Part of a series on word processing.
Business and Economics; Computer Science
Dist - CAMV

PFS - first publisher 48 MIN
VHS
Desktop publishing series
Color (J H C G)
$29.95 purchase _ #VP136V
Discusses PFS - First Publisher. Allows viewer to see keyboard and monitor simultaneously so that students can see the result of every keystroke. Part of two parts on desktop publishing.
Computer Science
Dist - CAMV

PFS - putting it all together level III 40 MIN
VHS
Spreadsheet series
Color (J H C G)
$29.95 purchase _ #VP139V
Offers advanced concepts in PFS dataabase and spreadsheet. Allows viewer to see keyboard and monitor simultaneously so that students can see the result of every keystroke. Part of a nine - part series on spreadsheets.
Business and Economics; Computer Science
Dist - CAMV

PFS series
Introduction to PFS - First Choice - the word processor 54 MIN
Introduction to PFS - First Publisher
PFS - First Choice level II - database and spreadsheet 50 MIN
PFS - First Choice level III - putting it all together 40 MIN
Dist - CARTRP

PG&E's state - of - the - art scheduling tool for hydro systems
VHS
Color (C PRO G)
$150.00 purchase _ #85.02
Reveals that a comprehensive hydro - scheduling system, HYSS, was developed for PG&E to produce optimal release policies for each of the 86 hydropower plants in the 23 - river basin hydroelectric system. Discloses that the use of HYSS has helped increase production of hydropower, resulting in a reduction of revenues required from ratepayers of an estimated $10 - $45 million each year. Pacific Gas and Electric Company. Yoshiro Ikura, George Gross, Gene S Hall.
Business and Economics; Social Science
Dist - INMASC

PH 21 MIN
VHS / U-matic
Fluids and electrolytes series
Color (PRO)
Discusses normal maintenance of acid - base balance and the body's buffering systems. Explains the chemistry of hydrogen in movements.
Health and Safety; Science; Science - Natural
Dist - BRA **Prod** - BRA

The pH meter 11 MIN
VHS
Chemistry master apprentice series
Color (H C)
$49.95 purchase _ #49 - 7206 - V
Uses a pH - ion meter and combination electrode to titrate an acid sample with standard base. Part of the Chemistry Master Apprentice series.
Science; Science - Physical
Dist - INSTRU **Prod** - CORNRS

Ph7 - 68 C Catalase Test for Mycobacterium Tuberculosis 5 MIN
U-matic
Color
LC 80-706132
Presents step - by - step procedures for performing a 68 degree C catalase test for mycobacterium tuberculosis, pointing out necessary precautions.
Health and Safety; Science
Dist - USNAC **Prod** - CFDISC 1978

Phacoemulsification 11 MIN
16mm / U-matic / VHS
Color (A)
Describes cataract formation, anatomy of the eye and the Phacoemulsification procedure. Details possible complications and benefits of this technique.
Health and Safety; Science - Natural
Dist - PRORE **Prod** - PRORE

Phacoemulsification 7 MIN
VHS
3 - part cataract series
Color (G)
$100.00 purchase, $40.00 rental _ #5312S, #5312V
Explains, using computer graphics, what the lens is, where it is and how clouding causes vision problems. Reveals that in phacoemulsification, an outpatient procedure, the lens is broken up, removed and replaced with a plastic lens; the surgery has a high success rate. Part of a three - part series.
Health and Safety; Science - Natural
Dist - AJN **Prod** - VMED

Phaethon 5 MIN
16mm / U-matic / VHS
Mythology of Greece series
Color (I J H)

LC 88-71594
Illustrates the tale of Phaethon who insisted upon steering the sun - god's chariot across the sky, only to kill himself and create havoc on earth.
Literature and Drama
Dist - BARR **Prod** - BRIANJ 1987

Phaethon 7 MIN
16mm
Color
LC 73-700689
Presents an experimental film directed to sensory stimulation. Features expanding and contracting superimposed concentric circles, kaleidoscopic images of geometrically patterned female torsos and exploding colors accompanied by electronic music.
Fine Arts; Psychology
Dist - CFS **Prod** - FRERCK 1972

Phaethon and Rhodes 11 MIN
VHS / 16mm
Greek and Roman Mythology in Ancient Art Series
Color (I)
LC 90708206
Surveys the myths of Helios and Phaethon. Theorizes about the origins of Rhodes.
Fine Arts; History - World; Religion and Philosophy
Dist - BARR

Phaeton 5 MIN
U-matic / VHS / 16mm
Mythology of Greece series
Color (I J H)
$115.00, $80.00, $110.00 _ #B509
Deals with the Greek myth about Phaeton's death to save the world.
Religion and Philosophy
Dist - BARR **Prod** - BARR 1987

Phagocytes - the Body's Defenders 10 MIN
16mm
Color (I)
LC FIA65-1700
Presents microphotographs of the circulatory system and the processes of mitosis and phagocytosis. Shows in detail how the body is protected from disease by white blood corpuscles, or phagocytes.
Health and Safety; Science - Natural
Dist - SF **Prod** - SF 1965

Phalaropes 3 MIN
16mm
Of all Things Series
Color (P I)
Discusses the birds known as phalaropes.
Science - Natural
Dist - AVED **Prod** - BAILYL

The Phans of Jersey City 49 MIN
16mm / U-matic / VHS
Color (H C A)
LC 81-700279
Introduces Mr Phan, a Vietnamese refugee who was a successful businessman in Saigon during the Vietnamese war but who now lives on welfare while his children hold menial jobs. Shows how a large refugee family is attempting to cope with an alien society.
History - United States; Sociology
Dist - FI **Prod** - HSP 1981

Phantasmagoria 8 MIN
16mm
B&W (C)
Illustrates an abstract expression of conflict, using ball bearings in weird, surrealistic settings. Evokes subjective responses.
Industrial and Technical Education; Religion and Philosophy
Dist - CFS **Prod** - OPLIN

Phantastron 26 MIN
16mm
B&W
LC 74-705352
Identifies phantastron circuit and states the purpose of each component. Constructs a time amplitude graph during explanation of circuit operation. (Kinescope).
Industrial and Technical Education; Science - Physical
Dist - USNAC **Prod** - USAF

Phantasy 5 MIN
16mm
Color; B&W (I)
LC 74-701547
Depicts the feeling of loneliness by using various objects and media found in a cellar in order to express a young girl's longing.
Guidance and Counseling; Psychology
Dist - CELLAR **Prod** - CELLAR 1970

A Phantasy 8 MIN
16mm / U-matic / VHS
Color (H C)
A surrealist abstract art film with pastel drawings and 'CUT - OUT' animation by Norman Mc Laren, saxophone music and synthetic sound by Maurice Blackburn.
Fine Arts
Dist - IFB **Prod** - NFBC 1952

Phantom India series
Bombay - the future India 52 MIN
Dream and reality 52 MIN
The Impossible camera 52 MIN
The Indians and the Sacred 52 MIN
A Look at the Castes 52 MIN
On the fringes of Indian society 52 MIN
Things seen in Madras 52 MIN
Dist - NYFLMS **Prod** - NYFLMS 1952

Phantom lake 25 MIN
VHS
Sparky's animation series
Color (P I R)
$19.95 purchase, $10.00 rental _ #35 - 817 - 2020
Uses a ghost story to teach the message that God's love can free people from fear.
Literature and Drama; Religion and Philosophy
Dist - APH **Prod** - ANDERK

Phantom of Liberty 104 MIN
16mm
Color (FRENCH (ENGLISH SUBTITLES))
Presents a comedy that contemplates man's survival in spite of his idiocies. Comprised of dozens of stories that lead from one to another with a dreamlike logic. Includes English subtitles.
Fine Arts; Foreign Language
Dist - TLECUL **Prod** - TLECUL

The Phantom of the bell tower 25 MIN
VHS
Detective stories for math problem solving series
Color (I J H)
$175.00 purchase _ #CG - 880 - VS
Reveals that the old bell tower at the edge of town, abandoned for 20 years, has started ringing again at the same time as a series of strange 'hauntings.' Shows that a pair of junior high detectives have uncovered a series of clues but students watching the video must solve the mystery. Includes a kit with clues and artifacts. Requires the breaking of a number - sequence code and the solving of a complex map problem. Part of a series.
Literature and Drama; Mathematics; Psychology; Social Science
Dist - HRMC **Prod** - HRMC

The Phantom of the Opera 79 MIN
16mm
B&W
Stars Lon Chaney as a scarred genius methodically plotting revenge in the Paris Opera House.
Fine Arts
Dist - KILLIS

The Phantom of the Opera 57 MIN
16mm
B&W
Presents the melodramatic horror tale of the embittered, disfigured composer who haunts the sewers beneath the Paris Opera House and takes a pretty young singer as his protege. Stars Lon Chaney, Mary Philbin and Norman Kerry.
Fine Arts
Dist - RMIBHF **Prod** - RMIBHF 1925

Phantom of the Opera 61 MIN
16mm
B&W
Presents a melodrama about a phantom who lives in the catacombs below the Paris opera house and tutors a young singer. Shows that, driven by hatred, the phantom kills a workman and is pursued to his lair.
Fine Arts
Dist - SF **Prod** - UPCI 1925

The Phantom of the Rue Morgue 84 MIN
16mm
Color
Based on Edgar Allan Poe's 'MURDERS IN THE RUE MORGUE.' Recreates the story of young girls being murdered in the 19th century streets of Paris.
Fine Arts
Dist - TWYMAN **Prod** - WB 1954

Phantoms of the Mind 26 MIN
U-matic / VHS
Breakthroughs Series
Color
Reveals how such everyday pursuits as flying, driving, swimming, eating or even walking are unattainable for thousands of people whose lifestyles are crippled by phobias. Gives case histories from the world's first phobic clinic.
Psychology
Dist - LANDMK **Prod** - NOMDFI

The Pharaoh awakes 50 MIN
VHS
Face of Tutankhamun series
Color; PAL (G)
PdS99 purchase
Presents the legend of the curse surrounding boy king Tutankhamun's tomb and treasures. Examines how the curse retains a powerful attraction for the occult world since the 1920s. Part four of a five - part series.
History - World
Dist - BBCENE

The Pharaohs 19 MIN
VHS / U-matic
Egypt series
Color (J H C)
$250.00 purchase _ #HP - 5808C
Covers the 2500 year reign of the god - king pharaohs of ancient Egypt. Starts in the Gallery of Kings at Abydos Temple. Presents the major Egyptian gods and supernatural beasts - Hapi, Anubis, Bastet, Sekhmet, Sobek, Horus, Bes, Tawaret - and explains their relationship to the Pharaohs and the rigidly hierarchial society. Examines the Egyptian preoccupation with life after death, funeral practices, mummification and the building of the pyramids, focusing on the treasures of Tutankhamen. Part of a series on ancient Egypt.
Civics and Political Systems; History - World; Religion and Philosophy
Dist - CORF **Prod** - BBCTV 1989

The Pharaoh's belt 43 MIN
16mm
Color (G)
$120.00 rental
Assembles collages of modern advertising images taken from a consumer culture's larger - than - life presentation of its products and their promised ecstasies. Intertwines these presences and their glowing colors in the characters'search for true love. Produced by Lewis Klahr.
Business and Economics; Fine Arts; Psychology; Sociology
Dist - CANCIN

The Pharaoh's daughter 5 MIN
VHS / U-matic
Write on series; Set 2
Color (J H)
Demonstrates how to make an outline.
English Language
Dist - CTI **Prod** - CTI

Phares O'Daffer
VHS / U-matic
Third R - Teaching Basic Mathematics Skills Series
Color
Discusses the importance of providing children with extensive experience in inductive discovery of geometric relationships that occur naturally.
Education; Mathematics
Dist - EDCPUB **Prod** - EDCPUB

The Pharmacist and Cancer 22 MIN
16mm
Color (PRO)
LC 75-706083
Shows the pharmacist's role in cancer control as a link between the public and physicians. Relates symptoms to actual cancers, which are shown, and demonstrates modern medical diagnostic and therapeutic procedures.
Health and Safety
Dist - AMCS **Prod** - AMCS 1969

Pharmacology 26 MIN
U-matic / VHS
Color
Contains 26 half - hour videotape on aspects of pharmacology.
Health and Safety
Dist - TELSTR **Prod** - TELSTR

Pharmacology - Administration of Drugs 12 MIN
BETA / VHS
Color
Discusses pharmacology and how drugs are administered.
Health and Safety
Dist - RMIBHF **Prod** - RMIBHF

Pharmacology and Clinical Use of Local Anesthetics 26 MIN
U-matic / VHS
Anesthesiology Clerkship Series
Color (PRO)
Describes the physiology and pharmacology of nerve conduction. Classifies the anatomy of individual neurons, and identifies the relationship between nerve fiber size and local anesthetics. Discusses the chemical structure of both the ester and amide local anesthetics. Covers complications associated with local anesthesia and their treatment.
Health and Safety
Dist - UMICHM **Prod** - UMICHM 1982

Pharmacology and physiology - Tape 1 57 MIN
VHS
Methamphetamines - Haight - Ashbury training series
Color (G)
$250.00 purchase
Presents segments on the history, pharmacology, effects and use of other drugs in relationship to amphetamines. Describes the newest methamphetamine phenomenon, ICE. Part one of a three - part series on methamphetamines.
Guidance and Counseling; Psychology
Dist - FMSP

Pharmacology - Drug Legislation and Standardization 15 MIN
BETA / VHS
Color
Health and Safety
Dist - RMIBHF **Prod** - RMIBHF

Pharmacology - General Principles 30 MIN
16mm
Pharmacology Series
B&W (C)
LC 73-703330
Health and Safety; Psychology
Dist - TELSTR **Prod** - MVNE 1971

Pharmacology of Antiarrhythmic Drugs, Pt 1 - Electrophysiology and Quinidine 22 MIN
U-matic / VHS
Color (PRO)
Develops an understanding of quinidine's pharmacological and electrophysiological effects upon the cardiovascular system.
Health and Safety
Dist - UMICHM **Prod** - UMICHM 1975

Pharmacology of Antiarrhythmic Drugs, Pt 3 - Propranolol and Bretylium 25 MIN
VHS / U-matic
Color (PRO)
Concentrates on the clinical pharmacology of propranolol and hretylium in their antiarrhythmic applications and contraindications.
Health and Safety
Dist - UMICHM **Prod** - UMICHM 1976

Pharmacology of Antiarrhythmic Drugs, Pt 2 - Procainamide, Lidocaine and DPH 30 MIN
U-matic / VHS
Color (PRO)
Discusses procainamides, lidocaine and diphenylhydantoin in terms of drug action, clinical use, administration, contraindications and the possibility of adverse effects. Compares the agents in this program with guinidine in both structure and action.
Health and Safety
Dist - UMICHM **Prod** - UMICHM 1975

The Pharmacology of Drug Abuse 48 MIN
16mm
Films and Tapes for Drug Abuse Treatment Personnel Series
Color (PRO)
LC 73-703450
Presents Dr Sidney Cohen, associate professor of psychiatry at the University of Southern California in Los Angeles, who discusses the pharmacology of various drugs of abuse. Includes definitions and explanations of how drug abuse affects the body, the psychopharmacology of the treatment of drug abuse and other related issues. Covers the nervous system in relation to drug abuse.
Health and Safety; Psychology; Science - Natural
Dist - NIMH **Prod** - NIMH 1973

Pharmacology of Neuromuscular Transmissions in Normal and Diseased States 52 MIN
U-matic
Intensive Course in Neuromuscular Diseases Series
Color (PRO)
LC 76-706074
Presents Dr David Grob lecturing on the pharmacology of neuromuscular transmissions in normal and diseased states.
Health and Safety; Science; Science - Natural
Dist - USNAC **Prod** - NINDIS 1974

Pharmacology of Oncologic Agents, Pt 1 24 MIN
VHS / U-matic
Color (PRO)
Details the general therapeutic principles which must be understood when administering oncologic agents, the chemotherapy program using cyclophosphamide, methotrexate, 5 - fluorouracil and Adriamycin, the acute and chronic toxicities of these agents and the way to minimize the occurrance of excessive toxicity of these agents by appropriate dose modification.
Health and Safety; Science
Dist - UMICHM **Prod** - UMICHM 1977

Pharmacology of Oncologic Agents, Pt 2 21 MIN
VHS / U-matic
Color (PRO)
Details the general therapeutic principles which must be understood when administering oncologic agents, the chemotherapy programs using bleomycin, vincristine, vinblastine, CCNU, BCNU and dacarbazine, the acute and chronic toxicities of these agents and the way to minimize the occurrence of excessive toxicity by appropriate dose modifications.
Health and Safety; Science
Dist - UMICHM **Prod** - UMICHM 1978

Pharmacology of Oncologic Agents, Pt 3 14 MIN
U-matic / VHS
Color (PRO)
Discusses types of bone marrow toxicity due to various chemotherapeutic agents, the appropriate management of bone marrow toxicity in the neutropenic cancer patient, and newer approaches to the management of the bone marrow toxicity such as platelet and granulocyte transfusion therapy.
Health and Safety; Science; Science - Natural
Dist - UMICHM **Prod** - UMICHM 1980

Pharmacology - Parenteral Administration 15 MIN
VHS / BETA
Color
Describes the administration of drugs by injection.
Health and Safety
Dist - RMIBHF **Prod** - RMIBHF

Pharmacology - Prescription 5 MIN
BETA / VHS
Color
Explains the abbreviations used and how to make out and phone in prescriptions.
Health and Safety
Dist - RMIBHF **Prod** - RMIBHF

Pharmacology Series

Adrenocorticorsteroids	30 MIN
Anticoagulants and hematinics	30 MIN
Antitubercular drugs and broad spectrum antibiotics	30 MIN
Cardiac depressants and vasodilators	30 MIN
Cardiac stimulants	30 MIN
Diuretics	30 MIN
General Anesthetics	30 MIN
Hematinics	30 MIN
Histamine, Antihistamine and Drugs used for Motion Sickness	30 MIN
Insulin and Oral Hypoglycemics	30 MIN
Local anesthetics	30 MIN
Narcotic and Non - Narcotic Analgesics	30 MIN
Parasympathomimetic Blocking Agents, Anticholinergics and Antispasmodics	30 MIN
Parasympathomimetics	30 MIN
Parkinsonism and Convulsive Disorders	30 MIN
Pharmacology - General Principles	30 MIN
Pituitary Hormones	30 MIN
Psychopharmacological Drugs - Pt 1	30 MIN
Psychopharmacological Drugs - Pt 2	30 MIN
Sedatives, Hypnotics and Alcohol	30 MIN
Sex hormones - oxytocics	30 MIN
Skeletal Muscle Relaxants, their Antagonists	30 MIN
Sulfonamides and penicillins	30 MIN
Sympathomimetic Blocking Agents, Ganglionic Blocking Agents and Anti - Hypertensive Agents	30 MIN
Sympathomimetics	30 MIN
Thyroid and antithyroid drugs	30 MIN

Dist - TELSTR

Pharmacy 15 MIN
VHS / 16mm
(H C A)
$24.95 purchase _ #CS213
Describes the skills necessary for a career in pharmacy. Features interviews with professionals working in the field.
Guidance and Counseling
Dist - RMIBHF **Prod** - RMIBHF

Pharmacy 15 MIN
VHS / U-matic / BETA
Career Success Series
(H C A)
$29.95 _ #MX213
Portrays occupations in pharmacy be reviewing required abilities and interviewing people employed in this field. Shows anxieties and rewards involved in pursuing a career as a pharmacist.
Education; Guidance and Counseling; Health and Safety; Science
Dist - CAMV **Prod** - CAMV

Pharmacy Communication Skills Series

Barriers to communication	16 MIN
Factors Affecting Pharmacist - Patient Communication	62 MIN
Interviewing Techniques and Communication Skills Test	21 MIN

Dist - HSCIC

Pharynx and Nasal Cavities - Unit 5 16 MIN
U-matic / VHS
Gross Anatomy Prosection Demonstration Series
Color (PRO)
Describes the pharynx as it relates to the superior and middle constrictors, as well as its internal aspects, shows parts of the nasal cavity, including the nasal septum, the lateral wall, and structures related to meatuses and conchae.
Health and Safety; Science - Natural
Dist - HSCIC **Prod** - HSCIC

The Pharynx Topographical Anatomy 9 MIN
8mm cartridge / 16mm
Anatomy of the Head and Neck Series
Color
LC 75-702061; 74-705353
Views the pharynx from the rear. Shows the extent and volume that edema may assume in these areas by injecting water into the submucosa.
Science - Natural
Dist - USNAC **Prod** - USVA 1969

The Pharynxtopographical Anatomy 9 MIN
U-matic
Anatomy of the Head and Neck Series
Color (PRO)
LC 78-706251
Shows the topography of the pharynx as viewed through the posterior neck. Illustrates the extent and volume that edema may assume in these areas.
Health and Safety; Science - Natural
Dist - USNAC **Prod** - USVA 1978

Phascolarctos Cinereus - the Koala 18 MIN
U-matic / VHS / 16mm
Color (J)
LC 75-702389
Provides a study of the habitat and behavior of the Australian koala.
Geography - World; Science - Natural
Dist - ALTSUL **Prod** - FLMAUS 1974

Phase Diagrams - Getting the Whole Picture 13 MIN
U-matic
Chemistry 102 - Chemistry for Engineers - Series
Color (C)
Explains the reading and use of phase diagrams. Shows that phase diagrams are plotted from measurements of the temperature dependence of vapor pressure.
Industrial and Technical Education; Science - Physical
Dist - UILL **Prod** - UILL 1981

Phase equilibria series

Free energy curves and binary phase diagrams	10 MIN
Generation of phase diagrams from free energy curves	22 MIN
Gibbs free energy - enthalpy and entropy	11 MIN
Isothermal Sections with Simple Ternary Eutectic	8 MIN
Isothermal Sections with Solid Solution	8 MIN
Reading ternary phase diagrams	8 MIN
Ternary diagrams derived from binaries	6 MIN

Dist - PSU

Phase one cardiac rehabilitation 20 MIN
VHS / U-matic
Color (PRO C)
$395.00 purchase, $80.00 rental _ #C901 - VI - 038
Shows how cardiac rehabilitation assists patient return to optimal wellbeing by providing structured exercise and formalized education to assist with behavior modification and lifestyle change. Follows Mr S through his pre - op and post - op event hospital stay to present a structured program of phase I in - hospital cardiac rehabilitation. Emphasizes an interdisciplinary approach to assist the patient in recovery and in educating patient and family to be better prepared for the adjustments and modifications a cardiac patient requires. Presented by Kay Baber, Judy Crown, RN, Carl Erickson, RN, Laurel Kratz, Cheryl Majeske and Renata C Sampson, RN, Medical College of Virginia, Virginia Commonwealth University.
Health and Safety
Dist - HSCIC

Phase One - Prince Charles Mountains 22 MIN
16mm
Color (H C A)
LC 73-709256
Shows a party of men from the Australian National Antarctic Research Expedition conducting a topographical and geological survey of the Prince Charles Mountains in Antarctica. Includes the scientists evaluation of the material collected and the construction of maps of the surveyed area.
Geography - World; Science - Physical; Social Science
Dist - AUIS **Prod** - ANAIB 1969

The Phase - Plane Method 37 MIN
U-matic / VHS
Nonlinear Vibrations Series
B&W
Illustrates the phase - plane method for simple linear systems.
Mathematics
Dist - MIOT **Prod** - MIOT

Phase Relationships 9 MIN
VHS / 16mm
Electrical Theory Series
Color (S)
$50.00 purchase _ #241319
Illustrates 22 concepts fundamental to the training of second year electrical apprentices using graphic animation. Introduces power, apparent power and reactive power and discusses power triangles and factors in 'Phase Relationships.'.
Education; Industrial and Technical Education; Psychology
Dist - ACCESS **Prod** - ACCESS 1983

Phase Relationships in Capacitive Circuits 5 MIN
VHS / 16mm
Electrical Theory Series
Color (S)
$50.00 purchase _ #241315
Illustrates 22 concepts fundamental to the training of second year electrical apprentices using graphic animation. Explains phase relationships in capacitive circuits and how current leads voltage by 90 degrees in 'Phase Relationships In Capacitive Circuits.'.
Education; Industrial and Technical Education; Psychology
Dist - ACCESS **Prod** - ACCESS 1983

Phase Relationships in Inductive Circuits 4 MIN
VHS / 16mm
Electrical Theory Series
Color (S)
$50.00 purchase _ #241310
Illustrates 22 concepts fundamental to the training of second year electrical apprentices using graphic animation. Discusses the phase differences between BEMF, current and voltage in 'Phase Relationships In Inductive Circuits.'.
Education; Industrial and Technical Education; Psychology
Dist - ACCESS **Prod** - ACCESS 1983

Phase Relationships in RL and C Circuits 6 MIN
VHS / 16mm
Electrical Theory Series
Color (S)
$50.00 purchase _ #241318
Illustrates 22 concepts fundamental to the training of second year electrical apprentices using graphic animation. Uses phasor diagrams to show the relationship between inductive and capacitive resistance in 'Phase Relationships In RL And C Circuits.'.
Education; Industrial and Technical Education; Psychology
Dist - ACCESS **Prod** - ACCESS 1983

Phase Shift Oscillator - VT 34 MIN
16mm
B&W
LC 74-705354
Describes the principle characteristics of the phase shift oscillator, with emphasis on its frequency range, stability and economy. Explains the effect of varying feedback as well as the frequency characteristics of the phase shift oscillator. (Kinescope).
Industrial and Technical Education; Science - Physical
Dist - USNAC **Prod** - USAF 1963

Phase Zero 30 MIN
VHS / 16mm
Solar Energy Series
Color (G)
$55.00 rental _ #SLRE - 101
Examines where solar technology is currently and the direction it is moving us.
Science - Physical; Social Science
Dist - PBS **Prod** - KNMETV

Phasemicroscopy of Normal Living Blood 28 MIN
16mm
Color
Compares the various circulating blood cells as they appear in a Wright's stained preparation and in the living state when examined with dark medium contrast phase objectives. Shows the unaltered blood platelet as wells as various stages in its transformation into the vesicular platelet.
Science - Natural
Dist - UWASHP **Prod** - RUBL 1954

Phases 6 MIN
16mm / U-matic / VHS
Color
LC 77-701826
Uses animation to show a man struggling with his inner self and adapting various animal forms.
Fine Arts; Health and Safety; Psychology
Dist - PHENIX **Prod** - SELIKC 1977

Pheasants and peacocks 27 MIN
U-matic / VHS / BETA
Stationary ark series
Color; PAL (G H C)
PdS50, PdS58 purchase
Discusses the recreation of humankind, nature and wildlife in part of a 12 - part series. Features Gerald Durrell. Filmed on location in Jersey, England.
Science - Natural
Dist - EDPAT

Phedre 93 MIN
VHS
Color (H C G) (FRENCH WITH SUBTITLES)
$99.00 purchase _ #DL139
Presents a French play written in the style of a classical Greek tragedy by Jean Baptiste Racine. Stars Marie Bell.
Fine Arts; History - World; Literature and Drama
Dist - INSIM

Phenelzine Sulfate 15 MIN
16mm
Color
Deals with the issue of taking drugs to cure psychological ills. Tells how a woman who relies on phenelzine sulfate to relieve depression, stops taking the drug and ends up in the hospital faced with the choice of resuming drug usage or facing reality.
Health and Safety; Psychology
Dist - TWOCH **Prod** - TWOCH 1979

Phenix 14 MIN
16mm
Color (G)
$45.00 rental
Features the Ljubljana Clinical Center in Yugoslavia, the filmmaker's home town. Pays homage to Zdravic's father, a plastic surgeon and holistic healer.
Fine Arts
Dist - CANCIN FLMKCO **Prod** - ZDRAVI 1975

The Phenix City Story 100 MIN
16mm
B&W (H C A)
Dramatizes the history of a small Alabama town.
Fine Arts; History - United States; Sociology
Dist - CINEWO **Prod** - CINEWO ,1955

Phenomena 1 30 MIN
U-matic
Phenomena Series
Color
Looks at a unique trigger film used by teachers of English to encourage writing skills.
English Language
Dist - UMITV **Prod** - UMITV 1981

Phenomena 10 29 MIN
U-matic
Phenomena Series
Color
Reports on toxic pollutants in the Great Lakes, basket weaving, bone playing and horticulture therapy for the aged.
Fine Arts; Sociology
Dist - UMITV **Prod** - UMITV 1981

Phenomena 11 29 MIN
U-matic
Phenomena Series
Color
Covers a variety of topics including a new library addition, a glass blower who makes scientific instruments for libraries, and a visiting pet program for geriatric patients.
Social Science; Sociology
Dist - UMITV **Prod** - UMITV 1981

Phenomena 2 30 MIN
U-matic
Phenomena Series
Color
Features Ken Yoshida using songs and games to teach English to foreign - born three - to five - year - old children. Includes discussions on mushrooms and the construction of the hologram.
English Language; Sociology
Dist - UMITV **Prod** - UMITV 1981

Phenomena 3 29 MIN
U-matic
Phenomena Series
Color
Reports on a university 'fitness lab' which helps people determine their own levels of fitness. Looks at the spherocentric artificial knee. Discusses the sinking of the Edmund Fitzgerald.
Health and Safety; Physical Education and Recreation; Social Science
Dist - UMITV **Prod** - UMITV 1981

Phenomena 4 29 MIN
U-matic
Phenomena Series
Color
Examines a hospital school and a school for firefighters. Looks at the cobalt camera.
Education; Health and Safety; Industrial and Technical Education; Social Science
Dist - UMITV **Prod** - UMITV 1981

Phenomena 5 29 MIN
U-matic
Phenomena Series
Color
Includes segments on the car shredder, Pointe Mouillee, Michigan, and sickle cell anemia.
Geography - United States; Health and Safety
Dist - UMITV **Prod** - UMITV 1981

Phenomena 6 29 MIN
U-matic
Phenomena Series
Color
Reports on student industrial design projects, the study of one of the martial arts, and a child care center where children play games that have been highly structured to provide useful learning experiences.
Education; Industrial and Technical Education; Physical Education and Recreation
Dist - UMITV **Prod** - UMITV 1981

Phenomena 7 29 MIN
U-matic
Phenomena Series
Color
Includes segments on the restoration of harpsicords, a camp for children with hemophilia, laboratory animal care and competitive rowing.
Fine Arts; Physical Education and Recreation; Science
Dist - UMITV **Prod** - UMITV 1981

Phenomena 8 29 MIN
U-matic
Phenomena Series
Color
Looks at The world of miniatures, hot air ballooning, a radio telescope, the value of exercise in slowing the aging process and a computer operated 'reading machine.'.
Mathematics; Physical Education and Recreation; Science - Physical
Dist - UMITV **Prod** - UMITV 1981

Phenomena 9 29 MIN
U-matic
Phenomena Series
Color
Contains segments on a variety of sports and games which teach many topics.
Physical Education and Recreation
Dist - UMITV **Prod** - UMITV 1981

Phenomena Series

Phenomena 1	30 MIN
Phenomena 10	29 MIN
Phenomena 11	29 MIN
Phenomena 2	30 MIN
Phenomena 3	29 MIN
Phenomena 4	29 MIN
Phenomena 5	29 MIN
Phenomena 6	29 MIN
Phenomena 7	29 MIN
Phenomena 8	29 MIN
Phenomena 9	29 MIN

Dist - UMITV

Phenomenal World Series

The Circle of life	21 MIN
Flowers are forever	21 MIN
The Mystery of Mesa Verde	22 MIN
Our Living Shield	21 MIN
Our Vanishing Marshland	22 MIN
The People Places	22 MIN
The River of Life	22 MIN
The Robot Revolution	22 MIN
Seasons of Survival	21 MIN
This Trembling Earth	22 MIN
Voyage to the Galapagos	21 MIN
When the Earth Explodes	22 MIN
The Winds of Change	22 MIN

Dist - EBEC

A Phenomenological Analysis of Catatonic Expression 35 MIN
16mm
B&W
Demonstrates the strange and rigid postures, and the fixed stance and stare of the catatonic patient. Shows the discrete shifts in this rigidity and demonstrates the effects of barbiturates on catatonic stupor.
Health and Safety; Science - Natural
Dist - USVA **Prod** - USVA 1960

Phenomenon no One 7 MIN
16mm
Color
Illustrates an opticular experiment in animation, making use of graphics that, when moved, produce optical illusions of color and form from black and white material.
Fine Arts; Industrial and Technical Education
Dist - VANBKS **Prod** - VANBKS 1965

Phenomenon of Thermoelastic Instability 14 MIN
16mm
Color (C)
Reports on oscillation frequency by thermal radiation and thermoelastic instability of boons.
Science - Physical
Dist - NASA **Prod** - NASA

Phenothiazines - 1 10 MIN
VHS
Focus on pharmacy series
Color (C PRO)
$200.00 purchase, $60.00 rental _ #4310S, #4310V
Presents basic information on phenothiazine for nurses. Uses a talk - show format between a nurse and a pharmacist who discuss key points of safe administration of the drug. Covers how phenothiazine is used, how to observe target symptoms for positive therapeutic outcomes and what side effects to anticipate. Emphasizes the importance of nursing documentation and its contribution to therapy success. Includes supporting materials. Part of a six - part series on commonly used drugs in long - term care produced by the American Society of Consultant Pharmacists.
Health and Safety
Dist - AJN

Phenylketonuria, a Preventable Cause of Mental Retardation 16 MIN
16mm
Color
Illustrates the manifestation of phenylketonuria. Discusses its detection and treatment.
Health and Safety; Psychology
Dist - CFI **Prod** - CRAF 1962

Pheochromocytoma 18 MIN
16mm
Color (PRO)
Illustrates the management of a patient with pheochromocytoma. Shows diagnostic measures, preoperative preparation and methods to control fluctuation in the blood pressure.
Health and Safety; Science
Dist - ACY **Prod** - ACYDGD 1955

Pheochromocytoma - Diagnosis, Localization, Preoperative Preparation and Anterior 18 MIN
16mm
Color (PRO)
LC 75-702238
Discusses diagnosis, tumor location and preoperative preparation of a patient with pheochromocytoma and shows surgery performed for transabdominal excision of the tumor.
Health and Safety; Science
Dist - EATONL **Prod** - EATONL 1974

Phil Black, Robin Black, Wade Goss and Alvin McDuffie 30 MIN
VHS / U-matic
Eye on Dance - Broadway Dance Series
Color
Shows how the dancer prepares for Broadway.
Fine Arts
Dist - ARCVID **Prod** - ARCVID

Phil Woods Quartet 60 MIN
VHS
Color (G)
#Shanacie 6305
Records the Phil Woods Quartet in the 1970s, when Woods moved back to the United States. Includes Song for Sisyphus; A Little Piece; Only When You're in My Arms; Shaw Nuff; How's Your Mama. Recorded in the Realtime - SP mode.
Fine Arts
Dist - ROUNDR

Philadelphia
VHS
Frugal gourmet - taste of America series
Color (G)
$19.95 purchase _ #CCP821
Shows how to prepare American food from Philadelphia. Features Jeff Smith, the Frugal Gourmet. Part of a ten - part series on American cooking.
Geography - United States; History - United States; Home Economics; Physical Education and Recreation
Dist - CADESF **Prod** - CADESF

Philadelphia 76 25 MIN
16mm
Color (A)
LC 77-700695
Presents highlights of the 26th annual meeting of the Mental Health Association, held in cooperation with the National Institute of Mental Health in Philadelphia, Pennsylvania.
Geography - United States; Health and Safety; Psychology
Dist - USNAC **Prod** - NIMH 1977

The Philadelphia story 112 MIN
VHS
B&W (H C)
$39.00 purchase _ #04479 - 126
Presents a comedy about a strong - willed Philadelphia woman and her mix - up with future and former husbands. Stars Katharine Hepburn and Cary Grant.
Fine Arts; Guidance and Counseling
Dist - GA **Prod** - GA

Philadelphia - the Good Life 20 MIN
U-matic / VHS / 16mm
Celebrates the images of a great city that is enjoying a renaissance as a tourist attraction, business center and a place to study. Shows sporting events, theater, art and science, museums, parades, hotels, restaurants, shops and convention facilities.
Geography - United States; History - United States
Dist - EXARC

The Philadelphia Woodwind Quintet 30 MIN
16mm / U-matic / VHS
World of Music Series
B&W (J)
Discusses the evolution of woodwind music from exclusive use outdoors to performances for the concert hall and illustrates this with examples of compositions from various periods played by the Philadelphia Woodwind Quintet.
Fine Arts
Dist - IU **Prod** - NET 1965

Philip Garrison - 2 - 27 - 75 31 MIN
VHS / Cassette
Poetry Center reading series
Color (G)
#102 - 76
Presents the writer Philip Garrison reading from his works at the Poetry Center, San Francisco State University, with an introduction by Kathleen Fraser. Available only for listening purposes at the Center; not for sale or rent.
Literature and Drama
Dist - POETRY **Prod** - POETRY 1975

Philip Glass and the Making of an Opera 87 MIN
16mm / VHS
Color (H C)
$975.00, $350.00 purchase, $150.00 rental
Allows us an intimate look at the inspiration, development, and production of Philip Glass's third opera 'Akhnaten'.
Fine Arts
Dist - BLACKW **Prod** - BLACKW 1985

Philip Guston - a Life Lived 58 MIN
16mm / VHS
Color (H C)
$875.00, $290.00 purchase, $110.00 rental
Documents the last ten year's of Philip Guston's life. The development of his work from figurative paintings to abstraction and back again.
Fine Arts
Dist - BLACKW **Prod** - BLACKW 1981

Philip Hall Likes Me
35mm strip / VHS / Cassette
Newbery Award - Winners Series
Color (I)
$66.00, $14.00 purchase
English Language; Literature and Drama
Dist - PELLER

Philip Knight - Nike, Oregon 47 MIN
VHS
Tycoons series
Color (J H G)
$225.00 purchase
Tells how his company, Blue Ribbon Sports, developed into the Nike sports clothing empire under the direction of Philip Knight.
Business and Economics; Physical Education and Recreation
Dist - LANDMK

Philip Kotler on competitive marketing series
New directions in differentiating and positioning - Part II 70 MIN
New directions in segmenting and targeting - Part I 50 MIN
Dist - VIDART

Philip Morris in 1976 14 MIN
16mm
Color (H C A)
LC 76-703153
Shows the world's largest and most modern cigarette manufacturing complex, the Philip Morris plant in Richmond, Va. Shows Philip Morris activities in beer brewing, housing and paper manufacture.
Business and Economics; Health and Safety
Dist - LYNCHV **Prod** - PHILMO 1976

The Philip Morris Way 16 MIN
16mm
Color
LC 75-703024
Surveys the history of tobacco. Shows the manufacturing process of cigarettes from leaf to finished product. Includes a tour of the Philip Morris Operations Center in Richmond, Virginia.
Business and Economics; Geography - United States; Health and Safety
Dist - PHILMO **Prod** - PHILMO 1975

Philip Pearlstein draws the artist's model 90 MIN
Videodisc / VHS / U-matic / BETA
Color (G)
$129.95, $69.95 purchase
Features Philip Pearlstein who demonstrates step - by - step the process of drawing the human figure. Produced by Horner - Stuart - Whiteley.
Fine Arts
Dist - ARTSAM

Philip Whalen - 11 - 10 - 65 37 MIN
VHS / Cassette
NET Outtake series
B&W (G)
$15.00, $125.00 purchase, $15.00 rental _ #192 - 149
Features the writer Philip Whalen in his San Francisco apartment reading a statement on poetics, Since You Asked; A Very Complicated Way of Saying Appearances Deceive; March 1964 - The Lost Poem; The Absolute Realty Company; and The Best of It. Discusses the unnatural separation between Eastern and Western philosophy and poetry. Part of a series of films composed of outtakes from the series USA - Poetry, which was produced in 1965 - 66 for National Educational Television, using all retrievable footage to provide rare glimpses of the poets in their own settings. Interviewed by Richard O Moore.
Guidance and Counseling; Literature and Drama
Dist - POETRY **Prod** - KQEDTV 1965

Philippe Genty - France - Pt 6 57 MIN
VHS
Jim Henson Presents the World of Puppetry Series
Color (I)
$49.00 purchase _ #064 - 9016
Travels the globe to meet some of the finest puppeteers on the planet. Features Muppet creator Jim Henson as host. Part 6 of six parts features Philippe Genty of France who uses every facaet of puppetry, from stringed marionettes to hand puppets.
Fine Arts; Geography - World; Health and Safety; Literature and Drama; Sociology
Dist - FI **Prod** - HENASS 1988

Philippians and Titus
VHS
The Bible - American Sign Language translation series
Color (S R)
Presents an American Sign Language translation of the New Testament books of Philippians and Titus. Available on a free - loan basis from the Lutheran Church - Missouri Synod's Deaf Ministry.
Guidance and Counseling; Literature and Drama; Religion and Philosophy
Dist - CPH **Prod** - LUMIS

Philippians - Rejoice in the Lord 22 MIN
16mm
Color
Presents Harold Songer, professor of New Testament interpretation at Southern Baptist TheologicaL Seminary, Louisville, Kentucky, outlining the book of Philippians.
Literature and Drama; Religion and Philosophy
Dist - BROADM **Prod** - BROADM 1981

A Philippine Diary 28 MIN
VHS
Color (I J H C A)
Talks about church workers who work among the poor in the Philippines. Produced by Maryknoll.
Religion and Philosophy; Sociology
Dist - CWS

Philippines 28 MIN
Videoreel / VHS
Marilyn's Manhattan series
Color
Presents an interview with Amabassador Alejandro Yango of the Philippines. Includes a film clip on the Philippines and the Manila Conference Center. Hosted by Marilyn Perry.
Business and Economics; Civics and Political Systems; Geography - World
Dist - PERRYM **Prod** - PERRYM

Philippines 29 MIN
Videoreel / VT2
International Cookbook Series
Color
Features home economist Joan Hood presenting a culinary tour of specialty dishes from around the world. Shows the preparation of Philippine dishes ranging from peasant cookery to continental cuisine.
Geography - World; Home Economics
Dist - PBS **Prod** - WMVSTV

Philippines 51 MIN
VHS
Asian insight series; Part 5
Color (S)
$79.00 purchase _ #118 - 9015
Introduces the people and the cultures of the Asian Pacific. Presents a balanced, objective interpretation of the region's history. Illuminates past and present social structure, mores, beliefs, art and architecture to give a well - rounded look at this newly influential area. Part 5 of six parts traces the history of Spanish and American colonization in the Philippines, shows how the complex social structure of the Spanish and the religious cult of Santo Nino are still found in Filipino life today.
Foreign Language; Geography - World; History - World; Religion and Philosophy
Dist - FI **Prod** - FLMAUS 1987

Philippines - Blackboard Newspaper 15 MIN
U-matic / VHS
Color (H C A)
Studies the people, their lives and their culture on a remote island in the Philippines where there is no TV and few radios. Tells how they keep informed by using a blackboard newspaper.
Geography - World; History - World
Dist - JOU **Prod** - JOU

The Philippines - Martial Law Ends 27 MIN
VHS / U-matic
Color (H C A)
Examines the effects of martial law on the Philippines. Discusses Philippine culture, politics and economy.
History - World
Dist - JOU **Prod** - UPI

The Philippines - Ricardo the Jeepney Driver 22 MIN
U-matic / VHS / 16mm
Color (J)
Follows the activities of Ricardo and his family during their day - to - day lives in the Philippines. Describes a jeepney, developed from the battle - scarred jeeps of World War II, and now the main form of transportation in the Philippines.
Geography - World; History - World; Social Science; Sociology
Dist - HANDEL **Prod** - HANDEL 1984

Philippines - the price of power 28 MIN
VHS / 16mm
Color (G)
$500.00, $390.00 purchase, $55.00 rental
Explores the struggle of the Igorots, traditional Filipino farmers, against a huge dam project threatening their land and culture.
Civics and Political Systems; Geography - World; History - World; Industrial and Technical Education; Science - Natural; Social Science
Dist - FIRS

Phill and Jean 5 MIN
16mm
B&W (G)
$8.00 rental
Depicts a commentary about a relationship. Produced by Victor Barbieri.
Fine Arts
Dist - CANCIN

Phillip and the White Colt 23 MIN
16mm / U-matic / VHS
Captioned; Color (P I J H A) (SPANISH)
LC 73-701593
Starts with a lonely boy, mute since age five, who falls in love with a wild colt. His power of speech is restored through working with the colt.
Literature and Drama; Psychology
Dist - LCOA **Prod** - LCOA 1973

Phillip Schlechty 29 MIN
VHS
Touching the future - dialogues on education series
Color (G)
$50.00 purchase, $11.50 rental _ #36273
Features Phillip Schlechty, president of the Center for Leadership and School Reform in Louisville, KY, and author of Schools for the Twenty - First Century. Says that schools must be organized around the needs of children rather than those of adult school employees. Reveals that Schlechty recognizes business as a model for organizing success - oriented educational leadership structures. Discusses the practical impact of legislation on education. Part of a series which interviews educational leaders on ways to improve American public school education. Features Dr Rodney Reed, dean of the College of Education at Penn State as host.
Education
Dist - PSU **Prod** - WPSXTV 1991

The Phillips Collection 40 MIN
16mm
Color (H A)
$600.00 purchase, $75.00 rental
Considers the genesis and growth of the private art collection of Duncan and Marjorie Phillips which became America's first public museum of modern art.
Fine Arts
Dist - AFA **Prod** - CHCFND 1986

The Philosopher prince - Pt 9 30 MIN
U-matic / VHS
Profiles in progress series
Color (H C)
$325.00, $295.00 purchase _ #V554
Focuses on Crown Prince Hassan of Jordan, younger brother of King Hussein, who has been entrusted with the task of economic development. Looks at his creation of a 'middle path' for Jordan, traditionally a moderate country in the volatile Middle East. Part of a 13 - part series on people who are moving their tradition - bound countries into modern times.
Business and Economics; Geography - World
Dist - BARR **Prod** - CEPRO 1991

Philosophers at work - capital punishment 29 MIN
VHS / 16mm
Moral question series
Color (C A G)
$90.00 purchase _ #BPN177904
Shows Walter Berns, author of 'For Capital Punishment', defending capital punishment before a panel consisting of philosophy professors Hugo Bedau - Tufts University - , Alan Donagan - University of Chicago, and Jonathan Glover - Oxford - .
History - World; Religion and Philosophy; Sociology
Dist - RMIBHF **Prod** - RMIBHF

Philosophers at Work - Capital Punishment 30 MIN
U-matic
Color (A)
Follows a discussion by a group of philosophers on the moral questions raised by capital punishment.
Religion and Philosophy; Sociology
Dist - TVOTAR **Prod** - TVOTAR 1985

Philosophers at work - moral philosophy 29 MIN
VHS / 16mm
Moral question series
Color (C A G)
$90.00 purchase _ #BPN177903
Discusses approaches to morality. Considers the utilitarian, contractarian, and Socratic stances with references to a concentration camp situation and the issue of abortion. Features philosophy professors David Gauthier - University of Pittsburgh - , A R C Duncan - Queen's University - , Alan Donagan - University of Chicago - , and Jonathan Glover - Oxford - . Hosted by T M Robinson.
Religion and Philosophy; Sociology
Dist - RMIBHF **Prod** - RMIBHF

Philosophers at Work - Moral Philosophy 30 MIN
U-matic
Color (A)
Follows a discussion by a group of philosophers on the approaches to morality. They consider the utilitarian, contractarian and Socratic stances with reference to a concentration camp situation and the issue of abortion.
Religion and Philosophy; Sociology
Dist - TVOTAR **Prod** - TVOTAR 1985

Philosophers at work - poverty and affluence 29 MIN
VHS / 16mm
Moral question series
Color (C A G)
$90.00 purchase _ #BPN177905
Discusses whether of not the world's wealthy nations are morally obliged to aid countries suffering from poverty. Features panelists Garrett Hardin of the Department of Biology, University of California; Henry Shue from the Washington D C, Center for philosophy and Public Policy; Jonathan Glover from Oxford, England; and Alan Donagan from the University of Chicago.
Business and Economics; Civics and Political Systems; History - World; Religion and Philosophy; Sociology
Dist - RMIBHF **Prod** - RMIBHF

Philosophers at Work - Poverty and Affluence 30 MIN
U-matic
Color (A)
Follows a discussion by a group of philosophers on the question of whether the world's wealthy nations are morally obligated to aid countries suffering from poverty.
Religion and Philosophy; Sociology
Dist - TVOTAR **Prod** - TVOTAR 1985

Philosophers at work - suicide and euthanasia 29 MIN
VHS / 16mm
Moral question series
Color (C A G)
$90.00 purchase _ #BPN177908
Questions whether people have a right to choose death for themselves or others. Features philosophy professors Marvin Kohl - State University of New York - , Philippa Foot - University of California - , Jonathan Glover and Alan Donagan.
History - World; Religion and Philosophy; Sociology
Dist - RMIBHF **Prod** - RMIBHF

Philosophers at Work - Suicide and Euthanasia 30 MIN
U-matic
Color (A)
Follows a discussion by a group of philosophers on the question of whether people have a right to choose death for themselves or others.
Religion and Philosophy; Sociology
Dist - TVOTAR **Prod** - TVOTAR 1985

Philosophers at work - the morality of war 29 MIN
VHS / 16mm
Moral question series
Color (C A G)
$90.00 purchase _ #BPN177906
Debates the morality of war. Features Michael Walzer of the Institute for Advanced Study in Princeton, NJ, and philosophy professors Jonathan Glover, Alan Donagan, and Richard Brandt.
History - World; Religion and Philosophy; Sociology
Dist - RMIBHF **Prod** - RMIBHF

Philosophers' ideas that changed the world - Christ, Marx, Darwin, Freud
VHS
Color (J H C)
$197.00 purchase _ #00239 - 126
Stresses that Christ, Marx, Darwin and Freud each initiated a revolution against established doctrines. Discusses how the perceptions of millions were changed about religion, politics, natural science and psychology. Includes teacher's guide and library kit. In two parts.
Civics and Political Systems; Psychology; Religion and Philosophy; Science - Natural; Sociology
Dist - GA **Prod** - GA

Philosophies of education series

The Classical realist approach to education	29 MIN
Education as intellectual discipline	29 MIN
Education for a free society	29 MIN
Education for cultural conservation	29 MIN
Education for cultural reconstruction	29 MIN
Education for life adjustment	29 MIN
Education for moral character	29 MIN
Education for psychological maturity	29 MIN
An Experimentalist Approach to Education	29 MIN

Dist - IU

Philosophies of Representation 30 MIN
U-matic / VHS
American Government 2 Series
Color (C)
Answers questions about congressional and senatorial representation.
Civics and Political Systems
Dist - DALCCD **Prod** - DALCCD

Philosophy and Concepts of Newborn Assessment with T Berry, MD 50 MIN
Videoreel / VHS
Brazelton Neonatal Behavioral Assessment Scale Films Series
B&W
Shows Dr T Berry Brazelton conducting a detailed examination of a neonate. Explains each step in using the scale and the scoring and its meaning. Provides an introduction to the scale and its uses.

Psychology
Dist - EDC **Prod** - EDC

Philosophy and faith 60 MIN
VHS / U-matic
Art of being human series
Color (H C A)
Discusses the connection between philosophy and faith.
Religion and Philosophy
Dist - FI **Prod** - FI 1978

Philosophy and human values
VHS / Cassette
Color (C A)
$149.95, $89.95 purchase _ #AI - B469
Presents eight lectures on views of the human condition as discussed by Socrates, Augustine, Kant, Hegel, Mill, Marx, Nietzche and Freud. Features Asst Prof Rick Roderick of Duke University as lecturer.
Religion and Philosophy
Dist - TTCO **Prod** - TTCO

Philosophy and literature 45 MIN
VHS
Men of ideas series
Color; PAL (H C A)
PdS99 purchase; Not available in Canada.
Explains in simple terms the main developments in Western philosophy from the 19th century to the present day. Features a contemporary thinker discussing his ideas on philosophy and literature with Bryan Magee. Part fourteen of a fifteen part series.
Literature and Drama; Religion and Philosophy
Dist - BBCENE

Philosophy and moral values 60 MIN
U-matic / VHS
Art of being human series
Color (H C A)
Discusses the connection between philosophy and moral values.
Religion and Philosophy
Dist - FI **Prod** - FI 1978

Philosophy and politics 45 MIN
VHS
Men of ideas series
Color; PAL (H C A)
PdS99 purchase; Not available in Canada.
Explains in simple terms the main developments in Western philosophy from the 19th century to the present day. Features a contemporary thinker discussing his ideas about philosophy and politics with Bryan Magee. Part thirteen of a fifteen part series.
Civics and Political Systems; Religion and Philosophy
Dist - BBCENE

Philosophy - eastern - western consciousness 60 MIN
U-matic / VHS
Art of being human series
Color (H C A)
Compares and contrasts Eastern and Western consciousness.
Religion and Philosophy
Dist - FI **Prod** - FI 1978

The Philosophy of Communications and the Arts 120 MIN
16mm
Philosophy Year Addresses and Responses Series
B&W
Presents Professor Richard Mc Keon of the University of Chicago in 'PHILOSOPHY OF COMMUNICATIONS AND THE ARTS' with response by Dr Kenneth Burke, visiting professor at Harvard University.
Fine Arts; Psychology; Religion and Philosophy; Social Science
Dist - SUNY **Prod** - SUNY 1968

The Philosophy of Ethics 120 MIN
16mm
Philosophy Year Addresses and Responses Series
B&W
Presents the address by visiting professor Milton Munitz, State University College at Brockport, with the response by Anthony Quinton, University lecturer, Oxford University.
Religion and Philosophy
Dist - SUNY **Prod** - SUNY

The Philosophy of Human Rights 120 MIN
16mm
Philosophy Year Addresses and Responses Series
B&W
Features the address by Professor Sidney Hook of New York University, 'REFLECTIONS ON HUMAN RIGHTS.'.
Civics and Political Systems; Religion and Philosophy; Sociology
Dist - SUNY **Prod** - SUNY

The Philosophy of language 45 MIN
VHS
Men of ideas series
Color; PAL (H C A)
PdS99 purchase; Not available in Canada.
Explains in simple terms the main developments in Western philosophy from the 19th century to the present day. Features a contemporary thinker discussing his ideas and beliefs about the philosophy of language with Bryan Magee. Part ton of a fifteen part series.
Foreign Language; Religion and Philosophy
Dist - BBCENE

The Philosophy of Logic and Language 120 MIN
16mm
Philosophy Year Addresses and Responses Series
B&W
Presents 'PHILOSOPHICAL PROGRESS IN LANGUAGE THEORY' by Professor W O Quine, Harvard University, with response by Professor Max Black, Cornell University.
English Language; Psychology; Religion and Philosophy
Dist - SUNY **Prod** - SUNY 1968

The Philosophy of Love 29 MIN
U-matic
Dickens World Series
Color
Traces Dickens' idea that love was the answer to the chaos he saw in the world.
Literature and Drama
Dist - UMITV **Prod** - UMITV 1973

The Philosophy of Mind 120 MIN
16mm
Philosophy Year Addresses and Responses Series
B&W
Features the address 'SOME PROBLEMS ABOUT THINKING' by Professor Gilbert Ryle, Oxford University, with response by Professor Stuart Hampshire, Princeton University.
Psychology; Religion and Philosophy
Dist - SUNY **Prod** - SUNY 1968

Philosophy of patient teaching 30 MIN
16mm
Nursing - patient teaching series; Part 1
B&W (C A)
LC 74-700199
Analyzes philosophical issues in developing a comprehensive patient teaching program.
Education; Health and Safety
Dist - NTCN **Prod** - NTCN 1971

The Philosophy of Practice 120 MIN
16mm
Philosophy Year Addresses and Response Series
Color
Records the address by Professor Charles Frankel, of Columbia University with a response by Professor Walter Kaufman, Princeton University.
Religion and Philosophy
Dist - SUNY **Prod** - SUNY

Philosophy of rehabilitation and its application - Pt 1 27 MIN
16mm
Directions for education in nursing via technology series; Lesson 79
B&W (PRO)
LC 74-701857
Identifies and discusses the physical and psychosocial effects of prolonged bed rest and immobilization. Discusses the nurse's role in the prevention of adverse effects.
Health and Safety; Psychology
Dist - WSUM **Prod** - DENT 1974

Philosophy of rehabilitation and its application - Pt 2 31 MIN
16mm
Directions for education in nursing via technology series; Lesson 80
B&W (PRO)
LC 74-701858
Presents the philosophy of rehabilitation as it relates to physical and physiological effects of immobility. Identifies the use of items within the patient's environment that promote patient safety.
Health and Safety; Psychology
Dist - WSUM **Prod** - DENT 1974

The Philosophy of Science 120 MIN
16mm
Philosophy Year Addresses and Response Series
Color
Presents Professor Ernest Nagel, Columbia University speaking on 'ISSUES IN THE LOGIC OF REDUCTIVE EXPLANATIONS.' Features the response given by Professor Richard Schlegel of Michigan State University.
Religion and Philosophy
Dist - SUNY **Prod** - SUNY 1968

The Philosophy of science 45 MIN
VHS
Men of ideas series
Color; PAL (H C A)
PdS99 purchase; Not available in Canada.
Explains in simple terms the main developments in Western philosophy from the 19th century to the present day. Features a contemporary thinker discussing his ideas on the philosophy of science with Bryan Magee. Part twelve of a fifteen part series.
Religion and Philosophy; Science
Dist - BBCENE

The Philosophy of Social Science 120 MIN
16mm
Philosophy Year Addresses and Responses Series
B&W
Records Professor H L A Hart, Oxford University, in his address, 'KELSEN'S DOCTRINE OF THE UNITY OF LAW' with response given by Professor R M Dworkin, Yale University.
Civics and Political Systems; Psychology; Religion and Philosophy; Social Science; Sociology
Dist - SUNY **Prod** - SUNY 1968

Philosophy of Supervision 17 MIN
16mm
Supervision and Management Series
Color
LC 70-712976
Presents a basic introduction to the principles of effective leadership. Explains the general philosophy of supervision and practical application in a nursing situation.
Business and Economics; Health and Safety; Psychology
Dist - TRNAID **Prod** - TRNAID 1969

The Philosophy of the Cartoonist 15 MIN
Videoreel / VT2
Charlie's Pad Series
Color
Fine Arts
Dist - PBS **Prod** - WSIU

The Philosophy of the Obvious 25 MIN
U-matic / VHS / 16mm
Gestalt Series
Color (H C)
LC 75-706493
Introduces the use of dreams in Gestalt therapy, examines our two levels of existence, the inner world and the outer world, and connects the Gestalt in our fantasy with the gestalt in the real world.
Psychology
Dist - FI **Prod** - AQUARP 1969

Philosophy - the Question of Man 18 MIN
U-matic / VHS / 16mm
Humanities Series
Color (H C)
LC 74-714099
Presents an introduction to the study of philosophy.
Religion and Philosophy
Dist - MGHT **Prod** - MGHT 1971

Philosophy - the social context 45 MIN
VHS
Men of ideas series
Color; PAL (H C A)
PdS99 purchase; Not available in Canada.
Explains in simple terms the main developments in Western philosophy from the 19th century to the present day. Features a contemporary thinker discussing his ideas on the social context of philosophy with Bryan Magee. Part fifteen of a fifteen part series.
Religion and Philosophy; Sociology
Dist - BBCENE

Philosophy Year Addresses and Response Series
The Philosophy of Practice 120 MIN
The Philosophy of Science 120 MIN
Dist - SUNY

Philosophy year addresses and responses - a series 8 MIN
16mm
Philosophy year addresses and responses - a series
Color
Presents a series of presentations by prominent scholars who participated in the International Philosophy Year Conference held at the State University College at Brockport, New York 1967 - 68. Philosophy Of Communications And The Arts, The; Philosophy Of Ethics, The; Philosophy Of Human Rights, The; Philosophy Of Logic And Language, The; Philosophy Of Mind, The; Philosophy Of Practice, The; Philosophy Of Science, The; Philosophy Of Social Science, The.
Religion and Philosophy
Dist - SUNY **Prod** - SUNY 1968

Philosophy year addresses and responses - a series
Philosophy year addresses and responses - a series 8 MIN
Dist - SUNY

Philosophy Year Addresses and Responses Series
The Philosophy of Communications and the Arts 120 MIN
The Philosophy of Ethics 120 MIN
The Philosophy of Human Rights 120 MIN
The Philosophy of Logic and Language 120 MIN
The Philosophy of Mind 120 MIN
The Philosophy of Social Science 120 MIN
Dist - SUNY

Phil's Friends 15 MIN
VHS / U-matic
Chemical People Educational Modules Series
Color (J)
Presents young television stars who discuss the value of friendship.
Psychology
Dist - CORF **Prod** - CORF

PHN - Public health nurse 25 MIN
16mm
B&W
LC FIA67-2147
Follows a public health nurse as she performs her duties in a clinic setting and in the patient's home. Illustrates that the variety and the personal nature of her work contribute to its appeal as a profession.
Guidance and Counseling; Health and Safety; Psychology
Dist - VADE **Prod** - VIRDH 1967

Phobias 28 MIN
U-matic / VHS
Color (G)
$249.00, $149.00 purchase _ #AD - 1246
Reveals that phobia, the terror that afflicts some people, is often seriously debilitating. Shows that self - help may consist of ignoring or avoiding the terrorizing situation. More serious manifestations require professional intervention - hypnosis or psychotherapy.
Health and Safety; Psychology; Sociology
Dist - FOTH **Prod** - FOTH

Phoebe and Jan 5 MIN
16mm
Color (G)
$8.00 rental
Features two women in the filmmaker's house in Mendocino, afternoons spent looking out over the field and ocean and interplay of the moving camera and subject through layered imagery.
Fine Arts; Geography - World; Sociology
Dist - CANCIN **Prod** - WALLIN 1968

Phoebe - Story of a Premarital Pregnancy 28 MIN
16mm / U-matic / VHS
B&W (H C A) (SPANISH)
Examines the emotional impact of a sensitive high school girl's premarital pregnancy. Reveals her relationship with the boy and her need for outside counseling.
Foreign Language; Guidance and Counseling; Psychology; Sociology
Dist - MGHT **Prod** - NFBC 1975

Phoebe - Story of a Premarital Pregnancy 28 MIN
U-matic / VHS / 16mm
B&W
Studies the emotional impact of premarital pregnancy on a sensitive high school girl. Reveals her relationships with the boy and her parents and stresses her need for outside counseling.
Health and Safety; Sociology
Dist - CRMP **Prod** - NFBC 1965

The Phoenix 22 MIN
16mm
Color
LC 75-702477
Explores the materials use cycle and its role in solid waste. Traces the collection, transportation and disposal of waste in Kansas and analyzes current attempts to recover materials and energy from the solid waste stream. Shows the roles consumers can play in solid waste disposal programs.
Health and Safety; Home Economics; Industrial and Technical Education; Science - Natural
Dist - USNAC **Prod** - KLWV 1975

Phoenix 55 MIN
VHS / U-matic
B&W
Highlights rejection and reinterpretation of roles. Protrays a Southern family.
Fine Arts; Sociology
Dist - KITCHN **Prod** - KITCHN

Phoenix and Finnegan 30 MIN
U-matic / VHS
Art of being human series; Module 12
Color (C)
History - World; Literature and Drama; Religion and Philosophy; Sociology
Dist - MDCC **Prod** - MDCC

Phoenix Country II 28 MIN
16mm
Color
LC 79-701022
Shows hang gliding in many countries, including the United States, Canada, Brazil, Chile, Argentina, Japan and Italy.
Physical Education and Recreation
Dist - BENARN **Prod** - BENARN 1979

A Phoenix Rises 15 MIN
VHS / U-matic
Explorers Unlimited Series
Color (P I)
Demonstrates the value of the scrap metal industry as it conserves and reclaims waste material.
Business and Economics; Science - Natural; Social Science
Dist - AITECH **Prod** - WVIZTV 1971

The Phone Call 24 MIN
16mm
Color (J H A)
LC 78-700210
Tells the story of courtship and the difficulty of reaching out to touch someone.
Guidance and Counseling; Psychology; Social Science; Sociology
Dist - EBEC **Prod** - BYU 1977

Phone - film portraits 6 MIN
VHS / 16mm
B&W (G)
$20.00 rental
Utilizes a telephone answering machine as the basic structure. Features a ten - second filmic portrait of the filmmaker's friends, with their phone messages to him used as a soundtrack. A statement of modern society and technology.
Fine Arts; Industrial and Technical Education; Psychology; Sociology
Dist - CANCIN FLMKCO **Prod** - ANGERA 1985

The Phone Freak 6 MIN
16mm
Color
LC 76-701353
Presents a satire of the Bell Telephone Company.
Business and Economics; Fine Arts; Industrial and Technical Education; Social Science; Sociology
Dist - CONCRU **Prod** - CONCRU 1975

The Phone Isn't Working 14 MIN
VHS / U-matic
Under the Yellow Balloon Series
Color (P)
Explains that when Jeff tries to talk to Steve, he can't. Presents a service technician explaining the machinery of the telephone and how people are needed to keep the phone system in order.
Industrial and Technical Education; Social Science
Dist - AITECH **Prod** - SCETV 1980

Phone power 53 MIN
VHS
Color (A PRO IND)
$54.95 purchase _ #S01933
Presents guidelines for communicating more effectively on the telephone. Covers subjects including scheduling of telephone appointments, opening statements, bolstering relations, and how to reduce time spent playing 'phone tag.' Hosted by George Walther.
Business and Economics; Industrial and Technical Education; Social Science
Dist - UILL

PhoneDisc USA eastern region
CD-ROM
(G)
$995.00 purchase _ #2901e
Includes the Eastern Region of PhoneDisc USA - zip codes 00001 - 47999. Provides access to millions of white pages telephone listings. Users can limit searches by area codes, zip codes, states, cities, and streets. Subscription includes a toll free help line. Updated semiannually. For IBM PCs and compatibles, requires 640K RAM, DOS 3.1 or later, one floppy disk drive - hard disk recommended, one empty expansion slot, and an IBM compatible CD - ROM drive.
Literature and Drama
Dist - BEP

PhoneDisc USA quarterly update
CD-ROM
(G)
$200.00 purchase _ #2901u
Includes quarterly updates to either the Western or Eastern editions of PhoneDisc USA. Provides access to millions of white pages telephone listings. Users can limit searches by area codes, zip codes, states, cities, and streets. Subscription includes a toll free help line. For IBM PCs and compatibles, requires 640K of RAM, DOS 3.1 or later, one floppy disk drive - hard disk recommended, one empty expansion slot, and an IBM compatible CD - ROM drive.
Literature and Drama
Dist - BEP

PhoneDisc USA residential
CD-ROM
(G)
$1850.00 purchase _ #2901n
Includes the National Edition of PhoneDisc USA. Provides access to millions of white pages telephone listings. Users can limit searches by area codes, zip codes, states, cities, and streets. Subscription includes a toll free help line. Updated semiannually. For IBM PCs and compatibles, requires 640K RAM, DOS 3.1 or later, one floppy disk drive - hard disk recommended, one empty expansion slot, and an IBM compatible CD - ROM drive.
Literature and Drama
Dist - BEP

PhoneDisc USA western region
CD-ROM
(G)
$995.00 purchase _ #2901w
Includes the Western Region of PhoneDisc USA - zip codes 48000 - 99999. Provides access to millions of white pages telephone listings. Users can limit searches by area codes, zip codes, states, cities, and streets. Subscription includes a toll free help line. Updated semiannually. For IBM PCs and compatibles, requires at least 640K RAM, DOS 3.1 or later, one floppy disk drive - hard disk recommended, one empty expansion slot, and an IBM compatible CD - ROM drive.
Literature and Drama
Dist - BEP

The Phonemaster 9000 call returning machine 8 MIN
VHS
Color (H A)
$125.00 purchase
Takes the concept of voice mail to its extreme in a humorous view of what might happen someday. Shows why inventors may live to regret their labor - saving inventions. For breaks or entertainment for conferences and similar meetings. Produced by Michael Addis.
Literature and Drama; Social Science
Dist - PFP

Phonetic Level Speech Evaluation 28 MIN
U-matic
Color (PRO)
LC 82-706187
Evaluates a 12 - year - old boy's hearing impairment to show procedures used to assess phonologic competence and to plan a remedial program.
Education; English Language; Psychology; Science - Natural
Dist - SYRCU **Prod** - MCGILL 1981

Phonetic Level Speech Teaching 55 MIN
U-matic
Color (PRO)
LC 82-706188
Presents the principles and practice of evoking and rehearsing speech patterns. Discusses strategies for evoking suprasegmental patterns, vowels and diphthongs, consonants and blends and alternative strategies.
Education; English Language; Psychology; Science - Natural
Dist - SYRCU **Prod** - MCGILL 1981

Phonework - life skills
VHS
Family - life skills video series
Color (H G A)
$89.00 purchase _ #ES888
Instructs on the basics of using the telephone. Includes reading and using the telephone directory, answering phones and machines, making calls and special services.
English Language; Industrial and Technical Education; Social Science
Dist - AAVIM **Prod** - AAVIM

Phonework - on the job
VHS
Family - life skills video series
Color (H G A)
$89.00 purchase _ #ES889
Teaches the importance of proper phone work on the job. Includes answering, dealing with customers, taking messages and using various phone options.
Business and Economics; Guidance and Counseling; Industrial and Technical Education; Social Science
Dist - AAVIM **Prod** - AAVIM

Phonics and word structure 15 MIN
U-matic / VHS / 16mm
Reading skills series; No 2
Color (P I)
Uses animated sequences of a 'WORD FACTORY' to put together the meaningful parts of words.
English Language
Dist - JOU **Prod** - GLDWER 1972

The Phonograph 30 MIN
16mm
B&W
LC FIA64-1141
Dramatizes how the communist revolution in Russia affected the life of a cobbler by making him realize the importance of freedom of worship on the sabbath and the menace of communism to individual liberties.
Civics and Political Systems; History - World; Religion and Philosophy
Dist - NAAJS **Prod** - JTS 1956

Phonologic Level Speech Development 40 MIN
U-matic
Color (PRO)
LC 82-706189
Examines problems of generalizing phonetic level speech skills into meaningful spoken language.
Education; English Language; Psychology; Science - Natural
Dist - SYRCU **Prod** - MCGILL 1981

Phonologic Level Speech Evaluation 20 MIN
U-matic
Color (PRO)
LC 82-706190
Describes sampling techniques, analysis of the spoken language sample and specifies phonologic and linguistic goals for a 12 - year - old boy with profound hearing impairment.
Education; English Language; Psychology; Science - Natural
Dist - SYRCU **Prod** - MCGILL 1981

Phonological Approach to Children's Speech and Sound Disorders 104 MIN
VHS / U-matic
Color
Discusses the diagnostic and remedial approaches for speech sound disorders in children.
Education; Psychology
Dist - PUAVC **Prod** - PUAVC

Phonological development 130 MIN
VHS / U-matic
Meeting the communications needs of the severely - profoundly handicapped series
Color
Discusses the different perspectives from which children's sound systems can be examined and the major stages of phonological development.
Psychology; Social Science
Dist - PUAVC **Prod** - PUAVC 1980

The Phony War 26 MIN
16mm / U-matic / VHS
Between the Wars Series
Color (H C)
Shows how Hitler's invasion of Poland triggered the Second World War. Explains that the 1930's ended with America still unconvinced that its destiny was intertwined with the rest of the world.
History - World
Dist - FI **Prod** - LNDBRG 1978

Phony war and F D R and Churchill - the human partnership
VHS
Between the wars - 1918 - 1941 series; Volume 7
Color (H C A)
$19.95 purchase
Reviews part of the history of the years between World War I and World War II. Focuses on the close working relationship that existed between Franklin Roosevelt and Winston Churchill. Includes excerpts from newsreels, soundtracks, and archival footage of the period. Hosted and narrated by Eric Sevareid.
History - World
Dist - PBS **Prod** - WNETTV

Photo album 14 MIN
16mm / U-matic / VHS
Color (G)
$350.00, $225.00, $125.00 purchase
Remembers the experiences of filmmaker Enrique Oliver as a young immigrant from Cuba. Stars his real family and demonstrates Oliver's ability to walk the tightrope between satire and parody. Offers a scene of his mother seeing a vision of the Virgin of Cubans in exile, his grandmother walking on her knees to church in gratitude, Oliver shouting, 'You're just doing this to embarrass me.' Produced and directed by Oliver.
Fine Arts; Literature and Drama; Sociology
Dist - FLOWER

Photo - Electric Effect 28 MIN
16mm
PSSC Physics Films Series
Color (H C)
Presents qualitative demonstrations of the photoelectric effect, employing the sun and a carbon arc as sources. Also shows an experiment measuring the kinetic energy of the photoelectrons emitted from a potassium surface.
Science; Science - Physical
Dist - MLA **Prod** - PSSC 1962

Photo - Electric Effect 28 MIN
16mm
PSSC Physics Series
B&W (SPANISH)
Shows qualitative demonstrations of photo - electric effect. Shows a quantitive experiment which measures kinetic energy of photo - electrons emitted from a potassium surface.
Foreign Language; Science; Science - Physical
Dist - MLA **Prod** - PSSC

Photo Opportunity 29 MIN
U-matic / VHS
Inside Story Series
Color
LC 83-706852
Explores the question of whether reporters have a moral or a professional obligation to intervene in stories they cover.
Fine Arts; Sociology
Dist - PBS **Prod** - PBS 1981

Photo processing 15 MIN
VHS
Career success series
Color (H C A)
$29.95 purchase _ #MX162
Presents an introduction to photo processing careers. Covers the necessary skills, and interviews people in these careers on the rewards and stresses involved.
Education; Industrial and Technical Education
Dist - CAMV **Prod** - CAMV

Photo Show Series

Accentuate the negative	29 MIN
A Change of Lens	29 MIN
Filters, Dodging and Burning	29 MIN
Hue and Eye	29 MIN
It's about Time	29 MIN
Let There be Light	29 MIN
Making Contacts	29 MIN
The Right Exposure	29 MIN
Starting to Print	29 MIN
Three Key Controls	29 MIN
To Choose a Camera	29 MIN
Tough Shots	29 MIN
What's in a Frame	29 MIN

Dist - PBS

A Photo Started it all 15 MIN
16mm
Color
Uses a yearbook staff photograph to help four junior high school students become acquainted with the basics of good grooming and dress.
Home Economics
Dist - MTP **Prod** - SEARS

Photo tips series

Architecture	7 MIN
Baby	2.55 MIN
Baseball	2.28 MIN
Caribbean vacation	5.45 MIN
Humor	4.04 MIN
Macro	7.03 MIN
Natural Light Portraits	5.34 MIN
Night	7.19 MIN
Vacation	3.05 MIN
Weddings	5.35 MIN

Dist - AITECH

Photocoupler applications 30 MIN
VHS / U-matic
Optoelectronics series; Pt I - Optoelectronic emitters, sensors and couplers
Color (PRO)
Uses the equivalent circuit to introduce photocoupler applications. Points out device capabilities in specific applications, including the important optical isolator application.
Industrial and Technical Education
Dist - TXINLC **Prod** - TXINLC

Photocouplers and their characteristics 30 MIN
U-matic / VHS
Optoelectronics series; Pt I - Optoelectronic emitters, sensors and couplers
Color (PRO)
Tells how photo couplers are emitters and sensors in the same package. Discusses effects of different fabrication types as well as the electrical characteristics with the sensor as a phototransistor or photodiode.
Industrial and Technical Education
Dist - TXINLC **Prod** - TXINLC

Photodegradable Polymers 20 MIN
U-matic
Breakthrough Series
Color (H C)
Examines the chemistry behind the production of artificial polymers and recent breakthroughs that will allow control of the rate of degradation.
Science; Science - Natural; Science - Physical
Dist - TVOTAR **Prod** - TVOTAR 1985

The Photofinishing Story 22 MIN
16mm
Color
Describes what happens to film that is sent for processing in a modern photofinishing plant. Shows the modern equipment and quality control procedures that produce beautiful prints and slides.
Industrial and Technical Education
Dist - EKC **Prod** - EKC 1983

The Photographer 15 MIN
VHS / 16mm
Harriet's Magic Hats IV Series
Color (P)
$175.00 purchase _ #207141
Presents thirteen new programs to familiarize children with more workers and their role in community life. Features Aunt Harriet's bottomless trunks of magic hats where Carrie has only to put on a particular hat to be whisked off to investigate the person and the role represented by the hat. 'The Photographer' discovers Ralph the parrot taking pictures. Ralph suggests that Carrie take the film to Sheila, a photographer, for developing. Sheila explains all about cameras, lighting, taking portraits, developing pictures and the many types of photographers.
Business and Economics; Guidance and Counseling; Industrial and Technical Education; Psychology
Dist - ACCESS **Prod** - ACCESS 1986

The Photographer 30 MIN
16mm
B&W (H C A)
LC FIE52-154
Shows the personality, philosophy, techniques and artistry of Edward Weston through scenes of the artist at home, on location and at work with his students.
Fine Arts; Industrial and Technical Education
Dist - USNAC **Prod** - USDS 1948

Photographers and their films 30 MIN
VHS
Color (G)
$24.95 purchase _ #S00937
Outlines the different kinds of Kodak films, explaining how each one is used.
Industrial and Technical Education
Dist - UILL **Prod** - EKC

The Photographer's Eye 29 MIN
U-matic / VHS
Creativity with Bill Moyers Series
Color (H C A)
Looks at the creative impulse in the art and practice of photography. Features the work of photographers Emmet Gowin and Garry Winogrand.
Fine Arts; Industrial and Technical Education; Psychology
Dist - PBS **Prod** - CORPEL 1982

Photographers of the American Frontier - 1860 - 1880 58 MIN
U-matic / VHS
Color
Shows how an inspired group of artists in the new medium of photography captured the American frontier. Features the work of Carleton Watkins, Eadweard Muybridge, A J Russell, William Henry Jackson and T H O'Sullivan.
Fine Arts
Dist - BLACKW **Prod** - BLACKW

Photographic Arts Centre 1 MIN
16mm
Color
LC 76-702042
Looks at the Photographic Arts Centre, one of Ryerson Polytechnical Institute's most popular buildings.
Education; Fine Arts; Industrial and Technical Education
Dist - RYERC **Prod** - RYERC 1975

Photographic design 90 MIN
VHS
On assignment - the video guide for photography series
Color (J H C G)

$29.95 purchase _ #MED101V VHS
Explains camera and lens choices. Discusses design elements and principles and light direction and quality. Part of an eight - part series hosted by nationally known photographer Brian D Ratty.
Fine Arts; Industrial and Technical Education
Dist - CAMV

Photographic light 90 MIN
VHS
On assignment - the video guide for photography series
Color (J H C G)
$29.95 purchase _ #MED102V VHS
Illustrates the principles of light. Shows how to control and manipulate light in photography. Part of an eight - part series hosted by nationally known photographer Brian D Ratty.
Fine Arts; Industrial and Technical Education; Science - Physical
Dist - CAMV

Photographic Processing 15 MIN
VHS / 16mm
(H C A)
$24.95 purchase _ #CS162
Describes the skills involved in a career in photographic processing. Features interviews with people employed in the field.
Guidance and Counseling
Dist - RMIBHF **Prod** - RMIBHF

Photographic Screen Printing 30 MIN
VHS
ArtSmart Series
Color (C)
LC 90708438
Depicts the processes and techniques of photographic screen printing in an effort to have students make immediate use of those processes and techniques. The fourth of ten installments of the ArtSmart Series.
Fine Arts; Industrial and Technical Education
Dist - GPN **Prod** - UNKNWN 1990

Photographic Study of Gold Flow 14 MIN
16mm
Color
LC 72-700476
Presents research on the character of gold flow. Demonstrates to dentists how gold actually fills a void and shows the function of the sprue.
Health and Safety
Dist - LOMA **Prod** - LOMA 1967

Photographic vision - all about photography series
The Camera 29 MIN
Dist - CAMV
CDTEL

Photographic vision - all about photography series
Artistic Expression 30 MIN
Controlling exposure 30 MIN
The Darkroom 30 MIN
The Film 30 MIN
Image and Impact 30 MIN
A Lifetime in Photography 30 MIN
The Marketplace 30 MIN
Photojournalism 30 MIN
Responding to Light 30 MIN
Structure within the Image 30 MIN
The Studio 30 MIN
Time and Motion 30 MIN
Visual Documents 30 MIN
A Visual Heritage 30 MIN
Dist - CDTEL

Photographic vision series
Artistic expression 29 MIN
Color 29 MIN
Controlling exposure 29 MIN
The Darkroom 29 MIN
The Film 29 MIN
Image and impact 29 MIN
A Lifetime of photography 29 MIN
The Marketplace 29 MIN
Photojournalism 29 MIN
Responding to light 29 MIN
Structure within the image 29 MIN
The Studio 29 MIN
Time and motion 29 MIN
Visual documents 29 MIN
A Visual heritage 29 MIN
Dist - CAMV

Photographic vision series
Landscape and cityscape 29 MIN
The Portrait 29 MIN
Reading photographs 29 MIN
Seeing with the camera 30 MIN
Dist - CAMV
CDTEL

Photographic vision series
Color 30 MIN
Dist - CDTEL

Photographics 30 MIN
VHS / U-matic
Antique Shop Series
Color
Presents guests who are experts in their respective fields who share tips on collecting and caring for antique photographics.
Fine Arts
Dist - MDCPB **Prod** - WVPTTV

Photographing people 30 MIN
VHS
Color (G)
$24.95 purchase _ #S00938
Describes techniques that can be used to make photographs of people seem more 'natural' than posed.
Fine Arts; Industrial and Technical Education
Dist - UILL **Prod** - EKC

Photography
U-matic / VHS
Career Builders Video Series
$95.00 purchase _ #ED109V
Uses actual professionals to talk about the job's demands, rewards, and frustrations. Shows the working environment of the career field.
Guidance and Counseling
Dist - CAREER **Prod** - CAREER

Photography 15 MIN
VHS
Career success series
Color (H C A)
$29.95 purchase _ #MX144
Presents an introduction to photography careers. Covers the necessary skills, and interviews people in these careers on the rewards and stresses involved.
Education; Industrial and Technical Education
Dist - CAMV **Prod** - CAMV

Photography 15 MIN
VHS / 16mm
(H C A)
$24.95 purchase _ #CS144
Describes the necessary skills involved in a career in photography. Features interviews with photographers.
Guidance and Counseling
Dist - RMIBHF **Prod** - RMIBHF

Photography 30 MIN
U-matic / VHS / 16mm
Media Probes Series
Color (H C A)
LC 82-700487
Profiles five photographers including photo - essayist Bruce Davidson, Pulitzer Prize winner David Kennerly, New York Daily News photojournalist Mary DiBiase, commercial photographer Michael O'Neill and wedding photographer Gil Amaral. Explains how a photographic image can take on a reality all its own. Narrated by Cheryl Tiegs.
Industrial and Technical Education
Dist - TIMLIF **Prod** - LAYLEM 1982

Photography 24 MIN
VHS / 16mm
Career Builders Video Series
Color
$85.00 purchase _ #V109
Examines a potential career choice by taking the viewer into the working environment and interviewing professionals on the demands, rewards and frustrations on the job.
Business and Economics; Industrial and Technical Education; Sociology
Dist - EDUCDE **Prod** - EDUCDE 1987

Photography - a History 24 MIN
VHS / 16mm
Color (I)
LC 90706253
Gives an overview of the history of photography. Presents basic concepts of black and white photography.
History - World; Industrial and Technical Education
Dist - BARR

Photography as an Art 29 MIN
U-matic / VHS / 16mm
Photography - the Incisive Art Series
B&W (H C A)
Presents Ansel Adams as he photographs Yosemite National Park. Explains how a sense of discovery and re - discovery is conveyed through his photography. Discusses his methods of teaching.
Education; Fine Arts; Industrial and Technical Education
Dist - IU **Prod** - NET 1960

Photography - Dorothea Lange - the Closer for Me 30 MIN
U-matic / VHS / 16mm
USA Series
B&W (J)
Mrs Dorothea Lange discusses a new photographic project for the present generation of photographers. Many of her photographs of American cities from various periods are presented.
Fine Arts; Industrial and Technical Education
Dist - IU **Prod** - NET 1966

Photography - Dorothea Lange - Under the Trees 30 MIN
16mm / U-matic / VHS
USA Series
B&W (J)
Shows Dorothea Lange at home making preparation for an exhibition of her work covering the past 50 years. Presents many of her photographs while she comments on the reasons and emotions that have moved her to photograph particular scenes.
Fine Arts; Industrial and Technical Education
Dist - IU **Prod** - NET 1966

Photography - How it Works 11 MIN
16mm
Color (I J H C)
Introduces the camera user to the basics of photography. Looks at the camera and its basic parts. Clarifies the interrelationship between lens opening and shutter speed in an explanation of how an automatic or adjustable camera compensates for various lighting conditions.
Industrial and Technical Education
Dist - EKC **Prod** - EKC 1979

Photography in Action 7 MIN
16mm
Color
LC 74-706381
Shows how slow motion, time - lapse and split - frame photography are used in obtaining engineering data at the Waterways Experiment Station.
Industrial and Technical Education
Dist - USNAC **Prod** - USAE 1969

Photography in the USAF - Optical Instrumentation at Vandenberg Air Force Base 17 MIN
16mm
Color
LC 74-706174
Depicts how optical instrumentation during missile launchings is achieved through engineering sequential photography. Pictures the cameras used and explains their characteristics and capabilities.
Industrial and Technical Education; Science - Physical
Dist - USNAC **Prod** - USDD 1961

Photography series
Presents a ten - part series on photography. Includes Action Photography, Advanced Existing - Light Photography, Nature Photography, Scenic Photography, The Way I See It, Creating the Image, Creating the Print, Images With Imagination, Glamour Photography, How to Take Better Pictures.
Creating the image 30 MIN
Creating the print 30 MIN
Glamour photography 30 MIN
How to take better pictures 30 MIN
Photography series 300 MIN
Dist - CAMV **Prod** - EKC 1961

Photography - the creative eye - darkroom techniques explained - how to develop film 31 MIN
VHS
Color (H C)
$219.00 purchase _ #00629 - 126
Demonstrates techniques of developing negatives. Explains how ASA ratings, film selection and bracketing can affect the final negative. Covers the actual development process with step - by - step instruction. Slides on video.
Industrial and Technical Education
Dist - INSTRU

Photography - the creative eye - darkroom techniques explained series
Effective darkroom techniques 29 MIN
How to develop film 31 MIN
How to print and enlarge 31 MIN
Dist - GA

Photography - the Daybooks of Edward Weston - How Young I was 30 MIN
U-matic / VHS / 16mm
USA Series
B&W (H C A)
LC FIA67-1841
Quotes from 'THE DAYBOOKS OF EDWARD WESTON' accompany photographs from his soft - focus portrait period, his abstract motifs and his work done in Mexico. Two of Weston's sons, his second wife and one of his former students discuss and evaluate the artist.

Fine Arts; Industrial and Technical Education
Dist - IU **Prod** - NET 1966

Photography - the Daybooks of Edward Weston - the Strongest Way of Seeing 30 MIN
U-matic / VHS / 16mm
USA Series
B&W (H C A)
LC FIA67-1842
Depicts various photographs by Edward Weston, such as his work on Point Lobos, California, his record of California and the Western United States, portraits of his cats, and samples from his satirical series and his civil defense series.
Fine Arts; Industrial and Technical Education
Dist - IU **Prod** - NET 1966

Photography - the Incisive Art Series
The Language of the Camera Eye 29 MIN
Photography as an Art 29 MIN
Points of View 29 MIN
Professional Photography 29 MIN
Technique 29 MIN
Dist - IU

Photography - which filter should I use 30 MIN
VHS
Color (H C)
$30.00 purchase _ #TIF - 01
Shows how the nature of photography has been dramatically changed by the invention of new filters to control light and make special effects. Covers fog, contrast diffusion, coral, sepia, gradiant color, polarizing, enhancing and star filters and more.
Industrial and Technical Education
Dist - INSTRU

Photojournalism 30 MIN
VHS / U-matic
Photographic Vision - all about Photography Series
Color
Industrial and Technical Education
Dist - CDTEL **Prod** - COAST

Photojournalism 29 MIN
VHS
Photographic vision series
Color (G)
49.95 purchase _ #RM117V-F
Features Baughman, who comments on truth, objectivity and ethics in photojournalism. Presents the technical aspects of photography clearly and simply, including principles of the camera and techniques for controlling exposure, the use of various kinds of lighting, selection of appropriate lenses and film and basic darkroom techniques. Focuses on the world of photographers and photography - its history and evolution, its uses for personal development and expression, and the impact of photography on the world. Part of a 20-part series examining all aspects of the field of photography.
Industrial and Technical Education
Dist - CAMV

Photojournalist 30 MIN
VHS / BETA
American Professionals Series
Color
Describes the life of photojournalist Vanessa Barns Hillian, who tries to create a dynamic image that sums up a whole story, as she records a piece of history for The Washington Post.
Guidance and Counseling; Industrial and Technical Education; Literature and Drama; Social Science
Dist - RMIBHF **Prod** - WTBS

Photons 19 MIN
16mm
PSSC Physics Films Series
B&W (H C)
Uses the photomultiplier and oscilloscope to demonstrate that light shows particle behavior.
Science - Physical
Dist - MLA **Prod** - PSSC 1960

Photons 10 MIN
U-matic
Wave Particle Duality Series
Color (H C)
Illustrates the roles of both the particle and wave models in explaining the behavior of light. Shows how the work of Compton and Tayor reinforced both models.
Science; Science - Physical
Dist - TVOTAR **Prod** - TVOTAR 1984

Photos 5 MIN
U-matic / VHS / 16mm
How It's made Series
Color (K)
Business and Economics
Dist - LUF **Prod** - HOLIA

Photosynthesis 60 MIN
VHS
Concepts in science - biology series
Color; PAL (J H)
PdS29.50 purchase
Uses 3 - D computer animation to show the dynamic process of photosynthesis at a molecular level. Examines the absorption of light by plants and follows the energy pathways to the production of carbohydrates and other organic materials. Divided into six ten - minute concepts - Seeing the Light; Absorbing the Light; The Light Reaction; The Dark Reaction; C 3 and C 4 Plants; and The Fluid Transport System. Part of a six - part series.
Industrial and Technical Education; Science; Science - Natural
Dist - EMFVL **Prod** - TVOTAR

Photosynthesis 20 MIN
U-matic / VHS / 16mm
Color (J H C) (SPANISH)
A Spanish language version of the film and videorecording Photosynthesis.
Foreign Language; Science - Natural
Dist - EBEC **Prod** - EBEC 1982

Photosynthesis
VHS
Basic science series
Color (J H) (ENGLISH AND SPANISH)
$39.95 purchase _ #MCV5023
Focuses on photosynthesis, presenting only basic concepts. Includes teacher's guide and review questions. Combines computer animation and the use of 'sheltered language' to help students acquire content vocabulary, become comfortable with scientific language and achieve success in science curriculum. Part of a series on basic science concepts.
Science; Science - Natural
Dist - MADERA **Prod** - MADERA

Photosynthesis 10 MIN
U-matic
Energy Flow Series
Color (H C)
Presents the science concepts of how chlorophyll in plants absorbs and transfers captured light energy to other molecules to eventually create energy storage molecules such as glucose.
Education; Science; Science - Physical
Dist - TVOTAR **Prod** - TVOTAR 1984

Photosynthesis 35 MIN
U-matic / VHS
Color
Discusses the location of different components of photo synthesis, from reaction centers, inputs and outputs to photosynthesis processes. Video version of 35mm filmstrip program, with live open and close.
Science - Natural; Science - Physical
Dist - CBSC **Prod** - BMEDIA

Photosynthesis - a demonstration series
Effect of chlorophyll and carbon dioxide on oxygen production 5 MIN
Effect of chlorophyll and carbon dioxide on starch formation 5 MIN
Effect of light on oxygen production 4 MIN
Dist - EDPAT

Photosynthesis and Assimilate Transport 15 MIN
U-matic / VHS
Experiment - Biology Series
Color (C)
$249.00, $149.00 purchase _ #AD - 1087
Demonstrates some techniques for studying photosynthetic metabolism and the translocation of the newly synthesized carbohydrates from the chloroplast to the various parts of the plant where it is utilized in growth and respiration. Part of a series on biology experiments.
Education; Psychology; Science - Natural
Dist - FOTH **Prod** - FOTH

Photosynthesis and muscular energy 13 MIN
VHS
Color; PAL (I J H)
Depicts a chlorophyll molecule enlarged several million times. Examines a leaf's cell structure which is open to sunlight, water and atmospheric carbon dioxide. Shows how sugar is produced and oxygen is liberated by photosynthesis triggered by sun energy. Sugar is readily absorbed by animals - bees, flies, horses and humans - and this chemical energy is converted into kinetic energy within the muscle fibers of animals, releasing carbon dioxide and water. Uses animated diagrams to show how the plant and animal world complement one another in a cycle of photosynthesis and muscular work.
Science - Natural
Dist - VIEWTH **Prod** - VIEWTH

Photosynthesis and respiration 29 MIN
U-matic
Introducing biology series; Program 5
Color (C A)
Discusses the sun as the place where photosynthesis begins. Gives detailed explanation of the photosynthesis equation. Covers cellular respiration.
Science - Natural
Dist - CDTEL **Prod** - COAST

Photosynthesis and Respiration 29 MIN
VHS
Basic Botany Series
Color (G)
$75.00 purchase _ #6 - 083 - 107P
Teaches basic botany. Shows how green plants take energy from the sun and convert it into chemical energy. Describes basic leaf structure and explains photosynthesis in detail. Looks at the production and role of glucose.
Agriculture; Science - Natural
Dist - VEP **Prod** - VEP

Photosynthesis - Chemistry of Food Making 18 MIN
U-matic / VHS / 16mm
Color (J H C)
Shows that through the process of photosynthesis, food is manufactured within the cells of green plants. Examines the chain of events that is responsible for the oxygen we breathe and the food we eat.
Science - Natural; Science - Physical
Dist - CORF **Prod** - CORF 1985

Photosynthesis - Energy from Light 52 MIN
VHS / U-matic
Color
LC 81-706670
Analyzes the process of photosynthesis with an explanation of the basic chemistry underlying the process.
Science - Natural
Dist - GA **Prod** - SCIMAN 1981

Photosynthesis in Purple Bacteria Series
Isolating Pure Cultures - Van Niel's Technique 5 MIN
Dist - IFB

Photosynthesis - maintenance in living things 20 MIN
VHS
Color (I J H)
$79.00 purchase _ #GW - 5095 - VS
Explains that air, water and sunlight are the raw materials from which green plants produce oxygen and food. Reveals that green plants produce oxygen as a byproduct of photosynthesis. Shows that carbon dioxide is the gas green plants need from the air in order to carry out photosynthesis and that photosynthesis is the process by which green plants use the energy of the sun to combine carbon dioxide and hydrogen to form food. Produced by EA Video Inc.
Science - Natural
Dist - HRMC

Photosynthesis - Pt 1; 2nd ed. 8 MIN
VHS / U-matic
Search for science series; Unit VIII - Plants
Color (I)
Explains that the green plant is the only organism on earth which produces its own food and describes how it does so.
Science - Natural
Dist - GPN **Prod** - WVIZTV

Photosynthesis - Pt 2; 2nd ed. 7 MIN
VHS / U-matic
Search for science series; Unit VIII - Plants
Color (I)
Explains that the green plant is the only organism on earth which produces its own food and describes how it does so.
Science - Natural
Dist - GPN **Prod** - WVIZTV

Photosynthesis - the flow energy from sun to man 15 MIN
VHS
Color (J H)
$39.75 purchase _ #49 - 8445 - V
Introduces the concepts of photosynthesis. Still frame.
Science - Natural
Dist - INSTRU **Prod** - CBSC

Photosynthetic Fixation of Carbon Dioxide, Pt 1 6 MIN
16mm
Plant Science Series
Color (H)

LC FIA66-170
Demonstrates measurement of the rate of photosynthesis using a radio - tracer technique. Uses green and white portions of verigated coleus leaves for a chlorophyl - non - chlorophyl variable and a light and dark chamber.
Agriculture; Science; Science - Natural
Dist - MLA **Prod** - IOWA 1964

Photosynthetic Fixation of Carbon Dioxide, Pt 2 6 MIN
16mm
Plant Science Series
Color (H)
Demonstrates measurement of the rate of photosynthesis using a radio - tracer technique. Uses green and white portions of verigated coleus leaves for a chlorophyl - non - chlorophyl variable and a light and dark chamber.
Agriculture; Science; Science - Natural
Dist - MLA **Prod** - IOWA 1964

Phototropism
VHS
Color (J H)
$59.95 purchase _ #193 W 2214
Considers phototropism - the movement of a plant toward or away from light.
Science - Natural; Science - Physical
Dist - WARDS **Prod** - WARDS

Phrase Reading Series
Advanced phrase reading - Pt 1 5 MIN
Advanced phrase reading - Pt 2 5 MIN
Advanced phrase reading - Pt 3 5 MIN
Advanced phrase reading - Pt 4 4 MIN
Advanced phrase reading - Pt 5 4 MIN
Advanced phrase reading - Pt 6 4 MIN
Beginning Phrase Reading, Pt 1, Alaska and Hawaii 5 MIN
Beginning Phrase Reading, Pt 2, Blue Whale 5 MIN
Beginning Phrase Reading, Pt 3, San Francisco 5 MIN
Intermediate Phrase Reading, Pt 1 7 MIN
Intermediate Phrase Reading, Pt 2 7 MIN
Intermediate Phrase Reading, Pt 3 7 MIN
Intermediate Phrase Reading, Pt 4 7 MIN
Intermediate Phrase Reading, Pt 5 6 MIN
Intermediate Phrase Reading, Pt 6 6 MIN
An Introduction to Phrase Reading - It's in the Phrase 8 MIN
Dist - AVED

Phrases 18 MIN
BETA / VHS
English and Speech Series
Color
English Language
Dist - RMIBHF **Prod** - RMIBHF

The Phyla 12 MIN
16mm
Color (J)
Deals with sea life from the protozoa to chordates, tracing the development of animals from the simplest forms to the most advanced. Shows unusual specimens appearing along the trail from sea creatures to man.
Science - Natural
Dist - MIAMIS **Prod** - REELA 1970

Phyllis Lamhut and Dan Wagoner 30 MIN
VHS / U-matic
Eye on Dance - on Your Own Series
Color
Fine Arts
Dist - ARCVID **Prod** - ARCVID

Phylogeny of Cellular Recognition 35 MIN
U-matic
Color
Presents a study of specific and nonspecific surveillance cells in protozoans and man.
Health and Safety; Science - Natural
Dist - UTEXSC **Prod** - UTEXSC

Physiatry - a Physician's Perspective 26 MIN
16mm
Color
Encourages a career in rehabilitative medicine.
Guidance and Counseling; Health and Safety
Dist - RIFL **Prod** - TOGGFI 1981

The Physical 25 MIN
VHS / U-matic
Color
Shows host Mario Machado undergoing a complete physical examination, during which viewers learn exactly what the doctor is looking for during the exam. Discusses symptoms of major diseases and preventive medicine 'tips' during the workup.
Health and Safety
Dist - MEDCOM **Prod** - MEDCOM

Physical Abuse 34 MIN
VHS / U-matic
Child Abuse Series
Color (PRO)
Provides in - depth information on physical abuse of children - its incidence, identification, and treatment. Teaches identification by physical examination and interviewing the child.
Health and Safety; Sociology
Dist - HSCIC **Prod** - HSCIC 1978

Physical Abuse of Children 30 MIN
VHS / U-matic
Child Abuse and Neglect Series
Color (H C A)
Home Economics; Sociology
Dist - GPN **Prod** - UMINN 1983

Physical activity and you 10 MIN
VHS / U-matic
Color (H G)
$195.00, $245.00 purchase, $60.00 rental
Introduces physical exercise and general physical fitness. Shows how to gradually build up to a full exercise regimen.
Physical Education and Recreation
Dist - NDIM **Prod** - UCALG 1992

Physical Adjustment to Dizziness 55 MIN
U-matic / VHS
Dizziness and Related Balance Disorders Series
Color
Health and Safety
Dist - GSHDME **Prod** - GSHDME

Physical and Biological Principles of Hyperthermia 50 MIN
U-matic
Color
Discusses the use of heat in treating cancer.
Health and Safety
Dist - UTEXSC **Prod** - UTEXSC

Physical and chemical changes 15 MIN
VHS / U-matic
Discovering series; Unit 3 - Chemistry
Color (I)
Science - Physical
Dist - AITECH **Prod** - WDCNTV 1978

Physical and Chemical Properties of the Elements Series
Group VIIA Elements - Chemical Properties 4 MIN
Group VIIA Elements - Physical Properties, Pt 1 4 MIN
Group VIIA Elements - Physical Properties, Pt 2 4 MIN
Dist - KALMIA

Physical and Chemical Properties of the
Group VIIA Elements - Manganese 4 MIN
Dist - KALMIA

Physical and Emotional Change as the Dance Artist Matures 30 MIN
U-matic / VHS
Dancers' Bodies Series
Color
Fine Arts
Dist - ARCVID **Prod** - ARCVID

Physical and Life Sciences 26 MIN
U-matic / VHS
Video Career Library Series
(H C A)
$69.95 _ #CJ112V
Covers duties, conditions, salaries and training connected with jobs in the physical and life sciences. Provides a view of employees in these occupations on the job, and gives information concerning the current market for such skills. Revised every two years.
Science; Science - Natural; Science - Physical
Dist - CAMV **Prod** - CAMV

Physical and Life Sciences 26 MIN
VHS / 16mm
Video Career Library Series
Color (H C A PRO)
$79.95 purchase _ #WW102
Shows occupations in physical and life sciences such as computer scientists, statisticians, physicists, chemists, meteorologists, geologists, forestry - conservation scientists, and others in the scientific field. Contains current occupational outlook and salary information.
Business and Economics; Guidance and Counseling; Science; Science - Physical
Dist - AAVIM **Prod** - AAVIM 1990

Physical and Occupational Therapy of the Burn Patient 13 MIN
16mm
Color
LC 74-706175
Deals with the physical and occupational therapy of the patient suffering from burns.
Health and Safety
Dist - USNAC **Prod** - USA 1973

The Physical and sexual aspects of relating 30 MIN
VHS / U-matic
Family portrait - a study of contemporary lifestyles series; Lesson 4
Color (C A)
Discusses attitudes toward sex. Compares research into human sexual behavior. Establishes patterns between social attitudes and sexual behavior.
Psychology; Sociology
Dist - CDTEL **Prod** - SCCON

Physical aspects 30 MIN
VHS
Tennis with Van der Meer series
Color (C A)
$95.00 purchase, $55.00 rental
Features tennis player and instructor Dennis Van der Meer in a presentation on physical aspects of the game. Uses freeze - frame photography and repetition to stress skill development. Serves as part eight of a 10 - part telecourse.
Physical Education and Recreation; Psychology
Dist - SCETV **Prod** - SCETV 1989

Physical assessment and patient history
VHS
Practical Spanish for health - care providers series
Color (A PRO) (SPANISH AND ENGLISH)
$700.00 purchase
Instructs in the basics of Spanish for health - care workers. Develops speaking ability to communicate with Spanish - speaking patients in physical assessment and patient history situations. Includes facilitator's guide, study guide and audiocassettes. Additional sets for students are available at a nominal charge.
Foreign Language; Health and Safety; Psychology
Dist - UARIZ **Prod** - UARIZ

Physical assessment - heart and lungs - series 102 MIN
BETA / VHS / U-matic
Physical assessment - heart and lungs - series
Color (C PRO)
$880.00 purchase _ #612
Presents a four - part series on the physical assessment of the heart and lungs. Includes the titles Percussion and Auscultation of the Lungs and Thorax - Parts 1 and 2; Auscultation of Heart Sounds; Eliminating Chaos During Code Blue.
Health and Safety; Science - Natural
Dist - CONMED

Physical assessment - heart and lungs series, Pgm 4
Assessing respirations 20 MIN
Dist - CONMED

Physical Assessment - Heart and Lungs Series Program 1
Inspection and palpation of the lungs and thorax 26 MIN
Dist - CONMED

Physical Assessment - Heart and Lungs Series Program 2
Percussion and auscultation of the lungs and thorax - Pt 1 20 MIN
Dist - CONMED

Physical Assessment - Heart and Lungs Series Program 3
Percussion and auscultation of the lungs and thorax - Pt 2 30 MIN
Dist - CONMED

Physical Assessment - Heart and Lungs Series Program 5
Initial assessment of the heart 27 MIN
Dist - CONMED

Physical Assessment - Heart and Lungs Series Program 6
Inspection and palpation of the anterior chest 25 MIN
Dist - CONMED

Physical Assessment - Neurologic System Series
Cranial Nerves, Pt 1
Cranial Nerves, Pt 2
Mental Status Exam
Motor Testing

Reflexes
Sensory Testing
Station, Gait and Cerebellar Function
Dist - CONMED

Physical Assessment of a Child 33 MIN
U-matic / VHS
Color
Demonstrates a head - to - toe approach to performing a physical exam on a young child. Covers four basic techniques of inspection, palpation, percussion and auscultation. Shows how to establish trust and positive rapport with child through a skillful and understanding nurse.
Health and Safety; Science; Science - Natural
Dist - AJN **Prod** - UCALGN

Physical assessment of an adult female 56 MIN
VHS
Color (PRO)
$275.00 purchase _ #6856
Shows how to conduct a physical assessment of the adult female including an examination of the reproductive system in an integrated and organized manner. Demonstrates the techniques of inspection, palpation, percussion and auscultation.
Health and Safety; Sociology
Dist - UCALG **Prod** - UCALG 1987

Physical Assessment of the Abdomen 9 MIN
U-matic / VHS
Physical Assessment Series
Color
Demonstrates the nurse making an assessment of the patient's abdominal status as she prepares him for discharge from the hospital.
Health and Safety; Science - Natural
Dist - AJN **Prod** - SUNHSC

Physical assessment of the adult - an interactive videodisc program
Videodisc
Color (PRO C)
$995.00 purchase _ #J22305, #J22303
Presents Head to Toe, a videodisc by UUTAH portraying physical assessment of an adult, coupled with software developed by AJN to provide a comprehensive interactive video program that teaches and tests the learner on all aspects of physical assessment. Incorporates video sequences and newly created graphics in each body module into sections on - anatomy review; assessment tools and techniques; a tutorial describing and providing a rationale for each aspect of the exam; behavior checklist; appropriate documentation; glossary terms; tests incorporating text and video. Requires IBM InfoWindow or compatible system with an InfoWindow emulator. Available in 5.25 or 3.5 supporting diskettes.
Health and Safety; Psychology
Dist - AJN **Prod** - AJN 1995

Physical Assessment of the Comatose Patient 107 FRS
27 MIN
VHS / U-matic
Comatose Patient Series
Color (PRO)
Identifies general physical and neurologic assessment of the comatose patient, relates metabolic causes of coma to abnormal physiologic states, separates etiology of coma into five categories and five critical signs during assessment.
Health and Safety; Science - Natural
Dist - BRA **Prod** - BRA

Physical Assessment of the Elderly 19 MIN
VHS / 16mm
(C)
$385.00 purchase _ #851V5001
Demonstrates how to properly examine the elderly patient. Shows how to overcome the barriers of physical and psychological impairment.
Health and Safety
Dist - HSCIC **Prod** - HSCIC 1985

Physical assessment of the frail elderly 25 MIN
VHS
Color (C PRO)
$285.00 purchase, $70.00 rental _ #4331S, #4331V
Demonstrates an efficient head - to - toe physical assessment on an elderly client performed by a nurse practitioner. Focuses on the unique aspects of assessing the frail elderly and the inherent problems encountered by health care professionals when assessing the very old. Covers common physical and functional problems seen in this population.
Health and Safety
Dist - AJN **Prod** - BELHAN

Physical assessment of the neonate series
Gestational age assessment 17 MIN
Physical examination 27 MIN
Dist - CONMED

Physical Assessment of the Newborn 32 MIN
VHS / U-matic
Color (PRO)
Shows how to perform a head - to - toe physical assessment of a newborn and to discriminate between normal and abnormal conditions. Demonstrates how to measure head circumference and length of an infant.
Health and Safety
Dist - UARIZ **Prod** - UARIZ

Physical assessment - Part 1 28 MIN
VHS / U-matic / BETA
Assessing the elderly series
Color (C PRO)
$280.00 purchase _ #617.2
Demonstrates, using live male and female models, a body system approach to a head - to - toe physical examination of an elderly patient, noting major differences between findings in the normal elderly and those of the normal adult. Introduces the exam and follows a patient through the general survey and head and neck examination, concluding with cardiac and respiratory examinations. Part one of two - parts on physical assessment and part of a five - part series on assessing the elderly produced by the School of Nursing, State University of New York at Stony Brook.
Health and Safety
Dist - CONMED

Physical assessment - Part 2 22 MIN
VHS / U-matic / BETA
Assessing the elderly series
Color (C PRO)
$280.00 purchase _ #617.3
Continues the head - to - toe examination of the first part, beginning with examination of the breast, abdomen and female genitalia. Reintroduces the famle for examination of the neuromuscular systems, and concludes with examination of the genitalia and rectum. Part two of two - parts on physical assessment and part of a five - part series on assessing the elderly produced by the School of Nursing, State University of New York at Stony Brook.
Health and Safety
Dist - CONMED

Physical assessment series
Presents a seven - part series providing step - by - step guides to physical assessment of various body systems for nursing students and professionals. Includes the titles Functional Health Assessment and Techniques of Physical Examination; Head and Neck - Parts I and II; Assessment of the Adbomen; Neurological Assessment; Neurological Assessment; Cardiovascular Assessment; and Respiratory Assessment.
Assessment of the abdomen 24 MIN
Assessment of the ears and auditory system 11 MIN
Assessment of the musculoskeletal system 21 MIN
The Breast exam 13 MIN
Cardiac examination 13 MIN
Cardiovascular assessment 30 MIN
Examination of the Eyes and Visual System 20 MIN
Examination of the Head and Neck 19 MIN
Examination of the male genitalia 13 MIN
Examination of the peripheral pulses 8 MIN
Examination of the pregnant abdomen 8 MIN
Examination of the thorax and lungs 15 MIN
Functional health assessment and techniques of physical examination 16 MIN
The Gynecological Examination 19 MIN
Head and neck - Part I 27 MIN
Head and neck - Part II 43 MIN
Neurological assessment 30 MIN
Neurological Assessment - Cerebellar Function, Motor Function, Reflexes and 20 MIN
Neurological Assessment - Cranial Nerves 17 MIN
Physical Assessment of the Abdomen 9 MIN
Respiratory assessment 30 MIN
Dist - AJN **Prod** - ANSELM

Physical Changes 30 MIN
U-matic
Transitions - Caught at Midlife Series
Color
Discusses the increased awareness of physical changes that occurs during mid - life.
Psychology; Sociology
Dist - UMITV **Prod** - UMITV 1980

Physical Changes 23 MIN
16mm / VHS
Facts, Feelings and Wonder of Life - the Early Stages Series
Color (I J PRO)
$295.00, $450.00 purchase, $50.00 rental _ #9977
Illustrates the four stages of growth. Offers strategies to help preteens deal with the stress and anxiety that often accompany growth.
Guidance and Counseling; Health and Safety; Science - Natural
Dist - AIMS **Prod** - PVGP 1988

Physical changes all about us 14 MIN
VHS
Color; PAL (P I J H)
Follows 11 - year - old Julie as she observes and experiments with familiar physical changes - blowing up a balloon, making lemonade, sawing wood. Leads to laboratory experiments which develop an understanding of physical changes in size, shape and appearance by such means as combination, separpation and heating and cooling.
Science - Physical
Dist - VIEWTH **Prod** - VIEWTH

Physical Changes all about Us 14 MIN
U-matic / VHS / 16mm
Color (I J)
$340, $240 purchase _ #3363
Shows different physical changes in size, shape, and appearance produced by different means.
Science - Physical
Dist - CORF

Physical Changes in Matter 15 MIN
VHS / U-matic
First Films on Science Series
Color (P I)
Shows that matter changes form according to the forces acting on it. Traces water as its molecules are changed by the action of heat from ice, a solid, to drinking water, a liquid, and then to water vapor, a gas. Points out that matter may undergo physical changes but that amount will always remain the same.
Science - Physical
Dist - AITECH **Prod** - MAETEL 1975

Physical characteristics - kinship - Parts 7 and 8 60 MIN
VHS / U-matic
French in action - part I series
Color (C) (FRENCH)
$45.00, $29.95 purchase
Looks at the expression of reality and appearance, describing oneself, talking about sports, numbers, questions in Part 7. Shows talking about family relationships, asking the identity of people and things, numbers, dates, partitive, possessive adjectives in Part 8. Parts of a 52 - part series teaching the French language, all in French, written by Pierre Capretz, Director of the Language Laboratory at Yale.
Foreign Language; History - World
Dist - ANNCPB **Prod** - YALEU 1987

Physical Chemistry of Immunohematology 30 MIN
16mm
Clinical Pathology Series
B&W (PRO)
LC 74-705356
Shows how immunological and immunochemical principles are reflected in the performance of routine immunochematologic tests performed in the clinical laboratory.
Health and Safety; Science; Science - Natural
Dist - NMAC **Prod** - NMAC 1968

Physical Conditioning for Prevention of Athletic Injuries 29 MIN
U-matic
Sports Medicine in the 80's Series
Color
Teaches the role of sports medicine as it relates to athlete, coach, trainer, team and school. Covers most kinds of injuries encountered in sports.
Health and Safety; Physical Education and Recreation
Dist - CEPRO **Prod** - CEPRO

Physical Conditions 26 MIN
VHS / U-matic
Right Way Series
Color
Tells how to deal effectively with handicapped and aged drivers.
Health and Safety
Dist - PBS **Prod** - SCETV 1982

Physical Controls 30 MIN
U-matic / VHS
Computer Security Techniques Series
Color
Provides basic measures and techniques for the physical protection of data processing resources.
Industrial and Technical Education
Dist - DELTAK **Prod** - DELTAK

Physical dangers of drug abuse
VHS
Color (J H C G A PRO)
$79.50 purchase _ #AH46313
Uses medical photography and art to demonstrate the medical damage caused by drug abuse. Focuses on the presentation of case histories and medical facts.
Guidance and Counseling; Health and Safety; Psychology; Science - Natural; Sociology
Dist - HTHED **Prod** - HTHED

Physical Development 21 MIN
U-matic / VHS / 16mm
Color (C A)
LC 78-701007
Discusses the physical development during the middle years when a child becomes an adult. Emphasizes the consolidation of growth and the building of strength.
Psychology; Science - Natural; Sociology
Dist - MGHT **Prod** - UCSD 1978

Physical Development 35 MIN
VHS / 16mm
Facts, Feelings and Wonder of Life - the Teenage Years Series
Color (I J H PRO)
$295.00 purchase, $50.00 rental _ #9973
Illustrates the four stages of physical development and answers the questions of teenagers about the changes they are experiencing.
Guidance and Counseling; Health and Safety; Science - Natural
Dist - AIMS **Prod** - PVGP 1988

Physical Development 0 - 3 Months 7 MIN
U-matic
Take Time Series
(A)
Demonstrates the influence of parents and others caring for pre - schoolers on the physical and emotional development of the child.
Health and Safety; Psychology; Sociology
Dist - ACCESS **Prod** - ACCESS 1976

Physical Development in the Middle Years 30 MIN
VHS / 16mm
Growing Years Series
Color (C A)
$85.00, $75.00 purchase _ 02 - 18
Describes the physical growth and nutritional considerations in child development.
Health and Safety; Psychology; Sociology
Dist - CDTEL **Prod** - COAST 1987

Physical Development 9 - 12 Months 7 MIN
U-matic
Take Time Series
(A)
Demonstrates the influence of parents and others caring for pre - schoolers on the physical and emotional development of the child.
Health and Safety; Psychology; Sociology
Dist - ACCESS **Prod** - ACCESS 1976

Physical Development of the Infant 29 MIN
VHS / U-matic
Tomorrow's Families Series
Color (H C A)
LC 81-706916
Explains that physical development of the infant is supported by appropriate nutrition, activity and medical care.
Health and Safety; Home Economics
Dist - AITECH **Prod** - MDDE 1980

Physical Development - Provisions for Growth 30 MIN
U-matic
Dimensions of Child Development Series
Color (PRO)
Identifies the interdependence of the physical skills of a young child including coordination, fine motor and complex skills. Discusses effective use of equipment.
Education
Dist - ACCESS **Prod** - ACCESS 1983

Physical Development 6 - 9 Months 7 MIN
U-matic
Take Time Series
(A)
Demonstrates the influence of parents and others caring for pre - schoolers on the physical and emotional development of the child.
Health and Safety; Psychology; Sociology
Dist - ACCESS **Prod** - ACCESS 1976

Physical Development, the Five Year Old 7 MIN
U-matic
Take Time Series
(A)
Demonstrates the influence of parents and others caring for pre - schoolers on the physical and emotional development of the child.
Health and Safety; Psychology; Sociology
Dist - ACCESS **Prod** - ACCESS 1976

Physical Development, the Four Year Old 7 MIN
U-matic
Take Time Series
(A)
Demonstrates the influence of parents and others caring for pre - schoolers on the physical and emotional development of the child.
Health and Safety; Psychology; Sociology
Dist - ACCESS **Prod** - ACCESS 1976

Physical Development, the One Year Old 7 MIN
U-matic
Take Time Series
(A)
Demonstrates the influence of parents and others caring for pre - schoolers on the physical and emotional development of the child.
Health and Safety; Psychology; Sociology
Dist - ACCESS **Prod** - ACCESS 1976

Physical Development, the Three Year Old 7 MIN
U-matic
Take Time Series
(A)
Demonstrates the influence of parents and others caring for pre - schoolers on the physical and emotional development of the child.
Health and Safety; Psychology; Sociology
Dist - ACCESS **Prod** - ACCESS 1976

Physical Development, the Two Year Old 7 MIN
U-matic
Take Time Series
(A)
Demonstrates the influence of parents and others caring for pre - schoolers on the physical and emotional development of the child.
Health and Safety; Psychology; Sociology
Dist - ACCESS **Prod** - ACCESS 1976

Physical Development 3 - 6 Months 7 MIN
U-matic
Take Time Series
(A)
Demonstrates the influence of parents and others caring for pre - schoolers on the physical and emotional development of the child.
Health and Safety; Psychology; Sociology
Dist - ACCESS **Prod** - ACCESS 1976

Physical Diagnosis - Examination of the Musculoskeletal System 27 MIN
U-matic / VHS / 16mm
Color (PRO)
Examines principles of physical diagnosis relating to the musculoskeletal system.
Science; Science - Natural
Dist - FEIL **Prod** - FEIL

Physical Diagnosis of the Ear, Nose and Throat 28 MIN
16mm
Color (H C)
Demonstrates the proper use of instruments in the examinations of the ear, nose and throat areas.
Health and Safety
Dist - OSUMPD **Prod** - OSUMPD 1960

Physical diagnosis series
The Ears 17 MIN
Dist - NMAC

Physical diagnosis series
The Adult abdomen 16 MIN(0001144)
Dist - WSUM

Physical Diagnosis - the Examination of the Neurological System 36 MIN
U-matic / VHS / 16mm
Color (PRO)
LC FIA67-19
Shows details of the technical aspects of the examination of the neurological system and interprets the meaning of the signs elicited. Uses brain slices and anatomical specimens of the nervous system, along with slides, to illustrate the changes or pathological conditions giving rise to the altered signs. Shows patients to illustrate alterations in gait, position sense and tremor.
Health and Safety; Psychology
Dist - FEIL **Prod** - CWRUSM 1964

Physical differences 20 MIN
BETA / VHS / U-matic
Pediatrics - physical care series
Color (C PRO)
$150.00 purchase _ #147.1
Presents a video transfer of a slide program which describes important physical differences between children and adults. Focuses on anatomic and physiologic differences in the pulmonary, cardiovascular and central nervous systems and emphasizes the implications for nursing care. Part of a series on physical care in pediatric nursing.
Health and Safety; Science - Natural
Dist - CONMED **Prod** - CONMED

Physical Distribution 30 MIN
VHS / U-matic
Marketing Perspectives Series
Color
Compares the advantages of shipping by air, rail and trucks. Shows means to differentiate a common carrier's transportation services from those of competitors.
Business and Economics; Education
Dist - WFVTAE **Prod** - MATC

Physical Education at Packwood School 15 MIN
16mm
B&W
Presents a record of the activities used with mentally subnormal adolescent boys. Illustrates use of the gymnastic table, strengthening activities, log exercises, road - work remedial gymnastics, partner work, special fitness activities and games.
Education; Physical Education and Recreation; Psychology
Dist - NYSED **Prod** - NYSED

Physical Education - Basic Skills 16 MIN
U-matic / VHS / 16mm
Color
Presents basic skills in six sports activities, including apparatus, basketball, football, soccer, softball and tumbling.
Physical Education and Recreation
Dist - AIMS **Prod** - AIMS

Physical Education in Elementary Schools 20 MIN
16mm
Color (C T)
LC FIA66-788
A training film for teachers of physical education in elementary schools. Shows teachers and students during physical education classes and an interview with a school principal.
Education; Physical Education and Recreation
Dist - FINLYS **Prod** - FINLYS 1964

Physical Education, Recreation and Leisure 30 MIN
U-matic
Primer Series
Color (A)
Explains that regardless of degree of mental handicap or age, a wide range of recreational programs and opportunities are necessary to foster health and growth.
Education; Psychology
Dist - ACCESS **Prod** - ACCESS 1981

The Physical Environment 11 MIN
16mm / U-matic / VHS
Biology - Unit 1 - Ecology - Spanish Series; Unit 1 - Ecology
Color (H) (SPANISH)
Illustrates ways in which organisms adapt to their environment.
Foreign Language; Science - Natural
Dist - EBEC **Prod** - EBEC

Physical Evidence Series
Gathering and Analysis 21 MIN
Search and Identification 15 MIN
Dist - CORF

Physical examination 27 MIN
BETA / VHS / U-matic
Physical assessment of the neonate series
Color (C PRO)
$280.00 purchase _ #602.1
Gives instruction in the immediate assessment of the newborn including examination of the head, neck, chest, abdomen, extremities, digits, back, genitals and anus. Helps personnel in concluding that the newborn is in stable condition. Produced by Golden West College.
Health and Safety
Dist - CONMED

The Physical Examination 15 MIN
U-matic / VHS
Color (K A) (SPANISH)
Explains a physical examination to children by taking them through the process.
Fine Arts; Foreign Language; Health and Safety; Sociology
Dist - SUTHRB **Prod** - SUTHRB

A Physical Examination 15 MIN
16mm
Color (K P)
LC 79-701089
Explains the routine procedures involved in a physical examination. Shows youngsters being given a blood test and urinalysis as well as having their heads, chests, abdomens, extremities and genitals checked.
Health and Safety
Dist - SUTHRB **Prod** - BROFLM 1979

Physical Examination of the Chest 20 MIN
U-matic / VHS / 16mm
Physical Respiratory Therapy Series
Color (C A)
Covers the basic elements of a physical examination of the chest, including observation, palpation, percussion and auscultation. Emphasizes the recognition and interpretation of different breathing sounds.
Health and Safety; Science; Science - Natural
Dist - TEF **Prod** - VISCI

Physical Examination of the Elderly 16 MIN
U-matic / VHS / 16mm
Color (PRO C)
$385.00 purchase _ #840VI082
Discusses and illustrates the unique aspects of examining the elderly patient. Demonstrates the left lateral position for rectal and pelvic - including speculum - examination for patients with musculoskeletal stiffness.
Health and Safety
Dist - HSCIC **Prod** - HSCIC 1984

Physical Examination of the Eye 12 MIN
VHS / U-matic / 16mm
Color (PRO C)
$330.00 purchase _ #490VI001
Introduces procedures for examining the eye.
Health and Safety; Science - Natural
Dist - HSCIC **Prod** - HSCIC 1977

Physical Examination of the Injured Athlete
VHS / U-matic
Sports Medicine Series
Color
Shows how to evaluate the severity of an athlete's injury and how to stabilize it until the injury can be properly treated off the field. Includes assessment of vital signs and how to minimize the risk of further injury in transportation of the injured athlete.
Health and Safety
Dist - VTRI **Prod** - VTRI

Physical Examination of the Musculoskeletal System 41 MIN
U-matic / VHS
Color (PRO)
Demonstrates the technique of performing a thorough and systematic examination of the joints. Shows a method to differentiate causes of joint pain and to diagnose specific pathologies of various joints.
Health and Safety; Science - Natural
Dist - UARIZ **Prod** - UARIZ

Physical Examination of the Newborn 18 MIN
VHS / 16mm
(C)
$385.00 purchase _ #870VI036
Shows a nurse performing a complete physical examination of a newborn.
Health and Safety
Dist - HSCIC **Prod** - HSCIC 1987

Physical examination of the newborn 18 MIN
VHS
Color (PRO C G)
$395.00 purchase _ #R870 - VI - 036
Shows a nurse performing a complete physical examination of the newborn. Demonstrates first the steps that begin the examination - observing the general appearance, checking the anterior fontanel, assessing the respiratory and cardiovascular systems, and examining the abdomen. Follows the performance of the rest of the examination, which can be done in any sequence.
Health and Safety
Dist - HSCIC **Prod** - UTXHSH 1987

Physical Examination of the Newborn 25 MIN
U-matic
Color (PRO)
LC 79-706518
Explains the importance of the initial clinical inspection of the newborn. Discusses how the examination should be carried out and what observations and findings should be made and recorded. Demonstrates a method for determining gestational age.
Health and Safety
Dist - UMMCML **Prod** - UMICH 1978

Physical Examination of the Newborn 33 MIN
16mm
Color
Discusses physical examination of the neonate, demonstrating the techniques for routine physical examinations and the techniques for the recognition of abnormalities which may be present. Shows a number of normal conditions which are often mistaken for defects.
Health and Safety
Dist - PFI **Prod** - PFI 1959

Physical Factors in the Parenthood Decision 29 MIN
U-matic / VHS
Tomorrow's Families Series
Color (H C A)
LC 81-706893
Tells how a mother's physical condition and the parents' genetic makeup affect the pregnancy and the child.
Health and Safety; Sociology
Dist - AITECH **Prod** - MDDE 1980

Physical Features 12 MIN
U-matic / VHS / 16mm
Map Skills Series
Color (I J)
$350 purchase - 16 mm, $250 purchase - video _ #5192C
Shows how a map indicates physical features, and how to determine land contour. Produced by Christianson Productions.
Social Science
Dist - CORF

Physical Features of India 26 MIN
16mm
B&W (I)
Gives a comprehensive picture of all three regions of India - the Himalayas, the Indo - gangetic plains and the Peninsular India.
Geography - World; History - World
Dist - NEDINF **Prod** - INDIA

Physical Fitness 13 MIN
U-matic / VHS / 16mm
Fun to be Fit Series
Color (I)
Defines physical fitness and the need for developing fitness in the areas of cardio - pulmonary endurance, muscle strength, muscle endurance, flexibility and body composition.
Physical Education and Recreation
Dist - CORF **Prod** - DISNEY 1983

Physical Fitness 19 MIN
U-matic / VHS / 16mm
Physical Fitness Series
Color (H C A)
LC 81-701107
Discusses the importance of keeping physically fit and shows that through proper diet and exercise a person can lose weight, reduce the risk of heart and blood vessel diseases, and achieve greater endurance and stamina.
Health and Safety; Physical Education and Recreation
Dist - JOU **Prod** - PRORE 1980

Physical Fitness 29 MIN
16mm
Big Picture Series
Color
LC 75-701193
Shows how the U S Army places much emphasis on physical fitness training in developing the soldier.
Civics and Political Systems; Physical Education and Recreation
Dist - USNAC **Prod** - USA 1967

Physical Fitness 30 MIN
U-matic / VHS
Here's to Your Health Series
Color (C T)
Explains that each individual must set his or her own goals to become physically fit. Discusses how planned programs succeed.
Health and Safety; Physical Education and Recreation
Dist - DALCCD **Prod** - DALCCD

Physical Fitness and Good Health 10 MIN
U-matic / VHS / 16mm
Color (I J H) (THAI)
Stresses the effect of physical fitness on social and mental health. Speaks on exercise, rest and proper diet.
Foreign Language; Health and Safety; Physical Education and Recreation
Dist - CORF **Prod** - DISNEY 1969

Physical Fitness and Good Health 10 MIN
U-matic / VHS / 16mm
Triangle of Health - Swedish Series
Color (I J H) (SWEDISH)
Stresses the effect of physical fitness on social and mental health. Speaks on exercise, rest and proper diet.
Foreign Language; Health and Safety; Physical Education and Recreation
Dist - CORF **Prod** - DISNEY 1969

Physical Fitness and Good Health 10 MIN
16mm / U-matic / VHS
Triangle of Health - Hungarian Series
Color (I J H) (HUNGARIAN)
Stresses the effect of physical fitness on social and mental health. Speaks on exercise, rest and proper dict.
Foreign Language; Health and Safety; Physical Education and Recreation
Dist - CORF **Prod** - DISNEY 1969

Physical Fitness and Good Health 10 MIN
U-matic / VHS / 16mm
Triangle of Health - Arabic Series
Color (I J H) (ARABIC)
Stresses the effect of physical fitness on social and mental health. Speaks on exercise, rest and proper diet.
Foreign Language; Health and Safety; Physical Education and Recreation
Dist - CORF **Prod** - DISNEY 1969

Physical Fitness and Good Health 10 MIN
U-matic / VHS / 16mm
Triangle of Health - German Series
Color (I J H) (GERMAN)
Stresses the effect of physical fitness on social and mental health. Speaks on exercise, rest and proper diet.
Foreign Language; Health and Safety; Physical Education and Recreation
Dist - CORF **Prod** - DISNEY 1969

Physical Fitness and Good Health 10 MIN
16mm / U-matic / VHS
Triangle of Health Series
Color (P I J H)
LC 70-712354
Discusses the importance of keeping the body physically fit and stresses the value of exercise to keep the heart and other muscles and organs functioning properly.
Physical Education and Recreation
Dist - CORF **Prod** - UPJOHN 1969

Physical Fitness and Good Health 10 MIN
16mm / U-matic / VHS
Triangle of Health - Spanish Series
Color (I J H) (SPANISH)
Stresses the effect of physical fitness on social and mental health. Speaks on exercise, rest and proper diet.
Foreign Language; Health and Safety; Physical Education and Recreation
Dist - CORF **Prod** - DISNEY 1969

Physical Fitness and Health
VHS
$139.00 purchase _ #HR101V
Features Dr James R White showing the benefits of fitness and how the cardiovascular system is affected by such things as hypertension, obesity and excessive use of alcohol, caffeine, and tobacco.
Health and Safety; Psychology
Dist - CAREER **Prod** - CAREER

Physical Fitness and Health
VHS
Color (J)
Demonstrates the benefits of fitness and the effects of various factors on cardiovascular system, including hypertension, obesity, alcohol, caffeine and tobacco.
Health and Safety; Physical Education and Recreation
Dist - HRMC **Prod** - HRMC 1986

Physical Fitness for WAVES - make - Up from the Neck Down 20 MIN
16mm
B&W
LC FIE52-1092
Presents a physical fitness program designed to persuade waves to exercise. Points out the value of sports but stresses the greater value of planned exercises and illustrates some of these exercises.
Civics and Political Systems; Physical Education and Recreation
Dist - USNAC **Prod** - USN 1944

Physical Fitness in the Later Years 23 MIN
U-matic / VHS / 16mm
Be Well - the Later Years Series
Color (C A)
LC 83-700399
Explains how exercise can help keep the body parts functioning, lessen pain and provide a feeling of well being. Describes different kinds of exercise programs, offers cautions, and suggests ways to motivate oneself.
Health and Safety; Physical Education and Recreation; Sociology
Dist - CF **Prod** - CF 1983

Physical Fitness - it Can Save Your Life 24 MIN
16mm / U-matic / VHS
Wide World of Adventure Series

Color (I J H)
Suggests a program of daily exercise and diet to overcome poor physical health, due to inactivity and overeating.
Health and Safety; Physical Education and Recreation; Social Science
Dist - EBEC **Prod** - AVATLI 1977

Physical Fitness Program for the United States Navy 25 MIN
U-matic
B&W
Shows exercises given the naval trainee and correlates their value with varied duties he will be called upon to perform afloat.
History - United States; Physical Education and Recreation
Dist - USNAC **Prod** - USNAC 1972

Physical Fitness Series
Physical Fitness 19 MIN
The Picture of Health 13 MIN
The Picture of Health - Genetic Platforms 13 MIN
Superjock 16 MIN
Superjock Scales Down 15 MIN
Dist - JOU

Physical Fitness Series
Tinikling - the Bamboo Dance 17 MIN
Dist - MMP

Physical Fitness - the New Perspective 10 MIN
VHS / 16mm / U-matic
Color (A)
Describes the adverse effects that sedentary lifestyles can have on physical fitness. Shows the positive aspects of being physically fit, and describes the simple ways to increase daily activity. Presented in animated cartoon format.
Physical Education and Recreation
Dist - PRORE **Prod** - PRORE

Physical Fitness Training - Navy Standard Physical Fitness Test 20 MIN
U-matic
B&W
Presents tests of strength, endurance, stamina and degree of agility, such as squat thrusts, sit - ups, push - ups, squat - jumps and pull - ups.
History - United States; Physical Education and Recreation
Dist - USNAC **Prod** - USNAC 1972

Physical Form 30 MIN
U-matic / VHS
Better Business Letters Series Lesson I; Lesson 1
Color
Discusses what letters should look like. Examines how letters show the corporate image.
Business and Economics; English Language
Dist - TELSTR **Prod** - TELSTR

Physical geography - for key stage 4 series
Physical geography series - for key stage 4 80 MIN
Dist - EMFVL

Physical geography of North America series
Presents a five - part series on the physical geography of North America. Includes the titles The East, The Pacific Edge, The Rocky Mountains, The Central Lowlands, The Northlands, The Western Drylands.
The Central lowlands 20 MIN
The East 20 MIN
The Northlands 20 MIN
The Pacific edge 20 MIN
The Rocky Mountains 20 MIN
The Western dry lands 20 MIN
Dist - NGS **Prod** - NGS

Physical geography of the continents series
Presents a six - part series on the physical geography of the continents. Includes the titles Europe, Antarctica, South America, Australia, Asia, Africa.
Africa 27 MIN
Antarctica 25 MIN
Asia 25 MIN
Australia 25 MIN
Europe 26 MIN
South America 25 MIN
Dist - NGS **Prod** - NGS

Physical geography series - for key stage 4 80 MIN
VHS
Physical geography - for key stage 4 series
Color; PAL (J H)
Features six programs including Ice Formation and Erosion; River Processes; Glacial Deposition and Landforms; Draining Basin Landforms; Coastal Processes; and Coastal Landforms. Presents a CV production from the United Kingdom. Price available on request.
Geography - World
Dist - EMFVL

Physical growth and motor development 19 MIN
BETA / VHS / U-matic
Human development - first 2.5 years series
Color (C PRO)
$280.00 purchase _ #616.1
Emphasizes individual differences by depicting a wide range or normal physical growth and motor development. Discusses ways in which environmental factors such as nutrition and the mother's health habits during pregnancy affect development. Traces developmental patterns and norms. Part of a four - part series on the first 2.5 years of human development.
Health and Safety; Psychology
Dist - CONMED **Prod** - CONMED

Physical growth and motor development 21 MIN
BETA / VHS / U-matic
Human development - 2.5 to 6 years series
Color (C PRO)
$280.00 purchase _ #620.1
Discusses the pattern of growth seen in the years between 2.5 and 6. Describes how the increased growth of various organs affects the child's ability to function. Examines gross motor development of the preschool child, including walking, running, jumping, skipping and stair climbing. Illustrates fine motor development and eye - hand coordination and discusses how these abilities aid the child in performing personal skills. Discusses how caretakers can maximize children's physical potentials. Part of a four - part series on human development, ages 2.5 to 6.
Health and Safety; Physical Education and Recreation; Psychology
Dist - CONMED **Prod** - CONMED

The Physical Hazards We Face 12 TO 18 MIN
VHS / U-matic
MSDS and you series
Color (IND)
Focuses on information provided on the MSDS about fire and safety hazards as well as reactivity hazards. Second in a three part series.
Health and Safety; Sociology
Dist - IFB **Prod** - BIOCON 1986

Physical Interpretation of the K and B Formulas 29 MIN
U-matic / VHS
Nonlinear Vibrations Series
B&W
Mathematics
Dist - MIOT **Prod** - MIOT

Physical Limitations 10 MIN
16mm
Safety and You Series
Color
Shows how awareness of physical limitations helps prevent accidents and errors in judgment.
Health and Safety; Psychology
Dist - FILCOM **Prod** - FILCOM

Physical Management of Psychiatric Patients 27 MIN
U-matic / VHS / 16mm
Color (PRO)
LC 77-701672
Presents a series of individual segments on managing the disturbed patient in rare instances where psychological techniques fail.
Psychology
Dist - USNAC **Prod** - USVA 1977

Physical Me 29 MIN
VHS / 16mm
Villa Alegre Series
Color (P T)
$46.00 rental _ #VILA - 131
Presents educational material in both Spanish and English.
Education; Psychology
Dist - PBS

Physical Metallurgy - Structure and Properties 50 MIN
BETA / VHS / U-matic
Color
$400 purchase
Presents physical makeup and dissimilarities between metals and nonmetals.
Science; Science - Physical
Dist - ASM **Prod** - ASM

Physical models - monolayer, bilayer and liposomes 17 MIN
VHS
Biological membranes series
Color (G C)
$110.00 purchase, $14.00 rental _ #23585
Discusses the physical properties of water and the interface behavior of emphipathic molecules which promote the organization of distinctive structures, as demonstrated in the hydrophobic - hydrophilic behavior of phospholipids. Reveals that monolayer, bilayer and liposomes are typical basic structures. Uses animated models to demonstrate their production and function. Part of a series on biological membranes.
Science - Natural
Dist - PSU **Prod** - IWIF 1979

Physical oceanography 19 MIN
Videodisc / VHS
Earth science library series
Color (J H)
$99.95, $69.95 purchase _ #Q18452
Stesses the relationship between the oceans, the atmosphere and the earth's crust. Features scientists in deep diving submersibles and investigates the ocean's mineral resources. Considers the growing impact of human activities such as oil spills and global warming.
Science - Physical; Sociology
Dist - CF

Physical oceanography 19 MIN
VHS
Earth science series
Color (J H)
$64.95 purchase _ #ES 8450
Explores the oceans from the biologically diverse continental shelves to the depths of the abyssal plains. Includes live footage from deep diving submersibles. Includes a teachers' guide. Part of a six - part series taking a contemporary look at Planet Earth, its natural resources and the human impact on global environment.
Science - Physical
Dist - INSTRU **Prod** - SCTRES

Physical Oceanography 15 MIN
VHS
Color (J)
$59.95 purchase _ #8450V
Explores the oceans. Travels from the biologically diverse continental shelves to the deep icy waters of the abyssal plains. Includes live footage from deep diving submersibles.
Geography - World; Science; Science - Physical
Dist - SCTRES **Prod** - SCTRES

Physical performing 30 MIN
VHS
Video guide to occupational exploration - the video GOE series
Color (J H C G)
$69.95 purchase _ #CCP1014V
Covers Sports and Physical Feats. Interviews a professional football player, tennis coach, baseball umpire, professional player, equestrian and a white water river guide. Part of a 14 - part series exploring occupational clusters.
Business and Economics; Guidance and Counseling; Physical Education and Recreation
Dist - CAMV **Prod** - CAMV 1991

Physical Properties and Molecular Structure 10 MIN
U-matic
Chemistry Videotape Series
Color
Introduces hydrogen bonding and its effects on solubility, melting point and boiling point. Demonstrates measurement techniques to determine melting and boiling points.
Science - Physical
Dist - UMITV **Prod** - UMITV

Physical rehabilitation 28 MIN
16mm
Color; B&W (C PRO)
Shows laymen, physical therapists, occupational therapists and physicians that rehabilitation therapy is not a luxury, but a practical and economical medical treatment. Demonstrates and describes fundamental methods.
Health and Safety
Dist - FO **Prod** - FO 1954

Physical respiratory therapy series
Breathing exercises - how and why 13 MIN
Introduction to chest physiotherapy 20 MIN
Pediatric Physiotherapy 14 MIN
Physical Examination of the Chest 20 MIN
Postural drainage and percussion 16 MIN
Dist - TEF

Physical Science - Chemical Energy 17 MIN
16mm / U-matic / VHS
Color (I J)
Considers the combining and separation of atoms in molecules that constitute chemical change and discusses how this differs from physical change. Shows means of causing chemical change, particularly by heat energy. Explains the importance of oxidation, providing examples ranging from explosive energy release to slow change in the human body.
Science - Physical
Dist - CF **Prod** - CF 1984

Physical science - electric currents and circuits 17 MIN
VHS
Color; PAL (H G)
Demonstrates how energy is continually transferred by electrical currents through intricate networks of circuits. Reveals that large circuits supply whole communties with electricity, smaller circuits supply individual buidlings, electrical devices or even exist on microscopic levels in computer chips. Looks at the concepts of voltage, current, resistance, series and parallel circuits and power.
Industrial and Technical Education; Science - Physical; Social Science
Dist - VIEWTH **Prod** - VIEWTH

Physical science - electrical energy 14 MIN
U-matic / VHS / 16mm
Color (I J)
$310.00 purchase, 16 mm; $230.00 purchase, video
Describes electrons and protons, discusses how an imbalance creates an electric charge, and shows how this can create static electricity or a flow of electrons in a battery. Demonstrates induction of a current with coil and how an electro - magnet spinning between two magnets causes the current to alternate.
Science - Physical
Dist - CF **Prod** - CF 1988

Physical science - electricity and magnetism 17 MIN
VHS
Color; PAL (H G)
Reveals that many devices which power technological civilization depend upon a relationship between motion and two basic properties of matter - electricity and magnetism. Uses animation to show how forces exerted by electric charges and magnets are related, how their interactions cause motion. Shows appllications in motors, generators and transformers and explores the relationship of the Earth's magnetic field, the aurora borealis and nuclear fusion.
Industrial and Technical Education; Science - Physical
Dist - VIEWTH **Prod** - VIEWTH

Physical Science - Energy at Work 13 MIN
U-matic / VHS / 16mm
Color (J H)
LC 83-700940
Introduces different kinds of energy, including mechanical, heat, light, chemical, electrical and nuclear. Explains concepts of input and output of energy.
Science - Physical
Dist - CF **Prod** - CF 1983

Physical Science Film Series
The Nature of Matter - an Atomic View 24 MIN
The Origin of the Elements 18 MIN
The States of Matter 18 MIN
Dist - CRMP

Physical science film series
Energy - a conversation 27 MIN
Dist - MGHT

Physical science - heat and energy transfer 13 MIN
VHS
Color; PAL (H G)
Shows that heat is a form of motion, a form of kinetic energy. Reveals that heat can be converted to other forms of energy and transferred through conduction, convection and radiation. Considers how all life depends upon heat energy.
Science - Physical; Social Science
Dist - VIEWTH **Prod** - VIEWTH

Physical science - heat energy 16 MIN
U-matic / VHS / 16mm
Color (J H)
$340.00 purchase, 16 mm; $255.00 purchase, video; LC 83-700941
Introduces heat energy and the way it is used. Describes changes in molecular motion when heat is added and demonstrates expansion in solids, liquids and gases when heated. Explains the difference between heat and temperature and ways of measuring temperature. Gives examples of the way heat energy is used.
Science - Physical
Dist - CF **Prod** - CF 1983

Physical science - heat, temperature and the properties of matter 17 MIN
VHS
Color; PAL (H G)
Explores visually how heat energy affects the properties of substances. Shows volume changes, changes in state and speed of reaction as related to heat. Distinguishes between the concepts of heat and temperature as well as the relationships of the Fahrenheit, Celsius and Kelvin scales.
Mathematics; Science - Physical
Dist - VIEWTH **Prod** - VIEWTH

Physical Science Learning Lab Series
Explores the world of physical science, especially the hidden world of particle structure and behavior. Uses a combination of models, live photography, animation, demonstrations and experiments that can be duplicated in the classroom. Explains many important scientific principles that are part of our everyday lives.
Energy Does Work 13.5 MIN
Magnetism and Fields of Force 13.5 MIN
Matter Changes 13.5 MIN
Matter is Everything 12 MIN
Physical Science Learning Lab Series
Dist - BARR **Prod** - BARR

Physical science - light and images 14 MIN
VHS
Color; PAL (H G)
Uses a jazz dance trio rehearsal before a mirror and photographer to investigate the nature of light. Illustrates reflection, refraction and absorption as well as how images are produced in cameras and the human eye. Examines light as wave and particle, as an energy form requiring no medium for transmission, but one that is affected by boundaries between mediums.
Industrial and Technical Education; Science - Physical
Dist - VIEWTH **Prod** - VIEWTH

Physical science - light and the electromagnetic spectrum 14 MIN
VHS
Color; PAL (H G)
Examines the relationship between light and other forms of electromagnetic radiation - cosmic rays, gamma rays, ultra - violet and infra - red rays, radio waves and light waves - through a televion broadcast of a videotape of jazz dancers. Shows how the generation and transmission of these waves has allowed scientists to probe the hidden regions of the human body and to explore the mysteries of the universe.
Fine Arts; Science - Physical
Dist - VIEWTH **Prod** - VIEWTH

Physical science - light, colour and the visible spectrum 13 MIN
VHS
Color; PAL (H G)
Views a colorfully costumed jazz group being videotaped. Observes the effects of using and mixing colored lights and filters, the principles of additive and subtractive color mixing. Shows that the color perceived by the human eye is determined by which wavelength of white light reaches the eye.
Science - Physical
Dist - VIEWTH **Prod** - VIEWTH

Physical Science - Light Energy 14 MIN
16mm / U-matic / VHS
Color (I J)
Explains that light sources occur by the transfers of other forms of energy into light energy. Discusses the theory of photons. Considers the wavelengths of light, their place in the electromagnetic spectrum, and various examples of the wave - particle characteristics of light.
Science - Physical
Dist - CF **Prod** - CF 1985

Physical Science - Mechanical Energy 15 MIN
U-matic / VHS / 16mm
Color (I J)
Describes how mechanical energy exerts a force in solid, liquid and gas states. Explains potential and kinetic energy and how machines provide mechanical energy.
Science - Physical
Dist - CF **Prod** - CF 1984

Physical science - secrets of science series - Set Three 188 MIN
VHS
Secrets of science series
Color (I J H C)
$159.00 purchase
Presents four videos on physical science. Includes The Mysteries of Motion and Power; Exploring Energy; Of Wheels and Wings; and Through the Looking Glass. Hosted by Discover Magazine Editor in Chief Paul Hoffman.
Industrial and Technical Education; Science - Physical; Social Science
Dist - EFVP **Prod** - DSCOVM 1994

Physical science - secrets of science series
Exploring energy - Video 11 47 MIN
The Mysteries of motion and power - Video 10 47 MIN
Of wheels and wings - Video 12 47 MIN
Dist - EFVP

Physical science series
Features a series of six programs that utilize descriptions, illustrations, and experiments to describe types of energy and how they are used. Focuses on chemical, light, mechanical, electrical, and heat energy. Considers how the basic principles of energy are the foundations for much of modern technology.
Chemical energy 17 MIN
Electrical energy 14 MIN
Heat energy 15 MIN
Light energy 14 MIN
Mechanical energy 15 MIN
Dist - CF

Physical Science Series
Electric Currents and Circuits 17 MIN
Electricity and Magnetism 17 MIN
Eletricity and magnetism 17 MIN
Heat and Energy Transfer 14 MIN
Heat, Temperature and the Properties of Matter 17 MIN
Light and Images 10 MIN
Light and the Electromagnetic Spectrum 14 MIN
Light, Color and the Visible Spectrum 13 MIN
Sound, Acoustics, and Recording 14 MIN
Sound, Energy and Wave Motion 14 MIN
Static and Current Electricity 16 MIN
Dist - CORF

Physical science - sound, acoustics and recording 14 MIN
VHS
Color; PAL (H G)
Uses an auditorium and a recording studio to demonstrate how interior surfaces affect sound waves. Illustrates how materials on these surfaces determine what is absorbed or reflected and how these materials are used to control echoes and reverberations.
Fine Arts; Science - Physical
Dist - VIEWTH **Prod** - VIEWTH

Physical science - sound, energy and wave motions 14 MIN
VHS
Color; PAL (H G)
Presents a jazz trio playing in an open field to give a sound demonstration of how energy moves from player to instrument to the surrounding air, is transferred by compressional waves to produce energy changes in the listener's ears. Examines musical instruments to illustrate the relationship between the pitch, frequency, loudness and amplitude of sound waves and explains how and why sounds of the same pitch and loudness can differ in quality to give instruments their characteristic sound.
Fine Arts; Science - Physical
Dist - VIEWTH **Prod** - VIEWTH

Physical Science (Spanish Series
El Origen De Los Elementos 18 MIN
La Energia 27 MIN
La Naturaliez De La Materia 24 MIN
Los Estados De La Materia 18 MIN
Dist - MGHT

Physical science - static and current electricity 16 MIN
VHS
Color; PAL (H G)
Uses experimentation and animation to demonstrate the causes, effects and application of static charges and their relation to an electric current and a complete circuit. Begins with the atom and its charged parts to show that electric charges result from positive and negative charges basic to the structure of matter.
Industrial and Technical Education; Science - Physical
Dist - VIEWTH **Prod** - VIEWTH

Physical sciences
Kit / Software / Videodisc
Newton's apple series
Color (I J) (ENGLISH AND SPANISH)
$225.00 purchase _ #T81285; $325.00 purchase _ #T81280
Introduces students to principles of physcial sciences, relating principles to everyday activities. Includes subjects - Buoyancy; Frisbee physics; Skydiving; Sideview mirror; Roller coaster; Doppler effect; Newton's laws; Slinky (Registered trademark) physics. Higher-priced kit includes software for use on Macintosh computers only.
Science - Physical
Dist - NGS

Physical Security, Pt 10 - Identification and Control 22 MIN
16mm
Color
LC 74-705359
Discusses purpose and techniques of ID and control procedures. Includes badges, access lists, duress codes and new equipment.

Business and Economics; Civics and Political Systems
Dist - USNAC **Prod** - USA 1971

Physical Security Surveys 30 MIN
16mm
B&W
LC 74-705358
Describes the purpose, fundamentals and procedures for a physical security survey of a military installation to uncover and correct security weakness.
Business and Economics; Civics and Political Systems
Dist - USNAC **Prod** - USA 1964

Physical Set - Up of the Letter 35 MIN
VHS / U-matic
Better Business Letters Series
Color
Business and Economics; English Language
Dist - DELTAK **Prod** - TELSTR

Physical Signs and Effects of Venereal Diseases 28 MIN
16mm / U-matic / VHS
Inner Woman Series
Color
Discusses several types of venereal diseases and emphasizes the importance of immediate medical attention.
Health and Safety
Dist - CRMP **Prod** - WXYZTV 1975
MGHT

Physical therapist
VHS
Vocational visions career series
Color (H A)
$39.95 purchase _ #CDS504
Interviews people who are physical therapists. Answers questions about the educational requirements and necessary skills for the occupation, as well as its career opportunities, salary range and outlook for the future. Part of a series which examines the potential of various occupations.
Business and Economics; Guidance and Counseling; Psychology; Science
Dist - CADESF **Prod** - CADESF 1989

Physical therapist
VHS
Day in a career series
Color (C H A J T G)
$89.00 purchase _ #VOC07V
Presents information about the occupation of physical therapist, of the careers that the United States Department of Labor projects as potentially successful by the year 2000. Profiles in detail the work day of a real person, with candid interviews and work situations and information about the educational requirements, credentials, job outlook, salaries, important associations, and contacts in the field. One of a series of ten videos, lasting 15 to 22 minutes, available individually or as a set.
Business and Economics; Guidance and Counseling; Health and Safety
Dist - CAMV

Physical therapist 19 MIN
VHS
Get a life - a day in the career guidance series
Color (H C A)
$89.00 purchase _ #886696-09-8
Takes viewers on a typical day in a physical therapy practice. Interviews the senior therapists and reveals the type of cases that they deal with frequently. Depicts the patients during the course of the day and their various therapies are explained. Addresses the kind of person it takes to be a therapist along with educational and credentialing requirements. Part of a ten-part series.
Business and Economics; Guidance and Counseling; Health and Safety
Dist - VOCAVD **Prod** - VOCAVD 1995

Physical therapy for arthritis - 1 16 MIN
VHS
Living well with arthritis series
Color (C PRO G)
$395.00 purchase _ #R911 - VI - 002
Discusses the two common types of arthritis - rheumatoid arthritis and osteoarthritis. Reveals that osteoarthritis is the most common, the causes of both types are unknown. Focuses on physical therpay intervention and the treatment of arthritis, how to instruct the patient on what treatment to follow when a problem arises and under what conditions a doctor should be notified. Part of a five - part series on arthritis.
Health and Safety
Dist - HSCIC **Prod** - BRMARH 1991

Physical Therapy for Suppurative Lung Disease Patients 42 MIN
U-matic
Color (PRO)
LC 80-706785
Explains the physical therapist's role in the treatment of suppurative pulmonary problems. Discusses therapeutic techniques.
Health and Safety
Dist - USNAC **Prod** - VAHSL 1980

Physical Therapy in the Treatment of Parkinsonism 15 MIN
16mm
Color
LC 75-702335
Presents a group physical therapy approach to the treatment of Parkinsonism which stresses alternating reciprocal movements of the limbs and trunk. Shows that the result of therapy is the re - establishment and retention of normal patterns by these patients.
Health and Safety
Dist - EATONL **Prod** - EATONL 1971

Physical Therapy in the Treatment of the Adult Hemiplegic Patient 26 MIN
16mm
Color
LC FIE67-84
Demonstrates physical therapy in the treatment of the adult hemiplegic patient, showing Bobath treatmenttechniques applied to a patient in the following positions - - supine, prone, sitting, kneeling, standing and walking.
Health and Safety; Psychology
Dist - USNAC **Prod** - USA 1962

Physical Therapy Management of a Bilateral Amputee 33 MIN
16mm
Color
LC 74-706176
Discusses the early management of above - knee and below - knee unilateral amputees, as well as rehabilitation of the bilateral amputee. Shows fitting of and training with protheses.
Health and Safety
Dist - USNAC **Prod** - USA 1964

Physical Therapy Management of Above - Knee and Below - Knee Amputees 23 MIN
16mm
Color
LC 79-701854
Highlights the major goals that the physical therapist wants the patient to achieve before being discharged from physical therapy care, including stump hygiene, bandaging, crutch walking, adequate range of motion, applying the prosthesis, functional strength, and correct gait ambulation. Details the steps involved in preprosthetic and prosthetic treatment.
Health and Safety; Psychology
Dist - USNAC **Prod** - WRAIR 1978

Physical therapy management of the patient with quadriplegia - Pt 1 30 MIN
U-matic
Color (PRO)
Presents therapeutic exercise programs for treating quadriplegia. Discusses treatment goals and demonstrates exercise regimes. Designed for therapists, students, patients and their families.
Health and Safety
Dist - RICHGO **Prod** - RICHGO

Physical Therapy Management of the Pre - and Post - Operative Open Heart Patient 14 MIN
16mm
Color
Depicts breathing exercise given to a patient prior to a heart operation and follow - up treatment after the operation.
Health and Safety
Dist - USNAC **Prod** - USPHS 1966

Physical therapy series
Presents a 19 - part series on physical therapy. Teaches effective techniques for minimizing pain and fatigue while enhancing the ability to perform daily activities. Produced by the physical therapy staff, St Luke's Hospital, Fargo, North Dakota.
Active range of motion exercises
Back strengthening exercises
Cervical traction in the sitting position
Cervical traction in the supine position
Contrast baths for the hands or feet
Heat and massage for the low back
Heat, massage and exercise for the neck and upper back
Heat, massage and quad setting for the knee
Low back extension exercises
Low back flexion exercises
Neck and back strengthening and stretching
Paraffin bath home program
Passive range of motion exercises for the lower extremity
Passive range of motion exercises for the upper extremity
Relaxation exercises
Self range of motion for lower extremity stretching
Shoulder mobilization exercises
Strengthening exercises for the lower extremity
Strengthening exercises for the upper extremity
Dist - HSCIC

Physical Therapy Techniques for Bulbar Involvement 26 MIN
16mm
Color
Discusses the anatomy of the jaw and bulbar region and points out malfunction caused by paralysis of the muscles involved. Offers techniques for the functional training of the muscles of the jaw, tongue, pharynx and larynx.
Health and Safety
Dist - RLAH **Prod** - RLAH

Physical Training in Sweden 10 MIN
16mm
B&W
Shows how the Swedes take an interest in every aspect of physical education.
Geography - World; Physical Education and Recreation
Dist - AUDPLN **Prod** - ASI

The Physical World of a Machine 13 MIN
VHS / 16mm
Industrial Hydraulic Technology Series
Color (H A)
$410.00 purchase, $110.00 rental
Demonstrates the relationship of physics to hydraulics - force, resistance, energy, work and power.
Industrial and Technical Education
Dist - TAT **Prod** - TAT 1976

Physically fit - faithfully yours 27 MIN
VHS
Color (A R)
$15.00 purchase _ #S10169
Shows how a Christian day school's wellness program eventually inspired the rest of the congregation. Includes discussion guide.
Guidance and Counseling; Literature and Drama; Religion and Philosophy
Dist - CPH **Prod** - LUMIS

The Physically Handicapped and Health Impaired Child in the Regular Classroom 30 MIN
U-matic / VHS
Promises to Keep Series Module 5
Color (T)
Considers selected physical conditions which may require special attention in the regular classroom. Discusses possible environmental and material accommodations along with guidelines for promoting acceptance in the classroom.
Education
Dist - LUF **Prod** - VPI 1979

Physically Handicapped Child in Foster Care 30 MIN
U-matic / VHS
Color
Looks at how one family has met the challenge of caring for three physically handicapped foster children.
Guidance and Counseling; Psychology; Sociology
Dist - CORF **Prod** - CORF 1984

Physically Impaired 20 MIN
U-matic
One Giant Step - the Integration of Children with Special Needs 'Series
Color (PRO)
Documents that the type of education physically handicapped children receive depends on their intellectual, sensory, physical and emotional characteristics.
Education
Dist - ACCESS **Prod** - ACCESS 1983

Physician 20 TO 30 MIN
U-matic
Opportunity Profile Series
(H C A)
$99.95 _ #AI207
Illustrates the daily activities involved in a career as a physician. Working professionals in related occupations describe the negative and positive aspects of such jobs.
Guidance and Counseling; Health and Safety
Dist - CAMV **Prod** - CAMV

Physician 25 MIN
VHS
Career encounters series
Color (J H C A)
$95.00 purchase _ #MG3401V-J
Presents a documentary-style program that explores a career as a physician. Features professionals at work, explaining what they do and how they got where they are. Emphasizes diversity of occupational opportunities and of men and women in the field. Offers information about new developments and technologies and about educational and certification requirements for entering the profession. One of a series of videos about professions available individually or as a set.
Business and Economics; Guidance and Counseling; Science
Dist - CAMV

Physician - Administrator Pressure Points 25 MIN
VHS / U-matic
Color
Examines sensitive and important aspects of hospital administration. Answers hard - hitting questions by a sequence of vignettes.
Health and Safety
Dist - TEACHM **Prod** - TEACHM

The Physician as a Community Consultant 30 MIN
U-matic / VHS
Color (PRO)
Stimulates discussion among doctors and medical students on the subject of community consultation.
Health and Safety; Social Science
Dist - HSCIC **Prod** - HSCIC 1980

The Physician Assistant - a Rural Profile 8 MIN
VHS / U-matic
Color
LC 80-706786
Focuses on a physician assistant working in the sparsely populated community of Hardin, Illinois.
Health and Safety
Dist - USNAC **Prod** - VAHSL 1980

The Physician Assistant - an Urban Profile 9 MIN
VHS / U-matic
Color
LC 80-707112
Offers a profile of a physician assistant in an urban, inner - city environment. Excerpted from the videorecording issued in 1977 under the title The Physician Assistant, New Member Of The Health Care Team.
Health and Safety
Dist - USNAC **Prod** - VAHSL 1980

The Physician Assistant - New Member of the Health Care Team 21 MIN
U-matic
Color
LC 79-707300
Describes the historical background, role, education and utilization of the physician's assistant.
Health and Safety; Science
Dist - USNAC **Prod** - VAHSL 1977

Physician Surplus 22 MIN
U-matic / VHS
Future of Nursing Series
Color (PRO)
Considers the consequences on health care and nursing with regard to an impending surplus of doctors.
Health and Safety
Dist - HSCIC **Prod** - HSCIC 1985

Physicians
VHS / U-matic
Opportunity Profile Series
$99.95 purchase _ #AJ106V
Provides advice on the skills and educational background desired by companies, the day to day activities of various careers, and the positive and negative aspects of various careers from corporate vice presidents, managers, and other working professionals.
Guidance and Counseling
Dist - CAREER **Prod** - CAREER

Physicians and AIDS - the ethical response - Part I 25 MIN
U-matic / VHS
Color (PRO)
$385.00 purchase, $65.00 rental, $695.00, $125.00 set
Dramatizes the dilemma of a surgeon on call, asked to perform gall bladder surgery on a man with HIV infection. Follows the surgeon as he discusses his concerns with colleagues and comes to terms with his own reservations. Treats the issue which has divided the medical community over whether or not a physician's refusal to treat HIV positive patients can be reconciled with the ethical responsibilities of the profession. Assesses the impact of major psychosocial barriers within the profession, including fear of contagion, confrontation with mortality, feelings of helplessness and hopelessness, and feelings of revulsion toward patients' lifestyles. Represents the first part of a two - part set.
Health and Safety
Dist - BAXMED **Prod** - BAXMED 1991

Physicians and AIDS - the ethical response - Part II 25 MIN
U-matic / VHS
Color (PRO)
$385.00 purchase, $65.00 rental, $695.00, $125.00 set
Presents candid interviews with physicians who have been treating patients who are HIV positive. Offers insights regarding common fears and feelings and provides personal and professional advice to colleagues who are wrestling with this issue. Designed to serve as a model for physicians to help resolve underlying psychosocial conflicts regarding care of seropositive patients. Represents the second part of a two - part set.
Health and Safety
Dist - BAXMED **Prod** - BAXMED 1991

Physicians and AIDS - the ethical response - Parts I and II 48 MIN
VHS / U-matic
Color (G PRO)
$695.00 purchase, $150.00 rental
Presents two parts on the debate over whether or not physician refusal to treat patients with HIV infection can be reconciled with the ethical responsibilities of the profession. Dramatizes the dilemma of a physician asked by an internist to remove the gallbladder of a man with HIV in Part I. Part II interviews physicians who have been treating patients with HIV and discusses their fears and feelings.
Health and Safety
Dist - BAXMED **Prod** - BAXMED

Physicians and health practitioners 30 MIN
VHS
Video career library series
Color (J H C)
$79.95 purchase _ #4368
Focuses on physicians and health practitioners. Describes job duties; working conditions; wages and salaries; job outlook; and training and education required. Part of an 18 - part series describing 165 occupations.
Business and Economics; Guidance and Counseling; Science
Dist - NEWCAR

Physicians and health practitioners 60 MIN
VHS
New medical and allied health series
Color (J H C)
$89.95 purchase _ #4338
Examines the occupations of chiropractor, dentist, pharmacist, physician, registered nurse, surgeon, physician's assistant and veterinarian. Part of a four - part series looking at medical and allied health careers.
Business and Economics; Guidance and Counseling; Science
Dist - NEWCAR

Physicians career encounters 28 MIN
VHS
Career encounters video series
Color (J H)
$89.00 purchase _ #4262
Offers a documentary on careers as physicians. Visits workplaces and hears professionals explain what they do, how they got where they are and why they find the work so rewarding. Emphasizes human diversity in the professions. Dispels myths, misconceptions and stereotypes and offers practical information about the requirements for entering the field. Part of a 13 - part series.
Business and Economics; Guidance and Counseling; Science
Dist - NEWCAR

Physician's data query
CD-ROM
Color (PRO)
$950.00 purchase _ #1483
Gives medical staff engaged in cancer treatment access to a comprehensive source of cancer treatment information. For IBM PCs and compatibles. Requires 640K RAM, DOS Version 3.1 or greater, one floppy disk drive - a hard drive is recommended, one empty expansion slot, and an IBM compatible CD - ROM drive.
Health and Safety
Dist - BEP

Physicians' desk reference
CD-ROM
(G PRO)
$595.00 purchase _ #1591
Contains the Physicians' Desk Reference - PDR, the PDR for Non - prescription Drugs, the PDR Drug Interaction and Side Effect Index, PDR Indications Index and the PDR for Ophthalmologists on one disc. Includes prescribing information on almost 3000 drugs that can be searched by name, indication, therapeutic category, interaction potential, side effects, active ingredient or manufacturer. For $895, an annual subscription that includes the Merck Manual is also available. For IBM PCs and compatibles, requires 640K of RAM, DOS 3.1 or later, one floppy disk drive - hard disk recommended, one empty expansion slot, and an IBM compatible CD - ROM drive.
Health and Safety; Literature and Drama
Dist - BEP

Physician's guide to managing back pain
VHS
Color (PRO)
#OR - 255
Presents a free - loan program which trains medical professionals. Contact distributor for details.
Health and Safety; Science - Natural
Dist - WYAYLA **Prod** - WYAYLA

Physicians - No 8 28 MIN
VHS / U-matic
Career encounters series
Color (H C)
$110.00, $95.00 purchase
Interviews doctors, interns and residents. Overviews the academic requirements for obtaining a medical degree.
Business and Economics; Guidance and Counseling; Health and Safety; Psychology
Dist - PLEXPU **Prod** - PLEXPU 1990

Physicians Under Fire - 220 30 MIN
U-matic
Currents - 1985 - 86 Season Series
Color (A)
Reveals that the exalted position once granted doctors is fast dwindling as the public perceives physicians to be in the business only for the money.
Health and Safety; Social Science
Dist - PBS **Prod** - WNETTV 1985

A Physician's update on managed care 14 MIN
VHS
Color (C PRO)
$30.00 purchase _ #OP111893PK
Overviews managed care and its effect on physician practice and patient care. Includes printed enclosure.
Health and Safety
Dist - AMEDA **Prod** - AMEDA 1995

The Physicists 22 MIN
16mm / VHS
Color (G)
$400.00, $300.00 purchase, $50.00 rental
Presents an introduction to modern physics. Shows how physicists are challenging our concepts of matter, space and time. Interview Freeman Dyson, Edwin Goldwasser, Richard Taylor, A R Thompson and Bernard Oliver.
Science; Science - Physical
Dist - CNEMAG **Prod** - DOCUA 1976

Physicists at work 39 MIN
VHS
Color (J H)
$130.00 purchase _ #A5VH 1427
Features astronaut Sally Ride, laser physicist Bahaa Saleh and nuclear physicist Gregory Moses. Introduces the history, the present and future of modern physics research.
Guidance and Counseling; Industrial and Technical Education; Science; Science - Physical
Dist - CLRVUE **Prod** - CLRVUE

Physicists at Work 45 MIN
U-matic / Kit / 35mm strip / VHS
Scientists at Work
Color (J H)
$109 three color sound filmstrips _ #C537 - 69684 - 9, $129 one
Interviews practicing physicists to provide an overview of careers in the field. Program is divided into three parts covering the past, present and future of the discipline which may be used in combination or alone.
Guidance and Counseling; Science; Science - Physical
Dist - RH

Physicists at work 34 MIN
VHS
Color (H C)
$129.00 purchase _ #601
Surveys the history of physics from Galileo and Newton, who radically changed how the world and the universe were viewed during the Renaissance, to Albert Einstein, Marie Curie, Nils Bohr and Ernest Rutherford, who led another revolution in the 20th century, in Part One, Physics, the Basic Science. Meets some of the outstanding physicists working today in Part Two.

Includes Donald Huffman, the physicist who, by serendipidity, discovered how to make bucky - balls; Sally Ride, the physicist who became America's first woman astronaut; and Don Eigler, the IBM physicist who was the first to move atoms one at a time.
Science; Science - Physical
Dist - HAWHIL **Prod** - HAWHIL 1995

Physicists at work series
Physics - the basic science, a brief history of physics from Galileo to Einstein 18 MIN
Dist - HAWHIL

The Physicists - Playing Dice with the Universe 22 MIN
16mm / U-matic / VHS
Color
Predicts that in the remainder of this century physicists will be experimenting with ideas which only few people can comprehend. Includes in these ideas mapping the tiniest structures, listening to the universe in an effort to discover and communicate with life and slowing time itself.
Science - Physical
Dist - CNEMAG **Prod** - DOCUA 1971

Physics and Astronomy - Careers for Women 30 MIN
VHS / 16mm
Women in Science Series
Color (I H A)
$150.00 purchase, $35.00 rental
Presents women role models in physics and astronomy both on the job and discussing various aspects of their chosen careers.
Psychology; Science - Physical; Sociology
Dist - AITECH **Prod** - UNMICH 1984

Physics and Chemistry of Water 21 MIN
U-matic / VHS / 16mm
Color (H C A)
LC FIA68-1
Shows how the nature of the water molecule determines the physical properties of water. Demonstrates that life is dependent on some of the unusual properties of water - - its slow rate of evaporation, its high surface tension, its powers of solution and its high fluid density.
Science - Physical
Dist - PHENIX **Prod** - LEVER 1967

Physics and consciousness 30 MIN
VHS / BETA
New physics and beyond
Color (G)
$29.95 purchase _ #S450
Extends the understanding of quantum physics as it applies to body and mind, suggesting that humans are inextricably connected with all that exists in the physical universe. Features Dr Fred Alan Wolf, author of 'Taking the Quantam Leap,' 'Starwave' and 'The Body Quantam.' Part of a four - part series on new physics and beyond.
Religion and Philosophy; Science - Physical
Dist - THINKA **Prod** - THINKA

Physics and fine art 30 MIN
VHS
Color (G)
PdS10.50 purchase _ #A4-300437
Goes behind the scenes at the National Gallery to show how scientific analysis increases knowledge of Old Master paintings. Explains how x-radiography, gas chromatography, and the scanning electron microscope help scientists and curators understand more about works by such artists as Botticelli, Rembrandt, Goya, and the German Romantic Caspar Friedrich.
Fine Arts
Dist - AVP **Prod** - NATLGL

Physics at the Indy 500 5 MIN
VHS
Color (I J H)
$95.00 purchase, $35.00 rental _ #38148
Uses five one - minute spots to demonstrate and explain five physics principles using scenes from the Indianapolis 500 car race. Employs animated graphics, actual race footage and special footage taped at the Indy Speedway to show the principles behind the conseration of energy, centripetal force, Newton's third law, the Doppler effect and the Bernoulli effect. Includes a 40 - page teacher's guide with less plans, physics background to support the video, additional samples of physics principles, experiments and demonstrations and suggested home assignments and quizzes. Produced by Ruth Howes, Nancy Carlson and Beverley Pitts, Ball State University.
Science - Physical
Dist - UCEMC

Physics Films Series
Mass of Atoms 47 MIN
Dist - MLA

Physics in Action Series
The Electromagnetic Spectrum 18 MIN
Electrostatics, Pt 1 18 MIN
Electrostatics, Pt 2 18 MIN
The Expansion of metals 18 MIN
The Generation of electricity - Pt 1 18 MIN
The Generation of Electricity, Pt 2 18 MIN
The Laws of Motion, Pt 1 18 MIN
The Laws of Motion, Pt 2 18 MIN
Radioactivity 18 MIN
Dist - LUF

Physics of Diving 29 MIN
Videoreel / VT2
Observing Eye Series
Color
Science - Physical; Sociology
Dist - PBS **Prod** - WGBHTV

Physics of GaAs and heterojunction electronic devices, part II - a series
Physics of GaAs and heterojunction electronic devices, part II series
B&W (PRO)
Focuses on quantum wells where dimensions approach the wavelenth of an electron in the solid. Notes under such conditions that quantum size effects tunneling and hot electron phenomena. Examines lasers, photodetectors, CCDs and entirely new types of solid state devices.
Industrial and Technical Education
Dist - AMCEE **Prod** - STITV

Physics of GaAs and heterojunction electronic devices, part II series
Physics of GaAs and heterojunction electronic devices, part II - a series
Dist - AMCEE

Physics of GaAs and heterojunction electronic devices, Pt I - a series
Physics of GaAs and heterojunction electronic devices, Pt I - a series
B&W (PRO)
Focuses on GaAs and heterojunction device physics and additional design freedom for optimization of semiconductor devices. Covers application of design principles to conventional device structures and ballistic transport devices for ultra - high - speed electronics.
Industrial and Technical Education
Dist - AMCEE **Prod** - STITV

Physics of GaAs and heterojunction electronic devices, Pt I - a series
Physics of GaAs and heterojunction electronic devices, Pt I - a series
Dist - AMCEE

Physics of optical communications 17 MIN
VHS / BETA / U-matic
Color; PAL (J H)
PdS15.00 purchase
Explains the scientific principles behind optical fiber technology. Demonstrates the development of lasers and optical fiber. Includes teachers' and students' notes. Contact distributor for free loan information.
Education; Industrial and Technical Education; Sociology
Dist - BTEDSE

Physics of sports
Videodisc
Color; CAV (J H)
$275.00 purchase _ #8L219
Analyzes body movements of athletes from a detailed record of over 20 athletic events, filmed expressly for scientific analysis. Considers the acceleration of a distance runner in comparison to a sprinter, the use of poles to achieve maximum vaulting height, whether a gymnast can gain energy from a trampoline, what determines the direction of a softball struck by a bat. Macintosh software is available separately to create an interactive lab.
Physical Education and Recreation; Science - Physical
Dist - BARR **Prod** - BARR 1992

Physics on Earth and in the heavens - Quad I 60 MIN
VHS
Mechanical universe - high school adaptation series
Color (H)
$75.00 purchase _ #MU - Q1
Presents four programs on physics. Includes - Newton's Laws which completed the kinematics of Galileo with dynamics and describes a theory of the causes of motion; The Apple and the Moon - how the universal law of gravitation emerged from Newton's efforts to reconcile Galileo's new kinematics with the new astronomy of Kepler; Harmonic Motion - presents simple harmonic motion as a model illustrating the scientific process of simple, underlying physical principles from complex behavior; Navigating in Space - introduces interplanetary travel as an application of the celestial mechanics of Kepler and Newton.
Science - Physical
Dist - INSTRU

Physics - the basic science, a brief history of physics from Galileo to Einstein 18 MIN
VHS
Physicists at work series
Color (H C)
$79.00 purchase _ #187
Shows how physics began with ideas and inventions such as the lever, the wheel, the catapult and the cannon. Demonstrates how physicists such as Galileo and Newton radically changed how the world and the universe were viewed during the Renaissance. Looks at physicists including Albert Einstein, Marie Curie, Nils Bohr and Ernest Rutherford who led another revolution in the 20th century. Part one. Includes guide.
Science; Science - Physical
Dist - HAWHIL **Prod** - HAWHIL 1995

Physiographic provinces of the United States 30 MIN
VHS
Color (J H C)
$39.95 purchase _ #IV260
Explores major physiolgraphic provinces as well as major landforms in the United States. Travels through the Superior Upland and the Atlantic Coast Plain region, from the New England Province to the Great Plains and Rocky Mountains to the Pacific Border. Overviews the great geomorphic diversity in the US and introduces geomorphology.
Geography - United States; Science - Physical
Dist - INSTRU

Physiologic Changes in Pregnancy
U-matic / VHS
Care of the Pregnant Patient Series
Color (PRO)
Health and Safety; Science - Natural
Dist - OMNIED **Prod** - OMNIED

Physiologic Manifestations of Stress 24 MIN
U-matic
Stress in Critical Illness Series Module 1
Color (PRO)
LC 80-707621
Discusses the body's reaction to stressful situations. Describes nursing interventions designed to assist the patient's efforts to resist or adapt to stress.
Health and Safety; Psychology
Dist - BRA **Prod** - BRA 1980

Physiologic Modulation of Pain 28 MIN
U-matic
Management of Pain Series Module 4
Color (PRO)
LC 80-707393
Health and Safety
Dist - BRA **Prod** - BRA 1980

Physiological and Behavioral Effects of Noise 8 MIN
16mm
Color (H C A)
LC 75-700199
Observes the behavior and cortisol levels of 12 rhesus monkeys who were exposed to loud, man - made noises for periods of one, three and five hours. Shows the aftereffects of noise on the monkeys.
Science - Natural; Science - Physical
Dist - PSUPCR **Prod** - WIRPRC 1974

Physiological and clinical aspects of cardiac
Subvalvular aortic stenosis 6 MIN
Dist - LIP

Physiological and Emotional Aspects of Pain 17 MIN
16mm
Patient as a Person Series
Color (PRO)
LC 73-712974
Portrays the characteristics of pain and shows the different reactions of individuals to its discomfort. Defines the four types of pain, the causes and physiological basis. Emphasizes the role of the nurse in responding to the patient in pain.
Health and Safety; Psychology
Dist - TRNAID **Prod** - TRNAID 1970

The Physiological and psychological challenge - osteoporosis 120 MIN
VHS
Virginia Geriatric Education Center Video Conference series

Color (G C PRO)
$149.00 purchase, $55.00 rental
Looks at causes, prevalence and risk factors associated with osteoporosis and diagnosis and intervention techniques that can prevent or successfully treat it.
Health and Safety
Dist - TNF **Prod** - VGEREC

Physiological aspects of sex 30 MIN
VHS / U-matic
Family portrait - a study of contemporary lifestyles series; Lesson 5
Color (C A)
Investigates the biological process of sex. Describes functions of the male and female reproductive organs. Discusses causes and treatment of infertility in men and women.
Health and Safety; Science - Natural
Dist - CDTEL **Prod** - SCCON

Physiological aspects of speech series
Normal Speech Articulation 25 MIN
Speakers with cerebral palsy 25 MIN
Speakers with cleft palates 30 MIN
Dist - UIOWA

The Physiological Effects of Cocaine 20 MIN
VHS / 16mm
Color (G)
$195.00 purchase, $50.00 rental _ #4014H, 4918H, 0500J, 0637J
Describes the history and physical properties of cocaine. Includes physicological and psychiatric toxicology information aimed at health professionals in emergency rooms and treatment centers. Features Randy Cox.
Guidance and Counseling; Health and Safety; Psychology; Sociology
Dist - HAZELB **Prod** - HAZELB

Physiological Limitations 11 MIN
16mm
Safety and You Series
Color
Examines the delicate balance human beings must maintain between their physical, biochemical and emotional make - up. Demonstrates how external and internal factors can affect this balance.
Guidance and Counseling; Health and Safety
Dist - FILCOM **Prod** - FILCOM

Physiological Responses of the Sexually Stimulated Female in the Laboratory 16 MIN
U-matic / VHS
Color
Provides observations of the physiological responses of the sexually stimulated female in the laboratory. Illustrates the vagina and external genitalia in orgasmic stages.
Health and Safety; Psychology; Sociology
Dist - MMRC **Prod** - MMRC

Physiological Responses of the Sexually Stimulated Male in the Laboratory 16 MIN
U-matic / VHS
Color
Features x - ray cinematography of physiological responses of the sexually stimulated male in the laboratory. Presented in a non - threatening, intellectual and clinical manner. Allows sex to be discussed in a comfortable nonjudgmental way.
Health and Safety; Psychology; Sociology
Dist - MMRC **Prod** - MMRC

Physiology - cell biology 51 MIN
VHS
Introductory principles of nutrition series
Color (C A PRO)
$70.00 purchase, $16.00 rental _ #50705
Examines tissue systems, cell structure and function, concepts of homeostasis, cellular energetics and nutrient functions. Part of a 20 - part series on nutrition. Emphasizes controversial nutritional issues and the principle instructional objectives.
Health and Safety; Science - Natural; Social Science
Dist - PSU **Prod** - WPSXTV 1978

Physiology of Conception 29 MIN
16mm
Nine to Get Ready Series no 2
B&W (C A)
LC 76-704215
Discusses physiology of conception, diagnosis and timing of ovulation, sperm migration, fertilization, early development of the fertilitzed ovum, infertility and female physiology and anatomy. Features Dr J Robert Bragonier and Leta Powell Drake.
Health and Safety; Science - Natural
Dist - UNEBR **Prod** - KUONTV 1965

The Physiology of Exercise 15 MIN
U-matic / VHS
Experiment - Biology Series
Color (C)
$249.00, $149.00 purchase _ #AD - 1092
Reveals that in order for active muscles to receive sufficient blood during exercise, cardiac imput must be increased. Shows that blood flow is redistributed by dilating some blood vessels and constricting others. Performs experiments to measure the increase in heart rate, systolic pressure, respiratory rate and tidal volume at different levels of exercise. Part of a series on biology experiments.
Physical Education and Recreation; Science - Natural
Dist - FOTH **Prod** - FOTH

Physiology of Food 15 MIN
16mm
Color
LC 74-706515
Explains human food requirements and how these requirements can be met by natural sources.
Health and Safety; Home Economics; Social Science
Dist - USNAC **Prod** - USN 1973

Physiology of Miscarriage and Abortion 28 MIN
U-matic / VHS / 16mm
Inner Woman Series
Color (H C A)
LC 77-702981
Presents the signs and causes of miscarriage and mentions the controversy about the effect of the IUD in causing abortions and infections. Discusses the induced abortion.
Health and Safety
Dist - MGHT **Prod** - WXYZTV 1975

Physiology of muscles 30 MIN
VHS
Perspectives - health and medicine - series
Color; PAL; NTSC (G)
PdS90, PdS105 purchase
Shows how greater understanding of the structure and function of muscles is helping doctors rebuild and replace them.
Health and Safety; Science - Natural
Dist - CFLVIS **Prod** - LONTVS

Physiology of Myocardial Ischemia - Angina Pectoris 51 MIN
U-matic / VHS
Color (PRO)
Shows how to apply knowledge of basic cardiovascular physiology in the diagnosis and treatment of ischemic heart disease.
Health and Safety; Science - Natural
Dist - HSCIC **Prod** - HSCIC 1982

The Physiology of neuromuscular blocking agents 18 MIN
VHS / U-matic
Anesthesiology clerkship series
Color (PRO)
Describes the physiology of the transmission of motor nerve impulses to skeletal muscle. Discusses the types of neuromuscular blockade and their electrophysiologic characteristics, as well as the pharmacology of drugs used to reverse neuromuscular blockade.
Health and Safety
Dist - UMICHM **Prod** - UMICHM 1982

The Physiology of Occlusion 30 MIN
16mm
Color (C)
LC 72-700940
Shows physiology examination techniques, including cineflouroscopy of speech and swallowing, gross dissection of the temporomandibular joint, palpation of muscles for kiagnostic purposes and examinations of occlusion (clinically and pantographycally) before and after equilibration.
Health and Safety; Psychology; Science
Dist - UIOWA **Prod** - UIOWA 1972

Physiology of Pregnancy and Labor 29 MIN
16mm
Nine to Get Ready Series no 5
B&W (C A)
LC 70-704216
Explains the physiology of pregnancy and labor, discussing the vital placenta, cardiovascular physiology, respiratory physiology, causes of onset of labor and physiology of labor and effects on the fetus. Features Dr J Robert Bragonier and Leta Powell Drake.
Health and Safety; Science - Natural
Dist - UNEBR **Prod** - KUONTV 1965

Physiology of the Ear 49 MIN
U-matic / VHS
Color (PRO)
Presents the physiology of the ear. Discusses early experiments and correlation of physiology to clinical conditions.
Health and Safety; Science - Natural
Dist - HOUSEI **Prod** - HOUSEI

Physiology of the Larynx Under Daily Stress 23 MIN
16mm
Larnyx and Voice Series
Color
Explores complexity of laryngeal function in everyday life. Relates physiological changes to clinical reality, vibratory function, biphasic pattern of laryngeal vibrations, effect of intensity, air pressure on components of vibratory cycle and the significance of secondary waves.
Health and Safety; Science - Natural
Dist - ILAVD **Prod** - ILAVD 1958

Physiology Series
Arterial Blood Pressure Regulation 19 MIN
The Cochlear Nerve - Recording with Microelectrodes 21 MIN
Microelectrodes in Muscle 19 MIN
The Milk Ejection Reflex 21 MIN
The Muscle Spindle 19 MIN
What Makes Muscle Pull - the Structural Basis of Contraction 9 MIN
Dist - MEDIAG

Piaget in new perspective patron 20 MIN
U-matic / VHS / BETA
Color; PAL (T PRO)
PdS40, PdS48 purchase
Psychology
Dist - EDPAT

Piaget on Piaget 42 MIN
16mm / VHS
Color (FRENCH)
LC 78-701564
Presents Jean Piaget, who discusses his theories on child development and his interpretations of experiments involving Swiss children.
Psychology
Dist - YUMDS **Prod** - YUMDS 1978

Piaget's developmental theory series
Classification 17 MIN
Conservation 28 MIN
Formal reasoning pattterns 32 MIN
Growth of Intelligence in the Preschool Years 31 MIN
Jean Piaget - memory and intelligence 44 MIN
Memory and Intelligence 45 MIN
Morality - the Process of Moral Development 28 MIN
Dist - DAVFMS

Pianissimo 8 MIN
16mm
Color (H C A)
Demonstrates abstractions of color and patterns of sounds, with a piano and an old phonograph.
Fine Arts; Industrial and Technical Education
Dist - GROVE **Prod** - GROVE 1963

The Piano 27 MIN
16mm
Color
Looks into the music created by and the history of the piano, including its evolution since the 18th century. Discusses how it is constructed and the physics of its sound patterns.
Fine Arts
Dist - FLMLIB **Prod** - CANBC 1982

Piano lab 58 MIN
VHS
Key changes - a seminar for music educators series
Color (T A PRO)
$69.95 purchase _ #1263 - 0010
Presents part eight of a 13 - part telecourse for music educators seeking renewal of their certification. Combines lecture and discussion on piano.
Education; Fine Arts
Dist - SCETV **Prod** - SCETV 1990

Piano Legends 63 MIN
VHS
Color (S)
$39.95 purchase _ #055 - 9002
Presents 23 legends of keyboard jazz from the private collection of David Chertok. Features Chick Corea as host and a few of the folks are Earl 'Fatha' Hines, Mary Lou Williams, 'Fats' Waller, Oscar Peterson, Thelonious Monk, Dave Brubeck, Duke Ellington, Count Basie, Keith Jarrett and Cecil Taylor.
Fine Arts
Dist - FI **Prod** - VAI 1988

The Piano Movers 7 MIN
16mm
Color
Presents a musical joke in which a young girl begins to play a Mozart exercise and in the course of a few minutes her piano is moved out of the house and replaced by a new

one. Contrasts the beauty of the music with the muscle and sweat that accompany the work that goes into moving a heavy piano.
Fine Arts; Literature and Drama
Dist - VIEWFI **Prod** - NFBC

Piano players rarely ever play together 76 MIN
U-matic / VHS
Color (G)
$600.00, $350.00 purchase
Celebrates New Orleans piano - playing. Features Professor Longhair, 'Tuts' Washington and Allen Toussaint. Produced by Stevenson Palfi. Available also in 60 minute version.
Fine Arts
Dist - FLOWER

The Piano Show 30 MIN
U-matic / VHS
Musical Encounter Series
Color (P I)
Features three young pianists of different ages who are in different stages of musical proficiency and who excel in different musical styles. Presents a fourth pianist, Tony Barone, who provides an example of what discipline and hard work can accomplish. Hosted by Rheda Becker.
Fine Arts
Dist - GPN **Prod** - MDCPB 1983

Pianos 30 MIN
U-matic
Today's Special Series
Color (K P)
Develops language arts skills in children. Programs are thematically designed around subjects of interest to youngsters. Action takes place in a department store where people, mannequins, puppets, comic characters and special guests present a light hearted approach to language arts.
Fine Arts; Literature and Drama; Psychology
Dist - TVOTAR **Prod** - TVOTAR 1985

Picasso 90 MIN
VHS
Color (H C A)
$39.95
Examines the varied works created by Picasso and collected in his Musee Picasso. Presents the development of his art throughout his life.
Fine Arts
Dist - ARTSAM **Prod** - RMART

Picasso 81 MIN
VHS
Color (S)
$39.95 purchase _ #833 - 9176
Captures on film the Picasso collection of the Musee Picasso in the Hotel Sale in Paris during the opening of the museum. Reveals that this particular collection is composed of the paintings Picasso kept for himself. Tells the artist's story through an in - depth look at these important works along with location footage of the places that inspired them.
Fine Arts; History - World
Dist - FI **Prod** - RMART 1989

Picasso 1881 - 1973 85 MIN
VHS
Color (G)
PdS22 purchase _ #ML-0887003
Profiles one of the twentieth century's most important artists - Pablo Picasso. Traces Picasso's development through several styles and as a leader in many revolutionary events in the art world. Notes the importance of the contrasts of the Minotaur - part savage, part human - in his work. Describes the use of dualism in Picasso's work and how his work speaks more about him than does any book or documentary. Directed by well-known art film director Didier Baussy with the help of the Musee Picasso in Paris.
Fine Arts
Dist - AVP

Picasso - a Painter's Diary, Pt 1 - the Formative Years 35 MIN
U-matic / VHS / 16mm
Color (H C A)
LC 80-701620
Re - creates the times, places, experiences and personalities that shaped Pablo Picasso's early years.
Biography; Fine Arts
Dist - CORF **Prod** - WNETTV 1981

Picasso - a Painter's Diary, Pt 3 - a Unity of Variety 21 MIN
16mm / U-matic / VHS
Color (H C A)
LC 81-700779
Examines the variety and significance of works produced by Pablo Picasso, using the artist's own words and those of his family and friends. Includes period photographs and archival footage.
Biography; Fine Arts
Dist - CORF **Prod** - WNETTV 1981

Picasso - a Painter's Diary, Pt 2 - from Cubism to Guernica 35 MIN
U-matic / VHS / 16mm
Color (H C A)
LC 81-700778
Examines Pablo Picasso's life and work during his cubist phase, including the creation of the painting entitled Guernica. Uses rare film sequences, unpublished photographs and interviews with friends and art historians to capture the artist's outlook during this period.
Biography; Fine Arts
Dist - CORF **Prod** - WNETTV 1981

Picasso - a Painter's Diary Series
The Formative years Part 1 35 MIN
From Cubism to Guernica - Pt 2 34 MIN
A Unity of Variety - Part 3 21 MIN
Dist - CORF

Picasso - an Exhibition at Walker Art Center 29 MIN
VHS / U-matic
Color
Features an exhibition at Minneapolis' Walker Art Center which contains over 160 works from the estate of artist and painter Pablo Picasso.
Fine Arts
Dist - PBS **Prod** - KTCATV 1980

Picasso and the Circus 7 MIN
16mm
Color
Shows a young girl visiting an exhibit of Picasso's paintings of jugglers, bareback riders, harlequins and clowns. Reveals the exhibit as it gradually gives way to scenes of a Parisian circus the kind Picasso attended.
Fine Arts
Dist - USNGA **Prod** - USNGA

Picasso, Artist of the Century 54 MIN
16mm
Color (H C A)
LC 76-701259
Examines the artwork of Pablo Picasso through study and analysis of color reproductions of his paintings. Covers a full range of his paintings, places where he lived while producing them and some photographs of the artist at work and recreation. Made in France.
Fine Arts
Dist - FI **Prod** - BBCTV 1976

Picasso, Artist of the Century - Pt 1 - Picasso, 1900 to Cubism 12 MIN
16mm
Color (H C A)
LC 76-701259
Examines the artwork of Pablo Picasso through study and analysis of color reproductions of his paintings. Covers a full range of his paintings, places where he lived while producing them and some photographs of the artist at work and recreation. Made in France.
Fine Arts
Dist - FI **Prod** - MACM 1976

Picasso, Artist of the Century - Pt 3 - Picasso, 1940's and After 25 MIN
16mm
Color (H C A)
LC 76-701259
Examines the artwork of Pablo Picasso through study and analysis of color reproductions of his paintings. Covers a full range of his paintings, places where he lived while producing them and some photographs of the artist at work and recreation. Made in France.
Fine Arts
Dist - FI **Prod** - MACM 1976

Picasso, Artist of the Century - Pt 2 - Picasso, Volcanic Thirties 17 MIN
16mm
Color (H C A)
LC 76-701259
Examines the artwork of Pablo Picasso through study and analysis of color reproductions of his paintings. Covers a full range of his paintings, places where he lived while producing them and some photographs of the artist at work and recreation. Made in France.
Fine Arts
Dist - FI **Prod** - MACM 1976

Picasso is 90 51 MIN
16mm / U-matic / VHS
Color; Captioned
LC 72-700682
Traces the highlights of the life and work of Picasso, and presents comments of personal friends, one of Picasso's sons and one of his ex - wives. Includes film clips showing scenes of Gertrude Stein, Georges Braque, the Spanish Civil War, the bombing of Guernica and Russian communists applauding the political sympathies of Picasso.
Biography; Fine Arts; History - World
Dist - CAROUF **Prod** - CBSTV 1971

Picasso - Joie De Vivre - 1881 - 1976 13 MIN
16mm
Color
Shows how the town of Antibes, on France's Riviera, offered the aging Picasso their ancient castle for a museum and he responded by filling the rooms with vibrant murals and bright pottery.
Fine Arts
Dist - ROLAND **Prod** - ROLAND

Picasso - Romancero Du Picador - 1881 - 1976 13 MIN
16mm
Color
Shows how Picasso, in swift sketches, makes the despised picador on his padded horse into a true knight, faithful to his duty and alone in his pleasures as he weakens the bull with his harsh lance.
Fine Arts
Dist - ROLAND **Prod** - ROLAND

Picasso - sculptor - painter 25 MIN
VHS
Color (G)
PdS15.50 purchase _ #A4-300492
Presents Picasso's career as a sculptor from Head of a Woman in 1906 to his metal sculptures of the early 1960s. Tours the Tate Gallery exhibition of Picasso's most famous sculptures and rarities from private collections, including Picasso's family.
Fine Arts
Dist - AVP **Prod** - NATLGL

Picasso - the man and his work 90 MIN
VHS
Color (H C A)
$79.95 purchase
Combines film and photography to portray the life and work of Pablo Picasso. Produced by Edward Quinn, a longtime friend of Picasso.
Fine Arts
Dist - PBS **Prod** - WNETTV

Picasso - the Man and His Work - 1881 - 1937 - Pt 1 45 MIN
VHS
Picasso - the Man and His Work Series
Color (J)
$39.95 purchase _ #HV - 915
Presents actual footage of Picasso at work and play. Reveals unknown facets of his life and art. Includes over 600 works and many sequences of Picasso explaining his art in process. Part 1 of a two - part series on Picasso.
Fine Arts; History - World
Dist - CRYSP **Prod** - CRYSP

Picasso - the Man and His Work - 1938 - 1973 - Pt 2 45 MIN
VHS
Picasso - the Man and His Work Series
Color (J)
$39.95 purchase _ #HV - 916
Presents actual footage of Picasso at work and play. Reveals unknown facets of his life and art. Includes over 600 works and many sequences of Picasso explaining his art in process. Part 2 of a two - part series on Picasso.
Fine Arts; History - World
Dist - CRYSP **Prod** - CRYSP

Picasso - the man and his work - Parts 1 and 2 90 MIN
VHS
Color (H C G T A)
$79.95 purchase _ #S00854
Portrays the art and life of Pablo Picasso. Features more than 600 of his works, along with footage from his life. Focuses on Picasso's artistic development and influences.
Fine Arts
Dist - UILL **Prod** - UILL

Picasso - The Man and his work - Pt 1 45 MIN
VHS
Color (H C A)
$39.95 each part, $79.95 set
Presents an intimate look at the life and works of artist Pablo Picasso. Makes use of home movies and photos to show the progress of his life and the development of his art in parallel. Shows many of his works. Part one of a set of two videos.
Fine Arts
Dist - ARTSAM

Picasso - The Man and his work - Pt 2 45 MIN
VHS
Color (H C A)

$39.95 each part, $79.95 set
Presents an intimate look at the life and works of artist Pablo Picasso. Makes use of home movies and photos to show the progress of his life and the development of his art in parallel. Shows many of his works. Part two of a set of two videos.
Fine Arts
Dist - ARTSAM

Picasso - the Man and His Work Series
Picasso - the Man and His Work - 1881 - 1937 - Pt 1 — 45 MIN
Picasso - the Man and His Work - 1938 - 1973 - Pt 2 — 45 MIN
Dist - CRYSP

Picasso - the Saltimbanques — 30 MIN
16mm
Color
Presents paintings of circus people painted by Pablo Picasso during his Rose Period. Traces the process through which E A Carmean Jr, curator of twentieth century art at the National Art Gallery and Ann Hoenigswald of the Gallery's conservation laboratory, discovered earlier compositions beneath the surface of Picasso's major painting Family Of Saltimbanques.
Fine Arts
Dist - USNGA **Prod** - USNGA

Picasso - War, Peace, Love — 51 MIN
VHS
Color (J H C G)
$24.95 purchase _ #HV - 683
Profiles the work of Picasso beginning with the anti - war Guernica mural. Documents his later works, travelling to museums, galleries, and private collections to explore both well known and little known pieces.
Fine Arts; History - World; Sociology
Dist - CRYSP **Prod** - CRYSP
ARTSAM

Picasso - War, Peace, Love — 50 MIN
VHS
Museum Without Walls Series
Color (C)
LC 90713079
Depicts the works of Picasso as found in 22 museums, 11 private collections and seven galleries. Gives tribute to the artist. Fourth installment of eight in the Museum Without Walls Series.
Fine Arts
Dist - GPN

PICC - Insertion procedure — 13 MIN
VHS
Color (C PRO)
250.00 purchase, $70.00 rental _ #4322S, #4322V
Answers common questions about peripherally inserted central catheters, an innovation in venous access. Begins set - up and preparation and discusses the equipment needed and the types of catheters used. Shows two insertion methods, including break - away needle and peel away sheath. Demonstrates the procedure on a patient, using clear graphics that show why particular veins are chosen, how to locate them and how to insert the catheter. Discusses use of equipment, maintaining sterility and correct procedures, with rationale for each action. Ends with guidelines for dressing changes and removing the cather. Produced by Perivascular Nurse Consultants.
Health and Safety; Science - Natural
Dist - AJN

Piccolo Saxo and Company — 10 MIN
16mm
Color (K P I)
LC 71-701331
Uses animation to describe each instrument of a symphony orchestra as a member of a family. Each gives a solo so that the listener can identify the sound with the instrument. Concludes with live symphony orchestra music, with each instrumental group contributing to the music being played.
Fine Arts
Dist - MLA **Prod** - MLA 1967

Pick a story, choose a language - 1
VHS
Color; PAL (P I)
PdS29.50 purchase
Tells five stories including Katie Morag and the Tiresome Ted; Not now, Bernard; Kimi and the Watermelon; Maybe it's a Tiger; and The Paper Bag Princess. Part one of two parts.
English Language; Literature and Drama
Dist - EMFVL

Pick a story, choose a language - 2
VHS
Color; PAL (P I)
PdS29.50 purchase
Tells five stories including Phoebe and the Hot Water Bottles; The White Crane; Sampeep and the Parrots; Jamine and the New Baby; and Cat on the Mat. Part two of two parts.
English Language; Literature and Drama
Dist - EMFVL

Pick and Choose - Pt 1 — 15 MIN
16mm / U-matic / VHS
Color (I)
Shows that good nutrition can be fun as well as necessary. Animated characters and live people tell the audience that they should pick and choose what they eat to help make their daily lives better.
Home Economics; Social Science
Dist - CORNRS **Prod** - CUETV 1978

Pick and Choose - Pt 2 — 15 MIN
U-matic / VHS / 16mm
Color (I)
Points out shopper strategy that results in getting the most food value for your money.
Home Economics; Social Science
Dist - CORNRS **Prod** - CUETV 1978

Pick - in by the River — 59 MIN
Videoreel / VT2
B&W
Captures roving troubadours and provides glimpses of history. Features John Rippey, president of the Brownville Historical Society, recounting the early days of the riverfront town when 13 saloons were supported by the brisk river trade. Includes musicians Ferlin Puny and the Blue Grass Boys, picker John Walker and fiddler Gene Wells.
Fine Arts; History - World
Dist - PBS **Prod** - NETCHE

Pick Me Up at Peggy's Cove — 25 MIN
16mm / U-matic / VHS
Color (I J) (FRENCH)
LC 83-700564
Tells of a boy who intentionally gets into trouble while visiting his aunt in the hopes that it will reunite his parents. Reveals that when the scheme fails, he emerges more knowledgeable about himself and more secure with the love of his friends and family.
Literature and Drama; Psychology; Sociology
Dist - BCNFL **Prod** - ATLAP 1982

Pick of the Crop — 30 MIN
VHS / BETA
Victory Garden Series
Color
Gives tips on making the most of the fall harvest. Presents the winner of The Fifth Annual Victory Garden Contest.
Agriculture; Physical Education and Recreation
Dist - CORF **Prod** - WGBHTV

Pick the Winner — 30 MIN
BETA / VHS
Victory Garden Series
Color
Reviews the choices for winner of The Victory Garden Contest.
Agriculture; Physical Education and Recreation
Dist - CORF **Prod** - WGBHTV

Pick - Up Notes, Michael Row the Boat Ashore, on Top of Old Smokey — 20 MIN
U-matic / VHS
Guitar, Guitar Series
Color (J H)
Fine Arts
Dist - GPN **Prod** - SCITV 1981

Pick Your Safety Target
16mm / 8mm cartridge
B&W
Explains how to use accident statistics for accident prevention.
Business and Economics; Health and Safety
Dist - NSC **Prod** - NSC

Picker Upper — 8 MIN
16mm / VHS
Muppet Meeting Films Series
Color (PRO)
$550.00 purchase, $300.00 rental, $30.00 preview
Presents Jim Henson's muppets who introduce and humorously comment on business meetings and breaks. Consists of three to four segments each approximately two and a half minutes.
Business and Economics; Psychology; Sociology
Dist - UTM

Picker - Upper — 8 MIN
16mm
Muppet Meeting Series
Color (A)
Presents Muppet characters in humorous vignettes which deal with the most trying parts of a business meeting. Includes stories dealing with introductions, announcements and the final speech.
Business and Economics; Psychology
Dist - HENASS **Prod** - HENASS 1981

Picking and Persuading a Jury Series Program 1
Selecting a Jury - a Demonstration — 150 MIN
Selecting a Jury - a Demonstration, Pt 1 — 50 MIN
Selecting a Jury - a Demonstration, Pt 2 — 50 MIN
Selecting a Jury - a Demonstration, Pt 3 — 50 MIN
Dist - ABACPE

Picking and Persuading a Jury Series Program 2
Selecting a Jury - a Critique — 60 MIN
Dist - ABACPE

Picking and Persuading a Jury Series Program 6
Persuading the Jury — 35 MIN
Dist - ABACPE

Picking and persuading a jury series
Case and community analysis — 45 MIN
The Juror's perspective — 40 MIN
Language and Communication — 30 MIN
Dist - ABACPE

Picking it Up — 24 MIN
U-matic
Homemade American Music Series
Color
LC 80-707483
Fine Arts
Dist - LAWREN **Prod** - AGINP 1980

Picking the Blue Crab — 8 MIN
16mm
Color
Presents a description and demonstration of the correct procedures for removing the flake, lump (backfin) and claw meat of the blue crab. Explains that one of the reasons this delicacy is ignored is because of inadequate consumer instructional information on the correct procedures for picking crabs.
Home Economics
Dist - VPI **Prod** - VPI 1982

Picking the next move — 45 MIN
VHS / U-matic
Artificial intelligence series; Fundamental concepts, Pt 1; Pt 1
Color (PRO)
Features mini - max, combinatorial explosion, alpha - beta algorithm, heuristic pruning, look - ahead horizon.
Mathematics
Dist - MIOT **Prod** - MIOT

Picking the Winner — 22 MIN
16mm
Color
Explains the development of corn hybrids by the world's largest corn breeding organization using the science of genetics.
Agriculture; Science - Natural
Dist - MTP **Prod** - MTP

Picking Tribes — 7 MIN
16mm / VHS
B&W (G)
$200.00, $125.00 purchase, $40.00 rental
Uses vintage photographs and watercolor animation to look at a woman born in the 1940s as she establishes her own identity between her dual origins of Black and Native American heritages. Reveals that she identifies with her grandfather's Indian heritage until the 1960s when she sheds her feathers for an Afro and dashiki.
Fine Arts; Psychology; Sooiology
Dist - WMEN **Prod** - SSHARP 1988

Picking - Up and Edges — 29 MIN
Videoreel / VT2
Busy Knitter I Series
B&W
Home Economics
Dist - PBS **Prod** - WMVSTV

Picking Up the Pieces — 30 MIN
U-matic
Family and the Law Series
(H C A)
Deals with the problems of a woman whose husband dies suddenly without a will which creates both legal and financial burdens.
Civics and Political Systems; History - World
Dist - ACCESS **Prod** - ACCESS 1980

Picking Up the Pieces — 60 MIN
VHS / 16mm
Making Sense of the Sixties Series
Color (G)
$59.95 purchase _ #MSIX - N903
Examines the end of the decade. Shows how minorities of every description put to work the techniques of the civil rights and anti - war movements to win political

empowerment. Considers the return of Vietnam vets, the persecution of the Black Panthers and the birth of two new movements, the environmentalists and the feminists. Part of a six - part series on the Sixties.
Civics and Political Systems; History - United States; Sociology
Dist - PBS **Prod** - WETATV 1990

Picking Up the Pieces - Living with Alcoholic Parents 48 MIN
VHS
Color (I)
$225.00 purchase
Shows teens that their own survival is what counts - an alcoholic parent is not their responsibility. Portrays Patty who says, 'Mom is an alcoholic and no one in my family talks.' Her father denies the reality of their dysfunctional family and Patty is trapped in the cover - up. Patty is introduced to Alateen, a support group for teen - aged children of alcoholics. She finds out she is not alone or unique. Stars Joanna Pettet and Ellie Cornell.
Health and Safety; Psychology; Sociology
Dist - MEDIAI **Prod** - MEDIAI

Picking up the pieces - 3 mistakes 11 MIN
16mm
Color (G)
$25.00 rental
Experiments with a 17 - image exercise using freeze frames of a tenement hallway in a Ken Kobland production.
Fine Arts
Dist - CANCIN

Picking Up the Tab 30 MIN
VHS / U-matic
Loosening the Grip Series
Color (C A)
Health and Safety
Dist - GPN **Prod** - UMA 1980

A Pickle for a Nickel 6 MIN
U-matic / VHS / 16mm
Golden Book Storytime Series
Color (P)
Relates that a quiet man with a quiet parrot is dismayed when a boy teaches the bird to talk.
Literature and Drama
Dist - CORF **Prod** - CORF 1977

Pickles 11 MIN
U-matic / VHS / 16mm
Zagreb Collection Series
Color (H C A)
LC 73-701431
Comments on the many absurd predicaments of day to day living. Uses irony, metaphor and satire to focus on some not - so - self evident truths.
Guidance and Counseling; Literature and Drama; Sociology
Dist - PHENIX **Prod** - PHENIX 1973

Pickles and Relishes 30 MIN
U-matic / VHS
Food Preservation Series
Color
Explains how to can pickles and relishes.
Home Economics
Dist - MDCPB **Prod** - UGATV

Pickling 29 MIN
VHS / 16mm
Food Preserving Series
Color (G)
$55.00 rental _ #FODP - 009
Home Economics
Dist - PBS **Prod** - WSWPTV

Pickpocket 75 MIN
16mm
B&W (FRENCH (ENGLISH SUBTITLES))
LC 77-701046
Presents an analysis of a criminal's compulsions and conscience, showing the agitation and transformation of a pickpocket. Includes English subtitles.
Fine Arts; Foreign Language; Sociology
Dist - NYFLMS **Prod** - NYFLMS 1963

Picnic 28 MIN
VHS
Elephant show series
Color (P I)
$95.00 purchase, $45.00 rental
Presents program 3 in the Sharon, Lois and Bram's Elephant Show series. Teaches reading readiness and social skills while engaging children in making music. Each program explores a new theme through adventure, fantasy, mystery and song with recording artists Sharon, Lois and Bram. Uses traditional materials which stress participation - action songs, sing - along songs, story songs, clapping songs, singing games, playground chants and folk songs from many different traditions. Includes teacher's guide co - authored by a music education specialist.
Fine Arts; Sociology
Dist - BULFRG **Prod** - CAMBFP 1988

Picnic 10 MIN
16mm / VHS
Color (K P I)
$120.00, $235.00 purchase, $25.00 rental _ #VC306V, #MP306
Presents the story from the book, Picnic, by Emily Arnold McCully. Members of a mouse family go for a picnic in the country.
Health and Safety; Literature and Drama; Psychology
Dist - WWS **Prod** - WWS 1989

Picnic 4 MIN
U-matic / VHS
Color; Mono (K P I)
Presents a glorious day for a picnic. The sky is bright, the hills are lush green, and all the members of an extended mouse family pile into a big red pickup for the ride to the country. The nine little mice are the first out of the truck. But wait, are there nine? Somebody is missing, and nobody will be happy until she is found.
English Language; Fine Arts; Guidance and Counseling; Literature and Drama; Sociology
Dist - WWS **Prod** - WWS 1985

The Picnic 30 MIN
16mm / U-matic
B&W
Documents the life of a Latin prisoner at Rahway State Prison in New Jersey. Explores prison life and life outside prison for the Latin population. Focuses on an hour - long picnic behind bars with family and friends.
Sociology
Dist - BLKFMF **Prod** - BLKFMF

Picnic 115 MIN
16mm
Color (C A)
Stars William Holden, Kim Novak and Rosalind Russell in the earthy story of a stranger in town and the havoc he creates in the lives of its people, especially its women, in one 24 - hour visit.
Fine Arts
Dist - TIMLIF **Prod** - CPC 1956

Picnic 8 MIN
16mm / U-matic / VHS
Starting to Read Series
Color (K P)
LC 72-702455
Introduces words and concepts to the youngest readers and pre - readers. Includes lively pictures and songs.
English Language
Dist - AIMS **Prod** - BURGHS 1972

A Picnic on the River - Paddington Dines Out 11 MIN
U-matic / VHS / 16mm
Paddington Bear Series
Color (K P I)
LC 80-700955
Discusses Paddington's adventures on the family picnic and at a family restaurant. Based on chapters one and seven of the book Paddington Helps Out by Michael Bond.
Literature and Drama
Dist - ALTSUL **Prod** - BONDM 1980

Pico - Union - Urban Community Development 30 MIN
16mm
Color
LC 72-702860
Highlights citizen involvement activities in the Pico - union community in downtown Los Angeles.
Civics and Political Systems; Sociology
Dist - UCLA **Prod** - UCLA 1971

A Pictorial Geography 14 MIN
16mm
Land of the Bible Series
Color; B&W (I)
Shows the geographical importance of the land of Palestine in world history, and particularly in Biblical history. Depicts the natural geographical environment of our Bible.
Geography - World; History - World; Religion and Philosophy
Dist - FAMF **Prod** - FAMF 1960

Pictorial Parade Series
New Zealand's Day with LBJ 15 MIN
Dist - NZNFU

Pictorial Views - Sketches 10 MIN
BETA / VHS
Color (IND)
Demonstrates the two basic types of pictorial views used by a draftsman or person making a freehand sketch for illustrating an object for more clarification. Illustrates isometric and oblique views.
Mathematics; Psychology
Dist - RMIBHF **Prod** - RMIBHF

The Picture 58 MIN
16mm
Color (H C A)
Presents a story in which the relentless pursuit of the buck demeans the artist and degrades art to a species of confection and erotic pastry.
Fine Arts
Dist - GROVE **Prod** - GROVE

Picture atlas of the world
CD-ROM
Color (I J H G)
$99.00 purchase _ #80602
Offers high resolution maps of every nation and photographs of each country's people, places and landforms. Requires IBM system. Contact distributor for hardware requirements.
Geography - World
Dist - NGS **Prod** - NGS 1992

A Picture book of Martin Luther King Jr 9 MIN
35mm strip / VHS
Color (P)
$34.95, $29.95 purchase
Presents a video version of the David A Adler book 'A Picture Book Of Martin Luther King Jr,' which captures the life and times of Dr King.
Biography; Civics and Political Systems; History - United States
Dist - LIVOAK **Prod** - LIVOAK

A Picture Book of Martin Luther King, Jr
VHS / 16mm
Color (K)
$33.33 purchase _ #LV VC9
Recounts the events of Dr. Martin Luther King's times, for young viewers.
Health and Safety; History - United States
Dist - EDUCRT

Picture book parade series
Stories from many lands
This is New York 12 MIN
Dist - WWS

Picture book park green module series
Folktales 15 MIN
Dist - AITECH

Picture Book Park Series Blue Module
That's Right Edie 15 MIN
What Mary Jo Shared 15 MIN
Dist - AITECH

Picture Book Park Series Brown Module
Happy Birthday 15 MIN
Presents 15 MIN
Zoo 15 MIN
Dist - AITECH

Picture Book Park Series Green Module
Mice are Nice 15 MIN
Mighty hunters 15 MIN
Dist - AITECH

Picture Book Park Series Red Module
Lovable Lyle 15 MIN
Dist - AITECH

Picture book park series
Alfred 15 MIN
Bedtime for Frances 15 MIN
Benjie 15 MIN
From Japan 15 MIN
Dist - AITECH

A Picture for Harold's Room 7 MIN
U-matic / VHS / 16mm
Mono; Color (K P)
LC 74-713209
A story about a boy who draws a picture on his wall, steps into his picture to draw the moon and begins to travel as a giant.
Literature and Drama
Dist - WWS **Prod** - WWS

Picture framing 42 MIN
VHS
Color (G)
PdS19.95 purchase _ #A4-ARG13
Demonstrates the equipment needed to build a variety of picture frames. Shows beginners how to choose and cut the card for mounting a picture. Features Bill Davies.
Fine Arts
Dist - AVP **Prod** - ARGUS

The Picture Gallery 9 MIN
16mm
B&W (I)
LC 74-701510
Uses animation techniques in a fanciful exploration of the characteristics of ten famous paintings.
Fine Arts
Dist - CONNF **Prod** - CONNF 1973

Picture in Your Mind 17 MIN
VHS / U-matic
Color (J)
Explores the roots of prejudice in animation and delves into the anthropological and pyschological origins of man's misconceptions of other men.
Psychology; Sociology
Dist - IFF **Prod** - IFF

Picture Interest Exploration Survey - P I E S
VHS / 35mm strip / U-matic / BETA
(J H C A)
$350.00 _ #CCP300 slide, #CCP300F filmstrip, CCP300V vhs, #CCP300B
Based on the Occupational Outlook Handbook and referenced to the Dictionary of Occupation Titles. Presents thirteen career clusters made up of twelve different views to depict the various vocational interests that might apply to students considering a career.
Business and Economics; Education; Guidance and Counseling
Dist - CAMV **Prod** - CAMV

Picture Interest Exploration Survey - PIES
VHS / 35mm strip
$350.00 filmstrip or VHS purchase _ #013 - 215 film, #013 - 234 VHS
Examines career interests using a visual inventory of occupations. Focuses on the task rather than on the person performing it by showing only workers' hands.
Guidance and Counseling
Dist - CAREER **Prod** - CAREER

Picture Interest Exploration Survey - PIES
BETA / VHS
Color (H G)
#CCP300B
Helps students investigate their vocational interests and apply this information to their career goals. Features occupations represented by workers' hands performing tasks representative of their occupations.
Guidance and Counseling
Dist - CADESF **Prod** - CADESF 1987

Picture Making at the Gang Age 6 MIN
U-matic / VHS / 16mm
Color (I)
Shows how to encourage children in grades five and six to make original compositions which reflect their own interests.
Education; Fine Arts; Psychology
Dist - IFB **Prod** - IFB 1951

Picture Making by Teenagers 11 MIN
U-matic / VHS / 16mm
Color (J H)
Illustrates self - expression and creativeness as well as problems in picture making by teenagers. Shows various media used. Correlated with 'ART EDUCATION DURING ADOLESCENCE' by C D and M R Gaitskill.
Education; Fine Arts; Psychology
Dist - IFB **Prod** - IFB 1956

A picture of celebration - Video 3
VHS
Video trilogy series
Color (H C G A R)
$25.00 purchase, $10.00 rental _ #35 - 89013 - 784
Tells the story of a man who regains his ability to savor life when he recovers from an attack on his person. Produced by Paul Keller and Stan Kloth.
Religion and Philosophy
Dist - APH

The Picture of Dorian Gray 111 MIN
VHS
B&W (G J H)
$24.95 purchase _ #S00193; $39.00 purchase _ #05921-126
Tells the story of a handsome young man whose portrait ages while he remains young. Stars Hurd Hatfield as Gray and George Sanders as Lord Henry Wotton. Co - stars Donna Reed, Peter Lawford, and Angela Lansbury. Based on the story by Oscar Wilde.
Fine Arts; Literature and Drama
Dist - UILL **Prod** - GA
CA

A Picture of health 52 MIN
VHS
First Tuesday series
Color; PAL (H C G)
PdS30 purchase
Shows that while money may not buy happiness in Britain it certainly helps wealthier people to stay healthier and live ten times longer than their poorer neighbors. Reveals that the startling health - wealth divide is based on studies in one of Great Britain's poorest regions to the northeast of England. First Tuesday tests the facts and visits four families in the town of Middlesborough and discovers that the area has some of the worst health and highest death rates in Britain. Spina bifida, heart disease, infant mortality and asthma are all more common in this once prosperous region, and an expert says that death rates in 1991 are as bad as in the 1930s depression. Contact distributor about availability outside the United Kingdom.
Health and Safety; History - World; Sociology
Dist - ACADEM **Prod** - YORKTV

The Picture of Health 13 MIN
U-matic / VHS / 16mm
Physical Fitness Series
Color (J)
LC 80-700253
Discusses the role heredity plays in determining individual health.
Health and Safety; Science - Natural
Dist - JOU **Prod** - ALTSUL 1979

A Picture of Health 20 MIN
16mm / U-matic / VHS
Color
LC 83-700652
Emphasizes the need for people to take responsibility for their own health through behavior patterns which reduce risk of disease and increase self - esteem. Examines the health regimens of Dr Kenneth Cooper's aerobics program, Dr Nathan Pritikin's Longevity Center and Dr Bill Connors family nutrition project.
Health and Safety
Dist - CORF **Prod** - MITCHG 1983

The Picture of Health - Genetic Platforms 13 MIN
U-matic / VHS / 16mm
Physical Fitness Series
Color (J)
Discusses the role heredity plays in determining individual health.
Health and Safety; Science - Natural
Dist - JOU **Prod** - ALTSUL 1979

A picture of rebirth - Video 2
VHS
Video trilogy series
Color (H C G A R)
$25.00 purchase, $10.00 rental _ #35 - 89012 - 784
Tells the story of a man who finds healing when he retraces his failures of the past. Produced by Paul Keller and Stan Kloth.
Religion and Philosophy
Dist - APH

A picture of sin - Video 1
VHS
Video trilogy series
Color (H C G A R)
$25.00 purchase, $10.00 rental _ #35 - 89011 - 784
Uses a Charlie Chaplin - type character to illustrate the sin of self - centeredness. Produced by Paul Keller and Stan Kloth.
Religion and Philosophy
Dist - APH

Picture Perfect - How to Become a Model 30 MIN
VHS
(H C A)
$24.95 purchase _ #CH300V
Explains how to develop a career in modeling. Discusses portfolio, go sees, rejections, and how to sell yourself. Details different types of models.
Home Economics
Dist - CAMV

The Picture programme 30 MIN
VHS
Perspectives - transport and communication - series
Color; PAL; NTSC (G)
PdS90, PdS105 purchase
Examines a box of magic tricks from video effects specialists.
Industrial and Technical Education
Dist - CFLVIS **Prod** - LONTVS

Picture this 14 MIN
U-matic / VHS
Writer's Realm Series
Color (I)
$125.00 purchase,$25.00 rental
Gives hints on how to improve characterization so that the reader can 'picture' the images clearly.
English Language; Literature and Drama; Social Science
Dist - AITECH **Prod** - MDINTV 1987

Picture Trouble - Trouble on the Beach - A Visit to the Theatre 16 MIN
U-matic / VHS / 16mm
Paddington Bear Series
Color (K P I)
LC 80-700956
Focuses on Paddington's encounter with a seaside photographer and his adventures at the beach. Describes his evening at the theatre. Based on chapters six and seven of the book A Bear called Paddington by Michael Bond.
Literature and Drama
Dist - ALTSUL **Prod** - BONDM 1980

Picture Yourself a Marine 12 MIN
16mm
Color (H C)
LC 76-702715
Shows the many activities, opportunities and responsibilities of today's woman Marine. Compares these aspects of military life with civilian life.
Civics and Political Systems; Guidance and Counseling; Sociology
Dist - USNAC **Prod** - USMC 1975

Picture Yourself in St Petersburg 22 MIN
16mm
Color
Features St Petersburg, Florida, an entertainment and cultural center which looks to the future without abandoning its past.
Geography - United States; History - United States; Physical Education and Recreation
Dist - FLADC **Prod** - FLADC

Picturebook classics on filmstrip series
Adam's smile
The Beast in the bathtub
Five secrets in a box
The Porcelain Cat
Dist - PELLER

Picturephone in Education 10 MIN
16mm
Color
Presents a short, spontaneous report on the use of a televised telephone hookup as an aid in teaching. Shows a child working on the famous 'TALKING TYPEWRITER' assisted by a paraprofessional and monitored vai picturephone. Treats the problem of how paraprofessionals in education can be trained and supervised using the advanced technology of picturephone.
Education
Dist - MATHWW **Prod** - MATHWW 1971

Pictures 3 MIN
16mm
Color (G)
$150.00 purchase, $25.00 rental
Presents a collage of paintings of women from all periods of history which are added to photos of women of all cultures. Uses gradually increasing speed in assemblage as the film's historical time line grows closer to the present. Produced by Janet Benn.
Fine Arts; History - World; Sociology
Dist - WMEN

Pictures 20 MIN
16mm
All that I Am Series
B&W (C A)
Fine Arts; Guidance and Counseling
Dist - NWUFLM **Prod** - MPATI

Pictures at an Exhibition 10 MIN
16mm
B&W
Illustrates a Moussorgsky tone poem with episodes from the composer's childhood in Russia and Alexander Alexeieff's memories of his own childhood there, using two pinboards, a small one that revolves and a stable one behind it. Introduced in English by Alexeieff.
Fine Arts
Dist - STARRC **Prod** - STARRC 1972

Pictures for Barbara 10 MIN
16mm
Color (G)
$20.00 rental
Delves into a friendship between two women who exchange letters and Polaroid pictures. Focuses on women's strength, spirituality and the violence of the external world.
Fine Arts; Sociology
Dist - CANCIN **Prod** - BARHAM 1981

Pictures from a revolution 92 MIN
35mm / 16mm / VHS
Color (G) (ENGLISH AND SPANISH WITH SUBTITLES)
$300.00, $400.00 rental
Travels with Susan Meiselas who returns to Nicaragua ten years after photographing the Sandinista victory for the New York Times. Observes a people living in the wake of political turmoil who have seen their hopes nad dreams destroyed by the reality of everyday life. Directed by Susan Meiselas, Alfred Guzzetti and Richard P Rogers.
Geography - World; History - World
Dist - KINOIC

Pictures from a Story 6 MIN
16mm
Color
LC 76-700405
Shows faces which are abstracted in a divisionistic manner.
Fine Arts
Dist - LILYAN **Prod** - LILYAN 1976

Pictures from camp 24 MIN
VHS
Color (G)
$195.00 purchase, $100.00 rental _ #CJ - 113
Chronicles the experiences of a group of kids aged 6 to 18 in summer camp, all of them knowing the trials and challenges of having cancer. Features music by Bob Marley, Enya, John Hiatt, Sounds of Soweto and Viveza. Produced by Braun Farnon and Jeth Weinrich of Red Motel Pictures for the Canadian Cancer Society.
Health and Safety
Dist - FANPRO

Pictures in a Patient 27 MIN
16mm / U-matic / VHS
Perspective Series
Color (C A)
Discusses the medical uses of ultrasonic scanning, nuclear magnetic resonance and radioactive isotopes. Describes the ways in which these methods enable health professionals to 'see' inside people.
Health and Safety; Science
Dist - STNFLD **Prod** - LONTVS

Pictures in Your Mind 30 MIN
U-matic
Read all about it - One Series
Color (I)
Teaches reading and writing skills as it continues a story in which Chris's friends Sam and Lynne are sent to the Planet of Maze with the help of Doctor Couplet.
Education; English Language; Literature and Drama
Dist - TVOTAR **Prod** - TVOTAR 1982

Pictures of Horyuji Born Again 45 MIN
16mm
Color (JAPANESE)
A Japanese language film. Points out that Horyuji Temple is Japan's oldest and largest wooden structure. Explains that this national property was destroyed by fire in 1952 including the pictures decorating the walls. Shows how Japan's topranking artists used their utmost efforts to restore these valuable pictures to their original state.
Fine Arts; Foreign Language
Dist - UNIJAP **Prod** - UNIJAP 1969

Pictures on pink paper 35 MIN
VHS / 16mm
Color (G)
$60.00 rental, $250.00 purchase
Weaves together numerous threads and layers to question who benefits from the apparent inevitability of the 'natural' and the immutability of the 'normal.'
Fine Arts; Religion and Philosophy
Dist - WMEN **Prod** - LIRHO 1982

Pictures Out of My Life
16mm
(H C A)
#2X39 N
Presents the drawings and recollectgions of Inuit Indian artist Pitseolak, the most famous member of the Cape Dorset artist colony and cooperative. Based on the book by Dorothy Eber.
Fine Arts; Social Science
Dist - CDIAND **Prod** - NFBC 1973

The Pictures that Moved 45 MIN
16mm
History of the Australian Cinema Series
B&W (H C A)
LC 71-709226
Traces the history of Australian film - making from 1896 to 1920. Uses excerpts from early films, stills and interviews to trace the growth of the silent film in Australia.
Fine Arts; Geography - World
Dist - AUIS **Prod** - FLMAUS 1968

Pictures to Serve the People 22 MIN
16mm / U-matic / VHS
Color (J)
LC 75-703257
Traces the American art of lithography, emphasizing the art's inexpensiveness and accessibility.
Fine Arts; Industrial and Technical Education
Dist - AIMS **Prod** - AAS 1975

A Picture's worth a thousand words - interpreting visual information
VHS
Color (J H C)
$197.00 purchase _ #00319 - 126
Demonstrates graphically how visual images, photographs and illustrations are used to present individual views of reality. Explains visual codes such as graphs and maps which have been developed to preserve and convey information. Discusses the possibility of distortion in such mediums. Includes teacher's guide and library kit. In two parts.
Fine Arts; Industrial and Technical Education; Mathematics; Social Science
Dist - GA **Prod** - GA

Picturing Oriental girls - a - re - educational videotape 12 MIN
VHS
Body, soul and voice - new work by women series
Color (G)
Offers a visual compendium of Asian women in American film and television. Juxtaposes text from 'mail - order bride' catalogs and men's magazines with clips from over 25 films and television programs to expose the 'orientalism' and exoticism prevalent in mass media images of Asian American women. Directed by Valerie Soe.
Sociology
Dist - CROCUR

Pidio ch'waryong
VHS
Color (G)
$80.00 _ #42090
Teaches the viewer how to use a video camera.
Industrial and Technical Education
Dist - PANASI

Piece Mandala - End War 5 MIN
16mm
Color; Silent (C)
$135.00
Experimental film by Paul Sharits.
Fine Arts
Dist - AFA **Prod** - AFA

Piece of Cake 26 MIN
16mm / U-matic / VHS
Color (J)
LC 82-700449
Tells of two retired friends who arrange to catch a goose for Christmas dinner. Reveals that although the dinner is ostensibly for one of the men's daughter, she has really been dead for several years.
Health and Safety; Literature and Drama; Sociology
Dist - LCOA **Prod** - AUSFLM 1982

A Piece of Sunshine 18 MIN
U-matic / VHS / 16mm
Color (P I)
LC 84-706801
Shows how, with the aid of a magical time machine, two youngsters are able to travel back through time to learn about man's sources of energy in history. Animated.
Science - Physical; Social Science
Dist - PHENIX **Prod** - EEPOH 1983

A Piece of the Cake 58 MIN
16mm
B&W (H C A)
LC 70-704653
Describes the successful hiring, training and retaining of the hard - core unemployed by the Westinghouse Electric Corporation plant in east Pittsburgh, PA. Explains that the company is hiring 23 men each month and that 90 per cent of these people remain on the job beyond an initial six - month period.
Business and Economics; History - United States; Psychology; Sociology
Dist - IU **Prod** - NET 1969

A Piece of the Pie 19 MIN
16mm
Color
Tells the story of four minority group members who are in business for themselves. Provides insights into what the minority business owner must do to succeed in today's business world.
Business and Economics; History - United States; Sociology
Dist - MTP **Prod** - EXXON

Piece touchee 15 MIN
16mm
B&W (G)
$45.00 rental
Reproduces an 18 - second sequence originally from a fifties American B movie frame by frame. Alters its temporal and spatial progression. Produced by Martin Arnold.
Fine Arts; Mathematics
Dist - CANCIN

Piece - Wise Linear Systems 33 MIN
VHS / U-matic
Nonlinear Vibrations Series
B&W
Mathematics
Dist - MIOT **Prod** - MIOT

Pieces of eight and the watchdogs 30 MIN
VHS
Davey and Goliath series
Color (P I R)
$19.95 purchase, $10.00 rental _ #4 - 8824
Presents two 15 - minute 'Davey and Goliath' episodes. 'Pieces of Eight' tells how Davey 'borrows' money from his sister's piggy bank to replace lost money. 'The Watchdogs' describes how Davey learns the importance of the Golden Rule in refusing to get involved as a crime witness. Produced by the Evangelical Lutheran Church in America.
Literature and Drama; Religion and Philosophy
Dist - APH

Pieces of silence 56 MIN
VHS / U-matic / BETA
Co - dependency series
Color (G)
$280.00 purchase _ #801.5
Tells the story of the family of author and psychologist Robert Subby which has suffered the effects of an alcoholic parent. Features Subby who narrates and discusses addiction, co - dependency and gives his own perspective on being part of such a family. Includes interviews with family members to illustrate the pain, guilt and frustration of life in a dyfunctional family. Part of a five - part series on co - dependency. Produced by Family Systems, Inc and the Subby family.
Guidance and Counseling; Health and Safety; Psychology; Sociology
Dist - CONMED

The Pieces of the Puzzle 30 MIN
U-matic / VHS
Money Puzzle - the World of Macroeconomics Series Module 1
Color
Introduces the viewer to the subject of economics. Emphasizes macroeconomics and what it covers.
Business and Economics; Sociology
Dist - MDCC **Prod** - MDCC

Pieces to peace series
Deals with marriage and divorce issues. Presents insights on why people marry and why they divorce. Suggests coping skills for life after a divorce. Consists of two videocassettes.
Breaking points - Part 1 46 MIN
New beginnings - Part 2 46 MIN
Dist - APH **Prod** - NEWLIB

The Pied Piper of Hamelin 29 MIN
16mm / U-matic / VHS
Color (I)
Uses poetry, music, dance film and puppet animation to produce a sophisticated, mystical rendition of the medieval legend of the Pied Piper of Hamelin. After the piper of Hamelin rid the town of rats, its citizens refused to pay him. His revenge was to lead their children away forever.
Literature and Drama
Dist - MEDIAG **Prod** - THAMES 1983

The Pied Piper of Hamelin 15 MIN
VHS / U-matic
Gather Round Series
Color (K P)
Literature and Drama
Dist - CTI **Prod** - CTI

The Pied Piper of Hamelin 18 MIN
U-matic / VHS / 16mm
Color (I J)
$49.95 purchase _ #L10912
Tells the story of a man who makes the children in a small town disappear when the council refuses to pay him for ridding the town of rats. Recited by Orson Welles. Animated. A Pied Piper Production.
Literature and Drama
Dist - CF

The Pied Piper of Hamelin 17 MIN
U-matic / VHS / 16mm
Color (I J)
LC 73-708669
An animated film of Robert Browning's narrative poem of the legend of the Pied Piper. Symbolizes the conflict between greed and honor.
Literature and Drama
Dist - PHENIX **Prod** - ARGO 1970

The Pied Piper of Hamelin 18 MIN
16mm
Color (I)
LC 83-700126
Relates what happens when the Council of Hamelin fails to pay the Pied Piper for ridding their town of rats and finds their children disappearing into an enchanted mountain.
Literature and Drama
Dist - PPIPER **Prod** - PPIPER 1982

The Pied Piper of Hamelin - a German Tale 11 MIN
16mm / U-matic / VHS
Favorite Fairy Tales and Fables Series
Color (K P)
$280.00, $195.00 purchase _ #4145
Presents the German tale The Pied Piper Of Hamelin. Shows how the Pied Piper uses his enchanting music to lure the rats away from Hamelin. Tells how he plays one more tune to take away the children when the town refuses to pay.
Literature and Drama
Dist - CORF **Prod** - CORF 1980

Pieper - zoology prelab dissections - series
VHS
Pieper - zoology prelab dissections - series
Color (J H C)
$925.00 purchase _ #CG - 886 - VS
Presents a 15 - part series on zoological lab dissection, including a lab safety review, produced by Bill Pieper. Includes Ascaris; Cnidaria and Ctenophora; Crayfish; Dogfish Shark; Earthworm; Fresh Water Clam; Grass Frog; Grasshopper; Perch; Platyhelminthes, Rotifer and Tardigrada; Porifera and Sea Star.
Health and Safety; Science; Science - Natural
Dist - HRMC

Pier Marton - Happy Medium 2 MIN
U-matic / VHS
Color
Presented by Pier Marton.
Fine Arts
Dist - ARTINC **Prod** - ARTINC

Pier Marton - Heaven is what I've Done, for My Fellow Beings 3 MIN
VHS / U-matic
Color
Features a public service announcement dealing with distractions and dilemmas.
Fine Arts
Dist - ARTINC **Prod** - ARTINC

Pier Marton - Hope You Croak Before Me 3 MIN
VHS / U-matic
Color
Presented by Pier Marton.
Fine Arts
Dist - ARTINC **Prod** - ARTINC

Pier Marton - Say I'm a Jew 28 MIN
U-matic / VHS
Color
Features interviews with Jews who grew up in post - war Europe. Presents a manifesto - like affirmation of Jewish identity.
Fine Arts; Sociology
Dist - ARTINC **Prod** - ARTINC

Pier Marton - Tapes 15 MIN
U-matic / VHS
Color
Explores images of excessive anguish. Presents the horrible with humor.
Fine Arts
Dist - ARTINC **Prod** - ARTINC

Pier Marton - Telepathos 3 MIN
VHS / U-matic
Color
Presented by Pier Marton.
Fine Arts
Dist - ARTINC **Prod** - ARTINC

Pier Marton - Unity through Strength 7 MIN
VHS / U-matic
Color
Deals with unity through strength.
Fine Arts
Dist - ARTINC **Prod** - ARTINC

The Pierced sky 50 MIN
VHS
Nomads of the wind series
Color (A)
PdS99 purchase _ Unavailable in USA or Canada
Combines wildlife footage with drama and documentary in exploring the fundamental relationship between humans and nature across the world's largest ocean - the Pacific. Explores the Maori, who were settled in New Zealand for almost 1000 years before the coming of the Europeans changed the course of the islands' natural history.
Geography - World
Dist - BBCENE

Piercing, Cutting Holes and Cutting 45 - Degree Bevels with the Cutting Torch
U-matic / VHS

Oxyacetylene Welding - Spanish Series
Color (SPANISH)
Foreign Language; Industrial and Technical Education
Dist - VTRI **Prod** - VTRI

Piero Della Francesca - 1416 - 1498 10 MIN
16mm
Color
Shows how Piero Della Francesca, a painter of the High Renaissance, used his art to convey his sense of sublime contemplation of a harmonious universe.
Fine Arts
Dist - ROLAND **Prod** - ROLAND

Pierre Bonnard 55 MIN
VHS
Color (H C A)
$39.95 purchase
Provides a close look at paintings by Pierre Bonnard to illustrate his unique style.
Fine Arts
Dist - ARTSAM **Prod** - RMART

Pierre Bonnard and the Impressionist vision 12 MIN
U-matic / VHS
Color (G)
$100.00, $29.95 purchase _ #BON-02, #BON-01
Examines the poetic, impressionistic paintings and prints by French artist Pierre Bonnard. Shows how he developed his own distinct style, combining his love of color with the simple forms and compositions he admired in Japanese woodblock prints and the work of Paul Gauguin. Focuses on several works - Bonnard's Dining Room in the Country - 1913; Vuillard's Place St Augustin - 1912-13; Pissaro's Place du Theatre Francais, Rain - 1898 - to explore his relationship with his contemporaries and his desire to depict the 'poetry' of life in his art.
Fine Arts
Dist - ARTSAM **Prod** - MIA

Pierre Bonnard - In search of pure colour 49 MIN
VHS
Color (H C A)
$39.95 purchase _ #BON-03
Looks at works by Pierre Bonnard to illustrate his individual style. Reveals that Bonnard was inspired by Gauguin and Cezanne, befriended by Renoir and Matisse, and scorned by Picasso. Takes a close look at paintings gathered for a retrospective at the Centre Georges Pompidou in Paris. Includes footage of the artist at a seaside resort in the period just before his death.
Fine Arts
Dist - ARTSAM **Prod** - RMART
FI

Pierre Lefevre on acting 39 MIN
VHS
Color (G C H)
$169.00 purchase _ #DL492
Demonstrates the use of neutral and character masks for the exploration of the physical, vocal, and inner life of a character. Shows Lefevre's methods of coaching students, demonstrating techniques, and providing constructive criticism.
Fine Arts
Dist - INSIM

Pierre Valliers 33 MIN
16mm
Color (G)
$40.00 rental
Features a political documentary about Pierre Valliers, a Quebec revolutionary who spent three years in jail without a trial. Concentrates on close - ups, to eliminate distractions, of Pierre raising the consciousness of workers in Mount Laurier, Quebec.
Fine Arts; Sociology
Dist - CANCIN **Prod** - WIELNJ 1972

Pierrefonds and Viollet - Le - Duc 26 MIN
U-matic / VHS
Castles of France Series
Color (C) (FRENCH (ENGLISH SUBTITLES))
$249.00, $149.00 purchase _ #AD - 1507
Reveals that architect Eugene - Emmanuel Viollet - le - Duc led the Gothic revival in 19th - century France and is famous for his restorations of historic cathedrals and medieval buildings. Focuses on Pierrefonds as an example of his passion and esthetics. Part of a six - part series on castles of France. In French with English subtitles.
Fine Arts; Foreign Language; Geography - World; History - World
Dist - FOTH **Prod** - FOTH

Pierrot and Lightning and Thunder 5 MIN
U-matic / VHS / 16mm
Weather Science Series
Color (P)
$150, $105 purchase _ #3866
Talks about the causes of thunder, lightning, and thunderstorms.
Science - Physical
Dist - CORF

Pierrot and Rain and Snow 7 MIN
U-matic / VHS / 16mm
Weather Science Series
Color (P)
$150, $105 purchase _ #3865
Discusses the weather cycle, focussing on clouds, rain, and snow.
Science - Physical
Dist - CORF

Pierrot and the Rainbow 6 MIN
U-matic / VHS / 16mm
Weather Science Series
Color (P)
$150, $105 purchase _ #3864
Shows how a rainbow is formed.
Science - Physical
Dist - CORF

Pierrot and the Sun 6 MIN
16mm / U-matic / VHS
Weather Science Series
Color (P)
$150, $105 purchase _ #3869
Shows the sun's physical characteristics and their effect on the earth.
Science - Physical
Dist - CORF

Pierrot and the Wind 4 MIN
U-matic / VHS / 16mm
Weather Science Series
Color (P)
$150, $105 purchase _ #3867
Shows what causes wind. Explains that certain land forms cause air masses to move in certain ways.
Science - Physical
Dist - CORF

Pies 13 MIN
U-matic / VHS / 16mm
Color (J A G)
Tells a universal tale of how human understanding can overcome prejudice. Uses humor to introduce discussions of ethnic stereotyping, urban versus rural life, problem solving, and dealing with interpersonal conflicts.
Fine Arts; Guidance and Counseling
Dist - DIRECT **Prod** - NFBC 1985

Piet Mondriaan 18 MIN
16mm / U-matic / VHS
Color
LC 75-703528
Presents a visual statement about the works of Piet Mondriaan, tracing his development from naturalism through cubism to pure abstraction. Uses photographs and other documents to depict his surroundings and activities.
Fine Arts
Dist - IFB **Prod** - IFB 1973

Piet Mondriaan - a film - essay 18 MIN
U-matic / VHS / BETA
Color; PAL (G H C)
PdS50, PdS58 purchase
Covers the work of the Netherlands' most important painter.
Fine Arts
Dist - EDPAT

The Pig 11 MIN
U-matic / VHS / 16mm
Animal Families Series
Color (K P I)
$275, $195, $225 purchase _ #B418
Shows the eating habits, basic anatomy, and playfulness of young and adult pigs. Shows little piglets feeding, frolicking, and nuzzling each other with their snouts.
Science - Natural
Dist - BARR **Prod** - BARR 1986

Pig Bird - a Film for Safety Training 4 MIN
VHS / 16mm
Color (C A)
$310.00 purchase, $110.00 rental _ #163
Depicts what could happen if people don't abide by health and safety regulations. Animated, no narrative. Includes Leader's Guide.
Geography - United States; Health and Safety
Dist - SALENG **Prod** - NFBC 1981

Pig heart dissection 15 MIN
VHS
Dissection video II series
Color (J H)

$150.00 purchase _ #A5VH 1223
Shows the dissection of a pig heart, start - to - finish. Provides clear and detailed presentations of the external anatomy, the correct procedures used for dissection and a review of the internal anatomy and physiological systems. Includes a dissection manual and a written examination. Part of a series on dissection.
Science - Natural
Dist - CLRVUE **Prod** - CLRVUE

Pig power 6 MIN
16mm
B&W (G)
$10.00 rental
Features an impressionistic piece on riots and marches in the late 1960s. Records brief remarks by the participants. Represents revolutionary filmmakers in the 1960s whose work provides a window to that period.
Civics and Political Systems; Fine Arts; History - United States; Sociology
Dist - CANCIN **Prod** - SINGLE

Pig Power 6 MIN
16mm
Color
Shows how the forces of order illustrate Mayor Daley's thesis that the police are there to 'PRESERVE DISORDER,' as the students take to the streets in New York and Berkeley.
Social Science; Sociology
Dist - CANWRL **Prod** - CANWRL

Pig Projects make Profits 29 MIN
16mm
Color
Illustrates practices essential to successful hog raising. Covers purchase, record keeping, health factors, and the training and showing of pigs.
Agriculture
Dist - UDSR **Prod** - UDSR

Pigbird 6 MIN
16mm
Color
Relates how a cagey citizen's success at getting a forbidden animal through customs has disastrous consequences for him and the rest of the population.
Fine Arts
Dist - NFBC **Prod** - NFBC 1982

Pigeon Feathers 40 MIN
U-matic / VHS / 16mm
Color (H C A)
$750 purchase - 16 mm, $250 purchase - video _ #5800C
Talks about a teenager who learns how to understand his own mortality by caring for the pigeons in his father's barn. Based on the story by John Updike.
Sociology
Dist - CORF

Pigeon feathers 45 MIN
VHS
Color (J H C)
$29.00 purchase _ #04637 - 126
Adapts a John Updike story of a young man's search for meaning and his discovery of nature.
Fine Arts; Literature and Drama; Sociology
Dist - GA **Prod** - GA

The Pigeon that Came Home - a Story of the Fjord Country 20 MIN
U-matic / VHS / 16mm
Color (P I)
LC 74-711606
The story of how a pigeon aids in the rescue of a young Norwegian boy. Through the story some geographic concepts are explored and the need to follow safety rules in all outdoor activities is stressed.
Geography - World; Health and Safety
Dist - PHENIX **Prod** - SVEK 1964

The Pigeon that Worked a Miracle 47 MIN
U-matic / VHS / 16mm
Color (I)
LC FIA67-1288
Tells the story of a boy whose love for his pigeon works a miraculous cure and forces him from the confinement of his wheelchair.
Psychology
Dist - CORF **Prod** - DISNEY 1964

The Pigeon that Worked a Miracle - Pt 1 24 MIN
U-matic / VHS / 16mm
Color (I)
LC FIA67-1288
Tells the story of a boy whose love for his pigeon works a miraculous cure and forces him from the confinement of his wheelchair.
Health and Safety
Dist - CORF **Prod** - DISNEY 1964

The Pigeon that Worked a Miracle - Pt 2 24 MIN
U-matic / VHS / 16mm
Color (I)
LC FIA67-1288
Tells the story of a boy whose love for his pigeon works a miraculous cure and forces him from the confinement of his wheelchair.
Health and Safety
Dist - CORF **Prod** - DISNEY 1964

Pigeons, doves, hummingbirds - Volume 3 60 MIN
VHS
Audubon society videoguides to the birds of North America series
Color (G)
$29.95 purchase
Combines live footage and color photography in an Audubon Society bird watching program. Focuses on pigeons, doves, hummingbirds, and several other bird types. Uses bird sights and sounds, visual graphics, and maps to aid in the identification of bird types. Narrated by Michael Godfrey.
Science - Natural
Dist - PBS **Prod** - WNETTV

The Piggy in the puddle - No 87
VHS
Reading rainbow series
Color; CC (K P)
$39.95 purchase
Goes with host LeVar Burton behind the scenes as the book Piggy In The Puddle by Charlotte Pomerantz, illustrated by James Marshall, is brought to life through clay animation. Reveals the secrets of 'claymation' from painting and sculpting the characters, to the painstaking process of filming the action frame by frame. Part of a series offering a multicultural approach to generating reading enthusiasm with cross - curricular applications, hosted by LeVar Burton.
English Language; Literature and Drama
Dist - GPN **Prod** - LNMDP

Pigs 11 MIN
U-matic / VHS / 16mm
Animals Series
Color (P I)
$49.95 purchase _ #Q10515; LC FIA68-791
Follows a farmer on his rounds as he feeds the pigs. Shows the faces, personalities and the varied textures of the pigs. Discusses their habits and their behavior.
Agriculture
Dist - CF **Prod** - DF 1967

Pigs 12 MIN
VHS
Color (P I J H)
Looks at pigs. Observes them scratching, eating, fighting, playing, running, lumbering, slumbering.
Agriculture; Science - Natural; Sociology
Dist - VIEWTH **Prod** - VIEWTH

Pigs and Hippos 13 MIN
U-matic / VHS / 16mm
Looking at Animals Series
Color (P I)
Describes the physical appearance, natural habitat and feeding habits of domesticated pigs, wild boars, wart hogs and peccaries. Compares pigs to hippos and demonstrates the unique ability of hippos to stay submerged in water.
Science - Natural
Dist - IFB **Prod** - IFB 1973

Pigs no more 29 MIN
Videoreel / VT2
Turning points series
Color
Reports on the progress of a Fort Smith, Arkansas youth center created specifically to improve communications between the city's youth and the local police force.
Geography - United States; Social Science; Sociology
Dist - PBS **Prod** - KETSTV

Pigs of the Past 30 MIN
16mm
Great Plains Trilogy Series; In the beginning - the primitive man
B&W (H C A)
Presents the geologic story of pig - like mammals. Describes world's largest hog from Sioux County, Nebraska. Shows how fossil remains demonstrate evolution in mammals.
Science - Natural
Dist - UNEBR **Prod** - KUONTV 1954

The Pig's Picnic
VHS / 35mm strip
Children's Sound Filmstrips Series
Color (K)
$33.00 purchase
Adapts a children's story by K Kasza. Part of a series.
English Language; Literature and Drama
Dist - PELLER

The Pigs Vs the Freaks 15 MIN
16mm / U-matic / VHS
Color (J)
LC 75-700314
Features a football game between campus longhair students at Michigan State University and the local town police. Presents an event in which two conflicting lifestyles meet.
Education; Sociology
Dist - PFP **Prod** - EPPSJ 1975

The Pig's wedding and other stories 35 MIN
VHS
Children's circle collection series
Color (K P I)
$14.95 purchase _ #WK1177
Contains the title story along with The Selkie Girl; The Happy Owls; A Letter to Amy; and The Owl and the Pussycat.
Fine Arts; Literature and Drama
Dist - KNOWUN

The Pigskin Palooka 11 MIN
16mm
B&W
Tells how Alfalfa's boasts about his prowess as a gridiron star get him into trouble. A Little Rascals film.
Fine Arts
Dist - RMIBHF **Prod** - UNKNWN 1937

Pike on Language Series
Into the Unknown 29 MIN
The Music of Speech - Pitch and Poetry 29 MIN
Voice at Work 29 MIN
Waves of Change 29 MIN
Way We Know - the Value of Theory in Linguistic Study 29 MIN
Dist - UMITV

Pikes Paradise 25 MIN
16mm
Color
Shows fisherman Ed Ebbinger fishing for Northern pike using the Cardinal 4 and 808 reels in the wilderness of northern Ontario. Includes information on the feeding and breeding habits of pike and information about local wildlife and history.
Geography - World; Physical Education and Recreation
Dist - KAROL **Prod** - BRNSWK

Pilafs 30 MIN
U-matic / VHS
Cooking Now Series
(C A)
$19.95 _ #CH270V
Features Franco Palumbo, former chef of Weight Watchers International, as he demonstrates simple, methodical recipes for preparing pilafs.
Home Economics; Industrial and Technical Education
Dist - CAMV **Prod** - CAMV

Pilafs, Pilavs and Perloos 5 MIN
16mm
Color
Shows easy and elegant pilaf dishes from around the world ranging from the traditional Middle Eastern pilaf to a Spanish arroz con pollo.
Home Economics
Dist - MTP **Prod** - MTP 1982

Pilferage, Cargo Theft and Shoplifting 13 MIN
16mm / U-matic / VHS
Security Officer Series
Color (PRO)
Discusses techniques to stop pilferage, cargo theft and shoplifting.
Civics and Political Systems; Social Science; Sociology
Dist - AIMS **Prod** - AIMS 1976

Pilgramage of remembrance - Jews in Poland today 48 MIN
VHS
Jewish life around the world series
Color (G)
$49.95 purchase _ #111
Reveals that of the 3.5 million Jews who lived in Poland on the eve of World War II only 6,000 remain. Visits 15 different cities in Poland to meet the survivors and examine their Jewish identity and relationship with other Poles. Directed by Yaron Shemer.
History - World; Sociology
Dist - ERGOM **Prod** - ERGOM

Pilgramage to the West 24 HRS
VHS
Color (G) (MANDARIN CHINESE)
$360.00 purchase _ #6038X
Presents a Mandarin Chinese language television program produced in the People's Republic of China.
Geography - World; Industrial and Technical Education; Literature and Drama
Dist - CHTSUI **Prod** - CHTSUI

The Pilgrim Adventure 54 MIN
16mm / U-matic / VHS
Saga of Western Man Series
Color (J)
LC FIA66-1494
Describes the Pilgrims' flight from Europe to America. Cites reasons for the emigration, hazards of the journey and difficulties of settlement.
History - United States; History - World
Dist - MGHT **Prod** - ABCTV 1968

The Pilgrim Adventure - Pt 1 27 MIN
U-matic / VHS / 16mm
Saga of Western Man Series
Color (J)
LC FIA66-1494
Describes the Pilgrims' flight from Europe to America. Cites reasons for the emigration, hazards of the journey and difficulties of settlement.
Dist - MGHT **Prod** - ABCTV 1966

The Pilgrim Adventure - Pt 2 27 MIN
U-matic / VHS / 16mm
Saga of Western Man Series
Color (J)
LC FIA66-1494
Describes the Pilgrims' flight from Europe to America. Cites reasons for the emigration, hazards of the journey and difficulties of settlement.
History - United States
Dist - MGHT **Prod** - ABCTV 1966

Pilgrim Farewell 110 MIN
U-matic / VHS
Color (H C A)
Introduces Kate, who is dying of cancer and is concerned about the estrangement between her and her daughter, whom she walked out on years before.
Sociology
Dist - FI **Prod** - FI 1982

Pilgrim journey 24 MIN
U-matic / VHS
Young people's specials series
Color
Looks at the voyage of the Mayflower as seen through the eyes of a young girl.
Fine Arts; History - United States; Sociology
Dist - MULTPP **Prod** - MULTPP

The Pilgrim must embark - living in community 25 MIN
VHS
Color (T PRO C G)
$125.00 purchase
Shows how people in crisis establish and maintain a sense of community. Documents communication practices in a residential facility for persons living with AIDS, Bonaventure House in Chicago. Focuses on the inherent tensions of community living that permeate the practical, personal and communal lives of residents. Combines interviews of staff and residents with footage of the home environment to illustrate the diversity of the membership, everyday living routines, house maintenance, group governance, communication practices, social attachment, death and dying and rituals for grieving. Developed by Mara Adelman and Peter Shultz, Seattle University.
Psychology; Social Science; Sociology
Dist - ERLBAU

The Pilgrim - Pielgrzym 80 MIN
VHS
Color (G A) (POLISH)
$24.95 purchase _ #V123
Presents an independent documentary made during the first visit to Poland of Pope John Paul II in June 1979.
Fine Arts; History - World; Religion and Philosophy
Dist - POLART

The Pilgrim - Pocahontas, the Landing of the Pilgrims Fathers, the First Thanksgiving, Southern Ships and Settlers 15 MIN
VHS / 16mm
Stories and Poems from Long Ago Series
Color (I)
Uses the character of a retired sea captain to tell stories from The Pilgrim - Pocahontas, The Landing Of The Pilgrims Fathers, The First Thanksgiving, Southern Ships And Settlers. The eighth of 16 installments of the Stories And Poems From Long Ago Series, which is intended to encourage young viewers to read and write.
Literature and Drama
Dist - GPN **Prod** - CTI 1990

Pilgrimage 30 MIN
U-matic / VHS
Journey into the Himalayas Series
Color (J S C A)
MV=$195.00
Shows the hundreds of thousands of Hindus who journey across India to the Himalayas where the sacred river, the Ganges, starts.
Geography - World; History - World; Religion and Philosophy
Dist - LANDMK **Prod** - LANDMK 1986

Pilgrimage to a Hindu Temple 14 MIN
16mm
Hindu Religion Series no 6; No 6
Color
LC 70-712495
Shows a middle - aged Tengalai Sri - vaisnava Brahmin getting off the bus in the village of Sriperumbudur. Features the pilgrim moving to the temple tank where he bathes and changes into garbs appropriate for worship, going into the temple and circumambulating the precincts, making his way through the shadowy passages and pillared courts to the innermost shrine in the sanctum. Concludes with the man completing his visit to the temple and is shown returning to the bus - stop for his trip back home from the pilgrimage.
Geography - World; Religion and Philosophy
Dist - SYRCU **Prod** - SMTHHD

Pilgrimage to a Mountain Peak 4 MIN
16mm
Screen news digest series; Vol 7; Issue 10
B&W (J)
LC FIA68-2097
Chronicles the conquest of Mt Kennedy, the highest unclimbed peak in North America, by an expedition which included Robert F Kennedy, brother of the late President.
Biography; Geography - United States
Dist - HEARST **Prod** - HEARST 1965

Pilgrimage to Freedom 21 MIN
16mm
B&W (I)
Recounts the inspiring story of India's struggle for independence from 1857, when the first banner of revolt was raised, to 1947, when independence was realized.
History - World
Dist - NEDINF **Prod** - INDIA

Pilgrimage to Mecca 28 MIN
Videoreel / VHS
International Byline Series
Color
Presents a short interview with the Minister of Information of Saudi Arabia, Dr Mohammad Abdo Yamani, as he discusses the role played by his government in assisting the visit of the pilgrims. Includes a film clip of Mecca and the Hajj ceremonies.
Business and Economics; Civics and Political Systems; Geography - World
Dist - PERRYM **Prod** - PERRYM

The Pilgrims 22 MIN
16mm / U-matic / VHS
B&W (I J H)
Follows the Pilgrims from England to Holland and to New England. Discusses the Mayflower compact and the hardships in the New World.
History - United States; History - World
Dist - EBEC **Prod** - EBEC 1955

The Pilgrims 8 MIN
16mm / U-matic / VHS
A Nation is Born Series
Color (P I)
Shows the explorers who followed Columbus, coming from Spain, Portugal, France, Holland and England in search of glory, wealth and adventure. Explains that, after a long struggle, the colonists came to settle and build a better life for themselves. Presents the story of the Pilgrims, who came from England in a small ship called 'THE MAYFLOWER,' and who landed on Plymouth Rock in Massachusetts.
History - United States; History - World
Dist - LUF **Prod** - PIC 1973

The Pilgrims 9MIN
16mm / VHS
Nation is Born Series
Color (P)
$195.00, $95.00 purchase
Reveals that after Columbus showed the way, many other explorers followed, including the colonists. Focuses on one group, the Pilgrims, who reached America on the Mayflower.
Biography; Geography - United States; History - United States; History - World; Sociology
Dist - LUF **Prod** - LUF

Pilgrims and puritans 30 MIN
VHS / U-matic
American story - the beginning to 1877 series
Color (C)
History - United States
Dist - DALCCD **Prod** - DALCCD

The Pilgrims at Plymouth 23 MIN
U-matic / 16mm / VHS
Color (I)
$575.00, $425.00, $395.00 purchase _ #A634
Recreates the first years of the Pilgrims in America. Portrays the voyage on the Mayflower, the search for a village site, the first harvest, the feast of Thanksgiving.
History - United States; Social Science
Dist - BARR **Prod** - VIDDIA 1991

Pilgrim's progress 135 MIN
VHS
Color; PAL (I J)
PdS30 purchase
Presents a series of nine 15 - minute programs portraying the John Bunyan allegory of one man's journey from this world to the next, brought to life in music, words and illustrations. Includes teacher's notes compiled by the Farmington Institute for Christian Studies. Contact distributor about availability outside the United Kingdom.
Fine Arts; Literature and Drama; Religion and Philosophy
Dist - ACADEM

Pilgrim's progress 72 MIN
VHS
Color (J H C G A R)
$59.95 purchase, $10.00 rental _ #35 - 825 - 2020
Presents a version of John Bunyan's classic allegory of the Christian life, 'Pilgrim's Progress.' Documents Bunyan's 12 years in prison, during which he wrote the book.
Literature and Drama; Religion and Philosophy
Dist - APH **Prod** - ANDERK

Pilgrim's Progress 40 MIN
16mm
Color
Presents a remake in color animation of John Bunyan's classic story of Pilgrim's Progress. Shows his epic journey from the City of Destruction to the Celestial City, a story that has had major effect on thousands of lives throughout the world. Notes that the immortal classic has given Christians a new vision of the Lord in the story that has as powerful an impact today as when it was written 300 years ago.
Literature and Drama
Dist - OMEGA **Prod** - OMEGA

Pilgrim's progress 9 MIN
16mm
Color (G)
$27.00 rental
Features a discourse on marketing through images. Experiments with the surface as an abstract potpourri of polyrhythms and recognizable 'named' items.
Business and Economics; Fine Arts; Psychology
Dist - CANCIN **Prod** - AVERYC 1985

Pilgrim's progress 40 MIN
VHS
Color (J H C G A R)
$12.99 purchase _ #35 - 850365 - 979
Presents an animated version of the classic allegory 'Pilgrim's Progress' by John Bunyan.
Literature and Drama; Religion and Philosophy
Dist - APH **Prod** - TYHP

Pilgrims to the West series
After Cortez 20 MIN
Dist - AITECH

The Pill 50 MIN
VHS
Timewatch series
Color (H C A)
PdS99 purchase _ Not available in the United States or Canada
Features three generations of women discussing the history of birth control pills. Notes that, rather than becoming acceptable birth control for developing countries, the pill has been associated with Western nations' development of irresponsible attitudes toward sex.
Health and Safety; Science - Natural
Dist - BBCENE

The Pill
VHS / U-matic
Color
Details the normal monthly cycle without and with use of the pill. Explains how to use the pill properly.
Sociology
Dist - MIFE **Prod** - MIFE

The Pill 7 MIN
U-matic / VHS
Color (SPANISH)
LC 78-730127
Describes in detail the way in which the pill prevents pregnancy and the manner in which it is obtained and used.
Guidance and Counseling; Sociology
Dist - MEDCOM **Prod** - MEDCOM

The Pill 10 MIN
16mm
Obstetrics and Gynecology Series
Color (H C A)
LC 75-700054
Presents a patient counseling film on birth control pills.
Health and Safety; Sociology
Dist - MIFE **Prod** - MIFE 1974

The Pill - a young woman's guide 11 MIN
VHS
Sex ed series
Color (J H G)
$175.00 purchase, $35.00 rental
Focuses specifically on the birth control pill - advantages and disadvantages, contraindications for use, how and when they should be taken, what to do if one forgets to take one as scheduled, why not to share pills with a friend, warning signs that require seeing a doctor. Suitable for use with diverse audiences. Part of four parts on reproductive health.
Health and Safety
Dist - POLYMR

The Pill poppers 20 MIN
U-matic / VHS / 16mm
Color (J H C)
Communicates certain facts about Dropping Pills. Tells the stories of three teenagers caught up in drug use.
Health and Safety; Psychology
Dist - AIMS **Prod** - DAVP 1971

The Pill, Population and Family Planning 29 MIN
Videoreel / VT2
University of Chicago Round Table Series
Color
Sociology
Dist - PBS **Prod** - WTTWTV

Pillar of salt 58 MIN
16mm
Sephardic Jewry series
Color (G) (HEBREW WITH ENGLISH SUBTITLES)
Captures the cultural richness and social complexity of a Jewish boy's life in Tunisia, North Africa. Reveals the unique customs of life there and the conflicting pressures from surrounding French and Arab societies. Based on the autobiographical novel by sociologist Albert Memmi. Part three of program two of the Sephardic Jewry series which illuminates the histories of the Sephardic Diaspora communities and addresses the social and political issues confronting the Sephardim in the 20th century. Not available separately.
Fine Arts; History - World; Literature and Drama; Religion and Philosophy; Sociology
Dist - NCJEWF

Pillars of Modern Drama 145 MIN
U-matic
University of the Air Series
Color (J H C A)
$750.00 purchase, $250.00 rental
Profiles five major dramatists, Ibsen, Chekov, Strindberg, Pirandello and Brecht. Program contains a series of five cassettes 29 minutes each.
Fine Arts; Literature and Drama
Dist - CTV **Prod** - CTV 1974

Pillows, Crates, and Boxes 20 TO 25 MIN
VHS
If You Paint, You See more Series
Color (P)
Shows children filling their paper with patches of color in the shape of pillows, crates and boxes. Demonstrates them then making human figures from the shapes and being asked to think about the human form in a new way.
Education; Fine Arts
Dist - AITECH

Pilobolus 60 MIN
U-matic / VHS
Dance in America Series
Color (H C A)
Presents members of the Pilobolus Dance Theatre performing Walklyndon, Momix, Alraune and Molly's Not Dead. Questions whether the group's dance style is slapstick, mime, gymnastics, theatrics or tableau vivant.
Fine Arts
Dist - FI **Prod** - WNETTV

Pilot 4 MIN
16mm
B&W (G)
$10.00 rental
Says filmmaker Wendy Blair, 'Amidst the speed of confusion, blind to our compass, where do we seek the clear bell of our own pilot.'
Fine Arts
Dist - CANCIN

Pilot 30 MIN
BETA / VHS
American Professionals Series
Color
Describes the life of Cliff Flood, 54, who has been flying for well over half of his life. He has accumulated hundreds of flight stories from the thirty years he has flown as a commercial pilot for Eastern Airlines.
Guidance and Counseling; Social Science
Dist - RMIBHF **Prod** - WTBS

Pilot down, presumed dead 15 MIN
VHS
Storybound series
Color (I)
#E375; LC 90-713100
Tells the story, 'Pilot Down, Presumed Dead' by Marjorie Phleger, of a young man's struggle to survive on an uninhabited island after his plane crashes. Part of a 16 - part series designed to lead viewers to the library to find and finish the stories they encounter in the series.
English Language; Literature and Drama; Social Science
Dist - GPN **Prod** - CTI 1980
CTI

Pilot for Glacier Skiers 25 MIN
16mm
Color
Presents Mr Mike Buckland, chief pilot of the Mount Cook Air Service and describes his job, carrying tourists and skiers to the glaciers by ski - plane. Portrays the difficult landings on the glaciers and the very beautiful scenery from the air. Tells the history of ski - plane.
Geography - World; Industrial and Technical Education; Physical Education and Recreation
Dist - UNIJAP **Prod** - UNIJAP 1967

Pilot, Patriot and 20th Century Pioneer - Eddie Rickenbacker's Machine Age America 24 MIN
VHS
American Lifestyles II - Singular American Series
Color (I)
$70.00 purchase, $50.00 rental _ #9886
Narrates how the many automotive and aeronautical innovations of Eddie Rickenbacker led the world into the Machine Age and how his courage and enthusiasm for life inspired millions. Features Hugh Downs as host.
Biography; History - United States; Industrial and Technical Education
Dist - AIMS **Prod** - COMCO 1986

Pilot Traverse 15 MIN
VHS / U-matic
Color (A)
LC 84-706451
Demonstrates the standard pilot tube method for determining average linear velocity and the volume of air flow through ducts. Describes the equipment used, how to find a sample point in the duct, measurement technique and data collection and calculation procedures.
Industrial and Technical Education; Mathematics
Dist - USNAC **Prod** - USNAC 1978

The Pilot - Value of Honesty 25 MIN
16mm / U-matic / VHS
Color (J H)
Tells the story of a teenage girl who overcomes shyness by breakdancing. Explores development of self - esteem and the value of honesty.
Literature and Drama; Psychology
Dist - MEDIAG **Prod** - PAULST 1985

Pilot Watershed 22 MIN
16mm
Color (H C A)
Considers the conservation land treatment, flood water retarding structures, and the cost and financial responsibilities.
Agriculture; Science - Natural
Dist - UNEBR **Prod** - UNL 1955

Piloted Operated Pressure Control Valves 15 MIN
U-matic / VHS
Industrial Hydraulic Technology Series Chapter 10; Chapter 10
Color (IND)
Examines valve characteristics, pump unloading and terms associated with pilot operated pressure control valves.
Education; Industrial and Technical Education; Science - Physical
Dist - TAT **Prod** - TAT

Piloting, Surface 33 MIN
16mm
B&W
LC FIE52-980
Stresses the importance of accurate piloting and discusses briefly the use of the bearing circle, compass repeater and alidade in securing bearings.
Industrial and Technical Education; Social Science
Dist - USNAC **Prod** - USN 1943

Pimentel Discusses Chemical Bonding 27 MIN
16mm
CHEM Study Teacher Training Series
B&W
Amplifies the idea that attraction of one or more electrons for two or more nuclei accounts for bond formation. Presents the virial theorem.
Science; Science - Physical
Dist - MLA **Prod** - MLA

Pimentel Discusses the Hydrogen Atom 32 MIN
16mm
B&W
LC FIA67-4
Professor George C Pimentel discusses the shortcomings of the planetary model in terms of its inconsistency with experiment and with quantum mechanics. Provides a basis for understanding the significance of the Schroedinger equation.
Science - Physical
Dist - MLA **Prod** - CHEMED 1964

Pin - Retained Foundation for a Full Crown 11 MIN
16mm
Color (PRO)
LC 77-700817
Demonstrates how a pin - retained foundation is added to a tooth so badly broken that insufficient tooth structure remains for preparation for a full crown restoration.
Health and Safety; Science
Dist - USNAC **Prod** - VADTC 1977

Pin - Retained Foundation for an Amalgam Restoration 14 MIN
VHS / U-matic
Color (PRO)
LC 81-706364
Illustrates various items of armamentarium which are utilized with the technique of amalgam restoration. Emphasizes the preparation of the pin - channels by means of a limited depth twist - drill and proper placement of the two - in - one, self - shearing threaded pins.
Health and Safety
Dist - USNAC **Prod** - VADTC 1978

Pin Retention for a Class V Restoration 7 MIN
16mm
Color (PRO)
LC 77-703350
Demonstrates the use of special superminiature threaded pins as retention for a Class V restoration.
Health and Safety; Science
Dist - USNAC **Prod** - VADTC 1976

Pinata 10 MIN
U-matic
Get it together series
Color (P I)
Teaches children how to make a Mexican pinata from newspaper, paste and a balloon.
Fine Arts
Dist - TVOTAR **Prod** - TVOTAR 1978

Pinata 24 MIN
U-matic / VHS / 16mm
Color
LC 78-700433
Tells the story of a small Mexican boy who strives to attain a beautiful pinata. Shows how he is able to reconstruct the pinata after it has been destroyed and how his efforts are rewarded.
Literature and Drama; Social Science
Dist - MCFI **Prod** - SWAIN 1977

The Pinata Makers 16.5 MIN
VHS / 16mm / U-matic
Color (I J H)
$305 _ #A531
Features a Mexican family engaged in the craft of pinata making. Provides an awareness of how immigrants from Mexico adapted to American life. Describes how a pinata is made.
History - United States; Sociology
Dist - BARR **Prod** - BARR 1988

Pinatas, posadas y pastorelas 25 MIN
VHS
Color (G) (SPANISH)
$49.95 purchase _ #W1454, #W1455
Highlights Mexican Christmas celebration traditions in Mexico City and in some of the rural states, pointing out the mix of Spanish and Indian cultural rituals. Includes script.
Foreign Language
Dist - GPC

Pinball Parlour 4 MIN
16mm
Color
LC 74-703004
Presents a look inside a pinball parlour.
Physical Education and Recreation
Dist - CANFDC **Prod** - INSCA 1973

The Pinballs 31 MIN
U-matic / VHS / 16mm
Afterschool specials series
Color (I J H)
LC 77-703089
Adapted from the novel THE PINBALLS by Betsy Byars, about three lonely foster children who learn to care about themselves and each other.
Guidance and Counseling; Psychology; Sociology
Dist - CORF **Prod** - TAHSEM 1977

The Pinballs 15 MIN
VHS
Storybound series
Color (I)
#E375; LC 90-713291
Tells the story, 'Pinballs' by Betsy Byars, of three children in a foster home. Part of a 16 - part series designed to lead viewers to the library to find and finish the stories they encounter in the series.
English Language; Literature and Drama; Social Science
Dist - GPN **Prod** - CTI 1980
CTI

Pincers - August 1944 - March 1945 52 MIN
U-matic / VHS / 16mm
World at War Series
Color (H C A)
Describes how the Allies invaded southern France from the west between August 1944 and March 1945. Russia invaded from the east and this tandem movement, known as Operation Anvil, drove Hitler's armies back across German borders and beyond.
History - World
Dist - MEDIAG **Prod** - THAMES 1973
USCAN

The Pinch 12 MIN
VHS / 16mm / U-matic
Magic circle series
Color (P)
Discusses the concept of role playing in terms of young children. Asks children to talk about something which made them angry.
Education; Guidance and Counseling
Dist - ECUFLM **Prod** - UMCOM 1975

Pinch 15 MIN
VHS
Storybound series
Color (I)
#E375; LC 90-713285
Tells the story, 'Pinch' by Larry Callen, of a clever lad and his champion pig. Part of a 16 - part series designed to lead viewers to the library to find and finish the stories they encounter in the series.
English Language; Literature and Drama; Social Science
Dist - GPN **Prod** - CTI 1980
CTI

Pinch pleated draperies 60 MIN
VHS
Yes you can video series
Color (H C G)
$39.00 purchase _ #TMCV105V
Demonstrates measuring a window, tool requirements, cutting different kinds of fabric and much more. Part of a five - part series on custom slipcovering and drapery, cushion and pillow making.
Home Economics
Dist - CAMV

The Pinch Singer 17 MIN
16mm
B&W
Shows Spanky holding tryouts for someone to represent the Gang on a radio station's talent contest. A Little Rascals film.
Fine Arts
Dist - RMIBHF **Prod** - ROACH 1936

Pinchas Zuckerman and the St Paul Chamber Orchestra 29 MIN
VHS
Creativity with Bill Moyers series
Color (G)
$49.95 purchase _ #CWBM - 107C
Interviews Pinchas Zuckerman, famed violinist, who directs the St Paul, Minnesota Chamber Orchestra. Presents Zuckerman's perspectives on music and the relationship between the conductor and orchestra members. Hosted by Bill Moyers.
Fine Arts
Dist - PBS **Prod** - CELED 1981

Pinched cheeks and slurs in a language that avoids her 11 MIN
VHS
Color (G)
$40.00 purchase
Layers a prosy momologue with a static image of a mirror reflecting a table, a woman and a young girl. Uses the girl's voice - over to recount a hazy 1970 Sunday sky. Explores her sense of belonging and estrangment to a culture and a language that is both familiar and alien to her. An Armenian woman reads coffee grounds offering mystery and wisdom that challenge racial slurs. Produced by Tina Bastajian.
Fine Arts; Sociology
Dist - CANCIN

Pine beauty 25 MIN
VHS
Color (H C G)
$245.00 purchase, $46.00 rental
Illustrates techniques used to study and control an introduced moth which has been defoliating forests in England. Examines mating - disruption techniques.
Agriculture; Geography - World; Science - Natural
Dist - MEDIAG **Prod** - MEDIAG 1987

Pine Point - a Lead - Zinc Deposit 25 MIN
VHS / 16mm
Earth's Physical Resources Series
Color (S)
$200.00 purchase _ #236206
Presents a global view of the earth's resource potential. Features footage filmed in Britain, Europe and North America. 'Pine Point - A Lead - Zinc Deposit' describes the discovery, exploration and geology of the Pine Point ore body and surrounding region.
History - World; Science - Physical; Social Science
Dist - ACCESS **Prod** - BBCTV 1984

Pine Point - Ore to Metal 24 MIN
VHS / 16mm
Earth's Physical Resources Series
Color (S)
$200.00 purchase _ #236208
Presents a global view of the earth's resource potential. Features footage filmed in Britain, Europe and North America. 'Pine Point - Ore To Metal' uses the model of the ore body at Pine Point derived from exploration and assessment to generate data on the relative effectiveness of various methods of ore extraction. The processing of the extracted ore is then examined and compared in terms of capital, efficiency and output with the Roman smelter at Derbyshire shown in 'Copper Resources And Reserves.'.
History - World; Industrial and Technical Education; Science - Physical; Social Science
Dist - ACCESS **Prod** - BBCTV 1984

Pine Point - Origin and Exploration 25 MIN
VHS / 16mm
Earth's Physical Resources Series
Color (S)
$200.00 purchase _ #236207
Presents a global view of the earth's resource potential. Features footage filmed in Britain, Europe and North America. 'Pine Point - Origin And Exploration' gives a detailed examination of the physical and chemical basis for the formation of the Pine Point ore body and a description of the procedures involved in delineating the extent of the commercially viable ore.
History - World; Science - Physical; Social Science
Dist - ACCESS **Prod** - BBCTV 1984

Pine Tree Camp 13 MIN
16mm
Color
LC 70-713208
Shows everyday life at Pine Tree Camp, emphasizing the rapport between campers and staff and the happiness that the camp can bring to a handicapped child.
Guidance and Counseling; Psychology; Sociology
Dist - ENVIC **Prod** - ENVIC 1970

Ping Chong and Douglas Dunn 30 MIN
U-matic / VHS
Eye on Dance - the Experimentalists Series
Color
Fine Arts
Dist - ARCVID **Prod** - ARCVID

Pink cadillac 46 MIN
VHS / U-matic / Cassette
Florida through the decades as seen by High - Sheriff Jim Turner 'series
Color; PAL (G)
$79.95, $24.95, $9.95 purchase _ #1050
Portrays the life of a former High - Sheriff of Levy County, Florida, Jim Turner. Recalls Turner's ongoing skirmishes with Willie Star, black survivor of the Rosewood Race Massacre, who has grown up to be a 'Bolita Runner' and petty criminal. Despite their differences, Turner lets Star off on a charge of 'justified' homicide. Part five of an eleven - part historical docudrama.
Civics and Political Systems; Fine Arts; History - United States; Sociology
Dist - NORDS **Prod** - NORDS 1991

Pink Porpoise 27 MIN
16mm
Color
Follows an expedition into the Amazon wilds of Peru to collect fresh water porpoise for Marineland of St Augustine.
Geography - World; Science - Natural
Dist - FLADC **Prod** - FLADC

Pink Rink 7 MIN
16mm
Color
Presents the Pink Panther in a story designed to show that productivity can be improved with capital investments and innovation. Shows that higher productivity comes from working smarter not harder.
Business and Economics; Fine Arts
Dist - MTP **Prod** - EXXON 1982

Pink roll 15 MIN
16mm
Diaries - 1979 - 1983 series
Color (G)
$20.00 rental
Features part of an eight - part series by Andras Szirtes.
Fine Arts; Literature and Drama
Dist - CANCIN

Pink Triangles 35 MIN
U-matic
Color
Studies prejudice against lesbians and gay men and challenges some of our most deeply rooted feelings, people's people's attitudes toward homosexuality. Synthesizes many disparate ideas and elements.
Sociology
Dist - CMBRD **Prod** - CMBRD

Pink Triangles - a Study of Prejudice Against Lesbians and Gay Men 34 MIN
16mm
Color (H C)
LC 81-701655
Takes a look at the nature of discrimination against lesbians and gay men and challenges some of society's attitudes toward homosexuality. Examines historical and contemporary patterns of racial, religious, political and sexual persecution.
Sociology
Dist - CMBRD **Prod** - CMBRD 1982

Pinkfoot 19 MIN
U-matic / VHS / 16mm
RSPB Collection Series
Color (I J H)
Shows how pink - footed geese fly north to their breeding grounds in Iceland and Greenland each spring. Follows their hazardous journey, then focuses on one pair's stuggle to hatch and raise their young before winter drives them south again.
Science - Natural
Dist - BCNFL **Prod** - RSFPB 1983

The Pinks and the Blues 57 MIN
16mm / U-matic / VHS
Nova Series
Color (A)
LC 81-700857
Probes the subtle ways in which parents and teachers introduce sex roles to young children so that by the age of four there are distinct behavioral differences between boys and girls.
Psychology; Sociology
Dist - TIMLIF **Prod** - WGBHTV 1981

Pinlay Abutments 26 MIN
16mm
Color
LC 74-705361
Demonstrates clinically, the pinlay abutment technique used in restoration of interior teeth.
Science
Dist - USNAC **Prod** - USA 1964

Pinlays using the Loma Linda Parallelometer 17 MIN
16mm
Color
LC 75-700807
Describes the techniques involved in the preparation, impression and fabrication of pinlays for anterior teeth using the Loma Linda parallelometer. Illustrates the technical, clinical and laboratory procedures.
Health and Safety; Science
Dist - USNAC **Prod** - USVA 1965

Pinnacle - Fred DeLuca 30 MIN
VHS
Color (G A)

$19.95 purchase _ #TCO109OE
Profiles Fred DeLuca, founder and president of Subway Sandwiches and Salads. Shows how DeLuca and his partner, Peter Buck, worked up from a part - time job to owning a chain with more than 4,000 shops and 25 new ones opening each week. Hosted by CNN correspondent Beverly Schuch.
Business and Economics; Home Economics
Dist - TMM **Prod** - TMM

Pinnacle - Leonard Stern 30 MIN
VHS
Color (G A)
$19.95 purchase _ #TCO108OE
Profiles Leonard Stern, president of the Hartz Corporation. Discusses how he and his company bitterly fought competitors during the 1970s and 1980s, and how he now participates actively in charitable causes. Hosted by CNN correspondent Beverly Schuch.
Business and Economics; Science - Natural
Dist - TMM **Prod** - TMM

Pinning Combinations 20 MIN
U-matic / VHS / 16mm
Wrestling Series no 4
Color
LC 79-700808
Demonstrates pinning combinations in the sport of wrestling.
Physical Education and Recreation
Dist - ATHI **Prod** - ATHI 1976

Pinocchio
VHS
Disney classics on video series
Color (K P I)
$29.95 purchase _ #DIS239
Presents the Disney version of Pinocchio on video.
Fine Arts; Literature and Drama
Dist - KNOWUN **Prod** - DISNEY

Pinocchio 72 MIN
16mm
Color (P I)
Presents Pinocchio in a live - action and animated puppet version.
Fine Arts
Dist - FI **Prod** - FI

Pinocchio
U-matic / VHS
Color (P I)
Presents an enactment of the classic fairy tale Pinocchio.
Literature and Drama
Dist - GA **Prod** - GA

Pinocchio - a lesson in honesty 8 MIN
U-matic / VHS / 16mm
Disney's animated classics - lessons in living series
Color (P I)
LC 78-701722
Tells how seven - year - old Bobby learns that lying is wrong, with the help of his friend and neighbor, Uncle Phil and a scene from the animated film Pinocchio.
Fine Arts; Guidance and Counseling
Dist - CORF **Prod** - DISNEY 1978

Pinocchio's Birthday Party 76 MIN
16mm
Color
LC 76-701354
Combines live action and animation to tell the story of Pinocchio's birthday party.
Literature and Drama
Dist - KTEL **Prod** - KTEL 1974

Pinocchio's Birthday Party - Pt 1 38 MIN
16mm
Color
LC 76-701354
Combines live action and animation to tell the story of Pinocchio's birthday party.
Literature and Drama
Dist - KTEL **Prod** - KTEL 1974

Pinocchio's Birthday Party - Pt 2 38 MIN
16mm
Color
LC 76-701354
Combines live action and animation to tell the story of Pinocchio's birthday party.
Literature and Drama
Dist - KTEL **Prod** - KTEL 1974

Pinoy 30 MIN
U-matic
Pearls Series
Color (H C A)
Features a 74 - year - old Filipino housing activist recalling the early days of Filipino immigration to America.
History - United States; Sociology
Dist - GPN **Prod** - EDFCEN 1979

Pinpointing and recording patient behavior 30 MIN
16mm
Nursing - cues behavior consequences series; No 2
B&W
LC 76-700927
Describes the application of behavior modification techniques in caring for patients. Features the selection of significant behaviors, defining them and recording their frequency.
Health and Safety; Psychology
Dist - UNEBR **Prod** - NTCN 1973

Pins and Needles 37 MIN
16mm
Color (A)
LC 80-701975
Explores the effects of multiple sclerosis through the account of Genni Batterham, an Australian communications student who contracted the disease. Presents an unveiled look at Batterham's changed life, her visits to the hospital and the multiple aspects of her relationship with her husband.
Health and Safety
Dist - FLMLIB **Prod** - FLMLIB 1980

Pins and Needles 1 Series
Program 14 - Basic Sewing Equipment 29 MIN
Program 15 - Basic Sewing Equipment 29 MIN
Program 16 - Basic Sewing Equipment 29 MIN
Program 17 - Basic Sewing Equipment 29 MIN
Program 18 - Basic Sewing Equipment 29 MIN
Program 19 - Basic Sewing Equipment 29 MIN
Program 21 - Basic Sewing Equipment 29 MIN
Program 22 - Basic Sewing Equipment 29 MIN
Program 23 - Basic Sewing Equipment 29 MIN
Program 24 - Basic Sewing Equipment 29 MIN
Program 25 - Basic Sewing Equipment 29 MIN
Program 26 - Basic Sewing Equipment 29 MIN
Program 5 - Basic a - Line Skirt Fitting 29 MIN
Program 4 - Basic a - Line Skirt Assembly 29 MIN
Program 6 - Tailored Skirt 29 MIN
Program 3 - Basic a - Line Skirt 29 MIN
Program 20 - Basic Sewing Equipment 29 MIN
Program 2 - Measurement Taking 29 MIN
Dist - RMIBHF

Pins and Needles - One Series
Program 1 30 MIN
Program 10 30 MIN
Program 11 30 MIN
Program 12 30 MIN
Program 13 30 MIN
Program 14 30 MIN
Program 15 30 MIN
Program 16 30 MIN
Program 17 30 MIN
Program 18 30 MIN
Program 19 30 MIN
Program 2 30 MIN
Program 20 30 MIN
Program 21 30 MIN
Program 22 30 MIN
Program 23 30 MIN
Program 24 30 MIN
Program 25 30 MIN
Program 26 30 MIN
Program 3 30 MIN
Program 4 30 MIN
Program 5 30 MIN
Program 6 30 MIN
Program 7 30 MIN
Program 8 30 MIN
Program 9 30 MIN
Dist - TVOTAR

Pins and Needles 2 Series
Program 11 - Basic Sewing Equipment 29 MIN
Program 12 - Basic Sewing Equipment 29 MIN
Program 13 - Basic Sewing Equipment 29 MIN
Program 8 - Basic Sewing Equipment 29 MIN
Program 5 - Basic Sewing Equipment 29 MIN
Program 4 - Basic Sewing Equipment 29 MIN
Program 9 - Basic Sewing Equipment 29 MIN
Program 1 - Basic Sewing Equipment 29 MIN
Program 7 - Basic Sewing Equipment 29 MIN
Program 6 - Basic Sewing Equipment 29 MIN
Program 10 - Basic Sewing Equipment 29 MIN
Program 3 - Basic Sewing Equipment 29 MIN
Program 2 - Basic Sewing Equipment 29 MIN
Dist - RMIBHF

Pinscreen 40 MIN
U-matic / VHS / 16mm
Color (H C A)
LC 77-701103
Features animator Alexandre Alexieff demonstrating and discussing the technique of pinscreen animation to a group of the world's leading animators. Shows how the pinscreen animation screen can create an intimate range of visual images and perspectives.
Fine Arts
Dist - PFP **Prod** - NFBC 1977

Pinstriping made Easy
VHS
(G)
$49.95 _ PL100
Presents step by step instruction for do it yourself penstriping.
Industrial and Technical Education
Dist - AAVIM **Prod** - AAVIM 1989

A Pint of life - fact and fiction 15 MIN
VHS
Color (G)
$250.00 purchase, $100.00 rental
Alleviates fear and negative feelings about being a blood donor. Asks why only 5 percent of people over the age of 17 give blood. Follows with a montage of answers from people approached randomly and asked about their reasons for donating or not donating blood. Those who have not donated blood express dislike of needles and pain, worries about screening and disease. Demonstrates some of the things done with a pint of blood and features 'testimonials' of people whose lives have been saved by donated blood. Produced by the Health Care Education Network, Stanford University Medical Center.
Science - Natural
Dist - BAXMED

Pinter People 58 MIN
16mm
Color (H C A)
LC 72-707492
Features an interview with Harold Pinter and five early Pinter 'REVIEW SKETCHES' in animated form, with the voices of Vivien Merchant, Donald Pleasence and Harold Pinter.
Biography
Dist - GROVE **Prod** - POTPRO 1969

Pinto for the Prince 16 MIN
16mm
Color (H C A)
#2X10I
Depicts the history and tradition of the Blood Indians and their relationship to Treaty No 7 and the Crown over the past hundred years.
Social Science
Dist - CDIAND **Prod** - NFBC 1979

Pints, Quarts and Pottles 15 MIN
VHS / U-matic
Math Mission 2 Series
Color (P)
LC 82-706354
Presents a math teacher who explains liquid measurements, including such old - fashioned units of liquid measure as pottles. Features a space robot demonstrating different quantities of liquid to his puppet assistant by using different measuring containers.
Mathematics
Dist - GPN **Prod** - WCVETV 1980

The Pioneer Blacksmith 11 MIN
16mm / U-matic / VHS
Pioneer Life Series
Color; B&W (I)
Shows an authentic blacksmith shop at old Sturbridge Village, Massachusetts. Illustrates how the blacksmith contributed to life in a small community in the early 1800's.
History - United States; Social Science
Dist - IU **Prod** - IU 1962

Pioneer Journey Across the Appalachians 14 MIN
16mm / U-matic / VHS
Color
$350.00, $245.00 purchase _ #4020
Follows a North Carolina family on a journey across the Appalachians before the Revolutionary War. Considers why the early settlers moved West and how they travelled.

History - United States
Dist - CORF Prod - CORF 1982
INSTRU

Pioneer life series
Canals - towpaths west 17 MIN
Long Journey West - 1820 15 MIN
New England Sea Community 17 MIN
Northeast Farm Community 15 MIN
The Pioneer Blacksmith 11 MIN
Pioneer Mill 12 MIN
Pioneer Spinning and Weaving 9 MIN
Dist - IU

Pioneer Living - Education and Recreation 11 MIN
U-matic / VHS / 16mm
Pioneer Living Series
Color (I J H)
LC 77-709703
Shows how pioneer communities in the early 1800's conducted school and enjoyed recreational activities including quilting bees, box socials and hay rides.
Education; History - United States; Physical Education and Recreation
Dist - CORF Prod - CORF 1970

Pioneer Living - Home Crafts 11 MIN
U-matic / VHS / 16mm
Pioneer Living Series
Color (I J H)
LC 76-709699
Shows how a pioneer family had to know such crafts and skills as sheep shearing, cloth making, hooking and braiding, woodworking and others.
History - United States
Dist - CORF Prod - CORF 1970

Pioneer Living - Preparing Foods 11 MIN
U-matic / VHS / 16mm
Pioneer Living Series
Color (I J H)
LC 76-709700
Shows pioneer preparations for the winter, including smoking meat, peeling and preserving apples, churning butter, making maple sugar and baking bread.
History - United States; Home Economics
Dist - CORF Prod - CORF 1970

Pioneer Living Series
Education and recreation 11 MIN
The Farm 10 MIN
The Home 11 MIN
Home crafts 10 MIN
Pioneer Living - Education and Recreation 11 MIN
Pioneer Living - Home Crafts 11 MIN
Pioneer Living - Preparing Foods 11 MIN
Pioneer Living - the Farm 11 MIN
Pioneer Living - the Home 11 MIN
Pioneer Living - the Village 11 MIN
Preparing Foods 10 MIN
The Village 11 MIN
Dist - CORF

Pioneer Living - the Farm 11 MIN
16mm / U-matic / VHS
Pioneer Living Series
Color (I J H)
LC 70-709701
Shows pioneers clearing and plowing the fields, planting crops, harvesting, threshing and grinding grain into flour, working at the flour mill and processing flax.
Agriculture; History - United States
Dist - CORF Prod - CORF 1970

Pioneer Living - the Home 11 MIN
U-matic / VHS / 16mm
Pioneer Living Series
Color (I J H)
LC 72-709698
Shows how a pioneer family of the early 1800's selected a site, built a log cabin, cooked, made soap and candles and did other household tasks.
History - United States; Psychology; Social Science
Dist - CORF Prod - CORF 1970

Pioneer Living - the Village 11 MIN
U-matic / VHS / 16mm
Pioneer Living Series
Color (I J H)
LC 73-709702
Observes women buying and bartering at the general store, and the blacksmith, cobbler, newspaperman and broommaker at work.
History - United States
Dist - CORF Prod - CORF 1970

Pioneer Mill 10 MIN
16mm
Color (I H C G)
Describes how corn was ground into meal in early pioneer homes or at larger water powered mills. Shows Midwestern farmers bringing their sacks of corn by horseback to the miller who runs the mill. Explains the miller's importance and function as he goes through each step of the grinding process.
Agriculture; History - United States
Dist - VIEWTH Prod - GATEEF

Pioneer Mill 12 MIN
16mm / U-matic / VHS
Pioneer Life Series
Color (P I)
LC 72-702790
Points out that corn meal was an important food to early settlers and describes how they ground corn in their home. Shows the operation and activities connected with larger water - powered mills used by early farmers in the Midwest. Explains the miller's importance and function as he goes through each step of the grinding process.
Agriculture; History - United States; Home Economics; Social Science
Dist - IU Prod - IU 1972

Pioneer of color - a conversation with Mal Goode 60 MIN
VHS
Color (C H G A)
$69.95 purchase _ #PCMG-000-WC95
Describes the life of Mal Goode, a grandson of slaves who became the first African American news correspondent for a major television network. Explains, in a series of interviews, his years working for the American Broadcasting Corporation (ABC). Includes footage from his career and news reports from 1962 to 1972.
Fine Arts; History - United States
Dist - PBS

Pioneer of Labor 20 MIN
U-matic
Truly American Series
Color (I)
Discusses the life of labor leader Samuel Gompers.
Biography
Dist - GPN Prod - WVIZTV 1979

Pioneer of the sea 60 MIN
VHS
Jacques Cousteau series
Color; CC (G)
$19.95 purchase _ #3046
Presents a biographical film salute to Jacques Cousteau upon his 75th birthday. Features rare photograghs and remarkable footage from his expeditions. Part of a series by Cousteau featuring narration by actors and actresses who speak American English.
Geography - World; History - World
Dist - APRESS

Pioneer Spinning and Weaving 9 MIN
16mm / U-matic / VHS
Pioneer Life Series
Color; B&W (I)
Shows how flax was processed into linen thread through retting, drying, braking, switcheling, hatcheling and spinning. Shows how fleece was changed into wool yarn after shearing, cleaning, carding and spinning.
History - United States
Dist - IU Prod - IU 1960

Pioneer Trails, Indian Lore and Bird Life of the Plains 14 MIN
U-matic / VHS / 16mm
Vanishing Prairie Norwegian Series
Color (I J H) (NORWEGIAN)
Explains the origins of Indian dance forms. Shows pioneer wagon trails. Describes bird life on the prairie.
Foreign Language; Science - Natural
Dist - CORF Prod - DISNEY 1963

Pioneer Trails, Indian Lore and Bird Life of the Plains 14 MIN
U-matic / VHS / 16mm
Vanishing Prairie Series
Color (I)
LC FIA63-15
Describes the vanishing American prairie, the area between the Mississippi River and the Rocky Mountains. Explains origins of Indian dance forms and describes types of bird life on the prairie.
Geography - United States; Science - Natural; Social Science
Dist - CORF Prod - DISNEY 1963

Pioneer Trails, Indian Lore and Bird Life of the Plains 14 MIN
U-matic / VHS / 16mm
Vanishing Prairie Portuguese Series
Color (I J H) (PORTUGUESE)
Explains the origins of Indian dance forms. Shows pioneer wagon trails. Describes bird life on the prairie.
Foreign Language; Science - Natural
Dist - CORF Prod - DISNEY 1963

Pioneer village 28 MIN
VHS
Elephant show series
Color (P I)
$95.00 purchase, $45.00 rental
Presents program 22 in the Sharon, Lois and Bram's Elephant Show series. Teaches reading readiness and social skills while engaging children in making music. Each program explores a new theme through adventure, fantasy, mystery and song with recording artists Sharon, Lois and Bram. Uses traditional materials which stress participation - action songs, sing - along songs, story songs, clapping songs, singing games, playground chants and folk songs from many different traditions. Includes teacher's guide co - authored by a music education specialist.
Fine Arts; Sociology
Dist - BULFRG Prod - CAMBFP 1989

Pioneer Village 20 MIN
16mm
Color (I J)
LC FIA67-1447
Depicts the growth and development of a northeastern pioneer village, covering the years 1790 to 1840. Shows the activities of a typical pioneer family.
History - United States
Dist - SF Prod - MORLAT 1966

Pioneer Women of Today 29 MIN
U-matic
American Women - Echoes and Dreams Series
Color
Shows interviews with four contemporary women who discuss solving problems, dealing with self - doubt and stress, and sexual discrimination.
Biography; History - World; Sociology
Dist - HRC Prod - OHC

Pioneering Research in Hypertension 24 MIN
VHS / U-matic
Color (PRO) (FRENCH)
Discusses the treatment of hypertension disease and the current concepts in the etiology of this disease, with emphasis on the role of the sympathetic nervous system activity and how this can be modulated by the use of the centrally acting sympatholytic agent, clonidine. Features four specialists. (Also available in French, German, Italian, Japanese and Spanish).
Health and Safety; Science - Natural
Dist - WFP Prod - WFP

The Pioneers 59 MIN
16mm
Masters of Modern Sculpture Series no 1
Color
LC 78-701407
Examines sculpture from the late 19th century to the beginning of World War I, illustrating the breakdown of the classical view of art. Shows works by Rodin, Maillol, Lehmbruck, Matisse, Picasso, Lipschitz and Brancusi.
Fine Arts
Dist - BLACKW Prod - BLACKW 1978

Pioneers and Modern Rockets 24 MIN
U-matic / VHS / 16mm
Man into Space - the Story of Rockets and Space Science Series
Color (I)
LC 76-707907
Presents an account of the technological advances in rocketry during the first half of the 20th century, with particular emphasis on the efforts of engineering technology to reach the levels of scientific knowledge. Describes the establishment of rocket research and interplanetary societies in europe and the U S during the 1920's.
Science - Physical
Dist - AIMS Prod - ACI 1970

Pioneers in the earth sciences 16 MIN
VHS
Earth scientists at work series
Color (H C)
$79.00 purchase _ #152
Begins with the first humans who learned to make a map, navigate a ship or mine for copper, gold and iron ore. Takes a field trip to the Tilt River in the Highlands of Scotland where a profession of geology, James Hutton, first learned that the Earth was much older than previously thought - not a few thousand years old, but millions of years old. Includes material on Aggasiz and his discovery of the glacial past of the Earth and the 20th - century discovery that the world floats on continental - sized plates that slip and move, causing earthquakes and more. Includes guide.
Science; Science - Physical
Dist - HAWHIL Prod - HAWHIL 1995

Pioneers O Pioneers 60 MIN
VHS / 16mm
Story of English Series
Color (C)
PdS99 purchase
Examines the contributions to the evolution of American English of immigrants, Native Americans, and those who expanded the American Frontier. Part 6 of the series.
English Language
Dist - BBCENE **Prod** - BBCTV 1986
FI
PSU

Pioneers of photography series
Examines the contributions made by pioneers in photography. Profiles work by Talbot, Niepce, Daguerre, Cameron, Muybridge, and Lumiere, among others. An eight-part series that traces the development of paper prints, photography as art, astronomical and landscape photography, portrait photography, and color photography.
Colour and the camera 25 MIN
Famous men and fair women 25 MIN
Fleeting image 25 MIN
Mirror with a memory 25 MIN
Nadar the great 25 MIN
Pencil of nature 25 MIN
Sun pictures 25 MIN
Traveling man 25 MIN
Dist - BBCENE

Pioneers of the Southwest 15 MIN
U-matic / VHS / 16mm
American Scrapbook Series
Color (I)
Depicts a reconstructed pioneer village in the Southwest, showing the Indian and Spanish influences on its architecture. Discusses early life in a pioneer town.
History - United States
Dist - GPN **Prod** - WVIZTV 1977

Pioneers of the Vertical 24 MIN
16mm
Color
LC 74-706179
Shows the training and care of primates, pointing out their vital use in decompression and radiation studies, blood analysis and experimental medicine.
Health and Safety; Science
Dist - USNAC **Prod** - USAF 1967

The Pioneers - Pt 1 30 MIN
16mm
Masters of Modern Sculpture Series no 1
Color
LC 78-701407
Examines sculpture from the late 19th century to the beginning of World War I, illustrating the breakdown of the classical view of art. Shows works by Rodin, Maillol, Lehmbruck, Matisse, Picasso, Lipschitz and Brancusi.
Fine Arts
Dist - BLACKW **Prod** - BLACKW 1978

The Pioneers - Pt 2 29 MIN
16mm
Masters of Modern Sculpture Series no 1
Color
LC 78-701407
Examines sculpture from the late 19th century to the beginning of World War I, illustrating the breakdown of the classical view of art. Shows works by Rodin, Maillol, Lehmbruck, Matisse, Picasso, Lipschitz and Brancusi.
Fine Arts
Dist - BLACKW **Prod** - BLACKW 1978

The Pioneers - the far east Pacific coast 52 MIN
VHS
Icebreaker - family life in the Soviet Union series
Color (I J H)
$295.00 purchase
Visits the Korets family, the only purely Russian family in the series who have settled in Nadhodka, a major commercial port on the Pacific Coast just behind Japan and ten days away on the Trans - Siberian Express. Reveals that Igor works on the docks, his wife is a nurse and they have an 8 - year - old son. Part of a six - part series on ethnically different families in the Soviet Union.
Geography - World; Sociology
Dist - LANDMK **Prod** - LANDMK 1989

Pioneers - vision of Zion 50 MIN
VHS
B&W (G)
$90.00 purchase
Captures scenes of Jerusalem, Tel Aviv, Rishon LeZion, and old Jaffa as well as rural settlements and activities throughout the land. Provides an historical document of pre - state Israel. Incorporates rare footage from four early films of Yaakov Ben Dov recently preserved in a joint project by The National Center of Jewish Film and The Israel Film Archive. Directed by Yaakov Gross.
Fine Arts; Geography - World; History - World; Religion and Philosophy; Sociology
Dist - NCJEWF **Prod** - NCJEWF 1995

Pipe and tubing series
Seamless modern - general pipe making 13 MIN
USS Line Pipe 9 MIN
USS Mechanical and Pressure Tubing 10 MIN
USS Oil Country Goods 11 MIN
USS Standard Pipe 9 MIN
USS Structural Tubing 11 MIN
Dist - USSC

Pipe Dreams 15 MIN
16mm
Color
LC 79-700369
Traces one man's purchase of a pipe by showing what he looks for in a quality pipe, the various tobaccos offered and how he starts a collection.
Health and Safety
Dist - KLEINW **Prod** - KLEINW 1979

Pipe Fabrication
U-matic / VHS
Drafting - Piping Familiarization Series
Color (IND)
Industrial and Technical Education
Dist - GPCV **Prod** - GPCV

Pipe Fabrication Drawings
U-matic / VHS
Drafting - Blueprint Reading Basics Series
Color (IND)
Industrial and Technical Education
Dist - GPCV **Prod** - GPCV

Pipe fabrication with jigs 22 MIN
16mm
Shipbuilding skills series; Pipefitting; 7
B&W
LC FIE52-246
Explains the purpose of the jig. Shows how to lay out and assemble targets for a jig, set hangers and targets using a pipe section as a template and fabricate pipe on the jig.
Industrial and Technical Education
Dist - USNAC **Prod** - USOE 1944

The Pipe is the Alter 13 MIN
U-matic / BETA / VHS
Wyld Ryce Series
Color; Stereo (J S C A G)
Shows spiritual leader Amos Owen in his daily prayer ritual using his ceremonial pipe to establish communication with the Universe and the Great Spirit.
Social Science
Dist - UCV **Prod** - TCPT 1979

Pipe Trades 15 MIN
16mm / U-matic / VHS
Career Awareness
(I)
$130 VC purchase, $240 film purchase, $25 VC rental, $30 film rental
Presents an empathetic approach to career planning, showing the personal as well as professional qualities of pipe trade personnel. Highlights the importance of career education.
Guidance and Counseling
Dist - GPN

Pipe welding
VHS
Shielded metal arc welding training systems
$445.00 purchase _ #MJ093129V
Provides training for achieving proficiency in the field of pipe welding.
Education; Industrial and Technical Education
Dist - CAREER **Prod** - CAREER

Pipe Welding 90 MIN
VHS / 35mm strip
(H A IND)
#911XV7
Advances a welder into skilled welding on all types of pipes using oxyacetylene, arc, TIG and MIG. Includes joint preparation, oxyacetylene welding and brazing, shielded metal arc, out of postion techniques, TIG and MIG, and qualification testing (6 tapes). Prerequisites required. Includes a Study Guide.
Education; Industrial and Technical Education
Dist - BERGL

Pipe welding - qualifying for all positions 20 MIN
U-matic / BETA / VHS
Welding training series
Color (IND G)
$495.00 purchase _ #821 - 09
Trains welders. Instructs on the seven steps of welding in the 6G position. Part of a series on welding.
Health and Safety; Industrial and Technical Education; Psychology
Dist - ITSC **Prod** - ITSC 1990

Pipefit - Plumbing 15 MIN
BETA / VHS / U-matic
Career Success Series
(H C A)
$29.95 _ #MX126
Portrays occupations in pipefitting and plumbing by reviewing required abilities and interviewing people employed in these fields. Tells of anxieties and rewards invloved in pursuing a career as a plumber.
Education; Guidance and Counseling; Industrial and Technical Education
Dist - CAMV **Prod** - CAMV

Pipefitter
VHS
Career connections video series
Color (J H C G)
$39.95 purchase _ #CCP0205V
Examines career options as a pipefitter. Looks at educational requirements, skills needed, safety considerations, advancement opportunities and related occupations. Interviews workers and shows on - the - job footage to overview the work. The last segment provides a brief summary of how to use the Occupational Outlook Handbook - OOH and the Dictionary of Occupational Titles - DOT. Part of a six - part series on occupations.
Business and Economics; Guidance and Counseling; Industrial and Technical Education
Dist - CAMV **Prod** - CAMV 1993

Pipefitter - steamfitter 5 MIN
U-matic
Good work series
Color (H)
Provides useful, up to date information on various occupations to aid high school students in career selection. Available in five series of ten jobs each.
Education; Guidance and Counseling; Industrial and Technical Education
Dist - TVOTAR **Prod** - TVOTAR 1981

Pipefitter - steamfitter 5 MIN
VHS / 16mm
Good works 4 series
Color (A PRO)
$40.00 purchase _ #BPN225802
Presents the occupation of a pipefitter - steamfitter. Gives a profile of a young person who is either undergoing an apprenticeship or has recently completed training in this field. Takes the viewer on a tour of this person's workplace and explains the practical skills and training offered by employers and schools. Gives a better understanding of the demand for skilled workers today and the potential for personal growth.
Guidance and Counseling
Dist - RMIBHF **Prod** - RMIBHF

Pipefitting and plumbing 15 MIN
VHS
Career success series
Color (H C A)
$29.95 purchase _ #MX126
Presents an introduction to pipefitting and plumbing careers. Covers the necessary skills, and interviews people in these careers on the rewards and stresses involved.
Education; Industrial and Technical Education
Dist - CAMV

Pipefitting and Plumbing 15 MIN
VHS / 16mm
(H C A)
$24.95 purchase _ #CS126
Describes the requisite skills for a career pipefitting and plumbing. Features interviews with professionals in the field.
Guidance and Counseling
Dist - RMIBHF **Prod** - RMIBHF

Pipefitting, Bell and Spigot 19 MIN
16mm
Color
Shows how to measure cast iron soil pipe, how to make cuts, and to use all the various yarning irons for good yarning with the oakum. Views the procedures for making vertical and horizontal joints, including proper safety practices and caulking.
Industrial and Technical Education
Dist - MOKIN **Prod** - MOKIN

Pipefitting - Cutting - Reaming - Threading 18 MIN
16mm
Color (IND)
Shows how to correctly cut, ream and thread pipe. Stresses the correct thread length for good tight screwed connections, removing the burr after the pipe is cut, the use of sharp dies and proper cutting oil.
Industrial and Technical Education
Dist - MOKIN **Prod** - MOKIN

Pipefitting - cutting - reaming - threading 18 MIN
U-matic / VHS
Marshall maintenance training programs series; Tape 9
Color (IND)
Shows how to correctly cut, ream and thread pipe. Stresses correct length for good tight screw connection, use of sharp dies and proper cutting oil.
Industrial and Technical Education
Dist - LEIKID **Prod** - LEIKID

Pipeline 28 MIN
16mm
Color
LC 78-701441
Tells the story of the Trans - Alaskan pipeline from the initial legal and environmental concerns, through construction problems, to successful completion of the project.
Business and Economics; Industrial and Technical Education; Social Science
Dist - MTP **Prod** - ALYSKA 1978

Pipeline, Alaska, a Lifeline
VHS / U-matic
Alaska Series
Color
Profiles the pipeline and the people who work on the edge of the Arctic Sea, one of the most unusual and chilling environments in the world.
Geography - United States; Physical Education and Recreation; Science - Natural
Dist - WCCOTV **Prod** - WCCOTV 1982

A Pipeline - and Animals 28 MIN
16mm
Color
Shows how well animals are living along the route of the Trans Alaska pipeline.
Geography - United States; Industrial and Technical Education; Social Science
Dist - MTP **Prod** - MTP

Piper Alpha - the human price of oil 40 MIN
VHS
Panorama series
Color; PAL (G)
PdS65 purchase
Asks questions about the standards of design and engineering of oil rig platforms following the 'Piper Alpha' disaster that claimed 167 lives. Investigates the attitudes to safety in the oil industry. Presents the necessary changes and how they may effect the economics of the oil industry and the future of the North Sea.
Business and Economics; Industrial and Technical Education
Dist - BBCENE

Pipes and Pipe Fitting 60 MIN
VHS
Piping and Valves Series
Color (PRO)
$600.00, $1500.00 purchase _ #GMPPF
Introduces techniques for pipe inspection and installation. Describes pipes, pipe fittings and demonstrates the use of pipe threading equipment. Part of a six - part series on piping and valves, which is part of a set on general and mechanical maintenance. Includes 10 textbooks and an instructor guide which provide four hours of instruction.
Education; Industrial and Technical Education; Psychology
Dist - NUSTC **Prod** - NUSTC

The Pipes are Calling 29 MIN
16mm / VHS
Color (G)
$425.00, $250.00 purchase, $50.00 rental
Portrays a summer bagpipe school in Coeur d'Alene, Idaho, where piping enthusiasts from all over North America gather to learn the music and the craft of bagpiping. Interviews chief instructor Evan MacRae from Scotland and students who discuss their desire to preserve a 300 - year - old cultural tradition.
Fine Arts; History - World
Dist - CNEMAG **Prod** - CNEMAG 1990

Pipetting - I 8 MIN
VHS
Chemistry master apprentice series
Color (H C)
$49.95 purchase _ #49 - 7203 - V
Illustrates the proper steps to deliver accurate, reproducible volumes with a volumetric transfer pipet fitted with a short piece of rubber tubing to a plastic syringe to generate the suction required to rinse and fill the volumetric pipet. Shows how to inspect the pipet for cleanliness and then rinse and fill it with solution. Demonstrates the errors that result from parallax and the proper filling and emptying procedures. Part of the Chemistry Master Apprentice series.
Science; Science - Physical
Dist - INSTRU **Prod** - CORNRS

Pipetting - II 9 MIN
VHS
Chemistry master apprentice series; Pgm 104
Color (H C)
$49.95 purchase _ #49 - 7204 - V
Illustrates the proper steps to deliver accurate, reproducible volumes with a volumetric transfer pipet. Shows how to inspect the pipet for cleanliness and then rinse and fill it with solution, using a pipet aid - vinyl bulb, polyethylene tip. Demonstrates the errors that result from parallax and the proper filling and emptying procedures. Part of the Chemistry Master Apprentice series.
Science; Science - Physical
Dist - INSTRU **Prod** - CORNRS
CORNRS CUETV

Pipetting III 8 MIN
VHS / U-matic
Chemistry - Master - Apprentice Series; Pgm 100
Color (C A)
LC 82-706046
Illustrates the proper steps required to deliver accurate, reproducible volumes with a volumetric transfer pipet. Uses a Fisher brand pipet filler to draw liquid into the pipet.
Health and Safety; Science; Science - Physical
Dist - CORNRS **Prod** - CUETV 1981

Piping 240 MIN
U-matic / VHS
Mechanical Equipment Maintenance - Spanish Series
Color (IND) (SPANISH)
Features tubing and piping. Covers strainers, filters, traps and heat exchangers.
Foreign Language; Industrial and Technical Education
Dist - ITCORP **Prod** - ITCORP

Piping 240 MIN
U-matic / VHS
Mechanical Equipment Maintenance Series
Color (IND)
Features tubing and piping. Covers strainers, filters, traps and heat exchangers.
Industrial and Technical Education
Dist - ITCORP **Prod** - ITCORP

Piping and auxiliaries 60 MIN
VHS
Equipment operations series
Color (PRO)
$600.00 - $1500.00 purchase _ #OTPA1
Focuses on the concepts involved in plant process piping and fittings and on pipe and pipe fitting classifications. Follows and identifies process pipelines on flow diagrams. Part of a twenty - part series on equipment operation. Includes ten textbooks and an instructor guide to support four hours of instruction.
Health and Safety; Industrial and Technical Education; Psychology
Dist - NUSTC **Prod** - NUSTC

Piping and Valves Series

Motor Operators	60 MIN
Pipes and Pipe Fitting	60 MIN
Safety Valves - 1	60 MIN
Safety Valves - 2	60 MIN
Valve Maintenance - 1	60 MIN
Valve Maintenance - 2	60 MIN

Dist - NUSTC

Piping Auxiliaries 60 MIN
VHS
Piping Auxiliaries and Insulation Series
Color (PRO)
$600.00, $1500.00 purchase _ #GMPAU
Identifies and explains the operation of various piping auxiliaries, including filters and strainers, pipe hangers and supports, hydraulic and mechanical snubbers and protective devices for shock and expansion. Part of a three - part series on piping auxiliaries and insulation, which is part of a set on general and mechanical maintenance. Includes 10 textbooks and an instructor guide which provide four hours of instruction.
Education; Industrial and Technical Education; Psychology
Dist - NUSTC **Prod** - NUSTC

Piping Auxiliaries and Insulation Series

Piping Auxiliaries	60 MIN
Steam Traps	60 MIN
Thermal insulation	60 MIN

Dist - NUSTC

Piping design draftsperson 5 MIN
VHS / 16mm
Good works 1 series
Color (A PRO)
$40.00 purchase _ #BPN195801
Presents the occupation of a piping design draftsperson. Gives a profile of a young person who is either undergoing an apprenticeship or has recently completed training in this field. Takes the viewer on a tour of this person's workplace and explains the practical skills and training offered by employers and schools. Gives a better understanding of the demand for skilled workers today and the potential for personal growth.
Guidance and Counseling
Dist - RMIBHF **Prod** - RMIBHF

Piping design draftsperson 5 MIN
U-matic
Good work series
Color (H)
Provides useful, up to date information on various occupations to aid high school students in career selection. Available in five series of ten jobs each.
Education; Guidance and Counseling; Industrial and Technical Education
Dist - TVOTAR **Prod** - TVOTAR 1981

Piping Drawings - Detail Dimensioning and Symbology
VHS / U-matic
Drafting - Blueprint Reading Basics Series
Color (IND)
Industrial and Technical Education
Dist - GPCV **Prod** - GPCV

Piping Drawings - Fittings and Orthographic Projections
VHS / U-matic
Drafting - Blueprint Reading Basics Series
Color (IND)
Industrial and Technical Education
Dist - GPCV **Prod** - GPCV

Piping Drawings - Terms and Equipment
VHS / U-matic
Drafting - Blueprint Reading Basics Series
Color (IND)
Industrial and Technical Education
Dist - GPCV **Prod** - GPCV

Piping Drawings - Valves, Flanges and Pipe
U-matic / VHS
Drafting - Blueprint Reading Basics Series
Color (IND)
Industrial and Technical Education
Dist - GPCV **Prod** - GPCV

Piping Fabrication for Shipboard High Temperature Steam Systems - Bending and 10 MIN
U-matic
B&W
LC 79-707969
Emphasizes the care and skills required in the bending and stalling phases of working with chrome - molybdenum piping. Issued in 1958 as a motion picture.
Industrial and Technical Education
Dist - USNAC **Prod** - USN 1979

Piping Fabrication for Shipboard High Temperature Steam Systems - Introduction 13 MIN
U-matic
B&W
LC 79-707968
Emphasizes the care and skill required for the handling, fabrication and installation of chrome - molybdenum piping in shipboard high temperature, high - pressure steam systems. Issued in 1958 as a motion picture.
Industrial and Technical Education
Dist - USNAC **Prod** - USN 1979

Piping Isometrics
VHS / U-matic
Drafting - Piping Familiarization Series
Color (IND)
Industrial and Technical Education
Dist - GPCV **Prod** - GPCV

Piping Preparation and Installation 60 MIN
U-matic / VHS
Mechanical Equipment Maintenance, Module 17 - Advanced Pipefitting 'Series
Color (IND)
Industrial and Technical Education
Dist - LEIKID **Prod** - LEIKID

Pippi Goes on Board 84 MIN
16mm
Color (P I)
Presents robbers who are out to get Pippi's survival money.
Fine Arts
Dist - FI **Prod** - FI

Pippi in the South Seas 85 MIN
16mm
Color (P I)
Presents Pippi as she rescues her sea captain father.
Fine Arts
Dist - FI **Prod** - FI

Pippi Longstocking 99 MIN
16mm
Color (P I)
Presents the story from the book by Astrid Lindgrer.
Fine Arts
Dist - FI **Prod** - FI

Pippi on the Run 97 MIN
16mm
Color (P I)
Presents Pippi and friends as they run away and have many fanciful adventures.
Fine Arts
Dist - FI **Prod** - FI

Pirandello's Six Characters in Search of an Author 60 MIN
U-matic / VHS
Drama - play, performance, perception series; Module 4
Color (C)
Fine Arts; Literature and Drama
Dist - MDCC **Prod** - MDCC

Piranesi 29 MIN
Videoreel / VT2
Museum Open House Series
Color
Fine Arts; Geography - World
Dist - PBS **Prod** - WGBHTV

The Pirates of Penzance 112 MIN
VHS
Color (H C G)
$49.00 purchase _ #DL194
Presents the 1982 film production of The Pirates of Penzance by Gilbert and Sullivan, starring Kevin Kline, Linda Ronstadt and Angela Lansbury.
Fine Arts
Dist - INSIM

The Pirate's Treasure 23 MIN
16mm
B&W
Presents an episode of the serial The Perils Of Pauline. Shows what happens when Pauline is trapped on a ship with a time - bomb about to explode. Stars Pearl White.
Fine Arts
Dist - KILLIS **Prod** - UNKNWN 1914

Pirate's week - Cayman, October 30 MIN
VHS
Scuba World series
Color (G)
$24.90 purchase _ #0446
Visits Pirate's Week on Grand Cayman Island, Brac and Little Cayman Islands, which occurs in October.
Geography - World; Physical Education and Recreation
Dist - SEVVID

Pirates's dagger 30 MIN
VHS
Color (J H)
$250.00 purchase, $50.00 rental
Offers a story about a 12 - year - old boy named Sam who, after being confined to his room as punishment by his mother, escapes in his imagination to a series of fantastic adventures with his friend, a fierce pirate captain. Conveys a message about the dangers of greed and of following a self - centered, violent leader. Directed by Steven Sorenson.
Literature and Drama
Dist - CNEMAG

The Pirogue maker 14 MIN
16mm
Color (G)
$40.00 rental
Records the making of a pirogue, a dugout canoe fashioned from red cypress, used by the Cajuns of Louisiana to navigate their marshy bayou country. Uses authentic Cajun music sung by Susan Reed. The filmmaker was on location with Robert Flaherty who was making his classic documentary The Louisiana Story in 1947, when they began to search for a pirogue to use in the film. A long search ensued and Flaherty's interest in preserving old crafts caused him to instruct Eagle in recording the actual making of the canoe. This is a new version, 1975, created from the original material, which had become unprintable.
Fine Arts; Geography - United States
Dist - CANCIN **Prod** - EAGLE 1947

Pirosmani 84 MIN
35mm / 16mm
Color (G) (RUSSIAN WITH ENGLISH SUBTITLES)
$250.00, $300.00 rental
Offers a visual meditation on the life of primitive Georgian artist Niko Pirosmanashuili, who was born in 1862 and died of alcoholism and starvation in 1919. Directed by Georgi Shengelaya.
Fine Arts; History - World
Dist - KINOIC **Prod** - IFEX 1971

Pisa - Story of a Cathedral Square - 1000 - 1300 A D 10 MIN
16mm
Color
Presents the story of the Pisa Cathedral Square from 1000 to 1300 A D.
Fine Arts; History - World
Dist - ROLAND **Prod** - ROLAND

Pista - the many Faces of Stephen Deutch 28 MIN
16mm
Color
LC 80-700272
Traces the life of Hungarian photographer - sculptor Stephen Deutch. Reveals his attitudes toward art, music and family.
Fine Arts
Dist - TATLOC **Prod** - TATLOC 1979

The Pistol 10 MIN
16mm
Color (H C A)
LC 70-710167
A wry commentary on man's tendency to solve problems with a gun.
Psychology; Sociology
Dist - VIEWFI **Prod** - URCHS 1970

Pistol Pete's ball handling 60 MIN
VHS
Pistol Pete's homework basketball series
Color (G)
$39.95 purchase _ #LA140V
Features the late 'Pistol' Pete Maravich teaching the basics of handling the basketball. Presents a variety of drills to develop ball handling skills, including the tap drill, 'squeeze the banana,' 'around the world,' the 'flip roll,' and others.
Physical Education and Recreation
Dist - CAMV **Prod** - CAMV 1987

Pistol Pete's dribbling 60 MIN
VHS
Pistol Pete's homework basketball series
Color (G)
$39.95 purchase _ #LA120V
Features the late 'Pistol' Pete Maravich teaching the basics of dribbling the basketball. Emphasizes the importance of a proper stance and use of wrist snap. Demonstrates various exercises which develop speed, agility, and particular dribbling skills.
Physical Education and Recreation
Dist - CAMV **Prod** - CAMV 1987

Pistol Pete's homework basketball series
Presents four programs on basketball skills. Includes Shooting, Dribbling, Passing and Ball Handling.

Pistol Pete's ball handling	60 MIN
Pistol Pete's dribbling	60 MIN
Pistol Pete's homework basketball series	205 MIN
Pistol Pete's passing	45 MIN
Pistol Pete's shooting	40 MIN

Dist - CAMV

Pistol Pete's passing 45 MIN
VHS
Pistol Pete's homework basketball series
Color (G)
$39.95 purchase _ #LA130V
Features the late 'Pistol' Pete Maravich teaching the basics of passing the basketball. Presents both basic and advanced skills. Explains and demonstrates various types of passes, including the basic chest, chest bounce, overhead, baseball, behind - the - back, between - the - legs, and the alley - oop.
Physical Education and Recreation
Dist - CAMV **Prod** - CAMV 1987

Pistol Pete's shooting 40 MIN
VHS
Pistol Pete's homework basketball series
Color (G)
$39.95 purchase _ #LA110V
Features the late 'Pistol' Pete Maravich teaching the basics of shooting the basketball. Covers the mechanics, psychological aspects, and techniques. Presents slow - motion footage of the jump shot, set shot, lay - up, and hook shot.
Physical Education and Recreation
Dist - CAMV **Prod** - CAMV 1987

Pistol Shooting Fundamentals 15 MIN
16mm / U-matic / VHS
Rifle Shooting Fundamentals Series
Color (J)
Presents World Pistol Champion Bill Blankenship and Women's World Air Pistol Champion Ruby E Fox demonstrating the fundamentals of pistol marksmanship. Covers sight alignment, breath control, hold control, trigger control and follow through with a strong emphasis on safety.
Physical Education and Recreation
Dist - ATHI **Prod** - ATHI 1982

Piston and Liner Removal 12 MIN
16mm
B&W
LC FIE52-1367
Tells how to remove connecting rod bearings, fork rod piston assembly, blade rod piston assembly and opposite liners.
Industrial and Technical Education
Dist - USNAC **Prod** - USN 1945

The Pit and the Pendulum 80 MIN
16mm
Color (H A)
Presents the gothic horror tale of lovers who plan to drive her brother mad. The brother responds by locking them in his torture chamber. Based on the Edgar Allan Poe story. Stars Vincent Price.
Fine Arts; Literature and Drama
Dist - TIMLIF **Prod** - AIP 1961
FI

The Pit and the Pendulum 8 MIN
16mm
Color
LC 76-701474
Presents an adaption of Edgar Allan Poe's short story The Pit And The Pendulum.
Fine Arts; Literature and Drama
Dist - CCAAT **Prod** - CCAAT 1975

Pit - Stop 28 MIN
16mm
Color
LC 76-702848
A driver - education film for high school students. Uses scenes of races and race - car drivers to explain that safe practices on the track are similar to safe practices on the highway.
Health and Safety; Social Science
Dist - CMI **Prod** - COCA 1968

Pitch 15 MIN
U-matic
Music Box Series
Color (K P)
Demonstrates pitch by tapping on bottles of water.
Fine Arts
Dist - TVOTAR **Prod** - TVOTAR 1971

Pitch Buttoning and Blocking 30 MIN
16mm
B&W
LC FIE52-383
Demonstrates the blocking of large convex lenses, blocking with pagoda tool, the use of the ring button, buttoning and blocking with pitch points and the pitch buttoning and blocking of very small lenses.
Industrial and Technical Education
Dist - USNAC **Prod** - USOE 1944

The Pitch of Grief 30 MIN
VHS / 16mm
Color (G)
$295.00 purchase, $100.00 - $50.00 rental
Looks at the emotional process of grieving through interviews with four bereaved men and women.
Guidance and Counseling; Sociology
Dist - FANPRO **Prod** - FANPRO 1989

Pitchers of fire and muscleman - Volume 7 45 MIN
VHS
Superbook series
Color (K P I R)
$11.99 purchase _ #35 - 86612 - 979
Uses an animated format to tell the story of Chris and Joy and their time travels through Biblical places and events. 'Pitchers Of Fire' tells the story of Gideon and his army, while 'Muscleman' tells the story of Samson.
Literature and Drama; Religion and Philosophy
Dist - APH **Prod** - TYHP

Pitchers, spouts and handles 12 MIN
16mm / U-matic / VHS
Art and the artist series
Color (A)
LC 73-700120
Deals with thrown pitcher forms, including addition of suitable spouts and handles. Stresses the value of practice in achieving hand coordination. Explains how to handle the fushly thrown pitcher so as to form a spout that is both pleasing and functional.
Mathematics
Dist - PHENIX **Prod** - CINCPR 1968

Pitching
VHS
Baseball Skills and Drills Series
(J H C)
$39.95 _ #TP120V
Explains the five phases of the pitching motion, proper position to avoid injury, and how to throw change up and curve balls in baseball.
Physical Education and Recreation
Dist - CAMV **Prod** - CAMV

Pitching
VHS
N C A A instructional video series
Color (H C A)
$39.95 purchase _ #KAR1151V
Presents the first of a two - part series on softball. Focuses on pitching techniques.
Physical Education and Recreation
Dist - CAMV **Prod** - NCAAF

Pitching 29 MIN
VHS / U-matic
Basically Baseball Series
Color
Presents George Bamberger, Oriole pitching coach and players Dave Mc Nally, Jim Palmer, Grant Jackson and Eddie Watt, teaching stance and foot position, wind - up, concealing pitches, 3/4 delivery, overhand, side - arm, follow - through/balance fastball - curve ball, change - up/slider/knuckler, sinker/screw ball, covering first and bunt coverage/backing bases.
Physical Education and Recreation
Dist - MDCPB **Prod** - MDCPB

Pitching, chipping and bunker play
VHS
N C A A instructional video series
Color (H C A)
$39.95 purchase _ #KAR2353V
Presents the third of a four - part series on golf. Focuses on pitching, chipping, and bunker play.
Physical Education and Recreation
Dist - CAMV **Prod** - NCAAF

Pitching development 75 MIN
VHS
Color (G T)
$59.95 purchase _ #TRS202V-P
Shows softball coaches how to further develop their pitching prospects through practice sessions and proper technique. Includes pitcher development using the wall, practice routine, teaching 'stuff,' pregame preparation, first inning corrections, and game strategies for the pitcher.
Physical Education and Recreation
Dist - CAMV

Pitching drills
VHS
NCAA instructional video series
Color (H C A)
$39.95 purchase _ #KAR1105V
Presents the second of a four - part series on defensive baseball. Focuses on pitching drills.
Physical Education and Recreation
Dist - CAMV **Prod** - NCAAF

Pitching essentials
VHS
N C A A instructional video series
Color (H C A)
$39.95 purchase _ #KAR1104V
Presents a four - part series on defensive baseball. Focuses on the essentials of pitching.
Physical Education and Recreation
Dist - CAMV **Prod** - NCAAF

Pitching for kids
VHS
Color (G)
$29.95 purchase _ #PE1006V
Features New York Mets pitching coach Mel Stottlemyre teaching basic pitching techniques. Covers subjects including throwing techniques, grips, body and footing positioning, pitching from the stretch position, and more. Breaks down the pitching motion into the individual motions - step - back, pivot, and stride.
Physical Education and Recreation
Dist - CAMV **Prod** - CAMV 1987

Pitching for the Yankees 15 MIN
16mm
Color (J H C)
New York Yankee players, such as Whitey Ford and Al Downing, talk about their approach to various aspects of pitching in baseball.
Physical Education and Recreation
Dist - MOKIN **Prod** - SBRAND 1965

Pitching mechanics 75 MIN
VHS
Color (G T)
$59.95 purchase _ #TRS201V-P
Provides softball coaches with teaching progressions to teach fast pitch pitching. Includes critical coaching considerations, essential mechanical concepts, teaching the grip, mechanics of the windmill, mechanics of the slingshot, and infallible coaching cues.
Physical Education and Recreation
Dist - CAMV

The Pitchpipe 13 MIN
16mm
B&W (T)
Illustrates the purpose and use of the pitch pipe. Introduces major key signatures and their key tones.
Fine Arts
Dist - MLA **Prod** - JHP 1955

Pitfalls in Biliary Tract Surgery 38 MIN
16mm
Color
LC FIA65-851
Reviews the anatomy of the biliary tract, demonstrates the common mechanisms of vascular and ductile injury occurring during cholecystectomy and illustrates the techniques of safe cholocystectomy.
Health and Safety
Dist - ACY **Prod** - ACYDGD 1964

Pitfalls in Stapes Surgery 19 MIN
16mm
Color (PRO)
Illustrates the difficult problems that may confront the surgeon in performing the stapes operation to correct hearing loss due to otosclerosis.
Health and Safety
Dist - EAR **Prod** - EAR

Pitfalls in Stapes Surgery 18 MIN
U-matic / VHS
Color (PRO)
Presents the pitfalls in stapes surgery.
Guidance and Counseling; Health and Safety; Science - Natural
Dist - HOUSEI **Prod** - HOUSEI

The Pitfalls of Textbook Adoption - and How to Avoid Them 40 MIN
U-matic
Color (T)
Separates the textbook adoption process into three stages and identifies the pitfalls that can occur. Accompanied by a users' guide containing support materials designed to assist school districts.
Education
Dist - AFSCD **Prod** - AFSCD 1986

Pithole, USA 14 MIN
16mm
B&W (H C A)
Documents the first roistering days of the oil industry in the 1800's.
Business and Economics; History - United States
Dist - USSC **Prod** - USSC

Pits, peaks and passes - a lecture on critical point theory - Pt 1 48 MIN
16mm
MAA individual lecturers series
Color (H C T)
LC FIA66-1272
Professor Marston Morse, with models and animation, derives the simple formula relating the number of pits, peaks and passes on an island with a single shoreline. An account of the professor's career and a discussion on the relationship between mathematics, physics and the arts are included.
Mathematics
Dist - MLA **Prod** - MAA 1966

Pits, peaks and passes - a lecture on critical point theory - Pt 2 26 MIN
16mm
MAA individual lecturers series
Color (H C T)
LC FIA66-1265
Presents a lecture by Professor Marston Morse in which he analyzes the critical points of continuous functions over compact, orientable 3 - manifolds. He defines the degree of stability in N - dimensions and presents applications to electrodynamics.
Mathematics
Dist - MLA **Prod** - MAA 1966

Pittsburgh - an American Industrial City 43 MIN
16mm
Color
LC 80-701370
Reviews the history of the Pittsburgh, Pennsylvania, area and examines the people, places and industries that have contributed to the development of this region. Includes archival lithographs, photographs and film footage.
Geography - United States; History - United States; Social Science
Dist - MAGIC **Prod** - MAGIC 1980

Pittsburgh - an American Industrial City - Pt 1 22 MIN
16mm
Color
LC 80-701370
Reviews the history of the Pittsburgh, Pennsylvania, area and examines the people, places and industries that have contributed to the development of this region. Includes archival lithographs, photographs and film footage.
Geography - United States
Dist - MAGIC **Prod** - MAGIC 1980

Pittsburgh - an American Industrial City - Pt 2 21 MIN
16mm
Color
LC 80-701370
Reviews the history of the Pittsburgh, Pennsylvania, area and examines the people, places and industries that have contributed to the development of this region. Includes archival lithographs, photographs and film footage.
Geography - United States
Dist - MAGIC **Prod** - MAGIC 1980

Pituitary Hormones 30 MIN
16mm
Pharmacology Series
B&W (C)
LC 73-703350
Reviews pituitary anatomy and physiology and shows the mechanism of action, classification and clinical uses of pituitary hormones. Classifies oxytoxic agents.
Health and Safety; Psychology
Dist - TELSTR **Prod** - MVNE 1971

Pituitary, Thyroid, Parathyroid 26 MIN
VHS / 16mm
Histology review series; Unit XII
(C)
$330.00 purchase _ #821VI052
Identifies the pituitary, thyroid and parathyroid glands, using original drawings and photomicrographrs. Part of the Endocrine System Unit.
Health and Safety
Dist - HSCIC **Prod** - HSCIC 1983

The Pivot Point - WP - 5 12 MIN
U-matic
Word Processing Series
(PRO)
$235.00 purchase
Presents the psychology of and difficulties associated with change in the organizational structure. Explains the direct benefits of word processing used wisely within the organizational structure, through the testimony of managers and professionals.
Business and Economics
Dist - MONAD **Prod** - MONAD

A Pixel is Worth a Thousand Words 30 MIN
U-matic / VHS / 16mm
Mr Microchip Series
Color (I J H)
Demonstrates how a computer reads and forms pictures, how pictures are stored in the computer and how animation is done. Discusses resolution (image quality) and computer monitors.
Mathematics
Dist - JOU **Prod** - JOU

Pizza 6 MIN
U-matic / VHS
Cooking with Jack and Jill Series
Color (P I)
$95.00
Portrays the skills of twins Jack and Jill as they cook nutritious and delicious snacks that are easy to prepare. Kitchen safety is emphasized. Animated.
Home Economics
Dist - LANDMK **Prod** - LANDMK 1986

Pizza 5 MIN
16mm
Color
Shows pizza lovers how to make their own pizzas.
Home Economics
Dist - EXARC **Prod** - EXARC

Pizza 32 MIN
VHS
Cookbook videos series
Color (G)
$19.95 purchase _ #ALW122
Shows how to prepare pizza in short, easy - to - learn segments. Lists each ingredient as it is added in subtitles and visually reinforces spoken instructions. Gives recipe background and nutritional facts. Part of the Cookbook Videos series.
Home Economics; Social Science
Dist - CADESF **Prod** - CADESF

Pizza 32 MIN
VHS
Cookbook videos series; Vol 12
Color (G)
$19.95 purchase
Shows how to make pizza using bread, rolls or frozen dough. Includes a basic pizza dough recipe. Includes printed abstract of recipes. Part of a series.
Home Economics; Social Science
Dist - ALWHIT **Prod** - ALWHIT

The Pizza perfect caper 30 MIN
VHS
Detective stories for math problem solving series
Color (I J H)
$175.00 purchase _ #CG - 955 - VS
Reveals that someone has been hiding diamond bracelets in pizza ingredients and smuggling them into Pleasantville, and Billie and Jodie have been enlisted to find out how it's done and to capture the culprits. Asks which ingredient is being used to conceal the contraband, which pizza parlor is acting as the 'fence,' and how do they keep all the secret shipments from showing up on the books. Billie, Jodie and students watching the video will have to use all of their statistical problem - solving skills. Requires sorting through mountains of invoices, preference surveys, sales charts and four mystery graphs to uncover the smuggler's trail of suspicious patterns. Includes clue kit. Part of a series.
Literature and Drama; Mathematics; Psychology
Dist - HRMC **Prod** - HRMC 1992

Pizza Pizza Daddy - O 18 MIN
16mm / U-matic / VHS
B&W (C A)
LC 78-712935
An anthropological and folkloric record of singing games played by Afro - American girls in the fourth grade of a school in Los Angeles.
Fine Arts; History - United States; Sociology
Dist - UCEMC **Prod** - HAWESB 1969

PKU - Preventable Mental Retardation 16 MIN
U-matic / VHS / 16mm
Color (PRO)
LC 73-707250
Reports on the effectiveness of present procedures used in diagnosing PKU. Includes information on new blood tests and new techniques for testing urine that can be used at home.
Education; Health and Safety; Psychology
Dist - IFB **Prod** - IFB 1967

PKU - Retardo Mental Evitable 15 MIN
U-matic / VHS / 16mm
Color (H C) (SPANISH)
LC 73-707251
Spanish version uses a series of actual case histories to emphasize the need for the universal examination of all children for phenylketonuria. Illustrates a simple test for PKU which can be made at home.
Foreign Language; Health and Safety; Psychology
Dist - IFB **Prod** - IFB 1962

The Place between Our Bodies 33 MIN
U-matic / VHS
Color (C A)
Comes to grips with the issues involved in one gay man's sexuality. Progresses from sexual observation, cruising, fantasy and pornography films to a lover relationship.
Health and Safety; Psychology; Sociology
Dist - MMRC **Prod** - MMRC

A Place Called Ardoyne 40 MIN
16mm
Color
Depicts a Catholic community in Belfast, Northern Ireland. Portrays the traumatic changes in the people's lives since Ardoyne came under Protestant attack in 1968.
Geography - World; History - World; Sociology
Dist - IMPACT **Prod** - THMPSN

A Place called Brunei 45 MIN
U-matic / VHS / BETA
Color; PAL (G H C)
PdS60, PdS68 purchase
Travels to Brunei. Looks at the palace, geography and more.
Fine Arts; Geography - World
Dist - EDPAT

A Place called home 27 MIN
VHS
Color (G)
$69.95 purchase _ #4913
Records the efforts of a group of citizens in Washington, DC who reached out to a group of homeless children in their community. Shows how their act of compassion and charity changed their lives - and the lives of the children - forever. Shows a social worker and a local theater director producing plays with shelter residents who held performances all over the city. Produced by Virginia Wolf.
Fine Arts; Sociology
Dist - CWLOA

A Place called lovely 20 MIN
VHS
Works of Sadie Benning series
Color (A)
$200.00 purchase, $50.00 rental
Recalls the difficult childhood memories of Sadie Benning. Questions societal standards which allow violence to exist. Part of a series produced by Benning.
Literature and Drama; Religion and Philosophy; Sociology
Dist - WMEN

A Place for Aunt Lois 17 MIN
16mm / U-matic / VHS
Color (J)
LC 74-700108
Examines traditional stereotypes of the major goals given to girls. Shows the capacity of the young to determine the value of other human beings, tells how nine - year - old Kathy grows to understand and respect her childless, husband - less Aunt Lois and sees that Lois's particular situation in no way lessens her value as a total human being.
Guidance and Counseling; Psychology; Sociology
Dist - WOMBAT **Prod** - WOMBAT 1973

A Place for Everything 15 MIN
VHS / U-matic
Math Mission 2 Series
Color (P)
LC 82-706320
Uses a space robot and his puppet assistant in a visit to a math class to explain the concepts of place value and zero. Tells how the robot and his assistant show the development of a system to write numbers down and then teach a game which explores number relationships using place value pieces.
Mathematics
Dist - GPN **Prod** - WCVETV 1980

A Place for Growing 15 MIN
16mm
Color; B&W
Highlights the conversion of an anti - social youngster through membership in a boy's club. Illustrates how unsupervised activity may get youth into trouble. Presents an entertaining review of the national youth organization's activities in story form.
Guidance and Counseling; Psychology
Dist - BCLA **Prod** - BCLA

A Place for no Story 59 MIN
VHS / 16mm
Color (G)
$70.00 rental _ #PFNS - 000
Features an environmental look at the California coastline. Moves from Mt Shasta to Los Angeles.
Geography - United States; Science - Natural
Dist - PBS **Prod** - KQEDTV 1974
KQEDTV

Place in Europe Series

Braemar Castle, Scotland	26 MIN
Burg Clam, Austria	26 MIN
Egeskov, Denmark	26 MIN
Goodwood house, England	26 MIN
The Island of Hydra, Greece	26 MIN
Jerez De La Fontera - the House of Domecq, Spain	26 MIN
Palazzo Giustiniani, Venice	26 MIN
Plas Newydd - Anglesey, Wales	26 MIN
The Royal Palace, Stockholm	26 MIN
Schloss Johannisberg, Germany	26 MIN
Schloss Valduz - Liechtenstein	26 MIN
Vaux - Le Vicomte, France	26 MIN

Dist - MEDIAG

A Place in History 28 MIN
U-matic / VHS / 16mm
Color
Depicts the life of Dwight Eisenhower, emphasizing his role in World War II and his White House years. Narrated by Lorne Greene.
Biography; History - United States
Dist - USNAC **Prod** - USNAC

A Place in Our World 14 MIN
16mm
Color
LC 76-702665
Shows how the acoupedic approach teaches deaf children to hear. Demonstrates techniques with children in different phases of the program.
Education; Guidance and Counseling; Psychology
Dist - TPA **Prod** - TPA 1976

A Place in the sun 122 MIN
VHS
B&W (H C)
$39.00 purchase _ #04482 - 126
Stars Montgomery Clift and Elizabeth Taylor in a film adaptation of the novel by Theodore Dreiser.
Literature and Drama; Sociology
Dist - GA **Prod** - GA

A Place in the Sun 52 MIN
U-matic / VHS / 16mm
Destination America Series
Color (J)
Describes how the first Italians in America were stigmatized for their colored skin, their unfamiliar language and the mafiosa label that lingers today. Four million Italians and Sicilians entered America in a twenty - year period, the most concentrated migration of all European countries and originally the least welcomed.
History - United States; Sociology
Dist - MEDIAG **Prod** - THAMES 1976

Place in Time 34 MIN
16mm
B&W
Presents a comedy satire in the silent film tradition of Charlie Chaplin and Buster Keaton. Tells the story of a young street portrait painter. Touches on themes of crime, apathy and alienation in urban society, and the struggles of the artist.
Fine Arts; Psychology; Sociology
Dist - BLKFMF **Prod** - BLKFMF

A Place Just Right 30 MIN
16mm
Color
LC 80-701483
Presents the story of city people moving to the country and their realization that they cannot carry city life with them and that they must learn to adapt to the ways of the backwoods if they are to survive.
Fine Arts; Sociology
Dist - PSU **Prod** - GUTKND 1980

Place mattes 8 MIN
16mm / VHS
B&W; Color (G)
$25.00 rental, $30.00 purchase
Embodies traveling mattes of the artist's torso, limbs and extremities in Puget Sound, Yosemite and the Yucatan. Presents her figure and the Earth as two planal relationships, made two - dimensional through optical printing. The artist is unable to touch the natural environment.
Fine Arts
Dist - CANCIN **Prod** - BARHAM 1987

Place name index - Mac
CD-ROM
Color (G A)
$795.00 purchase _ #1945m
Gives more than one million place names collected from the quadrangle maps of the US Geological Survey. For Macintosh Plus, SE and II computers. Requires at least one M of RAM, one floppy disk drive, and an Apple compatible CD - ROM drive.
Geography - World; Literature and Drama; Social Science
Dist - BEP

Place name index - PC
CD-ROM
Color (PRO)
$795.00 purchase _ #1351p
Collects more than one million place names from the quadrangle maps of the US Geological Survey. For IBM PCs and compatibles. Requires 640K RAM, DOS Version 3.1 or greater, one floppy disk drive - a hard drive is recommended, one empty expansion slot, and an IBM compatible CD - ROM drive.
Geography - World; Literature and Drama; Social Science
Dist - BEP

A Place of Being 12 MIN
16mm
Color
LC FIE68-20
Describes the recreational facilities available in the Lake Mead National Recreation Area, California.
Geography - United States; Science - Natural
Dist - USNAC **Prod** - USNPS 1967

Place of Change 30 MIN
U-matic
Read all about it - One Series
Color (I)
Teaches reading and writing skills as it continues a story in which Chris and his friend Lynn escape from Trialviron and help Sam with the second edition of the newspaper, Chronicle.
Education; English Language; Literature and Drama
Dist - TVOTAR **Prod** - TVOTAR 1982

A Place of Dreams - the National Air and Space Museum 35 MIN
59 MIN
16mm / VHS / U-matic
Color (J)
LC 80-700130; 80-701968
Presents a tour through the National Air and Space Museum in Washington, D C, which is dedicated to the men and women who made air and space flight possible.
Fine Arts; Geography - United States; Industrial and Technical Education; Science - Physical; Social Science
Dist - LCOA **Prod** - PAPPVA 1980

Place of Power in French Polynesia - Pt 3 28 MIN
VHS
Human Face of the Pacific Series
Color (S)
$79.00 purchase _ #118 - 9003
Looks behind the romance and mystery of the islands of the South Seas to reveal the islands as they really are - a heterogeneous group of countries and colonies struggling to meet the challenges of the modern world while trying to preserve their cultural identities. Part 3 of six parts reveals that the Polynesian culture of Tahiti was nearly extinguished by years of French rule. However, a recent cultural reemergence has revived traditional arts and rituals.
Foreign Language; Geography - World; History - World; Religion and Philosophy; Sociology
Dist - FI **Prod** - FLMAUS 1987

A Place of rage 52 MIN
VHS / 16mm
Color (G)
$295.00 purchase, $130.00, $90.00 rental
Celebrates African American women and their achievements. Interviews Angela Davis, June Jordan and Alice Walker. Examines the societal contributions of Rosa Parks and Fannie Lou Hamer. Includes a 1970 prison interview of Angela Davis recounting her involvement with the Black Panthers and the communist party, civil rights footage and archival photos, the poetry of June Jordan, insights from Alice Walker and filmmaker Trinh T Minh - ha, music by Prince, Janet Jackson, the Neville Brothers and the Staple Singers.
Civics and Political Systems; History - United States
Dist - WMEN **Prod** - PARMAR 1991

Place of weeping 88 MIN
VHS
Color (G)
$79.95 purchase _ #S01380
Portrays a white South African journalist and a black pacifist who seek justice for the murder of a black worker by a white farmer. Deals with the issues of apartheid and the black South African struggle for freedom.
Fine Arts; Geography - World; Sociology
Dist - UILL

Place that Comma 19 MIN
16mm / U-matic / VHS
Color (J)
Uses the format of a television game show to introduce, repeat and reinforce the rules of comma placement.
English Language
Dist - PFP **Prod** - PFP 1979

A Place to be 60 MIN
VHS
Color (G)
$49.95 purchase _ #PLTB - 000
Features the East Building of Washington's National Gallery of Art, a highly praised piece of architecture. Documents the construction process from the design efforts of I M Pei to the selection and placement of artwork by Henry Moore, Joan Miro, Jean Dubuffet and Alexander Calder. Presented by Charles Guggenheim.
Fine Arts
Dist - PBS **Prod** - GUG 1979

A Place to be 59 MIN
VHS / 16mm
Color (G)
$70.00 rental _ #PLTB - 000
Documents the design and construction of the East Building of the National Gallery of Art in Washington, D C Traces the process from blueprint to finished product.
Fine Arts
Dist - PBS **Prod** - WETATV

A Place to be all You Can be 10 MIN
16mm
Color
Shows many of the career opportunities available to young people in today's Army including dental technician, a tugboat crewperson, a Military Policewoman, a newscaster, a vehicle driver and a pilot.
Civics and Political Systems; Guidance and Counseling; Sociology
Dist - MTP **Prod** - USA

A Place to be Human 30 MIN
16mm
Color (J H C A)
Illustrates ways of humanizing and beautifying the purely commercial, bringing out the variety and value of older architecture, producing communities with individuality.
Industrial and Technical Education; Social Science
Dist - UILL **Prod** - UILL 1972

A Place to be Me 13 MIN
16mm
Color
Presents the many opportunities available to women in the U S Army. Includes such widely diverse jobs as dental technician, aviation crew chief and truck driver with emphasis on future opportunities. Stresses recreation, economical living conditions and the camaraderies that exist in the service.
Civics and Political Systems; Guidance and Counseling; Sociology
Dist - MTP **Prod** - USA

A Place to be - the Construction of the East Building of the National Gallery of Art 60 MIN
16mm
Color
LC 80-700188
Follows the creation of the East Building of the National Gallery of Art in Washington, DC, from the time it was designed by architect I M Pei to the final placement of artworks. Includes views of construction workers pouring concrete and shows meetings between artists, the architect, and museum staff.
Fine Arts; Geography - United States; Industrial and Technical Education
Dist - USNGA **Prod** - GUG 1979

A Place to be - the Construction of the East Building of the National Gallery of Art - Pt 1 30 MIN
16mm
Color
LC 80-700188
Follows the creation of the East Building of the National Gallery of Art in Washington, DC, from the time it was designed by architect I M Pei to the final placement of artworks. Includes views of construction workers pouring concrete and shows meetings between artists, the architect, and museum staff.
Fine Arts
Dist - USNGA **Prod** - GUG 1979

A Place to be Yourself 29 MIN
VHS / 16mm
Sonrisas Series
Color (T P) (SPANISH)
$46.00 rental _ #SRSS - 111
Shows how one of the children wants to be alone and how he discovers another room in the Carriage House. In Spanish and English.
Sociology
Dist - PBS

A Place to Belong 9 MIN
16mm
B&W
LC 73-700609
Tells how a community organization in a depressed neighborhood sets up a boxing association to help keep teenagers off the streets. Shows how their plans are hampered after the group loses its building to an urban renewal project.
Social Science
Dist - TEMPLU **Prod** - TEMPLU 1972

A Place to Call Home 13 MIN
16mm
Color (C A)
LC 72-702023
Shows the kinds of programs and activities offered in nursing homes which care for both the young mentally retarded and elderly residents.
Health and Safety; Psychology; Sociology
Dist - UKANS **Prod** - UKANS 1972

A Place to call home - Posadas 30 MIN
VHS
Maryknoll video magazine presents series
Color (G) (SPANISH)
$14.95 purchase
Focuses on a center in Veracruz, Mexico that provides friends, recreation and resources for young adults. Highlights the Mexican celebration of Posadas, in which Mary and Joseph search for a place to rest at the time of Jesus' birth.
Religion and Philosophy
Dist - MARYFA

A Place to Get Well 20 MIN
16mm
Color (P I)
Portrays the hospital and its routines through the eyes of a child in an effort to show children that hospitals are not to be feared. Includes doctors, nurses, the admissions procedure, the separation of child from parent, the children's ward, play therapy, meals, the operating room and other features.
Health and Safety; Sociology
Dist - MESHDO **Prod** - MESHDO 1970

A Place to Go 10 MIN
16mm
B&W
A free cinema essay on an espresso coffee house, the patrons and the proprietors, the way they look and what they do.
Fine Arts
Dist - NWUFLM **Prod** - KAJMRD 1960

A Place to Go 15 MIN
16mm / U-matic / VHS
Color (A)
LC 82-700373
Reveals the often ignored problem of wifebeating, a crime to which nearly two million American females annually fall victim. Observes women sharing their experiences and show ways communities can aid battered women. Hosted by Dan Rather and originally shown on the program 60 Minutes.
Sociology
Dist - CORF **Prod** - CORF 1981

A Place to Go 25 MIN
16mm
B&W
Discusses the adjustment of the aged to nursing homes and the role of the nurses aide in helping make that sometimes difficult adjustment possible.
Health and Safety; Psychology; Sociology
Dist - HF **Prod** - UHOSF 1966

A Place to Learn 19 MIN
16mm
Color (A)
LC 73-700692
Deals with the multipurpose services of a vital, growing community college learning resource center.
Education; Sociology
Dist - DUPAGE **Prod** - DUPAGE 1972

A Place to Live 27 MIN
16mm
Color
Tells the story of the rebirth of an American city and what the citizens accomplished between World War II and today.
Geography - United States; Psychology; Social Science; Sociology
Dist - GUG **Prod** - SLOUIS 1960

A Place to live 26 MIN
VHS
Alcohol - breaking the habit series
Color (G)
$149.00 purchase, $75.00 rental _ #UW3293
Shows how a group of recovering alcoholics are coming to terms with the elements in their environment, their personalities and their physiological makeups that caused them to become alcoholics. Looks at the steps they are learning to rejoin society. Part of a four - part series on alcoholism, how alcohol affects the body, how much alcohol can be safely consumed and how to break the alcohol habit.
Guidance and Counseling; Health and Safety; Psychology; Sociology
Dist - FOTH

Place to Live Series

Life in the Past	15 MIN
Life in the Valley	15 MIN
On the Ground	15 MIN
Spring in the Woods	15 MIN

Dist - JOU

A Place to Meet - a Way to Understand 35 MIN
16mm
Color
LC 74-705372
Documents a unique experiment in American life. Presents the idea that children and the occupational world of most adults do not need to remain apart.
Sociology
Dist - USNAC **Prod** - USSRS 1971

A Place to Meet - a Way to Understand 27 MIN
U-matic / VHS / 16mm
B&W
Explains an experiment in which two groups of children, one from the slums and another from middle income families, went into the plant of the Detroit Free Press and observed and participated in all stages of the production of the

newspaper. Shows how this brought children and adults back into each other's lives.
Guidance and Counseling; Psychology; Social Science; Sociology
Dist - CORNRS **Prod** - CUETV 1972

Place to Place 12 MIN
U-matic
Color (P)
Tells how two competing villages try to outdo one another in making a new mileage counter for an automobile executive. Introduces the concept of place value.
Mathematics
Dist - GA **Prod** - DAVFMS

A Place to Stand 11 MIN
U-matic / VHS / 16mm
Vignettes Series
Color (J)
LC 73-701781
Presents vignettes dealing with ecology, law enforcement and war to clarify the relationship between personal commitment and social responsibility.
Guidance and Counseling; Sociology
Dist - PAULST **Prod** - PAULST 1973

A Place to Work 24 MIN
16mm
Color (H)
Illustrates some of the basic factors influencing location decisions for industry in Europe, such as power, labor and marketing factors. Covers industrial linkage and inertia.
Business and Economics; Social Science
Dist - VIEWTH **Prod** - VIEWTH

A Place to Work 25 MIN
16mm
B&W
Discusses the challenges, opportunities and rewards of a career as a nurses aide.
Guidance and Counseling; Health and Safety; Psychology
Dist - HF **Prod** - UHOSF 1966

Place Value 15 MIN
U-matic / VHS
Math Cycle Series
Color (P)
Discusses place value in the base ten system.
Mathematics
Dist - GPN **Prod** - WDCNTV 1983

Place Value and Addition 30 MIN
16mm
Mathematics for Elementary School Teachers Series no 5
Color (T)
Discusses the properties of closure, commutativity and associativity under addition. Describes the additive identity. To be used following 'NUMERATION SYSTEMS.'.
Mathematics
Dist - MLA **Prod** - SMSG 1963

Place Value and Fractions 29 MIN
U-matic
Infinity Factory Series
Color (I)
Mathematics
Dist - PBS **Prod** - EDC 1976

Place Value Extended 15 MIN
U-matic / VHS
Math Cycle Series
Color (P)
Introduces students to the concepts of place value and five places in the base ten decimal system.
Mathematics
Dist - GPN **Prod** - WDCNTV

Place Value, Face Value 15 MIN
U-matic
Math Factory, Module III - Number Patterns Series
Color (P)
Explains the concept of place value and the meaning of two and three digit numbers.
Mathematics
Dist - GPN **Prod** - MAETEL 1973

Place Value - Know Your Place 20 MIN
U-matic / VHS / 16mm
Mathscore One Series
Color (I J)
Discussses aspects of place value.
Mathematics
Dist - FI **Prod** - BBCTV

Place Value - Pt 1 15 MIN
U-matic
Measure Up Series
Color (P)
Explains how to read and write numbers up to 99.
Mathematics
Dist - GPN **Prod** - WCETTV 1977

Place Value - Pt 2 15 MIN
U-matic
Measure Up Series
Color (P)
Tells how to state the order of two two - digit numbers. Explains how to complete a sequence counting by ones, twos, fives and tens.
Mathematics
Dist - GPN **Prod** - WCETTV 1977

Place Value - Pt 3 15 MIN
U-matic
Measure Up Series
Color (P)
Tells how many tens there are in sets of hundreds and how to read and write three - digit numbers.
Mathematics
Dist - GPN **Prod** - WCETTV 1977

Place Value - Take it Away 20 MIN
16mm / U-matic / VHS
Mathscore Two Series
Color (I)
Discusses aspects of place value.
Mathematics
Dist - FI **Prod** - BBCTV

Place Value - the Teens 15 MIN
U-matic
Measure Up Series
Color (P)
Explains how to read and write numbers to 20, when given sets of objects.
Mathematics
Dist - GPN **Prod** - WCETTV 1977

Place value through hundreds
VHS
Lola May's fundamental math series
Color (P I)
$45.00 purchase _ #10272VG
Shows how to state the value of each digit in a three - digit number. Teaches place value into the hundreds and how to find the rule in a sequence and then determine a missing number. Comes with a teacher's guide and blackline masters. Part 22 of a 30 - part series.
Mathematics
Dist - UNL

Place Values - Ones, Tens, Hundreds 10 MIN
U-matic / VHS / 16mm
Color (P)
$265, $185 purchase _ #4005
Shows the functions of place values in counting, illustrating the concept with cookie baking.
Mathematics
Dist - CORF

The Placement Service 27 MIN
U-matic / VHS / 16mm
Insight Series
Color (J)
Depicts two men outside the gates of heaven who must review their lives. Shows that one pompous man is proud to have done things his way and opts for a solitary suite while another man, although a sinner, opts to spend eternity trying to make others happy. Stars Jack Carter.
Guidance and Counseling; Psychology; Religion and Philosophy
Dist - PAULST **Prod** - PAULST

The Placental and Foetal Membranes 24 MIN
U-matic / VHS
Color (C A)
Demonstrates the early development of the embryo and its associated membranes. Describes how the placenta develops. Discusses placental circulation. Shows specimen fetuses in development. Illustrates fresh single and twin placentas following birth.
Health and Safety; Science - Natural
Dist - TEF **Prod** - UTORMC

Placental Circulation 18 MIN
16mm
Color (PRO)
Studies the pattern of placental vasculature and the dynamics of placental circulation, based on the results of radioangiographic studies in rhesus monkeys. Examines serial and cine radiograms after injection of a radiopaque medium into the maternal and fetal circulation.
Health and Safety
Dist - SQUIBB **Prod** - SQUIBB

Placental Circulation 20 MIN
VHS / U-matic
Color
Demonstrates the growth of endometrial sporal arteries, implantation of the blastocyst, trophoblastic penetration of the endometrium, tapping of maternal blood bessels and establishment of circulation in the intervillous space. Shows serial and cine radiograms made after injection of a radiopaque medium into the maternal or the fetal circulation or both simultaneously.
Health and Safety
Dist - AMCOG **Prod** - AMCOG

Places for the soul - the architecture of Christopher Alexander 29 MIN
VHS / 16mm
Color (H C G)
$595.00, $195.00 purchase, $45.00 rental _ #11399, #37239
Portrays original architect, thinker, and radical humanist Christopher Alexander. Reveals that he is also a passionate critic of contemporary architecture. Explores his ideas and his attempts to introduce a new approach to design and construction by focusing on two of his major projects - a school project in Japan and a shelter for the homeless in California. Produced by Ruth Landy.
Biography; Fine Arts; Religion and Philosophy
Dist - UCEMC

Places Pattern 16 MIN
16mm
PANCOM Beginning Total Communication Program for Hearing Parents of 'Series Level 1
Color (K)
LC 77-700504
Education; Guidance and Counseling; Psychology; Social Science; Sociology
Dist - JOYCE **Prod** - CSDE 1977

Places people live series

Arctic people	14 MIN
Boat families	14 MIN
Desert people	14 MIN
The Family farm	14 MIN
Forest people	13 MIN
Highland People	13 MIN
Island People	14 MIN
Mountain People	14 MIN
Plains People	14 MIN
Rainforest People	14 MIN
River people	12 MIN
Seacoast people	14 MIN

Dist - SF

Places, Places, Special Places 10 MIN
U-matic / VHS
Book, Look and Listen Series
Color (K P)
Focuses on the realization that children, as well as adults, often need a special place where they can be alone.
English Language; Literature and Drama
Dist - AITECH **Prod** - MDDE 1977

Places, Please 58 MIN
U-matic / VHS
Color (C)
$89.95 purchase _ #EX2182
Examines educational theater through the theater program at Hamden High School, Connecticut. Interweaves rehearsals and performance with interviews with teachers, students and individuals in the audience.
Education; Fine Arts
Dist - FOTH **Prod** - FOTH

Places to Visit 29 MIN
Videoreel / VT2
Children's Fair Series
B&W (K P)
Science
Dist - PBS **Prod** - WMVSTV

Places We Eat in 29 MIN
16mm
Food for Youth Series
Color
LC 76-701593
Takes a look at how children feel about their mealtime environment and discusses why they feel this way. Applies this information to school lunchrooms and discusses portion sizes for children of different ages and management of school dining rooms.
Health and Safety; Home Economics; Social Science
Dist - USNAC **Prod** - USFNS 1974

Places Where People Live 20 MIN
U-matic / VHS
Terra - Our World Series
Color (I J)
Considers the advantages and disadvantages of rural, urban and suburban living and discusses planned communities.
Science - Natural; Sociology
Dist - AITECH **Prod** - MDDE 1980

The Places within 58 MIN
VHS / 16mm / U-matic
Pride of place series
Color (C)
$40.00, $24.50 rental _ #50828; $89.95 purchase _ #EX984
Reveals how the interior space of American public places are not only functional but are also symbolic of

preoccupations with power, nature and the past. Part of an eight - part series hosted by architect Robert Stern.
Fine Arts; Geography - United States; Home Economics; Sociology
Dist - PSU **Prod** - FOTH 1986
FOTH

Placido - a Year in the Life of Placido Domingo 105 MIN
VHS
Color (G)
$19.95 purchase _ #1119
Travels around the world with Placido Domingo during a year in his busy schedule. Reveals that he had already sung a total of 1753 performances in 106 cities in 24 countries. Films Domingo in concert in opera houses in Barcelona, Milan, Madrid, Paris, London and Mexico City singing excerpts from Puccini's 'Tosca,' 'Manon Lescaut,' 'La Fanciulla Del West,' Verdi's 'Otello,' 'Ernani' and 'La Traviata.'.
Fine Arts; Geography - World
Dist - KULTUR

Placido Domingo - a musical life 90 MIN
VHS
Color (G)
$29.95 purchase_#1402
Documents every part of Placido Domingo's career and extraordinary musical life. Follows Domingo at work and at play. Includes excerpts of performances in La Traviata, Rigoletto with Carreras and Pavarotti, Lohengrin, and Perhaps Love with John Denver.
Fine Arts
Dist - KULTUR

Placido Domingo - Zarzuela royal gala concert 69 MIN
VHS
Color (G)
$24.95 purchase_#1314
Presents tenor Placido Domingo performing for King Juan Carlos of Spain and the royal family. Abounds with music and rhythms of old Spain. An all - star cast and the Ballet Espanol join the tenor in concert.
Fine Arts
Dist - KULTUR

Placido grandisimo 60 MIN
VHS
Color (G)
$24.95 purchase_#1313
Presents tenor Placido Domingo in concert with soprano Julia Migenes at Seville Stadium. Features Domingo and Migenes singing duets of favorite Spanish songs and an aria from Carmen. Also features Ms. Migenes singing a selectionfrom Puccini's La Rondine and Summertime from Gershwin's Porgy & Bess.
Fine Arts
Dist - KULTUR

Placido in Prague 94 MIN
VHS
Color (G)
$19.95 purchase_#1405
Stars tenor Placido Domingo in concert at the Prague Concert Hall in the new Czech Republic. Features also soprano Angela Gheorghiu joining Domingo in performing selections from favorite operas including arias and duets by Puccini, Verdi, Donizetti, Mozart and others.
Fine Arts
Dist - KULTUR

Placing the right man on the job 13 MIN
16mm
Problems in supervision series
B&W (SPANISH)
LC 74-705373
Dramatizes cases of five different workers who are unsatisfactory in their jobs and are reassigned to positions more suitable to their abilities and capacities.
Business and Economics; Psychology
Dist - USNAC **Prod** - USOE 1944

Plagiarism 10 MIN
16mm
Color (G)
$25.00 rental
Pulsates with the New York 'language poets' on their own turf. Presents a raw documentary featuring Bruce Andrews and Charles Bernstein, co - editors of L=A=N=G=U=A=G=E, James Sherry and Hanna Weiner. Produced by Henry Hills.
Fine Arts; Literature and Drama
Dist - CANCIN

Plague in Sylvatic Areas 26 MIN
16mm
Color
LC FIE61-17
Traces the world history of plague and its introduction into the United States. Explains the importance of the control of transmission agents, including the rodent - borne fleas. Discusses methods of rapid diagnosis and treatment.
Health and Safety
Dist - USNAC **Prod** - USPHS 1961

Plague of Locusts 45 MIN
U-matic / VHS
Color (C)
$279.00, $179.00 purchase _ #AD - 2125
Looks at an exceptionally severe outbreak of locusts which is endangering large areas surrounding the Sahara Desert and which also threatens the Western Hemisphere. Reveals that the species, which normally infests a region for several years, has adapted to route efforts to control it. Huge swarms have crossed the Atlantic and invaded some Caribbean territory and may threaten global food supplies.
Agriculture; Geography - World; Home Economics; Science - Natural; Social Science
Dist - FOTH **Prod** - FOTH

A Plague on Our Children - Pt 1 - Dioxins 57 MIN
U-matic / VHS / 16mm
Nova Series
Color (H C A)
LC 79-701710
Discusses Dioxins defoliants, like Sylvex sprayed on Oregon forests or Agent Orange dropped on Vietnam, which have caused miscarriages, cancers and disease. Looks at studies which show these herbicides cause serious health problems and describes theories that the Dioxin molecules fit into the basic DNA structure, altering it and causing mutations.
Business and Economics; Health and Safety; Sociology
Dist - TIMLIF **Prod** - WGBHTV 1980

A Plague on Our Children - Pt 2 - PCBs 57 MIN
U-matic / VHS / 16mm
Nova Series
Color (H C A)
LC 79-701710
Discusses how banning toxic chemicals has not solved the problem because no solution has been found to clean up chemical dumps or to break down their non - biogradable structure. Points out that over 90 per cent of all toxic wastes are dumped unsafely, illegally and secretly. Discusses the Hooker Chemical and Plastic Company in Love Canal, New York, which knew toxic chemicals were leaking out of drums they had buried on land they had sold for a school playground.
Business and Economics; Health and Safety; Sociology
Dist - TIMLIF **Prod** - WGBHTV 1980

A Plague upon the Land 24 MIN
Videoreel / VHS
Color (I J H C A)
Talks about the cause of 'river blindness' in West Africa, and international efforts to eradicate the disease.
Health and Safety; Sociology
Dist - CWS **Prod** - WORLDB 1984

A Plague upon the land 24 MIN
VHS
Color; PAL (I J H A)
$35.95 purchase _ #30918
Depicts the economic and social upheaval that comes with the occurrence of 'river blindness.' Focuses on West Africa where as many as 75 percent of a village can be infected by the debililating disease. In other villages, adult men are so incapacitated that they can no longer work and young boys must shoulder their responsibilities. Features experts who comment on the results of a massive international program to eradicate the illness. Includes teaching notes.
Geography - World; Guidance and Counseling; Health and Safety; Sociology
Dist - WB **Prod** - WB

Plagues 60 MIN
VHS
Color (G)
$59.95 purchase _ #PLAG - 000
Reviews the history of epidemics such as Spanish flu and malaria, giving historical and scientific background. Compares AIDS to past epidemics. Hosted by medical historian Dr. Baruch Blumberg.
Health and Safety
Dist - PBS **Prod** - WHYY 1988

Plain Indexing and Cutting a Spur Gear 26 MIN
16mm
Machine Shop Work - Operations on the Milling Machine Series no 4
B&W
LC FIE51-521
Explains diametral pitch and the parts of a gear tooth, the use of the dividing head for spacing teeth and the operations of a milling machine in the cutting of a spur gear.
Industrial and Technical Education
Dist - USNAC **Prod** - USOE 1941

Plain Journal Bearings 60 MIN
U-matic / VHS
Mechanical Equipment Maintenance, Module 4 - Bearings and 'Lubrication Series
Color (IND)
Industrial and Technical Education
Dist - LEIKID **Prod** - LEIKID

A Plain White Envelope 20 MIN
U-matic / VHS / 16mm
Color; B&W (I J)
LC FIA66-12
Tells the story of a boy who, wanting very badly to win a spelling contest, accidentally finds a white envelope with the contest words inside and faces the problem of cheating.
English Language; Guidance and Counseling; Psychology
Dist - PHENIX **Prod** - UMCOM 1965

Plain Wrap Exercise - Men 43 MIN
BETA / VHS
Color
Presents a series of exercises for men which can be done in the home.
Physical Education and Recreation
Dist - MOHOMV **Prod** - MOHOMV

Plain Wrap Exercise - Women 50 MIN
BETA / VHS
Color
Presents a home fitness program for women. Includes exercises such as wall stretches, indoor running, leg raises, push - ups and sit - ups.
Physical Education and Recreation
Dist - MOHOMV **Prod** - MOHOMV

The Plains 28 MIN
16mm
Spadework for History Series
Color (C A)
Tells of the problems involved in the excavation by the Smithsonian Institution of a fortified earth - lodge village of prehistoric Indians on the Missouri River in South Dakota in the Oahe Reservoir area. Shows at first hand how the archeologist decides where and how to dig in order to gain maximum amount of information from an archeological site.
Geography - United States; History - World; Science - Physical; Social Science; Sociology
Dist - UTEX **Prod** - UTEX 1963

The Plains 30 MIN
VHS / 16mm
Our Natural Heritage Series
Color (G)
$14.44 purchase _ #HSV4028
Explores lifestyles of flora and fauna in deserts, prairies, and meadows.
Psychology; Science - Natural
Dist - EDUCRT

The Plains 30 MIN
U-matic / VHS
Land and the People Series
Color
Explores the relationship between what people know, see and do and the plains around them.
Science - Natural
Dist - MDCPB **Prod** - EKC

Plains and Plateaus 10 MIN
16mm / U-matic / VHS
Color; B&W (P I)
LC FIA68-1967
Uses maps of several areas of the United States to depict the physical features which distinguish plains and plateaus. Illustrates the effects which the physical features have on land uses for each landform.
Science - Natural; Science - Physical; Social Science
Dist - IU **Prod** - IU 1968

Plains and Plateaus 10 MIN
16mm
Color (J H C G)
Discusses how plains and plateaus were formed and how their characteristics affect the population, transport, and the location of towns and industries. Illustrates concepts with examples from North America.
Geography - World
Dist - VIEWTH **Prod** - GATEEF

Plains Indian Girl 13 MIN
16mm
Color (P I J H)
Presents an Indian girl who hears stories of her ancestors, sees dances and imagines herself living in olden times, but decides it is more fun to be an Indian today.
Literature and Drama; Social Science
Dist - YALEDV **Prod** - YALEDV

Plains People 14 MIN
16mm
Places People Live Series
Color (I)
LC 78-713009
Describes the life of the Masai, a proud tribe of semi - nomadic herdsmen who live along the great Rift Valley of Kenya and Tanganyika and subsist on the milk, meat and blood of their livestock. Compares the way of life of the Cheyenne and Crow Indians living on the North Cheyenne Reservation in southeastern Montana for whom the ranch is a family enterprise and everyone works for it.
Psychology; Science - Natural; Social Science; Sociology
Dist - SF **Prod** - SF

Plainsmen of the Past 30 MIN
16mm
Great Plains Trilogy, 2 Series Nomad and Indians - Early Man on the 'Plains; Nomad and Indians - early man on the plains
B&W (H C A)
Traces the prehistory of the Great Plains, from the entrance of man to the arrival of the Europeans. Shows how archaeologists work, presenting photographs, diagrams, specimens and interpretations of finds.
History - United States; Science - Physical; Social Science
Dist - UNEBR **Prod** - KUONTV 1954

Plaintiff and Defendant Opening Statements 37 MIN
U-matic / VHS
Trial of a Civil Lawsuit Series
Color (PRO)
Civics and Political Systems
Dist - ABACPE **Prod** - SBWI

The Plan 54 MIN
U-matic / VHS / 16mm
Color
Documents the everyday life story of Utah's 'Young Mother Of The Year' for 1978, Michele Meservy. Follows this young Mormon mother's attempts to organize and control the chaos created by five young children aged five, four, three, two and ten months.
Sociology
Dist - CNEMAG **Prod** - CNEMAG 1980

A Plan for Living 29 MIN
16mm
Giving Birth and Independence Series
Color (H C A)
LC 81-701580
Dramatizes the problems of parents with handicapped children, focusing on parental guilt and the negative effects that these can have on marriage and family life. Concludes showing the parents seeking genetic counseling.
Education; Home Economics; Sociology
Dist - LAWREN **Prod** - JRLLL 1981

A Plan for Living 17 MIN
16mm
Color
LC 78-701631
Presents a parody dealing with the transformation of a man from a failure to a success.
Fine Arts
Dist - MORBRA **Prod** - MORBRA 1978

Plan for Prevention 10 MIN
16mm
Safety Management Series
Color
Business and Economics; Health and Safety
Dist - NSC **Prod** - NSC

Plan for Security 12 MIN
VHS / U-matic
Professional Security Training Series Module 1B
Color
Presents security as an organized approach to preventing loss of assets. Observes how security works, how the tools of security are used and how the security officer is the vital link in the total protection plan.
Health and Safety; Sociology
Dist - CORF **Prod** - CORF

Plan for Tomorrow 29 MIN
Videoreel / VT2
Environment - Today and Tomorrow Series
Color
Science - Natural; Sociology
Dist - PBS **Prod** - KRMATV

Plan, Till and Plant 30 MIN
VHS / U-matic
Corn - Planning to Harvest Series
Color
Details a series of management decisions which need to be made before the corn is planted. Demonstrates the best compromise of weed, moisture and erosion control, and discusses selection of the proper variety of seed and planting procedures.
Agriculture
Dist - NETCHE **Prod** - NETCHE 1981

Plan your dream wedding 80 MIN
VHS
Color (G)
$24.95 purchase _ #HT04
Covers everything from choosing the ring to choosing the honeymoon.
Sociology
Dist - SVIP

Plan your slinging 16 MIN
VHS
Color; PAL; NTSC (G IND)
PdS57, PdS67 purchase
Demonstrates precautions and planning necessary in the professional movement of equipment and materials which require a 'sling.' Illustrates the full lifting procedure laid out in seven significant steps - which sling to use, what signals to give the crane driver and how to move a load safely.
Health and Safety
Dist - CFLVIS

The Planar double pendulum 28 MIN
U-matic / VHS / BETA
Color; PAL (G H C)
PdS50, PdS58 purchase
Uses the examples of the planar double pendulum to demonstrate the principle of chaotic behavior. Features computer graphics to show periodic, quasi periodic and chaotic motion and to generate a Poincare section that illustrates how to distinguish between these motions.
Computer Science; Mathematics
Dist - EDPAT **Prod** - IWIF

Plane Crash 8 MIN
16mm
Spanish Newsreel Series Vol 45, no 54
B&W (SPANISH)
A Spanish language film. Shows the Polaris missile launching from the USS Ethan Allen, John Glenn's address to Congress and the American Airlines astrojet crossing.
Foreign Language
Dist - TWCF **Prod** - TWCF

Plane Geometry 20 MIN
U-matic
Mainly Math Series
Color (H C)
Explains and identifies basic geometric elements and relationships.
Mathematics
Dist - GPN **Prod** - WCVETV 1977

Plane Sense 19 MIN
16mm 20 MIN
Color
LC 74-705376
Acquaints the prospective pilot and airplane owner with the fundamentals of owning and operating an airplane. Offers hints about buying a used aircraft, outlines responsibilities in maintaining and recording the maintenance of the aircraft and engine and shows how to keep abreast of current FAA regulations concerning the operation and maintenance of an airplane.
Social Science
Dist - USNAC **Prod** - FAAFL 1968

Planer, Disc Sander, Drill Press, Grinder Safety
VHS / 35mm strip
Wood Safety Series
$28.00 purchase _ #TX1B8 filmstrip, $58.00 purchase _ #TX1B8V VHS
Teaches safety and use of the planer, disc sander, drill press, and grinder.
Industrial and Technical Education
Dist - CAREER **Prod** - CAREER

Planes 14 MIN
16mm
Hand Tools for Wood Working Series
Color (J H A)
Planes for wood work - - construction of common planes, jack plane, smoothing plane, jointer planes, block plane, rabbet plane and router plane.
Industrial and Technical Education
Dist - SF **Prod** - MORLAT 1967

Planes 15 MIN
VHS / U-matic / 16mm
Goofy's field trips series
Color (P)
$425.00, $280.00 purchase _ #JC - 67244
Stars Goofy who takes two youngsters on a behind - the - scenes tour of an airport where they investigate both passenger and cargo transportation. Teaches about the many types of airport workers and services. Looks at safety procedures, piloting, and the importance of the control tower. Part of a series on transportation.
Industrial and Technical Education; Social Science
Dist - CORF **Prod** - DISNEY 1989

Planes in the Sky, Ships in the Sea 28 MIN
16mm
Color
LC 74-705377
Portrays the role of the Naval Ships Research and Development Center and affiliated laboratories in developing modern Naval ships and equipment.
Civics and Political Systems; Industrial and Technical Education; Social Science
Dist - USNAC **Prod** - USN 1970

The Planet Earth - a Scientific Model 24 MIN
U-matic / VHS / 16mm
Color (H C A)
Uses a three - dimensional model of the earth - moon system and animation to give a truer picture of the earth's place and movements in the solar system. Reconstructs the classic Foucault pendulum experiment by hanging a pendulum from the dome of St Paul's Cathedral in London.
Science; Science - Physical
Dist - MEDIAG **Prod** - MEDIAG 1981

Planet Earth, our home - Video 5 47 MIN
VHS
Earth and space science - secrets of science series
Color (I J H C)
$49.95 purchase
Presents two parts in two segments each, overviewing the physical and chemical characteristics of Earth, the causes of air pollution, global warming and ozone destruction, how waste is contaminating the Earth, and the physics of earthquakes. Includes There's No Place Like Home and Polluting Our Atmosphere in Part I, Wasting Our Planet and When the Ground Quakes in Part II. Hosted by Discover Magazine Editor in Chief Paul Hoffman. First of five parts on Earth and space science.
Science - Physical; Sociology
Dist - EFVP **Prod** - DSCOVM 1994

Planet earth series
Presents the complete seven - part Planet Earth series. Features atmospheric chemist James Lovelock - creator of the Gaia theory, geologist James Hayes - predictor of future ice ages, astrophysicist Rich Mulle, who postulated the death star theory, and physicist Robin Stebbins - discoverer of sunquakes.
The Blue planet - Part 2 60 MIN
The Climate puzzle - Part 3 60 MIN
Fate of the Earth - Pt 7 60 MIN
Gifts from the sea - Part 5 60 MIN
The Living machine - Part 1 60 MIN
The Solar sea - Part 6 60 MIN
Tales from other worlds - Part 4 60 MIN
Dist - ANNCPB **Prod** - WQED 1994

Planet Earth Series
The Blue planet 60 MIN
The Climate puzzle 60 MIN
Fate of the Earth 60 MIN
Gifts from the Earth 60 MIN
The Living machine 60 MIN
The Solar Sea 60 MIN
Tales from Other Worlds 60 MIN
Dist - FI

Planet for the taking series
Mythmakers 52 MIN
A Planet for the Taking - Vol I 105 MIN
A Planet for the Taking - Vol II 106 MIN
A Planet for the Taking - Vol III 105 MIN
A Planet for the Taking - Vol IV 105 MIN
The Runaway brain 52 MIN
Dist - FI

A Planet for the Taking - Vol I 105 MIN
VHS
Planet for the Taking Series
Color (S)
$198.00 purchase _ #386 - 9001, #386 - 9002
Chronicles the strange paradox on earth - instead of working with nature, humans have always tried to master it, a tendency that could result in the destruction of all living things. Reveals that at the same time, our growing technology yields wondrous insights into the mysteries of matter and life. Volume I of four volumes has two parts. 'Human Nature' looks at the origins of the human species, the biological links with other life - forms, and the evolution of the tools that enabled humans to dominate the entire planet. 'Mythmakers' uncovers the foundations of science which have formed our ideas about human origins and destiny.
History - World; Religion and Philosophy; Science; Science - Natural; Science - Physical
Dist - FI **Prod** - CANBC 1988

A Planet for the Taking - Vol II 106 MIN
VHS
Planet for the Taking Series
Color (S)
$198.00 purchase _ #386 - 9003, #386 - 9004
Chronicles the strange paradox on earth - instead of working with nature, humans have always tried to master it, a tendency that could result in the destruction of all living things. Reveals that at the same time, our growing technology yields wondrous insights into the mysteries of matter and life. Volume II of four volumes has two parts. 'Subdue The Earth' shows how humans see themselves as supreme over all other forms of life in a relentless battle for survival. Suggests the natural order could be peaceful coexistence. 'Who Needs Nature' explores the human exploitation of animals - bullfights, experimentation, pets - the impulse to love, the desire to dominate.
Science - Natural; Science - Physical; Sociology
Dist - FI **Prod** - CANBC 1988

A Planet for the Taking - Vol III 105 MIN
VHS
Planet for the Taking Series
Color (S)
$198.00 purchase _ #386 - 9005, #386 - 9006
Chronicles the strange paradox on earth - instead of working with nature, humans have always tried to master it, a tendency that could result in the destruction of all living things. Reveals that at the same time, our growing technology yields wondrous insights into the mysteries of matter and life. Volume III of four volumes has two parts. 'The Ultimate Slavery' reveals that for thousands of years we have bred animals to serve us. This program suggests that humans, too, may be willingly enslaved by the same forces of science and technology. 'Improving On Nature' considers that in most of the world, the birth and survival of each child still depends on nature. In Western society, science is intervening more and more in human reproduction.
Health and Safety; Psychology; Science - Natural; Science - Physical; Sociology
Dist - FI **Prod** - CANBC 1988

A Planet for the Taking - Vol IV 105 MIN
VHS
Planet for the Taking Series
Color (S)
$198.00 purchase _ #386 - 9007, #386 - 9008
Chronicles the strange paradox on earth - instead of working with nature, humans have always tried to master it, a tendency that could result in the destruction of all living things. Reveals that at the same time, our growing technology yields wondrous insights into the mysteries of matter and life. Volume IV of four volumes has two parts. 'At War With Death' considers Western Culture's isolation from the concept of death, unlike other cultures. Is death a challenge for science to conquer, or a reminder that our power to control has limits? 'The Runaway Brain' asks if humans can begin to see themselves not as the dominators, but as just one part of the complex pattern of life on earth.
Science - Natural; Science - Physical; Sociology
Dist - FI **Prod** - CANBC 1988

Planet Mars 29 MIN
16mm
Color
LC 79-701510
Discusses what has been learned about Mars from Earth - based telescopes, observations from the fly - by Mariner spacecraft, and through the Viking landing and orbiter experiments.
History - World; Science - Physical
Dist - USNAC **Prod** - NASA 1979

Planet Ocean 15 MIN
16mm
Color
LC 75-703530
Shows how oceans of liquid water make the Earth a unique life sustaining environment.
Science - Natural
Dist - GRAF **Prod** - GRAF 1975

The Planet of Junior Brown
35mm strip / VHS / Cassette
Newbery Award - Winners Series
Color (I)
$66.00, $14.00 purchase
English Language; Literature and Drama
Dist - PELLER

Planet of man series
Animal, vegetable, mineral 29 MIN
Cosmic Connection 29 MIN
Jigsaw fit 26 MIN
Mountain Heritage - the Appalachians 29 MIN
Sharks - terror, truth, death 28 MIN
Shield of plenty 29 MIN
Trail of the Ice Age Blues 29 MIN
Uneventful Day 29 MIN
Dist - FI

The Planet of Maze 30 MIN
U-matic
Read all about it - One Series
Color (I)
Teaches reading and writing skills as it continues a story in which Chris's friends Sam and Lynne help Chris and his uncle escape from the dreaded Planet of Maze by answering the riddling questions of Mistress Maze.
Education; English Language; Literature and Drama
Dist - TVOTAR **Prod** - TVOTAR 1982

Planet phylon series
Syllabication skills, Pt 2 15 MIN
Dist - GPN

Planet pylon series
Adjectives 15 MIN
Antonyms and synonyms 15 MIN
Capitalization 15 MIN
Contractions 15 MIN
General Review 15 MIN
Homophones 15 MIN
Long Vowel Sounds 15 MIN
Nouns 15 MIN
Parts of a Book 15 MIN
Past - Present Tense 15 MIN
Plurals - S, Ss, Ch, Sh, Z, F - Ves, O - Oes 15 MIN
Possessives - nouns and pronouns 15 MIN
Prefixes and suffixes - Pt 2 15 MIN
Prefixes and Suffixes, Pt 1 15 MIN
Pronouns 15 MIN
Sentences - telling and asking 15 MIN
Short vowel sounds 15 MIN
Silent Letters - Kn, Wh, Wr, Mb 15 MIN
Syllabication Skills, Pt 1 15 MIN
Three Rules (1 - 1 - 1, Doubling, Silent E) 15 MIN
Verbs 15 MIN
Dist - GPN

The Planet that Got Knocked on its Side 58 MIN
U-matic / VHS
Nova Series
Color (H C A)
$250 purchase _ #5122C
Discusses the scientific information and theories about the planet Uranus. Produced by WGBH Boston.
Science - Physical
Dist - CORF

Planet water 15 MIN
VHS
Our wondrous oceans series
CC; Color (I J)
$69.95 purchase _ #10401VG
Explores ocean currents, the water cycle, and how humans have affected the oceans. Looks at the properties of water. Comes with an interactive video quiz, teacher's guide and a set of blackline masters. Part two of a two - part series.
Geography - World; Science - Natural; Science - Physical
Dist - UNL

Planetaria - Let's Go to the Planetarium 20 MIN
VHS
(I J)
$50 purchase
Explains planetaria to sixth through ninth grade level students. Focuses on space and astronomy. Narrated by Pat Boone.
Science - Physical
Dist - GPN

Planetary Circulation of the Atmosphere 28 MIN
16mm
B&W
LC 75-702522
Uses simple laboratory experiments to illustrate planetary circulation of heat, the ultimate source of heat, the action of gravity on latitudinal density and the relationship of the rotation of the earth to planetary circulation.
Science; Science - Physical
Dist - MLA **Prod** - EDS 1968

Planetary Gears, Principles of Operation - Pt 1 - Single Sets 18 MIN
16mm
B&W
Describes the use and operation of planetary gears, covering the basic components, the laws of mechanical operation and the results. Uses a scale model to show the mechanics of planetary gears.
Science - Physical
Dist - USNAC **Prod** - USA 1953

Planetary Gears, Principles of Operation - Pt 2 - Multiple Sets 15 MIN
16mm
B&W
LC FIE53-629
Uses a scale model to show the principles of operation governing multiple sets of planetary gears.
Science - Physical
Dist - USNAC **Prod** - USA 1953

Planetary Motion 9 MIN
16mm / VHS
Color (C)
$80.00, $34.95 purchase _ #194 E 0081, 193 E 2081
Demonstrates with specially constructed animation Keppler's three laws of planetary motion.
Science - Physical
Dist - WARDS **Prod** - AAS

Planetary motion 10 MIN
VHS
Astronomy series
Color (J H)
$34.95 purchase _ #193 W 0054
Studies Kepler's three laws of planetary motion. Uses dramatic animation complimented by specially created artwork. Part of a six - part series presenting a single concept about astronomy.
Science; Science - Physical
Dist - WARDS **Prod** - WARDS

Planetary Motion and Kepler's Laws 8 MIN
16mm
Explorations in Space and Time Series
Color (H C A)
LC 75-703979
Uses computer animation to examine the dynamic properties of the solar system. Relates these dynamics to Kepler's laws of planetary motion.
Science - Physical
Dist - HMC **Prod** - HMC 1974

Planetary motion, Keppler's laws 10 MIN
VHS
Astronomy series
Color (J H)
$24.95 purchase _ #S9102
Examines planetary motion in relationship to Keppler's laws. Part of a six - part series on astronomy using single - concept format and incorporating NASA footage.
Science - Physical
Dist - HUBDSC **Prod** - HUBDSC

Planetary Motions and Space Travel 10 MIN
16mm / U-matic / VHS
Color (I J)
LC 72-711111
Consists of an animated film that explains and shows the effect of the planets' orbits upon the projected routes toward them. Uses diagrams to describe these routes.
Science - Physical
Dist - PHENIX **Prod** - DOUGDR 1971

A Planetary Village 30 MIN
VHS / 16mm
Conquest of Space Series
Color (G)
Discusses the growing network of communications satellites.
Fine Arts; Industrial and Technical Education
Dist - FLMWST

Planets 24 MIN
16mm / U-matic / VHS
Space Science Series
Color (I J H)
$540, $250 purchase _ #4618C
Discusses the solar system and the space probes used to investigate it.
Science - Physical
Dist - CORF

The Planets 52 MIN
U-matic / VHS / 16mm
Color (H C A)
LC 78-700570
Looks at America's space program. Discusses the objectives of NASA, the results of its space flights and techniques used, such as space photography, communication and radiometric dating. Includes accounts of the geologic history of the moon and the planning of the U S Viking mission.
Science; Science - Physical
Dist - FI **Prod** - BBCTV 1976

The Planets 11 MIN
16mm / U-matic / VHS
Color (I J)
LC FIA67-1681
Discusses the movements of the planets around the sun, describing their comparative sizes, solar distances, axial rotations and satellite systems.
Science - Physical
Dist - IFB **Prod** - EDMNDS 1961

Planets 20 MIN
Videodisc / VHS
Earth science videolab series
Color (J H)
$179.95, 149.95 purchase _ #Q18547
Features an interdisciplinary, multi - learning approach to space studies. Explains planetary motion and the processes that created the planets. Demonstrates how to create a scale model of the solar system. Includes hands - on activities, teacher's guide, and enough materials to teach multiple sections of students. Part of a series of five programs.
Science
Dist - CF

Planets in Orbit - the Laws of Kepler 10 MIN
U-matic / VHS / 16mm
B&W (J H)
Explains some of the ancient beliefs regarding the movements of the planets. Shows how Tycho Brahe made the first accurate measurements of the position of the stars. Explains Kepler's work and his laws.
Science - Physical
Dist - EBEC **Prod** - EBEC 1960

Planets Mars and Mercury 52 MIN
VHS
Color (G)
$29.95 purchase _ #V8
Traces the evolving, sometimes imaginative theories about Mars from its discovery in 1669 to the historic Viking landing on its surface in the first program. Reveals planet Mercury in startling detail with photographs and finds from the Mariner 10 mission in the second. Includes animation, high - resolution photography and geological comparisons of both planets.
Science - Physical
Dist - INSTRU

Planets - new discoveries 20 MIN
VHS
Color (J H)
$64.95 purchase _ #GW - 5125 - VS
Offers the latest information on the celestial neighbors of Earth based on the newest generation of high tech space probes. Combines animated sequences with recent Voyager, Magellan and Galileo imagery.
History - World; Science - Physical
Dist - HRMC **Prod** - SCTRES

Planets - new discoveries 20 MIN
Videodisc / VHS
Earth sciences video library series
Color (J H)
$99.95, $69.95 purchase _ #ES8520
Travels through the solar system. Includes recent photos from Voyager, Magellan and Galileo and dramatic computer - simulated fly - bys of Mars and Venus. Part of a series which takes a contemporary look at Planet Earth, its natural resources and the human impact on the global environment.
Industrial and Technical Education; Science - Physical
Dist - INSTRU

Planets - new discoveries 20 MIN
Videodisc / VHS
Earth science library series
Color (J H)
$99.95, $69.95 purchase _ #Q18522
Combines animated sequences with recent Voyager, Magellan and Galileo imagery to explain the latest scientific discoveries about the solar system. Includes teacher's guide.
Science - Physical
Dist - CF

Planets of Gas 26 MIN
U-matic / VHS
Planets Series
Color (C)
$249.00, $149.00 purchase _ #AD - 1146
Reveals that Galileo was the first to study Jupiter in detail, which is why they space probe of Jupiter is named after him. Features NASA scientist Richard Terrile who discusses the rings of Jupiter. Part of a seven - part series on planets.
History - World; Industrial and Technical Education; Science - Physical
Dist - FOTH **Prod** - FOTH

Planets of the Sun 9 MIN
U-matic / VHS / 16mm
Color (I J)
Uses special effects to simulate a trip through the solar system. Examines the characteristics of the sun and its planets. Narated by Leonard Nimoy.
Science - Physical
Dist - AIMS **Prod** - DEADYK 1974

Planets series
The Angry red planet 26 MIN
Are we alone 26 MIN
The Blue planet 26 MIN
Mercury and Venus 26 MIN
Planets of Gas 26 MIN
The Search for Planet X 26 MIN
Dist - FOTH

Planing a Dovetail Slide 28 MIN
16mm
B&W
LC FIE51-574
Demonstrates how to set up the workpiece, cutting tools and machine, make rough and finished cuts in the clearance slot and make angle cuts.
Industrial and Technical Education
Dist - USNAC **Prod** - USOE 1945

Planing a flat surface 22 MIN
16mm
Machine shop work - operations on the planer series
B&W (SPANISH)
LC FIE51-575
Explains the function of a planer. Shows how to mount the workpiece, set the tool and table for the cut and make a first and second roughing cut and a first and second finishing cut.
Industrial and Technical Education
Dist - USNAC **Prod** - USOE 1945

Planing Machines
VHS
Woodworking Power Tools Series
(C G)
$59.00 _ CA184
Demonstrates the handling and operation of planing machines.
Industrial and Technical Education
Dist - AAVIM **Prod** - AAVIM 1989

Planing Machines 15 MIN
VHS / BETA
Woodworking Power Tools Series
Color (IND)
Industrial and Technical Education; Psychology
Dist - RMIBHF **Prod** - RMIBHF

Planing Rough Surfaces to Dimensions 17 MIN
16mm
B&W
LC FIE52-53
Describes how to prepare wood for planing and how to plane stock to uniform thickness, determine the amount of cut to be made, regulate the speed of feeding and adjust the surfacer to cut straight surfaces.
Industrial and Technical Education
Dist - USNAC **Prod** - USOE 1945

Plankton 12 MIN
U-matic / VHS / 16mm
Bio - Science Series
Color (H C A)
Offers a view of the wondrous variety of plants and animals which compose the ocean's plankton community. Takes a close look at 'plankton soup' and reveals what some of these forms of marine life look life and how they function. Shows how planktonic plants and animals are joined in complex food webs, with planktonic plants at the bottom of a web that may end with planktonic animals as large and complex as jellyfish.
Science - Natural
Dist - NGS **Prod** - NGS 1976

Plankton and the Open Sea 19 MIN
U-matic / VHS / 16mm
Biology Series Unit 2 - Ecosystems; Unit 2 - Ecosystems
Color; B&W (H)
Pictures typical forms of plankton and demonstrates the importance of minute plankton organisms to marine food chains. Photomicrography and laboratory experiments show how plankton is studied.
Science; Science - Natural
Dist - EBEC **Prod** - EBEC 1962

Plankton - Floaters and Drifters 30 MIN
VHS / U-matic
Oceanus - the Marine Environment Series Lesson 15
Color
Contrasts planktonic and nektonic lifestyles. Discusses the places on earth where plankton is most successful and abundant.
Science - Natural; Science - Physical
Dist - CDTEL **Prod** - SCCON

Plankton - Floaters and Drifters 28 MIN
U-matic / VHS
Oceanus - the Marine Environment Series
Color (C A)
Science - Natural; Science - Physical
Dist - SCCON **Prod** - SCCON 1980

Plankton - Life of the Sea 25 MIN
16mm
Color
LC 74-706552
Shows how the study of plankton is making major contributions toward an understanding of the ocean environment.
Science - Natural; Science - Physical
Dist - USNAC **Prod** - USN 1972

Plankton - The Breathing sea 26 MIN
VHS / U-matic / 16mm
Color (H G)
$280.00, $330.00, $475.00 purchase, $50.00 rental
Features a comprehensive exploration of plankton and sub - plankton, including recent studies on how they have altered knowledge of the sea, of evolution, of weather patterns and the environment.
Science - Natural; Science - Physical
Dist - NDIM **Prod** - CANBC 1986

Planned Economy - a Solution 30 MIN
U-matic
Realities
Color (A)
Delves into the political, social, economic and cultural trends of the 1980s. Probes a wide range of contemporary concerns. Each segment includes a guest speaker who is an expert in the field under discussion.
Business and Economics; Civics and Political Systems; Social Science; Sociology
Dist - TVOTAR **Prod** - TVOTAR 1985

Planned obsolessons 6 MIN
16mm
Color (G)
$10.00 rental
Witnesses a crowd of champagne - riddled art patrons reacting to the unveiling of a fountain sculpted by Richard See and the filmmaker; the fountain collapsed the night this film premiered.
Fine Arts
Dist - CANCIN **Prod** - WENDTD 1972

Planned Parenthood 9 MIN
16mm
B&W (I)
Contrasts the unhappy life of a large family with the happiness of a small one that has chosen to limit its size voluntarily. Emphasizes the need for planned parenthood.
Guidance and Counseling; Sociology
Dist - NEDINF **Prod** - INDIA

Planned Pethood 5 MIN
16mm
Color
Describes problems of pet parenthood and shows how to help prevent the birth of unwanted cats and dogs that will probably have to be destroyed.
Guidance and Counseling; Science - Natural
Dist - MTP **Prod** - AMVMA

Planned re - entry 25 MIN
U-matic / VHS
Caring community - alcoholism and drug abuse series
Color
Explains the on - going nature of the recovery process of the chemically dependent and the need to plan for its long - term implementation.
Psychology; Sociology
Dist - VTRI **Prod** - VTRI

A planned response 20 MIN
VHS
Color (A R)
$12.50 purchase _ #S11763
Describes the different forms of stewardship available to Missouri Synod Lutherans - regular congregational giving, Church Extension Fund investments, and wills and deferred gifts through the LCMS Foundation.
Guidance and Counseling; Literature and Drama; Religion and Philosophy
Dist - CPH **Prod** - LUMIS

Planned Workplace Inspections - Hotel and Food Service 9 MIN
VHS / 16mm
Color (A IND)
LC 91705454
Promotes safety in hotel and food service by detailing the three steps recommeded in any safety inspection - what to do before the inspection, during the inspection, and afterwards.
Health and Safety; Psychology
Dist - IFB

Planned Workplace Inspections - Municipal 10 MIN
VHS / 16mm
Color (A IND)
LC 91705463
Promotes safety awareness in the municipal workplace by detailing the steps recommended in any safety inspection - what to do before the inspection, during the inspection, and afterwards.

Health and Safety; Psychology
Dist - IFB

Planned workshop inspections - hotel & food service 9 MIN
16mm / VHS / BETA / U-matic
Color; PAL (IND)
PdS110, PdS118 purchase
Provides specific steps for safety inspection - before, during and after.
Health and Safety; Industrial and Technical Education; Social Science
Dist - EDPAT

Planning 15 MIN
VHS / U-matic / BETA
Job Catch Series
Color; Stereo (H)
Shows planning means preparation for a successful campaign to get a job. This covers creative paperwork preparation reports, references, resumes, letters, clear picture of the job, and clear picture of self to present to employer.
Guidance and Counseling
Dist - SEVDIM **Prod** - SEVDIM 1985

Planning 9 MIN
VHS / U-matic
Management of Work Series Module 2
Color
Shows what planning is, why it's so important and discusses both short - range and long - range planning.
Business and Economics; Psychology
Dist - RESEM **Prod** - RESEM

Planning 20 MIN
U-matic / VHS
Effective Manager Series
Color
Business and Economics; Guidance and Counseling; Psychology
Dist - DELTAK **Prod** - DELTAK

Planning 20 MIN
U-matic
Calling Captain Consumer Series
Color (P I J)
Emphasizes the necessity of planning before shopping.
Business and Economics; Home Economics
Dist - TVOTAR **Prod** - TVOTAR 1985

Planning
VHS / U-matic
Essentials of Management Series Unit II; Unit II
Color
Teaches managers and supervisors how they can apply planning procedures to their daily work and job and how they can participate in planning the work of their own management team.
Business and Economics; Psychology
Dist - AMA **Prod** - AMA

Planning 27 MIN
VHS
Minding my own business series
Color (G)
$225.00 purchase
Features women entrepreneurs who have developed businesses. Discusses their planning before starting the business. Part of a six - video series that highlights the personal experiences of business owners in getting started.
Business and Economics; Psychology
Dist - LANDMK

Planning 25 MIN
U-matic / VHS
How to be more Successful in Your Own Business Series
Color (G)
$279.00, $179.00 purchase _ #AD - 2003
Addresses the issues and techniques of planning. Features Susan Garber, director, Pennsylvania Small Business Development Center at the Wharton School. Part of an eight - part series on successful business management moderated by David Susskind.
Business and Economics; Psychology
Dist - FOTH **Prod** - FOTH

Planning a Lesson 12 MIN
VHS / 16mm
English as a Second Language Series
Color (A PRO)
$165.00 purchase _ #290307
Demonstrates key teaching methods for English as a Second Language - ESL teachers. Features a teacher - presenter who introduces and provides a brief commentary on the techniques, then demonstrates the application of the technique to the students. 'Planning A Lesson' demonstrates the principles of effective lesson planning. Using a team approach, a lesson plan is criticized and rewritten. Teachers are offered a simple acronym to assist them in evaluating their own lesson plans.
Education; English Language; Mathematics
Dist - ACCESS **Prod** - ACCESS 1989

Planning a New Business 30 MIN
16mm / U-matic / VHS
Color (C A)
Explores the kinds of planning and the various sources of assistance and advice necessary to start a new business or take over an existing business.
Business and Economics
Dist - GPN **Prod** - NETCHE

Planning a Persuasive, Realistic Proposal Budget 55 MIN
U-matic / VHS
Winning Grants series
(G)
$1,795 member purchase, $1,995 non member purchase
Presents seminars on successful grant writing. Focuses on setting up a realistic proposal budget. Eighth in a series of ten.
Business and Economics; Education
Dist - GPN

Planning a Persuasive, Realistic Proposal - Budget 60 MIN
U-matic / VHS
Winning Grants Series
Color (A)
Business and Economics; Education
Dist - GPN **Prod** - UNEBR

Planning a Program 18 MIN
VHS / U-matic
On Camera Series
Color (H C A)
LC 84-708013
Employs a television news report riddled with technical problems to illuminate errors and their avoidance. Presents a better planned version of the same report to further emphasize the value of proper planning.
Fine Arts
Dist - FI **Prod** - BBCTV 1984

Planning a Programme - Pt 2 17 MIN
VHS / 16mm
On Camera Series
Color (H)
$21.50 rental _ #23642
Depicts an ill - prepared television crew's efforts to shoot a retirement ceremony and compares those results with the results of a better prepared effort. Part of the On Camera Series, which provides instruction in the use of video equipment.
Fine Arts; Industrial and Technical Education
Dist - PSU **Prod** - FI

Planning a Project and Building Your Project Team 30 MIN
VHS / 16mm
Project Management Series
Color (PRO)
$400.00 purchase, $100.00 rental
Includes Elements of the Planning Process, Project Definition Statement, Project Phases, Selection of Project Team, Communication Formats and Initial Team Meeting. Part of a six - part series on project management.
Business and Economics; Industrial and Technical Education; Psychology
Dist - ISA **Prod** - ISA

Planning a Project and Building Your Project Team 30 MIN
U-matic / VHS
Project Management Series
Color
Identifies elements of the planning process. Covers project phases, selection of a project team and communication formats.
Business and Economics; Psychology
Dist - ITCORP **Prod** - ITCORP

Planning a Technical Presentation 15 MIN
VHS / U-matic
Effective Technical Presentations Series
Color
Industrial and Technical Education
Dist - DELTAK **Prod** - DELTAK

Planning a trip 5 MIN
VHS
English plus series
(J H A)
Presents travel vocabulary, indirect object pronouns, and days of the week.
English Language
Dist - AITECH **Prod** - LANGPL 1985

Planning a wedding to remember 35 MIN
VHS
Color (H C G)
$29.95 purchase _ #WK1125V
Helps to plan and organize a wedding to be remembered regardless of budget size. Features experts who offer practical guidance on budgets, bridal gowns, wedding party attire, photographers, invitations, flowers, wedding video, caterers, the ceremony, transportation, the reception and musicians.
Home Economics; Sociology
Dist - CAMV

Planning ahead series
Chile Pequin 30 MIN
Sister of the Bride 30 MIN
Dist - UCEMC

Planning and anticipating - Parts 3 and 4 60 MIN
VHS / U-matic
French in action - part I series
Color (C) (FRENCH)
$45.00, $29.95 purchase
Covers salutations, health, expressing surprise, decisiveness and indecisiveness, planning, anticipating, subject pronouns, the gender of adjectives, articles, future tenses, gender and number agreement, 'aller,' 'etre,' present indicative of ' - er' verbs in Parts 3 and 4. Parts of a 52 - part series teaching the French language, all in French, written by Pierre Capretz, Director of the Language Laboratory at Yale.
Foreign Language; History - World
Dist - ANNCPB **Prod** - YALEU 1987

Planning and Building a Retrieval Chart 20 MIN
16mm
B&W (P I J H)
Illustrates steps to take in assisting children to develop conceptual ideas for a retrieval chart.
Education
Dist - AWPC **Prod** - AWPC 1968

Planning and Control 30 MIN
VHS / U-matic
Organizational Transactions Series
Color
Shows control as the ultimate organizational glue. Demonstrates the birth, development and use of policy. Looks at how to improve control.
Psychology
Dist - PRODEV **Prod** - PRODEV

Planning and Decision Making 3 MIN
VHS / U-matic
Microcomputer at School Series Program Three
Color
Provides many practical, classroom - tested ideas related to issues which face education.
Mathematics
Dist - EDCORP **Prod** - EPCO

Planning and Drafting Irrevocable Trusts 120 MIN
U-matic / Cassette / VHS / 16mm
Color; Mono (PRO)
Features three estate planning attorneys as they discuss planning, drafting and funding the four most important irrevocable trusts, minors' trust, Crummey trust, Clifford trust and irrevocable insurance trust. Emphasizes the income, gift and estate tax consequences of each arrangement.
Civics and Political Systems
Dist - CCEB **Prod** - CCEB

Planning and Drafting Revocable Trusts 240 MIN
VHS / U-matic / Cassette
Color; Mono (PRO)
Reviews the advantages and disadvantages of the revocable living trust, including avoidance of probate, ease of later changes in asset disposition plans, convenience in property management and savings in income and estate taxes. Discusses specific trust clauses and how to use the power to revoke, provisions for distribution and provisions for administration.
Civics and Political Systems
Dist - CCEB **Prod** - CCEB

Planning and Estimating 20 MIN
VHS
Wallboard Series
Color (J H C A)
Reviews the important first steps to take in planning and estimating the amount of time and materials needed to wallboard a room.
Home Economics; Industrial and Technical Education
Dist - COFTAB **Prod** - AMHOM 1985

Planning and Laying Out Work 10 MIN
16mm
Problems in Supervision Series
B&W

LC FIE52-96
The story of a boy who has built a boat too large to go through the basement door, is used to explain the importance of planning a job in advance.
Business and Economics
Dist - USNAC **Prod** - USOE 1944

Planning and resourcing 30 MIN
U-matic / VHS
Sow seeds - trust the promise series
Color (J A)
Covers the planning process, community resources, early American handtools, no - trace campfires, folklore interview and group development. Features Robert Cagle and Marina Herman.
Religion and Philosophy
Dist - ECUFLM **Prod** - UMCOM

Planning and Scheduling of Maintenance 13 MIN
16mm
Color (IND)
Discusses how a good maintenance crew must keep half a day ahead of pressing maintenance matters.
Industrial and Technical Education
Dist - MOKIN **Prod** - MOKIN 1966

Planning and Selecting High Payoff Applications 45 MIN
U-matic / VHS
User Responsibilities in Information Management Series
Color
Explores the steps in planning the groundwork in information system development and the environmental factors which affect that process.
Industrial and Technical Education
Dist - DELTAK **Prod** - DELTAK

Planning and the Management Process 30 MIN
U-matic / VHS
Business Management Series Lesson 5; Lesson 5
Color (C A)
Focuses on the need for organizations to plan. Studies planning as it relates to organizations and to a manager's position in the organizational hierarchy.
Business and Economics; Psychology
Dist - SCCON **Prod** - SCCON

Planning around your congregation's life cycle 20 MIN
VHS
Congregational planning series
Color (G A R)
$39.95 purchase, $10.00 rental _ #35 - 876 - 2076
Suggests that church congregations have life cycles, and that it is necessary to determine a church's location in that cycle before renewal can take place. Hosted by Dr Margaret Wold. Produced by Seraphim.
Religion and Philosophy
Dist - APH

Planning babysitting 13 MIN
16mm
Babysitter series; Unit 2
Color (J)
LC 80-700510
Demonstrates how to perform some of the basic babysitting tasks, such as bathing, changing, and feeding infants and small children.
Guidance and Counseling; Home Economics
Dist - FILCOM **Prod** - SOCOM

Planning Better Behavior 30 MIN
U-matic / VHS
Developing Discipline Series
Color (T)
Emphasizes the correct response to inappropriate behavior, a response that leads to responsible, productive behavior.
Education; Guidance and Counseling; Psychology; Sociology
Dist - GPN **Prod** - SDPT 1983

Planning Classroom Tests 28 MIN
16mm
Nursing - Effective Evaluation Series
B&W (C A)
LC 74-700192
Identifies strengths and weaknesses in objective tests and offers practice in creating different types of objective test questions. Explains elements to be used in planning a test.
Education; Health and Safety
Dist - NTCN **Prod** - NTCN 1971

Planning Clinical Experiences 30 MIN
16mm
Nursing - Where are You Going, How will You Get There Series
B&W (C A)
LC 74-700181
Defines concept teaching and shows examples of how it may be implemented in a nursing curriculum.
Education; Health and Safety
Dist - NTCN **Prod** - NTCN 1971

Planning, Control and Reliability 180 MIN
U-matic
Software Engineering for Micro and Minicomputer Systems Series
Color (IND)
Discusses project planning and control, including defining measurable milestones, gaining software visibility, planning - control feedback loops, and techniques for controlling schedule, budget and performance. Speaks on reliability and verification.
Computer Science
Dist - INTECS **Prod** - INTECS

The Planning Environment 30 MIN
VHS / U-matic
Business Management Series Lesson 7; Lesson 7
Color (C A)
Compares centralized and participatory approaches to planning. Discusses how successful planning demands an environment in which information flows smoothly and quickly to the right people.
Business and Economics; Psychology
Dist - SCCON **Prod** - SCCON

Planning for a Place 20 MIN
16mm
Color (C A)
LC 83-700102
Offers a dramatized case study of a severely handicapped student's mother as she explores the possibilities of vocational training for her daughter with a special educator, a special education vocational counselor and an employer of handicapped workers.
Education; Guidance and Counseling
Dist - HUBDSC **Prod** - PEABC 1983

Planning for aging and incapacity 315 MIN
VHS
Color (PRO)
$97.00, $175.00 purchase, $69.00 rental _ #ES-54119, #ES-64119
Instructs in how to counsel clients in planning for the future, with consideration of public resources for health care such as Medicare. Details benefits planning with emphasis on incapacity or disability. Includes a handbook.
Civics and Political Systems
Dist - CCEB

Planning for Bomb Threats 16 MIN
U-matic / VHS
Color
Covers the nature of bomb threats, search and evacuation procedures, communications and recognition.
Civics and Political Systems; Sociology
Dist - CORF **Prod** - WORON 1984

Planning for Change 29 MIN
U-matic / VHS / 16mm
Teaching Children to Read Series
Color (T)
Presents reading authorities William Glasser, Vivian Windley and Madeline Hunter discussing ways of implementing new reading instruction techniques.
Education; English Language
Dist - FI **Prod** - MFFD 1975

Planning for data collection 16 MIN
VHS
Tools for continual improvement - two series
Color (IND PRO)
$395.00 purchase _ #ELI02
Teaches employee skills to improve performance. Includes trainer's notes, wall charts and reference cards. Available in healthcare and general business versions. Produced by Executive Learning, Inc.
Business and Economics
Dist - EXTR

Planning for Disaster 15 MIN
U-matic / VHS
Color (C)
$249.00, $149.00 purchase _ #AD - 1515
Shows a full - scale disaster exercise involving a fire and partial building collapse simulated by the Prince George's County Fire Department, the Maryland Institute for Emergency Medical Services Systems and other agencies in the greater Washington, DC area. Discusses preparational emergencies and drills.
Health and Safety; History - World; Social Science
Dist - FOTH **Prod** - FOTH

Planning for Discharge from the Hospital 14 MIN
U-matic
Color
Provides information that a hospitalized patient needs to know prior to the patient's discharge from the hospital in order to have a satisfactory continuity of care.
Health and Safety
Dist - UWISN **Prod** - UWISN

Planning for Dunya and Akhirah
VHS
Color (G)
$15.00 purchase _ #110 - 041
Features Dr Jamal Badawi, Imam M Sharif Himatov - Tajikistan - and Dr Mohammad Yunus.
Religion and Philosophy
Dist - SOUVIS **Prod** - SOUVIS

Planning for Effective Training 30 MIN
VHS / U-matic
Training the Trainer Series
Color (T)
Deals with conducting needs, job and task analysis.
Education; Psychology
Dist - ITCORP **Prod** - ITCORP

Planning for Financial Success 25 MIN
U-matic / VHS
Money Smart - a Guide to Personal Finance Series
Color (H C A)
Explains how changes in society motivate individuals to begin planning financial strategies linked to life plans.
Business and Economics; Education; Home Economics
Dist - BCNFL **Prod** - SOMFIL 1984

Planning for Floods 28 MIN
16mm
Color
Compares the 1973 Mississippi River flood with the 1972 Rapid City, South Dakota flood. Suggests that structural flood control violates intelligent land use policy and may result in an increase in the loss of life and property.
Science - Natural; Social Science
Dist - AMHRST **Prod** - AMHRST 1974

Planning for Impact 40 MIN
VHS / U-matic
Meeting Leading Series
Color
Business and Economics; English Language; Psychology
Dist - DELTAK **Prod** - PRODEV

Planning for Impact and Control 30 MIN
VHS / U-matic
Meeting Leading Series
Color
Discusses why a meeting should be held. Includes making a participant profile which helps anticipate support, attitudes and perhaps hidden agendas.
Business and Economics; Psychology
Dist - PRODEV **Prod** - PRODEV

Planning for improvement - a model 20 MIN
U-matic / VHS
Performance appraisal training series
Color
Fine Arts; Psychology
Dist - DELTAK **Prod** - DELTAK

Planning for Microcomputers 30 MIN
VHS / U-matic
Ready or not Series
Color
Discusses involving the right people in the planning process, finding out what computers can do, knowing sources of good information, learning from others' successes and failures, and setting goals.
Industrial and Technical Education; Mathematics
Dist - PCATEL **Prod** - NCSDPI

Planning for Personal Goals
U-matic / VHS
Employability Skills Series
Color
Shows how to select and describe realistic non - vocational goals, to specify and develop the steps necessary to accomplish these goals and how to apply time management and planning skills in order to achieve them.
Guidance and Counseling
Dist - CAMB **Prod** - ILCS

Planning for Profit 11 MIN
16mm
Running Your Own Business Series
Color
Demonstrates how to manipulate variable and fixed costs and adjust the break even point when sales begin to falter. Offers insights into the retirement of the principal of businesses loans, and the effect different courses can have on the balance sheet.
Business and Economics
Dist - EFD **Prod** - EFD

Planning for Retirement 25 MIN
VHS / U-matic
Money Smart - a Guide to Personal Finance Series
Color (H C A)
Shows how to assess financial needs for retirement and invest money.
Business and Economics; Education; Home Economics; Sociology
Dist - BCNFL **Prod** - SOMFIL

Planning for survival 20 MIN
VHS
Color; PAL (H C G)
Describes the World Conservation Strategy as 'an arrow aimed at a paradox,' as humans increase their demands upon the Earth to support them, they are reducing the Earth's capacity to do so. Looks at the three principal objectives of WCS - to maintain the Earth's ability to support life, to preserve genetic diversity through the conservation of animal and plant species, to ensure the sustainable use of all natural resources. Produced by the International Centre for Conservation Education.
Science - Natural; Science - Physical
Dist - VIEWTH

Planning for the Patient's Discharge 30 MIN
16mm
Color
Stresses the importance of returning as many patients as possible to their homes and communities.
Health and Safety; Social Science
Dist - USVA **Prod** - USVA 1956

Planning for Tomorrow 30 MIN
U-matic / VHS
Time's Harvest - Exploring the Future Series
Color (C)
Sociology
Dist - MDCPB **Prod** - MDCPB

Planning for Wellness System Series
A Personal Plan for Wellness 30 MIN
The Wellness Lifestyle 30 MIN
Dist - CORF

Planning Highway Access 32 MIN
U-matic / VHS / 16mm
Color (A)
Shows how Wisconsin counties, towns, villages and cities can preserve their highways as travel corridors without sacrificing safety or restricting business development or access to properties along them.
Geography - United States; Industrial and Technical Education
Dist - USNAC **Prod** - USDA 1981

Planning informal investigation and formal discovery 50 MIN
VHS
Training the advocate - The Pretrial stage series
Color (C PRO)
$95.00 purchase, $71.25 rental _ #PTA03
Presents lectures and demonstrations of the steps of the pretrial stage. Covers techniques of informal investigation and formal discovery.
Civics and Political Systems
Dist - NITA **Prod** - NITA 1985

Planning Lessons 30 MIN
VHS / U-matic
Educational Objectives Series
Color
Takes the objectives set down and organizes them into hierarchies and units.
Education
Dist - NETCHE **Prod** - NETCHE 1972

Planning Manufacturing Capacity 60 MIN
VHS / BETA
Manufacturing Series
(IND)
Includes methods for measuring capacity, levels of capacity planning and strategies for capacity planning.
Business and Economics
Dist - COMSRV **Prod** - COMSRV 1986

Planning Manufacturing Lot Sizes 60 MIN
BETA / VHS
Manufacturing Series
(IND)
Describes the relationship between the costs of ordering and the costs of carrying inventory and discusses how these factors affect lot sizing decisions.
Business and Economics
Dist - COMSRV **Prod** - COMSRV 1986

Planning patient teaching 30 MIN
16mm
Nursing - patient teaching series; Part 1
B&W (C A)
LC 74-700203
Illustrates specific elements in teaching patients. Concentrates on details of planning for patient teaching.
Education; Health and Safety
Dist - NTCN **Prod** - NTCN 1971

Planning - Preparing for Action 26 MIN
VHS / U-matic
Management Skills for Nurses Series
Color
Focuses on planning, such as the scheduling of staff time, nurse assignments and coverage when and emergency occurs.
Guidance and Counseling; Health and Safety
Dist - AJN **Prod** - INTGRP

Planning - Pt 1 43 MIN
U-matic / VHS
Project Management Series
Color (PRO)
Discusses the nature of planning, necessity for three plans and the relationship between planning and control.
Industrial and Technical Education; Mathematics
Dist - MIOT **Prod** - MIOT

Planning - Pt 2 45 MIN
U-matic / VHS
Project Management Series
Color (PRO)
Discusses earliest and latest start and finish, PERT time estimating, bar chart formats for network diagrams, cost estimating, project cost accounting, resource allocation, cost versus time trade - offs and contingency.
Industrial and Technical Education; Mathematics
Dist - MIOT **Prod** - MIOT

Planning, Scheduling, Organizing Work and Work Improvement 30 MIN
16mm
Success in Supervision Series
B&W
LC 74-706180
Discusses how supervisors can plan and organize work and tells about a simple approach to simplifying many jobs.
Business and Economics; Psychology
Dist - USNAC **Prod** - WETATV 1965

Planning successful rehearsals 58 MIN
VHS
Key changes - a seminar for music educators series
Color (T A PRO)
$69.95 purchase _ #1263 - 0015
Presents the final part of a 13 - part telecourse for music educators seeking renewal of their certification. Combines lecture and discussion on how to plan successful rehearsals.
Education; Fine Arts
Dist - SCETV **Prod** - SCETV 1990

Planning Technical Activities 30 MIN
U-matic / VHS
Management for Engineers Series
Color
Business and Economics; Industrial and Technical Education; Psychology
Dist - SME **Prod** - UKY

Planning Techniques 30 MIN
U-matic / VHS
Business Management Series Lesson 6; Lesson 6
Color (C A)
Looks at various quantitative and qualitative approaches to planning, and at tools designed to increase a manager's understanding of the future environment. Uses real world examples to illustrate master schedules, break - even analyses, Delphi and scientific management techniques.
Business and Economics; Psychology
Dist - SCCON **Prod** - SCCON

Planning the Future and the Opportunities for Your Enterprise Series
Setting your strategic goals 70 MIN
Your Operational Action Plan - Module 4 70 MIN
Your Planning Control - Module 5 70 MIN
Dist - VENCMP

Planning the future and the opportunities for your enterprise series
Developing your information data base - module 1 70 MIN
Developing your mission strategy - Module 2 70 MIN
Dist - VENCMP

Planning - the Future's First Step 20 MIN
U-matic / VHS
Supervisory Management Course, Pt 1 Series Unit 2
Color
Provides an introduction to the concept of planning and outlines the basic steps in making and implementing a plan.
Business and Economics; Psychology
Dist - AMA **Prod** - AMA

Planning - the Future's First Step 18 MIN
VHS / U-matic
Color
Provides managers with a step - by - step analysis of the elements that make up a successful plan.
Business and Economics; Psychology
Dist - AMA **Prod** - AMA

Planning the Land 24 MIN
16mm / U-matic / VHS
Color (J)
LC 76-701562
Shows how citizens can influence local governments to plan successful land - use policies in their communities. Outlines several legal methods for preserving open space, such as purchase of land by private nonprofit groups, leaseback agreements installment buying and other methods.
Civics and Political Systems; Sociology
Dist - AIMS **Prod** - CIASP 1975

Planning the Netherlands' water resources
VHS
Color (C PRO G)
$150.00 purchase _ #84.01
Shows how an integrated system of models was developed to evaluate mixes of new facilities, changes in operating rules and adjustments to prices and regulations. Reveals that the system has resulted in a national water management policy, with savings in the hundreds of millions of dollars in investment expenditures and over $10 million in estimated annual savings. The Netherlands Rijkswaterstaat. Bruce F Goeller.
Business and Economics; Social Science
Dist - INMASC

Planning - the Primary Function
VHS / U-matic
Principles of Management Series
Color
Defines and explains the importance of planning. Describes the manager's role in the development and application of different types of plans.
Business and Economics; Psychology
Dist - RMIBHF **Prod** - RMIBHF

Planning - the Process
U-matic / VHS
Principles of Management Series
Color
Highlights the basic steps in the planning process. Includes an explanation of the process for implementing a plan.
Business and Economics; Psychology
Dist - RMIBHF **Prod** - RMIBHF

Planning the Small Estate 24 MIN
VHS / U-matic / Cassette
Color; Mono (PRO)
Discusses the initial client interview, probate procedures, role of fiduciaries, will drafting and general estate planning in the small estate.
Civics and Political Systems
Dist - CCEB **Prod** - CCEB

Planning the Story 30 MIN
16mm
Starting Tomorrow Series Unit 1 - New Ways in Composition
B&W (T)
Presents ideas on developing creative writing in children in elementary grades.
Education; English Language
Dist - WALKED **Prod** - EALING

Planning the Use of Money 9 MIN
16mm
Color (I J)
Discusses the relationship between money and time and explains that young people as well as families must plan the use of their money.
Business and Economics; Social Science
Dist - SF **Prod** - MORLAT 1970

Planning Your Estate 25 MIN
U-matic / VHS
Your Money Matters Series
Color
Outlines the basics of setting up an estate. Discusses wills, executors, probate and common mistakes.
Business and Economics; Sociology
Dist - FILMID **Prod** - FILMID

Planning your financial future 60 MIN
VHS
Color (H C A)
$39.95 purchase
Covers the basic principles of financial planning. Explores such concepts as evaluation of net worth, expenses, budgeting, and goal - setting. Explains the six areas of financial planning - insurance, taxes, estates, investments, and more.
Business and Economics
Dist - PBS **Prod** - WNETTV

Planning your future
VHS
Job strategies set
Color (G A)

$69.50 purchase _ #ES110V
Focuses on the importance of proper planning to determine and attain life and employment goals. Differentiates between skilled and unskilled jobs, and explains the education and training required for each type.
Business and Economics; Psychology
Dist - CAMV

Planning Your Future
VHS / 35mm strip
Pre - Employment Planning Series
$43.50 film purchase, $69.50 VHS purchase _ #XY141 film, #XY151 VHS
Guidance and Counseling
Dist - CAREER **Prod** - CAREER

Planning your house
VHS
Architectural drafting series
(C G)
$59.00 _ CA150
Gives basic principles of design and layouts of living rooms, dining rooms, kitchens, bedrooms, and bathrooms.
Fine Arts; Industrial and Technical Education
Dist - AAVIM **Prod** - AAVIM 1989

Planning your speech 13 MIN
U-matic / VHS / 16mm
Art of communication series
Color (H C A)
$315.00, $215.00 purchase _ #78521; LC 79-701658
Takes a look at the process of planning a speech by showing how a speaker prepares prior to addressing a group.
English Language; Social Science
Dist - CORF **Prod** - CENTRO 1979

Planning Your Time
U-matic / VHS
Time Management - a Practical Approach Series
Color
Business and Economics; Psychology
Dist - DELTAK **Prod** - PACPL

Planning Your Wedding - the Expert's Guide 60 MIN
VHS
(H C A)
$39.95 purchase _ #MHE100V
Provides guidelines for planning a wedding. Explains how to chose a gown, hair, make up, flowers, and shoes, music, location, caterer, announcements, and more. Discusses how to deal with pre wedding stress and costs.
Sociology
Dist - CAMV

The Plans 15 MIN
VHS / U-matic
La Bonne Aventure Series
Color (K P)
Deals with French - Americans. Shows that the unforeseen can be rewarding.
Foreign Language
Dist - GPN **Prod** - MPBN

Plans and Elevations 4 MIN
16mm
Color (C)
$123.00
Experimental film by Al Jarnow.
Fine Arts
Dist - AFA **Prod** - AFA 1980

Plans and planning 30 MIN
VHS
Effective teacher telecourse series
Color (T)
$69.95 purchase, $50.00 rental
Discusses curriculum planning and lesson plans. Hosted by Dr Loren Anderson.
Education; Psychology
Dist - SCETV **Prod** - SCETV 1987

Plans for Success
BETA / VHS / U-matic
Vocational and Career Planning Series
Color (J H C A)
#PSV 102
Explains how to reach career goals by planning with timelines, educational or training requirements and resources. Comes with manual.
Guidance and Counseling
Dist - CADESF **Prod** - CADESF 1988

Plans for Success
VHS
Vocational and Career Planning Series
$98.00 purchase _ #VP101V
Discusses how to create a career plan that leads to success. Talks on realistic goals, training, education required for reaching those goals, a time - line, and resources.
Guidance and Counseling
Dist - CAREER **Prod** - CAREER

Plans for Success 18 MIN
VHS / 16mm
Vocational and Career Planning Series
(J H)
#FM212V
Shows how to set realistic goals based on abilities and skills, and how to set timetables to achieve career goals.
Guidance and Counseling
Dist - JISTW

Plans for Success 25 MIN
VHS / U-matic
Vocational and Career Planning Video Series
(J H C)
$98.00 _ #CD1110V
Uses dramatizations to instruct viewers on striving to accomplish career goals. Covers the difference between ability and skill, and other career issues. Includes accompanying manual.
Business and Economics; Education; Guidance and Counseling
Dist - CAMV **Prod** - CAMV

The Plant 13 MIN
16mm / U-matic / VHS
Color (I)
Presents the story of an extraordinary plant which demands attention and delights in music.
Literature and Drama
Dist - LUF **Prod** - LUF

Plant a Seed 3 MIN
16mm / U-matic / VHS
Color (P I)
LC 77-701010
Shows, through the use of music and lyrics, the positive effect that window boxes can create in a city.
Agriculture; Sociology
Dist - PHENIX **Prod** - ROSENJ 1977

Plant Anatomy and Function 56.58 MIN
VHS
Plants Series
Color (J H C)
LC 88-700285
Aids students in the study of the anatomy of plants to learn how plants function, use photosynthesis and reproduce.
Science - Natural
Dist - SRA **Prod** - SRA 1986

Plant anatomy collection series
Presents a three - part series introducing the structures and functions of plant anatomy. Includes The Primary Plant Body; The Secondary Plant Body; Plant Cells and Tissues.

Plant cells and tissues - Part 3	36 MIN
The Primary plant body - Part 1	35 MIN
The Secondary plant body - Part 2	20 MIN

Dist - CLRVUE **Prod** - CLRVUE 1986

Plant and animal life distribution - the natural world 18 MIN
U-matic / VHS
Natural science specials series; Module green
Color (I)
Examines factors that influence plant and animal growth and distribution. Visits different geological regions where various forms of life flourish.
Science - Natural; Science - Physical
Dist - AITECH **Prod** - COPFC 1973

Plant - animal communities - ecological succession 14 MIN
VHS
Color; PAL (H)
Looks at ecological succession, the long term replacement of one form of vegetation by another, which follows a predictable pattern that can be traced from either a bare rock stage or a water environment to the appearance of a forest. Reveals that succession is controlled to a major extent by climate and landform, but may also be accelerated, interrupted and retarded by humans.
Science - Natural
Dist - VIEWTH **Prod** - VIEWTH

Plant Care 29 MIN
Videoreel / VT2
Dig it Series
Color
Features Tom Lied discussing different types of ground cover and how they can be used. Offers tips on caring for these plants and how to use ornamental materials, such as bark and gravel.
Science - Natural
Dist - PBS **Prod** - WMVSTV

The Plant Care Quiz 15 MIN
16mm
Color
Presents horticulture expert Ralph Snodsmith who answers consumer questions about plant care.
Agriculture; Home Economics
Dist - KLEINW **Prod** - KLEINW

Plant cell and male and female flower parts 11 MIN
16mm / U-matic / VHS
Life cycle of a flowering plant series; No 1
Color
LC 73-703052
Uses the apple tree as a model to explain the characteristics of the plant cell, the male and female flower parts, genes, DNA and sexual and asexual reproduction.
Science - Natural
Dist - LUF **Prod** - SCHLAT 1971

Plant cells
VHS
Basic science series
Color (J H) (ENGLISH AND SPANISH)
$39.95 purchase _ #MCV5017
Focuses on plant cells, presenting only basic concepts. Includes teacher's guide and review questions. Combines computer animation and the use of 'sheltered language' to help students acquire content vocabulary, become comfortable with scientific language and achieve success in science curriculum. Part of a series on basic science concepts.
Science; Science - Natural
Dist - MADERA **Prod** - MADERA

Plant Cells and Tissues 35 MIN
U-matic / VHS
Color
Introduces major cell and tissue types found in vascular plants. Presents concept of cell specialization in multicullular organisms and examples of various specialized plant cells and tissues.
Science - Natural
Dist - CBSC **Prod** - BMEDIA

Plant cells and tissues - Part 3 36 MIN
VHS
Plant anatomy collection series
Color (J H)
$60.00 purchase _ #A5VH 1032
Explores the major cell and tissue types of vascular plants including meristematic cells, parenchyma, sclerenchyma, fibers, sylem, phloem and epidermis. Part three of a three - part series introducing the structures and functions of plant anatomy.
Science - Natural
Dist - CLRVUE **Prod** - CLRVUE

Plant Coordinate Systems
VHS / U-matic
Drafting - Blueprint Reading Basics Series
Color (IND)
Industrial and Technical Education
Dist - GPCV **Prod** - GPCV

Plant Defenses 28 MIN
U-matic / VHS
Life of Plants Series
Color (C)
$249.00, $149.00 purchase _ #AD - 1679
Shows that plants have a host of ingenious protective devices - spines and thorns, insecticides, caffeine, chemicals that interfere with hormone production in insects. Reveals how predators adapt to plant defenses. Part of a series on plants.
Science - Natural
Dist - FOTH **Prod** - FOTH

Plant doctor
CD-ROM
Color (PRO)
$129.00 purchase _ #2854
Offers a database on trees, turf, flowers, shrubs, and other plantings that flourish in an urban environment. Lists hundreds of plant disorders and cures. For IBM PCs and compatibles. Requires 640K RAM, DOS Version 3.1 or greater, one floppy disk drive - a hard drive is recommended, one empty expansion slot, and an IBM compatible CD - ROM drive.
Agriculture
Dist - BEP

Plant foods 30 MIN
U-matic / VHS
Home gardener with John Lenanton series; Lesson 5
Color (C A)
Identifies 16 elements essential for plant growth. Explains how to tell what nutrients a gardener might need for his or her particular soil. Teaches how to apply fertilizer.
Agriculture
Dist - CDTEL **Prod** - COAST

Plant Growth in Compensated Fields 7 MIN
16mm
Color
LC FIE67-132
Points out that plant growth is controlled by a sensitive mechanism which responds to brief and minute stimulation. Describes the operation and use of the mechanical servo - system which neutralizes stimuli on plants for experimental purposes.
Agriculture; Science - Natural
Dist - USNAC **Prod** - USNRC 1967

Plant growth regulators 12 MIN
VHS
Color (H C)
$39.95 purchase _ #49 - 8473 - V
Explains the physiology of plant growth hormones. Still frame.
Science - Natural
Dist - INSTRU **Prod** - CBSC

Plant growth requirements - Volume III 23 MIN
VHS
Tropical plants for the interiorscape series
Color (G)
$89.95 purchase _ #6 - 302 - 317A
Explains the needs of tropical plants for light, water, nutrients and growing media. Shows how to select environmentally sound containers for tropical plants. Demonstrates trimming, testing for nutrient needs, scheduling water and using both natural and artificial light to enhance plant health and appearance. Part of a series on using tropical plants for interior decoration.
Agriculture; Home Economics; Science - Natural
Dist - VEP **Prod** - VEP 1993

The Plant kingdom 16 MIN
35mm strip / VHS
Five kingdoms series
Color (I J H)
$49.95 purchase _ #193 Y 6438, #70 Y 6438
Reveals that the first tiny green multicellular beings lived in the aquatic environment of their protistan ancestors, but some developed adaptations which allowed them to 'creep out' onto land. Shows how various plant groups exploited the opportunities presented by life on land. Part of a six - part series on the kingdoms of life.
Science - Natural
Dist - WARDS **Prod** - WARDS 1990

The Plant Kingdom - a World of Green
U-matic / VHS
Color (H)
Discusses organisms that were once aquatic and have adapted to life on land. Details all types of plant forms, describing size, form, nature and reproductive systems, and relating them to their various aquatic or land environments.
Science - Natural
Dist - GA **Prod** - GA

Plant Life at Work 13 MIN
VHS / 16mm
Color (I J H)
LC 76-702110
Uses time - lapse photography to show the processes of plant life. Reveals the impressive energy of plants as they move, grow, reproduce and manufacture food through photosynthesis.
Science - Natural
Dist - MIS **Prod** - MIS 1976

Plant Life Cycles - Alternation of Generations in Plants 19 MIN
U-matic / VHS
Color
Presents a basic discussion of alternations of generations in plants, stressing the variety of patterns found in the haploid/diploid forms. Video version of 35mm filmstrip program, with live open and close.
Science - Natural
Dist - CBSC **Prod** - BMEDIA

Plant movement and transport 29 MIN
U-matic
Introducing biology series; Program 8
Color (C A)
Describes intricacies of external and internal plant movement. Uses time - lapse photography.
Science - Natural
Dist - CDTEL **Prod** - COAST

Plant Movement and Transport 29 MIN
VHS
Basic Botany Series
Color (G)
$75.00 purchase _ #6 - 083 - 108P
Teaches basic botany. Explores the intricacies of internal and external plant movement. Studies xylem and phloem and uses time - lapse video to show how materials move through a plant. Explains osmosis and transpiration.
Agriculture; Science - Natural
Dist - VEP **Prod** - VEP

Plant movements 16 MIN
VHS
Color; PAL (I J H)
PdS29
Explains the time - lapse technique in cinematography and its use in the study of plant movements. Contrasts the movement of plants with that of animals and use of movement by plants to meet their needs. Illustrates phototropism in cress plants, geotropism in bean roots and thigmotropism with twining stems and tendrils. Follows with an experiment designed to illustrate the hormonal mechanism by which plant movements are coordinated and controlled. Demonstrates movements which result from non - directional stimuli, the nastic movements, by shots of the Venus fly trap and the sensitive plant. Shows the diurnal movements of cultivated shamrock flowers.
Industrial and Technical Education; Science - Natural
Dist - BHA

Plant nutrition 29 MIN
U-matic
Introducing biology series; Program 7
Color (C A)
Identifies structures that enable a plant to make its own food. Discusses water, gas exchange and soil. Includes plants with unusual adaptations for obtaining nutrients.
Science - Natural
Dist - CDTEL **Prod** - COAST

Plant Nutrition 29 MIN
VHS
Basic Botany Series
Color (G)
$75.00 purchase _ #6 - 083 - 109P
Teaches basic botany. Identifies plant structures and their functions for making food. Uses animation to illustrate how the xylem conducts water and minerals up through the plant, and the phloem carries food down. Explains the two major types of soil.
Agriculture; Science - Natural
Dist - VEP **Prod** - VEP

Plant or Animal 15 MIN
VHS / U-matic
Color (K P)
Explores the two major kingdoms of living things - plants and animals. Shows the major differences between plants and animals, and reveals how each is nourished and reproduced.
Science - Natural
Dist - NGS **Prod** - NGS

Plant Populations 14 MIN
U-matic / VHS
Hands on, Grade 5 - Our Environment Series
Color (I)
Studies various plant populations.
Science - Natural
Dist - AITECH **Prod** - WHROTV 1975

Plant problem diagnosis - Volume IV 24 MIN
VHS
Tropical plants for the interiorscape series
Color (G)
$89.95 purchase _ #6 - 302 - 318A
Focuses on how to recognize, diagnose and treat disease and pest problems common in tropical interiorscape plants. Matches recommended treatments to insect or disease problems. Explains environmental and cultural conditions harmful to plant health and expands on plant pruning and grooming. Part of a series on using tropical plants for interior decoration.
Agriculture; Home Economics
Dist - VEP **Prod** - VEP 1993

Plant Propagation at the Iowa State Forest Nursery 19 MIN
VHS / 16mm
Color (H C A)
Documents the mission of the Iowa State Forest Nursery and provides a detailed look at the annual propagation cycle for some 15 species of conifers and deciduous trees.
Agriculture; Science - Natural
Dist - IOWA **Prod** - IOWA 1988

Plant Propagation - from Seed to Tissue Culture 27 MIN
16mm
Color
LC 78-700299
Shows various means of propagating plants in order to demonstrate the scientific priniciples involved. Introduces the technique of tissue culture by which tissue sections of a single plant, under controlled circumstances, can reproduce the parent plant hundreds of times.
Agriculture; Science; Science - Natural
Dist - FI **Prod** - HUAA 1977

Plant propagation series
Illustrates seven different methods of propagating plants in a two - part video series.
Plant propagation - Vol I 22 MIN
Plant propagation series 42 MIN
Plant propagation, Vol II 20 MIN
Dist - VEP **Prod** - VEP 1977

Plant propagation - Vol I 22 MIN
VHS
Plant propagation series
Color (G)
$89.95 purchase _ #6 - 044 - 001P
Shows four popular methods of plant propagation - by seed, by division, by bulbs and tubers, and one of the newest methods, micropropagation. Part one of a two - part series.
Agriculture; Science - Natural
Dist - VEP **Prod** - VEP

Plant propagation, Vol II 20 MIN
VHS
Plant propagation series
Color (G)
$89.95 purchase _ #6-044-002P
Shows three methods of plant propagation - cuttings of hardwood, semi - hardwood, softwood and herbaceous plants, layering, grafting and budding. Part two of a two - part series.
Agriculture; Science - Natural
Dist - VEP **Prod** - VEP

Plant pruning 30 MIN
U-matic / VHS
Consumer education for the deaf adult series
Captioned; Color (S) (AMERICAN SIGN)
Discusses the reason for pruning trees, plants and shrubs. Demonstrates pruning techniques and tools.
Guidance and Counseling; Psychology; Science - Natural
Dist - GALCO **Prod** - GALCO 1975

Plant Reproduction 29 MIN
VHS
Basic Botany Series
Color (G)
$75.00 purchase _ #6 - 083 - 110P
Teaches basic botany. Uses time - lapse photography to illustrate the female and male flower parts of a tulip and show how fertilization takes part. Explains angiosperms and gymnosperms and shows how pollen is transported. Looks at special adaptations of seeds for aid in their dispersal.
Agriculture; Science - Natural
Dist - VEP **Prod** - VEP

Plant reproduction 29 MIN
U-matic
Introducing biology series; Program 27
Color (C A)
Presents basic features and processes involved in plant reproduction. Details various methods of pollination.
Science - Natural
Dist - CDTEL **Prod** - COAST

Plant Safety 12 MIN
16mm / U-matic / VHS
Color (J)
Demonstrates the need for industrial safety regulations by telling the story of a man who is determined to win his plant's safety contest.
Health and Safety
Dist - GA **Prod** - XEROXF 1979

Plant Safety Series
Fire Safety 60 MIN
Hazardous Substances 60 MIN
Personal Safety 60 MIN
Respiratory Protection 60 MIN
Dist - NUSTC

Plant Science - 1 60 MIN
VHS
Basic Theory and Systems
Color (PRO)
$600.00 - $1500.00 purchase _ #OTPS1
Introduces basic scientific principles and their applications in a process facility. Considers units of measurement for length, time, mass, temperature, flow and level. Part of a twenty - part series on basic theory and systems. Includes ten textbooks and an instructor guide to support four hours of instruction.
Industrial and Technical Education; Mathematics; Psychology; Science - Physical
Dist - NUSTC **Prod** - NUSTC

Plant Science - 2 60 MIN
VHS
Basic Theory and Systems
Color (PRO)
$600.00 - $1500.00 purchase _ #OTPS2
Focuses on the properties of matter. Considers solids, liquids and gases. Demonstrates how these properties

influence process system operation. Part of a twenty - part series on basic theory and systems. Includes ten textbooks and an instructor guide to support four hours of instruction.
Industrial and Technical Education; Psychology; Science - Physical
Dist - NUSTC **Prod** - NUSTC

Plant Science - 3 60 MIN
VHS
Basic Theory and Systems
Color (PRO)
$600.00 - $1500.00 purchase _ #OTPS3
Teaches the principles of heat transfer, the effects of heat, the relationship between temperature and thermal energy and the effects of temperature on heat transfer. Part of a twenty - part series on basic theory and systems. Includes ten textbooks and an instructor guide to support four hours of instruction.
Ihdustrial and Technical Education; Psychology; Science - Physical
Dist - NUSTC **Prod** - NUSTC

Plant Science - 4 60 MIN
VHS
Basic Theory and Systems
Color (PRO)
$600.00 - $1500.00 purchase _ #OTPS4
Introduces the principles and operating characteristics of liquid, gas and vapor systems. Describes the main parts of a fluid system and the effects of pressure related to static fluids and steady - state flowing fluids. Part of a twenty - part series on basic theory and systems. Includes ten textbooks and an instructor guide to support four hours of instruction.
Industrial and Technical Education; Psychology; Science - Physical
Dist - NUSTC **Prod** - NUSTC

Plant Science - 5 60 MIN
VHS
Basic Theory and Systems
Color (PRO)
$600.00 - $1500.00 purchase _ #OTPS5
Examines the principles of electricity. Introduces the terms of voltage, current, resistance, electromagnetic force, induction and motor action. Teaches Ohm's law, the elements of Ohm's law formula and the interaction between electricity and magnetism. Part of a twenty - part series on basic theory and systems. Includes ten textbooks and an instructor guide to support four hours of instruction.
Industrial and Technical Education; Psychology; Science - Physical
Dist - NUSTC **Prod** - NUSTC

Plant Science Series
Algal syngamy - isogamy in chlamydomonas 3 MIN
Algal syngamy - oogamy in oedogonium 3 MIN
Algal syngamy - zygote formation in pandorina 3 MIN
Early development of the shoot in 'quercus' 3 MIN
Effect of red and far - red light on internode length 4 MIN
Liberation of Zoospores in the Alga Basicladia 4 MIN
Liberation of Zoospores in the Alga Oedogonium 4 MIN
Photosynthetic Fixation of Carbon Dioxide, Pt 1 6 MIN
Photosynthetic Fixation of Carbon Dioxide, Pt 2 6 MIN
Dist - MLA

Plant Selection 22 MIN
VHS
Color (G)
$89.95 purchase _ #6 - 102 - 100P
Explores the considerations for selecting landscaping plants. Shows how to select plants for specific functions, locations and environmental considerations, including safety. Teaches about information and plant sources. Uses extensive examples in a wide variety of locations to illustrate principles.
Agriculture; Science - Natural
Dist - VEP **Prod** - VEP

Plant selection and identification - Volume II 19 MIN
VHS
Tropical plants for the interiorscape series
Color (G)
$89.95 purchase _ #6 - 302 - 316A
Shows how to match plants to various interiorscape applications. Shows the most commonly used tropicals as well as the newest plants on the interiorscape market. Illustrates the use of tropicals to control traffic flow or enhance architectural features. Includes a primer on basic tropical plant identification and interiorscape use. Part of a series on using tropical plants for interior decoration.
Agriculture; Home Economics; Science - Natural
Dist - VEP **Prod** - VEP 1993

Plant survival series
Adaptation in plants 17 MIN
Dist - IU

Plant systems
U-matic / VHS
Industrial training series; Power production; Module 4
Color (IND VOC)
Includes circulating water systems, the condenser and condensate system.
Industrial and Technical Education
Dist - LEIKID **Prod** - LEIKID

Plant Tissue Culture - Pt I 21 MIN
VHS
Plant Tissue Culture Series
Color (G)
$89.95 purchase _ #6 - 101 - 100P
Introduces the concept of plant tissue culture. Explores new developments in the field - gene transfer, embryo rescue and encapsulation. Visits a lab and teaches the purpose and uses of common equipment and looks at the four stages of the tissue culture process. Part I of two parts.
Agriculture; Science - Natural
Dist - VEP **Prod** - VEP

Plant Tissue Culture - Pt II 20 MIN
VHS
Plant Tissue Culture Series
Color (G)
$89.95 purchase _ #6 - 101 - 200P
Reviews briefly the four stages of plant tissue culture covered in part I. Uses the African violet and the Syngonium as subjects for demonstrating the process of tissue culture. Shows inexpensive alternatives for undertaking tissue culture. Part II of two parts.
Agriculture; Science - Natural
Dist - VEP **Prod** - VEP

Plant tissue culture series
Introduces and expands on the concept of plant tissue culture. Looks at new developments in the field and tissue culture performed in a lab. Demonstrates the propagation of the African violet and Syngonium through the process of tissue culture and inexpensive alternatives in equipment and materials. Includes two videocassettes and a teaching guide.
Plant Tissue Culture - Pt I 21 MIN
Plant Tissue Culture - Pt II 20 MIN
Dist - VEP **Prod** - VEP

Plant Tissue Culture - the Basic Concepts 27 MIN
U-matic / VHS
Color
Describes conditions needed to start tissue cultures, different types of plant tissue cultures, and some advantages of certain tissue culture techniques. Video version of 35mm filmstrip program, with live open and close.
Science - Natural
Dist - CBSC **Prod** - BMEDIA

Plant Traps - Insect Catchers of the Bog Jungle 11 MIN
U-matic / VHS / 16mm
Color; B&W (J H C)
Reveals the behavior of carnivorous plants, such as pitcher plant, sundew and Venus flytrap. Formerly titled 'INSECT CATCHERS OF THE BOG JUNGLE.'.
Science - Natural
Dist - EBEC **Prod** - HARL 1955

Plant tropisms and other movements 10 MIN
VHS
Color; PAL (J H C)
Shows a variety of plants in time - lapse photography to illustrate movements of plants in response to internal or external stimuli. Differentiates the three different types of movement - tropisms such as phototropism, geotropism and thigmotropism; nastic movements such as mycinasty and thermonasty; and nutational movements such as circumnutation.
Science - Natural
Dist - VIEWTH CORF **Prod** - VIEWTH

The Plant world
VHS
Color (J H)
$175.00 purchase _ #49 - 8447 - V
Traces the development of plant life from its origins in the sea. Describes plant structure and discusses photosynthesis. Explores pollination and plant adaptations. Includes teacher's manual and duplicating masters. Five programs on two videocassettes. Still frame.
Science - Natural
Dist - INSTRU **Prod** - UNL

Plant your future 13 MIN
VHS
Color (G)
$49.95 purchase _ #6 - 211 - 100A
Takes a fast - paced tour of the plant science industry. Shows the diversity of career opportunities available, including genetics, biotechnology, agronomy, physiology, biochemistry, pathology, entomology, soil science, computer science, production, management, education.
Agriculture; Guidance and Counseling; Science - Natural
Dist - VEP **Prod** - VEP

Plantanos 23 MIN
U-matic / VHS
Color (PRO)
Shows four ways of cooking plantains - boiled, baked, sauteed and fried as patties.
Home Economics; Industrial and Technical Education
Dist - CULINA **Prod** - CULINA

Plantar Aspect of the Foot 15 MIN
U-matic / VHS / 16mm
Guides to Dissection Series
Color (C A)
Demonstrates the dissection of the plantar aspect of the foot.
Health and Safety; Science - Natural
Dist - TEF **Prod** - UCLA

Plantation Beach, Honduras 30 MIN
VHS
Scuba World series
Color (G)
$24.90 purchase _ #0441
Visits Chochonis Grande Island near Honduras. Finds a diver's dream with remote villages, mountain paths, unusual diving scenery.
Geography - World; Physical Education and Recreation
Dist - SEVVID

Plantation Boy 85 MIN
16mm
B&W (PORTUGUESE (ENGLISH SUBTITLES))
An English subtitle version of the Portuguese language film. Relates the story of young Carlinho who is sent to live on his grandfather's sugar plantation after his mother's violent death. Depicts the Brazil of 1920 and shows the country and society in a state of transition.
Fine Arts; Foreign Language; History - World
Dist - NYFLMS **Prod** - NYFLMS 1965

Plantation in Peru 10 MIN
16mm / U-matic / VHS
Color; B&W (J H)
Depicts the cultivation of sugar by irrigation in an almost rainless desert located between the Andes and the Pacific where thousands of Peruvians live and work under a system of tenant farming.
Geography - World; Social Science
Dist - IFB **Prod** - IFB 1950

Planting and Transplanting 22 MIN
U-matic / VHS
Color (A)
Demonstrates the essential techniques of planting and transplanting. Includes soil preparation, potting, root and top pruning.
Agriculture
Dist - BBG **Prod** - BBG 1975

Planting seeds for peace 23 MIN
VHS
Color (J H C G)
$81.00 purchase, $40.00 rental _ #840; $75.00 purchase, $40.00 rental
Chronicles the experiences of Israeli and Arab teenagers who toured American summer camps in 1988 to conduct workshops for youngsters on the Arab - Israeli conflict. Studies intercultural communication through cross - cultural perspectives to show what can be done about conflict. Includes a leader's guide, program summary, facilitator guidelines, questions for discussion groups and a list of reading and teaching resources. Produced by Legacy International.
Psychology; Sociology
Dist - INCUL EFVP

Planting Techniques Part 1 - Trees and Shrubs 26 MIN
VHS
Start Plants Right Video Series
Color (G)
$89.95 purchase _ #6 - 079 - 100P
Shows how proper plant selection, correct site preparation, use of appropriate planting techniques and proper follow - up care ensure successful growth and development of newly installed landscape plants. Focuses on woody plants in containers. Illustrates staking trees, bare root trees and shrubs and balled and burlapped plants. Part of a four - part series.
Agriculture
Dist - VEP **Prod** - VEP

Planting Techniques Part 2 - Herbaceous Plants and Ground Covers 25 MIN
VHS
Start Plants Right Video Series
Color (G)
$89.95 purchase _ #6 - 079 - 200P
Covers planting techniques for herbaceous plants, including bulbs and ground covers. Looks at plant selection, site preparation - including weed eradication and chemical handling safety - appropriate planting techniques and after care. Features Jim Harrigan. Part of a four - part series.
Agriculture
Dist - VEP **Prod** - VEP

Plants 57 MIN
35mm strip / VHS
Color (H)
$168.00 purchase _ #PE - 494794 - X, #PE - 512759 - 8
Gives an overview of how all plants function, reproduce and use photosynthesis. Highlights the importance of plants in producing oxygen. Filmstrip version includes four filmstrips, four cassettes and teacher's guide.
Science - Natural
Dist - SRA **Prod** - SRA

Plants 29 MIN
VHS / 16mm
Villa Alegre series
Color (K P T) (ENGLISH AND SPANISH)
$46.00 rental _ #VILA - 127
Presents educational material about plants in both Spanish and English.
Education; Science - Natural
Dist - PBS

Plants 10 MIN
U-matic
Take a Look Series
Color (P I)
Explores garden plants and show root, stem, leaf and flower and their function. Visits a greenhouse.
Science; Science - Natural
Dist - TVOTAR **Prod** - TVOTAR 1986

Plants 15 MIN
VHS / 16mm
Challenge Series
Color (I)
$125.00 purchase, $25.00 rental
Covers the functions of the parts of a plant and reveals facts about plants in a tropical greenhouse.
Agriculture; Science; Science - Natural
Dist - AITECH **Prod** - WDCNTV 1987

Plants and animals 63 MIN
35mm strip / VHS
Color (I J H)
$70.00 purchase _ #ACL495 - CV, #ACL - 495 - C
Introduces the classification of plant and animal life. Shows representative phyla that students may later be expected to understand and define. Examines the relationship of individual cell division to the reproduction of multicellular organisms, including both mitosis and meiosis. Covers evolutionary theory, presenting Darwin's work graphically while providing an historic perspective.
Science - Natural
Dist - CLRVUE **Prod** - CLRVUE

Plants and animals 24 MIN
VHS
Video guide to occupational exploration - the video GOE series
Color (J H C G)
$69.95 purchase _ #CCP1003V
Discusses careers which center on plants and animals. Interviews a landscape gardener, forester, horse trainer, farrier - blacksmith, and a groundskeeper. Part of a 14 - part series exploring occupational clusters.
Agriculture; Business and Economics; Guidance and Counseling; Physical Education and Recreation
Dist - CAMV **Prod** - CAMV 1991

Plants and Animals Depend on each Other 12 MIN
U-matic / VHS / 16mm
Color (P)
LC 74-703362
Uses the example of the relationship of plants and animals in an aquarium in order to explore plant and animal relationships in other environments, including ponds, grasslands and woodlands.
Science - Natural
Dist - CORF **Prod** - CORF 1974

Plants and animals depend on each other 12 MIN
U-matic / VHS / 16mm
Color (P)
$295, $210 purchase _ #3326
Shows the interdependence of plants and animals.
Science - Natural
Dist - CORF

Plants and Animals Share Space and Food 10 MIN
16mm / U-matic / VHS
Color (I)
LC 76-700277
Describes how many plants and animals manage to live together in the same environments. Discovers how they share nonliving things, such as sunlight, water and soil. Portrays a rabbit eating grass and a spider's web on a plant as an example of direct animal - plant dependence.
Science - Natural
Dist - CORF **Prod** - CORF 1976

Plants and Insects 28 MIN
U-matic / VHS
Life of Plants Series
Color (C)
$249.00, $149.00 purchase _ #AD - 1680
Looks at the interrelationship of plants and insects. Shows leafcutter ants protecting trees from other insects, butterflies camouflaged to look like leaves to feed and lay their eggs, flowers growing in gardens cultivated by ants. Part of a series on plants.
Science - Natural
Dist - FOTH **Prod** - FOTH

Plants and people 29 MIN
VHS / 16mm
Villa Alegre series
Color (P T) (ENGLISH & SPANISH)
$46.00 rental _ #VILA - 132
Presents educational material about plants and people in both Spanish and English.
Education
Dist - PBS

Plants and their Importance 11 MIN
U-matic / VHS / 16mm
Color (P I)
LC 71-704203
Presents basic concepts about plants and points out their importance in many phases of daily life.
Psychology; Science - Natural; Social Science
Dist - ALTSUL **Prod** - FILMSW 1969

Plants - angiosperms 29 MIN
VHS
Biology live series
Color (I J)
$149.00 purchase _ #GW - 5104 - VS
Shows the importance of angiosperm. Identifies the parts of a typical flower. Part of a 13 - part series on biology which uses high resolution animation, live - action photography and interesting narrative to teach a core curriculum in biological science.
Science - Natural
Dist - HRMC

Plants are different and alike 11 MIN
U-matic / VHS / 16mm
Color (P)
$280.00 purchase - video, $195.00 purchase - video _ #1820; LC FIA67-128
Two children in a nursery learn that plants have similar needs, but differ in physical appearance and characteristics, in usefulness to humans and in the ways in which they obtain food.
Science - Natural
Dist - CORF **Prod** - CORF 1967

Plants are different and alike 15 MIN
VHS / U-matic / 16mm
Color (P)
$420.00, $250.00 purchase _ #HP - 5709C
Teaches that all green plants require a minimum of essential elements in order to grow. Reveals that differences in root, stem and leaf systems allow green plants to flourish in a variety of climates and conditions. Shows that green plants, unlike animals, are capable of making their own food from water, sunlight, air and nutritients in the soil. Produced by Mike Carlson.
Science - Natural
Dist - CORF

Plants as a Food Source 20 MIN
16mm
Color
LC 74-706554
Shows how plant life can be utilized for all body food requirements.
Health and Safety; Home Economics; Science - Natural
Dist - USNAC **Prod** - USN 1973

Plants at work and seeds in motion 28 MIN
Videodisc
Color (I J H)
$295.00 purchase
Contains two segments on one disk. Uses time - lapse photography to show the development of plants from seed. Shows normally unseen aspects of plant life in 'Plants at Work' and 'Seeds in Motion.'
Science - Natural
Dist - PFP

Plants can be found everywhere 13 MIN
VHS
Debbie Greenthumb series
CC; Color (P I)
$59.95 purchase _ #1113VG
Shows the variety of plants and the environments they live in. Explains how plants have adapted to their surroundings from deserts to tundra. Comes with a teacher's guide and four blackline masters. Part one of a four - part series.
Science - Natural
Dist - UNL

Plants - green, growing, giving life 22 MIN
VHS
Color (P I)
$89.00 purchase _ #RB857
Examines the diversity of plants. Shows how plants, like other living things, require food for energy and growth. Looks at how plants reproduce and respond to stimuli in the environment, and are different from other life forms in their ability to manufacture their own food through photosynthesis. Examines plant anatomy.
Science - Natural
Dist - REVID **Prod** - REVID 1991

Plants - gymnosperms 28 MIN
VHS
Biology live series
Color (I J)
$149.00 purchase _ #GW - 5103 - VS
Defines a seed. Discusses the first plants that produced seeds, gynosperms. Part of a 13 - part series on biology which uses high resolution animation, live - action photography and interesting narrative to teach a core curriculum in biological science.
Science - Natural
Dist - HRMC

Plants in Action 10 MIN
VHS / U-matic
Color (J H)
Uses time - lapse photography to reveal that plants, although mostly rooted, do move, act and react. Shows leaves opening by day and closing at night, flowers and clover opening to or pursuing sunlight climbing tendrils looking for support.
Science - Natural
Dist - EDMI **Prod** - EDMI 1983

Plants in Action 10 MIN
16mm / VHS
Color (I J H C A)
$175.00, $210.00 purchase, $30.00 rental _ #8022
Uses time - lapse photography to show the activity of plants growing and responding to changes in their environment.
Agriculture; Science - Natural
Dist - AIMS **Prod** - EDMI 1983

Plants in Action 30 MIN
U-matic / VHS
Home Gardener with John Lenanton Series Lesson 22; Lesson 22
Color (C A)
Uses time - lapse photography to show plants growing. Demonstrates the function of the plants 'plumbing system,' the roots, trunk, leaves and buds. Describes photosynthesis.
Agriculture
Dist - CDTEL **Prod** - COAST

Plants in Peril 26 MIN
U-matic / VHS
Color (C)
$249.00, $149.00 purchase _ #AD - 1900
Explains the need for preserving plants that may become a source of food and medicine. Considers also the preservation of plants to ensure the development of genetically - diverse crop strains. Looks at efforts to save vanishing species.
Agriculture; Health and Safety; Science - Natural
Dist - FOTH **Prod** - FOTH

Plants in the Scheme of Things 28 MIN
U-matic / VHS
Life of Plants Series
Color (C)
$249.00, $149.00 purchase _ #AD - 1671
Presents a capsule history of life on Earth. Follows the flow of life into its progressively more complex forms, from bacteria to algae and photosynthesis. Demonstrates how photosynthesis works to create living matter that is 98 percent energy - efficient. Part of a series on plants.

Science - Natural
Dist - FOTH **Prod** - FOTH

Plants make Food 13 MIN
16mm / U-matic / VHS
Color (I J)
LC 81-700986
Shows how plants make food through the process of photosynthesis. Examines the functioning of roots, stems and leaves, and explains the transforming of water, minerals, and carbon dioxide into foods.
Science - Natural
Dist - CF **Prod** - CF 1981

Plants make Food ; 2nd ed. 13 MIN
U-matic / VHS / 16mm
Color (I J)
$49.95 purchase _ #Q10015
Illustrates the process of photosynthesis by examining the · functions of roots, stems and leaves; how water, minerals, and carbon dioxide are transformed into foods; and the role of sunlight. Describes how fats and proteins are stored in plants.
Science - Natural
Dist - CF

Plants Need Love Too Series
Orchids - 49 2 MIN
Dist - TVSS

Plants of the Galapagos 15 MIN
VHS
Color (J H C)
$39.95 purchase _ #49-8166-V
Documents the many plants found on the Galapagos Islands, and reviews the geology of these islands made famous by Charles Darwin. Shows how the islands formed and how the plants found there have evolved and survived. Still frame.
Science - Natural
Dist - INSTRU **Prod** - CBSC

The Plants of the Saltmarsh 12 MIN
VHS / 35mm strip
Color; Audible or Automated Advance (I J H C P)
$34.00 _ #52 - 3428 ; $43.95 purchase _ #52 3428
Presents the natural history of the Spartina salt marsh plants of the North American Atlantic region. Emphasizes cordgrass, its ecological importance, and its adaptation to life in salt water. Includes a teacher's guide.
Science - Natural
Dist - CBSC **Prod** - CBSC

Plants of the Sea 13 MIN
16mm / U-matic / VHS
Color (I J H)
LC 80-700119
Examines plant life in the ocean, including plankton, kelp, red algae and grasses. Describes their importance to other living things. Tells how much of the energy that is trapped from the Sun is converted to forms useful to people by the algae of the sea.
Science - Natural; Science - Physical
Dist - PHENIX **Prod** - BEANMN 1980

Plants or animals 15 MIN
VHS / U-matic
Animals and such series; Module green - animals and plants
Color (I J)
Considers the similarities of and differences between animals and plants, pointing out that some creatures have features of both.
Science - Natural
Dist - AITECH **Prod** - WHROTV 1972

Plants Series
Part Four - Photosynthesis and Plant Activities 56.58 MIN
Part One - Everywhere on Earth 56.58 MIN
Plant Anatomy and Function 56.58 MIN
Reproduction 56.58 MIN
Dist - SRA

Plants that climb 12 MIN
VHS
Color; PAL (K P)
PdS29
Shows why some plants climb and how they do so. Starts with a clear visual explanation of the importance of sunlight to plants. Uses time - lapse photography to show the methods by which plants climb through twining stems and different kinds of tendril.
Science - Natural
Dist - BHA

Plants that grow from leaves, stems and roots 15 MIN
U-matic / VHS / 16mm
Color (J H)
$355.00 purchase - 16mm, $250.00 purchase - video _ #4380
Describes how, from the simple act of planting a bulb to new methods of cloning, new plants can be grown from a single parent, passing along the same favorable characteristics from one generation to the next. Features experiments which show how entire plants can be grown from a single cell, also known as cloning.
Science - Natural
Dist - CORF VIEWTH **Prod** - CORF VIEWTH 1983

Plants that have no flowers or seeds 11 MIN
U-matic / VHS / 16mm
Color (I J)
$270.00 purchase - 16mm, $190.00 purchase - video _ #1214; LC FIA67-2495
Features microscopic and time - lapse photography and artwork in a study of plants that have neither flowers nor seeds. Investigates how such plants as algae, mosses, ferns and fungi reproduce and obtain food.
Science - Natural
Dist - CORF **Prod** - CORF 1967

Plaque and Prevention 9 MIN
U-matic / VHS / 16mm
Dental Health Series
Color (I)
Explains and demonstrates the various methods recommended for the prevention of plaque build - up.
Health and Safety
Dist - JOU **Prod** - JOU 1972

Plaque and Prevention 11 MIN
16mm / 8mm cartridge
Color (PRO) (SPANISH)
Teaches a program for preventing plaque through oral hygiene, including flossing, brushing, disclosing tablets and water - irrigating devices.
Foreign Language; Health and Safety
Dist - PRORE **Prod** - PRORE

Plaque control - flossing 7 MIN
16mm / VHS / BETA / U-matic
UK dental care series; Pt 3
Color; PAL (G)
PdS60, PdS68 purchase
Explains why dental floss is necessary and how to use it in part of a four - part series.
Health and Safety
Dist - EDPAT

Plaque control - toothbrushing 8 MIN
16mm / VHS / BETA / U-matic
UK dental care series; Pt 2
Color; PAL (G)
PdS60, PdS68 purchase
Helps determine viewer's choice of toothbrush and the most effective ways to use it in part of a four - part series.
Health and Safety
Dist - EDPAT

Plaque - the facts 7 MIN
16mm / VHS / BETA / U-matic
UK dental care series; Pt 1
Color; PAL (G)
PdS60, PdS68 purchase
Looks at why plaque control is vital to healthy teeth and gums in part of a four - part series.
Health and Safety
Dist - EDPAT

Plas Newydd - Anglesey, Wales 26 MIN
U-matic / VHS / 16mm
Place in Europe Series
Color (H C A)
Presents the beautiful and useful eighteenth - century country home, which is located on Anglesey, the island where the Roman legions ended their conquest of Europe and the merchant navy located a school. A nearby oil refinery provides income but detracts from the naturalness of the grounds.
Geography - World
Dist - MEDIAG **Prod** - THAMES 1975

Plasma Deposition of Other Microelectronic Films 35 MIN
U-matic / VHS
Plasma Sputtering, Deposition and Growth of Microelectronic Films 'for VLSI Series
Color (IND)
Extends plasma deposition from oxide and nitride films into other electronic films such as oxynitride, aluminum oxide, aluminum nitride, zinc oxide and indium tinoxide.
Industrial and Technical Education; Science - Physical
Dist - COLOSU **Prod** - COLOSU

Plasma deposition of silicon oxide and silicon nitride - Pt I 35 MIN
U-matic / VHS
Plasma sputtering, deposition and growth of microelectronic films'for VLSI series
Color (IND)
Looks at low temperature plasma deposition of both silicon nitride and silicon oxide films on both Si and III - V substrates for use as an interlayer dielectric, doping mask and encapsulation layer. Gives advantages and disadvantages of plasma deposition of both silicon compounds.
Industrial and Technical Education; Science - Physical
Dist - COLOSU **Prod** - COLOSU

Plasma deposition of silicon oxide and silicon nitride - Pt II 35 MIN
U-matic / VHS
Plasma sputtering, deposition and growth of microelectronic films'for VLSI series
Color (IND)
Discusses plasma deposited oxides in terms of their breakdown voltage, index of refraction, pinhole density, deposition rate and physical film qualities such as adhesion, stress and step coverage.
Industrial and Technical Education; Science - Physical
Dist - COLOSU **Prod** - COLOSU

Plasma Etching and Pattern - for VLSI Fabrication Series
Al - Si - Cu dry - plasma etching 35 MIN
Dry - Plasma Etching - Physical and Chemical Mechanisms 35 MIN
Patterned Films - Dry - Plasma Etching, I 35 MIN
Patterned Films - Dry - Plasma Etching, II 35 MIN
Patterned Films - Wet Chemical Etching, II 35 MIN
Dist - COLOSU

Plasma Etching and Pattern Transfer - for VSLI Fabrication Series
Patterned Films - Wet Chemical Etching, I 35 MIN
Dist - COLOSU

Plasma Frequency, Mobility, Conductivity and Dielectric Constant
VHS / U-matic
Plasma Process Technology Fundamentals Series
Color (IND)
Presents concepts of mobility and conductivity to describe charged - particle motion in plasma. Describes concept of electron motion in gas with collisions as mobility - limited motion. Gives sample calculations for accelerated electron motion in helium gas of low pressure, and develops conductivity of the plasma and its relation to electron mobility.
Industrial and Technical Education; Science - Physical
Dist - COLOSU **Prod** - COLOSU

The Plasma membrane 15 MIN
16mm / U-matic / VHS
Cell biology series
Color (H C)
$420 purchase - 16 mm, $250 purchase - video _ #5222C
Shows how the cell members acts as a gateway to molecular traffic. Explains the processes of diffusion, osmosis, active transport, and endocytosis.
Science - Natural
Dist - CORF

Plasma Probes for Electron - Distribution Properties and Optical Emissions for Atomic
U-matic / VHS
Plasma Process Technology Fundamentals Series
Color (IND)
Describes plasma probes, optical spectroscopy and mass spectroscopy techniques for measuring quantitative atomic species concentrations in the plasma. Outlines electrical characteristics of a metal probe inserted into the plasma. Measures plasma electron temperature, plasma - electron density and plasma potential itself.
Industrial and Technical Education; Science - Physical
Dist - COLOSU **Prod** - COLOSU

Plasma process technology fundamentals series
Basic collision processes and cross - section behavior with velocity
Cathode emission of beam electrons and secondary emission coefficients
Cathode sheaths
Debye shielding and plasma oscillation for ions and electrons
Derivation of the Boltzmann equation
Distribution functions and detailed balance
Electron density decay processes
Electron density steady - state solutions
Floating sheaths
Free Radicals

Gas Discharge Collision Processes, I
Gas Discharge Collision Processes, II
Gases, Free Radicals and Charged Particles
Langevin Equation, Distribution Function and Boltzmann Equation
Maxwellian and Druyvesteyn Distributions
Optical Spectroscopy for Diagnostics and Process Control
Plasma Frequency, Mobility, Conductivity and Dielectric Constant
Plasma Probes for Electron - Distribution Properties and Optical Emissions for Atomic
Plasmas as fluids - Pt I
Plasmas as fluids - Pt II
Transport Coefficients - Conductivity
Transport Coefficients - Mobility and Diffusion
Dist - COLOSU

Plasma sputtering, deposition and growth of microelectronic film for VLSI series
Chemical vapor deposition - practical aspects — 35 MIN
Dist - COLOSU

Plasma Sputtering, Deposition and Growth of Microelectronic Films for VLSI Series
Chemical Vapor Deposition - Basics — 35 MIN
Evaporation and Ion - Beam Deposition — 35 MIN
Gas Discharge Sputtering, I — 35 MIN
Gas Discharge Sputtering, II — 35 MIN
Ions Impacting Surfaces — 35 MIN
Magnetron Sputtering — 35 MIN
Plasma Deposition of Other Microelectronic Films — 35 MIN
RF Glow Discharges — 35 MIN
Secondary Particle Emissions from Surfaces, I — 35 MIN
Secondary Particle Emissions from Surfaces, II — 35 MIN
Sputter Deposition - an Overview — 35 MIN
Dist - COLOSU

Plasma sputtering, deposition and growth of microelectronic films for VLSI series
Aluminum film deposition via sputtering — 35 MIN
Glow discharges — 35 MIN
Plasma deposition of silicon oxide and silicon nitride - Pt I — 35 MIN
Plasma deposition of silicon oxide and silicon nitride - Pt II — 35 MIN
Dist - COLOSU

Plasma Sputtering, Depostion and Growth of Microelectronic Films for VLSI Series
Dry Plasma Development of Photoresist and Plasma Annealing — 35 MIN
Plasma - Surface Interactings — 23 MIN
Dist - COLOSU

Plasma - Surface Interactings — 23 MIN
U-matic / VHS
Plasma Sputtering, Depostion and Growth of Microelectronic Films for VLSI Series
Color (IND)
Presents beginning of interaction of plasmas with substrate surfaces. Describes surface topology in terms of macroscopic and microscopic defects, with special emphasis on crystalline silicon surfaces.
Industrial and Technical Education; Science
Dist - COLOSU **Prod** - COLOSU

Plasma - the Fourth State of Matter — 10 MIN
16mm / U-matic / VHS
Color (I)
LC FIA68-3182
Shows that as temperature increases, matter changes from one to another of the three familiar states - solid, liquid and gas. Explores the properties and potential uses of plasma, the fourth state of matter, in which energy causes the atoms themselves to break down into free electrons and protons or ions.
Science - Physical
Dist - PHENIX **Prod** - LUMAR 1968

Plasmas as fluids - Pt I
U-matic / VHS
Plasma process technology fundamentals series
Color (IND)
Views plasmas as multicomponent fluids in order to derive a macroscopic equation that includes density, temperature and pressure as variables rather than atomic cross sections. Shows how a fluid equation for plasmas is derived and compares to the classical Navier - Stokes equation.
Industrial and Technical Education; Mathematics; Science - Physical
Dist - COLOSU **Prod** - COLOSU

Plasmas as fluids - Pt II
VHS / U-matic
Plasma process technology fundamentals series
Color (IND)
Relates how moments of the Boltzmann equation yield three macroscopic equations - particle continuity, momentum conservation and energy conservation. Covers production and loss of electrons through excitation, ionization and recombination.
Industrial and Technical Education; Mathematics; Science - Physical
Dist - COLOSU **Prod** - COLOSU

Plasmasis — 14 MIN
16mm / U-matic / VHS
Color (A)
Portrays the evolution of the species in this modern ballet from Cuba.
Fine Arts; Geography - World; Science - Natural
Dist - CNEMAG **Prod** - CUBAFI 1974

Plaster — 4 MIN
16mm
Color (G)
$15.00 rental
Presents a performance film by sculptor Charley Ray.
Fine Arts
Dist - CANCIN **Prod** - HUDINA 1975

Plaster Casting — 25 MIN
16mm
B&W (H C)
Features Tylden W Streett, sculpture instructor and director of graduate schools of the Maryland Institute College of Art, who demonstrates the process of translating a clay portrait head into a plaster cast through the use of a one - time waste mold. Describes the techniques used, their underlying principles and the use of all of the necessary materials.
Fine Arts
Dist - HALLMK **Prod** - HALLMK

Plaster Dorsal Wrist Cockup Splint with Outrigger — 23 MIN
VHS / U-matic
Color (PRO)
Demonstrates the construction of a plaster dorsal wrist cockup splint with outrigger. Procedures for making a pattern, forming the splint and outrigger, and making and attaching finger loops and a support strap are covered in detail.
Health and Safety
Dist - HSCIC **Prod** - HSCIC

Plaster Sculpture in Color — 11 MIN
16mm / U-matic / VHS
Color (J H)
Discusses 3 - dimensional art activities. Encourages experimenting with ways to express ideas in sculptural form. Suggests materials for use.
Fine Arts
Dist - IFB **Prod** - IFB 1957

Plasterers, roofers, carpenters — 30 MIN
BETA / VHS
This old house series; The Dorchester series; Pt 1
Color
Shows the renovation of kitchen walls, the chimney and the front porch of an old house.
Industrial and Technical Education; Sociology
Dist - CORF **Prod** - WGBHTV

Plastic and Reconstruction Surgery of the Hand — 34 MIN
16mm
Color (PRO)
LC FIE52-1350
Illustrates cases of early traumatic wounds of the hands, methods of elective surgery of the hands and late reconstructive surgery.
Health and Safety; Science; Science - Natural
Dist - USNAC **Prod** - USN 1976

Plastic and Reconstructive Surgery — 19 MIN
U-matic / VHS
Color (C)
$249.00, $149.00 purchase _ #AD - 1429
Explains some of the more common cosmetic surgery procedures. Shows reconstructive surgery and how computer aided design is alleviating some of the complications of reconstructive surgery, as well as computer designed artificial joints, bones and sections of the skull.
Health and Safety; Science - Natural
Dist - FOTH **Prod** - FOTH

Plastic Deformation and Annealing of Metals I — 60 MIN
BETA / VHS / U-matic
Color
$400 purchase
Shows effects of plastic deformation on microstructure.
Science; Science - Physical
Dist - ASM **Prod** - ASM 1987

Plastic Deformation and Annealing of Metals II — 41 MIN
U-matic / BETA / VHS
Color
$400 purchase
Shows how dislocations effect mechanical properties.
Science; Science - Physical
Dist - ASM **Prod** - ASM 1987

Plastic fantastic — 20 MIN
VHS / U-matic
Color (H)
$280.00, $330.00 purchase, $50.00 rental
Explores biodegradable plastic, plastic recycling and other alternatives to the problems of plastic disposal. An ITV London production.
Industrial and Technical Education; Science - Natural
Dist - NDIM

Plastic fantastic — 30 MIN
VHS
QED series
Color (A PRO C)
PdS65 purchase _ Unavailable in Canada and USA
Details the work of Maurice Ward, a retired hairdresser, who has invented of a new kind of plastic called Starlite. Tells how his discovery has impressed the scientific world and attracted government departments and multi-national companies. Narrated by Alec Guinness.
History - World; Industrial and Technical Education
Dist - BBCENE

Plastic filler — 13 MIN
VHS / BETA / 16mm
Color (A IND VOC)
$68.50 purchase _ #KTI23
Covers how, where, and when to use plastic body filler.
Industrial and Technical Education
Dist - RMIBHF **Prod** - RMIBHF

Plastic haircut — 15 MIN
16mm
B&W (G)
$30.00 rental
Features sets by William Wiley and Robert Hudson with a soundtrack by Steve Reich.
Fine Arts
Dist - CANCIN **Prod** - NELSOR 1963

Plastic Isolators - New Tools for Bio - Medical Research — 14 MIN
16mm
Color
LC FIE64-108
Demonstrates how inexpensive plastic isolators protect laboratory animals from contamination during research studies and safeguard personnel from virulent organisms, noxious fumes and radioactive dusts.
Health and Safety; Industrial and Technical Education
Dist - USNAC **Prod** - USPHS 1964

Plastic Journey — 19 MIN
U-matic / VHS / 16mm
Color (H C A)
LC 76-700302
Shows how plastic materials were discovered, explains methods of transporting pellets and describes types of machines used and products made in the plastic injection molding process.
Business and Economics; Industrial and Technical Education
Dist - MCFI **Prod** - UMDME 1973

Plastic piping — 60 MIN
VHS / U-matic
Mechanical equipment maintenance series; Advanced pipefitting; Module 17
Color (IND VOC)
Industrial and Technical Education
Dist - LEIKID **Prod** - LEIKID

Plastic Surgery — 10 MIN
U-matic / VHS
Children's Medical Series
Color (P I)
Explores the question of self - image and children's concerns about becoming a new person after plastic surgery, as well as fears they may have about the operation itself.
Health and Safety
Dist - CORF **Prod** - HFDT 1982

Plastic Surgery 18 MIN
16mm
Doctors at Work Series
B&W (H C A)
LC FIA65-1357
A plastic surgeon explores the motives and emotional stability of a teen - age girl with a high - bridged nose before concluding that surgery is warranted. Shows the operation in progress and the reconstructed nose following surgery.
Health and Safety; Psychology
Dist - LAWREN **Prod** - CMA 1961

Plastic Surgery 25 MIN
VHS / U-matic
Color
Shows that reconstructive surgery is an area in medicine encompassing more than just face - lifts and nose jobs.
Health and Safety
Dist - MEDCOM **Prod** - MEDCOM

Plastic Surgery - Auto Accessories - Dog - Cat Food
U-matic / VHS
Consumer Survival Series
Color
Examines plastic surgery, auto accessories and dog and cat food.
Health and Safety; Home Economics; Industrial and Technical Education; Science - Natural
Dist - MDCPB **Prod** - MDCPB

Plastic surgery - facelift 45 MIN
VHS
Surgical procedures series
Color (C PRO G)
$149.00 purchase, $75.00 rental _ #UW4577
Focuses on a 51 - year - old patient, a former model who owns a public relations firm and is the mother of three. Watches Dr Neal Handel perform a rhytidectomy in which he removes excess skin from the neck and pulls the face back to make the skin tighter, and a blepharoplasty, in which excess skin is removed from the eye area. Part of a 17 - part series recording surgical procedures in detail, with specialists who explain the ailment, the anatomical function of the part of the body being operated on, how successful surgery might improve the patient's quality of life. Hosted by Dr Donna Willis.
Health and Safety
Dist - FOTH

Plastic world 29 MIN
VHS
FROG series; Series 2; 207
Color (P I J)
$100.00 purchase
Offers the seventh and final program in series 2 by Friends of Research and Odd Gadgets. Lifts science off the textbook page into the real world to show how enjoyable and challenging science can be. In this episode, the Froggers construct a totally cool plastic world, right down to the food on the table. Produced by Christopher Howard.
Industrial and Technical Education; Science - Physical
Dist - BULFRG **Prod** - OWLTV 1993

Plastics 21 MIN
VHS / 16mm
Manufacturing Materials Series
Color (I)
LC 90713863
Explains how plastic products are made. Surveys the various uses for plastics and considers their drawbacks.
Business and Economics; History - World; Industrial and Technical Education
Dist - BARR

Plastics 11 MIN
16mm / U-matic / VHS
Color (I J H)
Describes the versatility that has made plastics such an important part of our lives.
Industrial and Technical Education
Dist - PHENIX **Prod** - SANTER 1973

Plastics
VHS / U-matic
Color (J H)
Consists of 1 color filmstrip, cassette or 1 videocassette and a teacher's guide.
Industrial and Technical Education
Dist - CAREER **Prod** - CAREER 1977

Plastics and fiber glass series
Fiber glass 13 MIN
Thermoplastics 13 MIN
Dist - SF

Plastics Identification and Repair 29 MIN
BETA / VHS / 16mm
Color (A PRO)
$108.00 purchase _ #AB127
Discusses the identification and repair of plastics.
Industrial and Technical Education
Dist - RMIBHF **Prod** - RMIBHF

Plastics I - Layout, Cutting, Finishing, and Assembly 30 MIN
U-matic / VHS
Arts and Crafts Series
Color (H A)
LC 81-706993
Demonstrates layouts, cutting, finishing, and assembly techniques to be used with acrylic plastics.
Fine Arts
Dist - GPN **Prod** - GPN 1981

Plastics II - Heat Forming and Assembly 30 MIN
U-matic / VHS
Arts and Crafts Series
Color (H A)
LC 81-706995
Demonstrates how to create objects from plastics using cohesive solvents and heat - forming techniques.
Fine Arts
Dist - GPN **Prod** - GPN 1981

Plastics III - Casting Polyester and Cutting Plastic Foam 30 MIN
VHS / U-matic
Arts and Crafts Series
Color (H A)
LC 81-706997
Demonstrates how to use liquid polyester resin to encapsulate objects for display. Describes the technique of cutting polystyrene and styrofoam with a hot wire cutter.
Fine Arts
Dist - GPN **Prod** - GPN 1981

Plastics - Industrial Processes and Products 24 MIN
16mm
Color (J H C)
Uses animation and actual scenes of production to explain the principles of basic manufacturing processes of the plastics industry and their applications to the production of consumer goods.
Business and Economics; Industrial and Technical Education
Dist - STSU **Prod** - STSU 1963

Plastics Series no 10
Machining Laminated Plastics 19 MIN
Dist - USNAC

Plastics Series no 1
Origin and Synthesis of Plastics Materials 16 MIN
Dist - USNAC

Plastics Series no 2
Methods of Processing Plastics Materials 25 MIN
Dist - USNAC

Plastics Series no 7
Injection Molding, Pt 1, Setting Up the Press and Molding a Part 16 MIN
Dist - USNAC

Plastics Series no 8
Injection Molding, Pt 2, Cleaning and Servicing the Press 12 MIN
Dist - USNAC

Plastics Series no 9
Finishing Molded Parts 14 MIN
Dist - USNAC

Plastics series
Compression molding, Pt 1, preparing the charge and loading the mold 11 MIN
Compression molding, Pt 2, molding a simple part 10 MIN
Transfer Molding - Molding a Part with Inserts 10 MIN
Dist - USNAC

Plastics - the world of imagination 27 MIN
U-matic / VHS
Color (IND VOC G)
Emphasizes the important role of plastics in the modern world. Explores uses of the material in such diverse fields as flight, architecture, textiles, packaging, transportation, energy conservation and medicine.
Business and Economics; Industrial and Technical Education
Dist - MTP **Prod** - SPLENG SPLIND

Plastiphobia 10 MIN
16mm
Color (K P I J H)
LC 73-700973
Uses animation to show crazy characters and objects changing shape and turning into other things in a succession of scenes. Shows the limitless possibilities of clay.
Fine Arts
Dist - IFF **Prod** - NFUNZ 1973

Plate - coupled multivibrator - VT 40 MIN
16mm
B&W
LC 74-705381
Discusses the purpose of each component in the plate coupled multivibrator circuit, the construction of a waveform graph and how to maintain stability. Filmed in Kinescope.
Industrial and Technical Education; Science; Science - Natural
Dist - USNAC **Prod** - USAF

Plate cutting manual 8 MIN
BETA / VHS
Welding training comprehensive series; Oxy - acetylene welding
Color (IND)
Industrial and Technical Education; Psychology
Dist - RMIBHF **Prod** - RMIBHF

Plate detector 30 MIN
16mm
B&W (IND VOC A)
LC 74-705380
Discusses the purpose of each component in the plate detector circuit and explains how the circuit recovers ultrastructure of the megakaryocyte as well as the advantages and limitations of the plate detector with a reference to selectivity, sensitivity and signal handling ability. Filmed in Kinescope.
Industrial and Technical Education; Science; Science - Natural
Dist - USNAC **Prod** - USAF

Plate Tectonics 8 MIN
VHS / U-matic
Color
LC 80-706469
Shows puppets being used to explain the theory of plate tectonics to children visiting Rock Creek Park.
Science - Physical
Dist - USNAC **Prod** - USNPS 1979

Plate Tectonics 30 MIN
U-matic / VHS
Earth, Sea and Sky Series
Color (C)
Explores continental drift and sea floor spreading. Follows a scientifically outfitted deep sea drilling ship as it travels the world's oceans collecting data.
Science - Physical
Dist - DALCCD **Prod** - DALCCD

Plate tectonics 15 MIN
VHS
Basic concepts in physical geology video series
Color (J H)
$98.00 purchase _ #193 Y 0015
Traces the development of the modern theory of a dynamic Earth and interior structure, from Wegener's ideas on continental drift to the discoveries of the mid - ocean ridges, paleomagnetism, abyssal trenches, sea - floor spreading, transform faults and the global pattern of shifting tectonic plates. Part of a ten - part series on physical geology.
Science - Physical
Dist - WARDS **Prod** - WARDS 1990

Plate tectonics 52 MIN
U-matic / VHS
Earth's interior series; Basic and petroleum geology for non - geologists
Color (IND)
Industrial and Technical Education; Science - Physical
Dist - GPCV **Prod** - PHILLP

Plate Tectonics 6 MIN
U-matic / VHS / 16mm
Color (I J)
$150, $105, $135 purchase _ #B428
Uses live action and animation to describe the study of plate tectonics, and present a cinematic timeline showing our planet's long and continuing history of continental drift. Shows how continental drift has helped shape our planet's physical and evolutionary faces.
Science - Physical
Dist - BARR **Prod** - BARR 1986

Plate Tectonics 55 MIN
U-matic / VHS
Basic Geology Series
Color (IND)

Industrial and Technical Education; Science - Physical
Dist - GPCV **Prod** - GPCV

Plate Tectonics 28 MIN
VHS / U-matic
Oceanus - the Marine Environment Series
Color (C A)
Science - Natural; Science - Physical
Dist - SCCON **Prod** - SCCON 1980

Plate Tectonics - a Revolution in the Earth Sciences 28 MIN
VHS / U-matic
Earth Explored Series
Color
Illustrates how mountain building occurs and how animals migrate, Uses animation and visits to the Alps and active volcanic areas.
Geography - World; Science - Natural; Science - Physical
Dist - PBS **Prod** - BBCTV

Plate tectonics series
The Global mosaic 25 MIN
Mountain building in the Western Himalayas 25 MIN
Volcanoes of the Kenya Rift 28 MIN
Dist - CORF

Plate tectonics - the puzzle of the continents 18 MIN
VHS
Earth science series
Color (J H)
$59.95 purchase _ #ES8420; $99.95, $69.95 purchase _ #Q18422; $64.95 purchase _ #ES8420
Considers the fundamentals of the Plate Tectonics Theory from the observations of Alfred Wegener on continental drift to the latest computer analysis of movements at plate boundaries. Includes a teachers' guide. Part of a six - part series taking a contemporary look at Planet Earth, its natural resources and the human impact on global environment.
Science - Physical
Dist - SCTRES **Prod** - SCTRES
CF
INSTRU

Plate tectonics videodisc
Videodisc
Color; CAV (I J H)
$375.00 purchase _ #A5LD 1311
Allows instant access to hundres of photographs, diagrams and video sequences on every major aspect of plate tectonics, including - sea - floor spreading, paleomagnetism, subduction, convection, transform faults, hot spots and plumes, volcanoes, earthquakes, prediction and planning and plate motions. Enables use of resources in a number of ways detailed in accompanying teacher's guide. Correlated lab activities packs available separately.
Science - Physical
Dist - CLRVUE **Prod** - CLRVUE 1992

Plate welding - Pt I
VHS
Shielded metal arc welding training systems series
$445.00 purchase _ #MJ093125V
Provides an introduction for beginners to upgrade their skills in plate welding.
Education; Industrial and Technical Education
Dist - CAREER **Prod** - CAREER

Plate welding - Pt II
VHS
Shielded metal arc welding training systems series
$445.00 purchase _ #MJ093127V
Provides training in the area of plate welding for advanced welders.
Education; Industrial and Technical Education
Dist - CAREER **Prod** - CAREER

Plateau and Pacific 28 MIN
16mm
Color (C A)
Tells about the work of a field school of archeological students who excavated two sites in southeastern Washington. Explains that by combining the information from the two sites a history of the reservoir area stretching over more than 8,000 years is being developed.
Geography - United States; History - United States; Science - Physical
Dist - UTEX **Prod** - UTEX 1963

Plateau Farmers in France 15 MIN
U-matic / VHS / 16mm
Man and His World Series
Color (P I J H C)
LC 77-705491
Shows the contrast between traditional and modern farming techniques and mechanization in France.
Agriculture; Geography - World
Dist - FI **Prod** - FI 1969

Plateaued - Solutions to career gridlock 29 MIN
VHS
Color (PRO G A)
$545.00 purchase, $140.00 rental
Encourages management recognition of employees' achievements when promotion is not possible, pointing out that motivation leads to accomplishment.
Business and Economics; Guidance and Counseling; Psychology
Dist - EXTR **Prod** - DARTNL

Platelet aggregation - clot retraction - platelet factor 3 18 MIN
U-matic / VHS
Blood coagulation laboratory techniques series
Color
LC 79-707605
Demonstrates the instrumentation and procedure for assessment of platelet aggregation, a quantitative clot retraction method using platelet - rich plasma and a platelet factor 3 assay in which platelets are stimulated with epinephrine and kaolin to induce platelet factor 3 release and the recalcification time of the plasma is measured.
Health and Safety; Science
Dist - UMICH **Prod** - UMICH 1977

Plates and platemaking 13 MIN
VHS
Color (H C)
$69.95 purchase _ #SE - 13
Discusses light sources, vacuum time, plate processors, Newton rings, metal plates, electrostatic plates, chemistry, integrators, time - saving steps and money - saving hints. Demonstrates plate storage, the gray scale, the sensitivity guide, checking exposure time, developing the plate and developing the electrostatic plate.
Industrial and Technical Education
Dist - INSTRU

Platform Safety and Emergency Shutdown Procedures 24 MIN
U-matic / VHS
Color (IND)
Covers the steps to take to abandon a platform and what to do if an employee goes overboard. Describes firefighting equipment, shutdown systems and general safety rules and procedures.
Business and Economics; Health and Safety; Industrial and Technical Education; Social Science
Dist - UTEXPE **Prod** - UTEXPE

Platform to the stars 11 MIN
16mm
Screen news digest series; Vol 22; Issue 7
Color
Presents the space shuttle and its role in space exploration.
Industrial and Technical Education; Science - Physical
Dist - AFA **Prod** - AFA 1980

Plating operations 14 MIN
BETA / VHS / U-matic
Hazard communication series
Color (IND G)
$395.00 purchase _ #820 - 12
Informs employees of the types of materials used in plating operations, the potential health hazards, routes of entry of materials into the body, physical hazards, appropriate work practices, personal protective equipment and emergency procedures. Emphasizes the importance of consulting the Material Safety Data Sheet - MSDS - for complete physical and health hazard information on for a particular hazardous material. Part of a series on hazard communication.
Health and Safety; Industrial and Technical Education; Psychology
Dist - ITSC **Prod** - ITSC

Platinum 21 MIN
VHS / U-matic
Color (J)
Tells about the mining and use of platinum, an important metal widely used today in medicine, industry and fine jewelry construction. Commences with platinum's discovery and use as the standard metric measure in the 19th century, and shows how it is formed, mined, refined and used.
Industrial and Technical Education; Mathematics; Science - Physical
Dist - EDMI **Prod** - GAZEL 1981

Platinum Blonde 91 MIN
16mm
B&W
Tells how a man must choose between his aristocratic wife and a fellow newspaper reporter, played by Loretta Young. Stars Robert Williams and Jean Harlow. Directed by Frank Capra.
Fine Arts
Dist - TWYMAN **Prod** - CPC 1931

Platinum Jewelry Workshop I 30 MIN
U-matic
Platinum Jewelry Workshop Series
Color (J C)
Shows a detailed view of individual pieces presented by each artist with commentary on design, aesthetic motivation and specific use of platinum. Artists appear in the following order - Leslie Leupp, Helen Shirk, Gary Nemchock, Vickie Sedman, David Keens, Hiroko Pijanowski, Gene Pijanowski, Gary Griffin.
Fine Arts; Industrial and Technical Education
Dist - SDSC **Prod** - SDSC 1979

Platinum Jewelry Workshop II 30 MIN
U-matic
Platinum Jewelry Workshop Series
Color (J C)
Shows continuation of Tape #1 with the following artists - Jane Groover, Marcia Lewins, Fred Woell, Arline Fisch. Concluding remarks and general observations by Projector Director, Arline Fisch.
Fine Arts; Industrial and Technical Education
Dist - SDSC **Prod** - SDSC 1979

Platinum Jewelry Workshop III 30 MIN
U-matic
Platinum Jewelry Workshop Series
Color (J C)
Discussion of the specialized tools needed for working in platinum. Demonstrations of various technical procedures by participants as follows - tolls, Arline Fisch - chasing, Marcia Lewins - forging, Dieter Muller - Stach - soldering, Gary Nemchock - twisted wire and sheet metal folding, Gene Pijanowski.
Fine Arts; Industrial and Technical Education
Dist - SDSC **Prod** - SDSC 1979

Platinum Jewelry Workshop IV 30 MIN
U-matic
Platinum Jewelry Workshop Series
Color (J C)
Demonstrations of the cold forging of wire, annealing and a variety of Japanese inlay techniques including specialized tools required for these particular processes. Techniques discussed as follows - forging and annealing, Gary Griffin - Japanese inlay techniques, Hiroko Pijanowski.
Fine Arts; Industrial and Technical Education
Dist - SDSC **Prod** - SDSC 1979

Platinum Jewelry Workshop Series
Platinum Jewelry Workshop I 30 MIN
Platinum Jewelry Workshop II 30 MIN
Platinum Jewelry Workshop III 30 MIN
Platinum Jewelry Workshop IV 30 MIN
Platinum Jewelry Workshop V 30 MIN
Dist - SDSC

Platinum Jewelry Workshop V 30 MIN
U-matic
Platinum Jewelry Workshop Series
Color (J C)
Discussion of the fusion and granulation potentials of platinum, fusing being an effective process but granulation a difficult and unsuccessful experiment. Demonstration of fusion joints by welding, David Keens. A detailed discussion of the casting process and its specifications for platinum, Fred Woell - finishing and polishing procedures for platinum, Helen Shirk.
Fine Arts; Industrial and Technical Education
Dist - SDSC **Prod** - SDSC 1979

The Platinum rainbow 120 MIN
VHS
Color (COR G)
$119.00 purchase _ #605
Takes an inside look at the ingredients of success in the music industry. Features over 50 interviews with top industry executives. Focuses on the overlapping roles and responsbilities of producers, managers, attorneys, agents, publishers, distributors and others in shaping an artist's career. Based on the book The Platinum Rainbow. Produced by Mike Craven.
Business and Economics; Fine Arts
Dist - FIRLIT

Plato 45 MIN
VHS
Great philosophers series
Color; PAL (H C A)
PdS99 purchase
Introduces the concepts of Western philosophy and one of its greatest thinkers, Plato. Features a contemporary philosopher who, in conversation with Bryan Magee, discusses him and his ideas. Part one of a fifteen part series.
Education; Religion and Philosophy
Dist - BBCENE

Plato in Amerika 20 MIN
16mm
B&W (C A)

LC FIA66-517
The escapades of a first generation Greek caught between two cultures.
History - United States
Dist - NYU **Prod** - NYU 1965

Plato - Pt 5 - Dualism 30 MIN
U-matic
From Socrates to Sartre Series
Color
Discusses the concept of dualism in the work of Plato.
History - World; Religion and Philosophy
Dist - MDCPB **Prod** - MDCPB

Plato - Pt 4 - Tripartite Soul and Contemporary Psychology 30 MIN
U-matic
From Socrates to Sartre Series
Color
Describes Plato's theory of a tripartite soul and its relation to 20th century psychology.
History - World; Religion and Philosophy
Dist - MDCPB **Prod** - MDCPB

Plato - Pt 1 - the Death of Socrates 30 MIN
U-matic
From Socrates to Sartre Series
Color
Deals with the death of Socrates.
History - World; Religion and Philosophy
Dist - MDCPB **Prod** - MDCPB

Plato - Pt 3 - Theory of Knowledge 30 MIN
U-matic
From Socrates to Sartre Series
Color
Discusses the theory of knowledge in Plato's works.
History - World; Religion and Philosophy
Dist - MDCPB **Prod** - MDCPB

Plato - Pt 2 - the Republic, the Socratic Method, the Allegory of the Cave 30 MIN
U-matic
From Socrates to Sartre Series
Color
Looks at The Republic, the Socratic Method, and the Allegory of the Cave.
History - World; Religion and Philosophy
Dist - MDCPB **Prod** - MDCPB

Plato's Apology 58 MIN
Videoreel / VT2
Dialogue of the Western World Series
Color
Features Dean Robert A Goldwin of St John's College of Annapolis and three of his students discussing Plato's Apology with a special guest.
Literature and Drama; Religion and Philosophy
Dist - PBS **Prod** - MDCPB

Plato's Apology 60 MIN
VHS
Great Ideas Series
Color (H)
$14.00 rental _ #60923
Features Mortimer J. Adler in the third of five seminars of his Great Ideas Series, which exposes a group of high school students to the most important literary works of Western civilization. This installment examines Plato's Apology.
Education; Literature and Drama; Religion and Philosophy
Dist - PSU **Prod** - EBEC 1987

Plato's Apology - the Life and Teachings of Socrates 30 MIN
U-matic / VHS / 16mm
Humanities - Philosophy and Political Thought Series
Color (H C)
A study of Socrates, a man whose influence on the minds of men still endures.
Biography; Religion and Philosophy
Dist - EBEC **Prod** - EBEC 1962

Plato's Cave 20 MIN
16mm / U-matic / VHS
Color (J)
LC 74-703223
Presents an adaptation of Plato's allegory of the cave from the seventh book of the Republic. With dialog in classical Greek.
Literature and Drama
Dist - PFP **Prod** - GOULDA 1974

Plato's Crito 58 MIN
Videoreel / VT2
Dialogue of the Western World Series
Color
Features Dean Robert A Goldwin of St John's College of Annapolis and three of his students discussing Plato's Crito with a special guest.
Literature and Drama; Religion and Philosophy
Dist - PBS **Prod** - MDCPB

Plato's Meno 58 MIN
Videoreel / VT2
Dialogue of the Western World Series
Color
Features Dean Robert A Goldwin of St John's College of Annapolis and three of his students discussing Plato's Meno with a special guest.
History - World; Literature and Drama; Religion and Philosophy
Dist - PBS **Prod** - MDCPB

Plato's The Cave 10 MIN
VHS
Color (J H C G) (SPANISH)
$235.00, $79.00 purchase, $60.00 rental
Offers an excerpt from Plato's Republic, Book VII, narrated by Orson Welles. Portrays prisoners in a cave who mistake shadows for reality. One prisoner who is released learns to understand the nature of real things in contrast with their shadows. He returns to the cave to share his enlightenment.
Religion and Philosophy
Dist - CF **Prod** - BOSUST 1975

The Platte Valley - America's Great Road West 30 MIN
16mm
Great Plains Trilogy, 3 Series Explorer and Settler - the White Man 'Arrives; Explorer and settler - the white man arrives
B&W (J)
Portrays the Platte Valley as a natural highway to the West, and as a fur trade route. Discusses national expansion. Describes the Oregon Trail through Nebraska, the Mormon emigration, the California Gold Rush and the rugged life along the trail.
History - United States
Dist - UNEBR **Prod** - KUONTV 1954

Platyhelminthes, Rotifer and Tardigrada
VHS
Pieper - zoology prelab dissections - series
Color (J H C)
$95.00 purchase _ #CG - 968 - VS
Presents dissection instruction and an anatomy review of the Platyhelminthes, Rotifer and Tardigrada. Includes a brief post test to gauge student retention. Part of a 15 - part series on zoological lab dissection, including a lab safety review, produced by Bill Pieper.
Science; Science - Natural
Dist - HRMC

Platypus 25 MIN
U-matic
Animal Wonder Down Under Series
Color (I J H)
Takes an underwater look at the behavior of the duck - billed platypus.
Geography - World; Science - Natural
Dist - CEPRO **Prod** - CEPRO

Platypus - Ornithorhynchus Anatinus 22 MIN
16mm
Color (J)
LC 74-703289
Gives a comprehensive account of the platypus, the rare animal which is found only in Australia.
Geography - World
Dist - AUIS **Prod** - ANAIB 1973

Play 29 MIN
VHS / 16mm
Everybody's children series
(G)
$90.00 purchase _ #BPN16108
Explores the meaning of play and its development in children. Part of a series which examines child raising in modern society.
Psychology; Sociology
Dist - RMIBHF TVOTAR **Prod** - RMIBHF TVOTAR

The Play 13 MIN
U-matic / VHS / 16mm
Color (H C)
Shows two children at play as they fantasize and act out the aggressions of their adult environment.
Psychology
Dist - FI **Prod** - ZAGREB

Play 29 MIN
U-matic
Everybody's Children Series
Color (PRO)
Explores the meaning of play and its development in children.
Home Economics; Psychology; Sociology
Dist - TVOTAR **Prod** - TVOTAR 1985

Play - along games and songs 30 MIN
VHS
Sesame street home video series
Color (K P)
$14.95 purchase; $19.95 purchase _ #S01557
Features Oscar, Big Bird, and the rest of the Sesame Street gang as they present the popular Sesame Street games and songs, which teach skills such as reading, counting, and reasoning.
English Language; Fine Arts; Literature and Drama; Mathematics
Dist - PBS UILL **Prod** - WNETTV

Play and Cultural Continuity Series Part 2
Southern Black Children 27 MIN
Dist - CFDC

Play and Cultural Continuity Series Part 3
Mexican - American Children 27 MIN
Dist - CFDC

Play and Cultural Continuity Series Part 4
Montana Indian Children 27 MIN
Dist - CFDC

Play and cultural continuity series
Appalachian children 25 MIN
Dist - CFDC

Play and defend - Volume III
VHS
Bridge player's video library series
Color (G)
$29.95 purchase _ #RV005
Presents 'Life Master' Audrey Grant explaining bridge for beginner and advanced.
Physical Education and Recreation
Dist - SIV

Play and Personality 45 MIN
16mm
B&W (C T)
An actual record of a group of preschool children whose mothers have severe neuroses. Demonstrates that children's anxieties are revealed in play, that the anxieties are related to their mothers', and that a child tries to master his fears in play.
Physical Education and Recreation; Psychology; Sociology
Dist - NYU **Prod** - CASH 1964

Play Ball 25 MIN
U-matic
Not Another Science Show Series
Color (H C)
Explains the scientific principles of bowling, pool, baseball, and tennis.
Physical Education and Recreation; Science
Dist - TVOTAR **Prod** - TVOTAR 1986

Play Ball 15 MIN
U-matic / VHS
Explorers Unlimited Series
Color (P I)
Observes preparations for a major league baseball game at Cleveland Stadium.
Physical Education and Recreation; Social Science
Dist - AITECH **Prod** - WVIZTV 1971

Play Ball, Kate 8 MIN
U-matic / VHS
Giant First Start Series
Color (K P)
$29.95 purchase _ #VP012
Presents an adaptation of Play Ball, Kate. Contains a 32 page hardcover book and a video.
English Language; Literature and Drama
Dist - TROLA

Play Ball, Play Safe 14 MIN
16mm
Color
LC FIA66-520
Emphasizes the importance of safety precautions in sports. Features a young baseball team that loses a championship because of injuries, and experienced players who demonstrate techniques used to avoid injuries on the field.
Health and Safety; Physical Education and Recreation
Dist - AETNA **Prod** - AETNA 1965

Play Better Hockey 19 MIN
16mm
B&W (I)
Shows the basic skills and the strategy of attack and defense in hockey, as demonstrated by some of the Indian Olympic team players.
Physical Education and Recreation
Dist - NEDINF **Prod** - INDIA

Play bluegrass banjo by ear 60 MIN
VHS

Color (G)
$39.95 purchase _ #VD - KEI - BJ01
Features Bill Keith who teaches basic music theory, including techniques for finding melody and harmony notes. Shows how to combine these techniques with basic rolls to create bluegrass solos. Examines the banjo fingerboard, including details of right - hand rolls, harmonized scales, pentatonic runs and licks and more.
Fine Arts
Dist - HOMETA **Prod** - HOMETA

Play Bridge - Omar Sharif 55 MIN
VHS / BETA
$39.95 purchase _ #870
Takes you methodically through the bidding and playing of fifteen challenging bridge games.
Physical Education and Recreation
Dist - BESTF **Prod** - BESTF

Play Bridge Series

Bidding problem hands	30 MIN
Clear signals	30 MIN
Defensive Strategy	30 MIN
Double Talk	30 MIN
Fooling the opponents	30 MIN
Judgement in Bidding	30 MIN
No Trump Bidding and Play	30 MIN
Playing the Hand	30 MIN
Safety Plays and End Plays	30 MIN
The Simple Overcall	30 MIN
Slams - Bidding and Play	30 MIN
Take - Out Doubles	30 MIN
Using the Clues	30 MIN
When they Interfere	30 MIN

Dist - KYTV

Play Bridge with the Experts Series Pt 14
Lew Mathe 30 MIN
Dist - GPN

Play Bridge with the Experts Series Pt 15
Dr George S Dawkins 30 MIN
Dist - GPN

Play bridge with the experts series pt 20
Carol Sanders, Pt 1 30 MIN
Dist - GPN

Play Bridge with the Experts Series Pt 23
Alfred Sheinwold, Pt 2 30 MIN
Dist - GPN

Play Bridge with the Experts Series Pt 3
Dr Frank Hoadley - Pt 1 30 MIN
Dist - GPN

Play Bridge with the Experts Series Pt 8
Emma Jean Hawes, Pt 1 30 MIN
Dist - GPN

Play Bridge with the Experts Series Pt 9
Emma Jean Hawes, Pt 2 30 MIN
Dist - GPN

Play bridge with the experts series

Alfred Sheinwold, Pt 1	30 MIN
Betty Ann Kennedy, Pt 1	30 MIN
Betty Ann Kennedy, Pt 2	30 MIN
Bob Hamman - Pt 1	30 MIN
Bob Hamman - Pt 2	30 MIN
Bobby Goldman - Pt 1	30 MIN
Bobby Goldman - Pt 2	30 MIN
Bobby Goldman - Pt 3	30 MIN
Bobby Nail	30 MIN
Bobby Wolff - Pt 1	30 MIN
Bobby Wolff - Pt 2	30 MIN
Carol Sanders - Pt 2	30 MIN
Dan Morse	30 MIN
Dr Frank Hoadley - Pt 2	30 MIN
Jim Jacoby, Pt 1	30 MIN
Jim Jacoby, Pt 2	30 MIN
Julius Rosenblum, Pt 1	30 MIN
Julius Rosenblum, Pt 2	30 MIN
Paul Hodge	30 MIN

Dist - GPN

Play Experiences during Hospitalization 15 MIN
U-matic
Color (PRO)
LC 79-707731
Demonstrates a variety of play sessions which health professionals can utilize in caring for hospitalized children. Depicts diagnostic play, therapeutic play, and school activity sessions, emphasizing that play sessions allow children to express and master fears, release tension and learn.
Health and Safety
Dist - UMMCML **Prod** - UMICHM 1976

Play fair - voluntary compliance - political science 15 MIN
U-matic / VHS
Two cents' worth series
Color (P)
Shows that when Johnny and his sister Dionne accidentally break a window playing baseball, their first impulse is to run.
Civics and Political Systems; Guidance and Counseling; Sociology
Dist - AITECH **Prod** - WHATV 1976

Play guitar overnight - basics 32 MIN
VHS
Color (J H C G)
$19.95 purchase _ #THA2001V
Teaches the basics of guitar. Shows how to select an instrument, tuning, tablature and accessories. Illustrates chord progressions in country, folk and rock styles.
Fine Arts
Dist - CAMV

Play guitar overnight - basics and rock 64 MIN
VHS
Color (J H C G)
$35.95 purchase _ #THA2003SV
Presents two video cassettes which teach basic and rock guitar. Teaches guitar fundamentals in the basic video. Focuses exclusively on electric guitar in the rock video.
Fine Arts
Dist - CAMV

Play guitar overnight - rock 32 MIN
VHS
Color (J H C G)
$19.95 purchase _ #THA2002V
Teaches rock guitar. Focuses exclusively on electric guitar. Introduces the chords, fingerings, scales and right - hand techniques of rock guitar. Includes songbook.
Fine Arts
Dist - CAMV

A Play Half Written - the Energy Adventure 26 MIN
16mm
Color
LC 79-701445
Explores the relationship between energy and human achievement in the arts and technology. Examines energy sources in use during the 1970's and shows sources being developed for the future.
Social Science; Sociology
Dist - MTP **Prod** - AIF 1979

Play - Ibsen's Peer Gynt 60 MIN
VHS / U-matic
Drama - play, performance, perception series; Module 1
Color (C H)
Fine Arts; Literature and Drama
Dist - MDCC **Prod** - MDCC

Play in ten easy lessons - Video One 90 MIN
VHS
Kid's guitar series
Color (K P I J)
$24.95 purchase _ #VD - MAX - KI01
Presents 10 guitar lessons for children on an easy - to - follow video. Features Marcy Marxer as instructor. Includes the songs Down by the Riverside; Skip to My Lou; Buffalo Gals; 100 Bottles of Pop on the Wall; Polly Wolly Doodle; It Ain't Gonna Rain No More; Michael Row the Boat Ashore; Grandpa's Farm; Happy Birthday. Includes chords. Part one of a two - part series.
Fine Arts
Dist - HOMETA **Prod** - HOMETA

Play in ten easy lessons - Video One 55 MIN
VHS
Ukelele for kids series
Color (K P I J)
$24.95 purchase _ #VD - MAX - UK01
Teaches the parts of the ukelele and how to hold and tune the instrument. Teaches finger coordination, ear training and basic theory. Uses on - screen graphics to illustrate fingerings for the five basic chords taught. Includes the songs Row, Row, Row Your Boat; Mary Had a Little Lamb; Skip to My Lou; If You're Happy and You Know It; Old MacDonald; Oh Susannah; It Ain't Gonna Rain No More; On Top of Spaghetti; Bingo. Features Marcy Marxer as instructor. Book and progress chart included. Part one of a two part series.
Fine Arts
Dist - HOMETA **Prod** - HOMETA

Play in the hospital 50 MIN
16mm
Color (PRO)
LC 73-702921
Focuses on the fears and anxieties that confront the hospitalized child and demonstrates how a professionally supervised play program helps to provide outlets for these feelings.
Health and Safety; Psychology
Dist - CFDC **Prod** - CFDC 1972

Play is the Work of Young Children 14 MIN
U-matic / VHS / 16mm
Color
Illustrates the educational philosophy of Lenore Wilson, a specialist in early childhood education. Discusses her belief that young children learn to play with one another in a manner simulating the adult world. Talks about ways to bring out the uniqueness of each child.
Education; Psychology
Dist - UCEMC **Prod** - CROMIE 1974

Play - is Trying Out 25 MIN
U-matic / VHS / 16mm
Color (C A)
Shows two children at play, trying out new skills and new ways of combining means and ends to develop a rich repertory of actions and a more flexible approach to achieving goals.
Psychology
Dist - MEDIAG **Prod** - WILEYJ 1973

Play it out series

Darren - 1 - Karen - 2 - Unit 1	45 MIN
Kevin - 5 - Paul - 6 - Unit 3	45 MIN
Maria - 3 - Amina - 4 - Unit 2	45 MIN

Dist - EMFVL

Play it Safe 15 MIN
U-matic / 16mm
Color (P J)
LC 75-702893
Demonstrates how to be safe on a bike, walking, swimming, on the playground and in a car. Teaches children safe places to play and how to deal with people who try to touch private parts of their bodies. Tells how to act around wild or stray animals.
Health and Safety
Dist - USNAC **Prod** - USCPSD 1975

Play it Safe - Electrically 14 MIN
U-matic / VHS / 16mm
Color (K P I J)
Teaches children safety awareness when playing outdoors. Explains warning signs and gives safety advice.
Health and Safety; Science - Physical
Dist - BCNFL **Prod** - BORTF 1983

Play it safe, keep it clean 12 MIN
BETA / VHS / U-matic
Color (IND VOC)
#FC45
Introduces hospital foodservice personnel to on - the - job safety and hygiene.
Health and Safety; Industrial and Technical Education
Dist - CONPRO **Prod** - CONPRO

Play it safe - keep it clean 15 MIN
16mm / VHS / BETA / U-matic
Color; PAL (VOC IND)
PdS115, PdS123 purchase
Covers the area of food handling, infectious bacteria, proper attire and more in this program designed for kitchen workers in food service and hospital industries.
Industrial and Technical Education
Dist - EDPAT

Play it safe - making playtime safe for your child
VHS
Color (T F)
$59.95 purchase _ #CCP0143V
Provides specific instructions on how to ensure that playtime is safe time. Asks about the safety of toys, play area safety. Guides parents, babysitters and day care providers on ensuring that toys and play environments are safe for children. Offers explanations of manufacturers' labels, how to test toys for safety and how to decide what toys are safe for children of different ages. Shows how to childproof indoor and outdoor play areas and what to do to keep visits to friends and relatives safe. Demonstrates ways to teach children pool safety, bicycle safety, playground safety and toy safety.
Health and Safety
Dist - CAMV **Prod** - CAMV 1993

Play like a pro - ping pong 51 MIN
VHS
Color (H C G)
$39.95 purchase _ #OLY101V
Shows basic and advanced instruction in ping pong, covering footwork, strokes, timing, serves and more.
Physical Education and Recreation
Dist - CAMV

Play mah jongg
VHS
Color (G)
$29.95 purchase _ #MJA000
Includes booklet with English translations of the jargon.

Physical Education and Recreation
Dist - SIV

A Play on Belgium 26 MIN
16mm
Color
LC 78-700666
Highlights cities and sights of Belgium, including visits to Brussels, Bruges, Liege, Ghent, Antwerp, Dinant, and the war memorial at Bastogne.
Geography - World
Dist - MCDO **Prod** - BNTO 1978

Play Safe 11 MIN
U-matic / VHS / 16mm
Color (P I)
Encourages safety at school and at playgrounds. Uses stop - action photography - when an accident occurs, the narrator says 'Let's try it again' and correct safety procedures are reviewed for the accident sequences.
Health and Safety
Dist - ALTSUL **Prod** - FILMSW 1968

Play Safe Video
VHS
Color (P)
$99.95 purchase _ #5704
Instructs teachers and youth leaders in safe playing behavior.
Education; Guidance and Counseling; Health and Safety
Dist - HAZELB

Play sax - from day one 61 MIN
VHS
Color (J H C G)
$39.95 purchase _ #CCP02V
Offers a complete introduction to the saxophone for the beginner. Overviews each type of sax - soprano, alto, tenor. Shows how to put the horn together, use reeds, demonstrates fingering techniques, tone production, and covers reading music, daily practice routines and more. Includes instructional booklet.
Fine Arts
Dist - CAMV **Prod** - CAMV 1991

Play Series
As You Like It 30 MIN
Cyrano De Bergerac 30 MIN
The Front Page 30 MIN
The Inspector General 30 MIN
Life with Father 30 MIN
Oedipus Rex 30 MIN
Our Town 30 MIN
Winterset 30 MIN
Dist - GPN

Play the accordion 60 MIN
VHS
Video music lesson series
Color (J H C G)
$29.95 purchase _ #TMV11V
Offers step - by - step accordion instruction. Features studio musicians, composers, arrangers and educators who lend hands - on instruction about chord progressions, smooth and fluent style, timing and finger exercises, common note combinations, instrument set - up, special sound techniques. Includes examples of chord and scale theory, examples for technical improvement and songs to teach the principles of the instrument. Includes booklet. Part of a 16 - part series on musical instruction.
Fine Arts
Dist - CAMV

Play the Legend 52 MIN
U-matic / VHS
West of the Imagination Series
Color (G)
$279.00, $179.00 purchase _ #AD - 1106
Shows the West as the subject of popular culture and show business. Considers circus acts, dime novels, Buffalo Bill's Wild West Show, movie cowboys and the country singer. Part of a six - part series on the West of imagination, as reported by artists, writers and photographers who went to the frontiers and reported what they saw - or wished they had seen.
Fine Arts; Geography - United States; Industrial and Technical Education; Literature and Drama
Dist - FOTH **Prod** - FOTH

Play the shopping game 20 MIN
U-matic / VHS / 16mm
Consumers in a changing world series
Color (J)
LC 78-700837
Demonstrates good shopping techniques, using a television game show format to point out the knowledge a consumer needs in the marketplace.
Home Economics; Psychology
Dist - EBEC **Prod** - EBEC 1977

Play therapy with mentally handicapped children 20 MIN
U-matic / VHS
Color
Utilizes play therapy to convey the handicapped child's natural medium of self - expression by providing an opportunity to express his/her feelings or frustrations.
Psychology; Sociology
Dist - UWISC **Prod** - LASSWC 1979

Play time 17 MIN
VHS
Baby care workshop series
Color (T F) (SPANISH)
$175.00 purchase
Demonstrates simple, enjoyable activities for parents to share with their infants. Encourages flexibility and spontaneity in play activities, using readily available household items without need to purchase special equipment.
Guidance and Counseling; Health and Safety; Home Economics; Sociology
Dist - PROPAR **Prod** - PROPAR 1988

Play to win - for men and women 60 MIN
U-matic / VHS
Subliminal series
Stereo (A)
Shows relaxation techniques, affirmations, subliminal messages.
Psychology
Dist - BANTAP **Prod** - BANTAP

Play with Me - Play Therapy with Young Children 45 MIN
VHS
Color (C A)
$140.00 purchase, $20.00 rental
Focuses on three 4 - year old girls. Illustrates how the therapist's mode of intervention is tailored to help each child work through difficult issues that stand in the way of social and intellectual development.
Psychology
Dist - CORNRS **Prod** - BLOOF 1985

Play with the Fire 13 MIN
U-matic / VHS / 16mm
Color (J)
Uses the technique of cut - out silhouette animation to create the story of a girl and a boy who chance to meet a friendly imp and discover his lair where he makes diamonds, rubies and emeralds.
Fine Arts
Dist - PHENIX **Prod** - TRICFD

Play your best tennis - Vol one 82 MIN
VHS / BETA
Color
LC 84-706141
Presents mini - lessons in various levels of tennis. Discusses rackets, personal playing improvement and other topics.
Physical Education and Recreation
Dist - CARAVT **Prod** - CARAVT

Play your best tennis - Vol two 67 MIN
VHS / U-matic
Color
Provides instruction on how to play tennis. Focuses on strokes and strategies.
Physical Education and Recreation
Dist - CARAVT **Prod** - CARAVT

Play your hand 40 MIN
VHS
Color (G COR A) (FRENCH)
$150.00 purchase _ #PV114, #PV117
Portrays situations in which employees' personal problems can create problems for managers and unions. Shows practical methods of recognizing and managing these situations.
Guidance and Counseling; Psychology
Dist - ARFO **Prod** - ARFO 1985

Playful pandas 10 MIN
U-matic / VHS / 16mm
Color (K P)
$215.00, $155.00 purchase _ #3576
Talks about the pandas at the National Zoo in Washington D C which were imported from China.
Science - Natural
Dist - CORF **Prod** - CORF 1975

Playful Relaxers 10 MIN
Videoreel / VT2
Janaki Series
Color
Physical Education and Recreation
Dist - PBS **Prod** - WGBHTV

Playground 11 MIN
U-matic / VHS / 16mm
Color
LC 75-700295
Uses the example of three creative playgrounds in Denmark and England to show how children, under the guidance of a leader, enjoy building houses, bridges, towers, windmills and other structures, from junk materials donated by industries, junk collectors, parents and others. Includes descriptions of legal and practical considerations in founding a creative playground.
Education; Fine Arts; Social Science
Dist - UCEMC **Prod** - GRISTR 1974

Playground 7 MIN
U-matic / VHS / 16mm
Starting to Read Series
Color (K P)
LC 73-713458
Introduces the youngest readers and pre - readers to words and concepts, including pictures and songs.
English Language
Dist - AIMS **Prod** - BURGHS 1971

Playground Discipline - a Positive Approach 20 MIN
U-matic / VHS / 16mm
Color (T)
Demonstrates how to select and train older students to handle most of the conflicts that occur daily on the playground.
Education
Dist - FI **Prod** - MFFD

Playground fun 20 MIN
U-matic / 16mm / VHS
Mickey's safety club series
Color (P)
$450.00, $325.00 purchase _ #JC - 67192
Features Mickey Mouse who introduces playground safety experts Huey, Dewey and Louie as they take a 'safety first' tour of the playground. Describes safe playground behavior and equipment usage. Teaches the concepts of courtesy and respect for others, using the buddy system, what to do in case of an emergency, and thinking for oneself. Part of the Mickey's Safety Club series.
Health and Safety; Sociology
Dist - CORF **Prod** - DISNEY 1989

Playground in Six Acts 22 MIN
16mm
Color
LC 74-702757
Presents an experimental film which depicts man as a child in a playground, still in the infancy of development.
Industrial and Technical Education
Dist - CANFDC **Prod** - YORKU 1973

Playground Safety 15 MIN
U-matic / VHS
Safer You Series
Color (P I)
Demonstrates playground safety with the help of two mimes. Shows the proper ways to play on swings, slides, seesaws and climbing bars.
Health and Safety
Dist - GPN **Prod** - WCVETV 1984

Playground safety 11 MIN
U-matic / VHS / 16mm
Color (P I)
$265.00, $185.00 purchase _ #1736; LC FIA66-1751
Shows how to be safe on a playground by following three rules - be sure the play area is safe, keep out of the way of others, and learn how to play correctly. Demonstrates the violent force of moving objects.
Health and Safety
Dist - CORF **Prod** - CORF 1966

Playground Safety 10 MIN
U-matic / VHS / 16mm
Color (P I)
$265, $185 purchase _ #1736
Shows how to use playground equipment safely.
Health and Safety
Dist - CORF

Playground Safety - as Simple as A,B,C 14 MIN
16mm / U-matic / VHS
Color (P I)
$350, $245 purchase _ #75522
Shows the safety hazards that can arise during ball games, racing, and roughhousing.
Health and Safety
Dist - CORF

Playground Safety - the Peeperkorns 10 MIN
16mm / U-matic / VHS
Color (P I)
Explains that common sense is a child's best playground protection. Features different characters in the Peeperkorn family who typify the do's and don'ts of playground behavior.

Health and Safety
Dist - MGHT **Prod** - NSC 1975

Playground Science 10 MIN
U-matic
Take a Look Series
Color (P I)
Shows gravity and balance points using playground equipment.
Science; Science - Physical
Dist - TVOTAR **Prod** - TVOTAR 1986

The Playhouse 20 MIN
16mm
B&W (J)
Stars Buster Keaton.
Fine Arts
Dist - TWYMAN **Prod** - MGM 1921

The Playhouse series
Presents six programs for preschoolers and other young children on issues related to alcohol and drug abuse. 'You're A Wonderful Person to Know' stresses the importance of self - esteem, while 'The Pills' documents the potentially harmful effects of abusing prescription drugs. 'Healthy and Clean' gives an overview of health and hygiene concerns, and 'It's Just Not Safe' details the harmful effects of smoking. Conflict resolution is the focus of 'Friends Are Kind,' while 'Tell Someone' encourages children to discuss problems with adults. Uses a musical theater format, including children, puppets and music, to emphasize these messages.
The Playhouse series 80 MIN
Dist - SCETV **Prod** - SCETV 1921

Playing 15 MIN
16mm
I Am, I Can, I will, Level I Series
Color (K P S)
LC 80-700561
Presents Mr Rogers playing in the sand with a seven - year - old boy. Encourages the use of pretending, fantasy and creative play.
Guidance and Counseling; Psychology
Dist - HUBDSC **Prod** - FAMCOM 1979

Playing a part 15 MIN
VHS
Color (P I J H)
Shows actor Richard Pasco creating the character of Fagin from 'Oliver Twist' prior to a play's first performance, using movement, speech techniques, make - up and costume.
Fine Arts
Dist - VIEWTH **Prod** - VIEWTH

Playing basketball 13 MIN
U-matic / VHS / 16mm
Sports for elementary - Spanish series
Color (I J) (SPANISH)
Demonstrates techniques and skills necessary for developing and improving playing skills in the game of basketball. Explains methods for passing, catching, dribbling, pivoting and shooting.
Foreign Language; Physical Education and Recreation
Dist - AIMS **Prod** - CINEDU 1975

Playing Basketball 13 MIN
U-matic / VHS / 16mm
Sports for Elementary Series
Color (P I)
LC 75-703670
Demonstrates the skills and techniques necessary for playing basketball. Covers passing, catching, dribbling, pivoting and shooting.
Physical Education and Recreation
Dist - AIMS **Prod** - CINEDU 1975

Playing by ear 29 MIN
U-matic
Beginning piano - an adult approach series; Lesson 15
Color (H A)
Reviews A - major scales and chords. Introduces E - major scale. Demonstrates circle of fifths. Reviews earlier pieces. Begins discussion of playing by ear.
Fine Arts
Dist - CDTEL **Prod** - COAST

Playing Communication Games 30 MIN
VHS / U-matic
Principles of Human Communication Series
Color (H C A)
Focuses on how people can influence whether communication with another person will be positive or negative in style and outcome. Shows how an individual can influence the direction and tone of communication.
English Language; Psychology
Dist - GPN **Prod** - UMINN 1983

Playing Doubles
VHS
Tennis by Vic Braden Series
(J H C)
$29.95 _ #HSV7058V
Explains the team concept and team communication. Examines net play and working the baseline, cutting off the angles and attacking the ball.
Physical Education and Recreation
Dist - CAMV

Playing Doubles 29 MIN
U-matic / VHS
Vic Braden's Tennis for the Future Series
Color
Physical Education and Recreation
Dist - PBS **Prod** - WGBHTV 1981

Playing Folk Guitar 60 MIN
BETA / VHS
Color (J)
LC 83-706331
Assumes familiarity with the rudiments of guitar playing and emphasizes techniques, advancing from the basic folk chord progression into blues, flatpicking, country and western, bending tones, and barre chords. Each of the numerous, focused lessons is demonstrated by a professional guitar teacher.
Fine Arts
Dist - VIPRO **Prod** - VIPRO

Playing for Keeps 89 MIN
Videoreel / VT2
Color
Features 125 people playing reverse roles as citizens of Penn City, an imaginary middle - sized American city torn by racial conflict and created by the Presbyterian Synod of Pennsylvania as an experiment in human behavior.
Sociology
Dist - PBS **Prod** - WITFTV

Playing for Keeps 26 MIN
VHS / U-matic
Color (I J H)
Tells the story of John Spender, a high school basketball star, who comes to Tennessee State University on a partial basketball scholarship, and encounters academic difficulties.
Guidance and Counseling
Dist - NGS **Prod** - NGS

Playing for the future 52 MIN
U-matic / VHS
Color (H J)
$249.00, $149.00 purchase _ #AD - 1153
Purports to show the odyssey of a teenager traveling through real and fantasy environments to determine how interests, talents and personality can guide in career choices.
Guidance and Counseling; Psychology; Sociology
Dist - FOTH **Prod** - FOTH

Playing for Time
VHS / BETA
Color
Tells the story of a group of women prisoners in Auschwitz who save their lives by playing in the camp orchestra. Stars Jane Alexander and Vanessa Redgrave.
History - World; Sociology
Dist - GA **Prod** - GA

Playing Hooky - Truancy 20 MIN
VHS / U-matic
Color
$335.00 purchase
Education; Sociology
Dist - ABCLR **Prod** - ABCLR 1983

Playing in the Park 16 MIN
16mm
PANCOM Beginning Total Communication Program for Hearing Parents of deaf children series; Level 2
Color (K P)
LC 77-700504
Education; Guidance and Counseling; Psychology; Sociology
Dist - JOYCE **Prod** - CSDE 1977

Playing it Safe 10 MIN
VHS / 16mm
Sexuality - AIDS - Social Skills for Teens Series
Color (J)
$100.00 purchase
Shows teenagers modeling refusal skills, self - control and assertiveness. Presents a vignette on each skill showing a young adult communicating her or his decision on personal sexual issues. Includes leader's guide.
Guidance and Counseling; Health and Safety; Psychology; Sociology
Dist - CHEF **Prod** - CHEF

Playing it safe 15 MIN
U-matic / VHS / 16mm
Healthwise series
Color (K P I)
$355.00, $250.00 purchase _ #7009
Features the Healthwise puppets, who learn that playing it safe around the house means being on the lookout for common carelessness. Shows how to play it safe outside by driving with seatbelts buckled, crossing the street at the corner, and staying out of culverts and refrigerators.
Health and Safety
Dist - CORF **Prod** - CORF 1982

Playing large intervals 29 MIN
U-matic
Beginning piano - an adult approach series; Lesson 12
Color (H A)
Reviews the odd - even technique of reading large intervals. Introduces a new piece in the key of D major that uses broken intervals.
Fine Arts
Dist - CDTEL **Prod** - COAST

Playing Softball 11 MIN
16mm / U-matic / VHS
Sports for Elementary Series
Color (P I)
LC 75-703669
Demonstrates basic techniques for playing softball. Covers pitching, catching, batting, running, throwing and stopping around hits.
Physical Education and Recreation
Dist - AIMS **Prod** - CINEDU 1975

Playing softball 11 MIN
16mm / U-matic / VHS
Sports for elementary - Spanish series
Color (I J) (SPANISH)
Demonstrates softball techniques for pitching, catching, battling, running, stopping ground hits and throwing.
Foreign Language; Physical Education and Recreation
Dist - AIMS **Prod** - CINEDU 1975

Playing Tennis and Going Swimming 8 MIN
16mm
Crystal Tipps and Alistair Series
Color (K P)
LC 73-700459
Follows Crystal and Alistair as they play a few rounds of tennis. Explains that they are so hot from their exertions that they invite Flutter and Fancy to join them at a swimming pool.
Guidance and Counseling; Literature and Drama
Dist - VEDO **Prod** - BBCTV 1972

Playing the Cello 23 MIN
16mm
Color (J)
LC 73-701742
Begins with the fundamentals of playing the cello, such as holding the bow, body position, bowing, fingering exercises and vibrato control. Demonstrates through more advanced techniques shown by Peter Faroll as he teaches cellists. Deals with four students of varying ability.
Fine Arts
Dist - UILL **Prod** - UILL 1970

Playing the drum set 60 MIN
VHS
Video music lesson series
Color (J H C G)
$29.95 purchase _ #TMV14V
Offers step - by - step drum set instruction. Features studio musicians, composers, arrangers and educators who lend hands - on instruction about timing, rhythms, stroke exercises, instrument set - up, special sound techniques. Includes examples for technical improvement and songs to teach the principles of the instrument. Includes booklet. Part of a 16 - part series on musical instruction.
Fine Arts
Dist - CAMV

Playing the Guitar I - Course Review 29 MIN
Videoreel / VT2
Playing the Guitar I Series
Color
Fine Arts
Dist - PBS **Prod** - KCET

Playing the Guitar I - Lesson Review 29 MIN
Videoreel / VT2
Playing the Guitar I Series
Color
Fine Arts
Dist - PBS **Prod** - KCET

Playing the Guitar I Series
Arpeggio practice in a piece 29 MIN
Arpeggio techniques 29 MIN
Beginning to Play 29 MIN
Buying a guitar 29 MIN
Early history of the guitar 29 MIN
Flamenco forms 29 MIN
Greensleeves, Pt 1 29 MIN
Greensleeves, Pt 2 29 MIN
The Half - Bar and Second Position 29 MIN

Learning to Read Music 29 MIN
Ligado Technique 29 MIN
Music in Two Parts 29 MIN
Notes on the Fifth String 29 MIN
Notes on the First Two Strings 29 MIN
Notes on the Fourth String 29 MIN
Notes on the Sixth String 29 MIN
Notes on the Third String 29 MIN
Playing the Guitar I - Course Review 29 MIN
Playing the Guitar I - Lesson Review 29 MIN
Playing the Guitar I - the Final Lesson 29 MIN
Position and Tuning 29 MIN
Sharps, Flats, Keys and Scales 29 MIN
Sight Reading and Playing 29 MIN
Simple Chords 29 MIN
Styles in Song Accompaniment 29 MIN
Tone Production, Vibrato and Dynamics 29 MIN
Dist - PBS

Playing the Guitar I - the Final Lesson 29 MIN
Videoreel / VT2
Playing the Guitar I Series
Color
Fine Arts
Dist - PBS **Prod** - KCET

Playing the Guitar II - Course Review 29 MIN
Videoreel / VT2
Playing the Guitar II Series
Color
Fine Arts
Dist - PBS **Prod** - KCET

Playing the Guitar II Series
A Complete Sevillana 29 MIN
Completion of the fifth position 29 MIN
Correction of Common Faults 29 MIN
Guitar Makers 29 MIN
Increasing speed 29 MIN
Introduction to Flamenco Techniques 29 MIN
A More Difficult Solo 29 MIN
Notes of the Fifth Position 29 MIN
Playing the Guitar II - Course Review 29 MIN
Sight Reading in Two Parts 29 MIN
Song Accompaniment - Pt 1 29 MIN
Song Accompaniment - Pt 2 29 MIN
Song Recital 29 MIN
Study in A and vibrato technique 29 MIN
Dist - PBS

Playing the Hand 30 MIN
U-matic / VHS
Play Bridge Series
Color (A)
Physical Education and Recreation
Dist - KYTV **Prod** - KYTV 1983

Playing the Percentages 30 MIN
VHS / U-matic
Adult Math Series
Color (A)
Education; Mathematics
Dist - KYTV **Prod** - KYTV 1984

Playing the Selective College Admissions Game 47 MIN
16mm
Color
LC 83-701061
Presents Dick Moll, the Dean of Admissions at the University of California at Santa Cruz, who discusses the complex process of applying to college. Offers a look at how colleges actually make their decisions.
Education
Dist - AUTUMN **Prod** - AYDA

Playing the stock market around the world 30 MIN
U-matic
Adam Smith's money world series; 124
Color (A)
Attempts to demystify the world of money and break it down so that small as well as large businesses and businesspeople can understand and adjust to new social and economic trends. Reports on the major economic stories and discoveries of the day.
Business and Economics
Dist - PBS **Prod** - WNETTV 1985

Playing the Thing 16 MIN
16mm
Color (I)
LC 73-702806
Presents an informative musical experience with an accent on the history and development of the harmonica as a means of personal expression.
Fine Arts
Dist - SCREEI **Prod** - MORC 1973

Playing the Viol 29 MIN
U-matic
Color
Provides a clear demonstration of the basic principles of playing the viol. Shows many of the older viols and manuscripts.
Fine Arts
Dist - UWASHP **Prod** - UWASHP

Playing to win for backs and receivers 60 MIN
VHS
Tom Landry football series
(J H C)
$39.95 purchase _ #MXS130V
Presents Archie Griffin, who discusses the duties of tailbacks and fullbacks in football. Demonstrates techniques for running, pass receiving, and blocking.
Physical Education and Recreation
Dist - CAMV **Prod** - CAMV

Playing to Win for Widebacks and Receivers 59 MIN
VHS / BETA
Football Fundamentals Series
Color
Demonstrates proper techniques for the tailback and fullback and for a pass receiver.
Physical Education and Recreation
Dist - MOHOMV **Prod** - MOHOMV

Playing to Win - Fran Tarkenton's Business Strategies for Success 12 MIN
16mm / VHS
Color (PRO)
$250.00 purchase, $150.00 rental, $75.00 preview
Presents famed quarterback Fran Tarkenton describing his leadership principles and strategies for success. Stresses the importance of team effort and thinking ahead.
Business and Economics; Education; Physical Education and Recreation; Psychology
Dist - UTM **Prod** - UTM

Playing touch football 12 MIN
U-matic / VHS / 16mm
Sports for elementary - Spanish series
Color (I J) (SPANISH)
Highlights actions important to playing the game of touch football, such as passing, receiving, punting, place kicking and running skills.
Foreign Language; Physical Education and Recreation
Dist - AIMS **Prod** - CINEDU 1975

Playing Touch Football 12 MIN
16mm / U-matic / VHS
Sports for Elementary Series
Color (P I)
LC 75-703671
Demonstrates basic techniques for playing touch football. Covers passing, receiving, punting, place kicking and running skills.
Physical Education and Recreation
Dist - AIMS **Prod** - CINEDU 1975

Playing with a film camera 30 MIN
U-matic / VHS / BETA
Color; PAL (G H C)
PdS50, PdS58 purchase
Reveals the magic of simple cinematic effects. Includes the segments Spirit of St Louis; Gran Prix; Creation of the Sun; Meteorites; Sheer Magic. Produced in Belgium.
Fine Arts
Dist - EDPAT

Playing with Fire 75 MIN
U-matic
Color (C)
$400.00 purchase, $70.00, $100.00 rental
Presents the story of an orphan with no personality until she comes under the guardianship of a fearful but loving woman. Depicts how she learns about her body, sexuality, and her identity within and outside of society. Produced by the feminist collective Emma Productions and Marusia Bociurkiw.
Fine Arts; Psychology; Sociology
Dist - WMENIF

Playing with Fire 28 MIN
U-matic / VHS
Life of Plants Series
Color (C)
$249.00, $149.00 purchase _ #AD - 1681
Discloses that transplanting, cross - breeding, artificial pollination all seem like good ideas, but have unforseen side effects. Uses the example of the potato which was introduced in Europe to end food shortages. Instead, when it was wiped out by a fungus, famine resulted. Part of a series on plants.
History - World; Science - Natural
Dist - FOTH **Prod** - FOTH

Playing with Numbers
16mm
B&W
Examines the types of numbers possible. Illustrates rational, algebraic, and irrational numbers.
Mathematics
Dist - OPENU **Prod** - OPENU

Playing with problems - 6 78 MIN
VHS
Creating therapeutic change series
Color; PAL; SECAM (G PRO T)
$95.00 purchase
Features Richard Bandler in the sixth part of a seven - part series on creating therapeutic change using advanced NLP, neuro - linguistic programming. Reveals that just solving problems often isn't enough and that time distinctions can be used to interlace beliefs, feeling states and 'chains' into complexes that generatively reorganize fundamental attitudes throughout a person's life. Recommends that tapes be viewed in order. Uses some profanity.
Psychology
Dist - NLPCOM **Prod** - NLPCOM

Playing with scorpions 4 MIN
VHS / 16mm
San - Ju - Wasi series
Color (G)
$120.00, $100.00 purchase, $20.00 rental
Observes San children playing with scorpions and tempting fate. Part of a series by John Marshall about the Kung in Namibia and Botswana.
Geography - World; History - World; Sociology
Dist - DOCEDR **Prod** - DOCEDR

Playing, writing and arranging - concepts for jazz - rock piano 70 MIN
VHS
Color (G)
$49.95 purchase _ #VD - DON - JP01
Features pianist Donald Fagen with Warren Bernhardt. Explores the process that went into the writing and arranging of Steely Dan songs, as well as solo works from the Kamakiriad album. Uses tunes with familiar blues and R&B structures as source material and shows how, by altering the bass line and chord qualities, an ordinary blues is transformed into a sophisticated jazz - rock tune. Traces the development of increasingly complex pieces as Fagen and Bernhardt reveal each tune's singular structures, harmonic and rhythmic characteristics, intro ideas and other devices. Includes the songs Chain Lightning, Peg, Josie, On the Dunes, and Teahouse on the Tracks.
Fine Arts
Dist - HOMETA **Prod** - HOMETA

Playmaking 16 MIN
VHS / 16mm
Drama reference series
Color (T)
$150.00 purchase _ #268412
Implements elementary drama curriculum. Presents drama content, teaching strategies and resources, and demonstrated drama activities for the classroom. 'Playmaking' focuses on playmaking as a sequence of originating, shaping and communicating scenes from familiar stories.
Education; English Language; Fine Arts; Literature and Drama; Mathematics
Dist - ACCESS **Prod** - ACCESS 1987

Playmates 12 MIN
U-matic / VHS
Color (C A)
Shows how sexual playfulness and communication enliven the relationship of a couple obviously sensitive to each other's desires.
Health and Safety; Psychology
Dist - MMRC **Prod** - NATSF

Playmation 6 MIN
16mm
Color (G)
$12.00 rental
Consists of a trilogy of separate projects in claymation. Pokes fun at elaborate Hollywood productions; follows the development of human creation with poetic narration; and portrays a metamorphic character as the filmmaker, Karl Horvath.
Fine Arts
Dist - CANCIN

Plays 15 MIN
U-matic / VHS
Zebra Wings Series
Color (I)
Presents the elements of playwriting and shows children critiquing three original plays.
English Language; Literature and Drama
Dist - AITECH **Prod** - NITC 1975

Plays 30 MIN
U-matic
Today's Special Series
Color (K P)
Develops language arts skills in children. Programs are thematically designed around subjects of interest to youngsters. Action takes place in a department store where people, mannequins, puppets, comic characters and special guests present a light hearted approach to language arts.
Fine Arts; Literature and Drama; Psychology
Dist - TVOTAR **Prod** - TVOTAR 1985

Plays of Shakespeare Series
Othello 29 MIN
Dist - UMITV

The Play's the thing 15 MIN
VHS
Field trips series
Color (I J)
$34.95 purchase _ #E337; LC 90-708564
Observes the many aspects of the theater - staging, set design and construction, lighting, costuming, rehearsal, direction. Culminates with a scene performed before a live audience. Part of a series which provides visual opportunities for children to 'visit' a variety of locations and activities as if they were on a field trip.
Education; Fine Arts
Dist - GPN **Prod** - MPBN 1983

The Play's the thing 10 MIN
VHS / U-matic
Book, look and listen series
Color (K P)
Focuses on the skills needed to interpret story dramatizations and to follow the story line of a play.
English Language; Literature and Drama
Dist - AITECH **Prod** - MDDE 1977

The Play's the thing 15 MIN
U-matic / VHS
Hidden treasures series; No 12
Color (T)
LC 82-706552
Uses the adventures of a pirate and his three friends to explore the many facets of language arts. Focuses on creative imagination and encourages its use in writing.
English Language
Dist - GPN **Prod** - WCVETV 1980

Playspace 28 MIN
VHS / U-matic
Learning through play series
(T)
$180.00 purchase
Compares and assesses indoor and outdoor playspaces for children and examines how surroundings may affect their learning. Focuses on the benefits of a stimulating, flexible environment and shows how ordinary living space can be made into a play area for children.
Home Economics; Psychology; Sociology
Dist - AITECH **Prod** - TORMC 1980
UTORMC UTORMC

Playwright profiles - David Mamet 30 MIN
VHS
Color (H C G)
$99.00 purchase _ #DL265
Combines interviews with David Mamet, excerpts from his works and discussions with actors who have performed Mamet's works.
Fine Arts; Literature and Drama
Dist - INSIM

Playwright profiles - John Guare 30 MIN
VHS
Color (H C G)
$99.00 purchase _ #DL266
Combines interviews with John Guare, excerpts from his works and discussions with actors who have performed Guare's works.
Fine Arts; Literature and Drama
Dist - INSIM

Playwright profiles - Wendy Wasserstein 30 MIN
VHS
Color (H C G)
$99.00 purchase _ #DL267
Combines interviews with Wendy Wasserstein, excerpts from her works and discussions with actors who have performed Wasserstein's works.
Fine Arts; Literature and Drama
Dist - INSIM

Playwrights 15 MIN
U-matic / VHS
Word Shop Series
Color (P)
Literature and Drama
Dist - WETATV **Prod** - WETATV

Plaza 15 MIN
16mm
Color
LC 79-701237
Uses experimental techniques to explore narrative forms in uncovering the facts surrounding a murder.
Fine Arts
Dist - VANOSD **Prod** - VANOSD 1977

The Plaza - Since 1907 13 MIN
16mm
Color
LC 75-703607
Follows the activities of an out - of - town couple staying at the Plaza Hotel in New York City to attend a convention.
Geography - United States; History - United States; Sociology
Dist - PLAZAH **Prod** - PLAZAH 1975

The PLC - Campus and Corps 14 MIN
16mm
Color (H C A)
LC 77-700083
Discusses the advantages of joining the Marine Corps platoon leaders class program.
Civics and Political Systems
Dist - USNAC **Prod** - USMC 1974

The Plea 15 MIN
U-matic / VHS / 16mm
Under the Law Series
Color (J H C)
LC 74-703798
Presents the story of a young woman who, when upset at hearing news of her husband's death, becomes a hit - and - run driver. Points out the special circumstances surrounding the case as they relate to her treatment in the criminal justice system.
Civics and Political Systems; Sociology
Dist - CORF **Prod** - USNEI 1974

Plea Bargaining - an American Way of Justice 60 MIN
16mm
B&W (H C A)
LC 80-701459
Documents the plea bargaining process, a hidden but persuasive aspect of the American criminal justice system. Shows plea bargaining as it takes place in courtrooms, in judges' chambers, in jails and in backrooms.
Civics and Political Systems
Dist - THURFL **Prod** - THURFL 1980

A Plea for help 15 MIN
U-matic
Color (I)
Teaches writing skills while telling the story of Chris and his friends who hear a voice calling for help from the pages of Cinderella. They magically disappear into Book World to attempt a rescue.
Education; English Language; Literature and Drama
Dist - TVOTAR **Prod** - TVOTAR 1982

Please at least leave me the sun 10 MIN
U-matic / VHS / 16mm
Color
Presents drawings showing what children believe their world will be like.
Science - Natural; Sociology
Dist - CAROUF **Prod** - CHAGOL

Please Believe Me - Rheumatoid Arthritis and Young Adults 29 MIN
U-matic
Color
Focuses on four rheumatoid arthritis patients who share their experiences and problems with the disease at different stages of their lives.
Health and Safety
Dist - UMITV **Prod** - UMITV 1978

Please Construct 27 MIN
16mm
Color (IND)
Describes the building of commercial aviation's newest jet aircraft, the Airbus - A300B, which was built by several companies in West Germany, France, the Netherlands and Spain, The wings were manufactured in Britain and the engines in the United States, with the final assembly in Toulouse, France.
Civics and Political Systems; Science - Physical; Social Science
Dist - WSTGLC **Prod** - WSTGLC

Please do not Adjust Your Set 25 MIN
U-matic
Not Another Science Show Series
Color (H C)
Tells how the television pictures travel from the studio to the home. Shows how signals are transmitted, how cable TV works and what makes color.
Fine Arts; Science
Dist - TVOTAR **Prod** - TVOTAR 1986

Please don't hit me, Mom 46 MIN
U-matic / VHS
Color
Reveals the story of an eight - year - old boy who is physically beaten by his mother. Features Patty Duke Astin and Sean Astin.
Sociology
Dist - EMBASY **Prod** - EMBASY

Please don't tease 30 MIN
VHS
Our friends on Wooster Square series; Vol 10
Color (K P I R)
$34.95 purchase, $10.00 rental _ #35 - 87259 - 460
Presents religious concepts through storylines, songs and Scripture. Features puppet characters including Smedly, Troll and Sizzle.
Literature and Drama; Religion and Philosophy
Dist - APH **Prod** - FRACOC

Please hurry 14 MIN
16mm
Color
LC 77-705641
Describes the service of the 911 emergency communications system in cutting the response time between the report of an emergency and the arrival of police help. Includes scenes of the New York Police Department communications room where emergency calls are received and answered.
Civics and Political Systems; Social Science; Sociology
Dist - NYTELE **Prod** - NYTELE 1969

Please Let Us Help 18 MIN
16mm
Color
LC 80-701865
Describes a typical Veterans Administration Drug Dependence Treatment Program. Demonstrates the program's practice of comprehensive assessment and focuses on vocational retraining as a new client moves through the reception and initial evaluation procedures. Emphasizes that the VA program wants to help as a specialized treatment resource for other community programs and for self - referred veterans with self - abuse problems.
Health and Safety; Psychology; Sociology
Dist - USNAC **Prod** - USVA 1980

Please look after this bear - A bear in hot water - Paddington goes underground 17 MIN
16mm / U-matic / VHS
Paddington bear series
Color (K P I)
LC 77-700664
Presents an animated adaptation of chapters 1 - 3 of the children's book A Bear Called Paddington by Michael Bond.
Fine Arts; Literature and Drama
Dist - ALTSUL **Prod** - BONDM 1977

Please Mr. Elephant - Prosze slonia 67 MIN
VHS
Color (K P) (POLISH)
$17.95 purchase _ #V161
Presents the story of a young elephant living with a family as a household pet.
Fine Arts; Literature and Drama; Sociology
Dist - POLART

Please, play, done 10 MIN
U-matic
Readalong one series
Color (K P)
Introduces reading and spelling for preschoolers and children in grades 1 to 3 with animation, puppets, humor and music. Comes with teacher's guide and kit.
Education; English Language; Literature and Drama
Dist - TVOTAR **Prod** - TVOTAR 1975

Please Stand by
VHS / U-matic
Color
Uses humor in a presentation of a film projector that goes berserk.
Fine Arts; Literature and Drama
Dist - MEETS **Prod** - BBB

Please Stand by - a History of Radio 900 MIN
U-matic / VHS
(C A)
Describes the history of radio, which presents the inventions that gave radio its voice, the development of radio broadcasting as a business, and the types of programming that made radio an information/entertainment medium of great social and cultural significance.

Fine Arts; History - United States; Psychology; Sociology
Dist - SCCON **Prod** - SCCON 1986

Please Stand by - a History of Radio Series
All in the game 28 MIN
All things remembered 28 MIN
And now - the news 28 MIN
Case closed 28 MIN
Child's play 28 MIN
Days of Discord 18 MIN
A Dramatic Production 28 MIN
The End of the Beginning 28 MIN
Entertainment tonight 28 MIN
The Gang's all Here 28 MIN
Growing Pains 28 MIN
In a Family Way 28 MIN
In the Beginning 28 MIN
Law and Order 28 MIN
Listen and Learn 28 MIN
The Little Black Box 28 MIN
Make 'Em Laugh 28 MIN
The Melody Lingers on 28 MIN
New and Improved 28 MIN
News - the War Years 28 MIN
The Other Networks 28 MIN
Panic 28 MIN
Reviewing the Situation 28 MIN
Something to Hear 28 MIN
The Sounds of Time 28 MIN
Tall in the Studio 28 MIN
Tune in Tomorrow 28 MIN
A Voice in the Wilderness 28 MIN
Winning Ways 28 MIN
A Word from the Sponsor 28 MIN
Dist - SCCON

Please Take Care of Your Teeth 10 MIN
16mm / U-matic / VHS
Color
Uses a lighthearted approach to oral hygiene which encourages eating nutritiously, brushing and flossing daily and visiting the dentist regularly. Tells who develops cavities, demonstrates proper brushing and flossing techniques and assures that the dentist is a friendly person dedicated to the health of their patients' gums and teeth.
Health and Safety
Dist - PFP **Prod** - WHITS 1982

Pleasure 16 MIN
VHS
Fresh talk series
Color (H)
$150.00 purchase, $40.00 rental
Discusses power and gender roles; fantasy; alternatives to intercourse; and communication in consensual relationships. Helps young people develop critical attitudes about the sexual messages in pop culture, learn how to articulate their own sexual feelings and how to communicate them effectively and with respect for others. Part of a four - part series featuring thirty young men and women, ages 15 - 24, who share their reflections on sexuality and growing up. After one or more interviews in any segment, video may be stopped to enable discussion. Directed by Teresa Marshall and Craig Berggold. Study guide available.
Psychology; Sociology
Dist - CNEMAG

Pleasure boating
VHS
Color (G)
$39.80 purchase _ #0774
Teaches the basics of pleasure boating. Covers boating basics, basic navigation and rules of the road, preparation for getting under way, rough water handling, anchoring and mooring, fire aboard.
Health and Safety; Physical Education and Recreation
Dist - SEVVID **Prod** - CAMV

Pleasure boating 60 MIN
VHS
(A G)
$39.95 purchase _ #BM363V; $39.80 purchase _ #0774
Offers a guide to the basics of boating and safe navigation. Explains knot tying, line storage, fire hazards, anchoring and mooring. Discusses navigation skills such as using charts, compasses and depth sounders.
Physical Education and Recreation
Dist - CAMV **Prod** - CAMV
SEVVID

Pleasure Drugs - the Great American High 52 MIN
16mm / U-matic / VHS
Color (J)
LC 82-701131
Examines the pervasiveness and implications of the use of cocaine, marijuana, quaaludes and alcohol in the United States. Includes personal stories and testimonies of a medical examiner, a researcher and legal officials. Shows police - produced tapes of automobile accidents in which the drivers were under the influence of these substances.
Health and Safety; Sociology
Dist - FI **Prod** - NBCNEW 1982

Pleasure of finding things out 50 MIN
VHS
Horizon series
Color; PAL (H C A)
PdS99 purchase; Not available in the United States
Presents Richard Feynman as one of the world's outstanding scientists. Describes his passion for knowledge and his ability to transfer that excitement for discovery to others. Explores how all the parts of the world are linked by the laws of nature.
Science
Dist - BBCENE

The Pleasure of finding things out 57 MIN
VHS / U-matic
Nova series
Color (J H C)
LC 83-706602
Presents physicist Richard Feynman talking about his childhood and the influence of his father, his feelings about having participated in the development of the atomic bomb, the influence of scientific logic on his perceptions and philosophies, and his seemingly unorthodox teaching methods.
Religion and Philosophy; Science; Science - Physical
Dist - TIMLIF **Prod** - BBCTV 1982
AMBROS AMBROS

The Pleasure of Play 39 MIN
U-matic / VHS
Color
Demonstrates the use of expressive language, creative dramatic play and play therapy activities in developing learning skills and the expression of feelings in special - needs children. Guides the viewer through a number of actual play sessions with therapists and groups of children.
Psychology; Sociology
Dist - PSU **Prod** - PITTSG

The Pleasure of Your Company 15 MIN
16mm
Color
LC 80-701049
Tells of the services of hotels and motels and how the public can get the most from them.
Home Economics
Dist - KLEINW **Prod** - KLEINW 1977

The Pleasure principle 98 MIN
35mm
Color; PAL (G)
Portrays Dick, a medical journalist who, given a hard time by neurosurgeon Judith, seeks comfort with Sammy, then turns to Judith again just in time to be invited to her wedding, where he meets Charlotte. Introduces Dick's ex - wife Anne who gives steady, if sometimes doubtful, support. Directed by David Cohen for Psychology News. Contact distributor about price and availability outside the United Kingdom.
Fine Arts; Sociology
Dist - BALFOR

Pleasure profits 29 MIN
U-matic / VHS
Color
Intercuts an interview with the woman president of a sexual aids company with footage from a women's home sales party. Presented by John Orentlicher and Carol Porter.
Business and Economics; Fine Arts
Dist - ARTINC **Prod** - ARTINC

The Pleasure seekers - a surf odyssey 20 MIN
16mm
Color (R)
Shows two Malibu surfers setting out around the world to find the perfect beach. Illustrates that during their search they pass hungry children, people living in sickness and squaler, and human beings destined to live their lives in hopelessness. Portrays their apathy, and relates it to Jesus' statement, 'They have eyes to see, but do not see.'
Guidance and Counseling
Dist - FAMF **Prod** - FAMF

The Pleasures of chinese cooking 20 MIN
16mm
Color
Presents a sampling of easily prepared Chinese meals.
Home Economics
Dist - BUGAS **Prod** - BUGAS

Pleasuring 16 MIN
VHS / U-matic
Becoming Orgasmic - a Sexual Growth Program Series
Color
Continues to explore ways women can pleasure themselves by experimenting with techniques including erotic body movements.
Health and Safety; Psychology; Sociology
Dist - MMRC **Prod** - MMRC

Pleasuring 12 MIN
VHS / U-matic
EDCOA Sexual Counseling Series
Color
Describes a couple's feelings about behaviors in which they engage and discuss pleasuring as an end in itself.
Health and Safety; Psychology
Dist - MMRC **Prod** - MMRC

The Pledge and the Anthem - Behind the Words
U-matic / VHS / 16mm
Color
Shows how the U S National Anthem was written and the reasons for its words. Focuses on the meaning behind the Pledge of Allegiance and the National Anthem.
Civics and Political Systems; Social Science
Dist - HIGGIN **Prod** - HIGGIN

The Pledge of Allegiance 8 MIN
U-matic / VHS / 16mm
American Values for Elementary Series
Color (P I)
LC 71-713401
Defines the Pledge of Allegiance as a commitment of individual responsibility to uphold the laws and principles of America.
Civics and Political Systems
Dist - AIMS **Prod** - EVANSA 1971

Pledge of allegiance 5 MIN
U-matic / VHS / 16mm
Color (P I J)
Takes the Pledge of Allegiance and explains the words used in the verse, their individual meanings, the overall importance of the pledge and the reason for its use.
Civics and Political Systems
Dist - PHENIX **Prod** - GOULDA 1980

Plein Air 30 MIN
VHS
Tom Keating on painters series
Color (J H C G)
$195.00 purchase
Focuses on the painting style of Plein Air. Features Tom Keating who recreates the painting style as done in the original work and gives biographical information. Part of a six - part series on painters.
Fine Arts
Dist - LANDMK **Prod** - LANDMK 1987

Pleins Feux Sur La Revolution 1789 - 1799
VHS
Color (G) (ENGLISH AND FRENCH)
$34.95 purchase _ #V72162
Recounts French history through use of graphic illustrations, historic documents and narration. Includes a transcript in English and a historical guide in French.
Foreign Language; History - World
Dist - NORTNJ

Plena is Work, Plena is Song 37 MIN
16mm / VHS
Color (G)
$450.00, $295.00 purchase, $60.00 rental; LC 89715654
Examines the cultural and political history of 'plena,' a Puerto Rican musical blend of African and Spanish idioms. Directed by Pedro A Rivera and Susan Zeig.
Fine Arts; Geography - United States; History - United States; Sociology
Dist - CNEMAG **Prod** - CNEMAG 1989

Plessy vs Ferguson
U-matic / VHS / 35mm strip
Supreme Court decisions that changed the nation series
(J H C)
$59.00 purchase - filmstrip, $69.00 purchase - video _ #06810 94
Explores the lasting impact of the Plessy versus Ferguson Supreme Court decision that gave legal justification to segregation, invoking the concept 'separate but equal.'
Civics and Political Systems; Sociology
Dist - ASPRSS **Prod** - GA
GA

Pliable materials 30 MIN
VHS / U-matic
Learning through play series; Module 2
Color (H C A)
Discusses pliable materials. Presents five illustrations, including two and three year - olds at a daycare sandtable and ten year - olds constructing a fort out of junk in a back alley.

Psychology
Dist - UTORMC Prod - UTORMC 1980

Pliers 12 MIN
16mm
Hand Operations - Woodworking Series
Color
LC 76-700147
Describes common types of pliers.
Industrial and Technical Education
Dist - SF Prod - MORLAT 1974

Pliers and screw drivers 15 MIN
16mm / U-matic / VHS
Care and use of hand tools series; No 2
B&W
LC FIE52-1537
Shows correct use of pliers and screw drivers.
Industrial and Technical Education
Dist - USNAC Prod - USWD 1943

The Plight of Soviet ewry - let my people go 28 MIN
16mm
B&W
Points out that there are three million Jews living in Soviet Russia today, but Jewish religious and cultural life is not evident. Contends that Jewish identity is still strong and many Jews would like to emigrate to Israel, but notes that only a few have been allowed to leave Russia.
Geography - World; Religion and Philosophy; Sociology
Dist - ALDEN Prod - ALDEN

The Plight of the Afternoon Newspapers 29 MIN
U-matic / VHS
Inside Story Series
Color
Profiles the efforts of the Minneapolis Star to reverse the trend of declining readership for afternoon newspapers in America.
Literature and Drama; Social Science
Dist - PBS Prod - PBS 1981

Plight of the condor 13 MIN
VHS
Color (H C G)
$59.00 purchase _ #5524F
Examines the struggle of the California condor for survival. Depicts the bird in its natural habitat while explaining its slide toward extinction and the steps being taken to preserve it.
Science - Natural
Dist - INSTRU

Plimoth plantation 30 MIN
VHS
VideoTours history series
Color (G I J H)
$19.95 purchase _ #HC02
Visits Plimoth Plantation in Massachussetts. Tours the museum that commemorates the first white settlers of what is now the United States.
History - United States
Dist - SVIP

Plimoth plantation
VHS
Color (H C A)
$19.95 purchase
Tours the Plimoth Plantation, a museum that celebrates the first white settlers of what is now the United States. Tells some of the stories of the men and women who settled the New World, the Indians who befriended them, and the ways in which the settlers survived the wilderness.
History - United States
Dist - PBS Prod - WNETTV

Plimouth Plantation 30 MIN
VHS
Color (I J)
$19.95 purchase _ #ST - VT1007
Explores the significance of the year 1627 at Plimouth Plantation. Portrays the people who settled there and shares their views of politics, religion and survival in the wilderness.
History - United States; Sociology
Dist - INSTRU

Plimpton - at the wheel 52 MIN
U-matic / VHS / 16mm
Color (J H G)
Presents George Plimpton exploring the world of auto racing, where drivers and machines are driven to the limit and where the challenge of speed brings with it the threat of injury or death. Studies the driving technique of Grand Prix driver Jackie Stewart.
Literature and Drama; Physical Education and Recreation
Dist - FI Prod - WOLPER 1974

Plimpton - the Great Quarterback Sneak 52 MIN
U-matic / VHS / 16mm
Color (J)
Recounts the experiences of writer George Plimpton as he joins the world champion NFL Baltimore Colts for a month of pre - season training and then guides the team as a quarterback for four plays against the Detroit Lions in an exhibition game.
Physical Education and Recreation
Dist - FI Prod - WOLPER 1974

Plimpton - the man on the flying trapeze 52 MIN
16mm
Color (J H G)
LC 71-712183
George Plimpton enters the secret, back - stage world of the circus and attempts, in ten days, to become a death - defying, high flying aerialist. Provides insights into the personalities of circus performers.
Biography; Literature and Drama; Physical Education and Recreation
Dist - WOLPER Prod - DUPONT 1971

Plisetskaya dances 70 MIN
VHS
B&W (G)
$29.95 purchase _ #1196
Documents the dance career of Maya Plisetskaya, prima ballerina of Moscow's Bolshoi Ballet. Includes archival footage of Plisetskaya as a child and highlights from some of her greatest roles, scenes from Swan Lake, Sleeping Beauty, Spartacus, The Little Humpbacked Horse, Raymonda, The Stone Flower, Romeo And Juliet and Don Quixote.
Fine Arts; Geography - World
Dist - KULTUR

The Plot against Harry 81 MIN
35mm
B&W; PAL (G)
Witnesses Harry's adjustment to society after nine months in prison, including his discoveries that his income has dramatically fallen; his former lieutenant taken over his operation; and he's lost his contacts with the mob to regain his job. Continues with his revelation to go straight when he sees a friend's kosher catering hall; the plot thickens as fate - or is it certain people - may be out to get him. A King Screen Production. Contact distributor about price and availability outside the United Kingdom.
Health and Safety; Religion and Philosophy; Sociology
Dist - BALFOR

Plot in Science Fiction 25 MIN
16mm
Literature of Science Fiction Series
Color (H C T)
LC 72-700535
Paul Anderson discusses the role of plot in science fiction with James Gunn, president of the Science Fiction Writers of America.
Literature and Drama
Dist - UKANS Prod - UKANS 1970

Plot plans and landscape plans
VHS
Architectural drafting series
(VOC IND)
$59.00 _ #CA154
Gives legal requirements for plot plans and shows how property lines are identified. Also describes how buildings and various parts of buildings are contructed in a particular pattern.
Fine Arts; Industrial and Technical Education
Dist - AAVIM Prod - AAVIM 1989

Plotting your strategy - effective management of time and money 55 MIN
U-matic / VHS
Winning grants
(PRO COR T)
$1,795.00 member purchase, $1,995.00 non member purchase
Presents seminars on successful grant writing. Focuses on planning and managing time and money resourcefully. Seventh in a series of ten programs.
Business and Economics; Education
Dist - GPN

Plov Og Plojning - Plough and Ploughing 17 MIN
16mm
B&W (J H G) (DANISH)
Describes the development of the plough from the first primitive digging stick to the most modern farm implements. Demonstrates various ploughing methods, and shows a big moorland plough.
Agriculture; Sociology
Dist - STATNS Prod - STATNS 1951

The Plow that Broke the Plains 21 MIN
U-matic / VHS / 16mm
Color
LC 75-702991
Traces the social and economic history of the Great Plains from the time of the settlement of the prairies by cattlemen and farmers through the World War I boom to the years of depression and drought.
Business and Economics; Geography - United States; History - United States
Dist - USNAC Prod - USRA 1936

The Plow that Broke the Plains 25 MIN
U-matic / VHS / 16mm
B&W
LC 79-706027
Traces the social and economic history of the Great Plains from the settlement of the prairies to the years of depression and drought. Issued in 1936 as a motion picture.
History - United States
Dist - USNAC Prod - USRA 1978

Plowshare 28 MIN
16mm
Color
LC FIE66-11
Uses motion pictures and animation to explain the development and aims of the Plowshare Program, the Atomic Energy Commission's program for the safe use of nuclear explosives for civilian applications. Discusses the potential uses of nuclear explosives for mining, earth - moving and excavation projects and scientific investigations.
Business and Economics
Dist - USNAC Prod - USNRC 1965

Plucked Instruments 30 MIN
U-matic / VHS
Early Musical Instruments Series
Color
Presents the history and development of several musical instruments related to the guitar.
Fine Arts
Dist - FOTH Prod - GRATV

Plug - back cementing 33 MIN
U-matic / Slide / VHS / 16mm
Color (IND VOC)
$150.00 purchase _ #11.1123, $160.00 purchase _ #51.1123
Examines techniques and equipment used to plug back oil or gas wells with an emphasis on plugging to abandon.
Business and Economics; Industrial and Technical Education
Dist - UTEXPE Prod - UTEXPE 1978

Plug Us in 16 MIN
16mm
Color
LC 81-700457
Explains how older job seekers can project a positive image during interviews.
Psychology; Sociology
Dist - AFAEME Prod - AFAEME 1980

Plugging and Patching Drums 20 MIN
VHS
Hazardous Materials Containment Series
Color (G PRO)
$125.00 purchase _ #35355
Shows how to safely contain leaks in low - pressure drums. Presents techniques for controlling and containing spills, leaks and releases of hazardous materials. Stresses safety while demonstrating effective containment techniques using everyday tools and materials. Designed specifically for firefighters who may be called as first responders to hazardous materials incidents.
Health and Safety; Psychology; Social Science; Sociology
Dist - OKSU Prod - OKSU

Plugging in 60 MIN
VHS
History of rock 'n' roll series
Color (G)
$19.99 purchase _ #0 - 7907 - 2428 - 6NK
Watches Bob Dylan go electric at Newport - Maggie's Farm. Reveals that the Beatles continue to battle the Beach Boys. Features Monterrey pop hits by Janis Joplin - Ball and Chain; Jimi Hendrix - Like a Rolling Stone; and the Who - My Generation. Part of a ten - part series unfolding the history of rock music. May contain mature subject matter and explicit song lyrics.
Fine Arts
Dist - TILIED

Plugging the Holes 30 MIN
U-matic
Energy Efficient Housing Series
(A)
Explains different types of windows and ways of sealing them as well as hatches and electrical openings.
Industrial and Technical Education; Social Science
Dist - ACCESS Prod - SASKM 1983

Plum 19.5 MIN
16mm
Color; Silent (C)
$448.00
Experimental film by James Herbert.
Fine Arts
Dist - AFA **Prod** - AFA 1972

Plum Island Afternoon 13 MIN
16mm
B&W
LC 78-701442
Tells how a woman goes to the beach with her daughters on a cold, blustery day and experiences a series of flashbacks concerning significant moments in her life.
Fine Arts; Sociology
Dist - TATLOC **Prod** - TATLOC 1977

Plum Pudding 22 MIN
16mm
Color (K P I)
Presents a series of animated designs made by children, including pixillation, clay, flip cards and mache.
Fine Arts; Literature and Drama
Dist - YELLOW **Prod** - YELLOW 1969

Plum pudding in danger 30 MIN
VHS
Tales from the map room
Color; PAL (H C A)
PdS65 purchase; Not available in the United States
Features actors who re - create significant events in the history of cartography. Focuses on the controversies of mapping frontiers and lands. Fifth in a series of six programs.
Geography - World
Dist - BBCENE

Plumb line 18 MIN
16mm
Color (G)
$50.00 rental
Features an interpretation of a relationship breaking up edited from scrap diary footage shot in 8mm and hand printed as 16mm. Approximates the interior memory of the experience, which the viewer see and hears. Produced by Carolee Schneemann.
Fine Arts; Psychology
Dist - CANCIN

Plumber 5 MIN
U-matic
Good work series
Color (H)
Provides useful, up to date information on various occupations to aid high school students in career selection. Available in five series of ten jobs each.
Education; Guidance and Counseling; Industrial and Technical Education
Dist - TVOTAR **Prod** - TVOTAR 1981

Plumber 5 MIN
VHS / 16mm
Good works series
Color (VOC IND)
$40.00 purchase _ #BPN205606
Presents the occupation of a plumber. Gives a profile of a young person who is either undergoing an apprenticeship or has recently completed training in this field. Takes the viewer on a tour of this person's workplace and explains the practical skills and training offered by employers and schools. Gives a better understanding of the demand for skilled workers today and the potential for personal growth.
Guidance and Counseling
Dist - RMIBHF **Prod** - RMIBHF
TVOTAR TVOTAR

Plumber
VHS
Career connections video series
Color (J H C G)
$39.95 purchase _ #CCP0204V
Examines career options as an plumber. Looks at educational requirements, skills needed, safety considerations, advancement opportunities and related occupations. Interviews workers and shows on - the - job footage to overview the work. The last segment provides a brief summary of how to use the Occupational Outlook Handbook - OOH and the Dictionary of Occupational Titles - DOT. Part of a six - part series on occupations.
Business and Economics; Guidance and Counseling; Industrial and Technical Education
Dist - CAMV **Prod** - CAMV 1993

Plumbing 42 MIN
VHS
$39.95 purchase _ #DI - 320
Investigates bathroom and laundry installation of rough plumbing for water supply and waste lines. Examines installation of toilet, vanity faucet, sink, tub, shower, washer, and dryer. Provides instruction in safety, codes, tools, materials, sweating and hanging copper pipe, and assembling and gluing plastic pipe.
Industrial and Technical Education
Dist - CAREER **Prod** - CAREER

Plumbing 61 MIN
VHS
Home improvement video series
Color (G)
$39.95 purchase _ #204
Shows bathroom and laundry installation of rough plumbing for water supply and waste lines, installation of a toilet, vanity faucet and sink, tub and shower, washer and drier. Discusses safety codes, tools, materials, sweating, hanging copper pipe and assembling and gluing plastic pipe.
Home Economics; Industrial and Technical Education
Dist - DIYVC **Prod** - DIYVC

Plumbing
VHS
Home Improvement Series
(H C G A IND)
$39.95 _ SH320
Includes bathroom and laundry installation of rough plumbing for water supply and waste lines plus toilet installation, installation of the vanity faucet and sink, tub, shower, washer, and dryer.
Home Economics; Industrial and Technical Education
Dist - AAVIM **Prod** - AAVIM 1989

Plumbing 42 MIN
VHS / 16mm
Do it Yourself Series
(G)
$39.95 purchase _ #DIY320
Shows bathroom and laundry installation of rough plumbing for water and waste lines. Includes installation of toilet, vanity faucets, sink, tub, shower, and a washer and dryer. Covers safety codes, tools, and materials.
Home Economics
Dist - RMIBHF **Prod** - RMIBHF

Plumbing
VHS
Construction - Basic Principles Series
(C G)
$59.00 _ CA193
Gives basic principles regarding major water subsystems, water pressure, materials used in residential and industrial plumbing systems.
Education; Industrial and Technical Education
Dist - AAVIM **Prod** - AAVIM 1989

Plumbing and electrical 45 MIN
VHS
Color (A)
$19.95 purchase _ #S00425
Covers plumbing and electrical home improvement projects.
Home Economics; Industrial and Technical Education
Dist - UILL

Plumbing - Joints 13 MIN
16mm
Color (H C A)
Uses close - ups to take the student 'INSIDE' various joints, stressing aspects which make for a sound, water - tight fixture. Explains terms and measurements and how to calculate thread and fitting allowances. Shows copper soldered joints, methods of checking for a good joint, techniques of soldering, mechanical joints, use of inside and outside irons threaded joints and plastic pipe joints.
Industrial and Technical Education
Dist - SF **Prod** - SF 1969

Plumbing material and tool identification 47 MIN
VHS
Color (G H VOC)
$89.95 purchase _ #CEV00842V-T
Describes the most common plumbing tools and helps students identify and explain the use of each. Includes information on couplings; elbow joints; reducer bushings; female and male adaptors; gate and globe valves; common uses of galvanized steel and copper and plastic piping; and twenty-seven different tools. Discusses the tools in relation to the materials previously introduced.
Industrial and Technical Education
Dist - CAMV

Plumbing - Traps and Vents 14 MIN
U-matic / VHS
Color (H C A)
Shows the trap, parts of the trap, types, functions, stack vent, vents and terminals.
Industrial and Technical Education
Dist - SF **Prod** - SF 1970

Plump Jack - Shakespeare's Henry IV - Prince Hal's Rejection of Falstaff 45 MIN
U-matic / VHS
Survey of English Literature I Series
Color
Analyzes Prince Hal's rejection of Falstaff in Shakespeare's Henry IV.
Literature and Drama
Dist - MDCPB **Prod** - MDCPB

Plunge cut grinding 15 MIN
16mm
Machine shop work series; Operations on the center - type grinder; No 4
B&W
LC FIE51-560
Shows how to mount a bushing on a mandrel, dress the side of the grinding wheel, set a dial snap gage for the production grinding of bushings, and rough - and finish - grind a bushing. Stresses rhythm in grinding.
Industrial and Technical Education
Dist - USNAC **Prod** - USOE 1944

Plurals - S, Ss, Ch, Sh, Z, F - Ves, O - Oes 15 MIN
VHS
Planet Pylon Series
Color (I)
LC 90712900
Uses character Commander Wordstalker from Space Station Readstar to develop language skills in the area of plurals. Includes a worksheet exercise for students to complete with assistance of series characters. Fourth in a 23 - part series.
Education; English Language
Dist - GPN

Plus and Minus 15 MIN
U-matic / VHS
Math Mission 2 Series
Color (P)
LC 82-706316
Shows how a space robot's puppet assistant learns how to count money when she wants to buy some candy. Tells how the space robot helps her count it with a review of naming numbers and counting by tens, followed by an introduction to arithmetic drills on 'higher decade' addition facts.
Mathematics
Dist - GPN **Prod** - WCVETV 1980

Plus time served
16mm / U-matic / VHS
Insight series
Color (H C A)
Describes how an arrogant newscaster becomes the mediator for a group of prisoners after a riot. Tells how he grows beyond his ego - centered existence. Stars Jim Farentino, Don Stroud and Gregory Sierra.
Fine Arts; Guidance and Counseling
Dist - PAULST **Prod** - PAULST

Plutonium - an Element of Risk 59 MIN
VHS / 16mm
Color (G)
$70.00 rental _ #PEOR - 000
Investigates the proposals to expand the use of plutonium for nuclear fuel. Jack Lemmon narrates.
Science - Physical
Dist - PBS **Prod** - KCET

The Plutonium Connection 59 MIN
U-matic / VHS / 16mm
Nova Series
Color (H C A)
LC 78-700561
Explains that plutonium is the processed waste product of nuclear reactors and that it is becoming increasingly difficult to control the growing plutonium supply. Examines the complex problems resulting from the general availability of both the technical information and the plutonium needed for constructing an atomic bomb.
Science - Physical; Social Science; Sociology
Dist - TIMLIF **Prod** - WGBHTV 1976

The Plutonium Incident 90 MIN
U-matic / VHS
Color (H C A)
Offers the story of a woman who works as a technician at the Northern Oregon Nuclear facility and discovers that the safety procedures are woefully negligent. Stars Janet Margolin and Powers Boothe.
Fine Arts; Health and Safety; Social Science
Dist - TIMLIF **Prod** - TIMLIF 1983

Pluto's Christmas Tree 7 MIN
16mm / U-matic / VHS
Color (K P I J)
LC 72-700154
An animated cartoon picturing the antics of the chipmunks, Chip and Dale, who live in the fir tree which Mickey Mouse and Pluto chop down and decorate for Christmas.
Literature and Drama
Dist - CORF **Prod** - DISNEY 1971

Pluto's Surprise Package 8 MIN
U-matic / VHS / 16mm
Tales of Pluto Series
Color
Describes Pluto's trip to pick up some mail which becomes a harrowing experience when a turtle emerges from one of the packages and runs off with some letters.
Fine Arts; Literature and Drama
Dist - CORF **Prod** - DISNEY

Plymouth colony - the first year 16 MIN
U-matic / VHS / 16mm
Color (I J H)
$370.00, $250.00 purchase _ #4029; LC 80-701612
Portrays the events which forced the Pilgrims to leave Europe on the Mayflower, the difficulties of the trip, and the establishment of a settlement in America.
History - United States
Dist - CORF **Prod** - CORF 1980

Plyometrics
VHS
Coaching women's track and field series
Color (H C G)
$59.95 purchase _ #TRS1108V
Features women's field and track coaches Bob Meyers and Meg Ritchie on plyometrics. Demonstrates and discusses various plyometric drills utilized by women's field and track athletes. Includes - in place jumps; strength training; meso - power jumps; short - end jump; meso - endurance jumps; and longer jumps. Part of a nine - part series.
Physical Education and Recreation
Dist - CAMV

PM - 3A Nuclear Power Plant - Antarctica 20 MIN
16mm
Color (C A)
LC FIE64-159
Shows the construction of the first nuclear power station in the Antarctic, a 1500 kilowatt station at Mc Murdo Sound.
Geography - World; Industrial and Technical Education; Science - Physical
Dist - USERD **Prod** - USNRC 1963

PM of Hydraulic Systems 13 MIN
16mm
Color
Discusses the proper handling, storage and usage of hydraulic fluids and the vital importance of maintaining cleanliness throughout.
Industrial and Technical Education
Dist - MOKIN **Prod** - MOKIN

PM of Mobile Equipment 10 MIN
16mm
Color (IND)
Shows the vital components of any over - the - road vehicle that should be inspected before being driven and the items that should be checked while on the road.
Industrial and Technical Education
Dist - MOKIN **Prod** - MOKIN

PMS and Endometriosis 19 MIN
U-matic / VHS
Color (C)
$249.00, $149.00 purchase _ #AD - 1414
Explains the nature of PMS and its various treatments. Examines the pertinent facts about endometriosis.
Health and Safety; Psychology; Sociology
Dist - FOTH **Prod** - FOTH

PMS relief - unwinding naturally 20 MIN
VHS
Color (H C A)
$19.95 purchase
Features Jane Fryer in an introduction to natural techniques for relieving the stress and symptoms of PMS, premenstrual syndrome. Combines acupressure and Iyengar - style yoga to show women how to take control of their cycles, and balance their emotional and physical flows.
Health and Safety; Physical Education and Recreation; Sociology
Dist - YOGAJ **Prod** - YOGAJ

Pneuma 28 MIN
16mm
Color (G)
$60.00 rental
Incorporates Stoic philosophy, in which 'pneuma' is the soul or fiery wind permeating the body which survives the deaty of the body as impersonal energy. Recycles out - dated raw stock that has been processed without being exposed. Produced by Nathaniel Dorksy.
Fine Arts; Industrial and Technical Education
Dist - CANCIN

Pneumatic Actuators and Positioners 60 MIN
VHS
Pneumatic Systems and Equipment Series
Color (PRO)
$600.00 - $1500.00 purchase _ #ICPAP
Examines the main parts of a diaphragm and piston actuator, force - balance and motion - balance positioner. Covers how they work, how a force - balance positioner is adjusted and how a diaphragm actuator and a valve are stroked. Part of an eleven - part series on pneumatic systems and equipment, which is part of a 49 - unit set on instrumentation and control. Includes five workbooks and an instructor guide to support four hours of instruction.
Education; Industrial and Technical Education; Mathematics; Psychology
Dist - NUSTC **Prod** - NUSTC

Pneumatic Air Supplies and Regulators
U-matic / 16mm
Instrumentation Maintenance Series
Color (IND)
Covers filters, air dryers and dew point measurement. Explains troubleshooting of regulators.
Mathematics
Dist - ISA **Prod** - ISA

Pneumatic Control Equipment - 1 60 MIN
VHS
Pneumatic Systems and Equipment Series
Color (PRO)
$600.00 - $1500.00 purchase _ #ICPC1
Covers the basic types and functions of pneumatic instruments. Describes input, error detector and output - balancing mechanisms for various pneumatic control devices. Explains how these mechanism enable an instrument to balance itself automatically. Part of an eleven - part series on pneumatic systems and equipment, which is part of a 49 - unit set on instrumentation and control. Includes five workbooks and an instructor guide to support four hours of instruction.
Education; Industrial and Technical Education; Psychology
Dist - NUSTC **Prod** - NUSTC

Pneumatic Control Equipment - 2 60 MIN
VHS
Pneumatic Systems and Equipment Series
Color (PRO)
$600.00 - $1500.00 purchase _ #ICPC2
Focuses on the operating principles underlying common types of force and motion balance instruments. Part of an eleven - part series on pneumatic systems and equipment, which is part of a 49 - unit set on instrumentation and control. Includes five workbooks and an instructor guide to support four hours of instruction.
Education; Industrial and Technical Education; Mathematics; Psychology
Dist - NUSTC **Prod** - NUSTC

Pneumatic Control Equipment - 3 60 MIN
VHS
Pneumatic Systems and Equipment Series
Color (PRO)
$600.00 - $1500.00 purchase _ #ICPC3
Focuses on the function, purpose and operation of five pneumataic control instruments - transmitters, recorders, converters, indicators and hand - auto control stations. Explains how to identify correct output conditions, given instrument input conditons and how to calibrate the instruments. Part of an eleven - part series on pneumatic systems and equipment, which is part of a 49 - unit set on instrumentation and control. Includes five workbooks and an instructor guide to support four hours of instruction.
Education; Industrial and Technical Education; Mathematics; Psychology
Dist - NUSTC **Prod** - NUSTC

Pneumatic Controllers
16mm / U-matic
Instrumentation Maintenance Series
Color (IND)
Deals with the Ziegler - Nichols method of tuning, tuning cascade control loop and troubleshooting control problems.
Mathematics
Dist - ISA **Prod** - ISA

Pneumatic Controllers 60 MIN
VHS
Pneumatic Systems and Equipment Series
Color (PRO)
$600.00 - $1500.00 purchase _ #ICPCO
Explains the differences between the following control modes - proportional, proportional - plus - reset, proportional - plus - rate and proportional - plus - reset - plus - rate. Part of an eleven - part series on pneumatic systems and equipment, which is part of a 49 - unit set on instrumentation and control. Includes five workbooks and an instructor guide to support four hours of instruction.
Education; Industrial and Technical Education; Psychology
Dist - NUSTC **Prod** - NUSTC

Pneumatic Instrument Tubing 60 MIN
VHS
Pneumatic Systems and Equipment Series
Color (PRO)
$600.00 - $1500.00 purchase _ #ICPIT
Shows how to install pipe and tubing runs. Includes sizing pipe and tubing. Identifies various pipe and tube fittings. Part of an eleven - part series on pneumatic systems and equipment, which is part of a 49 - unit set on instrumentation and control. Includes five workbooks and an instructor guide to support four hours of instruction.
Education; Industrial and Technical Education; Psychology
Dist - NUSTC **Prod** - NUSTC

Pneumatic Instruments - Sensors, Indicators, Transmitters
U-matic / 16mm
Instrumentation Maintenance Series
Color (IND)
Teaches calibration of pressure gages and maintenance and calibration of differential pressure transmitters. Explains temperature transmitters.
Mathematics
Dist - ISA **Prod** - ISA

Pneumatic Systems and Controls 27 MIN
U-matic / VHS
Color (IND)
Discusses equipment, operation and circuitry used to pneumatically control drilling rig equipment.
Industrial and Technical Education; Social Science
Dist - UTEXPE **Prod** - UTEXPE 1968

Pneumatic Systems and Equipment Series

Basic pneumatic control systems	60 MIN
Basic pneumatic systems and diagrams	60 MIN
Multi - Element Pneumatic Control Systems	60 MIN
Pneumatic Actuators and Positioners	60 MIN
Pneumatic Control Equipment - 1	60 MIN
Pneumatic Control Equipment - 2	60 MIN
Pneumatic Control Equipment - 3	60 MIN
Pneumatic Controllers	60 MIN
Pneumatic Instrument Tubing	60 MIN
Troubleshooting pneumatic instrument systems	60 MIN
Tuning Pneumatic Control Systems	60 MIN

Dist - NUSTC

Pneumatic Transducers, Computing Relays
16mm / U-matic
Instrumentation Maintenance Series
Color (IND)
Explains amplifying and computer relays and maintenance and calibration of square root extractors.
Mathematics
Dist - ISA **Prod** - ISA

Pneumatics Explained 58 MIN
VHS / 35mm strip
(H A IND)
#530XV7
Explains the basic principles and applications of Pneumatic pressure and control. Includes gas laws for Pneumatic systems, pipe and compressor sizing, air compressors and compressor control, and system components, switches, relays and operators (4 tapes). Prerequisite required. Includes a Study Guide.
Education; Industrial and Technical Education
Dist - BERGL

Pneumonectomy for Carcinoma 35 MIN
16mm
Color (PRO)
Deals with the diagnosis, pathology and surgical technique of total pneumonectomy for primary carcinoma of the lung. Emphasizes roentgenological diagnosis and pathological characteristics through the use of X - ray studies and studies of the surgical specimens of five patients with this disease.
Health and Safety; Science
Dist - ACY **Prod** - ACYDGD 1953

Pneumothorax and hemothorax 20 MIN
VHS / U-matic
Emergency management - the first 30 minutes series; Vol 1
Color
Discusses pneumothorax and hemothorax, giving definitions and classifications, symptoms and techniques for posterior drainage.
Health and Safety; Science - Natural
Dist - VTRI **Prod** - VTRI

PNF - Assisting to Postures and Application in Occupational Therapy Activities 60 MIN
U-matic
Proprioceptive Neuromuscular Faciliation Series

Color (PRO)
Demonstrates the PNF procedure for assisting patients to various postures. Suggests occupational therapy activities that may be used in each posture.
Health and Safety
Dist - RICHGO **Prod** - RICHGO

PNF - diagonal patterns and their application to functional activities 45 MIN
U-matic
Proprioceptive neuromuscular facilitation series
Color (PRO)
Demonstrates the diagonal patterns of the head, neck, trunk and extremities. Gives examples of how each pattern occurs in functional activities and how it may be used as a basis for designing treatment activities.
Health and Safety
Dist - RICHGO **Prod** - RICHGO

Poached fish - stuffed sole to creole scallop casserole 30 MIN
VHS
International cooking school with Chef Rene series; Lesson 18
Color (G)
$69.00 purchase
Presents classic methods of cooking poached fish that stress essential flavor. Part of a series that introduces newer, lighter foods.
Home Economics
Dist - LUF **Prod** - LUF

Poaching 9 MIN
8mm cartridge / 16mm
Modern basics of classical cooking series; Lesson 5
Color (A)
#MB05
Presents information on the four kinds of poaching - in water, in stock, in a waterbath with agitation and in the double boiler with stirring. Part of a series developed in cooperation with the Swiss Association of Restauranteurs and Hoteliers to train foodservice employees. Includes five instructor's handbooks, a textbook by Eugene Pauli, 20 sets of student tests and 20 sets of student information sheets.
Home Economics; Industrial and Technical Education
Dist - CONPRO **Prod** - CONPRO

Poaching and steaming 30 MIN
VHS
Gourmet techniques series
Color (H C G)
$19.95 purchase _ #IVN045V
Features expert chef instructors from the California Culinary Academy in San Francisco who share their secrets on poaching and steaming. Part of a three - part series on gourmet techniques.
Home Economics
Dist - CAMV

Pocahontas 15 MIN
VHS / U-matic
Stories of America series
Color (P)
Traces the childhood of Pocahontas, her contributions to Colonial Virginia and later life in England.
Biography; History - United States; Social Science
Dist - AITECH **Prod** - OHSDE 1976

Pocket billiards 30 MIN
16mm
B&W (A G)
Demonstrates concepts and applications in the game of pocket billiards.
Physical Education and Recreation
Dist - SFI **Prod** - SFI

Pocket billiards series
Advanced skills of billiards 11 MIN
Fundamentals of billiards 11 MIN
Dist - ATHI

The Pocket Gopher - Adaptations for Living Underground 13 MIN
U-matic / VHS / 16mm
Aspects of Animal Behavior Series
Color (I)
Uses the pocket gopher as a model for analyzing fossorial life in rodents. Follows pocket gophers underground to show movement through the burrow and use of the feet and teeth in digging.
Science - Natural
Dist - UCEMC **Prod** - UCLA 1977

Pocket sweat suit 16 MIN
VHS
No sweat sewing projects series
Color (A H)
$39.95 purchase _ #SWE761V-H
Demonstrates with easy-to-understand instructions how to make a child's garment from a recycled adult's sweat shirt. Students learn basic measuring, cutting, conventional and serger sewing, attaching cuffs, installing a zipper and adding pockets.
Home Economics
Dist - CAMV

Pocket Watches 30 MIN
VHS / U-matic
Antique Shop Series
Color
Presents guests who are experts in their respective fields who share tips on collecting and caring for antique pocket watches.
Fine Arts
Dist - MDCPB **Prod** - WVPTTV

Pocketful of miracles 137 MIN
VHS
Color (G)
$19.95 purchase _ #S02084
Presents Frank Capra's final movie, in which a Broadway 'down - and - outer' poses as a society matron to impress her daughter. Stars Bette Davis, Glenn Ford, Peter Falk, and Ann - Margret in her first film role.
Fine Arts; History - United States
Dist - UILL

Pockets of Hate 26 MIN
U-matic / VHS
Color (G)
$249.00, $149.00 purchase _ #AD - 1940
Examines the increase in racial crime. Seeks to determine where young people are picking up their racist attitudes and why they are becoming more comfortable in acting out their prejudices.
Sociology
Dist - FOTH **Prod** - FOTH

Poco and friends - Volume 1 30 MIN
VHS
Uncle Nick and the magic forest series
Color (K P)
$14.95 purchase
Encourages the development of self - esteem, tolerance and physical coordination through storytelling, music and dance. Features Nick Felix, former dance choreographer of 'Barney and the Backyard Gang,' as Uncle Nick, neighborhood storyteller, who helps kids overcome personal problems like learning disabilities, unusual appearance or lack of coordination.
Literature and Drama
Dist - HFDANC **Prod** - MAGFOR 1994

Podiatric medicine 25 MIN
VHS
Career encounters series
Color (J H C A)
$95.00 purchase _ #MG3410V-J; $89.00 purchase _ #4270
Presents a documentary-style program that explores a career in podiatric medicine. Features professionals at work, explaining what they do and how they got where they are. Emphasizes diversity of occupational opportunities and of men and women in the field. Offers information about new developments and technologies and about educational and certification requirements for entering the profession. One of a series of videos about professions available individually or as a set
Guidance and Counseling
Dist - CAMV
NEWCAR

Podiatric medicine career encounters 28 MIN
VHS
Career encounters video series
Color (J H)
$89.00 purchase _ #4270
Offers a documentary on careers in the field of podiatric medicine. Visits workplaces and hears professionals explain what they do, how they got where they are and why they find the work so rewarding. Emphasizes human diversity in the professions. Dispels myths, misconceptions and stereotypes and offers practical information about the requirements for entering the field. Part of a 13 - part series.
Business and Economics; Guidance and Counseling; Science
Dist - NEWCAR

Poem of Rodia 4 MIN
16mm
B&W (I)
Presents an exploration of visual poetry inherent in the primitive handmade monument, Watts Towers, constructed by Simon Rodia from four generations of discarded junk.
Fine Arts
Dist - UWFKD **Prod** - UWFKD

Poemfield no 1 6 MIN
16mm
Color (J)
LC 73-701191
Presents a visual experiment with language.
English Language; Fine Arts; Literature and Drama
Dist - VANBKS **Prod** - VANBKS 1972

Poemfield no 2 5 MIN
16mm
Poemfield Series
Color
Combines modern music with brightly colored computer art.
Fine Arts
Dist - VANBKS **Prod** - VANBKS 1965

Poemfield no 3 8 MIN
16mm
Poemfield Series
Color
English Language; Fine Arts; Literature and Drama
Dist - VANBKS **Prod** - VANBKS

Poemfield no 4 10 MIN
16mm
Poemfield Series
Color
English Language; Fine Arts; Literature and Drama
Dist - VANBKS **Prod** - VANBKS

Poemfield no 5 8 MIN
16mm
Poemfield Series
Color
English Language; Fine Arts; Literature and Drama
Dist - VANBKS **Prod** - VANBKS

Poemfield no 7 9 MIN
16mm
Poemfield Series
Color
English Language; Fine Arts; Literature and Drama
Dist - VANBKS **Prod** - VANBKS

Poemfield Series
Poemfield no 2 5 MIN
Poemfield no 3 8 MIN
Poemfield no 4 10 MIN
Poemfield no 5 8 MIN
Poemfield no 7 9 MIN
Dist - VANBKS

Poems about Animals 13 MIN
U-matic / VHS / 16mm
Poetry for Fun Series
Color (P I J)
$325, $235 purchase _ #71046
Shows poetry as a visual, not just aural, experience. Animation. Live action.
Literature and Drama
Dist - CORF

Poems as Descriptions 15 MIN
U-matic / VHS
Word Shop Series
Color (P)
Literature and Drama
Dist - WETATV **Prod** - WETATV

Poems as Rhythm 15 MIN
U-matic / VHS
Word Shop Series
Color (P)
Literature and Drama
Dist - WETATV **Prod** - WETATV

Poems as Sounds 15 MIN
VHS / U-matic
Word Shop Series
Color (P)
English Language; Literature and Drama
Dist - WETATV **Prod** - WETATV

Poems as Stories 15 MIN
VHS / U-matic
Word Shop Series
Color (P)
Literature and Drama
Dist - WETATV **Prod** - WETATV

Poems for children - Wiersze dia dzieci 64 MIN
VHS
Color (P I J) (POLISH)
$17.95 purchase _ #V169
Features poems for children written by Jan Brzechwa, Konstanty Ildefons Galczynski and Julian Tuwin and recited by well - known Polish actors.
Fine Arts; Literature and Drama
Dist - POLART

Poems in their places 70 MIN
VHS
Color (A)
PdS99 purchase
Features the work of seven poets - A E Housman, Edward Thomas, Thomas Gray, W B Yeats, Dylan Thomas, Thomas Hardy, and John Clare. Puts their work into its geographical and social context. The program is a compliation of seven 10-minute segments.

English Language; Fine Arts; Literature and Drama
Dist - BBCENE

Poesie de la francophonie 100 MIN
VHS
Color (G) (FRENCH)
$49.95 purchase _ #W3601
Introduces French poetry with readings of 67 works from all over the French - speaking world, accompanied by music and animated illustrations.
Fine Arts; Literature and Drama
Dist - GPC

Poet and Hero - Milton's Paradise Lost - the Triumph of Human Love 45 MIN
Videoreel / VT2
Survey of English Literature I Series
Color
Features Dr Thomas Sheye of Loyola College discussing the significance, conflicts, themes and characters of Milton's PARADISE LOST as well as its place in Renaissance literature. Explains how Milton continued and brought to a conclusion the Renaissance search for a hero.
Literature and Drama
Dist - MDCPB **Prod** - MDCPB

Poet - Helen Harrington 12 MIN
VHS
Color (J H C G)
$150.00 purchase, $25.00 rental
Delves into the life of a poet and a farmer from Iowa whose work celebrates the Earth and the self. Looks at her inspiration which comes from the reality and practicality of farm life as well as the endless possibilities of the human spirit. A visual essay with poems set before a backdrop of nature sequences and laced with insightful comments from Harrington. Produced by Kelli Bixler.
Biography; Fine Arts; Literature and Drama; Social Science
Dist - CANCIN

Poet - Irving Layton observed 52 MIN
VHS
Creative process series
Color (G)
$89.85 purchase _ #S01986
Interviews Canadian poet Irving Layton.
Literature and Drama
Dist - UILL **Prod** - NFBC

Poet of his people - Pablo Neruda 13 MIN
16mm
Color
LC 78-701691
Offers a symbolic representation of the life of Chilean poet Pablo Neruda as portrayed in his poem La Barcarola.
Fine Arts; Literature and Drama
Dist - LILYAN **Prod** - LILYAN 1978

Poet, racer, dragon chaser 10 MIN
U-matic / VHS
Book, look and listen series
Color (K P)
Discusses the various occupations in which people are engaged.
English Language; Guidance and Counseling; Social Science
Dist - AITECH **Prod** - MDDE 1977

The Poetic nationalist and The spirit of Spain 57 MIN
VHS
Guitarra series; Vol II; Pts 5 and 6
Color (S)
$39.95 purchase _ #833 - 9071
Traces the evolution of the Spanish guitar from 1500 to the present day. Features world - renowned classical guitarist Julian Bream as host and musician. Volume III of the four - volume series performs Granado's 'Spanish Dances No 4 and 5,' 'Dedicatoria,' 'Maja de Goya' and 'Valsas Poeticas' at Ronad, Seville, Barcelona and Zahara in Part 5. Bream plays pieces from Albeniz's 'Iberia' cycle - 'Cadiz,' 'Granada,' 'Seville' and 'Cordova' at the cities of the same name in Part 6.
Fine Arts; Foreign Language; Geography - World; History - World
Dist - FI **Prod** - RMART 1986

The Poetry 30 MIN
VHS / U-matic
Black Poetry of the Midwest Series
Color
Presents the works of poets David Rice, Inua Fuller and Benjamin Franklin Gardner.
History - United States; Literature and Drama
Dist - NETCHE **Prod** - NETCHE 1977

Poetry 15 MIN
U-matic / VHS
Through the pages series; No 4
Color (P)
LC 82-707367
Introduces Grace Butcher and Leonard Trawick reading their poetry and discussing their work with librarian Phyllis Syracuse who seeks to inspire children to read, and especially to write, poetry.
English Language; Literature and Drama
Dist - GPN **Prod** - WVIZTV 1982

Poetry, a beginner's guide 26 MIN
16mm / U-matic / VHS
Color (H C)
$85.00 purchase; $540.00, $250.00 purchase _ #4909C
Shows how poetry reflects global emotions and everyday experiences. Includes poets Jim Wayne Miller and Joy Bale Boone reading from their own works, as well as material derived from Hopkins, Tennyson, and others.
Literature and Drama
Dist - UWKY **Prod** - UWKY 1986
CORF

Poetry - a beginner's guide 26 MIN
VHS
Color (H C G)
$85.00 purchase
Examines the presentation of poetry within the framework of the 'everyday,' the experiences common to all people. Features working poets Jim Wayne Miller and Joy Bale Boone of Kentucky, as well as material derived from Hopkins, Tennyson and others.
History - United States; Literature and Drama
Dist - UWKY **Prod** - UWKY 1984

Poetry and Arts 30 MIN
VHS / 16mm
Say Brother National Edition Series
Color (G)
$55.00 rental _ #SBRO - 110
Sociology
Dist - PBS **Prod** - WGBHTV

Poetry and Hidden Poetry 53 MIN
U-matic / VHS
Royal Shakespeare Company Series
Color
Reveals the hidden poetry in seemingly unpoetic lines and demonstrates how polysyllables trip easily off the tongue while monosyllabic lines and words are packed with thoughts and feelings in Shakespeare. Uses examples from King Lear, All's Well That Ends Well, King John and Othello.
Literature and Drama
Dist - FOTH **Prod** - FOTH 1984

Poetry - Brother Antonius and Michael Mc Clure 30 MIN
U-matic / VHS / 16mm
USA Series
B&W (J)
LC 76-704396
Describes the poetry of Michael Mc Clure. Discusses his use of hallucinogenic drugs to achieve poetry directly from the emotions. Introduces Brother Antonius, a Dominican lay brother known for his combination of poetry reading and dramatic encounters with audiences.
Literature and Drama
Dist - IU **Prod** - NET 1966

Poetry by Americans series
Edgar Allan Poe 9 MIN
James Weldon Johnson 12 MIN
Robert Frost 10 MIN
Walt Whitman 10 MIN
Dist - AIMS

Poetry Center reading series
Abigail Child - 9 - 8 - 84
Ai - 11 - 14 - 74 36 MIN
Alan Bernheimer - 2 - 25 - 82 30 MIN
Alan Davies - 11 - 4 - 82 30 MIN
Alan Davies - 2 - 25 - 88
Alan Davies - 2 - 26 - 88
Allen Ginsberg - 5 - 9 - 74 48 MIN
Allen Ginsberg - 9 - 28 - 78 50 MIN
Alta - 10 - 10 - 76 36 MIN
Amiri Baraka - 10 - 23 - 84 83 MIN
Amiri Baraka - 3 - 2 - 77 45 MIN
Amiri Baraka - 2 - 27 - 87 38 MIN
Amy Gerstler - 3 - 29 - 87 30 MIN
Ana Castillo - 10 - 16 - 86 23 MIN
Angela Davis - 10 - 24 - 80 16 MIN
Anita Barrows - 12 - 3 - 87 40 MIN
Anita Desai - 12 - 13 - 89
Anita Desai - 12 - 14 - 89
Anne Finger - 5 - 10 - 80 60 MIN
Anne Valley Fox - 5 - 22 - 75 10 MIN
Arkadii Dragomoshchenko - 3 - 13 - 88 90 MIN
Asian - American reading - 5 - 16 - 77 130 MIN
Barbara Einzig - 10 - 15 - 87 50 MIN
Barbara Guest - 5 - 16 - 79 60 MIN
Barbara Guest - 1 - 9 - 83
Barbara Guest - 2 - 14 - 74 25 MIN
Basil bunting - 4 - 29 - 76 23 MIN
Beau Beausoleil - 11 - 19 - 81 30 MIN
Ben Bova - 7 - 25 - 77
Bernard Gershenson - 9 - 1 - 87 40 MIN
Beverly Dahlen - 4 - 13 - 85 72 MIN
Beverly Dahlen - 4 - 4 - 74
Beverly Dahlen - 4 - 7 - 83 35 MIN
Beverly Dahlen - 10 - 12 - 89 45 MIN
Bill Berkson - 5 - 5 - 83
Bill Berkson - 10 - 10 - 74 30 MIN
Boadiba - 3 - 17 - 88 25 MIN
Bruce Andrews - 5 - 19 - 85 40 MIN
Bruce Andrews - 3 - 14 - 79 60 MIN
Bruce Boone - 11 - 8 - 84 29 MIN
Buff Bradley - 9 - 11 - 80 30 MIN
Buriel clay - 4 - 5 - 78 111 MIN
California one 27 MIN
Canyon - 5 - 10 - 80 60 MIN
Carl Dennis - 3 - 4 - 80 60 MIN
Carlos Fuentes - 9 - 3 - 87 76 MIN
Carol Berge - 12 - 5 - 74 24 MIN
Carol Frost - 2 - 13 - 80 30 MIN
Carolyn Burke - 11 - 7 - 87 102 MIN
Carolyn Forche - 5 - 10 - 80 48 MIN
Carroll Arnett - 9 - 29 - 83 25 MIN
Charles Amirkhanian - 6 - 22 - 73 30 MIN
Charles Amirkhanian - 3 - 7 - 74 40 MIN
Charles Bernstein - 10 - 6 - 84 41 MIN
Charles Bernstein - 2 - 28 - 79 46 MIN
Charles Bukowski - 12 - 6 - 73 30 MIN
Chris Tysh - 11 - 7 - 87 102 MIN
Christopher Dewdney - 2 - 25 - 82 30 MIN
Christy Taylor - 10 - 4 - 87 120 MIN
Cid Corman - 12 - 13 - 78 37 MIN
Clark Coolidge - 5 - 5 - 76 53 MIN
Clark Coolidge - 3 - 16 - 85 50 MIN
Clayton Eshleman - 12 - 5 - 79 60 MIN
Clayton Eshleman - 2 - 13 - 86 76 MIN
Coleman Barks - 2 - 6 - 80 30 MIN
Conyus - 2 - 18 - 84 50 MIN
Cyrus Cassells - 10 - 16 - 81 20 MIN
Daniel Davidson - 10 - 29 - 87
David Antin - 5 - 26 - 73
David Benedetti - 3 - 6 - 86 32 MIN
David Bromige - 11 - 15 - 90 90 MIN
David Bromige - 4 - 30 - 87 52 MIN
David Bromige - 10 - 11 - 78 60 MIN
David Gitin - 5 - 9 - 79 31 MIN
Debora Greger - 12 - 4 - 80 30 MIN
Dennis Cooper - 11 - 9 - 89 33 MIN
Dennis Cooper - 10 - 31 - 82 25 MIN
Diane Di Prima - 12 - 4 - 86 44 MIN
Diane Di Prima - 6 - 17 - 74 96 MIN
Diane Di Prima - 6 - 21 - 74 51 MIN
Diane Di Prima - 3 - 17 - 76
Diane Glancy - 9 - 22 - 88
Dick Gallup - 3 - 3 - 76 30 MIN
Dodie Bellamy - 10 - 3 - 85 40 MIN
Donald Hall - 4 - 20 - 86 54 MIN
Donald Hall - 10 - 27 - 76 43 MIN
Dorianne Laux - 11 - 14 - 85 20 MIN
Ebbe Borregaard - 2 - 11 - 76 30 MIN
Ed Dorn - 4 - 28 - 76 40 MIN
Ed Dorn - 9 - 19 - 74 45 MIN
Edward Field - 12 - 8 - 76
Eileen Corder - 7 - 28 - 80
Elizabeth Abel - 4 - 13 - 85 80 MIN
Ellery Akers - 4 - 13 - 89 50 MIN
Ernest J Gaines - 3 - 6 - 74 56 MIN
Ernesto Cardenal - 11 - 8 - 90 90 MIN
Etel Adnan - 3 - 10 - 88 37 MIN
Fernando Alegria - 12 - 11 - 81 30 MIN
Fielding Dawson - 11 - 22 - 83
Fielding Dawson - 10 - 22 - 75 30 MIN
Flora Arnstein - 4 - 4 - 74 30 MIN
Flora Arnstein - 6 - 18 - 73
Francisco Alarcon - 3 - 28 - 85 39 MIN
Francisco Alarcon - 2 - 7 - 89 20 MIN
Frank Bidart - 2 - 17 - 83 40 MIN
Frank Chin - 9 - 14 - 89 73 MIN
Gail Layton - 10 - 4 - 87 120 MIN
Garielle Daniels - 5 - 10 - 80 60 MIN
George Barlow - 4 - 2 - 87 36 MIN
George Butterick - 3 - 6 - 79 75 MIN
George Evans - 11 - 20 - 86 35 MIN
Georgette Cerutti - 5 - 22 - 75 17 MIN
Gloria Anzaldua - 9 - 15 - 88 40 MIN
Gloria Frym - 10 - 20 - 83 37 MIN
Harold Norse - 11 - 14 - 85 80 MIN
Harvey Stein - 10 - 29 - 87
Helen Adam - 11 - 2 - 77 30 MIN
Helen Gardner - 10 - 8 - 87
Henk Bernlef - 5 - 4 - 82 30 MIN
Ian Grand - 6 - 20 - 74 103 MIN
J M Coetzee - 2 - 21 - 86 50 MIN
Jack Collom - 10 - 20 - 76 37 MIN
Jack Gilbert - 11 - 1 - 78 60 MIN

James Anthony - 10 - 29 - 87
James Broughton - 11 - 12 - 89 80 MIN
James Broughton - 11 - 8 - 73 50 MIN
James Broughton - 11 - 2 - 77 30 MIN
James Broughton - 5 - 15 - 74 120 MIN
James Broughton - 10 - 4 - 87 120 MIN
James Leigh - 12 - 5 - 79 30 MIN
Jane Cooper - 3 - 20 - 75 34 MIN
Jean Day - 3 - 24 - 83 58 MIN
Jerry Estrin - 10 - 6 - 83 25 MIN
Jessica Grim - 2 - 22 - 90 37 MIN
Jessica Hagedorn and West Coast Gangster Choir - 10 - 30 - 75 55 MIN
Jill Breckenridge - 11 - 19 - 87 39 MIN
Jim Carroll - 10 - 10 - 74 30 MIN
Jim Gustafson - 11 - 8 - 78 30 MIN
Jim Gustafson - 2 - 9 - 77
Jimmy Santiago Baca - 2 - 16 - 89 29 MIN
Joan Didion - 2 - 3 - 77 90 MIN
Joanne Feit Diehl - 4 - 14 - 85 93 MIN
Johanna Drucker - 9 - 8 - 84 70 MIN
John Ashbery - 12 - 5 - 84 56 MIN
John Ashbery - 5 - 16 - 73 60 MIN
John Ashbery - 9 - 13 - 90 45 MIN
John Balaban - 10 - 28 - 82 40 MIN
John Beecher - 11 - 23 - 77 120 MIN
John Beecher - 12 - 1 - 75 30 MIN
John Beecher - 7 - 1 - 77
John Felstiner - 10 - 15 - 81 60 MIN
John Giorno - 11 - 4 - 74 40 MIN
Jon Anderson - 5 - 2 - 74 39 MIN
Jonathan Greene - 4 - 25 - 85 32 MIN
Jonathan Griffin - 10 - 28 - 75 53 MIN
Jorie Graham - 10 - 22 - 81 30 MIN
Joseph Chaikin - 6 - 1 - 78 40 MIN
Joy Cutler - 10 - 29 - 87
Joy Harjo - 9 - 26 - 85 32 MIN
Judy Grahn - 11 - 14 - 85 80 MIN
Judy Grahn - 4 - 13 - 85 45 MIN
Judy Grahn - 4 - 14 - 83
Judy Grahn - 9 - 15 - 88 46 MIN
Judy Grahn - 10 - 4 - 79 30 MIN
Judy Grahn - 10 - 2 - 74 25 MIN
Justine Fixel - 10 - 4 - 87 120 MIN
Karen Brennan - 11 - 19 - 81 30 MIN
Karen Brodine - 11 - 5 - 81 60 MIN
Karen Brodine - 5 - 10 - 80 60 MIN
Karen Brodine - 4 - 14 - 85 34 MIN
Karen Brodine - 3 - 28 - 85 31 MIN
Karina Epperlein - 1 - 1 - 84 20 MIN
Kathleen Fraser - 5 - 9 - 80 30 MIN
Kathleen Fraser - 9 - 28 - 82 45 MIN
Kathleen Fraser - 1 - 1 - 74 23 MIN
Kathleen Fraser - 6 - 21 - 74 30 MIN
Kathleen Fraser - 6 - 22 - 73
Kathleen Fraser - 2 - 25 - 76 50 MIN
Kathleen Fraser - 2 - 7 - 88 120 MIN
Kathleen Fraser - 2 - 7 - 89 15 MIN
Kathy Acker - 10 - 23 - 86 46 MIN
Kathy Acker - 2 - 9 - 77 57 MIN
Kay Boyle - 12 - 10 - 75 60 MIN
Keith Abbott - 3 - 6 - 75 27 MIN
Kenward Elmslie - 11 - 10 - 83 45 MIN
Kenward Elmslie - 3 - 1 - 90 60 MIN
Kenward Elmslie - 3 - 6 - 75 50 MIN
Killarney Clary - 12 - 6 - 90 30 MIN
Larry Eigner - 11 - 29 - 84
Larry Fagin - 4 - 27 - 77 40 MIN
Larry Goodell - 5 - 8 - 75 27 MIN
Laura Chester - 3 - 29 - 87 35 MIN
Laura Chester - 3 - 20 - 75 40 MIN
Laurie Duggan - 10 - 8 - 87
Lawrence Ferlinghetti - 3 - 5 - 76 30 MIN
Lawrence Fixel - 10 - 4 - 87 120 MIN
Lennart Bruce - 2 - 13 - 75 30 MIN
Lennart Bruce - 2 - 7 - 85 30 MIN
Leslie Campbell - 5 - 9 - 80 60 MIN
Linda Gregg - 3 - 11 - 82 30 MIN
Lori Callies - 11 - 14 - 85 80 MIN
Lorna Dee Cervantes - 4 - 24 - 85 34 MIN
Lorna Dee Cervantes - 10 - 24 - 80 16 MIN
Louis Ginsberg - 5 - 9 - 74 35 MIN
Louise Bernikow - 11 - 20 - 80 60 MIN
Louise Gluck - 5 - 10 - 90 29 MIN
Louise Gluck - 2 - 25 - 76 35 MIN
Lucha Corpi - 11 - 30 - 89 42 MIN
Lucia Berlin - 2 - 24 - 84 18 MIN
Luis Alfaro - 9 - 23 - 90 40 MIN
Lydia Davis - 2 - 21 - 85 37 MIN
Lynne Dreyer - 4 - 9 - 85
Madeline Gleason - 5 - 15 - 74 120 MIN
Manlio Argueta - 11 - 13 - 86 67 MIN
Margaret Atwood - 5 - 3 - 78 60 MIN
Margaret Cesa - 9 - 11 - 80 30 MIN
Margaret Crane - 9 - 28 - 89 15 MIN
Marilyn Chin - 10 - 26 - 89 40 MIN
Marilyn Hacker - 5 - 4 - 77 50 MIN
Mark Linenthal - 10 - 4 - 87 120 MIN
Mei - Mei Berssenbrugge - 4 - 21 - 76 41 MIN
Mei - Mei Berssenbrugge - 9 - 28 - 82 30 MIN
Mei - Mei Berssenbrugge - 2 - 22 - 90 40 MIN
Michael Amnasan - 10 - 27 - 88
Michael Brownstein - 10 - 8 - 75 37 MIN
Michael Davidson - 4 - 24 - 86 37 MIN
Michael Davidson - 4 - 10 - 75 28 MIN
Michael Dennis Browne - 2 - 19 - 86 30 MIN
Michael Gottlieb - 9 - 22 - 83 34 MIN
Michael McClure - 10 - 4 - 87 120 MIN
Michelle Cliff - 10 - 9 - 86 39 MIN
Millicent Dillon - 5 - 9 - 80 60 MIN
Millicent Dillon - 4 - 2 - 87 45 MIN
Nicole Brossard - 10 - 23 - 86 72 MIN
Nikki Giovanni - 12 - 4 - 84 61 MIN
Nina Cassian - 5 - 10 - 82 36 MIN
Norma Cole - 9 - 22 - 88
Norman Fischer - 9 - 30 - 82 30 MIN
Nzinga Asele - 2 - 18 - 84 33 MIN
Olga Broumas - 4 - 12 - 85 25 MIN
Opal Palmer Adisa - 11 - 17 - 83 30 MIN
Otis Brown - 10 - 30 - 75 30 MIN
Pablo Fernandez - 11 - 13 - 81 45 MIN
Pamela Edwards - 5 - 22 - 75 17 MIN
Pat Dienstfrey - 4 - 14 - 88 45 MIN
Patricia Goedicke - 10 - 8 - 81 30 MIN
Patricia Hampl - 2 - 6 - 80 30 MIN
Paul Auster - 3 - 16 - 89 60 MIN
Paul Sherman - 11 - 1 - 78
Paula Gunn Allen - 3 - 21 - 85 28 MIN
Paula Gunn Allen - 2 - 26 - 87 67 MIN
Peter Everwine - 5 - 10 - 73 25 MIN
Philip Garrison - 2 - 27 - 75 31 MIN
Q R Hand - 2 - 25 - 83 15 MIN
Quinton Duval - 3 - 25 - 82 60 MIN
Rachel Blau DuPlessis - 11 - 8 - 86 49 MIN
Rachel Blau DuPlessis - 11 - 9 - 86 63 MIN
Rachel Blau DuPlessis - 5 - 6 - 82 100 MIN
Rachel Blau DuPlessis - 5 - 10 - 80 60 MIN
Rae Armantrout - 5 - 2 - 85 60 MIN
Ralph Adamo - 2 - 18 - 82 30 MIN
Ralph Angel - 4 - 9 - 87 38 MIN
Rebecca Brown - 3 - 31 - 76 31 MIN
Richard Barnes - 10 - 24 - 74 31 MIN
Richard Caddel - 11 - 7 - 85 36 MIN
Richard Grossinger - 5 - 12 - 76 65 MIN
Rita Dove - 3 - 5 - 87 31 MIN
Robert Bly - 3 - 20 - 84 100 MIN
Robert Creeley - 11 - 15 - 73 28 MIN
Robert Creeley - 11 - 1 - 78
Robert Creeley - 5 - 9 - 78 45 MIN
Robert Creeley - 9 - 24 - 83 34 MIN
Robert Creeley - 3 - 27 - 83 20 MIN
Robert Duncan - 11 - 1 - 78
Robert Duncan - 5 - 17 - 74 120 MIN
Robert Duncan - 5 - 9 - 78 42 MIN
Robert Duncan - 9 - 22 - 84 109 MIN
Robert Duncan - 10 - 4 - 87 120 MIN
Robert Duncan - 2 - 22 - 73 42 MIN
Robert Gluck - 11 - 14 - 85 80 MIN
Robert Gluck - 11 - 8 - 84 36 MIN
Robert Gluck - 4 - 3 - 75 37 MIN
Robert Grenier - 11 - 27 - 88 30 MIN
Robert Grenier - 2 - 21 - 79 53 MIN
Robert Grenier - 2 - 21 - 85 60 MIN
Roberto Bedoya - 10 - 25 - 90 30 MIN
Robin Blaser - 11 - 9 - 83
Robin Blaser - 9 - 29 - 88 90 MIN
Robin Blaser - 2 - 11 - 76 30 MIN
Rosalie Moore - 10 - 4 - 87 120 MIN
Ruth Witt - Diamant Memorial Reading - 10 - 4 - 87 120 MIN
Sam Shepard - 6 - 1 - 78 40 MIN
Sandra Gilbert - 5 - 6 - 82 50 MIN
Sandra Gilbert - 4 - 13 - 85 90 MIN
Sharon Doubiago - 10 - 16 - 81 60 MIN
Shirley Taylor - 10 - 4 - 87 120 MIN
Sister Goodwin - 3 - 2 - 85 40 MIN
Stephan Gaskin - 5 - 13 - 76
Stephen Emerson - 11 - 22 - 83
Stephen Witt - Diamant - 10 - 4 - 87 120 MIN
Steve Benson - 3 - 10 - 83
Steven Gilmartin - 11 - 10 - 88
Suky Durham - 5 - 10 - 80 60 MIN
Summer Brenner - 11 - 16 - 76
Summer Brenner - 5 - 18 - 77 30 MIN
Summer Brenner - 5 - 1 - 75 25 MIN
Summer Brenner - 3 - 15 - 84 30 MIN
Susan Gevirtz - 10 - 12 - 89 35 MIN
Susan Griffin - 5 - 15 - 75 30 MIN
Susan Griffin - 3 - 21 - 79 50 MIN
Susan Griffin - 2 - 15 - 90 40 MIN
Susan Hansell - 11 - 17 - 88
Susan Stanford Friedman - 4 - 13 - 85 90 MIN
Ted Berrigan - 4 - 25 - 79 30 MIN
Ted Berrigan - 3 - 6 - 75 40 MIN
Ted Greenwald - 11 - 10 - 76 43 MIN
Tess Gallagher - 3 - 11 - 82 30 MIN
Theodore Enslin - 2 - 12 - 87 40 MIN
Thom Gunn - 11 - 22 - 86 34 MIN
Thom Gunn - 11 - 20 - 74 31 MIN
Thom Gunn - 12 - 13 - 90 34 MIN
Thulani Davis - 4 - 13 - 85 80 MIN
Tina Darragh - 11 - 29 - 84 29 MIN
Toi Derricotte - 10 - 9 - 86 40 MIN
Tom Clark - 10 - 25 - 73 60 MIN
Tom Clark - 10 - 27 - 76 30 MIN
Tom Clark - 3 - 12 - 87 70 MIN
Victor Hernandez Cruz - 12 - 11 - 81 30 MIN
Victor Hernandez Cruz - 3 - 3 - 76 28 MIN
Victor Hernandez Cruz - 3 - 3 - 83 35 MIN
Virginia de Araujo - 12 - 5 - 79 30 MIN
Wanda Coleman - 10 - 14 - 82 40 MIN
Wendell Berry - 3 - 3 - 77 43 MIN
Wilfredo Castano - 12 - 4 - 74 37 MIN
Wilfredo Castano - 9 - 29 - 83 28 MIN
Wilfredo Castano - 10 - 24 - 80 8 MIN
Wilfredo Castano - 10 - 25 - 78 20 MIN
William Bathurst - 2 - 18 - 76 61 MIN
William Benton - 11 - 20 - 74 40 MIN
William Benton - 3 - 26 - 74 25 MIN
William Dickey - 11 - 14 - 85 18 MIN
William Dickey - 4 - 17 - 75 33 MIN
William Dickey - 9 - 19 - 87 40 MIN
William Dickey - 10 - 18 - 78 39 MIN
William Dickey - 3 - 2 - 82 60 MIN
William Dickey - 2 - 7 - 89 12 MIN
William Everson - Brother Antoninus - 12 - 15 - 76 45 MIN
William Everson - Brother Antoninus - 5 - 15 - 74 120 MIN
William Gibson - 11 - 9 - 89 40 MIN
William S Burroughs - 11 - 4 - 74 39 MIN
William S Burroughs - 2 - 24 - 83
Xam Cartier - 11 - 17 - 88 30 MIN
Xam Cartier - 2 - 7 - 89 16 MIN
Yehuda Amichai - 11 - 22 - 77 45 MIN

Dist - POETRY

Poetry - Denise Levertov and Charles Olson 30 MIN
U-matic / VHS / 16mm
USA Series
B&W (J)
LC 70-704397
Denise Levertov discusses her reasons for being a poet and her methods of work and reads some of her poetry. Charles Olson describes his concept of open verse composition and recites several of his poems.
Literature and Drama
Dist - IU **Prod** - NET 1966

Poetry for Fun - Dares and Dreams 13 MIN
16mm / U-matic / VHS
Color (I J)
LC 74-701069
Introduces children to poetry. Presents six poems, illustrated by cartoon animation and live - action photography, including The Cave Boy, The Pirate Don Durk of Dowdee, The Fairies and others.
Fine Arts; Literature and Drama
Dist - CORF **Prod** - CENTRO 1974

Poetry for fun - poems about animals 13 MIN
16mm / U-matic / VHS
Color (P I J)
LC 72-702509
Presents eight poems for fun and appreciation. Includes The Camel's Lament, A Night With A Wolf, The Spangled Pandemonium, Lone Dog and Ogden Nash's An Introduction To Dogs.
English Language; Literature and Drama
Dist - CORF **Prod** - CENTEF 1972
CENTRO

Poetry for Fun - Poetry about Animals 13 MIN
U-matic / VHS / 16mm
Color (P I J)
Features eight poems written just for fun.
Literature and Drama
Dist - CORF **Prod** - CENTRO

Poetry for Fun Series
Dares and dreams 13 MIN
Poems about Animals 13 MIN
Trulier Coolier 11 MIN
Dist - CORF

Poetry for Fun - Trulier Coolier 11 MIN
16mm / U-matic / VHS
Color (P I J)
LC 78-701786
Presents eight humorous poems dealing with what children do, what they think about and how they feel, accompanied by animated cartoons, live - action photography, music and sound effects.
Literature and Drama
Dist - CORF **Prod** - CENTRO 1978

Poetry for people who hate poetry series
About words 16 MIN
e e cummings 17 MIN
Shakespeare 12 MIN
Dist - CF

Poetry for People who Hate Poetry with Roger Steffens
U-matic / VHS / 16mm
Color (J H C A)
$770 purchase - 16 mm (entire set), $235 purchase - video (entire set)
Portrays poet Roger Steffens presenting poetry for people who do not know much about it. Steffens/Shedd Poetry Films.
Literature and Drama
Dist - CF

Poetry for People who Hate Poetry with Roger Steffens Series
Shakespeare 12 MIN
Dist - CF

Poetry - Frank O'Hara and Ed Sanders 30 MIN
16mm / U-matic / VHS
USA Series
B&W (J)
LC 73-704398
Poet Frank O'Hara reads from his poems and works on a poetical script for a movie. Poet Ed Sanders discusses his pacifism, describes 'Literary Rock - And Roll,' and explains why the content of his poetry often creates a scandal.
Literature and Drama
Dist - IU **Prod** - NET 1966

Poetry I 15 MIN
VHS / U-matic
Zebra Wings Series
Color (I)
Presents poetry as a pleasurable way to express feelings and describe experiences.
English Language; Literature and Drama
Dist - AITECH **Prod** - NITC 1975

Poetry II 15 MIN
VHS / U-matic
Zebra Wings Series
Color (I)
Introduces figurative language and discusses the haiku form of poetry.
English Language; Literature and Drama
Dist - AITECH **Prod** - NITC 1975

Poetry in motion 90 MIN
VHS
Color (G)
$39.95 purchase _ #S02286
Presents a video poetry anthology in which the poets read their poetry aloud. Features poets William Burroughs, Anne Waldman, Ted Berrigan, Charles Bukowski, Ntozake Shange, and others.
Literature and Drama
Dist - UILL

Poetry in Motion 145 MIN
VHS / U-matic
Documentaries on Art Series
Color (G)
$360.00, $320.00 purchase, $135.00, $120.00 rental
Includes portraits of Robert Bly, 'A Man Writes To A Part Of Himself,' Frederick Manfred, 'American Grizzly,' and Thomas McGrath, 'The Movie At The End Of The World.' Produced by the Center for International Education.
Biography; Education; Literature and Drama
Dist - IAFC

Poetry is Alive and Well and Living in America Series
The Poetry of Edward Field 10 MIN
The Poetry of G C Oden 10 MIN
The Poetry of May Swenson 10 MIN
Dist - MPI

Poetry is words that sing 28 MIN
VHS
Color (C G)
$195.00 purchase, $35.00 rental _ #37792
Features the Pacific Poetry Ensemble which teaches poetry to children by demonstrating the power of poetry to enchant. Interweaves classroom scenes, rehearsals, interviews and live performances to show how the Ensemble develops and presents a spellbinding classroom show that opens the ears and minds of children to the magic of poetry. Includes discussion guide. Produced by Jon Herbst and Paul Shain.
Fine Arts; Literature and Drama
Dist - UCEMC

Poetry - Louis Zukofsky 30 MIN
U-matic / VHS / 16mm
USA Series
B&W (J)
LC 77-704400
Objectivist poet Louis Zukofsky describes the circumstances under which his first poem was published, explains the form and philosophy underlying his poetry, and reads from several of his works.
Literature and Drama
Dist - IU **Prod** - NET 1966

The Poetry of Edward Field 10 MIN
16mm
Poetry is Alive and Well and Living in America Series
Color (I J H C)
LC 76-706086
A visualization of two poems read by Edward Field. Shows the poet in his environment discussing his work.
Literature and Drama
Dist - MPI **Prod** - MPI 1969

The Poetry of G C Oden 10 MIN
16mm
Poetry is Alive and Well and Living in America Series
Color (I J H C)
LC 70-706087
A visualization of two poems read by the poet, G C Oden. Shows the poet in his environment discussing his work.
Literature and Drama
Dist - MPI **Prod** - MPI 1969

The Poetry of May Swenson 10 MIN
16mm
Poetry is Alive and Well and Living in America Series
Color (I J H C)
LC 73-706088
A visualization of two poems read by the poet, May Swenson. Shows the poet in her environment discussing her work.
Literature and Drama
Dist - MPI **Prod** - MPI 1969

The Poetry of Robert Frost 45 MIN
16mm
Color
LC 77-700022
Presents dramatizations of 12 of Robert Frost's poems. Explores Frost's view of man and nature.
Literature and Drama
Dist - CWRU **Prod** - CWRU 1977

The Poetry of Robert Frost - Pt 1 23 MIN
16mm
Color
LC 77-700022
Presents dramatizations of 12 of Robert Frost's poems. Explores Frost's view of man and nature.
Literature and Drama
Dist - CWRU **Prod** - CWRU 1977

The Poetry of Robert Frost - Pt 2 22 MIN
16mm
Color
LC 77-700022
Presents dramatizations of 12 of Robert Frost's poems. Explores Frost's view of man and nature.
Literature and Drama
Dist - CWRU **Prod** - CWRU 1977

The Poetry of Rock - a Reflection of Human Values
VHS / U-matic
Color (H C)
Examines the emotional content and poetic techniques found in rock lyrics. Uses hit songs from the 1950's to the 1970's to illustrate poetic tools such as simile, metaphor, hyperbole, symbolism and allegory, and lyric, dramatic and narrative poetic forms.
Fine Arts; Literature and Drama
Dist - GA **Prod** - GA

Poetry - Philip Whalen and Gary Snyder 30 MIN
U-matic / VHS / 16mm
USA Series
B&W (J)
LC 70-704401
Provides an introduction to the poetry of Gary Snyder and Philip Whalen and the reasons behind their work. Each poet comments on his poetry and reads selections.
Literature and Drama
Dist - IU **Prod** - NET 1966

Poetry Playhouse 24 MIN
16mm
Color
LC 78-701492
Dramatizes poems about love.
Literature and Drama
Dist - BERKS **Prod** - BERKS 1978

Poetry please 15 MIN
VHS
Magic library series
Color (P)
LC 90-707947
Tells a story about poetry. Raises children's awareness of a sense of story in order to enrich and motivate language, reading and writing skills. Includes teacher's guide. Part of a series.
English Language; Literature and Drama
Dist - TVOTAR **Prod** - TVOTAR 1990

Poetry - Richard Wilbur and Robert Lowell 30 MIN
U-matic / VHS / 16mm
USA Series
B&W (J)
LC 74-704402
Poet Richard Wilbur explains his interest in the formal means of poetic expression and reads several of his poems. Poet Robert Lowell reads some of his poems and describes the origin of the ideas behind them.
Literature and Drama
Dist - IU **Prod** - NET 1966

Poetry - Robert Creeley 30 MIN
16mm / U-matic / VHS
USA series
B&W (J H G)
LC 78-704403
Robert Creeley tells how other literary figures influenced his works, explains his own method of working, reminisces about his youth and reads several of his poems - La Noche, The First Time, The Place and Someplace.
Biography; Literature and Drama
Dist - IU **Prod** - NET 1966

Poetry - Robert Duncan and John Wieners 30 MIN
16mm / U-matic / VHS
USA Series
B&W (J)
LC 71-704404
Studies the return of the spirit of romance to contemporary poetry, as exemplified by Robert Duncan and John Wieners. Both poets discuss and read examples of their works.
Literature and Drama
Dist - IU **Prod** - NET 1966

Poetry - so many kinds 14 MIN
U-matic / VHS / 16mm
Color (J H)
$340.00, $240.00 purchase _ #3147
Examines poetry and its imagery, focusing on different poets and their works. Includes selections from Tennyson, Poe, Shakespeare, Robert and Elizabeth Browning, Frost, and Lewis Carroll.
Literature and Drama
Dist - CORF **Prod** - CORF 1972

Poetry - the Art of Words 18 MIN
16mm
Humanities Series
Color (J H C)
LC 70-714098
Presents an introduction to the study of poetry.
Literature and Drama
Dist - JOSHUA **Prod** - MGHT 1971

Poetry - the Essence of Being Human 18 MIN
U-matic / VHS / 16mm
Color (J H)
Shows how the poet fuses words, images and rhythms to startle the viewer into sharing his vision. Includes narration only to introduce the poetry. Presents poems which discuss man's most basic emotions and his most lofty strivings. Includes poems of love, hate, joy, despair, hope, ecstasy and the mysteries of God, nature and life.
Literature and Drama
Dist - MGHT **Prod** - MGHT 1972

Poetry Today 30 MIN
U-matic / VHS
Engle and Poetry Series
Color
Describes contemporary poetry as being in a period of extremes in form, technique and intent, but which, at the root, is still the experience of the real world transformed into art.
Literature and Drama
Dist - NETCHE **Prod** - NETCHE 1971

Poetry - William Carlos Williams 30 MIN
16mm
USA Series
B&W (J)
Presents an essay on the life and work of Dr William Carlos Williams, poet and Pulitzer Prize winner.
Literature and Drama
Dist - IU **Prod** - NET 1966

Poets 15 MIN
U-matic / VHS
Word Shop Series

Color (P)
Literature and Drama
Dist - WETATV **Prod** - WETATV

The Poets 30 MIN
U-matic / VHS
Black poetry of the Midwest series
(J H G)
Discusses the poetry and other works of Black midwestern writers. Features poets Inua Fuller and Estrella Sales, poet - critic Fr Joseph Brown, critic Dr Lillian Anthony and moderator Chester Fontenot.
History - United States; Literature and Drama
Dist - NETCHE **Prod** - NETCHE 1977

Poets and poetry 28 MIN
U-matic / BETA / VHS
Communication skills 2 - advanced series
Color (H C G)
101.95, $89.95 purchase _ #CA - 25
Looks at poetry as another way of getting messages to the reader. Defines poetry, examines its purposes and identifies some of poetry's important elements. Part of a 26 - part series.
Literature and Drama; Social Science
Dist - INSTRU

The Poet's Eye - Shakespeare's Imagery 16 MIN
U-matic / VHS / 16mm
Color (J)
LC 76-703606
Illustrates Shakespeare's unique imagery, presenting graphic examples of his method. Shows how all human activity appealed to Shakespeare as a source of imagery, using his plays as examples.
Literature and Drama
Dist - FOTH **Prod** - BIGRF 1976

Poet's Journal 25 MIN
VHS / U-matic
Process - Centered Composition Series
Color (T)
LC 79-706303
Presents a poet who talks about the relationship of his journal to his writing.
English Language; Literature and Drama
Dist - IU **Prod** - IU 1977

Poets Talking Series
Carolyn Kizer 29 MIN
Donald Hall 29 MIN
Galway Kinnell 29 MIN
Gregory Orr 29 MIN
Howard Norman 29 MIN
Jerome Rothenberg 29 MIN
Joyce Peseroff 29 MIN
Larry Fagin 29 MIN
Lawrence Raab 29 MIN
Louis Simpson 29 MIN
Marvin Bell 29 MIN
Robert Bly 29 MIN
Robert Hayden 29 MIN
W S Mervin 29 MIN
Wendell Berry 29 MIN
Dist - UMITV

A Poet's World 14 MIN
16mm
Color
LC 73-701620
Helps foster sensitivity to the poetic possibilities of familiar objects, such as clouds, trees, wind and water.
English Language; Literature and Drama
Dist - CWRU **Prod** - CWRU 1973

Pohinahina - Boy from the Sun 11 MIN
16mm
Color (J G)
Tells one of the legends of Hawaii in which the boy from the sun elects to remain on earth with his friend and is turned into the silversword plant.
Geography - United States; History - United States; Literature and Drama; Religion and Philosophy; Sociology
Dist - CINEPC **Prod** - TAHARA 1986

The Point 75 MIN
U-matic / VHS / 16mm
Color (I)
Uses animation and music to illustrate a fantasy about Oblio who lives in a kingdom where everything has a point, including people's heads. Shows how he is a victim of prejudice because his head is not pointed.
Guidance and Counseling; Sociology
Dist - FI **Prod** - ABC 1973

Point Bonita Lighthouse 13 MIN
VHS
Color (I J G)
$125.00 purchase, $30.00 rental _ #38149
Traces the history of one of America's most important lighthouses - Point Bonita Lighthouse at the entrance to San Francisco Bay. Uses old photos, quotes from memoirs and letters, anecdotes and stories to bring the history of the lighthouse to life and its role in historical events. Covers the period from the Gold Rush until the recent past when automation put an end to attended lighthouses. Produced by Kathleen McDonough.
History - United States
Dist - UCEMC

Point Conditioning 17 MIN
U-matic / VHS
Probability and Random Processes - Random Variables Series
B&W (PRO)
Teaches that conditioning is extended to point - conditioning which leads to the definition of conditional distribution functions of random variables.
Industrial and Technical Education; Mathematics
Dist - MIOT **Prod** - MIOT

Point Control of Traffic 32 MIN
16mm
B&W
LC FIE60-376
Explains that point control of traffic is essential for the smooth and rapid movement of troops and supplies. Demonstrates various procedures in effective point control of traffic.
Civics and Political Systems; Social Science
Dist - USNAC **Prod** - USA 1955

Point coordinates - quadrant one 13 MIN
16mm
Mathematics - graphing series
Color
LC 72-703443
Shows the need for a method to locate the position of a point on a plane and follows the step - by - step construction of the elements of the Cartesian coordinate system in quadrant one. Gives definitions of abcissa and ordinate and the point coordinate notation.
Mathematics
Dist - PHM **Prod** - UNISYS 1972

Point counterpoint - Georges Seurat 74 MIN
VHS
Color (H C A)
$49.95 purchase _ #SEU-01
Defines the life and work of Georges Seurat, one of the most influential artists of the Postimpressionist generation. Converses with artists Henry Moore and Bridget Riley to provide a close look at the creator of the pointillist technique.
Fine Arts
Dist - ARTSAM FI **Prod** - RMART 1986

The Point Ellice Bridge Disaster, May 26, 1896 10 MIN
16mm
Color
LC 76-703328
Uses old stills to re - create the Point Ellice Bridge disaster of May 26, 1896, in Victoria, British Columbia, where 55 people drowned when a streetcar overloaded the bridge's center span and fell into the harbor during the Queen's birthday celebrations.
History - World
Dist - BCPM **Prod** - BCPM 1974

Point of convergence 15 MIN
16mm
Color (J H C) (SPANISH)
LC 73-702050
Examines the cultures and artifacts of three early pre - Columbian cultures of Costa Rica.
Geography - World; History - World
Dist - PAN **Prod** - PAN 1973

The Point of Decimals 30 MIN
VHS / U-matic
Adult Math Series
Color (A)
Shows adult math students learning the rules about decimals.
Education; Mathematics
Dist - KYTV **Prod** - KYTV 1984

Point of Departure 28 MIN
16mm
B&W
LC 76-703794
Presents the story of a young man's realization that running away from difficulties will not solve or change them.
Guidance and Counseling; Psychology
Dist - SFRASU **Prod** - SFRASU 1976

Point of Entry 19 MIN
16mm
Color (J)
LC 79-700530
Discusses quarantine procedures and research facilities at arrival points in Australia.
Geography - World; Health and Safety
Dist - AUIS **Prod** - FLMAUS 1975

Point of no Return 10 MIN
16mm
Key Man Series
B&W
Analyzes an accident step - by - step and discusses how good supervision could prevent it.
Business and Economics; Health and Safety
Dist - NSC **Prod** - NSC

Point of order 46 MIN
16mm / VHS
Color (G IND)
$5.00 rental
Presents two parts on conducting meetings and the group process. Describes the rules of parliamentary procedure, using cartoon figures to show the sequence of motions and amendments in a properly conducted union meeting in the first part, 25 minutes. The second part, The Psychology Of Leadership, analyzes four types of behavior which can help or hinder the group process during meetings. Produced by the American Federation of State, County and Municipal Employees, AFL - CIO.
Business and Economics; Guidance and Counseling; Psychology; Social Science
Dist - AFLCIO **Prod** - AFLCIO 1988

Point of order 97 MIN
16mm
B&W
Presents a documentary composed of memorable events of the Army - Mc Carthy hearings of 1954.
Civics and Political Systems; Fine Arts; History - United States
Dist - NYFLMS **Prod** - ASTF 1961

Point of Pines 22 MIN
16mm
Color (H C)
Deals with the excavation of prehistoric Indian sites. Shows in detail the techniques of archaeology.
History - World; Science - Physical; Social Science; Sociology
Dist - NYU **Prod** - ARCHIA 1957

Point of return 24 MIN
16mm / U-matic / VHS
B&W (C A)
LC FIA67-759
Recounts events culminating in a suicide attempt. Includes comments from a panel discussing the incidence of suicide, the effect on survivors and the need for preventive programs.
Psychology; Sociology
Dist - IFB **Prod** - UOKLA 1965

Point of the stick 30 MIN
U-matic / VHS / BETA
Color; PAL (G H C)
PdS40, PdS48 purchase
Introduces the techniques of conducting with Sir Adrian Boult and the London Philharmonic Orchestra.
Fine Arts
Dist - EDPAT

Point of veiw 5 MIN
U-matic / 16mm / VHS
Color; Mono (G)
MV $85.00 _ MP $170.00 purchase, $50.00 rental
Tours Toronto's busy harbour and surveys its involvement with both industry and recreation. Includes musical accompaniment.
Geography - World
Dist - CTV **Prod** - MAKOF 1982

Point of View 23 MIN
16mm
Color
LC FIA67-1093
Dramatizes how routine hospital procedures such as blood withdrawal, X - ray and surgery can have residual psychological impact on young children.
Health and Safety; Psychology; Sociology
Dist - CMHOSP **Prod** - CMHOSP 1967

Point of view 41 MIN
16mm
B&W
LC FIE63-94
Demonstrates the discovery method as applied to the teaching of English. Shows Louis C Zahner leading a class of seventh graders to see the implications of point of view in writing and speaking.
English Language
Dist - USNAC **Prod** - USOE 1962

Point of View 19 MIN
16mm
B&W
LC FIA65-1708
Satirizes cigarette smoking and ridicules the smoking habit, pointing out its deleterious effects.
Guidance and Counseling; Health and Safety
Dist - AMLUNG **Prod** - NTBA 1965

Point of view 5 MIN
16mm
Song of the ages series
B&W (H C A R)
LC 78-702129
Presents a modern interpretation of Psalm 54 using a dramatization about the divorce of a couple.
Psychology; Religion and Philosophy; Sociology
Dist - FAMLYT **Prod** - FAMLYT 1964

Point of view dog 5 MIN
16mm
B&W
LC 74-701989
Shows the world as perceived through the eyes and ears of a dog.
Psychology; Science - Natural
Dist - CANFDC **Prod** - CANBC 1973

Point Pelee 30 MIN
U-matic / VHS
Color
Demonstrates the variety and complexity of relationships on the wildlife sanctuary of Point Pelee in Canada.
Geography - World; Science - Natural
Dist - JOU **Prod** - CANBC

The Point two percent solution 6 MIN
16mm / U-matic / VHS
Color
Shows students taking part in a self - applied fluoride program. Demonstrates a weekly rinse method which can be carried out in school.
Health and Safety; Science - Natural
Dist - USNAC **Prod** - USHHS

Point zero eight 25 MIN
VHS / U-matic / 16mm
Color; Mono (J H C A)
$50.00 Rental
Ilustrates the extreme effects of alcohol on eight expert drivers. Shows drivers' ability as their blood alcohol content was raised to .08% under medical supervision, while their responses were studied by a supervisory team. Significant impairment was noted at the .05% level.
Health and Safety
Dist - CTV **Prod** - CTV 1968

Pointe by point 45 MIN
VHS
Color (K P I)
$19.95 purchase_#1235
Provides lessons with Barbara Fewster - former associate director and Ballet Principal of the Royal Ballet School - showing young dancers how to begin pointe work and avoid bad habits which may lead to injury. Discusses the different types of feet and the proper preparation of a ballet shoe. Concludes with course study for beginning and elementary dancers.
Fine Arts; Physical Education and Recreation
Dist - KULTUR

Pointers 30 MIN
U-matic / VHS
Pascal - pt 2 - intermediate Pascal series
Color (H C A)
LC 81-706049
Reviews structured data types and introduces the pointer concept. Gives examples of tables and linked lists. Shows procedures for list initialization, list search and list insertion.
Industrial and Technical Education; Mathematics; Sociology
Dist - COLOSU **Prod** - COLOSU 1980

Pointers and addresses
VHS / U-matic
'C' language programming series
Color
Defines the use of the terms 'pointer' and 'address' in 'C' language and identifies the type of value contained in a pointer variable. Describes a string constant in terms of pointers and addresses.
Industrial and Technical Education; Mathematics; Sociology
Dist - COMTEG **Prod** - COMTEG

Pointless Pollution 28 MIN
U-matic / VHS / 16mm
Color (J)
$275.00, $250.00 purchase, $50.00 rental
Describes how nonpoint source pollution, the runoff pollutants not coming from a single source, accounts for 80 percent of America's water contamination. Reveals that oil and trash from streets, fertilizers and pesticides from farms and lawns fall under this category of pollutants.
Agriculture; Home Economics; Social Science; Sociology
Dist - BULFRG **Prod** - LCRA 1989

Points and line 20 MIN
VHS / U-matic
Math topics - geometry series
Color (J H C)
Mathematics
Dist - FI **Prod** - BBCTV

Points and line segments 15 MIN
U-matic
Math factory - geometry series
Color (P)
Introduces the geometric ideas of point, line, line segment and curve. Module II of the series.
Mathematics
Dist - GPN **Prod** - MAETEL 1973

Points in Space 55 MIN
VHS
Color (G)
$39.95 purchase _ #1245
Presents the famous collaboration of dancer Merce Cunningham and composer John Cage. Features the Merce Cunningham Dance Company performing.
Fine Arts; Physical Education and Recreation
Dist - KULTUR

Points, lines, planes 30 MIN
16mm
Mathematics for elementary school teachers series
Color (T)
Explains the geometric elements of points, lines and planes. Follows film on Sentences, Number Line. Number 13 in the series.
Mathematics
Dist - MLA **Prod** - SMSG 1963

Points of convergence 15 MIN
16mm
Color (J H C) (SPANISH)
LC 82-700848
Shows an extensive panorama of pre - Columbian art and culture in Costa Rica.
Fine Arts; History - World
Dist - MOMALA **Prod** - OOAS 1973

Points of View 29 MIN
U-matic / VHS / 16mm
Photography - the Incisive Art Series
B&W (H C A)
Shows Ansel Adams as he photographs an old house and its inhabitants. Explains his point of view as he photographs from many different perspectives to suit many purposes.
Fine Arts; Industrial and Technical Education
Dist - IU **Prod** - NET 1960

Poise and the art of job interviewing - tactics and techniques 30 MIN
BETA / VHS
Color (H C A)
Designed for entry - level job seekers and those intimidated by the interview process or needing to brush - up on interviewing skills.
Guidance and Counseling
Dist - BENNUP **Prod** - BENNUP 1987

Poison 88 MIN
35mm
Color; B&W; PAL (G)
Features three separate but interrelated and intercut stories inspired by the work of Jean Genet. Presents Hero, a mother's account of her son's disappearance; Horror, in which scientist's experiments lead to contagion and decay; and Homo, which depicts a prisoner who falls in love with a fellow inmate. Directed by Todd Haynes for Bronze Eye Productions. Contact distributor about price and availability outside the United Kingdom.
Literature and Drama; Sociology
Dist - BALFOR

Poison 25 MIN
U-matic / VHS
Color
Covers various sources of poisoning from snakebites, plants, spiders and fish through poisons that are swallowed. Includes tips on prevention.
Health and Safety
Dist - MEDCOM **Prod** - MEDCOM

Poison 14 MIN
U-matic / VHS / 16mm
Color (A)
LC 74-707254
Demonstrates that the natural curiosity of children sometimes leads to poisoning and that such an event can be avoided only by the care and diligence of parents. Shows measures to prevent and counteract poisoning of small children.
Health and Safety; Home Economics
Dist - IFB **Prod** - ALDPH 1968

Poison and the Pentagon 58 MIN
VHS
Frontline series
Color; Captioned (G)
$150.00 purchase _ #FRON - 608K
Reveals that the Pentagon has been one of America's worst polluters, but has done little to clean up its own toxic wastes. Focuses on two situations in Jacksonville, Florida and Tucson, Arizona, where cancer - causing agents contaminated a landfill and groundwater.
Health and Safety; Sociology
Dist - PBS **Prod** - DOCCON 1988

Poison animals of the United States 15 MIN
16mm / U-matic / VHS
Color (I J H)
LC 78-700916
Deals with the myths and realities concerning the dangers of bees and wasps as well as other venomous animals in the United States. Includes a brief description of treatments and preventive measures.
Health and Safety; Science - Natural
Dist - PHENIX **Prod** - BAYERW 1978

Poison in the Rockies 54 MIN
U-matic / VHS / 16mm
Color (H)
$275.00, $250.00 purchase, $85.00 rental
Depicts how past and present mining operations in the West are damaging sub - alpine ecosystems in the Rockies, which provide much of the water supplies for the West.
Geography - United States; Industrial and Technical Education; Science - Natural; Science - Physical; Sociology
Dist - BULFRG **Prod** - ERTHI 1990

Poison is queen 60 MIN
16mm / U-matic / VHS
I, Claudius series
Color (C A)
Tells how Claudius' revelation of Livia's plots not only fails to save the succession, but brings him under his grandmother's deadly scrutiny. Number five in the series.
History - World
Dist - FI **Prod** - BBCTV 1977

Poison Ivy 13 MIN
16mm / U-matic / VHS
Color (J)
LC 81-700790
Tells about Ivy Granstrom, nicknamed Poison Ivy, who has only two and one half percent vision yet manages to lead an energetic life. Shows her at sixty - six years of age, jogging, gardening and skiing. Emphasizes how she expresses her approach to life, as she says, the best way she knows how.
Health and Safety; Psychology; Sociology
Dist - PHENIX **Prod** - NFBC 1980

Poison Prevention for Primary 12 MIN
U-matic / VHS / 16mm
Color (P I)
Points out potential poison hazards in the home. Shows how to make the home poison - proof.
Health and Safety
Dist - AIMS **Prod** - HALPRM 1977

The Poison Problem 10 MIN
U-matic / VHS / 16mm
Color (K P I)
LC 78-700633
Points out the many potentially dangerous substances found around the home. Explains the danger warnings that appear on labels and the directions for correct and safe use.
Health and Safety
Dist - AIMS **Prod** - ASSOCF 1978

The Poisoned Room 22 MIN
16mm
B&W
Presents an episode from the serial The Exploits of Elaine. Shows Pearl Buck fighting the dreaded Clutching Hand.
Fine Arts
Dist - KILLIS **Prod** - UNKNWN 1914

Poisoned winds of war 58 MIN
VHS / U-matic
Nova series
Color (H C A)
$250.00 purchase _ #HP - 6375C
Recalls that in 1925, 40 nations, appalled by gas warfare in World War I that killed or injured more than a million soldiers and civilians, signed the Geneva Protocol - prohibiting the use, but not the production or stockpiling, of chemical weapons. Reveals that because chemical weaponry is cheaper and more easily produced than nuclear weapons, they are the weapons of choice of developing nations. Looks at past and present use of the weapons and the particular vulnerability of civilians when they are used.
History - World; Sociology
Dist - CORF **Prod** - WGBHTV 1990

Poisoning 5 MIN
16mm / U-matic / VHS
Emergency first aid training series
Color (A)
LC 81-700834
Discusses various types of poisoning and demonstrates first aid techniques for dealing with poison victims.
Health and Safety
Dist - IFB **Prod** - CRAF 1980

Poisoning by Accident 15 MIN
16mm / U-matic / VHS
Color (J H C G T A)
$25 rental _ #4050
Alerts the public to the causes of accidental poisoning and teaches essential lifesaving techniques that can be performed in an emergency.
Health and Safety
Dist - AIMS **Prod** - AIMS 1977

Poisoning by Accident 15 MIN
U-matic / VHS / 16mm
Color (J)
Shows the causes of accidental poisoning and demonstrates techniques the layman can perform in an emergency.
Health and Safety
Dist - AIMS **Prod** - NORMBP 1977

Poisoning by accident 15 MIN
VHS
Color (I J H G)
$49.95 purchase _ #AM4050
Alerts the public to the causes of accidental poisoning. Teaches essential lifesaving techniques that can be performed in an emergency. Points out potential killers found in the home and steps to be taken for poisons taken internally, inhaled or absorbed through the skin.
Health and Safety; Sociology
Dist - AAVIM **Prod** - NORMBP 1992

The Poisoning of a Mexican community 18 MIN
VHS
Color (G PRO)
$20.00 purchase
Tells about the joint efforts of the citizens of Matamoros, Mexico and the US based Coalition for Justice in the Maquiladoras to force a cleanup at the Stepan chemical plant in Matamoros.
Business and Economics; Geography - World; Sociology
Dist - CJM **Prod** - CJM 1992

The Poisoning of Michigan 65 MIN
U-matic / VHS / 16mm
Color (H C A)
Relates how during the summer of 1973, thousands of Michigan farm animals were poisoned by a chemical substance they ate. Tells how it spread throughout the Michigan food chain into the human population. The chemical was PBB, which can cause cancer, birth defects and genetic changes in humans.
Geography - United States; Sociology
Dist - MEDIAG **Prod** - THAMES 1977

Poisonous Currents of Air and Sea 18 MIN
VHS / 16mm
Fragile Planet Series
Color (J)
$139.00 purchase, $75.00 rental _ #0D - 2325
Explains how poisons released anywhere in the world spread from a single region to pollute the entire planet. The final of six installments of The Fragile Planet Series.
Sociology
Dist - FOTH

Poisonous Plants 12 MIN
16mm / VHS
Color (J H A)
$240.00, $290.00 purchase, $50.00 rental _ #8033
Identifies familar plants which are also dangerously poisonous. Produced by Norman Bean.
Health and Safety; Science - Natural
Dist - AIMS

Poisonous Plants 26 MIN
U-matic / VHS / 16mm
Color
LC 77-700746
Warns against the dangers of a variety of poisonous plants found in the northern section of the United States.
Guidance and Counseling; Health and Safety; Science - Natural
Dist - TEXFLM **Prod** - HUAA 1974

Poisons
VHS / U-matic
Chemsafe series
Color
Discusses the different forms of poisons, safe handling procedures and proper storage. Emphasizes personal protection, emergency methods and first - aid.
Health and Safety; Science - Physical
Dist - BNA **Prod** - BNA

Poisons 60 MIN
VHS
Color (IND)
$52.00 purchase _ #35430
Helps viewer identify various types of poisons. Discusses toxicity levels of poisons. Explains safe handling procedures.
Health and Safety; Sociology
Dist - OKSU **Prod** - CHEMMA

Poisons all Around Us 11 MIN
U-matic / VHS / 16mm
Color
LC 77-700041
Reviews common poisonous substances found in nature and in the average home. Provides instructions on how to handle accidental poisoning.
Health and Safety
Dist - HIGGIN **Prod** - HIGGIN 1977

Poisons and drug overdose 28 MIN
VHS
First aid video series
Color (J H G)
$165.00 purchase _ #60141 - 126; $189.00 purchase _ #AH45299
Shows how to deal with poisons and drug overdose. Includes vignettes of first aid situations, demonstrations of first aid procedures, dialogue between instructor and students and checkpoint quizzes. Part of a four - part series on first aid.
Health and Safety
Dist - GA **Prod** - HRMC
HTHED HTHED

Poisons - module 5 10 MIN
BETA / VHS / U-matic
Chemsafe series
Color (IND G A)
$546.00 purchase, $125.00 rental _ #POI005
Discusses the different forms of poisons. Considers that some poisons are gaseous and others can kill through skin contact. Focuses on health and safety precautions to take when working with poisons such as the critical factors of proper storage, and safe handling procedures. Emphasizes personal protection and emergency procedures and first aid. Part of a nine - part series which provides basic understanding of chemical safety and training in specific hazard categories. Each module dramatizes key points and is designed to support a one - hour training session.
Health and Safety; Psychology
Dist - ITF **Prod** - BNA

Poisons - Module 5 7 MIN
VHS / U-matic / BETA
Chemsafe series
Color; PAL (IND G) (SPANISH DUTCH ITALIAN)
$175.00 rental _ #CSF - 500
Discusses different types of toxic chemicals. Emphasizes proper handling and storage, as well as emergency and first aid procedures. Part of a comprehensive nine - part series on chemical safety in the workplace. Includes leader's guide and 10 workbooks which are available in English only.
Business and Economics; Health and Safety; Psychology; Science - Physical
Dist - BNA **Prod** - BNA

Poisons - V ; Rev. 7 MIN
8mm cartridge / VHS / BETA / U-matic
Chemsafe 2000 series
Color; CC; PAL (IND G)
$395.00 purchase, $175.00 rental _ #CS2 - 500
Discusses the different forms of toxic chemicals. Emphasizes proper handling and storage requirements, as well as emergency and first - aid procedures. Part of a nine - part series providing comprehensive training in chemical safety. Includes a trainer's manual and ten participant handouts.
Health and Safety; Psychology; Science - Physical
Dist - BNA **Prod** - BNA 1994

Poisson distribution
VHS
Probability and statistics series
Color (H C)
$125.00 purchase _ #8023
Provides resource material about Poisson distributions to support the study of probability and statistics. Part of a series of 60 videos, each part 25 to 30 minutes long, that explain and reinforce concepts using definitions, theorems, examples and step - by - step solutions to tutor the student.
Mathematics
Dist - LANDMK

The Poka - yoke system 47 MIN
Slide / VHS
Color (A PRO IND)
$749.00 purchase _ #V6 - 721, #S6 - 721
Explains the Poka - yoke system concept as created by Shigeo Shingo. Shows how this system can be used in conjunction with Zero Quality Control to develop a 100 percent inspection system. Includes facilitators' guides.
Business and Economics; Psychology
Dist - PRODUC **Prod** - PRODUC

Poker 21 MIN
16mm / VHS
Color (G)
LC 90709581
Presents a film by Gaspar Hernandez III. Stars Dean Briggs, Rick Masters, Jack Harrison and Jeff Hutchinson.
Fine Arts; Literature and Drama
Dist - CNEMAG **Prod** - CNEMAG 1990

Poker Game 28 MIN
16mm / U-matic / VHS
Insight Series
Color; B&W (H C A) (SPANISH)
Tells how a Christ - like hippie comedian invites himself to a regular poker game, treating the poker players with so much interest and concern that they soon begin to reveal their true personalities. Stars Beau Bridges, Bill Bixby and Jeffrey Hunter.
Fine Arts; Religion and Philosophy
Dist - PAULST **Prod** - PAULST

The Poky Little Puppy 8 MIN
16mm / U-matic / VHS
Color (K P)
LC 75-700398
Tells the story of the poky little puppy who outwits the four other puppies in the family and eats all of the dessert each night. Explains that the four puppies decide to do as their mother would have them do and are given their dessert before they go to bed. Shows that the poky little puppy is very surprised when he gets home and must go to bed without any dessert. Develops an awareness of numbers and the use of printed symbols to represent spoken language.
English Language; Literature and Drama; Mathematics
Dist - BARR **Prod** - WPES 1974

Poland 25 MIN
VHS / U-matic / 16mm / BETA
Changing faces of Communism series
Color (J H G)
$390.00, $110.00 purchase _ #C50548, #C51393
Witnesses the changes from pre - war agrarian Poland through its communist period to the rise of Solidarity, open elections and a noncommunist Prime Minister. Part of a three - part series on the changing status of Communism.
Civics and Political Systems; Geography - World; History - World
Dist - NGS **Prod** - NGS 1990

Poland
VHS
Dances of the world series
Color (G)
$39.95 purchase _ #FD800V
Presents performances of dances from Poland. Interviews the dancers.
Fine Arts; Geography - World; Physical Education and Recreation
Dist - CAMV **Prod** - CAMV

Poland 26 MIN
U-matic / VHS / 16mm
Today's history series
Color (H C)
Examines how the Poles see themselves, and what their role in history has been. Notes how the Polish state has changed many times during the past thousand years, how Poland's leaders have had a common style, and how Poland has struggled alone for freedom after having fought in other countries' battles.
History - World
Dist - JOU **Prod** - JOU 1984

Poland 25 MIN
U-matic / 16mm
Untamed world series
Color; Mono (J H C A)
$400.00 film, $250.00 video, $50.00 rental
Focuses on the Polish National Park and its various plants and animals, such as the black stork and European bison.
Geography - World; History - World; Science - Natural
Dist - CTV **Prod** - CTV 1973

Poland 27 MIN
16mm
Color (I J H C)
LC FIA68-1574
Portrays Poland's history by animation. Uses real photography to show the prewar years, and gives a thorough, intimate picture of modern Polish life.
Geography - World; History - World
Dist - IFF **Prod** - IFF 1965

Poland 29 MIN
Videoreel / VT2
International Cookbook Series
Color
Features home economist Joan Hood presenting a culinary tour of specialty dishes from around the world. Shows the preparation of Polish dishes ranging from peasant cookery to continental cuisine.
Geography - World; Home Economics
Dist - PBS **Prod** - WMVSTV

Poland - a new nightmare 13 MIN
16mm
Screen news digest series
Color
Shows a graphic and historical chronology of the heroic struggle of the Polish people for freedom and independence. Volume 24, issue 6 in the series.
History - World; Sociology
Dist - AFA **Prod** - AFA 1982

Poland - a New Nightmare 14 MIN
VHS / U-matic
Color
Presents a 200 year chronology of the heroic struggles of the Polish people that culminates with the internal crisis of 1981. Portrays a nation in pain.
Geography - World; History - World
Dist - KINGFT **Prod** - KINGFT

Poland - a proud heritage 60 MIN
VHS
European collection series
Color (J H C G)
$29.95 purchase _ #IVN109V-S; $24.95 purchase _ #V133
Tours many of the sites of Poland. Includes Warsaw, Gdansk, the Bialowieza Forest, Auschwitz, and the Jasna Gora monastery. Part of a 16-part series on European countries. Also part of a larger series entitled Video Visits that travels to six continents.
Geography - World
Dist - CAMV **Prod** - WNETTV
POLART

Poland - a year of Solidarity 25 MIN
U-matic / VHS
Color (J H)
Charts the history of the Solidarity movement in Poland and discusses the concessions it has obtained. Views the pressures, both internal and external, facing the Polish government.
Geography - World; History - World; Sociology
Dist - JOU **Prod** - JOU

Poland - an unforgettable nation - Polska 31 MIN
VHS
Color (G A)
$19.95 purchase _ #V283
Depicts a nation with a reputation for Slavic hospitality and a rich tradition of courage and resilience. Visits Warsaw, Malbork, Torun, Gdansk, Wroclaw and Kakow.
Geography - World
Dist - POLART

Poland - Church and a nation - Panorama Tysiaclecia 36 MIN
VHS
Color (G A) (POLISH)
$19.95 purchase _ #V293, #V292
Gives a history of Poland and the Polish Catholic church over the centuries. Shows the Church as a leader of spiritual movements in the country's rich history. Also available with Polish narration.
Fine Arts; History - World; Religion and Philosophy
Dist - POLART

Poland - martial law and Solidarity 19 MIN
VHS / U-matic
Color (H C A)
Presents a report on the Solidarity Movement in Poland, the people, the government and the leaders of the Polish people. Produced just prior to Lech Walesa's release from prison.
Geography - World; History - World; Sociology
Dist - JOU **Prod** - JOU

Poland Report 28 MIN
VHS / U-matic
Color (H C A)
Examines Poland's economy, politics, religion, social development, and history since World War II. Analyzes the dramatic changes which occurred after the Polish workers' strike.
Geography - World; History - World
Dist - JOU **Prod** - UPI

Poland - the Morning After 60 MIN
VHS
Frontline Series
Color; Captioned (G)
$300.00 purchase, $95.00 rental _ #FRON - 808K
Discusses the changes in Poland that came with the fall of Communism. Reveals the economic consequences of the shift to free - market capitalism, including significantly higher prices. Questions whether the Solidarity - led government of Lech Walesa will be able to handle the changeover.
Civics and Political Systems; History - World
Dist - PBS **Prod** - DOCCON 1990

Poland - the News in Uniform 29 MIN
VHS / U-matic
Inside Story Series
Color
Examines the situation in which Polish journalists now find themselves compared with the relative freedom they enjoyed for 16 months under Solidarity.
Geography - World; Literature and Drama
Dist - PBS **Prod** - PBS 1981

Poland - the will to be 26 MIN
16mm / VHS / U-matic
James Michener's World Series
Color
LC 79-700966; 79-700997
Features author James Michener taking a trip through Poland, where he examines the nation's history, heritage and people.
Geography - World; History - World; Sociology
Dist - PFP **Prod** - EMLEN 1979

Polar bear 60 MIN
VHS
Color (G)
$24.95 purchase _ #S01999
Portrays the great white, or 'polar,' bears in their Arctic habitats.
Science - Natural
Dist - UILL **Prod** - SIERRA

Polar bear 11 MIN
U-matic / VHS / 16mm
OWL animal studies series
Color (P I J)
Views a unique polar bear tagging program in Tuktoyatktuk, Northwest Territories. Shows scientists studying the impact of encroaching civilization on polar bear populations. Participates in an aerial survey and visits a lab in Edmonton, Alberta where on going research takes place.
Guidance and Counseling; Science - Natural
Dist - BULFRG **Prod** - OWLTV 1987

Polar bear alert 60 MIN
VHS
National Geographic video series
Color (G)
$29.95 purchase
Tells the story of the people of Churchill, Manitoba, and how every fall they must deal with polar bears passing through town, migrating northward.
Science - Natural
Dist - PBS **Prod** - WNETTV

Polar bear alert 60 MIN
VHS
Color; Captioned (G)
$29.95 purchase _ #S01394
Tells how the residents of Churchill, Manitoba have learned to live with the annual migration of polar bears through their town. Narrated by Jason Robards.
Geography - World; Science - Natural; Sociology
Dist - UILL **Prod** - NGS

Polar bears 15 MIN
VHS
Animal profile series
Color (P I)
$59.95 purchase _ #RB8102
Visits some polar bears in their refurbished exhibit at the Washington Park Zoo. Includes behind - the - scenes looks at the exhibit and footage of the bears entering their home for the first time. Part of a series on animals which looks at examples from the mammal, snake and bird classes, filmed in their natural habitat.
Science - Natural
Dist - REVID **Prod** - REVID 1990

Polar Bears 25 MIN
16mm / U-matic / VHS
Untamed World Series
Color; Mono (J H C A)
$400.00 film, $250.00 video, $50.00 rental
Follows a four week expedition to the Arctic to witness the counting and tagging of the threatened polar bear population.
Science - Natural
Dist - CTV **Prod** - CTV 1973

Polar Bears - Soft, White and Deadly
VHS / U-matic
Color
Focuses on a small port town trying to solve a problem with polar bears which congregate near their town every fall waiting to feed on seal.
Science - Natural
Dist - NWLDPR **Prod** - NWLDPR

Polar Coordinate Program 19 MIN
U-matic / VHS
Numerical Control/Computerized Numerical Control - Advanced 'Programming Series Module 2
Color (IND)
Covers polar coordinates, programming drilling on a radius and programming milling using polar coordinates.
Business and Economics; Industrial and Technical Education
Dist - LEIKID **Prod** - LEIKID

Polar coordinates 30 MIN
VHS
Trigonometry series
Color (H)
$125.00 purchase _ #5015
Explains polar coordinates. Part of a 16 - part series on trigonometry.
Mathematics
Dist - LANDMK **Prod** - LANDMK

Polar coordinates 20 MIN
VHS
Calculus series
Color (H)
LC 90712920
Examines polar coordinates. The 50th of 57 installments of the Calculus Series.
Mathematics
Dist - GPN

Polar coordinates 30 MIN
U-matic / VHS
Calculus of several variables - vector - - calculus series; Vector calculus
B&W
Mathematics
Dist - MIOT **Prod** - MIOT

Polar coordinates 15 MIN
U-matic / VHS / 16mm
Color (H)
Describes a system for using polar coordinates for graphing functions such as the equations for circles and rose curves. An angle measured from a base line and a distance from a pole (point) from an ordered pair which lables a point in the same way that an ordered pair (X, Y) label a point in the Cartesian coordinate system. Shows how the two systems are related.
Mathematics
Dist - PHENIX **Prod** - BOSUST 1970

Polar coordinates 30 MIN
VHS
Mathematics series
Color (J)
LC 90713155
Discusses polar coordinates. The 108th of 157 installments of the Mathematics Series.
Mathematics
Dist - GPN

The Polar Express
VHS / 35mm strip
Caldecotts on Filmstrip Series
Color (K)
$35.00 purchase
Presents a children's story. Part of the Caldecott Series.
English Language; Literature and Drama
Dist - PELLER

Polar oceans 25 MIN
VHS / U-matic
Oceanography series
Color (H C)
$250.00 purchase _ #HP - 5743C
Looks at the crucial impact of polar oceans on regulating physical, chemical, meteorological and biological systems all over the planet. Looks at the origins and evolution of polar oceanographic experimentation in the 20th century. Uses recent and historic footage to present the basics of polar ice formation. Shows the differences and similarities of the Arctic and Antartic. Studies polar wave action, water temperature, salinity and light penetration in polar waters. Part of a series on oceanography.
Geography - World; Science - Physical
Dist - CORF **Prod** - BBCTV 1989

Polar Regions - Hunters and Herders 17 MIN
U-matic / VHS / 16mm
Color (P I)

LC 78-702057
Describes the location and unique features of the polar regions and explains how the Eskimos and Lapps have learned to live in these frigid lands. Discusses ways in which technology has affected these ancient cultures.
Geography - World; Science - Natural; Social Science; Sociology
Dist - PHENIX **Prod** - BAYERW 1978

The Polar seas 30 MIN
U-matic / VHS
Oceanus - the marine environment series
Color
Looks at the arctic and Antarctic regions. Outlines a brief history of the exploration of the polar regions. Discusses several oceanographic aspects of the regions. Lesson 24 in the series.
Science - Natural; Science - Physical
Dist - CDTEL **Prod** - SCCON

Polaris, Blue and Gold 10 MIN
16mm
Color
LC FIE63-10
Depicts a typical Polaris submarine and shows the vital role each man plays in its operation.
Civics and Political Systems; Social Science
Dist - USNAC **Prod** - USN 1962

Polaris to Poseidon 15 MIN
16mm
Color
LC 74-705383
Presents one of the Navy's major contributions to world peace, the Polaris missile and the men who operate her. Depicts the men training to be polaris submariners and shows a practice launch.
Civics and Political Systems
Dist - USNAC **Prod** - USN 1966

Polarization of Single Photons 15 MIN
16mm
B&W (C)
LC 73-702778
Investigates the quantum behavior of polarized photons. Demonstrates that single polarized photons follow the statistical prediction of the cosine squared law.
Science - Physical
Dist - EDC **Prod** - MIOT 1972

Polarized Light 10 MIN
U-matic / VHS
Introductory Concepts in Physics - Light Series
Color (C)
$229.00, $129.00 purchase _ #AD - 1216
Introduces the concept of polarized light through experiments with polarizing plates and applies the theory of polarized light to the composition of minerals.
Science - Physical
Dist - FOTH **Prod** - FOTH

Pole line construction - pt 3 - erecting poles and attaching crossarms 26 MIN
16mm
B&W
LC FIE60-169
Demonstrates the use of the earth borer and the manual method of installing telephone poles and attaching double crossarms, sidearms and 'H' fixtures. Stresses the selection of the most suitable type of crossarm installation to safely support communication circuits.
Industrial and Technical Education; Social Science
Dist - USNAC **Prod** - USA

Pole replacement - pt 1
VHS / U-matic
Live line maintenance series
Color (IND)
Shows how to lift and secure conductors to a new pole using rubber gloves and an aerial device.
Industrial and Technical Education
Dist - LEIKID **Prod** - LEIKID

Pole replacement - pt 2
U-matic / VHS
Live line maintenance series
Color (IND)
Shows one method of installing a new electric pole, placing it beside one that is to be replaced.
Industrial and Technical Education
Dist - LEIKID **Prod** - LEIKID

Pole Vault APPROXIMATELY 60 MIN
VHS / U-matic
Frank Morris Instructional Videos Series
Color; B&W; Silent; Mono; Stereo (H C A)
Instructs athletes how to execute and improve performance of the pole vault. Prroduced and Narrated by coach Frank Morris.
Physical Education and Recreation
Dist - TRACKN **Prod** - TRACKN 1986

Pole vault
VHS
Coaching men's field and track series
Color (H C G)
$59.95 purchase _ #TRS1256V
Features men's field and track coach Rick Sloan on pole vaulting. Views the pole vault from bar level as well as from ground level. Shows the mechanics of the pole vault step - by - step in slow motion and stop action. Part of a nine - part series.
Physical Education and Recreation
Dist - CAMV

Pole vault 30 MIN
VHS
Track and field techniques series
Color (H C G)
$29.95 purchase _ #WK1102V
Features pole vaulter Jan Johnson who discusses the skill and improving performance. Part of a series.
Physical Education and Recreation
Dist - CAMV

Pole vault conditioning 16 MIN
VHS
Bill Dellinger's championship track and field series
Color (H C A)
$39.95 purchase _ #WES1713V
Features Bill Dellinger and the University of Oregon coaching staff, who teach the basic techniques of pole vault conditioning. Presents drills to develop an athlete's potential and correct common errors in technique. Uses slow - motion film and on - screen graphics.
Physical Education and Recreation
Dist - CAMV

Pole vault conditioning
U-matic / VHS
Bill Dellinger's championship track and field videotape training library series.
Color (H C)
Notes how the pole vault combines sprinter speed, shot putter strength and acrobatic ability. Banks on Dennis Whitby's experience with world class vaulters to prove helpful for beginners and seasoned veteran pole vaulters.
Physical Education and Recreation
Dist - CBSC **Prod** - CBSC

Pole vault technique
U-matic / VHS
Bill Dellinger's championship track and field videotape training library series.
Color (H C)
Dissects all aspects of pole vaulting so they may be identified, studied and mastered. Dennis Whitby details action in each phase, while TV special effects outline critical areas and show proper performance.
Physical Education and Recreation
Dist - CBSC **Prod** - CBSC

Pole vault techniques 27 MIN
VHS
Bill Dellinger's championship track and field series
Color (H C A)
$39.95 purchase _ #WES1702V
Features Bill Dellinger and the University of Oregon coaching staff, who teach the basic techniques of the pole vault. Presents drills to develop an athlete's potential and correct common errors in technique. Uses slow - motion film and on - screen graphics.
Physical Education and Recreation
Dist - CAMV

Pole vaulting with Douf Lytle 30 MIN
U-matic / VHS
John Powell associates videos series
Color (J H C A)
Provides technical instruction on pole vaulting. Includes drills and optional weight training components. Features expert Doug Lytle.
Physical Education and Recreation
Dist - TRACKN **Prod** - TRACKN 1985

Poleo and Poetic Figuration 28 MIN
16mm
Color (J) (SPANISH FRENCH)
LC 82-700849
Describes the life and works of Venezuelan painter Poleo.
Fine Arts; History - World
Dist - MOMALA **Prod** - OOAS 1977

The Poles - the parish and the immigrant 9 MIN
VHS
Columbus legacy series
Color (J H C G)
$40.00 purchase, $11.00 rental _ #12332
Reveals the dominant role of the Roman Catholic church in the life of Polish immigrants, providing moral authority, schooling and a social context for thousands of immigrant families. Part of a 15 - part series commemorating the 500th anniversary of Columbus' journeys to the Americas - journeys that brought together a constantly evolving collection of different ethnic groups. Examines the contributions of 15 distinct groups who imprinted their heritage on the day - to - day life of Pennsylvania.
History - United States; Religion and Philosophy; Sociology
Dist - PSU **Prod** - WPSXTV 1992

Poletop rescue breathing with closed chest heart massage 28 MIN
16mm
Color (IND)
LC FIA63-1231
Describes procedures to be followed when a lineman is electrocuted at a work location on a 40 - foot power pole. Explains safety procedures, shows rescue and resuscitation techniques to be followed, and describes emergencies which can occur pole - top and on the ground, such as suffocation, convulsive seizures and heart stoppage.
Health and Safety; Science - Natural
Dist - RBFA **Prod** - HERMAN 1962

Police 28 MIN
16mm
B&W (I A)
Features Charlie Chaplin in the 1916 slapstick comedy film in which a prisoner just released from the pen meets a former cell - mate and once again strays from the straight and narrow.
Fine Arts
Dist - RMIBHF **Prod** - MSENP 1916

Police 30 MIN
U-matic
Today's special series
Color (K P)
Develops language arts skills in children. Presents programs thematically designed around subjects of interest to youngsters. Action takes place in a department store where people, mannequins, puppets, comic characters and special guests present a light hearted approach to language arts.
English Language; Literature and Drama; Psychology
Dist - TVOTAR **Prod** - TVOTAR 1985

The Police 58 MIN
16mm
Color (H C A)
Presents a satire about a country where every citizen loves the government except one. Points out the necessity of the secret police to turn up revolutionaries even when there aren't any or find itself out of business.
Civics and Political Systems; Sociology
Dist - GROVE **Prod** - GROVE

Police 25 MIN
U-matic / VHS / 16mm
Charlie Chaplin Comedy Theater Series
B&W (I)
Features Charlie Chaplin as a man just released from prison and persuaded by reformers to go straight. Explains that old cronies soon talk him into a robbery, until he meets 'the girl' who sets him on the road to redemption.
Fine Arts
Dist - FI **Prod** - MUFLM 1916

Police Chief Speaks Out 30 MIN
U-matic
Decision Makers Series
Color
Features an interview with Richard G Hostuick, police chief of Reading, Ohio. Discusses leadership style, career development and problems.
Biography; Civics and Political Systems
Dist - HRC **Prod** - OHC

Police Civil Liability Series Part 1
Negligent Operation of Motor Vehicles 24 MIN
Dist - CORF

Police Civil Liability Series Part 2
Negligent Use of Firearms 24 MIN
Dist - CORF

Police Civil Liability Series Part 3
Limits of Physical Force 19 MIN
Dist - CORF

Police Civil Liability Series Part 6
Intentional Use of Deadly Force 22 MIN
Dist - CORF

Police civil liability series
Civil rights violations 23 MIN
Supervisory liability, management responsibility and accountability 24 MIN
Dist - CORF

Police dog 50 MIN
U-matic / VHS / 16mm
Color (I)
Describes the training of police dog Duke and tells the story of the day he saved his master's life. Presents re - enactments of true stories of police dogs at work, including searching for a lost child, narcotics, explosives, evidence of a crime, apprehending criminals and preventing an attack on an officer.

Civics and Political Systems; Science - Natural
Dist - HANDEL **Prod** - HANDEL 1972

Police dog - Pt 1 25 MIN
U-matic / VHS / 16mm
Color (I)
Describes the training of police dog Duke, and tells the story of the day he saved his master's life.
Civics and Political Systems; Science - Natural; Social Science; Sociology
Dist - HANDEL **Prod** - HANDEL 1972

Police dog - Pt 2 25 MIN
U-matic / VHS / 16mm
Color (I)
Presents reenactments of true stories of police dogs at work, including searching for a lost child, narcotics, explosives, evidence of a crime, apprehending criminals and preventing an attack on an officer.
Civics and Political Systems; Science - Natural; Social Science; Sociology
Dist - HANDEL **Prod** - HANDEL 1972

Police estimate - The Two worlds of Max Roach 29 MIN
U-matic
Interface series
Color
Presents a two - part program dealing with police relations in the ghetto and with a jazz drummer named Max Roach.
Fine Arts; Social Science; Sociology
Dist - PBS **Prod** - WETATV

Police - local 15 MIN
VHS / 16mm
(H C A)
$24.95 purchase _ #CS312
Describes the skills involved in being a local police officer. Features interviews with people working in the field.
Civics and Political Systems; Guidance and Counseling
Dist - RMIBHF **Prod** - RMIBHF

The Police marriage - family issues 20 MIN
16mm / U-matic / VHS
Color (A)
LC 76-702275
Examines the special problems that police officers and their children encounter because of the work. Discusses absence because of odd hours, potential emotional barriers, problems of authoritarianism and unrealistic expectations placed on children of police officers.
Civics and Political Systems; Guidance and Counseling; Social Science; Sociology
Dist - CORF **Prod** - HAR 1976

The Police marriage - husband, wife personal issues 20 MIN
16mm / U-matic / VHS
Color (A)
LC 76-702273
Focuses on the kinds of marital problems posed by the police officer's work. Considers the spouse's need to adapt to this work and its usual pressures while forming his or her own identity.
Civics and Political Systems; Guidance and Counseling; Social Science; Sociology
Dist - CORF **Prod** - HAR 1976

Police marriage - social issues 20 MIN
16mm / U-matic / VHS
Color (A)
LC 76-702274
Considers the social and psychological problems the police officer, spouse, and children may have in relating to friends, relatives and the public. Examines sources of conflict in informal settings and off - duty demands and expectations arising from the officer's role.
Civics and Political Systems; Guidance and Counseling; Psychology; Social Science; Sociology
Dist - CORF **Prod** - HAR 1976

Police Officer 20 MIN
U-matic / VHS
Rights and Responsibilities Series
Color (J H)
Shows two truant officers encountering juveniles involved in burglary, truancy, marijuana violations and driving without a license.
Civics and Political Systems; Guidance and Counseling; Social Science; Sociology
Dist - AITECH **Prod** - VAOG 1975

The Police officer 14 MIN
U-matic / VHS / 16mm
Color (P I)
Introduces the services performed by the police in a community. Explains how police officers' major responsibility is law enforcement and how they function as community helpers. Highlights the importance of teamwork in police operations, and the special skills and equipment used by the police department.
Social Science
Dist - EBEC **Prod** - EBEC 1981

Police officer exams
VHS / 16mm
Test preparation video series
Color (H)
$39.95 _ VAI 118
Reviews police officer examinations. Offers testing strategies and problem solving techniques.
Business and Economics; Civics and Political Systems; Guidance and Counseling; Psychology
Dist - CADESF **Prod** - CADESF

Police Officers 13 MIN
U-matic / VHS / 16mm
Community Helpers Series
Color (P I)
$325, $235 purchase _ #79522
Shows the many different functions and responsibilities of police officers.
Civics and Political Systems
Dist - CORF

Police Officers - Day and Night 12 MIN
16mm / U-matic / VHS
Color (P I)
LC 83-700079
Follows a police officer through a typical day, discussing the routine of police work and the training. Shows the police officer as a well - trained, intelligent and competent family man who cares about his family and community, and who wants to protect and serve the people.
Social Science
Dist - AIMS **Prod** - CAHILL 1981

Police on campus I 18 MIN
U-matic / VHS / 16mm
Color
Presents vignettes which explore such topics as racial conflict, dormitory theft, communication problems with foreign students, an arrest during a class session and a rape response. Designed to increase communication skills for campus security officers.
Civics and Political Systems; Education; Social Science
Dist - CORF **Prod** - BARPJ 1976

Police on campus II 10 MIN
U-matic / VHS / 16mm
Color
Presents six vignettes which explore security officer discretion, parking problems, a supervisor conflict, an off - campus arrest, city police/campus police conflict and a surprise situation. Shows how these situations are handled by campus police officers.
Civics and Political Systems; Education; Social Science
Dist - CORF **Prod** - BARPJ 1976

Police Pursuit 19 MIN
16mm
Color
LC 75-703028
Demonstrates techniques and procedures for the safe driving of pursuit vehicles, focusing on police pursuit.
Civics and Political Systems; Health and Safety
Dist - FILCOM **Prod** - FILCOM 1974

Police - school relations 28 MIN
U-matic / VHS / 16mm
Color (T)
Discusses how inappropriate police involvement in school campus incidents can lead to more, rather than less, tension. Examines a model memorandum of agreement between local law enforcement agencies and a school system.
Education; Sociology
Dist - PHENIX **Prod** - PHENIX 1984

Police station 10 MIN
VHS
Stop, look, listen series
Color; PAL (P I J)
Follows two children who find a lost dog and the one child who takes it to the police station. Observes the different kinds of police, a police officer with a panda car, a motorcycle police officer and mounted police. Part of a series of films which start from some everyday observation and show more of what is happening, how and why. Builds vocabulary and encourages children to be more observant.
Civics and Political Systems; English Language; Social Science
Dist - VIEWTH

The Police station 15 MIN
BETA / VHS / U-matic / 16mm
Your town I series
Color (K P)
$245.00, $68.00 purchase _ #C50627, #C51438
Examines the multitude of services provided by police officers - patrolling neighborhoods, governing traffic flow, ensuring street - crossing safety for young students. Looks at the special gear carried by the police because their work can be dangerous. Part of a five - part series on community services.
Health and Safety; Social Science; Sociology
Dist - NGS **Prod** - NGS 1990

Police story 12 MIN
VHS / U-matic
Color
LC 81-707113
Depicts the administrative organization and functions of hospital police officers at the Veterans Administration Hospital in Memphis, Tennessee.
Health and Safety; Social Science
Dist - USNAC **Prod** - VAHMT 1981

The Police tapes 90 MIN
U-matic / VHS
B&W
Reports on a police precinct in the South Bronx and its officers' daily confrontations with crime. Surveys urban crime, violence, brutality and cynical despair.
Civics and Political Systems
Dist - KITCHN **Prod** - KITCHN
VIDVER

Police Tapes 49 MIN
U-matic / VHS / 16mm
B&W
Offers a cinema verite look at urban police work and ghetto crime by portraying life at New York City's 44th Precinct. Details the pressures, stress, frustration, violence and brutality that must be faced and how the officers learn to cope.
Civics and Political Systems; Fine Arts; Social Science
Dist - CORF **Prod** - CORF

Police Tattoo 14 MIN
16mm
B&W
Presents a pageant staged by the Malaysian police held once every five years to raise funds for police welfare.
Geography - World; Social Science
Dist - PMFMUN **Prod** - FILEM 1961

Police technology 29 MIN
VHS / 16mm
Discovery digest series
Color (S)
$300.00 purchase _ #707614
Explores a vast array of science - related discoveries, challenges and technological breakthroughs. Profiles and 'demystifies' research and development currently underway in many fields. The film scrutinizes a bomb disposal robot, computerized finger printing, how radar works and forensic analysis of car paint to trace a hit - and - run driver.
Civics and Political Systems; Computer Science; Mathematics; Science
Dist - ACCESS **Prod** - ACCESS 1989

Police technology 30 MIN
VHS / U-matic
Innovation series
Color
Discusses innovations in law enforcement, pointing out that it takes different types of detective skills to investigate computer crimes.
Civics and Political Systems; Mathematics; Sociology
Dist - PBS **Prod** - WNETTV 1983

Police - the human dimension - authority - Pt A 23 MIN
16mm / U-matic / VHS
Police - the human dimension series
Color (C)
LC 75-700176
Focuses on the exercise of authority. Shows policemen acting out situations.
Civics and Political Systems; Education; Social Science; Sociology
Dist - CORF **Prod** - FLORSU 1975

Police - the human dimension - authority - Pt B 20 MIN
U-matic / VHS / 16mm
Police - the human dimension series
Color (C)
LC 75-700182
Explains the importance of correct ethical behavior by police officers in applying the law. Offers five vignettes of police behavior.
Civics and Political Systems; Social Science; Sociology
Dist - CORF **Prod** - FLORSU 1975

Police - the human dimension - community - Pt A 20 MIN
U-matic / VHS / 16mm
Police - the human dimension series
Color (C)
LC 75-700180
Explains the importance of proper police behavior.
Civics and Political Systems; Social Science; Sociology
Dist - CORF **Prod** - FLORSU 1975

Police - the human dimension - community - Pt B 20 MIN
16mm / U-matic / VHS
Police - the human dimension series
Color (C)
LC 75-700183
Examines the professional responsibility and the possibility of strains on a policeman's relations with his community.
Civics and Political Systems; Social Science; Sociology
Dist - CORF **Prod** - FLORSU 1975

Police - the human dimension - ethics - Pt A 23 MIN
16mm / U-matic / VHS
Police - the human dimension series
Color (C)
LC 75-700175
Focuses on ethical problems a policeman may face. Shows policemen acting out situations.
Civics and Political Systems; Education; Social Science; Sociology
Dist - CORF **Prod** - FLORSU 1975

Police - the human dimension - ethics - Pt B 20 MIN
16mm / U-matic / VHS
Police - the human dimension series
Color (C)
LC 75-700181
Explains the importance of correct ethical behavior by police officers.
Civics and Political Systems; Social Science; Sociology
Dist - CORF **Prod** - FLORSU 1975

Police - the Human Dimension - Minorities 23 MIN
U-matic / VHS / 16mm
Police - the Human Dimension Series
Color (C)
LC 75-700179
Focuses on problems involving minority groups in law enforcement situations. Shows policemen acting out situations.
Civics and Political Systems; Education; Social Science; Sociology
Dist - CORF **Prod** - FLORSU 1975

Police - the human dimension series
Police - the human dimension - authority - Pt A 23 MIN
Police - the human dimension - authority - Pt B 20 MIN
Police - the human dimension - community - Pt A 20 MIN
Police - the human dimension - community - Pt B 20 MIN
Police - the human dimension - ethics - Pt A 23 MIN
Police - the human dimension - ethics - Pt B 20 MIN
Police - the Human Dimension - Minorities 23 MIN
Police - the Human Dimension - Stress 23 MIN
Dist - CORF

Police - the Human Dimension - Stress 23 MIN
U-matic / VHS / 16mm
Police - the Human Dimension Series
Color (C)
LC 75-700178
Focuses on problems causing stress in law enforcement situations. Shows policemen acting out situations.
Civics and Political Systems; Education; Social Science; Sociology
Dist - CORF **Prod** - FLORSU 1975

Police - the legal dimension - Pt 1 - search and seizure without a warrant 22 MIN
U-matic / VHS / 16mm
Color
Illustrates the areas in which an officer's actions could jeopardize a case. Deals with situations involving search during temporary detention, search incidental to lawful arrest, search without consent and vehicle searches.
Civics and Political Systems; Social Science
Dist - CORF **Prod** - HAR

Police - the legal dimension - Pt 2 - admissions and confessions 22 MIN
U-matic / VHS / 16mm
Color
Demonstrates how the admissability of statements made by suspects during and after arrest frequently hinges on the behavior of officers and the conditions under which the statements were obtained.
Civics and Political Systems; Social Science
Dist - CORF **Prod** - HAR

Police Training Films Series
Officer Down, Code 3 25 MIN
Dist - CORF

Police unit 2a26 18 MIN
16mm
Color (I)
LC 78-701243
Follows two policemen through the activities of a typical day. Includes scenes of their families, and shows one of the men as he competes in the Police Olympics.
Social Science
Dist - AMEDFL **Prod** - DUNLF 1968

Policeman 12 MIN
U-matic / VHS / 16mm
Color (P I)
Demonstrates how safeguarding lives is the police officer's major responsibility and his or her most important tool is his knowledge of people. Includes vignettes depicting the law officer as a human being who cares about others.
Civics and Political Systems; Social Science
Dist - LUF **Prod** - LUF 1979

The Policeman and his job 13 MIN
U-matic / VHS / 16mm
Color; B&W (I J)
LC FIA68-2111
Presents the work of a police officer in the communications division trying to assist people with various needs.
Civics and Political Systems; Psychology; Social Science; Sociology
Dist - PHENIX **Prod** - BRAVC 1963

Policeman - he is there to help 11 MIN
16mm
Color (K P I)
LC 72-702928
Presents the police officer as a person whose job is helping people in a great variety of ways. Depicts officers at street crossings, checking shop doors at night, helping stranded motorists, answering calls and comforting lost children. Tells of the training necessary for police officers.
Civics and Political Systems; Social Science; Sociology
Dist - ASPTEF **Prod** - ASPTEF 1970

Policemen 28 MIN
U-matic
Are you listening series
Color (J H C)
LC 80-707149
Presents Chicago policemen discussing their life and work.
Civics and Political Systems; Social Science
Dist - STURTM **Prod** - STURTM 1972

Policewoman 11 MIN
16mm / U-matic
CTV reports series
Color; Mono (J H C A)
$200.00 film, $200.00 video, $50.00 rental
Describes the changing role of women in the Canadian Police Forces focusing on the future expectations of women in law enforcement today.
Social Science; Sociology
Dist - CTV **Prod** - CTV 1977

Policies and Procedures 60 MIN
BETA / VHS
Manufacturing Series
(IND)
Answers questions about policies and procedures and shows why they are important to the successful operation of all departments in a company.
Business and Economics
Dist - COMSRV **Prod** - COMSRV 1986

Policies and Programs of Other Governments 34 MIN
VHS / U-matic
Technology, Innovation, and Industrial Development Series
Color
Business and Economics
Dist - MIOT **Prod** - MIOT

Policies of Transition 30 MIN
VHS
American South Comes of Age Series
Color (J)
$95.00 purchase, $55.00 rental
Considers the rise of the Republican party in the American South. Part of a fourteen - part series on the economic, social and political transformation of the South since World War II.
Civics and Political Systems; Geography - United States; History - United States; Psychology; Sociology
Dist - SCETV **Prod** - SCETV 1985

Policing the peace (1948 to 1951) 24 MIN
16mm / U-matic / VHS
American chronicles series
Color (J H C G T A)
$75 rental _ #9820
Shows various international events, including the proclamation of Israel as a state, India's winning independence, and Gandhi's assassination.
Geography - World; History - World
Dist - AIMS **Prod** - AIMS 1986

Policy management - an overview - Pt 1 11 MIN
VHS
Breakthrough improvement in quality series; Pt 1
Color (PRO IND A)
$495.00 purchase, $175.00 rental _ #GP133A
Presents part one of a five - part series developed by Florida Power and Light's - Qualtec Quality Service. Discusses the principles that make up policy management and gives organizations a resource to help achieve and keep a competitive advantage.
Business and Economics
Dist - EXTR **Prod** - GPERFO

Polio and post - polio syndrome 28 MIN
VHS
Color (G)
$149.00 purchase, $75.00 rental _ #UW4229
Reveals that many polio survivors are facing new problems - after years of dormancy, their pain and disability are returning in a condition called post - polio syndrome. Reviews the history of polio, looks at the syndrome and examines worldwide polio eradication programs.
Health and Safety
Dist - FOTH

Polish Americans 30 MIN
VHS
Multicultural peoples of North America series
Color (J H C G)
$49.95 purchase _ #LVCD6684V - S
Celebrates the heritage of Polish Americans. Traces the history of their emigration to North America and shows the unique traditions they brought with them. Discusses why and when they emigrated, where they settled, their occupations and their important leaders. Focuses on a Polish American family and explains the importance of cultural identity. Part of a 15 - part series on multiculturalism in North America.
History - United States; Sociology
Dist - CAMV

The Polish experience - 10 51 MIN
VHS
Eastern Europe - breaking with the past series
Color (H C G)
$50.00 purchase
Presents three segments on Poland - Be Aware, historical footage from the first Solidarity Congress in 1980; From the Life of Monuments, which documents the destruction of a communist symbol in Warsaw, the statue of Feliks Dzierzinski, Polish founder of the Soviet Secret Police; and All That Is Alive, a look at the severe pollution problems in the Silesia region of Poland. Part ten of 13 parts.
Civics and Political Systems; History - World; Science - Natural
Dist - GVIEW **Prod** - GVIEW 1990

The Polish kitchen
VHS
Frugal gourmet international cooking I series
Color (G)
$19.95 purchase _ #CCP804
Shows how to prepare Polish food. Features Jeff Smith, the Frugal Gourmet. Part of a ten - part series on international cooking.
Home Economics; Physical Education and Recreation
Dist - CADESF **Prod** - CADESF

The Polish Kitchen 30 MIN
BETA / VHS
Frugal Gourmet Series
Color
Features traditional Polish dishes including Polish sausage and Pierogi.
Health and Safety; Home Economics; Psychology
Dist - CORF **Prod** - WTTWTV

Polish republic unknown - Rzeczypospolita nieznana 180 MIN
VHS
Color; B&W (G A) (POLISH)
$59.95 purchase
Contains six episodes on three tapes devoted to Warsaw, Lvov, Vilnus, Poznan, Katowice and COP. Features Polish historians who narrate and discuss various aspects of the cultural and economic aspects of life in these cities from 1918 to 1939. Uses original footage from the period.
Fine Arts; History - World
Dist - POLART

Polishing 15 MIN
U-matic
Scaling techniques series
Color (PRO)
LC 77-706009
Provides instruction in the mixing of abrasive agents used for polishing teeth. Discusses instrument speed and pressure used when applying the agent to tooth surfaces. Number ten in the series.
Health and Safety; Science; Science - Natural
Dist - USNAC **Prod** - UTENN 1976

Polishing 28 MIN
16mm
B&W
LC FIE52-381
Explains how to make a concave or convex polishing shell, trim the polishing shell to size and cut breathers.
Industrial and Technical Education
Dist - USNAC **Prod** - USOE 1944

Polishing 30 MIN
U-matic / VHS
Introduction to Technical and Business Communication Series
Color (H C A)
Business and Economics; English Language
Dist - GPN **Prod** - UMINN 1983

Polishing, Soldering, Applying the Handle 30 MIN
U-matic / VHS
How to Build a Knife Series
Color
Shows how to polish, solder and apply the handle when building a knife.
Industrial and Technical Education
Dist - MDCPB **Prod** - UGATV

Polishing the Apple 30 MIN
VHS / 16mm
Marketing Series
Color (C A)
$130.00, $120.00 purchase _15 - 17
Demonstrates the promotional mix practiced by Apple Computer, Inc.
Business and Economics
Dist - CDTEL **Prod** - COAST 1989

Polishing the Big Apple
VHS
Color (C PRO G)
$150.00 purchase _ #85.03
Shows how management science has played a critical role in increasing the ability of New York's Dept of Sanitation to clean the city's streets. Reveals that not only has the department achieved five consecutive years of improved cleanliness ratings but current ratings are near record levels. To achieve ratings equal to the highest ever recorded, the city will need approximately 400 fewer cleaners than previously, equivalent in financial terms to $12 million a year in salaries and fringe benefits.
Business and Economics; Geography - United States; Health and Safety
Dist - INMASC

The Politburo Presents 25 MIN
BETA / VHS / U-matic
Our Man in China Series
Color; Mono (H C A)
$200.00 purchase, $50.00 rental
Investigates the state of the arts in modern day China. Only the government decides who is an artist, thus many dissident artists are shunned by society. Dennis McIntosh interveiws a group of dissident artists who are aware that they share an uncertain future, as the government maintains strict control of the arts.
Geography - World; History - World
Dist - CTV **Prod** - CTV 1982

Politeness and enthusiasm 38 MIN
U-matic / VHS / 16mm
Christians series
Color (H C A)
LC 78-701659
Contrasts the two strands of Christianity that emerged in the 19th century, that of the educated classes and that of revivalist enthusiasm. Episode ten in the series.
History - World; Religion and Philosophy
Dist - MGHT **Prod** - GRATV 1978

Political Action Kit 30 MIN
U-matic / VHS
Making Government Work
(H)
Uses dramatizations and interviews to familiarize high school students with the functions of government. Focuses on political action committees.
Civics and Political Systems
Dist - GPN

Political Advertisement - 1956 - 84 35 MIN
U-matic / VHS
Color
Examines media landscape. Presented by Antonio Muntadas and Marshall Reese.
Fine Arts; Sociology
Dist - ARTINC **Prod** - ARTINC

Political and Social Comment in Dance Series
Black Choreographers' Social Comment in their Work 30 MIN
Contemporary Dancers' Social and Political Concerns 30 MIN
Dance and Social Consciousness in the 1930's and 1940's 30 MIN
Performance and Dance Theatre 30 MIN
Dist - ARCVID

The Political animal 60 MIN
VHS
Ark series; Episode 3
Color (G)
$290.00 purchase, $50.00 rental
Observes less glamorous animals being removed from Regent's Park Zoo in London while a blaze of publicity surrounds the one new arrival, Ming Ming, a giant panda from China who will hopefully bring 50,000 additional visitors. Contrasts this commercial endeavor with neglect in breeding the Partula Snail, one of the world's rarest animals. Meanwhile, a secret coup is planned. Part of a series on the Zoo which has been told that, due to the market economy, it must now pay its own way. Records events at the Ark for over a year as a cost conscious management team moves in, slashing expenditures, including 90 people and 1200 animals - 40 percent of the zoo's stock.
Business and Economics; Fine Arts; Science - Natural
Dist - FIRS **Prod** - DINEEN 1993

The Political candidate 29 MIN
Videoreel / VT2
Our street series
Color
Civics and Political Systems; Sociology
Dist - PBS **Prod** - MDCPB

The Political Cartoon 15 MIN
Videoreel / VT2
Charlie's Pad Series
Color
Fine Arts
Dist - PBS **Prod** - WSIU

Political Chicago 82 MIN
16mm
Color (G)
$65.00 rental
Presents a special rental package containing America's in Real Trouble; Love it - Leave it; Campaign; Anderson - Loosely; and Marquette Park I.
Civics and Political Systems; Fine Arts; Physical Education and Recreation; Sociology
Dist - CANCIN **Prod** - PALAZT

Political corruption 30 MIN
U-matic / VHS
America - the second century series
Color (H C)
$34.95 purchase
Uses the Grant, Harding and Nixon administrations as case studies of political corruption in America. Part of a 30-part series focusing on political, economic, and social issues in the United States since 1875.
History - United States
Dist - DALCCD **Prod** - DALCCD
GPN

The Political executives 29 MIN
16mm
Government story series
Color (H C)
LC 78-707184
Explains why the President's top advisers are political appointees, and discusses their problems in representing the President in his dealings with Congress and the federal departments. Number 29 in the series.
Civics and Political Systems
Dist - WBCPRO **Prod** - WBCPRO 1968

Political Idealogies of the Twentieth Century - Understanding the Isms Series
Liberalism and Conservatism
Dist - ASPRSS

Political Idelogies of the Twentieth Century - Understanding the Isms.
What is Communism?
Dist - ASPRSS

Political Ideologies of the Twentieth Century - Understanding the Isms Series
What is Capitalism?
What is Fascism?
What is Socialism?
Dist - ASPRSS

Political ideologies of the Twentieth century - understanding the isms series
Comparative political systems - the United States, the United Kingdom and the Soviet Union
Dist - ASPRSS

Political Leadership and Stability 30 MIN
U-matic
China After Mao Series
Color (CHINESE)
Focuses on fluctuations within Chinese politics.
Civics and Political Systems; Geography - World
Dist - UMITV **Prod** - UMITV 1980

Political Morality in America 29 MIN
U-matic
Interface Series
Color
Explores the civil rights movement and asks how it has been affected by the assassinations of black leaders and by the Watergate scandals.
History - United States
Dist - PBS **Prod** - WETATV

Political organization 30 MIN
U-matic
Faces of culture - studies in cultural anthropology series
Color (C A)
Describes major types of political organizations in the world. Includes decentralized and centralized systems and looks at the cultures in which these systems are usually found. Lesson 17 in the series.
Sociology
Dist - CDTEL **Prod** - COAST

Political Participation 30 MIN
U-matic / VHS
American Government Series; 1
Color (C)
Analyzes voting behavior and political participation.
Civics and Political Systems
Dist - DALCCD **Prod** - DALCCD

Political Participation 30 MIN
VHS / 16mm
Government by Consent - a National Perspective Series
Color (I J H C A)
Demonstrates how and why people participate in the political process and illustrates why participation is vital to our political system.
Civics and Political Systems
Dist - DALCCD **Prod** - DALCCD 1990

Political Participation of the Handicapped 30 MIN
VHS / U-matic
American Government Series; 1
Color (C)
Provides a case study of the handicapped with a focus on 'socialization' and 'political socialization.'.
Civics and Political Systems
Dist - DALCCD **Prod** - DALCCD

Political parties 30 MIN
VHS / U-matic
American government series; 1
Color (C)
Accounts for the development of today's political parties with their basic philosophical differences. Explores the historical stereotypes of the 'typical Republican' and the 'typical Democrat.'.
Civics and Political Systems
Dist - DALCCD **Prod** - DALCCD

Political parties 30 MIN
U-matic / VHS
Making government work
(H)
Uses dramatizations and interviews to familiarize high school level students with the functions of government. Focuses on political parties.
Civics and Political Systems
Dist - GPN

Political parties 30 MIN
VHS / 16mm
Government by consent - a national perspective series
Color (I J H C A)
Examines the role of the parties in selecting candidates. Illustrates the importance of volunteers in parties and evaluates the future of the Democratic and Republican parties.
Civics and Political Systems
Dist - DALCCD **Prod** - DALCCD 1990

Political Parties in America - Getting the People Together 20 MIN
U-matic / VHS / 16mm
Color (J H)
LC 76-701797
Presents candid interviews which probe the structure, workings and effects of American political parties. Includes interviews of workers in the street, political observers, social commentators, and elected representatives.
Civics and Political Systems
Dist - EBEC **Prod** - EBEC 1976

Political Parties in the United States 17 MIN
16mm / U-matic / VHS
Color (J)
LC 76-703178
Answers questions about the two - party political system in the United States, pointing out its advantages and disadvantages. Includes a discussion of the importance of third parties and splinter groups within the two parties.
Civics and Political Systems
Dist - PHENIX **Prod** - MEDFO 1976

Political Parties - Women's Clout 29 MIN
U-matic
Woman Series
Color
Suggests that the national political conventions of 1972 created a new awareness of political power by women.
Civics and Political Systems; Sociology
Dist - PBS **Prod** - WNEDTV

Political posture 2 MIN
U-matic / VHS
Color (H C A)
Offers a satire of political advertisements.
Civics and Political Systems; Psychology
Dist - IFEX **Prod** - IFEX

Political protest - the splinter groups 15 MIN
16mm
Color (H)
Discusses disssent within political parties. Explains that dissent takes many forms, beginning with the founding fathers, themselves violent dissenters. The evolution of the American two - party political system has not been immune from protest, to the extent that the United States has had three or more party systems in the 20th Century alone.
Civics and Political Systems
Dist - REAF **Prod** - INTEXT

Political Science 15 MIN
BETA / VHS / U-matic
Career Success Series
(H C A)
$29.95 _ MX312
Portrays occupations in political science by reviewing required abilities and interviewing people employed in this field. Tells of anxieties and rewards involved in pursuing a career as a political scientist.
Civics and Political Systems; Education; Guidance and Counseling
Dist - CAMV **Prod** - CAMV

Political Socialization 30 MIN
U-matic / VHS
American Government Series; 1
Color (C)
Displays different political options citizens have in their daily lives and shows how political attitudes and behavior may be influenced by families, social class, peer groups, schools and churches.
Civics and Political Systems
Dist - DALCCD **Prod** - DALCCD

Political spots 30 MIN
U-matic / VHS / 16mm
Media probes series
Color (H C A)
Offers a primer on the techniques used by political media makers. Shows media spots from across the country, representing several parties and many levels of government. Accompanies two media consultants into their editing rooms as they explain the process in making vote - winning TV commercials.
Civics and Political Systems; Fine Arts; Psychology; Social Science
Dist - TIMLIF **Prod** - LAYLEM 1982

Political systems 30 MIN
VHS
Color (H C)
$89.95 purchase _ #TSI - 123
Examines various forms of governments - including autocracy, totalitarianism and democracy - showing how governmental power is abused and used by the powerful. Illustrates how people can gain power and change government.
Civics and Political Systems; Sociology
Dist - INSTRU

The Politicians 19 MIN
VHS
Decade of destruction - classroom version series
Color (J H)
$150.00 purchase, $25.00 rental
Encapsulates the fight which has begun to save the world's richest heritage of biodiversity and evolution - the rainforest. Tells about how the World Bank financed the operation to pave the main road in the rainforest so exploitation of Brazil's raw materials could be achieved more efficiently. Hundreds of thousands of square miles of the forest were burned. The president and minister of the environment, elected in 1989, have pledged to cease further destruction.
Fine Arts; Science - Natural
Dist - BULFRG **Prod** - COWELL 1991

The Politician's life 60 MIN
VHS
Color & B&W (G)
$29.95 purchase
Features a mock documentary about a stormy congressional primary race in California in 1956 with a young novice candidate. Begins with 17 maverick Republicans in the running but when Thomas Preston Wilson, a big cheese with a dazzling record, announces his candidacy, all the others bow out - except for young Gary Martin. Martin's Kennedy - like flair for showmanship ignites what has been called one of the greatest congressional primary races ever held. Written, produced and directed by R J Thomas, who also stars as the inexperienced Martin.
Civics and Political Systems; Fine Arts
Dist - CANCIN

Politics - 6 29 MIN
VHS
Interactions in Science and Society - Teacher Programs - Series
Color (T PRO)
$150.00 purchase
Scrutinizes the role of government and military needs in shaping the development of science and technology since World War II. Considers genetic engineering, acid rain and regulation of hazardous materials as issues forcing legislators to reconcile differences and govern highly technical processes.
Civics and Political Systems; Education; History - United States; History - World
Dist - AITECH **Prod** - WHATV 1990

Politics and Conflict 15 MIN
U-matic / VHS
By the People Series
Color (H)
Examines causes and effects of political conflict. Shows how conflict is managed through the political process.
Civics and Political Systems; Social Science
Dist - CTI **Prod** - CTI

Politics and the arts 30 MIN
U-matic / VHS
Update - topics of current concern series
Color
Civics and Political Systems; Fine Arts; Sociology
Dist - ARCVID **Prod** - ARCVID

Politics and the Individual 15 MIN
VHS / U-matic
By the People Series
Color (H)
Illustrates how the political process in a democracy provides ways to protect the individual.
Civics and Political Systems; Social Science
Dist - CTI **Prod** - CTI

Politics and the Military - American Lifestyles II Series
George C Marshall - the Determined Victor 24 MIN
Dist - AIMS
UILL

Politics and Youth 15 MIN
U-matic / VHS / 16mm
Color (J H)
LC 73-701492
Presents interviews with young people from all across the country, all races, walks of life and political persuasions, talking about politics.
Civics and Political Systems; Social Science; Sociology
Dist - AIMS **Prod** - COP 1973

Politics of Age
16mm
Aging in the Future Series
Color
Urges legislators, professionals in the aging field and older people to consider the political interests and activities of older persons. Looks at the roles of organizations of older people and the prospects of an older people's political party.
Health and Safety; Sociology
Dist - UMICH **Prod** - UMICH

Politics of aging 15 MIN
U-matic
Aging in the future series
Color
Shows older people taking an active role in the politics of age. Focuses on older legislators and those politicians who advise older citizens to help their own interests by being active politically.
Civics and Political Systems; Sociology
Dist - UMITV **Prod** - UMITV 1981

The Politics of fear 48.30 MIN
VHS / U-matic / 16mm
Russian - German War series
Color; Mono (H C A)
MV $250.00 _ MP $350.00 purchase, $50.00 rental
Presents the events of June 21, 1941, the day that the war between Germany and Russia began. Portrays Germany as a proud and arrogant country and Russia as a country that was disciplined and had a sense of purpose. Describes Germany's surprise attack on Russia and indicates that irreparable damage was done to Russia's equipment and forces.
Geography - World; History - World
Dist - CTV **Prod** - CTV 1974

The Politics of food 100 MIN
VHS
Color; PAL (J H)
PdS30 purchase
Presents five programs of 20 minutes each examining the paradox of the world - more food is produced than is consumed, yet every day 35,000 people die of hunger and 100 million others, most of them children, are literally starving to death. Includes the programs USA 1 - the Food Machine; USA 2 - The Hunger Business; Asia - A Question of Aid; Sudan - The Avoidable Famine; Brazil - Sharing the Land. Contact distributor about availability outside the United Kingdom.
Civics and Political Systems; Geography - World; Social Science; Sociology
Dist - ACADEM

The Politics of food 208 MIN
VHS
Color; PAL (H C G)
PdS50 purchase
Presents four 52 - minute programs which reveal that on a daily global basis 35,000 people die of hunger, while 100 million others - most of them children - are literally starving to death. Considers the paradox of starvation on a planet which produces and consumes more food than it needs. Includes the titles Sudan - The Avoidable Famine; USA - The Hunger Machine; Brazil - Battle for the Land; Asia - The Aid Trap. Contact distributor about availability outside the United Kingdom.
Social Science; Sociology
Dist - ACADEM **Prod** - CFTV

The Politics of Genetics 29 MIN
U-matic
Issue at Hand Series
Color
Features a discussion between a science critic and a research scientist on the wisdom of genetic research. Focuses on recombinant DNA.
Psychology; Science; Science - Natural; Sociology
Dist - UMITV **Prod** - UMITV 1976

The Politics of hunger in America 29 MIN
Videoreel / VT2
University of Chicago round table series
Color
Health and Safety; Social Science; Sociology
Dist - PBS **Prod** - WTTWTV

Politics of love 55 MIN
VHS
Color (A PRO)
$25.00 purchase _ #138VU
Features Leo Buscaglia in an examination of the power of love in one's life. Encourages viewers to free themselves from labels, hang - ups and trivial matters. Stresses the importance of teaching love to one's children.
Psychology; Religion and Philosophy
Dist - NIGCON **Prod** - NIGCON

The Politics of military spending 30 MIN
VHS
America's defense monitor series; Politics and economics
Color (J H C G)
$29.95 purchase _ #ADM319V
Examines the politics of military spending in the United States. Part of a five - part series on the politics and economics of American military affairs.
Business and Economics; Civics and Political Systems
Dist - CAMV

The Politics of peace making 14 MIN
16mm / U-matic / VHS
World War I series
Color (J H C)
$300, $210 purchase _ #4238
Shows the different goals that delegates at Versailles had, and how this led to a treaty that helped to bring about World War II.
Civics and Political Systems; History - World
Dist - CORF

Politics of Poison 53 MIN
16mm
Color
LC 79-701011
Focuses on herbicide spraying in the United States and shows how the Environmental Protection Agency is dealing with this problem.
Agriculture; Science - Natural; Sociology
Dist - KRONTV **Prod** - KRONTV 1979

Politics of poison - Pt 1 27 MIN
16mm
Color
LC 79-701011
Focuses on herbicide spraying in the United States and shows how the Environmental Protection Agency is dealing with this problem.
Agriculture; Science - Natural
Dist - KRONTV **Prod** - KRONTV 1979

Politics of poison - Pt 2 26 MIN
16mm
Color
LC 79-701011
Focuses on herbicide spraying in the United States and shows how the Environmental Protection Agency is dealing with this problem.
Agriculture; Science - Natural
Dist - KRONTV **Prod** - KRONTV 1979

The Politics of Privacy 60 MIN
VHS
Color (C)
$8.00 rental _ #60871
Discusses how much of the private lives of public figures, especially politicians, should be revealed to the public. Features Harvard law professor Charles Nesson who heads a panel consisting of former vice presidential candidate Geraldine Ferraro, UN representative Jeane Kirkpatrick, Senator Alan Simpson, media analyst Jeff Greenfield and gossip columnist Liz Smith.
Religion and Philosophy; Sociology
Dist - PSU

The Politics of Regulation 60 MIN
VHS / U-matic
Bill Moyers' Journal Series
Color
Reports on the Federal Trade Commission and the battle in Congress over the power of the regulatory agencies.
Business and Economics; Civics and Political Systems
Dist - PBS **Prod** - WNETTV 1980

The Politics of Unreason - Right - Wing Extremism in America, 1790 - 1970 28 MIN
16mm
Color
Traces the efforts of the right - wing extremists to preserve their status by advocating the denial of rights to minority groups. Discusses movements including the anti - Masonic party of the 1820's and 1830's, the Know - Nothings, the anti - Catholic American Protective Association of the 1890's, the emergence of anti - Semitism in the 1890's, the Ku Klux Klan and the John Birch Society. Analyzes the impact of these movements on the mainstream of American two - party politics.
Civics and Political Systems; Sociology
Dist - ADL **Prod** - ADL

Politics of Violence 27 MIN
U-matic / VHS / 16mm
Seventies Series
Color (J)
LC 81-700252
Studies the emergence of international terrorism during the 1970's. Looks at the far - reaching effects of several terrorist organizations.
History - World; Sociology
Dist - JOU **Prod** - UPI 1980

The Politics of Working Together in a Gifted and Talented Program 28 MIN
U-matic / VHS
Successful Teaching Practices Series
Color (C A)
$75.00 purchase _ #1480
Presents parents, teachers, and administrators as they talk about how Sally Reis has involved them in planning and implementing a successful and satisfying Talented and Gifted (TAG) program at East School in Torrington, Connecticut.
Education
Dist - EBEC

Politics - Part 2 120 MIN
VHS
Chinese series
Color (C A)
Covers the Chinese political system, focusing on ideology, organization, and the relationship between the individual and the state. Filmed on location, and interviews Chinese people. Consists of parts three and four of a 13 - part telecourse on China. Includes two related videos - Believing, focusing on political ideology and organization, and Correcting, which deals with the relationship between the state and the individual. Additional educational materials available.
Civics and Political Systems; Geography - World
Dist - SCETV **Prod** - SCETV 1984

Politics, power and the public good 20 MIN
16mm / U-matic / VHS
Searching for values - a film anthology series
B&W (J)
LC 73-700114
Tells how a long - term popular politician, proud of 'getting things done for the people,' fights to retain his office with a panoply of unethical tactics.
Civics and Political Systems; Guidance and Counseling; Psychology; Sociology
Dist - LCOA **Prod** - LCOA 1972

Politics, privacy and the press - Pt 10 60 MIN
U-matic / VHS
Ethics in America series
Color (G)
Features 1984 candidate for Vice President Geraldine Ferraro, Washington Post publisher Katharine Graham, Peter Jennings and Mike Wallace. Debates 'the public's right to know' and the relevance of the conduct of public officials. Part ten of a ten - part series on ethics in America, produced by Fred W Friendly.
Civics and Political Systems; Literature and Drama
Dist - ANNCPB **Prod** - COLMU 1989
PSU

Politics - Soviet Style 27 MIN
U-matic / VHS / 16mm
Soviet Style Series
Color (J)
Provides a brief background on the Russian Revolution and examines the tumultuous history of politics in post - Czarist Russia. Looks at the role of Lenin in the establishment of the Soviet State, Stalin's role in World War II and after, and the function of Party members in contemporary Soviet politics.
Civics and Political Systems; Geography - World; History - World
Dist - JOU **Prod** - JOU 1982

Politics - the high cost of conviction 5 MIN
16mm / U-matic / VHS
Citizenship - whose responsibility - 1 - series; Set 1
Color (H C)
LC FIA65-400
Questions whether a successful business person has the obligation to publicly endorse a Senatorial candidate whom he considers to be the 'best' even though such endorsement may adversely affect his business.
Civics and Political Systems; Guidance and Counseling; Psychology
Dist - IFB **Prod** - HORIZN 1964

Polka 60 MIN
VHS
Kathy Blake dance studios - let's learn how to dance series
Color (G A)
$39.95 purchase
Features dance instructors Kathy Blake and Gene Russo, who instruct viewers on the basics of polka dancing.
Fine Arts
Dist - PBS **Prod** - WNETTV

Polka Dot Door Series

Air	30 MIN
All in a row	30 MIN
All of me and you	30 MIN
Alphabet	30 MIN
Autumn	30 MIN
Birds and animals	30 MIN
Bits and Pieces	30 MIN
Cars, boats, planes and trains	30 MIN
Christmas	30 MIN
Containers	30 MIN
Dreams	30 MIN
Exploring	30 MIN
Feelings	30 MIN
Friends and neighbors	30 MIN
Growing Week	30 MIN
Hands and Feet	30 MIN
Heads and Tails	30 MIN
Here, There, Everywhere	30 MIN
Hide and Seek	30 MIN
Holes and Circles	30 MIN
Houses and buildings	30 MIN
Land and Water	30 MIN
Messages	30 MIN
Moving about	30 MIN
Music	30 MIN
Night and Day	30 MIN
Numbers	30 MIN
Paper Week	30 MIN
Push Pull	30 MIN
Same and Different	30 MIN
Shows and Tell	30 MIN
Sound and Rhythm	30 MIN
Space	30 MIN
Spring	30 MIN
Summer	30 MIN
Things to do	30 MIN
This a Way, that a Way	30 MIN
Time	30 MIN
Up and Away	30 MIN
Winter	30 MIN

Dist - TVOTAR

Polka Dot Leaves on a Purple Tree 27 MIN
16mm
Color
LC 78-713400
Pictures a studio workshop where children are stimulated by color, design, texture and sound to create their own works of art by using ordinary household materials.
Fine Arts
Dist - HALMRK **Prod** - HALMRK 1971

Polkas, jigs and slides - Video One 90 MIN
VHS
Learn to play Irish fiddle series
Color (G)
$49.95 purchase _ #VD - BUR - FI01
Features Kevin Burke who covers rhythmic devices and other variations, including grace notes, ornaments, rolls, double - stops. Includes the songs Saddle the Pony; The Connaughtman's Rambles; The King of the Fairies; Bill Sullivan's Polka; Johnny Leary's Slide; Micho Russell's Slide and more. Includes music. Part one of a two - part series.
Fine Arts
Dist - HOMETA **Prod** - HOMETA

Pollination 23 MIN
U-matic / VHS / 16mm
Color (I J)
Shows the process of pollination and the various creatures involved in it. Reveals the reproductive parts of a flower and differentiates between self - pollination and cross - pollination. Discusses wind pollination, water pollination and co - evolution of insects and flowering plants.
Science - Natural
Dist - NGS **Prod** - NGS 1983

Pollination Mechanisms 12 MIN
U-matic / VHS / 16mm
Many Worlds of Nature Series
Color (I)
Discusses various pollination mechanisms, such as cross - pollination and self - pollination.
Science - Natural
Dist - CORF **Prod** - SCRESC

Pollination - the insect connection 15 MIN
VHS
Natural history series
Color (I J H)
$80.00 purchase _ #A5VH 1104
Shows the relationship between flowering plants and pollinating insects. Includes footage of orchids that mimic female wasps, flowers scented like rotting flesh and lilies that gather pollen by drowning insects. Part of a series on natural history.
Science - Natural
Dist - CLRVUE **Prod** - CLRVUE

Pollution 3 MIN
16mm
Color
LC 76-702525
Uses music and cartoon satire to show the growing hazards of air and water pollution in American cities. An animated film.
Health and Safety; Science - Natural; Sociology
Dist - USC **Prod** - USC 1967

Pollution 14 MIN
U-matic / VHS / 16mm
Your Chance to Live Series
Color (J H T)
Shows the effects of all types of pollution. Presents the neccessity of positive action to insure the future of mankind.

History - World; Science - Natural; Science - Physical; Sociology
Dist - CORF Prod - USDCPA 1972

Pollution Below 14 MIN
16mm
Rediscovery Series
Color
LC 75-703731
Presents stories of three widely separated people who are caught up in dangerous situations caused by unexpected pollution.
Guidance and Counseling; Science - Natural
Dist - USNAC Prod - NASA 1975

Pollution control 30 MIN
VHS
Inside Britain 1 series
Color; PAL; NTSC (G) (BULGARIAN CZECH HUNGARIAN . SPANISH POLISH ROMANIAN RUSSIAN SLOVAK UKRAINIAN ENGLISH WITH ARABIC SUBTITLES)
PdS65 purchase
States that international cooperation is crucial to combat pollution. Reveals that the British government has introduced an integrated approach to pollution control, tackling all kinds of pollution and placing the onus of payment for such controls on those responsible for the pollution.
Science - Natural; Sociology
Dist - CFLVIS Prod - CUTTIN 1991

Pollution - How Much is a Clean Environment Worth 30 MIN
U-matic / VHS
Economics USA Series
Color (C)
Business and Economics; Science - Natural; Sociology
Dist - ANNCPB Prod - WEFA

Pollution is Personal 14 MIN
16mm
Color
Takes a look at industrial and human pollution.
Science - Natural; Sociology
Dist - TASCOR Prod - TASCOR 1975

Pollution - Land - Air - Water - Noise 17 MIN
16mm
Color (P I J H C)
LC 78-713041
Examines the causes and conditions of four types of pollution - - air, land, water and noise.
Science - Natural; Sociology
Dist - ACA Prod - ACA 1971

Pollution liability - Managing the challenges of coverage and defense in 1991 210 MIN
VHS
Color (C PRO A)
$140.00, $200.00 purchase _ #M793, #P272
Presents an update of what happened in 1990 in the area of pollution liability as well as answers and solutions that are gaining acceptance in the rapidly evolving field of dispute resolution, pollution management and insurance litigation. Provides an overview of the federal environmental laws that create the obligation to pay, e.g. CERCLA, RCRA, SARA, UST and the Clean Air Act Amendments. Also discusses of the different types of relevant insurance policies.
Civics and Political Systems; Sociology
Dist - ALIABA Prod - ALIABA 1991

Pollution of the Upper and Lower Atmosphere 17 MIN
U-matic / VHS / 16mm
Environmental Sciences Series
Color (J)
LC 74-703806
Shows how auto emissions are changing the physical and chemical composition of the atmosphere. Examines the effects these changes might have on the Earth's climate and on man's health.
Science - Natural; Science - Physical; Sociology
Dist - LCOA Prod - DAVFMS 1975

Pollution Solution 15 MIN
16mm
Environmental Series - Landsat - Satellite for all Seasons Series
Color (J H A)
LC 77-700805
Discusses how Landsat's remote sensing capabilities can aid in resolving environmental quality problems. Shows that the satellite can locate and monitor strip - mining operations to facilitate land reclamation programs, help solve meteorological mysteries by tracking the path of airborne pollution and monitor the course of industrial wastes and garbage dumped in lakes, rivers and coastal areas.
Science - Natural; Science - Physical
Dist - USNAC Prod - NASA 1977

Pollution Solution 30 MIN
U-matic / VHS
K I D S - a Series
Color (H)
Describes the dilemma of Suzanne, a `gung - ho' ecologist whose father works for the worst chemical plant polluter in the whole town. Shows how, with help of friends, Suzanne uncovers evidence that changes her father's mind and affects the town.
Science - Natural
Dist - GPN Prod - CPOD

Pollution Solution 30 MIN
VHS / U-matic
K - I - D - S
Captioned (H)
Dramatizes the importance of individual responsibility in cleaning up the environment. Third in a five part series.
Science - Natural
Dist - GPN Prod - CPOSI 1981 - 1983

Pollution - world at risk 25 MIN
BETA / VHS / U-matic / 16mm
Color (H G P I J)
$390.00, $110.00 purchase _ #C50462, #C51355; $385.00, $99.95 purchase
Considers nearly every major environmental pollution issue facing the world from illegal dumping of toxic wastes to global warming and ocean pollution.
Business and Economics; Science - Natural; Sociology
Dist - NGS Prod - NGS 1989

Pollyanna 134 MIN
U-matic / VHS / 16mm
Color
Tells how an orphan girl's upbeat philosophy touches the hearts of a group of cynical adults.
Fine Arts; Literature and Drama
Dist - FI Prod - DISNEY 1960

Polo 3 MIN
16mm
Of all Things Series
Color (P I)
Discusses the sport of polo.
Physical Education and Recreation
Dist - AVED Prod - BAILYL

PolTox I - NLM, CSA, IFIS
CD-ROM
Cambridge Information series
(G PRO C)
$1495.00 purchase _ #1484a
Encompasses 10 years of data from the National Library of Medicine's TOXLINE subfile, Pollution Abstracts, Ecology Abstracts, Toxicology Abstracts, Health and Safety Science Abstracts, Aquatic Sciences and Fisheries Abstracts Part3 and Food Science and Technology Abstracts. Includes over 800,000 citations and abstracts covering toxic substances and environmental health. Quarterly updates. IBM PCs and compatibles require at least 640k RAM, DOS 3.1 or later, one floppy disk drive - hard disk recommended, one empty expansion slot, and an IBM compatible CD - ROM drive.
Health and Safety; Literature and Drama; Sociology
Dist - BEP

PolTox II - Excerpta Medica
CD-ROM
Cambridge Information series
(G PRO C)
$995.00 purchase _ #1484b
Includes 10 years of data from EMBASE, a biomedical and pharmacological database. Covers articles on environmental pollution and toxicology from over 3,500 medical journals. Quarterly updates. IBM PCs and compatibles require at least 640k of RAM, DOS 3.1 or later, one floppy disk drive - hard disk recommended, one empty expansion slot, IBM compatible CD - ROM drive.
Health and Safety; Literature and Drama; Sociology
Dist - BEP

PolTox III - CAB
CD-ROM
Cambridge Information series
(G PRO C)
$1295.00 purchase _ #1484c
Gives access to the agricultural dimensions of environmental issues with a database of over 92,000 citations and abstracts. Covers a seven year period. Produced by CAB International. Quarterly updates. IBM PCs and compatibles require at least 640k of RAM, DOS 3.1 or later, one floppy disk drive - hard disk recommended, one empty expansion slot, IBM compatible CD - ROM drive.
Agriculture; Literature and Drama; Sociology
Dist - BEP

Polyelectrolytes - examples - titration curves - electrophoresis 38 MIN
U-matic / VHS
Colloids and surface chemistry - lyophilic colloids series
B&W
Science - Physical
Dist - MIOT Prod - MIOT

Polyelectrolytes - Viscosity - Light scattering - osmotic pressure - sedimentation 49 MIN
U-matic / VHS
Colloids and surface chemistry - lyophilic colloids series
B&W
Science - Physical
Dist - MIOT Prod - MIOT

Polyelectrolytes - viscosity - light scattering - osmotic pressure - sedimentation 49 MIN
VHS / U-matic
Colloid and Surface Chemistry - Lyophilic Colloids Series
Color
Science; Science - Physical
Dist - KALMIA Prod - KALMIA

Polyester Fiberglass Fracture Repair 28 MIN
BETA / VHS / 16mm
Color (A PRO)
$106.00 purchase _ #KTI32
Shows damage preparation and complete repair on a small fracture in a Corvette door to illustrate polyester fiberglass fracture repair techniques.
Industrial and Technical Education
Dist - RMIBHF Prod - RMIBHF

Polyester Yarn 15 MIN
VHS / U-matic
Explorers Unlimited Series
Color (P I)
Visits an American Cyanamid plant to learn how polyester yarn is made.
Home Economics; Social Science
Dist - AITECH Prod - WVIZTV 1971

Polyethylene 20 MIN
U-matic / VHS
Chemistry in Action Series
Color (C)
$249.00, $149.00 purchase _ #AD - 1112
Demonstrates the polymerization of ethylene at different pressures and in the presence of different catalysts, depending on the intended end use of the polyethylene.
Industrial and Technical Education; Science - Physical
Dist - FOTH Prod - FOTH

Polygamy 20 MIN
U-matic / VHS
Color
$335.00 purchase
From the ABC TV program, Nightline.
Sociology
Dist - ABCLR Prod - ABCLR 1984

Polygons and angles 30 MIN
16mm
Mathematics for elementary school teachers series
Color (T)
Describes the geometric elements of angles and polygons. To be used following Points, Lines And Planes.
Mathematics
Dist - MLA Prod - SMSG 1963

The Polygraph - Demonstration and Discussion 43 MIN
U-matic / VHS
Scientific Evidence - the Polygraph Series
Color (PRO)
LC 80-707190
Explains the polygraph and how it works. Discusses the theory behind its development, its use in various tests, and how the test results are interpreted.
Civics and Political Systems
Dist - ABACPE Prod - ABACPE 1977

The Polygraph - Useful Tool or Dangerous Weapon 58 MIN
VHS / U-matic
Scientific Evidence - the Polygraph Series
Color (PRO)
LC 80-707191
Presents a panel discussion on the legal and scientific issues involved in using the polygraph. Covers the scientific reliability of the polygraph, competency of polygraph examiners, admitting polygraph results in court, and other related topics.
Civics and Political Systems
Dist - ABACPE Prod - ABACPE 1977

Polymer properties - meeting high technology challenges - Pt I 180 MIN
VHS
Color (C PRO)
$400.00 purchase _ #V - 4400 - 16991
Introduces current applications of elastomeric, radiation - sensitive and nonlinear optical qualities of polymers in high technology, including the ability to record or transmit information. James E Mark, Paras W Prasad and Jean M Frechet instruct. Includes three videos and a course study guide.
Industrial and Technical Education; Science - Physical
Dist - AMCHEM **Prod** - AMCHEM 1989

Polymer properties - meeting high technology challenges - Pt II 180 MIN
VHS
Color (C PRO)
$400.00 purchase _ #V - 4400 - 16991
Shows how to use structure - property relationships in polymers to develop materials with specific mechanical properties and how to develop and test new polymer systems. Looks at how to process conductive polymers and how organic polymers can be rendered conductive; why polymer composites are more than simple technology and how filled polymer composites could replace fiber - reinforced composites; and how to obtain desirable mechanical properties from heterophase polymer systems. Dale J Meier, Gary E Wnek and Paul D Calvert instruct. Includes two videotapes and study guide.
Industrial and Technical Education; Science - Physical
Dist - AMCHEM **Prod** - AMCHEM 1990

Polymer Synthesis - the Importance of Polymers - their Specific Role 55 MIN
U-matic / VHS
Colloids and Surface Chemistry - Lyophilic Colloids Series
B&W
Science - Physical
Dist - MIOT **Prod** - MIOT

Polymer Synthesis, the Role and Importance of Polymers 55 MIN
VHS / U-matic
Colloid and Surface Chemistry - Lyophilic Colloids Series
Color
Science; Science - Physical
Dist - KALMIA **Prod** - KALMIA

Polymer test technician 5 MIN
VHS / 16mm
Good works 2 series
Color (H VOC)
Presents the occupation of a polymer test technician. Gives a profile of a young person who is either undergoing an apprenticeship or has recently completed training in this field. Takes the viewer on a tour of this person's workplace and explains the practical skills and training offered by employers and schools. Gives a better understanding of the demand for skilled workers today and the potential for personal growth.
Education; Guidance and Counseling; Industrial and Technical Education
Dist - RMIBHF **Prod** - RMIBHF
TVOTAR

Polymers 23 MIN
U-matic
Chemistry 102 - Chemistry for Engineers - Series
Color (C)
Cites unique properties of polymers with specific types of technological progress to which they contribute.
Industrial and Technical Education; Science - Physical
Dist - UILL **Prod** - UILL 1984

Polymyositis and Related Disorders 50 MIN
U-matic
Intensive Course in Neuromuscular Diseases Series
Color (PRO)
LC 76-706075
Reviews Dr Darryl C Devino's discussion on polymyositis and related disorders.
Health and Safety; Science - Natural
Dist - USNAC **Prod** - NINDIS 1974

Polyneuropathies and Nerve Conduction Studies in Neuromuscular Diseases 42 MIN
U-matic
Intensive Course in Neuromuscular Diseases Series
Color (PRO)
LC 76-706076
Presents Dr Peter J Dyck lecturing on polyneuropathies and nerve conduction studies in neuromuscular diseases.
Health and Safety; Science - Natural
Dist - USNAC **Prod** - NINDIS 1974

Polynomial and rational inequalities 30 MIN
VHS
Mathematics series
Color (J)
LC 90713155
Describes polynomial and rational inequalities. The 74th of 157 installments of the Mathematics Series.
Mathematics
Dist - GPN

Polynomial and rational inequalities 30 MIN
VHS
College algebra series
Color (C)
$125.00 purchase _ #4012
Explains polynomial and rational inequalities. Part of a 31 - part series on college algebra.
Mathematics
Dist - LANDMK **Prod** - LANDMK

Polynomial Functions 30 MIN
VHS
Mathematics Series
Color (J)
LC 90713155
Explains polynomial functions. The 83rd of 157 installments of the Mathematics Series.
Mathematics
Dist - GPN

Polynomial functions 30 MIN
VHS
College algebra series
Color (C)
$125.00 purchase _ #4021
Explains polynomial functions. Part of a 31 - part series on college algebra.
Mathematics
Dist - LANDMK **Prod** - LANDMK

Polynomials 15 MIN
U-matic
Graphing mathematical concepts series
(H C A)
Uses computer generated graphics to show the relationships bewtwen physical objects and mathematical concepts, equations and their graphs. Relates theoretical concepts to things in the real world.
Computer Science; Mathematics
Dist - ACCESS **Prod** - ACCESS 1986

Polynomials and equations 15 MIN
VHS
Power of algebra series
Color (J)
LC 90712872
Uses computer animation and interviews with professionals who use algebra to explain polynomials and equations. The sixth of 10 installments of The Power Of Algebra Series.
Mathematics
Dist - GPN

Polypharmacy in the elderly 30 MIN
VHS
Color (PRO C)
$285.00 purchase, $70.00 rental _ #6525
Examines age - related changes and risk factors that affect medications and influences medication - taking behaviors of older adults. Discusses age - related changes such as changes in body composition; cardiac output; renal functions and delayed gastric emptying. Examines risk factors such as lack of information, functional impairements and disease - related factors affecting vision and memory, and interactions with other drugs. Explains the need to take an accurate and complete medication history and the importance of developing an appropriate medication management system.
Health and Safety
Dist - AJN **Prod** - HESCTV

Polyphemus 6 MIN
16mm
Color (G)
$10.00 rental
Captures a camera engaging a mirror that reflects it. Creates a film that becomes a meditation on its own substance.
Fine Arts
Dist - CANCIN **Prod** - OSBONS 1974

Polyps of colon and rectum 29 MIN
16mm
Color (PRO)
Discusses the incidence and transproctoscopic management of polyps in the rectum and lower sigmoid. Demonstrates the surgical technique of transabdominal management of patients with familial polyposis, adenomas, adenovillous and villous tumors.
Health and Safety; Science - Natural
Dist - ACY **Prod** - ACYDGD 1969

Polyps of the large intestine 18 MIN
16mm
Color (PRO)
Shows four cases, including solitary benign adenomatous polyp, familial polyposis, multiple polyps with double primary carcinoma and inflammatory polyposis due to ulcerative colitis.
Health and Safety; Science - Natural
Dist - ACY **Prod** - ACYDGD 1951

The Polyptych of San Francesco at Sansepolcro 30 MIN
VHS
Palette series
Color (G C)
$70.00 purchase, $12.50, rental _ #36404
Reveals that in 1444, Sassetta completed a double - sided altar piece of wood as commissioned by an Italian church, with one side addressed to the congregation and the other to the monks. Discloses that today, 26 fragments of this narrative - art masterpiece are dispersed through ten museums worldwide and may never be reassembled. Part of a 13 - part series which examines great paintings by moving into their creative spaces and spending time with the characters and their surroundings. Uses special video effects to investigate artistic enigmas and studies material, technique, style and significance. Narrated by Marcel Cuvelier, directed by Alain Jaubert.
Fine Arts
Dist - PSU **Prod** - LOUVRE 1992

Polysulfide Base Industrial Sealants 14 MIN
16mm
Color
Describes industrial use of Thiokol Polysulfides for sealing trailers, buildings, aircraft and tanks.
Business and Economics; Industrial and Technical Education
Dist - THIOKL **Prod** - THIOKL 1963

Polysulfide for Industry 18 MIN
16mm
Color
Shows the properties of Thiokol Polysulfide Liquid Polymer and uses of compounds based on this synthetic rubber, including sealants for windows, buildings, tanks, aircraft and truck trailers.
Business and Economics; Industrial and Technical Education
Dist - THIOKL **Prod** - THIOKL 1961

Polytome pantopaque study 13 MIN
16mm
Color (PRO)
LC 74-705643
Describes the indications of acoustic neuroma and the technique for performing the polytome pantopaque study of the posterior fossa in patients suspected of having this condition.
Health and Safety; Science - Natural
Dist - EAR **Prod** - EAR

Polytome pantopaque study 20 MIN
16mm / U-matic / VHS
Color (PRO)
Demonstrates the use of the pantopaque dye solution to outline tumors hidden within the internal auditory canal by the temporal bone by way of polytome x - ray.
Health and Safety; Science - Natural
Dist - HOUSEI **Prod** - HOUSEI

Polytrauma 26 MIN
16mm / VHS
Color (H C A)
$165.00 purchase
Dramatizes a town's procedures for emergency response to a single - victim car crash. Introduces high school and general audiences to a range of health care careers.
Guidance and Counseling; Health and Safety
Dist - FANPRO **Prod** - FANPRO 1989

Pomeroy Takes a Sex History 35 MIN
U-matic / VHS
Color (C A)
Demonstrates the sex history - taking procedure integral to therapy and research. Demonstrates the importance of ordering questions properly.
Health and Safety; Psychology
Dist - MMRC **Prod** - NATSF

The Pommel horse
VHS
N C A A instructional video series
Color (H C A)
$39.95 purchase _ #KAR2602V
Presents the second of a four - part series on gymnastics. Focuses on the pommel horse.
Physical Education and Recreation
Dist - CAMV **Prod** - NCAAF

Pomo basketweavers - a tribute to three elders 77 MIN
VHS
Pomo basketweavers - a tribute to three elders series
Color (G)
$112.50 purchase
Features a three - part series on the history of the Pomo nation of northern California. Looks at their basket weaving, culture and history. Includes Program 1 with Laura Somersal; Program 2 with Elsie Allen; and Program 3 with Mabel McKay. See individual titles for descriptions. Produced by Creative Light Productions.
Fine Arts; Social Science
Dist - NAMPBC

Pomo basketweavers - a tribute to three elders series
Pomo basketweavers - a tribute to three elders 77 MIN
Program 1 - Laura Somersal 29 MIN
Program 3 - Mabel McKay 29 MIN
Program 2 - Elsie Allen 29 MIN
Dist - NAMPBC

Pomo shaman 20 MIN
VHS / 16mm
B&W (C G)
$410.00, $195.00 purchase, $40.00 rental _ #6464, #37439
Records the second and final night of a shamanistic curing ceremony among the Kashia group of Southwestern Pomo Indians. Reveals that the Indian 'sucking doctor' is a prophet of the Bole Maru religion and the spiritual head of the community.
Health and Safety; Religion and Philosophy; Social Science
Dist - UCEMC **Prod** - HEICK 1964

Pompeii 3 MIN
16mm
Of all Things Series
Color (P I)
Discusses the city of Pompeii in Italy.
Geography - World
Dist - AVED **Prod** - BAILYL

Pompeii, AD 79 23 MIN
U-matic / VHS / 16mm
Color
Looks at the ancient city of Pompeii, which was buried by the volcanic eruption of Mt Vesuvius on August 24, AD 79. Shows how the remains of this age - old civilization create a bridge from past to present and points out that people, the heart of any civilization, remain much the same over the years.
History - World
Dist - CNEMAG **Prod** - DOCUA

Pompeii and Vesuvius 11 MIN
U-matic / VHS / 16mm
Color (I J H)
Pictures an actual eruption of Mt Vesuvius and the ruins of the city of Pompeii destroyed in 79 A D. Shows life in present - day Naples.
Geography - World; History - World; Social Science
Dist - EBEC **Prod** - EBEC 1951

Pompeii - city of painting (200 BC - 79 AD) 11 MIN
16mm
Color
Shows how the fact that the prosperous Roman city of Pompeii was buried in the volcanic lava of Vesuvius was their tragedy but our good fortune, for we are left with a perfect record of the life and art of their time dating from 200 BC to 79 A D.
Fine Arts; History - World
Dist - ROLAND **Prod** - ROLAND

Pompeii - daily life of the ancient Romans 45 MIN
U-matic / VHS
Color (C)
$279.00, $179.00 purchase _ #AD - 2094
Explains the history of Pompeii and its relationship to Rome. Examines its customs, lifestyles, moral and religious values and the volcanic cataclysm that buried the city and suffocated its entire population.
History - World; Sociology
Dist - FOTH **Prod** - FOTH

Pompeii - frozen in fire 29 MIN
VHS / 16mm
Color (G)
$55.00 rental _ #PFIF - 000
Tours the Pompeii AD 79 exhibition, which displays relics, jewelry, silverware, sculpture, mosaics, tools and simple pottery. Includes information about the attitudes of Pompeii's citizens toward topics such as religion and sex.
History - World
Dist - PBS **Prod** - WGBHTV

Pompeii - once there was a city 25 MIN
16mm / U-matic / VHS
Color (J H C A) (SPANISH)
LC 73-708188;
Juxtaposes life in ancient Pompeii with the quality of life in contemporary America. Poses the timeless question of whether man has learned anything from the past.
Geography - World; History - World
Dist - LCOA **Prod** - LCOA 1970

The Ponce Project - Petrochemicals in Puerto Rico 25 MIN
16mm
Color
LC 73-700611
Shows the problems encountered by Bechtel Corporation in constructing a petrochemical complex in Puerto Rico and the management and engineering techniques used in overcoming these problems.
Business and Economics; Geography - World; Industrial and Technical Education; Social Science
Dist - BECHTL **Prod** - BECHTL 1972

The Pond 20 MIN
16mm / U-matic / VHS
Living Science Series
Color (J H)
LC FIA65-268
Studies members of a pond community as they affect other members. Observes life forms above and below the surface of the water.
Science - Natural
Dist - IFB **Prod** - IFB 1961

The Pond 15 MIN
VHS / U-matic
Up close and natural series
Color (P I)
$125.00 purchase
Documents the changes that environment and animal undergo in the spring season.
Science - Natural
Dist - AITECH **Prod** - NHPTV 1986

The Pond - a First Film 11 MIN
U-matic / VHS / 16mm
Color (P I)
LC 72-703177
Examines the community of living things that grows in a pond. Shows that the community changes as the pool changes with the seasons. Points out that over a long period of time, the pool takes on a different form, and life in the pool community is altered to fit the new conditions.
Science - Natural
Dist - PHENIX **Prod** - PHENIX 1972

Pond and waterfall 15 MIN
16mm
Color (G)
$30.00 rental
Utilizes the camera like an amphibian that sees on two different levels during a journey from a pond's calm underwater to a turbelent ocean. Establishes a sense of intimacy and connection to a natural ecosystem.
Fine Arts; Geography - World
Dist - CANCIN **Prod** - BARHAM 1982

Pond Animals 11 MIN
U-matic / VHS / 16mm
Color (P I J H)
Demonstrates methods of collecting pond animals and analyzes the pond animals found in an ordinary pond on the outskirts of London.
Science - Natural
Dist - VIEWTH **Prod** - GATEEF

Pond life - a place to live series 44 MIN
VHS
Pond life - a place to live series
Color (I J H)
$307.00 purchase _ #CG - 865 - VS
Presents a three - part series which looks at life in and around a typical pond in intimate detail. Includes the titles Snails and Scorpions, A Tiger in the Pond and Wings Over the Pond.
Science - Natural
Dist - HRMC **Prod** - HRMC

Pond - Life Food Web 10 MIN
U-matic / VHS / 16mm
Bio - Science Series
Color (H C A)
Examines the microscopic world of a pond, identifying its inhabitants and observing some of the ways in which they relate to one another. Shows several food chains that are part of a pond's intricate food web, beginning with the countless tiny organisms that form the first link, absorbing the sun's energy and using it to produce plant tissue. Shows that the concept of a food web describes conditions in the pond better than that of a food chain, since numerous food chains exist and overlap.
Science - Natural
Dist - NGS **Prod** - NGS 1976

Pond succession - a circle of life 17 MIN
U-matic / VHS
Natural science specials series
Color (I)
Traces the history of a pond, from the creation of a basin to its disappearance as sediment. Explains that this process causes the pond to become more and more shallow. Module blue of the series.
Science - Natural
Dist - AITECH **Prod** - COPFC 1973

Pond water - Pt 1 20 MIN
16mm
Elementary science study series
Color (T)
LC 74-702016
Shows a sixth grade class on Long Island, New York, on a field trip to a nearby pond. Shows the children's study, experimentation, classification and discussion of the pond life they collect.
Science; Science - Natural
Dist - EDC **Prod** - EDC 1971

Pond water - Pt 2 19 MIN
16mm
Elementary science study series
Color (T)
LC 74-702016
Shows a sixth grade class on Long Island, New York, on a field trip to a nearby pond. Shows the children's study, experimentation, classification and discussion of the pond life they collect.
Science; Science - Natural
Dist - EDC **Prod** - EDC 1971

Pondicherry Ashram 8 MIN
16mm
B&W (I)
Provides glimpses of the Aurobindo Ashram at Pondicherry, where the one - time revolutionary Aurobindo set up an Ashram and became a 20th century saint and yogi. Discusses various activities of institutions like the Aurobindo International Centre of Education.
Biography; History - World; Religion and Philosophy
Dist - NEDINF **Prod** - INDIA

Pong San T'al Chum 32 MIN
U-matic / VHS
Color
Shows performances of traditional masked drama of Northern Korea.
Fine Arts; Geography - World
Dist - UWASHP **Prod** - UWASHP

Pong San T'al Chum - Northern Korean Masked Drama 32 MIN
16mm
Ethnic Music and Dance Series
Color (I)
LC 72-700243
Describes T'al Chum, a form of masked drama originating around Ping San in North Korea. Explains that the plays are performed outdoors, without a stage, and tells that they consist of short satires on the monks or the ruling class.
Geography - World; Literature and Drama
Dist - UWASHP **Prod** - UWASH 1971

Ponies 15 MIN
16mm / U-matic / VHS
Color (I J A)
LC 73-700508
Shows, without narration, the birth of a foal, ponies frolicking, horses eating, drinking and sleeping and a pony being groomed and winning a ribbon in the show ring.
Agriculture; Science - Natural
Dist - AIMS **Prod** - MORLAT 1972

Ponies of Miklaengi 25 MIN
U-matic / VHS / 16mm
Color; Captioned (K P I)
LC 79-700497
Tells the story of two children in Iceland who, while searching for lost sheep, wander far from home with their horses and witness the birth of a foal during an earthquake. Based on the book Ponies Of Mykillengi by John lonzo Anderson.
Fine Arts; Literature and Drama
Dist - PHENIX **Prod** - EVRGRN 1979
UILL

The Pons 15 MIN
VHS / U-matic
Neurobiology series
Color (PRO)
Identifies the macroscopic structures of the pons using brain specimens and diagrams. Discusses briefly its physiology and pathology.
Health and Safety; Science - Natural
Dist - HSCIC **Prod** - HSCIC

Pontiac pours it on 28 MIN
16mm
Color (J)
Presents a tour of an auto assembly plant. Shows all phases of auto manufacture, from casting the engine block to final assembly of the completed car along with the many inspections and tests made to assure quality and reliability.
Business and Economics; Industrial and Technical Education
Dist - GM **Prod** - GM 1971

Pony 24 MIN
16mm
Color (C)
$900.00
Experimental film by James Herbert.
Fine Arts
Dist - AFA **Prod** - AFA 1981

The Pony 46 MIN
VHS / U-matic / Cassette
Florida through the decades as seen by High - Sheriff Jim Turner 'series
Color; PAL (G)
$79.95, $24.95, $9.95 purchase _ #1090
Portrays the life of a former High - Sheriff of Levy County, Florida, Jim Turner. Focuses on Turner's wife, Martha, who loses her heart to a fatherless boy she cares for. When the boy's mother remarries and takes the boy, Martha turns to the bottle. Part nine of an eleven - part historical docudrama.
Civics and Political Systems; Fine Arts; Health and Safety; History - United States; Psychology; Sociology
Dist - NORDS **Prod** - NORDS 1991

The Pony Express 15 MIN
U-matic / VHS / 16mm
Color (I J H)
LC 78-700917
Deals with the history of the Pony Express and conditions in the United States which demanded fast, efficient mail service to the West.
History - United States; Social Science
Dist - PHENIX **Prod** - CALVIN 1977

The Pony express 16 MIN
VHS
Color (I J)
$89.00 purchase _ #RB840
Reveals that the pony express was in existence for only 19 months and that it led to the bankruptcy of the three men who started it. Recalls that it provided a vital link between California and the northern states at the onset of the Civil War.
History - United States; Social Science
Dist - REVID **Prod** - REVID

Pony Penning on Chincoteague 24 MIN
16mm
Color; B&W (I)
Shows a community custom dating from Colonial times - the round - up, penning and sale of the Chincoteague wild ponies.
Geography - United States; Social Science
Dist - VADE **Prod** - VADE 1955

The Pony, the table and the stick 8 MIN
VHS / U-matic
Timeless tales series
Color (P I)
$110.00, $160.00 purchase, $60.00 rental
Tells the story of a poor unhappy lad who leaves home and works hard, becoming the recipient of a magic pony, table and stick. Follows his adventures as he is tricked out of his gifts by greedy people but perseveres and reclaims them.
Literature and Drama
Dist - NDIM **Prod** - TIMTAL 1993

Pooh's Great School Bus Adventure 14 MIN
16mm
Color (K P I)
Clarifies safety rules in the three important areas of waiting for the bus, loading and riding the bus, and unloading.
Health and Safety
Dist - CORF **Prod** - DISNEY 1986

Pool 26 MIN
16mm
Color (I)
LC 74-701558
Presents a series of 12 motion pictures made by children ages seven to 16, using animation and live action techniques.
Fine Arts
Dist - CELLAR **Prod** - CELLAR 1968

Pool of thanatos 17 MIN
16mm
Color (G)
$34.00 rental
Exemplifies thanatos or death personified as a philosophical notion. Dramatizes a girl who watches as her sister is killed by a train. She dreams the journey of her sister's soul in a surreal mosaic of images. The film comprises eight parts - Querents Card, Ring of Changes, Tower of Secrets, Deep Time, Destiny of Departure, Fisherman's Ferry, Four Pillars and Pool of Thanatos. Produced by Peter McCandless.
Fine Arts; Sociology
Dist - CANCIN

Pool school
VHS
Color (G)
$29.95 purchase _ #RV001
Features pool champions Jim Rempe and Loree Jon Jones showing the fundamentals of pool.
Physical Education and Recreation
Dist - SIV

Pool school special package
VHS
Color (G)
$85.35 _ #RV100
Offers all three videos, Pool School, Power Pool and Trick Shots, at a special price.
Physical Education and Recreation
Dist - SIV

Pools 8 MIN
16mm
B&W; Color (G)
$30.00 rental
Features spectacular swimming pools at W R Hearst's San Simeon designed by architect Julia Morgan. Uses an underwater camera in these pools which are normally off - limits to all visitors. Made with Barbara Klutinis.
Fine Arts; Geography - United States
Dist - CANCIN **Prod** - BARHAM 1981

Poon - Tang Trilogy 8 MIN
16mm
B&W (C)
Presents a dadaistic new American film exercise.
Fine Arts
Dist - CFS **Prod** - CFS 1967

Poor dear series
Investigates the motives and methods of the charity industry. Explores the attitudes of disabled people to charities and the way the organizations influence public beliefs and feelings about disability. Focuses on advertising, the traditional role of the charity industry, and the search for cures for disabilities. Three videos that can be purchased separately constitute this series.
Cure 30 MIN
Images 30 MIN
Kindness of strangers 30 MIN
Dist - BBCENE

The Poor Glassblower 24 MIN
U-matic / VHS / 16mm
Color (K P)
LC 79-701276
Tells a story about a poor man who finds a genie who grants him his every wish. Shows how he becomes greedy and asks for power over nature itself. Based on the story The Fisherman And His Wife by the Brothers Grimm.
Fine Arts; Literature and Drama
Dist - CAROUF **Prod** - LONNEM 1979

Poor little rich man and The Greatest - Volume 5 45 MIN
VHS
Flying house series
Color (K P I R)
$11.99 purchase _ #35 - 8954 - 979
Uses an animated format to present events from the New Testament era, as three children, a professor and a robot travel in the 'flying house' back to that time. Poor Little Rich Man tells the story of the prodigal son, while The Greatest profiles two of Jesus' disciples, James and John.
Literature and Drama; Religion and Phlosophy
Dist - APH **Prod** - TYHP

Poor man, rich man 75 MIN
VHS
Color (G A R)
$10.00 rental _ #36 - 846 - 8516
Features Michael Orphelin in a portrayal of St Francis of Assisi. Reviews the life of St Francis, emphasizing how he gave up his privileged life to serve God.
Religion and Philosophy
Dist - APH **Prod** - VISVID

The Poor pay more 60 MIN
16mm
NET journal series
B&W (H C A)
LC FIA67-5070
Examines the special hardships of the poor in consumer purchasing. Explores pricing practices of supermarket chains, techniques of food freezer salesmen and methods of furniture and appliance stores and finance companies. Presents officials from various private and governmental programs outlining problems and show how they are being confronted.
Business and Economics; History - United States; Psychology; Sociology
Dist - IU **Prod** - NET 1967

The Poor pay more - Pt 1 30 MIN
16mm
NET journal series
B&W (H C A)
LC FIA67-5070
Examines the special hardships of the poor in consumer purchasing. Explores pricing practices of supermarket chains, techniques of freezer salesman, and methods of furniture and appliance stores and finance companies. Presents officials from various private and governmental programs outlining these problems.
Business and Economics; Psychology; Sociology
Dist - IU **Prod** - NET 1967

The Poor pay more - Pt 2 30 MIN
16mm
NET journal series
B&W (H C A)
LC FIA67-5070
Examines the special hardships of the poor in consumer purchasing. Explores pricing practices of supermarket chains, techniques of freezer salesman, and methods of furniture and appliance stores and finance companies. Presents officials from various private and governmental programs outlining these problems.
Business and Economics; Psychology; Sociology
Dist - IU **Prod** - NET 1967

The Poor princess 8 MIN
VHS / U-matic
Timeless tales series
Color (P I)
$110.00, $160.00 purchase, $60.00 rental
Tells the story of a beautiful princess who takes only a ballgown with her when she is cast out by her father. Continues with her working as a kitchen servent in a grand castle, secretly donning the gown and dancing with the King, who falls in love with her even after he learns her identity.
Literature and Drama
Dist - NDIM **Prod** - TIMTAL 1993

Pooter Safari 15 MIN
U-matic
Know Your World Series
(I J)
Studies small animal life with the construction of an aspirator.
Science
Dist - ACCESS **Prod** - ACCESS 1981

Pop 15 MIN
VHS
Art history - century of modern art series
Color (I)
$125.00 purchase
Discusses American Pop Artists Roy Lichtenstein, Andy Warhol, James Rosenquist, Wayne Thiebaud, Claes Oldenburg and Robert Indiana. Considers selected works, comments on the artists' personal histories and points out their distinctive styles and subjects.
Fine Arts
Dist - AITECH **Prod** - WDCNTV 1988

Pop Art 14 MIN
U-matic / VHS
Young at Art Series
Color (P I)
Discusses pop art.
Fine Arts
Dist - AITECH **Prod** - WSKJTV 1980

Pop Art 29 MIN
U-matic
Artist at Work Series
Color
Discusses effects of advertising and packaging materials on modern day art.
Fine Arts
Dist - UMITV **Prod** - UMITV 1973

Pop Goes the Revolution 25 MIN
BETA / 16mm / VHS
Color
LC 77-702519
Presents correspondent Michael Maclear interviewing pop star Dean Reed, who discusses his music and politics.
Civics and Political Systems; Fine Arts
Dist - CTV **Prod** - CTV 1976

Pop - pop video - general hospital, olympic women speed skating 6 MIN
VHS / U-matic
Color
Juxtaposes the cross - over in Olympic Women Speed Skating and 'whites' in General Hospital. Combines exertion and frustration.
Fine Arts
Dist - KITCHN **Prod** - KITCHN

Pop - Pop Video - Kojak, Wang 4 MIN
U-matic / VHS
Color
Brings the violence of corporate America to life with shots from the television show Kojak and from the television commercial about the Wang Corporation.
Fine Arts
Dist - KITCHN **Prod** - KITCHN

Pop show 8 MIN
16mm
Color (J)
Presents a fast - paced barrage of animated comic strips, campy film clips, pop art constructions and live action sequences letting us know what's 'in' and what's 'out.'
Literature and Drama
Dist - VIEWFI **Prod** - PFP

Popcorn 20 MIN
U-matic / VHS
$335.00 purchase
Fine Arts; Sociology
Dist - ABCLR **Prod** - ABCLR 1983

Popcorn lady 11 MIN
16mm / U-matic / VHS
Color (I)
LC 73-701210
Visits a small town in upstate New York to which change has come slowly. Portrays one of the town's most famous residents, the popcorn lady and shows her steam popcorn machine of 1925 vintage.
Geography - United States; Sociology
Dist - LUF **Prod** - SCHLAT 1973

Popcorn obstacles 15 MIN
16mm
Color (A)
$20.00 rental
Depicts a catastrophe at a movie theatre, where everything that can go wrong does. Shows the projectionist searching for loose ends while treating the crowd to a horror film, Thanksgiving II, a porno film titled Volley For Serve, and other accidental movies.
Fine Arts; Literature and Drama
Dist - CANCIN **Prod** - MICHAL 1984

Popcorn trailers 6 MIN
16mm
B&W (G)
$10.00 rental
Depicts trailers designed to increase popcorn consumption in repertory cinemas. Includes subjects such as Cave Men, Gangsters, A Red Neck Bar, Philip Marlowe and the Popcorn Eating Championship of the World. A Mike Quinn production.
Fine Arts
Dist - CANCIN

The Pope and his vatican 48 MIN
VHS / U-matic
Color
$455.00 purchase
From an ABC TV special.
Religion and Philosophy
Dist - ABCLR **Prod** - ABCLR 1983

The Pope from Afar 45 MIN
VHS / BETA
Color
Covers the life of Pope John Paul II and his initial impact on the Catholic Church.
Biography; Religion and Philosophy
Dist - DSP **Prod** - DSP

Pope Gregory 30 MIN
VHS
Saints and legions series
Color (H)
$69.95 purchase
Profiles Pope Gregory. Part 17 of a twenty - six part series which introduces personalities, movements and events in ancient history responsible for the beginnings of Western Civilization.
Biography; Civics and Political Systems; History - World; Religion and Philosophy
Dist - SCETV **Prod** - SCETV 1982

The Pope in America - with Liberty and Justice for all 24 MIN
16mm / U-matic / VHS
Color
LC 80-701782
Records the week Pope Paul II visited the United States in 1979, stressing the central message of justice, world peace and the common goals of all peoples which this spiritual leader brought to America.
History - United States; Religion and Philosophy
Dist - CORF **Prod** - ABCVID 1980

Pope John Paul II - a Pilgrimage of Faith, Hope, and Love
Celebration of life in Jesus Christ (B C Place Stadium) 60 MIN
Triumph of the Cross (Martyr's Shrine, Midland) 60 MIN
Yes to life - Montreal stadium youth rally 92 MIN
Dist - CANBC

Pope John Paul II at the United Nations 28 MIN
Videoreel / VHS
International byline series
Color
Interviews Mr Robert Muller, co - ordinator of the Pope's visit to the United Nations. Includes film clips of the Pope's address to the General Assembly, his walk in the U N Gardens and his visit to the office of Secretary - General Kurt Waldheim.
Civics and Political Systems; Geography - World; Religion and Philosophy
Dist - PERRYM **Prod** - PERRYM

Pope John Paul II - Pilgrim to Lourdes 27 MIN
BETA / VHS
Color
Follows Pope John Paul II on a visit to Lourdes.
Biography; Religion and Philosophy
Dist - DSP **Prod** - VATTV

Pope John Paul II
Slovak Byzantine Cathedral - Unionville Mass 58 MIN
Dist - CANBC

Pope John Paul's third pilgimage to his homeland - III Pielgrzymka Jana Pawla II do ojczyzny 120 MIN
VHS
Color (G A) (POLISH)
$24.95 purchase _ #V124
Documents the third visit of Pope John Paul II to Poland in June 1987.
Fine Arts; History - World; Religion and Philosophy
Dist - POLART

Pope John XXIII, 1881 - 1963 16 MIN
16mm
B&W
LC FI67-1005
Highlights the life of Pope John XXIII. Includes his election, the meeting of the Vatican Ecumenical Council in 1962 and his audiences with world leaders.
Biography; Geography - United States; Religion and Philosophy
Dist - TWCF **Prod** - MOVIET 1963

Pope John XXIII - the Good Shepherd 27 MIN
BETA / VHS
Color
Covers the life of Pope John XXIII who convoked the Second Vatican Council.
Biography; Religion and Philosophy
Dist - DSP **Prod** - DSP

Pope - new cardinals 8 MIN
16mm
Spanish newsreel series
B&W (SPANISH)
Shows Pope John XII creating ten new cardinals, De Gaulle appealing for support of his France - Algerian truce, Buddhist fire rites in Northern Japan and the Israeli - Syrian border dispute. Volume 45, number 57 in the series.
History - World
Dist - TWCF **Prod** - TWCF

The Pope - Pilgrim of Peace 38 MIN
16mm / U-matic / VHS
Color
Questions whether religion and revolution can co - exist by reviewing Pope John Paul II's controversial visit to Nicaragua in 1983. Interviews Ernesto Cardenal, a priest and Minister of Culture of the Sandinista government and Miguel Concha, a Mexican theologian and member of the Dominican order.
History - World; Religion and Philosophy
Dist - ICARUS **Prod** - REITIR 1983

Pope Pius XII 26 MIN
16mm
History makers of the 20th century series
B&W (J)
LC FIA66-1356
Presents the life story and deeds of Pope Pius XII.
Biography; Religion and Philosophy
Dist - SF **Prod** - WOLPER 1965

The Popes and their art - the Vatican collections 60 MIN
VHS
Color (G J H C)
$29.95 purchase _ #MHV02V
Journeys through the Vatican Collections with actor James Mason. Views a collection centuries in the making, a look through art history.
Fine Arts
Dist - CAMV

The Popes and their Art - the Vatican Collections 52 MIN
U-matic / VHS / 16mm
Color (J)
Views a great portion of the Vatican art collection which includes works by such masters as Michelangelo, da Vinci, Raphael, Bernini and Caravaggio. Shows the work necessary to maintain it against the effects of modern pollution and age.
Fine Arts; Religion and Philosophy
Dist - FI **Prod** - NBCNEW 1983

Popliteal region and leg - unit 24 29 MIN
VHS / U-matic
Gross anatomy prosection demonstration series
Color (PRO)
Covers the popliteal fossa, the anterior and posterior compartments of the leg, including the muscles of the superficial and deep layers and the neurovascular bundles, the lateral compartment and the knee.
Health and Safety; Science - Natural
Dist - HSCIC **Prod** - HSCIC

Popol Vuh - the creation myth of the Maya 60 MIN
VHS / 16mm
Color (I J H C G) (SPANISH)
$995.00, $410.00, $295.00 purchase, $60.00 rental _ #11380, #37902, #38183
Presents an animated film using authentic imagery from ancient Maya ceramics to depict Popol Vuh, the Maya creation myth and the foundation of most Native American religious, philosophical and ethical beliefs. Introduces the Maya and relates the entire tale, beginning with the creation of the world and concluding with the victory of the Hero Twins over the evil lords of the Underworld. Includes logical stopping places at quarter - hour intervals to facilitate viewing by young students. Includes teacher's guide. Produced by Patricia Amlin and Prof James A Fox, Stanford University.
History - World; Religion and Philosophy; Social Science; Sociology
Dist - UCEMC

The Popovich Brothers of South Chicago 60 MIN
16mm
Color (H A)
$800.00 purchase, $115.00 rental
Explores the social, cultural and religious activities of the close - knit Serbian - American community in the South Side of Chicago. Focuses on 'The Popovich Brothers' who perform tamburitza music.
Fine Arts
Dist - AFA

Poppa's Legacy 3 MIN
16mm
Color
LC 78-701323
Combines live action and animation in telling the story of a father who wills his three sons a claim check. Tells how after a lengthy search the sons discover their reward from their father's estate.
Fine Arts; Sociology
Dist - RODGR **Prod** - RODGR 1978

POPS multimedia complete set - modules 1 - 4
VHS
Color (K P I J H T)
$595.00 purchase _ #PO5Z
Presents the complete four - part series on Positively Solving Problems. Includes a set of two video tapes for teacher presentation to students and two motivational audio tapes for teachers for each part as well as a manual of instructions for activities, scripts for classroom presentations, music sheets for motivational songs. Includes the issues of self - awareness, goals and expectations, enthusiasm and coping, making a difference.
Education; Health and Safety; Psychology
Dist - PCI **Prod** - PCI 1990

POPS multimedia module 4 - making a difference
VHS
Color (K P I J H T)
$150.00 purchase _ #PO4Z
Presents a set of two video tapes for teacher presentation to students and two motivational audio tapes for teachers on making a difference for students. Offers a structure for problem solving with people. Includes a manual of instructions for activities, scripts for classroom presentations, music sheets for motivational songs. Part of a four - part series on Positively Solving Problems.
Education; Health and Safety; Psychology
Dist - PCI **Prod** - PCI 1990

POPS multimedia module 1 - self - awareness
VHS
Color (K P I J H T)
$150.00 purchase _ #PO1Z
Presents a set of two video tapes for teacher presentation to students and two motivational audio tapes for teachers on the issue of self - awareness in students. Offers a structure for problem solving with people. Includes a manual of instructions for activities, scripts for classroom presentations, music sheets for motivational songs. Part of a four - part series on Positively Solving Problems.
Education; Psychology
Dist - PCI **Prod** - PCI 1990

POPS multimedia module 3 - enthusiasm and coping
VHS
Color (K P I J H T)
$150.00 purchase _ #PO3Z
Presents a set of two video tapes for teacher presentation to students and two motivational audio tapes for teachers on the issue of enthusiasm and coping skills for students. Offers a structure for problem solving with people. Includes a manual of instructions for activities, scripts for classroom presentations, music sheets for motivational songs. Part of a four - part series on Positively Solving Problems.
Education; Health and Safety; Psychology
Dist - PCI **Prod** - PCI 1990

POPS multimedia module 2 - goals and expectations
VHS
Color (K P I J H T)
$150.00 purchase _ #PO2Z
Presents a set of two video tapes for teacher presentation to students and two motivational audio tapes for teachers on the issue of goals and expectations for students. Offers a structure for problem solving with people. Includes a manual of instructions for activities, scripts for classroom presentations, music sheets for motivational songs. Part of a four - part series on Positively Solving Problems.
Education; Psychology
Dist - PCI **Prod** - PCI 1990

Popsicle 10 MIN
U-matic / VHS / 16mm
Color
LC 71-701244
Points out that motorcycling is one of the fastest growing sports in America. Includes scenes of motorcycles on racetracks, climbing hills and on pleasure outings.
Industrial and Technical Education; Social Science
Dist - AMEDFL **Prod** - GRENWL 1969

Popular Culture in Dance Series
Black Dancers and Choreography in Films 30 MIN
How Popular Dance Came to the Stage 30 MIN
World of 'Hip Hop,' the - Rapping, Break Dancing and Electric Boogie 30 MIN
Dist - ARCVID

The Popular Dickens 29 MIN
U-matic
Dickens World Series
Color
Explores the life, success and philosophy of Charles Dickens.
Literature and Drama
Dist - UMITV **Prod** - UMITV 1973

Popular massage
VHS
Color (G) (MANDARIN CHINESE)
$29.95 purchase _ #9018
Presents a Mandarin Chinese language television program produced in the People's Republic of China.
Geography - World; Health and Safety; Industrial and Technical Education; Literature and Drama; Physical Education and Recreation
Dist - CHTSUI **Prod** - CHTSUI

Science - Natural
Dist - CBSC **Prod** - BMEDIA

Population et pollution 17 MIN
U-matic / VHS / 16mm
Color (J H C) (FRENCH)
A French - language version of the motion picture Population And Pollution.
Science - Natural
Dist - IFB **Prod** - IFB 1971

Population - future quest 36 MIN
VHS
Future quest series
Color; CC (J H C)
$79.00 purchase _ #318
Promotes critical thinking about population issues. Presents the many views on population, featuring experts in ecology, economics, environmental studies and land use research. Includes a guide. Part of a ten - part series.
Science; Sociology
Dist - HAWHIL **Prod** - HAWHIL

Population Growth 30 MIN
U-matic / VHS
Living Environment Series
Color (C)
Discusses the ability of humankind to control the earth's population and to increase the earth's capacity to carry more people.
Science - Natural
Dist - DALCCD **Prod** - DALCCD

Population, Patterns and Technology 20 MIN
VHS / 16mm
You, Me and Technology Series
Color (J H A)
$150.00 purchase, $30.00 rental
Discusses how improvements in health and hygiene have lowered the death rate in the Third World and how birth control and emigration have stabilized the growth of population.
Science - Natural; Social Science; Sociology
Dist - AITECH **Prod** - NJN 1988

The Population picture 10 MIN
U-matic
Organic evolution series
Color (H C) (FRENCH)
Traces the development of various theories of evolution beginning with the Biblical account of creation and going on to discuss Darwin, Mendel and others. Ties together the microscopic and macroscopic, genetics and heredity, cell reproduction and breeding populations. Available in French. Comes with teacher's guide.
Science; Science - Natural
Dist - TVOTAR **Prod** - TVOTAR 1986

The Population problem 20 MIN
VHS
Color; PAL (H)
States that the resources of the Earth are finite and that areas of natural vegetation are essential to the climate. Reveals that the global population is growing at an ever - accelerating rate and the pressure for more land to grow food and more wood for housing and for fuel is causing climatic changes and decreasing agricultural returns. Improved hygiene and medical care are making the situation worse because the birth rate has not decreased. Urges action to reduce the birth rate and achieve a balance between human demands and the Earth's capacity to renew itself.
Science - Natural; Social Science; Sociology
Dist - VIEWTH

Population Problem Series
Brazil - the Gathering Millions 30 MIN
The European Experience 30 MIN
India - Writings on the Sand 30 MIN
Japan - Answer in the Orient 30 MIN
USA - Seeds of Change 30 MIN
Dist - IU

Population Problems Series
The Gift of Choice 30 MIN
Dist - IU

Population statistics
CD-ROM
Color (PRO)
$1,200.00 purchase _ #1583
Gives the full range of population and housing characteristics from the 1980 census for the US, including all states, metropolitan areas, counties, places of 10,000 people or more, and congressional districts. For IBM PCs and compatibles. Requires at least 640K RAM, DOS Version 3.1 or greater, one floppy disk drive - a hard drive is recommended, one empty expansion slot, and an IBM compatible CD - ROM drive.
Civics and Political Systems; Social Science
Dist - BEP

Popular songs 18 MIN
16mm
Color (G)
$35.00 rental
Explains filmmaker Barnett, 'Junkfilm assemblage with favorites from Italian opera.'
Fine Arts
Dist - CANCIN **Prod** - BARND 1979

Popularity Game 30 MIN
U-matic
Color (I J)
Shows the force of peer pressure on children.
Psychology; Sociology
Dist - TVOTAR **Prod** - TVOTAR 1986

Popularity Storage - Planning the Storage Layout 20 MIN
16mm
Color
LC 75-700874
Discusses planning the storage layout in popularity storage. Shows storage space, layout, control of space, material positioning and the design of a stock location system.
Business and Economics; Psychology
Dist - USNAC **Prod** - USN 1958

Popularity Storage - Principles of Stock Positioning 18 MIN
16mm
Color
LC 75-700572
Shows basic principles of popularity storage, including similarity, size, characteristics and the advantage of stock positioning at all levels of the supply system.
Business and Economics; Psychology
Dist - USNAC **Prod** - USN 1958

Population and Pollution 17 MIN
U-matic / VHS / 16mm
Color (J H C)
LC 75-712271
Discusses the problems of population and pollution.
Science - Natural
Dist - IFB **Prod** - IFB 1971

Population and the American future - Pt 1 30 MIN
16mm
Color (H C)
LC 73-701825
Reports the findings of the President's Commission on Population Growth and the American Future. Discusses the economic, social, political, environmental and ethical aspects of past and present population trends and future population growth in the United States. Examines the consequences of unlimited population increase on various facets of U S society and shows why the population should become stabilized.
Sociology
Dist - FFG **Prod** - FFG 1973

Population and the American future - Pt 2 30 MIN
16mm
Color (H C)
LC 73-701825
Reports the findings of the President's Commission on Population Growth and the American Future. Discusses the economic, social, political, environmental and ethical aspects of past and present population trends and future population growth in the United States. Emphasizes the need for education of the population regarding consequences of unlimited growth and stresses the ideal of family planning.
Sociology
Dist - FFG **Prod** - FFG 1973

Population Crisis - India 16 MIN
U-matic / VHS
Color (H C A)
Points out that if India is to solve her economic and social problems, the population growth must be sharply reduced. Interviews India's Health Minister.
Geography - World; Sociology
Dist - JOU **Prod** - UPI

Population ecology 19 MIN
16mm / U-matic / VHS
Biology series
Color (H) (SPANISH)
Analyzes the effects of environment as they relate to birth rates, showing the influence of natural enemies, food and other environmental factors on population. Unit one of the series focuses on ecology.
Science - Natural; Sociology
Dist - EBEC **Prod** - EBEC

Population Ecology
U-matic / 35mm strip
Color (H C)
$43.95 purchase _ #52 3411
Discusses population ecology in theory, in the lab, and in nature. Examines population density, distribution, and growth. Considers environmental factors that limit these qualities. Includes a teacher's guide.

A Population story - collision with the future 24 MIN
U-matic / VHS / 16mm
Color (J H C)
Reveals startling facts about population growth.
Sociology
Dist - EBEC **Prod** - EBEC 1984

Population - the world's concern - 12 52 MIN
VHS
EarthScope series
Color (J H C G)
$50.00 purchase
Looks at population as an environmental issue. Part 12 of a 12 - part series hosted by Robert Siegel of NPR.
Science - Natural; Sociology
Dist - GVIEW **Prod** - GVIEW 1990

Population - whose problem is it? 29 MIN
U-matic
Issue at hand series
Color
Examines birth control, economics, food production, resource consumption and attitudes of third world countries.
Sociology
Dist - UMITV **Prod** - UMITV 1976

Populations 30 MIN
U-matic
Aspects of Ecology Series
(H)
Demonstrates concepts of limiting factors, carrying capacity, growth curves and open and closed populations through wildlife and plant studies.
Science - Natural
Dist - ACCESS **Prod** - ACCESS 1984

Populations and data
VHS
Probability and statistics series
Color (H C)
$125.00 purchase _ #8001
Provides resource material about collecting population data for help in the study of probability and statistics. Presents a 60 - video series, each part 25 to 30 minutes long, that explains and reinforces concepts using definitions, theorems, examples and step - by - step solutions to tutor the student.
Mathematics
Dist - LANDMK

The Populist challenge 30 MIN
VHS
America in perspective - US history since 1877 series
Color (H C G)
$99.00 purchase _ #AIP - 6
Examines how political leaders, political parties and the political system in general responded to industrialization. Assesses the effects to the populist challenge to the established political order. Part of 26 - part series.
Civics and Political Systems; History - United States; Social Science
Dist - INSTRU **Prod** - DALCCD 1991

Por Primera Vez 10 MIN
16mm
B&W
Explains how the Cuban Film Institute sends mobile film units into the rural provinces and how villagers delight in seeing movies for the first time.
Fine Arts; Sociology
Dist - CANWRL **Prod** - CANWRL

Por que Juanito 20 MIN
16mm
Color
Presents the problem of protein hunger among children of Latin America. Designed primarily for heads of state and policy making specialists in nutrition, economics and agriculture.
Geography - World; Health and Safety; Social Science
Dist - USNAC **Prod** - USAID 1966

Por que me llama 30 MIN
VHS
Grammar music videos series
Color (G) (SPANISH)
$49.95 purchase _ #W1451
Uses comic dialogue and rhythmic music to help beginning language students practice interrogatives. Includes video, audiocassette, exercise pages and teacher's guide.
Foreign Language
Dist - GPC

Porcelain 28 MIN
Videoreel / VT2
Wheels, kilns and clay series
Color
Features Mrs Peterson describing certain ceramic processes for her classroom at the University of Southern California. Demonstrates how to work with porcelain.
Fine Arts
Dist - PBS **Prod** - USC

The Porcelain Cat
VHS / 35mm strip
Picturebook Classics on Filmstrip Series
Color (P)
$44.95 purchase
Tells of an old sorcerer who turns a porcelain cat into a real cat to catch the rats that are gnawing on his books. Part of a series.
English Language; Literature and Drama
Dist - PELLER

Porcelain - fused - to - gold crowns and bridges - Pt 2 - gingival retraction and die preparation 9 MIN
8mm cartridge / 16mm
Color
LC 75-701666; 75-700810
Shows that accurately fitting gingival margins can be achieved by carefully adhering to the principles and details of gingival retraction. Demonstrates the impression technique and die preparation.
Health and Safety; Science
Dist - USNAC **Prod** - USVA 1972

Porcelain - Fused - to - Gold Fixed Partial Denture - Esthetics Control System, Pt 2 - 8 MIN
16mm
Color
LC 75-701320
Discusses the preparation of a fixed partial denture. Describes the laboratory procedures for developing wax patterns whose dimensions and contours are controlled by preoperative stents.
Health and Safety; Science
Dist - USNAC **Prod** - USVA 1974

Porcelain - fused - to - gold fixed partial denture - esthetics control system - Pt 1 17 MIN
16mm
Color
LC 75-701319
Discusses the examination of the patient and tooth preparation. Demonstrates an extraoral method for constructing a temporary restoration that protects the involved teeth.
Health and Safety; Science
Dist - USNAC **Prod** - USVA 1974

Porcelain - fused - to - metal, vita system - Pt 1 - a single crown 17 MIN
U-matic
Color (PRO)
LC 78-706283
Demonstrates procedures for making porcelain - fused - to - metal crowns, from application and condensation to firing and cooling. Considers esthetic factors such as color, translucency and labial contour age.
Health and Safety; Science
Dist - USNAC **Prod** - USVA 1978

Porcelain - fused - to - metal, vita system - pt 2 - multiple unit restoration 17 MIN
U-matic
Color (PRO)
LC 78-706284
Demonstrates techniques of multiple - unit porcelain - veneer restoration.
Health and Safety; Science
Dist - USNAC **Prod** - USVA 1978

Porcelain jacket crown - porcelain build - up 17 MIN
16mm
Color (PRO)
LC 77-703286
Describes the proper manipulation of the materials used in building up a porcelain jacket crown.
Health and Safety; Science
Dist - USNAC **Prod** - VADTC 1977

Porcelain jacket crown - Pt 1 - the matrix 9 MIN
U-matic / VHS
Color (PRO)
LC 81-706366
Depicts the laboratory steps involved in the fabrication of a porcelain jacket crown.
Health and Safety; Science
Dist - USNAC **Prod** - VADTC 1977

Porcelain jacket crown - Pt 2 - porcelain build - up 17 MIN
VHS / U-matic
Color (PRO)
LC 81-706367
Describes the proper manipulation of the materials used in building up a porcelain jacket crown.
Health and Safety; Science
Dist - USNAC **Prod** - VADTC 1977

Porcelain jacket crown - the matrix 9 MIN
16mm
Color (PRO)
LC 77-703285
Depicts the laboratory steps involved in the fabrication of a porcelain jacket crown.
Health and Safety; Science
Dist - USNAC **Prod** - VADTC 1977

Porcelain protected surface wiring 19 MIN
16mm
Electrical work - wiring series
B&W
LC FIE52-101
Demonstrates how to make an electrical entrance to a building, install wiring and porcelain fittings, support and insulate wires and prepare and connect wires for service. Number nine in the series.
Industrial and Technical Education
Dist - USNAC **Prod** - USOE 1944

Porcupine Quill Work - Un Decours En Piquants De Porc Epic 10 MIN
16mm
Color (G) (FRENCH)
#2X84I
Discusses the almost universal use of porcupine quills for decorative art work among the Indians of North America. Presents the work of artist Bernadette Pangawish as she decorates a box in traditional geometric design.
Social Science
Dist - CDIAND **Prod** - NAIFL 1977

Porifera
VHS
Pieper - zoology prelab dissections - series
Color (J H C)
$95.00 purchase _ #CG - 966 - VS
Presents dissection instruction and an anatomy review of Porifera. Includes a brief post test to gauge student retention. Part of a 15 - part series on zoological lab dissection, including a lab safety review, produced by Bill Pieper.
Science; Science - Natural
Dist - HRMC

Pork and lamb cuts judging 26 MIN
VHS
Carcass and cuts judging series; Set A
(C A)
$79.95 _ CV103
Surveys parts of hams and loins and describes principles of judging six cut classes, and gives oral reasons for six classes as well as principles of judging questions classes. Set A of the series.
Agriculture
Dist - AAVIM **Prod** - AAVIM 1989

Pork Dishes - Roast Loin to Medallions - Lesson 19 30 MIN
VHS
International Cooking School with Chef Rene Series
Color (G)
$69.00 purchase
Presents classic methods of cooking that stress essential flavor. Introduces newer, lighter foods. Lesson 19 focuses on pork.
Fine Arts; Home Economics; Psychology; Social Science; Sociology
Dist - LUF **Prod** - LUF

Pork Retail Cuts Identification 40 MIN
VHS
Color (G)
$79.95 purchase _ #6 - 040 - 113P
Uses a pork carcass to relate major bones, muscles and wholesale cuts to retail cut identification. Identifies and explains 34 pork retail cuts. Gives accepted industry names, size, color, shape, anatomical location and recommended cooking methods for each cut.
Agriculture; Business and Economics; Social Science
Dist - VEP **Prod** - VEP

Pork retail cuts identification 27 MIN
VHS
Retail cut identification series
(C)
$79.95 _ CV112
Includes a live hog, skeleton, and pork side, and relates major bones and retail cuts as well as 45 fresh, smoked and cured retail cuts. Set C of the series.
Agriculture; Home Economics
Dist - AAVIM **Prod** - AAVIM 1989

Porklips Now 22 MIN
U-matic / VHS / 16mm
Color (H C A)
Offers a satire of the film Apocalypse Now.
Fine Arts
Dist - PFP **Prod** - PFP 1980

The Porning of America - 207 30 MIN
U-matic
Currents - 1985 - 86 Season Series
Color (A)
Discusses the concerns about the amounts of pornography that are available in the country.
Social Science; Sociology
Dist - PBS **Prod** - WNETTV 1985

The Pornographers 128 MIN
VHS
B&W (G) (JAPANESE WITH ENGLISH SUBTITLES)
$35.95 purchase _ #CVC1030
Offers a black comedy which delivers a scathing attack on Japan's harsh yet vague anti - pornography laws. Directed by Shohei Imamura.
Fine Arts; Sociology
Dist - CHTSUI

Pornography 29 MIN
U-matic
Woman series
Color
Presents a discussion of the effects of pornography on children, crime rates and morality.
Psychology; Sociology
Dist - PBS **Prod** - WNEDTV

Pornography - the double message 28 MIN
VHS
Color (H C G)
$295.00 purchase, $55.00 rental
Explores the effect of hardcore pornography. Asks if people become desensitized by images of rape, domination and bondage. Surveys research studies which show how attitudes change after continued exposure to sado - masochistic images. A University of Wisconsin test group was less sympathetic to the victim at a rape trial after viewing pornography. Looks at efforts of legislators, censors and community groups to control the problem. Contains explicit material.
Sociology
Dist - FLMLIB **Prod** - CANBC 1987

Pororoca - the Backward Flow of the Amazon 30 MIN
U-matic / VHS
Color (C)
$249.00, $149.00 purchase _ #AD - 2089
Scrutinizes Pororoca - the powerful backward flow of the Amazon which is an annual phenomenon. Reveals that it is the world's largest tidal bore and that it has swamped camera crews from the US and Germany attempting to photograph it. Explains the natural forces at work.
Geography - World; Science - Physical
Dist - FOTH **Prod** - FOTH

Porosity 11 MIN
VHS
Hydrology concept series
Color (H C)
$24.95 purchase _ #S9019
Shows how spaces between individual particles vary in a single - concept format. Part of an 8 - part series covering water and soil topics.
Science - Physical
Dist - HUBDSC **Prod** - HUBDSC

Porosity and Permeability 26 MIN
16mm
B&W (C A)
Defines porosity and permeability and distinguishes between the two. Discusses and categorizes origin and kinds of voids and describes the sequence of development that rock history will have on the development of porosity and permeability in sandstone, limestone and lime mud.
Science - Physical
Dist - UTEX **Prod** - UTEX 1960

A Porpoise with a purpose 5 MIN
16mm
Screen news digest series
B&W (J H)
Tells how Navy scientists are studying, training and testing a porpoise to discover characteristics that can be adapted to submarines, torpedoes and the development of a sonar system as accurate as that of a porpoise. Volume four, issue nine of the series.
Civics and Political Systems; Science - Natural
Dist - HEARST **Prod** - HEARST 1962

Porque 10 MIN
VHS / 16mm
Color (G IND) (SPANISH)
$5.00 rental
Introduces the basic concepts of workplace safety and health. Discusses hazards ranging from chemicals and gases to stress, as well as remedies and legal rights.
Health and Safety; Social Science; Sociology
Dist - AFLCIO **Prod** - AFLCIO 1988

Port - A - Cath - an intravenous access system - 1 6 MIN
VHS
Nursing skills series
Color (C PRO G)
$395.00 purchase _ #R930 - VI - 020
Discusses Port - A - Cath, an intravenous access system that requires surgical implantation. Reveals that it is placed with its catheter tip in the superior vena cava or right atrium by way of the subclavian vein. When properly done, this procedure causes very little discomfort and increases a client's independence. It assures reliable access for short or long - term intravenous therapy without interfering with a client's lifestyle. Describes the procedure for preparing the site and placing the catheter. Part of a three - part series on nursing skills produced by Lander Univ Nursing Education, Greenwood, South Carolina.
Health and Safety; Science - Natural
Dist - HSCIC

A Port for the Prairies 30 MIN
U-matic
(A)
Explains the time and costs saved by the opening of the Prince Rupert Grain Terminal in Western Canada and shows its operation.
Agriculture; Geography - World
Dist - ACCESS **Prod** - ACCESS 1985

Port Fuel Injection 45 MIN
VHS / 16mm
Color (H A)
$239.00 purchase _ A21
Explains the advantages of fuel injection by reviewing combustion. Introduces basic components and details simple repair procedures.
Industrial and Technical Education
Dist - BERGL **Prod** - BERGL 1988

Port fuel injection series
Presents an introduction to the concepts and repair of port fuel injection systems. Discusses subjects including the advantages of fuel injection, how the parts operate, and troubleshooting. Consists of three videocassettes and a study guide.
Port fuel injection series
Dist - CAMV

Port Moresby 9 MIN
16mm
Color (J)
Presents a day in the life of Port Moresby, New Guinea.
Geography - World; Social Science
Dist - AUIS **Prod** - ANAIB 1971

Port Noarlunga Reef 10 MIN
16mm
Ecology of the Ocean Series
Color (I)
LC 78-709355
Tours the only marine sanctuary on the southern Australian coast, 22 miles from Adelaid, the capital of South Australia. Shows the visit of three skin divers.
Geography - World; Science - Natural
Dist - AMEDFL **Prod** - STEEND 1970

Port of Call 15 MIN
U-matic / VHS
Explorers Unlimited Series
Color (P I)
Summarizes the role of the Great Lakes as a transportation link.
Geography - United States; Social Science
Dist - AITECH **Prod** - WVIZTV 1971

Port of Preparedness 23 MIN
16mm
Color
LC 74-705385
Shows how port managements from coast to coast and from the Great Lakes to the Gulf are now making preparations to meet emergencies.
Business and Economics; Geography - United States
Dist - USNAC **Prod** - USOCD 1967

Port safety - vessel inspection 23 MIN
16mm
Color (A)
LC 77-702237
Shows inspection procedures for vessels and explains the legal responsibilities of the U S Coast Guard's captain of the port for the inspection of cargo and tank vessels.
Business and Economics; Civics and Political Systems; Social Science
Dist - USNAC **Prod** - USCG 1977

Port safety - waterfront facilities inspection 15 MIN
16mm
Color (A)
LC 77-702206
Discusses duties and legal responsibilities of the Coast Guard's captain of the port. Shows how the Coast Guard inspects waterfront facilities and informs owners of violations.
Business and Economics; Civics and Political Systems; Social Science
Dist - USNAC **Prod** - USCG 1972

The Portable computer
VHS
Computer series
Color (G)
$29.95 purchase _ #IV - 018
Looks at the different kinds of portable computers available, and the methods by which even the smallest computer can accomplish many of the functions that once only larger models were able to perform.
Computer Science; Education
Dist - INCRSE **Prod** - INCRSE

Portable electric sander 13 MIN
16mm
Woodwork - machine tools series
Color (J)
Presents six concepts dealing with the portable electric sander - - types of sanders, abrasive belts, parts of the belt sander, coarse sanding - belt sander, fine sanding - belt sander, and orbital sander.
Industrial and Technical Education
Dist - SF **Prod** - SF 1967

Portable electric saws 22 MIN
U-matic / VHS / 16mm
Color (A) (SPANISH)
Demonstrates the metal frame and plastic frame saw and discusses the advantages of each. Covers ripping, cross - cutting, bevelcutting of wood, and use of saws in cutting metals and masonry.
Industrial and Technical Education
Dist - PHENIX **Prod** - PHENIX 1969

Portable - emergency equipment 60 MIN
VHS
Equipment operations series
Color (PRO)
$600.00 - $1500.00 purchase _ #OTPEE
Focuses on portable and emergency equipment such as respirators, portable meters, analyzers, pumps, lubrication, filtration and fire equipment. Part of a twenty - part series on equipment operation. Includes ten textbooks and an instructor guide to support four hours of instruction.
Health and Safety; Industrial and Technical Education; Psychology
Dist - NUSTC **Prod** - NUSTC

Portable extinguisers
VHS / U-matic
Marine firefighting series
Color (IND) (KOREAN)
Opens with explanation of how fire extinguishers are rated and their expected delivery rate. Looks at different types available, their use, importance of technique and how to use extinguishers most effectively. Part two of the series.
Health and Safety; Social Science
Dist - GPCV **Prod** - GPCV

Portable extinguishers 30 MIN
VHS
Firefighter II - III video series
Color (G PRO)
$145.00 purchase _ #35252
Explains clearly how to select and use extinguishers for different types of fires. Includes AFFF, dry chemical, carbon dioxide and Halon extinguishers.
Health and Safety; Psychology; Social Science
Dist - OKSU **Prod** - OKSU

Portable extinguishers
VHS / U-matic
Marine firefighting series
Color (IND) (ITALIAN)
Opens with explanation of how fire extinguishers are rated and their expected delivery rate. Looks at different types available, their use, importance of technique and how to use exxtinguishers most effectively. Part two of the series.
Health and Safety; Social Science
Dist - GPCV **Prod** - GPCV

Portable extinguishers 18 MIN
VHS
Firefighter I series
Color (IND)
$130.00 purchase _ #35636
Presents one part of a 19 - part series that is the teaching companion for IFSTA's Essentials of Fire Fighting manual. Defines the rating system for portable extinguishers. Demonstrates how to select and use correct types of extinguishers. Based on Chapter 2.
Health and Safety; Science - Physical; Social Science
Dist - OKSU **Prod** - ACCTRA

Portable Fire Extinguishers 20 MIN
16mm
Color (J)
LC 75-700915
Examines different kinds of fire extinguishers, giving their classifications and providing instruction on their use.
Health and Safety
Dist - FILCOM **Prod** - IOWA 1966

The Portable Garden 29 MIN
Videoreel / VT2
Making Things Grow III Series
Color
Agriculture
Dist - PBS **Prod** - WGBHTV

Portable grinder safety 10 MIN
VHS / U-matic / BETA
Color (IND G A)
$510.00 purchase, $125.00 rental _ #POR019
Looks at portable industrial grinders which are used extensively to remove excess metal from castings or welds. Presents a step - by - step review of safety precautions for preparing and operating offset or side grinders. Includes work area safety, use of personal protective equipment, pre - operation checks and operating the grinder.
Health and Safety; Industrial and Technical Education; Psychology
Dist - ITF **Prod** - ERF 1991

Portable ladders 12 MIN
VHS / U-matic / BETA
Color; PAL (IND G)
$175.00 rental _ #AEB - 104
Reveals that the improper use of ladders is a source of many needless accidents. Illustrates the safe way to use straight, extension and step ladders. Shows how to select the right ladder for the job and outlines inspection procedures to ensure that the ladder is safe. Includes leader's guide and 10 workbooks or PAL.
Business and Economics; Health and Safety; Psychology
Dist - BNA **Prod** - BNA

Portable Ladders 6 MIN
VHS / U-matic
Take Ten for Safety Series
Color (IND)
Depicts the variety of hazards involved in using unsafe ladders or work habits.
Health and Safety; Industrial and Technical Education
Dist - CORF **Prod** - OLINC

A Portable life 30 MIN
U-matic / VHS
Color (PRO)
LC 83-706167
Introduces the executive and spouse to the realities of living overseas and problems of adjusting to different cultures and conditions. Describes the experiences of four wives who have lived on four continents.
Psychology; Social Science; Sociology
Dist - SYRCU **Prod** - MCGILL 1982

The Portable phonograph 29 MIN
Videoreel / VT2
Just generation series
Color (H C A)
Presents Walter Van Tilburg Clark's story about survivors of the world's final holocaust, adapted into an original drama.
Literature and Drama; Sociology
Dist - PBS **Prod** - WITFTV 1972

The Portable Phonograph by Walter Van Tilburg Clark 24 MIN
U-matic / VHS / 16mm
Humanities - Short Story Showcase Series
Color; B&W (J)
Presents The Portable Phonograph by Walter Van Tilburg Clark in which four survivors of a devastating war gather in a dugout built by soldiers to hear the portable phonograph one of them has saved.
Fine Arts; Literature and Drama
Dist - EBEC **Prod** - EBEC 1977

Portable Power Saw 37 MIN
VHS / 35mm strip
(H A IND)
#709XV7
Explains the safe use and operating procedures of the portable power saw when crosscutting and ripping lumber. Includes setting up and crosscutting, miter cuts, bevel cuts and ripping, and pocket cuts, dadoes and grooves (3 tapes). Includes a Study Guide.
Education; Industrial and Technical Education
Dist - BERGL

Portable power tools 17 MIN
U-matic / VHS / 16mm
Color (SPANISH)
Demonstrates the electric drill belt sander, orbital sander and saber saw and emphasizes safety. Shows each in detailed working operation.
Health and Safety; Industrial and Technical Education
Dist - PHENIX **Prod** - PHENIX 1968

Portable power tools - Volume III 23 MIN
VHS
Power tool principles - safety and technique series
Color (G)
$99.00 purchase _ #6 - 202 - 106A
Focuses on the circular saw. Discusses the sabre saw, miter saw and chop saw. Shows how to avoid hand and leg injuries, why safety guards should not be tampered with, correct selection and installation of blades and and proper grounding of electrical cords.
Health and Safety; Industrial and Technical Education
Dist - VEP **Prod** - VEP 1993

Portable power tools - Volume IV 23 MIN
VHS
Power tool principles - safety and technique series
Color (G)
$99.00 purchase _ #6 - 202 - 107A
Looks at sanders, drills, screw drivers, routers and planers. Highlights the importance of a clutter - free work area, the danger of damaged or improper extension cords, why safety guards should not be tampered with.
Health and Safety; Industrial and Technical Education
Dist - VEP **Prod** - VEP 1993

Portable Sander - Grinder Operation 23 MIN
BETA / VHS
Color (IND)
Demonstrates the operation of a sander - grinder, with different types of grinding wheel attachments.
Industrial and Technical Education; Psychology
Dist - RMIBHF **Prod** - RMIBHF

Portable wood power tools 35 MIN
VHS
Safety and operation series
Color (H A T)
$79.95 purchase _ #CV995
Discusses safety and proper operating procedures for the sabre saw, portable belt sander, portable router, orbital sander, electric drill and portable circle saw. Shows various types of cuts and uses for each tool. Features Charles Jedlicka.
Health and Safety; Industrial and Technical Education
Dist - AAVIM **Prod** - AAVIM 1992

Portal Decompression 30 MIN
16mm
Color (PRO)
Uses animation to depict the anatomy and physiology of hepatic circulation and to explain the etiologic factors responsible for portal hypertension. Presents a case study of a patient for whom portal decompression is indicated and shows the surgical procedure.
Health and Safety; Science; Science - Natural
Dist - SQUIBB **Prod** - SQUIBB

Portal hypertension 30 MIN
U-matic / VHS
Color
Discusses the diagnosis and management of bleeding varices and the selection of the proper type of shunt to prevent recurrent hemorrhage without impairment of liver function.
Health and Safety
Dist - ROWLAB **Prod** - ROWLAB

Portals of Vision 3 MIN
16mm
Color
LC 81-700398
Combines abstract sound and images to form reality in one continuous take.
Fine Arts
Dist - MARGAR **Prod** - MARGAR 1980

Porter springs 3 7 MIN
16mm
Color (G)
$35.00 rental
Uncovers animated reflections which were shot in ECO which is unstable and turned blue before the filmmaker could make an internegative. Warns the viewer that this is one of only three prints existing. Produced by Henry Hills.
Fine Arts
Dist - CANCIN

Portfolios - Tape 2 40 MIN
VHS
Redesigning assessment series
Color (A C PRO)
$350.00 purchase, $120.00 rental _ #614 - 226X01
Emphasizes performance - based assessment with a variety of test strategies. Explains the use of portfolios to demonstrate a student's progress in a class over time. Includes leader's guide. Part of a series.
Education
Dist - AFSCD

Portia Mansfield Motion Pictures on the Dance Series
Conchero Dancers of Mexico, the, Reel 1 10 MIN
Dist - SCHMUN

Portion control - a team effort 12 MIN
16mm / U-matic / VHS
Professional food preparation and service program series
Color
Introduces the basic economics of restaurant portion control as it affects jobs and careers. Demonstrates proper techniques of measuring, weighing, preparing and serving food.
Industrial and Technical Education
Dist - NEM **Prod** - NEM 1983

Portion control - using scoops and ladles 20 MIN
VHS / BETA
Color (G PRO)
$59.00 purchase _ #QF12
Describes various scoops, ladles and institutionally packed cans which aid the food service worker in portion control. Demonstrates portioning and ladling products.
Industrial and Technical Education
Dist - RMIBHF **Prod** - RMIBHF

Portland Cement Concrete Field Sampling and Testing 26 MIN
16mm
Color
LC 81-700880
Illustrates techniques for the sampling and testing of Portland cement concrete. Includes tests for air, slump, yield, casting of cylinders for compressive strength, making of beams for flexural strength, and the ball and chase indicator for entrained air.
Industrial and Technical Education; Social Science
Dist - USNAC **Prod** - USDTFH 1977

Portland glass 30 MIN
U-matic
Antiques series
Color
Fine Arts
Dist - PBS **Prod** - NHMNET

The Portrait 30 MIN
16mm / VHS
Color (H A)
$395.00, $495.00 purchase, $75.00 rental _ #9928
Deals with suicidal feelings in the young. Dramatizes the life of Julie, a young art student who feels intense pressure to be perfect. Portrays her suicide attempt and hospital recovery where she meets a terminally ill patient who still has enthusiasm for life.
Psychology; Sociology
Dist - AIMS **Prod** - MACROL 1987

The Portrait 29 MIN
VHS
Photographic vision series
Color (G)
$49.95 purchase _ #RM114V-F
Looks at the tradition and evolution of the photographic portrait. Presents the technical aspects of photography clearly and simply, including principles of the camera and techniques for controlling exposure, the use of various kinds of lighting, selection of appropriate lenses and film and basic darkroom techniques. Focuses on the world of photographers and photography - its history and evolution, its uses for personal development and expression, and the impact of photography on the world. Part of a 20-part series examining all aspects of the field of photography.
Industrial and Technical Education
Dist - CAMV **Prod** - COAST
CDTEL

The Portrait 30 MIN
VHS / 16mm
Focus on Watercolor Series
Color (C A)
$85.00, $75.00 purchase _ 21 - 11
Explains working with a model, equation for developing form, use of white paint, dry brush technique, and reflected light.
Fine Arts
Dist - CDTEL **Prod** - COAST 1987

Portrait 7 MIN
16mm
Color (H C)
LC 70-711401
Shows men, machinery and laboratory techniques in a research and development laboratory concerned with materials, processes and testing.
Industrial and Technical Education; Science
Dist - SANDIA **Prod** - SANDIA 1970

Portrait 20 MIN
16mm
Color
LC 75-703531
Portrays the rejection of an artist.
Fine Arts; Guidance and Counseling
Dist - WILLMD **Prod** - WILLMD 1975

Portrait - Angus Wilson 30 MIN
U-matic
Color
Features novelist and professor Angus Wilson as he discusses preparation for writing.
English Language; Literature and Drama
Dist - UMITV **Prod** - UMITV 1979

Portrait de Moliere 62 MIN
VHS
Color (H C G A) (FRENCH WITH SUBTITLES)
$250.00 purchase _ #DL406
Weaves together scenes from Moliere's plays and commentary by Jean - Louis Barrault, Madeleine Renard and Jean Desailly to evoke the life and character of playwright Moliere. Includes scenes from Le Tartuffe, Le Misanthrope, Le Malade Imaginaire, L'Avare, Don Juan, L'Ecole des Femmes and Le Bourgeois Gentilhomme.
Fine Arts; History - World; Literature and Drama
Dist - INSIM **Prod** - TRANSW 1972
TRANSW

Portrait drawing 60 MIN
VHS
Learning to paint with Carolyn Berry series
Color (H G)
$49.95 purchase
Offers a step - by - step method for creating a finished painting or drawing from a blank canvas. Presents part of an eight - part series designed by Carolyn Berry covering everything from arranging or selecting subjects to an explanation of the material needed and the specific techniques to be applied. Addresses needs of students, hobbyists, amateur painters and professionals seeking new tips. Produced by Artists Video and directed by Christian Surette; 1991 - 1994. Video jackets available.
Fine Arts
Dist - CNEMAG

Portrait drawing 26 MIN
VHS
ArtSmart drawing series
Color (J H C G)
$49.95 purchase _ #IBX01080V
Begins with a historical introduction to portrait drawing. Continues with straightforward examples of the three basic poses - frontal, profile and three - quarters view - appropriate for a beginner. Observes an artist drawing the portrait of a young girl, emphasizing the ideas of design, mood, texture and form within the portrait. Part of a series on drawing.
Fine Arts
Dist - CAMV

Portrait in black - A Philip Randolph 10 MIN
16mm / VHS
Color (G IND)
$5.00 rental
Interviews civil rights leader and former president of the Brotherhood of Sleeping Car Porters, A Philip Randolph, who tells the story of his long crusade for black equality. Recalls the struggle to organize black workers and historic confrontations with Presidents Franklin D Roosevelt and John F Kennedy.
Business and Economics; Civics and Political Systems; History - United States; Social Science
Dist - AFLCIO **Prod** - REPRO 1970
REPRO

A portrait in grief 6 MIN
16mm
B&W/Color (G)
$15.00 rental
Conveys, through imagery and editing, the pain of loss and the futility of grief. Communicates the shame of weeping, the quest for answers and the silence from which individuals attempt to hear them. By Lee Bridgers - Musiek.
Fine Arts; Sociology
Dist - CANCIN

Portrait in Pastel 29 MIN
U-matic
Artist at Work Series
Color
Focuses on facial bone structure. Demonstrates how to create a convincing face with pastels.
Fine Arts
Dist - UMITV **Prod** - UMITV 1973

Portrait - Joseph Heller 30 MIN
U-matic
Color
Interviews Joseph Heller, author of Catch 22 and Something Happened, as he discusses his novels, the thirteen - year interim between them and the creative pressures that resulted in his second novel.
Literature and Drama
Dist - UMITV **Prod** - UMITV 1975

Portrait - Maggie Kuhn 30 MIN
U-matic
Color
Features Maggie Kuhn, leader of the Gray Panther Network, an organization dedicated to eliminating ageism, as she discusses projects, issues, achievements and aspirations of the Gray Panthers.
Sociology
Dist - UMITV **Prod** - UMITV 1979

Portrait of a Blind Man 5 MIN
16mm
B&W
LC 76-702043
Depicts the everyday life of a blind man living in Montreal.
Geography - World; Guidance and Counseling; Psychology; Sociology
Dist - CONCRU **Prod** - CONCRU 1975

Portrait of a city 21 MIN
16mm
B&W (I)
Presents views of the people in the city of Calcutta.
Geography - World; Social Science; Sociology
Dist - NEDINF **Prod** - INDIA

Portrait of a City - Washington, DC 28 MIN
16mm
Color
Familiarizes the viewer with the nation's capital and the meaning behind the historic monuments and buildings.
Geography - United States
Dist - EKC **Prod** - EKC 1976

Portrait of a Coal Miner 15 MIN
U-matic / VHS / 16mm
Community Life in America Series
Color (I)
LC 80-700152
Offers a portrait of a West Virginia coal miner and his family.
Social Science
Dist - NGS **Prod** - NGS 1980

Portrait of a coast 29 MIN
16mm
Color (C A)
LC 82-700934
Details the natural and human - exacerbated causes of the erosion which is making the east coast of United States sink at the rate of one foot every 100 years.
Science - Natural; Science - Physical
Dist - COPRO **Prod** - COPRO 1982

Portrait of a Conductor 43 MIN
16mm
Color
LC 81-700420
Focuses on conductor David Zinman.
Fine Arts
Dist - SHWFI **Prod** - SHWFI 1981

Portrait of a deaf city 15 MIN
16mm
Color (J)
LC 72-702846
Presents the powerful and the powerless citizens and how they view their city. Features several insights, from the deputy mayor, the Black militant, the police officer, the poverty lawyer, the community organizer, the suburbanite and the businessman.
Psychology; Social Science; Sociology
Dist - SF **Prod** - REPRO

Portrait of a Disciplinarian 30 MIN
U-matic / VHS
Wodehouse Playhouse Series
Color (C A)
Presents an adaptation of the short story Portrait Of A Disciplinarian by P G Wodehouse.
Literature and Drama
Dist - TIMLIF **Prod** - BBCTV 1980

Portrait of a fisherman 15 MIN
U-matic / VHS / 16mm
Community life in america series
Color (K P I)
LC 81-700978
Follows New England fisherman John Sanfillippo and his crew as they go fishing. Examines life in a fishing town.
Geography - United States; Industrial and Technical Education
Dist - NGS **Prod** - NGS 1981

Portrait of a Horse 8 MIN
16mm
Color
LC 71-712463
Presents the story of a freedom - loving horse and the man who tries to subdue it.
Literature and Drama
Dist - VIEWFI **Prod** - GIERSZ 1970

Portrait of a killer 18 MIN
16mm
Color
Details symptoms and signs of Reye's Syndrome, a fatal disease in children.
Health and Safety
Dist - MTP **Prod** - MTP
NRSF

Portrait of a Mime 11 MIN
16mm
B&W
LC 76-701355
Takes a look at the work of a mime artist.
Fine Arts
Dist - YORKU **Prod** - YORKU 1975

Portrait of a Minority Group - Americans of Hispanic Heritage in the United States 37 MIN
16mm
B&W
LC 75-701356
Portrays Spanish - speaking Americans in the United States, the nation's second largest minority with a population of ten million in the United States and three million in Puerto Rico. Shows three different groups - Puerto Ricans, Mexican Americans and Latin Americans - describing the similarities and differences of each group.
Sociology
Dist - USNAC **Prod** - USCSC 1973

Portrait of a muckraker - the stories of Jessica Mitford 52 MIN
VHS
Color (H C G)
$445.00 purchase, $75.00 rental
Portrays outspoken British activist Jessica Mitford, whose expose of the funeral industry gained her instant notoriety. Reviews her other works and her life. Shows that Mitford's life is interwoven with American social issues - civil rights, communism and the anti - war movement. Produced by Stephen Evans, Ida Landauer and James Morgan in association with KQED.
Civics and Political Systems; History - World; Literature and Drama; Religion and Philosophy
Dist - FLMLIB **Prod** - KQEDTV 1987

Portrait of a Nurse 28 MIN
16mm
Color
LC 77-702123
Depicts the role of the nurse as the profession moves toward assuming greater responsibility in the delivery of health care.
Guidance and Counseling; Health and Safety; Sociology
Dist - BFF **Prod** - BFF 1976

Portrait of a poison 50 MIN
VHS
Horizon series
Color; PAL (G)
PdS99 purchase
Investigates the poisonous herbicide by - product dioxin and presents research showing its relation to a number of wasting diseases. Looks at poisons, particularly toxic chemicals made by humans in the chemical revolution since World War II. Focuses on the invisible, little understood chemicals, such as dioxin which is 4000 times more deadly than arsenic.
Health and Safety; Science - Physical
Dist - BBCENE

Portrait of a President - Lyndon Baines Johnson 17 MIN
16mm
Screen news digest series; Vol 6; Issue 6
B&W (J A)
LC FIA68-2077
Traces the life of Lyndon Baines Johnson from his birth in 1908 to his presidency in 1963.
Biography; History - United States
Dist - HEARST **Prod** - HEARST 1964

Portrait of a profession 30 MIN
U-matic / VHS
Accounting series; Pt 1
Color (C)
Gives an overview of the accounting profession.
Business and Economics; Guidance and Counseling
Dist - GPN **Prod** - UMA 1980

Portrait of a Railroad 26 MIN
16mm
Color
LC 73-701621
Offers a look at the people and operations of the nation's longest railroad, the Burlington Northern.

Social Science
Dist - THOMPN **Prod** - THOMPN 1973

Portrait of a Rebel - Margaret Sanger 96 MIN
VHS / U-matic
Color (H C A)
Details the efforts of Margaret Sanger to repeal the Comstock Act which forbade the dissemination of birth control information. Details her relationship with psychologist Havelock Ellis. Stars Bonnie Franklin and David Dukes.
Biography; History - World; Sociology
Dist - TIMLIF **Prod** - TIMLIF 1982

Portrait of a Sensei 30 MIN
16mm
Color
LC 73-700903
Presents a portrait of the art of Amanji Inoue, a Japanese Sensei and master porcelain potter.
Fine Arts
Dist - TOURTE **Prod** - TOURTE 1973

A Portrait of a small hydro 28 MIN
U-matic / VHS / 16mm
Color (J)
Looks at the experiences of three hydroelectric entrepreneurs who have bought up old dam sites and are rebuilding them for the production of power.
Business and Economics; Social Science
Dist - BULFRG **Prod** - LIVNGN 1984

Portrait of a steelworker 15 MIN
U-matic / VHS / 16mm
Community life in America series
Color (I J)
Looks at one of the steel mills in southwestern Pennsylvania and introduces a steelworker and his family.
Business and Economics; Geography - United States; Sociology
Dist - NGS **Prod** - NGS 1981

Portrait of a teenage drug abuser 23 MIN
U-matic / VHS / 16mm
Color (I J H C G)
$510.00, $355.00, $385.00 purchase _ #A439
Presents the individual and collective experiences of six young adults who are all recovering drug abusers. Presents insights into the causes and tragic fates of teenage drug abusers.
Health and Safety; Psychology
Dist - BARR **Prod** - BARR 1987

Portrait of a Teenage Shoplifter 47 MIN
16mm / U-matic / VHS
Teenage Years Series
Color (I J H)
Tells the story of Karen, a teenage shoplifter, who steals clothes and makeup she can't afford to attract her boyfriend, the school basketball star. Reveals that when she is finally caught, she must face the consequences.
Guidance and Counseling; Sociology
Dist - TIMLIF **Prod** - ALAMAR 1984

Portrait of a university 20 MIN
16mm
Color (J)
LC 74-701397
Presents a guided tour through the campus of West Virginia University. Describes the university's functions of education, research and service to the state.
Education; Geography - United States
Dist - WVAU **Prod** - WVAU

Portrait of a vandal 13 MIN
U-matic / VHS / 16mm
Color (I J)
$315.00, $220.00 purchase _ #76577; LC 78-701787
Tells the true story of three young boys who vandalize a classmate's home. Shows the effect on the boys and their parents.
Guidance and Counseling; Sociology
Dist - CORF **Prod** - CENTEF 1978

Portrait of a Wheat Farmer 15 MIN
U-matic / VHS / 16mm
Community Life in America Series
Color (I)
LC 80-700151
Offers a portrait of a family living on a farm in the Midwestern United States.
Social Science
Dist - NGS **Prod** - NGS 1980

Portrait of America series
Offers a 55-part series which visits all 50 states of the United States and its territories. Offers extensive research into each state's history. Presents segments on each state's history, government, education, folklore, science, journalism, sociology, industry, agriculture and business. Shows what is unique about each state and what is distinctive about its regional culture. Includes teacher study guides.

Alabama 60 MIN
Alaska 60 MIN
Arizona 60 MIN
Arkansas 60 MIN
Colorado 60 MIN
Delaware 60 MIN
Georgia 60 MIN
Hawaii 60 MIN
Idaho 60 MIN
Illinois 60 MIN
Indiana 60 MIN
Kansas 60 MIN
Kentucky 60 MIN
Louisiana 60 MIN
Maine 60 MIN
Maryland 60 MIN
Massachussetts 60 MIN
Michigan 60 MIN
Minnesota 60 MIN
Mississippi 60 MIN
Missouri 60 MIN
Montana 60 MIN
Nebraska 60 MIN
Nevada 60 MIN
New Hampshire 60 MIN
New York 60 MIN
North California 60 MIN
North Carolina 60 MIN
North Dakota 60 MIN
Ohio 60 MIN
Oklahoma 60 MIN
Pennsylvania 60 MIN
Rhode Island 60 MIN
South Carolina 60 MIN
South Dakota 60 MIN
Tennessee 60 MIN
Texas 60 MIN
Utah 60 MIN
Vermont 60 MIN
Washington 60 MIN
West Virginia 60 MIN
Wisconsin 60 MIN
Wyoming 60 MIN
Dist - CAMV

Portrait of America series
Connecticut 60 MIN
Florida 60 MIN
Iowa 60 MIN
New Jersey 60 MIN
New Mexico 60 MIN
Oregon 60 MIN
Virginia 60 MIN
Dist - CAMV
TBSESI

Portrait of America Series
Georgia
Indiana
Nevada
Texas
Dist - TBSESI

Portrait of an American Town 30 MIN
U-matic / VHS
Color
Provides a brief history of the city of Upper Arlington, Ohio, a deliberately - planned suburban community.
History - United States; Sociology
Dist - HRC **Prod** - OHC

Portrait of an Artist 28 MIN
16mm / VHS
Color (G)
$500.00, $250.00 purchase, $65.00 rental
Captures the work and life of artist Doris Chase. Spans thirty years of her career as a painter, sculptor and pioneer video artist.
Fine Arts
Dist - WMEN **Prod** - ROSCH 1984

Portrait of an Early American Village 10 MIN
16mm
Color (I)
LC FIA66-1688
Depicts life in an early American village. Shows villagers going to church, working on the farm and doing the household chores. Pictures a town meeting.
History - United States; Social Science
Dist - AVED **Prod** - VILF 1964

Portrait of an election 60 MIN
16mm
Artist as a reporter series
Color
Depicts the 1972 primary elections, the Democratic and Republican Conventions and the campaigns to election day. Features paintings from CBS convention coverage.
Civics and Political Systems; Fine Arts
Dist - ROCSS **Prod** - ROCSS 1973

Portrait of an island
VHS
Color (G)
$34.95 purchase _ #0781
Visits Mt Desert Island and Acadia National Park off the coast of Maine.
Geography - United States
Dist - SEVVID

Portrait of Antarctica 23 MIN
16mm
Color
LC FIE63-9
Discusses the Navy's support of scientific efforts being conducted in the Antarctic during Operation Deepfreeze. Shows logistic support operations, scientific surveys and activities of the traverse and winteringover parties on the icebound continent.
Geography - World; Science
Dist - USNAC **Prod** - USN 1962

Portrait of Bermuda 29 MIN
16mm
Color (I J)
Visits the island of Bermuda, showing its many attractions.
Geography - World
Dist - MTP **Prod** - BDOT

Portrait of Cape Cod 17 MIN
16mm
Color
Offers a portrait of Cape Cod including Heritage Plantation, Hyannisport, Provincetown, and the many golf courses, beaches, candle factories and artist colonies.
Geography - United States; Geography - World
Dist - MTP **Prod** - CCCOC

A Portrait of Charles M Russell - preserver of the Old West 60 MIN
VHS
Color (G)
$35.00 purchase _ #2519
Features many of the paintings of Charles M Russell. Includes historical movie footage and rare photographs. Interviews art historians, artists and people who knew Russell to explore the man, his growth as an artist and his passionate love of the West.
Biography; Fine Arts
Dist - MTHISO

Portrait of Christine 25 MIN
16mm / U-matic / VHS
Color
LC 77-702612
Tells the story of a young disabled woman. Shows how she enjoys life with enthusiasm, getting around in cities designed for the healthy and fit.
Psychology; Sociology
Dist - WOMBAT **Prod** - FIARTS 1977

Portrait of Christine 26 MIN
U-matic / VHS / 16mm
Color (C A)
Tells how an orthopedically handicapped 28 - year - old has become a fully involved member of society.
Psychology
Dist - WOMBAT **Prod** - FILMRT

Portrait of civilization 30 MIN
VHS
Color (G)
$29.95 purchase, $15.00 rental
Watches the creation of a fresco at the Churches of the Frescos in North Carolina with descriptive commentary by the artist, Jeff Mims. Traces the process from the cartoon tracing and sketching, to 'punching and pouncing,' to the actual painting of a wet wall surface. Demonstrates the mixing and use of earth pigments plus the use of aged, slaked lime in preparation of frescos. Covers the history of frescos from ancient Minoan culture and suggests that today's frescos will offer future civilizations a continuing portait of humanity.
Fine Arts
Dist - ARTSAM **Prod** - ERTVF

Portrait of Dame Mary Gilmore 9 MIN
16mm
Australian Eye Series
Color
LC 80-700787
Evokes the way a portrait painter approaches his subject, using the voice - overs of William Dobell, artist, Dame Mary Gilmore, subject and James Gleeson, the artist's friend and biographer.
Fine Arts
Dist - TASCOR **Prod** - FLMAUS 1978

Portrait of Diana - Portrait of Andrew Noren 8 MIN
16mm
Color; Silent (C)

$200.00
Experimental film by Barry Gerson.
Fine Arts
Dist - AFA **Prod** - AFA 1972

Portrait of Earth 27 MIN
VHS / U-matic
Color (H A)
LC 84-706407
Explores the history of the artificial satellite, discussing the key roles played by satellites in communication, meteorology, and other scientific and environmental disciplines.
Industrial and Technical Education; Science - Physical
Dist - USNAC **Prod** - NASA 1981

A Portrait of Elie Wiesel 60 MIN
VHS
Color (G)
$59.95 purchase _ #CELW - 000
Profiles Elie Wiesel, author, philosopher and Holocaust survivor. Traces his life from his birth in Hungary, through his study of Hasidic Judaism as a youth, his time in a concentration camp and his life as an adult. Presents Wiesel's work as an author and philosopher.
Biography; History - World
Dist - PBS **Prod** - WHYY 1988

Portrait of four women 28 MIN
16mm
B&W (G)
$60.00 rental
Presents four short films produced between 1968 and 1973 - Breakaway, featuring dance and vocals by Toni Basil; Vivian, portraying Vivian Kurz; The White Rose, depicting the removal of the painting of the same title by Jay De Feo; and Marilyn Times Five, scrutinizing the image of Marilyn Monroe. Available for rental in group packages only.
Fine Arts
Dist - CANCIN **Prod** - CONNER 1973

A Portrait of Giselle 97 MIN
U-matic / VHS / 16mm
Color (J)
LC 82-700335
Presents choreographer Sir Anton Dolin interviewing ballerinas on their interpretations of the role of Giselle. Includes the comments of Natalia Makarova, Yvette Chauvire, Alicia Alonso, Galina Ulanova, Alicia Markova, Carla Fracci, Olga Spessivtzeva and Tamara Karasavina.
Fine Arts
Dist - WOMBAT **Prod** - ABCVID 1982

Portrait of Grandpa Doc 28 MIN
U-matic / VHS / 16mm
Color
Describes the relationship between a grandfather and his grandson. Discusses intergenerational relationships.
Health and Safety; Sociology
Dist - CCNCC **Prod** - CCNCC 1985
APH PFP
UILL PHENIX
PHENIX

Portrait of Haiti 14 MIN
16mm / U-matic / VHS
Color (I)
LC 79-701793
Presents the history, culture and religion of Haiti as viewed through the eyes of a painter of primitive art.
Fine Arts; Geography - World
Dist - MCFI **Prod** - SWAIN 1977

Portrait of Holland 12 MIN
16mm
Color (J)
Shows Dutch paintings of the 17th century which have been photographed from the originals in full color with shape and scale indicated. Studies one of Jan Steen's country fairs, landscapes by Jan van der Heyden and Jacob Ruisdael, Frans Hals' portrait of Swalmius, still - lifes by Pieter Claesz and Nicholas Van Heussen. Emphasizes Rembrandt's work and examines The Visitation, a Biblical scene in which he introduced Dutch types and details of life.
Fine Arts; Geography - World
Dist - RADIM **Prod** - DETRIA 1955

Portrait of hope 24 MIN
VHS
Color (H C A)
$195.00 purchase
Presents Ellen Kingsley describing her experience when first diagnosed with breast cancer and when undergoing treatment. Provides information about cancer, treatment choices, the effects of the disease and treatments, and how family members are affected by the condition, with emphasis on the importance of early detection. For patient and family education.
Health and Safety
Dist - PFP

Portrait of Imogen 28 MIN
U-matic / 16mm / VHS
B&W (G)
$495.00, $295.00 purchase, $60.00 rental
Focuses on photographer Imogen Cunningham, who presents more than 250 of her photographs. Traces her 75 - year career. Produced by Meg Partridge for Pacific Arts Entertainment.
Biography; Fine Arts
Dist - NEWDAY

Portrait of Ivan Majdrakoff 9 MIN
16mm
Color & B&W (G)
$20.00 rental
Portrays Ivan Majdrakoff, the filmmaker's friend and teacher at the San Francisco Art Institute. Delves into Ivan's daily life in his studio.
Fine Arts
Dist - CANCIN **Prod** - WONGAL 1968

A Portrait of Jamie 29 MIN
VHS / 16mm
Color (G)
$55.00 rental _ #PORJ - 000
Studies the painter Jamie Wyeth. Discusses with Wyeth his influences and inspiration.
Biography; Fine Arts
Dist - PBS **Prod** - NETCHE

Portrait of Jason 105 MIN
16mm
B&W
Tells the story of Jason Holliday, a black male prostitute and sometime nightclub performer. Provokes him to reveal hidden aspects of his personality.
Guidance and Counseling; Sociology
Dist - NYFLMS **Prod** - NYFLMS 1967

A Portrait of Katherine Mansfield - a woman and a writer 54 MIN
VHS
Color (H C G)
$295.00 purchase, $75.00 rental
Follows the life of Katherine Mansfield, a romantic, brilliant and formidable woman who left her native New Zealand at age 18 and was soon the center of the literary scene in London. Produced by Sue Kedgley and Julienne Stretton.
Literature and Drama
Dist - FLMLIB

A Portrait of Mexico 34 MIN
16mm / U-matic / VHS
Color (J H A)
LC FIA62-1378
A group of students, visiting Mexico City and the surrounding area, view such things as the Palace of Fine Arts, the University, the market places and archeological remains of the Toltec and Mayan civilizations.
Geography - World
Dist - IFB **Prod** - UARIZ 1962

Portrait of Moliere 62 MIN
16mm
Color (J H C A) (FRENCH (ENGLISH SUBTITLES))
Presents a series of scenes from Moliere's plays which evoke the life and character of the French playwright. Includes scenes from Le Tartuffe, Le Misanthrope, Le Medecin Malgre Lui, Le Malade Imaginaire, L'Avare, Dom Juan, L'Ecole Des Femmes and Le Borugeois Gentihomme.
Literature and Drama
Dist - TRANSW **Prod** - IFB 1972
IFB

Portrait of Nelson Mandela 20 MIN
16mm / U-matic / VHS
Color
Documents Nelson Mandela and his leadership of the African National Congress of South Africa. Includes an interview with Mandela filmed in 1961 before his sentence to life imprisonment.
Civics and Political Systems; History - World
Dist - NEWTIM **Prod** - NEWTIM

Portrait of Polynesia 38 MIN
VHS
Color (G)
$24.95 purchase
Visits the Polynesian Cultural Center in Oahu, Hawaii. Explores the ancient cultures of Samoa, Tonga, Fiji, New Zealand, Tahiti, the Marquesas, and the Hawaiian islands.
Geography - United States; History - World
Dist - PBS **Prod** - WNETTV

A Portrait of Power 14 MIN
16mm
Color
Concentrates on mining techniques used to extract coal from the earth.
Industrial and Technical Education; Social Science
Dist - MTP **Prod** - AMAX

Portrait of Ramona 26.5 MIN
16mm
Color (C)
$571.00
Experimental film by George Kuchar.
Fine Arts
Dist - AFA **Prod** - AFA 1971

A Portrait of Samson Raphaelson 29 MIN
VHS
Creativity with Bill Moyers series
Color (G)
$49.95 purchase _ #CWBM - 103C
Focuses on the life and work of playwright Samson Raphaelson. Emphasizes his collaborations with director Ernst Lubitsch, including the film Trouble In Paradise. Hosted by Bill Moyers.
Fine Arts; Literature and Drama
Dist - PBS **Prod** - CORPEL 1981

A Portrait of the artist as a young man
VHS
Color (G)
$29.95 purchase
Presents a film version of the James Joyce novel A Portrait Of The Artist As A Young Man. Stars Bosco Hogan, T P McKenna, and John Gielgud.
Fine Arts; Literature and Drama
Dist - PBS **Prod** - WNETTV

A Portrait of the Artist as a Young Man 93 MIN
U-matic / VHS / 16mm
Color (H C)
LC 81-700034
Traces the childhood, schooldays, adolescence and early adulthood of an Irish poet - scholar. Based on the novel A Portrait Of The Artist As A Young Man by James Joyce.
Literature and Drama
Dist - TEXFLM **Prod** - TEXFLM 1978

A Portrait of the Artist as a Young Man - Pt 1 46 MIN
U-matic / VHS / 16mm
Color (H C)
LC 81-700034
Traces the childhood, schooldays, adolescence and early adulthood of an Irish poet - scholar. Based on the novel A Portrait Of The Artist As A Young Man by James Joyce.
Biography
Dist - TEXFLM **Prod** - TEXFLM 1978

A Portrait of the Artist as a Young Man - Pt 2 47 MIN
U-matic / VHS / 16mm
Color (H C)
LC 81-700034
Traces the childhood, schooldays, adolescence and early adulthood of an Irish poet - scholar. Based on the novel A Portrait Of The Artist As A Young Man by James Joyce.
Biography
Dist - TEXFLM **Prod** - TEXFLM 1978

Portrait of the Artist as an Old Lady 27 MIN
16mm
Color
Presents a portrait of Russian born 81 year old artist Paraskeva Clark. Narrated by Germaine Greer.
Fine Arts
Dist - NFBC **Prod** - NFBC 1982

Portrait of the Orient 27 MIN
16mm
Color (I)
LC 77-706089
Portrays nine countries of the Orient, showing examples of modernization as well as ancient temples, customs and dances.
History - World; Psychology; Sociology
Dist - MCDO **Prod** - JAPAL 1969

Portrait of the poet as James Broughton - Part One and Two 40 MIN
16mm
Color (G)
$60.00 rental
Pays homage to the concept of artistic cinema begun by Jean Cocteau in his famous trilogy, and continued through poet James Broughton. Contains voices and natural sound recorded, edited and tape - altered. Augments, by extensive optical printing, in - camera superimposition which created complex images. Part one was six years in the making and is a self - contained film although it will reveal deeper meanings when part two is completed. A John Luther Schofill production.
Fine Arts; Literature and Drama
Dist - CANCIN

Portrait of the press, warts and all - by John Chancellor 50 MIN
U-matic / VHS

Color (H C A)
Explores journalism in terms of the American standard of fairness, accuracy and objectivity and how the American public views journalists. Examines charges that the press is arrogant, negative, biased, and overly ambitious. Shows how decisions are made and stories covered in the newsroom.
Literature and Drama; Religion and Philosophy
Dist - FI **Prod** - NBCNEW

A Portrait of the Sculptor 30 MIN
U-matic
Color
Interviews sculptor and artist John Mills who discusses his work and the factors which influence his art while he sculpts a portrait of the host, Andrew Watson.
Fine Arts
Dist - UMITV **Prod** - UMITV 1979

Portrait of the Soviet Union Series
The Baltic style 60 MIN
Country of Revolution 60 MIN
The End of all the Earth 60 MIN
The Golden road 60 MIN
Mother Russia 60 MIN
Siberia - Ice on Fire 60 MIN
Swords and Ploughshares 60 MIN
Dist - AMBROS

Portrait of two artists 29 MIN
16mm / U-matic / VHS
Were you there series
Color (I)
LC 83-706600
Features Black American artists Hughie Lee - Smith and Jacob Lawrence. Shows their work and looks in on a class taught by Mr. Lee - Smith. Visits the artists in their studios and includes animated sequences of the illustrations of Mr. Lawrence's children's book Harriet And The Promised Land.
Fine Arts; History - United States
Dist - BCNFL **Prod** - NGUZO 1982

Portrait one - Earl James Barker 18 MIN
16mm
B&W (G)
$20.00 rental
Details Earl Bodien's portraiture of Earl James Barker.
Fine Arts
Dist - CANCIN

Portrait painting 60 MIN
VHS
Color (G)
PdS19.95 purchase _ #A4-MC2
Presents a working conversation with the Salford artist Harold Riley while he paints a portrait and offers information about the nature of the three-way relationship among the artist, the sitter, and the onlooker. Discusses the method, the materials, and the objective approach to portraiture. Produced by Master Class.
Fine Arts
Dist - AVP

Portrait painting 60 MIN
VHS
Learning to paint with Carolyn Berry series
Color (H G)
$49.95 purchase
Offers a step - by - step method for creating a finished painting or drawing from a blank canvas. Features part of an eight - part series covering everything from arranging or selecting subjects to an explanation of the material needed and the specific techniques to be applied. Professional art instructor Carolyn Berry designed this series for students, hobbyists, amateur painters and professionals seeking new tips. Produced by Artists Video and directed by Christian Surette; 1991 - 1994. Video jackets available.
Fine Arts
Dist - CNEMAG

Portrait - The Blue Angels 14 MIN
16mm
Color
LC 79-700262
Presents the U S Naval Flight Demonstration Squadron displaying aerobatic maneuvers in high - powered Skyhawks.
Civics and Political Systems; Physical Education and Recreation
Dist - MCDO **Prod** - MCDO 1979

Portrait two, the young lady 3 MIN
16mm
B&W (G)
$5.00 rental
Shows filmmaker Earl Bodien's 'framed portrait,' in which the purported subject, the young lady, is the frame. Presents Bodien's philosophy of art.
Fine Arts
Dist - CANCIN

Portraits 30 MIN
VHS / U-matic
Stage at a time
(K P I)
$180 VC purchase, $30 VC five day rental, $110 self dub
Uses theater to teach students self awareness, values and ethics. Explores the concepts of beauty and friendship. Third in a four part series.
Fine Arts; Psychology; Sociology
Dist - GPN **Prod** - WUFT 1983

Portraits 30 MIN
U-matic / VHS
Stage at a time series
Color (P)
Presents Sara, a model, Bill, a sculptor, and Mr. Finster, a writer, who have won a trip around the world, conditional on reporting to Studio Z for a test. Shows the three struggling to pass the test gaining a new understanding of 'beauty' and gaining friendship among themselves.
Literature and Drama
Dist - GPN **Prod** - WUFT

Portraits 30 MIN
VHS / U-matic
Taking better pictures series
Color (G)
Uses an antebellum home setting to show how to work with a portrait subject. Helps beginning and intermediate photographers use 35 mm equipment effectively. Focuses on creative portraiture - capturing an individual's personality on film.. Tenth in a ten - part series.n the studio how to capture an individual's personality on film.
Industrial and Technical Education
Dist - GPN **Prod** - GCCED

Portraits 28 MIN
16mm
Color
LC 78-701443
Shows Exxon employees from the 1930s to the 1970s and discusses the company's benefit program.
Business and Economics; Sociology
Dist - EXXON **Prod** - EXXON 1978

Portraits 28 MIN
U-matic / 16mm / VHS
Painter's world series
Color (H C A)
$595.00, $250.00 purchase _ #HP - 6095C
Examines the art of portraits, which involves exploration, choice and pictorial invention. Examines the conventions of portrait art. Compares portraits since the Renaissance with the present work of painters Philip Pearlstein and Yolanda Sonnabend and photographers Joel Meyerowitz and Jo Spence. Studies the impact of photography upon portraiture and changing fashions in stereotyping. Part of a series on painters.
Fine Arts
Dist - CORF **Prod** - WGBHTV 1989

Portraits 22 MIN
U-matic
Neighbours - a training program for community volunteers series
Color (A)
Interviews four people with differing ESL needs about their language ability and personal interests.
English Language; Social Science
Dist - ACCESS **Prod** - ACCESS 1985

The Portraits 25 MIN
VHS
Exploring photography series
Color (A)
PdS65 purchase
Illustrates the visual challenge of portrait photography. Presents the work of portrait photographers Arnold Newman and Duffy and Griffin. Explores the creative possibilities of still photography. Covers the major topics of interest to any photographer. Part of a six-part series hosted by Bryn Campbell.
Fine Arts; Industrial and Technical Education
Dist - BBCENE

Portraits in black 60 MIN
VHS
Color (H C A)
$39.95 purchase
Presents three programs exploring the cultural heritage of Black America. Program Paul Laurence Dunbar tells the story of America's first Black poet, while Two Centuries Of Black American Art covers Black artists from slavery to the present day. Gift Of The Black Folk profiles Tubman, Douglass, and Vesey.
Biography; Fine Arts; History - United States
Dist - PBS **Prod** - WNETTV

Portraits in watercolor - Pt i 60 MIN
VHS
Portraits in watercolor series
Color (J)
$39.95 purchase _ #HV - 677
Develops perceptual, drawing and painting skills in watercolor. Shows mirror and contour drawings. Leads to demonstrations of controlled and uncontrolled watercolor in portraits. Part I of a two - part series by James Kirk.
Fine Arts
Dist - CRYSP **Prod** - CRYSP

Portraits in watercolor - Pt ii 60 MIN
VHS
Portraits in watercolor series
Color (J)
$39.95 purchase _ #HV - 678
Explores shape, color and value with wet - into - wet watercolors. Emphasizes interpretation over realism, and artistic content over illustration. Part II of a two - part series by James Kirk.
Fine Arts
Dist - CRYSP **Prod** - CRYSP

Portraits in watercolor series
Portraits in watercolor - Pt i 60 MIN
Portraits in watercolor - Pt ii 60 MIN
Dist - CRYSP

Portraits of aging 28 MIN
U-matic / VHS / 16mm
Color (J H C A)
$615.00, $250.00 purchase _ #78528; LC 79-707584
Deals with aging as a positive process, presenting profiles of older people who have found that the later years can be most enriching and satisfying.
Health and Safety; Sociology
Dist - CORF **Prod** - MILPRO 1979

Portraits of America - the national parks
VHS
International travel films from Doug Jones series
Color (G H)
$19.95 purchase _ #IT05
Explores United States national parks.
Geography - United States; Social Science
Dist - SVIP

Portraits of American Presidents 225 MIN
VHS
Color (I J H)
$59.95 purchase _ #QV2276
Takes a look at the office of the United States Chief Executive and the people who have served in the office. Places all of the presidents within the context of their times, gives a brief assessment of their characters, their families and the social and political influences at work on them. Contains three videos - The Presidents of a New Nation 1789 - 1829; The Presidents of a National Struggle 1829 - 1901; The Presidents of a World Power 1901 - 1992. Includes a booklet on 15 presidential decisions that shaped America.
Biography; Civics and Political Systems; History - United States
Dist - KNOWUN
CAMV

Portraits of anorexia (original version) 51 MIN
U-matic / VHS / 16mm
Color (J H C A)
$595.00 purchase - 16 mm, $425.00 purchase - video
Talks about the eating disorder anorexia nervosa, which affects two million Americans. A film by Wendy Zheutlin.
Psychology
Dist - CF

Portraits of anorexia (short version) 28 MIN
U-matic / VHS / 16mm
Color (J H C A)
$490.00 purchase - 16 mm, $370.00 purchase - video
Shows interviews with six anorectics.
Psychology
Dist - CF

Portraits of Eternity 29 MIN
Videoreel / VT2
Museum Open House Series
Color
Fine Arts
Dist - PBS **Prod** - WGBHTV

Portraits of goodbye series
Deborah
Harriet
Island
Marilyn and Orrin
The Spencers
Dist - ECUFLM

Portraits of the great Far East
VHS
International travel films from Doug Jones series
Color (G H)
$19.95 purchase _ #IT03
Explores the Far East.
Geography - World
Dist - SVIP

Portraits - Pt 1 2 MIN
16mm
Color (G)
$10.00 rental
Creates 'moving paintings' by shooting over 200 in - camera double exposures on one roll of film.
Fine Arts; Psychology
Dist - CANCIN **Prod** - MICHAL 1987

Ports of Call motor vessel - Cayman Brac 30 MIN
VHS
Scuba World series
Color (G)
$24.90 purchase _ #0445
Boards the Ports of Call to explore the waters of Little Cayman in the Caribbean.
Geography - World; Physical Education and Recreation
Dist - SEVVID

The Portsmouth story 23 MIN
16mm
B&W
LC FIE58-45
Describes the construction of the gaseous diffusion plant at Portsmouth, Ohio.
Geography - United States; Industrial and Technical Education
Dist - USNAC **Prod** - USNRC 1958

Portugal 30 MIN
VHS
Essential history of Europe
Color; PAL (H C A)
PdS65 purchase; Not available in Denmark
Presents the history and culture of Portugal from an insider's perspective. Tenth in a series of 12 programs featuring the history of European Community member countries.
Geography - World; History - World
Dist - BBCENE

Portugal 60 MIN
VHS
Color (G)
$29.95 purchase _ #ST - IV1802
Visits one of the oldest countries in Europe, and examines its history of kings, religion and exploration. Observes a bullfight and the wines of the Douro.
Geography - World; History - World
Dist - INSTRU

Portugal 60 MIN
VHS
Traveloguer Southern Europe series
Color (J H C G)
$29.95 purchase _ #QC119V
Visits Portugal and its cities. Illustrates notable landmarks, special events in history and the legends that are part of Portuguese culture. Part of a four part series on Southern Europe.
Geography - World; History - World
Dist - CAMV

Portugal
VHS / 16mm
(J H)
Shows Portugal's main industries which are agriculture, shipbuilding and ocean commerce, and, like many other European countries, tourism. Examines major agricultural products including cork, wheat, and port wine. Demonstrates the great contrasts of Portuguese society, ranging from villages still using the horse and buggy to modern sea ports such as Lisbon.
Geography - World; History - World
Dist - BARR **Prod** - BARR 1988

Portugal ; 1986 19 MIN
16mm
Modern Europe series
Color (I J)
LC 88-712598; 88-712600
Illustrates the geography, industry and the history of Portugal.
History - World
Dist - JOU **Prod** - PIHLFM 1986

Portugal and the Azores 55 MIN
VHS
Traveloguer series
Color (G H)
$24.95 purchase _ #TC19
Travels to Portugal and the Azores, showing maps, geography, museums, sports, landmarks, historical figures, cuisine, etc. Comes with reference booklet.
Geography - World
Dist - SVIP

Portugal and the sea 29 MIN
VHS / 16mm
Countries and peoples series
Color (H C G)
$90.00 purchase _ #BPN128118
Gives a history of Portugal's navigational feats and its modern industries of fishing, shipbuilding, and cork and wine production. Reveals the central place of Portugal's Catholic religion. Includes film segments of the people's elaborate ceremonial processions.
Business and Economics; Geography - World; History - World
Dist - RMIBHF TVOTAR **Prod** - RMIBHF TVOTAR

Portugal - Azores 60 MIN
VHS
Color (G)
$29.95 purchase _ #QU021
Presents a video vacation of Portugal and the Azores combining history, geography, scenery and people.
Geography - World
Dist - SIV

Portugal - land of discovery 60 MIN
VHS
Video visits series; European collection
Color (J H C G)
$29.95 purchase _ #IVN122V-S
Teaches about the people, culture and history of Portugal. Visits historic buildings, monuments and landmarks. Examines the physical topography of the country. Part of a 16-part series on European countries. Also part of a larger series entitled Video Visits that travels to six continents.
Geography - World; History - World
Dist - CAMV **Prod** - WNETTV

Portugal - Lisbon 15 MIN
U-matic / VHS
Color (I)
Familiarizes third through fifth grade pupils with other nations' cultures. Builds understanding by studying differences that might divide or cause confusion between various ethnic groups.
Sociology
Dist - GPN

Portugal - Nazare to Coimbra 15 MIN
VHS / U-matic
Color (I)
Familiarizes third through fifth grade pupils with other nations' cultures. Builds understanding by studying differences that might divide or cause confusion between various ethnic groups.
Sociology
Dist - GPN

Portugal - Porto to Visen 15 MIN
VHS / U-matic
Color (I)
Familiarizes third through fifth grade pupils with other nations' cultures. Builds understanding by studying differences that might divide or cause confusion between various ethnic groups.
Sociology
Dist - GPN

Portugal - the Algarve 15 MIN
U-matic / VHS
Color (I)
Familiarizes third through fifth grade pupils with other nations' cultures. Builds understanding by studying differences that might divide or cause confusion between various ethnic groups.
Sociology
Dist - GPN

Portugal - the North 15 MIN
VHS / U-matic
Color (I)
Familiarizes third through fifth grade pupils with other nations' cultures. Builds understanding by studying differences that might divide or cause confusion between various ethnic groups.
Sociology
Dist - GPN

Portuguese cooking 30 MIN
U-matic
World in your kitchen series
Color (G)
Gives instructions on cooking Portuguese vegetable soup and baked fish with olives.
Home Economics; Social Science
Dist - TVOTAR **Prod** - TVOTAR 1985

Portuguese cooking 28.5 MIN
VHS / 16mm
World in your kitchen series
Color (G)
$90.00 purchase _ #BPN003781
Shows how to use traditional Portuguese ingredients to make a vegetable soup and baked fish. Features Mary Melo.
Home Economics
Dist - RMIBHF **Prod** - RMIBHF

The Portuguese man - of - war 10 MIN
VHS
Natural history series
Color (I J H)
$60.00 purchase _ #A5VH 1105
Brings the Portuguese man - of - war into the classroom to observe it as it feeds on organisms killed by its poisonous tentacles. Reveals that the colonial organism is a member of phylum Cnidaria and shows how each member performs a specific duty - catching food, digesting food, producing sperm and eggs for reproduction. Part of a series on natural history.
Science - Natural
Dist - CLRVUE **Prod** - CLRVUE

Posie grows up - Bug Hollow 26 MIN
VHS / U-matic
Color (K)
$325.00, $295.00 purchase _ #V522
Depicts Posie the Caterpillar who is told by Sammy the Snake that she is a worm. Shows that she learns to trust her own feelings and know that she is indeed, a caterpillar. Includes songs and humorous insights from Bug Hollow residents.
Fine Arts; Literature and Drama
Dist - BARR **Prod** - CEPRO 1991

Posie is born - Bug Hollow 27 MIN
U-matic / VHS
Color (K)
$325.00, $295.00 purchase _ #V521
Depicts Posie the Caterpillar who hatches from her egg and looks forward to becoming a beautiful butterfly. Features songs and insights from Bug Hollow residents.
Fine Arts; Literature and Drama
Dist - BARR **Prod** - CEPRO 1991

Position and Tuning 29 MIN
Videoreel / VT2
Playing the Guitar I Series
Color
Fine Arts
Dist - PBS **Prod** - KCET

Position classification 16 MIN
16mm
Color
LC 75-703071
Explains fundamental concepts of position classification in the U S Federal Government and how it affects both supervisors and employees. Recorded in filmograph style.
Business and Economics; Civics and Political Systems
Dist - USNAC **Prod** - NASA 1968

Position management or position madness 23 MIN
U-matic / VHS
Position management series; 0333328
Color (A)
Discusses how individual employees and staff advisors solve problems. Emphasizes good position management.
Business and Economics; Guidance and Counseling; Psychology
Dist - USNAC **Prod** - USOPMA 1984

Position management series
The Classification process 27 MIN
Position management or position madness 23 MIN
Writing position descriptions - a helping hand 22 MIN
Dist - USNAC

A Position of faith 17 MIN
16mm / U-matic / VHS
Color (C A)
LC 73-702514
Tells the story of William Johnson, a student for the United Church of Christ Ministry, who declared himself to be a homosexual only a short time before ordination. Documents the events that followed, including the seminary's refusal to ordain, the debate within the congregation and the final vote to approve his ordination or not.
Guidance and Counseling; Religion and Philosophy; Sociology
Dist - MGHT **Prod** - RHODES 1972

The Position of the Moon 8 MIN
16mm
Basic Facts about the Earth, Sun, Moon and Stars Series
Color (K P)
Discusses the Moon, its rotation and revolution, its light source, its location and the relative size of the sun, moon and earth.
Science - Physical
Dist - SF **Prod** - MORLAT 1967

Position Paper - Brantford 58 MIN
16mm
Color (C A)
#3X68 I
Documents the presentation of the Position Paper of the Association of Allied Iroquois to the Minister Of Indian Affairs.

Social Science
Dist - CDIAND **Prod** - AKOP 1975

Positional Injuries in Surgery 13 MIN
U-matic / VHS
Anesthesiology Clerkship Series
Color (PRO)
Describes the most common causes of muscle and nerve damage occurring from malpositioning. Stresses prevention and recognition.
Health and Safety
Dist - UMICHM **Prod** - UMICHM 1976

Positional welding 46 MIN
VHS / 35mm strip
Color (H A IND)
#904BXV7
Explains the fundamentals of positional welding techniques and their application. Includes arc welding in the flat position, horizontal position, vertical position, and overhead position (4 tapes). Includes a Study Guide.
Education; Industrial and Technical Education
Dist - BERGL

Positioning 13 MIN
VHS
Clinical nursing skills - nursing fundamentals - series; 17
Color (C PRO G)
$395.00 purchase _ #R890 - VI - 057
Outlines the systematic method for proper positioning of the patient in bed to maximize patient comfort and good body alignment. Demonstrates the various bed positions and techniques for facilitating the changes - supine, side - lying, prone, Sims' and Fowler's positions. Shows proper placement of support pillows, rolls and bed elevation. Part of a 23 - part series on clinical nursing skills.
Health and Safety
Dist - HSCIC **Prod** - CUYAHO 1989

Positioning a patient confined to bed 30 MIN
16mm
Directions for education in nursing via technology series; Lesson 12
B&W (PRO)
LC 74-701786
Demonstrates positioning a patient in the dorsal, lateral and prone positions. Reviews and makes application of the principles of body mechanics to correct body alignment of the patient and the activities of the nurse. Includes demonstrations on the use of footboard, hand roll and trochanter roll.
Health and Safety
Dist - WSUM **Prod** - DENT 1974

Positioning aerial apparatus 20 MIN
VHS
Aerial apparatus series
Color (IND)
$135.00 purchase _ #35449
Presents one of a five - part series that is a teaching companion for IFSTA's Fire Department Aerial Apparatus. Shows typical positioning procedures. Displays four tactical uses of aerials. Emphasizes safety factors.
Health and Safety; Science - Physical; Social Science
Dist - OKSU **Prod** - ACCTRA

Positioning and handling the high risk infant - staff development 15 MIN
U-matic
NICU video series
Color (PRO)
$175.00 purchase
Illustrates how positioning and handling can be used to normalize a premature infant's muscle tone and movement patterns. Part of a seven - part series on developmental intervention for infants in the neonatal intensive care unit.
Health and Safety
Dist - POLYMR **Prod** - POKORJ

Positioning Apparatus 30 MIN
VHS
Pumping Apparatus Video Series
Color (G PRO)
$125.00 purchase _ #35409
Discusses positioning of pumping apparatus for different functions. Shows what is involved in determining positioning, demonstrates correct positioning, what to consider in special operations. Defines and demonstrates staging procedures, and presents safety and tactical considerations on limited access highways. Trains firefighting personnel.
Agriculture; Health and Safety; Psychology; Social Science
Dist - OKSU **Prod** - OKSU

Positioning for infants and young children with motor problems 29 MIN
VHS / 16mm
Childcare providers collection series
Color (A PRO)
$180.00 purchase, $50.00 rental
Stresses the importance of proper positioning, need for therapy, definition of hypertonic and hypotonic muscles and developmental stages.
Health and Safety
Dist - AITECH **Prod** - UCOLO 1988

Positioning for neurosurgical anesthesia 20 MIN
VHS / U-matic
Color (PRO C)
$395.00 purchase, $80.00 rental _ #C891 - VI - 029
Demonstrates techniques for preparing the operating table as well as proper procedure for the four positions commonly used in neurosurgery. Presented by Drs Sidney J Aidinis and John C Drummond, Judy Jonilonis, RN, and Drs Harvey M Shapiro and Consezione Tommasino.
Health and Safety
Dist - HSCIC

Positioning patient for comfort and safety 7 MIN
VHS / U-matic
Color (PRO) (SPANISH)
LC 77-731353
Emphasizes the exact conditions between correct standing - up posture and lying - down posture. Explains the development, causes and common locations of body deformities and contractures in a bedridden patient and describes the positioning and exercising of the patient that will prevent contractures. Provides instructions for the home nurse to be able to avoid strain or injury while caring for the patient.
Health and Safety; Physical Education and Recreation
Dist - MEDCOM **Prod** - MEDCOM

Positioning the patient 13 MIN
VHS / 16mm
Color (PRO)
$295.00 purchase, $60.00 rental
Diagrams and demonstrates four bed positions - Fowler's and Semi - Fowler's, supine or back lying, prone and semi - prone or Sims, and side lying or lateral. Presents indications and rationale for use of each position.
Health and Safety
Dist - FAIRGH **Prod** - FAIRGH 1987

Positioning the patient for surgery 27 MIN
16mm
Color (PRO)
Stresses the basic principles involved in positioning the patient for surgery and demonstrates how the nurse practitioner fulfills the responsibility for proper body posture of the patient. Shows dorsal recumbent, trendelburg, lithotomy, lateral and prone positions.
Health and Safety; Science
Dist - ACY **Prod** - ACYDGD 1957

Positioning the Player and His Cello - the Fusion of the Right Hand and the Bow 30 MIN
U-matic / VHS
Cello Sounds of Today Series
Color (J H A)
Fine Arts
Dist - IU **Prod** - IU 1984

Positioning the surgical patient 22 MIN
VHS
Color (PRO C G)
$395.00 purchase _ #R871 - VI - 021
Addresses briefly the effects of anesthesia on positioning and the preparations for a surgical procedure. Focuses on describing the various surgical positions - dorsal recumbent or supine, Trendelenburg, reverse Trendelenburg, lithotomy, prone, jackknife and the lateral. Includes with the description of each position examples of surgeries in which the procedure is used, information about the position itself and instructions for maneuvering the patient into position. Produced at St Joseph Hospital, Creighton Univ, Omaha, NE.
Health and Safety; Science - Natural
Dist - HSCIC

Positioning, turning, and transferring 60 MIN
U-matic / VHS
Color (PRO)
Provides basic training in the proper positioning and safe turning and transferring of persons with physical disabilities. Teaches recognizing a client's needs, describing these needs to a clinical specialist, and following a specialist's directions for client care are included.
Health and Safety; Psychology
Dist - UNEBO **Prod** - UNEBO

Positions and Draping of Patients for Physical Exams 14 MIN
VHS / BETA
Color
Describes the positions and draping of patients for physical exams.
Health and Safety
Dist - RMIBHF **Prod** - RMIBHF

Positive 80 MIN
16mm
Color (G)
Documents the struggle between homosexuals and people with AIDS on one hand, and a society and government perceived as indifferent on the other. Shows the response to AIDS by homosexual men in New York. Details the struggle of a minority which has organized itself to influence state and city policy. Presents an independent production by Rosa von Praunheim in collaboration with Phil Zwickler.
Health and Safety; Sociology
Dist - FIRS

Positive action series
Energy direction - Vol 2 3 MIN
It's OK to have Feelings, Vol 1 3 MIN
Dist - PROSOR

The Positive and Negative Numbers 15 MIN
VHS
Power of Algebra Series
Color (J)
LC 90712872
Uses computer animation and interviews with professionals who use algebra to explain positive and negative numbers. The fourth of 10 installments of The Power Of Algebra Series.
Mathematics
Dist - GPN

A Positive approach to the psychiatric patient 30 MIN
16mm
B&W
Shows the treatment in Veterans Administration Hospitals for psychiatric patients emerging from acute episodes of mental illness. Stresses the roles of the nurse, aide and physician.
Guidance and Counseling; Health and Safety; Psychology
Dist - USNAC **Prod** - USVA 1955

Positive approaches to fitness series
Positive approaches to nutrition - weighing the choices 22 MIN
Positive approaches to stress management - taking it in your stride 28 MIN
Positive approaches to well - being - health & lifestyle 28 MIN
A Sporting chance 25 MIN
Dist - EDPAT

Positive approaches to nutrition - weighing the choices 22 MIN
16mm / VHS / BETA / U-matic
Positive approaches to fitness series; No 2
Color; PAL (G PRO)
PdS150, PdS158 purchase
Deals with how to make positive choices. Presents part of a five - part series on fitness.
Health and Safety; Physical Education and Recreation; Social Science
Dist - EDPAT

Positive approaches to stress management - taking it in your stride 28 MIN
16mm / VHS / BETA / U-matic
Positive approaches to fitness series; No 4
Color; PAL (G PRO)
PdS150, PdS158 purchase
Focuses on solutions and skills for coping with stress. Teaches how to manage stress productively. Presents part of a five - part series on fitness.
Guidance and Counseling; Psychology
Dist - EDPAT

Positive approaches to well - being - health & lifestyle 28 MIN
16mm / VHS / BETA / U-matic
Positive approaches to fitness series; No 3
Color; PAL (G PRO)
PdS150, PdS158 purchase
Promotes the concept that the individual has a responsibility for the quality of his or her own life. Includes a guide to stress management, nutrition and weight control and the psychology of dependence. Presents part of a five - part series on fitness.
Health and Safety; Physical Education and Recreation; Social Science
Dist - EDPAT

Positive Aspects in Teaching African History 50 MIN
VHS / U-matic
Blacks, Blues, Black Series
Color
Education; History - United States; Sociology
Dist - PBS **Prod** - KQEDTV

Positive attitude - as I choose a better way 60 MIN
Software / VHS
Attributes for successful employability series; Module 3
Color (H)
$395.00 purchase
Presents work situations which call for choices. Indicates that while some choices are better than others, often there is no right answer. Includes scenes filmed at a variety of work environments. Provides learner with the opportunity to view, review and experiment with alternative solutions to problems presented. Stresses the importance of a pleasant personality, a sense of humor, proper grooming, communication, stress control, attitudes and customer - client relations.
Business and Economics; Guidance and Counseling; Psychology
Dist - AITECH **Prod** - BLUNI 1990

Positive attitudes I - getting a job
VHS
Career process series
Color (G A)
$84.95 purchase _ #ES1110V
Portrays interview situations which show how a positive attitude and high self - confidence help the chances of employment.
Business and Economics; Guidance and Counseling
Dist - CAMV

Positive attitudes I - getting a job 15 MIN
VHS / 16mm
Color (H C A PRO)
Emphasizes having a positive attitude in preparing for a job search. Presents tips for keeping a positive attitude - being on time, having a good appearance, stressing good points and being willing to learn.
Business and Economics; Guidance and Counseling
Dist - AAVIM **Prod** - AAVIM 1990
JISTW JISTW
CAREER CAREER

Positive Attitudes II - Keeping a Job 15 MIN
VHS / 35mm strip
Emphasizes the positive attitudes needed to keep a job. Stresses the need to accept constructive criticism, keep a good appearance, improve skills, and be considerate of co - workers.
Business and Economics; Guidance and Counseling
Dist - CAREER **Prod** - CAREER
JISTW JISTW
AAVIM AAVIM

Positive credit 30 MIN
VHS
Credit series
Color (H A C)
$79.95 purchase _ #CCPO158V
Addresses issues related to credit. Teaches viewers the basics of making a budget, what savings and assets are, how to become eligible for credit, and more. Features interviews with financial planners and loan officers. Part of a three-part series.
Business and Economics; Home Economics; Social Science
Dist - CAMV

Positive Discipline in the Classroom 28 MIN
U-matic / VHS
Successful Teaching Practices Series
Color (A C)
$75.00 purchase _ #1491
Features Bill Rose, special program teacher, as he emphasizes and demonstrates a caring and continuing attitude toward positive discipline that contributes to students' positive self - image. Includes views of students who discuss this attitude.
Education; Psychology
Dist - EBEC

Positive discipline - the key to building self - image 60 MIN
VHS
Teaching teachers series
Color (R T C G)
$49.95 purchase _ #TTBL2
Shows teachers in Roman Catholic schools the importance of setting professional goals, of caring, of having professional ethics and of having a sense of humor. Demonstrates ways in which teachers can create an atmosphere for positive discipline and student motivation and help students to develop a good self - image. Features teacher trainer Bob Lento, who is also a Catholic school teacher and principal. Part two of two parts.
Education; Religion and Philosophy; Sociology
Dist - CTNA **Prod** - CTNA

Positive - Displacement Downhole Mud Motors 20 MIN
VHS / U-matic
Color (IND)
Discusses the advantage of the Dyna - Drill downhill motor. Shows how it operates and how it is used for drilling both straight and directional holes.
Business and Economics; Industrial and Technical Education; Social Science
Dist - UTEXPE **Prod** - UTEXPE 1970

Positive displacement pumps - Pt 1 60 MIN
VHS
Pumps series
Color (PRO)
$600.00, $1500.00 purchase _ #GMPD1
Details the operation of various types of positive displacement pumps - gear, screw, lobe and reciprocal - and associated components. Describes pump seals and troubleshooting problems. Part of a seven - part series on pumps, which is part of a set on general and mechanical maintenance. Includes 10 textbooks and an instructor guide.
Education; Health and Safety; Industrial and Technical Education; Psychology
Dist - NUSTC **Prod** - NUSTC

Positive displacement pumps - Pt 2 60 MIN
VHS
Pumps series
Color (PRO)
$600.00, $1500.00 purchase _ #GMPD2
Focuses on the specifics of overhauling a positive displacement pump - job preparation, safety, disassembly, rotor and bearing inspection, casing inspection, clearances, reassembly and mechanical seal replacement. Part of a seven - part series on pumps, which is part of a set on general and mechanical maintenance. Includes 10 textbooks and an instructor guide.
Education; Health and Safety; Industrial and Technical Education; Psychology
Dist - NUSTC **Prod** - NUSTC

Positive images 58 MIN
VHS / 16mm
Color (G)
$295.00 purchase, $75.00 rental
Provides a positive, realistic picture of the lives of women with disabilities and the social, economic and political issues they face. Focuses on three strong and articulate women, their loves, work and politics. Offers role models for women and girls with disabilitities. Produced by Julie Harrison and Harilyn Rousso.
Fine Arts; Health and Safety; Psychology; Sociology
Dist - WMEN **Prod** - HR 1989

A Positive Look at Negative Numbers 10 MIN
16mm
Color (I J)
LC FIA65-281
Uses animation to construct a number line with points marked to represent positive and negative numbers and zero. Analogies from bookkeeping and from reading a thermometer help clarify the negative number concept.
Mathematics
Dist - FILCOM **Prod** - SIGMA 1964

Positive mental health for children
VHS
Color (P)
$65.00 purchase _ #V013
Introduces Rational - Emotive Therapy concepts to children. Demonstrates the relationship between thinking and feeling in a variety of everyday situations.
Guidance and Counseling; Psychology; Sociology
Dist - IRL **Prod** - IRL

Positive modalities - music and activity therapy for the aged 49 MIN
U-matic / VHS
Color (PRO C G)
$395.00 purchase, $80.00 rental _ #C861 - VI - 038
Contains excerpts from a three - day workshop of therapeutic treatment for physical, social and cognitive problems of the aged. Presented by Ronald McKorkle and Share Bane.
Health and Safety
Dist - HSCIC

Positive motion 37 MIN
VHS
Color (C G)
$195.00 purchase, $50.00 rental _ #38151
Follows an HIV - AIDS dance group in San Francisco led by pioneering dancer Anna Halprin. Shows a group of men using the crisis of AIDS and HIV infection as a resource for expressive movement. Records seven months of the group's workshops and shows how dance can be therapeutic to the dancer. of health. Details benefits to individuals and their communities. Produced by Andy Abrahams Wilson.
Fine Arts; Health and Safety; Sociology
Dist - UCEMC

Positive motivation strategies - Pt 1 57 MIN
VHS
Building and maintaining generalizations series
Color; PAL; SECAM (G)
$60.00 purchase
Features Richard Bandler in the first part of a six - part series on building and maintaining generalizations using submodalities from advanced NLP, neuro - linguistic programming. Shows how people are motivated, learn, become convinced and generalize. Contains the first recorded descriptions of Bandler's time model. Contains some profanity.
Health and Safety; Psychology
Dist - NLPCOM **Prod** - NLPCOM

Positive parenting 60 MIN
VHS
Color (H A)
$39.95 purchase _ #BPG500V
Presents a comprehensive, five - part program for helping children grow. Covers subjects including developing optimism, positive role models, being a child's best friend, and more.
Health and Safety
Dist - CAMV

Positive parenting 60 MIN
VHS
Color (A G)
$39.95 purchase _ #S02184
Suggests guidelines for parents to encourage confidence and self - esteem in their children. Covers subjects including self - esteem, role models, self - determination, self - discipline and optimism. Hosted by Dr Denis Waitley.
Health and Safety; Psychology; Sociology
Dist - UILL
APH

Positive parenting series
How to get results with kids - Tape One 54 MIN
How to manage conflict and build positive behavior - Tape Two 49 MIN
Dist - NLPCOM

Positive Patient Safety through Simplified Operating Room Nursing Techniques 33 MIN
16mm
Color (PRO)
Illustrates simplified, uncomplicated operating room nursing techniques used to limit, confine and destroy bacteria in the operating room and surrounding environment. Emphasizes the relationship of the nurse to the patient and other team members.
Health and Safety; Science
Dist - ACY **Prod** - ACYDGD 1961

Positive Philosophy of Life Series
The Joy of Communication 18 MIN
Dist - DANA

Positive planning for defensive practice session 27 MIN
U-matic / VHS
Joe Paterno - coaching 'winning football' series
Color (C A)
$49.00 purchase _ #3772
Demonstrates how to best utilize available resources, practice time, and practice schedules while emphasizing the importance of practice organization in football. Conducted by Joe Paterno, head coach of the Penn State football team.
Physical Education and Recreation
Dist - EBEC

Positive prescription - supervisory training for healthcare providers 18 MIN
VHS / BETA / U-matic
Color (G)
$475.00 purchase, $130.00 rental
Shows supervisors how to balance criticism with praise, give sincere, positive recognition both verbally and nonverbally, effectively recognize individual and group achievement for future improvement and understand the importance of evaluation.
Business and Economics; Psychology
Dist - AMEDIA **Prod** - AMEDIA

Positive Pressure Ventilation Series
Principles and Basic Set - Up 27 MIN
Principles and basic set - up - Pt 1 27 MIN
Set - up variations and fire attack 27 MIN
Set - up variations and fire attack 27 MIN
Dist - OKSU

Positive Pressure Ventilation Videos 54 MIN
VHS
Color (PRO G)
$250.00 purchase _ #35416
Presents a two - part video series on the principles, theory, equipment selection and basic set - up for positive

pressure ventilation. Demonstrates positive pressure during fire attack, salvage and overhaul. Includes instructor and study guides.
Health and Safety; Psychology; Social Science
Dist - OKSU **Prod** - OKSU

Positive reconditioning of neurological injuries 21 MIN
U-matic
Biofeedback strategies series; Pt 3
Color (PRO)
Shows how dual - channel EMG training is integrated with other neurodevelopmental techniques for muscle re - education.
Health and Safety; Psychology
Dist - AOTA **Prod** - AOTA 1981

Positive Reinforcement 40 MIN
U-matic / VHS
Learning and Liking it Series
Color (T)
Describes the strategies for use and selection of reinforcers to encourage children.
Education; Psychology
Dist - MSU **Prod** - MSU

Positive reinforcement 10 MIN
U-matic / VHS
Protocol materials in teacher education - the process of teaching, 'series; Pt 2
Color (T)
Education; Psychology
Dist - MSU **Prod** - MSU

Positive self - determination
VHS
Psychology of winning learning system series
Color (A PRO)
$85.50 purchase _ #5710VU
Presents the Denis Waitley approach to winning through positive self - determination. Uses the concept of 'synergistic' learning. Set includes a video, a review audiocassette and an action guide.
Psychology; Sociology
Dist - NIGCON **Prod** - NIGCON

Positive self - dimension
VHS
Psychology of winning learning system series
Color (A PRO)
$85.50 purchase _ #5740VU
Presents the Denis Waitley approach to winning through positive self - dimension. Uses the concept of 'synergistic' learning. Set includes a video, a review audiocassette and an action guide.
Psychology; Sociology
Dist - NIGCON **Prod** - NIGCON

Positive self - discipline
VHS
Psychology of winning learning system series
Color (A PRO)
$85.50 purchase _ #5730VU
Presents the Denis Waitley approach to winning through positive self - discipline. Uses the concept of 'synergistic' learning. Set includes a video, a review audiocassette and an action guide.
Psychology; Sociology
Dist - NIGCON **Prod** - NIGCON

Positive self - expectancy
VHS
Psychology of winning learning system series
Color (A PRO)
$85.50 purchase _ #5720VU
Presents the Denis Waitley approach to winning through positive self - expectancy. Uses the concept of 'synergistic' learning. Set includes a video, a review audiocassette and an action guide.
Psychology; Sociology
Dist - NIGCON **Prod** - NIGCON

Positive shortage prevention series
The Dollar drain 16 MIN
Dist - SAUM

The Positive Show 28 MIN
16mm
Special Delivery Series
Color (P I)
LC 79-701077
Illustrates the things that handicapped people can do which others might not expect them to be able to accomplish.
Education; Psychology
Dist - LAWREN **Prod** - WNVT 1979

Positive thinking 25 MIN
VHS
Lowdown series
Color; PAL (G F)
PdS45 purchase
Tackles the subject of AIDS and HIV by listening to the children who are both infected and affected by the virus. Documents the experiences of about 400 children in Great Britain who are infected with HIV as they learn about the risks involved in everyday living.
Health and Safety
Dist - BBCENE

Positive vibes 10 MIN
VHS / U-matic
Color (A)
Shows University of South Carolina head basketball coach Bill Foster focusing on the importance of creating a winning attitude, both on the court and off.
Physical Education and Recreation
Dist - SFTI **Prod** - SFTI

Positive work habits - what they didn't tell you at school
VHS
Color (H G)
$98.00 purchase _ #JOB-500A; $98.00 purchase _ #CDJOB500V
Features advice about the qualities that give employers confidence in their employees. Illustrates crucial 'do's and 'don't's for the first - time employee. Covers appearance, being on time, being a good listener, having a good attention span, and being familiar with one's job description.
Business and Economics; Guidance and Counseling
Dist - CFKRCM **Prod** - CFKRCM
CAMV

Positively Change Your Life - for Men 60 MIN
VHS / U-matic
Self Help Subliminal Series
Stereo (C)
Gives subliminal suggestions on how to actively change your life for the better.
Health and Safety; Psychology
Dist - BANTAP **Prod** - BANTAP 1986

Positively Change Your Life - for Women 60 MIN
VHS / U-matic
Self Help Subliminal Series
Stereo (C)
Gives subliminal suggestions on how to actively change your life for the better.
Health and Safety; Psychology
Dist - BANTAP **Prod** - BANTAP 1986

Positively Yoga 62 MIN
Cassette / VHS
Color (G)
$19.95, $11.95 purchase _ #407, #214
Opens the lines of communication between body and mind through yoga. Features James Gagner and meditations by Louise L Hay.
Health and Safety; Physical Education and Recreation; Psychology
Dist - HAYHSE **Prod** - HAYHSE

Possessive nouns and pronouns 10 MIN
VHS / BETA
English and speech series
Color
English Language
Dist - RMIBHF **Prod** - RMIBHF

Possessives and Plurals of Nouns 14.27 MIN
VHS / U-matic
Grammar Mechanic
(I J)
Designed to help intermediate students apply the rules of grammar. Focuses on formation and usage of plurals and possessives. Fifth in a series of 16.
English Language
Dist - GPN **Prod** - WDCNTV

Possessives - nouns and pronouns 15 MIN
VHS
Planet pylon series
Color (I P)
LC 90712897
Uses character Commander Wordstalker from Space Station Readstar to develop language arts skills. Studies the possessive forms of nouns and pronouns. Includes worksheet to be used by student with help from series characters. Intended for third graders.
Education; English Language
Dist - GPN

Possibilities 12 MIN
U-matic / VHS
Color (C A)
Portrays a male quadraplegic's sexual relationship with emphasis on the couple's warm feelings for each other and pleasuring techniques. Talks about the injury's impact on his sex life.
Health and Safety; Psychology
Dist - MMRC **Prod** - NATSF

Possibilities in Clay 25 MIN
U-matic / 8mm cartridge
Color (H C A)
LC 76-701240
Examines four different approaches to working with clay and ceramics.
Fine Arts
Dist - IU **Prod** - IU 1976

Possible cures for FUNARG problems 50 MIN
U-matic / VHS
Computer languages series; Pt 1
Color
Industrial and Technical Education; Mathematics; Sociology
Dist - MIOT **Prod** - MIOT

The Possible dream - the quest for racial and ethnic harmony in American schools 45 MIN
VHS
Color (I J H C)
$69.95 purchase _ #FP100V - S
Features a group of students discussing racial differences and looking for solutions to problems found at schools throughout the United States. Reveals that after a racial brawl at their school, the participants in the discussion felt a racial war was imminent and that the American dream was a 'joke.' Joins psychiatrist Dr Alvin Poussaint, who helps students confront their anger, fears and differences, and to discover new confidence that they can make a difference and change the United States for the better. Includes a foreword by US Attorney General Janet Reno and a lesson guide.
Psychology; Social Science; Sociology
Dist - CAMV

The Possible Human 58 MIN
VHS / 16mm
Color (G)
$495.00 purchase, $175.00 rental ; $395.00 purchase, $100.00 rental
Features Dr Jean Houston, educator, consultant and author. Discusses ways to develop and expand learning capacities.
Psychology
Dist - PROSOR

The Possible Presidents - Vice Presidents and Third Parties 52 MIN
U-matic / VHS / 16mm
Presidency Series
Color (J)
Looks at five men who have served as Vice President and then as President. Examines how they achieved this position.
Biography; Civics and Political Systems
Dist - LUF **Prod** - CORPEL 1976

Possible Programs and Policies of the U S 27 MIN
VHS / U-matic
Technology, Innovation, and Industrial Development Series
Color
Business and Economics
Dist - MIOT **Prod** - MIOT

The Possible role of sex hormones in gynecological cancer 55 MIN
U-matic
Color
Describes a research development concerning steroid hormones and their relationship to gynecologic cancer.
Health and Safety
Dist - UTEXSC **Prod** - UTEXSC

Possible solution 30 MIN
U-matic / VHS
Ecology - our road to survival series
Color
Discusses solutions to environmental problems, which must include education and awareness.
Science - Natural; Sociology
Dist - NETCHE **Prod** - NETCHE 1971

Possibly in Michigan 12 MIN
VHS / U-matic
Cecilia Condit Series
Color (G)
$250.00, $200.00 purchase, $50.00 rental
Follows two female friends who go shopping in a mall and are followed home by a creepy man. In an ironic climax of victim reversal, the women consume their pursuer. Plays in a macabre way on the concepts of consumerism and consumption.
Fine Arts; Literature and Drama
Dist - WMEN **Prod** - CECON 1985

Possibly so, Pythagoras 14 MIN
U-matic / VHS / 16mm
Color; Captioned (J H) (ARABIC)
Investigates the Pythagorean theorem through induction as well as through formal deductive proof. Captioned for the hearing impaired.

Mathematics
Dist - IFB **Prod** - IFB 1963

The Possum 13 MIN
16mm
Color (C A)
Documents the feeling of a segment of time, a moment on a highway after a storm.
Fine Arts
Dist - CANCIN **Prod** - VIERAD 1975

Possum opossum 28 MIN
U-matic / VHS
Color
Takes a witty and affectionate look at a town and the people who dispense stories about the mythological possum.
Literature and Drama
Dist - SOFOLK **Prod** - KILLMR

The Possum that Didn't 11 MIN
16mm / U-matic / VHS
Color; B&W (K P I J)
LC 72-700695
Deals with superficial values, insensitivity and self - aggrandizement disguised as concern for others.
Guidance and Counseling; Literature and Drama; Psychology; Sociology
Dist - PHENIX **Prod** - PHENIX 1972

Possum trot - the life and work of Calvin Black 29 MIN
16mm / U-matic / VHS
Color
LC 77-700568
Documents the art of Calvin Black, a folk artist of the Mojave Desert who has created over 80 wooden, nearly life - size dolls, each with its own personality, function and costume. Shows how he built the theater where the dolls perform and sing in voices recorded by Black.
Fine Arts
Dist - PHENIX **Prod** - POSSUM 1977
SARLGT SARLGT

Post - anesthesia assessment 28 MIN
VHS
Color (PRO C)
$285.00 purchase, $70.00 rental _ #6511
Discusses the purpose, components and documentation of post - anesthesia assessment. Stresses the importance of getting the anesthesia report with complete information. Explains the post - anesthesia recovery scoring systems - PAR. Describes five sample PACU nursing care plans and discusses their use in helping to determine the appropriate nursing diagnosis for the patient and to plan the patient's care.
Health and Safety
Dist - AJN **Prod** - HESCTV

Post - anesthesia nursing - guidelines for care 28 MIN
VHS / U-matic
Color (PRO)
$275.00 purchase, $60.00 rental _ #7528S, #7528V
Presents guidelines for delivery of skilled post - anesthesia care according to standards developed by the American Society for Post - Anesthesia Nurses - ASPAN. Explores pre and postoperative assessment, stressing supportive, instructive communications, the types and effects of anesthesia, the Aldrete Scoring System used in assessment and decision making and factors requiring postoperative monitoring. Covers nursing diagnosis and care plan and implementation. Demonstrates the process through evaluation and discharge of patients from the postanesthesia care unit - PACU.
Health and Safety
Dist - AJN **Prod** - HOSSN 1985

Post colonial waltz - Pt 1 55 MIN
VHS
Slow boat from Surabaya series
Color (J H C)
$225.00 purchase
Travels the colonial trail. Takes a look at the British in Malaysia and Singapore, the Dutch in Indonesia, the Spanish in the Philippines, the French in Vietnam and the later incursion of Americans in the Philippines. Part one of a six - part series on Southeast Asia covering the Philippines, Thailand, Singapore, Indonesia, Malaysia, Vietnam and Kampuchnea.
History - World
Dist - LANDMK **Prod** - LANDMK 1992

Post Coronary Care 16 MIN
U-matic / VHS / 16mm
Color (PRO) (SPANISH)
Reviews causes of myocardial infarction and explains how the heart heals.
Health and Safety; Science - Natural
Dist - PRORE **Prod** - PRORE

The Post coronary patient
U-matic / VHS
Color (SPANISH)
Describes a heart attack patient who resumes living with a few modifications in his lifestyle. Describes his rehabilitation from hospital to home to work. Covers eating, exercise and regular check - ups. Stresses resuming an active, healthier life.
Health and Safety; Science - Natural
Dist - MIFE **Prod** - MIFE

Post - harvest care of cut flowers 16 MIN
VHS
Flower industry series
Color (G)
$89.95 purchase _ #6 - 109 - 100A
Reveals that cut flowers need specialized care to arrive fresh to the consumer. Shows how to properly care for cut flowers from harvest to retail. Part of a series on the flower industry.
Agriculture; Science - Natural
Dist - VEP **Prod** - VEP 1993

Post - impressionism 20 MIN
VHS
ARTV series
Color (J)
$44.95 purchase _ #E323; LC 90-708452
Offers music videos which feature the art works of Vincent Van Gogh, Paul Gauguin, Seurat and Lautrec. Part of a ten - part ARTV series which uses TV format, including 'commercials' which sell one aspect of an artist's style and a gossip columnist who gives little known facts about the artists.
Fine Arts
Dist - GPN **Prod** - HETV 1989

Post - impressionism to Cubism 20 MIN
VHS
ARTV series
Color (J)
$44.95 purchase _ #E323; LC 90-708453
Offers music videos which discuss the art works of Paul Cezanne - 'End of the Century' and Pablo Picasso - 'Can You Imagine,' and the works of Matisse and Kandinsky. Part of a ten - part ARTV series which uses TV format, including 'commercials' which sell one aspect of an artist's style and a gossip columnist who gives little known facts about the artists.
Fine Arts
Dist - GPN **Prod** - HETV 1989

The Post - impressionists 25 MIN
U-matic / VHS / BETA
Color; PAL (G H C)
PdS50, PdS58 purchase
Surveys the aims, influences and techniques of Cezanne, Gauguin, Van Gogh, Seurat and Toulouse Lautrec. Concludes with a statement of how the experiments and the work of these artists led to different movements in painting. Produced with George Barford, Illinois State University.
Fine Arts
Dist - EDPAT **Prod** - IFB

Post Industrial Fiddle 23 MIN
U-matic / VHS / 16mm
Color (A)
Discusses the relationship between work and music for Down East Style Fiddle player Gerry Morrell.
Fine Arts
Dist - CNEMAG **Prod** - CNEMAG 1982

Post - mastectomy exercises - Pt 1 10 MIN
VHS / U-matic
Mastectomy education series
Color (PRO C G)
$195.00 purchase _ #C890 - VI - 080
Presents the first part of two parts on post - mastectomy exercises. Provides a regimen of simple and light exercises to perform while still in the hospital. Allows the patient to work gradually toward strengthening the upper body and toward increasing mobility in the arm on the affected side. Part of a five - part series on mastectomy education presented by physical therapist Jan Anthes, Zaira Becker, RN, Linda Waldren, RN, Pilar Gonzalez, RN and Leatha Ross, RN.
Health and Safety
Dist - HSCIC

Post - mastectomy exercises - Pt 2 30 MIN
VHS / U-matic
Mastectomy education series
Color (PRO C G)
$195.00 purchase _ #C890 - VI - 081
Presents the second part of two parts on post - mastectomy exercises. Provides a more rigorous series of exercises designed to be performed with increasing intensity in order to allow the mastectomy patient to return to complete freedom of function. Part of a five - part series on mastectomy education presented by physical therapist Jan Anthes, Zaira Becker, RN, Linda Waldren, RN, Pilar Gonzalez, RN and Leatha Ross, RN.
Health and Safety; Physical Education and Recreation
Dist - HSCIC

Post - modern daydream 3 MIN
16mm / VHS
B&W (G)
$10.00 rental
Blends picture and sound to convey a sense of the 1906 San Francisco earthquake. A Larry Kless production made six months prior to the 1989 earthquake that shook the San Francisco Bay area.
Fine Arts; Geography - United States
Dist - CANCIN

Post - Mortem 15 MIN
16mm
Color
LC FIA67-1124
Uses dramatized incidents to portray the effect of common everyday drugs on automobile drivers and their contribution to traffic accidents.
Health and Safety
Dist - CINEA **Prod** - CINEA 1967
AIMS

Post Mortem 18 MIN
U-matic / VHS
Color (H C A)
Presents scientific evidence that Napoleon did not die of natural causes but was poisoned intentionally. Features a Canadian businessman and Napoleon buff, Ben Weider, discussing the evidence and the reasons he believes this information to be true.
History - World
Dist - JOU **Prod** - JOU

Post mortem 24 MIN
16mm / VHS / BETA / U-matic
Color; PAL (G)
PdS120, PdS128 purchase
Deals with the reality of misused prescription drugs.
Health and Safety; Psychology
Dist - EDPAT

Post Mortem Inspection - Cattle Heads 18 MIN
16mm
Color (IND)
LC 77-700954
Shows post mortem inspection procedures for examining the heads of cattle as a means of assuring their health quality.
Agriculture; Health and Safety; Science
Dist - USNAC **Prod** - USDA 1968

Post Mortem Inspection - Cattle Viscera and Carcass 17 MIN
16mm
Color (IND)
LC 77-700955
Shows post mortem health check and quality control inspection of cattle viscera.
Agriculture; Health and Safety; Science
Dist - USNAC **Prod** - USDA 1968

Post Mortem Inspection - Sheep and Calves 13 MIN
16mm
Color (IND)
LC 77-700956
Shows health check and quality control techniques recommended for post mortem inspection of sheep and calves.
Agriculture; Health and Safety; Science
Dist - USNAC **Prod** - USDA 1968

Post Mortem Inspection - Swine 11 MIN
16mm
Color (IND)
LC 77-700957
Shows health check and quality control techniques recommended for post mortem inspection of swine.
Agriculture; Health and Safety; Science
Dist - USNAC **Prod** - USDA 1968

Post moves
VHS
N C A A instructional video series
Color (H C A)
$39.95 purchase _ #KAR1253V
Presents the third of a three - part series on women's basketball. Focuses on post moves.
Physical Education and Recreation
Dist - CAMV **Prod** - NCAAF

Post - natal care 14 MIN
U-matic / VHS / 16mm
Woman talk series
Color (H C A)
Explains the importance of getting back into good physical condition after the birth of a baby. Reviews the first months, which can be very tiring as the new mother

adjusts to a new schedule and additional household duties. A mime demonstrates several post - natal exercises which can be started right in the hospital bed.
Health and Safety; Sociology
Dist - CORF **Prod** - CORF 1983

Post - Natal Care of a Song 29 MIN
U-matic
Song Writer Series
Color
Demonstrates the many steps between the birth of the song and the royalty checks.
Fine Arts
Dist - UMITV **Prod** - UMITV 1977

Post no Bills 9 MIN
16mm
Color (J H A)
LC 72-700410
A satire on the subject of commitment as revealed in an account about a man who destroys billboards as an act of civil disobedience, becomes a hero and is exploited in an advertisement which is ironically put on a billboard.
Psychology
Dist - MMA **Prod** - AISONE 1970

Post office 30 MIN
VHS
How do you do - learning English series
Color (H A)
#317718
Shows how CHIPS, a robot, learns about the many services offered by the post office. Demonstrates how to make different inquiries at a post office. Part of a series that helps newcomers learn English or improve their ability. Includes viewer's guide with grammar explanations and vocabulary drills, worksheets and two audio cassettes.
English Language
Dist - TVOTAR **Prod** - TVOTAR 1990

The Post office 15 MIN
VHS / U-matic / 16mm / BETA
Your town I series
Color (K P)
$245.00, $68.00 purchase _ #C50711, #C51472
Follows a birthday card through its postal handling Shows how mail is collected, carried, sorted, transported and delivered. Part of a five - part series on community services.
Social Science
Dist - NGS **Prod** - NGS 1991

Post office clerk 15 MIN
U-matic / 16mm / VHS
Career awareness
(I)
$130.00 VC purchase, $240.00 film purchase, $25.00 VC rental, $30.00 film rental
Presents an empathetic approach to career planning, showing personal as well as professional attributes of post office clerks. Highlights the importance of career education.
Civics and Political Systems; Guidance and Counseling; Social Science
Dist - GPN

Post office exams
VHS / 16mm
Test preparation video series
Color (H)
$39.95 _ VAI 116
Reviews post office examinations. Offers testing strategies and problem solving techniques.
Business and Economics; Guidance and Counseling; Psychology
Dist - CADESF **Prod** - CADESF

Post - operative care 15 MIN
VHS / 16mm
Licensed practical nursing assistant refresher series
Color (C)
$75.00 purchase _ #270507
Helps nursing assistants make the transition back to their chosen career after an extended absence. Updates nursing techniques and procedures which have changed substantially in the last decade. Provides a practical demonstration of step - by - step nursing procedures. Details the procedures used to tend to a surgical patient. Covers transferring, scheduled vital readings, pain assessment, mouth care, bed bath and exercises.
Health and Safety
Dist - ACCESS **Prod** - ACCESS 1989

Post Partum 36 MIN
16mm
Color (PRO)
LC 79-701728
Illustrates the role of the nurse clinician in caring for the post partum patient and her family, using the problem oriented approach as a method of analyzing, categorizing, synthesizing and utilizing data from medical records.
Demonstrates use of a paper chart in conjunction with centralized computer storage.
Health and Safety
Dist - USNAC **Prod** - NMAC 1979

Post partum depression 28 MIN
16mm / U-matic / VHS
Color (A)
LC 80-701651
Presents two couples who worked their way through post partum depression with the help of a psychiatrist. Looks at the symptoms and causes of the illness.
Health and Safety; Psychology
Dist - PEREN **Prod** - NFBC 1978

Post - placement counseling 25 MIN
16mm
Counseling the mentally retarded series; No 5
Color (PRO)
LC 72-702022
Illuminates the problems of retarded persons in social and work situations in the community through interviews with teachers, counselors, employers and parents of retarded persons.
Psychology; Sociology
Dist - NMAC **Prod** - UKANS 1968

Post - Prostatectomy Urinary Incontinence 20 MIN
16mm
Color (PRO)
LC 75-702294
Presents a cine - cystourethrographic demonstration of the mechanism of continence and incontinence and the endoscopic findings in a patient with postprostatectomy urinary incontinence. Discusses methods of treatment and illustrates a recommended procedure in detail.
Health and Safety; Science; Science - Natural
Dist - EATONL **Prod** - EATONL 1968

Post reinforcement for anterior teeth - Pt 1 - composite core 13 MIN
16mm
Color (PRO)
LC 79-700979
Shows preparation of the post channel and auxiliary pin channels and cementation of a stainless - steel post and two cemented - type pins. Demonstrates placement and preparation for the composite filing material to create a post - reinforced composite core to serve as the foundation for the full crown.
Health and Safety
Dist - USNAC **Prod** - VADTC 1978

Post reinforcement for anterior teeth - Pt 3 - indirect cast core 14 MIN
16mm
Color (PRO)
LC 79-700981
Shows various steps in making a one - piece, post - reinforced cast core for an anterior tooth using an indirect technique. Demonstrates preparation of the post and pin channels, fitting a smooth plastic post and pins to the channels, impressionmaking, pouring the cast and use of a resin pattern material to fabricate a pattern indirectly on the cast.
Health and Safety
Dist - USNAC **Prod** - VADTC 1978

Post reinforcement for anterior teeth - Pt 2 - direct cast core 13 MIN
16mm
Color (PRO)
LC 79-700980
Demonstrates a direct technique for fabricating a one - piece, post - reinforced cast core for an anterior tooth. Shows how a precious - metal post and two precious - metal pins are fitted to the prepared post channel and pin channels. Reveals how a resin pattern material is added directly against the tooth, shaped to the desired dimension, sprued and cast, and the resulting core is polished and cemented to the tooth.
Health and Safety
Dist - USNAC **Prod** - VADTC 1978

Post Reinforcement for Bicuspid Teeth 13 MIN
16mm
Color (PRO)
LC 79-701427
Demonstrates three methods of achieving a post reinforced amalgam core for bicuspid teeth using root canals and stainless steel posts and/or pins. Shows how amalgam is packed around the posts and/or pins and, at a subsequent visit, is prepared for a full - crown foundation.
Health and Safety
Dist - USNAC **Prod** - VADTC 1978

Post Reinforcement for Molar Teeth 13 MIN
16mm
Color (PRO)
LC 79-700988
Shows how to accomplish a post - reinforced amalgam core for mandibular and maxillary molars using stainless - steel posts and auxiliary pins. Demonstrates a copper - band matrix with interproximal wedging, packing amalgam material around posts and pins, and preparation of the amalgam core to provide a full - crown foundation.
Health and Safety
Dist - USNAC **Prod** - VADTC 1978

Post Reinforcement of Tooth with Endodontics and Full Crown Preparation 13 MIN
16mm
Color (PRO)
LC 79-700989
Demonstrates how the root canal is prepared to create a post channel, with parallel sides which extend one - half to two - thirds of the length of the root. Shows cementation of a cylindrical, stainless - steel, serrated vented post within the channel to reinforce the tooth.
Health and Safety
Dist - USNAC **Prod** - VADTC 1978

Post reinforcement - principles and armamentarium 14 MIN
16mm
Color (PRO)
LC 79-701428
Explains how to use post reinforcement, improved techniques of root - canal therapy and other methods of periodontal surgery to contribute to preventive dentistry procedures. Describes the different sizes of color - coded drills and the variety of mated accessories, and lists their indications and use.
Health and Safety
Dist - USNAC **Prod** - VADTC 1978

Post - shooting trauma 38 MIN
VHS
Crime to court procedural specials series
Color (PRO)
$99.00 purchase
Details symptoms and treatment for trauma - induced stress. Includes a dramatization of an officer who shoots and kills a felon and interviews with other officers involved in shootings. Trains law enforcement personnel. Part of an ongoing series which looks in depth at topics presented in 'Crime To Court.' Produced in conjunction with the South Carolina Criminal Justice Academy and the National Sheriffs' Association.
Civics and Political Systems; Psychology; Sociology
Dist - SCETV **Prod** - SCETV

Post synchronization - the editor's role 28 MIN
VHS
Color (PRO G)
$149.00 purchase, $49.00 rental _ #765
Shows the shooting of a period scene on a noisy location. Follows three possible dialog replacement procedures - the orginal method in which the film and guide track are cut into short loops, the 'rock and roll' procedure using synchronous rollback, and the modern Automatic Dialogue Replacement or ADR method. Shows how guide tracks are prepared for each procedure, how the recording session is executed and how the new tracks are integrated with sound effects and music to create a polished final track. Produced by the Australian Film, Television and Radio School.
Fine Arts; Industrial and Technical Education
Dist - FIRLIT

Post vaginal colpotomy 10 MIN
U-matic / VHS
Color (PRO)
Discussion and illustration of his approach to post vaginal colpotomy by Dr Johnnie Betson.
Health and Safety
Dist - WFP **Prod** - WFP

The Post - war era - film noir and the Hollywood ten 20 MIN
U-matic / VHS / 16mm
Life goes to the movies series; Pt 3
Color
LC 77-701543
Discusses the films which reflected the concerns of the post - World War II era by exploring themes such as crime, prejudice, mental illness, alcoholism and drugs. Examines the effects of the Cold War and Mc Carthyism on the entertainment industry.
Fine Arts; History - United States; Sociology
Dist - TIMLIF **Prod** - TIMLIF 1976

Post - war politics and art 30 MIN
VHS
Art America series
Color (H C)
$43.00 purchase
Considers the role of art in the United States after World War I, looking at its use for social criticism. Provides

background information about US social and cultural history of the period. Part of a 20-part series on art in America.
Fine Arts; History - United States
Dist - GPN

Post - war problems beyond - Pt 3 107 MIN
VHS
March of time - post - war problems and solutions series
B&W (G)
$24.95 purchase _ #S02131
Presents the third installment of a five - part series of newsreel excerpts covering the post - World War II era in the United States and abroad. Segments include The New US Frontier, Palestine Problem, and 18 Million Orphans.
History - United States; History - World
Dist - UILL

Post - war problems beyond - Pt 4 125 MIN
VHS
March of time - post - war problems and solutions series
B&W (G)
$24.95 purchase _ #S02132
Presents the fourth installment of a five - part series of newsreel excerpts covering the post - World War II era in the US and abroad. Segments include World Food Problem, The Soviets' Neighbor, Czechoslovakia, and Germany - Handle With Care.
History - United States; History - World; Social Science
Dist - UILL

Post War Russia Under Stalin 29 MIN
Videoreel / VT2
Course of Our Times II Series
Color
History - World
Dist - PBS **Prod** - WGBHTV

Post - War Years - the Far East 30 MIN
VHS / U-matic
Historically Speaking Series; Pt 24
Color (H)
Reviews Mao Tse Tung's peasant - based communist revolution in China, the Western reaction to the wars in Korea and Vietnam, Gandhi's non - violent movement in India and problems resulting from India's independence.
History - World
Dist - AITECH **Prod** - KRMATV 1983

Post - War Years - the West 30 MIN
U-matic / VHS
Historically Speaking Series; Pt 23
Color (H)
Analyzes the Soviet Union and the United States as superpowers in the cold war. Looks at the problem of Berlin and the Berlin Wall, and problems in the Near East and their significance in international affairs.
History - United States; History - World
Dist - AITECH **Prod** - KRMATV 1983

Postal Service 29 MIN
VHS / 16mm
Washington Connection Series
Color (G)
$55.00 rental _ #WACO - 107
Civics and Political Systems; Social Science
Dist - PBS **Prod** - NPACT

Postal service - a letter to a football hero 17 MIN
U-matic / 16mm / VHS
Color (P I)
LC 78-700580
A revised edition of the 1966 motion picture Our Post Office. Demonstrates the workings of the U S postal system by telling a true story about a boy with a hearing disability and his correspondence with a professional football player with the same problem. Shows the correct way to address letters and highlights postal workers and postal machinery.
Social Science
Dist - EBEC **Prod** - EBEC 1977

Postal workers 11 MIN
U-matic / VHS / 16mm
Community helpers series
Color (P I)
$280.00, $195.00 purchase _ #79512
Shows the complex system of machines and people that the United States postal service needs to operate efficiently.
Civics and Political Systems; Social Science
Dist - CORF

Postcards from Nicaragua - Postales de Nicaragua libre 50 MIN
VHS
Color (G)
$40.00 purchase
Shows arts and crafts, skills and labor, ceremonies and public statements from Nicaragua, summer 1984. Includes musicians, restaurants, straw market, market women in Masaya; saddle makers, rock gathering, washing, Sandinista vice - presidential candidate Sergio Ramirez campaigning, burial of a combatant, in Esteli. Also features three videos about Nicaragua by Julia Lesage in Spanish entitled Lamento; La Escuela; and Parque Wilfredo Valenzuela. Produced by Chuck Kleinhans.
Fine Arts; Geography - World
Dist - CANCIN

Postcode 10 MIN
VHS
Stop, look, listen series
Color; PAL (P I J)
Documents a class of children as they write letters and prepare them for mailing. Follows the letters to a mailbox and through their collection and machine sorting. Part of a series of films which start from some everyday observation and show more of what is happening, how and why. Builds vocabulary and encourages children to be more observant.
English Language; Social Science
Dist - VIEWTH

The Posterior Abdominal Wall 17 MIN
U-matic / VHS / 16mm
Guides to Dissection Series
Color (C A)
Focuses on the abdominal region. Demonstrates the dissection of the posterior abdominal wall.
Health and Safety; Science - Natural
Dist - TEF **Prod** - UCLA

Posterior abdominal wall 19 MIN
U-matic / VHS
Gross anatomy prosection demonstration series; Unit 19
Color (PRO)
Depicts the lecturer gaining access to the posterior abdominal wall, pointing out various structures along the way, (several of which are related to the kidney). Shows the muscles and nerves of the posterior abdominal wall.
Health and Safety; Science - Natural
Dist - HSCIC **Prod** - HSCIC

The Posterior and Superior Mediastina 10 MIN
U-matic / VHS / 16mm
Guides to Dissection Series
Color (C A)
Focuses on the thoracic region. Demonstrates the dissection of the posterior and superior mediastina.
Health and Safety; Science - Natural
Dist - TEF **Prod** - UCLA

Posterior Aspect of the Leg (Calf) 9 MIN
16mm / U-matic / VHS
Guides to Dissection Series
Color (C A)
Demonstrates the dissection of the posterior aspect of the leg.
Health and Safety; Science - Natural
Dist - TEF **Prod** - UCLA

Posterior Aspect of the Thigh 10 MIN
16mm / U-matic / VHS
Guides to Dissection Series
Color (C A)
Demonstrates the dissection of the posterior aspect of the thigh.
Health and Safety; Science - Natural
Dist - TEF **Prod** - UCLA

Posterior cervical spine stabilization 16 MIN
U-matic / VHS
Color (PRO C)
$395.00 purchase, $80.00 rental _ #C871 - VI - 045
Demonstrates techniques designed to obtain stability in flexion, extension and rotation for posterior cervical spine stabilization. Identifies specialized instruments used in the procedure and discusses proper soft tissue dissection. Looks at wire placement procedures and preparation and positioning of the bone graft. Presented by Dr E Shannon Stauffer.
Health and Safety; Science - Natural
Dist - HSCIC

Posterior Dissection of the Pharynx 19 MIN
VHS / U-matic
Hollinshead Dissection Series
Color (PRO)
Demonstrates the anatomy of the pharynx as seen in posterior dissection and identifies the anatomical relationship of nerves and blood vessels to the pharynx. Shows anatomical features from different perspectives.
Health and Safety; Science - Natural
Dist - HSCIC **Prod** - HSCIC

Posterior resection of the rectum for large villous adenoma 19 MIN
16mm
Color (PRO)
Presents resection and end - to - end anastomosis of lower and middle third of the rectum for large benign villous adenoma by means of a modified Kraske posterior transcoccygeal approach.
Health and Safety; Science
Dist - ACY **Prod** - ACYDGD 1968

The Posterior triangle of the neck 12 MIN
U-matic / VHS / 16mm
Guides to dissection series
Color (C A)
Focuses on the head and neck. Demonstrates the dissection of the posterior triangle of the neck.
Health and Safety; Science - Natural
Dist - TEF **Prod** - UCLA

Posters 15 MIN
U-matic / VHS
Expressions
(I J)
$130.00 purchase, $25.00 rental
Designed to interest fifth through ninth graders in art. Emphasizes creativity and experimentation. Features graphic designer Momi Cazimero demonstrating postermaking. Ninth in an 18 part series.
Fine Arts
Dist - GPN

Posters 15 MIN
VHS
Rediscovery - art media series
Color (SPANISH)
$69.95 purchase _ #6185
Shows how design principles can be applied to achieve striking results using a variety of materials to make posters.
Fine Arts
Dist - AIMS **Prod** - AIMS

Posters 15 MIN
16mm / U-matic / VHS
Rediscovery - art media series
Color (I)
Explains the basic concepts and methods of poster design.
Fine Arts
Dist - AIMS **Prod** - ACI 1968

Postman Pat and the magpie hen 14 MIN
VHS
Postman Pat series
Color (P I)
$175.00 purchase
Tells the story of Postman Pat, who falls asleep while picnicking, allowing some mischievous hens to eat his food and steal his keys. Shows that after some misadventures, Pat finds the keys and other things stolen by the birds. Part of a 13 - part animated puppet series which teaches values.
Guidance and Counseling; Literature and Drama
Dist - LANDMK **Prod** - LANDMK 1991

Postman Pat series
Presents a 13 - part animated puppet series about Postman Pat in the friendly village of Greendale who is accompanied by a black and white cat named Jess.

Letters on ice	14 MIN
Pat goes sledding	14 MIN
Pat's difficult day	14 MIN
Pat's foggy day	14 MIN
Pat's rainy day	14 MIN
Pat's thirsty day	14 MIN
Pat's tractor express	14 MIN
Pat's windy day	14 MIN
Postman Pat and the magpie hen	14 MIN
Postman Pat takes a message	14 MIN
Postman Pat's finding day	14 MIN
Postman Pat's secret	14 MIN
The Sheep in the clover field	14 MIN

Dist - LANDMK **Prod** - LANDMK 1991

Postman Pat takes a message 14 MIN
VHS
Postman Pat series
Color (P I)
$175.00 purchase
Reveals that trees and telephone wires have been blown down by heavy winds. Shows that Postman Pat delivers a very important message using roller skates and a bicycle. Part of a 13 - part animated puppet series which teaches values.
Guidance and Counseling; Literature and Drama
Dist - LANDMK **Prod** - LANDMK 1991

Postman Pat's finding day 14 MIN
VHS
Postman Pat series
Color (P I)
$175.00 purchase
Tells the story of Katy Pottage's birthday and her lost favorite doll. Shows that Postman Pat searches for the doll and finds it in time to attend her birthday party. Part of a 13 - part animated puppet series which teaches values.
Guidance and Counseling; Literature and Drama
Dist - LANDMK **Prod** - LANDMK 1991

Postman Pat's secret 14 MIN
VHS
Postman Pat series
Color (P I)
$175.00 purchase
Tells of Postman Pat's birthday and his surprise that everyone sends him cards. Part of a 13 - part animated puppet series which teaches values.
Guidance and Counseling; Literature and Drama
Dist - LANDMK **Prod** - LANDMK 1991

Postmark Impressions 22 MIN
16mm
Color (J)
Shows Papua and New Guinea through its stamps.
Geography - World; Social Science
Dist - AUIS **Prod** - ANAIB 1971

Postmark - Terror 15 MIN
U-matic / VHS / 16mm
Color (ARABIC FRENCH SPANISH)
Deals with all aspects of package bombs. Helps develop proper awareness and attitudes that could save lives.
Social Science; Sociology
Dist - CORF **Prod** - CORF

Postmenopausal vaginitis 7 MIN
U-matic / VHS
Take care of yourself series
Color
Explains the symptoms and treatment for postmenopausal vaginitis and encourages patient compliance in treatment.
Health and Safety
Dist - UARIZ **Prod** - UARIZ

Postmortem abnormalities of beef 26 MIN
16mm
Color
Examines postmortem abnormalities caused by disease, injury, genetics or careless handling of the live animal or carcass. Discusses the effects of these abnormalities on carcass yields. Follows inspection procedures from evisceration to chilling, illustrating various abnormalities that can be detected during this time.
Agriculture; Home Economics; Industrial and Technical Education; Social Science
Dist - UWISCA **Prod** - UWISCA 1985

Postmortem employee benefit planning, including IRAs and IRC section 403 (b) plans 53 MIN
VHS / U-matic
Postmortem tax planning after ERTA series
Color (PRO)
Gives an overview of planning for death benefits, explains the impact of TEFRA and discusses what facts must be obtained for effective planning.
Civics and Political Systems; Social Science
Dist - ABACPE **Prod** - ABACPE

Postmortem income tax planning and how it fits into the overall planning picture 55 MIN
VHS / U-matic
Postmortem tax planning after ERTA series
Color (PRO)
Provides a guide for the tax planner who must prepare a decedent's return. Discusses relationship between decedent's income and the marital deduction and shows the impact of choice of accounting period and alternative valuation elections.
Civics and Political Systems
Dist - ABACPE **Prod** - ABACPE

Postmortem tax planning after ERTA series
Postmortem employee benefit planning, including IRAs and IRC section 403(b) plans 53 MIN
Postmortem income tax planning and how it fits into the overall planning picture 55 MIN
Postmortem tax strategies for paying the tax which is due 50 MIN
Postmortem tax strategies for the surviving spouse's estate and the next generation 56 MIN
Special Use of Valuation - How and When to Use it 51 MIN
Use of Disclaimers in Postmortem Planning 54 MIN
Dist - ABACPE

Postmortem tax strategies for paying the tax which is due 50 MIN
U-matic / VHS
Postmortem tax planning after ERTA series
Color (PRO)
Discusses sections 302 and 303 redemptions and the impact of the Subchapter S Revision Act. Explains tax deferral periods and sections 6161 and 6166 and looks at the relationship between sections 6166 and 303.
Civics and Political Systems
Dist - ABACPE **Prod** - ABACPE

Postmortem tax strategies for the surviving spouse's estate and the next generation 56 MIN
U-matic / VHS
Postmortem tax planning after ERTA series
Color (PRO)
Provides postmortem tax strategies for the surviving spouse and the next generation. Enumerates seven reasons for moving from the deferral option to payment or partial payment of estate taxes.
Civics and Political Systems
Dist - ABACPE **Prod** - ABACPE

Postnatal development of the skeleton - Pt 1 - the skull 21 MIN
U-matic / VHS / 16mm
Skeletal and topographic anatomy series
Color (C A)
Health and Safety; Science - Natural
Dist - TEF **Prod** - UTEXMH

Postnatal development of the skeleton - Pt 3 - deciduous and permanent dentition 21 MIN
16mm / U-matic / VHS
Skeletal and topographic anatomy series
Color (C A)
Health and Safety; Science - Natural
Dist - TEF **Prod** - UTEXMH

Postnatal development of the skeleton - Pt 2 - vertebral column and extremities 22 MIN
16mm / U-matic / VHS
Skeletal and topographic anatomy series
Color (C A)
Health and Safety; Science - Natural
Dist - TEF **Prod** - UTEXMH

Postoperative Care 14 MIN
16mm
B&W
LC FIE60-90
Describes the duties and responsibilities of hospital corpsmen in caring for patients immediately after surgery.
Health and Safety
Dist - USNAC **Prod** - USN 1959

Postoperative disturbances of visually controlled behavior in the cat 14 MIN
16mm
B&W (C T)
Shows that cats deprived of visual projection areas display no impairment of pupillary reflexes, blinking, righting reactions or optic movements. The cats, however, lose visual placing reactions and cannot descend from a slightly elevated surface or avoid obstructions. They also lose the ability to discriminate brightness under conditions of light adaptation but retain the ability to discriminate brightness under conditions of low illumination.
Psychology
Dist - PSUPCR **Prod** - PSUPCR 1936

The Postoperative patient - nursing assessment 15 MIN
U-matic / VHS
Color (PRO)
LC 81-730133
Presents guidelines for assessment of the patient who is returning from surgery. Outlines signs and symptoms of postoperative complications and gives guidelines for nurse's initial observations and interactions with the patient. Gives examples of systematic assessment the nurse can use in the care of the patient following surgery.
Health and Safety
Dist - MEDCOM **Prod** - MEDCOM

Postpartum 14 MIN
U-matic / VHS
Color (SPANISH)
LC 77-73135
Stresses new mother's need for rest, proper diet, adequate amount of fluids and moderate exercise following delivery. Covers common problems such as urinating difficulty, constipation, and 'after - pains,' and explains breast care for both nursing and non - nursing mothers. Gives special attention to the importance of the six - week checkup.
Health and Safety
Dist - MEDCOM **Prod** - MEDCOM

Postpartum - a bittersweet experience 30 MIN
VHS
Color (A)
$59.95 purchase _ #LCP400V-K
Uses footage from a parenting class and discussions with new parents to educate viewers about postpartum adjustment. Covers the mother's sadness, the father's baby blues, the couple's feeling of estrangement, sexuality after the baby is born, adjusting to chaotic lives, and the mother's return to work.
Psychology; Sociology
Dist - CAMV

Postpartum blues 19 MIN
VHS / 16mm
Color (G)
$149.00, $249.00, purchase _ #AD - 1462
Profiles two women who learned how to combat postpartum depression. Each endured it after the birth of the first child, and learned from the experience to deal with the second birth. Explains the physical and hormonal changes that take place during pregnancy and childbirth. Shows a class where expectant parents learn to prepare themselves for the shock of parenthood.
Psychology; Sociology
Dist - FOTH **Prod** - FOTH 1990

Postpartum care 13 MIN
VHS
Color (PRO G) (ARABIC SPANISH)
$250.00 purchase _ #OB - 99
Gives practical care guidelines to the new mother from delivery through postpartum check - up. Covers dealing with the pains and discomforts immediately following birth, postpartum blues, the adjustments required in the early weeks at home and regaining strength.
Health and Safety; Sociology
Dist - MIFE **Prod** - MIFE 1991

Postpartum Depression 28 MIN
VHS / 16mm
Color (G)
$149.00, $249.00, purchase _ #AD - 1225
Focuses on depression after childbirth which is still often regarded as due to a woman's overly emotional nature. Shows that it in fact has a chemical as well as psychological cause. Explains that postpartum depression can range from a slight case of the blues to a severe delusional psychosis. Indicates to family members when medical intervention is warranted.
Health and Safety; Psychology
Dist - FOTH **Prod** - FOTH 1990

Postpartum depression - you're not alone 23 MIN
VHS / U-matic
Color (PRO C G)
$195.00 purchase _ #C900 - VI - 015
Reveals that eight out of ten women expreience some type of depression after the birth or adoption of a child. Interviews several women about expectations and experiences surrounding the births of their children. Explores reasons depression may occur and ways of resolving it. Presented by Honey Watts and Joan Stauffer.
Health and Safety; Psychology; Sociology
Dist - HSCIC

Postpartum nursing assessment - the twelve point check 22 MIN
VHS
Color (C PRO G)
$395.00 purchase _ #R871 - VI - 022
Introduces maternal health nurses to common characteristics of postpartum changes and a means to assess progress. Outlines the postpartum assessment in twelve steps with the standard time intervals between assessment provided. Presents appropriate techniques for patients who have delivered vaginally or by caesarean section.
Health and Safety
Dist - HSCIC **Prod** - UKANMC 1987

Postpartum period series
Presents a five - part series which informs women recovering from childbirth, their partners, childbirth educators and obstetrical staff. Features new parents in real situations. Hosted by Dr Linda Reid. Five - part series includes the titles Emotional Adjustment; Sexuality After Childbirth; Weight Loss, Diet and Exercise; Recuperation from Vaginal Delivery; and Cesarean Section Recovery.
Cesarean section recovery - 5 14 MIN
Emotional adjustment - 1 11 MIN
Postpartum period series 64 MIN
Recuperation from vaginal delivery - 4 13 MIN
Sexuality after childbirth - 2 14 MIN
Weight loss, diet and exercise - 3 13 MIN
Dist - CF **Prod** - HOSSN 1987

Postpartum self care - su cuidado en el post parto 10 MIN
VHS
Having a baby series
Color (H G PRO) (SPANISH)
$195.00 purchase _ #E910 - VI - 034, #E910 - VI - 046
Explains what happens to a woman's body after birth and what to do if she should experience any side effects postpartum. Eases the transition from pregnancy to motherhood through knowledge about bodily changes

after childbirth. Early recognition of these symptoms can help decrease the risk of having a preterm baby. Part of a six - part series on all aspects of birth, from prenatal to postnatal care of the mother and care of the newborn infant.
Health and Safety; Psychology
Dist - HSCIC **Prod** - UTXHSH 1991

Postponing sexual involvement - a proven effective curriculum for middle school - series
Postponing sexual involvement for parents of preteens 29 MIN
Postponing sexual involvement for parents of young teens 23 MIN
Postponing sexual involvement for preteens 39 MIN
Postponing sexual involvement for young teens 36 MIN
Dist - ETRASS

Postponing sexual involvement for parents of preteens 29 MIN
VHS
Postponing sexual involvement - a proven effective curriculum for 'middle school - series
Color (G)
$80.00 purchase _ #B009 - V8
Presents part of a two - part series for parents of preteens and young teens shown to create lasting behavioral change. Discusses peer and other pressures and shows parents how to help youth use assertive responses; learn where to go for information; and postpone sexual involvement. Helps parents reinforce learning from the preteen video. Includes 67 - page manual.
Guidance and Counseling; Health and Safety; Sociology
Dist - ETRASS **Prod** - ETRASS

Postponing sexual involvement for parents of young teens 23 MIN
VHS
Postponing sexual involvement - a proven effective curriculum for 'middle school - series
Color (G)
$80.00 purchase _ #B011 - V8
Presents part of a two - part series for parents of preteens and young teens shown to create lasting behavioral change. Helps parents to understand peer and other pressures and help youth deal with them through assertive responses; learn where to go for information; and postpone sexual involvement. Helps parents to reinforce the other videos in the series. Includes 67 - page manual.
Guidance and Counseling; Health and Safety; Sociology
Dist - ETRASS **Prod** - ETRASS

Postponing sexual involvement for preteens 39 MIN
VHS
Postponing sexual involvement - a proven effective curriculum for 'middle school - series
Color (I J)
$80.00 purchase _ #B008 - V8
Presents part of a two - part series for preteens and young teens shown to create lasting behavioral change. Helps students to understand peer and other pressures and deal with them through assertive responses; learn where to go for information; and postpone sexual involvement. Helps ages 10 - 12 understand their natural curiosity about sex, and develop assertiveness skills. Includes 93 - page manual.
Guidance and Counseling; Health and Safety; Sociology
Dist - ETRASS **Prod** - ETRASS

Postponing sexual involvement for young teens 36 MIN
VHS
Postponing sexual involvement - a proven effective curriculum for 'middle school - series
Color (I J)
$80.00 purchase _ #B010 - V8
Presents part of a series for preteens and young teens shown to create lasting behavioral change. Helps students to understand peer and other pressures and deal with them through assertive responses; learn where to go for information; and postpone sexual involvement. Includes five sessions that help ages 13 - 16 examine the motivations behind sexual pressures and develop skills to respond effectively to them. Includes 80 - page manual.
Guidance and Counseling; Health and Safety; Sociology
Dist - ETRASS **Prod** - ETRASS

Postscript 15 MIN
16mm
Color (FRENCH)
LC 74-703437
Studies the discrepancy between the image of reality presented by the mass media and the reality actually experienced by presenting the story of a young couple trying to get an apartment.
Sociology
Dist - YORKU **Prod** - YORKU 1973

Postscript to a War - the Indo - Chinese in America 28 MIN
VHS
Color (H C A)
$59.95 purchase, $16.00 rental _ #85798
Examines the plight of some of the 700,000 Indo - Chinese refugees now in America. Describes the church sponsorship process and a specific family protected by this process, contrasting with a Buddhist monk, also a refugee, who objects to the Christian proselytizing that is a part of church sponsorship. Explores the prejudice and resentment the Indo - Chinese face, and shows what happens when the sponsorship process breaks down.
Geography - World; History - United States; Sociology
Dist - UILL **Prod** - UILL 1985

Postulates and basic terms 30 MIN
VHS
Geometry series
Color (H)
$125.00 purchase _ #7001
Explains the postulates and basic terms of geometry. Part of a 16 - part series on geometry.
Mathematics
Dist - LANDMK **Prod** - LANDMK

Postulates and basic terms 30 MIN
VHS
Mathematics series; No 142
Color (J)
LC 90713155
Examines postulates and basic terms.
Mathematics
Dist - GPN

Postural drainage and percussion 16 MIN
U-matic / VHS / 16mm
Physical respiratory therapy series
Color (C A)
Teaches proper positions and techniques used in postural drainage, clapping and vibrating. Includes correct terminology, precautions, indications and contraindications.
Health and Safety; Science - Natural
Dist - TEF **Prod** - VISCI

Postural Drainage - Patient Positioning 9 MIN
16mm
Color
LC 74-705387
Demonstrates the various positions of the body which are used to drain the lung segments of the patient with chronic obstructive pulmonary disease.
Health and Safety; Science - Natural
Dist - NMAC **Prod** - NMAC 1968

Posture 15 MIN
VHS / 16mm
All Fit with Slim Goodbody Series
Color (P I)
$125.00 purchase, $25.00 rental
Demonstrates exercises to improve posture and muscle efficiency.
Health and Safety; Physical Education and Recreation; Science - Natural
Dist - AITECH **Prod** - GDBODY 1987

Posture 7 MIN
VHS / U-matic
Color (I)
$165.00, $215.00 purchase, $40.00 rental
Offers a program for students to improve posture. Includes detailed teacher's guide. Produced by Elizabeth Gilbert.
Physical Education and Recreation
Dist - NDIM

Posture 29 MIN
Videoreel / VT2
Maggie and the Beautiful Machine - Backs Series
Color
Physical Education and Recreation
Dist - PBS **Prod** - WGBHTV

Posture 9 MIN
16mm / U-matic / VHS
Good Grooming Series
Color (H)
Teen - age models demonstrate good posture in standing, sitting, walking and ascending stairs. The models' movements and stances are analyzed and the relationship of good posture to good health is indicated.
Health and Safety; Home Economics; Physical Education and Recreation
Dist - IFB **Prod** - IFB 1961

Posture and pain 30 MIN
VHS
Perspectives - health and medicine - series
Color; PAL; NTSC (G)
PdS90, PdS105 purchase
Shows how the Alexander Technique can be used to correct posture.
Health and Safety; Physical Education and Recreation
Dist - CFLVIS **Prod** - LONTVS

Posture and the keyboard 15 MIN
16mm
Color (J H)
Shows the fine points and adjustments to good posture, demonstrating the interrelationship between the typist, the typewriter and the copy as well as the position of the hands on the keyboard and striking action of the fingers. Uses examples to dramatize the importance of posture, the home row, rhythmic speed and striking action.
Business and Economics; Health and Safety
Dist - SF **Prod** - SF 1969

Posture of the dental assistant 6 MIN
U-matic / VHS
Color (C PRO)
$395.00 purchase, $80.00 rental _ #D861 - VI - 020
Discusses the benefits of good posture and the hazards of bad posture for dental assistants. Reveals that maintaining a straight spine decreases stress on muscles and pressures on body cavities. Explains how the dental assistant's posture differs from that of the dentist and demonstrates a seated working posture that is effortless and easy to maintain for long periods. Presented by Dr Deborah Romano.
Health and Safety; Physical Education and Recreation
Dist - HSCIC

Posture of the dentist 10 MIN
VHS / U-matic
Color (C PRO)
$395.00 purchase, $80.00 rental _ #D861 - VI - 021
Discusses the benefits of good posture and the hazards of bad posture for dentists. Reveals that maintaining a straight spine decreases stress on muscles and pressures on body cavities. Demonstrates in detail proper positions for the dentist's trunk and head, legs and arms. Presented by Dr Deborah Romano.
Health and Safety; Physical Education and Recreation
Dist - HSCIC

Posture Perfect with Harv and Marv 11 MIN
U-matic / VHS / 16mm
Color (P I)
LC 79-701662
Explains how a young boy learns to develop good posture habits and tells why good posture is important in helping him to look, feel and perform better.
Health and Safety; Physical Education and Recreation
Dist - HIGGIN **Prod** - HIGGIN 1979

Posture - Thinking Tall 12 MIN
16mm / U-matic / VHS
Color (I J H)
LC 79-700004
Uses examples of excellent body control in a variety of human activities to demonstrate that good posture contributes to performance, well - being and durability. Shows what is important in developing concepts and habits of good posture.
Physical Education and Recreation
Dist - PHENIX **Prod** - WINTNC 1978

Postures 23 - 73 - Tape 2 45 MIN
VHS
Imagination becomes reality series
Color (G)
$29.95 purchase _ #1182
Teaches the Yang style T'ai chi ch'uan of 93 - year - old T T Liang. Features Stuart A Olson, Liang's adopted son, who executes postures 23 - 73 in slow motion with a voiceover. Part two of a three - part series.
Physical Education and Recreation
Dist - WAYF

Postures 74 - 150 - Tape 3 45 MIN
VHS
Imagination becomes reality series
Color (G)
$29.95 purchase _ #1183
Teaches the Yang style T'ai chi ch'uan of 93 - year - old T T Liang. Features Stuart A Olson, Liang's adopted son, who executes postures 74 - 150 in slow motion with a voiceover. Part three of a three - part series.
Physical Education and Recreation
Dist - WAYF

Postwar hopes, cold war fears 58 MIN
VHS / U-matic
Walk through the 20th century with Bill Moyers series
Color
Tells of the 1950s, a time of nostalgia and neuroses, when factories were pouring out goods, the dollar was strong and the United States was filled with optimism. Characterizes the 1950s as the age of the lowering of the Iron Curtain in Eastern Europe, the loss of China to communism, and the Korean War and the Red Scare which divided Americans at home.
Civics and Political Systems; History - United States; History - World
Dist - PBS **Prod** - CORPEL 1982

Postwar Japan - 40 Years of Change 56 MIN
U-matic / VHS
Color (G)
$279.00, $179.00 purchase _ #AD - 2134
Provides Japanese answers to Western questions about the Japanese economic miracle and Japanese attitudes toward growing friction in economic areas with the West. Documents Japan's rise from its loss in World War II and the results of its policy of promoting economic growth.
Business and Economics; History - World
Dist - FOTH **Prod** - FOTH

Postwar Japan - 40 years of economic recovery 60 MIN
VHS
Anatomy of Japan - wellsprings of economic power series
Color (H C G)
$250.00 purchase
Traces the efforts of Japanese individuals and companies for economic recovery after the defeat of the Japanese in World War II. Explains how Japan emerged as the second largest economy over the past 40 years. Part of a 10 - part series on the current relations between Japan and the world.
Business and Economics; History - World
Dist - LANDMK **Prod** - LANDMK 1989

The Postwar period 11 MIN
VHS
American Revolution series
Color (J H)
$59.00 purchase _ #MF - 3771
Shows how the United States Constitution evolved out of the call for liberty and vision of the Revolution's leaders, out of the unity achieved in the Declaration of Independence, out of the suffering and sacrifice of war, out of colonial victory and out of the troubles of seven years without an effective central government.
Civics and Political Systems; History - United States
Dist - INSTRU **Prod** - CORF
CORF

Postwar Period 20 MIN
16mm / U-matic / VHS
Civil War Series
Color (J H C)
$465.00, $250.00 purchase _ #4394
Discusses the political reorganization of the South, the passing of the Fourteenth Amendment, and the confrontation between the Congress and President Johnson.
Geography - United States; History - United States
Dist - CORF

Postwar politics and art 30 MIN
U-matic / VHS
Art America series
Color (H C A)
Examines the influence of Regionalists, Precisionists and Magic Realists on American art.
Fine Arts
Dist - CTI **Prod** - CTI

Pot 30 MIN
VHS / U-matic
Color
Details the effect of THC on the human body. Explains the altered time perception and apparent need for higher sensory input of chronic marijuana users.
Health and Safety; Psychology
Dist - WHITEG **Prod** - WHITEG

Pot Bellies 29 MIN
Videoreel / VT2
Maggie and the Beautiful Machine - Bellies Series
Color
Physical Education and Recreation
Dist - PBS **Prod** - WGBHTV

The Pot problem 30 MIN
Videoreel / VT2
Making things grow I series
Color
Features Thalassa Cruso discussing different aspects of gardening. Shows various types and sizes of pots and matches them with appropriate plants.
Agriculture; Science - Natural
Dist - PBS **Prod** - WGBHTV

Potassium 34 MIN
VHS / U-matic
Fluids and electrolytes series
Color (PRO)
Describes importance of potassium as a vehicle for maintaining smoothly functioning neuromuscular system. Discusses location and function of this vital element and the pathophysiology of potassium imbalances.
Science - Natural
Dist - BRA **Prod** - BRA

Potassium - induced ulcer - strictures of the small intestine 28 MIN
16mm
Color (PRO)
Illustrates the operative findings of a potassium - induced ulcer - stricture in the small intestine, which had caused vague symptoms of anemia and small bowel obstruction. Presents other benign and malignant ulcer strictures.
Health and Safety; Science - Natural
Dist - ACY **Prod** - ACYDGD 1967

Potato dishes - from baked stuffed to Spanish fries 30 MIN
VHS
International cooking school with Chef Rene series; Lesson 14
Color (G)
$69.00 purchase
Presents classic methods of cooking that stress essential flavor. Introduces newer, lighter foods. Lesson 14 presents a variety of ways to prepare potatoes.
Home Economics; Psychology; Social Science
Dist - LUF **Prod** - LUF

The Potato farm 15 MIN
VHS
Field trips series
Color (P I J)
$34.95 purchase _ #E337; LC 90-708552
Visits potato growing areas in all seasons - planting, growing, harvesting and storage. Explains and observes the entire process of growing potatoes. Part of a series which provides visual opportunities for children to 'visit' a variety of locations and activities as if they were on a field trip.
Agriculture
Dist - GPN **Prod** - MPBN 1983

Potato Late Blight - Epidemiology 13 MIN
16mm / U-matic / VHS
Color (C A)
Introduces concepts of plant disease epidemiology. Uses potato late blight to illustrate the dynamics of the development of epidemics.
Agriculture
Dist - CORNRS **Prod** - CUETV 1982

Potato Planters 17 MIN
16mm
Faces of Change - Bolivia Series
Color
Shows an Aymara Indian family planting potatoes, preparing and eating a meal, and discussing the religious and astronomical forces that control their destiny. Contrasts the stark routine of a typical planting day with the complexity of their beliefs.
Geography - World; Social Science; Sociology
Dist - WHEELK **Prod** - AUFS

Potatoes 27 MIN
U-matic / VHS / 16mm
Color (J)
LC 77-703180
Presents a documentary which takes a look at potato farmers in New Brunswick, Canada, and focuses on huge food processors as the cause of the farmers' increasing financial problems.
Agriculture; Geography - World
Dist - BULFRG **Prod** - NFBC 1977

Potatoes 30 MIN
VHS
Perspective 10 series
Color; PAL; NTSC (G)
PdS90, PdS105 purchase
Discusses importance of potato in the human diet and international economy. Notes scientific advances in genetic engineering of food and subsequent changes in disease resistance and flavor of engineered potatoes.
Agriculture; Home Economics; Social Science
Dist - CFLVIS **Prod** - LONTVS 1993

Potatoes au gratin 6 MIN
U-matic / VHS
Cooking with Jack and Jill series
Color (P I)
$95.00
Portrays twins Jack and Jill as they cook nutritious and delicious snacks that are easy to prepare. Emphasizes kitchen safety. Animated.
Home Economics; Social Science
Dist - LANDMK **Prod** - LANDMK 1986

Potatoes - blessing and curse of Pacha Mama 15 MIN
VHS
Fruits of the earth series
Color (G)
$175.00 purchase
Looks at the current conditions in the Peruvian highlands, where areas for potato cultivation are diminishing. Considers what is necessary to increase production of this agriculturally important plant. Part of a series of 15 videos that describe everyday conditions in regions throughout the earth and look at plants available for environmentally sound, economically productive development.
Agriculture; Home Economics
Dist - LANDMK

Potemkin 50 MIN
16mm
B&W
Depicts a mutiny aboard one of the Russian Czar's battleships in 1905. Directed by Sergei Eisenstein.
Fine Arts; History - World
Dist - REELIM **Prod** - ESNSTN 1925

Potemkin 67 MIN
16mm / U-matic / VHS
B&W (J H C) (RUSSIAN WITH ENGLISH SUBTITLES)
Tells of an incident which occurred on the Russian ship Prince Potemkin during the Russian uprising of 1905. Produced in Russia in 1925 by Sergei Eisenstein. Music and Russian prologue added in 1951. Released in U S with English subtitles.
Fine Arts; History - World
Dist - FI **Prod** - BF 1954

Potemkin - a Multi - Media Film Study 10 MIN
16mm
B&W (J H C)
LC 76-700268
Presents the Odessa steps sequence from Eisenstein's 1925 motion picture Potemkin and offers an analysis of the cinematic content of the sequence.
Fine Arts
Dist - LSEC **Prod** - LSEC 1976

Potemkin - Pt 1 21 MIN
U-matic / VHS / 16mm
B&W (J H C) (RUSSIAN WITH ENGLISH SUBTITLES)
Tells of an incident which occurred on the Russian ship Prince Potemkin during the Russian uprising of 1905. Produced in Russia, 1925. Music and Russian prologue added in 1951. Released in U S with English subtitles.
History - World
Dist - FI **Prod** - BF 1954

Potemkin - Pt 2 21 MIN
16mm / U-matic / VHS
B&W (J H C) ((ENGLISH SUBTITLES))
Tells of an incident which occurred on the Russian ship Prince Potemkin during the Russian uprising of 1905. Produced in Russia, 1925. Music and Russian prologue added in 1951. Released in U S with English subtitles.
History - World
Dist - FI **Prod** - BF 1954

Potemkin - Pt 3 26 MIN
16mm / U-matic / VHS
B&W (J H C) ((ENGLISH SUBTITLES))
Tells of an incident which occurred on the Russian ship Prince Potemkin during the Russian uprising of 1905. Produced in Russia, 1925. Music and Russian prologue added in 1951. Released in U S with English subtitles.
History - World
Dist - FI **Prod** - BF 1954

Potential Applications and Limitations of Microprocessors 30 MIN
VHS / U-matic
Designing with Microprocessors Series
Color (PRO)
Defines types of systems suitable for microprocessor applications. Discusses main parameters of several equipment types now on market designed with microprocessors. Shows how microprocessors can lower costs, shorten design cycles, and improve performance and reliability in practical applications.
Industrial and Technical Education
Dist - TXINLC **Prod** - TXINLC

Potential Differences 10 MIN
U-matic
Electricity Series
Color (H C) (FRENCH)
Covers the fundamentals of electrostatics and current electricity and helps students formulate mental imgages of abstract concepts. Available in French. Comes with teacher's guide.
Science; Science - Physical
Dist - TVOTAR **Prod** - TVOTAR 1986

Potential energy 30 MIN
16mm / U-matic / VHS
Mechanical universe series
Color (C A)
Explains potential energy as a clue to understanding why the world has worked the same way since the beginning of time.
Science - Physical
Dist - FI **Prod** - ANNCPB

Potential energy 5 MIN
U-matic
Eureka series
Color (J)
Demonstrates the energy of position which is called potential energy.
Science - Physical
Dist - TVOTAR **Prod** - TVOTAR 1980

Potential Energy and Kinetic Energy 10 MIN
U-matic / VHS
Introductory Concepts in Physics - Dynamics Series
Color (C)
$229.00, $129.00 purchase _ #AD - 1189
Introduces mechanical energies. Shows the relationship between potential and kinetic energy and the law of conservation of energy.
Science - Physical
Dist - FOTH **Prod** - FOTH

Potential for Contamination of Groundwater by Abandoned Landfills 18 MIN
VHS
Color (C A)
$60.00 purchase, $20.00 rental
Shows how to pull together information provided by aerial photographs to assess potential groundwater contamination by abandoned landfills.
Science - Natural
Dist - CORNRS **Prod** - CORNRS 1988

Potential for infection - critical care challenge 28 MIN
VHS / U-matic
Color (PRO)
$275.00 purchase, $60.00 rental _ #7623S, #7623V
Gives an understanding of epidemiology that can be integrated into daily practice. Covers host defenses, signs and symptoms, invading organisms, transmission modes and sources of infection. Gives special attention to the critical care unit's high - tech equipment, a major potential reservoir. Pinpoints the most common sites for nosocomial infections - the respiratory system, urinary tract, blood and surgical and cutaneous wounds. Includes guidelines from the Centers for Disease Control on handwashing, soaps, and when to wear gloves.
Health and Safety
Dist - AJN **Prod** - HOSSN 1988

Potential Transformers 7 MIN
VHS / U-matic
Electrical Safety Series
Color (IND)
Cites electrical backfeed as major hazard associated with PTs. Details recommended steps for clearing ALL energy sources from the circuit.
Health and Safety; Industrial and Technical Education
Dist - GPCV **Prod** - GPCV

Potentially Yours 31 MIN
VHS / U-matic
Color
Presents techniques for developing human potential through humanistic psychology.
Psychology; Religion and Philosophy
Dist - HP **Prod** - HP

Potentiometric titrations, hydrolysis, acids and bases 57 MIN
VHS / U-matic
Electrochemistry series; Thermodynamics of galvanic cells; Pt III
Color
Discusses potentiometric titrations, hydrolysis and acids and bases.
Science; Science - Physical
Dist - KALMIA MIOT **Prod** - KALMIA MIOT

Potlatch - a Strict Law Bids Us Dance 53 MIN
16mm
Color (H C A)
#5X6 I
Discusses how through centuries the Kwakiutl Indians of the Northwest Pacific have developed a sophisticated culture based on the ceremonial giving away of surplus wealth harvested from the rich coastal areas, called Potlatch. Explains how this tradition was the basis of an indigenous social and economic ecology before the Canadian government outlawed the Potlatch in the Indian Act. Documents how the Indians attempt to maintain this important tradition in secrecy.
Social Science
Dist - CDIAND **Prod** - UMISTA 1975

Potlatch Country 28 MIN
16mm
Color; B&W (G)
Potlach, an American Indian word meaning 'distribution of gifts,' is a location in Idaho that many people visit annually.
Geography - United States; Physical Education and Recreation
Dist - FO **Prod** - FO 1968

Potlatch people 26 MIN
U-matic / VHS / 16mm
Native Americans series
Color (G)
Describes the thriving economy, rich culture and rigid class structure of the early Indians of the Pacific Northwest coast. Examines their near disappearance and the current efforts to revive and reconstruct Indian life as it was before the coming of the white man.
History - United States; Social Science
Dist - CNEMAG **Prod** - BBCTV

The Potlatch story 28 MIN
16mm
Color; B&W (G)
Describes lumber mill operation in the town of Lewiston, Idaho. Features the world's largest white pine mill, located at this sawmill in Lewiston.
Agriculture; Geography - United States; Social Science
Dist - FO **Prod** - FO 1957

Potluck 21 MIN
16mm
Color (P I)
Follows the Chiffy kids as they go camping near a haunted house. Portrays them as they busy themselves around the campsite, Magpie disappears and someone's bones are found cooking in the pot.
Literature and Drama
Dist - LUF **Prod** - LUF 1979

Poto and Cabengo 77 MIN
16mm
Color
Focuses on twin girls who converse in their own imaginary language. Describes the media attention given to these girls. Directed by Jean - Pierre Gorin.
Fine Arts; Psychology
Dist - NYFLMS **Prod** - UNKNWN 1979

Potomac - American Reflections 60 MIN
VHS
Color (G)
$49.95 purchase _ #PARE - 000
Traces the history and significance of the Potomac River. Takes viewers on a journey down the entire length of the river, emphasizing historical sites. Produced by Robert Cole Films.
Geography - United States
Dist - PBS

Potomac fever 58 MIN
U-matic / VHS
Frontline series
Color
Follows two newly - elected Congressmen from their homes to Washington where they experience the rewards and the frustrations of making the transition from citizen to Congressman.
Civics and Political Systems
Dist - PBS **Prod** - DOCCON

Potpourri 29 MIN
U-matic
House Botanist Series
Color
Exhibits and discusses a variety of unrelated house plants.
Agriculture; Science - Natural
Dist - UMITV **Prod** - UMITV 1978

Potpourri 9 MIN
16mm
B&W (J H C)
Presents a psychedelic animated film.
Fine Arts
Dist - CFS **Prod** - CFS 1969

Potpourri - the many views of marijuana - Pt 1 88 MIN
Videoreel / VT2
Potpourri - the many views of marijuana series
B&W
Presents social and economic information about marijuana and its impact on society. Includes satirical essays, a picture history of the use of the plant and panel discussions.
Health and Safety; Psychology; Sociology
Dist - PBS **Prod** - KCET

Potpourri - the many views of marijuana - Pt 2 90 MIN
Videoreel / VT2
Potpourri - the many views of marijuana series
Color
Presents the social and economic facts on marijuana and its impact on society. Includes satirical essays, a picture history of the use of the plant and panel discussions.
Health and Safety; Psychology
Dist - PBS **Prod** - KCET

Potpourri - the many views of marijuana series
Potpourri - the many views of marijuana - Pt 1 88 MIN
Potpourri - the many views of marijuana - Pt 2 90 MIN
Dist - PBS

Pot's a put - on 10 MIN
16mm
Color (I J)
Presents a parody of the arguments in favor of marijuana use and satirizes those who smoke it.
Health and Safety; Psychology
Dist - PROART **Prod** - PROART 1969

Potted Plant Production 25 MIN
VHS
Greenhouse Production Series
Color (G)
$89.95 purchase _ #6 - 094 - 100P
Looks at the marketing, crop selection, general guidelines for production, photoperiodic plants, bulbs, gesneriads in regard to the production of potted plants. Part of a three - part series on greenhouse production.
Agriculture
Dist - VEP **Prod** - VEP

Potted Psalm 25 MIN
16mm
B&W; Silent (C)
$300.00
Experimental film by Sidney Peterson.
Fine Arts
Dist - AFA **Prod** - AFA 1946

The Potter 15 MIN
VHS / 16mm
Harriet's magic hats IV series
Color (P)
$175.00 purchase _ #207146
Presents a program that familiarizes children with workers and their role in community life. Features Aunt Harriet's bottomless trunks of magic hats. Tells of Carrie's adventures, including a visit to Sharon, a potter. Sharon demonstrates how to 'throw' or mold clay, using the potter's wheel and explains the electric kiln and the use of glaze.
Fine Arts; Literature and Drama
Dist - ACCESS **Prod** - ACCESS 1986

The Potter
VHS
Video Biblical illustrator series
Color (H C G A R)
$24.99 purchase, $10.00 rental _ #35 - 83598 - 533
Portrays a master potter taking a broken lump of clay and turning it into a useful vessel. Likens this to the Biblical parable of the potter and the clay.
Literature and Drama; Religion and Philosophy
Dist - APH **Prod** - WORD

Potter
VHS
Vocational visions career series
Color (H A)
$39.95 purchase _ #CDS510
Interviews potters. Answers questions about the educational requirements and necessary skills for the occupation, as well as its career opportunities, salary range and outlook for the future. Part of a series which examines the potential of various occupations.
Fine Arts; Guidance and Counseling; Psychology
Dist - CADESF **Prod** - CADESF 1989

The Potter and his craft 20 MIN
16mm
B&W (I)
Shows how potters have carried on their craft for centuries. Explores potters' co - operatives as a way to gain the latest know - how and improve products.
Fine Arts
Dist - NEDINF **Prod** - INDIA

Potter at the wheel 15 MIN
VHS / U-matic
Expressions
(I J)

$130.00 purchase, $25.00 rental
Designed to interest fifth through ninth graders in art. Emphasizes creativity and experimentation. Features potter David Kuraoka showing how to use a potter's wheel. Eleventh in an 18 part series.
Fine Arts
Dist - GPN

Potters at Work 29 MIN
U-matic / VHS / 16mm
Color (H C A)
LC 77-703346
Examines the pottery of Japanese craftsmen, focusing on the daily circumstances out of which the pieces emerge.
Fine Arts; Geography - World
Dist - PHENIX **Prod** - GROSSM 1977

The Potters of Buur Heybe, Somalia 25 MIN
VHS
Color (H C G)
$295.00 purchase, $55.00 rental
Travels to the small village of Buur Heybe in southern Somalia where only men make pottery, although their legends give credit to a woman for first finding the clay. Shows how the men transform mounds of clay into drinking and cooking vessels. Produced by Tara Belkin.
Fine Arts; History - World; Sociology
Dist - FLMLIB

Potters of Hebron 30 MIN
16mm / VHS / U-matic
Color (J)
LC 76-703574; 76-703571
Shows potters demonstrating their crafts in a workshop in the Hebron Hills, southeast of Jerusalem. Focuses on processes employed by the potters in making earthenware water jugs called zirs.
Fine Arts; Geography - World
Dist - PHENIX **Prod** - HABERR 1976

The Potters of Mata Ortiz 47 MIN
VHS
Color (C G)
$30.00 purchase
Documents the ceramic tradition of Mata Ortiz, Mexico. Explores the ancient and contemporary pottery of the region and examines the methods of pottery production employed in the village. Discusses the history of the region and the evolution of Mata Ortiz from an agricultural community to a pottery producing center. Includes information about Juan Quezeda, an unknown, self - taught potter, who revived the ancient Casas Grandes ceramic tradition.
Fine Arts; History - World
Dist - GOFFIN **Prod** - GOFFIN

A Potter's Song - the Art and Philosophy of Paul Soldner 16 MIN
16mm
Color
LC 76-702868
Shows ceramic artist Paul Soldner presenting his views on trends in the art of ceramics and its relationship to the environment.
Fine Arts
Dist - CRYSP **Prod** - CRYSP 1976

The Potter's wheel 28 MIN
Videoreel / VT2
Wheels, kilns and clay series
Color
Describes certain ceramic processes used at the University of Southern California. Illustrates the use of the potter's wheel.
Fine Arts
Dist - PBS **Prod** - USC

The Potter's wheel 10 MIN
16mm
Color (J)
Demonstrates the method of throwing a pitcher and other shapes on a potter's wheel. Features Richard Petterson, head of Ceramic Studio at Scripps College, who describes the process in detail, from hollowing - out the clay to the final glaze firing.
Fine Arts
Dist - AVED **Prod** - ALLMOR 1951

Pottery 28 MIN
16mm / U-matic / VHS
Stop, look, listen series
Color; B&W; PAL (P I J)
Visits a pottery factory to watch mugs being made. Observes children learning to make simple shapes in clay and having their first lesson in throwing a pot on the potter's wheel. Watches a professional potter making a vase. Part of a series of films which start from some everyday observation. Builds vocabulary and encourages children to be more observant.
Fine Arts
Dist - VIEWTH

Pottery - an Introduction 17 MIN
16mm
Color
LC 75-701915
Provides an introduction to the techniques of making pottery.
Fine Arts
Dist - MORLAT **Prod** - MORLAT 1973

Pottery decoration - traditional techniques
VHS
Pottery series
Color (J H C G)
$49.95 purchase _ #THO03V
Shows viewers how to use a variety of decorating techniques with demonstrations and examples from the work of many different potters. Includes incising and carving, using and make stamps, added decoration, slip trailing, sgraffito and inlay, wax resist, marbled and mosaic patterns and more. Part of a two - part series.
Fine Arts
Dist - CAMV

Pottery making - Tajik 15 MIN
16mm
Mountain peoples of Central Asia series
B&W (P)
LC 73-702414
Shows expert potters bringing clay down from the hills to be pulverized, sifted, cleaned and prepared for women to make into pots, bowls and water jugs in the village of Kulala in Afghanistan.
Fine Arts; Geography - World; Social Science
Dist - IFF **Prod** - IFF 1972

Pottery series
Presents two parts on advanced pottery techniques. Includes Advanced Throwing - Projects and Techniques, and Pottery Decoration - Traditional Techniques.
Advanced throwing - projects and techniques
Pottery decoration - traditional techniques
Pottery series
Dist - CAMV

Pottery, stoneware and the southern crafts 30 MIN
U-matic
Antiques series
Color
Fine Arts
Dist - PBS **Prod** - NHMNET

Pottery techniques - slab building 15 MIN
U-matic / VHS
B&W
Shows a potter demonstrating hand building by slab construction and lists the tools needed.
Fine Arts
Dist - BUSARG **Prod** - BUSARG

Pottery techniques - surface decoration 15 MIN
U-matic / VHS
B&W
Shows a potter demonstrating methods of surface decoration such as mishima, incision and slip decoration.
Fine Arts
Dist - BUSARG **Prod** - BUSARG

Pottery techniques - the pinch pot 16 MIN
VHS / U-matic
B&W
Shows a potter demonstrating pinch pot (hand building) techniques and lists the tools needed.
Fine Arts
Dist - BUSARG **Prod** - BUSARG

Potting 30 MIN
Videoreel / VT2
Making Things Grow I Series
Color
Features Thalassa Cruso discussing different aspects of gardening. Shows how to pot plants.
Agriculture
Dist - PBS **Prod** - WGBHTV

Potting Houseplants 30 MIN
VHS / U-matic
Even You Can Grow Houseplants Series
Color
Discusses the potting of houseplants.
Agriculture
Dist - MDCPB **Prod** - WGTV

Potting Mixes for Houseplants 30 MIN
U-matic / VHS
Even You Can Grow Houseplants Series
Color
Discusses potting mixes for houseplants.
Agriculture
Dist - MDCPB **Prod** - WGTV

Poul Jorgensen on fly tying - my favorite fishing flies - Vol I 100 MIN
VHS
Color (G)
$24.95 purchase _ #SF07
Shows how to tie flies.
Physical Education and Recreation
Dist - SVIP

Poul Jorgensen on fly tying - my favorite fishing flies - Vol II 100 MIN
VHS
Color (G)
$24.95 purchase _ #SF08
Shows how to tie flies.
Physical Education and Recreation
Dist - SVIP

Poultry 45 MIN
VHS
Le Cordon Bleu cooking series
Color (H C G)
$24.95 purchase _ #LCB007V
Details methods needed of preparing an assortment of poultry. Features the chefs of Le Cordon Bleu's teaching staff. Part of an eight - part series.
Home Economics
Dist - CAMV

Poultry
U-matic
Matter of taste series; Lesson 14
Color (H A)
Introduces poultry as a complete protein food. Explains that poultry is classified according to age. Demonstrates how to cut poultry into individual serving pieces.
Home Economics
Dist - CDTEL **Prod** - COAST

Poultry 60 MIN
U-matic / VHS
Way to cook with Julia Child
(C A)
$34.95 _ #KN100V
Features chef and cooking teacher Julia Child as she demonstrates various recipes for poultry.
Home Economics; Industrial and Technical Education
Dist - CAMV **Prod** - CAMV
CAREER CAREER

Poultry cookery 21 MIN
16mm
Color
LC 74-706556
Illustrates in detail how to cook poultry.
Home Economics
Dist - USNAC **Prod** - USN 1965

Poultry dressings 29 MIN
VHS
Cookbook videos series; Vol 5
Color (G)
$19.95 purchase
Shows how to make basic bread poultry dressing. Includes printed abstract of recipes. Part of a series.
Home Economics
Dist - ALWHIT **Prod** - ALWHIT

Poultry dressings 29 MIN
VHS
Cookbook videos series
Color (G)
$19.95 purchase _ #ALW108
Shows how to prepare poultry dressings in short segments. Lists each ingredient as it is added in subtitles and visually reinforces spoken instructions. Gives recipe background and nutritional facts.
Home Economics
Dist - CADESF **Prod** - CADESF

Poultry judging series
Egg grading 50 MIN
Evaluating ready - to - cook poultry 45 MIN
Dist - AAVIM

Poultry Judging (Set S) Series
Introduction to Poultry Judging 20 MIN
Judging Pullets and Hens 38 MIN
Practice Poultry Judging - I 33 MIN
Practice Poultry Judging - II 25 MIN
Dist - AAVIM

Poultry - killing and dressing 56 MIN
U-matic
Color (J)
LC 81-707367
Shows how to kill, scald, pluck, eviscerate and package poultry in a small - scale operation. Explains in detail each step in the processing procedure and gives reasons for processing in a particular way.
Agriculture; Home Economics; Social Science
Dist - CORNRS **Prod** - NYSCAG 1979

Poultry - laying it on the line 11 MIN
U-matic / VHS / 16mm
Color (I J)
LC 75-701499
Examines the processing procedures of the automated poultry industry in the United States. Traces the development of specialized breeds of chickens and shows work in a modern hatchery, brooder, egg factory and processing plant.
Agriculture; Social Science
Dist - CORF **Prod** - CENTEF 1975

Poultry Processing Inspection 18 MIN
16mm
Color
LC FIE56-308
Outlines poultry processing procedures required by the U S Department of Agriculture, U S Public Health Service and medical services of the Army and Air Force. Explains duties of Air Force veterinary officers in checking cleanliness and handling of birds.
Agriculture
Dist - USNAC **Prod** - USAF 1956

The Pound theory - why everyone's special 12 MIN
U-matic / VHS / 16mm
Color (P I)
LC 78-700918
Presents an animated fable featuring storks - in - training, who learn why every baby is different, but equally valuable. Shows a stuffy flight instructor and his star pupil visiting the baby factory and being shown that everyone has desirable traits.
Guidance and Counseling; Sociology
Dist - PHENIX **Prod** - CREEDM 1977

Pour a pond 15 MIN
U-matic
Know your world series
(I J)
Teaches children to study the life within a small amount of pond water. Shows the construction of a portable pond.
Science; Science - Natural
Dist - ACCESS **Prod** - ACCESS 1981

Pour it on 29 MIN
16mm / U-matic / VHS
Color (PRO)
LC 73-701002
Features hockey star Bobby Hull teaching principles of success that motivate salesmen and stimulate them to achieve more.
Business and Economics; Psychology
Dist - DARTNL **Prod** - DARTNL 1972

Pour tout dire 60 MIN
VHS
Color (S) (FRENCH)
$398.00 purchase _ #101 - 9211
Presents examples of everyday spoken French for intermediate studentsin true - to - life situations of interest to teenagers. Demonstrates the use and importance of body language for communicating in foreign cultures. Divided into three 10 - minute programs. Modules available separately.
Foreign Language; Geography - World; History - World
Dist - FI **Prod** - NFBC 1989

Pouring Babbitt Bearings 17 MIN
16mm
Color (IND)
Shows how to pour a perfect bearing the first time. Discusses melting out the old bearings, the clean - up, good safety practices, installing the wood plugs, spaces and fillers, pre - heating, blackening and preventing leaks. Details how to pour, how to bore and scrape the bearing, and how to cut the oil grooves and the finger slots.
Industrial and Technical Education
Dist - MOKIN **Prod** - MOKIN

Pourquoi n'est - il pas la 13 MIN
16mm
Les Francais chez vous series; Set II; Lesson 22
B&W (I J H) (FRENCH)
LC 73-704477
Foreign Language
Dist - CHLTN **Prod** - PEREN 1967

Poussaint, Alvin 30 MIN
U-matic
Like it is series
Color
Discusses the negative psychological effects of discrimination on Blacks.
History - United States; Sociology
Dist - HRC **Prod** - OHC

Poussin - Le Deluge 8 MIN
16mm / U-matic
Through artists' eyes series
Color (H A)
$225.00 purchase, $45.00 rental
Views the work of Nicolas Poussin through the eyes of contemporary art historian Avigdor Arikha.
Fine Arts
Dist - AFA **Prod** - ASDA 1986

Poussin - the Seven Sacraments 21 MIN
16mm
Color (H A)
$425.00 purchase, $50.00 rental
Features the second version of The Seven Sacraments by Nicolas Poussin, 1593 - 1665.
Fine Arts
Dist - AFA **Prod** - ACGB 1968

Poverty 30 MIN
VHS / U-matic
Focus on society series
Color (C)
Discusses the character and limitations of poverty.
Sociology
Dist - DALCCD **Prod** - DALCCD

Poverty 18 MIN
U-matic / VHS / 16mm
Color (H C A)
$350 purchase - 16 mm, $200 purchase - video, $50 rental
Examines the problem of poverty in America. Features an interview with Michael Harrington.
Business and Economics; Sociology
Dist - CNEMAG **Prod** - DOCUA 1988

Poverty - closing the gap 18 MIN
U-matic / VHS / 16mm
Color
Shows that with the advance of civilization, the margins between the 'haves' and the 'have - nots' have widened to the point where there is an almost total breakdown in communication within these two classes. Presents interviews with Charles Dennison, a successful industrialist, and authors Michael Harrington and John Sewell who describe their remedies for this problem.
Sociology
Dist - CNEMAG **Prod** - DOCUA

Poverty in America 14 MIN
35mm strip / VHS
In our time series
Color (J H C T A)
$81.00, $48.00 purchase _ #MB - 540368 - 4, #MB - 509936 - 5
Examines the growth in poverty in the United States during the 1980s. Suggests that the nature of American poverty has changed, and that new solutions will be required. Includes excerpts from speeches by Franklin Roosevelt, Lyndon Johnson, Ronald Reagan, and Jesse Jackson.
Biography; History - United States; Sociology
Dist - SRA **Prod** - SRA 1988

Poverty in America 30 MIN
VHS / U-matic
America - the second century series
Color (H C)
$34.95 purchase
Offers historical analyses of poverty in America in 'hard times' as well as 'good times.' Part of a 30-part series covering topics from politics through social issues in the United States since 1875.
History - United States; Sociology
Dist - DALCCD **Prod** - DALCCD
GPN

Poverty shock - any woman's story 29 MIN
VHS / U-matic
Color (J H A)
$320.00, $295.00 purchase _ #V334
Focuses on real - life situations in which women's lifestyles have been severely disrupted. Looks at the economic consequences of divorce, loss of a husband's income or teen pregnancy. Stresses the importance of career goals for young girls.
Business and Economics; Guidance and Counseling; Psychology; Sociology
Dist - BARR **Prod** - CEPRO 1986
CEPRO

The Poverty showdown 56 MIN
U-matic / VHS
Poverty trilogy series
Color
Features Dr Joseph Lowery and Dr Walter Williams in a panel discussion on poverty, allowing professors and students to ask the speakers questions about poverty and its solutions.
Sociology
Dist - WORLDR **Prod** - WORLDR

Poverty - the Great Obstacle 56 MIN
16mm
Color (H C)
Deals with the effect of poverty on human welfare and urban development.
Sociology
Dist - SF **Prod** - SF 1973

The Poverty trap 30 MIN
16mm
Color (H C A)
Examines how the agencies which work with the poor present regulatory obstacles which keep their clients poor by limiting job opportunities, encouraging dependency, and controlling their economic and personal freedoms.
Sociology
Dist - WORLDR **Prod** - WORLDR 1982

Poverty trilogy series
The Poverty showdown 56 MIN
Dist - WORLDR

Pow - wow! 16 MIN
U-matic / VHS / 16mm
Color (I J H C A)
$375.00, $250.00 purchase _ #78007; LC 80-700969
Introduces ceremonies, songs, dances and other rituals as seen at an intertribal gathering of North American Indians. Includes interviews with the participants who express their resolve to pass along this heritage to their children.
Social Science
Dist - CORF **Prod** - CENTRO 1980

Pow Wow 5 MIN
16mm
Color (H C A)
#1X51 I
Documents the Pow Wow held in Winterburn, Alberta during the 1973 Elders Celebration.
Social Science
Dist - CDIAND **Prod** - ANCS 1974

Powder hound 14 MIN
16mm
Color
Introduces Powder Hound plummeting down high mountain ridges and plunging into deep powder chutes doing the 'Ski Wheelie.' Tells how he lives in a tent in the high mountains for peaceful solitude and the perfect descent. Shows how, in the end, Powder Hound is tamed by the charms of a local ski instructor who irreverently plants her tent next to his.
Physical Education and Recreation
Dist - EDFLM **Prod** - EDFLM

Powder keg in the Congo - a special report 5 MIN
16mm
Screen news digest series; Vol 3; Issue 8
B&W (J H)
Reports on the crisis in the Congo which occurred when it received its independence from Belgium in 1960. Follows the crisis from the seating of the new parliament to the military revolt and subsequent U N intervention, renewed violence and U N discussion.
Civics and Political Systems; Geography - World; History - United States; History - World
Dist - HEARST **Prod** - HEARST 1961

Powder metallurgy 14 MIN
U-matic / VHS
Manufacturing materials and processes series
Color
Covers steps in conventional powder metallurgy, its advantages and disadvantages and typical defects.
Industrial and Technical Education; Science - Physical
Dist - WFVTAE **Prod** - GE

Powder metallurgy 15 MIN
16mm
Color
Describes the science of powder metallurgy and its applications. Shows the advantages of the use of metal in a powder form.
Industrial and Technical Education; Science - Physical
Dist - MTP **Prod** - MTP

Powder metallurgy - manufacture of porous bronze bearings 15 MIN
U-matic
Engineering series
B&W
LC 79-706437
Discusses the manufacturing process by which metal powders are fabricated into porous bronze bearings and impregnated with oil. Issued in 1945 as a motion picture.
Industrial and Technical Education; Science - Physical
Dist - USNAC **Prod** - USOE 1979

Powder metallurgy - principles and uses 19 MIN
U-matic
Engineering series
B&W
LC 79-706436
Describes the principles of powder metallurgy, including powder, pressure and heat. Deals with major industrial applications of powder metallurgy and the laboratory process of combining silver and nickel powders. Issued in 1945 as a motion picture.

Industrial and Technical Education; Science - Physical
Dist - USNAC Prod - USOE 1979

Powder metallurgy - Pt 1 - principles and uses 19 MIN
16mm
Engineering series
B&W
LC FIE52-174
Discusses the principles of powder metallurgy and its major industrial applications. Depicts the laboratory process of combining silver and nickel powders.
Industrial and Technical Education
Dist - USNAC Prod - USOE 1945

Powder metallurgy - Pt 2 - manufacture of porous bronze bearings 15 MIN
16mm
Engineering series
B&W
LC FIE52-175
Shows how metal powders are fabricated into porous bronze bearings and impregnated with oil.
Industrial and Technical Education
Dist - USNAC Prod - USOE 1945

Powell - gunslingers 30 MIN
VHS
Vietnam home movies series
Color (J H C G)
$29.95 purchase _ #BV151V
Features actual footage shot by soldiers during their tours of duty in Vietnam. Tells the story of one soldier in his own words, the combat missions, his friends, his joy after a successful rescue, the devastation after an enemy raid, the sounds of war. Offers footage aboard a UH1 Huey helicopter gunship. Part of a four - part series.
History - United States; Sociology
Dist - CAMV

Power 30 MIN
U-matic / VHS
Making Government Work
(H)
Uses dramatizations and interviews to familiarize high school level students with the functions of government. Focuses on the use of power.
Civics and Political Systems
Dist - GPN

Power 34 MIN
U-matic / VHS / 16mm
Color (A)
LC 73-702748
Portrays a seance in a dark cellar where people are being taught the satanic skill of power and imposing one's will on others, releasing the evil hidden behind man's subconscious.
Psychology; Religion and Philosophy
Dist - PHENIX Prod - DUNAV 1973

Power 25 MIN
VHS
Fresh talk series
Color (H)
$150.00 purchase, $40.00 rental
Discusses sexism, homophobia, racism and sexual abuse. Helps young people develop critical attitudes about the sexual messages in pop culture, learn how to articulate their own sexual feelings and how to communicate them effectively and with respect for others. Part of a four - part series featuring thirty young men and women, ages 15 - 24, who share their reflections on sexuality and growing up. Directed by Teresa Marshall and Craig Berggold. Study guide available.
Sociology
Dist - CNEMAG

Power 30 MIN
VHS / 16mm
Solar energy series
Color (G)
$55.00 rental _ #SLRE - 104
Examines how the sun creates energy and how we can harness it.
Science - Physical; Social Science
Dist - PBS Prod - KNMETV

Power 10 MIN
VHS
Inside Acts series
Color (G R)
$14.95 purchase
Presents a study of experiences of Peter and John in Bible chapters Acts 3 and 4. Features student interviews, drama and historical events. Includes study questions. Part of a two - part series.
Literature and Drama; Religion and Philosophy
Dist - GF

Power - 1966 - 1968 60 MIN
VHS
Eyes on the prize series
Color; Captioned (G)
$59.95 purchase _ #EYES-203
Portrays the efforts of urban Black Americans to empower themselves. Highlights the election of Cleveland Mayor Carl Stokes, the first Black mayor of a major city. Shows the formation of the Black Panther Party in Oakland. Records how Black and Hispanic parents sought community control of Brooklyn schools. Part of a series on the Black civil rights movement.
Civics and Political Systems; History - United States; Sociology
Dist - PBS Prod - BSIDE 1990

Power - 1966 - 1968 and The promised land - 1967 - 1968 120 MIN
VHS
Eyes on the prize series
Color & B&W (G)
$19.95 purchase _ #PBS 1057
Presents three stories in the Power episode which capture the essence of the Civil Rights Movement in the late 1960s - the election of Carl Stokes as the first Black mayor of a major city, the rise of the Black Panther Party, and the uprising in the Ocean Hill - Brownsville section of Brooklyn. Looks in The Promised Land at the issues of war, poverty and economic justice as the war in Vietnam becomes a flashpoint. Martin Luther King, Jr, is assassinated in Memphis and the Poor People's Campaign comes to Washington DC.
Civics and Political Systems; History - United States; Sociology
Dist - INSTRU Prod - PBS

Power across the Sound 23 MIN
16mm
Color (I)
Shows the fabrication of worlds longest underwater cable in a factory in Italy, the transporting of the cables to New York and its installation between Norwalk, Connecticut and Northport, Long Island.
Industrial and Technical Education
Dist - LILC Prod - LILC

Power amplifier IC applications 30 MIN
U-matic / VHS
Linear integrated circuits series; Linear and interface integrated circuits; Pt 1
Color (IND VOC)
Shows how integrated circuit power amplifiers increase output power. Accomplishes variations by adjusting bandwidth for good communications, head phone and stereo amplifiers.
Industrial and Technical Education
Dist - TXINLC Prod - TXINLC

Power and Conflict in the Organization - We Can Work it Out 26 MIN
U-matic / VHS / 16mm
Human Resources and Organizational Behavior Series
Color
Points out that power struggles exist in all organizations and at all levels. Examines what skills are necessary for managing such struggles. Documents an actual training lab session, with participants developing an understanding of the dynamics of conflict and its resolution.
Business and Economics; Psychology
Dist - CNEMAG Prod - DOCUA

Power and Corruption 34 MIN
16mm / U-matic / VHS
Great Themes of Literature Series
Color (H C A)
LC 73-702550
Presents an edited version of the film Macbeth directed by Roman Polanski. Explores the theme of why men are attracted to power and the influence power, once gained, has upon their natures.
Civics and Political Systems; Guidance and Counseling; Literature and Drama; Sociology
Dist - LCOA Prod - LCOA 1973

Power and hand tool safety 21 MIN
VHS
Color (IND) (SPANISH FRENCH)
$365.00 purchase, $125.00 rental _ #TAT04
Demonstrates proper methods of selection, inspection, and use of hand tools and portable power tools both on the job and at home. Offers employee guides separately.
Health and Safety
Dist - EXTR Prod - TAT

Power and partnership - the church and development in Zimbabwe and One small story of success 60 MIN
VHS
Color (G)
Presents two 30 - minute videos about the changing role of the church and the nature of its development work in Zimbabwe.
Geography - World; Religion and Philosophy; Sociology
Dist - ASTRSK Prod - ASTRSK 1988

Power and Power Factor 34 MIN
16mm
B&W
LC 74-705390
Explains the difference between true power and apparent power in a series RC or RL circuit. Gives the power factor, with the equations for both true and apparent power. (Kinescope).
Industrial and Technical Education; Mathematics; Science - Physical
Dist - USNAC Prod - USAF

The Power and the Glory 52 MIN
U-matic / VHS
Testament - the Bible and History Series
Color (G)
$279.00, $179.00 purchase _ #AD - 1730
Looks at the Bible as the sole allowed source of learning and as justification for social order during the Dark Ages. Ends in 1453 when Constantinople fell and Gutenberg printed his first Bible. Part of a seven - part series on the Bible and history.
History - World; Literature and Drama; Religion and Philosophy
Dist - FOTH Prod - FOTH

Power and the Land 38 MIN
16mm
B&W
LC FIE52-403
Portrays a farm family in Pennsylvania before and after the electrification of their farm. Shows the formation of an electrical cooperative by a farm group. Illustrates savings and benefits brought by electricity.
Agriculture; Social Science
Dist - USNAC Prod - USDA 1948

Power and the Land 40 MIN
U-matic
B&W
LC 79-706462
Portrays a farm family in Pennsylvania before and after electrification of their farm. Contrasts farm duties and tasks with and without electricity and discusses how to form a farmers' electrical cooperative. Issued in 1951 as a motion picture.
Agriculture; Social Science
Dist - USNAC Prod - USDA 1979

Power and the Press 24 MIN
16mm
American Challenge Series
B&W
Uses an extract from the motion picture Citizen Kane to illustrate the use, misuses and power of the newspaper medium. Shows how Kane uses the press as an instrument of reform and power. Stars Orson Welles and Joseph Cotton.
Fine Arts; Social Science; Sociology
Dist - FI Prod - RKOP 1975

The Power and the Quest 27 MIN
16mm
Color
LC 75-700315
Gives a history of the American aircraft industry as seen through the eyes of pioneer engine manufacturers. Shows how aircraft progressed from piston engines up to the present - day jet aircraft manufactured by Pratt and Whitney Aircraft.
Business and Economics; Industrial and Technical Education
Dist - PWA Prod - PTRSEN 1975

Power and Wheels 17 MIN
U-matic / VHS / 16mm
Color (I J H)
LC 72-701972
Surveys the social and cultural impact of the car and investigates its relationship to the American economy.
Business and Economics; Home Economics; Industrial and Technical Education; Psychology; Sociology
Dist - EBEC Prod - EBEC 1972

Power and Wheels - the Automobile in Modern Life 17 MIN
VHS / U-matic
Color (J C)
$49.00 purchase _ #3502
Examines the influence of the automobile on American culture as seen through the eyes of two visitors from outer space. Shows the industries cars have created and the problems they have caused such as pollution, accidents, and congestion.
Industrial and Technical Education
Dist - EBEC

Power Basics of Auto Racing 78 MIN
U-matic / VHS / 16mm
(A PRO)
_ #VV1
Gives a methodical guide to road racing, stock racing, and off road racing. Hosted by Parnelli Jones, Rick Knoop and Rick McCray.
Physical Education and Recreation
Dist - RMIBHF **Prod** - RMIBHF

Power Basics of Baseball 80 MIN
U-matic / VHS
Power Basics of Sports Series
Color
Features demonstrations by Jerry Reuss and others of basics such as pitching windup and grip, batting stance and pivot, baserunning, stealing, infield and outfield. Includes pitching, batting, fielding and baserunning.
Physical Education and Recreation
Dist - ATHI **Prod** - ATHI

Power Basics of Baseball
VHS / BETA
Sports - Power Basics Series
Color (A)
Physical Education and Recreation
Dist - RMIBHF **Prod** - RMIBHF

Power Basics of Sports Series
Power Basics of Baseball 80 MIN
Dist - ATHI

Power Bending Conduit 17 MIN
16mm
Electrical Work Series
B&W
LC FIE52-142
Demonstrates how to assemble and operate a floor bender and a portable bender, make a 45 - degree bend in a three inch conduit, make an offset in a one and one - half inch conduit and make and offset in a conduit already installed.
Industrial and Technical Education
Dist - USNAC **Prod** - USOE 1940

The Power Beneath the Land - a Portrait of Power 15 MIN
16mm
Color
LC 79-701307
Focuses on techniques used in surface and deep mining of coal in the Midwest and shows how land is reclaimed.
Geography - United States; Industrial and Technical Education; Social Science
Dist - VISION **Prod** - AMAX 1979

The Power Beneath the Land - Westward Coal 14 MIN
16mm
Color
LC 79-701308
Shows the techniques involved in surface mining of coal, reclamation of land, and transportation of coal.
Industrial and Technical Education; Social Science
Dist - VISION **Prod** - AMAX 1979

Power Blower
VHS
Landscape Equipment Maintenance Series
Color (G) (SPANISH)
$65.00 purchase _ #6 - 073 - 100P, #6 - 073 - 200P - Spanish
Presents proper procedures on maintenance, safety and operation of the gas - powered blower for landscaping. Part of a five - part series on landscaping which is also available in Spanish.
Agriculture; Health and Safety
Dist - VEP **Prod** - VEP

Power by design 23 MIN
VHS
Color; PAL (I J H)
PdS15 purchase _ #1015
Charts the evolution of nuclear technology in Britain since 1945 in relation to social and economic factors. Includes teacher's guide.
Social Science
Dist - UKAEA

The Power Close 16 MIN
16mm / VHS
(PRO)
$150.00 rental
Tackles the problem of salespeople failing to ask for an order after a sales presentation. Discusses the vital elements for a successful close and illustrates five keys to getting more sales.
Business and Economics; Industrial and Technical Education; Psychology
Dist - DARTNL

The Power close 16 MIN
VHS
Color (A PRO)
$520.00 purchase, $150.00 rental
Discusses five key factors in successful selling.
Business and Economics; Psychology
Dist - VLEARN **Prod** - DARTNL

Power Considerations in Resistive Circuits 5 MIN
VHS / 16mm
Electrical Theory Series
Color (S)
$50.00 purchase _ #241303
Illustrates 22 concepts fundamental to the training of second year electrical apprentices using graphic animation. Defines the basic components of all electrical circuits and the relationship between work, energy, power and current in 'Power Considerations.'.
Education; Industrial and Technical Education; Psychology
Dist - ACCESS **Prod** - ACCESS 1983

Power, Control, and Decision Making 40 MIN
VHS / U-matic
Missiles of October - a Case Study in Decision Making Series
Color
Business and Economics; Civics and Political Systems; History - World
Dist - DELTAK **Prod** - LCOA

Power Distribution Systems 8 MIN
U-matic / VHS
Electrical Safety Series
Color (IND)
Shows how to be sure a circuit is de - energized before work begins, and how one - lines, work orders and communication are all essential for maintenance of distribution systems.
Health and Safety; Industrial and Technical Education
Dist - GPCV **Prod** - GPCV

Power Drills for Woodwork 13 MIN
16mm
Woodwork - Machine Tools Series
Color (J)
LC 74-713059
Presents seven concepts dealing with power drills - drill press - parts, drill press - bits, drill press - adjustments, drill press - operation, drill press - sanding drums, portable drill - parts and bits, and portable drill - operation. The projector may be stopped after each concept.
Industrial and Technical Education
Dist - SF **Prod** - SF 1967

Power Equipment Safety
VHS / 35mm strip
Wood Safety Series
$28.00 purchase _ #TX1B3 filmstrip, $58.00 purchase _ #TX1B3V VHS
Teaches power equipment safety and use.
Industrial and Technical Education
Dist - CAREER **Prod** - CAREER

Power Factor Correction 7 MIN
VHS / 16mm
Electrical Theory Series
Color (S)
$50.00 purchase _ #241320
Illustrates 22 concepts fundamental to the training of second year electrical apprentices using graphic animation. Illustrates how capacitance can be used to increase the ratio of true power to apparent power in 'Power Factor Correction.'.
Education; Industrial and Technical Education; Psychology
Dist - ACCESS **Prod** - ACCESS 1983

Power for the Moonship 28 MIN
16mm
B&W (J)
LC 78-708122
Shows working models of the fuel cell for the Apollo spacecraft and discusses possible uses of the cell here on Earth.
Industrial and Technical Education; Science - Physical
Dist - USNAC **Prod** - NASA 1966

Power from Coal 24 MIN
16mm
Color
LC 80-700864
Shows the resurrection of the New South Wales coal industry from a strife - ridden and backward assortment of coal producers into an efficient and highly productive coal industry. Discusses the vital role of coal as the cornerstone of civilization and living standards.
Geography - World; Industrial and Technical Education; Social Science
Dist - TASCOR **Prod** - IMPACT 1978

Power from Fusion - the Principles 29 MIN
16mm
Color (J)
Discusses the principles of the production of energy by nuclear fusion, including problems still to be solved. Covers thermonuclear research in Britain.
Geography - World; Industrial and Technical Education; Science - Physical; Social Science
Dist - UKAEA **Prod** - UKAEA 1964

Power from fusion - the problem of containment - Pt 2 40 MIN
16mm
Color
Describes the theory of the fusion process and the nature of a plasma. Defines the required conditions in terms of the temperature and the density times time product for the containment of the plasma. Illustrates a number of experiments, starting with the pinch effect, and considers in detail the instabilities which arise. Considers the thetatron system, followed by magnetic cages and the Phoenix experiment. Warns that although the major instabilities appear to have been overcome, other less violent instabilities may now be revealed.
Industrial and Technical Education; Science - Physical
Dist - UKAEA **Prod** - UKAEA 1965

Power from the Earth 13 MIN
16mm / U-matic / VHS
Color
Shows eight scientists, engineers and managers describing various aspects of obtaining thermal energy from the earth for the production of electrical power.
Social Science
Dist - USNAC **Prod** - USERD

Power from the Earth
U-matic / VHS / BETA
Search encounters in science series
Color; PAL (G H C)
PdS25, PdS33 purchase
Brings modern research efforts of the world's leading scientists into the classroom. Features one of a series of 24 mini - documentaries. Each film is 5 - 7 minutes in length.
Science; Science - Physical; Social Science
Dist - EDPAT **Prod** - NSF

Power from the Sun 5 MIN
16mm
Screen news digest series; Vol 4; Issue 4
B&W (J H)
Describes experiments to find new ways of harnessing solar power. Shows America's first solar home in which sun rays serve as the source of heat and power.
Science - Physical
Dist - HEARST **Prod** - HEARST 1961

Power from water 15 MIN
VHS
Field trips series
Color (I J)
$34.95 purchase _ #E337; LC 90-708555
Presents a brief review of the movement of water in nature. Identifies the three major sources of electric energy and traces the principle of falling water to its origin in solar energy. Explains how this energy is harvested by humans. Part of a series which provides visual opportunities for children to 'visit' a variety of locations and activities as if they were on a field trip.
Education; Geography - United States; Social Science
Dist - GPN **Prod** - MPBN 1983

Power Game Series
Focuses on the workings of the United States government. Analyzes government institutions including Congress, the presidency and the Pentagon, as well as lobbying groups. Four - part series is based on the book of the same name by Hedrick Smith, who also hosts the programs.
The Congress 60 MIN
The Pentagon 60 MIN
The Presidency 60 MIN
The Unelected 60 MIN
Dist - PBS **Prod** - MPTPB 1983

Power generators - Pt 1
U-matic / VHS
Industrial training - Power Production Series - Module 4; Module 4 - Power production
Color (IND)
Includes principles, frequency, construction and excitation of power generators.
Industrial and Technical Education
Dist - LEIKID **Prod** - LEIKID

Power Generators, Pt 2
VHS / U-matic
Industrial Training, Module 4 - Power Production Series; Module 4 - Power production

Color (IND)
Studies several aspects of power generators including cooling, hydrogen cooling and operation.
Industrial and Technical Education
Dist - LEIKID **Prod** - LEIKID

Power Hacksaw and Band Saw 12 MIN
16mm / U-matic / VHS
Color (J H A) (SPANISH)
LC 79-708038
Demonstrates the correct technique for accurate cutting with each machine and emphasizes the safety practices and proper maintenance of the band saw blades. Discusses the kinds of blades available and their safe installation.
Foreign Language; Health and Safety; Industrial and Technical Education
Dist - PHENIX **Prod** - BROSEB 1969

Power Hitting in Softball 30 MIN
VHS
(H C A)
$29.95 _ #SIM8917V
Presents the secret hitting tips of five power hitters in softball. Discusses stance, grip, positioning, conditioning, and weight training. Explains the need for consistent practice and mental concentration.
Physical Education and Recreation
Dist - CAMV

Power imbalances - Tape 5
VHS
Law and persons with mental disability series
Color (C PRO G)
$95.00 purchase
Analyzes the power imbalances in forensic cases as well as in cases involving the therapeutic process. Explains judicial and juror responses to these imbalances and offers some thoughts as to how they may be 'played out' in future cases. Part of a six - part series featuring Michael I Perlin, JD, on the law and persons with mental disability. Serves as a resource for attorneys practicing mental disability law, advocates working with mentally disabled individuals, mental health professionals, hospital administrators and other care providers subject to legal regulation.
Civics and Political Systems; Psychology
Dist - BAXMED

Power in parenting - the adolescent and the family under fire - Tape 2 98 MIN
VHS
Turn your heart toward home series
Color (H C G A R)
$10.00 rental _ #36 - 89982 - 533
Features Dr James Dobson and his wife Shirley in two presentations on issues affecting the family. 'Power in Parenting - The Adolescent' stresses the need for healthy father - daughter and mother - son relationships. 'The Family Under Fire,' intended for adults only, considers issues of abortion, pornography and government actions as they affect the family.
Psychology; Sociology
Dist - APH **Prod** - WORD

The Power in plants - Busy as a bee - It's a small world 30 MIN
VHS
Moody science adventures series
Color (R P I)
$14.95 purchase _ #6164 - 6
Uses time - lapse photography to reveal the mechanisms of plants. Follows hard - working bees through their daily routines. Examines the complex society living in a drop of water. Credits all of these activities to the creative aspects of the Christian deity. Part of a series.
Literature and Drama; Religion and Philosophy; Science - Natural
Dist - MOODY **Prod** - MOODY

Power in the land 104 MIN
VHS
Color; PAL (H)
PdS50 purchase
Presents a series of four programs of 26 minutes each examining the profound upheaval experienced by the British countryside. Considers the new forces at play - political power and profit. Shows how such changes affect the land itself and the people who live and work on the land. Charts some of the changes in four rural communities in England, Wales and Scotland. Raises important questions about how human manage their environment. Includes the titles Highland, Dreamland, Dairyland and No Man's Land. Contact distributor about availability outside the United Kingdom.
Geography - World
Dist - ACADEM

Power interviewing 55 MIN
VHS
(H C G)
$45.95 purchase _ #WAT100V
Shares the professional expertise of an executive recruiter who takes viewers step - by - step through writing and circulating a resume; researching a company and preparing for an interview; power interviewing; and following up after the interview.
Business and Economics; Guidance and Counseling
Dist - CAMV

Power lawn mower safety 15 MIN
16mm / U-matic / VHS
Color (J H C A)
$385.00, $250.00 purchase _ #80547
Shows how to avoid hazardous situations when using a power lawn mower.
Health and Safety
Dist - CORF **Prod** - CENTRO 1982

Power Mechanics Series

The Air Vane Governor	7 MIN
The Carburetor	8 MIN
The Four - Cycle engine	9 MIN
How to Adjust the Breaker Points	7 MIN
How to inspect and replace the valves	8 MIN
How to Remove the Valves	8 MIN
How to Time the 2 - Cycle Engine	8 MIN
How to Trouble Shoot a Small Engine	9 MIN
Magneto Ignition	6 MIN
Reading the Micrometer	10 MIN
Taking Inside Measurements	9 MIN
The Two - Cycle Engine	4 MIN
Use of a Torque Wrench	4 MIN
Use of Thickness Gauges	10 MIN
Valve Timing the 4 - Cycle Engine	8 MIN

Dist - CAROUF

Power Network - Pt 1
U-matic / VHS
Industrial Training, Module 4 - Power Production Series; Module 4 - Power production
Color (IND)
Covers load and demand, synchronising and reactance.
Industrial and Technical Education
Dist - LEIKID **Prod** - LEIKID

Power network - Pt 2
VHS / U-matic
Industrial training - power production series - Module 4; Module 4 - Power production
Color (IND)
Includes the Power factor, generators in parallel, sharing load, and reactive and three phase connections.
Industrial and Technical Education
Dist - LEIKID **Prod** - LEIKID

Power network - Pt 3
VHS / U-matic
Industrial Training, Module 4 - Power Production Series; Module 4 - Power production
Color (IND)
Covers direct current supply, motor and generator protection, and network protection.
Industrial and Technical Education
Dist - LEIKID **Prod** - LEIKID

The Power of a magnet - Pt 2 9 MIN
VHS
Magnets series
Color; PAL (P I J)
Examines the differing magnetic properties of magnets of varying shapes and the operation of magnetic force over distance. Part two of a five - part series on magnets.
Science - Physical
Dist - VIEWTH **Prod** - VIEWTH

The Power of addiction 19 MIN
VHS / 16mm
Color (H G)
$149.00, $249.00 purchase _ #AD - 1976
Covers both chemical and behavioral addiction. Describes the signs of compulsive behavior and analyzes such possible causes as neurotransmitter imbalance, genetic, and environmental factors. Profiles several recovered addicts and discusses recovery factors.
Psychology
Dist - FOTH **Prod** - FOTH 1990

Power of Algebra Series

Basic properties	15 MIN
Factoring, Pt 1	15 MIN
Factoring, Pt 2	15 MIN
Fractions	15 MIN
Inverse Operations	15 MIN
Order of Operations	15 MIN
Polynomials and equations	15 MIN
The Positive and Negative Numbers	15 MIN
Using Positive Exponents	15 MIN
Words into Symbols	15 MIN

Dist - GPN

The Power of Asia's media - a force for unity 30 MIN
VHS
Color (G)
$15.00 purchase _ #V94 - 22
Presents a seminar on international media issues. Part of a series on freedom of the press, free speech and free spirit.
Literature and Drama; Sociology
Dist - FREEDM **Prod** - FREEDM 1994

The Power of attention 59 MIN
VHS
Color (G R)
$29.95 purchase _ #C048
Features spiritual teacher Tara Singh.
Psychology; Religion and Philosophy
Dist - LIFEAP **Prod** - LIFEAP

Power of attorney for health care 14 MIN
VHS
Color (C PRO G)
$250.00 purchase, $70.00 rental _ #4336S, #4336V
Explains the 1991 Patient Self - Determination Act which mandates that every health care organization qualified for Medicare or Medicaid must advise all admitted patients in writing of their right to refuse treatment and to prepare an advance directive, along with the facility's policies for carrying out such a directive. Describes both living wills and the power of attorney for health care, explains the reasons for such documents and how to create them. Vignettes clarify issues. Produced by Rogue Valley Medical Center.
Civics and Political Systems; Health and Safety
Dist - AJN

Power of change series
Features Dr Gerald Ross and Michael Kay in a two - part series. Includes the titles The Management Revolution and Reinventing the Organization.
The Management revolution - I
Reinventing the organization - II
Dist - AMEDIA **Prod** - AMEDIA 1993

The Power of Choice 60 MIN
VHS / 16mm
Power of Choice Series
(H)
$99.95 _ #LW101V
Explains the use of the VIP formula - using Vision, Initiative and Perspective as tools for making the best choices.
Guidance and Counseling
Dist - JISTW

The Power of Choice 60 MIN
VHS
Power Of Choice Series
Color (G)
$79.95 purchase _ #CHOI - 101
Shows teenagers that they have the power to make many choices. Gives guidelines for good decision making. Applies these guidelines to some of the issues facing teenagers.
Guidance and Counseling; Psychology; Sociology
Dist - PBS **Prod** - LWIRE 1988

The Power of choice 60 MIN
VHS / U-matic
Power of choice series
Color (I J H)
$79.95, $89.95, $99.95 purchase _ #LWV100V, #LWV100-G, #HH - 6336M, #60285 - 025, #8809, #8808
Presents teen counselor and comedian Richard Pritchard who shows young people how to use Vision, Initiative, and Perspective to make the kind of choices that put them in control of their lives. Deals with many issues, including self esteem, peer pressure, parent relations, teen pregnancy, and drug and alcohol use.
Psychology
Dist - CAMV **Prod** - PBS
CORF ELSW
GA GA
HAZELB

The Power of Choice 25 MIN
VHS
FFA (Set X) Series
(H C)
$39.95 _ CV194
Presents a motivational talk targeted for recruiting vocational education students.
Education; Psychology
Dist - AAVIM **Prod** - AAVIM 1989

Power of choice - drugs and alcohol - Pt I 30 MIN
VHS
Color (J H G)
$64.95 purchase
Interviews groups of teens across the nation to discuss why teenagers choose to use drugs and alcohol and why they choose not to use drugs. Features Michael Pritchard as host. Produced by Victory Video. Part one of two parts.

Guidance and Counseling; Psychology; Sociology
Dist - BRODAT

Power of choice - drugs and alcohol - Pt II 30 MIN
VHS
Color (J H G)
$64.95 purchase
Explores what happens when friends or family members abuse drugs. Examines the impact of chemical abuse on relationships, and what can and cannot be done to help the abuser. Features Michael Pritchard as host. Produced by Victory Video. Part two of two parts.
Guidance and Counseling; Psychology; Sociology
Dist - BRODAT

Power of choice series
The Power of choice 60 MIN
Dist - CAMV
CORF
GA
HAZELB

Power of choice series
Presents the complete Power of Choice series, featuring Michael Pritchard who uses humor to promote positive, life - affirming values and empowers young people to take charge of their lives. Show how to be a 'VIP' by using Vision, Initiative and Perspective as tools for making the best choices. Discusses values, parents, pressures, drugs and alcohol, friendship and dating, sex, and self esteem.
Acting on your values 30 MIN
Communicating with parents 30 MIN
Depression and suicide 30 MIN
Drinking and driving 30 MIN
Drugs and alcohol - Part I 30 MIN
Drugs and alcohol - Part II 30 MIN
Friendship and dating 30 MIN
Raising your parents 30 MIN
Self esteem 30 MIN
Dist - CORF **Prod** - ELSW 1988

Power of choice series
Coping with pressures 30 MIN
Dist - CORF
GA
JISTW

Power of choice series
Sex 30 MIN
Dist - CORF
GA
JISTW
PBS

Power of choice series
Features comedian - teen counselor Michael Prichard in a twelve - part series on making choices. Helps young people realize that they are responsible for the choices they make, that they owe it to themselves to choose the best. Discusses values, self - esteem, coping with pressures, the abuse of drugs and alcohol, drinking and driving, sex, dating and friendship, depression and suicide, and having better relationships with parents.
Acting on your values 30 MIN
Communicating with parents 30 MIN
Drinking and driving 30 MIN
Drugs and alcohol - when someone you care about is hooked 30 MIN
Drugs and alcohol...and you 30 MIN
Friendship and dating 30 MIN
Raising your parents - making your relationships better 30 MIN
Self - esteem 30 MIN
Dist - GA **Prod** - GA 1988

Power of choice series
Depression and suicide 30 MIN
Dist - GA
JISTW

Power of choice series
Acting on your values 30 MIN
Communication with parents 30 MIN
Self - Esteem 30 MIN
Dist - HAZELB

Power of Choice Series
Presents a series of personal guidance videos narrated by a probation officer turned stand - up comic who talks to a group of kids about choices. Available as a series or as individual titles.
Acting on values 30 MIN
Communicating with your parents 30 MIN
Drinking and Driving 30 MIN
Drugs and Alcohol 30 MIN
Drugs and Alcohol,_Part 002 30 MIN
The Power of Choice 60 MIN
Raising Your Parents 30 MIN
Self Esteem 30 MIN
Dist - JISTW

Power Of Choice Series
Deals with issues facing teenagers. Considers topics such as depression, drug and alcohol use, peer pressure, dating and sex. Series consists of 12 episodes, each dealing with a different topic. Hosted by comedian and teen counselor Michael Pritchard.
Acting on your values 30 MIN
Communicating with parents 30 MIN
Coping with pressures 30 MIN
Depression and suicide 30 MIN
Drinking and Driving 30 MIN
Drugs and Alcohol - Part I 30 MIN
Drugs and Alcohol - Part II 30 MIN
Friendship and dating 30 MIN
The Power of Choice 60 MIN
Raising Your Parents 30 MIN
Self - Esteem 30 MIN
Dist - PBS **Prod** - LWIRE 1988

The Power of Christian love - Pt 3
VHS
Keith Miller - new wine series
Color (H C G A R)
$10.00 rental _ #36 - 87403 - 533
Proposes the theory that living one's faith can provide good opportunities for evangelism. Based on the Keith Miller book 'A Taste of New Wine.'
Religion and Philosophy
Dist - APH **Prod** - WORD

The Power of customer service 45 MIN
Cassette / VHS
Color (G)
$95.00 purchase _ #6 - 401 - 111Q
Reveals the keys to obtaining repeat business from customers. Features Paul Timm. Includes videocassette, audiocassette and softcover application guide.
Business and Economics; Psychology
Dist - VEP

Power of delta blues guitar series
Presents a two - part series featuring guitarist Rory Block, Mississippi Delta blues stylist, who passes on her favorite techniques and tunes. Breaks each song down phrase by phrase while teaching the use of regular and open tunings, treble melodies, bass runs, slides, string bending and a variety of pounding and strumming styles. Teaches intros, solos, turnarounds and endings. Includes blues songs by Booker White, Charlie Patton, Rory Block, Robert Johnson, Mattie Delaney and Charlie Spann.
The Power of delta blues guitar - Video One 60 MIN
The Power of delta blues guitar - Video Two 60 MIN
Dist - HOMETA **Prod** - HOMETA

The Power of delta blues guitar - Video One 60 MIN
VHS
Power of delta blues guitar series
Color (G)
$49.95 purchase _ #VD - ROR - PW01
Features guitarist Rory Block, Mississippi Delta blues stylist, who passes on her favorite techniques and tunes. Breaks each song down phrase by phrase while teaching the use of regular and open tunings, treble melodies, bass runs, slides, string bending and a variety of pounding and strumming styles. Teaches intros, solos, turnarounds and endings. Includes Moon's Goin' Down by Charlie Patton; Patton's Blues, based on Charlie Patton's Pea Vine Blues and Milk Cow Blues by Robert Johnson; Crossroads Blues by Robert Johnson and Travelin's Blues by Mattie Delaney. Part one of two parts.
Fine Arts
Dist - HOMETA **Prod** - HOMETA

The Power of delta blues guitar - Video Two 60 MIN
VHS
Power of delta blues guitar series
Color (G)
$49.95 purchase _ #VD - ROR - PW02
Features guitarist Rory Block, Mississippi Delta blues stylist, who passes on her favorite techniques and tunes. Breaks each song down phrase by phrase while teaching the use of regular and open tunings, treble melodies, bass runs, slides, string bending and a variety of pounding and strumming styles. Teaches intros, solos, turnarounds and endings. Includes Fixin' to Die by Booker White; Love My Blues Away and Leavin' Here by Block; When You've Got a Good Friend by Robert Johnson; The Water is Wide, a traditional arranged by Block; and My Train is Waiting by Charlie Spann. Part two of two parts.
Fine Arts
Dist - HOMETA **Prod** - HOMETA

The Power of dialogue 65 MIN
VHS / Cassette
Beyond fragmentation - memory of the whole series
Color; PAL (G C PRO)
$150.00, $25.00 purchase _ #V9331, #T9331
Features William Isaacs who explores the ways in which dialog can develop collective skills of thinking beyond existing paradigms to foster space for new thought and action - in effect transforming the ground out of which thinking and acting emerge. Part one of three parts on breaking down the myth that human relationships can be separated into their constituent parts and showing how this myth is slowly being replaced by an appreciation for interconnectedness and the integrity of the whole.
Business and Economics; Psychology
Dist - PEGASU

The Power of Enthusiasm 30 MIN
U-matic / VHS / 16mm
B&W (PRO)
Spells out how a salesman can create and maintain an enthusiastic 'ORDER - WINNING' attitude. Shows the belief in salesmen's enthusiasm describing 'WHEN A SALESMAN GETS EXCITED, BUYERS GET EXCITED, AND ORDERS ARE THE RESULT.'.
Business and Economics; Psychology; Social Science; Sociology
Dist - DARTNL **Prod** - DARTNL

The Power of green 30 MIN
VHS / U-matic
Forests of the world series
Color (J H G)
$270.00, $320.00 purchase, $60.00 rental
Uses a coastal tree plantation of enormous size in Brazil to show how commercial plantations can provide wood pulp and paper needs and reduce the pressure to log the tropical rain forests. Shows how a well - managed tree plantation may provide for jobs, health care, schools and a sustained community.
Geography - World; Science - Natural
Dist - NDIM **Prod** - NRKTV 1993

The Power of healing 50 MIN
VHS
First Tuesday series
Color; PAL (H C G)
PdS30 purchase
Examines the belief in faith healers or cranks, quacks and charlatans as they are called by skeptics. Shows that, for some people, this particular form of alternative medicine will always be treated with suspicion, while others swear that the effects of 'healing' can be miraculous. Contact distributor about availability outside the United Kingdom.
Health and Safety; History - World
Dist - ACADEM **Prod** - YORKTV

The Power of image 37 MIN
VHS
Color (J H C G A R)
$39.95 purchase, $10.00 rental _ #35 - 858346 - 93
Scrutinizes the influence of the mass media on U S culture. Hosted by Alaina Reed Hall of 'Sesame Street' and '227' fame.
Religion and Philosophy; Sociology
Dist - APH **Prod** - FRPR

The Power of independence 28 MIN
VHS
Color; Captioned (G)
$35.00 purchase
Demonstrates the importance of assistive technology for people with disabilities. Discusses legislation, employment and the Utah Assistive Technology Program.
Health and Safety
Dist - UATP **Prod** - UATP 1990

Power of Involvement 30 MIN
U-matic / VHS
Developing Discipline Series
Color (T)
Points out that through involvement with a caring person, a weak individual can be helped toward a strong, successful identity.
Education; Guidance and Counseling; Psychology; Sociology
Dist - GPN **Prod** - SDPT 1983

Power of linking spreadsheets
VHS
Lotus video series
Color (G J H C)
$49.95 purchase _ #LPVO002V _#LP007
Teaches the key features of linking spreadsheets in Lotus software. Involves beginning to advanced users in the learning process with simple illustrations and colorful analogies. Shows how Lotus software reacts to commands as students follow along at their keyboards. Part of an eight - part series on Lotus.
Computer Science
Dist - CAMV
SIV

The Power of Listening 26 MIN
U-matic / VHS / 16mm
Color (H C A) (SPANISH)
Explores the meaning and benefits of active listening and points out the deterrents to good listening.
English Language; Foreign Language; Psychology
Dist - MGHT **Prod** - MGHT 1978

The Power of listening 26 MIN
U-matic / VHS / 16mm
Behavior in business series
Color (H C A) (ENGLISH & SPANISH)
LC 78-700877
Explores the meaning and benefits of active listening and points out the deterrents to good listening.
English Language; Psychology
Dist - MGHT **Prod** - MGHT 1978

Power of Listening 26 MIN
VHS / 16mm
(C PRO)
$625.00 purchase, $125.00 rental
Shows managers and supervisors how improved productivity results from learning how to listen.
Education
Dist - VLEARN **Prod** - CRM

Power of Listening 24 MIN
VHS / 16mm
Color (C)
$28.50, $13.50 rental _ 35261
Examines barriers to effective listening and provides techniques to improve listening skills.
Business and Economics; Education; English Language; Guidance and Counseling; Social Science; Sociology
Dist - PSU **Prod** - CRMP

The Power of myth
VHS / Cassette
Color (G)
$149.95, $179.70, $44.95 purchase _ #VHXSET, #E9XSET, $688
Features Bill Moyers with anthropologist and storyteller Joseph Campbell. Explores the eternal themes of literature and religion. Includes the titles 'The Hero's Adventure,' 'The Message Of The Myth,' 'The First Storytellers,' 'Sacrifice And Bliss,' 'Love And The Goddess' and 'Masks Of Eternity' on six cassettes. The video version is complete and unabridged, the audio version is a specially edited version broadcast on American Public Radio.
Literature and Drama; Religion and Philosophy; Sociology
Dist - AUDIOE **Prod** - AUDIOE
PBS WNETTV
YELMON

Power of Myth Series
The First storytellers
The Hero's Journey
Love and the Goddess
Masks of Eternity
The Message of the Myth
Sacrifice and Bliss
Dist - BKPEOP

Power of Myth Series
The First storytellers
The Hero's Journey 58 MIN
Masks of Eternity 58 MIN
The Message of the Myth 58 MIN
Sacrifice and Bliss 58 MIN
58 MIN
Dist - GAINST

Power of Myth Series
Love and the Goddess 58 MIN
Dist - GAINST
PBS
YELMON

Power of myth series
First storytellers
The Hero's adventure 60 MIN
Love and the goddess
Masks of eternity
Message of the myth
Sacrifice and bliss
Dist - PBS

Power of Myth series
The First storytellers - Vol 3 60 MIN
The Hero's adventure, vol 1 60 MIN
Masks of eternity, vol 6 60 MIN
The Message of the myth, vol 2 60 MIN
Sacrifice and bliss, vol 4 60 MIN
Dist - YELMON

Power of no - the wizard returns 23 MIN
VHS / U-matic / BETA / 16mm
Color (I)
$525.00, $425.00 purchase _ #JR - 5887M
Uses live action and animation to demonstrate that alcohol is an equal opportunity destroyer that can be passed down from one generation to the next, wreaking havoc with lives and shattering dreams. Portrays 11 - year - old Alice who meets the magical Wizard of No and learns that acknowledging her feelings, believing in the power of dreams and making informed choices can help overcome the crutch of alcohol in her family.
Health and Safety; Psychology; Sociology
Dist - CORF **Prod** - MITCHG 1989

The Power of nursing 25 MIN
U-matic / VHS
Color (C PRO)
%i $275.00 purchase, $75.00 rental _ #42 - 2453, #42 - 2452, #42 - 2453R, #42 - 2452R
Discusses the nature of power. Offers a rare glimpse into the private and professional lives of three women who began their careers as nurses and became outstanding national leaders - Sheila Burke, Rae Grad and Maria Mitchell. Identifies the components of power and explains how to use power effectively.
Business and Economics; Civics and Political Systems; Guidance and Counseling; Health and Safety
Dist - NLFN **Prod** - NLFN

The Power of Objective Setting 30 MIN
VHS / U-matic
Decision Analysis by Kepner - Tregoe Series
Color
Business and Economics; Education; Psychology
Dist - DELTAK **Prod** - KEPTRG

The Power of PACs 30 MIN
VHS / 16mm
Government by Consent - a National Perspective Series
Color (I J H C A)
Examines the purpose of Political Action Committees and their relationship to interest groups. Explores the role of PACs in our democracy.
Civics and Political Systems
Dist - DALCCD **Prod** - DALCCD 1990

The Power of parenting - parent and child interaction
VHS
Family literacy training videos series
Color (G)
$60.00 purchase
Demonstrates the power of interaction sessions between parents and children. Includes footage of activities and staff and parent reactions. Includes a supplementary manual which is also available separately. Part of two parts.
English Language; Social Science; Sociology
Dist - NCFL **Prod** - NCFL

The Power of People 28 MIN
16mm
Color
LC 73-702359
Traces the relationship of all links of the cooperative system to the system as a whole and describes its relationship to individual members.
Sociology
Dist - FAMACO **Prod** - FAMACO 1973

The Power of Positive Reinforcement 28 MIN
U-matic / VHS / 16mm
Color (H C A)
Demonstrates behavior modification techniques and documents their successful use in organizations.
Business and Economics; Psychology
Dist - CRMP **Prod** - CRMP 1978

The Power of positive reinforcement 28 MIN
16mm / U-matic / VHS
Behavior in business series
Color (C A) (SPANISH)
Documents the systematic on - site application of behavior management and its emphasis on positive reinforcement. Examines its use in the Valley Fair Amusement Park in Minnesota, on the defensive line of the Minnesota Vikings and in the streets of Detroit, Michigan, with the Sanitation Department. Portrays behavior modification as a powerful tool for managing human performance.
Business and Economics; Foreign Language; Psychology; Sociology
Dist - MGHT **Prod** - MGHT 1978

Power of Positive Students (POPS) Self Esteem Builder for Children K - 4 480 MIN
VHS
Color (K)
$450.00 purchase
Presents four modules, each consisting of two audiocassettes and two videocassettes, aimed at combatting self destructive behavior in young children. Uses animation, drama, music, and stories from real life to focus on themes of self awareness, goals and expectations, enthusiasm and coping skills, and making a difference. Includes written support materials for teachers and parents.
Guidance and Counseling; Psychology; Sociology
Dist - UNKNWN

Power of positive students series - POPS
VHS
Power of positive students series
Color (K P I T)
$595.00 purchase _ #B016 - V8
Presents four modules of a series giving children K - 5 the foundation for lasting self - esteem, self - awareness, confidence, and positive decision - making skills. Introduces students to real - life problems. Begins with the Positively Solving Problems segment, which guides through a problem - solving skills sequence. Students practice this sequence to resolve the dilemma presented, and eventually apply it to their own problems. Includes 8 videos, 8 audiocassettes for teachers, a Teacher's Video Guide, and a Parent's Planner with 30 activities for parents and kids.
Guidance and Counseling; Psychology
Dist - ETRASS **Prod** - ETRASS

Power of positive students series
Module 4 - Making a difference
Module 1 - Self awareness
Module 3 - Enthusiasm and coping skills
Module 2 - Goals and expectations
Power of positive students series - POPS
Dist - ETRASS

The Power of publicity 120 MIN
Cassette / VHS
Color (PRO G)
$29.95 purchase
Gives precise, detailed information on how to carry out a publicity campaign from writing press releases to making the most of radio and TV interviews. Shows how to field relevant questions and control the focus of interviews, plug products, services and events without being blatantly commercial. Includes a publicity resource booklet.
Business and Economics; Social Science
Dist - CATPUB **Prod** - CATPUB 1984

The Power of Questioning 15 MIN
VHS / 16mm
Survivor's Guide to Learning Series
Color (S)
$185.00 purchase _ #288801
Introduces general processes and pointers through interviews with study skills specialists and students who have mastered the techniques. Covers five theme areas and includes five booklets which deal with each theme. 'The Power Of Questioning' considers true learning which involves the processes of synthesic, analysis and evaluation, in contrast with memorization.
Agriculture; Education; Psychology
Dist - ACCESS **Prod** - ACCESS 1989

The Power of ritual 30 MIN
VHS / BETA
Working with the unconscious series
Color (G)
$29.95 purchase _ #S340
Recognizes dancing and other ritual activities as a method for becoming aware of inner negativity and transforming the power of such negativity into a healing experience. Features Anna Halprin, director of the Tamalpa Institute, who draws on her own experience battling cancer to discuss the psychological value of body movement and symbolic action. Part of a four - part series about working with the unconscious.
Fine Arts; Health and Safety; Religion and Philosophy
Dist - THINKA **Prod** - THINKA

Power of Speech 25 MIN
U-matic / VHS / 16mm
Children Growing Up Series
Color (H C A)
Discusses the development of language in the child.
Psychology
Dist - FI **Prod** - BBCTV 1981

Power of Speech 26 MIN
16mm / U-matic / VHS
Children Growing Up Series
Color (C A)
Explores the problem of speech, and shows how it can be overcome, based on current ideas of speech development.
English Language; Home Economics; Psychology; Sociology
Dist - FI **Prod** - BBCTV 1971

The Power of Stories 17 MIN
16mm / U-matic / VHS
Color (T)
Underscores the importance of literature in children's educational, artistic and intellectual growth. Shows nursery rhymes and poetry being shared to the delight of children in a variety of settings.
Education
Dist - WWS **Prod** - IECS 1984

The Power of suggestion 24 MIN
VHS
Color (G A)
$450.00 purchase _ #VSUG - 721
Presents a two - part program outlining the importance of suggestion systems within organizations. Shows how both management and lower - level employees can participate in suggestion programs. Uses dramatizations and interviews to further support the concepts. Consists of two videocassettes.
Business and Economics; Guidance and Counseling; Psychology
Dist - PRODUC **Prod** - PRODUC

The Power of teams 28 MIN
VHS
Color (PRO IND A)
$495.00 purchase, $95.00 rental _ #BBP158
Uses examples from the corporate world - Chrysler, Weyerhaeuser and CSX Railways. Demonstrates the success of teams in today's business world and shows supervisors how teams improve business by making them more efficient, productive, profitable and quality - conscious.
Business and Economics; Psychology
Dist - EXTR **Prod** - BBP

The Power of the past - Florence 90 MIN
U-matic / VHS
Color; Captioned (A G)
$79.95, $99.95 purchase _ #POBM - 000
Travels with Bill Moyers to Florence to explore how the city's rich Renaissance legacy affects the way people think and feel today. Examines the power of the past through informal conversations with people for whom the Renaissance is a living presence - modern artisans, author Umberto Eco, film director Franco Zeffirelli and historian Federico Zeri. Features the works of Renaissance masters. Produced by David Gruben Productions in association with WETA, Washington, DC.
Fine Arts; History - World
Dist - PBS

Power of the playwright 15 MIN
VHS
Panorama of African - American theater series
Color (G C H)
$99.00 purchase _ #DL484
Traces the development of African - American theater from the 1820s to the present.
Fine Arts; History - United States; Sociology
Dist - INSIM

Power of the press 50 MIN
VHS
Look series
Color (A)
PdS99 purchase _ Unavailable in the USA
Reveals the clout fashion journalists wield. Strips away the glitz and glamor of the fashion business to look behind the scenes. Explores the mystique of the designer label and debates the meaning of style. Reveals the mysteries of material and unveils the interdependence between the fashion industry, the media, financiers, and the consumer. Part of a six-part series.
Home Economics
Dist - BBCENE

The Power of the purse 20 MIN
VHS
Color (J H C T A)
$81.00 purchase _ #MB - 540341 - 2
Examines the power of Congress to allocate Federal spending. Questions whether Congress actually has too much power. Features CNN video excerpts from past budget debates. Includes activities package.
Civics and Political Systems; History - United States
Dist - SRA **Prod** - SRA 1989

The power of the resurrection 60 MIN
16mm
Color & B&W (H A C)
Pictures the aged Peter in prison with other Christians, awaiting unknown tortures and possible death, comforting and reassuring a young man by telling him the story of his own faith. Portrays the proud, boastful Peter, turning into a coward and a traitor the night he betrays his beloved Lord. Shows the fearful man becoming Peter, the rock, as the power of the Holy Spirit comes upon him and the true meaning of the Resurrection becomes a living reality in his life.
Guidance and Counseling; Religion and Philosophy
Dist - FAMF **Prod** - FAMF
YALEDV YALEDV

The Power of the situation - constructing social reality - Parts 19 and 20 60 MIN
U-matic / VHS
Discovering psychology series
Color (C)
$45.00, $29.95 purchase
Presents parts 19 and 20 of the 26 - part Discovering Psychology series. Examines the effect of situational forces on belief and behavior. Looks at how social psychologists interpret human behavior within its broader social context. Considers how mental processes color interpretations of reality and how understanding such factors can help individuals become more empathetic and independent members of society. Two thirty - minute programs hosted by Professor Philip Zimbardo of Stanford University.
Psychology; Sociology
Dist - ANNCPB **Prod** - WGBHTV 1989

The Power of the Team 28 MIN
16mm
Color
LC 76-701539
Uses scenes of football plays to express the idea that teamwork can also be found throughout the Navy.
Civics and Political Systems
Dist - USNAC **Prod** - USN 1975

The Power of the Tongue 30 MIN
16mm
Eternal Light Series
B&W (H C A) (HEBREW)
LC 70-700974
Tells the story of Eliezer - Ben - Yehuda, presented in commemoration of the forty - fifth anniversary of his death. Portrays Ben - Yehuda's efforts to revive the Hebrew language. (Kinescope).
Foreign Language; Religion and Philosophy
Dist - NAAJS **Prod** - JTS 1968

The Power of the word 50 MIN
VHS
Arabs - a living history series
Color (H C G)
$250.00 purchase
Visits war - torn Lebanon, the meeting place and refuge and publishing center of contemporary intellectual thought in the Arab world. Discovers the origins of Arab theater and poetry and shows how Arab writers have responded to the challenges of the modern world. Part of a ten - part series on Arab history, culture and society from within and through the lives and opinions of Arabs today.
Geography - World; History - World
Dist - LANDMK **Prod** - LANDMK 1986

The Power of the Word - 6th Century BCE to 2nd Century CE - Pt 2 60 MIN
VHS / 16mm
Heritage - Civilization and the Jews Series
Color (J)
$800.00, $49.00 purchase _ #405 - 9122
Explores more than 3000 years of the Jewish experience and its intimate connections with the civilizations of the world. Uses all available resources to weave an extraordinary tapestry of the Jewish history and people. Hosted by Abba Eban, Israel's former ambassador to the UN and the US. Part 2 shows the consolidation of the Jewish people and their law. Their creataive interaction with the ancient Greeks and Romans permanently altered all three cultures.
History - World; Psychology; Religion and Philosophy; Sociology
Dist - FI **Prod** - WNETTV 1984

The Power of the world 50 MIN
U-matic / VHS
Arabs - a living history series
Color (H C A)
MV=$495.00
Explores Arab theatre, poetry and writing in the chaos of Lebanon.
Geography - World; History - World
Dist - LANDMK **Prod** - LANDMK 1986

The Power of TV news 10 MIN
VHS / U-matic
Inside television news series
Color (J H C)
$125.00, $175.00 purchase, $40.00 rental
Explores the impact of television images. Looks at how news coverage is molded by tragedies and certain kinds of dramatic stories and the ethical issues that confront news as entertainment and a TV rating medium.
Fine Arts; Religion and Philosophy; Sociology
Dist - NDIM **Prod** - LETHRV 1990

The Power of water 59 MIN
VHS
Color; CC (G)
$50.00 purchase - #A51639
Considers problems in the US related to the supply of fresh, clean water. Looks at diminishing supplies in the Midwest and Southwest, pollution cleanup in the Northeast, and conflicting needs in the Pacific Northwest. Presents some solutions to these problems. This television special includes closed - circuit telecast rights for educational institutions.
Civics and Political Systems; Science - Natural; Social Science
Dist - NGS **Prod** - NGS 1994

The Power of Words 15 MIN
U-matic
You Can Write Anything Series
Color (P I)
Teaches writing techniques through Amanda who is told how writers can influence perceptions through their choice of works.
Education; English Language
Dist - TVOTAR **Prod** - TVOTAR 1984

Power Operated Hoists and Cranes 60 MIN
VHS / U-matic
Mechanical Equipment Maintenance, Module 1 Rigging and Lifting 'Series
Color (IND)
Industrial and Technical Education
Dist - LEIKID **Prod** - LEIKID

Power over people - classic and modern political theory
VHS / Cassette
Color (C A)
$149.95, $89.95 purchase _ #AI - B448
Presents eight lectures on the impact of Plato, Aristotle, Machiavelli, Rousseau, Marx, Freud, Hitler, Gandhi. Features Prof Dennis Dalton of Barnard College and Columbia University as lecturer.
Civics and Political Systems; History - World; Religion and Philosophy
Dist - TTCO **Prod** - TTCO

Power pack series
Accelerated learning 30 MIN
Attract love and create a successful relationship 30 MIN
Increase self - discipline 30 MIN
Self - Healing 30 MIN
Dist - VSPU

Power Packed Selling 30 MIN
VHS / U-matic
Color (SPANISH)
Analyzes the concepts of consultative selling. Explores the relationship between customers and salesperson.
Business and Economics
Dist - CREMED **Prod** - CREMED

Power packed workout 60 MIN
VHS
Voigt fitness series
Color (G)
$19.95 purchase _ #GHM10002V
Offers a high - low impact aerobic workout for experienced exercisers. Features Karen Voigt as instructor. Part of a five - part series.
Physical Education and Recreation
Dist - CAMV

The Power pinch - sexual harassment in the workplace 28 MIN
VHS / U-matic / 16mm
(G A PRO)
$575.00 purchase _ #AG - IV01
Provides an inquiry into the extent and variety of sexual harassment, reasons it occurs, and how to deal with it. Hosted by Ken Howard.
Business and Economics; Psychology; Sociology
Dist - CORF **Prod** - IVS 1981 ^ 1982
VIEWTH CORF
VIEWTH

Power Plant Fire Fighting 60 MIN
U-matic
Fire Protection Training Series Tape 2; Tape 2
Color (IND)
LC 80-706024
Describes fire safety procedures for power plants, covering topics such as extinguisher systems, personnel and housekeeping safety, fire strategies, foam selection, and fire suppression.
Health and Safety
Dist - ITCORP **Prod** - ITCORP 1977

Power Plant Thermodynamics 30 TO 40 MIN
VHS
Heat Rate Improvement Series
Color (PRO)
$600.00 - $1500.00 purchase _ #HROO3
Examines thermodynamics as it applies to power plants. Considers the first and second law of thermodynamics, entropy and efficiency, and efficiency of plant processes. Includes one textbook and instructor guide to support two hours of instruction.
Education; Industrial and Technical Education; Psychology
Dist - NUSTC **Prod** - NUSTC

Power Play 60 MIN
U-matic
Vista Series
Color (H C A)
Describes the electrical power grid system shared by Canada and the United States, focusing on the complex business of selling electrical energy and the environmental risks involved.

Business and Economics; Industrial and Technical Education; Science
Dist - TVOTAR **Prod** - TVOTAR 1985

Power point 3.0 231 MIN
VHS
Color (G PRO)
$995.00 purchase, $250.00 rental
Shows how to use Power Point 3.0, a powerful and easy - to - use desktop presentation graphics package. Includes creating text charts and 3 - D graphics, importing and exporting data in many different file formats, and using the outlining features and the Slide Master. Includes two videos.
Computer Science; Psychology
Dist - AMEDIA **Prod** - AMEDIA

Power pool
VHS
Color (G)
$29.95 purchase _ #RV000
Features pool champions Jim Rempe and Loree Jon Jones showing tournament techniques that go beyond the basics shown in the video 'Pool School.'
Physical Education and Recreation
Dist - SIV

Power press guarding - yours to keep and protect 16 MIN
U-matic / VHS / 16mm
Color (IND A)
$375.00 purchase, $50.00 one week rental
Examines protective devices for punch and power presses. Highlights the fixed barrier guard, the gate guard, pull back devices, two handed controls and electronic sensing devices. Stresses accident prevention and the importance of safety measures.
Health and Safety; Industrial and Technical Education
Dist - IFB **Prod** - IAPA 1978

Power presses - Parts 1 & 2 40 MIN
VHS
Color; PAL; NTSC (IND G)
PdS120, PdS140 purchase
Presents two parts devoted to the safety of mechanical power presses, including brake presses. Introduces the basic components of such presses, in particular the flywheel, clutch and brake. Part two discusses using these machines safely and refers briefly to the Power Press Regulations 1965 and 1972, United Kingdom.
Health and Safety; Science - Physical
Dist - CFLVIS

Power series 30 MIN
VHS
Calculus series
Color (C)
$125.00 purchase _ #6051
Explains power series. Part of a 56 - part series on calculus.
Mathematics
Dist - LANDMK **Prod** - LANDMK

Power Series Solutions 33 MIN
VHS / U-matic
Calculus of Differential Equations Series
B&W
Mathematics
Dist - MIOT **Prod** - MIOT

Power sewing 120 MIN
VHS
Color (G)
$34.95 purchase _ #S01854
Provides a wide variety of sewing tips, including fabric and pattern compatibility, needles, lapels, and more. Hosted by Sandra Betzina. Not for beginners.
Fine Arts; Home Economics
Dist - UILL

Power Sewing 19 MIN
U-matic
Occupations Series
B&W (J H)
Describes a graduate's job of running a high speed sewing machine and the course that prepared her for it.
Guidance and Counseling
Dist - TVOTAR **Prod** - TVOTAR 1985

Power Shears
VHS
Landscape Equipment Maintenance Series
Color (G) (SPANISH)
$65.00 purchase _ #6 - 076 - 100P, #6 - 076 - 200P - Spanish
Presents proper procedures on maintenance, safety and operation of gasoline powered shears for landscaping. Part of a five - part series on landscaping.
Agriculture; Health and Safety
Dist - VEP **Prod** - VEP

Power Shovel Productivity 30 MIN
16mm
Color
LC 73-703379
Highlights the job conditions that determine the yardage output of power shovels on highway grading work and demonstrates how production is affected by the speed of the dipper cycle, size of dipper load and frequency and duration of delays.
Industrial and Technical Education
Dist - USNAC **Prod** - USDTFH 1969

Power struggle 58 MIN
VHS
Color (H C G)
$350.00 purchase, $85.00 rental
Discusses energy supply and efficiency and takes the view that nuclear power is disastrous in terms of costs and wastes. Looks at alternative energy sources.
Social Science
Dist - BULFRG **Prod** - BULFRG 1986

Power struggle series
Energy efficiency 22 MIN
Energy supply 34 MIN
Dist - BULFRG

Power Supplies 20 MIN
16mm
B&W
LC 74-705391
Solves for peak inverse voltage in half and full wave rectifier circuits using a capacitor input filter. Defines bleeder resistor and states the purpose of a permanent load. (Kinescope).
Industrial and Technical Education; Science - Physical
Dist - USNAC **Prod** - USAF

Power supplies 60 MIN
VHS
Electronic systems and equipment series
Color (PRO)
$600.00 - $1500.00 purchase _ #ICPSU
Explains the operation of transformers, rectifiers, filters, regulators and voltage multipliers and dividers. Part of a nineteen - part series on electronic systems and equipment, which is part of a 49 - unit set on instrumentation and control. Includes five workbooks and an instructor guide to support four hours of instruction.
Education; Industrial and Technical Education; Psychology
Dist - NUSTC **Prod** - NUSTC

Power Supplies 60 TO 90 MIN
VHS
Fundamentals of Digital Electronics Module Series
Color (PRO)
$600.00 - $1500.00 purchase _ #DEPSU
Identifies and describes the operation of linear power supplies, switching poewr supplies and switching regulators. Part of a twelve - part series on fundamentals of digital electronics. Includes five student guides, five workbooks and an instructor guide.
Computer Science; Industrial and Technical Education; Psychology
Dist - NUSTC **Prod** - NUSTC

Power Supplies and Filters - Troubleshooting 25 MIN
16mm / U-matic / VHS
B&W
Discusses problems in three commonly used power supply circuits, half - wave, full - wave and bridge rectifier. Explains the effects of open and shorted components on output voltage, ripple amplitude and ripple frequency.
Industrial and Technical Education; Science - Physical
Dist - USNAC **Prod** - USAF 1983

Power Supplies - Equipment Selection 47 MIN
BETA / VHS / U-matic
Color
$400 purchase
Shows different types of fixed and variable frequency power sources that include line frequency, frequency multipliers, motor generator sets, solid state, and radio frequency.
Industrial and Technical Education; Science; Science - Physical
Dist - ASM **Prod** - ASM

Power system
U-matic / VHS
Industrial training - power production series - Module 4; Module 4 - Power production
Color (IND)
Discusses the basic network, distribution system and the in - house generator.
Industrial and Technical Education
Dist - LEIKID **Prod** - LEIKID

Power Take Off (PTO) 21 MIN
VHS / U-matic
Agricultural Accidents and Rescue Series
Color
Dramatizes a scene where a farmer slips and is entangled in the power take off. Shows how the difficult disentanglement process is complicated by the tractor's three - point hitch.
Agriculture; Health and Safety
Dist - PSU **Prod** - PSU

Power talking
VHS
Individual success series
Color (G)
$79.95 purchase _ #CF011
Shows how to use powerful words and phrases to evoke a positive response.
Business and Economics; English Language; Social Science
Dist - SIV

Power teaching - how to develop creative teaching techniques using CD - ROM technology to supercharge your classroom
VHS
Color (C PRO G T)
$89.00 purchase _ #504
Teaches the basics of CD - ROM technology and how to find features of CDs that are used for more effective, creative teaching. Views samples of CD - ROM material and its application to the curriculum. Shows how this technology is used as a tool for successful remediation and why CD - ROMs are the ultimate in resource material. Features Rich Ryba as instructor.
Computer Science
Dist - EDREGR **Prod** - EDREGR 1995

The Power to Change 28 MIN
16mm
Color
LC 79-701836
Discusses appropriate technology solutions to significant social and economic problems. Describes solutions used by an agricultural marketing project in Tennessee, a land reclamation project in the Bronx, a bottle recycling center in California, a solar energy project on a farm in Nebraska, a housing project in California, a wind - powered electric car built in Ann Arbor, an alternative energy company in Berkeley and a windmill raising project in Massachusetts.
Sociology
Dist - THIRD **Prod** - SIMONJ 1980

The Power to change 44 MIN
VHS
Les Brown series
Color (G)
$69.95 purchase _ #TVL 1014
Teaches the 'do it now' techniques that enable individuals to take charge of their lives as they reach their true potential at work and in society.
Guidance and Counseling; Psychology
Dist - JWAVID **Prod** - JWAVID

Power to Change - Pt 3 60 MIN
VHS
Local Heroes - Global Change Series
Color (H)
$75.00 purchase, $40.00 rental
Shows that development is not an economic process with social effects. Reveals that first people change their notions of themselves and of their place in the world and then take a more active role in their own destiny. Part 3 of a four - part series on reducing world hunger.
Business and Economics; Civics and Political Systems; Health and Safety; History - World; Social Science; Sociology
Dist - SCETV **Prod** - SCETV 1990

The Power to Choose 20 MIN
VHS / 16mm
Color (H)
$150.00 purchase, $30.00 rental
Explores the issues of power and violence in teenage dating relationships in five short, compelling scenes.
Guidance and Counseling; Health and Safety; Psychology; Sociology
Dist - AITECH **Prod** - NCJW 1988

Power to do Work 15 MIN
VHS / 16mm
Challenge Series
Color (I)
$125.00 purchase, $25.00 rental
Illustrates potential and kinetic energy.
Science; Science - Physical
Dist - AITECH **Prod** - WDCNTV 1987

Power to Save 15 MIN
16mm / U-matic / VHS

Color (P)
Reports on controlling power consumption and costs. Provides examples of waste.
Science - Natural; Social Science
Dist - KLEINW **Prod** - KLEINW

The Power to tax 30 MIN
16mm
Structure and functions of American government - second semester' - Pt VI, Lesson 5
B&W
LC 70-700008
Discusses the conflict between state and federal government which has arisen over the concurrent powers of taxation.
Business and Economics; Civics and Political Systems
Dist - NBCTV **Prod** - NBCTV 1963

Power to the People 10 MIN
16mm
B&W
Shows a machine that goes nowhere. Concludes with one of the workers walking away, carelessly kicking the electric plug that supplies power to the machine.
Science - Physical; Sociology
Dist - UPENN **Prod** - UPENN 1970

Power to the People 25 MIN
U-matic
Not Another Science Show Series
Color (H C)
Shows how electrical power is generated, transmitted and distributed from hydroelectric, coal and nuclear plants. Explains turbines, generators and the relationship of volts, amps and watts.
Industrial and Technical Education; Science
Dist - TVOTAR **Prod** - TVOTAR 1986

Power to the people - Pt III 52 MIN
VHS
Energy alternatives - a global perspective series
Color (H C G)
$295.00 purchase, $75.00 rental
Focuses on the developing world where the energy debate is carried on against a background of grinding poverty, limited resources and rapidly growing population. Demonstrates affordable solutions and advocates the 'end - use approach,' stressing using energy more efficiently rather than increasing the supply. Part two of a three - part series produced by Grampian Television and INcA based on a five - year study, 'Energy for a Sustainable World.'
Geography - World; Science - Natural; Social Science; Sociology
Dist - FLMLIB

Power tool operation and safety 15 MIN
VHS
Firefighter II series
Color (IND)
$100.00 purchase _ #35656
Presents one part of a 14 - part series that is the teaching companion for IFSTA's Essentials of Fire Fighting manual. Demonstrates how to operate common hand and power tools used in fire service operations. Presents the proper service and maintenance of portable power plants and lighting equipment. Based on Chapter 19.
Health and Safety; Science - Physical; Social Science
Dist - OKSU **Prod** - ACCTRA

Power tool principles - safety and technique series

Drill Press, Bench Sander and Others , Vol II	
Portable power tools - Volume III	23 MIN
Portable power tools - Volume IV	23 MIN
Stationary Power Saws, Vol I	

Dist - VEP

Power Tools 13 MIN
U-matic / VHS / 16mm
Safety in the Shop Series
Color (H C A)
$325, $235 purchase _ #3152
Shows how to use woodworking and metalworking machines safely.
Industrial and Technical Education
Dist - CORF

Power Tools 60 MIN
VHS
Handtools and Hardware Series
Color (PRO)
$600.00, $1500.00 purchase _ #GMPOT
Presents power tools typically found in a plant. Shows how to select the most appropriate tool for a given job and operate it safely. Includes pneumatic and electric tools, portable power grinders, power saws and snips, impact wrenches and others. Part of a seven - part series on handtools and hardware, part of a larger set on general and mechanical maintenance. Includes 10 textbooks and an instructor guide which provide four hours of instruction.
Education; Health and Safety; Industrial and Technical Education; Psychology
Dist - NUSTC **Prod** - NUSTC

Power Tools and Forcible Entry 30 MIN
VHS
Firefighter II - III Video Series
Color (G PRO)
$145.00 purchase _ #35253
Demonstrates use of power tools for entering through doors, windows, roofs, ceilings, floors and other barriers. Emphasizes proper care and use of tools and stresses the importance of safety and discretion while using these tools at the fireground.
Agriculture; Health and Safety; Psychology; Social Science
Dist - OKSU **Prod** - OKSU

Power Train 13 MIN
16mm / U-matic / VHS
Color (H C A J) (SPANISH)
LC 70-70008
A fully animated explanation of the working of each of the components of the autombile transmission system - - clutch, gearbox, drive shaft and differential.
Foreign Language; Industrial and Technical Education
Dist - ALTSUL **Prod** - FILMSW 1968

Power transformers 10 MIN
VHS / U-matic
Electrical safety series
Color (IND)
Presents basics of power transformer design and application, and details the safe work practices that maintenance and operation personnel should follow when working with this equipment.
Health and Safety; Industrial and Technical Education
Dist - GPCV **Prod** - GPCV

Power Transmission Physics 20 MIN
VHS
Power Transmission Series I - PT Products Series
Color (A)
$225.00 purchase, $50.00 rental _ #57964
Gives an overview of the principles operative in the transmission of power through mechanical devices. Covers direct, fixed speed and variable speed drives. Defines vocabulary (ratio, horse power, work, efficiency, rotary motion, torque) and explains formulas which are applicable to common drive configurations.
Industrial and Technical Education; Science - Physical
Dist - UILL **Prod** - MAJEC 1986

Power transmission products I series

DC variable speed drives	20 MIN

Dist - UILL

Power Transmission Series I - PT Products Series

AC variable speed drives	20 MIN
Ball bearings	15 MIN
Basic electricity	18 MIN
Clutches and Brakes	MIN
Conveyor components	14 MIN
Electric Motors	23 MIN
Gear Reducers	21 MIN
Power Transmission Physics	20 MIN
Power Transmission Service Factors	14 MIN
Roller Bearings	10 MIN
Roller Chain and Sprockets	18 MIN
Shaft Couplings	16 MIN
Synchronous Belt Drives	10 MIN
V - Belts and Sheaves	22 MIN
Variable Speed Drives	19 MIN

Dist - UILL

Power Transmission Series II - Selection, Application and Maintenance Series

AC motor options and variations	15 MIN
Anti friction bearing lubrication	21 MIN
Ball bearing maintenance and failure analysis	19 MIN
Maintenance of Precision Roller Chain Drives	17 MIN
Roller Chain Drive Selection	18 MIN
Selection of Mounted Bearings	MIN
Shaft Coupling Alignment	18 MIN
Shaft Coupling Selection	16 MIN
V - Belt Drive Installation and Maintenance	19 MIN
V - Belt Drive Selection	16 MIN

Dist - UILL

Power transmission series II - selection, application and maintenance series

Spherical bearing installation and maintenance	13 MIN

Dist - UILL

Power Transmission Series

Gears - 1	60 MIN
Gears - 2	60 MIN

Dist - NUSTC

Power Transmission Service Factors 14 MIN
VHS
Power Transmission Series I - PT Products Series
Color (A)
$225.00 purchase, $50.00 rental _ #57966
Explains the purposes of service factors and design horsepower as being to select the most appropriate equipment for the job, and to produce maximum equipment life. Lists elements that enter into service factoring, and shows how to use service factor tables in selecting equipment and replacement components.
Industrial and Technical Education
Dist - UILL **Prod** - MAJEC 1986

The Power Trilogy 13 MIN
VHS / 16mm
Color (PRO)
$210.00 purchase, $35.00 preview
Offers ways to enhance the potential of employees, to inspire teamwork, to develop organizational skills, and to realize ideas. Includes three videotapes for complete three hour program.
Education; Psychology
Dist - UTM **Prod** - UTM

Power Under Control 22 MIN
U-matic / VHS / 16mm
Three for the Road Series
Color (H C A)
LC 83-700091
Shows the director of a driving school for racers discussing defensive driving techniques and giving other safe driving tips. Presents demonstrations that illustrate difficult driving conditions and the actual scene of a near head - on collision between an automobile and a large truck.
Health and Safety
Dist - IFB **Prod** - OMTC 1982

Power up - energy in our environment 22 MIN
VHS
Color (P I J)
$89.00 purchase _ #RB862
Focuses on the relationship between energy and environment. Looks at the greenhouse effect, air pollution, acid rain and energy conservation. Examines how energy is used, its sources, what fossil fuels are and their effects upon the environment.
Science - Natural; Social Science
Dist - REVID **Prod** - REVID 1990

Power Volleyball - Individual Defensive Skills 11 MIN
U-matic / VHS / 16mm
Women's Power Volleyball Series
Color (J)
Offers a look at the techniques top women volleyball players use when executing a block, dig, dive, roll or sprawl.
Physical Education and Recreation
Dist - ATHI **Prod** - ATHI

Power Volleyball - Individual Offensive Skills 11 MIN
16mm / U-matic / VHS
Women's Power Volleyball Series
Color (J)
Examines the individual skills of volleyball offense and shows how to improve techniques on the serve, the serve reception, the set and the attack.
Physical Education and Recreation
Dist - ATHI **Prod** - ATHI

Power vs the people 36 MIN
16mm / U-matic / VHS
Color (H C A)
LC 77-700498
Presents a record of the hearings conducted by the Equal Employment Opportunity Commission in Houston Texas. Records the testimonies of workers and officials of several corporations whose hiring and promotion practices violate Title VII of the Civil Rights Act, which prohibits discrimination against individuals based on race, ethnic origin, sex or religion.
Business and Economics; Civics and Political Systems; Guidance and Counseling; Sociology
Dist - GREAVW **Prod** - USEEOC 1975

Power Without End 16 MIN
U-matic / VHS / 16mm
Color (I J H)
LC 77-703420
Explores energy sources which cannot be exhausted, such as the sun, wind, geothermal energy and the tides. Shows current efforts to harness these energy sources.
Science - Physical; Social Science
Dist - GA **Prod** - XEROXF 1977

Power Without End
VHS / U-matic
(J H C)
$109.00 purchase _ #05210 94
Examines the inexhaustible sources of energy that are provided by the earth, including solar, wind, water, tides, and the earth's internal heat. States the need for enlightened thinking and methods of conservation.

Science - Natural; Social Science
Dist - ASPRSS **Prod** - WHARTI

Power writing - the key to success
VHS
Success series
Color (G)
$79.95 purchase _ #CO001
Shows how to overcome writer's block and to achieve desired results through writing skills.
Business and Economics; English Language; Social Science
Dist - SIV

Powerboat navigation 68 MIN
VHS
Color (G)
$49.80 purchase _ #0753
Covers all aspects of navigating recreational boats. Includes the use of electronic aids such as Loran - C, radar and the radio direction finder. Produced in association with the US Coast Guard. Features John Rousmaniere.
Health and Safety; Physical Education and Recreation
Dist - CREPRI SEVVID CTI **Prod** - CREPRI SEVVID 1988

Powerboat Navigation with John Rousmaniere 68 MIN
VHS
Color (A)
LC 90712273
Provides instruction in powerboat navigation. Features author and sailor John Rousmaniere.
Health and Safety; Physical Education and Recreation
Dist - CTI

Powered by Ford 30 MIN
VHS
Color; Stereo (G)
$19.98 purchase _ #TT8090
Relives the history of Henry Ford and his influence on motor racing.
Industrial and Technical Education; Literature and Drama; Physical Education and Recreation
Dist - TWINTO **Prod** - TWINTO 1990

Powered equipment in the warehouse 12 MIN
16mm / VHS
Safety on the job series
Color (C A PRO)
$245.00, $295.00 purchase, $75.00 rental _ #8177
Emphasizes important safety procedures for the correct operation and maintenance of warehouse equipment.
Health and Safety; Psychology
Dist - AIMS **Prod** - AIMS 1990

Powered equipment in the warehouse 12 MIN
VHS
Safety on the job series
Color (G IND)
$99.95 purchase _ #6 - 203 - 020A
Outlines safety procedures for correct operation and maintenance of warehouse equipment. Shows techniques for handling equipment on loading docks, including forklifts, hoists and conveyers. Stresses wearing protective gear and precautions when handling chemicals. Part of a series on job safety.
Health and Safety
Dist - VEP **Prod** - VEP 1993

Powerful medicine 48 MIN
VHS
Color (S)
$79.00 purchase _ #386 - 9053
Looks at herbal medicine and its future role in finding cures for cancer, AIDS, and other diseases. Considers that after years of dismissing medications based on natural compounds from plants, scientists are once again exploring the curative power of plants.
Business and Economics; Health and Safety; Psychology; Science; Science - Natural; Sociology
Dist - FI **Prod** - CANBC 1988

Powerful, Mountains, Danger 10 MIN
U-matic
Readalong Three Series
Color (P)
Provides reading instruction for third grade students. Uses animation, humor, music, repetition and audience participation. Comes with teacher's guide and kit.
Education; English Language; Literature and Drama
Dist - TVOTAR **Prod** - TVOTAR 1977

A Powerful thang 51 MIN
16mm / VHS
Color (G)
$350.00 purchase, $130.00 rental
Pits the desire for sexual intimacy against the need for love. Portrays the relationship of African - identified Yasmine Allen and music teacher Craig Watkins. Reveals that Allen wishes to end her self - imposed celibacy after her son's birth, but Watkins isn't ready. Explores the theme 'Sex is a powerful thang' through animation and Afro - Haitian dance.
Fine Arts; Guidance and Counseling; Psychology
Dist - WMEN **Prod** - ZDAVIS 1991

Powerful ways to persuade people 42 MIN
VHS
Color (PRO A)
$79.95 purchase
Shows how to be persuasive and sell ideas. Gives tips and techniques on the four keys to powerful persuasion, the perfect presentation; five types of clinching arguments; six ways to get someone to do something for you; when to use humor to persuade; and recognizing persuasive personalities. Offers dozens of ideas on presenting effectively, writing persuasive proposals, selling ideas, anticipating audience constraints, and more.
Business and Economics; Social Science
Dist - SIV CAMV

Powerhead 5 MIN
16mm
B&W
LC FIE52-1085
Shows adjustment of the speeder spring and construction and operation of the powerhead. Demonstrates the speed - setting control of the governor.
Industrial and Technical Education
Dist - USNAC **Prod** - USN 1943

The Powerhouse 60 MIN
VHS
Man on the rim - the peopling of the Pacific series
Color (H C)
$295.00 purchase
Examines the long history of China to observe 2,000 years of imaginative innovations and inventions - silk production, steel making, the box bellows, printing and gunpowder. Part of an 11 - part series on the people of the Pacific rim.
History - World; Sociology
Dist - LANDMK **Prod** - LANDMK 1989

Powerhouse series

Big devil	30 MIN
Celebration	30 MIN
Cheers	30 MIN
Fit to be tied	30 MIN
Help wanted	30 MIN
Life or Breath	30 MIN
Master of the Art	30 MIN
Name of the Game	30 MIN
One of the Gang	30 MIN
The Short Life of Lolo Knopke	30 MIN
Something for Nothing	30 MIN
Something Ventured	30 MIN
What have You Got to Lose	30 MIN
With a Little Help from My Friends, Pt 1	30 MIN
With a Little Help from My Friends, Pt 2	30 MIN
You make Me Sick	30 MIN

Dist - GA

Powering Apollo 5 MIN
U-matic
Apollo digest series
Color
LC 79-706986
Explains the major parts of the Saturn 5 rocket. Issued in 1969 as a motion picture.
Industrial and Technical Education; Science - Physical
Dist - USNAC **Prod** - NASA 1979

Powerless politics 28 MIN
VHS
Color (G)
$55.00 purchase
Takes a look at the structure of tribal governments and how they fit into the scheme of state and federal governmental systems. Examines the fact that Native American tribes have no political advocate because of the structure of the Dept of Interior and the Bureau of Indian Affairs, where Indians compete with powerful interest groups. Notes current political struggles over land and water.
Civics and Political Systems; Social Science
Dist - UPSTRE **Prod** - UPSTRE

Powerless politics 30 MIN
U-matic
Color
$55.00 purchase
Takes a look at the structure of tribal governments and how they fit into the scheme of state and federal governmental systems. Examines the fact that Native American tribes have not political advocate because of the structure of the Department of Interior and the Bureau of Indian Affairs where Indians compete with powerful interest groups. Notes current political struggles over land and water. Part of KNBC series on the life of modern American Indians.
Social Science
Dist - ADL UPSTRE **Prod** - UPSTRE

Powerman 5 MIN
16mm
Color (G)
$5.00 rental
Pays homage to the superhero with animation. Features the song 'Powerman,' performed by Rogue Streib's East Bay Symphony, with the filmmaker singing the lead.
Fine Arts
Dist - CANCIN **Prod** - LIPTNL 1966

Powers of Ten 9 MIN
U-matic / VHS / 16mm
Color (J) (SPANISH SWEDISH GERMAN FINNISH FRENCH)
Presents an adventure in magnitudes, starting at a picnic by the lakeside in Chicago, and progressing to the edges of the universe and into the micro - world of cells, molecules, and atoms. Describes the universe, using the best available evidence and scientific speculation.
Foreign Language; Industrial and Technical Education; Religion and Philosophy; Science - Natural; Science - Physical
Dist - PFP **Prod** - EAMES

Powers of ten - 1978 9 MIN
16mm / U-matic / VHS
Color (J)
LC 78-700367
A revised edition of the 1968 motion picture Powers Of Ten. Shows a linear view of the universe, increasing time and distance in increments of ten. Travels into the microworld of cells, DNA molecules and the nucleus of an atom.
Science - Natural; Science - Physical
Dist - PFP **Prod** - EAMES 1978

Powers of Ten - a Rough Sketch 8 MIN
U-matic / VHS / 16mm
Color (I)
LC 75-706836
Presents a linear view of our universe from the human scale to the sea of galaxies, then directly down to the nucleus of a carbon atom. Uses an image, a narration and a dashboard, to give a clue to the relative size of things and what it means to add another zero to any number.
Mathematics
Dist - PFP **Prod** - EAMES 1968

Powers of Ten - Decimal Conversion and Multiplication 20 MIN
16mm
B&W
LC 74-705393
Develops the need for powers of ten, shows the procedures for converting large and small numbers to powers of ten and explains the rules for multiplying powers of ten. (Kinescope).
Mathematics
Dist - USNAC **Prod** - USAF 1972

Powers of Ten - Division and Prefixes 25 MIN
16mm
B&W
LC 74-705394
States rules of division and introduces prefixes. Shows how to convert from prefix to power of ten and from power of ten to standard prefix. (Kinescope).
Mathematics
Dist - USNAC **Prod** - USAF 1972

The Powers of the Presidency - Armed Intervention 23 MIN
U-matic / VHS / 16mm
Color (J H)
LC 73-703312
Examines when, if ever, the interests of the United States are so vitally affected by events in another country that military intervention is required. Shows how the President must choose a course of action in an international crisis quickly and on the basis of swiftly changing and often conflicting information.
Civics and Political Systems
Dist - BARR **Prod** - WILETS 1973

The Powers of the Presidency - Economic Controls 23 MIN
U-matic / VHS / 16mm
Color (J)
LC 75-702805
Examines the extent of the President's constitutional authority to order wage and price controls without the sanction of Congress. Raises questions concerning potential effects of such controls on America's complex economy.
Business and Economics; Civics and Political Systems
Dist - BARR **Prod** - WILETS 1975

Powers of trig functions - Pt 1
U-matic
Calculus series
Color
Mathematics
Dist - MDCPB **Prod** - MDDE

Powers of trig functions - Pt 2
U-matic
Calculus series
Color
Mathematics
Dist - MDCPB **Prod** - MDDE

The Powers that be 52 MIN
U-matic / VHS / 16mm
Shock of the New Series
Color (C A)
LC 80-700985
Examines Western art during the period after World War I, including Dada And German Expressionism. Points out that some artists sought an active political role.
Fine Arts
Dist - TIMLIF **Prod** - BBCTV 1980

The Pproject 6 MIN
VHS / U-matic / 16mm
What should I do series
Color (P)
$195.00, $120.00 purchase _ #JC - 67812; LC 78-714361
Uses animation to portray Susie, leader of a project, who enlists the help of Billy and Doug. Teaches positive attitudes about the need for cooperation. Part of a series which dramatizes real life situations, gives possible options, alternatives and consequences, then leaves the final solution to students - for a learning situation which lasts.
Psychology; Sociology
Dist - CORF **Prod** - DISNEY 1970

PR 24 MIN
U-matic / VHS
Young people's specials series
Color
Depicts the life of a Puerto Rican boy in New York. Explores the reasons for his immigration from an island to crowded city streets.
Fine Arts; Sociology
Dist - MULTPP **Prod** - MULTPP

Prabhu Guptara 45 MIN
VHS
Color (H C G)
$79.00 purchase
Features the writer discussing with Naseem Khan the place in British literature held by Black writers. Talks about his book entitled Black British Literature, a history and bibliography of Black writing in Britain.
Literature and Drama
Dist - ROLAND **Prod** - INCART

Practical Application of Modern Urodynamic Equipment in the Urologist's Office 25 MIN
16mm
Color (PRO)
LC 78-701377
Shows the practical application, in an office setting, of cystometric equipment and tests to determine problems of patients who have underlying urological dysfunction problems.
Health and Safety; Science
Dist - EATONL **Prod** - EATONL 1978

Practical Applications 11 MIN
U-matic / VHS
Introductory Concepts in Physics - Magnetism and Electricity Series
Color (C)
$229.00, $129.00 purchase _ #AD - 1181
Conducts experiments within a one - cubic - meter magnetic field produced by a large and very powerful magnet using wheels on a railroad track, an electric swing and the manufacture of a bipolar motor to explain the operative force when an electric current flows through a magnetic field.
Science - Physical
Dist - FOTH **Prod** - FOTH

Practical applications of ESP 30 MIN
BETA / VHS
Developing intuition series
Color (G)
$29.95 purchase _ #S260
Describes the methods used for 'remote viewing' and the potential practical applications of such techniques. Features psychologist Dr Keith Harary, psychic practitioner in ESP - extrasensory perception, researcher and coauthor of 'The Mind Race.' Part of a four - part series on developing intuition.
Psychology; Religion and Philosophy
Dist - THINKA **Prod** - THINKA

Practical Applications of Sensitometry 29 MIN
U-matic / VHS
Automatic Film Processor Quality Control Series
Color (C A)
Health and Safety; Industrial and Technical Education; Science
Dist - TEF **Prod** - BCAMRT

Practical applications - Pt 1 19 MIN
VHS / U-matic / BETA
Nursing diagnosis and care planning series
Color (C PRO)
$150.00 purchase _ #144.4
Presents a video transfer from slide program which presents the first part of two programs of exercises in which the learner is given assessment data by six nurses in different patient care areas - pediatrics, home care, medical, critical care, psychiatry and surgical nursing. Requires learners to record pertinent data they will use later to formulate nursing diagnoses for each patient as each patient situation unfolds. Learners test their diagnostic skills by comparing their diagnoses with those selected by the nurse caring for the patient. Part of a series on nursing diagnosis and care planning.
Health and Safety
Dist - CONMED **Prod** - CONMED

Practical applications - Pt 2 19 MIN
BETA / VHS / U-matic
Nursing diagnosis and care planning series
Color (C PRO)
$150.00 purchase _ #144.5
Presents a video transfer from slide program which presents the second part of two programs of exercises in which the learner is given assessment data by six nurses in different patient care areas - pediatrics, home care, medical, critical care, psychiatry and surgical nursing. Requires learners to record pertinent data they will use later to formulate nursing diagnoses for each patient as each patient situation unfolds. Learners test their diagnostic skills by comparing their diagnoses with those selected by the nurse caring for the patient. Part of a series on nursing diagnosis and care planning.
Health and Safety
Dist - CONMED **Prod** - CONMED

A Practical Approach to a High Fiber Diet 10 MIN
VHS / U-matic
Color (J H C G T A)
How the role of dietary fiber in the human diet became the subject of increasing public attention, due in large part to the positive correlation between the consumption of fiber and the absence of disease. Defines dietary fiber and provides many specific examples of common foods that contain it. The relationship between a variety of diseases and fiber intake, how to add fiber to diets, and the difference between dietary fiber and crude fiber also are discussed.
Health and Safety; Home Economics
Dist - PSU **Prod** - PSU 1984

A Practical Approach to Acid - Base Balance 22 MIN
U-matic / VHS
Color (PRO)
Discusses the delicate balance of acid - base chemistry in the blood. Outlines a very practical and clinically useful technique of managing patients with acid - base disorders.
Health and Safety; Science
Dist - UMICHM **Prod** - UMICHM 1973

Practical Approach to Understanding 20 MIN
VHS / U-matic
Personality Styles Series
Color
Presents an understanding of the forces that shape behavior. Describes why people respond as they do when a situation becomes stressful or antagonistic and why these same people can operate differently when a situation becomes favorable. Describes behavioral response in a four - dimensional model including dominance, inducement, steadiness and compliance.
Psychology; Sociology
Dist - AMA **Prod** - AMA

A Practical approach to wrongful termination 120 MIN
VHS
Color (PRO)
$65.00, $119.00 purchase, $49.00 rental _ #MI-54300, #MI-64300
Demonstrates conducting initial interviews, beginning discovery, and starting negotiations before deciding to sue for wrongful termination. Talks about witness credibility, the client interview, personnel policies, causes of action, damages, depositions, dispute resolution, and effective strategies. Includes program material.
Civics and Political Systems; Guidance and Counseling
Dist - CCEB

Practical approaches to laboratory waste management 180 MIN
VHS
Color (C PRO)
$498.00 purchase _ #V - 5700 - 2456X
Offers a low - cost and effective approach to waste management. Looks at common waste management issues for laboratory managers and administrators, as well as for bench chemists. James M Harless and Russell W Phifer coordinate the seminar; John E Cole, Jr, Alan Corson, Matthew Finucane and Sharon Harless serve as panelists. Includes two videos and a manual.
Industrial and Technical Education; Science; Sociology
Dist - AMCHEM **Prod** - AMCHEM 1992

Practical care for hearing aids 10 MIN
VHS / U-matic
Color (C PRO)
$395.00 purchase, $80.00 rental _ #C921 - VI - 037
Shows how a hearing aid works, the placement of and use of several common types of hearing aids and basic maintenance requirements. Presented by Dr Kathleen Campbell and Elaine Kadakia.
Health and Safety; Science - Natural
Dist - HSCIC

Practical Chinese readers - Book 1
VHS / Cassette
Practical Chinese readers series
Color (C) (CHINESE)
$49.95 purchase _ #0 - 88727 - 086 - 7
Supports Book 1 of the Practical Chinese Reader which is available separately. Identifies fundamental grammatical patterns.
Foreign Language
Dist - CHTSUI **Prod** - CHTSUI

Practical Chinese readers - Book 2
VHS / Cassette
Practical Chinese readers series
Color (C) (CHINESE)
$49.95 purchase _ #0 - 88727 - 087 - 5
Supports Book 2 of the Practical Chinese Reader which is available separately. Reviews fundamental grammatical patterns.
Foreign Language
Dist - CHTSUI **Prod** - CHTSUI 1992

Practical Chinese readers series
Practical Chinese readers - Book 1
Practical Chinese readers - Book 2
Dist - CHTSUI

Practical Complete Denture Reline Technique 11 MIN
U-matic / VHS
Color (PRO)
Demonstrates a laboratory technique for relining complete dentures that can be done in a dental office using autopolymerizing acrylic and a reline jig.
Health and Safety; Science
Dist - USNAC **Prod** - VADTC

Practical Computing Systems - Operating Systems and Procedures
16mm
Color
Looks at the operating system and the sort of computing procedures used in a large company.
Mathematics
Dist - OPENU **Prod** - OPENU

Practical Considerations 8 MIN
VHS / 16mm
Electrical Theory Series
Color (S)
$50.00 purchase _ #241301
Illustrates 22 concepts fundamental to the training of second year electrical apprentices using graphic animation. Provides an overview of electrical circuits and the concepts of resistance, inductance and capacitance in 'Practical Considerations.'.
Education; Industrial and Technical Education; Psychology
Dist - ACCESS **Prod** - ACCESS 1983

Practical Drafting Series
Hand Tools
Dist - AAVIM

Practical examination in neuroanatomy - Pt I 56 MIN
VHS / U-matic
Neuroanatomy series
Color (C A)
Health and Safety; Science - Natural
Dist - TEF **Prod** - UWO

Practical examination in neuroanatomy - Pt II 34 MIN
U-matic / VHS
Neuroanatomy series

Color (C A)
Health and Safety; Science - Natural
Dist - TEF **Prod** - UWO

Practical film making 19 MIN
U-matic / VHS / 16mm
Color (J C)
$49.00 purchase - #3154; LC 73-700471
Traces the essential elements of filmmaking by presenting the steps to the production of a film. Emphasizes ways to cut costs. Presents the importance of well coordinated production and preproduction preparation.
Fine Arts; Guidance and Counseling
Dist - EBEC **Prod** - JULF 1972

Practical guide to modeling series
Presents a three - part series on careers in modeling. Includes the titles How to Become a Model; On the Set - Preparing for Pictures; Designing Your Portfolio.
Designing your portfolio 30 MIN
How to Become a Model 30 MIN
Preparing for pictures 30 MIN
Dist - CAMV **Prod** - CAMV 1972

Practical Information for Job Hunters 20 MIN
VHS / U-matic
Color
Gives practical information to job hunters via phone calls from viewers to a panel of three experts.
Guidance and Counseling
Dist - WCCOTV **Prod** - WCCOTV 1982

Practical M B O Series
Analyzing problems and alternatives 10 MIN
Are you ready for it 15 MIN
Categories of objectives 8 MIN
Identifying Key Result Areas 6 MIN
New or Innovative Areas 10 MIN
Obtaining Agreement on Objectives 10 MIN
Personal Development Objectives - Appraisal by Results 12 MIN
Regular - Routine Responsibilities 7 MIN
Setting Overall Objectives 7 MIN
Starting the System 13 MIN
The Step - by - Step Process 6 MIN
What is M B O 13 MIN
Dist - DELTAK

Practical math 22 MIN
VHS
Basic skills for food service workers series
Color (H G)
$129.00 purchase _ #31388 - 027
Discusses importance of accuracy. Explains basic measurement terms and abbreviations, shows conversion systems and how to compute cost per unit. Part of a two - part series.
Industrial and Technical Education; Mathematics
Dist - GA

Practical Parenting Series
Adolescence
The Art of Communication
Child management
School Days
Single Parenting
So You're Going to be a Parent
Dist - CAREER

Practical parenting series
Presents a group of 12 programs aimed at different aspects of parenting. Features Dick Van Patten and Dr Bill Wagonseller. Comes with 12 facilitator's guides.
Adolescence 27 MIN
Blended families - yours, mine, and ours 29 MIN
Single parenting - one - parent families 27 MIN
So you want to be a parent 29 MIN
Teenage pregnancy 29 MIN
Violence prevention - what every parent should know 29 MIN
Violence prevention - what middle school teachers and students should know 29 MIN
Violence prevention package 58 MIN
Dist - UNL

A Practical - Performance Examination for Emergency Medical Technicians (Basic Level) 92 MIN
U-matic
Color
LC 78-706079
Offers instructions for the organization and execution of the standardized practical - performance examination for basic level emergency medical technicians.
Health and Safety
Dist - USNAC **Prod** - USHRA 1977

Practical - performance examination for emergency medical technicians - Pt 1 46 MIN
U-matic
Color
LC 78-706079
Offers instructions for the organization and execution of the standardized practical - performance examination for basic level emergency medical technicians.
Health and Safety
Dist - USNAC **Prod** - USHRA 1977

Practical Planning 15 MIN
VHS / U-matic
Making it Work Series
Color (H A)
Shows Mary learning to plan ahead to prevent babysitting emergencies while Connie helps Lucy understand why others resent her behavior on the job and helps her plan how to do better.
Guidance and Counseling
Dist - AITECH **Prod** - ERF 1983

Practical Prevention for a Healthy You 55 MIN
U-matic
Color
Discusses fact and fiction about commerical products that are said to produce cancer and offers tips on how to keep healthy.
Health and Safety
Dist - UTEXSC **Prod** - UTEXSC

The Practical Princess 20 MIN
16mm
Color (K P I)
LC 73-700904
Presents the story 'The Practical Princess' by Jay Williams. Stimulates reading and classroom discussion of plot, character development, emotions and other elements of writing. Filmed in and around a castle in Llewellyn Park, New Jersey.
Literature and Drama
Dist - SF **Prod** - SF 1973

The Practical Princess 10 MIN
U-matic / VHS / 16mm
Color (P I)
LC 80-701656
Uses animation to tell the story of a princess blessed with beauty, brains and common sense. Shows how she outsmarts a dragon, her royal father and an unacceptable suitor. Based on the children's book The Practical Princess by Jay Williams.
Literature and Drama
Dist - CF **Prod** - BOSUST 1980

Practical Procedures of Measurement 48 MIN
16mm
Radioisotope Series no 3
B&W
LC FIE53-26
Discusses purposes of measurement, operational principles of the electroscope, ionization chamber, proportional counter and the Geiger - Muller counter.
Science; Science - Physical
Dist - USNAC **Prod** - USA 1953

Practical Rheumatology
VHS / U-matic
Color
Discusses a comprehensive approach to all aspects of the patient with a rheumatic disease. Discusses the soft tissue rheumatic syndromes.
Health and Safety
Dist - AMEDA **Prod** - AMEDA

Practical self defense 90 MIN
VHS
Color (G)
$39.95 purchase _ #MA - 07
Shows how to use the force of an aggressor in counterattack, control an aggressor's attention and balance and neutralize the force of aggression.
Physical Education and Recreation; Religion and Philosophy
Dist - ARVID **Prod** - ARVID

Practical Shop Metallurgy 60 MIN
VHS
Welding Series
Color (PRO)
$600.00, $1500.00 purchase _ #GMPSM
Presents concepts of shop metallurgy. Identifies metals and their properties and where and how these metals are used in the plant. Demonstrates various heat - treating processes and how to identify the causes of metal failures. Part of a three - part series on welding, which is part of a set on general and mechanical maintenance. Includes 10 textbooks and an instructor guide which provide four hours of instruction.
Education; Health and Safety; Industrial and Technical Education; Psychology; Science - Physical
Dist - NUSTC **Prod** - NUSTC

Practical Spanish for health - care providers series
Overview module - Spanish language basics
Physical assessment and patient history
Survival Spanish for general patient care
Survival Spanish for hospital admissions staff
Survival Spanish for labor and delivery personnel
Dist - UARIZ

Practical strategies for structuring charitable gifts 50 MIN
VHS
Color (A PRO C)
$95.00 purchase _ #Y502
Examines practical ways to structure gifts of tangible personal property, life insurance and closely held stock. Looks at the provisions of Section 170 of the Internal Revenue Code.
Business and Economics; Civics and Political Systems; Sociology
Dist - ALIABA **Prod** - CLETV 1992

Practical Stress Management with Dr Barry Alberstein Series
Assertiveness for stress management 32 MIN
An Introduction to Stress Management 37 MIN
Relaxation as a Form of Stress Management 32 MIN
Straight Thinking for Stress Management 32 MIN
Time Management for Managing Stress 27 MIN
Dist - DELTAK

Practical Suggestions and Personal Stories 45 MIN
U-matic / VHS
Dizziness and Related Balance Disorders Series
Color
Health and Safety
Dist - GSHDME **Prod** - GSHDME

Practical tax shelters - Pt I 25 MIN
U-matic / VHS
Your money matters series
Color
Answers commonly asked questions about individual retirement and Keogh accounts. Features banker and tax attorney.
Business and Economics; Social Science; Sociology
Dist - FILMID **Prod** - FILMID

Practical tax shelters - Pt II 25 MIN
U-matic / VHS
Your money matters series
Color
Discusses oil and gas, equipment leasing and real estate partnerships as tax shelters for those in the 50 per cent tax bracket.
Business and Economics; Social Science
Dist - FILMID **Prod** - FILMID

Practical Tips on Organizing 15 MIN
VHS / U-matic
Put it in Writing Series
Color
English Language
Dist - DELTAK **Prod** - DELTAK

Practical Use of Logarithms 30 MIN
16mm
Trigonometry Series
B&W (H)
Describes the rule for the characteristic of a logarithm of a number less than one. Shows the technique of adding and subtracting 10 to obtain a positive characteristic. Presents various applications of the use of logarithms.
Mathematics
Dist - MLA **Prod** - CALVIN 1959

Practical Uses of Multi - Media Techniques
U-matic / VHS
Independent Study in Human Sexuality Series
Color (PRO)
Health and Safety; Psychology
Dist - MMRC **Prod** - MMRC

A Practical View of Syphilis 30 MIN
16mm
Color; B&W (PRO)
LC FIE65-90
Presents significant aspects of modern syphilis diagnosis and management.
Health and Safety
Dist - USNAC **Prod** - USPHS 1963

Practical Woodworking
U-matic / VHS
Color (J H)
Presents the basics of woodworking for use in and out of the profession.
Guidance and Counseling; Industrial and Technical Education
Dist - CAREER **Prod** - CAREER 1973

Practical Woodworking Series
Construction - Joinery
Design
Intro to Woodworking
Machine Tools
Dist - AAVIM

Practice 30 MIN
VHS
Tennis with Van der Meer series
Color (C A)
$95.00 purchase, $55.00 rental
Features tennis player and instructor Dennis Van der Meer in a presentation on practice in tennis skills. Uses freeze - frame photography and repetition to stress skill development. Serves as the final part of a 10 - part telecourse.
Physical Education and Recreation; Psychology
Dist - SCETV **Prod** - SCETV 1989

Practice and coaching techniques 25 MIN
VHS
Color (H C A)
$39.95 purchase _ #GOF500V
Features former wrestling star Greg Shoemaker with an instructional video on wrestling coaching techniques. Explains and demonstrates various drills for developing wrestling skills.
Physical Education and Recreation
Dist - CAMV

Practice beef carcass judging 40 MIN
VHS
Color (H C A PRO)
$69.95 purchase _ #CV220
Includes five beef carcass practice classes, five questions on each class, official placings, cuts, answers and oral reasons by Judge G W Davis, Texas Tech U.
Agriculture
Dist - AAVIM **Prod** - AAVIM 1990

Practice beef wholesale cuts judging - I 32 MIN
VHS
Color (H C A PRO)
$69.95 purchase _ #CV245
Includes five beef wholesale cuts classes - beef rounds, beef loins, oven prepared ribs, beef shortloins, beef ribs, five questions on each class, official placings, cuts, answers and oral reasons by Judge GW Davis, Texas Tech U.
Agriculture
Dist - AAVIM **Prod** - AAVIM 1990

Practice beef wholesale cuts judging - II 32 MIN
VHS
Color (H C A PRO)
$69.95 purchase _ #CV246
Includes six beef wholesale cuts classes - oven prepared ribs, beef loins, two classes of beef ribs, two classes of beef rounds, five questions on each class, official placings, cuts, answers and oral reasons by Judge GW Davis, Texas Tech U.
Agriculture
Dist - AAVIM **Prod** - AAVIM 1990

Practice Beef Yield Grading 44 MIN
VHS
Beef Grading (Set B) Series
(C)
$69.95 _ CV108
Provides an opportunity for students to view a total of fifty practice carcasses ranging from A to E maturity as well as P D to M A in marbling degrees. Includes official grading data for each carcass.
Agriculture
Dist - AAVIM **Prod** - AAVIM 1989

Practice breed identification I
VHS
Practice breed identification series
Color (H A T)
$79.95 purchase _ #CV411
Shows representatives of 35 different cattle breeds. Presents each animal on screen for 30 seconds and provides a video key at the end of the tape.
Agriculture
Dist - AAVIM **Prod** - AAVIM 1992

Practice breed identification II
VHS
Practice breed identification series
Color (H A T)
$79.95 purchase _ #CV412
Shows representatives of 35 different cattle breeds. Presents each animal on screen for 30 seconds and provides a video key at the end of the tape.
Agriculture
Dist - AAVIM **Prod** - AAVIM 1992

Practice breed identification III
VHS
Practice breed identification series
Color (H A T)
$79.95 purchase _ #CV413
Shows representatives of 35 different cattle breeds. Presents each animal on screen for 30 seconds and provides a video key at the end of the tape.
Agriculture
Dist - AAVIM **Prod** - AAVIM 1992

Practice breed identification IV
VHS
Practice breed identification series
Color (H A T)
$79.95 purchase _ #CV414
Shows representatives of 35 different cattle breeds. Presents each animal on screen for 30 seconds and provides a video key at the end of the tape.
Agriculture
Dist - AAVIM **Prod** - AAVIM 1992

Practice breed identification series
Practice breed identification I
Practice breed identification II
Practice breed identification III
Practice breed identification IV
Dist - AAVIM

Practice carcass judging I
VHS
Practice carcass judging series
Color (T H A)
$69.95 purchase _ #CV319
Presents one class each of beef, pork and lamb carcasses followed by ten practice questions - 30 total. Features Dr Gordon Davis formerly of Texas A&M University, University of Tennessee and Texas Tech University. Provides official placing and cuts along with sample sets of reasons for each class. Uses quad - split video to exhibit all four carcasses simultaneously for comparative judging.
Agriculture; Business and Economics
Dist - AAVIM **Prod** - AAVIM 1992

Practice carcass judging II
VHS
Practice carcass judging series
Color (T H A)
$69.95 purchase _ #CV320
Presents one class each of beef, pork and lamb carcasses followed by ten practice questions - 30 total. Features Dr Gordon Davis formerly of Texas A&M University, University of Tennessee and Texas Tech University. Provides official placing and cuts along with sample sets of reasons for each class. Uses quad - split video to exhibit all four carcasses simultaneously for comparative judging.
Agriculture; Business and Economics
Dist - AAVIM **Prod** - AAVIM 1992

Practice carcass judging III
VHS
Practice carcass judging series
Color (T H A)
$69.95 purchase _ #CV321
Presents one class each of beef, pork and lamb carcasses followed by ten practice questions - 30 total. Features Dr Gordon Davis formerly of Texas A&M University, University of Tennessee and Texas Tech University. Provides official placing and cuts along with sample sets of reasons for each class. Uses quad - split video to exhibit all four carcasses simultaneously for comparative judging.
Agriculture; Business and Economics
Dist - AAVIM **Prod** - AAVIM 1992

Practice carcass judging IV
VHS
Practice carcass judging series
Color (T H A)
$69.95 purchase _ #CV322
Presents one class each of beef, pork and lamb carcasses followed by ten practice questions - 30 total. Features Dr Gordon Davis formerly of Texas A&M University, University of Tennessee and Texas Tech University. Provides official placing and cuts along with sample sets of reasons for each class. Uses quad - split video to exhibit all four carcasses simultaneously for comparative judging.
Agriculture; Business and Economics
Dist - AAVIM **Prod** - AAVIM 1992

Practice carcass judging series
Practice carcass judging I
Practice carcass judging II
Practice carcass judging III
Practice carcass judging IV
Dist - AAVIM

Practice Cattle Judging 39 MIN
VHS
Cattle Judging (Set F) Series; Set F
(C)
$69.95 CV126
Gives students a chance to practice cattle judging by including two mixed market steer classes, one class of limousin heifers, one class of progress steers, and one class of Brahmousin heifers which are shown in various positions.
Agriculture
Dist - AAVIM **Prod** - AAVIM 1989

Practice dairy judging - Cows - I 31 MIN
VHS
Dairy cattle judging Set T series; Set T
(C)
$69.95 _ CV174
Including four year old Jersey Cows, three year old Holstein Cows, Aged Brown Swiss Cows, two year old Jersey Cows, and four year old Holstein Cows, this film gives students a chance to practice dairy judging.
Agriculture
Dist - AAVIM **Prod** - AAVIM 1989

Practice dairy judging - Heifers - II
VHS
Dairy cattle judging Set T series; Set T
(C)
$69.95 _ CV175
Gives students a chance to practice dairy judging by presenting clear views of the heifer's rear, walking, posing, and top.
Agriculture
Dist - AAVIM **Prod** - AAVIM 1989

Practice ham and loin judging 32 MIN
VHS
Color (H C A PRO)
$69.95 purchase _ #CV244
Includes four fresh ham and two fresh pork loin classes, five questions on each class, official placings, cuts, answers and oral reasons by Judge GW Davis, Texas Tech U.
Agriculture
Dist - AAVIM **Prod** - AAVIM 1990

Practice horse judging series
Reining 31 MIN
Dist - AAVIM

Practice Horse Judging Set Z - 1 Series
Halter 39 MIN
Hunter Under Saddle 26 MIN
Western Pleasure 22 MIN
Western Riding 35 MIN
Dist - AAVIM

Practice in lay life 60 MIN
VHS / BETA
Color; PAL (G)
PdS25, $50.00 purchase
Features a speech by the Venerable Sumedho Bhikkhu at the Amaravati Buddhist Centre, September and October 1986.
Fine Arts; Religion and Philosophy
Dist - MERIDT

Practice Lamb Carcass Judging 40 MIN
VHS
Color (H C A PRO)
$69.95 purchase _ #CV222
Includes five lamb carcass practice classes, five questions on each class, official placings, cuts, answers and oral reasons by Judge GW Davis, Texas Tech U.
Agriculture
Dist - AAVIM **Prod** - AAVIM 1990

Practice Livestock Judging - I 44 MIN
VHS
Practice Livestock Judging (Set J) Series
(C)
$59.95 _ CV140
Includes a class of market swine, market lambs, market steers, breeding gilts and yearling bulls to provide practice for students in livestock judging.
Agriculture
Dist - AAVIM **Prod** - AAVIM 1989

Practice Livestock Judging - II 38 MIN
VHS
Practice Livestock Judging (Set J) Series
(C)
$59.95 _ CV141
Gives students practice for placing and oral reasons including two classes of heifers, a class of market hogs, and two classes of breeding gilts.
Agriculture
Dist - AAVIM **Prod** - AAVIM 1989

Practice Livestock Judging III 45 MIN
VHS
Color (H C A PRO)
$69.95 purchase _ #CV240
Includes a class of crossbred market steers, Suffolk breeding ewe lambs, Blackface crossbred market lambs, Yorkshire gilts, and crossbred market hogs. Each video class is edited to 6.5 minutes with five angles shown - scan of class together, walking, rear, top, and front views. Classes were placed and a 1.5 minute set of oral reasons is provided by Judge Jim Jenkins.
Agriculture
Dist - AAVIM **Prod** - AAVIM 1990

Practice Livestock Judging IV 45 MIN
VHS
Color (H C A PRO)
$69.95 purchase _ #CV241
Includes a class of market steers, Suffolk market lambs, Hampshire yearling ewes, Hampshire gilts, and crossbred market hogs. Five angles are shown of each animal. Judge Jim Jenkins presents oral reasons after each class.
Agriculture
Dist - AAVIM **Prod** - AAVIM 1990

Practice livestock judging IX 43 MIN
VHS
Practice livestock judging series
Color (T H A)
$69.95 purchase _ #CV315
Shows three practice classes of livestock in side, front, rear, top and walking views. Includes Hereford Steers, Crossbred Market Lambs and Yorkshire Market Hogs. Features Dr John Edwards of Texas A&M University as critic. Part of a series of practice livestock judging videocassettes.
Agriculture; Business and Economics
Dist - AAVIM **Prod** - AAVIM 1992

Practice livestock judging series
Practice livestock judging IX 43 MIN
Practice livestock judging V 45 MIN
Practice livestock judging VI 44 MIN
Practice livestock judging VII 42 MIN
Practice livestock judging VIII 43 MIN
Practice livestock judging X
Practice livestock judging XI 44 MIN
Practice livestock judging XII 42 MIN
Dist - AAVIM

Practice Livestock Judging (Set J) Series
Practice Livestock Judging - I 44 MIN
Practice Livestock Judging - II 38 MIN
Dist - AAVIM

Practice livestock judging V 45 MIN
VHS
Practice livestock judging series
Color (T H A)
$69.95 purchase _ #CV311
Shows three practice classes of livestock in side, front, rear, top and walking views. Includes Light Weight Crossbred Market Steers, Light Weight Berkshire Market Hogs and Southdown Market Lambs. Features Jim Jenkins of South Plains College as critic. Part of a series of practice livestock judging videocassettes.
Agriculture; Business and Economics
Dist - AAVIM **Prod** - AAVIM 1992

Practice livestock judging VI 44 MIN
VHS
Practice livestock judging series
Color (T H A)
$69.95 purchase _ #CV312
Shows three practice classes of livestock in side, front, rear, top and walking views. Includes Heavy Weight Shorthorn Steers, Light Weight Finewool Market Lambs and Duroc Market Hogs. Features Dr John Edwards of Texas A&M University as critic. Part of a series of practice livestock judging videocassettes.
Agriculture; Business and Economics
Dist - AAVIM **Prod** - AAVIM 1992

Practice livestock judging VII 42 MIN
VHS
Practice livestock judging series
Color (T H A)
$69.95 purchase _ #CV313
Shows three practice classes of livestock in side, front, rear, top and walking views. Includes Hereford Steers, Medium Wool Market Lambs and Crossbred Market Hogs. Features Dr John Edwards of Texas A&M University as critic. Part of a series of practice livestock judging videocassettes.
Agriculture; Business and Economics
Dist - AAVIM **Prod** - AAVIM 1992

Practice livestock judging VIII 43 MIN
VHS
Practice livestock judging series
Color (T H A)
$69.95 purchase _ #CV314
Shows three practice classes of livestock in side, front, rear, top and walking views. Includes Light Weight Crossbred Steers, Medium Wool Market Lambs and Crossbred Market Hogs. Features Dr John Edwards of Texas A&M University as critic. Part of a series of practice livestock judging videocassettes.
Agriculture; Business and Economics
Dist - AAVIM **Prod** - AAVIM 1992

Practice livestock judging X
VHS
Practice livestock judging series
Color (T H A)
$69.95 purchase _ #CV316
Shows three practice classes of livestock in side, front, rear, top and walking views. Includes Shorthorn Steers, Medium Wool Market Lambs and Hampshire Market Hogs. Features Dr John Edwards of Texas A&M University as critic. Part of a series of practice livestock judging videocassettes.
Agriculture; Business and Economics
Dist - AAVIM **Prod** - AAVIM 1992

Practice livestock judging XI 44 MIN
VHS
Practice livestock judging series
Color (T H A)
$69.95 purchase _ #CV317
Shows three practice classes of livestock in side, front, rear, top and walking views. Includes Heavy Weight Charolais Steers, Medium Wool Market Lambs and Crossbred Market Hogs. Features Dr John Edwards of Texas A&M University as critic. Part of a series of practice livestock judging videocassettes.
Agriculture; Business and Economics
Dist - AAVIM **Prod** - AAVIM 1992

Practice livestock judging XII 42 MIN
VHS
Practice livestock judging series
Color (T H A)
$69.95 purchase _ #CV318
Shows three practice classes of livestock in side, front, rear, top and walking views. Includes Charolais Heifers, Southdown Market Lambs and Crossbred Market Hogs. Features Dr John Edwards of Texas A&M University as critic. Part of a series of practice livestock judging videocassettes.
Agriculture; Business and Economics
Dist - AAVIM **Prod** - AAVIM 1992

Practice makes perfect 13 MIN
VHS / U-matic
En Francais series
Color (H C A)
Features an engineer in the Allevard steel works and a village blacksmith who has run out of horses to shoe.
Foreign Language; Geography - World
Dist - AITECH **Prod** - MOFAFR 1970

Practice makes perfect soccer series
Art of goalkeeping 30 MIN
Championship ball skills 90 MIN
Coach to win 120 MIN
The Winning kick 90 MIN
Dist - CAMV

The Practice of meditation 30 MIN
VHS / BETA
Personal and spiritual development series
Color (G)
$29.95 purchase _ #S315
Suggests that through quieting the mind one becomes aware of unconscious tensions and that the act of awareness serves to heal those tensions. Features Dr Jack Kornfield, clinical psychologist, Buddhist teacher of Vipassana - mindfulness - meditation and author of 'Living Master of Buddhism' and 'A Clear Forest Pool.' Part of a four - part series on personal and spiritual development.
Psychology; Religion and Philosophy
Dist - THINKA **Prod** - THINKA

Practice of nursing series
Blueprints for excellence - clinical practice guidelines
Career encounters - advanced practice nursing
Meet NIC - the nursing interventions classification system
Nursing research - the state of the art
Dist - NLFN

Practice organization 32 MIN
VHS
VIP softball series
Color (G)
$29.95 purchase _ #ASAT06V
Covers the basics of organizing softball practice sessions. Shows how to keep all the players interested and involved. Taught by Bobby Simpson, Cindy Bristow and Buzzy Keller.
Physical Education and Recreation
Dist - CAMV **Prod** - CAMV

Practice Pork Carcass Judging 40 MIN
VHS
Color (H C A PRO)
$69.95 purchase _ #CV221
Includes two pork carcass, one fresh loin and two fresh ham practice classes, five questions on each class, official placings, cuts, answers and oral reasons by Judge GW Davis, Texas Tech U.
Agriculture
Dist - AAVIM **Prod** - AAVIM 1990

Practice Poultry Judging - I 33 MIN
VHS
Poultry Judging (Set S) Series
(C)
$69.95 _ CV181
Introduces poultry judging and gives students a chance to practice judging.
Agriculture
Dist - AAVIM **Prod** - AAVIM 1989

Practice Poultry Judging - II 25 MIN
VHS
Poultry Judging (Set S) Series
(C)
$69.95 _ CV182
Explains poultry judging and includes practice classes on broiler grading, turkey placing, breaded patty placing, poultry parts identification, and poultry examination with questions and answers.
Agriculture
Dist - AAVIM **Prod** - AAVIM 1989

Practice rating exercises 5 - 8 20 MIN
U-matic / BETA / 16mm / VHS
Color; Silent (A PRO)
$200.00, $275.00 purchase, $10.00 rental
Offers four separate films to be used in conjunction with Fair Day's Work Concepts to develop rating skills in the apparel and lighter industries. Silent feature permits seminar leaders to inject appropriated comments.
Business and Economics; Psychology
Dist - TAMMFG **Prod** - TAMMFG

Practice Retail Cut Identification I 30 MIN
VHS
Color (H C A PRO)
$69.95 purchase _ #CV211
Incluces 75 retail cuts - five classes - presented on a rotating tray for 25 seconds each. Beef, lamb and pork cuts were selected from the 1988 - 90 Natl FFA Meats Evaluation and Management Contest approved list of 126 cuts.
Agriculture
Dist - AAVIM **Prod** - AAVIM 1990

Practice Retail Cut Identification II 30 MIN
VHS
Color (H C A PRO)
$69.95 purchase _ #CV212
Includes 75 retail cuts - five classes - shown from all angles for 25 seconds each. The red meat cuts were selected from the 1988 - 90 Natl FFA Meats Evaluation and Management Contest approved list of 126 cuts.
Agriculture
Dist - AAVIM **Prod** - AAVIM 1990

Practice Retail Cuts Judging 40 MIN
VHS
Color (H C A PRO)
$69.95 purchase _ #CV223
Includes three beef - Porterhouse, T - bone, Blade steaks, two pork - loin and blade chops, two lamb - loin and blade chops, five questions on each class, official placings, cuts, answers and oral reasons by Judge GW Davis, Texas Tech U.
Agriculture
Dist - AAVIM **Prod** - AAVIM 1990

Practice Sheep Judging
VHS
Sheep Judging (Set H) Series
(C)
$69.95 _ CV134
Provides opportunity students to practice sheep judging.
Agriculture
Dist - AAVIM **Prod** - AAVIM 1989

Practice Swine Judging 42 MIN
VHS
Swine Judging (Set G) Series
(C)
$69.95 _ CV130
Provides students a chance to practice swine judging by including three classes of crossbred barrows, one class of Duroc gilts, one class of crossbred gilts.
Agriculture
Dist - AAVIM **Prod** - AAVIM 1989

Practice to Theory to Practice 240 MIN
VHS
Generativity Project Series
Color (A PRO)
$150.00 purchase _ #79301
Reviews student development theories and their potential usefulness in practice and presents the 11 - step P - T - P model created by Lee Knefelkamp.
Guidance and Counseling
Dist - AACD **Prod** - AACD

Practice Tree Identification 35 MIN
VHS
Color (H C A PRO)
$69.95 purchase _ #CV602
Includes 40 hardwood trees and timber - forage relationships, shows each specimen's leaves and bark up close and an identification key after each class of 10 specimens.
Agriculture; Social Science
Dist - AAVIM **Prod** - AAVIM 1990

Practice Under the Bankruptcy Code 240 MIN
U-matic / Cassette / VHS / 16mm
Color; Mono (PRO)
Features two bankruptcy attorneys and a judge as they discuss court structure and jurisdiction in bankruptcy cases. Covers Chapter 7 cases, Chapter 11 reorganizations, consumer bankruptcy and Chapter 13.
Civics and Political Systems
Dist - CCEB **Prod** - CCEB

Practice Under the New California Revised Limited Partnership Act 120 MIN
VHS / U-matic / Cassette
Color; Mono (PRO)
Features experienced law practitioners as they explain the law of July 1, 1984, which covers limited partnership. Emphasizes how the law expands management participation by limited partners, new voting rights, reservation of name, new filing requirements and conditions for continuity.
Business and Economics; Civics and Political Systems
Dist - CCEB **Prod** - CCEB

Practice with the Pros
VHS
Tennis by Vic Braden Series
(J H C)
$29.95 _ #HSV7055V
Presents coach Braden who demonstrates the lob, overhead, approach shot, and half volley in tennis. Features slow motion photography to demonstrate proper body form.
Physical Education and Recreation
Dist - CAMV

Practicing and performing - a pianist's guide 75 MIN
VHS
Color (G)
$29.95 purchase _ #VD - ABR - PP01
Features concert pianist and composer Daniel Abrams. Shows players of all levels and styles how to get maximum results from minimum time spent at the keyboard. Covers relaxation, inspiration, breathing, focus, attitude and interpretation, as well as phrasing, scales, wrist action, pedaling and understanding chords. Demonstrates what to do when mistakes are made and how to isolate, practice and master difficult passages.
Fine Arts
Dist - HOMETA **Prod** - HOMETA

Practicing in California under the new rules of professional conduct 45 MIN
VHS
Color (PRO)
$19.00, $49.00 purchase, $19.00 rental _ #MI-52920, #MI-62920
Discusses rules of professional conduct that affect contacting opposing parties, representing corporations, conflict of interest, client marketing, selling a law practice, and other issues of legal practice in California.
Civics and Political Systems
Dist - CCEB

Practicing mathmatical skills 18 MIN
16mm
Project on interpreting mathematics education research series
Color
LC 74-705395
Illustrates suitable materials for practicing mathematical skills, describes use of a computer terminal, and deals with techniques for promoting interest and ways of identifying appropriate items for drill.
Mathematics
Dist - USNAC **Prod** - USOE 1970

Practicing the heart of healing series
Wisdom, freedom and compassion 120 MIN
Dist - MERIDT

A Practitioner's Guide to Determining Beneficiaries 35 MIN
U-matic / VHS
Practitioner's Guide to Preventing Probate Litigation Series
Color (PRO)
Examines how to prevent malpractice exposure in intestate distribution. Gives a lesson in genealogy and proof of heirship.
Civics and Political Systems
Dist - ABACPE **Prod** - ABACPE

Practitioner's guide to preventing probate litigation series
Anticipating the defense of will contests 42 MIN
A Practitioner's Guide to Determining Beneficiaries 35 MIN
Dist - ABACPE

Practitioner's guide to recent developments in copyright law - New protections, standards and formalities 50 MIN
VHS
Color (C PRO A)
$95.00 purchase _ #Y154
Examines new copyright protections for architectural works; moral rights of attribution and integrity for works of visual art; notice and registration reforms; changes in the 'works made for hire' and 'fair use' doctrines; the repeal of the 'sweat of the brow' doctrine and other issues pertaining to federal legislation introduced between 1988 and 1991.
Civics and Political Systems
Dist - ALIABA **Prod** - CLETV 1991

The Prado - 3 80 MIN
VHS / BETA
Grand museum series
Color (G)
$29.95 purchase
Visits the Prado. Offers close - up views of paintings with informative narrative rich in artistic and historic detail. Includes a chronological list of the works and artists shown. Part three of a three - parts series on famous art museums produced by Vistar.
Fine Arts
Dist - ARTSAM

Pragmatic development 112 MIN
VHS / U-matic
Meeting the communications needs of the severely - profoundly handicapped 1980 series
Color
Describes the normal sequences of pragmatic development and their relationship to Piaget's stages of sensorimotor development. Explores the application of pragmatics to communication assessment and intervention with severely/profoundly handicapped individuals.
Psychology; Social Science
Dist - PUAVC **Prod** - PUAVC

Pragmatic development 146 MIN
VHS / U-matic
Meeting the communication needs of the severely - profoundly handicapped 1981 series
Color
Addresses the central role of pragmatics in communication development and intervention. Describes normal sequences of pragmatic development and their relationship to Piaget's stages of sensorimeter development.
Psychology; Social Science
Dist - PUAVC **Prod** - PUAVC

Prague Castle 13 MIN
16mm / U-matic / VHS
Color
Features the Prague Castle, one of the oldest and best - preserved castles in Europe.
Geography - World; History - World
Dist - KAWVAL **Prod** - KAWVAL

The Prairie 19 MIN
U-matic / VHS / 16mm
Color (I J H)
Examines typical animal forms of the semi arid North American prairie against a background of the dominant plant species and grasses. Describes two microseres, the dung feeders and the carrion eaters, as integral parts of the grassland ecosystem.
Science - Natural
Dist - IFB **Prod** - CMPBL 1982

The Prairie - 1 15 MIN
U-matic / 16mm / VHS
Natural science series
Color (P I J)
$325.00, $260.00, $230.00 purchase _ #A290
Overviews North America's vast prairie grasslands which feature nutrient - rich soil which forms one of the most productive farming areas in the world. Shows prairie dogs, coyotes, insects, bison, pronghorn antelope, birds and plants which form the richly varied prairie community. Offers clear explanations of the prairie ecosystem. Part of a three - part series on natural history.
Geography - United States; Science - Natural
Dist - BARR **Prod** - CASDEN 1980

The Prairie - America's Grassland 12 MIN
U-matic / VHS
Color
Explores both tall and short - grass prairies with a close look at virgin prairie areas.
Science - Natural
Dist - CBSC **Prod** - CBSC

Prairie cabin - a Norwegian pioneer woman's story 17 MIN
Cassette / U-matic / BETA / VHS
Women's history and literature media series
Color (P I J H G)
$95.00 purchase, $40.00 rental
Uses the personal narratives of several pioneer Norwegian - American women to portray one woman's life after immigrating to the Midwestern prairie country. Illustrates Norwegian - American artifacts, foods and clothing. Part of a series about women's history and literature created by Jocelyn Rile. Resource guide available separately.
History - United States; History - World
Dist - HEROWN **Prod** - HEROWN 1992

Prairie Coulee 15 MIN
U-matic / VHS / 16mm
Animals and Plants of North America Series
Color (J)
LC 81-700950
Shows the plants and animals that inhabit the 'prairie coulee,' a steep - walled valley made by water during a glacial period.
Science - Natural
Dist - LCOA **Prod** - KARVF 1981

Prairie Fire 30 MIN
U-matic / VHS
B&W
Brings to life a time in American history when farmers organized to protect their way of life and fight against the abuses of Eastern grain, banking and railroad trusts.
History - United States; Sociology
Dist - NFPS **Prod** - NFPS

The Prairie giant - Le Geant de la prairie 21 MIN
U-matic / VHS / 16mm
Color (J A H) (FRENCH)
LC FIA68-2896
Tells the story of the Canada goose and of other birds. Shows geese in flight, nesting, raising their young and migrating south.
Science - Natural
Dist - IFB **Prod** - COTTEN 1968

A Prairie home companion final performance
VHS / Cassette
Color (G H A)
$16.95, $29.95 purchase _ #18624, #12809
Presents the last live performance and broadcast of 'A Prairie Home Companion' with Garrison Keillor. Audio version captures the entire radio broadcast, running 2 hours and 42 minutes long, while the video is a shorter version.
Fine Arts; Literature and Drama
Dist - WCAT **Prod** - WCAT

A Prairie Home Companion - the 2nd Annual Farewell Performance 260 MIN
Cassette / VHS
Color (G)
$29.95, $16.95 purchase _ #12810, #10795
Presents the June 4, 1988, performance at Radio City Hall. Reunites Garrison Keillor, Chet Atkins, Leo Kottke, the Everly Brothers.
Fine Arts; Literature and Drama
Dist - WCAT **Prod** - WCAT

Prairie Killers 30 MIN
16mm / U-matic / VHS
Our Vanishing Wilderness Series no 2
Color (H C A)
LC 76-710655
Describes the white man's invasion of the Great Plains, the displacement of the Indians and the annihilation of the buffalo. Explains how ranchers are changing the ecological balance by killing coyotes and prairie dogs. Points out how the destruction of one part of life relates to the eventual extermination of the whole.
Science - Natural; Social Science
Dist - IU **Prod** - NET 1971

Prairie Pronghorn 13 MIN
16mm
Color
Shows much of the wildlife in the regions of the plains of central Wyoming.
Geography - United States; Science - Natural
Dist - SFI **Prod** - SFI

Prairie Pronghorns 15 MIN
16mm
Color
Archer stalks fleet antelope through sparse cover in central Wyoming.
Geography - United States; Physical Education and Recreation
Dist - SFI **Prod** - SFI

Prairie quilts 15 MIN
Cassette / U-matic / BETA / VHS
Women's history and literature media series
Color (P I J H G)
$95.00 purchase, $40.00 rental
Illustrates the work of 31 quilters who interpret the flowers, grasses and wildlife of the prairies in a wide variety of artistic expression. Includes Scandinavian folk music for the background. Part of a series about women's history and literature created by Jocelyn Rile. Resource guide available separately.
Fine Arts; History - World; Home Economics; Science - Natural
Dist - HEROWN **Prod** - HEROWN 1991

Prairie Roadsides 14 MIN
16mm
Color (J H C)
LC 74-700139
Describes an experimental program using native prairie plants to control weeds and erosion on roadsides. Shows that the reintroduction of native plants can provide functional, low - maintenance roadside cover vegetation. Illustrates the advantages of a more ecological approach to the maintenance of highway right - of - way.
Science - Natural; Social Science
Dist - IOWA **Prod** - IOWA 1973

Prairie School Architecture 28 MIN
U-matic / VHS
Color (H C A)
LC 84-707061
Capsulizes the principles of the Prairie School of Architecture. Visits the midwestern heartland to buildings sparked by the vision of master architect Louis Sullivan under the influence of Frank Lloyd Wright.
Fine Arts
Dist - UCV **Prod** - UCV 1984

Prairie School Architecture 28
16mm / VHS
Color (H A)
$250.00 purchase, $65.00 rental
Provides a view of the first American architecture, the small banks and private residences of the Prairie School. Presents the visions of Louis Sullivan and Frank Lloyd Wright. This radical approach to design revolutionized American architecture and decorative art at the turn of the century.
Fine Arts
Dist - AFA **Prod** - UMINN 1983

Prairie Slough 15 MIN
16mm / U-matic / VHS
Animals and Plants of North America Series
Color (J)
LC 81-700951
Describes the role of prairie marshes in providing food and sanctuary for thousands of waterfowl as they migrate to and from breeding grounds.
Science - Natural
Dist - LCOA **Prod** - KARVF 1981

Prairie Storm 57 MIN
U-matic / VHS
Color
Discusses the issue of abortion and the effect the opening of North Dakota's first abortion clinic has on one midwestern community.
Sociology
Dist - WCCOTV **Prod** - WCCOTV 1982

The Prairie that was 19 MIN
16mm / U-matic / VHS
Color (I J H C)
LC 75-703688
Takes a look at the grasslands and wildlife found in parks and wildlife refuges which preserve the North American prairie in its original habitat.
Geography - United States; Science - Natural
Dist - AIMS **Prod** - GALATR 1975

Prairie towns a - boomin' 30 MIN
16mm
Great plains trilogy - explorer and settler - the White man'arrives - 3 series; Explorer and settler - the white man arrives
B&W (H C A)
Describes the life of the agricultural state as reflected in its towns. Discusses the county seat struggles, the urban boom, and the cities, schools and churches. Pictures social life in Omaha and on the farm.
History - United States
Dist - UNL **Prod** - KUONTV 1954

Prairie War 29 MIN
16mm
Al Oeming - Man of the North Series
Color
LC 77-702872
Portrays Al Oeming's journey to southern Saskatchewan in an experiment to introduce two kit foxes, bred at his game farm, back into the wilderness.
Geography - World; Science - Natural
Dist - NIELSE **Prod** - NIELSE 1977

The Prairies 25 MIN
U-matic / VHS / 16mm
Untamed World Series
Color; Mono (J H C A)
$400.00 film, $250.00 video, $50.00 rental
Features the varied wildlife of the North American prairies stretching from central Canada down through the United States.
Geography - United States; Geography - World; Science - Natural
Dist - CTV **Prod** - CTV 1971

The Prairies 48.30 MIN
U-matic / 16mm / VHS
Canada - Five Portraits Series
Color; Mono (G) (FRENCH)
MV $350.00 _ MP $475.00 purchase, $50.00 rental
Traces the plight of the people who settled the unforgiving Prairies of Western Canada. This film follows the people from the resistance movement of Louis Riel, the decline of the fur trade, to the survival of the wheat industry.
Geography - World
Dist - CTV **Prod** - CTV 1973

Prairies to Peaktops 22 MIN
U-matic / VHS
Aerie Nature Series
Color (I J H)
Introduces important concepts in ecology and behavior of wildlife by exploring the life zones of the Rocky Mountains.
Science - Natural
Dist - CEPRO **Prod** - CEPRO 1982

Praise 60 MIN
16mm / VHS
Color
Portrays Praise, a young, black street boy with incredible raw intelligence, who is haunted by peer pressure and his own heritage.
Fine Arts
Dist - TLECUL **Prod** - TLECUL

Praise and rewards subseries 40 MIN
VHS / U-matic
Parents and children series
Color (G C A)
$440.00 purchase _ #C840 - VI - 020P
Presents a two - part subseries which teaches parents how to use praise and rewards to the greatest advantage. Part of a ten - part series on parents and children presented by Dr Carolyn Webster - Stratton.
Health and Safety; Psychology; Sociology
Dist - HSCIC

Praise and rewards subseries
The Art of effective praising - Part I 25 MIN
Tangible rewards - Part II 15 MIN
Dist - HSCIC

Praise house 25 MIN
VHS
Color (G)
$65.00 rental, $250.00 purchase
Combines elements of theater, dance and music based on the rhythms and rituals of Africa. Brings together Julie Dash, director of 'Daughters of the Dust,' and Jawole Willa Jo Zollar, found and choreographer of Urban Bush Women, to explore the source of creativity and its effect on three generations of African - American women. Shows the emotional prison so many people live in, even as it celebrates the persistence of belief and creativity and the splendid legacies African Americans have preserved against all odds.
Fine Arts; History - United States; Sociology
Dist - WMEN **Prod** - JUDA 1991

Praise the Lord 58 MIN
VHS
Frontline Series
Color; Captioned (G)
$59.95 purchase _ #FRON - 601K
Investigates the scandals connected with the PTL ministries of Jim and Tammy Bakker. Shows how the Bakkers used much of the money raised to live a lavish lifestyle. Suggests that federal authorities knew of the financial irregularities in PTL several years before the scandal broke in 1987, but failed to act.
Religion and Philosophy; Sociology
Dist - PBS **Prod** - DOCCON 1988

Praise the Lord and pass the ammunition 30 MIN
VHS
America in World War II - The home front series
Color (G)
$49.95 purchase _ #AWWH - 102
Shows how the American government and people pursued the war effort after the Pearl Harbor incident brought the U.S. into World War II. Focuses on the explosive industrial growth that the war promoted. Portrays popular culture and how it sought to divert Americans. Narrated by Eric Sevareid.
History - United States
Dist - PBS

Praisin' His Name - the Gospel Soul Children of New Orleans 60 MIN
U-matic / VHS
Color
Presents the Gospel Soul Children who perform such gospel favorites as Wounded For Me, Call Him Up, If Jesus Goes With Me and I Love The Lord.
Fine Arts
Dist - MDCPB **Prod** - WYESTV

Pranks 30 MIN
VHS
Color (G)
$24.00 purchase
Explores the strange and wonderful phenomenon of pranks. Features five artists - pranksters who extreme and funny subversive acts challenge the boundaries of social and artistic acceptability. Interviews Joe Coleman, painter and performance artist; Mark Pauline, founder of Survival Research Laboratories; Karen Finley, controversial New York performance artist; Frank Discussion, leader of San Francisco's seminal punk band, the Feederz; and Boyd Rice, perpetrator of all practical jokes. Produced by Re - Search Publications.
Fine Arts; Literature and Drama
Dist - CANCIN

A Prarie home companion with Garrison Keillor - the last show 120 MIN
VHS
Color (G)
$29.95 purchase _ #S01457
Presents a video version of the last Prarie Home Companion radio show by humorist and author Garrison Keillor. Reveals that Keillor performed the show before a live audience for 13 years.
Fine Arts; History - United States; Literature and Drama
Dist - UILL

Pratibha Parmar Series
Emergence 18 MIN
Memory Pictures 24 MIN
Sari red 12 MIN
Dist - WMEN

Pravda
CD-ROM
Color (G A)
$249.00 purchase _ #1505
Presents the entire English translation of Pravda from 1986 - 87. For IBM PCs and compatibles. Requires 640K RAM, DOS Version 3.1 or greater, one floppy disk drive - a hard drive is recommended, one empty expansion slot, and an IBM compatible CD - ROM drive.
Foreign Language; Sociology
Dist - BEP

Prayer 2 MIN
16mm
Meditation Series
Color (I)
LC 80-700755
Touches on every form of prayer through the quiet reflections of a young woman.
Religion and Philosophy
Dist - IKONOG **Prod** - IKONOG 1974

Prayer 5 MIN
16mm
Color (HEBREW)
LC 76-700407
Shows the movements and atmosphere in Jewish prayer. Includes a morning service in a synagogue of a chassidic community, the welcoming of the Sabbath and a cantorial psalm.

Religion and Philosophy; Sociology
Dist - URIELI **Prod** - URIELI 1975

Prayer 9 MIN
16mm
Cuba - a view from inside series
B&W (G)
$150.00 purchase, $25.00 rental
Juxtaposes Marilyn Monroe's life with contemporaneous political events by employing Ernesto Cardenal's poem, 'A Prayer for Marilyn Monroe.' Features part of a 17 - part series of shorts by and about Cuban women. Directed by Marisol Trujillo. Illustrated catalog available. Contact distributor for programming advice and discount package rental fees.
Civics and Political Systems; Fine Arts; Literature and Drama
Dist - CNEMAG

A Prayer before birth 20 MIN
VHS
Color (G)
$75.00 rental, $275.00 purchase
Chronicles the filmmaker's experience of coming to terms with multiple sclerosis with disturbing intensity and creative vitality. Looks at the physical and emotional traumas of a young lesbian's journey from able - bodied exuberance to the acceptance of disability. Shows how vulnerability, fear of disability and issues around health and autonomy apply to us all. Produced by Jacqui Duckworth.
Fine Arts; Health and Safety; Psychology; Sociology
Dist - WMEN

A Prayer from the Abyss 27 MIN
16mm / U-matic / VHS
Insight Series
Color; B&W (H A)
LC 75-713918
A dramatization about a girl who attempts suicide and a young psychiatric intern who tries to help the girl on the long return to reality.
Psychology; Religion and Philosophy; Sociology
Dist - PAULST **Prod** - PAULST 1971

Prayer in the classroom 28 MIN
VHS
This Constitution - a history series
Color (H C G)
$180.00 purchase, $19.00 rental _ #35739
Describes controversial efforts to bring prayer into public schools. Discusses the conflict between the Free Exercise Clause and the Establishment Clause of the First Amendment. Outlines several Supreme Court cases on the establishment of religion, including Cantwell v Connecticut; Engel v Vitale and Wallace v Jeffree. Part of a five - part series on the philosophical origins, drafting and interpretation of the US Constitution and its effect on American society, produced by the International University Consortium and Project '87.
Civics and Political Systems
Dist - PSU

Prayer shield
VHS
Color (R)
$29.99 purchase _ #SPCN 85116.00620
Focuses on aggressively invoking God for the protection of leaders. Features Peter Wagner who illustrates Biblical ways to make the prayer life of Christians - both individually and as leaders of corporations - more targeted and fruitful. Includes two videos.
Religion and Philosophy
Dist - GOSPEL **Prod** - GOSPEL

Prayer - the ultimate conversation 30 MIN
VHS
Color (G A R)
$39.95 purchase, $10.00 rental _ #35 - 81 - 2076
Presents Lutheran theologian Joseph Sittler in an examination of prayer.
Religion and Philosophy
Dist - APH

Prayer to Virachocha 5 MIN
VHS
Color (J H G)
$99.00 purchase, $40.00 rental
Uses animation to portray the conflict between the Catholicism brought over by the Conquistadors and the religion of the native people of Latin America. Produced by Alan Fountain and Sue Shephard.
History - World; Religion and Philosophy
Dist - FLMLIB **Prod** - CFTV 1993

The Praying Mantis 11 MIN
U-matic / VHS / 16mm
Animal Families Series
Color (I J)
$275, $195, $225 purchase _ #B423
Offers a lesson on the anatomy and life cycle of one of nature's insects.
Science - Natural
Dist - BARR **Prod** - BARR 1986

Praying mantis Kung - Fu 94 MIN
VHS
Color (G)
$39.95 purchase _ #MA - 06
Demonstrates the praying mantis form of Kung - Fu from northern China. Illustrates the form from two angles.
Physical Education and Recreation; Religion and Philosophy
Dist - ARVID **Prod** - ARVID

Pre - algebra 90 MIN
VHS
Color (I J)
$29.95 purchase _ #S01792
Presents an introduction to algebra concepts. Covers subjects including evaluation of algebraic expressions, signed numbers and polynomials. Includes workbook, with additional workbooks available at an extra charge.
Mathematics
Dist - UILL

Pre - algebra 95 MIN
VHS
Video tutor basic math series
Color (I J H)
$29.95 purchase _ #VIT104V
Introduces concepts of algebra, including linear equations, signed numbers and polynomial operations. Uses computer graphics and an electronic chalkboard to illustrate the concepts. Includes a workbook. Part of a seven - part series on basic mathematics.
Mathematics
Dist - CAMV

Pre and Post Conferences 30 MIN
16mm
Nursing - Where are You Going, How will You Get There Series
B&W (C A)
LC 74-700184
Employs dramatization to illustrate pre and post conference teaching principles.
Education; Health and Safety
Dist - NTCN **Prod** - NTCN 1971

Pre and Post Operative Breathing Exercises
VHS / U-matic
Color (ARABIC SPANISH)
Explains how patients can help ensure their own recovery by practicing respiratory exercises before their operation.
Health and Safety; Physical Education and Recreation
Dist - MIFE **Prod** - MIFE

Pre and post operative care - Part II 30 MIN
VHS
Caring for the transplant patient series
Color (PRO C)
$225.00 purchase, $70.00 rental _ #6531
Covers a range of issues important to nurses who care for transplant patients. Discusses and demonstrates preoperative preparation of the organ recipient. Covers the pathophysiology and nursing interventions for these patients. Examines immunosuppressive medications, steroids and other medications and their side effects. Reviews possible complications after surgery and gives information on signs and symptoms of rejection and infection. Features actual family members and patients discussing their transplant experiences. Part two of three parts on transplant patient care.
Health and Safety
Dist - AJN **Prod** - HESCTV

Pre and post - operative education 25 MIN
U-matic / VHS
Mastectomy education series
Color (PRO C G)
$195.00 purchase _ #C890 - VI - 077
Prepares mastectomy patients with a detailed outline of what to expect leading up to and following sugery. Describes each step from admission to recovery. Discusses common questions and concerns. Part of a five - part series on mastectomy education presented by physical therapist Jan Anthes, Zaira Becker, RN, Linda Waldren, RN, Pilar Gonzalez, RN and Leatha Ross, RN.
Health and Safety
Dist - HSCIC

Pre and post - operative patient management 18 MIN
VHS / U-matic
Psychosocial care series
Color (PRO C)
$395.00 purchase, $80.00 rental _ #C851 - VI - 067
Features Norman Cousins, Norma Wylie and Dr Roland Folse who discuss the essential features of clear communication with the patient. Discusses telling the patient and the family the truth, being willing to repeat telling until the details are clear, giving the patient the sense that fighting the disease is a challenge, and learning to listen or sit in silence or intervene when necessary. Part of a six - part series presented by Norma A Wylie, RN.
Health and Safety
Dist - HSCIC

Pre and postnatal yoga 35 MIN
VHS
Color (H C A)
$29.95 purchase
Features Jennie Arndt instructing in yoga techniques designed for women who are pregnant or recovering from pregnancy. Focuses on preparing for the birth of a baby, as well as how to get back into shape afterwards.
Health and Safety; Physical Education and Recreation
Dist - YOGAJ **Prod** - YOGAJ

Pre - calculus
VHS
Color (H C)
$159.95 purchase _ #VAD029
Presents four videocassettes teaching pre - calculus. Includes step - by - step instruction on the theory of equations, matrix algebra, determinants, conics, sequences and series.
Mathematics
Dist - SIV

Pre - Cleaning 7 MIN
VHS / BETA / 16mm
Color (A PRO)
$53.50 purchase _ #KTI99
Shows entry level masking techniques. Covers different tape widths, use of apron taper, and other procedures in pre - cleaning.
Industrial and Technical Education
Dist - RMIBHF **Prod** - RMIBHF

Pre - Columbian Art of Costa Rica 15 MIN
16mm
Color (J H C) (SPANISH)
Deals with an extensive panorama of pre - Columbian art objects of Costa Rica.
Fine Arts; Foreign Language
Dist - PAN **Prod** - PAN

Pre - Columbian Civilizations 30 MIN
U-matic / VHS
Historically Speaking Series Part 2; Pt 2
Color (H)
Looks at the first arrivals to America. Studies the Olmecs, the Mayas, the Aztecs and the Incas.
History - World; Social Science
Dist - AITECH **Prod** - KRMATV 1983

Pre - Delivery Adjustment of Casting - Laboratory Procedure 9 MIN
16mm
Color (PRO)
LC 75-700811
Presents the alteration procedures involved in removable partial denture casting. Describes the areas that require adjustment.
Health and Safety; Science
Dist - USNAC **Prod** - USVA 1968

Pre - Delivery Adjustment of Casting - Laboratory Procedure 10 MIN
U-matic
Removable Partial Dentures, Clasp Type - Clinical and Laboratory 'Procedures Series
Color (PRO)
LC 78-706182
Explains that certain arbitrary relief procedures should be accomplished on the removable partial denture casting to remove potential interferences that may resist complete sealing of the appliance. Describes area adjustment problems and methods to obtain necessary alterations. Issued in 1967 as a motion picture.
Health and Safety
Dist - USNAC **Prod** - USVA 1978

Pre - Employment Planning
VHS / 35mm strip
Pre - Employment Planning - Set of Six Filmstrips or Six VHS Tapes -'Series
$239.00 film purchase, $369.00 VHS purchase _ #XY140 film, #XY150 VHS
Guidance and Counseling
Dist - CAREER **Prod** - CAREER

Pre - employment planning series
Completing an application
Developing your resume
Good money management
Planning Your Future
While at Work
Dist - CAREER

Pre - Employment Planning - Set of Six Filmstrips or Six VHS Tapes - Series
Pre - Employment Planning
Dist - CAREER

Pre - Employment Planning
Interviewing for the Job
Dist - CAREER

Pre - Fire Planning 30 MIN
VHS
Firefighter II - III Video Series
Color (G PRO)
$145.00 purchase _ #35273
Explains pre - fire planning for structures in the community. Identifies key elements of a pre - fire plan and explains their strategic importance.
Health and Safety; Psychology; Social Science
Dist - OKSU **Prod** - OKSU

Pre - Fire Planning for Tankers 30 MIN
VHS
Tanker Operations Series
Color (G PRO)
$125.00 purchase _ #35371
Covers the pre - fire preparation for efficient utilization of resources, equipment and personnel involved with tankers. Trains firefighting personnel.
Health and Safety; Psychology; Social Science
Dist - OKSU **Prod** - OKSU

Pre - Flight 29 MIN
Videoreel / VT2
Discover Flying - Just Like a Bird Series
Color
Industrial and Technical Education; Social Science
Dist - PBS **Prod** - WKYCTV

The Pre - Game Stretch 25 MIN
U-matic / VHS
Color
Shows California Angel Bill Singer and his teammates detailing a new form of stretching exercises that can be useful for everyone.
Physical Education and Recreation
Dist - MEDCOM **Prod** - MEDCOM

A Pre - Kindergarten Program - a Camera Visit to New Haven 30 MIN
16mm
B&W
Describes a Head Start - like program for disadvantaged children operated by a public school system in a community center. Follows the childrens' unrehearsed activities while the director of the program is being interviewed.
Education; Psychology; Sociology
Dist - NYU **Prod** - VASSAR 1965

Pre - Malignant and Malignant Lesions of the Breast and Colon 90 MIN
16mm
B&W (PRO)
Presents a panel of doctors discussing simple versus radical mastectomy, surgical procedures, radiation therapy and opinions about biopsies. Shows three actual breast and colon cases and a neurosurgeon demonstrating a hypophysectomy.
Health and Safety; Science - Natural
Dist - UPJOHN **Prod** - UPJOHN

Pre - Manufacture Notification Rule (EPA, may 1983 Series
Highlights of the June 23, 1983 PMN Seminar in Washington, DC 43 MIN
How to Complete the PMN Form 18 MIN
Questions and answers about EPA's final PMN rule 21 MIN
Dist - USNAC

Pre - menstrual syndrome 52 MIN
VHS
Color; PAL (G)
PdS20 purchase
Presents a straightforward, instructive program to help sufferers come to terms with PMS - premenstrual syndrome. Combines medical facts and advice with basic self - help information. Features a barrister and sociologist who discuss the social implications. Contact distributor about availability outside the United Kingdom.
Psychology; Sociology
Dist - ACADEM

Pre - Natal Care 15 MIN
U-matic / VHS / 16mm
Woman Talk Series
Color (H C A)
Emphasizes the role of the doctor in pre - natal counseling, and also the importance of good nutrition and moderation in drinking, smoking and use of medications. Features a mime demonstrating several simple exercises useful in alleviating some of the discomfort usually associated with an advancing pregnancy.
Health and Safety; Sociology
Dist - CORF **Prod** - CORF 1983

Pre - natal care
VHS / U-matic
Color (A) (ARABIC FRENCH SPANISH)
Describes what happens on the first pre - natal care visit. Covers history taking, examination, various tests, diet and health care tips, activities, what to expect and what to be concerned about.
Health and Safety; Sociology
Dist - MIFE **Prod** - MIFE

Pre - natal care - vaccinations 30 MIN
U-matic / VHS
Health, safety and well - being series
Color
Health and Safety
Dist - CAMB **Prod** - MAETEL

The Pre - natal crisis 30 MIN
U-matic
Parent puzzle series
(A)
Shows a couple planning and preparing for their first child which involves coping with pressures from well meaning relatives and friends while making adjustments in lifestyle and working out new roles.
Psychology; Sociology
Dist - ACCESS **Prod** - ACCESS 1982

Pre - natal diagnosis by amniocentesis 26 MIN
16mm
Color (PRO) (ENGLISH, SPANISH)
Portrays two genetic counseling situations in which amniocentesis is suggested, one concerning the risk of a biochemical defect and the other concerning the risk of a chromosomal defect. Explains the facts of amniocentesis and shows the technique used to withdraw amniotic fluid from the uterus.
Psychology; Science - Natural; Sociology
Dist - MIFE **Prod** - NFMD 1973

Pre - natal diagnosis - to be or not to be 45 MIN
16mm
Color (A)
LC 81-701614
Shows the scientific techniques involved in prenatal diagnosis of genetic abnormalities and examines the responsibilities and decisions facing both physicians and parents as they weigh the risks of the tests against the findings. Includes interviews with parents of children afflicted with genetic abnormalities and observations of genetic specialists.
Health and Safety
Dist - FLMLIB **Prod** - CANBC 1981

Pre - number ideas 30 MIN
16mm
Mathematics for elementary school teachers series
Color (A)
Provides an overview of modern mathematics, and presents some fundamental concepts about sets. Number one in the series.
Mathematics
Dist - MLA **Prod** - SMSG 1963

Pre - op 29 MIN
U-matic / VHS / 16mm
Footsteps Series
Color (A)
Brings attention to the emotional needs of children when they are ill and need hospitalization. Dramatizes the situation in the fictional Tristero family, in which Ann Marie's own fears of sickness and hospitals frighten her young son Paul. Includes a brief introduction and commentary by real - life families and child development experts.
Health and Safety; Psychology; Sociology
Dist - USNAC **Prod** - USDED 1980

Pre - Op - Illness and Hospitalization 23 MIN
16mm / U-matic
Footsteps Series
Color
Deals with helping sick or injured children understand what is happening to their bodies. Shows that easing fears and anxieties is as important as providing physical care.
Health and Safety; Psychology
Dist - PEREN **Prod** - PEREN

Pre - Operative Admissions 11 MIN
VHS / 16mm
Licensed Practical Nursing Assistant Refresher Series
Color (C)
$75.00 purchase _ #270503
Helps nursing assistants make the transition back to their chosen career after an extended absence. Updates nursing techniques and procedures which have changed substantially in the last decade. Provides a practical demonstration of step - by - step nursing procedures. 'Pre - Operative Admissions' instructs in the techniques of preparing a patient for surgery. Points covered include communication skills, information gathering and pre - operative procedures.
Health and Safety; Science
Dist - ACCESS **Prod** - ACCESS 1989

Pre - operative and post - operative thoracotomy care 47 MIN
VHS / U-matic
Color
LC 81-706298
Emphasizes the importance of good preoperative teaching by the nursing staff. Discusses the care needed during the early postoperative period of a thoracotomy patient.
Health and Safety
Dist - USNAC **Prod** - USVA 1980

Pre - operative experience 22 MIN
U-matic / VHS
Color (PRO C G)
$195.00 purchase _ #C891 - VI - 017
Reduces patient anxiety by familiarizing them with hospital surgical routine. Features a patient as narrator who uses a generous amount of humor to put the viewer at ease while discussing each stage of the surgical procedure. Highlights basic procedures and experiences the day before surgery, the night before surgery, the morning of surgery and in the recovery room. Presented by the Educational Service Dept, the Credit Valley Hospital.
Health and Safety
Dist - HSCIC

Pre - operative instruction 20 MIN
U-matic
Color
Provides general information for the patient having general elective surgery, including management of pain and excercises to improve recovery following surgery.
Health and Safety
Dist - UWISN **Prod** - UWISN

Pre - Operative Interviews 35 MIN
16mm
Color
LC 74-702664
Clarifies for the nursing staff what can be accomplished via the pre - operative visit. Focuses on three patient interviews, identified by operating room nurses as being difficult to manage, the hostile patient, the depressed patient and the patient who denies illness.
Guidance and Counseling; Health and Safety; Sociology
Dist - AMCSUR **Prod** - ACYDGD 1974

Pre - operative problems in regional enteritis 26 MIN
16mm
Color (PRO)
Explains that regional enteritis should be treated medically until complication of obstruction, fistula formation, hemorrhage or recurrent attacks require operation. Points out that recurrence is common and illustrates various late complications.
Health and Safety
Dist - ACY **Prod** - ACYDGD 1961

The Pre - organizing drive 100 MIN
U-matic
How to keep your company union free series
Color (A)
Tells management that employee communications, proper supervisory training and a nine step action plan are needed to keep their company union free.
Business and Economics
Dist - VENCMP **Prod** - VENCMP 1986

Pre - participation physical examination of the athlete
VHS / U-matic
Sports medicine series
Color
Offers a guide to conducting a thorough examination of aspiring athletes before actual participation. Discusses specifics to look for and presents the physical examination as an important tool for the prevention of injury to athletes.
Health and Safety; Physical Education and Recreation
Dist - VTRI **Prod** - VTRI

Pre - Post Test 19 MIN
U-matic / VHS
Reading approach to math series
Color (J H)
Contains a test of 21 questions which is given to students before viewing the series and then again after they have seen the series.
Mathematics
Dist - GPN **Prod** - WNVT 1979

Pre - Primer Sanding of Fill Material 7 MIN
BETA / VHS / 16mm
Color (A PRO)
$53.50 purchase _ #KTI109
Covers the proper leveling and feathering of fill material in relationship to the panel itself.
Industrial and Technical Education
Dist - RMIBHF **Prod** - RMIBHF

Pre - production 5.17 MIN
VHS
On location
(J)
$180.00 series purchase, $50.00 rental, $110.00 self dub
Demonstrates video production skills for small format student productions. Focuses on the importance of careful planning and production coordination. Fifth in an eight part series.
Fine Arts
Dist - GPN **Prod** - NCGE

The Pre - purchase survey no 1 55 MIN
VHS
Pre - purchase survey series
Color (G A)
$39.95 purchase _ #0897
Shows how to perform a pre - purchase survey of a boat. Covers underwater machinery, thruhull fittings, coring systems, deck and cockpit moldings, blisters - delaminations, hull construction, keels - rudders, hull to deck joints, deck hardware, propane lockers, corrosion, stiffening systems, masts - rigging, sails. Part one of a two - part series on boat buying.
Home Economics; Physical Education and Recreation
Dist - SEVVID

The Pre - purchase survey no 2 55 MIN
VHS
Pre - purchase survey series
Color (G A)
$39.95 purchase _ #0898
Shows how to perform a pre - purchase survey of a boat. Covers propulsion machinery, electronics, auxiliary, generators, 110 Volt AC - 12 Volt DC systems, wiring, pumping, tankage, domestic system, accommodations, safety, sea trial, fire fighting, instrumentation, spares. Part two of a two - part series on boat buying.
Home Economics; Physical Education and Recreation
Dist - SEVVID

Pre - purchase survey series
The Pre - purchase survey no 1 55 MIN
The Pre - purchase survey no 2 55 MIN
Dist - SEVVID

The Pre - Raphaelite Revolt 30 MIN
U-matic / VHS / 16mm
Color
LC 73-712016
Traces the movement of the pre - Raphaelite Brotherhood, which protested the outmoded academic conventions of the day and wanted to emulate the naturalism of the Italian Renaissance painters before Raphael. Studies the early works of Ford Madox Brown, John Everett Millais, John Ruskin, Holman Hunt, Arthur Hughs and Dante Gabriel Rossetti.
Fine Arts
Dist - FI **Prod** - BCACGB 1967

Pre - Retirement Planning 25 MIN
VHS / U-matic
Your Money Matters Series
Color
Outlines steps that lead to a leisurely and worry - free retirement. Presented by a Social Security representative and a planning firm.
Business and Economics; Sociology
Dist - FILMID **Prod** - FILMID

Pre - Retirement Planning - it Makes a Difference 15 MIN
16mm / U-matic / VHS
Color (A)
Uses four examples of retirees to illustrate the need to plan ahead for a successful retirement.
Business and Economics; Sociology
Dist - USNAC **Prod** - USSSA

The Pre - Roosevelt era 59 MIN
VHS
History machine series
B&W (H C G)
Documents the first airplane purchased by the US Army in 1909, the American homefront in 1917 - 1918, the Versailles Peace Conference and its consequences in 1919, actions of the United States during the Russian Civil War in 1918 - 1920, Harding and Coolidge in 1921 - 1929, the economic revolution, social and cultural trends of the 1920s, the flight of Charles A Lindbergh in 1927 and a biography of Herbert Hoover, 1874 - 1964. Part of a seven - part series on American history produced by Arthur M Schlesinger, Jr, and a team of historians and film editors.
Biography; History - United States; Industrial and Technical Education
Dist - VIEWTH

The Pre - School 22 MIN
U-matic / VHS / 16mm
Color (H C A)
LC 74-702026
Presents a day's visit to a pre - school, illustrating the positive learning environment and long term benefits that can result from pre - school education.
Education; Psychology; Social Science
Dist - AIMS **Prod** - JARBRI 1973

Pre - school readiness - foundation for learning
U-matic / VHS
Vital link series
Color (A)
Suggests ways parents can prepare children for experiences encountered in school.
Education; Guidance and Counseling; Psychology; Social Science; Sociology
Dist - EDCC **Prod** - EDCC

Pre - speech evaluation and therapy 17 MIN
16mm
B&W (PRO)
Illustrates the techniques utilized by Helen Mueller of Swtizerland for evaluation of lip, tongue, jaw control, sucking, swallowing and chewing and breathing problems in the young child. Demonstrates procedures aimed to overcome deficits. Presents the findings in the abnormal child as compared to those in the normal child.
English Language; Psychology
Dist - UCLA **Prod** - UCLA 1970

Pre - supervisory training series 35 MIN
35mm strip / U-matic / VHS / Slide
Pre - supervisory training series
Color (G)
$265.00, $235.00 purchase
Presents three modules on training employees in various supervisory skills before they actually assume a supervisory position. Includes the titles The Need for Pre - Supervisory Training, Determining Pay - Off Areas, The Training Activity.
Business and Economics; Psychology
Dist - RESEM **Prod** - RESEM

Pre - Supervisory Training Series Module 1
The Need for Pre - Supervisory Training 61 FRS
Dist - RESEM

Pre - Supervisory Training Series Module 2
Determining Pay - Off Areas 12 MIN
Dist - RESEM

Pre - Supervisory Training Series Module 3
The Training Activity 69 FRS
Dist - RESEM

Pre - supervisory training series
Pre - supervisory training series 35 MIN
Dist - RESEM

Pre - test market models - Validation and managerial implications
VHS
Color (C PRO G)
$150.00 purchase _ #83.03
Focuses on the assessor model developed to test and evaluate new consumer products before the expenditure of a test market. Reveals that the predictive value of the model has saved clients $126 million on 450 tested products. Management Decision Systems Inc. Glen L Urban, Gerald M Katz, Thomas E Hatch, Alvin J Silk.
Business and Economics; Computer Science; Sociology
Dist - INMASC

Pre - trip truck inspection 23 MIN
VHS
Color (IND)
$295.00 purchase, $95.00 rental _ #800 - 24
Provides a comprehensive 7 - step inspection routine to incorporate into a driver's daily schedule. Includes leader's guide.
Health and Safety
Dist - ITSC **Prod** - ITSC

Pre - Vasectomy Family Consultation 13 MIN
U-matic / VHS
Urology Series
Color (PRO)
Health and Safety; Science - Natural; Sociology
Dist - MSU **Prod** - MSU

Pre - Verbal Communication 16 MIN
16mm
Under Fives Series
Color (C A)
Shows how dependent an eight - month - old baby is on her mother to interpret her gestures and noises. Demonstrates that they can still communicate even when they can only see each other on a television monitor.
Psychology
Dist - FLMLIB **Prod** - GRATV 1982

Pre - War German Featurettes Series
Becoming an Army
Honor of Work
Three Years of Adolf Hitler
Yesterday and today
Dist - IHF

The Preacher 20 MIN
VHS / U-matic
French Revolution - revolutionary witness series
Color (H C)
$250.00 purchase _ #HP - 5958C
Dramatizes the life of radical priest Jacques Roux from St Nicholas, the poorest parish in Paris, as portrayed by Alan Rickman. Portrays what may have been his last sermon, spoken with a dagger in his belt and his dog at his feet. Reveals that Roux has been charged with revolutionary excess and is to be judged the next day by a tribunal whose authority he does not recognize. Part of a four - part series on the French Revolution written by playwright Peter Barnes.
History - World
Dist - CORF **Prod** - BBCTV 1989

The Preacher 1 MIN
16mm
Color (J)
LC 74-702119
Satirizes the communication gap between the Church and the world and the problems of misguided though well - intentioned communication of any kind.
Civics and Political Systems; Psychology; Religion and Philosophy
Dist - MMA **Prod** - MMA 1972

The Preamble 3 MIN
U-matic / 35mm strip
America Rock Series
Color (I P)
LC 76-730444
Considers the ideas embodied in the preamble to the Constitution and shows how these ideas have been reflected in the development of America.
Civics and Political Systems; History - United States
Dist - GA **Prod** - ABCTV 1976

Precambrian and Paleozoic Eras 24 MIN
VHS
Grand Canyon Chronicles Series
Color
$69.95 purchase _ #9698
Shown and explained are details of the earliest life on earth, the appearance of the first sea animals, plants, and land animals, and the Age of Fishes. Narrated by Orson Welles, the video features a specially commissioned musical score.
History - World; Science - Physical
Dist - AIMS **Prod** - AIMS

Precambrian Shield - the Bones of the Earth 30 MIN
U-matic
Landscapes Series
(J H C A)
Examines the Precambrian Shield of northeastern Alberta which is composed of rocks that are two billion years old. Looks at the stunted pine forests and a variety of isolation loving animals that live there and in the nearby sandy areas.
Science - Natural; Science - Physical
Dist - ACCESS **Prod** - ACCESS 1984

Precast Concrete Bridge 18 MIN
16mm
Color
LC 74-705399
Uses construction scenes and animated drawings to show casting of beams, deck slabs and curb sections, driving of piles and construction of bent caps, placement of precast units and final operations in completing a three - span bridge structure.
Industrial and Technical Education
Dist - USNAC **Prod** - USDTFH 1955

Precautionary Measures in Isolation
U-matic / 35mm strip
Infection Control III Series
Color
Presents the rationale and illustrates four precautionary measures in isolation, namely handwashing, assigning an appropriate room, protective apparel and handling of contaminated items.
Health and Safety
Dist - CONMED **Prod** - CONMED

Precautions Against Fanatics 11 MIN
16mm
B&W (GERMAN (ENGLISH SUBTITLES))
Presents an elaborate on - camera practical joke involving German celebrities and a one - armed, self - appointed protector of racehorses. Directed by Werner Herzog. With English subtitles.
Fine Arts; Foreign Language
Dist - NYFLMS **Prod** - UNKNWN 1969

Precautions in the Resection of the Colon for Carcinoma 29 MIN
16mm
Color (PRO)
Illustrates two precautions in resection of the colon which might minimize the possibility of recurrence. Deals with the possibility of implantation of cancer cells in the suture line and with prevention of venous metastasis incident to manipulation of the tumor during the resection.
Health and Safety; Science
Dist - ACY **Prod** - ACYDGD 1954

Precinct 94 - 142 22 MIN
16mm / U-matic / VHS
Color (T)
Looks at how attitudes, feelings and interpersonal communication can affect education for the handicapped.
Education; Psychology
Dist - CORF **Prod** - CORF

A Precious balance - the Christmas Meadows story 18 MIN
BETA / U-matic / VHS
Color (J H G)
$29.95, $130.00 purchase _ #LSTF25
Chronicles the successful symbiotic relationship between an oil exploration company and environmentalists. Reveals that after a well was drilled in an environmentally sensitive area, part of the land was reclaimed and part was improved into a recreational area. Produced by Panacom, Inc.
Science - Natural; Social Science
Dist - FEDU

Precious Blood 60 MIN
VHS / U-matic
Color
Fine Arts; Literature and Drama
Dist - ABCLR **Prod** - ABCLR

Precious Cargo 15 MIN
16mm
Color
Illustrates and interprets the inter - country adoption program supported by WAIF/ISS.
Sociology
Dist - HF **Prod** - HF

The Precious envelope - the chemistry of the Earth - Pts 17 and 18 60 MIN
VHS / U-matic
World of chemistry series
Color (C)
$45.00, $29.95 purchase
Presents parts 17 and 18 of the 26 - part World of Chemistry series. Examines the chemistry of the earth's atmosphere. Explains theories of chemical evolution, ozone depletion and the greenhouse effect. Investigates the forces which distribute mineral resources from the center to the surface of the Earth. Looks at elements and focuses on silicon which has become a cornerstone of modern high - tech industry. Two thirty - minute programs hosted by Nobel laureate Roald Hoffmann.
Science - Physical; Social Science
Dist - ANNCPB **Prod** - UMD 1990

Precious Metal 4 MIN
16mm
Color (C)
$112.00
Experimental film by David Ehrlich.
Fine Arts
Dist - AFA **Prod** - AFA 1980

Precious Tissue 10 MIN
16mm
Color (PRO)
Depicts the uses of blood components and derivatives in highly technical terms.
Science; Science - Natural
Dist - ARMPHC **Prod** - ARMPHC 1970

Precipitation Equilibria 9 MIN
U-matic
Chemistry Videotape Series
Color
Introduces solubility, precipitation and saturated solution equilibria. Demonstrates common ion effect.
Science; Science - Physical
Dist - UMITV **Prod** - UMITV

Precipitation Hardening 45 MIN
BETA / VHS / U-matic
Color
$300 purchase
Shows heat treatment of nonferrous alloys.
Industrial and Technical Education; Psychology; Science - Physical
Dist - ASM **Prod** - ASM

Precisely So 20 MIN
16mm
B&W (H C A)
Traces the development of modern standards of accuracy from ancient times. Illustrates scientific instruments which measure time to the thousandth part of a second, weigh a dot of a lead pencil on a piece of paper and split a hair - breadth measurement into hundreds of parts.
Mathematics; Science
Dist - GM **Prod** - HANDY 1940

Precision casting for high performance 18 MIN
16mm
Color
Examines the production of jet engine turbine blades from the first to final steps in their manufacture.
Business and Economics; Industrial and Technical Education
Dist - GM **Prod** - GM

Precision Football 28 MIN
16mm
Color; B&W (J)
LC 78-701640
Illustrates most major areas of high school football rules. Emphasizes scrimmage violations, pass interference encroachment, free kicks, false starts and live and dead ball fouls.
Physical Education and Recreation
Dist - NFSHSA **Prod** - NFSHSA 1978

Precision Football 29 MIN
VHS / U-matic
Color
LC 79-707710
Designed to provide an understanding of the rules and officiating procedures used in football by focusing on such topics as pass interference, encroachment and free kicks.
Physical Education and Recreation
Dist - NFSHSA **Prod** - NFSHSA 1979

Precision gage blocks 18 MIN
16mm
Machine shop work - precision measurement No 6 series
B&W
LC FIE51-553
Discusses the various uses of gage blocks in setting inspection gages. Shows how to calculate, clean and assemble gage blocks.
Industrial and Technical Education
Dist - USNAC **Prod** - USOE 1945

Precision measuring instruments - the micrometer caliper - ITP practical project 30 MIN
VHS / U-matic
Aviation technician training program series
Color (IND)
Acquaints students with the most popular precision measuring instument, the micrometer caliper. Shows how the instrument is made and how it is used, especially in conjunction with the telescoping and ball gauge. Includes, also, explanations of use of the inside and depth micrometers plus care and handling of these precision instruments.
Industrial and Technical Education
Dist - AVIMA **Prod** - AVIMA

Precision Measurment Tools 16 MIN
U-matic / VHS
Introduction to Machine Technology, Module 1 Series; Module 1
Color (IND)
Teaches how to read precision measurement tools such as the micrometer, vernier caliper and depth gauge.
Industrial and Technical Education
Dist - LEIKID **Prod** - LEIKID

Precision mechanical measuring series
Presents a series of training videos on the use of various precision mechanical measuring devices.
Advanced technology 16 MIN
Applying measurement skills 14 MIN
Calipers 15 MIN
Introduction to Measurements 22 MIN
Micrometers 18 MIN
Dist - TAT **Prod** - TAT

Precision of Articulation in Hearing Children 17 MIN
16mm
Color
LC 74-705400
Interprets a sound spectrogram in order to analyze the precision of a child's speech represented as a function of age.
English Language; Psychology
Dist - USNAC **Prod** - USHHS

Precision wood machining - operations on a spindle shaper series
Rabbeting and shaping an edge on straight stock 18 MIN
Dist - USNAC

Precision Wood Machining - Operations on the Jointer Series no 4
Jointing an Edge for Gluing - Installing Knives 21 MIN
Dist - USNAC

Precision wood machining - operations on the spindle shaper - a series
Precision wood machining series
B&W
Cutting Grooves With Circular Saw Blades; Rabbeting And Shaping An Edge On Straight Stock; Shaping After Template And Shaping Curved Edges.
Industrial and Technical Education
Dist - USNAC **Prod** - USOE 1945

Precision wood machining, operations on the variety saw series
Cutting cove molding and a corebox 19 MIN
Dist - USNAC

Precision Wood Machining Series Fundamentals of Pattern Making, no 1
Making a One - Piece Flat Pattern 22 MIN
Dist - USNAC

Precision Wood Machining Series Fundamentals of Patternmaking, no 8
Making a Matchboard Pattern 21 MIN
Dist - USNAC

Precision wood machining series operations on the band saw, no 2
Sawing a reverse curve and a bevel reverse curve 18 MIN
Dist - USNAC

Precision Wood Machining Series Operations on the Cutter Grinder, no 2
Sharpening a Plain Helical Milling Cutter 16 MIN
Dist - USNAC

Precision wood machining series operations on the jointer series
Beveling, stop chamfering and tapering square stock 20 MIN
Dist - USNAC

Precision wood machining series - operations on the jointer
Face planing uneven surfaces 13 MIN
Dist - USNAC

Precision Wood Machining Series Operations on the Spindle Shaper, no 2
Shaping After Template and Shaping Curved Edges 17 MIN
Dist - USNAC

Precision wood machining series operations on the variety saw, series
Beveling, mitering, rabbeting and dadoing 19 MIN
Dist - USNAC

Precision Wood Machining Series Operations on the Wood Lathe
Face Turning a Collar 16 MIN
Turning a Cylinder between Centers 17 MIN
Turning a Cylinder between Centers and Turning Work on a Face Plate 30 MIN
Turning Work in a Chuck and Face Turning a Collar 30 MIN
Turning Work on a Face Plate 15 MIN
Dist - USNAC

Precision Wood Machining Series Problems in Patternmaking
Making a Pattern for a Machine Molded Steel Globe and Angle Valve 14 MIN
Making a Pattern Requiring Segmental Construction 13 MIN
Redesigning a Pattern for Production Purposes 11 MIN
Dist - USNAC

Precision Wood Machining Series
Cutting grooves with circular saw blades 22 MIN
Cutting tenons and segments 15 MIN
Jointing Edges and Ends 90 Degrees to Face 17 MIN
Precision wood machining - operations on the spindle shaper - a series
Ripping and crosscutting 19 MIN
Sawing with Jig and Changing Band 20 MIN
Dist - USNAC

Preconception care and diagnosis of pregnancy 29 MIN
16mm
Nine to get ready - No 1 series
B&W (C A)
LC 73-704217
Tells about annual physical examinations, cancer detection by cytology, prevention of fetal loss and mental retardation by optimal health at time of conception, physiologic changes of early pregnancy and older biologic and newer imminologic pregnancy tests.
Health and Safety
Dist - UNEBR **Prod** - KUONTV 1965

Precursors - Cezanne, Gauguin, Van Gogh 26 MIN
U-matic / VHS / 16mm
Color (H C)
LC 79-712674
Portrays the influence of impressionism on artists Cezanne, Gauguin and Van Gogh, as exemplified in Cezanne's preoccupation with construction by volume, Gauguin's use of descriptive backgrounds and bright color, and Van Gogh's attempt to evoke emotion rather than display craftsmanship.
Fine Arts
Dist - IFB **Prod** - LFLMDC 1971
IFB

Predation 20 MIN
U-matic / VHS
Color
Surveys the behavioral and structural adaptations shown by predators in pursuit of prey. Covers such adaptations as hunting in groups and construction of traps, and structural adaptations such as keen senses, sharp breaks, talons, and the ejection of poisons. A video version of 35mm filmstrip program with live open and close.
Science - Natural
Dist - CBSC **Prod** - REXERC

The Predator 50 MIN
VHS
Horizon series
Color; PAL (H C A)
PdS99 purchase
Describes the Partula, a Polynesian tree snail that is the most endangered species on Earth. Discusses the Partula's predators, which are the African Land Snail and the Euglandina. Traces the international relief efforts that are focused on saving the Partula. Part of the Horizon series.
Science - Natural
Dist - BBCENE

The Predators 50 MIN
16mm 26 MIN
Color
LC 78-700300
A shortened version of The Predators. Depicts predators as an important part of a balanced ecosystem. Emphasizes that they are beautiful and fascinating and deserve protection as much as any other animal. Narrated by Robert Redford.
Science - Natural
Dist - STOUFP **Prod** - STOUFP 1977

Predators 27 MIN
U-matic / VHS / BETA
Stationary ark series
Color; PAL (G H C)
PdS50, PdS58 purchase
Discusses the recreation of humankind, nature and wildlife in part of a 12 - part series. Features Gerald Durrell. Filmed on location in Jersey, England.
Science - Natural
Dist - EDPAT

The Predators 60 MIN
U-matic / 16mm / VHS
Last Frontier Series
Color; Mono (G)
MV $225.00 _ MP $550.00
Describes the many species of predators that roam the coral reefs. Shows some unique encounters with the moray eel.
Science - Natural
Dist - CTV **Prod** - MAKOF 1985

The Predators 58 MIN
16mm / U-matic / VHS
Crossroads of Civilization Series
Color (A)
Discusses the discovery of oil in the Middle East and the raids by the West on the resources of the East. Examines the possibility of overcoming the gulf between East and West, and Persia's survival of the ambitions of British and Russian imperialism.
Business and Economics; History - World; Social Science
Dist - CNEMAG **Prod** - CNEMAG 1978

Predators and Prey 9 MIN
U-matic / VHS / 16mm
Life Science for Elementary Series
Color (P I) (SPANISH)
LC 76-700812
Examines the predator and prey relationships among a variety of animals, including a fox, roadrunner, pocket gopher and striped skunk.
Science - Natural
Dist - AIMS **Prod** - PEDF 1976

Predators and Scavengers 25 MIN
U-matic / VHS / 16mm
Untamed World Series
Color; Mono (J H C A)
$400.00 film, $250.00 video, $50.00 rental
Shows many of the wild kingdom's creatures whose food source depends on the killing or devouring of other living creatures.
Science - Natural
Dist - CTV **Prod** - CTV 1968

Predators of North America 12 MIN
16mm / U-matic / VHS
Color (I J)
Looks at North American animals that must kill to survive. Reveals some of the adaptations that aid predators in obtaining prey and the tremendous diversity among predators.
Science - Natural
Dist - NGS **Prod** - NGS 1981

Predators of the Desert 22 MIN
U-matic / VHS / 16mm
Living Desert Series
Color (I J H)
LC 74-703788
Edited from the 1953 motion picture The Living Desert. Shows confrontations between predator and prey in a struggle for survival in the desert.
Science - Natural
Dist - CORF **Prod** - DISNEY 1974

Predatory Behavior of Snakes 16 MIN
U-matic / VHS / 16mm
Aspects of Animal Behavior Series
Color (H C A)
Examines the roles of vision, olfactory and heat senses for the location of prey by snakes. Discusses the adaptations of the skulls of pythons and pit vipers for capturing and swallowing prey. Explores the snakes' procedures of seizing, striking, invenomating and constricting prey.
Science - Natural
Dist - UCEMC **Prod** - UCLA 1978

Predatory Behavior of the Grasshopper Mouse 10 MIN
U-matic / VHS / 16mm
Aspects of Animal Behavior Series
Color (H C A)
LC 75-702964
Uses slow - motion photography to examine how the grasshopper mouse attacks its prey. Evaluates the role of experience in its handling of beetles, crickets and scorpions.
Science - Natural
Dist - UCEMC **Prod** - UCLA 1974

A Predictable Disaster 32 MIN
U-matic / VHS / 16mm
Nova Series
Color (H C A)
LC 78-700586
Focuses on the development of techniques to predict earthquakes.
History - World; Science; Science - Physical
Dist - TIMLIF **Prod** - WGBHTV 1976

Predicting at Random 43 MIN
16mm
MAA Individual Lecturers Series
Color (H C T)
LC FIA66-1271
Professor David Blackwell solves a problem in which a source sequentially generates 0's or 1's and one must predict against it, with a knowledge of success or failure after each prediction.
Mathematics
Dist - MLA **Prod** - MAA 1966

Predicting electric circuits 15 MIN
U-matic / VHS
Hands on - Grade 4 - cars, cartoons, etc - Unit 4 series'Inferring/Predicting; Unit 4 - Inferring, predicting
Color (I)
Gives experience in predicting electric circuits.
Science
Dist - AITECH **Prod** - WHROTV 1975

Predicting here, there, and everywhere 15 MIN
VHS / U-matic
Hands on - Grade 4 - cars, cartoons, etc - Unit 4 - 'inferring and predicting series; Unit 4 - Inferring and predicting
Color (I)
Gives experience in predicting future events.
Science
Dist - AITECH **Prod** - WHROTV 1975

Predicting Oscillations
16mm
B&W
Looks at differential equations that describe free and forced oscillations of an undamped mass spring system.
Mathematics
Dist - OPENU **Prod** - OPENU

Predicting plant growth 15 MIN
VHS / U-matic
Hands on - Grade 3, Unit 4 - inferring, predicting series; Unit 4 - Inferring, predicting
Color (P)
Science; Science - Natural
Dist - AITECH **Prod** - VAOG 1975

Predicting Reliability during Development Test 30 MIN
U-matic / VHS
Reliability Engineering Series
Color (IND)
Describes use of Duane plots to predict reliability at customer release from failure data obtained during development test.
Industrial and Technical Education
Dist - COLOSU **Prod** - COLOSU

Predicting shadow lengths 15 MIN
U-matic / VHS
Hands on - Grade 3, Unit 4 - inferring, predicting series; Unit 4 - Inferring, predicting
Color (P)
Science; Science - Physical
Dist - AITECH **Prod** - VAOG 1975

Predicting the Weather 30 MIN
U-matic / VHS
Earth, Sea and Sky Series
Color (C)
Explains how television weathermen collect data and organize their weather reports. Discusses the ways the weather affects different people and businesses.
Science - Physical
Dist - DALCCD **Prod** - DALCCD

Predicting through Sampling 10 MIN
16mm / U-matic / VHS
Color (I J H)
LC 71-706598
Develops the basic principles of good sampling through a practical problem.
Psychology
Dist - PHENIX **Prod** - BOUNDY 1969

Predicting tracks 14 MIN
U-matic / VHS
Hands on - Grade 4, Unit 4 - cars, cartoons, etc - inferring and'predicting series; Unit 4 - Inferring, predicting
Color (I)
Gives experience in predicting tracks.
Science
Dist - AITECH **Prod** - WHROTV 1975

Predicting weather 15 MIN
U-matic / VHS
Hands on - Grade 3, Unit 4 - inferring, predicting series; Unit 4 - Inferring, predicting
Color (P)
Science; Science - Physical
Dist - AITECH **Prod** - VAOG 1975

Prediction 18 MIN
16mm
Search for Solutions Series
Color (J)
LC 79-701462
Explains how prediction in scientific investigation helps to foresee and manipulate consequences in order to get a headstart on a future problem. Narrated by Stacy Keach.
Science
Dist - KAROL **Prod** - PLYBCK 1979

Prediction - a Tool for Safe and Reliable Operation
16mm / U-matic
Color (A)
Outlines a three - phase ongoing program of safe and reliable operation of equipment, describes the different detection instruments and delves into the cooperation needed between workers and the specialists who perform the tests.
Health and Safety
Dist - BNA **Prod** - BNA 1983

Prediction Initiative - Cerebral Cortex and its Areas 18 MIN
U-matic / VHS / 16mm
Anatomical Basis of Brain Function Series
Color (PRO)
Science - Natural
Dist - TEF **Prod** - AVCORP

Prediction intervals
VHS
Probability and statistics series
Color (H C)
$125.00 purchase _ #8048
Provides resource material about prediction intervals for help in the study of probability and statistics. Presents a 60 - video series, each part 25 to 30 minutes long, that explains and reinforces concepts using definitions, theorems, examples and step - by - step solutions to tutor the student. Videos are also available in a set.
Mathematics
Dist - LANDMK

Prediction of Dangerousness 30 MIN
U-matic / VHS
Color
Presents a two - part program on the prediction of dangerousness in a violent patient. Takes a look at the current state of the art of predicting violence in the future in the first part. Identifies dangerous patient in the second part.
Health and Safety; Psychology
Dist - HEMUL **Prod** - HEMUL

Prediction of Wound Disruption by the Use of the Healing Ridge 16 MIN
16mm
Color (PRO)
Explains that a reliable harbinger of wound disruption would be of considerable clinical value since this complication usually presents as a precipitous calamity. Points out that the state of the indurated ridge, palpable beneath healing laparotomy wounds, may be depended upon to accurately forbode the probability or improbability of wound disruption.
Health and Safety; Science
Dist - ACY **Prod** - ACYDGD 1962

Predictions and reflections 15 MIN
U-matic / VHS
Math mission 2 series
Color (P)
LC 82-706355
Presents a space robot and his puppet assistant as they explore the concept of prediction through examples of geometric properties found in designs on a balloon and a piece of paper. Shows how they decide which designs are symmetrical.
Mathematics
Dist - GPN **Prod** - WCVETV 1980

A Predominantly Black College 13 MIN
16mm
College Selection Film Series
Color (J)
LC 79-713044
Presents black students who talk about how their education helps them to succeed in a white world, and discuss how they can serve the black community. Filmed at Hampton Institute.
Education; History - United States; Psychology; Sociology
Dist - VISEDC **Prod** - VISEDC 1971

Preeclampsia - reducing the risk 11 MIN
VHS
Color (PRO G) (SPANISH)
$200.00 purchase _ #OB - 74
Focuses on a teenager and a woman over 30 to explain how high blood pressure developed during pregnancy can endanger the health of mother and child. Reviews early detection, bed rest and continuous monitoring. Informs patients about possible hospitalization when home management is ineffective.
Health and Safety
Dist - MIFE **Prod** - MIFE

Preemie development - the first two years of life
VHS
Color (PRO)
#IF - 999
Presents a free - loan program which trains medical professionals. Contact distributor for details.
Health and Safety; Social Science
Dist - WYAYLA **Prod** - WYAYLA

Preemies - the Price Tag 16 MIN
U-matic / VHS
Color
Probes the delicate, difficult ethical issues surrounding saving the prematurely born. Brings up crucial issues of who decides to begin treatment and discontinue treatment.
Health and Safety; Psychology
Dist - AJN **Prod** - CANBC

Preemies - the untold tragedy 53 MIN
VHS
Color (G)
$149.00 purchase, $75.00 rental _ #UW4592
Follows the story of babies who survived premature birth. Shows that many of the medicines and techniques used in neonatal wards are still classified as experimental. Reveals that many survivors suffer lifelong health problems and grow up with severely disabling conditions.
Health and Safety
Dist - FOTH

Prefaces - Mutiny - Covert action 30 MIN
VHS
Is this what you were born for series
Color & B&W (G)
$75.00 purchase
Features three films, produced between 1981 - 1984, from the ongoing series Is This What You Were Born For. Investigates aggressions of the twentieth century. See separate titles for description and availability for rental in 16mm format.
Fine Arts; Sociology
Dist - CANCIN **Prod** - CHILDA

Prefaces - Part 1 10 MIN
VHS
Is this what you were born for series
Color (G)
$35.00 rental
Plays with formalist elements in a wide range of images resulting in an abstract work where the rapid - fire cross cutting of images is extended to the fragmented sound track. Weaves a collage of 'female' sounds with snippets from vocal music, conversations, poetry readings.
Fine Arts
Dist - CANCIN **Prod** - CHILDA 1981

Preference for reference 20 MIN
U-matic / VHS
Tomes and talismans series
(I J)
$145.00 purchase, $27.00 rental, $90.00 self dub
Uses a science fantasy adventure to define, illustrate and review basic library research concepts. Designed for sixth, seventh and eighth graders. Discusses special subject reference sources. Eighth in a 13 part series.
Education
Dist - GPN **Prod** - MISETV

Preferential Treatment for High Occupancy Vehicle 21 MIN
16mm
Color
LC 74-706182
Shows systematic ways to make more efficient use of urban highways, including special lanes for buses and carpools, curb lanes on arterial streets and parking facilities outside congested areas for commuters. Illustrates a design of interchanges and approaches which allows limited access to reversible lanes.
Science - Natural; Social Science; Sociology
Dist - USNAC **Prod** - USDTFH 1973

Preferred Stock 25 MIN
16mm
Color
Depicts the growth of stock car racing from its beginnings in cow pasture dirt tracks to the Silver Anniversary 500 at Daytona International Speedway.
Physical Education and Recreation
Dist - MTP **Prod** - SEARS

Prefixes and suffixes 15 MIN
U-matic / Kit / VHS
Space station readstar series
(P)
$130 purchase, $25 rental, $75 self dub
Teaches phonics in a series designed to supplement second grade reading programs. Explains the use of prefixes and suffixes. Nineteenth in a 25 part series.
English Language
Dist - GPN

Prefixes and Suffixes, Pt 1 15 MIN
VHS
Planet Pylon Series
Color (I)
LC 90712897
Uses character Commmander Wordstalker from the Space Station Readstar to develop language arts skills. Studies prefixes and suffixes. Includes a worksheet that students can finish with the help of series characters. Intended for grade level three.
Education; English Language
Dist - GPN

Prefixes and suffixes - Pt 2 15 MIN
VHS
Planet Pylon Series
Color (I)
LC 90712897
Uses character Commander Wordstalker from Space Station Readstar to develop language arts skills. Continues the study of prefixes and suffixes. Includes a worksheet intended to be used by student with help from series characters. Aimed at third grade level.
Education; English Language
Dist - GPN

Prefixes / Suffixes 23 MIN
VHS / BETA
Color
Teaches basic vocabulary skills. Uses stories and visuals.
English Language
Dist - PHENIX **Prod** - PHENIX

Preflight inspection series
Engine 13 MIN
Dist - USNAC

Prefrontal Lobotomy in Chronic Schizophrenia 21 MIN
16mm
Color; B&W (PRO)
Illustrates improvement that may be obtained by prefrontal lobotomy in chronic schizophrenia. Presents our cases and shows behavior before and after lobotomy. The film does not show operation itself. Showings restricted.
Psychology
Dist - PSUPCR **Prod** - PSUPCR 1943

Prefrontal lobotomy in the treatment of mental disorders - psychosurgery 13 MIN
16mm
B&W (PRO)
Shows the locations of incisions and structures encountered in a prefrontal lobotomy on skull and brain specimens. The operation is shown in full detail. Showings restricted.
Psychology
Dist - PSUPCR **Prod** - PSUPCR 1942

Pregnancies and STDs 16 MIN
VHS
Price tag of sex series
Color (H J T)
$89.95 purchase _ #UL901V; $89.95 purchase _ #10377VG
Features Pam Stenzel, a speaker with whom teens relate. Stresses the advantages of sexual abstinence and promotes positive interaction and discussion. Deals with pregnancy issues; teen parents - growing up fast; what if guys had babies; and straight talk between guys and girls.
Health and Safety; Sociology
Dist - CAMV
UNL

Pregnancy 30 MIN
VHS
At time of diagnosis series
Color (G)
$19.95 purchase _ #1 - 5757 - 7023 - 7NK
Provides pregnant patients and their families with thorough, comprehensive and understandable information. Examines what is going on in the body. Explains the type of medical professionals a patient may encounter and how pregnancy is monitored. Explores care options, including medication and lifestyle changes. Looks at practical issues surrounding pregnancy and answers the most common questions. Part of an ongoing series to provide the in - depth medical information patients and their families need to know.
Health and Safety
Dist - TILIED **Prod** - TILIED 1996

Pregnancy 26 MIN
BETA / VHS / U-matic
Human development - conception to neonate series
Color (C PRO)
$280.00 purchase _ #618.1
Follows a couple through their pregnancy from conception until birth. Describes the emotional and psychological reactions of the couple and the physical changes that occur in both the mother and the fetus. Discusses the developmental tasks that confront the couple as they await the birth of their first child. Part of a three - part series on human development from conception to birth.
Health and Safety; Science - Natural
Dist - CONMED **Prod** - CONMED

Pregnancy 30 MIN
VHS / U-matic
Consumer survival series; Health
Color
Presents tips on maintaining health during pregnancy.
Health and Safety; Home Economics
Dist - MDCPB **Prod** - MDCPB

Pregnancy
VHS / U-matic
Parenthood - Bringing New Life into the World Series
Color
Explains the three trimesters of pregnancy and the changes in both mother and fetus. Expectant parents relate their anxieties and emotional changes, and feelings of expectancy and worry in the later stages.
Health and Safety; Home Economics; Science - Natural
Dist - GA **Prod** - GA

Pregnancy - 1st trimester 24 MIN
VHS
Baby video library series
Color (G)
$29.95 purchase _ #MMI001V-K
Uses scenarios to show prospective parents what to expect with the birth process. Explains the advantages of careful prenatal care. Part of a 12-part series on giving birth and a child's first 18 months.
Health and Safety; Sociology
Dist - CAMV

Pregnancy - 2nd trimester 24 MIN
VHS
Baby video library series
Color (G)
$29.95 purchase _ #MMI002V-K
Uses scenarios to show prospective parents what to expect with the birth process. Explains the advantages of careful prenatal care. Part of a 12-part series on giving birth and a child's first 18 months.
Health and Safety; Sociology
Dist - CAMV

Pregnancy - 38 weeks and labor 24 MIN
VHS
Baby video library series
Color (G)
$29.95 purchase _ #MMI004V-K
Uses scenarios to show prospective parents what to expect with the birth process. Explains the advantages of careful prenatal care and covers labor and childbirth. Part of a 12-part series on giving birth and a child's first 18 months.
Health and Safety; Sociology
Dist - CAMV

Pregnancy - 3rd trimester 24 MIN
VHS
Baby video library series
Color (G)
$29.95 purchase _ #MMI003V-K
Uses scenarios to show prospective parents what to expect with the birth process. Explains the advantages of careful prenatal care. Part of a 12-part series on giving birth and a child's first 18 months.
Health and Safety; Sociology
Dist - CAMV

Pregnancy - a Time of Change 16 MIN
U-matic
Color (C H)
Covers health topics important to pregnant women.
Health and Safety
Dist - CEPRO **Prod** - CEPRO

Pregnancy - a Time of Change 16 MIN
VHS
Color (C A)
Designed to be shown to pregnant woman and expectant couples. Discusses mood changes, sexual activity, smoking, use of alcohol and medications.
Health and Safety
Dist - CEPRO **Prod** - CEPRO 1989

Pregnancy After 35 19 MIN
VHS / 16mm
Color (G)
$149.00, $249.00, purchase _ #AD - 1989
Looks at some of the risks of pregnancy after 35, including diabetes, hypertension, premature delivery, and Down's Syndrome. Follows three women over 35 through their pregnancies and explores the medical technology now being now being used to minimise those risks.
Health and Safety; Science - Natural
Dist - FOTH **Prod** - FOTH 1990

Pregnancy After 35 14 MIN
16mm / U-matic / VHS
Color (A)
Discusses concerns and misconceptions facing women past 35 who decide to have children. Provides information about prenatal care, amniocentesis, relative risks to mother and child and personal adjustment after birth.
Health and Safety
Dist - PRORE **Prod** - PRORE

Pregnancy After 35 29 MIN
U-matic
Woman Series
Color
Takes a look at the facts, myths and misunderstandings about the pregnancies of women over 35.
Health and Safety
Dist - PBS **Prod** - WNEDTV

Pregnancy after thirty - five 30 MIN
U-matic / VHS
Here's to your health series
Color (C T)
Examines the positive and negative aspects of pregnancy after thirty - five. Presents benefits as well as risks. Explains social, environmental and physical aspects of a pregnancy later in the female cycle.'
Health and Safety; Science - Natural
Dist - DALCCD **Prod** - DALCCD

Pregnancy and childbirth 30 MIN
U-matic / VHS
Family portrait - a study of contemporary lifestyles series; Lesson 25
Color (C A)
Describes the functions of the female body during pregnancy and the stages of fetal development. Stresses that the mother's diet, health, age and emotional condition are important factors in childbirth.
Science - Natural
Dist - CDTEL **Prod** - SCCON

Pregnancy and childbirth 20 MIN
U-matic / Kit / VHS
Growing up
(J)
Discusses pregnancy and childbirth, stressing prenatal care and nutrition. The effects of drug, alcohol and tobacco use. Fifth in a six part series.
Health and Safety; Science - Natural; Sociology
Dist - GPN

Pregnancy and Childbirth 1 MIN
16mm 60 MIN
Color
LC 77-702616
Discusses pregnancy and childbirth.
Health and Safety; Science - Natural; Sociology
Dist - CRAF **Prod** - DALHSU 1976

Pregnancy and Childbirth Series

Before Pregnancy	9 MIN
Labor and Delivery	19 MIN
Special Cases	13 MIN

Dist - IFB

Pregnancy and nutrition 12 MIN
VHS
Parents - to - be series
Color (J H C)
$150.00 purchase _ #CG - 921 - VS
Discusses the importance of nutrition during pregnancy. Part of a six - part series answering many of the questions and concerns of parents - to - be and new parents regarding the safety and care of their children - before and after birth.
Health and Safety
Dist - HRMC **Prod** - HRMC

Pregnancy and nutrition 12 MIN
VHS
Color (PRO G) (SPANISH)
$250.00 purchase _ #OB - 77
Explains how pregnancy changes nutritional needs and offers practical advice on how to meet these new dietary goals. Discusses the four food groups and gives examples of healthful meals and snacks. Teaches patients the importance of adequate fluid intake and the rate and amount of weight gain they should expect. Lists foods to be avoided including 'junk food', caffeine and sugar substitutes. Includes warnings against the use of alcohol, cigarettes and drugs. Provides tips on coping with discomforts such as nausea and constipation.
Health and Safety
Dist - MIFE **Prod** - MIFE

Pregnancy and substance abuse 28 MIN
VHS
Color (J H G)
$149.00 purchase, $75.00 rental _ #UW2882
Follows several couples through pregnancy and prenatal care. Features former United States Surgeon General C Everett Koop talking about the risks of smoking, and Michael Dorris, author of The Broken Cord, discussing raising an adopted son with fetal alcohol syndrome. Shows a media campaign in Vermont that reaches out to the poor and uninsured to persuade them to get the necessary prenatal care to prevent birth defects and cope with problem pregnancies.
Health and Safety
Dist - FOTH

Pregnancy and the Family 20 MIN
U-matic / 35mm strip
Color (PRO)
LC 81-730246;
Discusses changes in the role of the maternity nurse. Explains the increasing emphasis now placed on nursing care to meet the needs of the pregnant woman. Describes the many variations in the form and structure of the family.
Health and Safety; Psychology; Sociology
Dist - MEDCOM **Prod** - MEDCOM

Pregnancy and the Newborn Child 72 MIN
VHS / BETA
Color
Demonstrates pregnancy exercises and care of a newborn baby. Deals with choosing a doctor, labor and birthing.
Health and Safety; Home Economics
Dist - VIPRO **Prod** - VIPRO

Pregnancy and the pre - natal period
VHS
Childbirth - from inside out series
Color (H A T)
Presents comprehensive, medically sound information that deals simply and honestly with the many aspects of childbirth. Answers sensitive questions of parents-to-be, enables them to formulate a list of concerns to discuss with their physician and promotes a healthier, safer pregnancy. A six-phase program takes the viewer from the planning stages to the actual delivery room procedures. Part of a two-part series which includes two videos, interactive pregnancy test, program guide and a checklist for each phase. aspects of childbirth. Graphic depictions of the birthing process may not be suitable for children.
Health and Safety; Science - Natural; Sociology
Dist - AAVIM **Prod** - AAVIM 1992
CAMV

Pregnancy and work 14 MIN
VHS
Color (PRO G)
$100.00 purchase _ #OB - 67
Reviews many concerns women have about working while pregnant. Follows three typical women at various levels of activity - sedentary, standing or walking and real physical exertion. Women discuss how they cope with the minor discomforts on the job. Mentions the Pregnancy Discrimination Act and environmental hazards in the work place.
Health and Safety
Dist - MIFE **Prod** - MIFE

Pregnancy, birth, and first weeks of life 45 MIN
VHS
Touchpoints series
Color (G)
$34.95 purchase _ #COV201V-K
Offers advice from Dr T Berry Brazelton about managing touchpoints, predictable times in the first years of life when bursts of rapid growth and learning occur. Recommends videos for new parents, so they can anticipate and recognize the touchpoints. Part one of a three-part series.
Psychology; Sociology
Dist - CAMV

Pregnancy - Caring for Your Unborn Baby 20 MIN
16mm / U-matic / VHS
Color (H C G T A)
$50 rental _ #9788
Spotlights the needs of the gestating child. Encourages prospective parents to properly care for their unborn child.
Guidance and Counseling; Health and Safety
Dist - AIMS **Prod** - AIMS 1984

Pregnancy Exercise Program 50 MIN
VHS
(H C A)
$49.95 purchase _ #FF222V
Explains exercises to tone up the abdomen during pregnancy.
Health and Safety
Dist - CAMV **Prod** - CAMV

Pregnancy - mom and the unborn baby 70 MIN
VHS
Color (G)
$39.95 purchase _ #MMI100V
Provides thorough and detailed coverage of the changes a woman experiences during each trimester of her pregnancy. Shows four different women at different stages of their pregnancy with their personal doctors. Alleviates fears and misconceptions about pregnancy and physical exams, especially for first time mothers.
Health and Safety; Sociology
Dist - CAMV

Pregnancy - nine special months 35 MIN
VHS
Women's health series
Color (G)
$49.00 purchase _ #WHV5
Offers the most - up - to - date medical information on pregnancy, reviewed and approved by a national panel of health care professionals. Features medical correspondent Dr Holly Atkinson of NBC News Today. Part of an eight - part series.
Health and Safety; Sociology
Dist - GPERFO **Prod** - AMEDCO

Pregnancy Occurs 29 MIN
VHS / U-matic
Tomorrow's Families Series
Color (H C A)
LC 80-706999
Describes why becoming a parent is an emotional and physiological event that begins with conception.
Health and Safety; Sociology
Dist - AITECH **Prod** - MDDE 1980

Pregnancy on the Rocks 25 MIN
U-matic / VHS
Color (J A)
LC 84-707293
Focuses on birth defects caused by liquor intake of pregnant women. Explains that even moderate intake can precipitate defects.
Health and Safety; Psychology; Sociology
Dist - SUTHRB **Prod** - SUTHRB

Pregnancy on the Rocks - the Fetal Alcohol Syndrome 26 MIN
16mm / VHS
Color (G)
$425.00 purchase, $70.00 rental _ #4300, 4302, 0510J, 0531J
Educates on the Fetal Alcohol Syndrome - FAS. Interviews families worldwide and examines children with the syndrome.
Guidance and Counseling; Health and Safety; Psychology; Sociology
Dist - HAZELB **Prod** - GLAWSP

Pregnancy over 35 13 MIN
VHS
Color (PRO G) (SPANISH)
$150.00 purchase _ #OB - 63
Examines specific health problems of pregnancy over age 35 to the mother - increased risk of anemia, high blood pressure, preclampsia, eclampsia - and to the fetus - risks of birth defects or inherited diseases. Reviews specific tests and procedures - ultrasound, amniocentesis and fetal monitoring - used to reassure the new gravida about the health of her baby.
Health and Safety
Dist - MIFE **Prod** - MIFE

Pregnancy prevention and sex hygiene series
Contraception - alternatives for today 19 MIN
VD - it is Your Problem 14 MIN
Dist - USNAC

Pregnancy Prevention - Options 17 MIN
U-matic / VHS / 16mm
Color (J H)
LC 81-700729
Interviews typical teenagers to reveal common misconceptions about birth control. Describes the various birth control techniques and emphasizes the importance of responsibility.
Health and Safety; Sociology
Dist - AIMS **Prod** - CAHILL 1980

Pregnant and fit 60 MIN
VHS
Color (G)
$29.95 purchase _ #KAR500
Shows comfortable and energizing exercises for pregnant women. Uses stretching exercises and low impact aerobics. Follows the American College of Obstetricians and Gynecologists guidelines.
Physical Education and Recreation; Sociology
Dist - CADESF **Prod** - CADESF

Pregnant but Equal 24 MIN
16mm / U-matic / VHS
Color
Interviews doctors, lawyers, workers and union officials who discuss the problems of enforcing the Pregnancy Discrimination Act which makes it illegal for employers to discriminate against pregnant workers in hiring, firing, seniority or benefits.
Business and Economics; Sociology
Dist - ICARUS **Prod** - POMRJ 1983

Pregnant but equal - the fight for maternity benefit 24 MIN
16mm
Color (G IND)
$5.00 rental
Records the history of the fight to pass the 1978 Pregnancy Discrimination Act. Focuses on the organizing effort of a group of factory workers to improve conditions for pregnant women at their plant. Reveals that although the law is in force, many companies fail to comply with the law and women frequently are not aware of their rights.
Business and Economics; Social Science; Sociology
Dist - AFLCIO **Prod** - POMRJ 1981

Pregnant Teens - Taking Care 22 MIN
U-matic / VHS / 16mm
Color (J H C)
$435 purchase - 16 mm, $325 purchase - video
Provides complete prenatal care information for pregnant teenagers. Explains the need for early medical care, the hazards of alcohol, drugs, and cigarettes, and the emotional aspects of preparation for parenthood. Directed by Ed Schuman.
Health and Safety; Sociology
Dist - CF

Pregnant Teens - Taking Care 22 MIN
U-matic / VHS / 16mm
Color (H)
Offers complete prenatal care information for pregnant teenagers. Covers such topics as nutrition, fetal development and the effects of drug and alcohol use. Emphasizes regular medical attention during pregnancy.
Health and Safety
Dist - PEREN **Prod** - PEREN 1983

Pregnant with dreams - 4th feminist encuentro - prenados de suenos 48 MIN
U-matic / VHS
Color (G)
$225.00 purchase, $60.00 rental
Documents the 4th Encuentro Feministo Latinoamericano y del Caribe which brought together 1200 Latin American women for a week in Mexico in 1987. Reveals that daily workshops brought forth resolutions on issues such as church and state, the labor movement, male violence and political repression. Less formal gatherings in the evening confronted profound divisions between the mainstream women's movement and those in the radical feminist struggle.
Business and Economics; History - World; Sociology
Dist - WMEN

The Pregnant woman 28 MIN
VHS
Human body - reproduction - series
Color (J H G)
$89.95 purchase _ #UW4185
Shows the interrelated causes and effects of hormonal changes. Follows the course of a pregnancy from the moment of conception to the birth. Discusses lifestyle factors a woman should take into consideration during her pregnancy. Part of a 39 - part series featuring computer animation, medical photography, electron micrography, full - color drawings and diagrams and three - dimensional working models to cover the workings of the human body from head to toe and inside out.
Health and Safety; Science - Natural; Sociology
Dist - FOTH

Preheating Prior to Hot Working 55 MIN
BETA / VHS / U-matic
Color
$400 purchase
Shows static, multistage, and in line heating.
Industrial and Technical Education; Science
Dist - ASM **Prod** - ASM

Prehistoric Animals of the Tar Pits 14 MIN
U-matic / VHS / 16mm
Color (I J H) (FRENCH)
Introduces the tar pits at Rancho La Brea and the skeletons of some of the animals taken from them. Illustrates the methods used by paleontologists in identifying and assembling fossil materials.
Geography - United States; Science; Science - Natural; Science - Physical
Dist - PHENIX **Prod** - FA 1957

Prehistoric animals, reptiles, and amphibians - Volume 12 30 MIN
VHS
Tell me why series
Color (K P I)
$19.95 purchase
Presents Volume 12 of the 'Tell Me Why' video encyclopedia series. Teaches children the facts about prehistoric animals, reptiles, and amphibians.
Science - Physical
Dist - PBS **Prod** - WNETTV

Prehistoric farmers 30 MIN
16mm
Great Plains trilogy - Nomad and Indians - early man on the Plains - 2 series; Nomad and Indians - early man on the plains
B&W (H C A)
Describes native crops, new types of houses and specialized tools brought in by new groups of people pushing into the plains. Takes a look at primitive social organization as suggested by archaeology.
Social Science; Sociology
Dist - UNL **Prod** - KUONTV 1954

Prehistoric Fish 22 MIN
16mm
Color
Depicts Homer Circle angling for some fish which are prehistoric throwbacks, such as the bowfin, alligator gar, paddlefish and sturgeon.
Physical Education and Recreation
Dist - KAROL **Prod** - BRNSWK

Prehistoric Humans 17 MIN
16mm / U-matic / VHS
Color (J)
LC 80-700458
Focuses on several prehistoric relatives of modern man.
History - World; Science - Natural; Sociology
Dist - PHENIX **Prod** - MATVCH 1980

Prehistoric Images - the First Art of Man 17 MIN
U-matic / VHS / 16mm
Color (I J H C)
An exploration of the prehistoric caves of France and Spain, examination of the paintings found there and some conjecture as to the character of the men who created the paintings. Produced in France.
Fine Arts; History - World
Dist - FI **Prod** - ROWETL

Prehistoric Magic 14 MIN
U-matic / VHS
Young at Art Series
Color (P I)
Discusses prehistoric art.
Fine Arts
Dist - AITECH **Prod** - WSKJTV 1980

Prehistoric Mammals 16 MIN
U-matic / VHS / 16mm
Color (I J H)
LC 81-700236
Describes the large mammals which once roamed the Earth.
Science - Natural
Dist - PHENIX **Prod** - MATVCH 1981

Prehistoric Man 17 MIN
U-matic
Color (H)
Traces the development of the Indians in the American West from prehistoric times until the Spanish arrived in the 16th century.
Social Science
Dist - GA **Prod** - BARBRE

Prehistoric man 50 MIN
VHS
Discoveries underwater series
Color; PAL (G)
PdS99 purchase
Observes archaeologists as they search for prehistoric settlements in lakes and lochs. Looks at the growing science of underwater archaeology. Part three of an eight - part series.
Geography - World; History - World; Social Science
Dist - BBCENE

Prehistoric Man in Colorado 17 MIN
VHS / BETA
Color
Traces the development of prehistoric cultures from across the Bering Strait to the great Pueblo period in Mesa Verde.
Science - Physical; Sociology
Dist - CBSC **Prod** - CBSC

Prehistoric Man in Europe 23 MIN
16mm / U-matic / VHS
Color (I)
LC FIA67-1682
Relates the story of the probable development of man based on agreed archeological deductions. Shows products, tools and progress by periods to the Roman rule.
History - World; Science - Physical; Sociology
Dist - IFB **Prod** - BHA 1965

Prehistoric times 10 MIN
VHS / U-matic
Color (J H)
$59.00 purchase _ #MF - 3522
Examines the long history of planet Earth and the beginnings of life. Uses dioramas, fossil remains, examples of terrain and models to illustrate the many eras that passed before the existence of human life.

Science - Natural; Science - Physical
Dist - CORF **Prod** - CORF
INSTRU

Prehistoric world 30 MIN
VHS
Color (G)
$19.95 purchase _ #S02020
Presents unusual facts about paleontology. Focuses on prehistoric mammals. Takes viewers to various sites including Los Angeles' La Brea tar pits and New Mexico's ice caves. Hosted by Gary Owens and Eric Boardman.
History - World; Science - Natural; Science - Physical
Dist - UILL

Prehistoric World 30 MIN
VHS
Color; Stereo (K)
$14.98 purchase _ #TT8081
Features the Saber Toothed Tiger, the Woolly Mammoth and other predators and early mammals of the past.
History - World; Science - Natural
Dist - TWINTO **Prod** - TWINTO 1990

Prejudice 25 MIN
U-matic / VHS
Color (J H C A)
Examines the modern day exploits of the Ku Klux Klan. Features interviews with the chief counsel and Grand Wizard of the KKK, James R Venable, and with a Nashville reporter who infiltrated the Klan and authored a book, My Life With The Clan.
Psychology; Sociology
Dist - GERBER **Prod** - SIRS

Prejudice 75 MIN
VHS
ABC News collection series
Color (G)
$29.98 purchase _ #6302461898
Features broadcast journalist Peter Jennings who leads a studio audience of young people on an exploration of prejudice and the stereotypes that divide the human race.
Sociology
Dist - INSTRU **Prod** - ABCNEW 1992

Prejudice 30 MIN
VHS
Social psychology series
Color (C G PRO)
$180.00 purchase, $19.00 rental _ #35760
Displays and reviews stereotypes and emotions that underlie prejudice. Offers four scenarios which provide evidence of prejudicial behavior. Discusses remedial intervention and methods for reducing discrimination. Part of an eight - part series on social psychology produced by the International University Consortium.
Psychology; Sociology
Dist - PSU

Prejudice 75 MIN
VHS
Color (G)
$24.95 purchase _ #ST - MP6364
Discusses the question of whether or not all human beings have to be the same or equal. Considers human differences and provides viewers with a greater understanding of themselves and an appreciation of differences.
Sociology
Dist - INSTRU **Prod** - ABCNEW

Prejudice - a lesson to forget 20 MIN
U-matic / VHS / BETA
Color; PAL (J H C G)
PdS50, PdS58 purchase
Explores this learned emotion and how a person can change his or her attitude. Shows examples of racial and religious prejudice.
Psychology; Sociology
Dist - EDPAT

Prejudice - a Lesson to Forget 16 MIN
16mm / U-matic / VHS
Color (J)
LC 73-702628
Attempts to separate discrimination, a symptom, from prejudice, its cause. Illustrates a general history of the prejudices that scorched the American melting pot. Uses vignettes to demonstrate how children learn prejudice from each other and from their parents and teachers.
Guidance and Counseling; Sociology
Dist - AMEDFL **Prod** - DUNLF 1973

Prejudice and Racism 145 MIN
U-matic
University of the Air Series
Color (J H C A)
$750.00 purchase, $250.00 rental
Considers the cause and effect of prejudice and racism, the measurement and development of prejudice in children and youth and the continuing effects of prejudice in print and pictures. Program contains a series of five cassettes, 29 minutes each.
Sociology
Dist - CTV **Prod** - CTV 1974

Prejudice - answering children's questions 75 MIN
VHS
Color (P I J)
$19.95 purchase _ #MP6364
Features Peter Jennings who leads an investigation of prejudice before an audience of young children. Includes a panel of experts which conducts enlightening experiments with the children to help them better understand the roots of prejudice and the influences that shape opinion.
Sociology
Dist - KNOWUN **Prod** - ABCNEW 1991

Prejudice - Causes, Consequences, Cures 24 MIN
U-matic / VHS / 16mm
Social Science Film Series
Color (H C A)
LC 74-703308
Takes a look at the nature of prejudice in its many forms, including racial, sexual, educational and economic prejudice, and delves into the root causes of this devastating social illness. Demonstrates the various ways in which our need to classify groups can be subverted into negative prejudice. Presents examples of prejudice including the problems of double standards, overgeneralized observations, territorial and economic group conflicts, severe and punitive upbrining and conformity and socialization.
Guidance and Counseling; Sociology
Dist - CRMP **Prod** - CRMP 1974

The Prejudice Film 29 MIN
16mm
Color (I)
LC 73-700612
Examines the historical origins of prejudice and illustrates contemporary forms of prejudice.
Guidance and Counseling; Psychology; Sociology
Dist - MTVTM **Prod** - AVANTI 1972

Prejudice in Humor / Locked in these Rooms / Pat and Evy 29 MIN
U-matic
As We See it Series
Color
Presents three looks at racial issues. Shows how ethnic humor perpetuates misunderstandings. Profiles Asian - American parents who don't want their children to leave San Francisco's Chinatown. Features a young woman's fantasy that she can eliminate people she doesn't like by snapping her fingers, and describes her realization that she has too many prejudices.
Education; Sociology
Dist - PBS **Prod** - WTTWTV

Prejudice - Perceiving and Believing 28 MIN
U-matic / VHS / 16mm
Color (H C A)
LC 76-703716
Shows that stereotyped classification by race, religion, ethnicity or sex, rather than by individual worth, prevents positive personal interactions. Reveals that prejudice is seen as prejudgment based upon what one expects to perceive, rather than what exists in reality. Narrated by Ed Asner.
Business and Economics; Psychology; Sociology
Dist - CORF **Prod** - MTVTM 1977

Prejudice - tolerance
VHS
Color (G)
$79.00 purchase _ #CCP0224V-G
Discusses prejudice and its effect on individuals and society. Provides examples of different kinds of stereotypes and reveals that few are 'prejudice free.' Asserts that what is learned can be unlearned and uses interviews, narration, and questions to viewers. Encourages discussion of personal prejudices and rethinking of beliefs. Explains how biases are formed and reinforced and how the roots of all prejudices are the same.
Sociology
Dist - CAMV

Prejudice, USA series
Divided we stand 28 MIN
Dist - ADL

Prejudices, stereotyping, biases 30 MIN
VHS / U-matic
Interaction - human concerns in the schools series
Color (T)
Analyzes prejudices, stereotypes and biases in an educational setting.
Education; Sociology
Dist - MDCPB **Prod** - MDDE

Preliminary, beginning, and work phases 96 MIN
U-matic
Skills of helping series; Program 1
Color (C A)
LC 80-707458
Tells how social workers can tune in, respond to indirect communication, contract, elaborate, empathize, and share worker feelings.
Psychology; Sociology
Dist - SYRCU **Prod** - MCGILU 1980

Preliminary, beginning, and work phases - Pt 1 48 MIN
U-matic
Skills of helping series; Program 1
Color (C A)
LC 80-707458
Tells how social workers can tune in, respond to indirect communication, contract, elaborate, empathize, and share worker feelings.
Psychology; Sociology
Dist - SYRCU **Prod** - MCGILU 1980

Preliminary, Beginning, and Work Phases - Pt 2 48 MIN
U-matic
Skills of Helping Series
Color (C A)
LC 80-707458
Tells how social workers can tune in, respond to indirect communication, contract, elaborate, empathize, and share worker feelings. Program one of the series.
Psychology; Sociology
Dist - SYRCU **Prod** - MCGILU 1980

Preliminary Examination and Procedures for Diagnosis 12 MIN
U-matic
Removable Partial Dentures, Clasp Type - Clinical and Laboratory 'Procedures Series
Color (PRO)
LC 78-706183
Presents extra - oral inspection and examines soft and hard intraoral tissues, preliminary impressions and the interocclusal record to mount the study casts. Issued in 1967 as a motion picture.
Health and Safety
Dist - USNAC **Prod** - USVA 1978

Preliminary Hearing of a Criminal Case 161 MIN
U-matic / VHS
Trial of a Criminal Case Series
Color (PRO)
Covers preliminary hearing of a criminal case.
Civics and Political Systems
Dist - ABACPE **Prod** - SBWI

Preliminary impressions for complete dentures 14 MIN
16mm
Color (PRO)
LC 78-701358
A revised version of the motion picture Preliminary Impressions For Complete Dentures - Alginate Method. Demonstrates a simple and efficient method of using wax modifications of stock trays to obtain preliminary denture impressions with alginate.
Health and Safety; Science
Dist - USNAC **Prod** - VADTC 1978

Preliminary impressions in complete denture prosthodontics 22 MIN
16mm / U-matic / VHS
Color (PRO)
Presents a technique for obtaining physiologically acceptable preliminary impressions using four different commercially available impression trays and an alginate substitute that consists of two pastes.
Health and Safety
Dist - USNAC **Prod** - USVA 1984

Preliminary survey of study casts, tentative design and detailed treatment planning 11 MIN
U-matic
Removable partial dentures, clasp type - clinical and laboratory'procedures series
Color (PRO)
LC 78-706184
Discusses the kinds of information upon which planning for treatment is based, including that achieved from mounted study casts, oral examination, radiographs, general patient information and accurate survey of casts. Covers tentative design of the appliance compatible with the oral conditions and biological requirements. Issued in 1967 as a motion picture.
Health and Safety; Science
Dist - USNAC **Prod** - USVA 1978

Preliminary title reports, title policies and closing procedures 120 MIN
VHS / U-matic / Cassette
Color (PRO)
Focuses on the different types of title insurance and what lawyers should know about lenders' and owners' policies. Includes such topics as selecting a title company, evaluating preliminary title reports, closing and funding the transaction, and getting the title insurance policy issued.
Business and Economics; Civics and Political Systems
Dist - CCEB **Prod** - CCEB

Prelude 1 MIN
16mm
Color (G)
$10.00 rental
Deals with light and aggression and heat and religion.
Fine Arts; Religion and Philosophy
Dist - CANCIN **Prod** - KIRBYL 1982

Prelude 4 MIN
16mm
Color (J H C)
Presents an abstract film exercise using colored lights, wire forms and abstract sculpture.
Fine Arts
Dist - CFS **Prod** - CFS 1954

Prelude - Dog Star Man 27 MIN
16mm
Color; Silent (C)
$885.00
Presents an experimental film by Stan Brakhage.
Fine Arts
Dist - AFA **Prod** - AFA 1964

Prelude - Przygrywka 175 MIN
VHS
Color (P I J H) (POLISH)
$34.95 purchase _ #V164
Presents a six - part series, on two tapes, from Polish television for children and teenagers that tells the story of four children who, unexpectedly left on their own, look after their farm.
Fine Arts; Literature and Drama; Sociology
Dist - POLART

Prelude to deduction 30 MIN
16mm
Teaching high school mathematics - first course series; No 26
B&W (T)
Mathematics
Dist - MLA **Prod** - UICSM 1967

Prelude to power 25 MIN
U-matic / VHS / 16mm
B&W (J H C)
LC FIA67-5541
Relates the story of the life of Michael Faraday and his work in the field of electromagnetism.
Biography; Science; Science - Physical
Dist - IFB **Prod** - OECD 1965

Prelude to proof - making 40 MIN
16mm
Teaching high school mathematics - first course series
B&W (T)
Presents number 28 in the series.
Mathematics
Dist - MLA **Prod** - UICSM 1967

Prelude to Revolution 13 MIN
U-matic / VHS / 16mm
Color (J H)
LC 75-702355
Uses watercolors by A N Wyeth to recount events that slowly transformed the American colonists' limited resistance to British rule into a struggle for the rights and principles outlined in the Declaration of Independence.
History - United States
Dist - EBEC **Prod** - EBEC 1975

Prelude to revolution 17 MIN
U-matic / VHS / 16mm
American history - birth of a nation series; No 3
Color (I)
$69.95 purchase _ #1983; $69.95 purchase _ #SO1502; LC FIA68-1117
Discusses Parliament's repeal of the Townshend Acts and the gradual return of heavy taxes, resulting in the burning of the British ship, the Gaspree, by the colonists. Reviews the events leading to the Boston Tea Party and the meeting of the first Continental Congress in 1774, in opposition to the new Intolerable Acts. Number three in the series.
History - United States
Dist - AIMS **Prod** - CAHILL 1967
UILL

Prelude to Taps 11 MIN
16mm
B&W
LC 75-701196
Presents a display of military pageantry in commemoration of two centuries of American heroes who died fighting for their country.
Civics and Political Systems
Dist - USNAC **Prod** - USDD 1964

Prelude to Vietnam 52 MIN
U-matic / VHS
B&W (G)
$239.00, $139.00 purchase _ #AD - 1484
Documents the rise and fall of the French in Indochina. Considers the political outcome of the loss of Dien Bien Phu.
History - United States; History - World; Sociology
Dist - FOTH **Prod** - FOTH

Prelude to war 60 MIN
VHS
B&W (G)
$19.95 purchase _ #S00384
Presents an account of the events leading up to World War II. Used as training film for US servicemen in World War II. Produced by Frank Capra.
History - United States; History - World
Dist - UILL

Prelude to war 54 MIN
16mm
Why we fight series
B&W (GERMAN)
LC FIE52-1709
Describes the events leading up to World War II. Shows the development of Fascism in Germany, Italy and Japan, and the beginning of Japanese aggression in Manchuria. Dwells on the rise of Nazism in Germany.
History - World
Dist - USNAC **Prod** - USWD 1942

Prelude to War (1935 to 1939) 22 MIN
16mm / U-matic / VHS
American Chronicles Series
Color (J H C G T A)
$75 rental _ #9815
Shows Hitler rallying the German youth, imprisoning Jews, forming the Axis alliance with Italy, and retaking the Rhineland.
History - World; Social Science
Dist - AIMS **Prod** - AIMS 1986

Prelude to World War I 45 MIN
VHS / U-matic / 35mm strip / Kit
Western man and the modern world in video
Color (J H C)
$1378.12 the 25 part series _ #C676 - 27347 - 5, $89.95 the individual; $72.00, $72.00 purchase _ #MB - 510394 - X, #MB - 510263 -3
Traces the growth of militarism, colonial ambitions and diplomatic maneuvering that made World War I all but inevitable. Explains how the assassination at Sarajevo activated key alliances and began global mobilization.
History - World
Dist - RH
SRA

Premature 55 MIN
16mm
Color (H C A)
LC 81-701555
Records the personal crisis endured by a family when their first child was born prematurely by cesarean section and given a one percent chance of surviving without physical or mental defects. Tells how an unexpected pregnancy six months later and a second cesarean birth caused further stress.
Health and Safety; Sociology
Dist - BNCHMK **Prod** - PARRYD 1981

Premature babies 30 MIN
VHS
Perspectives - health and medicine - series
Color; PAL; NTSC (G)
PdS90, PdS105 purchase
Reveals that more and more premature babies are surviving.
Health and Safety
Dist - CFLVIS **Prod** - LONTVS

Premature baby 30 MIN
U-matic
Health care today series
Color (H A)
Compares the attachment of the mother of a full term infant to her baby with that of the mother of a premature infant.
Health and Safety
Dist - TVOTAR **Prod** - TVOTAR 1985
RMIBHF

The Premature baby 17 MIN
VHS
Color (PRO A)
$200.00 purchase _ #OB - 114
Discusses the difficulties preterm babies have in adjusting to life outside the womb. Shows parents how to understand their premature baby by explaining what is normal for a preterm infant including skin color, crying, eye contact, feeding and sleep patterns. Explains that parents may want to have a neonatal - behavior professional assess their baby on an individual basis in order to help them recognize the signs and signals their baby uses to display its needs. Produced by Perinatal Innovations.
Health and Safety; Sociology
Dist - MIFE

Premature Burial 79 MIN
16mm
Color (H A)
Tells the tale of a man who fears being buried alive but suffers that very fate. Directed by Roger Corman. Stars Ray Milland.
Fine Arts
Dist - TIMLIF **Prod** - AIP 1961

Premature ejaculation
VHS / U-matic
Color
Outlines a 12 to 15 visit treatment program for a husband's premature ejaculation. Includes education on the male and female reproductive organs, genitalia, arousal cycles and a progressive series of home exercises including 'sensate Focus' training and the 'Squeeze Technique.'.
Health and Safety; Psychology
Dist - MIFE **Prod** - MIFE

The Premature Infant with Esophageal Atresia and Tracheoesophageal Fistula 17 MIN
U-matic / VHS
Color (PRO)
Describes the premature infant with esophageal atresia and tracheoesophageal fistula.
Health and Safety
Dist - WFP **Prod** - WFP

Premature parents, miracle babies 18 MIN
VHS
Color (H C A PRO) (SPANISH)
$160.00 purchase, $50.00 rental
Interviews four couples whose premature babies spent time in the neonatal intensive care unit. Reveals that the babies now live normal childhoods.
Health and Safety
Dist - UARIZ **Prod** - UARIZ

Prematurely yours - premature infant behavior and personality 15 MIN
U-matic / VHS
Color (PRO)
LC 83-706810
Provides encouragement for parents and hospital staff by showing how one can respond in a positive manner to the premature infant. Examines the needs of the newborn and of the parents.
Health and Safety; Sociology
Dist - POLYMR **Prod** - POLYMR 1983

Premenstrual syndrome
VHS
Mosby cameo series; Volume 2
Color (C PRO G)
$150.00 purchase
Features nurse researcher Dr Nancy Fugate Woods and her work. Part of a series featuring the work of outstanding nurse researchers.
Health and Safety
Dist - MOSBY **Prod** - SITHTA

Premenstrual syndrome 15 MIN 18 MIN
VHS
Color (G C PRO) (SPANISH)
$175.00 purchase _ #OB - 123; $200.00 purchase _ #OB - 59
Explores the problems of women who suffer severely from PMS - premenstrual syndrome - and focuses on how PMS affects one woman's daily routine. Includes group discussions with other PMS sufferers talking about their own personal struggles.
Health and Safety; Sociology
Dist - MIFE **Prod** - MIFE

Premenstrual syndrome 26 MIN
U-matic / VHS
Color (C)
$249.00, $149.00 purchase _ #AD - 1899
Examines the physical and emotional problems experienced by some women before menstruation. Explores misconceptions about PMS and the various treatments available. Considers the controversy surrounding PMS as a legal defense.

Health and Safety; Psychology; Sociology
Dist - FOTH **Prod** - FOTH

Premenstrual syndrome 11 MIN
VHS
Color (G PRO C) (SPANISH)
$200.00 purchase _ #OB - 59
Defines and differentiates PMS from other menstrual conditions. Makes it clear that many women have symptoms but not every woman has premenstrual syndrome. Shows that PMS is a combination of biological and behavioral symptoms and lets women who suffer from the syndrome know that they are not alone. Stresses the importance of an accurate diagnosis and discusses treatment options such as medication, dietary changes, exercise, stress reduction, improved communication skills and anger management.
Health and Safety; Sociology
Dist - MIFE **Prod** - MIFE 1993

The Premie and the NICU environment - staff development 16 MIN
U-matic
NICU video series
Color (PRO)
$175.00 purchase
Explains the various ways in which premies react to stress. Illustrates typical self - comforting behaviors. Describes ways in which medical care staff can reduce the excessive stimulation that often occurs in the NICU, and how they can help facilitate a premie's self - comforting. Part of a seven - part series on developmental intervention for hospitalized infants in the neonatal intensive care unit.
Health and Safety
Dist - POLYMR **Prod** - POKORJ

Premie development - an overview - staff development 14 MIN
VHS / U-matic
NICU video series
Color (PRO)
$175.00 purchase
Outlines the various stages of premie development, including behavioral states, physiological and motor responses and attentional reactions of premies. Part of a seven - part series on developmental intervention for hospitalized infants in the neonatal intensive care unit.
Health and Safety
Dist - POLYMR **Prod** - POKORJ

Premiere 10 MIN
16mm
B&W
Uses an applause and 'after the opening' party to frame a view of the inner conflicts of an actress who is in search of her own sense of self as she wanders through the city trying to 'see' herself in windows, museums and cameras.
Fine Arts; Guidance and Counseling; Psychology
Dist - UPENN **Prod** - UPENN 1971

Premonition 11 MIN
16mm
B&W (H C A)
$35.00 rental
Admires the aesthetics of modernity and its colossal feats of engineering that surround us: highways, buildings, bridges. Compares the human ego with the overwhelming presence of the rest of the world. Directed by Dominic Angerame.
Geography - World; Sociology
Dist - CANCIN

Prenatal 21 MIN
U-matic / VHS / 16mm
Color (H C A)
LC 80-700672
Examines changes in the mother's body and the development of the fetus during pregnancy. Demonstrates the techniques of correct breathing and proper posture and details the usual indications that the time for delivery is approaching.
Health and Safety; Science - Natural
Dist - IFB **Prod** - DALHSU 1977

Prenatal - 2 21 MIN
16mm / VHS / BETA / U-matic
Canadian hospitals Pregnancy - birth series
Color; PAL (PRO G)
PdS90, PdS98 purchase
Examines the development of the fetus during pregnancy. Stresses the danger of cigarettes, importance of grooming, exercise and recreation. Correct breathing and posture and common problems such as leg cramps are studied. Part of a four - part series.
Health and Safety; Physical Education and Recreation
Dist - EDPAT

Prenatal care
VHS
Color (PRO G)
$250.00 purchase _ #OB - 108
Follows several women through prenatal visits and answers the most common questions patients have about pregnancy. Presents guidelines for developing good nutrition and exercise habits and stresses the importance of avoiding substances such as cigarettes, alcohol and illegal drugs. Discusses the need to be cautious about over - the - counter medications. Explains safety precautions, such as prevention of toxoplasmosis and the proper use of seat belts. Mentions the importance of learning the warning signs of preterm labor and the advantages of prepared childbirth classes.
Health and Safety; Physical Education and Recreation
Dist - MIFE **Prod** - MIFE 1991

Prenatal care 12 MIN
VHS
Parents - to - be series
Color (J H C A)
$119.00 purchase _ #CG - 922 - VS
Discusses the importance of prenatal care. Part of a six - part series answering many of the questions and concerns of parents - to - be and new parents regarding the safety and care of their children - before and after birth.
Health and Safety; Sociology
Dist - HRMC **Prod** - HRMC

Prenatal care 12 MIN
VHS
Color (J H G) (SPANISH)
$295.00 purchase, $35.00 rental
Focuses on instructing women early in their pregnancy. Explains what happens during prenatal visits. Covers history taking, a complete physical exam and presents easy - to - understand guidelines for nutrition, diet and exercise. Answers many questions asked by pregnant women. Reviews the normal changes that occur in women's bodies during pregnancy, as well as the warning signs that indicate a doctor should be called. Discusses the harmful effects of smoking, alcohol and drugs.
Guidance and Counseling; Health and Safety; Psychology
Dist - POLYMR

Prenatal care 29 MIN
16mm
Nine to get ready series
B&W (C A)
LC 77-704218
Tells about prenatal care, mortality and morbidity rates, nutrition, dental care, emotional aspects, physical aspects and prenatal visit to the doctor. Number four in the series.
Health and Safety
Dist - UNL **Prod** - KUONTV 1965

Prenatal care 24 MIN
16mm / U-matic / VHS
Color (A) (ARABIC SPANISH)
LC 77-701104
Presents basic information on prenatal care. Covers normal body changes during pregnancy, medical care, necessary precautions, preparations for birth and possible complications. Shows expectant mothers and fathers, an obstetrician and a childbirth specialist demonstrating what to do, from the first indications of pregnancy to the onset of labor.
Health and Safety; Psychology; Science - Natural; Sociology
Dist - PFP **Prod** - BURN 1977

Prenatal Care - the Early Months 12 MIN
16mm / U-matic / VHS
Prepared Childbirth and Parenting Series
Color
Explores the importance of proper medical care, nutrition and dealing with common annoyances during the first few months of pregnancy.
Health and Safety
Dist - JOU **Prod** - JOU 1979

Prenatal detection of genetic disorders in man 30 MIN
U-matic / VHS
Choice to know series
Color
Discusses genetic amniocentesis, through which doctors are learning more about genetic disease. Outlines several genetic diseases and provides a detailed demonstration of genetic amniocentesis.
Health and Safety; Science - Natural
Dist - NETCHE **Prod** - NETCHE 1976

Prenatal development 30 MIN
U-matic
Growing years series
Color
Presents the stages of prenatal development and the environmental influences on the infant - to - be.
Health and Safety; Psychology
Dist - CDTEL **Prod** - COAST

Prenatal Development 23 MIN
U-matic / VHS / 16mm
Developmental Psychology Today Film Series
Color (H C A)
LC 74-703309
Explores the biology and the psychology of the developing fetus. Presents the latest theories and information about the fetus and the environmental influences within the mother's uterus.
Health and Safety; Psychology; Science - Natural
Dist - CRMP **Prod** - CRMP 1974

Prenatal Exercises 19 MIN
U-matic / 8mm cartridge
Color (A)
Emphasizes physical and psychological conditioning during pregnancy. Suggests a program of exercise, breathing and movement.
Health and Safety
Dist - PRORE **Prod** - PRORE

Prenatal management 8 MIN
U-matic / VHS / 16mm
Prepared childbirth and parenting series
Color (ENGLISH, SPANISH)
Portrays the physical changes that develop as pregnancy advances. Discusses normal discomforts, danger signals and substances to be avoided.
Health and Safety
Dist - JOU **Prod** - JOU 1969
PRORE

Prenatal nutrition 12 MIN
VHS
Color (J H C G)
$59.95 purchase _ #NHV200V - K
Reveals that pregnant women can suffer complications during and after pregnancy if they are not aware of their body's nutritional needs and their babies' nutritional needs for growing and developing correctly. Discusses energy needs and weight gain for the mother, folic acid, iron, protein, calcium, fluids and sodium. Shows how to overcome morning sickness, constipation, heart burn and craving. Gives special advice to pregnant teens on proper eating habits since teens are still growing and developing themselves.
Health and Safety; Social Science
Dist - CAMV

Preoccupied 22 MIN
U-matic
Color (G)
$375.00 purchase, $75.00, $60.00 rental
Examines the pros and cons of motherhood. Presented by Solrun Hoaas.
Sociology
Dist - WMENIF **Prod** - WMENIF 1985

Preoperative care 16 MIN
16mm
B&W
LC FIE60-91
Presents the duties and responsibilities of hospital corpsmen in preparing a patient for surgery in the 16 to 24 hour period immediately preceding the operation.
Health and Safety
Dist - USNAC **Prod** - USN 1952

Preoperative Evaluation of Cancer Patients at M D Anderson 45 MIN
U-matic
Color
Dr Hollis Bivens discusses preoperative requirements, evaluation and patient information for patients at the University of Texas M D Anderson Hospital.
Health and Safety
Dist - UTEXSC **Prod** - UTEXSC

The Preoperative Patient - Consent, Preparation and Transfer 13 MIN
U-matic / 35mm strip
Color (PRO)
LC 80-730132;
Explains guidelines to planning and implementing of the patient's preparation for surgery. Identifies such nursing responsibilities as helping prepare the patient for surgical consent, coordinating surgical preparation, orienting the patient to surgical preparation and preparing the patient for transfer to the operating room.
Health and Safety
Dist - MEDCOM **Prod** - MEDCOM

The Preoperative Patient - Nursing Assessment 19 MIN
VHS / U-matic
Color (PRO)
LC 80-730130
Explains the nurse's preoperative assessment of the surgical patient. Presents the nurse's data collection and analysis and goals of the preoperative assessment. Describes the methods for obtaining information about the patient's physical needs, emotional needs and learning needs in preparation for surgery.

Health and Safety
Dist - MEDCOM **Prod** - MEDCOM

The Preoperative Patient - Nursing Care 18 MIN
U-matic / VHS
Color (PRO)
LC 80-730134
Presents guidelines for nursing care of the surgical patient during postoperative recovery. Presents specific responsibilities to promote the patient's participation in care, to promote adequate ventilation and circulation, to promote wound healing, to promote elimination and nutrition and to plan for the patient's discharge.
Health and Safety
Dist - MEDCOM **Prod** - MEDCOM

The Preoperative Patient - Teaching and Anticipatory Guidance 15 MIN
U-matic / 35mm strip
Color (PRO)
LC 80-730131;
Explains guidelines for planning and implementing preoperative teaching and anticipatory guidance. Identifies elements of the nurse's written teaching plan and shows guidelines for meeting individual learning needs.
Health and Safety
Dist - MEDCOM **Prod** - MEDCOM

Prepackaged Liquid Rocket Motor 26 MIN
16mm
Color
Shows how a prepackaged liquid motor works and how it is fitted to the missile.
Industrial and Technical Education
Dist - THIOKL **Prod** - THIOKL 1967

Preparaciones rapidas de cromosomas 7 MIN
U-matic / VHS / 16mm
Biological techniques - Spanish series
Color (H C) (ENGLISH, SPANISH)
Presents laboratory techniques demonstrating a simple method of making slides to study mitosis. Uses onion root tips and flower buds.
Science
Dist - IFB **Prod** - THORNE 1960

Preparation
U-matic / 16mm
Art of negotiating series
Color (A)
Goes into fact finding, hidden assumptions, the opening and closing, subject matter objectives, issues, positions, team composition, agenda, implementation, self - evaluation, checklists, preparation and applications of negotiations. Module two of the series.
Business and Economics; Psychology
Dist - BNA **Prod** - BNA 1983

The Preparation 21 MIN
U-matic / VHS
Negotiating sales series
Color
Exposes and analyzes the most frequent and costly errors of untrained negotiators and establishes four basic principles for successful negotiating. Part one of the series.
Business and Economics
Dist - VISUCP **Prod** - VISUCP

Preparation 10 MIN
BETA / VHS / U-matic
Young job seekers series
Color; Stereo (H)
Highlights the importance of references, resumes and reports in the job interview preparation.
Guidance and Counseling; Psychology
Dist - SEVDIM **Prod** - SEVDIM 1984

The Preparation 25 MIN
VHS / U-matic
So You Want to be a Success at Selling Series Pt I
Color
Reveals the work and techniques required for one to sell effectively. Covers research, setting objectives and using proper questioning.
Business and Economics; Psychology
Dist - VISUCP **Prod** - VIDART

Preparation - 1 47 MIN
VHS
Working with Japan series
Color (C PRO G)
$395.00 purchase, $175.00 rental _ #820
Examines the differences between Western and Japanese values that dramatically affect the conduct of business. Offers detailed information and recommendations on market research in Japan, quality assurance, avoiding pitfalls in strategic planning, team development, proper introductions through effective go - betweens, planning meeting arrangements, presenting and packaging ideas, the appropriate form and etiquette of business cards and gifts. Part one of a six - part series on business relations with Japan. Produced by Intercultural Training Resources, Inc.
Business and Economics; Civics and Political Systems; Geography - World; Home Economics; Psychology
Dist - INCUL

Preparation - Administration of oral medication 8 MIN
U-matic / VHS
Basic nursing skills series
Color (PRO)
Health and Safety
Dist - BRA **Prod** - BRA

Preparation and delivery 30 MIN
VHS
Oral communicating - content and confidence series
Color (I J H)
$85.00 purchase _ #GW - 5102 - VS; $85.00 purchase _ #1723VG
Provides techniques for dealing with stage fright and the fear of presenting in front of an audience. Presents relaxation techniques and stresses the importance of planning ahead of time. Demonstrates practice as a positive approach to feeling comfortable about a presentation. First of two parts. Comes with a teacher's guide and blackline masters.
English Language
Dist - HRMC **Prod** - UNL 1990
UNL

Preparation and staining of blood films 17 MIN
16mm
Malaria control series
Color
Illustrates smearing and staining procedures for preparing thick and thin blood films for use by technicians in ascertaining the presence of malaria parasites. Includes technique of preparing giemsa and Wright's stains.
Health and Safety; Science
Dist - USPHS **Prod** - USPHS 1946

Preparation and staining of fecal smears for parasitological examination 8 MIN
16mm
Color
LC FIE67-55
Demonstrates the trichrome staining technique for the detection of intestinal parasites.
Health and Safety; Science
Dist - USNAC **Prod** - USPHS 1965

Preparation and use of graphics 30 MIN
U-matic / VHS
Video - a practical guide and more series
Color
Lists the dimensional limitations of television. Discusses devices including marker pens and computerized graphics. Explains how to combine words and pictures for best effect.
Fine Arts; Industrial and Technical Education
Dist - VIPUB **Prod** - VIPUB

Preparation - developing a quality assurance, risk management program - Pt II 20 MIN
VHS / U-matic
Color
Continues the discussion on how to help small or rural hospitals develop a program that meets quality assurance requirements.
Business and Economics; Health and Safety; Psychology
Dist - AHOA **Prod** - AHOA 1981

Preparation - financing capital investments 20 MIN
VHS / U-matic
Color
Addresses the unique financing problems faced by small or rural hospitals.
Business and Economics; Health and Safety; Psychology
Dist - AHOA **Prod** - AHOA 1981

Preparation for docking with keel and bilge blocks 14 MIN
16mm
B&W
LC FIE52-1196
Examines the graving dock and demonstrates the placement of keel and bilge blocks according to the docking plan.
Physical Education and Recreation; Social Science
Dist - USNAC **Prod** - USN 1944

Preparation for Functional Activities - Exercise and Ambulation 28 MIN
VHS / U-matic
Color
Health and Safety
Dist - UMDSM **Prod** - UMDSM

Preparation for Homecoming 29 MIN
U-matic / VHS
Tomorrow's Families Series
Color (H C A)
LC 81-706902
Points out that equipment for the baby's needs and a support system for the mother's recovery must be ready by the time the baby is born.
Home Economics; Sociology
Dist - AITECH **Prod** - MDDE 1980

Preparation for mainstreaming 60 MIN
U-matic / VHS
Teaching strategies for the development of auditory verbal communication series
Color
Shows development of listening skills for the classroom. Depicts kindergarten child with severe to profound hearing loss participating in activities such as phonics and use of tape recorder. Shows his eight year old brother, who has a profound hearing loss and is mainstreamed, demonstrating the same activities on a second to third grade level.
Education; English Language; Psychology
Dist - BELLAG **Prod** - BELLAG 1981

Preparation for Negotiations 26 MIN
U-matic
Basic Procurement Course Series
Color
LC 80-706737
Shows how to prepare documentation and strategies in anticipation of negotiations on federal government contracts.
Business and Economics; Civics and Political Systems
Dist - USNAC **Prod** - USGSFC 1978

Preparation for oral surgery 12 MIN
VHS / U-matic
Preparation for oral surgery series
Color (PRO C)
$395.00 purchase, $80.00 rental _ #C920 - VI - 037
Shows how to set up the work area, scrub, prepare the evacuation systems and assemble the tray top materials. Stresses that carefully following the procedures shown will help to ensure the safety of surgeon and patient. Part of a three - part series on oral surgery presented by Mary Ann Adkisson, RN, and Dr James B Sweet, University of Texas, Health Science Center at Houston, Dental Branch.
Health and Safety
Dist - HSCIC

Preparation for oral surgery series
Presents a three - part series on oral surgery. Includes the titles Preparation for Oral Surgery; Surgical Scrub and Gloving; Principles of Asepsis, Draping the Patient, Final Preparation Prior to Surgery and Post - Operative Handling of Instruments and Materials. Stresses that carefully following the procedures shown will help to ensure the safety of surgeon and patient. Presented by Mary Ann Adkisson, RN, and Dr James B Sweet, University of Texas, Health Science Center at Houston, Dental Branch.

Preparation for oral surgery	12 MIN
Principles of asepsis, draping the patient, final preparations prior to surgery and post - operative handling of instruments and materials	15 MIN
Surgical scrub and gloving	12 MIN

Dist - HSCIC

Preparation for Overnight Camping 30 MIN
VHS / U-matic
Roughing it Series
Color
Discusses preparation for overnight camping as an outdoor activity that requires 'roughing it.'.
Physical Education and Recreation
Dist - KYTV **Prod** - KYTV 1984

Preparation for permanent waving - No 2
U-matic / VHS
Color
Covers all areas of preparation, such as analysis for lotion strength, the ruffle test, porosity and conditioning, elasticity, density and blocking patterns and rod selection for the wave form desired. Explains all supplies and equipment needed.
Education; Home Economics
Dist - MPCEDP **Prod** - MPCEDP 1984

Preparation for Spring 30 MIN
BETA / VHS
Victory Garden Series
Color
Shows how to prepare the garden for spring planting using cold frames and cloches. Introduces cool weather vegetables such as cabbage and broccoli.

Agriculture; Physical Education and Recreation
Dist - CORF Prod - WGBHTV

Preparation - Governance in Small Rural Hospital 20 MIN
VHS / U-matic
Color
Focuses on the role of trustees in small or rural hospitals and illustrates how corporate board management techniques can be used to meet the trustees' increasing responsibilities.
Business and Economics; Health and Safety; Psychology
Dist - AHOA Prod - AHOA 1980

Preparation - improving hospital management board, medical staff, and administrative staff 20 MIN
U-matic / VHS
Color
Discusses problems in managerial relationships and methods for promoting better relationships between members of hospital board, medical staff and administrative staff.
Health and Safety; Psychology
Dist - AHOA Prod - AHOA 1981

Preparation - New Responsibilities for Middle Management 19 MIN
U-matic / VHS
Color
Shows how hospital department managers can prepare for their responsibilities as leaders. Focuses on how to set goals, reach objectives and evaluate performance. Stresses communication skills and personal motivation techniques.
Health and Safety; Psychology
Dist - AHOA Prod - AHOA 1980

Preparation of a culture medium 14 MIN
16mm
Laboratory diagnosis of tuberculosis series
B&W
Shows the necessity for bacteriologic diagnosis of TB. Discusses the Lowenstein medium - - its advantages, ingredients, preparation, tubing, inspissating, testing and storing. Shows the appearance of colonies on the medium.
Health and Safety; Science
Dist - USNAC Prod - USPHS 1949

Preparation of Audio - Visual Materials Series
Better bulletin boards 13 MIN
Lettering Instructional Materials 22 MIN
Dist - IU

Preparation of gypsum casts 12 MIN
VHS / U-matic
Color (PRO C)
$395.00 purchase, $80.00 rental _ #C901 - VI - 085
Demonstrates three of the most common methods for mixing gypsum powder to make dental models and casts. Describes and demonstrates techniques of hand spatulation, hand - mechanical spatulation and power - driven mechanical spatulation. Shows materials and instruments and procedures for pouring the gypsum mix into molds. Presented by Drs M Borecki, L Smith and J Powers University of Texas Health Science Center at Houston, Dental Branch.
Health and Safety; Science
Dist - HSCIC

Preparation of items for sterilization in the dental office 16 MIN
BETA / VHS
Color (PRO)
Discusses dental instruments and sterilization.
Health and Safety; Science
Dist - RMIBHF Prod - RMIBHF

Preparation of less tender beef cuts 7 MIN
16mm
Food and nutrition series
Color (J)
LC 72-702650
Identifies the less tender wholesale cuts of beef. Demonstrates two methods of cooking with moist heat and shows three methods of tenderizing by physically altering the tissue.
Home Economics
Dist - IOWA Prod - IOWA 1971

Preparation of medication - ampule 5 MIN
U-matic / VHS
Basic skills - nursing series
Color (PRO)
Demonstrates how to prepare medication in an ampule.
Health and Safety
Dist - IU Prod - NICEPR

Preparation of medication - oral 5 MIN
U-matic / VHS
Basic skills - nursing series
Color (PRO)
Demonstrates how to prepare oral medication.
Health and Safety
Dist - IU Prod - NICEPR

Preparation of medication - reconstitution 5 MIN
U-matic / VHS
Basic skills - nursing series
Color (PRO)
Demonstrates how to prepare medication which is to be reconstituted.
Health and Safety
Dist - IU Prod - NICEPR

Preparation of medication - vial 4 MIN
VHS / U-matic
Basic skills - nursing series
Color (PRO)
Demonstrates how to prepare medication in a vial.
Health and Safety
Dist - IU Prod - NICEPR

Preparation of Primary Mammalian Kidney Cell Cultures 13 MIN
16mm
Color
LC 75-702069; FIE67-56
Demonstrates preparation of primary cell cultures from monkey kidney tissue. Shows preparation of the animal, surgical procedures to remove the kidneys, techniques of dissecting the tissue and treatment with trypsin to obtain a cell suspension. Explains how to determine cell concentration by microscopic means.
Science; Science - Natural
Dist - USNAC Prod - USPHS 1965

Preparation of sputum specimens 67 FRS 16 MIN
16mm
Laboratory diagnosis of tuberculosis series
Color; B&W
LC FIE53-196
Shows the technique of sputum preparation used in laboratory diagnosis of TB to simplify diagnostic methods and to supplement mass X - ray programs.
Health and Safety; Science
Dist - USNAC Prod - USPHS 1949

Preparation of surfaces - planing 63 MIN
Videoreel / VHS
Woodworking series
Color
Suggests staying with hand planing, rather than using power tools. Demonstates the technique.
Industrial and Technical Education
Dist - ANVICO Prod - ANVICO

Preparation of tender beef cuts 11 MIN
16mm
Food and nutrition series
Color (J)
LC 72-702649
Identifies the tender wholesale cuts of beef and demonstrates five methods of cooking with dry heat.
Home Economics
Dist - IOWA Prod - IOWA 1971

Preparation of the newborn for transport 14 MIN
VHS / U-matic
Color (PRO)
Covers communication between community hospital and referral center ICU, care of the infant prior to transport, preparing the parents for infant transfer and transfer of information and interactions among community hospital staff and the transfer team.
Health and Safety
Dist - UMICHM Prod - UMICHM 1983

Preparation of the participants 60 MIN
VHS
Teaching teachers series
Color (R T C G)
$49.95 purchase _ #TTBL1
Shows teachers in Roman Catholic schools the importance of setting professional goals, of caring, of having professional ethics and of having a sense of humor. Demonstrates ways in which teachers can create an atmosphere for positive discipline and student motivation and help students to develop a good self - image. Features teacher trainer Bob Lento, who is also a Catholic school teacher and principal. Part one of two parts.
Education; Religion and Philosophy
Dist - CTNA Prod - CTNA

Preparation of the root canal system 13 MIN
VHS / U-matic
Color (C PRO)
$395.00 purchase, $80.00 rental _ #D871 - VI - 024
Shows the basic techniques and instrumentation used in removing bacteria and necrotic tissue from the root canal and shaping the root canal in preparation for the filling material. Presented by Drs Ming W Wang, Jeffrey Hoover and Richard M Madden.
Health and Safety
Dist - HSCIC

Preparation of Thick and Thin Blood Films 6 MIN
16mm
Color
LC 74-705404
Demonstrates techniques of preparing blood films for detection of blood parasites and shows examples of good and poor films.
Health and Safety; Science; Science - Natural
Dist - USNAC Prod - USPHS 1967

The Preparation - Part 1 23 MIN
U-matic / VHS
Negotiating profitable sales series
Color (C A PRO)
$695.00 purchase, $205.00 rental
Shows that knowledge of negotiation can be more profitable than any other sales skill. Analyzes the most frequent and costly mistakes of negotiation in sales. Establishes crucial techniques and presents the four commandments of negotiations. Part one of a two - part series on negotiating profitable sales.
Business and Economics
Dist - VIDART Prod - VIDART

Preparation - Performance Measurements 20 MIN
U-matic / VHS
Color
Presents successful methods for measuring performance and quality control in a small or rural hospital.
Business and Economics; Health and Safety; Psychology
Dist - AHOA Prod - AHOA 1980

Preparation - physician recruitment 18 MIN
VHS / U-matic
Color
Offers practical recruitment and retention methods to enhance the physician recruitment process.
Guidance and Counseling; Health and Safety
Dist - AHOA Prod - AHOA 1980

Preparation - Pt one 16 MIN
VHS
Cardiac surgery - a new beginning series
Color (G PRO)
$195.00 purchase _ #E930 - VI - 029
Gives vital preoperative information to both patients and their spouses, including ways to cope with fears associated with cardiac surgery and practical advice about preparing for surgery. Part of a three - part series on cardiac surgery.
Health and Safety
Dist - HSCIC

Preparation - sharing and diversifying hospital services 20 MIN
U-matic / VHS
Color
Presents a nationwide perspective on activities and arrangements that small or rural hospitals are implementing. Discusses how a particular hospital is diversifying its services.
Health and Safety; Psychology
Dist - AHOA Prod - AHOA 1981

Preparation - the Chief Executive Officer as a Professional 19 MIN
U-matic / VHS
Color
Discusses the role of the chief executive officer of a small or rural hospital. Outlines methods for transferring responsibilities and developing management skills at department levels.
Business and Economics; Health and Safety; Psychology
Dist - AHOA Prod - AHOA 1980

Preparation - the Hospital as a Center for Community Health 20 MIN
VHS / U-matic
Color
Demonstrates how a hospital offering health awareness and promotion programs can become a center for community health.
Health and Safety; Sociology
Dist - AHOA Prod - AHOA 1981

The Preparatory 24 MIN
16mm
Color
Deals with life in a Catholic boys' boarding school, demonstrating a boy's adaptation to that life and the interpersonal relationships that develop among him and the older students and teacher - priests.
Fine Arts; Religion and Philosophy
Dist - USC Prod - USC

Preparatory techniques for gravlee jet washer endometrial specimens 17 MIN
16mm
Upjohn vanguard of medicine series
Color
LC 73-701867
Features obstetrician - gynecologist - pathologist Dr George Wied and cytotechnologist Margaret Harris of the University of Chicago, who demonstrate various laboratory procedures for preparing endometrial specimens for both histologic and cytologic analysis.
Health and Safety; Science
Dist - UPJOHN **Prod** - UPJOHN 1973

Prepare the Learner 29 MIN
16mm
Job Instructor Training Series
B&W (IND)
LC 77-703324
Business and Economics; Psychology
Dist - EDSD **Prod** - EDSD

Prepare the man 25 MIN
16mm
Color
LC 74-706183
Explains concepts in selective recruiting, proper placement, and specialized training of personnel. Points out the continuing need for missile crews, pilots, electronic specialists, scientists and related high level personnel.
Civics and Political Systems; Psychology
Dist - USNAC **Prod** - USDD 1962

Prepare to Win 18 MIN
U-matic / VHS / 16mm
Color (J H C)
Introduces the 1984 U S Olympic team's basketball coach. Reveals his secrets for winning championships.
Physical Education and Recreation
Dist - KLEINW **Prod** - KLEINW

Prepare with care 15 MIN
16mm
Color
LC 74-705405
Provides an informational and motivational look at modern main handling machines used in many U S Post Offices. Explains the importance of preparing U S Government mail properly for maximum service.
Social Science
Dist - USNAC **Prod** - USPOST 1969

Prepare your halter horse for show 60 MIN
VHS
Horse care and training series
Color (H C A PRO)
Covers the feeding, conditioning and schooling necessary to get a horse ready to compete at halter. Features a section on Arabians for attaining the ideal head and neck position.
Agriculture; Physical Education and Recreation
Dist - AAVIM **Prod** - AAVIM 1990
MOHOMV

Prepared childbirth 15 MIN
VHS
Color (PRO G)
$250.00 purchase _ #OB - 91
Acquaints viewers with the prepared childbirth experience. Follws one couple through their Lamaze preparation, showing the value of pre - natal classes and relaxation techniques. Climaxes with the couple's actual labor and delivery experience.
Health and Safety; Sociology
Dist - MIFE **Prod** - MIFE 1991

Prepared childbirth 29 MIN
VHS / 16mm
Health care today
Color (H C G)
Presents three couples discussing the issue of preparations for childbirth. Contemplates the father's role, what community organizations can help at this time, and the physician's role. Features commentary by two medical professionals.
Health and Safety
Dist - RMIBHF **Prod** - RMIBHF
TVOTAR

Prepared childbirth 16 MIN
16mm / U-matic / VHS
Prepared childbirth and parenting series
Color
LC 80-700071
Uses animation, dialogue scenes and documentary footage to explain the advantages and leading methods of prepared childbirth.
Health and Safety; Sociology
Dist - JOU **Prod** - PRORE 1979

Prepared Childbirth and Parenting Series
And spare the child 11 MIN
The Birth of Your Baby 14 MIN
Cesarean Childbirth 16 MIN
Fathers 16 MIN
It's not an Illness 24 MIN
A Moveable Feast - a Film about Breastfeeding 22 MIN
Prenatal Care - the Early Months 12 MIN
Prepared childbirth 16 MIN
Stress and the Child 10 MIN
Understanding Labor 11 MIN
Weight, Nutrition and Exercise during Pregnancy 8 MIN
Dist - JOU

Prepared childbirth and parenting series
Prenatal management 8 MIN
Dist - JOU
PRORE

Prepared childbirth and parenting series
Anatomy and physiology of pregnancy 6 MIN
Dist - PRORE

Prepared for health care 12 MIN
VHS
Color (G)
$149.00 purchase
Presents a video and workbook offering patients the skills they need to actively share in health care decisions. Teaches eight key areas - Procedure - course of action recommended by doctor; Reason - reason for procedure; Expectation - what benefits are expected; Probability - odds of getting hoped for benefit; Alternatives - other choices available; Risk - possible complications; Expense - costs; Decision - patient participation in making the decision. Produced by HealthCare Works.
Health and Safety; Home Economics
Dist - GPERFO

Preparing a case for trial - the last 180 days 180 MIN
VHS
Color (PRO)
$65.00, $125.00 purchase, $49.00 rental _ #CP-53130, #CP-63130
Emphasizes that setting the trial location and time; holding pretrial, status, and arbitration conferences; completing discovery; and proposing pretrial motions are necessary steps in preparing for trial. Includes a handbook with the audio or the video program.
Civics and Political Systems
Dist - CCEB

Preparing a case for trial - the last one hundred days 120 MIN
VHS / U-matic / Cassette
Color (PRO)
Shows the steps that may have to be taken before a law case is actually tried. Discusses pretrial strategy and provides tips on how to proceed from the filing of the at issue memorandum to the moment when the trial begins.
Civics and Political Systems
Dist - CCEB **Prod** - CCEB

Preparing a Child for a Renal Transplant
U-matic
Staff Development Series
Color (PRO)
Provides a program for showing how to teach a child who is about to undergo renal transplant what the operation is like. Includes kidney anatomy and functions, the use of dramatic play techniques, the question of kidney donors and post - operative appearance.
Guidance and Counseling; Health and Safety; Home Economics
Dist - CFDC **Prod** - CFDC

Preparing a Child for an Appendectomy
U-matic
Staff Development Series
Color (PRO)
Presents a program of teaching children about having an appendectomy. Discusses collecting teaching aids, the function of an appendix, post - operative appearance, physiology of the GI tract and the use of a body outline.
Guidance and Counseling; Health and Safety; Home Economics
Dist - CFDC **Prod** - CFDC

Preparing a Child for Anesthesia, or, Recovery Room and ICU
U-matic
Staff Development Series
Color (PRO)
Presents the essential points to be covered in a pre - operative teaching session for preparing a child for anesthesia. Treats such topics as no food before the operation, scrubbing, hospital clothing, parent participation and recovery room. The first of two parts.
Guidance and Counseling; Health and Safety; Home Economics
Dist - CFDC **Prod** - CFDC

Preparing a Child for Herniorrhaphy
U-matic
Staff Development Series
Color (PRO)
Presents a program for teaching the parents of a child about to undergo a herniorrhaphy how to teach their child about it. Demonstrates the use of teaching equipment, including the use of a body outline for discussing anatomy, operative site and post - operative appearance.
Guidance and Counseling; Health and Safety; Home Economics
Dist - CFDC **Prod** - CFDC

Preparing a cupola for charging 21 MIN
16mm
B&W
LC FIE52-146
Explains how to recognize the end of a heat. Follows the procedure for dropping bottom and for preparing a cupola for its next heat.
Industrial and Technical Education
Dist - USNAC **Prod** - USOE 1945

Preparing a custody case 51 MIN
U-matic / VHS
Preparing and trying a custody case series
Color (PRO)
Shares insights from two experienced family lawyers on how to prepare a custody case. Explores how to conduct the initial interview, obtain a case history and evaluate a case.
Civics and Political Systems; Sociology
Dist - ABACPE **Prod** - ABACPE

Preparing a Hem 5 MIN
16mm
Clothing Construction Techniques Series
Color (J)
LC 77-701231
Demonstrates the necessary first steps for achieving an inconspicuous hem on the right side of a garment. Shows how to keep an even and appropriate width that is parallel to the floor.
Home Economics
Dist - IOWASP **Prod** - IOWA 1976

Preparing a roast 20 MIN
BETA / VHS / 16mm
Color (G PRO)
$59.00 purchase _ #QF05
Shows how to prepare a rib roast for the oven. Describes the three types of heat transfer and the steps used to prepare a meat product for the roasting process.
Home Economics; Industrial and Technical Education
Dist - RMIBHF **Prod** - RMIBHF

Preparing a technical presentation 15 MIN
U-matic / VHS
Effective technical presentations series
Color
English Language; Industrial and Technical Education
Dist - DELTAK **Prod** - DELTAK

Preparing a working outline 30 MIN
VHS
Color (H C G)
$69.95 purchase _ #RWR - 6
Shows how to organize ideas into phrase or sentence outlines, maintaining balance with supportive statements. Discusses rearranging main points with subheadings, fine - tuning and reformulating the thesis, such as dealing with the problem of finding new information or disagreement between sources and the lack of supporting evidence.
English Language
Dist - INSTRU **Prod** - FLCCJA 1991

Preparing and examining expert witnesses 180 MIN
in civil litigation
VHS
Color (PRO)
$65.00, $125.00 purchase, $49.00 rental _ #CP-53215, #CP-63215
Provides information about how to choose and make use of expert witnesses in civil court proceedings. Explains how to use inspections, tests, and demonstrative evidence as well as how to handle opposing experts. Discusses preparing and cross-examining the witness. A handbook is included with either the audio or the video program.
Civics and Political Systems
Dist - CCEB

Preparing and setting a keelblock and bottom cradle 18 MIN
16mm
B&W
LC FIE52-191
Demonstrates the use of base line, vertical centerline, buttock lines, waterlines and frame lines in checking dimensions during ship construction. Shows how to lay a keelblock, use templates to make spauls and erect a ship cradle.

Industrial and Technical Education; Physical Education and Recreation; Social Science
Dist - USNAC Prod - USOE 1942

Preparing and Trying a Custody Case Series

Developing trial strategy in a custody case 46 MIN
Preparing a custody case 51 MIN
Trial Techniques in a Custody Case 74 MIN
Dist - ABACPE

Preparing and Trying a Medical Malpractice Case Series

Cross - examination of the medical expert 44 MIN
Direct Examination of the Medical Expert 66 MIN
Evaluation and Preparation of a Malpractice Case from the Defendant's Perspective 76 MIN
Evaluation and Preparation of a Malpractice Case from the Plaintiff's Perspective 82 MIN
Substantive Law - Consent to Treatment 51 MIN
Substantive Law - Vicarious Liability and Hospital Records 99 MIN
Substantive Law of the Physician - Patient Relationship 50 MIN
Dist - ABACPE

Preparing and using microscope slides
VHS
Science laboratory technique series
Color (J H)
$79.95 purchase _ #193 W 2201
Presents brief but thorough coverage showing the preparation of a permanently mounted slide. Part of a series on laboratory technique, including proper use and handling of equipment, preparation of materials and recording observations. Includes a supplementary teaching guide.
Science
Dist - WARDS Prod - WARDS

Preparing and using microscopic slides 19 MIN
VHS
Color (J H)
$145.00 purchase _ #A5VH 1009
Uses very clear photography to illustrate common laboratory techniques to prepare fresh - mount microscopic slides. Includes a brief but thorough section showing the preparation of a permanently mounted slide and a reference bank of commonly viewed commercially prepared slides.
Science; Science - Natural
Dist - CLRVUE Prod - CLRVUE

Preparing buffet foods 46 MIN
VHS
Buffets and banquet series
Color (H G)
$129.00 purchase _ #31175 - 027
Describes the roles of the staff, how to set up the room, how to schedule and coordinate serving. Illustrates preparation of cold buffet entrees, vegetables and salads emphasizing fresh ingredients and colorful display. Part of a three part series.
Education; Home Economics; Industrial and Technical Education
Dist - GA

Preparing chicken Cordon Bleu 20 MIN
VHS / BETA
Color (G PRO)
$59.00 purchase _ #QF20
Describes the step - by - step preparation of chicken Cordon Bleu, including how to fill, roll and present this entree.
Home Economics
Dist - RMIBHF Prod - RMIBHF

Preparing children for the hospital experience 28 MIN
U-matic / VHS
Color (PRO)
$275.00 purchase, $60.00 rental _ #7514S, #7514V
Shows nursing staff how to prepare their pediatric patients for a stay in the hospital. Reviews child cognitive developmental levels to help staff key their explanations to the level of understanding of each child. Demonstrates the use of books, diagrams, dolls and actual hospital equipment in patient teaching.
Health and Safety
Dist - AJN Prod - HOSSN 1985

Preparing Fabric 4 MIN
16mm
Clothing Construction Techniques Series
Color (J)
LC 77-701168
Identifies grain and bias directions and illustrates straightening of the fabric ends by tearing or pulling a crosswise yarn. Discusses preshrinking washable and nonwashable fabrics.
Home Economics
Dist - IOWASP Prod - IOWA 1976

Preparing flatfish to be served whole
U-matic / VHS
How to fillet fish series
Color
Home Economics; Industrial and Technical Education
Dist - CULINA Prod - CULINA

Preparing Foods 10 MIN
U-matic / VHS / 16mm
Pioneer Living Series
Color (I J H)
$265, $185 purchase _ #3131
Shows how settlers lived on food provided by forests and farms and how they stored food for winter.
History - United States; Home Economics
Dist - CORF

Preparing for a deposition 57 MIN
Cassette
Faster, more effective depositions in business cases series
Color (PRO)
$125.00, $30.00 purchase, $50.00 rental _ #DEP3-002, #ADE3-002
Emphasizes that changes in federal and local discovery rules resulting from the Civil Justice Reform Act of 1990 give courts greater control over the extent of discovery, while at the same time clients are demanding more efficiency, accountability and results, forcing effective business litigators to rethink their deposition strategies and practices. Shows how some of the nation's outstanding litigators develop their discovery and trial strategies and conduct depositions in a fraud case. Includes study guide.
Business and Economics; Civics and Political Systems
Dist - AMBAR Prod - AMBAR 1993

Preparing for a job interview 13 MIN
U-matic / VHS / 16mm
Color (G)
$20 rental
Presents the elements of preparation in a concise and realistic fashion. Features an unemployed job seeker as he goes through the process of preparing for a successful job interview. Addresses such topics as job research, networking, dependability, personal appearance and positive attitude.
Business and Economics; Guidance and Counseling; Social Science; Sociology
Dist - BRAURP Prod - BRAURP 1987

Preparing for and Conducting Effective Performance Reviews 40 MIN
U-matic / VHS
Performance Improvement Program Series
Color
Demonstrates how the performance review can be handled effectively, using positive role models and to plan future improvement in job expectations and requirements.
Business and Economics; Psychology
Dist - PRODEV Prod - PRODEV

Preparing for and taking depositions 56 MIN
VHS
Business litigation series
Color (C PRO)
$95.00 purchase, $71.25 rental _ #LBC04
Provides guidelines for preparing for and taking depositions in business litigation cases.
Civics and Political Systems
Dist - NITA Prod - NITA 1987

Preparing for Bed 16 MIN
16mm
PANCOM Beginning Total Communication Program for Hearing Parents of 'Series Level 2
Color (K)
LC 77-700504
Education; Guidance and Counseling; Psychology; Sociology
Dist - JOYCE Prod - CSDE 1977

Preparing for childbirth - a family affair 26 MIN
16mm
Color (H C A)
LC 75-702602
Shows how both a mother and father train and prepare for the birth of the family's third child. Emphasizes the roles of both parents in making the birth a success.
Health and Safety; Sociology
Dist - CRTVLC Prod - CINEMN 1975

Preparing for childbirth - a nine month experience
VHS / U-matic
Color (ARABIC SPANISH)
Emphasizes pre - natal visits and covers birth preparation classes on diet, exercise and relaxation techniques. Concludes with labor onset, birth and bonding.
Health and Safety; Sociology
Dist - MIFE Prod - MIFE

Preparing for Christmas I 60 MIN
VHS
Color (G R)
$24.95 purchase, $10.00 rental _ #35 - 87155 - 460
Presents four Advent themes, one for each week - Waiting, Hoping, Preparing, and Giving And Receiving. Utilizes Scripture, stories and music to further encourage the Christmas spirit. Hosted by Father Anthony Scannell.
Religion and Philosophy
Dist - APH Prod - FRACOC

Preparing for Christmas II 60 MIN
VHS
Color (G R)
$29.95 purchase, $10.00 rental _ #35 - 87184 - 460
Presents four reflections on the Advent season - The Child In Us, Santa Clausing, The Perfect Gift, and Journey To Bethlehem. Hosted by Father Anthony Scannell.
Religion and Philosophy
Dist - APH Prod - FRACOC

Preparing for College 20 MIN
U-matic / VHS / 16mm
Color (J)
LC 81-700016
Explains what the first year of college might be like and shows how students can prepare for their application to college.
Education
Dist - CRMP Prod - CBSTV 1981

Preparing for competition 14 MIN
VHS
Sports science series
Color; PAL (T J H)
PdS29.50 purchase
Reviews and summarizes important points about training and fitness, including setting realistic goals, practice and more. Features part of a seven - part series on the science behind sports and physical activity, suitable for health and physical education courses, coaching and fitness programs. Visual only; without narration.
Physical Education and Recreation
Dist - EMFVL

Preparing for Competition - 7 8 TO 37 MIN
VHS
Sports Science Series
Color (H)
$75.00 purchase
Presents the science behind sports and physical activity, including training, acquiring new motor skills and preventing injuries. Alternates scenes of athletes in practice and competition with views of anatomical models, commentary and graphics that explain the science and physiology behind movements. Program 7 reviews and summarizes important points about training and fitness, including setting realistic goals, practice, motivation and equipment.
Health and Safety; Physical Education and Recreation; Science - Natural
Dist - AITECH

Preparing for Dinner 16 MIN
16mm
PANCOM Beginning Total Communication Program for Hearing Parents of 'Series Level 2
Color (K)
LC 77-700504
Education; Guidance and Counseling; Psychology; Sociology
Dist - JOYCE Prod - CSDE 1977

Preparing for downsizing - Part I 45 MIN
VHS
Change in the workplace series
Color (G C PRO)
$695.00 purchase, $35.00 preview
Presents part one of a three - part series guiding managers and employees through downsizing. Includes an 18 - minute managerial video and a 27 - minute employee video.
Business and Economics; Psychology
Dist - FI Prod - FLILN 1995

Preparing for mainstreaming 60 MIN
VHS / U-matic
Teaching strategies for the development of auditory verbal communication series

Color
Shows a kindergarten child with severe to profound hearing loss and demonstrates ways of developing listening skills. An 8 year old mainstreamed child demonstrates the same activities on a second to third grade level.
Guidance and Counseling; Psychology
Dist - BELLAG **Prod** - BELLAG 1981

Preparing for negotiation 42 MIN
VHS / U-matic
Art of negotiating series
Color
Business and Economics; Psychology
Dist - DELTAK **Prod** - DELTAK

Preparing for negotiations 50 MIN
U-matic / VHS
Negotiation lectures series
Color (PRO)
Explains the benefit of getting background information, holding practice negotiation sessions and creating the proper atmosphere for negotiation.
Civics and Political Systems; Psychology
Dist - ABACPE **Prod** - NITA

Preparing for parenthood
U-matic / VHS
Parenthood - bringing new life into the world series
Color
Presents the feelings, beliefs, attitudes and experiences of a diverse group of parents. Compares and contrasts varied concepts of parental responsibilities and roles, discusses financial and emotional problems and examines the child - parent relationship during the formative years.
Guidance and Counseling; Science - Natural; Sociology
Dist - GA **Prod** - GA

Preparing for parenthood 15 MIN
16mm
Color (A)
#2X112
Discusses prenatal care for the Native American family. Deals with diets, exercise, alcohol, and drugs.
Health and Safety; Social Science
Dist - CDIAND **Prod** - BTFS 1981

Preparing for pictures 30 MIN
VHS
Practical guide to modeling series
(H C)
$29.95 purchase _ #FO200V
Explains the basics of photography modeling for the budding model. Discusses the importance of photography and the application of makeup before a shoot.
Home Economics; Industrial and Technical Education
Dist - CAMV **Prod** - CAMV

Preparing for success - the organization of your church - Tape 1 60 MIN
VHS
Management skills for church leaders series
Color (G R PRO)
$10.00 rental _ #36 - 81 - 223
Discusses the importance of organization. Covers reasons for training clergy and volunteers.
Business and Economics; Religion and Philosophy
Dist - APH

Preparing for successful sales relationships - Part 1 35 MIN
VHS
Real selling series
Color (A PRO)
$395.00 purchase, $150.00 rental
Presents the first of a five - part series on sales. Portrays real sales persons on sales calls. Covers subjects including establishing contacts, referrals, gathering sales leads by phone, and more.
Business and Economics; Psychology; Social Science
Dist - VLEARN

Preparing for, taking, and using depositions 360 MIN
VHS
Color (PRO)
$97.00, $175.00 purchase, $69.00 rental _ #CP-53262, #CP-63262
Demonstrates how to take and use depositions in commercial and personal injury cases, with practical advice for defense attorneys in such cases. Includes a handbook with either the audio or the video program.
Civics and Political Systems
Dist - CCEB

Preparing for the 21st century - the challenge of critical thinking 29 MIN
VHS
Color (H C T PRO)
$65.00 purchase, $35.00 rental
Features a high school teacher, Mr Halstead, who for 18 years has taught his students to think critically about issues of war, peace, and conflict resolution. Includes excerpts from his classroom presentations and interviews with students, parents and other teachers. Comes with process and course outlines. Produced by Ian Thiermann.
History - World; Psychology; Sociology
Dist - EFVP **Prod** - EFVP 1988

Preparing for the Conference 67 FRS
U-matic / VHS
Conference Leading Skills Series
Color
Covers the four steps of preplanning a conference and outlines steps for pinpointing precise conference objectives.
Business and Economics; English Language; Psychology
Dist - RESEM **Prod** - RESEM

Preparing for the future - implications of sea level rise 10 MIN
VHS
Color (G)
#V - 1
Presents facts and predictions for the future on rising sea levels. Looks at the effect global warming is having on the rise in our oceans due to ice caps melting. The Corps of Engineers predicts that the United States will need major coastal renovation to deal with this problem in the coming century. Discusses career opportunities for civil engineers. Contact distributor for information on loan arrangements.
Fine Arts; Geography - World; Industrial and Technical Education; Science - Physical
Dist - CZONEF **Prod** - YELCAT 1989

Preparing for the Interview - Program 7 25 MIN
VHS / 16mm
Job Search - How to Find and Keep a Job
Color (H C A PRO)
$720.00 purchase _ #SD100
Presents recommended answers for 16 common interview questions and cautions about body language. This program only available as part of the complete series. Part 7 of 12 parts.
Business and Economics; Guidance and Counseling
Dist - AAVIM **Prod** - AAVIM 1990

Preparing for the interview - Pt 001 25 MIN
VHS / 16mm
Job search - how to find and keep a job series
(H)
$69.00 _ #PA107V
Gives guidelines for answering questions and an overview of the interview process.
Guidance and Counseling
Dist - JISTW

Preparing for the Interview_Part 002 25 MIN
VHS / 16mm
Job Search - How to Find and Keep a Job Series
(H)
$69.00 _ #PA108V
Gives guidelines for answering questions and an overview of the interview process.
Guidance and Counseling
Dist - JISTW

Preparing for the Job Interview - Resume Writing, Research Methods, and Physical Appearance 30 MIN
VHS / BETA
Color (J H C)
Demonstrates those aspects of the job search process that job hunters should be concerned with prior to the interview.
Guidance and Counseling
Dist - BENNUP **Prod** - BENNUP 1987

Preparing for the Jobs of the 1990's - what You Should Know
VHS / U-matic
Color (H)
Explores factors that change the job market and the computer revolution, and tells how to keep pace with expanding technology. Attempts to develop a flexible approach to career preparation and outlines informational resources.
Industrial and Technical Education; Psychology
Dist - GA **Prod** - GA

Preparing for the review 35 MIN
U-matic / VHS
Appraisals in action series; Ses 2
Color
Focuses on the 'how' of the appraisal process. Prepares both employee and manager for the appraisal. Shows how to write specific objectives.
Business and Economics; Guidance and Counseling; Psychology
Dist - DELTAK **Prod** - PRODEV

Preparing for the summer hunt 20 MIN
VHS / U-matic
We are one series
Color (G)
Shows the village preparing for the hunt. The elderly and the sick will remain behind. Others will stay to protect and care for those who cannot go. Hi'bthaska has been assigned to stay because he has a grandmother who had chosen not to go on the hunt. Mi'onbathin begs Grandmother to find a way to go on the hunt and offers the use of travois but grandmother declines saying she will walk proudly to her death and not be pulled. Consequently Ni'bthaska will not earn 'warrior' status from participation in the hunt.
Social Science; Sociology
Dist - NAMPBC **Prod** - NAMPBC 1986

Preparing for Tomorrow's World 26 MIN
16mm
Careers in Nuclear Science and Nuclear Engineering Series
Color
LC 70-706769
Discusses the education necessary for a career in the nuclear field. Stresses the value of building a firm foundation in science, mathematics and English. States that government agencies, industry, and educational and research institutions engaged in a wide variety of projects all need nuclear scientists and engineers.
Science; Science - Physical
Dist - USNAC **Prod** - USNRC 1970

Preparing for Variable Modular Scheduling 25 MIN
16mm
Color (C T)
LC 76-710821
Discusses considerations in planning for the implementation of a variable program. Portrays the changes in learning behavior, teaching method, curriculum and facility design that have taken place in schools across the country on this type of schedule. Emphasizes the structural concepts of variable scheduling, the ways that time can be varied, performance and demand curriculum, individualized learning and the concept of teacher as director of learning.
Education; Guidance and Counseling
Dist - EDUC **Prod** - EDUC 1970

Preparing for Winter 9 MIN
16mm / U-matic / VHS
Primary Language Development Series
Color (K P I)
Presents scenes of animals preparing for winter.
English Language; Science - Natural
Dist - AIMS **Prod** - PEDF 1975

Preparing for Your Surgery 11 MIN
U-matic / 35mm strip
Color
LC 81-730135;
Introduces the patient to the basic feature of this preoperative care and describes the operating room environment. Discusses the consent form, preoperative testing and preparations immediately before a surgery.
Health and Safety
Dist - MEDCOM **Prod** - MEDCOM

Preparing lay readers 30 MIN
VHS
Color (H C G A R)
$39.95 purchase, $10.00 rental _ #35 - 865 - 2076
Teaches the high office of reading the Scriptures aloud in church. Covers topics including overcoming nervousness, rehearsal and exercises for voice and diction. Produced by Seraphim.
Religion and Philosophy
Dist - APH

Preparing meals 13 MIN
16mm
Cooking, home economics series
Color (J)
LC FIA68-1376
Presents five concepts dealing with meal preparation - planning the menu, breakfast, luncheon, dinner and snacks. The projector may be stopped after each part.
Home Economics
Dist - SF **Prod** - MORLAT 1968

Preparing Meals - the Last Step 26 MIN
U-matic / VHS
Food for Youth Series
Color (J H A)
Industrial and Technical Education; Social Science; Sociology
Dist - CORNRS **Prod** - CUETV 1975

Preparing Meals - the Last Step 27 MIN
16mm
Food for Youth Series
Color
LC 76-701594
Outlines quantity food preparation techniques and offers basic school lunch program aids which ensure that the children get maximum nutritional value.
Health and Safety; Home Economics; Social Science
Dist - USNAC **Prod** - USFNS 1974

Preparing medication from a vial 16 MIN
BETA / VHS / U-matic
Parenteral medication administration series
Color (C PRO)
$280.00 purchase _ #622.3
Begins with an explanation of the vial as a packaging container and describes how to access the vial. Presents techniques for withdrawing medication from a vial and expelling air bubbles. Demonstrates how to reconstitute medication in powdered form. Illustrates essential steps for combining medications from two vials into one syringe and highlights the procedure for combining insulins in one syringe. Part of a four - part series on parenteral medication administration produced by Healthcare Media.
Health and Safety
Dist - CONMED

Preparing medication from an ampule 13 MIN
BETA / VHS / U-matic
Parenteral medication administration series
Color (C PRO)
$280.00 purchase _ #622.2
Illustrates in detail the correct techniques for handling glass ampules. Demonstrates basic skills essential to withdrawing medications from ampules, including proper handling of the syringe and needle and safety factors. Part of a four - part series on parenteral medication administration produced by Healthcare Media.
Health and Safety
Dist - CONMED

Preparing NOW for success in the future 25 MIN
VHS
Careers 2000 series
Color (J H)
$95.00 purchase _ #FYI3A
Emphasizes personal information gathering, career exploration, and preparing for a future career. Discusses the importance of careful planning when pursuing educational and training options. Features high school programs, apprenticeships, military, junior and 4 - year colleges, proprietary schools and professional - graduate schools. Includes workbook. Part 3 of a 3 - part series.
Business and Economics; Guidance and Counseling
Dist - CFKRCM **Prod** - CFKRCM

Preparing old buildings for wiring 21 MIN
16mm
Electrical work - wiring series
B&W
LC FIE52-99
Discusses how to plan the wiring paths, visualizing the obstructions, and how then to prepare the paths for the wiring runs.
Industrial and Technical Education
Dist - USNAC **Prod** - USOE 1945

Preparing pattern for layout 29 MIN
Videoreel / VT2
Sewing skills - tailoring series
Color
Features Mrs Ruth Hickman demonstrating how to prepare the pattern for layout.
Home Economics
Dist - PBS **Prod** - KRMATV

Preparing petitions for certiorari to the US Supreme Court 35 MIN
Cassette
Effective argument to the court series
Color (PRO)
$125.00, $30.00 purchase, $50.00 rental _ #EAC1-005, #AEAC-005
Describes how to prepare petitions for certiorari to the US Supreme Court. Includes study guide.
Civics and Political Systems
Dist - AMBAR **Prod** - AMBAR 1989

Preparing professional notes and reports 15 MIN
U-matic / VHS
Health care security training series
Color (PRO)
Teaches the legal and operational importance of accurate notes and reports.
Health and Safety
Dist - CORF **Prod** - GREESM

Preparing Projected Materials 15 MIN
U-matic / VHS / 16mm
Color (C T)
LC FIA66-5
Illustrates the growth of the audio - visual field by contrasting the old magic lantern with the modern projection materials. Discusses the use of projectors, 2 X 2 cameras, polaroid copying stand and thermofax copier.
Education
Dist - PHENIX **Prod** - VEF 1964

Preparing Ration - Dense Foods 17 MIN
16mm
Color
LC 76-700475
Shows how to prepare ration - dense food items using standard Navy galley equipment afloat or ashore.
Civics and Political Systems; Home Economics; Industrial and Technical Education
Dist - USNAC **Prod** - USN 1976

Preparing the all - important business plan 57 MIN
VHS
How to start your own business series
Color (H A T)
$69.95 purchase _ #NC124
Looks at business strategy. Part of a ten - part series on starting a business.
Business and Economics
Dist - AAVIM **Prod** - AAVIM 1992

Preparing the Burn Patient for Transport 19 MIN
U-matic / VHS
Color (PRO)
LC 81-730383
Identifies the nurse's role in continuing physical support and preparation for transport of the burn patient. Discusses continuing physical support in terms of respiratory support, cardiovascular support, gastrointestinal support and other support measures which will assist the patient before transport.
Health and Safety
Dist - MEDCOM **Prod** - MEDCOM

Preparing the college application package
VHS / U-matic
(H A)
$29.95 _ #CVT100V
Presents a discussion of many aspects of the college admissions process. Provides insights into the steps involved in making decisions and gives advice on increasing one's chances of being admitted into the college of his or her choice. Based on interviews with officials from West Point, Princeton, Villanova and other universities.
Education
Dist - CAMV **Prod** - CAMV

Preparing the college application package 57 MIN
VHS
Color (H C A)
$19.95 purchase _ #S02195
Interviews admissions officers from 12 colleges, who tell what they look for in students and what can be done to increase chances of being admitted.
Education
Dist - UILL

Preparing the dancer for broadway 30 MIN
U-matic / VHS
Broadway dance series
Color
Fine Arts; Industrial and Technical Education; Physical Education and Recreation
Dist - ARCVID **Prod** - ARCVID

Preparing the deponent 50 MIN
VHS
Training the advocate - The Pretrial stage series
Color (C PRO)
$95.00 purchase, $71.25 rental _ #PTA06
Presents lectures and demonstrations of the steps of the pretrial stage. Covers strategies and techniques for receiving testimony from a deponent.
Civics and Political Systems
Dist - NITA **Prod** - NITA 1985

Preparing the expert deponent 48 MIN
VHS / Cassette
Taking depositions - VideoLaw seminar - series
Color (PRO)
$125.00, $30.00 purchase, $50.00 rental _ #DEP2-003, #ADEP-003
Teaches the fundamental skills involved in preparing for, taking and defending depositions. Includes demonstrations of preparing and deposing expert witnesses with Professor James McElhaney. Includes study guide.
Civics and Political Systems
Dist - AMBAR **Prod** - AMBAR 1988

Preparing the financial expert for deposition 59 MIN
VHS
Using financial experts in business litigation series
Color (C PRO)
$195.00 purchase, $95.00 rental _ #Z0402
Gives a broad perspective on the use of financial experts in business litigation cases. Features business litigation attorneys and financial experts in a joint analysis of an imaginary case. Presents guidelines for preparing financial experts for depositions.
Business and Economics; Civics and Political Systems
Dist - NITA **Prod** - NITA 1988

Preparing the food 24 MIN
U-matic
Occupations series
B&W (J H)
Shows the skills and knowledge required to prepare the food served in a restaurant.
Guidance and Counseling; Industrial and Technical Education
Dist - TVOTAR **Prod** - TVOTAR 1985

Preparing the halter horse for show 61 MIN
VHS / 16mm
(G)
$39.95 purchase _ #VT1069
Covers the feeding, conditioning, and schooling necessary to prepare a horse for halter competition in the show ring. Part of a series on horse care and training.
Agriculture; Physical Education and Recreation
Dist - RMIBHF **Prod** - RMIBHF

Preparing the Interview - Program 8 26 MIN
VHS / 16mm
Job Search - How to Find and Keep a Job
Color (H C A PRO)
$720.00 purchase _ #SD100
Continues Program 7 and deals with more difficult question in interviews. This program only available as part of the complete series. Part 8 of 12 parts.
Business and Economics; Guidance and Counseling
Dist - AAVIM **Prod** - AAVIM 1990

Preparing the lay witness for the deposition 47 MIN
Cassette
Taking Depositions - VideoLaw seminar - series
Color (PRO)
$125.00, $30.00 purchase, $50.00 rental _ #DEP2-001, #ADEP-001
Teaches the fundamental skills involved in preparing for, taking and defending depositions. Includes demonstrations of preparing and deposing lay witnesses with Professor James McElhaney. Includes study guide.
Civics and Political Systems
Dist - AMBAR **Prod** - AMBAR 1988

Preparing the loom 29 MIN
Videoreel / VT2
Exploring the crafts - weaving series
Color
Fine Arts; Home Economics; Industrial and Technical Education
Dist - PBS **Prod** - NHN

Preparing the Patient for Normal Delivery 13 MIN
VHS / U-matic
Color (PRO)
Shows how to prepare a patient for normal delivery of the infant.
Health and Safety
Dist - HSCIC **Prod** - HSCIC 1977

Preparing the second draft - revising, revising and revising 30 MIN
VHS
Color (H C G)
$69.95 purchase _ #RWR - 13
Shows how to review the contents of a paper for overall organization, factual accuracy and paragraph unity. Discusses recognizing slant vs bias, checking for precision and detail, looking for contradictions. Suggests techniques for reworking and polishing the introduction and conclusion.
English Language
Dist - INSTRU **Prod** - FLCCJA 1991

Preparing the Sensory and Visual Perceptual Motor Prerequisites for Communication 50 MIN
VHS / U-matic
Meeting the Communications Needs of the Severely/Profoundly Handicapped 1980 Series
Color
Discusses various abnormal reflexes that interfere with the communication development of cerebral palsied individuals.
Psychology; Social Science
Dist - PUAVC **Prod** - PUAVC

Preparing the way
VHS
Sell it to me series
Color; CC (IND PRO)
$870.00 purchase, $250.00 rental _ #VAR149
Gives pointers on sales approaches. Includes a leader's guide and briefcase booklet. Part of a two - part series.
Business and Economics; Psychology; Social Science
Dist - EXTR **Prod** - VIDART

Preparing the way - Pt 1 23 MIN
VHS
Sell it to me - Video, workshop and CD-i program series
Color (IND PRO COR A)
$870.00 purchase, $250.00 rental, $50.00 preview
Gives both new and experienced salespeople the chance to sharpen their skills. Novice and veteran sales representatives are presented with familiar lessons to learn such as, he fails to ask open questions, she makes too many assumptions, he loses control of his presentation, she doesn't listen to her customer.
Business and Economics
Dist - VIDART

Preparing theatre dance productions 30 MIN
U-matic / VHS
Broadway dance series
Color
Fine Arts
Dist - ARCVID **Prod** - ARCVID

Preparing thickening agents, making a roux 20 MIN
VHS / BETA / 16mm
Color (G PRO)
$59.00 purchase _ #QF17
Demonstrates how to prepare a roux and cornstarch mixture for use as a thickening agent. Gives helpful hints.
Home Economics
Dist - RMIBHF **Prod** - RMIBHF

Preparing to coach an effective offense 27 MIN
U-matic / VHS
Joe paterno - coaching 'winning football' series
Color (C A)
$49.00 purchase _ #3769
Shows the frequently overlooked details essential to an effective offense. Conducted by Joe Paterno, head coach of the Penn State football team.
Physical Education and Recreation
Dist - EBEC

Preparing to cook 13 MIN
16mm
Cooking, home economics series
Color (I)
LC FIA68-1377
Presents five concepts dealing with preparation for cooking - - selection of foods, cleanliness and storage, measuring and terms, ways of cooking and steps in getting ready to cook. The projector may be stopped after each concept.
Home Economics
Dist - SF **Prod** - MORLAT 1967

Preparing to dance 15 MIN
16mm / U-matic / VHS
Dance experience - training and composing series
Color (J H C)
Deals with the preparation of the dancer in studio classes that will develop technique and awareness of space, time and energy.
Fine Arts; Physical Education and Recreation
Dist - ATHI **Prod** - ATHI 1984

Preparing to give birth
VHS / U-matic
Parenthood - bringing new life into the world series
Color
Reviews, through case histories, pregnancy testing, childbirth, methods of delivery, the father's involvement and selection of a medical facility and personnel. Shows a childbirth education class and discusses the importance of psychological preparation.
Guidance and Counseling; Science - Natural; Sociology
Dist - GA **Prod** - GA

Preparing to perform Shakespeare 50 MIN
VHS / U-matic
Color
Shows director John Barton of the Royal Shakespeare Company working on a scene from Troilus And Cressida with actors Alan Howard, Michael Pennington, Ian McKellen, Patrick Stewart and David Suchet. Presents Ian McKellen describing the thoughts and ideas that run through an actor's mind as he prepares for a major soliloquy.
Fine Arts; Literature and Drama
Dist - FOTH **Prod** - FOTH 1984

Preparing to Speak 17 MIN
U-matic / 35mm strip
Effective Speaking Series
Color
Discusses the tools of development, organization and method of delivery of a speech. Offers six steps for preparing an oral presentation.
English Language; Psychology
Dist - RESEM **Prod** - RESEM

Preparing today for the challenges of tomorrow 56 MIN
VHS
Color (A PRO IND)
$69.95 purchase _ #S02007
Explores the 'balanced strategy concept' of management. Focuses on practicality, comprehensiveness, and intensiveness of implementation. Hosted by Dr Pete Johnson.
Business and Economics; Guidance and Counseling; Psychology
Dist - UILL

Preparing Training Objectives 12 MIN
U-matic / 35mm strip
Supervisor and OJT Series Module 2
Color
Shows supervisors how to develop sound training objectives with emphasis on preplanning and the significance of carefully stated objectives that cover action, standards and conditions.
Business and Economics; Psychology
Dist - RESEM **Prod** - RESEM

Preparing witnesses for deposition and trial 120 MIN
VHS / U-matic / Cassette
Color; Mono (PRO)
Presents practical tips and strategies for preparing witnesses. Includes such topics as attorney preparation, selecting witnesses to testify, preparing witnesses for examination, and handling uncooperative witnesses.
Civics and Political Systems
Dist - CCEB **Prod** - CCEB 1984^1984

Preparing Witnesses for Deposition and Trial 160 MIN
U-matic / VHS
Color
Discusses various considerations in preparing lay witnesses for deposition and trial, and methods for preparing expert witnesses.
Civics and Political Systems; Guidance and Counseling; Social Science
Dist - ABACPE **Prod** - CCEB

Preparing your home for sale 25 MIN
VHS
Color (A)
$19.95 purchase _ #S01573
Features host Les Cizek in a discussion of ways to prepare a home for sale. Covers topics including how to create the impression of space, how to tone down the overwhelming personal feeling of some rooms, and the importance of being completely honest with potential buyers.
Business and Economics; Home Economics
Dist - UILL

Preparing your home for sale 25 MIN
VHS
Color (A G)
$39.95 purchase _ #SH561
Walks the viewer through two homes, one professsionally prepared for sale, the other unprepared. Starts at the curb and goes through each room to discuss what should be considered in packaging and preparing the home for the broadest range of potential buyers and correcting any shortcomings in the home that might turn off the buyer.
Business and Economics; Home Economics
Dist - AAVIM **Prod** - AAVIM

Preparing your home health agency for the Joint Commission Accreditation Survey 30 MIN
VHS
Color (PRO C)
$195.00 purchase, $70.00 rental _ #4387
Demonstrates a 'mock survey' of a home health agency. Gives agency staff members the opportunity to see what is expected. Uses a question and answer format to provide realistic practice in addressing JCAHO survey concerns.
Health and Safety
Dist - AJN **Prod** - BELHAN

Preparing Your Home to Sell 45 MIN
VHS
Color (G)
$19.95 purchase _ #6111
Shares the secrets pros use to make homes sell faster and at better prices.
Agriculture; Business and Economics; Home Economics; Sociology
Dist - SYBVIS **Prod** - HOMES

Preparing your home to sell 45 MIN
VHS
Better homes and gardens video library series
(A)
Features an array of tips and suggestions for presenting a home in the most attractive and inviting manner. Teaches ideas for attracting buyers and introduces home improvement techniques useful to any homeowner. Demonstrates enhancing an entryway, arranging furniture, ridding a house of odors and performing simple repairs. Includes guidebook.
Business and Economics; Home Economics
Dist - PBS **Prod** - WNETTV
CAMV

Preparing your house for sale 25 MIN
VHS
Real estate video series
Color (G)
$39.95 purchase _ #261; $39.95 purchase _ #SH561
Walks the viewer through two homes - one professionally prepared for sale, the other unprepared. Starts at the curb and goes through each room and discusses what should be considered in packaging and preparing the home for the broadest range of potential buyers and correcting any shortcomings that might turn off the buyer. Features Les Cizek.
Business and Economics; Home Economics
Dist - DIYVC
AAVIM

Preparing Your Speech 28 MIN
VHS / U-matic
Business of Effective Speaking Series
Color
Tells how to prepare a business - related speech.
Business and Economics; English Language
Dist - KYTV **Prod** - KYTV

Preparing your students for the A C T 120 MIN
U-matic / VHS
A C T exam preparation series
Color (H)
Education
Dist - KRLSOF **Prod** - KRLSOF 1985

Preparing Your Students for the S A T 120 MIN
U-matic / VHS
SAT Exam Preparation Series
Color
Education
Dist - KRLSOF **Prod** - KRLSOF 1985

Preplacement interview 37 MIN
VHS
Sexually abused children in foster care training videotapes series
Color (PRO A C G)
$9.95 purchase _ #V515
Models a meeting between a foster parent and a caseworker in which the caseworker is placing a sexually abused child in the home. Provides both foster parents and caseworkers a perspective on the kinds of information that should be shared before placement. Part of an eight - part series training foster parents on the care of sexually abused children.
Guidance and Counseling; Sociology
Dist - FFBH **Prod** - FFBH 1993

Preplanning 28 MIN
U-matic / VHS
Business of Effective Speaking Series
Color
Suggests preplanning makes business - related speeches more effective.
Business and Economics; English Language
Dist - KYTV **Prod** - KYTV

Preplanning and Objectives 11 MIN
U-matic / 35mm strip
Supervisor as a Classroom Instructor Series Module 3
Color
Stresses the importance of formulating a set of objectives before starting any training session. Offers some practical help on developing sound objectives.
Business and Economics; Education; Psychology
Dist - RESEM **Prod** - RESEM

Prepositions 10 MIN
U-matic / VHS / 16mm
Wizard of Words Series
Color (P I)
Explains the basics of using prepositions.
English Language
Dist - MGHT **Prod** - MGHT 1976

Prepositions I - the strike - 18 30 MIN
VHS
English 101 - Ingles 101 series
Color (H) (ENGLISH, SPANISH)

$125.00 purchase
Presents a series of thirty 30 - minute programs in basic English for native speakers of Spanish. Focuses on a specific topic in order to emphasize a particular grammatical point or set of idioms. English is used from the beginning as the primary language of instruction but Spanish translations are included to ensure understanding. Part 18 identifies identification, prepositions of place - in, on, at.
English Language
Dist - AITECH **Prod** - UPRICO 1988

Prepositions II - the negotiation - 19 30 MIN
VHS
English 101 - Ingles 101 series
Color (H) (ENGLISH, SPANISH)
$125.00 purchase
Presents a series of thirty 30 - minute programs in basic English for native speakers of Spanish. Focuses on a specific topic in order to emphasize a particular grammatical point or set of idioms. English is used from the beginning as the primary language of instruction but Spanish translations are included to ensure understanding. Part 19 identifies prepositions of time - in, on, at, and prepositions of manner - by, like, with.
English Language
Dist - AITECH **Prod** - UPRICO 1988

Preprocessor
U-matic / VHS
'C' Language Programming Series
Color
Defines the preprocessor in 'C' language and how it works, what its effects are and how it performs these effects. Describes the syntax and usage of preprocessor token replacement and illustrates the syntax and use of conditional compilations.
Computer Science; Mathematics; Sociology
Dist - COMTEG **Prod** - COMTEG

Prerequisite to communication 22 MIN
16mm
Teaching high school mathematics - first course series; No 21
Color; B&W (T)
Mathematics
Dist - MLA **Prod** - UICSM 1967

Preschool articulation screening 18 MIN
16mm
Color (PRO)
LC 78-700817
Provides practice exercises for those who will be administering the Denver articulation screening exam. Supplements the slide/tape program Preschool Articulation Screening.
Education; English Language; Psychology
Dist - USNAC **Prod** - NMAC 1977

Preschool Child 41 MIN
VHS / U-matic
Infancy through Adolescence Series
Color
Shows the rapid development of gross motor skills and beginning development of fine motor skills through the medium of play activities. Discusses the emergence of the child as a social being.
Psychology; Sociology
Dist - AJN **Prod** - WSUN

The Preschool experience 30 MIN
U-matic
Growing years series
Color
Discusses the effect of early schooling on a child's development and the role of preschools in society.
Psychology
Dist - CDTEL **Prod** - COAST

The Preschool Experience - Four Programs 22 MIN
16mm / U-matic / VHS
Developmental Psychology - Infancy to Adolescence Series
Color (H C A)
LC 78-701012
Discusses the programs and goals of four preschools.
Education; Psychology
Dist - MGHT **Prod** - UCSD 1978

A Preschool Lesson in Cued Speech 7 MIN
16mm
Color
LC 74-705407
Presents a short teaching segment that incorporates manipulative visuals, hand signs and language to two - to three - year - old hearing impaired children.
Education; English Language; Guidance and Counseling; Psychology
Dist - USNAC **Prod** - USBEH 1972

Preschool mental development 30 MIN
U-matic
Growing years series
Color
Shows the preschool child's growing ability to use symbols and manipulate information. Discusses Piaget's stage of pre - operational thought.
Psychology
Dist - CDTEL **Prod** - COAST

Preschool personality 30 MIN
U-matic
Growing years series
Color
Discusses the personality development of the three - to six - year - old child.
Psychology
Dist - CDTEL **Prod** - COAST

Preschool Physical Development 30 MIN
U-matic
Growing Years Series
Color
Shows the physical growth of the three - to six - year - old child and discusses motor skills and physical and perceptual coordination.
Psychology
Dist - CDTEL **Prod** - COAST

Preschool Story Programs 20 MIN
U-matic
Access Series
Color (T)
LC 76-706250
Presents basic techniques for working with preschoolers in a library. Discusses how to select materials, present a story program and deal with problems that might arise.
Education
Dist - USNAC **Prod** - UDEN 1976

The Preschooler 15 MIN
VHS
Feeding with love and good sense series
Color (G)
$59.95 purchase _ #BUL004V
Discusses practical tips for preschoolers who want to get better at everything, including eating. Part of a four - part series featuring real parents, child care providers and children who show what works and doesn't work in feeding, as well as helping children to eat well, staying out of eating struggles with children, understanding feeding from the child's perspective and knowing when to hold the line.
Health and Safety; Sociology
Dist - CAMV

Prescribing Fluoride Supplements in Dental Practice 16 MIN
16mm
Color
Describes the rationale for prescribing dietary fluoride supplements for children in areas with fluoride deficient drinking water, ways to maximize longterm compliance and recommended dosages.
Health and Safety
Dist - MTP **Prod** - MTP

Prescription 7 MIN
16mm
Bellevue Volunteers Series
B&W
Describes the hospitals in New York City in need of volunteer services and discusses their physical plants and locations, and explains the procedures to follow in applying for volunteer assignments.
Health and Safety; Social Science
Dist - NYU **Prod** - NYU

Prescription and over - the - counter drugs 30 MIN
VHS / U-matic
Contemporary health issues series; Lesson 18
Color (C A)
Examines the rapidly growing drug industry in the United States. Investigates the effectiveness of government regulation of the drug industry. Studies the role of the physician in prescribing drugs. Gives special attention to the responsibility of the patient.
Health and Safety
Dist - CDTEL **Prod** - SCCON

Prescription drugs - advertising - adoption
VHS / U-matic
Consumer survival series
Color
Discusses various aspects of prescription drugs, advertising and adoption.
Business and Economics; Health and Safety; Home Economics; Sociology
Dist - MDCPB **Prod** - MDCPB

Prescription Drugs / Travel Tips / Air Conditioning
U-matic / VHS
Consumer Survival Series
Color
Discusses various aspects of prescription drugs, travel tips and air conditioning.
Geography - World; Health and Safety; Home Economics
Dist - MDCPB **Prod** - MDCPB

Prescription for a Profession - a Program on Physician Well - Being 16 MIN
U-matic / VHS
Color (PRO)
Stimulates discussion of causes, identification and prevention of physician impairment. Explores attitudes of affected colleagues and family.
Health and Safety; Sociology
Dist - HSCIC **Prod** - HSCIC 1984

Prescription for change 30 MIN
VHS / 16mm
Color (G)
$195.00 purchase, $60.00 rental
Probes the profession of nursing. Considers that many hospitals in the US are now owned by corporations as profit producing entities rather than as agencies of healthcare. Nursing staffs are being cut back, leaving remaining staff with long hours and total responsibility for patient care. Interviews nurses from a variety of hospitals who question the conditions that prevent providing responsible, quality healthcare and who present a prescription for change. Produced by Tami Gold and Lyn Goldfarb.
Business and Economics; Health and Safety; Sociology
Dist - WMEN **Prod** - GOGO 1986

Prescription for complaints 21 MIN
U-matic / VHS
Color (A)
Gives employees a 6 - stage strategy for handling any complaint. Uses a light touch to show right and wrong ways of dealing with complaints in the business world.
Business and Economics; Psychology
Dist - XICOM **Prod** - XICOM

Prescription for Complaints 20 MIN
VHS / U-matic
Color
Illustrates the six stages for handling complaints with special focus on the danger points.
Business and Economics
Dist - VISUCP **Prod** - VISUCP

Prescription for life 48 MIN
8mm cartridge / 16mm
Color (PRO H C A)
LC FIA 67-564; 73-700473; 73-700183
Presents detailed instructions in cardiopulmonary resuscitation, including artificial respiration, artificial circulation and definite treatment of all forms of cardiac arrest.
Health and Safety
Dist - BANDEL **Prod** - AHA 1967

Prescription for Profit 35 MIN
VHS / U-matic
Color
Examines what contributes to the rising costs which threaten to crush the health care system.
Business and Economics; Health and Safety; Social Science
Dist - WCCOTV **Prod** - WCCOTV 1981

Prescription narcotics 30 MIN
VHS
Video encyclopedia of psychoactive drugs series
Color (J H G)
$44.95 purchase _ #LVP6619V
Presents research in clinical and laboratory studies on prescription narcotics. Discusses the effects of prescription narcotics on the mind and body, addiction and abuse, recovery and rehabilitation, medical uses, importation and distribution facts, user methodology and trends. Part of a series.
Guidance and Counseling; Health and Safety; Psychology
Dist - CAMV

The Prescription Trap 38 MIN
U-matic / VHS
Color
Demonstrates that prescription drugs can be addictive and recovering alcoholics and drug abusers must avoid taking any mood altering chemical, whether wet or dry.
Health and Safety; Psychology; Sociology
Dist - WHITEG **Prod** - WHITEG

Prescription trap update 34 MIN
VHS
Color (H C G)
$500.00 purchase
Features Dr David Ohlm who explains the hidden dangers to recovering chemical dependents who use prescription and non - prescription drugs. Discusses polydrug or cross -

addiction and explains in clear language the dynamics of alcohol and drug withdrawal.
Guidance and Counseling; Health and Safety; Psychology
Dist - FMSP

Prescriptions for learning 30 MIN
16mm
Color (C A) (NAVAJO)
LC 75-702927
Pictures Navajo Indian children in special learning situations in order to show methods used in evaluating, testing and correcting learning disabilities.
Education; Psychology; Social Science
Dist - AVED **Prod** - USBIA 1975

Prescriptions for profit 60 MIN
VHS
Frontline series
Çolor; Captioned (G)
$300.00 purchase, $95.00 rental _ #FRON - 707K
Examines the pharmaceutical industry. Shows that developing new drugs takes large amounts of both time and money, with tremendous pressure to make money on their investments. Relates the importance of marketing.
Business and Economics; Health and Safety
Dist - PBS **Prod** - DOCCON 1989

The presence 4 MIN
16mm
Color (G)
$10.00 rental, $155.00 purchase
Shows the 'ratchety Japanese wood block style' - a short 'spook movie.'
Fine Arts
Dist - CANCIN

The Presence of Self
U-matic
Growth and Development - a Chronicle of Four Children Series Series '5
Color
Describes growth and development of a child from 15 to 16 months.
Psychology
Dist - LIP **Prod** - JUETHO

The Presence of Self - Gregory, 15 Months 7 MIN
16mm
Growth and Development - a Chronicle of Four Children Series Series '5
Color
LC 78-700686
Psychology
Dist - LIP **Prod** - JUETHO 1976

The Presence of Self - Joseph, 16 Months 7 MIN
16mm
Growth and Development - a Chronicle of Four Children Series Series '5
Color
LC 78-700686
Psychology
Dist - LIP **Prod** - JUETHO 1976

The Presence of Self - Melissa, 15 Months 6 MIN
16mm
Growth and Development - a Chronicle of Four Children Series Series '5
Color
LC 78-700686
Psychology
Dist - LIP **Prod** - JUETHO 1976

The Presence of Self - Terra, 16 Months 7 MIN
16mm
Growth and Development - a Chronicle of Four Children Series Series '5
Color
LC 78-700686
Psychology
Dist - LIP **Prod** - JUETHO 1976

The Presence of the past 30 MIN
VHS / BETA
Number, form and life series
Color (G)
$29.95 purchase _ #S505
Applies evolutionary theory to physics, chemistry and cosmology. Views all laws of the universe as habits developed over time. Features biologist Dr Rupert Sheldrake, author of 'A New Science of Life' and 'The Presence of the Past.' Part of a four - part series on number, form and life.
Religion and Philosophy; Science - Natural; Science - Physical
Dist - THINKA **Prod** - THINKA

Present 6 MIN
16mm / U-matic / VHS
Color (H C A)
Presents an animated film in which a bottle of liquid serves as payment for services. Shows how the bottle is passed along from one person to another without ever being opened. Tells of the tragic results when the bottle is finally opened.
Fine Arts; Guidance and Counseling
Dist - PHENIX **Prod** - SFTB

The Present chaos 30 MIN
U-matic / VHS
How wars end series
Color (G)
$249.00, $149.00 purchase _ #AD - 915
Looks at the legacy of World War II - dispossessed Germans, Hungarians and Czechs, a divided Germany, Poland a trouble spot and the threat of nuclear warfare. Offers the reassurance of historian Taylor, 'The Third World War will be the last.' Part of a six - part series on how wars end, hosted by historian A J P Taylor.
History - United States; History - World; Sociology
Dist - FOTH **Prod** - FOTH

The Present continuous tense - 5 30 MIN
VHS
English 101 - Ingles 101 series
Color (H) (ENGLISH, SPANISH)
$125.00 purchase
Presents a series of thirty 30 - minute programs in basic English for native speakers of Spanish. Focuses on a specific topic in order to emphasize a particular grammatical point or set of idioms. English is used from the beginning as the primary language of instruction but Spanish translations are included to ensure understanding. Part 5 considers formation, usage, time expressions.
English Language
Dist - AITECH **Prod** - UPRICO 1988

Present continuous tense - special spelling rules - 6 30 MIN
VHS
English 101 - Ingles 101 series
Color (H) (ENGLISH, SPANISH)
$125.00 purchase
Presents a series of thirty 30 - minute programs in basic English for native speakers of Spanish. Focuses on a specific topic in order to emphasize a particular grammatical point or set of idioms. English is used from the beginning as the primary language of instruction but Spanish translations are included to ensure understanding. Part 6 considers negative sentences, yes - no questions, information questions, spelling rules.
English Language
Dist - AITECH **Prod** - UPRICO 1988

A Present for Gramps - Volume 17 30 MIN
VHS
Our friends on Wooster Square series
Color (K P I R)
$34.95 purchase, $10.00 rental _ #35 - 87266 - 460
Presents religious concepts through storylines, songs and Scripture. Features puppet characters including Smedly, Troll and Sizzle.
Fine Arts; Literature and Drama; Religion and Philosophy
Dist - APH **Prod** - FRACOC

Present from Gondwanaland 30 MIN
VHS
Up a tree with David Bellamy series
Color; PAL (H C A)
PdS65 purchase
Travels around Australia and looks at the flora and fauna of the continent. Explores the ways in which the plants and animals have evolved in 200 million years of isolation from other species. Employs David Bellamy as a tour guide. Part five of a five part series.
Geography - World; History - World; Science - Natural
Dist - BBCENE

Present memory 88 MIN
16mm / VHS
Color (H C G)
$1200.00, $350.00 purchase, $200.00, $75.00 rental
Examines the many facets of ethnic and cultural Jewish life in America. Examines the effects of the Holocaust and the establishment of the state of Israel on American Jews. Interviews attorney Alan Dershowitz, the late Rabbi Meire Kahane of the JDL who sounds surprisingly moderate, and a young New Hampshire backwoodsman who quotes the Talmud at town meetings. Produced by Full Moon Productions.
History - United States; History - World; Sociology
Dist - FLMLIB

The Present situation - doubts and reassessment 40 MIN
VHS
Architecture at the crossroads series
Color (A)
PdS99 purchase _ Unavailable in Europe
Examines the main themes running through the world of architecture. Explores the exciting changes taking place in architecture in the late 20th century.The first program in a ten-part series.
Fine Arts; Industrial and Technical Education
Dist - BBCENE

Present tense 27 MIN
16mm
Color; B&W (G A)
$50.00 rental
Presents the work of filmmaker Jack Walsh. Defines Walsh's homosexual identity through the interplay of power relationships drawn from historical, personal and cultural contexts. Utilizes intellectual and physical travel in the modern state, both Amerian and European, to examine issues of attraction and death, torture and genocide, family relationships and gender.
Fine Arts; History - World; Industrial and Technical Education; Sociology
Dist - PARART **Prod** - CANCIN 1987

Present tense of verbs - 15 30 MIN
VHS
English 101 - Ingles 101 series
Color (H) (ENGLISH, SPANISH)
$125.00 purchase
Presents a series of thirty 30 - minute programs in basic English for native speakers of Spanish. Focuses on a specific topic in order to emphasize a particular grammatical point or set of idioms. English is used from the beginning as the primary language of instruction but Spanish translations are included to ensure understanding. Part 15 looks at simple present tense, verb forms, usage of simple present tense, pronouncing the ' - s' form.
English Language
Dist - AITECH **Prod** - UPRICO 1988

Present tense of verbs - negative 'do' and 'does' - 16 30 MIN
VHS
English 101 - Ingles 101 series
Color (H) (ENGLISH, SPANISH)
$125.00 purchase
Presents a series of thirty 30 - minute programs in basic English for native speakers of Spanish. Focuses on a specific topic in order to emphasize a particular grammatical point or set of idioms. English is used from the beginning as the primary language of instruction but Spanish translations are included to ensure understanding. Part 16 looks at simple present tense, auxiliaries 'do' and 'does,' negative sentences, word order, negative contractions.
English Language
Dist - AITECH **Prod** - UPRICO 1988

Present tense of verbs - questions and answers - 17 30 MIN
VHS
English 101 - Ingles 101 series
Color (H) (ENGLISH, SPANISH)
$125.00 purchase
Presents a series of thirty 30 - minute programs in basic English for native speakers of Spanish. Focuses on a specific topic in order to emphasize a particular grammatical point or set of idioms. English is used from the beginning as the primary language of instruction but Spanish translations are included to ensure understanding. Part 17 looks at simple present tense, yes - no questions, information questions, word order.
English Language
Dist - AITECH **Prod** - UPRICO 1988

Present the Operation 29 MIN
16mm
Job Instructor Training Series
B&W (IND)
LC 77-703324
Business and Economics; Psychology
Dist - EDSD **Prod** - EDSD

Present worth method 30 MIN
VHS / U-matic
Engineering econony series
Color (IND) (ENGLISH & JAPANESE)
Introduces an evaluation method which converts all cash flows to an equivalent amount today. Uses present value of a U S Treasury Bond as example.
Business and Economics
Dist - COLOSU **Prod** - COLOSU

The Presentation 26 MIN
U-matic / VHS
So You Want to be a Success at Selling Series Pt II
Color
Illustrates techniques for dealing with sales objections and points out the importance of watching for buying signals and then asking for the order.

Business and Economics
Dist - VISUCP **Prod** - VIDART

Presentation
U-matic
Matter of taste series; Lesson 20
Color (H A)
Shows viewers how to develop their own original ideas for presenting food with style. Discusses simple methods of stylish presentation. Demonstrates preparation of a meal served in edible containers.
Home Economics
Dist - CDTEL **Prod** - COAST

Presentation 50 MIN
U-matic / VHS
Training the trainer series
Color (IND)
Looks at lesson plans, classroom equipment, classroom presentation and using the overhead projector.
Education; Psychology
Dist - LEIKID **Prod** - LEIKID

Presentation 10 MIN
BETA / VHS / U-matic
Young job seekers series
Color; Stereo (H C)
Looks at the suitability of appearance, manner and attitude of three job applicants.
Guidance and Counseling; Psychology
Dist - SEVDIM **Prod** - SEVDIM 1984

Presentation excellence 77 MIN
U-matic / 16mm / VHS
Color (G PRO A)
$1295.00, $1095.00, $995.00 purchase, $350.00, $250.00 rental
Illustrates principles and techniques for presenting ideas to one person or to a group. Uses film clips and video segments of exceptional moments in presentation history. Features Walter Cronkite who shows how to master the skills of great presenters and how to tailor such skills to personal use.
Business and Economics; English Language; Psychology; Social Science
Dist - MAGVID **Prod** - MAGVID 1984

Presentation Excellence 77 MIN
VHS / 16mm
(C PRO)
$995.00 purchase, $350.00 rental
Presents examples of presentation skills by some recognized political, business and film personalities. Narrated by Walter Cronkite.
Education
Dist - VLEARN **Prod** - VPHI

Presentation Excellence 77 MIN
BETA / 16mm
Color (A)
Features Walter Cronkite, former CBS national news anchor, explaining techniques for making presentations, both to individuals and to large groups.
English Language; Guidance and Counseling; Psychology
Dist - CBSFOX **Prod** - CBSFOX

Presentation of the meal - are you being stared at
VHS
Meal presentation and etiquette video basics series
Color (G)
$39.95 purchase _ #CDKIT142V-H
Offers many ideas for preparing meals for groups and how to feel comfortable and confident when entertaining. Looks at the role esthetics plays in presenting a meal. Discusses the use of sauces to enhance a plate.
Home Economics
Dist - CAMV

Presentation reel of films on smoking and health 19 MIN
16mm
Color (H C A)
Presents highlights of American Cancer Society films on smoking and health.
Health and Safety
Dist - AMCS **Prod** - AMCS

Presentation reel of public education films 21 MIN
16mm
Color (H C A)
Promotes a broader use of films on cancer by showing a presentation of short excerpts from selected American Cancer Society public education films.
Guidance and Counseling; Health and Safety
Dist - AMCS **Prod** - AMCS

Presentation Reel of School Films 20 MIN
16mm
Color (H C A)
Presents footage put together by the national office of the American Cancer Society related to cigarette smoking and health.

them avoid sexual exploitation, and talking about touching for preschoolers. Age - appropriate delivery of key messages are modeled, and alternatives for handling difficult questions are presented.
Health and Safety; Psychology; Sociology
Dist - AIMS **Prod** - SICACC 1987

Presenting and arguing damages in tort cases 90 MIN
VHS
Color (A PRO C)
$95.00 purchase _ #Y801
Focuses on presenting and refuting damage theories in tort cases, demonstrated by two renowned litigators, S Gerald Litvin and Perry S Bechtle, both of Philadelphia.
Civics and Political Systems
Dist - ALIABA **Prod** - CLETV 1992

Presenting and cross examining the damages claim 56 MIN
VHS / Cassette
Winning the business jury trial series
Color (PRO)
$125.00, $30.00 purchase, $50.00 rental _ #BUS1-007, #ABUS-007
Provides sophisticated trial skills training for the business litigator. Demonstrates business cases including lender liability, securities fraud and antitrust. Explains how to present and cross examine the damages claim, giving the viewer an analytical framework in which to view subsequent demonstrations and discussions. Gives an insider's look at nationally recognized business litigators as they plan their strategies. Includes a psychologist who specializes in persuasive communication strategies and decision-making processes providing analysis based on empirical research and juror interviews. Includes study guide.
Business and Economics; Civics and Political Systems
Dist - AMBAR **Prod** - AMBAR 1992

Presenting Documentary and Demonstrative Evidence Effectively 120 MIN
VHS / U-matic
Color
Covers collection of evidence, getting evidence admitted and employing the evidence most effectively during trial.
Civics and Political Systems; Social Science
Dist - ABACPE **Prod** - CCEB

Presenting One - Third 15 MIN
U-matic
Math Factory, Module V - Fractions Series
Color (P)
Introduces the concepts of thirds and their relationship to a whole.
Mathematics
Dist - GPN **Prod** - MAETEL 1973

Presenting the Bayeux Tapestry 13 MIN
VHS
Color; PAL (G)
Examines closely the Bayeux Tapestry to point out details. Looks at the differences between Norman and English haircuts, the styles of dress, and marginal details. Relates historical events to their depiction in the main panels of the tapestry.
Fine Arts; History - World; Industrial and Technical Education
Dist - VIEWTH

Presenting the case 32 MIN
16mm
We can help series
Color (PRO)
LC 77-703247
Dramatizes a social worker's testimony in a child abuse hearing before the juvenile court.
Civics and Political Systems; Home Economics; Sociology
Dist - USNAC **Prod** - NCCAN 1977

Presenting the Story 61 FRS
VHS / U-matic
Basic Sales Series
Color
Focuses on the best way to communicate benefits to the customer. Emphasizes careful preparation and practice as keys to success.
Business and Economics; Psychology
Dist - RESEM **Prod** - RESEM

Presenting Your Sales Case Convincingly 30 MIN
16mm / U-matic / VHS
B&W (PRO)
Explains that no matter how well salesmen or dealers know their product, or the answers to whatever objection a prospect might raise, unless they are able to present their sales case convincingly, nothing happens. Demonstrates skills used by sales champions to convince skeptics.

Health and Safety; Psychology
Dist - AMCS **Prod** - AMCS

Presentation skills 30 MIN
VHS / U-matic
Communication skills for managers series
Color (A)
Demonstrates how to make a presentation and gives many pointers on projecting an overall favorable image in any business situation. Gives principles for preparing and conducting a formal presentation. Hosted by Richard Benjamin and Paula Prentiss.
Business and Economics; English Language; Psychology
Dist - TIMLIF **Prod** - TIMLIF 1981

Presentation skills - hook, line, sinker 50 MIN
VHS
Color (A PRO IND)
$199.00 purchase _ #S01130
Teaches skills in making presentations. Covers subjects including the four levels of communication and how to use them, organizing the presentation, and making presentations with minimal anxiety. Hosted by communication consultant Tom Mira.
English Language; Psychology; Social Science
Dist - UILL

Presentation techniques - teaching in three domains - no 5 60 MIN
U-matic
Training the trainer series
Color (PRO)
Presents training sessions for professional training personnel. Includes goal selection, design and presentation of training material and evaluation and reports.
Education; Industrial and Technical Education
Dist - VTRI **Prod** - VTRI 1986

Presentations and explanations 30 MIN
VHS
Effective teacher telecourse series
Color (T)
$69.95 purchase, $50.00 rental
Covers lesson presentations and explanations. Hosted by Dr Loren Anderson.
Education; Psychology
Dist - SCETV **Prod** - SCETV 1987

Presentations that work
VHS / 16mm
(PRO)
Teaches viewer how to prepare, deliver, and illustrate a presentation.
Business and Economics; English Language
Dist - MRCC **Prod** - MRCC

Presente Series

Alpaca breeders of Chimboya	29 MIN
First look - Pt I	29 MIN
First look - Pt II	29 MIN
Manos a La Obra - the Story of Operation Bootstrap - Pt I	28 MIN
Manos a La Obra - the Story of Operation Bootstrap - Pt II	29 MIN
Manuel Jimenez - Woodcarver	29 MIN
The Mexican Tapes - a Chronicle of Life Outside the Law - Pt I - El Gringo	29 MIN
The Mexican Tapes - a Chronicle of Life Outside the Law - Pt II - El Rancho Grande	29 MIN
The Mexican Tapes - a Chronicle of Life Outside the Law - Pt III - the Winner's	29 MIN
The Mexican Tapes - a Chronicle of Life Outside the Law - Pt IV - La Migra	29 MIN
Moon Shadows	29 MIN
Nicaragua - the Other Invasion	29 MIN
Sojourn Earth	29 MIN

Dist - KCET

The Presenter - a videodisc utility
Videodisc
(G)
$59.00 purchase _ #VID5501 - 5
Allows the computer screen to be used as a paper outline and the videodisc player a slide or movie projector when composing interactive outlines for video lectures or presentations. Requires an Apple IIe, IIc, or IIGS computer, a Pioneer videodisc player in the LD - V6000 or LD - V4200 series and an Apple Super Serial Card.
Computer Science; Education
Dist - MECC **Prod** - MECC

Presenting a Personal Safety Curriculum 30 MIN
VHS / 16mm
Color (C A PRO)
$145.00 purchase, $50.00 rental _ #9875
Shows three lessons - talking about touching for elementary age children to prevent child abuse, personal safety and decision - making for intermediate - age children to help

Business and Economics; Psychology; Social Science; Sociology
Dist - DARTNL Prod - DARTNL

Presents 90 MIN
16mm
Color (C)
$4000.00
Offers an experimental film by Michael Snow.
Fine Arts
Dist - AFA Prod - AFA 1981

Presents 15 MIN
VHS / U-matic
Picture Book Park Series Brown Module; Brown module
Color (P)
Presents the children's stories Ask Mr Bear by Marjorie Flack and Mr Rabbit And The Lovely Present by Charlotte Zolotow.
Literature and Drama
Dist - AITECH Prod - WVIZTV 1974

Presents, Beautiful 10 MIN
U-matic
Readalong Two Series
Color (P)
Provides young viewers with a flexible range of reading experiences through active involvement in reading and writing. Comes with teacher's guide and kit.
Education; English Language; Literature and Drama
Dist - TVOTAR Prod - TVOTAR 1976

Preservation and adaption 40 MIN
VHS
Architecture at the crossroads series
Color (A)
PdS99 purchase _ Unavailable in Europe
Examines the main themes running through the world of architecture. Details how old buildings are given a new lease of life. The eighth program in a ten-part series.
Fine Arts; Industrial and Technical Education
Dist - BBCENE

Preservation of bacteria by desiccation in vacuo 11 MIN
16mm
B&W (PRO)
LC FIE52-2233
Demonstrates the technique for desiccation in vacuo as a method of preservation for most bacteria. For professional use.
Health and Safety
Dist - USNAC Prod - USPHS 1949

Preservation of pair bonds through rival inhibitation in hamadryas baboons 27 MIN
VHS / U-matic
Color (C G T A)
Examines field studies undertaken to construct detailed hypotheses concerning the inhibitory mechanisms that to a great extent prevent Hamadryas baboon males from stealing one another's mates, thus enabling physically inferior males to possess a harem. Shows hypotheses retested in cage experiments.
Health and Safety; Psychology; Science - Natural
Dist - PSU Prod - PSU 1975

Preserve 5 MIN
16mm
B&W
LC 72-702419
Shows wild African animals in a game preserve and in their reactions to human visitation. Explores commerical values and the peculiar relationship of 'caged' people viewing 'free' wildlife.
Fine Arts; Science - Natural
Dist - USC Prod - USC 1972

Preserving Egypt's Past 23 MIN
U-matic / VHS / 16mm
Color (J)
Looks at the monuments, temples and tombs that have survived since the days of ancient Egypt. Shows how agriculture, population, changing weather conditions and even tourists are endangering the monuments.
History - World; Science - Physical
Dist - NGS Prod - NGS 1982

Preserving flowers and foliages 61 MIN
VHS / 16mm
(G)
$39.95 purchase _ #VT1045
Shows how to preserve garden flowers in silica gel using a microwave oven technique. Gives tips on preserving foliage in glycerine solution and the art of pressing flowers.
Fine Arts; Science - Natural
Dist - RMIBHF Prod - RMIBHF

Preserving flowers and foliages 61 MIN
VHS / BETA
Crafts and decorating series
Color
Demonstrates pressing flowers. Shows how to preserve flowers in silica gel using a microwave oven. Tells how to preserve foliages in glycerine solution.
Science - Natural
Dist - MOHOMV Prod - MOHOMV

Preserving Flowers and Foliages 61 MIN
VHS
Morris Flower Series
(A)
$29.95 _ #MX1315V
Teaches the viewer how to preserve flowers and foliage using various mediums and methods.
Science - Natural
Dist - CAMV Prod - CAMV

Preserving Holland's Tidal Ecology 16 MIN
U-matic / VHS / 16mm
One Second Before Sunrise - Search for Solutions, Program 1 Series
Color (J)
$110.00, $85.00 purchase, $25.00 rental
Describes how a specially designed dike built in the 1960s prevents storms from threatening the Eastern Scheldt Delta of Holland's North Sea coast.
Geography - World; Industrial and Technical Education; Science - Natural; Science - Physical; Social Science; Sociology
Dist - BULFRG Prod - HCOM 1990

Preserving the landscape 30 MIN
VHS / U-matic
Art America series
Color (H C A)
$43.00 purchase
Examines the development of Luminism in American art and the interest in the preservation of the land. Part of a 20-part series.
Fine Arts
Dist - CTI Prod - CTI
GPN

Preserving the past 26 MIN
VHS / U-matic
Color (C G)
$149.00 purchase _ #EX1884
Focuses on the restoration and preservation of art, historic documents and buildings. Visits on - going preservation projects at the Winterthur Museum in Wilmington, Delaware, Princeton University's rare book collection, and a century - old county courthouse whose stone, wood and marble are all being restored.
Fine Arts
Dist - FOTH Prod - FOTH

Preserving the past to ensure the future 15 MIN
VHS
Color (I J H G)
$175.00 purchase
Visits Yad Vashem, a memorial complex of museum, art and archives housed in Jerusalem and dedicated to collecting and preserving documentation of the Holocaust of World War II. Includes the Children's Memorial in memory of the 1.5 million children killed in the Holocaust. Looks at children's drawings and poems recovered from some of the death camps and historical film and slides.
History - World; Sociology
Dist - LANDMK Prod - LANDMK 1992

Preserving the past to ensure the future 15 MIN
VHS
B&W (I J H G)
$29.95 purchase _ #620
Visits Yad Vashem museum in Jerusalem and its Children's Memorial to the 1.5 million children who perished in the Holocaust because they were Jewish. Produced by Ray Errol Fox.
History - World; Sociology
Dist - ERGOM Prod - ERGOM

Preserving your sight 15 MIN
VHS
Color (G PRO C)
$200.00 purchase _ #EY - 19
Educates older patients and their families and makes them aware of the physical changes and common eye disorders associated with aging. Discusses the medical, surgical and optical techniques that can help patients retain good vision for a lifetime.
Health and Safety; Science - Natural
Dist - MIFE Prod - MIFE

The Presidency 17 MIN
VHS
More perfect union - the three branches of the federal government series
Color (J H C G)
Reviews the powers and responsibilities of the President of the United States. Looks at some critical issues surrounding presidential decision - making. Part of a three - part series on the branches of the federal government.
Civics and Political Systems
Dist - CAMV

The Presidency 17 MIN
VHS
More perfect union series
Color (I J)
$55.00 purchase _ #4010VD
Reviews the powers and duties of the United States President. Takes a look at some critical issues surrounding presidential decision - making. Includes a guide. Part of a three - part series on the three branches of the federal government.
Civics and Political Systems
Dist - KNOWUN Prod - KNOWUN 1992

The Presidency 19 MIN
VHS / U-matic / BETA / 16mm
Focus on the Constitution series
Color (J H C A)
$425.00, $250.00 purchase _ #JY - 4905M
Considers the President of the United States as the most powerful and influential person in the world. Looks at specific powers granted to the President by the Constitution. Considers the expansion of Presidential authority unforeseen by the framers of the Constitution. Examines checks on Presidential power. Surveys the development of the presidency from the swearing in of George Washington to the fall of Richard Nixon and his 'imperial presidency.' Part of a series on the United States Constitution.
Biography; Civics and Political Systems; History - United States
Dist - CORF Prod - CORF 1987

The Presidency 60 MIN
VHS
Power Game Series
Color; Captioned (G)
$59.95 purchase _ #TPGE - 104
Considers the role of the president in American government. Proposes that a successful president is a combination of economist, diplomat and 'regular guy' all rolled into one. Suggests that there has been a growing trend toward management of media coverage, and that this has actually hurt policy making. Hosted by Hedrick Smith.
Civics and Political Systems; History - United States; Sociology
Dist - PBS Prod - MPTPB 1988

The Presidency 18 MIN
35mm strip / VHS
US government in action series
Color (J H C T A)
$57.00, $45.00 purchase _ #MB - 510778 - 3, #MB - 509992 - 6
Examines the executive branch of the US government. Emphasizes the Constitutional concept of checks and balances. Uses archival and modern graphics.
Civics and Political Systems
Dist - SRA Prod - SRA 1988

The Presidency 28 MIN
16mm
B&W
LC 74-705409
Depicts the evolution of the constitutional powers and day - to - day duties of the President of the United States. Explains how presidential decision making has become almost too burdensome for one person. Discusses the relationship of the executive, legislative and judicial branches of government.
Civics and Political Systems
Dist - USNAC Prod - USDD 1967

The Presidency 30 MIN
VHS / 16mm
Government by Consent - a National Perspective Series
Color (I J H C A)
Describes the organization, structure and powers of the Presidency and assesses why individual presidents may emphasize one or more roles over others.
Biography; Civics and Political Systems
Dist - DALCCD Prod - DALCCD 1990

The Presidency 12 MIN
16mm
Senator Sam Ervin, Jr - the Constitution Series
Color (J H)
Discusses Article II of the Constitution, which deals with Executive powers.
Civics and Political Systems
Dist - COUNFI Prod - CHILBE

The Presidency - 100 Days of Jimmy Carter 29 MIN
VHS / 16mm
Color (G)
$55.00 rental _ #POJC - 000
Assesses the first 100 days of Jimmy Carter's Presidency.
Civics and Political Systems
Dist - PBS Prod - WGBHTV

The Presidency - how much alone 29 MIN
VHS / 16mm
Color (G)
$55.00 rental _ #PHMA - 000
Analyzes the ways in which the office of the President works within its limitations and through the strength of other political forces. Examines President Jimmy Carter's difficulties with Congress and demonstrates similar power limitations experienced by other past presidents.
Civics and Political Systems
Dist - PBS **Prod** - WGBHTV

Presidency Series
The Perfect President - a Man for His Time 52 MIN
The Possible Presidents - Vice Presidents and Third Parties 52 MIN
The Private President - the Man and , His Family 52 MIN
The Public President - Wit and Warmth in the White House 52 MIN
Dist - LUF

The Presidency, the Press and the People 120 MIN
VHS
Color (G)
$89.95 purchase _ #PRPP - 000
Interviews the press secretaries of former Presidents Kennedy, Johnson, Nixon, Ford, Carter and Reagan. Explores the question of whether press secretaries are communicators or image makers, with the participants disagreeing about the answer. Hosted by NBC commentator John Chancellor.
Civics and Political Systems; History - United States; Sociology
Dist - PBS **Prod** - KPBS 1990

The Presidency - Volume I 28 MIN
VHS
Who, what, where, why and when series
B&W (G)
$14.95 purchase _ #FV - 816
Traces the historical evolution of the constitutional powers and day to day duties of the President of the United States. Starts with George Washington and proceeds through Lyndon B Johnson. Includes dramatizations and archival footage of recent presidents.
Biography; Civics and Political Systems; History - United States
Dist - INCRSE

The President and Congress 30 MIN
VHS / 16mm
Government by Consent - a National Perspective Series
Color (I J H C A)
Examines and illustrates the deliberate nature of conflict and cooperation between the legislative and executive branches of the U S government. Issues used as examples are the federal budget and war making powers.
Civics and Political Systems
Dist - DALCCD **Prod** - DALCCD 1990

President Gerald Ford, the Oath and Straight Talk among Friends 12 MIN
16mm
Great Decisions Series
Color (J)
LC 75-702938
Documents the inauguration of Gerald Ford as president. Includes the oath of office and the acceptance speech.
Biography; Civics and Political Systems
Dist - AMEDFL **Prod** - ACME 1974

President, press and public 29 MIN
16mm
Government story series; No 33
Color
LC 71-707185
Discusses the ways in which the President communicates with the public through the press and broadcast media, and examines such questions as the credibility gap, the white lie and managed news.
Civics and Political Systems; Psychology; Social Science
Dist - WBCPRO **Prod** - WBCPRO 1968

A President remembered 5 MIN
16mm
Screen news digest series
B&W (J A)
LC FIA68-2098
A tribute to the late President Kennedy. Reveals plans for his permanent grave marker at Arlington National Cemetery. Volume seven, issue five of the series.
Biography; History - United States
Dist - HEARST **Prod** - HEARST 1964

President Ronald Reagan's farewell address - Wednesday, January 11, 1989 30 MIN
VHS
Nightline series
Color (H C G)
$14.98 purchase _ #MP6171
Marks the final public address of Ronald Reagan as President of the United States.
Biography; Fine Arts
Dist - INSTRU **Prod** - ABCNEW 1989

The President versus congress - executive privilege and the delegation of power 60 MIN
VHS / U-matic
Constitution - that delicate balance series
Color
Questions whether a President is bound by congressional limits he does not choose to honor and what Congress can do if he ignores them. Offers a hypothetical case concerning presidential appointees whose views conflict with congressional intentions for their agencies.
Civics and Political Systems
Dist - FI **Prod** - WTTWTV 1984

The President versus congress - war powers and covert action 60 MIN
VHS / U-matic
Constitution - that delicate balance series
Color
Offers a hypothetical case involving the War Powers Act which explores whether the Constitution has - or has ever had - relevance in the implementation of foreign policy.
Civics and Political Systems
Dist - FI **Prod** - WTTWTV 1984

Presidential and state designs 30 MIN
VHS / 16mm
Art of decorating cakes series
(G)
$49.00 purchase _ #BCD21
Instructs in the art of cake decorating. Illustrates patriotic cake decorating techniques. Shows how to make state seals and presidential seals out of piping gel on parchment paper and transfer to cake, also using presidential borders. Taught by Leon Simmons, master cake decorator.
Home Economics; Industrial and Technical Education
Dist - RMIBHF **Prod** - RMIBHF

Presidential Campaign of 1952 9 MIN
8mm cartridge / 16mm
U S Presidential Elections 1928 - 1968 Series
B&W (C)
LC 75-703328
Biography; Civics and Political Systems; History - United States
Dist - KRAUS **Prod** - KRAUS 1975

Presidential Campaign of 1956 9 MIN
16mm
U S Presidential Elections 1928 - 1968 Series
B&W (C)
LC 75-703330
Biography; Civics and Political Systems; History - United States
Dist - KRAUS **Prod** - KRAUS 1975

Presidential Campaigning 30 MIN
VHS / 16mm
Government by Consent - a National Perspective Series
Color (I J H C A)
Describes the factors, especially scheduling, polling and fundraising, that influence presidential campaigns.
Civics and Political Systems
Dist - DALCCD **Prod** - DALCCD 1990

Presidential Campaigns and the Influence of Music, 1840 - 1916 27 MIN
16mm
Color
LC 76-702870
Shows what Presidential campaigning was like before the advent of radio and television. Explains how music was an integral part of campaigning by influencing the emotions of the voters.
Civics and Political Systems; Fine Arts; History - United States; Psychology; Sociology
Dist - DANA **Prod** - DANA 1976

Presidential Character 30 MIN
U-matic / VHS
American Government Series; 1
Color (C)
Discusses a theory that childhood, relationships with parents and peers and successes and failures make permanent imprints on leaders. Examines several Presidents.
Civics and Political Systems
Dist - DALCCD **Prod** - DALCCD

Presidential debates 30 MIN
U-matic
Adam Smith's money world series; 106
Color (A)
Attempts to demystify the world of money and break it down so that small as well as large businesses and their workers understand and adjust to new social and economic trends. Reports on major economic stories and discoveries.
Business and Economics
Dist - PBS **Prod** - WNETTV 1985

Presidential Election of 1928 7 MIN
8mm cartridge / 16mm
U S Presidential Elections 1928 - 1968 Series
B&W (C)
LC 75-703322
Biography; Civics and Political Systems; History - United States
Dist - KRAUS **Prod** - KRAUS 1975

Presidential Election of 1960 16 MIN
16mm
U S Presidential Elections 1928 - 1968 Series
B&W (C)
LC 75-703331
Biography; Civics and Political Systems; History - United States
Dist - KRAUS **Prod** - KRAUS 1975

Presidential Election of 1964 10 MIN
16mm
U S Presidential Elections 1928 - 1968 Series
B&W (C)
LC 75-703332
Biography; Civics and Political Systems; History - United States
Dist - KRAUS **Prod** - KRAUS 1975

Presidential Election of 1968 9 MIN
8mm cartridge / 16mm
U S Presidential Elections 1928 - 1968 Series
B&W (C)
LC 75-703333
Biography; Civics and Political Systems; History - United States
Dist - KRAUS **Prod** - KRAUS 1975

The Presidential persuaders 29 MIN
16mm
Government story series
Color
LC 75-707186
Stephen Horn talks with Presidential special assistants Joseph A Califano and Bryce Harlow about the ways in which the President leads and lobbies Congress to get his program enacted into law. Number 28 in the series.
Biography; Civics and Political Systems
Dist - WBCPRO **Prod** - WBCPRO 1968

Presidential power 30 MIN
VHS / U-matic
American government 2 series
Color (C)
Explores the ability of the President to control and shape government activity. Shows how personality, political environment and external factors, such as war and Watergate, affect a President's power.
Civics and Political Systems
Dist - DALCCD **Prod** - DALCCD

Presidential summer 14 MIN
16mm
Color
Focuses on the preparations made for the 1972 Democratic and Republican political conventions in Miami Beach, Florida.
Civics and Political Systems; Geography - United States; History - United States
Dist - FLADC **Prod** - FLADC

Presidential Tour 28 MIN
16mm
Color (J)
LC FIA68-1746
Records the visit to Australia in 1966 by United States President Lyndon B Johnson, from touch down at Canberra to his departure from Townsville, Queensland.
Biography; Geography - World
Dist - AUIS **Prod** - ANAIB 1966

Presidents and Politics with Richard Strout 58 MIN
VHS / U-matic
Walk through the 20th Century with Bill Moyers Series
Color
Focuses on newsman Richard Strout, who has covered Washington and the White House since the administration of Warren G Harding. Strout reflects about presidents from Harding to Reagan, Congressional lions and famous speeches.
Biography; Civics and Political Systems; History - United States; History - World; Literature and Drama
Dist - PBS **Prod** - CORPEL 1982

Presidents and Power, Pt 1 60 MIN
U-matic / VHS
Bill Moyers' Journal Series
Color
Presents an interview with Clark Clifford, former Secretary of State and advisor to Presidents Harry Truman, John Kennedy and Lyndon Johnson. Clifford talks about the men for whom he worked, looking at their contributions and weaknesses, their use and abuse of power, their characters and personalities, and their place in history.
Biography; Civics and Political Systems; History - United States
Dist - PBS **Prod** - WNETTV 1981

Presidents and Power, Pt 2 60 MIN
U-matic / VHS
Bill Moyers' Journal Series
Color
Presents an interview with Clark Clifford, former Secretary of State and advisor to Presidents Harry Truman, John Kennedy and Lyndon Johnson. Clifford talks about the men for whom he worked, looking at their contributions and weaknesses, their use and abuse of power, their characters and personalities, and their place in history.
Biography; Civics and Political Systems; History - United States
Dist - PBS **Prod** - WNETTV 1981

The President's Budget 30 MIN
U-matic / VHS
American Government 2 Series
Color (C)
Looks at the budget as an important political statement disguised as a dull economic document. Provides insight into the way the budget influences government.
Civics and Political Systems
Dist - DALCCD **Prod** - DALCCD

President's committee on mental retardation in action 9 MIN
16mm
Color (PRO)
LC 78-701606
Describes the work and the mission of the President's Committee on Mental Retardation.
Biography; Psychology
Dist - UKANS **Prod** - UKANS 1974

President's Day 15 MIN
VHS
America's special days series
Color (K P) (SPANISH)
$23.95 purchase
Shows visits to Washington, DC, including the Washington Monument and the Lincoln Memorial. Looks at Mount Vernon, Washington's home, and Lincoln's homes in Illinois. Challenges students to learn more about American presidents.
Civics and Political Systems; Social Science
Dist - GPN **Prod** - GPN 1993

Presidents' Day
VHS
Color (K P I)
$69.95 purchase _ #10013VG
Shows the lives and accomplishments of George Washington and Abraham Lincoln, and why Presidents' Day is celebrated. Gives facts and legends about the two presidents. Includes a guide.
Biography; Civics and Political Systems
Dist - UNL

The Presidents - it all started with George
CD-ROM
Color (I J H A)
$99.00 purchase _ #80605; $185.00 purchase _ #T80716
Profiles the American presidents. Offers more than 1200 photos, presidential trivia game, photo essays on the presidency and politics, 33 video clips of historical moments, glossary and political party index. Requires IBM system. Contact distributor for hardware requirements.
Biography; Civics and Political Systems; History - United States
Dist - NGS

The President's program 29 MIN
16mm
Government story series; No 27
Color
LC 79-707187
Discusses how the President chooses his program and the political and personal factors which affect his choice. points to the President's State of the Union Address and the executive budget as reflections of his program.
Biography; Civics and Political Systems
Dist - WBCPRO **Prod** - WBCPRO 1968

The Press 29 MIN
VHS / 16mm
Washington Connection Series
Color (G)
$55.00 rental _ #WACO - 104
Civics and Political Systems; Social Science
Dist - PBS **Prod** - NPACT

Press and the White House 29 MIN
U-matic / VHS
Inside Story Series
Color
Examines the attempt by the White House to control the flow and the content of news from the Reagan Administration. Includes Hodding Carter, Jack Anderson, Barry Dunsmore and John Lofton.
Civics and Political Systems; Fine Arts; Literature and Drama; Social Science; Sociology
Dist - PBS **Prod** - PBS 1981

Press Brake Changing Dies 13 MIN
VHS / BETA
Color (IND)
Explains how a set of press brake dies are removed and different ones installed and adjusted.
Industrial and Technical Education; Psychology
Dist - RMIBHF **Prod** - RMIBHF

Press Brake Demonstration 50 MIN
VHS / BETA
Color (IND)
Discusses the basic operating procedure for using a mechanical press brake with an air electric clutch and three - speed transmission on the drive mechanism.
Industrial and Technical Education; Psychology
Dist - RMIBHF **Prod** - RMIBHF

Press brake guarding - they can be guarded 16 MIN
U-matic / VHS / 16mm
Color (ENGLISH, SPANISH)
$375.00 purchase, $50.00 one - week rental
Introduces and examines safety equipment now used on press brakes including clear, acrylic fixed barrier guards, hold - back cables and two - handed control panels.
Health and Safety; Industrial and Technical Education
Dist - IFB **Prod** - IAPA 1978

Press for Success - First Time Job Seekers and Re - entry Adults 53 MIN
U-matic / VHS
JIST Conference Presentations Series
(C A P)
$60 _ #JWCV66V
Highlights Joyce Lain Kennedy, Syndicated Careers Columnist, as she speaks on career issues.
Business and Economics; Sociology
Dist - JISTW **Prod** - JISTW

Press Mold Ceramics 10 MIN
16mm
Color; B&W (J)
AdA Korsakaite, west coast artist, uses the press mold method to demonstrate the process of making a ceramic, from carving a plaster of paris slab in readiness to receive the clay, to the final bisque - firing.
Fine Arts
Dist - AVED **Prod** - ALLMOR 1955

Presses
VHS / U-matic
Pulp and Paper Training, Module 3 - Papermaking Series
Color (IND)
Presents aspects of papermaking presses. Includes principles of water removal, rolls and felts and press arrangements.
Business and Economics; Industrial and Technical Education; Social Science
Dist - LEIKID **Prod** - LEIKID

Presses, Production and Protection 13 MIN
U-matic / VHS / 16mm
Machine Tool Safety Series
Color (IND)
Health and Safety; Industrial and Technical Education
Dist - NATMTB **Prod** - NATMTB

Pressing and Construction Details 28 MIN
U-matic / VHS
Clothing Construction Techniques Series
Color (C A)
Covers pressing techniques, stay - stitching and directional stitching - making darts, tucks, and pleats - making gathers, finishing garment edges, using hand stitches - layering, trimming, clipping, and notching seam allowances - matching stitching techniques.
Home Economics
Dist - IOWASP **Prod** - IOWASP

Pressing defense 11 MIN
16mm
B&W (J H)
Coach Benington explains proper techniques in use and execution of a pressing defense.
Physical Education and Recreation
Dist - COCA **Prod** - BORDEN

Pressing Out Fatigue 10 MIN
Videoreel / VT2
Janaki Series
Color
Physical Education and Recreation
Dist - PBS **Prod** - WGBHTV

Pressing Techniques 3 MIN
16mm
Clothing Construction Techniques Series
Color (J)
LC 77-701171
Shows pressing darts and curved seams over a pressing cushion, seams on a seam roll, corners and points on a point presser and napped fabric on a needle board or turkish towel.
Home Economics
Dist - IOWASP **Prod** - IOWA 1976

Pressman 15 MIN
U-matic / 16mm / VHS
Career Awareness
(I)
$130 VC purchase, $240 film purchase, $25 VC rental, $$30 film rental
Presents an empathetic approach to career planning, showing the personal as well as professional attributes of pressmen. Highlights the importance of career education.
Guidance and Counseling; Industrial and Technical Education
Dist - GPN

Pressure 60 MIN
VHS / 16mm
Industrial measurement series
Color (PRO)
$695.00 purchase, $125.00 rental
Includes Introduction to Pressure, Pressure Measurement, Manometers, Mechanical Pressure Transducers, Electrical Pressure Elements, Electronic Pressure Elements and Installation Considerations. Part of a five - part series on industrial measurement.
Industrial and Technical Education; Mathematics
Dist - ISA **Prod** - ISA

Pressure and Current 13 MIN
16mm
Electricity Series
Color (I)
Discusses the electric current in terms of amperes and volts, circuit concepts, switches and parallel series.
Science - Physical
Dist - SF **Prod** - MORLAT 1967

Pressure and Humidity 10 MIN
U-matic / VHS / 16mm
Weather - Air in Action Series
Color (I J)
Studies the variations in air pressure and humidity. Explains the function of the barometer and hygrometer and describes the formation of clouds and fog.
Science - Physical
Dist - AIMS **Prod** - CAHILL 1965

Pressure and level measurement concepts
Software / BETA
Liquid level measurement series
Color (PRO)
$600.00 - $1500.00 purchase _ #IDPLM
Describes the basic principles of pressure as they apply to liquid level of measurement. Part of a six - part series on liquid level measurement. Interactive training system includes course administrator guide, videodisc and computer software.
Industrial and Technical Education; Mathematics; Psychology; Science - Physical
Dist - NUSTC **Prod** - NUSTC

Pressure and Pressure Measurement 60 MIN
VHS
Fundamentals of Instrumentation and Control Series
Color (PRO)
$600.00 - $1500.00 purchase _ #ICPPM
Shows how to discuss pressure in practical terms, use a manometer to take a pressure measurement - observing standard practice for reading liquid levels, convert pressure measurements from one unit to another and identify and explain basic operating principles of various types of pressure elements and transducers. Part of a nineteen - part series on the fundamentals of instrumentation and control, which is part of a 49 - unit set on instrumentation and control. Includes five workbooks and an instructor guide to support four hours of instruction.
Industrial and Technical Education; Mathematics; Psychology
Dist - NUSTC **Prod** - NUSTC

Pressure and Pressure Measurement Series
Gauge Calibration - Absolute Pressure, Retard and Compound Gauges
Gauge Calibration - Rotary - Geared, Bellows and Bourdon Tube Gauges
Gauge Calibration Basics
Head Compensation and Gauge Protection Devices
Introduction to Pressure and Pressure Measurement
Pressure Elements
Dist - NUSTC

Pressure buildup and drawdown analysis 720 MIN
U-matic / VHS
Color
Teaches systematic analysis and design procedures for . pressure buildup and drawdown tests for petroleum engineers. Available to SPE organizations only.
Industrial and Technical Education
Dist - SPE **Prod** - SPE

Pressure control devices 15 MIN
16mm
Color (H C)
Shows the application of pressure devices on the job. Discusses types of pressure - sensing elements, differential pressure meters, pressure controls, pilot regulators and pressure distribution systems in large installations.
Industrial and Technical Education; Mathematics
Dist - SF **Prod** - SF 1970

Pressure Control Valves 24 MIN
U-matic / VHS
Industrial Hydraulic Technology Series Chapter 9; Chapter 9
Color (IND)
Discusses pressure adjustment, drains and flow. Studies terms and idioms associated with pressure control valves.
Education; Industrial and Technical Education; Science - Physical
Dist - TAT **Prod** - TAT

Pressure controls 60 MIN
U-matic / VHS
Hydraulic systems series
Color
Discusses pressure control valve operation. Highlights sequence and pressure reducing valves.
Industrial and Technical Education
Dist - ITCORP **Prod** - ITCORP

Pressure controls
VHS
Refrigeration training seminars by Bob Graham series
Color (G IND)
$55.00 purchase
Presents the proper installation techniques as they pertain to high and low - pressure controls. Part of a series of refrigeration training seminars by Bob Graham.
Industrial and Technical Education; Psychology; Science - Physical
Dist - AACREF **Prod** - AACREF 1990

Pressure defensive basketball 17 MIN
16mm
Color; B&W (J H C)
Shows defensive basketball, starting out with the basic stance in defending and progressing through drills and the application of the skills in game situations. Highlights one - on - one drills, switching drill, trapping drills and cutting of dribbling and passing lanes.
Physical Education and Recreation
Dist - SPORTF **Prod** - SPORTF

Pressure Elements
Software / BETA
Pressure and Pressure Measurement Series
Color (PRO)
$600.00 - $1500.00 purchase _ #IDPRE
Describes the operating principles of the Bourdon tube, bellows, metal diaphragm and limp, or slack, diaphragm pressure elements. Part of a six - part series on pressure and pressure measurement. Interactive training system includes course administrator guide, videodisc and computer software.
Education; Industrial and Technical Education; Psychology
Dist - NUSTC **Prod** - NUSTC

Pressure Gauges and Calibration - 1 60 MIN
VHS
Fundamentals of Instrumentation and Control Series
Color (PRO)
$600.00 - $1500.00 purchase _ #ICPG1
Demonstrates how to read pressure gauges, remove gauges and return gauges to service. Part of a nineteen - part series on the fundamentals of instrumentation and control, which is part of a 49 - unit set on instrumentation and control. Includes five workbooks and an instructor guide to support four hours of instruction.
Industrial and Technical Education; Mathematics; Psychology
Dist - NUSTC **Prod** - NUSTC

Pressure Gauges and Calibration - 2 60 MIN
VHS
Fundamentals of Instrumentation and Control Series
Color (PRO)
$600.00 - $1500.00 purchase _ #ICPG2
Shows how to calibrate gauges. Includes retard, absolute and compound gauges. Part of a nineteen - part series on the fundamentals of instrumentation and control, which is part of a 49 - unit set on instrumentation and control. Includes five workbooks and an instructor guide to support four hours of instruction.
Industrial and Technical Education; Mathematics; Psychology
Dist - NUSTC **Prod** - NUSTC

Pressure gradient prophylaxis of thrombosis 12 MIN
16mm
Color (PRO)
LC 79-700452
Gives reasons for some blood clots in veins and shows the use of reduced venous stasis stockings.
Health and Safety; Science - Natural
Dist - PD **Prod** - HFH 1978

Pressure Groups in Action 20 MIN
16mm
Government and Public Affairs Films Series
B&W (C A)
Dr Marbury Ogle, professor of Government, Purdue University, shows the need for pressure groups in our democratic political system.
Civics and Political Systems
Dist - MLA **Prod** - RSC 1960

Pressure Groups in Action - Dr Marbury Ogle 20 MIN
16mm
Building Political Leadership Series
B&W (H C)
Civics and Political Systems
Dist - MLA **Prod** - RCS 1960

Pressure of Light 23 MIN
16mm
PSSC Physics Films Series
B&W (H C)
Discusses the role of light pressure in the universe. Shows how light pressure on a thin foil suspended in a high vacuum sets the foil into oscillation. Includes a discussion of the Crookes radiometer.
Science - Physical
Dist - MLA **Prod** - PSSC 1959

Pressure point 15 MIN
16mm
Color (C)
LC 76-701577
Informs college - age men and women about becoming aviation officer candidates in the U S Navy. Suggests ways to select the field for which they are best suited.
Civics and Political Systems; Guidance and Counseling
Dist - USNAC **Prod** - USN 1973

Pressure point control tactics 19 MIN
VHS / U-matic
Color (PRO)
$200.00, $250.00 purchase, $50.00 rental
Demonstrates simple physical restraint techniques useful in subduing criminals or suspects in potentially violent situations. Features a Partners Against Substance Abuse production.
Civics and Political Systems
Dist - NDIM

Pressure Points - Oman, South Yemen, North Yemen 21 MIN
U-matic / VHS / 16mm
Oil and American Power Series
Color (H C A)
Discusses the politics of Oman, South Yemen and North Yemen, showing how America has been forced into a relationship with countries with which it has no long - standing political partnership. Extracted from the NBC television show No More Vietnams, But.
Civics and Political Systems; History - World; Social Science
Dist - FI **Prod** - NBCTV 1979

Pressure, shear and friction - assessing risk 21 MIN
VHS / U-matic / BETA
Immobility - preventing complications series
Color (C PRO)
$280.00 purchase _ #625.3
Discusses the incidence of pressure ulcers and their enormous cost, both monetarily and in terms of human suffering. Discusses principles of pressure, shear and friction, illustrates how they occur in the health care setting and describes the type of tissue damage they inflict. Describes staging of pressure ulcers, cites facets that place a patient at risk for developing pressure ulcers and concludes with a discussion of commonly used assessment tools. Part one of two parts on pressure, shear and friction and part of a four - part series on preventing the complications of immobility produced by VPC Publishing.
Health and Safety; Physical Education and Recreation
Dist - CONMED

Pressure, shear and friction - prevention and intervention 27 MIN
BETA / VHS / U-matic
Immobility - preventing complications series
Color (C PRO)
$280.00 purchase _ #625.4
Describes general nursing measures such as frequent position changes to reduce pressure for patients in both bed and wheelchair. Illustrates more advanced techniques such as 'bridging' for patients who require complete relief of pressure. Discusses measures to reduce shear and friction. Describes some pressure - reducing equipment - mattresses, mattress overlays, mattress replacements and specialty beds. Emphasizes discharge planning and patient teachiing necessary to prevent or heal pressure ulcers at home. Part two of two - parts on pressure, shear and friction and part of a four - part series on preventing the complications of immobility produced by VPC Publishing.
Health and Safety; Physical Education and Recreation
Dist - CONMED

Pressure sores 19 MIN
U-matic / VHS
Breaking the chain of nosocomial infections series
Color (C PRO)
$395.00 purchase, $80.00 rental _ #C930 - VI - 002
Helps medical students, nurses, doctors and other hospital and nursing home staff to reduce the risk factors that cause pressure sores. Demonstrates techiques and suggests types of drug therapy to lessen the chances of infection. Part of a five part series on nosocomial infections presented by Crescent Counties Foundation for Medical Care.
Health and Safety
Dist - HSCIC

Pressure systems and wind 19 MIN
16mm
Color
LC FIE64-20
Explains phenomena of pressure systems and wind flow, and how they affect weather and flight conditions.
Science - Physical
Dist - USNAC **Prod** - USAF 1963

Pressure testing the cooling system 4 MIN
16mm
Color
LC FI68-210
Describes the use of the pressure test pump to discover leaks in the cooling system.
Industrial and Technical Education
Dist - RAYBAR **Prod** - RAYBAR 1966

Pressure ulcer prevention 14 MIN
VHS
Color (G)
$99.00 purchase
Illustrates pressure ulcers and shows how shear and pressure can cause bedsores. Explains nine prevention techniques and the importance of turning. Instructs nurse aides and family care givers. Includes fact sheet, teacher's guide and broadcast rights documentation.
Health and Safety
Dist - FAMHEA **Prod** - FAMHEA 1992

Pressure Vessels
U-matic / VHS
Drafting - Piping Familiarization Series
Color (IND)
Industrial and Technical Education
Dist - GPCV **Prod** - GPCV

Pressure, volume and Boyle's law 4 MIN
16mm
Kinetic theory by computer animation series
Color (H C A)
LC 73-703241
Displays impulses imparted to a wall by a single particle in a box on an oscilloscope and pressure meter. Shows that as the number of particles increases, the pressure increases and becomes steadier.
Science; Science - Physical
Dist - KALMIA **Prod** - KALMIA 1973

The Pressure's on 28 MIN
16mm
Color
LC 80-701335
Dramatizes four cases of hypertension to show how pervasive this disease is. Discusses the nature of high blood pressure and tells how it can be detected and treated.
Health and Safety
Dist - MTP **Prod** - PICA 1979

Pressures to Smoke 15 MIN
16mm
Color (I J)
LC 81-700656
Features two junior high school students exploring the problems of smoking and the social, family and media pressures leading to the habit. Shows the effects of smoking on carbon monoxide levels in the body, on nicotine levels in saliva and on those who inhale the smoke of others.
Health and Safety; Psychology
Dist - USNAC **Prod** - USNIH 1979

Pressworking 25 MIN
VHS / U-matic
Technical Studies Series
Color (H C A)
Discusses aspects of pressworking.
Industrial and Technical Education
Dist - FI **Prod** - BBCTV 1981

Prestressed Concrete Pavement Construction 25 MIN
16mm
Color
LC 74-705410
Shows a pictorial record of the first substantial section of prestressed concrete highway pavement built in the United States.
Industrial and Technical Education; Social Science
Dist - USNAC **Prod** - USDTFH 1973

Presumed Innocent 60 MIN
U-matic / VHS / 16mm
B&W (J)
Exposes conditions for pre - trial jail inmates and examines how the bail system affects the poor and the consequent social, constitutional and legal implications of detention.
Civics and Political Systems; Sociology
Dist - CNEMAG **Prod** - TVGDAP 1980

Presumption of Innocence 89 MIN
16mm 39 MIN
Color (J)
LC 73-702517; 73-702516
Presents an actual criminal court trial. Follows the defendant's feelings through the cross - currents of question and answer, examination and cross - examination as prosecution and defense put the case before the jury.
Civics and Political Systems; Sociology
Dist - SCREEI **Prod** - SCREEI 1973

The Presumptuous Mr Nobody 110 MIN
VHS
Color (G) (CHINESE)
$45.00 purchase _ #6071C
Presents a film from the People's Republic of China.
Geography - World; Literature and Drama
Dist - CHTSUI

Presuppositions and hypnosis - 3 63 MIN
VHS
Submodalities and hypnosis series
Color; PAL; SECAM (G)
$60.00 purchase
Features Richard Bandler in the third part of a five - part series on submodalities and hypnosis, from a seminar, March, 1987. Uses advanced NLP, neuro - linguistic programming. Recommended that tapes be viewed in order. Bandler sometimes uses profanity for emphasis, which may offend some people.
Health and Safety; Psychology
Dist - NLPCOM **Prod** - NLPCOM

Pretend, Picture 10 MIN
U-matic
Readalong Two Series
Color (P)
Provides young viewers with a flexible range of reading experiences through active involvement in reading and writing. Comes with teacher's guide and kit.
Education; English Language; Literature and Drama
Dist - TVOTAR **Prod** - TVOTAR 1976

Pretend the Picture is Rosy 7 MIN
16mm
B&W
Examines the life of an old man wandering alone in the inner city. Emphasizes his fight to face reality and to maintain human dignity by presenting his views and thoughts on the world around him.
Fine Arts; Guidance and Counseling; Psychology; Sociology
Dist - USC **Prod** - USC

Pretend world 25 MIN
VHS / U-matic
Blizzard's wonderful wooden toys series
Color (H C A)
Shows how to build a large playhouse and the furniture to go inside it.
Fine Arts; Industrial and Technical Education
Dist - FI **Prod** - BBCTV

Pretend You're Wearing a Barrel 10 MIN
U-matic / VHS / 16mm
Color (H C A)
LC 81-700791
Presents a portrait of Lynn Ryan, a woman on welfare, who learned to become a welder and found a job in order to support her five children. Emphasizes how she was able to take practical steps to achieve something better for herself and her children.
Sociology
Dist - PHENIX **Prod** - NFBC 1980

Pretending 21 MIN
16mm
I Am, I Can, I will, Level II Series
Color (K P S)
LC 80-700570
Presents Mr Rogers using a puppet show to emphasize the importance of separating fantasy from reality. Explains that pretending can be used to have fun, to explore, and to express and test feelings in fanciful yet controlled ways.
Guidance and Counseling; Psychology
Dist - HUBDSC **Prod** - FAMCOM 1979

Preterm labor
VHS
Color (PRO G)
$150.00 purchase _ #OB - 113
Helps patients understand how serious the consequences of preterm labor can be. Explains that it can be treated if the warning signs are detected early enough. Stresses that all pregnant women should be familiar with these warning signs.
Health and Safety
Dist - MIFE **Prod** - MIFE 1991

Preterm labor - diagnosis and treatment 23 MIN
U-matic / VHS
Color (C PRO)
$395.00 purchase, $80.00 rental _ #C911 - VI - 045
Provides physicians with necessary information about the signs and symptoms, risk assessment and diagnosis and management of preterm labor. Reveals that preterm birth is a leading cause of adverse perinatal outcome but when healthcare providers are educated about preterm labor, premature birth rates decrease as much as 40 percent. Presented by Drs Robert K Creasy, Valerie Parisi and Bernard Gonik.
Health and Safety
Dist - HSCIC

Pretrial Conferences and Opening Statements in an Antitrust Case 170 MIN
U-matic / VHS
Trial of an Antitrust Case Series
Color (PRO)
Offers opening statements presented by two skilled litigators in an antitrust case. Analyzes the methodologies used by the attorneys, the judge's control of the pretrial conference and jury selection procedures.
Civics and Political Systems
Dist - ABACPE **Prod** - ABACPE

Pretrial strategies 58 MIN
VHS
Business litigation series
Color (C PRO)
$95.00 purchase, $71.25 rental _ #LBC05
Outlines appropriate pretrial strategies for business litigation cases.
Civics and Political Systems
Dist - NITA **Prod** - NITA 1987

Pretrial strategies - discovery and deposition 53 MIN
VHS / Cassette
Medical malpractice litigation - new strategies for a new era series
Color (PRO)
$125.00, $30.00 purchase, $50.00 rental _ #MED2-002, #AME2-002
Discusses and demonstrates innovative litigation strategies and techniques developed in response to the rapidly changing climate in which medical malpractice cases are litigated. Outlines the pretrial strategies of discovery and deposition. Includes demonstrations by skilled trial lawyers, interviews of those conducting the demonstrations and panel discussions. Includes study guide.
Civics and Political Systems
Dist - AMBAR **Prod** - AMBAR 1987

Pretty as a Picture - Graduation and Prom Dresses 29 MIN
Videoreel / VT2
Designing Women Series
Color
Home Economics
Dist - PBS **Prod** - WKYCTV

A Pretty Good Class for a Monday 26 MIN
16mm
One to Grow on Series
Color (T)
LC 73-701936
Presents a study of three uniquely different high school students in a single history class. Shows how each participates in the class with his own special set of motives, needs and values.
Education; Psychology
Dist - USNAC **Prod** - NIMH 1973

A Pretty Good Class for a Monday 25 MIN
U-matic / VHS
One to Grow on Series
Color; B&W (T)
LC 80-706189
Examines the different ways in which three pupils participate in a high school history class.
Education
Dist - USNAC **Prod** - NIMH 1979

Pretty Insects 30 MIN
VHS / 16mm
Our Natural Heritage Series
Color (G)
$14.44 purchase _ #HSV4029
Explores the life cycles of butterflies and aphid eaters.
Psychology; Science - Natural
Dist - EDUCRT

A Pretty Kettle of Fish 20 MIN
U-matic / VHS / 16mm
Color (K P I J)
LC 74-703648
Presents a story about a young French girl who decides to fish for her supper rather than play with the other children. Explains that when she falls asleep at the fishing place a gypsy boy helps her land her catch.
Literature and Drama; Sociology
Dist - PHENIX **Prod** - INTERA 1974

The Pretty Lady and the Electronic Musicians 15 MIN
U-matic
Color (I J H)
Uses animation to show two musicians competing for the same pretty lady by inventing and playing increasingly complex electronic instruments.
Fine Arts
Dist - GA **Prod** - BOSUST

Pretty Poison 23 MIN
VHS / U-matic
Color
Traces the fragile - looking Monarch Butterfly. Shows where they hibernate for the winter after a long journey.
Science - Natural
Dist - NWLDPR **Prod** - NWLDPR

Pretty, Swim, Away 10 MIN
U-matic
Readalong One Series
Color (K P)
Introduces reading and spelling for preschoolers and children in grades 1 to 3 with animation, puppets, humor and music. Comes with teacher's guide and kit.
Education; English Language; Literature and Drama
Dist - TVOTAR **Prod** - TVOTAR 1975

The Preventable disaster - static electricity 14 MIN
U-matic / BETA / VHS
Color (IND G)
$395.00 purchase _ #600 - 03
Instructs employees on the dangers of static electricity in the continuous process industries which handle flammable liquids. Emphasizes safety while loading tankers.
Health and Safety; Industrial and Technical Education; Psychology
Dist - ITSC **Prod** - ITSC

Preventable Forms of Kidney Disease 25 MIN
VHS / U-matic
Color (PRO)
Presents the fact that kidney disease can be prevented or minimized by recognition and treatment of diseases which cause it and classifies these diseases according to the specific anatomic site of the kidney they affect.
Health and Safety
Dist - UMICHM **Prod** - UMICHM 1978

Preventative and Protective Taping and Wrapping 29 MIN
U-matic
Sports Medicine in the 80's Series
Color (G)
Teaches the role of sports medicine as it relates to athlete, coach, trainer, team and school. Covers most kinds of injuries encountered in sports.
Health and Safety; Physical Education and Recreation
Dist - CEPRO **Prod** - CEPRO

Preventative management series
Why Employees don't do what they're supposed to do 25 MIN
Dist - CCCD

Preventative management series
The First time around 29 MIN
Dist - CCCD
FI
VLEARN

Preventing accidents involving lead - acid batteries 12 MIN
VHS / U-matic / BETA
Color (IND G A)
$670.00 purchase, $125.00 rental _ #PRE049
Demonstrates correct emergency jump - start procedures, as well as how to safely handle and maintain 12 - volt lead - acid batteries.
Health and Safety; Industrial and Technical Education; Psychology; Sociology
Dist - ITF **Prod** - ERF 1991

Preventing and resolving conflicts
VHS
Big changes, big choices series
Color (I J)
$69.95 purchase _ #LVB - 7A
Looks at how a typical conflict develops in a middle school and what stands in the way of peaceful resolution. Encourages basic rules of good communication, such as listening instead of insulting. Part of a 12 - part video series designed to help young adolescents work their way though the many anxieties and issues they face. Encourages them to make positive and healthful life choices. Features humorist and youth counselor Michael Pritchard.
Psychology; Social Science
Dist - CFKRCM **Prod** - CFKRCM

Preventing back injuries 24 MIN
VHS
Safety on the job series
Color (G IND) (SPANISH)
$79.95 purchase _ #6 - 203 - 013A, #6 - 203 - 014A
Reveals that back problems keep millions away from their jobs on a daily basis. Features Backman, program host, who shows the proper way to life and move objects, how to get in and out of vehicles, how to bend, reach and use equipment properly and how to sit at a desk. Part of a series on job safety.
Health and Safety; Science - Natural
Dist - VEP **Prod** - VEP

Preventing Back Injuries 24 MIN
16mm / VHS
Safety on the Job Series
Color (H C PRO)
$395.00, $495.00 purchase, $75.00 rental _ #9877
Covers the proper way to lift and move heavy objects, how to get in and out of vehicles, how to bend, reach and use equipment properly and how to sit at a desk. Emphasizes the importance of safety procedures to prevent accidents and points out that stress and fatigue can be the cause of back injury.
Health and Safety; Psychology
Dist - AIMS **Prod** - AIMS 1987

Preventing burnout
VHS
Personal action system series
Color (G)
$149.00 purchase _ #V218
Teaches employees about how to prevent job burnout. Part of a 13 - part series to educate employees on the importance of health.
Health and Safety; Psychology
Dist - GPERFO

Preventing burnout - Tape 1 25 MIN
VHS
Church leaders under fire series
Color (A R PRO)
$10.00 rental _ #36 - 81 - 222
Presents the symptoms, causes and solutions to burnout among church leaders. Includes personal accounts from leaders who have been burnout victims.
Religion and Philosophy
Dist - APH

Preventing burns in the kitchen
U-matic / VHS / 16mm
Professional food preparation and service program series
Color
Views the burn dangers of steam, gas, boiling, bubbling fats and hot foods. Shows how to handle steam equipment safely. Explains safe procedures at the stove and what to watch out for to avoid burns in a commercial kitchen.
Industrial and Technical Education
Dist - NEM **Prod** - NEM 1983

Preventing Child Abuse 31 MIN
VHS
Safe Child Program - K - 3 - Series
Color (A)
$895.00 purchase
Presents a Parent - Teacher seminar to show how to teach primary children prevention of sexual, emotional and physical abuse. Combines teacher training for consistent presentation of program, parental involvement to reinforce program goals, videotapes to guarantee accurate introduction of concepts to children, and classroom role - playing to develop individual mastery of safety skills. Part of a seven videotape program adapted from 'The Safe Child Book' by Sherryll Kraizer, K - 3.
Education; Health and Safety; Psychology; Sociology
Dist - LUF **Prod** - LUF 1989

Preventing Childhood Poisonings 14 MIN
U-matic / VHS
Color
LC 81-706269
Discusses ways to poison - proof the home and respond to emergency situations in which children have ingested harmful substances.
Health and Safety; Home Economics
Dist - USNAC **Prod** - USFDA 1981

Preventing Cross Contamination in Removable Prosthodontics - Delivery - Adjustments 15 MIN
U-matic / VHS
Color
Presents and demonstrates an ordered, systematic approach to handling dentures from the insertion through the adjustment phases to prevent the possibility of cross contamination.
Health and Safety; Science
Dist - AMDA **Prod** - VADTC 1978

Preventing Cutting and Welding Fires 14 MIN
16mm
Color
Uses live action and animation to illustrate the safety measures that should be used to prevent fires before, during and after cutting and welding operations. Covers the use of approved equipment, sprinkler systems and the use of permit systems.
Health and Safety
Dist - FILCOM **Prod** - FILCOM

Preventing disease transmission in personal service worker occupations
VHS / Slide
Color (A PRO)
$47.00 purchase _ #TCA18031
Presents a multi - media kit on infection control for personal service workers. Defines personal service workers as including acupuncturists, cosmetologists, electrologists, tattooists, hairdressers, barbers, and others. Includes 52 color slides, a videocassette, and a 52 - page set of guidelines for conducting workshops.
Health and Safety
Dist - USNAC

Preventing electrical injuries - Part 1 22 MIN
U-matic / VHS
Safety action for employees series
Color (IND)
Shows the potential hazards of electricity and demonstrates proper rescue techniques in an emergency situation.
Health and Safety
Dist - GPCV **Prod** - GPCV

Preventing electrical injuries - Part 2 21 MIN
VHS / U-matic
Safety action for employees series
Color (IND)
Discusses safety practices on the job, care and use of electrical tools, and personal protective equipment.
Health and Safety
Dist - GPCV **Prod** - GPCV

Preventing emergencies in the process industries 28 MIN
BETA / VHS / U-matic
Color (IND G A)
$903.00 purchase, $125.00 rental _ #PRE036
Trains in emergency planning for process industries. Emphasizes discussion and group participation.
Health and Safety; Psychology
Dist - ITF **Prod** - GPCV

Preventing employee lawsuits - 12 ways to stay out of court 23 MIN
VHS
Color (IND)
$350.00 purchase, $95.00 rental _ #SON01
Trains supervisors to treat employees fairly and avoid the most common types of employee lawsuits. Includes a leader's guide, transparency masters, a post training follow - up memo, wallet cards and a quiz. Produced by Sonalysts Studios.
Business and Economics; Guidance and Counseling
Dist - EXTR

Preventing Employee Theft 12 MIN
U-matic / VHS / 16mm
Cashiering and Security Programs Series
Color (H C A)
LC 74-700228
Shows ways to reduce employee pilferage and embezzlement, a multibillion dollar a year problem faced by all organizations. Illustrates reducing temptation, limiting opportunity, establishing controls and communication. Emphasizes a coordinated program of prevention involving communication and control on every level, from use of simple locks to proper accounting procedures.
Business and Economics; Psychology; Sociology
Dist - NEM **Prod** - NEM 1972

Preventing falls and other injuries in the elderly 17 MIN
VHS / U-matic
Color (PRO C G)
$195.00 purchase _ #C881 - VI - 062
Reveals that falls and instability are among the most serious problems facing the older population and that the pain or injury caused by a fall may mean a loss of independence requiring expensive care or premature nursing home placement. Presents effective measures for preventing falls in the home by identifying environmental risks that can be diminished. Demonstrates precautions in accessing hard - to - reach places and the proper use of step ladders. Gives guidelines for handrail placement. Presented by Dr Molly Engle.
Health and Safety
Dist - HSCIC

Preventing falls and strains 10 MIN
VHS
Color (IND PRO COR VOC)
$395.00 purchase, $100.00 five - day rental, $30.00 three - day preview _ #SF2
Presents information on prevention of negligent, unnecessary accidents that can be prevented by following basic safety procedures. Teaches correct lifing techniques to prevent back or leg injuries. Demonstrates proper methods of cleaning spills and correct use of stepladders to prevent falling. Includes facilitator's guide and materials for 25 trainees, as well as other materials.
Health and Safety
Dist - ADVANM

Preventing Fires in the Hospital 16 MIN
U-matic / VHS
Color (PRO)
LC 80-731001
Explains principles of fire prevention, beginning with the conditions necessary for a fire to start in a hospital. Presents examples of combustible and flammable materials in the hospital and sources of fire ignition and support. Emphasizes the importance of applying fire prevention guidelines.
Health and Safety
Dist - MEDCOM **Prod** - MEDCOM

Preventing Food Spoilage 15 MIN
16mm / U-matic
Food Service Employee Series
Color (IND)
LC 75-707352
Discusses the causes of food spoilage and tells what the food service worker can do to prevent it.
Health and Safety; Science - Natural
Dist - COPI **Prod** - COPI 1969

Preventing heart attack 38 MIN
VHS
Color (G)
$24.95 purchase; $29.95 purchase _ #AMI100V
Takes a comprehensive look at heart attacks. Features two Harvard physicians who discuss the causes and prevention of coronary heart disease. Also considers medical treatments, cardiac catheterization, coronary angioplasty, and coronary bypass surgery.
Health and Safety
Dist - PBS **Prod** - WNETTV 1989

Preventing injuries 26 MIN
VHS
Color (G)
$149.00 purchase, $75.00 rental _ #UW2358
Covers the most common areas of danger and makes some very basic points about common sense and risk - taking. Divides injury prevention into major categories - wearing seat belts, using safe toys, taking care in sports and avoiding winter hazards.
Health and Safety
Dist - FOTH

Preventing Legal Malpractice 4 MIN
VHS / U-matic
Color (PRO)
Presents dramatizations followed by panel discussion of typical problems and pitfalls faced by attorneys which could lead to malpractice.
Civics and Political Systems
Dist - ABACPE **Prod** - ABACPE

Preventing legal malpractice - a guide for estate planners 52 MIN
VHS / Cassette
Preventing legal malpractice series
Color (PRO)
$125.00, $30.00 purchase, $50.00 rental _ #PLM4-001, #APL4-001
Reveals that, during the last decade, clients have become increasingly willing to sue their lawyers for alleged malpractice. Presents part of a series designed to sharpen the ability of viewers to perceive potential malpractice problems in their own practice. Helps to develop systems and safeguards for a loss prevention program for firms. Dramatizes a lawyer - client meeting, asking the viewer to scrutinize the situation portrayed for its malpractice implications. Later a panel of experts analyzes the potential malpractice problems in the dramatization and alerts viewers to other situations that often result in malpractice claims. Includes study guide.
Civics and Political Systems
Dist - AMBAR **Prod** - AMBAR 1988

Preventing legal malpractice - a guide for family lawyers 56 MIN
Cassette
Preventing legal malpractice series
Color (PRO)
$125.00, $30.00 purchase, $50.00 rental _ #PLM3-001, #APLM-001
Reveals that during the last decade, clients have become increasingly willing to sue their lawyers for alleged malpractice. Presents part of a series designed to sharpen the ability of viewers to perceive potential malpractice problems in their own practice. Helps to develop systems and safeguards for a loss prevention program for firms. Dramatizes a lawyer - client meeting, asking the viewer to scrutinize the situation portrayed for its malpractice implications. Later a panel of experts analyzes the potential malpractice problems in the dramatization and alerts viewers to other situations that often result in malpractice claims. Includes study guide.
Civics and Political Systems
Dist - AMBAR **Prod** - AMBAR 1988

Preventing Legal Malpractice - a Guide for General Practitioners 50 MIN
U-matic / VHS
Preventing Legal Malpractice - a Practitioner's Guide Series
Color (PRO)
Dramatizes a client asking his lawyer to draft an agreement transferring partial ownership of the client's company to the business manager. Covers such issues as deciding when to refer a case and recognizing conflicts of interest.
Civics and Political Systems
Dist - ABACPE **Prod** - ABACPE

Preventing Legal Malpractice - a Guide for Litigators 50 MIN
U-matic / VHS
Preventing Legal Malpractice - a Practitioner's Guide Series
Color (PRO)
Explores the issues surrounding the case of an employer being sued by an employee who has been fired. Includes work control calendaring and potential conflicts of interest. Suggests ways litigators can reduce malpractice vulnerability.
Civics and Political Systems
Dist - ABACPE **Prod** - ABACPE

Preventing Legal Malpractice - a Guide for Real Property Probate and Trust Practitioners 55 MIN
VHS / U-matic
Preventing Legal Malpractice - a Practitioner's Guide Series
Color (PRO)
Dramatizes the sale of an apartment building. Includes discussion about the use of checklists in real estate transactions and the doctrine of judgmental immunity.
Civics and Political Systems
Dist - ABACPE **Prod** - ABACPE

Preventing legal malpractice - a guide for the larger law firms 57 MIN
Cassette
Preventing legal malpractice series
Color (PRO)
$125.00, $30.00 purchase, $50.00 rental _ #PLM3-002, #APLM-002
Reveals that during the last decade, clients have become increasingly willing to sue their lawyers for alleged malpractice. Presents part of a series which sharpens the ability of viewers to perceive potential malpractice problems in their own practice. Helps to develop systems and safeguards for a loss prevention program for firms. Dramatizes a lawyer - client meeting, asking the viewer to scrutinize the situation portrayed for its malpractice implications. Later a panel of experts analyzes the potential malpractice problems in the dramatization and alerts viewers to other situations that often result in malpractice claims. Includes study guide.
Civics and Political Systems
Dist - AMBAR **Prod** - AMBAR 1988

Preventing legal malpractice - a guide to practice management 56 MIN
Cassette
Preventing legal malpractice series
Color (PRO)
$125.00, $30.00 purchase, $50.00 rental _ #PLM3-003, #APLM-003
Reveals that during the last decade, clients have become increasingly willing to sue their lawyers for alleged malpractice. Presents part of a series designed to sharpen the ability of viewers to perceive potential malpractice problems in their own practice. Helps to develop systems and safeguards for a prevention program for firms. Dramatizes a lawyer - client meeting, asking the viewer to scrutinize the situation portrayed for its malpractice implications. Later a panel of experts analyzes the potential malpractice problems in the dramatization and alerts viewers to other situations that often result in malpractice claims. Includes study guide.
Civics and Political Systems
Dist - AMBAR **Prod** - AMBAR 1988

Preventing Legal Malpractice - a Practitioner's Guide Series
Preventing Legal Malpractice - a Guide for General Practitioners 50 MIN
Preventing Legal Malpractice - a Guide for Litigators 50 MIN
Preventing Legal Malpractice - a Guide for Real Property Probate and Trust Practitioners 55 MIN
Dist - ABACPE

Preventing legal malpractice - Pt 4 - standard of care 30 MIN
U-matic
Color (PRO)
LC 80-707193
Presents dramatizations of typical malpractice problems faced by practicing attorneys, followed by analyses by a panel of experts.
Civics and Political Systems
Dist - ABACPE **Prod** - ABACPE 1978

Preventing legal malpractice - Pt 1 - client relations 29 MIN
U-matic
Color (PRO)
LC 80-707193
Presents dramatizations of typical malpractice problems faced by practicing attorneys, followed by analyses by a panel of experts.
Civics and Political Systems
Dist - ABACPE **Prod** - ABACPE 1978

Preventing legal malpractice - Pt 3 - conflicting interests 28 MIN
U-matic
Color (PRO)
LC 80-707193
Presents dramatizations of typical malpractice problems faced by practicing attorneys, followed by analyses by a panel of experts.
Civics and Political Systems
Dist - ABACPE **Prod** - ABACPE 1978

Preventing legal malpractice - Pt 2 - office procedures 28 MIN
U-matic
Color (PRO)
LC 80-707193
Presents dramatizations of typical malpractice problems faced by practicing attorneys, followed by analyses by a panel of experts.
Civics and Political Systems
Dist - ABACPE **Prod** - ABACPE 1978

Preventing legal malpractice series
Preventing legal malpractice - a guide for estate planners 52 MIN
Preventing legal malpractice - a guide for family lawyers 56 MIN
Preventing legal malpractice - a guide for the larger law firms 57 MIN
Preventing legal malpractice - a guide to practice management 56 MIN
Dist - AMBAR

Preventing long term complications of diabetes 14 MIN
VHS
AADE patient education video series
Color; CC (G C PRO)
$175.00 purchase _ #DB - 28
Stresses recognition and prevention of damage to blood vessels and nerves due to hyperglycemia. Explains how this may lead to diabetic retinopathy, foot problems, damage to sexual organs, kidney disease or heart disease. Part of an eight - part series produced in cooperation with the American Association of Diabetes Educators. Contact distributor for special purchase price on multiple orders.
Health and Safety; Science - Natural
Dist - MIFE

Preventing low birth weight - a nurse's guide 30 MIN
VHS
Color (PRO)
$295.00 purchase, $50.00 rental
Reveals that low birth weight is associated with nearly 70 percent of all neonatal deaths and is the most common factor in newborn illness and death - these infants are 40 times more likely to die during their first month of life than are normal birth weight infants. Stresses the role nurses play in assessment, patient education and support. Explains how nurses can encourage patients to taken an active part in reducing risk factors leading to low birth rate, recognize signs of preterm labor and help to delay preterm delivery. Discusses risk factors increasing the risk of going into preterm labor and appropriate prenatal care for high - risk patients. Includes a study guide summarizing program content which can be photocopied as a handout.
Health and Safety
Dist - POLYMR **Prod** - SPECTP

Preventing Malnutrition by Reinforcing Improved Diets 28 MIN
16mm
Color (C)
LC 80-701546
Documents a field experiment in the Philippines in which mothers are reinforced for helping improve their children's growth rate.
Health and Safety
Dist - PSUPCR **Prod** - GUTHGH 1980

Preventing Organizational Burnout
VHS / 16mm
Burnout Prevention Series
(PRO)
$80.00 purchase _ #PMT1006
Looks at the prevention of and recovery from organizational burnout. Features Dr Steve Asbell, PhD, psychologist.
Business and Economics; Psychology
Dist - RMIBHF **Prod** - RMIBHF

Preventing Organizational Burnout
VHS
$80.00 purchase _ #RP1005
Points out how every organization can suffer the damaging effects of burnout. Provides helpful suggestions for prevention and recovery.
Guidance and Counseling; Health and Safety
Dist - CAREER **Prod** - CAREER

Preventing our kids from using drugs and alcohol 46 MIN
VHS
Over the influence series
Color (J H C A)
$95.00 purchase
Highlights programs available that encourage children and teens to choose a drug - free lifestyle and help them understand the effects of alcohol and drug abuse. Part of a two - part series.
Guidance and Counseling; Health and Safety; Psychology
Dist - PFP **Prod** - ASHAP

Preventing Patient Falls in a Health Care Facility 30 MIN
U-matic / VHS
Color
Illustrates a 'safe - environment awareness' on the part of all health care personnel. Identifies patients most likely to fall and the precautions that will reduce incidents.
Health and Safety
Dist - FAIRGH **Prod** - FAIRGH

Preventing Pressure Sores 21 MIN
16mm
Color (PRO) (SPANISH)
LC 76-702871
Uses clinical examples to illustrate preventive measures against pressure sores in immobile patients.
Health and Safety
Dist - MMAMC **Prod** - MMAMC 1976

Preventing Pressure Sores 40 FRS
U-matic / VHS
Color (PRO)
Explains how and why bedsores occur and gives procedures for preventing and healing them. Shows how the body's weight is concentrated on a few areas when the patient is in a reclining position. Emphasizes the necessity for frequent position changes, also considers dangers from prolonged sitting without position change.
Health and Safety
Dist - WFP **Prod** - WFP

Preventing Probate Litigation
VHS / U-matic
Color (PRO)
Serves as a practical guide for attorneys involved in will preparation and probate administration. Discusses how to prepare a will in such a way as to prevent later litigation. , Contains a sample of a videotaped will.
Civics and Political Systems
Dist - ABACPE **Prod** - ABACPE

Preventing reading failure 29 MIN
U-matic / VHS / 16mm
Color (C T) (SPANISH)
LC 74-714072
Covers a reading lesson for young children with reading problems. Involves both group and individual work, demonstrating the Marianne Fostig Center of Educational Therapy's remedial approach, which can be used in regular classrooms as well as special groups.
Education; English Language; Psychology
Dist - AIMS **Prod** - HORNE 1971

Preventing relapse - Part II 48 MIN
VHS
Treating cocaine addiction successfully series
Color (H C G)
$225.00 purchase
Offers a guide to help patients stay off cocaine and other drugs. Features Dr Arnold M Washton in part one of a two - part series.
Guidance and Counseling; Psychology
Dist - FMSP

Preventing sexual harassment - a management responsibility - 1 27 MIN
U-matic / VHS / BETA
Preventing sexual harassment series
Color; CC; PAL (PRO G IND)
Contact distributor about price
Shows the consequences of sexual harassment in the workplace. Outlines the responsibilities of managers to prevent it. Uses dramatizations, interviews with legal and HR experts and on-screen narration to show the specific nature of sexual harassment and the errors that organizations and managers can make. Covers passage of the 1991 Civil Rights Act and the adoption of the 'Reasonable Woman' standard. Part of a 3-part program, two parts for training managers and an employee program. Includes trainer's manual and 20 participant manuals with pre- and post-tests, training acknowledgement forms and more.
Business and Economics; Psychology; Social Science; Sociology
Dist - BNA **Prod** - BNA

Preventing sexual harassment - a shared responsibility - 2 24 MIN
U-matic / VHS / BETA
Preventing sexual harassment series
Color; CC; PAL (PRO G IND)
Contact distributor about price
Outlines clearly the responsibilities of managers to maintain a workplace free of sexual harassment. Puts employees on notice that harassment is forbidden. Details internal complaint procedures for organizations enabling employees to resolve complaints within an organization rather than through an attorney or the EEOC. Covers passage of the 1991 Civil Rights Act and the adoption of the 'Reasonable Woman' standard. Part of a three - part program with two parts training managers and an employee program. Includes a trainer's manual and 20 participant manuals with pre - and post - tests, training acknowledgment forms and more.
Business and Economics; Psychology; Social Science; Sociology
Dist - BNA **Prod** - BNA

Preventing sexual harassment - employee version 15 MIN
U-matic / VHS / BETA
Preventing sexual harassment series
Color; CC; PAL (PRO G IND)
Contact distributor about price
Defines what sexual harassment is and what distinguishes harassment from friendly behavior. Puts employees on notice that harassment is forbidden. Details internal complaint procedures for organizations enabling employees to resolve complaints within an organization. Discusses important documentation forms, including Acknowledgment of Receipt and Understanding of the No - Harassment Policy. Covers passage of the 1991 Civil Rights and adoption of the 'Reasonable Woman' standard. Part of a 3-part program, two parts for training managers and an employee program. Includes a trainer's manual and 20 participant manuals with pre- and post-tests, training acknowledgement forms and more.
Psychology; Social Science; Sociology
Dist - BNA **Prod** - BNA

Preventing Sexual Harassment in the Workplace Series
The Law 68 MIN
The Preventive Action Plan 72 MIN
Dist - VENCMP

Preventing sexual harassment series
Presents a 3-part program, two parts for training managers and an employee program on sexual harassment in the workplace. Covers passage of the 1991 Civil Rights Act and adoption of the 'Reasonable Woman' standard. Shows managers how to identify sexual harassment and reduce organization liability and employees how to prevent harassment and resolve complaints within the organization. Includes trainer's manuals and 40 participant manuals with pre- and post-tests, training acknowledgement forms and more. Produced by the Employers' Reserve Group in association with a major labor law firm.
Preventing sexual harassment - a management responsibility - 1 27 MIN
Preventing sexual harassment - a shared responsibility - 2 24 MIN
Preventing sexual harassment - employee version 15 MIN
Dist - BNA **Prod** - BNA

Preventing Sexual Harrassment in the Workplace Series
The Nature of the Problem 66 MIN
Dist - VENCMP

Preventing Teen Pregnancy 28 MIN
VHS / 16mm
Color (G)
$149.00, $249.00, purchase _ #AD - 1438
Points out that a statistically unwarranted number of teen pregnancies result in mentally retarded infants and many medical problems for the mother. Recommends that sex education should begin in the pre - teens and makes a case for abstinence by teenagers.
Health and Safety
Dist - FOTH **Prod** - FOTH 1990

Preventing the Final Mistake 15 MIN
Videoreel / U-matic / VT3
Search for Common Ground Series
(G)
$75.00 purchase, $35.00 rental
Portrays the threat of accidental or unintentional nuclear war and shows how the common ground approach can be extended to crisis control.
Guidance and Counseling; Sociology
Dist - EFVP **Prod** - EFVP 1986

Preventing the nightmare - Part II 23 MIN
U-matic / VHS / BETA
Jack Cade's nightmare - a supervisor's guide to laws affecting the 'workplace series
Color; CC; PAL (IND PRO G)
$595.00 purchase
Presents ten simple rules that, if followed, will keep supervisors out of trouble. Shows how easy it is to violate various labor laws - sometimes by merely complying with an employee request. Reveals that supervisors have special responsibilities and that these ten rules can help. Hones the expertise of an experienced supervisor and offers orientation for the newly promoted or hired supervisor. Part two of two parts on workplace law.
Business and Economics; Guidance and Counseling
Dist - BNA **Prod** - BNA 1994

Preventing the Reality of Rape 53 MIN
U-matic / VHS / 16mm
Color (H C A)
Shows a positive approach to preventing rape in America. Profiles typical assailants and typical victims, examines the most frequent times and places where rape occurs and tells what a person can do if assaulted.
Sociology
Dist - FI **Prod** - PROSOR 1983

Prevention
VHS
Suicide - Causes and Prevention Series
Color
Describes the warning signs of potential suicide. Provides guidelines for intervention to help a potential suicide.
Psychology; Sociology
Dist - IBIS **Prod** - IBIS

Prevention 30 MIN
16mm
Color
Offers sensible decisions for those who choose to drink.
Health and Safety; Psychology
Dist - KELLYP **Prod** - FMARTN

Prevention 30 MIN
VHS / Cassette
Color; Mono (G)
$250.00, $10.00 purchase
Discusses decision - making for those who drink alcohol. Drawn from the work of Father Joseph C Martin.
Guidance and Counseling; Health and Safety; Psychology
Dist - KELLYP **Prod** - KELLYP

Prevention 12 MIN
VHS
Color (J H)
$99.00 purchase
Features six young people who have suffered the consequences of alcohol and other drug use and share their experiences, including addiction, accidents, suicide, pregnancy and crime.
Guidance and Counseling; Health and Safety; Psychology
Dist - FMSP

Prevention and Care of Decubiti 17 MIN
16mm
Nurse's Aide, Orderly and Attendant Series
Color (IND)
LC 73-701054
Describes the appearance of decubiti (bedsores), the types of patients who are prone to develop decubiti and the methods for prevention and care of decubiti.
Health and Safety
Dist - COPI **Prod** - COPI 1971

Prevention and Control of Air Leaks Following Segmental Pulmonary Resection 20 MIN
16mm
Color (PRO)
Presents a modification of conventional pulmonary segmental resection techniques both in cadavers and during an operation. Shows that air spaces and leaks have been almost completely eliminated.
Health and Safety; Science
Dist - ACY **Prod** - ACYDGD 1967

Prevention and Control of Distortion 20 MIN
16mm
Color (IND)
Explains controlling distortion in Arc Welding.
Industrial and Technical Education
Dist - LECO **Prod** - DISNEY

Prevention and early detection of cancer 22 MIN
VHS
Color (C A)
$225.00 purchase
Explains causes, common symptoms and methods to prevent cancer of the lung, colon and rectum, skin, breast, cervix and testicles. Emphasizes important lifestyle changes and precautions that can help prevent cancer. By Ralph Rosenthal and Russell Knightley.
Health and Safety
Dist - PFP

Prevention and Field Management of Head and Neck Injuries 23 MIN
VHS / U-matic
Sports Medicine Series
Color (C A)
$69.00 purchase _ #1469
Focuses on the life - threatening potential of head and neck injuries and provides examination and emergency treatment as well as preventative measures.
Health and Safety; Physical Education and Recreation
Dist - EBEC

Prevention and Identification of Premature Labor 12 MIN
VHS / U-matic
Color (PRO)
Discusses identification of true premature labor, medical and obstetric conditions which cause premature labor, indications for intervention, arrest of labor with ritadrine and the use of cerclage.
Health and Safety
Dist - UMICHM **Prod** - UMICHM 1983

Prevention and regression of coronary atherosclerosis - Volume 16
VHS / 8mm cartridge
Cardiology video journal series
Color (PRO)
#CA - 38
Presents a free - loan program, part of a series on cardiology, which trains medical professionals. Contact distributor for details.

Health and Safety
Dist - WYAYLA **Prod** - WYAYLA

Prevention and Therapy of Infectious Complications of Cancer and their Treatment 50 MIN
U-matic
Color
Discusses prophylactic management of infection for patients undergoing cancer chemotherapy.
Health and Safety
Dist - UTEXSC **Prod** - UTEXSC

The Prevention and treatment of childhood injuries 50 MIN
VHS
Color (G)
$39.95 purchase _ #ACV300V
Reviews the primary causes of personal injuries to children - drowning, choking, and burns. Provides prevention and first - aid treatment through explicit visual reenactment. Discusses traffic safety, poisoning, fractures, sprains, dislocations, bites, stings and more. Includes safety tips for the home and soft cover book.
Health and Safety
Dist - CAMV

Prevention and Treatment of Decubitus Ulcers 15 MIN
16mm
Color
LC 76-712972
Defines decubitus ulcers, shows how they develop and describes what specific measures to follow in order to prevent their occurrence.
Health and Safety; Science; Science - Natural
Dist - TRNAID **Prod** - TRNAID 1970

Prevention and Treatment of Five Complications of Diabetes 14 MIN
U-matic / VHS
Color (PRO)
Describes the usefulness of the publication, The Prevention and Treatment of Five Complications of Diabetes - A Guide for Primary Care Practitioners, in the day to day management of the patient with diabetes. Demonstrates clinical applications of the principles advocated in the Guide in five brief case studies. Discusses visual impairment, adverse pregnancy outcome, foot problems, kidney problems and acute hyperglycemia and ketoacidosis, all complications of diabetes.
Health and Safety
Dist - UMICHM **Prod** - UMICHM 1983

Prevention and Treatment of Foot Injuries 25 MIN
U-matic / VHS
Sports Medicine Series
Color (C A)
$69.00 purchase _ #1461
Teaches techniques for diagnosing and treating a variety of foot disorders caused by flat feet, high arches, blisters, calluses, nail hypertrophy, and shin splints.
Health and Safety; Physical Education and Recreation
Dist - EBEC

Prevention and treatment of heart disease
VHS
Color (J H C G T A PRO)
$79.50 purchase _ #AH46317
Gives numerous examples of preventable and treatable heart diseases. Stresses the relationship between lifestyle and heart disease.
Health and Safety; Science - Natural
Dist - HTHED **Prod** - HTHED

Prevention and treatment of pressure ulcers 28 MIN
VHS
Wound care series
Color (PRO C)
$285.00 purchase, $70.00 rental _ #4403
Focuses on pressure ulcer prevention strategies, risk assessment and early intervention techniques. Reviews the physiology of the skin and explains the dynamics of a pressure ulcer, how it develops and the risks of aging skin. Explains the guidelines for preventions of pressure ulcers. Demonstrates pressure - relieving devices such as mattress overlays, as well as indirect preventive strategies. Focuses on the depth of tissue damage and assessment of the ulcer for staging pressure ulcers. Covers comprehensively risk evaluation and prevention strategies. Part three of three parts on wound care.
Health and Safety
Dist - AJN **Prod** - AJN 1995

Prevention and Treatment of Sports Injuries 23 MIN
VHS
Color (J)
$49.95 purchase _ #V2222 - 10
Presents role of coach in prevention of injuries. Presents guidelines for returning an athlete to competition and studies how ice and heat are used in healing of injuries.
Health and Safety; Physical Education and Recreation
Dist - SCHSCI

Prevention and treatment of sports injuries 23 MIN
VHS
Color (J H A)
$69.95 purchase _ #DH400V
Examines prevention and treatment of sports injuries. Stresses the critical role of the coach in injury prevention and in dealing effectively with injury when it occurs.
Health and Safety; Physical Education and Recreation; Science - Natural
Dist - CAMV

Prevention and Work with Natural Helpers 7 MIN
U-matic
Child Welfare Learning Laboratory Materials Series
Color
Introduces the idea that prevention should be aimed at the person - at - risk in child welfare situations. Emphasizes the use of informal and semi - formal helpers in social work.
Guidance and Counseling; Sociology
Dist - UMITV **Prod** - UMITV

The Prevention Factor 28 MIN
16mm
Color
Documents a brief episode in the life of an unusual man, who is successful, loved, driven to achieve and yet indifferent to his health. Stars Gary Merrill.
Health and Safety
Dist - MTP **Prod** - AMLUNG

The Prevention Factor 27 MIN
16mm
Color
LC 79-700453
Uses flashbacks to tell a story about a man who neglects to take care of himself when he catches a cold and develops pneumonia as a result.
Health and Safety
Dist - WSTGLC **Prod** - KNIFED 1979

Prevention health series - pounds off 55 MIN
VHS
Prevention health series
Color (J H C G)
$29.95 purchase _ #BV760V
Offers a complete 25 - minute exercise routine that can be done everyday to help lose weight permanently, trim inches, tone muscles and increase the energy level. Discusses three common eating errors, the yo - yo syndrome and other diet pitfalls, how to achieve a realistic weight goal, calorie dense foods and other cooking tips and the benefits of drinking water.
Health and Safety; Home Economics; Physical Education and Recreation; Social Science
Dist - CAMV **Prod** - PREVEN

Prevention health series
Prevention health series - pounds off 55 MIN
Dist - CAMV

Prevention I
VHS
Color (K P)
$85.00 purchase _ #K45188
Educates parent and children ages 1 - 6 about basic oral hygiene, complete care of children's teeth for new mothers and the first visit to a dentist.
Health and Safety
Dist - HTHED **Prod** - HTHED

Prevention II
VHS
Color (K P I J H)
$85.00 purchase _ #K45189
Presents concepts in dental care to children aged 6 - 18. Addresses oral hygiene, nutrition, topical fluoride and pit and fissure sealants. Accompanies Prevention I video.
Health and Safety
Dist - HTHED **Prod** - HTHED

Prevention is Better than Cure 19 MIN
U-matic / VHS / 16mm
Color (A)
Shows examples of industrial occupational hazards such as fumes, noise, toxic material and more. Gives suggestions on elimination, isolation or substitution of these hazards, and stresses worker protection.
Health and Safety; Psychology; Sociology
Dist - IFB **Prod** - MILLBK

Prevention of accidents at home - Part 1 23 MIN
VHS / U-matic / 16mm
Safety for seniors series
Color (G)
$450.00, $400.00 purchase
Points out fifty hazardous areas in the home. Gives simple safety measures which can be used at little or no cost to prevent injuries to the elderly. Part of a three - part series on safety for the elderly.
Health and Safety; Sociology
Dist - HANDEL **Prod** - HANDEL 1985

Prevention of Cancer Dissemination in the Operating Room 24 MIN
U-matic
Color
Discusses various methods which are employed in the operating room to avoid spreading cancer during surgery.
Health and Safety
Dist - UTEXSC **Prod** - UTEXSC

Prevention of Child Abuse and Neglect 30 MIN
VHS / U-matic
Child Abuse and Neglect Series
Color (H C A)
Home Economics; Sociology
Dist - GPN **Prod** - UMINN 1983

Prevention of complications of bed rest 29 MIN
16mm
Directions for education in nursing via technology series; Lesson 11
B&W (PRO)
LC 74-701785
Identifies changes which predispose to complications involving the pulmonary, circulatory, musculo - skeletal system, and mental processes brought about by bed rest. Demonstrates motion exercises and the use of footboard, hand roll and trochanter roll.
Health and Safety
Dist - WSUM **Prod** - DENT 1974

Prevention of Contamination in Removable Posthodontics Delivery Adjustments 14 MIN
16mm
Color (PRO)
LC 78-701359
Demonstrates a systematic method of handling dentures from the insertion through the adjustment phases, emphasizing simple precautions for preventing cross - contamination.
Health and Safety
Dist - USNAC **Prod** - VADTC 1978

Prevention of Cross - Contamination in Removable Prosthodontics Delivery Adjustments 14 MIN
U-matic
Color (PRO)
LC 78-706209
Demonstrates a systematic method of handling dentures from the insertion through the adjustment phases, emphasizing simple precautions for preventing cross - contamination.
Health and Safety
Dist - USNAC **Prod** - USVA 1978

Prevention of Drowning 26 MIN
U-matic / VHS / 16mm
Color (A)
Describes how to avoid getting into tactical military or recreational situations that might lead to drowning. Shows the drown - proof method of staying afloat.
Civics and Political Systems; Health and Safety
Dist - USNAC **Prod** - USA 1984

Prevention of Heat Casualties 25 MIN
16mm
Color
LC FIE60-82
Introduces the problem of heat stress and the principal types of heat illness that may occur when men are subjected to heavy work output in conditions of severe climatic heat.
Health and Safety
Dist - USNAC **Prod** - USN 1959

Prevention of Heat Injury 21 MIN
16mm
Color
LC 80-700958
Covers troop operations in jungle and desert environments and gives proper dress and other precautions to prevent heat injury.
Civics and Political Systems; Health and Safety
Dist - USNAC **Prod** - USA 1976

Prevention of Learning Disabilities 30 MIN
VHS / U-matic
Characteristics of Learning Disabilities Series
Color (C A)
Discusses the value of early recognition of learning disorders.
Education; Psychology
Dist - FI **Prod** - WCVETV 1976

Prevention of occupational injury and disease through control technology 40 MIN
U-matic / VHS
Safety, health, and loss control - managing effective programs series
Color (IND)
LC 81-706518
Shows Walter Haag, who describes the National Institute for Occupational Safety and Health's hazard control technology program as it relates to occupational safety. Describes the impact of engineering and monitoring controls, personal protective equipment and improved work practices.
Health and Safety
Dist - AMCEE **Prod** - AMCEE 1980

Prevention of Pulmonary Embolism by Partial Occlusion of Inferior Vena Cava 18 MIN
16mm
Color (PRO)
Illustrates the application of a smooth edged, partially occluding teflon clip to the inferior vena cava and types of venous pathology sometimes encountered.
Health and Safety; Science
Dist - ACY **Prod** - ACYDGD 1968

Prevention of rutting and stripping in asphalt pavements 22 MIN
VHS / U-matic
Color (IND)
$80.00, $110.00 purchase _ #TCA17762, #TCA17761
Defines and shows examples of rutting and stripping in asphalt pavements. Offers possible solutions to eliminate rutting and stripping. Includes two technical reports.
Civics and Political Systems; Industrial and Technical Education; Social Science
Dist - USNAC **Prod** - USDTFH 1989

Prevention of stuttering - Pt 1 - identifying the danger signs 33 MIN
16mm
Color (T)
LC 75-703894
Introduces and distinguishes normal from abnormal disfluencies in the speech of young children. Points out danger signs of developing stuttering behavior, indicating the severity of the problem.
Education; English Language; Psychology
Dist - SOP **Prod** - SOP 1975

Prevention of stuttering - Pt 2 - parent counseling and elimination of the problem 44 MIN
16mm
Color (T)
LC 75-703895
Shows stutterers, from two to six years of age, interacting in stressful situations with parents and shows counseling sessions with parents which emphasize the parent's role in helping to eliminate the problem.
Education; English Language; Psychology
Dist - SOP **Prod** - SOP 1975

Prevention of Suicide 28 MIN
U-matic / VHS
Color (PRO)
Discusses how nursing staffs can recognize and prevent the suicide - prone patient. Presents a 'psychogical autopsy' of such patients, and advises on how to assess and manage the depressed inpatient.
Health and Safety; Sociology
Dist - USNAC **Prod** - VAMCSL 1984

Prevention of suicide 28 MIN
VHS / U-matic
Color (PRO C)
$395.00 purchase, $80.00 rental _ #C861 - VI - 073
Opens with a nurse on rounds who discovers a patient who has hanged himself. Follows with a meeting of the patient's treatment team for a 'psychological autopsy.' Makes health care teams aware of the factors that lead to suicide and encourages teams to work together in helping and assessing patients. Presented by Ruth Chen, RN, Dr Patrick Gannon, Christine Warfield, RN, Nadine Ward, RN, and Dr Willian Danton.
Health and Safety
Dist - HSCIC **Prod** - VAMCSL 1986

Prevention - Pt 2 12 MIN
VHS
Coronary heart disease series
Color (J H A C)
$195.00 purchase
Talks about the risks of developing heart disease, with emphasis on high risk behavior. Calls attention to ways to reduce the risk of heart disease.
Health and Safety; Science - Natural
Dist - PFP

Prevention - the Epidemiological Approach to Cancer 31 MIN
VHS / 16mm
Cancer Prevention Series
Color (C PRO)
$250.00 purchase _ #635302
Presents the risk factors and prevention strategies for the five most common types of cancer - colo - rectal (bowel), lung, skin, breast and cervical. Offers two programs, one of which is aimed at general interest audiences while the other contains information relevant to medical students and professionals. 'Prevention' takes the epidemiological approach to present a model for clinical intervention in the five most common forms of cancer. Teaches health care professionals about the five most common cancer sites, detecting cancer in its early stages, and motivating clients to adopt a healthier lifestyle.
Health and Safety; Psychology; Sociology
Dist - ACCESS **Prod** - ACCESS 1987

The Preventive Action Plan 72 MIN
U-matic
Preventing Sexual Harassment in the Workplace Series
Color (A)
Aids business people in developing a preventive action plan to minimize and eventually eliminate sexual harrassment in the workplace. Includes a sample written policy which may be used as a guideline and gives instructions on how to conduct an investigation into a complaint.
Business and Economics; Sociology
Dist - VENCMP **Prod** - VENCMP 1986

Preventive and Predictive Maintenance 30 MIN
U-matic / VHS
Maintenance Management Series
Color
Deals with balancing preventive and corrective maintenance. Identifies critical equipment. Highlights predictive maintenance.
Business and Economics; Psychology
Dist - ITCORP **Prod** - ITCORP

Preventive Antitrust - Corporate Compliance Program Series
Negotiating with the Government 72 MIN
Overview of Preventive Antitrust Activities 89 MIN
Uncovering, remedying and reporting antitrust violations 176 MIN
Dist - ABACPE

Preventive Antitrust - Corporate Compliance Programs Series
Corporate Antitrust Compliance Programs 187 MIN
Dist - ABACPE

Preventive approaches - Part III 8 MIN
VHS / U-matic
Handling misbehavior subseries
Color (G C A)
$220.00 purchase _ #C840 - VI - 020J
Teaches parents preventive approaches to misbehavior. Part three of a three - part subseries on handling misbehavior and part of a ten - part series on parents and children presented by Dr Carolyn Webster - Stratton.
Health and Safety; Psychology; Sociology
Dist - HSCIC

Preventive Dental Care 15 MIN
16mm / U-matic / VHS
Color (J)
LC 81-701108
Describes methods of keeping teeth healthy and preventing serious dental problems. Stresses the importance of careful and proper brushing and flossing of the teeth, cutting down on sweets and regular dental examinations as ways of achieving dental health.
Health and Safety
Dist - PRORE **Prod** - PRORE 1978

Preventive Dental Care for the Handicapped Child 17 MIN
16mm
Color (A)
LC 78-700007
Describes preventive dental techniques for handicapped children, including tooth treatment, bacteria removal, food choice and positioning techniques for brushing and flossing.
Education; Health and Safety; Psychology
Dist - VCI **Prod** - VCI 1974

Preventive Dentistry - a Hospital Based Program 18 MIN
16mm
Color (PRO)
LC 77-700818
Describes the approach and methodology of formulating a preventive dontistry program in a hospital.
Health and Safety
Dist - USNAC **Prod** - VADTC 1977

Preventive Dentistry for the Handicapped Patient 17 MIN
16mm
Color
LC 79-701725
Focuses on oral hygiene problems of the severely handicapped, with emphasis on education and encouragement of the patient by the health - care team.
Health and Safety; Psychology
Dist - USNAC **Prod** - VADTC 1979

Preventive dentistry - Pt 2 - professional responsibility 24 MIN
16mm
Color (PRO)
LC 74-706557
Discusses how the U S Navy's preventive dentistry program enables its professional dental staff to cope with the demands for adequate dental care for Navy personnel.
Civics and Political Systems; Health and Safety
Dist - USNAC **Prod** - USN 1966

Preventive Dentistry - the Prevention of Oral Disease 16 MIN
U-matic / VHS / 16mm
Color
Discusses prevention of tooth decay and gum disease as well as beginning, progression and destruction of healthy tissue resulting from neglect.
Health and Safety
Dist - USNAC **Prod** - USN 1979

Preventive Dentistry - the Prevention of Oral Disease 16 MIN
U-matic / VHS / 16mm
Color (SPANISH)
LC 74-705412
Shows prevention of tooth decay and gum disease as well as beginning, progression and destruction of healthy tissue resulting from neglect.
Foreign Language; Health and Safety
Dist - USNAC **Prod** - USN 1963

Preventive Health Care 20 MIN
U-matic / VHS / 16mm
Woman Talk Series
Color (H C A)
Describes breast self - examination, pelvic examination and pap smear and emphasizes the importance of their regular application. Includes a section on venereal disease and discusses the various forms of the disease, from herpes and venereal warts to syphilis. Discusses measures that should be taken to prevent their spreading.
Health and Safety; Sociology
Dist - CORF **Prod** - CORF 1983

Preventive Lifeguarding 9 MIN
16mm
Lifesaving and Water Safety Series
Color (I)
LC 76-701570
Defines the duties of the lifeguard, emphasizing that while the ability to make rescues is important, the lifeguard's main job is to prevent accidents, injuries and aquatic emergencies.
Health and Safety
Dist - AMRC **Prod** - AMRC 1975

Preventive Maintenance of Signal Equipment for Commanders 15 MIN
16mm
B&W
Explains the procedures to be followed in the maintenance of ground signal equipment when in storage at Army depots.
Civics and Political Systems; Industrial and Technical Education; Social Science
Dist - USNAC **Prod** - USA 1951

Preventive maintenance - Pt 1 60 MIN
U-matic / VHS
Mechanical equipment maintenance, module 12 - diesel engines series
Color (IND)
Industrial and Technical Education
Dist - LEIKID **Prod** - LEIKID

Preventive maintenance - Pt 2 60 MIN
U-matic / VHS
Mechanical equipment maintenance, module 12 - diesel engines series
Color (IND)
Industrial and Technical Education
Dist - LEIKID **Prod** - LEIKID

Preventive Marriage Counselling 145 MIN
U-matic
University of the Air Series

Color (J H C A)
$750.00 purchase, $250.00 rental
Features a look at marriage counselling and the possible benefits for couples in trouble. Program contains a series of five cassettes 29 minutes each.
Guidance and Counseling
Dist - CTV **Prod** - CTV 1974

Preview 3 MIN
16mm
Color (G)
$10.00 rental
Combines several kinds of imagery and two kinds of sound to reveal the ambiguity of personal and cultural significations once they are removed from their usual contexts. Features a J J Murphy production.
Fine Arts
Dist - CANCIN

Preview 5 MIN
VHS
Color (G)
$20.00 rental
Highlights excerpts of performances and impersonations for the camera. Includes a rooftop Cinderella, a political protest of US imperialism in Haiti and old Coke ads with childhood memories.
Fine Arts
Dist - CANCIN **Prod** - LEVINE 1989

Preview Program 30 MIN
VHS / U-matic
Meeting Leading Series
Color
Business and Economics; Psychology
Dist - PRODEV **Prod** - PRODEV

Preview/Overview of Learning System Design
VHS / U-matic
Learning System Design Series Unit 1
Color (T)
Education; Psychology
Dist - MSU **Prod** - MSU

Prewriting, Pt 1 29 MIN
U-matic / VHS
Teaching Writing - a Process Approach Series
Color
Provides a structure for organizing thought before the writer begins to write. Examines the first three of five stages in prewriting - why, what and who.
Education; English Language
Dist - PBS **Prod** - MSITV 1982

Prewriting, Pt 2 29 MIN
U-matic / VHS
Teaching Writing - a Process Approach Series
Color
Emphasizes that by approaching writing as a process, the fears, hesitation and obstacles to writing become diminished. Examines the last two of five stages in prewriting - where and how.
Education; English Language
Dist - PBS **Prod** - MSITV 1982

Prey of innocence 28 MIN
16mm
Color (H C A)
$50.00 rental
Tells the story of a punch drunk knuckle breaker who unknowingly kidnaps a seven-year-old girl from her drug addict mother in an attempt to start a family. Presents a dark, character-driven, fast-paced comedy. Features Dom DeLuise and Ruth Buzzi. Produced by Michael DeLuise.
Fine Arts; Sociology
Dist - CANCIN

The Price 38 MIN
VHS
Color (A)
$525.00 purchase
Tells of Walt Ames, a sales manager who became involved in price - fixing, bid rigging and other illegal practices. Details the Justice Department's methods of building an antitrust case against such practices, and the penalties for individuals and companies involved. An updated 1990s version.
Business and Economics; Civics and Political Systems; Education
Dist - COMFLM **Prod** - COMFLM

The Price of Change 26 MIN
U-matic / VHS / 16mm
Women in the Middle East Series
Color
Examines the consequences of employment for five Egyptian women and presents a picture of changing attitudes regarding work, the family, sex and women's place in society.
History - World; Sociology
Dist - ICARUS **Prod** - ICARUS 1982

The Price of Democracy - Pt 8 58 MIN
VHS
Struggle for Democracy Series
Color (S)
$49.00 purchase _ #039 - 9008
Explores the concept of democracy and how it works. Features Patrick Watson, author with Benjamin Barber of 'The Struggle For Democracy,' as host who travels to more than 30 countries around the world, examining issues such as rule of law, freedom of information, the tyranny of the majority and the relationship of economic prosperity to democracy. Part 8 examines a fundamental contradiction within democratic societies - uncontrolled wealth promotes injustice while controlled wealth limits freedom, and at the same time, the health of democracy seems to be directly related to the existence of economic prosperity.
Business and Economics; Civics and Political Systems; History - World; Social Science; Sociology
Dist - FI **Prod** - DFL 1989

Price of Free Speech 29 MIN
U-matic / VHS
Inside Story Series
Color
Focuses on the use of libel suits that threaten many small town newspapers.
Literature and Drama; Social Science
Dist - PBS **Prod** - PBS 1981

The Price of Freedom 28 MIN
16mm
Color
LC 75-703837
Gives some historical background on ideas behind battle monuments. Presents scenes of World War I and World War II, along with current footage of various battle monuments maintained by the American Battle Monuments Commission.
History - United States; History - World
Dist - USNAC **Prod** - AMBAT 1973

The Price of freedom 60 MIN
VHS
Inside the FBI series
Color (G)
$79.95 purchase
Discloses that the FBI is charged with guarding national security. Reveals that it must strike a delicate balance, protecting the nation but not at the expense of people's freedoms. Examines the counterintelligence work of the FBI and illustrates how and why the agency has been criticized for interfering in the political process. Part of a four - part series investigating the Federal Bureau of Investigation.
Civics and Political Systems
Dist - PBS **Prod** - PBS 1995

The Price of Gold 60 MIN
16mm / U-matic / VHS
Making of a Continent Series
Color (H C A)
Reveals that when the Sierra Nevada range was pushed upward, minerals were exposed including the small amount of gold that resulted in the 1849 gold rush in California. Shows that this geologic action was also responsible for the rich soil that resulted in the agriculture industry of the region.
Science - Physical
Dist - FI **Prod** - BBCTV 1983

The Price of hunger 21 MIN
VHS
Color (G)
$49.95 purchase _ #ST - BR2318
Discusses the causes of world hunger and possible solutions. Examines the economic policies of Third World governments and new farming methods that do not depend on expensive energy, chemicals and technology and foreign investments.
Business and Economics; Sociology
Dist - INSTRU

The Price of imperialism 30 MIN
U-matic / VHS
America - the second century series
Color (H C)
$34.95 purchase
Comments on significant diplomatic happenings of the pre - World War I years in America. Part of a 30-part series on political, social, diplomatic and economic issues in the United States since 1875.
History - United States
Dist - DALCCD **Prod** - DALCCD
GPN

The Price of Life 12 MIN
U-matic / VHS / 16mm
Vignettes Series
Color (J)
LC 73-701989
Presents three vignettes in which the rights of civilians collide with combat necessity, those of the retarded with social expediency and those of the unborn with societal pressures. Encourages value judgments on the importance of human life.
Sociology
Dist - PAULST **Prod** - PAULST 1973

Price of Power 29 MIN
U-matic
Like no Other Place Series
Color (J H)
Looks at the construction of the largest hydroelectric plant in North America. Three workers weigh the project's benefits against the environmental damage and discuss the staggering financial cost and the effects on the native people of the regions.
Geography - World; History - World
Dist - TVOTAR **Prod** - TVOTAR 1985

The Price of power - money in politics 30 MIN
VHS
Contemporary political campaign series
Color (J H G)
$69.95 purchase _ #CCP0126V
Zeroes in on the price political candidates pay to win election to office. Discusses the costs for media during a campaign and how a candidate's chances are determined by the amount of campaign expenditures, the quest for money being as demanding on a candidate's time as the quest for votes. Investigates where candidates get their money and what they trade in their quest for political power. Takes a look at wealth and its influence on American first amendment rights and analyzes the role of money in local, state and national races. Part of a two - part series.
Civics and Political Systems
Dist - CAMV **Prod** - CAMV 1993

The Price of Progress 54 MIN
U-matic / VHS / 16mm
Color (H)
$375.00, $350.00 purchase, $75.00 rental
Examines social, environmental and economic costs of resettlement efforts sponsored by the World Bank in India, Indonesia and Brazil.
Business and Economics; Education; Geography - World; Sociology
Dist - BULFRG **Prod** - CITV 1989

The Price of Progress 54 MIN
VHS / 16mm
(I A)
$75.00 rental
Investigates three resettlement schemes in India, Indonesia and Brazil, sponsored by the World Bank. Analyzes the social, environmental and economic costs of some of the bank's policies. Narrated by Bob Geldor.
Business and Economics; Social Science; Sociology
Dist - BULFRG **Prod** - CTVS 1989

The Price of progress 60 MIN
VHS
Inside the FBI series
Color (G)
$79.95 purchase
Looks at the changing faces of modern day crime. Follows an FBI property seizure in the home of a woman found guilty of embezzling over $1.5 million. Explores the positive and negative aspects of using sophisticated technology to assist in law enforcement. Includes stories of FBI operations gone wrong. Part of a four - part series investigating the Federal Bureau of Investigation.
Civics and Political Systems; Sociology
Dist - PBS **Prod** - PBS 1995

The Price of smile
VHS
Frontiers series
Color; PAL (G)
PdS20 purchase
Reveals that industrial research has led to the development of new and exciting materials for use in dentistry. Discusses the increasing use of specialized equipment and hypnotherapy which may mean pain - free visits in the future. Includes support material. Part of a series examining how developments at the frontiers of science, technology and psychology have had a major impact on a range of health and medical issues. Contact distributor about availability outside the United Kingdom.
Health and Safety
Dist - ACADEM

The Price of Survival 28 MIN
16mm
Color
LC 75-701357
Depicts the reactions of a hospital staff and local citizens to disaster. Portrays the preparation and planning neccssary to correct the weak points in a hospital's disaster plan and illustrates a successful test of an improved disaster plan.

Health and Safety; Science - Natural; Sociology
Dist - USNAC **Prod** - USDEHS

Price of Survival 27 MIN
U-matic
Emergency Techniques Series
Color (PRO)
Presents a discussion of community disaster programs.
Health and Safety; History - World; Social Science
Dist - PRIMED **Prod** - PRIMED

Price - quality relationship - speed reading - retirement homes
U-matic / VHS
Consumer survival series
Color
Deals with various aspects of price - quality relationship, speed reading and retirement homes.
English Language; Health and Safety; Home Economics
Dist - MDCPB **Prod** - MDCPB

Price tag of sex series
Presents a series of four videos that address teen sexuality and the consequences of sexual indulgence. Features a speaker who stresses the advantages of abstinence and promotes positive interaction and discussion. Series includes modules on pregnancy and STDs; incurable diseases; emotions and sexuality and self-esteem; and issues surrounding alcohol and sex, abortion and adoption, date rape.

The Incurables	18 MIN
More than just a body	16 MIN
Pregnancies and STDs	16 MIN
Sex is no game	15 MIN

Dist - CAMV
UNL

The Price you pay 29 MIN
VHS / U-matic
Color (G)
$150.00 purchase, $50.00 rental
Explores the rich cultural heritage of the Vietnamese, Laotion and Khmer people. Conveys the pain and frustration of resettlement of the resettlement of the refugees from the war in Southeast Asia. Produced and directed by Christine Keyser.
History - United States; History - World; Sociology
Dist - CROCUR

The Priceless Laboratory 25 MIN
16mm
Color (H C A)
Records the activity of men and equipment dispatched to the frozen laboratory of Antarctica. Explores the animal life and land of the area and emphasizes the rewards in terms of scientific research and historical significance.
Geography - World; Science - Natural; Science - Physical
Dist - MCDO **Prod** - MCDO 1963

The Priceless treasures of Dresden 59 MIN
U-matic / VHS / 16mm
Color (H C A)
LC 79-700098
Examines the rich array of art and artifacts gathered by Saxon kings and wealthy merchants of Dresden over a 500 - year period. Reviews the many perils which have threatened the survival of the collection.
Fine Arts
Dist - IU **Prod** - WNETTV 1978

Prices 15 MIN
U-matic / VHS
Common Cents Series
Color (P)
Looks at the elements that determine how much goods and services cost. Introduces the concept of expenses, supply and demand, and competition, and considers how prices change.
Business and Economics
Dist - AITECH **Prod** - KETCTV 1977

Price/Value 12 MIN
VHS / U-matic
Color (IND)
Examines various parts of Ansul brand dry chemical cartridge - operated fire extinguishers.
Health and Safety
Dist - ANSUL **Prod** - ANSUL 1980

Pricing 30 MIN
VHS / U-matic
Accounting Series; Pt 11
Color (C)
Discusses pricing as it applies to accounting.
Business and Economics; Guidance and Counseling
Dist - GPN **Prod** - UMA 1980

Pricing 10 MIN
U-matic
Calling Captain Consumer Series
Color (P I J)
Discusses all the costs that go into pricing a product, the fluctuations of prices and the services of different stores with different prices for the same objects.
Business and Economics; Home Economics
Dist - TVOTAR **Prod** - TVOTAR 1985

Pricing and promotional decisions - legal implications of alternative approaches 120 MIN
U-matic / VHS
Antitrust counseling and the marketing process series
Color (PRO)
Explores the legal implications of a manager's pricing and promotional strategies, focusing on the Robinson - Patman Act. Covers issues relating to price and promotional discrimination.
Business and Economics; Civics and Political Systems
Dist - ABACPE **Prod** - ABACPE

Pricing and sales strategy 59 MIN
VHS
How to start your own business series
Color (H A T)
$69.95 purchase _ #NC123
Considers pricing and other sales strategies. Part of a ten - part series on starting a business.
Business and Economics
Dist - AAVIM **Prod** - AAVIM 1992

Pricing Strategies 30 MIN
U-matic / VHS
Marketing Perspectives Series
Color
Focuses on the role of price in the marketing mix, product pricing sequence, effects on pricing of the product's position in the product lifecyIce, corporate pricing objectives and other pricing strategies.
Business and Economics; Education
Dist - WFVTAE **Prod** - MATC

Pricing Theories 30 MIN
VHS / U-matic
Marketing Perspectives Series
Color
Correlates the supply and the demand curve. Covers the benefits of multiple - point pricing, break - even concept and marginal cost theory.
Business and Economics; Education
Dist - WFVTAE **Prod** - MATC

Pride 29 MIN
Videoreel / VT2
Our Street Series
Color
Sociology
Dist - PBS **Prod** - MDCPB

PRIDE - '69 - '89 28 MIN
U-matic / VHS
Color (G)
Documents Gay and Lesbian Pride Weekend in New York City in 1989, on the 20th anniversary of the Stonewall riots.
History - United States; Sociology
Dist - ACTUP **Prod** - DIVATV 1990

Pride and Prejudice
U-matic / VHS
Color (J C I)
Presents Jane Austen's comedy of manners. Stars Greer Garson and Laurence Olivier.
Fine Arts; Literature and Drama
Dist - GA **Prod** - GA

Pride and prejudice 118 MIN
VHS
B&W (G)
$24.95 purchase _ #S00532
Presents the 1944 film adaptation of Jane Austen's novel 'Pride and Prejudice.' Tells the story of a woman who seeks husbands for her five daughters. Stars Greer Garson and Laurence Olivier.
Fine Arts; Literature and Drama
Dist - UILL

Pride and Prejudice 44 MIN
16mm
B&W (I J H)
LC FIA52-4976
Portrays Jane Austen's comedy of 18th - century provincial England society. Stars Greer Garson, Laurence Olivier and Maureen O'Sullivan.
Literature and Drama
Dist - FI **Prod** - PMI 1940

Pride and prejudice - a history of black culture in America
VHS
Color (I J H)
$55.00 purchase _ #5486VD
Tells the story of the impact of African Americans upon United States culture. Looks at their contributions to the world of ideas, the arts and ways of life. Includes a resource guide with background information, lesson ideas, bibliographies and more.
History - United States
Dist - KNOWUN **Prod** - KNOWUN 1993

Pride and principle 17 MIN
16mm / U-matic / VHS
Searching for values - a film anthology series
Color (J)
LC 73-700115
Tells how under the extreme conditions of a Japanese prison camp, two intransigent men meet and clash over the question of principle, leaving questionable the 'rightness' of the winner's behavior.
Guidance and Counseling; Psychology; Religion and Philosophy; Sociology
Dist - LCOA **Prod** - LCOA 1972

Pride and the power to win 30 MIN
VHS / U-matic
Color (G)
$49.95 purchase, $35.00 rental
Tells the success story of Baboquivari High School in Sells, Arizona, a Tohono O'Odham community, in which the entire town joined forces to turn the school from the lowest ranked high school in Arizona to one with graduates who now compete with graduates of any school in the state. Looks at how the people used their traditional tribal - consensus method of problem solving. Documents the process with interviews of students and school officials leading to an emotional graduation day.
Education; Psychology; Social Science
Dist - NAMPBC

Pride and Workmanship 9 MIN
U-matic / VHS / 16mm
Color (I J H C)
LC 75-703687
Examines the work of an immigrant woodcarver whose life work has been devoted to carving animals for carousels.
Fine Arts; Industrial and Technical Education
Dist - AIMS **Prod** - WSMRCB 1975

A Pride in Belonging 28 MIN
16mm
Color
LC 75-704424
Depicts the changing role of women and the occupations available for women in today's military. Presents women discussing the benefits of military life and the changes that have taken place.
Civics and Political Systems; Sociology
Dist - USNAC **Prod** - USOIAF 1975

Pride of Place - Building the American Dream Series
Dist - FOTH
PSU

Pride of Place - Building the American Dream Series

The Campus - a place apart	58 MIN
The Places within	58 MIN
Proud towers	58 MIN
The Search for a usable past	58 MIN

Dist - PSU

Pride of place - building the American dream

Dream houses	58 MIN
The Garden and the grid	58 MIN
Resorts - paradise reclaimed	58 MIN

Dist - PSU

Pride of Place Series
Dist - FOTH

Pride of place series
Presents the story of American architecture - which is also the story of America and its aspiration as told by its buildings and builders. Consists of eight parts, each 58 minutes. Includes: The Search for a Usable Past; The Campus - A Place Apart; Dream Houses; Suburbs - Arcadia for Everyone; Resorts - Paradise Reclaimed; The Places Within; Proud Towers; and The Garden and the Grid.

The Campus - a place apart	58 MIN
Dream houses	58 MIN
The Garden and the grid	58 MIN
The Places within	58 MIN
Proud towers	58 MIN
Resorts - paradise reclaimed	58 MIN
The Search for a usable past	58 MIN
Suburbs - Arcadia for everyone	58 MIN

Dist - FOTH **Prod** - FOTH 1975
PSU

The Pride of the Yankees 128 MIN
U-matic / VHS / 16mm
B&W
Presents a biography of Lou Gehrig, who had to give up baseball at the height of his career due to illness. Stars Gary Cooper and Teresa Wright.
Fine Arts; Physical Education and Recreation
Dist - FI **Prod** - MGM 1942

Pride on Parade 13 MIN
16mm
Color
LC 79-701188
Offers a look at the Oscar Mayer Company by juxtaposing day - to - day operations against the disciplines of a musical art form.
Business and Economics
Dist - MTP **Prod** - OMAY 1979

Pride - Preface to Politics 29 MIN
Videoreel / VT2
Black Experience Series
Color
Civics and Political Systems; History - United States
Dist - PBS **Prod** - WTTWTV

The Priest and the Girl 89 MIN
16mm
B&W (PORTUGUESE (ENGLISH SUBTITLES))
An English subtitle version of the Portuguese language film. Tells the story of a country priest who falls in love with a young girl who is jealously guarded by her stepfather. Follows the couple from their elopement to their tragic end.
Fine Arts; Foreign Language
Dist - NYFLMS **Prod** - NYFLMS 1966

The Priest Know - all 27 MIN
U-matic / VHS / 16mm
Storybook International Series
Color
Present the Norwegian tale of a simple peasant who is mistaken for a priest and is taken to a royal convention of ecclesiastes. Shows that when he is made to predict the sex of the queen's unborn child and she luckily gives birth to twins, he is ordained a bishop.
Guidance and Counseling; Literature and Drama
Dist - JOU **Prod** - JOU 1982

The Primacy of learning - Profiles of Greek American educators 28 MIN
VHS
Illuminations series
Color (G R)
#V - 1044
Documents the historic Greek regard for education, pointing to the claims by some that Greek Americans are the most highly educated ethnic group in the U S. Explores the responsibilities and challenges that educators face today. Features the 1989 National Teacher of the Year, Mary Biconvaris.
Education; Fine Arts
Dist - GOTEL **Prod** - GOTEL 1990

The Primal furnace 22 MIN
VHS / U-matic
Color (H C)
$280.00, $330.00 purchase, $50.00 rental
Covers the history of geothermal energy. Defines and views the different kinds of geothermal energy available in the United States and elsewhere in the world. Looks at how that energy can be harnessed to serve humankind.
Social Science
Dist - NDIM **Prod** - EPRI 1988

The Primal Mind 58 MIN
16mm / U-matic / VHS
Color
Identifies the important distinctions between Native American and Western or European - based people. Looks at some of their shared legacies.
History - United States; Social Science
Dist - CNEMAG **Prod** - BERMNL

Primal Therapy 19 MIN
16mm / VHS
Color (G)
$365.00, $300.00 purchase, $50.00 rental
Interviews Arthur Janov, author of 'Primal Scream.' Discusses primal therapy as a method for dealing with neurotic patients.
Psychology
Dist - CNEMAG **Prod** - DOCUA 1976

Primal Therapy - in Search of the Real You 19 MIN
16mm / U-matic / VHS
Color
Explains that primal therapy asserts that within everyone there is a state of being with which we are unfamiliar. Describes this state as being free of tensions and defenses and knowing no split between conscious and sub - conscious awareness. Points out that in order to reach this state, the patient must go back, uncover the hurts of childhood, relive them and free the real person.
Health and Safety; Psychology
Dist - CNEMAG **Prod** - DOCUA

Primaries 3 MIN
16mm
Color (G)
$10.00 rental
Looks at the body as a fragile object and how it is united with the elements - physical, aural and visual - yet at times paralyzed. Reveals that the machine, camera, has the power of motion while the body is frozen. Produced by Linda Tadic.
Fine Arts; Sociology
Dist - CANCIN

Primary 54 MIN
16mm
Living camera series
B&W (H C A)
An example of the 'cinema verite' approach to filmmaking which gives a behind - the - scenes account of the primary fight in Wisconsin between candidates John Kennedy and Hubert Humphrey. The emotional reactions of the candidates and of the public are emphasized.
Civics and Political Systems; Fine Arts; History - United States
Dist - DIRECT **Prod** - DREW 1961

Primary adventure 42 MIN
16mm
Color (C T)
LC 73-700971
Depicts life in the primary schools of England. Emphasizes the 'open plan' principle, the easy relationship between children and teachers and the variety of successful teaching methods.
Education; Geography - World; Sociology
Dist - NYU **Prod** - TARAL 1972

Primary Art Series

Bugs, bees and butterflies	15 MIN
Changing Faces	15 MIN
Deep down	15 MIN
Meeting Artists	15 MIN
Odds and Ends	15 MIN
Paint	15 MIN
Paint to Music	15 MIN

Dist - AITECH

Primary Batteries, Secondary Batteries, Fuel Cells 52 MIN
VHS / U-matic
Electrochemistry Series
Color
Science; Science - Physical
Dist - KALMIA **Prod** - KALMIA

Primary batteries - secondary batteries - storage cells, accumulators - fuel cells 52 MIN
U-matic / VHS
Electrochemistry - Pt V - electrokinetics series
Color
Science; Science - Physical
Dist - MIOT **Prod** - MIOT

Primary Cancer of Bone 22 MIN
16mm
Color (PRO)
LC 77-701317
Surveys the five most important classes of malignant bone tumors and outlines how they are differentiated. Emphasizes the importance of early diagnosis and treatment in improving the chance of successful outcome.
Health and Safety; Science
Dist - AMCS **Prod** - AMCS 1973

Primary Care Management of Common Eye Problems
U-matic / VHS
Color
Reviews the correlation of the anatomy and functions of the eye with frequently seen disorders. Outlines relevant medical information to be elicited from the patient. Offers guidelines to the physician in performing physical examinations of the eye and its related structures.
Health and Safety
Dist - AMEDA **Prod** - AMEDA

Primary Care Nursing II 119 MIN
VHS / U-matic
Color (PRO)
LC 81-706299
Presents reasons for and against going to another system of nursing care. Discusses the pros and cons of primary care.
Health and Safety
Dist - USNAC **Prod** - USVA 1980

Primary Cementing 24 MIN
VHS / U-matic
Color (A PRO IND)
$150.00 purchase _ #11.1121, $160.00 purchase _ #51.1121
Explains the procedures and equipment used to properly cement casing in an oil or gas well.
Industrial and Technical Education; Social Science
Dist - UTEXPE **Prod** - UTEXPE 1976

Primary Cementing 21 MIN
U-matic / VHS / 16mm
Color (IND)
Covers the basic theory and the latest equipment and procedures involved in cementing an oil or gas well.
Business and Economics; Industrial and Technical Education; Social Science
Dist - UTEXPE **Prod** - UTEXPE 1982

The Primary Circuit 10 MIN
16mm
Color
Illustrates the assembly of the primary circuit of the steam generating heavy water reactor at Winfrith, Dorset.
Industrial and Technical Education; Science - Physical
Dist - UKAEA **Prod** - UKAEA 1966

Primary circuit testing 60 MIN
VHS
Ignition system troubleshooting series
Color (H A)
$409.00 purchase _ #VMA31358V
Examines primary circuit testing procedures for Ford, Chrysler and General Motors vehicles. Consists of four videocassettes and a program guide.
Industrial and Technical Education
Dist - CAMV

Primary Circuit Testing
VHS
Troubleshooting the Ignition System - Testing and Service Series
$409.00 purchase _ #IE31358V
Explores high energy and integrated ignition systems. Demonstrates methods for testing secondary and primary circuits.
Education; Industrial and Technical Education
Dist - CAREER **Prod** - CAREER

Primary Closure of the Perineal Wound in Abdominiperineal Resections 27 MIN
16mm
Color (PRO)
Illustrates the operative method used for primary closure of the perineal wound in abdominoperineal resections and the results obtained.
Health and Safety; Science
Dist - ACY **Prod** - ACYDGD 1966

Primary Colors - the Story of Corita 60 MIN
VHS / 16mm
Color (G)
$49.95 purchase _ #CRTA - N903
Chronicles the life of Frances Elizabeth Kent who entered the Order of the Immaculate Heart Community and was renamed Sister Mary Corita. Reveals that she became a world famous artist and creator of the top - selling 'Love' stamp. In the 1960s Corita joined the civil rights and anti - war movements. After her political activities were scrutinized by conservative Cardinal McIntyre, Corita left the Roman Catholic church. Narrated by Eva Marie Saint and produced in association with the Saint - Hayden Company.
Civics and Political Systems; Fine Arts; History - World; Religion and Philosophy; Sociology
Dist - PBS **Prod** - SCETV 1990

Primary distribution systems
VHS / U-matic
Distribution system operation series; Topic 4
Color (IND)
Examines the primary distribution system in detail. Describes its function, design and features of construction. Includes substations, overhead primary and underground primary.
Industrial and Technical Education
Dist - LEIKID **Prod** - LEIKID

Primary grades - Tape 2 22 MIN
VHS
Making meaning - integrated language arts series
Color (C A PRO)
$295.00 purchase, $125.00 rental _ #614 - 230X01
Emphasizes a whole - language approach to teaching reading, writing, speaking and listening skills in the classroom. Visits classrooms to show how whole - language principles are applied in kindergarten and early grade classrooms. Includes teacher's guide and text.
Education; English Language
Dist - AFSCD

Primary Health Care Series

Health - Communicable Diseases	10 MIN

Dist - AIMS

Primary Health Series

Health - Ear Care	9 MIN
Health - Eye Care	11 MIN
Health - Food and Nutrition	11 MIN
Health - Our Picture of Ourselves	11 MIN

Health - Personal Cleanliness 8 MIN
Health - Your Senses and their Care 11 MIN
Health - eye care 15 MIN
Dist - AIMS

Primary Isolation of Mycobacteria using the N - acetyl - L Cysteine - Na - Oh Method 10 MIN
U-matic
Color
LC 80-706597
Demonstrates the laboratory technique for the primary isolation of mycobacteria using the N - acetyl - L cysteine - Na - Oh method.
Health and Safety; Science
Dist - USNAC **Prod** - CFDISC 1979

Primary Language Development Series
The Gila Monster 9 MIN
The Ground Squirrel Family 10 MIN
The Mouse Takes a Chance 9 MIN
Preparing for Winter 9 MIN
The Spider Takes a Trip 9 MIN
Dist - AIMS

Primary Nursing 28 MIN
VHS / 16mm
Color (C PRO)
$275.00 purchase, $60.00 rental _ #7619S, #7619V
Describes roles of primary nurse, associate nurse, and support departments, highlighting ways in which primary nursing can facilitate assessment, planning, implementation, and evaluation of care. Approved for CE credit. Includes study guide.
Health and Safety
Dist - AJN **Prod** - HOSSN 1990

Primary Nursing - Accountability for Care 14 MIN
U-matic / VHS
Color (PRO)
LC 80-730070
Demonstrates elements of nursing care that promote accountability of the primary nurse, such as direct provision of care, patient evaluation, nursing - care review and discharge summary.
Health and Safety
Dist - MEDCOM **Prod** - MEDCOM

Primary Nursing - Continuity of Care 14 MIN
U-matic / VHS
Color (PRO)
LC 80-730070
Demonstrates methods for achieving continuity of care in primary nursing. Explains and illustrates important factors such as nursing orders for associate nurses, communication with other hospital departments and with the patient's attending physician, nursing - care conferences and discharge planning.
Health and Safety; Psychology
Dist - MEDCOM **Prod** - MEDCOM

Primary Nursing - Planning and Validation 12 MIN
U-matic / VHS
Color (PRO)
LC 80-730070
Illustrates cooperative planning in primary nursing. Demonstrates important features of nurse - patient communications.
Health and Safety; Psychology
Dist - MEDCOM **Prod** - MEDCOM

Primary Pilot Navigation 27 MIN
16mm
Color
LC FIE56-195
Emphasizes the importance of a flying cadet's first cross - country solo. Includes the pre - flight preparations and all details of the flight plan and the flight.
Civics and Political Systems; Industrial and Technical Education
Dist - USNAC **Prod** - USAF 1955

The Primary Plant Body 36 MIN
U-matic / VHS
Color
Presents the organization of the apical meristems and the products of these meristems. Discusses the external form and the tissues of roots, stems and leaves, and reviews variation of the structure of these organs. Video version of 35mm filmstrip program, with live open and close.
Science - Natural
Dist - CBSC **Prod** - BMEDIA

The Primary plant body - Part 1 35 MIN
VHS
Plant anatomy collection series
Color (J H)
$60.00 purchase _ #A5VH 1033
Examines the organization and function of the apical meristems as well as the various forms and tissues of roots, stems and leaves. Part one of a three - part series introducing the structures and functions of plant anatomy.
Science - Natural
Dist - CLRVUE **Prod** - CLRVUE

Primary prevention of atherosclerosis in the role of lipids - Parts I, II and III
VHS
Color (PRO)
#IF - 454
Presents a free - loan program which trains medical professionals. Contact distributor for details.
Health and Safety
Dist - WYAYLA **Prod** - WYAYLA

Primary problems of Fizz and Martina series
Presents a two - part series featuring cross - curricular experiences including reading, storytelling, art, writing and mathematics and utilizing a cooperative learning method that inspires students to explain and justify their problem - solving process. Includes the titles Fizz and Martina Buddies for Life and Fizz and Martina and the Caves of Blue Falls. Each program includes blackline masters, award cards, 30 student workbooks and a Big Book featuring four stories without endings for students to finish.
Fizz and Martina - buddies for life 30 MIN
Fizz and Martina and the caves of Blue Falls 30 MIN
Dist - HRMC

The Primary Production of Heather 15 MIN
U-matic / VHS
Experiment - Biology Series
Color (C)
$249.00, $149.00 purchase _ #AD - 1095
Shows that energy flow and nutrient recycling are two important areas of ecological investigation. Asseses the growth rate and net primary production of heather, Calluna vulgaris L, as a basis for estimating energy flow and nutrient uptake. Part of a series on biology experiments.
Science - Natural
Dist - FOTH **Prod** - FOTH

Primary Pulmonary Hypertension - Diagnosis and Treatment 36 MIN
U-matic / VHS
Color (PRO)
Covers the major clinical features of primary pulmonary hypertension. Reviews current thoughts about the pathogenesis of this condition and these are linked to the major therapeutic efforts available. Presents the rationale for and initial results with the therapeutic use of calcium channel blockers. Emphasizes the importance of recognizing and treating right heart failure. Discusses special issues in the etiology and treatment of primary pulmonary hypertension.
Health and Safety
Dist - UMICHM **Prod** - UMICHM 1982

Primary safety - school and playground 11 MIN
U-matic / 16mm / VHS
Color (P)
$275.00 purchase _ #3403 MP, $185.00 purchase _ #3403 MV; LC 80-701614
Presents safety practices to be used at school and on the playground. Includes walking down sidewalks, making sure the play area is safe and the proper use of playground equipment.
Health and Safety
Dist - CORF **Prod** - CORF 1980

Primary school bus safety 15 MIN
U-matic / VHS / 16mm
Color (P I)
$355.00, $255.00 purchase _ #76505; LC 76-703615
Introduces rules of safe conduct for young children traveling to and from school by bus. Uses the concept of an invisible safety circle in which children apply safety rules to the area surrounding them.
Guidance and Counseling; Health and Safety; Social Science
Dist - CORF **Prod** - CENTRO 1976

Primary science series
Presents an 11 - part series on primary science. Includes the titles of 'Air,' 'Clouds,' 'Earth,' 'Electricity,' 'Fire,' 'Light,' 'Magnifying Glass,' 'Rain,' 'Snow,' 'The Sun' and 'Water.'
Air 10 MIN
Air - 1 10 MIN
Clouds 10 MIN
Clouds - 2 10 MIN
Earth 10 MIN
Earth - 3 10 MIN
Electricity 10 MIN
Electricity - 4 10 MIN
Fire 10 MIN
Fire - 5 10 MIN
Light 10 MIN
Light - 6 10 MIN
Magnifying glass 10 MIN
Magnifying glass - 7 10 MIN
Rain 10 MIN
Rain - 8 10 MIN
Snow 10 MIN
Snow - 9 10 MIN
Sun 10 MIN
The Sun - 10 10 MIN
Water 10 MIN
Water - 11 10 MIN
Dist - BARR **Prod** - GREATT 1976

Primary sedimentary features 15 MIN
VHS
Color (J H C)
$29.95 purchase _ #IV802
Looks at the principles of sedimentation and how geologists are able to decipher in the rocks the exact process of sedimentation. Explores the principle of superpostion where rocks on the bottom are older than those above unless they have been overturned by distrophism. Explores graded bedding and examines some of the principal formations usually found in sedimentary rocks.
Science - Physical
Dist - INSTRU

Primary Tenorrhaphy in no Man's Land 39 MIN
VHS / U-matic
Color (PRO)
Shows symptoms and diagnosis of primary tenorrhaphy in no man's land, as well as surgical repair and post - operative care.
Health and Safety
Dist - HSCIC **Prod** - HSCIC 1984

Primary, Total and Near Total Colectomy for Cancer of the Colon Including Experiences 29 MIN
16mm
Color (PRO)
Explains that occult polyps and silent colic cancers are encountered beyond the reach of the conventional hemicolectomy or segmental colic resection frequently enough to justify the performance of total or near total colectomy as a primary operative procedure in most colic cancers.
Health and Safety; Science
Dist - ACY **Prod** - ACYDGD 1955

Primate 105 MIN
U-matic / VHS / 16mm
B&W (C A)
LC 74-703501
Shows some of the routine events at a primate research center. Examines the scientific programs designed to study primate physical and mental development, primate manual and language skills and primate sexual and aggressive behavior.
Psychology; Science; Science - Natural
Dist - ZIPRAH **Prod** - WISEF 1974

Primate Growth and Development - a Gorilla's First Year 22 MIN
16mm
Color
A record of the growth and development during the first year of a gorilla raised by the attendants at the San Diego Zoo. Presents comparisons to chimpanzee and human children.
Science - Natural
Dist - PHM **Prod** - PH 1968

The Primates 20 MIN
16mm
Color
Traces the origin of man two million years ago until the dawn of civilization.
Social Science; Sociology
Dist - BARSUM **Prod** - BARSUM

Primates 15 MIN
U-matic
Tell Me what You See Series
Color (P)
Presents an examination of a Capuchin monkey and a comparison of the skeletons of monkey and man.
Science - Natural
Dist - GPN **Prod** - WVIZTV

Primates 25 MIN
U-matic / VHS / 16mm
Untamed World Series
Color; Mono (J H C A)
$400.00 film, $250.00 video, $50.00 rental
Explores the realm of primates and looks at the major findings of modern scientific research concerned with them.
Science; Science - Natural
Dist - CTV **Prod** - CTV 1971

The Primates - Pt 25 30 MIN
16mm
Life on Earth series; Vol VII
Color (J)
$495.00 purchase _ #865 - 9046
Blends scientific data with wildlife photography to tell the story of the development of life. Features wildlife expert David Attenborough as host. Part 25 of 27 parts is entitled 'The Primates.'
Science; Science - Natural; Science - Physical
Dist - FI **Prod** - BBCTV 1981

The Prime Minister, the junkie and the boys on death row 52 MIN
VHS
First Tuesday series
Color; PAL (H C G)
PdS30 purchase
Reveals that carrying drugs in Malaysia is dangerous, as little as a spoonful of illegal drugs can cost the carrier's life. Discloses that seven years ago Malaysia was accused worldwide of barbarism when it hanged two Australians for drug offenses. Looks at Malaysia's drug problem from three different points of view - Prime Minister Mahatir; junkie Aris, an addict for 20 years; and convicted drug offenders waiting to die in Kajang prison. Asks if the hard - hitting drug legislation of Malaysia is catching the real criminals. Contact distributor about availability outside the United Kingdom.
Civics and Political Systems; Health and Safety
Dist - ACADEM **Prod** - YORKTV

Prime rib - lesson 24 30 MIN
VHS
International cooking school with Chef Rene series
Color (G)
$69.00 purchase
Presents classic methods of cooking that stress essential flavor. Introduces newer, lighter foods. Lesson 24 focuses on prime rib.
Home Economics; Psychology; Social Science; Sociology
Dist - LUF **Prod** - LUF

Prime Time 16 MIN
16mm
Color
Offers a large - scale, role - playing simulation of the business of television. Counterpoints the simulation with the activities of a professional television executive.
Fine Arts
Dist - UPITTS **Prod** - UPITTS 1974

Prime Time 10 MIN
U-matic
Color (P)
Describes the multi - headed residents of the planet Herkey, explaining that only the creatures with a prime number of heads are peaceful. Demonstrates a method of testing for primeness and distinguishing between prime and composite numbers.
Mathematics
Dist - GA **Prod** - DAVFMS

Prime time for parents video series
An eating adventure with Buddy Goodhealth 28 MIN
Every child is special 28 MIN
Fears and feelings 28 MIN
Hold them close and let them go 28 MIN
Parents are human too 28 MIN
Self worth in children and parents 28 MIN
Sparing the rod won't spoil the child 28 MIN
Talk so they listen, listen so they talk 28 MIN
Dist - CADESF

Prime time series
Dilema for democracy 13 MIN
Flotsam of the China Sea 12 MIN
The Invisible Epidemic 9 MIN
Ira and Vicki 18 MIN
Nyiregyhazi - Return of the Prodigy 33 MIN
Teenage suicide 12 MIN
Dist - CTV

Prime Time Series
Coping with change 28 MIN
Inner Strengths 28 MIN
Interdependent Relationships 28 MIN
Learning to Enjoy 28 MIN
Dist - MTP

Primel - Kleines Madchen Zu Verleihen 86 MIN
16mm
Color (GERMAN (ENGLISH SUBTITLES))
A German language film with English subtitles. Tells the story of Primel, a nine - year - old girl, who is cared for by the seven tenants of a house when her mother visits her sick grandmother. Continues as the tenants describe how Primel brightens their lives, gets to know each one of them well, and, in the end, creates a togetherness and friendship hitherto unknown in this house community.
Fine Arts; Foreign Language
Dist - WSTGLC **Prod** - WSTGLC 1971

Primer for Professionals 19 MIN
16mm
Color
Deals with nitrogen fertility in the soil, one of agriculture's most basic topics. Explains the use of anhydrous ammonia as the source of nitrogen for crop growth.
Agriculture
Dist - DCC **Prod** - DCC 1957

A Primer for psychiatric nurses
VHS
Color (C PRO)
$1200.00 purchase _ #42 - 2368
Presents eight 20 to 30 - minute videos augmenting the mental health curriculum in nursing programs. Includes an instructor's guide, a 12 - chapter text, accompanying workbook and two versions of a standardized test - five copies of each - that can be used as a pre - test or post - test and to qualify for CEUs.
Health and Safety
Dist - NLFN **Prod** - NLFN

A Primer of Poison Ivy 18 MIN
U-matic / VHS / 16mm
Color (I J)
LC 80-700440
Offers information about poison ivy, poison oak and poison sumac, explaining how to avoid harmful contact with these plants.
Health and Safety; Science - Natural
Dist - TEXFLM **Prod** - CHVANP 1979

Primer Series
Causes and characteristics of mental retardation 30 MIN
Community services and normalization 30 MIN
Familial, Social and Sexual Aspects of Mental Retardation 30 MIN
Learning and Development - Part 1 - Birth through Childhood 30 MIN
Learning and Development - Part 2 - Adolescence through Maturity 30 MIN
Physical Education, Recreation and Leisure 30 MIN
Professional Support Services and Mental Retardation 30 MIN
Dist - ACCESS

Primeros Alimentos 14 MIN
U-matic / VHS
Color (SPANISH)
A Spanish language version of the film First Foods. Offers information on how to introduce semi - solid foods to babies. Portrays parents and babies from a variety of ethnic and social groups.
Health and Safety; Home Economics
Dist - SNUTRE **Prod** - SNUTRE

Primeros auxilios orientados hacia la prevencion de accidentes - a series
U-matic / VHS / 16mm
Primeros auxilios orientados hacia la prevencion de accidentes - a'series
Color (C A) (SPANISH)
A Spanish - language version of the motion picture series Safety - Oriented First Aid Multimedia Course. Deals with injury prevention and the causes and effects of accidents. Primeros Auxilios Orientados Hacia La - - ; Primeros Auxilios Orientados Hacia La - - ; Primeros Auxilios Orientados Hacia La - - ; Primeros Auxilios Orientados Hacia La - - .
Foreign Language; Health and Safety
Dist - IFB **Prod** - CRAF

Primeros auxilios orientados hacia la prevencion de accidentes - a series
Primeros auxilios orientados hacia la prevencion de accidentes - a series
Dist - IFB

Primeros auxilios orientados hacia la prevencion de accidentes - Unidad 1 29 MIN
U-matic / VHS / 16mm
Primeros auxilios orientados hacia la prevencion de accidentes'series
Color (C A) (SPANISH)
A Spanish - language version of the motion picture Safety - Oriented First Aid Multimedia Course, Unit 1. Deals with such first aid topics as respiratory emergencies and artificial respiration, indirect methods of artificial respiration, bleeding, embedded foreign objects, dressings and bandages.
Foreign Language; Health and Safety
Dist - IFB **Prod** - CRAF

Primeros auxilios orientados hacia la prevencion de accidentes - Unidad 2 22 MIN
16mm / U-matic / VHS
Primeros auxilios orientados hacia la prevencion de accidentes'series
Color (C A) (SPANISH)
A Spanish - language version of the motion picture Safety - Oriented First Aid Multimedia Course, Unit 2. Deals with such first aid topics as shock, fractures and dislocations of the upper and lower limbs, and chest injuries.
Foreign Language; Health and Safety
Dist - IFB **Prod** - CRAF

Primeros auxilios orientados hacia la prevencion de accidentes - Unidad 3 28 MIN
16mm / U-matic / VHS
Primeros auxilios orientados hacia la prevencion de accidentes'series
Color (C A) (SPANISH)
A Spanish - language version of the motion picture Safety - Oriented First Aid Multimedia Course, Unit 3. Deals with such first aid topics as head, neck and back injuries, burns and scalds, eye injuries, handling and moving casualties, and poisoning.
Foreign Language; Health and Safety
Dist - IFB **Prod** - CRAF

Primeros auxilios orientados hacia la prevencion de accidentes - Unidad 4 10 MIN
U-matic / VHS / 16mm
Primeros auxilios orientados hacia la prevencion de accidentes'series
Color (C A) (SPANISH)
A Spanish - language version of the motion picture Safety - Oriented First Aid Multimedia Course, Unit 4. Deals with casualty management.
Foreign Language; Health and Safety
Dist - IFB **Prod** - CRAF

Primeros auxilios orientados hacia la prevencion de accidentes series
Primeros auxilios orientados hacia la prevencion de accidentes - Unidad 1 29 MIN
Primeros auxilios orientados hacia la prevencion de accidentes - Unidad 2 22 MIN
Primeros auxilios orientados hacia la prevencion de accidentes - Unidad 3 28 MIN
Primeros auxilios orientados hacia la prevencion de accidentes - Unidad 4 10 MIN
Dist - IFB

Primers, Surfacers, Sealers 10 MIN
BETA / VHS
Color (A PRO)
$61.00 purchase _ #KTI46
Deals with auto body repair. Explains the applications of primers, surfacers and sealers.
Industrial and Technical Education
Dist - RMIBHF **Prod** - RMIBHF

Primers Surfacers Sealers 10 MIN
VHS / 16mm
(A PRO)
$61.00 purchase _ #KTI46
Deals with the applications of various primers, surfacers and sealers.
Industrial and Technical Education
Dist - RMIBHF **Prod** - RMIBHF

Priming and Block Sanding 20 MIN
BETA / VHS / 16mm
Color (A PRO)
$86.00 purchase _ #AB156
Illustrates the correct method of priming and block sanding a repair.
Industrial and Technical Education
Dist - RMIBHF **Prod** - RMIBHF

Priming the Productivity Engine - the Federal Rule in Advanced Electronics 29 MIN
VHS / U-matic
Color (A)
Discusses the development of the micro - electronics and computer industries and their influence on the American economy, and the potential threat of foreign competition and its impact an U S markets.
Business and Economics; Industrial and Technical Education
Dist - USNAC **Prod** - USNAC 1985

Primitive Beliefs 29 MIN
Videoreel / VT2
Who is Man Series
Color
Features Dr Puryear and Dr Van de Castle who examine the origins and consequences of the beliefs of certain primitive tribes and early man. Shows Dr Van de Castle

displaying and explaining a number of artifacts he collected while studying a Central American Indian tribe.
Psychology; Religion and Philosophy; Social Science; Sociology
Dist - PBS **Prod** - WHROTV

Primitive Man in a Modern World 23 MIN
16mm / VHS
Color (J H)
LC 76-704676
Acquaints the student with data concerning the Mayan and Inca civilizations. Shows small, isolated groups of people living virtually untouched by progress surrounding them in the modern world.
History - World; Sociology
Dist - MIS **Prod** - MIS 1969

Primitive plants - the algae 16 MIN
VHS
Cell biology series
Color (J H)
$70.00 purchase _ #ACL400 - 2CV
Examines the importance and diversity of algae. Looks at many varieties. Discusses photosynthesis, mutualism, locomotion, the oxygen cycle and the food chain. Part of a series on cell biology featuring Dr Jeremy Pickett - Heaps.
Science - Natural
Dist - CLRVUE **Prod** - CLRVUE

Primitives 30 MIN
U-matic / VHS
Antique Shop Series
Color
Presents guests who are experts in their respective fields who share tips on collecting and caring for primitive antiques.
Fine Arts
Dist - MDCPB **Prod** - WVPTTV

Primordial Soup 10 MIN
U-matic / VHS
Color
Features Julia Child preparing a primordial soup. The recipe shows how simple inorganic chemicals may have been transformed into complex organic chemicals, the building blocks of life. This batch is mixed in a special laboratory apparatus made to simulate the conditions of ancient Earth.
Science; Science - Natural; Science - Physical
Dist - USNAC **Prod** - NASM

The Primordial tradition 30 MIN
VHS / BETA
Living philosophically series
Color (G)
$29.95 purchase _ #S048
Delineates the common threads which run through all spiritual traditions. Reveals that the notion of a human soul and spirit persists despite the fact of conflict with a modern, materialistic world view. Features Dr Huston Smith, philosopher and author of 'Forgotten Truth' and 'The Religions of Man.' Part of a four - part series on living philosophically.
Religion and Philosophy
Dist - THINKA **Prod** - THINKA

Primum Non Nocere 18 MIN
16mm
Color
LC 77-702124
Demonstrates an alternative to hospital childbirth by showing a woman giving birth to her first child at home.
Health and Safety; Sociology
Dist - CINMD **Prod** - CINMD 1976

The Prince 58 MIN
Videoreel / VT2
Dialogue of the Western World Series
Color
Features Dean Robert A Goldwin of St John's College of Annapolis and three of his students discussing The Prince with a special guest.
Literature and Drama; Religion and Philosophy
Dist - PBS **Prod** - MDCPB

The Prince and the Pauper 93 MIN
U-matic / VHS / 16mm
Color
Relates the experiences of two boys destined to look alike. Explains that they meet and exchange places, each wishing to see how the other lives.
Fine Arts; Literature and Drama
Dist - FI **Prod** - DISNEY 1964

The Prince and the Pauper 28 MIN
U-matic / VHS / 16mm
Films as literature, series 1 series
Color
Presents a shortened version of the motion picture The Prince And The Pauper. Relates the experiences of two look - alike boys, in very different social positions, who change places. Based on the novel The Prince and the Pauper by Mark Twain.
Fine Arts; Literature and Drama
Dist - CORF **Prod** - DISNEY

Prince Caspian and the voyage of the dawn treader 174 MIN
VHS
Chronicles of Narnia - Wonderworks collection series
Color (I J H)
$29.95 purchase _ #PRI02
Presents a segment from the C S Lewis fantasy in which animals speak, mythical creatures roam and children fight an epic battle against evil.
Guidance and Counseling; Literature and Drama
Dist - KNOWUN **Prod** - PBS

Prince Hazelnut 13 MIN
16mm
Color
LC 73-706881
A story about a king who must decide which of his sons will inherit his crown is used to stimulate oral language skills.
English Language; Fine Arts
Dist - MLA **Prod** - DBA 1969

Prince Igor 110 MIN
VHS
Color (G) (RUSSIAN (ENGLISH SUBTITLES))
$39.95 purchase _ #1286
Presents a Soviet movie version of the opera 'Prince Igor' by Alexander Borodin as produced by the Kirov Opera. Filmed in 1969.
Fine Arts
Dist - KULTUR **Prod** - KULTUR 1991

Prince in the Apple Town 28 MIN
16mm / U-matic / VHS
Insight Series
Color; B&W (H A)
LC 79-705438
Presents Lunt and Fontaine who, after giving their last performance return to the stage where they reminisce and ask themselves if it has all been worth it.
Fine Arts; Guidance and Counseling; Psychology
Dist - PAULST **Prod** - PAULST 1969

The Prince who Learned a Trade 7 MIN
16mm
Color (P I)
Shows what happens when a princess refuses to marry a prince until he learns a trade.
Literature and Drama
Dist - SF **Prod** - SF 1980

Princes and Prelates 41 MIN
16mm / U-matic / VHS
Christians Series Episode 6; Episode 6
Color (H C A)
LC 78-701655
Reviews the low point for the Papacy, the Council of Constance, caused when an emperor deposed three popes and arranged the choice of a fourth. Tells how the greatest glories of the Renaissance in Rome flowered after this event.
History - World; Religion and Philosophy
Dist - MGHT **Prod** - GRATV 1978

Princess 28 MIN
16mm / U-matic / VHS
Insight Series
Color (J)
Examines the way in which the divorce of her parents shatters the life of a girl whose life until then had been unusually happy. Demonstrates that divorce can strengthen the lives of the children involved. Stars Lenora May and Richard Jaeckel.
Guidance and Counseling; Psychology; Religion and Philosophy; Sociology
Dist - PAULST **Prod** - PAULST

The Princess and the Pea 15 MIN
U-matic / VHS / 16mm
Children's Classic Story Series
Color (K P I)
LC FIA67-736
Dramatizes the Hans Christian Andersen story of a princess who proves she is as delicate as royalty should be.
Literature and Drama
Dist - MGHT **Prod** - SCHWAR 1966

The Princess and the People 50 MIN
VHS
Color (S)
$29.95 purchase _ #781 - 9007
Reveals that during her first year of marriage to Prince Charles, Princess Diana traveled the world as representative of the British Crown and grew from a shy, reluctant celebrity into a confident world figure. Presents an intimate portrait filmed during her tours of Australia, New Zealand and Canada.
Civics and Political Systems; Geography - World; History - World
Dist - FI **Prod** - BBCTV 1987

Princess, Large, Small 10 MIN
U-matic
Readalong One Series
Color (K P)
Introduces reading and spelling for preschoolers and children in grades 1 to 3 with animation, puppets, humor and music. Comes with teacher's guide and kit.
Education; English Language; Literature and Drama
Dist - TVOTAR **Prod** - TVOTAR 1975

Princess Margaret 26 MIN
16mm
History Makers of the 20th Century Series
B&W (I)
LC FI67-267
Views the life of Princess Margaret.
Biography; History - World
Dist - SF **Prod** - WOLPER 1965

The Princess of the Full Moon 15 MIN
U-matic
Magic Carpet Series
Color (P)
Presents a West African folk tale.
Literature and Drama
Dist - GPN **Prod** - SDCSS 1977

The Princess of Tomboso 29 MIN
16mm / U-matic / VHS
(K P I)
#650 77 03
Presents a fairy tale about a young prince and a wicked princess, with lessons on greed and vanity, valor and innocence.
Literature and Drama
Dist - CANBC **Prod** - FLMLIB

Princess Scargo and the birthday pumpkin 30 MIN
VHS
Rabbit Ears series
Color (K P)
$9.95 purchase _ #PRI - 01
Tells about a young girl who gives up a precious birthday gift in order to help her people. Captures the spirit of giving and the importance of selflessness. Narrated by Geena Davis, music by Michael Hedges.
Literature and Drama
Dist - ARTSAM **Prod** - RABBIT 1993

Princess Tam Tam 77 MIN
VHS / 35mm / 16mm
B&W (G)
$250.00, $300.00 rental
Presents Josephine Baker in a Pygmalian - like musical comedy about a native woman who is transformed into a princess. Directed by Edmond Greville.
Fine Arts
Dist - KINOIC

The Princess who never laughed 60 MIN
VHS
Faerie tale theatre series
Color; CC (K P I J)
$19.95 purchase _ #CBS6847
Stars Ellen Barkin and Howie Mandel.
Literature and Drama
Dist - KNOWUN

Princess Yang Kwei Fei 91 MIN
VHS
Color (G) (JAPANESE WITH ENGLISH SUBTITLES)
$79.95 purchase _ #NYV07983
Offers a love story about a servant girl who becomes a princess. Directed by Kenji Mizoguchi.
Fine Arts; Literature and Drama
Dist - CHTSUI NYFLMS **Prod** - NYFLMS 1955

Princeton
VHS
Campus clips series
Color (H C A)
$29.95 purchase _ #CC0069V
Takes a video visit to the campus of Princeton University in New Jersey. Shows many of the distinctive features of the campus, and interviews students about their experiences. Provides information on the composition of the student body, professors, academics, social life, housing, and other subjects.
Education
Dist - CAMV

Princeton Forrestal Village - Plainsboro, New Jersey - Vol 18, No 11 12 MIN
VHS
Project reference file - PRF - series
Color (G A PRO)

$60.00 purchase _ #P42
Examines an open-air shopping center developed in Plainsboro, New Jersey. Features Norbert Young, a member of the development team.
Business and Economics; Geography - United States
Dist - ULI **Prod** - ULI

The Principal as Instructional Leader - Reflections on Effectiveness 60 MIN
U-matic
Color (T)
Discusses the qualities which demonstrate effectiveness in a school principal. Available with captions.
Education
Dist - AFSCD **Prod** - AFSCD 1986

Principal Dimensions - Reference Surfaces, and Tolerances 12 MIN
U-matic
Machine Shop Work - Fundamentals of Blueprint Reading Series
B&W
LC 79-707977
Explains the relationship between a blueprint and a rough and finished casting. Shows how to use a blueprint to select reference surfaces, interpret tolerances, and check the accuracy of finished product. Issued in 1945 as a motion picture.
Fine Arts; Industrial and Technical Education
Dist - USNAC **Prod** - USOE 1979

Principal Dimensions, Reference Surfaces and Tolerances 12 MIN
16mm
Machine Shop Work Series Fundamentals of Blueprint Reading, no 3
B&W
LC FIE51-503
Discusses the relationship between the blueprint and a rough and finished casting. Describes how to use a blueprint in selecting reference surfaces, interpret tolerance and check the accuracy of the finished work.
Industrial and Technical Education
Dist - USNAC **Prod** - USOE 1945

Principle of Moments 23 MIN
16mm
Engineering Series Fundamentals of Mechanics
B&W
LC FIE52-166
Explains the concept of moment of a force and presents the formula for finding its numerical value. Discusses the principle of moments as applied to all coplanar force systems.
Industrial and Technical Education; Science - Physical
Dist - USNAC **Prod** - USOE 1945

Principles 57 MIN
U-matic / VHS
Proprioceptive Neuromuscular Facilitation Series
Color
Health and Safety
Dist - UMDSM **Prod** - UMDSM

The Principles and Applications of Atomic Spectra 23 MIN
16mm
Color (H C)
Begins with a brief survey of the electromagnetic spectrum and then makes the point when electrons in atoms lose or gain energy, radiation with wavelengths ranging from the X ray to the near infrared region is emitted or absorbed. Discusses all aspects of atomic spectra and their measurement.
Science - Physical
Dist - VIEWTH **Prod** - MULLRD

Principles and Basic Set - Up 27 MIN
VHS
Positive Pressure Ventilation Series
Color (G PRO)
$125.00 purchase _ #35368
Covers the principles, theory, equipment selection and basic set - up for postive pressure ventilation. Trains firefighting personnel.
Health and Safety; Psychology; Social Science
Dist - OKSU **Prod** - OKSU

Principles and basic set - up - Pt 1 27 MIN
VHS
Positive pressure ventilation series
Color (PRO IND)
$125.00 purchase _ #35368
Covers the theory, equipment selection and basic set - up of positive pressure ventilation equipment. Trains firefighters. Part of a two - part series which includes instructor and study guides.
Industrial and Technical Education; Psychology; Social Science
Dist - OKSU **Prod** - OKSU

Principles and Body Movement 13 MIN
16mm
Combative Measures - Judo Series
B&W
LC 75-700827
Shows parrying, striking and throwing in defensive and counteroffensive grappling in judo.
Civics and Political Systems; Physical Education and Recreation
Dist - USNAC **Prod** - USAF 1955

Principles and discovery in algebraic manipulation - Pt 4 - some other common cases 29 MIN
16mm
Teaching high school mathematics - first course series; No 35
B&W (T)
Mathematics
Dist - MLA **Prod** - UICSM 1967

Principles and discovery in algebraic manipulation - Pt 1 - equivalent expressions 21 MIN
16mm
Teaching high school mathematics - first course series; No 32
B&W (T)
Mathematics
Dist - MLA **Prod** - UICSM 1967

Principles and discovery in algebraic manipulation - Pt 3 - manipulating fractions 39 MIN
16mm
Teaching high school mathematics - first course series; No 34
B&W (T)
Mathematics
Dist - MLA **Prod** - UICSM 1967

Principles and discovery in algebraic manipulation - Pt 2 - simplification 31 MIN
16mm
Teaching high school mathematics - first course series; No 33
B&W (T)
Mathematics
Dist - MLA **Prod** - UICSM 1967

Principles and Metallurgy 60 MIN
U-matic / VHS
Welding Training Series
Color (IND)
Goes into basic definition, metallurgy, effects of heat and weld defects.
Education; Industrial and Technical Education
Dist - ITCORP **Prod** - ITCORP

Principles and Methods of Teaching a Second Language Series

Modern Techniques in Language Teaching	32 MIN
The Nature of Language and How it is Learned	32 MIN
The Organization of Language	33 MIN
The Sounds of Language	32 MIN
Words and their Meaning	32 MIN

Dist - IU

Principles and Operation of Glcol Dehydrators 26 MIN
U-matic / VHS
Color (IND)
Explains the basic principles of glycol dehydration. Describes a typical flow pattern of a glycol dehydration system.
Industrial and Technical Education; Social Science
Dist - UTEXPE **Prod** - UTEXPE 1973

Principles and operation of production separators 32 MIN
Slide / VHS
Color (IND PRO)
$265.00, $255.00 purchase _ #55.1164, #15.1164
Explains how production separators work. Shows how to maintain them. Describes common operating problems and how to overcome these problems. Includes non illustrated script.
Industrial and Technical Education; Psychology
Dist - UTEXPE **Prod** - UTEXPE 1986

Principles and operation of production separators - Pts 1 and 2 35 MIN
VHS / U-matic
Color (IND)
Shows construction, operation and troubleshooting problems with production separators. Covers procedures an operator should follow to overcome the problems of high and low liquid level and high or low pessure in the separator.
Industrial and Technical Education; Social Science
Dist - UTEXPE **Prod** - UTEXPE 1973

The Principles and Practice of Zen 100 MIN
U-matic / VHS
Color (G)
$349.00, $199.00 purchase _ #AD - 1669
Seeks to explain the process leading to satori - enlightenment - using the principles of Zen Buddhism. Demonstrates the rigors and esthetic delicacy, the personal abnegation and the devotion to principles inexpressible in words.
Geography - World; History - World; Religion and Philosophy
Dist - FOTH **Prod** - FOTH

Principles and selected procedures for eye care 27 MIN
16mm
Directions for education in nursing via technology series; Lesson 66
B&W (PRO)
LC 74-701842
Reviews the anatomy and physiology of the eye and identifies guidelines for procedures performed on the eye. Demonstrates eversion of the eye lid, irrigation, instillation of liquid and ointment medications, application of eye compresses and the use of eye pads and shields.
Health and Safety; Science; Science - Natural
Dist - WSUM **Prod** - DENT 1974

Principles and Techniques of MIG 60 MIN
VHS / U-matic
Welding Training Series
Color (IND)
Covers safety, equipment, plate welding and pipe welding.
Education; Industrial and Technical Education
Dist - ITCORP **Prod** - ITCORP

Principles - Fire Pump Operation and Maintenance 30 MIN
VHS
Color (PRO IND)
$35.00 purchase _ #35353
Reviews the theory and operation of a mid - ship pump with common accessories. Covers routine service and maintenance in detail. Includes a summary of scheduled maintenance. From the Waterous Fire Pump Company for training firefighters.
Industrial and Technical Education; Psychology; Social Science
Dist - OKSU

Principles for positioning immobilized patients - Part 2 28 MIN
VHS / U-matic
Patient transfer and positioning series
Color (PRO)
$275.00 purchase, $60.00 rental _ #7640S, #7640V
Demonstrates four basic positions - supine, prone, side - lying and Fowler's - along with correct methods for moving patients from one position to another. Stresses prevention of complications such as pressure sores, loss of muscle tone and decreased circulation. Provides guidelines for documentation. Part of two - parts on patient transfer and positioning.
Health and Safety
Dist - AJN **Prod** - HOSSN 1987

Principles for Positioning Immobilized Patients

Patient Transfer and Positioning - Part 2	28 MIN

Dist - AJN

Principles in Oral Examination for the Medical Student 31 MIN
VHS / 16mm
(C)
$385.00 purchase _ #850VI065
Shows how to perform a basic oral examination as part of the routine physical exam. Shows how to use palpation and careful observation to assess musculature, joint movement and the general health of the face and mouth.
Health and Safety
Dist - HSCIC **Prod** - HSCIC 1985

Principles in Practice - Standards of Conduct for Federal Procurement Personnel 39 MIN
U-matic / VHS
Color
LC 80-707195
Dramatizes some of the common ways Federal Government procurement workers might unknowingly develop practices of fraud and waste.
Civics and Political Systems
Dist - USNAC **Prod** - USFAI 1980

Principles of achievement - Part 2 23 MIN
VHS
Legacy of achievement series
Color (PRO IND A)
$595.00 purchase, $195.00 rental _ #JHP01B
Features Denis Kimbro, motivational speaker and co - author of 'Think and Grow Rich - A Black Choice,' with a message of hope and fulfillment transcending differences of race, gender and culture. Presents concepts, based on interview research, for developing one's own achievement. Motivates reevalution of goals, setting priorities, using personal abilities to maximize career and life opportunities. By Joan Holman Productions.
Business and Economics; Psychology
Dist - EXTR

Principles of administration of medications 26 MIN
16mm
Directions for education in nursing via technology series; Lesson 16
B&W (PRO)
LC 74-701791
Demonstrates the basic principles related to the administration of medications.
Health and Safety
Dist - WSUM **Prod** - DENT 1974

Principles of Alternating Current 30 MIN
VHS / U-matic
Basic Electricity, AC Series
Color (IND)
Provides theory and functions of AC in simple, logical steps. Begins with introduction to alternation and frequency and continues through effective values of current, voltage and apparent and true power. Uses animation to explain concept of phase angle.
Industrial and Technical Education; Science - Physical
Dist - AVIMA **Prod** - AVIMA

Principles of asepsis, draping the patient, final preparations prior to surgery and post - operative handling of materials 15 MIN
U-matic / VHS
Preparation for oral surgery series
Color (PRO C)
$395.00 purchase, $80.00 rental _ #C920 - VI - 039
Shows the proper procedures for assuring a sterile working environment, draping the patient, preparing for surgery and handling instruments and materials after performing the surgery. Stresses that carefully following the procedures shown will help to ensure the safety of surgeon and patient. Part of a three - part series on oral surgery presented by Mary Ann Adkisson, RN, and Dr James B Sweet, University of Texas, Health Science Center at Houston, Dental Branch.
Health and Safety
Dist - HSCIC

The Principles of Bed Exercising with the Arthritis Patient 7 MIN
8mm cartridge / 16mm
Color
LC 75-701670; 75-704049
Demonstrates exercises for regaining and maintaining body use. Presents exercises which can be performed by the patient alone and those which require nurse or therapist assistance.
Health and Safety
Dist - USNAC **Prod** - ARHEUM 1968

The Principles of blood typing 17 MIN
U-matic / VHS
Color (PRO C)
$395.00 purchase, $80.00 rental _ #C891 - VI - 037
Describes and demonstrates the techniques used for typing blood by ABO and Rh groups. Provides a full explanation of agglutination and lysing. Presented by Drs Rita C Zachariasen and Stewart D Turner.
Health and Safety; Science; Science - Natural
Dist - HSCIC

Principles of Body Mechanics / Moving the Patient in Bed / Assisting the Patient Out of bed - Pt 3
U-matic / VHS
We Care Series
Color
Demonstrates how to understand good posture and how to lift and move patients and objects in a safe and correct manner, illustrates how to change the position of the patient and shows proper procedures for assisting a patient in and out of bed.
Health and Safety
Dist - VTRI **Prod** - VTRI

Principles of Boiler Safety Systems 18 MIN
U-matic / VHS / 16mm
Boiler Control Series
Color (IND)
Covers some of the important dynamics of boiler safety, including fuel valve position, purging, air/fuel flow, water level, pressure limits, flame detection and ignition. Depicts control permissives and various safety interlock systems as part of practical approach to proper safety measures.
Industrial and Technical Education
Dist - ISA **Prod** - ISA

Principles of Caste 24 MIN
16mm / U-matic / VHS
Color
Interprets the principles of caste held in the central India village of Singhara. Pictures the caste system as rules derived from the polar concepts of purity and pollution, whereby people whose traditional occupations are considered low are themselves tainted.
Geography - World; History - World; Sociology
Dist - MEDIAG **Prod** - OPENU 1982

Principles of coaching 20 MIN
VHS
VIP softball series
Color (G)
$29.95 purchase _ #ASAT07V
Covers the basics of coaching softball. Features Bobby Simpson in discussions of communication, winning, positive attitudes, and more. Taught by Bobby Simpson, Cindy Bristow and Buzzy Keller.
Physical Education and Recreation
Dist - CAMV **Prod** - CAMV

Principles of Computer Memory - 1 60 TO 90 MIN
VHS
Microprocessors Module Series
Color (PRO)
$600.00 - $1500.00 purchase _ #MIPC1
Focuses on the concepts common to all memories. Differentiates between basic types of memory circuits. Primarily concerned with RAM. Part of an eleven - part series on microprocessors. Includes five student guides, five workbooks and an instructor guide.
Computer Science; Education; Industrial and Technical Education; Psychology
Dist - NUSTC **Prod** - NUSTC

Principles of Computer Memory - 2 60 TO 90 MIN
VHS
Microprocessors Module Series
Color (PRO)
$600.00 - $1500.00 purchase _ #MIPC2
Focuses on integrated circuit memory - ROM, PROM, EPROM, EAROM and EEPROM memories - not discussed in the first unit. Part of an eleven - part series on microprocessors. Includes five student guides, five workbooks and an instructor guide.
Computer Science; Education; Industrial and Technical Education; Psychology
Dist - NUSTC **Prod** - NUSTC

Principles of Continuous Process Control 30 MIN
VHS / 16mm
Continuous Process Control Series
Color (PRO)
$495.00 purchase, $100.00 rental
Discusses Characteristics of a Continuous Process, Functions of Process Control, Process and Product Characteristics Subject to Measurement and Control, Final Control Elements, Central Algorithms, Data Communications, Feedback and Feedforward Control and Use of Mathematical Models. Part of a four - part series on continuous process control, each of which is an independent unit of information.
Home Economics; Industrial and Technical Education
Dist - ISA **Prod** - ISA

Principles of Cross - Examination 39 MIN
U-matic / VHS
Principles of Examination - Lectures by John a Burgess Series
Color (PRO)
Civics and Political Systems
Dist - ABACPE **Prod** - ABACPE

Principles of cross examination 39 MIN
VHS
Advocacy lectures series
Color (C PRO)
$50.00 rental _ #LSX03
Presents lectures from various law school professors on principles of trial advocacy. Focuses on principles of cross examination.
Civics and Political Systems
Dist - NITA **Prod** - NITA

Principles of cutting - off 15 MIN
BETA / VHS
Machine shop - engine lathe series; No 22
Color (IND)
Explains how to grind and install the blade - type cutoff tool and position it to the workpiece. Emphasizes proper speed and feed relationships and application of cutting fluid to prevent chatter and binding.
Industrial and Technical Education; Psychology
Dist - RMIBHF **Prod** - RMIBHF

Principles of Democracy 30 MIN
VHS / U-matic
American Government Series; 1
Color (C)
Discusses the basic American democratic values of individualism, liberty, equality and majority rule. Considers these issues from contrasting philosophical viewpoints.
Civics and Political Systems
Dist - DALCCD **Prod** - DALCCD

Principles of design 30 MIN
Videoreel / VT2
Designing home interiors series; Unit 4
Color (C A)
Looks at proportion, scale, balance, rhythm, emphasis and harmony. Shows how these six principles of design were used in designing a model home.
Home Economics
Dist - CDTEL **Prod** - COAST

The Principles of Diagnosis and Treatment 30 MIN
U-matic / VHS
Cyriax on Orthopaedic Medicine Series
Color
Presents an introduction of orthopaedic medicine diagnosis and treatment. Covers passive movements, resisted movements, specimen examination, referred pain, palpation, extrasegementally referred pain/spinal pain, history, treatment.
Health and Safety; Science - Natural
Dist - VTRI **Prod** - VTRI

Principles of direct examination 44 MIN
VHS
Advocacy lectures series
Color (C PRO)
$50.00 rental _ #LSX02
Presents lectures from various law school professors on principles of trial advocacy. Focuses on principles of direct examination.
Civics and Political Systems
Dist - NITA **Prod** - NITA

Principles of Direct Examination 44 MIN
U-matic / VHS
Principles of Examination - Lectures by John a Burgess Series
Color (PRO)
Civics and Political Systems
Dist - ABACPE **Prod** - ABACPE

Principles of Dry Friction 17 MIN
16mm
Engineering Series
B&W
LC FIE52-167
Explains advantages and disadvantages of friction, forces involved in friction and calculation of the forces of static and kinetic friction.
Industrial and Technical Education; Science - Physical
Dist - USNAC **Prod** - USOE 1945

Principles of Electricity 20 MIN
16mm
Color (J H C)
LC FIA66-758
Uses animation to describe basic concepts of electrons and electron flow, positive and negative charges, current, voltage, resistance, and fundamental methods of generating electricity.
Industrial and Technical Education; Science - Physical
Dist - GE **Prod** - GE 1966

Principles of Endocrine Activity 16 MIN
U-matic / VHS / 16mm
Human Physiology Series
Color (H C)
LC 80-701071
Introduces the endocrine system and indicates the better known glands and the effects of gland secretions. Studies the chemical coordination in man, animals and plants. Uses roosters and a pea plant to show the effects of hormones.
Science - Natural
Dist - IU **Prod** - IU 1960

Principles of Ethylene Oxide Gas Sterilization and Aeration 18 MIN
U-matic / VHS
Color (PRO)
Gives comprehensive overview of proper ethylene oxide (EO) gas sterilization in the hospital. Discusses how EO works, preparing items for EO sterilization, how to aerate and operator safety.
Health and Safety
Dist - MMAMC **Prod** - MMAMC

Principles of Evaluation 28 MIN
16mm
Nursing - Effective Evaluation Series
B&W (C A)
LC 74-700189
Reviews general principles of evaluation. Stresses the relationship of behavioral objectives to evaluation and sources of unreliability.
Education; Health and Safety
Dist - NTCN **Prod** - NTCN 1971

Principles of Examination - Lectures by John a Burgess Series
Principles of Cross - Examination 39 MIN
Principles of Direct Examination 44 MIN
Dist - ABACPE

The Principles of Extrication 40 MIN
VHS
Extrication Video from Carbusters Series
Color (G PRO)
$149.95 purchase _ #35341
Creates the foundation of knowledge for the rest of the series. Focuses on safety and reducing extrication time to under 15 minutes. Presents elements common to every extricaton and offers solutions. Includes basic terminology, the action circle, tool staging and establishing command.
Health and Safety; Psychology; Social Science
Dist - OKSU

Principles of Flying 9 MIN
16mm / U-matic / VHS
Color (P I J)
LC 74-703172
Explains the principles of flight and man's early flying efforts.
Science - Physical; Social Science
Dist - ALTSUL **Prod** - CRAIGF 1973

Principles of Fracture Reduction 30 MIN
VHS / U-matic
Fracture Management Series
Color (PRO)
Health and Safety
Dist - WFP **Prod** - WFP

Principles of Frequency Response 37 MIN
16mm
Color (IND)
LC FIA65-22
Explores the basic elements of frequency responses. Gives a practical example showing how a frequency response analysis is performed.
Industrial and Technical Education; Mathematics; Science
Dist - ISA **Prod** - ISA 1958

Principles of Gas - Filled Tubes 15 MIN
16mm
B&W
LC FIE52-187
Explains the theory of ionization applied to gas filled tubes and control of current in circuits employing gas - filled tubes.
Science - Physical
Dist - USNAC **Prod** - USOE 1945

Principles of Gearing - an Introduction 18 MIN
16mm
Engineering Series Fundamentals of Mechanics
B&W
LC FIE52-172
Discusses friction gears and toothed gears. Explains the law of gearing, positive driving, pressure angle, involute profiles, cycloid profiles, velocity rates and circular pitch.
Industrial and Technical Education
Dist - USNAC **Prod** - USOE 1945

Principles of harmonic motion 22 MIN
VHS
Color (G)
$50.00 purchase
Looks at the process of actively engaging in perception and how individuals oscillate between forgetting and remembering that activeness as they age. Takes a painterly approach to the image. In 3 parts - Part 1 - If with those eyes and ears; Part 2 - No Green at ease in the margins; and part 3 - Principles of harmonic motion and epilogue - white picket fence.
Fine Arts; Psychology
Dist - CANCIN **Prod** - PIERCE 1991

Principles of Heat Transfer 30 TO 40 MIN
VHS
Heat Rate Improvement Series
Color (PRO)
$600.00 - $1500.00 purchase _ #HROO2
Introduces the fundamentals of heat transfer. Relates the fundamentals to component and plant efficiency. Explains how heat transfer occurs and identifies factors that affect transfer. Includes one textbook and instructor guide to support two hours of instruction.
Education; Industrial and Technical Education; Psychology
Dist - NUSTC **Prod** - NUSTC

Principles of Heterocyclic Chemistry
16mm
Color (C)
LC 79-701625
Explains the difference between heterocycles and homocycles and examines the relationship between structural, chemical and physical properties of heterocyclic compounds. Contains 24 reels totalling 1,260 minutes.
Science - Physical
Dist - AMCHEM **Prod** - KODAKC 1974

Principles of Human Communication Series
And the people merely players 30 MIN
The Interpersonal Bond 30 MIN
Knowing the Rules 30 MIN
Learning the Process 30 MIN
Playing Communication Games 30 MIN
What do You Mean 30 MIN
Who Listens 30 MIN
Dist - GPN

Principles of Indexing 86 MIN
U-matic / VHS
Color
Discusses the principles and techniques of indexing journal articles for input to the Medline data base and explains how these same theories and practices may be used in searching Medline.
Education; Health and Safety; Industrial and Technical Education; Mathematics; Sociology
Dist - USNAC **Prod** - USHHS

Principles of Industrial Calibration 60 MIN
VHS / 16mm
Instrument Calibration Series
Color (PRO)
$595.00 purchase, $125.00 rental
Presents Instrument Performance, Instrument Errors and Calibration Procedure. Part of a three - part series on instrument calibration.
Industrial and Technical Education; Mathematics
Dist - ISA **Prod** - ISA

Principles of interior landscape design - Volume I 21 MIN
VHS
Tropical plants for the interiorscape series
Color (G)
$89.95 purchase _ #6 - 302 - 315A
Lays a foundation for the use of tropicals in interiorscapes. Discusses plant functions in interior environments and their impact on space, mood, feel and design. Uses dramatic examples from commercial buildings and homes to illustrate the design principles discussed. Part of a series on using tropical plants for interior decoration.
Agriculture; Home Economics; Science - Natural
Dist - VEP **Prod** - VEP 1993

Principles of Investment 25 MIN
VHS / U-matic
Money Smart - a Guide to Personal Finance Series
Color (H C A)
Shows methods of evaluating financial vehicles and developing financial strategies.
Business and Economics; Education; Home Economics
Dist - BCNFL **Prod** - SOMFIL 1985

The Principles of Kwanzaa 12 MIN
VHS
Color (I J)
$79.95 purchase _ #10348VG
Shows the seven principles and African foundations of the Kwanzaa holiday celebration. Describes how each principle can be applied in the African - American youngster's daily life. Through animation and live - action, takes viewers to ancient African kingdoms. Ties in Swahili terms to enhance the linguistic heritage. Includes a guide.
History - United States; Religion and Philosophy
Dist - UNL

Principles of Ladder Diagrams 30 MIN
U-matic / VHS
Programmable Controllers Series
Color
Sketches principles of ladder diagrams. Covers switches, relays and symbols.
Industrial and Technical Education; Sociology
Dist - ITCORP **Prod** - ITCORP

Principles of Ladder Logic Programming 30 MIN
U-matic / VHS
Programmable Controllers Series
Color
Introduces principles of ladder logic programming. Points out limitations.
Industrial and Technical Education; Sociology
Dist - ITCORP **Prod** - ITCORP

The Principles of landscape design - Vol I 22 MIN
VHS
Landscape design series
Color (G)
$89.95 purchase _ #6 - 045 - 001P
Discusses the value of well - planned landscapes. Defines the professions of both landscape designer and landscape architect. Looks at the artistic principles and elements of landscape design. Explores the scientific and technical disciplines which make a design successful. Part one of a two part series.
Agriculture; Home Economics
Dist - VEP **Prod** - VEP

Principles of learning 30 MIN
16mm
Nursing - patient teaching series; Part 1
B&W (C A)
LC 74-700200
Describes essential principles related to patient learning. Examines learning levels which patients may be capable of achieving.
Education; Health and Safety
Dist - NTCN **Prod** - NTCN 1971

Principles of Learning 23 MIN
16mm
Military Instruction Series no 1
B&W
LC FIE56-248
Explains six principles of learning - - motivation, objective, doing, realism, background and appreciation - emphasizing the importance of understanding and applying them during all phases of instruction.
Civics and Political Systems; Education; Psychology
Dist - USNAC **Prod** - USA 1956

Principles of Learning and Instruction 30 MIN
U-matic / VHS
Instructional Technology Introduction Series
Color (C A)
Defines the application of educational pyschology to the use of learning materials, wherein four mental processes come are developed - cognition, memory, motivation and attitude. Lists external conditions affecting the learning process, including stating objectives, establishing content, guiding learning, providing practice and giving feedback. Documents how such 'learning events' create learning sequences that guide students' integration of knowledge, and how the concepts work in both teacher - based and media - based instruction.
Education
Dist - BCNFL **Prod** - MCGILU

Principles of Lubrication 23 MIN
U-matic / VHS / 16mm
Captioned; Color (H C)
Shows the major principles involved when two moving surfaces meet. Demonstrates simple laws of friction experimentally and explains them in terms of the geometric nature of solid surfaces. Explores three ways of reducing friction and wear.
Science - Physical
Dist - IFB **Prod** - BARRAN 1978

Principles of Lubrication 16 MIN
16mm
Engineering Series
B&W
LC 80-700111
Discusses the need for lubrication, the properties, action and viscosity of lubricants, and conditions that determine proper viscosity.
Industrial and Technical Education
Dist - USNAC **Prod** - USOE 1945

Principles of machinery guarding 12 MIN
VHS
Color; PAL; NTSC (IND G)
PdS57, PdS67 purchase
Presents an outline guide to the requirements of the Health and Safety at Work Act, United Kingdom. Addresses the provision, maintenance and correct use of machine guarding. Provides definitions of various types of guards and illustrates their use.
Health and Safety; Science - Physical
Dist - CFLVIS

Principles of Management Series
Approaches to management thought
Change and Conflict
Communication - the thread of unity
Controlling - the thermostat
The Informal Organization
The Job of Management
Leadership - Working with People
Managerial Decision Making
Motivation - Why Employees Work
Organizing - the Structuring Function
Planning - the Primary Function
Planning - the Process
Staffing - Developing the Employee
Dist - RMIBHF

Principles of Mechanical Troubleshooting 60 MIN
U-matic / VHS
Troubleshooting Series
Color
Outlines principles of troubleshooting. Stresses preventing future trouble. Deals with troubleshooting under pressure.
Education; Industrial and Technical Education
Dist - ITCORP **Prod** - ITCORP

Principles of microwave cookery 38 MIN
VHS
Color (H G)
$99.00 purchase _ #31064 - 027
Explains the concepts of microwave energy and shows how the components operate. Includes a discussion of microwave containers and illustrates specific cooking techniques.
Education; Home Economics; Industrial and Technical Education
Dist - GA

Principles of MRO Inventory Management
U-matic / VHS
Effective Inventory Control Series
Color (IND)
Discusses objectives of inventory management, identifies most important questions a manager considers when setting up a system and defines performance measures. Considers prerequisites for successful inventory management and explains importance of a good classification or numbering system.
Business and Economics
Dist - GPCV **Prod** - GPCV

Principles of Neurological Epidemiology Series
General concepts of analytic epidemiology 55 MIN
General Concepts of Descriptive Epidemiology 48 MIN
General Concepts of Experimental and Theoretical Epidemiology - Review 31 MIN
Investigating an Epidemic - Cohort Analysis in Descriptive Epidemiology 42 MIN
Dist - USNAC

Principles of Neuromotor Assessment 19 MIN
U-matic / VHS
Pediatric Assessment Series
Color
Health and Safety; Psychology
Dist - UMDSM **Prod** - UMDSM

Principles of Orbit 11 MIN
U-matic / VHS / 16mm
Space Science Series
Color (I J H)
Investigates how the laws of inertia and universal gravitation govern the flight of an orbiting satellite, demonstrating the behavior of a satellite, both in circular and elliptical orbits.
Science - Physical
Dist - JOU

Principles of Paper Work Management - Managing Your Forms 17 MIN
16mm
Color
LC FIE61-108
Describes the efficient design and use of Navy forms and shows common errors. Outlines the procedures for obtaining well - designed forms.
Business and Economics; English Language; Guidance and Counseling
Dist - USNAC **Prod** - USN 1960

Principles of Paperwork Management 13 MIN
16mm
Color
LC FIE61-111
Describes the qualities of efficient, effective letterwriting and suggests ways of obtaining these qualities.
Business and Economics; English Language; Guidance and Counseling
Dist - USNAC **Prod** - USN 1960

Principles of Paperwork Management - Better Correspondence Practices 11 MIN
16mm
Color
LC 74-705416
Describes nine ways of saving time and money in correspondence management.
Business and Economics; English Language; Guidance and Counseling
Dist - USNAC **Prod** - USN 1960

Principles of Paperwork Management - Managing Your Reports 11 MIN
16mm
Color
LC FIE61-107
Describes common deficiencies that occur in reports and in reporting procedures. Describes areas of possible improvements such as quality of content, frequency and timing, preparation procedures and cost.
Business and Economics
Dist - USNAC **Prod** - USN 1961

Principles of Paperwork Management - Moving the Mail 14 MIN
16mm
Color
LC FIE61-110
Describes common deficiencies which occur in reports and in reporting procedures. Describes areas of possible improvement such as quality of content, frequency and timing, preparation procedures and cost.
Business and Economics; English Language; Guidance and Counseling
Dist - USNAC **Prod** - USN

Principles of Paperwork Management - Records Disposal 15 MIN
16mm
Color
LC FIE61-106
Discusses the administrative and supervisory problem of moving mail quickly and economically. Shows 15 ways of improving mail movement.
Business and Economics; Guidance and Counseling; Social Science
Dist - USNAC **Prod** - USN

Principles of Parent - Child Programs for the Pre - School Hearing Impaired 28 MIN
16mm
B&W (C T S)
LC FIA68-1959
Illustrates pre - school programs for children with impaired hearing. Indicates the importance of parental cooperation in these programs.
English Language
Dist - PSUPCR **Prod** - PSU 1967

Principles of Pharmacokinetics 40 MIN
U-matic
Color (PRO)
LC 79-707946
Presents basic principles associated with the process of absorption, distribution, metabolism, and excretion of drugs and other chemicals.
Health and Safety
Dist - USNAC **Prod** - ORMAC 1978

Principles of Picture Design 15 MIN
VHS / 16mm
Drawing with Paul Ringler Series
Color (I H)
$125.00 purchase, $25.00 rental
Offers suggestions for using balance, repetition, gradation, dominance, harmony, contrast, alternation and unity in visual design.
Fine Arts; Industrial and Technical Education
Dist - AITECH **Prod** - OETVA 1988

Principles of Picture Design - 11 15 MIN
VHS
Drawing with Paul Ringler Series
Color (I)
$125.00 purchase
Presents suggestions for using balance, repetition, gradation, dominance, harmony, contrast, alternation and unity. Emphasizes the drawing process, for older students, rather than drawing specific objects. Part of a thirty - part series.
Fine Arts
Dist - AITECH **Prod** - OETVA 1988

Principles of plant growth - Set 3 24 FRS
VHS / Slide / Cassette
Western fertilizer handbook series
Color (G)
$32.95, $40.00, $8.50 purchase _ #1 - 580 - 603P, #1 - 580 - 203P, #1 - 580 - 533P
Looks at principles of plant growth. Part of a fourteen - part series based on the Western Fertilizer Handbook.
Agriculture
Dist - VEP **Prod** - VEP

Principles of Process and Servo Control 4 2/3HR
VHS / 16mm
Color (A IND)
$2900.00 purchase
Focuses in seven videotapes on the components of electronic process control systems. Also teaches system analysis, programming and testing. Textbook available.
Computer Science; Industrial and Technical Education
Dist - SME **Prod** - SME 1989

Principles of Pump Operations and Maintenance 30 MIN
VHS
Color (G PRO)
$35.00 purchase _ #35353
Reviews theory and operation of a midship pump with common accessories. Covers routine service and maintenance. Summarizes scheduled maintenance. Trains firefighting personnel.
Agriculture; Health and Safety; Industrial and Technical Education; Psychology; Science - Physical; Social Science
Dist - OKSU **Prod** - OKSU

Principles of Quality Concrete 26 MIN
16mm
Color
LC 82-700033
Deals with the fundamental principles of quality concrete and procedures for the design of mixes. Explains and illustrates the water - cement - ratio hypothesis, the process of hydration, and the effects of aggregates and air entrainment on concrete.
Industrial and Technical Education
Dist - PRTLND **Prod** - PRTLND 1980

Principles of Quality Concrete 26 MIN
16mm
Color
Presents a Canadian metric version of a film on the fundamentals of quality concrete and design of mixes, explaining the water/cement ratio hypothesis and demonstrating mix design and calculations. Explains hydration and the effects of aggregate characteristics on plastic and hardened concrete, with emphasis on air entrainment.
Industrial and Technical Education; Science - Physical
Dist - PRTLND **Prod** - PRTLND 1977

Principles of Refrigeration 20 MIN
16mm
Engineering Series
B&W
LC FIE52-171
Explains the basic physics of heat transfer. Uses animation to show the compression and the absorption systems of refrigeration.
Industrial and Technical Education
Dist - USNAC **Prod** - USOE 1944

Principles of respiratory mechanics - Pt 1 22 MIN
16mm
Color (PRO)
Demonstrates the process of breathing using a healthy subject in contrast to one with various functional and organic disorders. Explains basic concepts such as elastic and resistive properties of the lungs and pressure - volume relationships.
Science - Natural
Dist - AMEDA **Prod** - HSPUBH 1954

Principles of respiratory mechanics - Pt 2 21 MIN
16mm
Color (PRO)
Demonstrates the process of breathing using a healthy subject in contrast to one with various functional and organic disorders. Explains basic concepts such as work of breathing and the value of mechanical measurements.
Science - Natural
Dist - AMEDA **Prod** - HSPUBH 1956

The Principles of rocketry 28 MIN
VHS
Color (J H C)
$14.95 purchase _ #NA065
Industrial and Technical Education
Dist - INSTRU **Prod** - NASA

Principles of Seed Processing Series
Air screen cleaner 5 MIN
Specific gravity separator 3 MIN
Spiral Separator 3 MIN
Velvet Roll Separator 3 MIN
Dist - IOWA

Principles of shade and ornamental tree pruning and pruning standards for shade trees
VHS
Color (G)
$162.00 purchase _ #6 - 205 - 001P
Covers the methods, equipment and reasons for pruning. Discusses the limits and criteria for arboricultural work. Reviews the four classes of pruning - fine, standard, hazard and crown reduction pruning. In two parts produced by the National Arborist Association.
Agriculture; Psychology; Science - Natural
Dist - VEP

Principles of shade and ornamental tree pruning and pruning standards for shade trees series
Pruning practices and standards
Pruning tools and techniques
Dist - VEP

Principles of SNA 35 MIN
U-matic / VHS
SNA Management Considerations Series
Color
Presents the concepts, structure and components of System Network Architecture (SNA) and the relationship of SNA to other IBM products and to non - IBM products as well.
Industrial and Technical Education
Dist - DELTAK **Prod** - DELTAK

Principles of Solubility 18 MIN
U-matic
Chemistry 102 - Chemistry for Engineers - Series
Color (C)
Relates solubility of two substances to their relative polarities. Attractive forces between the molecules of the pure substances must be broken for a solution to form.
Industrial and Technical Education; Science - Physical
Dist - UILL **Prod** - UILL 1981

Principles of Teaching Speech After Laryngectomy 21 MIN
16mm
Color (PRO)
Discusses the advantages and disadvantages of various methods of teaching speech after laryngectomy. Explores the anatomical and physiological changes that result from larynegectomy and examines the associated psychological, social and economic aspects of total rehabilitation.
English Language; Health and Safety; Psychology; Science - Natural
Dist - AMCS **Prod** - AMCS 1970

The Principles of the spiritual path 240 MIN
VHS / BETA
Color; PAL (G)
PdS55, $110.00 purchase
Explains the three fundamental features of the spiritual path of the Great Vehicle - the development of renunciation; the wish to gain liberation from suffering; the activation of the awakening mind; the motivation to attain the highest perfection of mind, enlightenment, in order to help all others; and cultivating the correct view of reality, the awareness of emptiness, the void nature of all distorting projections. Recorded at the Lam Rim Centre, Wales. Translated by the Venerable Geshe Namgyal Wangchen.
Fine Arts; Religion and Philosophy
Dist - MERIDT

The Principles of Tibetan medicine 300 MIN
VHS / BETA
Color; PAL (G)
PdS62, $124.00 purchase
Covers the underlying features of the causes of illness, the process of diagnosis and the treatment of sickness in traditional Buddhist medicine. Explains how illness results from the interplay of the entire physical, emotional and even astrological state of the individual; the cause is treated rather than the symptom of an illness. Although based on the Indian Ayurvedic system, Tibetan medicine includes treatments such as acupuncture and moxabustion. Presented by Dr Tenzin Choedak, personal physician to the Dalai Lama, who trained and practiced in Tibet before the Communist invasion in 1959 and was subsequently imprisoned by the Chinese for years before being allowed to leave the country. Recorded at Rikon, Switzerland. Translated by Elio Guarisco.
Fine Arts; Religion and Philosophy
Dist - MERIDT

Principles of TIG 60 MIN
U-matic / VHS
Welding Training Series
Color (IND)
Focuses on safety, equipment, electrodes, shield gas, starting arc, techniques and shutdown.
Education; Industrial and Technical Education
Dist - ITCORP **Prod** - ITCORP

Principles of Time Management 30 MIN
VHS / U-matic
Time Management for Management Series Pt 1
Color (A)
Explains a time management process which can be followed to help meet goals in the time available. Emphasizes the need to distinguish between goals and activities.
Business and Economics; Psychology
Dist - TIMLIF **Prod** - TIMLIF 1981

Principles of Traction 20 MIN
U-matic / VHS
Traction Series
Color
Reviews the basics of traction. Discusses the three classifications of traction, including skin, skeletal and manual, along with a review of the principles of traction a application.
Health and Safety
Dist - FAIRGH **Prod** - FAIRGH

Principles of training 27 MIN
VHS
Sports science series
Color; PAL (T J H)
$29.50 purchase _ #1 - 580
Presents ways to put theory into practice according to the requirements of different sports; measuring physical capacities; aggressive overload with specific exercises for training effects; and more. Features part of a seven - part series on the science behind sports and physical activity, suitable for health and physical education courses, coaching and fitness programs.
Physical Education and Recreation
Dist - EMFVL

Principles of Training - 4 8 TO 37 MIN
VHS
Sports Science Series
Color (H)
$75.00 purchase
Presents the science behind sports and physical activity, including training, acquiring new motor skills and preventing injuries. Alternates scenes of athletes in practice and competition with views of anatomical models, commentary and graphics that explain the science and physiology behind movements. Program 4 puts theory into practice, according to the the requirements of different sports, measuring physical capacity, adaptation as the role of training, principles of progressive overload and other training specifics.
Health and Safety; Physical Education and Recreation; Science - Natural
Dist - AITECH

Principles of translation 50 MIN
U-matic / VHS
Computer languages series; Pt 1
Color
Discusses relation of translation to interpretation, efficiency advantages of translation and translation of AEs to LISP in computer languages.
Industrial and Technical Education; Mathematics; Sociology
Dist - MIOT **Prod** - MIOT

Principles of Visual Training 30 MIN
VHS / U-matic
Training the Trainer Series
Color (T)
Describes types of visual aids used in training. Discusses principles of visual learning.
Education; Psychology
Dist - ITCORP **Prod** - ITCORP

PRINT Again, Finding Largest Values and String Variables 60 MIN
U-matic / VHS
Introduction to BASIC Series Lecture 7; Lecture 7
Color
Industrial and Technical Education; Mathematics
Dist - UIDEEO **Prod** - UIDEEO

Print generation 50 MIN
16mm
Color (G)
$75.00 rental
Builds a picture from an abstract pattern of dots. Transforms shimmering red points of light into whites, then blue - green and finally combining secondary colors. Produced by J J Murphy.
Fine Arts
Dist - CANCIN

Print Reading and Use 60 MIN
VHS
Maintenance Practices Series
Color (PRO)
$600.00, $1500.00 purchase _ #GMPRU
Shows how to read simple prints with the aid of reference material. Gives examples of piping system, hydraulic system, pneumatic system and machine prints. Part of a two - part series on maintenance practices, part of a set on general and mechanical maintenance. Includes 10 textbooks and an instructor guide which provide four hours of instruction.
Education; Health and Safety; Industrial and Technical Education; Psychology
Dist - NUSTC **Prod** - NUSTC

Print Shop 3 MIN
16mm
Color
LC 77-702617
Presents the day - to - day workings of a small print shop owned and operated by poet - printer Tim Inkster.
Business and Economics; Industrial and Technical Education; Literature and Drama
Dist - CANFDC **Prod** - MIRUS 1976

PRINT using subroutine 60 MIN
U-matic / VHS
Introduction to BASIC series; Lecture 13
Color
Industrial and Technical Education; Mathematics
Dist - UIDEEO **Prod** - UIDEEO

Printed Circuit
VHS / 35mm strip
Electronic Soldering Series
$42.00 purchase _ #LXES3 filmstrip, $62.00 purchase _ #LXES3V VHS
Shows the mounting and soldering of components using the clinching, swagging, and clipping methods. Shows the manufacturing of the printed circuit - PC - board by two processes.
Education; Industrial and Technical Education
Dist - CAREER **Prod** - CAREER

Printed Circuit Board Conductor Repair 8 TO 15 MIN
VHS
High - Reliability Soldering Series
Color (PRO)
$600.00 - $1500.00 purchase _ #TRPCR
Concentrates on determining printed circuit board conductor damage, repairing cracked or broken PCBs, repairing delaminated or missing PCB conductors and repairing or replacing damaged PCB pads. Part of an eighteen - part series on high - reliability soldering. Requires a solid understanding of digital electronics. Includes one textbook and an instructor guide to support 45 minutes of instruction.
Education; Health and Safety; Industrial and Technical Education; Psychology
Dist - NUSTC **Prod** - NUSTC

Printed Circuit Board Conformal Coatings 8 TO 15 MIN
VHS
High - Reliability Soldering Series
Color (PRO)
$600.00 - $1500.00 purchase _ #TRPCC
Identifies and describes six conformal coatings used on printed circuit boards. Describes three methods for removing conformal coatings from a PCB. Part of an eighteen - part series on high - reliability soldering. Requires a solid understanding of digital electronics. Includes one textbook and an instructor guide to support 45 minutes of instruction.
Education; Health and Safety; Industrial and Technical Education; Psychology
Dist - NUSTC **Prod** - NUSTC

Printed Circuit Board Construction Fundamentals 8 TO 15 MIN
VHS
High - Reliability Soldering Series
Color (PRO)
$600.00 - $1500.00 purchase _ #TRPCF
Describes the three parts of a circuit board. Identifies various type of printed circuit boards. Describes the three phases of constructing a board. Defines 'conformal coating.' Part of an eighteen - part series on high - reliability soldering. Requires a solid understanding of digital electronics. Includes one textbook and an instructor guide to support 45 minutes of instruction.
Education; Health and Safety; Industrial and Technical Education; Psychology
Dist - NUSTC **Prod** - NUSTC

Printed Circuit Board Laminate Repair 8 TO 15 MIN
VHS
High - Reliability Soldering Series
Color (PRO)
$600.00 - $1500.00 purchase _ #TRPCL
Identifies and describes materials used to make up a printed circuit board substrate. Describes damage that can occur to a PCB substrate, damage analysis and repair. Part of an eighteen - part series on high - reliability soldering. Requires a solid understanding of digital electronics. Includes one textbook and an instructor guide to support 45 minutes of instruction.
Education; Health and Safety; Industrial and Technical Education; Psychology
Dist - NUSTC **Prod** - NUSTC

Printed Circuit Board Repair Task Analysis 8 TO 15 MIN
VHS
High - Reliability Soldering Series
Color (PRO)
$600.00 - $1500.00 purchase _ #TRPCR
Presents the seven steps required in a printed circuit board repair task analysis. Part of an eighteen - part series on high - reliability soldering. Requires a solid understanding of digital electronics. Includes one textbook and an instructor guide to support 45 minutes of instruction.
Education; Health and Safety; Industrial and Technical Education; Psychology
Dist - NUSTC **Prod** - NUSTC

Printed Circuits and their Repair 28 MIN
16mm
Color
LC FIE62-77
Explains that the accomplishment of many Air Force missions is dependent upon the reliability of printed circuits. Shows how to manufacture, clean, coat and dry printed circuits. Describes methods and tools used in their repair. Demonstrates how to remove and replace a faulty transistor and some types of emergency repair.
Business and Economics; Industrial and Technical Education
Dist - USNAC **Prod** - USAF 1961

Printed Flowers 10 MIN
U-matic / VHS / 16mm
Inventive Child Series
Color (P I)
Depicts the situation which occurs when Boy decides to paint a house and gets some clumsy help from a friend. Shows that by turning mistakes into advantages and by putting some common materials to inventive use, he finds a way to make his task easier.
History - World; Home Economics
Dist - EBEC **Prod** - POLSKI 1983

Printed Flowers and Barking Plate 20 MIN
U-matic / VHS
Inventive Child Series
Color (P I J)
$89.00 purchase _ #1581
Shows two partners as they face some trouble while attempting to paint a house and how they make their task easier using imagination (1st part). Shows some of the steps involved in the invention of the phonograph (2nd part). Stresses the importance of problem - solving skills and creativity.
Psychology
Dist - EBEC

Printing 15 MIN
VHS / U-matic / BETA
Career Success Series
Color (H C A)
$29.95 _ #MX163
Portrays occupations in printing by reviewing required abilities and interviewing people employed in this field. Tells of anxieties and rewards involved in pursuing a career in printing.
Education; Guidance and Counseling; Industrial and Technical Education
Dist - CAMV **Prod** - CAMV

Printing 15 MIN
VHS / 16mm
(H C A)
$24.95 purchase _ #CS163
Describes the skills involved in a career in printing. Features interviews with people working in this field.
Guidance and Counseling
Dist - RMIBHF **Prod** - RMIBHF

Printing
U-matic / VHS
Work - a - Day America
$59.95 purchase _ #VV117V
Helps students achieve career vocational preparation. Stresses the four main points of career awareness and exploration, specific skills intended, employability skills needed, and real people sharing on the job experiences.
Guidance and Counseling
Dist - CAREER **Prod** - CAREER

Printing 15 MIN
U-matic / VHS
Art cart series
Color (P I)
LC 79-708040
Describes glue printing and object printing and shows how to design a pattern to be printed or stamped.
Fine Arts
Dist - AITECH **Prod** - WBRATV 1979

Printing and Fractur 29 MIN
Videoreel / VT2
Commonwealth Series
Color
History - United States; Industrial and Technical Education
Dist - PBS **Prod** - WITFTV

Printing and writing series

Printing - Printed Capital Letters a - M	30 MIN
Printing - Printed Capital Letters N - Z	30 MIN
Printing - Printed Small Letters a - m	30 MIN
Printing - Printed Small Letters N - z	30 MIN
Writing - Cursive Capital Letters a - M	30 MIN
Writing - Cursive Capital Letters N - Z	30 MIN
Writing - cursive small letters a - m	30 MIN
Writing - cursive small letters n - z	30 MIN

Dist - KITTLC

Printing basics for non - printers 1 - an abridged guide to printing fundamentals 60 MIN
VHS
Graphic specialties series
Color (J H C G)
$39.95 purchase _ #GFG2070V
Demystifies the various steps leading to the printing of simple and complex projects for designers, production artists and buyers of printed materials. Shows how to talk to printers in their own language and how to save money on printing by properly preparing materials for the job. Part of a four - part series on graphic specialties.
Industrial and Technical Education
Dist - CAMV

Printing Card Punch 15 MIN
16mm
Color (H C A)
Follows a card through the entire process of recording data on the key punch machine. Indicates the design, purpose and function of the keyboard, its keys, switches and other manipulative parts. Describes the hopper, stacker, feeding station and reading station. Demonstrates card duplication and shows how data can be printed as the card is punched.
Mathematics; Psychology; Sociology
Dist - SF **Prod** - SF 1968

Printing - Platen Press Makeready 15 MIN
U-matic / VHS / 16mm
B&W (J H A)
Depicts each step in platen press makeready. Identifies parts of the press.
Industrial and Technical Education
Dist - IFB **Prod** - STSC 1960

Printing - Printed Capital Letters a - M 30 MIN
U-matic / VHS
Printing and Writing Series
Color
English Language
Dist - KITTLC **Prod** - KITTLC

Printing - Printed Capital Letters N - Z 30 MIN
VHS / U-matic
Printing and Writing Series
Color
English Language
Dist - KITTLC **Prod** - KITTLC

Printing - Printed Small Letters a - m 30 MIN
U-matic / VHS
Printing and Writing Series
Color
English Language
Dist - KITTLC **Prod** - KITTLC

Printing - Printed Small Letters N - z 30 MIN
U-matic / VHS
Printing and Writing Series
Color
English Language
Dist - KITTLC **Prod** - KITTLC

Printing Techniques 30 MIN
U-matic
Media and Methods of the Artist Series
Color (H C A)
Demonstrates several techniques for printing including aquatint, mezzotine and colograph.
Fine Arts
Dist - TVOTAR **Prod** - TVOTAR 1971

Printing the Positive 19 MIN
16mm
Fundamentals of Photography Series
B&W
Shows hand and machine methods of making photographic prints. Emphasizes cleanliness, timing, temperature, testing of solutions and drying.
Industrial and Technical Education
Dist - USNAC **Prod** - USN 1950

Printing transforms knowledge - Program 4 52 MIN
VHS
Day the universe changed series
Color (H C G)
$695.00, $300.00 purchase, $75.00 rental
Reveals that the Medieval world was transformed by Gutenberg's discovery of printing. Shows how learning, restricted largely to memorization and the spoken word, was made available to people outside of monasteries, who learned to read. Mass production of information through print contributed to the Protestant Reformation and the beginnings of nationalism. Part of a ten - part series on Western thought hosted by James Burke.
Civics and Political Systems; History - World; Religion and Philosophy; Sociology
Dist - CF **Prod** - BBCTV 1986

Printmaking 60 MIN
VHS / 16mm
Children's Crafts Series
(K P)
$39.00 purchase _ #VT1117
Shows how to printmake using various items such as vegetables, toys, kitchen tools, keys, or coins. Teaches how to overlap, create good design, and turn your prints into gifts. Taught by Julie Abowitt, Multi - Arts Coordinator for the Seattle Public Schools.
Fine Arts
Dist - RMIBHF **Prod** - RMIBHF

Printmaking 15 MIN
VHS / U-matic
Expressions
(I J)
$130 purchase, $25 rental, $75 self dub
Designed to interest fifth through ninth graders in art. Emphasizes creativity and experimentation. Features printmaker Elly Tepper demonstrating serigraphy. Seventh in an 18 part series.
Fine Arts; Industrial and Technical Education
Dist - GPN

Printmaking - 10 31 MIN
U-matic / VHS
Think new series
Color (C G)
$129.00, $99.00 purchase _ #V585
Gives theoretical motivation and practical ideas about printmaking. Draws content from mathematics, science, history, human feelings, every human endeavor. Part of an 11 - part series that treats art as an essential mode of learning.
Fine Arts; Industrial and Technical Education
Dist - BARR **Prod** - CEPRO 1991

Printmaking - four artists, four media 19 MIN
16mm / U-matic / VHS
Color (A)
LC FIA68-1195
Explains that printmaking can be divided into four basic methods - - serigraph, woodcut, lithograph and intaglio. Shows four printmakers in their workshops. Pictures how each method progresses from sketch to finished print, including the special equipment and skills required by each method. Contrasts the differences in producing each kind of print and the differences in appearance of the finished artwork.
Fine Arts; Industrial and Technical Education
Dist - PHENIX **Prod** - EDDLES 1968

Prints 15 MIN
VHS
Rediscovery Art Media Series
Color
$69.95 purchase _ #4398
Presented are several processes that can be carried out with simple, easily available materials.
Fine Arts
Dist - AIMS **Prod** - AIMS

Prints 15 MIN
U-matic / VHS / 16mm
Rediscovery - Art Media
Color (I) (SPANISH)
Presents a number of printmaking processes that can be carried out with the use of readily available materials.
Fine Arts; Foreign Language
Dist - AIMS **Prod** - ACI 1966

Prints 30 MIN
U-matic / VHS
Antique Shop Series
Color
Presents guests who are experts in their respective fields who share tips on collecting and caring for antique prints.
Fine Arts
Dist - MDCPB **Prod** - WVPTTV

Prints 15 MIN
16mm / U-matic / VHS
Rediscovery - Art Media Series
Color (I)
LC FIA67-566
Illustrates print - making processes involving simple materials like vegetables, string, crayon graffito and cardboard. Emphasizes each method's potential in stimulating creativity and individual exploration.
Fine Arts
Dist - AIMS **Prod** - ACI 1966

Prints and reproductions 25 MIN
VHS
Artists in print series
Color (A)
PdS65 purchase
Introduces the art of printmaking and illustrates basic printmaking techniques. Artists talk about their approach to the medium and are seen at all stages of making a print. Asks what a print is and explains the difference between an 'original' and a reproduction. Part of a five-part series.

Fine Arts; Industrial and Technical Education
Dist - BBCENE

Prior claim 28 MIN
VHS
Moody science classics series
Color (R I J)
$19.95 purchase _ #6117 - 4
Credits the creation of the Venus Fly Trap, archer fish, trapdoor spider and other animals to the Christian deity. Features part of a series on creationism.
Literature and Drama; Religion and Philosophy
Dist - MOODY **Prod** - MOODY

The Prioress' Tale 30 MIN
Videoreel / VT1
Canterbury Tales Series
B&W (A)
History - World; Literature and Drama
Dist - UMITV **Prod** - UMITV 1967

Priorities 12 MIN
U-matic / VHS / 16mm
Vignettes Series
Color (J)
LC 73-701990
Presents three vignettes leading to an assessment of personal values.
Guidance and Counseling; Sociology
Dist - PAULST **Prod** - PAULST 1973

Priorities - freedom from the tyranny of the urgent - Tape 1
VHS
Strengthening your grip series
Color (H C G A R)
$10.00 rental _ #36 - 892001 - 533
Features Chuck Swindoll in a discussion of priorities for Christians.
Religion and Philosophy
Dist - APH **Prod** - WORD

Priorities in Hospital Fire Procedure 13 MIN
VHS / U-matic
Color (PRO)
LC 80-731001
Defines priorities for action during a hospital fire. Emphasizes the importance of using good judgement and explains factors which influence appropriate actions. Reviews an evacuation procedure.
Health and Safety
Dist - MEDCOM **Prod** - MEDCOM

The Prioritization matrices - Part 5 34 MIN
VHS
Memory jogger plus series
Color (PRO IND A)
$495.00 purchase _ #GO01E
Presents part five of a seven - part series featuring Michael Brassard. Uses an interactive format giving viewers hands - on experience with topic. By Goal - QPC. Includes extensive workshop materials.
Business and Economics; Psychology
Dist - EXTR

Priority Highway Facilities for Carpools and Buses 28 MIN
16mm
Color (A)
LC 77-702238
Shows how urban traffic congestion can be solved with the use of bus priority projects and special facilities for carpools.
Industrial and Technical Education; Social Science
Dist - USNAC **Prod** - USDTFH 1977

Priority 1 - drug free workplace 28 MIN
VHS
Color (A PRO IND)
$120.00 purchase _ #TCA18110
Presents the personal experiences and testimony of three transit professionsals recovering from drug and alcohol dependency. Interviews counselors on th specifics of abuse, dependency, and recovery. Includes four booklets, with additional booklets available at an extra charge. Co - produced by the Metropolitan Atlanta Rapid Transit Authority - MARTA - and the U S Department of Transportation's Urban Mass Transportation Administration.
Guidance and Counseling; Industrial and Technical Education; Psychology
Dist - USNAC

Priority Setter 15 MIN
U-matic / VHS
Modern President Series
Color (H C)
$250 purchase
Talks about the major priorities of different presidents. Shows how political maneuvering and world and national events influence priority setting. Produced by Focus Enterprises.

Biography; Civics and Political Systems
Dist - CORF

Priory - the Only Home I've Got 29 MIN
U-matic / VHS / 16mm
Color (H C A)
LC 81-700792
Focuses on the Priory, a public extended - care hospital in Victoria, British Columbia, which helps those suffering from chronic geriatric illnesses to regenerate some physical independence and find a sense of self - worth.
Health and Safety; Sociology
Dist - PHENIX **Prod** - NFBC 1980

Priscilla's yoga maintenance routine 38 MIN
VHS
Color (G)
$23.95 purchase
Presents a yoga maintenance routine for the experienced yoga student. Features Priscilla Patrick as instructor.
Physical Education and Recreation
Dist - PRIPAT **Prod** - PRIPAT 1991

Prism 8 MIN
16mm
Color (G)
$10.00 rental
Sketches a prism of light moving over surfaces in a room in a Caroline Savage - Lee production.
Fine Arts; Science - Physical
Dist - CANCIN

Prisms and cones
VHS
Now I see it geometry video series
Color (J H)
$79.00 _ #60253 - 026
Connects with students' lives and interests by linking lessons to everyday objects ranging from automobiles to ice cream cones, stereos to honeycombs. Includes reproducible worksheet book and answer key. Part of a nine - part series.
Education; Mathematics
Dist - GA

Prisms - some Properties 12 MIN
U-matic / VHS / 16mm
Color (I J)
LC FIA68-3183
Reviews the basic properties of three - dimensional objects. Uses an examination of a conventional triangular glass prism, to introduce the viewer to the basic properties of prisms. Shows other prisms and examines their properties.
Mathematics; Science - Physical
Dist - PHENIX **Prod** - BOUNDY 1968

The Prison Break 1 MIN
U-matic / VHS / 16mm
Coffee Breaks I Series
Color (A)
Presents a funny announcement which lets professionals break out of the room and head for the coffee pots during business meetings.
Business and Economics; Literature and Drama
Dist - CORF **Prod** - MBACC 1983

The Prison Community 29 MIN
U-matic / VHS / 16mm
Penitentiary Staff Training Series
B&W (PRO)
LC FIA67-131
Health and Safety; Psychology; Sociology
Dist - IFB **Prod** - NFBC 1966

Prison guards 28 MIN
U-matic
Are you listening series
Color (J)
LC 80-707151
Features a group of North Carolina prison guards speaking about the changes they have noticed in the prison system and about how their jobs have altered as a result.
Sociology
Dist - STURTM **Prod** - STURTM 1973

Prison Reform - Gruvberget 15 MIN
U-matic / VHS
Color (H C A)
Looks at a prison without guards, where inmates live with their wives and children in order to acclimate them to living in society. Explains that no one has ever tried to escape.
Sociology
Dist - JOU **Prod** - UPI

Prison Without Bars 27 MIN
Videoreel / VT2
Color
Explains that alternatives to prison are being tried in Pennsylvania. Explores the pros and cons offered by community treatment centers, including supervised homes in the neighborhood where non - dangerous offenders learn to adjust to society.
Geography - United States; Sociology
Dist - PBS **Prod** - WLVTTV

The Prisoner 91 MIN
16mm
B&W (J)
Stars Alec Guinness and Jack Hawkins. Portrays the conflict between two strong - willed, brilliant minds - a cardinal and former resistance leader who is arrested and charged with treason and an interrogator determined to extract a confession.
Fine Arts
Dist - TWYMAN **Prod** - CPC 1955

The Prisoner 27 MIN
16mm / U-matic / VHS
Insight Series
Color (H C A)
Gives an account of the true story of Maximillian Kolbe, a prisoner in Auschwitz, who volunteers to take the place of an embittered man in a starvation box. Reveals that after Kolbe dies, the embittered man opens up and begins to love again. Stars Jack Klugman.
Guidance and Counseling; History - World; Psychology; Religion and Philosophy
Dist - PAULST **Prod** - PAULST

Prisoner Counseling 26 MIN
16mm / U-matic / VHS
Color
Explains the different phases of confinement and the counseling used as a major part of the Army rehabilitation program.
Civics and Political Systems; Health and Safety; Psychology; Sociology
Dist - USNAC **Prod** - USA

Prisoner of the past 54 MIN
VHS
Red empire series
Color (J H C G)
$19.98 purchase _ #FFO9610V
Reveals that Lenin's ideal of individual rights has still not materialized in the Soviet Union and the people are restless. Discloses that Brezhnev crushes the rebellion at home and invades Czechoslovakia. Brezhnev, Andropov and Konstantin Chernenko all die within a three - year period. Mikhail Gorbachev comes to power with ideas for a new revolution. Part of a seven - part series tracing Russian history from the fall of the Tsar and rise of Lenin, through World War I, the internal war for communism, the emergence of the brutal and ruthless Stalin, World War II, Krushchev, Brezhnev and Gorbachev.
Civics and Political Systems; History - World; Sociology
Dist - CAMV

Prisoner or patient 50 MIN
VHS
Color (C G PRO)
$198.00 purchase, $24.00 rental _ #50864
Examines the treatment of the mentally ill criminal. Interviews psychiatrists, prison authorities and prisoners.
Psychology; Sociology
Dist - PSU **Prod** - BBC 1986

Prisoners 28 MIN
16mm
Are you listening series
Color (J)
LC 80-701125
Features white and black prisoners expressing their views on morals, self - respect, sex, homosexuality and the prison process which they feel strips them of their self - esteem.
Sociology
Dist - STURTM **Prod** - STURTM 1973

Prisoners of Chance 23 MIN
16mm / U-matic / VHS
Color; Captioned (J)
LC 78-702047
Dramatizes the problems, philosophies and lifestyles of several teenagers who became parents due to their lack of sexual responsibility. Emphasizes their unrealistic views toward their futures.
Guidance and Counseling; Health and Safety; Sociology
Dist - ALTSUL **Prod** - ALTSUL 1979

Prisoners of childhood - exploring the inner child 52 MIN
VHS
Color (H C G)
$445.00 purchase, $75.00 rental
Presents the intimate memories of five actors as they explore childhood memory. Reveals that professional therapists Marcia Karp, Dr Petruska Clarkson and Sue Fish work with the actors to help them put aside their

professional selves and to engage the real life child they had been. Often with vivid pain, they discover lost feelings that are finally allowed to surface and have power over and relevancy to the present. Inspired by The Drama of the Gifted Child by Dr Alice Miller.
Psychology
Dist - FLMLIB **Prod** - MKNZM 1992

Prisoners of Conscience 45 MIN
16mm
B&W
Examines the human rights situation in India, focusing on the State of Emergency imposed by Indira Gandhi from June, 1975, to March, 1977.
Civics and Political Systems; Geography - World; History - World
Dist - ICARUS **Prod** - ICARUS 1977

Prisoners of conscience 30 MIN
16mm / U-matic / VHS
Color
Dramatizes international human rights with the stories of Gustavo Westerkamp in Argentina and Danylo Shumuk in the Soviet Union, both imprisoned for their beliefs. Shows efforts of Amnesty International to help obtain release of these two prisoners.
History - World; Sociology
Dist - CNEMAG **Prod** - AMNSTY

Prisoners of Debt - Global Banking Crises 59 MIN
16mm
Color
#106C 0183 010N
Geography - World
Dist - CFLMDC **Prod** - NFBC 1983

Prisoners of Hope - Multiple Sclerosis 50 MIN
U-matic / VHS / 16mm
Color (C A)
Looks at the treatment and outlook for people with multiple sclerosis. Recounts the ineffective efforts to treat the disease through spinal pacemakers and a drug which proved to be carcinogenic.
Health and Safety
Dist - FI **Prod** - BBCTV 1980

Prisoners of Incest
VHS / U-matic
Color (C G T A)
Examines the effects of incest on a family - the secrecy, guilt, fear, and lack of communication that distort the structure of a family's relationships. A family created from the experiences of social workers and psychiatrists at London's Hospital for Sick Children participate in a typical therapy session in which all of the family members discuss the father's actions and the effects of the situation.
Psychology; Sociology
Dist - PSU **Prod** - PSU 1985

Prisoners of Propaganda 58 MIN
VHS
Color (S)
$79.00 purchase _ #118 - 9024
Uncovers the facts behind the film made in 1943 by the Imperial Japanese Army Secret Service and Australian servicemen to show the 'exemplary conditions' prisoners of war supposedly enjoyed at the hands of their Japanese captors. Tells how the film was also intended to prepare the Australian public for Japanese occupation.
Geography - World; History - United States; Sociology
Dist - FI **Prod** - FLMAUS 1988

Prisoners of the Dunes 23 MIN
U-matic / VHS
Color (K)
Focuses on a strange community of insects, lizards and primitive mammals. Shows how these life forms have survived since prehistoric times.
Science - Natural
Dist - NWLDPR **Prod** - NWLDPR 1982

Prisoners of the sun 150 MIN
VHS
Natural world series
Color; PAL (H C A)
PdS150 purchase; Not available in the United States, Canada or Japan
Explores the idea that all life on earth is controlled by the sun. Provides images that contrast the power of nature with our man-made world. Includes sections on fuel rations, tight budgets, and energy wars.
Science - Natural; Science - Physical
Dist - BBCENE

Prisoners of the sun - Natural world series
Energy wars 50 MIN
Fuel rations 50 MIN
Tight budgets 50 MIN
Dist - BBCENE

Prisons for Profit - 208 30 MIN
U-matic
Currents - 1985 - 86 Season Series
Color (A)
Reveals the growing trend of private companies running prisons for the states and making a profit at it. Discusses the concerns this raises among some civil rights groups and politicians.
Social Science; Sociology
Dist - PBS **Prod** - WNETTV 1985

The Privacy Act of 1974 32 MIN
VHS / U-matic / 16mm
Color (PRO)
$340.00, $125.00 purchase _ #TCA16526, #TCA16527, #TCA16533
Outlines the provisions of the Privacy Act of 1974. Stresses the fact that people have a right of access to records that are kept on them. Shows that personal information does have limited access overall, however.
Business and Economics; Civics and Political Systems
Dist - USNAC **Prod** - USDD 1987

The Privacy Act of 1974 and its Relevancy to Medical Records 16 MIN
U-matic
Color
LC 79-708081
Gives an overview of the Privacy Act of 1974, explaining how it affects access to medical records and what its implications are for the staffs of VA health care facilities.
Civics and Political Systems; Health and Safety
Dist - USNAC **Prod** - VAHSL 1976

Privacy and the Press, Pt 10 60 MIN
VHS
Ethics in America Series
Color (C)
$8.00 rental _ #60870
Discusses how much the public has the right to know about a public official's conduct. Features journalists Peter Jennings, Mike Wallace and Katharine Graham, who join Geraldine Ferraro, former candidate for vice president, in a debate on the issue.
Civics and Political Systems; Fine Arts; Literature and Drama; Social Science
Dist - PSU

Privacy - can you buy it 20 MIN
U-matic / VHS / 16mm
Color
Examines various aspects of the increasing intrusion into people's privacy. Looks at some bugging devices, including a two - microphone unit built into a woman's bra which gives stereo sound. Shows that the use of the polygraph or lie - detector prior to hiring is becoming widespread in the United States.
Guidance and Counseling; Sociology
Dist - CNEMAG **Prod** - DOCUA

Privacy - homebuying - hotels - motels
VHS / U-matic
Consumer survival series
Color
Discusses various aspects of privacy, homebuying, and hotels and motels.
Business and Economics; Home Economics
Dist - MDCPB **Prod** - MDCPB

Privacy in the workplace - Unreasonable intrusion or legitimate interest 50 MIN
VHS
Color (A PRO C)
$95.00 purchase _ #Y161
Examines a number of privacy issues, such as drug screening, that arise in both the private and public employment sectors. Describes the judicial balancing test that should be applied by employers as a precaution when assessing the reasonableness, and legality, of workplace searches, testing and surveillance.
Civics and Political Systems; Sociology
Dist - ALIABA **Prod** - ALIABA 1992

Privacy rights vs the common good - new constitutional issues 18 MIN
35mm strip / VHS
Color (J H C T A)
$57.00, $48.00 purchase _ #MB - 540339 - 0, #MB - 540025 - 1
Examines the debate over privacy rights and the Constitution. Considers the Third, Fourth, Fifth and Ninth Amendments in terms of their impact on privacy.
Civics and Political Systems
Dist - SRA **Prod** - NYT 1989

Privacy - the Press at Your Door 29 MIN
U-matic / VHS
Inside Story Series
Color
Discusses the question of invasion of privacy by the press. Includes the parents of former hostage Richard Queen talking about how the press invaded their privacy when the news broke that their son was to be released from Iran.
Fine Arts; Literature and Drama; Social Science; Sociology
Dist - PBS **Prod** - PBS 1981

Private and Public Service - Cosmetic and Personal Services
VHS
Video Career Series
$29.95 purchase _ #MD303V
Shows students going 'on the job' to learn the variety of skills required for this occupation and the special training or educational requirements. Discusses various hiring procedures and what is involved in joining a professional association or union.
Education; Guidance and Counseling
Dist - CAREER **Prod** - CAREER

Private and Public Service - Fire Prevention and Firefighting
VHS
Video Career Series
$29.95 purchase _ #MD304V
Shows students going 'on the job' to learn the variety of skills required for this occupation and the special training or educational requirements. Discusses various hiring procedures and what is involved in joining a professional association or union.
Education; Guidance and Counseling
Dist - CAREER **Prod** - CAREER

Private and Public Service - Nursing and Paramedical
VHS
Video Career Series
$29.95 purchase _ #MD311V
Shows students going 'on the job' to learn the variety of skills required for this occupation and the special training or educational requirements. Discusses various hiring procedures and what is involved in joining a professional association or union.
Education; Guidance and Counseling
Dist - CAREER **Prod** - CAREER

Private and Public Service - Retailing and Merchandising
VHS
Video Career Series
$29.95 purchase _ #MD218V
Shows students going 'on the job' to learn the variety of skills required for this occupation and the special training or educational requirements. Discusses various hiring procedures and what is involved in joining a professional association or union.
Education; Guidance and Counseling
Dist - CAREER **Prod** - CAREER

Private Contentment 90 MIN
U-matic / VHS
Color (H C A)
LC 84-706189
Deals with the conflicts and emotions experienced by a young GI in 1945, who discovers his father's secret when he returns home for his mother's funeral before he is shipped overseas to fight the war.
Fine Arts; History - United States
Dist - FI **Prod** - WNETTV 1983

Private conversations on the set of Death of a Salesman 82 MIN
VHS
Color (H C G)
$89.00 purchase _ #DL73
Eavesdrops on heated discussions among actor, director and playwright. Shows how various interpretations of the play emerge and gives viewers insight into how each role contributed to the final production.
Fine Arts
Dist - INSIM **Prod** - PBS 1986

The Private Eyes 97 MIN
U-matic / VHS
Color (H C A)
Portrays two bumbling detectives, Doctor Tart and Inspector Winslip as they try to solve a complex double murder. Shows what happens when the two bumblers receive a letter from the victims authorizing them to investigate the homicide. Stars Tim Conway and Don Knotts.
Fine Arts
Dist - TIMLIF **Prod** - TIMLIF 1982

The Private history of a campaign that failed
VHS / U-matic
Films - on - video series
Color (G C J)
$59 purchase _ #05922 - 85
Re - enacts the story by Mark Twain concerning the doomed military campaign of a squad of soldiers during the Civil War.

Literature and Drama
Dist - CHUMAN

A Private Junior College 12 MIN
16mm
College Selection Film Series
Color (J)
LC 70-713110
Presents students of Mitchell Junior College who discuss the heavy academic support and structured lifestyle at a two - year school which serves as a stepping stone to four - year colleges. Shows that close student - teacher relationships and minimal social activities predominate.
Education; Guidance and Counseling; Sociology
Dist - VISED **Prod** - VISEDC 1971

Private life 102 MIN
16mm
Color (C A) (RUSSIAN (ENGLISH SUBTITLES))
LC 83-700202
Presents the story of a manager of a large Soviet factory who has spent all his time and energy on work and is now facing retirement. Shows him taking stock of his role as husband and father and of the many things he has neglected as he attempts to acquire a private life.
Fine Arts; Foreign Language
Dist - IFEX **Prod** - MOSFLM 1983

Private Life of a Cat 20 MIN
16mm
B&W (P)
Shows the female cat approaching labor and the birth of her five kittens, and then as she feeds and cares for them in the learning and growing process.
Science - Natural
Dist - GROVE **Prod** - HAMMID 1947

The Private life of Henry VIII 97 MIN
VHS
B&W (G)
$19.95 purchase _ #S00274
Presents a dramatic historically - based account of the life of King Henry VIII of England. Features period costumes. Stars Charles Laughton as Henry, with Elsa Lanchester as Anne of Cleves. Directed by Alexander Korda.
Civics and Political Systems; Fine Arts; History - World; Literature and Drama
Dist - UILL **Prod** - LONDON 1933
TWYMAN
VIDIM

The private life of plants 300 MIN
VHS
Color; PAL (A)
PdS300 series; not available in USA, Canada
Examines plant behavior in a six - part series of videos hosted by David Attenborough. Focuses on survival problems faced by plants. Includes episodes on the abilities of plants to move and colonize; trap energy and get sustenance from the air; use flowers to attract animals; compete for limited resources; grow in unlikely surroundings and survive in extreme conditions. Episodes are available individually.
Science - Natural
Dist - BBCENE

The private life of plants
Flowering 50 MINS.
Growing
Living together 50 MINS.
The social struggle 50 MINS.
Surviving 50 MINS
Travelling 50 MINS.
Dist - BBCENE

The Private life of the kingfisher 25 MIN
16mm / U-matic / VHS
Private lives series
Color (J H)
Traces the life cycle of the kingfisher, a bird found throughout the world. Follows a pair of birds through the year, from mating season and nesting to rearing their young until they are capable of self - sufficiency.
Science - Natural
Dist - FI **Prod** - BBCTV 1967

Private life - Pt 1 34 MIN
16mm
Color (C A) (RUSSIAN (ENGLISH SUBTITLES))
LC 83-700202
Presents the story of a manager of a large Soviet factory who has spent all his time and energy on work and is now facing retirement. Shows him taking stock of his role as husband and father and of the many things he has neglected as he attempts to acquire a private life.
Fine Arts
Dist - IFEX **Prod** - MOSFLM 1983

Private life - Pt 2 34 MIN
16mm
Color (C A) (RUSSIAN (ENGLISH SUBTITLES))
LC 83-700202
Presents the story of a manager of a large Soviet factory who has spent all his time and energy on work and is now facing retirement. Shows him taking stock of his role as husband and father and of the many things he has neglected as he attempts to acquire a private life.
Fine Arts
Dist - IFEX **Prod** - MOSFLM 1983

Private life - Pt 3 34 MIN
16mm
Color (C A) (RUSSIAN (ENGLISH SUBTITLES))
LC 83-700202
Presents the story of a manager of a large Soviet factory who has spent all his time and energy on work and is now facing retirement. Shows him taking stock of his role as husband and father and of the many things he has neglected as he attempts to acquire a private life.
Fine Arts
Dist - IFEX **Prod** - MOSFLM 1983

Private Lives of Americans Series
Mike and Lee Moore 28 MIN
Dist - KQEDTV

Private lives series
The Private life of the kingfisher 25 MIN
Dist - FI

Private pain - public burden 15 MIN
VHS
Color (G IND)
$95.00 purchase _ #SHA16337
Explores the issue of seat belts from economic and social perspectives. Offers a convincing argument for wearing seat belts.
Health and Safety; Industrial and Technical Education
Dist - USNAC **Prod** - NHTSA 1986

Private parts 17 MIN
16mm / VHS
Color (G)
$35.00 rental
Portrays Blake Sitney on summer days in this third in the series of in - camera edited films.
Biography; Fine Arts
Dist - CANCIN **Prod** - KELLEM 1988

Private Places 30 MIN
VHS / U-matic
In Our Own Image Series
Color (C)
Fine Arts
Dist - DALCCD **Prod** - DALCCD

Private Practices 20 MIN
U-matic / VHS
Color (C A)
Documents the experiences of a sexual surrogate and two of her clients. Profiles each client's progress.
Health and Safety; Psychology
Dist - MMRC **Prod** - KIRBDP

Private practices - the story of a sex surrogate 75 MIN
VHS / 16mm
Color (G)
$150.00 rental
Records the work of sex surrogate Maureen Sullivan. Directed by Kirby Dick.
Fine Arts; Psychology
Dist - KINOIC

The Private President - the Man and His Family 52 MIN
U-matic / VHS / 16mm
Presidency Series
Color (J)
Presents the wives of six presidents offering their behind - the - scenes views of life in the White House. Depicts some of the famous and infamous moments involving the women who have shared the office of the President.
Biography; Civics and Political Systems
Dist - LUF **Prod** - LUF 1976

Private property 20 MIN
16mm
Good life series
Color (S)
LC 81-700270
Uses a TV game show format to stress the importance of respecting others' possessions and taking care of one's own.
Guidance and Counseling; Social Science
Dist - HUBDSC **Prod** - DUDLYN 1981

A Private University 15 MIN
16mm
College Selection Film Series
Color (J H A)
LC 75-713106
Explores the strong influences of locale and climate on the atmosphere and programs of a university, using the University of Miami as an example. Shows that where the surrounding area offers interesting activities, students tend to use them for educational and extracurricular activities.
Education; Guidance and Counseling
Dist - VISEDC **Prod** - VISEDC 1971

Private victories 114 MIN
U-matic / VHS
K - 12 drug prevention video series
Color; Captioned (H)
$45.00, $84.00 purchase _ #TCA17526, #TCA17525
Presents four dramas on how drugs can affect school work, health, and family. Includes teacher's guide and information guide.
Guidance and Counseling; Health and Safety; Psychology
Dist - USNAC **Prod** - USDED 1988

Private victories - Episode 4 - Todd 25 MIN
VHS
Private victories - win one for yourself series
CC; Color (J H)
$99.00 purchase _ #10174VG
Tells the story of Todd, a teen drug pusher who learns hard lessons about what drug use does to him and his friends. Presents teens with information on drug abuse and how to prevent it. Includes a teacher's guide, discussion questions, and student activities. Part four of a four - part series.
Psychology
Dist - UNL

Private victories - Episode 1 - Bobby 25 MIN
VHS
Private victories - win one for yourself series
CC; Color (J H)
$99.00 purchase _ #10171VG
Presents the story of Bobby, a championship athlete who becomes involved with cocaine and ends up in a coma after a heart attack. Shows students the effects of drug use and how to prevent it. Includes a teacher's guide, discussion questions and student activities. Part one of a four - part series.
Psychology
Dist - UNL

Private victories - Episode 3 - Jackie and Stacy 25 MIN
VHS
Private victories - win one for yourself series
CC; Color (J H)
$99.00 purchase _ #10173VG
Features two friends, one of whom gets involved with crack. Presents the effects of drug use on oneself and on relationships. Includes a teacher's guide, discussion questions, and student activities. Part three of a four - part series.
Guidance and Counseling; Psychology
Dist - UNL

Private victories - Episode 2 - Hank 25 MIN
VHS
Private victories - win one for yourself series
CC; Color (J H)
$99.00 purchase _ #10172VG
Tells the story of Hank, a new student who confronts drug dealers and users. Shows how Hank and other students form a rock band and deal with peer drug users. Includes a teacher's guide, discussion questions, and student activities. Part two of a four - part series.
Psychology
Dist - UNL

Private victories - win one for yourself series 100 MIN
VHS
Private victories - win one for yourself series
CC; Color (J H)
$297 purchase _ #10170VG
Presents four stories of teens who became involved in drugs and their problems. Addresses the negative aspects of drug use through the stories of an athlete who took cocaine; a new student who faces pressure to use drugs; a girl involved with crack; and a teen drug pusher. Includes four videos, teacher's guide, discussion questions and activities.
Guidance and Counseling; Psychology
Dist - UNL

Private victories - win one for yourself series
Private victories - Episode 4 - Todd 25 MIN
Private victories - Episode 1 - Bobby 25 MIN
Private victories - Episode 3 - Jackie and Stacy 25 MIN
Private victories - Episode 2 - Hank 25 MIN
Private victories - win one for yourself series 100 MIN
Dist - UNL

A Private view - National Gallery series
VHS
Private view - National Gallery series
Color (G)
#A4-ODY136-175
Presents a six-part survey of the history of European art by art critic Edward Mullins. Examines various styles, schools, and key personalities of European art illustrated through the collection of London's National Gallery. Includes works about the birth of European painting; early Renaissance in Italy and the northern Renaissance; the age of Titian and the age of Leonardo; the age of Rubens and the age of Rembrandt; El Greco to Goya and the Baroque in France and Italy; and the British achievement and the road to Modern art. Videos available separately. Produced by Odyssey.
Fine Arts
Dist - AVP

Private violence - public crisis series
Acquaintance violence 16 MIN
Discussion openers 22 MIN
Domestic violence 17 MIN
Teen violence 29 MIN
Dist - CORF

The Private world of Emily Dickinson 27 MIN
VHS
Color (J H)
$99.00 purchase _ #06219 - 026
Explores the passion, precision and variety of Dickinson's poetry through excerpts from her verse, letters and notes to friends. Looks at her personal relationships, exposure to transcendentalism, quiet rebellion against religious orthodoxy and self - imposed isolation. Includes teacher's guide and library kit.
Education; Literature and Drama
Dist - GA

Private Yankee Doodle 28 MIN
VHS
While soldiers fought series
Color (H C G)
$180.00 purchase, $19.00 rental _ #35751
Looks at the rigorous life of a Revolutionary War soldier to underscore evolving perceptions of warfare from the 18th to the 20th centuries. Part of a seven - part series which examines the impact of war on American society from historical, literary, artistic and philosophical perspectives. Produced by the International University Consortium.
History - United States; Sociology
Dist - PSU

Private Yankee Doodle 30 MIN
U-matic / VHS
Color
Discusses the American Revolution with special emphasis on the daily routine of the common soldier. Recreates an entire Continental Army Camp with 250 soldiers.
History - United States
Dist - MDCPB **Prod** - MDCPB

Privatisation 30 MIN
VHS
Inside Britain 1 series
Color; PAL; NTSC (G) (BULGARIAN CZECH HUNGARIAN SPANISH POLISH ROMANIAN RUSSIAN SLOVAK UKRAINIAN ENGLISH WITH ARABIC SUBTITLES)
PdS65 purchase
Asks if privatization is an answer to an ailing economy and falling profits. Reveals that in the United Kingdom many public services have been taken out of the state sector to be run on behalf of their shareholders. British Steel and the National Freight Corporation stand as particularly successful examples.
Business and Economics
Dist - CFLVIS **Prod** - INFVIS 1991

Privilege 26 MIN
VHS / U-matic
Two by Forsyth Series
Color
Presents the story of a dealer in rare stamps who takes the law into his own hands when he is libeled by an unscrupulous newspaper columnist. Stars Milo O'Shea and Patrick Bedford.
Literature and Drama
Dist - FOTH **Prod** - FOTH 1984

The Privilege of Walking 50 MIN
16mm
B&W (PRO)
Shows several children undergoing procedures to help them walk normally, including a boy with scoliosis who has a cast applied to help straighten his spine, a baby with congenital hip dislocation who is placed in traction, a boy with Perthes disease who must wear a shoebar to help restore his hip joint and a boy with osteochondroma who has bony growths removed surgically.
Health and Safety
Dist - LAWREN **Prod** - CMA

Privileges for the trial and business lawyer 120 MIN
VHS / Cassette / U-matic
Color; Mono (PRO)
Features three trial attorneys as they discuss the procedures for handling privileges in the context of both California and federal law. Emphasizes attorney and client privileges, the attorney - work product rule and the special problems that arise with joint clients, expert witenesses and consultants, and internal corporate investigations.
Civics and Political Systems
Dist - CCEB **Prod** - CCEB
ABACPE

The Prize 73 MIN
16mm / VHS / U-matic
Color (H A)
$49.95 video purchase, $66.00 film rental
Tells how a free style skier rediscovers his Christian faith.
Physical Education and Recreation; Religion and Philosophy
Dist - CAFM **Prod** - CAFM 1978
OUTRCH OUTRCH

The Prize 15 MIN
VHS / U-matic
La bonne aventure series
Color (K P)
Deals with French - Americans. Focuses on family rivalries.
Guidance and Counseling; Sociology
Dist - GPN **Prod** - MPBN

The Prize and pawn of empires 22 MIN
VHS
Mississippi River series
Color (I J)
$89.00 purchase _ #RB830
Traces the history of the Mississippi River from the time of the Moundbuilders through the War of 1812 up to the steamboat era. Part of a series on the Mississippi River.
Geography - United States; History - United States
Dist - REVID **Prod** - REVID

The Prize that was won and lost and another life - Volume 4 45 MIN
VHS
Flying house series
Color (K P I R)
$11.99 purchase _ #35 - 8953 - 979
Uses an animated format to present events from the New Testament era, as three children, a professor and a robot travel in the 'Flying House' back to that time. 'The Prize That Was Won and Lost' reviews the life of John the Baptist, while 'Another Life' tells the story of Jairus' daughter being raised from the dead.
Literature and Drama; Religion and Philosophy
Dist - APH **Prod** - TYHP

Prize - winning pictures 30 MIN
VHS
Color (G)
$24.95 purchase _ #S00939
Features two photo experts with advice to photographers on how to improve the quality of their picture.
Business and Economics; Industrial and Technical Education
Dist - UILL **Prod** - EKC

The Prizewinners 59 MIN
16mm
Color
LC 79-700110
Focuses on Rosalyn Yallow, Roger Guillemin and Andrew Schally, the Veterans Administration's Nobel laureates of 1977. Presents a portrait of their personalities and describes their scientific backgrounds, research methods and the impact of their research on patient care.
Biography; Health and Safety
Dist - USNAC **Prod** - USVA 1978

The Prizewinners - Pt 1 30 MIN
16mm
Color
LC 79-700110
Focuses on Rosalyn Yallow, Roger Guillemin and Andrew Schally, the Veterans Administration's Nobel laureates of 1977. Presents a portrait of their personalities and describes their scientific backgrounds, research methods and the impact of their research on patient care.
History - World
Dist - USNAC **Prod** - USVA 1978

Pro and con 8 MIN
VHS
Color (H C A)
$195.00 purchase
Combines animated graphic images and interviews with a professional corrections officer and a prisoner serving 15 years for armed robbery to highlight the stark realities of prison life. Puts a human face on the facts and fiction of incarceration without being judgmental and opens the door for discussion. Useful for viewing by at - risk youth, criminal justice professionals and sociology classes. Produced by Joanna Priestly and Joan Gratz.
Sociology
Dist - PFP

The Pro Arte String Quartet in Rehearsal 15 MIN
VHS / U-matic
Chamber Music - the String Quartet Series
Color (I J H)
Fine Arts
Dist - AITECH **Prod** - NETCHE 1977

Pro blackjack - winning techniques
VHS
Color (G)
$29.95 purchase _ #IV003
Presents professional Nick Daniels playing actual games and discussing winning decisions.
Physical Education and Recreation
Dist - SIV

Pro Bowl Classic 27 MIN
16mm
Color (J)
LC FIA68-1409
Highlights the activities surrounding the 1967 NFL Pro Bowl game in which the East defeated the West by a score of 20 to 10.
Physical Education and Recreation
Dist - NFL **Prod** - NFL 1967

Pro Bowl Classic - 1959 through 1962 Series
Pro Bowl Classic - 1960 30 MIN
Dist - NBCTV

Pro Bowl Classic - 1960 30 MIN
16mm
Pro Bowl Classic - 1959 through 1962 Series
B&W
Physical Education and Recreation
Dist - NBCTV **Prod** - NBCTV

Pro chess - Volume 1 120 MIN
VHS
Video chess mentor series
Color (G)
$29.95 purchase _ #IV001
Presents Grandmaster Yasser Seirawan explaining basics to beginners and 14 tactics to intermediate players.
Physical Education and Recreation
Dist - SIV

Pro chess - Volume 2 120 MIN
VHS
Video chess mentor series
Color (G)
$29.95 purchase _ #IV002
Presents Grandmaster Yasser Seirawan explaining advanced concepts to intermediate players and presenting master players with tips on subtler maneuvers.
Physical Education and Recreation
Dist - SIV

Pro - chess - Volumes 1 & 2 240 MIN
VHS
Video chess mentor series
Color (G)
$59.90 _ #IV100
Presents lessons on playing chess from basic concepts to advanced, subtle maneuvers.
Physical Education and Recreation
Dist - SIV

Pro Driving Attitudes 16 MIN
16mm / U-matic / VHS
Color (H C A)
LC 79-700038
Shows why professional automobile drivers have better safety records and demonstrates four attitudes characteristic of professional drivers.
Health and Safety
Dist - AIMS **Prod** - PORTA 1977

Pro driving attitudes 16 MIN
U-matic / VHS / 16mm
Color (H C A) (SPANISH)
Shows why professional automobile drivers have better safety records and demonstrates four attitudes characteristic of professional drivers.
Health and Safety
Dist - AIMS **Prod** - AIMS 1977

Pro Driving Tactics 15 MIN
16mm / U-matic / VHS
Color (H C A) (SPANISH)
LC 79-7900881
Uses animation to dramatize tactics that can be used to avoid hazardous driving situations.
Health and Safety
Dist - AIMS **Prod** - PORTA 1977

Pro Football - Mayhem on a Sunday Afternoon 58 MIN
16mm
Color
LC FIA66-1728
Surveys the history of football as a game, a business and a sociological phenomenon from 14th - century England to the present. Shows football teams in their training camps, class sessions and locker rooms. Includes highlights of a game between the Cleveland Browns and the San Francisco Forty - niners.
Physical Education and Recreation
Dist - WOLPER **Prod** - MMAMC 1965

Pro - karate championships
U-matic / VHS
Color
Physical Education and Recreation; Sociology
Dist - MSTVIS **Prod** - MSTVIS

Pro Ski Racers 13 MIN
16mm
Color
LC 77-702618
Shows Spider Sabich and others competing in the world championship dual slalom and giant slalom ski races in Montreal.
Physical Education and Recreation
Dist - CANFDC **Prod** - FLTHMK 1975

Pro Sports 15 MIN
VHS / U-matic / BETA
Career Success Series
(H C A)
$29.95 _ #MX214
Portrays occupations in professional sports by reviewing required abilities and interviewing people employed in this field. Tells of the anxieties and rewards involved in pursuing a career in professional sports.
Education; Guidance and Counseling; Physical Education and Recreation
Dist - CAMV **Prod** - CAMV

Pro Ten - Different and Better 8 MIN
16mm
Color
LC 77-700403
Explains the research, development and testing of Pro Ten pre - tendered beef products.
Business and Economics; Home Economics
Dist - CINEMR **Prod** - CINEMR 1976

Proactive customer service
VHS
Telephone doctor series
Color; CC (A PRO)
Features Nancy Friedman, customer service consultant, to help CSRs represent their organization well. Offers numerous tips and practice guidelines. Part eight of a 16-part series of humorous programs for training in telephone skills that are designed to enhance long-term behavior modification. Includes leader's guide and participant workbook.
Business and Economics; Social Science; Sociology
Dist - EXTR **Prod** - TELDOC

ProArt Professional Art Library
ProArt trilogy 1
ProArt trilogy 2
ProArt trilogy 3
Dist - BEP

ProArt Professional Library
ProArt trilogy 4
Dist - BEP

ProArt trilogy 1
CD-ROM
ProArt Professional Art Library
(G)
$375.00 purchase _ #1552
Contains a selection of illustrations from Multi - Ad Services, Inc using Adobe Illustrator software. Includes 300 images in the following subject areas - business, holidays, and sports. Illustrations are in the Encapsulated PostScript - EPS - format, and can be scaled up or down. For IBM PCs and compatibles, requires at least 640K RAM, DOS 3.1 or later, one floppy disk drive - hard disk recommended, one empty expansion slot, and an IBM compatible CD - ROM drive. For Macintosh Classic, Plus, SE and II computers, requires 1MB of RAM, one floppy drive, and an Apple compatible CD - ROM drive.
Computer Science; Industrial and Technical Education
Dist - BEP

ProArt trilogy 2
CD-ROM
ProArt Professional Art Library
(G)
$375.00 purchase _ #1553
Contains a selection of illustrations from Multi - Ad Services, Inc using Adobe Illustrator software. Includes 300 images in the following subject areas - food, people, and borders and headings. Illustrations are in the Encapsulated PostScript - EPS - format, and can be scaled up or down. For IBM PCs and compatibles, requires at least 640K RAM, DOS 3.1 or later, one floppy disk drive - hard disk recommended, one empty expansion slot, and an IBM compatible CD - ROM drive. For Macintosh Classic, Plus, SE and II computers, requires 1MB of RAM, one floppy drive, and an Apple compatible CD - ROM drive.
Computer Science; Industrial and Technical Education
Dist - BEP

ProArt trilogy 3
CD-ROM
ProArt Professional Art Library
(G)
$375.00 purchase _ #1554
Contains a selection of illustrations from Multi - Ad Services, Inc using Adobe Illustrator software. Includes 300 images in the following subject areas - religious images, Christmas, and generic products. Illustrations are in the Encapsulated PostScript - EPS - format, and can be scaled up or down. For IBM PCs and compatibles, requires 640K RAM, DOS 3.1 or later, one floppy disk drive - hard disk recommended, one empty expansion slot, and an IBM compatible CD - ROM drive. For Macintosh Classic, Plus, SE and II computers, requires 1MB of RAM, one floppy drive, and an Apple compatible CD - ROM drive.
Computer Science; Industrial and Technical Education
Dist - BEP

ProArt trilogy 4
CD-ROM
ProArt Professional Library
(G)
$375.00 purchase _ #1555
Contains a selection of illustrations from Multi - Ad Services, Inc using Adobe Illustrator software. Includes 300 images in the following subject areas - education, business, health and medicine. Illustrations are in the Encapsulated PostScript - EPS - format, and can be scaled up or down. For IBM PCs and compatibles, requires at least 640K RAM, DOS 3.1 or later, one floppy disk drive - hard disk recommended, one empty expansion slot, and an IBM compatible CD - ROM drive. For Macintosh Classic, Plus, SE and II computers, requires 1MB of RAM, one floppy drive, and an Apple compatible CD - ROM drive.
Computer Science; Industrial and Technical Education
Dist - BEP

The Probabilities of Zero and One 11 MIN
U-matic / VHS / 16mm
Color (I J)
LC 75-703101
Demonstrates how situations which involve chance are stated as probabilities. Presents basic concepts of probability.
Mathematics
Dist - PHENIX **Prod** - BAILEY 1969

Probabilities, Pt 1 20 MIN
U-matic
Mainly Math Series
Color (H C)
Discusses the various conditions and characteristics of probabilities. Identifies the value of using numbers to predict occurrences and extend statistics.
Mathematics
Dist - GPN **Prod** - WCVETV 1977

Probabilities, Pt 2 20 MIN
U-matic
Mainly Math Series
Color (H C)
Introduces probabilities and the Fundamental Counting Principle.
Mathematics
Dist - GPN **Prod** - WCVETV 1977

Probability
VHS
Color (H C)
$79.95 purchase _ #VAD007
Presents two videocassettes teaching probability. Includes step - by - step instruction in 142 probability problems.
Mathematics
Dist - SIV

Probability 15 MIN
U-matic
Mathematical relationship series
Color (I)
Looks at the odds with a view to predicting probabilities both mathematical and empirical.
Mathematics
Dist - TVOTAR **Prod** - TVOTAR 1982

Probability 11 MIN
VHS
Children's encyclopedia of mathematics - pre - algebra series
Color (I)
$49.95 purchase _ #8369
Discusses probability. Part of a nine - part series about preparing the student for algebra.
Mathematics
Dist - AIMS **Prod** - DAVFMS 1991

Probability - an Introduction 9 MIN
U-matic / VHS / 16mm
Color (I J)
LC 76-700650
Explains some of the fundamental principles of probability, using a disc, a lettered cube, a set of numbered cards and several everyday situations. Demonstrates how the verbal description of a probability may be written as a simple equation.
Mathematics
Dist - PHENIX **Prod** - BOUNDY 1969

Probability and its Uses 13 MIN
U-matic / 16mm / VHS
Color (I J)
$315, $220 purchase _ #3161; LC 73-700819
Discusses mathematical probability and its use in predicting the likelihood of future events. Defines such probability terms as event, outcome, sample space, tree diagram and sampling.
Mathematics
Dist - CORF **Prod** - CORF 1972

Probability and random processes - elementary probability theory - a series
Probability and random processes - elementary probability theory'series
B&W (PRO)
Reveals the widespread applicability of probability theory. Conditional Probability; Conditional Probability (2); Conditional Probability - A Digital - ; Elementary Set Theory; Formulation Of Mathematical Models (1); Formulation Of Mathematical Models (2); Introduction To Probability; Joint Probability; Probablistic Models; Product Spaces And Statistically Independent - ; Proof By Induction; Statistical Independence; Theorem Proving.
Mathematics
Dist - MIOT **Prod** - MIOT

Probability and Random Processes - Elementary Probability Theory Series
Conditional Probability - a Digital Communications Example 29 MIN
Conditional Probability (1) 18 MIN
Conditional Probability (2) 26 MIN
Introduction to Probability 35 MIN
Joint Probability 19 MIN
Probablistic models 45 MIN
Product Spaces and Statistically Independent Experiments 17 MIN
Proof by Induction 16 MIN
Statistical Independence 19 MIN
Theorem Proving 18 MIN
Dist - MIOT

Probability and random processes - elementary probability theory series
Elementary set theory 29 MIN
Formulation of mathematical models 1 22 MIN
Formulation of mathematical models 2 30 MIN
Probability and random processes - elementary probability theory - a series
Dist - MIOT

Probability and Random Processes Introduction to Random Processes Series
Binary transmission wave 32 MIN
Introduction to Random Processes 33 MIN
The Role of the Covariance Function in Estimation 22 MIN
Second - Moment Characterizations 38 MIN
Dist - MIOT

Probability and random processes introduction to random processes series
Fixed - form random processes 34 MIN
Random processes - basic concepts and definitions 28 MIN
Random telegraph wave 24 MIN
Dist - MIOT

Probability and random processes - limit theorems and statistics - a series
Probability and random processes - limit theorems and statistics - a'series
B&W (PRO)
Discusses limit theorems and statistics. Central Limit Theorem; Estimation Of The Moments Of A Random - ; Estimation Of The Parameter Of A Probability - ; Estimation Of The Probability Density Of A -; Gaussian Approximation, The; Introduction To Statistical Inference; Performance Bounds - The Cramer Rao - ; Relative Frequency; Sample Means And The Weak Law Of Large Numbers.

Mathematics
Dist - MIOT **Prod** - MIOT

Probability and random processes - limit theorems and statistics - a series
Probability and random processes - limit theorems and statistics - a series
Dist - MIOT

Probability and Random Processes - Limit Theorems and Statistics Series
Central Limit Theorem 35 MIN
Estimation of the Moments of a Random Variable 37 MIN
Estimation of the Parameter of a Probability Density 27 MIN
Estimation of the Probability Density of a Random Variable 36 MIN
The Gaussian Approximation 33 MIN
Introduction to Statistical Inference 18 MIN
Performance Bounds - the Cramer Rao Inequality 28 MIN
Sample Means and the Weak Law of Large Numbers 30 MIN
Dist - MIOT

Probability and random processes - limit theorems and statistics series
Relative frequency 18 MIN
Dist - MIOT

Probability and Random Processes - Linear Systems Series
Complex exponential inputs - frequency domain analysis 28 MIN
Convolution integral 16 MIN
Fourier Series Demonstration 15 MIN
Fourier Transform Properties 42 MIN
Fourier Transforms 33 MIN
Linear System Descriptions 40 MIN
Measurement of Impulse Response 11 MIN
Periodic Inputs and Fourier Series 28 MIN
Sampling theorem 28 MIN
System Classification 27 MIN
System Descriptions 22 MIN
System Functions 35 MIN
Dist - MIOT

Probability and Random Processes - Random Variables Series
Canonical Random Variables 11 MIN
Conditioning 15 MIN
Conditioning by Sets 16 MIN
Continuous Random Variables 34 MIN
A Digital communication application 49 MIN
Functions of a Random Variable 22 MIN
Functions of Vector Random Variables - 1 19 MIN
Functions of Vector Random Variables - 2 11 MIN
Impulsive Densities 18 MIN
Mixed Random Variables 30 MIN
Multiple Random Variables - Discrete 34 MIN
Point Conditioning 17 MIN
Random variables - Pt 1 26 MIN
Random variables - Pt 2 20 MIN
Reliability Applications 30 MIN
Statistically - Independent Random Variables 25 MIN
Dist - MIOT

Probability and Random Processes - Statistical Averages Series
Characteristic Functions 25 MIN
The Chebyshev inequality 29 MIN
Conditional Expectation 13 MIN
Estimation of Random Variables 23 MIN
Expectations of Functions of a Random Variable 23 MIN
Joint Moments - Correlation 27 MIN
Linear Estimation 44 MIN
Minimum Mean - Square Error Estimation 18 MIN
Moments of a Random Variable 18 MIN
Statistical Averages - Expectation of a Random Variable 19 MIN
Dist - MIOT

Probability and Statistics
U-matic / VHS
Color
Teaches the computation of chance or probability. Discusses predicting events using probability. Describes how to collect and organize data and present information on charts, tables and graphs.
Mathematics
Dist - EDUACT **Prod** - EDUACT

Probability and statistics series
Provides resource material for help in the study of probability and statistics. Presents a 60 - video series, each part 25 to 30 minutes long, that explains and reinforces concepts using definitions, theorems, examples and step - by - step solutions to tutor the student. Videos are also available separately.
Bayes theorem
Binomial distribution
Central limit theorem
Coefficient correlation
Combinations
Conditional probability
Confidence intervals and hypothesis tests I
Confidence intervals and hypothesis tests II
Confidence intervals and hypothesis tests III
Confidence intervals and hypothesis tests IV
Confidence intervals for difference of means
Confidence intervals for proportions
Confidence intervals for variance and chi - square
Confidence intervals with variance known
Continuous random variables and densities
Expectations of random variables
Frequency distributions
Goodness of fit
Hypothesis testing
Hypothesis tests about mean
Hypothesis tests for difference of means
Hypothesis tests of proportions
Hypothesis tests of variance
Hypothesis tests with variance unknown
Independent events
Independent random variables
Index of predictive association
Mean
Means, medians, and modes of grouped data
Mode, median, and midrange
Model of equally likely outcomes
Multiplication principle for counting
Normal approximation to binomial
Normal distribution and distribution and standardization
Normality test
One - way analysis of variance
Permutations and factorials
Poisson distribution
Populations and data
Prediction intervals
Probability laws and gambling odds
Random variables and distributions
Rank test
Runs test
Sample spaces and events
Sampling distribution to mean
Sign test
Spearman rank correlation
Standard error of mean
Standard error of regression
T - distribution and confidence intervals
Tchebychev's approximation
Two - sample design
Two - way analysis of variance I
Two - way analysis of variance II
Two variance goodness of fit and independence
Variance and standard deviation
Variance of random variables
Visual display of data
Dist - LANDMK

Probability and the binomial distribution 30 MIN
U-matic / VHS
Engineering statistics series
Color (IND)
Incorporates a general introduction to probability rules, and discusses development of the binomial probability distribution and the underlying distribution for the proportion defective in a process.
Industrial and Technical Education; Mathematics
Dist - COLOSU **Prod** - COLOSU

Probability and uncertainty 57 MIN
Videoreel / VHS
Feynman lectures - the character of physical law series
B&W
Considers the behavior of electrons and photons according to the theories of quantum mechanics. Discusses single and double slit experiments.
Science - Physical
Dist - EDC **Prod** - EDC

Probability And\Random Processes - Averages Series
Joint Characteristic Functions 25 MIN
Dist - MIOT

Probability distributions
U-matic / VHS
Statistics for managers series
Color (IND)
Continues discussion of go/no - go data where sample sizes are large or small. Discusses use of the normal and Poisson distributions to approximate the binomial, along with general use of the Poisson and hypergeometric distributions.
Business and Economics; Mathematics; Psychology
Dist - COLOSU **Prod** - COLOSU

Probability for decision analysis 1 - fundamentals 55 MIN
U-matic / VHS
Decision analysis series
Color
Mathematics
Dist - MIOT **Prod** - MIOT

Probability for Decision Analysis 2 - Random Variables 57 MIN
VHS / U-matic
Decision Analysis Series
Color
Mathematics
Dist - MIOT **Prod** - MIOT

Probability I 14 MIN
VHS / U-matic
Math Matters Series Green Module
Color (I J)
Presents the basic concepts of probability using a gumball machine, a gypsy fortuneteller and a probability counseling booth.
Mathematics
Dist - AITECH **Prod** - KRLNTV 1975

Probability I 20 MIN
U-matic / VHS
Math Topics - Statistics Series
Color (J H C)
Mathematics
Dist - FI **Prod** - BBCTV

Probability II 20 MIN
U-matic / VHS
Math Topics - Statistics Series
Color (J H C)
Mathematics
Dist - FI **Prod** - BBCTV

Probability II 14 MIN
VHS / U-matic
Math Matters Series Green Module
Color (I J)
Shows how the possibility of winning a free meal at a restaurant called Fat Chance draws the characters into a challenging probability exercise.
Mathematics
Dist - AITECH **Prod** - KRLNTV 1975

Probability laws and gambling odds
VHS
Probability and statistics series
Color (H C)
$125.00 purchase _ #8009
Provides resource material about probability laws, the meaning of odds, and how to figure them for help in the study of probability and statistics. Part of a 60 - video series, each part 25 to 30 minutes long, that explains and reinforces concepts using definitions, theorems, examples and step - by - step solutions to tutor the student. Videos are also available in a set.
Mathematics
Dist - LANDMK

Probability - possible outcomes 15 MIN
VHS / U-matic
Math works series
Color (I)
Looks at the relationship between possible outcome and probability in examples that include both one out of five and two out of five.
Mathematics
Dist - AITECH **Prod** - AITECH

Probable cause and the scope of searches 50 MIN
U-matic / VHS
Criminal procedure and the trial advocate series
Color (PRO)
Explains the requirements of a valid warrant, probable cause and the scope of a search. Discusses who may issue the warrant and the implications of a flaw in the warrant.
Civics and Political Systems
Dist - ABACPE **Prod** - ABACPE

Probable cause - search and seizure 25 MIN
U-matic / VHS / 16mm
Law enforcement - patrol procedures series
Color (PRO)
Covers how police can determine probable cause to search, seize and arrest with or without a warrant. Shows how to obtain eyewitness information, use a police informant and obtain a warrant.
Civics and Political Systems
Dist - CORF **Prod** - MTROLA 1973

The Probable Passing of Elk Creek 60 MIN
VHS / U-matic
Color (G)
Focuses on a contemporary controversy to encourage viewers to think about the forces that shape our society. The little town of Elk Creek and the Grindstone Indian Reservation are both located in a small valley in Northern California. The state government plans to build a reservoir over the valley, which will force both whites and Native Americans to leave their homeland. Ironically, the law gives the Native Americans the power to decide whether or not the dam will be built.
Social Science
Dist - NAMPBC **Prod** - NAMPBC 1984

The Probable Passing of Elk Creek 60 MIN
16mm / U-matic / VHS
Color (J)
Portrays a controversy in Elk Creek, California, in which the state government plans to build a reservoir in a valley that would force the white people and the Indians to leave their homes. Reveals that the Indians have the power to decide whether the the dam is built.
Social Science; Sociology
Dist - CNEMAG **Prod** - TOCAYO 1982

Probableman 14 MIN
U-matic
Color (P)
Explores the exploits of a part - time superhero named Probableman. Introduces the relative frequency notion of probability.
Mathematics
Dist - GA **Prod** - DAVFMS

Probablistic models 45 MIN
U-matic / VHS
Probability and random processes - elementary probability theory 'series
B&W (PRO)
Covers the five basic axioms of probability theory.
Mathematics
Dist - MIOT **Prod** - MIOT

Probe 7 MIN
U-matic / VHS
Color
Introduces a group of women discussing personal sexual experiences related to vibrators. Presented by Carol Porter and Joan Valdes.
Psychology; Sociology
Dist - ARTINC **Prod** - ARTINC

Probe labelling strategies and cloning techniques 96 MIN
VHS
DNA technology in forensic science series
Color (A PRO)
$50.00 purchase _ #TCA17407
Presents two lectures on DNA technology in forensic science. Covers subjects including isotopic and nonisotopic labelling methods, recombinant DNA technology, screening genomic libraries, and more.
Science - Natural; Sociology
Dist - USNAC **Prod** - FBI 1988

PROBE - pattern recognition of behavioral events 14 MIN
16mm
Color (H C)
LC 80-700557
Describes the application of computer pattern recognition programs to the study of primate behavior and shows how such data can be correlated with morphological changes. Demonstrates the sensitivity of the method in detecting alterations of spontaneous behavior by toxicologic and pharmacologic insults.
Mathematics; Psychology
Dist - IOWA **Prod** - ISURF 1979

Probing a new domain 45 MIN
U-matic / VHS
Artificial intelligence series; Fundamental concepts, Pt 1
Color (PRO)
Helps in understanding success and failure, moving from ad hoc heuristics to constraint - based algorithms, and an illustration.
Mathematics
Dist - MIOT **Prod** - MIOT

Probing for the Sale 20 MIN
U-matic / 16mm / VHS
Color (H C A) (SPANISH)
LC 81-706213; 81-700329
Depicts Art asking Claire, a successful salesperson, about her selling style and customer contacts.
Business and Economics
Dist - CRMP **Prod** - CRMP 1981

Probing Mind 29 MIN
U-matic
B&W
Describes the uses of new educational media, such as films, television, recordings, teaching machines and well equipped laboratories in the teaching of high school science.
Education; Science
Dist - USNAC **Prod** - USNAC 1972

A Probing mind 29 MIN
16mm
B&W (C T)
Illustrates the uses of new educational media - films, television, recordings and teaching machines. Explains the importance of well - equipped laboratories for teaching high school science classes.
Education
Dist - USNAC **Prod** - USOE 1961

Probing planetary processes 15 MIN
16mm
Science in action series
Color (C)
Examines the possible explanations for the formation and evolution of the earth and moon. Utilizes data provided by the Apollo Lunar Missions and the Glomar Challenger Drilling Project.
Science; Science - Physical
Dist - COUNFI **Prod** - ALLFP

Probing - Questions that Help You Sell 10 MIN
U-matic / VHS / 16mm
Color
LC 79-706195
Demonstrates a technique of asking questions to find out why, what and how much a prospective customer will buy.
Business and Economics; Psychology
Dist - SALENG **Prod** - SALENG 1979

Probing the Continental Margin 23 MIN
16mm
Color (J)
LC 72-701524
Describes life and work on board two ships as men survey the Australian continental shelf and slopes.
Geography - World; Science; Science - Physical
Dist - AUIS **Prod** - ANAIB 1971

Probing the Mysteries of Sleep
VHS
Ater of the Night - the Science of Sleep and Dreams Series
Color
Examines sleep deprivation, REM and non - REM sleep, and myths about normal lengths of sleep. Traces the progress of a volunteer through a night at a sleep lab.
Health and Safety; Psychology
Dist - IBIS **Prod** - IBIS

Probing the Secrets of the Stomach 18 MIN
16mm
Color
Depicts the functions and organisms of the stomach of a mammal using a microscope. Shows the secretions of gastric acid by the mucous membrane and hydrochloric acid and pepsinogen by the cells. Follows the changes that occur in the secretions when acetylcholine and gastrin come into contact with these cells.
Science - Natural
Dist - UNIJAP **Prod** - UNIJAP 1969

The Problem 13 MIN
U-matic / VHS / 16mm
Color
An animated puppet film that centers on the question of what color the trash box in a large organization should be painted. Examines the dehumanizing effect of bureaucracies and raises questions concerning the nature of responsibility and the individual's reaction to it.
Guidance and Counseling; Sociology
Dist - FI **Prod** - BF 1966

The Problem 30 MIN
U-matic / VHS
Ecology - our road to survival series
Color
Discusses the complexity of contemporary environmental problems, for example, man's use of chemical pesticides which are beginning to have effects they were never intended to have on the environment.
Science - Natural; Sociology
Dist - NETCHE **Prod** - NETCHE 1971

Problem children 20 MIN
16mm
B&W (C)
Presents the story of two junior high school boys and how their personalities are affected by their relationships in home and school. Illustrates how parents and teachers can and should work together.
Education; Psychology; Sociology
Dist - PSUPCR **Prod** - ODPW 1947

The Problem class 30 MIN
16mm
B&W (T)
Records the strategies used by a University Elementary School staff teacher to overcome severe behavior problems in an inner - city classroom. Includes Dr Madeline Hunter's comments on the episodes to point out the power of basic learning principles in the hands of a teacher who understands how to use those principles.
Education; Psychology
Dist - SPF **Prod** - SPF

Problem Diagnosis 35 MIN
U-matic / VHS
Situation Management Series
Color
Business and Economics; Psychology
Dist - DELTAK **Prod** - EXECDV

Problem dogs 30 MIN
VHS / U-matic
Training dogs the Woodhouse way
Color (H C A)
Shows Barbara Woodhouse's method of handling problem dogs.
Physical Education and Recreation; Science - Natural
Dist - FI **Prod** - BBCTV 1982

Problem Drinker - Driver 6 MIN
16mm
Color
LC 75-703699
Shows how a center in Nassau County, New York, aids drivers who have drinking problems. Discusses several cases and suggests how they can be helped.
Health and Safety; Psychology; Sociology
Dist - USNAC **Prod** - USHTSA 1974

Problem exercises - staff - inmate relations 18 MIN
VHS / 16mm
Correctional officer series
Color (PRO)
$345.00 purchase, $75.00 rental _ #8157
Dramatizes problem situations correctional officers encounter on the job.
Computer Science; Psychology; Sociology
Dist - AIMS **Prod** - AIMS 1990

Problem identification - determining the underlying issues of a conflict 22 MIN
U-matic / VHS / 16mm
Officer survival - an approach to conflict management series
Color (PRO)
LC 76-702279
Explains how to identify the underlying causes of disputes by calm, orderly information gathering.
Civics and Political Systems
Dist - CORF **Prod** - HAR 1976
HAR

A Problem of Acceptance 47 MIN
16mm
Psychodrama in Group Process Series
B&W
Features the psychodramatic exploration of a teenager's attempt to deal with her homosexuality.
Psychology; Sociology
Dist - NYU **Prod** - NYU

The Problem of community 60 MIN
VHS
Europe and America in the modern age - 1776 to the present series
Color (H C PRO)
$95.00 purchase
Presents a lecture by James Sheehan. Focuses on a critical period in European and American history and on leaders of the time. Part of a 20 - part series that looks at the last two centuries in Europe and America. Series presents lectures by David M Kennedy and James Sheehan of Stanford University on such figures as Adam Smith, Marx, Lincoln, Washington, Jefferson, Freud, Margaret Sanger, Susan B Anthony and Jane Adams and their impact on the events of their day. For history resource material and continuing education courses.
Civics and Political Systems; Guidance and Counseling; History - United States; History - World
Dist - LANDMK

Problem of Evil 25 MIN
VHS / U-matic
Introduction to Philosophy Series
Color (C)
Religion and Philosophy
Dist - UDEL **Prod** - UDEL

The Problem of evil 30 MIN
VHS / U-matic
Art of being human series; Module 6
Color (C)
History - World; Religion and Philosophy
Dist - MDCC **Prod** - MDCC

A Problem of feelings 15 MIN
U-matic / VHS
La bonne aventure series
Color (K P)
Deals with French - American culture. Focuses on caring for others and self.
Guidance and Counseling; Psychology
Dist - GPN **Prod** - MPBN

The Problem of Hookworm Infection 8 MIN
16mm
Color
LC FIE54-126
Pictures the life cycle of the hookworm and shows the conditions in a rural home conducive to hookworm infection. Depicts the effects of hookworm disease in a young girl.
Health and Safety; Science - Natural
Dist - USNAC **Prod** - USPHS 1954

A Problem of power 45 MIN
16mm
Color
LC 79-705001
Illustrates the general social and economic situation in Latin America, using Colombia as the representative nation. Includes views of the agrarian culture, the urban poor, and various individuals working for change in Latin America.
Geography - World; Psychology; Sociology
Dist - CCNCC **Prod** - CCNCC 1970

The Problem of refuse disposal 16 MIN
U-matic / VHS / 16mm
Color (H C G)
Introduces the problem of how to dispose of the ever increasing amount of refuse that modern society produces. Surveys contemporary methods of dealing with solid waste including composting, tipping, incineration and pulverization.
Sociology
Dist - VIEWTH **Prod** - GATEEF

The Problem of water 15 MIN
16mm / U-matic / VHS
American legacy series
Color (I)
Visits California's Mojave Desert and recounts the explorations of Jedediah Smith. Examines the water dependence of the Imperial Valley and of Los Angeles.
Geography - United States; History - United States; Social Science
Dist - AITECH **Prod** - KRMATV 1983

The Problem on our hands 19 MIN
16mm
Color
Presents unrehearsed interviews with nurses, doctors, aides and personnel of the U S Public Health Service discussing the problem of inadequate hand decontamination in hospitals.
Health and Safety
Dist - JAJ **Prod** - JAJ 1967

Problem - oriented medical record 30 MIN
16mm
Directions for education in nursing via technology series
Color (PRO)
LC 76-703340
Defines and demonstrates the problem - oriented medical record as a systemic process for documenting, monitoring and evaluating the quality of health care provided by nursing service.
Health and Safety
Dist - WSUM **Prod** - DENT 1976

Problem - Oriented Medical Record 4 MIN
VHS / BETA
Typing - Medical Series
Color
Business and Economics; Health and Safety
Dist - RMIBHF **Prod** - RMIBHF

The Problem - Oriented Medical Record - Dental Utilization 18 MIN
8mm cartridge / 16mm
Color (PRO)
LC 75-703839; 75-703838
Describes the method by which the Veterans Administration Dental Services utilizes and implements the medical records of its patients. Shows how this system permits recording of the patient's history, problems, assessment, plan for treatment and continuing treatment record on the same medical record chart.
Health and Safety
Dist - USNAC **Prod** - USVA 1975

Problem oriented record 16 MIN
U-matic / VHS
Color (PRO)
Provides a detailed description of the use of the problem oriented record and details its use in individualizing patient care.
Health and Safety
Dist - UMICHM **Prod** - UMICHM 1978

The Problem Pit 30 MIN
U-matic
Read all about it - One Series
Color (I)
Teaches reading and writing skills as it continues a story in which Chris's friends, Samantha and Lynne, meet Duneedon, ruler of the galaxy Trialviron and become trapped in the Problem Pit.
Education; English Language; Literature and Drama
Dist - TVOTAR **Prod** - TVOTAR 1982

Problem Prevention 26 MIN
VHS / U-matic
Situation Management Series
Color
Business and Economics; Psychology
Dist - DELTAK **Prod** - EXECDV

The Problem Solvers - an Opportunity 11 MIN
16mm
Color
Looks at the profession of internal auditing providing an overview of responsibilities and activities by visiting a practicing internal auditor.
Business and Economics; Guidance and Counseling
Dist - MTP **Prod** - IIA

Problem solving 29 MIN
16mm
Interviewing for results series
B&W (IND)
LC 73-703323
Business and Economics; Psychology
Dist - EDSD **Prod** - EDSD 1968

Problem Solving 10 MIN
16mm
Parent Education - Attitude Films Series
B&W
Education; Guidance and Counseling; Sociology
Dist - TC **Prod** - TC

Problem Solving 15 MIN
U-matic
Math Makers One Series
Color (I)
Presents the math concepts of word problem interpretation, formula creation and use, ratio use, and multiplication grid.
Education; Mathematics
Dist - TVOTAR **Prod** - TVOTAR 1979

Problem solving 8 MIN
U-matic / VHS
ASSET - a social skills program for adolescents series; Session 5
Color (J H)
LC 81-706054
Presents problem - solving techniques which adolescents can use in their dealings with parents, teachers, peers and others.
Guidance and Counseling; Psychology
Dist - RESPRC **Prod** - HAZLJS 1981

Problem solving
VHS / 16mm
(C PRO)
165.00 rental
Teaches the management processes of situation analysis and problem solving through logical methods. Includes full print materials and transparencies.
Business and Economics; Education
Dist - VLEARN

Problem solving
VHS
Algebra 1 series
Color (J H)
$125.00 purchase _ #A5
Teaches the concepts involved in solving mathematical problems. Part of a series of 16 videos, each between 25 and 30 minutes long, that explain and reinforce 89 basic concepts of algebra. Includes a stated objective for each segment. Tutors the student through definitions, theorems, step - by - step solutions and examples. Videos are also available in a set.
Mathematics
Dist - LANDMK
GPN

Problem solving 31 MIN
U-matic / VHS
Hub of the wheel series
Color (G)
$249.00, $149.00 purchase _ #AD - 1566
Addresses the creative and efficient channeling of energy to resolve problems. Describes a unique five - step method for solving problems. Presents detailed exercises. Part of a ten - part series for office professionals.
Business and Economics; Psychology
Dist - FOTH **Prod** - FOTH

Problem solving 10 MIN
U-matic
Geography skills series
Color (J H)
Shows how to recognize patterns which in turn helps to solve problems. Solving geography problems needs practice and method.
Computer Science; Education; Geography - World
Dist - TVOTAR **Prod** - TVOTAR 1985

Problem Solving
VHS / U-matic
Organizational Quality Improvement Series
Color
Provides ten steps to problem solving. Addresses pitfalls and teamwork.
Psychology
Dist - BNA **Prod** - BNA

Problem solving 30 MIN
VHS
A House for all seasons series
Color (G)
$49.95 purchase _ #AHFS - 309
Features a superinsulated house located in a turn - of - the - century St Louis neighborhood. Gives guidance on buying and installing skylights. Tours a 400 - square - foot solar cottage.
Home Economics; Industrial and Technical Education; Science - Natural; Sociology
Dist - PBS **Prod** - KRMATV 1986

Problem Solving - a Demonstration in Social Studies 30 MIN
VHS / U-matic
Teaching for Thinking - Creativity in the Classroom Series
Color (T PRO)
$180.00 purchase,$50.00 rental
Employs the subject of the depression to demonstrate the use of individual creativity in the classroom.
Education; English Language
Dist - AITECH **Prod** - WHATV 1986

Problem solving - a process for managers 16 MIN
U-matic / VHS / 16mm
Professional management program series
Color (SPANISH)
Teaches problem - solving methods for managers and supervisors.
Business and Economics; Foreign Language; Psychology
Dist - NEM **Prod** - NEM

Problem solving - a process for managers 20 MIN
U-matic / VHS / 16mm
Color (A)
LC 82-700804
Shows eight young managers who gather in a theater setting to role - play problems they have faced and to share principles they have learned. Demonstrates a simple process for solving the problems of managers and supervisors.
Business and Economics; Psychology
Dist - NEM **Prod** - NEM 1981

Problem solving and conflict resolution 28 MIN
VHS
Management skills series
Color (C PRO)
$285.00 purchase, $70.00 rental _ #6002S, #6002V
Uses realistic, health care - based examples to show how conflicts can be resolved and how, if managed correctly, conflicts can lead to new options. Discusses the different types of conflict - I win - you lose; lose - lose; win - win. Shows the advantages of win - win resolutions and methods of achieving such resolutions. Part of a five - part series on management skills produced by Health and Sciences Network.
Business and Economics; Health and Safety
Dist - AJN

Problem - solving and decision - making 30 MIN
U-matic / VHS
Organizational transactions series
Color
Demonstrates the opportunity for release of leadership potential in problem - solving and decision activities. Develops basic functions and requirements of organizations. Identifies crucial requirements which must be met for the functions to be effectively carried out.
Business and Economics; Psychology
Dist - PRODEV **Prod** - PRODEV

Problem solving and decision making 17 MIN
U-matic / VHS
Applied management series
Color
Business and Economics
Dist - DELTAK **Prod** - ORGDYN

Problem Solving and Decision Making 20 MIN
U-matic / VHS
Effective Manager Series
Color
Business and Economics; Guidance and Counseling; Psychology
Dist - DELTAK **Prod** - DELTAK

Problem solving and decision - making 30 MIN
U-matic / VHS
Teaching for thinking - creativity in the classroom series
Color (T PRO)
$180.00 purchase,$50.00 rental
Features a computer simulation to help teach students how to obtain skill in making decisions.
Education; English Language; Psychology
Dist - AITECH **Prod** - WHATV 1986

Problem solving and forgiveness - Volume 5 60 MIN
VHS
Families - quality relationships in changing times series
Color (G R)
$29.95 purchase, $10.00 rental _ #35 - 83743 - 1
Consists of two 30 - minute sessions. Covers the importance of resolving differences, as well as the five steps involved in forgiveness. Hosted by seminary professor Dr Roland Martinson.
Psychology; Religion and Philosophy; Sociology
Dist - APH

Problem solving and program design - programming languages - Parts 15 and 16 60 MIN
VHS / U-matic
New literacy - an introduction to computers
Color (G)
$45.00, $29.95 purchase
Discusses problems of programming and how flowcharts, debugging and testing create the end product in Part 15. Explores the distinguishing characteristics of FORTRAN, COBOL, PL - I, BASIC, Pascal, APL and RPG in Part 16. Parts of a 26 - part series on computing machines.
Computer Science; Mathematics
Dist - ANNCPB **Prod** - SCCON 1988

Problem solving by objectives 29 MIN
16mm
Management by objectives series
B&W (IND)
LC 70-703325
Business and Economics; Psychology
Dist - EDSD **Prod** - EDSD

Problem solving - calculating formatting and filing 60 MIN
U-matic / VHS
Computer tutor series
Color
Teaches math functions, explains formatting data, teaches writing to disk and recovering data from text files and presents overview of VisiCalc and Apple Writer (R).
Computer Science; Industrial and Technical Education; Mathematics; Sociology
Dist - FILMID **Prod** - FILMID 1983

Problem solving - calculating, formatting and filing 57 MIN
U-matic / VHS
Computer tutor series
Color
Covers math functions, formats, filing and word processing. Teaches writing to disk and recovering data from text files. Gives applications for the Apple II and IIe.
Computer Science; Industrial and Technical Education; Mathematics
Dist - PSU **Prod** - PSU 1984

Problem solving - drawing and interpreting tables and diagrams 15 MIN
VHS / U-matic
Mathematics for the '80s - grade six series
(I)
$125.00 purchase
Discusses the proper usage of tables and diagrams for problem solving.
Mathematics; Psychology
Dist - AITECH **Prod** - AITECH 1987

Problem solving for first line supervisors 20 MIN
VHS
Correctional officer series
Color (PRO)
$395.00 purchase, $75.00 rental _ #8340
Allows brand new and experienced first line supervisors to improve their problem - solving skills in the non - threatening environment of the classroom. Portrays 16 situations that a supervisor may encounter on the job and allows participants to evaluate the situation and explore possible solutions.
Business and Economics; Psychology; Sociology
Dist - AIMS **Prod** - SKIDJ 1991

Problem solving - guess - check - revise 15 MIN
U-matic / VHS
Mathematics for the '80s - grade six series
(I)
$125.00 purchase
Talks on the use of guessing as an active nonalgorithmic strategy.
Mathematics
Dist - AITECH **Prod** - AITECH 1987

Problem Solving - Identifying the Problem 15 MIN
U-matic / VHS
Math Works Series
Color (I)
Teaches problem solving by re - stating the problem, changing the context, discarding unnecessary information and indicating what is given and what is needed.
Mathematics
Dist - AITECH **Prod** - AITECH

Problem solving in groups 25 MIN
16mm / U-matic / VHS
Management development series
B&W (C A)
LC FIA63-1258
Outlines functions of management committees. Describes methods of improving group problem - solving procedure and decision - making procedure. Illustrates advantages and difficulties of group problem solving.
Business and Economics; Guidance and Counseling; Psychology
Dist - UCEMC **Prod** - UCLA 1961

Problem - solving in groups 25 MIN
VHS / U-matic
B&W
Brings a situation to a problem - solving group in which in - laws have decided to visit a student for the first time. Helps to develop a satisfactory plan to deal with student's stressful situation.
Psychology; Sociology
Dist - UWISC **Prod** - VRL 1980

Problem solving in mathematics
U-matic / VHS
Color (J)
Presents strategies for solving math problems that cover five categories - whole numbers, fractions, decimals, percent and combined computational skills. Uses everyday problems to help students find hidden questions and key words to simplify problem solving.
Mathematics
Dist - GA **Prod** - PATED

Problem solving in science 40 MIN
VHS
Color (J H)
$100.00 purchase _ #A1VH 9432
Offers an interactive program to involve students in solving historical scientific problems. Challenges students to duplicate Galileo's observations of the moons of Jupiter, decide whether his findings indicate that the sun or the Earth is the center of the universe, compare NASA's three alternatives for reaching the moon and determine which has the most chance for success, plot the course of a hurricane to determine whether to issue an evacuation order. In two parts. Includes reproducible worksheets, activity sheets and teacher's guide.
History - World; Science; Science - Physical
Dist - CLRVUE **Prod** - CLRVUE

Problem solving in the job world
VHS
Color (J H S)
$99.00 purchase _ #ES893
Offers a job retention video for adolescents and young adults who are trying to learn skills necessary to progress in their careers. Improves interpersonal communications, problem solving skills and conflict resolution. Includes three vignettes to stimulate discussion and analysis, and a teacher's guide.
Business and Economics; Guidance and Counseling; Psychology; Social Science
Dist - EDAS

Problem solving - looking for a pattern 15 MIN
U-matic / VHS
Math works series
Color (I)
Explains how a pattern helps solve a problem and how to find a pattern by looking at data from different perspectives.
Mathematics
Dist - AITECH **Prod** - AITECH

Problem - solving 1 - the basic skill
U-matic / VHS
Third r - teaching basic mathematics skills series
Color (T)
Focuses on a variety of problem - solving processes and strategies. Features five elementary school children applying these strategies.
Education; Mathematics
Dist - EDCORP **Prod** - EPCO

Problem solving process
VHS / U-matic
Implementing quality circles series
Color
Shows how to establish and use standard guidelines for problem solving.
Business and Economics; Psychology
Dist - BNA **Prod** - BNA

Problem Solving Selling
VHS / U-matic
Making of a Salesman Series Session 5
Color
Introduces 19 vignettes that depict situations using problem solving, preventive problem solving and contingency planning. Includes kinds of obstacles, responses to obstacles, the 'lost order,' problem solving methods and competitor - prepared specs.
Business and Economics; Psychology
Dist - PRODEV **Prod** - PRODEV

Problem solving - simplifying the problem 15 MIN
U-matic / VHS
Math works series
Color (I)
Shows how to simplify a problem by decreasing the size of numbers or the number of variables or by taking one step at a time.
Mathematics
Dist - AITECH **Prod** - AITECH

Problem solving - solving a simpler problem 15 MIN
U-matic / VHS
Mathematics for the '80s - grade six series
(I)
$125.00 purchase
Looks at the use of smaller numbers, forming a simpler model and breaking the problem into steps.
Mathematics
Dist - AITECH **Prod** - AITECH 1987

Problem solving strategies - the Synectics approach 28 MIN
16mm / U-matic / VHS
Color (C A)
LC 79-701492
Shows a problem - solving session held at Synectics, Inc, a consulting firm specializing in exploring creative alternatives and solutions. Presents strategies to stimulate organizational creativity and streamline problem - solving.
Business and Economics; Psychology
Dist - CRMP **Prod** - CRMP 1980
MGHT

Problem Solving Techniques 30 MIN
U-matic / VHS
Statistical Process Control Series
Color (PRO)
Provides an interactive video applications oriented training program that focuses on the role of the control chart as a powerful tool in monitoring quality. Lessons are designed to introduce shop floor operators, supervisors and technical personnel to the techniques of statistical process control.
Business and Economics; Mathematics
Dist - ITCORP **Prod** - ITCORP 1986

Problem solving through QC circles 18 MIN
VHS
(PRO)
Shows the seven representative tools of Quality Control, or QC, used in problem solving.
Business and Economics; Psychology
Dist - TOYOVS **Prod** - JPC 1987

Problem solving to make ideas happen 30 MIN
VHS
Color (G A)
$645.00 purchase _ #VSOLVE - 721; $645.00 purchase, $150.00 rental
Discusses how to encourage organizational creativity in order to aid problem solving. Suggests methods of analyzing opportunities and problems, turning ideas into solutions, and taking advantage of workplace diversity to encourage innovation. Offers case studies from corporate executives at Gillette, Fisher - Price Toys, Kimberly - Clark, Lotus, and other companies. Includes an 85 - page learning guide.
Business and Economics; Psychology
Dist - PRODUC **Prod** - PRODUC VLEARN

Problem - Solving Unit
U-matic / VHS
Management Skills for Supervisors Series
Color (A)
Shows how managers can identify a problem, determine what has gone wrong, decide what to do about it and take corrective action. Gives specifics for anticipating difficulties, stating goals, brainstorming and other problem - solving skills and techniques.
Business and Economics; Psychology
Dist - TIMLIF **Prod** - TIMLIF 1984

Problem solving - using diagrams and models 15 MIN
VHS / U-matic
Math works series
Color (I)
Shows how flow charts, models, assembly plans and blueprints simplify, clarify, abstract or make concrete.
Mathematics
Dist - AITECH **Prod** - AITECH

Problem Solving - using Graphs 15 MIN
VHS / U-matic
Math Works Series
Color (I)
Focuses on how to choose the right kind of graph to convey a particular point. Compares situations in which bar, circle or line graphs are most appropriate.
Mathematics
Dist - AITECH **Prod** - AITECH

Problem solving - using logical reasoning 15 MIN
U-matic / VHS
Mathematics for the '80s - grade six series
(I)
$125.00 purchase
Instructs on how to organize information carefully to avoid jumping to conclusions.
Mathematics
Dist - AITECH **Prod** - AITECH 1987

Problem solving - using maps 15 MIN
U-matic / VHS
Math works series
Color (I)
Focuses on reading and interpreting a map that someone else has prepared. Shows how to find a particular location, to determine the distance between two points and to plan a route by noting the region covered, the directions, the coordinates, the scale and the key to symbols.
Mathematics
Dist - AITECH **Prod** - AITECH

Problem Solving - using Tables 15 MIN
U-matic / VHS
Math Works Series
Color (I)
Reviews different kinds of tables and explains how to read and how to make a table.
Mathematics
Dist - AITECH **Prod** - AITECH

Problem Solving - using the Hen as an Educational Tool 29 MIN
U-matic / VHS / 16mm
Color (J H A)
Demonstrates a technique for solving problems using a real life problem - whether or not a hen is in laying condition at a given time. Describes the five basic steps taken in solving this problem.
Science
Dist - CORNRS **Prod** - CUETV 1974

Problem Solving - using Your Head Creatively 45 MIN
VHS
Color (J H)
Uses everyday situations, to which your students can easily relate, to stress the importance of approach and imagination in finding inventive solutions to one's problems. Presents problem solving as a learnable skill, to be developed and refined.
Psychology
Dist - HRMC **Prod** - HRMC 1978

Problem solving - using your head creatively
VHS / 35mm strip
$199.00 purchase _ #HR631 filmstrip, $199.00 purchase _ #HR631V VHS
Points out that problem solving is a skill everyone can acquire by using natural creativity and imagination.
Psychology
Dist - CAREER **Prod** - CAREER

Problem solving with peer counseling - students helping students 45 MIN
VHS
Color (H)
$209.00 purchase _ #60198 - 126
Teaches young people the communication skills necessary to help their peers with teenage problems such as life choices, self - esteem and sexual identity. Shows how to talk with peers, listen to them and be sensitive to the feelings of others as techniques in problem solving.
Guidance and Counseling; Psychology; Social Science; Sociology
Dist - GA **Prod** - GA 1992

The Problem with exhaustion 28 MIN
VHS / 16mm
Sonrisas series
Color (T P) (SPANISH)
$46.00 rental _ #SRSS - 129
Shows how Garven's new car threatens the environment.
Sociology
Dist - PBS

A Problem with sex 43 MIN
VHS
Color (C G PRO)
$198.00 purchase, $24.00 rental _ #40441
Documents programs at St George's Hospital Medical School, London, and St Clements Hospital, Ipswich, for understanding and treating mental and physical problems related to sexual behavior. Focuses on the case work of Dr Elizabeth Stanly with married couples at St George's. Details education programs for medical students and postgraduate counselors, social workers, physicians, probation officers and health professionals.
Health and Safety
Dist - PSU **Prod** - BBC 1986

The Problem with water is people 30 MIN
16mm / U-matic / VHS
Color (I)
LC FIA66-1496
Traces the Colorado River watershed from the snowcovered Rockies to the delta in Baja California. Discusses water usage and equitable division of water, especially between California and Arizona. Narrated by Chet Huntley.
Geography - United States; Science - Natural
Dist - MGHT **Prod** - NBCTV 1964

Problem Witness Tactics - a Lecture with Demonstrations 28 MIN
VHS / U-matic
Color (PRO)
Presents 12 common problems and possible solutions that lawyers face during trial. Discusses and demonstrates different methods for resolving problems and methods by which a witness' recollection can be refreshed.
Civics and Political Systems
Dist - ABACPE **Prod** - ABACPE

Problems 15 MIN
U-matic
Color (I)
Teaches writing skills while telling the story of Chris and his friends who are unhappy that Samantha will have to leave town when her father accepts a new job.
Education; English Language; Literature and Drama
Dist - TVOTAR **Prod** - TVOTAR 1982

Problems and challenges for office support 30 MIN
U-matic / VHS
Impact of office automation on people series
Color
Examines how office automation is changing the office support function and the attitudes and abilities of people in support positions. Points out steps that management must take to avoid the serious problems that may arise with the introduction of automated technologies.
Business and Economics; Industrial and Technical Education; Psychology
Dist - DELTAK **Prod** - DELTAK

Problems and practices for the disadvantaged 30 MIN
VHS / U-matic
Educating the disadvantaged series
Color
Examines government programs for the disadvantaged, beginning with emergency nursery care during the Depression and the growth of the Head Start program.
Civics and Political Systems; Education; Psychology
Dist - NETCHE **Prod** - NETCHE 1972

Problems and prospects in cognitive intervention in learning disabilities
VHS
Cognition and learning series
Color (T)
$49.95 purchase
Reviews cognitive interventions with learning disabled students in reading comprehension and writing. Examines problems in cognitive research. Looks at the future of cognitive intervention in learning disabilities. Presented by Dr Bernice Wong of the University of British Columbia. Part of a six - part series on recent theoretical and empirical work done on cognition and learning.
Education; English Language; Psychology
Dist - UCALG **Prod** - UCALG 1991

Problems and solutions 42 MIN
16mm / VHS
Water supply and sanitation in development series
Color (H C A)
$650.00, $170.00 purchase, $30.00 rental _ #NC1825
Presents in detail the situations presented in People And Problems, another part in this series, reviewing the numerous enteric pathogens that thrive under unsanitary conditions and showing through animation how they are transmitted. Presents plans for construction of several low - cost systems of sanitary control.
Health and Safety; Science - Natural
Dist - IU **Prod** - NFBC 1985

Problems, Crises and Opportunities 13 MIN
U-matic / VHS
Thinking in Action Series Module 4
Color (A)
Shows how problems can be solved in a business environment by defining them, breaking them down and looking beyond the first and most obvious adequate answer.
Business and Economics; Psychology
Dist - FI **Prod** - BBCTV 1983

Problems encountered by the home visitor 15 MIN
U-matic / VHS
B&W (PRO)
Shows typical problems encountered by the home visitor, such as a mother annoyed because the visitor arrives late, constant interruptions by the father and absence of the parent at the appointed time.
Education; Sociology
Dist - HSERF **Prod** - HSERF

Problems in academic tasks performance - Pt 1 7 MIN
16mm
Systems for precise observations for teachers series
Color
LC 74-705420
Illustrates problems of the multiply, physically handicapped and demonstrates supportive devices for task performance. Includes auditory sound production of written letter cues, letter production of auditory cues, blending sound and word reading.
Education; English Language; Psychology
Dist - USNAC **Prod** - USOE 1970

Problems in Diagnosis and Management of Hypothyroidism 40 MIN
16mm
Boston Medical Reports Series
B&W
LC 74-705421
Presents a patient with severe myxedema secondary to pituitary tumor. Describes the clinical procedure and laboratory findings common to primary and pituitary myxedema. Explains etiologies and importance of differential diagnosis. (Kinescope).
Health and Safety; Science
Dist - USNAC **Prod** - NMAC 1964

Problems in geriatric pharmacy 24 MIN
U-matic / VHS
Color (C PRO)
$395.00 purchase, $80.00 rental _ #C850 - VI - 032
Uses 11 vignettes to illustrate medication - based problems commonly experienced by ambulatory geriatric patients. Supports each scene with comments from elderly citizens who have experienced the same or related difficulties. Presented by Drs Edward Sumner and Ron Durand.
Health and Safety
Dist - HSCIC

Problems in harmonic analysis related to oscillatory integrals and curvature 60 MIN
VHS
ICM Plenary addresses series
Color (PRO G)
$49.00 purchase _ #VIDSTEIN - VB2
Presents Elias M Stein who discusses problems in harmonic analysis related to oscillatory integrals and curvature.

Mathematics; Science - Physical
Dist - AMSOC **Prod** - AMSOC

Problems in High Risk Pregnancy, Pt II
Management of the Postdate Pregnancy 10 MIN
Dist - HSCIC

Problems in high risk pregnancy series
Dating the pregnancy - some consequences of post maturity, Pt 1 15 MIN
Dist - HSCIC

Problems in Job Enrichment 13 MIN
U-matic / 35mm strip
Job Enrichment Series
Color
Covers the many problems that arise when a job enrichment program is installed and suggests some ways to prevent them.
Business and Economics; Psychology
Dist - RESEM **Prod** - RESEM

Problems in Supervision Series
Employing Blind Workers in Industry 17 MIN
Employing Disabled Workers in Industry 20 MIN
Establishing Working Relations for the Disabled Worker 14 MIN
Every minute counts 10 MIN
Instructing the Blind Worker on the Job 17 MIN
Instructing the Disabled Worker on the Job 14 MIN
Instructing the Worker on the Job 14 MIN
Introducing the New Worker to His Job 16 MIN
Maintaining Good Working Conditions 9 MIN
Maintaining Quality Standards 10 MIN
Maintaining Workers' Interest 13 MIN
A New Supervisor Takes a Look at His Job 13 MIN
Placing the right man on the job 13 MIN
Planning and Laying Out Work 10 MIN
Relaciones entre supervisores 8 MIN
Supervising Women Workers 11 MIN
Supervising workers on the job 10 MIN
The Supervisor as a Leader 27 MIN
The Supervisor as a leader - Pt 1 14 MIN
The Supervisor as a leader - Pt 2 13 MIN
Dist - USNAC

Problems in Supervision - Spanish Series
Buenas condiciones en el trabajo 9 MIN
Conserve El Interes De Sus Empleados 13 MIN
Dist - USNAC

Problems in the surgical management of hyperparathyroidism 19 MIN
16mm
Color (PRO)
Points out that when the diagnosis of primary hyperparathyroidism has been made, many of the surgeon's problems have really just begun. Explains that the obscure and variable positions of the parathyroid glands require for their search and identification adequate exposure, meticulous hemostasis, careful dissection and a detailed working knowledge of the anatomical relationships and anomalies of the neck and mediastinum.
Health and Safety
Dist - ACY **Prod** - ACYDGD 1962

Problems in transporting the handicapped 27 MIN
16mm
Color (A)
Discusses problems in transporting the physically handicapped.
Education; Health and Safety
Dist - VISUCP **Prod** - VISUCP 1978

The Problems of confederation 30 MIN
VHS
American adventure series
Color (G)
$150.00 purchase _ #TAMA - 109
Discusses the conflicts Americans had over what form of government was best for the Confederation. Explores controversial issues of the time, including church - state relations and exploration of lands to the west.
History - United States
Dist - PBS

Problems of conservation - forest and range 14 MIN
16mm / U-matic / VHS
Environmental studies series
Color (J H) (SPANISH)
Describes the struggle to retain large areas of undeveloped forest and range while the demands of rapidly expanding population press upon these areas. Illustrates the 'multiple use' programs of protection and management that lead to effective use of resources.
Science - Natural; Social Science
Dist - EBEC **Prod** - EBEC

Problems of conservation - our natural resources 11 MIN
U-matic / VHS / 16mm
Environmental studies series
Color (J H) (SPANISH)
Provides an overview of the developing crises in natural resources stemming from reliance on, and misuse of them. Documents efforts to conserve resources in the twentieth century.
Science - Natural; Social Science
Dist - EBEC **Prod** - EBEC

Problems of conservation - soil 14 MIN
U-matic / VHS / 16mm
Environmental studies series
Color; B&W (J H)
LC 76-704834
Discusses the nature of soil, what it is and how it was formed. Illustrates the damaging effects of water and wind erosion when the ground cover of vegetation is stripped away and notes the loss of nutrients in the soil. Describes the origin of the U S Soil Conservation Service which was established by Congress to help combat these problems. Shows on - the - spot examples of its technical assistance of projects that range from contour plowing to land - use planning.
Science - Natural; Science - Physical
Dist - EBEC **Prod** - EBEC 1969

Problems of conservation - wildlife 13 MIN
VHS / 16mm / U-matic
Environmental studies series
Color (J H) (SPANISH)
Depicts how survival becomes more difficult for wildlife as man changes the earth to suit his needs. Identifies endangered species, examines efforts to conserve wildlife and emphasizes the importance of every species in the biosphere.
Science - Natural
Dist - EBEC **Prod** - EBEC

Problems of Emerging Nations 11 MIN
16mm
Color (I)
Explores social and economic problems of the emerging African nations, such as communication, education, national unity, cultural conflict and poverty.
Geography - World; History - United States; Psychology; Sociology
Dist - AVED **Prod** - CBF 1962

Problems of Hydramatic Transmission 30 MIN
VHS / 35mm strip
(H A IND)
#437XV7
Includes hydraulic failures and troubleshooting techniques and mechanical failures and what the dipstick can tell you (2 tapes). Includes a Study Guide.
Education; Industrial and Technical Education
Dist - BERGL

Problems of internal combustion engine 58 MIN
VHS / 35mm strip
(H A IND)
#409XV7
Includes compression leaks, oil pressure problems, excessive oil consumption, and unusual engine problems. Includes a Study Guide.
Education; Industrial and Technical Education
Dist - BERGL

Problems of scarcity and choice 45 MIN
U-matic / VHS
Economic perspectives series
Color
Deals with the economic problems of scarcity and choice.
Business and Economics
Dist - MDCPB **Prod** - MDCPB

Problems of the allocation of scarce life - saving therapy 59 MIN
U-matic
Ethics and medicine series
Color
Discusses who should have access to scarce life - saving therapies. Covers the pros and cons of various solutions.
Health and Safety; Religion and Philosophy
Dist - HRC **Prod** - OHC

Problems of the G - machine 50 MIN
U-matic / VHS
Computer languages series; Pt 1
Color
Gives a review of G - machine algorithms in computer languages.
Computer Science; Industrial and Technical Education; Mathematics; Sociology
Dist - MIOT **Prod** - MIOT

Problems of the Middle East 21 MIN
U-matic
Color (J H)
LC 77-704660
Depicts the history and culture of the Middle East area from antiquity, explaining the basic forces molding its destiny. Provides essential concepts of principal problems - minorities, Arab unity, agriculture, industralization, Westernization and education.
Civics and Political Systems; Geography - World; History - World; Sociology
Dist - ATLAP **Prod** - ATLAP 1967

Problems of the Therapeutic Symbiosis - Helplessness, Self - Doubt and Feelings of 16 MIN
VHS / U-matic
Treatment of the Borderline Patient Series
Color
Points out that borderline patients provoked by the calmness of the therapist are driven to knock him off his omnipotent pedestal that can lead the therapist to feel irrelevant. Presents the implications of therapeutic symbiosis.
Health and Safety; Psychology
Dist - HEMUL **Prod** - HEMUL

Problems of the young married 30 MIN
16mm
B&W (J H T R)
Tells a story to point out the dangers of overemphasis on material things during the first years of marriage.
Psychology; Sociology
Dist - FAMF **Prod** - FAMF

Problems of Working Women 24 MIN
U-matic / VHS
Color (G)
$249.00, $149.00 purchase _ #AD - 1529
Examines the pressures on working women with small children. Considers their salaries which are too low to pay for proper child care, inadequate or unavailable child care facilities, inadequate or absent household help.
Sociology
Dist - FOTH **Prod** - FOTH

Problems of World Order Series
Communication satellites 10 MIN
Hijacking 10 MIN
Our Cultural Heritage 10 MIN
World Health 10 MIN
Dist - AGAPR

Problems, problems 25 MIN
VHS
Supervisors series
Color (A)
PdS50 purchase
Looks at the disciplinary issues facing supervisors. Interviews some supervisors who explain how they tackle discipline. Part of an eight-part series designed to help supervisors - particularly newly-appointed ones - understand the demands of their individual roles through the experience of established supervisors who offer personal insights and strategies from within a framework of good practice.
Business and Economics; Psychology; Sociology
Dist - BBCENE

Problems, Problems, Problems 30 MIN
U-matic / VHS / 16mm
Mr Microchip Series
Color (I J H)
Discusses how the computer solves problems, using information and following certain rules, and whether or not computers can make mistakes.
Mathematics
Dist - JOU **Prod** - JOU

Problems to solve 20 MIN
U-matic
Exploring our nation series
Color (I)
Discusses some of the problems confronting large cities in the United States. Focuses on inadequate housing, unemployment, pollution and transportation. Proposes a number of solutions to each problem.
Sociology
Dist - GPN **Prod** - KRMATV 1975

Procainamide in the management of acute ventricular arrhythmias - pharmacodynamic 30 MIN
16mm
Color (PRO)
Studies ventricular arrhythmias that occur in almost 90 percent of the patients who survive myocardial infarction long enough to reach a hospital. Examines the effectiveness of Procainamide as a highly useful and versatile agent in the management of these ventricular arrhythmias.

Health and Safety; Science - Natural
Dist - SQUIBB **Prod** - SQUIBB

Procedural questions in an insurance arbitration 21 MIN
BETA / VHS / U-matic
Color (PRO)
$90.00 purchase
Presents 15 different procedural questions that could arise during the course of an arbitration. Helps counsel for both sides prepare for arbitration of a dispute. Includes a discussion guide.
Business and Economics; Psychology
Dist - AARA **Prod** - AARA

Procedure for permanent waving
U-matic / VHS
Color
Covers the entire permanent wave procedure, from the client consultation to after - care advice. Details wrapping techniques, including angle, end papers, control and placement. Outlines processing and neutralizing. Gives specifics of test curling. Shows all client protection measures and illustrates all working sequences.
Education; Home Economics
Dist - MPCEDP **Prod** - MPCEDP 1984

Procedure of Choice in Duodenal Ulcer Problems 23 MIN
16mm
Color (PRO)
Explains that time has clarified the relative advantages and disadvantages of the newer procedures for duodenal ulcer. Discusses the physiological basis of ulcer surgery and the choice of procedure indicated in specific situations.
Health and Safety; Science
Dist - ACY **Prod** - ACYDGD 1960

Procedures
U-matic / VHS
PASCAL - a modern programming language series
Color
Introduces modular programming concept, global vs local variables, passing parameters, value vs variable parameters, and comments.
Computer Science; Industrial and Technical Education; Mathematics
Dist - EDUACT **Prod** - EDUACT

Procedures 30 MIN
U-matic / VHS
Pascal, Pt 1 - Beginning Pascal Series
Color (H C A)
LC 81-706049
Introduces the generalized Pascal subprogram, the procedure. Discusses actual arguments and formal parameters, and variables. Provides examples. Concludes with discussion of Pascal block structure and scope of variables.
Computer Science; Industrial and Technical Education; Mathematics; Sociology
Dist - COLOSU **Prod** - COLOSU 1980

Procedures common to most pyeloplasties - Pt 1 15 MIN
16mm
Surgical correction of hydronephrosis - Pt 3 - procedures common to most pyeloplasties series
Color
LC 75-702266
Illustrates the steps required in a pyeloplasty operation including patient positioning and draping, incision and kidney exposure, evaluation of obstruction, the importance of ureteral length, pyelotomy placement and division of the ureter.
Health and Safety; Science
Dist - EATONL **Prod** - EATONL 1972

Procedures common to most pyeloplasties - Pt 2 15 MIN
16mm
Surgical correction of hydronephrosis - Pt 3 - procedures common to most pyeloplasties series
Color
LC 75-702267
Discusses the technique of ureteral calibration and its value in splint selection and placement.
Health and Safety; Science
Dist - EATONL **Prod** - EATONL 1972

Procedures common to most pyeloplasties - Pt 3 15 MIN
16mm
Surgical correction of hydronephrosis - Pt 3 - procedures common to most pyeloplasties series
Color
LC 75-702268
Illustrates the steps required in a pyeloplasty operation including nephrostomy technique, ureteral splint placement, surgical pelvic reduction, nephropexy, drain placement, wound closure and the tube fixation.
Health and Safety; Science
Dist - EATONL **Prod** - EATONL 1972

Procedures for Entering and Leaving the Isolation Unit 14 MIN
U-matic / 8mm cartridge
Housekeeping Personnel Series
Color (IND)
LC 73-701047
Outlines the care and procedures entailed in entering and leaving the isolation unit.
Health and Safety
Dist - COPI **Prod** - COPI 1970

Procedures for hypodermoclysis 12 MIN
VHS
Color (PRO)
$395.00 purchase _ #N900VI043
Demonstrates the equipment and procedures for initiating, maintaining and discontinuing hypodermoclysis, a procedure for infusing fluids and medication under the skin to stabilize symptoms or to treat dehydration and electrolyte imbalance. Discusses the use of hypodermoclysis with debilitated geriatric, pediatric and palliative care patients when other procedures are inappropriate.
Health and Safety
Dist - HSCIC

Procedures for Mixing Dental Cements 13 MIN
VHS / U-matic
Color
Shows methods for mixing cements for use as temporary cements, permanent cements and base material and demonstrates using the chemical preparations zinc phosphate, polycarboxylate, zinc oxide eugenol and calcium hydroxide (Dycal). Manual included.
Health and Safety; Science - Natural
Dist - UWASH **Prod** - UWASH

Procedures for Monitoring the Preterm Infant 15 MIN
VHS / U-matic
Color (PRO)
Details principles and techniques of monitoring and interpreting temperature, heart rate, respiratory rate, blood pressure, skin color, oxygenation, and activity level and urine output in the preterm infant.
Health and Safety
Dist - UMICHM **Prod** - UMICHM 1983

Procedures for Rat Muscle Experiments 15 MIN
U-matic / VHS
Color (PRO)
Shows how to perform a rat muscle experiment, together with the set - up, calibration, and operation of a polygraph.
Health and Safety; Science; Science - Natural
Dist - HSCIC **Prod** - HSCIC 1981

Procedures for the Family Physician Series
Presents a six - part series on procedures for the family physician presented by Dr Peter Coggan. Includes Application of a Lower Leg Cast, Application of a Short Arm Cast, Audiography, Performance of an EKG, Removal of Cerumen - through Irrigation and The Vitalogram.

Application of a lower leg cast	21 MIN
Application of a short arm cast	21 MIN
Audiography	26 MIN
Performance of an EKG	21 MIN
Removal of Cerumen - through irrigation	8 MN
The Vitalogram	19 MIN

Dist - HSCIC

Procedures - INSET video - 7 20 MIN
VHS
Design and technology starters series
Color; PAL (J H)
PdS29.50 purchase
Begins with a search for worthwhile design possibilities within a particular real - world context. Suggests ways in which pupils might start thinking about certain artifacts, systems and environments, and how well they meet the needs and desires of different people who might use them. Part seven of a seven - part series.
Fine Arts; Home Economics; Sociology
Dist - EMFVL

The Process 9 MIN
16mm
Color; Silent (C)
$291.20
Presents an experimental film by Stan Brakhage.
Fine Arts
Dist - AFA **Prod** - AFA 1972

Process Analysis
VHS / U-matic
Implementing Quality Circles Series
Color
Shows how to uncover hidden costs, delays and shortages using process analysis.
Business and Economics; Psychology
Dist - BNA **Prod** - BNA

Process and analysis 30 MIN
U-matic / VHS
Write course - an introduction to college composition series
Color (C)
Shows the second of four lessons on how to write a practical paper using the process and analysis pattern. Explores the uses of the process/analysis pattern for writing outside of the classroom.
Education; English Language
Dist - DALCCD **Prod** - DALCCD 1984
FI

Process and analysis - definition - Parts 13 and 14 60 MIN
U-matic / VHS
Write course - an introduction to college composition
Color (C)
$45.00, $29.95 purchase
Prepares the student for writing a practical paper by focusing on diction and sentence skills in part 13. Presents several methods of writing extended definitions through examples from academic and nonacademic writing in part 14. Two parts of a 30 - part series on college composition.
Education; English Language
Dist - ANNCPB **Prod** - DALCCD 1984

Process - Capability Analysis 30 MIN
U-matic / VHS
Quality Control Series
Color
Discusses how Q C affects process capability analysis. Describes the steps in performing a process - capability analysis.
Business and Economics; Industrial and Technical Education
Dist - MIOT **Prod** - MIOT

Process - Centered Composition Series

Nine - Step Writing Process in Class	37 MIN
Organizing Your Writing Course	31 MIN
Poet's Journal	25 MIN
A Professional Talks about Interviewing	25 MIN
Report, Analyze, Evaluate	58 MIN
The Student as Interviewer	53 MIN
Students as their Own Editors	40 MIN
Using the Journal, Pt 1	50 MIN
Using the Journal, Pt 2	44 MIN

Dist - IU

Process charts 16 MIN
U-matic / 16mm / VHS
B&W; Mono (C A)
Shows how a process chart is made and how work can be systematically simplified through its use.
Business and Economics; Industrial and Technical Education
Dist - UIOWA **Prod** - UIOWA 1953

Process chemistry 60 MIN
VHS
Systems operations series
Color (PRO)
$600.00 - $1500.00 purchase _ #RCPCH
Demonstrates the use of material balancing in process systems. Presents principles of process chemistry. Covers process variables that affect reaction rates and the role of catalysts in process system operation and reversible reactions. Includes ten textbooks and an instructor guide to support four hours of instruction.
Education; Industrial and Technical Education; Psychology; Science - Physical
Dist - NUSTC **Prod** - NUSTC

Process Control 20 MIN
U-matic / VHS
Statistics for Technicians Series
Color (IND)
Introduces the concepts of X, R and P control charts. Notes how these charts are most informative as to manufacturing processes, and emphasizes chart interpretation.
Business and Economics; Mathematics; Psychology
Dist - COLOSU **Prod** - COLOSU

Process control 30 MIN
U-matic / VHS
UNIX series
Color (IND)
Concludes UNIX lecture series with following commands - ps, kill, sleep, wait, and at.
Computer Science; Industrial and Technical Education; Mathematics; Sociology
Dist - COLOSU **Prod** - COLOSU

The Process decision program chart - Part 7 23 MIN
VHS
Memory jogger plus series
Color (PRO IND A)
$495.00 purchase _ #GO01G
Presents part seven of a seven - part series featuring Michael Brassard. Uses an interactive format giving viewers hands - on experience with topic. By Goal - QPC. Includes extensive workshop materials.
Business and Economics; Psychology
Dist - EXTR

Process disturbances and dynamics
Software / BETA
Basic process control series
Color (PRO)
$600.00 - $1500.00 purchase _ #IDPDD
Covers feedback and feedforward control in manual and automatic control systems. Describes step input, resistance capacitance, dead time, lag and time constant. Part of a six - part series on basic process control. Interactive training system includes course administrator guide, videodisc and computer software.
Industrial and Technical Education; Psychology
Dist - NUSTC **Prod** - NUSTC

Process library function
U-matic / VHS
'C' language programming series
Color
Discusses the concept and use of the standard library functions in 'C' language programs and describes the relationship of standard library functions to actual libraries.
Computer Science; Industrial and Technical Education; Mathematics; Sociology
Dist - COMTEG **Prod** - COMTEG

Process of Aging - a Discussion Trigger 39 MIN
VHS / 16mm
(C)
$385.00 purchase _ #860VI038
Presents several important issues involved in the study of the aging process. Shows the significance of health on the daily experiences of older adults and the importance of reminiscence.
Health and Safety
Dist - HSCIC **Prod** - HSCIC 1986

Process of catheterization with a foley catheter 25 MIN
VHS / U-matic
Color
Presents the indications for catheterization of the urinary bladder using a Foley catheter and shows the equipment used in the process. Demonstrates techniques used for male and female patients.
Health and Safety; Science - Natural
Dist - AJN **Prod** - WSUN

Process of catheterization with a foley catheter 28 MIN
16mm
Directions for education in nursing via technology series; Lesson 108
B&W (PRO)
LC 74-701887
Demonstrates the process of catheterization with a Foley catheter on a female and a male patient.
Health and Safety
Dist - WSUM **Prod** - DENT 1974

The Process of communication 46 MIN
16mm
Communication theory and the new educational media series
B&W (SPANISH)
LC 74-705427
Explores the process of communication beginning with an animated theoretical model, followed by sequences that progressively elaborate and illuminate the theory through illustrations drawn from communications networks in military, industrial, research and teaching settings.
Civics and Political Systems; English Language; Psychology; Social Science
Dist - USNAC **Prod** - USOE 1966

Process of Engineering Production 20 MIN
U-matic / VHS
Engineering Crafts Series
Color (H C A)
Industrial and Technical Education
Dist - FI **Prod** - BBCTV 1981

The Process of growth - Section A 48 MIN
U-matic / VHS
Management by responsibility series
Color
Psychology
Dist - DELTAK **Prod** - TRAINS

The Process of Growth (Section B) 28 MIN
U-matic / VHS
Management by Responsibility Series
Color
Psychology
Dist - DELTAK **Prod** - TRAINS

The Process of Newspaper Production 13 MIN
16mm
Color
LC 80-701374
Gives a brief history of printing and explains the steps in publishing a newspaper, from writing the story to publishing the paper.
Literature and Drama; Social Science
Dist - COLOSU **Prod** - COLOSU 1980

The Process of pollination 16 MIN
VHS
Color; PAL (I J H)
PdS29
Considers the function of pollination and the methods by which it occurs. Illustrates and compares the characteristics of wind - and insect - pollinated flowers. Looks at the mechanisms used by plants to avoid self - pollination. Uses familiar garden examples and exploits the resources of cine - macrography and time - lapse photography.
Science - Natural
Dist - BHA

The Process of professional collections
Videodisc
Color; CAV (G)
Trains collection representatives. Develops interpersonal skills and positive collection techniques. Includes leader's guide. participant manual and role - play manual and a Level II interactive video disc.
Psychology; Social Science
Dist - ADVET **Prod** - ADVET 1987

The Process of professional telemarketing
Videodisc
Color; CAV (G)
Develops telemarketing skills. Includes leader's guide. participant manual and role - play manual and Level II interactive video disc.
Business and Economics; Social Science
Dist - ADVET **Prod** - ADVET 1985

Process of Reading - more than Meets the Eye 15 MIN
U-matic
Process of Reading Series
Color
Uses Poe's Telltale Heart to examine words and their meanings, structure and pattern. Reveals that reading is not primarily a visual activity, much meaning is derived from the readers themselves.
English Language; Literature and Drama
Dist - TVOTAR **Prod** - TVOTAR 1976

Process of Reading Series
Beware the frumious bandersnatch 15 MIN
Bringing the Text to Life 15 MIN
An Intelligent Guessing Game 15 MIN
Process of Reading - more than Meets the Eye 15 MIN
Visions and Revisions 15 MIN
Windows into the Mind 15 MIN
Dist - TVOTAR

The Process of recovery
VHS
Color (A)
$99.95 purchase _ #8133
Examines recovery from chemical dependency as it relates to children of alcoholics.
Health and Safety; Psychology; Sociology
Dist - HAZELB

Process of taking temperature, pulse and respiration 27 MIN
16mm
Directions for education in nursing via technology series; Lesson 9
B&W (PRO)
LC 74-701783
Demonstrates methods of taking oral, axillary and rectal temperatures, as well as apical rate and apical - radial pulse. Discusses the parts, types and operational principles of equipment.
Health and Safety
Dist - WSUM **Prod** - DENT 1974

The Process of television news 15 MIN
16mm
Color
Reveals the people and forces at work behind a television news show. Examines the roles of anchormen, reporters, producers, editors and minicams.
Fine Arts; Literature and Drama
Dist - COLOSU **Prod** - COLOSU 1977

Process Operations Troubleshooting 60 MIN
VHS
Systems Operations Series
Color (PRO)
$600.00 - $1500.00 purchase _ #OTPOT
Introduces different types of troubleshooting techniques. Describes how these methods can be used to troubleshoot problems in various types of process operations. Part of a seventeen - part series on systems operations. Includes ten textbooks and an instructor guide to support four hours of instruction.
Education; Industrial and Technical Education; Psychology
Dist - NUSTC **Prod** - NUSTC

Process Reactor Fundamentals 60 MIN
VHS
Systems Operations Series
Color (PRO)
$600.00 - $1500.00 purchase _ #RCPRF
Examines various types of reactors such as vapor, liquid phase and catalyst. Considers plant batch and continuous reactor operations and reactor applications as well as basic operator responsibilities. Includes ten textbooks and an instructor guide to support four hours of instruction.
Education; Industrial and Technical Education; Psychology
Dist - NUSTC **Prod** - NUSTC

Process safety for plant personnel 19 MIN
VHS
Color (IND)
$495.00 purchase, $95.00 rental _ #800 - 81
Shows realistic in - plant scenarios highlighting the five aspects of process safety most influenced by plant personnel - process documentation, training and performance, process and equipment integrity and human factors. Motivates plant personnel to become active members of the process safety team. Includes leader's guide.
Business and Economics; Health and Safety
Dist - ITSC **Prod** - ITSC

Process safety management - an introduction 13 MIN
VHS
Color (IND G)
$395.00 purchase _ #150
Helps to sell the concept of process safety management to senior managers. Provides information about the specific requirements for the OSHA Process Safety Standard. Includes leader guide.
Business and Economics; Health and Safety; Psychology
Dist - GOVINS

Process safety management - it's just good business 30 MIN
VHS
Color (IND G)
$495.00 purchase _ #155
Provides an overview of OSHA's new Process Safety Standard to help with compliance efforts. Describes key aspects of the Standard and shows examples. Includes leader guide.
Business and Economics; Health and Safety; Psychology
Dist - GOVINS

Process safety management - OSHA compliance - 29 CFR 1910.119 16 MIN
VHS
Color (IND)
$495.00 purchase, $95.00 rental _ #800 - 90
Provides an overview and key aspects of OSHA's Process Safety Standard, to help with compliance.
Business and Economics; Health and Safety
Dist - ITSC **Prod** - ITSC

Process safety management - process safety information 17 MIN
VHS
Color (IND G)
$450.00 purchase _ #151
Gives detailed information on how to gather process safety information for use in a process hazard analysis. Informs about types of information to be gathered and where to get it. Covers chemical hazard information, technology of the process, equipment in the process. Includes leader guide.
Business and Economics; Health and Safety; Psychology
Dist - GOVINS

Process sampling 60 MIN
VHS
Basic theory and systems
Color (PRO)
$600.00 - $1500.00 purchase _ #OTPSA
Looks at the importance of safety when process materials are sampled. Demonstrates techniques for sampling liquids, solids and gases, with emphasis on nonhazardous materials. Notes safety considerations when sampling

hazardous materials. Part of a twenty - part series on basic theory and systems. Includes ten textbooks and an instructor guide to support four hours of instruction.
Health and Safety; Industrial and Technical Education; Psychology; Sociology
Dist - NUSTC **Prod** - NUSTC

Process Unit Operations Series
Alkylation operations 60 MIN
Blending Operations 60 MIN
Fluid catalytic cracking operations 60 MIN
Hydrotreating and Catalytic Reforming - 1 60 MIN
Hydrotreating and Catalytic Reforming - 2 60 MIN
Treating and Sulfur Recovery Operations 60 MIN
Dist - NUSTC

Processed meats 15 MIN
U-matic
Meats in canada series
(A)
Examines the various cutting methods employed in the preparation of processed meats and the types of packaging.
Agriculture; History - World; Home Economics; Social Science
Dist - ACCESS **Prod** - ACCESS 1983

Processes of aging - a discussion trigger 39 MIN
VHS / U-matic
Color (PRO C)
$395.00 purchase, $80.00 rental _ #C860 - VI - 038
Presents several important issues involved in the study of the process of aging. Interviews two women in their nineties to examine the effect of history on life experiences of older adults, the continuity of personality and values throughout life, the importance of memories and the uniqueness of the very old. Presented by Dr Karen Kapke and John Gray.
Health and Safety
Dist - HSCIC

Processing 10 MIN
VHS
Commercial chicken production series
Color (G)
$39.95 purchase _ #6 - 050 - 104A
Discusses the processing of poultry. Part of a six - part series on commercial chicken production.
Agriculture; Social Science
Dist - VEP **Prod** - UDEL

Processing 30 MIN
U-matic / VHS
Interaction - Human Concerns in the Schools Series
Color (T)
Shows how processing is done in an educational setting.
Education
Dist - MDCPB **Prod** - MDDE

Processing files
16mm
B&W
Explores the nature of computer files. Illustrates how files can be organized on tape and discs and shows a simple model of sequential updating.
Computer Science; Mathematics
Dist - OPENU **Prod** - OPENU

Processing for quality 17 MIN
16mm / VHS / BETA / U-matic
Quality series
Color; PAL (PRO IND)
PdS135, PdS143 purchase
Explores the needs of managers and decision - makers in a wide variety of companies. Part of a three - part series.
Business and Economics; Psychology
Dist - EDPAT

Processing States and Exception 30 MIN
VHS / U-matic
MC68000 Microprocessor Series
Color (IND)
Describes three system control systems in the 68000 - HALT, RESET, and bus error (BERR). Discusses normal, halted and exception processing states including privileged states and interrupts.
Industrial and Technical Education; Mathematics; Sociology
Dist - COLOSU **Prod** - COLOSU

Processing with Daceasy 4.3
VHS
Daceasy 4.3 series
Color (G)
$29.95 purchase _ #VIA052
Explains data processing with Daceasy 4.3.
Computer Science
Dist - SIV

Procession - Contemporary Directions in American Dance 19 MIN
16mm / U-matic / VHS
B&W (J H C)
Presents Ann Halpern and the Dancers Workshop Company of San Francisco performing selections from Procession, a dance from their experimental repertoire. Examines the group's theory of the dance and 'total theater' as the dancers adapt to their constantly changing environment, collaborating with all of its elements and accompanied by electronic sound.
Fine Arts
Dist - UCEMC **Prod** - UCEMC 1967

Processione - a Sicilian Easter 28 MIN
VHS
Color (H C G)
$195.00 purchase, $40.00 rental _ #37872
Portrays the 400 - year - old Good Friday ritual procession, the annual 'Procession of the Mysteries' in Trapani, Sicily, in which townsmen carry one - ton statues depicting the Stations of the Cross through old Trapani. Explores the psychology of ritual - why a community has for centuries staged a religious celebration as a public theater of grief and communally shared mourning. Produced by Susan C Lloyd.
History - World; Religion and Philosophy
Dist - UCEMC

Processor maintenance 35 MIN
VHS
Color (H C)
$59.95 purchase _ #SE - 14
Shows in detail the daily, weekly, monthly, three - month and yearly maintenance needed to keep a processor in excellent condition. Uses a LogE LD - 24 processor to demonstrate.
Industrial and Technical Education; Science - Physical
Dist - INSTRU

Procrastination 30 MIN
VHS
Insights - topics in contemporary psychology series
Color (H C G)
$89.95 purchase _ #ARG - 110
Presents two experts in the area of overcoming procrastination who share why procrastinators are stuck, what to do when living or working with one, and what a procrastinator can do to move beyond the problem. Shares important lessons. Part of a four - part series on contemporary psychology.
Health and Safety; Psychology
Dist - INSTRU

Proctosigmoidoscopy 9 MIN
U-matic / VHS
Medical Skills Films Series
Color (PRO)
Health and Safety
Dist - WFP **Prod** - WFP

Proctosigmoidoscopy - a Part of the Physical Examination 22 MIN
16mm
Color (PRO)
Presents a convincing case for extensive use of proctosigmoidoscopy to detect asymptomatic cancer of the colon and rectum. Demonstrates technical points and safeguards of the examination using endoscopic photography.
Health and Safety
Dist - AMCS **Prod** - AMCS 1963

Proctosigmoidoscopy - a Part of the Routine Physical Examination 23 MIN
VHS / U-matic
Color (PRO)
Attempts to persuade physicians in general practice to use the proctosigmoidoscope as part of the routine physical examination. Shows endoscopic views of areas of the colon as the physician sees them.
Health and Safety
Dist - WFP **Prod** - WFP

Procurement performance measurement 60 MIN
BETA / VHS
Manufacturing series
(IND)
Points out ways that buyers and purchasing departments are evaluated in a strong purchasing performance measurement system.
Business and Economics; Psychology
Dist - COMSRV **Prod** - COMSRV 1986

Procurement Planning and Contracting 60 MIN
BETA / VHS
Manufacturing Series
(IND)
Shows how to collect requirements for purchased items and services, identify qualified suppliers, develop requests for quotes and negotiate and award contracts.
Business and Economics
Dist - COMSRV **Prod** - COMSRV 1986

Procurement Source Selection 20 MIN
16mm
Color
LC 74-705428
Explains how the Defense Department and the Army select the source of a major procurement.
Civics and Political Systems
Dist - USNAC **Prod** - USA 1967

The Prodigal father 27 MIN
16mm / U-matic / VHS
Insight series
Color; B&W (H C A)
Scrutinizes the reunion of a man with his father who had deserted his family. Discloses that although the father's absence caused a lot of misery, the younger man cannot hate the person who gave him life. Stars Jim McMullan.
Guidance and Counseling; Psychology; Religion and Philosophy; Sociology
Dist - PAULST **Prod** - PAULST

Prodigal Son 15 MIN
16mm
Color (P I J)
Presents the Parable of the Prodigal Son, dramatized with the use of puppets.
Guidance and Counseling; Literature and Drama
Dist - YALEDV **Prod** - YALEDV

Prodigies - Great Expectations 52 MIN
U-matic / VHS
Color (G)
$249.00, $149.00 purchase _ #AD - 1513
Examines the problems and privileges of brilliant children who are gifted with intellectually mature minds, yet are still often emotionally and physically immature. Considers the social consequences of being exceptionally intelligent.
Health and Safety; Psychology
Dist - FOTH **Prod** - FOTH

Producers and Consumers 15 MIN
VHS / U-matic
Common Cents Series
Color (P)
Compares the roles of producers and consumers, defines income, and discusses the value of productive work.
Business and Economics
Dist - AITECH **Prod** - KETCTV 1977

Producing a Videotape 30 MIN
VHS / U-matic
Video - a Practical Guide and more Series
Color
Follows a production from conceptualization through post - production. Explains story treatments, scripts, storyboards, budgets, production boards, shooting schedules and more.
Fine Arts; Industrial and Technical Education
Dist - VIPUB **Prod** - VIPUB

Producing Accurate Orifice Meter Charts 21 MIN
Slide / VHS / 16mm
Color (A IND)
$210.00, $220.00 purchase _ #15.1181, #55.1181
Illustrates techniques for creating and maintaining accurate orifice meter charts. Focuses on role of lease operators and pipeline workers.
Industrial and Technical Education; Mathematics; Social Science
Dist - UTEXPE

Producing an Ad 23 MIN
16mm
Introduction to Commercial Art Series
Color
LC 79-701848
Demonstrates the production of an advertisement as it concerns the commercial artist. Shows the five layout steps followed in producing an ad, using the creation of a school poster as an example.
Business and Economics; Fine Arts
Dist - SF **Prod** - SF 1979

Producing an instructional videotape - ear surgery 10 MIN
U-matic / VHS
Color (PRO C)
$395.00 purchase, $80.00 rental _ #C851 - VI - 061
Illustrates how to initiate and follow through with the production of an instructional videotape examining production sequence, video cameras and optics and techniques for shooting and editing the videotape. Presented by Dr Richard M Bass and Thomas R Penrose.
Education; Health and Safety; Industrial and Technical Education
Dist - HSCIC

Producing and Transmitting Messages 15 MIN
VHS / 16mm
Exploring Technology Series
Color (I J)

$180.00 purchase, $25.00 rental
Shows the role of computers in the print industry at USA Today, and communication of the Live Aid concert by satellite.
Business and Economics; Computer Science; Fine Arts; Psychology
Dist - AITECH **Prod** - AITECH 1990

Producing and Transmitting Messages - 3 17 MIN
VHS
Exploring Technology Education - Communication - Series
Color (I)
$180.00 purchase
Visits USA TODAY to show the central role of computers in preparing and transmitting information. Discloses that typesetting, laser scanning for color pictures and transmission by facsimile scanners all make use of digital signals so that identical papers can be printed simultaneously at plants across the country. Builds the technological literacy vital for current and future careers. Part of the Exploring Technology Series.
Education; Industrial and Technical Education; Social Science
Dist - AITECH **Prod** - AITECH 1990

Producing better learning series Module 1
Let the student come first 7 MIN
Dist - RESEM

Producing Better Learning Series Module 3
Good Techniques for Teaching 7 MIN
Dist - RESEM

Producing better learning series
Presents three modules on fundamental teaching theory and practice. Includes the titles Let the Student Come First, Helping Learning Happen, Good Techniques for Teaching.
Helping learning happen 52 FRS
Dist - RESEM **Prod** - RESEM 1990

Producing Dance Documentaries 30 MIN
U-matic / VHS
Glances at the Past Series
Color
Fine Arts; Industrial and Technical Education
Dist - ARCVID **Prod** - ARCVID

Producing Dance Specials for the Mass Market 30 MIN
U-matic / VHS
Dance on Television - Lorber Series
Color
Fine Arts; Industrial and Technical Education
Dist - ARCVID **Prod** - ARCVID

Producing Miracles Everyday 23 MIN
VHS / 16mm
Documentaries by Adobe Foundations Series
Color (G)
$195.00 purchase, $50.00 rental
Shows Latin Americans of all ages who turn misery into miracles by creating their own forms of income and employment through hard work and ingenuity - children fill potholes in the street, old men and old women fashion sandals out of old tires and professional mourners are on call at cemeteries. Celebrates the resourcefulness of impoverished people throughout the developing world for whom economic necessity is truly the mother of invention.
Geography - World; Psychology; Social Science; Sociology
Dist - CNEMAG **Prod** - ADOF 1990

Producing Oil 25 MIN
U-matic / VHS
Color (IND)
LC 76-700850
Shows in a nontechnical manner how oil and gas are formed, produced and processed for delivery from the well to the pipeline.
Industrial and Technical Education; Science - Natural; Social Science
Dist - UTEXPE **Prod** - UTEXPE 1974

Producing reproducers 44 MIN
VHS
Building the family of God series
Color (R G)
$29.95 purchase _ #6109 - 3
Shows how ordinary Christians can change their world through discipleship. Features Dr John MacArthur.
Literature and Drama; Religion and Philosophy
Dist - MOODY **Prod** - MOODY

Producing the Product 29 MIN
U-matic / VHS
Business File Series
Color
Business and Economics
Dist - PBS **Prod** - PBS

Product 30 MIN
VHS / 16mm
Growing a Business Series
(H C)
$99.95 each, $1,295.00 series
Explores the issues of quality and quantity in big business production.
Business and Economics
Dist - AMBROS **Prod** - AMBROS 1988

Product and Competitive Knowledge 9 MIN
U-matic / VHS
Telemarketing for Better Business Results Series
Color
Business and Economics; Psychology
Dist - DELTAK **Prod** - COMTEL

The product and quotient rules 30 MIN
VHS
Calculus series
Color (C)
$125.00 purchase _ #6009
Explains product and quotient rules. Part of a 56 - part series on calculus.
Mathematics
Dist - LANDMK **Prod** - LANDMK

The Product and Quotient Rules 30 MIN
VHS
Mathematics Series
Color (J)
LC 95713155
Examines product and quotient rules. The 118th of 157 installments of the Mathematics Series.
Mathematics
Dist - GPN

Product and Quotient Rules for Derivatives 20 MIN
VHS
Calculus Series
Color (H)
LC 90712920
Discusses product and quotient rules for derivatives. The eighth of 57 installments of the Calculus Series.
Mathematics
Dist - GPN

Product Costs - What's in Them 14 MIN
U-matic / VHS / 16mm
Color (H C A)
LC 79-700447
Shows some of the costs that go into the final price of a product. Uses the situation of a shopper at his local grocery store to demonstrate why the same or similar products can have widely varying prices.
Business and Economics; Home Economics
Dist - PHENIX **Prod** - GREENF 1979

Product Definition 60 MIN
BETA / VHS
Manufacturing Series
(IND)
Introduces the first two phases of the product design methodology, product initiation and analysis.
Business and Economics
Dist - COMSRV **Prod** - COMSRV 1986

Product Development 60 MIN
BETA / VHS
Manufacturing Series
(IND)
Describes the use of models, computers and other tools to generate drawings and specifications which will be used to create the engineering prototype.
Business and Economics
Dist - COMSRV **Prod** - COMSRV 1986

Product development 30 MIN
VHS / U-matic
Marketing perspectives series
Color
Covers primary sources for new product concepts, product development sequences, ways that product introductions affect existing product lines and role of corporate management in product development.
Business and Economics; Education
Dist - WFVTAE **Prod** - MATC

Product development 58 MIN
VHS / U-matic
Management of microprocessor technology series
Color
Lectures on information sources, the project team and management guidelines in product development.
Business and Economics; Industrial and Technical Education; Mathematics
Dist - MIOT **Prod** - MIOT

Product Liability 26 MIN
U-matic / VHS
Quality Control Series
Color
Describes the current status of product liability in the U S and the impacts on quality control specifications and procedures.
Business and Economics; Industrial and Technical Education
Dist - MIOT **Prod** - MIOT

Product Liability and the Reasonably Safe Product 55 MIN
U-matic / VHS
Color
Stresses that designing for safety from the start avoids product liability suits and rising insurance rates. Explains the definitions of defects, warnings, and disclaimers in today's legal system.
Business and Economics; Health and Safety; Industrial and Technical Education
Dist - SME **Prod** - SME

Product Management 30 MIN
U-matic / VHS
Marketing Perspectives Series
Color
Shows five stages of the product lifecycle. Compares the growth curve to the profit - loss curve in the product lifecycle. Shows ways to expand the product line and to extend the product's lifecycle.
Business and Economics; Education
Dist - WFVTAE **Prod** - MATC

Product of two negative numbers 7 MIN
VHS
Children's encyclopedia of mathematics - pre - algebra series
Color (I)
$49.95 purchase _ #8370
Discusses the product of two negative numbers. Part of a nine - part series about pre - algebra.
Mathematics
Dist - AIMS **Prod** - DAVFMS 1991

Product Producibility 60 MIN
BETA / VHS
Manufacturing Series
(IND)
Describes the process of design which includes considerations which will affect manufacturing, inventory control, procurement, and marketing.
Business and Economics
Dist - COMSRV **Prod** - COMSRV 1986

Product Release 60 MIN
VHS / BETA
Manufacturing Series
(IND)
Describes the release of a product to manufacturing and production departments. Reviews the design engineering process.
Business and Economics
Dist - COMSRV **Prod** - COMSRV 1986

Product Spaces and Statistically Independent Experiments 17 MIN
U-matic / VHS
Probability and Random Processes - Elementary Probability Theory 'Series
B&W (PRO)
Extends the concept of statistical independence.
Industrial and Technical Education; Mathematics
Dist - MIOT **Prod** - MIOT

Production 15 MIN
VHS / 16mm
Econ and Me Series
Color (P)
$95.00 purchase, $25.00 rental
Tells how producers combine resources to make goods and services. To make good choices about what to produce and what resources to use, producers need to consider costs and benefits.
Business and Economics
Dist - AITECH **Prod** - AITECH 1989

Production
VHS
Dynamics of business series
Color (H C A)
$139.00 purchase _ #MAS05V
Explores basic production concepts. Considers subjects including planning and inventory, production control, purchasing and procurement, and the law and personnel.
Business and Economics
Dist - CAMV

Production 15 MIN
VHS / U-matic
Pennywise Series no 5
Color (P)

LC 82-706007
Uses the format of a television program to explain the basic economic principle of production. Demonstrates that both goods and services are produced and that their production is carried out by people for the most part.
Business and Economics
Dist - GPN **Prod** - MAETEL 1980

Production 30 MIN
U-matic
It's Everybody's Business Series Unit 5, Operating a Business
Color
Business and Economics
Dist - DALCCD **Prod** - DALCCD

Production and general control 30 MIN
U-matic / VHS
Business of management series lesson 20; Lesson 20
Color (C A)
Focuses on control devices, methods and procedures that are used to collect and distribute information to various management information systems. Discusses new trends in control and management information systems.
Business and Economics; Psychology
Dist - SCCON **Prod** - SCCON

Production and inventory control 15 MIN
16mm
Color (A)
LC 80-701484
Introduces the American Production And Inventory Control Society, emphasizing its history, why it developed and what it does.
Business and Economics
Dist - MTP **Prod** - APICS 1979

Production and Printing 30 MIN
U-matic
Maps - Horizons to Knowledge Series
Color
Explains early processes such as wood blocks and copper plates and the more recent use of offset lithography in map making.
Geography - United States; Geography - World; Social Science
Dist - UMITV **Prod** - UMITV 1980

Production and technology 25 MIN
VHS
Tech prep careers of the future video series
Color (J H C G)
$149.00 purchase _ #CDTEC204V
Examines careers in production and technology in a program developed in conjunction with the Carl Perkins Applied Technology Act. Discloses what the technical preparatory, vocational student or community college graduate can expect from the work place and how the student's interests, values and skills relate to each of the clusters presented. Balances relevant career data with what to expect from the day to day workplace. Features three in - depth interviews. Part of a five - part series on careers.
Business and Economics; Guidance and Counseling
Dist - CAMV

Production Art
U-matic / VHS
Work - a - Day America
$59.95 purchase _ #VV118V
Helps students achieve career vocational preparation. Stresses the four main points of career awareness and exploration, specific skills intended, employability skills needed, and real people sharing on the job experiences.
Guidance and Counseling
Dist - CAREER **Prod** - CAREER

Production employee training - the do's and don'ts 18 MIN
U-matic / BETA / VHS
Color (A PRO)
$100.00 purchase
Takes the viewer into the shop and goes through the problems encountered in training two new employees on a simple drill - press job. Shows what happens when a poor job of training new operators is done, and the results obtained when a really thorough job is done.
Business and Economics; Psychology
Dist - TAMMFG **Prod** - TAMMFG

Production I 28 MIN
VHS / 16mm
Video career library series
Color (H C A PRO)
$79.95 purchase _ #WW115
Shows occupations in production such as layout workers, precision typesetters, lithographers, photoengravers, bookbinders, hand tailors, dressmakers, upholsterers, water and sewage plant operators, power and chemical plant operators. Contains occupational outlook and salary information.
Business and Economics; Guidance and Counseling
Dist - AAVIM **Prod** - AAVIM 1990

Production I 28 MIN
U-matic / VHS
Video career library series
(H C A)
$69.95 _ #CJ125V
Covers duties, conditions, salaries and training connected to jobs in the production field. Provides a view of employees in production related occupations, and gives information on the current market for such skills. Revised every two years.
Guidance and Counseling
Dist - CAMV **Prod** - CAMV

Production II 32 MIN
U-matic / VHS
Video career library series
(H C A)
$69.95 _ #CJ126V
Covers duties, conditions, salaries, and training connected with jobs in the production field. Provides a view of employees in production related occupations, and gives information concerning the market for such skills. Revised every two years.
Education; Guidance and Counseling
Dist - CAMV **Prod** - CAMV

Production II 32 MIN
VHS / 16mm
Video career library series
Color (H C A PRO)
$79.95 purchase _ #WW116
Shows occupations in production such as tool and die makers, machinists, sheet metal workers, cabinet and bench carpenters, opticians, precision electronic equipment assemblers, industrial machine operators, welders, cutters, and assemblers. Contains occupational outlook and salary information.
Business and Economics; Guidance and Counseling
Dist - AAVIM **Prod** - AAVIM 1990

Production - minded management series 51 MIN
35mm strip / U-matic / VHS / Slide
Production - minded management series
Color (G)
$305.00, $270.00 purchase
Presents four modules on production efficiency. Includes the titles Inflation and Productivity, How to Improve Production, Attitudes Toward Production, What Difference Does It Make.
Business and Economics
Dist - RESEM **Prod** - RESEM

Production - Minded Management Series Module 1
Inflation and Productivity 66 FRS
Dist - RESEM

Production - Minded Management Series Module 2
How to Improve Production 13 MIN
Dist - RESEM

Production - Minded Management Series Module 4
What Difference Does it make? 13 MIN
Dist - RESEM

The Production possibilities frontier 60 MIN
VHS
Macroeconomics series
Color (H C G)
$89.00 purchase _ #GSU - 304
Discusses the production possibility curve, differing economic systems. Introduces the market system and interviews Frank Galman, President of House of Lamantia, Chicago. Part of a 24 - part series instructed by Dr Edward F Stuart, Northwestern University, which focuses on a description of the major economic policy - making bodies in the United States and their interrelationships.
Business and Economics
Dist - INSTRU

Production Process 15 MIN
U-matic / VHS
Common Cents Series
Color (P)
Introduces the concept of risk and profit, explains assembly line production, looks at some responsibilities of producers, and reinforces the theme of economic interdependence.
Business and Economics
Dist - AITECH **Prod** - KETCTV 1977

Production - Shooting Tips 8.55 MIN
VHS
On Location
(J)
$180 series purchase, $50 rental, $110 self dub
Demonstrates video production skills for small format student productions. Focuses on shooting on location. Highlights techniques, equipment, and basic camera movements and transitions. Sixth in an eight part series.
Fine Arts
Dist - GPN **Prod** - NCGE

Production technology
VHS
School to work - communications connections for the real world 'series
Color (J H C G)
$149.00 purchase _ #CDCOM112V
Discusses why communications skills are a vital part of careers in production technology. Meets the requirements for integrating academic communication skills with the vocational work world of the Carl Perkins Applied Technology Act. Part of a ten - part series.
Business and Economics; Guidance and Counseling; Social Science
Dist - CAMV

Productive Discipline Series Module 1
Why Discipline? 10 MIN
Dist - RESEM

Productive Discipline Series Module 2
Why Employees Don't Perform 12 MIN
Dist - RESEM

Productive discipline series
Presents three modules on practical and realistic discipline in supervision. Includes the titles Why Discipline, Why Employees Don't Perform, How to Do Productive Discipline.
How to do productive discipline 68 FRS(0237180)
Dist - RESEM **Prod** - RESEM 1993

Productivity
U-matic / VHS
Color
Satirizes well - known rules for improving employee productivity.
Business and Economics; Fine Arts; Literature and Drama
Dist - MEETS **Prod** - BBB

Productivity 20 MIN
16mm
Color
Business and Economics
Dist - CINE **Prod** - CINE

Productivity 30 MIN
VHS / U-matic
Economics exchange series; Program 5
Color (T)
LC 82-706417
Presents Dr Willard M Kniep of Arizona State University instructing teachers in the strategies and skills of teaching children economics and consumer education concepts. Focuses on the topic of productivity by explaining it and then demonstrating specific approaches that teachers can use in their classrooms.
Business and Economics; Education; Home Economics
Dist - GPN **Prod** - KAETTV 1981

Productivity - an American Challenge 18 MIN
U-matic / VHS / 16mm
Color (C A)
LC 84-706179
Presents Dr Frank Wagner analyzing the Hawthorne studies film and commenting on America's failure in recent years to match the productivity levels of other nations.
Business and Economics; Psychology
Dist - SALENG **Prod** - SALENG 1984

Productivity and Performance by Alex K 24 MIN
16mm / U-matic / VHS
Developing Your Potential Series
Color (I J H)
Shows a lazy young man who strives to become a highly motivated person. Uses humor to point out that productivity has to be understood and adopted at a personal and practical level.
Guidance and Counseling; Psychology
Dist - JOU **Prod** - SCCL

Productivity and performance improvement - management and - a series
Productivity and performance improvement - management series
Color
Presents three one - hour recordings of a live teleconference held September 30, 1982. Helps educators develop strategies and action plans for improving productivity and performance in a health care setting.
Health and Safety; Psychology
Dist - AHOA **Prod** - AHOA

Productivity and performance improvement - management series
Productivity and performance improvement - management and - a series
Dist - AHOA

Productivity and the Self - Fulfilling Prophecy - the Pygmalion Effect 30 MIN
U-matic / VHS / 16mm
Behavior in Business Film Series
Color (H C A)
LC 75-700171
Shows how the powers of expectation, or the Pygmalion effect, can be used as a positive or negative influence on behavior. Illustrates the way this process occurs and show how management can use it as a tool for the benefit of both the organization and the individual.
Business and Economics; Psychology
Dist - CRMP **Prod** - CRMP 1974

Productivity and the self fulfilling prophecy - the Pygmalion effect; 2nd 30 MIN
16mm / VHS
(PRO)
#109102 - 5 3/4
Demonstrates how a manager's expectations can dramatically improve a worker's performance.
Business and Economics; Guidance and Counseling
Dist - MGHT

Productivity Breakthroughs - Begin with Results Instead of Preparation 28 MIN
VHS / U-matic
Color
Explains why managers can't wait for more motivated employees, increasingly cooperative unions, newer equipment or low cost power, but must make dramatic productivity gains with resources available now.
Business and Economics
Dist - SME **Prod** - SME

Productivity - Can We Get more for Less 30 MIN
U-matic / VHS
Economics USA Series
Color (C)
Business and Economics
Dist - ANNCPB **Prod** - WEFA

Productivity challenge in the decade of the 80s 43 MIN
VHS / U-matic
Color
Identifies some of the changes companies can make to dramatically increase productivity. Discusses the part that a sense of a national spirit, unity and pride play in effectively dealing with lagging productivity.
Business and Economics
Dist - SME **Prod** - SME

The Productivity Dilemma 30 MIN
U-matic / VHS
Business of Management Series Lesson 25; Lesson 25
Color (C A)
Features academicians and managers as they discuss the dimensions of productivity and the numerous factors that have contributed to the productivity slowdown in the United States.
Business and Economics; Psychology
Dist - SCCON **Prod** - SCCON

Productivity in Motion 14 MIN
16mm
Color
Documents the importance of the conveyor industry to America's industrialization.
Business and Economics
Dist - MTP **Prod** - CEMA

Productivity - It's a Personal Matter 19 MIN
16mm / U-matic / VHS
Color (IND)
LC 84-7067178
Explores the idea of work, what it means to people, how its meaning has changed for many and how that change has hurt some people. Argues that people need to rediscover the value of work for their own individual benefit as well as that of their company and their country.
Psychology
Dist - SALENG **Prod** - CCS 1983

Productivity - Key to America's Economic Growth 28 MIN
16mm
Color; B&W (H)
LC FIA65-567
Provides an introduction to the American economic system. Explains the relationship between productivity and wages and between productivity and the standard of living. Cites causes of economic growth.
Business and Economics
Dist - SUTHLA **Prod** - SLOAN 1965

Productivity - key to progress 20 MIN
16mm
Exploring basic economics series
B&W (H A)
LC FI67-368
Discusses the factor of productivity as related to economic growth. Illustrates how savings and investments create capital and how increasingly efficient tools add to increased productivity.
Business and Economics
Dist - MLA **Prod** - RSC 1964

Productivity measurement 60 MIN
BETA / VHS
Manufacturing series
(IND)
Defines the work center supervisor's role in productivity measurement activities and the importance of these measurements in supervision.
Business and Economics
Dist - COMSRV **Prod** - COMSRV 1986

Productivity of Japanese Industry 30 MIN
VHS / U-matic
Business Nippon Series
Color (A)
LC 85-702162
Business and Economics; History - World
Dist - EBEC **Prod** - JAPCTV 1984

Productivity - Pygmalion; 2nd 25 MIN
VHS / 16mm
(C PRO)
$625.00 purchase, $125.00 rental
Applies the Pygmalion principle to self expectations showing the power of self motivation.
Business and Economics; Education
Dist - VLEARN **Prod** - CRM

Productivity - Pygmalion effect 29 MIN
VHS / 16mm
(C PRO)
$625.00 purchase, $125.00 rental
Illustrates the self fulfilling prophecy or Pygmalion Effect, wherein employees tend to perform in accordance with what their leaders expect of them.
Business and Economics; Education
Dist - VLEARN **Prod** - CRM

Productivity - Quality of Work Life Series
The Moving and the Stuck 20 MIN
Dist - DELTAK

Productivity through People 29 MIN
VHS / 16mm
Management Action Program Series
Color (A PRO)
$310.00 purchase
Encourages productivity in personnel. Stresses removal of their 'fear of failure.' Features North American Tool & Die. Part of a three - part series on customer service, featuring Bob Waterman, author of 'In Search of Excellence.' Each program includes workshop materials.
Business and Economics
Dist - VIDART **Prod** - NATTYL 1990

Products and services
Videodisc
Financial FLASHFAX product knowledge series
(H A)
$1995.00
Explains differences and features among over 40 different financial products and services, improving an employee's ability to match a customer with the most appropriate investments and services. Can be customized for a particular financial institution.
Business and Economics
Dist - CMSL **Prod** - CMSL

Products, People and Ideas 15 MIN
16mm
Color
Tells the story of the National Housewares Manufacturers Association through its annual exposition. Stresses marketing and merchandising in the housewares industry.
Business and Economics
Dist - MTP **Prod** - NATHMA 1982

Profession education series
Homefires 28 MIN
Dist - IFB

The Profession of Accounting is 25 MIN
U-matic
Color
Describes the challenges and rewards of the accounting profession. Discusses the skills and education needed. Narrated by Ed Herlihy.
Business and Economics; Education; Guidance and Counseling
Dist - MTP **Prod** - AICPA

The Profession of Arms 60 MIN
U-matic / VHS / 16mm
War Series
Color (C A)
Deals with the professional soldier, career officers in every country who devote their lives to maintaining military organizations. Features officers from the Israeli, American, Soviet and Canadian forces describing battles they have fought and the special characteristics needed to pursue their career, discussing how they reconcile themselves to their mandate to kill and the knowledge that they may be killed.
Civics and Political Systems; Sociology
Dist - FI **Prod** - NFBC

Profession of Authorship in America 30 MIN
VHS
Modern American Literature Eminent Scholar - Teachers Video Series
Color (C)
$95.00 purchase
Corrects the misapprehension that writing books is a way to fame and fortune in American culture. Focuses on the business of publishing, stressing the effects of marketing considerations, competing media and financial arrangements. The 30th of 34 installments of the Modern American Literature Eminent Scholar - Teachers Video Series.
Business and Economics; Guidance and Counseling; Literature and Drama
Dist - OMNIGR

The Professional 30 MIN
16mm / U-matic / VHS
Color (PRO)
No descriptive information available.
Business and Economics
Dist - DARTNL **Prod** - DARTNL 1969

Professional attitudes 15 MIN
VHS / U-matic
Safety for oilfield contractors series
Color
Presents the story of a man with a hangover who comes to work on heavy equipment, doing about everything wrong, wearing no hardhat, showing improper equipment sense and finally coming to a tragic end.
Health and Safety
Dist - FLMWST **Prod** - FLMWST

Professional Attitudes 15 MIN
VHS / 16mm
(A PRO)
$165.00 purchase _ #40.0149
Follows the plight of a heavy equipment operator who reports to work with a hangover. Shows how, after doing almost everything wrong, he finally meets a tragic end.
Industrial and Technical Education; Social Science
Dist - UTEXPE **Prod** - UTEXPE 1982

The Professional Counselor in School Settings 33 MIN
VHS / U-matic
Color (A)
Discusses through panel guests the problems and future challenges that school counselors are facing.
Education
Dist - AACD **Prod** - AACD 1984

Professional development in the clinical laboratory 18 MIN
U-matic / VHS
Color (PRO C)
$395.00 purchase, $80.00 rental _ #C870 - VI - 051
Presents vignettes based on the learning vector model which proposes that clinical instruction can influence a student's professional development in a series of progressive stages. Shows how a student's attitude and psychosocial and social characteristics develop in the exposure, acquisition and integration stages. Presented by Susan J Beck, Debbie Cowan, Nancy Hymel, Barbara Hawthorne and Frank Stritter.
Business and Economics; Health and Safety; Psychology
Dist - HSCIC

Professional Drug Films Series
Drug Dialogue - Orientation 16 MIN
Rick, File X - 258375 11 MIN
Dist - USNAC

The Professional Education Program of the American Cancer Society 22 MIN
16mm
Color
Shows the roles of volunteers from health professions and American Cancer Society staff members in planning and carrying out cancer education by and for professionals. Shows this program in action at unit, division and national levels. Examines projects conducted for developing attitudes and clinical techniques to promote the early detection of cancer and its prompt and adequate

treatment. Demonstrates the effective uses of professional publications, films and exhibits and shows how programs are adapted to local community needs.
Health and Safety; Sociology
Dist - AMCS **Prod** - AMCS 1973

Professional Engineering Review Series
CE 1
CE 2
CE 3
CHE 1 9 MIN
CHE 2 9 MIN
EEc 1 6 MIN
ME 1 6 MIN
ME 2 7 MIN
Dist - AMCEE

Professional excellence 40 MIN
VHS
Color (A PRO IND)
$395.00 purchase, $130.00 rental
Discusses motivation for professionals. Suggests that motivational tactics must consider how professionals are usually driven by professional pride, responsibility, and a desire for autonomy. Based on a book by Peter Burgher.
Business and Economics; Guidance and Counseling; Psychology
Dist - VLEARN **Prod** - CVIDE

Professional food preparation and service program series
The Art of broiler cookery
Banquet service 15 MIN
Bar management - internal controls 17 MIN
Bartending 14 MIN
Buffet layout and service 12 MIN
Cafeteria service 10 MIN
Care and cleaning of kitchen equipment 12 MIN
Carving the rib roast 8 MIN
A Cool head for salads 8 MIN
Courtesy - food service is people service 8 MIN
Courtesy - the inside story 8 MIN
Creative hamburger sandwich preparation
Dining room safety 8 MIN
Dish machine operator 8 MIN
The Efficient busperson - assisting the server
Fast food service 15 MIN
Fast sandwich making 8 MIN
Food purchasing, Pt 1 - general principles 13 MIN
Food purchasing, Pt 2 - let the buyer beware 14 MIN
Give your eggs a break 8 MIN
Handwashing of kitchen utensils and glassware
Hosting
How do you look when it counts 8 MIN
Kitchen fire safety
Kitchen knives - safe and efficient use 11 MIN
Kitchen safety - preventing cuts and strains 8 MIN
Kitchen safety - preventing falls 8 MIN
Kitchen safety - preventing machine injuries 8 MIN
The Microwave oven 11 MIN
Portion control - a team effort 12 MIN
Preventing burns in the kitchen
Rush hour service 10 MIN
Sandwich preparation and presentation 8 MIN
Sanitation - rodent and insect control 10 MIN
Sanitation and hygiene - basic rules
Sanitation and hygiene - why the importance
Sanitation and hygiene for dining room personnel
Sauteing and pan frying 12 MIN
Serving food and beverage
Short order cookery 10 MIN
Simmering and poaching 10 MIN
Soup preparation 15 MIN
Stopping foodservice waste
Suggestive selling for waiters and waitresses
Table settings 8 MIN
Using standardized recipes 9 MIN
Vegetable preparation 10 MIN
Dist - NEM

Professional food preparation and service programs series
Waiters and waitresses - basic responsibilities 15 MIN
Dist - NEM

Professional Hotel and Tourism Program Series
Front Desk Courtesy 11 MIN
Hotel fire safety 30 MIN
Hotel Security 25 MIN
Dist - NEM

Professional hotel and tourism programs series
The Bellman 10 MIN
Making up the room 9 MIN
Room Service 10 MIN
Dist - NEM

The Professional Image 20 MIN
VHS / U-matic
Color (A)
Shows how to create an effective business wardrobe for both men and women. Based on book The Professional Image by Susan Bixler.
Business and Economics; Home Economics; Psychology
Dist - AMEDIA **Prod** - AMEDIA

The Professional Image - Unit 4 15 MIN
VHS / 16mm
Essentials of Professionalism Series
Color (PRO)
$325.00 purchase, $150.00 rental, $35.00 preview
Trains bank employees. Presents step by step methods for creating a good first impression. Includes support materials.
Business and Economics; Home Economics; Psychology; Sociology
Dist - UTM **Prod** - UTM

Professional Management Program Series
Delegate - don't abdicate 12 MIN
Discipline - a Matter of Judgment 12 MIN
Eye of the supervisor 12 MIN
Flight plan 13 MIN
The Manager and the Law 19 MIN
The Peter Hill Puzzle 31 MIN
Problem solving - a process for managers 16 MIN
Profile of a Manager 14 MIN
Strategy for Winning 20 MIN
The Supervisor - motivating through insight 12 MIN
Supervisor - motivating through insight 13 MIN
The Time Game 14 MIN
The Training Memorandum 12 MIN
Dist - NEM

Professional management program - Spanish series
Flight plan 14 MIN
Profile of a Manager 14 MIN
Dist - NEM

The Professional Nature of Selling
U-matic / VHS
Strategies for Successful Selling Series Module 1
Color
Identifies the main elements that must be managed in all selling situations.
Business and Economics
Dist - AMA **Prod** - AMA

Professional occupations - part 1
VHS
Profiles - people and jobs series
Color (H G)
$50.00 purchase _ #POCC - 1V
Presents part of a series of 6 videos that introduce high school students to high demand, rewarding occupations of the future. Looks at the careers of Occupational Therapist; Physical Therapist; Respiratory Therapist; Registered Nurse; Elementary School Teacher; Secondary School Teacher. Series is based on the Occupational Outlook Handbook.
Business and Economics; Guidance and Counseling
Dist - CENTER **Prod** - CENTER

Professional occupations - part 2
VHS
Profiles - people and jobs series
Color (H G)
$50.00 purchase _ #POCC - 2V
Presents part of a series of 6 videos that introduce high school students to high demand, rewarding occupations of the future. Looks at the careers of Civil Engineer; Electronic Engineer; Operations Research Analyst; Social Worker; Computer Systems Analyst; Human Services Worker. Series is based on the Occupational Outlook Handbook.
Business and Economics; Guidance and Counseling
Dist - CENTER **Prod** - CENTER

Professional Patrol 14 MIN
VHS / U-matic
Professional Security Training Series Module 2
Color
Stresses the importance of the routine patrol, illustrating proper tactics and procedures. Covers various patrol requirements and decision - making skills.
Health and Safety; Sociology
Dist - CORF **Prod** - CORF

Professional Photography 29 MIN
16mm / U-matic / VHS
Photography - the Incisive Art Series
B&W (H C A)
Presents Ansel Adams and Milton Halberstadt discussing photography as a profession. Mr Adams applies his imagination and techniques to industrial, promotional and portrait photography.
Guidance and Counseling; Industrial and Technical Education; Psychology
Dist - IU **Prod** - NET 1960

Professional photography
CD-ROM
Color (G A)
$149.00 purchase _ #2371
Offers 100 high resolution photos covering a wide range of subjects - with unlimited reproduction rights. Presents photos in TIFF format, stored both as 24 bit color and 8 bit black and white files. For Macintosh Plus, SE and II computers. Requires at least one M of RAM, one floppy disk drive, and an Apple compatible CD - ROM drive.
Computer Science; Fine Arts; Industrial and Technical Education
Dist - BEP

Professional Planning for Pairs 27 MIN
U-matic
Color (H C A)
LC 81-707368
Explores how married couples cope with the difficulties encountered with dual careers. Interviews three couples who discuss such topics as children, part - time employment and problems presented by new job opportunities.
Guidance and Counseling; Sociology
Dist - CORNRS **Prod** - CUETV 1979

Professional Planting 51 MIN
BETA / VHS / U-matic
Color (G)
$49.95 _ #MA2211
Teaches about outdoor plant propagation by experts from the Brooklyn Botanical Gardens. Shows how to improve your lawn by planting a variety of flora that can be grown from seeds and tissue cultures.
Agriculture
Dist - BAKERT

Professional presence 24 MIN
VHS
Color (PRO A G)
$595.00 purchase, $130.00 rental
Updates the video The Professional Image with tips on business etiquette. Provides advice for men and women about clothing and personal care for a polished, professional appearance. Features Susan Bixler and includes a book and summary fact sheets.
Guidance and Counseling; Home Economics; Psychology
Dist - EXTR **Prod** - AMEDIA

Professional presence 26 MIN
VHS
Color (A PRO IND)
$595.00 purchase, $130.00 rental
Provides tips for improving one's professional image. Covers subjects including wardrobe, grooming, and business manners. Updates the film 'The Professional Image.'
Business and Economics; Guidance and Counseling; Home Economics; Social Science; Sociology
Dist - VLEARN **Prod** - AIMS

Professional Realism - Pt 1 56 MIN
VHS
Professional Realism Series
Color (J)
$29.95 purchase _ #HV - 670
Shows how to design compositions and landscapes in oil and watercolor using light and values. Part 1 of a two - part series by Quinten Gregory.
Fine Arts
Dist - CRYSP **Prod** - CRYSP

Professional Realism - Pt 2 56 MIN
VHS
Professional Realism Series
Color (J)
$29.95 purchase _ #HV - 671
Shows how to design compositions and landscapes in oil and watercolor using light and values. Part 2 of a two - part series by Quinten Gregory.
Fine Arts
Dist - CRYSP **Prod** - CRYSP

Professional Realism Series
Professional Realism - Pt 1 56 MIN
Professional Realism - Pt 2 56 MIN
Dist - CRYSP

Professional Security Training Series Module 1B
Plan for Security 12 MIN
Dist - CORF

Professional Security Training Series Module 1
The Security Story 12 MIN
Dist - CORF

Professional Security Training Series Module 2
Professional Patrol 14 MIN
Dist - CORF

Professional Security Training Series Module 3
Notes, Reports, and Communications 14 MIN
Dist - CORF

Professional Security Training Series Module 4
Security and the Law 14 MIN
Dist - CORF

Professional Security Training Series Module 5
Fire 14 MIN
Dist - CORF

Professional Security Training Series
Public Relations in Security 12 MIN
Dist - CORF

Professional Selling Practices Series I Series
Moment of Decision 11 MIN
Dist - SAUM

Professional Selling Practices Series 1 Series
Know Your Facts 9 MIN
One Minute Please 8 MIN
Personalize Your Presentation 9 MIN
Dist - SAUM

Professional Selling Practices Series 2 Series
No One Told Me 8 MIN
Test Your Suggestability 8 MIN
They Know what they Want 8 MIN
Think Tall - Sell Up to Quality 8 MIN
Dist - SAUM

Professional Shoplifting 18 MIN
16mm / U-matic / VHS
Color (A)
Discusses the psychology of the shoplifter. Demonstrates the shopping bag, garment hanger and other concealment methods used by the shoplifter. Alerts to the team techniques used by thieves.
Sociology
Dist - RTBL **Prod** - RTBL

Professional Skills for Secretaries Series Pt 1
We're Counting on You 30 MIN
Dist - TIMLIF

Professional Skills for Secretaries Series Pt 3
Working with Others 30 MIN
Dist - TIMLIF

Professional skills for secretaries series
Coping with change 30 MIN
Getting the job done 30 MIN
Dist - TIMLIF

Professional sports 15 MIN
VHS
Career success series
Color (H C A)
$29.95 purchase _ #MX214
Presents an introduction to professional sports careers. Covers the necessary skills, and interviews people in these careers on the rewards and stresses involved.
Education; Physical Education and Recreation
Dist - CAMV

Professional Sports 15 MIN
VHS / 16mm
(H C A)
$24.95 purchase _ #CS214
Describes the skills involved in a career in professional sports. Features interviews with people working in this field.
Guidance and Counseling
Dist - RMIBHF **Prod** - RMIBHF

Professional sports training for kids series
Baseball with Ken Griffey, Jr
Football with Dan Fouts
Dist - MIRMP

Professional style 60 MIN
VHS
Color (H C A)
$29.95 purchase
Provides advice in choosing the most appropriate wardrobe for business. Stresses the importance of choosing the right sort of wardrobe for one's body type and profession, and covers subjects including alterations and accessorizing. Produced by Esquire magazine.
Home Economics
Dist - PBS **Prod** - WNETTV

Professional Style - Dressing Well as Part of Career Success 60 MIN
VHS
(H C A)
$39.95 _ #EQ100V
Discusses the ways in which a man can develop a professional and attention getting image through dress. Features interviews with many successful men who discuss how wardrobe and grooming affects business success.
Home Economics
Dist - CAMV **Prod** - CAMV

Professional style - dressing well as part of career success 60 MIN
VHS
Color (H C G)
$39.95 purchase _ #EQ100V
Shows business men how to develop an image for a competitive business environment. Interviews successful men who reveal how their appearance helped them. Discusses choosing the right wardrobe for an occupation, putting together wardrobe components to create a powerful look, personal grooming for success. Aids male job hunters.
Home Economics
Dist - CAMV **Prod** - ESQUIR

Professional Style - Dressing Well for Career Success 60 MIN
U-matic / VHS
(H C)
$69.95 _ PC3V
Features experts on dress and grooming who comment on strategies for dressing well for job interviews, and give specific hints.
Business and Economics; Education
Dist - JISTW **Prod** - JISTW

Professional Support Services and Mental Retardation 30 MIN
U-matic
Primer Series
Color (A)
Shows that some types of retardation are only detectable in a child's early developmental years, hence the urgency of parents acquiring such support as medical, legal, specialized therapy and rehabilitative services.
Education; Psychology
Dist - ACCESS **Prod** - ACCESS 1981

A Professional Talks about Interviewing 25 MIN
U-matic / VHS
Process - Centered Composition Series
Color (T)
LC 79-706302
Discusses techniques for interviewing, including the structuring of questions and taking notes.
English Language
Dist - IU **Prod** - IU 1977

Professional Techniques 60 MIN
VHS / U-matic / BETA
Color (A G)
$49.94 _ #MA2212
Shows the secret of obtaining natural dyes from plants, sophisticated pruning techniques, how to reap a bountiful harvest with help from specialists at the Brooklyn Botanical Garden.
Agriculture
Dist - BAKERT

Professional Techniques
VHS / U-matic
Color
Agriculture
Dist - MSTVIS **Prod** - MSTVIS

Professional telephone skills series
Presents a two - part series on professional telephone skills. Discusses how to gain callers' trust and loyalty, how to keep the human touch in every call, how to utilize advanced telephone technologies including voice mail, call - waiting and conference calls, and more.
Professional telephone skills series 161 MIN
Dist - CAMV

Professional telephone skills series
Professional telephone skills - Vol I 81 MIN
Professional telephone skills - Vol II 91 MIN
Dist - CARTRP

Professional telephone skills - Vol I 81 MIN
VHS
Professional telephone skills series
Color (G)
$99.95 purchase _ #20096
Features Debra Smith. Shows how to identify a caller's objectives and objections and how to win and keep new customers. Reveals rapport building through getting on the same 'wavelength' and the specific words and phrases which sabotage a presentation. Part one of two parts.
Business and Economics; Psychology
Dist - CARTRP **Prod** - CARTRP

Professional telephone skills - Vol I and II 172 MIN
VHS
Color (G)
$149.95 purchase _ #20096, #20100
Features Debra Smith. Offers strategies for making every telephone contact more positive.
Business and Economics; Industrial and Technical Education; Psychology; Social Science
Dist - CARTRP **Prod** - CARTRP

Professional telephone skills - Vol II 91 MIN
VHS
Professional telephone skills series
Color (G)
$99.95 purchase _ #20100
Features Debra Smith. Reveals the benefits of voice mail and the advantage of each, as well as how to make conference calls more productive. Offers telemarketing tips, how to remember names and ways to make every caller feel special. Part two of two parts.
Business and Economics; Psychology
Dist - CARTRP **Prod** - CARTRP

Professional telephone skills - Volume 1 81 MIN
VHS
Color (H C A)
$99.95 purchase _ #CTKTEL1V
Presents the first of a two - part series on professional telephone skills. Discusses how to keep callers satisfied, how to increase one's confidence and effectiveness, how to deal with angry and abusive callers, and more.
Business and Economics; Education; Psychology
Dist - CAMV

Professional telephone skills - Volume 2 80 MIN
VHS
Color (H C A)
$99.95 purchase _ #CTKTEL2V
Presents the second of a two - part series on professional telephone skills. Discusses how to gain callers' trust and loyalty, how to keep the human touch in every call, and how to utilize advanced telephone technologies including voice mail, call - waiting and conference calls.
Business and Economics; Education; Psychology
Dist - CAMV

Professional tips for easy wallpapering
VHS
Around the home series
Color (G)
$29.95 purchase _ #IV - 043
Shows all aspects of wallpapering in hands - on applications.
Home Economics
Dist - INCRSE **Prod** - INCRSE

Professional tree care safety
VHS
Color (G) (SPANISH)
$270.00, $320.00 purchase _ #6 - 204 - 001P, #6 - 204 - 002P -
Presents a four - part series on tree worker safety. Discusses work terminology, protective gear and positioning around equipment, the safe use of aerial lifts, chippers, stump cutters and power tools, safety habits for common tree care procedures. Produced by the National Arborist Association.
Agriculture; Health and Safety; Psychology; Science - Natural
Dist - VEP

Professional tree care safety series
Equipment procedures
General requirements
Operational practices
Personal protection
Dist - VEP

Professional tree pruning in the xerisphere 27 MIN
VHS
Color (G)
$89.95 purchase _ #6 - 302 - 312S
Shows the correct way to prune water saving trees. Includes specific tips for maintaining the natural looks of dry - land trees, work safety tips, the objectives of pruning and the three stages of growth when pruning is necessary.
Agriculture; Health and Safety; Science - Natural
Dist - VEP **Prod** - VEP 1991

Professional Turf Management 26 MIN
VHS
Color (G)
$89.95 purchase _ #6 - 056 - 100P
Examines the growth patterns of various turfgrass varieties and site assessment for turf management. Covers mowing, irrigation, soil fertility and fertilization, cultural practices and control of weeds, insects and other pests.
Agriculture
Dist - VEP **Prod** - VEP

Professional Turf Management 26 MIN
VHS
Color (H C A IND)
LC 88-700128
Presents an explanation of the necessary care for various types of grasses.
Agriculture; Science - Natural
Dist - CSPC **Prod** - CSPC 1987

Professional Write 2.2 series
Presents two videos on Professional Write 2.2, teaching beginning and advanced word processing.
Advanced using Professional Write 2 .2
Learning Professional Write 2.2
Dist - SIV

Professionalism at Every Level of Banking - Unit 3 31 MIN
VHS / 16mm
Essentials of Professionalism Series
Color (PRO)
$295.00 purchase, $175.00 rental, $35.00 preview
Trains bank employees. Describes 20 aspects of being a professional. Includes support materials.
Business and Economics; Home Economics; Psychology; Sociology
Dist - UTM **Prod** - UTM

The Professionals 27 MIN
16mm
Color
LC 76-701356
Takes a look at the work of firemen and considers a number of fire prevention tips.
Guidance and Counseling; Health and Safety; Social Science; Sociology
Dist - OOFM **Prod** - OMSG 1975

The Professionals 117 MIN
16mm
Color (H C A)
Gives an account of what happens when a band of adventurers is hired to rescue a railroad tycoon's daughter from her kidnapper. Stars Burt Lancaster, Lee Marvin and Robert Ryan.
Fine Arts
Dist - TIMLIF **Prod** - CPC 1966

Professionals and their interactions with families 56 MIN
U-matic / VHS
Color (C)
$170.00, $150.00 purchase _ #85856
Proposes a basic change in the approach used in counseling with families, appealing to the audience to begin as students rather than as teachers, allowing the family to teach them. Advises trying to be with the entire family rather than just with the child. Asserts in particular that if the therapist is able to hear the mother's cry for help in her situation the mother is then enabled to hear the cry of the child. Shows instances of success with this innovative indirect method.
Guidance and Counseling; Psychology; Sociology
Dist - UILL **Prod** - IPIN 1986

Professional's Guide to Lawn Mower Safety 24 MIN
VHS
Color (G)
$89.95 purchase _ #6 - 202 - 103P
Examines the safe operation of lawn mowers. Includes general safety precautions, push mowers and riding mowers.
Agriculture; Health and Safety
Dist - VEP **Prod** - VEP

The Professionals - the Baltic republic of Estonia 52 MIN
VHS
Icebreaker - family life in the Soviet Union series
Color (I J H)
$295.00 purchase
Visits the four - member Sibul family of Estonia who live in the coastal capital, medieval Talinn. Reveals that they are a well - off successful family, with a large private home on the coast, a late - model family car, a private sauna and a dog. They belong to the local yacht club, they travel extensively, their friends are artists, writers, musicians and medical colleagues. Part of a six - part series on ethnically different families in the Soviet Union.
Geography - World; Sociology
Dist - LANDMK **Prod** - LANDMK 1989

Professor 20 MIN
16mm
B&W
Presents a psychology professor at the University of Pennsylvania who declares himself a revolutionary. Shows him in class, at home with his wife and children, and interacting with his students in his office and on campus. Explores the professor's view of what it means to be a revolutionary in today's academic context, his relations with his faculty colleagues and the nature of his choices between normal academic pursuits, and the values of revolutionary behavior as he sees them.
Education; Psychology
Dist - UPENN **Prod** - UPENN 1971

Professor Balthazar Series
Clown Daniel 5 MIN
Sporting life 5 MIN
Dist - IFB

Professor Bonner and the slime molds 50 MIN
U-matic / VHS
Color (H C A)
Introduces slime molds, simple soil - dwelling protozoans with properties of both plants and animals, that aggregate together and metamorphose into plant - like stalks which split open and discharge thousands of new one - celled slime molds. Explains how the development of these molds may teach us more about the development of the human embryo.
Science - Natural
Dist - FI **Prod** - BBCTV

Professor Bunruckle's Guide to Pixilation 16 MIN
16mm / VHS
Animation Series
Color (J H A)
$295.00, $370.00 purchase, $50.00 rental _ #8008
Describes pixilation.
Fine Arts
Dist - AIMS **Prod** - EDMI 1988

Professor Erik Erikson - Pt 1 50 MIN
16mm / U-matic / VHS
Notable Contributors to the Psychology of Personality Series
B&W (C G T A)
Discusses his involvement with psychoanalysis and his theory of the eight stages of psychosocial development.
Biography; Psychology
Dist - PSUPCR **Prod** - PSUPCR 1966

Professor Erik Erikson - Pt 2 50 MIN
U-matic / VHS / 16mm
Notable Contributors to the Psychology and Personality Series
B&W (C G T A)
Discusses libido theory, ego identity, identity crisis, positive and negative identity, existentialism, and cross cultural research.
Biography; Psychology
Dist - PSUPCR **Prod** - PSUPCR 1966

Professor Greenthumb Good Gardening 60 MIN
VHS / U-matic / BETA
Color (A G)
$15.25 _ #KA165
Teaches about soil preparation and conditioning, seeding and transplanting, fertilization and more.
Agriculture
Dist - BAKERT

Professor Greenthumb's guide to good gardening 60 MIN
VHS
Color (A)
$14.95 purchase _ #S00993
Demonstrates basic gardening techniques. Covers 11 different areas, including soil preparation, seeding, watering, pruning and more. Hosted by Britain's 'Professor Greenthumb,' John Lenanton.
Agriculture
Dist - UILL

Professor Ya - Ya's Memoirs 8 MIN
16mm / U-matic / VHS
Tales of Hoffnung Series
Color
LC 81-701026
Takes a sentimental journey in animated fashion with Professor Ya - Ya who, on his birthday, sits down on his favorite easy chair to peruse his family photograph album and recall all his charming and unusual relatives. Based on the cartoons by Gerald Hoffnung.
Fine Arts
Dist - PHENIX **Prod** - HALAS 1981

Profile Descent and Metering 13 MIN
U-matic / VHS
Color (A)
Describes new operational procedures in effect as of 1979 at terminals serving high performance aircraft. Shows profile descent and metering program as an air traffic management concept for safety enhancement.
Industrial and Technical Education
Dist - AVIMA **Prod** - FAAFL

Profile Descent and Metering 20 MIN
16mm
Color (PRO)
LC 77-701300
Offers a look at the profile descent and metering program, a comprehensive air traffic management concept designed to enhance safety and efficiency in air traffic handling, conserve fuel and reduce noise over airport communities. Describes new operational procedures that are expected to be in effect at all terminals served by high performance aircraft by 1979.
Industrial and Technical Education; Science - Natural; Social Science
Dist - USNAC **Prod** - USFAA 1977

Profile - health series
Eat defensively 29 MIN
Dist - BRGNHS

Profile mapping 8 MIN
VHS
Map reading series
Color (I J)
$24.95 purchase _ #S9050
Examines the mapping of varying elevations of ground surface. Part of a five - part series teaching mapping skills in single - concept format.
Geography - World; Science - Physical; Social Science
Dist - HUBDSC **Prod** - HUBDSC

Profile of a British corporate raider 30 MIN
VHS
Adam Smith's money world series
Color (H C A)
$79.95 purchase
Profiles British corporate raider Sir James Goldsmith. Features host Jerry Goodman, also known as 'Adam Smith,' and his guests Goldsmith, Geoffrey Wansell and Jacob Rothschild.
Business and Economics
Dist - PBS **Prod** - WNETTV

Profile of a Drug Dealer 28 MIN
VHS
Crime to Court Procedural Specials Series
Color (PRO)
$99.00 purchase
Interviews a convicted drug dealer who tells how he got into the business and evaded arrest for over nine years. Trains law enforcement personnel. Part of an ongoing series which looks in depth at topics presented in 'Crime To Court.' Produced in conjunction with the South Carolina Criminal Justice Academy and the National Sheriff's Association.
Civics and Political Systems; Health and Safety; Psychology; Social Science; Sociology
Dist - SCETV **Prod** - SCETV

Profile of a Manager 14 MIN
16mm / U-matic / VHS
Professional Management Program (Spanish Series
Color (SPANISH)
Dramatizes the experiences of a new manager. Shows basic management skills.
Business and Economics; Foreign Language
Dist - NEM **Prod** - NEM

Profile of a Manager 14 MIN
U-matic / VHS / 16mm
Professional Management Program Series
Color (H C A)
LC 77-700929
Explores the attitudes, skills and knowledge required of an effective manager.
Business and Economics; Psychology
Dist - NEM **Prod** - NEM 1977

Profile of a Middle School 25 MIN
U-matic
Color (T)
Focuses on the role of the administration and staff in the operation of a middle school. Shows interdisciplinary team meetings, teacher/advisory sessions, teacher planning, and reading lab use.
Education
Dist - AFSCD **Prod** - AFSCD 1986

Profile of a President - Richard Milhous Nixon 15 MIN
16mm
Screen news digest series; Vol 11; Issue 4
B&W (J H)
LC 77-703470
Presents a biographical sketch of America's 37th President, Richard Nixon.
Biography; History - United States
Dist - HEARST **Prod** - HEARST 1968

Profile of a Problem Drinker 29 MIN
16mm
B&W (J H C A)
#3X69 I
Dramatizes the life of a problem drinker. Shows how a drinking problem starts and is perpetuated and the tragic consequences it can bring about for a family.

Sociology
Dist - CDIAND **Prod** - NFBC 1957

Profile of a Winning Competitor 30 MIN
U-matic / VHS
Successful Strategies for Manufacturing Management Series
Color
Examines the critical factors of success and looks at what the winners are doing with their new systems and technology for manufacturing and materials.
Business and Economics; Industrial and Technical Education
Dist - DELTAK **Prod** - DELTAK

Profile of an Accident - and Then There were Two 13 MIN
16mm
Color
LC 82-700306
Depicts two helicopter crashes which happen on the same day, not because of chance or fate, but because of carelessness and hastiness. Outlines procedures by the accident investigation board as to why the mishaps occurred and how they could have been prevented.
Civics and Political Systems
Dist - USNAC **Prod** - USA 1980

A Profile of an aging person 30 MIN
16mm
Directions for education in nursing via technology series; Lesson 82
B&W (PRO)
LC 74-701860
Demonstrates that the aging process is an individual matter. Provides a profile of the aged person in American society.
Health and Safety; Sociology
Dist - WSUM **Prod** - DENT 1974

Profile of an artist - Moriziu Gottlieb 40 MIN
VHS
B&W (G)
$34.95 purchase _ #707
Captures the life of Polish Jewish artist Moriziu Gottlieb who died tragically at the age of 23 near the end of the 19th century.
Fine Arts; Sociology
Dist - ERGOM **Prod** - ERGOM

Profile of Community 42 MIN
16mm
Color
LC 80-700441
Looks at a group called the Community of the Christian Spirit, in which the liturgy, written by the members, is the focal point. Shows people celebrating God and each other as they explain their reasons for participating in the Community.
Religion and Philosophy
Dist - TEMPLU **Prod** - TEMPLU 1979

Profile of community - Pt 1 21 MIN
16mm
Color
LC 80-700441
Looks at a group called the Community of the Christian Spirit, in which the liturgy, written by the members, is the focal point. Shows people celebrating God and each other as they explain their reasons for participating in the Community.
Religion and Philosophy
Dist - TEMPLU **Prod** - TEMPLU 1979

Profile of community - Pt 2 21 MIN
16mm
Color
LC 80-700441
Looks at a group called the Community of the Christian Spirit, in which the liturgy, written by the members, is the focal point. Shows people celebrating God and each other as they explain their reasons for participating in the Community.
Religion and Philosophy
Dist - TEMPLU **Prod** - TEMPLU 1979

Profile - the Petroleum Industry 30 MIN
U-matic / VHS / 16mm
Color (A PRO)
$450.00 purchase _ #30.0121, $425.00 purchase _ #50.0121
Presents a fundamental overview of the petroleum industry from exploration to refining.
Industrial and Technical Education; Science - Physical; Social Science
Dist - UTEXPE **Prod** - UTEXPE 1981

Profile - Three Nurses 25 MIN
U-matic / VHS
Color
Explores the responsibilities and emotions involved in being a nurse. Follows three nurses, one who cares for children, another who cares for critically ill patients in the Intensive Care Unit, and one who is the head nurse on a medical - surgical floor.
Health and Safety
Dist - MEDCOM **Prod** - MEDCOM

Profiles in American art series
Bob Kuhn 30 MIN
Conrad Schwiering 30 MIN
Donald Teague 30 MIN
Edward Fraughton 30 MIN
Eric Sloane 30 MIN
George Carlson 30 MIN
Glenna Goodacre 30 MIN
John Clymer 30 MIN
John Stobart 30 MIN
Sergei Bongart 30 MIN
William Whitaker 30 MIN
Wilson Hurley 30 MIN
Dist - KAWVAL

Profiles in change - valuing diversity - Part VII 60 MIN
VHS
Valuing diversity series
Color (A PRO IND)
$995.00 purchase, $100.00 rental
Presents the final part of a seven - part series on diversity in the workplace. Argues that diversity can be a strength if properly handled. Dramatizes situations leading to conflict and poor performance, showing how they can be better handled. Profiles companies that have successfully capitalized on diversity in their workforces.
Business and Economics; Guidance and Counseling; Sociology
Dist - VLEARN

Profiles in courage series
Alexander William Doniphan 51 MIN
Alexander William Doniphan, Pt 1 25 MIN
Alexander William Doniphan, Pt 2 25 MIN
Andrew Johnson 51 MIN
Andrew Johnson - Pt 1 25 MIN
Andrew Johnson - Pt 2 25 MIN
Anne Hutchinson 51 MIN
Anne Hutchinson, Pt 1 24 MIN
Anne Hutchinson, Pt 2 24 MIN
Benjamin B Lindsey, Pt 1 25 MIN
Benjamin B Lindsey, Pt 2 25 MIN
Benjamin Barr Lindsey 51 MIN
Charles Evans Hughes 51 MIN
Charles Evans Hughes - Pt 1 25 MIN
Charles Evans Hughes - Pt 2 25 MIN
Daniel Webster 51 MIN
Daniel Webster, Pt 1 25 MIN
Daniel Webster, Pt 2 25 MIN
Edmund Ross 51 MIN
Edmund ross - Pt 1 25 MIN
Edmund ross - Pt 2 25 MIN
Frederick Douglass 50 MIN
Frederick Douglass - Pt 1 25 MIN
Frederick Douglass, Pt 2 25 MIN
George Mason 51 MIN
George Mason, Pt 1 25 MIN
George Mason, Pt 2 25 MIN
George Norris 51 MIN
George W Norris 50 MIN
George W Norris, Pt 1 25 MIN
George W Norris, Pt 2 25 MIN
Grover Cleveland 51 MIN
Grover Cleveland, Pt 1 25 MIN
Grover Cleveland, Pt 2 25 MIN
Hamilton Fish 50 MIN
Hamilton Fish, Pt 1 25 MIN
Hamilton Fish, Pt 2 25 MIN
John Adams 50 MIN
John Adams, Pt 1 25 MIN
John Adams, Pt 2 25 MIN
John M Slaton 51 MIN
John M Slaton, Pt 1 25 MIN
John M Slaton, Pt 2 25 MIN
John Marshall 51 MIN
John Marshall, Pt 1 25 MIN
John Marshall, Pt 2 25 MIN
John Peter Altgeld 51 MIN
John Peter Altgeld, Pt 1 25 MIN
John Peter Altgeld, Pt 2 25 MIN
John Quincy Adams 48 MIN
John Quincy Adams, Pt 1 24 MIN
John Quincy Adams, Pt 2 24 MIN
Mary S Mc Dowell 50 MIN
Mary S Mc Dowell, Pt 1 25 MIN
Mary S Mc Dowell, Pt 2 25 MIN
Oscar W Underwood 51 MIN
Prudence Crandall 51 MIN
Prudence Crandall - Pt 1 25 MIN
Prudence Crandall - Pt 2 25 MIN
Richard T Ely 51 MIN
Richard T Ely - Pt 1 25 MIN
Richard T Ely - Pt 2 25 MIN
Robert A Taft 51 MIN
Robert A Taft - Pt 1 25 MIN
Robert A Taft - Pt 2 25 MIN
Sam Houston 51 MIN
Sam Houston - Pt 1 25 MIN
Sam Houston - Pt 2 25 MIN
Thomas Corwin 51 MIN
Thomas Corwin - Pt 1 25 MIN
Thomas Corwin - Pt 2 25 MIN
Thomas Hart Benton 50 MIN(0123198)
Thomas Hart Benton - Pt 1 25 MIN
Thomas Hart Benton - Pt 2 25 MIN
Woodrow Wilson 50 MIN
Woodrow Wilson, Pt 1 25 MIN
Woodrow Wilson, Pt 2 25 MIN
Dist - SSSSV

Profiles in journalism series
Alfred Balk 29 MIN
Arnold Gingrich 29 MIN
Francoise Giroud 29 MIN
Dist - UMITV

Profiles in Management
VHS / 16mm
(C PRO)
$595.00 purchase, $175.00 rental
Covers leadership and motivation.
Education
Dist - VLEARN

Profiles in Management Series
On Leadership - Part 1 23 MIN
On Motivation - Part 2 16 MIN
Dist - SALENG

Profiles in Power Series
Catherine the Great - a profile in power 26 MIN
Gandhi - a Profile in Power 25 MIN
Hitler - a Profile in Power 26 MIN
Joan of Arc - a Profile in Power 25 MIN
Queen Victoria - a Profile in Power 26 MIN
Dist - LCOA

Profiles in Power (Spanish Series
Gandhi - a Profile in Power 25 MIN
Joan of Arc - a profile in power 25 MIN
Queen Victoria - a profile in power 26 MIN
Sitting Bull - a Profile in Power 26 MIN
Dist - LCOA

Profiles in progress series
Presents a 13 - part series on people who are moving their tradition - bound countries into modern times. Looks at Morocco, Malaysia, India, Jordan, Indonesia, Singapore, Nepal, Belize and other Third World countries and efforts to combine industrialization with ecologic responsibility, the emerging role of women and family planning in economic viability, and the growth of tourism.
Casablanca drive - Pt 1 30 MIN
The Delicate balance - Pt 2 30 MIN
Designing women - lifting the veil - Pt 3 30 MIN
Indonesia's doctor of happiness - Pt 4 30 MIN
Marketing mystique - Pt 5 30 MIN
Mastering money - Pt 6 30 MIN
A Matter of people - Pt 7 30 MIN
Nepal - on top of the world - Pt 8 30 MIN
The Philosopher prince - Pt 9 30 MIN
Russi Mody - India's man of steel - Pt 10 30 MIN
School story - Pt 11 30 MIN
A Search in the sun - Pt 12 30 MIN
Singapore - toward tomorrow - Pt 13 30 MIN
Dist - BARR **Prod** - CEPRO

Profiles of achievement - Part I 41 MIN
VHS
Legacy of achievement series
Color (PRO IND A)
$695.00 purchase, $250.00 rental _ #JHP01A
Features Dennis Kimbro, motivational speaker and co - author of 'Think and Grow Rich - A Black Choice,' with a message of hope and fulfillment transcending differences of race, gender and culture. Interviews Arlene DeCandia - founder of Riverwood Conference Center, artist Dean Mitchell, Scott Olson - founder of Rollerblade Inc, Tom Gegax - CEO of Tires Plus, and Dr Reatha Clark King - president of General Mills Foundation - all sharing their own keys to success. By Joan Holman Productions.
Business and Economics; Psychology
Dist - EXTR

Profiles - people and jobs series
Professional occupations - part 1
Professional occupations - part 2
Service occupations - Pt 1
Service occupations - Pt 2
Technical occupations - part 1
Technical occupations - part 2
Dist - CENTER

Profiling the Blade 30 MIN
VHS / U-matic
How to Build a Knife Series
Color
Shows how to profile a blade when building a knife.
Industrial and Technical Education
Dist - MDCPB **Prod** - UGATV

Profils des Francais 60 MIN
VHS
VideoFrance series
Color (H C) (FRENCH)
$119.95 purchase _ #E1471 - X
Offers profiles and portraits of ordinary French people such as radio announcers, taxi drivers, children, and policemen as they talk about their lives and attitudes. For intermediate through advanced students of French. Includes teacher's manual.
Foreign Language
Dist - NTCPUB **Prod** - NTCPUB

Profit 20 MIN
16mm
Color
Business and Economics
Dist - CINE **Prod** - CINE

Profit - a lure, a risk 8 MIN
U-matic / VHS / 16mm
Color (J H C)
$49.00 purchase _ #3540; LC 77-703469
Explains the principles of financial investment, profit and risk using a song - and - dance extravaganza format.
Business and Economics
Dist - EBEC **Prod** - SUTHLA 1977

Profit and Laws 27 MIN
VHS / U-matic
Color (G)
Gives antitrust information.
Business and Economics; Civics and Political Systems
Dist - VPHI **Prod** - VPHI 1986

Profit Forecasting 30 MIN
16mm
That's Business Series
Color (H C A)
LC 79-700658
Discusses the concepts of gross profit, pre - tax profit, net profit and overhead. Explains how to calculate and forecast profit and elaborates on the accrual concept of matching revenues with expenses to determine profit. Based on the book Profit And Cash Flow Management For Non - Financial Managers by John A Welsh and Jerry F White.
Business and Economics
Dist - OWNMAN **Prod** - WELSHJ 1978

Profitable Direct Mail Programs 30 MIN
U-matic / VHS
Business of Direct Mail Series
Color
Gives the characteristics of profitable direct mail programs.
Business and Economics
Dist - KYTV **Prod** - KYTV 1983

Profitable pork selection 12 MIN
16mm
Color
Describes what to look for in a modern meat hog. Features 'Jasper,' a 225 pound chest white - Hampshire cross - bred barrow, donated to Purdue University for study and carcass evaluation.
Agriculture
Dist - MTP **Prod** - ADAC

Profits and Bosses 25 MIN
16mm / VHS / BETA
Color
LC 77-702520
Examines regimented forms of management that are used by Japanese firms to pursue the highest profit margins possible. Notes that these and related mind - conforming techniques are widely copied and enforced by North American business firms.
Business and Economics
Dist - CTV **Prod** - CTV 1976

Profits and Interest - Where is the Best Return 30 MIN
U-matic / VHS
Economics USA Series
Color (C)
Business and Economics
Dist - ANNCPB **Prod** - WEFA

Profits, Capital, Equipment and Economic Growth 17 MIN
16mm
Exploring Basic Economics Series
B&W (H A)
LC FI67-367
Tells how professional management of labor and capital can make wages, productive output and profits increase simultaneously. Gives the factors needed for growth. Emphasizes the role of manager and entrepreneur.
Business and Economics
Dist - MLA **Prod** - RSC 1963

Profits from Poison 46 MIN
VHS / 16mm
Protecting the Global Environment Series
Color (G)
$295.00 purchase, $90.00 rental; LC 90707380
Shows how harmful pesticides and other manmade chemicals banned from use in developed countries are still being used and sold in Third World nations. Examines Thailand and the Philippines to consider the complex issue of pesticides, demonstrating the long - term effects of pesticide abuse on the entire world and showing alternatives now available. Part of a series which highlights the urgent need for international cooperation to deal with threats to the world's basic ecosystem.
Agriculture; Business and Economics; Geography - World; Home Economics; Sociology
Dist - CNEMAG **Prod** - BWORLD 1989

Profits in the bag 9 MIN
16mm
Color (I J H)
Demonstrates the fundamentals of proper grocery bag packing through animation and 'hip' narration.
Business and Economics
Dist - CALVIN **Prod** - CALVIN 1966

Profits of doom - Volume I 26 MIN
VHS / U-matic / BETA
Into the boardroom series
Color (C A G)
$870.00 purchase, $240.00 rental
Unravels the mysteries of company finances. Explains clearly that what the accounts do not reveal is often more important than what they actually show. Shows how published company results can mislead both investors and managers. Demonstrates a couple of ratios for testing a firm's short - term viability and how to check the debt - equity ratio, interest cover and availability of ready cash. Produced jointly by The Economist and Video Arts.
Business and Economics
Dist - VIDART **Prod** - VIDART 1993

Progeny 18 MIN
VHS / U-matic
Color
Involves the subjective framing of space. Presented by Steina and Woody Vasulka and Barbara Smith.
Fine Arts
Dist - ARTINC **Prod** - ARTINC

Prognosis - Fire 20 MIN
U-matic / VHS
Color
Presents employee's responsibilities for fire prevention, fire control and emergency action.
Health and Safety
Dist - FPF **Prod** - FPF

Prognosis - Safety 22 MIN
U-matic / VHS
Color
Teaches employees how to prevent occupational injuries or illness from falls, strains, electric shock, needle punctures and other hazards.
Health and Safety
Dist - FPF **Prod** - FPF
Home Economics
Dist - TVOTAR **Prod** - TVOTAR 1985

Program 1 15 MIN
U-matic
Computer Room Series
Color (I J)
Explains modems and how they allow computers to talk to each other.
Computer Science; Education
Dist - TVOTAR **Prod** - TVOTAR 1984

Program 2 15 MIN
U-matic
Computer Room Series
Color (I J)
Explains modems, computer assisted design and computer games.
Computer Science; Education
Dist - TVOTAR **Prod** - TVOTAR 1984

Program 3 15 MIN
U-matic
Computer Room Series
Color (I J)
Features an after school program where kids play educational computer games. Shows a factory where Macintosh computers are made.
Computer Science; Education
Dist - TVOTAR **Prod** - TVOTAR 1984

Program 4 15 MIN
U-matic
Computer Room Series
Color (I J)
Takes the viewer inside an Apple computer and demonstrates how computers can make music.
Computer Science; Education
Dist - TVOTAR **Prod** - TVOTAR 1984

Program 5 15 MIN
U-matic
Computer Room Series
Color (I J)
Demonstrates an automatic bank teller and how it operates.
Business and Economics; Computer Science; Education
Dist - TVOTAR **Prod** - TVOTAR 1984

Program 6 15 MIN
U-matic
Computer Room Series
Color (I J)
Shows that computers, satellites and cables are used to distribute telephone signals and that computers record sales in stores.
Computer Science; Education
Dist - TVOTAR **Prod** - TVOTAR 1984

Program 7 15 MIN
U-matic
Computer Room Series
Color (I J)
Shows how to use word processing to write error free reports and how computers are used by reporters, editors and printers to put out a newspaper.
Computer Science; Education
Dist - TVOTAR **Prod** - TVOTAR 1984

Program 8 15 MIN
U-matic
Computer Room Series
Color (I J)
Shows how computers are used to create special effects used in movies. Storage of computer data is also explained.
Computer Science; Education
Dist - TVOTAR **Prod** - TVOTAR 1984

Program 9 15 MIN
U-matic
Computer Room Series
Color (I J)
Looks at how a microchip is created and demonstrates computer graphics and environmental control with computers.
Computer Science; Education
Dist - TVOTAR **Prod** - TVOTAR 1984

Program 10 15 MIN
U-matic
Computer Room Series
Color (I J)
Looks at computer use in space, shows the use of a light pen and how to design the pictures that flash across giant billboards.
Computer Science; Education
Dist - TVOTAR **Prod** - TVOTAR 1984

Program 1 - Basic Sewing Equipment 29 MIN
VHS / 16mm
Pins and Needles 2 Series
Color (G PRO)
$90.00 purchase _ #BPN211401
Taught by Montreal couturiere Angelina Di Bello.
Home Economics
Dist - RMIBHF **Prod** - RMIBHF

Program 2 - Basic Sewing Equipment 29 MIN
VHS / 16mm
Pins and Needles 2 Series
Color (G PRO)
$90.00 purchase _ #BPN211402
Taught by Montreal couturiere Angelina Di Bello.
Home Economics
Dist - RMIBHF **Prod** - RMIBHF

Program 3 - Basic Sewing Equipment 29 MIN
VHS / 16mm
Pins and Needles 2 Series
Color (G PRO)
$90.00 purchase _ #BPN211403
Taught by Montreal couturiere Angelina Di Bello.
Home Economics
Dist - RMIBHF **Prod** - RMIBHF

Program 4 - Basic Sewing Equipment 29 MIN
VHS / 16mm
Pins and Needles 2 Series
Color (G PRO)
$90.00 purchase _ #BPN211403

Taught by Montreal couturiere Angelina Di Bello.
Home Economics
Dist - RMIBHF **Prod** - RMIBHF

Program 5 - Basic Sewing Equipment 29 MIN
VHS / 16mm
Pins and Needles 2 Series
Color (G PRO)
$90.00 purchase _ #BPN211405
Taught by Montreal couturiere Angelina Di Bello.
Home Economics
Dist - RMIBHF **Prod** - RMIBHF

Program 6 - Basic Sewing Equipment 29 MIN
VHS / 16mm
Pins and Needles 2 Series
Color (G PRO)
$90.00 purchase _ #BPN211406
Taught by Montreal couturiere Angelina Di Bello.
Home Economics
Dist - RMIBHF **Prod** - RMIBHF

Program 7 - Basic Sewing Equipment 29 MIN
VHS / 16mm
Pins and Needles 2 Series
Color (G PRO)
$90.00 purchase _ #BPN211407
Taught by Montreal couturiere Angelina Di Bello.
Home Economics
Dist - RMIBHF **Prod** - RMIBHF

Program 8 - Basic Sewing Equipment 29 MIN
VHS / 16mm
Pins and Needles 2 Series
Color (G PRO)
$90.00 purchase _ #BPN211408
Taught by Montreal couturiere Angelina Di Bello.
Home Economics
Dist - RMIBHF **Prod** - RMIBHF

Program 9 - Basic Sewing Equipment 29 MIN
VHS / 16mm
Pins and Needles 2 Series
Color (G PRO)
$90.00 purchase _ #BPN211409
Taught by Montreal couturiere Angelina Di Bello.
Home Economics
Dist - RMIBHF **Prod** - RMIBHF

Program 10 - Basic Sewing Equipment 29 MIN
VHS / 16mm
Pins and Needles 2 Series
Color (G PRO)
$90.00 purchase _ #BPN211410
Taught by Montreal couturiere Angelina Di Bello.
Home Economics
Dist - RMIBHF **Prod** - RMIBHF

Program 11 - Basic Sewing Equipment 29 MIN
VHS / 16mm
Pins and Needles 2 Series
Color (G PRO)
$90.00 purchase _ #BPN211411
Taught by Montreal couturiere Angelina Di Bello.
Home Economics
Dist - RMIBHF **Prod** - RMIBHF

Program 12 - Basic Sewing Equipment 29 MIN
VHS / 16mm
Pins and Needles 2 Series
Color (G PRO)
$90.00 purchase _ #BPN211412
Taught by Montreal couturiere Angelina Di Bello.
Home Economics
Dist - RMIBHF **Prod** - RMIBHF

Program 13 - Basic Sewing Equipment 29 MIN
VHS / 16mm
Pins and Needles 2 Series
Color (G PRO)
$90.00 purchase _ #BPN211413
Taught by Montreal couturiere Angelina Di Bello.
Home Economics
Dist - RMIBHF **Prod** - RMIBHF

Program 14 - Basic Sewing Equipment 29 MIN
VHS / 16mm
Pins and Needles 1 Series
Color (G PRO)
$90.00 purchase _ #BPN147214
Taught by Montreal couturiere Angelina Di Bello.
Home Economics
Dist - RMIBHF **Prod** - RMIBHF

Program 15 - Basic Sewing Equipment 29 MIN
VHS / 16mm
Pins and Needles 1 Series
Color (G PRO)
$90.00 purchase _ #BPN147215
Taught by Montreal couturiere Angelina Di Bello.
Home Economics
Dist - RMIBHF **Prod** - RMIBHF

Program 16 - Basic Sewing Equipment 29 MIN
VHS / 16mm
Pins and Needles 1 Series
Color (G PRO)
$90.00 purchase _ #BPN147216
Taught by Montreal couturiere Angelina Di Bello.
Home Economics
Dist - RMIBHF **Prod** - RMIBHF

Program 17 - Basic Sewing Equipment 29 MIN
VHS / 16mm
Pins and Needles 1 Series
Color (G PRO)
$90.00 purchase _ #BPN147217
Taught by Montreal couturiere Angelina Di Bello.
Home Economics

Program 18 - Basic Sewing Equipment 29 MIN
VHS / 16mm
Pins and Needles 1 Series
Color (G PRO)
$90.00 purchase _ #BPN147218
Taught by Montreal couturiere Angelina Di Bello.
Home Economics
Dist - RMIBHF **Prod** - RMIBHF

Program 19 - Basic Sewing Equipment 29 MIN
VHS / 16mm
Pins and Needles 1 Series
Color (G PRO)
$90.00 purchase _ #BPN147219
Taught by Montreal couturiere Angelina Di Bello.
Home Economics
Dist - RMIBHF **Prod** - RMIBHF

Program 20 - Basic Sewing Equipment 29 MIN
VHS / 16mm
Pins and Needles 1 Series
Color (G PRO)
$90.00 purchase _ #BPN147220
Taught by Montreal couturiere Angelina Di Bello.
Home Economics
Dist - RMIBHF **Prod** - RMIBHF

Program 21 - Basic Sewing Equipment 29 MIN
VHS / 16mm
Pins and Needles 1 Series
Color (G PRO)
$90.00 purchase _ #BPN147221
Taught by Montreal couturiere Angelina Di Bello.
Home Economics
Dist - RMIBHF **Prod** - RMIBHF

Program 22 - Basic Sewing Equipment 29 MIN
VHS / 16mm
Pins and Needles 1 Series
Color (G PRO)
$90.00 purchase _ #BPN147223
Taught by Montreal couturiere Angelina Di Bello.
Home Economics
Dist - RMIBHF **Prod** - RMIBHF

Program 23 - Basic Sewing Equipment 29 MIN
VHS / 16mm
Pins and Needles 1 Series
Color (G PRO)
$90.00 purchase _ #BPN147224
Taught by Montreal couturiere Angelina Di Bello.
Home Economics
Dist - RMIBHF **Prod** - RMIBHF

Program 24 - Basic Sewing Equipment 29 MIN
VHS / 16mm
Pins and Needles 1 Series
Color (G PRO)
$90.00 purchase _ #BPN147225
Taught by Montreal couturiere Angelina Di Bello.
Home Economics
Dist - RMIBHF **Prod** - RMIBHF

Program 25 - Basic Sewing Equipment 29 MIN
VHS / 16mm
Pins and Needles 1 Series
Color (G PRO)
$90.00 purchase _ #BPN147226
Taught by Montreal couturiere Angelina Di Bello.
Home Economics
Dist - RMIBHF **Prod** - RMIBHF

Program 26 - Basic Sewing Equipment 29 MIN
VHS / 16mm
Pins and Needles 1 Series
Color (G PRO)
$90.00 purchase _ #BPN147227
Taught by Montreal couturiere Angelina Di Bello.
Home Economics
Dist - RMIBHF **Prod** - RMIBHF

Program 1 30 MIN
U-matic
Pins and Needles - One Series
Color (G)
Offers an explanation of the functions of basic sewing equipment and accessories essential for proper measurement, cutting, pressing and fabric assembly.
Home Economics
Dist - TVOTAR **Prod** - TVOTAR 1985

Program 2 30 MIN
U-matic
Pins and Needles - One Series
Color (G)
Gives an introductory lesson in measurement taking, an essential element for correct fit.
Home Economics
Dist - TVOTAR **Prod** - TVOTAR 1985

Program 3 30 MIN
U-matic
Pins and Needles - One Series
Color (G)
Gives instructions on pattern adjustment for correct fit, style modification and proper fabric choice for a basic A line skirt.

Program 4 30 MIN
U-matic
Pins and Needles - One Series
Color (G)
Gives instructions on assembly of an A line skirt cut from the basic pattern.
Home Economics
Dist - TVOTAR **Prod** - TVOTAR 1985

Program 5 30 MIN
U-matic
Pins and Needles - One Series
Color (G)
Gives instructions on fitting, zipper installation and waist band application for an A line skirt.
Home Economics
Dist - TVOTAR **Prod** - TVOTAR 1985

Program 6 30 MIN
U-matic
Pins and Needles - One Series
Color (G)
Gives instructions on choosing the proper weight of lining and underlining for various fabrics and a demonstration in economical pattern layout for a tailored skirt.
Home Economics
Dist - TVOTAR **Prod** - TVOTAR 1985

Program 7 30 MIN
U-matic
Pins and Needles - One Series
Color (G)
Gives instructions on underlining, marking and basting a tailored skirt.
Home Economics
Dist - TVOTAR **Prod** - TVOTAR 1985

Program 8 30 MIN
U-matic
Pins and Needles - One Series
Color (G)
Gives instructions on underlining attachment, zipper installation, assembly and waistband preparation for a tailored skirt.
Home Economics
Dist - TVOTAR **Prod** - TVOTAR 1985

Program 9 30 MIN
U-matic
Pins and Needles - One Series
Color (G)
Gives instructions on custom made garments, correct cutting, ease stitching and pressing techniques.
Home Economics
Dist - TVOTAR **Prod** - TVOTAR 1985

Program 10 30 MIN
U-matic
Pins and Needles - One Series
Color (G)
Gives instructions on proper measurement, cutting, application of a classic couturier waistband and the importance of waistband proportions for a tailored skirt.
Home Economics
Dist - TVOTAR **Prod** - TVOTAR 1985

Program 11 30 MIN
U-matic
Pins and Needles - One Series
Color (G)
Gives instructions on the secrets of haute couture finishing and details of handsewn zippers and waist bands.
Home Economics
Dist - TVOTAR **Prod** - TVOTAR 1985

Program 12 30 MIN
U-matic

Pins and Needles - One Series
Color (G)
Gives instructions on final fitting, techniques for finishing raw fabric edges and stitching hems for a tailored skirt.
Home Economics
Dist - TVOTAR **Prod** - TVOTAR 1985

Program 13 30 MIN
U-matic
Pins and Needles - One Series
Color (G)
Gives instructions on the preparation and use of bias tape on edges that fray excessively and hemming a skirt and lining.
Home Economics
Dist - TVOTAR **Prod** - TVOTAR 1985

Program 14 30 MIN
U-matic
Pins and Needles - One Series
Color (G)
Gives instructions on taking one's own measurements and checking them against commercial pattern dimensions.
Home Economics
Dist - TVOTAR **Prod** - TVOTAR 1985

Program 15 30 MIN
U-matic
Pins and Needles - One Series
Color (G)
Gives instructions on the modification of a commercial bodice pattern at neck and shoulder lines for individual fit without destroying the original design.
Home Economics
Dist - TVOTAR **Prod** - TVOTAR 1985

Program 16 30 MIN
U-matic
Pins and Needles - One Series
Color (G)
Gives instructions on the modification of a commercial pattern for specific figure problems with shoulders and bust line.
Home Economics
Dist - TVOTAR **Prod** - TVOTAR 1985

Program 17 30 MIN
U-matic
Pins and Needles - One Series
Color (G)
Gives instructions on the modification of a commercial pattern for specific figure problems with sleeves, back and waistline.
Home Economics
Dist - TVOTAR **Prod** - TVOTAR 1985
Dist - RMIBHF **Prod** - RMIBHF

Program 18 30 MIN
U-matic
Pins and Needles - One Series
Color (G)
Gives instructions on important elements of haute couture and the secrets of hand rolled hems and French buttonholes.
Home Economics
Dist - TVOTAR **Prod** - TVOTAR 1985

Program 19 30 MIN
U-matic
Pins and Needles - One Series
Color (G)
Gives instructions on buttonhole preparation and a selection of easy to make hats.
Home Economics
Dist - TVOTAR **Prod** - TVOTAR 1985

Program 20 30 MIN
U-matic
Pins and Needles - One Series
Color (G)
Gives instructions on techniques for making a broad brimmed organza hat, a one piece circle skirt and matching halter top.
Home Economics
Dist - TVOTAR **Prod** - TVOTAR 1985

Program 21 30 MIN
U-matic
Pins and Needles - One Series
Color (G)
Gives instructions on measurement taking and pattern modification for making pants.
Home Economics
Dist - TVOTAR **Prod** - TVOTAR 1985

Program 22 30 MIN
U-matic
Pins and Needles - One Series
Color (G)
Gives instructions on making children's pants by modification of the basic pattern.
Home Economics
Dist - TVOTAR **Prod** - TVOTAR 1985

Program 23 30 MIN
U-matic
Pins and Needles - One Series
Color (G)
Gives instructions on adding a fly extension, pockets and elasticized waistband to a pattern shell of men's sports slacks.
Home Economics
Dist - TVOTAR **Prod** - TVOTAR 1985

Program 24 30 MIN
U-matic
Pins and Needles - One Series
Color (G)
Gives instructions on fabric needs, pattern layout, marking and cutting for men's sport slacks.
Home Economics
Dist - TVOTAR **Prod** - TVOTAR 1985

Program 25 30 MIN
U-matic
Pins and Needles - One Series
Color (G)
Gives instructions on construction procedures for waistband, pockets, fly extension and zipper for men's sport slacks.
Home Economics
Dist - TVOTAR **Prod** - TVOTAR 1985

Program 26 30 MIN
U-matic
Pins and Needles - One Series
Color (G)
Gives instructions on construction procedures for completing the zipper and applying the elasticized waistband for men's sport slacks.
Home Economics
Dist - TVOTAR **Prod** - TVOTAR 1985

Program 1 10 MIN
U-matic
Telefrancais Series
Color (I J)
Features a talking pineapple and a musical group called the Squelettes.
Education; Foreign Language
Dist - TVOTAR **Prod** - TVOTAR 1985

Program 2 10 MIN
U-matic
Telefrancais Series
Color (I J)
Features a flight over Quebec and a parachute jump.
Education; Foreign Language
Dist - TVOTAR **Prod** - TVOTAR 1985

Program 3 10 MIN
U-matic
Telefrancais Series
Color (I J)
Features a camping trip, in which the children get lost.
Education; Foreign Language
Dist - TVOTAR **Prod** - TVOTAR 1985

Program 4 10 MIN
U-matic
Telefrancais Series
Color (I J)
Features a search for children lost in the forest. Their rescuer sings them a song about bravery.
Education; Foreign Language
Dist - TVOTAR **Prod** - TVOTAR 1985

Program 5 10 MIN
U-matic
Telefrancais Series
Color (I J)
Features a test for children which turns out to be unfair so some of them refuse to take it. The Squelettes sing Je deteste les tests.
Education; Foreign Language
Dist - TVOTAR **Prod** - TVOTAR 1985

Program 6 10 MIN
U-matic
Telefrancais Series
Color (I J)
Follows children looking for a job so they can buy a badminton set and the difficulties they encounter.
Education; Foreign Language
Dist - TVOTAR **Prod** - TVOTAR 1985

Program 7 10 MIN
U-matic
Telefrancais Series
Color (I J)
Follows children looking for a way to earn money to buy a badminton set and then being given one as a gift.
Education; Foreign Language
Dist - TVOTAR **Prod** - TVOTAR 1985

Program 8 10 MIN
U-matic
Telefrancais Series
Color (I J)
Follows children as one of them receives an invition to dinner and the others try to sneak in with a delivery of fruit.
Education; Foreign Language
Dist - TVOTAR **Prod** - TVOTAR 1985

Program 9 10 MIN
U-matic
Telefrancais Series
Color (I J)
Follows children trying to sneak into a dinner disguised as a bouquet of flowers.
Education; Foreign Language
Dist - TVOTAR **Prod** - TVOTAR 1985

Program 10 10 MIN
U-matic
Telefrancais Series
Color (I J)
Presents children being coached for a spelling championship between schools.
Education; Foreign Language
Dist - TVOTAR **Prod** - TVOTAR 1985

Program 11 10 MIN
U-matic
Telefrancais Series
Color (I J)
Presents children winning a spelling test and are invited to meet the prime minister.
Education; Foreign Language
Dist - TVOTAR **Prod** - TVOTAR 1985

Program 12 10 MIN
U-matic
Telefrancais Series
Color (I J)
Presents children being excited when they receive an invitation, being disappointed when it announces another test but after a treasure hunt, they change their minds about tests.
Education; Foreign Language
Dist - TVOTAR **Prod** - TVOTAR 1985

Program 13 10 MIN
U-matic
Telefrancais Series
Color (I J)
Presents children seeking pledges for a 20K run for the blind.
Education; Foreign Language
Dist - TVOTAR **Prod** - TVOTAR 1985

Program 14 10 MIN
U-matic
Telefrancais series
Color (I J)
Shows a child getting tired after running a few kilometers in a race and being encouraged by a friendly bat.
Education; Foreign Language
Dist - TVOTAR **Prod** - TVOTAR 1985

Program 15 10 MIN
U-matic
Telefrancais series
Color (I J)
Follows children as one of them is moving to Paris and a friend wants to go too. He hides in her suitcase but an observant inspector discovers him.
Education; Foreign Language
Dist - TVOTAR **Prod** - TVOTAR 1985

Program 16 10 MIN
U-matic
Telefrancais Series
Color (I J)
Follows children as a new neighbor moves in who looks like a gorilla. They find it is only a costume.
Education; Foreign Language
Dist - TVOTAR **Prod** - TVOTAR 1985

Program 17 10 MIN
U-matic
Telefrancais Series
Color (I J)
Shows children visiting a museum where they find out that a big dinosaur lies buried beneath their town.
Education; Foreign Language
Dist - TVOTAR **Prod** - TVOTAR 1985

Program 18 10 MIN
U-matic
Telefrancais Series
Color (I J)
Shows children trying to reconstruct the skeleton of a huge dinosaur from bones they have uncovered.
Education; Foreign Language
Dist - TVOTAR **Prod** - TVOTAR 1985

Program 19 10 MIN
U-matic
Telefrancais Series
Color (I J)
Follows children as a friend returns home after a trip to Paris and they buy her presents.
Education; Foreign Language
Dist - TVOTAR **Prod** - TVOTAR 1985

Program 20 10 MIN
U-matic
Telefrancais Series
Color (I J)
Follows children playing video games while waiting for a friend at the airport.
Education; Foreign Language
Dist - TVOTAR **Prod** - TVOTAR 1985

Program 21 10 MIN
U-matic
Telefrancais series
Color (I J)
Shows children looking through a telescope and finding a new comet.
Education; Foreign Language
Dist - TVOTAR **Prod** - TVOTAR 1985

Program 22 10 MIN
U-matic
Telefrancais Series
Color (I J)
Shows children with their friend, a pineapple who found a new comet. He is made an honorary member of the Astronomers Society.
Education; Foreign Language
Dist - TVOTAR **Prod** - TVOTAR 1985

Program 23 10 MIN
U-matic
Telefrancais Series
Color (I J)
Shows children who have found a monkey's paw being told that it has magical powers.
Education; Foreign Language
Dist - TVOTAR **Prod** - TVOTAR 1985

Program 24 10 MIN
U-matic
Telefrancais Series
Color (I J)
Shows children who have a magic monkey's paw making wishes they do not really want.
Education; Foreign Language
Dist - TVOTAR **Prod** - TVOTAR 1985

Program 25 10 MIN
U-matic
Telefrancais Series
Color (I J)
Shows children rehearsing for the play The Three Musketeers.
Education; Foreign Language
Dist - TVOTAR **Prod** - TVOTAR 1985

Program 26 10 MIN
U-matic
Telefrancais Series
Color (I J)
Shows children rehearsing for the play The Three Musketeers and risking an encounter with the villainous Duc.
Education; Foreign Language
Dist - TVOTAR **Prod** - TVOTAR 1985

Program 27 10 MIN
U-matic
Telefrancais Series
Color (I J)
Shows children learning about photography.
Education; Foreign Language
Dist - TVOTAR **Prod** - TVOTAR 1985

Program 28 10 MIN
U-matic
Telefrancais Series
Color (I J)
Follows children as their pineapple friend discovers a shipment of grapefruit has arrived.
Education; Foreign Language
Dist - TVOTAR **Prod** - TVOTAR 1985

Program 29 10 MIN
U-matic
Telefrancais Series
Color (I J)
Follows children as their pineapple friend falls in love with famous singer Brigitte Banane.
Education; Foreign Language
Dist - TVOTAR **Prod** - TVOTAR 1985

Program 30 10 MIN
U-matic
Telefrancais series
Color (I J)
Follows children as a city order closes Telefrancais but everyone finds a new interest.
Education; Foreign Language
Dist - TVOTAR **Prod** - TVOTAR 1985

Program Acquisition
U-matic
Visual Learning Series Session 5
Color (T)
Explains how to preview and acquire television programs for classroom use. Discusses the media - related services available to schools.
Education; Fine Arts
Dist - NYSED **Prod** - NYSED

Program Control 30 MIN
U-matic / VHS
Hands - On with the 68000 Series
Color (IND)
Demonstrates JMP.RTR and RESET instructions. Shows how main program FLASHAWORD calls subroutine FLASH to illustrate simple program control features of the 68000.
Industrial and Technical Education; Mathematics; Sociology
Dist - COLOSU **Prod** - COLOSU

Program Development Conference 29 MIN
U-matic
Launching Civil Service Reform Series
Color
LC 79-706272
Outlines the events leading to the passage of the Civil Service Reform Act and explains the purpose of the Ocean City, Maryland, program development conference. Includes excerpts from addresses on the issues and points out the challenges of civil service reform.
Civics and Political Systems
Dist - USNAC **Prod** - USOPMA 1978

Program development in the kindergarten series
The Learning environment 30 MIN
Dist - GPN

Program Documentation 30 MIN
VHS / U-matic
Programmable Controllers Series
Color
Examines the function and procedures of program documentation. Reports on types of documents.
Industrial and Technical Education; Sociology
Dist - ITCORP **Prod** - ITCORP

Program Execution - a Grey Code - Counter Implementation 30 MIN
U-matic / VHS
Microprocessors for Monitoring and Control Series
Color (IND)
Describes program execution, and shows how a simple counting program is designed and a delay used to slow down program operation. Notes that Grey counter is designed as Class 2 machine and program is provided for implementation.
Industrial and Technical Education; Mathematics; Sociology
Dist - COLOSU **Prod** - COLOSU

Program Exercises 30 MIN
VHS / U-matic
MC68000 Microprocessor Series
Color (IND)
Examines four problems and various solutions to each, using bytes, words and long words, making a good working demonstration of the 68000.
Industrial and Technical Education; Mathematics; Sociology
Dist - COLOSU **Prod** - COLOSU

Program 5 - Basic a - Line Skirt Fitting 29 MIN
VHS / 16mm
Pins and Needles 1 Series
Color (G PRO)
$90.00 purchase _ #BPN147205
Shows fitting, zipper installation, and application of the waistband of the basic A - line skirt. Taught by Montreal couturiere Angelina Di Bello.
Home Economics
Dist - RMIBHF **Prod** - RMIBHF

A Program for Grades 4 - 7 30 MIN
16mm / U-matic / VHS
Child Sexual Abuse - what Your Child Should Know Series
Color (J)
Tells children about problem situations involving touching. Explores problems with babysitters, sex role stereotypes, and communications. Prescreening advised.
Psychology; Sociology
Dist - IU **Prod** - WTTWTV 1983

A Program for Grades K - 3 30 MIN
16mm / U-matic / VHS
Child Sexual Abuse - what Your Child Should Know Series
Color (K P T)
Teaches children about touching, the meaning of good touches, bad touches, or touches that may be uncomfortable or confusing. Prescreening advised.
Psychology; Sociology
Dist - IU **Prod** - WTTWTV 1983

A Program for Grades 7 - 12 60 MIN
16mm / U-matic / VHS
Child Sexual Abuse - what Your Child Should Know Series
Color (J)
Illustrates the problems of adolescence. Helps growing people to examine the risks in dating and the growing up process that may leave them vulnerable to sexual assault and abuse. Prescreening advised.
Psychology; Sociology
Dist - IU **Prod** - WTTWTV 1983

A Program for Parents 90 MIN
U-matic / VHS / 16mm
Child Sexual Abuse - what Your Child Should Know Series
Color (C A)
Explains sexual abuse of children, who falls victim, who are the perpetrators, and what the viewer can do to prevent it. Prescreening advised.
Psychology; Sociology
Dist - IU **Prod** - WTTWTV 1983

A Program for Senior High 60 MIN
16mm / U-matic / VHS
Child Sexual Abuse - what Your Child Should Know Series
Color (H C T)
Explores issues confronting adolescents. Discusses understanding of sexual assault, how it happens, who is the victim, and who is the assailant. Prescreening advised.
Psychology; Sociology
Dist - IU **Prod** - WTTWTV 1983

A Program for Training in Human Sexuality 60 MIN
VHS / U-matic
Color
Describes a conceptual approach for training in sexuality for practioners in medicine, psychology, social work, nursing and education. Presents a training design which examines the cognitive, affective and communication skills necessary for preparing health professionals for effective delivery of sexual health care.
Health and Safety; Psychology; Sociology
Dist - HEMUL **Prod** - HEMUL

Program for Victory 10 MIN
U-matic / VHS
Color (A)
Presents Tom Osborne, football coach at Nebraska and holder of a PhD in psychology, explaining the importance of sound preparation in motivating a team. Stresses care, understanding and sharing goals.
Physical Education and Recreation; Psychology
Dist - SFTI **Prod** - SFTI

Program 4 - Basic a - Line Skirt Assembly 29 MIN
VHS / 16mm
Pins and Needles 1 Series
Color (G PRO)
$90.00 purchase _ #BPN147204
Shows how to assemble a basic A - line skirt cut from the basic pattern. Taught by Montreal couturiere Angelina Di Bello.
Home Economics
Dist - RMIBHF **Prod** - RMIBHF

Program I 40 MIN
VHS / U-matic
Othello - a Stage Production Series
Color
Establishes the characters of Shakespeare's `Othello' and ends with Othello's transfer to Cyprus.
Literature and Drama
Dist - NETCHE **Prod** - NETCHE 1984

Program II 43 MIN
U-matic / VHS
Othello - a stage production series
Color
Centers on Iago's plot of revenge in Shakespeare's 'Othello.'
Literature and Drama
Dist - NETCHE **Prod** - NETCHE 1984

Program III 39 MIN
VHS / U-matic
Othello - a stage production series
Color
Involves Emilia establishing her innocence as the network of suspicion builds to close all avenues of escape for the guiltless Desdemona in Shakespeare's 'Othello.'

Literature and Drama
Dist - NETCHE **Prod** - NETCHE 1984

The Program in action 22 MIN
VHS
Perspectives in science series
Color (J H C G)
Offers an introductory video which describes the series. Explains how to make the best use of the interactive model. Included with both videodisc and videocassette series
Computer Science; Science - Natural; Sociology
Dist - BULFRG **Prod** - NFBC 1991

Program IV 44 MIN
VHS / U-matic
Othello - a Stage Production Series
Color
Presents the final scene of Shakespeare's 'Othello,' of the preparation for bed and the deaths of Desdemona and Othello.
Literature and Drama
Dist - NETCHE **Prod** - NETCHE 1984

Program management video
VHS
Color (G T PRO)
$299.00 purchase _ #91125
Presents a 3 - part management training series produced by LVA and Laubach. Looks at board development, long range planning, program evaluation, public relations, fund development, and board assessment. Leader's handbook and notes for participants available separately.
Business and Economics; Education; English Language; Psychology
Dist - LITERA

Program Manipulation Instructions 30 MIN
U-matic / VHS
MC68000 Microprocess Series
Color (IND)
Describes very special instructions including the decrement and branch until condition true. Tells about LINK and UNLINK, powerful subroutine instructions, in a typical compiler exercise.
Industrial and Technical Education; Mathematics; Sociology
Dist - COLOSU **Prod** - COLOSU

Program of songs by Lightnin' Sam Hopkins 8 MIN
16mm
Ethnic music and dance series
B&W (J)
LC 72-700242
Presents an informal performance of three songs by Lightnin' Sam Hopkins, a country - blues guitarist who carries on a characteristic banter between each song.
Fine Arts
Dist - UWASHP **Prod** - UWASH 1971

Program One 14 MIN
U-matic / 16mm
Feeling Yes, Feeling no Series
Color
Teaches children basic skills to protect themselves against sexual assault. Differentiates good touching and bad touching. Encourages children to use their right to say NO.
Health and Safety; Psychology; Sociology
Dist - PEREN **Prod** - NFBC

Program 1 - Gangs - decisions and options 18 MIN
VHS
What about gangs series
Color (I J H)
$85.95 purchase _ #10137VG
Shows how three youngsters from different backgrounds grapple with their decision to join a gang or reject membership. Covers issues of low self - esteem, dysfunctional families, and fears of gang violence. Part one of a two - part series. Includes a teacher's guide.
Sociology
Dist - UNL

Program 1 - Laura Somersal 29 MIN
VHS
Pomo basketweavers - a tribute to three elders series
Color (G)
$49.95 purchase
Features Laura Somersal who presents an overview of the Pomoan people and their culture. Looks at the internationally - acclaimed baskets of the Pomo and reveals the different types and styles and the techniques used in their making. Part of a three - part series on the history of the Pomo nation of northern California. Produced by Creative Light Productions.
Fine Arts; Social Science
Dist - NAMPBC

Program Planning 30 MIN
U-matic / VHS
Basic Education - Teaching the Adult Series
Color (T)
Discusses program planning when teaching adult basic education students.
Education
Dist - MDCPB **Prod** - MDDE

Program planning 29 MIN
VHS / 16mm
Breaking the unseen barrier series
Color (C)
$180.00, $240.00 purchase _ #269702
Demonstrates through vignettes effective teaching strategies to help students with learning disabilities reach their full potential. Offers insight into integrating learning disabled students into the classroom. Illustrates the cycle of assessment, diagnosis, individual educational planning, teaching and further assignment in the story of Dan, an elementary student. This process has proven to be successful in helping learning disabled students fit into the regular classroom routine.
Education; Mathematics; Psychology
Dist - AITECH **Prod** - ACCESS 1988

Program planning - Pt 1 12 MIN
U-matic
Color
LC 79-708057
Focuses on the planning of instructional programs. Discusses identifying and developing objectives.
Education
Dist - USNAC **Prod** - VAHSL 1976

Program planning - Pt 2 11 MIN
U-matic
Color
LC 79-708057
Focuses on the planning of instructional programs. Discusses developing an instructional task analysis.
Education
Dist - USNAC **Prod** - VAHSL 1976

Program Preparation 16 MIN
U-matic / VHS
Numerical Control/Computerized Numerical Control, Module 1 - 'Fundamentals Series
Color (IND)
Focuses on required operations, selecting appropriate tools and identifying methods to fix the parts.
Business and Economics; Industrial and Technical Education
Dist - LEIKID **Prod** - LEIKID

Program 6 - Tailored Skirt 29 MIN
VHS / 16mm
Pins and Needles 1 Series
Color (G PRO)
$90.00 purchase _ #BPN147206
Shows how to choose the proper weight of lining and underlining for various fabrics for the tailored skirt. Demonstrates economical pattern layout. Taught by Montreal couturiere Angelina Di Bello.
Home Economics
Dist - RMIBHF **Prod** - RMIBHF

Program Structures 20 MIN
U-matic / VHS
Basic Power Series
Color (H C A)
Examines some fundamental structures. Shows how to create branching and looping structures.
Industrial and Technical Education; Mathematics; Sociology
Dist - UCEMC **Prod** - VANGU

Program testing - Pt 1 30 MIN
VHS / U-matic
Software engineering - a first course series
Color (IND)
Defines some program - testing terminology. Distinguishes various types of testing. Discusses unit - testing concepts of functional testing, structural testing and test - coverage criteria.
Industrial and Technical Education; Mathematics
Dist - COLOSU **Prod** - COLOSU

Program testing - Pt 2 30 MIN
U-matic / VHS
Software engineering - a first course series
Color (IND)
Covers system - integration strategies and testing techniques, including structural walk - through, static analysis and dynamic testing. Concludes with discussion of current issues in testing.
Industrial and Technical Education; Mathematics
Dist - COLOSU **Prod** - COLOSU

Program Three 16 MIN
16mm / U-matic
Feeling Yes, Feeling no Series
Color
Deals with the subject of the sexual assault of children by family members or other trusted persons.
Health and Safety; Psychology; Sociology
Dist - PEREN **Prod** - NFBC

Program 3 - Basic a - Line Skirt 29 MIN
VHS / 16mm
Pins and Needles 1 Series
Color (G PRO)
$90.00 purchase _ #BPN147203
Shows how to adjust patterns, modify styles, and choose fabrics for making a basic A - line skirt. Taught by Montreal couturiere Angelina Di Bello.
Home Economics
Dist - RMIBHF **Prod** - RMIBHF

Program 3 - Mabel McKay 29 MIN
VHS
Pomo basketweavers - a tribute to three elders series
Color (G)
$49.95 purchase
Features Mabel McKay, a dream weaver and Pomo nation doctor. Looks at the Pomo people and basketry plants they have cultivated. Reveals their spiritual rules and responsibility to the natural world. Part of a three - part series on the history of the Pomo nation of northern California. Produced by Creative Light Productions.
Fine Arts; Social Science
Dist - NAMPBC

Program Two 14 MIN
16mm / U-matic
Feeling Yes, Feeling no Series
Color
Shows children how to recognize sexual assault by strangers. Shows how children can ensure their safety before saying yes or no to a request from a stranger.
Health and Safety; Physical Education and Recreation; Psychology; Sociology
Dist - PEREN **Prod** - NFBC

Program 2 - Elsie Allen 29 MIN
VHS
Pomo basketweavers - a tribute to three elders series
Color (G)
$49.95 purchase
Features Elsie Allen who highlights the progressive changes in the art of Pomo basket weaving. Includes the Warm Springs Dam project of the 1970s. Part of a three - part series on the history of the Pomo nation of northern California. Produced by Creative Light Productions.
Fine Arts; Social Science
Dist - NAMPBC

Program 2 - Measurement Taking 29 MIN
VHS / 16mm
Pins and Needles 1 Series
Color (G PRO)
$90.00 purchase _ #BPN147202
Gives an introduction to measurement taking. Taught by Montreal couturiere Angelina Di Bello.
Home Economics
Dist - RMIBHF **Prod** - RMIBHF

Program 2 - Recognizing, containing and eliminating gangs - strategies for educators 40 MIN
VHS
What about gangs series
Color (T)
$94.00 purchase _ #10139VG
Presents a discussion on recognizing, containing and eliminating gangs in schools. Features advice for educators from a variety of experts on gangs and juvenile crime. Includes a teacher's guide. Part two of a two - part series.
Sociology
Dist - UNL

Program types - stereotyping 15 MIN
VHS / U-matic
Tuned - In series; Lesson 4
Color (J H)
Explains why information in television news stories is often edited out. Reveals that the ninth - grade students come to the conclusion that this editing may be a plot against kids and are therefore challenged to produce better television, complete with drama, news and commercials.
Fine Arts; Sociology
Dist - FI **Prod** - WNETTV 1982

Programmable Controller I - O Devices 60 TO 90 MIN
VHS
Programmable Controllers Module Series
Color (PRO)
$600.00 - $1500.00 purchase _ #PCPCI
Covers the basic operation of common I - O modules, including descrete input and output modules, analog I - O modules and special I - O modules. Part of a seven - part

series on programmable controllers. Includes five student guides, five workbooks and an instructor guide.
Computer Science; Education; Industrial and Technical Education; Psychology
Dist - NUSTC **Prod** - NUSTC

Programmable Controller - Programming 1 60 TO 90 MIN
VHS
Programmable Controllers Module Series
Color (PRO)
$600.00 - $1500.00 purchase _ #PCPC1
Describes the basic organization of ladder language programming and its devices. Part of a seven - part series on programmable controllers. Includes five student guides, five workbooks and an instructor guide.
Computer Science; Education; Industrial and Technical Education; Psychology
Dist - NUSTC **Prod** - NUSTC

Programmable Controller - Programming 2 60 TO 90 MIN
VHS
Programmable Controllers Module Series
Color (PRO)
$600.00 - $1500.00 purchase _ #PCPC2
Introduces Boolean programming language. Covers documentation and peripherals used in the maintenance of programmable controllers. Part of a seven - part series on programmable controllers. Includes five student guides, five workbooks and an instructor guide.
Computer Science; Education; Industrial and Technical Education; Psychology
Dist - NUSTC **Prod** - NUSTC

Programmable Controller Systems 60 TO 90 MIN
VHS
Programmable Controllers Module Series
Color (PRO)
$600.00 - $1500.00 purchase _ #PCPCS
Looks at aspects of programmable controller systems such as system classifications and characteristics, communication techniques, system documentation, installation procedures and startup procedures. Part of a seven - part series on programmable controllers. Includes five student guides, five workbooks and an instructor guide.
Computer Science; Education; Industrial and Technical Education; Psychology
Dist - NUSTC **Prod** - NUSTC

Programmable controllers 27 MIN
VHS / 16mm
Manufacturing insights series
Color (A IND)
$200.00, $190.00 purchase _ #VT254, #VT254U
Explains the benefits of using programmable controllers in several different manufacturing situations.
Business and Economics; Computer Science; Industrial and Technical Education
Dist - SME **Prod** - SME 1987

Programmable Controllers Module Series
Basic concepts of programmable controllers 60 TO 90 MIN
Elements of discrete control systems 60 TO 90 MIN
Programmable Controller I - O Devices 60 TO 90 MIN
Programmable Controller Programming - 1 60 TO 90 MIN
Programmable Controller Programming - 2 60 TO 90 MIN
Programmable Controller Systems 60 TO 90 MIN
Troubleshooting Programmable Controllers 60 TO 90 MIN
Dist - NUSTC

Programmable Controllers - PLC's Series
Presents a series of training programs to familiarize the student with PC hardware, programs, functions and systems, as well as troubleshooting techniques used to isolate problems.
Control devices 22 MIN
Number Systems 24 MIN
PC Hardware and Ladder Logic 23 MIN
PC's - Specialized Computers 24 MIN
Troubleshooting PCs - Pt 1 27 MIN
Troubleshooting PCs - Pt 2 21 MIN
Dist - TAT **Prod** - TAT 1987

Programmable Controllers Series
Analog and special input - output modules 30 MIN
Central Processing Unit 30 MIN
Communication fundamentals 30 MIN
Developing a program 30 MIN
Discrete Input, Output Modules 30 MIN
Installation Considerations 30 MIN
Interpreting Ladder Diagrams 30 MIN
Introduction to Programmable Controllers 30 MIN
Networking 30 MIN
Numbering Systems, Numbering Codes, and Logic Concepts 30 MIN
Principles of Ladder Diagrams 30 MIN
Principles of Ladder Logic Programming 30 MIN
Program Documentation 30 MIN
Programming 30 MIN
Programming - Analog and PID 30 MIN
Programming - Data Comparison and Arithmatic Functions 30 MIN
Programming - Times and Counters 30 MIN
Programming Devices and Peripheral Equipment 30 MIN
Sizing and Selection 30 MIN
Troubleshooting Field Device Malfunctions 30 MIN
Troubleshooting P C Malfunctions 30 MIN
Troubleshooting Techniques 30 MIN
Dist - ITCORP

Programmable controllers series
Automatic control systems 24 MIN
Dist - TAT

Programmed Instruction in Medical Interviewing Series
Programmed Interview Instruction, no 1 - Mrs Adams 20 MIN
Programmed Interview Instruction, no 2 - Mr Barrett 20 MIN
Programmed Interview Instruction, no 3 - Mrs Carson 18 MIN
Programmed Interview Instruction, no 4 - Mr Dunn 17 MIN
Programmed Interview Instruction, no 5 - Mr Egan 20 MIN
Programmed Interview Instruction, no 6 - Miss Frazer 18 MIN
Programmed Interview Instruction, no 8 - Miss Hadkell 20 MIN
Programmed Interview Instruction, no 9 - Miss Ingram 12 MIN
Programmed Interview Instruction, no 10 - Mrs Jackson 15 MIN
Programmed Interview Instruction, no 11 - Mr King 14 MIN
Programmed Interview Instruction, no 12 - Mr Lloyd 15 MIN
Dist - NMAC

Programmed instruction in medical interviewing series
Programmed interview instruction - No 7 - Mrs Goodrich 20 MIN
Dist - NMAC
USNAC

Programmed Instruction - the Development Process 19 MIN
16mm
Color; B&W (T) (SPANISH)
LC 74-705430; 74-705429
Introduces the major stages in the development of programmed instructional materials, emphasizing student tryouts and revisions leading to lasting and influential effects on education.
Education; Foreign Language
Dist - USNAC **Prod** - USOE

Programmed instruction - the teacher's role series
Eighth grade mathematics 10 MIN
Fifth grade geography 10 MIN
First grade reading 10 MIN
Fourth Grade Vocabulary 13 MIN
Third grade science 11 MIN
Dist - USNAC

Programmed Interview Instruction, no 11 - Mr King 14 MIN
16mm
Programmed Instruction in Medical Interviewing Series
B&W
LC 74-706199
Follows an interview with a patient, pausing at intervals to ask a multiple - choice question on the correct response for each situation. Serves as a test film to measure cognitive learning.
Guidance and Counseling; Health and Safety; Psychology
Dist - NMAC **Prod** - USCSM 1970

Programmed Interview Instruction, no 12 - Mr Lloyd 15 MIN
16mm
Programmed Instruction in Medical Interviewing Series
B&W
LC 74-706200
Follows an interview with a patient, pausing at intervals to give the audience a multiple - choice question on the correct response for each situation.
Guidance and Counseling; Health and Safety; Psychology
Dist - NMAC **Prod** - USCSM 1970

Programmed Interview Instruction, no 8 - Miss Hadkell 20 MIN
16mm
Programmed Instruction in Medical Interviewing Series
B&W
LC 74-706196
Demonstrates how the interviewer selects and sequences interventions to exercise the least possible explicit control over the patient and to obtain medical information which is difficult for the patient to talk about.
Guidance and Counseling; Health and Safety; Psychology
Dist - NMAC **Prod** - USCSM 1970

Programmed Interview Instruction, no 5 - Mr Egan 20 MIN
16mm
Programmed Instruction in Medical Interviewing Series
B&W
LC 74-706192
Reviews a case of an industrial accident victim to demonstrate that accuracy in communication is facilitated when the interviewer avoids suggesting patient responses by wording and by demeanor, tone of voice and other nonverbal acts.
Guidance and Counseling; Health and Safety; Psychology
Dist - NMAC **Prod** - USCSM 1970

Programmed Interview Instruction, no 4 - Mr Dunn 17 MIN
16mm
Programmed Instruction in Medical Interviewing Series
B&W
LC 74-706191
Combines the use of confrontation, facilitation and silence to show that relevant communication occurs when opportunity is provided for it to emerge. Deals with an anxious, overweight professional man who reports two recent cases of tachycardia.
Guidance and Counseling; Health and Safety; Psychology
Dist - NMAC **Prod** - USCSM 1970

Programmed Interview Instruction, no 9 - Miss Ingram 12 MIN
16mm
Programmed Instruction in Medical Interviewing Series
B&W
LC 74-706197
Demonstrates the technique of creation of an emotional climate conducive to a successful interview in the case of a hostile patient.
Guidance and Counseling; Health and Safety; Psychology
Dist - NMAC **Prod** - USCSM 1970

Programmed Interview Instruction, no 1 - Mrs Adams 20 MIN
16mm
Programmed Instruction in Medical Interviewing Series
B&W
LC 74-706188
Demonstrates the technique of facilitation in an interview with a patient who complains of chronic fatigue. Shows how the interviewer encourages the flow of information from the patient without requiring him to speak or to specify the content expected.
Guidance and Counseling; Health and Safety; Psychology
Dist - NMAC **Prod** - USCSM 1970

Programmed interview instruction - No 7 - Mrs Goodrich 20 MIN
16mm
Programmed instruction in medical interviewing series
B&W
LC 74-706195
Demonstrates how the interviewer discourages an overtalkative patient from communicating redundant or irrelevant information in the interest of permitting the emergence of new or more relevant information within time limits of the interview.
Guidance and Counseling; Health and Safety; Psychology
Dist - NMAC **Prod** - USCSM 1970
USNAC

Programmed Interview Instruction, no 6 - Miss Frazer 18 MIN
16mm
Programmed Instruction in Medical Interviewing Series
B&W
LC 74-706193
Points out how the interviewer avoids suggesting patient responses by the timing of his participation. Involves the case of a suggestive young woman who has developed conversion reaction on the job.
Guidance and Counseling; Health and Safety; Psychology
Dist - NMAC **Prod** - USCSM 1970

Programmed Interview Instruction, no 10 - Mrs Jackson 15 MIN
16mm

Programmed Instruction in Medical Interviewing Series
B&W
LC 74-706198
Demonstrates how the interviewer arouses the patient's confidence in the physician and his recommendations, as well as limits the patient's dependency on the physician.
Guidance and Counseling; Health and Safety; Psychology
Dist - NMAC **Prod** - USCSM 1970

Programmed Interview Instruction, no 3 - Mrs Carson 18 MIN
16mm
Programmed Instruction in Medical Interviewing Series
B&W
LC 74-706190
Demonstrates the effective use of silence to permit a harassed housewife with continuous headaches to speak on her own initiative and contribute to an understanding of her complaint.
Guidance and Counseling; Health and Safety; Psychology
Dist - NMAC **Prod** - USCSM 1970

Programmed Interview Instruction, no 2 - Mr Barrett 20 MIN
16mm
Programmed Instruction in Medical Interviewing Series
B&W
LC 74-706189
Demonstrates the technique of confrontation designed to elicit significant verbal and nonverbal information from a businessman who tries to discuss only his peptic ulcer and denies that he has emotional problems.
Guidance and Counseling; Health and Safety; Psychology
Dist - NMAC **Prod** - USCSM 1970

Programmed Learning in the United States Air Force 26 MIN
16mm
Color
LC 74-705433
Describes principles of programmed learning and explains how the Air Force is using this revolutionary teaching method to increase quality and quantity of Air Force instructions with a decrease in training cost.
Education
Dist - USNAC **Prod** - USAF 1963

Programmed Preventive Maintenance 27 MIN
U-matic / VHS
Color (IND)
Discusses the advantages, scope, design, implementation, follow - up and modification of a programmed preventive maintenance plan for a well production system.
Industrial and Technical Education; Social Science
Dist - UTEXPE **Prod** - UTEXPE 1974

A Programmer's introduction to C 180 MIN
VHS / U-matic
(A PRO)
$400.00
Covers applications of structured programming and C fundamentals.
Computer Science
Dist - VIDEOT **Prod** - VIDEOT 1988

A Programmer's Introduction to C
VHS / U-matic
(A PRO)
$400
Covers C's advanced features such as variable scope and structures.
Computer Science
Dist - VIDEOT **Prod** - VIDEOT 1988

Programmer's ROM
CD-ROM
Color (G A)
$125.00 purchase _ #1942
Gives a wide range of routines, tools and source codes for Basic, C, Fortran, Cobol, Prolog, ADA, etc. Presents most files compressed in the PKware ZIP format. For IBM PCs and compatibles. Requires 640K RAM, DOS Version 3.1 or greater, one floppy disk drive - a hard drive is recommended, one empty expansion slot, and an IBM compatible CD - ROM drive.
Computer Science
Dist - BEP

Programmer's ROM
CD-ROM
(G)
$149.00 purchase
Presents hundred of Megabytes of DOS based public domain source code, programming libraries and applications. Includes ADA, Assembler, Basic, Quick Basic, C (Turbo, Lattice, Microsoft, Aztec, Desmet), dBase, Lotus, Pascal, Turbo Pascal applications. Many files compressed in the PKware ZIP format. Catalogs each file with a one line description including file name, byte size, date and description.
Computer Science
Dist - QUANTA **Prod** - QUANTA

Programmer's Workbench
VHS / U-matic
UNIX Overview Series Unit 5
Color
Describes the four major UNIX applications, the five primary stages of the application development cycle, the four major programmer's workbench tools and shows how major tools can be applied to office automation, engineering and management information applications.
Business and Economics; Industrial and Technical Education; Mathematics; Sociology
Dist - COMTEG **Prod** - COMTEG

Programming 30 MIN
U-matic / VHS
Programmable Controllers Series
Color
Considers logical operations and data manipulation.
Industrial and Technical Education; Sociology
Dist - ITCORP **Prod** - ITCORP

Programming - Analog and PID 30 MIN
U-matic / VHS
Programmable Controllers Series
Color
Deals with analog and PID.
Industrial and Technical Education; Sociology
Dist - ITCORP **Prod** - ITCORP

Programming and problem - solving - BASIC 30 MIN
U-matic / VHS
On and about instruction - microcomputers
Color (T A PRO)
$180.00 purchase, $30.00 rental
Designed to provide teachers with information for a one hour course on computer literacy. Focuses on programming and problem solving using BASIC. Thirteenth in a 16 part series.
Computer Science
Dist - GPN

Programming and problem - solving - LOGO 30 MIN
U-matic / VHS
On and about instruction - microcomputers
Color (T A PRO)
$180.00 purchase, $30.00 rental
Designed to provide teachers with information for a one hour course on computer literacy. Focuses on programming and problem solving using LOGO. Fourteenth in a 16 part series.
Computer Science
Dist - GPN **Prod** - VADE 1984 - 1985

Programming C N C - Absolute 14 MIN
BETA / VHS
Machine Shop - C N C Machine Operations Series
Color (IND)
Industrial and Technical Education; Psychology
Dist - RMIBHF **Prod** - RMIBHF

Programming C N C, Circular Interpolation 20 MIN
BETA / VHS
Machine Shop - C N C Machine Operations Series
Color (IND)
Industrial and Technical Education; Psychology
Dist - RMIBHF **Prod** - RMIBHF

Programming C N C, Drilling Cycles 19 MIN
BETA / VHS
Machine Shop - C N C Machine Operations Series
Color (IND)
Industrial and Technical Education; Psychology
Dist - RMIBHF **Prod** - RMIBHF

Programming C N C - Incremental 23 MIN
VHS / BETA
Machine Shop - C N C Machine Operations Series
Color (IND)
Industrial and Technical Education; Psychology
Dist - RMIBHF **Prod** - RMIBHF

Programming C N C, Special Milling Cycles 16 MIN
VHS / BETA
Machine Shop - C N C Machine Operations Series
Color (IND)
Industrial and Technical Education; Psychology
Dist - RMIBHF **Prod** - RMIBHF

Programming - Data Comparison and Arithmatic Functions 30 MIN
U-matic / VHS
Programmable Controllers Series
Color
Covers data comparison and arithmatic functions.
Industrial and Technical Education; Sociology
Dist - ITCORP **Prod** - ITCORP

Programming Devices and Peripheral Equipment 30 MIN
VHS / U-matic
Programmable Controllers Series
Color
Explores programming devices and peripheral equipment. Highlights I O simulators.
Industrial and Technical Education; Sociology
Dist - ITCORP **Prod** - ITCORP

Programming dilemma 30 MIN
U-matic / VHS
Application development without programmers series
Color
Describes how application development tools can help meet the increasing demand for computer application that directly affect a business' growth.
Industrial and Technical Education; Psychology
Dist - DELTAK **Prod** - DELTAK

The Programming environment - operating systems - Parts 17 and 18 60 MIN
VHS / U-matic
New literacy - an introduction to computers
Color (G)
$45.00, $29.95 purchase
Discusses the ever - increasing costs of program development and maintenance and the role of chief programmer in Part 17. Reviews operating systems, including on - line direct - access systems, multiprogramming and multiprocessing in Part 18. Parts of a 26 - part series on computing machines.
Computer Science; Mathematics
Dist - ANNCPB **Prod** - SCCON 1988

Programming for microcomputers series

Alphanumeric expressions - numeric operations	30 MIN
Branching and looping	29 MIN
Designing a program	29 MIN
Double subscripted variables	29 MIN
Format and edit commands - storing and retrieving programs	30 MIN
Functions	29 MIN
Introduction - getting started	30 MIN
More about program construction	29 MIN
Nested loops and more about program design	30 MIN
READ - DATA Statements - Strings	30 MIN
Single subscripted variables	29 MIN
Subroutines - program construction	30 MIN
Variables - input statement	30 MIN

Dist - IU

Programming language - understanding BASIC
U-matic / VHS
Computer literacy - computer language series
Color
Illustrates the computer language BASIC for use in programming computers.
Industrial and Technical Education; Mathematics
Dist - LIBFSC **Prod** - LIBFSC

Programming Languages - Apple LOGO
VHS
$59 purchase _ #RM6360V
Teaches students about programming languages through the use of pictorial displays of commands. Discusses how computer commands relate to computer operations.
Computer Science
Dist - CAREER **Prod** - CAREER

Programming Languages - Apple Logo 29 MIN
VHS / BETA
Computer Education / Programming / Operations Series
Color
Business and Economics; Industrial and Technical Education; Mathematics
Dist - RMIBHF **Prod** - RMIBHF

Programming languages - Apple Logo
VHS / U-matic
Computer literacy - computer language series
Color
Contains the common primitive LOGO and TURTLE commands and gives demonstration programs and examples in computer programming.
Industrial and Technical Education; Mathematics
Dist - LIBFSC **Prod** - LIBFSC

Programming languages - Apple Pascal
U-matic / VHS
Computer literacy - computer language series
Color
Offers an introductory overview of the Apple II adaptation of the UCSD Pascal Operating System.
Industrial and Technical Education; Mathematics
Dist - LIBFSC **Prod** - LIBFSC

Programming Languages - Apple PASCAL
VHS
$59 purchase _ #RM6363V
Teaches students about programming languages through the use of pictorial displays of commands. Discusses how computer commands relate to computer operations.
Computer Science
Dist - CAREER **Prod** - CAREER

Programming Languages - Apple Pascal 25 MIN
BETA / VHS
Computer Education / Programming / Operations Series
Color
Business and Economics; Industrial and Technical Education; Mathematics
Dist - RMIBHF **Prod** - RMIBHF

Programming languages - Atari Pilot - Text
U-matic / VHS
Computer literacy - computer language series
Color
Introduces PILOT programming language and covers the basic CORE PILOT commands required to write text programs (without graphics). Explains and demonstrates all commands.
Industrial and Technical Education; Mathematics
Dist - LIBFSC **Prod** - LIBFSC

Programming languages - Atari Pilot - Turtle Graphics and Sound
U-matic / VHS
Computer literacy - computer language series
Color
Presents all necessary commands needed to create interesting and exciting color graphics displays. Covers PILOT sound capabilities to add a dimension to TEXT and TURTLE graphic programs using Atari PILOT. Explains the commands and shows the programs and examples.
Industrial and Technical Education; Mathematics
Dist - LIBFSC **Prod** - LIBFSC

Programming Languages - Basic
VHS
$59 purchase _ #RM6352V
Teaches students about programming languages through the use of pictorial displays of commands. Discusses how computer commands relate to computer operations.
Computer Science
Dist - CAREER **Prod** - CAREER

Programming Languages - Basic 22 MIN
BETA / VHS
Computer Education / Programming / Operations Series
Color
Business and Economics; Mathematics
Dist - RMIBHF **Prod** - RMIBHF

Programming Microprocessors Series
Input/Output 30 MIN
Software 30 MIN
What is a Microprocessor? 30 MIN
Dist - COLOSU

Programming Perspectives 28 MIN
VHS / U-matic
Next Steps with Computers in the Classroom Series
Color (T)
Business and Economics; Industrial and Technical Education; Mathematics
Dist - PBS **Prod** - PBS

Programming Perspectives 360 MIN
U-matic / VHS
Next Steps with Computers in the Classroom Series
Color (C T)
Computer Science; Education; Mathematics
Dist - UEUWIS **Prod** - UEUWIS 1985

Programming the Key Punch 14 MIN
16mm
Color (H C A)
Illustrates the preparation of different program cards for the key punch. Shows how the star wheels of the program unit read the cards and cause the keypunch to change shifts, ship or duplicate. Introduces the verifier, which checks punched cards to detect errors.
Mathematics; Psychology; Sociology
Dist - SF **Prod** - SF 1968

Programming - Times and Counters 30 MIN
U-matic / VHS
Programmable Controllers Series
Color
Examines programming timers and counters. Describes cascading functions.
Industrial and Technical Education; Sociology
Dist - ITCORP **Prod** - ITCORP

Programming your personal computer
VHS
Computer series
Color (G)
$29.95 purchase _ #IV - 009
Explains the basic workings of the computer. Emphasizes the conversion of ordinary user's language to computer language, or binary code.
Computer Science
Dist - INCRSE **Prod** - INCRSE

Programs - Helicopter Example 45 MIN
VHS / U-matic
Modern Control Theory - Deterministic Optimal Linear Feedback Series
Color (PRO)
Industrial and Technical Education; Mathematics
Dist - MIOT **Prod** - MIOT

Programs with Hazel Henderson series
Worth quoting - Videocassette 1 90 MIN
Worth quoting - Videocassette 2 60 MIN
Worth quoting - Videocassette 3 60 MIN
Worth quoting - Videocassette 4 60 MIN
Worth quoting series 243 MIN
Dist - BULFRG

Progress Against Cancer 28 MIN
16mm
Color
LC 74-706560
Explains how modern research has solved many of the mysteries of cancer and improved the cancer victim's chance to survive.
Health and Safety; Science
Dist - USNAC **Prod** - USHHS 1974

Progress, but who is it for 20 MIN
16mm / U-matic / VHS
Brazil Series
Color (J H)
Points out that coffee used to dominate the Brazilian economy, but the products of a growing industrial sector are just as important, if not more so. Discusses who benefits from progress in Brazil, showing that the production line worker at the Fiat plant outside Belo Horizonte can rarely afford a car and that plantation workers are the people who gain the least from the sugar cane being made into motor fuel.
Business and Economics; Geography - World; History - World
Dist - FI **Prod** - BBCTV 1982

Progress Explosion - 106 30 MIN
U-matic
Currents - 1984 - 85 Season Series
Color (A)
Explores the risks of industrial society to the environment and the individual.
Business and Economics; Social Science
Dist - PBS **Prod** - WNETTV 1985

Progress in all Traffic Control 20 MIN
16mm
Color
LC 74-705435
Reviews the history of air traffic control and depicts techniques and systems presently in operation. Describes plans for improved future control and conservation of air space to handle increasing air traffic.
Industrial and Technical Education; Social Science
Dist - USNAC **Prod** - USAF 1966

A Progress report from the process consultants - what have YOU done 60 MIN
U-matic / VHS
Color; PAL (C G PRO)
$89.95, $69.95 purchase _ #92AST - V - W55
Shows how process consulting helps businesses identify the source of some of their difficulties by looking at how they do business rather than just what they do. Discusses the parallel experiences of Kate Butler and Madeline F Finnerty as internal and external practitioners, identifies critical skills for process consultants and shows participants how to develop these skills in themselves and maximize their effectiveness. Highlights the predictable phases of process consultation and analyzes case studies of process consulting successes and failures. Butler is the Executive Director of American Humanagement Association, Flemington NJ; Finnerty is the General Employee Involvement Manager, United Telephone Co, Mansfield OH.
Business and Economics; Psychology
Dist - MOBILE **Prod** - ASTD 1992

Progress! Technology on the Move Set - Venture Read - Alongs 66 MIN
VHS / U-matic
Venture Read - Alongs Series
(P I)
Contains a read along cassette and 8 paperbacks.
Industrial and Technical Education
Dist - TROLA **Prod** - TROLA 1986

Progress through Performance - Iowa's Swine Testing Stations 14 MIN
16mm
Color (H C)
LC 83-700621
Illustrates how the four Iowa Swine Testing Stations identify genetically superior pigs by measuring feed efficiency, average daily weight gain and back fat levels under carefully controlled environmental conditions.
Agriculture
Dist - IOWA **Prod** - IOWA 1982

Progress Towards Mach 3 11 MIN
16mm
Color (J)
Highlights the first 9 XB - ?0a test flights.
Social Science
Dist - RCKWL **Prod** - NAA

Progression and continuity - 5
VHS
Teaching for tomorrow series
Color; PAL (C T)
PdS20 purchase
Uses real teachers and schools to evaluate ideas and support professional development for primary and secondary teachers in the area of progression and continuity. Stimulates discussion on classroom management, handling curriculum changes and developing new teaching techniques. Contact distributor about availability outside the United Kingdom.
Education
Dist - ACADEM

Progressions, Sequences and Series 29 MIN
16mm
Intermediate Algebra Series
B&W (H)
Develops the law of formation for arithmetic and geometric progressions and shows how to find a series from known terms. The problem of finding the sum of N terms in a series is worked out analytically for both arithmetic and geometric progressions.
Mathematics
Dist - MLA **Prod** - CALVIN 1959

The Progressive Development of Movement Abilities in Children 13 MIN
16mm / U-matic / VHS
Color (C A)
LC 82-700037
Defines the three developmental stages of children's physical maturity. Uses high - speed, normal, and stop - action cinematography to show individuals at each of the three stages engaged in a variety of activities. Emphasizes a hierarchical approach to categorizing children's development and identifies developmental anomalies.
Psychology
Dist - IU **Prod** - IU 1982

Progressive Dies - Proven Design Principles and Applications 240 MIN
VHS / 16mm
Color (A IND)
$1800.00
Illustrates hundreds of proven designs and gives tips for efficient die operations. Design principles and application examples. Includes five reference guides.
Education; Industrial and Technical Education
Dist - SME **Prod** - SME 1988

Progressive discipline - you be the judge 18 MIN
VHS / U-matic / BETA
Color (G IND)
$495.00 purchase, $95.00 rental _ #DHL8
Trains supervisors in the process of progressive discipline.
Business and Economics; Psychology; Sociology
Dist - BBP **Prod** - BBP 1989
VLEARN

The Progressive impulse 30 MIN
VHS
America in perspective - US history since 1877 series
Color (H C G)
$99.00 purchase _ #AIP - 8
Examines the motives of the progressive reformers at the turn of the 20th century. Assesses the successes and limitations of progressive reform at the municipal and state levels. Part of a 26 - part series.
Civics and Political Systems; History - United States; Sociology
Dist - INSTRU **Prod** - DALCCD 1991

Progressive Maintenance Diesel Propulsion Engine Series
Disassembly of the 8 - 268a Engine 27 MIN
Dist - USNAC

Progressive maintenance diesel propulsion series
Bearing removal and inspection, B - 268A engine 17 MIN
Dist - USNAC

Progressive maintenance on the General Motors B - 268A diesel engine series
Bearings 9 MIN
Dist - USNAC

The Progressive Muscular Dystrophies 48 MIN
U-matic
Intensive Course in Neuromuscular Diseases Series
Color (PRO)
LC 76-706077
Presents Dr Lewis P Rowland lecturing on the progressive muscular dystrophies.
Health and Safety; Science - Natural
Dist - USNAC Prod - NINDIS 1974

The Progressive presidents 30 MIN
VHS
America in perspective - US history since 1877 series
Color (H C G)
$99.00 purchase _ #AIP - 9
Discusses United States' national progressive reform, particularly as expressed during the presidencies of Theodore Roosevelt and Woodrow Wilson. Analyzes the significance and limits of progressivism. Part of a 26 - part series.
Civics and Political Systems; History - United States
Dist - INSTRU Prod - DALCCD 1991

Progressive Relaxation Training 20 MIN
VHS / U-matic
Color (PRO)
Presents techniques to reduce stress by progressive relaxation procedures.
Health and Safety; Psychology
Dist - BAXMED Prod - BAXMED 1986

Progressive Relaxation Training 20 MIN
16mm
Color
Portrays the subtleties of progressive relaxation procedures by showing a counseling session in which a therapist directs a client to the stages of relaxation. Discusses why progressive relaxation works, the importance of the therapist's voice, the proper physical setting and nonverbal communication during relaxation.
Psychology
Dist - RESPRC Prod - RESPRC

Progressive resistance exercise 34 MIN
VHS
Color (J H C G)
$195.00 purchase, $40.00 rental _ #37947
Introduces the scientific principles and safe techniques to athletes and those who wish to increase their physical strength and fitness. Covers the principles and types of weight training, its effects on basic muscle groups and rules of safety. Demonstrates specific exercises for each major muscle group and suggests some overall routines for different purposes. Produced for Andrew Ertl, Dept of Physical Education, by Instructional Media, University of California, Davis.
Health and Safety; Physical Education and Recreation
Dist - UCEMC

The Progressives 25 MIN
16mm / U-matic / VHS
American History Series
Color (J H)
LC 78-702074
Traces the progressive movement from its beginning in 1890 through World War I. Notes that it was a revolt of the American conscience in the cities and on the state and federal levels against corruption, poverty, prejudice and other social evils.
Civics and Political Systems; History - United States; Psychology; Sociology
Dist - MGHT Prod - PSP 1969

Progressives, Populists and Reform in America (1890 - 1917) 32 MIN
U-matic / VHS
Color
LC 81-706676
Presents reform activists Jesse Jackson and Heather Booth relating past social problems and reformers to modern - day struggles for racial justice and to other contemporary social conditions.
History - United States
Dist - GA Prod - GA 1981

Prohibition and pot 15 MIN
16mm
Color
Discusses whether the parallels in public attitudes toward prohibition in the 20s and toward pot now are valid comparisons.
Health and Safety; History - United States; Psychology; Sociology
Dist - REAF Prod - INTEXT

Projecct planning
VHS
Advanced woodworking series
(C G)
$59.00 _ CA170
Discusses the building of a project that serves the function for which it was designed, is structurally sound, and is aesthetically pleasing.
Industrial and Technical Education
Dist - AAVIM Prod - AAVIM 1989

The Project 30 MIN
16mm
Color (J H T R)
LC FIA66-1335
Dramatizes two high school boys who are undertaking a science project in a garage. Shows the importance of friendship.
Guidance and Counseling; Psychology; Science; Social Science
Dist - FAMF Prod - FAMF 1966

The Project 35 MIN
U-matic / VHS
Color
Points out the keys to successful project management using an entertaining vehicle of a band of white - collar criminals planning and carrying out a crime.
Business and Economics
Dist - VISUCP Prod - MELROS

Project A - Ko 86 MIN
VHS
Color (A) (JAPANESE WITH ENGLISH SUBTITLES)
$39.95 purchase _ #CPM1015
Presents a Japanese animated film. Viewer discretion is advised as some films contain strong language or violence.
Fine Arts
Dist - CHTSUI

Project a professional image 15 MIN
VHS
Color (R)
$295.00 purchase, $95.00 rental
Teaches clerical personnel the importance of their maintaining a highly professional image. Covers both mental and physical aspects of such an image.
Business and Economics; Guidance and Counseling; Home Economics
Dist - VLEARN

Project Acorn 14 MIN
16mm
Color (A)
Tells the story of a middle - and low - income housing project in Oakland in which both the building crew and occupants are totally integrated.
History - United States; Sociology
Dist - AFLCIO Prod - ACBCTC 1969

Project Apollo 15 MIN
16mm
Color
Shows pre - Apollo flight plans and animated drawings of how Apollo flights will be made by manned space vehicles.
Industrial and Technical Education; Science; Science - Physical
Dist - THIOKL Prod - THIOKL 1965

Project Apollo - Manned Flight to the Moon 100 FRS
13 MIN
35mm strip / 16mm
Color (J H C)
LC FIE67-519; 74-704125
Shows the Gemini spacecraft and Titan booster, and the Apollo spacecraft and the Saturn 1, 1b and 5 boosters. Depicts the sequence of events for a manned lunar landing using Saturn 5 booster and Apollo spacecraft.
Industrial and Technical Education; Science - Physical
Dist - USNAC Prod - NASA 1963

Project apollo - mission to the moon 18 MIN
16mm
Screen news digest series
B&W
Reports on the rendezvous in space between Geminis 6 and 7, and explains its relation to America's proposed manned flight to the moon. Vol 10, Issue 5.
Science - Physical
Dist - HEARST Prod - HEARST

Project Aware 27 MIN
VHS / 16mm / U-matic
Color (J H)
Presents ex - felon David Crawford who relates his experiences and mistakes both on the streets and in prison. Encourages people to think twice before engaging in unlawful behavior.
Health and Safety; Sociology
Dist - PEREN Prod - CRAWDA

Project Bilingual Series
Everything You do 7 MIN
Happy 8 MIN
How do we look 7 MIN
Other People at School 7 MIN
Temores 8 MIN
Un Viaje a Mexico 9 MIN
Unpleasant Feelings 7 MIN
Dist - SUTHLA

Project children - Pt 1 60 MIN
VHS / U-matic
Project children series
Color
Deals with the problems of children such as growing up in the eighties, divorce, new family structures, changing culture, stress, the punk subculture, changing schools, juvenile justice and rejection.
Sociology
Dist - WCCOTV Prod - WCCOTV

Project children - Pt 2 23 MIN
VHS / U-matic
Project children series
Color
Focuses on mental health, spare time, children and Reaganomics, and looking to the future for the children of the 80's.
Health and Safety; Sociology
Dist - WCCOTV Prod - WCCOTV

Project children series
Project children - Pt 1 60 MIN
Project children - Pt 2 23 MIN
Dist - WCCOTV

Project compassion 29 MIN
16mm
This is the life series
Color
Presents a young woman who panics when her grandmother suffers a stroke and the ensuing personality change. Shows how working in a volunteer program in a nursing home helps the young woman deal with her feelings.
Health and Safety; Psychology; Social Science
Dist - LUTTEL Prod - LUTTEL 1982

Project deep probe 28 MIN
U-matic / VHS / 16mm
Color (H C A)
LC 70-705973
Describes the work of scientists associated with the deep sea drilling project as they work aboard the ship Glomar Challenger, which is capable of sending a probe 20,000 feet to retrieve samples of the ocean floor for analysis, in an attempt to determine what the earth looked like millions of years ago. Hypothesizes that the earth was once a single body of land.
Science - Physical
Dist - IU Prod - NET 1969

Project Discovery - a Demonstration in Education 28 MIN
U-matic / VHS / 16mm
Color (C)
LC FIA67-1244
Describes project discovery, an examination of audiovisual materials as the primary element of instruction. Describes classroom utilization of audio - visual materials.
Education
Dist - EBEC Prod - EBEC 1965

Project Discovery II Series
Let Them Learn 27 MIN
Dist - EBEC

Project future series
Presents a six - part series in three programs on teen pregnancy, childbirth and parenting coproduced by the National Organization of Gynecologic, Obstetric and Neonatal Nurses. Includes the titles Your Pregnancy, Your Plan; Giving Birth to Your Baby; Your New Baby, Your New Life.
Giving birth to your baby - 2 43 MIN
Project future series 144 MIN
Your new baby, your new life - 3 58 MIN
Your pregnancy, your plan - 1 43 MIN
Dist - VHC Prod - VHC 1965

Project G 15 MIN
16mm
B&W (C T)
Consists of a documentary record of gambling behavior in a variety of situations which include teen - age groups in tenement districts and pool rooms and adults at race tracks. Attempts to indicate some of the psychological causes of gambling.
Physical Education and Recreation; Psychology; Sociology
Dist - CCNY Prod - PSUPCR 1956

Project Galileo - a Jovian odyssey 4 MIN
VHS
Color (J H C)
$14.95 purchase _ #NA705
History - World; Science - Physical
Dist - INSTRU **Prod** - NASA

Project Gemini Mission Review 1965 20 MIN
U-matic
Color
Highlights the six Gemini missions in 1965, including the Gemini II verification of spacecraft reentry, the first manned mission by astronauts Grissom and Young in Gemini III, the stroll in space by astronaut White of Gemini V and the first dual missions of Gemini VII in which two spacecrafts rendezvoused in space.
Industrial and Technical Education; Science; Science - Physical
Dist - NASA **Prod** - NASA 1972

Project Gemini series
Project Gemini videos - Primary - INSET
Project Gemini videos - Secondary - INSET
Project Gemini videos series - INSET
Dist - BTEDSE

Project Gemini - the Next Step in Space 9 MIN
16mm
Screen news digest series; Vol 6; Issue 2
B&W (J A)
LC FIA68-2074
Animated. Explains Project Gemini, America's next step into space. Introduces astronauts who will fly Gemini missions.
Science - Physical
Dist - HEARST **Prod** - HEARST 1963

Project Gemini videos - Primary - INSET
VHS / BETA / U-matic
Project Gemini series
Color; PAL (T)
PdS9.99 purchase _ #GCP
Consists of five projects based in primary schools which investigated the benefits of electronic communications to support children's learning including the telephone; electronic mail; fax; the accessing of remote databases; computer conferencing; audio graphics; and video conferencing. Includes snapshots of classroom activities, animated explanations of technologies, and lively interviews with teachers and pupils along with a comprehensive set of notes. Contact distributor for free loan. Part of a two - part series.
Education; Industrial and Technical Education; Sociology
Dist - BTEDSE

Project Gemini videos - Secondary - INSET
VHS / BETA / U-matic
Project Gemini series
Color; PAL (T)
PdS9.99 purchase _ #GCS
Consists of five projects based in secondary schools which investigated the benefits of electronic communications to support children's learning including the telephone; electronic mail; fax; the accessing of remote databases; computer conferencing; audio graphics; and video conferencing. Includes snapshots of classroom activities, animated explanations of technologies, and lively interviews with teachers and pupils along with a comprehensive set of notes. Contact distributor for free loan. Part of a two - part series.
Education; Industrial and Technical Education; Sociology
Dist - BTEDSE

Project Gemini videos series - INSET
VHS / BETA / U-matic
Project Gemini series
Color; PAL (T)
PdS18.00 purchase _ #GCP & GCS
Consists of ten projects based in primary and secondary schools which investigated the benefits of electronic communications to support children's learning including the telephone; electronic mail; fax; the accessing of remote databases; computer conferencing; audio graphics; and video conferencing. Includes snapshots of classroom activities, animated explanations of technologies, and lively interviews with teachers and pupils along with a comprehensive set of notes. Contact distributor for free loan. Part of a two - part series.
Computer Science; Education; Industrial and Technical Education; Sociology
Dist - BTEDSE

Project Hardsite 14 MIN
16mm
Color
Depicts the launching of the rocket - like F - 100 A/C.
Civics and Political Systems; Industrial and Technical Education
Dist - RCKWL **Prod** - NAA

Project management 25 MIN
VHS
Color (PRO IND A)
$495.00 purchase, $150.00 rental _ #CR133
Teaches project management from idea through implementation stages. Shares the experience of supervisors who have used the techniques of charting, time estimation and project monitoring - helping employees complete projects on time and within budget. Based on the book by Marion E Haynes.
Business and Economics
Dist - EXTR **Prod** - CRISP
DHB

Project Management 720 MIN
U-matic / VHS
(A PRO)
$2,880.00 purchase, $999.00 rental
Shows steps involved in operating a successful project under the triple constraints of schedules, budgets and project specifications.
Computer Science
Dist - VIDEOT **Prod** - VIDEOT 1988

Project Management 170 MIN
VHS / 16mm
(C PRO)
$3000.00 purchase, $950.00 rental
Follows the life cycle of a project through conceptualization, planning, implementation and completion. Stresses communication and motivation as well as planning, organization and control techniques.
Education
Dist - VLEARN

Project management 60 MIN
VHS
Color (PRO IND A) (DUTCH FRENCH)
$695.00 purchase _ #VIM22
Takes a human resources approach in outlining the framework and phases of project management. Provides help for managers responsible for large or small projects in industry or service areas. Features Prof Daniel Muzkyka.
Business and Economics
Dist - EXTR

A Project management approach to course development - from idea to draft to AV materials - Diana Booher 75 MIN
VHS
Color; PAL (C G PRO)
$89.95, $69.95 purchase _ #92AST - V - W28
Discloses that the project management approach to developing course materials is an effective, repeatable, nine - step process that significantly decreases development time. Shows how to organize a wealth of materials and avoid common pitfalls in course design. Offers clear and concise guidelines for systematically crating an integrated training program from flipcharts to overheads to participants' manuals and instructor notes. Features Dianna Booher, owner and president, Booher Consultants, Euless TX.
Business and Economics; Education; Psychology
Dist - MOBILE **Prod** - ASTD 1992

Project Management for Engineers 360 MIN
U-matic / VHS
(A PRO)
$2,160.00 purchase, $750.00 rental
Teaches project management responsibilities and how to succeed with timing and budget constraints.
Computer Science
Dist - VIDEOT **Prod** - VIDEOT 1988

Project Management - Keep Projects on Time and within Budget, Vol I 58 MIN
VHS
Project Management Series
Color (G)
$99.95 purchase _ #20160
Features Larry Johnson. Considers the seven traits of a successful project manager and how to identify a project's real objectives. Reveals negotiating tips for getting the resources necessary to complete a project. Part one of two parts.
Business and Economics; Computer Science; Psychology
Dist - CARTRP **Prod** - CARTRP

Project Management - Keep Projects on Time and within Budget, Vol II 79 MIN
VHS
Project Management Series
Color (G)
$99.95 purchase _ #20162
Features Larry Johnson. Looks at four ways to chart a project's flow so that staff members know what to do and when. Shows how to make timely corrections in a project's progress. Reveals how to do a 'What If' analysis to keep problems to a minimum. Two of two parts.
Business and Economics; Computer Science; Psychology
Dist - CARTRP **Prod** - CARTRP

Project Management Series
Project Management - Keep Projects on Time and within Budget, Vol I 58 MIN
Project Management - Keep Projects on Time and within Budget, Vol II 79 MIN
Dist - CARTRP

Project Management Series
Implementing and Controlling Your Project 30 MIN
Man - Loading and Budgeting in Project Planning 30 MIN
Managing People for Project Success 30 MIN
Organizing for Successful Project Management 30 MIN
Planning a Project and Building Your Project Team 30 MIN
Using Networking and Bar Charting in Project Scheduling 30 MIN
Dist - ISA

Project Management Series
Implementing and Controlling Your Project 30 MIN
Managing People for Project Success 30 MIN
Manloading and Budgeting in Project Planning 30 MIN
Organizing for Successful Project Management 30 MIN
Planning a Project and Building Your Project Team 30 MIN
Using Networking and Bar Charting in Project Scheduling 30 MIN
Dist - ITCORP

Project management series
Completion 34 MIN
Control 42 MIN
Definition 48 MIN
Implementation 40 MIN
Planning - Pt 1 43 MIN
Planning - Pt 2 45 MIN
Dist - MIOT

Project Management, Vol I and II 137 MIN
VHS
Color (G)
$149.95 purchase _ #20160, #20162
Features Larry Johnson. Shows how to organize complex projects, get people to work and report as a team, and keep projects on the critical path to successful completion.
Business and Economics; Computer Science; Psychology
Dist - CARTRP **Prod** - CARTRP

Project manager or product manager 30 MIN
U-matic / VHS
Changing role of the information systems manager series
Color
Points out that the Information Systems manager must function as a product manager as well as a project manager. Reveals that a product manager takes a broader perspective, considering issues such as operational costs, maintenance, enhancement, marketing and education as they relate to products and services.
Industrial and Technical Education; Psychology
Dist - DELTAK **Prod** - DELTAK

Project Mercury 28 MIN
16mm
Color
Presents animated sequences of a Mercury orbital manned mission, demonstrating the rigors of astronaut training and the complexities of the program.
Industrial and Technical Education; Science - Physical
Dist - NASA **Prod** - NASA

Project on Interpreting Mathematics Education Research Series
Practicing mathmatical skills 18 MIN
Solving Verbal Problems in Mathematics 21 MIN
Using a Mathematics Laboratory Approach 15 MIN
Using Diagnosis in a Mathematics Classroom 15 MIN
Dist - USNAC

Project ORBIS in Ankara, Turkey - a Secondary Implant 17 MIN
U-matic / VHS
Project ORBIS Videotape Subscription Series

Color (PRO)
Demonstrates Dr Leiske technique for secondary lens implantation.
Health and Safety; Science - Natural
Dist - HSCIC **Prod** - HSCIC 1982

Project ORBIS in Berlin - Corneal Wedge Resection 30 MIN
U-matic / VHS
Project ORBIS Videotape Subscription Series
Color (PRO)
Shows corneal wedge resection performed by Dr Troutman. Demonstrates the use of a prototypical, double - bladed diamond knife.
Health and Safety; Science - Natural
Dist - HSCIC **Prod** - HSCIC 1982

Project ORBIS in Berlin - Penetrating Keratoplasty 28 MIN
U-matic / VHS
Project ORBIS Videotape Subscription Series
Color (PRO)
Shows a corneal transplant performed by Dr Troutman and provides surgeons with the rationale behind each of the steps performed.
Health and Safety; Science - Natural
Dist - HSCIC **Prod** - HSCIC 1982

Project ORBIS in Birmingham, England - clear corneal Iridectomy and Trabeculectomy 25 MIN
U-matic / VHS
Project ORBIS videotape subscription series
Color (PRO)
Complete title is Project ORBIS In Birmingham, England - Clear Corneal Iridectomy And Trabeculectomy. Shows Dr Cairns performing a clear corneal iridectomy on one patient and a trabeculectomy on a second.
Health and Safety; Science - Natural
Dist - HSCIC **Prod** - HSCIC 1982

Project ORBIS in Birmingham, England - Molteno Long Tube Implant 26 MIN
VHS / U-matic
Project ORBIS Videotape Subscription Series
Color (PRO)
Discusses Dr Cairns' technique for inserting the Molteno tube and anchoring it at the back of the eye.
Health and Safety; Science - Natural
Dist - HSCIC **Prod** - HSCIC 1982

Project ORBIS in Birmingham, England - two methods of cataract extraction and intraocular lens implantation 24 MIN
U-matic / VHS
Project ORBIS videotape subscription series
Color (PRO)
Features Dr Barnet implanting an iris clip intraocular lens, while Dr McCannel implants a Leiske - type anterior chamber lens.
Health and Safety; Science - Natural
Dist - HSCIC **Prod** - HSCIC 1982

Project ORBIS in Canton, China - Silica Bead Cataract Extraction 20 MIN
U-matic / VHS
Project ORBIS Videotape Subscription Series
Color (PRO)
Demonstrates Dr McIntyre performing a simple Chinese method of cataract extraction.
Health and Safety; Science - Natural
Dist - HSCIC **Prod** - HSCIC 1982

Project ORBIS in Cartagena, Colombia - Vitrectomy for Cysticercus 39 MIN
U-matic / VHS
Project ORBIS Videotape Subscription Series
Color (PRO)
Demonstrates Dr Ronald Michels performing the removal of a retinal cysticercus.
Health and Safety; Science - Natural
Dist - HSCIC **Prod** - HSCIC 1982

Project ORBIS in Kingston - extracapsular cataract extraction with intraocular lens implantation 33 MIN
VHS / U-matic
Project ORBIS Videotape Subscription Series
Color (PRO)
Demonstrates Dr Praeger's techniques for performing an extracapsular cataract extraction and intraocular lens implantation.
Health and Safety; Science - Natural
Dist - HSCIC **Prod** - HSCIC 1982

Project ORBIS in Kingston - Senile Ptosis Repair 30 MIN
U-matic / VHS

Straw Hill - Manchester, New Hampshire - Vol 17, No 18 9 MIN
Dist - ULI

Project Renewal 25 MIN
U-matic / VHS
Color (I J H)
Shows the American Indian enduring profound cultural change over the years, leading to pressures that have often resulted in loss of traditional values. Some, lacking community support, turned to alcohol and drugs. Documents effort of an abuse prevention pilot program called Project Renewal. It portrays positive cultural regeneration through involvement of elders and youth in a wooded summer camp environment. Also illustrates the effectiveness of interagency cooperation.
Social Science; Sociology
Dist - SHENFP **Prod** - SHENFP 1987

Project Shoal 18 MIN
16mm
Color
LC FIE64-144
A non - technical film on the underground Project Shoal detonation, an experiment conducted by the Department of Defense with the participation of the Atomic Energy Commission. Describes the selection of the test site near Fallon, Nevada, the pre - shot preparations to insure public safety and the efforts to inform the citizens of Fallon of the proposed shot, the reaction of various city groups to the test, the Seismic Station Program, instrumentation and the results of the detonation.
Civics and Political Systems; Health and Safety; Science - Physical
Dist - USNAC **Prod** - USNRC 1964

Project Skill 15 MIN
16mm
Color
LC 76-701596
Shows how a two - year project in the state of Wisconsin has developed, tested and demonstrated methods and procedures for employing less severely mentally and emotionally handicapped persons. Points out that state agencies are using the hire first, train later concept and that such employees will be absorbed in regular work settings with the nonhandicapped.
Business and Economics; Education; Geography - United States; Health and Safety
Dist - USNAC **Prod** - USETA 1975

Project Slush 21 MIN
16mm
Color
LC 74-705438
Reports tests conducted at NAFEC using the 850 jet aircraft to determine the effects of slush on jet aircraft accelerating for take off.
Industrial and Technical Education; Social Science
Dist - USNAC **Prod** - FAAFL 1963

Project Solo 28 MIN
16mm
Color
Presents a look at a new program that uses individualized computer programming to expand the horizons of high school math, physics and chemistry. Features students who demonstrate and explain their programs and give spontaneous reactions to the new technology. Discusses Project Solo's design, its aims and the role of staff members and teachers in making the project work.
Education; Mathematics
Dist - MATHWW **Prod** - MATHWW 1971

Project spot series
Devices for self - help task performance 8 MIN
Dist - USNAC

Project STRETCH series

Art and the exceptional child	30 MIN
Art and the exceptional student	30 MIN
Assessment	30 MIN
Behavior modification	30 MIN
Career education	30 MIN
Classroom management	30 MIN
Counseling parents of exceptional children	30 MIN
Grouping	25 MIN
Increasing teacher effectiveness through peer tutoring	29 MIN
Individualized instruction	30 MIN
Label the behavior, not the child	30 MIN
Language experience approach	30 MIN
Learning styles	30 MIN
Mainstreaming	30 MIN
Mathematics and the special child	29 MIN
Questioning skills	30 MIN
Reading in the content area	30 MIN
Simulation - the next best thing to being there	30 MIN

Project ORBIS Videotape Subscription Series
Color (PRO)
Demonstrates Dr Iliff's technique for ptosis repair. Provides ongoing commentary on the anatomical and technical aspects of the procedure.
Health and Safety; Science - Natural
Dist - HSCIC **Prod** - HSCIC 1982

Project ORBIS in Munich - extracapsular cataract extraction with intraocular lens implantation 20 MIN
U-matic / VHS
Project ORBIS videotape subscription series
Color (PRO)
Demonstrates Dr McIntyre's microsurgical technique for extracapsular cataract extraction.
Health and Safety; Science - Natural
Dist - HSCIC **Prod** - HSCIC 1982

Project ORBIS in Munich - phacoemulsification of a cataract with posterior chamber intraocular lens implantation 17 MIN
U-matic / VHS
Project ORBIS videotape subscription series
Color (PRO)
Introduces medical students, residents in ophthalmology, and ophthalmologists to a technique for phacoemulsification of a cataract.
Health and Safety; Science - Natural
Dist - HSCIC **Prod** - HSCIC 1982

Project ORBIS Videotape Subscription Series

Project ORBIS in Ankara, Turkey - a Secondary Implant	17 MIN
Project ORBIS in Berlin - Corneal Wedge Resection	30 MIN
Project ORBIS in Berlin - Penetrating Keratoplasty	28 MIN
Project ORBIS in Birmingham, England - clear corneal Iridectomy and Trabeculectomy	25 MIN
Project ORBIS in Birmingham, England - Molteno Long Tube Implant	26 MIN
Project ORBIS in Birmingham, England - two methods of cataract extraction and intraocular lens implantation	24 MIN
Project ORBIS in Canton, China - Silica Bead Cataract Extraction	20 MIN
Project ORBIS in Cartagena, Colombia - Vitrectomy for Cysticercus	39 MIN
Project ORBIS in Kingston - extracapsular cataract extraction with intraocular lens implantation	33 MIN
Project ORBIS in Kingston - Senile Ptosis Repair	30 MIN
Project ORBIS in Munich - extracapsular cataract extraction with intraocular lens implantation	20 MIN
Project ORBIS in Munich - phacoemulsification of a cataract with posterior chamber intraocular lens implantation	17 MIN

Dist - HSCIC

Project Pride - a Positive Approach to Vandalism 17 MIN
16mm
Color (A)
Shows how one elementary school district cut vandalism costs by more than half by turning students on to school improvement projects.
Education; Sociology
Dist - LAWREN **Prod** - PARKRD

Project Puffin 13 MIN
16mm / U-matic / VHS
Color (J)
LC 82-700444
Shows the effort being made to induce the puffin to recolonize their former breeding sites.
Science; Science - Natural
Dist - LCOA **Prod** - NAS 1982

Project reference file - PRF - series

Crocker Center - Boca Raton, Florida - Vol 18, No 2	15 MIN
Fair Lakes - Fairfax, Virginia - Vol 18, No 5	12 MIN
Nottingham - Fairfax County, Virginia - Vol 19, No 4	15 MIN
Princeton Forrestal Village - Plainsboro, New Jersey - Vol 18, No 11	12 MIN
Riverplace - Portland, Oregon - Vol 18 - No 3	15 MIN
Seaside - Walton County, Florida - Vol 16, No 16	15 MIN

Spelling - visualization, the key to spelling success 30 MIN
Value clarification 30 MIN
Dist - HUBDSC

Project STRETCH - Strategies to Train Regular Educators to Teach Children with Handicaps Series
Grouping and special students 30 MIN
Learning centers 30 MIN
Mathematics and the special student 30 MIN
Peer tutoring 30 MIN
Simulation 30 MIN
Spelling 30 MIN
Dist - HUBDSC

Project 20 Series
End of the Trail - the American Plains Indians, Pt 2 27 MIN
The Great War - 1914 - 1917 52 MIN
The Innocent Years - 1901 - 1914 54 MIN
The Jazz Age - 1919 - 1929, Pt 1 25 MIN
The Jazz Age - 1919 - 1929, Pt 2 25 MIN
Dist - CRMP

Project 20 Series
The Great War - 1914 - 1917, Pt 1 26 MIN
The Great War - 1914 - 1917, Pt 2 26 MIN
The Innocent Years 52 MIN
Island Called Ellis, the, Pt 1 26 MIN
Island Called Ellis, the, Pt 2 27 MIN
The Jazz Age 52 MIN
Not So Long Ago - 1945 - 1950 54 MIN
Not So Long Ago - 1945 - 1950, Pt 1 27 MIN
Not So Long Ago - 1945 - 1950, Pt 2 27 MIN
Dist - CRMP
MGHT

Project 20 series
He is risen 29 MIN
Dist - FI

Project 20 Series
End of the Trail - the American Plains Indian 53 MIN
The Island Called Ellis 53 MIN
Jazz Age, the, Pt 1 26 MIN
Jazz Age, the, Pt 2 26 MIN
Life in the Thirties 52 MIN
Life in the Thirties, Pt 1 26 MIN
Life in the Thirties, Pt 2 26 MIN
Mark Twain's America 54 MIN
Mark Twain's America, Pt 1 27 MIN
Mark Twain's America, Pt 2 27 MIN
Nightmare in Red 55 MIN
Nightmare in Red, Pt 1 27 MIN
Nightmare in Red, Pt 2 27 MIN
The Real West 54 MIN
The Real West - Pt 1 27 MIN
The Real West - Pt 2 27 MIN
The Twisted Cross 55 MIN
The Twisted cross - Pt 1 27 MIN
The Twisted cross - Pt 2 28 MIN
Dist - MGHT

Project 20 Series
Meet George Washington, Pt 1 26 MIN
Meet George Washington, Pt 2 26 MIN
Dist - NBCTV

Project Universe - Astronomy Series Lesson 2
Historical Perspectives 29 MIN
Dist - CDTEL

Project Universe - Astronomy Series Lesson 3
Lunar Aspects 29 MIN
Dist - CDTEL

Project Universe - Astronomy Series Lesson 4
Electromagnetic Radiation 29 MIN
Dist - CDTEL

Project Universe - Astronomy Series Lesson 7
Lunar Geology 29 MIN
Dist - CDTEL

Project Universe - Astronomy Series Lesson 8
Mercury and Venus 29 MIN
Dist - CDTEL

Project Universe - Astronomy Series Lesson 9
Mars 29 MIN

Project universe - astronomy series lesson 11
Saturn 29 MIN
Dist - CDTEL

Project Universe - Astronomy Series Lesson 12
Uranus, Neptune, and Pluto 29 MIN
Dist - CDTEL

Project Universe - Astronomy Series Lesson 13
Solar System Debris 29 MIN
Dist - CDTEL

Project Universe - Astronomy Series Lesson 14
The Solar Image 29 MIN
Dist - CDTEL

Project Universe - Astronomy Series Lesson 15
The Solar Interior 29 MIN
Dist - CDTEL

Project Universe - Astronomy Series Lesson 17
The Message of Starlight 29 MIN
Dist - CDTEL

Project universe - astronomy series lesson 18
Binary stars 29 MIN
Dist - CDTEL

Project Universe - Astronomy Series Lesson 19
The Milky Way Discovered 29 MIN
Dist - CDTEL

Project Universe - Astronomy Series Lesson 20
The Milky Way Structure 29 MIN
Dist - CDTEL

Project Universe - Astronomy Series Lesson 23
Stars - the Nuclear Furnace 29 MIN
Dist - CDTEL

Project Universe - Astronomy Series Lesson 26
Black Holes 29 MIN
Dist - CDTEL

Project Universe - Astronomy Series Lesson 29
The Expanding Universe 29 MIN
Dist - CDTEL
Dist - CDTEL

Project universe - astronomy series
The Astronomer's universe 29 MIN
Astronomical observations 29 MIN
Earth - the water planet 29 MIN
Extraterrestrial communication 29 MIN
Galaxies 29 MIN
Jupiter 29 MIN
Relativity 29 MIN
Supernovas and pulsars 29 MIN
Surveying the Stars 29 MIN
White Dwarfs and Red Giants 29 MIN
Dist - CDTEL

Project universe - lesson 28 - astronomy series
Quasars 29 MIN
Dist - CDTEL

Project universe series
The Big Bang 30 MIN
Dist - CDTEL

Projectile Motion
U-matic / VHS
Experiments in Space Series
Color
Shows interesting examples of flight in a weightless space.
Science - Physical
Dist - EDMEC **Prod** - EDMEC

Projectile Motion 15 MIN
U-matic / VHS
Experiment - Physics Level 1 Series
Color (C)
$249.00, $149.00 purchase _ #AD - 1961
Demonstrates the laws of projectile motion in one and two dimensions. Makes measurements of position as a function of time and compares with the predictions of the equations of motion under constant acceleration. Part of a series of videos demonstrating physics experiments which are impractical to perform in a classroom laboratory.
Education; Psychology; Science - Physical
Dist - FOTH **Prod** - FOTH

Projecting a Professional Image 15 MIN
U-matic / VHS
Hub of the Wheel Series
Color (G)
$249.00, $149.00 purchase _ #AD - 1561
Focuses on the physical and mental aspects of professional image. Encourages thinking about image on the job. Part of a ten - part series for office professionals.
Business and Economics; Home Economics
Dist - FOTH **Prod** - FOTH

Projecting the Ball 15 MIN
U-matic / VHS
Leaps and Bounds Series no 14
Color (T)
Explains how to teach primary students to strike a ball with various parts of their body and about the application of force, and about the relationship of impact to desired direction.
Physical Education and Recreation
Dist - AITECH

Projecting visions 25 MIN
VHS / U-matic
Developmental biology series
Color (H C)
$250.00 purchase _ #HP - 5979C
Overviews the problems of nerve regeneration. Shows how nervous system cells know when and where to migrate for purposes of repair. Uses photomicrography to examine what determines cell uniqueness and why the instigation of nerve fiber regrowth is more difficult than the connecting of nerves. Part of a four - part series on biology which addresses regeneration, internal and external structures, cellular communication, gender influences, growth and stability of form.
Science; Science - Natural
Dist - CORF **Prod** - BBCTV 1990

The Projection of Australia 59 MIN
16mm
Color (J)
Presents a compilation of excerpts from productions of the Commonwealth Film Unit made over the past 21 years.
Geography - World; History - World
Dist - AUIS **Prod** - ANAIB

Projections 35 MIN
16mm
Color (H C A)
LC 79-701622
Tells a story about a photographer who discovers he is dying of cancer and dreams that all his photographs of children turn into symbols of death. Concludes with his discovery of life's possibilities after he is visited by his niece.
Fine Arts; Sociology
Dist - JURMAR **Prod** - JURMAR 1979

Projections for the Future Series
A Behavior Model 18 MIN
A Growth Model 17 MIN
A Humanist Model 20 MIN
Dist - CRYSP

Projective Generation of Conics 16 MIN
U-matic / VHS / 16mm
Color (H C)
Presents conic sections which may be developed in various ways. Introduces the eccentricity definition which was known to the ancient Greeks and then focuses on the several projective definitions, namely those that are devoid of metric notions. Exhibits the methods of construction developed by Pascal, Maclaurin, Braikenridge, Poncelet and Steiner.
Mathematics
Dist - IFB **Prod** - UMNAV 1971

Projects Mean People
16mm
Color
Looks at three case studies involving computers and business.
Business and Economics; Mathematics
Dist - OPENU **Prod** - OPENU

Prokofiev - Cinderella ballet 75 MIN
VHS
Color (G)
$39.95 purchase _ #S01576
Presents a ballet version of the classic fairy tale 'Cinderella.' Features Hannelore Bey as Cinderella and Rolan Gawlick as the prince. Includes the musical score by Prokofiev.
Fine Arts
Dist - UILL

Proliferative diabetic retinopathy 9 MIN
VHS
Color (PRO A)
$250.00 purchase _ #EY - 29
Explains conditions, treatments, risks and possible complications of proliferative diabetic retinopathy. Gives patients an overview of pre and post - operative routines. Complements physician personal patient counseling by giving patients a basic understanding of their condition and the terminology so they can ask informed questions. For use in the private physician's office, hospitals, outpatient or ambulatory surgery centers and clinics providing ophthalmological care.
Health and Safety; Science - Natural
Dist - MIFE **Prod** - MIFE 1991

The Prologue 21 MIN
16mm
Peggy and Fred in Hell Series
Color (G)
$450.00 purchase, $60.00 rental
Introduces the on - going epic about two children, Peggy and Fred. Follows them through a densely cluttered, technological - consumer jumble of late 20th - century icons. By Leslie Thornton.
Fine Arts; Psychology; Sociology
Dist - WMEN **Prod** - LETH

Prologue in Masonry 24 MIN
16mm
B&W (H C A)
LC 75-701979
Explores some of the history of bricklaying and clay masonry structures made from brick.
Industrial and Technical Education
Dist - SCPI **Prod** - SCPI

Prologue - the Lion and the Crown; 2nd Ed 7 MIN
16mm
Of Stars and Men Series
Color (J)
LC 76-701274
A revised version of the 1964 film Of Stars And Men. Presents a fable about forest animals who observe the miracles of man and are so awed by him that they present him with a crown. Shows how he gives up his hum - drum existence to seek truth through a philosophical quest.
Literature and Drama; Religion and Philosophy; Science - Physical
Dist - RADIM **Prod** - HUBLEY 1976

A Prologue to Chaucer 29 MIN
U-matic / VHS
Color (C) (ENGLISH AND MIDDLE ENGLISH)
$249.00, $149.00 purchase _ #AD - 998
Combines period art, location photography which retraces the Canterbury pilgrimage, excerpts read from various tales, and the beginning of 'The Canterbury Tales' read in Middle English to introduce Chaucer. Written by Velma B Richmond, produced by the University of California, Berkeley.
Fine Arts; Literature and Drama; Religion and Philosophy
Dist - FOTH **Prod** - FOTH

A Prologue to Chaucer 29 MIN
VHS / 16mm
Color (H) (ENGLISH AND MIDDLE ENGLISH)
$14.00 rental _ #35255
Relates the characters and themes of Chaucer's Canterbury Tales to everyday life in late 14th century England. Combines rich period art with on - location photography to retrace the pilgrimage to Archibishop Becket's shrine, and offers oral excerpts, including the familiar prologue in Middle English.
Fine Arts; History - World; Literature and Drama
Dist - PSU

Prologue to Peace 16 MIN
16mm
B&W
Shows a delegation of peace from Malaysia, headed by Malaysian Deputy Premier Tun Abdul Razak, arriving in Bangkok, Thailand, on May 29, 1966, to meet with an Indonesian delegation, headed by Indonesian Deputy Premier Adam Malik. Tells how they were hosted by Thai Foreign Minister Tun Thanat Khoman and met to discuss ways and means of ending the Indonesian confrontation and to restore friendly relations between the two countries.
Civics and Political Systems; Geography - World; History - World
Dist - PMFMUN **Prod** - FILEM 1966

Prologue to Tomorrow 19 MIN
16mm
Color
LC 77-701829
Shows how advance planning helped provide sufficient energy during an extremely harsh winter.
Home Economics; Social Science
Dist - CONPOW **Prod** - CONPOW 1977

Prometheus 10 MIN
U-matic / VHS / 16mm
Mythology of Greece series
Color (I J H)
$425.00, $295.00, $325.00 purchase _ #A508; LC 88-713592
Portrays account of how Prometheus defied Zeus by giving humanity the ability to use fire for security and warmth.
History - World; Literature and Drama; Religion and Philosophy
Dist - BARR **Prod** - BRIANJ 1987

Prometheus 18 MIN
VHS / U-matic / 16mm
Mythology of Greece Series
Color (I J H)
$425, $295, $325 _ #A508
Recounts the Greek myth of Prometheus which talks about compassion for humanity. Animated film is used.
Religion and Philosophy
Dist - BARR **Prod** - BARR 1987

Prometheus and the Gift of Fire
VHS / 35mm strip
Timeless Tales - Myths of Ancient Greece - Set I
Color (I)
$39.95, $28.00 purchase
Recreates the myth of Prometheus and the gift of fire. Part of a five - part series on Greek mythology.
English Language; History - World; Literature and Drama; Religion and Philosophy
Dist - PELLER

Promise 14 MIN
16mm
Color (I)
LC 80-700758
Tells how a young woman looks back in her life and realizes that the promises of others to her and her promises to others have given her a fuller life. States that God has also used promises to enrich human life.
Religion and Philosophy
Dist - IKONOG **Prod** - IKONOG 1974

The Promise 29 MIN
U-matic
As We See it Series
Color
Focuses on problems faced by Native American students in South Dakota.
Education; Social Science; Sociology
Dist - PBS **Prod** - WTTWTV

The Promise 15 MIN
16mm / U-matic / VHS
Bloomin' Human Series
Color (I J)
LC 77-703309
Presents a story about a girl and her unhappiness when she learns that the horse she has been caring for is to be sold.
Guidance and Counseling; Science - Natural
Dist - MEDIAG **Prod** - PAULST 1977

The Promise and Danger of Genetic Engineering
VHS
Genetic Engineering - Prospects of the Future Series
Color
Weighs potential benefits and risks of genetic engineering. Explores ethical ramifications of eugenics, cloning and genetic screening.
Science; Science - Natural
Dist - IBIS **Prod** - IBIS

The Promise and the Challenge 18 MIN
16mm
Color
Discusses Dow's Texas division and how it produces many basic intermediates that serve as working tools for chemists and manufacturers.
Business and Economics; Science - Physical
Dist - DCC **Prod** - DCC

A Promise broken 30 MIN
VHS
Saying goodbye - on bereavement series
Color (H C G)
$295.00 purchase, $55.00 rental
Shows the friends and family of a teenage suicide victim as they grapple with grief, guilt and anger. Discusses the difficulty of averting suicide without professional intervention and the importance of having a funeral at which those affected can express their grief. Part of a series on bereavement produced in cooperation with Insight Production.
Guidance and Counseling; Sociology
Dist - FLMLIB **Prod** - TVOTAR 1990

Promise City 29 MIN
Videoreel / VT2
Synergism - Cities and Towns Series
B&W
Portrays a small Iowa farming community and explores its past, present and people that are a part of both.
Social Science; Sociology
Dist - PBS **Prod** - IEBNTV

Promise for the Future 16 MIN
16mm
Color (FRENCH GERMAN ITALIAN SPANISH)
LC 76-703154
Uses split - screen opticals to show division of work, employees and products of Rockwell International. Includes information on the company's space shuttle and B - 1 bomber.
Business and Economics; Foreign Language; Industrial and Technical Education
Dist - RCKWL **Prod** - RCKWL 1976

The Promise fulfilled and the promise broken 52 MIN
U-matic / 16mm / VHS
America - a personal history of the United States series; No 10
Color (J) (SPANISH)
LC 74-701580
Presents Alistair Cooke, who shows how the Depression came after the war to end all wars and after the promise of unlimited prosperity symbolized by a Model - T Ford and a mail order catalogue. Explains how the mills stayed closed until the United States returned to war.
Business and Economics; History - United States
Dist - TIMLIF **Prod** - BBCTV 1973

The Promise Fulfilled and the Promise Broken 52 MIN
16mm / VHS
America Series
(J H C)
$99.95 each, $595.00 series
Looks at the changes America went through after World War I, from the prosperity and happiness of the roaring '20's to the big stock market crash, and the the Depression.
Geography - United States; History - United States
Dist - AMBROS **Prod** - AMBROS 1973

The Promise fulfilled and the promise broken - Pt 1 26 MIN
U-matic / 16mm
America - a personal history of the United States series; No 10
Color (J)
LC 74-701580
Presents Alistair Cooke who shows how the Depression came after the war to end all wars and after the promise of unlimited prosperity symbolized by a Model - T Ford and a mail order catalog. Explains how the mills stayed closed until the United States returned to war.
History - United States
Dist - TIMLIF **Prod** - BBCTV 1972

The Promise fulfilled and the promise broken - Pt 2 26 MIN
U-matic / 16mm
America - a personal history of the United States series; No 10
Color (J)
LC 74-701580
Presents Alistair Cooke who shows how the Depression came after the war to end all wars and after the promise of unlimited prosperity symbolized by a Model - T Ford and a mail order catalog. Explains how the mills stayed closed until the United States returned to war.
History - United States
Dist - TIMLIF **Prod** - BBCTV 1972

Promise her anything but give her the kitchen sink 3 MIN
16mm
Color (G)
$10.00 rental
Discloses filmmaker's diary which shows her love for her husband, babies, friends and California. Combines a melange of domestic, maternal and personal symbols. Produced by Freude.
Fine Arts; Sociology
Dist - CANCIN

A Promise kept 46 MIN
VHS
Color (H G)
$375.00 purchase, $75.00 rental
Recounts the story of the extraordinary relationship between Karin Donnan and her husband Blair, who discovered he had AIDS just months before their wedding. Features Karin candidly revealing the shared anguish and loss of coping with his illness and the dignity and joy they discover as their unconditional love grew. When Blair died, Karin honored his last wish - that she go public with their story as a means to fight the ignorance and fear that still surrounds AIDS. Personal and intense, she spares no details of the terrible emotional and physical toll taken by AIDS. Produced by R Alan Gough and Lawrence Zack.
Fine Arts; Health and Safety; Psychology; Religion and Philosophy; Sociology
Dist - FIRS

The Promise of life 29 MIN
16mm
Color
Describes the history and purposes of the order of the Knights of Columbus. Focuses on the social and humanitarian works of the order in various parts of the United States, Canada and Mexico.
History - World; Religion and Philosophy; Sociology
Dist - MTP **Prod** - KNICOL

Promise of Plato 7 MIN
16mm / U-matic / VHS
Color (I)
LC 74-703354
Shows the diversity of learning experiences possible with computer - assisted education and points out that this individualized instruction helps to meet the needs of each student.

Education
Dist - AMEDFL **Prod** - NSF 1974

The Promise of Sociology 30 MIN
U-matic / VHS
Focus on Society Series
Color (C)
Examines the discipline of sociology, one which examines the many groups and relationships in which individuals participate.
Sociology
Dist - DALCCD **Prod** - DALCCD

The Promise of Space 14 MIN
16mm
Color (A)
LC 77-700778
Describes the diverse activities of the Marshall Space Flight Center in Alabama.
Industrial and Technical Education; Science - Physical
Dist - USNAC **Prod** - NASA 1976

Promise of spring 26 MIN
16mm
Audubon wildlife theatre series
Color (I)
Portrays the changing patterns of spring in plants, animals and elements from the shores of Vancouver Island to the Alpine meadows of the Canadian Rockies, to the rich valleys of the interior. Points out that from grizzly to ground squirrel, mountain glacier to mountain stream nothing escapes the changes wrought on the varied British Columbia scene by spring.
Geography - World; Science - Natural
Dist - AVEXP **Prod** - AVEXP

Promise of spring 18 MIN
16mm
Color (C A)
Demonstrates how to get best results from world famous imported Holland spring flowering bulbs.
Agriculture; Science - Natural
Dist - NATDIS **Prod** - NATDIS 1955

Promise of the Land 25 MIN
16mm
Color (H)
Presents the story of how the Bureau of Land Management works to satisfy the multitude of demands made on the lands it manages.
Civics and Political Systems; Science - Natural
Dist - MTP **Prod** - USDILM

The Promise of the land 60 MIN
VHS
Smithsonian world series
Color; Captioned (G)
$49.95 purchase _ #SMIW - 304
Examines modern agricultural practices such as man - made irrigation and pesticides, questioning whether they are destructive. Reviews the history of agriculture from the turn of the century to the present.
Agriculture
Dist - PBS **Prod** - WETATV

A Promise shared - women in Israeli society 25 MIN
16mm / VT2
Color
Presents working women in Israel, including labor union officials, a kibbutz secretary, an attorney and a newspaper publisher, who takes a hard look at the legal and social status of women in their country. Features divergent opinions based on differences in age, experienceand expectation and an analysis of the women's movement in the United States as it affects Israel.
Geography - World; Sociology
Dist - ADL **Prod** - WOSUTV
PBS

The Promised Land 112 MIN
16mm
B&W
_ *#106B 0159 025N*
Geography - World
Dist - CFLMDC **Prod** - NFBC 1959

The Promised Land - 1967 - 1968 60 MIN
VHS
Eyes On The Prize - Part II - Series
Color; Captioned (G)
$59.95 purchase _ #EYES - 204
Reviews the final year of the life of Martin Luther King Jr. Shows his organizing efforts against poverty and in support of striking black sanitation workers in Memphis. Describes how his staff attempted to continue his work after his assasination. Part of a series on the black civil rights movement.
Biography; History - United States; Sociology
Dist - PBS **Prod** - BSIDE 1990

Promised Land - Images of Canada
16mm
Color
_ *#106C 0176 043*
Geography - World
Dist - CFLMDC **Prod** - NFBC 1976

Promised land - Montgomery, Alabama, two decades after Martin Luther King, Jr 50 MIN
VHS
Color (H C G)
$445.00 purchase, $75.00 rental
Portrays current tensions and frustrations, hopes and fears of the divided city that was at the center of the civil rights struggles in the 1950s and 1960s. Interviews Vanzetta, a lawyer, who recounts how whites fled when she moved into their middle - class neighborhood; Harold and Lloyd, brothers who own a hairdressing shop and one of the few black businesses to survive in Montgomery; Paget, who took her employees at a fast food shop to court after she was fired becuase white customers complained that there were too many black employees; and the Rev Ralph Abernathy who voices the suspicion that Martin Luther King's involvement in the poor people's campaign was the cause of King's death. Produced by Otmoor.
Civics and Political Systems; Geography - United States; History - United States; Sociology
Dist - FLMLIB **Prod** - BBCTV 1993

Promised land, troubled land 14 MIN
16mm
Screen news digest series
B&W
LC 74-701523
Tells of major events during the centuries of smouldering conflict that have shaped history in the Middle East from ancient days to modern times. Vol. 16, No. 4.
History - World
Dist - HEARST **Prod** - HEARST 1973

Promised Lands 55 MIN 87 MIN
16mm
Color
Documents the October, 1973, war between Israel and its Arab neighbors. Emphasizes the Jewish struggle for survival throughout history. Explains that Israel is a land promised to many peoples.
Geography - World; History - World; Religion and Philosophy
Dist - NYFLMS **Prod** - NYFLMS 1973

The Promised People 15 MIN
16mm
Color
Tells the story of Kiryat - Gat, a typical Israeli town, as a microcosm of Israel's hopes and problems.
Geography - World; Sociology
Dist - ALDEN **Prod** - UJA

Promises 21 MIN
16mm
Color
LC 78-701468
Uses satires on television commercials to explore the influence of advertising.
Business and Economics; Fine Arts
Dist - SUTHRB **Prod** - RAMFLM 1978

Promises of Pluto - 8
U-matic / VHS / BETA
Search encounters in science series
Color; PAL (G H C)
PdS25, PdS33 purchase
Brings modern research efforts of the world's leading scientists into the classroom. Features one of a series of 24 mini - documentaries. Each film is 5 - 7 minutes in length.
Science; Science - Physical
Dist - EDPAT **Prod** - NSF

Promises - Profile of an Alcoholic 30 MIN
U-matic / VHS / 16mm
Color
Tells the true story of a successful theater producer during one crucial period in his life. Shows that he cannot control his drinking and that his problems with alcohol are slowly beginning to destroy every facet of his life. Demonstrates that his wife also has serious emotional problems that contribute to her husband's drinking.
Psychology; Sociology
Dist - PFP **Prod** - ELKIND 1982

Promises, promises
VHS
Bippity boppity bunch series
Color (K P I R)
$14.95 purchase _ #35 - 816 - 8579
Tells how Maxine and the rest of the Bippity Boppity Bunch break their promises, and how they learn that God's promises are always kept.
Literature and Drama; Religion and Philosophy
Dist - APH **Prod** - FAMF

Promises, promises - the 100 percent test 23 MIN
VHS / U-matic / BETA
Color (IND PRO G)
$495.00 purchase, $95.00 rental _ #PHN6
Trains supervisors in avoiding legal problems through 'broken promises.' Shows how to improve production, delivery dates and customer relations.
Business and Economics; Psychology
Dist - BBP **Prod** - BBP 1989
VLEARN

Promises to Keep 60 MIN
16mm
Color (G)
Presents an independent production by Ginny Durrin. Documents the four - year struggle of the late Mitch Snyder with the federal bureaucracy to help the homeless. Features Martin Sheen as narrator.
History - United States; Sociology
Dist - FIRS

Promises to Keep Series Module 11
Instructional and Behavior Management 30 MIN
Dist - LUF

Promises to Keep Series Module 12
Guidelines for Teaching the Handicapped Child in the Regular Classroom 30 MIN
Dist - LUF

Promises to Keep Series Module 1
An Introduction to Teaching the Handicapped 30 MIN
Dist - LUF

Promises to Keep Series Module 2
The Mentally Retarded and Slow Learning Child 30 MIN
Dist - LUF

Promises to Keep Series Module 3
Specific Learning Disabilities 30 MIN
Dist - LUF

Promises to Keep Series Module 4
Behavior Disorders 30 MIN
Dist - LUF

Promises to Keep Series Module 5
The Physically Handicapped and Health Impaired Child in the Regular Classroom 30 MIN
Dist - LUF

Promises to Keep Series Module 8
Speech and Language Disorders 30 MIN
Dist - LUF

Promises to Keep Series
Classroom assessment of student needs 30 MIN
The Hearing Impaired Child 30 MIN
Related services for the handicapped 30 MIN
The Visually Impaired 30 MIN
Dist - LUF

The Promoter - The Card 87 MIN
VHS
B&W (G)
$39.95 purchase _ #PRO020
Features a comedy in which an enterprising and often unscrupulous young man is determined to succeed at whatever the cost, and appears unstoppable until confronted by an equally deceptive man. Directed by Ronald Neame.
Fine Arts; Psychology; Religion and Philosophy; Sociology
Dist - HOMVIS **Prod** - JANUS 1952

Promoting Concerts from Rock to Pop 30 MIN
VHS / 16mm
(PRO G)
$89.95 purchase _ #DGP39
Talks about the nuts and bolts of promoting headline concert events. Hosted by Dick Goldberg.
Business and Economics
Dist - RMIBHF **Prod** - RMIBHF

Promoting good behaviour - 9
VHS
Teaching for tomorrow series
Color; PAL (C T)
PdS20 purchase
Uses real teachers and schools to evaluate ideas and support professional development for primary and secondary teachers in the area of classroom management. Stimulates discussion on classroom management, handling curriculum changes and developing new teaching techniques. Contact distributor about availability outside the United Kingdom.
Education
Dist - ACADEM

Promoting normal growth in the hospitalized child 12 MIN
U-matic / VHS
Color (PRO)
$200.00 purchase, $60.00 rental _ #4269S, #4269V
Details developmental stages of children from infancy to adolescence. Emphasizes the particular care appropriate for each stage in a hospitalized child - infants need comfort and stimulation, toddlers should have a safe environment which encourages exploration.
Health and Safety; Psychology; Sociology
Dist - AJN **Prod** - CNCEV 1986

Promoting the development of infants with prolonged hospitalization - staff development 13 MIN
U-matic
Pediatric video series
Color (PRO)
$175.00 purchase
Presents a variety of ways for promoting an infant's development during a stay in the pediatric unit. Shows how to use play, adjusting routines to suit the needs of the child, the use of proper positioning and handling techniques and by involving the family in day - to - day care. Part of a three - part series on infants with prolonged hospitalization.
Health and Safety; Sociology
Dist - POLYMR **Prod** - POKORJ

Promoting the independence of older adults through the use of assistive devices 120 MIN
VHS
Virginia Geriatric Education Center Video Conference series
Color (G C PRO)
$149.00 purchase, $55.00 rental
Calls attention to over 17,000 devices available to help older adults and their family members, with information on how health professionals can choose those items that best meet the needs of an individual. Uses case histories to illustrate appropriate choices.
Health and Safety
Dist - TNF **Prod** - VGEREC

Promoting urinary continence - who and how 21 MIN
U-matic / VHS
Understanding and treating incontinence series
Color (PRO C)
$395.00 purchase, $80.00 rental _ #C891 - VI - 007
Presents three cases in which noninvasive techniques are used to treat patients with urinary incontinence. Includes a 67 - year - old woman with urgency problems who is trained by a home nurse to use volume frequency - time charts to help with bladder retraining, an 80 - year - old incontinent male patient with dementia whose nurse develops an individualized toilet training regimen for him, and an elderly male patient with mobility problems that cause nocturnal incontinence - environmental barriers are removed to improve his ability to reach the toilet in time. Part of a seven - part series on incontinence presented by J C Brocklehurst and Bernadette M Ryan - Wooley.
Health and Safety; Science - Natural
Dist - HSCIC

Promoting wholesome sibling relationships
VHS
Color (H A G)
$45.00 purchase _ #MC238
Looks at rivalry and jealousy among siblings. Suggests methods for dealing with problems.
Business and Economics; Sociology
Dist - AAVIM **Prod** - AAVIM

Promotion of QC Circle Activities 30 MIN
VHS
Seven Steps to TQC Promotion Series
(PRO) (JAPANESE)
 # C106
Discusses Quality Control circle activities. Covers ideas such as 'voluntarism,' 'total participation,' 'improving the physical constitution of a company,' and 'respecting humanity.' Features Dr Kaoru Ishikawa.
Business and Economics
Dist - TOYOVS **Prod** - TOYOVS 1987

Promotion - solving the puzzle
VHS
Small business video library series
Color (PRO J H C G)
$39.95 purchase _ #VPR003V
Presents promotional and public relations strategies for the small business person, with special emphasis on free or low - cost sources of critical information and assistance. Combines instruction, case studies, personal insights and informal panel discussions. Includes a comprehensive workbook to stimulate thinking and provide step - by - step instructions for writing, analyzing, planning and implementing constructive change for any business. Part of a four - part series for budding entrepreneurs.
Business and Economics
Dist - CAMV

Promotion - solving the puzzle - Volume 3 56 MIN
VHS
Small business video library series
Color (G)
$29.95 purchase _ #BC03
Shows how to promote a business. Includes a workbook. Part of a series for small businesses, sole proprietors and students. Developed by the Small Business Administration and Bell Atlantic.
Business and Economics
Dist - SVIP

Prompting 25 MIN
VHS / 16mm
Teaching People with Developmental Disabilities Series
Color (A PRO)
$150.00 purchase, $55.00 rental _ #3130VHS
Demonstrates prompting techniques for people with developmental disabilities.
Mathematics; Psychology
Dist - RESPRC **Prod** - OREGRI 1988

Proms and pacifiers 15 MIN
VHS
Teen issues video series
Color (I J H)
$99.00 purchase _ #ES752V
Explores the consequences of teenage pregnancy, including the realities of parenthood; balancing school, work and finances; the effects on family and social relationships; and the parenting skills needed as child development issues arise. Part of a three - part series confronting the issues of teen pregnancy prevention, the confusions and misconceptions as teens face the pressures of dating, the realities of being a parent and parenting skills.
Guidance and Counseling; Health and Safety; Sociology
Dist - CAMV

Pronoun Anaphora 15 MIN
VHS / Software / U-matic
Storylords Series
Color (P)
$125.00 purchase,$240.00 software purchase
Depicts a fictional situation in which the children interact to learn the basic association between pronouns and their antecedents.
English Language
Dist - AITECH **Prod** - WETN 1986

Pronoun Usage 14.28 MIN
VHS / U-matic
Grammar Mechanic
(I J)
Designed to help intermediate students apply the rules of grammar. Focuses on the correct use of pronouns, highlighting agreement problems and solutions. Tenth in a series of 16.
English Language
Dist - GPN **Prod** - WDCNTV

Pronouns 15 MIN
VHS
Planet Pylon Series
Color (I)
LC 90712897
Uses character Commander Wordstalker from Space Station Readstar to develop language arts skills. Studies pronouns. Includes a worksheet for student to complete with help from series characters. Intended for the third grade level.
Education; English Language
Dist - GPN

Pronunciation Difficulties 8 MIN
U-matic / VHS
Better Spelling Series
Color
English Language
Dist - DELTAK **Prod** - TELSTR

Pronunciation of Medical Terminology 15 MIN
VHS / U-matic
Medical Terminology Series
Color (PRO)
Discusses and demonstrates pronunciation of medical terminology and gives viewers examples to follow. Helps the learner feel comfortable pronouncing medical terminology by showing the similarities between the medical vocabulary and the English language.
Health and Safety
Dist - HSCIC **Prod** - HSCIC

Proof 24 MIN
16mm
Color
LC 81-701143
Relates how a young man surprises his friends by parachuting out of an airplane and proving his manhood.
Fine Arts
Dist - USC **Prod** - USC 1981

Proof by Induction 16 MIN
U-matic / VHS
Probability and Random Processes - Elementary Probability Theory 'Series
B&W (PRO)
Continues theorem proving. Illustrates in detail proof by induction.
Industrial and Technical Education; Mathematics
Dist - MIOT **Prod** - MIOT

Proof of causation and damages in toxic tort cases 210 MIN
VHS
Color (C PRO A)
$67.20, $200.00 purchase _ #M727, #P236
Emphasizes the most controversial aspects of toxic tort litigation, the proof of causation and damages. Covers the legal proof and the role of the expert, risk injury, emotional distress claims, medical monitoring damages and an update of court decisions, all from the viewpoint of both plaintiffs' and defense counsel.
Civics and Political Systems
Dist - ALIABA **Prod** - ALIABA 1988

Proofreading and editing skills series
Presents a three - part series on proofreading and editing. Discusses spotting common typographical errors; reviews basic sentence structure and looks at spelling errors.

Proofreading and editing - Volume 1 77 MIN
Proofreading and editing - Volume 2 62 MIN
Proofreading and editing - Volume 3 59 MIN

Dist - CAMV **Prod** - CARTRP 1988

Proofreading and editing - Volume 1 77 MIN
VHS
Proofreading and editing skills series
Color (J H C G)
$99.95 purchase _ #CTK20248V
Discusses how to spot common typographical errors and how to correct writing without changing the meaning, how to create a comfortable environment for proofreading and more in Volume 1. Part of a three - part series on proofreading and editing.
English Language; Industrial and Technical Education
Dist - CAMV **Prod** - CARTRP 1992

Proofreading and editing - Volume 2 62 MIN
VHS
Proofreading and editing skills series
Color (J H C G)
$99.95 purchase _ #CTK20249V
Reviews basic sentence structure. Shows how to fix run - on sentences, the rules of subject - verb agreement, the most essential rules for commas, how and when to use colons and more in Volume 2. Part of a three - part series on proofreading and editing.
English Language; Industrial and Technical Education
Dist - CAMV **Prod** - CARTRP 1992

Proofreading and editing - Volume 3 59 MIN
VHS
Proofreading and editing skills series
Color (J H C G)
$99.95 purchase _ #CTK20250V
Offers a fun spelling test. Shows how to use a word processor's spell checker correctly, when to use numbers and when to use words, 200 frequently misspelled words, the most commonly confused word pairs and more in Volume 3. Part of a three - part series on proofreading and editing.
English Language; Industrial and Technical Education
Dist - CAMV **Prod** - CARTRP 1992

Proofs of Claims Hearing 58 MIN
VHS / U-matic
Remedies Phase of an EEO Case - Class Back Pay and Proof of Claims 'Series Pt 1
Color (PRO)
Presents a hypothetical formal hearing on proof of claims. Covers the language and form of the notice, the best methods of its distribution and the proper stage at which plaintiff's attorney can contact unnamed class members. Includes cost considerations and discouraging of fraudulent claims.
Civics and Political Systems
Dist - ABACPE **Prod** - ALIABA

A Propaganda Message 13 MIN
U-matic / VHS / 16mm
Color

LC 73-703700
Uses animation to spoof the many regional and cultural differences of Canadians. Shows that in spite of these differences, Canadians make their kind of governmental federalism work.
Civics and Political Systems; Geography - World; Sociology
Dist - PHENIX **Prod** - INFOCA 1973

Propaganda Message Revised 14 MIN
16mm
Color (FRENCH)
_ #106C 0373 077N
Geography - World
Dist - CFLMDC **Prod** - NFBC 1973

A Propaganda Message (Un Message De Propagande) 13 MIN
16mm / U-matic / VHS
Color (H C A)
LC 73-702700
Presents a cartoon film about the whole heterogenous mixture of Canada and Canadians. Views the way the invisible, adhesive force called federalism makes it all cling together.
Geography - World; Sociology
Dist - PHENIX **Prod** - NFBC 1973

Propaganda Parade 55 MIN
VHS / U-matic
B&W
Looks at various propaganda shorts from the 1940s and 1950s including some recently declassified footage.
Sociology
Dist - IHF **Prod** - IHF

Propagation 1 30 MIN
U-matic / VHS
Home gardener with John Lenanton series
Color (C A)
Discusses plant reproduction. Demonstrates simpler methods of propogation such as layering methods. Lesson 27.
Agriculture
Dist - CDTEL **Prod** - COAST

The Propagation of Waves 9 MIN
U-matic / VHS
Introductory Concepts in Physics - Wave Motion Series
Color (C)
$229.00, $129.00 purchase _ #AD - 1202
Demonstrates the phenomenon of resonance using a string pendulum. Shows structural vibration from earthquakes caught as waves on seismograpph to demonstrate specific vibration resonance. Polarization and high - speed, stop - motion photography demonstrate how an elastic wave propagates through a solid body.
Science - Physical
Dist - FOTH **Prod** - FOTH

Propane, butane and propylene 29 MIN
VHS
Color (IND PRO)
$395.00 purchase, $150.00 rental
Examines liquefied petroleum gas problems. Studies dangerous properties of LPG, safe storage and handling and safe response to emergencies involving leaks and fires. These three LPGs are highly flammable and when exposed to fire their containers can fail with explosive force. This video offers everything you need to know to handle LPG emergencies.
Health and Safety; Science - Physical; Sociology
Dist - JEWELR

Propane - LPG 16 MIN
BETA / VHS / U-matic
Forklift operator training series
Color (IND G)
$395.00 purchase _ #817 - 26
Trains forklift operators. Covers technical information about and the properties of propane. Identifies cylinder components and purposes, inspection of cylinders, recommendations and procedures for changing cylinders and specific safety tips. Part of a series on skills in forklift operation.
Health and Safety; Industrial and Technical Education; Psychology
Dist - ITSC **Prod** - ITSC

Propellant - Plus Heat 20 MIN
16mm
Color
A safety film on the handling characteristics of propellants.
Industrial and Technical Education
Dist - THIOKL **Prod** - THIOKL 1962

Proper implementation of the ABG procedure - arterial blood gases - a technical instruction for respiratory therapists 19 MIN
VHS
Color (PRO C G)
$395.00 purchase _ #R871 - VI - 028
Shows viewers how to draw blood for the measurement of arterial blood gases. Explains and demonstrates the procedure in 12 steps. Notes the differences in performing the procedure on a CPR patient. Uses a humorous but serious example of a technician taking an ABG from a patient to illustrate parts of the procedure that are often poorly or incorrectly. Includes a barbershop quartet's rousing rendition of The Procedure Polka to help viewers remember the 12 steps. Produced at St Paul Medical Center, Dallas, Texas.
Health and Safety
Dist - HSCIC

Proper Laboratory Techniques 59 MIN
VHS / U-matic
Digital Electronics Series
Color (PRO)
Industrial and Technical Education; Mathematics
Dist - MIOT **Prod** - MIOT

Proper operating room attire 24 MIN
16mm
AORN film series
Color (PRO)
LC 75-703020
Explains the controversy over what is worn in the operating room. Designed to inform persons who must enter a surgical suite area with the proper policies and procedures relating to operating room dress.
Health and Safety
Dist - ACY **Prod** - AORN 1975

The Proper Place for Women in the Church 29 MIN
U-matic
Woman Series
Color
Discusses the changing role of women in the Catholic church.
Religion and Philosophy; Sociology
Dist - PBS **Prod** - WNEDTV

A Proper Place in the World 59 MIN
U-matic / VHS
Japan Series
Color (H C A)
$125 purchase _ #5847C
Shows the political and economic factors leading to World War II. Examines modern Japanese problems of overcrowding, overindustrialization, and a competitive lifestyle. A production of WTTW, Chicago.
History - World
Dist - CORF

Proper Summer Bush Clothing 10 MIN
16mm
Survival in the Wilderness Series
Color (I)
LC FIA67-1444
Shows two boys who dress differently for a fishing trip and the resulting differences in comfort and well - being.
Guidance and Counseling; Physical Education and Recreation
Dist - SF **Prod** - MORLAT 1967

Proper Training and Hole Fill Procedure 9 MIN
U-matic / VHS
Blowout Prevention and Well Control Series
Color (IND)
Details procedure before tripping out, keeping the fluid level from falling below 30 meters from the top of the hole, and minimum intervals when flow checks should be performed.
Business and Economics; Industrial and Technical Education; Social Science
Dist - GPCV **Prod** - CAODC

Proper use and disposal of personal protective clothing 9 MIN
U-matic / BETA / VHS
Color (IND G)
$395.00 purchase _ #826 - 13
Informs on the proper use and disposal of personal protective equipment. Trains employees who are required to work near or around asbestos - containing material. Discusses proper donning, decontaminating and disposing of gloves and disposable full - body protection.
Health and Safety; Industrial and Technical Education; Psychology
Dist - ITSC **Prod** - ITSC 1990

Proper Winter Clothing 13 MIN
16mm
Outdoor Recreation - Winter Series
Color (I)
LC FIA68-1290
Shows that skiers, hikers and other winter outdoor people learn quickly that it is not how much you have on but what you wear and how you wear it. Provides the necessary clues to keeping warm during outdoor travel in the winter.
Home Economics; Physical Education and Recreation
Dist - SF **Prod** - SF 1967

Properties and Grain Structure 20 MIN
U-matic / VHS
Engineering Crafts Series
Color (H C A)
Industrial and Technical Education
Dist - FI **Prod** - BBCTV 1981

Properties and Uses of Redwood 25 MIN
16mm
Color (I)
Explores the properties of the redwood tree, including its durability, fire - resistance and beauty. Illustrates the architectural uses of different redwood grades, patterns and grains.
Agriculture; Science - Natural; Social Science
Dist - CRA **Prod** - CRA

Properties of air; 2nd ed. 15 MIN
U-matic
Search for science series; Unit VI - Air and weather
Color (I)
Shows that although air is a colorless fluid, it exerts force and has weight.
Science - Physical
Dist - GPN **Prod** - WVIZTV

Properties of Becquerel Rays 10 MIN
U-matic
Nuclear Physics Series
Color (H C)
Recreates the experiments of Becquerel and the Curies on radioactive sources. Experiments by Rutherford illustrate the properties of the three types of radiation, alapha, beta and gamma.
Science; Science - Physical
Dist - TVOTAR **Prod** - TVOTAR 1986

Properties of cardiac muscle - Pt 5 - Sino - atrial block in the frog heart 2 MIN
16mm
Dukes physiology film series; No 10
Color
LC 77-710193
Demonstrates a blocking of excitatory impulses from the sinus venosus in a frog heart and compares the normal heart beat, the beat with a sino - atrial block and the impaired beat with the blocking ligature removed.
Health and Safety; Science; Science - Natural
Dist - IOWA **Prod** - IOWA 1971

Properties of cardiac muscle - Pt 4 - cardiac response to an artificial pacemaker 2 MIN
16mm
Dukes physiology film series; No 9
Color
LC 70-710194
Demonstrates the response of an isolated turtle ventricle to artificial stimulation. Illustrates the staircase effect as the degree of response to rhythmical application of stimuli.
Health and Safety; Science; Science - Natural
Dist - IOWA **Prod** - IOWA 1971

Properties of cardiac muscle - Pt 1 - heart responses to stimuli 2 MIN
16mm
Dukes physiology film series; No 6
Color
LC 71-710197
Uses electrical stimulation of an isolated turtle heart to demonstrate the all or nothing response of cardiac muscle, the induction of premature beats and the compensatory pauses.
Health and Safety; Science; Science - Natural
Dist - IOWA **Prod** - IOWA 1971

Properties of cardiac muscle - Pt 3 - cardiac muscle contrasted with skeletal muscle 2 MIN
16mm
Dukes physiology film series; No 8
Color
LC 74-710195
Uses the ventricle muscle from a turtle heart and the gastronemius muscle of the frog to compare the latent periods and the contraction and relaxation periods of cardiac and skeletal muscles under various rates of stimulation. Suggests physiological advantages for each type of muscle response.
Health and Safety; Science; Science - Natural
Dist - IOWA **Prod** - IOWA 1971

Properties of cardiac muscle - Pt 2 - isolation of the cardiac pacemaker 2 MIN
16mm
Dukes physiology film series; No 7
Color

LC 78-710196
Demonstrates the location and function of the cardiac pacemaker in an isolated turtle heart by successively separating less rhythmic parts from those in which auto - rhythm is most developed.
Health and Safety; Science; Science - Natural
Dist - IOWA **Prod** - IOWA 1971

Properties of Enzymes I - Flexibility 24 MIN
U-matic / VHS / 16mm
Color
Presents eminent biochemist Daniel Koshland's work in the field of enzymes. Postulates the concept of the flexible enzyme, called the induced fit theory of enzyme action.
Science - Natural
Dist - MEDIAG **Prod** - OPENU 1978

Properties of Enzymes II - Cooperativity 24 MIN
U-matic / VHS / 16mm
Color
Develops the idea of the flexible enzyme in connection with the cooperativity factor of enzymes, an important factor in the regulation of enzyme activity. Details the two major theories about the various kinds of cooperativity, the sequential or concerted model and the symmetry model.
Science - Natural
Dist - MEDIAG **Prod** - OPENU 1978

The Properties of Heat 21 MIN
U-matic / VHS
Introduction to Energy and Heat Series
Color (H C A)
Introduces the subject of heat, the BTU, calorie and kilocalorie. Rates various substances in terms of their abilities to absorb and store heat. Shows the ways heat is transferred from one place to another.
Science - Physical
Dist - MOKIN **Prod** - NCDCC

The Properties of Light 9 MIN
U-matic / VHS
Introductory Concepts in Physics - Light Series
Color (C)
$229.00, $129.00 purchase _ #AD - 1204
Examines the relationship between light and sight. Considers light's property of moving in a straight line and the difference between sunlight and electric light.
Science - Physical
Dist - FOTH **Prod** - FOTH

Properties of Matter 15 MIN
U-matic / VHS / 16mm
B&W
Defines matter and shows examples of matter in different states. Shows how a material can be tested to see if it is a conductor or insulator, and how materials exhibit different characteristics when subjected to extreme voltages or when impurities are added.
Industrial and Technical Education; Science - Physical
Dist - USNAC **Prod** - USAF 1983

Properties of Petroleum Fluids 300 MIN
U-matic / VHS
Color
Available to SPE organizations only. Provides a better understanding of the properties that characterize oil, gas and water encountered in the oil patch, and the ability to estimate values of these properties for use in other engineering calculations.
Industrial and Technical Education
Dist - SPE **Prod** - SPE

Properties of Plastics 25 MIN
U-matic / VHS
Technical Studies Series
Color (H C A)
Discusses the properties of plastics.
Industrial and Technical Education
Dist - FI **Prod** - BBCTV 1981

Properties of radiation 68 MIN
16mm
Radioisotope series; 2
B&W
Explains the characteristics and properties of primary and secondary nuclear radiations in terms of their ionizing effects. Describes the effect of matter on radiation, showing that absorbing materials can be used to measure radiation characteristics or to shield against their biological effects.
Science - Physical
Dist - USNAC **Prod** - USA 1953

Properties of radiation 30 MIN
U-matic
Understanding the atom - 1970s - series; 05
B&W
Presents a lecture - demonstration by Dr Ralph T Overman discussing general problems of radiation decay, standard deviations in experimental counts, the energy spectrum from alpha and beta emitters, the use of absorption curves to study energy distribution of beta radiation, as well as the problems of self - absorption, specific activity and backscattering of radiation.
Science; Science - Physical
Dist - USNAC **Prod** - USNRC 1972

Properties of the Definite Integral 20 MIN
VHS
Calculus Series
Color (H)
LC 90712920
Examines the properties of the definite integral. The 26th of 57 installments of the Calculus Series.
Mathematics
Dist - GPN

Properties of zero and one 15 MIN
VHS / U-matic
Math matters series
Color (I J)
Expresses the concept of an additive identity and multiplicative identity by demonstrating their existence and illustrating with examples. Shows how to change fractions to equivalent fractions. Blue Module.
Mathematics
Dist - AITECH **Prod** - STETVC 1975

Property 92 MIN
VHS / U-matic
Color
Celebrates the exuberance of a nonconformist group from the Sixties caught in the world of Seventies corporate America. Combines fact and fiction as real characters act out an event close to their own lives. Focuses on a collection of likeable marginals and eccentrics who attempt to buy up their block from real estate developers and secure their way of life within the mainstream.
Social Science; Sociology
Dist - FIRS **Prod** - MEDIPR 1978

Property and Liability Insurance 25 MIN
VHS / U-matic
Money Smart - a Guide to Personal Finance Series
Color (H C A)
Outlines methods of avoiding financial loss due to property damage or suit for negligence.
Business and Economics; Education; Home Economics
Dist - BCNFL **Prod** - SOMFIL 1985

Property and Liability Insurance 29 MIN
U-matic
You Owe it to Yourself Series
Color (G)
$55.00 rental _ #YOIY - 007
Business and Economics
Dist - PBS **Prod** - WITFTV

Property Identification and Theft Insurance 30 MIN
U-matic / VHS
Burglar - Proofing Series
Color
Discusses property identification in the event of theft insurance.
Health and Safety; Sociology
Dist - MDCPB **Prod** - MDCPB

Property Rights and Pollution 19 MIN
U-matic / VHS / 16mm
People on Market Street Series
Color (H A)
LC 77-702443
Shows how the exchange of well - defined property rights can direct goods to their highest valued applications. Contrasts this situation with one in which difficulties are encountered because property rights are not well defined or exchangeable. Illustrates these principles in the context of air and water usage.
Business and Economics
Dist - CORF **Prod** - FNDREE 1977

Prophecy 48 MIN
U-matic / VHS / 16mm
Color (A)
LC 84-706163
Presents views of the explosions and the aftermath of the atomic bombing of Hiroshima and Nagasaki. Views the anguish of the survivors and the horror of the 90,000 people who were killed.
Civics and Political Systems; History - World
Dist - FI **Prod** - FI 1983

Prophesy 30 MIN
VHS / 16mm
Marketing Series
Color (C A)
$130.00, $120.00 purchase _15 - 04
Focuses on market research as practiced by the Preview House company.
Business and Economics
Dist - CDTEL **Prod** - COAST 1989

The Prophet and the people around Him
VHS
Video lectures of Khurram Murad series
Color (G)
$15.00 purchase _ #110 - 031
Features Islamic lecturer Khurram Murad who reveals that mercy and compassion were essential characteristics of the Prophet's dealings with Muslims and non - Muslims alike, that these virtues played a major role in winning the hearts of humanity. Analyzes how the spirit of the Prophet's teachings can be implemented on the American scene, that Muslims must follow the example of the Prophet Muhammad to relate to American society and its people.
Religion and Philosophy
Dist - SOUVIS **Prod** - SOUVIS

Prophet for all Seasons - Aldo Leopold 59 MIN
VHS / U-matic
Color
Presents Lorne Greene narrating a biography of Aldo Leopold, following his life and career as a naturalist, biologist and agriculturalist.
Literature and Drama; Science - Natural
Dist - PBS **Prod** - WETN 1980

Prophet from Tekoa 30 MIN
16mm
Color (R)
Shows how God punishes a nation that fails to heed warnings to overcome evil and renew allegiance to God. Describes how Amos went to Israel, witnessed against the people's sins and lashed out against them. Shows people in modern - day America committing the particular sin of which Amos speaks.
Guidance and Counseling; Religion and Philosophy
Dist - BROADM **Prod** - BROADM 1961

Prophet of peace - the story of Dr Martin Luther King, Jr 23 MIN
VHS
Color (P I J G)
$195.00 purchase, $35.00 renta _ #37262
Presents a cartoon - strip - style biography of Dr Martin Luther King, Jr, as told by the kids of the nationally syndicated 'Wee Pals' cartoon strip. Produced by Harold Lawrence, drawings by Morrie Turner.
Biography; Civics and Political Systems; Literature and Drama
Dist - UCEMC

Prophet of truth - Volume 10 30 MIN
VHS
Jesus of Nazareth series
Color (I J H C G A R)
$29.95 purchase, $10.00 rental _ #35 - 8323 - 1502
Presents excerpts from the Franco Zeffirelli film on the life and ministry of Jesus. Surveys the events of Jesus' ministry to the adulterous woman, Jesus and Nicodemus, the Roman centurion and Jesus' continued conflicts with the Pharisees.
Literature and Drama; Religion and Philosophy
Dist - APH **Prod** - BOSCO

Prophet Series
The Dancing Prophet 15 MIN
Dist - FRACOC

Prophet unheard 30 MIN
VHS
Business matters series
Color (A)
PdS65 purchase
Reveals that American intellectual Dr W Edwards Deming was regarded in Japanese business circles as the original management guru, and that few Westerners realize that it was an American who introduced the basics of quality control to Japan. Profiles Deming's unique management philosophy.
Business and Economics
Dist - BBCENE

Prophets and Promise of Classical Capitalism 60 MIN
U-matic / VHS / 16mm
Age of Uncertainty Series
Color (H C A)
LC 77-700660
Discusses the birth of classical capitalism in Britain and France, generated by the theories of Adam Smith. Based on the book The Age Of Uncertainty by John Kenneth Galbraith.
Business and Economics; History - World
Dist - FI **Prod** - BBCL 1977

Prophets and Promise of Classical Capitalism, Pt 1 30 MIN
U-matic / VHS / 16mm
Age of Uncertainty Series
Color (H C A)

LC 77-700660
Discusses the birth of classical capitalism in Britain and France generated by the theories of Adam Smith. Based on the book The Age Of Uncertainty by John Kenneth Galbraith.
Business and Economics
Dist - FI **Prod** - BBCL 1977

Prophets and Promise of Classical Capitalism, Pt 2 30 MIN
16mm / U-matic / VHS
Age of Uncertainty Series
Color (H C A)
LC 77-700660
Discusses the birth of classical capitalism in Britain and France generated by the theories of Adam Smith. Based on the book The Age Of Uncertainty by John Kenneth Galbraith.
Business and Economics
Dist - FI **Prod** - BBCL 1977

The Prophets - Pont - Aven, the Nabis, and Toulouse - Lautrec 18 MIN
U-matic / VHS / 16mm
Pathways of Modern Painting Series
Color (H C)
LC 72-712675
Presents the works of the Nabis - - Builldard, Denis Serusier, Ranson, Roussel and Bonnard - - whose basic principle was that the picture is not a description and should differ from the model. Compares the Nabis' work with the work of Toulouse - Lautrec to show how both confirmed the change in painting and helped open the way for modern painting.
Fine Arts
Dist - IFB **Prod** - LFLMDC 1971

The Prophet's village - Pt 1 50 MIN
VHS
Diary of a Maasai village series
Color (G)
$350.00 purchase, $50.00 rental
Examines the problem of maintaining enough cattle to supply milk and meat vs selling off cattle for cash to purchase maize, antibiotics and pesticides. Reveals that cash is also needed to pay legal fees for Rerenko, the Laibon's son. Part of a five-part series by Melissa Llelewyn - Davis, her diary of a 7-week visit to a single village in Kenya - Tanzania which examines a village life centered around the senior man - the most important prophet and magician - the Laibon, who has 13 wives living in the village, a large number of children, 20 daughters-in-law and 30 grandchildren.
Geography - World; History - World; Sociology
Dist - DOCEDR BBCENE **Prod** - BBCTV 1984

Prophylactic antibiotics - uses and abuses for physicians and dentists 30 MIN
U-matic / VHS
Color (PRO C)
$395.00 purchase, $80.00 rental _ #C920 - VI - 008
Reveals that dentists give antibiotics before procedures to patients with cardiac valvular and congenital abnormalities in order to prevent bacterial endocarditis. Reviews current research and recent recommendations concerning prophylactic antibiotic use by dental patients. Presented by Drs C Daniel Dent, Walter Paulsen and Edward Wong, Virginia Hospital Television Network, Office of Continuing Education, Medical College of Virginia, Virginia Commonwealth University, Richmond.
Health and Safety
Dist - HSCIC

Propogation 2 30 MIN
VHS / U-matic
Home Gardener with John Lenanton Series Lesson 28; Lesson 28
Color (C A)
Discusses some of the more difficult techniques of plant reproduction including stem cuttings, root cuttings and leaf - bud cuttings. Includes suggestions for easy ways to create a humid environment for newly planted cuttings.
Agriculture
Dist - CDTEL **Prod** - COAST

Proportion 29 MIN
U-matic
Sketching techniques series
Color (C A)
Considers how relative size of body parts affects the size of an entire creature. Shows how relative size is used to inject humor. Demonstrates the use of proportion. Lesson 9.
Fine Arts
Dist - CDTEL **Prod** - COAST

Proportion at Work 12 MIN
16mm / U-matic / VHS
Color (J H)
LC FIA65-365
Introduces ratio and proportion as practical tools for solving problems by direct measurement.
Mathematics
Dist - IFB **Prod** - VEF 1960

Proportions in Drawing - Pt 22 15 MIN
VHS / 16mm
Drawing with Paul Ringler Series
Color (I H)
$125.00 purchase, $25.00 rental
Defines and demonstrates proportions - drawing objects, singly or together as the eye sees them. Part of a 30 - part series.
Fine Arts; Industrial and Technical Education
Dist - AITECH **Prod** - OETVA 1988

A Propos De Jivago 8 MIN
16mm
B&W
Presents the Russian - born artist - filmmaker, Alexander Alexeieff, and his American wife, Claire Parker, who show and explain how they create pictures on the pinboard, l'ecran d'epingles, which they invented.
Fine Arts
Dist - STARRC **Prod** - STARRC 1960

The Proposal 25 MIN
U-matic / VHS
Color
Shows how a salesman makes all of the most common mistakes in proposal writing before he learns the simple five - part structure and sees how to present the proposal in terms of the needs of a customer.
Business and Economics
Dist - VISUCP XICOM **Prod** - VIDART

Proposal for Expansion 30 MIN
VHS / BETA
This Old House, Pt 2 - Suburban '50s Series
Color
Presents a 1950s ranch - style tract house. Discusses possibilities for creating space in it.
Industrial and Technical Education; Sociology
Dist - CORF **Prod** - WGBHTV

Proposal for 'QUBE' 10 MIN
VHS / U-matic
Color
Concerns the QUBE system - two - way cable television in Columbus, Ohio.
Fine Arts; Sociology
Dist - KITCHN **Prod** - KITCHN

Proposal preparation 796 MIN
U-matic / VHS
Color (C PRO)
$995.00 purchase _ #V9000 - 40
Develops a comprehensive knowledge of proposal preparation for companies and government agencies. Trains in the art and science of organizing, developing, writing and evaluating proposals. Includes - Introduction; Marketing and Proposal Preparation; Analysis of the Statement of Work; Requests for Proposals; Source Selection Processes; Organization for Proposal Preparation; Proposal Preparation Procedures; Development of Key Issues and Themes; Modular Proposal Techniques; Writing and Publishing the Proposal; Executive Summary - Proposal Formats; The Technical Proposal; The Management Proposal; The Cost Proposal; Proposal Review and Follow - Up. Includes proposal preparation manual and detailed lesson plans.
Business and Economics
Dist - AGUPA

Proprioceptive Neuromuscular Faciliation Series
PNF - Assisting to Postures and Application in Occupational Therapy Activities 60 MIN
Dist - RICHGO

Proprioceptive neuromuscular facilitation - PNF - Evaluation and treatment in occupational therapy - hemiplegic patient in relative recovery series
Evaluation - Tape I 30 MIN
Treatment - Tape II 23 MIN
Dist - RICHGO

Proprioceptive neuromuscular facilitation series
PNF - diagonal patterns and their application to functional activities 45 MIN
Dist - RICHGO

Proprioceptive Neuromuscular Facilitation Series
Geriatric CVA - Resistive Gait Program 26 MIN
Geriatric CVA - Resistive Mat Exercises 30 MIN
Geriatric CVA - Table Exercises 39 MIN
History and Philosophy 26 MIN
Principles 57 MIN
Resistive Gait Program 26 MIN
Resistive Mat Exercises I 33 MIN
Resistive Mat Exercises II 32 MIN
Table Treatment 41 MIN
Dist - UMDSM

Propulsion Systems 16 MIN
U-matic / VHS / 16mm
Color (I J)
Discusses propulsion systems, pointing out that the history of man is closely correlated to the history of propulsion. Tells how the horse - drawn vehicle opened up the American West and the steam engine in locomotives welded the entire continent. Describes how the gasoline engine of the Model T Ford revolutionized transportation, how the gasoline engine spawned air transportation and how rockets made it possible to leave the earth's gravity and conquer space.
Industrial and Technical Education; Science - Physical
Dist - HANDEL **Prod** - HANDEL 1981

Propulsion systems - 2 101 MIN
VHS
Creating therapeutic change series
Color; PAL; SECAM (G)
$95.00 purchase
Features Richard Bandler in the second part of a seven - part series on creating therapeutic change using advanced NLP, neuro - linguistic programming. Reveals that just solving problems often isn't enough and that time distinctions can be used to interlace beliefs, feeling states and 'chains' into complexes that generatively reorganize fundamental attitudes throughout a person's life. Recommended that tapes be viewed in order. Bandler sometimes uses profanity for emphasis, which may offend some people.
Health and Safety; Psychology
Dist - NLPCOM **Prod** - NLPCOM

Pros and cons 30 MIN
VHS
Business matters series
Color (A)
PdS65 purchase
Reveals that in 1993, the Business Matters team had unique access to HMP Strangeways before its proposed privization. Profiles three of the seven companies competing to run the refurbished jail - HM Prison service led by the Governor Robin Halward, Group 4 and and the Correction Corporation of America - CCA. In seeking to discover what privization will mean for a prison like Strangeways, the team visits Wolds Remand Prison in Humberside - in 1993 the United Kingdom's only privately-run prison, by Group 4, and Leavenworth, Kansas in the United States, which is run by CCA.
Sociology
Dist - BBCENE

Pros and Cons 28 MIN
VHS / U-matic
Metric Education Video Tapes for Pre and Inservice Teachers (K - 8 'Series
Color
Addresses teacher attitudes towards the metric system and promotes the generation of a positive attitude.
Mathematics
Dist - PUAVC **Prod** - PUAVC

Pros and Cons 30 MIN
U-matic
Speakeasy Series
(J H)
Charts the progress of a formal debate from stating the resolution through affirmative and negative contentions, logic and plausible evidence.
English Language
Dist - ACCESS **Prod** - ACCESS 1981

Pros in conflict 13 MIN
VHS
Peacemakers series
CC; Color (I)
$89.95 purchase _ #10390VG
Instructs students in peer mediation and conflict resolution. Uses three easy steps with actual elementary students modeling the process of mediation. Includes a teacher's guide and blackline masters. Part three of a three - part series.
Psychology
Dist - UNL

Prospect of Petroleum - Beaufort Sea Project 16 MIN
16mm
Color (H C A)
#3X119 N
Discusses how if Canada finds no new energy resources, it will face a serious and immediate energy crisis.
Social Science
Dist - CDIAND **Prod** - CREA 1977

Prospect of Turkey 32 MIN
16mm
Color
LC 74-705440
Presents a study of the condition of present - day Turkey, its successive cultures through the ages, its technical and economic developments, and its military contribution to western collective security.
Business and Economics; Geography - World; History - World
Dist - USNAC **Prod** - NATO 1967

Prospecting and Planning 7 MIN
VHS / U-matic
Telemarketing for Better Business Results Series
Color
Business and Economics; Psychology
Dist - DELTAK **Prod** - COMTEL

Prospective Pricing - Management Strategies 10 MIN
VHS / U-matic
Color
Offers the management team a comprehensive review of the major events and key legislative provisions leading to Medicare payment on a cost - per - case basis. Addresses such issues as hospitals' financial concerns and the impact of the Prospective Payment Commission and Professional Review Board on the new Medicare payment system.
Business and Economics; Civics and Political Systems; Health and Safety
Dist - AHOA **Prod** - AHOA

Prospects for humanity series

Community and culture	59 MIN
Consciousness and Health	59 MIN
Energy and technology	59 MIN
Evolution and Education	60 MIN
Justice and Religion	60 MIN

Dist - HRC

Prosperity
VHS
Synergy subliminal series
Color (G)
$19.98 purchase
Focuses on prosperity. Combines the nature cinematography of David Fortney with radiant, kaleidoscopic dances of color by Ken Jenkins, wilderness scenes by Blair Robbins, abstract animation by Jordan Belson and ethereal patterns of light created by Jason Loam. Features filmmaker Richard Ajathan Gero who integrates all of the foregoing imagery with subliminal visual affirmations and the music of Steven Halpern.
Fine Arts; Industrial and Technical Education; Religion and Philosophy; Sociology
Dist - HALPER **Prod** - HALPER

Prosperity ahead 103 MIN
VHS
March of time - the great depression series
B&W (G)
$24.95 purchase _ #S02139
Presents newsreel excerpts covering the period from September to December of 1936. Covers events including political extremism in the US, the effect of the bad English economy on tithing, Nazi occupation of the Rhine, and more. Part five of a six - part series.
History - United States
Dist - UILL

Prostaglandins - Tomorrow's Physiology 22 MIN
16mm
Color (PRO)
LC 74-702505
Examines the discovery, current status and clinical potential of prostaglandins.
Health and Safety; Science; Science - Physical
Dist - UPJOHN **Prod** - UPJOHN 1974

The Prostate, a Patient's View 19 MIN
16mm
Color
LC 78-701378
Encourages early diagnosis and treatment for prostate conditions.
Science - Natural
Dist - EATONL **Prod** - EATONL 1978

Prostate cancer 30 MIN
VHS
At time of diagnosis series
Color (G)
$19.95 purchase _ #1 - 5757 - 7007 - 5NK
Provides patients who have just been diagnosed with prostate cancer and their families with thorough, comprehensive and understandable information. Examines what is going on in the body and what might have caused the condition. Explains the type of medical professionals a patient may encounter and how the condition is monitored. Explores treatment options, including medication, surgery and lifestyle changes. Looks at practical issues surrounding the illness and answers the most common questions. Part of an ongoing series to provide the in - depth medical information patients and their families need to know.
Health and Safety
Dist - TILIED **Prod** - TILIED 1995

Prostate Cancer 19 MIN
U-matic / VHS
Color (C)
$249.00, $149.00 purchase _ #AD - 1548
Reveals that more than 24,000 men in the US die from prostate cancer in a year. Shows that these deaths could have been avoided had these men overcome their reluctance to undergo a simple examination. Shows how early detection together with radiotherapy and modified surgical techniques enable men with precancerous and malignant growths to avoid impotence and incontinence.
Health and Safety; Psychology; Science - Natural; Sociology
Dist - FOTH **Prod** - FOTH

Prostate cancer - treat to control 7 MIN
VHS
Color (PRO C G)
$200.00 purchase, $60.00 rental _ #5326
Educates the patient whose prostate cancer has spread beyond the prostate. Provides an objective discussion of the therapeutic modalities available, various approaches to hormonal therapy, chemotherapy, 'watchful waiting,' and on - going clinical trials. Emphasizes that, while a complete cure may not be possible, the disease can often be controlled and the patient can lead a comfortable life.
Health and Safety; Sociology
Dist - AJN **Prod** - LPRO 1995

Prostate cancer - treat to cure 24 MIN
VHS
Color (PRO C G)
$250.00 purchase, $70.00 rental _ #5325
Educates the patient with early stage, curable prostate cancer. Gives the basic information patients and their families need to know. Outlines the available options, including total prostatectomy, radiation therapy and 'watchful waiting.' Includes clear explanations and three - dimensional animated graphics to help patients understand the anatomy and pathophysiology of the disease.
Health and Safety; Sociology
Dist - AJN **Prod** - LPRO 1995

Prostate disorders 30 MIN
VHS
At time of diagnosis series
Color (G)
$19.95 purchase _ #1 - 5757 - 7012 - 1NK
Provides patients who have just been diagnosed with a prostate disorder and their families with thorough, comprehensive and understandable information. Examines what is going on in the body and what might have caused the condition. Explains the type of medical professionals a patient may encounter and how the condition is monitored. Explores treatment options, including medication, surgery and lifestyle changes. Looks at practical issues surrounding the illness and answers the most common questions. Part of an ongoing series to provide the in - depth medical information patients and their families need to know.
Health and Safety
Dist - TILIED **Prod** - TILIED 1996

Prostate Surgery 9 MIN
VHS / U-matic
Color
Describes the two most common 'open' procedures for prostate surgery. Prepares the patient both for hospitalization and operative procedures.
Health and Safety; Science - Natural
Dist - MEDCOM **Prod** - MEDCOM

Prostate Surgery 18 MIN
16mm
Doctors at Work Series
B&W (H C A)
LC FIA65-1358
Shows how an X - ray pyelogram reveals an enlargement of the prostate gland in an elderly man. Describes corrective surgery for the prostate condition, including a discussion on the anatomy of the prostate gland, and a clarification of misconceptions concerning the disorder.
Health and Safety; Science - Natural
Dist - LAWREN **Prod** - CMA 1961

Prostate - ultrasound and biopsy 6 MIN
VHS
Color (C PRO G)
$250.00 purchase
Uses tasteful visuals and clear graphics to present an unpleasant procedure in a pleasant way. Helps to prepare the patient and improve his acceptance of the exam.
Health and Safety; Sociology
Dist - LPRO **Prod** - LPRO

Prostatitis 7 MIN
U-matic / 35mm strip
Color
Alerts the adult male population to this very common problem among men. Discusses medical intervention, including antibiotic therapy, sitz baths, and the need for diminished activity during the acute phase.
Health and Safety; Science - Natural
Dist - MEDCOM **Prod** - MEDCOM

Prostheses 30 MIN
VHS
Perspectives - health and medicine - series
Color; PAL; NTSC (G)
PdS90, PdS105 purchase
Reveals that, a century ago, a wooden leg, a hook or a glass eye were the common prostheses. Shows that today, sophisticated joints and limbs are being created as prosthetics approaches the performance of nature.
Health and Safety
Dist - CFLVIS **Prod** - LONTVS

The Prosthesis Implant - a Surgical Treatment for Temporomandibular Joint Disease 19 MIN
16mm
Color
LC 77-702408
Describes the headaches, dizziness and other symptoms of jaw joint disease and shows X - rays of the surgical repair of the jaw by a metal prosthesis.
Health and Safety; Science; Science - Natural
Dist - WFP **Prod** - WFP 1977

Prosthesis Plus Technique Equals Independence - Pt 1 30 MIN
Videoreel / VHS
Color
Features a bilateral upper extremity amputee explaining and demonstrating techniques for bathing, shampooing, dressing and other personal hygiene activities.
Health and Safety; Psychology
Dist - UNDMC **Prod** - UNDMC

Prosthesis Plus Technique Equals Independence - Pt 2 37 MIN
Videoreel / VHS
Color
Features a bilateral upper extremity amputee explaining and demonstrating techniques for cooking, driving, working and participating in leisure time activities.
Health and Safety; Psychology
Dist - UNDMC **Prod** - UNDMC

Prosthetic Above - Knee Sockets 9 MIN
16mm
Color
LC 74-705441
Describes the quadrilateral or anatomical socket used with above - knee amputations and shows the importance of having the socket fit the stump correctly. Shows three different methods of suspension.
Health and Safety
Dist - USNAC **Prod** - NYUIMR 1969

Prosthetic Below - Knee Sockets 6 MIN
16mm
Color
LC 74-705443
Explains the various qualities of three different below - knee prosthetic sockets and shows each of these being worn by a patient.
Health and Safety
Dist - USNAC **Prod** - NYUIMR 1969

Prosthetic Checkout 12 MIN
U-matic / VHS
B&W
Shows step - by - step checkouts of two below knee prostheses, one a PTS prothesis and the other a PTB prosthesis.
Health and Safety
Dist - BUSARG **Prod** - BUSARG

Prosthetic Foot Components 7 MIN
16mm
Color
LC 74-705444
Reviews the various aspects of four types of foot - ankle components and presents patients wearing each of these types.
Health and Safety
Dist - USNAC **Prod** - NYUIMR 1969

Prosthetic Knee Components 8 MIN
16mm
Color

LC 74-705445
Describes the various qualities of five different knee joints that may be used by the patient with an above - knee amputation.
Health and Safety
Dist - USNAC **Prod** - NYUIMR 1969

Protect the Patient 12 MIN
16mm
Color
Presents six methods of carrying a hospital patient from a room in an emergency. Includes information on notifying the fire department.
Health and Safety
Dist - UIOWA **Prod** - UIOWA 1976

Protect your hearing in a noisy environment 13 MIN
U-matic / VHS / BETA
Color; PAL (G T)
PdS140, PdS148 purchase
Convinces employees that the danger of hearing loss is a real one. Takes a look at the measures that will protect your hearing.
Guidance and Counseling; Health and Safety
Dist - EDPAT

Protect Yourself - a Woman's Guide to Self Defense 60 MIN
VHS
(H C A)
$24.95 purchase _ #CH100V
Teaches women how to defend themselves through simple defense techniques. Discusses mental attitude, self concept, and inner strength.
Health and Safety; Physical Education and Recreation
Dist - CAMV

Protect yourself - HIV - AIDS education program 46 MIN
VHS
Color (I J H A T)
$125 purchase _ #10088VG
Presents facts on AIDS prevention and HIV infections to parents, teachers and students. Avoids complex medical terms in teaching protection and understanding of AIDS. Shares the story of four students who each face situations where the virus or an HIV infection may be involved. Includes a leader's guide, information for parents, and blackline masters.
Education; Health and Safety
Dist - UNL

The Protected School 6 MIN
16mm
B&W
Tells the story of the United Consolidated High School in Webb County, Texas - - about the architects, school board, teachers, administrators and the students who work in this fallout protected school. Emphasizes the advantages of this two - story type building.
Education; Fine Arts; Health and Safety
Dist - USNAC **Prod** - USOCD 1965

Protecting Endangered Animals 15 MIN
U-matic / VHS / 16mm
Color (I J)
Discusses animals that have become extinct or are in danger of extinction such as the dinosaur, the passenger pigeon, the black - footed ferret, the Devil's Hole pupfish, the manatee and the bald eagle. Looks at animals that have been saved from extinction such as the bison and the whooping crane.
Science - Natural
Dist - NGS **Prod** - NGS 1984

Protecting our environment series
Recycle 16 MIN
Reduce 14 MIN
Reuse 13 MIN
Dist - AIMS

Protecting the environment - it's everybody's business 13 MIN
BETA / VHS / U-matic
Color (IND G)
$495.00 purchase _ #600 - 36
Overviews RCRA and hazardous waste disposal regulations as they impact operations and maintenance personnel at waste generating sites. Explains how and why certain wastes are defined as hazardous. Reviews training requirements, inspection procedures, waste analysis, contingency plans, security and recordkeeping.
Industrial and Technical Education; Psychology; Science - Natural; Sociology
Dist - ITSC **Prod** - ITSC

Protecting the Family Members from Germs and Infection 8 MIN
U-matic / VHS
Color (SPANISH)
LC 77-731353; 77-731356
Provides a clear, easily understood definition of microorganisms and preventing the spread of infection. Explains difference between harmless and harmful microorganisms and conditions required for growth of microorganisms. Shows ways how germ may be spread from person to person and step - by - step instruction for preventing such spread.
Foreign Language; Health and Safety; Home Economics
Dist - MEDCOM **Prod** - MEDCOM

Protecting the global environment series
Presents a four - part documentary series. Highlights the urgent need for international cooperation to deal with threats to the world's basic ecosystems. Each episode examines a different ecological threat and suggests ways in which the average citizen can respond. Titles are Can Polar Bears Tread Water, global warming trends and the greenhouse effect; Chico Mendes - Voice of the Amazon, environmentalist and rubber tapper who started a modern movement to protect Brazil's rainforests; Jungle Pharmacy, Amazon tribes share knowledge of medicinal plants; and Profits from Poison, banned pesticides sold and used in Third World nations. Viewer Action Guide available free of charge.
Can Polar Bears Tread Water 58 MIN
Chico Mendes - Voice of the Amazon 57 MIN
Jungle Pharmacy 53 MIN
Profits from Poison 46 MIN
Dist - CNEMAG **Prod** - BWORLD

Protecting the web 14 MIN
VHS
Color (I J)
$225.00 purchase
Promotes respect for all forms of life, encouraging choices that help rather than hurt other creatures of the Earth. Teaches that all life is part of the Earth's ecosystem, using the metaphor of a spider's web. Produced for the Anti - Cruelty Society of Chicago.
Science - Natural
Dist - PFP **Prod** - FRIEDL

Protecting your back - for healthcare employees 19 MIN
BETA / U-matic / VHS
Color (G)
$395.00 purchase, $95.00 rental
Prescribes for a healthy back - posture, exercise, body mechanics, common sense. Shows how to avoid injury through proper body mechanics. Offers back - strengthening exercises and shows how to avoid injury during patient transfer.
Health and Safety; Physical Education and Recreation; Psychology; Science - Natural
Dist - AMEDIA **Prod** - AMEDIA

Protecting your eyes 12 MIN
VHS
Color (A PRO IND)
$249.00 purchase, $100.00 rental
Provides a preventive approach to eye safety in the workplace.
Business and Economics; Health and Safety; Psychology
Dist - VLEARN **Prod** - EBEC

Protecting Your Hearing in a Noisy World 13 MIN
U-matic / VHS
Color (A)
LC 84-707798
Explains the nature of sound and its transmission, pointing out how exposure to very loud noise can cause hearing loss. Demonstrates sound - insulated booths and protection devices such as ear muffs and plugs. Recommends yearly testing.
Health and Safety; Science - Physical; Sociology
Dist - IFB **Prod** - KOHLER

Protecting your property interests in computer software 50 MIN
VHS
Color (C PRO A)
$95.00 purchase _ #Y127
Provides instruction on the fundamentals of patent, trade secret and copyright protection as applied to computer software.
Civics and Political Systems; Computer Science
Dist - ALIABA **Prod** - CLETV 1990

Protecting yourself against bloodborne pathogens 15 MIN
VHS
Color (IND COR T PRO)
$159.00 purchase _ #BPY/IB
Conveys information about taking precautions against the spread of viral diseases. Discusses bloodborne pathogens and their transmission, demonstrates safe handling of bio - hazardous wastes, and shows on - the - job safety guidelines. Also explains what to do if exposed to bloodborne pathogens. Includes Employer's Compliance Manual, Employee Safety Facts, and Employer Proof - of - Training Quiz.
Health and Safety
Dist - ADVANM

Protection 24 MIN
VHS
Video guide to occupational exploration - the video GOE series
Color (J H C G)
$69.95 purchase _ #CCP1004V
Discusses careers which center on protection. Interviews a private investigator, a chief of police, corrections officer and a fire fighter. Part of a 14 - part series exploring occupational clusters.
Business and Economics; Guidance and Counseling; Social Science
Dist - CAMV **Prod** - CAMV 1991

Protection Against Infection - the Inside Story of the Immune System and AIDS 15 MIN
VHS / 16mm
Inside Story with Slim Goodbody Series
Color (P I)
$125.00 purchase, $25.00 rental
Explains in a way appropriate for younger elementary children what AIDS is, the health hazards of AIDS and major causes of AIDS.
Health and Safety
Dist - AITECH **Prod** - GDBODY 1988

Protection Against Nuclear Radiation 8 MIN
16mm
Color
LC 74-706202
Examines factors that reduce the hazards of nuclear radiation. Emphasizes the value of fallout shelters in a nuclear emergency.
Health and Safety; History - World; Industrial and Technical Education
Dist - USNAC **Prod** - USOCD 1968

Protection Against Radioactivity in Uranium Mines 27 MIN
16mm
Color
LC 74-705447
Presents a general description of the radon daughter hazards in uranium mines and outlines the environmental control, principles and procedures that have proven effective in mitigating the hazard.
Health and Safety; Science - Natural
Dist - USNAC **Prod** - USBM 1969

Protection against the odds - Video II 32 MIN
VHS
Introduction to chemical laboratory safety series
Color; PAL (C PRO)
$695.00 purchase _ #V - 4802 - 18102
Concentrates on containment methods and hazard elimination techniques. Shows how to eliminate hazards by substituting materials; reduce risk by changing the process or scale of a procedure. Illustrates the proper use of ventilation and containment equipment; when and why to use eye protection; tested and proven respiratory protection techniques; personal protective equipment. Part two of four parts on chemical lab safety. Technical advisor, George D Heindel.
Health and Safety; Science; Science - Physical
Dist - AMCHEM

Protection equipment
VHS / U-matic
Distribution system operation series; Topic 8
Color (IND)
Introduces the concept of electrical faults. Shows details of operation of various types of protective relays and devices. Includes maintenance considerations.
Industrial and Technical Education
Dist - LEIKID **Prod** - LEIKID

Protection for Sale - the Insurance Industry 52 MIN
U-matic / VHS / 16mm
Color (H C A)
Looks at the vastness of the insurance industry and questions whether the public needs more federal protection from their supposed protectors.
Business and Economics
Dist - FI **Prod** - NBCNEW 1982

Protection in Neighborhoods 15 MIN
U-matic / VHS
Neighborhoods Series
Color (P)
Looks at the issue of protection in neighborhoods.
Sociology
Dist - GPN **Prod** - NEITV 1981

Protection in the Nuclear Age 24 MIN
16mm
Color
LC 78-701475
Shows what individuals can do to improve chances for survival if a nuclear crisis or enemy attack should occur. Covers major aspects of protection, from avoidance of blast effects and fallout to emergency shelter and supplies.
Health and Safety
Dist - USNAC **Prod** - USDCPA 1978

Protection of client confidences 38 MIN
VHS
Understanding modern ethical standards series
Color (C PRO)
#UEX01
Analyzes the American Bar Association's Model Rules of Professional Conduct. Emphasizes issues of client confidentiality, applying ABA standards to both attorneys and paralegals. Not available for separate sale or rental.
Civics and Political Systems
Dist - NITA **Prod** - NITA 1985

Protection of Proprietary Information (POPI) 23 MIN
16mm / U-matic / VHS
Color (SPANISH FRENCH)
Discusses employees' important role in protecting their organization's intellectual assets including patents, trade secrets and commercial information. Includes a discussion of classification, marking and duplication of sensitive materials, access control, confidentiality procedures, handling the press, and employee and family gossip.
Business and Economics; Foreign Language
Dist - CORF **Prod** - SOREG

The protection racket 30 MIN
VHS
Nature by design series
Color (A PRO C)
PdS65 purchase _ Unavailable in USA and Canada
Deals with protection in the world of design. Part of a series which utilizes a visual style blending natural history footage, graphics and video effects - moving back and forth between science and nature. Emphasizes that good design is essential for the success of any product, in the natural world and today's high-tech world.
Psychology
Dist - BBCENE

Protectionism - can saving jobs cost us jobs 30 MIN
U-matic
Adam Smith's money world series; 107
Color (A)
Attempts to demystify the world of money and break it down so that small as well as large businesses and it's people understand and adjust to new social and economic trends. Reports on the major economic stories and discoveries of the day.
Business and Economics
Dist - PBS **Prod** - WNETTV 1985

Protective Breathing Apparatus 30 MIN
VHS
Firefighter Video Series
Color (G PRO)
$115.00 purchase _ #35060
Shows the use, features, limitations and proper maintenance of protective breathing apparatus. Uses live footage.
Health and Safety; Psychology; Social Science
Dist - OKSU **Prod** - OKSU

Protective clothing 25 MIN
VHS
Hazmat emergency series
Color (IND PRO)
$265.00 purchase
Presents one of three videos in the Hazmat Emergency series. Looks at specialized protective clothing and equipment and how it is designed to protect against such dangers as thermal, asphyxiation, chemical or mechanical hazards. Teaches proper use of SCBA, protective clothing for structural fire fighting and chemical protective clothing, and how to select protective clothing by matching the protective equipment to the hazard. Also covers decontamination.
Health and Safety; Sociology
Dist - JEWELR

Protective Coloration 13 MIN
U-matic / VHS / 16mm
Many Worlds of Nature Series
Color
LC 75-703253
Shows the relationships between an animal's coloration and its habitat and behavior. Discusses camouflage, disguise, warning, coloration and Batesian mimicry.
Science - Natural
Dist - CORF **Prod** - MORALL 1975

Protective coloration 18 MIN
16mm
Color (G)
$50.00 rental
Generates a succession of visual and aural 'notes' by the patterns in animals' hides, which are arranged and re - edited into a complex musical architecture. Views elements of sand, dirt, light and shadow. The animals' fur patterns, which evolved naturally as camouflage to hide them from predators, ironically now make them more visible to human predators, who are attracted by their exotic uniqueness. Produced by Scott Stark.
Fine Arts; Science - Natural
Dist - CANCIN

Protective relaying, tape 16a
U-matic / VHS
Electric power system operation series
Color (IND)
Covers fundamentals, overcurrent, voltage, pilot wire, primary and backup, targets, distance relays, phase and ground faults, load shedding and trip and block relays.
Industrial and Technical Education
Dist - LEIKID **Prod** - LEIKID

Protective relaying, tape 16b
U-matic / VHS
Electric power system operation series
Color (IND)
Covers fundamentals, overcurrent, voltage, pilot wire, primary and backup, targets, distance relays, phase and ground faults, load shedding and trip and block relays.
Industrial and Technical Education
Dist - LEIKID **Prod** - LEIKID

Protective Relays, Tape 1 - Protective Relaying Fundamentals, Relay Testing 60 MIN
U-matic / VHS
Electrical Equipment Maintenance Series
Color (IND) (SPANISH)
Industrial and Technical Education
Dist - ITCORP **Prod** - ITCORP

Protective Services 58 MIN
U-matic / VHS
Legal Training for Children Welfare Workers Series; Part III
Color
Focuses on due process rights for parents, protective proceedings, jurisdictional and residency requirements, problems in dealing with emotional neglect, psychological abuse in the legal system and the child abuse reporting laws.
Civics and Political Systems; Sociology
Dist - UWISC **Prod** - UWISC 1975

The Protective Tariff Issue - 1816 - 1833 - Pt 2 15 MIN
U-matic / VHS
Taxes in US History Series
Color (J)
Centers on the influence of tax policy on economic behavior by featuring the protectionist tariffs of the 1830s. Designed to protect industry more than to raise revenue, these laws marked the beginnings of extreme sectional controversies over tariff policy. Part 2 of a three - part series which presents the economics of taxation within the context of key events in the American past.
Business and Economics; Civics and Political Systems; History - United States
Dist - AITECH **Prod** - AITECH 1991

The Protectors - preparing offensive linemen 25 MIN
VHS
Color (H C A)
$39.95 purchase _ #BYU100V
Presents the Brigham Young University football coaching staff and players in a video outlining the offensive line techniques that have made BYU one of the nation's top offensive powers. Demonstrates stance, foot positioning, hand positioning, and other relevant techniques.
Physical Education and Recreation
Dist - CAMV

Protein from the Sea 26 MIN
16mm
Color
LC 81-700425
Documents the construction of a seafood processing ship in Seattle which is owned by a Native American organization and stationed in Cold Bay, Alaska.
History - United States; Industrial and Technical Education; Social Science
Dist - ANFP **Prod** - ANFP 1980

Protein - IV 6 MIN
VHS / U-matic
It's never too late to change series
Color (PRO C G)
$195.00 purchase _ #C881 - VI - 027
Discusses protein requirements in the diets of older people. Promotes discussion and participation in group activities and motivates older citizens to adopt healthier nutrition and exercise habits. Part of a nine - part series aimed at retirement home communities, senior citizen organizations and community health centers presented by Dr Molly Engle and Melissa Galvin.
Health and Safety; Physical Education and Recreation; Social Science
Dist - HSCIC

Protein - Pt 1 30 MIN
VHS / U-matic
Food for Life Series
Color
Home Economics; Social Science
Dist - MSU **Prod** - MSU

Protein - Pt 2 30 MIN
VHS / U-matic
Food for Life Series
Color
Home Economics; Social Science
Dist - MSU **Prod** - MSU

Protein Quality of Foods - James Adkins , PHD 20 MIN
U-matic
Food and Nutrition Seminars for Health Professionals Series
Color (PRO)
LC 78-706164
Discusses aspects of the Food and Drug Administration's regulations governing labeling of food and nutritional quality guidelines.
Social Science
Dist - USNAC **Prod** - USFDA 1976

Protein - Structure and Function 16 MIN
16mm / U-matic / VHS
Color
Shows how proteins work in our bodies. Explains the structure of protein and illustrates the interactions that bring about three - dimensiomal proteins and how enzymes work. Describes how proteins play a major part in the structure of living things and how, as catalysts, they control life's chemical reactions.
Science - Natural
Dist - MEDIAG **Prod** - WILEYJ

Protein Synthesis 20 MIN
U-matic / 35mm strip
Color (H C)
$43.95 purchase _ #52 2515
Discusses the basic types of RNA and the stucture and function of ribosomes as components in the process of photosynthesis. Analyzes tRNA charging, initiation, elongation, and termination in photosynthesis. Explains the structure and function of polysomes.
Science - Physical
Dist - CBSC **Prod** - BMEDIA

Protein Synthesis Series

DNA - the molecule of heredity	10 MIN
DNA replication - the repeating formula	10 MIN
Protein - the Stuff of Life	10 MIN
Ribosomal RNA - the Protein Maker	10 MIN
RNA Synthesis - the Genetic Messenger	10 MIN
Transfer RNA - the Genetic Messenger	10 MIN

Dist - TVOTAR

Protein systhesis 60 MIN
VHS
Concepts in science - biology series
Color; PAL (J H)
PdS29.50 purchase
Explores the importance of proteins as the basic building blocks of life and the fundamental role that protein synthesis plays in all living things. Divided into six ten - minute concepts - Protein - The Stuff of Life; DNA - The Molecule of Heredity; DNA Replication - The Repeating Formula; RNA Synthesis; Transfer RNA; and Ribosomal RNA. Part of a six - part series.
Industrial and Technical Education; Science; Science - Natural
Dist - EMFVL **Prod** - TVOTAR

Protein - the Stuff of Life 10 MIN
U-matic
Protein Synthesis Series
Color (H C)
Explores the varied protein compounds and their biological functions, the way they bind and how organisms synthesize the complex chains of amino acids that make up proteins.

Science; Science - Natural; Science - Physical
Dist - TVOTAR Prod - TVOTAR 1984

Proteins - 1 36 MIN
VHS
Introductory principles of nutrition series
Color (C A PRO)
$70.00 purchase, $16.00 rental _ #40400
Presents the first part of two parts on proteins. Part of a 20 - part series on nutrition. Emphasizes controversial nutritional issues and the principle instructional objectives.
Health and Safety; Social Science
Dist - PSU Prod - WPSXTV 1978

Proteins - 2 45 MIN
VHS
Introductory principles of nutrition series
Color (C A PRO)
$70.00 purchase, $16.00 rental _ #50702
Presents the second part of two parts on proteins. Part of a 20 - part series on nutrition. Emphasizes controversial nutritional issues and the principle instructional objectives.
Health and Safety; Social Science
Dist - PSU Prod - WPSXTV 1978

Proteins, Immunoglobulins and Antibodies 22 MIN
U-matic / VHS
Immunology Series
Color (C A)
Health and Safety; Science; Science - Natural
Dist - TEF Prod - ESSMED

Proteins - structure and function - the genetic code - Parts 23 and 24 60 MIN
VHS / U-matic
World of chemistry series
Color (C)
$45.00, $29.95 purchase
Presents parts 23 and 24 of the 26 - part World of Chemistry series. Reveals that proteins are polymers built of amino acids and that there are only 20 basic amino acids. Investigates the structure and role of the nucleic acids DNA and RNA. Two thirty - minute programs hosted by Nobel laureate Roald Hoffmann.
Science - Natural; Science - Physical
Dist - ANNCPB Prod - UMD 1990

Protest and Communication 52 MIN
U-matic / VHS / 16mm
Civilisation Series; No 6
Color (J)
LC 78-708453
Surveys the development of Western civilization in the 16th century in the north as evidenced in the use of the printing press and in the Reformation, Protestantism and especially in the works of Erasmus, Sir Thomas More, Durer, Holbein, Luther, Cranach and Shakespeare.
Fine Arts; History - World; Religion and Philosophy
Dist - FI Prod - BBCTV 1970

Protest and Communication - Pt 1 24 MIN
U-matic / VHS / 16mm
Civilisation Series; No 6
Color
LC 78-708453
Surveys the development of Western civilization in the 16th century in the north as evidenced in the use of the printing press and in the Reformation, Protestantism and especially in the works of Erasmus, Sir Thomas More, Durer, Holbein, Luther, Cranach and Shakespeare.
History - World
Dist - FI Prod - BBCTV 1970

Protest and Communication, Pt 2 28 MIN
16mm / U-matic / VHS
Civilisation Series no 6; No 6
Color
LC 78-708453
Surveys the development of Western civilization in the 16th century in the north as evidenced in the use of the printing press and in the Reformation, Protestantism and especially in the works of Erasmus, Sir Thomas More, Durer, Holbein, Luther, Cranach and Shakespeare.
History - World
Dist - FI Prod - BBCTV 1970

Protest and Reform 40 MIN
16mm / U-matic / VHS
Christians Series; Episode 7
Color (H C A)
LC 78-701656
Surveys the history of the Reformation, focusing on developments within the Christian church.
History - World; Religion and Philosophy
Dist - MGHT Prod - GRATV 1978

Protest on the Campus - Columbia University 1968 15 MIN
16mm
Protest Series
Color (H)
What is the meaning of the extreme behavior of students at the ivy - covered Columbia campus. This film puts your class in the arena for a first - hand view of the age - old conflict between generations. Helps the young discover for themseleves a broadened viewpoint of how a faculty and administration reacted to the passion and needs of their students.
Civics and Political Systems
Dist - REAF Prod - INTEXT

Protest Series
All of the people against some of the people 15 MIN
Anti - war protest 15 MIN
The Assassins 15 MIN
Black Power 15 MIN
Confrontation in Washington - Resurrection City 15 MIN
Protest on the Campus - Columbia University 1968 15 MIN
Dist - REAF

Protestant Spirit USA 52 MIN
U-matic / VHS / 16mm
Long Search Series; 1
Color (H C A)
LC 78-700470
Visits various Protestant churches in Indianapolis and observes how services are conducted. Examines the reasons for the vigor of religious expression among both Black and white American Protestants.
Religion and Philosophy; Sociology
Dist - TIMLIF Prod - BBCTV 1977
AMBROS

Protestant Women in Ministry 21 MIN
U-matic / VHS
Color
$80 rental
Profiles two women who are pastors, one is Presbyterian, one is Baptist. Discusses their different backgrounds, one is white, married, and is a sole minister, the other is black, single, and an assistant. Discusses the problem of male domination in the ministry.
Religion and Philosophy; Sociology
Dist - CCNCC Prod - CCNCC 1986

Prothalamion 4 MIN
16mm
Color (G)
$8.00 rental
Records a friend's wedding ceremony in the bride's ancestral Charlotte, North Carolina home one rainy December 1977.
Fine Arts; Sociology
Dist - CANCIN Prod - BALLGO 1978

Prothesis Films Series
Shoulder Prosthesis for Four Part Fracture 19 MIN
Surgical Technique for Multiplex Total Knee Replacement 32 MIN
Universal Proximal Femur Prosthesis 20 MIN
Dist - WFP

Protist behavior 11 MIN
16mm / VHS
Inhabitants of the planet Earth series
Color (H C) (FRENCH)
$176.00, $132.00 purchase, $25.00 rental _ #194 W 2015, #193 W 2004, #140 W 2015
Considers the origins of animal behavior at the protistan level. Reveals that each protist examined shows its own unique form of behavioral adaptation - Paramecium exhibits stereotyped avoidance and aggregation responses, Euglena moves along a light beam into areas of optimal light intensity. Examines didinium and suctorians. Part of a series on microorganisms.
Science - Natural
Dist - WARDS Prod - RUSB 1975
MLA

The Protist Kingdom 14 MIN
U-matic / VHS / 16mm / 8mm cartridge
Color (I) (SPANISH)
LC FIA65-570
Discusses protists, one - celled animals or plants, which scientists have divided into six major groups - sarcodina, ciliates, flagellates, slime mold, sporozoa and bacteria. Illustrates how these microscopic, one - celled organisms can carry on activities found in multicellular living things.
Science - Natural
Dist - PHENIX Prod - FA 1965

Protist physiology 13 MIN
16mm / VHS
Inhabitants of the planet Earth series
Color (H C) (FRENCH)
$208.00, $156.00 purchase, $25.00 rental _ #194 W 2010, #193 W 2003, #140 W 2010
Illustrates the complex inner workings of living cells. Examines the methods used by Amoeba and Paramecium to capture and digest food by phagocytosis, the saprozoic lifestyle of Chilomonas, and Euglena which can live as an autotroph or exist saprozoically. Uses high magnification to follow the functioning contractile vacuole. Part of a series on microorganisms.
Science - Natural
Dist - WARDS Prod - RUSB 1975
MLA

Protist reproduction 10 MIN
16mm / VHS
Inhabitants of the planet Earth series
Color (H C) (FRENCH)
$160.00, $120.00 purchase, $25.00 rental _ #194 W 2020, #193 W 2005, #140 W 2020
Shows the reproductive methods of protists, including fission, specialized forms of budding, sexual processes and the production of eggs and sperm of colonial protists. Part of a series on microorganisms.
Science - Natural
Dist - WARDS Prod - RUSB 1973
MLA

Protista - Protozoa and Algae 14 MIN
U-matic / VHS / 16mm
Modern Biology Series
Color (H C)
Presents a microscopic look at the Protistans, which include all the single - celled organisms. Classifies protozoans into four groups according to their method of locomotion.
Science - Natural
Dist - BNCHMK Prod - BNCHMK 1985

Protists - Form, Function, and Ecology 23 MIN
U-matic / VHS / 16mm
Color (J H)
Guides viewers through the kingdom protista with light and electron microscopes. Examines distinguishing behavior and physiology of this kingdom which includes protozoa, algae, and slime molds. Includes teachers guide.
Science - Natural
Dist - EBEC Prod - EBEC 1984

Protists - Threshold of Life 12 MIN
16mm / U-matic / VHS
Bio - Science Series
Color (I J H C)
Tells how thousands of tiny organisms called protists may be found within a single drop of stagnant water. Shows the Euglena, which has both plant and animal characteristics and the amoeba's puzzling movement. Discovers that seemingly featureless ooze from the ocean floor is composed of billions of discarded shells and skeletons of marine protists.
Science - Natural
Dist - NGS Prod - NGS 1977

Protocol Materials in Teacher Education - Interpersonal Communication Skills Series
Responsible Feedback, Pt 1 15 MIN
Responsible Feedback, Pt 2 15 MIN
Dist - MSU

Protocol Materials in Teacher Education - the Process of Teaching, Pt 1 Series
Tasks of Teaching, Pt 1 30 MIN
Tasks of Teaching, Pt 2 20 MIN
Dist - MSU

Protocol Materials in Teacher Education - the Process of Teaching, Pt 2 Series
Modeling 10 MIN
Negative Reinforcement 5 MIN
Operant Learning 10 MIN
Respondent learning 10 MIN
Shaping 5 MIN
Dist - MSU

Protocol materials in teacher education - the process of teaching, series
Positive reinforcement 10 MIN
Dist - MSU

Protozoa 15 MIN
VHS
Biology live series
Color (I J) (SPANISH)
$129.00 purchase _ #GW - 5071 - VS, #GW - 5071 - SP
Looks at the four major classes of protozoa - sarcodina, flagellates, ciliates and sporozoa in part of a 13 - part series on biology which uses high resolution animation, live - action photography and interesting narrative to teach a core curriculum in biological science.
Science - Natural
Dist - HRMC

The Protozoa 30 MIN
U-matic / VHS

Color
Depicts the micro - world of the protozoa. Captures the structures and functions of four of the main phyla represented by the Amoeba, Paramecium, Euglena and Plasmodium. Includes ten follow - up questions at the end of the program.
Science - Natural
Dist - EDMEC **Prod** - EDMEC

Protozoa 20 MIN
VHS
Color (J H)
$130.00 purchase _ #A5VH 1611
Introduces protozoa. Illustrates the four major classes of protozoa - sacrodina, flagellata, ciliata and sporozoa. Shows the various structures of protozoa, how they capture and digest food and how they reproduce both sexually and asexually. Details the malaria cycle and observes other protozoa that cause disease and affect human life.
Health and Safety; Science - Natural
Dist - CLRVUE **Prod** - CLRVUE 1992

Protozoa - Structures and Life Functions 17 MIN
16mm / VHS / U-matic
Major Phyla Series
Color (J H C)
$395, $250 purchase _ #1092; LC FIA65-325
Uses photomicrography to show the living specimens of the four classes of protozoa - - rhizopods, flagellates, ciliates and sporozoans. Pictures structural adaptations which enable these animals to get food, reproduce and respond to stimuli.
Science - Natural
Dist - CORF **Prod** - CORF 1965

Protozoans - Part One 10 MIN
VHS
Microscopy prelab series
Color (J H C)
$95.00 purchase _ #CG - 910 - VS
Explains that protozoans are in the Kingdom Protista. Examines Phyla Sarcodina and Mastigophora. Looks at a specimen of Amoeba proteus in a living culture as well as in a prepared slide. Examines Entamoeba, Euglena, Volvox, Chlamydomanas and Trypanosoma as representatives of Matigophora. Part one of two parts on Protozans and part of a five - part series on microscopy prelab produced by Bill Pieper.
Science; Science - Natural
Dist - HRMC

Protozoans - Part Two 9 MIN
VHS
Microscopy prelab series
Color (J H C)
$95.00 purchase _ #CG - 909 - VS
Focuses on Phyla Ciliophora and Sporozoa, animals which illustrate the specialization needed by unicellular organisms to carry out all of the life processes. Examines the Paramecium in depth, as well as other ciliates such as Stentor, Voricella and Blepharisma. Looks at parasitic and nonmotile sporozoans, particularly Plasmodium, the cause of malaria. Part one of two parts on Protozans and part of a five - part series on microscopy prelab produced by Bill Pieper.
Science; Science - Natural
Dist - HRMC

Proud Barns of North America 8 MIN
16mm
Color
LC 79-700362; 79 - 700362
Examines the architecture, construction and use of several old barns in North America.
Fine Arts; Industrial and Technical Education
Dist - DEERE **Prod** - DEERE 1978

The Proud Breed
BETA / VHS
Color
Depicts Arabian horses. Hosted by Wayne Newton.
Physical Education and Recreation
Dist - EQVDL **Prod** - EQVDL

Proud Free Men 26 MIN
VHS / 16mm
Color (G)
$55.00 rental _ #PFMN - 000
Examines how the 19th century free people of color in New Orleans flourished within their tight coterie between 1840 - 1880. Looks at how these people of mixed race lived and explains their contributions.
History - United States
Dist - PBS **Prod** - WYESTV

Proud to be me - developing self - esteem
VHS
Color (H)
$209.00 purchase _ #06829 - 025
Combines interviews with dramatic scenarios to give insights on how teens can control the way they feel about themselves. Encourages teens to evaluate and accept their strengths and weaknesses and discover how to make changes to get through tough times. In four parts. Includes teacher's guide, library kit and 25 subscriptions to Time magazine for 12 weeks and 12 weekly guides.
Health and Safety; Psychology; Sociology
Dist - GA **Prod** - GA 1992

Proud towers 58 MIN
16mm / VHS / U-matic
Pride of place series
Color (C)
$40.00, $24.50 rental _ #50823; $89.95 purchase _ #EX985
Examines the skyscraper as an expression of national and corporate pride. Follows the development of the skyscraper from the Gothic Woolworth Building, to the glass boxes of the international style, up to the Transco Tower and PPG Place, which share the spirit of past skyscrapers. Part of an eight - part series hosted by architect Robert Stern.
Business and Economics; Fine Arts; Geography - United States; Industrial and Technical Education
Dist - PSU **Prod** - FOTH
FOTH

Proudly we hail 45 MIN
VHS
Color (I J)
$29.95 purchase _ #ST - BG9000
Examines the symbolism and history of the United States flag.
Civics and Political Systems
Dist - INSTRU

Proven strategies for competitive success series
Presents four programs on competitive success strategy. Includes 'Competing Through Technology,' 'Michael Porter on Competitive Strategy,' 'Competing Through Quality' and 'Rosabeth Moss Kanter on Synergies, Alliances and New Ventures.'

Competing through information technology	112 MIN
Competing through quality	102 MIN
Michael Porter on competitive strategy	146 MIN
Rosabeth Moss Kanter on synergies, alliances and new ventures	93 MIN

Dist - NATTYL **Prod** - HBS

Provence and the Riviera 20 MIN
U-matic / VHS
Color (J)
LC 82-706760
Shows the romantic and enchanting regions of Provence and the Riviera that once attracted artists, such as Picasso, Cezanne and Fragonard. Visits the cities of Saint Tropez, Cannes and Marseilles. Also shows the native flower markets and cafes which help to make this area a special place to visit.
Geography - World; History - World
Dist - AWSS **Prod** - AWSS 1981

Provide for the Common Defense 24 MIN
16mm
B&W
LC FIE58-80
Discusses national defense. Emphasizes its importance to security.
Civics and Political Systems
Dist - USNAC **Prod** - USDD 1957

Providence College
VHS
Campus clips series
Color (H C A)
$29.95 purchase _ #CC0105V
Takes a video visit to the campus of Providence College in Rhode Island. Shows many of the distinctive features of the campus, and interviews students about their experiences. Provides information on the composition of the student body, professors, academics, social life, housing, and other subjects.
Education
Dist - CAMV

Providing a Focus and Developing and Creating 29 MIN
VHS / 16mm
Diversity in Communication Series
Color (C)
$200.00 purchase _ #277202
Catalogues motivational 'beginnings' for instructional projects. Focuses on language - communication - arts. 'Providing A Focus' examines a few of the diverse methods for motivating students.
Education; Mathematics; Psychology; Social Science
Dist - ACCESS **Prod** - ACCESS 1989

Providing care at home - Tape IV 30 MIN
VHS
All about aging series
Color (A G)
$195.00 series purchase, $25.00 series rental
Describes how to make the home a safe and efficient place in which to provide care for an aged person. Illustrates useful medical equipment. Part four of a four - part series not available separately. Includes workbook and provider's guide.
Guidance and Counseling; Health and Safety; Home Economics; Sociology
Dist - AGEVI **Prod** - AGEVI 1990

Providing Feedback 19 MIN
VHS / U-matic
Videosearch Behavior Skill Model Series
Color
Fine Arts; Psychology
Dist - DELTAK **Prod** - DELTAK

Providing foot care - Part III 23 MIN
VHS
Foot care for the older adult series
Color (C PRO G)
$395.00 purchase _ #R921 - VI - 012
Shows how to perform foot care for the older patient. Reveals that many of these patients have long, thick tonails, excessively dry skin and other conditions that warrant attention. Illustrates how foot care by nurses can prevent and - or reduce the discomfort and decreased mobility which can accompany foot problems. Presents procedures involved in providing proper foot care such as trimming toenails, buffing corns and calluses and massaging the skin. Stresses that providing foot care can help in the detection of skin, circulatory and neuromuscular problems, resulting in a prompt referral to a primary care specialist. Part of a four - part series on foot care for the elderly.
Health and Safety; Sociology
Dist - HSCIC **Prod** - CESTAG 1993

Providing for Family Needs 15 MIN
U-matic / VHS
Across Cultures Series
Color (I)
Shows how family needs are met by the Tarahumara Indians of Mexico, the Baoule of West Africa and the Japanese. Reveals that the Tarahumara and the Baoule grow their own food or grow cash crops which can be sold for money to buy goods. Contrasts this with the Japanese who must buy all their goods, either on the local or international market.
Geography - World; Social Science; Sociology
Dist - AITECH **Prod** - POSIMP 1983

Providing medical and nursing care for the dying patient 60 MIN
VHS
Hospice ... living with dying series
Color (R G)
$49.95 purchase _ #HOLD1
Trains clergy and pastoral ministers, physicians and nurses, social workers and therapists, counselors and volunteers and others who provide care and outreach to seriously ill patients and their families. Informs those who want information about options for care of their seriously ill family members. Features the Visiting Nurse Service of New York's Hospice Care Team and some of the patients and families under their care, as well as Dr Patrick Del Zoppo. Part of three parts on hospice care.
Guidance and Counseling; Health and Safety; Religion and Philosophy
Dist - CTNA **Prod** - CTNA

Providing professional bell service 22 MIN
VHS
Color (H C A IND)
LC 90-716349
Trains employees in the hotel industry in proper bell service to guests. Produced by Media Magic.
Business and Economics; Psychology
Dist - EIAHM

Provinces and People 14 MIN
16mm / U-matic / VHS
Canada's Provinces and People Series
Color (I J H)
The second edition of Canada - Geography Of The Americas. Shows the land and people of Canada. Emphasizes the relation of Canada's natural resources to the lives of its people.
Geography - World
Dist - CORF **Prod** - CORF

Proving generalizations - Pt 1 - test pattern principle 32 MIN
16mm
Teaching high school mathematics - first course series; No 29
B&W (T)
Mathematics
Dist - MLA **Prod** - UICSM 1967

Proving generalizations - Pt 2 - classroom examples 31 MIN
16mm

Teaching high school mathematics - first course series; No 30
B&W (T)
Mathematics
Dist - MLA **Prod** - UICSM 1967

Proving Meters with Open Tank Provers 28 MIN
Slide / VHS / 16mm
Color (A IND)
$240.00, $250.00 purchase _ #13.2980, #53.2980
Reviews procedures for using open tank provers to prove meters. Presents roles of those who must perform or witness provings.
Industrial and Technical Education; Mathematics; Psychology; Social Science
Dist - UTEXPE

Proving Meters with Pipe Provers 34 MIN
U-matic / VHS
Color (IND)
Describes the components in a bidirectional U - type pipe prover and their functions. Shows a typical meter proving with a pipe prover and covers filling out a proving report. Conforms to current API Manual of Petroleum Measurement Standards.
Business and Economics; Industrial and Technical Education; Social Science
Dist - UTEXPE **Prod** - UTEXPE

Proving Personal Injury Claims to Arbitrators 120 MIN
U-matic / Cassette / VHS / 16mm
Color; Mono (PRO)
Covers proof of personal injury claims in four arbitration settings; judicial arbitration, arbitration by private agreement, unisured motorist arbitration and federal judicial arbitration.
Civics and Political Systems
Dist - CCEB **Prod** - CCEB

Provisions Affecting Qualified Plans 30 MIN
VHS / U-matic
Tax Reform Act of 1984 Series
Color (PRO)
Business and Economics; Civics and Political Systems; Social Science
Dist - ALIABA **Prod** - ALIABA

Prowler, the Lone Trailer Story 12 MIN
16mm
Color
LC 76-702608
Documents how the first Prowler Travel Trailer television commercial was made.
Business and Economics; Fine Arts; Psychology; Social Science
Dist - FLTWDE **Prod** - FLTWDE 1976

Prowling with the mighty polar bear 24 MIN
VHS
Wild refuge series
Color (G)
$39.95 purchase
Records a polar bear and her cubs playing in the Arctic tundra. Witnesses baby harp seals clubbed to death for fashionable furs in the gulf of the St Lawrence River. Part of a thirteen - part series on the North American wilderness. Each episode documents a different area and shows how animal species cope with their surroundings to survive.
Geography - World; Science - Natural
Dist - CNEMAG **Prod** - HOBELP 1976

Proxemics - Distance 30 MIN
U-matic / VHS
Language and Meaning Series
Color (C)
English Language; Psychology
Dist - GPN **Prod** - WUSFTV 1983

Proxyhawks 80 MIN
16mm
B&W
LC 74-701248
Relates a story about the relationship between a woman, a man and their animals.
Guidance and Counseling; Psychology; Sociology
Dist - CANFDC **Prod** - CFDEVC 1971

Prudence Crandall 51 MIN
U-matic / VHS / 16mm
Profiles in Courage Series
B&W (I J H)
LC 83-706542; FIA65-1424
Describes Prudence Crandall's importance in civil rights activities on the behalf of black Americans in the 1783 to 1860 period. Based on book Profiles In Courage by John F Kennedy.
Biography; Civics and Political Systems; History - United States
Dist - SSSSV **Prod** - SAUDEK 1965

Prudence Crandall - Pt 1 25 MIN
16mm
Profiles in Courage Series
B&W (J)
LC FIA65-1424
Describes a school teacher who insisted on the right of every American child, regardless of color, to be educated. Considers equal opportunity in education and the status of women and Blacks in America.
Civics and Political Systems
Dist - SSSSV **Prod** - SAUDEK 1966

Prudence Crandall - Pt 2 25 MIN
16mm
Profiles in Courage Series
B&W (J)
LC FIA65-1424
Describes a school teacher who insisted on the right of every American child, regardless of color, to be educated. Considers equal opportunity in education and the status of women and Blacks in America.
Civics and Political Systems
Dist - SSSSV **Prod** - SAUDEK 1966

Prudhoe Bay - or Bust 30 MIN
16mm / U-matic / VHS
Our Vanishing Wilderness Series
Color (J H A)
Points out that monetary interests and ecological and conservation interests are at odds over the issue of building 800 miles of hot oil pipeline through the Arctic tundra in Alaska.
Business and Economics; Geography - United States; Science - Natural
Dist - IU **Prod** - NET 1970

Pruning 47 MIN
VHS / U-matic / BETA
Color (A G)
$14.95 _ #MR608
Teaches how, when and where to prune trees, as well as why to prune. All types of bushes and trees, including deciduous and evergreen varieties are covered.
Agriculture
Dist - BAKERT

Pruning 29 MIN
Videoreel / VT2
Dig it Series
Color
Features Tom Lied detailing what should be done with various types of woody plants to give them better appearance and better health.
Agriculture
Dist - PBS **Prod** - WMVSTV

Pruning 47 MIN
VHS / BETA
Lawn and Garden Series
Color
Shows how to prune a variety of trees and bushes. Demonstrates the proper tools to use. Explains when to prune trees.
Agriculture
Dist - MOHOMV **Prod** - MOHOMV

Pruning 48 MIN
BETA / VHS / 16mm
Color (G)
$39.95 purchase _ #VT1106
Shows how, when, and where to prune trees, and tells why. Demonstrates the proper techniques and tools. Covers a wide variety of trees and bushes. Taught by Ed Hume.
Agriculture
Dist - RMIBHF **Prod** - RMIBHF

Pruning 47 MIN
VHS
Garden Design Series
(H C A)
$159.60 series of 8 purchase _ #MX600SV
Presents garden expert Ed Hume who explains how, when, why, and where to prune plants in the garden. Discusses a wide variety of trees and bushes, pruning equipment, techniques, and more.
Agriculture
Dist - CAMV

Pruning Grapes 6 MIN
VHS
Color (A)
$45.00 purchase, $16.00 rental
Shows, step - by - step, the process of pruning grapevines. Includes the rationale for each step.
Agriculture
Dist - CORNRS **Prod** - CORNRS 1986

Pruning of Woody Plants 29 MIN
U-matic
Grounds Maintenance Training Series
Color
Demonstrates how to prune shrubs, small trees, vines, hedges and evergreens. Includes definitions, identification of pruning tools and when to use them.
Agriculture
Dist - UMITV **Prod** - UMITV 1978

Pruning practices and standards
VHS
Principles of shade and ornamental tree pruning and pruning 'standards for shade trees series
Color (G)
$90.00 purchase _ #6 - 205 - 201P
Covers the limits and criteria for arboricultural work. Reviews the four classes of pruning - fine, standard, hazard and crown reduction pruning. Part of two - parts on principles of shade and ornamental tree pruning. Produced by the National Arborist Association.
Agriculture; Psychology; Science - Natural
Dist - VEP

Pruning Practices at the Brooklyn Botanic Garden 22 MIN
U-matic / VHS
Color (A)
Demonstrates the proper pruning techniques for shrubs, deciduous and evergreen trees. Includes the Japanese art of cloud pruning.
Agriculture
Dist - BBG **Prod** - BBG 1975

Pruning Techniques 49 MIN
VHS
Color (G)
$160.00 purchase _ #6 - 067 - 000P
Offers a two - video tape series on pruning. Presents basic concepts of pruning in part one. Part two shows how to apply the concepts learned in part one. Includes teaching guide.
Agriculture; Science - Natural
Dist - VEP **Prod** - VEP

Pruning techniques series
Advanced pruning 20 MIN
Elements of pruning 26 MIN
Dist - VEP

Pruning tools and techniques
VHS
Principles of shade and ornamental tree pruning and pruning 'standards for shade trees series
Color (G)
$90.00 purchase _ #6 - 205 - 101P
Covers the methods, equipment and reasons for pruning trees. Part of two - parts on principles of shade and ornamental tree pruning. Produced by the National Arborist Association.
Agriculture; Psychology; Science - Natural
Dist - VEP

PS - Caring for Pretty Special Children 90 MIN
VHS
Color (H)
$79.95 purchase
Trains caregivers of abused and neglected children. Presents six 15 - minute dramatized segments - an overview of the series, description of abused children and their behavior, encouraging group particpation by such children, appropriate behavior for staff, screening methods for psychological and physical abuse and pointers on working with the families of abused children. Features Alaina Reed of Sesame Street as moderator.
Guidance and Counseling; Sociology
Dist - SCETV **Prod** - SCETV 1989

Psalm 104 7 MIN
16mm
Color (I)
LC 71-705156
Presents an iconographic interpretation of a time painting to show Psalm 104 as an esthetic, visual, verbal and musical experience.
Fine Arts; Guidance and Counseling; Psychology
Dist - SIM **Prod** - SCHNDL 1969

PSAT and national merit scholarship qualifying test preparation - a series
PSAT and national merit scholarship qualifying test preparation - series
Dist - KRLSOF

PSAT and national merit scholarship qualifying test preparation - series
PSAT and national merit scholarship qualifying test preparation - a'series
Color
Offers tutoring for the PSAT and National Merit Scholarship Qualifying Test exam, in two versions. The school version consists of nine 2 hr lessons. The home version consists of the first five lessons. Math - All Skill Areas And Problem Types; Math - Quantitative Comparison; Model Examination - I With Explanations; Model Examination - II With Explanations; Model Examination - III With Explanations; Preparing Your Students For The SAT; PSAT And NMSQT Overview And Test Taking - - ; Reading Comprehension; Vocabulary And Word Analogies.

Education
Dist - KRLSOF **Prod** - KRLSOF 1985

PSAT and National Merit Scholarship Qualifying Test Preparation Series
Model Examination - I with Explanations 120 MIN
Model Examination - II with Explanations 120 MIN
Model Examination - III with Explanations 120 MIN
PSAT and NMSQT Overview and Test Taking Strategy 120 MIN
Dist - KRLSOF

PSAT and NMSQT Overview and Test Taking Strategy 120 MIN
VHS / U-matic
PSAT and National Merit Scholarship Qualifying Test Preparation 'Series
Color
Education
Dist - KRLSOF **Prod** - KRLSOF

Pseudo - Rabies Eradication - a Producer's Program 18 MIN
VHS / 16mm
Color (H C A)
Visits with three pork producers whose swine herds have been infected with the pseudo - rabies virus. Describes the national program to eradicate the disease.
Agriculture; Health and Safety
Dist - IOWA **Prod** - IOWA 1989

PSI - Boundaries of the Mind 17 MIN
U-matic / VHS / 16mm
Science - New Frontiers Series
Color (H C A)
LC 76-702966
Presents experiments being conducted to explore and define the phenomena of PSI, an unexplained, extra sensory type of communication.
Psychology
Dist - PHENIX **Prod** - PHENIX 1976

Psoriasis 21 MIN
VHS / U-matic
Color (PRO)
Provides information which differentiates psoriasis from eczema, pityriasis rosea, syphilis, and Bowen's carcinoma. Describes the clinical course of the disease, including time of onset, hereditary factors, waxing and waning course and exacerbation following trauma. Includes treatment with topical steroids, occlusion, intralesional injections of steroids, tar therapy and maintenance with methotrexate.
Health and Safety
Dist - UMICHM **Prod** - UMICHM 1976

Psoriasis 25 MIN
VHS / U-matic
Color (PRO)
Describes the lesions of psoriasis and defines treatment procedures.
Health and Safety; Science - Natural
Dist - PRIMED **Prod** - PRIMED

PSSC College Physics Films Series
Time Dilation - an Experiment with Mu - Mesons 36 MIN
The Ultimate Speed - an Exploration with High Energy Electrons 38 MIN
Dist - MLA

PSSC physics films series
Behavior of Gases 15 MIN
Change of Scale 23 MIN
Collisions of hard spheres 19 MIN
Conservation of Energy 27 MIN
Coulomb Force Constant 34 MIN
Coulomb's Law 28 MIN
Counting Electrical Charges in Motion 22 MIN
Crystals 25 MIN
Definite and multiple proportions 30 MIN
Deflecting forces 30 MIN
E M F 20 MIN
Elastic Collisions and Stored Energy 27 MIN
Electric Fields 25 MIN
Electric Lines of Force 7 MIN
Electrical Potential Energy and Potential Difference 54 MIN
Electrical Potential Energy and Potential Difference, Pt 1 27 MIN
Electrical Potential Energy and Potential Difference, Pt 2 27 MIN
Electromagnetic Waves 33 MIN
Electrons in a uniform magnetic field 10 MIN
Elementary charges and transfer of kinetic energy 34 MIN
Elements, compounds and mixtures 33 MIN
Elliptic Orbits 19 MIN
Energy and work 28 MIN
Forces 23 MIN
Frames of Reference 28 MIN
Free Fall and Projectile Motion - Falling Bodies 27 MIN
Inertia 26 MIN
Inertial Mass 19 MIN
Interference of Photons 13 MIN
Introduction to Optics 23 MIN
Long Time Intervals 25 MIN
A Magnet Laboratory 20 MIN
The Mass of atoms - Pt 1 20 MIN
The Mass of atoms - Pt 2 27 MIN
Measurement 21 MIN
Measuring Large Distances 29 MIN
Measuring Short Distances 20 MIN
Mechanical Energy and Thermal Energy 22 MIN
Millikan Experiment 30 MIN
A Million to One 5 MIN
Moving with the Center of Mass 26 MIN
Periodic Motion 33 MIN
Photo - Electric Effect 28 MIN
Photons 19 MIN
Pressure of Light 23 MIN
Random events 31 MIN
Rutherford Atom 40 MIN
Short Time Intervals 21 MIN
Simple Waves 27 MIN
Sound Waves in Air 35 MIN
Speed of Light 21 MIN
Straight Line Kinematics 34 MIN
Time and Clocks 28 MIN
Universal Gravitation 31 MIN
Vector Kinematics 16 MIN
Dist - MLA

PSSC Physics Series
Behavior of Gases 13 MIN
Photo - Electric Effect 28 MIN
Dist - MLA

Psst - Hammerman's after you 28 MIN
16mm / U-matic / VHS
Afterschool specials series
Color (I J H)
LC 77-703088
Adapted from the novel The 18th emergency by Betsy Byars, about Mouse, a timid 11 - year - old boy who provokes the school bully. Shows how Mouse learns a lesson in honor and self - respect when he faces the consequences of his actions.
Guidance and Counseling; Psychology; Sociology
Dist - CORF **Prod** - TAHSEM 1977

Psychedelic Wet 8 MIN
U-matic / VHS / 16mm
Color (J)
LC FIA68-847
Presents an impressionistic view of water. Views reflections on the ceiling of the sea off the Bahamas, a pretty girl in a pool and great waves off the north shore in Oahu, Hawaii.
Fine Arts
Dist - AIMS **Prod** - GROENG 1968

Psychiatric Evaluation 41 MIN
U-matic / VHS
Psychiatry Learning System, Pt 1 - Assessments Series
Color (PRO)
Gives Norman Kagan's view to assessment and the mental status examination.
Guidance and Counseling; Health and Safety; Psychology
Dist - HSCIC **Prod** - HSCIC 1982

Psychiatric intervention and care series
Presents a three - part series on psychiatric intervention and care. Includes the titles The Art of Intervention - Preventing Aggression in Mental Health Facilities; Dynamics of Treatment Planning; Group Work - Fundamentals of Group Process.
The Art of intervention - preventing aggression in mental health facilities 24 MIN
Dynamics of treatment planning 22 MIN
Group work - fundamentals of group process 26 MIN
Dist - CONMED **Prod** - CALDMH 1982

The Psychiatric interview - Module II
Videodisc
Psychiatric interview series
Color (PRO C)
$1300.00 purchase _ #C891 - IV - 022
Presents selected segments from the initial interview between a psychiatrist and a young woman admitted to the psychiatric ward the night before after attempting suicide with aspirin tablets. Allows students to place themselves in the role of the psychiatrist by requiring them to answer questions or select responses related to the segments. Provides confirmation and reinforcement for appropriate physician responses and remediation by returning to the appropriate segment of the interview. Requires an IBM InfoWindow Touch Display Monitor, a 20MB hard disk and a Pioneer LD - V6000 videodisc player or equivalent. Contact distributor for other requirements.
Guidance and Counseling; Health and Safety
Dist - HSCIC

Psychiatric interview series
The Psychiatric interview - Module II
Dist - HSCIC

Psychiatric Medical Records - Treatment Plan 27 MIN
U-matic
Color (PRO)
LC 77-706084
Presents a basic review of the essential content of psychiatric medical records. Features Dr George J Weinstein and a resident psychiatrist discussing medical records and their role in quality of care, research and avoidance of litigation.
Civics and Political Systems; Psychology
Dist - USNAC **Prod** - USVA 1977

Psychiatric mental health
VHS
Mosby cameo series; Volume 9
Color (C PRO G)
$150.00 purchase
Presents the study by nurse researcher Dr Kathleen Buckwalter of psychiatric mental health clients in rural settings. Examines her successful outreach program for home care of rural clients. Part of a series featuring the work of outstanding nurse researchers.
Health and Safety
Dist - MOSBY **Prod** - SITHTA

Psychiatric - Mental Health Nursing Series
Anxiety - concept and manifestations 30 MIN
The Depressed client 30 MIN
The Long - Term Psychiatric Patient 40 MIN
The Manipulative Client 30 MIN
Nursing in a Multi - Cultural Society 30 MIN
Psychogeriatrics 40 MIN
Psychosocial Assessment - Pt I 30 MIN
Psychosocial Assessment - Pt II 30 MIN
Psychotherapeutic Interview 30 MIN
The Suspicious Client 30 MIN
The Withdrawn Client 30 MIN
Dist - AJN

The Psychiatrist 2 MIN
U-matic / VHS / 16mm
Coffee Breaks I Series
Color (A)
Offers a humorous tale designed to introduce coffee breaks in which a man on the psychiatrist's couch thinks he's a cup of coffee, and the doctor helps couch an ordinary announcement in unusual terms.
Business and Economics; Literature and Drama
Dist - CORF **Prod** - MBACC 1983

The Psychiatrist in the community 22 MIN
16mm / VHS
Documentaries for learning series
B&W (C G PRO)
$70.00 purchase, $31.00 rental _ #24270
Offers excerpts from lectures delivered in a 1965 seminar by the late Dr Erich Lindemann, a pioneer in community psychiatry who surveyed the developing field of social psychiatry. Contains material of historical importance which remains relevant to the mental health field. Part of a series produced for use by health care professionals and educators.
Health and Safety; Psychology
Dist - PSU **Prod** - MASON 1967

Psychiatry and Law - How are they Related - Pt 1 29 MIN
16mm
Concepts and Controversies in Modern Medicine Series
B&W
LC 75-701277
Presents Dr Thomas S Szasz, Dr Bernard Diamond and Dr Alexander D Brooks discussing the role of the psychiatrist in the courtroom and in prison.
Civics and Political Systems; Health and Safety; Psychology; Sociology
Dist - USNAC **Prod** - NMAC 1970

Psychiatry and the System 25 MIN
VHS / U-matic
Color
Examines the psychiatrists's role as well as that of the doctor in society, using Dr Seymour Pollack, Professor of Psychiatry at USC School of Medicine, and John Miner, a lawyer who was formerly Deputy DA in charge of medical legal matters in Los Angeles. Shows them, with host Mario Machado, as they discuss the ways doctors are

involved in practicing medicine in deciding who is a threat to society because of mental illness, as well as the psychiatrist's function in court.
Health and Safety; Psychology
Dist - MEDCOM **Prod** - MEDCOM

Psychiatry comes of age 24 MIN
VHS
Meaning of madness series
Color (C G PRO)
$175.00 purchase, $19.00 rental _ #35078
Describes the emergence of social psychiatry outside the asylum system and its incorporation into conventional psychiatric practice during the period between the two world wars. Highlights development of treatment for battle neurosis by the US military and the concept of the therapeutic community at Cassel Hospital in London. Part of a four - part series which traces the history of psychiatry in a societal context from the mid - 1800s to modern - day England.
History - World; Psychology; Sociology
Dist - PSU **Prod** - BBC 1982

Psychiatry learning system - disorders - Pt 2 series
Anxiety disorders 34 MIN
Dist - HSCIC

Psychiatry Learning System, Pt 1 - Assessments Series
Psychiatric Evaluation 41 MIN
Psychodynamic Considerations and Defense Mechanisms 23 MIN
Psychological Evaluation 21 MIN
Psychosocial Factors in Physical Illness 27 MIN
Dist - HSCIC

Psychiatry Learning System, Pt 2 - Disorders Series
Affective disorders 62 MIN
Behavioral Treatment 56 MIN
Disorders of Infancy, Childhood, and Adolescence 85 MIN
Impulse Control Disorders 27 MIN
Organic Mental Disorders 30 MIN
Other Treatment Modalities 18 MIN
Personality Disorders 66 MIN
Psychopharmacology
Psychosexual Disorders 78 MIN
Psychosocial Treatments
Schizophrenic Disorders, Psychoses not Elsewhere Classified, and Paranoid Disorders 66 MIN
Sleep Disorders
Somatoform and Dissociative Disorders 70 MIN
Dist - HSCIC

Psychiatry learning system series
Substance use disorders
Dist - HSCIC

Psychic and spiritual healing 30 MIN
VHS / BETA
Perspectives on healing series
Color (G)
$29.95 purchase _ #S334
Features Dr Stanley Krippner, psychologist, who tells of his experiences with native shamans and healers in the Americas and Asia. Asks if the methods and ideas of native spiritual healers can be incorporated into modern psychological and medical practice. Part of a series giving alternative perspectives on healing.
Health and Safety; Psychology; Religion and Philosophy; Social Science
Dist - THINKA **Prod** - THINKA

Psychic confessions 41 MINS
VHS
Color (J H C G A R)
$49.95 purchase, $10.00 rental _ #35 - 847 - 8516
Features Christian magician Danny Korem in an expose of an alleged psychic's tactics. Interviews the exposed psychic to demonstrate the methods he used.
Religion and Philosophy
Dist - APH **Prod** - VISVID

The Psychic Parrot 19 MIN
U-matic / VHS / 16mm
Color (J)
Deals with a TV - viewing family of apartment dwellers watching the drama unfolding of portended end of the world as foretold by a psychic parrot. Focuses on a group of people selected by the President to rocket to the moon to permit survival of the human race which is treated as a news event by TV reporters. Shows reactions of apartment dwellers to TV reporting as 'the end' nears.
Fine Arts; Social Science; Sociology
Dist - BCNFL **Prod** - PARROT 1979

Psychic Phenomena and the Occult 30 MIN
U-matic / VHS
Ethics in America Series
Color (H C A)
Shows professional conjurer James Randi, professor of psychology Ray Hayman, author Ethel Grodzins and psycho - physicist Wilbur Franklin discussing paranormal and psychic phenomena, and taking sides in regard to its validity.
Psychology; Religion and Philosophy; Sociology
Dist - AMHUMA **Prod** - AMHUMA

Psychics, Saints and Scientists 33 MIN
16mm / VHS / U-matic
Color (H C A)
LC 72-700930
Presents parapsychologist Thelma Moss who introduces the field of psychic phenomena and acts as Mistress of Ceremonies for a discussion by scientists who are responsible for particular areas of study, such as healing, bio - feedback training, psychokinesis, telepathy and extrasensory perception. Explains that only recently has parapsychology gained respect as a field of serious scientific consideration.
Psychology; Religion and Philosophy; Science
Dist - HP **Prod** - HP 1972

Psychling 25 MIN
16mm / U-matic / VHS
#107779 - 0 3/4
Chronicles the record - breaking cross - country bicycle trip of John Marino, and shows how the techniques of goal setting, personal motivation, and crisis management that made his feat possible can apply to the workplace as well.
Business and Economics; Guidance and Counseling; Physical Education and Recreation
Dist - MGHT
ATHI

Psycho 109 MIN
VHS
B&W (G)
$59.95 purchase _ #S00905
Presents the Alfred Hitchcock suspense thriller about a lonely motel, multiple murders, and money stolen from a bank. Stars Anthony Perkins, Janet Leigh, Vera Miles, John Gavin, and others.
Fine Arts; Literature and Drama
Dist - UILL

Psycho - Educational Assessment 24 MIN
16mm
League School for Seriously Disturbed Children Series
Color
LC 75-702424
Shows how children are admitted to the League School for seriously disturbed children and tells how they are initially and progressively evaluated by staff clinicians representing a variety of disciplines.
Education; Psychology
Dist - USNAC **Prod** - USBEH 1973

Psycho Mein Amour 38 MIN
16mm
Color
Presents Douglas Davis' film entry selected from the 1985 Whitney Biennial Film and Video Exhibition.
Fine Arts
Dist - AFA **Prod** - AFA 1986

Psychoactive 28 MIN
VHS
Color (J H C G A) (SPANISH)
$79.95 purchase _ #AH45508
Documents how nine systems of the body are negatively affected by the use of psychoactive drugs. Deals with issues of tolerance, withdrawal and dependence. Available in Spanish - language version only.
Guidance and Counseling; Health and Safety; Psychology; Sociology
Dist - HTHED **Prod** - HTHED

Psychoactive 29 MIN
U-matic / VHS / 16mm
Color (J)
LC 76-702873
Uses actor George Carlin's comedy routine to show how the nine systems of the human body are affected by each of the five classifications of psychoactive drugs. Explores tolerance, withdrawal and dependence.
Health and Safety; Psychology; Sociology
Dist - PFP **Prod** - COHNW 1976

Psychoactive prescription drugs and human physiology 18 MIN
VHS / 16mm
Color (H C G)
$445.00, $360.00 purchase, $75.00 rental _ #8278
Describes the types of psychoactive drugs and shows how they work in the human body. Explores the dangers of abusing these medications. Reveals that the margin between therapeutic dose and overdose can be slim.
Guidance and Counseling; Psychology
Dist - AIMS **Prod** - AIMS 1991

The Psychobiology of Stress 10 MIN
VHS / 16mm
Stress - Unwinding the Spring Series
Color (H C A PRO)
$195.00 purchase, $75.00 rental _ #8074
Considers the physiological as well as the psychological manifestations of stress.
Health and Safety; Psychology
Dist - AIMS **Prod** - HOSSN 1988

Psychodelics - the bad trip 26 MIN
U-matic / VHS
Color (G)
$249.00 purchase _ #7491
Features Joe and Denny, former users of psychedelics or hallucinatory drugs. Reviews the physical and psychological effects on users of mind - altering drugs which can be emotionally addictive and discusses the unpredictability of the effects of acid, crystal, angel dust and white lightning.
Guidance and Counseling; Health and Safety; Psychology; Sociology
Dist - VISIVI **Prod** - VISIVI 1991

Psychodrama in Group Process Series
Interstaff Communications 42 MIN
A Problem of Acceptance 47 MIN
Dist - NYU

Psychodynamic Considerations and Defense Mechanisms 23 MIN
U-matic / VHS
Psychiatry Learning System, Pt 1 - Assessments Series
Color (PRO)
Deals with theories of the unconscious and with some of the ways the unconscious is manifested verbally and behaviorally.
Psychology
Dist - HSCIC **Prod** - HSCIC 1982

Psychodynamic vs behaviorial, Jane Kessler vs Richard Whelan 30 MIN
VHS
Video training workshops on child variance series
Color (T PRO)
$135.00 purchase _ #M199h
Presents discussion between Jane Kessler and Richard Whelan representing psychodynamic and behavioral viewpoints respectively. Part of a six - part series produced by William C Morse and Judith M Smith.
Psychology; Sociology
Dist - CEXPCN **Prod** - CEXPCN

The Psychodynamics of liberation 90 MIN
VHS / BETA
Innerwork series
Color (G)
$49.95 purchase _ #W068
Reveals that under the apparent separation of individuals there is a level of unity and interconnectedness. Features Dr Kathleen Speeth who suggests that true liberation involves attaining an awareness of the level of interconnectedness.
Guidance and Counseling; History - United States; History - World; Psychology
Dist - THINKA **Prod** - THINKA

Psychodynamics of Neurosis 56 MIN
U-matic
Color (C)
Contains a comprehensive overview of the psychodynamics of neurotic behavior.
Health and Safety; Science - Natural
Dist - UOKLAH **Prod** - UOKLAH 1980

Psychodynamics of Pain 19 MIN
U-matic
Management of Pain Series
Color (PRO)
LC 80-707393
Module 2 on Management of pain series.
Health and Safety
Dist - BRA **Prod** - BRA 1980

The Psychoeducational Profile - introduction to scoring the PEP 33 MIN
U-matic / VHS
PEP subseries - Autism series
Color (C PRO)
$395.00 purchase, $80.00 rental _ #C850 - VI - 132
Demonstrates how to administer and score the PEP by showing a variety of children being tested. Reveals that the PEP test has three purposes - to assess a child's functional skills in seven different areas, to evaluate the presence or absence of pathological behavior, and to allow for individualized educational planning based on the emerging skills the child demonstrates. Part of a three - part subseries on PEP - PsychoEducational Profile - presented by Dr Eric Schopler, which is part of a series on autism.
Health and Safety; Psychology
Dist - HSCIC

The Psychoeducational Profile test tape - scoring the PEP 55 MIN
VHS / U-matic
PEP subseries - Autism series
Color (C PRO)
$395.00 purchase, $80.00 rental _ #C850 - VI - 135
Shows an edited version of the PsychoEducational Profile being given to an eight - year - old autistic child. Allows viewers to score each test item, then provides correct answers. Part of a three - part subseries on PEP presented by Dr Eric Schopler, which is part of a series on autism.
Health and Safety; Psychology
Dist - HSCIC

Psychogenic Diseases in Infancy 20 MIN
16mm
Film Studies of the Psychoanalytic Research Project on Problems in 'Infancy Series
B&W (C T)
Illustrates a series of psychogenic diseases and attempts to relate them to the infants' relationships with their mothers.
Health and Safety; Psychology; Sociology
Dist - NYU **Prod** - SPITZ 1952

Psychogeriatrics 40 MIN
16mm / U-matic
Psychiatric - Mental Health Nursing Series
Color (PRO)
LC 76-701624
Presents interviews with patients of nursing homes which illustrate the dynamics of two major psychiatric syndromes of the elderly, chronic brain syndrome and depression. Discusses nursing assessment and related planning for care of the elderly to minimize these problems.
Health and Safety; Sociology
Dist - AJN **Prod** - AJN 1976

Psychokillers 70 MIN
16mm
B&W (G) (FRENCH WITH ENGLISH SUBTITLES)
$120.00 rental
Satirizes cheap horror classics including gags from American horror films. Portrays a punk heroine who falls into strange real - life horror scenes which include a carnivorous plant, giant bean pods and living brains. The music is 'pure psychobilly.' A Jackie Leger production.
Fine Arts; Literature and Drama
Dist - CANCIN

Psychokinesis, or mind - over - matter 30 MIN
BETA / VHS
Exploring parapsychology series
Color (G)
$29.95 purchase _ #S285
Reveals that to learn psychokineses, it helps to attain a Zen - like state of both 'focus on' and 'indifference to' the experimental task. Features Dr Julian Isaacs, professor of parapsychology. Part of a four - part series on exploring parapsychology.
Psychology
Dist - THINKA **Prod** - THINKA

Psychokinesis (Russia and Here) 29 MIN
Videoreel / VT2
Who is Man Series
Color
Features Dr Charles Thomas Cayce and Dr Puryear who show and explain a film made on a recent research trip when Dr Puryear met and observed at work two women especially gifted in the practice of psychokinesis.
Geography - World; Religion and Philosophy
Dist - PBS **Prod** - WHROTV

Psychologic Stress in Critical Illness 26 MIN
U-matic
Stress in Critical Illness Series
Color (PRO)
LC 80-707622
Reviews physiologic responses identified with stress and discusses the stages of the psychologic general adaptation syndrome. Describes appropriate nursing intervention during this stage. Module 2 on the Stress in critical illness series.
Health and Safety; Psychology
Dist - BRA **Prod** - BRA 1980

Psychological Adjustment to College 43 MIN
16mm
B&W
LC 77-714204
Frederick Coons describes for beginning college students the major developmental tasks that they will encounter during their college years.
Education; Guidance and Counseling; Psychology; Sociology
Dist - IU **Prod** - IU 1971

Psychological Adjustment to Dizziness 50 MIN
VHS / U-matic
Dizziness and Related Balance Disorders Series
Color
Health and Safety
Dist - GSHDME **Prod** - GSHDME

Psychological and Emotional Habits
VHS / BETA / 16mm
RMI Stress Management Series
(PRO)
$80.00 purchase _ #RSM1003
Looks at psychological and emotional habits and the role they play in creating and dealing with stress.
Business and Economics; Psychology
Dist - RMIBHF **Prod** - RMIBHF

Psychological and spiritual blindspots 30 MIN
BETA / VHS
Critical self - awareness series
Color (G)
$29.95 purchase _ #S115
Suggests that with a return to innocence, one can rediscover one's connection with the world in a healing manner. Features Patricia Sun, spiritual teacher and expert in conflict resolution, who believes that the fear of confronting the self and those around the self leads to unnecessary suppression of the higher powers. Part of a four - part series on critical self - awareness.
Health and Safety; Psychology; Religion and Philosophy
Dist - THINKA **Prod** - THINKA

Psychological Aspects 25 MIN
U-matic / VHS
Right Way Series
Color
Tells how to cope with emotional reactions and frustrating situations while driving.
Health and Safety
Dist - PBS **Prod** - SCETV 1982

Psychological Aspects 28 MIN
VHS / U-matic
Color (J A)
Explores the thinking and psychology of the heavy drinker.
Health and Safety; Psychology; Sociology
Dist - SUTHRB **Prod** - SUTHRB

Psychological Aspects of Coma 90 FRS
U-matic / VHS
Comatose Patient Series
Color (PRO)
Studies psychological and emotional needs of comatose patient, family, and health professionals.
Health and Safety; Science - Natural
Dist - BRA **Prod** - BRA

Psychological Aspects of Dance Performance and Competition 30 MIN
VHS / U-matic
Dancers' Bodies Series
Color
Fine Arts; Psychology
Dist - ARCVID **Prod** - ARCVID

Psychological defenses - A series
Psychological defenses - Series A 43 MIN
Dist - HRMC
IBIS

Psychological defenses - B series
Psychological defenses - series B
Dist - HRMC

Psychological defenses - Series A 43 MIN
VHS / 35mm strip
Psychological defenses - A series
Color (J H C)
$139.00 purchase _ #FG - 614 - VS
Presents three parts that explain how defense mechanisms help people deal with everyday stress and how the unconscious affects behavior. Includes Introduction - Repression on conscious, preconscious, and unconscious awareness as the basis of defense mechanisms; Avoidance - Denial on hiding from unwanted experience and tuning out reality; and Regression - Undoing which demonstrates that both behaviors involve resorting to immature behavior and minimizing one's guilt over a secret wish. Part one of two parts. Filmstrip on video.
Psychology; Sociology
Dist - HRMC **Prod** - HRMC 1980
IBIS

Psychological defenses - series B
VHS
Psychological defenses - B series
Color (J H C)
$139.00 purchase _ #FG - 615 - VS
Presents three parts that explain how defense mechanisms help people deal with everyday stress and how the unconscious affects behavior. Includes Projection - Rationalization which distinguishes healthy from unhealthy projection and negative from positive aspects of rationalization; Identification - Displacement which describes mimicking someone else's behavior; and Reaction Formation - Sublimation which explains the expression of attitudes opposed to one's true feelings and the channeling of unconscious desires into socially acceptable forms of expression. Part two of two parts. Filmstrip on video.
Psychology; Sociology
Dist - HRMC **Prod** - HRMC 1994

Psychological development of gifted youngsters
VHS
Giftedness - research and practice series
Color (T)
$49.95 purchase
Focuses on the social and emotional needs of gifted youngsters. Discusses developmental issues, personality adjustment, emotional and moral sensitivities, family issues and interactions. Presented by Dr Nicholas Colangelo of the University of Iowa. Part of a six - part series on gifted children.
Education; Psychology
Dist - UCALG **Prod** - UCALG 1991

Psychological Dialogue with Playwright Arthur Miller - Pt 1 50 MIN
U-matic / VHS / 16mm
Notable Contributors to the Psychology of Personality Series
B&W (C G T A)
Discusses the interplay between psychology and the creation of drama. Subjects include motivation, reactions to psychological analysis of the author, psychological impact on the audience, and attitudes toward psychological theories and methods.
Biography; Literature and Drama; Psychology
Dist - PSUPCR **Prod** - PSUPCR 1964

Psychological Dialogue with Playwright Arthur Miller - Pt 2 51 MIN
16mm / U-matic / VHS
Notable Contributors to the Psychology of Personality Series
B&W (C G T A)
Continues with his reactions to major personality theories, art versus science, nature of the message, and reflections on contemporary problems.
Biography; Literature and Drama; Psychology
Dist - PSUPCR **Prod** - PSUPCR 1964

Psychological Dimensions of Pregnancy, Labor and Delivery, 56 MIN
VHS / 16mm
Awakening and Growth of the Human - Studies in Infant Mental Health 'Series
Color (C A)
$150.00, $170.00 purchase _ #85850
Gives a descriptive and diagnostic assessment of normal feelings, thoughts and impressions in the mother during the course of a pregnancy. Deals with ambivalence, listing specific psychological "work" to be done. Mentions influences that may change the course of the progress of this work and affect the parent's feelings toward the child. Also lists signs which may indicate to the therapist the presence of a possible problem, to which he can then bring help.
Health and Safety; Psychology
Dist - UILL **Prod** - IPIN 1986

Psychological Evaluation 21 MIN
VHS / U-matic
Psychiatry Learning System, Pt 1 - Assessments Series
Color (PRO)
Reviews the use of various psychological tests in assessment evaluation. Addresses issues of reliability and validity of tests.
Guidance and Counseling; Psychology
Dist - HSCIC **Prod** - HSCIC 1982

Psychological Factors and Ethical Considerations in Negotiations 50 MIN
U-matic / VHS
Negotiation Lectures Series
Color (PRO)
Explains how to handle racial, ethnic, gender and age differences that may affect negotiations. Includes discussion of provisions of the ABA Code Of Professional Responsibility.
Civics and Political Systems
Dist - ABACPE **Prod** - NITA

Psychological Growth and Spiritual Development
BETA / VHS
Color (G)
Explores the interrelationship of psychological growth and spiritual development as seen by Father Benedict Groeschel, who holds a Doctorate in Psychology. Includes study guide.
Psychology; Religion and Philosophy
Dist - DSP **Prod** - DSP

Psychological growth and spiritual development series
The Awakening 45 MIN
The Dark night of the soul 45 MIN
Defense mechanisms and anxiety 45 MIN
The Healing Call of Grace 45 MIN
How to Assess Spiritual Growth 45 MIN
The Illuminative Way 45 MIN
Mature Faith 45 MIN
Personality, Normality, and Adjustment 45 MIN
Personality Types 45 MIN
The Religious experience 45 MIN
Spiritual Progress and Psychological Growth 45 MIN
The Three Ways and the Levels of Maturity 45 MIN
Trust in Darkness 45 MIN
The Unitive Way 45 MIN
Dist - DSP

Psychological Growth and Spritual Development Series
Moral Integration 45 MIN
Dist - DSP

Psychological Hazards in Infancy 22 MIN
16mm
Head Start Training Series
B&W (J)
Describes the types of psychological damage that may be done to infants and suggests means of prevention.
Home Economics; Psychology
Dist - NYU **Prod** - VASSAR

Psychological Implications of Behavior during the Clinical Visit 20 MIN
16mm
Film Studies on Integrated Development Series
B&W (C T)
Illustrates that clues to a child's emotional attitudes are seen from its overt behavior while awaiting examination, during physical and dental examinations and at play.
Health and Safety; Psychology
Dist - NYU **Prod** - FRIWOL 1944

Psychological implications of divorce 30 MIN
U-matic / VHS
Family portrait - a study of contemporary lifestyles series; Lesson 22
Color (C A)
Examines major problems faced by divorced persons and their families.
Psychology; Sociology
Dist - CDTEL **Prod** - SCCON

Psychological Issues in the Rehabilitation Process 56 MIN
VHS / 16mm
Medical Aspects of Disability - Course Lecture Series
Color (PRO)
$50.00, $65.00 purchase _ #8826
Presents one part of a course lecture series on the medical aspects of disability. Discusses psychological issues in the rehabilitation process.
Health and Safety; Psychology
Dist - RICHGO **Prod** - RICHGO 1988

Psychological Limitations 11 MIN
16mm
Safety and You Series
Color
Explores emotional limits and how they affect people. Shows that caution is a psychological process that evolves through learning, and that humans can only learn so much so fast. Points out that knowing psychological limitations can help prevent accidents.
Guidance and Counseling; Health and Safety; Psychology
Dist - FILCOM **Prod** - FILCOM

The Psychological make - Up of a Customer
VHS / U-matic
Strategies for Successful Selling Series
Color
Stresses that people don't buy from people they don't trust and that sales success depends heavily on one's ability to build a personal rapport with the customer. Module 2 on the Strategies for successful selling series.
Business and Economics
Dist - AMA **Prod** - AMA

Psychological maltreatment of children - assault on the psyche 19 MIN
VHS / 16mm
Color (C G PRO)
$290.00, $150.00 purchase, $19.00, $16.50 rental _ #23541
Presents a dramatized portrayal of the emotional effects of verbal abuse on children to stimulate discussion. Includes the analysis of Dr James Garbarino and his recommendations for intervention. Produced by Garbarino and Dr John Merrow.
Psychology; Sociology
Dist - PSU **Prod** - WPSXTV 1985

Psychological Romance 10 MIN
16mm
Color
LC 81-700392
Concerns a young man's fantasies about a girl he wants to date. Shows his reactions when he finally meets her.
Fine Arts
Dist - NUCCI **Prod** - NUCCI 1981

Psychological symptoms of the sexually abused child 39 MIN
VHS
Sexually abused children in foster care training videotapes series
Color (PRO A C G)
$10.95 purchase _ #V520
Features Dr Paul M Fine of the Creighton Univ School of Medicine and Univ of Nebraska Medical Center who presents a team - approach model that includes the foster parent, protective services worker and the mental health professional working with a sexually abused child in foster care. Talks about behaviors children in this population may manifest in foster care, related psychological patterns and psychiatric symptoms. Uses excerpts from sessions between Dr Fine and sexually abused children in foster care to illustrate certain points. Part of an eight - part series training foster parents on the care of sexually abused children.
Psychology; Sociology
Dist - FFBH **Prod** - FFBH 1993

Psychological Testing 30 MIN
VHS / U-matic
Psychology of Human Relations Series
Color
Focuses on achievement tests, aptitude tests, cognitive style mapping, criteria of a good test and other psychological testing.
Psychology
Dist - WFVTAE **Prod** - MATC

The Psychologically Safe Environment 30 MIN
U-matic / VHS
Teaching for Thinking - Creativity in the Classroom Series
Color (T PRO)
$180.00 purchase,$50.00 rental
Explores methods of creating discussion and question and answer sessions to promote a deeper understanding of presented material.
Education; English Language
Dist - AITECH **Prod** - WHATV 1986

Psychology 29 MIN
U-matic / VHS
Vic Braden's Tennis for the Future Series
Color
Physical Education and Recreation
Dist - PBS **Prod** - WGBHTV 1981

Psychology 25 MIN
VHS
Career encounters series
Color (J H C A)
$95.00 purchase _ #MG3411V-J
Presents a documentary-style program that explores a career in psychology. Features professionals at work, explaining what they do and how they got where they are. Emphasizes diversity of occupational opportunities and of men and women in the field. Offers information about new developments and technologies and about educational and certification requirements for entering the profession. One of a series of videos about professions available individually or as a set.
Business and Economics; Guidance and Counseling; Psychology
Dist - CAMV

Psychology 15 MIN
VHS / U-matic / BETA
Career Success Series
(H C A)
$29.95 _ #MX246
Portrays occupations in psychology be reviewing required skills and interviewing people employed in this field. Tells of the anxieties and rewards involved in pursuing a career as a psychologist.
Education; Guidance and Counseling; Psychology
Dist - CAMV **Prod** - CAMV

Psychology 48 MIN
U-matic / VHS
Color
Includes 48 half - hour videotape lessons on several aspects of psychology.
Psychology
Dist - TELSTR **Prod** - TELSTR

Psychology 15 MIN
VHS / 16mm
(H C A)
$24.95 purchase _ #CS246
Describes the skills necessary for a career in psychology. Features interviews with professionals in this field.
Guidance and Counseling
Dist - RMIBHF **Prod** - RMIBHF

Psychology, a Science 30 MIN
U-matic / VHS
Psychology of Human Relations Series
Color
Outlines the applications of the scientific method in psychology and the purposes of psychological research.
Psychology
Dist - WFVTAE **Prod** - MATC

Psychology and Movement 30 MIN
U-matic / VHS
Health and Well - Being of Dancers Series
Color
Fine Arts; Health and Safety; Physical Education and Recreation
Dist - ARCVID **Prod** - ARCVID

Psychology and Spirituality 360 MIN
VHS / BETA
Color
Introduces practical religious psychology. Highlights personality development, how to cope with everyday neuroses, self acceptance and fulfillment.
Psychology; Religion and Philosophy
Dist - DSP **Prod** - DSP

Psychology and the World of Work 30 MIN
U-matic / VHS
Psychology of Human Relations Series
Color
Focuses on applications of psychological theory in work settings, elements of rational - emotive therapy applied to work - related problems, positive reinforcement in work situations and psychological consulting in business and industry.
Psychology
Dist - WFVTAE **Prod** - MATC

Psychology career encounters 28 MIN
VHS
Career encounters video series
Color (J H)
$89.00 purchase _ #4272
Offers a documentary on careers in the field of psychology. Visits workplaces and hears professionals explain what they do, how they got where they are and why they find the work so rewarding. Emphasizes human diversity in the professions. Dispels myths, misconceptions and stereotypes and offers practical information about the requirements for entering the field. Part of a 13 - part series.
Business and Economics; Guidance and Counseling; Psychology
Dist - NEWCAR

The Psychology of Aging, Dying and Death 145 MIN
U-matic
University of the Air Series
Color (J H C A)
$750.00 purchase, $250.00 rental
Explores how our views on aging, dying and death change from childhood to old age. Program contains a series of five cassettes of 29 minutes each.
Psychology; Sociology
Dist - CTV **Prod** - CTV 1978

The Psychology of attraction 14 MIN
VHS
System of change series
Color (PRO G A)
$465.00 purchase, $130.00 rental
Focuses on positive aspects of change. Provides a formula for dealing with attitudes toward change. Part of Changing People, Unit 3.
Business and Economics; Guidance and Counseling; Psychology
Dist - EXTR **Prod** - CCCD

A Psychology of creativity 31 MIN
VHS / 16mm
Notable contributors to the psychology of personality series
Color (C G PRO)
$455.00, $60.00 purchase, $24.50, $12.00 rental _ #33815
Features Richard I Evans, professor of psychology at the University of Houston. Part of a series of interviews with the world's foremost psychologists.
Fine Arts; Psychology
Dist - PSU **Prod** - RIE 1972

Psychology of Disability - Working with and Motivating the Difficult Client 57 MIN
VHS / 16mm
Medical Aspects of Disability - Course Lecture Series
Color (PRO)
$50.00, $65.00 purchase _ #8826
Presents one part of a course lecture series on the medical aspects of disability. Presents ways for the health care professional to deal with difficult and unmotivated patients.
Health and Safety; Psychology
Dist - RICHGO **Prod** - RICHGO 1988

Psychology of human relations series
Abnormal behavior 30 MIN
Adult life stages 30 MIN
Aging and death 30 MIN
Applied learning 30 MIN
Assertiveness training 30 MIN
B F Skinner on behaviorism 30 MIN
Career choice 30 MIN
Career development 30 MIN
Communication and language 30 MIN
Coping 30 MIN
Emotion, Mind and Body 30 MIN
Groups in Action 30 MIN
How do we feel 30 MIN
Information Processing 30 MIN
Intergroup Relations 30 MIN
Interpersonal Relations 30 MIN
The Motives in Our Lives 30 MIN
Perception 30 MIN
Psychological Testing 30 MIN
Psychology, a Science 30 MIN
Psychology and the World of Work 30 MIN
Pychotherapy 30 MIN
Social Roles 30 MIN
What is Psychology? 30 MIN
Why We do what We do 30 MIN
Dist - WFVTAE

The Psychology of Mass Persuasion 47 MIN
VHS
Color (J H)
Equips students to cope with attempts at persuasion by showing them how it works and under what circumstances it succeeds. Probes personal psychological phenomenon of attitude, the role of advertising in politics and selling, and how advertising and propaganda compare.
Business and Economics; Education; Guidance and Counseling; Psychology; Sociology
Dist - HRMC **Prod** - HRMC 1981

Psychology of Parenting 19 MIN
U-matic / VHS
Color (G)
$249.00, $149.00 purchase _ #AD - 1409
Explores some of the problems of being a parent. Visits a workshop where parents share the joys and pains of child rearing and explain their problems. Offers solutions for better communication with teenagers.
Health and Safety; Psychology; Sociology
Dist - FOTH **Prod** - FOTH

Psychology of Personal and Professional Goal Setting 30 MIN
VHS / U-matic
High Performance Leadership Series
Color
Psychology
Dist - DELTAK **Prod** - VIDAI

The Psychology of Personal Constructs, an Introduction - Pt 1 52 MIN
VHS / U-matic
Personal Construct Psychology Series
Color (C PRO)
$75.00, $69.95 purchase
Introduces the concepts of personal construct theory. Part 1 of a twelve part series on personal construct psychology, a cognitive theory of personality formulated by George A Kelly.
Psychology
Dist - SCETV **Prod** - SCETV 1986

The Psychology of Persuasion
VHS / U-matic
Strategies for Successful Selling Series
Color
Introduces sales people to the master methods of overcoming a customer's objection. Module 6 on the Strategies for successful selling series.
Business and Economics
Dist - AMA **Prod** - AMA

Psychology of religious experience 30 MIN
BETA / VHS
Roots of consciousness series
Color (G)
$29.95 purchase _ #S030
Discusses the relation between psychedelic experience and religious practice, the god within and the cultivation of psychic experiences within religious and shamanic traditions. Features Dr Huston Smith, author of 'The Religions of Man.' Part of a four - part series on the roots of consciousness.
Psychology; Religion and Philosophy; Social Science
Dist - THINKA **Prod** - THINKA

The Psychology of resistance 11 MIN
VHS
System of change series
Color (PRO G A)
$465.00 purchase, $130.00 rental
Discusses emotional reactions to changes in the work setting. Explains why people resist making adjustments and suggests ways to overcome opposition. Part of Changing People, Unit 3.
Business and Economics; Guidance and Counseling; Psychology
Dist - EXTR **Prod** - CCCD

The Psychology of self - management 54 MIN
VHS
Color (A PRO)
$69.95 purchase _ #S01549
Covers principles of self - management. Shows how to eliminate distractions and how to organize tasks according to their importance. Stresses delegation. Hosted by Dr John Lee.
Business and Economics; Guidance and Counseling; Psychology
Dist - UILL

Psychology of Sport 19 MIN
16mm
Coaching Development Programme Series
Color
LC 76-701040
Introduces applications of sports psychology. No 3 on the Coaching development programme series.
Physical Education and Recreation
Dist - SARBOO **Prod** - SARBOO 1974

Psychology of Sports 25 MIN
VHS / 16mm / U-matic
Sports Medicine Series
Color (T C)
$69.00 purchase _ #1467
Discusses the importance of psychological factors in motivating athletes to perform at their best, how to communicate through positive reinforcement, how to be a good listener and the importance of skill improvement.
Health and Safety; Physical Education and Recreation
Dist - EBEC **Prod** - UNIDIM 1982

The Psychology of Successful Retirement - Positive Preparation for a Major Life Transition 27 MIN
VHS / 16mm
Color (PRO)
$525.00 purchase, $110.00 rental, $35.00 preview
Discusses negative stereotypes about retirement and aging. Features Lois Haynes, counselor and therapist. Offers a positive perspective and advice on how to successfully make the transition into retirement. Available with optional personal preretirement inventory.
Business and Economics; Guidance and Counseling; Psychology; Sociology
Dist - UTM **Prod** - UTM

The Psychology of the Bible - Pt 1 30 MIN
16mm
B&W
Maurice Samuel and Mark Van Doren discuss the psychological connotations of various episodes in the Bible. (Kinescope).
Religion and Philosophy
Dist - NAAJS **Prod** - JTS 1963

The Psychology of the Bible - Pt 2 30 MIN
16mm
B&W
LC FIA65-1101
Features Maurice Samuel and Mark Van Doren discussing the psychological connotations of several biblical episodes.
Psychology
Dist - NAAJS **Prod** - JTS 1965

A Psychology of the soul - spiritual beings in human form 120 MIN
VHS
Color (G)
$34.95 purchase _ #P22
Explores some of the key concepts of psychospiritual psychology. Features author Jacquelyn Small, MSSW speaking of healing that occurs when the shadow self is honored.
Literature and Drama; Psychology
Dist - HP

Psychology of Trading 30 MIN
U-matic / VHS
Commodities - the Professional Trader Series
Color (C A)
Presents experts discussing the use of discipline in overcoming emotions which interfere with objective trading.
Business and Economics
Dist - VIPUB **Prod** - VIPUB

The Psychology of weight loss - resolving emotional eating for a lighter, healthier you 47 MIN
VHS
Color (A C)
Reveals the subconscious dynamics of food and substance addictions. Shows people describing their struggle with eating disorders. The hosts provide insights about emotional eating, subconscious programming, body image, low self-esteem, and trauma from childhood abuse. Includes booklet on eating disorder symptoms. Hosted by hypnotherapist John Zulli and MFCC Pamela Scott.
Health and Safety; Social Science
Dist - SVIP
CAMV

The Psychology of Winning 20 MIN
16mm
Color
LC 81-700722
Explores the characteristics of successful people in all walks of life, including astronauts, returning POW's, and sports figures.
Psychology
Dist - SOLIL **Prod** - SOLIL 1981

The Psychology of winning in action 58 MIN
VHS
Color (G)
$49.95 purchase _ #S01797; $49.95 purchase
Features Dr Denis Waitley in a discussion of how to put the psychology of winning in life. Stresses the importance of developing self - esteem and of not being defeated by past failures.
Business and Economics; Guidance and Counseling; Psychology
Dist - UILL **Prod** - WNETTV
PBS

Psychology of winning learning system series
Positive self - determination
Positive self - dimension
Positive self - discipline
Positive self - expectancy
Dist - NIGCON

Psychology - the Emotions Series
Shy, Withdrawn and Bashful 10 MIN
Dist - SUMHIL

Psychology - the study of human behavior series
VHS / 16mm
Psychology - the study of human behavior series
Color (C A)
Reveals the broad sweep of research and analylsis by featuring many renowned psychologists, emphasizes the importance of critical thinking, and identifies the diversity of human beings and human behavior.
Psychology
Dist - CDTEL **Prod** - COAST 1990

Psychology Today Films Series
Aspects of behavior 31 MIN
Information Processing 28 MIN
The Sensory World 33 MIN
Social Psychology 33 MIN
Dist - CRMP

Psychoneurological Aspects of AIDS for the Primary Care Provider 20 MIN
VHS
AIDS Education and Training Series
Color (G PRO)
$195.00 purchase, $97.50 members _ N910 - VI - 008
Describes broad range of behavior and cognitive problems related to HIV infection. Covers diagnosis of HIV - related organic brain disease, challenges for providing optimal clinical care, and possible behavioral and pharmacological interventions for management of these conditions. Includes videotaped interview segments with patients, conducted by two staff psychiatrists from University of Michigan Medical School.
Health and Safety
Dist - HSCIC

Psychopathologies - descriptions and interventions series
Abnormal behavior - origins 17 MIN
Abnormal behavior - overview 22 MIN

Anxiety disorders - Part 1 22 MIN
Anxiety disorders - Part 2 23 MIN
Personality disorders 25 MIN
Schizophrenia - acute care 23 MIN
Schizophrenia - causation 20 MIN
Schizophrenia - rehabilitation 17 MIN
Schizophrenia - symptomology 22 MIN
Dist - CONMED

Psychopathology - diagnostic vignettes series
Bipolar affective disorders (case numbers 5 - 8) 32 MIN
Dysthymic disorder and major affective disorders - case numbers 1 - 4 38 MIN
Schizophrenic disorders - case numbers 9 - 12 35 MIN
Dist - IU

Psychopathology - psychotherapy - Parts 21 and 22 60 MIN
U-matic / VHS
Discovering psychology series
Color (C)
$45.00, $29.95 purchase
Presents parts 21 and 22 of the 26 - part Discovering Psychology series. Defines and explores schizophrenia, phobias and affective disorders. Examines the factors which can lead to mental and behavioral disorders. Shows how historical, cultural and social forces have influenced attitudes toward the mentally ill. Two thirty - minute programs hosted by Professor Philip Zimbardo of Stanford University.
Health and Safety; Psychology
Dist - ANNCPB **Prod** - WGBHTV 1989

Psychopharmacological Drugs - Pt 1 30 MIN
16mm
Pharmacology Series
Color (C)
LC 73-703336
Health and Safety; Psychology
Dist - TELSTR **Prod** - MVNE 1971

Psychopharmacological Drugs - Pt 2 30 MIN
16mm
Pharmacology Series
Color (C)
LC 73-703337
Health and Safety; Psychology
Dist - TELSTR **Prod** - MVNE 1971

Psychopharmacology
U-matic / VHS
Psychiatry Learning System, Pt 2 - Disorders Series
Color (PRO)
Serves as a good guide to the use of psychoactive drugs.
Health and Safety; Psychology
Dist - HSCIC **Prod** - HSCIC 1982

Psychos in love 88 MIN
16mm
Color (A)
$125.00 rental
Tells of the romance that blossoms as a psychopathic killer falls in love with a psychotic killer when he finds that she doesn't like grapes. Chronicles their lives together as their drains clog up from getting rid of their victims. But all ends well when they discover that the plumber is a cannibal. Directed by Gorman Bechard.
Fine Arts; Literature and Drama
Dist - CANCIN

Psychoses - schizophrenia and unspecified psychoses - Part V 21 MIN
VHS / U-matic
Simulated psychiatric profiles series
Color (PRO C)
$250.00 purchase _ #C871 - VI - 006
Examines cases of schizophrenia and unspecified psychoses to illustrate theories about those illnesses. Demonstrates therapeutic techniques such as clarification, confrontation and interpretation. Part five of a five - part series progressing from adjustment disorders to major psychoses presented by Dr Donald C Fidler.
Health and Safety; Psychology
Dist - HSCIC

Psychosexual Disorders 78 MIN
VHS / U-matic
Psychiatry Learning System, Pt 2 - Disorders Series
Color (PRO)
Teaches how to recognize common myths about sexuality and to recall information to dispel these myths. Identifies the gender identity disorders, paraphilias, and psychosexual dysfunctions. Considers diagnosis and treatment.
Health and Safety; Psychology
Dist - HSCIC **Prod** - HSCIC 1982

Psychosis - a Family Intervention 13 MIN
VHS / U-matic
Crisis Intervention Series
Color (PRO)
Tells of the methods emergency medical technicians employ to calm a psychotic who is threatening family members.
Health and Safety; Psychology; Sociology
Dist - GPN **Prod** - SBG 1983

Psychosocial Aspects of Death 39 MIN
U-matic / VHS / 16mm
B&W
LC 73-712773
Presents a dramatized story about a nurse who faces the death of a patient for the first time, in order to show the impact of the death of a patient on a nurse and to examine the nurse - patient relationship.
Health and Safety; Psychology; Sociology
Dist - IU **Prod** - IU 1971

Psychosocial Assessment - Pt I 30 MIN
16mm
Psychiatric - Mental Health Nursing Series
Color (PRO)
LC 76-701626
Surveys the aims, content areas and methods of obtaining data for a nursing psychosocial assessment. Shows the importance of the initial psychiatric interview.
Health and Safety
Dist - AJN **Prod** - AJN 1976

Psychosocial Assessment - Pt II 30 MIN
16mm
Psychiatric - Mental Health Nursing Series
Color (PRO)
LC 76-701626
Explores the initial psychiatric interview as an investigative and therapeutic method in the nurse's assessment of psychosocial problems. Illustrates and evaluates four common interview techniques.
Health and Safety
Dist - AJN **Prod** - AJN 1976

Psychosocial care series
Presents a six - part series presented by Norma A Wylie, RN. Includes The Artistry of Medicine, The Breast Cancer Patient, The Cancer Patient, Coping with Loss, Instructing Medical Students, Pre and Post - Operative Patient Management.
The Artistry of medicine 19 MIN
The Breast cancer patient 18 MIN
The Cancer patient 18 MIN
Coping with loss 18 MIN
Instructing medical students 15 MIN
Pre and post - operative patient management 18 MIN
Dist - HSCIC

Psychosocial development 23 MIN
VHS / U-matic / BETA
Human development - 2.5 to 6 years series
Color (C PRO)
$280.00 purchase _ #620.3
Begins by discussing the tasks which are crucial to a preschooler's emotional and social development. Describes Erikson's stages pertaining to preschool children and Rene Spitz's stages of how children deal with frustration. Addresses self - awareness, self - esteem, sexuality and attainment. Gives information on sibling rivalry and discipline to caregivers. Part of a four - part series on human development, ages 2.5 to 6.
Health and Safety; Psychology
Dist - CONMED **Prod** - CONMED

Psychosocial Factors in Physical Illness 27 MIN
U-matic / VHS
Psychiatry Learning System, Pt 1 - Assessments Series
Color (PRO)
Contains material on the relationship between the mind and the body.
Psychology
Dist - HSCIC **Prod** - HSCIC 1982

Psychosocial intervention in AIDS 25 MIN
U-matic / VHS
Color (G)
$250.00 purchase, $100.00 rental
Clarifies the complex interrelationship among medical, psychological and social challenges that add to psychological distress in people with HIV. Synthesizes the latest information on the clinical course of HIV infection and suggests stages at which people with AIDS or other HIV - related infections are most likely to encounter problems - suspected high - risk contact, HIV antibody testing, development of ARC or other HIV disease symptoms, AIDS diagnosis, symptom progression, acute terminal illness.
Health and Safety
Dist - BAXMED **Prod** - BAXMED

The Psychosocial nursing assessment - a holistic approach 30 MIN
VHS
Color (PRO C)
$285.00 purchase, $70.00 rental _ #6528
Stresses the importance of establishing a trusting nurse - patient relationship. Discusses the holistic approach to nursing which can help nurses accurately assess patient psychosocial needs and provide nurses with opportunities to identify present stressors in patient life, as well as past and present coping methods. Demonstrates several interviews by a nurse of a patient and family to show how the mental status, suicidal potentials, substance abuse history and current support systems of the patient can be explored. Shows how nurses can use a holistic approach to foster a relationship of trust, privacy, confidentiality and safety.
Health and Safety
Dist - AJN **Prod** - HESCTV

Psychosocial nursing diagnoses - descriptions and interventions series
Focus on altered family processes 17 MIN
Focus on hopelessness 16 MIN
Focus on powerlessness 15 MIN
Dist - CONMED

Psychosocial sexual development - adolescent, aged 30 MIN
16mm
Directions for education in nursing via technology series
Color (PRO)
LC 76-703344
Presents the development of sexuality from adolescence through adult age, with emphasis on behavioral aspects of sexual development.
Health and Safety; Psychology
Dist - WSUM **Prod** - DENT 1976

Psychosocial sexual development - infant, pre - adolescent 30 MIN
16mm
Directions for education in nursing via technology series
Color (PRO)
LC 76-703343
Defines what constitutes being sexually healthy. Depicts the development of sexuality in children from birth through preadolescence, with emphasis on behavioral components that are characteristic of each phase.
Health and Safety; Psychology
Dist - WSUM **Prod** - DENT 1976

Psychosocial Survival in Burn Trauma 26 MIN
U-matic / 35mm strip
Burn Trauma Series
Color (PRO)
Reveals effects of burn trauma in terms of sudden, catastrophic, physiologic or psychologic assault on patient. Shows two main sections, each dealing in detail with massive psychologic and sociologic insults to burn victims life - style and personal integrity.
Health and Safety; Psychology
Dist - BRA **Prod** - BRA

Psychosocial Treatments
VHS / U-matic
Psychiatry Learning System, Pt 2 - Disorders Series
Color (PRO)
Goes beyond the traditional individual psychotherapy to include family therapy and group therapies.
Guidance and Counseling; Psychology
Dist - HSCIC **Prod** - HSCIC 1982

Psychosomatic Disorders 36 MIN
VHS
Color (J H)
Discusses how the interaction of mind and body produces real physical ailments, of which the origins are mental and emotional. Explores causes and surveys available methods of treatment. Helps make your students aware of their own psychosomatic tendencies.
Health and Safety; Psychology
Dist - HRMC **Prod** - HRMC 1980

Psychosomatics of Experimental Drug Dissociation 14 MIN
16mm
B&W (C T)
Presents an experiment in which conditioned responses to tone and light stimuli are developed in dogs given erythroidine, a curare - like drug which produces paralysis. An electric shock is used as an unconditioned stimulus. Conditioned responses produced during the drug state cannot be elicited after recovery but reappear spontaneously when the animal is again given the drug.
Psychology
Dist - PSUPCR **Prod** - PSUPCR 1946

Psychosynthesis 8 MIN
16mm
Color (G)
$15.00 rental
Fuses filmmaker's personalities of herself, her baby, athlete, witch and artist. Bonds all facets of herself through the healing powers of natural touchstone.
Fine Arts; Sociology
Dist - CANCIN **Prod** - BARHAM 1975

Psychotherapeutic Interview 30 MIN
16mm
Psychiatric - Mental Health Nursing Series
Color (PRO)
LC 76-701625
Uses the beginning and middle stages of an actual therapy relationship to present the nurse's conduct of individual psychotherapy. Describes the process by which the patient is helped to observe personal behavior, identify patterns of experience and make connections between present and past life events.
Health and Safety
Dist - AJN **Prod** - AJN 1976

Psychotherapeutic Interviewing Series
An approach to understanding dynamics 34 MIN
A Clinical picture of anxiety hysteria 26 MIN
A Clinical Picture of Claustrophobia 31 MIN
Non - Verbal Communication 27 MIN
Dist - USNAC

Psychotherapy 26 MIN
U-matic / VHS / 16mm
Color (H C A)
LC 78-700212
Explains basic concepts underlying most psychotherapeutic techniques as well as the role of the therapist. Uses dramatizations of several therapy sessions to illustrate the process of psychotherapy.
Psychology
Dist - CRMP **Prod** - DAVFMS 1978

Psychotherapy and Medication 30 MIN
VHS / U-matic
Management and Treatment of the Violent Patient Series
Color
Presents a two - part program on working with violent persons. Discusses psychotherapy treatment in the first part and medication in the second part.
Health and Safety; Psychology
Dist - HEMUL **Prod** - HEMUL

Psychotherapy and spiritual paths 30 MIN
BETA / VHS
Spiritual psychology quartet series
Color (G)
$29.95 purchase _ #S045
Features Dr Seymour Boorstein, author of 'Transpersonal Psychotherapy,' who discusses his personal transformation from a conventional psychiatrist to a student of spirituality. Reveals that meditation may harm individuals with poorly developed ego structures because of the possibility of dissolution of ego boundaries through intense spiritual practices. Part of a series on spiritual psychology.
Psychology; Religion and Philosophy
Dist - THINKA **Prod** - THINKA

Psychotherapy Begins - the Case of Mr Lin 53 MIN
16mm
B&W (C T)
Documents the first interview with a young male student concerned about his homosexuality. Shows him exploring his problem and beginning to realize that perhaps homosexuality is not the central difficulty. He realizes he has many personality difficulties and reviews some of his attempts to resolve these problems.
Guidance and Counseling; Psychology; Sociology
Dist - PSUPCR **Prod** - PSUPCR 1955

Psychotherapy I 29 MIN
U-matic
Understanding Human Behavior - an Introduction to Psychology Series
Color (C A)
Illustrates and evaluates wide range of therapies being used to treat mental disorders. Focuses on and critically examines the psychoanalytic and humanistic approaches. Lesson 25 on the Understanding human behavior - an introduction to psychology series.
Psychology
Dist - CDTEL **Prod** - COAST

Psychotherapy II 29 MIN
U-matic
Understanding Human Behavior - an Introduction to Psychology Series
Color (C A)
Describes group and environmental therapies. Compares types of therapies in terms of claims for success, cost, duration and basis for choice. Lesson 26 on the Understanding human behavior - an introduction to psychology series.
Psychology
Dist - CDTEL **Prod** - COAST

Psychotherapy in Process - the Case of Miss Mun 57 MIN
16mm
B&W (C T)
Follows a complete therapeutic interview of a young woman client who is suffering from fatigue, depression, tenseness and psychosomatic ailments. She is deeply involved in therapy and her emotional responses are supplemented by spontaneous reactions from the therapist. The client weeps as she expresses her complete aloneness in her fears and expresses positive feelings as she realizes that the therapist understands her. The reactions of the therapist are recorded at the end.
Guidance and Counseling; Psychology
Dist - PSUPCR **Prod** - PSUPCR 1955

Psychotherapy of the Schizophrenic 60 MIN
U-matic / VHS
Schizophrenia Series
Color
Gives the step - by - step approach used by Dr Silvano Arieti with patients suffering with hallucinations, delusions and thought disorders. Integrates his theories and techniques with traditional psychodynamics.
Health and Safety; Psychology; Sociology
Dist - HEMUL **Prod** - HEMUL

Psychotherapy Pro and Con 28 MIN
U-matic / VHS
Color (G)
$249.00, $149.00 purchase _ #AD - 1245
Examines psychotherapy. Considers whether psychotherapy helps with problems, to what extent, and whether it is necessary at all. Asks if psychotherapy is a crutch, a drain on the wallet, a never - ending series of sessions or a valuable way to enable individuals to deal with their lives. Features Phil Donhaue.
Health and Safety; Psychology; Sociology
Dist - FOTH **Prod** - FOTH

Psychotherapy vignettes 95 MIN
VHS / U-matic
Color (PRO C)
$395.00 purchase, $80.00 rental _ #C870 - VI - 056
Uses actors in 22 short scenes to simulate key episodes in the psychotherapeutic process. Shows several patients interacting with therapists during various phases of evaluation and treatment. Stimulates discussion of aspects of psychotherapy - dreams, supportive and exploratory psychotherapy, therapeutic interventions, therapeutic contracts and terminating therapy. Presented by Dr Donald C Fidler.
Health and Safety
Dist - HSCIC

The Psychotic Assaultive Patient
VHS / U-matic
Crisis Intervention Series
Color
Shows how the violent patient can be controlled by applying expert technique. Places emphasis on verbal, personal intervention to help the patient regain internal control. Presents recommended applications and appropriate cautions in the administration of medication.
Psychology
Dist - VTRI **Prod** - VTRI

The Psychotic Assaultive Patient 20 MIN
U-matic / VHS
Medical Crisis Intervention Series
Color (PRO)
Show how to effectively and efficiently recognize and provide initial treatment and disposition of psychotic assaultive patients. Discusses typical precipitating factors, management techniques, how to test patient's level and control and behavioral characteristics.
Health and Safety; Psychology
Dist - LEIKID **Prod** - LEIKID

The Psychotic Child 25 MIN
16mm
B&W (C A)
LC FIA68-2699
Pictures a seven - year - old psychotic child who actively resists a variety of relationships, displaying autistic defenses and ritualistic, compulsive behavior. Indicates that his motor skill has developed to that of a two or three year - old. Shows the child exhibiting rebellious and frustrated behavior.
Education; Psychology
Dist - PSUPCR **Prod** - PSU 1967

Psychotic Disorders 30 MIN
VHS / 16mm
Psychology - the Study of Human Behavior Series
Color (C A)
$99.95, $89.95 purchase _ 24 - 21
Discusses schizophrenia, its treatment and causes.
Psychology
Dist - CDTEL **Prod** - COAST 1990

Psychotropic Drugs and the Health Care Professional Series
Adjunctive medications 22 MIN
Antidepressants and Lithium 24 MIN
Anxiolytic sedatives 11 MIN
Management issues 28 MIN
Neuroleptic Drugs and Adjunctive Medications 29 MIN
Dist - UWASHP

Psychotropic Drugs and the Hyperkinetic Syndrome 24 MIN
16mm
B&W (PRO)
LC 78-701607
Focuses on a research project conducted at the Kansas Center for Mental Retardation and Human Development, which examines psychotropic drug effects on the memory and academic performance of hyperactive, mentally retarded children.
Psychology
Dist - UKANS **Prod** - UKANS 1974

Psychotropics 20 MIN
VHS / U-matic
Color (PRO)
LC 77-730541
Defines psychotropic drugs and briefly reviews the nervous system. Employs a case - study technique to demonstrate the use of psychotropic drugs in treating anxiety, depression and psychosis. Introduces the patient for each of these conditions, describes his complaints, specifies the types of drugs that might be used, explains their intended actions and depicts important nursing considerations.
Health and Safety; Psychology
Dist - MEDCOM **Prod** - MEDCOM

PT - 109 140 MIN
U-matic / VHS / 16mm
Color (I)
Stars Cliff Robertson in the story of John F Kennedy's heroism during World War II. Pictures naval combat in the Pacific and life aboard Lieutenant Kennedy's battle - scarred PT - 109.
Biography; Fine Arts; History - World
Dist - FI **Prod** - WB 1963

Pterodactyl 12 MIN
16mm
Color (G)
$20.00 rental
Terrifies with a pre - historic reptile that invades and almost destroys the US, particularly the Marine Corps and television.
Fine Arts; Literature and Drama; Science - Natural
Dist - CANCIN **Prod** - PEARLY

Pterodactyls Alive 25 MIN
U-matic / VHS / 16mm
Color (J)
Explores the possibility of the existence of pterodactyls, the prehistoric flying reptiles from the age of dinosaurs. Presents living clues among reptiles, bats and birds around the world which exhibit similar characteristics.
Science - Natural
Dist - FI **Prod** - BBCTV

The Pterygopalatine Fossa 16 MIN
U-matic / VHS / 16mm
Cine - Prosector Series
Color (PRO)
Points out the distribution of nerves and vessels of the middle face.
Science - Natural
Dist - TEF **Prod** - AVCORP

Pterygopalatine Fossa 9 MIN
U-matic / VHS
Skull Anatomy Series
Color (C A)
Describes the boundaries, demonstrates the bones and identifies the boney regions of the pterygopalatine fossa.
Health and Safety; Science - Natural
Dist - TEF **Prod** - UTXHSA

P'tit Canada - Nouvelle Angleterre 28 MIN
16mm
Color (FRENCH)
_ #106C 0281 027

Geography - World
Dist - CFLMDC **Prod** - NFBC 1981

P'tit Jean S'en Va Aux Chantiers 16 MIN
16mm / U-matic / VHS
Color (P I) (FRENCH)
LC 75-702707
A French language version of Ti - Jean Goes Lumbering. Presents a French - Canadian folk tale about a mysterious stranger who behaves like a young Paul Bunyan.
Fine Arts; Foreign Language; Literature and Drama
Dist - IFB **Prod** - NFBC 1953

Puberty
VHS
Understanding yourself and your body series
Color (I J)
$89.00 purchase _ #MC316
Discusses the process of sexual maturation.
Health and Safety; Psychology; Sociology
Dist - AAVIM **Prod** - AAVIM 1992

Puberty 18 MIN
VHS
Let's talk about it series
Color; PAL (I J)
PdS29.50 purchase
Discusses body changes and sex characteristics at puberty. Focuses particularly on menstrustration and 'wet dreams.' Part of a five - part series on sex education.
Health and Safety
Dist - EMFVL

The Puberty years 33 MIN
VHS
Color (I J)
$199.00 purchase _ #661 - SK
Uses humorous vignettes, animation, and group discussion to examine the changes that occur during puberty for boys and girls. Considers bodily changes, social and emotional 'growing pains,' and the emerging sexuality. Stresses the fact that puberty is a normal part of growing up. Includes teacher's guide.
Education; Health and Safety; Psychology
Dist - SUNCOM **Prod** - HRMC

The Puberty years - Program 1 33 MIN
VHS
Sex education series
Color (I J H)
$199.00 purchase _ #CG - 829 - VS
Presents two parts on puberty. Portrays Alfred, Jamie and Steve who look at male changes in puberty in part one. Uses a humorous sketch and animation to discuss emotional and physical changes. Part two features Lynn, Kerry and Hilary who discuss the emotional and physical changes of female puberty. Includes a humorous sketch about the first period and getting a bra. Part one of a five - part series on sex education.
Health and Safety
Dist - HRMC **Prod** - HRMC

Public agenda foundation series
AIDS at issue - coping with an epidemic 22 MIN
Crisis in the work force - help wanted 22 MIN
Environment at issue 22 MIN
Exploring alternatives to prison and probation 22 MIN
The United States and the Soviet Union - looking to the future 28 MIN
What should we do in school today 22 MIN
Dist - FLMLIB

Public and Personal Services 35 MIN
VHS / 16mm
Video Career Library Series
Color (H C A PRO)
$79.95 purchase _ #WW111; $69.95 purchase _ #CJ121V
Shows public and personal service occupations such as firefighters, police officers, correctional officers, bartenders, waitpeople, chefs, barbers, cosmetologists, child care workers, flight attendants, gardeners, butchers and meatcutters. Contains current occupational outlook and salary information.
Business and Economics; Guidance and Counseling; Industrial and Technical Education
Dist - AAVIM **Prod** - CAMV 1990
CAMV

Public broadcast laboratory series
Anacostia - museum in the ghetto 18 MIN
Civil disorder - the Kerner Report - Pt 3 24 MIN
Civil disorder - the Kerner Report - Pt 1 and 2 56 MIN
Confrontation - Dialogue in Black and White 35 MIN
Defense and domestic needs - contest for tomorrow 77 MIN
Do You Think a Job is the Answer 68 MIN
The Frustrated Campus 49 MIN
Goodbye and good luck 30 MIN
Journalism - Mirror, Mirror on the World 52 MIN
Mexican - Americans - the Invisible Minority 38 MIN
The People Left Behind 31 MIN
Stop Ruining America's Past 22 MIN
Television - a Political Machine 14 MIN
A View of America from the 23rd Century 21 MIN
The Violent Universe 148 MIN
The Whole World is Watching 55 MIN
Dist - IU

Public Broadcast Laboratory
Gift of Life - Right to Die 15 MIN
Dist - IU

Public Data Networks 45 MIN
U-matic / VHS
Network Architectures - a Communications Revolution Series
Color
Covers such topics as the structure of an Advanced Communications Service (ACS) network, ACS services, possible uses for ACS, relationship between ACS and other architectures and the storage of programs and data in an ACS network.
Industrial and Technical Education; Social Science
Dist - DELTAK **Prod** - DELTAK

Public dducation - at whose expense 29 MIN
Videoreel / VT2
Turning points series
Color
Examines methods of public school financing in light of the 1971 California Supreme Court ruling which declared revenue raised from property taxes unconstitutional as a source of funds for public education.
Education
Dist - PBS **Prod** - NETCHE

Public debt - international effects 60 MIN
VHS
Macroeconomics series
Color (H C G)
$89.00 purchase _ #GSU - 317
Discusses the effects of fiscal policy on international trade and the balance of payments. Examines aggregate demand and supply revisited. Interviews Prof Robert Eisner, Dept of Economic, Northwestern University. Part of a 24 - part series instructed by Dr Edward F Stuart, Northwestern University, which focuses on a description of the major economic policy - making bodies in the United States and their interrelationships.
Business and Economics
Dist - INSTRU

Public education - it's a bull market 30 MIN
VHS
Color (H C G)
$295.00 purchase, $55.00 rental
Looks at big business influence on public education. Combines educator and business interviews with media clips to show corporate influence on curricula and policy. Reveals that films sponsored by corporations often were propaganda for nuclear energy and pesticides and corporate 'adoption' of schools was actually subtle coercion - giving them high - tech equipment and expecting endorsement of their products. Shows that some educators resent imposing corporate values on the goals of education, such as free market strategies encouraging parents to 'shop around' for the best schools, resulting in floods of applications to the most desirable schools, decreased access to quality education for poor and minority students. Produced by Hobart Swan.
Business and Economics; Education; Guidance and Counseling; Sociology
Dist - FLMLIB

Public Enemy Number One 55 MIN
16mm
Color (A)
LC 81-700963
Introduces 70 - year - old Australian journalist Wilfred Burchett, who has found himself unwelcome in his own country because of his unconventional reporting on World War II, Korea and Vietnam.
Biography; Geography - World; Literature and Drama
Dist - FLMLIB **Prod** - FLMLIB 1981

Public gardens and trees
VHS
Gardens of the world series
Color (H C G)
$24.95 purchase _ #GW06
Features host Audrey Hepburn and narrator Michael York. Explores Mt Vernon. Relates the story of the greening of Paris. Part of a six - part series on gardens.
Agriculture; Science - Natural
Dist - SVIP **Prod** - AUVICA 1993

Public Goods and Responsibilities - How Far Should We Go 30 MIN
VHS / U-matic
Economics USA Series
Color (C)
Business and Economics
Dist - ANNCPB **Prod** - WEFA

Public Health and the U S Army Veterinarian 15 MIN
16mm
Color
LC 78-700253
Explains the role played by United States Army veterinarians in maintaining public health. Shows the interrelationship between human and animal well - being.
Civics and Political Systems; Health and Safety; Science; Sociology
Dist - USNAC **Prod** - USA 1977

The Public Health Nurse and the Mentally Retarded Child 24 MIN
U-matic / VHS / 16mm
Color (C T)
LC FIA65-1488
Shows how a public health nurse can help the parents of retarded children. Traces one case from the detection of the abnormal condition to the education given parents to cope with training situations.
Education; Health and Safety; Psychology; Sociology
Dist - IFB **Prod** - UOKLA 1959

Public Health Problems in Mass Evacuation 13 MIN
16mm
B&W
LC FIE57-85
Explains the public health problems attending the mass evacuation of an urban population, including mass feeding, water supply, medical care, waste and sewage disposal and disease outbreaks. Supplement with current data.
Health and Safety; Science - Natural; Sociology
Dist - USNAC **Prod** - USPHS 1957

Public health science - bioenvironmental health series
Air and water pollution 30 MIN
Dist - GPN

Public health science - epidemiology series
Glimpse of reality 30 MIN
Dist - GPN

Public health science series unit III - introduction to epidemiology
Associates can cause happenings - control them 30 MIN
Dist - GPN

Public Health Science Series Unit IV - Intro to Community Organ for Health Services
The Contemporary Community Scene 30 MIN
Dist - GPN

Public Man and Private Man 29 MIN
U-matic
Social Animal Series
Color
Examines public roles and private roles that each person has.
Sociology
Dist - UMITV **Prod** - UMITV 1974

Public mind series
Presents a series of four videos with Bill Moyers that examines the impact on democracy of a mass culture whose basic information comes from image - making, the media, public opinion polls, public relations and propaganda. Produced by Alvin H Perlmutter, Inc and Public Affairs TV, Inc, New York.
Consuming images 60 MIN
Illusions of news 60 MIN
Leading questions 60 MIN
Public mind series 240 MIN
Dist - PBS

Public Opinion 30 MIN
U-matic / VHS
American Government Series; 1
Color (C)
Reviews the origin, nature and impact of public opinion on political matters.
Civics and Political Systems
Dist - DALCCD **Prod** - DALCCD

Public Places 17
16mm / VHS
Color (H A)
$400.00 purchase, $55.00 rental
Explores the 'dearchitecture' of SITE, a New York - based architectural firm, by documenting seven structures that appear to tilt, crumble, peel, and grow. These innovative edifices, located in otherwise ordinary commercial

shopping centers throughout America, challenged expectations and created controversy. Shows local citizens expressing their opinions about the structures.
Fine Arts
Dist - AFA **Prod** - HOSIL 1980

Public Places and Monuments 60 MIN
VHS
America by Design Series
Color (H)
$11.50 rental _ #60949, VH
Features architectural historian Spiro Kostof speaking about public areas, urban renewal, restoration, recreation and preservation. Explains how architecture and design have shaped the American environment. Encourages debate about future land use.
Fine Arts; Sociology
Dist - PSU **Prod** - PBS

Public Places Series
The Zoo 6 MIN
Dist - PHENIX

The Public President - Wit and Warmth in the White House 52 MIN
16mm / U-matic / VHS
Presidency Series
Color (J)
Focuses on the wit and charm of Presidents Roosevelt, Truman, Eisenhower and Kennedy.
Biography; Civics and Political Systems
Dist - LUF **Prod** - CORPEL 1976

Public Relations 20 MIN
U-matic
Access Series
Color (T)
LC 76-706251
Stresses that good public relations are a matter of filling unmet needs of the community. Shows how, in different ways, four libraries have done this and as a consequence have earned strong community support.
Education
Dist - USNAC **Prod** - UDEN 1976

Public Relations in Security 12 MIN
VHS / U-matic
Professional Security Training Series
Color
Shows the importance of courtesy, good manners, tact and personal deportment in dealing with the public as a security officer. Module 1C on the Professional security training series.
Health and Safety; Sociology
Dist - CORF **Prod** - CORF

Public - School Library Cooperation 40 MIN
U-matic
Access Series
Color (T)
LC 76-706253
Presents experiences and ideas on cooperative library programs. Discusses issues, trends and possible programs involved with public - school library cooperation.
Education
Dist - USNAC **Prod** - UDEN 1976

Public Schools - How are they Doing? 29 MIN
U-matic
Issue at Hand Series
Color
Discusses racism in the schools, sexism, teacher accountability, and the causes of vandalism and violence.
Education; Sociology
Dist - UMITV **Prod** - UMITV 1976

The Public Sector I 45 MIN
VHS / U-matic
Economic Perspectives Series
Color
Discusses the effect of the public sector on the economy.
Business and Economics
Dist - MDCPB **Prod** - MDCPB

The Public Sector II 45 MIN
U-matic / VHS
Economic Perspectives Series
Color
Discusses the effect of the public sector on the economy.
Business and Economics
Dist - MDCPB **Prod** - MDCPB

The Public Sector Integrity Program 50 MIN
U-matic / VHS
Color
Trains federal employees to be more aware of waste, fraud and abuse in their jobs and identifies their responsibilities as public servants working under standards of conduct.
Business and Economics; Civics and Political Systems; Psychology; Religion and Philosophy
Dist - USNAC **Prod** - USDJ

Public Service 10 MIN
U-matic
Color (P)
Presents a National Weather Service forecaster explaining the detailed work behind local and national weather reports.
Guidance and Counseling; Science - Physical
Dist - GA **Prod** - MINIP

Public Service 6 MIN
16mm / U-matic / VHS
Kingdom of Could be You Series
Color (K P I)
Guidance and Counseling
Dist - EBEC **Prod** - EBEC 1974

Public Service Announcement 2 MIN
16mm
Color
LC FIA67-572
Presents an experimental film which shows an expert black soccer player, representing all men, kicking a ball, symbolizing the world. Uses titles to convey the uniqueness of each moment and the world itself. Includes a musical background consisting of a plaintive Zulu chant.
History - United States; Psychology; Sociology
Dist - GROENG **Prod** - GROENG 1966

Public service announcements
VHS
Color (G)
Offers four public service announcements about assistive technology for the disabled and four on the Americans with Disabilties Act. Allows the customization with organization name and number. Call distributor for more information.
Health and Safety
Dist - UATP **Prod** - UATP

Public Service Announcements - Bandes Annonce 3 MIN
16mm
Color (G) (FRENCH)
#1X61 I
Presents three Canadian public television announcements concerning park wardens, journalists, and athletes.
Fine Arts
Dist - CDIAND **Prod** - NFBC 1978

Public Service Commercial 1 MIN
16mm
Color
$30.00 rental
Depicts the Association for Children with Down Syndrome, Inc.
Health and Safety
Dist - ADWNSS **Prod** - ADWNSS

Public Spaces 30 MIN
VHS / U-matic
In Our Own Image Series
Color (C)
Fine Arts
Dist - DALCCD **Prod** - DALCCD

The Public speaker and the audience 28 MIN
U-matic / BETA / VHS
Communication skills 1 - basic series
Color (H C G)
$101.95, $89.95 purchase _ #CA - 41
Examines the importance of effective public speaking. Dissects the process of public speaking into various parts and discusses the first two - the speaker and the audience. Part of a series on communication.
English Language; Social Science
Dist - INSTRU

Public Speaking 16 MIN
U-matic / VHS
Communication Series
Color (H C A)
Teaches the characteristics of a purpose sentence as a preliminary step in the creation of a public speech. Provides students practice in critiquing sample purpose sentences.
English Language; Psychology
Dist - MSU **Prod** - MSU

Public speaking fundamentals 13 MIN
VHS
Color (H)
Uses live action demonstrations to examine public speaking in terms of the speech, the audience and the speaker. Focuses on research and organization, watching audience reactions and practicing.
English Language
Dist - VIEWTH **Prod** - VIEWTH

Public trust, private interests - Part 3 60 MIN
VHS / U-matic
Ethics in America series
Color (G)
$45.00, $29.95 purchase
Features Jeane Kirkpatrick, Joseph A Califano, Jr, Senator Alan Simpson, Peter Jennings and others. Addresses the problems of trust - within government, between one public official and another, and between the government and the public. Part three of a ten - part series on ethics in America, produced by Fred W Friendly.
Business and Economics; Civics and Political Systems; Religion and Philosophy; Sociology
Dist - ANNCPB **Prod** - COLMU 1989

A public voice. . .95: juvenile violence, immigration 60 MIN
VHS
A public voice. . .'95 series
Color (C H G A)
$39.95 purchase _ #APUL-101-WC95
Describes current issues facing the United States. Presents several United States Senators, and journalists Suzanne Fields, Georgie Ann Geyer, Robert Siegel along with scholars and Daniel Yankelovich of Public Agenda discussing immigration, and juvenile violence.
Sociology
Dist - PBS

A public voice. . .'95 series
A public voice. . .95: juvenile violence, immigration 60 MIN
Dist - PBS

Public works 15 MIN
BETA / VHS / U-matic / 16mm
Your town II series
Color (K P)
$245.00, $68.00 purchase _ #C50735, #C51491
Shows that a city's public works department provides many services to help keep a community running smoothly - clean water, collecting and recycling trash, maintaining streets, traffic lights, bridges. Part of a five - part series on community services.
Industrial and Technical Education; Social Science; Sociology
Dist - NGS **Prod** - NGS 1992

Publicity 20 MIN
U-matic
Access Series
Color (T)
LC 76-706256
Discusses the different ways local radio and newspapers can be used to publicize the library.
Business and Economics; Education; Social Science
Dist - USNAC **Prod** - UDEN 1976

The Public's View 60 MIN
VHS / U-matic
Every Four Years Series
Color (H C A)
LC 81-706050
Examines public perceptions of the presidency and the kind of person people say they want in that office. Focuses on the 1980 political campaign.
Civics and Political Systems
Dist - AITECH **Prod** - WHYY 1980

Publique arte
CD-ROM
Color (G A)
$179.00 purchase _ #2853
Offers thousands of 600 DPI PCX images in the public domain and royalty free. Presents a convenient viewing program along with ZIP sections for bulletin board users. For IBM PCs and compatibles. Requires 640K RAM, DOS Version 3.1 or greater, one floppy disk drive - a hard drive is recommended, one empty expansion slot, and an IBM compatible CD - ROM drive.
Computer Science; Industrial and Technical Education
Dist - BEP

Publish and Print 15 MIN
U-matic / VHS
Explorers Unlimited Series
Color (P I)
Shows the complex process of preparing and printing a magazine.
Literature and Drama; Social Science
Dist - AITECH **Prod** - WVIZTV 1971

A Publisher is Known by the Company He Keeps 25 MIN
U-matic / VHS / 16mm
B&W
LC 74-701564
Presents a series of sequences about famous writers using footage from the personal film library of Alfred A Knopf.
Biography; Literature and Drama
Dist - PHENIX **Prod** - DEROCH 1974

Puccini 113 MIN
VHS
Color (S)
$39.95 purchase _ #833 - 9178
Unfolds the tragic involvement of Puccini in a scandal that nearly ruined his career. Features Robert Stephens and Virginia McKenna in the dramatic segments and excerpts from a recent production of the unfinished masterpiece 'Turandot' which shows parallels between the composer's work and life.
Fine Arts
Dist - FI **Prod** - RMART 1987

Puce moment 7 MIN
16mm
Color (G)
$12.00 rental
Evokes the Hollywood of the 1920s. Uses a fragment of an abandoned film to feflect the filmmaker's interest in the myths and decline of Hollywood.
Fine Arts
Dist - CANCIN **Prod** - ANGERK 1949

Puddling and Running Beads with Oxyacetylene
U-matic / VHS
Oxyacetylene Welding - Series
Color (SPANISH)
Industrial and Technical Education
Dist - VTRI **Prod** - VTRI

Pudd'nhead Wilson
U-matic / VHS
Films - on - Video Series
Color (G C J)
$59 purchase _ #05924 - 85
Screens the film version of Mark Twain's story that examines slavery, injustice, and human folly. Stars Ken Howard. Filmed in Harpers Ferry, West Virginia.
Fine Arts; Literature and Drama
Dist - CHUMAN

Pudd'nhead Wilson 87 MIN
VHS
(G)
$39.95 purchase _ #S00534; $39.00 purchase _ #05924-126
Presents a film version of the Mark Twain story Pudd'nhead Wilson. Set in pre - Civil War days, tells how a mulatto slave switches her mixed race child with the child of her master to keep her child out of slavery. Stars Ken Howard and Lise Hilboldt. Filmed in West Virginia.
History - United States; Literature and Drama
Dist - UILL **Prod** - GA
GA

Pueblitos De Mexico 10 MIN
U-matic / VHS / 16mm
Color (J H) (SPANISH)
LC 71-700247
A Spanish language film. Shows the visit of an American woman to a Mexican family. Includes scenes of typical village life, a music class in a modern school and children selling shell necklaces.
Foreign Language
Dist - IFB **Prod** - IFB 1963

The Pueblo Affair 106 MIN
U-matic / VHS / 16mm
Color (J)
Looks at the seizure of the American intelligence ship Pueblo by North Korean gunboats. Examines the treatment of the captain and crew as well as the tangled bureaucracy that precipitated the affair. Stars Hal Holbrook.
Civics and Political Systems; Fine Arts; History - United States
Dist - LUF **Prod** - LUF 1976

Pueblo Andaluz 14 MIN
U-matic / VHS / 16mm
Viajando Por Mexico Y Espana Series
Color; B&W (J H A) (SPANISH)
LC FIA67-1245
A Spanish language film. Depicts life in a southern village through the eyes of a young boy. To be used after lesson 10 of level II, 'Emilio en Espana.'.
Foreign Language
Dist - EBEC **Prod** - EBEC 1966

Pueblo of Laguna - Elders of the Tribe 14 MIN
16mm
Color
LC 81-700733
Documents the development and delivery of the Laguna tribe's comprehensive program of services to the elderly, including transportation, housing, nutrition, health, recreation, social services and community involvement.
Social Science
Dist - USNAC **Prod** - USHHS 1981

Pueblo peoples - first encounters 30 MIN
VHS / U-matic / VT1
Color (G)
$49.95 purchase, $35.00 rental
Captures the reaction of the Pueblo peoples to the first Spanish invaders in 1539 and 1540. Interweaves historic accounts with contemporary Pueblo interpretations of events. Explores the spiritual and cultural dimensions of the first confrontation with Europeans. Shows the Pueblo experience through stories by elders, historic pueblos, archival photographs and footage, dramatic readings, Pueblo art and music.
History - United States; History - World; Social Science
Dist - NAMPBC **Prod** - KNMETV 1991

Pueblo Renaissance 26 MIN
16mm / U-matic / VHS
Native Americans Series
Color
Provides an overview of the sacred traditions, ancient religious and agricultural ceremonies of the Pueblo people. Points out that, unlike other American Indians, the Southwest Indians were never removed from their homeland. Shows that while retaining the ancient traditions, many inhabitants of the Pueblo work at the Meson Physics Facility at Los Alamos.
Social Science; Sociology
Dist - CNEMAG **Prod** - BBCTV

Pueden Ser Protegidos 16 MIN
U-matic / VHS / 16mm
Color (IND) (SPANISH)
A Spanish language film. Trains workers to use press brakes safely. Introduces safety equipment used on press brakes. Examines fixed barrier guards, hold - back cables, two - handed control panels and electronic sensing devices.
Foreign Language; Health and Safety; Psychology
Dist - IFB **Prod** - BLLHOW

Puerto Rican folkart expression - las artesanias de Puerto Rico - a series
Puerto Rican folkart expression series
Color
Life Of Christ As Seen By A Puerto Rican.
Fine Arts; Geography - United States
Dist - CASPRC **Prod** - CASPRC 1979

Puerto Rican Folkart Expression - Las Artesanias De Puerto Rico Series
The Life of Christ as seen by a Puerto Rican woodcarver 47 MIN
The Life of Christ as Seen by a Puerto Rican Woodcarver - Pt 1 24 MIN
The Life of Christ as Seen by a Puerto Rican Woodcarver - Pt 2 23 MIN
Dist - CASPRC

Puerto Rican folkart expression series
Puerto Rican folkart expression - las artesanias de Puerto Rico - a series
Dist - CASPRC

Puerto Rican Women's Federation 29 MIN
U-matic
Woman Series
Color
Examines the goals of the Puerto Rican Women's Foundation, which is intended to change discriminatory laws and eradicate social inequities in Puerto Rico.
Geography - United States; Sociology
Dist - PBS **Prod** - WNEDTV

Puerto Ricans 30 MIN
VHS
Multicultural peoples of North America series
Color (J H C G)
$49.95 purchase _ #LVCD6685V - S
Celebrates the heritage of Puerto Ricans. Traces the history of their emigration to North America and shows the unique traditions they brought with them. Discusses why and when they emigrated, where they settled, their occupations and their important leaders. Focuses on a Puerto Rican family and explains the importance of cultural identity. Part of a 15 - part series on multiculturalism in North America.
History - United States; Sociology
Dist - CAMV

The Puerto Ricans - art as cultural expression 8 MIN
VHS
Columbus legacy series
Color (J H C G)
$40.00 purchase, $11.00 rental _ #12341
Looks at the past and present difficulties of the Puerto Rican community in Pennsylvania. Visits the Taller Puertorriqueno art center, where art is used as a means of self - expression and as a tool to educate children. Shows and discusses a rare display of Puerto Rican art. Part of a 15 - part series commemorating the 500th anniversary of Columbus' journeys to the Americas - journeys that brought together a constantly evolving collection of different ethnic groups and examining the contributions of 15 distinct groups who imprinted their heritage on the day - to - day life of Pennsylvania.
History - United States; Sociology
Dist - PSU **Prod** - WPSXTV 1992

Puerto Rico
VHS
Dances of the world series
Color (G)
$39.95 purchase _ #FD1500V
Presents performances of dances from Puerto Rico. Interviews the dancers.
Fine Arts; Geography - United States
Dist - CAMV **Prod** - CAMV

Puerto Rico 28 MIN
16mm / U-matic / VHS
Captioned; Color (A) (SPANISH (ENGLISH SUBTITLES))
Presents a socio - economic analysis of Puerto Rico, and discusses the history of U S involvement in Puerto Rico and the anti - colonialist struggle. Spanish dialog with English subtitles. In two parts.
Fine Arts; History - United States
Dist - CNEMAG **Prod** - CUBAFI 1975

Puerto Rico 79 MIN
16mm
B&W (H C A) (SPANISH (ENGLISH SUBTITLES))
$895 purchase, $95 rental
Presents a socio economic analysis of Puerto Rico. Shows archival footage, reenactments of key historical events, and interviews with participants in the Puerto Rico independence movement. Coproduced by the Cuban Film Institute and Tirabuzon Rojo.
Business and Economics; History - World
Dist - CNEMAG

Puerto Rico - a Colony the American Way 27 MIN
U-matic / VHS / 16mm
Color
Portrays Puerto Rico and its long relationship with the U S. Examines Puerto Rico's emerging economic crisis, reviews the transformation of the island in the 50's under Operation Bootstrap and shows demonstrators protesting U S naval bombardment and artillery practice on the off - shore islands.
Geography - United States; History - United States
Dist - CNEMAG **Prod** - TERRP

Puerto Rico - art and identity 56 MIN
VHS
Color (H G)
$350.00 purchase, $95.00 rental
Surveys the work of plastics artists in Puerto Rico during the 20th century, focusing on the artists' expression of national identity. Combines illustrations of hundreds of art works with interviews with a dozen major art critics. Directed by Sonia Fritz.
Fine Arts; History - United States; Social Science
Dist - CNEMAG

Puerto Rico Es Asi 22 MIN
U-matic / VHS / 16mm
Color (I J H) (SPANISH)
A Spanish language version of Puerto Rico - The Caribbean Americans. Describes the land and people of Puerto Rico. Introduces Rafael Gonzalez, one of many Puerto Ricans who came to the United States to make a better life, then returned to the island of his birth.
Foreign Language; Geography - United States
Dist - IFB **Prod** - ABCNEW 1970

Puerto Rico - history and culture 25 MIN
VHS
Hispanic culture video series
Color (J H)
$49.95 purchase _ #VK45361
Surveys the history of Puerto Rico from the 15th century to the 1990s. Presents part of a six - part series that examines the background and history of Spanish influences on the history, culture and society of different parts of the world.
History - United States; History - World
Dist - KNOWUN

Puerto Rico, Isle of Guernsey, United States 27 MIN
16mm
Big Blue Marble - Children Around the World Series
Color (P I)
LC 76-700624
Describes sports activities of children in Puerto Rico, the Isle of Guernsey and New Jersey. Presents a Puerto Rican folk tale about a red hat. Program M on the Big blue marble - children around the world series.
Geography - United States; Geography - World; Literature and Drama; Social Science
Dist - VITT **Prod** - ALVEN 1975

Puerto Rico Libre 26 MIN
U-matic
Interface Series
Color
Asks whether Puerto Rico should remain a Commonwealth of the United States or become independent.
Geography - United States
Dist - PBS **Prod** - WETATV

Puerto Rico - Migration 9 MIN
16mm
Color (I J H)
Explains that large numbers of Puerto Ricans left their homeland to settle in some of the larger cities in the United States. Depicts the problems these people faced in the course of their migration. Parallels the Puerto Ricans with the Europeans who came to the United States during the late 19th and early 20th century.
History - United States; Sociology
Dist - SF **Prod** - SF 1972

Puerto Rico - more or Less 22 MIN
16mm
Color (SPANISH)
LC 76-703678; 74-705448
Shows the many beauties of Puerto Rico and the work of the Institute of Tropical Forestry and the research that is being carried on to improve the forests of Puerto Rico.
Agriculture; Foreign Language; Geography - World
Dist - USNAC **Prod** - USDA 1972

Puerto Rico - Our Right to Decide 28 MIN
U-matic / VHS / 16mm
Color
Examines the social reality behind most Americans' image of Puerto Rico, primarily as a pleasant vacation spot. Describes Puerto Ricans as disenfranchised US Citizens who cannot vote in national elections and have no representation in the Congress. Traces the island's history from Spanish colonials' destruction of Indian natives to revolts quelled by US troops to the unsolved questions of today - Puerto Rican destiny and right to determine their own future.
Geography - United States; History - United States
Dist - CNEMAG **Prod** - BOMME 1981

Puerto Rico - Paradise Invaded 30 MIN
16mm / U-matic / VHS
Captioned; Color (A) (SPANISH (ENGLISH SUBTITLES))
Portrays the history and present - day reality of Puerto Rico. Discusses the relationship with the United States, the impact of industrialization, the economic exile and life in New York City, and the Puerto Rican independence movement. Includes interviews with Puerto Ricans and rare documentary and news reel footage of the 1898 invasion by the Marines. Spanish dialog with English subtitles.
Fine Arts; History - United States
Dist - CNEMAG **Prod** - BEATOA 1977

Puerto Rico - progress in the Caribbean 25 MIN
VHS / U-matic / 16mm
Color (J H C A)
$525.00 purchase
Examines the Caribbean island of Puerto Rico, a commonwealth of the US which is trying to decide its future status - as a state, an independent nation, or continuation of its present status.
Geography - United States; History - United States; History - World
Dist - HANDEL **Prod** - HANDEL 1988

Puerto Rico - south coast diving - Gil Gerard 30 MIN
VHS
Scuba World series
Color (G)
$24.90 purchase _ #0450
Joins Scuba World and television star Gil Gerard on a diving expedition in the virgin reefs off the south coast of Puerto Rico. Experiences the history and culture of the island.
Geography - World; Physical Education and Recreation
Dist - SEVVID

Puerto Rico USA 24 MIN
16mm
Color
LC 80-701557
Looks at the Puerto Rican people, discussing culture, lifestyles, spirit, and commitment. Emphasizes the benefits of investing in Puerto Rico.
Geography - United States
Dist - EDAPR **Prod** - EDAPR 1980

Puerto Rico, USA - Profile of a People 23 MIN
16mm
Color
Pictures Puerto Rico as a land where economic growth has created a unique partnership between government and industry. Shows that the family remains the centerpiece of life in Puerto Rico.
History - World
Dist - MTP **Prod** - PROT

Pues, Alfredo 28 MIN
16mm / U-matic / VHS
Career Job Opportunity Film Series
B&W
LC 74-706516
Informs Spanish - American junior and senior high school students and veterans of the basic requirements and opportunities available in apprenticeship.
Guidance and Counseling; Sociology
Dist - USNAC **Prod** - USDLMA 1969

Puff and the Incredible Mr Nobody 24 MIN
16mm / U-matic / VHS
Puff Series
Color (K P I)
When Terry needed a friend who thought in the same intellectual way he did, he invented Nobody - a duck with a sauce - pan hat and a wild imagination. When Terry's parents urged him to let Nobody go, he felt lost without his friend. Puff, the Magic Dragon took Terry on a fantastic odyssey through the Fantaverse, and he realized that the children at school didn't understand how special he was. He found Nobody and learned something about Somebody.
Fine Arts; Literature and Drama; Psychology
Dist - PERSPF **Prod** - PERSPF 1984
CORF VIEWTH
VIEWTH

Puff Pastry Dough 9 MIN
U-matic / VHS
Color (PRO)
Demonstrates the long method and the Blitz or Scottish Method of making puff pastry.
Home Economics; Industrial and Technical Education
Dist - CULINA **Prod** - CULINA

Puff Pastry - Pt 1
VHS / U-matic
Puff Pastry Series
Color
Home Economics; Industrial and Technical Education
Dist - CULINA **Prod** - CULINA

Puff Pastry - Pt 2
VHS / U-matic
Puff Pastry Series
Color
Home Economics; Industrial and Technical Education
Dist - CULINA **Prod** - CULINA

Puff Pastry Series
Puff Pastry - Pt 1
Puff Pastry - Pt 2
Dist - CULINA

Puff Series
Puff and the Incredible Mr Nobody 24 MIN
Puff the Magic Dragon 24 MIN
Puff the Magic Dragon in the Land of Living Lies 24 MIN
Dist - CORF
PERSPF
VIEWTH

Puff the Magic Dragon 24 MIN
16mm / U-matic / VHS
Puff Series
Color (K P I)
Presents an animated story with the voice of Burgess Meredith as Puff. Tells how doctors despair of ever curing Jackie of his shyness until Puff takes him on an incredible journey to the land of Hona Lee. Eventually Jackie makes contact with the real world again so he no longer needs to retreat into the world of his imagination to cover his shyness.
Fine Arts; Literature and Drama; Psychology
Dist - PERSPF **Prod** - PERSPF 1984
CORF VIEWTH
VIEWTH

Puff the Magic Dragon in the Land of Living Lies 24 MIN
U-matic / 16mm / VHS
Puff Series
Color (K P I)
Tells how when Sandy's parents were divorced, she assumed guilt and responsibility and resolved these feelings by telling fictitious tales which appeared to be lies. When Puff, a genuine imaginary dragon, took her on a magical journey to the Land of Living Lies, Sandy realized that the divorce wasn't her fault and learned the difference between harmless fantasy and falsehood.
Fine Arts; Literature and Drama; Psychology
Dist - PERSPF **Prod** - PERSPF 1984
CORF VIEWTH
VIEWTH

Puffed out 7 MIN
16mm / VHS / BETA / U-matic
Color; PAL (I J)
PdS80, PdS88 purchase; LC 81-700711
Takes youngsters down into the sordid little ashtray world of Bill and Betty and out into their own world of running, dancing and surfing. Lets children know that smoking doesn't just cause cancer, it also slows down their reflexes considerably. An animated production by Film Victoria.
Health and Safety; Sociology
Dist - EDPAT **Prod** - VICCOR 1981
TASCOR

The Puffed - Up Dragon 10 MIN
16mm
Color (K P I)
LC FIA66-1179
The story of a friendly, vegetarian dragon, who visits a medieval kingdom and eats wagon - loads of food each day while the townspeople try to get rid of him. The story is told with animated paper cut - outs and music.
Literature and Drama
Dist - SF **Prod** - VIKING 1966

Puffins 25 MIN
U-matic / VHS / 16mm
Untamed Frontier Series
Color; Mono (J H C A)
$400.00 film, $250.00 video, $50.00 rental
Features the habits and behavior of the Puffin bird.
Science - Natural
Dist - CTV **Prod** - CTV 1975

Puffins 10 MIN
VHS / U-matic
Eye on Nature Series
Color (I J)
$250 purchase
Shows the social life of puffins and the efforts to protect them from extinction. Produced by the BBC.
Science - Natural
Dist - CORF

Puffins and Ladybirds 10 MIN
VHS
Tiny tales series
Color (K P I)
$195.00 purchase
Presents two short animated stories narrated in rhyme by Ivor the spider. Tells a story about puffins in The Story of Humphrey the Puffin and about ladybirds in Color Me Red.
Literature and Drama
Dist - LANDMK **Prod** - LANDMK

Puffins, Predators and Pirates 28 MIN
16mm
Nature of Things Series
Color (I J H)
LC 79-700961
Views the struggle between two species, the North American Puffin and the Herring Gull. Describes their life on the Great Island near Newfoundland and explains that their delicate population balance has been upset by man's pollution of the coastal waters.
Science - Natural
Dist - FLMLIB **Prod** - CANBC 1979

The Pugnacious Sailing Master 30 MIN
16mm
B&W
Presents the story of Uriah P Levy, who was responsible for the elimination of corporal punishment in the U S Navy, and who refused to conceal his Jewish origin in the face of anti - semitic taunting from members of the crew. Tells how Levy later become a commodore. (Kinescope).
Religion and Philosophy
Dist - NAAJS **Prod** - JTS 1954

Pulaskis, Shovels and Men 25 MIN
16mm
Color (PRO)
Tells the story of the organization of a crew for the suppression of a watershed fire.
Health and Safety; Social Science
Dist - LAFIRE **Prod** - LAFIRE

Pulcinella 11 MIN
16mm
Color
LC 74-701037
Presents an animated cartoon about the uproarious adventures of Pulcinella, the Tuscan version of the puppet Punch.
Literature and Drama
Dist - CONNF **Prod** - CONNF 1973

Pull My Daisy 29 MIN
16mm
B&W (A)
Presents a slice of beatnik life in a New York Bowery loft with Allan Ginsberg, Gregory Corso, Peter Orlovsky and Larry Rivers. Documents the subculture of the 1950's and features narration by author Jack Kerouac.

Fine Arts; Literature and Drama; Sociology
Dist - NYFLMS **Prod** - NYFLMS 1959

Pull ourselves up or die out 26 MIN
VHS
San - Ju - Wasi series
Color (G)
$150.00 purchase, $20.00 rental
Presents a field report on the situation of the Kung San people at TshumKwi in Namibia. Looks at economic issues, the possible establishment of a game reserve, development of the cattle industry and conflicts over water rights. Part of a series by John Marshall about the Kung in Namibia and Botswana.
Geography - World; History - World; Sociology
Dist - DOCEDR **Prod** - DOCEDR

Pull out - fallout 4 MIN
16mm
Color (G)
$10.00 rental
Explains filmmaker Barnett, 'Junkfilm assemblage from 50 prints of a trailer for a James Bond film.'
Fine Arts
Dist - CANCIN **Prod** - BARND 1974

Pull through Intra - Urethral Bladder Flap - a New Surgical Treatment of Post 25 MIN
U-matic
Color (PRO)
Shows an intra - urethral bladder flap operation on a patient who is incontinent after a suprapubic prostatectomy and who has perineal urethral fistula due to erosion of a bulbous urethra after using a Kaufman III prothesis.
Health and Safety
Dist - USNAC **Prod** - VAHSL 1976

Pull together 4 MIN
VHS / U-matic
Color (G)
$250.00 purchase, $125.00 rental
Uses women and men in racing shells, rowing as a synchronized single unit, with a single purpose but with collective strengths and skills. Demonstrates teamwork. Produced by NVC.
Business and Economics; Guidance and Counseling; Literature and Drama; Psychology
Dist - VLEARN

The Pulley 11 MIN
16mm
Color (P I J)
Describes the function and operation of the pulley and at the same time develops the concepts of force, work and mechanical advantage. Shows the fixed pulley, the moveable pulley and the block and tackle.
Science - Physical
Dist - VIEWTH **Prod** - CENCO

The Pulley 5 MIN
U-matic
Eureka Series
Color (J)
Shows how a pulley works to lift a heavy object. If the number of ropes supporting the weight is doubled the mechanical advantage is also doubled.
Science; Science - Physical
Dist - TVOTAR **Prod** - TVOTAR 1980

Pulley - a Simple Machine 15 MIN
VHS / U-matic
Why Series
Color (P I)
Discusses the characteristics of a pulley.
Science - Physical
Dist - AITECH **Prod** - WDCNTV 1976

Pulley Bar 15 MIN
U-matic / VHS
Blueprint Reading for Machinists Series
Color (IND)
Shows basics of reading blueprints. Demonstrates how to identify dimensions and other vital characteristics of the part to be produced.
Industrial and Technical Education
Dist - LEIKID **Prod** - LEIKID

Pulley Bar (Basic)
U-matic / VHS
Blueprint Reading Series
Color (SPANISH)
Industrial and Technical Education
Dist - VTRI **Prod** - VTRI

Pulleys 12 MIN
U-matic / VHS / 16mm
Simple Machines Series
Color (I J)
$315, $215 purchase _ #4482
Shows the different parts of a pulley and its uses.
Industrial and Technical Education
Dist - CORF

Pulleys and Work Load 14 MIN
U-matic / VHS / 16mm
Color (I)
LC FIA68-2112
Explores what the pulley, a typical, simple machine, can and cannot do. Shows that pulleys do not create energy, but can be used to make a small force exert a large force.
Science - Physical
Dist - PHENIX **Prod** - IWANMI 1968

Pulling and Installing Cable and Packing Terminal Tubes 16 MIN
16mm
B&W
LC FIE52-210
Demonstrates how to pull, strap and straighten cable, prepare cable for pushing and for pulling with a rope and how to pack terminal tubes.
Industrial and Technical Education
Dist - USNAC **Prod** - USOE 1945

Pulling Flowers 29 MIN
VHS / 16mm
A Different Understanding Series
Color (G)
$90.00 purchase _ #BPN230603
Dramatizes the parental practice of pressuring children into becoming superachievers. Shows the dangers of pushing too hard.
Psychology; Sociology
Dist - RMIBHF TVOTAR **Prod** - RMIBHF TVOTAR 1985

Pulling it all together 30 MIN
Videoreel / VT2
Designing home interiors series; Unit 28
Color (C A)
Discusses when architectural changes are appropriate in the sequence of an interior design plan.
Home Economics
Dist - CDTEL **Prod** - COAST

Pulling Together 9 MIN
16mm / U-matic / VHS
Color (P I)
LC 78-700788
Tells the story of a little boy and his friend, the Squiggle, and how they rescue their friend, the Puffy, from a bubble gum pond. Focuses on individual strengths and working together.
Guidance and Counseling; Sociology
Dist - BARR **Prod** - BARR 1978

Pulmonary Anastomosis 33 MIN
16mm
Color (PRO)
Illustrates the operative technique of aortic - pulmonary anastomosis for tetralogy of fallot. Summarizes follow - up results in the first 100 patients operated upon six to eight years ago.
Health and Safety; Science
Dist - ACY **Prod** - ACYDGD 1955

Pulmonary Arterial Catheterization 9 MIN
U-matic / VHS
Color (PRO)
Demonstrates pulmonary catheterization in the intraoperative and postoperative monitoring of a critically ill patient using the Swan - Ganz, flow directed catheter. Utilizes an oscilloscope to determine its location.
Health and Safety; Science - Natural
Dist - UARIZ **Prod** - UARIZ

Pulmonary Artery Banding 24 MIN
U-matic / VHS
Cardiovascular Series
Color
Health and Safety; Science - Natural
Dist - SVL **Prod** - SVL

Pulmonary artery cannulation - anatomical considerations 17 MIN
VHS / U-matic
Color (PRO C)
$395.00 purchase, $80.00 rental _ #C870 - VI - 010
Provides an anatomical review of the veins used for cannulation - the basilic, subclavian, internal and external jugular, cephalic and femoral veins. Shows them in relation to significant structures. Discusses the advantages, disadvantages and complications of various venous sites. Presented by Dr Jon Grossman and Bruce M Smith.
Health and Safety
Dist - HSCIC

The Pulmonary Artery Catheter and the Nurse 28 MIN
VHS / 16mm
Color (PRO)
$295.00 purchase, $60.00 rental
Discusses the pulmonary artery catheter, often referred to as the Swan Ganz. Describes when and why this procedure is used - nursing responsibilities, catheter maintenance, normal values for PAP, PCWP and cardiac output as well as potential complications.
Health and Safety
Dist - FAIRGH **Prod** - FAIRGH 1988

Pulmonary artery catheter insertion - nursing care 28 MIN
VHS / U-matic
Pulmonary artery catheters series
Color (PRO)
$275.00 purchase, $60.00 rental _ #7524S, #7524V
Presents a comprehensive study of pulmonary artery catheter insertion. Features Terri Forshee, critical care nurse specialist, and Dr A J C Swan, co - originator of the catheter. Details nursing responsibilities before and during insertion procedure and components and functions of the catheter. Considers potential complications. Uses graphics to demonstrate insertion. Part of a two - part series.
Health and Safety
Dist - AJN **Prod** - HOSSN 1986

Pulmonary artery catheters series
Presents a two - part series on pulmonary artery catheters. Details insertion procedures and nursing management on indwelling catheters.
Indwelling pulmonary artery catheters - nursing management 28 MIN
Pulmonary artery catheter insertion - nursing care 28 MIN
Dist - AJN **Prod** - HOSSN 1986

Pulmonary Complications in Shock 17 MIN
16mm
Upjohn Vanguard of Medicine Series
Color (PRO)
LC 75-700366
Demonstrates the shock lung phenomenon, using in vivo cinematography of a dog's lung. Explains the correct step - by - step program required to prevent this pulmonary edema in a human patient in severe shock.
Health and Safety; Science - Natural
Dist - UPJOHN **Prod** - UPJOHN 1974

Pulmonary Complications of Fire and Smoke 22 MIN
VHS / U-matic
Color (PRO)
Provides information which aids physicians in diagnosing smoke inhalation from the minute signs and symptoms, determining the severity of pulmonary damage from the physical exam, determining the existence of carbon monoxide intoxication, managing the airway, treating progressive bronchiolitis and infections if pulmonary infiltrates appear on chest x - rays and performing pulmonary hygiene to treat accompanying bronchospasm.
Health and Safety
Dist - UMICHM **Prod** - UMICHM 1976

Pulmonary Cryptococcosis 16 MIN
16mm
Clinical Pathology Series
B&W
LC 74-705449
Presents a review of the epidemiology of pulmonary cryptococcosis as well as the clinical and radiologic findings. Discusses the laboratory techniques for the isolation and identification of the etiologic agent. (Kinescope).
Science
Dist - USNAC **Prod** - NMAC 1969

Pulmonary Disease - the Hidden Enemy 25 MIN
U-matic / VHS
Killers Series
Color
Looks at America's most deadly, yet most preventable illness, pulmonary disease. Explains what causes respiratory disease, who's likely to be afflicted and what can be done to prevent it. Fosters new understanding, through on - the - scene reports from clinics and hospitals and respect for the efforts and achievements of science in combating pulmonary ailments.
Health and Safety; Sociology
Dist - MEDCOM **Prod** - MEDCOM

Pulmonary Embolism 18 MIN
VHS / U-matic
Emergency Management - the First 30 Minutes, Vol II Series
Color
Discusses pulmonary embolism, including pre - disposing factors, signs of thrombophlebitis, ventilation perfusion lung scan, pulmonary angiography, arterial blood gas analysis and treatment with heparin therapy.
Health and Safety; Science
Dist - VTRI **Prod** - VTRI

Pulmonary Function Testing 1 - Lung Volumes and Capacities using ' Collins' Spirometer 14 MIN
VHS / BETA
Color (PRO)
Mathematics; Science - Natural
Dist - RMIBHF **Prod** - RMIBHF

Pulmonary Histoplasmosis 30 MIN
16mm
Clinical Pathology Series
B&W
LC 74-705453
Discusses pulmonary histoplasmosis, its spectrum etiology, epidemiology, distribution, clinical forms and radiologic findings. Shows techniques for the isolation and identification of H capsulatum and treatment. (Kinescope).
Health and Safety; Science
Dist - USNAC **Prod** - NMAC 1969

Pulmonary Manifestations of Cardiovascular Disease 27 MIN
U-matic
Radiology of the Respiratory System - a Basic Review Series
Color (C)
Presents disorders of the cardiovascular system as they are reflected in the lung.
Health and Safety; Industrial and Technical Education; Science - Natural
Dist - UOKLAH **Prod** - UOKLAH 1978

Pulmonary Mycosis - Pt 1 - Blastomycosis 12 MIN
16mm / U-matic
Clinical Pathology Series
B&W
LC 74-705454; 76-706082
Defines blastomycosis as a chronic granulomatous mycosis primarily in the lungs. Presents early symptomatology. Discusses epidemiology and concurrent factors, such as race, sex and age. (Kinescope).
Health and Safety
Dist - USNAC **Prod** - NMAC 1969

Pulmonary Resection 29 MIN
16mm
Color (PRO)
Explains that meticulous dissection of the vascular and bronchial anatomy at the pulmonary hilum greatly increases the safety of pulmonary resectional procedures. Shows a number of techniques, including a rapid pneumonectomy utilizing vascular clamps.
Health and Safety; Science
Dist - ACY **Prod** - ACYDGD 1967

Pulp 7 MIN
16mm
B&W
LC 75-703222
Satirizes the content of modern 'pulp' magazines. Shows the effect of these magazines' exaggerated style of writing on a leather jacketed youth who is viewing the world as the magazine writers do.
Literature and Drama; Psychology; Social Science; Sociology
Dist - USC **Prod** - USC

Pulp and Paper Training - Kraft Pulping Series
Pulp Treament - Pt 2
Dist - LEIKID

Pulp and Paper Training, Module 1 - Kraft Pulping Series
Kraft Pulping, Pt 1
Kraft Pulping, Pt 3
Kraft Pulping, Pt 4
Pulp Treatment - Pt 1
Pulp Treatment - Pt 3
Wood, Pt 1
Wood, Woodyard and Pulping
Dist - LEIKID

Pulp and paper training, module 3 - papermaking series
Cylinder machine
Dryers
Finishing and Shipping
Fourdrinier machine, Pt 1
Fourdrinier machine, Pt 2
Papermaking, Pt 1
Papermaking, Pt 2
Papermaking, Pt 3
Presses
White Water and Broke
Dist - LEIKID

Pulp and Paper Training, Module 2 - Chemcial - - Recovery Series
Black Liquor Systems, Pt 1
Dist - LEIKID

Pulp and Paper Training, Module 2 - Chemical Recovery Series
Black Liquor Systems Operation
Black Liquor Systems, Pt 2
Recovery boiler - Pt 1
Recovery boiler - Pt 2
Recovery Boiler Operation
The Recovery Process
Smelt Recovery Operation
Smelt Recovery, Pt 1
Smelt Recovery, Pt 2
Dist - LEIKID

Pulp and Paper Training - Thermo - Mechanical Pulping Series
Introduction to TMP
Materials Handling
Operation and Process Control
Pulp Treatment
Refining Principles
Steam and Water Recovery and Effluent Treatment
TMP Equipment
Dist - LEIKID

Pulp Treament - Pt 2
VHS / U-matic
Pulp and Paper Training - Kraft Pulping Series
Color (IND)
Covers refiners, handling rejects and pulp washers. Module 1 on the Pulp and paper training - kraft pulping series.
Business and Economics; Industrial and Technical Education; Social Science
Dist - LEIKID **Prod** - LEIKID

Pulp Treatment
VHS / U-matic
Pulp and Paper Training - Thermo - Mechanical Pulping Series
Color (IND)
Shows treatment of pulp after refining. Includes screening and cleaning, objectives, latency treatment, handling and refining of rejects, and thickening of the pulp for storage.
Industrial and Technical Education
Dist - LEIKID **Prod** - LEIKID

Pulp Treatment - Pt 1
U-matic / VHS
Pulp and Paper Training, Module 1 - Kraft Pulping Series
Color (IND)
Covers several aspects of the pulp treatment process such as the purpose, coarse and fine screens and knot breakers.
Business and Economics; Industrial and Technical Education; Social Science
Dist - LEIKID **Prod** - LEIKID

Pulp Treatment - Pt 3
U-matic / VHS
Pulp and Paper Training, Module 1 - Kraft Pulping Series
Color (IND)
Includes several aspects of pulp treatment such as wash water, thickeners, pulp storage and treatment systems.
Business and Economics; Industrial and Technical Education; Social Science
Dist - LEIKID **Prod** - LEIKID

Pulse 11 MIN
16mm
B&W (P I J H C)
LC 72-702045
An experimental film which combines a succession of still drawings of abstract shapes with a sound track of electronic synthesized sounds.
Fine Arts; Industrial and Technical Education
Dist - CFS **Prod** - BYMPRO 1972

Pulse
16mm
Color
Presents an experimental film done entirely in animation.
Fine Arts; Industrial and Technical Education
Dist - CANCIN **Prod** - CANCIN

Pulse 10 MIN animation.
16mm
B&W
Fine Arts; Industrial and Technical Education
Dist - CANCIN **Prod** - CANCIN 1969

Pulse code modulation 10 MIN
VHS / BETA / U-matic
Color; PAL (J H)
PdS15.00 purchase
Shows how a signal can be converted into a coded string of electrical pulses for transmission and then decoded at the receiver. Includes teachers' notes. Contact distributor for free loan information.
Education; Industrial and Technical Education
Dist - BTEDSE

Pulse Modulation 26 MIN
16mm
B&W
LC 74-705455
Discusses the basic principles of pulse modification with emphasis on these terms - pulse repetition frequency, pulse width, peak power, average power, duty cycle and pulse repetition time. Explains the block diagram of a pulse modulated transmitter showing the waveshapes out of each block. (Kinescope).
Industrial and Technical Education; Science - Physical
Dist - USNAC **Prod** - USAF 1965

Pulse oximetry 15 MIN
VHS / U-matic / BETA
High tech skills in nursing series
Color (C PRO)
$280.00 purchase _ #608.1
Contrasts arterial blood gases - ABG - and pulse oximetry, including data obtained, efficiency and efficacy of the procedures, and implications for the patient. Describes the relationship between SaO2 and PaO2 on the oxygen - hemoglobin dissociation curve, and discusses the general principles underlying pulse oximetry. Shows use of equipment and gives guidelines to help nurses interpret information. Part of a five - part series.
Health and Safety; Science - Natural
Dist - CONMED **Prod** - CONMED

Pulsing and Patterning, Leading and Directing 29 MIN
VHS / 16mm
Encounters Series
Color (I)
$200.00 purchase _ #269207
Presents a ten - part series on art. Introduces art concepts, encourages students to visually explore their world and the world of art, and demonstrates art techniques such as drawing, printmaking, photography, clay and wire sculpture, painting and fabric arts to motivate art expression. 'Pulsing And Patterning, Leading And Directing' explores the many different patterns and rhythms in the environment and in art. Teaches how to create pattern and rhythm in art compositions through repetition and movement.
Computer Science; Fine Arts
Dist - ACCESS **Prod** - ACCESS 1988

Pultrusion and pulforming 50 MIN
BETA / VHS / U-matic
Composites I the basics series
Color
$400 purchase
Presents pultrusion of composites versus extrusion of metals.
Industrial and Technical Education; Science; Science - Physical
Dist - ASM **Prod** - ASM

Pump and Valve Packing 60 MIN
VHS / U-matic
Mechanical Equipment Maintenance, Module 3 - Packing and Seals 'Series
Color (IND)
Industrial and Technical Education
Dist - LEIKID **Prod** - LEIKID

Pump Assembly 60 MIN
U-matic / VHS
Mechanical Equipment Maintenance, Module 5 - Centrifugal Pumps 'Series
Color (IND)
Industrial and Technical Education
Dist - LEIKID **Prod** - LEIKID

Pump Disassembly 60 MIN
U-matic / VHS
Mechanical Equipment Maintenance, Module 5 - Centrifugal Pumps 'Series
Color (IND)
Industrial and Technical Education
Dist - LEIKID **Prod** - LEIKID

Pump failure 30 MIN
U-matic
Acute myocardial infarction series; Unit 2
Color (PRO)
LC 77-706060
Describes normal and abnormal left ventricular function curves and explains the importance of measuring the pulmonary capillary wedge pressure, cardiac output and systemic resistance in patients with acute myocardial infarction complicated by pump failure.
Health and Safety; Science - Natural
Dist - USNAC **Prod** - NMAC 1977

Pump Island Serviceman 24 MIN
U-matic
Occupations Series
B&W (J I)
Shows the work done by a graduate of an occupational course who is a saleman at an automotive service station.

Guidance and Counseling
Dist - TVOTAR **Prod** - TVOTAR 1985

Pump Operations, Centrifugal Pumps 60 MIN
VHS / U-matic
Equipment Operation Training Program Series
Color (IND)
Identifies the major parts of a centrifugal pump and tells how it works. Defines net positive suction, head available and suction head required. Shows how to read and interpret a pump normal operating curve as well as a pump system characteristic curve.
Industrial and Technical Education
Dist - ITCORP **Prod** - ITCORP

Pump Operations, Positive Displacement Pumps 60 MIN
U-matic / VHS
Equipment Operation Training Program Series
Color (IND)
Describes the operation of a rotary positive displacement pump. Highlights performing an emergency pump shutdown. Tells how a reciprocating positive displacement pump works.
Industrial and Technical Education
Dist - ITCORP **Prod** - ITCORP

Pump Operator 26 MIN
16mm
Color (PRO)
Depicts the development of the pump apparatus, how it is placed in service, how men are trained to use it, spotting for hookups, routine, and fire maintenance, driving, and handling and tips on drafting and firefighting procedures.
Health and Safety; Social Science
Dist - FILCOM **Prod** - LACFD 1955

Pump Packing 7 MIN
16mm
Color (IND)
Shows how to remove old ring packing, how to cut new packing rings, how to install new rings for long life, what the function of the lantern ring is and how to tighten packing glands.
Industrial and Technical Education
Dist - MOKIN **Prod** - MOKIN

Pumpdown, Evacuation and Charging 60 MIN
U-matic / VHS
Air Conditioning and Refrigeration - Training Series
Color (IND)
Teaches about system pump down, system evacuation and charging.
Education; Industrial and Technical Education
Dist - ITCORP **Prod** - ITCORP

Pumping Apparatus Video Series
Presents a four - part video series on pumping apparatus for training firefighting personnel. Includes operation, positioning, operating pumps and maintenance and inspection. Comes with instructor's guides.

Apparatus maintenance and inspection	30 MIN
Operating Emergency Vehicles	30 MIN
Operating Fire Pumps	30 MIN
Positioning Apparatus	30 MIN

Dist - OKSU **Prod** - OKSU

Pumping hormones 45 MIN
VHS / U-matic
Color (J H G)
$270.00, $320.00 purchase, $60.00 rental
Discusses the role hormones play in many aspects of human physiology. Covers many of the different hormones in the body and how they influence bodily functions.
Psychology
Dist - NDIM **Prod** - CANBC 1993

Pumping iron II - the women 107 MIN
35mm / 16mm
Color (G)
Examines the effect of the weightlifting phenomenon on women. Features four very different women and documents their preparations for the Caesar's Palace Women's World Cup in Las Vegas, Nevada. Looks at the issue of femininity, asking whether it's possible to be both sexy and strong. Directed by George Butler. Stars Rachel McLish, Lori Bowen, Carla Dunlap and Bev Francis. Contact distributor for price.
Fine Arts; Physical Education and Recreation; Sociology
Dist - OCTOBF

Pumping life - the heart and circulatory system 22 MIN
VHS
Color (P I J)
$89.00 purchase _ #RB847
Follows the functions of the circulatory system. Emphasizes the importance of blood and the roles of red and white blood cells. Uses graphics to show the functions of the heart, its four chambers and the journey of blood.
Science - Natural
Dist - REVID **Prod** - REVID

The Pumpkin Eater 114 MIN
16mm / U-matic / VHS
B&W
Based on the novel of the same name by Penelope Mortimer. Delves into the problems of a contempory marriage with all its possible ramifications. Studies the relationships of men and women through infidelity, multiple divorce, the population explosion, and psychiatric sessions. Stars Anne Bancroft.
Fine Arts
Dist - FI **Prod** - CPC 1964

The Pumpkin who Couldn't Smile 23 MIN
16mm / U-matic / VHS
Color (K P I)
Describes what happens when Raggedy Ann and Raggedy Andy bring together a glum pumpkin and a sad boy during the Halloween season.
Fine Arts; Literature and Drama; Social Science
Dist - CORF **Prod** - CORF 1981

Pumps - 1 60 MIN
VHS
Equipment operations series
Color (PRO)
$600.00 - $1500.00 purchase _ #OTPU1
Introduces the functions and uses of pumps in systems providing fluid flow in plant operations. Considers positive displacement and centrifugal pumps. Part of a twenty - part series on equipment operation. Includes ten textbooks and an instructor guide to support four hours of instruction.
Health and Safety; Industrial and Technical Education; Psychology
Dist - NUSTC **Prod** - NUSTC

Pumps - 2 60 MIN
VHS
Equipment operations series
Color (PRO)
$600.00 - $1500.00 purchase _ #OTPU2
Focuses on the various types of positive displacement pumps available to industry. Covers major components, basic operating principles for each type and operator responsibilities. Part of a twenty - part series on equipment operation. Includes ten textbooks and an instructor guide to support four hours of instruction.
Health and Safety; Industrial and Technical Education; Psychology
Dist - NUSTC **Prod** - NUSTC

Pumps - 3 60 MIN
VHS
Equipment operations series
Color (PRO)
$600.00 - $1500.00 purchase _ #OTPU3
Presents the wide scope of single - stage and multistage centrifugal pump use in industry. Examines the functions of major centrifugal pump components. Part of a twenty - part series on equipment operation. Includes ten textbooks and an instructor guide to support four hours of instruction.
Education; Industrial and Technical Education; Psychology
Dist - NUSTC **Prod** - NUSTC

Pumps and Actuators - no 3 60 MIN
U-matic
Hydraulic Technology Series
Color (PRO)
Teaches hydraulic technology to professionals working in the field.
Industrial and Technical Education
Dist - VTRI **Prod** - VTRI 1986

Pumps and Compressors
U-matic / VHS
Drafting - Piping Familiarization Series
Color (IND)
Industrial and Technical Education
Dist - GPCV **Prod** - GPCV

Pumps and their lubrication 14 MIN
BETA / VHS / U-matic
Color (IND G)
$295.00 purchase _ #800 - 15
Intructs operating personnel in the fundamental principles of centrifugal, reciprocating and rotary pumps. Overviews preventive maintenance practices.
Health and Safety; Industrial and Technical Education; Psychology
Dist - ITSC **Prod** - ITSC

Pumps series

Centrifugal Pumps - 1	60 MIN
Centrifugal Pumps - 2	60 MIN
Gaskets, packing and mechanical seals	60 MIN
Mechanical Seals	60 MIN
Multistage Centrifugal Pumps	60 MIN
Positive displacement pumps - Pt 1	60 MIN
Positive displacement pumps - Pt 2	60 MIN

Dist - NUSTC

Punch and Jonathan 9 MIN
16mm
Color (P I)
LC 72-702191
Describes how a young boy's desire to play with the puppet Punch which he sees in a show on an English beach leads him to an adventure.
English Language; Literature and Drama
Dist - CONNF **Prod** - CONNF 1972

Punch Press Guarding 11 MIN
16mm / U-matic / VHS
Color (A)
Shows guards for punch press operations and stresses that protection is provided only when the guard is properly adjusted.
Industrial and Technical Education
Dist - IFB **Prod** - IFB 1957

Punching and Editing 16 MIN
VHS / U-matic
Numerical Control/Computerized Numerical Control - 'Fundamentals series; Module 1
Color (IND)
Discusses operating the terminal in the local mode, loading a program through the terminal and editing a program.
Business and Economics; Industrial and Technical Education
Dist - LEIKID **Prod** - LEIKID

Punctuation and conventions in mathematics - Pt 1 - punctuation 29 MIN
16mm
Teaching high school mathematics - first course series; No 8
B&W (T)
Mathematics
Dist - MLA **Prod** - UICSM 1967

Punctuation and conventions in mathematics - Pt 2 - conventions 33 MIN
16mm
Teaching high school mathematics - first course series; No 9
B&W (T)
Mathematics
Dist - MLA **Prod** - UICSM 1967

Punctuation - Colon, Semicolon and Quotation Marks 14 MIN
U-matic / VHS / 16mm
Color (I J)
LC 77-703197
Uses innovative visuals and effects to illustrate the use of colons, semicolons and quotation marks.
English Language
Dist - CORF **Prod** - CENTRO 1977

Punctuation - Mischievous Marks - Parentheses 15 MIN
U-matic / VHS / 16mm
Color (I J)
LC 77-703198
Uses innovative visuals and effects to illustrate the uses of dashes and parentheses to interrupt a sentence and the use of the apostrophe in contractions and in forming possessives.
English Language
Dist - CORF **Prod** - CENTRO 1977

Punctuation series

Colon, semicolon, and quotation marks	14 MIN
Mischievous Marks - ( )'s	15 MIN
Putting commas between	16 MIN
Stop that period - period that stop	18 MIN
Taking Commas Aside	18 MIN

Dist - CORF

Punctuation - Stop that Period - Period that Stop 18 MIN
U-matic / VHS / 16mm
Color (I J)
LC 77-703200
Shows the two parts of a simple sentence and tells how to use the correct end stops.
English Language
Dist - CORF **Prod** - CENTRO 1977

Punctuation - Taking Commas Aside 18 MIN
16mm / U-matic / VHS
Color (I J)
LC 77-703201
Uses innovative visuals and effects to demonstrate how commas are used to set off parenthetical elements, nonrestrictive elements, words in apposition and a direct address.
English Language
Dist - CORF **Prod** - CENTRO 1977

Punctuation with Ralph and Stanley 14 MIN
16mm / U-matic / VHS
Writing Skills Series
Color (P I)
LC 79-700003
Tells a story about a boy who makes arrangements to take a UFO to Jupiter until he receives extraterrestrial messages that are missing punctuation marks. Teaches how various types of punctuation marks give meaning to the written word.
English Language
Dist - PHENIX **Prod** - BEANMN 1978

The Punctuation wizard 24 MIN
VHS / U-matic / 16mm
Color (K P I)
$540.00, $410.00, $380.00 purchase _ #A365
Tells about Wimbleton who lives in a kingdom where punctuation is forbidden. Reveals that he uses magic to add punctuation to sentences and is captured and placed in a dungeon. Finally, the king recognizes the impossibility of life without punctuation and Wimbleton is made the Royal Punctuator. Written by Brent Maddock.
English Language
Dist - BARR **Prod** - CHODZK 1984

Punishment 44 MIN
U-matic / VHS
Learning and Liking it Series
Color (T)
Covers the effects of punishment. Examines whether or not a teacher should use it.
Education; Psychology
Dist - MSU **Prod** - MSU

Punitive Damages 120 MIN
VHS / U-matic
Color (PRO)
Discusses the kinds of cases in which punitive damages may be available, and focuses on the pleading and proof of punitive damages and the arguments for and against them.
Civics and Political Systems
Dist - ABACPE **Prod** - CCEB

Punitive Damages 120 MIN
U-matic / Cassette / VHS / 16mm
Color; Mono (PRO)
Features personal injury litigators who discuss the kinds of cases in which punitive damages may be available. Focuses on the pleading and proof of punitive damages the and arguments for and against them.
Civics and Political Systems
Dist - CCEB **Prod** - CCEB

Punk rock 60 MIN
VHS
History of rock 'n' roll series
Color (G)
$19.99 purchase _ #0 - 7907 - 2433 - 2NK
Travels from Elvis Costello to Nirvana as a new wave of artists reclaim rock. Features the Sex Pistols, Talking Heads, Velvet Underground, the Ramones, Green Day and clips of Lollapalooza. Part of a ten - part series unfolding the history of rock music. May contain mature subject matter and explicit song lyrics.
Fine Arts
Dist - TILIED

Punk Rock and the Elvis Legend 15 MIN
U-matic / VHS
Color
Focuses on the Elvis Presley legend, discusses the Elvis imitators and the mini - industry of Presley mementos, and looks at the devotees of punk rock.
Biography; Fine Arts
Dist - JOU **Prod** - UPI

Punking Out 25 MIN
16mm
B&W
LC 79-700263
Documents the punk rock music scene at the CBGB club in New York City.
Fine Arts
Dist - CARMAG **Prod** - CARMAG 1978

Punktlichkeit Ist Alles 15 MIN
U-matic / VHS / 16mm
Guten Tag Wie Geht's Series
Color (H C) (GERMAN)
A German language film. Features Hans who is put on the bench because he is always late for hockey practice and Gabi trying the same tactics on him.
Foreign Language
Dist - IFB **Prod** - BAYER 1973

A Punt, a Pass and a Prayer 76 MIN
VHS / U-matic
Color
Offers a play written by David Mark about the aspirations, obsessions and ironic conflicts that delineate the life of a star quarterback seeking to make a comeback. Stars Hugh O'Brien and Betsy Palmer.
Fine Arts; Literature and Drama
Dist - FOTH **Prod** - FOTH 1984

Punt Gunning for Ducks 29 MIN
16mm
Color (J)
LC 74-703695
Examines many aspects of punt - gunning for ducks, including the preparation and loading of shot, the mounting of the stanchion gun on the punt, the stalking of water fowl and the firing of the large gun at a flock of ducks.
Physical Education and Recreation
Dist - VEDO **Prod** - ASHLEY 1975

Punting
VHS
Color (H C A)
$39.95 purchase _ #CVN1200V
Features San Francisco 49ers punter Barry Helton instructing in the techniques of punting. Emphasizes the importance of concentration and the correct application of style.
Physical Education and Recreation
Dist - CAMV

Punting
VHS
Championship football coaching series
Color (J H C G)
$39.95 purchase _ #CBV48KV
Features Coach Bill Renner of the Green Bay Packers. Shows basic skills and drills, successful techniques and strategies, expert demonstration of punting in football.
Physical Education and Recreation
Dist - CAMV

Punting and kicking
VHS
NCAA football instructional videos series
Color (H C A)
$39.95 purchase _ #KAR1308V
Features Notre Dame head football coach Lou Holtz teaching various skills and drills for punters and kickers. Produced by the National Collegiate Athletic Association.
Physical Education and Recreation
Dist - CAMV **Prod** - NCAAF

Punting and kicking
VHS
NCAA football videos - defensive series
Color (A G T)
$39.95 purchase _ #KAR1308V-P
Presents instruction on skills and drills given by NCAA coaches. Features Lou Holtz explaining punting and kicking. One of a series of videos that provide coaching tips to offensive and defensive players and coaches. Series is available as individual cassettes, a set of offensive series, a set of defensive series, or both series combined.
Physical Education and Recreation
Dist - CAMV

Punto De Encuentro 15 MIN
16mm
Color
LC 74-700625
Surveys pre - Columbian culture in Costa Rica.
History - World; Social Science; Sociology
Dist - PAN **Prod** - OOAS 1973

Punto De Ignicion 21 MIN
16mm / U-matic / VHS
Color (IND) (SPANISH)
A Spanish - language version of the motion picture Flashpoint. Dramatizes the events leading to a chemical explosion and fire in a chemical laboratory. Shows the safety precautions which should have been taken.
Foreign Language; Health and Safety; Science
Dist - IFB **Prod** - MILLBK 1980

Punts, Passes and Plies 20 MIN
VHS / U-matic
Color
Presents an ABC TV health and safety program on athletics and dancing.
Health and Safety; Physical Education and Recreation
Dist - ABCLR **Prod** - ABCLR 1984

Puny Petunia, a Canine Venus 16 MIN
16mm
B&W
Presents five visual 'stories' in a surrealistic manner - - scenes about a young girl who finds and cherishes a clothing store dummy, a man who gets caught and strangles in the strings growing on an abacus, a nude girl who rides a unicycle, a photographer who tries to pose his model and a dancer who does a dance to a cook book recipe.
Fine Arts; Industrial and Technical Education; Literature and Drama
Dist - UPENN **Prod** - UPENN 1967

Pupfish of the Desert 18 MIN
U-matic / VHS / 16mm
Color (J H)
Explains how the desert pupfish adapt to environmental changes. Shows the conditions that exist on deserts, expecially in isolated areas of Mexico and the southwestern states.
Science - Natural
Dist - STANF **Prod** - STANF 1975

Pupil diversity - 6
VHS
Teaching for tomorrow series
Color; PAL (C T)
PdS20 purchase
Uses real teachers and schools to evaluate ideas and support professional development for primary and secondary teachers in multicultural classrooms. Stimulates discussion on classroom management, handling curriculum changes and developing new teaching techniques. Contact distributor about availability outside the United Kingdom.
Education
Dist - ACADEM

Pupil Interactions 30 MIN
U-matic / VHS
Interaction - Human Concerns in the Schools Series
Color (T)
Looks at pupil interactions in an educational setting.
Education
Dist - MDCPB **Prod** - MDDE

Puppet Animation 16 MIN
16mm / VHS
Animation Series
Color (J H A)
$295.00, $370.00 purchase, $50.00 rental _ #8006
Demonstrates simple techniques of puppet animation.
Fine Arts; Industrial and Technical Education
Dist - AIMS **Prod** - EDMI 1985

Puppet Magic 12 MIN
16mm / U-matic / VHS
Color (P I)
LC 80-700666
Gives a brief history of puppetry and details each step in the construction of marionettes. Shows the puppeteer at work making the marionettes come alive.
Fine Arts
Dist - IFB **Prod** - INTNEW 1977

Puppet on a String 15 MIN
16mm
Color
LC 80-701050
Provides consumer information on batteries, telling how to buy them for each use, how to store them, and what to expect of them. Discusses their diversity and battery safety and convenience.
Home Economics
Dist - KLEINW **Prod** - KLEINW 1979

Puppet Plays 0 MIN
U-matic
Teachers Teaching Writing Series
Color (T)
Demonstrates classroom techniques of several teachers who have been judged superior in their methods of teaching writing. Each of the six programs, which were taped in regular classes, features a single teacher conducting an actual writing process.
Education; English Language
Dist - AFSCD **Prod** - AFSCD 1986

Puppet Preparation for Surgery 10 MIN
16mm
Color
LC 71-711407
Demonstrates modes of operation as hospital employees, including doctors, nurses, recreation workers and others work with the hospitalized child. Shows the interaction between volunteer and patient, and explains the surgical procedure by using puppets and mock - ups of the equipment.
Health and Safety; Psychology; Science
Dist - AMEDA **Prod** - CMHOSP 1970

The Puppet Proposition 26 MIN
16mm
Color
LC 76-700411
Takes a look at several kinds of puppets used in marionette theater and how a puppet show is planned and performed.
Fine Arts
Dist - LMT **Prod** - LMT 1976

Puppeteer 15 MIN
U-matic
Harriet's Magic Hats II Series
(P I J)
Shows the different types of puppets, how they are made and how they work.
Guidance and Counseling
Dist - ACCESS **Prod** - ACCESS 1983

The Puppeteers 50 MIN
VHS
Gladio - Timewatch series
Color; PAL (H C A)
PdS99 purchase
Reports on the secret terrorist groups that were originally set up to face the Communist threat but who later developed into the enemies' established political order. Documents a series of inexplicable bombings which revealed the existence of an 'invisible government' in Italy. Part two of a three part series.
History - World; Sociology
Dist - BBCENE

Puppetry 13 MIN
VHS / 16mm
Drama reference series
Color (C)
$150.00 purchase _ #268408
Implements elementary drama curriculum. Presents drama content, teaching strategies and resources, and demonstrated drama activities for the classroom. Illustrates puppetry in eight stages from pretending to be a puppet to transferring personality traits to puppets constructed in class.
Education; Fine Arts; Literature and Drama; Mathematics
Dist - ACCESS **Prod** - ACCESS 1987

Puppets 15 MIN
U-matic / VHS / 16mm
Rediscovery - art media (spanish series
Color (K P I J H C) (SPANISH)
Presents various methods of making puppets ranging from simple stick puppets to more involved processes including the use of sawdust and glue, shaped cloth and paper mache.
Fine Arts
Dist - AIMS **Prod** - ACI 1967

Puppets 11 MIN
16mm
B&W
Presents a puppet actor who steps out of his role in a marionette performance of 'Julius Caesar' to provide a lesson on totalitarianism and conformity. Introduces infamous charlatans and despots and the victims who suffered through their treachery. Reveals how these villains used the scapegoat technique to gain adherence from their followers while duping them into relinquishing their freedom.
Civics and Political Systems; Literature and Drama; Sociology
Dist - ADL **Prod** - ADL

Puppets 10 MIN
U-matic
Get it together series
Color (P I)
Teaches children how to make hand and string puppets from modelling dough.
Fine Arts
Dist - TVOTAR **Prod** - TVOTAR 1978

Puppets 15 MIN
VHS
Rediscovery Art Media Series
Color
$69.95 purchase _ #4067
Shows artists encouraged to experiment and discover ways to make puppets out of unusual and everyday materials.
Fine Arts
Dist - AIMS **Prod** - AIMS

Puppets - 5 34 MIN
U-matic / VHS
Think new series
Color (C G)
$129.00, $99.00 purchase _ #V580
Gives theoretical motivation and practical ideas about puppets. Draws content from mathematics, science, history, human feelings, every human endeavor. Part of an 11 - part series that treats art as an essential mode of learning.
Fine Arts
Dist - BARR **Prod** - CEPRO 1991

Puppets and the Poet 59 MIN
Videoreel / VT2
Color
Features the National Theatre of Puppet Arts in an adaptation of Excerpts From Shakespeare. Includes dramatizations of scenes from Macbeth, Taming of the Shrew, Richard III and Hamlet.
Fine Arts; Literature and Drama
Dist - PBS **Prod** - MAETEL

Puppet's Dream 9 MIN
16mm
Color (K)
LC FIA68-636
Presents motion, light and shadow effects with the linear shapes of puppet - like figures on evolving plane and surfaces.
Fine Arts
Dist - FILCOM **Prod** - SIGMA 1967

Puppets - How they Happen 18 MIN
VHS / 16mm
Color (P)
$425.00, $380.00 purchase, $45.00 rental _ #C - 505; LC 86708184
Tells the story of a group of summer workshop students who when introduced to the art of puppetry discover that they each have some special talent they never knew existed. Produced by Don MacDonald.
Fine Arts; Literature and Drama; Psychology; Sociology
Dist - ALTSUL

Puppets of Jiri Trnka 26 MIN
U-matic / VHS / 16mm
Color (K)
LC 73-702702
Brings to life several puppets in the world of fairy tale, using various film techniques.
Fine Arts; Literature and Drama
Dist - PHENIX **Prod** - CFET 1973

Puppies 30 MIN
VHS / U-matic
Training Dogs the Woodhouse Way
Color (H C A)
Shows Barbara Woodhouse's method of handling puppies.
Home Economics; Science - Natural
Dist - FI **Prod** - BBCTV 1982

The Puppy 30 MIN
VHS
Join in series
Color (K P)
#322601
Tells how Zack tries to make a magic spell work while Nikki agonizes over how she will reconcile her promise to care for a friend's puppy with the rule that no pets are allowed in the workshop. Jacob tells the story of Barney the Blue Dog. Part of a series about three artist - performers who share studio space in a converted warehouse.
Fine Arts; Literature and Drama
Dist - TVOTAR **Prod** - TVOTAR 1989

Puppy Dogs' Tails 29 MIN
16mm
Color
LC 75-711408
A promotional and fund raising film for the Crippled Children's Society of Los Angeles County which shows a group of crippled children, aged seven to nine years, going to camp for the first time.
Health and Safety; Psychology; Sociology
Dist - CCSLAC **Prod** - CCSLAC 1971

The Puppy saves the circus 23 MIN
U-matic / VHS / 16mm
Color (K P I)
$515.00, $250.00 purchase _ #4387
Presents an animated film about Petey, the circus elephant, who has amnesia, and his owner Tommy. Tells how villain clowns plot to destroy the circus but the circus animals unite to catch the culprits.
Fine Arts; Literature and Drama
Dist - CORF **Prod** - CORF 1983

The Puppy who wanted a boy 23 MIN
U-matic / VHS / 16mm
Color (K P I)
$515.00, $520.00 purchase _ #4021
Tells a story about a puppy who waits impatiently for the day he will be adopted and who watches as his brothers and sisters are carried off while he is left behind. Shows his adventures when he runs off to the city to find a boy of his own.
Literature and Drama; Science - Natural
Dist - CORF **Prod** - RSPRO 1978

The Puppy's Amazing Rescue 23 MIN
U-matic / VHS / 16mm
Color (P I)
$515.00, $250.00 purchase _ #4116
Tells the story of some puppies who rescue a boy and his father who get lost in the mountains.
Literature and Drama
Dist - CORF

Puppy's Amazing Rescue 23 MIN
U-matic / VHS / 16mm
Color (K P I)
Presents the animated story of two puppies who save their master and his father after they are trapped on a mountain by an avalanche.
Fine Arts
Dist - CORF **Prod** - RSPRO 1980

The Puppy's great adventure 24 MIN
U-matic / VHS / 16mm
Color (P I)
$515.00, $250.00 purchase _ #4059
Tells the story of a lost puppy who searches for his master and has many adventures.
Literature and Drama
Dist - CORF

Puppy's Great Adventure - further Adventures of Petey 24 MIN
U-matic / VHS / 16mm
Color (K P I)
Tells how a puppy is separated from his young master and sets out to find him, encountering diamond thieves and puppy love along the way.
Fine Arts
Dist - CORF **Prod** - RSPRO 1979

Pups is Pups 19 MIN
16mm
B&W
Describes how the Gang enters their unruly pets in a posh hotel pet show, while one of the kids scours the city for his missing flock of puppies. A Little Rascals film.
Fine Arts
Dist - RMIBHF **Prod** - ROACH 1930

Purcell, the Trumpet and John Wilbraham and Michael Laird 26 MIN
16mm / U-matic / VHS
Musical Triangle Series
Color (J)
States that British composer Henry Purcell (1659 - 1695) held the prestigious post of organist at London's Westminster Abbey for several years. Presents professional musicians John Wilbraham and Michael Laird playing Purcell's trumpet music.
Fine Arts
Dist - MEDIAG **Prod** - THAMES 1975

Purcell's Fanfare in C - Bach's Toccata in D minor
VHS
Music in motion series
Color (J H C G)
$75.00 purchase _ #MUS01V
Expresses visually what is heard in the two musical pieces. Teaches classical music appreciation, develops interest and enhances listening enjoyment. Includes manual with suggestions for presenting the video, questions for discussion, research projects, correlations with other subject areas and listening and reading lists. Part of an eight - part series.
Fine Arts
Dist - CAMV **Prod** - MUSLOG

Purchasing Material and Service Cost 60 MIN
VHS / BETA
Manufacturing Series
(IND)
Teaches how to translate manufacturing data into their financial equivalent.
Business and Economics
Dist - COMSRV **Prod** - COMSRV 1986

Purchasing - resupply - lead time
U-matic / VHS
Effective inventory control series
Color (IND)
Discusses components and statistics of lead time and a system for tracking and forecasting. Cites importance of understanding combined effects of usage and lead time uncertainty.
Business and Economics
Dist - GPCV **Prod** - GPCV

Purdue
VHS
Campus clips series
Color (H C A)
$29.95 purchase _ #CC0030V
Takes a video visit to the campus of Purdue University in Indiana. Shows many of the distinctive features of the campus, and interviews students about their experiences. Provides information on the composition of the student body, professors, academics, social life, housing, and other subjects.
Education
Dist - CAMV

Purdue Eye Camera 10 MIN
16mm
B&W (C T)
Photographs the eye movements of a person looking at advertisements. Special drawings show localization of eyes, experienced investigators indicate the areas of the

advertisement to which the person devoted time and the subject verifies these interpretations by saying which elements interested him.
Business and Economics; Psychology
Dist - PSUPCR **Prod** - PSUPCR 1940

Pure and simple 60 MIN
VHS
Man on the rim - the peopling of the Pacific series
Color (H C)
$295.00 purchase
Documents the determination of Japan to remain distinctive from the dominance of China and to conserve its cultural identity. Part of an 11 - part series on the people of the Pacific rim.
History - World; Sociology
Dist - LANDMK **Prod** - LANDMK 1989

Pure and simple stretch 35 MIN
VHS
Voigt fitness series
Color (G)
$19.95 purchase _ #GHM20003V
Shows how to increase flexibility and release tension. Features Karen Voigt as instructor. Part of a five - part series.
Physical Education and Recreation; Psychology
Dist - CAMV

Pure Dance - a Demonstration 58 MIN
U-matic / VHS
Color
Demonstrates 'pure dance' as performed by Barbara Mettler and her five - member dance company.
Fine Arts
Dist - METT **Prod** - METT

Pure enantiomers - separation, synthesis, analysis 180 MIN
VHS
Color (C PRO)
$1100.00 purchase _ #V - 5600 - 21952
Discusses the challenges of and cutting - edge developments in ontaining enantiomerically pure compounds and analyzing the degree of purity. Opens with a discussion of the key methods of obtaining chiral non - racemic molecules, including separation and enantioselective synthesis. Overviews how to analyze enantiomer mixtures. Features Ernest L Eliel, Samuel H Wilen, John J Partridge and Joel Hawkins. Includes two videos and a course manual.
Science - Physical
Dist - AMCHEM **Prod** - AMCHEM 1992

Purification by fire - the passage through pain 26 MIN
U-matic / VHS
Conscious living - conscious dying - the work of a lifetime series
Color
Describes fear of physical and emotional pain. Recounts work with a young man immobilized and in intractable pain who was able to use the pain to transform his life.
Sociology
Dist - PELICN **Prod** - ORGNLF

Purification of Amphibian Oovacyte Promoting Factor 60 MIN
U-matic
Color
Studies the human cell cycles and amphibian cell cycles to show the changes that occur in cancer cells.
Health and Safety
Dist - UTEXSC **Prod** - UTEXSC

Purim 15 MIN
16mm
Color
Shows how the festival of Purim is celebrated in Israel.
Geography - World; Religion and Philosophy; Social Science
Dist - ALDEN **Prod** - ALDEN

The Purimspieler 90 MIN
VHS
B&W (G)
$72.00 purchase
Features a musical comedy set in a Galician shtetl prior to WWII. Focuses on three characters - the sad vagabond peasant Getsel; a vaudeville performer in a traveling circus; and a shoemaker's daughter, whose father tried to marry her into a prominent family in the community when he unexpectedly becomes wealthy. Climaxes during a traditional Purim celebration when the performers drive off the rich suitor's family. Stars Miriam Kressyn, Hymie Jacobson, Zygmunt Turkow, Issac Samberg. Produced and directed by Joseph Green in his native country of Poland.
Fine Arts; Religion and Philosophy; Social Science; Sociology
Dist - NCJEWF

The Puritan Experience - Forsaking England 28 MIN
16mm / U-matic / VHS
Color (J I) (SPANISH)
LC 75-702920
Presents the story of one family, the Higgins, and their decision to leave the land they love and head for America. Describes the main ideas of Puritanism and depicts the experiences lived by many immigrants.
Fine Arts; Foreign Language; History - United States
Dist - LCOA **Prod** - LCOA 1975

The Puritan Experience - Making a New World 31 MIN
U-matic / VHS / 16mm
Color (I J) (SPANISH)
LC 75-702921;
Continues the Higgins' chronicle in Massachusetts. Presents factual information on Puritan beliefs, culture and life.
History - United States; Religion and Philosophy; Social Science
Dist - LCOA **Prod** - LCOA 1975

Puritan family of early New England 11 MIN
16mm / U-matic / VHS
Color (P I J)
$270.00, $290.00 purchase _ $4040; LC 80-701613
Depicts the many activities of a Puritan family living in a small New England coastal village.
History - United States
Dist - CORF **Prod** - CORF 1980

The Puritan revolution - Cromwell and the rise of parliamentary democracy 33 MIN
16mm / U-matic / VHS
Western Civilization - majesty and madness series
Color (H C)
LC 72-715346
Shows how the revolt of Parliament against Charles I in the 1640s, under the leadership of Oliver Cromwell and the Puritans, destroyed the absolute power of the English monarchy and directed the country on the road to parliamentary democracy.
Civics and Political Systems; History - World; Religion and Philosophy
Dist - LCOA **Prod** - LCOA 1972

A Puritan way 30 MIN
VHS
American adventure series
Color (G)
$150.00 purchase _ #TAMA - 103
Highlights the mass migration of English Puritans to the Massachusetts Bay region. Discusses Puritan ideals and their influence on American culture. Features the scenery of New England.
History - United States
Dist - PBS

Purity, and After 5 MIN
16mm
Color (G)
$201.00 purchase, $10.00 rental
Presents two short films, the first on the search for purity, the second on the reverberations of the search.
Fine Arts
Dist - CANCIN **Prod** - BRAKS 1978

Purlie Victorious, Daris, Dee and Alda
U-matic / VHS
Color
History - United States
Dist - MSTVIS **Prod** - MSTVIS

Purple Adventures of Lady Elaine Fairchilde Series Program 1
Lady Elaine Flies to Jupiter 29 MIN
Dist - HUBDSC

Purple Adventures of Lady Elaine Fairchilde Series Program 2
Lady Elaine Discovers Planet Purple 25 MIN
Dist - HUBDSC

Purple Adventures of Lady Elaine Fairchilde Series Program 3
Lady Elaine Wants Everything to be as it is on Planet Purple 24 MIN
Dist - HUBDSC

Purple Adventures of Lady Elaine Fairchilde Series Program 4
Purple Visitors to the Neighborhood of make - Believe 25 MIN
Dist - HUBDSC

Purple Adventures of Lady Elaine Fairchilde Series Program 5
Things Begin to Change on Planet Purple 28 MIN
Dist - HUBDSC

The Purple coat - 50
VHS
Reading rainbow series
Color; CC (K P)
$39.95 purchase
Reveals that every year Grampa makes Gabrielle a navy blue coat, but this year she wants something new in a story by Amy Hest, narrated by Jack Gilford. Visits the garment district of New York City with LeVar where he has a coat made specially for him. Visits the Fashion Institute of Technology to explore the world of design. Part of a series offering a multicultural approach to generating reading enthusiasm with cross - curricular applications, hosted by LeVar Burton.
English Language; Home Economics; Literature and Drama
Dist - GPN **Prod** - LNMDP

The Purple Gang 85 MIN
16mm
B&W (H C A)
Dramatizes the career of the Purples, a gang that terrorized Detroit in the prohibition era.
Fine Arts
Dist - CINEWO **Prod** - CINEWO 1960

Purple Heart 1 MIN
16mm
Color (J)
Presents an anti - war comment.
Psychology; Sociology
Dist - CFS **Prod** - CFS 1970

Purple pirate blues 25 MIN
16mm
Color (A)
$40.00 rental
Comments on the sadness that comes from a society that can't get beyond its immature preoccupation with the sex drive. Looks at found 'cheesecake' footage spliced together with refilmed footage of pornography that was hand - developed in a bucket. Difficult visuals due to flicker format. A Kon Petrochuk production. Note - Sound is on cassette.
Psychology; Sociology
Dist - CANCIN

Purple Turtle 14 MIN
16mm / U-matic / VHS
Color (K P T)
LC FIA68-124
Shows kindergarten children at work with various art mediums. Captures the intensity, delight and skill with which four - and five - year - olds take to paint. Shows why art is one of the most important means of development.
Education; Fine Arts; Psychology
Dist - AIMS **Prod** - ACI 1962

Purple Visitors to the Neighborhood of make - Believe 25 MIN
16mm
Purple Adventures of Lady Elaine Fairchilde Series Program 4
Color (K P S)
LC 80-700581
Presents Mr Rogers talking, singing and using puppets to tell what happens when three visitors arrive from Planet Purple. Discusses individual differences, handicaps, uniqueness and change.
Fine Arts; Guidance and Counseling; Literature and Drama
Dist - HUBDSC **Prod** - FAMCOM 1979

Purpose and Audience 30 MIN
U-matic / VHS
Effective Writing for Executives Series
Color (C A)
LC 80-707552
Focuses on techniques involved in planning and getting started writing correspondence. Shows how to define the purpose of correspondence and where to place important ideas to get the reader's attention, taking into account his needs. Describes those situations in which it is more desirable to call or see someone in person. Hosted by Ed Asner.
Business and Economics; English Language
Dist - TIMLIF **Prod** - TIMLIF 1980

The Purpose of meditation 120 MIN
VHS / BETA
Color; PAL (G)
$70.00 purchase _ #PdS35
Features the Venerable Lama Thubten Zopa explaining, with great humor, how neither friends, money nor reputation are the key to happiness and satisfaction. Elucidates the importance of compassion and gives a very clear explanation of emptiness.
Fine Arts; Religion and Philosophy
Dist - MERIDT **Prod** - MERIDT

Purpose of Satsang 60 MIN
U-matic / VHS
Color
Presents Sri Gurudev answering a series of questions including 'what is the difference between needs and desires?' and 'how can love grow without attachment?'
Religion and Philosophy
Dist - IYOGA **Prod** - IYOGA

Purpose, types, application and removal - Part 1 28 MIN
U-matic / VHS
Nursing care of patients with casts series
Color (PRO)
$275.00 purchase, $60.00 rental _ #7625S, #7625V
Details nursing care from the time a cast is applied to its removal. Informs on the purpose of casts, common types, casting materials, how applied and removed. Describes potential problems related to nursing care. Part of a two - part series.
Health and Safety
Dist - AJN **Prod** - HOSSN 1986

The Purposes and Techniques of Joint Aspiration 20 MIN
U-matic / VHS
Color (PRO)
Demonstrates the technique for aspiration of the knee, ankle, wrist and shoulder with emphasis on aseptic technique, anatomical landmarks, positioning of the patient and handling of the specimen in order to obtain maximum diagnostic information. Gives special consideration to identification of crystals and to noting the pressure of cells associated with specific diseases.
Health and Safety
Dist - UMICHM **Prod** - UMICHM 1974

Purposes of Family Planning 15 MIN
U-matic / VHS / 16mm
Color (H C A) (SPANISH)
Presents reasons for practicing family planning. Includes motivations of health, emotional maturity, economic stability and the need to provide each child with individual love and attention.
Sociology
Dist - AIMS **Prod** - MORLAT 1973

Purposes of Family Planning 15 MIN
16mm / U-matic / VHS
Family Planning and Sex Education Series
Color (H C A)
LC 73-702455
Presents the different reasons why people choose to practice family planning. Points out that among the motivations for choosing to practice family planning are health, emotional maturity, economic stability and the need to provide each child with individual love and attention.
Sociology
Dist - AIMS **Prod** - MORLAT 1973

The Purse 13 MIN
16mm / U-matic / VHS
B&W (H C A)
LC FIA67-1186
Dramatizes the discovery of a lost purse containing a large sum of money to stimulate discussion about conscience and its motivation and principles of honesty and integrity.
Guidance and Counseling; Psychology
Dist - IFB **Prod** - NFBC 1967

Purse Seining 11 MIN
16mm
Color; B&W (P I J)
Shows the operation of a purse seine boat and the duties of its crew in locating schools of fish, setting the net, hauling in and refigerating the catch.
Industrial and Technical Education
Dist - MLA **Prod** - JHP 1949

The Pursuit of Cleanliness 14 MIN
16mm
Color (J H A)
Depicts the evolution and importance of cleanliness from ancient Rome to today. Traces the history of soap.
Guidance and Counseling; Health and Safety; Home Economics
Dist - MTP **Prod** - SOAPDS

The Pursuit of Efficiency 25 MIN
U-matic / VHS / 16mm
Color (A)
LC 80-701515
Tells the story of a tea lady who pushes her cart through an office, dispensing observations on office management along with the refreshments. Stresses the importance of taking a fresh and critical look at one's duties.
Psychology
Dist - RTBL **Prod** - RANKAV 1980

The Pursuit of equality 28 MIN
VHS
This Constitution - a history series
Color (H C G)
$180.00 purchase, $19.00 rental _ #35740
Considers the nature and historical development of the idea of equality in the context of federal civil rights policies of the past 20 years. Examines Brown v the Board of Education; the Civil Rights Act of 1964; the Voting Rights Act of 1965; Title VII; and the creation of the Equal Opportunity Commission. Includes a discussion of racial discrimination and the direction of affirmative action. Part of a five - part series on the philosophical origins, drafting and interpretation of the US Constitution and its effect on American society, produced by the International University Consortium and Project '87.
Civics and Political Systems; Education
Dist - PSU

The Pursuit of Excellence 50 MIN
16mm
Color
LC 79-701054
Profiles two of America's top long - distance runners, Bill Rodgers and Frank Shorter, as they prepare for the 1978 Boston Marathon.
Physical Education and Recreation
Dist - WQED **Prod** - WQED 1978

The Pursuit of excellence - Pt 1 25 MIN
16mm
Color
LC 79-701054
Profiles two of America's top long - distance runners, Bill Rodgers and Frank Shorter, as they prepare for the 1978 Boston Marathon.
Physical Education and Recreation
Dist - WQED **Prod** - WQED 1978

The Pursuit of Excellence - Pt 2 25 MIN
16mm
Color
LC 79-701054
Profiles two of America's top long - distance runners, Bill Rodgers and Frank Shorter, as they prepare for the 1978 Boston Marathon.
Physical Education and Recreation
Dist - WQED **Prod** - WQED 1978

The Pursuit of Happiness 52 MIN
U-matic / VHS / 16mm
Civilisation Series no 9; No 9
Color (J)
LC 79-708456
Surveys the development of Western civilization during the 18th century as evidenced in the music of Bach, Handel, Mozart and Haydn, the architecture of Neumann and the paintings and etchings of Tiepolo.
Fine Arts; History - World
Dist - FI **Prod** - BBCTV 1970

The Pursuit of happiness - Pt 1 24 MIN
U-matic / VHS / 16mm
Civilisation series no 9; No 9
Color (J H C)
LC 79-708456
Surveys the development of Western civilization during the 18th century as evidenced in the music of Bach, Handel, Mozart and Haydn, the architecture of Neumann and the paintings and etchings of Tiepolo.
Fine Arts; History - World
Dist - FI **Prod** - BBCTV 1970

The Pursuit of happiness - Pt 2 28 MIN
16mm / U-matic / VHS
Civilisation series no 9; No 9
Color (J H C)
LC 79-708456
Surveys the development of Western civilization during the 18th century as evidenced in the music of Bach, Handel, Mozart and Haydn, the architecture of Neumann and the paintings and etchings of Tiepolo.
Fine Arts; History - World
Dist - FI **Prod** - BBCTV 1970

Pursuit of life - visual impairment 5 MIN
U-matic / VHS
Assistive technology series
Color (C PRO G)
$195.00 purchase _ #N921 - VI - 049
Introduces the accessibility and adaptation strategies of a man handicapped by macular degeneration of the eyes. Features Art who is a woodworker who can no longer do such work because of his visual impairment. Discusses the social agencies he turned to for help and the types of equipment he has procured to help him function in his environment and to keep working. Part of nine parts produced by Southern Illinois University School of Medicine.
Guidance and Counseling; Health and Safety
Dist - HSCIC

The Pursuit of the ideal 30 MIN
VHS / U-matic
Art of being human series; Module 11
Color (C)
History - World; Literature and Drama; Religion and Philosophy
Dist - MDCC **Prod** - MDCC

Pursuit to the Rhine - Volume 5 35 MIN
VHS
War chronicles series
B&W (G)
$14.95 purchase _ #S01095
Presents the fifth segment of an eight - part series on World War II. Covers General Patton's successful 'Operation Cobra,' in which Allied forces forced Hitler's armies to retreat.
History - United States
Dist - UILL

Push 10 MIN
U-matic / VHS / BETA
Color; PAL (J H C G)
PdS30, PdS38 purchase
Confronts our push - button world using a visual essay. Suggests that in achieving mastery over nature, we have lost our most basic resource - the ability to reach each other.
Psychology; Social Science
Dist - EDPAT

Push and pull - simple machines at work 20 MIN
VHS
Color (P I)
$89.00 purchase _ #RB852
Examines the six types of simple machines - the lever, the wheel and axle, the pulley, the inclined plane, the screw and the wedge. Reveals that all machines, no matter how complicated, are all made up of combinations of simple machines.
Science - Physical
Dist - REVID **Prod** - REVID 1991

Push hands - Kung Fu's greatest training secret 120 MIN
VHS
Color (G)
$39.95 purchase _ #MA - 05
Demonstrates a two - person Chinese exercise which develops fluidity, internal energy - chi, concentration and the ability to neutralize aggression. Shows how to read the intentions of an aggressor before those intentions materialize physically.
Physical Education and Recreation; Religion and Philosophy
Dist - ARVID **Prod** - ARVID

The Push hands video manual 38 MIN
VHS
Color (G)
$49.95 purchase _ #1137
Teaches the Chinese martial art of push hands, both fixed and moving step. Shows applications as well as a segment where host Sam Masich uses push hands against an attacker.
Physical Education and Recreation
Dist - WAYF

Push Pull 30 MIN
U-matic
Polka Dot Door Series
Color (K)
Presents a variety show for pre - school children. Includes songs, mime, stories, film sequences, talk, dance and fantasy figures. Each show emphasizes a particular theme such as numbers, feelings, exploring, music or time. Comes with parent teacher guide.
Fine Arts; Literature and Drama
Dist - TVOTAR **Prod** - TVOTAR 1985

Push - Pull Amplifier 32 MIN
16mm
B&W
LC 74-705457
Lists the requirements for push - pull operation. Explains how bias affects class of operation and compares classes as to fidelity, harmonics and efficiency. (Kinescope).
Industrial and Technical Education; Science - Physical
Dist - USNAC **Prod** - USAF

Pushbuttons and People 10 MIN
VHS / U-matic
Screen news digest series
B&W
Shows a study of automation and its effects on industry and workers.
Industrial and Technical Education; Social Science
Dist - AFA **Prod** - AFA 1986

Pushed to the edge 50 MIN
VHS
ABC News collection series

Color (G)
$29.98 purchase _ #6302316545
Presents a special edition of ABC's 20 - 20. Features Barbara Walters, Hugh Downs, Lynn Sherr and Tom Jarriel who report on the growing number of cases in which American women fight back against abusive partners and rapists.
Sociology
Dist - INSTRU **Prod** - ABCNEW 1992

Pushed to the Limit 28 MIN
U-matic / VHS / 16mm
Understanding Space and Time Series
Color
Shows how the speed of light was measured and that Newton's universal laws have certain limitations.
Science - Physical
Dist - UCEMC **Prod** - BBCTV 1980

Pushing Back the Darkness 27 MIN
VHS
Color (G)
$75.00 purchase
Chronicles the evolution of Santee Cooper, South Carolina's state - owned electric utility. Starts with the connection of the Santee and Cooper Rivers with a diversion canal and reaches fruition with the building of a small canal and a hydro - generating unit in 1934.
Geography - United States; History - United States; Industrial and Technical Education; Social Science; Sociology
Dist - SCETV **Prod** - SCETV 1989

Pushing the Limits - an IBM Information Technology Report 27 MIN
16mm
Color
LC 78-701347
Presents a view of computer technology research and development in IBM laboratories around the world.
Business and Economics; Industrial and Technical Education
Dist - MTP **Prod** - IBMCOP 1978

Pushmi - Pullyu 11 MIN
16mm
Peppermint Stick Selection Series
Color (P I)
LC 76-701277
An excerpt from the motion picture Doctor Dolittle. Tells how Doctor Dolittle receives a pushmi - pullyu, a rare llama with a head on each end, as a gift to help him raise money for his search for the great pink sea snail. Based on the book Doctor Dolittle by Hugh Lofting.
English Language; Fine Arts; Literature and Drama
Dist - FI **Prod** - FI 1976

Pushtu tribe series
Baking unleavened bread 10 MIN
Boys' games 5 MIN
Making felt rugs 9 MIN
Dist - EDPAT

Pushtu tribe series
Men's dance 11 MIN
Dist - EDPAT
IFF

Puss in boats - a french fairy tale 11 MIN
16mm / U-matic / VHS
Favorite fairy tales and fables series
Color (K P)
$280.00, $195.00 purchase _ #4144
Presents the French fairy tale Puss In Boots. Tells the story of Jacques, who has nothing to his name but the clothes on his back, a pair of old, red boots and the loyalty of Puss, his very clever cat. Shows how, with Puss' help, Jacques becomes a rich, landowning noble.
Literature and Drama
Dist - CORF **Prod** - CORF 1980

Puss in Boots 16 MIN
16mm / U-matic / VHS
B&W (P I)
Retells the fairy tale with animated puppets made by the Dietz Brothers. Uses stop - motion photography.
Literature and Drama
Dist - EBEC **Prod** - EBEC 1958

Puss in boots 12 MIN
VHS / 16mm
Literature - fairy tales series
Color (P)
$295.00, $265.00 purchase, $30.00 rental
Presents the fairytale Puss in Boots by Perrault. Part of a series on fairytales.
Literature and Drama
Dist - BNCHMK **Prod** - BNCHMK

Puss in Boots 10 MIN
16mm
Lotte Reiniger's Animated Fairy Tales Series
B&W
Uses animated paper silhouettes to illustrate the children's story Puss In Boots. Based on live shadow plays produced by Lotte Reiniger for BBC Television.
Fine Arts; Literature and Drama
Dist - MOMA **Prod** - PRIMP 1934

Puss in Boots 98 MIN
VHS
Color (K)
$29.95 purchase _ #278 - 9002
Evokes a storybook world of castles, monsters and damsels in distress in a production of 'Puss In Boots' by the National Ballet of Marseilles. Features Patrick Dupond in the lead, choreography by Roland Petit and music by Tchaikovsky.
Fine Arts; Physical Education and Recreation
Dist - FI **Prod** - INTERA 1988

Puss - in - Boots 26 MIN
VHS / 16mm
Children's Classics Series
Color (P)
$195.00 purchase
Recreates the classic 'Puss - In - Boots.'
Fine Arts; Literature and Drama
Dist - LUF **Prod** - BROVID

Puss'n Boots 70 MIN
U-matic / VHS / 16mm
Color
Presents the children's tale 'Puss'N Boots,' about a talking, thinking, ever - so - clever cat and his young master.
Literature and Drama; Science - Natural
Dist - FI **Prod** - AIM

Pussycat that Ran Away 21 MIN
U-matic / VHS / 16mm
Color (P I)
Gives an impression of life on a farm and views of the Norwegian countryside. Includes importance of obeying parents and being kind to little brothers.
Geography - World; Guidance and Counseling; Psychology; Social Science
Dist - PHENIX **Prod** - SVEK 1958

Pustular Psoriasis 14 MIN
16mm
Case Presentations on Film Series
Color (PRO)
LC 70-701966
Describes and illustrates an atypical form of psoriasis vulgaris through the use of charts and a case history.
Health and Safety; Science; Science - Natural
Dist - SQUIBB **Prod** - SQUIBB 1966

Put a medal on the man 5 MIN
16mm
Color (H C A)
Presents a scathing political - social commentary to the words of Phil Ochs' 'Is There Anybody Here.'
Literature and Drama; Sociology
Dist - UWFKD **Prod** - UWFKD

Put a Smile in Every Aisle 9 MIN
U-matic / VHS
(PRO)
$450.00 purchase, $125.00 rental
Presents tips on improving customer service. Emphasizes knowledge of store and products. Stresses importance of extra effort towards helping a customer.
Business and Economics
Dist - CREMED **Prod** - CREMED 1987

Put Another Quarter in 9 MIN
U-matic / VHS / 16mm
Color (J H C A)
Comments on present day entertainment and that of the past as it moves from the video game to the abandoned opera house.
Sociology
Dist - BRAURP **Prod** - BRAURP

Put it all together 30 MIN
VHS
Color (G)
$565.00 purchase, $150.00 rental _ #91F6020
Reveals how Joe Paterno, Gene Cernan and Janet Guthrie use the same basic formula for success and how their philosophy can be applied to selling.
Business and Economics; Psychology
Dist - DARTNL **Prod** - DARTNL

Put it in Writing 15 MIN
U-matic / VHS
Writer's Realm Series
Color (I)
$125.00 purchase
Focuses on the everyday use of writing as a natural part of social interaction.
English Language; Literature and Drama; Social Science
Dist - AITECH **Prod** - MDINTV 1987

Put it in Writing 15 MIN
U-matic
Keys to the Office Series
Color (H)
Offers help on writing skills needed in business and information on word processing techniques now in use.
Business and Economics
Dist - TVOTAR **Prod** - TVOTAR 1986

Put it in Writing Series
Changing some Old Attitudes 20 MIN
Clarity - your first objective 27 MIN
The Finishing Touches of the Pros 20 MIN
How to Outsmart the Deadline 15 MIN
Measuring Your Clarity 13 MIN
Practical Tips on Organizing 15 MIN
Dist - DELTAK

Put it on Poles 18 MIN
16mm
Color
Illustrates the problem of space including space for display, raw material storage and servicing extensive machines. Offers an answer in pole building.
Industrial and Technical Education
Dist - DCC **Prod** - DCC

Put more leadership into your style 30 MIN
U-matic / VHS / 16mm
Color (C PRO)
$595.00, $445.00, $415.00 purchase; $690.00 purchase, $140.00 rental
Explores the fundamentals of leadership - communication, mutual reward, power, decision making, and positive force.
Psychology
Dist - VLEARN **Prod** - BARR

Put more leadership into your style 30 MIN
U-matic / 16mm / VHS
Color (C A G H)
$595.00, $445.00, $415.00 purchase _ #C395
Shares the five fundamental principles of the leadership pyramid of George Franklin. Looks at communication, mutual reward, power, decision making and positive force. Explains the importance of mission to provide unity and meaning. Written by Carolyn Miller and based upon the book by Elwood N Chapman.
Business and Economics; Guidance and Counseling; Psychology; Social Science
Dist - BARR **Prod** - CHODZK 1985

Put the Kettle on 11 MIN
16mm / U-matic / VHS
Reading and Word Play Series
Color (P)
Uses vignettes of train trips, boat rides, amusement park attractions, a kettle, a clown and a magician to reinforce the words get, find, put, on, off and help.
English Language
Dist - AIMS **Prod** - PEDF 1976

Put Them Together - a Saturday Adventure 11 MIN
16mm / U-matic / VHS
Read on Series
Color (P)
LC 76-701556
Uses a story about a young boy's adventures in an imaginary jungle to encourage the use of descriptive words and phrases in describing experiences.
English Language
Dist - AIMS **Prod** - ACI 1971

The Put - Together Look 29 MIN
Videoreel / VT2
Designing Women Series
Color
Home Economics
Dist - PBS **Prod** - WKYCTV

Put - Togetherer 15 MIN
U-matic / VHS
Strawberry Square II - Take Time Series
Color (P)
Fine Arts
Dist - AITECH **Prod** - NEITV 1984

Put wings on your career 15 MIN
16mm
Color (H)
Illustrates the diversity of jobs in aviation maintenance, both in government and private industry. Outlines the basic technical requirements and points interested people in the right direction for more specific career information.
Guidance and Counseling; Industrial and Technical Education
Dist - MTP **Prod** - FAAFL

Put Wings on Your Career 15 MIN
16mm

Color
LC 78-701644
Illustrates the diversity of jobs associated with aviation maintenance, both in government and in private industry. Outlines the basic technical requirements of this field and enumerates various sources of more specific career information.
Guidance and Counseling; Industrial and Technical Education
Dist - USNAC **Prod** - USFAA 1978

Put your business on the Web - create your own home pages
VHS
Color (C PRO G)
$89.00 purchase _ #507
Shows how to develop your own business presence on the Web by creating an effective Home Page. Includes text editing, setting up links, graphics editing, scanning, zap shot, video, character formatting, fill - in forms, clickable graphics maps, hardware and software, and resources. Features Rich Enderton as instructor.
Business and Economics; Computer Science
Dist - EDREGR **Prod** - EDREGR 1995

Put Your Hand in My Hand 15 MIN
16mm
Color (I J H)
LC 77-701857
Shows several foreign youths on a cultural exchange program to the United States discussing differences in customs and explains how visiting their American peers has affected their perception of the country.
Sociology
Dist - CASTOP **Prod** - CASTOP 1975

Put your hands on the top of your head 4 MIN
U-matic / VHS / 16mm
Most important person - body movement series
Color (K)
Presents a song game where the hands are put on top of the head and the body moves to a rousing song, to learn the parts of the body.
Physical Education and Recreation; Science - Natural
Dist - EBEC **Prod** - EBEC 1972

Put your show on the road 50 MIN
VHS
Color (G)
$29.95 purchase _ #VDZ - PU01
Offers dozens of tips from music business professionals on how to present oneself, how to construct a winning promo kit, how to get gigs, which publications are 'must - haves' and more.
Fine Arts
Dist - HOMETA **Prod** - HOMETA 1994

Put your show on the road 51 MIN
VHS
Color (G)
$29.95 purchase
Shows how to make a living as a professional musician. Discusses five steps to getting gigs; the elements of a winning promotional kit; six must - have publications; mistakes to avoid on the road.
Business and Economics; Fine Arts
Dist - TOMKAT **Prod** - TOMKAT 1994

Putney Swope 84 MIN
35mm / 16mm
Color (G)
$150.00, $200.00 rental
Portrays a mild - mannered black yuppie in a staid, white Madison Avenue advertising firm who is accidentally elected chair of the board. Reveals that the conservative office is shocked into life when the new chair decides to introduce a little Afro - American culture into the corporation. Directed by Robert Downey.
Fine Arts; History - United States; Sociology
Dist - KINOIC

Putting Animals in Groups 13 MIN
16mm / U-matic / VHS
Color (I J H)
Stresses that children can classify animals by observing their structure. Shows distinctive characteristics of mammals, birds, reptiles, amphibians, fishes and insects.
Science - Natural
Dist - IFB **Prod** - IFB 1956

Putting Aside Pesticides 26 MIN
U-matic / VHS
Color (C)
$249.00, $149.00 purchase _ #AD - 1826
Explores alternative pest control methods. Looks at biological pesticides, genetically - engineered microbes that kill selected insects, using natural insect predators and breeding plant strains that produce their own anti - pest toxins.
Agriculture; Home Economics; Science - Natural
Dist - FOTH **Prod** - FOTH

Putting back the pieces 22 MIN
VHS
Color (PRO A G)
$125.00 purchase _ #PM - 01
Portrays the stress related events and problems encountered by families of brain injured individuals. Familiarizes the family members with the health care professionals, situations, responses, treatments, equipment, procedures and therapies involved in rehabilitation.
Health and Safety; Science - Natural
Dist - MIFE **Prod** - LOMAM

Putting commas between 16 MIN
U-matic / VHS / 16mm
Punctuation series
Color (I J)
$385.00, $250.00 purchase _ #76532
Shows the different uses of commas and the importance of using them to separate items in a series.
English Language
Dist - CORF

Putting ethics to work 22 MIN
35mm strip / VHS
Color (J H C A)
$93.00, $93.00 purchase _ #MB - 909783 - 9, #MB - 909784 - 7
Examines ethics in the business world. Questions how honesty can be achieved in the face of intense pressures to succeed. Covers ethics on the job and in the marketplace.
Psychology; Sociology
Dist - SRA **Prod** - SRA 1990

Putting Fruit by - the Solar Way 15 MIN
U-matic / VHS / 16mm
Color
Shows the steps for dehydrating fruits, from building a solar box to storing the product.
Home Economics
Dist - BULFRG **Prod** - ODECA

The Putting game
VHS
N C A A instructional video series
Color (H C A)
$39.95 purchase _ #KAR2354V
Presents the fourth of a four - part series on golf. Focuses on putting.
Physical Education and Recreation
Dist - CAMV **Prod** - NCAAF

Putting - Golf's End Game 13 MIN
16mm
Modern Golf Instruction in Motion Pictures Series
Color (H C A)
LC 76-703596
Explains the geometric factors involved in putting. Details methods of putting and the importance of establishing a routine approach.
Physical Education and Recreation
Dist - NGF **Prod** - NGF 1974

Putting - Golf's End Game 12 MIN
Videoreel / VT2
Modern Golf Instruction in Motion Pictures Series Unit 5
Color (H C A)
LC 76-703596
Explains geometrical factors of putting and fundamentals for developing a dependable putting technique. Demonstrates methods of stroking and putting across, up and down slopes.
Physical Education and Recreation
Dist - NGF **Prod** - NGF 1944

Putting high school to work for you 30 MIN
VHS
Color (J H)
$89.00 purchase _ #CCP0018V
Focuses on effectively designing an educational plan for the high school years. Emphasizes selecting high school courses that will provide the vehicle for successfully pursuing future educational and career goals in three segments. The first segment illustrates the importance of planning ahead. Segment two explains types of curricular programs. The final segment shows how to design a sound educational plan.
Education; Guidance and Counseling
Dist - CAMV

Putting Ideas in Order - Outlining Skills
U-matic / VHS / 35mm strip
Study Skills Series
(G J C)
$109.00 purchase _ #00330 - 85
Shows students how to create useful and effective outlines from lecture notes or books. Reviews the standard system of numerals and letters, and explores other systems of organization.
Education
Dist - CHUMAN

Putting ideas in order - outlining skills
VHS
Color (H)
$119.00 purchase _ #00330 - 126
Helps students create useful and effective outlines from lecture notes and books. Shows how to categorize information according to the customary system of numbers and letters, and how to identify and use patterns such as lists, chronology, cause - effect and compare - contrast. Includes teacher's guide, library kit, 25 subscriptions to Time magazine for six weeks, six weekly guides. Part of a two - part series.
Education
Dist - GA **Prod** - GA 1992

Putting it all into practice - Video Two 90 MIN
VHS
Branching out on bluegrass banjo series
Color (G)
$49.95 purchase _ #VD - WER - BO02
Features Pete - Dr Banjo - Wernick who shows how to apply techniques covered in Video One plus dozens of new licks, runs, back - ups, modulations, scales, chords, breaks and more. Shows how to create improvisations and solos while teaching bluegrass classics such as Soldier's Joy; The Wild Ride; High on a Mountain; If I Should Wander Back Tonight; Radio Boogie; Walk the Way the Wind Blows; Gone Fishing; Nellie Kane and Foggy Mountain Special. Includes tablature. Part two of a two - part series.
Fine Arts
Dist - HOMETA **Prod** - HOMETA

Putting it all together 28 MIN
U-matic / BETA / VHS
Communication skills 2 - advanced series
Color (H C G)
$101.95, $89.95 purchase _ #CA - 09
Identifies proper and improper participation in symposiums, panels and forums. Includes leader introduction of topics and speakers. Illustrates proper transitions between topics and speakers and logical and timely conclusions to discussions, as well as effective handling of questions and responses. Focuses on leader and member participation as it relates to effective presentations. Part of a 26 - part series.
Guidance and Counseling; Social Science
Dist - INSTRU

Putting it all Together 18 MIN
U-matic / VHS
Color (PRO)
Provides an orientation to community health nursing through a typical student's experiences as she visits several families. Utilizes interviewing and interpersonal skills with a broad range of families and ages. Emphasizes nursing experiences to which students are exposed and the personal and professional growth that results.
Health and Safety
Dist - UMICHM **Prod** - UMICHM 1975

Putting it all Together
VHS / U-matic
Organizational Quality Improvement Series
Color
Examines how to reduce costs and increase quality. Shows how to set up a system of checks and balances with quality audits. Deals with establishing goals.
Business and Economics; Psychology
Dist - BNA **Prod** - BNA

Putting it all Together 28 MIN
VHS / 16mm
Serving the Gifted and Talented Series
Color (C)
$200.00 purchase _ #276302
Assists teachers in identifying, assessing, managing and programming for gifted and talented students. 'Putting It All Together' shows how to plan a program, covering topics like steering committees, program philosophy, design - regular classroom, catalyst teacher, clustering, partial and complete pull - out, extra credit - special subjects - and suggested resources.
Education; Mathematics; Psychology
Dist - ACCESS **Prod** - ACCESS 1988

Putting it all Together 15 MIN
16mm
Color (J)
Explores different attitudes toward music and presents interviews with people whose interests in the musical world range from student teaching to performing, including jazz musicians and Clark Terry and Bobby Columbi of the rock group Blood, Sweat and Tears.
Fine Arts
Dist - MTP **Prod** - MAGSD

Putting it all Together - Action Plans 26 MIN
16mm
Color

LC 75-701358
Illustrates how definable steps in a chosen strategy are put into the work stream of an organization. Examines two new activities for their fiscal and manpower implications.
Business and Economics; Education; Guidance and Counseling; Psychology
Dist - USNAC **Prod** - USOE 1973

Putting it all Together - Evaluation 30 MIN
16mm
Color
LC 75-701361
Discusses principles of evaluation in a managerial context with programs, students, teachers and administrators as a part of the total system. Emphasizes that evaluation is corrective and not punitive.
Business and Economics; Education; Guidance and Counseling; Psychology; Sociology
Dist - USNAC **Prod** - USOE 1973

Putting it all Together - Farmers and their Cooperatives 22 MIN
16mm
Color
LC 79-701239
Explains the cooperative system in American agriculture and the significance of this system to the family farmer and the consumer.
Agriculture; Social Science; Sociology
Dist - AMIC **Prod** - AMIC 1979

Putting it all Together - Integrating Your Objectives 22 MIN
16mm
Color
LC 75-701362
Demonstrates a top - down, deductive means of developing a hierarchy of objectives. Shows that a hierarchy is useful to relate objectives to the fundamental purpose of a school system.
Business and Economics; Education; Psychology; Sociology
Dist - USNAC **Prod** - USOE 1973

Putting it all Together - Introduction to Planning 12 MIN
16mm
Color
LC 75-701363
Points out the consequences of the absence of planning and indicates the necessity for a rational approach to planning.
Business and Economics; Education; Psychology
Dist - USNAC **Prod** - USOE 1973

Putting it all Together - it all Depends 18 MIN
16mm
Color
LC 75-701364
Stresses the importance of understanding the situation before setting objectives or committing resources when planning. Provides guidance for structuring an analysis of the situation to make it useful in decision - making.
Business and Economics; Education; Psychology
Dist - USNAC **Prod** - USOE 1973

Putting it all Together - Organization 22 MIN
16mm
Color
LC 75-701366
Describes the concepts of organization, the tools for organizing and the impact of good organization.
Business and Economics; Education; Psychology
Dist - USNAC **Prod** - USOE 1973

Putting it all Together - Pitfalls of Planning 29 MIN
16mm
Color
LC 75-701368
Discusses seven of the most critical reasons why planning fails and offers suggestions to prevent failure.
Business and Economics; Education; Psychology
Dist - USNAC **Prod** - USOE 1973

Putting it all Together - Planning 57 MIN
16mm
Color
LC 75-701369
Presents the principles of management, emphasizing the differences between management activities and technical activities. Includes concepts of a system of management in which planning is stressed.
Business and Economics; Education; Psychology
Dist - USNAC **Prod** - USOE 1973

Putting it all Together - Policies 16 MIN
U-matic
Color
LC 76-706092
Shows how an organization analyzes its goals and chooses to channel its activities in one direction rather than another. Demonstrates how articulating such policies can avoid conflict.
Business and Economics; Psychology
Dist - USNAC **Prod** - USOE 1973

Putting it all Together - Summary and Conclusion 15 MIN
VHS / U-matic
Clyde Frog Show Series
Color (P)
Presents a summary of how to use The Clyde Frog Show Series.
Education
Dist - GPN **Prod** - MAETEL 1977

Putting it all Together - the Concept of Strategy 25 MIN
16mm
Color
LC 75-701360
Shows how alternative means may be devised to achieve management objectives. Describes ways of developing priorities among the strategies.
Business and Economics; Education; Psychology
Dist - USNAC **Prod** - USOE 1973

Putting it all Together - the Nature of Objectives 14 MIN
16mm
Color
LC 75-701365
Presents the criteria for evaluating a management objective. Emphasizes the problem of evaluating the validity of an objective and the problem of tying an objective to a specific position in the organization.
Business and Economics; Education; Psychology
Dist - USNAC **Prod** - USOE 1973

Putting it all Together - Values in Planning 14 MIN
16mm
Color
LC 75-701371
Demonstrates the value of a visible system of beliefs and assumptions in the management of a school system. Provides a discussion of the basic issues involved in the management of a school system.
Business and Economics; Education; Psychology
Dist - USNAC **Prod** - USOE 1973

Putting it all together - Video Three 60 MIN
VHS
You can play jazz guitar series
Color (G)
$49.95 purchase _ #VD - DEM - GT03
Features jazz guitarist Mike DeMicco. Starts with DeMicco's bebop - oriented tune, Boptology, to show how to build creative solos while challenging the viewer to find an individual voice. Reveals that the melody of this tune is a complete study tool as it illustrates a synthesis of several jazz styles. Takes apart the classic Victor Young standard, Love Letters, to fully discuss chord melodies and new ideas for soloing. Includes music and diagrams. Part three of a three - part series.
Fine Arts
Dist - HOMETA **Prod** - HOMETA

Putting it Straight 14 MIN
U-matic / VHS / 16mm
Color (I J H)
Dramatizes the basic facts about teeth, their care and orthodontic treatment.
Health and Safety; Science - Natural
Dist - IFB **Prod** - NFBC 1957

Putting Learning Back in the Classroom 45 MIN
U-matic / VHS
Milton Friedman Speaking Series Lecture 11
Color (C)
LC 79-708071
Presents economist Milton Friedman examining schooling in the United States.
Education
Dist - HBJ **Prod** - HBJ 1980

Putting learning back in the classroom - Pt 1 23 MIN
U-matic / VHS
Milton Friedman speaking series lecture 11
Color (C)
LC 79-708071
Presents economist Milton Friedman examining schooling in the United States.
Business and Economics
Dist - HBJ **Prod** - HBJ 1980

Putting learning back in the classroom - Pt 2 22 MIN
VHS / U-matic
Milton Friedman speaking series lecture 11
Color (C)
LC 79-708071
Presents economist Milton Friedman examining schooling in the United States.
Business and Economics
Dist - HBJ **Prod** - HBJ 1980

Putting Microbes to Work
VHS
Genetic Engineering - Prospects of the Future Series
Color
Focuses on the role of bacteria in genetic engineering and the creation of new kinds of bacteria by scientists. Examines recombinant DNA techniques used in producing insulin and interferon.
Science; Science - Natural
Dist - IBIS **Prod** - IBIS

Putting Microprocessors to Work 180 MIN
U-matic
Microprocessors - a Comprehensive Introduction Series
Color (A)
Presents the major impacts of microprocessors, discussing reduction of manufacturing costs, system capability and flexibility, rapid response to market changes, and the product family concept. Features application case histories illustrating consumer products, process control and automation, and distributed data processing. Presents the status and future trends in microelectronics, hardware and software costs, and 8 - , 16 - , and 32 - bit micros. Discusses the impact on telecommunications.
Computer Science
Dist - INTECS **Prod** - INTECS

Putting on the Dog 8 MIN
16mm
Color (J)
LC 80-700737
Dramatizes the importance of perseverance, as well as occasional compromise in the pursuit of happiness. Tells the story of a woman who dresses up in odds and ends and waltzes around town, fantasizing that she is a beautiful lady. Shows how she accidentally finds a solution and dances happily away to the country.
Fine Arts; Guidance and Counseling
Dist - KINMIK **Prod** - INSDEA 1980

Putting Pants on Philip 20 MIN
16mm / U-matic / VHS
B&W (J)
Stars Laurel and Hardy attempting to get Ollie's Scottish immigrant cousin out of kilts and into pants.
Fine Arts
Dist - FI **Prod** - ROACH 1928

Putting power, punch and pizzaz in your training - Robert W Pike 90 MIN
VHS
Color; PAL (C G PRO)
$89.95, $69.95, $16.00 purchase _ #91AST - V - S22, #91AST - S22
Shows how to increase participants' retention and get them more involved in the training process and applying skill and content back on the job. Demonstrates 19 ways to improve trainer's transfer and five techniques for creating high - impact visuals. Features the President of Creative Training Techniques International, Eden Prairie MN.
Business and Economics; Education; Psychology
Dist - MOBILE **Prod** - ASTD 1991

Putting psychotherapy on the couch 30 MIN
BETA / VHS
Therapeutic alternatives series
Color (G)
$29.95 purchase _ #S121
States that to achieve personal transformation through psychotherapy, one must be motivated to work hard and make difficult and disturbing changes in one's life. Features Dr Bernie Zilbergeld, author of 'The Shrinking of America' and 'Mind Power.' Part of a four - part series on therapeutic alternatives.
Psychology
Dist - THINKA **Prod** - THINKA

Putting Sleeves on the Coat 29 MIN
Videoreel / VT2
Sewing Skills - Tailoring Series
Color
Features Mrs Ruth Hickman demonstrating how to put sleeves on a coat.
Home Economics
Dist - PBS **Prod** - KRMATV

Putting the Atom to Work 25 MIN
16mm
Color
Presents basic information on nuclear fission, how this is applied to generate power, the present nuclear generating stations now operating or under construction for Britain's power program, the advanced gas - cooled reactor, the Dounreay fast breeder reactor and what radioisotopes are and how they are used.

Industrial and Technical Education; Science - Physical
Dist - UKAEA **Prod** - UKAEA 1966

Putting the bars behind you 23 MIN
VHS
Color (H C G)
$149.00 purchase _ #JW0972V
Teaches the ex - offender new job search methods designed to reduce job search time and lessen the risk of being 'screened out' before having a chance to interview. Shows how to answer tough interview questions and the proper way to act during an interview. Features ex - offenders who tell their stories and offer advice on what to expect from employers in the interview and job search process. Includes the book Getting the Job You Really Want.
Business and Economics; Guidance and Counseling
Dist - CAMV **Prod** - JISTW 1993

Putting the one minute manager to work 59 MIN
U-matic / 16mm / VHS
One minute management system series
Color (G PRO A)
$1295.00, $995.00, $895.00 purchase, $375.00, $325.00 rental
Presents Dr Ken Blanchard who shows how to put his 'one minute manager' system to work.
Business and Economics; Psychology
Dist - MAGVID **Prod** - MAGVID 1984

Putting the One Minute Manager to Work 60 MIN
16mm / BETA
Color (A)
Presents Dr Ken Blanchard and Dr Robert Lorber, business consultants, explaining how to implement management theory in a work setting. Expands on the ideas of the book The One Minute Manager. Emphasizes goal setting and judicious praising and reprimands.
Business and Economics; Psychology
Dist - CBSFOX **Prod** - CBSFOX

Putting the one minute manager to work
U-matic
$1150.00 purchase, $250.00 rental
Discusses the secrets of Putting the One Minute Manager to Work and some live examples of how their concepts have actually been incorporated in major corporations worldwide.
Business and Economics
Dist - BLNCTD **Prod** - BLNCTD

Putting the Pieces Together - 30 30 MIN
VHS
English 101 - Ingles 101 Series
Color (H)
$125.00 purchase
Presents a series of thirty 30 - minute programs in basic English for native speakers of Spanish. Focuses on a specific topic in order to emphasize a particular grammatical point or set of idioms. English is used from the beginning as the primary language of instruction but Spanish translations are included to ensure understanding. Part 30 reviews simple present tense, prepositions, simple past tense.
English Language; Foreign Language
Dist - AITECH **Prod** - UPRICO 1988

Putting the Rules Together 14 MIN
U-matic / VHS / 16mm
Reading Skills, Set 2 Series no 3
Color (P I)
LC 73-700985
Shows that the rules for pronouncing the long and short sounds of a single vowel can be put together and reduced to a few simple understandings.
English Language
Dist - JOU **Prod** - GLDWER 1972

Putting the sun to work 5 MIN
U-matic / VHS / 16mm
Search - encounters with science series
Color (I)
LC 74-702823
Describes the work of scientists and engineers from government and private industry in their search for ways to produce electrical energy from the sun.
Science; Social Science
Dist - AMEDFL **Prod** - NSF 1973

Putting - Volume 1 55 MIN
VHS
Name of the game is golf series
(H C A)
$49.95 purchase _ #SWC410V
Discusses the basics of golf, including how to select a putter, proper grip, uphill and downhill puts and more. Features slow motion photography.
Physical Education and Recreation
Dist - CAMV

Putting Your Financial Plan into Action 25 MIN
U-matic / VHS
Money Smart - a Guide to Personal Finance Series
Color (H C A)
Explains how individuals set aside money for investment. Includes budgeting, developing good spending habits, finding suitable investments and using professional help.
Business and Economics; Education; Home Economics
Dist - BCNFL **Prod** - SOMFIL 1984

Puuc - Mayan history
VHS
Color (J H G) (SPANISH)
$44.95 purchase _ #MCV5005, #MCV5006
Presents a program on the history of the Maya of Mexico.
History - World; Social Science
Dist - MADERA **Prod** - MADERA

The Puzzle 6 MIN
U-matic / VHS / 16mm
This Matter of Motivation Series
Color (IND)
LC 75-703992
Discusses the problem of dealing with a good employee who suddenly becomes hard to get along with and sloppy when he transfers to another department.
Business and Economics; Psychology
Dist - DARTNL **Prod** - CTRACT 1971

The Puzzle children 60 MIN
16mm
Color (H C A G)
$125.00 purchase _ #PLZC - 000; LC 77-701035
Discusses learning disabilities in children and identifies some of the myths that prevent an accurate understanding of these problems. Profiles four children with specific learning handicaps, including comments by their parents, teachers and special educators. Hosted by Julie Andrews and Bill Bixby.
Education; Psychology
Dist - IU **Prod** - WQED 1977

The Puzzle of Pain 145 MIN
U-matic
University of the Air Series
Color (J H C A)
$750.00 purchase, $250.00 rental
Considers the psychology of pain, clinical pain syndromes or phantom limb pain, the physiology, theories and treatment of pain. Program contains a series of five cassettes 29 minutes each.
Health and Safety; Psychology
Dist - CTV **Prod** - CTV 1977

Puzzling Problems 15 MIN
VHS / U-matic
Math Mission 2 Series
Color (P)
LC 82-706317
Tells how a space robot and his detective friend help unravel mysterious numbers and a secret message by translating and finding the answers to several different types of word problems, picture problems, and number stories.
Mathematics
Dist - GPN **Prod** - WCVETV 1980

pV Isotherms of CO2 - 1 15 MIN
U-matic / VHS
Experiment - Physics Level 2 Series
Color (C)
$249.00, $149.00 purchase _ #AD - 1075
Illustrates changes in the isothermal pressure over volume relationship for a gas under a range of pressures. Measures the volume of a constant mass of CO2 confined in a tube immersed in a bath held at 0 degrees C as a function of the pressure exerted by a column of mercury behind the gas. Part of a series of videos demonstrating physics experiments which are impractical to perform in a classroom laboratory.
Education; Psychology; Science - Physical
Dist - FOTH **Prod** - FOTH

pV Isotherms of CO2 - 2 15 MIN
U-matic / VHS
Experiment - Physics Level 2 Series
Color (C)
$249.00, $149.00 purchase _ #AD - 1076
Measures additional pV isotherms for CO2 below and above critical temperature. Part of a series of videos demonstrating physics experiments which are impractical to perform in a classroom laboratory.
Education; Psychology; Science - Physical
Dist - FOTH **Prod** - FOTH

Pyatachok 58 MIN
VHS
Color (G C)
$200.00 purchase, $19.00 rental _ #61397
Traces the history of the pyatachok in Moscow, from its beginnings in the 1920s when young Russian immigrants forced to find city employment began a migration process into Moscow that went on for decades. Reveals that, seeking diversion from hard weekday work, these immigrants made the pyatachok a common weekend event in the capital's main parks. The celebrants dance to lively music accompanied by the spontaneous, bursting recitation of humorous, testimonial verse, and tell of the oppression that drove them from the villages. Produced by Dr Alexei Khanyutin.
Fine Arts; Sociology
Dist - PSU **Prod** - CDFS 1987

Pychotherapy 30 MIN
U-matic / VHS
Psychology of Human Relations Series
Color
Presents the psychoanalytic approach, client - centered therapy, gestalt therapy, transactional analysis, psychiatric drugs, services offered by counselor, psychologists, clinical social workers and psychiatrists.
Psychology
Dist - WFVTAE **Prod** - MATC

Pyeloplasty by Modified Ureteroneopyelostomy 25 MIN
16mm
Color
LC 75-702300
Presents three cases to illustrate that the method of pyeloplasty best suited to the individual case must be determined at the time of surgical intervention. Illustrates the classical approach, in case one, used with high ureteral insertion with no intrinsic stricture at the uretero - pelvic junction. Portrays the preservation of an aberrant blood vessel supplying a major portion of the kidney in case two. Depicts the utilization of the Schwyzer - Foley modification combined with ureteroneopyelostomy in the correction of a uretero - pelvic junction stricture.
Health and Safety; Science
Dist - EATONL **Prod** - EATONL 1966

Pygmalion
VHS / BETA
B&W
Presents a 1938 adaptation of Shaw's play Pygmalion, starring Wendy Miller and Leslie Howard.
Fine Arts; Literature and Drama
Dist - GA **Prod** - GA

Pygmalion 95 MIN
VHS
B&W (G)
$39.95 purchase _ #S00535
Presents a 1938 version of George Bernard Shaw's play, in which a professor teaches a Cockney flower girl to be a lady. Stars Leslie Howard, Wilfred Lawson, and Wendy Hiller. Directed by Anthony Asquith.
Literature and Drama
Dist - UILL

Pygmalion 96 MIN
16mm
B&W
Presents the classic story of Professor Henry Higgins, who bets his companion Colonel Pickering that he can transform a Cockney flower girl into a lady after only a few months instruction. Shows what happens when Higgins chooses hapless Eliza Doolittle as his subject. Features Leslie Howard, Wendy Hiller and Wilfrid Lawson. Directed by Anthony Asquith. Based on the play Pygmalion by George Bernard Shaw.
Fine Arts; Literature and Drama
Dist - LCOA **Prod** - MGM 1938

Pygmies 25 MIN
U-matic / VHS / 16mm
Untamed World Series Series
Color; Mono (J H C A)
$400.00 film, $250.00 video, $50.00 rental
Studies the nomadic existance of the Mbutu pygmies in the jungles of Africa.
Geography - World; Sociology
Dist - CTV **Prod** - CTV 1969

The Pygmies of the Ituri Forest 19 MIN
U-matic / VHS / 16mm
Color (J H)
LC 75-700239
Examines the life and customs of the Efe Pygmies as observed and photographed by the anthropologist Jean - Pierre Hallet.
Social Science; Sociology
Dist - EBEC **Prod** - HALLTJ 1974

Pygmies of the Rain Forest 51 MIN
16mm / U-matic / VHS
Color (I)
LC 77-701105
Portrays the life of the nomadic Mbuti pygmies of Zaire, Africa. Shows their primal world of hut building, food gathering and bull elephant hunting.
Geography - World; Social Science; Sociology
Dist - PFP **Prod** - DUFFY 1976

The Pygmies - People of the Forest 14 MIN
16mm / U-matic / VHS
Color (I J)
LC 75-700240
Examines the life and customs of Pygmies in the African forest. Shows how they adapt their way of life to their environment from which they take all their basic supplies and materials.
Social Science; Sociology
Dist - EBEC **Prod** - HALLTJ 1975

Pyloric Stenosis 9 MIN
U-matic / VHS
Pediatric Series
Color
Health and Safety
Dist - SVL **Prod** - SVL

Pyloric Stenosis 13 MIN
16mm
Doctors at Work Series
B&W (PRO)
LC FIA65-1359
Uses drawings and a stomach model to explain the anatomy of the stomach region and the area involved in the treatment of pyloric stenosis. Shows a pediatrician performing surgery on a six - week old infant.
Health and Safety
Dist - LAWREN **Prod** - CMA 1962

Pyloric Stenosis 28 MIN
16mm
Color (PRO)
Points out that the modern operative technique for pyloroplasty varies little from that described by Conrad Ramstedt in 1912. Explains that improved preparation for operation coupled with improved anesthesia and after - care are the major factors contributing to a now extremely low mortality.
Health and Safety; Science
Dist - ACY **Prod** - ACYDGD 1963

Pyramid 60 MIN
VHS
Color (J)
$13.00 rental _ #60897
Uses animated story about life in ancient Egypt with modern - day visits to Valley of the Kings and the Egyptian Museum in Cairo to understand how the great pyramids were built. Based on host David Macaulay's book.
Civics and Political Systems; Fine Arts; History - World
Dist - PSU **Prod** - PBS

Pyramid 60 MIN
VHS / 16mm
Color (G H)
$59.95 purchase _ #PYRM - 000H; $13.00 rental _ #60897
Combines an animated story about life in ancient Egypt with live - action footage of the Valley of the Kings and the Egyptian Museum in Cairo. Transports viewers to the Fourth Dynasty of ancient Egypt, circa 2500 BC, to view the planning and construction of the Great Pyramid of Giza, tomb of King Khufu. Based on host David Nacaulay's book.
History - World
Dist - PBS

Pyramid Layout Radial Line Method 7 MIN
BETA / VHS
Color (IND)
Demonstrates the application of the radial line method for developing the patterns for pyramid shapes.
Industrial and Technical Education; Psychology
Dist - RMIBHF **Prod** - RMIBHF

Pyramid of Success 25 MIN
16mm / VHS
Color (PRO)
$595.00, $500.00 purchase, $150.00 rental, $75.00 preview
Presents famed coach John Wooden's philosophy for contributing, achieving, and succeeding in life. Encourages the development of enthusiasm and honest working habits.
Psychology
Dist - UTM **Prod** - UTM

Pyramid Probe 6 MIN
U-matic / VHS / 16mm
Color
LC 79-701481
Focuses on a search for an Egyptian pharoah's secret burial chamber. Explains how cosmic radiation from space was used to X - ray the pyramid.
Science - Physical; Sociology
Dist - AMEDFL **Prod** - NSF 1975

Pyramid probe - cosmic radiation - 4
U-matic / VHS / BETA
Search encounters in science series
Color; PAL (G H C)
PdS25, PdS33 purchase
Brings modern research efforts of the world's leading scientists into the classroom. Features one of a series of 24 mini - documentaries. Each film is 5 - 7 minutes in length.
Science; Science - Physical
Dist - EDPAT **Prod** - NSF

Pyramid School Kit 60 MIN
VHS
Color (G)
$125.00 purchase _ #PYRK - 000
Discusses ancient Egyptian history. Uses animation and live action film sequences to present information on history, geography, culture and customs, religion, archaeology, mythology, science and art of the period. Includes instructional materials.
History - World
Dist - PBS

Pyramids 60 MIN
VHS
Muscle building series
Color (G)
$39.99 purchase _ #MFV009V
Presents a body building workout program based on the Oxford Method of weight training. Utilizes a system of 100 percent - 66 percent - 50 percent decrease of the maximum lift over the sets for each exercise. Recommends at least six months of previous weight training experience due to the strenuousness of the program.
Physical Education and Recreation; Science - Natural
Dist - CAMV **Prod** - CAMV 1988

The Pyramids and the cities of the pharaohs 60 MIN
VHS
Great cities of the ancient world series
Color (G)
$29.95 purchase _ #QV2338V-S
Travels back 5,000 years to view the awakening of Egypt and its civilization that created colossal structures with simple tools and manpower. Includes two of the seven wonders of the ancient world, the Pyramids and the Lighthouse at Alexandria. Part of a three-part series.
History - World; Sociology
Dist - CAMV

Pyramids of the sun and the moon 20 MIN
U-matic / VHS
Color (SPANISH)
Presents a comprehensive panorama of Teotihuacan and the Aztec art.
Fine Arts
Dist - MOMALA **Prod** - MOMALA

The Pyramids of the Sun and the Moon 20 MIN
16mm
Color (SPANISH)
Offers a panorama of Teotihuacan and the Aztec art, filmed on location and at the Museum of Anthropology of Mexico City.
Fine Arts; History - World; Social Science
Dist - MOMALA **Prod** - OOAS 1983

Pysanka - the Ukrainian Easter Egg 14 MIN
U-matic / VHS / 16mm
Color
Explains the myth and magic behind the craft of Easter egg design. Follows an artist as she creates a design on a naked egg.
Fine Arts
Dist - CORF **Prod** - NOWYTS 1975

Pythagoras' theorem - Pt 1 - diagrammatic proof 7 MIN
16mm
B&W (J H C)
Uses animation to diagrammatically prove the Pythagorean theorem for the relationship among the three sides of a right triangle.
Mathematics
Dist - VIEWTH **Prod** - GATEEF

Pythagoras' theorem - Pt 2 - an extension of the proof 7 MIN
16mm
B&W (J H C)
Extends the Pythagorean theorem to the field of trigonometry showing its application to acute angled triangles as a special case of the cosine formula.
Mathematics
Dist - VIEWTH **Prod** - GATEEF

The Pythagorean theorem and graphing equations - parabolas 30 MIN
VHS
Beginning algebra series
Color (J H)
$125.00 purchase _ #M34
Explains the Pythagorean theorem and how to graph equations - parabolas. Features Elayn Gay. Part of a 19 - part series on beginning algebra.
Industrial and Technical Education; Mathematics
Dist - LANDMK **Prod** - MGHT

Pyza adventures - Vol 1 - Wedrowki Pyzy - Cz 1 68 MIN
VHS
Color (P I J) (POLISH)
$17.95 purchase _ #V168A
Offers the animated Pyzy adventures for children.
Fine Arts; Literature and Drama
Dist - POLART

Pyza adventures - Vol 2 - Wedrowki Pyzy - Cz 2 68 MIN
VHS
Color (P I J) (POLISH)
$17.95 purchase _ #V168B
Offers a continuation of the animated Pyzy adventures for children.
Fine Arts; Literature and Drama
Dist - POLART

Q

Q A Documentation 60 MIN
U-matic / VHS
Quality Assurance Series
Color (IND)
Presents vendor qualification, traceability, document control and conducting an audit.
Business and Economics; Industrial and Technical Education
Dist - LEIKID **Prod** - LEIKID

Q A Programs 60 MIN
U-matic / VHS
Quality Assurance Series
Color (IND)
Presents details of management's responsibility, regulatory bodies and standards. Discusses dominance, inspection and nonconformance.
Business and Economics; Industrial and Technical Education
Dist - LEIKID **Prod** - LEIKID

Q is for Quest 20 MIN
16mm
Color (I J)
Tells of 10 - year - old Kathy who feels that her dreams of knighthood will never come true after she goes to live with an embittered old aunt who vows to turn her into a proper young lady. Shows how she gets her opportunity for knighthood and in the process revises her aunt's opinions on the roles of men and women.
Fine Arts
Dist - USC **Prod** - USC 1983

Q it up 16 MIN
U-matic / VHS
Color (G)
$75.00 purchase, $40.00 rental
Explores the issue of drug abuse among Asian American adolescents. Reveals that Eddie struggles to win peer acceptance by getting 'high' on quaaludes and, at the same time, longs to be understood by his traditional family. Features Dennis Dun, Kelvin Han Yee, Cora Miao and Victor Wong. Produced by the Chinatown Youth Center.
Psychology; Sociology
Dist - CROCUR

Q R Hand - 2 - 25 - 83 15 MIN
VHS / Cassette
Poetry Center reading series
Color (G)
$15.00, $45.00 purchase, $15.00 rental _ #522 - 442
Features the African American writer reading his works at the Poetry Center, San Francisco State University.
Literature and Drama
Dist - POETRY **Prod** - POETRY 1983

Qaddafi's warning - Monday, January 13, 1986 30 MIN
VHS
Nightline series
Color (H C G)
$14.98 purchase _ #MP6152
Focuses on the pugnacious ruler of Libya, Colonel Muammar Qaddafi, and his threats against the United States.
Civics and Political Systems; Fine Arts
Dist - INSTRU **Prod** - ABCNEW 1986

Qallunaani 10 MIN
16mm
Color (G)

#5X9
Portrays the emotions and experiences of Inuit Indian students caught between two cultures in a Canadian city.
Social Science
Dist - CDIAND **Prod** - ANDPVA 1981

Qari Abdul Basit on video
VHS
Color (G)
$20.00 purchase _ #129 - 003
Presents the following Surahs - Surah Al - Hashr - 18 - 24, Surah Al - Infitar, Ash - Shams, Ad - Duha, Al - Inshirah, Al - Mutaffifin - 18 - 28, An - Nasr, Al - Qamar 49 - 55, Ar - Rahman - 1 - 23, At - Tahrim - 8 - 12, At - Tariq - 2 recited by Qari Abdul Basit Abdul Samad before a live audience.
Foreign Language; Religion and Philosophy
Dist - SOUVIS **Prod** - SOUVIS

Qatar - quest for excellence 28 MIN
U-matic / VHS / BETA
Color; PAL (G H C)
PdS50, PdS58 purchase
Portrays the relationship between cultural environment and modern technology. Combines visual images with an musical score without commentary.
Fine Arts; Geography - World
Dist - EDPAT

QE2 sails New Zealand and Australia
VHS
International travel films from Doug Jones series
Color (G H)
$19.95 purchase _ #IT06
Sails on the Queen Elizabeth II to New Zealand and Australia.
Geography - World
Dist - SVIP

QED series

Another little drink won't do us any harm	30 MIN
The bike	30 MIN
Casualties of the wild	30 MIN
Cot death	40 MIN
Craig's boot	30 MIN
Curse of the killer bug	30 MIN
Deaf whale, dead whale	50 MIN
Fall from grace	30 MIN
Invisible killer	30 MIN
Lifeline express	60 MIN
Little monsters	30 MIN
My best friend's a computer	30 MIN
Panic attack	30 MIN
Plastic fantastic	30 MIN
Sleeping it off	30 MIN
The 300 million years war	30 MIN
Trauma	50 MIN

Dist - BBCENE

QED

Family game	40 MINS.
Food fights	30 MINS.
Is love enough?	55 MINS.

Dist - BBCENE

Q'eros - the shape of survival 53 MIN
16mm / VHS
Color (C G)
$995.00, $295.00 purchase, $70.00 rental _ #11418, #38167
Depicts the way of life of the Q'eros Indians of Peru who have lived in the Andes for more than 3,000 years. Shows that their economy is nearly self - sufficient and their location at an altitude of 14,000 feet is well adapted for raising alpacas - for wool - and llamas - beasts of burden. Discloses that the Q'ero employ the same agricultural methods, play the same panpipes and flutes and weave cloth using the same patterns as those described by Spanish chroniclers in the 16th century. Presents Q'ero music in its shepherdic and religious functions and shows weaving as an integral part of family life.
Fine Arts; Social Science; Sociology
Dist - UCEMC **Prod** - COHNJ 1979

Qeros - the Shape of Survival 50 MIN
16mm / U-matic / VHS
Color (H C A)
Looks at the lifestyle of the Qeros Indian who have lived in the Peruvian Andes for over 3,000 years. Shows their ecological consciousness as they adapt crops to different altitudes, use natural materials and play flutes which echo Andean winds.
Geography - World; History - World; Social Science
Dist - FI **Prod** - COHEN 1979

Qeros - the Shape of Survival 53 MIN
16mm / U-matic / VHS
Color
Illustrates the life of the Qeros Indians in the high Andes Mountains of Peru. Describes their culture as far older than that of the Incas. Portrays them as rural and agricultural and doomed to extinction, primarily because of vulnerability to disease.
Agriculture; Social Science; Sociology
Dist - CNEMAG **Prod** - CNEMAG 1979

Qi gong '18 style' video - for health and longevity 60 MIN
VHS
Color (G)
$32.00 purchase _ #V - QG
Presents 18 exercises for internal health from a system practiced in China for over 2000 years.
Physical Education and Recreation
Dist - WHOLEL

Qilaluganiatut - Whale Hunting 10 MIN
16mm
Color (J H A)
#1X33 N
Visits with six Inuit Indian whale hunters in their pursuit of a Beluga whale near Frobisher Bay, Canada.
Social Science
Dist - CDIAND **Prod** - NFBC 1977

Qimmiq 24 MIN
16mm
Color (G)
#3X14
Discusses how the Eskimo dog has been a part of northern Canadian life for more than 2,000 years. Describes the accomplishments of dog breeder William Carpenter.
Agriculture; Science - Natural; Social Science
Dist - CDIAND **Prod** - NFBC 1982

Qiu hai tang 450 MIN
VHS
Color (G) (MANDARIN)
$150.00 purchase _ #5098
Presents television programming produced in the People's Republic of China. Includes four videocassettes.
Geography - World
Dist - CHTSUI

Qiu Jin - a revolutionary 110 MIN
VHS
Color (G) (MANDARIN WITH ENGLISH SUBTITLES)
$45.00 purchase _ #1046A
Presents a movie produced in the People's Republic of China.
Fine Arts
Dist - CHTSUI

The Quack - Znachor 132 MIN
VHS
Color (G A) (POLISH WITH ENGLISH SUBTITLES)
$39.95 purchase _ #V098
Presents a melodrama, set in Poland in the 1930s, in which a famous surgeon loses his memory and wanders alone through Poland's eastern frontier. Follows him on his adventures, including an amorous escapade. Directed by Jerzy Hoffman.
Fine Arts; Religion and Philosophy
Dist - POLART

Quackery - a side effect of arthritis 12 MIN
U-matic
Arthritis series
Color
LC 79-707861
Features discussions between patients and health professionals regarding the hazards of quackery and patients' reasons for trying unproven remedies.
Health and Safety
Dist - UMICH **Prod** - UMICH 1978

Quackgrass - the Perennial Guest 17 MIN
16mm
Color
Explains that quackgrass is a difficult and costly problem for farmers. Shows how scientific development can increase yields, improve crop quality and facilitate crop tillage.
Agriculture
Dist - DCC **Prod** - DCC

Quacky, Wacky and Buzz Bee 30 MIN
VHS
Color (K P R)
$9.99 purchase _ #SPCN 85116.00345
Presents a story by Ethel Barrett which teaches children that they are special and that they should respect authority.
Religion and Philosophy
Dist - GOSPEL **Prod** - GOSPEL

Quad Graphics 30 MIN
VHS / 16mm
Growing a Business Series
(H C)
$99.95 each, $1,295.00 series
Points out the successful business tactics used by Quad Graphics, a printing company in Milwaukee, as a means of exemplifying innovative thinking in managerial situations.
Business and Economics
Dist - AMBROS **Prod** - AMBROS 1988

Quadragla 3 MIN
16mm
B&W
LC 74-703007
Presents an experimental film with action and stop - action effects.
Industrial and Technical Education
Dist - CANFDC **Prod** - UTORMC 1973

Quadratic equations 60 MIN
VHS
Algebra I series; Volume 6
Color (I J H C A)
$29.95 purchase _ #S02152
Covers algebraic concepts of quadratic equations. Encourages students to use sight, sound and writing skills in learning the material. Uses modern electronic and computer graphics to illustrate many of the concepts. Includes a workbook, with additional workbooks available at an extra charge.
Mathematics
Dist - UILL

Quadratic Equations 29 MIN
16mm
Intermediate Algebra Series
B&W (H)
Analyzes the standard form for the quadratic expression in order to find various conditions that make it solvable. Describes a second way of solving by completing the square.
Mathematics
Dist - MLA **Prod** - CALVIN 1959

Quadratic equations 30 MIN
VHS
Beginning algebra series
Color (J H)
$125.00 purchase _ #M33
Explains quadratic equations. Features Elayn Gay. Part of a 19 - part series on beginning algebra.
Mathematics
Dist - LANDMK **Prod** - MGHT

Quadratic equations and applications 30 MIN
VHS
Intermediate algebra series
Color (H)
$125.00 purchase _ #M44
Explains quadratic equations and applications. Features Elayn Gay. Part of a 27 - part series on intermediate algebra.
Mathematics
Dist - LANDMK **Prod** - MGHT

Quadratic Forms
16mm
B&W
Looks at the problem of classifying stationary values of a function of two variables. Introduces Taylor's series for a function of two variables by demonstrating how to find linear and quadratic approximations to a surface at a point.
Mathematics
Dist - OPENU **Prod** - OPENU

The Quadratic formula - 4
VHS
Quadratics series
Color; PAL (J H G)
Introduces quadratic equations and their corresponding functions on the Cartesian plane. Uses computer animation. Part four of a six - part series.
Industrial and Technical Education; Mathematics
Dist - EMFVL **Prod** - TVOTAR

Quadratic functions 30 MIN
VHS
College algebra series
Color (C)
$125.00 purchase _ #4020
Explains quadratic functions. Part of a 31 - part series on college algebra.
Mathematics
Dist - LANDMK **Prod** - LANDMK

Quadratic Functions 30 MIN
VHS
Mathematics Series
Color (J)
LC 90713155
Explains quadratic functions. The 82nd of 157 installments of the Mathematics Series.
Mathematics
Dist - GPN

Quadratic functions - Pt 1 30 MIN
U-matic
Introduction to mathematics series
Color (C)
Mathematics
Dist - MDCPB **Prod** - MDCPB

Quadratic functions - Pt 2 30 MIN
U-matic
Introduction to mathematics series
Color (C)
Mathematics
Dist - MDCPB **Prod** - MDCPB

Quadratics 15 MIN
U-matic
Graphing Mathematical Concepts Series
(H C A)
Uses computer generated graphics to show the relationships between physical objects and mathematical concepts, equations and their graphs. Relates theoretical concepts to things in the real world.
Computer Science; Mathematics
Dist - ACCESS **Prod** - ACCESS 1986

Quadratics series
Applications of quadratics - 6
Completing the square - 3
Complex roots - 5
Factoring quadratics - 2
The Quadratic formula - 4
Zeros and roots - 1
Dist - EMFVL

Quadricepsplasty - a technique for restoration of muscle function in cases of fibrous adhesions folllowing injury 18 MIN
16mm
Color (PRO)
Examines quadricepsplasty, a technique for restoration of muscle function in cases of fibrous adhesions following injury. Presents the case study of a patient with a 'stiff knee' gait who undergoes surgery and regains 90 degrees of flexion at the knee through the quadricepsplasty technique.
Health and Safety; Science; Science - Natural
Dist - SQUIBB **Prod** - SQUIBB

Quadrilaterals 30 MIN
VHS
Mathematics Series
Color (J)
LC 90713155
Discusses quadrilaterals. The 148th of 157 installments of the Mathematics Series.
Mathematics
Dist - GPN

Quadrilaterals 15 MIN
U-matic / VHS
Math Matters Series Blue Module
Color (I J)
Identifies, squares, rectangles and rhombi and points out the special characteristics of each. Distinguishes between parallelograms, trapezoids and other quadrilaterals.
Mathematics
Dist - AITECH **Prod** - STETVC 1975

Quadrilaterals 30 MIN
VHS
Geometry series
Color (H)
$125.00 purchase _ #7007
Explains quadrilaterals. Part of a 16 - part series on geometry.
Mathematics
Dist - LANDMK **Prod** - LANDMK

Quadriplegia - Car Transfer 15 MIN
VHS / U-matic
Color
Deals with car transfer of quadriplegics, but can be applied to persons with other disabilities. Focuses on making the patient completely independent in transferring himself and his wheelchair in and out of a standard automobile.
Health and Safety
Dist - PRIMED **Prod** - PRIMED

Quadriplegia car transfer - Pt 3 15 MIN
16mm
Color (PRO)
Shows the complete independence of a patient transferring himself and his wheelchair in and out of a standard production automobile.
Education; Health and Safety
Dist - RLAH **Prod** - RLAH

Quadriplegia - Driver Training 15 MIN
U-matic / VHS
Color
Demonstrates the type of equipment needed for quadraplegic driver and begins the process of teaching the patient to drive.
Health and Safety
Dist - PRIMED **Prod** - PRIMED

Quadriplegia driver training - Pt 4 15 MIN
16mm
Color (PRO)
Demonstrates the potential for training the quadriplegic to drive an automobile. Shows the actual training of the quadriplegic.
Education; Health and Safety
Dist - RLAH **Prod** - RLAH

Quadriplegic Functional Skills - Bowel and Bladder Techniques 14 MIN
16mm
Color
LC 75-701725
Presents methods that may be utilized by the quadriplegic to achieve independence in the management of bowel and bladder functions. Shows variations in drainage clamps and urinary connectors, management of catheter irrigation and external collectors and adaptations in clothing.
Health and Safety; Psychology; Science - Natural
Dist - USNAC **Prod** - UILL 1974

Quadriplegic Functional Skills - Dressing 18 MIN
16mm
Color
LC 75-701727
Demonstrates ways for quadriplegics to achieve independence in clothing themselves.
Health and Safety; Psychology
Dist - USNAC **Prod** - UILL 1974

Quadriplegic Functional Skills - Driving 19 MIN
16mm
Color
LC 75-701728
Demonstrates methods quadriplegics can use without assistance in transferring to and from a car and getting a wheelchair in and out of a car. Shows driving with hand controls and adaptations.
Health and Safety; Psychology
Dist - USNAC **Prod** - UILL 1974

Quadriplegic Functional Skills - Showering and Grooming 16 MIN
16mm
Color
LC 75-701729
Demonstrates ways for the quadriplegic to achieve independence in personal hygiene. Shows how to transfer to and from a wheelchair to a shower seat in a tub and a shower stall. Illustrates bathing, shaving and dental and hair care.
Health and Safety; Psychology
Dist - USNAC **Prod** - UILL 1974

Quadriplegic Functions Skills Series
Bowel and bladder techniques 14 MIN
Dressing
Driving 18 MIN
Showering and grooming 16 MIN
Dist - UILL

The Quadruparetic Patient - Changing Position and Sitting Up in Bed 7 MIN
16mm
Color
LC 74-705459
Depicts how the quadruparetic patient can move to one side and roll over in bed. Shows how a patient can learn to sit up.
Health and Safety
Dist - USNAC **Prod** - USPHS 1968

The Quadruparetic Patient - Sitting Balance in Bed 9 MIN
16mm
Color
LC 74-705460
Illustrates how the quadruparetic patient can learn to move his extremities and trunk while sitting in bed.
Health and Safety
Dist - USNAC **Prod** - USPHS 1968

The Quadruparetic Patient - Transfer from Bed to Wheelchair using a Sliding Board 7 MIN
16mm
Color
LC 74-705461
Depicts techniques used in transfer of the quadruparetic patient between bed and wheelchair with the use of a sliding board.
Health and Safety
Dist - USNAC **Prod** - USPHS 1968

The Quadruparetic Patient - Transfer from Wheelchair to Car and Reverse using Sliding 8 MIN
16mm
Color
Demonstrates use of the sliding board for transfer between wheelchair and car.
Health and Safety
Dist - USNAC **Prod** - NMAC 1970

Quaint Cafe 10 MIN
U-matic / VHS
Color (H C A)
Presents comedy by the Brave New World Workshop of the Twin Cities.
Literature and Drama
Dist - UCV **Prod** - BRVNP

Qualification Test Programs 30 MIN
U-matic / VHS
Reliability Engineering Series
Color (IND)
Describes test programs to estimate mean time to failure of devices that fail according to either the normal (wearout) or exponential (chance) distributions. Presents confidence limits for MTTF as well.
Industrial and Technical Education
Dist - COLOSU **Prod** - COLOSU

Qualification Tests - Examples 30 MIN
VHS / U-matic
Reliability Engineering Series
Color (IND)
Contains numerical examples to estimate parameters of the normal and exponential distributions and their confidence intervals.
Industrial and Technical Education
Dist - COLOSU **Prod** - COLOSU

Qualifying the expert 54 MIN
VHS
The Art of advocacy - expert witnesses series
Color (C PRO)
$90.00 purchase, $67.50 rental _ #Z0103
Presents techniques for qualifying expert witnesses. Uses courtroom demonstrations to illustrate the techniques.
Civics and Political Systems
Dist - NITA **Prod** - NITA 1988

Qualitative analytical techniques 17 MIN
VHS
Chemistry master apprentice series
Color (H C)
$49.95 purchase _ #49 - 7210 - V
Demonstrates basic techniques of semi - micro qualitative analysis relevant to transfer, addition and mixing of chemicals. Shows techniques related to precipitation - centrifugation, decantation, testing for completeness of precipitation and washing - and safe methods of heating solutions. Part of the Chemistry Master Apprentice series.
Health and Safety; Science; Science - Physical
Dist - INSTRU **Prod** - CORNRS

Qualitatively Different Program 30 MIN
U-matic / VHS
Simple Gifts Series no 6
Color (T)
Education; Psychology
Dist - GPN **Prod** - UWISC 1977

Qualities of high performance 30 MIN
VHS / BETA
Optimal performance series
Color (G)
$29.95 purchase _ #S196
Reveals that qualities of success - goal setting, high self - esteem and a passion for life - can be developed in anyone. Features Dr Lee Pulos, clinical psychologist, who identifies the characteristics held in common by outstanding achievers in athletics and business. Part of a four - part series on optimal performance.
Psychology
Dist - THINKA **Prod** - THINKA

Qualities of Light 30 MIN
U-matic / VHS
Taking Better Pictures Series
Color (A)
Stresses various qualities of light as being a vital element in creating good photographs. Shows how light can be used to transform an ordinary scene into one of special beauty.
Industrial and Technical Education
Dist - GPN **Prod** - GCCED

Qualities of light 30 MIN
U-matic / VHS
Taking better pictures
(G)
$180.00 purchase, $30.00 rental
Designed to help beginning and intermediate photographers use 35 mm equipment effectively. Focuses on the creative use of light. Fourth in a ten part series.
Industrial and Technical Education
Dist - GPN

Quality, access and cost - the nursing solution 90 MIN
VHS
Color (C PRO)
$295.00 purchase, $85.00 rental _ #42 - 2426, #42 - 2426R
Joins O Marie Henry and Sara Berger during National Nurses' Week 1991 on a panel of a national interactive teleconference on the PBS Adult Learning Satellite Service. Focuses on assessment of the health crisis in the United States and how nursing centers offer solutions to the pressing issues of quality, access and cost in health care. Includes a question and answer session with nurses from around the country, as well as video clips from nursing centers. Includes a detailed seminar description, content outline, references, related articles, biographies of panelists and a bibliography of additional recommended reading and texts. CEUs available.
Health and Safety
Dist - NLFN **Prod** - NLFN

Quality and Cost Control
VHS / 35mm strip
Food Service - Skills and Equipment Series
$219.00 purchase _ #PX1134 filmstrip, $219.00 purchase _ #PX1134V VHS
Discusses the first in, first out principle of storage. Stresses coordination of workers. Portrays how to achieve portion control. Shows measuring devices and converting recipes for a greater or lesser yield.
Industrial and Technical Education
Dist - CAREER **Prod** - CAREER

Quality and productivity in service organizations 50 MIN
U-matic / VHS
Deming videotapes - quality, productivity, and competitive series
Color
Discusses the differences and similarities between service industries and manufacturing concerns.
Business and Economics
Dist - MIOT **Prod** - MIOT
SME

Quality and Quantity - 'do it Right' - Module 2 60 MIN
Software / VHS
Attributes for Successful Employability Series
Color (H)
$395.00 purchase
Presents four 60 - minute Level III interactive video modules - available for Macintosh and IBM InfoWindow - dealing with realistic work situations which call for choices. Makes it clear that while some choices are better than others, often there is no right answer, just different answers with different results. Each module includes five scenes filmed at a variety of work environments. Each scene includes a computerized dictionary of terms which define the attributes demonstrated in the scene. The learner views, reviews and experiments with alternative solutions to problems presented. Module 2 discusses quality and quantity of work, balancing work and social lives, understanding workplace standards, decision making, following instructions and safety.
Business and Economics; Education; Guidance and Counseling; Psychology
Dist - AITECH **Prod** - BLUNI 1990

Quality and the Consumer 50 MIN
VHS / U-matic
Deming Video Tapes - Quality, Productivity and the Competitive 'Series
Color
Business and Economics
Dist - SME **Prod** - MIOT

Quality and value in home furnishing series
Quality and value in home furnishings - Pt 1 - aesthetics in the home 20 MIN
Quality and value in home furnishings - Pt 2 - selecting furniture 20 MIN
Dist - IOWA

Quality and value in home furnishings - Pt 1 - aesthetics in the home 20 MIN
VHS / 16mm
Quality and value in home furnishing series
Color (H C A)
Helps the viewer recognize the need for quality aesthetic experiences in the home environment. Includes interviews with a professor of philosophy and an interior designer.
Home Economics
Dist - IOWA **Prod** - IOWA 1989

Quality and value in home furnishings - Pt 2 - selecting furniture 20 MIN
VHS / 16mm
Quality and value in home furnishing series
Color (H C A)
Teaches the viewer to become a wiser consumer when purchasing furniture. Includes a tour of the International Design Center in Minneapolis and visits with Pirkko Stenros, leading Finnish furniture designer.
Home Economics
Dist - IOWA **Prod** - IOWA 1989

Quality assurance in drug administration
VHS
Color (C A PRO)
$75.00 purchase, $25.00 rental _ #600, #601
Trains health care staff in ensuring accuracy of drug distribution to make drug therapy safer and more effective. Covers federal regulations, identifying situations leading to errors in medication, describing the appropriate procedure for drug administration, listing situations for soap and water handwashing, categories of medications that should not be crushed and determining the significance of a medication error. Includes discussion guide.
Health and Safety; Psychology
Dist - CATHHA

Quality Assurance is the Essence of TQC 28 MIN
VHS
Seven Steps to TQC Promotion Series
(PRO) (JAPANESE)
#C104
Explains fundamental thought behind quality assurance. Stresses process control and the development of new products as a way to progress. Features Dr Kaoru Ishikawa.
Business and Economics
Dist - TOYOVS **Prod** - TOYOVS 1987

Quality Assurance Series
International Standards 60 MIN
Measuring and Calibration 60 MIN
Q a Documentation 60 MIN
Q a Programs 60 MIN
Testing 60 MIN
Why Q A 60 MIN
Dist - LEIKID

Quality at work 20 MIN
VHS
Color (A PRO)
$495.00 purchase, $150.00 rental
Emphasizes characteristics of quality work and its relationship to workers' personal standards. Teaches ten steps to establishing higher standards in the workplace.
Business and Economics
Dist - DHB **Prod** - CRISP

Quality Audits 30 MIN
VHS / U-matic
Quality Control Series
Color
Discusses how audits can make the success difference. Describes the purposes of quality audits and lists some items for audit.
Business and Economics; Industrial and Technical Education
Dist - MIOT **Prod** - MIOT

Quality Circles
U-matic / VHS
Organizational Quality Improvement Series
Color
Describes how to involve employees in the program for organizational quality improvement.
Business and Economics; Psychology
Dist - BNA **Prod** - BNA

Quality Circles - First Year in Review 42 MIN
U-matic / VHS
Color
Explains a tried and proven concept, 'people involvement', which has added to employee morale and productivity improvement. Discusses why management must listen to, as well as direct, the work force.
Business and Economics; Psychology
Dist - SME **Prod** - SME

Quality Circles - Problem - Solving Tools for Educators 30 MIN
U-matic
Color (T)
Describes the four - part quality circle process including problem selection, problem analysis, solution selection and presentation to management.
Education; Psychology
Dist - AFSCD **Prod** - AFSCD 1986

The Quality Connection 22 MIN
VHS / 16mm
Color (PRO)
$695.00 purchase, $150.00 rental, $40.00 preview
Presents business consultant John Gaspari who teaches managers how they can educate their employees to see everything from the customer's point of view. Shows how to create an organization which rewards customer - oriented ideas. Includes leader's guide.
Business and Economics; Education; Psychology
Dist - UTM **Prod** - UTM

The Quality Connection 22 MIN
VHS / 16mm
(PRO IND)
$150.00 rental
Shows management how to overcome resistance to quality improvement efforts. Helps employees understand the link between their responsiblities and the customer's perceptions. Leader's guide included.
Business and Economics; Psychology
Dist - FI **Prod** - AMA 1989

The Quality Connection
VHS
Guaspari Series
Color (G)
$695.00 purchase, $150.00 rental
Provides a blueprint for looking at quality from a customer's point of view and providing that level of quality. Part of three videos on books written by John Guaspari.
Business and Economics
Dist - VLEARN

The Quality connection 22 MIN
VHS
Color (A PRO IND)
$695.00 purchase, $150.00 rental
Encourages employees to focus on the customers' point of view. Hosted by John Guaspari.
Business and Economics; Guidance and Counseling; Psychology
Dist - VLEARN **Prod** - EFM

Quality control - an American idea takes root in Japan 30 MIN
VHS
Anatomy of Japan - wellsprings of economic power series
Color (H C G)
$250.00 purchase
States that the concept of quality control - QC - was born in the United States but it has flowered in Japan. Investigates the history of quality control and how it is managed in Japan. Part of a 10 - part series on the current relations between Japan and the world.
Business and Economics; History - World; Psychology
Dist - LANDMK **Prod** - LANDMK 1989

Quality control and failure analysis 55 MIN
BETA / VHS / U-matic
Color
$400.00 purchase
Presents statistical sampling and evaluation, dye penetration and radiography.
Science; Science - Physical
Dist - ASM **Prod** - ASM

Quality Control Circles - a Lasting Impact? 70 MIN
BETA / 16mm
Color (A)
Features Robert Cole, sociology professor at the University of Michigan, discussing quality control circles as a key factor in Japan's phenomenal productivity. Explains how they can be adopted in American business.
Business and Economics; Geography - World
Dist - CBSFOX **Prod** - CBSFOX

Quality control series
Concepts of Acceptance Sampling Plans 33 MIN
Continuous Sampling Plans 29 MIN
Control charts for defectives 31 MIN
Control charts for mean and range 35 MIN
Control of continuous processes 30 MIN
Dodge - Romig sampling plans 37 MIN
Process - Capability Analysis 30 MIN
Product Liability 26 MIN
Quality Audits 30 MIN
Specifications and tolerances 32 MIN
Variable Sampling (MIL - STD - 414) 30 MIN
Vendor Certification and Rating 33 MIN
Dist - MIOT

Quality customer service 25 MIN
VHS
Color (A PRO)
$495.00 purchase, $150.00 rental
Shows how to enhance customer service for client retention through examples taken from real life. Demonstrates ways to learn and meet customer's needs.
Business and Economics; Social Science
Dist - DHB **Prod** - CRISP 1993

Quality customer service 22 MIN
VHS
Color (A PRO IND)
$395.00 purchase
Trains employees in the skills of customer service. Covers skills including developing a positive attitude, identification and satisfaction of customer needs, and cultivating repeat business. Includes leader's guide and five workbooks.

Business and Economics; Guidance and Counseling; Psychology
Dist - VLEARN

Quality Data Collection and Analysis 30 MIN
VHS / U-matic
Quality Planning Series
Color
Reviews several forms used by a company to collect and analyze quality data.
Business and Economics; Industrial and Technical Education
Dist - MIOT **Prod** - MIOT

Quality Day Care - It's Your Choice 60 MIN
U-matic
(A)
Deals with the different needs of different families and focuses on one vital common factors, the need for good staff - parent communications. Comes with guide.
Health and Safety; Sociology
Dist - ACCESS **Prod** - ACCESS 1984

The Quality Difference 14 MIN
16mm
Color
LC 82-700179
Advises on the assessment and selection of quality and confidence - building clothing by showing the artistry and craftsmanship that goes into the creation of a finely - tailored suit.
Home Economics; Psychology
Dist - MTP **Prod** - MTP 1981

Quality for all Seasons 18 MIN
16mm
Color (J)
LC 76-703702
Presents an overview of fruit and vegetable marketing, from harvest through packing, grading and distribution to wholesale markets. Shows how fresh fruits and vegetables are inspected for quality by the U S Department of Agriculture and cooperating state departments of agriculture.
Agriculture
Dist - USNAC **Prod** - USDA 1974

Quality function deployment and the competitive challenge 390 MIN
VHS
Color (PRO A G)
$4250.00 purchase _ #VQFD - 622
Presents nine videocassettes on quality function deployment. Produced by the American Supplier Institute.
Business and Economics; Psychology
Dist - PRODUC

Quality in Design 29 MIN
U-matic
Kirk - American Furniture Series
Color
Fine Arts; Home Economics
Dist - PBS **Prod** - WGBHTV

Quality in the Making 23 MIN
16mm
Color
Highlights the production and quality control of ball bearings at General Motors, New Departure Division.
Business and Economics
Dist - GM **Prod** - GM

Quality in the office 20 MIN
VHS
Color (PRO IND A)
$695.00 purchase, $190.00 rental _ #AMA56
Helps employees to use five key quality principles as a basis for viewing their work procedures. Utilizes interviews to show factory and office workers that application of these principles can lead to an improvement of their work quality.
Business and Economics
Dist - EXTR **Prod** - AMA

The Quality innovation process 15 MIN
BETA / U-matic / VHS
Total quality leadership series
Color (G PRO)
$395.00, $250.00 rental _ #QU0226 - 14
Features Dr Richard Ruhe in a consultant role in a staged quality team meeting. Includes numerous on - site interviews with public and private sector quality role models. Part of ten parts.
Business and Economics
Dist - BLNCTD **Prod** - BLNCTD

The Quality leader - Volume XVI
U-matic / VHS
Deming library series
Color (G)
$595.00 purchase, $150.00 rental
Presents volume XVI of a sixteen - part series on the business philosophy of Dr W Edwards Deming.
Business and Economics; Guidance and Counseling
Dist - VLEARN **Prod** - FI

The Quality leader - Volume XVI 25 MIN
VHS
Deming library series
Color (PRO A G)
$595.00 purchase, $150.00 rental
Explains the three bases for managerial authority and outlines the need for direction in any attempt to achieve. Discusses the effort to achieve quality as seen by Dr. Edwards Deming. Part of a sixteen - volume series.
Business and Economics; Psychology
Dist - EXTR **Prod** - FI

The Quality Man 30 MIN
U-matic / VHS / 16mm
Color (C A)
Presents the views of Philip B Crosby, who has been associated with quality in business and industry for 30 years, on the need for effective quality management. Lays out the philosophy that the key to quality is an attitude that must be generated from those at the top and points the way to quality improvements.
Business and Economics; Psychology
Dist - FI **Prod** - BBCTV

Quality meetings 15 MIN
VHS / BETA / U-matic
Total quality leadership series
Color (G PRO)
$395.00, $250.00 rental _ #QU0244 - 14
Features Dr Richard Ruhe in a consultant role in a staged quality team meeting. Includes numerous on - site interviews with public and private sector quality role models. Part of ten parts.
Business and Economics
Dist - BLNCTD **Prod** - BLNCTD

The Quality of a Nation 30 MIN
16mm
Color
Celebrates Canada's 100th anniversary of confederation.
Geography - World; History - World
Dist - CFI **Prod** - CRAF

The Quality of Care 35 MIN
16mm
Color (PRO)
Examines British attempts to find more humane ways to deal with the problems of the chronic schizophrenic. Focuses on the new and different problems created by the advent of antipsychotic drugs and discusses the long - acting fluphenazine decanoate known in the United States as Prolixin Decanoate.
Health and Safety; Psychology
Dist - SQUIBB **Prod** - SQUIBB

Quality of Life 20 MIN
U-matic / VHS
Terra - Our World Series
Color (I J)
Deals with the effects of noise, air and visual pollution.
Sociology
Dist - AITECH **Prod** - MDDE 1980

Quality of Life 30 MIN
U-matic / VHS
Family Planning Series
Color
Discusses the extent to which quality of life in any society is dependent on the society's population density. Explains how the decision to change the ideal family size affects lifestyles, patterns of behavior, birth control methods and sex education.
Science - Natural; Sociology
Dist - NETCHE **Prod** - NETCHE 1970

The Quality of Life 58 MIN
U-matic
Moneywatchers Series
Color
Examines the influence of economics on the overall quality of life in America.
Business and Economics; Sociology
Dist - PBS **Prod** - SCIPG

Quality of mercy - a case for better pain management 53 MIN
VHS
Color (H C G)
$445.00 purchase, $75.00 rental
Reveals that despite advances in pharmacology and pain research, many patients still suffer needlessly. Looks at pediatric surgery where major procedures are done without anaesthesia because of the rationale that newborns do not feel pain and that anesthetics might seriously harm ill infants - both proven untrue. Examines research in burn treatment and the widespread refusal of hospitals to give priority to pain control. Produced by Richard J Adler.
Health and Safety
Dist - FLMLIB

Quality of time - an introduction to hospice 25 MIN
VHS / U-matic / BETA
Color (G C PRO)
$150.00 purchase _ #705.2
Acquaints patients considering home hospice care and their family members with the specifics of that care. Gives an in - depth look at the two major facets of successful home hospice care - the family member who acts as the primary caregiver for the patient and the hospice team - physician, nurse, social worker, home health aide, chaplain, volunteer and auxiliary personnel - who provide 24 - hour physical and psychological care and support to both patient and primary caregiver. Appropriate for healthcare professionals and those in support education.
Health and Safety
Dist - CONMED **Prod** - KAISP

The Quality of your life 120 MIN
VHS
Color (G R)
$49.95 purchase _ #354
Offers advice and exercises on how to improve the psychological, physical and spiritual quality of life in a Christian context for adult Roman Catholics who are experiencing difficulty in dealing with the pressure of daily existence on the job, in relationships and in community involvement. Features Dr Richard Issel, Steven Humowiecki, MD, Father John Canary and Brother James Zullo.
Guidance and Counseling; Health and Safety; Psychology; Religion and Philosophy
Dist - ACTAF **Prod** - ACTAF

Quality on the job 40 MIN
VHS
Color (G)
$495.00 purchase, $140.00 rental _ #91F6111C
Presents a two - step training program for maximizing the effectiveness of employees.
Business and Economics; Psychology
Dist - DARTNL **Prod** - DARTNL

Quality, Our Competitive Edge 28 MIN
16mm
Color
LC 77-700570
Explains the problem of terminal maintenance that was causing severe interruption in phone service in New York City and gives instructions for repair by telephone company service people.
Social Science
Dist - NILCOM **Prod** - NYTELE 1976

Quality - pass it on 20 MIN
U-matic / VHS
Color (IND)
Illustrates the importance of having customers satisfied with the complete service call. Presents an action plan to reduce the number of unhappy customers. Helps technicians realize that good customer relations are vital to the security of their jobs. Shows elements of successful customer relations techniques.
Business and Economics; Home Economics; Industrial and Technical Education; Sociology
Dist - WHIRL **Prod** - WHIRL

Quality Planning Series
Designing quality into a product 26 MIN
Developing quality mindedness 31 MIN
Diagnostic Techniques to Identify the Causes of Poor Quality 31 MIN
Economics of quality 31 MIN
Improving the Quality Image by Customer Relations 23 MIN
Interfacing Quality and Reliabliity 32 MIN
Organization 31 MIN
Quality Data Collection and Analysis 30 MIN
Selling Quality to Management 32 MIN
What is Quality? 30 MIN
Dist - MIOT

Quality Practice 56 MIN
VHS / U-matic
Color (PRO)
Responds to 1979 poll which found that almost half of all lawyers face difficulties in operating and managing their practices. Includes interviews with consumers, a dramatized lawyer - client consultation and a display of modern office equipment.
Business and Economics; Civics and Political Systems
Dist - ABACPE **Prod** - ABACPE

Quality problem solving 15 MIN
BETA / U-matic / VHS
Total quality leadership series
Color (G PRO)

$395.00, $250.00 rental _ #QU0250 - 14
Features Dr Richard Ruhe in a consultant role in a staged quality team meeting. Includes numerous on - site interviews with public and private sector quality role models. Part of ten parts.
Business and Economics; Psychology
Dist - BLNCTD **Prod** - BLNCTD

Quality, Production and Me Series
Me and We 17 MIN
Me and You 12 MIN
Dist - RTBL

Quality - productivity series 98 MIN
VHS
Quality - productivity series
Color (PRO G A)
$1995.00 purchase
Presents methods for building commitment and implementing quality control principles in work settings. Based on work by Dr. Richard Chang. Includes four videos, Building Commitment, Teaming Up, Applied Problem Solving and Self - directed Evaluation.
Business and Economics; Psychology
Dist - EXTR **Prod** - DOUVIS

Quality programs and inspection system requirements - quality program 29 MIN
16mm
B&W
LC 74-705462
Shows the military and civilian panel review of Department of Defense specifications for a contractor's quality program and inspection system.
Business and Economics; Civics and Political Systems
Dist - USNAC **Prod** - USAF 1964

The Quality revolution 22 MIN
VHS
Color (PRO IND A)
$495.00 purchase, $95.00 rental _ #BBP140
Takes a look at three American manufacturers which have turned focus on quality into profitability. Uses Ford Motor Company, Globe Metallurgical and Eastman Kodak Copier Products Division as motivational examples of quality management. Includes Companion Leader's Guide.
Business and Economics
Dist - EXTR **Prod** - BBP

The Quality revolution 51 MIN
VHS / U-matic
Color (G)
$795.00 purchase _ #HH - 6323M
Profiles the Ford, Globe Metallurgical and Kodak companies and their focus on quality. Investigates the state of service - oriented businesses in America. Features Collin Siedor as host. Produced by Dystar Television.
Business and Economics
Dist - CORF

The Quality revolution - Part 2 22 MIN
VHS
Competing to win series
Color (PRO IND A)
Features David Kearn of Xerox, Roger Milliken of Milliken Textiles and John Grettenberger of Cadillac Motors, all recent winners of the Malcolm Baldridge Quality Award. Part of a series on international business.
Business and Economics
Dist - CORF **Prod** - CORF 1990

Quality Science Education Versus Creationism
VHS / Cassette
Humanist Voices Speak Out Series
(G)
$49.95, $9.00 purchase
Discusses the problem of presenting quality science education when such education is under attack by religious minorities who embrace a belief in creationism. Features Laurie Godfrey, John R Cole, Ronnie Hastings and Steven Schafersman. Part of a series which discusses social issues in humanist terms.
Education; Guidance and Counseling; Religion and Philosophy; Science
Dist - AMHUMA **Prod** - AMHUMA

Quality series
Creating quality 20 MIN
Marketing quality 15 MIN
Processing for quality 17 MIN
Dist - EDPAT

Quality service in the public sector 24 MIN
VHS
Color (PRO IND A)
$550.00 purchase, $275.00 rental _ #AMI125
Focuses on discerning customer needs and how to provide quality service to customers and co - workers. Aids employees in improving customer service skills and caring for the customer. Includes Training Leader's Guide.
Business and Economics
Dist - EXTR **Prod** - AMEDIA

Quality supervision for industry 25 MIN
VHS
Color (PRO IND A)
Dramatizes a new boss being told about certain important supervisory skills - organization, delegation, communication - needed to motivate workers.
Business and Economics; Guidance and Counseling; Psychology; Social Science
Dist - AMEDIA **Prod** - AMEDIA 1990

Quality supervision for industry 24 MIN
BETA / U-matic / VHS
Color (G IND)
$595.00 purchase, $130.00 rental
States that supervisors influence employee morale, commitment and turnover, that they determine the degree of teamwork that can be achieved and affect product and service quality. Shows how to communicate, discipline, organize, delegate and motivate as a manager.
Business and Economics; Psychology; Sociology
Dist - AMEDIA **Prod** - AMEDIA

Quality - the big picture 17 MIN
VHS / 16mm
Color (C A PRO)
$625.00 purchase, $150.00 rental _ #196
Overviews the 'total quality management' process as it relates to organizational development in the current business environment. Includes Leader's Guide.
Business and Economics; Guidance and Counseling; Psychology
Dist - SALENG **Prod** - SALENG 1990

Quality - the only way 30 MIN
VHS
Color (A PRO IND G)
$795.00 purchase, $185.00 rental
Tells the story of a man who is satisfied with his second - rate work effort until he goes on vacation and receives poor service.
Business and Economics; Guidance and Counseling; Psychology
Dist - VLEARN **Prod** - MELROS

Quality through excellence 3 MIN
U-matic / VHS
Color (G)
$200.00 purchase, $75.00 rental
Blends visuals, lyrics and music to celebrate craftsmanship.
Business and Economics; Fine Arts; Psychology
Dist - VLEARN **Prod** - PROTC

Quality through people - Volume I 59 MIN
BETA / VHS / U-matic
In Search of quality series
Color (C A G)
$795.00 purchase, $225.00 rental
Details four of the seven steps of the Baldridge Criteria that distinguish an organization - customer satisfaction, quality results, human resource utilization and leadership. Features Bob Waterman, coauthor of In Search of Excellence.
Business and Economics
Dist - VIDART **Prod** - VIDART

Quality through systems - Volume II 65 MIN
BETA / VHS / U-matic
In Search of quality series
Color (C A G)
$795.00 purchase, $225.00 rental
Details three of the seven steps of the Baldridge Criteria that distinguish an organization - strategic quality planning, information and analysis, and quality assurance. Features Bob Waterman, coauthor of In Search of Excellence.
Business and Economics
Dist - VIDART **Prod** - VIDART

Quality tools 15 MIN
BETA / U-matic / VHS
Total quality leadership series
Color (G PRO)
$395.00, $250.00 rental _ #QU0256 - 14
Features Dr Richard Ruhe in a consultant role in a staged quality team meeting. Includes numerous on - site interviews with public and private sector quality role models. Part of ten parts.
Business and Economics
Dist - BLNCTD **Prod** - BLNCTD

The quality transformation in health care - the Parkview experience 30 MIN
VHS
Color (IND PRO)
$595.00 purchase, $195.00 rental _ #XEE01
Profiles Parkview Episcopal Medical Center, a 300 - bed hospital that is considered a benchmark for care quality initiatives. Includes a leader's discussion guide and sample package of Parkview's care quality initiative materials. Produced by Xee Media.
Business and Economics; Health and Safety
Dist - EXTR

Quality video 3 MIN
VHS
Meeting opener motivation videos series
Color (G)
$89.00 purchase _ #MV1
Presents a video which incorporates cinematography, music and lyrics to create a mood that enhances the impact of the desired message.
Business and Economics; Psychology
Dist - GPERFO

Quality - why bother 8 MIN
VHS / U-matic
Meeting breaks series
Color (C A PRO)
$295.00 purchase
Features comedian Lenny Henry who tries to present a serious message on quality, but production disasters that trip him up illustrate that everyone on the team must do their job right. Produced by Playback.
Business and Economics; Literature and Drama; Psychology
Dist - VIDART

Quality, why bother 9 MIN
VHS
Color (A PRO IND)
$450.00 purchase, $95.00 rental
Stars Lenny Henry as a television news anchorman let down by staff people who did their jobs in less than quality fashion. Reveals that the staff's lack of effort made everyone look bad.
Business and Economics; Guidance and Counseling; Psychology
Dist - VLEARN **Prod** - CRMF

Quality - you don't have to be sick to get better 22 MIN
VHS
Color (PRO IND A)
$695.00 purchase, $345.00 rental _ #AMI126
Recognizes the good work being performed by employees, but also motivates them to define and improve quality at all organizational levels. Helps workers to define and exceed customer needs and to assess current work processes through the use of Dr Richard Chang's Continuous Improvement Model.
Business and Economics
Dist - EXTR

The Quality/Reliability Function 180 MIN
U-matic
Electronics Testing, Quality/Reliability and Manufacturing Control 'Series
Color (IND)
Defines quality and reliability as applied to electronics manufacture, and discusses failure rates, quality control, quality levels and budgets.
Business and Economics; Industrial and Technical Education
Dist - INTECS **Prod** - INTECS

Quantitative Approaches to Decision Making Series
Assessing the value of information 29 MIN
Decision making - rationality or intuition 29 MIN
Decision making under risk 29 MIN
Decision making under uncertainty 29 MIN
Key Elements in the Decision Making Process 29 MIN
Systems Analysis - Means - Ends Diagnosis 29 MIN
Dist - EDSD

Quantitative Metallography II 57 MIN
BETA / VHS / U-matic
Color
$400.00 purchase
Provides guidelines for measuring structural gradients.
Science; Science - Physical
Dist - ASM **Prod** - ASM 1987

The Quantum Idea 10 MIN
U-matic
Wave Particle Duality Series
Color (H C)
Looks at Planck's theory of energy emissions as bundles, which he called quanta, and Einstein's explanation of the photoelectric effect. Describes how these discoveries led to the use of both the particle and the wave models to describe the behaviour of light.
Science; Science - Physical
Dist - TVOTAR **Prod** - TVOTAR 1984

Quantum leaps through unfolding potential
VHS
Individual success series
Color (G)
$29.95 purchase _ #CF012
Features Dr Vern Woolf who shows how to focus the life force to achieve full potential.

Business and Economics; Psychology
Dist - SIV

Quantum numbers 30 MIN
U-matic / VHS / BETA
Color (T)
$39.95 purchase _ #5203
Offers a grahic illustration of quantum numbers and their description of an element and its structure. Explains how quantum numbers are related to the structure of the periodic table. Part of a series teaching teachers of senior high students and up how to teach chemistry. Covers important concepts, assists substitute teachers. Shows how to deal with student absenteeism, compensating for differences in learning rates, improving preparation time and review lessons.
Science - Physical
Dist - INSTRU

Quantum Numbers 20 MIN
VHS
(PRO A H C)
$163.00 purchase _ E1VH6671
Illustrates the four quantum numbers through graphics. Explains how quantum numbers describe an element's electron orbitals, and discusses how they verify the periodic system of elements.
Mathematics; Science - Physical
Dist - EAV **Prod** - EAV 1987

Quantum Numbers 20 MIN
U-matic / VHS
Color
Illustrates the four quantum numbers. Develops possible values for the quantum numbers.
Science - Physical
Dist - EDMEC **Prod** - EDMEC

The Quantum universe 60 MIN
VHS
Smithsonian world series
Color; Captioned (G)
$49.95 purchase _ #SMIW - 505
Deals with the emerging field of quantum physics. Interviews scientists and artists on this new area of science.
Science - Physical
Dist - PBS **Prod** - WETATV

Quarks 8 MIN
U-matic / VHS
Color
Analyzes broadcast television. Presents layers of sounds, images and written texts ironically juxtaposed with TV patter.
Fine Arts
Dist - KITCHN **Prod** - KITCHN

Quarks and the universe with Murray Gell - Mann 30 MIN
U-matic / VHS
World of ideas with Bill Moyers, season 2 series
Color; Captioned (A G)
$39.95, $59.95 purchase _ #WIWM - 226
Approaches elementary particle physics from the point of view of naturalist Murray Gell - Mann, winner of the 1969 Nobel Prize in physics for his discovery of the particles he named 'quarks'. Discusses the simplicity and complexity of the universe. Part of a series with Bill Moyers featuring some of the most important and inventive minds of the 20th century who explore the ideas and values shaping our future.
Science - Physical
Dist - PBS **Prod** - PATV 1990

Quarter Horses 3 MIN
16mm
Of all Things Series
Color (P I)
Discusses the horses known as quarter horses.
Physical Education and Recreation; Science - Natural
Dist - AVED **Prod** - BAILYL

Quarter panel replacement - Pt 1 30 MIN
BETA / VHS / 16mm
Color (A PRO)
$110.00 purchase _ #AB133
Discusses quarter panel replacement, in the first of two tapes.
Industrial and Technical Education
Dist - RMIBHF **Prod** - RMIBHF

Quarter panel replacement - Pt 2 42 MIN
VHS / BETA / 16mm
Color (A PRO)
$140.00 purchase _ #AB133B
Discusses quarter panel replacement, in the second of two tapes.
Industrial and Technical Education
Dist - RMIBHF **Prod** - RMIBHF

The Quarterback
VHS
NCAA football instructional videos series
Color (H C A)
$39.95 purchase _ #KAR1302V
Features college football coach Doug Scovil teaching various skills and drills for quarterbacks. Produced by the National Collegiate Athletic Association.
Physical Education and Recreation
Dist - CAMV **Prod** - NCAAF

The Quarterback
VHS
NCAA football videos - offensive series
Color (A G T)
$39.95 purchase _ #KAR1302V-P
Presents instruction on skills and drills given by NCAA coaches. Features Doug Scovil explaining quarterback techniques. One of a series of videos that provide coaching tips to offensive and defensive players and coaches. Series is available as a set of offensive series, defensive series, or both combined.
Physical Education and Recreation
Dist - CAMV

Quarterback and receiver camp series
Quarterback and wide receiver 20 MIN
Quarterback skills and drills 20 MIN
Wide receiver skills and drills 20 MIN
Dist - CAMV

Quarterback and wide receiver 20 MIN
VHS
Quarterback and receiver camp series
Color (H C A)
$39.95 purchase _ #QRC300V
Teaches skills and drills for both quarterbacks and wide receivers. Stresses the importance of quarterbacks and receivers working together to read coverages, find open seams, and recognize weaknesses in the defense.
Physical Education and Recreation
Dist - CAMV

Quarterback - fundamentals and techniques 60 MIN
VHS
Color (H C A)
$29.95 purchase _ #KOD405V
Explains and demonstrates the fundamentals and techniques of quarterbacking. Covers subjects including grip, quarterback - center exchange, quarterback pivots, passing techniques, and aiming points. Hosted and taught by University of Maryland head football coach Joe Krivak and three of his former quarterbacks - Boomer Esaison, Frank Reich, and Stan Gelbaugh.
Physical Education and Recreation
Dist - CAMV

Quarterback skills and drills 20 MIN
VHS
Quarterback and receiver camp series
Color (H C A)
$39.95 purchase _ #QRC100V
Teaches skills and drills for quarterbacks. Covers subjects including the quarterback - center exchange, dropping back, and seven drills used to improve skills.
Physical Education and Recreation
Dist - CAMV

Quarterbacking to Win 56 MIN
BETA / VHS
Football Fundamentals Series
Color
Demonstrates such details of quarterbacking as the drop back pass, the rollout, handing off, and faking and reading the defense.
Physical Education and Recreation
Dist - MOHOMV **Prod** - MOHOMV

Quarterbacking to win 60 MIN
VHS
Tom Landry football series
(J H C)
$39.95 _ #MXS140V
Presents former N F L player Jim Zorn who teaches football skills for quarterbacks, including defense reading, cadence count, and passing skills.
Physical Education and Recreation
Dist - CAMV **Prod** - CAMV

Quarterbacks 60 MIN
VHS
One on one coaching series
(J H C)
$39.95 _ #CVN1020V
Features football coach Schnellenberger who explains special techniques for quarterbacks, including the correct passing stance, hand - offs, drops, deep passing games, pass patterns, and more drills.
Physical Education and Recreation
Dist - CAMV **Prod** - CAMV

Quartermaster quality control for clothing and textile items 17 MIN
16mm
B&W
LC FIE59-262
Discusses a new system of quality control inspection of the U S Army. Describes its application to the manufacture of clothing and textile items.
Business and Economics; Civics and Political Systems; Home Economics; Social Science
Dist - USNAC **Prod** - USA 1959

Quartermaster Quality Control for General Supplies and Parts 17 MIN
16mm
B&W
LC FIE59-263
Discusses a new system of quality control inspection of the U S Army and describes its application to the manufacture of general supplies and equipment.
Business and Economics; Civics and Political Systems
Dist - USNAC **Prod** - USA 1959

Quartermaster Quality Control for Subsistence Items 18 MIN
16mm
B&W
LC FIE59-264
Discusses a new system of quality control inspection of the U S Army and describes its application to the production of food and other subsistence items.
Civics and Political Systems; Social Science
Dist - USNAC **Prod** - USA 1959

The Quarters guard 4 MIN
16mm
Ceremonial drill series
Color
LC 77-702844
Demonstrates the military drill known as the Quarters Guard.
Civics and Political Systems
Dist - CDND **Prod** - CDND 1976

Quartet 120 MIN
VHS
Color (G)
$39.95 purchase _ #S02193
Presents dramatizations of four W Somerset Maugham short stories - 'The Facts of Life,' 'The Alien Corn,' 'The Kite,' and 'The Colonel's Lady.' Stars Dirk Bogarde, Honor Blackman, Sir Felix Aylmer, Hermione Baddeley, and many others. Each story is introduced by Maugham himself.
Literature and Drama
Dist - UILL

Quasars 29 MIN
U-matic
Project universe - lesson 28 - astronomy series
Color (C A)
Reviews initial discovery of quasi - stellar radio objects, or quasars. Describes radio and Suzfert galaxies.
Science - Physical
Dist - CDTEL **Prod** - COAST

Quasars, Pulsars and Black Holes 29 MIN
35mm strip / VHS
Color (H)
$84.00 purchase _ #PE - 540783 - 3, #PE - 512800 - 4
Examines the fusion process which forms stars, relating gravity, nuclear force and electromagnetism to star growth and death. Traces transformation of stars leading to formation of white dwarf, black dwarf and pulsar states. Discusses the possible existence of black holes. Filmstrip version includes two filmstrips, two cassettes and teacher's guide.
Science - Physical
Dist - SRA **Prod** - SRA

Quasi at the Quackadero 10 MIN
16mm
Color (H C A)
LC 76-700714
Features Quasi, a science fiction boy who lives in a progressive household with his grownup friend Anita and little robot friend Rollo. Follows them on a day's outing to Quackadero, the Coney Island of the future.
Literature and Drama
Dist - SERIUS **Prod** - CRUIKS 1976

Quasiconformal mappings 60 MIN
VHS
ICM Plenary addresses series
Color (PRO G)
$49.00 purchase _ #VIDGEHRING - VB2
Presents Frederick W Gehring who discusses quasiconformal mappings.
Mathematics
Dist - AMSOC **Prod** - AMSOC

Quattro pro
VHS / BETA / U-matic
MS - DOS training video series
Color (G)
$1195.00 purchase, $275.00 rental
Offers introductory and advanced training in Quattro Pro by Borland International. Looks at editing, formatting, printing spreadsheets, working with databases, creating 3 - D graphs, customizing program windows and creating presentations.
Computer Science; Psychology
Dist - AMEDIA **Prod** - AMEDIA

Quattro Pro 4.0 series
Presents two videos teaching about beginning and advanced Quattro Pro 4.0 spreadsheets.
Advanced
Introduction
Quattro Pro 4.0 series
Dist - SIV

Que Fais - Tu Aujourd'hui 10 MIN
U-matic / VHS
Salut - French Language Lessons Series
Color
Focuses on pastimes, intonation questions, inversion questions, and question formulas with inversion.
Foreign Language
Dist - BCNFL **Prod** - BCNFL 1984

Que Hacer 90 MIN
16mm / U-matic / VHS
Color
Deals with the Salvador Allende election campaign in Chile. Combines fiction and documentary technique. Filmed during the 1970 elections in Chile.
Civics and Political Systems; Sociology
Dist - NEWTIM **Prod** - NEWTIM

Que Hacer 90 MIN
16mm
Color
Depicts the different roads to revolution including the reality of Chile, Allende's election victory and the CIA and a fictional story about a Peace Corps girl, a murdered priest and a political kidnapping.
Geography - World; History - World
Dist - IMPACT **Prod** - LOBO 1972

Que pasa, U S A series
The Farewell party 30 MIN
Here comes the bride 30 MIN
Dist - MDCPB

Que pasa, U S A series
Computer friend 29 MIN
Fiesta de quince 28 MIN
Gato Encerrado 29 MIN
Iay, Abuela 29 MIN
Los Novios 29 MIN
Malas Companias 29 MIN
Noche Cubana 29 MIN
Super chaperone 29 MIN
We Speak Spanish 28 MIN
Dist - PBS

Que Pasa, USA Series
Growing Pains 29 MIN
Dist - PBS

Que Viva Mexico 85 MIN
16mm
B&W (RUSSIAN (ENGLISH SUBTITLES))
A Russian language film with English subtitles. Presents a history of Mexico, divided into four separate novellas. Includes an exposition of the Tehuantepec jungles and the peculiarly quiet and peaceful lifestyles of the inhabitants, a love story of a poor peon and his wife, a novel devoted to bullfighting and romantic love, and a view of the 1910 Revolution.
Fine Arts; Foreign Language; History - World
Dist - IFEX **Prod** - MOSFLM 1931

Que viva Mexico 85 MIN
16mm / 35mm
Films of Sergei Eisenstein series
Color (G)
$250.00, $300.00 rental
Presents an epic celebration of Mexico's history and people directed by Sergei Eisenstein, who was unable to complete the project. Assembled and edited by Grigori Alexandrov and Nikita Orlov. Includes musical score.
Fine Arts; History - World
Dist - KINOIC

Quebec and the Atlantic Provinces 60 MIN
VHS
AAA travel series
Color (G)
$24.95 purchase _ #NA17
Explores Quebec and the Atlantic provinces.
Geography - World
Dist - SVIP

Quebec Kandahar 23 MIN
16mm
B&W (FRENCH)
LC 76-702048
Presents a French language film on skiing.
Foreign Language; Physical Education and Recreation
Dist - RYERC **Prod** - RYERC 1974

Quebec Kandahar 23 MIN
16mm
B&W (ENGLISH & FRENCH)
LC 76-702048
Presents a film on skiing in French and English.
Foreign Language; Physical Education and Recreation
Dist - RYERC **Prod** - RYERC 1975

Quebec - masters in our own house 50 MIN
VHS
Blood and belonging series
Color (A)
PdS99 purchase _ Available in UK only
Features host Michael Ignatieff taking a dramatic journey of discovery to examine nationalism in Quebec. Looks at two nationalistic conflicts in one state. Contrasts the politics of language dividing the French and English and the Cree people's claim for nation status in the icy North.
Civics and Political Systems; History - World; Social Science
Dist - BBCENE

Quebec - the Citadel City 14 MIN
16mm
New Candian City Series
Color
LC FIA68-1224
Surveys Quebec and its surroundings and points out why the city is a tourist attraction.
Geography - World
Dist - MORLAT **Prod** - MORLAT 1968

Quebec - the French disconnection 28 MIN
U-matic / VHS / 16mm
Color (H C A)
Features Canada's province of Quebec - its history of French and English nationalistic rivalry and its present-day French separatist sentiments movement. An 80 percent majority has a specific viewpoint that will have an effect on the British community and on the future of the province.
Geography - World
Dist - MEDIAG **Prod** - THAMES 1977

The Quechua 51 MIN
VHS
Disappearing world series
Color (G C)
$99.00 purchase, $14.00 rental _ #51157
Focuses on the Quechua who live in an isolated region of the Peruvian Andes. Reveals that, unlike many tribes in remote areas, they desperately want a road to link them with the outside world and its benefits, especially the tourist trade. Features anthropologist Michael Sallnow. Part of a series working closely with anthropologists who lived for a year or more in societies whose social structures, beliefs and practices are threatened by the expansion of technocratic civilization.
Sociology
Dist - PSU **Prod** - GRANDA 1974

The Quechua - Pt 9 51 MIN
VHS
Disappearing World Series
Color (S)
$99.00 purchase _ #047 - 9009
Provides a precious record of the social structure, beliefs and practices of societies now threatened with imminent extinction by the pressures of our expanding technocratic civilization. Travels to the remote corners of three continents and features film crews who worked in close association with anthropologists who had spent a year or more living among the societies concerned. Part 9 considers the Quechua who live in the Andes Mountains in an isolated part of Peru. Unlike many tribes in remote areas, they desperately want a road to link them with the outside world and its benefits, especially tourist trade.
Geography - World; History - World; Industrial and Technical Education; Psychology; Social Science; Sociology
Dist - FI **Prod** - GRATV 1989

The Queen 68 MIN
16mm
Color (H C A)
LC 73-707582
A documentary film about a transvestite beauty pageant. Includes scenes of the contestants as they prepare for the pageant.
Psychology; Social Science; Sociology
Dist - GROVE **Prod** - LITVIS 1968

The Queen and Prince Philip 60 MIN
16mm / U-matic / VHS
Royal Heritage Series
Color (H C A)
Reviews the history of the art collections of Queen Elizabeth, explained by members of the Royal Family themselves. Features Prince Philip who talks about the modernization of the royal farms and the redecoration of the Edward III tower. Presents Prince Charles who shows his collection of Eskimo sculpture from Canada. Shows the Holbein Room at Windsor Castle, which contains the core of the collection.
Civics and Political Systems; History - World
Dist - FI **Prod** - BBCTV 1977

Queen Bea 14 MIN
16mm
Color
LC 80-701258
Presents the story of Bea Farber, who abandoned her career as a legal secretary to enter the sport of harness racing.
Biography; Physical Education and Recreation
Dist - LANGED **Prod** - USTROT 1980

Queen Elizabeth II 26 MIN
16mm
Biography series
B&W
LC FI67-269
Highlights the life of Queen Elizabeth II of England. Includes her life as a princess of the royal family, her marriage to Philip Mountbatten and her coronation in 1952.
Biography; Geography - World
Dist - SF **Prod** - WOLPER 1962

Queen Esther 50 MIN
16mm
B&W (J)
Describes religious misunderstanding and prejudice. Reveals the message that God never fails those who love and serve him, and presents the book of Esther.
Religion and Philosophy
Dist - CAFM **Prod** - CAFM

Queen for a Day 30 MIN
16mm
Footsteps Series
Color
LC 79-701426
Show how young children go about defining themselves and how this effort can affect their relationships with other family members. Tells how parents can ease this process, and, with help, the child will paint a picture of himself that is clear and strong.
Home Economics; Psychology; Sociology
Dist - USNAC **Prod** - USOE 1978

Queen in Arabia 47 MIN
U-matic / VHS / BETA
Color; PAL (G H C)
PdS60, PdS68 purchase
Tours the Middle East. Looks at the history and changes in Quatar, UAE, Bahrain, Oman and Saudi Arabia.
Fine Arts; Geography - World; History - World
Dist - EDPAT

Queen Isabel and Her Spain 32 MIN
U-matic / VHS / 16mm
Color (H C A)
LC 79-700656
Studies key events during the reign of Isabel I of Spain, centering on the year 1492 when she consolidated her power. Shows the distinctive palaces, monasteries and towns that were constructed during this era.
Civics and Political Systems; History - World
Dist - IFB **Prod** - PILGRM 1978

Queen Kelly 95 MIN
VHS / 35mm / 16mm
B&W (G)
$200.00, $250.00 rental
Stars Gloria Swanson as a convent girl who falls in love with a prince but, as revealed by recently discovered footage, ends up in a seedy African brothel and is forced to marry a crippled trader portrayed by Tully Marshall. Directed by Erich von Stroheim, restored by Dennis Doros in 1985. Includes musical soundtrack.
Fine Arts
Dist - KINOIC

Queen Lear 60 MIN
U-matic / VHS
Sixty Minutes on Business Series
Color (G)
Business and Economics
Dist - VPHI **Prod** - VPHI 1984

Queen Lear (Lear Fan)
U-matic / VHS
Sixty Minutes on Business Series
Color
One of ten segments selected from the reality of the business world, and chosen from key '60 Minutes' telecasts to provide insight into vital issues affecting business today. Includes sourcebook.

Business and Economics; Industrial and Technical Education; Psychology
Dist - CBSFOX **Prod** - CBSFOX

Queen Mary's dolls' house 50 MIN
VHS
Color (G)
$29.95 purchase _ #QUE05
Tours the miniature craftsmanship of Queen Mary's Dolls' House in England. Views Chippendale chairs and a handwritten book of poems by Rudyard Kipling, in miniature.
Fine Arts; History - World
Dist - HOMVIS **Prod** - BBCTV 1990

Queen Mother 89 MIN
VHS
Color (G)
$29.95 purchase _ #QUE06
Celebrates the 90th birthday of the Queen Mother of England.
Civics and Political Systems; History - World
Dist - HOMVIS **Prod** - BBCTV 1990

Queen of Apollo 12 MIN
16mm
Color
Features the 1970 debutante - queen of Apollo, an Exclusive New Orleans Mardi Gras ball, on her big night. By Richard Leacock.
Fine Arts
Dist - PENNAS **Prod** - PENNAS

Queen of Autumn - the Chrysanthemum in Japan 22 MIN
U-matic / VHS / 16mm
Color (A)
LC 70-706202
Shows various forms of the chrysanthemum as they are grown in Japan each year. Photographs of six shows - - Hirakata Park, Nagoya Castile, Hibiya Park, Shinjuku - Guoen, Yasukuni and Meiju Shrines.
Geography - World; Science - Natural
Dist - IFB **Prod** - IFB 1969

Queen of Falcon 25 MIN
VHS
Color (G C)
$165.00 purchase, $45.00 rental
Focuses on an active elderly woman who plays many roles in her small town - post - mistress, newspaper columnist, leader. Presents a positive view of aging.
Health and Safety
Dist - TNF

Queen of hearts 113 MIN
35mm / 16mm
Color (G)
Travels to Italy where, twenty years ago, Dinilo's former rival for Rosa's hand in marriage was Barbariccia. Barbariccia becomes a successful club owner and tracks Dinilo and Rosa down, hoping to win her back. Examines the complexity of human feelings through a story of hope and despair, true love and betrayal. Directed by Jon Amiel. Contact distributor for price.
Fine Arts; Psychology; Religion and Philosophy; Sociology
Dist - OCTOBF

Queen of Heaven 60 MIN
U-matic / VHS / 16mm
I, Claudius - No 7 series; No 7
Color (C A)
Relates how Tiberius' empire declines and Claudius learns all of Livia's secrets, including his own eventual rule as Emperor.
Civics and Political Systems; History - World
Dist - FI **Prod** - BBCTV 1977

Queen of night gotta box of light 4 MIN
16mm
Color (G)
$10.00 rental
Pursues a Cambridge - Boston night scene. Stars Vivian Kurz.
Fine Arts; Geography - United States
Dist - CANCIN **Prod** - LEVINE 1965

Queen of Outer Space 80 MIN
16mm
Color (J)
Features Zsa Zsa Gabor in a science fiction tale of a planet populated and ruled by beautiful women.
Fine Arts; Literature and Drama
Dist - CINEWO **Prod** - CINEWO 1958

The Queen of spades 102 MIN
VHS
Color; Dolby stereo (G) (RUSSIAN ENGLISH SUBTITLES)
$39.95 purchase _ #1283
Presents a 1960 production of 'The Queen of Spades' by Tchaikovsky produced by the Bolshoi Opera, Theatre, Orchestra and Choir.
Fine Arts
Dist - KULTUR **Prod** - KULTUR 1991

The Queen of spades 15 MIN
VHS
Short story series
Color (J H)
#E373; LC 90-713154
Tells of a ruthless gambler who loses everything in 'The Queen of Spades' by Russian writer Alexander Pushkin. Part of a 16 - part series which introduces American and European short story writers and discusses the technical aspects of short story structure.
Guidance and Counseling; Literature and Drama
Dist - GPN **Prod** - CTI 1978

The Queen of spades by Alexander Pushkin 15 MIN
U-matic / VHS / 16mm
Short story series
Color (J H C A)
LC 83-706230; 83-700056
Presents a tale of the supernatural in which a greedy gambler meets a fitting fate at the hands of a former victim. Based on the short story The Queen of Spades by Alexander Pushkin.
Guidance and Counseling; Literature and Drama
Dist - IU **Prod** - IITC 1982

Queen of Spades 'Pique Dame' - Bolshoi Opera 174 MIN
VHS
Color (G) (RUSSIAN (ENGLISH SUBTITLES))
$59.95 purchase _ #1164
Presents the complete 'Queen Of Spades' by Tchaikovsky for the first time on videocassette. Stars Yelena Obraztsova, Vladimir Atlantov and Tamara Milashkina and features the Bolshoi Chorus and Corps de Ballet.
Fine Arts; Geography - World
Dist - KULTUR

Queen of the Cascades 26 MIN
16mm
Audubon wildlife theatre series
Color (I)
Presents Mount Rainier, the superb landmark towering 14,410 feet above the Pacific Northwest, which allows Ty Hotchkiss to photograph wildlife in four different life zones without leaving the mountain environment. Reveals a broad range of plants and animals that otherwise would be spread across hundreds of miles of northward travel.
Geography - United States; Geography - World; Science - Natural
Dist - AVEXP **Prod** - AVEXP

Queen Victoria - a Profile in Power 26 MIN
16mm / U-matic / VHS
Profiles in Power Series
Color (H C A)
LC 76-702970
Explores, through the use of an imaginary historical interview, the life and role of Queen Victoria of England.
Biography; Civics and Political Systems; History - World
Dist - LCOA **Prod** - LCOA 1976

Queen Victoria - a profile in power 26 MIN
U-matic / VHS / 16mm
Profiles in power - Spanish series
Color (H C A) (SPANISH)
Portrays Queen Victoria and her accomplishments.
Biography; Civics and Political Systems; History - World
Dist - LCOA **Prod** - LCOA 1977

Queen Victoria and British History - 1837 - 1901 28 MIN
U-matic / VHS / 16mm
World Leaders Series
B&W (H C A)
$525, $250 purchase _ #76572
Discusses the highlights of Queen Victoria's reign, including the Crimean War, Darwin's Origin of Species, and the Great Exhibition.
Biography; Civics and Political Systems; History - World
Dist - CORF

Queen Victoria and the Indians 11 MIN
VHS / U-matic
Color (P I J)
Presents an animated adaptation of a true story by American George Catlin about a group of American Indians who danced for Queen Victoria.
History - United States; History - World; Social Science
Dist - CEPRO **Prod** - CEPRO 1986

Queen Victoria - Pt 2 30 MIN
VHS
Late Great Britons
Color; PAL (C H)
PdS65 purchase
Presents many misconceptions about Queen Victoria. Provides information to counter the contention that the Queen was prudish. Suggests that she may have disliked many of her children. Second in the six - part series Late Great Britons, which covers the lives of six important figures in British history.
Civics and Political Systems; History - World
Dist - BBCENE

Queena Stovall - Life's Narrow Space 19 MIN
16mm
Color (J)
LC 80-701591
Presents 90 - year - old Queena Stovall reminiscing about her life and the rural Virginia atmosphere captured in her paintings.
Fine Arts
Dist - BOWGRN **Prod** - BOWGRN 1980

The Queen's Birthday Parade 96 MIN
VHS
Color (S)
$29.95 purchase _ #781 - 9008
Presents the Household Division, the guards of Buckingham Palace, who honor the Queen's birthday every year by 'Trooping the Colour.' Features their seven bands providing military music, footage of the Grenadier Guards on active duty in Northern Ireland and an interview with the late Lord Louis Mountbatten.
Civics and Political Systems; Geography - World; History - World; Social Science
Dist - FI **Prod** - BBCTV 1987

The Queen's pictures - royal collectors through the centuries 27 MIN
VHS
Color (G)
PdS15.50 purchase _ #A4-300424
Examines the Royal Collection, containing over 6,000 paintings. Traces the collection's history from the reign of Henry VIII to Queen Victoria. Visits Hampton Court Palace, Windsor Castle, Kensington Palace, Osborne House, and the Banqueting House in Whitehall, with a ceiling painted by Rubens for Charles I.
Fine Arts
Dist - AVP **Prod** - NATLGL

The Queens's award 30 MIN
VHS
Inside Britain 4 series
Color; PAL; NTSC (G) (BULGARIAN CZECH HUNGARIAN SPANISH POLISH ROMANIAN RUSSIAN SLOVAK UKRAINIAN LITHUANIAN)
PdS65 purchase
Shows how the Queen's award recognizes British companies achieving outstanding commercial success. Examines the history of the award and a selection of winners.
Business and Economics
Dist - CFLVIS **Prod** - GREYST 1993

A quel prix la publicite 25 MIN
VHS
Les jeunes entrepreneurs series
Color (I J H) (FRENCH)
$29.95 purchase _ #W5462
Continues the story of young teens, the robot they built, and the new - generation robot constructed. Develops intermediate - level language students' listening, comprehending, reading, writing and speaking skills through exercises and follow - up activities based on the story. Comes with video and teacher's guide with class activity material.
Foreign Language
Dist - GPC

Quelle blague 25 MIN
VHS
Paroles d'echanges 1 series
Color (J H) (FRENCH AND ENGLISH FRENCH)
#350101; LC 91-707557
Follows Hector, a teenager from rural, English - speaking Ontario, as he learns about life in Quebec City, where he stays with a French - speaking family and is forced to use his limited French. Part of a series that gives viewers a taste of authentic French - Canadian culture.
Foreign Language; Geography - World; Sociology
Dist - TVOTAR **Prod** - TVOTAR 1990

Quelle Chance 10 MIN
16mm / U-matic / VHS
B&W (J H) (FRENCH)
A French language film. Portrays incidents and dialogue in a cafe.
Foreign Language
Dist - IFB **Prod** - EFVA 1955

Quenelles and Meat Dumplings 30 MIN
BETA / VHS
Frugal Gourmet Series
Color
Shows how to prepare dumplings using pork, liver and fish.
Health and Safety; Home Economics; Psychology
Dist - CORF **Prod** - WTTWTV

Quentin Bell 41 MIN
VHS
Color (H C G)
$79.00 purchase
Features the British writer with Edward Blishen discussing writing mystery novels and the roles of humor and morality in fiction. Talks about his works including his biography of Virginia Woolf, and his sculpture and pottery as well.
Literature and Drama
Dist - ROLAND **Prod** - INCART

Quentin Blake 36 MIN
VHS
Color (H C G)
$79.00 purchase
Features the British writer and illustrator with Heather Neill discussing how to choose a format, rhyme of prose, and how to develop illustrations for your own or someone else's work. Talks about his works including Mister Magnolia, Angelo, The Story of the Dancing Frog, and collaborative works The Enormous Crocodile, Revolting Rhymes, Dirty Beasts, and others.
Literature and Drama
Dist - ROLAND **Prod** - INCART

Querelle
VHS
Color (G) (FRENCH (ENGLISH DUBBING))
$59.90 purchase _ #0322
Presents the French film 'Querelle,' the last feature directed by Rainer Werner Fassbinder. Tells of a proud and tough sailor, a loner, who learns softness and vulnerability. Stars Brad Davis, Franco Nero, Jeanne Moreau, Laurent Malet.
Fine Arts; Literature and Drama
Dist - SEVVID

Queremos Paz! We Want Peace! 27 MIN
VHS / U-matic
Color (J H C A)
Discusses a Witness for Peace Group of Methodists who visit Nicaragua. Includes visits to Christian base communities and a soap making collective. Produced by Esperanza Videos.
Religion and Philosophy; Sociology
Dist - CWS

The Quest 28 MIN
16mm
Color
LC 80-700072
Explores the progress in the field of medicine during the last 25 years, which has been the result of the work of many scientists, including those in the pharmaceutical industry.
Health and Safety; Science
Dist - GOLDST **Prod** - HOFLAR 1979

Quest 30 MIN
U-matic / VHS / 16mm
Color
Presents a short fiction story by Ray Bradbury.
Fine Arts
Dist - PFP **Prod** - BASSS 1983

A Quest 8 MIN
16mm
Color
LC 77-702285
Presents a montage of words, photography and music featuring sailing boats and water birds.
Fine Arts; Industrial and Technical Education
Dist - SUTHRB **Prod** - SUTHRB 1977

The Quest 37 MIN
16mm / U-matic / VHS
B&W (A)
Depicts Dr Frederick Banting and Charles Best and their struggle in the discovery of insulin.
Health and Safety; Science
Dist - IFB **Prod** - NFBC 1958

The Quest - an Artist and His Prey 22 MIN
16mm
Color
Accompanies artist Guy Coheleach as he watches lions and leopards, giraffes and gazelles, bison and elk. Examines his wildlife paintings.
Fine Arts; Science - Natural
Dist - ACORN **Prod** - ACORN

Quest Beyond Time 52 MIN
U-matic / VHS
Winners from Down Under Series
Color (K)
$349.00, $249.00 purchase _ #AD - 1357
Reveals that an innocent flight on a hang glider sends Mike a thousand years into the future. Shows that after many adventures, new friends and much self - discovery, Mike must decide whether to return to his own century. Part of an eight - part series on children's winning over their circumstances produced by the Australian Children's Television Foundation.
Fine Arts; Literature and Drama; Mathematics
Dist - FOTH **Prod** - FOTH

Qu'est - ce que c'est 13 MIN
16mm
Les Francais chez vous series; Set I; Lesson 3
B&W (I J H)
Foreign Language
Dist - CHLTN **Prod** - PEREN 1967

Qu'est - ce qu'il y a 13 MIN
16mm
Les Francais chez vous series; Set I; Lesson 6
B&W (I J H)
Foreign Language
Dist - CHLTN **Prod** - PEREN 1967

Quest for Flight 13 MIN
U-matic / VHS
Color (J C)
$59.00 purchase _ #3427
Follows the history of humans' attempts to imitate the bird - from Icarus' featured wings to the Supersonic Transport system.
Industrial and Technical Education
Dist - EBEC

Quest for Flight 23 MIN
16mm / U-matic / VHS
Wide World of Adventure Series
Color (I J)
LC 76-703647
Uses animation in simulating scenes from aviation history. Includes an account of Leonardo da Vinci's 15th - century helicopter.
History - World; Industrial and Technical Education; Social Science; Sociology
Dist - EBEC **Prod** - AVATLI 1976

The Quest for Integration in Europe 29 MIN
Videoreel / VT2
Course of Our Times III Series
Color
Civics and Political Systems; History - World
Dist - PBS **Prod** - WGBHTV

Quest for life - A Year with Petrea King 53 MIN
VHS
Color (H C G)
$195.00 purchase, $75.00 rental
Looks at Petrea King, diagnosed with terminal leukemia several years ago and told she only had weeks to live, and her counseling techniques for those with life - threatening diseases. Portrays her beliefs that humans become aware of the uniqueness of life only through extreme circumstances. Offers not medical advice but wisdom to deal with the feelings of anger, guilt, injustice and helplessness that individuals confront when ill. Her positive therapy allows her patients to discover an intense joy in life and a transformed outlook on the world. Produced by 220 Productions. A film by Julian Russell and Tony Gailey.
Fine Arts; Guidance and Counseling; Health and Safety; Sociology
Dist - CANCIN

Quest for Mars 60 MIN
VHS
Space age series
Color (J H)
$24.95 purchase _ #SPA060
Addresses the challenges that must be met to put people on Mars in the 21st century. Features Patrick Stewart as host. Part of a 3 - part series on the space age.
History - World; Science - Physical
Dist - KNOWUN

Quest for peace series

Albert Ellis, psychology	29 MIN
B F Skinner, psychology	29 MIN
Carl R Rogers, psychology, Pt 1	29 MIN
Carl R Rogers, psychology, Pt 2	29 MIN
Daniel Ellsberg, Government, Education	29 MIN
F Sherwood Rowland, Chemistry	29 MIN
H Jack Geiger, Community Medicine, Pt 1	29 MIN
H Jack Geiger, Community Medicine, Pt 2	29 MIN
Harold Willens, business	29 MIN
Helen Caldicott, pediatrics	29 MIN
Herbert F York, physics, government	29 MIN
Jerome D Frank, Psychology, Psychiatry	29 MIN
Jessie Bernard, Sociology	29 MIN
John Kenneth Galbraith, Economics, Government	29 MIN
John Marshall Lee, Military	29 MIN
John W Gardner, Psychology, Government, Public Service	29 MIN
Julian Bond, Government	29 MIN
Karl Menninger, Psychiatry, Education	29 MIN
Kenneth B Clark, Psychology	29 MIN
Norman Cousins, Education, Public Service	29 MIN
Paul R Ehrlich, Biology	29 MIN
Rollo may, Psychology	29 MIN
Sheila Tobias, Political Science, Education	29 MIN
Theodore M Hesburgh, education, religion - Pt 2	29 MIN
William Sloan Coffin, Jr, Religion	29 MIN

Dist - AACD

Quest for Perfection 10 MIN
16mm
Color
LC 80-701485
Presents the story of Linda Fratianne's hard work and efforts to win the gold medal in women's figure skating at the 1980 Winter Olympics. Emphasizes her achievements although she did not win the gold medal.
Physical Education and Recreation
Dist - STEEGP **Prod** - IBM 1980

Quest for planet Mars - 1
VHS
Space age series
Color (G)
$24.95 purchase _ #SPA060
Examines the possibilities of the exploration of the planet Mars. Looks at technology that may be used in the exploration. Features Patrick Stewart as host. Part one of a six - part series.
History - World; Science - Physical
Dist - INSTRU **Prod** - NAOS

Quest for Power - Sketches of the American New Right 50 MIN
U-matic / VHS / 16mm
Color
Examines the radical right - wing movement in the United States.
Civics and Political Systems; History - United States; Sociology
Dist - NEWTIM **Prod** - STDC

Quest for Quality
VHS
Color (G)
$395.00 purchase, $125.00 rental
Chronicles the ups and downs of the journey of a manufacturing company as it successfully puts quality theory to work.
Business and Economics; Psychology
Dist - VLEARN

The Quest for quality 15 MIN
BETA / U-matic / VHS
Total quality leadership series
Color (G PRO)
$395.00, $250.00 rental _ #QU0214 - 14
Features Dr Richard Ruhe in a consultant role in a staged quality team meeting. Includes numerous on - site interviews with public and private sector quality role models. Part of ten parts.
Business and Economics
Dist - BLNCTD **Prod** - BLNCTD

The Quest for self 30 MIN
U-matic
Humanities through the arts with Maya Angelou - Lesson 1 series; Lesson 1
Color (C A)
Studies how values are revealed in seven different art forms. Defines terms used in critical evaluation of art forms.
Fine Arts; Religion and Philosophy
Dist - CDTEL **Prod** - COAST

Quest for Tannu Tuva 45 MIN
VHS
Horizon series
Color (C PRO H A)
PdS99; Not available in USA
Tells about Richard Feynman's love of science and passion for adventure, which extended beyond the laboratory and classroom. Relates the story of Feynman's fascination with a country few Westerners have seen - Tannu Tuva, on the Mongolian - USSR border. Discusses the part Feynman played in pinpointing the cause of the 1986 space shuttle disaster.
Biography; Science
Dist - BBCENE

Quest for the Best 10 MIN
VHS / U-matic
Color
Goes into women's track and field as top amateur athletes tell their stories of dedication to the accomplishment of their goals.
Physical Education and Recreation
Dist - KAROL **Prod** - KAROL

Quest for the best series
Biography 20 MIN
Dist - GPN

Quest for the Killers Series
The Kuru Mystery 60 MIN
The Last Outcasts 60 MIN
The Last Wild Virus 60 MIN
Vaccine on trial 60 MIN
Dist - PBS

Quest Into Matter 30 MIN
U-matic
Dimensions in Science - Chemistry Series
Color (H C)
Examines the significance of symmetry and shape at the molecular level and the relationship between the molecular structure of materials and their general properties.
Science; Science - Physical
Dist - TVOTAR **Prod** - TVOTAR 1979

Quest into matter 30 MIN
U-matic / VHS / 16mm
Dimensions in science - Pt 1 series
Color (H C)
Considers the significance of symmetry and shape at the molecular level. Introduces the relationship between the molecular structure of materials and their general properties.
Science - Physical
Dist - FI **Prod** - OECA 1978

The Quest of Robert Goddard 24 MIN
16mm
Color
Presents Robert Goddard, pioneer genius of rocketry, and his wife Ester and combines their color photography of space flights with records of experiments they have done over a 30 - year period.
Biography; Industrial and Technical Education; Science; Science - Physical
Dist - REAF **Prod** - INTEXT

The Question 36 MIN
VHS
Color (J H R)
$59.95 purchase, $10.00 rental _ #35 - 82 - 8937
Portrays a teenager who must come to terms with his brother's suicide and struggles with the meaning of life. Shows that he is forced to do so only days before he addresses his high school graduating class.
Religion and Philosophy; Sociology
Dist - APH **Prod** - MARHLL

The Question 10 MIN
16mm / U-matic / VHS
Color (J)
LC 75-702068
Uses animation to show how a little man seeks the answer to the meaning of life in religion, politics, science, money, psychology and war, and eventually finds it in love.
Fine Arts; Guidance and Counseling; Psychology
Dist - MGHT **Prod** - HALAS 1969

Question 7 107 MIN
16mm
B&W (H C A)
Sets an example for every young person who must someday decide between what is easy and expedient and what is right and honorable, and for every parent who wishes to instill faith in God and respect for the freedom and dignity of man.
Religion and Philosophy
Dist - CPH **Prod** - CPH

The Question and the holy instant - Pt 1 60 MIN
VHS
Nothing real can be threatened series
Color (G R)
$29.95 purchase _ #C040
Addresses the fundamental issue of fear which is at the root of most of the problems of humanity. Considers insecurity, anger, depression, blame, ambition and unfulfillment. Features spiritual teacher Tara Singh. Part one of a four - part workshop series on 'A Course in Miracles' by Dr Helen Shucman.
Health and Safety; Psychology; Religion and Philosophy
Dist - LIFEAP **Prod** - LIFEAP 1990

Question - Answer Relationships 15 MIN
VHS / Software / U-matic
Storylords Series
Color (P)
$125.00 purchase,$240 software purchase
Teaches reading theory to children by allowing them to take part in the adventures of a storybook character.
Education; English Language
Dist - AITECH **Prod** - WETN 1986

A Question of AIDS 25 MIN
VHS
Color; PAL (I J H)
PdS29.50 purchase
Features a group of students who question Dr Michael Adler, a professor at the Middlesex Hospital, London, about AIDS. Voices their concerns.
Fine Arts; Health and Safety; Sociology
Dist - EMFVL

A Question of Attitude 12 MIN
16mm
Color (H C A)
LC 70-709831
Examines the reluctance that many firms have towards the employment of physically hanicapped people. Shows that once the initial reluctance is overcome, it is found that the handicapped become loyal and productive employees who are capable of doing a fine job without any special considerations.
Business and Economics; Guidance and Counseling; Health and Safety; Psychology
Dist - AUIS **Prod** - ANAIB 1970

A Question of authority 25 MIN
VHS
Horizons in bioethics series
Color (G)
$49.95 purchase _ #860
Tells of a young mother of two who in an advanced state of pregnancy suffers a terrible fall. Tells how she is rushed to a hospital and is kept alive by a respirator inspite of the fact that she has been declared brain dead. Doctors want to deliver the baby by cesarean section to save its life. The father resists because he is afraid that the baby may have also suffered brain damage. The question of who has the authority to determine whether the baby will live or die arises. Refers to Jewish law - halacha. Developed by the Jerusalem Religious Council.
Religion and Philosophy
Dist - ERGOM **Prod** - ERGOM 1992

A Question of Balance 29 MIN
16mm
Energy - an Overview Series
Color (J H)
Explains the role of the electric power industry in maintaining an adequate power supply in an era of increasing demand, fuel shortage, opposition to nuclear power and the need to protect the environment.
Home Economics; Industrial and Technical Education; Science - Physical; Social Science
Dist - CONPOW **Prod** - CENTRO

A Question of balance 30 MIN
VHS
Perspective - agriculture - series
Color; PAL; NTSC (G)
PdS90, PdS105 purchase
Shows how natural methods are used to feed agricultural land and protect it from insect invaders and fungi.
Agriculture
Dist - CFLVIS **Prod** - LONTVS

A Question of balance - art and redevelopment in old Pasadena 30 MIN
VHS
Color (H C G)
$195.00 purchase, $45.00 rental _ #37740
Explores the impact on the resident artistic community in Old Pasadena, near Los Angeles, of recent efforts to redevelop and 'gentrify' the area. Investigates the responses of the various interests involved and examines some of the suggestions made to help maintain the longtime artistic character of the area and incorporate the arts into the revitalization process. Produced by Robert J Richards.
Geography - United States; Social Science; Sociology
Dist - UCEMC

The Question of causation - experimental design - Parts 11 and 12 60 MIN
U-matic / VHS
Against all odds - inside statistics series
Color (C)
$45.00, $29.95 purchase
Presents parts 11 and 12 of 26 thirty - minute programs on statistics hosted by Dr Teresa Amabile of Brandeis University. Observes that association may or may not represent causation. Illustrates Simpson's paradox. Distinguishes between observation studies and experiments. Examines design - comparison, randomization and replication. Produced by the Consortium for Mathematics and Its Applications - COMAP - and the American Statistical Association and American Society of Quality Control.
Mathematics; Psychology
Dist - ANNCPB

A Question of Codes 29 MIN
U-matic
A Different Understanding Series
Color (PRO)
Discusses the methods used by several organizations in Ontario to detect defective learning skills in children.
Psychology
Dist - TVOTAR **Prod** - TVOTAR 1985

A Question of Codes 29 MIN
VHS / 16mm
A Different Understanding Series
Color (G)
$90.00 purchase _ #BPN164103
Discusses several Ontario organizations that are developing techniques to detect defective learning skills in children.
Education; Psychology
Dist - RMIBHF **Prod** - RMIBHF

A Question of Confidence 29
VHS / 16mm
A Different Understanding Series
Color (G)
$90.00 purchase _ #BPN227801
Documents the effects of economic recession on Terra Steel, a small manufacturing business in Ontario. Discusses the history and current financial difficulties of the company and why it faces bankruptcy. Explores possible ways to keep the plant operating.
Business and Economics
Dist - RMIBHF **Prod** - RMIBHF

A Question of confidence 29 MIN
U-matic
A Different understanding series
Color (PRO)
Examines how the owners, employees and other concerned indivduals attempt to save a small manufacturing business facing bankruptcy.
Business and Economics
Dist - TVOTAR **Prod** - TVOTAR 1985

A Question of conscience 47 MIN
VHS
Color (G)
$325.00 purchase, $75.00 rental
Tells the story behind the 1989 slayings of six Jesuit priests, Ignacio Ellacuria - a liberation theologian, their cook and her daughter at San Salvador's University of Central America. Juxtaposes the priests' story, told by their surviving colleague and the story of Jesuit - educated murderer, Lt Jose Espinoza Guerra. A chilling conclusion reveals the terrible logic behind the killings for which Espinoza was sentenced to three years in prison, and his superior officer to 30 years.
Civics and Political Systems; Fine Arts
Dist - FIRS **Prod** - ZIVILN 1990

Question of consent - rape 20 MIN
U-matic / VHS / 16mm
Color
Examines a court case in which a rape victim invites her assailant into her apartment causing attorneys to argue over the issue of consent.
Civics and Political Systems; Sociology
Dist - CORF **Prod** - WORON

A Question of Custody 19 MIN
U-matic / VHS
Child Training Tapes Series
Color
Attempts to determine what is in the best interests of the child when it comes to custody. Shows an interview between a social worker and a father who is filing for custody of his son, presently in custody of the mother.
Sociology
Dist - UWISC **Prod** - OHIOSU

Question of doping - Pt 3 30 MIN
VHS
Human element series
Color; PAL (G)
PdS65 purchase; Not available in the United States or Canada
Examines doping in horse racing and the methods used to detect drugs. Follows show - jumper David Broome as he sets out to discover why his horse failed a routine drug test. Provides a human look at the world of science, showing that there is more to chemistry than meets the eye. Part three of a five - part series.
History - World; Physical Education and Recreation; Psychology
Dist - BBCENE

A Question of Duty 26 MIN
16mm / U-matic / VHS
Color
Describes humans' responsibility to all wildlife.
Fine Arts
Dist - KAWVAL **Prod** - KAWVAL

A Question of ethics 24 MIN
VHS
Color (J H)

$295.00 purchase
Depicts a young man who tries to pass off a friend's work as his in order to maintain his chance for a scholarship. Challenges viewers' concepts of what is ethical, honest and trustworthy behavior. Produced by BC Productions - Creative Youth Resources.
Guidance and Counseling; Religion and Philosophy; Social Science
Dist - PFP

A Question of future time 12 MIN
VHS
Color (G R)
$12.50 purchase _ #S16066
Stresses the importance of churches planning for the future. Includes a message from Lutheran Church - Missouri Synod President Ralph Bohlmann.
Guidance and Counseling; Literature and Drama; Religion and Philosophy
Dist - CPH **Prod** - LUMIS

A Question of Growth 30 MIN
U-matic / VHS
Time's Harvest - Exploring the Future Series
Color (C)
Sociology
Dist - MDCPB **Prod** - MDCPB

The Question of heating Pt 1 30 MIN
BETA / VHS
This Old house - the Dorchester series
Color
Looks at the bedroom closets of an old house being renovated and at the heating plant in the basement. Discusses baseboard heat.
Industrial and Technical Education; Sociology
Dist - CORF **Prod** - WGBHTV

A Question of hope - deciding on rhizotomy 15 MIN
VHS
Color (G)
$75.00 purchase
Discusses the procedure of rhizotomy - the surgical cutting of spinal nerve roots - for parents of children with cerebral palsy and anyone who works with these patients.
Health and Safety
Dist - RICHGO **Prod** - RICHGO 1989

A Question of hunting 29 MIN
16mm
Color
LC 75-700156
Examines the controversies surrounding hunting for sport in America. Presents arguments used by critics of hunting and shows, points of view from defenders, and insights on the contributions made to wildlife conservation by sportsmen.
Physical Education and Recreation; Psychology; Science - Natural
Dist - MTP **Prod** - RARMS 1974

A Question of intimacy 19 MIN
16mm
Color
LC 81-700426
Presents nine people sharing their feelings and thoughts, their frustrations and their fears about intimate relationships.
Psychology
Dist - ECUFLM **Prod** - UMCOM 1981

A Question of justice 28 MIN
16mm
B&W
LC 76-702200
Considers several recent court cases and studies which dramatize the problem of unpunished rapes. Shows that society and the criminal justice system often punish women for using violence in defending themselves against assaults.
Civics and Political Systems; Sociology
Dist - PBS **Prod** - WNETTV 1975

A Question of learning 60 MIN
VHS / U-matic
Discovery of animal behavior series
Color (H C A)
Re - creates Ivan Pavlov's experiments which led to the discovery of the conditioned reflex. Looks at the investigation by Otto Pfungst of Clever Hans, a horse whose apparent knowledge of arithmetic was actually a response to subtle signals from his trainer.
Science; Science - Natural
Dist - FI **Prod** - WNETTV 1982

A Question of Life 29 MIN
16mm
Color (J H A)
LC 77-700806
Reviews the history of Mars, describes its present surface topography and considers its capacity to sustain life as we know it.
History - World; Science - Physical
Dist - USNAC **Prod** - NASA 1977

A Question of Loyalty 50 MIN
16mm / U-matic / VHS
Yesterday's Witness in America Series
Color (H C A)
Describes the internment of Japanese - Americans in camps during World War II out of fear that they might help the enemy. Presents interviews with people who were actually interned at the Manzanar camp in California.
History - United States; Sociology
Dist - TIMLIF **Prod** - BBCTV 1982

A Question of management 35 MIN
16mm / VHS
Color (C A)
$595.00 purchase, $150.00 rental _ #183
Includes Leader's Guide. Reviews the history of management theory and practice from Frederick Taylor, the Hawthorne Studies and Maslow to the present. Excellent overview, relevant to today's managers.
Business and Economics; Guidance and Counseling; Psychology
Dist - SALENG **Prod** - SALENG 1986

Question of Management - a Historical Perspective 35 MIN
VHS / 16mm
(C PRO)
$595.00 purchase, $250.00 rental
Presents a historical persective on the history of management theory and practice.
Education
Dist - VLEARN

A Question of numbers 28 MIN
16mm / VHS
Women's lives and choices series
Color (G)
$50.00, $65.00 rental, $195.00 purchase
Uses the Ibu Eze ceremony in Nigeria to highlight how family planning issues often conflict with traditional family ideals. Looks at this ceremony which celebrates women who have given birth to large numbers of children. Points out that Nigeria is Africa's most populous country, yet has one of the highest infant and maternal mortality rates in the world. Part of a three - part series dealing with women's health and the social, cultural and economic factors underlying reproductive choices.
Fine Arts; Religion and Philosophy; Sociology
Dist - WMEN **Prod** - RIESEN
MACART

A Question of power 58 MIN
VHS
Color (H C G A)
$45.00 purchase, $30.00 rental
Focuses on the controversial Diablo Canyon nuclear plant in California, which environmental activists have fought to keep from opening. Suggests that the plant has many significant safety problems. Profiles individuals who have fought against the plant. Narrated by actor Peter Coyote. Produced by David L Brown, Jane Kinzler, and Tom Anderson.
Civics and Political Systems; Health and Safety; Social Science
Dist - EFVP

A Question of Quality 29 MIN
16mm
Color (A)
LC 78-700947
Examines forests and areas of wilderness, noting man's effect on their existence and development. Points out that the wilderness experience, land resources and ultimately human life are questions of quality.
Science - Natural; Sociology
Dist - USNAC **Prod** - USNPS 1977

A Question of quality - Program 2 45 MIN
VHS
Advanced television lighting - a seminar with Bill Millar, BBC - TV 'series
Color (PRO G)
$149.00 purchase, $49.00 rental _ #711
Examines sophisticated lighting techniques used by Bill Millar in several BBC period productions. Shows how Millar orchestrates a sunset that lasts 45 minutes and mimics the lighting of Rembrandt and Vermeer. Part two of a four - part series on advanced television lighting featuring Bill Millar of BBC - TV. Produced by the Australian Film, Television and Radio School.
Fine Arts; Industrial and Technical Education
Dist - FIRLIT

The Question of re - election 29 MIN
16mm
Government story series; No 4
Color
LC 76-707189
Discusses how campaigning for election and re - election affects the working Congress, pointing out the advantages of the incumbents over the challengers.
Civics and Political Systems
Dist - WBCPRO **Prod** - OGCW 1968

A Question of respect 11 MIN
VHS / U-matic / BETA
Color (J H C G)
$119.95, $69.95 purchase
Discusses the concept of having respect for all animal life. Touches on several situations where killing animals is taken for granted, such as in schools where frogs, cats, pigs and other animals are routinely killed for dissection. Describes alternatives to these practices.
Guidance and Counseling; Religion and Philosophy; Science - Natural
Dist - VARDIR **Prod** - ASPCA 1989

The Question of Television Violence 56 MIN
U-matic / VHS / 16mm
Color (H C A)
LC 73-702703
Reports on the hearings of the United States Senate Subcommittee on Communications investigating the effects of televised violence. Explains that the hearings confirmed a correlation between violence on the screen and violence in real life.
Education; Psychology; Sociology
Dist - PHENIX **Prod** - NFBC 1973

A Question of Values 24 MIN
16mm / U-matic / VHS
Color (H C A)
Describes Down's syndrome and some of the moral problems it raises. Presents three infants and three children, ranging in age from five years to 21 years, with their families. Includes information about the physical and psychological characteristics and the range of variation in a population of persons with Down's syndrome.
Health and Safety; Psychology; Science - Natural
Dist - FEIL **Prod** - CWRU 1973

A Question of Values 28 MIN
16mm
Color (I)
LC 74-701899
Probes the attitudes of people in Searsport, Maine, as they confront a proposal to build an oil refinery on their bay. Presents arguments from both proponents and opponents of the refinery.
Guidance and Counseling; Psychology
Dist - NEWFLM **Prod** - NEWFLM 1972

A Question of values 29 MIN
U-matic
Everybody's children series
Color (PRO)
Dramatizes the problem children face in weighing the values of their families against those of the outside world.
Psychology; Sociology
Dist - TVOTAR **Prod** - TVOTAR 1985

A Question of Values 29 MIN
VHS / 16mm
Everybody's Children Series
(G)
$90.00 purchase _ #BPN16112
Appraises the process of developing a personal value system. Demonstrates children in a value testing situation. Comprises part of a series which examines child raising in modern society.
Education; Psychology; Sociology
Dist - RMIBHF **Prod** - RMIBHF

The Question of Video Display Terminals 27 MIN
VHS / U-matic
Color (IND)
Mathematics; Social Science
Dist - PLACE **Prod** - PLACE 1982

The Question of War 19 MIN
16mm
Color (I J H)
LC 80-701984
Uses animation to trace the history of war from the first armed conflict between primitive men to the highly complex nature of war in the 1970's.
Sociology
Dist - CGWEST **Prod** - CGWEST 1980

Questioning 10 MIN
VHS / 16mm
English as a second language series
Color (A PRO)

$165.00 purchase _ #290302
Demonstrates key teaching methods for English as a Second Language - ESL teachers. Features a teacher - presenter who introduces and provides a brief commentary on the techniques, then demonstrates the application of the technique to the students. Shows several methods of questioning which teachers can use to promote communication in ESL classes.
Education; English Language; Mathematics
Dist - ACCESS **Prod** - ACCESS 1989

Questioning 29 MIN
16mm
Real Revolution - Talks by Krishnamurti Series
B&W
LC 73-703037
Features a dialog between Indian spiritual leader Krishnamurti and the boys of Thacher school, Ojai, California. Contains his encouragement to question life and understand themselves, warns them against the traditional intellectual and argumentative approach to questioning. Comments on war as a way of life and acceptance of death and world problems such as hunger and poverty.
Guidance and Counseling; Religion and Philosophy
Dist - IU **Prod** - KQEDTV 1968

Questioning 30 MIN
U-matic / VHS
Teaching Reading Comprehension Series
Color (T PRO)
$180.00 purchase,$50.00 rental
Explores the possibilities of allowing the students to operate the question and answer sessions in the classrooms.
Education; English Language
Dist - AITECH **Prod** - WETN 1986

Questioning skills 30 MIN
16mm
Project STRETCH series; Module 1
Color (T)
LC 80-700608
Demonstrates types of creative questions that require students to formulate ideas rather than simply recall facts.
Education; Psychology
Dist - HUBDSC **Prod** - METCO 1980

Questioning techniques and gender - Unit H 59 MIN
VHS
Drama forum series
Color; PAL (T)
PdS35.00 purchase
Features Malcolm Morrison with a fourth - year GCSE class in a boys' school using drama to explore the working environment and the status of women in the early twentieth century. Presents unit seven of a ten - unit series of observational material on the work of drama teachers.
Education; Fine Arts; Sociology
Dist - EMFVL

Questioning Techniques and Probing 29 MIN
VHS / U-matic
Strategies of Effective Teaching Series
Color (T)
Deals with a teaching strategy called probing, which is aimed at increasing reflexive thinking in students. Demonstrates different types of probing questions.
Education
Dist - AITECH **Prod** - GSDE 1980

Questioning techniques for developing drama activities - Unit J 55 MIN
VHS
Drama forum series
Color; PAL (T)
PdS35.00 purchase
Features Malcolm Morrison with a fifth - year boys' school GCSE class using drama to analyze concepts of winning and losing, and achievement and success. Presents unit eight of a ten - unit series of observational material on the work of drama teachers.
Education; Fine Arts; Psychology
Dist - EMFVL

Questions
U-matic / 16mm
Art of negotiating series; Module 5
Color (A)
Deals with how to formulate and use questions, the five functions of questions, the question matrix, the question map for preparation and applications.
Business and Economics; Psychology
Dist - BNA **Prod** - BNA 1983

Questions 20 MIN
16mm
Color
LC 74-706384
Presents a high school student discussion on smoking. Focuses on the social pressures that impel them to smoke and the emotional attitudes that make them receptive to those pressures.
Guidance and Counseling; Health and Safety; Psychology
Dist - USNAC **Prod** - USHHS 1969

Questions 29 MIN
Videoreel / VT2
Synergism - in Today's World Series
Color
Presents information on teenage smoking.
Sociology
Dist - PBS **Prod** - WETATV

Questions and Answers 33 MIN
16mm
School Board Debates - Career Education Series
Color
LC 79-700356
Presents scenes in which representatives from every segment in a community have an opportunity to ask questions about a proposed comprehensive career education program. Shows experts answering the questions and the school board voting on the program.
Education
Dist - SWRLFF **Prod** - NSBA 1978

Questions and answers 30 MIN
VHS
New faces on make - up series
Color (G A)
$24.95 purchase _ #PRO207V
Provides professional answers to the most commonly asked questions about make - up.
Home Economics
Dist - CAMV

Questions and answers about EPA's final PMN rule 21 MIN
VHS / U-matic
Pre - manufacture notification rule - EPA, May 1983 series
Color (A)
LC 84-706424
Jack McCarthy, director of the Toxic Substances Control Act Assistance Office of the Environmental Protection Agency, chairs a panel discussion of the EPA's May 1983 ruling on final Premanufacture Notification. Covers the most important elements of the rule, information changes, requirements for importers and exporters, and how a manufacturer can determine whether or not a specific chemical substance is on the inventory.
Business and Economics; Civics and Political Systems; Science - Physical
Dist - USNAC **Prod** - USEPA 1983

Questions and Answers - Globes 13 MIN
VHS / U-matic
Under the Blue Umbrella Series
Color (P)
Presents an interview show in which a panel of experts provides information on the globe.
Social Science
Dist - AITECH **Prod** - SCETV 1977

Questions and Answers I 29 MIN
Videoreel / VT2
Who is Man Series
Color
Features Dr Puryear who examines and answers questions sent by viewers from all over the country during the broadcast of the Who Is Man series.
Psychology
Dist - PBS **Prod** - WHROTV

Questions and Answers II 29 MIN
Videoreel / VT2
Who is Man Series
Color
Features Dr Puryear who examines and answers questions sent by viewers from all over the country during the broadcast of the Who Is Man series.
Psychology
Dist - PBS **Prod** - WHROTV

Questions and answers III - making things grow III 29 MIN
Videoreel / VT2
Making things grow III series
Color
Agriculture
Dist - PBS **Prod** - WGBHTV

Questions and Answers IV - Making Things Grow III 29 MIN
Videoreel / VT2
Making Things Grow III Series
Color
Agriculture
Dist - PBS **Prod** - WGBHTV

Questions and Answers - Making Things Grow I 30 MIN
Videoreel / VT2
Making Things Grow I Series
Color
Features Thalassa Cruso discussing different aspects of gardening and answering questions.
Agriculture
Dist - PBS **Prod** - WGBHTV

Questions and Answers - Making Things Grow II 30 MIN
Videoreel / VT2
Making Things Grow II Series
Color
Features Thalassa Cruso discussing different aspects of gardening and answering questions.
Agriculture
Dist - PBS **Prod** - WGBHTV

Questions and Answers - Maps 14 MIN
U-matic / VHS
Under the Blue Umbrella Series
Color (P)
Offers information on maps.
Geography - World; Social Science
Dist - AITECH **Prod** - SCETV 1977

Questions Answered 36.24 MIN
VHS
Truth about AIDS Series
Color (J H C)
LC 88-700284
Discusses questions that students commonly ask about Acquired Immune Deficiency Syndrome (AIDS). Deals with treatments, transmission, vaccines, prevention and more.
Health and Safety
Dist - SRA **Prod** - SRA 1986

Questions for the Statistician
16mm
B&W
Underlines the need for sampling. Chooses a sample statistic from a population of 52 permutations of a pack of playing cards and concludes by proving the formula for the variance of the binomial distribution using the new viewpoint of a sampling distribution.
Mathematics
Dist - OPENU **Prod** - OPENU

Questions for Thinking 28 MIN
U-matic / VHS / 16mm
Survival Skills for the Classroom Teacher Series
Color (C)
LC 72-700974
Explores what schools are doing, not doing, or could be doing to encourage students to think. Covers a lively public lecture by Dr William Glasser, author of 'SCHOOLS WITHOUT FAILURE' and 'THE IDENTITY SOCIETY.'.
Education; Psychology; Sociology
Dist - FI **Prod** - MFFD 1972

Questions most Frequently Asked 30 MIN
16mm
Color (H C A)
LC 80-701051
Provides information about funerals, telling which questions to ask funeral directors, various ways of dealing with arrangements, and other death customs.
Home Economics; Sociology
Dist - KLEINW **Prod** - KLEINW 1979

Questions of commitment 16 MIN
VHS
System of change series
Color (PRO G A)
$465.00 purchase, $130.00 rental
Explains how to achieve effective communication within a company in preparation for changes. Teaches managers to encourage a team approach to changes. Part of Implementing Change, Unit 2.
Business and Economics; Guidance and Counseling; Psychology
Dist - EXTR **Prod** - CCCD

Questions of faith III series
Remember sin and salvation
What about grace and miracles
What are the moral dilemmas
What do you mean by faith
What's religion got to do with sex
Why worship
Dist - APH

Questions of Hamlet - Why Does Hamlet Delay 45 MIN
VHS / U-matic
Survey of English Literature I Series
Color
Strives to answer the question of why Hamlet delayed in Shakespeare's play Hamlet.

Literature and Drama
Dist - MDCPB Prod - MDCPB

Questions of taste - A Panel discussion 28 MIN
U-matic / VHS
Color (H C A)
$75.00, $100.00 purchase, $40.00 rental
Shows a filmed discussion by Clement Greenburg, Walter Darby Bannard, Andre Emmerich, Kenworth Moffett, William O'Reilly and Pat Lipsky Sutton.
Fine Arts
Dist - ARTSAM

Questions of time 30 MIN
16mm / U-matic / VHS
World we live in series
Color (I J H)
LC 76-700240
Tells the story of time as the most elusive of all man's measurements.
Mathematics
Dist - MGHT Prod - TIMELI 1968

Questions that Help You Sell - Probing 10 MIN
16mm / U-matic / VHS
Color (C A)
LC 79-700503
Demonstrates the technique of asking the right questions to find out why, what and how much a prospective customer will buy.
Business and Economics; Psychology
Dist - SALENG Prod - SALENG 1979

Questions using Past Tense - 24 30 MIN
VHS
English 101 - Ingles 101 Series
Color (H)
$125.00 purchase
Presents a series of thirty 30 - minute programs in basic English for native speakers of Spanish. Focuses on a specific topic in order to emphasize a particular grammatical point or set of idioms. English is used from the beginning as the primary language of instruction but Spanish translations are included to ensure understanding. Part 24 considers interrogative sentences, word order in yes - no questions, word order in 'wh - ' questions.
English Language; Foreign Language
Dist - AITECH Prod - UPRICO 1988

The Questors 17 MIN
16mm
Color
LC 77-711411
Uses a story about a man and what happens to him during a family vacation to explain the need of man to give in order to receive even though giving is a matter of choice.
Guidance and Counseling; Psychology; Sociology
Dist - MATTCO Prod - MATTCO 1971

Quetzalcoatl 20 MIN
16mm
B&W
LC FIA52-424
Presents the legend of Quetzalcoatl, the fairest god of the Aztecs. Gods and mortals are portrayed by masks, statuettes and other artifacts made by preColumbian Indians of Mexico.
History - World; Literature and Drama
Dist - USC Prod - USC 1951

Quetzalcoatl 20 MIN
16mm
B&W (SPANISH)
LC 75-703224
Presents the legend of Quetzalcoatl, the fairest god of the Aztecs. Gods and mortals are portrayed by masks, statuettes and other artifacts made by preColumbian Indians of Mexico.
Foreign Language; History - World; Literature and Drama
Dist - USC Prod - USC 1954

Qui a Casse 13 MIN
16mm
En Francais, set 1 series
Color (J A)
Foreign Language
Dist - CHLTN Prod - PEREN 1969

Qui est - ce 13 MIN
16mm
Les Francais chez vous series
B&W (I J H)
Foreign Language
Dist - CHLTN Prod - PEREN 1967

Qui Jin - a Revolutionary 110 MIN
VHS
Color (G) (MANDARIN CHINESE (ENGLISH SUBTITLES))
$45.00 purchase _ #1046A
Presents a Mandarin Chinese language movie produced in the People's Republic of China.
Fine Arts; Geography - World; Literature and Drama
Dist - CHTSUI Prod - CHTSUI

Quiche Lorraine 29 MIN
Videoreel / VT2
French Chef - French Series
Color (FRENCH)
A French language videotape. Features Julia Child of Haute Cuisine au Vin demonstrating how to prepare Quiche Lorraine. With captions.
Foreign Language; Home Economics
Dist - PBS Prod - WGBHTV

Quick 98 MIN
16mm
B&W (GERMAN (ENGLISH SUBTITLES))
A German language film with English subtitles. Tells the story of a young girl who falls in love with a clown without ever having seen his face. As a result of mixups and mistaken identities, the original love story turns into a comedy with a very happy ending.
Fine Arts; Foreign Language
Dist - WSTGLC Prod - WSTGLC 1932

Quick and Easy Sewing Series
Craft - Gift Ideas 30 MIN
Redo a Room in a Weekend 30 MIN
Super Time Saving Tips 30 MIN
Wardrobe in a Weekend 30 MIN
Dist - CAMV

The Quick and the Dead 90 MIN
VHS
Color; Stereo (G)
$39.98 purchase _ #TT8032
Stars Stacy Keach in high - speed Formula One racing.
Literature and Drama; Physical Education and Recreation
Dist - TWINTO Prod - TWINTO 1990

Quick as Light 25 MIN
16mm
Start Here - Adventures and Science Series
Color
Features experiments which explain wavelength and color and shows that nothing travels faster than light.
Science - Physical
Dist - LANDMK Prod - VIDART 1983

Quick Billy 72 MIN
16mm
Color (C)
$1064.00
Experimental film by Bruce Baillie. Includes six uncut camera rolls - numbers 14, 41, 43, 46, 47, 52.
Fine Arts
Dist - AFA Prod - AFA 1970

Quick dog training 90 MIN
VHS
Color (G)
$59.95 purchase
Features dog trainer Barbara Wodehouse in a demonstration of effective dog training techniques and strategies.
Science - Natural
Dist - PBS Prod - WNETTV

Quick Esthetic Provisionalization during Crown and Bridge Therapy 10 MIN
U-matic / VHS / 16mm
Color (PRO)
Demonstrates how a preformed polypropylene splint is used to fabricate a temporary bridge intraorally. Discusses the principles of temporization.
Health and Safety
Dist - USNAC Prod - USVA 1984

Quick Flicks Series
Numbers in Sign Language 15 MIN
The Sign Language Alphabet 15 MIN
Dist - JOYCE

Quick opener 5 MIN
16mm
B&W (G)
$15.00 rental
Offers a short comedy dealing with baseball. Contains numerous referencesa to baseball players and the 1960 World Series, along with the 'world's longest baseball joke.' Produced by Brady Lewis, who advises that this plays well with The Suicide Squeeze and should be shown last in the progam.
Fine Arts; Physical Education and Recreation
Dist - CANCIN

Quick Relaxation 10 MIN
Videoreel / VT2
Janaki Series
Color
Physical Education and Recreation
Dist - PBS Prod - WGBHTV

A Quick Review 10 MIN
VHS / 16mm
Type it Up Series
Color (S)
$500.00 series purchase _ #270307
Features detailed introductory typing instruction at the high school - adult level. Presents amusing interplay between the private detective - novice typist 'Bogie' and his perfectionist instructor 'Sam.' Further understanding is gained by an explanation of what happens inside the typewriter whenever an activity is performed. 'A Quick Review' summarizes points made in the previous five programs including typewriter parts, home row keys, tabs and corrections.
Business and Economics; Education
Dist - ACCESS Prod - ACCESS 1986

Quick Rise 5 MIN
16mm
Color (K)
LC 78-714049
Uses stop - motion techniques to show the complete construction of a high rise office building.
Industrial and Technical Education; Social Science
Dist - VIEWFI Prod - GERGOR 1971

Quick skillet 28 MIN
VHS / 16mm
What's cooking series
Color (G)
$55.00 rental _ #WHAC - 110
Home Economics
Dist - PBS Prod - WHYY

Quick start to WordPerfect for Windows
VHS
WordPerfect 5.1 series
Color (G)
$39.95 purchase _ #VIA029
Teaches WordPerfect, version 5.1, and its applications in Windows.
Computer Science
Dist - SIV

Quick Tricks 40 MIN
U-matic / VHS
$19.95 purchase
Features magician Peter London as he teaches popular tricks such as making a spoon vanish, pulling a playing card from thin air, and others.
Fine Arts; Physical Education and Recreation
Dist - BESTF Prod - BESTF

Quick - Witted Hikoichi 16 MIN
16mm
Color (JAPANESE)
A Japanese language film. Tells the story of Japan's feudal age Hikoichi, the quick witted who saves his lord and province.
Foreign Language; Literature and Drama
Dist - UNIJAP Prod - UNIJAP 1970

Quicken, quick and easy
VHS
Color (G)
$29.95 purchase _ #VIA036
Teaches Quicken 5.0 accounting.
Computer Science
Dist - SIV

Quicker cleaning - for everyone who has better things to do than housework 40 MIN
VHS
Color (H C G)
$29.95 purchase _ #DSE200V
Features Don Aslett, the nation's number one house cleaner, who presents more tips on cleaning with the head, not the hands. Shows how to wash down a whole room in less than 30 seconds, wash enormous windows in seconds. Discloses the tricks of hotel maids in cleaning bathrooms. Reveals how to organize to clean.
Home Economics
Dist - CAMV

Quickest Draw in the West 12 MIN
16mm
Color (J)
Portrays the Strategic Air Command as sheriff guarding over the west, stretching from the Berlin Wall to the China coast.
Civics and Political Systems; Social Science
Dist - RCKWL Prod - NAA

Quicks - winning when it counts 43 MIN
VHS
Color (H C G)
$49.95 purchase _ #TMS010V
Features Coach Paul Billiard who has designed a series of training drills and exercises that provide a dynamic sports movement system to enhance natural athletic ability and improve agility for off - season training. Includes - the ready position; lead - up and basic movement; a method

of teaching the skills; and a designed time structure. Covers running, leg - hip steps and thrusts, bounding - plyometrics, eye - hand - foot coordination, lateral and angle movement, footwork and balance.
Physical Education and Recreation
Dist - CAMV

Quiddity Tree 17 MIN
16mm
Color (I)
LC 75-700000
Presents a fantasy film which illustrates the history of man's relationship with nature from the time of the Garden of Eden to the future.
Science - Natural; Sociology
Dist - MARALF **Prod** - WASDE 1975

Quiescence 10 MIN
16mm
Color (I J H)
LC 72-709994
Uses a sailing voyage among the islands and waterways of Northwestern Washington and British Columbia as the setting for a visual poem.
Fine Arts; Geography - United States
Dist - SOUND **Prod** - SOUND 1970

A Quiet afternoon with strangers 9 MIN
VHS / 16mm
Six interviews series
B&W (G)
$10.00 rental
Documents the year - round garage sale of an eccentric, elderly Ohio couple. Focuses, without sound, on their legacy of bric - a - brac, discarded appliances, and collected curiosities. Part four of a six - part series of 'interviews' from 1973 - 1981. Although not serial in content, the films should be shown in chronological order when viewed as a group. Produced by Tyler Turkle.
Fine Arts; Health and Safety
Dist - CANCIN
FLMKCO

Quiet Champion, the 59 MIN
U-matic / VHS
Captioned; Color (P A)
Presents Gallaudet College student Danny Fitzpatrick as he trains for and competes in World Games for the Deaf in Romania.
Guidance and Counseling; Physical Education and Recreation; Psychology
Dist - GALCO **Prod** - GALCO 1978

The Quiet Crisis 55 MIN
U-matic / VHS
Moore Report Series
Color (J)
LC 81-707441
Examines the use of water resources in transportation, industry, recreation, energy and food production. Discusses the issue of of a water crisis and emphasizes the need to attend to and correct negative trends before an irreversible freshwater shortage occurs.
Science - Natural; Social Science; Sociology
Dist - IU **Prod** - WCCOTV 1981

Quiet, Hunter, Noise 10 MIN
U-matic
Readalong Two Series
Color (P)
Provides young viewers with a flexible range of reading experiences through active involvement in reading and writing. Comes with teacher's guide and kit.
Education; English Language; Literature and Drama
Dist - TVOTAR **Prod** - TVOTAR 1976

Quiet Life 27 MIN
16mm
Color
Shows how the Japanese try to keep protecting beauty and a tranquil mind in the midst of this mechanical civilization. Points out that these attempts to regain a quiet life can be found in offices, urban construction sites, plants and in the lives of citizens. Explains that loving nature and a sense of beauty helps them understand the charms of the world, gives them composure of mind and increases their reserve of energy.
Business and Economics; Geography - World; Sociology
Dist - UNIJAP **Prod** - KAJIMA 1970

The Quiet Man 129 MIN
16mm
Color
Tells the story of a fighter who goes back to his hometown in Ireland to forget the tragic fight in which he killed a man. Stars John Wayne.
Fine Arts
Dist - TWYMAN **Prod** - REP 1952

Quiet Nacelle 17 MIN
16mm
Color
LC 75-701730
Depicts flight tests, complete with noise level recordings, which compare a 707 with untreated nacelles and an identical aircraft complete with treated nacelles. Uses animation to illustrate noise comparisons for approach and takeoff operations.
Industrial and Technical Education; Science - Natural
Dist - USNAC **Prod** - BOEING 1974

The Quiet one - Pt 1 34 MIN
16mm / U-matic / VHS
B&W
Tells the story of a mentally - disturbed Negro boy from the Harlem district of New York City who is sent for rehabilitation to the Wiltwyck School which was founded by the Protestant Episcopal church.
Health and Safety
Dist - TEXFLM **Prod** - FDOC 1948

Quiet passages - the Japanese - American war bride experience 27 MIN
BETA / U-matic / VHS
Color (H C)
Examines the experiences of Japanese - American war brides who came to the United States after World War II.
History - United States; Sociology
Dist - CEASUK

Quiet passages - the Japanese American war bride experience 26 MIN
VHS / U-matic
Color (G)
$150.00 purchase, $50.00 rental
Recalls how the lives of thousands of Japanese women were changed during the Occupation of Japan when they, in defiance of custom and law, married American servicemen. Reveals that in the early 1950s, the determination and perseverence of these couples helped to destroy the long - standing barriers to Japanese immigration to the United States. Combines archival photographs and film footage, personal photographs and interviews to record the journey of several Japanese American war brides to the American Midwest where they settled and raised their families. Produced by Chico Herbison and Jerry Shultz.
History - United States; Sociology
Dist - CROCUR

The Quiet Revolution 28 MIN
16mm
Color (K)
LC FIA67-1626
Depicts staffing patterns in five different schools that have initiated team teaching, flexible scheduling, non - graded elementary programs and other innovations. Explains that improvement in American education can only follow when the teacher has time to plan, analyze and teach. Suggests some alternatives for educators who desire action.
Education
Dist - EDUC **Prod** - NEAPRO 1967

Quiet Revolution 15 MIN
16mm
Color (H C A)
Depicts the revolution which has occurred in the Jacksonville area with the merging of the county and city government and other aspects of Florida living.
Geography - United States; Social Science
Dist - FLADC **Prod** - FLADC

A Quiet Revolution 60 MIN
U-matic / VHS / 16mm
Color (H C A)
$895 purchase - 16 mm, $495 purchase - video, $95 rental
Discusses Liberation Theology and citizens of Latin America who are organizing to fight against hunger, disease, umemployment, political oppression, and land distribution. Features interviews with community activists and religious leaders, including Reverend Gustavo Gutierrez, 'Father of Liberation Theology'. Directed by Audrey L. Glynn.
Civics and Political Systems; History - World; Sociology
Dist - CNEMAG

The Quiet Revolution of Mrs Harris 20 MIN
U-matic / VHS / 16mm
Color (H C A)
Gives a housewife's account of her gradual self - realization in becoming a person. Features Gloria Harris, talking about her dissatisfaction with her roles as mother, wife and housekeeper. Follows her efforts to establish her own identity by attending college and becoming a professional.
Sociology
Dist - MEDIAG **Prod** - CINELO 1976

A Quiet scream 34 MIN
VHS
First Tuesday series
Color; PAL (H C G)
PdS30 purchase
Reveals that Great Britain spends 90 million pounds a year on research into cancer treatment, but virtually nothing goes into the research and care of the emotional needs of patients facing up to painful treatments and the knowledge that there is no real cure. Looks at the level of care available in Britain and visits a city which leads the way in providing emotional support and understanding for cancer victims. Contact distributor about availability outside the United Kingdom.
Health and Safety; History - World
Dist - ACADEM **Prod** - YORKTV

The Quiet Summer 28 MIN
16mm
B&W
LC 74-705463
Describes how in 1965 a summer project operated by youths ended annual youth rioting in Hampton Beach, New Hampshire.
Sociology
Dist - USNAC **Prod** - USOJD 1965

The Quiet Warrior 28 MIN
16mm
Color
LC 74-705463
Tells the story of a Naval Air Reserve squadron. Shows how the reservist - citizens keep in readiness by training on weekends.
Civics and Political Systems
Dist - USNAC **Prod** - USN 1968

Quieting a noisy refrigerator 16 MIN
16mm
Refrigeration service - domestic units series
B&W
LC FIE52-228
Shows how to check and correct compressor and motor noises, noises caused by wear or looseness of parts and noises caused by high head pressure or an oil - logged evaporator. Number 10 in the Refrigeration service - domestic units series.
Industrial and Technical Education
Dist - USNAC **Prod** - USOE 1945

Quigley's village series

Always be thankful	30 MIN
Always tell the truth	30 MIN
Be kind to one another	30 MIN
Let's obey	30 MIN
Sharing with others	30 MIN
That's not fair	30 MIN

Dist - APH

The Quilt 10 MIN
VHS
Color (H G)
$75.00 purchase _ #E911 - VI - 050
Uses the quilt - laying event in Washington, DC, as a focus to raise the consciousness of viewers to a consideration of how many lives have been lost to AIDS and how many lives have been affected by each death.
Health and Safety; Psychology; Sociology
Dist - HSCIC

Quilt on the wall - a portrait of Jan Myers 28 MIN
U-matic / VHS
Color (G)
$100.00, $39.95 purchase
Observes contemporary textile artist Jan Myers constructing a patchwork quilt from planning, through dying the fabric, cutting, sewing and quilting.
Fine Arts; Home Economics
Dist - ARTSAM **Prod** - MIA

Quilted Friendship 6 MIN
U-matic / VHS
Color
Shows two women who have almost completed a quilt together when they discover that they have completely different views of their friendship.
Psychology; Sociology
Dist - WMEN **Prod** - WMEN

Quilting 51 MIN
VHS
Erica Wilson needle works series
Color (G)
$29.95 purchase
Presents basic quilting techniques, including shadow quilting, pinwheel quilting, the country bride quilt. Taught by Erica Wilson. Includes free pinwheel quilt templates.
Home Economics
Dist - PBS **Prod** - WNETTV

Quilting - a Video Guide 60 MIN
VHS
(H A)
$34.95 purchase _ #GV100V
Explains how to design and create handmade quilts. Illustrates all the stages of quilt production. Depicts many popular quilts.
Fine Arts; Home Economics
Dist - CAMV **Prod** - CAMV

Quilting and Basting in the Full Size Frame 60 MIN
VHS
Quilting with Joe Cunningham and Gwen Marston Series
(H A)
$39.95 purchase _ #BIQ003V
Demonstrates how to make and use a full size quilting frame and benefits for hoop quilters who baste in a full size frame.
Fine Arts; Home Economics
Dist - CAMV **Prod** - CAMV

Quilting party 2 MIN
16mm
Color
Presents an artistic view of quilting patterns set to the fiddle music of the Red Clay Ramblers.
Fine Arts
Dist - TRIF **Prod** - TRIF

Quilting - Patterns of Love 20 MIN
U-matic
Color
Traces the evolution of quilting from a necessary skill to a highly prized folk art. Takes a look at the use of quilts to express social concerns as well as the resurgence of quilting as a creative craft.
Fine Arts; Physical Education and Recreation
Dist - LAURON **Prod** - LAURON

Quilting with Erica Wilson 50 MIN
VHS
Erica Wilson's Craft Series
(H A)
$34.95 purchase _ #3M400V
Presents tips and techniques for making quilts. Uses an oval frame to demonstrate the basics. Discusses patch design, machine use, and hand painting.
Home Economics
Dist - CAMV **Prod** - CAMV

Quilting with Joe Cunningham and Gwen Marston Series
Basic piecing and applique 60 MIN
Caring for and Displaying Your Quilts 60 MIN
Making Quilt Designs - Vol 3 60 MIN
Quilting and Basting in the Full Size Frame 60 MIN
Sets and borders 60 MIN
Dist - CAMV

Quilting women 28 MIN
U-matic / 16mm
Color (G H C A)
LC 77 - 701992
Focuses on women artists who create works of art in textile. Traces the entire process of quiltmaking.
Fine Arts; Geography - United States; Home Economics
Dist - APPAL **Prod** - BARETE 1976

Quilting Women 27 MIN
16mm
Color (H C A)
LC 77-701992
Examines the art of quilting, showing women of previous generations, as well as of today, as they practice and comment on various aspects of the craft.
Fine Arts; Home Economics
Dist - APPAL **Prod** - BARETE 1976

Quinceaneras 23 MIN
U-matic / VHS
Images / Imagenes Series
Color
Explores the traditional ceremony and party held when a Chicana comes into womanhood.
Sociology
Dist - LVN **Prod** - TUCPL

Quingalik and the Sea 6 MIN
U-matic / VHS / 16mm
Inuit Legends Series
Color (K P)
Tells how the Eskimo hunter is accidentally set adrift on an ice floe during the Arctic spring. Shows how he remembers what an old hunter told him, improvises a raft and reaches home safely.
Geography - United States; Geography - World; Physical Education and Recreation; Science - Natural; Sociology
Dist - BCNFL **Prod** - ANIMET 1982

The Quinkins 11 MIN
16mm / U-matic / VHS
Color
LC 82-700604
Presents the story of two groups of Quinkins, the spirit people of the country of Cape York. Explains that one group consists of small, fat - bellied bad fellows who steal children and the other is comprised of humorous, whimsical spirits. Based on the book The Quinkins by Percy Trezise and Dick Roughsey.
Literature and Drama
Dist - WWS **Prod** - WWS 1982

Quinten Gregory - professional artist series
How professional artists paint realistic art that sells - Volume 1 60 MIN
How professional artists paint skies, clouds and atmosphere - Volume 3 60 MIN
How professional artists paint water - Volume 2 60 MIN
Dist - VICAV

Quinton Duval - 3 - 25 - 82 60 MIN
VHS / Cassette
Poetry Center reading series
Color (G)
$15.00, $45.00 purchase, $15.00 rental _ #483 - 410
Features the writer reading from his works at the Poetry Center, San Francisco State University, with an introduction by Tom Mandel.
Literature and Drama
Dist - POETRY

A Quip with Yip and friends - masters of light verse 45 MIN
VHS
Heritage poetry collection series
Color (J H)
$49.00 purchase _ #60305 - 126
Presents works by Ogden Nash, Dorothy Parker, Phyllis McGinley, e e cummings and Edgar 'Yip' Harburg.
Literature and Drama
Dist - GA **Prod** - GA 1992

Quiproquo 13 MIN
16mm
Color (G)
$35.00 rental
Creates an environment where nature and social - industry technology meet. Attempts a visual dialogue with - and critique of - mainstream society's concerns. Soundtrack by Katie O'Looney.
Fine Arts; Social Science; Sociology
Dist - CANCIN **Prod** - LOWDER 1992

Quit Kicking Sand in Our Faces 20 MIN
U-matic / VHS
Color
Presents vignettes which illustrate and satirize sexual stereotyping.
Fine Arts
Dist - KITCHN **Prod** - KITCHN

The Quite one - Pt 2 34 MIN
U-matic / VHS / 16mm
B&W
Tells the story of a mentally - disturbed Negro boy from the Harlem district of New York City who is sent for rehabilitation to the Wiltwyck School which was founded by the Protestant Episcopal church.
Health and Safety
Dist - TEXFLM **Prod** - FDOC 1948

The Quitter 7 MIN
VHS
Color (H C A)
$145.00 purchase
Encourages smokers to quit using an animated tale of a smoker who is known as a quitter in everything but smoking. Provides ideas for those who want to become ex - smokers.
Guidance and Counseling; Health and Safety; Psychology
Dist - PFP **Prod** - FERLIP

Quitting - Tips for Smokers 28 MIN
16mm
Color
Interviews Dr Donald T Frederickson, former director of the New York City Smoking Withdrawal Clinic and one of the nation's most successful smoking - cessation teachers on ways to quit smoking.
Health and Safety; Psychology
Dist - LAWREN **Prod** - LAWREN

The Quiver of Life 58 MIN
16mm / U-matic / VHS
Music of Man
(G)
#151 79 01
Features early music history. Shows prehistoric discoveries in Russia, the traditions of ancient Greece and India, and the primitive sounds of Africa.
Fine Arts
Dist - CANBC **Prod** - TIMELI

The Quiver of Life 57 MIN
16mm / U-matic / VHS
Music of Man Series
Color (H C A)
Explores the evolution of music by looking at how the ancient civilizations of China, Japan, Sumeria and Greece created music. Presents the primeval rhythms of Africa and shows the recent discoveries of prehistoric instruments. Demonstrates a soundscape, a gigantic mobile that emits a cacophony of unique sounds.
Fine Arts
Dist - TIMLIF **Prod** - CANBC 1981

Quixote 45 MIN
16mm
Color; B&W (C)
$672.00
Experimental film by Bruce Baillie.
Fine Arts
Dist - AFA **Prod** - AFA 1965

Quixote 45 MIN
VHS / 16mm
Color & B&W (G)
$75.00 rental, $50.00 purchase
Takes a year - long journey through the land of incessant progress. Researches those sources which have given rise twenty years later to the essential question of survival. In four parts on one reel.
Fine Arts; Sociology
Dist - CANCIN **Prod** - BAILB 1967

Quixote dreams 10 MIN
VHS / 16mm
Color (G)
$30.00 rental
Explores the Don Quixote myth in a surrealistic fantasy. Compares his character and mission to the seemingly hopeless landscape of the late 20th century. Produced in 1990 - 1991.
Fine Arts; Literature and Drama
Dist - CANCIN **Prod** - ALVARE

The Quiz master
VHS / BETA / U-matic
Vocational and career planning series
Color (J H C A)
#QMV 101
Asks students questions to test their retention of concepts found in the three tapes to the Vocational And Career Planning Series.
Education; Guidance and Counseling
Dist - CADESF **Prod** - CADESF 1988

The Quiz Master
U-matic / VHS
Vocational and Career Planning Video Series
(J H C)
$49.00 _ #CD1140V
Contains a set of questions regarding career planning, with a 20 second pause between each question for answering time. May be used by instructors to test students over knowledge obtained in the Vocational and Career Planning Video Series.
Business and Economics; Education; Guidance and Counseling
Dist - CAMV **Prod** - CAMV

Quiz Master
VHS
Vocational and Career Planning Series
$49.00 purchase _ #VP103V
Asks questions to test retention of concepts learned in the video series 'Vocational and Career Planning Series'.
Guidance and Counseling
Dist - CAREER **Prod** - CAREER

The Quiz Master
VHS / 16mm
Vocational and Career Planning Series
(J H)
$49.00 _ #FM214
Tests retention of vital concepts. Includes optional scorer with correct answers.
Guidance and Counseling
Dist - JISTW

Quo Vadis 3 MIN
U-matic / VHS / 16mm
Color (H C A)
LC 74-701712
Emphasizes the problem of overpopulation and an insufficient food supply. Shows cells dividing into more complex forms of life, culminating in the human face, which turns into many faces and then just many mouths. Pictures the earth being devoured by such hungry mouths.
Guidance and Counseling; Health and Safety; Social Science; Sociology
Dist - MGHT **Prod** - ZAGREB 1974

Quotation Marks, Programs, Deep, Dark, Dirty, Vanished 10 MIN
U-matic
Readalong Three Series
Color (P)
Provides reading instruction for third grade students. Uses animation, humor, music, repetition and audience participation. Comes with teacher's guide and kit.
Education; English Language; Literature and Drama
Dist - TVOTAR **Prod** - TVOTAR 1977

Quotations from Chairman Stu 22 MIN
16mm
B&W
Presents a story about an aluminum powder factory in New Jersey that is importing and exploiting Haitians. Tells how chaos ensues when the youngest son of the factory owner returns home from college espousing Maoist ideals and discovers the injustice.
Fine Arts
Dist - USC **Prod** - USC 1980

Quote, Unquote 15 MIN
U-matic / VHS
Magic Shop Series no 13
Color (P)
LC 83-706158
Employs a magician named Amazing Alexander and his assistants to explore the use of quotation marks.
English Language
Dist - GPN **Prod** - CVETVC 1982

The Quran - as it is as it was
VHS
Color (G)
$12.00 purchase _ #110 - 077
Features Khurram Murad, Ahmad von Denffer and Imam Al - Phaim Jobe who present the history of the Quran, its themes and its capacity to guide humanity until the Day of Judgment.
Religion and Philosophy
Dist - SOUVIS **Prod** - SOUVIS 1995

Quran on video - 1st and 2nd parts - juz 120 MIN
VHS
Quranic videos series
Color (G)
$20.00 purchase _ #129 - 006
Features Qari Ghulam Rasool as reciter.
Foreign Language; Religion and Philosophy
Dist - SOUVIS **Prod** - SOUVIS

Quran on video - 29th and 30th parts - juz 120 MIN
VHS
Quranic videos series
Color (G)
$20.00 purchase _ #129 - 005
Features Qari Ghulam Rasool as reciter.
Foreign Language; Religion and Philosophy
Dist - SOUVIS **Prod** - SOUVIS

Quran on video - complete quran 1800 MIN
VHS
Quranic videos series
Color (G)
$300.00 purchase _ #129 - 001
Presents the complete Quran recited by Qari Ghulam Rasool with the pointer moving on each word of the Quran.
Foreign Language; Religion and Philosophy
Dist - SOUVIS **Prod** - SOUVIS

Quran on video - Lesson 1 - Short surahs 120 MIN
VHS
Quranic videos series
Color (P I J G)
$20.00 purchase _ #129 - 004
Presents a Quran video for children recited by Qari Ghulam Rasool. Recites each word slowly three or four times to allow for easy memorization of short surahs. Includes Surah Ad - Duha to An - Nas.
Foreign Language; Religion and Philosophy
Dist - SOUVIS **Prod** - SOUVIS

Quran on video, the last 37 chapters 120 MIN
VHS
Color (G)
$20.00 purchase _ #129 - 002
Presents the entire 30th part of the Quran, from Surah An - Naba' to Surah An - Nas recited by Qari Abdul Basit Abdul Samad.
Foreign Language; Religion and Philosophy
Dist - SOUVIS **Prod** - SOUVIS

Quranic videos series
Quran on video - 1st and 2nd parts - juz 120 MIN
Quran on video - 29th and 30th parts - juz 120 MIN
Quran on video - complete quran 1800 MIN
Quran on video - Lesson 1 - Short surahs 120 MIN
Dist - SOUVIS

Quynh Lap Leprosarium 10 MIN
16mm
B&W/Color
Shows Quynh Lap leprosarium in Vietnam that has been bombed 106 times by U S planes. Shows the continued devastation of Vietnam.
Civics and Political Systems; Geography - World; Health and Safety
Dist - CANWRL **Prod** - CANWRL 1967

R

R 3 MIN
16mm
B&W (G)
$6.00 rental
Presents a silent film based on the rhythms of a Bach invention for two voices. By Yann Beauvais.
Fine Arts
Dist - CANCIN

R-1 - Ein formspiel 7 MIN
16mm
Color tint (G)
$22.00 rental
Combines two different films, Staffs and one of small fragments of different experiemnts such as wax, model planets, atoms which appears to be a revised version of the first.
Fine Arts
Dist - CANCIN **Prod** - FISCHF 1927

R - 101, a Business Survival System 7 MIN
VHS / U-matic
Color (IND)
Provides a non - technical introduction to automatic dry chemical restaurant fire protection systems. Illustrates how to extinguish a fire in a deep fat fryer.
Health and Safety
Dist - ANSUL **Prod** - ANSUL 1975

R-102 / Ansulex Fire Test Film 11 MIN
U-matic / VHS
Color (IND)
Shows the actual fire test procedures used in order to earn a listing from the Underwriters Laboratories.
Health and Safety
Dist - ANSUL **Prod** - ANSUL 1982

R-102/Ansulex Promotional Program 10 MIN
VHS
Color (IND)
Demonstrates the Ansul brand wet agent restaurant fire protection system. Includes installation techniques.
Health and Safety
Dist - ANSUL **Prod** - ANSUL

R a / Osteo - Two Different Diseases 17 MIN
16mm
Color
Deals with rheumatoid arthritis and osteoarthritis, two different diseases which attack different age groups. Defines both types of arthritis, appropriate techniques of diagnosis, and a general professional overview of current methods of treatment.
Health and Safety
Dist - WSTGLC **Prod** - WSTGLC

R - a - P - Radiological Assistance Program 27 MIN
16mm
Color
LC FIE66-12
Re - enacts three radiological emergencies to show the readiness and proficiency of radiological assistance teams as they put to work their specialized professional skills and equipment in dealing with accidents involving radiological materials.
Health and Safety; Science - Physical
Dist - USNAC **Prod** - USNRC 1965

R and D and innovation 45 MIN
U-matic / VHS
Technology, innovation, and industrial development series
Color (IND)
Business and Economics
Dist - MIOT **Prod** - MIOT

R-Base 115 MIN
VHS / Software / 16mm
Color (PRO)
$495.00 purchase, $40.00 preview
Introduces the R - Base computer software system. Explains basic concepts, how to create a database file, how to enter and edit data, how to query data, create a data form, print reports, use commands, and create applications.
Computer Science; Mathematics; Psychology
Dist - UTM **Prod** - UTM

R-BASE System V 120 MIN
U-matic / VHS
(A PRO)
$495.00 purchase, $595.00 purchase
Contains instruction on database management, creating a database and modifying data.
Computer Science
Dist - VIDEOT **Prod** - VIDEOT 1988

The R - blends - brooms and crutches, using the structure of the word 18 MIN
VHS / U-matic
Getting the word series; Unit II
Color (J H)
English Language
Dist - AITECH **Prod** - SCETV 1974

R Buckminster Fuller - Prospects for Humanity 30 MIN
16mm
Spectrum series
B&W (H C A)
Presents excerpts from speeches by R Buckminster Fuller during which Dr Fuller predicts the unification of humankind as a result of technology derived from space exploration, computer applications and systems analysis.
History - United States; Industrial and Technical Education; Psychology; Religion and Philosophy; Sociology
Dist - IU **Prod** - NET 1967

R C Gorman 20 MIN
U-matic / VHS
American Indian Artists Series
Color
Profiles American Indian artist R C Gorman, a Navajo painter and printmaker.
Fine Arts; Social Science
Dist - PBS **Prod** - KAETTV

R C Gorman 29 MIN
VHS / U-matic
American Indian artist series; Pt 1
Color (G)
Examines work of artist R C Gorman, who concentrates on mass and shape, challenging the conventional Native American decorative line work representation of the human figure. Portrays Gorman working in his Taos, New Mexico studio, executing one of the suite of paintings dedicated to his favorite subject, Navajo women. Tracks his jet set existence while Gorman discusses his life and work as a Native American and as an artist.
Fine Arts; Social Science
Dist - NAMPBC **Prod** - NAMPBC 1979

R D Laing 50 MIN
VHS
Color (H C G)
$79.00 purchase
Features writer R D Laing in an interview with Anthony Clare. Addresses Laing's controversial view of psychiatry, his questioning the basis of normality in society and his efforts to understand the family's role and its influence on individual personality. Talks about his books The Divided Self; The Self and Others; and The Politics of Experience.
Health and Safety; Literature and Drama; Psychology; Sociology
Dist - ROLAND **Prod** - INCART

R D Laing's discussion with Richard Evans - dilemma of mental illness 30 MIN
U-matic / VHS / 16mm
Notable contributors to the psychology of personality series
Color (C G T A)
Shows psychiatrist R D Laing reacting to Richard Evans's question concerning the problem of classifying mental disorders, the psychosomatic quandary, and the so - called double bind family. Deals with Laing's contention that the person who becomes mentally ill may have been the tragic victim of mixed signals of love and rejection from his family.
Biography; Psychology
Dist - PSUPCR **Prod** - PSUPCR 1975

R D Laing's Glasgow 25 MIN
16mm / U-matic / VHS
Cities Series
Color (H C A)
LC 80-701288
A shortened version of the motion picture R D Laing's Glasgow. Presents psychiatrist R D Laing on a tour of the city of Glasgow.
Geography - World; Sociology
Dist - LCOA **Prod** - NIELSE 1980

R D Laing's Glasgow 51 MIN
U-matic / VHS / 16mm
Cities Series
Color (I)
LC 78-701705
Presents R D Laing, psychiatrist and poet, as he tours his native city of Glasgow, Scotland.
Geography - World; Sociology
Dist - LCOA **Prod** - NIELSE 1978

R E Buff 25 MIN
U-matic / VHS
The View from My Room is Great
Color (H C)
Presents a video portrait of artist R. E. Buff.
Fine Arts
Dist - QUEENU **Prod** - KAA 1985

R I P Harry Sparks 21 MIN
16mm / U-matic / VHS
Harry Sparks Series
Color (IND) (SPANISH)
Stresses safety precautions such as inspecting tools and tagging those which are defective before tackling electrical repair jobs.
Health and Safety; Industrial and Technical Education
Dist - IFB **Prod** - IAPA 1972

R - influenced vowels 15 MIN
U-matic / Kit / VHS
Space station readstar series
(P)
$139 purchase, $25 vowels, $75 self dub
Teaches phonics in a series designed to supplement second grade reading programs. Highlights vowels whose sounds are changed by proximity to the letter r.
English Language
Dist - GPN

R is for rice 14 MIN
16mm / U-matic / VHS
Color; Captioned (P C)
Compares rice production in the U.S., which is highly mechanized, to production in other countries of the world. Explores the importance of rice as a food and explains its nutritional value. Examines the importance of rice and the harvest throughout history and its representation in folklore and art.
Health and Safety; Literature and Drama; Social Science
Dist - HANDEL **Prod** - HANDEL 1986

R M I Stress Management Series Series
Introduction and Overview
Personal Stress Management
Stress Relief Techniques
Dist - RMIBHF

R T Gribbon - interview on campus ministry 29 MIN
VHS / U-matic
Color (A)
Features R T Gribbon as he addresses the role of higher education and how churches can help students who are entering college.
Education; Religion and Philosophy
Dist - ECUFLM **Prod** - WHSPRO 1981

R T Techniques 30 MIN
U-matic / VHS
Dealing in Discipline Series
Color (T)
Education; Psychology
Dist - GPN **Prod** - UKY 1980

R W 26 MIN
16mm / U-matic / VHS
Color (I J)
LC 83-707158
Shows how people of all ages sometimes have difficulty grappling with their real worlds. Looks at an eleven - year old boy who was advanced to high school and is unable to fit in, his mother who has self doubts about returning to work, and his father who masks his own insecurities in a blustery, go - get - 'em attitude. Shows how they confront their problems.
Education; Psychology; Sociology
Dist - BCNFL **Prod** - ATLAF 1981

R W - Real World 26 MIN
U-matic / VHS / 16mm
Color (I J) (FRENCH)
The French version of the film and videorecording R W (Real World).
Foreign Language; Literature and Drama; Psychology; Sociology
Dist - BCNFL **Prod** - ATLAF 1983

R12 update - file interface commands 100 MIN
VHS
Autocad basics series
Color (G H VOC C PRO)
$49.95 purchase _ #AVT107V-T
Describes the basics of the new features contained in the 12th release of AutoCAD. Includes lessons on the use of FILES, NEW, OPEN, SAVEAS, QSAVE, SAVETIME, REINIT, SQL EXTENSIONS, PLOT OPTIONS, SOFT LOCKS, POST SCRIPT FONTS, PSIN, SPOUT, PSFILL, RASTER, SUPPORT SAVE and REPLAY IMAGE and other commands. Introduces the concepts of the use of the new file pull down menu.
Computer Science
Dist - CAMV

R12 update - workspace commands 120 MIN
VHS
Autocad basics series
Color (G H VOC C PRO)
$49.95 purchase _ #AVT106V-T
Describes the basics of the new features contained in the 12th release of AutoCAD. Includes lessons on the use of GUI, HELP, ENTITY SELECTION, DDSELECT, GRIPS, FILTERS, LOCKED LAYERS, DDMODIFY, DIGITIZER SCALING, BPLOY, BHATCH, PSLTSCALE, CAL-MATH, CAL-GEOMETRY, and CAL-ROUTINES. Explains the default settings of each command and the options available from that point.
Computer Science
Dist - CAMV

Ra - the path of the sun god 72 MIN
VHS
Color (G)
$29.95 purchase _ #V - RPSG
Starts at the dawn of civilization, uncovers the creative process, initiations into the rites and mysteries of the temples of ancient Egypt, the births of Pharaoh and incarnations of the gods and goddesses on Earth. Follows the Pharaoh's journey into the afterlife where he is challenged at the gates of Night, his deeds examined and his heart weighed before he can become one with Orisi and Ra. Uses animation and optical effects.
Fine Arts; History - World
Dist - WHOLEL

RAAF Heritage 28 MIN
16mm
Color (J)
LC 71-713558
Presents the history of the first fifty years of the Royal Australian Air Force. Includes scenes of action in World Wars I and II, Korea and Vietnam.
Civics and Political Systems; Geography - World; History - World
Dist - AUIS **Prod** - ANAIB 1971

Raananah - a World of our own 28 MIN
16mm / U-matic / VHS
Color (H C A)
$425 purchase - 16 mm, $295 purchase - video, $55 rental
Examines the Jewish summer colony of Raananah Park in New York State. Tells about the purpose of the colony, and features interviews with the surviving original members of the colony. Directed by Marlene Booth.
Sociology
Dist - CNEMAG

Rabbeting and shaping an edge on straight stock 18 MIN
16mm
Precision wood machining - operations on a spindle shaper series
B&W
LC FIE52-46
Explains the principles of the shaper operation. Shows how to set up a machine for cutting rabbets and for shape molding, and describes the process.
Industrial and Technical Education
Dist - USNAC **Prod** - USOE 1945

Rabbi from Tarsus 88 MIN
VHS
Color (G A R)
$49.99 purchase, $10.00 rental _ #35 - 83542 - 533
Presents a dramatic portrayal of the Apostle Paul in prison at age 60. Surveys Paul's life, teaching and character.
Literature and Drama; Religion and Philosophy
Dist - APH **Prod** - WORD

The Rabbit - 27 11 MIN
VHS / U-matic / 16mm
Animal families series
Color (K P I)
$275.00, $225.00, $195.00 purchase _ #B568
Follows several young rabbits as they learn to adapt to their new environment. Shows how a mother rabbit treats her young offspring as they develop their special skills of speed and sensitive hearing. Explains the basic life cycle of the typical rabbit. Part of a series on animal families.
Science - Natural
Dist - BARR **Prod** - GREATT 1989

Rabbit and Foxes on Wheels 13 MIN
16mm
Color (H C A)
LC 79-700088
Describes the U S Cycling Federation Competitive Stock - Bike Program, a nationwide program involving all municipalities in an amateur competitive cycling network.
Physical Education and Recreation
Dist - MENCI **Prod** - MENCI 1979

Rabbit ears collection series
The Boy who drew cats 30 MIN
Brer Rabbit and the wonderful tar baby 30 MIN
The Emperor and the nightingale 30 MIN
The Emperor's new clothes 30 MIN
Finn McCoul 30 MIN
The Fisherman and his wife 30 MIN
How the rhinoceros got his skin - How the camel got his hump 30 MIN
Jack and the beanstalk 30 MIN
Koi and the kola nuts 30 MIN
The Legend of Sleepy Hollow 30 MIN
The Marzipan pig 30 MIN
The Monkey people 30 MIN
Paul Bunyan 30 MIN
Red riding hood - Goldilocks 30 MIN
Rumpelstiltskin 30 MIN
The Tailor of Gloucester 30 MIN
The Tale of Mr Jeremy Fisher - The Tale of Peter Rabbit 30 MIN
The Three billy goats gruff - The Three little pigs 30 MIN
Thumbelina 30 MIN
Dist - KNOWUN

Rabbit Ears series
The Gingham dog and the calico cat 30 MIN
The Night before Christmas 30 MIN
Princess Scargo and the birthday pumpkin 30 MIN
Squanto and the first Thanksgiving 30 MIN
Dist - ARTSAM

A Rabbit for Alice 15 MIN
U-matic / VHS / 16mm
Color (P I)
Presents the story of Alice, who is lonely in the new neighborhood she and her family have moved to. Tells how her father buys her a rabbit named Peter and recounts the adventures they have together.
Literature and Drama
Dist - ALTSUL **Prod** - AMITAI 1984

Rabbit Hill 53 MIN
U-matic / VHS / 16mm
Color (K P S)
LC FIA68-1761
Tells how the small animals who live on Rabbit Hill are affected by the new owners who move into the big house and plant a garden.
Literature and Drama
Dist - MGHT **Prod** - NBCTV 1968

Rabbit Hill, Pt 1 26 MIN
U-matic / VHS / 16mm
Color (K P S)
LC FIA68-1761
Tells how the small animals who live on Rabbit Hill are affected by the new owners who move into the big house and plant a garden.
Fine Arts
Dist - MGHT **Prod** - NBCTV 1968

Rabbit Hill, Pt 2 27 MIN
16mm / U-matic / VHS
Color (K P S)
LC FIA68-1761
Tells how the small animals who live on Rabbit Hill are affected by the new owners who move into the big house and plant a garden.
Fine Arts
Dist - MGHT **Prod** - NBCTV 1968

Rabbit Stew 7 MIN
16mm
Color
Presents an animated story in which a brash, fearless rabbit is pitted against a human landowner.
Fine Arts
Dist - RMIBHF **Prod** - PORTER

Rabbits 11 MIN
U-matic / VHS / 16mm
Color (K P I)
LC 75-704204
Examines the habits and behavior of rabbits. Without narration.
Science - Natural
Dist - ALTSUL **Prod** - FILMSW 1969

Rabbits and Hares 11 MIN
U-matic / VHS / 16mm
Looking at Animals Series
Color (I J H)
LC FIA67-5542
Compares and contrasts rabbits and hares and discusses the burrowing, nesting and feeding habits of each.
Science - Natural
Dist - IFB **Prod** - BHA 1966

Rabbit's moon 7 MIN
16mm
Color (G)
$12.00 rental
Relates a fable of the Unattainable - the moon. Combines elements of commedia dell'arte with Japanese myth.
Fine Arts; Literature and Drama; Religion and Philosophy
Dist - CANCIN **Prod** - ANGERK 1972

Rabi - Pt 4 60 MIN
VHS
Developing stories series
Color (H C G)

$150.00 purchase, $75.00 rental
Documents the effects of the dislocated relationship of humans with the natural world. Uses traditional African storytelling techniques to present a modern day fable in which Rabi, a young boy in Burkina Faso, acquires a pet tortoise. The boy's fascination with nature manifests itself in turning his pet on its back and watching it struggle. He is heartbroken when he must set it free so he finds his own tortoise, which speaks to him so eloquently about his abuse that Rabi eventually sets it free. A film by Gaston Kabore for Cinecom Productions - BBC. Part of a six - part series highlighting debates of the Earth Summit.
Civics and Political Systems; Fine Arts; Geography - World; Literature and Drama
Dist - CANCIN **Prod** - BBCTV 1994

Rabies 13 MIN
U-matic / VHS
Color
LC 83-706974
Demonstrates, through a story of a rabies incident, the actions taken to save a child's life. Portrays current ways to curtail exposure to rabies disease and to discourage its existence.
Health and Safety; Home Economics
Dist - MTP **Prod** - AMVMA 1983

Rabies Can be Controlled 20 MIN
16mm
Color
Emphasizes the importance of protecting dogs against rabies by means of vaccination. Shows clinical cases of rabies in both humans and dogs and demonstrates methods of producing rabies vaccine for dogs as well as its use in mass vaccination programs.
Health and Safety; Science
Dist - LEDR **Prod** - ACYLLD 1954

Rabies Control in the Community 11 MIN
16mm
B&W
LC FIE56-141
Shows actual cases of rabies in both humans and dogs. Explains how the apathy of dog owners can permit rabies to become a community problem and how concerted community action can prevent rabies.
Health and Safety
Dist - USNAC **Prod** - USPHS 1956

Rabies F - a Staining 8 MIN
16mm
Color
LC 74-705466
Shows the technique of staining brain impressions with fluorescent antibody for the detection of negri bodies.
Health and Safety
Dist - USNAC **Prod** - USPHS 1966

Rabies - It's no Way for a Friend to Die 8 MIN
16mm / U-matic / VHS
Color (P I J)
Visits a veterinarian's office, some kennels, and a health clinic to witness the new painless rabies shots being administered. Shows symptoms of the disease and what preventive measures should be taken.
Health and Safety; Science; Science - Natural
Dist - BULFRG **Prod** - YNF 1985

The Rabies Threat 15 MIN
16mm
Color (J)
LC 74-703290
Deals with rabies, an animal disease which is foreign to Australia and outlines the work of the Animal Quarantine Service which functions to keep Australia free of all exotic animal diseases.
Agriculture; Health and Safety; Sociology
Dist - AUIS **Prod** - ANAIB 1974

Rabindranath Tagore 22 MIN
16mm
B&W (I)
Presents a biography of the Nobel laureate Rabindranath Tagore narrated through live shots, sketches, photographs, paintings and a dramatic impersonation of his early life. Shows the many - sided life of Gurudev Tagore as poet, painter, composer of songs and dances, educationist and patriot.
Biography
Dist - NEDINF **Prod** - INDIA

Raccoon 11 MIN
U-matic / VHS / 16mm
Color (P I J)
Describes how raccoons have good brains and nimble feet and manage to survive well in an assortment of environments, from forest den to the chimney of a suburban home.
Science - Natural
Dist - CENTEF **Prod** - CENTRO 1982

$15.00 purchase _ #110 - 039
Features Dr Ahmad Sakr, Greg Noakes and Imam Siraj Wahhaj.
Religion and Philosophy; Sociology
Dist - SOUVIS **Prod** - SOUVIS

Race and Residence - the Shaker Heights Model 30 MIN
U-matic
Color
Describes how the people of Shaker Heights, Ohio, have encouraged integration maintenance instead of resegregation.
History - United States; Sociology
Dist - HRC **Prod** - OHC

Race, ethnicity, language and religion work place issues 20 MIN
VHS
Diversity series
Color; CC (C PRO)
$425.00 purchase, $150.00 rental
Focuses on race, ethnicity, language and religion as part of the fundamental diversity issues of conflict resolution, communication styles and respecting those who are different. Features diversity experts, human resources professionals, managers and employees who outline the main messages. Part three of a four-part series with segments specifically addressing gender, sexual orientation, race, ethnicity, language, religion, age and physical ability as workplace issues. Includes facilitator's guide and handouts. Produced by Quality Media Resources.
Psychology; Social Science; Sociology
Dist - VTCENS
EXTR

Race, ethnicity, language & religion workplace issues - Pt 3 20 MIN
VHS
The diversity series
Color (PRO IND COR A)
$425.00 purchase, $150.00 rental, $50.00 preview
Profiles people pigeon-holed because of prejudice and fear. Examines resolving tensions and implementing a healthy philosophy of diversity.
Sociology
Dist - VIDART

Race for Gold 57 MIN
U-matic / VHS / 16mm
Nova Series
Color (H C A)
LC 79-701745
Discusses government - sponsored training for Olympic competitors. Considers whether training programs could help American amateur athletes, who only receive a ticket to the games and a uniform. Asks who should be responsible for the costs of new programs. Explores training methods in the United States and abroad to determine if drugs or training are responsible for the phenomenal success of certain athletes. Focuses on the possible use of anabolic steroids by competitors in the Olympic games.
Physical Education and Recreation; Psychology
Dist - TIMLIF **Prod** - WGBHTV 1979

Race for number one 54 MIN
16mm / U-matic / VHS
Jack London's tales of the Klondike series
Color (H C A)
$139.00 purchase _ #3745
Relates the spills, laughs and strange twists which occur in a Yukon dog sled race between Big Olaf and Smoke with a million dollars in gold waiting at the finish line. Based on the short story Race For Number One by Jack London.
Literature and Drama
Dist - EBEC **Prod** - NORWK 1982

Race for Number One 54 MIN
VHS / U-matic
Jack London's Tales of the Klondike Series
Color (C A)
$139.00 purchase _ #3745
Depicts a race between two men and their teams as they try to stake a single, unregistered mine claim. Characterized by humor and strange twists of fate as the two teams struggle to be the winner. Narrated by Jack London.
Literature and Drama
Dist - EBEC

The Race for the cup 60 MIN
VHS
Color (G)
$24.95 purchase
Looks at the 1988 America's Cup from the point of view of New Zealand.
Geography - World; Physical Education and Recreation
Dist - MYSTIC **Prod** - MYSTIC

Raccoon 11 MIN
U-matic / VHS / 16mm
Color (P I J)
$270, $190 purchase _ #81539
Discusses the physical characteristics and behavior of raccoons.
Science - Natural
Dist - CORF

Raccoon Story - a Menomini Indian Folktale 9 MIN
16mm / U-matic / VHS
Color (P)
LC 74-700233
Features two old blind men who live by a lake. Shows how a playful raccoon tricks the men and gets their food. Concludes with the blind men learning that if they had trusted each other the raccoon would not have been able to trick them.
Literature and Drama; Social Science
Dist - LUF **Prod** - SCHLAT 1974

Raccoons and ripe corn - 77
VHS
Reading rainbow series
Color; CC (K P)
$39.95 purchase
Draws inspiration from books by Jim Arnosky, including Deer at the Brook and Come Out, Muskrats for LeVar to learn about wildlife watching. Joins Arnosky for a day of exploration and finds out how to play detective in the wild. Part of a series offering a multicultural approach to generating reading enthusiasm with cross - curricular applications, hosted by LeVar Burton.
English Language; Literature and Drama; Science; Science - Natural
Dist - GPN **Prod** - LNMDP

The Race 14 MIN
U-matic / VHS / 16mm
Color (K P I J H C A)
Uses an inventive sound track instead of narration to show animated toys racing against each other while other toys look on and comment.
Fine Arts
Dist - IFB **Prod** - MINERV 1986

The Race 10 MIN
16mm / U-matic / VHS
Color (I J H)
LC 76-701427
Considers competitiveness and the meaning of being a winner in life with a story about a bicycle - racing champion who, holding triumph within his grasp, drops out of a race because winning suddenly becomes meaningless to him.
Guidance and Counseling; Physical Education and Recreation; Sociology
Dist - WOMBAT **Prod** - ZAGREB 1975

Race against death 15 MIN
U-matic / VHS
Book bird series
Color (I)
Tells of a true life heroic mission to bring antitoxin to a remote Alaskan village struck by diptheria. From the book by Seymour Reit.
English Language; Literature and Drama
Dist - CTI **Prod** - CTI

Race against prime time 58 MIN
VHS
Color (G)
$195.00 purchase, $75.00 rental
Goes behind the scenes of the newsrooms of three Miami network affiliates during the 1980 Liberty City riots. Reveals how the stations anointed spokespeople for the black community and invariably characterized whites as victims and blacks as rioters - although most of the dead were black, some attacked by white vigilantes. Coverage failed to place the riots within the historical context of deteriorating community - police relations and years of civic neglect. Produced by David Shulman.
Fine Arts; History - United States; Literature and Drama; Sociology
Dist - CANWRL

Race and ethnicity 30 MIN
VHS
Color (H C)
$89.95 purchase _ #TSI - 115
Shows the difference between prejudice, discrimination and racism, using historical and current examples. Explores the effects of prejudice and discrimination through the eyes of Asian, Hispanic and African American families.
Sociology
Dist - INSTRU

Race and justice in our society
VHS
Color (G)

The Race for the Cup - 1988 America's Cup 60 MIN
VHS
Color (G)
$24.95 purchase _ #0937
Documents the controversial 1988 America's Cup Race between Michael Fay and Dennis Conner. Represents the vantage point of New Zealand.
Physical Education and Recreation
Dist - SEVVID

Race for the future 21 MIN
VHS
Color (J H C G)
$195.00 purchase, $45.00 rental
Demonstrates the hope of the future with non - polluting, energy - efficient, solar and electric cars. Documents four major competitions for these cars with races run all over the US. Produced by Jim Arwood for the Energy Office of the Arizona Department of Commerce.
Fine Arts; Industrial and Technical Education; Social Science
Dist - BULFRG

Race for the Superconductor 58 MIN
U-matic / VHS
Nova Series
Color (H C A)
$250 purchase _ #5278C
Shows how superconductors generate and transmit energy. Shows the work of American and foreign physicists. Produced by WGBH Boston.
Science - Physical
Dist - CORF

Race for top quark 58 MIN
U-matic / VHS
Nova series
Color (H C A)
$250.00 purchase _ #HP - 6177C
Follows the race between physicists at the Fermilab and CERN to discover the smallest particle - the top quark. Witnesses the role of mammoth particle generators where physicists collide subatomic particles at the speed of light, measuring the resultant debris and energy. Part of the Nova series.
Science - Physical
Dist - CORF **Prod** - WGBHTV 1989

Race - gender - national origin issues - environment - 12 ; 2nd ed.
U-matic / VHS / BETA
Choices - a management training program in equal opportunity series
Color; CC; PAL (IND PRO G)
Contact distributor about price
Shows managers how to deal with racial, gender and national origin issues and the work environment. Trains both new managers and those with previous EEO training. Part of a 12 - part program providing managers with essential knowledge of EEO and enhancing their skills in in such areas as hiring, interviewing, selecting, performance appraisals and more.
Business and Economics; Guidance and Counseling
Dist - BNA **Prod** - BNA

Race - gender - national origin issues - environment - Pt 6; 2nd ed.
U-matic / VHS / BETA
Choices - a management training program in equal opportunity series
Color; CC; PAL (IND PRO G)
Contact distributor about price
Shows managers how to deal with racial, gender and national origins issues and the work environment. Trains both new managers and those with previous EEO training. Part of a 12 - part program providing managers with essential knowledge of EEO and enhancing their skills in in such areas as hiring, interviewing, selecting, performance appraisals and more.
Business and Economics; Guidance and Counseling
Dist - BNA **Prod** - BNA

Race, hatred and violence - searching for solutions 22 MIN
VHS
Color (J H C)
$169.00 purchase _ #CG - 903 - VS
Asks what caused Bensonhurst and Howard Beach to erupt into racial violence and killings. Explores the question of whether the community or individuals were to blame for the acts. Covers key events and interviews community leaders, social activists, politicians and legal and psychological experts. Produced by Fox Television Station WNYW.
History - United States; Sociology
Dist - HRMC

Race issues - promotion - Pt 4; 2nd ed.
U-matic / VHS / BETA
Choices - a management training program in equal opportunity series
Color; CC; PAL (IND PRO G)
Contact distributor about price
Shows managers how to deal with racial issues and promotion. Trains both new managers and those with previous EEO training. Part of a 12 - part program providing managers with essential knowledge of EEO and enhancing their skills in in such areas as hiring, interviewing, selecting, performance appraisals and more.
Business and Economics; Guidance and Counseling
Dist - BNA **Prod** - BNA

Race issues - selection - interview - Pt 1; 2nd ed.
U-matic / VHS / BETA
Choices - a management training program in equal opportunity series
Color; CC; PAL (IND PRO G)
Contact distributor about price
Shows how to recruit and retain the best employees without violating equal employment opportunity. Trains both new managers and those with previous EEO training. Part of a 12 - part program providing managers with essential knowledge of EEO and enhancing their skills in such areas as hiring, interviewing, selecting, performance appraisals and more.
Business and Economics; Guidance and Counseling
Dist - BNA **Prod** - BNA

Race movies - the popular art of the 1920s 20 MIN
U-matic / VHS
Color (G A)
$45.00, $95.00 purchase _ #TCA16475, #TCA16474
Reveals the contributions made by African - Americans to filmmaking during the 1920s. Focuses on the films and production companies of that era.
Fine Arts
Dist - USNAC **Prod** - SMITHS 1985

A Race of Horses 10 MIN
16mm / U-matic / VHS
Color (J H)
Shows the sport of horse racing which involves many people, such as strappers, trainers, jockeys, veterinarians and breeders. Features all of these people at work as the pace of the race and the quiet of routine are undercut.
Physical Education and Recreation
Dist - JOU **Prod** - JOU 1976

The Race of the century
VHS
Color (G)
$29.80 purchase _ #0100
Presents New York Yacht Club footage of the 1983 America's Cup.
History - United States; Physical Education and Recreation
Dist - SEVVID

The Race of the Century 46 MIN
VHS / 16mm
Color
Deals with the 1983 America's Cup races.
Physical Education and Recreation
Dist - OFFSHR **Prod** - SILVER

Race relations 15 MIN
16mm
B&W (A)
Explores today's Christian biggest problems - does the Christian attitude toward other races mean more than toleration and sympathetic understanding of national background, how and where do racial prejudice and bigotry begin and how can they be combated in the Christian home.
Religion and Philosophy; Sociology
Dist - CPH **Prod** - CPH

Race round Britain
VHS
Color (G)
$39.90 purchase _ #0407
Documents the sixth Round Britain and Ireland Race which was the stormiest sailing race on record.
Physical Education and Recreation
Dist - SEVVID

Race Symphony / Two - Penny Magic 10 MIN
16mm
B&W
Features Race Symphony, an excerpt from Hans Richter's study of a day at the races, in pre - Nazi Germany, and Two - Penny Magic, Richter's essay in rhyming images, made to advertise a picture magazine. Produced 1928 - 29.
Fine Arts
Dist - STARRC **Prod** - STARRC

Race - the world's most dangerous myth 60 MIN
VHS
Dealing with diversity series
Color (H C G)
$99.00 purchase _ #GSU - 106
Examines the concept of race from a scientific and cultural perspective. Discusses 'classifications' of race and the Racism Quotient Questionnaire. Features Dr Jerry Hirsch, Prof of Psychology, University of Illinois at Champaign. Includes studio guest Dr Bem Allen, Prof of Sociology, W Illinois U. Part of a 23 - part series hosted by Dr J Q Adams, Western Illinois University, which helps students to develop the awareness that society is strengthened by a free and unfettered expression of individuality in all its diverse manifestations.
Sociology
Dist - INSTRU

Race to Bermuda with Ted Turner
VHS
Color (G)
$35.90 purchase _ #0087
Races from Newport, Rhode Island to Bermuda with Ted Turner and his sailing crew.
Physical Education and Recreation
Dist - SEVVID

The race to breed 30 MINS.
VHS
Life in the freezer
Color; PAL (H G)
PdS65 purchase; not available in USA
Focuses on the process of reproduction among the plant and animal life of the Antarctic region. Highlights the aspects unique to this arctic environment. Third in the six - part Antarctic wildlife series, Life in the Freezer. Hosted by David Attenborough.
Science - Natural
Dist - BBCENE

Race to oblivion 28 MIN
U-matic / Kit / VHS
(J S A)
$69.95
Presents the case against nuclear war. Compiled by the Los Angeles Chapter of Physicians for Social Responsibility. Uses expert testimony by doctors, scientists and economists as well as an eyewitness account of nuclear destruction by a Hiroshima survivor. Narrated by Burt Lancaster.
Religion and Philosophy; Science - Physical; Sociology
Dist - RH

Race to oblivion 28 MIN
16mm
Color (H C A)
$245.00 purchase
Discusses nuclear war. Includes an interview with a Hiroshima survivor. A film by Physicians for Social Responsibility.
Civics and Political Systems; Sociology
Dist - CF **Prod** - PSR 1988

The Race to Perth
VHS
Color (G)
$39.90 purchase _ #0485
Tells the story of Buddy Melges the Heart of America campaign for the America's Cup. Includes footage of 12 meter racing in the snow off Chicago.
Physical Education and Recreation
Dist - SEVVID

A Race to Sell 10 MIN
U-matic
Calling Captain Consumer Series
Color (P I J)
Shows and explains a TV commercial with emphasis on the role of special effects.
Business and Economics; Home Economics
Dist - TVOTAR **Prod** - TVOTAR 1985

The Race - Trans - Am 15 MIN
16mm / U-matic / VHS
Color (J H)
LC 72-703366
Presents one of America's major series of auto racing, the Trans - Am. Builds excitingly from the arrival of the festive and excited spectators and the intense concentration of the drivers to the split - second precision of the pit crews and the sounds of the cars through high speed turns.
Industrial and Technical Education; Physical Education and Recreation
Dist - AIMS **Prod** - COUKLA 1972

A Race with Death 30 MIN
16mm
Color
LC 79-701012
Shows the work of the Maryland Institute for Emergency Medical Service Systems in Baltimore in combating trauma, the leading killer of people under 40. Follows several victims from rescue in police helicopters through

the trauma emergency rooms and postoperative critical care.
Health and Safety; Sociology
Dist - WJLATV **Prod** - WJLATV 1978

Race with Time - Pt 2 59 MIN
VHS
Saudi Arabia Series
Color (S)
$49.00 purchase _ #315 - 9002
Interweaves historical information with current footage of Arabian life, from the nomadic Bedouins to modern cities in this in - depth political, economic and cultural look at Saudi Arabia. Part 2 of three parts considers how the invasion of Western technology and culture poses a dilemma for people who want to preserve traditional Arab values.
Civics and Political Systems; Foreign Language; Geography - World; History - World; Religion and Philosophy; Social Science; Sociology
Dist - FI **Prod** - PP 1986

The Racer that Lost His Edge 30 MIN
16mm
Mulligan Stew Series
Color (I)
Tells the story of a fat race driver and his new bride who learn why a healthy diet is for champions.
Guidance and Counseling; Health and Safety; Social Science
Dist - GPN **Prod** - GPN

Racetrack 114 MIN
VHS / 16mm
Color (G)
$350.00 purchase, $150.00 rental
Profiles the Belmont Race Track, which is one of the world's leading race tracks for thoroughbred horse racing. Covers training, maintaining and racing of the horses.
Fine Arts; Physical Education and Recreation; Psychology
Dist - ZIPRAH **Prod** - WISEF

Racetrack Chaplain 25 MIN
16mm
Color
LC 79-701337
Follows Reverend Izzy Vega as he ministers to the needs of his unique congregation, the exercise boys, grooms, and stablehands on a thoroughbred racetrack. Describes special ministries and areas in which there are physical and spiritual needs.
Guidance and Counseling; Religion and Philosophy
Dist - FAMF **Prod** - FAMF 1979

Rachel 3 MIN
VHS
Color (G)
$25.00 purchase
Portrays a middle - aged man observing what appears to be traditional Jewish mourning rites for his daughter. Reveals in the last scene that she has not died, but has married in a church. Produced by The Institute for Jewish Life.
Fine Arts; Religion and Philosophy; Sociology
Dist - NCJEWF

Rachel 3 MIN
16mm
Color (I)
Uses a Jewish man who is mourning his daughter's 'death' as the hour of her church wedding approaches as the basis for discussing intermarriage.
Religion and Philosophy; Sociology
Dist - NJWB **Prod** - JEWMED 1974

Rachel - a difficult year - the death of a sibling 25 MIN
VHS
Citizen 2000 child development series
Color (H C G)
$295.00 purchase, $55.00 rental
Focuses on Rachel, daughter of Paul, a London taxi driver, and Paula. Reveals that Rachel's fourth year was traumatic. Her baby brother Stuart died suddenly at the age of seven months and his death has affected Rachel emotionally and physically. Follows her during the year as she comes to terms with her bereavement and charts her progress at a Jewish nursery school where she has learned to read before her fourth birthday. Part of a series on child development which is following a group of children over a period of 18 years - from their birth in 1982 until they become adults in the year 2000. Produced by Dove Productions for Channel 4.
Health and Safety; Psychology; Sociology
Dist - FLMLIB **Prod** - CFTV 1993

Rachel and Marla 24 MIN
U-matic / 16mm / VHS
Color (P I)
$540.00, $325.00 purchase _ #JC - 67277
Follows the growing friendship between Rachel, the new girl in school, and shy Marla, who is hiding a secret. Teaches youngsters the symptoms of physical and emotional abuse and the importance of confiding in others. Dramatizes the concepts of trust, loyalty and responsibility in realistic terms. Underscores the importance of telling a trusted adult if abuse is suspected.
Health and Safety; Sociology
Dist - CORF **Prod** - DISNEY 1990

Rachel and the stranger 82 MIN
VHS
B&W; CC (G)
$19.95 purchase _ #6127
Stars Loretta Young, William Holden and Robert Mitchum in a western about a man whose love for his wife is first arouses when a stranger played by Mitchum visits their home. Costars Sara Haden. Directed by Norman Foster.
Fine Arts; Literature and Drama
Dist - APRESS

Rachel at School 11 MIN
16mm
Exploring Childhood Series
B&W (J)
LC 76-701895
Shows Rachel and two of her friends engaged in a mild clash over who is to be included in their small group. Shows how the three solve their problem with little adult intervention.
Guidance and Counseling; Psychology; Sociology
Dist - EDC **Prod** - EDC 1975

Rachel Blau DuPlessis - 11 - 8 - 86 49 MIN
VHS / Cassette
Poetry Center reading series
Color (G)
$15.00, $45.00 purchase, $15.00 rental _ #723 - 581
Features the writer reading from Draft No 1 - It; Afterimage; Draft No 2 - She; and Writing, which is read with other writers at the Poetry Center, San Francisco State University, with an introduction by Frances Phillips.
Literature and Drama
Dist - POETRY

Rachel Blau DuPlessis - 11 - 9 - 86 63 MIN
VHS / Cassette
Poetry Center reading series
Color (G)
$15.00, $45.00 purchase, $15.00 rental _ #724 - 582
Features the writer presenting a talk entitled The Familiar Becomes the Extreme at the George Oppen Memorial Lecture at the Poetry Center, San Francisco State University, with an introduction by Frances Phillips.
Literature and Drama
Dist - POETRY

Rachel Blau DuPlessis - 5 - 6 - 82 100 MIN
VHS / Cassette
Poetry Center reading series
Color (G)
$15.00, $45.00 purchase, $15.00 rental _ #492 - 416
Features the writer reading her essay entitled Rewriting the Myth, discussing her process of writing pertaining to myth and talking about deconstructing culture through language at the Poetry Center, San Francisco State University.
Literature and Drama
Dist - POETRY

Rachel Blau DuPlessis - 5 - 10 - 80 60 MIN
VHS / Cassette
Poetry Center reading series
Color (G)
$15.00, $45.00 purchase, $15.00 rental _ #393 - 328
Features the writer participating in the Women Writers Union reading on the workplace and reading a section from her essay on H D and Family, Sexes, Psyche, along with poems, at the Poetry Center, San Francisco State University, with an introduction by Tom Mandel.
Literature and Drama; Sociology
Dist - POETRY

Rachel Runs for Office 26 MIN
U-matic / VHS / 16mm
Color (I J)
Describes the differing campaign strategies of Rachel Hewitt and Billy Martin, opposing candidates in a school election. Shows how Rachel refuses to use personal information against Billy.
Literature and Drama; Psychology; Sociology
Dist - BCNFL **Prod** - PLAYTM 1985

Racial Relationships 29 MIN
16mm
We're Number One Series
Color
LC 79-701398
Features representatives of groups who have suffered discrimination. Looks at the problem of racial discrimination from a Christian perspective.
Religion and Philosophy; Sociology
Dist - AMERLC **Prod** - AMERLC 1979

Racine - Phedre 110 MIN
U-matic / VHS
Color (C) (FRENCH)
$399.00, $249.00 purchase _ #AD - 1697
Presents 'Phedre' by Racine in French.
Foreign Language; History - World; Literature and Drama; Sociology
Dist - FOTH **Prod** - FOTH

Racing 1981
16mm
B&W; Silent (C)
$100.00
Experimental film Stuart Sherman.
Fine Arts
Dist - AFA **Prod** - AFA 1981

Racing Cars 7 MIN
16mm
Exploring Childhood Series
Color (J)
LC 76-701896
Shows five - year - old Enroue painting cars on an easel for the first time, although he has drawn cars with pencils, crayons or magic markers on horizontal surfaces. Illustrates his ability to conceive and follow a plan and to improvise when the plan runs into problems.
Education; Psychology
Dist - EDC **Prod** - EDC 1974

Racing for the moon - America's glory days in space 60 MIN
VHS
Color (I J H)
$24.98 purchase _ #MP1714
Tells about the United States' race into space, from the shock of Sputnik to John Glenn's first flight into the Earth's orbit, to Neil Armstrong's first steps on the surface of the moon.
History - World; Science - Physical
Dist - KNOWUN **Prod** - ABCNEW

Racing on Thin Air 30 MIN
Videoreel / VT2
Synergism - the Challenge of Sports Series
B&W
Relates the external challenge of Pikes Peak through its history and excitement of the Pikes Peak Auto Hill Climb. Interviews the winners of the 1966 race.
Physical Education and Recreation
Dist - PBS **Prod** - KRMATV

Racing Revolution 22 MIN
16mm
Color (I J H)
LC 72-702855
A documentary account of the development and use of gas turbine engines in vehicles. Includes the controversy over the use of turbine engines in automobile racing which resulted in barring turbine engines in competition at the Indianapolis Motor Speedway.
Industrial and Technical Education
Dist - STP **Prod** - STP 1968

Racing rules made easy 51 MIN
VHS
Color (G A)
$39.95 purchase _ #0947
Overviews the current sailboat racing rules of the United States Yacht Racing Union. Features Steve Colgate as host.
Physical Education and Recreation
Dist - SEVVID **Prod** - OFFSHR

Racing the winds of paradise
VHS
Color (G)
$29.80 purchase _ #0780
Documents the 1988 Kenwood Cup Series. Includes boat racing footage. Features Gary Jobson as host.
Physical Education and Recreation
Dist - SEVVID

Racing to win with Gary Jobson
VHS
Color (G A)
$49.80 purchase _ #0903
Uses computer animation and live action to teach racing strategies in sailboating. Covers starting, windward and downwind tactics. Features Gary Jobson. Also entitled Gary Jobson's Winner's Edge.
Physical Education and Recreation
Dist - SEVVID

Racing Tradition 14 MIN
16mm
Color
Features the Hialeah Park Racetrack in Florida.
Geography - United States; Physical Education and Recreation
Dist - FLADC **Prod** - FLADC

Racing under sail
VHS
Color (G)
$19.90 purchase _ #0246
Examines the racing capabilities of Maxiboats, 12 meters, multihulls, lasers, sailboards and IOR boats.
Physical Education and Recreation
Dist - SEVVID

Racism 50 MIN
U-matic
CTV Reports Series
Color; Mono (J H C A)
$350.00 purchase, $50.00 rental
Gives an account of the race problems around the world and tries to discover the cause and some possible solutions for the future.
Sociology
Dist - CTV **Prod** - CTV 1977

Racism 101 58 MIN
VHS
Frontline Series
Color; Captioned (G)
$300.00 purchase, $95.00 rental _ #FRON - 612K
Uses a racial confrontation at the University of Michigan to show how racism and violence appear to be increasingly common on college campuses.
Sociology
Dist - PBS **Prod** - DOCCON 1988

Racism 101 57 MIN
VHS
Color (H C G)
$300.00 purchase _ #PHC - 638
Visits college campuses marred by racial unrest. Interviews students of various ethnic backgrounds to explore why racism and bigotry persist.
Education; Sociology
Dist - ADL **Prod** - PBS 1991

Racism - cross colors 14 MIN
VHS
Color (J H)
$79.95 purchase _ #10226VG
Interviews teens from a variety of places around the United States about racism, race relations, prejudice, stereotyping, and hatred. Shows scenes from a KKK demonstration and a riot to illustrate ignorance, fear and media influence on racism. Includes a leader's guide and blackline masters.
Guidance and Counseling; Sociology
Dist - UNL

Racism - How Pervasive is it 30 MIN
VHS / U-matic
Afro - American Perspectives Series
Color (C)
Discusses the pervasiveness of racism in America.
History - United States
Dist - MDCPB **Prod** - MDDE

Racism in advertising - from Frito Bandito to Power - Master 13 MIN
VHS
Color (J H C)
$99.00 purchase _ #UMC-2
Reviews the historical neglect and mistreatment of people of color in advertising. Examines current improvements and the need for more progress. Offers basic information about racial and ethnic consumers and suggestions to generate more inclusive advertising and more interest and product loyalty in these rapidly increasing markets. Shows how the acknowledgement of the increasingly multicultural society of the United States can lead to exciting, creative possibilities - and better service to clients.
Business and Economics; Sociology
Dist - INSTRU **Prod** - UMCOM

Racism in America 26 MIN
U-matic / VHS
Color (G)
$249.00, $149.00 purchase _ #AD - 1919
Examines the resurgence of racially motivated violence and vandalism. Considers the reasons people vent anger against minorities, the social and economic implications of racist acts, and how a community successfully responded to its racial problems.
Sociology
Dist - FOTH **Prod** - FOTH

Racism in news 24 MIN
VHS
Color (J H C)
$99.00 purchase _ #UMC - 1
Explores the often overlooked or unrecognized level of racism in United States news organizations. Examines the causes and effects of such racism and presents recommendations for overcoming the attitudes and hiring practices that sustain it.
Sociology
Dist - INSTRU **Prod** - UMCOM

Racism in theory and practice 60 MIN
VHS
Europe and America in the modern age - 1776 to the present series
Color (H C PRO)
$95.00 purchase
Presents a lecture by James Sheehan. Focuses on a critical period in European and American history and on leaders of the time. Part of a 20 - part series that looks at the last two centuries in Europe and America. Series presents lectures by David M Kennedy and James Sheehan of Stanford University on such figures as Adam Smith, Marx, Lincoln, Washington, Jefferson, Freud, Margaret Sanger, Susan B Anthony and Jane Adams and their impact on the events of their day. For history resource material and continuing education courses.
Civics and Political Systems; History - United States; History - World; Sociology
Dist - LANDMK

Rack and Pinion Power Steering Gears and Pumps 25 MIN
U-matic / VHS
Color
Covers the operation, diagnosis and repair of rack and pinion steering systems used on Ford and other domestic vehicles. Describes use of special tools.
Industrial and Technical Education
Dist - FORDSP **Prod** - FORDSP

Racquetball 15 MIN
16mm
Color (I)
LC 82-700550
Looks at advanced racquetball. Uses voice - over commentaries by players Mike Yellen and Lindsay Myers to accompany scenes of their intense concentration during warm - up exercises and a game. Shows the manufacture of racquets and balls.
Physical Education and Recreation
Dist - DIRECT **Prod** - MERPI 1981

Racquetball fundamentals 11 MIN
U-matic / VHS / 16mm
Color (J)
LC 81-700759
Discusses the basic concepts of the sport of racquetball. Covers such topics as the ball, the racquet, the court, the basic grip, playing strokes, service and strategies.
Physical Education and Recreation
Dist - AIMS **Prod** - ASSOCF 1980

Racquetball - moving fast 15 MIN
16mm / U-matic / VHS
Color (J)
LC 78-701685
Explains the rules for playing racquetball and provides step - by - step instruction in the basic skills of the game. Demonstrates strokes, serves and returns, illustrating the strategic function of each.
Physical Education and Recreation
Dist - PHENIX **Prod** - CREEDM 1978

Racquetball Series no 3
Racquetball Serves and Serve Returns 10 MIN
Dist - ATHI

Racquetball Series no 4
Strategy for Singles, Doubles, Cut - Throat 10 MIN
Dist - ATHI

Racquetball series
Fundamentals of racquetball 10 MIN
Dist - ATHI

Racquetball Serves and Serve Returns 10 MIN
VHS / 16mm / U-matic
Racquetball Series no 3
Color (I)
LC 79-700791
Focuses on racquetball serves and serve returns.
Physical Education and Recreation
Dist - ATHI **Prod** - ATHI 1979

Racquetball - sports teaching video 25 MIN
VHS
Color (J H A)
$29.95 purchase _ #HSV8805V
Features professional racquetball player Al Chassard in an introduction to the sport. Covers subjects including proper racquet grip, forehand and backhand strokes, serving, and strategies for different on - court situations.
Physical Education and Recreation
Dist - CAMV

Racquetball with Dave Peck 60 MIN
VHS / BETA
Color
Offers neuro - muscular programming, using Dave Peck as the model for perfecting racquetball skills. Comes with four audiocassettes and personal training guide.
Physical Education and Recreation; Psychology
Dist - SYBVIS **Prod** - SYBVIS

Radar Contact 28 MIN
U-matic / VHS
Color (A)
Shows how radar operates, its capabilities and limitations, and cautions that radar does not replace pilot responsibility.
Industrial and Technical Education
Dist - AVIMA **Prod** - FAAFL

Radar eyes the weather - analysis of severe weather - Pt B 21 MIN
16mm
B&W
LC FIE61-200
Explains the necessary use of weather data from other sources in addition to radar scope readings when the approach of severe weather seems imminent. Shows how the meteorologist must be alert for areas of deception.
Civics and Political Systems; Industrial and Technical Education; Science - Physical
Dist - USNAC **Prod** - USAF 1961

Radar Eyes the weather - fundamentals of radar meteorology - Pt A 25 MIN
16mm
B&W
LC FIE61-199
Discusses the basic principles of radar meteorology. Explains reflectivity and factors affecting it, such as hydrometers and precipitation attentuation. Shows various types of clouds and describes their characteristics.
Science - Physical
Dist - USNAC **Prod** - USAF 1961

Radar men from the moon - Commando Cody, sky marshal of the universe 192 MIN
35mm
Republic cliffhanger serials series
B&W (G)
Features Commando Cody flying to the moon and discovering a hidden city. Offers 12 episodes, 16 minutes each. Contact distributor for rental price.
Fine Arts
Dist - KITPAR **Prod** - REP 1952

Radar navigation and collision avoidance
VHS
Color (G A)
$69.95 purchase _ #0472
Presents a home - study course and guide to radar observing techniques for the pleasure boat skipper and light commercial vessel captain.
Physical Education and Recreation
Dist - SEVVID

Radar Refraction and Weather - the Radar Weather Problem 15 MIN
16mm
Color
LC FIE56-361
Explains how weather information is used at three different levels - operational radar site, division or sector control center and staff level for planning purposes. Emphasizes the importance of teamwork at each level with the weather station.
Civics and Political Systems; Industrial and Technical Education; Science - Physical; Social Science
Dist - USNAC **Prod** - USAF 1956

Radar Set an - PPS - 5 - Operation and Manpacking 25 MIN
16mm
Color
LC 74-705467
Shows components, assembly and replacement of the set. Tells how it is operated to detect, locate and identify moving targets through visual and aural radar signals. Shows disassembly and manpacking the equipment for movement to the next surveillance site.
Industrial and Technical Education
Dist - USNAC **Prod** - USA 1968

Radar - Visions from space 27 MIN
VHS / U-matic
Color (J H)
$275.00, $325.00 purchase, $50.00 rental
Explains how developments in radar, since its beginnings in England in the 1930s, have heightened scientists' knowledge of climate patterns, geology and the environment. Looks at three - dimensional radar images of the globe and the planetary system.
Business and Economics; Science - Physical
Dist - NDIM **Prod** - CANBC 1990

Radha's Day - Hindu Family Life 17 MIN
16mm
Hindu Religion Series no 5; No 5
Color (H C)

LC 77-712494
Shows a Hindu girl in her late teens during a typical day doing such things as getting up, decorating the threshold, putting on her make - up and jewelry, shopping, cooking and performing other typical middle - class activities.
Geography - World
Dist - SYRCU **Prod** - SMTHHD 1969

Radial Arm and Band Saw Safety
VHS / 35mm strip
Wood Safety Series
Color
$28.00 purchase _ #TX1B5 filmstrip, $58.00 purchase _ #TX1B5V VHS
Teaches radial arm and band saw safety and use.
Health and Safety; Industrial and Technical Education
Dist - CAREER **Prod** - CAREER

Radial Arm Saw Joinery
VHS
Video Workshops Series
$39.95 purchase _ #FW400
Shows a master craftsman demonstrating his technique for doing radial arm saw joinery.
Education; Industrial and Technical Education
Dist - CAREER **Prod** - CAREER

Radial Arm Saw Joinery with Curtis Erpelding 110 MIN
VHS / BETA
Color (H C A)
Shows how to set up and fine tune a radial arm saw as well as use is to create a host of design possibilities. Comes with a booklet.
Industrial and Technical Education
Dist - TANTON **Prod** - TANTON

Radial Arm Saw - Operation and Safety
VHS
Woodworking Power Tools Videos Series
$89.00 purchase _ #LX6102
Provides instruction on basic and advanced operational techniques for the radial arm saw. Uses close up photograpy to show how each machine performs cutting, forming, or shaping operations. Stresses safety procedures and considerations including use of each machine's safety guards.
Industrial and Technical Education
Dist - CAREER **Prod** - CAREER

Radial Artery Cannulation 7 MIN
VHS / U-matic
Color (PRO)
Reviews pertinent anatomy and essential equipment. Presents step - by - step analysis of cannulation procedure on a critically ill patient.
Health and Safety; Psychology; Science - Natural
Dist - UWASH **Prod** - UWASH

Radial Drill no 1 - Familiarization and Basic Drill Operations 22 MIN
BETA / VHS
Machine Shop - Drill Press, Radial Drill, Drill Grinder Series
Color (IND)
Discusses methods of mounting work and drills, machine functions and controls. Explains the procedure for positioning the drill for spotting and drilling through and blind holes.
Industrial and Technical Education; Psychology
Dist - RMIBHF **Prod** - RMIBHF

Radial Drill no 2 - Production, Drilling, Reaming and Tapping 22 MIN
BETA / VHS
Machine Shop - Drill Press, Radial Drill, Drill Grinder Series
Color (IND)
Explains methods of locating and drilling a series of holes with emphasis on speed and accuracy. Includes reaming and tapping techniques.
Industrial and Technical Education; Psychology
Dist - RMIBHF **Prod** - RMIBHF

Radial keratotomy 11 MIN
VHS
Color (G PRO C)
$150.00 purchase _ #EY - 17
Covers all aspects of the surgical procedure, radial keratotomy. Includes the criteria for identifying the best candidates for RK surgery, operative risks and complications. Includes on - camera patient interviews.
Health and Safety; Science - Natural
Dist - MIFE **Prod** - MIFE

Radial Line - 180 Degree Shortcut Method 12 MIN
VHS / BETA
Metal Fabrication - Round Tapers Series
Color (IND)
Industrial and Technical Education; Psychology
Dist - RMIBHF **Prod** - RMIBHF

Radial Line Theory for Cone or Frustrum of Cone - Parallel Openings 20 MIN
VHS / BETA
Metal Fabrication - Round Tapers Series
Color (IND)
Industrial and Technical Education; Psychology
Dist - RMIBHF **Prod** - RMIBHF

Radiance - the Experience of Light 21 MIN
U-matic / VHS
Color
Relates the insight felt by Dorothy Fadiman after her 'experience of light'.
Religion and Philosophy
Dist - HP **Prod** - HP

Radiance - the Experience of light 22 MIN
16mm / U-matic / VHS
Color (I)
LC 78-701047
Uses nature photography, religious art, video images and kinetic mandalas to provide a visual illustration of the experience of inner light, a recurrent theme in religious and spiritual trends throughout the world.
Fine Arts; Industrial and Technical Education; Religion and Philosophy
Dist - PFP **Prod** - FADMND 1978

Radiant Energy - more than Meets the Eye 17 MIN
16mm / VHS
Color (I J H)
LC 79-700077
Gives an overview of visible light as a source of radiant energy within the electromagnetic spectrum. Examines various aspects of radiant energy, including its major forms, and tells how the relationship between wavelengths and frequency of light waves determines their color and how the reflection of light affects people's ability to see objects.
Science - Physical
Dist - MIS **Prod** - MIS 1978

Radiation 36 MIN
U-matic / Kit / 35mm strip / VHS
Time Space and Spirit
Color (J H)
$82 two color sound filmstrips _ #C537 - 81126 - 5N, one videocassette,
Investigates radiation. The first part covers the history of scientific discovery in the 19th and 20th centuries. The second part present information about radiation, focusing on its pros and cons.
Health and Safety; Science - Physical
Dist - RH

Radiation 5 MIN
16mm
B&W (G)
$10.00 rental
Leaves the door open for many interpretations including exploding orgasms or marching soldiers.
Fine Arts
Dist - CANCIN **Prod** - WHITJL 1977

Radiation 36 MIN
VHS
Color; CC (H C)
$129.00 purchase _ #114
Presents two parts about radiation. Shows how scientists such as Newton, Young, Maxwell, Becquerel and Curie discovered the basic facts about radiation in How Radiation was Discovered. Discusses the differences between radiation that is ionizing and radiation that is not in Radiation and You. Compares electromagnetic and nuclear radiation. Covers the concepts of electromagnetic spectrum; light as particle and as wave; wavelength; frequency; x rays; alpha and beta particles; gamma rays; radioactive isotopes; fission; fusion; rems; ozone; and cosmic rays. Includes a book of the same title from the Learning Power series.
Health and Safety; Science - Physical
Dist - HAWHIL **Prod** - HAWHIL 1994

Radiation 10 MIN
16mm
Color (G)
$25.00 rental
Couples a brief narrative introduction concerning the microwave irradiation of small animals with single - framed sequences combined with the rock group Damaged Life's soundtrack.
Fine Arts
Dist - CANCIN **Prod** - SONDHE 1988

Radiation accident patients 17 MIN
16mm
Color (J H A)
LC 76-703890
Describes how workers suffering from radioactive contamination can be effectively and safely treated within existing medical facilities. Presents techniques for proper handling of radiation accident patients, shows how to use simple detection instruments and discusses radiation injury aspects of first aid.
Health and Safety; Science - Physical; Social Science; Sociology
Dist - USNAC **Prod** - USNRC 1969

Radiation and environment 25 MIN
VHS
Color (I J H)
$120.00 purchase _ #A1VH 6669
Introduces Alpha particles, protons, neutrons, electron, cosmic rays and X - rays. Covers the origins, characteristics, uses and dangers of radiation. Provides a solid understanding of ratiation concepts essential to informed decisions on energy, health and environmental issues.
Health and Safety; Science - Natural; Science - Physical
Dist - CLRVUE **Prod** - CLRVUE

Radiation and matter 44 MIN
U-matic
Understanding the atom - 1970s - series; 02
B&W
Presents a lecture - demonstration by Dr Ralph T Overman considering the interaction of radiation with matter and the development of various processes by which alpha, beta and gamma radiation give up energy to their surroundings.
Science - Physical
Dist - USNAC **Prod** - USNRC 1972

Radiation and you 21 MIN
VHS
Color; CC (H C)
$79.00 purchase _ #914
Reveals that the world is made up of atoms and that it is powered by radiation. Helps students to understand electromagnetic and nuclear radiation, ionizing radiation and the effects of radiation on human health. Part 2 of the program Radiation. Includes a book of the same title from the Learning Power series.
Health and Safety; Science - Physical
Dist - HAWHIL **Prod** - HAWHIL 1994

Radiation and Your Environment 25 MIN
VHS
(PRO A C H)
$163.00 purchase
Introduces readioactive emissions, their origins, characteristics, uses and dangers. Gives information on radiation in relation to energy, health, and environmental issues.
Science - Physical
Dist - EAV **Prod** - EAV 1987

Radiation and Your Environment 25 MIN
U-matic / VHS
Color
Introduces radioactive emissions. Provides an understanding of radiation concepts essential to informed decisions on related energy, health and environmental issues. Includes ten review questions at the end of the program.
Science - Natural; Science - Physical
Dist - EDMEC **Prod** - EDMEC

Radiation and your environment 30 MIN
U-matic / VHS / BETA
Color (T)
$39.95 purchase _ #5402
Illustrates the use of radiation detection devices in detecting radiation present in the environment. Discusses different types of radiation in up - to - date terms. Discusses and illustrates some of the problems involved in handling radioactive materials. Part of a series teaching teachers of junior high students and up how to teach chemistry. Covers important concepts, assists substitute teachers.
Health and Safety; Science - Physical
Dist - INSTRU

Radiation - Boon and Bane 17 MIN
U-matic / VHS
Too Hot to Handle Series
Color (C)
$249.00, $149.00 purchase _ #AD - 1553
Discloses that Roentgen discovered the X - ray in 1895 and that it soon became a circus attraction. Reveals that X - rays were used to treat ringworm in children, bathwater, corsets, luminous watch dials, pick - me - up tonics and children's feet were irradiated, and no one knows how many deaths resulted. Looks at the work of Ernest Rutherford, Einstein's equation, the chain reaction in fission and the Manhatten Project. Part of a series on radioactivity.
Health and Safety; Industrial and Technical Education; Social Science; Sociology
Dist - FOTH **Prod** - FOTH

Radiation - Can We Control it? (Safety Precautions) 15 MIN
U-matic / VHS

Story of Radiation Series
Color (H C A)
Tells how many occupations involve exposure to potentially harmful radiation. Notes that advisory bodies and regulatory commissions have established safety standards and procedures.
Health and Safety; Science - Natural; Science - Physical
Dist - EDMI **Prod** - EDMI 1981

Radiation - can we use it - risks vs benefits 15 MIN
U-matic / VHS
Story of radiation series
Color (H C A)
Gives examples to help define what is meant by 'risk' and 'benefit.' Tells how risk factor is quantifiable to some extent, but often remains subjective. Notes that attempts are being made to analyze radiation effects to provide a sound basis for legislative control.
Science - Natural; Science - Physical
Dist - EDMI **Prod** - EDMI 1981

Radiation Carcinogenesis 59 MIN
U-matic
Color
Discusses radiation - related malignancies resulting from the Hiroshima and Nagasaki bombings.
Health and Safety
Dist - UTEXSC **Prod** - UTEXSC

Radiation Damage in Solids 30 MIN
16mm
B&W (C A)
LC 74-700176
Develops an understanding of the nature of solids using the simple atomic theory of matter. Discusses the use of radiation to investigate the properties of solids. Presents an experiment in which a sodium chloride is bombarded with three billionths of a second pulse of 600 kilovolt electrons.
Science; Science - Physical
Dist - UNL **Prod** - UNL 1969

Radiation detection by ionization 30 MIN
U-matic
Understanding the atom - 1980s - series; 03
B&W
LC 80-706619
Presents a lecture - demonstration by Dr Ralph T Overman describing basic principles of ionization detectors. Gives brief descriptions of ionization chambers, proportional counters and Geiger counters. Discusses the resolving tome of a counter, as well as the various components of practical instruments, including amplifiers and scalers.
Science; Science - Physical
Dist - USNAC **Prod** - USNRC 1980

Radiation detection by scintillation 30 MIN
U-matic
Understanding the atom - 1980s - series; 04
B&W
LC 80-706615
Presents a lecture - demonstration by Dr Ralph T Overman reviewing gamma interaction with matter. Describes the scintillation process and the efficiency of the conversion of gamma radiation to visible light by the scintillator. Describes the operation of a photomultiplier tube, the principles behind a pulse - height analyzer and the use of solid - state radiation detectors.
Science; Science - Physical
Dist - USNAC **Prod** - USNRC 1980

Radiation - does it affect us - human effects 15 MIN
U-matic / VHS
Story of radiation series
Color (H C A)
Shows how humans are exposed to approximately 100 millirads per year from both background of radiation and man - made radiation. Notes how knowledge of human effects is based on cases of severe exposure and that effects of small doses are still difficult to measure.
Science - Natural; Science - Physical
Dist - EDMI **Prod** - EDMI 1981

Radiation - fact or fiction 30 MIN
VHS
Bodymatters series
Color (H C A)
PdS65 purchase
Explains the effects of radiation on the body. Part of a series of 26 30-minute videos on various systems of the human body.
Health and Safety; Science - Natural
Dist - BBCENE

Radiation hazards 15 MIN
VHS
Chemical hazards identification and training
Color (IND) (SPANISH)
$395.00 purchase, $100.00 rental _ #8297
Distinguishes between several sources and types of radiation and discusses their potential for harm. Stresses proper labeling and storage techniques as well as the use of protective clothing and equipment, emergency and disposal procedures. Explains and complies with 'Right - to Know' laws protecting employees who work with or around hazardous chemicals. Enhances worker understanding of the need to be informed about hazardous materials. Part of a six - part series that helps companies comply with federal - OSHA - and state Right - to - Know laws ensuring safe work environments for employees, and introduces the Material Safety Data Sheet - MSDS - chemical reference guide.
Health and Safety; Sociology
Dist - AIMS **Prod** - MARCOM 1991

Radiation - Impact on Life 23 MIN
16mm / U-matic / VHS
Color (H C A)
LC 82-700654
Presents three experts who explain the most important physical and biological concepts regarding radiation, including stable and unstable elements, ionizing radiation, the half - life of radioactive materials, how radiation affects DNA and how its levels can be concentrated in the food chain.
Health and Safety; Science - Physical
Dist - BULFRG **Prod** - PUBCOM 1982

Radiation - in Sickness and in Health 28 MIN
16mm
Color (H C A)
Studies the constructive applications of radiation, explaining what radioactivity and ionizing radiation are. Examines the use of radiation for diagnostic purposes, in which radioactive materials are injected into the patient's body.
Health and Safety; Science
Dist - FI **Prod** - CANBC

Radiation - is it safe - interpretation of dose 15 MIN
U-matic / VHS
Story of radiation series
Color (H C A)
Tells how government committees try to assess results of low - level radiation on health, genetic inheritance and the unborn fetus. Notes how study of Hiroshima victims helped our knowledge of injuries resulting from radiation exposure. Explains how maximum doses are established.
Science - Natural; Science - Physical
Dist - EDMI **Prod** - EDMI 1981

Radiation Losses 34 MIN
U-matic / VHS
Integrated Optics Series
Color (C)
Discusses the radiation losses which occur in waveguides, especially in curved waveguides. Gives examples of the techniques used to measure waveguide losses.
Science - Physical
Dist - UDEL **Prod** - UDEL

Radiation - Naturally 29 MIN
16mm
Color
LC 81-701372
Explores radiation, its sources, applications, effects, benefits and risks. Includes an historical perspective, an animated trip from space to the heart of the atom, and visits nuclear research reactors and nuclear power generating plants.
Industrial and Technical Education; Science - Physical
Dist - MTP **Prod** - AIF 1981

Radiation Processing - a New Industry 14 MIN
16mm
Color (PRO)
LC 70-714174
Provides several examples - - including radiation sterilization, chemical processing and electron beam treatment of durable - press fabrics - - of the use of radiation for industrial processing and states the reasons for the rapid increase of its use.
Business and Economics; Industrial and Technical Education; Science - Physical
Dist - USERD **Prod** - BATELL 1971

Radiation Protection 20 MIN
U-matic
Breakthrough Series
Color (H C)
Focuses on new research which has demonstrated the effectiveness of the enzyme superoxide dismutase in preventing and repairing cellular and genetic damage associated with exposure to radiation.
Science; Science - Physical
Dist - TVOTAR **Prod** - TVOTAR 1985

Radiation Protection in Nuclear Medicine 43 MIN
16mm
Color
LC FIE62-21
Demonstrates the procedures devised for naval hospitals to protect against the gamma radiation emitted from materials used in radiation therapy. Shows that the principles are applicable in all hospitals.
Health and Safety; Science
Dist - SQUIBB **Prod** - USN 1961

Radiation Safety - Emergency Procedures 16 MIN
U-matic / VHS
Radiation Safety Series
Color (C A)
LC 83-706046
Contains re - enactments of a variety of laboratory accidents illustrating the basic principles for coping with emergency situations, including assist people first, monitor personnel, control area and call radiation safety.
Health and Safety; Science
Dist - IU **Prod** - IU 1982

Radiation Safety in Nuclear Energy Explorations 24 MIN
16mm
Color
LC FIE62-7
Depicts the activities of the division of radiological health of the Public Health Service, showing health programs designed for protection against radiation.
Health and Safety
Dist - USNAC **Prod** - USPHS 1962

Radiation Safety in the Laboratory 15 MIN
U-matic / VHS
Color
Shows a step by step response to a spill of radioactive material in the workplace.
Health and Safety; Science
Dist - UNKNWN

Radiation Safety - Introduction 16 MIN
VHS / U-matic
Radiation Safety Series
Color (C A)
LC 83-706044
Deals with the properties of radiation, its biololgical effects and the regulations governing the use of radioactive materials in the laboratory.
Health and Safety; Science
Dist - IU **Prod** - IU 1982

Radiation Safety - Laboratory Techniques 16 MIN
VHS / U-matic
Radiation Safety Series
Color (C A)
LC 83-706045
Describes a program for laboratory safety to be used when working with radioactive materials. Notes that such a program involves careful planning, safe working habits, routine monitoring, proper disposal of radioactive waste and utilization of radiation safety personnel.
Health and Safety; Science
Dist - IU **Prod** - IU 1982

Radiation Safety Series
Radiation Safety - Emergency Procedures 16 MIN
Radiation Safety - Introduction 16 MIN
Radiation Safety - Laboratory Techniques 16 MIN
Dist - IU

Radiation safety series
The Key to contamination detection - Part 2 21 MIN
Dist - UCALG

Radiation Safety - the Key to Contamination Control
U-matic / BETA / VHS
Color; Mono
Designed to help radiation workers work safely and efficiently with radioactive materials. Demonstrates a typical lab technique using radioactive markers, showing correct and incorrect techniques. This is repeated using black light fluorescence to show where contamination typically occurs.
Health and Safety; Science; Science - Physical
Dist - UCALG **Prod** - UCALG 1987

The Radiation Spectrum 5 MIN
U-matic
Eureka Series
Color (J)
Explains that the waves of heat energy radiated by the sun come in many forms which together make a band, or spectrum, of energy waves.
Science; Science - Physical
Dist - TVOTAR **Prod** - TVOTAR 1980

Radiation therapy - an option for early breast cancer 8 MIN
VHS
Color (G)
$250.00 purchase
Helps women to understand that radiation therapy in combination with breast - preserving surgery, offers the same rate of cure as mastectomy.
Health and Safety
Dist - LPRO **Prod** - LPRO

Radiation therapy - cancer and you 8 MIN
VHS / U-matic
Color (PRO)
$200.00 purchase, $60.00 rental _ #5286S, #5286V
Explains the uses of radiation therapy in the treatment of cancer clearly and simply. Covers internal and external therapy and combination therapy with hormones and chemotherapy. Shows discussion before treatment, the equipment used, skin markings to identify treatment area, shields and treatment schedules. Discusses skin care and side effects such as nausea.
Health and Safety
Dist - AJN **Prod** - LPRO 1989

Radiation Therapy for Cancer 25 MIN
16mm
Color (PRO)
LC 78-711414
Demonstrates the biophysical principles involved in radiation therapy dosage for cancer. Shows treatment planning and the clinical management of various cancer sites.
Health and Safety; Science
Dist - AMCS **Prod** - AMCS 1970

Radiation Therapy - Rays of Hope 15 MIN
VHS / 16mm
Color (H A PRO)
$260.00 purchase, $75.00 rental _ #9966
Explains what radiation therapy is and how it is used to kill cancer cells.
Health and Safety
Dist - AIMS **Prod** - LINEDS 1987

Radiation Waves 5 MIN
U-matic
Eureka Series
Color (J)
Explains that one of the chief ways in which heat energy moves is in the form of waves. This kind of heat transfer is called radiation.
Science; Science - Physical
Dist - TVOTAR **Prod** - TVOTAR 1980

Radiation - what does it do - inter - reaction with matter 15 MIN
U-matic / VHS
Story of radiation series
Color (H C A)
Outlines the basic idea of ionization through animation and interviews with experts, and reveals that harmful effects from radiation were discovered over the years. Explains how radiation interacts with matter and how it can be used.
Industrial and Technical Education; Science - Physical
Dist - EDMI **Prod** - EDMI 1981

Radiation - what effect does it have - biological effects 15 MIN
VHS / U-matic
Story of radiation series
Color (H C A)
Shows how differing life forms all have cells, whose characteristics are encoded in DNA, a chemical substance which may be affected by radiation. Notes how different radiation forms affect cells differently and shows radiation's role in causing leukemia.
Science - Natural; Science - Physical
Dist - EDMI **Prod** - EDMI 1981

Radiation - what is it - energy in motion 15 MIN
VHS / U-matic
Story of radiation series
Color (J)
Defines radiation as a form of energy, like sunlight, which can be natural or man - made. Shows how radiation can change living cells either harmfully or beneficially. Deals with alpha, beta, gamma and x - rays, and concludes it is up to us how we control and use radiation.
Science - Physical
Dist - EDMI **Prod** - EDMI 1981

Radiation - what is it made of - particles and waves 15 MIN
VHS / U-matic
Story of radiation series
Color (H C A)
Explains that radiation is the result of unstable atoms. Illustrates and describes gamma rays, x - rays, alpha and beta particles and neutron radiation. Notes how radiation in form of x - ray photos has been used since end of 19th century, but first self - sustaining nuclear reaction took place in 1942.
Industrial and Technical Education; Science - Physical
Dist - EDMI **Prod** - EDMI 1981

Radiation - where do we go from here - issues 15 MIN
VHS / U-matic
Story of radiation series
Color (H C A)
Notes how some interest groups are concerned about nuclear safety, disposal of radioactive waste and limitation of nuclear arms, and that many radiation questions are unresolved. Explains how Congressional committees reconcile the interests of the public, industry, science and medicine.
Science - Natural; Science - Physical
Dist - EDMI **Prod** - EDMI 1981

Radiation - where is it - measurement and detection 15 MIN
U-matic / VHS
Story of radiation series
Color (H C A)
Describes how radiation detecting instruments such as the Geiger Counter work. Examines others, too, such as scintillation detectors and personal monitoring devices.
Industrial and Technical Education; Mathematics; Science - Physical
Dist - EDMI **Prod** - EDMI 1981

Radiation work - reprocessing 29 MIN
VHS
Color (G)
$39.95 purchase
Tells the story of workers at the first United States commercial nuclear reprocessing plant in the state of New York. Reveals how the plant closed after several years in operation, leaving massive high - level and low - level dumps of radiactive materials.
History - United States; Social Science; Sociology
Dist - WMMI **Prod** - WMMI

Radical Americans series
Angry Negro 30 MIN
Dist - IU

Radical and quadratic equations 30 MIN
VHS
Intermediate algebra series
Color (H)
$125.00 purchase _ #M51
Explains radical and quadratic equations. Features Elayn Gay. Part of a 27 - part series on intermediate algebra.
Mathematics
Dist - LANDMK **Prod** - MGHT

Radical applications and applications
VHS
Beginning algebra series
Color (J H)
$125.00 purchase _ #2026
Teaches basic concepts of applying radical expressions to solve problems. Part of a 31 - video series, each part between 25 and 30 minutes long, that explains and reinforces fundamental concepts of beginning algebra. Uses definitions, theorems, examples and step - by - step solutions to instruct the student.
Mathematics
Dist - LANDMK

Radical equations
VHS
Intermediate algebra series
Color (J H)
$125.00 purchase _ #3023
Teaches basic concepts involved in solving radical equations. Part of a 31 - video series, each part 25 to 30 minutes long, that explains and reinforces concepts in intermediate algebra. Uses definitions, theorems, examples and step - by - step solutions to tutor the student. Videos also available in a set.
Mathematics
Dist - LANDMK

Radical Equations 30 MIN
VHS
Mathematics Series
Color (J)
LC 90713155
Explains radical equations. 54th of 157 installments of the Mathematics Series.
Mathematics
Dist - GPN

Radical Expressions 30 MIN
VHS
Mathematics Series
Color (J)
LC 90713155
Describes radical expressions. The 65th of 157 installments of the Mathematics Series.
Mathematics
Dist - GPN

Radical expressions 30 MIN
VHS
College algebra series
Color (C)
$125.00 purchase _ #4003
Explains radical expressions. Part of a 31 - part series on college algebra.
Mathematics
Dist - LANDMK **Prod** - LANDMK

Radical Hysterectomy Following Central Irradiation for Carcinoma of the Cervix 29 MIN
16mm
Color (PRO)
Gives a resume of the method used in the central irradiation. Depicts the details of the lymph node dissection, emphasizing the removal of the obturator group with reference to the prevention of troublesome bleeding.
Health and Safety; Science
Dist - ACY **Prod** - ACYDGD 1962

Radical Mastectomy 23 MIN
16mm
Color (PRO)
Deals with policy in the treatment of primary carcinoma of the breast. Illustrates briefly the place of mammography and details the technical operation of the conventional radical mastectomy.
Health and Safety; Science
Dist - ACY **Prod** - ACYDGD 1965

Radical Mastectomy 27 MIN
VHS / U-matic
Breast Series
Color
Health and Safety; Science - Natural
Dist - SVL **Prod** - SVL

Radical Mastectomy for Carcinoma of the Breast 26 MIN
16mm
Color
Depicts the technique of doing a biopsy in carcinoma of the breast and methods that decrease the likelihood of dissemination by biopsy. Shows the technique of radical mastectomy and excision of an internal mammary lymph node for biopsy.
Health and Safety; Science
Dist - ACY **Prod** - ACYDGD 1956

Radical Neck Dissection and Epiglottidectomy 36 MIN
U-matic / VHS
Head and Neck Series
Color
Health and Safety; Science - Natural
Dist - SVL **Prod** - SVL

Radical Operation for Carcinoma of the Vulva during Pregnancy 15 MIN
16mm
Color
LC 75-702325
Describes the treatment of a patient who was found to have invasive carcinoma of the vulva in the 24th week of pregnancy. Explains that she was treated with radical vulvectomy and bilateral groin lymphadenectomy at this stage in pregnancy and at the 38th week of pregnancy a Cesarean hysterectomy with bilateral pelvic lymphadenectomy was performed. Discusses the use of lymphography in the mangement of this patient.
Health and Safety; Science
Dist - EATONL **Prod** - EATONL 1967

Radical Pneumonectomy for Carcinoma of Lung 33 MIN
16mm
Color (PRO)
Explains that radical pneumonectomy, as described by Brock and others, follows accepted principles of cancer surgery, and makes even extensive tumor resectable with an accepted mortality. Depicts the technique for this procedure.
Health and Safety; Science
Dist - ACY **Prod** - ACYDGD 1969

The Radical Reformer 29 MIN
U-matic
Dickens World Series
Color
Looks at Charles Dickens as the radical defender of the poor and attacker of the law, church and schools.
Literature and Drama
Dist - UMITV **Prod** - UMITV 1973

Radical Resection of the Ischial Tuberosity 15 MIN
16mm
Color

LC FIA66-59
Illustrates the technique used in radical resection of the ischial tuberosity in a 21 - year - old paraplegic with a large ulcer proved to be refractory to healing for a year. Points out that the operation does not interfere with the use of braces and hastens rehabilitation.
Health and Safety; Psychology
Dist - EATONL **Prod** - EATONL 1963

The Radical romantic 53 MIN
16mm / VHS
Color (J H C G)
$795.00, $275.00 purchase, $80.00 rental
Portrays John Weinzweig, a musician and composer who has fought for 50 years for the cause of New Music. Tells of a visionary's struggle against a conformist world. Features an inside view of the compositional process and demystifies the unfamiliar sounds of modern classical music. Throughout, Weinzweig maintains the dry and often acerbic wit that sustains his music.
Biography; Fine Arts
Dist - CANCIN **Prod** - RHOMBS 1990

Radical Skull Resection for Congenital Skull Defects 24 MIN
U-matic / VHS
Color (PRO)
Demonstrates a radical skull resection in treating an infant with premature skull base and vault suture fusion known as kleeblatt - schadel or Cloverleaf skull. Shows the three - month follow - up.
Health and Safety; Science - Natural
Dist - UARIZ **Prod** - UARIZ

Radical Therapy - Techniques for Directed Change with will Handy 49 MIN
U-matic / VHS
Color
Presents guidelines for changing reactions to individual/internal and societal/external reinforcement patterns.
Sociology
Dist - UWISC **Prod** - NOTTH 1982

Radical Vulvectomy with Posterior Exenteration for Carcinoma of the Vulva 15 MIN
16mm
Color
LC 75-702324
Shows the technique of radical vulvectomy with bilateral pelvic inguinal lymphadenectomy. Shows pre - and post - operative lymphangiograms.
Science
Dist - EATONL **Prod** - EATONL 1967

Radical Wertheim Operation 26 MIN
16mm
Color (PRO)
Depicts in detail a personal technique of radical abdominal hysterectomy and bilateral pelvic lymphadenectomy as it has evolved over the last 20 years.
Health and Safety; Science
Dist - ACY **Prod** - ACYDGD 1960

Radicals and Conservatives 29 MIN
Videoreel / VT2
Black Experience Series
Color
History - United States
Dist - PBS **Prod** - WTTWTV

Radicals and the Real Number System 29 MIN
16mm
Intermediate Algebra Series
B&W (H)
Defines the concept of irrational numbers and lists some. Explains that the real number system includes all irrational and rational numbers, but does not include radicals of negative numbers.
Mathematics
Dist - MLA **Prod** - CALVIN 1959

Radicals - square roots 30 MIN
VHS
Beginning algebra series
Color (J H)
$125.00 purchase _ #M32
Explains radicals - square roots. Features Elayn Gay. Part of a 19 - part series on beginning algebra.
Mathematics
Dist - LANDMK **Prod** - MGHT

Radio 60 MIN
16mm
Color
Takes an up - tempo look at today's large radio fad. Emphasizes the radio's message and its influence on its youthful owners. Asks such questions as 'Can you own the big box and still succeed at your career objectives'.
Fine Arts; Guidance and Counseling; Psychology; Sociology
Dist - BLKFMF **Prod** - BLKFMF

Radio 29 MIN
U-matic / VHS / 16mm
American memoir series
B&W (H C A)
Features Dr Dodds discussing how the 'Radio Era' revolutionized life. Explains that from the '20s to the early '30s, radio was emerging as the 'poor man's' entertainment and that in the '30s radio entered the realm of serious programing. Concludes that today, in the era of television, radio has lost much of its mass appeal.
Biography; History - United States; Psychology; Social Science
Dist - IU **Prod** - WTTWTV 1961

Radio adios 12 MIN
16mm
Color (G)
$30.00 rental
Examines an intensely rhythmic and precise conversational and literary language. Promotes the idea that an overabundance of useless information effectively subdues freedom of speech. Condense and survive. Produced by Henry Hills.
Fine Arts
Dist - CANCIN

Radio and Television Production 15 MIN
VHS / 16mm
(H C A)
$24.95 purchase _ #CS164
Describes the requisite skills for a career in radio and television production. Features interviews with professionals in this field.
Guidance and Counseling
Dist - RMIBHF **Prod** - RMIBHF

Radio and TV production 15 MIN
VHS
Career success series
Color (H C A)
$29.95 purchase _ #MX164
Presents an introduction to radio and television production careers. Covers the necessary skills, and interviews people in these careers on the rewards and stresses involved.
Education; Fine Arts
Dist - CAMV

Radio Antennas, Creation and Behavior of Radio Waves 12 MIN
U-matic
B&W
LC 78-706317
Explains electric and magnetic fields, generation of electromagnetic waves, behavior of radio waves in space, ground wave, reflection and refraction, the ionosphere and causes of fading.
Industrial and Technical Education; Science - Physical
Dist - USNAC **Prod** - USAF 1978

Radio Antennas - Creation and Behavior of Radio Waves 12 MIN
16mm
B&W
LC FIE52-1474
Depicts electric and magnetic fields, behavior of radio waves in space, ground waves, reflection and refraction and the causes of fading.
Industrial and Technical Education; Science - Physical
Dist - USNAC **Prod** - USAF 1942

Radio Astronomers Probe the Universe 15 MIN
16mm
Science in Action Series
Color (C)
Shows how the study of radio signals given off in space is already transforming our picture of the universe. Explains that the sun emits blasts of radio energy which can be linked to disruptions of radio and TV communications. Tells how the Crab Nebula in the constellation Taurus gives off a pulsating signal generated by the imploded star within it.
Industrial and Technical Education; Science - Physical
Dist - COUNFI **Prod** - ALLFP

Radio Astronomy Explorer 30 MIN
16mm
Color (J H C)
LC FIE68-93
Describes the new radio astronomy spacecraft, whose 1500 - foot antennas will detect radio waves of various frequencies emitted by the sun, the earth and Jupiter.
Science - Physical
Dist - NASA **Prod** - NASA 1968

Radio Bikini 60 MIN
VHS / 16mm
American experience series
Color (H G)
$9.50 rental _ #60943; $59.95 purchase _#AMEX _ 102
Tells of Operation Crossroads, America's first unclassified testing of the atom bomb in 1946 on the Pacific islands of Bikini, using archival footage and testimony from witnesses. Planned as a major media event and hailed officially as a success, Operation Crossroads was in fact a disaster which left 162 Bikinians homeless, and exposed many Navy sailors to heavy doses of radiation.
Civics and Political Systems; Science - Physical; Sociology
Dist - PBS **Prod** - WGBHTV 1988

Radio Bikini 56 MIN
VHS
B&W (H A C)
$24.95 purchase _ #PAV683V-S
Presents the story of the 1946 testing of two atomic bombs near the Marshall Island of Bikini. Reveals that the United States evacuated the 162 natives of Bikini and installed 42,000 servicemen and 18 tons of photographic equipment to witness the blasts. The effects from the testing left the island a wasteland of contaminated soil, food, and wildlife. Contains footage formerly classified 'secret material.'
History - United States; History - World
Dist - CAMV

Radio Bikini 56 MIN
VHS
Color; CC (G)
$29.95 purchase _ #RABI
Uses excerpts from film formerly classified as secret material by the US government. Records the US testing of two atomic bombs on Bikini atoll in the Pacific Ocean in July, 1946. Reveals that over 42,000 servicemen were assigned to this operation and that natives were evacuated from the islands.
Civics and Political Systems; History - United States; History - World
Dist - APRESS

Radio Bikini 60 MIN
VHS
American Experience Series
Color; Captioned (G)
$59.95 purchase _ #AMEX - 102
Tells the story of the U.S. Navy's atomic bomb testing on the Bikini Islands. Reveals that many Navy sailors were exposed to heavy doses of radiation. Shows that the islands remain highly radioactive today.
Civics and Political Systems; Health and Safety; History - United States; Science - Physical
Dist - PBS **Prod** - WGBHTV 1988

Radio communications 16 MIN
VHS / BETA / U-matic
Color; PAL (J H)
PdS15.00 purchase
Introduces radio communications and demonstrates the creation of electromagnetic waves using a simple dipole aerial. Explains amplitude modulation and the ways in which different frequency waves travel through space. Useful for physics courses. Includes students' and teachers' notes. Contact distributor for free loan information.
Education; Industrial and Technical Education; Science - Physical; Sociology
Dist - BTEDSE

Radio days 88 MIN
16mm
B&W (G)
$150.00 rental
Evokes the Age of Radio in a Woody Allen production. Pays tribute to the medium that time forgot and spotlights both the people whose lives revolved around their favorite radio programs - a colorful Jewish family living in Rockaway Beach - and the people who created those aural fantasies - exemplified by Mia Farrow, a cigarette girl trying to hit the big time. Also stars Seth Green, Julie Kavner, Diane Keaton, Tony Roberts, Danny Aiello, Jeff Daniels, Josh Mostel and Dianne West.
Fine Arts; Religion and Philosophy; Sociology
Dist - NCJEWF

Radio Drama - Life and Rebirth 30 MIN
U-matic
Color
Focuses on the art of radio drama, its life in Europe and its revival in the United States.
Fine Arts
Dist - UMITV **Prod** - UMITV 1974

Radio drama with Shaun McLaughlin 55 MIN
VHS
Color (PRO G C)
$149.00 purchase, $49.00 rental _ #732
Features Shaun McLaughlin, director of BBC radio plays, who leads a master class at AFTRS in the rehearsal and production of a short radio drama. Watches the rehearsal and recording process in Part One as McLaughlin describes his approach and working methods. Part Two presents the finished radio drama played over a black

screen to consider its effect on the imagination. Part Three repeats the drama but includes visuals of the cast at work to illustrate how each ambience and effect is achieved. Produced by the Australian Film, Television and Radio School.
Fine Arts; Literature and Drama
Dist - FIRLIT

Radio Dynamics 4 MIN
16mm
B&W
LC 73-700559
Presents an interplay of shapes, colors and movement visualizing color - keyed moods, recurrent themes, contrapuntal melodies and staccato chords without the accompaniment of music.
Mathematics
Dist - CFS **Prod** - PFP 1972

Radio Dynamics 5 MIN
16mm
Color; Silent (C)
$123.00
Experimental film byl Oskar Fischinger.
Fine Arts
Dist - AFA **Prod** - AFA 1942

Radio Frequency Heater/Sealer Surveys 27 MIN
U-matic / VHS
Color (A)
Discusses a radio frequency heater/sealer survey. Emphasizes field measurement techniques. Introduces the basic methods of controlling employee exposure.
Health and Safety; Industrial and Technical Education; Science - Physical
Dist - USNAC **Prod** - USNAC 1983

Radio Frequency Radiation Hazards 18 MIN
U-matic / VHS / 16mm
Color
Explains the biological (personnel) and nonbiological (EED and fuel) effects of RF radiation. Explains the frequency spectrum and shows the difference between ionizing and non - ionizing radiation.
Health and Safety; Science - Physical
Dist - USNAC **Prod** - USAF

Radio Interference 60 MIN
U-matic
B&W
LC 78-706293
Explains the significance of radio interference in military operations and describes the nature and theory of radio interference. Shows how radio interference can be tracked down and how various kinds of interference can be suppressed. Issued in 1958 as a motion picture.
Industrial and Technical Education
Dist - USNAC **Prod** - USA 1978

Radio Interference from Rural Power Lines 45 MIN
16mm
B&W
LC FIE53-631
Demonstrates, using models, charts and blackboard, the causes of radio interference from power lines in rural areas. For the training of employees of rural electrification co - operatives.
Industrial and Technical Education
Dist - USNAC **Prod** - USDA 1953

Radio interference - Pt 1 30 MIN
U-matic / VHS / 16mm
B&W
Explains the significance of radio interference in military operations and describes the nature and theory of radio interference. Shows how radio interference can be tracked down and how various kinds of interference can be suppressed. Issued in 1958 as a motion picture.
Industrial and Technical Education
Dist - USNAC **Prod** - USA 1978

Radio interference - Pt 2 30 MIN
16mm / U-matic / VHS
B&W
Explains the significance of radio interference in military operations and describes the nature and theory of radio interference. Shows how radio interference can be tracked down and how various kinds of interference can be suppressed. Issued in 1958 as a motion picture.
Civics and Political Systems; Industrial and Technical Education
Dist - USNAC **Prod** - USA 1978

Radio Mathematics in Nicaragua 20 MIN
U-matic / VHS
Color
LC 81-707240
Explores a project in Nicaragua that combines radio and systematic instructional design to teach primary school mathematics in rural parts of the country. Shows how curriculum and lesson plans are developed and how Nicaraguan teachers support the project.
Education; Mathematics
Dist - USNAC **Prod** - USAID 1980

The Radio Priest 60 MIN
VHS
American Experience Series
Color (H)
$9.50 rental _ #60947; $59.95 purchase _ #HAMEX - 111
Portrays Father Charles Coughlin, Depression - era priest whose Sunday night radio program supported his role as leader of a popular protest against the country's economic and social system. Reveals that as he became increasingly unstable and supportive of fascists on his radio program, Coughlin became the subject of a debate on the freedom of the airwaves. Fourth installment of the American Experience Series.
Civics and Political Systems; Fine Arts; History - United States; Sociology
Dist - PSU **Prod** - PBS
PBS

Radio production - making a radio commercial 43 MIN
VHS
Color (PRO G C)
$149.00 purchase, $49.00 rental _ #733
Observes the production process of a humorous insurance commercial. Features producers Street Remly and Bob Dennis as narrators. Watches Remley and Dennis at work with the client and with the actors during the recording session. Looks at the editing process in detail and the addition of sound effects, the balance of aesthetic considerations against client needs. Produced by the Australian Film, Television and Radio School.
Business and Economics; Fine Arts
Dist - FIRLIT

Radio, Racism and Foreign Policy 26 MIN
16mm / U-matic / VHS
Between the Wars Series
Color (H C)
Describes how the United States tried to isolate herself after being disillusioned by the horrors of the First World War. Explains that there was a period of racism and ethnic discrimination during the 1920's.
Civics and Political Systems; History - United States
Dist - FI **Prod** - LNDBRG 1978

Radio, racism and foreign policy and the great depression
VHS
Between the wars - 1918 - 1941 series
Color (H C A)
$19.95 purchase
Reviews part of the history of the years between World War I and World War II. Focuses on the effects of the Great Depression, as well as how radio personalities of the day rallied against U S involvement abroad. Includes segments from newsreels, soundtracks, and archival footage of the period. Hosted and narrated by Eric Sevareid.
History - World
Dist - PBS **Prod** - WNETTV

Radio Relay Equipment an - Trc35 and 36, Pt 4 - System Lineup Procedures 24 MIN
16mm
B&W
LC FIE60-170
Describes the features and function of AN - TRC35 and 36. Gives procedures for radio system lineup and overall system lineup when radio relay equipment is used with telephone carrier equipment.
Civics and Political Systems; Industrial and Technical Education; Social Science
Dist - USNAC **Prod** - USA 1959

Radio Sets an - GRC 3, 4, 5, 6, 7, and 8 17 MIN
16mm
B&W
LC FIA53-126
Explains the characteristics, components and mechanical operation of the Army - Navy radio sets in the GRC classification.
Civics and Political Systems; Industrial and Technical Education; Social Science
Dist - USNAC **Prod** - USA 1952

Radio Shack TRS - 80 Model 2
VHS / U-matic
Basic Computer Operations Series
Color
Presents basic operation procedures for use of the Radio Shack micro - computer TRS - 80 Model II.
Industrial and Technical Education; Mathematics
Dist - LIBFSC **Prod** - LIBFSC

Radio Shack TRS - 80 Model 3
U-matic / VHS
Basic Computer Operations Series
Color
Presents basic operation procedures for use of the Radio Shack micro - computer TRS - 80 Model III.
Industrial and Technical Education; Mathematics
Dist - LIBFSC **Prod** - LIBFSC

Radio Shop Techniques 38 MIN
16mm
Radio Technician Training Series
B&W
LC FIE52-917
Shows tools used by radio technicians and demonstrates various procedures in making a regenerative receiver.
Industrial and Technical Education
Dist - USNAC **Prod** - USN 1943

Radio Technician Training - Elementary Electricity Series

Amperes, Volts and Ohms	8 MIN
Current and Electromotive Force	11 MIN

Dist - USNAC

Radio Technician Training Series

Audio oscillator operation and use	9 MIN
Capacitance	31 MIN
Elementary electricity - amperes, volts and ohms	8 MIN
Inductance	35 MIN
Oscillators	13 MIN
Periodic Functions	17 MIN
Radio Shop Techniques	38 MIN
RCL	34 MIN
RCL - resistance capacitance	34 MIN
Rectangular Coordinates	13 MIN
Rhythm, Speed and Accuracy in Hand Sending	12 MIN
Series and parallel circuits	8 MIN
Signal Generator Operation	9 MIN
Synchro Systems	28 MIN
Synchro systems, Pt 1	14 MIN
Synchro Systems, Pt 2	13 MIN
Tube Tester Operation	9 MIN
Vectors	12 MIN
Volt Ohmmeter Operation	12 MIN

Dist - USNAC

A Radio view of the universe 29 MIN
16mm
Color
Dr Morton S Roberts of the National Radio Astronomy Observatory in Green Bank, West Virginia, explains the use of the radio line of atomic hydrogen in determining the total hydrogen content of galaxies external to the Milky Way system. Dr Roberts then establishes the strong correlation between hydrogen content and galactic shape and raises the question as to whether this correlation can be used as an indicator of galactic evolution.
Science - Physical
Dist - MLA **Prod** - MLA 1967

Radioactive dating 13 MIN
U-matic / VHS / 16mm
Color (J H C)
$315.00, $220.00 purchase _ #4121
Describes radioactive dating and how carbon - 14 and potassium - 40 is used to date materials from recent past to times over 4.5 billion years ago.
Science; Science - Physical
Dist - CORF **Prod** - CORF 1981

Radioactive dating 12 MIN
VHS
History in the rocks series
Color (H C)
$24.95 purchase _ #S9819
Shows how rock age is determined through the measurement of radioactivity using single - concept format. Part of a ten - part series on rocks.
Science - Physical
Dist - HUBDSC **Prod** - HUBDSC

Radioactive dating 13 MIN
VHS
Color; PAL (H)
Describes the basis for radioactive dating in clear detail, with animation explaining the concepts of radioactive decay and half - life, and how scientists can make use of radioactive substances such as carbon - 14 and potassium - 40 to date minerals from the recent past to times when the Earth - and the moon - were first forming more than 4.5 billion years ago.
Science - Physical
Dist - VIEWTH **Prod** - VIEWTH

Radioactive Decay A - 1 3 MIN
16mm
Single - Concept Films in Physics Series

Color (H C)
Uses time - lapse photography to study radioactive decay. Shows a gamma - ray display of a 400 - channel analyzer indicating simultaneous decay of 12.8 hour CU - 64 for 1 half life, and 2.6 hour MN - 56 for 5 half lives.
Science - Physical
Dist - OSUMPD **Prod** - OSUMPD 1963

Radioactive fallout and shelter 28 MIN
16mm
Medical self - help series
Color (SPANISH)
LC 74-705471
Discusses the effects of radiation on people and emphasizes protective procedures against radiation. To be used with the course 'Medical Self-Help Training.'
Health and Safety
Dist - USNAC **Prod** - USHHS 1965
USPHS

Radioactive Medicine 50 MIN
16mm
B&W (PRO)
Details the use of radioisotopes in diagnosis and treatment. Shows a scintillation scanner providing a picture of a patient's thyroid gland as it detects radioactivity from the isotope, iodine 193. Depicts the use of isotopes in diagnosing blood diseases and in researching metabolic processes.
Health and Safety
Dist - LAWREN **Prod** - CMA

Radioactivity 29 MIN
U-matic
Nuclear Power and You Series
Color
LC 79-706951
Explains the nature, uses and perils of nuclear radioactivity. Shows the physiological dangers of radiation and the extraordinary measures taken by atomic power stations to contain the toxicity of atom fuels and wastes.
Social Science
Dist - UMAVEC **Prod** - UMAVEC 1979

Radioactivity 18 MIN
U-matic / VHS / 16mm
Physics in Action Series
Color (J H C)
Creates a short - lived radioactive isotope and shows how to plot its decay curve. Introduces the Diffusion Cloud Chamber.
Science - Physical
Dist - LUF **Prod** - LUF

Radioactivity - 34 40 MIN
VHS
Conceptual physics alive series
Color (H C)
$45.00 purchase
Discusses the differences between alpha, beta and gamma radiation, with some balancing of nuclear equations. Explains half life and techniques for radioactive dating. Part 34 of a 35 - part series adapted from the college and high school textbook Conceptual Physics by Professor Paul Hewitt.
Science - Physical
Dist - MMENTE **Prod** - HEWITP 1992

Radioactivity and drinking water - part 1 24 MIN
U-matic / VHS / BETA
Color (I J H G)
$29.95, $130.00 purchase _ #LSTF20
Provides basic concepts of nuclear physics for non - scientists with visual demonstrations, with emphasis on health effects.
Health and Safety; Science - Natural; Sociology
Dist - FEDU **Prod** - USEPA 1983

Radioactivity and drinking water - part 2 20 MIN
BETA / U-matic / VHS
Color (I J H G)
$29.95, $130.00 purchase _ #LSTF21
Provides basic concepts of nuclear physics for non - scientists, using visual demonstrations, with emphasis on health effects.
Health and Safety; Science - Natural; Sociology
Dist - FEDU **Prod** - USEPA 1984

Radioactivity and the Environment 15 MIN
VHS / U-matic
Matter and Motion Series Module Blue; Module blue
Color (I)
Explores the properties of radioactive materials.
Science - Natural
Dist - AITECH **Prod** - WHROTV 1973

Radiocarbon Dating 27 MIN
16mm
B&W
Discusses radioactive materials and their decay and describes the application of the radiocarbon count in dating archaeological materials.
Science; Science - Physical
Dist - NYU **Prod** - NYU

Radiochromatography - testing for radiochemical purity 18 MIN
U-matic / VHS
Color (PRO)
LC 83-706072
Discusses the factors involved in choosing a radiochromatography procedure, and the techniques and methodologies of various kits. Explores the evaluation of radiopharmaceutical quality and alternatives for reporting product defects.
Health and Safety; Industrial and Technical Education; Science
Dist - USNAC **Prod** - USHHS 1982

Radiographic Evaluation of the Lumbar Spine 31 MIN
U-matic
Evaluation of Low Back Pain Series
Color (C)
Discusses A/P, lateral, flexion and extension, oblique and spot view of the lumbo - sacral area.
Health and Safety; Science - Natural
Dist - UOKLAH **Prod** - UOKLAH 1978

Radiographic Processing Series Pt 10
Replenishment System 29 MIN
Dist - USNAC

Radiographic processing series Pt 11
Circulation - filtration system 29 MIN
Dist - USNAC

Radiographic Processing Series Pt 12
Drying System 29 MIN
Dist - USNAC

Radiographic Processing Series Pt 13
The Electrical System 30 MIN
Dist - USNAC

Radiographic Processing Series Pt 15
Artifact Film Interpretation 29 MIN
Dist - USNAC

Radiographic Processing Series Pt 1
Function of Processing 29 MIN
Dist - USNAC

Radiographic Processing Series Pt 2
Theory of Processing 29 MIN
Dist - USNAC

Radiographic Processing Series Pt 5
Chemistry System, Developer 29 MIN
Dist - USNAC

Radiographic Processing Series Pt 6
Chemistry System, Fixer and Wash 29 MIN
Dist - USNAC

Radiographic Processing Series Pt 7
Chemistry System, Archival Quality and Safety 29 MIN
Dist - USNAC

Radiographic Processing Series Pt 9
Temperature Control System 29 MIN
Dist - USNAC

Radiographic processing series
Basic sensitometry 29 MIN
Basics of consistent sensitometric quality 29 MIN
Maintenance, Lubrication and Troubleshooting 29 MIN
A Short story history of processors 29 MIN
Transport system 29 MIN
Dist - USNAC

Radiography of the Mandibular Ramus with the Panorex Unit 9 MIN
16mm / 8mm cartridge
Color (PRO)
LC 75-701672
Demonstrates a method of obtaining conventional panoramic radiographs of the maxillo - mandibular regions.
Health and Safety; Science
Dist - USNAC **Prod** - USVA 1973

Radioisotope Scanning in Medicine 16 MIN
U-matic / VHS / 16mm
Magic of the Atom Series no 30
Color (J H C)
LC FIA66-1072
Explains the principle of scanning with radioactive tracers for diagnostic purposes. Presents a case history of a lung scanning. Illustrates both photoscans and dot scans. Discusses future developments.
Health and Safety
Dist - HANDEL **Prod** - HANDEL 1965

Radioisotope Series no 13
Radioisotopes in General Science 46 MIN
Dist - USNAC

Radioisotope Series no 3
Practical Procedures of Measurement 48 MIN
Dist - USNAC

Radioisotope series
Fundamentals of radioactivity 59 MIN
Properties of radiation 68 MIN
Dist - USNAC

Radioisotoper applications in medicine 26 MIN
U-matic
Understanding the atom - 1980s - series; 10
B&W
LC 80-706616
Traces the development of the use of radioisotopes and radiation in the field of medicine from the early work by Hervesy to the present. Includes studies of atherosclerosis, cobalt - labeled vitamin b - 12, the use of iodine radioisotopes in determining thyroid physiology and pathology, the localization of brain tumors, determination of volume of body fluids and the measurement of red cell volume and life time. Discusses its use in treating disease, such as hyperthyroidism and cancer.
Health and Safety; Science; Science - Physical
Dist - USNAC **Prod** - USNRC 1980

Radioisotopes 16 MIN
U-matic
Chemistry 101 Series
Color (C)
Defines radioactivity and shows how it is measured with a Geiger counter and shows that common materials like gas mantles for lanterns give off ionizing radiation.
Science; Science - Physical
Dist - UILL **Prod** - UILL 1981

Radioisotopes for Medicine 11 MIN
16mm
Color (PRO)
LC FI68-220
Using a flow chart as a guide, depicts the main steps in the manufacturing of medotopes at the Squibb Radiopharmaceuticals Plant in New Brunswick, N. J. And traces events taking place when an order is received. Stresses testing for quality control.
Health and Safety
Dist - SQUIBB **Prod** - SQUIBB 1965

Radioisotopes in Agricultural Research 41 MIN
16mm
Radioisotopes Series no 12
B&W
LC FIE53-494
Traces the utilization of chemicals by plants and animals, and explains how the exact amounts needed are determined by radioactive chemicals. Shows the manufacture and uses of radioactive phosphate.
Agriculture; Science - Physical
Dist - USNAC **Prod** - USA 1952

Radioisotopes in biology and agriculture 26 MIN
U-matic
Understanding the atom - 1970s - series; 09
B&W
Discusses the applications of atomic energy in agriculture and biology. Shows how radioisotopic tracers are used in determining the structure and role of nucleic acids and other cellular components, including the specific structure of a proton. Includes examples of plant breeding projects, theories of aging, and other examples on the effect of radiation effects in living systems.
Agriculture; Science - Natural; Science - Physical
Dist - USNAC **Prod** - USNRC 1972

Radioisotopes in General Science 46 MIN
16mm
Radioisotope Series no 13
B&W
LC FIE52-2009
Gives nine illustrations of the radioisotope as an important research tool adaptable to tracer investigations in all branches of general science.
Science; Science - Physical
Dist - USNAC **Prod** - USA 1952

Radioisotopes in Medical Diagnosis and Investigation 30 MIN
16mm
Color
Shows the present day uses of radioisotopes in medical diagnosis and investigation, including dilution analysis, tracing studies, scanning and renography.
Health and Safety; Industrial and Technical Education; Science
Dist - UKAEA **Prod** - UKAEA 1967

Radioisotopes in the Diagnosis of Cancer 23 MIN
U-matic / VHS
Color
Describes the nature of radioisotopes and how their properties are applied in the diagnosis of cancer, by means of animation. Discusses and illustrates the most common clinical applications.
Health and Safety
Dist - WFP **Prod** - WFP

Radioisotopes in the Diagnosis of Cancer 22 MIN
16mm
Color (PRO)
LC 72-700180
Uses animation to describe to members of the medical profession the nature of radioisotopes. Shows through clinical photography how radioisotopes are used in cancer detection.
Business and Economics; Health and Safety; Science
Dist - AMCS **Prod** - AMCS 1971

Radioisotopes Series no 12
Radioisotopes in Agricultural Research 41 MIN
Dist - USNAC

Radiological Reporting - a New Approach 13 MIN
16mm
Color
LC 78-701565
Discusses a computerized radiological reporting system which eliminates the risk of lost X - ray records.
Business and Economics; Health and Safety; Mathematics
Dist - JHH **Prod** - JHH 1978

Radiology 25 MIN
VHS
Career encounters series
Color (J H C A)
$95.00 purchase _ #MG3408V-J
Presents a documentary-style program that explores a career in radiology. Features professionals at work, explaining what they do and how they got where they are. Emphasizes diversity of occupational opportunities and of men and women in the field. Offers information about new developments and technologies and about educational and certification requirements for entering the profession. One of a series of videos about professions available individually or as a set.
Business and Economics; Guidance and Counseling
Dist - CAMV

Radiology career encounters 28 MIN
VHS
Career encounters video series
Color (J H)
$89.00 purchase _ #4268
Offers a documentary on careers in the field of radiology. Visits workplaces and hears professionals explain what they do, how they got where they are and why they find the work so rewarding. Emphasizes human diversity in the professions. Dispels myths, misconceptions and stereotypes and offers practical information about the requirements for entering the field. Part of a 13 - part series.
Business and Economics; Guidance and Counseling; Science
Dist - NEWCAR

The Radiology Factor to DRGs 30 MIN
VHS / U-matic
Color (PRO)
Reveals ways to manage radiology cooperatively with physicians in the hospital.
Health and Safety; Psychology; Science
Dist - AMCRAD **Prod** - AMCRAD

Radiology of the Respiratory System - a Basic Review Series
Pulmonary Manifestations of Cardiovascular Disease 27 MIN
Dist - UOKLAH

Radiology of the Respiratory System - a Basic Review
Infections and Inhalation Disease of the Lung 28 MIN
Normal Radiographic Anatomy of the Chest 30 MIN
An Overview of Intrathoracic Neoplasia 24 MIN
Patterns of Intrathoracic Disease 23 MIN
Dist - UOKLAH

Radiology Practice in a Small Community 23 MIN
16mm
Color
LC 76-702198
Presents four practicing radiologists from small towns in Nebraska, New York and Pennsylvania who offer their impressions concerning practice in their areas.
Health and Safety; Psychology; Science
Dist - FILAUD **Prod** - AMCRAD 1976

Radiotherapy - High Dosage Treatment 17 MIN
16mm
Nursing Series
B&W
LC FIE52-361
Shows nature and physiological effects of high dosage X - rays, administration of X - ray treatment for carcinoma of the tongue, function and administration of radon seeds and factors in care of patients receiving X - ray therapy.
Health and Safety
Dist - USNAC **Prod** - USOE 1945

Radiotherapy of Breast Cancer 31 MIN
U-matic
Color
Summarizes the effectiveness of control dosages of radiation in the treatment of breast cancer.
Health and Safety
Dist - UTEXSC **Prod** - UTEXSC

Radium Decontamination 8 MIN
16mm
Color
LC 74-705472
Tells the story of the decontamination of a radium contaminated basement in a duplex frame house by the Pennsylvania Health Department and the U S Public Health Service during the summer of 1964 at Lansdowne, Pennsylvania.
Health and Safety; Science - Physical; Social Science
Dist - USNAC **Prod** - USPHS

Radon 26 MIN
U-matic / VHS
Color (C)
$249.00, $149.00 purchase _ #AD - 1822
Looks at the health implications of radon pollution. Shows methods homeowners can use to detect radon gas and what can be done to minimize radon hazards once it is found.
Health and Safety; Home Economics; Science - Natural; Sociology
Dist - FOTH **Prod** - FOTH

Radon Free 35 MIN
VHS
Color (G)
$24.95 purchase _ #6311
Shows how to detect and remove the poison of radon from the home.
Health and Safety
Dist - SYBVIS **Prod** - SYBVIS

Rae Armantrout - 5 - 2 - 85 60 MIN
VHS / Cassette
Poetry Center reading series
Color (G)
$15.00 purchase, rental _ #656 - 542
Features Armantrout reading from her manuscript Precedence and from Necromance at the Poetry Center, San Francisco State University.
Literature and Drama
Dist - POETRY **Prod** - POETRY 1985

The Rafer Johnson Story 55 MIN
16mm
B&W (I)
The story of Rafer Johnson, world decathlon champion, captain of the 1960 U S Olympic Team, honor student, president of his grade school, high school and college classes and first member of the Peace Corps.
Biography; History - United States; Physical Education and Recreation
Dist - SF **Prod** - SF 1963

The Raft 29 MIN
16mm / U-matic / VHS
Color (C A)
LC 74-701534
Tells how a family travels on a raft down the Parnaiba River in Brazil to sell their homemade earthenware and other merchandise in the city of Teresina, the journey taking approximately a month.
Geography - World; Social Science
Dist - PHENIX **Prod** - SLUIZR 1974

Rafter Construction 13 MIN
16mm
Color (J H A)
Explains rafter construction, including basic roof types, roof members and all types of rafters. Defines rafter layout terminology and presents layout of the common rafter with the framing square.
Industrial and Technical Education
Dist - SF **Prod** - SF 1969

Rafting the whitewater - Pt 1
U-matic / VHS
Rafting the whitewater series
Color
Shows what to look for in a raft, the pro's and con's of various raft designs and the advantages of different rafting materials.
Physical Education and Recreation
Dist - PBS **Prod** - KWSU 1981

Rafting the whitewater - Pt 2
U-matic / VHS
Rafting the whitewater series
Color
Shows how to equip a raft, taking a careful look at the difference in paddles.
Physical Education and Recreation
Dist - PBS **Prod** - KWSU 1981

Rafting the whitewater - Pt 3
VHS / U-matic
Rafting the whitewater series
Color
Demonstrates the maintenance of a raft with a step - by - step look at the repair of tears, a common occurence in the whitewater rafting.
Physical Education and Recreation
Dist - PBS **Prod** - KWSU 1981

Rafting the whitewater - Pt 4
VHS / U-matic
Rafting the whitewater series
Color
Summarizes the information in the first three programs, and prepares viewers for an extended trip on the river.
Physical Education and Recreation
Dist - PBS **Prod** - KWSU 1981

Rafting the whitewater series
Rafting the whitewater - Pt 1
Rafting the whitewater - Pt 2
Rafting the whitewater - Pt 3
Rafting the whitewater - Pt 4
Dist - PBS

Rag knit sweater 45 MIN
BETA / VHS
Color
Gives the basics of an inexpensive and easy way to knit. Features four sweater patterns.
Home Economics
Dist - HOMEAF **Prod** - HOMEAF

Rag Rugs 14 MIN
Videoreel / VT2
Living Better II Series
Color
Shows how to make a throw rug from strips of old clothing and burlap. Explains that the cloth strips are sewn to the burlap backing with a running stitch and additional information is given on hooking the rug.
Fine Arts; Home Economics
Dist - PBS **Prod** - MAETEL

Rag tag champs 48 MIN
U-matic / VHS / 16mm
Color (I J)
LC 78-701065
Tells the story of young Jake's search for a coach for his baseball team and how he finds a solution that helps the team win games. Points out that one often gets more by giving than by taking. Based on the book Jake by Alfred Slote.
Guidance and Counseling; Literature and Drama; Physical Education and Recreation
Dist - CORF **Prod** - ABCTV 1978

Rag Tapestry 11 MIN
16mm
Color (P I J H)
LC 78-702693
Follows a group of 25 children at a workshop at the Metropolitan Museum of Art in New York as they work on a rag tapestry from initial concept through drawings to production of the final work.
Fine Arts
Dist - IFF **Prod** - BRYAN 1969

Rage 20 MIN
16mm
Cellar Door Cine Mites Series
Color (I)
LC 74-701552
Fine Arts
Dist - CELLAR **Prod** - CELLAR 1972

Rage net 1 MIN
16mm
Color (G)
$138.00 purchase
Presents a hand - painted film by Stan Brakhage. Enlarges upon the theme of rage, as a meditation rather than a psychological entrapment.
Fine Arts; Guidance and Counseling
Dist - CANCIN **Prod** - BRAKS 1988

The Rage of a privileged class - why are middle - class blacks angry 30 MIN
VHS
Author's night at the Freedom Forum series
Color (G)
$15.00 purchase _ #V94 - 03
Focuses on Ellis Cose, author of the book of the same title, in part of a series on freedom of the press, free speech and free spirit.
History - United States; Social Science; Sociology
Dist - FREEDM **Prod** - FREEDM 1994

The Ragged Ragamuffins of the Continental Army 8 MIN
U-matic / VHS / 16mm
A Nation is Born Series
Color (P I)
Explains the beginnings of the Revolutionary War period, and the adoption of the Declaration of Independence on July 4, 1776. Shows the Colonists' long struggle for what they wanted - freedom from British rule and the freedom to build a life of their own.
History - United States
Dist - LUF **Prod** - PIC 1973

The Ragged Revolution - the Romance and the Reality of the Mexican Revolution, 1910 - 1920 37 MIN
U-matic / VHS / 16mm
B&W
Looks at the realities behind the romantic myths of the Mexican Revolution. Shows how the disastrous social and economic conditions in Mexico at the turn of the century paved the way for the revolution. Documents the Battle of Chihuahua and provides a portrait of Pancho Villa. Discusses the role of the United States and describes the influence of the Revolution on the work of the great Mexican muralists, such as Rivera, Orozco, and Siqueiros.
History - World
Dist - CNEMAG **Prod** - YORKTV

Raging Bull 129 MIN
16mm
B&W
Stars Robert DeNiro as middle - weight boxing champion Jake La Motta. Directed by Martin Scorsese.
Fine Arts
Dist - UAE **Prod** - UAA 1980

Raglan Shoulder Shaping and Decreasing 29 MIN
Videoreel / VT2
Busy Knitter I Series
B&W
Home Economics
Dist - PBS **Prod** - WMVSTV

Rags - 100 Years of the Apparel Industry in Northeastern Ohio 29 MIN
U-matic
Color
Presents a documentary about the apparel industry in northeastern Ohio for the past 100 years. Discusses its prospects for the future.
Business and Economics; History - United States
Dist - HRC **Prod** - OHC

Rags and buttons and lemonade stand 30 MIN
VHS
Davey and Goliath series
Color (P I R)
$19.95 purchase, $10.00 rental _ #4 - 8826
Presents two 15 - minute 'Davey and Goliath' episodes. 'Rags and Buttons' likens Sally's love for her imperfect doll to God's love for humans. 'Lemonade Stand' teaches Davey that his father loves both his children equally, just as God loves all people equally. Produced by the Evangelical Lutheran Church in America.
Literature and Drama; Religion and Philosophy
Dist - APH

Ragtime King 20 MIN
U-matic
Truly American Series
Color (I)
Explores the life of ragtime composer Scott Joplin.
Biography; Fine Arts; History - United States
Dist - GPN **Prod** - WVIZTV 1979

Raguira 9 MIN
VHS / U-matic
Life in Colombia series
Color (G)
Shows a remote mountain village, Raguira, in Colombia, where an old man reflects on his youth. While the old man reminisces, a small boy shows that things have changed little as major daily activities still include selling wood, making pottery, going to market and playing music. Exhibits the first effects of modernization on an old way of life.
Geography - World; History - World
Dist - IFF **Prod** - IFF

Rahway, Stay 'Way 27 MIN
U-matic / VHS / 16mm
Color (H C A)
Explains a program at Rahway State Prison which brings delinquency - prone teenagers inside the prison to learn what confinement is really like. Shows the prisoners graphically describing the horrors of prison life and the stunned reactions of the young people.
Sociology
Dist - FI **Prod** - WNETTV 1977

Raices De Felicidad 25 MIN
U-matic / VHS / 16mm
B&W (J H C) (SPANISH)
LC FIA56-760
A Spanish language film. Describes the nature of family relationships, particularly the role of the father in building and maintaining a happy family environment. Shows a family in Puerto Rico where mutual love and respect provide the mortar to build a firm structure of self - respect, independence and productivity.
Foreign Language; Guidance and Counseling; Psychology; Sociology
Dist - IFB **Prod** - MHFB 1955

Raid Commercial 1 MIN
VHS / U-matic
Color
Shows a classic animated television commercial.
Business and Economics; Psychology; Sociology
Dist - BROOKC **Prod** - BROOKC

Rail 10 MIN
VHS
Stop, look, listen series
Color; PAL (P I J)
Follows some children to the local railway station where they buy tickets and go for a ride on the train. Observes the engineer, railroad signals, and the train going round corners, through a tunnel, under bridge and beside a road. Part of a series of films which start from some everyday observation and show more of what is happening, how and why. Builds vocabulary and encourages children to be more observant.
English Language; Social Science
Dist - VIEWTH

Railroad 1 - a wild and impractical scheme - 1800 to 1845 14 MIN
VHS
Railroad series
Color (I J)
$89.00 purchase _ #RB827
Covers the early beginnings of the railroad in the United States. Part of a series on the railroad.
History - United States; Social Science
Dist - REVID **Prod** - REVID

Railroad Safety 34 MIN
16mm
B&W
LC FIE52-2092
Points out the importance of safety in all phases of railroad work, in the yards, on the trains, along the right - of - way and in the shops.
Health and Safety; Social Science
Dist - USNAC **Prod** - PENNRR 1952

Railroad series

The Golden age - 1880 - 1916	35 MIN
One nation indivisible - 1845 - 1865	14 MIN
Transcontinental - 1865 - 1880	16 MIN
A Wild and impractical scheme - 1800 - 1845	14 MIN

Dist - KAWVAL

Railroad series

Railroad 1 - a wild and impractical scheme - 1800 to 1845	14 MIN
Railroad 3 - transcontinental - 1865 to 1890	16 MIN
Railroad 2 - one nation - indivisible - 1845 to 1865	14 MIN

Dist - REVID

Railroad songs - Pt 1 15 MIN
U-matic / VHS
Song sampler series
Color (P)
LC 81-707034
Shows how to clap a steady beat and an off beat pattern, and recognize a tempo change. Presents the songs I've Been Working On The Railroad, Down At The Station and Get On Board.
Fine Arts; Social Science
Dist - GPN **Prod** - JCITV 1981

Railroad songs - Pt 2 15 MIN
U-matic / VHS
Song sampler series
Color (P)
LC 81-707034
Shows how to clap a steady beat and an offbeat pattern, and recognize a tempo change. Presents the songs I've Been Working On The Railroad, Down At The Station and Get On Board.
Fine Arts; Social Science
Dist - GPN **Prod** - JCITV 1981

Railroad 3 - transcontinental - 1865 to 1890 16 MIN
VHS
Railroad series
Color (I J)
$89.00 purchase _ #RB829
Looks at the growth of the railroad in the United States across the continent. Part of a series on the railroad.
History - United States; Social Science
Dist - REVID **Prod** - REVID

Railroad 2 - one nation - indivisible - 1845 to 1865 14 MIN
VHS
Railroad series
Color (I J)
$89.00 purchase _ #RB828
Looks at the importance of the railroad in the United States during the Civil War. Part of a series on the railroad.
History - United States; Social Science
Dist - REVID **Prod** - REVID

Railroad women 30 MIN
VHS / U-matic
Color (G)
$195.00 purchase, $50.00 rental
Documents the little - known history of women railroad workers in non - traditional jobs, from their first positions in the 19th century to the present. Shows a woman engineer and a brakewoman - switchwoman. Five retired railroad women get together to reminisce about the men's jobs they held during World War II. Includes historical photos and traditional railroad music. Produced by Sharon Genasci and Dorothy Velasco.
History - World; Sociology
Dist - WMEN

Railroads 20 MIN
VHS / U-matic
Color
Presents a documentary on the Soviet railroad system.
Geography - World; History - World; Social Science
Dist - IHF **Prod** - IHF

Railroads and Westward Expansion - 1800 - 1845 14 MIN
16mm / U-matic / VHS
Color (I)
LC 78-701051
Examines America's need for improved transportation in the early 19th century, discusses the industrial revolution and its effect on the development of the railroad, and shows the impact of the railroad on commerce, westward expansion and jobs in the first half of the 19th century.
Geography - United States; History - United States; Social Science
Dist - PHENIX **Prod** - CALVIN 1978

Railroads and Westward Expansion - 1845 - 1865 14 MIN
U-matic / VHS / 16mm
Color (I)
LC 78-701052
Examines the role of the railroad in the settlement of the prairies, the growth of cities and immigration during the period 1845 - 1865. Explains how the growth of the frontier led to the growth of the railroad and discusses the impact of rail power on the Civil War.
History - United States; Social Science
Dist - PHENIX **Prod** - CALVIN 1978

Railroads and Westward Expansion, 1865 - 1900 16 MIN
U-matic / VHS / 16mm
Color (I)
LC 78-701958
Explains how the desire for the resources of the West led to the building of the transcontinental railroad after the Civil War. Discusses the importance of the railroad in settling the Great Plains and Western states and its significance in unifying the nation. Examines the ways in which the transcontinental railroad affected commerce and the fabric of daily life in America.
History - United States; Social Science
Dist - PHENIX **Prod** - CALVIN 1978

Railroads - are we on the right track 30 MIN
U-matic
Adam Smith's money world series; 132
Color (A)
Attempts to demystify the world of money and break it down so that employees of small as well as large businesses can understand and adjust to new social and economic trends. Reports on the major economic stories and discoveries of the day.
Business and Economics
Dist - PBS **Prod** - WNETTV 1985

The Railrodder 25 MIN
16mm
Color (J)
Presents Buster Keaton as the 'Railrodder,' crossing Canada east to west on a railway track speeder.
Geography - World; Social Science
Dist - NFBC **Prod** - NFBC 1965

Rails across the summit 28 MIN
U-matic / VHS / 16mm
Color
LC 76-702666
Presents sights and sounds recorded on the 64 - mile narrow gauge railroad line between Chama, New Mexico, and Antonito, Colorado, in the San Juan Mountains.
Geography - United States; Social Science
Dist - MCFI **Prod** - MARLOV 1976

The Rails to hell - and back 66 MIN
VHS
Color (H)
$99.95 purchase, $50.00 rental _ #8173; LC 89716250
Recounts the ordeal of one family during the 1940s in Europe, emphasizing events leading up to the Holocaust.
History - World; Sociology
Dist - AIMS

The Rails to hell - and back 66 MIN
VHS / 16mm
Color (J H A)
$99.95 purchase, $50.00 rental _ #8173
Features David Bergman, a survivor of the Nazi concentration camps, who recounts the ordeal of his family and millions of other people who suffered under the Nazi war machine.
Business and Economics; History - United States; History - World
Dist - AIMS **Prod** - REMEM 1990

Rain 10 MIN
16mm / U-matic / VHS
Color (P I)
LC FIA65-371
Shows man's need for rain. Explains the water cycle and the phenomenon of the rainbow.
Science - Physical
Dist - IFB **Prod** - EDMNDS 1961

Rain 10 MIN
U-matic
Take a Look Series
Color (P I)
Explains why the water cycle is important for all living things. Demonstrates condensation and evaporation.
Science; Science - Physical
Dist - TVOTAR **Prod** - TVOTAR 1986

The Rain 8 MIN
16mm
B&W
Tells the story of a pregnant woman who, after the death of her husband, struggles with the decision to keep or abort her unborn child.
Fine Arts
Dist - USC **Prod** - USC 1981

Rain 10 MIN
U-matic / 16mm / VHS
Primary science series
Color (P I)
LC 91-705331
Illustrates how clouds and raindrops form. Describes how rain can be beneficial or destructive. Includes two teacher's guides. Part of a series on primary science produced by Fred Ladd.
Science; Science - Physical
Dist - BARR

Rain 6 MIN
16mm / U-matic / VHS
Starting to Read Series
Color (P)
LC 79-707905
Uses everyday situations in familiar environments to encourage the development of language skills. Teaches basic words through song, melody and repetition.
English Language
Dist - AIMS **Prod** - BURGHS 1971

Rain - 8 10 MIN
U-matic / 16mm / VHS
Primary science series
Color (K P I)
$265.00, $215.00, $185.00 purchase _ #B589
Explains how clouds and raindrops form. Teaches why rainfall is so important to farmers and how rain can cause problems for city dwellers. Shows how water flows in streams and how too much rain can cause floods. Part of an 11 - part series on primary science.
Science - Natural; Science - Physical
Dist - BARR **Prod** - GREATT 1990

Rain - a First Film 10 MIN
U-matic / VHS / 16mm
Color
LC 74-700073
Presents visual experiences which encourage students to look for interesting patterns in clouds and rain, while learning about the water cycle. Considers the information that can be gained from watching clouds and winds and the good and bad effects of rainstorms.
Science - Physical
Dist - PHENIX **Prod** - PHENIX 1973

Rain and Shine 103 MIN
16mm
Color (HUNGARIAN (ENGLISH SUBTITLES))
Details the encounter between dyspeptic city bureaucracy and voracious peasantry. Directed by Ferenc Andras. With English subtitles.
Fine Arts; Foreign Language
Dist - NYFLMS **Prod** - UNKNWN 1977

Rain forest 60 MIN
VHS
National Geographic video series
Color (G)
$29.95 purchase
Tours the rain forests of Costa Rica. Shows the unique environmental wonders that exist there.
Science - Natural
Dist - PBS **Prod** - WNETTV

Rain forest 60 MIN
VHS
Animal kingdom series
Color (J H C G)
$19.98 purchase _ #VV1056V - S
Explores the tropical rainforests of Costa Rica to encounter great and small biological wonders in a species - rich habitat under threat from human encroachment. Part of a series visiting remote regions of the world to study exotic wildlife.
Science - Natural
Dist - CAMV **Prod** - NGS

Rain forest 60 MIN
VHS
Color; Captioned (G)
$29.95 purchase _ #S01395
Portrays the plant and animal life of tropical rain forests. Reveals that the rain forests, now in danger of disappearing, are home to nearly half the animal species on earth.
Science - Natural; Social Science
Dist - UILL **Prod** - NGS

Rain forest 59 MIN
VHS / Videodisc / BETA
Color; CLV; Captioned (G)
$35.20, $24.20 purchase _ #C53515, #C50515
Science - Natural
Dist - NGS **Prod** - NGS

Rain forest ecology - Manu National Park, Peru 28 MIN
VHS / U-matic
Color (H C)
$325.00, $295.00 purchase _ #V540
Shows Manu National Park in Peru, the largest rain forest park in South America. Reveals that in 1977, the United Nations designated this area as a Global Biosphere Reserve. The park, over 2,000 miles in length, has the greatest diversity of living organisms anywhere on Earth and encompasses the entire Manu River.
Geography - World; Science - Natural
Dist - BARR **Prod** - CEPRO 1991

Rain Forests - a Part of Your Life
VHS / 35mm strip
Color (J)
$84.00 purchase _ #PE - 909744 - 8, #PE - 909469 - 4
Explains the role of rain forests in preserving plants and animals as well as in releasing oxygen into the atmosphere. Considers the economic factors contributing to destruction of the forests and suggests solutions to the problems. Filmstrip version includes two filmstrips, two cassettes and teacher's guide.
Science - Natural
Dist - SRA **Prod** - SRA 1990

The Rain forest's green hell 24 MIN
VHS
Wild refuge series
Color (G)
$39.95 purchase
Visits the Amazon rain forest. Finds monkeys, tapirs and Indians who still use poison darts and blow guns to hunt. Part of a thirteen - part series on the North American wilderness. Each episode documents a different area and shows how animal species cope with their surroundings to survive.
Geography - World; Science - Natural; Social Science
Dist - CNEMAG **Prod** - HOBELP 1976

Rain forests - proving their worth 31 MIN
VHS
Color (I J H C G A)
$85.00 purchase, $45.00 rental
Shows how products grown or made in the world's rain forests are gaining popularity. Describes the problems that remain, such as Brazil nut growers not getting fair prices. Features footage from various rain forest regions. Narrated by Jane Alexander. Produced by Interlock Media Associates.
Agriculture; Science - Natural; Social Science
Dist - EFVP

Rain in the City 14 MIN
U-matic / VHS / 16mm
B&W (J H A)
LC 79-712272
Presents the various activities of the people in various sections of Regen, a typical German city, during the rain. Shows the street life reawakening when the rain is over. Without narration.
Geography - World; Science - Physical; Social Science; Sociology
Dist - IFB **Prod** - HARTWF 1971

Rain on the Lion 28 MIN
VHS / U-matic
Contemporary Arts Series
Color (G)
$160.00, $110.00 purchase, $60.00, $40.00 rental
Features dramatic dance sequences and special effects to create a modern day urban fairy tale which explores time, space and the maturing self. Features unusual characters weaving fanciful moods and a curious story involving a young woman who acquires knowledge from an old woman and is transformed. Produced by Daniel Polsfuss.
Fine Arts; Literature and Drama
Dist - IAFC

Rain on the Turks 15 MIN
16mm
B&W
Shows rare footage.
Industrial and Technical Education
Dist - FCE **Prod** - FCE

Rain or shine - understanding the weather 15 MIN
VHS
Color (P I)
$89.00 purchase _ #RB804
Shows how weather predictions are made possible. Analyzes uneven atmospheric heating, cool and warm air masses, the use of barometers, the significance of clouds. Uses graphics and animation to clarify concepts.
Science - Physical
Dist - REVID **Prod** - REVID

The Rain People 106 MIN
16mm
Color
Follows the fortunes of a housewife who escapes to California. Directed by Francis Ford Coppola. Stars Shirley Knight, James Caan and Robert Duvall.
Fine Arts
Dist - TWYMAN **Prod** - WB 1969

Rain plague 30 MIN
VHS
Nature series
Color; PAL (H C A)
PdS65 purchase; Not available in the United States, Canada and Japan.
Examines the effects of an iodine deficient diet on more than half of the poplulation of Bangladesh. Presents UNICEF's plans to supplement iodine in people's diets by adding it to salt. Explains how political instability, poverty and religious convictions threaten to undermine the plan.
Health and Safety; Social Science
Dist - BBCENE

Rain, Rain, Go Away 15 MIN
U-matic
Two Plus You - Math Patrol One Series
Color (K P)
Presents the mathematical concepts of capacity, its conservation and units and the description and identification of shapes.
Education; Mathematics
Dist - TVOTAR **Prod** - TVOTAR 1976

Rain, Rain Go Away 11 MIN
16mm / U-matic / VHS
Reading and Word Play Series
Color (P)
Shows how a rainy morning turns into an action - packed sunshiny day where children, adults and animals work and play with the joy of language. Designed to reinforce the words work, play, hands, feet, big and little.
English Language
Dist - AIMS **Prod** - PEDF 1976

Rainbow Acres 26 MIN
16mm
Color (J)
LC 79-700732
Looks at Rainbow Acres, a ranch home for mentally retarded adults. Shows the growth and positive lifestyle achieved by living in this alternative setting.
Psychology
Dist - FMSP **Prod** - FMSP 1979

The Rainbow Bear 6 MIN
U-matic / VHS / 16mm
Color (K P I)
LC 72-700705
Uses animation to tell the story about the rainbow bear who awakes after several hundred years of slumber, returns to a world of warmth and sunshine to play a green flute and then vanishes into space and time.
English Language; Fine Arts; Literature and Drama
Dist - AMEDFL **Prod** - MELNDZ 1971

Rainbow Black 31 MIN
16mm
Color (H C A)
LC 77-701039
Presents a portrait of Black poet, critic and historian Sarah Webster Fabio. Includes readings of her works and interviews in which she discusses her approaches to writing, the relationship of the Black experience to her work and her early influences.
History - United States; Literature and Drama; Sociology
Dist - UCEMC **Prod** - FABIOC 1976

Rainbow goes to hospital 26 MIN
VHS
Color; PAL (K P)
PdS20 purchase
Follows a six - year - old to the hospital where he has a tonsillectomy. Answers the questions of children and their parents about going to the hospital. Contact distributor about availability outside the United Kingdom.
Fine Arts; Guidance and Counseling; Health and Safety; Literature and Drama
Dist - ACADEM

Rainbow has a new baby 26 MIN
VHS
Color; PAL (K)
PdS20 purchase
Helps children under age five to understand the arrival of a new baby in their home. Contact distributor about availability outside the United Kingdom.
Fine Arts; Sociology
Dist - ACADEM

Rainbow movie of the week series
Ann of the Wolf Clan 60 MIN
Billy loves Ali 60 MIN
College 60 MIN
JOB 60 MIN
Keiko 60 MIN
Mariposa 60 MIN
Pals 60 MIN
Silver City 60 MIN
Two of Hearts 60 MIN
Weekend 60 MIN
Dist - GPN

A Rainbow of my own 5 MIN
VHS
Color (K P)
$34.95 purchase
Presents a video version of the Don Freeman book 'A Rainbow Of My Own.' Tells the story of how a little boy who has spent all afternoon playing imaginary games with a rainbow returns home and finds a real rainbow awaiting him in his room.
Literature and Drama
Dist - LIVOAK **Prod** - LIVOAK

A Rainbow of My Own
35mm strip / VHS / Cassette
Storybook Library Series
Color (K)
$34.95, $32.00, $29.95 purchase
Offers another Corduroy, the favorite teddy bear, story by Don Freeman.
English Language; Literature and Drama
Dist - PELLER

Rainbow Pass 6 MIN
16mm
Color (J)
LC 75-704206
Presents an experimental film in which immobile shapes are combined with moving patterns to create a feeling of endless depth.
Fine Arts; Industrial and Technical Education
Dist - CFS **Prod** - DEMOS 1975

Rainbow quest series
Alexander Zelkin 52 MIN
The Beers Family 52 MIN
Bessie Jones and children from the Downtown Community School 52 MIN
Buffy Sainte - Marie 52 MIN
The Cajun Band 52 MIN
Clinch mountain boys and Cousin Emmy 52 MIN
Doc Watson, Clint Howard and Fred Price 52 MIN
Donovan and Rev Gary Davis 52 MIN
Elizabeth Cotton, Rosa Valentin and Rafael Martinez 52 MIN
Frank Warner 52 MIN
The Greenbriar Boys 52 MIN
Herbert Levy, K L Wong and Hilanders Steel Band 52 MIN
Herbert Manana 52 MIN
Jean Ritchie and Bernice Reagon 52 MIN
Jim and Hazel Garland 52 MIN
Judy Collins 52 MIN
Leadbelly 52 MIN
Len Chandler 52 MIN
Lino Manocchia, Ralph Marino and Federico Picciano 52 MIN
Malvina Reynolds and Jack Elliot 52 MIN
Martha Schlamme 52 MIN
Mimi and Richard Farina 52 MIN
New Lost City Ramblers 52 MIN
Norman Studer and Grant Rogers 52 MIN
Pat Sky and the Pennywhistlers 52 MIN
Paul Cadwell, Mississippi John Hurt 52 MIN
Paul Draper 52 MIN
Penny and Sonya Cohen 52 MIN
Pete Seeger - solo 52 MIN
Roscoe Holcomb and Jean Redpath 52 MIN
Ruth Rubin 52 MIN
Sonny Terry and Brownie McGhee 52 MIN
Steve Addiss and Bill Croft with Phan Duy 52 MIN
Theodore Bikel and Rashid Hussain 52 MIN
Tom Paxton, the Clancy Brothers and Tommy Makem 52 MIN
Woody Guthrie 52 MIN
Dist - NORROS

Rainbow quest sries
Sonia Malkine 52 MIN
Dist - NORROS

Rainbow Reel 15 MIN
16mm
Color (K P I J)
Presents a series of animated designs made by children, including flip cards, cells and cut - outs.
Fine Arts; Literature and Drama
Dist - YELLOW **Prod** - YELLOW 1968

Rainbow road - overview 30 MIN
VHS / U-matic
Rainbow road series - Pt 1
Color (A)
LC 82-707393
Surveys the various factors that make for a solid foundation in reading readiness such as visual and auditory discrimination, directionality, eye - hand coordination, attention span, teaching the alphabet, and physical, emotional and social awareness.
Home Economics; Sociology
Dist - GPN **Prod** - KAIDTV 1982

Rainbow Road - Review 30 MIN
U-matic / VHS
Rainbow Road Series Pt 4
Color (A)
LC 82-707396
Relates oral and written language with the development of a background of information and experiences on the part of the young child.
Home Economics; Sociology
Dist - GPN **Prod** - KAIDTV 1982

Rainbow road series - Pt 1
Rainbow road - overview 30 MIN
Dist - GPN

Rainbow Road Series Pt 2
Oral Language 30 MIN
Dist - GPN

Rainbow Road Series Pt 3
Written Language 30 MIN
Dist - GPN

Rainbow Road Series Pt 4
Rainbow Road - Review 30 MIN
Dist - GPN

The Rainbow Serpent 11 MIN
U-matic / VHS / 16mm
Color (P I)
LC 79-700546
Adapted from the book The Rainbow Serpent by Dick Roughsey. Presents an aboriginal legend about a serpent named Goorialla whose journey across Australia resulted in the creation of the geographical features and the animal and plant life found there.
Fine Arts; Literature and Drama; Religion and Philosophy; Social Science
Dist - WWS **Prod** - WWS 1979

Rainbow starts school 26 MIN
VHS
Color; PAL (K P)
PdS20 purchase
Presents a documentary about a child starting school. Contact distributor about availability outside the United Kingdom.
Education; Fine Arts; Sociology
Dist - ACADEM

Rainbow war 20 MIN
Videodisc
Color (G)
$295.00 purchase
Presents a multicultural and multinational view of peoples and societies of the world.
Sociology
Dist - PFP

Rainbowland 14 MIN
U-matic / VHS / 16mm
Captioned; Color (I)
Presents Philip Harmonic, the best harmonica player in Rainbowland, who is disgusted with the pollution, graffiti and noise that surround him. His journeys through other lands convince him, finally, that his home land is special, after all.
Fine Arts
Dist - LCOA **Prod** - ARTASI 1979

Rainbows and red skies 25 MIN
VHS
Lightly story series
Color (J H C)
$195.00 purchase
Covers the hows and whys of light - refraction, electromagnetism, dispersion and the wave theory of light. Part of a four - part series on the physics and perception of light.
Science - Physical
Dist - LANDMK **Prod** - LANDMK 1992

Raindace 16 MIN
16mm
Color (C)
$364.00
Experimental film by Standish D Lawder.
Fine Arts
Dist - AFA **Prod** - AFA 1972

Raindance 16 MIN
16mm
Color (G)
$30.00 rental
Uses a scrap of found footage of an old animated cartoon of falling rain. Plays directly on the mind through programmatical stimulation of the central nervous system in which individual frames are imprinted on the retina of the eye with intensity similar to Alpha Wave frequencies of the brain.
Fine Arts; Science - Natural
Dist - CANCIN **Prod** - LAWDRS 1972

Raindrops 90 MIN
16mm
B&W (G) (GERMAN WITH ENGLISH SUBTITLES)
$50.00 rental
Recounts the lives of the Goldbachs, a German - Jewish family forced to sell their business and leave their provincial town as Hitler rises to power. Follows their move to Cologne, where they study English and spend most of their remaining energy seeking visas from uncaring officials at the United States Consulate in Stuttgart. Based partly on co - director Harry Raymon's childhood recollections.
Civics and Political Systems; History - World; Religion and Philosophy; Social Science
Dist - NCJEWF

Raindrops and Frog Hops 15 MIN
VHS / U-matic
Mrs Cabobble's Caboose
(P)
Designed to teach primary grade students basic music concepts. Highlights melody, rhythm, harmony and the different families of instruments. Features Mrs. Fran Powell.
Fine Arts
Dist - GPN **Prod** - WDCNTV 1986

Raindrops and Soil Erosion 21 MIN
16mm
Color
LC FIE52-420
Shows the action of individual raindrops on uncovered soil and emphasizes the need for soil and water conservation methods.
Agriculture; Science - Natural
Dist - USNAC **Prod** - USDA 1947

The Rainforest 10
VHS
Decade of destruction - classroom version series
Color (J H)
$150.00 purchase, $25.00 rental
Uses time - lapse and satellite photography as visual aids to provide a basic understanding of the mechanics of the world's largest rainforest. Shows clouds formed at the coastline then drifting over the heart of the forest. Explains how three - fourths of the rain that falls in the forest is caught by trees and leaves and pumped back into the sky again in a symbiotic process.
Fine Arts; Science - Natural
Dist - BULFRG **Prod** - COWELL 1991

Rainforest 27 MIN
16mm
Color
Presents the premiere performance at the 1968 Buffalo Festival of the Arts of the Merce Cunningham ballet, with music by John Cage. By Richard Leacock and D A Pennebaker.
Fine Arts
Dist - PENNAS **Prod** - PENNAS

The Rainforest 30 MIN
VHS
Earth at risk environmental video series
Color (J H C G)
$49.95 purchase _ #LVPN6629V
Introduces and defines environmental terms and global ecological dilemmas in terms of rainforests. Presents current statistical information. Part of a ten - part series on environmental issues based on a series of books by Chelsea House Publishers and featuring former MTV host Kevin Seal.
Science - Natural
Dist - CAMV

A Rainforest grows in Manhattan 13 MIN
VHS
Color (K P I J)
$125.00 purchase, $45.00 rental
Documents a summer program at an ethnically diverse youth club in Manhattan which introduced students to the plight of the world's rainforests and the need for their actions to confront the situation. Shows that the environment of the club was decorated, painted and planted to recreate a tropical forest. Greenery was imported from the jungle to be transplanted and studies. Older plant experts shared their wisdom. A young man who lived among indigenous people told stories. Produced by Barbara Zahm and Jonathan Stack.
Science - Natural
Dist - FLMLIB

Rainforest People 14 MIN
16mm
Places People Live Series
Color (I)
LC 77-713006
Examines the isolation of people who live behind the barrier of dense vegetation. Tells how the tropical rainforest provides the pygmies of the Congo with all their basic needs. Shows the Waika indians who live along the Orinoco River in the rainforests of Southern Venezuela. Discusses their crops and points out that the river is their sole means of transportation to the outside world.
Geography - World; Social Science
Dist - SF **Prod** - SF 1970

Rainmaking 29 MIN
Videoreel / VT2
Weather Series
Color
Features meteorologist Frank Sechrist explaining how man can and does make rain through cloud seeding. Introduces a couple of theories, such as supercooling and coalescence showing how clouds can produce freezing water drops and then considers the moral and economic aspects of weather modification.
Science - Physical
Dist - PBS **Prod** - WHATV

The Rains Came 55 MIN
U-matic / VHS
Color (I H C A)
Portrays the rain and drought cycle in East Africa and its impact on the animals that live there.
Geography - World; Science - Natural
Dist - BNCHMK **Prod** - BNCHMK 1987

Rainshower 15 MIN
16mm / U-matic / VHS
Color (P I) (SPANISH)
LC FIA65-577
Shows a rainshower which comes to the plants and animals on a farm and to the people in a community.
Science - Physical
Dist - CF **Prod** - CF 1965

Rainshower 15 MIN
U-matic / VHS / 16mm
Color (P I)
$295.00 purchase - 16 mm, $220.00 purchase - video
Shows the sights, sounds, and rhythm of rain on a farm and in a community. Directed by Michael Murphy.
Science - Physical
Dist - CF

A Rainy Day 14 MIN
U-matic / VHS
Strawberry Square Series
Color (P)
Fine Arts
Dist - AITECH **Prod** - NEITV 1982

A Rainy Day 35 MIN
16mm / U-matic / VHS
Color (H C A)
LC 79-700953
Tells the story of a famous actress who returns home for her father's funeral and reminisces about the horrors of her overprotected childhood.
Fine Arts; Literature and Drama; Psychology; Sociology
Dist - LCOA **Prod** - AMERFI 1979

Rainy day 28 MIN
VHS
Elephant show series
Color (P I)
$95.00 purchase, $45.00 rental
Presents program 8 in the Sharon, Lois and Bram's Elephant Show series. Teaches reading readiness and social skills while engaging children in making music. Each program explores a new theme through adventure, fantasy, mystery and song with recording artists Sharon, Lois and Bram. Uses traditional materials which stress participation - action songs, sing - along songs, story songs, clapping songs, singing games, playground chants and folk songs from many different traditions. Includes teacher's guide co - authored by a music education specialist.
Fine Arts; Sociology
Dist - BULFRG **Prod** - CAMBFP 1988

A Rainy day story 13 MIN
U-matic / VHS / 16mm
Color (P I J)
$325.00, $235.00 purchase _ #71081
Discusses methods a child can use to create stories. A Centron film.
English Language; Fine Arts
Dist - CORF

A Rainy Night, a Sick Computer, an Estimate - Estimating to Tens and Hundreds 15 MIN
U-matic / VHS
Figure Out Series
Color (I)
Tells how Alice estimates prices to see if she has enough money for spare parts.
Mathematics
Dist - AITECH **Prod** - MAETEL 1982

Rainy Season in West Africa 14 MIN
U-matic / VHS / 16mm
Man and His World Series
Color (P)
LC 77-705483
Portrays the lives, religion and dress of West African villagers. Follows the planting and harvesting of crops in this dry land using centuries - old methods.
Geography - World; History - United States; Social Science; Sociology
Dist - FI **Prod** - FI 1969

Rainy Sunday 27 MIN
U-matic / VHS / 16mm
Ramona series
Color (P I)
$3795.00 purchase (entire set) - 16 mm, $435.00 purchase - 16 mm
Tells how Ramona and her family become bored and frustrated when their Sunday outing is spoiled by rain, and how a stranger helps them to see that every cloud has a silver lining. From Ramona Quimby, Age 8. A production of Atlantis Films, Ltd. in association with Lancit Media Productions, Ltd. and Revcom Television.
Literature and Drama
Dist - CF

Raise the red lantern 125 MIN
VHS
Color (G) (MANDARIN WITH ENGLISH SUBTITLES)
$79.98 purchase _ #ORN5068V
Portrays a beautiful young woman who has become the fourth wife to a wealthy man but she must compete with his three other wives for his affections. Reveals that every night the wives await the arrival of the red lantern which signifies which woman will be the master's chosen one for the night. Directed by Zhang Yimou.
Fine Arts; Sociology
Dist - CHTSUI

Raised in Anger 54 MIN
16mm / U-matic / VHS
Color (H C A)
LC 80-700185
Explains aspects of child abuse, including how it touches families throughout society and programs available to help parents deal with stress.
Psychology; Sociology
Dist - MEDIAG **Prod** - WQED 1979

A Raisin in the Sun 128 MIN
VHS
B&W (G)
$59.95 purchase _ #S00537
Tells the story of a black Chicago family who searches for understanding of their constrained lives. Based on the play by Lorraine Hansberry. Stars Claudia McNeil, Sidney Poitier, and Ruby Dee. Directed by Daniel Petrie.
Fine Arts; Sociology
Dist - UILL **Prod** - CPC 1961
TIMLIF

Raisin in the Sun
VHS / U-matic
Color (J C I)
Presents the drama of a black family's frustrating life in a crowded Chicago tenement. Stars Sidney Poitier and Ruby Dee.
Fine Arts; History - United States
Dist - GA **Prod** - GA

Raisin in the sun 171 MIN
VHS
Color (G C H)
$89.00 purchase _ #DL76
Presents the American Playhouse version.
Fine Arts
Dist - INSIM

Raising a child with spina bifida - an introduction 14 MIN
VHS
Color (PRO C G)
$250.00 purchase, $70.00 rental _ #4419
Offers the parents of children born with spina bifida the reassurance and information they need. Uses easy - to - understand explanations to define spina bifida and discusses its implications for the child. Covers the procedures that the infant may face, such as a ventricular shunt. Emphasizes the importance of early intervention. Contains footage of happy and healthy children with spina bifida and interviews with parents. Produced by the Children's Hospital of Alabama.
Health and Safety
Dist - AJN

Raising and Lowering Our Flag 11 MIN
16mm
Color (I J)
LC FIA65-1157
Shows the correct way to handle the American flag. Depicts a Marine Corps color detail in the traditional ceremonies of raising and of lowering the flag.
Civics and Political Systems
Dist - FILCOM **Prod** - SIGMA 1964

Raising baby lambs series
Assuring baby lamb survival 23 MIN
Castration, docking and identification 29 MIN
Raising Orphan Lambs 21 MIN
Sheep Obstetrics 29 MIN
Dist - HOBAR

Raising capital 90 MIN
VHS
Color (PRO)
$99.00 purchase _ #IBR30024V
Advises businesses on how to gain capital. Describes the mosaic approach to raising money; how to tap into the private equity market; acquiring capital through the power of negotiated value; shopping tips for finding the best bank to meet a business' needs; and more. Outlines the pitfalls of borrowing money and how to avoid them, as well as how to obtain operational financing.
Business and Economics
Dist - CAMV

Raising Children 59 MIN
VHS / U-matic
Young and Old - Reaching Out Series
Color
LC 80-707699
Explores contrasting views on discipline, religion, parental authority, and youthful rebellion.
Home Economics; Psychology
Dist - PBS **Prod** - CRFI 1979

Raising Children 60 MIN
VHS / U-matic
Color (J)
LC 80-707699
Presents the views of eight persons, half in their twenties and half over 60, as they discuss with their host various aspects of child rearing. Contrasts views on discipline, religion, parental authority, youthful rebellion and personal tragedy.
Guidance and Counseling; Psychology; Sociology
Dist - WINFBC **Prod** - WINFBC 1979

Raising good kids in bad times series
The American dream contest 47 MIN
New and improved kids 47 MIN
See Dick and Jane lie, cheat and steal - teaching morality to kids 47 MIN
Take me to your leaders 47 MIN
The Truth about teachers 47 MIN
Dist - PFP

Raising money and financing 36 MIN
VHS
How to start your own business series
Color (H A T)
$69.95 purchase _ #NC122
Looks at raising money and capital for starting a business. Part of a ten - part series on starting a business.
Business and Economics
Dist - AAVIM **Prod** - AAVIM 1992

Raising Orphan Lambs 21 MIN
U-matic / VHS
Raising Baby Lambs Series
Color
Focuses on how to take care of orphan lambs.
Agriculture
Dist - HOBAR **Prod** - HOBAR

Raising rainbow kids series
Discipline 30 MIN
Emotions 30 MIN
Self esteem 30 MIN
Dist - APH

Raising stewards 30 MIN
VHS
Color (G A R)
$39.95 purchase, $10.00 rental _ #35 - 864 - 2076
Features pastor Mervin Thompson in a presentation on stewardship.
Religion and Philosophy
Dist - APH

Raising Your Parents 30 MIN
VHS / 16mm
Power of Choice Series
(H)
$75.95 #LW112V
Demonstrates how you can make your relationship with your parents work better.
Guidance and Counseling
Dist - JISTW

Raising Your Parents 30 MIN
VHS
Power Of Choice Series
Color (G)
$64.95 purchase _ #CHOI - 112
Features teenagers discussing their relationships with their parents. Explores how the actions of teenagers can affect these relationships. Hosted by comedian and teen counselor Michael Pritchard.
Guidance and Counseling; Psychology; Social Science; Sociology
Dist - PBS **Prod** - LWIRE 1988

Raising your parents 30 MIN
U-matic / VHS
Power of choice series
Color (J H)
$64.95 purchase _ #HH - 6347M
Shows young people how they can affect their relationshps with their parents. Part of a series featuring Michael Pritchard who uses humor to promote positive, life - affirming values and empowers young people to take charge of their lives.
Psychology; Social Science; Sociology
Dist - CORF **Prod** - ELSW 1990

Raising your parents - making your relationships better 30 MIN
VHS
Power of choice series
Color (H)
$89.00 purchase _ #60296 - 025
Features comedian - teen counselor Michael Prichard who helps young people realize that they are responsible for the choices they make, that they owe it to themselves to choose the best. Discusses communication between teenagers and parents, and how to create better family relationships. Part of a twelve - part series on making choices.
Guidance and Counseling; Psychology; Social Science; Sociology
Dist - GA **Prod** - GA 1992

Raiz de Chile - Roots of Chile 50 MIN
VHS
Color (G)
$390.00 purchase, $75.00 rental
Compares the contemporary rural lives of the Aymara and the Mapuche, Chile's largest indigenous groups. Looks at how these cultures have blended their traditional ways with new customs from outside. Touches on the elders' fear of the loss of their children, who are sent away to school and lose interest in learning the languages or traditions. Produced by David Benavente.
Fine Arts; Social Science; Sociology
Dist - FIRS

Raj Gonds 55 MIN
U-matic / VHS / 16mm
Worlds apart series
Color (H C A)
Explains that the Raj Gonds were once a rich and powerful people in Central India, but now live as a tribal group outside the mainstream of Indian life on land owned by landlords. Portrays their annual festival of Dandari in which they cover themselves in dust and ashes and take a self-deprecating look at their present low status, as they make fun of landlords, Gods and bridegrooms.
History - World; Sociology
Dist - FI **Prod** - BBCTV 1982

Rajah Mahendra Pratap 28 MIN
U-matic / VHS / BETA
Faces of India series
Color; NTSC; PAL; SECAM (J H C G)
PdS58
Visits a rajah. Follows the camera into his home where it becomes a part of his environment. Part of a series of portraits on film presenting a cross section of characters from real life.
History - World
Dist - VIEWTH

Rajmohan Gandhi - encounters with truth 40 MIN
VHS / 16mm
Color (H C G)
$750.00, $395.00 purchase, $150.00, $65.00 rental
Portrays author, journalist and campaigner Rajmohan Gandhi, grandson of Mahatma Gandhi, nephew of Indira Gandhi and cousin to Rajiv Gandhi, all assassinated Indian leaders. Discusses the difficulties of India - rural poverty, inhuman housing, pollution, corruption, the caste system, divisiveness. Includes photography of India, original music by flutist Pandit Harisprasad Chaurasia. Produced by David Channer.
Geography - World; History - World; Sociology
Dist - FLMLIB

Raju - a guide from Rishikesh 20 MIN
VHS
Color; PAL (P I J H)
Chooses a boy of nine from the crowds of Rishikesh, India, to follow through a day's work, taking visitors on tour around town. Presents intimate knowledge of the lives of the ordinary people in Rishikesh through the boy's discussion of facts and figures and details of every object he sees. Directed by Yavar Abbas.
Geography - World; History - World
Dist - VIEWTH **Prod** - VIEWTH

Rajvinder - an East Indian Family 16 MIN
U-matic / VHS / 16mm
Color (J H C)
Documents the marriage preparations and wedding of Rajvinder, a young Sikh woman who lives in an East Indian community in North America. Reveals the Sikh culture through traditional activities as well as different stages of the wedding ceremony. Shows the couple's adaptation to living between two cultures.
Social Science; Sociology
Dist - BCNFL **Prod** - BCNFL 1984

The Rake's Progress
VHS / U-matic
Color (G) (ITALIAN (ENGLISH SUBTITLES))
Presents Leo Goeke as Tom Rakewell, Samuel Ramey, Felicity Lott and Rosalind Elias in the David Hockney production conducted by Bernard Haitink.
Fine Arts; Foreign Language
Dist - VAI **Prod** - VAI

Raku Glaze Firing 28 MIN
Videoreel / VT2
Wheels, Kilns and Clay Series
Color
Features Mrs Peterson describing certain ceramic processes for her classroom at the University of Southern California. Demonstrates raku glaze firing.
Fine Arts
Dist - PBS **Prod** - USC

Raku - the Ancient Art of Japanese Ceramics 10 MIN
16mm / U-matic / VHS
Color (J)
LC 72-701043
Covers the basic techniques involved in the ancient Raku process of making pottery.
Fine Arts; Geography - World; Social Science
Dist - AIMS **Prod** - CAHILL 1972

Rally - a Race Against Time 19 MIN
16mm
Color
Depicts a road rally from San Francisco to Sacramento to Reno showing the drivers, navigators and their equipment pitted against unrelenting terrain under the most demanding and varied conditions available.
Physical Education and Recreation
Dist - MTP **Prod** - GC

Rally for Bosnia
VHS
Color (G)
$10.00 purchase _ #110 - 063
Covers the historic Rally for Bosnia on May 15, 1993, in Washington DC. Reveals that more than 50,000 Muslims marched for Bosnia.
Fine Arts; Sociology
Dist - SOUVIS **Prod** - SOUVIS

Ralph 10 MIN
16mm
B&W (G)
$20.00 rental
Tells the story of Ralph who invested his entire life savings so he could go into business for himself despite his wife's vehement objections. Broaches the subject of the American dream versus spirit of the family. Produced by Paul Heilemann.
Fine Arts; History - United States; Sociology
Dist - CANCIN

Ralph Adamo - 2 - 18 - 82 30 MIN
VHS / Cassette
Poetry Center reading series
Color (G)
$15.00, $45.00 purchase _ #471 - 400
Features the poet reading his works at the Poetry Center, San Francisco State University.
Literature and Drama
Dist - POETRY **Prod** - POETRY 1982

Ralph Angel - 4 - 9 - 87 38 MIN
VHS / Cassette
Poetry Center reading series
Color (G)
$15.00, $45.00 purchase _ #753 - 601
Features the poet reading selections from Anxious Latitudes at the Poetry Center, San Francisco State University, with an introduction by Frances Phillips.
Literature and Drama
Dist - POETRY **Prod** - POETRY 1987

Ralph Erskine 58 MIN
16mm / VHS
Color (H C)
$875.00, $290.00 purchase, $110.00 rental
Portrays the British born architect, Ralph Erskine who has spent his professional years living and working in Sweden.
Biography; Fine Arts; Foreign Language
Dist - BLACKW **Prod** - BLACKW 1985

Ralph Fasanella, Song of the City 25 MIN
16mm
Color (H C A)
LC 79-701720
Describes the life and works of self - taught painter Ralph Fasanella. Emphasizes the themes that make up his work, including his troubled youth, hard - working immigrant parents and labor organizing activities.
Biography; Fine Arts
Dist - BOWGRN **Prod** - BOWGRN 1979

Ralph Kirkpatrick plays Bach 58 MIN
U-matic / VHS
Color (C)
$79.95 purchase _ #EX1334
Presents a performance by harpsichordist Ralph Kirpatrick of music by J S Bach. Features the Toccata in D, Chromatic Fantasy and Fugue, and Partita No 5 in G.
Fine Arts; History - World
Dist - FOTH **Prod** - FOTH

Ralph Nader - Opinion Leader 30 MIN
VHS / U-matic
American Government Series; 1
Color (C)
Illustrates the way consumer advocate Ralph Nader rose from relative obscurity to his position as a national opinion leader, as well as the reasons he is able to command national attention.
Civics and Political Systems
Dist - DALCCD **Prod** - DALCCD

Ralph Nader - up close 72 MIN
16mm / VHS
Color (G J H)
$995.00, $395.00 purchase, $100.00 rental
Profiles America's leading consumer advocate and author who has been responsible for the passage of dozen of major environmental, consumer and safety reforms. Blends archival footage and scenes of Nader with his staff at work in Washingon, DC. Includes interviews with Nader, his friends and adversaries. Also available for rental and purchase in 49 minute and 30 minute versions in film and video. Study guide available. Directed by Mark Litwak and Tiiu Lukk.
Fine Arts; Home Economics; Social Science
Dist - CNEMAG

Ralph S Mouse 40 MIN
VHS / Videodisc
Color (K P I)
$99.95, $59.95 purchase _ #L10408
Reveals that when Mountain View Inn is overrun with 'country mice,' Ralph must leave again on his third adventure. Follows Ralph and friend Ryan to school where Ralph inspires a class project on mice. Ryan meets the school bully and Ralph's beloved motorcycle is crushed, a TV journalist says that the school is infested with mice and the school janitor tries to catch Ralph with a diabolical trap. Will Ralph be snared by the janitor, will Ralph make it through the maze, what will Ryan do about the bully. Stars Robert Oliveri as Ryan, Karen Black as Miss Kuckenbacker, and Ray Walston as Matt, the crusty doorman with a soft spot for talking mice. From the book by Beverly Cleary, dimensional animation by John Matthews.
Literature and Drama
Dist - CF **Prod** - MATTHE 1990

Ralph Stanley's Bluegrass Festival 15 MIN
U-matic / VHS
Color
LC 84-707294
Captures Bluegrass performer Ralph Stanley's foot stomping, hand clapping, outdoor music festival and pays tribute to the Stanley family.
Fine Arts
Dist - AMBERO **Prod** - AMBERO 1984

Ralph Steadman 50 MIN
VHS
Color (H C G)
$79.00 purchase
Features the cartoonist and illustrator talking with Peter Fuller about drawing caricatures, using satire in pictures and illustrating children's books. Discusses his drawings for publications and for children Alice In Wonderland; The Jelly Book; and The Hunting of the Snark, among others. Also notes his collection of essays and his books on Sigmund freud and Leonardo da Vinci.
Fine Arts; Literature and Drama
Dist - ROLAND **Prod** - INCART

Ralph Votapek - Pianist 29 MIN
Videoreel / VT2
Young Musical Artists Series
Color
Presents the music of pianist Ralph Votapek.
Fine Arts
Dist - PBS **Prod** - WKARTV

Ralph Waldo Emerson - Self - Reliance, Emerson's Philosophy 30 MIN
Videoreel / VT2
B&W (J H)
Literature and Drama; Religion and Philosophy
Dist - GPN **Prod** - GPN

Ralph's arm 30 MIN
VHS
Short stories - video anthology series
Color (H G)
$59.95 purchase
Features the story of Ralph and his arm. Shows a world famous pianist stranded without his arm and forced to search the wilds of Beverly Hills for it. He finds it hiding in the hacienda of a blase Yuppie couple. Presents a film directed by Michelle Truffaut. Part of a sixteen - part anthology of short dramas by young American filmmakers.
Fine Arts; Literature and Drama
Dist - CNEMAG

Ralph's busy day 14 MIN
16mm
B&W (G)
$10.00 rental
Tells the story of a toy who comes to life and wanders San Francisco in search of a free lunch. Features tourists, street artists, cable cars and various objects, animate and inanimate. A modern silent comedy with piano sound track by Dr Real.
Fine Arts
Dist - CANCIN **Prod** - COHENK 1973

Ramakrishna 78 MIN
VHS
Color (G)
$29.95 purchase _ #V - RAMA
Presents information and rare footage portraying the life of Ramakrishna.
Religion and Philosophy
Dist - PACSPI

Rameau, the Harpsichord, and George Malcolm 26 MIN
16mm / U-matic / VHS
Musical Triangle Series
Color (J)
Presents French composer and theorist Jean Philippe Rameau (1683 - 1764), who composed both suites and operas for the harpsichord. Features professional musician George Malcolm who describes the harpsichord and plays several selections from some of Rameau's compositions.
Fine Arts
Dist - MEDIAG **Prod** - THAMES 1975

Rameau's nephew, by Diderot 240 MIN
16mm
Color
LC 74-703008
Presents an adaptation of Diderot's book Rameau's Nephew.
Fine Arts
Dist - CANFDC **Prod** - SNOWM 1973

Ramifications of normal value 50 MIN
U-matic / VHS
Computer languages series; Pt 1
Color
Discusses relativity of privileged names and implications of changes in order of evaluation in computer languages.
Industrial and Technical Education; Mathematics; Sociology
Dist - MIOT **Prod** - MIOT

Ramlila 13 MIN
16mm
B&W (I)
Presents the Ramlila celebrations as performed in Delhi where the legend of Rama and Sita is unfolded. Includes recitations from Tulsidas' 'Ramayana.'
History - World; Literature and Drama
Dist - NEDINF **Prod** - INDIA

Rammed earth construction 29 MIN
VHS
Ecology workshop series
Color (J H C G)
$195.00 purchase, $50.00 rental
Discusses the rammed earth construction method which is still in use in many parts of the world. Points out that this method of construction saves energy and produces beautiful structures.
Science - Natural; Science - Physical
Dist - BULFRG **Prod** - BULFRG 1987

Ramona 93 MIN
16mm
B&W (SPANISH)
A Spanish language film. Explores the story of an adopted Indian girl and the problems that develop when she falls in love and marries a young Indian man.
Fine Arts; Foreign Language
Dist - TRANSW **Prod** - TRANSW

Ramona - a Story of Passion and Protest 28 MIN
U-matic / VHS
Color (C)
$249.00, $149.00 purchase _ #AD - 1947
Uses feature film clips to recap the plot of 'Ramona' by Helen Hunt Jackson, and historical sources and sites to explain both the popularity of the book and its transformation into a mythic symbol of interaction between white and Indians in the West.
Fine Arts; Literature and Drama
Dist - FOTH **Prod** - FOTH

Ramona series
Presents ten episodes about 8 - year - old Ramona Quimby and her family from the stories by Beverly Cleary. Includes Ramona's Bad Day; The Great Hair Argument; New Pajamas; Squeakerfoot; Mystery Meal; Ramona the Patient; Rainy Sunday; Goodbye, Hello; The Perfect Day; and Siblingitis.

Goodbye, hello	27 MIN
The Great hair argument	27 MIN
Mystery Meal	27 MIN
New Pajamas	27 MIN
The Perfect Day	27 MIN
Rainy Sunday	27 MIN
Ramona the patient	27 MIN
Ramona's bad day	27 MIN
Siblingitis	27 MIN
Squeakerfoot	27 MIN

Dist - CF **Prod** - LNMDP

Ramona the patient 27 MIN
U-matic / VHS / 16mm
Ramona series
Color (P I)
$3795.00, $435.00 purchase
Tells how Ramona is afraid to go back to school after throwing up in front of her classmates, and how having a book report forces her to go back. From Ramona Quimby, Age 8. A production of Atlantis Films, Ltd. in association with Lancit Media Productions, Ltd. and Revcom Television.
Literature and Drama
Dist - CF

Ramona's bad day 27 MIN
U-matic / VHS / 16mm
Ramona series
Color (P I)
$3795.00, $435.00 purchase
Describes a day when everything seems to go wrong for Ramona. From Ramona and Her Mother. A production of Atlantis Fillms, Ltd. in association with Lancit Media Productions, Ltd. and Revcom Television.
Literature and Drama; Sociology
Dist - CF

Ramp metering - signal for success 17 MIN
U-matic / VHS
Color (A PRO)
$65.00, $95.00 purchase _ #TCA17495, #TCA17494
Deals with ramp metering, explaining how it works as a means of controlling traffic as it enters and drives on freeways.
Civics and Political Systems; Industrial and Technical Education; Social Science
Dist - USNAC **Prod** - USDTFH 1988

Rampaging Carbons 27 MIN
U-matic / VHS / 16mm
Perspective Series
Color (J)
Discusses the 'Greenhouse Effect' - the increase in the carbon dioxide content of the air - and its cause and its potential effects.
Science - Natural; Science - Physical
Dist - STNFLD **Prod** - LONTVS

The Ramsey trade fair 20 MIN
16mm
Color (H C A)
LC 74-702536
Visits the weekly flea market in Ramsey, West Virginia, where a variety of articles and gossip are traded in a spirit of fair play and hard bargaining.
Business and Economics; Geography - United States; Social Science
Dist - APPAL **Prod** - APPAL 1974

Ramus Endosseous Implant 20 MIN
16mm
Color (PRO)
Examines the use of the ramus endosseous implant and presents patients who have been using them for as many as three years.
Health and Safety
Dist - LOMAM **Prod** - LOMAM

Ran 160 MIN
Videodisc / VHS
Color (G) (JAPANESE WITH ENGLISH SUBTITLES)
$35.95, $44.98 purchase _ #FOX3732, #3732-80; $79.98 purchase _ #S00922
Tells the story of an aging leader in 16th - century Japan who attempts to peacefully divide his hard - won kingdom amongst his three sons. Directed by Akira Kurosawa.
Fine Arts
Dist - CHTSUI
UILL

Rana 19 MIN
16mm / U-matic / VHS
Color (J)
LC 78-700883
Follows the everyday activities of a young Moslem college student in Old Delhi. Points out the restrictions of her religion and includes interviews with her family.
Geography - World; Religion and Philosophy; Sociology
Dist - WOMBAT **Prod** - FLMAUS 1977

Ranch girl 16 MIN
U-matic / VHS / 16mm
Color (P I J)
LC 76-701559
Uses the snow capped Teton peaks as a background for a portrait of a self - reliant girl who helps with her family's occupation, ranching. Shows her spending the day riding, exploring and looking for Indian relics.
Agriculture; Sociology
Dist - AIMS **Prod** - GORKER 1972

Ranch Hand 15 MIN
16mm / U-matic / VHS
Career Awareness
(I)
$130 VC purchase, $240 film purchase, $25 VC rental, $30 film rental
Presents an empathetic approach to career planning, showing the personal as well as the professional attributes of ranch hands. Highlights the importance of career education.
Agriculture; Guidance and Counseling
Dist - GPN

A Ranch in South America - Venezuela 8 MIN
VHS
Nature's kingdom series; Pt 19
Color (P I J)
$125.00 purchase
Visits a ranch in Venzuela. Shows cattle with ornamental humps, tiny deer and capybara who surround gauchos who are struggling to control half - wild horses. Reveals that there are more than 10,000 animals on this ranch. Part of a 26 - part series on animals showing the habitats and traits of various species.
Agriculture; Geography - World
Dist - LANDMK **Prod** - LANDMK 1992

The Ranch - Pt 1 14 MIN
Videoreel / VT2
Muffinland Series
Color
Literature and Drama
Dist - PBS **Prod** - WGTV

The Ranch - Pt 2 14 MIN
Videoreel / VT2
Muffinland series
Color
Literature and Drama
Dist - PBS **Prod** - WGTV

Rancher Glen's Secrets 10 MIN
16mm
Color (P)
Rancher Glen, the healthy cowboy of the Tuberculosis Association, explains why and how the tuberculin skin test is given.
Health and Safety
Dist - WSUM **Prod** - WSUM 1961

Ranchero and gauchos in Argentina 17 MIN
16mm / U-matic / VHS
Man and his world series
Color (P I J H C)
LC 70-705492
Describes the ranch life on a beef ranch. Shows gauchos working with the herd and the use of scientific farming methods. Contrasts the affluence and poverty on the ranch. Examines Spanish architecture and furnishings.
Agriculture; Geography - World; Social Science
Dist - FI **Prod** - FI 1969

Ranching and Farming Series
The Danish Field 7 MIN
Spanish Ranching in Texas 7 MIN
Dist - UTXITC

Rancho La Puerta - yoga - meditation in action 54 MIN
VHS
Color (G)
$29.75 purchase
Presents a graduated series of yoga postures performed outdoors at Rancho La Puerta in Baja California, Mexico. Features Phyllis Pilgrim as instructor.
Health and Safety; Physical Education and Recreation
Dist - GODOOR **Prod** - GODOOR 1990

Rancho Notorious 89 MIN
U-matic / VHS / 16mm
Color (C A)
Stars Arthur Kennedy and Marlene Dietrich. Follows a rancher's search for the murderer of his fiancee.
Fine Arts
Dist - FI **Prod** - RKOP 1952

Random access memory applications - Pt 1 60 MIN
Videoreel / VT1
Semiconductor memories course series; No 9
Color (IND)
Gives application examples of systems ranging in size from small scratch pad memory systems to a minicomputer mainframe.
Industrial and Technical Education
Dist - TXINLC **Prod** - TXINLC

Random access memory applications - Pt 2 60 MIN
Videoreel / VT1
Semiconductor memories course series; No 10
Color (IND)
Details MOS random access memory applications. Emphasizes considerations unique to MOS, including drive requirements, refresh and clock timing.
Industrial and Technical Education
Dist - TXINLC **Prod** - TXINLC

Random access memory applications - Pt 3 60 MIN
Videoreel / VT1
Semiconductor memories course series; No 11
Color (IND)
Describes thoroughly the level cache, core, MOS, ECL and TTL memory systems. Emphasizes the comparison of these memory systems.
Industrial and Technical Education
Dist - TXINLC **Prod** - TXINLC

Random events 31 MIN
16mm
PSSC physics films series
B&W (H C)
Shows how the over - all effect of a very large number of random events can be very predictable. Several unusual games are played to bring out the statistical nature of this predictability. The predictable nature of radioactive decay is explained.
Mathematics; Science - Physical
Dist - MLA **Prod** - PSSC 1962

Random processes - basic concepts and definitions 28 MIN
U-matic / VHS
Probability and random processes - introduction to random processes' series
Color (PRO)
Mathematics
Dist - MIOT **Prod** - MIOT

Random telegraph wave 24 MIN
U-matic / VHS
Probability and random processes - introduction to random processes' series
B&W (PRO)
Considers the random telegraph wave and uses that example to introduce the minimum mean - square error (MMSE) prediction problem.
Mathematics
Dist - MIOT **Prod** - MIOT

Random variables and distributions
VHS
Probability and statistics series
Color (H C)
$125.00 purchase _ #8017
Provides resource material about random variables and distributions for help in the study of probability and statistics. Presents a 60 - video series, each part 25 to 30 minutes long, that explains and reinforces concepts using definitions, theorems, examples and step - by - step solutions to tutor the student. Videos are also available in a set.
Mathematics
Dist - LANDMK

Random variables - Pt 1 26 MIN
VHS / U-matic
Probability and random processes - random variables series
B&W (PRO)
Introduces random variables. Defines probability distributions and probability distribution functions.
Industrial and Technical Education; Mathematics
Dist - MIOT **Prod** - MIOT

Random variables - Pt 2 20 MIN
VHS / U-matic
Probability and random processes - random variables series
B&W (PRO)
Discusses random variables and probability density functions and their properties.
Industrial and Technical Education; Mathematics
Dist - MIOT **Prod** - MIOT

Randy 27 MIN
VHS / 16mm
Wediko series
B&W (C G PRO)
$400.00, $70.00 purchase, $36.00, $18.00 rental _ #35648
Records the attempts of four staff people at Camp Wediko to help Randy, an 11 - year - old boy whose beguiling but inconsistent behavior makes care difficult, with varying degrees of success. Includes print material. Part of a series recording spontaneous behavior at Camp Wediko, a pioneer facility for therapeutic camping in Hillsboro, New Hampshire.
Health and Safety; Physical Education and Recreation; Psychology
Dist - PSU **Prod** - MASON 1970

Randy's up - Randy's down 22 MIN
16mm
Color (C A)
LC 78-701608
Depicts a child's progress and regressions during the administration of contingent shock therapy for controlling self - abusive behavior in an institutional environment. Focuses on the child's behavior as well as the moods and attitudes of the workers and psychologists dealing with him day to day.
Health and Safety; Psychology
Dist - UKANS **Prod** - UKANS 1977

Range Allotment Analysis 47 MIN
16mm
Color
LC 75-701372
Shows the systematic method used by range managers in the U S Forest Service to collect information on which to base their management plans and decisions for the National Forests and National Grasslands.
Agriculture; Science - Natural
Dist - USNAC **Prod** - USDA 1965

Range Determination 21 MIN
16mm
B&W
LC 80-701839
Describes various range determination methods, such as binoculars, registration maps, and observation of flash and sound.
Civics and Political Systems
Dist - USNAC **Prod** - USA 1980

The Range of Change 15 MIN
U-matic
Landscape of Geometry Series
Color (J)
Examines transformation in nature and geometry. Explains translation, rotation and reflection.
Education; Mathematics
Dist - TVOTAR **Prod** - TVOTAR 1982

Range of motion 21 MIN
BETA / VHS / U-matic
Basic nursing skills series
Color (C PRO)
$280.00 purchase _ #621.1
Explains the objectives of range of motion. Defines key terminology for the understanding and performance of this skill. Shows examples of joints and illustrates joint movements. Discusses guidelines for implementing range of motion. Demonstrates step - by - step range of motion exercises. Produced by the Nursing Program, Indiana University - Purdue University. Part of a three - part series on basic nursing skills.
Health and Safety; Science - Natural
Dist - CONMED

Range of motion and positioning - Tape 2 26 MIN
VHS
Increased mobility for the elderly series
Color (PRO)
$80.00 purchase _ #876
Teaches nurses and health professionals about range of motion and positioning in acute rehabilitation of elderly patients or for long term care settings. Presents the work of W Griggs and K S Black.

Health and Safety; Sociology
Dist - RICHGO **Prod** - RICHGO 1985

Range of Motion for Physical Rehabilitation Series
Exercises to Mobilize the Shoulder 7 MIN
Joint Motion 6 MIN
Dist - PRIMED

Range of Motion - the Lower Extremity 19 MIN
U-matic / VHS
B&W
Shows a step - by - step demonstration of the range of motion exercises for the joints of the lower extremity.
Health and Safety
Dist - BUSARG **Prod** - BUSARG

Range of Motion - the Upper Extremity 24 MIN
U-matic / VHS
B&W
Shows a step - by - step demonstation of motion exercises for the joints of the upper extremity.
Health and Safety
Dist - BUSARG **Prod** - BUSARG

Rangelands - an American Heritage 24 MIN
16mm
Color
LC 77-702409
Emphasizes the importance of the American rangelands in providing clean water, recreational areas, vegetation for livestock and other natural resources.
Geography - United States; Science - Natural
Dist - SOCRM **Prod** - SOCRM 1977

Rangelands - the Silent Resources 24 MIN
16mm
Color
LC 77-702410
Stresses the importance of the American rangelands as a natural resource and explains techniques for proper range management.
Geography - United States; Science - Natural
Dist - SOCRM **Prod** - SOCRM 1977

Ranger 29 MIN
16mm
Big picture series
Color
LC 74-705476
Points out that the small unit leader must be resourceful and capable of directing operations under many types of geographic and climatic conditions. Shows how rangers are trained at Fort Benning, Georgia.
Agriculture; Business and Economics; Guidance and Counseling
Dist - USNAC **Prod** - USA 1968

Ranger 8 - television pictures of the moon 8 MIN
16mm
B&W
LC 74-706386
Shows the photographs of the moon taken by Ranger 8 on February 17, 1965. Gives a detailed description of selected photographs.
Industrial and Technical Education
Dist - USNAC **Prod** - NASA 1965

Ranger 7 - photographs of the moon 8 MIN
16mm
B&W
LC 74-706385
Describes the photographs of the moon taken by Ranger 7 on July 31, 1964. Gives a detailed description of selected photographs.
Industrial and Technical Education
Dist - USNAC **Prod** - NASA 1964

Ranger - the Ultimate Soldier 32 MIN
16mm
Color (A)
LC 77-700728
Describes the objectives and nature of ranger training offered in the U S Army, including physical conditioning, military mountaineering and guerilla warfare.
Education; Guidance and Counseling
Dist - USNAC **Prod** - USA 1968

Rangi and Papa (Maori creation myth) 8 MIN
VHS / U-matic
Color (J)
Shows in animation the story of the creation, based on ancient wood and stone carvings. Tells of the gods' struggle to separate themselves from their parents and, once free, to develop their creative powers and shape the universe.
Geography - World; Literature and Drama; Religion and Philosophy
Dist - IFF **Prod** - IFF

Rank test
VHS
Probability and statistics series
Color (H C)
$125.00 purchase _ #8059
Provides resource material about rank testing for help in the study of probability and statistics. Presents part of a 60 - video series, each part 25 to 30 minutes long, that explains and reinforces concepts using definitions, theorems, examples and step - by - step solutions to tutor the student. Videos are also available in a set.
Mathematics
Dist - LANDMK

Ransom 5 MIN
16mm
Color (P)
Uses animation in a story in which the kidnappers of a young girl struggle to spell a word in their ransom note, with a series of rather humorous variants resulting.
English Language
Dist - USC **Prod** - USC

Ransom note 2 MIN
16mm
Color (G)
$5.00 rental
Asks the audience to perform certain tasks. Presents an animated experiment on audience participation.
Fine Arts
Dist - CANCIN **Prod** - LEHE 1969

Ransom of Red Chief 24 MIN
U-matic / VHS / 16mm
Color (I J)
Recounts the tale of two scoundrels who kidnap a young boy with the hope of collecting a large ransom for his return. Reveals, however, that the boy turns out to be more trouble than they bargained for and the abductors gladly pay the boy's father to take back the mischievous child. Based on a short story by O Henry and produced for the ABC Weekend Specials.
Fine Arts; Literature and Drama
Dist - CORF **Prod** - ABCLR 1983

Raoul Dufy - painter and decorator 58 MIN
VHS
Color (H C A)
$39.95 purchase _ #833 - 9526
Reveals why many believe Raoul Dufy to be one of this century's most influential designers and an innovative painter who ranks alongside Matisse and Leger. Interviews Dufy's colleagues and critics and views a variety of his ceramics, wall hangings, furniture and fabric designs as evidence of his adventurous artistry.
Fine Arts; History - World
Dist - FI **Prod** - RMART 1989
ARTSAM

Raoul Wallenberg - Buried Alive 78 MIN
U-matic / VHS / 16mm
Color (J A G)
Focuses on the true story of the young Swedish man, Raoul Wallenberg who saved thousands of Hungarian Jews during the Nazi holocaust, only to vanish forever into Russian prisions at the end of WWII. Traces Wallenberg's almost superhuman efforts on behalf of the American Red Cross, as well as international attempts to free him, the film offers some answers to the mystery of this war hero who never fired a gun.
Biography; History - United States; History - World
Dist - DIRECT **Prod** - RUBCON 1984

Rap letters 39 MIN
16mm
Color (G)
Presents an Andras Szirtes production. Inquire for rental price.
Fine Arts
Dist - CANCIN

Rap - o - matics 12 MIN
VHS / U-matic
Color (J H)
$240.00, $290.00 purchase, $50.00 rental
Dramatizes the value of math and science to heighten student awareness.
Mathematics; Science
Dist - NDIM **Prod** - ITF 1992

Rape 40 MIN
VHS
40 minutes series
Color; PAL (H C A)
PdS65 purchase
Features the intersecting stories of Jane, a rape victim beginning a journey of recovery, and Paul, a rapist serving two life sentences for his crime. Documents the meeting between the two at the Grendon Underwood Prison, where Paul has volunteered to undergo ten weeks of therapy. Focuses on Jane's attempt to glean insight from her face - to -face encounter with a rapist.
Sociology
Dist - BBCENE

Rape 25 MIN
U-matic / VHS
Color
Includes interviews with four rape victims who explain their ordeal and how they dealt with it. Shows how to defend oneself when in a rape situation.
Civics and Political Systems; Sociology
Dist - MEDCOM **Prod** - MEDCOM

Rape - a new perspective 7 MIN
VHS
Color (H C G)
Looks at rape as the only crime in which the victim's innocence becomes an issue. Challenges the widely held premise that the victim's behavior in the crime of rape is a defense for the rapist. Uses the cross - examination of a robbery victim to contrast with the ordeal rape victims must face in courts of law.
Civics and Political Systems; Sociology
Dist - VIEWTH **Prod** - SUMHIL
CORF

Rape - a Preventive Inquiry 18 MIN
U-matic / VHS / 16mm
Color (J) (SPANISH)
Portrays four rape victims, a college student, a businesswoman, a secretary and a mother, who relate the circumstances surrounding their attacks and methods of escape in what the police call the four most common cases - hitchhiking, casual acquaintance, hot prowl and kidnapping.
Sociology
Dist - CORF **Prod** - MITCHG 1974

Rape Alert 17 MIN
16mm / U-matic / VHS
Color (J) (SPANISH)
LC 76-702133
Offers hints to women on defense against rape, including how to make the home secure, how to avoid hazards, how to use available weapons in case of attack and how to try to escape.
Health and Safety; Sociology
Dist - AIMS **Prod** - CAHILL 1975

Rape - an Act of Hate 30 MIN
VHS / 16mm
Color (G)
$149.00, $249.00, purchase _ #AD - 1055
Seeks to determine why people commit rape and shows potential victims how to protect themselves. Examines the history and mythology of rape, explains who are the most likely victims and contains interviews with experts in law enforcement, media, and sociology. Hosted by Veronica Hamel.
Health and Safety; Psychology; Sociology
Dist - FOTH **Prod** - FOTH 1990

Rape and the rapist 15 MIN
16mm / U-matic / VHS
Color (PRO)
LC 78-701162
Uses a series of vignettes to examine the psychology of the rapist, including research which indicates that rapists are primarily motivated by the desire to dominate and to inflict suffering.
Psychology; Sociology
Dist - CORF **Prod** - DAVP 1978

Rape by any name 60 MIN
VHS
Color (G)
$295.00 purchase, $75.00 rental
Interviews survivors of rape, counselors and male and female college students. Draws boundaries between coercive and consensual sex through testimony from three date rape survivors, in contrast with a male defense attorney's justification of 'casual' versus 'absolute' rape. Examines male socialization, lack of legal recognition and the victim's assumed culpability. Produced by Angelique LaCouer and Wade Hanks.
Guidance and Counseling; Health and Safety; Sociology
Dist - WMEN

Rape - Caring for the Adult Female Victim 29 MIN
U-matic / VHS / 16mm
Color (PRO)
Portrays the trauma of rape and demonstrates the procedures and approaches to be used by emergency room personnel in treating rape victims, emphasizing sensitivity to the needs of the victim.
Health and Safety; Sociology
Dist - USNAC **Prod** - USNAC

Rape / Crisis 87 MIN
U-matic / VHS / 16mm
Color (J)
Investigates the trauma of rape, documents the experience of the rape victim and provides insight into the root causes of sexual violence in society.
Sociology
Dist - CNEMAG **Prod** - SAMHUN 1983

Rape Culture 35 MIN
16mm
Color
Considers the phenomenon of rape in relation to the cultural and social forces that produce rapists and rape victims. Includes the opinions of convicted rapists, rape crisis center workers and others associated with the problem.
Psychology; Sociology
Dist - CMBRD **Prod** - CMBRD 1983

Rape - Escape Without Violence 18 MIN
U-matic / VHS / 16mm
Color (J)
Shows women how to stop a rapist in a non - violent manner. Emphasizes home security and planning travel routes for optimum safety.
Health and Safety; Sociology
Dist - PEREN **Prod** - COXBAR

Rape - face to face
VHS / U-matic
Color
Features a remarkable confrontation between four female rape victims and four young men who are undergoing treatment in a sex offenders program.
Psychology; Sociology
Dist - FLMLIB **Prod** - FLMLIB 1984

Rape is a social disease 28 MIN
U-matic
Color
Looks at the image of women and rape presented in classical art and modern day advertising. Dramatizes some of the most common myths surrounding rape to dispel the myths and pinpoint the facts. Analyzes how males are socialized into aggressive roles and women into passive roles.
Psychology; Sociology
Dist - WMENIF **Prod** - WMENIF

Rape is not an option 50 MIN
VHS
Color (G I J H)
$29.95 purchase _ #SD07
Makes a case for prevention of rape rather than helping victims after the fact. Discusses rapist profiles, how to remain in control during vulnerable situations and the classification of rape in Part 1. Part 2 discusses how to act rather than react, the stages of sexual assault, recognizing and avoiding situations, and redirecting the attacker's thinking. Presents several common - sense defense techniques that require no special skills. Includes a 35 - page booklet.
Sociology
Dist - SVIP

Rape - it Can Happen to You 17 MIN
U-matic / VHS / 16mm
Color (J)
Presents dramatic vignettes showing how five women were raped in ordinary circumstances in which they behaved naturally, but too trustingly. Helps teach women how to develop a self - protection program against rape.
Sociology
Dist - AIMS **Prod** - GORKER 1983

Rape - not always a stranger 25 MIN
VHS / U-matic / BETA / 16mm
Color (H G C)
Provides guidelines to minimize the risk of being raped.
Health and Safety; Sociology
Dist - AIMS **Prod** - AIMS 1991

The Rape of the lock
16mm
Stereo
Presents a selection from the works of Alexander Pope. Includes The Rape Of The Lock - Cantos I and II; An Essay On Man - Epistle II; The Dunciad - Book IV; Epistle To Dr Arbuthnot and Epistle To A Lady. Read by Sir Michael Redgrave.
Literature and Drama
Dist - CAEDMN **Prod** - CAEDMN

Rape prevention series
He loves me not 29 MIN
Dist - USNAC

Rape prevention - trust your instincts 18 MIN
BETA / VHS / U-matic
Color (H C G)
$275.00 purchase _ #KC - 5789M
Teaches women to raise their level of awareness to their surroundings and to project the kind of nonverbal assertiveness that discourages rapists. Instills an effective nonviolent approach to rape prevention.
Sociology
Dist - CORF **Prod** - FILMA 1989

Rape Relief 28 MIN
U-matic
Color
Presents a member of the Vancouver Rape Relief talking about the problem of rape and the work done by Rape Relief.
History - World; Sociology
Dist - WMENIF **Prod** - WMENIF

Rape response 31 MIN
VHS
Crime to court procedural specials series
Color (PRO)
$99.00 purchase
Scrutinizes an officer's initial personal response to a rape case and his involvement and evolution as the case progressed. Enables officers to better understand the crime and its emotional consequences. Trains law enforcement personnel. Part of an ongoing series to look in depth at topics presented in Crime To Court. Produced in cooperation with the South Carolina Criminal Justice Academy and the National Sheriff's Association.
Civics and Political Systems; Sociology
Dist - SCETV **Prod** - SCETV

Rape stories 25 MIN
VHS / U-matic
Color; B&W (G)
$250.00, $200.00 purchase, $50.00 rental
Reveals that in October, 1978, Margie Strosser was raped in the elevator of her apartment building. Tells how, two weeks later, she asked a friend to interview her about the rape. Ten years later she remembers and recounts the incident, integrating the experience over time and revealing the process of healing.
Sociology
Dist - WMEN **Prod** - MASTRO 1989

Rape - the boundaries of fear 30 MIN
U-matic
Color (H C A)
Examines the problem of rape today. Includes interviews and social action.
Sociology
Dist - CEPRO **Prod** - CEPRO

Rape - the community viewpoint 20 MIN
VHS / U-matic
B&W
Examines public sentiment about rape, raises questions about the treatment of rape victims and tackles some of the myths about rape.
Psychology; Sociology
Dist - NOVID **Prod** - NOVID

Rape - the right to resist 17 MIN
16mm / U-matic / VHS
Color (J)
LC 76-702134
Presents the positive options that a woman has available to her under attack or attempted rape conditions. Shows how to face an assailant and strategies to use in evading and escaping.
Health and Safety; Sociology
Dist - AIMS **Prod** - AIMS 1975

Rape - Victim or Victor 17 MIN
U-matic / VHS / 16mm
Color (H C A)
LC 79-700092
Deals with situations in which rapes occur and demonstrates precautions which women can take to reduce the risk of attack. Offers guidelines about how to avoid vulnerability, how to prevent an intruder from entering a home or automobile and how, if trouble arises, to attract attention and escape.
Health and Safety; Sociology
Dist - CORF **Prod** - LACSD 1978

Rape - Victim or Victor 17 MIN
16mm
Color
Emphasizes that there are no hard and fast rules to follow to avoid being raped, but there are things women can do to protect themselves and reduce the risk.
Sociology
Dist - MTP **Prod** - NCPCR

The Rape Victims 22 MIN
U-matic / VHS / 16mm
Color
LC 79-700264
Presents information on rape and an assessment of the act as a social problem. Includes a discussion of punishment for rapists, the history of rape and the psychology of the act of rape.
Sociology
Dist - MEDIAG **Prod** - MEDIAG 1978

Rapeutic Relationships Series
Therapeutic Silence 30 MIN
Dist - AJN

Raphael - Legend and legacy 60 MIN
U-matic
Color (H C A)
$39.95 purchase
Examines the work of Raphael in his later years as seen on location where he lived and worked. Written and narrated by David Thompson.
Fine Arts; History - World
Dist - ARTSAM **Prod** - RMART

Raphael Series
The Apprentice years - Pt 1 60 MIN
Legend and Legacy - Pt 3 60 MIN
Dist - ARTSAM
CRYSP
FI

Raphael - The Apprentice years 60 MIN
U-matic
Color (H C A)
$39.95 purchase
Examines the work of Raphael in his early years as seen on location where he lived and worked. Written and narrated by David Thompson.
Fine Arts; History - World
Dist - ARTSAM **Prod** - RMART

Raphael - The Prince of painters 60 MIN
U-matic
Color (H C A)
$39.95 purchase
Examines the work of Raphael in his middle years as seen on location where he lived and worked. Written and narrated by David Thompson.
Fine Arts; History - World
Dist - ARTSAM **Prod** - RMART

Rapid Frozen Section Techniques 6 MIN
16mm
Color
LC FIE67-512
A training film for hospital medical technologists in a rapid method of preparing tissue sections for examination by the hospital pathologists. Demonstrates how the specimen is identified, trimmed for sectioning, placed on the microtome and frozen. Shows how th frozen specimen is cut into thin sections, stained and finally prepared for examination by the pathologist.
Health and Safety; Science
Dist - USNAC **Prod** - USPHS 1966

Rapid option offense and delay game strategies - Trenkle
VHS
Basketball small college winners series
Color (H C G)
$29.95 purchase _ #SAM053V - P
Features Coach Trenkle who discusses rapid option offense and delay game strategies in basketball. Part of an 11 - part series featuring innovative basketball coaches at the small college level.
Physical Education and Recreation
Dist - CAMV

Rapid - paced aversive smoking - explanation and instructions 45 MIN
16mm
Comprehensive smoking cessation program series; Tape 5
Mono
Health and Safety; Psychology
Dist - BIOMON **Prod** - BIOMON

Rapid physical assessment of the critically ill patient 20 MIN
VHS
Color (C PRO)
$250.00 purchase, $70.00 rental _ #4335S, #4335V
Focuses on the most important areas in a quick assessment - the neurological, cardiovascular, respiratory and gastrointestinal systems. Demonstrates mental status assessment - cranial nerves, motor system, sensory system and reflexes; cardiac status assessment - auscultating for heart sounds and checking peripheral pulses; respiratory system assessment - inspection, palpation and auscultation, endotracheal placement; and abdominal assessment - auscultation, percussing and palpating. Produced by St Elizabeth Hospital Medical Center.
Health and Safety; Science - Natural
Dist - AJN

Rapid reading 29 MIN
VHS / U-matic
Speed learning series
Color (J H)
Discusses the place of rapid reading within the confines of learning. Demonstrates steps to developing reading rate as one part of overall reading efficiency. Uses runners as an analogy.
English Language
Dist - AITECH **Prod** - LEARNI 1982
DELTAK
LEARNI

Rapid review for the SAT
VHS
Color (H)
$39.95 purchase _ #VAD023
Offers tips, tricks and traps, insider strategies and relaxation hints for taking the Scholastic Aptitude Test.
Education
Dist - SIV

Rapid runway repair procedures 15 MIN
16mm
Color
LC 76-703704
Demonstrates how to repair a bomb - damaged runway in four hours or less. Shows how to clean the area around a crater and how to top it off with gravel and a metal patch that has been assembled beside it. Introduces new engineering techniques for performing these jobs.
Industrial and Technical Education
Dist - USNAC **Prod** - USAF 1975

Rapid Transit 10 MIN
U-matic / VHS / 16mm
Color
Offers an impressionistic view of the 1979 Transpac on board the 61 - foot sloop Rapid Transit.
Physical Education and Recreation
Dist - OFFSHR **Prod** - OFFSHR 1979

RapidRise Yeast 4 MIN
16mm
Color (A)
Demonstrates to homemakers how to use Fleischmann's RapidRise Yeast.
Home Economics
Dist - EXARC **Prod** - EXARC

Rapists - can they be stopped 55 MIN
VHS
Color (H C G)
$445.00 purchase, $75.00 rental
Focuses on a program in Oregon State Hospital for rehabilitating sex offenders. Describes the methods used and observes that few graduates have become repeat offenders. Produced by John Zaritsky.
Health and Safety; Sociology
Dist - FLMLIB

Rapp session - male responsibility 22 MIN
VHS / U-matic
Color (J H)
$260.00, $310.00 purchase, $50.00 rental
Addresses the problems, stereotypes and expectations in the world of today's teenagers in an upbeat, outspoken way. Focuses on Black teenagers, but appropriate for everyone.
Sociology
Dist - NDIM **Prod** - PARGRO 1989

Rappaccini's daughter 57 MIN
U-matic / VHS / 16mm
American short story series
Color (J H C)
Presents an adaptation of Nathaniel Hawthorne's short story Rappaccini's Daughter, set in 18th - century Italy, about a young man's romantic entanglement with a beautiful forbidden woman in a poisonous garden.
Fine Arts; Literature and Drama
Dist - CORF **Prod** - LEARIF 1980
CDTEL

Rappin' - the art of street talk 30 MIN
16mm
Stereo
Explores the urban verbal art form of rapping.
English Language; Psychology; Sociology
Dist - NAPURA **Prod** - NAPURA 1984

Rapping 15 MIN
U-matic / VHS / 16mm
Rapping and tripping series
Color (J H S)
LC 76-706670
Features a discussion among teenagers about why they take drugs and why they want to stop.
Guidance and Counseling; Health and Safety
Dist - ALTSUL **Prod** - ALTSUL 1969

Rapping and tripping series
Rapping 15 MIN
Tripping 15 MIN
Dist - ALTSUL

Rapping it up (student protest in other countries) 30 MIN
16mm
Today's challenge series; Pt 2
Mono (H A)
Education; Social Science; Sociology
Dist - NCAT **Prod** - UCOLO

Rapport 12 MIN
U-matic / VHS / 16mm
Vignettes Series
Color (J)
LC 73-701991
Presents three vignettes exploring the dynamics of the man - woman relationship to encourage reflection on the deeper aspects of contemporary marriage.
Sociology
Dist - MEDIAG **Prod** - PAULST 1973

Raptors - Birds of Prey 14 MIN
16mm / U-matic / VHS
Color (I J H)
LC 76-702117
Shows birds of prey such as the golden eagle, sparrow hawk, great horned owl, red tail hawk, falcon and osprey. Discusses their flying, nesting and feeding habits.
Science - Natural
Dist - PHENIX **Prod** - AFAI 1976

The Rapture 42 MIN
16mm
Color (R)
Portrays how a television network might handle the news events one day after Christ returns. Reveals what happens to those who are not ready for the return.
Guidance and Counseling; Religion and Philosophy
Dist - GF **Prod** - GF

Rapture 20 MIN
VHS
Color (G)
$50.00 purchase
Features a vision of a Dionysian experience. Explores the similarity between religious and visionary ecstasy and psychotic states.
Fine Arts; Psychology
Dist - CANCIN **Prod** - SHARIT 1987

The Rapture family 30 MIN
16mm
Color (H C A)
LC 79-700101
Discusses the history and meaning of a traditional Black form of worship known as 'in the rapture,' which dramatizes man's struggle to resist the temptations of Satan.
History - United States; Religion and Philosophy; Sociology
Dist - IU **Prod** - IU 1978

The Rapture of being 90 MIN
BETA / VHS
Innerwork series
Color (G)
$49.95 purchase _ #W052
Describes the Sufi path of beingness and Sufi dancing as an expression of the dynamic shifting equilibriums of life. Focuses on Sufi meditation techniques. Features Pir Valayat Inayat Khan.
Psychology; Religion and Philosophy
Dist - THINKA **Prod** - THINKA

Rapunzel 17 MIN
16mm
B&W
LC 78-701445
Tells how a young girl uses her long hair to help her rescuer climb into the tower where she has been imprisoned by a wicked witch. Based on the story Rapunzel by the Brothers Grimm.
Literature and Drama
Dist - HOOVJ **Prod** - HOOVJ 1978

Rapunzel 15 MIN
VHS / U-matic
Gather Round Series
Color (K P)
Literature and Drama
Dist - CTI **Prod** - CTI

Rapunzel 11 MIN
U-matic / VHS / 16mm
Color; B&W (P I)
Uses puppets to visualize the well - known fairy tale of Rapunzel.
Literature and Drama
Dist - PHENIX **Prod** - HARRY 1955

Rapunzel 10 MIN
VHS
Color (P)
Presents an animated version of the fairy tale Rapunzel.
Fine Arts; Literature and Drama
Dist - VIEWTH **Prod** - VIEWTH

Rapunzel
16mm
Anthology of children's literature series; Set 1
Mono (K P)
Literature and Drama
Dist - TROLA **Prod** - TROLA

Rapunzel 10 MIN
U-matic / VHS / 16mm
Color (K P I)
$265.00, $170.00 purchase _ #4083; LC 81-700070
Offers an animated adaptation of the fairy tale about the girl who uses her long golden hair to escape her fate.
Literature and Drama
Dist - CORF **Prod** - PERSPF 1980

Rapunzel and The golden bird 15 MIN
16mm
Stories are for fun series
Mono (P I)
Tells the story of Rapunzel, a beautiful girl with long hair, and the story of The Golden Bird, about an arrogant prince who is humanized by a golden song bird.
Literature and Drama
Dist - NCAT **Prod** - UTEX 1961

Rapunzel, Rapunzel 15 MIN
U-matic / VHS / 16mm
Brothers Grimm Folktales Series
Color (P)
Tells the famous Grimm Brothers folktale of Rapunzel.
Literature and Drama
Dist - DAVT **Prod** - DAVT

Rapunzel, Rapunzel 18 MIN
16mm / U-matic / VHS
Brothers Grimm Folktales Series
Color
LC 78-700150
Presents a live - action version of the Grimm Brothers' tale Rapunzel, placed in modern times with an American setting.
Fine Arts; Literature and Drama
Dist - DAVT **Prod** - DAVT 1978

Rare Chaplin 60 MIN
VHS
B&W (G)
$29.95 purchase
Presents three lesser - known comedies starring and directed by Charlie Chaplin. Includes The Bank, Shanghaied and A Night in the Show.
Fine Arts
Dist - KINOIC

Rare should not mean alone 35 MIN
VHS
Captioned; Color (PRO A)
Surveys individuals who have Treacher Collins Syndrome and their families, the physicians who provide treatment, the researchers conducting studies across the country, the the Treacher Collins Foundation. This closed caption video addressses issues faced by families at various times during the life cycle of an affected individual and is a comprehensive educational tool for families and professionals.
Health and Safety
Dist - TRECOL **Prod** - TRECOL 1995

Rascal 15 MIN
U-matic / VHS / 16mm
Film as Literature; Series 3
Color (I J H)
Tells the story of a young boy, his pet raccoon and their efforts to get along with each other.
Fine Arts; Literature and Drama
Dist - CORF **Prod** - DISNEY 1982

Rasgos Culturales Series
Siqueiros, El Maestro - March of Humanity in Latin America 14 MIN
Dist - EBEC

Rashomon 83 MIN
U-matic / VHS
B&W (JAPANESE (ENGLISH SUBTITLES))
Delves into the mysteries of truth by examining the contradictory stories of a murder and rape recounted by the murdered man, his ravished wife, the murderer, the arresting constable and a neutral bystander. Directed by Akira Kurosawa. Stars Toshiro Mifune, Machiko Kyo and Masayuki Mori. With English Subtitles.
Fine Arts; Foreign Language
Dist - IHF **Prod** - IHF
CHTSUI
UILL

Raspberry High 10 MIN
VHS / U-matic
Color (J H)
Represents a new concept for getting an audience to examine their own behavior. Shows a young man being urged by his fellow workers to drink more than he can hold.
Health and Safety; Psychology; Sociology
Dist - SUTHRB **Prod** - SUTHRB

Rasputin 104 MIN
16mm / 35mm
Color (G) (RUSSIAN WITH ENGLISH SUBTITLES)

$250.00, $300.00 rental
Captures Czarist Russia on the verge of collapse. Dramatizes the rise of Rasputin to power. Shows how, hypnotized by Rasputin's wicked presence and 'visions,' the royal family loses all control and the country is led into revolt. Directed by Elem Klimov.
Fine Arts; History - World
Dist - KINOIC **Prod** - IFEX 1984

Rasputin 83 MIN
16mm
B&W (GERMAN)
Surveys the life and death of the Siberian miracle monk Rasputin, who enjoys the unrestricted trust of the Imperial Family, but because of his many amorous affairs and his political influence, makes many enemies. Concludes with his death at the hand of a political assassin.
Civics and Political Systems; History - World
Dist - WSTGLC **Prod** - WSTGLC 1932

Rat Attack
16mm
Rats Series
Color
Health and Safety; Home Economics; Sociology
Dist - MLA **Prod** - MLA

Rat dissection 31 MIN
VHS
Dissection video series
Color (J H)
$160.00 purchase _ #A5VH 1224
Shows the dissection of a rat from start to finish. Provides detailed presentations of the external anatomy, the correct procedures used for dissection and a review of the internal anatomy and physiological systems. Includes a dissection manual and a written examination. Part of a series on dissection.
Science - Natural
Dist - CLRVUE **Prod** - CLRVUE

Rat dissection 30 MIN
VHS
Dissection videos series
Color (H C)
$153.95 purchase _ #193 W 0028
Covers dissection and external and internal anatomy of the rat. Includes dissection manual. Part of a series on dissection.
Science; Science - Natural
Dist - WARDS **Prod** - WARDS 1990

Rat Life and Diet in North America 14 MIN
16mm
Color
LC 75-704332
Presents a parable on political and economic repression in the United States and liberation in Canada.
Civics and Political Systems; Geography - World; Literature and Drama
Dist - CANFDC **Prod** - CANFDC 1973

Rate it X 93 MIN
VHS / 16mm
Color (G)
$350.00 purchase, $225.00 $150.00 rental
Asks what men really think of women. Talks to a cross - section of men who produce and profit from images of women. Visits banks, toy stores, a fundamentalist church, the nation's largest sex emporium and a suburban baker whose torso shaped cake is a best seller. Shows how sexism is rationalized through commmerce, religion and social values. Produced by Lynn Campbell, Claudette Charbonneau, Paula de Koenisberg and Lucy Winer.
Guidance and Counseling; Psychology; Sociology
Dist - WMEN

Rate of change 18 MIN
16mm
Acts of light trilogy
Color (G)
$36.00 rental
Presents a section having no original, no frames, only slow continuously shifting colors, cycling around the perimenter of the spectrum, with changes so slow as to be unseen, yet altering the perception of color. Part of the Acts of Light trilogy produced by Bill Brand.
Fine Arts
Dist - CANCIN

Rate of Change
16mm
B&W
Shows how the concepts of function, limit, and limit of a function can be drawn together to make a mathematical definition of instantaneous velocity.
Mathematics
Dist - OPENU **Prod** - OPENU

Rate of return method 30 MIN
U-matic / VHS
Engineering economy series
Color (IND) (JAPANESE)
Introduces evaluation method which solves for the prospective rate of return or invested capital. Uses a share of American Telephone and Telegraph Co common stock as an example problem.
Business and Economics
Dist - COLOSU **Prod** - COLOSU

Rates and equilibrium
Videodisc
Exploring chemistry series
Color (H A)
$350.00, $125.00 purchase
Allows chemistry lab students to perform controlled, varied experiments using interactive computer simulations that take less time and materials than actual laboratory work, permitting investigations that might not be feasible in a normal classroom setting. Provides lessons in rates and equilibrium. Part of a series of four discs. Available in videodisc format in either stand - alone or network version. Contact distributor for system requirements.
Computer Science; Science; Science - Physical
Dist - FALCSO

Rates and ramps - Program 2 18 MIN
VHS
Fraction action series
Color (I J H)
$175.00 purchase _ #CG - 920 - VS
Looks at how fractions are used to describe two important real - world phenomena - rates and ramps. Opens with a dramatization of two students buying marbles which leads to a discussion of rates and graphic segments applying this knowledge to new experiences, and to a series of concrete, hands - on activities for the classroom. Part two looks at how fractions are used to describe the slope of a ramp, serving as an introduction to coordinate geometry. Includes a teacher's activity book, overhead transparencies, student worksheets and markers and manipulatives for visualizing rates. Part of a two - part series.
Mathematics
Dist - HRMC **Prod** - HRMC

Rates of chemical reaction 13 MIN
VHS / 16mm
Chem study video - film series
Color (H C)
$208.00, $99.00 purchase, $23.00 rental _ #192 W 0815, #193 W 2034, #140 W 4121
Illustrates the mechanisms of some simple chemical reactions. Explains the effect of temperature, activation energy, geometry of collision and catalysis upon the rate of reaction. Uses the reactions between hydrogen and chlorine and hydrogen and iodine as examples Examines the relationship between the energy required for a reaction to occur and the relative position of the reaction particles before, during and after the collision. Part of a series for teaching chemistry to high school and college students.
Science - Physical
Dist - WARDS **Prod** - WARDS 1990

Rates of chemical reaction - effects of temperature and concentration 11 MIN
VHS
Color (H)
$245.00 purchase
Develops kinetic theory model showing effect of temperature on speed of molecules and variation in the speed of molecules at a fixed temperature.
Science - Physical
Dist - LUF **Prod** - LUF 1989

Ratio 8 MIN
VHS
Children's encyclopedia of mathematics - pre - algebra series
Color (I)
$49.95 purchase _ #8367
Discusses ratio. Part of a nine - part series about pre - algebra.
Mathematics
Dist - AIMS **Prod** - DAVFMS 1991

Ratio 15 MIN
U-matic
Mathematical Relationship Series
Color (I)
Provides insight into ratio by showing the ratio of the Wright brothers' plane compared with that of a Boeing 747.
Education; Mathematics
Dist - TVOTAR **Prod** - TVOTAR 1982

Ratio and proportion 30 MIN
VHS
Basic mathematical skills series
Color (J H)
$125.00 purchase _ #M10
Teaches about ratio and proportion. Features Elayn Gay. Part of a 15 - part series on basic math.
Mathematics
Dist - LANDMK **Prod** - MGHT

Ratio and proportion
VHS
Beginning algebra series
Color (J H)
$125.00 purchase _ #2020
Teaches fundamental concepts of ratio and proportion. Part of a series of 31 videos, each between 25 and 30 minutes long, that explain and reinforce basic concepts of algebra. Tutors the student through definitions, theorems, step - by - step solutions and examples. Videos are also available in a set.
Mathematics
Dist - LANDMK

Ratio and Trend Analysis 15 MIN
U-matic / VHS
Finance for Nonfinancial Managers Series
Color
Business and Economics
Dist - DELTAK **Prod** - DELTAK

Ratio - Forming Ratios 15 MIN
U-matic / VHS
Math Works Series
Color (I)
Demonstrates what a ratio is, how to express ratio in particular examples, when ratio might be used and what specific ratios mean in specific situations.
Mathematics
Dist - AITECH **Prod** - AITECH

Ratio, Proportion, Percent 15 MIN
VHS / U-matic
Mathematics for the '80s - Grade Six Series
(I)
$125.00 purchase
Examines the use of percentages, ratios and proportions as applied to figuring tips and sales prices.
Mathematics
Dist - AITECH **Prod** - AITECH 1987

Ratio, rate, percent 30 MIN
16mm
Mathematics for elementary school teachers series; No 24
Color (T)
Shows the techniques to be used in determining ratio, rate and percent. Explores the use of decimals. To be used following Decimals.
Mathematics
Dist - MLA **Prod** - SMSG 1963

Ratio test 20 MIN
VHS
Calculus series; Program 55
Color (H)
LC 90712920
Presents the ratio test.
Mathematics
Dist - GPN

Ratio test and root test 30 MIN
VHS
Calculus series
Color (C)
$125.00 purchase _ #6050
Explains ratio test and root test. Part of a 56 - part series on calculus.
Mathematics
Dist - LANDMK **Prod** - LANDMK

A Rational Approach to Newly Discovered Hypertension 18 MIN
U-matic / VHS
Color (PRO)
Presents the diagnostic criteria for the various types of hypertension, indications for differing forms of anti - hypertensive therapy, the potential morbidity and mortality associated with diagnostic procedures and the concept of utilizing the cost/benefit ratio in making diagnostic and therapeutic decisions.
Health and Safety
Dist - UMICHM **Prod** - UMICHM 1974

The rational approach to the patient with azotemia 12 MIN
U-matic / VHS
Color (PRO)
Uses logical procedures, including four major diagnostic categories, to lead the viewer to a definitive physio - logical diagnosis. Discusses the common causes and the historical, physical, physiological and biochemical findings which suggest a diagnosis of pre - renal azotemia. Shows the historical physical and roentgenographic findings which suggest post renal azotemia, and the means to differentiate between acute and chronic renal failure.
Health and Safety; Science
Dist - UMICHM **Prod** - UMICHM 1973

A rational approach to the square root of 2
16mm
B&W
Explains the algebraic techniques needed for finding the root of a polynomial which is irreducible over the rational numbers. Shows how a quotient field can be constructed in which a root lies.
Mathematics
Dist - OPENU **Prod** - OPENU

Rational emotive therapy 29 MIN
16mm / VHS
Color (C G PRO)
$495.00 purchase, $26.00, $16.00 rental _ #33631
Overviews 'rational emotive therapy,' originated by Dr Albert Ellis in 1955. Interviews Ellis, who explains why he rejected traditional therapies and discusses the evolution of RET. Visits the Institute for Rational Emotive Therapy in New York City during a five - day practicum in which Ellis and his staff offer clients an alternative to the destructive, irrational self - talk which RET practitioners believe to be responsible for emotional disturbance.
Psychology
Dist - PSU **Prod** - IRL 1982

Rational Emotive Therapy 30 MIN
16mm
Color (C A)
LC 82-700418
Presents a documentary overview of rational emotive therapy, a form of psychotherapy developed in the 1950's by Dr Albert Ellis. Discusses the evolution of RET and shows it in practice at a public workshop and in unstaged counseling sessions.
Psychology
Dist - RESPRC **Prod** - RESPRC 1982

Rational - emotive therapy - a documentary film featuring Dr Albert Ellis 30 MIN
16mm
Color
Discusses Rational - Emotive Therapy's basic tenets and their evolution and shows counseling sessions by Albert Ellis and other therapists. Demonstrates R E T's applications to guilt, anxiety and jealousy in an overview of R E T.
Fine Arts; Psychology
Dist - IRL **Prod** - IRL 1982

Rational exponents 30 MIN
VHS
College algebra series
Color (C)
$125.00 purchase _ #4004
Explains radical expressions. Part of a 31 - part series on college algebra.
Mathematics
Dist - LANDMK **Prod** - LANDMK

Rational exponents
VHS
Beginning algebra series
Color (J H)
$125.00 purchase _ #2028
Teaches basic concepts of rational exponents and how to work with expressions and equations involving them. Part of a 31 - video series, each part between 25 and 30 minutes long, that explains and reinforces fundamental concepts of beginning algebra. Uses definitions, theorems, examples and step - by - step solutions to instruct the student.
Mathematics
Dist - LANDMK

Rational exponents
VHS
Intermediate algebra series
Color (J H)
$125.00 purchase _ #3019
Teaches the concepts involved in using expressions or equations with rational exponents. Part of a set of 31 videos, each between 25 and 30 minutes long, that explain and reinforce concepts in intermediate algebra. Videos are also available in a set.
Mathematics
Dist - LANDMK

Rational exponents 30 MIN
VHS
Mathematics series; Program 50
Color (J)
LC 90713155
Explains rational exponents.
Mathematics
Dist - GPN

Rational exponents and complex numbers 30 MIN
VHS
Intermediate algebra series
Color (H)
$125.00 purchase _ #M49
Explains rational exponents and complex numbers. Features Elayn Gay. Part of a 27 - part series on intermediate algebra.
Mathematics
Dist - LANDMK **Prod** - MGHT

Rational expressions
VHS
Algebra 1 series
Color (J H)
$125.00 purchase _ #A10
Teaches the concepts involved in working with rational expressions. Part of a series of 16 videos, each between 25 and 30 minutes long, that explain and reinforce 89 basic concepts of algebra. Includes a stated objective for each segment. Tutors the student through definitions, theorems, step - by - step solutions and examples. Videos are also available in a set.
Mathematics
Dist - LANDMK
GPN

Rational expressions and complex fractions 30 MIN
VHS
Intermediate algebra series
Color (H)
$125.00 purchase _ #M45
Explains rational expressions and complex fractions. Features Elayn Gay. Part of a 27 - part series on intermediate algebra.
Mathematics
Dist - LANDMK **Prod** - MGHT

Rational expressions I
VHS
Beginning algebra series
Color (J H)
$125.00 purchase _ #2009
Teaches fundamental concepts of rational expressions. Part of a series of 31 videos, each between 25 and 30 minutes long, that explain and reinforce basic concepts of algebra. Tutors the student through definitions, theorems, step - by - step solutions and examples. Videos are also available in a set.
Mathematics
Dist - LANDMK

Rational expressions II
VHS
Beginning algebra series
Color (J H)
$125.00 purchase _ #2010
Teaches fundamental concepts of rational expressions. Part of a series of 31 videos, each between 25 and 30 minutes long, that explain and reinforce basic concepts of algebra. Tutors the student through definitions, theorems, step - by - step solutions and examples. Videos are also available in a set.
Mathematics
Dist - LANDMK

Rational expressions - Pt 1 30 MIN
VHS
Mathematics series; Program 25
Color (J)
LC 90713155
Discusses rational expressions. The first of two installments on rational expressions.
Mathematics
Dist - GPN

Rational Expressions, Pt 2 30 MIN
VHS
Mathematics Series
Color (J)
LC 90713155
Discusses rational expressions. The second of two installments on rational expressions. The 26th of 157 installments of the Mathematics Series.
Mathematics
Dist - GPN

Rational numbers and the square root of two 24 MIN
U-matic / VHS / 16mm
Color
Addresses what sort of number the square root of two is. Approaches question from the viewpoint of geometry and the viewpoint of calculation.
Mathematics
Dist - MEDIAG **Prod** - OPENU 1979

Rational root theorem 30 MIN
VHS
College algebra series
Color (C)
$125.00 purchase _ #4023
Explains rational root theorem. Part of a 31 - part series on college algebra.
Mathematics
Dist - LANDMK **Prod** - LANDMK

Rational root theorem 30 MIN
VHS
Mathematics series; Program 85
Color (J)
LC 90713155
Explains rational root theorem.
Mathematics
Dist - GPN

Rational Suicide 15 MIN
U-matic / VHS / 16mm
Color (C A)
LC 82-700422
Examines the controversial issue of suicide as a plausible option for the incurably - ill, rational person. Narrated by Mike Wallace and originally shown on the CBS program 60 Minutes.
Sociology
Dist - CAROUF **Prod** - CBSTV 1981

Rationale for Seeking Solutions 30 MIN
VHS / U-matic
Interaction - Human Concerns in the Schools Series
Color (T)
Reveals the rationale for seeking solutions in an educational setting.
Education
Dist - MDCPB **Prod** - MDDE

Ratios 18 MIN
U-matic
Basic Math Skills Series Proportions; Proportions
Color
Mathematics
Dist - TELSTR **Prod** - TELSTR

Ratios and Proportions 20 MIN
U-matic
Mainly Math Series
Color (H C)
Uses the dimensions of a television screen to illustrate ratios and proportions.
Mathematics
Dist - GPN **Prod** - WCVETV 1977

Ratios and proportions
VHS
Basic mathematical skills series
Color (I J H)
$125.00 purchase _ #1019
Teaches the concept of ratio and proportion. Presents part of a series that provides 27 videos, each between 25 and 30 minutes long, that explain and reinforce basic mathematical concepts. Tutors the student through definitions, theorems, step - by - step solutions and examples. Videos are also available in a set.
Mathematics
Dist - LANDMK

Ratopolis 57 MIN
16mm
Color (H C A) (FRENCH)
LC 74-702413
Studies the rat, focusing on its origins and its role in maintaining an ecological balance.
Foreign Language; Science - Natural
Dist - NFBC **Prod** - NFBC 1973

Rats and Mice 7 MIN
8mm cartridge / 16mm
Control of Pests for Food Service and Housekeeping Personnel Series
Color (A) (SPANISH)
LC 73-704828
Describes how rats and mice spread disease and what the hospital worker can do to make the hospital safe from these threats to the patient and to the worker.
Guidance and Counseling; Health and Safety; Home Economics
Dist - COPI **Prod** - COPI 1969

Rats Series
Minus One
Rat Attack
Dist - MLA

Rattle tattletail - Vol 18 30 MIN
VHS
Our friends on Wooster Square series
Color (K P I R)

$34.95 purchase, $10.00 rental _ #35 - 87267 - 460
Presents religious concepts through storylines, songs and Scripture. Features puppet characters including Smedly, Troll and Sizzle.
Fine Arts; Literature and Drama; Religion and Philosophy
Dist - APH **Prod** - FRACOC

Rattlesnake in a Cooler 60 MIN
VHS / U-matic
Color
Fine Arts; Literature and Drama
Dist - ABCLR **Prod** - ABCLR

Ravel 103 MIN
16mm / U-matic / VHS
Color; Stereo (H)
$1475.00, $520.00 purchase, $125.00 rental
Documents the Montreal Symphony's performance of music by Ravel. Features Alice de Larocha, Victoria de los Angeles, Jean - Phillipe Collard and Augustin Dumay among the performers.
Fine Arts
Dist - BULFRG **Prod** - RHOMBS 1989

Ravel 103 MIN
16mm / VHS
(J A)
$125.00 rental
Presents an homage to the French composer, Maurice Ravel, by many of his foremost interpreters. Includes home movie footage, photographs and unpublished letters giving insight into Ravel's life. Available in three parts for schools.
Biography; Fine Arts
Dist - BULFRG

The Raven 84 MIN
16mm
Color (H A)
Describes two 15th century conjurers who fight a deadly duel of magic. Stars Vincent Price, Peter Lorre, Boris Karloff and Jack Nicholson.
Fine Arts
Dist - TIMLIF **Prod** - AIP 1963

The Raven and other poems 19 MIN
U-matic / VHS
Edgar Allan Poe - the principal works series
Color (C)
$249.00, $149.00 purchase _ #AD - 1699
Features performances of The Raven, Annabel Lee and The Dream Within A Dream by Edgar Allan Poe. Features Conrad Pomerleau as presenter.
Fine Arts; Literature and Drama
Dist - FOTH **Prod** - FOTH

The Raven by Edgar A Poe 11 MIN
U-matic / VHS / 16mm
Color (I J H C)
LC 75-704400
Revised version of the 1951 film, The Raven. Uses the engravings of Gustave Dore to illustrate Poe's poem The Raven.
Literature and Drama
Dist - TEXFLM **Prod** - JACOBS 1976

The Raven - The Black cat 126 MIN
VHS
B&W (J H)
$59.00 purchase _ #04502 - 126
Stars Bela Lugosi and Boris Karloff in two macabre favorites by Edgar Allan Poe.
Literature and Drama
Dist - GA **Prod** - GA

Raven's End 99 MIN
16mm
B&W (SWEDISH)
Looks at Raven's End, a slum area of Sweden, in 1936, focusing on one family. Tells of the son who wants to become a writer and of the father who has lost hope for the future.
Fine Arts; Foreign Language; Sociology
Dist - NYFLMS **Prod** - NYFLMS 1964

The Ravens remain 26 MIN
16mm
Winston Churchill - the valiant years series; No 6
B&W
LC FI67-2111
Uses documentary footage to describe the Battle of Britain. Includes scenes of the Luftwaffe Blitz on RAF installations and industrial cities of northern England, the bombing of London and the resistance of members of the RAF.
History - World
Dist - SG **Prod** - ABCTV 1961

Raw fish and pickle - traditional rural and seafaring life 28 MIN
16mm
Human face of Japan series
Color (H C A)
LC 82-700642
Looks At Iwate, a rural area of Japan which has been transformed through the country's technological boom and new found prosperity.
Geography - World; History - World; Social Science; Sociology
Dist - LCOA **Prod** - FLMAUS 1982

Raw mash 29 MIN
VHS / 16mm
Color (H A)
$65.00 rental
Follows moonshiner Hamper McBee as he demonstrates the construction and use of a 'groundhog' still in the mountains near Chattanooga, Tennessee. Makes use of tall tales and ballads about moonshiners, revenuers and devil - may - care lovers.
Fine Arts
Dist - AFA

Raw Stock 27 MIN
16mm
Color
LC 76-701358
Explains the making of a motion picture.
Fine Arts
Dist - SFRASU **Prod** - SFRASU 1975

Ray Bradbury 30 MIN
16mm
Sun and the Substance Series
B&W (H C A)
LC FIA67-5004
Features Ray Bradbury, magazine, screenplay and story writer, who gives an interpretation of the creative writer's place in life and describes how the writer's role relaxes tensions formed by the demands of modern civilization. Filmed in Kinescope.
Biography; Fine Arts; Literature and Drama; Religion and Philosophy
Dist - MLA **Prod** - USC 1964

Ray Bradbury on Fantasy and Reality 29 MIN
VHS / 16mm
Color (G)
$55.00 rental _ #RBFR - 000
Fine Arts; Literature and Drama
Dist - PBS **Prod** - KPBS

Ray Gun Virus 14 MIN
16mm
Color (C)
$435.00
Experimental film by Paul Sharits.
Fine Arts
Dist - AFA **Prod** - AFA 1966

Ray Jefferson L999 60 MIN
VHS
Using Loran series
Color (G A)
$29.90 purchase _ #0784
Shows how to operate the Ray Jefferson L999 Loran nautical navigation model. Includes installation tips, initialization, calibration, chain selection, notch filters, signal - to - noise ratio, time differentials, Lat - Lon functions, selecting and programming waypoints, setting anchor and waypoint alarm, cross - track error, determining course to steer and distance to go. Part of a series on Loran models.
Physical Education and Recreation; Social Science
Dist - SEVVID

Ray Kroc - the Man Behind McDonald's 28 MIN
U-matic / VHS
Color (G)
$249.00, $149.00 purchase _ #AD - 2018
Interviews Ray Kroc, creator of the nationwide McDonald's food chain and inventor of the fast food formula. Adapts a Phil Donahue program.
Biography; Business and Economics; Home Economics
Dist - FOTH **Prod** - FOTH

Ray Lum - Mule Trader 18 MIN
16mm
Color (J)
LC 74-701911
Shows a day in the life of 82 - year - old trader, storyteller and auctioneer Ray Lum.
Biography; Geography - United States; Sociology
Dist - SOFOLK **Prod** - SOFOLK

A Ray of Hope 10 MIN
16mm
Color
LC 78-700301
Describes positive results achieved in the treatment of Hodgkin's disease by means of radiation therapy. Follows two young mothers' experiences as patients and after recovery. Shows their family lives, medical examinations and treatments.
Health and Safety
Dist - AMCS **Prod** - AMCS 1977

A Ray of hope 28 MIN
VHS / U-matic
Color (J H)
$245.00, $295.00 purchase, $50.00 rental
Reenacts how three scientists persevered in the face of possible ridicule to propound their then controversial findings regarding the danger from the hole in the ozone layer.
Science - Natural
Dist - NDIM **Prod** - YORKTV 1991

The Rayattam 18 MIN
16mm
B&W (H C)
Documents the dance worship of North Malabar in South India as performed in the courtyard of the village shrine in honor of the heroes that belong to legend, faith or family.
Fine Arts; Religion and Philosophy
Dist - RADIM **Prod** - JOHN 1960

Raybestos brake service clinic 40 MIN
16mm
Color (IND)
Discusses various aspects of automotive brake systems, including discs and drums, calipers, valves, master cylinder and power brakes, hydraulic systems, rotors and asbestos linings. Includes multiple choice tests.
Industrial and Technical Education
Dist - MTP **Prod** - MTP

RayJeff L 100
VHS
Loran operation guide series
Color (G A)
$29.90 purchase _ #0906
Teaches Loran C programming for the RayJeff L 100 in nautical navigation. Shows how to enter the correct Loran chain for specific positions, how to program positions, determine the accuracy of a Loran C 'fix' and how to deal with the intricacies of specific machines.
Physical Education and Recreation; Social Science
Dist - SEVVID

Raymond Briggs 45 MIN
VHS
Color (H C G)
$79.00 purchase
Features British writer and illustrator Raymond Briggs with Barry Took discussing telling a story through pictures and using friends for inspiration. Talks about his works including The Mother Goose Treasury; Gentleman Jim; When the Wind Blows; and The Tin Pot Foreign General and the Old Iron Woman, an allegory of the Falklands War.
Fine Arts; Literature and Drama
Dist - ROLAND **Prod** - INCART

Raymond Chandler's Los Angeles 28 MIN
U-matic / VHS
Color (C)
$249.00, $149.00 purchase _ #AD - 1948
Uses period newsreels and clips from feature films made from the stories of Raymond Chandler to recreate his observations of life in Los Angeles during the 1930s.
Fine Arts; Geography - United States; Literature and Drama
Dist - FOTH **Prod** - FOTH

Raymond Loewy - Father of Industrial Design 15 MIN
16mm / U-matic / VHS
Color (H C A)
LC 80-700606
Presents Morley Safer as he interviews Raymond Loewy, who discusses elements of good design, his design of NASA's Skylab capsule and the philosophy behind his work. Shows some of his designs, such as the original Coca - Cola dispenser and the Greyhound bus. Originally shown on the CBS television program 60 Minutes.
Fine Arts; Industrial and Technical Education
Dist - CAROUF **Prod** - CBSTV 1979

Raymond Williams 45 MIN
VHS
Color (H C G)
$79.00 purchase
Features writer Raymond Williams talking with Michael Ignatieff about culture and politics as themes in writing and the difficulty in recreating a historical period accurately. Discusses his writings including The Long Revolution; Towards 2000; and the novels Border Country and Fight for Manod.
Literature and Drama
Dist - ROLAND **Prod** - INCART

Raymonda 146 MIN
VHS
Color (G)
$39.95 purchase _ #1170
Presents the Bolshoi Ballet production of Raymonda in three acts. Stars Ludmila Semenyaka, Erek Moukhamedov and Gedeminas Taranda. Scored by Alexander Glazunov.

Fine Arts; Foreign Language; Geography - World; Physical Education and Recreation
Dist - KULTUR

RayNav 580
VHS
Loran operation guide series
Color (G A)
$29.90 purchase _ #0942
Teaches Loran C programming for the Raynav 580 in nautical navigation. Shows how to enter the correct Loran chain for specific positions, how to program positions, determine the accuracy of a Loran C 'fix' and how to deal with the intricacies of specific machines.
Physical Education and Recreation; Social Science
Dist - SEVVID

Raytheon RayNav 570, Apelco 6100, 6600 60 MIN
VHS
Using Loran series
Color (G A)
$29.90 purchase _ #0745
Shows how to operate the Raytheon RayNav 570 and Apelco 6100 and 6600 Loran nautical navigation models. Includes installation tips, initialization, calibration, chain selection, notch filters, signal - to - noise ratio, time differentials, Lat - Lon functions, selecting and programming waypoints, setting anchor and waypoint alarm, cross - track error, determining course to steer and distance to go. Part of a series on the most popular Loran models.
Physical Education and Recreation; Social Science
Dist - SEVVID

Razor Blades 25 MIN
16mm
Color; B&W (C)
$1092.00
Dual Screen Projection. Experimental film by Paul Sharits.
Fine Arts
Dist - AFA **Prod** - AFA 1968

RBBS in a box
CD-ROM
Color (G A)
$175.00 purchase _ #1937
Offers almost 9,000 popular shareware programs in PKzip version 1.02. May be used as a program archive or loaded as a fully functional on - line bulletin board. For IBM PCs and compatibles. Requires at least 640K RAM, DOS Version 3.1 or greater, one floppy disk drive - a hard drive is recommended, one empty expansion slot, and an IBM compatible CD - ROM drive.
Computer Science
Dist - BEP

The RBS express 19 MIN
16mm
Color
LC 74-706208
Presents operation of SAC mobile RADAR Bomb Scoring (RBS) trains. Reviews site selection and preparation. Features information about crew accommodations and community relations.
Civics and Political Systems; Science - Physical
Dist - USNAC **Prod** - USAF 1965

RC time constants 8 MIN
VHS / 16mm
Electrical theory series
Color (IND)
$50.00 purchase _ #241313
Illustrates 22 concepts fundamental to the training of second year electrical apprentices using graphic animation. Explains how increased capacitance requires more charging time to reach maximum voltage and its calculation in 'RC Time Constants.'.
Education; Industrial and Technical Education; Psychology
Dist - ACCESS **Prod** - ACCESS 1983

RC time constants 15 MIN
U-matic / VHS
Basic electricity and D C circuits - laboratory series
Color (IND)
Industrial and Technical Education; Science - Physical; Social Science
Dist - TXINLC **Prod** - TXINLC

RC transients 34 MIN
16mm
B&W (IND)
LC 74-705479
Gives several illustrations showing the importance of timing in radar circuits. Gives definitions for transient voltage, transient current, transient interval and waveshape. Illustrates the meaning of each of these terms, using a simple circuit consisting of a battery, switch, resistor and capacitor. Demonstrates the effect on charge time when the value of capacitance and resistance is charged and briefly explains the universal time constant chart. (Kinescope).
Industrial and Technical Education; Science - Physical
Dist - USNAC **Prod** - USAF

RCA Victor portable radio 1 MIN
U-matic / VHS
Color
Shows a classic television commercial with the famous RCA dog logo.
Business and Economics; Psychology; Sociology
Dist - BROOKC **Prod** - BROOKC

RCFX - radiation - causes and effects 23 MIN
VHS
Color; PAL (I J H)
PdS15 purchase _ #1008
Discusses radiation, in particular ionizing radiation. Covers natural and background radiation, possible risks to health and the many uses of radiation in the home, in medicine and in industry. Features Carol Vorderman as presenter and includes teacher's notes.
Health and Safety
Dist - UKAEA

RCL 34 MIN
U-matic
Radio technician training series
B&W (IND)
LC 78-706298
Explains current and voltage in relation to time and discusses voltage and current curves, the relationship of current and voltage, the measurement of voltage at source, the addition of phase components and the effect of impedance on resonance. Issued in 1943 as a motion picture.
Industrial and Technical Education
Dist - USNAC **Prod** - USN 1978

RCL - resistance capacitance 34 MIN
16mm
Radio technician training series
B&W (IND)
LC FIE52-915
Explains current and voltage in relation to time. Shows voltage and current curves, how current leads voltage and voltage leads current in different instances and the relation of current to voltage.
Industrial and Technical Education
Dist - USNAC **Prod** - USN 1943

Re - discovering America series

Goldrush country	18 MIN
St Augustine - the Oldest City	14 MIN
West Point on the Hudson	17 MIN

Dist - AIMS

Re - emerging goddess series

The Ancient goddess	30 MIN
The Ancient goddess - The Descent of the goddess - The Return of the goddess	90 MIN
The Descent of the goddess	30 MIN

Dist - HP

Re - energize yourself 30 MIN
VHS
Color (G PRO)
$79.95 purchase _ #736 - 67
Offers an array of practical tips for refocusing mental and physical resources to maximize performance on and off the job. Illustrates fitness tips to be used at a desk and specific guidelines and practical methods to improve performance, guard against burnout and turn stress into a positive motivator.
Physical Education and Recreation; Psychology
Dist - MEMIND **Prod** - AMA
CAMV

Re - entry 90 MIN
16mm
Color (G)
$150.00 rental
Presents a Carl E Brown production, sound by Kaiser Neitzche.
Fine Arts
Dist - CANCIN

Re - Evaluating Homemaking 28 MIN
U-matic / VHS
Color (G)
$249.00, $149.00 purchase _ #AD - 1589
Examines the feelings of women toward the traditional roles of homemaker and mother in a society that demeans and undervalues these responsibilities. Adapts a Phil Donahue program.
Home Economics; Sociology
Dist - FOTH **Prod** - FOTH

Re - inventing the fire 15 MIN
VHS
Color; PAL; NTSC (IND G)
PdS57, PdS67 purchase
Highlights the issues of disposing of industrial and domestic waste in an environmentally acceptable way. Pinpoints some solutions using the latest waste combustion technology. Examines the disposal of straw, wornout tires and hospital waste. Reveals that the energy recovered represents both a valuable resource in itself and a potential source of income for organizations involved in waste disposal.
Science - Natural; Social Science; Sociology
Dist - CFLVIS **Prod** - BRCOI 1991

Re - Making of Work Series

At home, at work - alternate work sites	30 MIN
For my own cause - quality circles	27 MIN
Modern Times - Revisited - Alternatives to Assembly Lines	29 MIN
More Time to Live - Flexible Working Time	30 MIN
Responsibility Shared - Autonomous Production Groups	28 MIN
Smarter Together - Autonomous Working Groups	29 MIN
A Terminal on My Desk - the Impact of Data Processing in the Office	29 MIN

Dist - EBEC

Re - run - 230 30 MIN
U-matic
Currents - 1985 - 86 Season Series
Color (A)
Explores the use of the re - run in television.
Fine Arts; Social Science
Dist - PBS **Prod** - WNETTV 1985

The Re - Selling of Tylenol
U-matic / VHS
Sixty Minutes on Business Series
Color
One of ten segments selected from the realities of the business world, and chosen from key '60 Minutes' telecasts to provide insight into vital issues affecting business today. Includes sourcebook.
Business and Economics; Psychology
Dist - CBSFOX **Prod** - CBSFOX

Re - Side Your House 30 MIN
VHS / 16mm
Build Your Own Series
Color (H C A PRO)
$15.00 purchase _ #TA219
Shows how to reside a structure with APS siding panels and a few simple tools.
Industrial and Technical Education
Dist - AAVIM **Prod** - AAVIM 1990

Re - Union 13 MIN
U-matic / BETA / VHS
(G)
$100.00
Reunites a Toronto bag lady and her long lost daughter.
Sociology
Dist - CTV **Prod** - CTV 1985

Re - use it or lose it 20 MIN
VHS
Color (G)
$15.00 rental
Examines the components of the solid waste stream and explains the reasons for recycling a wide range of materials. Looks at recycling programs in a number of communities, what they have achieved, the problems they are encountering. Produced by Doug Prose.
Science - Natural; Sociology
Dist - CMSMS **Prod** - SIERRA 1990

Re - use it or lose it - Reusarlo o perderlo 20 MIN
VHS
Color (J H C G) (SPANISH)
$175.00 purchase, $40.00 rental _ #38142, #38158
Reveals that Americans throw out more than 160 million tons of waste annually - enough to fill the New Orleans Superdome twice every day of the year. Discloses that this enormous amount of waste creates major social problems because most of the nation's landfills have closed in the last ten years and those remaining will be filled by the year 2000. Focuses on solutions to the waste problem. Shows how people in the San Francisco Bay Area have achieved one of the highest recycling rates in the world and how innovative recycling programs in the area have become models for communities nationwide. Produced by Doug Prose.
Science - Natural; Sociology
Dist - UCEMC

Re - work wiring techniques 15 MIN
VHS
Color (H A T)
$75.00 purchase _ #VC301
Teaches the specialized skills for installing electrical devices such as switches and receptacles into existing finished walls. Checks and lays out walls, cuts in boxes and fishes cable. Explains how to install conduit down finished walls and how to expand a single opening in a two - gang. Includes NEC references.

Industrial and Technical Education
Dist - AAVIM **Prod** - AAVIM 1992

Reach Beyond the Horizon - a History of Edwards Air Force Base 40 MIN
16mm
Color
LC 79-701538
Traces the history of Edwards Air Force Base in California. Shows many unusual aircraft in flight, including the XP - 59, the X - 1, the X - 15 mach 6 rocket plane, the X - 13 tail sitter, and the XC - 142 tilt wing.
Industrial and Technical Education
Dist - USNAC **Prod** - USAF

Reach for Fitness
VHS
(C A)
$24.95 _ #WW270V
Features specially designed workouts for the physically handicapped.
Physical Education and Recreation
Dist - CAMV **Prod** - CAMV

Reach for fitness 40 MIN
VHS
Color (G)
$24.95 purchase _ #WW270V
Features fitness expert Richard Simmons, who offers advice on nutrition and daily exercise in a program designed especially for the handicapped. Offers exercises suitable for individuals with a range of disabilities and health conditions, including multiple sclerosis, spina bifida, muscular dystrophy, asthma, diabetes and more. Exercises demonstrated by children and adults.
Health and Safety; Physical Education and Recreation
Dist - CAMV

Reach for the stars 26 MIN
VHS
Stars series
Color (I J H)
$195.00 purchase
Looks at the star - gazing techniques of several cultures and shows how they interpreted the skyscape. Describes how the sun rules the calendar and why the zodiac is 'slipping.' Uses computer animation to journey through outer space and observe the universe from the vantage point of an inter - stellar traveler. Part of a six - part series on astronomy.
History - World; Science - Physical
Dist - LANDMK **Prod** - LANDMK 1988

Reach for the summit 30 MIN
16mm
Color (R)
Introduces Lou Zamperini, who was unable to adjust to post - war life because of experiences in a Japanese prisoner - of - war camp. Shows how a Billy Graham crusade changed his life.
Guidance and Counseling; Religion and Philosophy
Dist - OUTRCH **Prod** - OUTRCH

Reach for tomorrow 15 MIN
16mm
Color
Shows Girl Scout participation in activities ranging from high ropes to bread baking. Represents all levels, from Daisy Girl Scouts to adults. Filmed on location at four different Girl Scout Councils.
Physical Education and Recreation; Psychology; Sociology
Dist - GSUSA **Prod** - GSUSA 1984

Reach into silence 15 MIN
16mm
Color
LC FIA63-1077
Attempts to recruit workers to work with handicapped children, especially those with defective hearing.
Health and Safety; Psychology; Sociology
Dist - USC **Prod** - USC 1956

Reach into Space 16 MIN
16mm
Color
LC 74-706209
Explains the military and scientific significance of space research. Describes the progress of various space projects and examines their future requirements.
Civics and Political Systems; Science - Physical
Dist - USNAC **Prod** - USAF 1964

Reach out 5 MIN
16mm / U-matic / VHS
Bill Martin's freedom series
Color (K P I)
LC 72-712659
Explores the concept of 'open mind' to accept new sights, sounds and people and to counteract the urge to settle for the comfort of the familiar.
Civics and Political Systems; Social Science; Sociology
Dist - ALTSUL **Prod** - LAWTNM 1971

Reach Out and Grow 28 MIN
16mm
Color (R)
Discusses why some churches are more successful than others and why some Christians seem to enjoy more useful and effective lives. Presents comments by Christian leaders on principles and practical applications of Biblical messages.
Religion and Philosophy; Sociology
Dist - GF **Prod** - GF

Reach out and touch 15 MIN
16mm
Color
LC 74-700524
Shows the human side of a hospital, emphasizing staff attitude rather than medical care.
Health and Safety; Psychology
Dist - VISION **Prod** - VISION 1973

Reach Out for Life 11 MIN
16mm
Color (A)
LC 80-701099
Relates the story of an elderly man who realizes that his preoccupation with job advancement and family expenses in his youth has prevented him from enjoying life. Shows that after attempting suicide and gaining control of his life, he comes to believe that people should not harbor unrealistic expectations about themselves and others.
Psychology; Sociology
Dist - FLMLIB **Prod** - EPIDEM 1980

Reach Out - Occupational Therapy in the Community 20 MIN
U-matic
Color
Presents occupational therapists providing services in the community. Includes home health services for the elderly, the progress of an adolescent spinal cord injury patient from the hospital to recovery, identification of developmental disabilities and living skills programs in special education.
Education; Health and Safety; Psychology
Dist - AOTA **Prod** - AOTA 1977

Reach out to help someone series
Dealing with people on the telephone 20 MIN
Handling Incoming Calls 20 MIN
Selling on the Telephone 20 MIN
Dist - AMEDIA

Reaching all your students 30 MIN
VHS
How children learn series
Color (G A R)
$39.95 purchase, $10.00 rental _ #35 - 871 - 2076
Proposes that teachers and students have dominant teaching styles which affect their classroom performance. Hosted by Sharon Lee. Produced by Seraphim.
Education; Health and Safety; Religion and Philosophy
Dist - APH

Reaching for the Gold, Pt 1 60 MIN
VHS / BETA
Color
Deals with horsemanship. Discusses posture, lunging, dressage saddles, breeds, gaits, training tests and transitions.
Physical Education and Recreation
Dist - EQVDL **Prod** - EQVDL

Reaching for the Gold, Pt 2 52 MIN
VHS / BETA
Color
Covers transitions, levels, piaf, passage and stretching involved in horsemanship.
Physical Education and Recreation
Dist - EQVDL **Prod** - EQVDL

Reaching for the trigger 6 MIN
16mm
B&W (G)
$12.00 rental
Fine Arts; Industrial and Technical Education
Dist - CANCIN **Prod** - MICHAL 1986

Reaching into Space 14 MIN
16mm / U-matic / VHS
Color (I J H)
Explains Newton's third law as it applies to rocket flight. Depicts the amount of force necessary for a satellite to orbit, the escape speed necessary to break through the earth's gravitational pull, weather surveys and other ramifications of space research.
Science - Physical
Dist - IFB **Prod** - VEF 1960

Reaching orgasm 17 MIN
16mm
Color (PRO)
Depicts a series of exercises for helping a pre - orgasmic woman learn about her body's sensations. Begins with observing exercises and progresses to tactile ones.
Guidance and Counseling; Health and Safety
Dist - DAVFMS **Prod** - DAVFMS 1974

Reaching Out 32 MIN
16mm / U-matic / VHS
Color (H C A)
LC 80-701095
Presents the story of two teenagers, one physically handicapped and the other emotionally handicapped, who learn to accept each other and themselves at the same time and fall in love.
Education; Fine Arts; Guidance and Counseling; Psychology; Sociology
Dist - LCOA **Prod** - CINEFL 1980

Reaching Out - a Story about Mainstreaming 13 MIN
U-matic / VHS / 16mm
Color (P I)
LC 82-700570
Portrays the first days of school for Mary Rivera, a multiply - handicapped girl who is entering a regular classroom for the first time. Shows both Mary's reactions and those of her classmates.
Education; Psychology
Dist - CORF **Prod** - BELLDA 1982

Reaching out - the library and the exceptional child 25 MIN
16mm
Color (P)
LC 72-701728
Shows how children with various handicaps respond to books and other materials. Demonstrates ways in which the use of these materials can contribute to their development.
Education
Dist - CONNF **Prod** - CHCPL 1968

Reaching out - the National Greek Orthodox Ladies Philoptochos Society 28 MIN
VHS
Illuminations series
Color (G R)
#V - 1027
Profiles the National Greek Orthodox Ladies Philoptochos Society, which is the official philanthropic society of the Greek Orthodox Church. Interviews Philoptochos members, who discuss some of the projects in which they are engaged.
Fine Arts; Religion and Philosophy; Sociology
Dist - GOTEL **Prod** - GOTEL 1988

Reaching out with Islam
VHS
Video lectures of Yusuf Islam series
Color (G)
$11.95 purchase _ #110 - 003
Features Islamic lecturer Yusuf Islam who advocates teaching Westerners about Islam. Encourages Muslims to call others to the Truth.
Religion and Philosophy
Dist - SOUVIS **Prod** - SOUVIS

Reaching Potential 26 MIN
U-matic / VHS / 16mm
Color (T)
Shows the integration into a regular school system of four children who are visually impaired to different degrees. Assesses the value of integration of visually impaired children from the point of view of teachers, school administrators, parents and other children. Stresses the importance of integration into a regular school system as a learning system that will facilitate the later adjustment of the visually impaired to life in the community at large.
Education
Dist - EBEC **Prod** - EBEC 1981

Reaching the Child within 30 MIN
U-matic / VHS
Color (H C A)
Portrays the intimate experiences of three families with autistic children, as well as the early warning sign of autism and the viewpoints of national experts working in the field.
Guidance and Counseling; Health and Safety; Psychology; Sociology
Dist - UEUWIS **Prod** - UEUWIS 1980

Reaching your golf potential
VHS
Color (G)
$39.99 purchase _ #BHV011
Presents 2 videos of golf lessons with Tom Kite.
Physical Education and Recreation
Dist - SIV

Reaching your reader 10 MIN
U-matic / VHS / 16mm
Effective writing series
Color (I)
$255.00, $180.00 purchase _ #81528
Discusses how to make written material more interesting to the reader. Suggests using words that stimulate the reader's memory, appeal to the five senses and create images with feeling and movement.
English Language
Dist - CENTEF **Prod** - CENTRO 1983
CORF

Reaching your reader 17 MIN
U-matic / VHS / 16mm
Color (J) (SPANISH)
Demonstrates methods the writer can use to reach the minds and emotions of the intended reader.
English Language
Dist - CORF **Prod** - CENTRO 1971

REACT - Review of Emergency Aid and CPR Training Series

Accident prevention and safety	15 MIN
Bandaging	15 MIN
Care for choking victim who is conscious	15 MIN
Care for choking victim who is unconscious	15 MIN
CPR for Babies and Children	15 MIN
Emergency Action Principles	15 MIN
Emergency Rescue and Transfer	15 MIN
First Aid for Burns	15 MIN
First Aid for Injuries to Bones, Muscles and Joints	15 MIN
First aid for specific injuries	15 MIN
First Aid for Sudden Illness	15 MIN
First Aid for Wounds	15 MIN
Mouth - to - Mouth Breathing	15 MIN
One Rescuer CPR	15 MIN
Respiratory Emergencies	15 MIN
Respiratory Emergencies - Babies and Children	15 MIN
Two Rescuer CPR	15 MIN

Dist - CORF

Reactance Tube Modulator 24 MIN
16mm
B&W
LC 74-705480
Points out the principles of operation of the reactance tube modulator and identifies and states the purpose of each component. (Kinescope).
Industrial and Technical Education; Science - Physical
Dist - USNAC **Prod** - USAF 1963

Reaction, brakes, time and space 9 MIN
16mm / U-matic / VHS
Color (H C A)
Presents an excerpt from Freeway Driving Tactics. Translates reaction time into reaction distance. Uses animation and a driving experiment to show that Tailgating At Any Speed Does Not Make Sense.
Health and Safety; Industrial and Technical Education
Dist - AIMS **Prod** - CAHILL 1965

Reaction, Braking and Stopping Distances 28 MIN
16mm
Sportsmanlike Driving Series no 19
B&W (H A)
LC FIA68-916
Illustrates the concept of car control and the need for a cushion of safety. Uses an AAA brake reaction detonator to show that it takes time and distance to bring a vehicle to a stop.
Health and Safety
Dist - GPN **Prod** - AAA 1967

Reaction kinetics 10 MIN
U-matic
Chemical equilibrium series
Color (H C)
Examines why some chemical reactions happen more quickly than others. Uses a chain mechanism model to show how energy released by reacting molecules influences other molecules and leads to a clearer understanding of exothermic and endothermic reactions.
Science; Science - Physical
Dist - TVOTAR **Prod** - TVOTAR 1984

Reaction Mechanisms 10 MIN
U-matic
Chemistry 102 - Chemistry for Engineers - Series
Color (C)
Explains the concept of mechanism by analogy, defining chemical reaction mechanism and intermediate. Shows how to use kinetic data to devise, test and evaluate proposed mechanisms, checking for consistency with the experimental rate law.
Industrial and Technical Education; Science - Physical
Dist - UILL **Prod** - UILL 1985

Reaction - Molecules - Molecular Symbols 60 MIN
U-matic / VHS
Chemistry Training Series
Color (IND)
Shows sulphur as an energy - rich raw material, the symbol for the molecules in water, how molecular symbols confirm one another, the size of the molecules in olive oil, the vaporization and electrolysis of water and its energy requirements.
Science; Science - Physical
Dist - ITCORP **Prod** - ITCORP

Reaction Orders 11 MIN
U-matic
Chemistry 102 - Chemistry for Engineers - Series
Color (C)
Defines molecularity showing how to determine it in a reaction. Introduces the elements of a rate law equation showing how the rate law of a reaction enables prediction of rate dependent on reactant concentration.
Industrial and Technical Education; Science - Physical
Dist - UILL **Prod** - UILL 1985

Reaction overpotential - crystallization overpotential 51 MIN
U-matic / VHS
Electrochemistry series; Pt 5
Color
Science; Science - Physical
Dist - MIOT **Prod** - MIOT
KALMIA KALMIA

Reaction Rates 18 MIN
U-matic
Chemistry 102 - Chemistry for Engineers - Series
Color (C)
Lists factors affecting chemical reaction rates; temperature, surface area and concentration. Demonstrates by a miniature simulation how explosions occur in grain elevators. Articulates the aim of kinetics studies.
Industrial and Technical Education; Science - Physical
Dist - UILL **Prod** - UILL 1985

Reaction rates and equilibrium 20 MIN
U-matic / VHS / 16mm
Chemistry series
Color (J H C)
$480.00, $250.00 purchase _ #4366
Teaches factors which influence the rates at which chemical reactions take place. Demonstrates equilibrium, how it can be upset and its role in the chemical industry.
Science; Science - Physical
Dist - CORF **Prod** - CORF

Reaction tendencies 10 MIN
U-matic
Chemical equilibrium series
Color (H C)
Introduces Le Chatelier's principle which states that if a system in equilibrium is subject to stress, the system tends to react in such a way as to oppose the effect of the stress. Observes the effects of two types of stress, change in temperature and change in pressure or volume.
Science; Science - Physical
Dist - TVOTAR **Prod** - TVOTAR 1984

Reactions and decisions of parents with hearing impaired children 36 MIN
U-matic / VHS
Color (PRO C G)
$195.00 purchase _ #C890 - VI - 044
Discusses the reactions, problems and decisions that parents of hearing - impaired children often encounter. Reveals that the training that speech - language pathologists, audiologists and teachers of hearing - impaired people receive often does not prepare them to interact with a hearing - impaired person's family. Discloses that knowledge of the variety of emotions these families experience will better prepare professionals to implement an effective aural rehabilitation program of which counseling is an essential component. Presented by Debby Bengala and Dr Gregg D Givens.
Guidance and Counseling; Health and Safety; Sociology
Dist - HSCIC

Reactive displays 6 MIN
16mm
Color (C A)
Describes the General Motors Research Laboratory computer which processes pictures instead of digits. Provides designers flexibility in manipulating shapes and forms on a readout screen to determine the best possible dimensions for a part.
Mathematics
Dist - GM **Prod** - GM

The Reactor 29 MIN
U-matic
Nuclear Power and You Series
Color
Tours the Enrico Fermi Nuclear Power Generating Plant II. Discusses the energy process.
Science - Physical; Social Science
Dist - UMITV **Prod** - UMITV 1979

Reactor Safety Research 15 MIN
16mm
Color (C A)
LC FIE64-147
Shows the characteristics, conservative design of nuclear power reactors and the elaborate safeguards that are incorporated into the design. Examines the progress of reactor safety research in studies of abnormal nuclear behavior, fission product release, chemical reactions, containment and vapor cleanup systems.
Health and Safety; Science; Science - Physical
Dist - USNAC **Prod** - ANL 1964

Reactors at Calder Hall 35 MIN
16mm
B&W
Presents a survey of the work carried out inside the reactor pressure vessel at Calder Hall, including cleaning, laying the graphite and installing the gas - sampling equipment.
Industrial and Technical Education; Science - Physical
Dist - UKAEA **Prod** - UKAEA 1957

Read 10 MIN
U-matic
Readalong One Series
Color (K P)
Introduces reading and spelling for preschoolers and children in grades 1 to 3 with animation, puppets, humor and music. Comes with teacher's guide and kit.
Education; English Language; Literature and Drama
Dist - TVOTAR **Prod** - TVOTAR 1975

Read all about it - One Series

The Accidental visitor	30 MIN
Closer to the Truth	30 MIN
The Coach House	30 MIN
An Evil Pirate	30 MIN
The First edition	30 MIN
Pictures in Your Mind	30 MIN
Place of Change	30 MIN
The Planet of Maze	30 MIN
The Problem Pit	30 MIN
Rhyme Time	30 MIN
Seek and Speak	30 MIN
The Showdown	30 MIN
Special Edition	30 MIN
The Stolen Message	30 MIN
Strange Discoveries	30 MIN
The Stranger	30 MIN
Time for action	30 MIN
To the Rescue	30 MIN
Voices in the Park	30 MIN

Dist - TVOTAR

Read and adjust toe - John Bear alignment machine 7 MIN
VHS / 16mm
Auto mechanics series
(IND)
$54.00 purchase _ #AM3
Shows how to read and adjust the toe on the John Bear alignment machine.
Industrial and Technical Education
Dist - RMIBHF **Prod** - RMIBHF

Read Before You Write 7 MIN
U-matic / VHS / 16mm
Consumer Education Series
Captioned; Color (J) (SPANISH)
LC 72-703427
Presents a young couple considering a typical installment purchase, a TV set. Follows them from their obvious enchantment outside the store window to a new awareness when they learn to really examine a contract before they sign it.
Business and Economics; Civics and Political Systems; Home Economics; Social Science
Dist - ALTSUL **Prod** - ALTSUL 1972

READ - DATA Statements - Strings 30 MIN
U-matic / VHS
Programming for microcomputers series; Unit 14 and 15
Color (J)
LC 83-707132
Teaches how to use 'read...data' statements and explains the data pointer. Discusses how data statements may be written and suggests their placement at the end of a program. Reveals how certain functions can be used to manipulate strings. Explains a number of these functions and introduces the ASCII character code. Illustrates the use of quotation marks and brackets.
Mathematics
Dist - IU **Prod** - IU 1983

Read English today 70 MIN
VHS
Color (H A G)

$49.95 purchase
Presents 15 lessons in beginning reading for English as a second language - ESL - students. Features Dr Mary 'Marisol' Samaras as instructor.
Education; English Language
Dist - NUVO **Prod** - NUVO 1993

Read music today 120 MIN
VHS
Color (J H C G)
$29.95 purchase _ #BSPRM2V
Teaches students how to read music. Offers a basic understanding of musical notes and composition that can be applied to all musical instruments. Uses computer graphics to explain step - by - step beginning through advanced topics. Includes note reading, scales, chords, intervals, triads, inversions and more.
Fine Arts
Dist - CAMV

Read My Arm 17 MIN
16mm
Color
Relates the actual experience of administering the Lederle Tuberculine Tine Test to several hundred migratory farm workers on a large farm. Demonstrates how state and local agencies can help to protect the health of migratory farm workers by bringing services directly into the field and indicates how a cooperative project, involving employers, churches, voluntary agencies and government agencies, can be applied to control other infectious diseases in both urban and rural situations.
Health and Safety; Sociology
Dist - LEDR **Prod** - ACYLLD 1962

Read on Series
And then what happened - starring Donna, Alice and you 10 MIN
From left to right - inversions and reversals 10 MIN
From Start to Finish - the Nature Trail 11 MIN
One and more than One - Birthday on a Farm 8 MIN
Put Them Together - a Saturday Adventure 11 MIN
Tell Me all about it - what Makes a Friend So Special 9 MIN
Dist - AIMS

Read the label
VHS
Right - to - know series
Color (H IND T)
$225.00 purchase _ #BM504
Trains educational market personnel about the potential chemical hazards they might encounter on the job.
Health and Safety; Psychology
Dist - AAVIM **Prod** - AAVIM 1992

Read the label - and live 13 MIN
U-matic / VHS / 16mm
Color (I J H)
LC 77-702128
Stresses reading the labels of commonly used household products. Details safe handling practices for foods, aerosol products, insecticides, paint thinners and medicines.
Health and Safety; Home Economics
Dist - HIGGIN **Prod** - HIGGIN 1977

Read the label - it's the law - lisez l'etiquette - c'est la loi 16 MIN
U-matic / BETA / VHS
Canadian specific programs series
Color (IND G) (FRENCH)
$495.00 purchase _ #820 - 50, #820 - 51
Discusses the WHMIS Requirements for labels on hazardous materials received from a supplier, as well as workplace and laboratory labels and other modes of identification. Covers work practices, Canadian hazard class symbols, bulk shipments and the responsibility of suppliers, employers and workers who handle controlled products. Produced by Innovative Video Training, Inc, of Canada.
Health and Safety; Psychology; Sociology
Dist - ITSC

Read the label, set a better table 14 MIN
16mm
Color (SPANISH)
LC 75-700573; 75-702479
Shows consumers how they can get more value for their food dollar by reading the new food labels. Explains that food packages now list many nutrients and encourages viewers to learn to set a better table.
Home Economics; Social Science
Dist - USNAC **Prod** - USFDA 1974

Read to me 15 MIN
VHS / U-matic
Color (G)
Emphasizes the importance of reading to babies to develop their language skills and imagination.
English Language; Psychology
Dist - GVLF **Prod** - GVLF

Readability 30 MIN
U-matic / VHS
Effective Writing Series
Color
English Language; Psychology
Dist - DELTAK **Prod** - TWAIN

Readabout - reading skills 150 MIN
VHS
Color; PAL (I)
PdS40 purchase
Helps young readers to understand and respond to all types of writing. Uses play, graphics, on - screen text and excerpts from books to convey concepts. Includes 10 programs of 15 minutes each and a supporting book. Contact distributor about availability outside the United Kingdom.
English Language; Literature and Drama
Dist - ACADEM

Readalong good time 10 MIN
U-matic
Readalong two series
Color (P)
Provides young viewers with a flexible range of reading experiences through active involvement in reading and writing. Comes with teacher's guide and kit.
Education; English Language; Literature and Drama
Dist - TVOTAR **Prod** - TVOTAR 1976

Readalong One Series
Book 10 MIN
Boy, Room, Stop 10 MIN
Careful, Front 10 MIN
Could, would, Should, who, Quick 10 MIN
Day, apple, push 10 MIN
Flowers 10 MIN
Friend, because, broken 10 MIN
Girl, Boot, Jump 10 MIN
Here, There 10 MIN
House, kick, ball 10 MIN
How, Why, what 10 MIN
Nice, Rain, Fish 10 MIN
Noise, Elephant, Forget 10 MIN
Nurse 10 MIN
Party, Dress, Game 10 MIN
Please, play, done 10 MIN
Pretty, Swim, Away 10 MIN
Princess, Large, Small 10 MIN
Read 10 MIN
Safety, Look, Rock 10 MIN
Sleep, Hole, Up, Down 10 MIN
Something, Nothing, Feelings 10 MIN
Teacher, Shaker, Sweet 10 MIN
True, False 10 MIN
When, Around, Sound 10 MIN
Where, Turn 10 MIN
Your touch 10 MIN
Dist - TVOTAR

Readalong Three Series
Advertise, advertising, advertisement, route, root, photographer, photo 10 MIN
Apology, apologize, apologized 10 MIN
Assistant, assist, kilometre 10 MIN
Audience, discouraged, encourage, introduce, introduction, courage, encouragement 10 MIN
Capital, Capitals 10 MIN
Celebrate, celebration, accept, except, admitted, admission, admittance, admit 10 MIN
Closer, Footsteps, Opened, Pointing 10 MIN
Concert 10 MIN
Direction, Wish, Guide 10 MIN
Editor, news 10 MIN
Explanation, Explain, Telephone, Telegram, Television Mystery, Mysterious, Dungeon 10 MIN
Famous, history, battle, rebuilt, recall , repaired, reopens, received, remain, retakes 10 MIN
Farewell, awards, shoe 10 MIN
Favorite, mistake, previews, autograph , preview, practice 10 MIN
Fortune, fortunate, unfortunately, would, record, wish 10 MIN
Future, final edition, graduation 10 MIN
Guarded, Guards, Guard, Approaches, Approach, Mislead, Mischief, Misunderstanding, Mistake 10 MIN
Hero, West 10 MIN
Powerful, Mountains, Danger 10 MIN
Quotation Marks, Programs, Deep, Dark, Dirty, Vanished 10 MIN
Report, Reporter, Deliver, New 10 MIN
Resist, Retreat, Mistaken, Listening 10 MIN
Sentence, characters, sinister, disappeared, vanished 10 MIN
Shiver, Shudder, Stairs, Secrets, Scream, Shriek, Yelling 10 MIN
Standing, Start, Starter 10 MIN
Straight, Huge, Gigantic, Enormous, Dinosaur, Curve 10 MIN
Suspect, Suspicious, Suspicions, Emergency, Rattled, Rattle, Gurgled, Clanked, Hissed 10 MIN
Terrific, Terrifically 10 MIN
Unusual 10 MIN
Dist - TVOTAR

Readalong Two Series
Adventure, interest 10 MIN
Adventure, interested 10 MIN
Afraid, collect, collector 10 MIN
Answer, know, luck 10 MIN
Beautiful, rainbow 10 MIN
Before, Wind, Unsafe 10 MIN
Bicycle 10 MIN
Cheer, whisper 10 MIN
Cloud, Cloudy 10 MIN
First review week 1 10 MIN
First review week 2 10 MIN
First review week 3 10 MIN
Fly, flying, begin, beginning 10 MIN
Forest, Better 10 MIN
Holiday, Decide, Weather 10 MIN
Idea, Amazing, Story 10 MIN
Little 10 MIN
Measure, Take, Pepper 10 MIN
Presents, Beautiful 10 MIN
Pretend, Picture 10 MIN
Quiet, Hunter, Noise 10 MIN
Readalong good time 10 MIN
Riding, Scared 10 MIN
Said, Asked 10 MIN
Second review week 1 10 MIN
Second review week 2 10 MIN
Second review week 3 10 MIN
Third Review Week 1 10 MIN
Third Review Week 2 10 MIN
Third Review Week 3 10 MIN
Dist - TVOTAR

Readers' Cube Series
The Me of the Moment 20 MIN
My World 20 MIN
Dist - AITECH

Reader's digest great national parks series
Grand canyon 55 MIN
Yellowstone 55 MIN
Yosemite 55 MIN
Dist - PBS

Reader's Digest in America 20 MIN
16mm
Color
Uses facts and figures to illustrate the impact of an advertising campaign in a national magazine of popular appeal. Shows how a selected readership in a specific economic level brings in a high rate of sales return for the advertising dollar.
Business and Economics; Literature and Drama; Psychology
Dist - CCNY **Prod** - READER

Reader's theatre 10 MIN
VHS / 16mm
Drama reference series
Color (C)
$150.00 purchase _ #268410
Implements elementary drama curriculum. Presents drama content, teaching strategies and resources, and demonstrates drama activities for the classroom. Teaches the ability to perform works of literature through interpretive reading.
Education; English Language; Fine Arts; Literature and Drama; Mathematics
Dist - ACCESS **Prod** - ACCESS 1987

Readers's Guide to Periodical Literature 7 MIN
U-matic / VHS
Library skills tapes series
Color
Shows how to locate magazine articles on a particular subject by using Reader's Guide to Periodical Literature.
Education
Dist - MDCC **Prod** - MDCC

Readin' and writin' ain't everything 25 MIN
16mm / U-matic / VHS
Color (A)
LC 75-703532
Presents a community - oriented view of mental retardation through the personal account of a retarded adult and three families with retarded children.

Education; Psychology; Sociology
Dist - STNFLD Prod - KCCMHS 1975

Readiness - Audience and Persona 30 MIN
VHS / U-matic
Writing for a Reason Series
Color (C)
English Language
Dist - DALCCD Prod - DALCCD

Readiness for Addition and Subtraction 15 MIN
U-matic
Measure Up Series
Color (P)
Introduces basic aspects of addition and subtraction.
Mathematics
Dist - GPN Prod - WCETTV 1977

Readiness for learning 30 MIN
16mm
Nursing - patient teaching series; Part 1
B&W (C A)
LC 74-700201
Differentiates between student readiness for learning to teach patients and patient readiness to learn self - care.
Education; Health and Safety
Dist - NTCN Prod - NTCN 1971

Reading 29 MIN
VHS / 16mm
Breaking the unseen barrier series
Color (C)
$180.00, $240.00 purchase _ #269703
Demonstrates through dramatic vignettes effective teaching strategies to help students with learning disabilities reach their full potential. Offers insight into integrating learning disabled students into the classroom. Focuses on Mark, a high school student, and Jill, a primary student, who are struggling with reading problems characteristic of learning disabilities. Suggests specific techniques and general principles to help Mark and Jill improve their individual reading abilities.
Education; English Language
Dist - AITECH Prod - ACCESS 1988

Reading 1974 - portrait of a city 56 MIN
VHS
Color (G)
$50.00 purchase
Captures the visual essence of the center of Pennsylvania Dutch culture immediately before its dissolution from rapidly encroaching suburban Philadelphia. Makes use of the City Symphony tradition that began in Europe in the 1920s and shares with these older films a basically formalist - experimental approach to montage and cinematography. With Gary Adlestein, Costa Mantis and Jerry Orr. Sound by Ida Orr.
Fine Arts; Geography - United States
Dist - CANCIN Prod - ORRJER 1975

Reading a Bibliography 20 MIN
VHS / 16mm
Study Research Library Skills Series
Color (J)
Presents a lesson on how to obtain information from a bibliography.
Education
Dist - COMEX Prod - COMEX 1987

Reading a Dictionary Entry 20 MIN
VHS / 16mm
Study Research Library Skills Series
Color (J)
Presents a lesson on uderstanding the information contained in a dictionry entry.
Education
Dist - COMEX Prod - COMEX 1987

Reading a drawing of a valve bonnet 20 MIN
16mm
Machine shop work series; Fundamentals of blueprint reading; No 5
B&W
LC FIE51-505
Explains how to interpret conventional symbols and tolerance specifications and how to use the blueprint in planning machine operations.
Education; Industrial and Technical Education
Dist - USNAC Prod - USOE 1944

Reading - a Language Experience Approach 33 MIN
16mm / U-matic
Stereo; Color
Presents the teaching of reading through resources such as dictated stories, experience charts, talking murals, word walls and book publishing to help develop the child's progression from speaking, to writing, to reading. Discusses the idea that reading skills are not sequenced, but develop best in clusters.
English Language; Psychology
Dist - PROMET Prod - PROMET

Reading a Lecture 16 MIN
U-matic / VHS
Developing Your Study Skills Series
Color (H C)
Outlines the different forms a lecture may take. Explains the necessity for students to assess the lecture and determine to what extent they are expected to participate. Presents an approach to effective note - taking.
Education
Dist - BCNFL Prod - UWO 1985

Reading a Map 20 MIN
U-matic
Understanding Our World, Unit I - Tools We Use Series
Color (I)
Features host John Rugg discussing basic concepts in map reading.
Geography - World; Social Science
Dist - GPN Prod - KRMATV

Reading a ruler 25 MIN
VHS / 16mm
Color (P I)
$149.00 purchase _ F10
Defines basic terminology and examines the decimal system as it applies to the nature of dollar.
Industrial and Technical Education; Mathematics
Dist - BERGL Prod - BERGL 1989

Reading a story to extend thinking 30 MIN
VHS / U-matic
Aide - ing in education series
Color
Demonstrates teachers' use of the six levels of thinking to extend students' thinking while listening to a story.
Education; English Language; Psychology
Dist - SPF Prod - SPF

Reading a three - view drawing 10 MIN
16mm
Machine shop work series; Fundamentals of blueprint reading
B&W (SPANISH)
LC FIE51-502; FIE62-66
Describes how to interpret and use a blueprint. Shows how to make a tool block according to specifications written on a blueprint.
Industrial and Technical Education
Dist - USNAC Prod - USOE 1945

Reading - an introduction 25 MIN
16mm
Jab reading series
Color (C T)
LC 75-701423
Presents examples of each of the four basic methods of teaching children to read as observed in actual classroom situations. Emphasizes reading on the elementary level.
Education; English Language
Dist - JBFL Prod - JABP 1974

Reading and adjusting caster and camber - John Bear alignment machine 7 MIN
VHS / 16mm
Auto mechanics series
(G PRO)
$53.00 purchase _ #AM2
Shows how to read and adjust the caster and camber on the John Bear alignment machine.
Industrial and Technical Education
Dist - RMIBHF Prod - RMIBHF

Reading and learning styles 28 MIN
U-matic / VHS
Integration of children with special needs in a regular classroom series
Color
Presents a program for elementary school children with learning disabilities. Emphasizes auditory and visual learning. Discusses remedial activities for the classroom.
Education
Dist - AITECH Prod - LPS 1975

Reading and sorting mail automatically 10 MIN
16mm
Color (IND)
LC 75-700574
Examines the operation of the new optical character reader used by the U S Post Office Department to recognize typed addresses and sort mail at high speeds.
Industrial and Technical Education; Social Science
Dist - USNAC Prod - USPOST 1970

Reading and understanding and Fostering comprehension 50 MIN
VHS
Extending literacy series; Cassette 3
Color; PAL (I H)
PdS35 purchase
Shows third year juniors learning to use a variety of resources - maps, documents, pictures and books and to find and organize the information they want. Features the teacher helping students make sense of what they read by helping them to link it with what they have learned from other sources and through discussion. Part of an eight - part series on four cassettes featuring children engaged in their classroom in a variety of interrelated learning experiences involving reading and writing.
English Language
Dist - EMFVL

Reading and word play series

Around you go	11 MIN
Come out to play	11 MIN
The Day begins	11 MIN
How do you do	11 MIN
Jack be quick	11 MIN
Ladybug, Ladybug	11 MIN
Put the Kettle on	11 MIN
Rain, Rain Go Away	11 MIN
Some Like it Cold	11 MIN
Up to the Moon	11 MIN

Dist - AIMS

Reading and Writing / Five Basic Skills 30 MIN
VHS / BETA
Color
Uses skits to demonstrate the importance of skills in reading, writing, speaking, listening and non - verbal communication.
English Language
Dist - PHENIX Prod - PHENIX

Reading Approach to Math Series

Estimating, Pt 1	19 MIN
Estimating, Pt 2	19 MIN
How to Read a Math Problem, Pt 1	19 MIN
How to Read a Math Problem, Pt 2	19 MIN
In - Service Program	29 MIN
Pre - Post Test	19 MIN
Words and Symbols	19 MIN

Dist - GPN

Reading as a Part of Life 29 MIN
16mm / U-matic / VHS
Teaching Children to Read Series
Color (T)
Identifies and discusses key thoughts on reading's broad context. Examines reading as a natural part of language development rather than as an isolated skill.
Education; English Language
Dist - FI Prod - MFFD 1975

Reading - assessment and programming 29 MIN
U-matic / VHS
Mainstreaming the exceptional child series
Color (T)
Discusses reading assessment and programming in a mainstreaming situation.
Education; English Language
Dist - FI Prod - MFFD

Reading Blood Pressure 10 MIN
U-matic
Human Sexuality Series
Color (PRO)
Discusses the method for reading blood pressure, including the palpation and audition of pulsating sounds in the brachial artery. Explains the sphygmomanometer.
Health and Safety; Science; Science - Natural
Dist - PRIMED Prod - PRIMED

Reading Chinese horoscopes
VHS
Color (G)
$29.95 purchase _ #VDG003
Demonstrates principles of the horoscope. Answers questions about hidden talents, career and romance.
Religion and Philosophy; Sociology
Dist - SIV

Reading comprehension 120 MIN
U-matic / VHS
SAT exam preparation series
Color
Education; English Language
Dist - KRLSOF Prod - KRLSOF 1985

Reading comprehension, analysis of situations - Lesson 2
U-matic / VHS
GMAT/Graduate Management Admission Test series
Color (C A)
Education; English Language
Dist - COMEX Prod - COMEX

Reading comprehension, analytical reasoning - Lesson 1
VHS / U-matic
GRE/Graduate Record Examination series
Color (H A)
Education; English Language
Dist - COMEX Prod - COMEX

Reading Comprehension from the Child's Perspective 29 MIN
VHS / U-matic

Reading Comprehension Series
Color (T)
Produced by Frank Smith for Heinemann Educational Books, Inc.
Education; English Language
Dist - HNEDBK **Prod** - IU

Reading comprehension introduction - preview 29 MIN
U-matic / VHS
Reading comprehension series
Color (T)
Education; English Language
Dist - HNEDBK **Prod** - IU

Reading comprehension series
Children's literature in a comprehension - centered reading program 29 MIN
The Comprehension - Centered Classroom - Making it Work 29 MIN
Comprehension - Centered Reading Curriculum 29 MIN
First encounters with written language 29 MIN
Learning about the Reader 29 MIN
Reading comprehension - the instructional connection 29 MIN
Reading Comprehension from the Child's Perspective 29 MIN
Reading comprehension introduction - preview 29 MIN
Strategies for a Comprehension - Centered Reading Program 29 MIN
The Teacher Variable - an Interview with Vera Milz 29 MIN
Dist - HNEDBK

Reading comprehension - the instructional connection 29 MIN
U-matic / VHS
Reading comprehension series
Color (T)
Produced by Jerome Harste for Heinemann Educational Books, Inc.
Education; English Language
Dist - HNEDBK **Prod** - IU .

Reading Diagrams 60 MIN
VHS
Basic Theory and Systems
Color (PRO)
$600.00 - $1500.00 purchase _ #OTRDI
Illustrates the various types of diagrams associated with process system opertions and the information presented on these diagrams. Part of a twenty - part series on basic theory and systems. Includes ten textbooks and an instructor guide to support four hours of instruction.
Education; Industrial and Technical Education; Psychology
Dist - NUSTC **Prod** - NUSTC

Reading disabilities 30 MIN
U-matic / VHS
Characteristics of learning disabilities series
Color (C A)
Characterizes various reading disorders.
Education; Psychology
Dist - FI **Prod** - WCVETV 1976

Reading drawings
U-matic / VHS
Drafting - blueprint reading basics series
Color (IND)
Industrial and Technical Education
Dist - GPCV **Prod** - GPCV

Reading efficiency series
Stars Bill Cosby in a three - part series which teaches basic reading skills. Targets support staff members.
Reading efficiency series
Dist - VLEARN

Reading electrical diagrams 23 MIN
VHS / 16mm
Applied electricity series
Color (H A)
$465.00 purchase, $110.00 rental
Identifies components and circuits found in common motor and machine control systems. Explains symbols used in schematics.
Industrial and Technical Education
Dist - TAT **Prod** - TAT 1987

Reading electrical diagrams - Pt 1 60 MIN
VHS
Electrical maintenance practices series
Color (PRO)
$600.00, $1500.00 purchase _ #EMRD1
Introduces four types of electrical diagrams - block, single - line, schematic and wiring diagrams. Reads simple examples of each. Applies diagram knowledge to troubleshooting situations. Part of a six - part series on electrical maintenance practices, which is part of a 29 unit set on electrical maintenance. Includes 10 textbooks and an instructor guide which provide four hours of instruction.
Education; Industrial and Technical Education; Psychology
Dist - NUSTC **Prod** - NUSTC

Reading electrical diagrams - Pt 2 60 MIN
VHS
Electrical maintenance practices series
Color (PRO)
$600.00, $1500.00 purchase _ #EMRD2
Covers connection and interconnection diagrams, raceway diagrams and logic diagrams. Shows how to read 'Raceway Schedule,' 'Raceway Notes, Symbols And Detail' books and truth tables. Part of a six - part series on electrical maintenance practices, which is part of a 29 unit set on electrical maintenance. Includes 10 textbooks and an instructor guide which provide four hours of instruction.
Education; Industrial and Technical Education; Psychology
Dist - NUSTC **Prod** - NUSTC

Reading electrical drawings
VHS / U-matic
Industrial training series; Electrical and instrumentation fundamentals; Module 3
Color (IND)
Covers indication and alarm diagrams, set - in - circuit and control diagrams.
Industrial and Technical Education
Dist - LEIKID **Prod** - LEIKID

Reading enrichment - the fun way to grow 30 MIN
U-matic / VHS
Reading is power series; No 7
Color (T)
LC 81-707522
Uses interviews and candid scenes from the classroom to show how teachers help children learn to express themselves through the creative arts.
English Language; Fine Arts
Dist - GPN **Prod** - NYCBED 1981

Reading films - junior high school level - a series
Reading films - junior high school level - a series
B&W (J)
Provides selections for a developmental reading program, ranging in speed from 90 to 300 words per minute. Includes Booker T Washington; The Caribou; The Castle; Comets From Afar; How Would You Decide The Case; Mountains Under The Sea; Peking Man; The Reign Of Reptiles; Socrates; Spinning Jennies; Using Your Eyes; and Why The British Burned Washington.
English Language; Psychology
Dist - PUAVC **Prod** - PUAVC 1961

Reading films - junior high school level - a series
Reading films - junior high school level - a series
Dist - PUAVC

Reading financial reports - the balance sheet 13 MIN
16mm / U-matic / VHS
Color (J H)
$400, $250.00 purchase _ #83601
Explains graphically how to read an annual report, including assets, liabilities, capital, accounts receivable and earned surplus.
Business and Economics; Home Economics
Dist - CENTEF **Prod** - CENTRO 1984
CORF

Reading Financial Reports - the Income Statement 12 MIN
U-matic / VHS / 16mm
Color (H C A)
$335, $240 purchase _ #83602
Discusses the income statement and business accounting.
Business and Economics
Dist - CORF

Reading for a Reason Series no 2
I Know the Reason 15 MIN
Dist - AITECH

Reading for a Reason Series no 3
There's a Message for You 15 MIN
Dist - AITECH

Reading for a Reason Series no 5
I Already Knew that 15 MIN
Dist - AITECH

Reading for a Reason Series no 7
The Way I Remember it 15 MIN
Dist - AITECH

Reading for a reason series
A Different kind of reading 15 MIN
Different subjects, different messages 15 MIN
Everything means something 15 MIN
Is that a fact 15 MIN
Dist - AITECH

Reading for Analysis 30 MIN
16mm 13 MIN
Individualizing in a Group Series
B&W (T)
A shortened version, without commentary, of the film Reading For Analysis. Presents a reading lesson in an upper grade classroom which provides examples of how a skillful teacher adjusts his expectations and instructional techniques to meet the individual needs of students.
Education; English Language; Psychology
Dist - SPF **Prod** - SPF

Reading graphs
VHS
Using maps, globes, graphs, tables, charts and diagrams series
Color (I J H)
$49.50 purchase _ #UL1053VJ
Shows how to read graphs. Presents part of a five - part series on basic globe skills and understanding data in charts, maps, tables, charts and other graphic representations.
Mathematics
Dist - KNOWUN

Reading in the content area 26 MIN
U-matic / VHS
Successful teaching practices series
Color (T)
Introduces teacher and reading specialist Norma McClean who demonstrates how she helps teachers fuse course content and the reading content into a holistic unit through remodeling existing activities, recognition, dealing with reading problems in the classroom and designing activities that encourage success.
Education; English Language; Psychology
Dist - EBEC **Prod** - UNIDIM 1982

Reading in the content area 30 MIN
16mm
Project STRETCH Series; Module 13
Color (T)
LC 80-700620
Shows a teacher who realizes many of her students are experiencing difficulty with reading and decides to view a videotape of an inservice session that gives practical suggestions for analyzing and adapting any reading task for maximum effectiveness.
Education; Psychology
Dist - HUBDSC **Prod** - METCO 1980

Reading in the content areas - interaction 22 MIN
16mm
Color
Demonstrates how student interaction helps students clarify their own ideas. Shows students working cooperatively on tasks and learning to help each other as well as learning from one another.
Education; English Language
Dist - SYRCU **Prod** - SYRCU 1978

Reading in the Content Areas - Preparation 22 MIN
16mm
Color (C T)
Focuses on preparing students for reading a selection or performing some related task. Demonstrates a lesson that teaches reading skills functionally and simultaneously with course content.
Education; English Language; Psychology
Dist - SYRCU **Prod** - HERBH 1976

Reading in the Content Areas - Process 21 MIN
16mm
Color (C T)
Demonstrates the development of four general processes, including vocabulary, comprehension, organization and reasoning.
Education; English Language; Psychology
Dist - SYRCU **Prod** - HERBH 1976

Reading is... 25 MIN
VHS / U-matic / 16mm
Color (I)
$565.00, $425.00, $395.00 purchase _ #C343
Motivates youngsters to spend more time reading. Tells the story of an unhappy girl who has shut everyone out of her life and made TV her escape. Reveals that the likable bookworm next door encourages her to discover the comfort to be found in reading - and through reading she learns the answers to some of her problems. Produced by Mark Chodzko.
English Language; Literature and Drama
Dist - BARR **Prod** - DONMAC 1983

Reading is believing 10 MIN
U-matic
Calling Captain Consumer series
Color (P I J)
Teaches consumer education by showing a man looking through a comic book and finding an ad that promises 17 records for only $2.27.

Business and Economics; Home Economics
Dist - TVOTAR **Prod** - TVOTAR 1985

Reading is Power Series no 2
Meeting Individual Needs 30 MIN
Dist - GPN

Reading is Power Series no 3
Organization - Stations, Everyone 30 MIN
Dist - GPN

Reading is Power Series no 4
Words, Words, Words 30 MIN
Dist - GPN

Reading is Power Series no 6
Content Area Reading - Getting it all Together 30 MIN
Dist - GPN

Reading is Power Series
Comprehension - the early stages 30 MIN
Diagnosis - getting to know you 30 MIN
Reading enrichment - the fun way to grow 30 MIN
Dist - GPN

Reading magic with Figment and Peter Pan 16 MIN
U-matic / 16mm / VHS
Color (P)
$400.00, $280.00 purchase _ #JC - 67253
Uses original animation, classic Disney clips and special effects to make the point that books can transport the reader to faraway lands, transform the reader into other characters and open up adventures. Stars the dragon Figment and his friend Amy and features an unexpected visit by Peter Pan who has lost his way to Wendy's house. Peter illustrates the problems of not being able to read when Figment starts to write down directions for Peter to find Wendy.
English Language; Literature and Drama
Dist - CORF **Prod** - DISNEY 1989

Reading Motivation Series
The Elephant eats, the penguin eats - nouns 10 MIN
Frogs are funny, frogs are fat - adjectives 10 MIN
Monkey See, Monkey do - Verbs 10 MIN
Squirrels are Up, Squirrels are Down - Adverbials of Place 10 MIN
What are Letters for - Initial Consonants 12 MIN
What are Letters for - Vowels 12 MIN
Dist - PHENIX

Reading nonverbal communications 42 MIN
U-matic / 16mm
Art of negotiating series; Module 8
Color (A)
Shows how to understand hidden verbal and nonverbal responses, gestures, gesture clusters and the nonverbal communications of environment, furniture, sitting arrangements and rooms.
Psychology
Dist - BNA DELTAK **Prod** - BNA DELTAK 1983

Reading, note - taking and recall 15 MIN
VHS / 16mm
Survivor's guide to learning series
Color (S)
$185.00 purchase _ #288803
Introduces general processes and pointers through interviews with study skills specialists and students who have mastered the techniques. Describes the basic skills that help students become more focused and effective readers, better at note - taking and memorization. Part of a series that covers five theme areas and includes five booklets which deal with the themes.
Education
Dist - ACCESS **Prod** - ACCESS 1989

Reading people right 56 MIN
VHS
Speaking of success series
Color (H C G)
$39.95 purchase _ #PD02
Features trainer Dr Tony Alessandra, who explains that good communication requires an understanding of the thinking styles and personality types of others. Describes the steps that can be taken to improve these skills. Part of a series.
Psychology; Social Science
Dist - SVIP **Prod** - AUVICA 1993

Reading photographs 29 MIN
VHS
Photographic vision series
Color (G)
$49.95 purchase _ #RM108V-F
Looks at the impact of visual communication. Presents the technical aspects of photography clearly and simply, including principles of the camera and techniques for controlling exposure, the use of various kinds of lighting, selection of appropriate lenses and film and basic darkroom techniques. Focuses on the world of photographers and photography - its history and evolution, its uses for personal development and expression, and the impact of photography on the world. Part of a 20-part series examining all aspects of the field of photography.
Industrial and Technical Education
Dist - CAMV CDTEL **Prod** - COAST

Reading piping drawings 17 MIN
VHS / U-matic
Marshall maintenance training programs series; Tape 44
Color (IND)
Reduces complicated piping drawings to simple terms. Covers symbols and notations, dimensional, elevation and plan drawings, and spool drawing. Designed for the pipefitter or millwright.
Industrial and Technical Education
Dist - LEIKID **Prod** - LEIKID

Reading poetry series
Annabel Lee 10 MIN
Casey at the bat 12 MIN
The Creation 12 MIN
Haiku 7 MIN
Mending Wall 10 MIN
O Captain, My Captain 12 MIN
Dist - AIMS

The Reading process 28 MIN
U-matic / BETA / VHS
Communication skills 1 - basic series
Color (H C G)
$101.95, $89.95 purchase _ #CA - 49
Helps the viewer to understand the reading process so that established reading habits can be changed and the viewer can become a more efficient reader. Offers a detailed and comprehensive examination of reading as it relates to the whole of the communication process. Part of a series on communication.
English Language; Social Science
Dist - INSTRU

Reading Rainbow Series no 10
The Gift of the Sacred Dog 30 MIN
Dist - GPN

Reading Rainbow Series no 11
Gregory the Terrible Eater 30 MIN
Dist - GPN

Reading Rainbow Series no 12
Three by the Sea 30 MIN
Dist - GPN

Reading Rainbow Series no 13
Arthur's Eyes 30 MIN
Dist - GPN

Reading Rainbow Series no 2
Miss Nelson is Back 30 MIN
Dist - GPN

Reading Rainbow Series no 4
Bringing the Rain to Kapiti Plain 30 MIN
Dist - GPN

Reading Rainbow Series no 5
Louis the Fish 30 MIN
Dist - GPN

Reading Rainbow Series no 7
Liang and the Magic Paintbrush 30 MIN
Dist - GPN

Reading Rainbow Series no 8
Gila Monsters Meet You at the Airport 30 MIN
Dist - GPN

Reading rainbow series
Abiyoyo - 35
The Adventures of Taxi Dog - 72
Alistair in outer space - 27
Alistair's time machine - 71
Amazing Grace - 91
And still the turtle watched - 99
Animal cafe - 26
Barn dance - 51
Bea and Mr Jones 30 MIN
Berlioz the bear - 90
Best friends - 43
The Bicycle man - 68
The Bionic bunny show - 46
Bored - nothing to do - 64
Brush - 49
Bugs - 47
A Chair for my mother - 20
Chickens aren't the only ones - 38
Come a tide - 86
The Day Jimmy's boa ate the wash 30 MIN
Desert giant - the world of the saguaro cactus - 62
Digging up dinosaurs 30 MIN
Dinosaur Bob and his adventures with the Family Lazardo - 60
Dive to the coral reefs - 61
Duncan and Dolores - 52
Feelings
Florence and Eric take the cake - 69
Follow the drinking gourd - 96
Fox on the job - 75
The Furry news - 92
Galimoto - 74
Germs make me sick - 34
Hill of Fire 30 MIN
Hot - air Henry - 16
Humphrey the lost whale - a true story - 56
If you give a mouse a cookie - 97
Imogene's antlers - 33
Is this a house for a hermit crab - 98
Jack, the seal and the sea
June 29, 1999 - 100
Kate Shelley and the Midnight Express
Keep the lights burning, Abbie - 37
Knots on a counting rope - 53
The Lady with the ship on her head - 78
The Legend of the Indian paintbrush - 73
The Life cycle of the honeybee - 36
Little Nino's pizzeria - 58
Ludlow laughs - 59
The Magic school bus inside the Earth - 66
Mama don't allow - 30
Meanwhile back at the ranch - 44
The Milk makers - 32
Mrs Katz and Tush
Mufaro's beautiful daughters - 55
Mummies made in Egypt - 54
My little island - 45
Mystery on the docks - 19
Opt - an illusionary tale - 76
Ox - cart man - 18
The Paper crane - 39
Patchwork Quilt 30 MIN
Paul Bunyan 30 MIN
Perfect the Pig 30 MIN
The Piggy in the puddle - No 87
The Purple coat - 50
Raccoons and ripe corn - 77
Rechenka's eggs - 84
The Robbery of the Diamond Dog Diner - 48
Rumpelstiltskin - 42
The Runaway duck - 40
The Salamander room - 94
Sam the sea cow - 82
Seashore surprises - 88
Silent Lotus - 95
Simon's book - 17
Snowy day - stories and poems - 80
Sophie and Lou - 85
Space case - 31
Sports pages - 65
Stay away from the junkyard - 57
Sunken treasure - 70
Tar beach - 81
Three Days on a River in a Red Canoe 30 MIN
A Three hat day - 41
Through moon and stars and night skies
Tight times 30 MIN
Tooth - gnasher superflash
The Tortoise and the Hare 30 MIN
Ty's one man band 30 MIN
The Wall - 82
Watch the stars come out - 29
Dist - GPN

Reading rainbow treasury series
Presents a six part series of animated children's stories which features Levar Burton as host. Includes Mummies Made in Egypt - Bringing the Rain to Kapiti Plain; Legend of the Indian Paintbrush - Lifecycle of the Honeybee; Dive to the Coral Reef - The Magic Schoolbus Under the Earth; Rumpelstiltskin - Snowy Day Stories and Poems; The Bicycle Man - Adventures of Taxi Dog; Opt - an Illusionary Tale - A Three - Hat Day.
The Bicycle man - Adventures of Taxi Dog
Dive to the coral reef - The Magic school bus under the Earth
Legend of the Indian Paintbrush - Lifecycle of the honeybees
Mummies made in Egypt - Bringing the rain to Kapiti Plain
Opt - an illusionary tale - A Three - hat day

Rumpelstiltskin - Snowy day stories and poems
Dist - KNOWUN **Prod** - PBS

Reading readiness - Part 2 30 MIN
VHS
Teaching early reading series
Color (K P I)
#E376; LC 90-712989
Provides a broad spectrum of teaching methods and materials for teaching beginning reading skills. Stresses that reading readiness is unique to each child based upon the child's maturity level. Part 2 of a six - part series on teaching early reading.
Education; English Language
Dist - GPN **Prod** - CTI 1978

Reading reinforcement series
Reinforces early reading skills of ESL and remedial as well as differently - paced students. Introduces initial consonants and provides practice in recognizing, writing, discriminating and pronouncing them in the first four videos. The fifth presents familiar phrases to encourage reading words in segments, gradually reducing the cues until the student can read a simple ghost story.
Reading reinforcement series 115 MIN
Dist - LANDMK

Reading self - improvement - interpretation 13 MIN
16mm / U-matic / VHS
Reading self - improvement series
Color (I J H)
Explores how to search for unstated meanings when reading. Tells how to understand the difference between denotive and connotative meanings, recognize figures of speech, identify assumptions and draw inferences.
English Language
Dist - CORF **Prod** - CORF 1979

Reading Self - Improvement Series
Competency skills 12 MIN
Comprehension 12 MIN
Interpretation 13 MIN
Reading self - improvement - interpretation 13 MIN
Variable Speeds 13 MIN
Word Recognition 11 MIN
Word Understanding 14 MIN
Dist - CORF

Reading Short Stories Series
The Big red barn 8 MIN
The Dead bird 13 MIN
Just Awful 8 MIN
One Kitten for Kim 16 MIN
Right Thumb, Left Thumb 9 MIN
Dist - AIMS

Reading sketch 10 MIN
16mm
Color (G)
$25.00 rental
Employs multiple exposure, single framing and experimental visual rhythms.
Fine Arts
Dist - CANCIN **Prod** - TARTAG 1972

Reading Skill, Set 3 Series
The Semi - Vowel Rule 15 MIN
Dist - JOU

Reading Skills Series
I Couldn't Put it Down - Hooked on Reading Adolescent Novels
Dist - CHUMAN

Reading skills series
The Double vowel rule 14 MIN
Phonics and word structure 15 MIN
Dist - JOU

Reading Skills, Set 1 (2nd Ed Series
Find the Vowels 11 MIN
The Vowel a 13 MIN
Vowel E, the 13 MIN
Vowel I, the 13 MIN
Vowel O, the 13 MIN
Vowel U, the 13 MIN
Vowels and their Sounds 12 MIN
Dist - JOU

Reading Skills, Set 2 Series no 1
The Long Vowel Sounds 15 MIN
Dist - JOU

Reading Skills, Set 2 Series no 3
Putting the Rules Together 14 MIN
Dist - JOU

Reading skills, set 2 series
The Short vowel sounds 12 MIN
Dist - JOU

Reading strategies 28 MIN
U-matic / BETA / VHS
Communication skills 1 - basic series
Color (H C G)
$101.95, $89.95 purchase _ #CA - 50
Discusses three types of reading rates. Explains that when discerning a general or main idea is the purpose, floating and surveying are recommended. For careful reading - at least 80 percent retention - a study system called SQ3R is suggested. Part of a series on communication.
English Language; Social Science
Dist - INSTRU

Reading Terminal Market - a celebration 28 MIN
VHS
Color (I J H)
$224.00 purchase
Views the history of Philadelphia, Pennsylvania as seen in the development of one of the city's public marketplaces called the Reading Terminal market. Features narrator Kevin Bacon telling of this landmark gathering - place for Philadelphia citizens.
Geography - United States; History - United States
Dist - LANDMK

Reading ternary phase diagrams 8 MIN
16mm
Phase equilibria series
Color (C)
LC 78-700706
Uses computer animation to show how to decipher data in a ternary phase diagram. Includes obtaining information about composition, primary fields of crystalization for each component and temperature in its relationship to isothermal lines.
Industrial and Technical Education; Science - Physical
Dist - PSU **Prod** - NSF 1976

Reading - the American Dinosaur 26 MIN
16mm / U-matic / VHS
Dealing with social problems in the classroom series
Color (C A)
Features English headmistress - teacher Lillian Thompson discussing her approach to teaching reading and raising questions about contemporary practices. Filmed at the Claremont Reading Conference.
Education; English Language
Dist - FI **Prod** - MFFD 1976

Reading the Blood Pressure Manometer 6 MIN
16mm
Color (PRO)
LC 74-705481
Shows six different 100 pressure readings - the viewer records his readings, and compares them to the correct readings given at the end of the film.
Health and Safety; Science; Science - Natural
Dist - USNAC **Prod** - USA 1971

Reading the Micrometer 10 MIN
U-matic / VHS / 16mm
Power Mechanics Series
Color (J)
LC 76-703250
Presents basic information about how to read a micrometer.
Industrial and Technical Education
Dist - CAROUF **Prod** - THIOKL 1969

Reading the moon's secrets 18 MIN
16mm
Color (H A)
Examines important aspects of lunar knowledge, using Apollo gained data.
History - World; Science - Physical
Dist - USNAC **Prod** - NASA 1976

Reading the rocks 30 MIN
U-matic
North of sixty degrees - destiny uncertain series
Color (H C)
Portrays life in the mines and mining towns in the northern part of Canada. Gives a brief history of the industry and its effects on the economy and society of the north.
Geography - United States; Geography - World; History - World
Dist - TVOTAR **Prod** - TVOTAR 1985

Reading the sky 20 MIN
VHS / U-matic
Color (J)
LC 82-706783
Discusses how the changing patterns and colors of the sky help make weather forecasts. Shows what different types of clouds mean and how to identify them.
Science - Physical
Dist - AWSS **Prod** - AWSS 1981

Reading the wind
VHS
Under sail with Robbie Doyle series
Color (G A)
$19.90 purchase _ #0476
Considers the important elements for sailing a course. Looks at navigation in relationship to the wind and teaches knot tying. Features Robbie Doyle.
Physical Education and Recreation
Dist - SEVVID

Reading to develop sight vocabulary 13 MIN
16mm 30 MIN
Individualizing in a group series
B&W (T)
Depicts the initial stages of developing sight vocabulary with a group of inner - city children who don't learn to read automatically, but who are successful when taught by a skillful teacher.
Education; English Language
Dist - SPF **Prod** - SPF

Reading Vocabulary Series
The Boat that Jack sailed 11 MIN
Dog gone 11 MIN
They were Cars 11 MIN
Dist - PHENIX

Reading Way Series
Consonant Digraphs 15 MIN
Sounds of Y 15 MIN
Special Consonant Combinations 15 MIN
Using `C' and `G' 15 MIN
Using `L' Blends 15 MIN
Using R with A and O 15 MIN
Using R with E, I and U 15 MIN
Using Short `A' and `I' 15 MIN
Using Short E Patterns 15 MIN
Using Short O and U 15 MIN
Using Silent E 15 MIN
Variant Vowels - Au, Ou and Aw 15 MIN
Variant Vowels - Ay and Ow 15 MIN
Vowel Digraphs 15 MIN
Vowel Diphthongs 15 MIN
Dist - AITECH

Reading - who needs it 19 MIN
U-matic / VHS / 16mm
Color (J H)
LC 82-700483
Dramatizes the common plight of high school students whose career ambitions are stymied by their illiteracy. Includes adults offering advice on how to overcome this problem.
English Language; Social Science
Dist - PHENIX **Prod** - ALLEND 1981

Reading - Why - the Ice Cream Stand 13 MIN
U-matic / VHS / 16mm
Color (K P)
LC 78-701796
Illustrates the importance of learning to read by presenting a story about two children whose desire to open an ice cream and cookie stand runs into trouble when the boy uses the wrong ingredients because of his reading problem.
English Language; Guidance and Counseling; Literature and Drama
Dist - HANDEL **Prod** - HANDEL 1978

Reading, Writing and Reefer 52 MIN
U-matic / VHS / 16mm
Color (J)
LC 79-700623
Reports on the use of marijuana by American teenagers and the effect it has on their lives. Narrated by Edwin Newman.
Health and Safety; Psychology; Sociology
Dist - FI **Prod** - NBCTV 1978

Reading, writing and revolvers - coping with teenage violence
VHS
Color (J H)
$89.95 purchase _ #CCP0142V
Provides students with specific skills they can apply if confronted with violence. Interviews students, parents and teachers at urban, suburban and rural schools to provide a firsthand look at the situation from the perspectives of people who cope with school violence on a day - to - day basis.
Education; Sociology
Dist - CAMV **Prod** - CAMV 1993

The Reading - Writing Relationship 30 MIN
VHS / U-matic
Teaching Reading Comprehension Series
Color (T PRO)
$180.00 purchase,$50.00 rental
Explores the utilization of the students own experiences in understanding the reading material.
English Language
Dist - AITECH **Prod** - WETN 1986

Reading Your Tires 30 MIN
VHS / BETA
Last Chance Garage Series
Color
Demonstrates how to 'read' tires. Discusses headlight alignment and rack - and - pinion steering. Features a 1926 Pierce Arrow.
Industrial and Technical Education
Dist - CORF **Prod** - WGBHTV

Readit series

Ben and me	14 MIN
Blue moose and the return of the moose	15 MIN
The Boxcar children	15 MIN
The Comeback dog	15 MIN
Deadwood City and the Third Planet from Altair	15 MIN
Give us a great big smile, Rosy Cole	14 MIN
A Grandmother for the orphelines	14 MIN
Groundhog's Horse	15 MIN
Have you seen Hyacinth Macaw	15 MIN
My Father's Dragon	15 MIN
My Robot Buddy and My Trip to Alpha I	14 MIN
The Rise and Fall of Ben Gizzard, the Parrot and the Thief and the Contests at Cowlick	15 MIN
Trouble for Lucy	14 MIN
Twenty and Ten	15 MIN
The Whistling Teakettle and the Witch of Fourth Street	14 MIN
Who's in Charge of Lincoln and the Lucky Stone	14 MIN

Dist - AITECH

ReadManager
VHS / BETA / U-matic
Color (G PRO)
$1545.00, $670.00 rental _ #ML0047, #ML0049
Presents a 12 - hour, 4 - unit program to help manage information through proven methods of organizing approaches to new information, increasing reading speed and increasing comprehension. Includes instructor's guide, two videocassettes, workbooks and reading materials for 10 participants.
Education; English Language
Dist - BLNCTD **Prod** - BLNCTD

Ready boots of Red Wing 28 MIN
16mm
Color (G)
Describes how boots are made.
Business and Economics; Industrial and Technical Education
Dist - BOYD **Prod** - RWSHOE

Ready for Edna 29 MIN
16mm
B&W
LC FIE67-59
Examines, through the experiences of a stroke victim, the range of health services needed to protect and promote the physical and mental health of the aged. Points out that the number of aged is increasing.
Health and Safety; Sociology
Dist - USNAC **Prod** - USPHS 1965

Ready for sea 14 MIN 29 MIN
16mm
B&W; Color
LC 74-706210
Presents a story of the preparation of navy supply officers through OCS and the Naval Supply Officer School at Athens, Georgia, ending with shipboard assignments showing the application of their training.
Civics and Political Systems; Guidance and Counseling
Dist - USNAC **Prod** - USN 1966

Ready for the Worst 40 MIN
U-matic / VHS
Color
Explains why the Red Cross has become a major force in disaster relief and what the future may hold in store. Features action, pathos, tragedy and ironic humor.
History - World; Sociology
Dist - AMRC **Prod** - AMRC

Ready, get set, go - subtraction via time 20 MIN
U-matic
Let's figure it out series
B&W (P)
Mathematics
Dist - NYSED **Prod** - WNYE 1968

Ready - made programs - Pt 2 30 MIN
U-matic / VHS
Bits and bytes series; Pt 2
Color (A)
Examines ready - made computer programs, shows everyday applications of computers in fields such as accounting, and introduces the computer as a teaching aid. Explains the differences between RAM and ROM.
Mathematics
Dist - TIMLIF **Prod** - TVOTAR 1984

Ready mades in Hades 7 MIN
16mm
Color (G)
$24.00 rental
Features East Somerville, Massachussetts, with an empty lot piled with garbage and remnants of the past lives of its nearby residents. Shows the laundry of a present set of inhabitants next door, with children roaming through involved in their own private play. Made in 1986 - 1987.
Fine Arts; Science - Natural
Dist - CANCIN **Prod** - AVERYC

Ready or not 23 MIN
16mm
Color (C A)
LC 72-702021
Describes the follow - through projects in Wichita and Topeka, Kansas. Explains that two different instructional models are used in the Kansas program. Shows children working under the models and describes the facets of the follow - through program which are carried on outside the classroom.
Education
Dist - UKANS **Prod** - UKANS 1972

Ready or not and Down on the farm 30 MIN
VHS
Davey and Goliath series
Color (P I R)
$19.95 purchase, $10.00 rental _ #4 - 8827
Presents two 15 - minute 'Davey and Goliath' episodes. 'Ready or Not' stresses the theme of stewardship of God's world, as Davey and his parents and friends work together to restore a park. 'Down on the Farm' features Davey as he works on his vegetable garden. Produced by the Evangelical Lutheran Church in America.
Literature and Drama; Religion and Philosophy
Dist - APH

Ready or not, here i come 52 MIN
U-matic / VHS
Color (H C A)
Probes the psychological and physical abuse of the elderly. Profiles the elderly through four tragic cases - lonely, helpless, isolated elderly people often mistreated to the point of death in nursing homes and by members of their family. Features a panel discussion by several experts on aging.
Health and Safety; Sociology
Dist - FI **Prod** - FI

Ready or not, here i come 4 MIN
U-matic / VHS
Multiplication rock series
Color (P I)
Uses songs and cartoons to explore the mathematical possibilities of the number five.
Mathematics
Dist - GA **Prod** - ABCTV 1974

Ready or not series

Administrative management in schools - case studies	30 MIN
Administrative management in schools - software	30 MIN
Courseware Review - the Criteria	30 MIN
Courseware Review - the Process	30 MIN
Managing Microcomputers - the Microcomputer Game	30 MIN
Micros and the Arts	30 MIN
Micros and the Writing Process	30 MIN
Planning for Microcomputers	30 MIN

Dist - PCATEL

Ready, set...goals - setting lifetime goals 30 MIN
VHS
Color (I J H)
$79.95 purchase _ #CCP0078V
Teaches students the purpose and importance of goals. Features people of all ages discussing what goals are, how goals have affected their lives, how they choose goals and forces that have influenced the fulfillment of their goals. Discusses the different types of goals that might be worked toward, people and things that might hinder the achievement of goals, how to choose and prioritize goals, how to evaluate goals and when to change goals. Stresses the importance of setting realistic and measurable goals and defines resources which help to achieve goals. Includes student manual.
Guidance and Counseling; Psychology
Dist - CAMV **Prod** - CAMV 1992

Ready - Story of the Marine Corps Reserves 15 MIN
16mm
Color
LC 74-705482
Documents the 50 - year history of the Marine Corps Reserves from World War I to World War II and Korea.
Guidance and Counseling; History - United States
Dist - USNAC **Prod** - USMC 1966

Ready to grow 29 MIN
U-matic / VHS
Color
Contains three segments about inexpensive activities for parents and their preschool - age children.
Psychology; Sociology
Dist - LVN **Prod** - LVN

Ready to live 60 MIN
VHS
People in motion - changing ideas about physical disability series
Color; CC (G)
$89.95 purchase _ #UW5678
Looks at ways adaptive technologies help people with disabilities find independence. Includes profiles of a world - class runner who uses an advanced prosthetic leg; a Bosnian refugee whose life was transformed by a pair of artificial hands; a national disability rights activist - once called a 'helpless cripple' - who became one of the founders of the Independent Living Movement; and a woman who inspired a revolution in wheelchair design. Part two of three parts.
Health and Safety
Dist - FOTH

Ready to love, ready to care
VHS
Color (G R)
$15.00 purchase _ #S10167
Uses personal stories to encourage Missouri Synod Lutherans to respond to those in need. Includes discussion guide and music 'When We Reach Out.'
Guidance and Counseling; Religion and Philosophy; Sociology
Dist - CPH **Prod** - LUMIS

Ready to Strike 29 MIN
16mm
Big Picture Series
Color
LC 74-706211
Shows the actions of the Tropic Lightning 25th Infantry Division in Vietnam.
Civics and Political Systems; History - United States; History - World
Dist - USNAC **Prod** - USA 1967

Ready to teach 26 MIN
VHS
Color (G A R)
$19.95 purchase, $10.00 rental _ #4 - 85071
Demonstrates effective teaching methods for church school classes. Features examples from classes at several different grade levels.
Religion and Philosophy
Dist - APH **Prod** - APH

Ready, willing and able - a videotape series
VHS
Ready, willing and able - a videotape series
Color (H A)
$348.00 purchase _ #RSG200
Presents a series package which looks at personal growth, education, career and employment problems and successes experienced by 12 women who have faced disabilities and struggled through restructuring their lives to gain a personal identity and job satisfaction. Includes titles To Be Me - coping skills; To Be Independent - career issues; and To Be Employed - the job search. Also includes workbook for students and clients and two - volume staff handbook.
Business and Economics; Guidance and Counseling; Sociology
Dist - CENTER **Prod** - CENTER

Ready, Wrestle - the Rules of Wrestling 17 MIN
16mm
National Federation Sports Films Series
Color (I)
LC 77-700469
Describes rules and procedures used in judging interscholastic wrestling competitions. Includes takedowns, reverses, technical violations, escapes, potentially dangerous holds, stalling, pinning situations and illegal holds.
Physical Education and Recreation
Dist - NFSHSA **Prod** - NFSHSA 1976

Reaffirmation and discovery - The First Pow - wow on Hawai'i 29 MIN
VHS
Color (G J H C)
$45.00 rental, $250.00 purchase
Tells the story of two women whose lives and vision come together in the creation of the first pow wow on the Big Island, Hawai'i. Looks at the connections made between Native Americans and Native Hawai'ians. Shows the continuance of ancient traditions through a coming out ceremony of two young girls during the pow wow. A portion of the proceeds of this video will go to the Indian Child Welfare Defense Fund.

Geography - United States; Social Science
Dist - SHENFP

Reagan at Midterm 52 MIN
U-matic / VHS
Color (J)
LC 83-706396
Assesses the presidency of Ronald Reagan at its halfway point, analyzing the president's effect on national defense, foreign affairs and economics. Includes interviews with politicians, economists, businesspersons and private citizens, as well as footage of the president in various settings.
Biography; Civics and Political Systems; History - United States
Dist - FI Prod - NBCNEW 1983

The Reagan years - in pursuit of the American dream 75 MIN
VHS
Color; B&W (G)
$29.95 purchase _ #S02085
Documents the life of Ronald Reagan, tracing his career from sports announcer to President of the United States. Includes footage from Reagan's Hollywood films, an interview with his brother Neil, and footage of the assassination attempt and major events in his presidency.
Biography; History - United States
Dist - UILL

Reagan's shield - Part 12 60 MIN
U-matic / VHS
War and peace in the nuclear age series
Color (G)
$45.00, $29.95 purchase
Focuses on the Strategic Defense Initiative, the heart of Ronald Reagan's nuclear program, and Reagan's major arms control initiatives. Part twelve of a thirteen - part series on war and peace in the nuclear age.
Civics and Political Systems; History - United States
Dist - ANNCPB Prod - WGBHTV 1989

Real and not So Real 29 MIN
VHS / 16mm
Encounters Series
Color (I)
$200.00 purchase _ #269209
Presents a ten - part series on art. Introduces art concepts, encourages students to visually explore their world and the world of art, and demonstrates art techniques such as drawing, printmaking, photography, clay and wire sculpture, painting and fabric arts to motivate art expression. 'Real And Not So Real' considers that the world is full of visual illusions and distortions. Explores the world of fun and fantasy and the techniques used to create visual illusions.
Fine Arts; Psychology
Dist - ACCESS Prod - ACCESS 1988

Real Estate 29 MIN
16mm
Corporation Series
B&W
LC 74-702415
Predicts the role of the corporation, one of the largest landowners in Quebec, in shaping the future of the cities and the way of life of their dwellers.
Business and Economics; Geography - World; Sociology
Dist - NFBC Prod - NFBC 1973

Real Estate 30 MIN
U-matic / VHS / 16mm
Enterprise Series
Color (H C A)
Looks at a real estate developer interested in drawing show business to Texas.
Business and Economics
Dist - CORF Prod - CORF

Real estate, boom or crash - Zuckerman's high stakes gamble 30 MIN
U-matic
Adam Smith's money world 1985 - 1986 season series; 212
Color (A)
Attempts to demystify the world of money and break it down so that small as well as large businesses and it's people understand and adjust to new social and economic trends. Reports on the major economic stories and discoveries of 1985 and 1986.
Business and Economics
Dist - PBS Prod - WNETTV 1986

Real Estate Broker 15 MIN
U-matic / 16mm / VHS
Career Awareness
(I)
$130 VC purchase, $240 film purchase, $25 VC rental, $30 film rental
Presents an empathetic approach to career planning, showing the personal as well as the professional attributes of real estate brokers. Highlights career education.
Business and Economics; Guidance and Counseling
Dist - GPN

Real Estate Investments 25 MIN
U-matic / VHS
Your Money Matters Series
Color
Outlines the groundwork for those thinking about owning or investing in income producing property.
Business and Economics; Social Science
Dist - FILMID Prod - FILMID

Real Estate Investments 30 MIN
VHS / U-matic
Personal Finance Series
Color (C A)
Describes the myths and facts about investing in real estate, including factors that can affect investments in income - producing property, vacant land and mortgages. Lesson 18 on the Personal finance series.
Business and Economics
Dist - CDTEL Prod - SCCON

Real Estate Investments 28 MIN
U-matic / VHS
Personal Finance and Money Management Series
Color (C A)
Business and Economics; Civics and Political Systems
Dist - SCCON Prod - SCCON 1987

Real Estate, Pt 1 - Getting Started
U-matic / VHS
Real Estate Series
Color (A)
Includes multiple learning techniques, visual instruction, written workbook exercises, related readings, job aids and follow - up checklists for retention.
Business and Economics
Dist - CORF Prod - CORF 1984

Real Estate, Pt 3 - the Real Estate Executive Series
VHS / U-matic
Real Estate Series
Color (A)
Presents a management program that heightens the ability to organize, prepare and direct a high - yield sales force. This program would be useful for a single office firm or a multi - office organization as part of a management training program.
Business and Economics
Dist - CORF Prod - CORF 1984

Real Estate, Pt 2 - the Real Estate Success Series
VHS / U-matic
Real Estate Series
Color (A)
Demonstrates solutions for the real estate salesperson in any situation. Stresses solid training and includes lectures, video instructions, dramatizations, written exercises and group discussion.
Business and Economics
Dist - CORF Prod - CORF 1984

Real Estate Series
Real Estate, Pt 1 - Getting Started
Real Estate, Pt 3 - the Real Estate Executive Series
Real Estate, Pt 2 - the Real Estate Success Series
Dist - CORF

Real estate video series
Preparing your house for sale 25 MIN
Dist - AAVIM
DIYVC

Real Inside 12 MIN
16mm / U-matic / VHS
Color (C A)
Presents a cartoon character tired of the animated life applying for an executive assistant position.
Literature and Drama
Dist - CORF Prod - NFBC

Real Italian pizza 12 MIN
16mm
Color (G)
$20.00 rental
Looks at a ten - minute eternity chronicling what takes place within the view of the lens of the camera, which is bolted to a window. Uses a typical New York pizza stand for the backdrop. The highlight occurs when a fire engine, with lights flashing, stops so the firefighters can dash in to grab some pizza to take to the fire.
Fine Arts
Dist - CANCIN Prod - RIMMER 1971

The Real Life of Ronald Reagan 90 MIN
VHS
Frontline Series
Color; Captioned (G)
$59.95 purchase _ #FRON - 701K
Analyzes the Reagan presidency. Interviews Reagan, his aides, media and political figures to gain insight into his private and political life. Examines the impact of Reagan's policies on the nation.
Civics and Political Systems; History - United States
Dist - PBS Prod - DOCCON 1989

The Real Malcolm X - an intimate portrait of the man 60 MIN
VHS
Color (J H C G)
$49.95 purchase _ #SVE5758V
Portrays Malcolm X in exclusive, never - before - shown footage and excerpts from his most important speeches. Interviews his widow, Betty Shabazz, Quincy Jones, Dick Gregory, Andrew Young and Lionel Hampton. Features contemporary artists Public Enemy and Malcolm Jamal Warner who discuss his legacy to the black community today. Features Dan Rather.
Biography; Civics and Political Systems; History - United States
Dist - CAMV

The Real Merle Travis guitar - like father , like son 90 MIN
VHS
Color (G)
$49.95 purchase _ #VD - BRE - GT01
Features Thom Bresh, son of guitarist Merle Travis, who gives an in - depth look at the Merle Travis techniques that changed the course of guitar history. Takes the viewer step - by - step through essential Travis techniques. Teaches Guitar Rag, Cannonball Rag, Walking the Strings, I'll See You in My Dreams, Bugle Call Rag, Farewell My Blue Belle and Hangin' With the Girls I Know. Includes music and tablature.
Fine Arts
Dist - HOMETA Prod - HOMETA

The Real Mr Ratty 25 MIN
U-matic / VHS / 16mm
Color (K P I J)
Features the life - style of one of Kenneth Grahame's characters from The Wind In The Willows, Ratty, the Water Vole. Shows the animal underground and underwater, among the wild creatures of the Devon river bank in western England and through the changing seasons.
Geography - World; Science - Natural
Dist - FI Prod - BBCTV

A Real Naked Lady 13 MIN
U-matic / VHS / 16mm
Color
LC 80-701333
Tells how three young boys visit an art school in order to satisfy their longing to see a nude woman.
Fine Arts
Dist - FI Prod - EISBEN 1980

The Real Numbers 30 MIN
16mm
Mathematics for Elementary School Teachers Series
Color (T)
Reviews the properties of rational numbers, and provides an introduction to irrational numbers. Restates the three major aspects of the arithmetic program - concepts, computations and application. To be used following 'Negative rational numbers.' No 3 on the Mathematics for elementary school teachers series.
Mathematics
Dist - MLA Prod - SMSG 1963

Real numbers - developing the concept 32 MIN
16mm
Teaching high school mathematics - first course series
B&W (T)
No 3 on Teaching high school mathematics - first course series.
Mathematics
Dist - MLA Prod - UICSM 1967

The Real People - a Series
VHS / U-matic
Real People Series
Color (G)
Presents this as the first television series made by and about American Indians. Choose highlights from the past and the important aspects of current life on and off the reservations. Designed for a family audience; presents a truly Indian point of view.
Social Science
Dist - NAMPBC Prod - NAMPBC 1976

Real people - coping with eating disorders 27 MIN
VHS
Color (J H C)
$169.00 purchase _ #2299 - SK
Documents the stories of three young people with eating disorders - anorexia, bulimia, and compulsive overeating. Shows how all three faced their problems and have learned to cope. Interviews expert Kay Pitsenberger on the underlying causes of eating disorders. Includes teacher's guide.
Health and Safety; Psychology; Social Science
Dist - SUNCOM **Prod** - SUNCOM

Real people - meet a teenage anorexic 18 MIN
VHS
Color (J H C)
$149.00 purchase _ #2304 - SK
Profiles 17 - year - old Staci, who is anorexic. Tells how her obsession with thinness led to her problem. Interviews expert Kay Pitsenberger, who examines the reasons for anorexia, the patterns it takes in a person's life, and the course of treatment.
Health and Safety; Psychology; Social Science
Dist - SUNCOM **Prod** - SUNCOM

Real people - meet a teenage drug addict 24 MIN
35mm strip / VHS
Color (I J H)
$169.00, $109.00 purchase _ #2270 - SK, #2269 - SK
Profiles Wendy, a teenager recovering from drug addiction. Tells her story of addiction, which began with alcohol and ended with cocaine. Covers the events that led her to recognize her problem and seek help. Shows that she has turned her life around. Includes teacher's guide.
Guidance and Counseling; Psychology; Sociology
Dist - SUNCOM **Prod** - SUNCOM

Real people - meeting a teenage mother 18 MIN
VHS
Color (I J H)
$149.00 purchase _ #GW - 3429 - VS
Meets 17 - year - old Lauri who became a mother at age 15. Takes a revealing look at the problems faced by a teenage single mother. Lauri relates her bitterness toward the young father who walked out on her even before she gave birth, her realization that she now has to find a way to support herself and her daughter, and her hopes and fears for the future. Details the support she has received from her own family, and the daycare program at her high school that makes it possible for her to complete her studies. Describes her social problems with her peers and ends with her message to other teenagers.
Guidance and Counseling; Health and Safety; Psychology
Dist - HRMC **Prod** - SUNCOM

Real People Series

Awakening	30 MIN
Buffalo, blood, salmon and roots	30 MIN
Legend of the Stick Game	30 MIN
Mainstream	30 MIN
Words of Life, People of Rivers	30 MIN

Dist - GPN

Real people series

Circle of song - Pt 1	28 MIN
Circle of song - Pt 2	29 MIN
A Season of grandmothers	29 MIN
Spirit of the wind	29 MIN

Dist - GPN
NAMPBC

Real people series

Awakening	29 MIN
Buffalo, blood, salmon, and roots	28 MIN
Legend of the Stick Game	29 MIN
Mainstream	25 MIN
The Real People - a Series	
Word of Life - People of Rivers	28 MIN

Dist - NAMPBC

Real people - Teens who chose abstinence 24 MIN
VHS
Color (J H)
$169 purchase No. 2424-YZ
Teaches students grades 7 - 12 that abstinence is a valid and enforceable choice. Real teenagers tell how they combat peer pressure and choose abstinence. Includes 24-minute video, teacher's guide.
Education; Psychology
Dist - SUNCOM **Prod** - SUNCOM

The Real princess 15 MIN
VHS
Magic library series
Color (P)
LC 90-707936
Tells about a princess. Raises children's awareness of a sense of story in order to enrich and motivate language, reading and writing skills. Includes teacher's guide. Part of a series.
Education; English Language
Dist - TVOTAR **Prod** - TVOTAR 1990

Real property law practice - recent developments - 1992 210 MIN
VHS / Cassette
CEB 1992 recent developments programs series
Color (PRO)
$169.00, $115.00 purchase, $79.00 rental _ #RE-65252, #RE-55252, #RE-65252-63
Shows how to adapt a practice to recent legislative and case law developments affecting real property matters. Includes handbook. 1991 version also available.
Business and Economics; Civics and Political Systems
Dist - CCEB **Prod** - CCEB 1992

Real Property Purchase and Sales Agreements 120 MIN
VHS / U-matic / Cassette
Color; Mono (PRO)
Focuses on the real estate sale and purchase agreement. Contrasts how a standard form deposit receipt might differ from a custom - drafted agreement in memorializing each element of the transaction. Discusses such topics as drafting the pertinent documents, the basics of tax free exchanges, cost recovery and tax loss allocations.
Business and Economics; Civics and Political Systems
Dist - CCEB **Prod** - CCEB

Real Property Remedies 240 MIN
VHS / U-matic / Cassette
Color; Mono (PRO)
Focuses on remedies in real property law. Discusses the range of legal and equitable remedies for breach of contracts relating to real property.
Business and Economics; Civics and Political Systems
Dist - CCEB **Prod** - CCEB

Real Property Secured Transactions 240 MIN
U-matic / Cassette / VHS / 16mm
Color; Mono (PRO)
Discusses basic real property law. Covers foreclosures, receiverships, deficiency judgments and documentation.
Business and Economics; Civics and Political Systems
Dist - CCEB **Prod** - CCEB

Real Revolution - Talks by Krishnamurti Series

Freedom from Fear	30 MIN
Meditation	29 MIN
Observing Ourselves	29 MIN
Questioning	29 MIN
What is Love	29 MIN

Dist - IU

The Real Rookies 28 MIN
16mm / U-matic / VHS
Color (A)
LC 81-700380
Follows a group of recruits from the time they enter the police academy through their first year on the force. Shows how police officers and their families respond to the rigors of training and the threat of violence on the job.
Civics and Political Systems; Social Science
Dist - CORF **Prod** - BELLDA 1979

The Real Saint Therese 45 MIN
BETA / VHS
B&W
Gives an account of the life of Saint Therese.
Biography; Geography - World; Religion and Philosophy
Dist - DSP **Prod** - DSP

Real selling series
Presents a five - part series on sales. Portrays real sales persons on sales calls. Covers subjects including establishing contacts, sales call strategies, deal negotiations, and more.

The Closing process - when and how - Part 4	36 MIN
Dealing with buying objectives - Part 3	37 MIN
Follow up service and sales - developing long - term customers - Part 5	32 MIN
Making effective sales calls - Part 2	47 MIN
Preparing for successful sales relationships - Part 1	35 MIN

Dist - VLEARN

The Real Star Wars - Defense in Space 50 MIN
U-matic / VHS
Color (H C A)
Discusses Reagan's Star Wars proposal and studies the exotic weapons involved, including the x - ray laser developed by Dr Edward Teller, father of the H - bomb. Presents a three - dimensional animation process using models of new weapons systems. Features several mini - debates between Secretary of Defense Weinberger, Robert McNamara, physicist Richard Garwin and scientist Robert Jastrow.
Civics and Political Systems
Dist - FI **Prod** - NBCNEW

The Real story behind the right - to - work 12 MIN
16mm / VHS
Color (G IND)
$5.00 rental
Punctures the myths about the right - to - work laws being introduced in state legislatures. Looks at the National Right to Work Committee which represents big business interests.
Business and Economics; Social Science
Dist - AFLCIO **Prod** - AFLCIO 1986

The Real stuff 58 MIN
VHS
Frontline series
Color; Captioned (G)
$59.95 purchase _ #FRON - 501K
Interviews Richard Covey and other space shuttle astronauts. Probes the difficulties and dangers of space flight.
History - World; Industrial and Technical Education; Science - Physical
Dist - PBS **Prod** - DOCCON 1987

Real Talking, Singing Action Movie about Nutrition 14 MIN
U-matic / VHS / 16mm
Color (P I J) (FRENCH SPANISH)
LC 73-701870
Discusses the impact of food and food choices on body development.
Health and Safety; Social Science
Dist - AIMS **Prod** - SUNKST 1973

The Real thing 36 MIN
16mm / VHS
Color (G)
$630.00, $360.00 purchase, $70.00 rental
Documents the abrupt closing of the Coca Cola bottling plant in Guatemala City in 1984 and the reaction of its 460 workers who, suspecting foul play when the owners claimed bankrupty, refused to leave the plant. Tells the union's story and the ultimately successful year long occupation of the plant. Examines the use of bankruptcy as a method to bust unions and the neglect of foreign responsibilities by United States - based multinationals. Narrated by Martin Sheen. Produced by Peter Schnall.
Business and Economics; Civics and Political Systems; Fine Arts
Dist - FIRS

The Real thing by Henry James 15 MIN
VHS / U-matic / 16mm
Short story series
Color (J H)
#E373; LC 90-713146; 83-700048; 83-706131
Explores the nature of reality and its relationship to art in 'The Real Thing' by Henry James. Part of a 16 - part series which introduces American short story writers and discusses the technical aspects of short story structure.
Literature and Drama; Religion and Philosophy
Dist - GPN **Prod** - CTI 1978
IU IITC

Real time dispatching and strategic pricing for truckload motor carriers
VHS
Color (C PRO G)
$150.00 purchase _ #87.02
Shows how a novel network model, LOADMAP, forecasts demands and capacity, decisions to move or to hold trucks and trailers to anticipate the market, also balancing marginal profitability between regions on a real time basis involving several thousand trailers. Reveals that by using dual variables output, each loaded and empty activity can be measured in terms of its total contribution and thus evaluate different markets and shippers and coordinate sales and operations. North Amer Vanlines. Warren B Powell, Yosef Sheffi, Kenneth S Nickerson, Kevin Butterbaugh.
Business and Economics; Social Science; Sociology
Dist - INMASC

Real Time Systems 57 MIN
U-matic / VHS
Management of Microprocessor Technology Series
Color
Discusses real time interrupts, human interaction considerations, developments in the man - machine interface and intelligent safeguards.
Industrial and Technical Education; Mathematics
Dist - MIOT **Prod** - MIOT

Real Time Teletype 19 MIN
16mm
Color
Describes the use by Chrysler Corporation of a GE Datanet 30 system as a communication processor in worldwide data communications. Explains that the system serves as a message switching center, replacing a tape system.
Mathematics; Social Science
Dist - HONIS **Prod** - GE

Real time video micrography series
Presents a nine - part series on the behavior and interactions of microorganisms. Discusses use of the microscope, bacteria and other one - celled microorganisms, coelenterates, flatworms, mollusks, annelids, arthropods and echinoderms.

The Annelids - 7 — 12 MIN
The Arthropods - 8 — 15 MIN
The Coelenterates - 4 — 12 MIN
The Echinoderms - 9 — 11 MIN
The Flatworms - 5 — 12 MIN
Imaging the hidden world - microscopy and videomicroscopy - 1 — 14 MIN
The Micro - life resource - Parts 1 - 2 — 26 MIN
The Micro - life resource - Parts 2 - 3 — 26 MIN
The Mollusks - 6 — 12 MIN
Dist - ENVIMC **Prod** - BIOMED

Real - time, wide area dispatch of petroleum tank trucks
VHS
Color (C PRO G)
$150.00 purchase _ #86.04
Reveals that at Mobil a highly automated, real - time dispatch system uses embedded optimization methods to replace manual operations and to substantially reduce dispatching staff and transportation costs. Shows that the system permitted Mobil to consolidate its nationwide light product dispatching operations, double individual dispatcher productivity and realize an estimated $2 million annual savings in product distribution costs. Mobil Oil Corp. Gerald G Brown, Carol J Ellis, Glen W Graves, David Ronen.
Business and Economics; Social Science
Dist - INMASC

The Real War in Space 52 MIN
U-matic / VHS
Color (H C A)
LC 80-706910
Presents General George Keegan, former Chief of U S Air Force Intelligence, who believes the Russians are developing the capacity to destroy intercontinental ballistic missiles by using high - energy lasers. Discusses the discovery that the Russians have been testing hunter - killer satellites capable of seeking out and destroying other satellites in space. Explains that both America and Russia may be on the verge of a costly arms race for the domination of space.
Civics and Political Systems; Industrial and Technical Education; Science - Physical
Dist - FI **Prod** - BBCTV 1980

The Real West 54 MIN
16mm / U-matic / VHS
Project 20 Series
B&W (J)
Uses still - picture animation to explore the social and economic developments of the expanding West from 1849 to 1900. Portrays the legends of the famous gunfighters and the conquest of the Plains Indians. Narrated by Gary Cooper.
History - United States
Dist - MGHT **Prod** - NBCTV 1961

The Real West - Pt 1 27 MIN
U-matic / VHS / 16mm
Project 20 Series
B&W (J)
Uses still - picture animation to explore the social and economic developments of the expanding West from 1849 to 1900. Portrays the legends of the famous gunfighters and the conquest of the Plains Indians. Narrated by Gary Cooper.
History - World; Literature and Drama
Dist - MGHT **Prod** - NBCTV 1961

The Real West - Pt 2 27 MIN
U-matic / VHS / 16mm
Project 20 Series
B&W (J)
Uses still - picture animation to explore the social and economic developments of the expanding West from 1849 to 1900. Portrays the legends of the famous gunfighters and the conquest of the Plains Indians. Narrated by Gary Cooper.
History - World; Literature and Drama
Dist - MGHT **Prod** - NBCTV 1961

Real world economic series
Barter, bank notes and beyond — 16 MIN
Macro models — 14 MIN
The Specialists — 15 MIN
What is scarcity — 17 MIN
Dist - NDIM

Real world economics series
Presents a series of 13 to 17 - minute programs introducing economics to the secondary school student. Hopes to bring real life situations filmed in the streets, motorways, shops, factories, offices and countryside into the classroom to help students make the connection between theory and reality. Titles include What is Scarcity; Market Structure; The Specialists; Economies of Scale; Barter, Bank Notes and Beyond; Getting the Right Mix; and Macro Models. Separate titles available for purchase or rent.

Economies of scale — 15 MIN
Getting the right mix — 13 MIN
Market structure — 13 MIN
Dist - NDIM **Prod** - REALWO 1961

The Real world of Andrew Wyeth 69 MIN
VHS
Color (H C A)
$39.95 purchase _ #HV-911
Presents an interview with artist Andrew Wyeth. Shows footage of the landscapes in Maine and Pennsylvania which inspired his work along with the works themselves.
Fine Arts
Dist - ARTSAM **Prod** - RMART 1986
CRYSP
FI

Real World of Insects Series
Dragonflies - Flying Hunters of the Waterside — 13 MIN
Gypsy moths - vandals of the forest — 10 MIN
Locusts - the Now and Ancient Plague — 10 MIN
Locusts - the Now and Ancient Plague — 9 MIN
Termites - Architects of the Underground — 9 MIN
Wasps - Paper Makers of the Summer — 10 MIN
Dist - LCOA

The Real World of Selling
VHS / U-matic
Making of a Salesman Series
Color
Gives numerous examples of customer contact problems in both plant penetration and account building. Aimed at projecting salespeople into a variety of field situations to develop strategies. Includes cold call strategies, tools for territory management, purchasing authority conflicts and the entertainment entrapment. Sesson 2 on Making of salesman series.
Business and Economics; Psychology
Dist - PRODEV **Prod** - PRODEV

The Real world of TV 12 MIN
VHS / U-matic / 16mm
Getting the most out of TV series
Color (P I J)
$195.00, $245.00 purchase, $50.00 rental
Considers the various forms of news programs available on TV. Asks how TV news relates to magazines, newspapers and other news formats. Part of a seven - part series.
Fine Arts; Industrial and Technical Education
Dist - NDIM **Prod** - YALEU 1981
CORF TAPPRO

The Real You 15 MIN
U-matic / VHS
Safer You Series
Color (P I)
Shows how others see us and how we see ourselves. Demonstrates how self - concept affects our lives.
Guidance and Counseling; Health and Safety
Dist - GPN **Prod** - WCVETV 1984

Realism 15 MIN
VHS
Art history - century of modern art series
Color (I H A)
$125.00 purchase; $25.00 rental
Discusses American Realists Edward Hopper, Ben Shahn, Jack Levine, Horace Pippin, Milton Avery, Andrew Wyeth, Grant Wood and Thomas Hart Benton. Considers selected works, comments on the artists' personal histories and points out their distinctive styles and subjects.
Fine Arts
Dist - AITECH **Prod** - WDCNTV 1988

Realism 20 MIN
VHS
ARTV series
Color (J)
$44.95 purchase _ #E323; LC 90-708450
Offers two music videos which feature the art works of Honore Daumier and Edouard Manet. Includes Courbet and Carot. Part of a ten - part ARTV series which uses TV format, including 'commercials' which sell one aspect of an artist's style and a gossip columnist who gives little known facts about the artists.
Fine Arts
Dist - GPN **Prod** - HETV 1989

Realism and Naturalism in American Literature 30 MIN
VHS
Modern American Literature Eminent Scholar - Teachers Video Series
Color (C)
$95.00 purchase
Explains the origins of the idea of realism in the 1850s, discriminates among the varieties of literary realism in fiction, and differentiates between the general literary method of realism and the deterministic concept of naturalism. The 21st of 34 installments of the Modern American Literature Eminent Scholar - Teacher Video Series.
Literature and Drama
Dist - OMNIGR

Realistic expectations and communication 30 MIN
VHS
Being good to each other series
Color (H C G A R)
$39.95 purchase, $10.00 rental _ #35 - 893 - 2076
Features Carol and Lowell Erdahl in a discussion of relationships, emphasizing marriage. Shows that the Erdahls believe that communication and mutual nurture are essential to a healthy relationship. Produced by Seraphim.
Guidance and Counseling; Psychology; Sociology
Dist - APH

Realities of Blindness - the Perkins Experience 29 MIN
16mm
Color (I)
LC 72-702330
Shows how the staff and pupils at the Perkins School for the Blind correct the opposing myths that the blind person is capable of anything or that he is helpless. Discusses the nature of blindness and various activities that make up a well - rounded education for blind children.
Education; Guidance and Counseling; Psychology
Dist - CMPBL **Prod** - CMPBL 1972

The Realities of Change 29 MIN
U-matic / VHS / 16mm
Dealing with Classroom Problems Series
Color (T)
Describes techniques, ideas and tips which have made change a positive experience for some teachers. Includes ideas on what to do about tests, texts and troublemakers, and on the creative uses of curriculum. Offers suggestions on how new ideas and techniques can most effectively be introduced into a school.
Education
Dist - FI **Prod** - MFFD 1976

Realities of chemotherapy 45 MIN
VHS
Home care video series
Color (G PRO C)
$100.00 purchase _ #ON - 03
Explains what chemotherapy is and answers the most common questions. Shows how to alleviate common side effects and discusses warning symptoms that necessitate physician contact. Available with or without a segment on Groshong catheter care. Includes a segment on a cancer support group. Part of a series on home care for cancer patients.
Health and Safety
Dist - MIFE **Prod** - SMRMC 1993

The Realities of Recycling 38 MIN
16mm
Color (J A)
LC 71-714058
Points out that recycling our solid wastes is basic to the protection of our environment, showing the inadequacy of many of today's systems. Discusses new ideas being developed, such as the CPU - 400 which is designed to burn 400 tons of refuse a day to produce up to 15,000 kilowatts of electricity and the zig - zag air classifier which sorts and separates refuse into specific categories. Intended for use by leaders and technicians who need a more comprehensive grasp of the potentials of recycling.
Science - Natural
Dist - FINLYS **Prod** - USEPA 1971

Realities series
Delves into the political, social, economic and cultural trends of the 1980s. Probes a wide range of contemporary concerns. Each segment includes a guest speaker who is an expert in the field under discussion.

Are you intelligent without knowing it — 30 MIN
Civil rights - how much is enough — 30 MIN
A Class act - born not made — 30 MIN
Crisis of higher education — 30 MIN
Crisis of humanities — 30 MIN
Economics - dilemma of a profession — 30 MIN
In defence of family — 30 MIN
In defence of the west — 30 MIN
Realities series — 0 MIN
Sex and the brain — 30 MIN
Dist - TVOTAR **Prod** - TVOTAR 1971

Realities

America's search for an effective foreign policy	30 MIN
The Anarchist utopia	30 MIN
And justice for all	30 MIN
Canada's First Lady in Washington	30 MIN
Christianity	30 MIN
Citizens party	30 MIN
A Czech Writer	30 MIN
Decoding the Soviet Union	30 MIN
The Disappearance of Childhood	30 MIN
The Disappearance of the Middle Class	30 MIN
Disciplining the Body - Freeing the Mind	30 MIN
Divergent conservatism	30 MIN
Do We Need Culture	30 MIN
Feminism today	30 MIN
Genetic Engineering - a Threat to who We are	30 MIN
Homosexuality	30 MIN
Israel After Begin	30 MIN
Judaism	30 MIN
Liberalism Under Attack	30 MIN
Libertarian Left	30 MIN
Living in the Age of Chaos	30 MIN
Martin Luther and Catholicism	30 MIN
Message of the Medium	30 MIN
Moral Conflicts - the same for Men and Women	30 MIN
The Morality of Geopolitics	30 MIN
New - Liberal View of the US	30 MIN
A New Private Eye	30 MIN
Nicaragua - a Failed Revolution	30 MIN
1984 revisited	30 MIN
Planned Economy - a Solution	30 MIN
Red Menace or Red Scare - Part 1	30 MIN
Red Menace or Red Scare - Part 2	30 MIN
Socialism in the Third World - Success or Failure	30 MIN
Socialist View of Reaganomics	30 MIN
The Soviet Threat	30 MIN
Supply Side Economics	30 MIN
The Turning Point in the Soviet Union	30 MIN
US and Canada	30 MIN
The Western Guilt and the Third World	30 MIN
Who Runs Washington	30 MIN
World Hunger	30 MIN

Dist - TVOTAR

Reality and America's dreams 98 MIN
VHS
March of time - the great depression series
B&W (G)
$24.95 purchase _ #S02140
Presents newsreel excerpts covering the period from January to May of 1937. Covers events including Turkish modernization, the development of 'swing' music, prohibitionists fighting against the bootleggers, the abdication of the English monarch, and more. Final part of a six - part series.
History - United States
Dist - UILL

Reality and Hallucinations of Jose Luis Cuevas 23 MIN
16mm / VHS / U-matic
Color (SPANISH)
LC 78-701324
Focuses on the life and works of Mexican artist Jose Luis Cuevas. Explores Cuevas' artistic beliefs through his commentary on the various themes that characterize his drawings.
Fine Arts; Foreign Language
Dist - MOMALA **Prod** - OOAS 1978

Reality and the also - ran van 22 MIN
U-matic / VHS
Dollar scholar series; Pt 2
Color (H)
LC 82-707401
Presents high school senior Jerry Malone giving tips on being a wise consumer.
Business and Economics; Home Economics
Dist - GPN **Prod** - BCSBIT 1982

The Reality of Dreams 22 MIN
U-matic
Color
Illustrates the World of Motion Pavillion at Disney World's Epcot Center. Focuses on transportation systems of the future.
Physical Education and Recreation; Social Science; Sociology
Dist - MTP **Prod** - GM

The Reality of imagination - an inquiry into human creativity 32 MIN
VHS
Color (J H)
$99.00 purchase _ #00259 - 026
Shows how imagination enables the coloring and reshaping of the world and expression of feelings about others. Suggests that reason can organize dreams and fantasies into new forms of communication. Uses excerpts from music and literature. Includes teacher's guide and library kit.
Education; Fine Arts; Psychology; Social Science
Dist - GA

Reality of Rape 10 MIN
U-matic / VHS / 16mm
Color
Recounts how a rapist negotiates for powerful control of his victim. Shows two police officers of varying sensitivity interviewing the victim after the rape.
Sociology
Dist - CORF **Prod** - FILMA

Reality Shock 21 MIN
U-matic
Nursing Preceptorship Series
(PRO)
Reveals that nurses go through three reactions to their first work experience; honeymoon, shock and resolution.
Health and Safety
Dist - ACCESS **Prod** - ACCESS 1983

The Reality Therapy Approach to School Discipline 29 MIN
16mm / U-matic / VHS
Human Relations and School Discipline Series
Color (C)
Documents teachers successfully using concepts developed by Dr William Glasser to achieve effective school discipline, along with a full explanation by Dr Glasser of his five - part approach to discipline and the seven steps of reality therapy.
Education; Psychology
Dist - FI **Prod** - MFFD 1974

Reality Therapy in High School 29 MIN
U-matic / VHS / 16mm
Dealing with Classroom Problems Series
Color (T)
Discusses Dr William Glasser's Reality Therapy approach to discipline as it is used at the Jersey Village High School in Houston, Texas. Presents the principal and staff describing how the use of Reality Therapy was introduced into the school and how discipline problems were reduced by over 80 percent the first year.
Education; Psychology
Dist - FI **Prod** - MFFD 1976

Really Rosie 26 MIN
U-matic / VHS / 16mm
Color (P I)
LC 76-701290
Uses animation to tell the story of Rosie who challenges all to believe that she's a star, terrific at everything and a fascinating personality. Shows how make - believe is not just a pastime, but a lifestyle.
Guidance and Counseling; Literature and Drama
Dist - WWS **Prod** - WWS 1976

Really start a business
VHS
Inc magazine business success program series
Color (H C A)
$39.95 purchase _ #KA038V
Examines what is necessary to get a business started. Interviews successful entrepreneurs on how they got started. Presents practical tips rather than textbook theory.
Business and Economics
Dist - CAMV

Realm of the alligator 60 MIN
VHS
National Geographic video series
Color (G)
$29.95 purchase
Portrays the alligators of the Okefenokee swamp. Provides scientific insights into this reptile.
Science - Natural
Dist - PBS **Prod** - WNETTV

Realm of the Alligator 55 MIN
U-matic / 16mm
Color (G)
$29.95 purchase _ #51296 ; $395.00 purchase _ #50198
Science - Natural
Dist - NGS

Realm of the white shark 26 MIN
VHS
Challenge of the seas series
Color (I J H)
$225.00 purchase
Reveals that the heaviest concentration of great white sharks in the world is just off San Francisco. Discloses that more attacks by great whites have taken place there than anywhere else on Earth. Interviews people who have been attacked and survived. Part of a 26 - part series on the oceans.
Geography - United States; Science - Natural; Science - Physical
Dist - LANDMK **Prod** - LANDMK 1991

Realm of the Wild 28 MIN
U-matic / VHS / 16mm
Color
LC FIE52-414
Pictures wild life in the national forests. Illustrates the work of the national forest service in the conservation of wild life, particularly the attempt to balance wild life population and the available food supply.
Geography - United States; Science - Natural
Dist - USNAC **Prod** - USDA 1945

Realms of light - the baroque - 5 60 MIN
VHS / U-matic
Art of the Western world series
Color (G)
$45.00, $29.95 purchase
Presents two thirty - minute programs on the Baroque period hosted by historian Michael Wood. Focuses on the campaign of the Roman Catholic Church to counter the Protestant Reformation through dramatic depictions of religious scenes by artists such as Caravaggio and Bernini in Part I. Part II looks at the royal courts of Spain and the wealthy burghers of the Netherlands who commissioned major paintings and shaped their content. Part 5 of a nine - part series on art of the Western world.
Civics and Political Systems; Fine Arts; History - World; Religion and Philosophy
Dist - ANNCPB **Prod** - WNETTV 1989

Reamer Sharpening between Centers
U-matic / VHS
Milling and Tool Sharpening Series
Color (SPANISH)
Industrial and Technical Education
Dist - VTRI **Prod** - VTRI

Reaming with Straight Hand Reamers 20 MIN
16mm
Machine Shop Work Bench Work Series
B&W
LC FIE51-532
Discusses types of reamers. Shows how to check the size of reamers and ream straight holes with straightfluted, helical - fluted and adjustable - blade reamers. No 4 on the Machine shop work bench work series.
Industrial and Technical Education
Dist - USNAC **Prod** - USOE 1942

Reaming with Taper Hand Reamers 15 MIN
16mm
Machine Shop Work Series Bench Work
B&W
LC FIE51-533
Describes how to hand ream a tapered hole through a shaft and collar and how to fit a taper pin in the reamed hole. Explains how to ream bearing caps for fitting dowel pins.
Industrial and Technical Education
Dist - USNAC **Prod** - USOE 1942

Rear End Collision, Unitized Body 14 MIN
VHS / BETA
Color (A PRO)
$71.00 purchase _ #KTI81
Deals with auto body repair. Shows body and uniframe deflection, using a Ford Pinto as an example.
Industrial and Technical Education
Dist - RMIBHF **Prod** - RMIBHF

Rear Legs and Udder, Vol V 26 MIN
VHS
Clipping Dairy Cattle Series
Color (G)
$49.95 purchase _ #6 - 099 - 105P
Discusses procedures for topline clipping of dairy cattle. Part 5 of a five - part series.
Agriculture
Dist - VEP **Prod** - VEP

Rear window 112 MIN
VHS
Color (G)
$24.95 purchase _ #S00906
Presents the Alfred Hitchcock tale of a news photographer who, while confined to his room by a broken leg, witnesses a murder in a nearby building. Stars James Stewart, Grace Kelly, and Raymond Burr.
Fine Arts
Dist - UILL

Rearing and Handling of Anopheles Mosquitoes 16 MIN
16mm
Malaria Control Series
Color; B&W
LC FIE52-2262
Depicts the insectary techniques used at the U S Public Health Service Malaria Research Laboratory, Columbia, S C, in supplying anopheles mosquitoes to health laboratories studying infection of foreign types of malaria.
Health and Safety; Science - Natural
Dist - USNAC **Prod** - USNAC 1945

Rearing Kibbutz Babies 27 MIN
16mm
Color (C T)
LC 74-701433
Observes infant rearing in an Israeli kibbutz organized around the activities of Hannah, seen both as a young mother and as a metapelet (care - giver) for four infants. Follows her weekday work as she cares for four under - a - year - old infants in their baby house from early morning to mid - afternoon and as she takes scheduled breaks to visit her own children in their nearby children's houses. Depicts Hannah's adroit blending of household tasks with tender, expert infant care and upbringing.
Geography - World; Home Economics; Psychology; Sociology
Dist - NYU **Prod** - VASSAR 1973

Reason and relationships
VHS
Baby's world series
Color (G)
$29.95 purchase _ #DIS24161V-K
Eavesdrops on toddlers as they think, reason, fantasize and relate to others. Shows how trial and error is replaced by planned action that goes far beyond instinct. Part of a three-part series that demonstrates the process of maturing from infancy into walking, talking, thinking human beings.
Health and Safety; Psychology
Dist - CAMV

A Reason for Confidence 28 MIN
16mm
Color
Depicts a day in the life of Nancy Taylor, homemaker and mother of three, as she and her family use a variety of foods, drugs, cosmetics and household chemicals. Takes the viewer behind the scenes to see what the food and drug administration does to protect the health and safety of every American.
Civics and Political Systems; Psychology; Social Science
Dist - USPHS **Prod** - USPHS

A Reason to buy 27 MIN
VHS
Color (G)
$598.00 purchase, $150.00 rental _ #91F0878
Teaches sales teams how to sell customer confidence.
Business and Economics; Psychology
Dist - DARTNL **Prod** - DARTNL 1991

A Reason to live 30 MIN
VHS
B&W (G)
$30.00 rental, $40.00 purchase
Delves into depression and despairing emotions against a huge meteorological background that brings inspiration and terror to the characters. Explores San Francisco and central Oklahoma.
Fine Arts; Geography - United States; Psychology
Dist - CANCIN **Prod** - KUCHAR 1976

The Reason Why 14 MIN
16mm / U-matic / VHS
Color (J)
LC 73-709666
Presents two cronies who sit before an isolated country house and gradually spill forth their personal feelings about the things they have killed during their lifetimes. Deals with the impulses of the human animal toward war, violence and murder. Features Eli Wallach and Robert Ryan. Written by Arthur Miller.
Fine Arts; Literature and Drama; Psychology; Religion and Philosophy
Dist - PHENIX **Prod** - PHENIX 1970

Reasonable doubt - the single bullet theory and the assassination of JFK 60 MIN
VHS
Color (H A)
$29.95 purchase _ #KU1626V-S; $29.95 purchase _ #1626
Examines in detail the controversy surrounding one of history's most tragic events - the assassination of President John F Kennedy. Takes students back to the source of the controversy, the Warren Commission's report on the assassination, in an attempt to answer the mystery's most basic question - Was Kennedy killed by a lone assassin or as a result of a conspiracy?
Biography; History - United States
Dist - CAMV
KULTUR

Reasonable limits - the Canadian Charter of Rights and Freedoms 30 MIN
VHS
Remaking of Canada - Canadian government and politics in the 1990s 'series
Color (H C G)
$89.95 purchase _ #WLU - 506
Discusses how the Charter of Rights and Freedoms has changed judicial review in Canada, how it has changed parliamentary supremacy and how it has changed the way Canadians think about each other. Part of a 12 - part series incorporating interviews with Canadian politicians and hosted by Dr John Redekop.
Civics and Political Systems; History - World
Dist - INSTRU **Prod** - TELCOL 1992

Reasons for Caring 21 MIN
16mm
Color (IND)
LC 75-704160
Describes correct fire prevention and emergency action procedures for hospital employees. Illustrates how a fire safety program applies to their work.
Health and Safety
Dist - NFPA **Prod** - NFPA 1975

Reasons for Implementing TQC 27 MIN
VHS
Seven Steps to TQC Promotion Series
(PRO) (JAPANESE)
 # C107
Gives reasons to implement Total Quality Control, or TQC, and recommendations on how to deal with various problems that might be encountered. Stresses goal that companies end low growth rates by promoting TQC.
Business and Economics
Dist - TOYOVS **Prod** - TOYOVS 1987

Reasons for Law - Le Cafe Politic 19 MIN
VHS / U-matic
Ways of the Law Series
Color (H)
Examines in depth, exactly why we need laws.
Civics and Political Systems
Dist - GPN **Prod** - SCITV 1980

The reasons people drown 25 MIN
VHS
Color (IND)
$295.00 purchase, $95.00 rental _ #805 - 30
Shows how drowning is the second leading cause of accidental death for ages 1 to 44. Shows how employees and their families can identify potential drowning victims and prevent tragedies.
Health and Safety
Dist - ITSC **Prod** - ITSC

Reasons to be cheerful - Part Three 5 MIN
16mm
Color (G)
$10.00 rental
Features a showdown between Britain's most manic rock 'n' roll entertainer and the toughest rhythm section in the world in a Laurie Lewis production.
Fine Arts
Dist - CANCIN

Reassemblage 40 MIN
16mm
Color (G)
$800.00 purchase, $90.00 rental
Studies the women of rural Senegal in Africa.
Agriculture; Fine Arts; Geography - World; History - United States; History - World
Dist - WMEN **Prod** - JPBOU 1982

Reassembling the engine 22 MIN
16mm
Aircraft work series; Power plant maintenance
B&W
LC FIE52-148
Shows how to reassemble the crankshaft and camshaft assemblies, crankcase section and gear case cover assembly, how to reinstall the oil sump and how to completely reassemble the engine.
Industrial and Technical Education
Dist - USNAC **Prod** - USOE 1945

Reassembly of Cylinder Head 14 MIN
16mm
B&W
LC FIE52-1241
Demonstrates how to reassemble and install the cylinder head. Explains each operation and the use of proper tools.
Industrial and Technical Education
Dist - USNAC **Prod** - USN 1944

Reassembly of the 8 - 268A Engine 36 MIN
16mm
B&W
LC FIE52-1050
Demonstrates how to reassemble the General Motors 8 - 268A diesel engine.
Industrial and Technical Education
Dist - USNAC **Prod** - USN 1943

Reassessing Goals - Transition and Flight 60 MIN
VHS
Group Work - Leading in the Here and Now Series
Color (A PRO)
$125.00 purchase _ #76502
Teaches reassessing group purpose and guiding groups through transition and "in flight".
Psychology
Dist - AACD **Prod** - AACD 1985

Rebecca 115 MIN
16mm / U-matic / VHS / BETA
B&W (J)
Stars Laurence Olivier and Joan Fontaine in the Daphne du Maurier novel 'Rebecca.' Concerns a young bride who comes to a mysterious manor in England, where she finds that the memory of her husband's first wife haunts her. Depicts how she tries to discover the secret locked in her husband's heart about the fate of his first wife.
Fine Arts; Literature and Drama
Dist - FI **Prod** - UAA 1940
GA

Rebecca Allen and Dianne McIntyre 30 MIN
VHS / U-matic
Eye on Dance - Dance on TV Series
Color
Discusses the interface of the choreographer and the new technology. Presents excerpts from the works of Allen and McIntyre. Shows Dianne McIntyre in 'Esoterica.'
Fine Arts
Dist - ARCVID **Prod** - ARCVID

Rebecca Brown - 3 - 31 - 76 31 MIN
VHS / Cassette
Poetry Center reading series
Color (G)
$15.00, $45.00 purchase, $15.00 rental _ #183 - 140AB
Features the writer reading from her works at the Poetry Center, San Francisco State University, with an introduction by Lewis MacAdams. Includes poetry and an excerpt from a novel in progress.
Literature and Drama
Dist - POETRY **Prod** - POETRY 1976

Rebel Earth 50 MIN
U-matic / VHS
B&W
Chronicles a prairie voyage as a 97 - year - old man goes out with a young farmer to look for the sites of his past.
Biography; History - United States
Dist - NFPS **Prod** - NFPS

The Rebel slave 24 MIN
U-matic / VHS
Young people's specials series
Color
Focuses on a young slave boy's involvement in the Civil War.
Fine Arts; History - United States; Sociology
Dist - MULTPP **Prod** - MULTPP

Rebel Without a Cause 111 MIN
U-matic / VHS / 16mm
Color (J)
Stars James Dean as a boy caught in the undertow of today's juvenile violence, disrespectful of his parents and contemptuous of the law and authority, who attempts to join a teenage gang with his girlfriend and best pal. Describes the death, violence and needless tragedy that follow before the chastened, saddened and wiser 'Rebel' is re - united with his parents.
Fine Arts
Dist - FI **Prod** - WB 1955

Rebids 30 MIN
VHS / U-matic
Bridge Basics Series
Color (A)
Physical Education and Recreation
Dist - KYTV **Prod** - KYTV 1982

Rebirth of a Nation 30 MIN
VHS / U-matic
Japan - the Changing Tradition Series
Color (H C A)
History - World
Dist - GPN **Prod** - UMA 1978

Rebirth of a region 30 MIN
VHS

Inside Britain 3 series
Color; PAL; NTSC (G) (BULGARIAN CZECH HUNGARIAN SPANISH POLISH ROMANIAN RUSSIAN SLOVAK UKRAINIAN ENGLISH WITH ARABIC SUBTITLES LITHUANIAN)
PdS65 purchase
Reveals that the traditional heavy industries of Northern England - coal mining, ship building, textiles and steel - have declined. Discloses that new businesses are moving in to rejuvenate derelict areas and to create new jobs. Features projects in the Dearne Valley, Consett and Halifax.
Business and Economics; History - World
Dist - CFLVIS **Prod** - GALILE 1993

The Rebirth of Atlantic Avenue 20 MIN
16mm
Color
Provides a historic look at Atlantic Avenue and discusses its history and possible future.
Sociology
Dist - BUGAS **Prod** - BUGAS

The Rebirth of Packy Rowe 25 MIN
U-matic / VHS / 16mm
Insight Series
Color (J)
LC 79-700646
Tells the story of an aggressive theatrical agent, who learns that he may enter heaven because of of his many acts of love.
Guidance and Counseling; Religion and Philosophy
Dist - PAULST **Prod** - PAULST 1978

Rebirth of the American City 17 MIN
16mm
Color
Records how Brooklyn Union Gas' award winning 'Cinderella' program helped spark the renaissance of downtown Brooklyn over the last decade. Includes a brief study of Brooklyn's development as a residential community in the late 1880s to its revival in the late 60s and 70s as a desirable place to live and work. Shows how other cities such as San Antonio, Texas, are beginning to experience similar rebirths.
Sociology
Dist - BUGAS **Prod** - BUGAS

Rebop Series
Kelly 9 MIN
Michael 9 MIN
Thanh 9 MIN
Dist - IU

Reborn in America - Pt 2 58 MIN
VHS
Struggle for Democracy Series
Color (S)
$49.00 purchase _ #039 - 9002
Explores the concept of democracy and how it works. Features Patrick Watson, author with Benjamin Barber of 'The Struggle For Democracy,' as host who travels to more than 30 countries around the world, examining issues such as rule of law, freedom of information, the tyranny of the majority and the relationship of economic prosperity to democracy. Part 2 takes Watson back to the Pilgrims on the Mayflower, the issuing of the Declaration of Independence, the drafting of the Constitution and the opening of the American West, for a consideration of American democracy.
Civics and Political Systems; History - United States; History - World
Dist - FI **Prod** - DFL 1989

Rebounding
VHS
NCAA basketball instructional video series
Color (G)
$39.95 purchase _ #KAR1202V
Features Louisville basketball coach Denny Crum in an instructional video on rebounding skills in basketball.
Physical Education and Recreation
Dist - CAMV **Prod** - NCAAF

Rebuilding a Master Cylinder 4 MIN
16mm
Color
LC FI68-222
Shows the method of disassembling the master cylinder, inspecting and honing the bore, installing new parts and refilling the reservoir before reinstalling the cylinder unit in the automobile.
Industrial and Technical Education
Dist - RAYBAR **Prod** - RAYBAR 1966

Rebuilding a Small Block Chevrolet Engine 103 MIN
VHS
Color (H C A PRO)
$89.95 purchase _ #VS100; $89.95 purchase _ #VL100V
Covers eight engine sizes in the Chevrolet small block series. Begins with a step by step breakdown of a 350 engine. Observes worn parts such as bearings. Includes close - up footage and diagrams.
Industrial and Technical Education
Dist - AAVIM **Prod** - CAREER 1990

The Rebuilding of Mascot Flats 59 MIN
VHS
Color (H C G)
$350.00 purchase, $75.00 rental
Tells about a group of homeless New Yorkers who set out to renovate an abandoned tenement building, helped by Habitat for Humanity. Shows inexperienced people becoming proficient carpenters and tenant - owners. Follows a group of ethnically diverse people overcoming bureaucracy, skepticism and lack of money to attain a decent affordable place to live over a three - year period.
Social Science; Sociology
Dist - FLMLIB **Prod** - DEANJ 1991

Rebuilding the American nation - 1865 - 1890 20 MIN
VHS
Color (J H)
$99.00 purchase _ #06029 - 026
Helps students understand how the social forces following the Civil War - emancipation, transfer of wealth from the South to the North and new technology - interacted with the political and economic structures to create Reconstruction and to overthrow it. Includes teacher's guide and library kit.
Education; History - United States
Dist - GA

Rebuilding the Body 29 MIN
VHS
Life Matters Series
Color (G)
$59.95 purchase _ #LIFM - 113
Focuses on 74 - year - old Milt Foreman, who had to fight off cancer that eventually destroyed most of the roof of his mouth. Shows how Foreman lives a reasonably normal life, although he must now use a mouth prosthesis.
Health and Safety
Dist - PBS **Prod** - KERA 1988

Rebuilding the body 29 MIN
U-matic / VHS
Life matters series
Color (G)
$49.95 purchase; $59.95 purchase _ #LIFM-113
Focuses on 74 - year - old Milt Forman who discovered a cancer that destroyed 85 percent of the roof of his mouth. Reveals that the discovery brought two terrors - how long he could live and whether he could be productive. He has had two surgeries and uses a carefully constructed prosthesis that allows him to eat and talk normally. Part of a 13 - part series that takes an in - depth look at the internal strength and convictions of people who live active and productive lives in spite of an illness that can be crippling or fatal.
Health and Safety
Dist - BAXMED **Prod** - KERA 1988
PBS

Rebuilding the Union 30 MIN
U-matic / VHS
American story - the beginning to 1877 series
Color (C)
History - United States
Dist - DALCCD **Prod** - DALCCD

Rebuilding Wheel Cylinders 16 MIN
VHS / 16mm
Automotive Tech Series
(G PRO)
$76.50 purchase
Shows how to rebuild wheel cylinders.
Industrial and Technical Education
Dist - RMIBHF **Prod** - RMIBHF

Rebuttal of the Selling of the Pentagon 22 MIN
16mm / U-matic / VHS
B&W (H A)
Presents a postscript to the original broadcast of 'The selling of the Pentagon,' with critical reactions from Vice President Agnew, Secretary of Defense Melvin Laird, F Edward Herbert, chairman of the House Armed Services Committee and Richard Salant, president of CBS News.
Biography; Civics and Political Systems
Dist - CAROUF **Prod** - CBSTV 1971

Recapitulation and I am working on a film 22 MIN
16mm
Films 1 - 37 series
B&W (G)
$35.00 rental
Attempts to condense the series Films 1 - 37 as a whole but fails; these two films exhaust themselves. Advises to rent with the other works from the series Films 1 - 37, of psychoanalytical content, dealing with the 'imaginary' and other phenomena and described as 'gritty and obsessive.'
Fine Arts; Psychology
Dist - CANCIN **Prod** - SONDHE 1981

Recapturing the Past - Pt 3 58 MIN
VHS
Treasure Houses of Britain Series
Color (S)
$29.95 purchase _ #362 - 9018
Transports the viewer to some of Great Britain's most magnificent houses from the fifteenth century to the twentieth. Features John Julius Norwich as narrator who interviews current owners to reveal the privileges and the problems of living in an historic house. Part 3 of the three - part series guides viewers through the splendid rooms of Belvoir Castle, Pas Newydd, Penrhyn Castle, Wightwick Manor, Haddon Hall and Lindisfarne Castle.
Fine Arts; Geography - World; History - World
Dist - FI **Prod** - NATLGL 1989

Receipt Administration 60 MIN
BETA / VHS
Manufacturing Series
(IND)
Highlights the buyer's role in receipt validation by outlining the purchasing cycle. Looks at typical receiving problems created by both the buyer and the supplier and how to prevent them.
Business and Economics
Dist - COMSRV **Prod** - COMSRV 1986

Receiver Alignment 37 MIN
16mm
B&W
LC 74-705486
Demonstrates the troubleshooting of a superheterodyne receiver. Shows how, after finding and replacing the defective component, the receiver is aligned using a signal generator for the signals. Explains proper test equipment and how alignment is reaccomplished. (Kinescope).
Industrial and Technical Education
Dist - USNAC **Prod** - USAF

Receiver Troubleshooting Procedure 21 MIN
16mm
B&W
LC 74-705487
Explains general troubleshooting procedures for receivers, stage - by - stage and half - split methods of troubleshooting and identifies basic test equipment. (Kinescope).
Industrial and Technical Education
Dist - USNAC **Prod** - USAF 1965

Receivers
VHS
Color (H C A)
$39.95 purchase _ #CVN1080V
Features Louisiana State assistant football coach Jerry Sullivan in instruction of pass receiving techniques. Covers techniques including reading coverage, stance, running routes, catching techniques, splitting defenders, and more.
Physical Education and Recreation
Dist - CAMV

Receiving 60 MIN
VHS / BETA
Manufacturing Series
(IND)
Analyzes how the receiving function works with other functions in a company.
Business and Economics
Dist - COMSRV **Prod** - COMSRV 1986

Receiving and donating organs 28 MIN
VHS
Color (G)
$149.00 purchase, $75.00 rental _ #UW4231
Reveals that, of the more than 6000 Americans waiting for a liver, heart or lung transplant, a quarter will die before they receive one. Examines how the organ transplant program works for both donors and recipients. Follows patients through a cornea and a kidney transplant, showing who will get what, and when.
Health and Safety
Dist - FOTH

Receiving Feedback Non - Defensively 17 MIN
Videoreel / VT2
Interpersonal Competence, Unit 02 - Communication Series; Unit 2 - Communication
Color (C A)
Features a humanistic psychologist who, by analysis and examples, discusses that receiving feedback is essential to self - improvement provided that it is done in a non - defensive manner.
Psychology; Sociology
Dist - TELSTR **Prod** - MVNE 1973

Receiving Help and Manipulating 27 MIN
Videoreel / VT2
Interpersonal Competence, Unit 04 - Helping Series; Unit 4 - Helping

Color (C A)
Features a humanistic psychologist who, by analysis and examples, discusses that it is as important to be capable of receiving help as giving it.
Psychology; Sociology
Dist - TELSTR **Prod** - MVNE 1973

Receiving Prosperity 60 MIN
Cassette / VHS
Conversations On Living Lecture Series
Color (G)
$19.95, $10.00 purchase _ #408, #217
Shows how to use the power of thought to attract what is wanted in life - money, fulfilling relationships, rewarding work. Features Louise L Hay. Part of a four - part series.
Health and Safety; Psychology; Social Science; Sociology
Dist - HAYHSE **Prod** - HAYHSE

Recent advances in crew pairing optimization
VHS
Color (C PRO G)
$150.00 purchase _ #90.03
Focuses on the many hundreds of flights per day at American Airlines which make crew pairing logistics extremely complex because of the additional factors of dealing with a variety of union and FAA work rules and pay guarantees. Reveals that the software developed by American Airlines Decision Technologies incorporates algorithmic improvements and more efficient data structure, reducing annual crew costs by $20 million. Amer Airlines Decision Technologies. Ranga Anbil, Eric Gelman, Bruce W Patty, Rajan M Tanga.
Business and Economics; Social Science
Dist - INMASC

Recent Advances in Folate - Antagonist Pharmacology 40 MIN
U-matic
Color
Discusses new developments in antifolate intercellular metabolism.
Health and Safety
Dist - UTEXSC **Prod** - UTEXSC

Recent Advances in Gastrointestinal Endoscopy 30 MIN
U-matic / VHS
Color
Describes the state of the art of gastrointestinal endoscopy. Reviews the techniques and usefulness of esophagogastroduodenoscopy, endoscopic retrograde cholangiopancreatography and colonoscopy with polypectomy.
Health and Safety
Dist - ROWLAB **Prod** - ROWLAB

Recent Advances in Reproductive Physiology 29 MIN
16mm
Nine to Get Ready Series
B&W (C A)
LC 70-704219
Discusses research in reproductive physiology, including biochemistry, endocrinology, electron microscopy, genetics and clinical pathology. Features Dr J Robert Bragonier and Leta Powell Drake. No 12 on the Nine to get ready series.
Science - Natural
Dist - UNL **Prod** - KUONTV 1965

Recent Cartoon Innovations 15 MIN
Videoreel / VT2
Charlie's Pad Series
Color
Fine Arts
Dist - PBS **Prod** - WSIU

Recent Developments in Business Law Practice 120 MIN
VHS / U-matic / Cassette
Color; Mono (PRO)
Presents a concentrated summary of the cases statutes and other developments in business law practice for 1984/1985.
Business and Economics; Civics and Political Systems
Dist - CCEB **Prod** - CCEB

Recent Developments in Civil Procedure 120 MIN
U-matic / Cassette / VHS / 16mm
Color; Mono (PRO)
Presents a concentrated summary of the cases, statutes and other developments in civil procedure for 1985.
Civics and Political Systems
Dist - CCEB **Prod** - CCEB

Recent Developments in Criminal Law Practice - Winter 1985 120 MIN
U-matic / Cassette / VHS / 16mm
Color; Mono (PRO)
Presents a concentrated summary of the cases, statutes and other developments in Criminal Law Practice since Winter of 1984.
Civics and Political Systems
Dist - CCEB **Prod** - CCEB 1985^1985

Recent Developments in Estate Planning and Administration - Fall 1984 120 MIN
VHS / U-matic / Cassette
Color; Mono
Presents a concentrated summary of the cases, statutes and other developments in estate planning and administration since the Fall of 1983.
Civics and Political Systems
Dist - CCEB **Prod** - CCEB 1985^1985

Recent Developments in Family Law Practice - Spring 1985 120 MIN
VHS / U-matic / Cassette
Color; Mono (PRO)
Presents a concentrated summary of the cases, statutes and other developments in family law practice since Spring of 1984.
Civics and Political Systems
Dist - CCEB **Prod** - CCEB 1985^1985

Recent developments in land use law 210 MIN
VHS
Color (C PRO A)
$140.00, $200.00 purchase _ #M786, #P270
Offers a course designed principally for attorneys. Presupposes some familiarity with the basic legal principles and fundamental court decisions in land use law and features faculty panelists from ALI - ABA's annual three - day Land Use Institute.
Business and Economics; Civics and Political Systems
Dist - ALIABA **Prod** - ALIABA 1991

Recent Developments in Our Knowledge of Serum Hepatitis 30 MIN
U-matic
Clinical Pathology Series
B&W (PRO)
LC 76-706098
Reviews developments in our knowledge of serum hepatitis resulting from the discovery of the serum hepatitis virus specific antigen (SH) or Australia antigen.
Health and Safety; Science - Natural
Dist - USNAC **Prod** - NMAC 1970

Recent Developments in Real Property Law Practice - Spring 1985 120 MIN
VHS / U-matic / Cassette
Color; Mono (PRO)
Presents a concentrated summary of the cases, statutes and other developments in Real Property Law practice since Spring of 1984.
Business and Economics; Civics and Political Systems
Dist - CCEB **Prod** - CCEB 1985^1985

Recent Developments in Tax Practice - Fall 1984 120 MIN
VHS / U-matic / Cassette
Color; Mono (PRO)
Looks at the cases, statutes and other developments in tax practice for the twelve months prior to Fall of 1984.
Business and Economics; Civics and Political Systems
Dist - CCEB **Prod** - CCEB

Recent Developments in Workers' Compensation Practice - Fall 1984 120 MIN
U-matic / Cassette / VHS / 16mm
Color; Mono (PRO)
Presents a concentrated summary of the cases, statutes and other developments in workers' compensation practice since Fall, 1984.
Business and Economics; Civics and Political Systems
Dist - CCEB **Prod** - CCEB 1984^1984

Recent Deveplopments in Torts Practice - Spring 1985 120 MIN
U-matic / Cassette / VHS / 16mm
Color; Mono (PRO)
Presents a concentrated summary of the cases, statutes and other developments in torts practice since Spring of 1984.
Civics and Political Systems
Dist - CCEB **Prod** - CCEB 1985^1985

Recent experimental narrative - Package A - Displaced realities 52 MIN
16mm
Color & B&W (G)
$114.00 rental
Features a collection of four experimental films that utililize contemporary editing styles and visual effects, which have changed the experience with narrative film. Notes that conceptual, visual, and aesthetic considerations take precedence over formulaic themes and standardized running times. Titles and production dates are - The Idea - 1990 - by Bill Knowland; Island Zoethrope - 1986 - by Al Hernandez; Avatar - 1990 - by Michael Moore and John Cazden; and Somber Accomodations - 1990 - by Thad Povey and Joe Bini. Films also available separately. Part one of a two - part package.
Fine Arts
Dist - CANCIN

Recent experimental narrative - Package B - Juxtaposed myth and ritual 87 MIN
16mm
Color & B&W (G)
$228.00 rental
Features a collection of five experimental films that utililize contemporary editing styles and visual effects, which have changed the experience with narrative film. Notes that conceptual, visual, and aesthetic considerations take precedence over formulaic themes and standardized running times. Titles and production dates are - Cinderella - 1986 - by Ericka Beckman; Flight - 1989 - by Marian Berges; Terrain Vague - 1987 - by Albert Gabriel Nigrin; Room in his Heart - 1985 - by Gary Adlestein; and Pool of Thanatos - 1990 - by Peter McCandless. Films also available separately. Part two of a two - part package.
Fine Arts
Dist - CANCIN

Recent Modifications of Convulsive Shock Therapy 20 MIN
16mm
Color; B&W (C T)
Demonstrates the use of curare and quinine methochloride in protecting patients from spinal fractures in metrazol and electrical convulsion therapies. Curare is administered to a young woman in extreme manic excitement and the result is a 'SOFT' convulsion. An X - ray photograph shows a fracture which occurred when older methods were used.
Psychology
Dist - PSUPCR **Prod** - PSUPCR 1941

Recent progress in arithmetic algebraic geometry 60 MIN
VHS
ICM Plenary addresses series
Color (PRO G)
$49.00 purchase _ #VIDFALTINGS - VB2
Presents Gerd Faltings who discusses recent progress in arithmetic algebraic geometry.
Mathematics
Dist - AMSOC **Prod** - AMSOC

Recent Results in X - Ray Astronomy 30 MIN
U-matic / VHS
Astronomy Series
Color
Discusses how x - ray astronomy has been able to pinpoint sources of x - radiation and information from the satellite 'Uhuru', which some consider to be strong evidence for the existence of black holes.
Science - Physical
Dist - NETCHE **Prod** - NETCHE 1973

Recent Trends in Manual Communication 60 MIN
U-matic / VHS
Color (S) (AMERICAN SIGN LANGUAGE)
Discusses major characteristics of sign language systems and reviews research of recent trends. Signed.
Education; Guidance and Counseling; Psychology
Dist - GALCO **Prod** - GALCO 1983

Recently bereaved parents - Part I 28 MIN
U-matic / VHS
Issues of cystic fibrosis series
Color (PRO C)
$395.00 purchase, $80.00 rental _ #C891 - VI - 046
Presents part one of a two - parts on a faclated group interview with recently bereaved parents of cystic fibrosis patients. Discusses decisions to bring the child home to die and efforts to raise a terminally ill child as normally as possible. Part of a 13 - part series on cystic fibrosis presented by Drs Ivan Harwood and Cyril Worby.
Health and Safety; Science - Natural; Sociology
Dist - HSCIC

Recently bereaved parents - Part II 28 MIN
VHS / U-matic
Issues of cystic fibrosis series
Color (PRO C)
$395.00 purchase, $80.00 rental _ #C891 - VI - 047
Presents part two of a two - part series on a facilitated group interview with recently bereaved parents of cystic fibrosis patients. Discusses how they, their dying child and the child's caregivers dealt with the dying - at - home phase of cystic fibrosis. Describes how their child protected them and shares memories of the last few days. Part of a 13 - part series on cystic fibrosis presented by Drs Ivan Harwood and Cyril Worby.
Health and Safety; Science - Natural; Sociology
Dist - HSCIC

Receptacle and switch wiring and installation 15 MIN
VHS
Color (H A T)
$95.00 purchase _ #VC302
Takes a thorough look at the wiring and installation of a variety of common switches and receptacles, including Duplex, Split Wired, Switched Outlets, Isolated Ground Receptacles - IGs, Ground Fault Circuit Interrupters - GFCIs, Snap Switches and Dimmers. Covers grounding, conductor termination, mounting, trim - out and circuit testing. Four common NEMA receptacle configurations are explained and includes NEC references.
Industrial and Technical Education
Dist - AAVIM **Prod** - AAVIM 1992

Reception 28 MIN
U-matic / VHS / 16mm
Penitentiary Staff Training Series
B&W (PRO)
LC FIA68-2893
Reviews procedures for receiving new inmates at the regional center for examination and allocation. Describes variations in the character, intelligence and training of the prisoners as well as variations in attitudes of the prison staff.
Psychology; Sociology
Dist - IFB **Prod** - NFBC 1967

The Receptionist 18 MIN
VHS
Color; PAL (IND G)
PdS95 purchase
Offers simple guidelines to make the job of receptionist more efficient and fulfilling. Stresses the importance of examining how one treats visitors to an organization. Presents six sections discussing first impressions, security, internal organization, emergencies and basic health and safety. Includes a booklet.
Business and Economics; Psychology
Dist - CFLVIS **Prod** - SCHWOP 1993

Recession as Opportunity - Smart Moves for Tough Times 60 MIN
U-matic / VHS / 16mm
Color (C PRO)
$695.00 purchase, $200.00 rental; $795.00, $695.00 purchase, $200.00 rental
Presents Tom Peters on strategy for dealing with recessionary forces. Urges business people to shift their mindsets and view recession as an opportunity to implement positive change and avoid the inadvertant destruction of hard - won trust and profitability.
Business and Economics
Dist - VPHI **Prod** - MAGVID 1990
MAGVID

Recette D'Abidjan, Une 11 MIN
16mm / U-matic / VHS
Color (H C)
Foreign Language
Dist - EBEC **Prod** - EBEC 1974

Recharging - Ansul Dry Chemical Hand Portable Extinguishers 6 MIN
VHS
Color (IND)
Reviews the proper recharging procedures for effective operation of fire extinguishers as listed by Underwriters Laboratories and approved by Factory Mutual.
Health and Safety
Dist - ANSUL **Prod** - ANSUL

Recharging - Ansul Dry Chemical Wheeled Extinguishers 8 MIN
VHS
Color (IND)
Reviews proper recharging procedures required to help assure effective operation of fire extinguishers as listed by Underwriters Laboratories and approved by Factory Mutual.
Health and Safety
Dist - ANSUL **Prod** - ANSUL

Recharging - Ansul Large Dry Chemical Hand Hose Line Systems 13 MIN
VHS
Color (IND)
Details the sequence of recharging a large dry chemical hand hose line fire fighting system.
Health and Safety
Dist - ANSUL **Prod** - ANSUL

Rechenka's eggs - 84
VHS
Reading rainbow series
Color; CC (K P)
$39.95 purchase
Features Patricia Polacco, author and illustrator of the story who demonstrates the traditional art of Ukrainian egg - painting, pysanky. Part of a series offering a multicultural approach to generating reading enthusiasm with cross - curricular applications, hosted by LeVar Burton.
English Language; Fine Arts; Literature and Drama
Dist - GPN **Prod** - LNMDP

The Recidivist 15 MIN
16mm
B&W (J)
LC 72-700409
Points out factors which could cause a man to become a repeated criminal offender by telling a story about a man, who was faced with loneliness and desperation after being released from prison. Shows how he steals a car, unconsciolsy hoping to be caught.
Psychology; Sociology
Dist - MMA **Prod** - MMA 1969

A Recipe for Happy Children 26 MIN
U-matic / VHS
Spoonful of Lovin' Series
Color (H C A)
LC 82-706064
Presents Reynelda Muse explaining how to guide children's behavior and stresses the necessity of having expectations that children can live up to. Shows day - care providers using supervisory skills to create stimulating environments for their charges. No 4 on the Spoonful of lovin' series.
Home Economics; Psychology
Dist - AITECH **Prod** - KRMATV 1981

Recipe for Marriage - Minded Career Women 30 MIN
U-matic / VHS
Color
Studies the problems of working women. Provides data regarding the conflicts which build up between marriage and career. Presents views of researcher Dr Sandra S Tangri, Professor of Psychology, Howard University. From the Syl Watkins television program.
Sociology
Dist - SYLWAT **Prod** - RCOMTV

A Recipe for Results 32 MIN
VHS / U-matic
Color
Shows how managing by objective can ensure organizational direction and improved employee morale.
Business and Economics
Dist - CREMED **Prod** - CREMED

The Recipe Maker 30 MIN
U-matic
Magic Ring I Series
(K P)
Making a sandwich leads to an explanation of the food groups, nutrition, and tours of a market garden, a farmer's market and a food fair.
Education; Literature and Drama
Dist - ACCESS **Prod** - ACCESS 1984

The Reciprocal Function - an Area for Revision 24 MIN
U-matic / VHS / 16mm
Color
Describes weighing shapes cut from the area under the graph of the reciprocal (1 over X) function. Explains that such areas add like logarithms.
Mathematics
Dist - MEDIAG **Prod** - OPENU 1979

Reciprocals - multiplicative inverses 10 MIN
VHS
Children's encyclopedia of mathematics - multiplication and division of fractions series
Color (I)
$49.95 purchase _ #8359
Discusses reciprocals and multiplicative inversions used with fractions. Part of a seven - part series on multiplication and division with fractions.
Mathematics
Dist - AIMS **Prod** - DAVFMS 1991

Reciprocating Air Compressor Operation 60 MIN
VHS / U-matic
Equipment Operation Training Program Series
Color (IND)
Identifies components and describes how an air compression system works. Covers monitoring of oil level and how to perform startup checks.
Education; Industrial and Technical Education; Psychology
Dist - LEIKID **Prod** - ITCORP

Reciprocating Gas Compressors 29 MIN
U-matic / VHS
Color (IND)
Explains compression fundamentals, operating principles and troubleshooting procedures for reciprocating compressors.
Social Science
Dist - UTEXPE **Prod** - UTEXPE 1973

Reciprocating Pump Opening for Inspection 21 MIN
16mm
B&W
LC FIE52-1233
Demonstrates, on a vertical simplex reciprocating pump, the proper procedures, marking of parts, use of standard machinist's tools and safety precautions.
Industrial and Technical Education
Dist - USNAC **Prod** - USN 1943

Recital 20 MIN
16mm
B&W (G)
$40.00 rental
Addresses the state of 'woman in love' from a feminist perspective. Produced by Stephanie Beroes.
Fine Arts; Religion and Philosophy; Sociology
Dist - CANCIN

Reckless 70 MIN
16mm
B&W (G) (FRENCH WITH ENGLISH SUBTITLES)
$120.00 rental
Plays with the Frence 'nouvelle vague' style of the Sixties and gags from Elvis musicals. Tells the story of a French Elvis lookalike who steals a car to go to America and hopes to entice his punk girlfriend in joining him. But she tries to outsmart him, stealing his car and money to head for Germany. Music is rare Fifties rock 'n' roll and rockabilly. A Jackie Leger production.
Fine Arts; Psychology
Dist - CANCIN

Reckless Romeo 10 MIN
16mm
B&W
Presents a Billy Dooley comedy.
Fine Arts
Dist - FCE **Prod** - FCE

The Reckless Years - 1919 - 1929
VHS / U-matic
Color (H)
Demonstrates how corruption, government inaction and a laissez - faire economic policy contributed to the worst depression in the nation's history. Discusses the profound changes that took place during that time.
Business and Economics; History - United States
Dist - GA **Prod** - GA

Reckon with the Wind 28 MIN
16mm / U-matic / VHS
Color
Documents the 1976 Victoria to Maui race on board the sailboat Impossible, captained by mountaineer Jim Whittaker.
Physical Education and Recreation
Dist - OFFSHR **Prod** - OFFSHR 1976

The Reckoning 26 MIN
16mm / VHS / U-matic
Color (G IND)
$5.00 rental
Looks at studies by Dr Harvey Brenner of John Hopkins University which show a correlation between joblessness and an increase in deaths from heart attacks, suicide, liver disease and other stress related illnesses.
Business and Economics; Psychology; Sociology
Dist - AFLCIO **Prod** - GRATV 1980
CANWRL

Reckoning - 1945 and After 52 MIN
U-matic / VHS / 16mm
World at War Series
Color (H C A)
Tells how after the war, world governments attempted to restore civilization. The order of the day included revenge, brutality and displaced and missing persons throughout the world who numbered in the tens of millions in Europe alone.
History - World
Dist - MEDIAG **Prod** - THAMES 1973
USCAN

Reclaimed 11 MIN
16mm
B&W (A)
Portrays the Christian Witness Pavilion of the Seattle World's Fair.
Guidance and Counseling; Religion and Philosophy
Dist - CPH **Prod** - CPH

Reclaiming our past, recreating our future - reflections on the chalice and the blade 90 MIN
VHS / BETA
Innerwork series
Color (G)
$49.95 purchase _ #W035
Features attorney and author Riane Eisler who reveals that humanity shifted from a 'partnership' model of social interaction to a 'dominator' model. Examines societies where women and men treated each other as equals,

fertility goddesses were the focus of worship and creation was valued more than destruction. Unfortified cities existed for milleniums. Burial grounds revealed equality in social roles and distribution of wealth. Suggests that as 'civilization' arose, warfare and male domination became established social institutions.
Social Science; Sociology
Dist - THINKA **Prod** - THINKA

Recognition and Management of Valvular Heart Disease 54 MIN
U-matic
Color (PRO)
LC 76-706099
Discusses mitral stenosis and describes aortic stenosis. Includes signs and symptoms, electrocardiographic features, radiographic features, catheterization and angiocardiography.
Health and Safety
Dist - USNAC **Prod** - WARMP 1969

Recognition and Management of Valvular Heart Disease - Pt 1 27 MIN
U-matic
Color (PRO)
LC 76-706099
Discusses mitral stenosis and describes aortic stenosis. Includes signs and symptoms, electrocardiographic features, radiographic features, catheterization and angiocardiography.
Health and Safety
Dist - USNAC **Prod** - WARMP 1969

Recognition and Management of Valvular Heart Disease - Pt 2 27 MIN
U-matic
Color (PRO)
LC 76-706099
Discusses mitral stenosis and describes aortic stenosis. Includes signs and symptoms, electrocardiographic features, radiographic features, catheterization and angiocardiography.
Health and Safety
Dist - USNAC **Prod** - WARMP 1969

Recognition and Prevention of Bedsores 8 MIN
VHS / U-matic
Color (PRO) (SPANISH)
LC 77-731353
Defines the conditions under which bed sores may develop and describes those persons most susceptible to the development of bed sores. Explains the stages of development of bed sores. Emphasizes the relative ease with which bed sores are prevented and the relative difficulty with which they are cured. Concludes with steps required to prevent the development of bed sores.
Foreign Language; Health and Safety
Dist - MEDCOM **Prod** - MEDCOM

Recognition and Prevention of Child Abuse 18 MIN
VHS / U-matic
Color (PRO)
Details the shared characteristics of abusive parents, the means to follow up the suspicion that abuse has occurred, the way to determine the triad of 'special parents,' 'special child,' and 'stressful home environment' and an effective way to encourage local supports to initiate a community - based child abuse prevention program.
Health and Safety; Sociology
Dist - UMICHM **Prod** - UMICHM 1975

Recognition and Treatment of Arrhythmias 76 MIN
U-matic
Color (PRO)
LC 76-706100
Discusses recognition and treatment of arrhythmias, including chronotropic agents, myocardial depressants, cardioversion and pacemaker therapy. Describes early recognition of the common arrhythmias associated with myocardial infarction, including observations which enable classification of arrhythmias.
Health and Safety
Dist - USNAC **Prod** - WARMP 1968

Recognition and Treatment of Arrhythmias - Pt 1 28 MIN
U-matic
Color (PRO)
LC 76-706100
Discusses recognition and treatment of arrhythmias, including chronotropic agents, myocardial depressants, cardioversion and pacemaker therapy. Describes early recognition of common arrhythmias associated with myocardial infarction, including observations which enable classification of arrhythmias.
Health and Safety
Dist - USNAC **Prod** - WARMP 1968

Recognition and Treatment of Arrhythmias - Pt 2 28 MIN
U-matic
Color (PRO)
LC 76-706100
Discusses recognition and treatment of arrhythmias, including chronotropic agents, myocardial depressants, cardioversion and pacemaker therapy. Describes early recognition of common arrhythmias associated with myocardial infarction, including observations which enable classification of arrhythmias.
Health and Safety
Dist - USNAC **Prod** - WARMP 1968

Recognition and Treatment of Arrhythmias - Pt 3 28 MIN
U-matic
Color (PRO)
LC 76-706100
Discusses recognition and treatment of arrhythmias, including chronotropic agents, myocardial depressants, cardioversion and pacemaker therapy. Describes early recognition of common arrhythmias associated with myocardial infarction, including observations which enable classification of arrhythmias.
Health and Safety
Dist - USNAC **Prod** - WARMP 1968

Recognition of Defects 24 MIN
U-matic / VHS
Supervisor's Role in Food Distribution Series
Color
Explores the realistic application of the federal Food, Drug and Cosmetic Act and the Good Manufacturing Practice regulation. Reviews handling of commodities, storage temperatures, and protection of facility and stock from adulteration.
Industrial and Technical Education; Social Science
Dist - PLAID **Prod** - PLAID

Recognition of Leprosy 13 MIN
16mm
Color (SPANISH)
LC FIE59-254; 74-705490
Illustrates the clinical manifestations of leprosy, using patients from the Public Health Service hospital at Carville, Louisiana. Shows the technique of taking and staining skin scrapings to demonstrate the etiologic agent, Mycobacterium leprae, and the technique of taking skin biopsies to determine pathology of peripheral nerves.
Health and Safety
Dist - USNAC **Prod** - USPHS 1959

The Recognition of Russia - a Climate of Mutual Distrust 26 MIN
U-matic / VHS / 16mm
Between the Wars Series
Color (H C)
Traces the relationship between the United States and Russia from 1917 to 1933. Explains that Cold War attitudes can be linked to this period and the national paranoia over Bolshevism.
Civics and Political Systems; History - United States; History - World
Dist - FI **Prod** - LNDBRG 1978

Recognition of Russia and Latin America - intervention - Volume 5
VHS
Between the wars - 1918 - 1941 series
Color (H C A)
$19.95 purchase
Reviews part of the history of the years between World War I and World War II. Focuses on the roles of Russia and Latin America. Includes segments from newsreels, soundtracks, and archival footage of the period. Hosted and narrated by Eric Severeid.
History - World
Dist - PBS **Prod** - WNETTV

Recognition of the sources of stress 60 MIN
VHS
Stress and the caregiver - Are we driving each other mad - series
Color (R G)
$49.95 purchase _ #SCGR2
Reveals that stress in the lives of Americans is causing immense suffering in the form of painful emotional and physical disease. Discloses that most stress is borne unnecessarily and can be prevented if one is willing to gain some self - knowledge and make changes in attitudes, beliefs and approaches to life. Presents the principles of emotional, physical and mental health that can be applied to daily situations. Features Father James Gill, MD, SJ, who examines ways of distinguishing the painful and disturbing emotions of anger, resentment, loss, anxiety and fear and replacing them with a healthy and energizing way of life. Part of four parts.
Guidance and Counseling; Health and Safety; Psychology; Religion and Philosophy
Dist - CTNA **Prod** - CTNA

Recognizing a Failure Identity 30 MIN
VHS / U-matic
Developing Discipline Series
Color (T)
Tells how to become aware of negative addictive behaviors in our self and others.
Education; Guidance and Counseling; Psychology; Sociology
Dist - GPN **Prod** - SDPT 1983

Recognizing and managing forest soil compaction problems 15 MIN
VHS / U-matic / Slide
Color (H C A)
$130.00 purchase, $25.00 rental _ #823
Discusses causes of forest soil compaction. Describes the effects of compaction on productivity. Introduces management alternatives for reducing compaction problems. Reviewed in 1985 and determined to contain appropriate and timely material.
Agriculture; Geography - United States; Industrial and Technical Education; Science - Natural; Social Science
Dist - OSUSF **Prod** - OSUSF 1981

Recognizing and Reacting 22 MIN
U-matic / VHS
Food Plant Supervisor - Understanding and Performing Inplant Food 'Safety Inspection Series
Color
Assists the supervisor with applied knowledge in the trained observation of food plant problems, emphasizing the coupling of seemingly unrelated problems to arrive at common sense corrections which save in terms of cost of repairs and down time.
Agriculture; Health and Safety; Industrial and Technical Education; Social Science
Dist - PLAID **Prod** - PLAID

Recognizing and Solving Capacity Problems 60 MIN
BETA / VHS
Manufacturing Series
(IND)
Distinguishes between priority and capacity planning. Describes the importance of long range planning and the significance of unbalanced queues.
Business and Economics
Dist - COMSRV **Prod** - COMSRV 1986

Recognizing chemical hazards 10 MIN
VHS / U-matic / BETA
Color (IND G A)
$548.00 purchase, $125.00 rental _ #REC040
Explains how to identify chemicals and their hazards. Shows how they should be handled, used or stored, and how to prevent exposure and respond to medical emergencies. Looks at cleanup after a spill. Educates employees without a chemistry background on the use of Material Safety Data Sheets - MSDS.
Health and Safety; Psychology
Dist - ITF **Prod** - ERF

Recognizing Common Communicable Diseases
VHS / U-matic
Color (PRO)
Helps the viewer gain skill and confidence in recognizing common communicable diseases of children. Focuses on the differentiation between measles, rubella, chickenpox, smallpox and scarlet fever.
Health and Safety
Dist - UMICHM **Prod** - UMICHM 1976

Recognizing, Confronting, and Helping the Alcoholic 40 MIN
VHS / U-matic
Color (PRO)
Acquaints users with principles of diagnosing and confronting the alcoholic. Excerpts the interview session and demonstrates the four CAGE questions to determine the alcoholic condition.
Health and Safety; Psychology; Sociology
Dist - HSCIC **Prod** - HSCIC 1982

Recognizing, containing and eliminating gangs - strategies for educators 40 MIN
VHS
Color (T PRO C A)
$94.95 purchase _ #RB8133
Presents an in - depth panel discussion on gangs led by Mara Tapp of National Public Radio. Offers common sense suggestions on what to do when encountering gang activities in communities.
Social Science; Sociology
Dist - REVID **Prod** - REVID 1993

Recognizing drug seeking behavior - an interview with Henry Douglas Matthews 20 MIN
U-matic / VHS

Color (PRO C)
$395.00 purchase, $80.00 rental _ #C891 - VI - 021
Introduces physicians, dentists and other health professionals who prescribe medicine to common drug seeking behavior patterns. Interviews a former 'professional patient' and addict to highlight the basic repertoire of techniques used to manipulate physicians into prescribing narcotics and other controlled substances. Provides recommendations for appropriate physician responses. Presented by Dr Charles Druckett.
Guidance and Counseling; Health and Safety; Psychology
Dist - HSCIC

Recognizing Food Spoilage 15 MIN
U-matic / 16mm
Food Service Employee Series
Color (IND)
LC 79-707353
Points out factors that indicate food spoilage and shows ways to prevent possible food poisoning.
Health and Safety; Science - Natural
Dist - COPI **Prod** - COPI 1969

Recognizing hazards 20 MIN
VHS
Hazmat emergency series
Color (IND PRO)
$265.00 purchase
Presents one of three videos in the Hazmat Emergency series. Teaches how to recognize the presence of dangerous substances and how to assess the hazards involved. Viewers learn how toxic materials can burn and how to use basic information - gathering techniques including DOT placards and labels, MSDS, shipping papers and witnesses. Information on CHEMTREC and other helpful resources provided.
Health and Safety
Dist - JEWELR

Recognizing intervals 29 MIN
U-matic
Beginning piano - an adult approach series; Lesson 11
Color (H A)
Introduces D - major scale and principal dynamic indication in music notation. Presents intervals of the sixth to the tenth.
Fine Arts
Dist - CDTEL **Prod** - COAST

Recognizing radiographic artifacts
Videodisc
Color (PRO C)
$1300.00 purchase _ #C900 - IV - 022
Allows users to view many X - rays which have unwanted features on them. Teaches how to recognize the artifacts on these X - rays. Offers a high level of individualized and self - paced practice opportunities and encourages the development of complex discrimination skills. Requires an IBM InfoWindow Touch Display Monitor, a 20MB hard disk and a Pioneer LD - V6000 videodisc player or equivalent. Contact distributor for other requirements.
Health and Safety
Dist - HSCIC

Recognizing the Obvious 25 MIN
U-matic / VHS
Computers in Control Series
Color (H C A)
Discusses the systems approach to a complex problem and the kind of sophisticated software which can be introduced in the more advanced systems. Concludes with a look at the future of robotics.
Industrial and Technical Education; Mathematics; Psychology
Dist - FI **Prod** - BBCTV 1984

Recognizing values - Part 2 21 MIN
VHS
Straight talk on teams series
Color (PRO IND A)
$450.00 purchase, $95.00 rental _ #BBP132B
Presents part two of a four - part series. Uses the expertise of Allan Cox to enable managers to take an in - depth look at team building. Includes a leader's guide and workbook.
Business and Economics; Guidance and Counseling; Psychology
Dist - EXTR **Prod** - BBP

Recollection 7 MIN
16mm
Color (G)
$20.00 rental
Explores death, birth and timelessness. Features storytelling by the filmmaker's grandparents, which is heard as a series of images poetically repeating and weaving through the narration and ambient sounds. A Dana Plays production.
Fine Arts; Sociology
Dist - CANCIN

Recommendations for a more Rational Use of Antipsychotic Drugs - Overview to the Series 5 MIN
U-matic
Recommendations for a more Rational Use of Antipsychotic Drugs 'Series
Color (PRO)
LC 80-706126
Emphasizes the importance of the sensible use of antipsychotic drugs, stating that physicians should reexamine their drug administration practices.
Health and Safety; Psychology
Dist - USNAC **Prod** - VAHSL 1979

Recommendations for a more rational use of antipsychotic drugs series
Antipsychotics and acute psychosis 20 MIN
Recommendations for a more Rational Use of Antipsychotic Drugs - Overview to the Series 5 MIN
Dist - USNAC

Reconciliation and Justice 30 MIN
16mm
Color (R)
Explores life in Zaire, the heartland of Africa, and the home of the largest independent African church, the Kimbanguist. Discusses the problems of ecumenism, tribal unity and Africanization.
Geography - World; Religion and Philosophy; Sociology
Dist - CCNCC **Prod** - CBSTV

Reconciliation in Zimbabwe 34 MIN
VHS
Color (G)
$250.00 purchase, $55.00 rental
Offers a historical overview of Zanu leader Robvert Mugabe and the newly independent nation of Zimbabwe, which emerged after 15 years of guerilla struggle against the white - ruled government of Rhodesia. Examines the first ten years and focuses on relations between the white minority and black majority citizens.
Civics and Political Systems; Fine Arts; History - World; Sociology
Dist - CNEMAG **Prod** - KAPM 1990

Reconciliatory need and the hope and healing - Volume 6 60 MIN
VHS
Divorce - from pain to hope series
Color (G A R)
$24.95 purchase, $10.00 rental _ #35 - 861158 - 1
Presents strategies for reconciliation after divorce. Covers the consequences of continued alienation.
Psychology; Sociology
Dist - APH **Prod** - ABINGP

Reconditioning a Cultivator 14 MIN
16mm
Farm Work Series
B&W
LC FIE52-326
Demonstrates replacement of a worn wheel boring. Explains how to adjust the yoke, check and adjust the shovels, check and lubricate the gang expansion and steering assemblies and lubricate all parts of a cultivator.
Industrial and Technical Education
Dist - USNAC **Prod** - USOE 1944

Reconditioning a Cylinder with a Portable Boring Bar 36 MIN
16mm
B&W
LC FIE52-1213
Traces a typical boring job to illustrate various checks, adjustments and alignments required to operate the boring bar. Covers types, uses, nomenclature, set - up and operation of the portable bar while demonstrating the reconditioning of a cylinder.
Industrial and Technical Education
Dist - USNAC **Prod** - USN 1944

Reconditioning a Grain Drill 31 MIN
16mm
B&W (H C A) (FRENCH)
Tells how to inspect and repair a typical grain drill, clean and lubricate the fertilizer and seeding mechanism, repair the disc furrow openers, drive chains, assemble a pawl and calibrate the seeding mechanism.
Agriculture; Foreign Language
Dist - USNAC **Prod** - USOE 1943

Reconditioning a Grain Drill 31 MIN
16mm
Farm Work Series Equipment Maintenance, no 4; No 4
B&W
LC FIE52-359
Shows how to inspect, repair and recondition a typical grain drill.
Agriculture
Dist - USNAC **Prod** - USOE 1943

Reconditioning a Mower, Pt 1 - Cutter Bar 21 MIN
16mm
Farm Work Series Equipment Maintenance, no 1; No 1
B&W
LC FIE52-324
Shows how to recondition, check and repair the cutter bar mechanism.
Agriculture
Dist - USNAC **Prod** - USOE 1943

Reconditioning a Mower, Pt 2 - Drive System 21 MIN
16mm
Farm Work Series Equipment Maintenance, no 2; No 2
B&W
LC FIE52-325
Shows how to clean, inspect and lubricate a reconditioned mower.
Agriculture
Dist - USNAC **Prod** - USOE 1943

Reconditioning the Fuel Pump 17 MIN
16mm
B&W
LC FIE52-1364
Shows how to install seal assembly, diaphragm, copper seal gasket, shim, setting bar and spacer in the fuel pump.
Industrial and Technical Education
Dist - USNAC **Prod** - USN 1945

Reconductoring or Upgrading Voltage
U-matic / VHS
Live Line Maintenance Series
Color (IND)
Demonstrates procedures for grounding an overhead disbtribution line on a tangent structure, a vertical running corner, and a vertical deadend.
Industrial and Technical Education
Dist - LEIKID **Prod** - LEIKID

Reconnaissance pilot 35 MIN
VHS / U-matic
B&W
Features William Holden as a P - 38 Lightning reconnaissance pilot in the South Pacific in 1942.
Civics and Political Systems; History - United States; Industrial and Technical Education
Dist - IHF **Prod** - IHF

Reconnective Surgery 20 MIN
16mm
Color
LC 83-700096
Discusses reconnective surgery. Describes the achievements of Dr Chen Chung Wei of China in reconstructing usable limbs after accidents and the work of Dr Ralph Mankeltow of Toronto General Hospital who performs intricate microsurgery. Presents a young man who has regained the use of his damaged hand telling about the dramatic change in his life since the surgery.
Health and Safety
Dist - FLMLIB **Prod** - CANBC

Reconsiderations 60 MIN
VHS
Americans, too - black experiences in rural America series
Color (J H C G)
$70.00 purchase, $12.50 rental _ #61561
Interviews subjects from two programs in the 'Americans, too' series who join producers to discuss their views on the series and what has happened since the documentaries were made. Includes a team of experts who also voice their views. Part of a six - part series visiting widely scattered geographic areas of Pennsylvania to interview and understand the rural black community.
Geography - United States; History - United States
Dist - PSU **Prod** - OCONEL 1992

Reconstructing the Nation - the Crucial Years 29 MIN
Videoreel / VT2
Black Experience Series 20024
Color
History - United States
Dist - PBS **Prod** - WTTWTV

Reconstructing the south 30 MIN
VHS
American adventure series
Color (G)
$150.00 purchase _ #TAMA - 125
Examines the early years of Reconstruction. Reviews Andrew Johnson's efforts to reunite the nation. Discusses the significance of the thirteenth, fourteenth and fifteenth amendments to the Constitution.
History - United States
Dist - PBS

Reconstruction 30 MIN
VHS / U-matic
American story - the beginning to 1877 series
Color (C)
History - United States
Dist - DALCCD **Prod** - DALCCD

Reconstruction of Early Ballet Repertory 30 MIN
U-matic / VHS
Passing on Dance Series
Color
Fine Arts; Industrial and Technical Education
Dist - ARCVID **Prod** - ARCVID

The Reconstruction of space 20 MIN
VHS
Center for Humanities seminars in modern art series
Color (J H)
$99.00 purchase _ #002642 - 026
Highlights a major category of modern art - Cubism. Traces the influence of Cezanne on Picasso and Braque. Looks at Cubism's emphasis on formal, geometric harmony that continues to have a profound effect on the present - day world. Part of a four - part series. Includes teacher's guide and library kit.
Education; Fine Arts
Dist - GA

Reconstruction of the Breast After Mastectomy 27 MIN
U-matic
Color
Discusses the advances made in breast reconstruction. Looks at the different methods of reconstruction after mastectomy.
Health and Safety
Dist - UTEXSC **Prod** - UTEXSC

Reconstruction of the Cervical Esophagus 25 MIN
16mm
Color (PRO)
Presents a technique of total excision of the laryngo - esophageal complex, with or without radical neck dissection and thyroidectomy, with a staged reconstruction as the most satisfactory method of obtaining significant cure rate and maintaining adequate patency.
Health and Safety; Science
Dist - ACY **Prod** - ACYDGD 1967

Reconstruction of the Common Bile Duct 26 MIN
16mm
Color (PRO)
Explains that if the two ends of the common bile duct can be found, an end - to - end anastomosis should be performed. Shows the techniques for two or three different types of anastomoses.
Health and Safety; Science
Dist - ACY **Prod** - ACYDGD 1965

Reconstruction of the Thumb 30 MIN
16mm
Cine Clinic Series
Color (PRO)
Illustrates transplantation of an index finger and utilization of a vestigial thumb to reconstruct the first web.
Health and Safety; Science
Dist - NMAC **Prod** - ACYDGD 1970

Reconstruction Techniques Related to Cancer - Breast Reconstruction 12 MIN
VHS / U-matic / BETA
(PRO)
Demonstrates one method of breast reconstruction and includes views of the patient before reconstruction, intraoperative views, and postoperative pictures.
Health and Safety
Dist - UTXAH **Prod** - UTXAH 1984

Reconstruction Techniques Related to Cancer - Chest - Wall Reconstruction 9 MIN
VHS / U-matic / BETA
(PRO)
Demonstrates one method of chest - wall reconstruction which involves chest resection and the inset of a contralateral rectus abdominus musculocutaneous flap to cover the defect.
Health and Safety
Dist - UTXAH **Prod** - UTXAH 1984

Reconstructive surgery 45 MIN
VHS
Surgical procedures series
Color (C PRO G)
$149.00 purchase, $75.00 rental _ #UW4576
Focuses on Maria, born with only a pinkie and four stubs on her left hand. Watches as Dr David Chiu - Columbia - Presbyterian Medical Ctr, NYC - performs an 8 - hour operation on the 14 - month - old patient to transplant the second toe of her left foot to her ring finger nub, connecting bones, veins and arteries to create a single but complete digit. The transplanted toe will look like a toe but have superior sensitivity because the brain will send messages to it as if it were a finger. Part of a 17 - part series recording surgical procedures in detail, with specialists who explain the ailment, the anatomical function of the part of the body being operated on, and how successful surgery might improve the patient's quality of life. Hosted by Dr Donna Willis.
Health and Safety
Dist - FOTH

The Record Business - not Just for the Big Guys 30 MIN
VHS / 16mm
(PRO G)
$89.95 purchase _ #DGP2
Explains the ins and outs of the recording business from the point of view of the owner and producer of a small recording company, Stephen Powers and Ben Sidran. Hosted by Dick Goldberg.
Business and Economics
Dist - RMIBHF **Prod** - RMIBHF

The Record of a tenement gentleman 72 MIN
16mm
B&W (JAPANESE)
Deals with the relationship between an aging woman and an abandoned child. Tells of the difficulties of their life together, the hostility of the woman and the exasperating ungratefulness of the child.
Fine Arts; Sociology
Dist - NYFLMS **Prod** - NYFLMS 1947

Record of orogeny 11 MIN
VHS
History in the rocks series
Color (H C)
$24.95 purchase _ #S9816
Discusses the process of interpreting rock history using single - concept format. Part of a ten - part series on rocks.
Science - Physical
Dist - HUBDSC **Prod** - HUBDSC

The Record of the Rocks 20 MIN
VHS / U-matic
Evolution Series
Color
Discusses determining the age of rocks and how to evaluate the results, Miller's experiment simulating the conditions of early Earth and ascending the layers of sedimentary rock in the Grand Canyon.
Science - Natural; Science - Physical
Dist - FOTH **Prod** - FOTH 1984

Record passage to Mobay - Jamaica's blue water challenge 60 MIN
VHS
Color (G)
$29.95 purchase _ #YS - 10
Features a retrospective of the 810 - mile Miami to Montego Bay Race from 1961 through 1980 centering on the racer Windward Passage, a 73 - foot Maxi which set the record in 1971. Includes racing scenes aboard the racer described by author, sailor and photographer Ted Jones.
Geography - World; Literature and Drama; Physical Education and Recreation
Dist - MYSTIC **Prod** - MYSTIC
SEVVID

The Record Ride for the Pony Express 22 MIN
U-matic / VHS / 16mm
You are There Series
Color (I J H)
LC 72-700120
Shows how hostile Indians, the refusal of a relief rider to take his turn and other emergencies do not keep Bob Haslam, one of the teen - age Pony Express riders, from riding 380 miles in 36 hours - a record ride for the Pony Express.
History - United States; Social Science
Dist - PHENIX **Prod** - CBSTV 1972

A Record Show 30 MIN
U-matic / VHS
Musical Encounter Series
Color (P I)
Presents young performers Ocie Davis and Robert Chen, who show that there are two sides to a record and that music is music whether it be rock, country, gospel, jazz or classical. Features violinist Nina Bodnar, winner of the Jacques Thibaud prize. Hosted by Florence Henderson.
Fine Arts
Dist - GPN **Prod** - KLCSTV 1983

Record structures 30 MIN
VHS / U-matic
Pascal, pt 2 - intermediate pascal series
Color (H C A)
LC 81-706049
Introduces the record data structure. Describes variables of record type as well as record types. Includes examples of code segments using records. Concludes with description of with statement.
Industrial and Technical Education; Mathematics; Sociology
Dist - COLOSU **Prod** - COLOSU 1980

Recorded Live 8 MIN
16mm / U-matic / VHS
Color (J)
LC 76-700414
Uses animation to show how a young man on a job interview at a television station is abruptly attacked by a huge, mobile mound of videotape, which pursues him, traps him and ultimately assimilates him.
Fine Arts
Dist - PFP **Prod** - USC 1978

Recorders 60 MIN
VHS
Fundamentals of instrumentation and control series
Color (PRO)
$600.00 - $1500.00 purchase _ #ICREC
Covers the construction and operation of typical circular chart and strip chart recorders. Shows the variety of designs and types of available recorders, types of input, print and chart drive sections and recorder printers. Part of a nineteen - part series on the fundamentals of instrumentation and control, which is part of a 49 - unit set on instrumentation and control. Includes five workbooks and an instructor guide to support four hours of instruction.
Education; Industrial and Technical Education; Mathematics; Psychology
Dist - NUSTC **Prod** - NUSTC

Recorders
U-matic / 16mm
Instrumentation Maintenance Series
Color (IND)
Covers drive and balance motors and multipoint, strip and circular recorders.
Mathematics
Dist - ISA **Prod** - ISA

Recording and Measuring Lengths 15 MIN
U-matic / VHS
Hands on, Grade 3 Series Unit 2 - Measuring; Unit 2 - Measuring
Color (P)
Mathematics; Science; Science - Physical
Dist - AITECH **Prod** - VAOG 1975

Recording Centric Relation, Graphic Methods, Pt 1, Intraoral Tracer 14 MIN
16mm / U-matic / VHS
Recording Centric Relation, Graphic Methods Series
Color (PRO)
Details the clinical use of an intraoral tracing device for recording centric relations during the fabrication of complete dentures. Demonstrates the fabrication of accurate stable record bases.
Health and Safety; Mathematics; Science
Dist - USNAC **Prod** - VADTC

Recording Centric Relation, Graphic Methods, Pt 2, Extraoral Tracer 10 MIN
U-matic / VHS / 16mm
Recording Centric Relation, Graphic Methods Series
Color (PRO)
Details the clinical use of the extraoral tracing device for recording centric relation during the fabrication of complete dentures. Compares intraoral and extraoral tracing devices.
Health and Safety; Mathematics; Science
Dist - USNAC **Prod** - VADTC

Recording Centric Relation, Graphic Methods Series
Recording Centric Relation, Graphic Methods, Pt 1, Intraoral Tracer 14 MIN
Recording Centric Relation, Graphic Methods, Pt 2, Extraoral Tracer 10 MIN
Dist - USNAC

Recording edentulous ridge contour - correctable wax impressions 16 MIN
16mm
Color (PRO)
LC 74-706517
Demonstrates the methodology for fluid wax impressions on edentulous ridges in distal extension removable partial dentures. Shows how this procedure enhances stability and retention of the prosthesis and reduces stress on the remaining teeth.
Health and Safety; Science
Dist - USNAC **Prod** - USVA 1969

The Recording Industry 30 MIN
U-matic / VHS
From Jumpstreet Series
Color (J H)
Looks at the influence Black artists have had on the recording industry by focusing on the contributions of George Benson and Quincy Jones.
Fine Arts; History - United States; Sociology
Dist - GPN **Prod** - WETATV 1979

Recording Observations 14 MIN
VHS / U-matic
Hands on, Grade 1 Series Unit 1 - Observing; Unit 1 - Observing
Color (P)
Science; Science - Natural; Science - Physical
Dist - AITECH **Prod** - VAOG 1975

Records 30 MIN
U-matic
Today's special series
Color (K P)
Develops language arts skills in children. Programs are thematically designed around subjects of interest to youngsters. Action takes place in a department store where people, mannequins, puppets, comic characters and special guests present a lighthearted approach to language arts.
Fine Arts; Literature and Drama; Psychology
Dist - TVOTAR **Prod** - TVOTAR 1985

Records in the Rocks 29 MIN
Videoreel / VT2
Observing Eye Series
Color
Science - Physical; Sociology
Dist - PBS **Prod** - WGBHTV

Records, Information and Micrographics Management 56 MIN
U-matic
Color (PRO)
Defines records and information management and how to organize these departments. Also describes how to develop and market cost and benefit analysis of records programs.
Business and Economics
Dist - CAPVID **Prod** - CAPVID 1985

Recourse for the Consumer 18 MIN
U-matic / VHS / 16mm
Color (J H)
LC 81-701387
Shows available alternatives when purchased merchandise proves to be defective.
Guidance and Counseling; Home Economics
Dist - CORF **Prod** - CENTRO 1981

Recovering from a heart attack 14 MIN
VHS
Color; CC (G C PRO)
$175.00 purchase _ #HA - 33
Explains what causes a heart attack and answers patients' most pressing questions about recovery. Describes what to expect during the hospital stay, including possible tests and procedures. Contact distributor for special purchase price on multiple orders.
Health and Safety
Dist - MIFE **Prod** - MIFE 1995

Recovering our kids from drugs and alcohol 46 MIN
VHS
Over the influence series
Color (J H C A)
$95.00 purchase
Highlights programs available that help children and teens recover from alcohol and drug abuse. Part of a two - part series.
Guidance and Counseling; Health and Safety; Psychology
Dist - PFP **Prod** - ASHAP

Recovering the Soul
VHS / Cassette
(G)
$29.95, $9.95 purchase
Presents an exploration at the crossroads of mysticism, healing, religion and physics.
Health and Safety; Psychology; Religion and Philosophy; Science - Physical
Dist - BKPEOP **Prod** - MFV

Recovery After Mastectomy 16 MIN
16mm
Color
Shows a Reach To Recovery volunteer visiting hospitalized mastectomy patients. Explains her role in helping patients to recuperate and demonstrates Reach To Recovery exercises.
Health and Safety
Dist - AMCS **Prod** - AMCS 1971

Recovery and human physiology - alcohol 15 MIN
VHS
Color (H C G)
$295.00 purchase, $100.00 rental _ #8387
Explains to recovering alcoholics some of the physical and mental symptoms they may experience as they withdraw from alcohol.
Guidance and Counseling; Health and Safety; Psychology
Dist - AIMS **Prod** - AIMS 1992

Recovery and human physiology - drug abuse 18 MIN
VHS
Color (H C G)
$345.00 purchase, $100.00 rental _ #8388
Tells recovering drug abusers what to expect. Details the physical and mental aspects of recovery from drugs which are snorted, smoked, injected or swallowed.
Guidance and Counseling; Psychology
Dist - AIMS **Prod** - AIMS 1991

Recovery and prevention of relapse 21 MIN
BETA / VHS / U-matic
Substance abuse assessment and intervention series
Color (G C PRO)
$280.00 purchase _ #805.4
Reveals that certain behaviors promote recovery while other behaviors and risk factors increase the chance of relapse. Demonstrates counseling techniques for helping a client recognize and circumvent negative patterns. Reviews the challenges of avoiding relapse and illustrates how a client can be helped to return to recovery. Part of a four - part series on assessment and intervention in substance abuse produced by M and M Productions.
Guidance and Counseling; Health and Safety; Psychology
Dist - CONMED

Recovery and the family
VHS
(G)
$250.00, $10.00 purchase
Encourages each family member to work at personal recovery from the effects of alcoholism as the first step towards family interaction and wellness.
Guidance and Counseling; Health and Safety; Sociology
Dist - KELLYP **Prod** - KELLYP

Recovery Boiler Operation
VHS / U-matic
Pulp and Paper Training, Module 2 - Chemical Recovery Series
Color (IND)
Includes startup and operation, operating problems and emergencies and safety procedures of recovery boiler operation.
Business and Economics; Health and Safety; Industrial and Technical Education; Science - Physical; Social Science
Dist - LEIKID **Prod** - LEIKID

Recovery Boiler Operations 60 MIN
VHS
Systems Operations Series
Color (PRO)
$600.00 - $1500.00 purchase _ #PKRBO
Describes the function of recovery boilers in the Kraft process and the function and operation of major boiler systems such as black liquor and auxiliary fuel systems. Outlines startup, operating and shutdown procedures for a typical recovery boiler in addition to emergency procedures for flameouts, blackouts and water tube leaks. Includes ten textbooks and an instructor guide to support four hours of instruction.
Education; Health and Safety; Industrial and Technical Education; Psychology
Dist - NUSTC **Prod** - NUSTC

Recovery boiler - Pt 1
U-matic / VHS
Pulp and paper training, module 2 - chemical recovery series
Color (IND)
Includes boiler construction, auxiliary fuel, air/gas flowpath and precipitator.
Business and Economics; Industrial and Technical Education; Science - Physical; Social Science
Dist - LEIKID **Prod** - LEIKID

Recovery boiler - Pt 2
U-matic / VHS
Pulp and paper training, module 2 - chemical recovery series
Color (IND)
Covers sootblowers, water and steam flowpath, steam and drum, and desuperheater.
Business and Economics; Industrial and Technical Education; Science - Physical; Social Science
Dist - LEIKID **Prod** - LEIKID

Recovery from a heart attack 16 MIN
VHS / U-matic
Color
LC 77-730434
Presents a typical recovery from a heart attack, beginning in the hospital and concluding six months afterward. Shows what one's own recovery will involve and why, and that recovery will take time, patience and restraint but, more importantly, that the patient can recover and return to a normal life.
Health and Safety; Science - Natural
Dist - MEDCOM **Prod** - MEDCOM

Recovery from Cocaine Addiction - the Message of Hope 24 MIN
VHS / 16mm
Color (J H A PRO)
$395.00 purchase, $75.00 rental _ #9972
Describes the six stages of recovery from cocaine addiction ranging from pre - detox to maintenance. Emphasizes the importance of support groups and twelve - step recovery programs. Discusses symptoms of relapse.
Guidance and Counseling; Psychology; Sociology
Dist - AIMS **Prod** - ADHAD 1988

Recovery from major disasters
U-matic / VHS
Electric power system operation series; Tape 19
Color (IND)
Includes sectionalization, cold load pick - up, resynchronization of islands, black start, operator co-ordination and frequency voltage control.
Health and Safety; Industrial and Technical Education
Dist - LEIKID **Prod** - LEIKID

The Recovery Process
U-matic / VHS
Pulp and Paper Training, Module 2 - Chemical Recovery Series
Color (IND)
Covers making pulp, black liquor, recovery boiler and smelt recovery.
Business and Economics; Industrial and Technical Education; Science - Physical; Social Science
Dist - LEIKID **Prod** - LEIKID

Recovery Room Care 22 MIN
U-matic / VHS
Anesthesiology Clerkship Series
Color (PRO)
Indicates a rationale for development of the recovery room. Identifies patients needing recovery room care. Discusses cardiorespiratory problems. Considers differential diagnosis of the anxious or restless recovery room patient, with special emphasis on postanesthetic pain relief.
Health and Safety
Dist - UMICHM **Prod** - UMICHM 1982

Recovery roulette - Can you gamble with drugs 22 MIN
VHS
Color (J H G)
$295.00 purchase
Reveals that a seemingly harmless cough syrup, tranquilizer or sleeping pill can lead to relapse. Discloses that people in recovery need to know that, for them, any mood - altering chemical is likely to create a new addiction or lead back to the old one. Uses humor in an animated film about visitors from a distant galaxy discovering and studying the disease of chemical dependency.
Guidance and Counseling; Psychology
Dist - FMSP

The Recovery Series - Complete Series - 55 MIN
VHS / 16mm
Recovery Series
(G)
$150/3 Day VHS/3/4
Presents the stories of five women who are recovering from their addictions to drugs and alcohol, showing how each has dealt with the recovery process in her own way. Four tapes include Debby and Sharon, Lorri, Delia, and Ruth.
Health and Safety; Psychology; Sociology
Dist - BAXMED **Prod** - NFBC 1989

Recovery Series
Debby and Sharon 15 MIN
Delia 12 MIN
Lorri 14 MIN
The Recovery Series - Complete Series - 55 MIN
Ruth 14 MIN
Dist - BAXMED

Recovery starts with us 32 MIN
VHS
Color (C PRO G)
$195.00 purchase
Uses dramatic portrayals to illustrate eight diagnostic situations in drug abuse treatment. Focuses on a different part0144410 of the assessment process in each interview. Helps to improve evaluation and treatment skills of staff - workers and counselors.

Guidance and Counseling; Psychology
Dist - FMSP

Recreating the Earliest Modern Dance 30 MIN
VHS / U-matic
Passing on Dance Series
Color
Fine Arts; Industrial and Technical Education
Dist - ARCVID **Prod** - ARCVID

Recreation 15 MIN
VHS / U-matic / 16mm / BETA
Your town II series
Color (K P)
$245.00, $68.00 purchase _ #C50741, #C51493
Joins citizens of all ages enjoying their leisure time at facilities maintained by their community's department of recreation. Shows that, no matter the season, these departments provide recreational opportunities for people to pursue their favorite pastimes. Looks at the organization of team sports and other indoor and outdoor activities. Part of a five - part series on community services.
Physical Education and Recreation; Social Science; Sociology
Dist - NGS **Prod** - NGS 1992

Recreation 2 MIN
16mm
Color (C)
$129.00
Presents an experimental film by Robert Breer.
Fine Arts
Dist - AFA **Prod** - AFA 1956

Recreation - Hospitality - Tourism 6 MIN
16mm / U-matic / VHS
Kingdom of Could be You Series
Color (K P I)
Guidance and Counseling
Dist - EBEC **Prod** - EBEC 1974

Recreation in Modern China 7 MIN
VHS / 35mm strip / U-matic
Modern China Series
Color; Sound
$25 each color sound filmstrip, $115 filmstrip series, $115 five
Explores the changes taking place in China. Focuses on how the Chinese people spend their leisure time. Includes camel races, wrestlers, sports, fishing, boating, visiting historical sites and parks, and Tai Chi Chuan, the performance of patterned body movements.
Geography - World; History - World; Social Science; Sociology
Dist - IFB

Recreation Leadership 23 MIN
16mm
B&W
LC FIE55-26
Portrays the procedures used by an army captain in developing a recreational program for a newly formed company.
Civics and Political Systems; Physical Education and Recreation; Psychology
Dist - USNAC **Prod** - USA 1953

Recreation - the Japanese Way 30 MIN
16mm
Color
Depicts the various recreational activities enjoyed by the Japanese including sumo wrestling, the Kabuki theatre and cherry blossom viewing.
Geography - World; Physical Education and Recreation
Dist - MTP **Prod** - MTP

Recreation therapy - developing a treatment plan 22 MIN
VHS
Color (C PRO G)
$395.00 purchase _ #R861 - VI - 040
Shows a 55 - year - old alcoholic working with a recreation therapist after being admitted to a VA medical center. Shows recreation therapy as a vital part of alcohol rehabilitation.
Guidance and Counseling; Health and Safety
Dist - HSCIC **Prod** - USVA 1986

Recreational and occupational therapy 13 MIN
16mm
B&W
LC FIE52-333
Points out recreational and occupational activities fitted to the patient's condition -- passive diversion during an immobile state, limited physical activities carried on in bed, individualized occupational therapy and social recreation projects.
Health and Safety; Psychology
Dist - USNAC **Prod** - USOE 1945

Recreational Development of Your Community Waterfront 30 MIN
VHS
Color (C A)
$45.00 purchase
Documents the re - development of three waterfront communities of New York's Lake Ontario coast and summarizes the key elements necessary for waterfront development projects to occur.
Geography - United States; Science - Natural; Social Science
Dist - CORNRS **Prod** - CORNRS 1988

Recreational Safety 20 MIN
16mm / VHS
Color (J H A)
$395.00, $450.00 purchase, $75.00 rental _ #9959
Teaches important safety rules for weekend trips and vacations.
Health and Safety; Physical Education and Recreation
Dist - AIMS **Prod** - SANDE 1988

Recruiting and Developing the D P Professional Series
The Decision to build or buy systems talent 30 MIN
The Interview Process 30 MIN
The Mark of the D P Professional 30 MIN
Recruiting and Hiring 30 MIN
Staff Development 30 MIN
Dist - DELTAK

Recruiting and Hiring 30 MIN
U-matic / VHS
Recruiting and Developing the D P Professional Series
Color
Business and Economics; Guidance and Counseling; Psychology
Dist - DELTAK **Prod** - DELTAK

Recruiting Life at Sea 20 MIN
16mm
Color (H C)
LC 77-703235
Depicts the life of men aboard ships, including their living quarters, chow call, recreation, medical care, religious services, military activities and drills.
Civics and Political Systems; Social Science
Dist - USNAC **Prod** - USN 1948

Recruiting - search and interviewing techniques 60 MIN
U-matic / VHS
Dynamics of sales management series; Session 6
Color
Discusses the use of selection effectiveness when expanding or replacing members of a sales force in order to lessen the training time needed in the future. Clarifies the 'can - do' versus the'will - do' components of the job matching. Includes cost of open territories, sales personnel planning, recruiting sources and how to avoid the ten biggest mistakes of interviewing.
Business and Economics; Psychology
Dist - PRODEV **Prod** - PRODEV

Recruiting Step by Step 13 MIN
16mm
Color
Demonstrates the six key steps for recruiting volunteers, and the benefits they gain by working with Girl Scout troops.
Social Science
Dist - GSUSA **Prod** - GSUSA 1980

Recruiting Talented People, J Kenneth Lund
U-matic / VHS
Management Skills Series
Color (PRO)
Business and Economics; Psychology
Dist - AMCEE **Prod** - AMCEE

Recruiting, training, and rewarding volunteers series
Identifies community sources for Expanded Food and Nutrition Education Program (EFNEP) volunteers. Discusses matching volunteer skills to jobs and providing positive and negative performance related feedback to volunteers and gives suggestions for recognizing good volunteer performance.
Recruiting, training, and rewarding volunteers series 33 MIN
Dist - UWISCA **Prod** - UEUWIS

Recruitment and Retention 30 MIN
U-matic / VHS
Basic Education - Teaching the Adult Series
Color (T)
Explains how to recruit and retain adult basic education students.
Education
Dist - MDCPB **Prod** - MDDE

Recruitment interviewing across cultures 40 MIN
VHS
Mosaic series
Color (A)
PdS50 purchase
Draws would-be interviewers' attention to differences in perception between different cultural groups. Films real life interviews to illustrate how people from various cultural backgrounds approach a job interview with different attitudes and expectations of the procedure. Shows how misunderstandings can be arrived at - and avoided.
Guidance and Counseling; Sociology
Dist - BBCENE

Recrystallization 21 MIN
VHS / U-matic
Organic Chemistry Laboratory Techniques Series
Color
Presents the theory and methods of selecting a solvent or solvent pair for a laboratory recrystallization.
Science; Science - Physical
Dist - UCEMC **Prod** - UCLA

Recrystallization - Pt 1 3 MIN
16mm
General chemistry laboratory techniques series
Color (H C A)
LC 72-708615
Demonstrates techniques for purifying a substance containing soluble and insoluble impurities. Shows preparation of solution and removal of insoluble impurities, the filtering of the hot solution through a funnel and flask and the ice bath where the filtrate and solvent bottle are placed to cool.
Science
Dist - KALMIA **Prod** - KALMIA 1970

Recrystallization - Pt 2 3 MIN
16mm
General chemistry laboratory techniques series
Color (H C A)
LC 76-708616
Shows the cold filtrate resulting from the procedure in part 1 which is now supersaturated. Shows the adding of seed crystals and the spreading of beautiful crystal 'needles.' Illustrates vacuum filtration and the cold solvent stage of the crystals. Concludes with the removing of the filter cake for viewing and drying.
Science
Dist - KALMIA **Prod** - KALMIA 1970

Rectal Bleeding 17 MIN
U-matic / VHS
Emergency Management - the First 30 Minutes, Vol III Series
Color
Presents evaluation, physical examination, diagnostic procedures and diagnostic techniques of rectal bleeding.
Health and Safety; Science
Dist - VTRI **Prod** - VTRI

Rectal Flap Repair (Beneventi - Cassebaum) of Prostato - Rectal Fistula 14 MIN
16mm
Color
LC 75-702244
Demonstrates rectal flap repair of the prostato - rectal fistula. Shows that with the patient in the jack knife position wide exposure of the fistula is obtained by linear incision of the posterior rectal wall and rectal sphincters.
Science
Dist - EATONL **Prod** - EATONL 1973

Rectal Polyp Regression with Surgical Management of Multiple Familial Polyposis 27 MIN
16mm
Color (PRO)
Illustrates the technique of colectomy and the need for low ileorectal anastomosis. Shows regression of rectal polyps after colectomy through the proctoscope and discusses the mechanism for polyp disappearance.
Health and Safety; Science
Dist - ACY **Prod** - ACYDGD 1967

Rectal Prolapse, Enterocele, and Uterine Prolapse Repair through Rectal and 23 MIN
16mm
Color (PRO)
Explains that complete rectal prolapse in women is associated with pelvic floor relaxation, sliding of the cul - de - sac, and uterine descensus. Presents a technique of repair, using a combined rectal and transvaginal approach.
Health and Safety; Science
Dist - ACY **Prod** - ACYDGD 1965

Rectangles and Right Angle 20 MIN
Videoreel / VT2
Mathemagic, Unit III - Geometry Series
Color (P)
Mathematics
Dist - GPN **Prod** - WMULTV

Rectangular Coordinates 13 MIN
16mm / U-matic / VHS
Radio Technician Training Series
Color
Demonstrates how to use coordinates in solving problems of time and distance. Shows how to locate a point using two coordinates. Issued in 1944 as a motion picture.
Industrial and Technical Education
Dist - USNAC **Prod** - USN 1978

Rectangular coordinates and graphing 30 MIN
VHS
Calculus series
Color (C)
$125.00 purchase _ #6001
Explains rectangular coordinates and graphing. Part of a 56 - part series on calculus.
Industrial and Technical Education; Mathematics
Dist - LANDMK **Prod** - LANDMK

Rectangular Coordinates and Graphing 30 MIN
VHS
Mathematics Series
Color (J)
LC 90713155
Explaines rectangular coordinates and graphing. The 110th of 157 installments of the Mathematics Series.
Mathematics
Dist - GPN

Rectangular solids
VHS
Now I see it geometry video series
Color (J H)
$79.00 _ #60252 - 026
Connects with students' lives and interests by linking lessons to everyday objects ranging from automobiles to ice cream cones, stereos to honeycombs. Includes reproducible worksheet book and answer key. Part of a nine - part series.
Education; Mathematics
Dist - GA

Rectangular to Larger Round Transition - Centered 15 MIN
BETA / VHS
Metal Fabrication - Square to Round Layout Series
Color (IND)
Industrial and Technical Education; Psychology
Dist - RMIBHF **Prod** - RMIBHF

Rectangular to Round Transition - Centered 20 MIN
BETA / VHS
Metal Fabrication - Square to Round Layout Series
Color (IND)
Industrial and Technical Education; Psychology
Dist - RMIBHF **Prod** - RMIBHF

Rectangular to Round Transition - Double Offset 37 MIN
BETA / VHS
Metal Fabrication - Square to Round Layout Series
Color (IND)
Industrial and Technical Education; Psychology
Dist - RMIBHF **Prod** - RMIBHF

Rectangular to Round Transition - Offset One - Way 34 MIN
VHS / BETA
Metal Fabrication - Square to Round Layout Series
Color (IND)
Industrial and Technical Education; Psychology
Dist - RMIBHF **Prod** - RMIBHF

Rectangular to Round Transition - Offset Two - Way 44 MIN
BETA / VHS
Metal Fabrication - Square to Round Layout Series
Color (IND)
Industrial and Technical Education; Psychology
Dist - RMIBHF **Prod** - RMIBHF

Rectangular to Triangular Transition - One Elevation, Sides of Openings Parallel 23 MIN
BETA / VHS
Exercise in Triangulating One - Piece Patterns Series
Color (IND)
Industrial and Technical Education; Psychology
Dist - RMIBHF **Prod** - RMIBHF

Rectifiers and power supplies 60 MIN
VHS / U-matic
Electrical maintenance training series; Module 7 - Solid - state devices
Color (IND)
Industrial and Technical Education
Dist - LEIKID **Prod** - LEIKID

Recuerdos de Flores Muertas 7 MIN
VHS
Color; Silent (G)
Contemplates mortality and memory. Uses El Paso's Concordia Cemetery as the landscape for a melancholic montage of gravestones which identify the inhabitants of this arid burial ground located beneath a freeway. Decaying and limbless statues, Christ figures, keep vigil over the dead while the wind batters the flowers left by mourners.
Fine Arts; Sociology
Dist - VARELA **Prod** - VARELA 1982

Recuperation from vaginal delivery - 4 13 MIN
VHS
Postpartum period series
Color (J H C G PRO)
$250.00 purchase, $60.00 rental
Discusses recovery for women who give birth vaginally. Informs women recovering from childbirth, their partners, childbirth educators and obstetrical staff. Features new parents in real situations. Hosted by Dr Linda Reid. Part of a five - part series.
Health and Safety
Dist - CF **Prod** - HOSSN 1989

Recurrence in Inguinal Hernia 21 MIN
16mm
Color (PRO)
Indicates the causes of recurrence of inguinal hernia and emphasizes the need for repair of the anatomical defects in the transversalis fascia as well as the inguinal canal. Demonstrates the use of a rectus sheath.
Health and Safety; Science
Dist - ACY **Prod** - ACYDGD 1960

Recurrent Anterior Dislocation of the Shoulder - Simplified Surgical Repair 13 MIN
16mm
Color (PRO)
LC 74-706213
Shows surgical techniques for repairing anterior dislocation of the shoulder. Explains the advantages of this method of operation and shows the postoperative recovery of a patient.
Health and Safety
Dist - USNAC **Prod** - USAF 1968

Recurrent Inguinal Hernia Repair with Fascial Sutures 26 MIN
16mm
Color (PRO)
Explains that recurrent inguinal hernia is the surgeon's bete noire. Demonstrates repairing recurrent inguinal hernia with fascial sutures.
Health and Safety; Science
Dist - ACY **Prod** - ACYDGD 1963

Recurrent Parotidectomy 20 MIN
U-matic / VHS
Head and Neck Series
Color
Health and Safety; Science - Natural
Dist - SVL **Prod** - SVL

A Recurring idea
16mm
B&W
Revises the way in which the theory of linear problems helps solve differential equations and systems of algebraic equations. Presents a banking problem and expresses it in terms of a recurrence relation.
Mathematics
Dist - OPENU **Prod** - OPENU

Recursion 40 MIN
U-matic / VHS
Computer languages series; Pt 2
Color
Explains and demonstrates the process of writing recursive programs, i.e., programs that invoke themselves in computer languages.
Industrial and Technical Education; Mathematics; Sociology
Dist - MIOT **Prod** - MIOT

Recursion 30 MIN
U-matic / VHS
Pascal, Pt 3 - Advanced Pascal Series
Color (H C A)
LC 81-706049
Introduces recursion as used in the Pascal compiler itself and user - written recursive algorithms. Describes execution of recursive code and defines variable scope in recursive procedures.
Industrial and Technical Education; Mathematics; Sociology
Dist - COLOSU **Prod** - COLOSU 1980

Recursion in G and S 50 MIN
VHS / U-matic
Computer languages series; Pt 1
Color
Gives examples demonstrating the implementation of recursive programs in global and stack environments in computer languages.
Industrial and Technical Education; Mathematics; Sociology
Dist - MIOT **Prod** - MIOT

Recursive function theory 50 MIN
U-matic / VHS
Computer languages series; Pt 1
Color
Continues the subject of computability by defining the computing scheme known as the recursive functions.
Industrial and Technical Education; Mathematics; Sociology
Dist - MIOT **Prod** - MIOT

Recycle 16 MIN
VHS / Videodisc / 16mm
Protecting our environment series
Color (I J H) (SPANISH)
$395.00, $295.00 purchase, $50.00 rental _ #8253, #8253 - LD
Explains the recycling process and provides a list of recyclable items. Follows several items through the process of breaking down, being recycled and manufactured into new products. Part of a series on the new '3Rs' of environmental protection - Reduce, Reuse and Recycle - produced by Century 21 Video.
Business and Economics; Science - Natural
Dist - AIMS

Recycle that trash 18 MIN
VHS
Color (P I)
$275.00 purchase
Takes a viewer along with a class studying how trash is picked up and then dumped in landfills or recycled. Emphasizes that trash pollutes the environment and that students can help deal with the problem. Produced by Jon and Alison Zuber.
Science - Natural
Dist - PFP

Recycled Reflections 12 MIN
U-matic / VHS / 16mm
Color (I)
LC 73-701084
Shows what is being done by the automobile industry to conserve resources by recycling automobile bumpers.
Science - Natural
Dist - ALTSUL **Prod** - SLOANM 1973

Recycling 30 MIN
VHS
Earth at risk environmental video series
Color (J H C G)
$49.95 purchase _ #LVPN6630V
Introduces and defines environmental terms and global ecological dilemmas in terms of recycling. Presents statistical information. Part of a ten - part series on environmental issues based on a series of books by Chelsea House Publishers and featuring former MTV host Kevin Seal.
Science - Natural
Dist - CAMV

Recycling 21 MIN
16mm
Color (J A)
LC 73-714061
Shows the inadequacy of today's systems for reclaiming and re - using steel, aluminum, glass, paper and others. Points out that recycling is the most important single principle which must be incorporated into future solid waste management systems to permit conservation of resources and easy and economical solid waste disposal. Discusses new ideas being developed. Intended for use by the general public, including conservationists and students.
Science - Natural
Dist - FINLYS **Prod** - FINLYS 1971

Recycling 15 MIN
VHS / U-matic
Pass it on Series
Color (K P)
Discusses paper and how it is made and why recycling is important.
Education; Science - Natural
Dist - GPN **Prod** - WKNOTV 1983

Recycling - a Way of Life 14 MIN
16mm
Color
Presents the story of aluminum recycling and its importance in a world where conservation of energy and material resources is a must. Shows facets of aluminum recycling from consumer collection to recycling of auto parts.

Science - Natural; Sociology
Dist - MTP **Prod** - ALUMA

Recycling - conserving natural resources 20 MIN
Videodisc / VHS
Earth science library series
Color (J H)
$99.95, $69.95 purchase _ #Q18582
Illustrates how raw materials are mined, milled and refined. Investigates why recycled waste is becoming an increasingly vital source of crude elements for new products and emphasizes how recycling lessens the demands placed on natural resources. Utilizes computer graphics and includes a teacher's guide; videodisc guides are barcoded for access of still frames and independent segmented lessons.
Science - Natural; Sociology
Dist - CF
VIEWTH

Recycling energy and materials 19 MIN
VHS
Life science - science in focus series
Color (J H)
$395.00 purchase, $40.00 rental
Reveals that recycling glass is cheaper than creating new glass out of sand because melting glass requires less energy than melting sand. Determines that recycling aluminum cans requires only 10 percent of the energy required to make cans from ore. Considers how various materials should be sorted out for recycling by using their physical properties and determining whether a material is worth recycling. Part of a five - part series on energy.
Science - Natural; Science - Physical
Dist - BNCHMK **Prod** - BNCHMK 1990

Recycling - furniture buying - marriage counselors
VHS / U-matic
Consumer survival series
Color
Discusses various aspects of recycling, furniture buying and picking a marriage counselor.
Home Economics; Science - Natural; Sociology
Dist - MDCPB **Prod** - MDCPB

Recycling in Action 14 MIN
U-matic / VHS / 16mm
Color (P)
Establishes the need for recycling solid waste products in a society of 'endless consumption.'.
Science - Natural; Sociology
Dist - ALTSUL **Prod** - AMITAI 1973

Recycling is fun 12 MIN
VHS
Color (K P I)
$315.00, $195.00 purchase, $25.00 rental
Explores the three Rs of recycling - reduce, recycle, reuse. Visits a landfill, a recycling center and a local supermarket to find out what can be done to help with the solid waste crisis. Narrated by three young children who discover their own power to recycle and choose what they buy. Produced by Stuart Perkin.
Science - Natural; Sociology
Dist - BULFRG **Prod** - YNF 1991

Recycling - it's everybody's job 20 MIN
VHS / U-matic / 16mm / BETA
Color (P I)
$280.50, $79.00 purchase _ #C50801, #C51513
Shows students getting down and dirty as they sort through family garbage for a class project. Discloses how they learn why recycling is the most logical solution to mounting garbage problems. Illustrates that it takes work to separate trash into paper, metal, plastic and glass, that it is expensive for factories to turn these materials back into useful items, but the alternatives - using up resources, cluttering the landscape with landfills - are far more costly.
Science - Natural; Sociology
Dist - NGS **Prod** - NGS 1992

Recycling Our Resources 10 MIN
U-matic / VHS / 16mm
Color (I J)
LC 73-701911
Shows why conservation is important and some significant ways that recycling contributes.
Science - Natural
Dist - AIMS **Prod** - COLLRD 1973

Recycling prosperity 30 MIN
VHS
Inside Britain 2 series
Color; PAL; NTSC (G) (BULGARIAN CZECH HUNGARIAN SPANISH POLISH ROMANIAN RUSSIAN SLOVAK UKRAINIAN ENGLISH WITH ARABIC SUBTITLES LITHUANIAN)
PdS65 purchase
Cautions that, while sustaining economic growth, industries should be aware of environmental issues. Shows that local councils, central government and individual households are working together and recycling all manner of things.
Business and Economics; Science - Natural
Dist - CFLVIS **Prod** - JACARA 1992

Recycling Roads with Asphalt Emulsions 22 MIN
16mm
Color
Highlights the methods and materials used throughout the United States to recycle low - volume roads' materials to construct asphalt - strengthened pavement bases. Shows both central plant and in - place operations.
Industrial and Technical Education
Dist - AI **Prod** - AI 1982

Recycling - the endless circle 25 MIN
VHS / U-matic / 16mm / BETA
Color (J H G)
$390.00, $110.00 purchase _ #C50804, #C51514
Examines a landfill 25 times larger than the Great Pyramid of Egypt. Explains how recycling returns used materials to the beginning of the consumption cycle, short - circuiting waste. Looks at the processes of recycling paper, aluminum and plastic. Emphasizes the need for a commitment to recycling.
Science - Natural; Sociology
Dist - NGS **Prod** - NGS 1992

Recycling Waste 12 MIN
16mm / U-matic / VHS
Captioned; Color
LC 71-712873
Shows how raw materials can be conserved and pollution curbed by turning waste materials back into useful products. Illustrates how paper, glass and metal can be recycled.
Science - Natural
Dist - JOU **Prod** - WER 1971

Red 6 MIN
16mm
Color
LC 74-713398
A departure from the traditional Little Red Ridinghood tale in which a little girl falls in love with a red wolf.
Literature and Drama
Dist - GCCED **Prod** - GCCED 1971

Red Africa 8 MIN
16mm
Color (G)
$45.00 rental
Portrays Robert Fulton, who came to the Art Institute in 1981 and inspired the filmmaker. Uses fast jump cuts, visual transitions as the main character discovers he cannot have his cake and eat it too.
Fine Arts
Dist - CANCIN **Prod** - WHITDL 1982

Red Alert 16 MIN
16mm
Color
LC 79-700822
Describes Federal Aviation Administration regulations relating to airplane crash and fire rescue operations. Illustrates basic principles and techniques and demonstrates new equipment protective suits and agents to extinguish fires.
Industrial and Technical Education
Dist - USNAC **Prod** - USFAA 1979

Red and Black 7 MIN
16mm / U-matic / VHS
Color (P I)
Uses unexpected plot twists and lively Spanish music to convert a funny parody of a bullfight into a setting for imagination.
Fine Arts
Dist - LUF **Prod** - LUF

Red and Black 6 MIN
16mm
Color (K P I)
LC FIA66-1180
A parody of a bullfight, effected through tricks of animation, color and light and accompanied by lively Spanish music.
Fine Arts
Dist - SF **Prod** - MINFS 1965

The Red and the white 92 MIN
VHS / 16mm
Miklos Jansco series
B&W (G) (HUNGARIAN WITH ENGLISH SUBTITLES)
$175.00 rental
Portrays the Civil War in Russia, 1918, in central Russia, near an abandoned monastery and a field hospital. Directed by Miklos Jansco.
Fine Arts; History - World
Dist - KINOIC

The Red Army 22 MIN
VHS / U-matic
B&W
Portrays the Soviet armed forces on the eve of World War II. Includes recruit training, Army, Navy and Air Force maneuvers, a performance by the Red Army Ensemble conducted by Professor Alexandrov and a military parade in Red Square.
Civics and Political Systems; History - World
Dist - IHF **Prod** - IHF

Red Auerbach 20 MIN
16mm
Sports Legends Series
Color (I J)
Features Red Auerbach, coach of the Boston Celtics, speaking candidly about his philosophy, some of the great players he has coached and other provocative issues in professional basketball.
Biography; Physical Education and Recreation
Dist - COUNFI **Prod** - COUNFI

The Red Badge of Courage
VHS / U-matic
Adolescent literature series
B&W (G C J)
$39.00 purchase _ #05987 - 85
Presents the 1951 adaptation of Stephen Crane's novel about the Civil War. Stars Audie Murphy. Directed by John Huston.
Fine Arts; Literature and Drama
Dist - CHUMAN

The Red badge of courage 69 MIN
VHS
Color (H)
$39.00 purchase _ #05987 - 126
Presents a film adaptation of the Stephen Crane novel directed by John Huston.
Fine Arts; History - United States; Literature and Drama
Dist - GA **Prod** - GA 1951

The Red Badge of Courage
Cassette / 16mm
Now Age Reading Programs, Set 1 Series
Color (I J)
$9.95 purchase _ #8F - PN681840
Brings a classic tale to young readers. The filmstrip set includes filmstrip, cassette, book, classroom materials and a poster. The read - along set includes an activity book and a cassette.
English Language; Literature and Drama
Dist - MAFEX

The Red Badge of Courage
U-matic / VHS
B&W (J H C A)
$39.00 purchase _ #05987 94
Enacts Stephen Crane's war novel The Red Badge Of Courage. Stars Audie Murphy. Directed by John Huston.
Fine Arts; Sociology
Dist - ASPRSS

The Red badge of courage 70 MIN
VHS
B&W (G)
$24.95 purchase _ #S00538
Presents the Stephen Crane story of a young soldier's experiences in the Civil War. Stars Audie Murphy. Directed by John Huston.
Literature and Drama
Dist - UILL

The Red Ball Attacks - 34th Infantry Division 21 MIN
16mm / U-matic / VHS
B&W (H A)
Discusses the history of the 34th Infantry Division, from its origin as Minnesota volunteers in the Civil War to division action in World Wars I and II.
Civics and Political Systems; History - United States
Dist - USNAC **Prod** - USA 1950

Red Ball Express 4 MIN
16mm / U-matic / VHS
Color
LC 76-700740
Uses animation to show a train changing shape and color. Describes how this is achieved by drawing directly on the film, a technique for fast - paced animated short films.
Industrial and Technical Education
Dist - CORF **Prod** - PERSPF 1975

Red Ball Express 3 MIN
U-matic / VHS / 16mm
Color (P I J H C A)
$105, $70 purchase _ #3800
Shows a train that changes color and shape and goes up and down and sideways. Animated. A Perspective film.
Fine Arts
Dist - CORF

The Red Balloon 34 MIN
U-matic / VHS / 16mm
Color (P I J H C)
A boy makes friends with a balloon and the balloon begins to live a life of its own. They play together in the streets of Montmartre and try unsuccessfully to elude the urchins who want to destroy the balloon.
English Language; Fine Arts; Literature and Drama
Dist - FI **Prod** - LAM 1956

The Red Baron 50 MIN
U-matic / 16mm / VHS
Color; B&W; Mono (J H C A)
$50.00 Rental
Relates the story of the World War One fighter pilot, the Red Baron. Manfred von Richtohofen left his cavalry position to join the flying squadron and quickly became a top fighter. After his 14th victory he painted his plane red, a symbol meant to strike fear in the hearts of the enemy. Production includes interviews with some of the men who commanded the early fighter planes.
History - United States; History - World
Dist - CTV **Prod** - CTV 1976

The Red bead experiment and life - Vol VII
VHS
Deming series
Color (G)
$595.00 purchase, $195.00 rental
Considers the 'red bead' experiment and life. Part of a nine - part series produced by Dr W Edwards Deming, Prof Robert Reich and Ford CEO Donald Peterson. Illustrates the principles and implementation of the Deming philosophy.
Business and Economics; Guidance and Counseling; Psychology
Dist - VLEARN

The Red bead experiment and life - Vol VII 25 MIN
VHS
Deming library series
Color (S)
$595.00 purchase, $150.00 rental _ #213 - 9012
Provides a plan of action for taking organizations into the future with confidence. Features business strategist and statistician Dr W Edwards Deming, journalist Lloyd Dobyn, producer Clare Crawford - Mason, Harvard Professor Robert B Reich and Ford Motor Company CEO Donald Petersen. Volume VII demonstrates the famous 'Red Bead Experiment' which shows that quality must be built into the system, the way products are made and services are performed, and that current American managerial techniques are not conducive to quality improvement.
Business and Economics; Psychology; Religion and Philosophy
Dist - FI **Prod** - CCMPR 1989

The Red bead experiment and life - Volume VII 25 MIN
U-matic / VHS
Deming library series
Color (G)
$595.00 purchase, $150.00 rental
Shows the Red Bead Experiment as it is done at four - day seminars led by Dr W Edwards Deming. Part of a sixteen - part series on the business philosophy of Dr Deming.
Business and Economics; Guidance and Counseling; Psychology
Dist - VLEARN **Prod** - FI

The Red bead experiment and life - Volume VII 25 MIN
VHS
Deming library series
Color (PRO A G)
$595.00 purchase, $150.00 rental
Shows through an experiment that standard managerial setups cannot produce quality, according to Dr. Edwards Deming. Advocates complete changes in business organization. Part of a sixteen - volume series.
Business and Economics; Psychology
Dist - EXTR **Prod** - FI

Red beard 185 MIN
VHS
B&W (G)
$39.95 _ #RED170
Depicts the touching and tumultuous relationship between a vain young doctor and a compassionate clinic director. Follows the changes that take place in the ambitious intern as he comes to cherish the lives of each of his destitute patients. Letterboxed, widescreen version in two tapes.
Fine Arts; Health and Safety; Sociology
Dist - HOMVIS **Prod** - JANUS 1965

Red beard 185 MIN
Videodisc
B&W; CLV (G) (JAPANESE WITH ENGLISH SUBTITLES)
$89.95 purchase _ #CC1252L
Examines the spiritual growth of a status - craving, money - hungry doctor who is assigned to an under - financed public clinic for the poor. Directed by Akira Kurosawa.
Guidance and Counseling; Literature and Drama; Religion and Philosophy
Dist - CHTSUI

Red Blood Cell Development 30 MIN
VHS / U-matic
Developmental Biology Series
Color
Deals with red blood cell development as a complex, vitally important phase of development in the embryo.
Science - Natural
Dist - NETCHE **Prod** - NETCHE 1971

The Red bowmen 58 MIN
16mm / VHS
Institute of Papua New Guinea studies series
Color (G)
$800.00, $400.00 purchase, $80.00, $60.00 rental
Reveals that every year the ida is performed by the Umeda people of the dense primary forest of the Waina - Sawanda district of West Sepik, Papua New Guinea. Discloses that the ida, the central social and cultural drama of the Umeda, is a fertility ritual with a dominant theme of the metamorphosis of the cassowaries. Part of a series by Chris Owen.
History - World; Religion and Philosophy; Sociology
Dist - DOCEDR **Prod** - IPANGS 1983

The Red Box 30 MIN
16mm
B&W
Dramatizes an episode in the life of Gershom Seixas, a rabbi who lived during the American Revolution and fought for freedom through his religious beliefs. (Kinescope).
Religion and Philosophy
Dist - NAAJS **Prod** - JTS 1958

The Red Carpet 10 MIN
16mm / U-matic / VHS
Color (K P)
An iconographic motion picture based on the children's book of the same title. Tells the story of a carpet that ran away to greet the Duke of Sultana. Camera techniques are used to give an illusion of motion to the original illustrations.
English Language; Literature and Drama
Dist - WWS **Prod** - WWS 1955

Red China Diary with Morley Safer 54 MIN
U-matic / VHS / 16mm
Color; B&W (H C A)
LC FIA68-1186
Takes a first - hand look at the cultural revolution of Chairman Mao Tse - tung. Examines the impact of Maoism and covers the five principal cities in Red China. Interviews students, factory workers and aggressive members of the Red Guard.
History - World
Dist - PHENIX **Prod** - CBSTV 1968

Red China Diary with Morley Safer, Pt 1 27 MIN
U-matic / VHS / 16mm
Color; B&W (H C A)
LC FIA68-1186
Takes a first - hand look at the cultural revolution of Chairman Mao Tse - Tung. Examines the impact of Maoism and covers the five principle cities in Red China. Interviews students, factory workers and members of the Red Guard.
Civics and Political Systems; Geography - World
Dist - PHENIX **Prod** - CBSTV 1968

Red China Diary with Morley Safer, Pt 2 27 MIN
16mm / U-matic / VHS
Color; B&W (H C A)
LC FIA68-1186
Takes a first - hand look at the cultural revolution of Chairman Mao Tse - Tung. Examines the impact of Maoism and covers the five principle cities in Red China. Interviews students, factory workers and members of the Red Guard.
Civics and Political Systems; Geography - World
Dist - PHENIX **Prod** - CBSTV 1968

The Red Danube 25 MIN
BETA / 16mm / VHS
Color
LC 77-702521
Presents correspondent Michael Maclear's examination of the Hungarian freedom fighters who rebelled against Soviet oppression in 1956. Discusses how these individuals have unwittingly become supporters of the Soviet regime.
Civics and Political Systems; History - World
Dist - CTV **Prod** - CTV 1976

Red Dawn 20 MIN
U-matic / VHS
History in Action Series
Color
Recounts the abdication of Czar Nicholas and Lenin's seizure of power.
History - World
Dist - FOTH **Prod** - FOTH 1984

The Red Deer 25 MIN
U-matic / VHS / 16mm
Color (J)
LC 80-700718
Uses the red deer of New Zealand as an example of man's folly in introducing an animal into an environment that isn't ready for it.
Science - Natural
Dist - JOU **Prod** - SPRKTF 1980

Red Deer Valley 26 MIN
16mm
Audubon wildlife theatre series
Color (I)
Shows many plants and animals of Red Deer Valley in Central Alberta. Portrays an unusual number of rare creatures and includes many sequences of seldom seen animal behavior.
Geography - World; Science - Natural
Dist - AVEXP **Prod** - AVEXP

The Red Dress 28 MIN
16mm / U-matic / VHS
Color
Tells the story of an Indian trapper and his daughter, illustrating both culture conflict and parental misunderstanding.
Fine Arts; Social Science
Dist - FI **Prod** - NFBC 1979

Red drives me nuts 50 MIN
VHS
Signs of the times series
Color (A)
PdS99 purchase
Takes viewers 'through the keyhole' into ordinary late 20th-century homes in Britain to see what people's perceptions of good and bad taste really are. Examines how single people's tastes are circumscribed by a host of subtle restraints. Part two of a five-part series.
Fine Arts; Home Economics; Industrial and Technical Education
Dist - BBCENE

Red empire series
Presents a seven - part series tracing Russian history from the fall of the Tsar and rise of Lenin, through World War I, the internal war for communism, the emergence of the brutal and ruthless Stalin, World War II, Krushchev, Brezhnev and Gorbachev. Includes Revolutionaries, Winners and Losers, Class Warriors, Enemies of the People, Patriots, Survivors, Prisoner of the Past.
Class warriors 54 MIN
Enemies of the people 54 MIN
Patriots 54 MIN
Prisoner of the past 54 MIN
Revolutionaries 54 MIN
Survivors 54 MIN
Winners and losers 54 MIN
Dist - CAMV

Red empire - the history of the Soviet Union 357 MIN
VHS
Color; PAL (H)
PdS80 purchase
Presents seven 51 - minute programs on the Soviet Union. Traces the history of Russia from the fall of the Tsars to the rise of Mikhail Gorbachev. Uses archival film, eye witness accounts and location filming in the USSR and a number of other countries. Contact distributor about availability outside the United Kingdom.
History - World
Dist - ACADEM

Red Eye, Pt 1 20 MIN
U-matic / VHS
Color (PRO)
Presents information to assist the primary care physician in recognizing and treating simple cases of red eye and indications for referral to an opthalmologist.
Health and Safety; Science - Natural
Dist - UMICHM **Prod** - UMICHM 1976

Red Eye, Pt 2 16 MIN
U-matic / VHS
Color (PRO)
Discusses the symptoms, causes and treatment of keratitis, keratoconjunctivitis sicca, iritis and acute angle closure glaucoma.
Health and Safety; Science - Natural
Dist - UMICHM **Prod** - UMICHM 1976

Red eyes - Volume 6 45 MIN
VHS
Bubblegum crisis series
Color (A) (JAPANESE WITH ENGLISH SUBTITLES)
$34.95 purchase _ #CPM91006
Presents a Japanese animated film. Viewer discretion is advised as some films contain strong language or violence.
Fine Arts
Dist - CHTSUI

Red firecracker, green firecracker 116 MIN
35mm / 16mm
Color (G)
$200.00 rental
Features a romantic ballad of sexual longing set in a remote town on the banks of the Yellow River during the early years of post - 1911 Republican China. Follows the Cais', an old established family in northern China whose name is identified with the production of firecrackers. Their daughter is the sole heir to the large business, and has always been treated as a boy, wearing male attire. When she falls in love with a visiting artist, her parents object, offering a unique suggestion for choosing her husband. Produced by Yung Naiming; directed He Ping; screenplay by Da Ying. Based on the novel by Feng Jicai.
Fine Arts; Psychology; Religion and Philosophy; Sociology
Dist - OCTOBF

Red Flag - to Fly and to Fight 25 MIN
16mm
Color
LC 78-701240
Depicts the importance of Tactical Air Command training programs. Shows how these programs attempt to help air crews and support personnel maintain a constant state of readiness.
Civics and Political Systems; Industrial and Technical Education
Dist - USNAC **Prod** - USAF 1978

Red flags in the critically unstable pediatric patient 28 MIN
VHS
Color (C PRO)
$285.00 purchase, $70.00 rental _ #7823S, #7823V
Offers nurses essential information on assessment of infants and young children at risk for arrest. Focuses on early identification and intervention and helps viewers develop perceptual acuity and to recognize signs of cardiopulmonary distress.
Health and Safety
Dist - AJN **Prod** - HOSSN

The Red Fox - a Predator 10 MIN
U-matic / VHS / 16mm
Color; B&W (I)
LC FIA67-5250
Follows the activities of a red fox and its family showing how they live, how they are adapted to be predators, and the characteristics of a red fox that place it in the group called mammals.
Science - Natural
Dist - EBEC **Prod** - EBEC 1967

The Red fox - a predator 11 MIN
U-matic / VHS
Color (I)
$59.00 purchase _ #2475
Looks at the activities of a red fox and its family to see how they live, thereby showing the importance of predators in the balance of nature.
Science - Natural
Dist - EBEC

Red Fox - Second Hanging 90 MIN
BETA / VHS
Color
Features a live performance of the play Red Fox / Second Hangin' written and produced by the Appalshop Roadside Theater. Presents a classic of Southern storytelling, based on oral history and trial transcripts from the 1880s. Evokes the history of the rural Southern United States.
Fine Arts; History - United States; Literature and Drama; Sociology
Dist - APPAL **Prod** - APPAL

Red Grooms talks about Dali Salad 4 MIN
U-matic / VHS
Color (H C A)
$29.95, $75.00 purchase
Shows how artist Red Grooms conceived, printed and assembled his portrait of Salvador Dali called 'Dali Salad.' Emphasizes the production process used in the three - dimensional print, made of ordinary things such as paper, aluminum, plastic and ping pong balls.
Fine Arts
Dist - ARTSAM

The Red Guards on Lake Hunghu 121 MIN
VHS
Color (G) (MANDARIN CHINESE (ENGLISH SUBTITLES))
$45.00 purchase _ #1026B
Presents a movie produced in the People's Republic of China.
Fine Arts; Geography - World; Literature and Drama
Dist - CHTSUI **Prod** - CHTSUI

The Red hen 11 MIN
U-matic / VHS / 16mm
Color (K P)
LC 79-701882
Presents the experience of a young boy who monitors the development of his red hen's baby chicks. Shows how the chicks learn to eat, drink and play.
Science - Natural
Dist - BARR **Prod** - BARR 1979

Red hot Chicago 26 MIN
VHS / U-matic
Color (J H G)
$225.00, $275.00 purchase, $50.00 rental
Studies Americana through that most American of popular foods - the hotdog. Traces the history and nuances of this edible ethnic cuisine and the city that has over 3,000 hot dog emporiums.
Home Economics
Dist - NDIM **Prod** - INTERA 1992

Red is green - Jud Fine 11 MIN
VHS
California artists series
Color (H C A)
$39.95
Presents artist Jud Fine and his work which focuses on the possibilities and impossibilities of communicating. Reflects the multilayered dimensions of his work.
Fine Arts
Dist - ARTSAM

Red letter edition - an evening with Jesus 42 MIN
VHS
Color (G A R)
$39.95 purchase, $10.00 rental _ #35 - 8656 - 1518
Features actor and author Curt Cloninger in a dramatic portrayal of Jesus. Presents the role in a contemporary setting.
Literature and Drama; Religion and Philosophy
Dist - APH **Prod** - SPAPRO

Red light - green light 45 MIN
BETA / VHS / U-matic
Color; Stereo (J S C A G)
Focuses on growing up female in the 1980s. Depicts the intermediate stage that adolescent girls endure as they try to understand what the future offers them. Questions about careers, boys, family and friends are shared. Includes a study guide.
Psychology; Sociology
Dist - UCV

Red Light Return 14 MIN
U-matic / VHS / 16mm
Color (H C A)
LC FIA66-533
Indicates what happens to windshields, doors and people in a 40 - miles per hour auto collision. Shows collision tests with various types of glass, door latches and seat belts and harnesses. Studies the similarity between the velocity of a car dropped from a helicopter and one involved in a collision.
Health and Safety; Industrial and Technical Education
Dist - AIMS **Prod** - CAHILL 1965

Red Line Promotional Program 15 MIN
VHS
Color (IND)
Demonstrates the hand portable Ansul brand Red Line Cartridge - Operated fire extinguisher.
Health and Safety
Dist - ANSUL **Prod** - ANSUL

Red lion 115 MIN
VHS
Color (G) (JAPANESE WITH ENGLISH SUBTITLES)
$55.95 purchase _ #VDAVA18
Stars Toshiro Mifune in a movie directed by Kihachi Okamoto.
Fine Arts
Dist - CHTSUI

Red Man and the Red Cedar 12 MIN
16mm
Man and the Forest Series
Color (I)
LC 78-707902
Shows how the coastal Indians used the Western red cedar for food, clothing, shelter, transportation and art. Portrays the relationship of present day Indians to the old culture through demonstrations of how things were done in the old culture.
Sociology
Dist - MMP **Prod** - MMP 1969

Red Menace or Red Scare - Part 1 30 MIN
U-matic
Realities
Color (A)
Delves into the political, social, economic and cultural trends of the 1980s. Probes a wide range of concerns. Each segment includes a guest speaker who is an expert in the field under discussion.
Business and Economics; Civics and Political Systems; Social Science; Sociology
Dist - TVOTAR **Prod** - TVOTAR 1985

Red Menace or Red Scare - Part 2 30 MIN
U-matic
Realities
Color (A)
Delves into the political, social, economic and cultural trends of the 1980s. Probes a wide range of contemporary concerns. Each segment includes a guest speaker who is an expert in the field under discussion.
Business and Economics; Civics and Political Systems; Social Science; Sociology
Dist - TVOTAR **Prod** - TVOTAR 1985

The Red Metal of Amarillo 24 MIN
16mm
Color
LC 77-700404
Shows the construction and operation of Asarco's new copper refinery.
Industrial and Technical Education
Dist - BECHTL **Prod** - BECHTL 1976

Red Nightmare 25 MIN
16mm
B&W
LC 74-705491
Deals with the nightmare of an American citizen who finds himself in a communist village and is rudely awakened to his civic responsibilities.
Civics and Political Systems; Geography - World; History - World
Dist - USNAC **Prod** - USDD 1965

Red Norvo
VHS
Color (G)
$29.95 purchase _ #1278
Showcases xylophonist Red Norvo in a trio with guitarist Tal Farlow and bassist Steve Novosel. Includes vocalist Mavis Rivers for 'Pennies From Heaven' and other favorites.
Fine Arts
Dist - KULTUR

The Red nose express 30 MIN
VHS
Color (K P I R)
$14.95 purchase _ #35 - 83006 - 8936
Follows the members of Gingerbrook Fare as they join a clown school and learn some lessons along the way. Teaches that understanding God's ways is more important than any clown stunt. Produced by Bridgestone.
Religion and Philosophy
Dist - APH

Red on Roundball
VHS / U-matic
(G)
$29.95 purchase
Demonstrates winning strategies and favorite plays in the game of basketball.
Physical Education and Recreation
Dist - BESTF **Prod** - BESTF

Red pandas 11 MIN
VHS
Animal profile series
Color (P I)
$59.95 purchase _ #RB8127
Studies the extremely rare and endangered red panda, mysterious tree climber from high altitude bamboo forests in Asia. Includes footage of a 30 - day - old red panda baby. Part of a series on animals which looks at examples from the mammal, snake and bird classes, filmed in their natural habitat.
Science - Natural
Dist - REVID **Prod** - REVID 1990

Red peony 105 MIN
VHS
Color (G) (MANDARIN CHINESE (ENGLISH SUBTITLES))
$45.00 purchase _ #1013A
Presents a movie produced in the People's Republic of China.
Fine Arts; Geography - World; Literature and Drama
Dist - CHTSUI **Prod** - CHTSUI

The Red Plague 21 MIN
16mm
Unbroken Arrow Series

Color (P I)
Presents an adventure set in the time of the Saxons which tells how old Wulfric is taking his sick granddaughter to the Friar when he is caught by the Baron's men, who accuse him of poaching. Relates how the men scramble for cover when convinced that the granddaughter's illness is catching.
Literature and Drama
Dist - LUF **Prod** - LUF 1977

The Red Planet - Mars 17 MIN
U-matic / VHS / 16mm
Color (J)
LC FIA68-2892
Interprets the changing appearance of the planet Mars, including its seasons, the growth and decay of the ice caps and the clouds in the atmosphere. Shows details of scientific experiments carried out by the Mariner 4 probe.
Science - Physical
Dist - IFB **Prod** - PLYMTH 1967

Red pomegranate 75 MIN
16mm / 35mm
Films of Sergei Paradjanov series
Color (G) (RUSSIAN WITH ENGLISH SUBTITLES)
$300.00, $400.00 rental
Uses the words of 17th - century poet Arutuin Sayadian, 'Sayat Nova' - King of Siam, in an eight - part portrait of his life and work. Directed by Sergei Paradjanov.
Fine Arts; Literature and Drama
Dist - KINOIC **Prod** - IFEX 1969

The Red Pony
VHS / U-matic
Color (J C I)
Presents and adaptation of John Steinbeck's novel about the relationship between a boy and his father. Features music by Aaron Copland.
Fine Arts; Literature and Drama
Dist - GA **Prod** - GA

The Red Pony
VHS / U-matic
Films - on - Video Series
Color (G C J)
$69 purchase _ #05650 - 85
Re - enacts John Steinbeck's novel about sensitive family relationships. Features a score by Aaron Copeland.
Fine Arts; Literature and Drama
Dist - CHUMAN

The Red Pony 101 MIN
16mm / U-matic / VHS
Color (I)
LC 76-702513
Based on the book The Red Pony John Steinbeck. Tells a story of a young boy and life on his father's ranch. Stars Henry Fonda and Maureen O'Hara.
Fine Arts; Literature and Drama; Sociology
Dist - PHENIX **Prod** - PHENIX 1976

The Red pony 89 MIN
VHS
Color (G)
$59.95 purchase _ #S00539
Presents a film account of John Steinbeck's novel The Red Pony. Tells the story of a ranch family involved in the birth and death of a pony. Stars Robert Mitchum, Myrna Loy, and Peter Miles. Directed by Louis Milestone. Musical score by Aaron Copland. Filmed in 1949.
Fine Arts; Literature and Drama
Dist - UILL

Red pride, red sorrow - Part 6 55 MIN
VHS
Slow boat from Surabaya series
Color (J H C)
$225.00 purchase
Examines the creative enterprises of the Vietnamese which hint of capitalism, revealing a culture of resilience and patience. Shows that neighboring Kampuchea remains in a state of unrest, that because of the genocidal regime of Pol Pot of Cambodia, half its population is dead or refugees in other countries. Part six of a six - part series on Southeast Asia covering the Philippines, Thailand, Singapore, Indonesia, Malaysia, Vietnam and Kampuchea.
Business and Economics; Civics and Political Systems; Geography - World; Sociology
Dist - LANDMK **Prod** - LANDMK 1992

Red psalm 88 MIN
16mm
Miklos Jansco series
Color (G) (HUNGARIAN WITH ENGLISH SUBTITLES)
$200.00 rental
Portrays the tragedy of a group of Hungarian farm workers on a labor strike. Directed by Miklos Jansco.
Agriculture; Fine Arts
Dist - KINOIC

A Red Ribbon 10 MIN
U-matic / VHS / 16mm
Color (P I)
LC 82-700448
Chronicles, without words, the making and testing of a kite by a small boy, as observed by a little girl, whom he ignores. Reveals that when he runs into problems, her hair ribbon saves the day.
Literature and Drama
Dist - TEXFLM **Prod** - TEXFLM 1981

Red Riding Hood 8 MIN
U-matic / 35mm strip
Color (K P I)
LC 85-700138
Presents an account of Little Red Riding Hood's visit to her sick grandmother. Features Edward Gorey's line drawings highlighted in brown with red accents to depict the verse of Beatrice Schenk de Regniers.
English Language; Literature and Drama
Dist - WWS **Prod** - WWS 1984

Red Riding Hood and the well - fed wolf 15 MIN
VHS
Color (P I)
$405.00, $295.00 purchase, $60.00 rental
Revamps the traditional Little Red Riding Hood story with a new twist - the ugly wolf is all dressed up in Grandma's clothing and looking forward to a tasty dinner of Red Riding Hood, but Red has a different idea. Reveals that she's convinced that Grandma looks so awful because her diet is terrible. Red and some articulate foods which appear from her bottomless basket explain about the four food groups and why the body needs them. She fixes the wolf a well - balanced meal and the wolf has to reluctantly agree that it's not bad at all.
Literature and Drama; Social Science
Dist - CF **Prod** - CF 1990

Red riding hood - Goldilocks 30 MIN
VHS
Rabbit ears collection series
Color; CC (K P I J)
$12.95 purchase _ #199773
Features actress Meg Ryan as narrator.
Literature and Drama
Dist - KNOWUN **Prod** - RABBIT

The Red River
VHS / U-matic
Body human series
Color
Looks inside the heart and bloodstream of a human fetus, examines human lungs and provides a guided tour through the inside of a 'hardened' artery. Includes cases of a 41 - year old man undergoing a delicate triple - bypass operation, a six - year - old girl with a leaking malformed heart undergoing surgery wherein her heart is stopped, rebuilt, and started again, a 16 - year - old girl, paralyzed and facing death from a rare growth of blood vessels obstructing her spinal cord, and a 61 - year - old man with severe blockage of his brain arteries.
Health and Safety; Industrial and Technical Education
Dist - MEDCOM **Prod** - MEDCOM

Red river of life 28 MIN
VHS
Moody science classics series
Color (R I J)
$19.95 purchase _ #6149 - 2
Compares metaphorically the human circulatory system with the religious consideration of the blood Christ shed as a source of life. Features part of a series on creationism.
Literature and Drama; Religion and Philosophy
Dist - MOODY **Prod** - MOODY

Red Road - Towards the Techno Tribal 27 MIN
U-matic / VHS
Color (J H C)
Presents and explores contemporary views of Native American philosophy, spirituality, and prophesy. Shows how traditional values and ancient cosmology can play an important role in today's world. Provides insights to a world view and philosophy largely invisible to the Americna public.
Religion and Philosophy; Social Science; Sociology
Dist - NAMPBC **Prod** - NAMPBC 1984

Red Room Riddle 24 MIN
U-matic / VHS / 16mm
Color (I)
Tells what happens when two children visit a haunted mansion and encounter a strange boy who traps them in a glowing red room peopled by menacing transparent people. Reveals that when the adventure is over, the boys admit that sometimes it feels good to say you're scared. Produced for the ABC Weekend Specials.
Literature and Drama
Dist - CORF **Prod** - ABCLR 1983

The Red Sea - David and Saul 26 MIN
VHS
Color (R P I)
$14.95 purchase _ #6138 - 9
Presents two bible stories with still illustrations and Mr Fixit and friends who show how scripture applies to daily life.
Literature and Drama; Religion and Philosophy
Dist - MOODY **Prod** - MOODY

Red shift 50 MIN
16mm
B&W (G)
$110.00 rental
Explores relationships, generations and time. Involves the filmmaker, her mother and her daughter portraying their emotional bond to one another.
Fine Arts; Psychology; Sociology
Dist - CANCIN **Prod** - NELSOG 1984

The Red Shoes 25 MIN
VHS / 16mm
Color (P)
$495.00, $295.00 purchase
Features the fairytale by Hans Christian Andersen in a modern setting. Tells of Lisa and her parents who win the lottery. Lisa, once a pleasant child, becomes a greedy brat who snubs her best friend Jenny. Alphonse, the cobbler, makes Jenny a pair of magic red ballet slippers to console her. Lisa sees the slippers in the cobbler's shop and steals them, puts them on and is forced to dance back to her old neighborhood where she learns humility and the importance of friendship.
Guidance and Counseling; Health and Safety; Literature and Drama; Psychology
Dist - LUF **Prod** - LUF 1989

Red shoes 136 MIN
VHS
Color (G A)
$19.95 purchase
Presents the 1948 film version of 'The Red Shoes,' a story based on a tale by Hans Christian Anderson. Stars Moira Shearer, Ludmilla Tcherina, and Marius Goring.
Fine Arts
Dist - PBS **Prod** - WNETTV

The Red Shoes 134 MIN
16mm
Color
Tells the story of ballerina Victoria Page, who is catapulted to stardom in the Ballet Russes. Shows the conflict which arises when she falls in love with the company's composer and must choose between art and romance. Stars Moira Shearer and Leonide Massine. Directed by Michael Powell and Emeric Pressburger.
Fine Arts
Dist - LCOA **Prod** - RANK 1948

The Red Shoes 10 MIN
16mm / U-matic / VHS
Classic Tales Retold Series
Color (P I)
LC 81-700077
Presents the Hans Christian Andersen story about a girl obsessed with obtaining a pair of red shoes.
Literature and Drama
Dist - PHENIX **Prod** - PHENIX 1981

Red sorghum 91 MIN
VHS
Color (G) (CHINESE WITH ENGLISH SUBTITLES)
$79.95 purchase _ #NYV55992
Explores the struggles of the individual against the forces of fate and community. Based on a short story by Mo Yan.
Fine Arts; Geography - World
Dist - CHTSUI

Red Squad 45 MIN
U-matic / VHS / 16mm
B&W
Presents a study of the New York Police Department's red squad and various agencies involved in domestic intelligence gathering. Depicts the filmmakers themselves as they become the target of investigation, harrassment and intimidation.
Civics and Political Systems; Social Science
Dist - CNEMAG **Prod** - PACSFM 1972

Red Star 60 MIN
16mm
World at War Series
Color (H C A)
LC 76-701778
History - World; Sociology
Dist - USCAN **Prod** - THAMES 1975

Red Star Over Kyber 58 MIN
BETA / VHS
Frontline Series
Color
Examines the complex and politically charged situation in Afghanistan and Pakistan. Traces the relationship between the two countries and the two superpowers behind them, Russia and the U S.
Civics and Political Systems; Geography - World
Dist - PBS **Prod** - DOCCON

Red Star - the Soviet Union, 1941 - 1943 52 MIN
16mm / U-matic / VHS
World at War Series
Color (H C A)
Describes Russia's massive, lonely war against Germany from 1941 to 1943, resulting in twenty million military and civilian casualties and equally staggering material losses. Russian military men demonstrated a heroic fighting spirit that became legendary.
History - World
Dist - MEDIAG **Prod** - THAMES 1973

Red Sunday 28 MIN
U-matic / VHS / 16mm
Color
LC 75-700354
Uses photographs, paintings and live action shots to illustrate the events, politics, personalities and tenor of the times that led to the Battle of the Little Big Horn in 1876.
History - United States
Dist - PFP **Prod** - HGFP 1975

Red swing 8 MIN
16mm
Color (G)
$20.00 rental
Looks at subjective experience. Creates a quiet mood by the interplay between the soundtrack and complex figure - ground relationships. Uses the point of view of a porch swing through a partially opened door to portray the image to which we constantly return as the tonic.
Fine Arts; Literature and Drama; Psychology
Dist - CANCIN **Prod** - PIERCE 1986

Red tape - government departments and non - departmental agencies 30 MIN
VHS
Remaking of Canada - Canadian government and politics in the 1990s 'series
Color (H C G)
$89.95 purchase _ #WLU - 504
Discusses Canada's bureaucracy and the structures and procedures which cause bureaucrats to think and act as they do. Part of a 12 - part series incorporating interviews with Canadian politicians and hosted by Dr John Redekop.
Civics and Political Systems; History - World
Dist - INSTRU **Prod** - TELCOL 1992

Red Tapes Series
Common knowledge 45 MIN
Local Color
Time Lag
Dist - KITCHN

The Red thread 15 MIN
16mm
Larry Gottheim series
Color (G A)
$60.00 rental
Presents the work of filmmaker Larry Gottheim. Recreates a Hindu legend and weaves a metaphorical labyrinth.
Fine Arts; History - United States; Industrial and Technical Education; Religion and Philosophy
Dist - PARART **Prod** - CANCIN 1987

The Red Trap 30 MIN
16mm
B&W (H A)
LC 72-701643
Exposes some of the subtle methods used by communist agents.
Civics and Political Systems
Dist - CPH **Prod** - CPH 1961

Red Tsar 20 MIN
U-matic / VHS
History in Action Series
Color
Documents how Stalin took power after the death of Lenin and eliminated his rivals and former comrades.
History - World
Dist - FOTH **Prod** - FOTH 1984

The Red Wagon 30 MIN
16mm / VHS
Color (P I J H A)
$395.00, $495.00 purchase, $50.00 rental _ #8050
Deals with the feelings of children whose parents are divorced. Uses a fantasy story about a talking red wagon.
Guidance and Counseling; Literature and Drama; Psychology; Sociology
Dist - AIMS **Prod** - JOJO 1988

Red, White and Blue 1 MIN
U-matic
Color
Discusses prejudice in America by use of animation. Made in a television spot announcement format.
Fine Arts; Sociology
Dist - ADL **Prod** - ADL

Red, White, Blue and Brown 29 MIN
16mm
Color
LC 75-701278
Briefs government supervisors, personnel directors, ethnic groups and the general public on the President's 16 - point program. Defines some of the problems faced by the Spanish surname minority.
Civics and Political Systems; Sociology
Dist - USNAC **Prod** - USN 1972

The Red - White Struggle 30 MIN
16mm
Great Plains Trilogy, 3 Series Explorer and Settler - the White Man 'Arrives; Explorer and settler - the white man arrives
B&W (H C A)
Discusses the Indian barrier to white settlement, the methods used to subdue the red man, military expeditions and posts and the Indian wars. Describes the Grattan Massacre and the conflict between military and civilian authority.
History - United States; Social Science
Dist - UNL **Prod** - KUONTV 1954

Red - Winged Blackbirds 3 MIN
16mm
Of all Things Series
Color (P I)
Discusses the birds known as red - winged blackbirds.
Science - Natural
Dist - AVED **Prod** - BAILYL

Red wolf 13 MIN
VHS
Northwest wild series
Color (J H C A)
$89.95 purchase _ #P11098
Investigates the human and environmental factors that have led to the demise of the red wolf. Considers how human attitudes toward predators and hunting are changing and why it is important to save the wolves from extinction. Follows a rescue mission and describes the captive breeding and relocation program. Part of a series of seven programs.
Science - Natural; Sociology
Dist - CF

Redecorating - Selecting the Right Carpet
VHS
$39.95 purchase _ #DI - 218
Features Cathy Crane, author of 'Personal Places' and 'What Do You Say to a Naked Room', discussing the basic decorating and design concepts to consider to make one's house feel like a home.
Home Economics
Dist - CAREER **Prod** - CAREER

Redecorating the House Before Crystal's Girlfriends Arrive 8 MIN
16mm
Crystal Tipps and Alistair Series
Color (K P)
LC 73-700452
Shows how Crystal's friends cooperate in redecorating the house before her girlfriends arrive to help her choose a dress for a party.
Guidance and Counseling; Literature and Drama
Dist - VEDO **Prod** - BBCTV 1972

The Redemption of Space 5 MIN
16mm
Color (J H A)
LC 80-700761
Tells how churches can use their buildings to meet the needs of the community for worship and for cultural, social and educational purposes.
Religion and Philosophy; Sociology
Dist - IKONOG **Prod** - IKONOG 1979

Redemption song series
Utilizes interviews with modern inhabitants to investigate the tumultuous history of the Caribbean in a series of seven programs. Covers the topics of British imperialism; slavery and voodoo in Haiti and Jamaica; racial tensions between blacks and Asians in Trinidad and Guyana; the role of Cuba and Fidel Castro; and prospects for the future in the Caribbean.
Following Fidel 50 MIN
Iron in the soul 50 MIN
Out of Africa 50 MIN
Paradise lost 50 MIN
Shades of freedom 50 MIN
Worlds apart 50 MIN
Dist - BBCENE

Redemption song
La grande illusion 50 MIN
Dist - BBCENE

Redesigning a Pattern for Production Purposes 11 MIN
16mm
Precision Wood Machining Series Problems in Patternmaking
B&W
LC FIE52-70
Shows how a pattern originally designed for casting a single piece is redesigned for quantity production.
Computer Science
Dist - USNAC **Prod** - USOE 1945

Redesigning and chaining states - 4 96 MIN
VHS
Submodalities and hypnosis series
Color; PAL; SECAM (G)
$95.00 purchase
Features Richard Bandler in the fourth part of a five - part series on submodalities and hypnosis, from a seminar, March, 1987. Uses advanced NLP, neuro - linguistic programming. Recommended that tapes be viewed in order. Bandler sometimes uses profanity for emphasis, which may offend some people.
Health and Safety; Psychology
Dist - NLPCOM **Prod** - NLPCOM

Redesigning Appliances 30 MIN
U-matic
Rethinking America Series
Color
Discusses the appliance industry's focus on efficiency of units versus sleek appearance.
Social Science
Dist - UMITV **Prod** - UMITV 1979

Redesigning assessment - Introduction - Tape 1 24 MIN
VHS
Redesigning assessment series
Color (T C PRO)
$278.00 purchase, $120.00 rental _ #614 - 225X01
Introduces the three - part series to teachers, administrators and parents. Explores why assessment should be changed and explains the rationale behind performance - based assessment. Describes the characteristics of such assessment and shows different types of assessment. Examines the issues surrounding the adoption of a performance - based approach. Interviews experts Grant Wiggins and Richard Stiggins. Includes a facilitator's guide.
Education
Dist - AFSCD **Prod** - AFSCD 1992

Redesigning assessment - Performance assessment - Tape 3 34 MIN
VHS
Redesigning assessment series
Color (T C PRO)
$350.00 purchase, $120.00 rental _ #614 - 227X01
Explains and demonstrates a variety of assessment strategies that measure student abilities while developing the skills they need outside of school. Illustrates how performance assessment communicates standards and criteria to students for establishing their best possible performance, focuses students on the essential outcomes of the curriculum, provides students with choices on how to demonstrate their knowledge and skills, and requires student synthesis, evaluation and use of other higher - level thinking skills. Includes a facilitator's guide. Part three of a three - part series on performance - based assessment.
Education
Dist - AFSCD **Prod** - AFSCD 1992

Redesigning assessment - Portfolios - Tape 2 40 MIN
VHS
Redesigning assessment series
Color (T C PRO)
$350.00 purchase, $120.00 rental _ #614 - 226X01
Shows how to develop and review portfolios and how to get started using them. Explains what portfolios are and features experienced teachers who describe how they have students create portfolios that exhibit a student's best work, show progress over time and demonstrate specific skills. Films classrooms to show how portfolios can be used in geometry, music, writing, art and language arts - social studies. Includes a facilitator's guide. Part two of a three - part series on performance - based assessment.
Education
Dist - AFSCD **Prod** - AFSCD 1992

Redesigning assessment series
Emphasizes performance - based assessment with a variety of test strategies. Broadens a teacher's repertoire of methods to determine student progress, with focus on portfolios, displays and exhibits. Includes three videotapes. Tape 1 - Redesigning Assessment - Introduction. Tape 2 - Portfolios. Tape 3 - Performance Assessment. Three leader's guides are included.
Portfolios - Tape 2 40 MIN

Portfolios - Tape 2 40 MIN
Performance assessment - Tape 3 34 MIN
Redesigning assessment - Introduction - Tape 1 24 MIN
Redesigning assessment - Portfolios - Tape 2 40 MIN
Redesigning assessment - Performance assessment - Tape 3 34 MIN
Dist - AFSCD

Redesigning the human machine 60 MIN
VHS
People in motion - changing ideas about physical disability series
Color; CC (G)
$89.95 purchase _ #UW5679
Explores the use of technological advances in creating mechanical substitutes for human joints, bones and nerves. Shows how virtual reality is being used as a learning tool for children with disabilities, as an assistive technology for Parkinson's Disease patients and as a form of empowerment. Examines the potential use of robotics to assist people with limited mobility. Explains cochlear implants, considered by some a controversial form of treatment although the implants help some people to hear. Part three of three parts.
Computer Science; Health and Safety
Dist - FOTH

Rediscover the Safety Belt 9 MIN
U-matic / VHS / 16mm
Color (H A)
Former Mercury astronaut Wally Schirra illustrates why business and community leaders will benefit from encouraging employees, constituents and others to wear safety belts. Features driving risks, safety belt facts and myths, and personal commentary.
Education; Health and Safety; Industrial and Technical Education; Psychology
Dist - USNAC **Prod** - NHTSA 1982

Rediscovering a forgotten legacy 8 MIN
VHS / BETA / U-matic
Color (G)
$59.95, $39.95 purchase
Traces the history of a rare collection of plaster casts which were exhibited at the Metropolitan Museum of Art from 1880 to 1938. Reveals that this collection was rediscovered in 1975 by the Queens Museum in storage in a warehouse under the Riverside Viaduct at 158th Street, New York. Shows the restoration of the historical casts with commentary by Chief Conservator Neal Martz. Produced by the Queens Museum.
Fine Arts
Dist - ARTSAM

Rediscovering America 30 MIN
U-matic / VHS
American story - the beginning to 1877 series
Color (C)
History - United States
Dist - DALCCD **Prod** - DALCCD

Rediscovering Herbs - Overview 28 MIN
U-matic / VHS / 16mm
Rediscovering Herbs Series
Color (H C A)
LC 81-701538
Describes the role of herbs in home remedies, cookies, potpourris, pest control in the garden, dyeing and home decorating.
Agriculture; Home Economics
Dist - BULFRG **Prod** - RPFD 1981

Rediscovering Herbs Series
Culinary Herbs 15 MIN
Dried Flower Arrangements 15 MIN
Rediscovering Herbs - Overview 28 MIN
Dist - BULFRG

Rediscovery - art media film series
Paper construction 15 MIN
Dist - AIMS

Rediscovery - Art Media - French Series
Stitchery 14 MIN
Watercolor 14 MIN
Weaving 14 MIN
Dist - AIMS

Rediscovery - Art Media Series
Basketry 15 MIN
Clay 15 MIN
Collage 16 MIN
Crayon 15 MIN
Enameling 15 MIN
Leather 15 MIN
Macrame 15 MIN
Papier Mache 15 MIN
Posters 15 MIN
Prints 15 MIN
Puppets 15 MIN
Silkscreen 15 MIN
Stitchery 14 MIN
Water Color 14 MIN
Watercolor 15 MIN
Weaving 14 MIN
Dist - AIMS

Rediscovery - art media - Spanish series
Clay 15 MIN
Crayon 15 MIN
Enameling 15 MIN
Puppets 15 MIN
Silkscreen 14 MIN
Stitchery 14 MIN
Watercolor 14 MIN
Weaving 14 MIN
Dist - AIMS

Rediscovery - Art Media
Prints 15 MIN
Dist - AIMS

Rediscovery series
Earthquake below 15 MIN
Flood below 14 MIN
Hurricane Below 14 MIN
Pollution Below 14 MIN
Tornado Below 15 MIN
Dist - USNAC

Redlands 28 MIN
VHS
Short stories - video anthology series
Color (H G)
$59.95 purchase
Delves into the relationship between two sisters, where one is forced to rethink her self - centered priorities and make a commitment to her retarded adult sibling. Presents a film directed by Joan Taylor. Part of a sixteen - part anthology of short dramas by young American filmmakers.
Fine Arts; Literature and Drama; Psychology; Religion and Philosophy
Dist - CNEMAG

Redo a Room in a Weekend 30 MIN
VHS
Quick and Easy Sewing Series
(H C A)
$59.80 purchase series of 4 _ #CH400SV
Demonstrates simple home decorating ideas that can be produced on the sewing machine.
Home Economics
Dist - CAMV

Redo a Room in a Weekend
VHS
$29.95 purchase _ #VK23185
Helps students learn to see the possibilities of redecorating and rearranging a room for a new look.
Fine Arts; Home Economics
Dist - CAREER **Prod** - CAREER

Redondo Beach - a stand against censorship 15 MIN
VHS
Color (G)
$20.00 purchase
Shows how a California community, Redondo Beach, stood up to attacks on the freedom to learn. Reveals that a group of activists, with the help of national organizations, tried to remove the 'Impressions' elementary reading series from the Redondo Beach public schools - even though the series was carefully chosen and widely praised for its ability to stir the imagination of children and present different cultures.
Civics and Political Systems; Religion and Philosophy; Sociology
Dist - PAMWAY **Prod** - PAMWAY 1990

Redox titration 16 MIN
VHS
Chemistry master apprentice series
Color (H C)
$49.95 purchase _ #49 - 7219 - V
Shows the use of a pH - ion meter as a potentiometer in the titration of ferrous ion with ceric ion using calomel and platinum electrodes. Part of the Chemistry Master Apprentice series.
Science; Science - Physical
Dist - INSTRU **Prod** - CORNRS

Reds, whites and booze 29 MIN
16mm
Color (H C)
Explores a few days in the life of a high school senior to examine cultural forces and everyday stimuli that influence individual attitudes regarding drugs.
Guidance and Counseling; Health and Safety; Psychology; Sociology
Dist - NINEFC **Prod** - LYNVIL

Redtail - the story of a hawk 25 MIN
16mm / U-matic / VHS
Color (J)
Covers a year in the life of a hawk from his birth in an oak tree to his migration to the Caribbean for winter in an environment of hummingbirds, orchids and palm trees to his return to his birthplace, a freezing wilderness where he must find food until spring comes.
Science - Natural
Dist - FI **Prod** - BBCTV

Reduce 14 MIN
VHS / Videodisc / 16mm
Protecting our environment series
Color (I J H) (SPANISH)
$395.00, $295.00 purchase, $50.00 rental _ #8255
Gives some concrete suggestions on how to reduce the amount of debris thrown away. Looks at shopping habits to reduce the purchase of over - packaged and disposable items, buying things with a longer service life and taking care of things to make them last longer. Part of a series on the new '3Rs' of environmental protection - Reduce, Reuse and Recycle - produced by Century 21 Video.
Business and Economics; Science - Natural
Dist - AIMS

Reduce, reuse, recycle 19 MIN
VHS / U-matic
Kidzone series
Color (I J)
$175.00, $225.00 purchase, $50.00 rental
Features different aspects of recycling and strategies for the reduction of trash and material waste.
Science - Natural
Dist - NDIM **Prod** - KNONET 1992

Reduce your stress on and off the job 30 MIN
VHS
Color (G)
$75.00 purchase
Features Dr Rick Shields who offers a training seminar on dealing with job - related stress.
Health and Safety; Psychology
Dist - BALLIV **Prod** - BALLIV

Reduced voltage starters 23 MIN
16mm
Electrical work - motor control series; No 3
B&W
LC FIE52-181
Explains the principle of the transformer. Shows the operation of a manual starting compensator, thermal overload relay and automatic starting compensator.
Industrial and Technical Education
Dist - USNAC **Prod** - USOE 1945

Reducers and Gearmotors 25 MIN
U-matic / VHS
Color (IND)
Gives introduction and requirements for reducers. Discusses advantages and disadvantages of parallel reducers and gear motors.
Education; Industrial and Technical Education
Dist - TAT **Prod** - TAT

Reducers and Generators 25 MIN
VHS / U-matic
Color (IND) (SPANISH)
Gives introduction and requirements for reducers. Discusses advantages and disadvantages of parallel reducers and gear motors.
Education; Foreign Language; Industrial and Technical Education
Dist - TAT **Prod** - TAT

Reducing Conflict in the Organization 66 FRS
U-matic / VHS
Supervisor and Interpersonal Relations Series Module 5
Color
Shows supervisors how to remove the threats, uncertainties and other causes of conflict in the work group. Deals with problems of competition and conflict between work groups.
Business and Economics; Psychology
Dist - RESEM **Prod** - RESEM

Reducing fats - III 6 MIN
VHS / U-matic
It's never too late to change series
Color (PRO C G)
$195.00 purchase _ #C881 - VI - 026
Discusses dietary fat reduction for older people. Promotes discussion and participation in group activities and motivates older citizens to adopt healthier nutrition and exercise habits. Part of a nine - part series aimed at retirement home communities, senior citizen organizations and community health centers presented by Dr Molly Engle and Melissa Galvin.
Health and Safety; Physical Education and Recreation; Social Science
Dist - HSCIC

Reducing Fractions 11 MIN
U-matic
Basic Math Skills Series Multiplying Fractions and Reducing; Multiplying fractions and reducing
Color
Mathematics
Dist - TELSTR **Prod** - TELSTR

Reducing inventory at Blue Bell
VHS
Color (C PRO G)
$150.00 purchase _ #84.02
Reveals that models for inventory targets, manufacturing requirements and production scheduling were used with a seasonal demand forecasting technique and diagnostic computer simulation to reduce inventories. Shows how inventory reduction over 18 months was more than $100 million. Blue Bell Inc. Jerry R Edwards, Harvey M Wagner, William P Wood.
Business and Economics
Dist - INMASC

Reducing logistics costs at General Motors
VHS
Color (C PRO G)
$150.00 purchase _ #86.03
Focuses on a General Motors optimization tool known as Transpart 2, an IBM PC application currently in use at over 40 GM facilities to minimize the sum of transportation and inventory costs. Reveals that Transpart 2 identifies solutions without the need for complex mathematical programming techniques and allows managers to easily and quickly examine the impact of changes on shipping decisions. Savings ranging from $35,000 to $500,000 per year per plant have been identified. GM Research Laboratories. Dennis E Blumenfeld, Lawrence D Burns, Michael C Frick, Carlos G Daganzo, Randolph W Hall.
Business and Economics
Dist - INMASC

Reducing Poverty - what have We Done 30 MIN
U-matic / VHS
Economics USA Series
Color (C)
Business and Economics; Sociology
Dist - ANNCPB **Prod** - WEFA

Reducing, reusing and recycling - environmental concerns 20 MIN
VHS
Color (P I)
$89.00 purchase _ #RB853
Focuses on the problems of solid waste. Reveals that natural resources are often the base for products that become solid waste, that many such resources are not renewable. Considers that trees, a renewable resource, are being consumed faster than they can be replaced. Looks at the problems of toxic wastes that leak into the soil surrounding dumps, the difficulty of finding new sites for waste disposal, how improper disposal of waste pollutes land, water and air.
Science - Natural; Sociology
Dist - REVID **Prod** - REVID 1990

Reducing risk factors 34 MIN
VHS / U-matic / BETA
Human development - conception to neonate series
Color (C PRO)
$280.00 purchase _ #618.3
Discusses environmental factors in pregnancy that contribute to low birth weight and birth defects. Focuses on those factors that have been shown to be preventable through intervention, primarily changes in lifestyle. Discusses the importance of delaying childbirth until after adolescence, obtaining information about personal risks, seeking early prenatal care and avoiding harmful substances. Part of a three - part series on human development from conception to birth.
Health and Safety; Science - Natural
Dist - CONMED **Prod** - CONMED

Reducing sugar and salt - VIII 6 MIN
VHS / U-matic
It's never too late to change series
Color (PRO C G)
$195.00 purchase _ #C881 - VI - 031
Discusses the importance of reducing sugar and salt in the diets of older people. Promotes discussion and participation in group activities and motivates older citizens to adopt healthier nutrition and exercise habits. Part of a nine - part series aimed at retirement home communities, senior citizen organizations and community health centers presented by Dr Molly Engle and Melissa Galvin.
Health and Safety; Physical Education and Recreation; Social Science
Dist - HSCIC

Reducing the risks of PCBs 12 MIN
VHS
Color (A IND G)
$95.00 purchase _ #SHA15051
Gives the history of PCBs and explains the use and health effects as they apply to EPA activities under the Toxic Substances Control Act. Discusses general provisions of the PCB rules such as disposal requirements, registration of PCB transformers with fire departments, notification of building owners, annual inventory report and other recordkeeping requirements.
Health and Safety
Dist - USNAC **Prod** - EPA 1986

Reduction and Fixation of Middle Third Fractures of the Face - Lateral Orbital Rim 13 MIN
16mm
Color
LC 74-705494
Demonstrates the reduction of a fracture of the middle third of the face by lateral orbital approach.
Science
Dist - USNAC **Prod** - USVA 1969

Reduction of Radio Interference - Shipboard Installation 17 MIN
16mm
Machine Workshop Series
B&W
Shows how poor installation practices contribute to radio interference and how good installation practices can eliminate such interferences.
Industrial and Technical Education
Dist - USNAC **Prod** - USN

Reduction of Zygomatic Arch Fracture, Gillies Approach 7 MIN
U-matic
Color (PRO)
LC 76-706221
Demonstrates reduction of a zygomatic arch fracture. Points out how access to the fracture is gained through an aurinculotemporal incision and how reduction is achieved by blind manipulation and touch.
Health and Safety
Dist - USNAC **Prod** - USVA 1969

Reductions in workforce - Legal rights and remedies in downsizing 210 MIN
VHS
Color (C PRO A)
$140.00, $200.00 purchase _ #M801, #P275
Examines the practical problems raised by reductions in force - RIFs - and the potential suits and defenses. Provides instruction for employment and labor law practitioners representing plaintiffs or defendants, litigators, in - house corporate counsel and general practitioners.
Civics and Political Systems; Social Science
Dist - ALIABA **Prod** - ALIABA 1991

Redwood summer 30 MIN
VHS
Color (J H C G)
$195.00 purchase, $45.00 rental
Documents a season of public demonstrations and civil disobedience actions against northern California timber corporations by the environmental action group, Earth First. Covers protests from small town Main Street to confrontations with bulldozers in an ancient redwood grove. Also chronicles events of the tragic bombing of two organizers in May 1990. Produced by Stuart Rickey - Redwood Summer Partners.
Fine Arts; Science - Natural; Social Science; Sociology
Dist - BULFRG

The Redwoods 20 MIN
U-matic / VHS / 16mm
Color (I)
LC FIA68-805
Surveys the future of a vanishing forest of Sequoia sempervirens, a link to the age of the dinosaurs and a testament to nature's power to create and of man's power to destroy.
Geography - United States; Science - Natural
Dist - PHENIX **Prod** - SIERRA 1972

Reed Instruments 30 MIN
U-matic / VHS
Early Musical Instruments Series
Color
Shows the development of reeds from those played by the Saracens to frighten the Crusaders' horses, to the 17th - century forerunners of modern orchestral reed instruments.
Fine Arts
Dist - FOTH **Prod** - GRATV

Reed - Insurgent Mexico 110 MIN
16mm
B&W (SPANISH (ENGLISH SUBTITLES))
Accompanies a left - wing American journalist, John Reed, on a tour through modern Mexico. Shows how he begins participating in revolutionary events, rather than merely reporting them.
Fine Arts; Foreign Language; Geography - World; Sociology
Dist - NYFLMS **Prod** - NYFLMS 1971

The Reef
VHS
Color (G)
$29.95 purchase _ #0273
Portrays a coral reef with its rays, pompano, grouper and sharks. Includes a background of classical music.
Geography - World; Science - Natural; Science - Physical
Dist - SEVVID

The Reef and the rainforest 30 MIN
VHS
Return to the sea series
Color (I J H G)
$24.95 purchase _ #RTS206
Reveals that the tiny country of Belize in Central America is trying to preserve its large tropical rainforest and the second largest barrier reef in the world as a prime source of tourism income. Part of a 13 - part series on marine life produced by Marine Grafics and University of North Carolina Public TV.
Geography - World; Science - Natural
Dist - ENVIMC

Reef at Heron Island 10 MIN
16mm
Ecology of the Ocean Series
Color (I)
LC 77-710536
Describes a reef as an intricate accumulation of organisms whose symbiotic relationships result in a seemingly indestructible barrier to sea and surf.
Science - Natural
Dist - AMEDFL **Prod** - AMEDFL

Reef at Michaelmas Cay 10 MIN
16mm
Ecology of the Ocean Series
Color (I)
LC 70-712314
Shows the beauty and importance of reefs through their evolution and formation throughout geologic history.
Science - Natural; Science - Physical
Dist - AMEDFL **Prod** - AMEDFL 1970

The Reef at the end of the road - Last days of the manatee 30 MIN
VHS
Return to the sea series
Color (I J H G)
$24.95 purchase _ #RTS107
Visits the state of Florida which is blessed with environmental wonders and cursed with environmental challenges. Discloses that pollution, damage by divers and boats, runoff and other environmental problems have assaulted Florida reefs, that the manatee, native to Florida's fresh and salt water ecosystems, is one of America's most endangered marine animals. Part of a 13 - part series on marine life produced by Marine Grafics and University of North Carolina Public TV.
Geography - United States; Science - Natural
Dist - ENVIMC

Reefer Madness 67 MIN
16mm
B&W (J)
Explains the evils of marijuana, previously called 'the devil's weed.' Discusses out - moded views that marijuana may lead to either insanity or death.
Fine Arts
Dist - KITPAR **Prod** - NLC 1936

Reefer madness revisited 29 MIN
VHS
America's drug forum second season series
Color (G)
$19.95 purchase _ #208
Considers that 20 million people in the United States use marijuana and that it is the second most valuable cash crop in the country, after corn. Reveals that critics consider marijuana to be a major health hazard, while advocates say it is less dangerous than alcohol. Discusses who the users are, the effects of marijuana upon them and what society should do with users. Features Dr Frederick Meyers, pharmacologist, University of California, San Francisco, William von Raab, former commissioner, US Customs Service, Dr Gabriel Nahas, drug researcher at Columbia University, Kevin Zeese, VP, Drug Policy Foundation.
Civics and Political Systems; Psychology
Dist - DRUGPF **Prod** - DRUGPF 1992

Reefs 27 MIN
16mm
B&W (C A)
Describes reefs, along with accompanying environment. Utilizes submarine photography to show various portions of a reef. Uses the late Paleozoic Horseshoe Atoll of West Texas as an example.
Science - Natural; Science - Physical
Dist - UTEX **Prod** - UTEX 1960

Reefs 5 MIN
VHS
Seahouse series
Color (K P)
$29.95 purchase _ #RB8152
Compares reefs to jungles where many plants and animals live in a very small space. Reveals that a reef is made up of thousands of tiny animals, coral, and that a reef provides homes for many other animals, large and small. Shows that coral reefs can be easily damaged or completely destroyed, which hurts all the living things which live there. Part of a series of ten parts on marine animals.
Geography - World; Science - Natural
Dist - REVID **Prod** - REVID 1990

Reefs, Deltas and Channels 30 MIN
U-matic / VHS
Basic and Petroleum Geology for Non - Geologists - Sedimentary Rocks Series; Sedimentary rocks
Color (IND)
Industrial and Technical Education; Science - Physical
Dist - GPCV **Prod** - PHILLP

Reefs - Past to Present 28 MIN
U-matic / VHS
Earth Explored Series
Color
Explores the 250 million - year history of the Capitan Reef in Texas, with geologists using microscopic analysis, topographic maps and cross - sectional drawings.
Geography - World; Science - Natural; Science - Physical
Dist - PBS **Prod** - BBCTV

The Reel Way to Lay Pipe 17 MIN
16mm
Color
LC 79-700266
Uses live action and animation to show the advantages of laying pipe on the ocean floor using the reel system.
Industrial and Technical Education
Dist - MARTB **Prod** - SFINTL 1978

The Reel world of news 58 MIN
U-matic / VHS
Walk through the 20th Century with Bill Moyers series
Color
Looks at newsreels, first seen in 1911, and their role in the evolution to televised news. Tells that newsreels disappeared in the mid - 1960s as televised news took over.
Fine Arts; History - United States; History - World; Literature and Drama; Sociology
Dist - PBS **Prod** - CORPEL 1982

Reels, jigs and gavottes - Video Two 105 MIN
VHS
Learn to play Irish fiddle series
Color (G)
$49.95 purchase _ #VD - BUR - FI02
Features Kevin Burke who examines more complex rolls, triplets, grace notes, bowing techniques, rhythmic timing and phrasing. Includes the songs The Cottage Grove; Bonnie Kate; Jenny's Chickens; The Man from Bundoran; The Miller of Droghan; Connie O'Connell's; Dan Collin's Father's Jig; Off to the Races; and three Breton gavottes. Includes music. Part two of a two - part series.
Fine Arts
Dist - HOMETA **Prod** - HOMETA

The Reengineering roadmap - a how - to approach 60 MIN
VHS
Color (G C PRO)
$995.00 purchase, $190.00 rental
Takes a step - by - step approach to successful reengineering with Dr Raymond L Manganelli, coauthor of The Reengineering Handbook. Uses a three - module video format to trace the three stages of reengineering and identify the skills needed for each. Includes case studies from Polaroid Corporation and other organizations.
Business and Economics; Psychology
Dist - FI **Prod** - AMA 1995

Reengineering the corporation - Dr Michael Hammer series 150 MIN
VHS
Reengineering the corporation - Dr Michael Hammer series
Color (G C PRO)
$2000.00 purchase
Presents a two - part series which delves into the six characteristics that distinguish reengineering from other business improvement programs and explores six reengineering guidelines. Discovers how reengineering transforms all aspects of an organization. Focuses on employee resistance and how to keep a program on track. Features Dr Michael Hammer, coauthor of Reengineering the Corporation - a Manifesto for Business Revolution. Includes videocassettes, audiocassettes, leader's and viewer's guides and discussion and self - assessment guides.
Business and Economics; Psychology
Dist - FI **Prod** - HAMMIC 1995

Reengineering the corporation - Dr Michael Hammer series
Reengineering the corporation - Dr Michael Hammer series 150 MIN
Succeeding at reengineering 65 MIN
Understanding reengineering 85 MIN
Dist - FI

Reeving 15 MIN
U-matic / VHS
Safety in Rigging
Color (A IND)
Defines reeving, passing ropes through sheaves in blocks to form an arrangement which gains mechanical advantage. Explains different methods of reeving and how they work. Tells how to determine the safe working load of a tackle system as well as details of selection, care, and inspection of a tackle system.
Health and Safety
Dist - IFB **Prod** - CSAO 1985

Referee 30 MIN
BETA / VHS
American Professionals Series
Color
Deals with the work of Jess Kersey, who has been blowing a whistle and calling the shots for basketball games across the country as a National Basketball Association Referee.
Guidance and Counseling; Physical Education and Recreation; Social Science
Dist - RMIBHF **Prod** - WTBS

Reference Collection
U-matic / VHS
College Library Series
Color
Education
Dist - NETCHE **Prod** - NETCHE 1973

Reference library
CD-ROM
(G)
$149.00 purchase _ #2233
Includes the full text of eight reference books - Webster's Dictionary 3rd College Edition, Webster's Thesaurus, The New York Public Library Desk Reference, The 20th Century History Guide, Business Forms, Webster's New World Dictionary of Quotable Definitions, National Five Digit Zip Code Directory, and The National Directory of Addresses and Telephone Numbers. For IBM PCs and compatibles, requires 640K RAM, DOS 3.1 or later, one floppy disk drive - hard disk recommended, one empty expansion slot, and an IBM compatible CD - ROM drive.
English Language; History - World; Literature and Drama
Dist - BEP

The Reference section 22 MIN
VHS / U-matic / 16mm
Library skills series
Color (P I J)
$500.00, $380.00, $350.00 purchase _ #A295
Shows how to find information in encyclopedias and dictionaries, almanacs and atlases, Current Biography and Who's Who. Looks at the Reader's Guide to Periodical Literature, Statistical Abstracts and other indices. Produced by S S Wilson. Part of a three - part series on library skills.
Education; Psychology; Social Science
Dist - BARR **Prod** - UNDERR 1980

Reference Works in Biology - Biological Abstracts 12 MIN
U-matic / 35mm strip
Color (H C)
$43.95 purchase _ #52 1008
Illustrates how to use the Biological Abstracts for a literature search. Includes a teacher's guide.
Literature and Drama; Science - Natural
Dist - CBSC **Prod** - BMEDIA

The Referral Process 30 MIN
VHS / U-matic
Teaching Children with Special Needs Series
Color (T)
Discusses the referral process used when dealing with children with special needs.
Education
Dist - MDCPB **Prod** - MDDE

Referred for underachievement 34 MIN
16mm / VHS
Documentaries for learning series
B&W (C G PRO)
$465.00, $70.00 purchase, $39.00 rental _ #32304
Records the interview of a 12 - year - old boy referred to a psychiatric clinic as an underachiever, along with his entire family of seven. Part of a series produced for use by health care professionals and educators.
Education; Guidance and Counseling; Health and Safety; Psychology
Dist - PSU **Prod** - MASON 1966

The Refiner's Fire 6 MIN
U-matic / VHS / 16mm
Color (P)
LC 77-701011
Presents an animated abstract ballet, without narration, which depicts the conflict that arises between an established society and its idealistic members who discover and preach a new truth. Uses squares and circles which take on human characteristics in the portrayal of the conflict.
Guidance and Counseling; Psychology; Sociology
Dist - PHENIX **Prod** - BGH 1977

Refinery 14 MIN
16mm
Color
LC 75-703611
Uses animation to explain the functions of a petroleum refinery.
Industrial and Technical Education; Social Science
Dist - MTP **Prod** - EXXON 1975

Refinery and Petrochemical Plant Fire Fighting 60 MIN
VHS / U-matic
Fire Fighting Training Series
Color (IND)
Covers special strategies and techniques, hose handling and tank fires.
Health and Safety; Industrial and Technical Education; Social Science
Dist - LEIKID **Prod** - LEIKID

Refinery and Petrochemical Plant Fires 60 MIN
VHS / U-matic
Fire Protection Training Series
Color
Health and Safety
Dist - ITCORP **Prod** - ITCORP

Refining Basics 60 MIN
VHS
Basic Theory and Systems Series
Color (PRO)
$600.00 - $1500.00 purchase _ #ROCRC
Explains the terminology associated with the operation of common refinery systems and the resulting products. Emphasizes raw materials and characteristics. Describes how petroleum and petroleum products are processed. Looks at the testing of intermediate and final products. Includes ten textbooks and an instructor guide to support four hours of instruction.
Education; Industrial and Technical Education; Psychology
Dist - NUSTC **Prod** - NUSTC

Refining Principles
VHS / U-matic
Pulp and Paper Training - Thermo - Mechanical Pulping Series
Color (IND)
Details refiner operation, loading, axial thrust, steam generation, feed problems, consistency and refiner plates.
Industrial and Technical Education
Dist - LEIKID **Prod** - LEIKID

Refining Your Search Techniques 35 MIN
U-matic / VHS
Computers in Legal Research Series
Color (PRO)
Explains advanced computer searching techniques for law - related material. Suggests ways of reducing the costs of computer research.
Industrial and Technical Education; Mathematics; Sociology
Dist - ABACPE **Prod** - ABACPE

Refinishing antiques - refinishing antiques, varnish - refinishing antiques, paint 30 MIN
BETA / VHS
Wally's workshop series
Color
Fine Arts; Home Economics; Industrial and Technical Education
Dist - KARTES **Prod** - KARTES

Refinishing furniture 57 MIN
VHS
Color (A)
$29.95 purchase _ #VH106V-H
Shows viewers the process of deciding if a piece should be refinished, choosing the appropriate process, stripping and refinishing a piece and repairing furniture. Viewers learn every step from choosing the correct tools to applying the finish. They also learn special tips on how to remove burns, stains, water marks, and scratches. From Better Homes & Gardens.
Industrial and Technical Education; Physical Education and Recreation
Dist - CAMV

Refinishing furniture 57 MIN
VHS
Better homes and gardens video library series
Color (G)
$19.95 purchase
Presents a comprehensive guide to furniture refinishing. Covers stripping, filling, staining, sealing, waxing, and the do's and don'ts of refinishing.
Home Economics; Industrial and Technical Education
Dist - PBS **Prod** - WNETTV

Refinishing Furniture 57 MIN
VHS
Color (G)
$19.95 purchase _ #6112
Goes through the whole process of refinishing furniture, including a variety of commonly needed refinishing repairs.
Home Economics; Industrial and Technical Education; Sociology
Dist - SYBVIS **Prod** - HOMES

The Reflectance map 45 MIN
U-matic / VHS
Artificial intelligence series; Computer vision, Pt 3
Color (PRO)
Features the reflectance map, properties of Lambertian surfaces, the photometric stereo technique, and needle diagrams and depth maps.
Psychology
Dist - MIOT **Prod** - MIOT

Reflectant Spectroscopy 9 MIN
U-matic / VHS
Color
LC 80-706814
Uses diagrams and actual equipment to teach the principles of operating a chemical reflectant photometer. Describes calibration and maintenance procedures.
Science
Dist - USNAC **Prod** - CFDISC 1979

Reflected Light 15 MIN
U-matic / VHS
Why Series
Color (P I)
Discusses reflected light.
Science - Physical
Dist - AITECH **Prod** - WDCNTV 1976

Reflecting on the Life Career of a Dancer 30 MIN
U-matic / VHS
Dancers' Survival Tactics Series
Color
Fine Arts; Guidance and Counseling
Dist - ARCVID **Prod** - ARCVID

Reflecting on the Moon 15 MIN
16mm / U-matic / VHS
Color (P I)
Deals with the moon's composition, gravity, lack of atmosphere, orbit, phases, exploration and effect on earth.
Science - Physical
Dist - NGS **Prod** - NGS 1982

Reflection - a Film about Time and Relatedness 57
16mm / VHS
Color (H A)
$950.00 purchase, $95.00 rental
Investigates the cosmological significance in the architectural design of apparently unrelated structures, including Chartres Cathedral, Stonehenge, and the Mandan Indian Lodge. Presented by Keith Critchlow.
Fine Arts
Dist - AFA **Prod** - ACGB 1978

Reflection - a Metaphoric Journey 9 MIN
16mm
Color
Presents a fable about one man's struggle to find meaning in life.
Fine Arts
Dist - HP **Prod** - HP

Reflection and refraction - 29 41 MIN
VHS
Conceptual physics alive series
Color (H C)
$45.00 purchase
Compares mirrored and diffuse reflections. Demonstrates refraction using a water tank. Explains rainbows, with a demonstration of their bow shape. Part 29 of a 35 - part series adapted from the college and high school textbook Conceptual Physics by Professor Paul Hewitt.
Science - Physical
Dist - MMENTE **Prod** - HEWITP 1992

Reflection of Light 9 MIN
U-matic / VHS
Introductory Concepts in Physics - Light Series
Color (C)
$229.00, $129.00 purchase _ #AD - 1205
Illustrates the scientific laws of angle of incidence and angle of reflection through experiments with light reflected from a mirror.
Science - Physical
Dist - FOTH **Prod** - FOTH

Reflections 29 MIN
16mm
Color
LC 76-702875
Presents a documentary on American life by examining the beliefs and values of residents of a seven - county region of Pennsylvania, with narrative in the words of the people themselves.
Geography - United States; Guidance and Counseling; Sociology
Dist - GITTFI **Prod** - GITTFI 1976

Reflections 25 MIN
16mm
Color (A)
LC 79-700926
Presents a group of eight people who regularly share sex together, giving their opinions and experiences, first in discussion and then in lovemaking in a mirrored room.
Psychology
Dist - NATSF **Prod** - NATSF 1976

Reflections 60 MIN
VHS / U-matic
Color
Presents Dr Carl Rogers discussing his development. Also presents Dr Warren Bennis, an expert in the field of group dynamics and organizational development.
Psychology
Dist - PSYCHF **Prod** - PSYCHF

Reflections 20 MIN
VHS / U-matic
Folk Book Series
Color (P)
Features folktales from Japan, Russia and Korea.
Literature and Drama
Dist - AITECH **Prod** - UWISC 1980

Reflections 16 MIN
U-matic / VHS / 16mm
Color (H C A)
LC 80-700307
Presents astronaut Rusty Schweickart's philosophical reactions to the grandeur of viewing the Earth during his incredible journey.
Industrial and Technical Education; Religion and Philosophy; Science - Physical
Dist - LCOA **Prod** - VARDIR 1980

Reflections 12 MIN
16mm
B&W w/color tint (H C A)
$30.00 rental
Journeys through a collection of past life experiences. Utilizes filtered light, shadows, multiple exposures, and film tinting to create a surrealistic, hypnotic effect. Resembles the late 1980s Behrens film entitled "Exposures". Produced by Jon Behrens with original music by Rubato.
Fine Arts; Religion and Philosophy
Dist - CANCIN

Reflections 17 MIN
U-matic / VHS
Witness to the Holocaust Series
B&W (J)
Presents survivors of the Jewish Holocaust reflecting on such questions as how the scope of Nazi atrocities grew beyond the Jewish question to include non - Jews and what universal lessons can be learned from the Holocaust.
History - World; Religion and Philosophy
Dist - CNEMAG **Prod** - HORECE 1983

Reflections 10 MIN
16mm
B&W
Shows the United States of America through the metaphor of a used car junk heap. Begins with 'artistic' close - ups of parts of old cars, and the huge machinery needed to make scrap out of them. Concludes with the steel teeth of the scrap derrick across a highway and the American flag waving in the midst of grain and storage tanks.
Fine Arts; Geography - United States; Social Science; Sociology
Dist - UPENN **Prod** - UPENN 1970

Reflections - a Cultural History 30 MIN
U-matic / VHS
Kaleidoscope Series
Color
Fine Arts
Dist - SCCOE **Prod** - KTEHTV

Reflections - a Japanese Folk Tale 19 MIN
U-matic / VHS / 16mm
Color (P I)
LC 75-703662
Presents an Oriental folk tale, showing different human responses to an unfamiliar experience, which exemplifies unresolved or unresolvable dilemmas.
Geography - World; Literature and Drama; Social Science
Dist - EBEC **Prod** - EBEC 1975

Reflections - a Metaphoric Journey 9 MIN
U-matic / VHS
Color
Presents one woman's struggle to find meaning in life. Told as a fable.
Religion and Philosophy; Sociology
Dist - HP **Prod** - HP

Reflections and Cast Shadows 15 MIN
VHS / 16mm
Drawing with Paul Ringler Series
Color (I H)
$125.00 purchase, $25.00 rental
Compares and contrasts reflections and cast shadows; demonstrates how they are drawn.
Fine Arts; Industrial and Technical Education
Dist - AITECH **Prod** - OETVA 1988

Reflections and cast shadows 15 MIN
VHS
Drawing with Paul Ringler Series; 14
Color (I)
$125.00 purchase
Shows how reflections and cast shadows are similar and different, and how they are drawn. Emphasizes the drawing process, for older students, rather than drawing specific objects. Part of a thirty - part series.
Fine Arts
Dist - AITECH **Prod** - OETVA 1988

Reflections at 75 31 MIN
VHS
Documentaries for learning series
Color (C G PRO)
$70.00 purchase, $28.00 rental _ #35643
Features 10 graduates of the Massachusetts Mental Health Center in the 1920s, including Karl Menninger, who recall experiences in their training to care for for the severely mentally ill. Provides a perspective on the history of mental health care in the United States. Part of a series produced for use by health care professionals and educators.
Health and Safety; History - United States; Psychology
Dist - PSU **Prod** - MASON 1987

Reflections, Carl Rogers 59 MIN
16mm
Color (C G)
Shows Warren Bennis, President of the University of Cincinnati, interviewing Carl Rogers. Presents Rogers' theories and how they were formed.
Guidance and Counseling; Psychology
Dist - AACD **Prod** - AACD 1976

Reflections - George Meany 52 MIN
16mm
Color (G IND) (ENGLISH, SPANISH)
Presents an intimate conversation with George Meany who reflects on his lifetime of service to American workers. Includes documentary footage, photographs and cartoons.
Biography; Business and Economics; History - United States; Social Science
Dist - AFLCIO USNAC **Prod** - ICA 1979

Reflections - George Meany - Pt 1 26 MIN
16mm
Color (C A) (ENGLISH, SPANISH)
LC 80-700514
Focuses on American labor leader George Meany.
Business and Economics; Social Science
Dist - USNAC **Prod** - USINCA 1979

Reflections - George Meany - Pt 2 26 MIN
16mm
Color (C A) (ENGLISH, SPANISH)
LC 80-700514
Focuses on American labor leader George Meany.
Civics and Political Systems; Social Science
Dist - USNAC **Prod** - USINCA 1979

Reflections - Imaginations 15 MIN
VHS
Color (G)
$29.95 purchase
Uses a journey through many lands as a metaphor for one's journey through life with the conclusion that love is the answer. Includes Imaginations, a short inspirational video on the creative uses of the imagination.
Fine Arts; Health and Safety; Literature and Drama; Religion and Philosophy
Dist - HP

Reflections in a golden eye 109 MIN
16mm
Color
Tells how an Army colonel hides his impotence from his nymphomaniacal wife, who in turn has an affair with another officer whose wife is losing her mind. Stars Marlon Brando, Julie Harris, Elizabeth Taylor and Brian Keith. Based on the novel Reflections in A Golden Eye by Carson McCullers. Directed by Carson McCullers.
Fine Arts
Dist - TWYMAN **Prod** - WB 1967

Reflections in a Pond 10 MIN
16mm / U-matic / VHS
Color (K P I J H C)
LC 76-715426
Presents a story about animal life of the pond, using free form music and sound effects to show a pair of swans during their courtship - nest building and other activities.
Science - Natural
Dist - JOU **Prod** - WER 1971

Reflections - Ireland 17 MIN
16mm
Color (H C A)
LC 79-701091
Depicts the sights of Ireland, showing landscape, greenery, animal life and sea.
Geography - World
Dist - CECROP **Prod** - ITO 1979

Reflections - Margaret Mead 58 MIN
16mm
Color (H C A)
LC 80-700166
Presents Margaret Mead discussing a wide range of subjects, including her childhood, her studies of primitive peoples, the evolution of women's suffrage, World War II, the atomic bomb, mental health and the environment.
Sociology
Dist - USNAC **Prod** - ICA 1975

Reflections - Margaret Mead, Pt 1 29 MIN
16mm
Color (H C A)
LC 80-700166
Presents Margaret Mead discussing a wide range of subjects, including her childhood, her studies of primitive peoples, the evolution of women's suffrage, World War II, the atomic bomb, mental health and the environment.
Social Science
Dist - USNAC **Prod** - ICA 1975

Reflections - Margaret Mead, Pt 2 29 MIN
16mm
Color (H C A)
LC 80-700166
Presents Margaret Mead discussing a wide range of subjects, including her childhood, her studies of primitive peoples, the evolution of women's suffrage, World War II, the atomic bomb, mental health and the environment.
Sociology
Dist - USNAC **Prod** - ICA 1975

Reflections, no 2 7 MIN
16mm
Color
Shows a moulding of light patterns into a controlled artistic expression. Presents an interplay of shapes and colors in building complexity.
Fine Arts; Science - Physical
Dist - RADIM **Prod** - DAVISJ

Reflections of a Good Life 15 MIN
16mm
Color
Points out the social and business opportunities available in Palm Beach, Florida.
Geography - United States; Physical Education and Recreation
Dist - FLADC **Prod** - FLADC

Reflections of Man 13 MIN
16mm
Color
LC 74-702846
Explores the basic universal nature of all men through an examination of chess pieces from all over the world.
Civics and Political Systems; Psychology; Sociology
Dist - USC **Prod** - USC 1974

Reflections of Spinal Cord Injuries 60 MIN
VHS / U-matic
B&W
Interviews a quadraplegic man and a paraplegice woman, both of whom were injured in their teens. Discusses their experiences as hospital patients undergoing rehabilitation and their lives since then.
Health and Safety; Psychology; Sociology
Dist - UWISC **Prod** - UWISC 1979

Reflections on elephants 59 MIN
VHS
Color; CC (G)
$24.20 purchase - #A51656
Presents film by Dereck and Beverly Joubert of the details of elephant life in northern Botswana. Shows how the large animals work together to find food and to protect each other. Includes unusual film of lions hunting elephants. Purchase includes closed - circuit rights for educational institutions to show this television special.
Science - Natural
Dist - NGS **Prod** - NGS 1994

Reflections on Richard Wright, native son 60 MIN
VHS
Europe and America in the modern age - 1776 to the present series
Color (H C PRO)
$95.00 purchase
Presents a lecture by David M Kennedy. Focuses on a critical period in European and American history and on leaders of the time. Part of a 20 - part series that looks at the last two centuries in Europe and America. Series presents lectures by David M Kennedy and James Sheehan of Stanford University on such figures as Adam Smith, Marx, Lincoln, Washington, Jefferson, Freud, Margaret Sanger, Susan B Anthony and Jane Adams and their impact on the events of their day. For history resource material and continuing education courses.
Civics and Political Systems; History - United States; History - World
Dist - LANDMK

Reflections on Suffering 20 MIN
16mm
Color
Presents a conversation between a doctor and a cancer victim who has come to terms with her illness.
Health and Safety; Psychology
Dist - NFBC **Prod** - NFBC 1982

Reflections on the Long Search 52 MIN
16mm / VHS
Long Search Series
(H C)
$99.95 each, $595.00 series
Summarizes the remainder of the movies in the Long Search Series.
Religion and Philosophy
Dist - AMBROS **Prod** - AMBROS 1978

Reflections on the long search 52 MIN
16mm / U-matic / VHS
Long search series; 13
Color (H C A)
LC 78-700483
Presents theater director Ronald Eyre discussing personal reflections on his pilgrimage through the world in which he explored the religious beliefs and experiences of various peoples.
Religion and Philosophy; Sociology
Dist - TIMLIF **Prod** - BBCTV 1978

Reflections on Time 22 MIN
U-matic / VHS / 16mm
Earth Science Program Series
Color (I J H)
LC 75-704192
Discusses subjective, objective and geological time. Follows a geologist down the Grand Canyon as he records his interpretation of the significance of each layer within the millions of years locked inside the rock formation.
Science - Physical
Dist - EBEC **Prod** - EBEC 1969

Reflections on Waves 24 MIN
U-matic / VHS
Discovering Physics Series
Color (H C)
Introduces key concepts about electromagnetism, waves, and resonance using a case study of a new airfield surveillance radar system under development. Describes how radar works and defines a radar signal.
Industrial and Technical Education; Science - Physical
Dist - MEDIAG **Prod** - BBCTV 1983

Reflections - returning to Vietnam 30 MIN
VHS
Color (G)
$125.00 purchase, $50.00 rental
Explores three individual perspectives of the Vietnamese diaspora since the fall of Saigon in 1975. Features Huy Le, Vu Duc Vuong and Thuy Vu who speak of the loss of family and friends, migration, feelings about their war - torn homeland, and the complex challenges faced by many Asian immigrants in American culture. Features San Francisco Bay area journalist Jan Yanehiro as host, produced by KCSM, San Mateo, California.
History - United States; Sociology
Dist - CROCUR

Reflections - Samuel Eliot Morison 58 MIN
U-matic / VHS / 16mm
Color
Profiles Samuel Eliot Morison, historian, discussing his early years, his 40 - year relationship with Harvard University and the influences that led him to become the biographer of Columbus, Magellan, John Paul Jones and others. Explores his interest in maritime history.
Biography; History - United States; Literature and Drama
Dist - USNAC **Prod** - USIA 1982

Reflections series
Girl on the edge of town 25 MIN
Dist - MEDIAG

Reflections Series
Chicken 28 MIN
A Family of winners 28 MIN
Friend in deed 30 MIN
It Can't Happen to Me 25 MIN
The Sex game 20 MIN
Soupman 25 MIN
This One for Dad 18 MIN
When, Jenny, When 25 MIN
Dist - PAULST

Reflets de la vie intellectuelle 19 MIN
16mm
Aspects de France series
Color (FRENCH)
A French language film. Traces France's intellectual creativity and expression through the centuries.
History - World
Dist - MLA **Prod** - WSUM 1966

Reflex hammer techniques 13 MIN
VHS / U-matic
Color (PRO C)
$395.00 purchase, $80.00 rental _ #C871 - VI - 044
Teaches proper techniques for the deep tendon reflexes commonly practiced in neurologic examinations - the knee, ankle, bicep and tricep reflexes. Shows how to test other important reflexes such as the abductor, pronator, abdominal, hamstring, finger flexion and jaw jerk reflexes. Presented by Dr Howard S Barrows.
Health and Safety
Dist - HSCIC

Reflex Klystron 40 MIN
16mm
B&W
LC 74-705496
Uses a mock - up to give a pictorial view of the construction and components of the reflex klystron. Shows the operation of the tube, emphasizing the bunching and catching action of the cavity. Shows how repeller plate voltage can be changed to obtain the different modes of operation. (Kinescope).
Industrial and Technical Education
Dist - USNAC **Prod** - USAF

Reflexes
U-matic / VHS
Physical Assessment - Neurologic System Series
Color
Health and Safety; Psychology
Dist - CONMED **Prod** - CONMED

Reflexes and conscious movement 28 MIN
VHS
Human body - the nervous system - series
Color (J H G)
$89.95 purchase _ #UW4174
Looks at the range of reflexive and controlled, conscious and unconscious movements of the human body. Shows how the controlling nerve impulses are originated and executed. Part of a 39 - part series featuring computer animation, medical photography, electron micrography, full - color drawings and diagrams and three - dimensional working models to cover the workings of the human body from head to toe and inside out.
Science - Natural
Dist - FOTH

Reflexes in the Cerebral Palsied Child 24 MIN
U-matic / VHS

B&W
Discusses the effect of the cortical, midbrain, brainstem and spiral level reflexes on the child with cerebral palsy.
Health and Safety
Dist - BUSARG **Prod** - BUSARG

Reflexions 4 MIN
VHS / U-matic
Color
Presents an abstract of nighttime water reflections. Uses hand - colored imagery. An experimental film.
Fine Arts; Industrial and Technical Education; Science - Physical
Dist - MEDIPR **Prod** - MEDIPR 1979

Reflux (Peptic) Esophagitis 30 MIN
U-matic / VHS
Color
Discusses causes and treatment of reflux esophagitis.
Health and Safety
Dist - ROWLAB **Prod** - ROWLAB

Reform and reaction 30 MIN
VHS / U-matic
America - the second century series
Color (H C)
$34.95 purchase
Discusses the political swings involved in reform and reaction in American politics. Part of a 30-part series on political, economic and social issues in the United States since 1875.
History - United States
Dist - DALCCD **Prod** - DALCCD
GPN

Reform at Last 22 MIN
16mm
Color (A)
Views the delay tactics of employers to prevent union organizing from the workers' perspective. Documents the weakness of the NLRB enforcement procedures.
Business and Economics; Civics and Political Systems; Psychology
Dist - AFLCIO **Prod** - AFLCIO 1977

The Reformation 14 MIN
16mm / U-matic / VHS
Color (J H C) (GERMAN)
Discusses how criticism of the Catholic Church, the cultural rebirth brought about by the Renaissance, the emergence of national states and new interpretations of the Scriptures combined to bring about the Reformation. Focuses on Martin Luther and the Protestant Reformation in Germany.
History - World; Religion and Philosophy
Dist - CORF **Prod** - CORF 1979

The Reformation 30 MIN
16mm
How should we then live - Dutch series; No 4
Color (DUTCH)
LC 77-702366
Surveys the contributions of the Reformation towards a reestablishment of man's spiritual integrity which had been threatened by the worldliness of the Renaissance. Based on the book How Should We Then Live by Francis A Schaeffer.
Foreign Language; Religion and Philosophy
Dist - GF **Prod** - GF 1977

The Reformation 20 MIN
VHS
Lutherans and their beliefs series
Color (J H C G A R)
$39.95 purchase, $10.00 rental _ #35 - 8107 - 2076
Features Dr Jerry L Schmalenberger in a consideration of Lutheran views on the Protestant Reformation. Produced by Seraphim.
Religion and Philosophy
Dist - APH

The Reformation 52 MIN
U-matic / VHS / 16mm
Color (H C A)
LC FIA67-1609
Explores the factors which prompted the development of the schism between Protestants and Roman Catholics during the 16th century.
History - World; Religion and Philosophy
Dist - MGHT **Prod** - NBCTV 1967

The Reformation 30 MIN
16mm
How should we then live series; Episode 4
Color
LC 77-702366
Surveys the contributions of the Reformation towards a reestablishment of man's spiritual integrity which had been threatened by the worldliness of the Renaissance. Based on the book How Should We Then Live by Francis A Schaeffer.
Religion and Philosophy
Dist - GF **Prod** - GF 1977

The Reformation 13 MIN
VHS
Color; PAL (H)
Traces the origins of the Reformation to four major factors - criticism of the leadership of the Catholic Church, the cultural rebirth of the Renaissance, the emergence of nation states, and radical new interpretations of the Scriptures. Looks at the work of Calvin, Zwingli and Knox, but focuses on Martin Luther and the Protestant Reformation in Germany.
Religion and Philosophy
Dist - VIEWTH

The Reformation 45 MIN
16mm / U-matic / VHS
Christians Series
Color (H A)
Discusses the Reformation of the church by such men as Luther and Calvin. Shows how although the Reformation movement had many great leaders, it did not have a consistent view.
Religion and Philosophy
Dist - MGHT **Prod** - GRATV 1978

The Reformation - age of revolt 24 MIN
16mm / U-matic / VHS
Humanities - philosophy and political thought series
Color (H C)
LC 73-701227
Introduces the political, social and religious climate that existed in Europe during the 16th century. Emphasizes the religious reforms of Martin Luther as indicators of the future trend and reflection of their historical context.
History - World; Religion and Philosophy
Dist - EBEC **Prod** - EBEC 1973

Reformation overview 180 MIN
VHS
Color (G R)
$99.95 purchase
Brings Reformation to life and introduces viewers to reformers - Wycliffe, Hus, Luther, Zwingli, Calvin, Anabaptists, Tyndale - and significant turning points. Features interspersed on-site segments from places where events occurred. Full curriculum package can be adapted to 6, 12, or 13-session format.
History - World; Religion and Philosophy
Dist - GF

The Reformation - Pt 1 26 MIN
16mm / U-matic / VHS
Color (H C A)
LC FIA67-1609
Explores the factors which prompted the development of the schism between Protestants and Roman Catholics during the 16th century.
History - World; Religion and Philosophy
Dist - MGHT **Prod** - NBCTV 1967

The Reformation - Pt 2 26 MIN
U-matic / VHS / 16mm
Color (H C A)
LC FIA67-1609
Explores the factors which prompted the development of the schism between Protestants and Roman Catholics during the 16th century.
Religion and Philosophy
Dist - MGHT **Prod** - NBCTV 1967

The Reformation - the rise of the middle class 60 MIN
VHS / U-matic
Western tradition - part II series; Pts 27 and 28
Color (G)
$45.00, $29.95 purchase
Presents two thirty - minute programs tracing the history of ideas, events and institutions which have shaped modern societies hosted by Eugen Weber. Explores the life and beliefs of Martin Luther, who shattered the unity of the Roman Catholic Church and ushered in Protestantism in part 27. Part 28 examines the impact of the growing middle class on religious life in European cities. Parts 27 and 28 of a 52 - part series on the Western tradition.
Geography - World; History - World; Religion and Philosophy; Sociology
Dist - ANNCPB **Prod** - WGBH 1989

Reforming the republic 30 MIN
VHS
American adventure series
Color (G)
$150.00 purchase _ #TAMA - 118
Describes the reform movement that swept the U S during Andrew Jackson's presidency. Illustrates the influence of the Transcendental and Utopian movements on American life.
History - United States
Dist - PBS

The Refracted image
VHS / BETA
Adult years - continuity and change series
Color (GREEK)
Examines representations of the human figure in Greek, Renaissance, and modern visual arts, and discusses the images of adulthood in these historical periods. Explores the role of the arts in conveying these images.
Fine Arts
Dist - OHUTC **Prod** - OHUTC

Refraction 6 MIN
16mm
From the Light Series
B&W (J H)
Covers refraction through various media, right angled prisms, periscopes and binoculars.
Science - Physical
Dist - VIEWTH **Prod** - GBI

Refraction of Light 10 MIN
U-matic / VHS
Introductory Concepts in Physics - Light Series
Color (C)
$229.00, $129.00 purchase _ #AD - 1206
Examines various applicable laws including effects of the degree of refraction through experiments with the refractive property of light.
Science - Physical
Dist - FOTH **Prod** - FOTH

Refraction of light by spherical lenses 10 MIN
16mm / U-matic / VHS
Optics of the human eye series
Color (C PRO)
Health and Safety; Science - Natural
Dist - TEF **Prod** - BAYCMO

Refraction of Light by Spherocylindrical Lenses 10 MIN
16mm / U-matic / VHS
Optics of the Human Eye Series
Color (H C A)
Health and Safety; Science - Natural
Dist - TEF **Prod** - BAYCMO

Refraction, Pt 2 22 MIN
16mm
Optics Series
B&W (H)
Continues the investigation of refraction beginning with the path of rays of light through a prism, followed by total internal reflection.
Science - Physical
Dist - GPN **Prod** - CETO

Refractions, no 1 7 MIN
16mm
Color
Shows how light passes through the transparent material of objects and is bent or refracted in a spectrum of colors.
Science - Physical
Dist - RADIM **Prod** - DAVISJ

Refractive Errors 25 MIN
VHS / U-matic
Color (PRO)
Defines preshyopia, myopia, hyperopia, astigmatism and cataracts and describes how these conditions affect vision. Discusses corrective procedures to modify these conditions, including the use of glasses and contact lenses.
Health and Safety; Science - Natural
Dist - UMICHM **Prod** - UMICHM 1976

The Refractory cast in removable partial denture construction 15 MIN
U-matic / VHS
; Pt I
Color (PRO)
Demonstrates the various steps involved in modifying the master cast, surveying, block out and its duplication, stressing the importance of this procedure in the production of accurate removable partial denture casting.
Health and Safety; Science
Dist - AMDA **Prod** - VADTC 1979

The Refractory cast in removable partial denture construction 5 MIN
16mm
Color (PRO)
LC 81-700643
Demonstrates the transfer of design, steps involved in modifying the master cast, surveying, block out and duplication for accurate removable partial denture casting.
Health and Safety; Science
Dist - USNAC **Prod** - VA 1980

Refractory heart failure - medical and surgical management 45 MIN
VHS / U-matic

Color (PRO C)
$395.00 purchase, $80.00 rental _ #C901 - VI - 082
Looks at management of congestive heart failure patients. Focuses on left ventricular afterload reductions using a drug management program designed especially for the control of super ventricular arrhythmias. Discusses the pros and cons of mechanical devices as a last measure to save the patient. Presented by cardiologists Drs Hermes A Kontos, Michael L Hess and Robert B Williams, Medical College of Virginia, Virginia Commonwealth University.
Health and Safety
Dist - HSCIC

Refractory Maintenance 60 MIN
VHS
Boiler Maintenance Series
Color (PRO)
$600.00, $1500.00 purchase _ #GMRMT
Describes various types of refractory and boiler wall construction to show how to select the proper type of refractory for a particular application. Explains refractory failure, causes, symptoms and repair techniques. Part of a six - part series on boiler maintenance, part of a larger set on general and mechanical maintenance. Includes 10 textbooks and an instructor guide which provide four hours of instruction.
Education; Industrial and Technical Education; Psychology
Dist - NUSTC **Prod** - NUSTC

Refrains of Paris 16 MIN
16mm
B&W (H C)
Presents Jacqueline Francois, French Chanteuse, singing three songs against a Parisian background. 'De La Madelein A L'Opera,' a satirical present - day ballad, is pantomimed as Georgette Plana sings.
Fine Arts
Dist - REMBRT **Prod** - ART 1955

Refresher course in chemical safety series
Presents a four - part series on chemical safety. Includes the titles Chemical Hazards - A Refresher Session; Spill Response - A Refresher Session; Hazardous Waste - A Refresher Session; Personal Protective - A Refresher Session. A trainer's manual and ten employee manuals accompanies each program.
Chemical hazards - a refresher session - I 14 MIN
Hazardous waste - a refresher session - III 17 MIN
Personal protective equipment - a refresher session - IV 16 MIN
Spill response - a refresher session - II 14 MIN
Dist - BNA **Prod** - BNA 1955

Refrigerated ammonia spill tests 22 MIN
16mm
Color
LC FI68-223
Shows controlled one - ton and ten - ton low - temperature spills designed to determine evaporation rates, concentration and spread of vapors, reaction to water and flammability under the test conditions.
Industrial and Technical Education; Science - Physical
Dist - PHILLP **Prod** - PHILLP 1965

Refrigeration - Compressor Controls 6 MIN
16mm
B&W
LC 73-701074
Depicts how the low pressure switch turns on and off the compressor motor via motor controller and how safety controls protect compressor and motor.
Industrial and Technical Education
Dist - USNAC **Prod** - USN 1957

Refrigeration - Condenser Controls 5 MIN
16mm
B&W
LC 73-701075
Shows controls for the condenser of a refrigeration system. Demonstrates how the refrigeration pressure in the high pressure line is used by the water - regulating valve to control the flow of water through the condenser. Tells how use of the water failure switch serves as protection for the compressor.
Industrial and Technical Education
Dist - USNAC **Prod** - USN 1957

The Refrigeration cycle
VHS
Refrigeration training seminars by Bob Graham series
Color (G IND)
$55.00 purchase
Presents the theory of refrigeration. Covers important concepts from beginning theory to the concept of superheat. Part of a series of refrigeration training seminars by Bob Graham.
Industrial and Technical Education; Psychology; Science - Physical
Dist - AACREF **Prod** - AACREF 1990

Refrigeration - Evacuating and Charging 13 MIN
16mm
Color
LC 74-705498
Demonstrates procedures for removing air and moisture from refrigeration lines and charging the unit with fresh refrigerant. Shows how to attach the manifold gauge assembly, evacuate the system and conduct a leak test prior to charging.
Industrial and Technical Education
Dist - USNAC **Prod** - USAF 1957

Refrigeration - Evaporator Controls 8 MIN
16mm
B&W
LC 74-705499
Examines how the thermostatic switch and solenoid valve work to deliver full flow refrigerant to the thermal expansion valve. Shows how the super head is used by the thermal expansion valve to control the flow of refrigerant into the evaporator coil and how the evaporator pressure regulator works to release refrigerant from the evaporator to the compressor.
Industrial and Technical Education
Dist - USNAC **Prod** - USN 1957

Refrigeration - Introduction to Control Mechanisms 10 MIN
16mm
B&W
LC 74-705500
Explains the function of the automatic controls in the refrigeration cycle and use of the manual control in emergencies.
Industrial and Technical Education
Dist - USNAC **Prod** - USN 1970

Refrigeration - Motors, Controls and Testing Them 16 MIN
VHS / U-matic
Color (H C A)
Shows the single phase motor compressors, single phase motors, capacitor start run, permanent split capacitor, meters and how to use them, locating terminals on unmarked dome, testing relays, capacitors and fuses.
Industrial and Technical Education
Dist - SF **Prod** - SF 1970

Refrigeration - Multiple Temperature Evaporator 16 MIN
VHS / U-matic
Color (H C A)
Presents an instructional film on installation and valves, surge tank and oil separator, thermostat and solenoid valve, short cycling of compressor and the sizing liquid reservoirs.
Industrial and Technical Education
Dist - SF **Prod** - SF 1970

Refrigeration service - commercial systems, No 1 series
Adjusting and repairing the thermo expansion valve 12 MIN
Dist - USNAC

Refrigeration service - Commercial systems No 3 series
Adjusting commercial thermostatic controls 12 MIN
Dist - USNAC

Refrigeration service - domestic units series
Adding or removing refrigerant 17 MIN
Adjusting and checking the expansion valve 21 MIN
Checking and replacing a float valve 19 MIN
Checking the electrical system 17 MIN
Checking the system - Pt 1 - general procedure 17 MIN
Checking the system - Pt 2 - trouble shooting 17 MIN
Locating and repairing leaks 17 MIN
Quieting a noisy refrigerator 16 MIN
Dist - USNAC

Refrigeration Service Fundamentals
VHS / 35mm strip
$295.00 purchase _ #DXRSF060 filmstrips, $295.00 purchase _
Provides instruction on the the tools, equipment and safety, ACR tubing, diagnosing refrigeration problems, and servicing refrigeration systems.
Education; Industrial and Technical Education
Dist - CAREER **Prod** - CAREER

Refrigeration Service Series Commercial Systems, no 5
Making and Repairing Tubing Connections 18 MIN
Dist - USNAC

Refrigeration service series commercial systems
Servicing water - cooled condensers 12 MIN
Dist - USNAC

Refrigeration service series
Removing and installing a compressor or condenser 17 MIN
Removing and installing a cooling unit 19 MIN
Dist - USNAC

Refrigeration systems - 1 60 MIN
VHS
Systems operations series
Color (IND)
$600.00 - $1500.00 purchase _ #OTRS1
Introduces the refrigeration process. Provides functional descriptions of typical refrigeration systems and components. Covers cooling systems. Part of a seventeen - part series on systems operations. Includes ten textbooks and an instructor guide to support four hours of instruction.
Industrial and Technical Education; Psychology
Dist - NUSTC **Prod** - NUSTC

Refrigeration systems - 2 60 MIN
VHS
Systems operations series
Color (IND)
$600.00 - $1500.00 purchase _ #OTRS2
Focuses on the functions and operation of heating, ventilating and air conditioning - HVAC - systems. Overviews the air conditioning process and typical dust and humidity control devices. Part of a seventeen - part series on systems operations. Includes ten textbooks and an instructor guide to support four hours of instruction.
Industrial and Technical Education; Psychology
Dist - NUSTC **Prod** - NUSTC

Refrigeration training seminars by Bob Graham series
Lube oil controls
Pressure controls
The Refrigeration cycle
Temperature controls - Pts 1 and 2
Dist - AACREF

Refuelling 32 MIN
16mm
Operating a Calder Hall Reactor Series
Color (PRO)
Illustrates the fuel channels in a Calder Hall reactor discharging spent fuel, preparation of new fuel elements and refuelling.
Industrial and Technical Education; Science - Physical
Dist - UKAEA **Prod** - UKAEA 1959

Refuge in the sea 26 MIN
VHS
Challenge of the seas series
Color (I J H)
$225.00 purchase
Reveals that kelp forests in the oceans are as huge as the giant redwoods and are home to creatures ranging from tiny fish to giant whales. Part of a 26 - part series on the oceans.
Science - Natural; Science - Physical
Dist - LANDMK **Prod** - LANDMK 1991

Refugee Road 59 MIN
16mm
Color
Follows a Laotian family from a refugee camp in Thailand to the United States. Illustrates the differences in cultures.
Sociology
Dist - HRC **Prod** - OHC

Refugees 23 MIN
U-matic / VHS
Color
Shows the arrival of the Hmong family in Minnesota, pointing out the difficulties of adapting to life in a new country.
Sociology
Dist - WCCOTV **Prod** - WCCOTV 1979

Refugees 30 MIN
VHS
Inside Britain 4 series
Color; PAL; NTSC (G) (BULGARIAN CZECH HUNGARIAN SPANISH POLISH ROMANIAN RUSSIAN SLOVAK UKRAINIAN LITHUANIAN)
PdS65 purchase
Reveals that Great Britain has accepted refugees for over 400 years. Profiles asylum seekers from Vietnam as they make new lives for themselves in Britain.
Sociology
Dist - CFLVIS **Prod** - LDNSCI 1993

Refugees - an Historical View 22 MIN
U-matic / VHS / 16mm

Color
Examines the history of world refugeeism by looking at the plight of such diverse groups as the Jews, Pilgrims and the displaced millions from the Russian Revolution and World Wars I and II. Discusses several solutions to refugeeism suggested by world leaders and organizations.
Sociology
Dist - CRMP **Prod** - UN

Refugees in our backyard 58 MIN
16mm / VHS
Color (G)
$895.00, $390.00 purchase, $125.00 rental
Looks at the controversies created by the arrival into the United States of so many undocumented aliens seeking refuge from violent civil wars and acute economic crises. Investigates the impact of civil strife on Central America and the enormous obstacles its people face as they attempt to escape into the US. Graphic scenes of destruction and violence in that region provide a jolting backdrop to the cautious words of US officials and the refugees' own stories. Produced by George Nahitchevansky and Helena Pollack Sultan.
Fine Arts; History - World; Sociology
Dist - FIRS

Refuse Disposal by Sanitary Landfills 13 MIN
16mm
Color
LC FIE57-8
Describes the faults of disposal methods such as open dumps and compares the hazards of these methods to those of landfills. Shows how to select a site and procedures to use.
Health and Safety
Dist - USNAC **Prod** - USPHS 1956

Refuse Disposal by Sanitary Landfills 13 MIN
16mm
Color (SPANISH)
LC 74-705501
Discusses the faults of disposal methods, such as open dumps, and compares the vector - borne disease and nuisance hazards of these methods to those of landfills. Shows how to select a site, types of equipment used, how to construct a landfill, different types of operating procedures and overall contributions of sanitary landfills to public health.
Foreign Language; Health and Safety
Dist - USNAC **Prod** - NMAC 1956

The Refuse Problem 14 MIN
16mm
Color (J H A)
Presents the problems of refuse storage, collection and disposal. Suggests how the individual can act to help solve some of these problems.
Health and Safety; Science - Natural; Social Science; Sociology
Dist - VADE **Prod** - VADE 1963

A Refusenik Diary 60 MIN
VHS
Color (G)
$59.95 purchase _ #REDI - 000
Features the story of Vladimir and Masha Slepak, Soviet Jewish 'refuseniks' who sought to emigrate to Israel. Reveals that this desire came at a great personal cost, including a breakup of the family, prison sentences and loss of their jobs. Concludes with an account of the Slepak family's eventual reunion.
Civics and Political Systems; History - World; Religion and Philosophy
Dist - PBS **Prod** - WHYY 1988

Refusing to say No - spinal cord injury 5 MIN
U-matic / VHS
Assistive technology series
Color (C PRO G)
$195.00 purchase _ #N921 - VI - 045
Introduces the accessibility and adaptation strategies of a man who is a quadriplegic because of a spinal injury. Features Jim who is a vice - president of the Illionois Chamber of Commerce and chair of the Springfield Disabilities Commission. Discusses adaptations Jim has made in his home and work environments. Notes agencies that can provide the physically challenged with practical and financial assistance. Part of nine parts produced by Southern Illinois University School of Medicine.
Health and Safety
Dist - HSCIC

Regatta de amigos
VHS
Color (G)
$100.00 rental _ #0421
Presents full race coverage on five boats over a 600 mile open ocean trip. Views Veracruz, Tuxpan and Isla de Lobos. Includes footage shot from helicopters and motor launches.
Physical Education and Recreation
Dist - SEVVID

Regen 14 MIN
16mm / U-matic / VHS
German cities series
B&W (H C) (GERMAN)
LC 70-707313
A German language film. Presents the various activities which occupy the people in a typical German city.
Geography - World
Dist - IFB **Prod** - IFB 1969

Regeneration 4 MIN
16mm
Color (C)
$157.00
Experimental film by Standish D Lawder.
Fine Arts
Dist - AFA **Prod** - AFA 1980

Regentropfen 89 MIN
16mm
B&W (GERMAN (ENGLISH SUBTITLES))
Deals with the hardships of an integrated Jewish family in a small German town at the beginning of the Nazi regime, and ending with the family being allowed to immigrate to the United States, leaving the father behind because he cannot pass the necessary health examination.
Fine Arts
Dist - WSTGLC **Prod** - WSTGLC 1980

Reggae 25 MIN
VHS / U-matic
Rockschool Series
Color (J)
Shows how the rise of reggae, based on a perfect symmetrical relationship between guitar, bass and drums, has influenced rock music. Explains the importance of a sense of discipline and precision to reggae musicians. Looks at the 'dub' technique.
Fine Arts
Dist - FI **Prod** - BBCTV

Regina - Gift of Vision 11 MIN
VHS / 16mm
Color (P I)
LC 79-700704
Focuses on an 11 - year - old blind girl who explains how she has learned to function effectively in the everyday world.
Education; Guidance and Counseling; Psychology
Dist - LRF **Prod** - LOYUDC 1978

Reginald Parse 5 MIN
U-matic / VHS
Write on, Set 1 Series
Color (J H)
Teaches correct word usage. Explains 'Imply' and 'Infer' and 'Continual' and 'Continuous'. Shows the distinction between 'Differ with' and 'Differ from'.
English Language
Dist - CTI **Prod** - CTI

Region of Tanach 28 MIN
16mm
Color
Tells the story of the Atlas Mountains Jews living in Israel.
Geography - World; Religion and Philosophy; Sociology
Dist - ALDEN **Prod** - ALDEN

Regional Enteritis 19 MIN
16mm
Color (PRO)
Describes the etiology, surgical anatomy and symptoms of regional ileitis. Presents the indications and contraindications for surgery. Illustrates microscopic and gross findings in diseased bowel.
Health and Safety; Science
Dist - ACY **Prod** - ACYDGD 1960

Regional Geography - British Isles Series
Central - Southern England 19 MIN
Northwest England 19 MIN
Southwest England 21 MIN
Dist - IFB

Regional geography of England series
East Anglia 20 MIN
The Fenlands 20 MIN
South - east England 20 MIN
Yorkshire 20 MIN
Dist - BHA

Regional Ileitis Treatment by Resection and Primary Anastomosis between the Ilium and mesentery 40 MIN
16mm
Color (PRO)
Demonstrates surgical problems encountered with the marked involvement of the terminal ileum, perforation and thickening of the mesentery. Shows the salient pathologic and X - ray features of regional ileitis as well as the clinical symptoms and course of the disease.
Health and Safety; Science
Dist - ACY **Prod** - ACYDGD 1952

Regional Intervention Program Series
Individual Tutoring 18 MIN
Language Preschool 19 MIN
That's what It's all about 29 MIN
Toddler management 19 MIN
Dist - USNAC

Regional Perfusion for Malignant Melanoma 15 MIN
16mm
Cine Clinic Series
Color (PRO)
Explains that a patient with melanoma of calf with clinically negative lymph nodes had extremity perfusion with phenylalanine nitrogen mustard and wide local excision of the melanoma.
Health and Safety; Science
Dist - NMAC **Prod** - ACYDGD 1970

Regional report series
From pot to psychedelics 32 MIN
Dist - IU

Regional Seminar on Development 10 MIN
16mm
B&W
Presents a seminar on economic development in Malaysia.
Business and Economics; Geography - World
Dist - PMFMUN **Prod** - FILEM 1968

Regional variations 28 MIN
16mm
Language - the social arbiter series; No 4
Color (J H)
LC FIA67-5264
Dr Frederic Cassidy, professor of English at the University of Wisconsin, and Dr Hood Roberts, of the Center for Applied Linguistics, discuss the major regional dialects in the United States.
English Language; Sociology
Dist - FINLYS **Prod** - FINLYS 1966

Regions of the United States 24 MIN
VHS / U-matic / 16mm
Color (P I J)
$550.00, $415.00, $385.00 purchase _ #A614
Examines the four major regions of the United States - the Northeast, the South, the North Central and the West. Explores the major industries, the landforms and climate of each. Shows how land and climate affect the way people live, work and play.
Geography - United States; History - United States
Dist - BARR **Prod** - CEPRO 1991

Regions of the world - Part One
VHS
Color (J H)
$105.00 purchase _ #UL215103
Introduces students to the physical geography, climates, economies, history, cultural patterns and politics of more than 50 countries. Covers Latin America and the Caribbean, 'Anglo' America, Europe and the Soviet Union. Includes a comprehensive teacher's guide and a set of duplicating masters. Part one of two parts.
Geography - United States; Geography - World
Dist - KNOWUN

Regions of the world - Part Two
VHS
Color (J H)
$105.00 purchase _ #UL215203
Introduces students to the physical geography, climates, economies, history, cultural patterns and politics of Asia, the Middle East and Northern Africa and the South Pacific. Discusses serious Third World problems such as population growth, unstable political situations and poverty. Includes a comprehensive teacher's guide and a set of duplicating masters. Part two of two parts.
Geography - World; Sociology
Dist - KNOWUN

Register and Vote 1 MIN
16mm
Color (H C A)
LC 75-701514
Encourages members of the black community in the United States to register and vote.
Civics and Political Systems; History - United States; Social Science
Dist - LEECC **Prod** - LEECC 1975

Regitel Training at Bullock's 15 MIN
16mm
Color
LC 72-700038
Presents the basic operational methodology of the American Regitel Corporation electronic computer - controlled point - of - sale cash register at Bullock's, a high - fashion department store.
Business and Economics; Industrial and Technical Education
Dist - CANCIN **Prod** - CANCIN 1971

Regression analysis
U-matic / VHS
Statistics for managers series
Color (COR)
Gives detailed explanation of the linear trend between one independent and dependent variable. Develops, discusses and tests the least square line. Makes predictions for mu sub - y/x, Y sub - x and Y sub - x. Cites possible problems relating to data gathered.
Business and Economics; Mathematics; Psychology
Dist - COLOSU **Prod** - COLOSU

Regret for the Past 107 MIN
VHS
Color (G) (MANDARIN CHINESE)
$45.00 purchase _ #1048A
Presents a movie produced in the People's Republic Of China.
Fine Arts; Geography - World; Literature and Drama
Dist - CHTSUI **Prod** - CHTSUI

Regular Homotopies in the Plane, Pt 1 16 MIN
U-matic / VHS / 16mm
Topology Series
Color (C)
LC 73-702051
Uses computer graphics to present a class of transformations on continuous curves and some of the mathematical properties associated with these transformations. Provides an example of the kinds of problems considered in topology, a branch of modern mathematics.
Mathematics
Dist - IFB **Prod** - EDC 1973

Regular Homotopies in the Plane, Pt 2 19 MIN
U-matic / VHS / 16mm
Topology Series
Color (C A)
Gives a constructive proof of the Whitney - Graustein Theorem which states that two regular curves in a plane are regularly homotopic if and only if they have the same rotation number.
Mathematics
Dist - IFB **Prod** - EDC 1975

A Regular Kid 15 MIN
16mm
Color (A)
LC 81-700361
Presents four vignettes involving children who have asthma to explain what causes the disease, how it affects children's lives, and how the child and parents cope with the disease.
Health and Safety; Psychology; Sociology
Dist - GEIGY **Prod** - AMLUNG 1981

A Regular Kid 16 MIN
U-matic
Color
Documents parents' and children's views on asthma. Explains how medicine and medical equipment help treat the problem.
Health and Safety
Dist - MTP **Prod** - GEIGYP

Regular lives 30 MIN
VHS
Color (T PRO)
$60.00 purchase _ #M349
Shows the integration of students with mental and physical disabilities into regular educational life. Includes a discussion guide with fact sheets and handouts and suggestions for conducting group sessions.
Education; Health and Safety
Dist - CEXPCN **Prod** - CEXPCN 1990

Regular Lives 30 MIN
VHS
Color; Captioned (G)
$39.95 purchase _ #RRLV - 000
Shows how people with disabilities can be allowed into regular schools, jobs and the community. Tells how this process, known as 'mainstreaming,' has generally been successful. Narrated by Martin Sheen.
Health and Safety; Psychology
Dist - PBS **Prod** - SACVP 1988

A Regular Rolling Noah
VHS / 35mm strip
ALA Notable Children's Filmstrips Series
Color (K)
$33.00 purchase
Presents a children's story. Part of the American Library Association series.
English Language; Literature and Drama
Dist - PELLER

Regular - Routine Responsibilities 7 MIN
U-matic / VHS
Practical M B O Series
Color
Business and Economics; Education; Psychology
Dist - DELTAK **Prod** - DELTAK

Regular Stochastic Matrices 30 MIN
U-matic
Introduction to Mathematics Series
Color (C)
Mathematics
Dist - MDCPB **Prod** - MDCPB

Regulated Power Supply 16 MIN
VHS / 16mm
Electronics Series
(C A IND)
$99.00 purchase _ #VCI11
Introduces the viewer to a variety of solid state devices used to regulate power supplies. Illustrates how Zener diodes, series transistors, and switching regulators function. Utilizes an additional workbook.
Industrial and Technical Education
Dist - RMIBHF **Prod** - RMIBHF

Regulated Power Supply
VHS
Industrial Electronics Training Program Series
$99.00 purchase _ #RPVCI11
Industrial and Technical Education
Dist - CAREER **Prod** - CAREER

Regulating body temperature 22 MIN
U-matic / VHS / 16mm
Biology series; Unit 8
Color (J H)
Presents the development, importance and physiology of body temperature regulation. Compares man's heat - regulating responses with that of other animals. Introduces the variety of physiological and behavior mechanisms that balance heat and cold in the body. Unit eight in the series focuses on human physiology.
Science - Natural
Dist - EBEC **Prod** - EBEC 1972

Regulation and Innovation 51 MIN
VHS / U-matic
Technology, Innovation, and Industrial Development Series
Color
Business and Economics
Dist - MIOT **Prod** - MIOT

The Regulation of Atomic Radiation 29 MIN
16mm
Color
LC FIE64-190
Surveys the work of the Atomic Energy Commission in licensing and regulating the use of nuclear materials. Examines the close control of radioactive materials from the time they leave the mines to be processed until they are again returned to the earth or to the sea as waste materials.
Civics and Political Systems; Health and Safety; Science - Physical
Dist - USNAC **Prod** - USNRC 1963

Regulation of Gene Expression in Eucaryotes 32 MIN
U-matic / VHS
Color
Introduces chromatin structure, chromosome puffs, and steroid hormone binding proteins to describe some current ideas on how nuclear genes in eucaryotic cells may be turned on and off. Compares gene regulation in eucaryotes and bacteria, and notes the complex molecular interactions required for correct, coordinated development of higher organisms. Video version of 35mm filmstrip program, with live open and close.
Science - Natural
Dist - CBSC **Prod** - BMEDIA

Regulation of heart beat in the mammal 4 MIN
16mm
Dukes physiology film series
Color (C)
LC 73-710192
Illustrates the relationship of nerve impulses to neurocellular junctions in the heart as regulators of the heart beat.
Science - Natural
Dist - IOWA **Prod** - IOWA 1971

Regulation of Normal and Leukemic Hematopoiesis in Humans 60 MIN
U-matic
Color
Discusses the regulation of normal and leukemic hematopoiesis in humans.
Health and Safety
Dist - UTEXSC **Prod** - UTEXSC

Regulation of the Microcirculation 50 MIN
U-matic / VHS
Color (PRO)
Familiarizes students with mechanisms of flow regulation in microcirculation.
Health and Safety; Science - Natural
Dist - HSCIC **Prod** - HSCIC 1982

Regulations 19 MIN
U-matic / VHS
Jobs - Seeking, Finding, Keeping Series
Color (H)
Tells how a worker balks at a tyrannical boss's order and is then fired. Explains how he gets his job back by going through grievance procedures.
Guidance and Counseling
Dist - AITECH **Prod** - MDDE 1980

Regulator Fundamentals 25 MIN
VHS / U-matic
Color (IND)
Describes the most common kinds of regulators and controllers used in the gas industry to control the pressure of gas. Tells how the regulators and controllers work.
Social Science
Dist - UTEXPE **Prod** - UTEXPE 1978

The Regulators 29 MIN
16mm
Government story series; No 34
Color
LC 70-707190
A discussion of the role of the independent regulatory agencies created by Congress and staffed by the President. Includes a picture history of the creation of the first agency, the Interstate Commerce Commission and the development of the seven major commissions and agencies which followed.
Civics and Political Systems
Dist - WBCPRO **Prod** - OGCW 1968

Regulators, excess flow valves, boosters, sequence valves 26 MIN
VHS / U-matic
Industrial pneumatic technology series; Chapter 10
Color (IND)
Illustrates and explains the operations of sequence values, pressure regulators, venting type regulators, pilot controlled regulators, differential pressure circuits, dual pressure circuits, air - to - oil booster circuits and excess flow values. Chapter 10 of the Industrial pneumatic technology series.
Education; Industrial and Technical Education
Dist - TAT **Prod** - TAT

The Regulators - our invisible government 50 MIN
U-matic / VHS / 16mm
Color (H C A)
LC 82-700620
Looks at the regulatory function of the U S government by focusing on the Environmental Protection Agency's drafting of one regulation which carries out a provision of the Clean Air Act. Illustrates the role of citizens in establishing governmental policy.
Business and Economics; Civics and Political Systems; Science - Natural; Social Science; Sociology
Dist - LCOA **Prod** - WVIATV 1982

The Regulatory agencies 18 MIN
35mm strip / VHS
US government in action series
Color (J H C T A)
$57.00, $45.00 purchase _ #MB - 510774 - 0, #MB - 509988 - 8
Examines the regulatory agencies, enforcers of actions taken by other branches of the US government. Emphasizes the Constitutional concept of checks and balances. Uses archival and modern graphics.
Civics and Political Systems
Dist - SRA **Prod** - SRA 1988

Rehabilitation 10 MIN
16mm
Criminal Justice Series
Color (J)
Defines rehabilitation as it relates to the offender and stresses modern concepts and different types of programs currently in operation.
Health and Safety; Sociology
Dist - GCCED **Prod** - GCCED 1971

Rehabilitation 30 MIN
VHS
Perspectives - health and medicine - series
Color; PAL; NTSC (G)
PdS90, PdS105 purchase
Shows how new materials, electronic gadgetry and a deeper knowledge of the body make the replacement of limbs and tissues possible.
Health and Safety
Dist - CFLVIS **Prod** - LONTVS

Rehabilitation - a Patient's Perspective 26 MIN
16mm
Color
LC 73-702361
Examines the psychological and emotional aspects of rehabilitation from the patient's point of view.
Health and Safety; Psychology
Dist - FLMLIB **Prod** - TOGGFI 1973

Rehabilitation After Myocardial Infarction
U-matic / VHS
Color
Provides detailed clinical guidelines for the rehabilitation of myocardial infarction patients, both during and after hospitalization. Presents the principles of patient selection and outlines a comprehensive rehabilitation program.
Health and Safety
Dist - AMEDA **Prod** - AMEDA

Rehabilitation - an inside view 29 MIN
16mm
Directions for education in nursing via technology series; Lesson 81
B&W (PRO)
LC 74-701859
Demonstrates facets of rehabilitation of patients with musculo - skeletal and visual problems and the laryngectomized patient. Shows activities of physical therapy, hydrotherapy and occupational therapy. Includes interviews with patients, a psychologist, a social worker and therapists.
Health and Safety; Science - Natural
Dist - WSUM **Prod** - DENT 1974

Rehabilitation Center 15 MIN
16mm
Color; B&W (J H C G T A)
Shows the process a rehabilitation center undergoes in the making of a rehabilitation hospital. Helps create a positive approach to physical rehabilitation. Film was produced at the 'turning point' in social attitudes toward the physically handicapped.
Health and Safety
Dist - FO **Prod** - FO 1960

Rehabilitation, Essential to Patient Care 60 MIN
VHS / U-matic
Color (PRO)
LC 81-706300
Emphasizes the three phases of rehabilitation. Illustrates the basic concepts of positioning, bowel and bladder training, and range of motion.
Health and Safety
Dist - USNAC **Prod** - USVA 1980

Rehabilitation II and character as a defense 23 MIN
VHS
Basic concepts in the law of evidence series
B&W (C PRO)
$90.00 purchase, $30.00 rental _ #EYX06
Features the late law professor Irving Younger in a presentation of basic concepts of the law of evidence. Discusses character defenses and concludes consideration of rehabilitation.
Civics and Political Systems
Dist - NITA **Prod** - NITA 1975

Rehabilitation Management of Below Knee Amputation 13 MIN
16mm
Color (PRO)
LC 74-706389; 74-706388
Discusses the amputation, beginning with the preoperative evaluation and following through to the postsurgical prosthetic training. Describes surgical techniques, application of rigid dressing, controlled weight - bearing and progressive ambulation.
Health and Safety
Dist - USNAC **Prod** - USVA 1971

Rehabilitation of dancer's injuries 30 MIN
U-matic / VHS
Care and feeding of dancers series
Color
Fine Arts; Health and Safety
Dist - ARCVID **Prod** - ARCVID

Rehabilitation of spinal cord injuries series
Body mechanics 10 MIN
Dist - PRIMED

Rehabilitation of the forequarter amputee 12 MIN
U-matic / VHS
Color (PRO)
Describes a forequarter amputation and various aspects of rehabilitation for patients who have had one. Includes a description of a post - operative program, a pre - prosthetic program, and the initial checkout of the prosthesis, as well as demonstrating a patient putting on the prosthesis and a description of prosthetic training programs.
Health and Safety
Dist - HSCIC **Prod** - HSCIC

Rehabilitation - Part Three 14 MIN
VHS
Cardiac surgery - a new beginning series
Color (G PRO)
$195.00 purchase _ #E930 - VI - 031
Takes the patient through the steps necessary for a successful return to a normal, active lifestyle. Part of a three - part of series on cardiac surgery.
Health and Safety
Dist - HSCIC

Rehabilitation Procedures, Part I and II 58 MIN
U-matic
Sports Medicine in the 80's Series
Color (G)
Teaches the role of sports medicine as it relates to athlete, coach, trainer, team and school. Covers most kinds of injuries encountered in sports.
Health and Safety; Physical Education and Recreation
Dist - CEPRO **Prod** - CEPRO

A Rehabilitation Team Conference 20 MIN
U-matic / VHS
Color (PRO)
Concerns the rehabilitation of a 48 - year - old male stroke patient. Shows how a rehabilitation team consisting of an occupational therapist, physical therapist, speech therapist, nurse, social worker, psychologist, and physician identify and rank the patient's problems and treatment.
Health and Safety
Dist - UMICHM **Prod** - UMICHM 1979

Rehabilitation - the Miracle in Us all 28 MIN
16mm
Color (C A)
Demonstrates the Liberty Mutual Insurance Company's commitment to provide the best medical care and to return the injured worker to a productive life. Portrays case histories and features actual claimants, rehabilitation nurses and four physicians associated with well - known hospitals and rehabilitation facilities.
Business and Economics; Health and Safety
Dist - MTP **Prod** - LIBMIC

Rehabilitative Patient Care Planning - a Team Approach 27 MIN
U-matic
Color (PRO)
LC 80-706787
Demonstrates the interaction and decision - making processes of a multidisciplinary stroke rehabilitation team. Shows how the team identifies the patient's needs and establishes goals for the treatment plan in order to insure effective rehabilitation.
Health and Safety
Dist - USNAC **Prod** - VAHSL 1980

The Rehearsal 23 MIN
U-matic / VHS
Color
Follows hospital staff and community emergency personnel as they rehearse together various methods of moving both ambulatory and bedfast patients.
Health and Safety
Dist - FPF **Prod** - FPF

Rehearsal 17 MIN
16mm
B&W (C A)
Dramatizes the story of a woman directing a play in a theater where actuality, memory and fantasy all intertwine.
Fine Arts
Dist - CANCIN **Prod** - VIERAD 1976

Rehearsal 29 MIN
U-matic
Music Shop Series
Color
Gives an insider's look at a rehearsal for a recording session.
Fine Arts
Dist - UMITV **Prod** - UMITV 1974

Rehearsal 25 MIN
U-matic / VHS / 16mm
Color (H C A)
LC 77-700877
Shows a psychologist in a juvenile home working with a group of teenaged offenders in an attempt to help them understand and cope with the emotions and hostilities governing their behavior.
Guidance and Counseling; Psychology; Sociology
Dist - MEDIAG **Prod** - PAULST 1977

Rehearsal for D - Day 26 MIN
U-matic / VHS
Color (G)
$249.00, $149.00 purchase _ #AD - 1739
Documents some of the rehearsals for D - Day - a wargame played for real that went tragically wrong, costing more than 750 American lives. Reveals that live ammunition was used in the rehearsals, 36 GIs were killed when mines exploded during a lecture. Provides another dimension to our knowledge of D - Day.
History - United States; History - World; Sociology
Dist - FOTH **Prod** - FOTH

Rehearsal - Strindberg's Miss Julie 60 MIN
U-matic / VHS
Drama - play, performance, perception series; Module 1
Color (C)
Fine Arts; Literature and Drama
Dist - MDCC **Prod** - MDCC

Rehearsals for Extinct Anatomies 14 MIN
16mm
B&W (G)
Presents an independent production by Timothy and Stephan Quay. Features inventive animation. Also available in 35mm film format.
Fine Arts
Dist - FIRS

Rehearsing a Dance Company 30 MIN
VHS / U-matic
Behind the Scenes Series
Color
Fine Arts
Dist - ARCVID **Prod** - ARCVID

Rehearsing the Text 53 MIN
U-matic / VHS
Royal Shakespeare Company Series
Color
Employs a scene from Twelfth Night to search for Shakespeare's clues to character, language and staging. Discusses text and subtext and how the verse itself is a clue to the meaning.
Literature and Drama
Dist - FOTH **Prod** - FOTH 1984

Reign of terror 60 MIN
U-matic / VHS / 16mm
I, Claudius series; No 8
Color (C A)
Describes how Claudius helps remove Sejanus as a threat to Tiberius and how the bloodbath that follows almost destroys him.
History - World
Dist - FI **Prod** - BBCTV 1977

Reign of the Wanderers 60 MIN
VHS
Triumph Of The Nomads Series
Color (G)
$49.95 purchase _ #TRON - 102
Reveals the nomadic life of the Australian Aborigines. Shows that the Aborigines were hunters, learned to use fire, and dealt with problems such as drought and disease successfully. Illustrates their attitudes toward old age and abortion.
History - World; Sociology
Dist - PBS **Prod** - NOMDFI 1989

Reincarnation 29 MIN
Videoreel / VT2
Who is Man Series
Color
Features Dr Puryear looking at the possibilities and beliefs with regard to theories of reincarnation and examines a number of documented case histories.
Religion and Philosophy
Dist - PBS **Prod** - WHROTV

The Reincarnation of Khensur Rinpoche 62 MIN
VHS / BETA
Color; PAL (G)
PdS25 purchase
Tells the story of a monk's search for the reincarnation of his dead master and the eventual discovery of a young boy who was recognised to be the one. Culminates with the new master returning to his monastery in south India.
Literature and Drama; Religion and Philosophy
Dist - MERIDT

Reindeer in the Arctic - a study in adaptation 25 MIN
VHS
Evolution series
Color (G C)
$150.00 purchase, $19.50 rental _ #36260
Takes a comparative look at the adaptive characteristics of Arctic and sub - Arctic reindeer. Reveals that each species exhibits characteristics that specially qualify it for life in its native environment. Part of a ten - part series exploring evolutionary selection and adaptation.

Science - Natural
Dist - PSU **Prod** - BBC 1992

The Reindeer people - the forests of Arctic Siberia 52 MIN
VHS
Icebreaker - family life in the Soviet Union series
Color (I J H)
$295.00 purchase
Visits a family of the Evenki people who are indigenous to Siberia, a mother, daughter and the daughter's son. Reveals that they share a log cabin in the village of Nakanno which is very isolated - its only contact to the outside world is the radio - telegraph and the small biplane which services the village. The eonomy of Nakanno revolves largely around fur trapping. Part of a six - part series on ethnically different families in the Soviet Union.
Geography - World; Sociology
Dist - LANDMK **Prod** - LANDMK 1989

The Reindeer queen - the story of Alaska's Sinrock Mary 28 MIN
VHS
Color (H C G)
$295.00 purchase, $55.00 rental
Documents the life of an Alaskan - Eskimo woman whose tenacity and spirit led her to play an important role in the history of Alaska's Arctic. Combines archival footage, stills and interviews with people who knew her to portray Sinrock Mary who played an important part in the introduction of Siberian reindeer into Alaska. She served as a Russian interpreter in Siberia in the Department of Interior project, introduced the first reindeer to Alaskan territory and became the owner of the largest herd in the North, although she was subjected to constant harassment and attempts to gain control of her herd because she was a woman of color. Produced by Maria Brooks.
Biography; History - United States; History - World; Social Science
Dist - FLMLIB

The Reindeer thief 13 MIN
VHS / 16mm
From the elders series
Color (G) (ENGLISH DUBBED OVER SIBERIAN YUPIK)
$260.00, $150.00 purchase, $25.00, $20.00 rental
Presents Pelaasi, an elder from Gambel who tells a mythical story about a man who goes in search of a reindeer thief, an ungipaghaq, a tale unchanged through generations and believed to be based on truth. Sets the story in Siberia where Churkchi, the Reindeer People, live. Produced by the Alaska Native Heritage Film Project.
Fine Arts; Religion and Philosophy; Social Science
Dist - DOCEDR

Reinforced Plastics - Inspection and Quality Control 20 MIN
16mm
Color
LC FIE58-24
Demonstrates inspection procedures, showing examples of various common defects and procedures leading to final acceptance of the finished parts by naval inspectors.
Civics and Political Systems; Industrial and Technical Education
Dist - USNAC **Prod** - USN 1957

Reinforced Plastics - Introduction 20 MIN
16mm
B&W
LC FIE58-23
Explains in general the nature of reinforced plastics and their composition and fabrication.
Industrial and Technical Education
Dist - USNAC **Prod** - USN 1957

Reinforcement 17 MIN
VHS / 16mm
Teaching People with Developmental Disabilities Series
Color (A PRO)
$150.00 purchase, $55.00 rental _ #3135VHS
Illustrates the use of reinforcers to strengthen behavior and improve student performance when teaching people with developmental disabilities.
Mathematics; Psychology
Dist - RESPRC **Prod** - OREGRI 1988

The Reinforcement Show 28 MIN
16mm
Special Delivery Series
Color (P I)
LC 79-701078
Shows handicapped people achieving difficult goals and effectively interacting with their nonhandicapped peers.
Education; Psychology
Dist - LAWREN **Prod** - WNVT 1979

Reinforcement Theory for Teachers 28 MIN
16mm
Translating Theory into Classroom Practices Series
B&W (C)
Features Dr Madeline Hunter discussing positive reinforcement, negative reinforcement, extinction and schedule of reinforcement. Suggests how the theory behind reward and punishment can be applied effectively in daily teaching.
Education
Dist - SPF **Prod** - SPF 1963

Reinheit Des Herzens 104 MIN
16mm
Color (GERMAN (ENGLISH SUBTITLES))
Shows how violence affects human relationships, through the story of a couple who had formerly lived together harmoniously but who are suddenly torn apart by an outside force. Describes how the partner who, during good times, was the strong one, falls apart, with the formerly dependent one taking over.
Fine Arts
Dist - WSTGLC **Prod** - WSTGLC 1980

Reining 31 MIN
VHS
Practice horse judging series; Set Z - 1
Color (H C A PRO)
$69.95 purchase _ #CV804
Contains two classes in practice horse judging - reining class. Features John Pipkin of Texas Tech U who places and critiques each class.
Agriculture; Physical Education and Recreation
Dist - AAVIM **Prod** - AAVIM 1990

The Reining Horse 25 MIN
16mm / U-matic / VHS
Color
Discusses the reining horse, the foundation for any performance event. Offers a definition of a reining horse, basic training, and the difference between East and West coast styles of competition. Deals with the snaffle - bit, hackamore and bit reining.
Physical Education and Recreation
Dist - AQHORS **Prod** - AQHORS

Reining I - a Progressive Approach 60 MIN
VHS
Horse Training By Video Series
Color (G)
$89.95 purchase _ #6 - 020 - 102P
Shows the progressive training approach for horse reining maneuvers by Al Dunning. Includes evaluation of good reining horse conformation, selection and fit of equipment, shoeing, turnarounds, rollbacks, stopping, lead changes, circles, rating speed, cadence. Part of a series on horse training.
Agriculture; Physical Education and Recreation; Psychology
Dist - VEP **Prod** - VEP

Reining II - Advanced Techniques 60 MIN
VHS
Horse Training By Video Series
Color (G)
$89.95 purchase _ #6 - 020 - 103P
Features Al Dunning who shows advanced techniques to use in progressing to the hackamore and bridle. Illustrates the tying of a hackamore, selection of bits, riding in the hackamore, the transition to riding with one hand and perfecting a horse's moves. Part of a series on horse training.
Agriculture; Physical Education and Recreation; Psychology
Dist - VEP **Prod** - VEP

The Reins of Command - Air Force Communications Service 28 MIN
16mm
Color
LC 74-705508
Portrays the mission of the Air Force Communications Service and its role in air force operations. Presents the highly complex and sophisticated techniques, equipment, global communications network and air traffic control system.
Civics and Political Systems; Social Science
Dist - USNAC **Prod** - USAF

Reinventing the organization - II
VHS
Power of change series
Color (G COR)
$895.00 purchase, $200.00 rental
Features Dr Gerald Ross and Michael Kay and three CEOs who have undertaken wrenching changes in the face of a hostile environment. Provides a four - point approach to change based on over a decade of working directly on deep seated change with thousands of organizations worldwide. Part one of two parts.
Business and Economics; Psychology; Sociology
Dist - AMEDIA **Prod** - AMEDIA 1993

The Reivers 107 MIN
VHS
Color (J H)
$89.00 purchase _ #05953 - 126
Presents the adventures of a 12 - year - old boy by William Faulkner.
Literature and Drama
Dist - GA **Prod** - GA

Rejected 30 MIN
16mm
Color (H A)
LC FIA68-1494
John Stubbins refuses to help Cliff Brown, a former friend, who has just completed a prison term for embezzlement. A tragic chain of events ensues for which John blames himself.
Guidance and Counseling; Psychology; Sociology
Dist - CPH **Prod** - CPH 1968

Rejection of Renal Transplant 18 MIN
16mm
Clinical Pathology Series
B&W (PRO)
LC 74-705509
Provides a general review of rejection theory followed by a discussion concerning types of rejections of renal homografts in man. Includes a brief survey of statistical data. (Kinescope).
Health and Safety; Mathematics
Dist - USNAC **Prod** - NMAC 1969

Relaciones entre supervisores 8 MIN
U-matic
Problems in supervision series
B&W (SPANISH)
LC 79-706960
A Spanish language version of Working With Other Supervisors. Discusses the importance of working harmoniously with other people. Issued in 1959 as a motion picture.
Business and Economics; Psychology
Dist - USNAC **Prod** - USOE 19791979

Relapse 45 MIN
U-matic / Cassette
Color (G)
$495.00, $10.00 purchase
Discusses warning signs to look for if one has the urge to drink or use drugs again.
Guidance and Counseling; Health and Safety; Psychology
Dist - KELLYP **Prod** - KELLYP

Relapse Prevention 25 MIN
VHS / 16mm
Color (A PRO)
$395.00 purchase, $75.00 rental _ #8106
Examines the causes of relapse into alcoholism and suggests methods of prevention.
Guidance and Counseling; Health and Safety; Psychology
Dist - AIMS **Prod** - BROFLM 1989

Relapse Prevention 30 MIN
U-matic
Action Options - Alcohol, Drugs and You Series
(H C A)
Examines how to accentuate personal power and how to develop healthy coping mechanisms.
Psychology; Sociology
Dist - ACCESS **Prod** - ACCESS 1986

Relapse prevention, patient module 42 MIN
VHS
Cocaine, treatment and recovery - Haight - Ashbury training series; Tape 3
Color (C G PRO)
$250.00 purchase
Explains the pharmacological basis of addiction. Examines tools, techniques and strategies to help people bond into treatment, control craving, prevent relapse and maintain long - term recovery. Teaches patients the HALT method - relapse may occur when the patient is Hungry, Angry, Lonely or Tired. Part of a three - part series on the treatment of cocaine addiction.
Guidance and Counseling; Health and Safety; Psychology
Dist - FMSP

Relapse prevention series
Presents a two - part series on relapse prevention. Includes the titles Relapse Prevention - the Facts, and Slipping into Darkness.
Relapse prevention - the facts 23 MIN
Slipping into the darkness 17 MIN
Dist - VISIVI **Prod** - VISIVI

Relapse prevention - the facts 23 MIN
VHS / U-matic
Relapse prevention series
Color (G)
$249.00 purchase _ #7458
Reveals that relapse in the process of recovery is a progressive, identifiable process that begins long before the actual use of drugs or alcohol. Discusses the dynamics of relapse which include denial, self - pity and blame. Part of a two - part series on relapse prevention.

Guidance and Counseling; Health and Safety; Psychology
Dist - VISIVI **Prod** - VISIVI 1991

Related Rates
U-matic
Calculus Series
Color
Mathematics
Dist - MDCPB **Prod** - MDDE

Related Rates 30 MIN
VHS
Mathematics Series
Color (J)
LC 90713155
Discusses related rates. The 128th of 157 installments of the Mathematics Series.
Mathematics
Dist - GPN

Related rates 30 MIN
VHS
Calculus series
Color (C)
$125.00 purchase _ #6019
Explains related rates. Part of a 56 - part series on calculus.
Mathematics
Dist - LANDMK **Prod** - LANDMK

Related services 62 MIN
VHS
Legal challenges in special education series; Tape 4
Color (G)
$90.00 purchase
Reveals that most impartial hearing requests involve related services - special transportation, medical diagnostic tests, psychological services, physical therapy, occupational therapy and recreation and leisure therapy. Examines the court decisions, giving answers to questions usch as how much physical therapy is enough and how to balance related services with the least restrictive environment requirement. Features Reed Martin, JD. Includes resource materials. Part of a 12 - part series on Public Law 94 - 142.
Education
Dist - BAXMED

Related services for the handicapped 30 MIN
U-matic / VHS
Promises to keep series; Module 9
Color (T)
Defines related services for the handicapped and the benefits from effective coordination for the handicapped child. Gives attention to selected specialists, their role and the services which each might provide. Presents a professional panel discussing the procedures for determining eligibility for Special Education services.
Education
Dist - LUF **Prod** - VPI 1979

Relating facts 15 MIN
16mm
PANCOM beginning total communication program for hearing parents of series; Level 1
Color (K)
LC 77-700504
Education; Guidance and Counseling; Psychology; Social Science; Sociology
Dist - JOYCE **Prod** - CSDE 1977

Relating multiplication and division 15 MIN
U-matic
Math factory - problem solving series; Module IV
Color (P)
Presents multiplication and division as inverse operations.
Mathematics
Dist - GPN **Prod** - MAETEL 1973

Relating semiconductors to systems 60 MIN
Videoreel / VT1
Understanding semiconductors course outline series; No 04
Color (IND)
Discusses electronic circuits by describing how their frequency, power and other requirements affect the choice of semiconductor devices used in the circuits. Includes explanations of inductance and capacitance.
Industrial and Technical Education
Dist - TXINLC **Prod** - TXINLC

Relating sets to numbers 11 MIN
16mm
Pathways to modern math series
Color (I J H)
LC FIA64-1444
Shows the meaning of a 'well - defined set' and 'member of a set.' Demonstrates methods of writing sets using braces to enclose a listing of the members. Emphasizes the meaning of 'empty set,' 'finite sets' and 'infinite sets,' and the meaning and difference between the concepts of number and numerals.

Mathematics
Dist - GE **Prod** - GE

The Relation of Mathematics to Physics 55 MIN
16mm
Character of Physical Law - Feynman Series
B&W (C)
LC 77-707488
Professor Richard Feynman, California Institute of Technology, discusses examples of how the logic of mathematics aids us in describing nature, and shows the use of models in formulating laws. Feynman emphasizes the contrast between physical laws and mathematical theorems.
Mathematics; Science; Science - Physical
Dist - EDC **Prod** - BBCTV 1965

The Relation of transfer functions and state variable representations 53 MIN
U-matic / VHS
Modern control theory - systems analysis series
Color
Industrial and Technical Education; Mathematics
Dist - MIOT **Prod** - MIOT

Relational Data Base 30 MIN
VHS / U-matic
SQL/DS and Relational Data Base Systems Series
Color
Provides a basic introduction to relational data base systems. Discusses current trends in data processing suggesting the need for improved data management tools and techniques and looks at various data base structures and the advantages and disadvantages associated with each.
Business and Economics; Industrial and Technical Education
Dist - DELTAK **Prod** - DELTAK

Relational Database 180 MIN
VHS / U-matic
Color (PRO)
Describes relational database and discusses its importance. Covers basic concepts, terminology, programmer and end - user access, data definition and manipulation, views, application programming, security and integrity, transaction processing, frontend systems and storage structures.
Industrial and Technical Education; Mathematics; Sociology
Dist - AMCEE **Prod** - AMCEE

Relational Databases 180 MIN
VHS / U-matic
(A PRO)
$990.00 purchase, $450.00 rental
Describes relational databases and their importance.
Computer Science
Dist - VIDEOT **Prod** - VIDEOT 1988

Relations 48 MIN
U-matic / VHS / 16mm
Color (T H)
LC 75-702965
Shows the relationship between students and teachers in the arts, using the examples of a Kentucky mountain fiddler, an instructor in primitive art and the conductor of the Seattle Youth Symphony.
Education; Fine Arts
Dist - PHENIX **Prod** - FERTIK 1975

Relations
16mm
B&W
Introduces the concept of a relation on a set and considers equivalence relations. Illustrates the partition of a set into disjoining equivalence classes under an equivalence relation.
Mathematics
Dist - OPENU **Prod** - OPENU

Relations and functions 30 MIN
VHS
Intermediate algebra series
Color (H)
$125.00 purchase _ #M60
Explains relations and functions. Features Elayn Gay. Part of a 27 - part series on intermediate algebra.
Mathematics
Dist - LANDMK **Prod** - MGHT

Relations - Ringing the Changes 25 MIN
U-matic / VHS / 16mm
Color
Discusses the 'Trinitas' symbol found in 13th century manuscripts, which depicts three rings locked together. Asks whether four rings can be linked in the same manner.
Mathematics
Dist - MEDIAG **Prod** - OPENU 1979

Relations with the World 30 MIN
U-matic
China After Mao Series
Color
Examines China's place in the world and its relationship with other countries.
Civics and Political Systems; Geography - World
Dist - UMITV **Prod** - UMITV 1980

Relationship Enhancement Program for Family Therapy and Enrichment 39 MIN
16mm / U-matic / VHS
Color (C G T A)
Demonstrates the application of an educational, skill training approach to family therapy. Examples of therapy sessions illustrate how an educator/therapist teaches family members to communicate more effectively with each other and solve family problems and conflicts. Emphasizes the importance of expressing one's feelings and listening empathically to other family members.
Psychology; Sociology
Dist - PSU **Prod** - PSU 1977

Relationship growth group series

The Family genogram - Pt 2	45 MIN
The Family grid demonstration - Pt 4	44 MIN
The Family grid discussion	32 MIN
Family interpersonal development, family development over time - general - Pt 5	42 MIN
Life Stances Genogram, Pt 7	41 MIN
Life Stances, Pt 6	45 MIN
Setting the Context, Pt 1	42 MIN
Termination - Pt 8	50 MIN

Dist - UWISC

Relationship of Conformation to Lameness 56 MIN
BETA / VHS
Color
Deals with plating, fractures, hoof wall wear, knock knees and other causes of lameness in a horse.
Health and Safety; Physical Education and Recreation
Dist - EQVDL **Prod** - EQVDL

The Relationship of Problems 22 MIN
VHS / U-matic
Food Plant Supervisor - Understanding and Performing Inplant Food 'Safety Insp Series
Color
Instructs the supervisor in determining the seriousness of observed food protection problems, determination of the sources, and establishing priorities for correction.
Agriculture; Health and Safety; Industrial and Technical Education; Social Science
Dist - PLAID **Prod** - PLAID

Relationship strategies 38 MIN
VHS
Color (COR PRO IND A)
$895.00 purchase, $300.00 rental
Utilizes the communication expertise of Dr Tony Alessandra to teach employees innovative techniques for successful interaction. Identifies and differentiates four behavioral styles - Dove, Owl, Eagle and Peacock. Part One is entitled Understand and Identify, and Part Two is entitled Adapt. Includes support materials.
Business and Economics; Psychology; Social Science
Dist - AMEDIA **Prod** - AMEDIA
EXTR

Relationship Styles 23 MIN
Videoreel / VT2
Interpersonal Competence, Unit 01 - the Self Series; Unit 1 - The self
Color (C A)
Features a humanistic psychologist who, by analysis and examples, discusses interpersonal relationships.
Psychology; Sociology
Dist - TELSTR **Prod** - MVNE 1973

Relationships 15 MIN
U-matic / VHS
Watch Your Language Series
Color (J H)
$125.00 purchase
Examines the use of language in the courtship process.
English Language; Social Science
Dist - AITECH **Prod** - KYTV 1984

Relationships
VHS / 16mm
Color (G)
$395.00 purchase, $70.00 rental _ #4972, 4976, 0438J, 0442J
Explains the dynamics of healthy and unhealthy relationships and how to prosper in intimacy. Produced by Earnie Larsen.
Guidance and Counseling; Health and Safety; Psychology; Sociology
Dist - HAZELB

Relationships
VHS
Inside Genesis series
Color (G R)
$14.95 purchase
Examines the reason for God's statement, 'It is not good for man to be alone.' Helps in individual study, small groups, and for teaching Bible concepts. 10 - 13 minutes in length. Part of a four - part series.
Psychology; Religion and Philosophy
Dist - GF

Relationships 57 MIN
U-matic
Challenge Series
Color (PRO)
Shows a discussion by six men on their personal adjustments and contributions to our rapidly changing society.
Psychology
Dist - TVOTAR **Prod** - TVOTAR 1985

Relationships 15 MIN
VHS / U-matic
Drug wise series; Module 4
Color (J)
Contrasts the alternatives of healthy relationships with people and an unhealthy relationship with chemreals.
Health and Safety; Psychology
Dist - GPN **Prod** - WDCNTV

Relationships 30 MIN
VHS
Survivor's pride - building resiliency in youth at risk series
Color (I J H T PRO C)
$60.00 purchase _ #SW - 05Z
Conducts reframing interviews with resilient teens from a variety of ethnic and socio - economic backgrounds. Features youngsters discussing their most personal issues - parental drug and alcohol use, physical and sexual abuse, abandonment and neglect. Focuses on relationships, one of the seven resiliencies Drs Steve and Sybil Wolin have identified in teens with survival instincts. Part of an eight - part series showing how to recognize and foster resiliency among students and how to help young people recognize their own inner strengths.
Guidance and Counseling; Health and Safety; Psychology; Social Science
Dist - SHENEL **Prod** - ATTAIN 1995

Relationships 15 MIN
VHS / U-matic
Drug wise series
(J)
$40 purchase, $25 rental, $75 self dub
Compares healthy relationships with people to unhealthy ways of interacting using drugs.
Health and Safety; Psychology
Dist - GPN **Prod** - NCGE 1984 - 1985

Relationships - Achieving the Rewards of Recovery 30 MIN
VHS
(A)
$395.00 _ #83220
Presents a seminar on alcohol addiction recovery by Earnie Larsen. Discusses the value of healthy relationships as part of recovery.
Guidance and Counseling; Health and Safety; Psychology
Dist - CMPCAR **Prod** - CMPCAR

Relationships among Structued Techniques 30 MIN
U-matic / VHS
Structured Techniques - an Overview Series
Color
Continues the introductory overview of structured techniques by investigating the relationships among the various structured techniques.
Industrial and Technical Education; Psychology
Dist - DELTAK **Prod** - DELTAK

Relationships and stress 30 MIN
16mm / U-matic / VHS
Coping with serious illness series; No 4
Color (H C A)
LC 80-701663
Explains how serious illness can materially change relationships and how people can cope with the emotion and strain that invariably follow the diagnosis of a serious illness.
Psychology
Dist - TIMLIF **Prod** - TIMLIF 1980

Relationships - knowing the good from the bad 36 MIN
VHS
Color (I J H C)
$189.00 purchase _ #FG - 116 - VS
Reveals that patterns of unhealthy, overly - dependent and even abusive relationships are usually begun in adolescence and that teens need to learn how to spot unhealthy trends in their relationships - over - dependence, physical, verbal or sexual abuse, drug abuser - enabler patterns. Teaches the key aspects of healthy relationships, including setting boundaries, communicating clearly and assertively and maintaining self - respect. Includes guidance on when to leave an unhealthy relationship and how to do it. Uses a real workshop with teens role - playing different types of relationship problems and their solutions with adolescent counselors and experts. Includes teacher's manual. Consultant - Dr Deborah Gatins.
Guidance and Counseling; Health and Safety; Psychology; Social Science; Sociology
Dist - HRMC **Prod** - HRMC 1994

Relationships of the elderly 30 MIN
U-matic / VHS
Family portrait - a study of contemporary lifestyles series; Lesson 29
Color (C A)
Presents the three phases of aging. Considers the physiological realities of aging and changes brought about by retirement in the individual and in the marriage relationship.
Sociology
Dist - CDTEL **Prod** - SCCON

Relationships with Other People - a World Without 15 MIN
VHS / U-matic
It's a Rainbow World
(P)
Designed to teach social studies to primary grade students. Explains concepts in terms of everyday situations. Focuses on awareness of handicapped people and their problems.
Psychology; Sociology
Dist - GPN

Relationships with Other People - Who's Your Hero? 15 MIN
U-matic / VHS
It's a Rainbow World
(P)
Designed to teach social studies to primary grade students. Explains concepts in terms of everyday situations. Focuses on hero worship.
Psychology; Sociology
Dist - GPN

Relative age dating 33 MIN
U-matic / VHS
Basic and petroleum geology for non - geologists - geologic age series; Geologic age
Color (IND)
Science - Physical
Dist - GPCV **Prod** - PHILLP

Relative and absolute age dating 27 MIN
VHS / U-matic
Basic geology series
Color (IND)
Science - Physical
Dist - GPCV **Prod** - GPCV

Relative Atomic Mass 10 MIN
U-matic
Mole Concept Series
Color (H C)
Introduces the mass spectrometer, the modern method of measuring atomic mass.
Science; Science - Physical
Dist - TVOTAR **Prod** - TVOTAR 1986

Relative Circular Motion 7 MIN
U-matic / VHS
Introductory Concepts in Physics - Dynamics Series
Color (C)
$229.00, $129.00 purchase _ #AD - 1197
Demonstrates that the motion of an object depends on the point of view through releasing a ball from a point on the circumference of a large revolving disk.
Science - Physical
Dist - FOTH **Prod** - FOTH

Relative frequency 18 MIN
U-matic / VHS
Probability and random processes - limit theorems and statistics series
B&W (C)
Defines relative frequency. Shows that the relative frequency of an event converges to the probability of that event.
Mathematics
Dist - MIOT **Prod** - MIOT

Relative Mass 10 MIN
U-matic
Mole Concept Series
Color (H C)
Looks at how to compare the masses of atoms in order to understand how they differ from one another.
Science; Science - Physical
Dist - TVOTAR **Prod** - TVOTAR 1986

Relative Motion
16mm
B&W
Discusses relative motion in the context of the observed retrograde motion of a planet, and introduces the concept of the derivative of a vector.
Mathematics
Dist - OPENU **Prod** - OPENU

Relative Movement, Pt 1 - Relative Movement and Interception 14 MIN
16mm
B&W
LC FIE52-985
Shows the basic principles of relative movement and interception between planes and ships.
Civics and Political Systems; Industrial and Technical Education; Science - Physical
Dist - USNAC **Prod** - USN 1944

Relative Movement, Pt 2 - Out and in Search, Relative Wind 13 MIN
16mm
B&W
LC FIE52-986
Covers relative movement, computing time speed when leaving and returning to a carrier, searching on a relative bearing to a carrier and relative wind.
Civics and Political Systems; Industrial and Technical Education; Science - Physical
Dist - USNAC **Prod** - USN 1944

Relative position 14 MIN
VHS / U-matic
Hands on, grade 2 - lollipops, loops, etc series; Unit 1
Color (P)
Gives experience in observing relative position.
Science
Dist - AITECH **Prod** - WHROTV 1975

Relative values series
Explores fine art as big business. In 1987 Van Gogh's 'Irisis' sold for PdS30 million and is just one of hundreds of works bought as an investment rather than for aesthetic appreciation. Interviews distinguished critics, collectors, and artists to discover just how art is perceived in the modern world, how it is valued and promoted, and why artists are more important than the art they produce.

The Agony and the ecstasy	50 MIN
Altered states	50 MIN
The Colour of money	50 MIN
Keeping up with the Medicis	50 MIN
The Last picture show	50 MIN
The Sweet smell of success	50 MIN

Dist - BBCENE

Relatively posed 3 MIN
16mm
Family series
Color (G)
$10.00 rental
Presents the first in a series of four short films that deal with an idiosyncratic, personal and conceptual view of aspects of familial relationships. Animates still photographs of a posed family portrait to release the characteristics of the subjects and their relationships to each other. A voice - over track names the various connections between the relatives. A Sandy Maliga production.
Fine Arts; Industrial and Technical Education; Literature and Drama; Sociology
Dist - CANCIN

The Relatives Came
VHS / 35mm strip
Caldecotts on Filmstrip Series
Color (K)
$35.00 purchase
Presents a children's story. Part of the Caldecott Series.
English Language; Literature and Drama
Dist - PELLER

Relativity 29 MIN
U-matic
Project universe - astronomy series
Color (C A)
Explains features of Einstein's special theory of relativity. Uses hypothetical examples and scientific observations to illustrate effects of uniform relative motion. Lesson 22 in the series.
Science - Physical
Dist - CDTEL **Prod** - COAST

The Relativity of Motion 9 MIN
U-matic / VHS
Introductory Concepts in Physics - Dynamics Series
Color (C)
$229.00, $129.00 purchase _ #AD - 1196
Shows that two balls, one in parabolic and the other in falling motion, can appear to an observer falling at the proper speed to be, respectively, at a standstill and moving horizontally.

Science - Physical
Dist - FOTH **Prod** - FOTH

Relax, Take it Easy 25 MIN
U-matic / VHS
Color
Focuses on stress and the stress - triggered diseases of high blood pressure, headaches and stomach upsets. Suggests that tension may be linked to everything from cancer to stiff necks.
Health and Safety
Dist - MEDCOM **Prod** - MEDCOM

Relax your mind 15 MIN
16mm
Color (G)
$40.00 rental
Dabbles with fun and games, both real and fantasized, at the zoo, the park and on the train. Features music by Buffy St Marie, Sandy Bull, Johnny Cash and an anonymous Swiss yodeler. Produced by Bob Giorgio.
Fine Arts; History - United States
Dist - CANCIN

Relaxation
VHS
Synergy subliminal series
Color (G)
$19.98 purchase
Focuses on relaxation. Combines the nature cinematography of David Fortney with radiant, kaleidoscopic dances of color by Ken Jenkins, wilderness scenes by Blair Robbins, abstract animation by Jordan Belson and ethereal patterns of light created by Jason Loam. Features filmmaker Richard Ajathan Gero who integrates all of the foregoing imagery with subliminal visual affirmations and the music of Steven Halpern.
Fine Arts; Industrial and Technical Education; Religion and Philosophy
Dist - HALPER **Prod** - HALPER

Relaxation and Imagination 20 MIN
U-matic / VHS
Creative Dramatics Series
Color (I)
Introduces drama as a means of communication, begins the relaxation process, and provides several imagination - stretching experiences.
Fine Arts; Physical Education and Recreation
Dist - AITECH **Prod** - NEWITV 1977

Relaxation and imagination 30 MIN
VHS / U-matic
Creative dramatics - teacher series
Color (T)
Shows classroom demonstrations of beginning creative drama techniques.
Fine Arts
Dist - AITECH **Prod** - NEWITV 1977

Relaxation and Inspiration
VHS
Color (G)
$24.95 purchase _ #U891109048
Presents a montage of gentle nature images backed by soothing music. Features Emmett E Miller, MD.
Health and Safety; Psychology; Religion and Philosophy
Dist - BKPEOP **Prod** - SOURCE 1989

Relaxation as a Form of Stress Management 32 MIN
VHS / U-matic
Practical Stress Management with Dr Barry Alberstein Series
Color
Psychology
Dist - DELTAK **Prod** - DELTAK

Relaxation exercises
VHS / U-matic
Physical therapy series
Color (PRO C G)
$195.00 purchase _ #C890 - VI - 014
Informs patient educators and patients about relaxation exercises. Teaches effective techniques for minimizing pain and fatigue while enhancing the ability to perform daily activities. Part of a series by the physical therapy staff, St Luke's Hospital, Fargo, North Dakota.
Health and Safety; Physical Education and Recreation
Dist - HSCIC

Relaxation Oscillations 30 MIN
VHS / U-matic
Nonlinear Vibrations Series
B&W
Mathematics
Dist - MIOT **Prod** - MIOT

The Relaxation Tape 30 MIN
U-matic / VHS
Color
Presents soothing music and sounds and a narration to help focus the mind for point by point relaxation, controlled breathing, autogenic training, meditation and concentration exercises.
Health and Safety; Physical Education and Recreation; Psychology
Dist - HP **Prod** - HP

Relaxation Techniques 45 MIN
U-matic / VHS
B&W
Discusses various types of stress and the effects of stress on muscle tensions. Offers techniques for relieving stress.
Psychology; Sociology
Dist - UWISC **Prod** - UWISC 1979

Relaxed body - an anti - tension workout 60 MIN
VHS
Color (A)
$19.95 purchase _ #S00995
Emphasizes breathing and relaxation techniques for reducing stress. Covers topics including the health effects of stress, headache healers and targeted relaxation exercises.
Health and Safety; Physical Education and Recreation; Psychology
Dist - UILL

Relaxing time 11 MIN
VHS / U-matic
Life's little lessons - self - esteem 4 - 6 series; No 47
Color (I)
$129.00, $99.00 purchase _ #V676
Portrays Sammy Higgins who worked for newspaper with the motto, 'You can either burn out or rust out.' Shows that Higgins took the motto too seriously and worked day and night - until he realized that his life needed some balance. Part of a 65 - part series on self - esteem.
Guidance and Counseling; Health and Safety; Physical Education and Recreation; Psychology; Sociology
Dist - BARR **Prod** - CEPRO 1992

The Relay 11 MIN
U-matic / VHS / 16mm
Athletics Series
Color (H C A)
LC 80-700342
Shows athletes demonstrating a relay trainig session in 4 - by 100 - meter and 4 - by 400 - meter races. Reveals, through slow - motion scenes, the details and precision of high - speed baton exchange. Concludes with a complete race in the European Cup Semi - Finals.
Physical Education and Recreation
Dist - IU **Prod** - GSAVL 1980

Relay running 30 MIN
VHS
Track and field techniques series
Color (H C G)
$29.95 purchase _ #WK1103V
Features relay runner David Hemery who discusses the skill and improving performance. Part of a series.
Physical Education and Recreation
Dist - CAMV

Relay technique
VHS / U-matic
Bill Dellinger's championship track and field videotape training library series.
Color (H C)
Stresses that relays are won or lost in exchange zones and outlines phases of 400 meter and mile relays to show desirability of one method of exchanging the baton over another.
Physical Education and Recreation
Dist - CBSC **Prod** - CBSC

Relay technique 22 MIN
VHS
Bill Dellinger's championship track and field series
Color (H C A)
$39.95 purchase _ #WES1710V
Features Bill Dellinger and the University of Oregon coaching staff, who teach the basic techniques of relay events. Presents drills to develop an athlete's potential and correct common errors in technique. Uses slow - motion film and on - screen graphics.
Physical Education and Recreation
Dist - CAMV

Relays 18 MIN
16mm
B&W
LC 74-705510
Discusses some uses of relays and explains their construction and purpose. Shows the symbol used to identify types of relays and tells how a relay operates. (Kinescope).
Industrial and Technical Education; Science - Physical
Dist - USNAC **Prod** - USAF

Relays and Vibrators 18 MIN
U-matic / VHS / 16mm
B&W
Discusses the principles, use and operation of a relay. Shows troubleshooting a relay for an open or shorted coil with an ohmmeter. Describes the vibrator as an intermittent relay and shows its operation and output waveshape. Includes animated sequences.
Industrial and Technical Education; Science - Physical
Dist - USNAC **Prod** - USAF 1983

Release of Burn Scar Contracture of the Knee 10 MIN
16mm
Color
LC 75-702315
Demonstrates the correction of an early post - burn contracture of the popliteal space. Shows that an excellent cosmetic and functional result is obtained by excision of the contracture and coverage of the defect with thick split thickness skin.
Health and Safety; Science
Dist - EATONL **Prod** - EATONL 1969

Release of Information - or Knowing When to Open Your Mouth and Close the File 39 MIN
U-matic
Color
LC 79-707304
Deals with the Privacy act, the Freedom of information act, statutes on drugs, alcohol and sickle cell anemia and the Veterans Administration confidentiality statute, 38 USC 3301.
Civics and Political Systems
Dist - USNAC **Prod** - VAHSL 1978

Releasing shoulder and neck tension
VHS
Acupressure Institute series
Color (G)
$29.95 purchase _ #ACU003
Presents the fourth of a series of four tapes explaining the ancient Oriental art of therapeutic acupressure and how it stimulates the body's natural healing abilities. Shows step - by - step instructions for preventing and relieving shoulder and neck tension, either for oneself or for others.
Health and Safety; Psychology
Dist - SIV

Releasing shoulder and neck tension 60 MIN
VHS
Color (G)
$29.95 purchase _ #V84
Features acupressure specialist Michael Reed Gach who demonstrates and explains simple and effective ways to relieve the pain of shoulder and neck tension quickly and easily.
Health and Safety; Psychology
Dist - LIBSOR

Releasing the spirits - a village cremation in Bali 45 MIN
VHS / 16mm
Color (G)
$650.00, $350.00 purchase, $60.00, $40.00 rental
Records a group of villagers in Central Bali who cooperated to carry out a group cremation in 1978. Reveals that it has been recommended by religious officials that all Balinese cleanse the island by cremating their dead in preparation for an exorcism and purification ceremony, Eka Dasa Rudra, to be held at Bali's main temple, Besakih, in 1979. Produced by Patsy Asch, Linda Connor and Timothy Asch.
Geography - World; History - World; Religion and Philosophy; Sociology
Dist - DOCEDR

Relevance and witnesses 33 MIN
U-matic / VHS
Evidence update series
Color (PRO)
Analyzes prohibition against evidence of subsequent remedial measures and discusses exceptions offered to prove ownership and control or feasibility of precautionary measures.
Civics and Political Systems
Dist - ABACPE **Prod** - ABACPE

Relevance and witnesses 33 MIN
VHS
Evidence update series
Color (C PRO)
$75.00 purchase _ #ERX01
Presents Cornell law professor Faust Rossi in a discussion of the law of evidence. Emphasizes topics of relevance and witnesses.
Civics and Political Systems
Dist - NITA **Prod** - NITA 1980

Reliability and risk 34 MIN
VHS
Color (J H C G T A)
$35.00 purchase, $30.00 rental
Reveals that computer systems are increasingly being used to make 'life or death' military decisions. Suggests that the inherent unreliability of these systems makes this a dangerous policy. Produced by Jonathan Schwartz, Computer Professionals for Social Responsibility.

Civics and Political Systems; Computer Science; Industrial and Technical Education; Sociology
Dist - EFVP

Reliability Applications 30 MIN
U-matic / VHS
Probability and Random Processes - Random Variables Series
B&W (PRO)
Introduces computation of reliability, standard configurations of networks and components in series and in parallel.
Industrial and Technical Education; Mathematics
Dist - MIOT **Prod** - MIOT

Reliability Apportionment and Growth 30 MIN
VHS / U-matic
Reliability Engineering Series
Color (IND)
Describes how the reliability of successive generations of a product should improve. Shows a dynamic programming procedure to direct efforts to activities with greatest reliability payoffs.
Industrial and Technical Education
Dist - COLOSU **Prod** - COLOSU

Reliability approach to safety - a management introduction
U-matic / 16mm
Color (A)
Describes the reliability approach to safety, illustrates its effectiveness, the techniques used and shows how it anticipates potential trouble spots before they become serious.
Business and Economics; Health and Safety; Industrial and Technical Education
Dist - BNA **Prod** - BNA 1983

Reliability - Economic Considerations in Reliability 20 MIN
16mm
Color
LC 74-705511
Shows applications of break - even analysis for use in selection from competing systems and for economic decisions when changes to a system are considered.
Industrial and Technical Education
Dist - USNAC **Prod** - USN 1965

Reliability - Elements of Reliability Prediction 30 MIN
16mm
Color
LC 74-705512
Shows how prediction techniques are used on major components of a weapon system. Describes how predictions are made in drawing - board phase and refined in bench test and prototype test phase.
Industrial and Technical Education
Dist - USNAC **Prod** - USN 1964

Reliability Engineering 25 MIN
U-matic / VHS
Color
Covers Reliability Engineering principles, times - to - failure acquisition, failure rate calculation, reliability, time - to - failure, and failure rate function determination for early, useful and wearout life periods.
Industrial and Technical Education
Dist - UAZMIC **Prod** - UAZMIC

Reliability Engineering - Introduction 30 MIN
VHS / U-matic
Reliability Engineering Series
Color (IND)
Provides introduction by defning reliability and describing various models to predict mode of failure. Describes graphical techniques to estimate failure distribution.
Industrial and Technical Education
Dist - COLOSU **Prod** - COLOSU

Reliability Engineering - Reliability Testing 30 MIN
16mm
Color
LC FIE62-46
Presents advanced methods of techniques of reliability analysis.
Civics and Political Systems; Industrial and Technical Education
Dist - USNAC **Prod** - USN 1961

Reliability engineering series

Chance Failures	30 MIN
Chance Failures - Examples	30 MIN
Comparison test programs	30 MIN
Comparison tests - examples	30 MIN
Designing reliability into a product	30 MIN
Lot Acceptance Sampling	30 MIN
Mil - STD - 781C - Examples	30 MIN
Optimum Burn - in	30 MIN
Predicting Reliability during Development Test	30 MIN
Qualification Test Programs	30 MIN
Qualification Tests - Examples	30 MIN
Reliability Apportionment and Growth	30 MIN
Reliability Engineering - Introduction	30 MIN
Series, Parallel, and Standby Systems	30 MIN
Software Reliability	30 MIN
Wearout Failure	30 MIN
Wearout Failure - Examples	30 MIN
Weibull Failure Model	30 MIN
Weibull Probability Paper - Example	30 MIN

Dist - COLOSU

Reliability - Fundamental Concepts, Pt 1 30 MIN
16mm
Color
LC FIE62-47
Presents some of the fundamental concepts of reliability engineering that shall be used by designers of national weapons systems to achieve maximum inherent reliability in the design.
Civics and Political Systems; Industrial and Technical Education
Dist - USNAC **Prod** - USN 1961

Reliability - Fundamental Concepts, Pt 2 30 MIN
16mm
Color
LC FIE62-48
Presents fundamentals of engineering that should be used by designers of naval weapons systems to achieve the maximum inherent reliability in the design.
Civics and Political Systems; Industrial and Technical Education
Dist - USNAC **Prod** - USN 1961

Reliability growth with applications 180 MIN
U-matic / VHS
Reliability growth with applications series
Color
Provides an overview of a very valuable reliability engineering and management tool, Reliability and MTBF Growth.
Business and Economics; Industrial and Technical Education
Dist - UNKNWN

Reliability growth with applications series

Reliability growth with applications	180 MIN

Dist - UNKNWN

The Reliability of Scripture 60 MIN
VHS
Color (G A R)
$10.00 rental _ #36 - 811179 - 533
Features Christian apologist Josh McDowell in a defense of the reliability of both the Old and New Testaments. Based on the film series 'Evidence for Faith.'
Literature and Drama; Religion and Philosophy
Dist - APH **Prod** - WORD

Reliability of semiconductor memories 60 MIN
Videoreel / VT1
Semiconductor memories course series; No 7
Color (IND)
Establishes failure rates of future semiconductor memory systems using basic reliability information on integrated circuits.
Industrial and Technical Education
Dist - TXINLC **Prod** - TXINLC

Reliability - Part and Parcel 28 MIN
U-matic / VHS / 16mm
Color
LC 74-705514
Describes reliability standards established within Air Force Systems and Logistics Commands. Explains how the standards serve as production requirements and management tools in procurement of electronic replacement parts. Shows how the standards reduce costs and increase product reliability.
Business and Economics; Industrial and Technical Education
Dist - USNAC **Prod** - USAF 1963

Reliability - Reliability Analysis 30 MIN
U-matic / VHS / 16mm
Color
Presents advanced methods and techniques of reliability analysis. Studies an actual problem and demonstrates regression techniques, design improvement analysis and the Monte Carlo technique.
Civics and Political Systems; Industrial and Technical Education
Dist - USNAC **Prod** - USN

Reliability - Reliability Monitoring 20 MIN
16mm
Color
LC 74-705515
Shows how a program is monitored from concept through use phase and shows how data is used.
Business and Economics; Civics and Political Systems; Industrial and Technical Education
Dist - USNAC **Prod** - USN 1964

Reliability - Reliability Testing 25 MIN
16mm
Color
LC 74-705516
Depicts fundamentals of reliability testing design.
Business and Economics; Industrial and Technical Education
Dist - USNAC **Prod** - USN 1962

Reliability - Specifications and Reliability Assurance 25 MIN
16mm
Color
LC 74-705517
Describes the philosophy and function of specifications in relation to achievement of reliability assurance, general and detailed specifications, environment, interferences, interactions and interfaces affecting system performance requirements.
Business and Economics; Industrial and Technical Education
Dist - USNAC **Prod** - USN 1963

Reliability - Statistical Concepts 25 MIN
16mm
Color
LC FIE62-45
Describes reliability engineering methods and demonstrates the basic concepts on which the analytical methods are based.
Civics and Political Systems; Industrial and Technical Education
Dist - USNAC **Prod** - USN 1961

Reliability Testing 28 MIN
VHS / U-matic
Color
Covers Reliability Testing principles, the failure rate concept, time - to - failure distribution, failure rate function and reliability function determination.
Industrial and Technical Education
Dist - UAZMIC **Prod** - UAZMIC

Reliability - the Application of Reliability Data 21 MIN
16mm
Color
LC 74-705518
Shows application of feedback to the solution of problems arising during the life cycle of a weapon system.
Business and Economics; Industrial and Technical Education
Dist - USNAC **Prod** - USN 1964

Relief 30 MIN
U-matic
Media and Methods of the Artist Series
Color (H C A)
Demonstrates techniques for woodcut, wood engraving and lino block printing.
Fine Arts
Dist - TVOTAR **Prod** - TVOTAR 1971

Relief from back pain 57 MIN
VHS
Color (G)
$19.95 purchase _ #SF06
Presents Dr Irene Lamberti, a doctor of chiropractic, with a three - part relief program. Offers techniques to relieve back pain in everyday life, a simple exercise program to safely build back and neck flexibility and strength, and comprehensive pain and stress management through techniques such as guided imagery. Provides information about creating a safe work environment including computer workstations, housework dos and don'ts, back comfort during sex, and safely playing with or lifting small children.
Science - Natural
Dist - SVIP

Relief of Obstruction of Superior Vena Cava by Venous Autografts 31 MIN
16mm
Color (PRO)
Shows excision of benign, calcific obstruction of the superior vena cava in a young woman. Shows that continuity is restored by femoral vein autografts between innominate veins and intra - pericardial vena cava.
Health and Safety; Science
Dist - ACY **Prod** - ACYDGD 1956

Relief painting 25 MIN
VHS
Artists in print series
Color (A)
PdS65 purchase
Introduces the art of printmaking and illustrates basic printmaking techniques. Artists talk about their approach to the medium and are seen at all stages of making a

print. Asks what a print is and explains the difference between an 'original' and a reproduction. Part of a five-part series.
Fine Arts; Industrial and Technical Education
Dist - BBCENE

Relief printing 25 MIN
U-matic / VHS
Artist in print series
Color (H C A)
Demonstrates a method of making a lino - cut flower print. Shows cutting, inking and printing cardboard to make a brightly colored interior scene.
Industrial and Technical Education
Dist - FI **Prod** - BBCTV

Relief printing 30 MIN
VHS
ArtSmart series
Color (J H T)
LC 90708444
Depicts the processes and techniques of relief printing in an effort to have students make immediate use of those processes and techniques. The tenth of ten installments of the ArtSmart Series.
Fine Arts; Industrial and Technical Education
Dist - GPN **Prod** - UNKNWN 1990

Relief Valves 120 MIN
U-matic / VHS
Mechanical Equipment Maintenance Series
Color (IND)
Features steam and gas safety valves. Highlights electrically operated relief valves.
Industrial and Technical Education
Dist - ITCORP **Prod** - ITCORP

Relief valves 120 MIN
U-matic / VHS
Mechanical equipment maintenance - Spanish series
Color (IND) (SPANISH)
Features steam and gas safety valves. Highlights electrically operated relief valves.
Foreign Language; Industrial and Technical Education
Dist - ITCORP **Prod** - ITCORP

The Religion 15 MIN
VHS / U-matic
Across Cultures Series
Color (I)
Examines the very special place religion has in the cultures of the Baoule of West Africa, the Tarahumara of Mexico and the Japanese.
Geography - World; Religion and Philosophy; Social Science; Sociology
Dist - AITECH **Prod** - POSIMP 1983

Religion 30 MIN
VHS
Color (H C)
$89.95 purchase _ #TSI - 121
Explores the various functions of religion, using several major religions. Shows how religion affects society and how it is involved with social change and social conflict.
Sociology
Dist - INSTRU

Religion 20 MIN
16mm
Color (H C A)
$365 purchase, $45 rental
Discusses the role of religion in today's society and examines the need for the church to offer relevant spiritual service. Examines current interest in Eastern philosophies.
Religion and Philosophy
Dist - CNEMAG **Prod** - DOCUA 1988

Religion 15 MIN
VHS / U-matic
America past series
(J H)
$125 purchase
Explains the diversity and similarities in the American religious tradition.
History - United States; Religion and Philosophy
Dist - AITECH **Prod** - KRMATV 1987

Religion and civilisation series
Origins - 1 20 MIN
Symbols - 2 20 MIN
Dist - EDPAT

Religion and ethnicity 28 MIN
VHS
Illuminations series
Color (G R)
#V - 1032
Explores the dual influences of ethnicity and religious tradition in Greek Orthodox life. Suggests that the two influences have not always been in harmony with one another. Discusses interfaith marriage and its possible influence on the future state of the church, whether to use Greek or English as the primary church language, and the possibility of 'American Orthodoxy' as a future identity for the church.
Religion and Philosophy; Sociology
Dist - GOTEL **Prod** - GOTEL 1989

Religion and magic 30 MIN
U-matic
Faces of culture - studies in cultural anthropology series; Lesson 19
Color (C A)
Describes a variety of religious practices. Includes the roles of gods and goddesses, worship of ancestral spirits, animism, and various rituals and ceremonies.
Sociology
Dist - CDTEL **Prod** - COAST

Religion and the Clergy 35 MIN
U-matic
Terminal Illness Series
B&W
Sociology
Dist - UWASHP **Prod** - UWASHP

Religion and Values 15 MIN
VHS / 16mm
Junior High Ethics Resource Package Series
Color (J)
$200.00, $250.00 purchase _ #278407
Presents a comprehensive series on ethics for educators, junior high students and concerned adults. Describes an ethics course introduced in Alberta, Canada, schools and suggests teaching strategies for educators. The last five programs are dramas for students to teach key ethical concepts. 'Religion And Values' features Krupad, an alien from the planet Garf, who creates quite a stir when he arrives on Earth for a fact - finding mission to learn about religion and the part it plays in the lives of humans. Krupad's objective, unbiased perspective and curiosity can be used as a model to encourage tolerance and respect and to motivate thinking about religion and values. Diverse and common elements are discovered in different religious groups.
Business and Economics; Guidance and Counseling; Psychology; Religion and Philosophy; Sociology
Dist - AITECH **Prod** - ACCESS 1989

Religion and Values, Student Discussion 15 MIN
VHS / 16mm
Junior High Ethics Resource Package Series
Color (J)
$200.00, $250.00 purchase _ #278408
Presents a comprehensive series on ethics for educators, junior high students and concerned adults. Describes an ethics course introduced in Alberta, Canada, schools and suggests teaching strategies for educators. The last five programs are dramas for students to teach key ethical concepts. 'Religion And Values, Student Discussion' includes students from a number of different religious backgrounds discussing aspects of their religious beliefs and values from a personal perspective. Their honest comments will encourage further reflection and classroom discussion on the topic of religion.
Business and Economics; Guidance and Counseling; Psychology; Religion and Philosophy; Sociology
Dist - AITECH **Prod** - ACCESS 1989

Religion in a post - Holocaust world series
Anti - Semitism in the New Testament 141 MIN
Defining the Holocaust 155 MIN
The German Church 120 MIN
Reshaping Values After the Holocaust 180 MIN
Dist - HRC

Religion in America 15 MIN
35mm strip / VHS
In our time series
Color (J H C T A)
$57.00, $48.00 purchase _ #MB - 540359 - 5, #MB - 540031 - 6
Examines the historical role of religion in American life. Discusses the principles of religious tolerance and freedom that emerged from early US life. Hosted by Dr Martin Marty, noted editor and religious historian.
Civics and Political Systems; Religion and Philosophy
Dist - SRA **Prod** - SRA 1988

Religion in America 30 MIN
VHS / U-matic
Focus on Society Series
Color (C)
Discusses the status and history of religion in America. Examines secularization as a complex and important process affecting organized religion.
Sociology
Dist - DALCCD **Prod** - DALCCD

Religion in Indonesia - the way of the ancestors 52 MIN
U-matic / VHS / 16mm
Long search series; No 8
Color (H C A)
LC 79-707795
Visits the Torajas of Indonesia to investigate the experience of primal worship. Explores the reasons for the survival of the Torajas' religion at a time when other primal religions are dying out as a result of contact with the outside world.
Geography - World; Religion and Philosophy; Social Science; Sociology
Dist - TIMLIF **Prod** - BBCTV 1978
AMBROS

Religion in Indonesia - the way of the ancestors - Pt 2 26 MIN
U-matic / VHS / 16mm
Long search series; No 8
Color (H C A)
LC 78-700478
Visits the Torajas of Indonesia to investigate the experience of primal worship. Explores the reasons for the survival of the Torajas' religion at a time when other primal religions are dying out as a result of contact with the outside world.
Geography - World; Religion and Philosophy; Social Science; Sociology
Dist - TIMLIF **Prod** - BBCTV 1978

Religion in Nigeria - Christianity 28 MIN
16mm
Color
Looks at Christianity as it is practiced in Nigeria and explores such issues as ways of bringing more cultural influence into the church, the secularization of education, the provision of social services, the role of women and the contributions of Christianity to contemporary Nigerian society.
History - World; Religion and Philosophy
Dist - CCNCC **Prod** - CBSTV

Religion in Nigeria - Islam 28 MIN
VHS
Color (A)
Looks at Islam, the dominant religion in Nigeria. Discusses its hundreds of year history and the varied ethnic groups that practice Islam in Nigeria today.
Geography - World; Religion and Philosophy
Dist - ECUFLM **Prod** - CBSTV 1982

Religion in Nigeria - Islam 30 MIN
U-matic / VHS
Color
$325 rental
Provides a 'primer' on Islam in Nigeria, which is practised by half of the population. Includes discussions by Islamic leaders and educators on the history of Islam in Nigeria, basic tenets of belief, and relationships between Moslems and Christians in Nigeria. Hosted by Douglas Edwards.
History - World; Religion and Philosophy
Dist - CCNCC **Prod** - CCNCC 1985

A Religion in Retreat 13 MIN
U-matic
Asians in America Series
Color (C H)
Documents the Communist suppression of the Buddhist religion in most of the countries of Asia. Several leading Buddhist teachers and scholars who now live in America describe the religious persecution they were forced to endure before their escape.
History - United States; History - World; Religion and Philosophy; Sociology
Dist - CEPRO **Prod** - CEPRO 1986

Religion in Roman life 18 MIN
VHS
Color (J H C)
LC 89-700174
Examines the development of religion in Rome, from the early days of the Roman Republic through the establishment of Christianity.
History - World; Religion and Philosophy
Dist - EAV **Prod** - EAV 1989

Religion in Russia 20 MIN
16mm
Russia Today Series
Color (J H)
LC 77-701843
Views religious festivals in Russia - - an anicent jewish wedding, Shamanism, celebrations in an old Russian monastery and a Christmas procession in snow at 20 degrees below zero.
Geography - World; Religion and Philosophy
Dist - IFF **Prod** - IFF 1969

Religion in the Soviet Union - Another Look 57 MIN
VHS / U-matic
Color
$300 rental
Examines the vitality of religion in the U. S. S. R. in an age of persecution by the state. Presents Protestant, Catholic, Jewish, and Orthodox viewpoints.
Religion and Philosophy; Sociology
Dist - CCNCC **Prod** - CCNCC 1986

Religion - life after death 25 MIN
U-matic / VHS
Color (J H C A)
Discusses religion with the Rev Pat Fenske in Philadelphia and Rabbi Ephraim Buchwald in New York. Describes a first - hand 'near death' experience.
Sociology
Dist - GERBER **Prod** - SIRS

Religious dishes
VHS
Frugal gourmet - ancient cuisines from China, Greece and Rome series
Color (G)
$19.95 purchase _ #CCP853
Shows how to prepare religious dishes from the cultures of ancient China, Greece and Rome. Features Jeff Smith, the Frugal Gourmet. Part of a five - part series on ancient cuisines.
History - World; Home Economics; Physical Education and Recreation
Dist - CADESF **Prod** - CADESF

Religious education 28 MIN
VHS
Illuminations series
Color (G R)
#V - 1036
Features a panel discussion on the importance of religious education. Suggests that it is a necessary tool for passing on faith and values.
Education; Religion and Philosophy
Dist - GOTEL **Prod** - GOTEL 1989

Religious education in secondary schools series
Abraham's journey - an investigation with first year mixed - ability pupils - Unit C 37 MIN
Being compared with first year mixed - ability pupils in a Jewish school - Unit E 36 MIN
Birth ceremonies with secondary mixed - ability pupils in a Roman Catholic school - Unit A 31 MIN
An Investigation into preparing for and welcoming a new baby with second - year pupils in a boys' school - Unit G 43 MIN
The Jewish Bar Mitzvah ceremony with fourth year GCSE mixed - ability group - Unit D 44 MIN
A Mixed - ability fourth year GCSE examination group in a Roman Catholic school - Unit B 32 MIN
Rules protect freedom with a fourth - year GCSE group in a Jewish school - Unit F 33 MIN
A Study of rules and their effects on our everyday life with third - year pupils in a boys' school - Unit H 38 MIN
Dist - EMFVL

The Religious Experience 17 MIN
U-matic / VHS / 16mm
Humanities Series
Color (H C A)
LC 78-713372
Explores the various facets of the religious experience, discusses the meaning of religion to man and portrays the forms and rituals of several religions.
Religion and Philosophy; Sociology
Dist - MGHT **Prod** - MGHT 1971

The Religious experience 45 MIN
VHS / BETA
Psychological growth and spiritual development series
Color (G)
Psychology; Religion and Philosophy
Dist - DSP **Prod** - DSP

Religious experience 25 MIN
U-matic / VHS
Introduction to philosophy series
Color (C)
Religion and Philosophy
Dist - UDEL **Prod** - UDEL

Religious Experience, Pt 1 30 MIN
VHS / U-matic
Japan - the Living Tradition Series
Color (H C A)
Examines the major religions in Japan.
History - World; Religion and Philosophy
Dist - GPN **Prod** - UMA 1976

Religious Experience, Pt 2 30 MIN
U-matic / VHS
Japan - the Living Tradition Series
Color (H C A)
Examines the major religions in Japan.
History - World; Religion and Philosophy
Dist - GPN **Prod** - UMA 1976

Religious liberty 30 MIN
U-matic / VHS
Moral values in contemporary society series
Color (J)
Presents Glenn L Archer of Americans United Foundation and C Stanley Lowell, Associate Director of Church And State magazine, talking about religious liberty.
Civics and Political Systems; Religion and Philosophy; Sociology
Dist - AMHUMA **Prod** - AMHUMA

Religious neighborhoods - city 15 MIN
VHS / U-matic
Neighborhoods series
Color (P)
Looks at religious neighborhoods in cities.
Sociology
Dist - GPN **Prod** - NEITV 1981

Religious neighborhoods - rural 15 MIN
U-matic / VHS
Neighborhoods series
Color (P)
Looks at rural religious neighborhoods.
Sociology
Dist - GPN **Prod** - NEITV 1981

Religious neighborhoods - town 15 MIN
U-matic / VHS
Neighborhoods series
Color (P)
Looks at religious neighborhoods in towns.
Sociology
Dist - GPN **Prod** - NEITV 1981

The Religious right - in their own words 8 MIN
VHS
Color (G)
$25.00 purchase
Documents the radical rhetoric of the Religious Right. Includes Pat Robertson, Jerry Falwell, Phyllis Schlafly, Pat Buchanan and Robert Simonds. Illustrates the views of these people on gay rights, women's rights, reproductive freedom, public education and more.
Civics and Political Systems; Religion and Philosophy
Dist - PAMWAY **Prod** - PAMWAY 1993

Reliving the Past - Alonzo Pond and the 1930 Logan African Expedition 45 MIN
U-matic
Color (H C A)
Covers the reunion of eight surviving members of a 1930 archeological expedition to Algeria. Includes original footage from the expedition.
Geography - World; History - World
Dist - CEPRO **Prod** - CEPRO

Relocation 22 MIN
U-matic / VHS
Dollar scholar series; Pt 8
Color (H)
LC 82-707406
Presents high school senior Jerry Malone discussing home ownership.
Business and Economics; Home Economics
Dist - GPN **Prod** - BCSBIT 1982

Relocations 15 MIN
VHS / U-matic
Color (G)
$99.00 purchase, $40.00 rental
Explores the issues of race, gender and sexuality from an Asian American perspective. Features Japanese American poet Daivd Mura who performs four pieces, one telling the story of his grandfather who was interned during World War II and later returned to Japan, scene two portraying a gay Japanese American, scene three relating an eyewitness account of the murder of Chinese American Vincent Chin in Detroit and scene four shows Mura arguing with his video double on whether racism affected his sexuality as a teenager. Produced and directed by Mark Tang.
History - United States; Sociology
Dist - CROCUR

The Reluctant astronaut 102 MIN
16mm
Color
Presents Don Knotts as an astronaut in an amusement park. Deals with a funny situation that arises when Knotts is sent to Washington for space duty.
Fine Arts
Dist - SWANK **Prod** - SWAMD

The Reluctant braider 8 MIN
16mm
Human side of supervision series
Color (IND)
LC 73-701928
Studies the development and recognition of attitudes and attitude changes that vitally affect any kind of production. Asks how much to monitor the work of the old hand who has an enviable work record and how to motivate this 'expert' into changing the technique.
Business and Economics; Psychology
Dist - VOAERO **Prod** - VOAERO 1972

The Reluctant Delinquent 24 MIN
U-matic / VHS / 16mm
Color (C A)
Examines the high correlation between learning disabilities and juvenile delinquency. Presents a positive case history of what can be done to help young people with undiagnosed learning disabilities avoid problems with the law.
Education; Psychology; Sociology
Dist - CORF **Prod** - EISBGI 1978

The Reluctant detectives 30 MIN
VHS
Color (J H C)
$195.00 purchase
Offers a critical perspective on environmental concerns. Pits expectations of the public about environmental scientists against working, human realities and discovers an important gulf between the two, ranging from conspiracy scenarios - scientists don't tell what they really know - to unthinking confidence that science will provide a quick fix for any problem.
Science - Natural
Dist - LANDMK **Prod** - LANDMK 1992

The Reluctant Dragon 19 MIN
16mm / U-matic / VHS
Color (K P I)
LC 79-700816
An edited version of the 1941 motion picture The Reluctant Dragon. Uses animation to tell the story of a dragon who is shy and poetic rather than ferocious. Based on the story The Reluctant Dragon by Kenneth Grahame.
Fine Arts; Literature and Drama
Dist - CORF **Prod** - DISNEY 1979

The Reluctant dragon 12 MIN
U-matic / VHS / 16mm
Misunderstood monsters series
Color (P I J)
LC 81-700987
Recounts the story of a boy who discovers that the terrifying dragon who lives in a cave near his village wants nothing more than to live peacefully and write poetry. Reveals that when a famous dragon slayer appears in the village, both he and the boy visit the dragon and agree to stage a mock battle in order to save their reputations and appease the villagers.
Literature and Drama
Dist - CF **Prod** - BOSUST 1981

The Reluctant Politician - the Life and Presidency of William Howard Taft 28 MIN
U-matic
Color
Dramatizes the life and political career of former President William Howard Taft.
Biography
Dist - HRC **Prod** - OHC

The Reluctant World Power 29 MIN
U-matic / VHS / 16mm
History of U S Foreign Relations Series
Color (J)
LC 74-701136
Portrays the agonizing process by which the United States assumed, then rejected, and then finally was obliged to accept the role of a major power.
Civics and Political Systems; History - United States
Dist - CORF **Prod** - USDS 1972

The Remainder in division 8 MIN
VHS
Children's encyclopedia of mathematics - multiplication and division of fractions series
Color (I)
$49.95 purchase _ #8361
Discusses the remainder in division with fractions. Part of a seven - part series on multiplication and division with fractions.
Mathematics
Dist - AIMS **Prod** - DAVFMS 1991

Remains 13 MIN
16mm
Color (G)
$35.00 purchase
Features a dark psychological sketch of Berlin's architecture in a production by Konrad Steiner.
Fine Arts
Dist - CANCIN

Remains to be Seen 7 MIN
16mm
Color
Presents Jane Aaron's film selected by John Hambardt, curator of film and video at the Whitney Museum of American Art, from the 1985 Whitney Bicennial Film and Video Exhibition.
Fine Arts
Dist - AFA **Prod** - AFA 1986

Remaking of Canada - Canadian government and politics in the 1990s series
Articulation, aggregation, integration - the minor political parties and interest groups 30 MIN
Heads of state and heads of government - the formal and political executives in Canada 30 MIN
In the shadow of the giant - Canadian political culture and the political socialization process 30 MIN
Masters in our own house - French and English relations in Canada 30 MIN
O Canada - an introduction to Canadian government and politics 30 MIN
Peace, order and good government - the Canadian Constitution and Canadian federalism 30 MIN
Reasonable limits - the Canadian Charter of Rights and Freedoms 30 MIN
Red tape - government departments and non - departmental agencies 30 MIN
Show time - the decline of the Canadian Parliament 30 MIN
The Sum of its parts - regions, nations, state 30 MIN
Tweedledum and Tweedledee - the party system and the major political parties 30 MIN
Winning and losing - the electoral process and electoral systems 30 MIN
Dist - INSTRU

The Remarkable Bandicoots 25 MIN
U-matic
Animal Wonder Down Under Series
Color (I J H)
Tells about the Rabbit Eared Bandicoot, a rare marsupial of Australia.
Science - Natural
Dist - CEPRO **Prod** - CEPRO

The Remarkable Mountain Goat 20 MIN
VHS / U-matic
Color (J)
Shows the mountain goat in the highest crags of the Rocky Mountains where no other large mammal lives year around. Depicts this remote home in the alpine areas where the mountain goats feeling the pressures of modern civilization as people seek minerals, timber and recreation.
Science - Natural
Dist - BERLET **Prod** - BERLET

The Remarkable Mr Wetherby 15 MIN
U-matic
Color (I)
Teaches writing skills while telling the story of Chris and Lynne who meet the ghost of Mr Wetherby who was a school principal.
Education; English Language; Literature and Drama
Dist - TVOTAR **Prod** - TVOTAR 1982

The Remarkable Phagocyte 22 MIN
VHS / U-matic
Color
Shows actions of granulocytes in response to various foreign bodies and micro - organisms by means of animation and scenes through a microscope.
Health and Safety; Science - Natural
Dist - WFP **Prod** - WFP

The Remarkable Riderless Runaway Tricycle 11 MIN
U-matic / VHS / 16mm
Color (P)
LC 82-700423
Tells a story of a tricycle whose young owner distractedly abandons it. Shows how it ends up in a dump, escapes, careens around town in a series of humorous hijinks and then returns, at last, to its downcast owner. Based on the book The Remarkable Riderless Runaway Tricycle by Bruce McMillan.
Literature and Drama
Dist - PHENIX **Prod** - EVRGRN 1982

The Remarkable Rocket 25 MIN
U-matic / VHS / 16mm
Color
Tells the story of a pompous - looking rocket who feels he is the most important part of a lavish fireworks display until he dampens his own fuse with his tears of pride. Features David Niven as narrator of this Oscar Wilde short story.
Literature and Drama
Dist - PFP **Prod** - READER 1975

Remarriage 30 MIN
VHS / U-matic
Family portrait - a study of contemporary lifestyles series; Lesson 23
Color (C A)
Discusses the readjustment of the family when a remarriage occurs following a divorce or death of a spouse.
Sociology
Dist - CDTEL **Prod** - SCCON

Rembitika 50 MIN
U-matic / VHS / 16mm
Color (J)
LC 84-706001
Introduces Rembitika, the often - melancholy music brought to Greece after the 1921 tragedy at Smyrna, Turkey and the subsequent Greek and Turkish exchange of minority religious groups. Presents the music being performed by master musicians and by contemporary groups, who have adopted past performers' styles or added new interpretations of the bousouki - accompanied songs.
Fine Arts; History - World
Dist - WOMBAT **Prod** - MONROS 1983

Rembrandt 7 MIN
U-matic / VHS / 16mm
Art awareness collection series
Color (J H C)
LC 78-701206
Concentrates on Rembrandt's aesthetic and dramatic use of light and shade. Considers Rembrandt's richly painted and sensitive portraits, then progresses to his etchings of New Testament scenes.
Fine Arts
Dist - EBEC **Prod** - USNGA 1974

Rembrandt 40 MIN
VHS
Three painters 3 series
Color (A)
PdS65 purchase
Explores the work of the painter Rembrandt, hosted by painter and critic Sir Lawrence Gowing. Based on the concept that Rembrandt's work represents a distinct stage in the development of European painting between the Renaissance and the present day. Discusses the historical and social backgrounds against which the artist worked, but concentrates on examining a small number of canvases. Includes views of the places which particularly inspired the artist.
Fine Arts
Dist - BBCENE

Rembrandt 29 MIN
U-matic
Meet the Masters Series
B&W
Discusses Rembrandt's genius. Reproduces a portion of Man in the Gold Helmet to show the master's technique.
Fine Arts
Dist - UMITV **Prod** - UMITV 1966

Rembrandt 30 MIN
VHS
Tom Keating on painters series
Color (J H C G)
$195.00 purchase
Focuses on the painter Rembrandt. Features Tom Keating who recreates the painting of Rembrandt exactly the way the original work was done and gives biographical information about the artist. Part of a six - part series on painters.
Fine Arts
Dist - LANDMK **Prod** - LANDMK 1987

Rembrandt and Velazquez 28 MIN
VHS
Color (I)
$29.95 purchase _ #HV - 648
Presents an in - depth look at '1660 Self - Portrait' by Rembrandt and the 1650 portrait of Juan de Pareja by Velasquez.
Fine Arts; History - World
Dist - CRYSP **Prod** - CRYSP

Rembrandt - Painter of Man 20 MIN
16mm
Color (J)
Presents selected canvases gathered from twenty - nine museums in twelve countries. These show Rembrandt's amazing ability in the use of light and shadow and his genius in expressing human compassion for his subjects. Made in commemoration of the 350th anniversary of Rembrandt's birth.
Biography; Fine Arts
Dist - CORF **Prod** - NETHIS 1958

Rembrandt - painter of stories 21 MIN
VHS
Color (G)
PdS15.50 purchase _ #A4-300428
Follows the development of Rembrandt van Rijn's art and chronicles his achievements in the art of storytelling. Notes his mastery in this area and speculates that in another age he might have been a movie director.
Fine Arts
Dist - AVP **Prod** - NATLGL

Rembrandt Van Rijn - a Self - Portrait 27 MIN
U-matic / VHS / 16mm
Color (J H C)
Uses Rembrandt's self - portraits to depict his life from the time he was a young cavalier to when he was an old man. Explains that he was one of Holland's most popular portrait painters, but gave up fame and wealth to follow his true artistic inclinations.
Biography; Fine Arts
Dist - EBEC **Prod** - EBEC 1955

Rembrandt's Christ (1606 - 1669) 40 MIN
16mm
B&W
Depicts the story of Christ as drawn by Rembrandt. Takes place in the houses, towns, canals, streets and fields of 17th century Holland.
Fine Arts
Dist - ROLAND **Prod** - ROLAND 1964

Remedial Reading Comprehension 5 MIN
16mm
Color (C)
$386.00
Experimental film by George Landow (aka Owen Land).
Fine Arts
Dist - AFA **Prod** - AFA 1970

Remedial Reading - who, what, Why and How 23 MIN
16mm
Jab Reading Series
Color (C S)
LC 75-701424
Offers explanations of corrective and remedial reading programs for students in elementary and secondary school levels, as well as possible causative factors leading to reading disability. Features Dr Albert J Mazurkiewicz in a reading clinic to show diagnosis and remedial situations in action. Shows examples of VAK VAKT and neurological impress techniques.
Education; English Language; Psychology
Dist - JBFL **Prod** - JABP 1975

Remedial Typing 11 MIN
16mm
Color (J H)
Demonstrates clear and concise information concerning reading, rhythm and pre - positioning, showing that the most common typing errors result from poor posture and finger positioning, a bad striking action and carriage return, unrhythmic typing and a generally careless attitude.
Business and Economics
Dist - SF **Prod** - SF 1969

Remedies for Breach of Contract 120 MIN
U-matic / VHS / Cassette
Color; Mono (PRO)
Focuses on breaches and potential breaches of contract and how to handle them. Features business planners and litigators as they analyze specific contract clauses and their consequences, pointing out how to anticipate possible trouble areas.
Civics and Political Systems
Dist - CCEB **Prod** - CCEB

Remedies Phase of an EEO Case - Class Back Pay and Proof of Claims Series Pt 1
Panel Discussions 49 MIN
Proofs of Claims Hearing 58 MIN
Dist - ABACPE

Remedies phase of an EEO case - Class back pay and proof of claims series
Class back pay 57 MIN
Dist - ABACPE

Remedies Phase of an EEO Case - Contested Settlement and Attorneys' Fees Trial Series Pt 3
Closing Arguments and Panel Discussion 42 MIN
Contested Settlement 57 MIN
Dist - ABACPE

Remedies Phase of an EEO Case - Individual Determinations Series Pt 2
Opening Statements and First Witness 43 MIN
Panel Discussion 37 MIN
Second and Third Witnesses 44 MIN
Dist - ABACPE

Remember 52 MIN
U-matic / VHS / 16mm
World at war series
Color (H C A)
States that the war is the most memorable experience in the lives of many men and women all over the world. Many veterans feel alienated from those who did not experience the war because they cannot or prefer not to understand it.
History - World; Sociology
Dist - MEDIAG **Prod** - THAMES 1973

Remember 60 MIN
16mm
World at War Series
Color (H C A)
LC 76-701778
History - World; Sociology
Dist - USCAN **Prod** - THAMES 1975

Remember Africville 35 MIN
VHS / U-matic
Color (C G)
$170.00 purchase, $35.00 rental _ #CC4523VU, #CC4523VH
Questions the wisdom of dismantling Africville, a black community, in the early 1970s, and the relocation of its residents to housing throughout Halifax, Novia Scotia. Uses archival stills, moving footage and interviews to depict a poor, but unified community through which a strong sense of identity is still maintained by its members. Contrasts these views with those of government officials who viewed Africville as an impoverished, segregated community which lacked essential public services such as paved roads, running water and sewers.
History - World; Sociology
Dist - IU **Prod** - NFBC 1991

Remember Me 15 MIN
U-matic / VHS / 16mm
Color
LC 79-701189
Presents portraits of children from around the world and the environments in which they live. Emphasizes the influence of environment on daily life.
Geography - World; Social Science; Sociology
Dist - PFP **Prod** - UNICEF 1979

Remember me 10 MIN
U-matic / VHS / 16mm
Color (H A) (SPANISH)
LC 81-701360
Looks at several typical examples of salesperson - customer interface and shows that it is not whether the customer's desired service can be fulfilled that is important, but the attitude with which the customer is treated.
Business and Economics; Psychology
Dist - CRMP **Prod** - CRMP 1981

Remember My Lai 60 MIN
VHS
Frontline Series
Color; Captioned (G)
$300.00 purchase, $95.00 rental _ #FRON - 714K
Documents the My Lai massacre in the Vietnam War. Explores how this incident affected American support for the war. Interviews servicemen and survivors involved.
History - United States; History - World; Sociology
Dist - PBS **Prod** - DOCCON 1989

Remember My Name 18 MIN
16mm
Color
LC 75-700575
Illustrates the frustrations of employees in lower level, deadended jobs. Stresses the need for management and supervisory actions to bring about equality of opportunity in employment and upward mobility within the Federal Government.
Business and Economics; Civics and Political Systems; Guidance and Counseling; Psychology; Sociology
Dist - USNAC **Prod** - USCSC 1972

Remember My Name 52 MIN
VHS / 16mm
Color (PRO G)
$179.00, $249.00, purchase _ #AD - 1978
Documents the assembly of a giant quilt in San Francisco from three foot by six foot panels, each bearing the name of an AIDS victim. Focuses on eleven individual stories which reflect the plight of children who are living with AIDS, the impact of AIDS on religion and community, the role of the family, and the effect of fear and stigma on private lives and public attitudes.
Health and Safety; Psychology; Sociology
Dist - FOTH **Prod** - FOTH 1990

Remember Pearl Harbor - America at War, 1941 - 45 17 MIN
16mm
Screen new digest series; Vol 9; Issue 5
B&W (J)
LC 70-700284
Recalls America's entry into World War II with the attack on Pearl Harbor, and her subsequent involvement in Guadalcanal, Europe and the Pacific. Shows effects of the war at home and the final Allied victories.
History - United States; History - World
Dist - HEARST **Prod** - HEARST 1966

Remember, remember 15 MIN
VHS
Color; PAL (H)
Discusses the Guy Fawkes Gunpowder Plot and how it has been historically viewed. Considers whether history written by victors in a political conflict is reliable.
Civics and Political Systems; History - World; Science
Dist - VIEWTH

Remember sin and salvation
VHS
Questions of faith III series
Color (J H C G A R)
$10.00 rental _ #36 - 84 - 217
Examines the meaning of sin and salvation. Features the perspectives of a wide variety of contemporary Christian and Jewish thinkers.
Religion and Philosophy
Dist - APH **Prod** - ECUFLM

Remember the Ladies - Women in America 1750 - 1815 25 MIN
16mm
Color
LC 77-702130
Documents the exhibition Remember The Ladies held at the Corcoran Art Gallery. Traces the changing lifestyle, position and concerns of colonial women through the art, artifacts and documents of the period.
Fine Arts; History - United States; History - World; Sociology
Dist - MTP **Prod** - PHILMO 1977

Remember the Witches 22 MIN
VHS
Color (C)
$550.00 purchase, $125.00, $160.00 rental
Documents withcraft in the Middle Ages and the resurgence of goddess worship. Discusses persecution of women healers through post - industrial society, the threat of the social and political power of women, the cult of rational science, and the impact of the Industrial Revolution. Depicts scenes of contemporary goddess worship in women's communities.
Civics and Political Systems; History - World; Religion and Philosophy; Sociology
Dist - WMENIF

Remember Tibet 60 MIN
VHS / BETA
Color; PAL (G)
PdS25 purchase
Commemorates the uprising of thousands of Tibetans in Lhasa against the Chinese garrisons that surrounded them on March 10, 1959. Features the Venerable Doboom Rinpoche, Director of Tibet House, New Delhi, speaking to the Tibetan community at Rigpa, London and Western friends about the contribution Tibetan society and Buddhism can make to the world. Mr Phuntsog Wangyal, His Holiness the Dalai Lama's representative in London, and a member of the second official delegation to Tibet in 1980, gives an illustrated talk on conditions inside Tibet today.
Fine Arts; Religion and Philosophy
Dist - MERIDT

Remember when 15 MIN
VHS / U-matic
Mrs Cabobble's caboose series
(P)
Designed to teach primary grade students basic music concepts. Highlights melody, rhythm, harmony and the different families of instruments. Features Mrs Fran Powell.
Fine Arts
Dist - GPN **Prod** - WDCNTV 1986

Remembering 57 MIN
U-matic / VHS / 16mm
Heart of the Dragon Series Pt 1; Pt 1
Color (H C A)
Gives a broad overview of historic and modern China.
Civics and Political Systems; Geography - World; History - World
Dist - TIMLIF **Prod** - ASH 1984

Remembering 57 MIN
16mm / VHS
Heart of the Dragon Series
(J H C)
$99.95 each, $595.00 series
Gives a broad look at historic and modern China.
Geography - World; History - World
Dist - AMBROS **Prod** - AMBROS 1984

Remembering 15 MIN
VHS / U-matic
Strawberry Square Series
Color (P)
Fine Arts
Dist - AITECH **Prod** - NEITV 1982

Remembering 1924 16 MIN
VHS
Bi - Folkal Remembering series
Color (G PRO)
$210.00, $220.00 purchase _ #TF101, #TF103
Reminisces over the sights and sounds, moods and music of the 20s. One of a series of kits designed to stimulate remembrance and conversation in the elderly - used in senior centers, retirement homes, nursing homes and with the young. Includes an 80 - slide carousel tray and cassette tape or a videocassette, plus two manuals, 25 booklets with nostalgic singalong songs, one or more skits, touch cards and paraphernalia from earlier eras and a kit bag.
Health and Safety; History - United States; Psychology
Dist - BFKLP **Prod** - BFKLP

Remembering and forgetting - cognitive processes 60 MIN
U-matic / VHS
Discovering psychology series; Pt 9 and 10
Color (C)
$45.00, $29.95 purchase
Presents parts 9 and 10 of the 26 - part Discovering Psychology series. Looks at the complex process of memory. Examines the 'cognitive revolution.' Two thirty - minute programs hosted by Professor Philip Zimbardo of Stanford University.
Psychology
Dist - ANNCPB **Prod** - WGBHTV 1989

Remembering automobiles 20 MIN
Slide
Color (G A PRO)
$35.00 purchase ; $210.00, $220.00 purchase _ #AU101, #AU103
Remembers the sights and sounds, moods and music of automobiles in the past. One of a series of kits designed to stimulate remembrance and conversation in the elderly - used in senior centers, retirement homes, nursing homes and with the young. Includes an 80 - slide carousel tray and cassette tape or a videocassette, plus two manuals, 25 booklets with nostalgic singalong songs, one or more skits, touch cards and paraphernalia from earlier eras and a kit bag.
Health and Safety; Industrial and Technical Education; Psychology; Sociology
Dist - BFKLP **Prod** - BFKLP

Remembering birthdays 10 MIN
VHS / BETA
Color (G PRO)
$210.00, $220.00 purchase _ #BD101, #BD103
Remembers the sights and sounds, moods and music of birthdays past and birthdays present. One of a series of kits designed to stimulate remembrance and conversation in the elderly - used in senior centers, retirement homes, nursing homes and with the young. Includes an 80 - slide carousel tray and cassette tape or a videocassette, two manuals, 25 booklets with nostalgic singalong songs, one or more skits, touch cards and paraphernalia from earlier eras and a kit bag.
Health and Safety; Psychology; Sociology
Dist - BFKLP **Prod** - BFKLP

Remembering County Fairs 20 MIN
Slide / VHS / BETA
Color (G PRO)
$210.00, $220.00 purchase _ #CF101, #CF103
Remembers the sights and sounds, moods and music of county fairs. One of a series of kits designed to stimulate remembrance and conversation in the elderly - used in senior centers, retirement homes, nursing homes, and with the young. Includes an 80 - slide carousel tray and cassette tape or a videocassette, two manuals, 25 booklets with nostalgic singalong songs, one or more skits, touch cards and paraphernalia from earlier eras and a kit bag.
Health and Safety; History - United States; Sociology
Dist - BFKLP **Prod** - BFKLP

Remembering Fall 62 FRS
VHS / BETA
Color (G PRO)
$210.00, $220.00 purchase _ #FA101, #FA103; LC 81-720021
Remembers the sights and sounds, moods and music of autumn in the early 20th century. One of a series of kits designed to stimulate remembrance and conversation in the elderly - used in senior centers, retirement homes, nursing homes and with the young. Includes an 80 - slide carousel tray and cassette tape or a videocassette, two manuals, 25 booklets with nostalgic singalong songs, one or more skits, touch cards and paraphernalia from earlier eras and a kit bag.
Health and Safety; History - United States; Sociology
Dist - BFKLP **Prod** - BFKLP

Remembering Farm Days 12 MIN
VHS / Slide
Color (G PRO)
$210.00, $220.00 purchase _ #FD101, #FD103; LC 80-720330
Remembers the sights and sounds, moods and music from farm life in the early 20th century. One of a series of kits designed to stimulate remembrance and conversation in the elderly - used in senior centers, retirement homes, nursing homes and with the young. Includes an 80 - slide carousel tray and cassette tape or a videocassette, two manuals, 25 booklets with nostalgic singalong songs, one or more skits, touch cards and paraphernalia from earlier eras and a kit bag.
Health and Safety; History - United States; Sociology
Dist - BFKLP **Prod** - BFKLP

Remembering Fun and Games 16 MIN
Slide / VHS
(J H A)
$220.00 video _ #FG103, $210.00 slides _ #FG101
Remembers childhood gaames. Offers a kit with visual media, sing - along songs and stories for discussion, includes 25 booklets, five writing exerciseses, scripts for two skits, the Game of Games board, 2 program manuals. Nostalgia kit for older adults.
Sociology
Dist - BFKLP **Prod** - BFKLP 1989

Remembering Jack Cole 30 MIN
VHS / U-matic
Broadway Series
Color
Fine Arts; Industrial and Technical Education
Dist - ARCVID **Prod** - ARCVID

Remembering Jackie Robinson 14 MIN
VHS / U-matic
Color
Examines the historical implications and social significance of Jackie Robinson's breaking the color barrier to become the first black man to play in the major leagues.
Biography; History - United States; Physical Education and Recreation
Dist - KINGFT **Prod** - KINGFT 1983

Remembering Life 28 MIN
U-matic / VHS / 16mm
Color (H C A)
Documents the history of Life magazine. Presents photographers and editors of Life who describe their experiences and Life's impact on the country and on modern journalism.
Literature and Drama; Social Science
Dist - CORF **Prod** - VARDIR

Remembering music 20 MIN
VHS
Bi - Folkal Remembering series
Color (G PRO)
$210.00, $220.00 purchase _ #MU101, #MU103
Remembers the sights and sounds, moods and music of decades past. One of a series of kits designed to stimulate remembrance and conversation in the elderly - used in senior centers, retirement homes, nursing homes, and with the young. Includes an 80 - slide carousel tray and cassette tape or a videocassette, two manuals, 25 booklets with nostalgic singalong songs, one or more skits, touch cards and paraphernalia from earlier eras and a kit bag.
Fine Arts; Sociology
Dist - BFKLP **Prod** - BFKLP

Remembering Names and Faces 17 MIN
VHS / 16mm / U-matic
Color (A) (DUTCH)
Portrays a salesman who cannot recall the name of an important customer. Shows him going to a memory expert who demonstrates how to fix a name firmly in the mind so that it can be recalled easily.
Business and Economics; Psychology
Dist - RTBL **Prod** - RTBL

Remembering, planning, intervening 111 MIN
VHS
Building and maintaining generalizations series; No 6
Color; PAL; SECAM (G)
$95.00 purchase
Features Richard Bandler in the sixth part of a six - part series on building and maintaining generalizations, using submodalities from advanced NLP, neuro - linguistic programming. Shows how people are motivated, learn, become convinced and generalize. Contains the first recorded descriptions of Bandler's time model. Recommended that tapes be viewed in order. Bandler sometimes uses profanity for emphasis, which may offend some people.
Health and Safety; Psychology
Dist - NLPCOM **Prod** - NLPCOM

Remembering school days 14 MIN
VHS
Bi - Folkal Remembering series
Color (G PRO)
$210.00, $220.00 purchase _ #SD101, #SD103
Remembers the sights and sounds, moods and music from school days in the early 20th century. One of a series of kits designed to stimulate remembrance and conversation in the elderly - used in senior centers, retirement homes, nursing homes and with the young. Includes an 80 - slide carousel tray and cassette tape or a videocassette, two manuals, 25 booklets with nostalgic singalong songs, one or more skits, touch cards and paraphernalia from earlier eras and a kit bag.
Health and Safety; Psychology; Social Science; Sociology
Dist - BFKLP **Prod** - BFKLP

Remembering summertime 10 MIN
VHS
Color (G PRO)
$210.00, $220.00 purchase _ #ST101, #ST103
Remembers the sights and sounds, moods and music of an old - time summertime. One of a series of kits designed to stimulate remembrance and conversation in the elderly - used in senior centers, retirement homes, nursing homes and with the young. Includes an 80 - slide carousel tray and cassette tape or a videocassette, two manuals, 25 booklets with nostalgic singalong songs, one or more skits, touch cards and paraphernalia from earlier eras and a kit bag.
Health and Safety; Psychology; Science - Natural; Sociology
Dist - BFKLP **Prod** - BFKLP

Remembering the depression 29 MIN
VHS
Bi - folkal remembering series
Color (G PRO)
$210.00, $220.00 purchase _ #DP101, #DP103
Reminisces over the sights and sounds, moods and folk music of the Great Depression. One of a series of kits designed to stimulate remembrance and conversation in the elderly - used in senior centers, retirement homes, nursing homes and with the young. Includes a 140 - slide carousel tray and cassette tape or a videocassette, two manuals, 25 booklets with nostalgic singalong songs, one or more skits, touch cards and paraphernalia from earlier eras and a kit bag.
Health and Safety; History - United States; Psychology; Sociology
Dist - BFKLP **Prod** - BFKLP

Remembering the fashion 15 MIN
VHS / BETA
Color (G PRO)
$210.00, $220.00 purchase _ #FS101, #FS103 ; $195.00 purchase _ #FS101
Reminisces over the fashions of past decades. One of a series of kits designed to stimulate remembrance and conversation in the elderly - used in senior centers, retirement homes, nursing homes and with the young. Includes an 80 - slide carousel tray and cassette tape or videotape, two manuals, 25 booklets of nostalgic singalong songs, one or more skits, touch cards and paraphernalia from earlier eras and bag.
Health and Safety; History - United States; History - World; Home Economics; Sociology
Dist - BFKLP **Prod** - BFKLP

Remembering the home front 20 MIN
VHS
Bi - Folkal Remembering series
Color (G PRO)
$210.00, $220.00 purchase _ #HF101, #HF103
Reminisces over the sights and sounds, moods and music of World War II. One of a series of kits designed to stimulate remembrance and conversation in the elderly - used in senior centers, retirement homes, nursing homes and with the young. Includes either an 80 - slide carousel tray and cassette tape or a videocassette, plus two manuals, 25 booklets with nostalgic singalong songs, one or more skits, touch cards and paraphernalia from earlier eras and a kit bag.
Health and Safety; History - United States; Psychology; Sociology
Dist - BFKLP **Prod** - BFKLP

Remembering Thelma 15 MIN
16mm / VHS
Color (G)
$295.00, $175.00 purchase, $50.00 rental
Documents the life of Thelma Hill, dance instructor, mentor and performer in the development of black dance in America. Contains rare film footage and photographs of Hill as a performer with the original Alvin Ailey Dance Theater and the New York Negro Ballet of the 1950s.
Fine Arts; History - United States
Dist - WMEN **Prod** - KSAND 1981

Remembering Thelma 15 MIN
16mm
Color
Documents the late dance instructor and performer, Thelma Hill, and her influence on the development of black dance in America. Includes film footage and photographs of her performances.
Biography; Fine Arts; Sociology
Dist - BLKFMF **Prod** - BLKFMF

Remembering train rides 20 MIN
VHS / BETA
Color (G PRO)
$210.00, $220.00 purchase _ #TR101, #TR103
Remembers the sights and sounds, moods and music of trains in the past, in contrast to traveling on the modern Amtrak. One of a series of kits designed to stimulate remembrance and conversation in the elderly - used in senior centers, retirement homes, nursing homes, and with the young. Includes an 80 - slide carousel tray and cassette tape or a videocassette, two manuals, 25 booklets with nostalgic singalong songs, one or more skits, touch cards and paraphernalia from earlier eras and a kit bag.
Health and Safety; History - United States; Social Science; Sociology
Dist - BFKLP **Prod** - BFKLP

Remembering Winsor McCay 20 MIN
U-matic / VHS / 16mm
Color (J)
LC 81-700884
Profiles American animation pioneer Winsor McCay and includes excerpts from some of his classic works, such as Gertie the Dinosaur, the Sinking of the Lusitania and Little Nemo.
Fine Arts
Dist - PHENIX **Prod** - CANEJ 1978

Remembering work life 20 MIN
VHS
Bi - Folkal Remembering series
Color (G PRO)
$210.00, $220.00 purchase _ #WL101, #WL103
Remembers the sights and sounds, moods and music of people at work. One of a series of kits designed to stimulate remembrance and conversation in the elderly - used in senior centers, retirement homes, nursing homes and with the young. Includes an 80 - slide carousel tray and cassette tape or a videocassette, two manuals, 25 booklets with nostalgic singalong songs, one or more skits, touch cards and paraphernalia from earlier eras and a kit bag.
Health and Safety; Psychology; Social Science; Sociology
Dist - BFKLP **Prod** - BFKLP

Remembrance 22 MIN
VHS / U-matic
Color (H C G)
$60.00, $40.00 purchase _ #EVC - 641, #EHC - 641
Documents the life of an elderly Chinese gentlemen in the Chinatown of Philadelphia. Reveals that the man migrated to the United States as a youth in search of a higher standard of living but died single and poor. Explores the Chinese heritage of the filmmaker and changes in Asian immigration to the United States.
History - United States; Sociology
Dist - ADL **Prod** - ADL 1991

Remembrance 5 MIN
16mm / VHS
Color (G)
$25.00 rental
Explores the narrator's obsession with strong female characters in Italian opera and in Hollywood movies. Consists of glimpses of an 8mm home movie and optically printed images of Bette Davis in All About Eve. Available for purchase in video format with Vocation for $50.00.
Fine Arts
Dist - CANCIN **Prod** - TARTAG 1990

Remembrance of Things Past - Pt 1 60 MIN
VHS
Story of Fashion Series
Color (S)
$29.95 purchase _ #833 - 9368
Traces fashion through the 20th century, illustrating that it is both the cause and effect of social and cultural developments. Quotes contemporary designer Karl Lagerfeld who said, 'You cannot define fashion. As soon as you do, it changes and you are out of fashon.' Part 1

follows the course of haute couture from Charles Worth in the late 19th century to Coco Chanel in the 20th. Famous women parade their extravagant wardrobes, reflecting the dramatic changes in fashion during the era.
Fine Arts; Geography - World; History - World; Home Economics
Dist - FI **Prod** - RMART 1988

Remington and AVA 59 MIN
VHS
Color (H C A)
$64.95 purchase
Profiles the life and work of the artist Frederic Remington, whose art focused on the American West. Also includes footage of the winners of the Awards in the Visual Arts - AVA.
Fine Arts
Dist - PBS **Prod** - WNETTV

Remington and AVA - American Art
VHS / U-matic
Color
Fine Arts
Dist - MSTVIS **Prod** - MSTVIS

Remington Shaver Shaving a Peach 1 MIN
U-matic / VHS
Color
Shows a classic television commercial.
Business and Economics; Psychology; Sociology
Dist - BROOKC **Prod** - BROOKC

Reminiscence 7 MIN
16mm
Color (G)
$15.00 rental
Views the world in two ways - as seen from a race car and a woman standing in a doorway looking out over a backyard picnic. Features music and text by Robert Ashley.
Fine Arts
Dist - CANCIN **Prod** - FERGCO 1980

Reminiscences of a Journey to Lithuania 82 MIN
16mm
Color (C)
$2200.00
Experimental film by Jonas Mekas.
Fine Arts
Dist - AFA **Prod** - AFA 1972

Remnants of a Race 18 MIN
16mm / U-matic / VHS
Color (I J H)
Explores the life of the Bushmen who live in the desolate Kalahari Desert of South - Central Africa. Shows these people in their search for food. Presents examples of their local art work.
Geography - World; History - United States; Sociology
Dist - EBEC **Prod** - KALAHR 1953

Remodeling the scars 12 MIN
VHS / U-matic
Color (PRO)
$245.00 purchase, $100.00 rental
Aids health professionals in getting burn patients to comply with wearing compression garments. Provides positive testimony from burn victims who have recovered successfully. Shows why it is important to wear the garments, how they are fitted, how to put them on, how it feels to wear them and how to take care of them. Produced by the Center for Educational Television, Southern Illinois University School of Medicine.
Health and Safety
Dist - BAXMED

Remodeling the scars - a patient's guide to compression garments 30 MIN
VHS / U-matic
Color (PRO C G)
$195.00 purchase _ #C890 - VI - 048
Reveals that an important part of recovery from a burn is wearing pressure garments. Shares the burn recovery experiences of burn victims and their families. Presents information on fitting and caring for the garments. Presented by Dr E Clyde Smoot.
Health and Safety
Dist - HSCIC

Remote control scale model ship regatta 20 MIN
VHS
Color (G)
$39.95 purchase _ #S01852
Features 'Shotgun Tom' Kelly in an introduction to boat and ship modeling. Interviews people who build model boats and ships, and shows their work.
Fine Arts; Sociology
Dist - UILL

Remote heat sensing 28 MIN
VHS / U-matic
Color (J H G)
$250.00, $300.00 purchase, $45.00 rental
Examines the multiplicity of uses of the infrared camera, such as revealing an oil slick in the middle of the night, disease in a farmer's field and mapping the globe.
Business and Economics
Dist - NDIM **Prod** - LONTVS 1985

Remote Possibilities 15 MIN
16mm
Landsat - Satellite for all Seasons Series
Color (H A)
LC 77-700808
Provides a description of the Landsat satellite, including an explanation of its design, purpose and potential value in the study and conservation of the Earth's resources.
Geography - World; Science; Science - Natural; Science - Physical
Dist - USNAC **Prod** - NASA 1977

Remote - remote 12 MIN
16mm
Color (H C A)
$35.00 rental
Presents the idea that human behavior is influenced by events in the past, and therefore there exists a psychic para-time parallel to the objective time. Produced by Valie Export.
Science - Natural; Sociology
Dist - CANCIN

Remote Sensing 30 MIN
VHS / U-matic
Earth, Sea and Sky Series
Color (C)
Explains the process and the value of remote sensing. Demonstrates some work with crop analysis, thermatic mapping, forestry, perma frost, hurricane damage and urban sprawl using Landsat images.
Science - Physical
Dist - DALCCD **Prod** - DALCCD

Remote sensing 30 MIN
VHS
Perspectives - transport and communication - series
Color; PAL; NTSC (G)
PdS90, PdS105 purchase
Shows that infrared cameras have multiple uses, from seeing at night to charting the Earth from space.
Industrial and Technical Education
Dist - CFLVIS **Prod** - LONTVS

The Remote Sensing Information System 30 MIN
U-matic / VHS
Introduction to Quantitative Analysis of Remote Sensing Data Series
Color
Provides a non - mathematical description of the multispectral technique and how it can be applied to obtain information from current satellite data as well as future satellites with more advanced sensors.
Industrial and Technical Education
Dist - PUAVC **Prod** - PUAVC

Remotely Piloted Vehicle 7 MIN
16mm
Color
LC 74-706563
Introduces the QF86H target system with details of the first successful flight as a real - size, all - attitude, highly - maneuverable, remotely - piloted vehicle.
Civics and Political Systems; Industrial and Technical Education
Dist - USNAC **Prod** - USN 1973

Removable Partial Denture Design - the RPI Clasp Assembly 14 MIN
16mm
Color (PRO)
LC 81-700736
Demonstrates the use of the RPI clasp assembly, which exhibits minimal tooth and gingival coverage and provides stress relief for abutment teeth that support extension base partial dentures. Gives the rationale for using the assembly and shows its proper design.
Health and Safety
Dist - USNAC **Prod** - VADTC 1979

Removable Partial Dentures 7 MIN
U-matic / 8mm cartridge
Color (A) (SPANISH)
Explains the application of a removable partial denture which replaces diseased or missing teeth.
Health and Safety
Dist - PRORE **Prod** - PRORE

Removable Partial Dentures 20 MIN
16mm
Color (PRO)
LC 74-706564
Describes how to develop wax - up for partial denture casting from a plain refractory cast. Emphasizes the important construction details.
Science
Dist - USNAC **Prod** - USN 1963

Removable Partial Dentures - Clasp Type, Clinical and Laboratory Procedures Series
Constructing the Occlusal Template, Arrangement of Teeth - Laboratory Procedure 12 MIN
Dist - NMAC

Removable Partial Dentures, Clasp Type - Clinical and Laboratory Procedures Series
Finishing, Occlusal Correction, Insertion, and Adjustment 13 MIN
Impression and Preparation of the Master Cast for the Laboratory 13 MIN
Pre - Delivery Adjustment of Casting - Laboratory Procedure 10 MIN
Preliminary Examination and Procedures for Diagnosis 12 MIN
Dist - USNAC

Removable partial dentures, clasp type - clinical and laboratory procedures series
Preliminary survey of study casts, tentative design and detailed treatment planning 11 MIN
Dist - USNAC

Removal from the water 6 MIN
16mm
Lifesaving and water safety series
Color (H G)
LC 76-701571
Demonstrates techniques of removing accident victims from the water, including the saddleback carry, the drag, the team lift and the use of a backboard for suspected neck or back injuries. Stresses the importance of starting artificial respiration in the water if necessary.
Health and Safety
Dist - AMRC **Prod** - AMRC 1975

Removal of a Superficial Foreign Body from the Eye 9 MIN
VHS / U-matic
Medical Skills Films Series
Color (PRO)
Presents a concise demonstration of removal of a superficial foreign body from the eye.
Health and Safety
Dist - WFP **Prod** - WFP

Removal of Cerumen - through irrigation 8 MN
VHS / U-matic
Procedures for the family physician series
Color (PRO C)
$395.00 purchase, $80.00 rental _ #C841 - VI - 133
Illustrates the removal of cerumen - ear wax - through irrigation. Part of a six - part series on procedures for the family physician presented by Dr Peter Coggan.
Health and Safety; Science - Natural
Dist - HSCIC

Removal of Corneal and Scleral Contact Lenses 9 MIN
16mm
Nursing Techniques for the Care of Patients with Impaired Vision 'Series
Color
LC 72-700351
Uses close - up photography to demonstrate emergency manual or suction cup removal of a patient's corneal or scleral contact lenses.
Health and Safety
Dist - OSUMPD **Prod** - OHIOSU 1971

Removal of Double Gallbladder - Technique of Sphincterotomy and Pancreatogram 26 MIN
16mm
Cine Clinic Series
Color (PRO)
Demonstrates removal of double gallbladders, cholangiogram through the two cystic ducts, a reliable simple method to facilitate transduodenal sphincterotomy and the technique of pancreatogram.
Health and Safety; Science
Dist - NMAC **Prod** - ACYDGD 1970

Removal of rust and metal treatment - Part Two 11 MIN
VHS
Using oxyacetylene welding to replace damaged sheet metal series
Color (H A T)
$62.95 purchase _ #SS601
Covers step two of the three - steps of 'patch panel replacement' - removal of rust and metal treatment. Shows the variety of tools used to clean up and prepare a damaged area for repair. Principles shown are appropriate for metal repair tasks utilizing the oxyacetylene welder. Emphasizes safety. Includes quiz and answer sheet.

Health and Safety; Industrial and Technical Education
Dist - AAVIM **Prod** - AAVIM

Removal of the Brain 18 MIN
U-matic / VHS / 16mm
Autopsy Dissection Technique - a Cinematographic Atlas Series
Color (PRO)
Demonstrates step - by - step procedures for dissection of the brain, from initial incision to total removal. Identifies the pituitary stalk and gland, various arteries and nerves, and the sinuses.
Health and Safety
Dist - USNAC **Prod** - MFIORH

Removal of the Eye 8 MIN
16mm
Autopsy Dissection Technique - a Cinematographic Atlas Series
Color (PRO)
LC 76-703705
Demonstrates the removal of an eye. Shows a technique, performed by Dr A H Friedman, that is similar to the one employed for the enucleation of the eye by opthalmologists. Includes reconstruction of a closed eye for embalming and viewing by mourners.
Health and Safety; Science; Science - Natural
Dist - USNAC **Prod** - NMAC 1976

Removal of the Spinal Cord 18 MIN
U-matic / VHS / 16mm
Autopsy Dissection Technique - a Cinematographic Atlas Series
Color (PRO)
Demonstrates a technique for removing the spinal cord, emphasizing the way in which the individual vertebral pedicles are identified and cut to facilitate the removal of the vertebrate column.
Health and Safety
Dist - USNAC **Prod** - MFIORH

Removal of the Spinal Cord - Anterior Approach 18 MIN
16mm
Autopsy Dissection Technique - a Cinematographic Atlas Series
Color (PRO)
LC 74-706219
Demonstrates the technique for removing the spinal cord by exposing it anteriorly after removal of the vertebral column from C4 to T5 inclusive. Emphasizes the way in which the individual vertebral pedicles are identified and cut to facilitate the removal of the vertebrate column.
Science; Science - Natural
Dist - NMAC **Prod** - HASSJ 1971

Removing a Section of Piping Aboard Ship 13 MIN
16mm
B&W
LC FIE52-1189
Explains the purpose of the piping system. Shows how to remove a section of pipe aboard ship and defines outside diameter, pitch diameter, pitch cord, bleeding point and backing - off.
Industrial and Technical Education
Dist - USNAC **Prod** - USN 1943

Removing and inspecting cylinders 18 MIN
16mm
Aircraft work series; Power plant maintenance
B&W
LC FIE52-253
Shows how to remove the cylinder assemblies from the engine, disassemble the cylinder assemblies, and clean, inspect and recondition the cylinders.
Industrial and Technical Education
Dist - USNAC **Prod** - USOE 1945

Removing and installing a compressor or condenser 17 MIN
16mm
Refrigeration service series; Domestic Units; No 5
B&W
LC FIE52-225
Shows how to evacuate and remove a compressor in a domestic refrigerator, evacuate a stuck compressor, install a compressor and remove and install a condenser. Number 5 in the Refrigeration service - domestic units series.
Industrial and Technical Education
Dist - USNAC **Prod** - USOE 1945

Removing and installing a cooling unit 19 MIN
16mm
Refrigeration service series; Domestic Units; No 6
B&W
LC FIE52-226
Discusses cooling unit disorders in a domestic refrigerator. Shows how to evacuate valved evaporators, remove an oil - logged evaporator, install the evaporator and install a direct expansion cooling unit. Number 6 in the Refrigeration service - domestic units series.
Industrial and Technical Education
Dist - USNAC **Prod** - USOE 1945

Removing and Replacing a Distributor 10 MIN
VHS / 16mm
Kirkwood Community College Auto Mechanics Series
(G PRO)
$61.00 purchase _ #KTI102
Covers removing a distributor, timing an engine from scratch, and installing the distributor.
Industrial and Technical Education
Dist - RMIBHF **Prod** - RMIBHF

Removing and replacing seat backrest trim 19 MIN
BETA / VHS / 16mm
Color (A IND)
$83.50 purchase _ #KTI59
Demonstrates removing and replacing seat backrest trim, using a GM bucket seat.
Industrial and Technical Education
Dist - RMIBHF **Prod** - RMIBHF

Removing and replacing seat cushion trim 18 MIN
BETA / VHS / 16mm
Color (A IND)
$81.00 purchase _ #KTI58
Demonstrates removing and replacing seat cushion trim, using a GM seat. Includes jcack stringers and complete envelope repair.
Industrial and Technical Education
Dist - RMIBHF **Prod** - RMIBHF

Removing defective rivets 15 MIN
16mm
Aircraft work series
B&W
LC FIE52-34
Pictures how an inspector marks defective rivets. Demonstrates how to drill the head of flushtype and brazier head rivets and remove the shand and head after drilling.
Industrial and Technical Education
Dist - USNAC **Prod** - USOE

Removing, examining and refitting a clutch - Unit C 36 MIN
VHS
Motor vehicle engineering crafts - workshop practice series
Color; PAL (J H IND)
PdS29.50 purchase
Shows workshop practice lessons with a class of second year public service engineering apprentices. Consists of an introduction and demonstration of removing, examining and refitting a clutch, followed by the students' own attempts. Part of a five - part series.
Industrial and Technical Education
Dist - EMFVL

Removing Frog Pituitary 2 MIN
U-matic / VHS / 16mm
Biological Techniques Series
Color (H C)
Illustrates an efficient method of location, identification and removal of the frog pituitary.
Science; Science - Natural
Dist - IFB **Prod** - THORNE 1960

Removing valves from cylinder head 8 MIN
VHS / 16mm
Auto mechanics series
(G IND)
$56.00 purchase _ #AM29
Shows how to remove the valves from a cylinder head.
Industrial and Technical Education
Dist - RMIBHF **Prod** - RMIBHF

Remy Charlip and Elaine Summers 30 MIN
VHS / U-matic
Eye on Dance - Dance and the Plastic Art Series
Color
Focuses on experimenting with the design of dance in different media. Hosted by Celia Ipiotis.
Fine Arts
Dist - ARCVID **Prod** - ARCVID

Remy, Grand Central - Trains and Boats and Planes 4 MIN
U-matic / VHS
Color
Involves a pretty girl, animated trains, updated Bacharach Muzak and pouring Remy.
Fine Arts
Dist - KITCHN **Prod** - KITCHN

The Renaissance 45 MIN
U-matic / Kit / VHS
Western Man and the Modern World in Video
Color (J H)
$1378.12 the 25 part series _ #C676 - 27347 - 5, $89.95 the individual
Evokes the Italian Renaissance. Highlights Florentine architecture, sculpture and paintings. Discusses the era's return to Greek ideals of classical humanism.
Fine Arts; History - World; Religion and Philosophy
Dist - RH

The Renaissance 30 MIN
16mm
How Should We Then Live Series Episode 3; Episode 3
Color
LC 77-702365
Juxtaposes the artistic accomplishments of the Renaissance with its spiritual bankruptcy, which resulted from an emphasis on humanism and a deemphasis of religion. Based on the book How Should We Then Live by Francis A Schaeffer.
History - World; Religion and Philosophy
Dist - GF **Prod** - GF 1977

The Renaissance 54.20 MIN
BETA / VHS
Color (I J H C)
LC 88-700020
Introduces students to the painting, sculpture, architecture, and other arts in relation to music in the Renaissance period.
Fine Arts; History - World
Dist - EAV **Prod** - EAV 1988

Renaissance 10 MIN
16mm
B&W (J)
LC 77-708686
An art film in which a mysterious piece of junk which has been filmed in monochrome vanishes with a flash and turns into a spectrum of colors, then explodes in various shades of blue.
Fine Arts; Industrial and Technical Education; Science - Physical
Dist - VIEWFI **Prod** - FORGJ 1970

Renaissance 16 MIN
16mm / U-matic / VHS
Color
LC 79-711669
Presents paintings which demonstrate the changes in styles and techniques, especially the development of perspective, during the early years of the Renaissance.
Fine Arts; History - World
Dist - TEXFLM **Prod** - SEABEN 1970

The Renaissance 30 MIN
16mm
How should we then live - Dutch series episode 3; No 3
Color (DUTCH)
LC 77-702365
Juxtaposes the artistic accomplishments of the Renaissance with its spiritual bankruptcy, which resulted from an emphasis on humanism and a deemphasis of religion. Based on the book How Should We Then Live by Francis A Schaeffer.
Foreign Language; History - World; Religion and Philosophy
Dist - GF **Prod** - GF 1977

The Renaissance 45 MIN
35mm strip / VHS
Western man and the modern world series - Unit II
Color (J H C T A)
$102.00, $102.00 purchase _ #MB - 510418 - 0, #MB - 510227 - 7
Examines the Renaissance and its impact on European society. Features numerous examples of paintings, sculptures and public buildings from the era. Notes the Renaissance concept of the dignity of the individual.
Fine Arts; History - World
Dist - SRA

The Renaissance 13 MIN
U-matic / VHS / 16mm
Color (I J H)
LC 78-700791
Examines the renewed interest in art and architecture, the discoveries in science and technology, the spirit of exploration and learning and the sense of the importance and potential of human beings that characterized the Renaissance. Discusses the men and women whose ideas were the backbone of this period.
Fine Arts; History - World
Dist - CORF **Prod** - CORF 1978

The Renaissance 60 MIN
VHS / U-matic
James Galway's Music in Time Series
Color (J)
LC 83-706264
Presents flutist James Galway discussing the importance of wealthy nobles, kings and the church as patrons of music. Shows how music moved away from the elaborate formality of the Gothic and found newer and purer forms.

Fine Arts
Dist - FOTH **Prod** - POLTEL 1982

The Renaissance and Resurrection - Pt 1 26 MIN
U-matic / VHS / 16mm
Color (J)
Presents author - historian Luigi Barzini discussing the artistic achievements of the Renaissance and how these works reflected the glory of God.
Fine Arts; History - World; Religion and Philosophy
Dist - MGHT **Prod** - ABCTV 1978

The Renaissance and Resurrection - Pt 2 29 MIN
16mm / U-matic / VHS
Color (J)
Presents author - historian Luigi Barzini discussing the artistic achievements of the Renaissance and how these works reflected the glory of God.
Fine Arts; History - World; Religion and Philosophy
Dist - MGHT **Prod** - ABCTV 1978

The Renaissance and the age of discovery - the Renaissance and the New World - Parts 25 and 26 60 MIN
VHS / U-matic
Western tradition - part I series
Color (G)
$45.00, $29.95 purchase
Presents two thirty - minute programs tracing the history of ideas, events and institutions which have shaped modern societies hosted by Eugen Weber. Examines the reemergence of knowledge and scholarship with Renaissance humanists who made man 'the measure of all things' in part 25. Part 26 considers the discovery of the continents in the Western Hemisphere and the impact of such discoveries on Europe. Parts 25 and 26 of a 52 - part series on the Western tradition.
Geography - World; History - World; Religion and Philosophy; Sociology
Dist - ANNCPB **Prod** - WGBH 1989

The Renaissance and the Resurrection 55 MIN
U-matic / VHS / 16mm
Color (J)
LC 78-700970
Presents author - historian Luigi Barzini discussing the artistic achievements of the Renaissance and how these works reflected the glory of God.
Fine Arts; History - World; Religion and Philosophy
Dist - MGHT **Prod** - ABCTV 1978

Renaissance architecture in Slovakia - 1500 - 1600 40 MIN
16mm
B&W
Presents the architecture of the High Renaissance that is often overwhelming in its perfection but shows how on the edge of the then civilized world the Slovaks softened the style to human scale, adding charming touches of their own.
Fine Arts; History - World
Dist - ROLAND **Prod** - ROLAND

The Renaissance Band 30 MIN
16mm
World of Music Series
B&W (J)
LC 73-703490
Presents music of the Renaissance played by the New York Pro Musica using authentic instruments of that period. Demonstrates these instruments using woodcuts and the instruments of the individual band members.
Fine Arts; History - World
Dist - IU **Prod** - NET 1965

Renaissance Center 9 MIN
16mm
Color
LC 76-702877
Shows the construction of the Detroit Renaissance Center and several models of the finished structures.
Fine Arts; Geography - United States
Dist - FORDFL **Prod** - RCP 1976

The Renaissance - its beginnings in Italy 26 MIN
16mm / U-matic / VHS
Color; B&W (J H C) (SPANISH)
Portrays the rise of the Renaissance in Europe. Photographed entirely in Italy and France. Pictures the achievements of the Renaissance by showing paintings, sculpture and architecture of the period.
Fine Arts; History - World
Dist - EBEC **Prod** - EBEC 1957

Renaissance of a River 20 MIN
16mm
Color (J A)
Shows that the Susquehanna River from its headwater tributaries to its mouth at the head of Chesapeake Bay has various specific problems which are to be solved by a proposed interstate compact.
Science - Natural
Dist - FINLYS **Prod** - FINLYS 1965

Renaissance Show 24 MIN
VHS / U-matic
Color
Takes a trip to the Renaissance Fair in Shakopee, Minnesota, to meet the kids there, including a group of unicycling youngsters, a kid dj and kids who eat bugs as a source of protein.
Geography - United States; Physical Education and Recreation; Sociology
Dist - WCCOTV **Prod** - WCCOTV 1981

Renal Angiography 19 MIN
16mm
Color (PRO)
Shows the preparation of the patient for a renal angiography and the proper technique for performing the procedure.
Health and Safety; Science
Dist - CORDIS **Prod** - CORDIS

Renal hypertension - bilateral nephrectomy kidney transplantation 23 MIN
16mm
Color (PRO)
Features three outstanding authorities in the field of renal hypertension, Dr William Kolff, Dr Irvine Page and Dr Harry Goldblatt.
Health and Safety; Science - Natural
Dist - UPJOHN **Prod** - UPJOHN

Renal Transplantation 15 MIN
U-matic / VHS
Color (PRO)
Demonstrates an actual renal transplantation. Covers anatomy and explains details of operation.
Health and Safety; Science - Natural
Dist - HSCIC **Prod** - HSCIC 1984

Renal tumors in children - Mac
CD-ROM
Color (PRO)
$150.00 purchase _ #1956m
Presents images scanned from the original slides of the National Wilm's Tumor Registry. Contains 240 full color images, including cytology and histology. For Macintosh Plus, SE and II computers. Requires at least one M of RAM, one floppy disk drive, and an Apple compatible CD - ROM drive.
Computer Science; Health and Safety
Dist - BEP

Renal tumors of children - PC
CD-ROM
Color (PRO)
$150.00 purchase _ #1956p
Presents images scanned from the original slides of the National Wilm's Tumor Registry. Contains 240 full color images, including cytology and histology, in a compact and easily retrievable format. For IBM PCs and compatibles. Requires 640K RAM, DOS Version 3.1 or greater, one floppy disk drive - hard disk drive recommended, one empty expansion slot, and an IBM compatible CD - ROM drive.
Computer Science; Health and Safety
Dist - BEP

Renal vascular access in hemodialysis 25 MIN
VHS / U-matic / Slide
Color (PRO)
$275.00, $195.00 purchase, $60.00 rental _ #4281S, #AT29, #4281V
Reviews the causes of kidney failure and the purposes of hemodialysis. Discusses internal and external access devices, such as the femoral vein catheter, subclavian vein catheter, A - V fistula and A - V graft. Shows how to inspect, palpate and percuss for signs of adequate flow, how to inspect for causes of inadequate perfusion, how to provide nursing care of the renal vascular access site and how to make appropriate decisions in an emergency situation.
Health and Safety
Dist - AJN **Prod** - UMCSN 1983

Renal Vascular Hypertension 26 MIN
U-matic
Color (PRO)
LC 76-706101
Discusses etiology and methods of diagnosing renal vascular hypertension. Describes surgical management and arteriography.
Health and Safety
Dist - USNAC **Prod** - WARMP 1969

Renaming Fractions and Addition of Fractions 12 MIN
U-matic / VHS / 16mm
Mathematics - an Animated Approach to Fractions Series Part 2
Color
Presents an animated story dealing with the renaming and addition of fractions.
Mathematics
Dist - FI **Prod** - FI

Renaming in Addition 16 MIN
U-matic / VHS
Math Cycle Series
Color (P)
Discusses renaming the ones and tens place.
Mathematics
Dist - GPN **Prod** - WDCNTV 1983

Renaming in Addition 15 MIN
U-matic
Math Factory - Module IV - Problem Solving Series
Color (P)
Introduces addition when regrouping of ones is required.
Mathematics
Dist - GPN **Prod** - MAETEL 1973

Renaming in Addition Extended 15 MIN
VHS / U-matic
Math Cycle Series
Color (P)
Explains an application of addition skills in a variety of problem - solving situations with varying degrees of difficulty.
Mathematics
Dist - GPN **Prod** - WDCNTV

Renaming in Multiplication 15 MIN
U-matic / VHS
Math Cycle Series
Color (P)
Introduces students to methods for renaming ones as tens and ones in multiplication.
Mathematics
Dist - GPN **Prod** - WDCNTV

Renaming in Subtraction 16 MIN
VHS / U-matic
Math Cycle Series
Color (P)
Discusses renaming the tens place.
Mathematics
Dist - GPN **Prod** - WDCNTV 1983

Renaming in Subtraction Extended 15 MIN
U-matic / VHS
Math Cycle Series
Color (P)
Shows how in the tens place students can review renaming in subtraction and extends renaming to the hundreds place to solve practical problems.
Mathematics
Dist - GPN **Prod** - WDCNTV

Renata Scotto - Prima Donna in Recital
VHS / U-matic
Color (G)
Presents Miss Scotto singing music of Verdi, Rossini, Puccini, Liszt, and others.
Fine Arts
Dist - VAI **Prod** - VAI

Renault Dauphin 1 MIN
VHS / U-matic
Color
Shows a classic television commercial that uses fast action and the line 'a better way to get around.'.
Business and Economics; Psychology; Sociology
Dist - BROOKC **Prod** - BROOKC

Rendering Plant Safety 12 MIN
U-matic / VHS
Color (A)
Discusses safety and health issues in the animal rendering industry.
Health and Safety; Science - Natural
Dist - USNAC **Prod** - USNAC 1981

Rendevous 90 Degrees South 28 MIN
16mm
Color
LC 74-705523
Depicts the role of the C - 130 Hercules in blazing an unrestricted supply line to the South Pole, heart of Antarctica.
Civics and Political Systems; Geography - World; Industrial and Technical Education
Dist - USNAC **Prod** - USAF 1961

Rendezvous 10 MIN
16mm
Color (A)
LC 77-700475
Presents frontier life of the American fur trapper in the 1820's with a description of trappers living in Teton Canyon, Wyoming, during that time.
History - United States
Dist - USNAC **Prod** - USIA 1976

Rendezvous 11 MIN
16mm / U-matic / VHS
Space Science Series
Color (I J H)
Presents a complete rendezvous maneuver when two spacecraft are in different orbits and on different planes. Discusses the similarities between the rendezvous maneuver and flight to the moon.
Science - Physical
Dist - JOU

Rendezvous 27 MIN
U-matic / VHS / 16mm
Insight Series
Color; B&W (H C A)
Reveals how a man encounters a woman who shows him that he has suppressed the feminine side of himself all his life. Stars James Farentino and Melinda Dillon.
Guidance and Counseling; Psychology; Religion and Philosophy
Dist - PAULST **Prod** - PAULST

Rendezvous 9 MIN
U-matic / 8mm cartridge
Color (H C A)
LC 77-703268
Takes the viewer on a high - speed Ferrari ride through the early morning streets of Paris, passing the most famous districts and giving split second glimpses of well - known monuments and buildings.
Geography - World
Dist - PFP **Prod** - LFILMT 1977

Rendezvous with freedom 37 MIN
16mm
Color (G)
$60.00 rental _ #JRF - 719
Traces the causes and effects of successive waves of Jewish immigration to the New World from the first arrivals in 1654 until the 20th century. Examines the central necessity for such migration - flight from persecution to a land which promised religious and personal freedom. Narrated by Herbert Kaplow with Sam Jaffe, Zero Mostel, George Segal and Marian Seldes.
History - United States; Sociology
Dist - ADL **Prod** - ABCNEW

The Rendille 53 MIN
VHS
Disappearing world series
Color (G C)
$99.00 purchase, $19.00 rental _ #51251
Reveals that camels enable the Rendille to survive in the harsh African desert in which they live. Discloses that because camels are so precious, every Rendille male must serve 14 years as a warrior herdsman before he is allowed to settle down in the village. Long droughts have rapidly decreased the herd, and the herdsmen are being lured to big city life in Nairobi. Features anthropologist Anders Grum. Part of a series working closely with anthropologists who lived for a year or more in societies whose social structures, beliefs and practices are threatened by the expansion of technocratic civilization.
Sociology
Dist - PSU **Prod** - GRANDA 1977

Rene and George Magritte 4 MIN
U-matic
Color
Presents a music video by Joan Logue for the Paul Simon song, Rene And George Magritte With Their Dog After The War.
Fine Arts; Industrial and Technical Education
Dist - IEEE **Prod** - IEEE

Rene Spitz - about his own work 15 MIN
U-matic / VHS / BETA
Color; PAL (T PRO)
PdS40, PdS48 purchase
Psychology
Dist - EDPAT

The Renegade 19 MIN
U-matic / VHS / 16mm
Color (J)
Presents an adaptation of a short story by Shirley Jackson. Concerns the trouble that results in a Vermont town when a family's dog begins killing neighbors' chickens.
Literature and Drama
Dist - PHENIX **Prod** - PHENIX

Renewable Energy 15 MIN
VHS / 16mm
Challenge Series
Color (I)
$125.00 purchase, $25.00 rental
Views a plant where garbage and other renewable energy sources provide heating and cooling for buildings, also views a solar facility.
Science; Science - Physical; Social Science
Dist - AITECH **Prod** - WDCNTV 1987

Renewable energy 30 MIN
VHS
Inside Britain 4 series
Color; PAL; NTSC (G) (BULGARIAN CZECH HUNGARIAN SPANISH POLISH ROMANIAN RUSSIAN SLOVAK UKRAINIAN LITHUANIAN)
PdS65 purchase
Examines the concept of renewable energy and what it has to offer. Investigates solar, hydro and geothermal energy, as well as biofuels and wind industry. Looks at their role as the technologies of the future.
Social Science
Dist - CFLVIS **Prod** - DUNSTN 1993

Renewable Energy Resources - Water and Solar Rays
U-matic / VHS / 35mm strip
(J H C)
$159.00 purchase, $179.00 purchase _ #01052 94
Explains how energy from the sun can supply power for heat, electricity and transportation by means of solar cells, solar towers and active or passive solar heating systems. Discusses other souces of renewable energy, including biomass, wind, falling water, and tides. In 4 parts.
Social Science
Dist - ASPRSS **Prod** - SCIMAN

Renewable Energy Resources - Wind, Water, and Solar Rays 48 MIN
VHS / U-matic
Color
LC 81-706669
Provides information about possible solutions to the energy problem.
Social Science
Dist - GA **Prod** - SCIMAN 1981

Renewable Resources 20 MIN
VHS / U-matic
Terra - Our World Series
Color (I J)
Describes resources that can maintain themselves or be replenished if managed wisely. Discusses the delicate balance that lets certain wildlife species survive.
Science - Natural; Social Science
Dist - AITECH **Prod** - MDDE 1980

Renewable Sources of Energy 13 MIN
16mm
Color (H C A)
Deals with German research into renewable sources of energy, and provides examples of government - supported research.
History - World; Science; Science - Physical
Dist - WSTGLC **Prod** - WSTGLC

The Renewable Tree 59 MIN
U-matic / VHS / 16mm
Nova Series
Color (H C A)
LC 78-700590
Explores solutions to the problem of conserving trees while meeting economic and social demands for paper.
Agriculture; Science - Natural; Social Science
Dist - TIMLIF **Prod** - WGBHTV 1976

The Renewal and Evaluation of Teaching - Preparing a Teaching Dossier 37 MIN
U-matic / VHS
Color (C A)
LC 83-706043
Presents Kenneth Gros Louis, a university executive officer with extensive experience helping faculty document their professional achievements, providing a detailed review of what a useful dossier should include and how faculty can prepare materials pertinent to reappointment, promotion and tenure decisions.
Education; Guidance and Counseling
Dist - IU **Prod** - IU 1982

The Renewal of Easter 50 MIN
VHS
Color (S)
$79.00 purchase _ #322 - 9303
Chronicles the modern observance of Easter from the Pope's observance of Holy Week in Rome to the 1000th anniversary of Christianity in Russia, and the South African Dutch Reformed Church's effort to revise its position on aparthied, as well as ceremonies in Los Angeles, California, and Selma, Alabama. Features NBC News correspondant Robert Abernathy as host joined by Stan Bernard, Sandy Gilmour, Mike Boettcher, Keith Morrison and Kenley Jones in other parts of the world.
Fine Arts; Geography - World; Religion and Philosophy; Sociology
Dist - FI **Prod** - NBCNEW 1988

Renewal through recycling 30 MIN
VHS / U-matic
Forests of the world series
Color (J H G)
$270.00, $320.00 purchase, $60.00 rental
Covers how forests and forest products are exploited and recycled. Approaches from a number of perspectives the ways the total log might be used to minimize waste and how it can be milled and processed in an environmentally clean fashion.
Science - Natural
Dist - NDIM **Prod** - NRKTV 1993

Renewing the family spirit 240 MIN
VHS
Color (G A R)
$249.95 purchase _ #35 - 8836 - 19
Profiles several families, showing how they change over several months. Considers subjects including personality clashes, emotions, differing backgrounds, and how to let God control family life. Includes leader's and participants' guides. Consists of two two - hour videocassettes.
Guidance and Counseling; Religion and Philosophy; Sociology
Dist - APH **Prod** - CPH

Renga 6 MIN
VHS
Color & B&W; Silent (G)
$20.00 purchase
Creates a filmic version of renga, a Japanese form of poetry or haikai. Follows the rules of composition, substituting camera shots for stanzas, filmmaker for poet and view for read. Enjoyment is a primary concern of renga - readers must enjoy a flow of sights from an imaginary landscape, sounds and insights as they tumble past. Produced by E S Theise.
Fine Arts; Literature and Drama
Dist - CANCIN

Rennsymphonie - Zweigroschenzauber 10 MIN
16mm
B&W
Features Race Symphony, an excerpt from Hans Richter's study of a day at the races, in pre - Nazi Germany, and Two - Penny Magic, Richter's essay in rhyming images, made to advertise a picture magazine. Produced 1928 - 29.
Fine Arts
Dist - STARRC **Prod** - STARRC

Renoir 7 MIN
16mm / U-matic / VHS
Art awareness collection series
Color (J H C)
LC 78-701207
Presents fifteen Renoir works, Uses narration adapted from Renoir's own observations about art.
Fine Arts
Dist - EBEC **Prod** - USNGA 1974

Renoir 30 MIN
VHS
Tom Keating on painters series
Color (J H C G)
$195.00 purchase
Focuses on the painter Renoir. Features Tom Keating who recreates the painting of Renoir exactly as the artist did the original work and gives biographical information. Part of a six - part series on painters.
Fine Arts
Dist - LANDMK **Prod** - LANDMK 1987

Reno's kids - 87 days plus 11 99 MIN
16mm
Color (J H C G)
LC 87-706952
Focuses on 20 year teaching veteran Reno Taini, who conducts an alternative, last chance high school class for potential dropouts and troublemakers in Daly City, California. Shows the youngsters interacting with the handicapped, feeding the homeless, meeting with civic leaders, teaching other teens, and learning responsibility, commitment and values in the process. Produced by Whitney Blake.
Education; Sociology
Dist - NEWDAY

Rensselaer Polytechnic Institute
VHS
Campus clips series
Color (H C A)
$29.95 purchase _ #CC0076V
Takes a video visit to the campus of Rensselaer Polytechnic Institute in New York. Shows many of the distinctive features of the campus, and interviews students about their experiences. Provides information on the composition of the student body, professors, academics, social life, housing, and other subjects.
Education
Dist - CAMV

Renting 30 MIN
U-matic / VHS
Personal Finance Series Lesson 11
Color (C A)
Stresses financial and legal factors that are involved in renting. Provides guidelines for assessing the pros and cons of renting versus buying, with regard to taxes, types of leases and rent control legislation.
Business and Economics; Sociology
Dist - CDTEL **Prod** - SCCON

Renting 28 MIN
VHS / U-matic
Personal Finance and Money Management Series
Color (C A)
Business and Economics; Civics and Political Systems
Dist - SCCON **Prod** - SCCON 1987

Renting Your Money for Profit 25 MIN
U-matic / VHS
Money Smart - a Guide to Personal Finance Series
Color (H C A)
Features use of debt instruments for financial growth.
Business and Economics; Education; Home Economics
Dist - BCNFL **Prod** - SOMFIL 1985

Reorienting occlusal relationships - Pt 2 27 MIN
16mm
Color
LC 74-705524
Presents a clinical demonstration of a correctly engineered restoration of a patient's upper teeth, with stress on accomplishment of proper occlusal balance.
Health and Safety; Science
Dist - USNAC **Prod** - USA 1963

Repainting a frame building 18 MIN
16mm
Farm work series painting - No 1; No 1
B&W
LC FIE52-287
Shows how to determine repairs on a building before painting and how to prepare a building for painting.
Agriculture
Dist - USNAC **Prod** - USOE 1944

Repair and maintenance of a sink - faucet assembly 32 MIN
VHS
Color (G H VOC)
$89.95 purchase _ #CEV00847V-T
Describes the correct procedures for repairing common problems that occur with home sinks and faucets. Includes information on tools, safety procedures, and how to recognize problems or potential problems. Explains how to repair and plunge clogged drains.
Industrial and Technical Education
Dist - CAMV

Repair and maintenance of a toilet 35 MIN
VHS
Color (G H VOC)
$89.95 purchase _ #CEV00846V-T
Describes the correct way to install, disassemble, assemble, and repair common problems with a toilet. Discusses the functions of toilet; removing a ball cock valve; installing a cup float valve; replacing water supply tubing; float valve repair; and disassembly and reassembly of the toilet tank and bowl.
Industrial and Technical Education
Dist - CAMV

Repair Cluster 15 MIN
U-matic / VHS
Vocational Visions Series
Color
Discusses the requirements and duties for such jobs as heating/air conditioning repairer, appliance/refrigeration repairer and radio/TV repairer.
Guidance and Counseling; Psychology
Dist - GA **Prod** - GA

Repair Fields 23 MIN
VHS / 16mm
Video Career Library Series
Color (H C A PRO)
$79.95 purchase _ #WW113
Shows occupations in repair fields such as industrial machinery repairers, communication and data processing equiplment repairers, home entertainment equipment and office machinery repairers, electical power installers, electrical and electronic repairers. Contains current occupational outlook and salary information.
Business and Economics; Guidance and Counseling; Industrial and Technical Education
Dist - AAVIM **Prod** - AAVIM 1990

Repair Fields 23 MIN
VHS / U-matic
Video Career Library Series
(H C A)
$69.95 _ #CJ123V
Covers duties, conditions, salaries and training connected with repair fields of work. Provides a view of employees in repair related occupations on the job, and gives information on the current market for such skills. Revised every two years.
Education; Guidance and Counseling; Industrial and Technical Education
Dist - CAMV **Prod** - CAMV

The Repair of Esophageal Hiatal Hernia using the Abdominal Approach 28 MIN
16mm
Color (PRO)
Shows that the abdominal approach for the repair of an esophageal hiatus hernia offers distinct advantages in selected patients. Illustrates the steps in operative technique employed in accomplishing the repair of such a hernia in an elderly patient with concomitant chronic cholecystitis and cholelithiasis.
Health and Safety; Science
Dist - ACY **Prod** - ACYDGD 1957

Repair of Flexor Tendon Injuries 60 MIN
U-matic / VHS
Color (PRO)
Presents a discussion of flexor tendon injuries and the method of repair. Uses diagrams and selected cases to present the principles involved in management of one of the most difficult problems in treatment of the injured hand.
Health and Safety
Dist - ASSH **Prod** - ASSH

Repair of Inguinal Hernia
U-matic / VHS
Color (SPANISH ARABIC)
Explains both congenital and direct hernias including a warning on incarcerated hernia. Discusses the choice of living with a hernia or having it surgically repaired.
Health and Safety
Dist - MIFE **Prod** - MIFE

Repair of Inguinal Hernia in Infancy 31 MIN
16mm
Color (PRO)
Presents the repair of inguinal hernia in infancy to show the pre - operative and operative findings and the technique of repair of a variety of infantile hernias, hydrocoeles and undescended testes.
Health and Safety; Science
Dist - ACY **Prod** - ACYDGD 1968

Repair of Median Episiotomies Including Third Degree Lacerations 28 MIN
16mm
Color (PRO)
Shows a method of repairing midline episiotomies with emphasis upon technical simplicity and the relief of postpartum pain. Explains the many advantages of midline episiotomy. Includes an anatomical technique for the repair of third degree lacerations.
Health and Safety; Science
Dist - ACY **Prod** - ACYDGD 1960

Repair of Old Complete Perineal Lacerations 14 MIN
16mm
Color
LC 75-702323
Demonstrates the classical layer type of repair of an old complete perineal laceration with careful anatomical restoration of the entire perineal body. Emphasizes the use of the paradoxical incision or anal sphincterotomy allowing partial decompression and careful pre - operative mechanical and antimicrobial bowel preparation.
Health and Safety; Science
Dist - EATONL **Prod** - EATONL 1973

Repair of Penoscrotal Urethral Fistula and Diverticulum 16 MIN
16mm
Color (PRO)
LC 75-702241
Illustrates a technique for treating diverticulum and fistula of the male urethra by urethrostomy or cystostomy drainage.
Health and Safety; Science; Science - Natural
Dist - EATONL **Prod** - EATONL 1974

Repair of Recurrent Urethrovaginal Fistula by Bladder Flap Advancement Technique 20 MIN
16mm
Color
LC 75-702252
Explains that the successful repair of recurrent urethrovaginal fistula requires the mobilization of tissue which contains a good blood supply. Shows that the advancement of a bladder flap by the technique illustrated provides tissue with excellent blood supply, normal urothelium and obviates a suture line in the area of repair. Points out that this technique also lends itself to the reconstruction of the urethra and to repair of urethral and vesical - rectal fistulae.
Science
Dist - EATONL **Prod** - EATONL 1973

Repair of the Injured Common Duct 30 MIN
16mm
Color (PRO)
Shows the steps in performing end - to - end anastomosis. Identifies, and frees the duct ends as the reconstruction of the duct is accomplished over a T - tube.
Health and Safety; Science
Dist - ACY **Prod** - ACYDGD 1959

Repair of urethane bumpers and grills 21 MIN
BETA / VHS
Color (A PRO)
$88.50 purchase _ #KT136
Deals with auto body repair. Shows gauge repair on a 'soft' bumper, using a 1976 Mustang bumper.
Industrial and Technical Education
Dist - RMIBHF **Prod** - RMIBHF

Repair of Ventral Hernia 25 MIN
16mm
Color (PRO)
Explains that the majority of incisional herniae occur in obese persons through vertical incisions. Emphasizes the fact that each repair is an individual problem and that no one method of repair is universally satisfactory.
Health and Safety; Science
Dist - ACY **Prod** - ACYDGD 1956

The Repair of Vesicovaginal Fistula - Transperitoneal Transvesical Approach 15 MIN
16mm
Color
LC 75-702326
Demonstrates a surgical procedure which produced cures with a single operation in 32 cases of complicated vesicovaginal fistula. Emphasizes the value of the transperitoneal, transvesical exposure, which allows complete visualization of all important structures, mobilization of fistula tract under direct vision, simplified closure of vaginal defect with peritonealization, closure of bladder without tension and deperitonealization of anterior vaginal wall to prevent recurrent fistula formation.
Health and Safety; Science
Dist - EATONL **Prod** - EATONL 1959

Repairing a Wooden Rib 24 MIN
16mm
B&W
LC FIE52-275
Shows how to remove gussets and broken rib parts, splice a section of cap strip, cut and finish a scarf joint, make a new truss member and make and assemble gussets and reinforcement plates.
Industrial and Technical Education
Dist - USNAC **Prod** - USOE 1945

Repairing Aircraft Tires 20 MIN
16mm
B&W
LC FIE52-236
Pictures the inspection of an airplane tire. Shows how the tire is removed, how the tube is vulcanized, how the cut in the tire is repaired and how the wheel is reinstalled.
Industrial and Technical Education
Dist - USNAC **Prod** - USOE 1945

Repairing aircraft tires 22 MIN
U-matic
Aircraft work series; Aircraft maintenance
B&W (IND)
LC 79-706792
Tells how to inspect an airplane tire, remove the tire and the tube, vulcanize the tube, repair a cut in the tire and reinstall the wheel. Issued in 1945 as a motion picture.
Industrial and Technical Education
Dist - USNAC **Prod** - USOE 1979

Repairing and Finishing 21 MIN
VHS
Hardwood Floors Series
$39.95 purchase _ #DI - 109
Discusses repairing, sanding, and refinishing hardwood floors already in existence.
Industrial and Technical Education
Dist - CAREER **Prod** - CAREER

Repairing and Relining Mechanical Brakes 21 MIN
16mm
B&W
LC FIE52-281
Demonstrates how to check brake action, remove the wheel and inspect the brakes, disassemble the wheel, remove brake lining, install new brake lining, replace brake cables and adjust the brakes.
Industrial and Technical Education
Dist - USNAC **Prod** - USOE 1945

Repairing Door Damage using the Door Stretcher 25.5 MIN
25 MIN
BETA / VHS
Color (A PRO)
$99.00 purchase _ #AB123
Deals with auto body repair.
Industrial and Technical Education
Dist - RMIBHF **Prod** - RMIBHF

Repairing Furniture 70 MIN
VHS
$29.95 purchase _ #011 - 419
Talks about various aspects of furniture repair. Discusses glues and their uses, disassembly and assembly, veneer repairs, cleaning the joints, building out a joint, and repairing broken parts.
Industrial and Technical Education
Dist - CAREER **Prod** - CAREER

Repairing furniture with Bob Flexner 70 MIN
BETA / VHS
Color (IND G)
$29.95 purchase _ #060019
Shows how to choose and use glue to repair furniture, how to clamp roundtables, ways to replace damaged veneer, how to construct molding and repair broken parts. Features carpenter Bob Flexner. Includes booklet.
Fine Arts; Industrial and Technical Education
Dist - TANTON **Prod** - TANTON 1987

Repairing structural tubing 20 MIN
16mm
Aircraft work series; Aircraft maintenance
B&W
LC FIE52-276
Shows how to straighten a bent tube, round out a tube, remove a damaged section of tube, prepare a replacement section, prepare internal reinforcing sleeves and assemble and weld the replacement section and sleeves.
Industrial and Technical Education
Dist - USNAC **Prod** - USOE 1945

Repairing the damage 30 MIN
VHS
Perspective 10 series
Color; PAL; NTSC (G)
PdS90, PdS105 purchase
Shows how profits have sometimes been pursued at the expense of the environment. Reveals that the legacies of such conduct can be poisoned land, infertile soil or treeless hillsides swept away by storms. However, with the right political and economic will, land can be cleansed, repaired and restored.
Business and Economics; Science - Natural
Dist - CFLVIS **Prod** - LONTVS 1993

Repairing the detached retina 11 MIN
VHS
Color (G PRO C)
$250.00 purchase _ #EY - 21
Outlines treatment methods as well as the risks and complications associated with each. Reminds patients that prognosis depends on how much detachment has taken place and each person's ability to heal. Reviews patient responsibility during recovery.
Health and Safety; Science - Natural
Dist - MIFE **Prod** - MIFE

Repeat after me 50 MIN
VHS
White heat series
Color; PAL (G)
PdS99 purchase; Not available in the United States or Canada
Examines the processes of standardization and simplification in technology. Utilizes unusual visual and musical elements to explore the ongoing drive to make technology simple to use. Part four of an eight - part series.
Business and Economics; Psychology
Dist - BBCENE

Repentance 151 MIN
VHS
Color (G) (RUSSIAN (ENGLISH SUBTITLES))
$79.95 purchase _ #S02279
Tells the story of a mysterious woman who is arrested for constantly digging up the body of a despotic local ruler. Set in a fictional Soviet province. Presents an allegory of the brutal repression of the Stalin era.
Civics and Political Systems; Fine Arts; History - World; Literature and Drama
Dist - UILL

Repercussions - a Celebration of African - American Music Series
Repercussions - a Celebration of African - American Music - Vol I 120 MIN
Repercussions - a Celebration of African - American Music - Vol II 124 MIN
Repercussions - a Celebration of African - American Music - Vol III 115 MIN
Repercussions - a Celebration of African - American Music - Vol IV 63 MIN
Dist - FI

Repercussions - a Celebration of African - American Music - Vol I 120 MIN
VHS
Repercussions - a Celebration of African - American Music Series
Color (S)
$39.95 purchase _ #833 - 9050
Celebrates America's musical legacy forged from the Old World music of Africa and Europe. Tells the story of the origins of jazz, soul, blues, gospel, funk, rock and reggae and other modern American musical forms. Volume I is divided into two parts - 'Born Musicians - Traditional Music From The Gambia' which focuses on professional musicians of the West African Savannah and the Mandrinka music of Gambia, and 'On The Battlefield - Gospel Quartets,' which considers the plantation orgins of gospel music.
Fine Arts; History - United States; History - World
Dist - FI **Prod** - RMART 1987

Repercussions - a Celebration of African - American Music - Vol II 124 MIN
VHS
Repercussions - a Celebration of African - American Music Series
Color (S)
$39.95 purchase _ #833 - 9052
Celebrates America's musical legacy forged from the Old World music of Africa and Europe. Tells the story of the origins of jazz, soul, blues, gospel, funk, rock and reggae and other modern American musical forms. Volume II is divided into two parts - 'Legends Of Rhythm And Blues' which features Big Mama Thornton, Lowell Fulson, Lloyd Glen and the Honeydrippers and others, and 'Sit Down And Listen - The Story Of Max Roach,' which captures postwar jazz on the East Coast through the life of one of its most articulate performers - drummer Max Roach.
Fine Arts; History - United States; History - World
Dist - FI **Prod** - RMART 1987

Repercussions - a Celebration of African - American Music - Vol III 115 MIN
VHS
Repercussions - a Celebration of African - American Music Series
Color (S)
$39.95 purchase _ #833 - 9054
Celebrates America's musical legacy forged from the Old World music of Africa and Europe. Tells the story of the origins of jazz, soul, blues, gospel, funk, rock and reggae and other modern American musical forms. Volume III is divided into two parts - 'The Drums Of Dagbon' which considers traditional West African drum music, the Dagbamba drummers of Ghana, and 'Caribbean Crucible,' shot in Jamaica and in the Dominican Republic to examine the roots of reggae.
Fine Arts; History - United States; History - World
Dist - FI **Prod** - RMART 1987

Repercussions - a Celebration of African - American Music - Vol IV 63 MIN
VHS
Repercussions - a Celebration of African - American Music Series
Color (S)
$29.95 purchase _ #833 - 9056
Celebrates America's musical legacy forged from the Old World music of Africa and Europe. Tells the story of the origins of jazz, soul, blues, gospel, funk, rock and reggae and other modern American musical forms. Volume IV, 'African Comeback - The Popular Music Of West Africa,' explores the diversity of African music and King Sunny Ade and Segun Adewale, popular musicians in Ghana.
Fine Arts; History - United States; History - World
Dist - FI **Prod** - RMART 1987

Reperfusion therapy for acute myocardial infarction - Volume 2
VHS / 8mm cartridge
Cardiology video journal series
Color (PRO)
#FSR - 505
Presents a free - loan program, part of a series on cardiology, which trains medical professionals. Contact distributor for details.
Health and Safety
Dist - WYAYLA **Prod** - WYAYLA

Repertory Grid Technique - Research and Assessment - Pt 2 52 MIN
VHS / U-matic
Personal Construct Psychology Series
Color (C PRO)
$75.00, $69.95 purchase
Considers research and assessment using personal construct theory. Part 2 of a twelve part series on personal construct psychology, a cognitive theory of personality formulated by George A Kelly.
Psychology
Dist - SCETV **Prod** - SCETV 1986

Repertory styles - how different is one ballet from another - a series
Repertory styles - how different is one ballet from another -˙series
Color
Presents programs from the New York City cable TV series Eye On Dance. All - Round Dancer, The - Swinging From Jazz To - - ; Demands Placed On Principal Dancers By - - ; Small Repertory Companies And The Importance - - .
Fine Arts
Dist - ARCVID **Prod** - ARCVID

Repertory styles - how different is one ballet from another series
The All - round dancer - swinging from jazz to ballet 30 MIN
Demands placed on principal dancers by choreographers 30 MIN
Repertory styles - how different is one ballet from another - a series
Small Repertory Companies and the Importance of Style 30 MIN
Dist - ARCVID

Repetition in sketching 29 MIN
U-matic
Sketching techniques series; Lesson 14
Color (C A)
Illustrates that repetition is one of the most prevalent and basic of all art elements. Shows examples of repetition in nature as well as in man - made objects.
Fine Arts
Dist - CDTEL **Prod** - COAST

Repetitive motion syndrome
Videodisc
Color; CAV (G)
Addresses the problem of repetitive motion injury, risk factors and prevention through the application of ergonomic principles. Includes a Level II interactive video disc which requires a Pioneer LD - V 8000 player.
Health and Safety; Physical Education and Recreation
Dist - ADVET **Prod** - ADVET 1990

Repetitive Programming 15 MIN
BETA / VHS
Machine Shop - C N C Machine Operations Series
Color (IND)
Industrial and Technical Education; Psychology
Dist - RMIBHF **Prod** - RMIBHF

Replacement of the Aortic Valve with a Homograft 28 MIN
16mm
Color (PRO)
Depicts the operative treatment of acquired aortic valve disease with a homograft. Presents certain other sequences illustrating ancillary material.
Health and Safety; Science
Dist - ACY **Prod** - ACYDGD 1968

Replacement Studies 30 MIN
VHS / U-matic
Engineering Economy Series
Color (IND) (JAPANESE)
Introduces methodology necessary to calculate the economic time to replace an asset that still has remaining physical life. Utilizes replacement of an automobile as example problem.
Business and Economics; Foreign Language
Dist - COLOSU **Prod** - COLOSU

Replacing a Window 30 MIN
VHS
Color (J H C A)
Teaches how to remove and replace an existing window in a stucco house.
Home Economics; Industrial and Technical Education
Dist - COFTAB **Prod** - AMHOM 1985

Replacing Exhaust Systems 22 MIN
VHS
Tune Up America - Home Video Car Repair Series
(A)
$24.95 _ #UMKHTR004V
Provides an instructional demonstration for the viewer on how to replace an exhaust system in a car.
Industrial and Technical Education
Dist - CAMV **Prod** - CAMV

Replacing Exhuast Systems 22 MIN
VHS
Color (G)
$19.95 _ TA106
Covers the inspection, repair, and replacement of exhaust system components.
Industrial and Technical Education
Dist - AAVIM **Prod** - AAVIM 1989

Replacing Shocks and Struts 40 MIN
VHS
Color (G)
$19.95 _ ta102
Gives fundamentals of replacing shocks and struts.
Industrial and Technical Education
Dist - AAVIM **Prod** - AAVIM 1989

Replacing Shocks and Struts 40 MIN
VHS
Tune Up America - Home Video Car Repair Series
(A)
$29.95 _ #UMKHTR005V
Provides an instructional demonstration for the viewer on how to replace shocks and struts on a car.
Industrial and Technical Education
Dist - CAMV **Prod** - CAMV

Replanning Solutions to Production Problems 60 MIN
BETA / VHS
Manufacturing Series
(IND)
Describes planner actions that may be appropriate in several different cases.
Business and Economics
Dist - COMSRV **Prod** - COMSRV 1986

Replantation at Level of the Metacarpus 20 MIN
VHS / U-matic / BETA
(PRO)
Demonstrates the replantation of a totally amputated hand through the shafts of the metacarpals sparing the thumb. Includes microsurgical techniques for vessel and nerve repair and the necessity of rigid bone fixation.
Health and Safety
Dist - ASSH **Prod** - ASSH 1985

Replantation Techniques - Indications and Contraindications 60 MIN
VHS / U-matic
Color (PRO)
Presents the techniques of replantation of the amputated extremity and revascularization of the partially severed extremity. Discusses the indications and contraindications for replantation. Narrated by Dr Harold E Kleinert.
Health and Safety
Dist - ASSH **Prod** - ASSH

Replanting the Tree of Life 20 MIN
VHS / U-matic / 16mm
Color (I)
$415.00, $275.00 purchase, $40.00 rental
Explains the importance of trees in human culture and history and the role trees play in purifying the planet's air and water.
Agriculture; Fine Arts; Literature and Drama; Science - Natural; Social Science
Dist - BULFRG **Prod** - ASTRSK 1987

Replay 8 MIN
16mm / U-matic / VHS
Color (J)
LC 71-711423
Documents the existence of the generation link. Shows that history repeats itself and change is very often a replay of past events.
History - World; Sociology
Dist - MGHT **Prod** - CUNLIM 1971

Replenishment System 29 MIN
U-matic
Radiographic Processing Series Pt 10
Color (C)
LC 77-706079
Shows how replenishing is necessary to sustain the chemical volume and activity in the radiographic processor. Discusses equipment function and problems, emphasizing factors involved in the calculation of correct replenishment rates. Describes replenishment pumps and those used in popular X - ray processors.
Health and Safety; Industrial and Technical Education; Science
Dist - USNAC **Prod** - USVA 1975

Repolarization Alterations 51 MIN
U-matic / VHS
Electrocardiogram Series
Color (PRO)
Emphasizes the lability of the ventricular repolarization phase (S - T segment and T wave) and illustrates factors that create ventricular repolarization alterations.
Health and Safety; Science; Science - Natural
Dist - HSCIC **Prod** - HSCIC 1982

The Report 30 MIN
VHS / U-matic
Writing for a Reason Series
Color (C)
English Language
Dist - DALCCD **Prod** - DALCCD

Report 13 MIN
16mm
B&W (G)
$600.00 purchase
Uses newsreel footage and radio tapes of President Kennedy's assassination to show how society thrives on violence and destruction, from bullfights to nuclear war. Produced between 1963 - 1967.
Fine Arts; Sociology
Dist - CANCIN **Prod** - CONNER

Report, Analyze, Evaluate 58 MIN
U-matic / VHS
Process - Centered Composition Series
Color (T)
LC 79-706299
Shows methods for teaching students to analyze and discuss writing.
English Language
Dist - IU **Prod** - IU 1977

Report and Proposal Writing 30 MIN
U-matic / VHS
Write Course - an Introduction to College Composition Series
Color (C A)
Discusses how to write proposals and reports using proper format. Studies audience appeal and occasion.
English Language
Dist - FI **Prod** - FI 1984

Report and Proposal Writing
U-matic / VHS
Write Course - an Introduction to College Composition Series
Color (C)
Studies how to write proposals and reports using proper format, audience appeal and occasion.
Education; English Language
Dist - DALCCD **Prod** - DALCCD

Report Card 12 MIN
16mm / U-matic / VHS
Critical Moments in Teaching Series
Color (C A)
LC FIA68-2462
An open - end film which examines the problem of the basis on which students should be graded.
Education; Psychology
Dist - PHENIX **Prod** - CALVIN 1967

The Report card - how does Ricardo feel 5 MIN
U-matic / VHS / 16mm
Color (P)
LC 76-712290
Tells a story about Ricardo, who gets a scolding instead of expected praise for a good report card. Shows Ricardo busy at school and proud of a good report card he knows will please his mother. But she is having a frustrating day - little brother is in her way, she pricks her finger, a pot boils over. So when Ricardo bursts into the kitchen and knocks over the scrub bucket, he becomes the target of an emotional tirade. The last scene shows Ricardo clutching his report card as he listens in hurt, confused astonishment.
Education; Psychology; Sociology
Dist - EBEC **Prod** - EBEC 1970

Report - Endeavour Anchor 14 MIN
16mm
Color (J)
LC 76-700570
Covers the recovery and restoration of the anchor abandoned by Captain James Cook on Australia's Great Barrier Reef in 1770.
Geography - World; History - World; Science - Physical
Dist - AUIS **Prod** - FLMAUS 1975

Report from Beirut - Summer of '82 20 MIN
U-matic / VHS / 16mm
Color
Documents the experiences of the people of Beirut, under siege by Israeli forces in the summer of 1982.
History - World; Sociology
Dist - NEWTIM **Prod** - NEWTIM

Report from China 90 MIN
16mm
Color
LC 70-710762
Portrays the apparent success of Mao Tse - Tung's cultural revolution in China. Explains Mao's philosophy and stresses the vast economic development that has occurred as a result of educating peasants and city workers to accept and participate in various degrees of industrialization.
Business and Economics; Civics and Political Systems; Geography - World; Religion and Philosophy; Social Science
Dist - RADIM **Prod** - IWANMI 1970

Report from the Aleutians 47 MIN
16mm / U-matic / VHS
Color
Documents the lives of soldiers in the Aleutians during World War II, and the bad weather, boredom and loneliness they encountered. Concludes with a bombing raid against Japanese - held Kiska Island. Written, narrated and directed by John Huston.
Civics and Political Systems; History - United States
Dist - USNAC **Prod** - USAPS

Report from Thiokol - Polysulfide Base Industrial Sealants 13 MIN
16mm
Color (IND)
LC FI67-949
Reviews the properties of polysulfide base sealants and discusses their applications in industry, in architecture and in marine and highway situations.
Business and Economics; Fine Arts; Science - Physical
Dist - THIOKL **Prod** - THIOKL 1963

Report from Wounded Knee 11 MIN
VHS / U-matic
Color (J)
Presents a short history of the government's attitude towards the American Indian culminating in the infamous massacre of Wounded Knee.
Social Science
Dist - SF **Prod** - SF

Report on Civilization 8 MIN
U-matic / VHS / 16mm
Color (J H C)
LC 84-706802
Presents an animated report on the negative aspects of humanity and the state of mankind today, told in a cartoon - like fashion.
Fine Arts; Guidance and Counseling; Sociology
Dist - PHENIX **Prod** - KRATKY 1983

Report on CORA 30 MIN
16mm
Color (R)
Reports on the Commission on Religion in Appalachia, CORA. Tries to instill an awareness of welfare rights and calls attention to the problem of strip mining in West Virginia.
Geography - United States; Industrial and Technical Education; Religion and Philosophy; Sociology
Dist - CCNCC **Prod** - CBSTV

Report on Drought 21 MIN
16mm
B&W (I)
Reports on the drought conditions of 1966 - 1967 in Bihar and Uttar Pradesh.
Agriculture; History - World; Science - Physical
Dist - NEDINF **Prod** - INDIA

A Report on German Morale 21 MIN
VHS / U-matic
B&W
Purports to examine methods used by the Nazi to control morale and includes original Nazi footage.
History - World; Sociology
Dist - IHF **Prod** - IHF

A Report on Serious Football Injuries 19 MIN
U-matic / VHS / 16mm

Color (J H C A)
Presents procedures on how coaches and administrators can protect themselves against lawsuits from football injuries. Explains the risks of playing football and offers information on physical conditioning.
Health and Safety; Physical Education and Recreation
Dist - ATHI **Prod** - ATHI 1985

Report, Reporter, Deliver, New 10 MIN
U-matic
Readalong Three Series
Color (P)
Provides reading instruction for third grade students. Uses animation, humor, music, repetition and audience participation. Comes with teacher's guide and kit.
Education; English Language; Literature and Drama
Dist - TVOTAR **Prod** - TVOTAR 1977

Report to the Nation 14 MIN
16mm
B&W
Presents a picture of United Cerebral Palsy's research, training and treatment program.
Psychology; Sociology
Dist - UCPA **Prod** - UCPA

Report Writing 27 MIN
U-matic / VHS / 16mm
Color
Shows how to write clear and accurate reports. Uses hospital and industry security as well as police training.
Civics and Political Systems; English Language; Guidance and Counseling
Dist - CORF **Prod** - MTROLA 1973

Report writing 20 MIN
VHS
Color (PRO IND A)
$690.00 purchase, $240.00 rental _ #VAR138
Teaches basic techniques for writing successful reports. Demonstrates, through tested examples, the ease of handling any report or proposal. Includes a leader's guide and briefcase booklet.
Business and Economics; Social Science
Dist - EXTR **Prod** - VIDART

Reportage - report 10 MIN
16mm
B&W (DANISH)
A Danish language film. Presents an experimental film based on the expressive prints of the young Danish painter, Soren Hansen. Portrays the cruel, tragic story of Jeftha, who, returning home victorious from war, must sacrifice his daughter to fulfill a promise to the Lord, which is taken from the book of Judges, chapter 11.
Fine Arts; Foreign Language
Dist - STATNS **Prod** - STATNS 1968

Reporters 101 MIN
16mm / U-matic / VHS
Color; Captioned (A) (FRENCH (ENGLISH SUBTITLES))
Portrays the lives of Parisian photojournalists in a humorous light. French dialog with English subtitles.
Fine Arts
Dist - CNEMAG **Prod** - CNEMAG 1983

The Reporter's Eye 29 MIN
U-matic
City Desk Series
Color
Discusses several aspects of news reporting.
Literature and Drama; Social Science; Sociology
Dist - UMITV **Prod** - UMITV

Reporting and briefing 16 MIN
U-matic / VHS / 16mm
Art of communication series
Color (H C A)
$375.00, $250.00 purchase _ #78508; LC 79-701659
Points out the importance of effective informative discourse and highlights characteristics of successful reporting.
English Language
Dist - CORF **Prod** - CENTRO 1979

Reports 15 MIN
U-matic
You Can Write Anything Series
Color (P I)
Teaches writing techniques through Keith who is told that to write a report he should write down all the questions that he wants to have answered before starting his research. He also learns how to set up a title page, illustrations and subheadings.
Education; English Language
Dist - TVOTAR **Prod** - TVOTAR 1984

Reports from Iran and Afghanistan 30 MIN
VHS / U-matic
Color
Depicts life in Tehran and other areas of Iran (circa the hostage crisis at the United States Embassy in Tehran). Portrays the Iranian culture as still pervaded by western influence and drug addiction despite the Shah's departure and Ayatolloh Khomenini's teaching. Includes footage shot while traveling with an Afghan rebel unit in Afghanistan.
Geography - World; Sociology
Dist - DCTVC **Prod** - DCTVC

The Reppies in concert at Universal Studios Florida 42 MIN
VHS
Color (G K)
$14.95 purchase _ #AC11
Features a group of reptilian characters singing about environmental concerns and love, helpfulness, discipline and respect.
Fine Arts; Science - Natural
Dist - SVIP

Representation and Gerrymandering 29 MIN
U-matic / VHS / 16mm
Our Election Day Illusions - the Beat Majority Series Part 1
B&W (J)
Discusses the problem of 'UNFAIR' representation in state legislatures. Uses animation to depict gerrymandering, the practice which results in districts being reshaped for political reasons.
Civics and Political Systems
Dist - CAROUF **Prod** - CBSTV

Representation of Linear Digital Networks 52 MIN
VHS / U-matic
Digital Signal Processing Series
Color (PRO)
Industrial and Technical Education; Mathematics
Dist - GPCV **Prod** - GPCV

Representations of reductive Lie groups 60 MIN
VHS
ICM Plenary addresses series
Color (PRO G)
$49.00 purchase _ #VIDVOGAN - VB2
Presents David A Vogan, Jr, who discusses representations of reductive Lie groups.
Mathematics
Dist - AMSOC **Prod** - AMSOC

Representative Beef Brisket, Short Plate and Flank Breakdown 5 MIN
16mm
Food and Nutrition Series
Color (J)
LC 72-702641
Shows a representative breakdown of the beef shank, brisket, short plate and flank, providing a basis for the indentification of retail cuts in the grocery store.
Home Economics
Dist - IOWA **Prod** - IOWA 1971

A Representative Beef Carcass Breakdown 9 MIN
16mm
Food and Nutrition Series
Color (J)
LC 72-702637
Shows a representative breakdown of a beef carcass half into the nine most common wholesale cuts. Gives the yield figures for the demonstration carcass and points out the tender wholesale cuts.
Home Economics
Dist - IOWA **Prod** - IOWA 1971

A Representative Beef Chuck Breakdown 7 MIN
16mm
Food and Nutrition Series
Color (J)
LC 72-702639
Shows a representative beef chuck breakdown of the wholesale cuts into the most common retail cuts, providing a basis for the identification of retail cuts in the grocery store.
Home Economics
Dist - IOWA **Prod** - IOWA 1971

A Representative Beef Rib Breakdown 4 MIN
16mm
Food and Nutrition Series
Color (J)
LC 72-702630
Shows a representative breakdown of the beef rib into the most common retail cuts, providing a basis for the identification of retail cuts in the grocery store.
Home Economics
Dist - IOWA **Prod** - IOWA 1971

A Representative Beef Round Breakdown 7 MIN
16mm
Food and Nutrition Series
Color (J)
LC 72-702648
Shows a representative breakdown of the beef round providing a basis for the identification of retail cuts in the grocery store.
Home Economics
Dist - IOWA **Prod** - IOWA 1971

A Representative Beef Short Loin Breakdown 5 MIN
16mm
Food and Nutrition Series
Color (J)
LC 72-702645
Shows a representative breakdown of the beef short loin providing a basis for the identification of retail cuts in the grocery store.
Home Economics
Dist - IOWA **Prod** - IOWA 1971

A Representative Beef Sirloin Breakdown 5 MIN
16mm
Food and Nutrition Series
Color (J)
LC 72-702647
Shows a representative breakdown of the beef sirloin providing a basis for the identification of retail cuts in the grocery store.
Home Economics
Dist - IOWA **Prod** - IOWA 1971

A Representative Hog Carcass Breakdown 5 MIN
16mm
Color
LC 70-710222
Describes typical breakdown of a hog carcass into primal cuts. Shows which cuts must be skinned and stresses the economic importance of skinning for gelatin production.
Agriculture; Business and Economics
Dist - IOWA **Prod** - IOWA 1970

Representing a client before a grand jury series
Client interviews - demonstration and discussion 137 MIN
Grand Jury lecture series 130 MIN
Grand Jury room - demonstration and discussion 201 MIN
Witness Preparation for the Grand Jury 175 MIN
Dist - ABACPE

Representing clients in computer software transactions 60 MIN
VHS
Color (C PRO A)
$95.00 purchase _ #Y129
Benefits attorneys who represent parties, typically the software developer, the distributor and the end - user - purchaser, in the common sale of a business computer system.
Civics and Political Systems; Computer Science
Dist - ALIABA **Prod** - CLETV 1990

Representing corporations in environmental criminal cases 50 MIN
VHS
Color (C PRO A)
$95.00 purchase _ #Y130
Targets the current surge in criminal prosecutions for violations of environmental laws that have resulted in both individual and corporate liability, such as fines and jail sentences. Features panelists who set forth steps that in - house counsel and outside corporate counsel should take when the government initiates an environmental crime investigation.
Civics and Political Systems; Sociology
Dist - ALIABA **Prod** - CLETV 1990

Representing Residential Landlords and Tenants 120 MIN
U-matic / VHS / Cassette
Color; Mono (PRO)
Offers an overview of various devices for resolving landlord tenant diputes under California law. Discusses such topics as damage actions and actions in unlawful detainer.
Business and Economics; Civics and Political Systems
Dist - CCEB **Prod** - CCEB

Representing the Individual Debtor 60 MIN
U-matic / VHS
Modern Bankruptcy Practice Series
Color (PRO)
Business and Economics; Civics and Political Systems
Dist - ABACPE **Prod** - ABACPE

Representing the State in Child Abuse and Neglect Proceedings 60 MIN
VHS / U-matic

Color (PRO)
Designed for training of attorneys representing child protective services agencies in court cases brought under state civil code child protective laws.
Civics and Political Systems
Dist - ABACPE **Prod** - ABACPE

Reprieve 22 MIN
16mm
Color
LC FIE67-61
Former President Eisenhower and other heart patients tell how sensible living habits and adherence to doctors orders have enabled them to return to active and useful living.
Health and Safety; Psychology
Dist - USNAC **Prod** - USPHS 1964

Reprieve 105 MIN
16mm
B&W (H C A)
Traces John Resko's actual rehabilitation at Dannemora prison through the efforts of the dedicated prison staff. Shows how Resko's aggressiveness was channelled into the study of art.
Biography; Fine Arts; Sociology
Dist - CINEWO **Prod** - CINEWO 1962

Reprise for the Lord 30 MIN
VHS
Color (J H C G A R)
$29.95 purchase, $10.00 rental _ #35 - 89 - 597
Shows that gospel singer Ketti Washington's faith was shaken when a throat ailment sent her to the hospital. Suggests that friends and family helped restore her faith.
Health and Safety; Religion and Philosophy
Dist - APH **Prod** - NEWLIB

Reprocessing of hemodialyzers 30 MIN
U-matic / VHS
Hemodialysis series
Color (C PRO)
$395.00 purchase, $80.00 rental _ #C911 - VI - 042
Describes the processes, both manual and automated, for effective reprocessing of hemodialyzers. Illustrates methods and techniques to reduce and eliminate problems that can occur from using improperly reprocessed dialyzers in hemodialysis. Highlights federal regulations governing the processes. Familiarizes health professionals with the recommended procedures as a basis for evalutating the program in their facility. Part of a four - part series on hemodialysis presented by the Health Industry Manufacturers Association, Food and Drug Administration, Renal Physicians' Association and American Nephrology Nurses' Association.
Health and Safety; Science - Natural
Dist - HSCIC

The Reproducer 15 MIN
16mm
Color (H C A)
Demonstrates several card reproducing techniques to show the integral functions of the reproducer. Examines the gang punch operation and the method of verifying matching cards and detecting and correcting unmatched cards. Discusses mark sensing, alone and in combination with gang punching and the method, purpose and application of end printing and summary punching. Introduces the principle of control panel wiring as it applies to the reproducer.
Mathematics; Psychology; Sociology
Dist - SF **Prod** - SF 1968

Reproduction 30 MIN
U-matic
Medical - Legal Issues Series
(A)
Reviews major ethical and legal issues arising from artifical insemination, in vitro fertilization, contraception, sterilization, prenatal care and childbirth.
Civics and Political Systems; Health and Safety; Sociology
Dist - ACCESS **Prod** - ACCESS 1983

Reproduction 56.58 MIN
VHS
Plants Series
Color (J H C)
LC 88-700285
Aids students in the study of the anatomy of plants to understand their functions, use of photosynthesis and reproduction.
Science - Natural
Dist - SRA **Prod** - SRA 1986

Reproduction - a New Life 26 MIN
16mm / U-matic / VHS
Living Body - an Introduction to Human Biology Series
Color
Looks at the events that lead from the fertilized cell to a human baby. Uses film of living fetuses in the womb to show how the familiar human shape is 'sculpted' out of the basic cell mass.
Science - Natural
Dist - FOTH **Prod** - FOTH 1985

Reproduction and Birth 25 MIN
16mm
Starting Tomorrow Series Unit 5 - Introducing Sex Education
B&W (T)
Presents an in - service program for elementary school teachers on the introduction of sex education.
Education; Health and Safety; Science - Natural; Sociology
Dist - WALKED **Prod** - EALING 1969

Reproduction and evolution 15-19 MIN
VHS
Fresh water invertebrates
Color (J H)
$99.95 purchase _ #Q11168
Examines fresh water invertebrates utilizing microphotography. Focuses on the sexual reproduction and evolution of macroscopic and microscopic organisms with an emphasis on the evolution of defense mechanisms. Presents a visual wrap - up which reiterates all technical names and major characteristics of each organism. Part of a series of three programs.
Science; Science - Natural
Dist - CF

Reproduction and Meiosis
VHS
Basic Biology And Biotechnology Series
Color (G)
$75.00 purchase _ #6 - 083 - 111P
Overviews reproduction. Examines asexual reproduction and fission in amoebas and budding in the stentor. Studies sponges, jellyfish and algae. Explains meiosis. Part of a series on basic biology.
Science - Natural
Dist - VEP **Prod** - VEP

Reproduction and meiosis 29 MIN
U-matic
Introducing biology series; Program 26
Color (C A)
Presents first of four lectures on reproduction in series. Provides overview of reproduction. Explains meiosis, the process underlying all forms of sexual reproduction. Defines chromosome.
Science - Natural
Dist - CDTEL **Prod** - COAST

Reproduction and Survival 20 MIN
16mm / U-matic / VHS
Exploring Science Series
Color (J H)
Shows that while the individuals of any species always die, the species live on. Points out that sufficient offspring must be born and survive to adulthood.
Science - Natural
Dist - FI **Prod** - BBCTV 1982

Reproduction - Coming Together 29 MIN
U-matic / VHS / 16mm
Living Body - an Introduction to Human Biology Series
Color
Discusses the physiological events that underly the process of reproduction.
Science - Natural
Dist - FOTH **Prod** - FOTH 1985

Reproduction Cycle of Angel Fish 10 MIN
U-matic / VHS / 16mm
Color (P I J H) (DANISH)
LC 71-710016;
Explains the reproduction cycle of an angel fish. Begins with the courtship and proceeds through the egg - laying, fertilization and incubation stages to the development of the newly - hatched fry.
Science - Natural
Dist - IFB **Prod** - IFB 1971

Reproduction in organisms 16 MIN
16mm / VHS
Color (J H C A)
$275.00, $340.00 purchase, $50.00 rental _ #8021
Develops the concept that all life is dependent upon reproduction for its continued existence. Divides the concept into three main parts - first, that most species produce an incredible amount of offspring, far more than the generation that produces them, secondly, explains sexual forms of reproduction, defining gametes and fertilization, thirdly, examines asexual forms of reproduction.
Science - Natural
Dist - AIMS **Prod** - EDMI 1982
EDMI

Reproduction in the Collared Lemming 13 MIN
16mm
B&W (C)
Shows the mating behavior of collared lemmings and the birth of a litter. Includes sequences on the growth of the young and retrieval behavior by the mother.
Science - Natural
Dist - PSUPCR **Prod** - UILL 1967

Reproduction - into the World 26 MIN
16mm / U-matic / VHS
Living Body - an Introduction to Human Biology Series
Color
Covers the tumultuous events of birth, using fetoscopy and models to show what happens from the baby's viewpoint. Shows the physiological events immediately following the birth.
Science - Natural
Dist - FOTH **Prod** - FOTH 1985

The Reproduction Kit Video Transfers
VHS
Color (G)
$80.90 purchase _ #1 - 413 - 100VT
Offers a set of two videotapes dealing with the latest technology in cattle reproduction. Illustrates the embryo transfer performed on beef and dairy cattle, showing preparations and procedures for removing and implanting an ovum from donor to surrogate beast on one tape. Explores the critical phases of artificial insemination on the second tape.
Agriculture; Science - Natural
Dist - VEP **Prod** - VEP

Reproduction of life - sex education 100 MIN
VHS
Color (J H)
$69.00 purchase _ #04508 - 126
Portrays human reproduction from conception through prenatal development to birth itself in graphic detail.
Guidance and Counseling; Health and Safety; Psychology; Science - Natural; Sociology
Dist - GA **Prod** - GA

Reproduction - Shares in the Future 26 MIN
U-matic / VHS / 16mm
Living Body - an Introduction to Human Biology Series
Color
Looks at how the male and female bodies are prepared for their task of increasing the human race. Shows the characteristics of sperm and ova and how each contains a partial blueprint for the future offspring. Uses micro - photography to show the mechanism of cell vision and describes the mechanisms of heredity.
Science - Natural
Dist - FOTH **Prod** - FOTH 1985

Reproduction - the Continuity of Life 49 MIN
VHS / Slide / U-matic
Color (J H)
$195.00 filmstrips, $209.00 sound slides purchase _ #01044 - 161
Shows how living organisms reproduce both sexually and asexually. Studies fission, mitotic cell division, budding, spore formation and propagation by runners, and illustrates evolutionary changes with comparisons of external and internal fertilization.
Science - Natural
Dist - GA **Prod** - SCIMAN

Reproductive and Social Behavior of Belding's Ground Squirrel 18 MIN
U-matic / VHS / 16mm
Aspects of Animal Behavior Series
Color
Follows the annual cycle of Belding's ground squirrel in the alpine environments of the Sierra Nevada and documents hibernation, aggressive behavior between males, female territoriality, feeding, copulation, nest construction, behavior of the young, the effects of predation and altruistic predator - warning behavior.
Science - Natural
Dist - UCEMC **Prod** - UCLA 1979

Reproductive Behavior in the African Mouth - Breeding Fish 35 MIN
16mm
Color (C T)
Points out characteristic markings which identify male and female African mouth - breeding fish (Tilapia macrocephilia). illustrates courtship patterns and the laying of eggs. Shows the eggs, stored in the male's mouth, at various stages of development - - eight days, ten days, two months, four months and eight months. Pictures the ovulation process in detail.
Science - Natural
Dist - PSUPCR **Prod** - PSUPCR 1959

Reproductive behavior of the brook trout 24 MIN
VHS / 16mm
Color (G C)
$380.00, $175.00 purchase, $17.50, $18.00 rental _ #22712
Details all behavioral activity involved in the spawning of brook trout in a natural environment. Includes coordinated sequences from an underwater observation tank and from the surface of the stream. Uses slow - motion photography to add to the clarity of movement. Produced by Robert L Butler.
Science - Natural
Dist - PSU

Reproductive Behavior of the Brook Trout 24 MIN
16mm
Color (C)
Demonstrates all behavioral activity leading up to, including, and following spawning of brook trout in their natural environment.
Science - Natural
Dist - PSUPCR **Prod** - PSUPCR 1971

Reproductive Behavior of the Brook Trout , Salvelinus Fontinalis 24 MIN
16mm
Color (H C A)
LC 76-713858
Shows the spawning of brook trout in their natural environment. Explains how phenologic environmental changes are related to the spawning period. Illustrates the initiatory cutting and probing of the female and her preparation of the redd. Shows the competitive behavior of males, the spawning act and the postnuptial dance.
Psychology; Science - Natural
Dist - PSUPCR **Prod** - SPTFRF 1971

Reproductive Behavior of the Guppy Poecilia Reticulata Peters 17 MIN
16mm
B&W (C)
Shows, using normal and slow - motion photographs, the movement patterns, displays and copulatory behavior of unreceptive and receptive female and normal and gonopodectomized male guppies.
Science - Natural
Dist - PSUPCR **Prod** - UBC 1967

Reproductive or Sexual Cycles in the Female I 11 MIN
16mm / U-matic / VHS
Human Embryology Series
Color (C A)
Health and Safety; Science - Natural
Dist - TEF **Prod** - UTORMC

Reproductive or Sexual Cycles in the Female II 11 MIN
16mm / U-matic / VHS
Human Embryology Series
Color (C A)
Health and Safety; Science - Natural
Dist - TEF **Prod** - UTORMC

Reproductive System 16 MIN
16mm / U-matic / VHS
Human Body Series
Color (J H C)
$380, $250 purchase _ #3964
Discusses how hormones from the pituitary gland control the maturation and functioning of the organs of the reproductive system and make reproduction possible.
Science - Natural
Dist - CORF

Reproductive Systems 25 MIN
VHS / U-matic
Human Body Series
Color (J H C A G)
$235.00 purchase _ #51309
Chronicles fertilization, the union of sex cells and the development of new life.
Science - Natural
Dist - NGS

Reproductive systems 20 MIN
VHS
Your body series
Color (I)
$80.00 purchase _ #A51610
Uses photography and animation to illustrate the beginning of human life, from fertilization through the first six weeks of development in the womb. Discusses both male and female reproductive anatomy and role in conception. Includes a teacher's guide.
Health and Safety; Science - Natural
Dist - NGS **Prod** - NGS 1994

Reptiles 15 MIN
VHS
Exploring environments series
Color (P I)
$250.00 purchase
Reveals that there are hundreds of different species of reptiles. Look at snakes, lizards, turtles, tortoises and crocodiles. Part of a four - part series looking at different environments.
Science - Natural
Dist - LANDMK **Prod** - LANDMK 1989

Reptiles 25 MIN
U-matic
Animal Wonder Down Under Series
Color (I J H)
Shows a giant crocodile, sea turtles and a variety of lizards and snakes.
Geography - World; Science - Natural
Dist - CEPRO **Prod** - CEPRO

Reptiles 29 MIN
Videoreel / VT2
Observing Eye Series
Color
Science - Natural; Sociology
Dist - PBS **Prod** - WGBHTV

Reptiles 14 MIN
VHS
Vertebrate series
Color; PAL (I J H)
Examines reptiles, descendents of the life form which dominated Earth for millions of years, and found today in virtually every environment. Introduces the five groups of reptiles - tuataras, lizards, snakes, turtles and crocodiles. Part of a series on vertebrate animals.
Science - Natural
Dist - VIEWTH
CORF

Reptiles 20 MIN
U-matic / VHS / 16mm
Color (I)
LC 72-702932
Presents a program on reptiles taken from the TV special 'REPTILES AND AMPHIBIANS.'.
Science - Natural
Dist - NGS **Prod** - NGS 1973

Reptiles 14 MIN
16mm / U-matic / VHS
Color; B&W (I J H C)
Introduces the five orders of reptiles remaining on earth - - lizards, turtles, tautaras, crocodilians and serpents. Describes the physical characteristics, reproductive processes, feeding habits and habitats.
Science - Natural
Dist - EBEC **Prod** - EBEC 1955

Reptiles 10 MIN
U-matic / VHS / 16mm
All about Animals Series
Color (P)
Shows the characteristics of reptiles through nature photography.
Science - Natural
Dist - AIMS **Prod** - BURGHS 1978

Reptiles - a First Film 12 MIN
U-matic / VHS / 16mm
Color (P I J)
Introduces the reptile family, which includes snakes, turtles and lizards, filmed in each species' natural habitat.
Science - Natural
Dist - PHENIX **Prod** - BEANMN 1983

Reptiles and amphibians 60 MIN
VHS
Animal kingdom series
Color (J H C G)
$19.98 purchase _ #VV5427V - S
Encounters the crocodile, komodo dragon, giant tortoise and poisonous sea snake in a study of the reptilian world. Part of a series visiting remote regions of the world to study exotic wildlife.
Science - Natural
Dist - CAMV **Prod** - NGS

Reptiles and amphibians 59 MIN
VHS / 16mm / BETA
Color; Captioned (G)
$225.00, $24.20 purchase _ #C53311, #C50404
Science - Natural
Dist - NGS **Prod** - NGS

Reptiles and birds 30 MIN
U-matic / VHS
Oceanus - the marine environment series lesson 17
Color
Looks at the three families of marine reptiles in the world today. Discusses the common ancestry of reptiles and birds. Compares the behavior and habits of several oceanic birds.
Science - Natural; Science - Physical
Dist - CDTEL **Prod** - SCCON 1980
SCCON

Reptiles are Interesting 10 MIN
U-matic / VHS / 16mm
Color (I J H C) (FRENCH)
Pictures various kinds of reptiles and the characteristics of each including the crocodilians, turtles, lizards, snakes and the group represented by the tautara.
Foreign Language; Science - Natural
Dist - PHENIX **Prod** - FA 1955

Reptiles - Part 1 10 MIN
VHS
Color; PAL (P I)
PdS29
Discusses reptiles as cold - blooded animals. Points out that reptiles are divided into four main groups. Depicts the characteristics and habits of various members of the tortoise group and the crocodile group. Part one of two parts.
Science - Natural
Dist - BHA

Reptiles - Part 2 11 MIN
VHS
Color; PAL (P I)
PdS29
Depicts the characteristics and habits of various members of the lizard group and the snake group. Part two of two parts.
Science - Natural
Dist - BHA

Republic cliffhanger serials series

The Adventures of Captain Marvel - return of Captain Marvel	216 MIN
The Crimson ghost	204 MIN
Dangers of the Canadian Mounted	204 MIN
Don Daredevil rides again	192 MIN
Federal operator 99	204 MIN
Ghost riders of the west - the phantom rider	204 MIN
Government agents vs. phantom legion	192 MIN
Jesse James rides again	208 MIN
Nyoka and the tigerman - perils of Nyoka	270 MIN
Panther girl of the Kongo	180 MIN
Radar men from the moon - Commando Cody, sky marshal of the universe	192 MIN
Trader Tom of the China Seas	180 MIN
Zorro's black whip	216 MIN

Dist - KITPAR

The Republic in a hostile world 30 MIN
VHS
American adventure series
Color (G)
$150.00 purchase _ #TAMA - 111
Reviews the early Federalist governments of George Washington and John Adams. Shows that the nation had conflicts both at home and abroad. Notes the accomplishments and failures of Federalist policies.
History - United States
Dist - PBS

The Republic of Colombia 11 MIN
U-matic / VHS / 16mm
Color; B&W (I J H)
Emphasizes the relationship of Colombia to the other American republics. Shows scenes of the natural beauty of the country, principal cities, coffee plantations and other farming activities and industries.
Geography - World
Dist - IFB **Prod** - PAU 1954

Republic of Guatemala 22 MIN
U-matic / VHS / 16mm
Color (I J H)
Shows the physical geography and culture of Guatemala. Portrays its pre - Columbian history, the Spanish conquest and colonization.
Geography - World
Dist - IFB **Prod** - PAU 1954

The Republican party 58 MIN
VHS
America's political parties series
Color (J H G)
$395.00 purchase, $75.00 rental _ #8335
Features U S News and World Report editor David Gergen who examines the activities of the Republican party since 1960. Focuses on presidential elections and the conservative western wing's wresting of control away from eastern moderates. Includes commentary by Barry Goldwater, William Bennett, Dick Cheney, Henry Kissinger, Newt Gingrich, Lowell Weicker, James Baker, Lee Atwater.

Civics and Political Systems; History - United States
Dist - AIMS **Prod** - MANIF 1991

The Republicans - 1960 - 1972 16 MIN
VHS
America's political parties series
Color (J H G)
$295.00 purchase, $75.00 rental _ #8336
Features U S News and World Report editor David Gergen who examines the rise of conservatives to control the Republican party and lead the country, 1960 - 1972. Focuses on presidential elections and Nixon's three campaigns for the presidency which were interrupted by the defeat of Goldwater in 1964. Includes commentary by Barry Goldwater, William Bennett, Dick Cheney, Henry Kissinger, Newt Gingrich, Lowell Weicker, James Baker, Lee Atwater.
Civics and Political Systems; History - United States
Dist - AIMS **Prod** - MANIF 1991

The Republicans - 1972 - 1988 30 MIN
VHS
America's political parties series
Color (J H G)
$295.00 purchase, $75.00 rental _ #8337
Features U S News and World Report editor David Gergen who examines the rise of conservatives to control the Republican party and lead the country, 1972 - 1988. Focuses on presidential elections and the domination of the party by Ronald Reagan and the conservatives. Includes commentary by Barry Goldwater, William Bennett, Dick Cheney, Henry Kissinger, Newt Gingrich, Lowell Weicker, James Baker, Lee Atwater.
Civics and Political Systems; History - United States
Dist - AIMS **Prod** - MANIF 1991

Repulsion - induction motor - general overhaul 25 MIN
16mm
Electrical work - motor maintenance and repair series; No 6
B&W
LC FIE52-180
Shows how to check a repulsion - induction motor for electrical and mechanical faults, dismantle it, remove a damaged coil, wind and insulate a new coil, and assemble and lubricate the motor.
Industrial and Technical Education
Dist - USNAC **Prod** - USOE 1945

Repulsion motor principles 11 MIN
16mm
Electrical work - electrical machinery series; No 5
B&W
Shows construction of a repulsion motor. Explains rotor circuits and effect of brush position, shortcircuiting and brush - lifting mechanism, and applications of repulsion motors.
Industrial and Technical Education
Dist - USNAC **Prod** - USOE 1945

Reputation 30 MIN
VHS
Skirt through history series
Color; PAL (H C A)
PdS65 purchase
Presents the life of Artemisia Gentilesshi, a painter who, in 1612, accused another artist of raping her. Notes that the trial verdict is missing from Vatican archives, but as a result of the trial, she was forced to leave Rome. Fifth in a series of six programs featuring women's history through their writings.
Fine Arts; History - World
Dist - BBCENE

Requesting anatomical gift donation - a nursing perspective 28 MIN
VHS / U-matic
Color (PRO)
$275.00 purchase, $60.00 rental _ #7812S, #7812V
Describes the role of the nursing staff in requesting anatomical donations and their sensitive, caring relationship with potential donors and their families. Describes the importance of assessing personal attitudes toward donor programs, developing knowledge of individual and family rights and the legal aspects of donor programs.
Health and Safety; Sociology
Dist - AJN **Prod** - HOSSN 1989

Requests for admission, discovery overseas, motions to compel, and sanctions 54 MIN
Cassette
Effective discovery techniques series
Color (PRO)
$100.00, $20.00 purchase, $50.00 rental _ #EDT1-002, #AEDT-002
Provides a basic understanding of all aspects of discovery prior to depositions. Designed to provide practical information for the attorney with minimal litigation experience. Covers requests for admission, discovery overseas, motions to compel, and sanctions. Includes study guide.
Civics and Political Systems
Dist - AMBAR **Prod** - AMBAR 1985

Requiem 2 MIN
16mm
B&W (G)
$5.00 rental
Resurrects myth in a play of light and shadow. Evokes images of epochs within short passages. Produced by Phil Costa Cummins. Requiem is included free of charge with rental of the three other films by Cummins - Fire, Handmade and Moondance.
Fine Arts
Dist - CANCIN

Requiem 4 MIN
16mm
Color
LC 73-702858
A tribute to Martin Luther King. Portrays the shame and horror of his death.
Biography; History - United States
Dist - MMM **Prod** - DELL 1968

Requiem for a faith 28 MIN
VHS
Color (G)
$89.00 purchase _ #HFRF
Tells the story of Tibetan Buddhism. Guides through a world of ancient rituals, continuous meditation, deep compassion and a profound faith in the divinity of man. Produced by Houston Smith.
Religion and Philosophy
Dist - SNOWLI **Prod** - SNOWLI

Requiem for a Faith 28 MIN
16mm
Color (H C)
LC FIA68-515
Huston Smith tells of the paths that lead to enlightenment according to Tibetan Buddhism and reveals the secret that is discovered. The film shows Tibetan monks and includes an interview with the Dalai Lama.
Geography - World; Religion and Philosophy
Dist - HP **Prod** - HP 1968

Requiem for a faith - The Sufi way - Islamic mysticism 60 MIN
VHS
Color (G)
$59.95 purchase
Offers two productions on one tape. Features Requiem for a Faith, which tells the story of Tibetan Buddhism in a remote Indian refugee camp, and The Sufi Way - Islamic Mysticism, an in - depth study of Islam and its mystical core, shot in locations from India to Morocco. Narrated by Huston Smith, professor of philosophy and religion and author of The Religions Of Man and The World's Religions.
Fine Arts; Literature and Drama; Religion and Philosophy
Dist - HP

Requiem for a Heavyweight 18 MIN
16mm
B&W
An abridged version of the motion picture Requiem For A Heavyweight. Gives a grim account of an honest, proud champion prizefighter forced into corruption and degradation when his ring career ends. Stars Anthony Quinn and Jackie Gleason.
Fine Arts
Dist - TIMLIF **Prod** - CPC 1982

Requiem for a Heavyweight 100 MIN
16mm
B&W
Features the story of the decline of an ex - champion prize fighter and his inability to adjust to the loss of fame, glory and dignity. Stars Mickey Rooney, Jackie Gleason and Jack Dempsey.
Fine Arts
Dist - TIMLIF **Prod** - CPC 1962

Requiem for a heavyweight 53 MIN
VHS
B&W (H C)
$39.00 purchase _ #04509 - 126
Presents a melodrama about the last bouts of a prize fighter who will not realize his career is over. Stars Anthony Quinn and Jackie Gleason.
Fine Arts; Literature and Drama; Physical Education and Recreation
Dist - GA **Prod** - GA

Requiem for an Alcoholic 19 MIN
16mm
Color
LC 77-700036
Portrays the desperate and purposeless existence of a hardened alcoholic.
Health and Safety; Psychology; Sociology
Dist - CFS **Prod** - AFFAC 1976

The Required dives 20 MIN
16mm / U-matic / VHS
Diving series
Color
LC 79-700785
Covers required dives, including forward, back and reverse dives.
Physical Education and Recreation
Dist - ATHI **Prod** - ATHI 1977

Requirements Analysis 30 MIN
U-matic / VHS
Software Engineering - a First Course Series
Color (IND)
Discusses system analysis, software requirements, analysis, analysis tools and techniques, and form and content of requirements documents.
Industrial and Technical Education; Mathematics
Dist - COLOSU **Prod** - COLOSU

Requirements for Television Bronchoscopy 15 MIN
16mm
Color (PRO)
LC 78-700721
Discusses equipment requirements for two types of television bronchoscopy systems, including a high - quality system for teaching programs and a more economical system for in - house use. Covers topics such as bronchoscopes, light sources, cameras, test and monitoring equipment, videotape recorder and tape storage.
Health and Safety; Industrial and Technical Education; Science - Natural
Dist - USNAC **Prod** - VAHLCF 1977

Resale price maintenance - legal issues in developing pricing policies 58 MIN
VHS / U-matic
Antitrust counseling and the marketing process series
Color (PRO)
Reviews the state of the law after a marketing manager requests legal help on how to respond to price cutting by distributors.
Business and Economics
Dist - ABACPE **Prod** - ABACPE

Rescue 20 MIN
VHS
Firefighter I Video Series
Color (PRO G)
$115.00 purchase _ #35088
Shows approved procedures for locating and rescuing people in burning structures. Demonstrates carries, drags, life nets, stretchers, life belts and other rescue equipment and techniques. Includes an instruction guide for review. Part of a video series on Firefighter I training codes to be used with complementing IFSTA manuals.
Health and Safety; Psychology; Social Science
Dist - OKSU **Prod** - OKSU

Rescue 32 MIN
VHS
Color (P I J R)
$19.95 purchase, $10.00 rental _ #35 - 827 - 2020
Describes how Nicky, on his way to a basketball tournament, stops to help Laura and her mother, who are in a desperate situation.
Literature and Drama
Dist - APH **Prod** - ANDERK

Rescue 20 MIN
U-matic / VHS
Color
Shows approved procedures for locating and rescuing people in burning structures. Demonstrates carries, drags, life nets, stretchers, life belts and other rescue equipment and techniques.
Health and Safety; Science - Physical; Social Science
Dist - OKSU **Prod** - OKSU

Rescue 20 MIN
VHS
Firefighter II series
Color (IND)
$130.00 purchase _ #35655
Presents one part of a 14 - part series that is the teaching companion for IFSTA's Essentials of Fire Fighting manual. Describes techniques and safety procedures for various rescue activities. Demonstrates the use of several rescue tools. Based on Chapter 5.

Health and Safety; Science - Physical; Social Science
Dist - OKSU **Prod** - ACCTRA

Rescue Breathing 22 MIN
16mm
Color
Uses laboratory experiments to explain the superiority of mouth - to - mouth or mouth - to - nose breathing techniques over manual methods of artificial respiration.
Health and Safety
Dist - RBFA **Prod** - HERMAN 1958

Rescue for River Runners 28 MIN
VHS / 16mm / U-matic
Color (J H A)
MP=$475.00
Demonstrates self - help and assisted rescue techniques for boaters. Explains all the normal paddling mishaps that may occur in white water. The causes of accidents are explained so that the dangers can be understood and avoided.
Health and Safety; Physical Education and Recreation
Dist - LANDMK **Prod** - LANDMK 1985

Rescue from Isolation 22 MIN
16mm
Color (A)
LC 79-700592
Depicts the activities of geriatric day hospitals which offer medical, social and psychiatric rehabilitation for elderly persons whose physical disabilities, negative outlook and personal loneliness have caused them to become increasingly isolated.
Health and Safety; Psychology; Sociology
Dist - POLYMR **Prod** - BLUMNO 1978

Rescue from Isolation - the Role of a Psychogeriatric Day Hospital 22 MIN
16mm
Color (C A)
LC 73-703365
Uses a series of interviews with old people to establish the need for some sort of half - way house between total isolation and total institutionalization. Points out that one answer to this need is a day hospital, an out - patient facility connected with a geriatric day hospital. Documents the activities of one such organization in the areas of physiotherapy and psychiatry.
Psychology; Sociology
Dist - ROLAND **Prod** - ROLAND 1973

Rescue of a river 29 MIN
Videoreel / VT2
Turning points series
Color
Looks at one of the nation's environmental success stories - the clean - up of Oregon's Willamette River, once one of the filthiest waterways in the Northwest. Traces the industrial and agricultural growth of the rich Willamette River, fabled in historic monographs as a land of milk and honey, and shows in vivid detail how man had polluted the river.
Science - Natural; Sociology
Dist - PBS **Prod** - KOAPTV

Rescue Party 20 MIN
U-matic / VHS / 16mm
Color (I J H C)
LC 78-700919
Presents a story about a spaceship from the Galactic Federation which is given a mission to rescue the inhabitants of Earth before the Sun explodes.
Literature and Drama
Dist - BARR **Prod** - WILETS 1978

Rescue Procedures Series
Before the Emergency 25 MIN
Water Rescue 13 MIN
Dist - PRIMED

Rescue Squad 14 MIN
16mm / U-matic / VHS
World of Work Series
Color (I J H)
LC 76-715513
Describes the danger, excitement and responsibility of a large city rescue team. Shows the squad as it is called to a fire and to assist in health emergencies.
Health and Safety; Sociology
Dist - EBEC **Prod** - EBEC 1971

Rescue Team Alert 21 MIN
U-matic / VHS / 16mm
Color (IND)
LC 81-700775
Tells how two men are trapped in a pit by a load of drums containing acid waste. Depicts their rescue, which is hampered because the rescue team lacks training. Encourages the establishment of factory rescue teams.
Health and Safety
Dist - IFB **Prod** - MILLBK 1980

Rescues for river runners 30 MIN
VHS
Color (G)
$275.00 purchase _ #6865
Presents a safety film for canoeists, kayakers and rafters who paddle white water. Explains the causes of accidents and demonstrates self - help and assisted rescue techniques.
Health and Safety; Physical Education and Recreation
Dist - UCALG **Prod** - UCALG 1983

Rescuing Everest
VHS / U-matic / BETA / 16mm
Everest connection series
Color (G)
$480.00, $292.00, $270.00 purchase
Details the crisis of deforestation in the Mount Everest region of Nepal which is causing disastrous consequences both locally and in India downstream which is experiencing flooding. Tells the story of Mingma Norbu, a young Sherpa forester, who is in charge of Mount Everest National Park and responsible for its new reforestation program. Shows him journeying with his family to Canada to further his studies on resource management. Features Sir Edmund Hillary.
Agriculture; Geography - World; Science - Natural; Social Science
Dist - MEDCIN **Prod** - MEDCIN

Rescuing Everest - 2 28 MIN
U-matic / VHS
Everest connection series
Color (H C)
$205.00, $175.00 purchase _ #V697
Details the crisis of deforestation in the Mount Everest region of Nepal and its disastrous consequences. Tells the personal story of Mingma Norbu, the Sherpa forester in charge of the reforestation program and chronicles his travel to Canada to study resource management. Part two of a three - part series on the Sherpa people of the Himalayan region.
Agriculture; Geography - World; Science - Natural; Social Science
Dist - BARR **Prod** - CEPRO 1991

Research and development 30 MIN
U-matic
It's everybody's business series - operating a business; Unit 5
Color
Business and Economics
Dist - DALCCD **Prod** - DALCCD

Research and Development - Interactive Computer Graphics for Intuitional Problem 41 MIN
VHS / U-matic
New Technology in Education Series
Color (J)
Complete title is Research And Development - Interactive Computer Graphics For Intuitional Problem Solving. Shows computer systems which explore the possibility that the skillful use of dynamic graphics may bring about qualitative changes in the educational process. Shows a system for animating algebra word problems that exercises intuitional rather than analytical problem solving.
Education; Industrial and Technical Education
Dist - USNAC **Prod** - USDOE 1983

A Research and Development Perspective 25 MIN
16mm
Color
LC 78-700819
Highlights research and development efforts of the U S Department of Transportation. Shows projects, such as a microwave landing system, vessel traffic control radar, linear induction motored rail vehicles and nondestructive tire testing.
Business and Economics; Industrial and Technical Education; Social Science
Dist - USNAC **Prod** - USDT 1978

Research and Development Progress Report Number Nine - Delong Piers 12 MIN
16mm
Color
LC 76-701540
Discusses the construction and installation of Delong piers to relieve logistical problems in Vietnam.
History - World; Industrial and Technical Education
Dist - USNAC **Prod** - USA 1967

Research and planning 30 MIN
16mm / U-matic / VHS
Advertising the small business series
(A)
$180.00, $450.00 purchase, $30.00
Pinpoints and discusses planning a small business. Focuses on identifying potential customers, the best places to advertise, and what information to present. First of two parts.
Business and Economics
Dist - GPN **Prod** - NETCHE 1981

Research and planning 30 MIN
VHS / U-matic
Advertising the small business series
Color
Examines profiling customers, preparing the message and selecting the media that best fits a particular business. Discusses the various methods of advertising, including radio, newspapers, direct mail, television, outdoor and point - of - purchase.
Business and Economics
Dist - NETCHE **Prod** - NETCHE 1981

Research and Preparation 50 MIN
U-matic / VHS
Training the Trainer Series
Color (IND)
Includes the trainer's role, job and task analysis and the course outline.
Education; Industrial and Technical Education; Psychology
Dist - LEIKID **Prod** - LEIKID

Research associate program - making technology transfer work 13 MIN
VHS / U-matic
Color (A PRO)
$50.00, $95.00 purchase _ #TCA17895, #TCA17894
Covers the National Institute of Standards and Technology's Research Associate Program, which allows federal laboratories to work with industry on projects of mutual interest.
Civics and Political Systems; Industrial and Technical Education; Science
Dist - USNAC

Research at the Interface 19 MIN
16mm
Color
LC 80-700444
Shows a scientific research expedition in the North Atlantic.
Geography - World; Science; Science - Physical
Dist - WOODHO **Prod** - GOLDMN 1980

Research in Animal Behavior 18 MIN
U-matic / VHS / 16mm
Color
LC 77-700932
Discusses six experiments in animal behavior in order to introduce significant research in this field, interdisciplinary methodology and experimental procedures.
Psychology
Dist - CORF **Prod** - HAR 1978

Research in Multiple Sclerosis 15 MIN
16mm
Color
Details how the National Multiple Sclerosis Society allocates three million dollars a year for research into the cause, prevention and cure of MS. Explains in lay terms some of the unsolved mysteries surrounding the virology, immunology and epidemology of MS Demonstrates how antibodies form in humans and animals and how they may contribute to the demyelination process in the central nervous system.
Health and Safety; Science; Science - Natural; Sociology
Dist - NMSS **Prod** - FLEMRP 1972

Research in Nursing 62 MIN
VHS / U-matic
Color (PRO)
LC 81-706301
Reviews the definition and purpose of research in nursing. Demonstrates the 16 major steps involved in the research process by using the hypothetical research study.
Health and Safety
Dist - USNAC **Prod** - USVA 1980

Research interview module - Session 1 20 MIN
VHS / 16mm
Interview techniques series
(H C A)
$280.00 - $300.00 purchase, $35.00 rental
Covers basic techniques of survey interviewing used in research data gathering, including how to handle an interview, how to gain entry, begin the interview, and conduct the actual interview. Emphasizes rapport and neutrality.
Business and Economics
Dist - CORNRS **Prod** - CORNRS 1978

Research interview module - Session 1 20 MIN
16mm / U-matic / VHS

Color (H A)
Covers basic techniques and how to handle an interview. Tells how to gain entry, begin the interview and conduct the actual interview.
Business and Economics; Guidance and Counseling
Dist - CORNRS **Prod** - CUETV 1978

Research interview module - Session 2 20 MIN
VHS / 16mm
Interview techniques series
(H C A)
$280.00 - $300.00 purchase, $35.00 rental
Details how to record information verbatim and probe to get full answers. Simulates interviews to demonstrate techniques, analyzes the simulations.
Business and Economics
Dist - CORNRS **Prod** - CORNRS 1978

Research interview module - Session 2 20 MIN
U-matic / VHS / 16mm
Color (H A)
Emphasizes how to record verbatim when the interviewer is writing and the subject is talking quickly. Includes simulated interviews demonstrating what the interviewer is doing correctly and not so correctly.
Business and Economics; Guidance and Counseling
Dist - CORNRS **Prod** - CUETV 1978

Research interview module - Session 3 20 MIN
VHS / 16mm
Interview techniques series
(H C A)
$280.00 - $300.00 purchase, $35.00 rental
Illustrates 3 problem areas in survey interviewing and three different approaches toward solving them. Includes entry problem, how to probe, and stress questions.
Business and Economics
Dist - CORNRS **Prod** - CORNRS 1978

Research interview module - Session 3 20 MIN
U-matic / VHS / 16mm
Color (H A)
Features three different interviewers handling three specific problems. Includes entry problem, how to probe and stress questions.
Business and Economics; Guidance and Counseling
Dist - CORNRS **Prod** - CUETV 1978

Research into Controlled Fusion 55 MIN
16mm
Color
LC FIE63-184
A technical report of fusion research programs at Princeton University, Oak Ridge National Laboratory, Los Alamos scientific laboratory and the University of California radiation laboratory. Outlines principal problems encountered and uses animation to explain research devices in detail.
Science; Science - Physical
Dist - USERD **Prod** - USNRC 1958

Research into High Blood Pressure 15 MIN
16mm
Science in Action Series
Color (C)
Deals with high blood pressure. Explains that this condition has no characteristic symptoms and in most cases the cause is unknown. Tells of the dangers of untreated high blood pressure including stroke, kidney failure and congestive heart failure.
Health and Safety; Science; Science - Natural
Dist - COUNFI **Prod** - ALLFP

Research Methods 30 MIN
VHS / 16mm
Psychology - the Study of Human Behavior Series
Color (C A)
$99.95, $89.95 purchase _ 24 - 02
Shows footage of lobotomy, autism, and cognitive interview techniques being adopted by police investigators.
Psychology
Dist - CDTEL **Prod** - COAST 1990

Research Methods and Probability 29 MIN
Videoreel / VT2
Who is Man Series
Color
Examines methods for scientific research with emphasis on mathematical probability as it applies to investigations into psychic phenomena.
Psychology
Dist - PBS **Prod** - WHROTV

Research on Family and Marital Therapy with Alan Gurman 60 MIN
VHS / U-matic
B&W
Discusses with Proffessor Alan Gurman his research on family and marital therapy. Presents information taken from an article he co - authored and includes a discussion of the pros and cons of statistical analysis.
Psychology; Sociology
Dist - UWISC **Prod** - UWISC 1978

Research on the Disadvantaged 30 MIN
U-matic / VHS
Educating the Disadvantaged Series
Color
Focuses on language skills, intelligence tests and the self - concept of the disadvantaged. Discusses recent concern with problems of health as a prerequisite for learning.
Education; Psychology
Dist - NETCHE **Prod** - NETCHE 1972

Research on training 30 MIN
VHS
Effective teacher telecourse series
Color (T)
$69.95 purchase, $50.00 rental
Discusses the latest research on training as it relates to school teachers. Hosted by Dr Loren Anderson.
Education; Psychology
Dist - SCETV **Prod** - SCETV 1987

The Research paper 28 MIN
U-matic / BETA / VHS
Communication skills 2 - advanced series
Color (H C G)
$101.95, $89.95 purchase _ #CA - 16
Overviews the benefits to be gained by writing a research paper. Identifies the six essential elements of a research paper and the requirements for each element - title page, introduction, body, conclusion, bibliography and citations. Part of a 26 - part series.
English Language; Social Science
Dist - INSTRU

The Research Paper 30 MIN
U-matic
Communicating with a Purpose Series
(H C A)
Illustrates the research paper, a non - fiction literary form. Demonstrates the preliminary steps which provide a logical method for writing a research paper.
Education; Literature and Drama
Dist - ACCESS **Prod** - ACCESS 1982

The Research Paper made Easy - from Assignment to Completion 55 MIN
U-matic / VHS
Color
LC 81-706679
Offers instruction in writing a research paper by focusing on such skills as defining a topic, making a thesis statement, preparing a bibliography, outlining, writing a draft and preparing the final paper.
Education; English Language
Dist - GA **Prod** - CHUMAN 1981

A Research Problem - Inert Gas Compounds 19 MIN
16mm
CHEM Study Films Series
Color (H)
Conveys the excitement and personal involvement of research involved in the synthesis of one of the inert gas compounds, krypton difluoride.
Science - Physical
Dist - MLA **Prod** - CHEMS 1962

The Research Process 26 MIN
U-matic / VHS
Color (C)
$249.00, $149.00 purchase _ #AD - 1892
Looks at research. Reveals that research has been codified into specific methodologies but it still allows for the unorthodox and the unexpected. Visits the laboratory of Thomas Edison to show how he operated. Illustrates contemporary examples of corporate and academic research. Considers the Japanese approach.
Business and Economics; Geography - World; Psychology; Science
Dist - FOTH **Prod** - FOTH

The Research Process 30 MIN
U-matic / VHS
Innovation Series
Color
Offers an in - depth look at research itself, a well - organized process that is still open enough to allow for the unexpected.
Science
Dist - PBS **Prod** - WNETTV 1983

Research Project X - 15 27 MIN
16mm
Color
LC FIE67-116
Shows the development of the experimental X 15 research airplane which took test pilots to the edge of space.
Industrial and Technical Education; Science - Physical
Dist - NASA **Prod** - NASA 1966

Research Reactors - U S A 38 MIN
16mm
Color
Uses live action and animation to present a semitechnical summary of the major types of research reactors and their uses in industry, chemistry, physics, metallurgy, biology and medicine.
Science - Physical
Dist - USERD **Prod** - USNRC 1958

Research Skills 11 MIN
U-matic / VHS / 16mm
Effective Writing Series
Color (J H)
$270, $190 purchase _ #1908
Shows the many different types of library resources that can be utilized to write research papers.
English Language; Social Science
Dist - CORF

Research - the Challenge to Survival 24 MIN
16mm
Color (H C A)
LC 83-700682
Studies the advances being made in the fight against leukemia.
Health and Safety
Dist - LEUSA **Prod** - LEUSA 1983

Research to Reality 29 MIN
16mm
Color
LC 75-700576
Shows the many capabilities of the Naval Ship Research and Development Center.
Civics and Political Systems; Science
Dist - USNAC **Prod** - USN 1973

Research with Disadvantaged Preschool Children 11 MIN
16mm
Color (C T)
LC 72-702020
Demonstrates research at the Juniper Gardens Children's Project of the University of Kansas Bureau of Child Research. Explains that the Turner House Preschool is designed to develop and investigate child behavior, particularly language behavior.
Education; English Language; Psychology
Dist - UKANS **Prod** - UKANS 1969

Researching public funding sources 55 MIN
U-matic / VHS
Winning grants
(G A)
$1,795.00 member purchase, $1995.00 non member purchase
Presents seminars on successful grant writing. Focuses on effective methods for researching public funding sources. Fourth in a series of ten.
Business and Economics; Education
Dist - GPN **Prod** - UNEBR

Resection and Reconstruction for Large Esthesioneuroblastoma Involving the Maxila, Anterior and Middle Cranial Fosa 15 MIN
VHS / 16mm
(C)
$385.00 purchase _ #851VI004
Demonstrates the resection of large esthesioneuroblastomas.
Health and Safety
Dist - HSCIC **Prod** - HSCIC 1985

Resection of Abdominal Aneurysm 23 MIN
16mm
Color (PRO)
Demonstrates the technique of resection of an abdominal aortic aneurysm. Discusses specific areas of technical difficulty as well as pre - and postoperative management.
Health and Safety; Science
Dist - ACY **Prod** - ACYDGD 1970

Resection of an Adrenal Tumor 10 MIN
VHS / U-matic
Pediatric Series
Color
Health and Safety
Dist - SVL **Prod** - SVL

Resection of arteriosclerotic aneurysms of the abdominal aorta and replacement by 26 MIN
16mm
Color (PRO)
Demonstrates two cases of arteriosclerotic aneurysm of the abdominal aorta and principles of excision therapy of aortic aneurysm. Considers technical aspects of the procedure and the method of preparation and use of vascular homografts for aortic replacement.

Health and Safety; Science
Dist - ACY **Prod** - ACYDGD 1953

Resection of Right Colon for Carcinoma 14 MIN
16mm
Color (PRO)
Points out that malignant lesions of the right colon should never have less than a resection of the entire right colon, with approximately 25 centimeters of the terminal ileum.
Health and Safety; Science
Dist - ACY **Prod** - ACYDGD 1950

Resemblances in expressive behavior 42 MIN
VHS
Mother - infant interaction series
B&W (C G A)
$195.00 purchase, $40.00 rental _ #38074
Shows a variety of mother - infant interactions that illustrate how the expressive behavior of infants is derived to an important extent, even at one year of age, from the maternal behavior to which they have become accustomed. Part of a six - part series on infant development.
Psychology; Sociology
Dist - UCEMC

Reserve for Tomorrow 13 MIN
U-matic / VHS
Color
LC 81-706426
Discusses the Strategic Petroleum Reserve, a supply of crude oil stored underground for emergency use in the event of an oil embargo.
Social Science
Dist - USNAC **Prod** - USERD 1981

Reserved for Tomorrow 13 MIN
16mm
Color (A)
LC 77-703405
Discusses the Strategic Petroleum Reserve, a supply of crude oil stored underground for emergency use in the event of an oil embargo.
Geography - United States; Industrial and Technical Education; Social Science
Dist - USNAC **Prod** - USERD 1977

Reservoir fluids and pressures 60 MIN
U-matic / VHS
Basic and petroleum geology for non - geologists - reservoirs and -·- series; Reservoirs
Color (IND)
Industrial and Technical Education; Science - Physical
Dist - GPCV **Prod** - PHILLP

Reservoir mechanics 33 MIN
VHS / U-matic
Basic and petroleum geology for non - geologists - drilling and -'series; Drilling
Color (IND)
Industrial and Technical Education; Science - Physical
Dist - GPCV **Prod** - PHILLP

Reservoir Mechanics and Secondary and Tertiary Recovery 27 MIN
U-matic / VHS
Petroleum Geology Series
Color (IND)
Industrial and Technical Education; Science - Physical
Dist - GPCV **Prod** - GPCV

Reservoir Rocks 37 MIN
U-matic / VHS
Petroleum Geology Series
Color (IND)
Industrial and Technical Education; Science - Physical
Dist - GPCV **Prod** - GPCV

Reservoir rocks - limestones 39 MIN
U-matic / VHS
Basic and petroleum geology for non - geologists - hydrocarbons and' - series; Hydrocarbons
Color (IND)
Industrial and Technical Education; Science - Physical
Dist - GPCV **Prod** - PHILLP

Reservoir rocks - sandstones 36 MIN
VHS / U-matic
Basic and petroleum geology for non - geologists - hydrocarbons and'- series; Hydrocarbons
Color (IND)
Industrial and Technical Education; Science - Physical
Dist - GPCV **Prod** - PHILLP

Reservoirs of strength 57 MIN
VHS
Color (H C A PRO)
$395.00 purchase
Illustrates the physiological, psychological, legal and personal challenges faced by those who have been burned. Looks at the range of experiences from emergency treatment through daily care to rehabilitation and dismissal from the hospital. Provides a source for staff training and can be used for patient education also. Produced by Marino Colmano with direction by Margot Tempereau.
Health and Safety
Dist - PFP

Reset, Rate and Combination Control
Software / BETA
Basic Process Control Series
Color (PRO)
$600.00 - $1500.00 purchase _ #IDRRC
Focuses on reset control action, rate and combination control. Part of a six - part series on basic process control. Interactive training system includes course administrator guide, videodisc and computer software.
Industrial and Technical Education; Psychology
Dist - NUSTC **Prod** - NUSTC

Reshaping Aquatic Environments 15 MIN
16mm
Science in Action Series
Color (C)
Examines the attempts of marine ecologists, scientists and engineers to regulate and understand various life - systems within aquatic environments. Includes the investigation of the energy systems of the Chesapeake Estuary, an attempt to monitor the migration of the shad and an examination of the experiment to control life - destroying pollution.
Science; Science - Natural
Dist - COUNFI **Prod** - ALLFP

Reshaping, Characterization and Glazing of Anterior Ceramometal Restorations 21 MIN
U-matic
Color
LC 79-706755
Demonstrates and explains each step in the procedure for reshaping, characterizing and glazing the porcelain in an anterior ceramo - metal restoration.
Health and Safety
Dist - USNAC **Prod** - MUSC 1978

Reshaping Values After the Holocaust 180 MIN
VHS
Religion in a Post - Holocaust World Series
B&W
Discusses the re - defining of post - Holocaust values.
History - World; Religion and Philosophy
Dist - HRC **Prod** - OHC

Resident Exile 30 MIN
16mm
Color (G)
Presents an independent production by Ross McElwee. Portrays a young Iranian who escaped the torture of the Shah only to find Houston isn't so nice either.
Civics and Political Systems; Fine Arts; Geography - United States; Geography - World; Sociology
Dist - FIRS

Residential construction 10 MIN
VHS
Skills - occupational programs series
Color (H C)
$49.00 purchase, $15.00 rental _ #316613; LC 91-712394
Profiles a house framer, a plumber, a drywall taper, an electrician, and a roofer. Part of a series that features occupations in the skilled trades, in service industries and in business leading to careers in areas of demand and future growth. Includes teacher's guide with reproducible worksheets.
Guidance and Counseling; Industrial and Technical Education; Psychology
Dist - TVOTAR **Prod** - TVOTAR 1990

Residential electrical wiring skills 60 MIN
VHS
Color (G H)
$79.95 purchase _ #CEV00858V-T
Describes the basics involved in the electrical wiring for residential construction. Demonstrates through a 'demonstration board' that gives students examples of the skills for wiring: receptavles, lighting fixtures, dimmer switches, three-way lights, circuit panel boxes, and testing procedures.
Education; Industrial and Technical Education
Dist - CAMV

The Residential fire problem - Pt 1
VHS / U-matic
International fire protection organizations conference series
Color
Health and Safety; Social Science
Dist - NFPA **Prod** - NFPA

The Residential fire problem - Pt 2
U-matic / VHS
International fire protection organizations conference series
Color
Health and Safety; Social Science
Dist - NFPA **Prod** - NFPA

Residential installation techniques 20 MIN
VHS
Toro landscape irrigation series
Color (G)
$75.00 purchase _ #6 - 051 - 103P
Follows how irrigation designers in both the eastern and western United States demonstrate proper methods for installing landscaping irrigation systems. Covers zoning, layout of the system, trenching, pulling pipe, valves, backflow prevention, types of pipe, wire and connectors, locating controllers, installing heads, professional customer service.
Agriculture; Home Economics
Dist - VEP

Residential plumbing
VHS / 35mm strip
Residential plumbing series
$295.00 purchase _ #DXPLR000 filmstrips, $295.00 purchase _
Discusses various aspects of residential plumbing.
Industrial and Technical Education
Dist - CAREER **Prod** - CAREER

Residential plumbing series
Residential plumbing
Residential plumbing - Unit I
Residential plumbing - Unit II
Residential plumbing - Unit III
Residential plumbing- Unit IV
Dist - CAREER

Residential plumbing - Unit I
VHS / 35mm strip
Residential plumbing series
$85.00 purchase _ #DXPLR010 filmstrips, $85.00 purchase _ #DXPLR010V
Talks about installing the Sewer, water service, and locating fixtures.
Industrial and Technical Education
Dist - CAREER **Prod** - CAREER

Residential plumbing - Unit II
VHS / 35mm strip
Residential plumbing series
$85.00 purchase _ #DXPLR020 filmstrips, $85.00 purchase _ #DXPLR020V
Discusses installing drain and waste pipes, vent pipes, and supply pipes.
Industrial and Technical Education
Dist - CAREER **Prod** - CAREER

Residential plumbing - Unit III
VHS / 35mm strip
Residential plumbing series
$85.00 purchase _ #DXPLR030 filmstrips, $85.00 purchase _ #DXPLR030V
Talks about testing the rough plumbing, installing the bathtub, installing the water heater, and completing the bathtub.
Industrial and Technical Education
Dist - CAREER **Prod** - CAREER

Residential plumbing- Unit IV
VHS / 35mm strip
Residential plumbing series
$85.00 purchase _ #DXPLR040 filmstrips, $85.00 purchase _ #DXPLR040V
Discusses installing the water closet, lavatory, sink, dishwasher and disposal.
Industrial and Technical Education
Dist - CAREER **Prod** - CAREER

Residential Styles 30 MIN
U-matic
Growing Old in Modern America Series
Color
Health and Safety; Sociology
Dist - UWASHP **Prod** - UWASHP

Residenz - Und Wagnerstadt Bayreuth 5 MIN
16mm / U-matic / VHS
European Studies - Germany - German Series
Color (H C A) (GERMAN)
A German - language version of the motion picture Bayreuth, Royal Residence And Wagner City. Examines Bayeuth, noted not only for Richard Wagner's festival hall, but for other historic and artistic landmarks as well.
Foreign Language; Geography - World; History - World
Dist - IFB **Prod** - MFAFRG 1973

Residual exceptions 57 MIN
VHS
Evidence update series
Color (C PRO)
$75.00 purchase _ #ERX03
Presents Cornell law professor Faust Rossi in a discussion of the law of evidence. Emphasizes the concept of residual exceptions.
Civics and Political Systems
Dist - NITA **Prod** - NITA 1980

Residual Exceptions 57 MIN
VHS / U-matic
Evidence Update Series
Color (PRO)
Explains erosion of the rule against hearsay. Points out that the federal rules provide for the admissibility of hearsay not falling within other exceptions.
Civics and Political Systems
Dist - ABACPE **Prod** - ABACPE

Resist - Resistance 10 MIN
16mm
B&W
Gives a general outline of the anti - draft work being done in the Boston - Cambridge area by National Resist and the New England Resistance.
Civics and Political Systems; Geography - United States; Psychology; Sociology
Dist - CANWRL **Prod** - CANWRL 1967

Resist, Retreat, Mistaken, Listening 10 MIN
U-matic
Readalong Three Series
Color (P)
Provides reading instruction for third grade students. Uses animation, humor, music, repetition and audience participation. Comes with teacher's guide and kit.
Education; English Language; Literature and Drama
Dist - TVOTAR **Prod** - TVOTAR 1977

The Resistance 7 MIN
16mm / U-matic / VHS
Color
LC 80-700457
Presents an animated story about conformity and rebellion which is expressed in the struggle of a hammer and other hand tools to force a nail into a piece of wood.
Fine Arts
Dist - IFB **Prod** - ZAGREB 1980

The Resistance 18 MIN
16mm
Color (G)
$25.00 rental
Presents film produced by Leonard Henny in cooperation with the Peace and Liberation Commune and the Committee for Draft Resistance in the San Francisco Bay area. Features a speech by David Harris and members of The Resistance. This film was made to be shown on the summer 1968 project of The Resistance in which a truck, equipped with projection screen and audio, travelled around the US in 1968 in order to enlighten people about their alternatives to the draft.
Sociology
Dist - CANCIN

Resistance 16 MIN
U-matic / VHS / 16mm
B&W
Shows how changes in length, diameter and temperature of a material affect its resistance. Shows the construction of several different resistors and their use in circuits.
Industrial and Technical Education; Science - Physical
Dist - USNAC **Prod** - USAF

Resistance 17 MIN
U-matic / VHS
Witness to the Holocaust Series
B&W (J)
LC 84-706508
Explores spiritual and armed resistance by the Jews to Nazi tyranny during World War II.
History - World; Religion and Philosophy
Dist - CNEMAG **Prod** - HORECE 1983

Resistance 20 MIN
U-matic / VHS
Introductory Concepts in Physics - Magnetism and Electricity Series
Color (C)
$229.00, $129.00 purchase _ #AD - 1186
Demonstrates the relationship between current and resistance and between the length and/or the thickness of the wire and the amount of resistance.
Science - Physical
Dist - FOTH **Prod** - FOTH

Resistance 10 MIN
U-matic
Electricity Series
Color (H C) (FRENCH)
Covers the fundamentals of electrostatics and current electricity and helps students formulate mental imgages of abstract concepts. Available in French. Comes with teacher's guide.
Science; Science - Physical
Dist - TVOTAR **Prod** - TVOTAR 1986

Resistance - no 3 60 MIN
U-matic
AC/DC Electronics Series
Color (PRO)
One of a series of electronic and electrical training sessions for electronics workers on direct and alternating current and how to work with each.
Industrial and Technical Education
Dist - VTRI **Prod** - VTRI 1986

Resistance Welding 12 MIN
16mm
How to Weld Aluminum Series
B&W
Shows aluminum welds made under heat and pressure, two types of spot - welding machines, the use of carbon electrodes in high - speed resistance welding and tests for checking the size and strength of welds.
Industrial and Technical Education
Dist - USDIBM **Prod** - USDIBM 1946

Resisting peer pressure 8 MIN
U-matic / VHS
ASSET - a social skills program for adolescents series; Session 4
Color (J H)
LC 81-706054
Presents methods of resisting peer pressure which adolescents can use in their dealings with peers.
Guidance and Counseling; Psychology
Dist - RESPRC **Prod** - HAZLJS 1981

Resisting Peer Pressure
U-matic / VHS
Asset Series
Color
Psychology; Sociology
Dist - RESPRC **Prod** - RESPRC

Resisting Pressures to Smoke 9 MIN
16mm / U-matic / VHS
Color (J H)
Presents strategies for students to resist the pressure to smoke, be it peer pressure, parental modeling or media advertising.
Health and Safety; Psychology
Dist - USNAC **Prod** - USHHS

Resistive Bridge Circuits 26 MIN
16mm
B&W
LC 74-705526
Identifies a simple resistive bridge circuit and discusses the specific characteristics of resistance ratio, voltage distribution and current flow. Differentiates between balanced and unbalanced bridges. Verifies voltage distribution and current flow direction and describes the application of the wheatstone bridge. (Kinescope).
Industrial and Technical Education; Science - Physical
Dist - USNAC **Prod** - USAF

Resistive Gait Program 26 MIN
VHS / U-matic
Proprioceptive Neuromuscular Facilitation Series
Color
Health and Safety
Dist - UMDSM **Prod** - UMDSM

Resistive Mat Exercises I 33 MIN
VHS / U-matic
Proprioceptive Neuromuscular Facilitation Series
Color
Health and Safety
Dist - UMDSM **Prod** - UMDSM

Resistive Mat Exercises II 32 MIN
U-matic / VHS
Proprioceptive Neuromuscular Facilitation Series
Color
Health and Safety
Dist - UMDSM **Prod** - UMDSM

Resistor Color Code 8 MIN
U-matic / VHS / 16mm
Basic Electricity Series
Color (H C A)
Shows how to identify the resistors in a circuit and explains color bands, tolerances and identification bands.
Science - Physical
Dist - IFB **Prod** - STFD 1979

Resistors - Color Code 33 MIN
16mm
B&W
LC 74-705527
Gives the purpose of color coding resistors, then explains and shows the relationship of the colors on a resistor. Gives the color code and describes the value indicated by each color. (Kinescope).
Industrial and Technical Education
Dist - USNAC **Prod** - USAF

Resistors - Construction 21 MIN
16mm
B&W
LC 74-705528
States the purpose of resistors and gives the types. Demonstrates the construction and uses of fixed, adjustable and variable resistors. (Kinescope).
Industrial and Technical Education
Dist - USNAC **Prod** - USAF

The Resolution of Mossie Wax
VHS / 16mm
Color (G)
$95.00 rental _ #ROMW - 000
Dramatizes the problems of the welfare system for the elderly and one woman's struggle for a dignified old age. Shows how Mossie Wax tries to survive in a world of public indifference.
Health and Safety; Sociology
Dist - PBS **Prod** - WITFTV

Resolution of the Eye 40 MIN
VHS / U-matic
Color
Presents themes and variations concerning perception, time and television. Originally aired on the Video - Film Review Series on PBS.
Fine Arts
Dist - KITCHN **Prod** - KITCHN

Resolution on Saturn 57 MIN
VHS / U-matic
Nova Series
Color (H C A)
LC 83-706022
Shows pictures of Saturn and its moons taken on the Voyager I mission. Uses interviews with scientists, along with computer graphics and animation to explain such phenomena as why there are numerous rings around Saturn and how tiny moons help keep the rings in place.
Science - Physical
Dist - TIMLIF **Prod** - BBCTV 1982

Resolution - the recovering family - 8 11 MIN
VHS / U-matic
Adolescent alcoholism - recognizing, intervening and treating series
Color (PRO C)
$195.00 purchase _ #C901 - VI - 014
Focuses on the recovering families of adolescent alcoholics. Provides a framework for caregiver awareness. Presents facts and information and outlines current thinking regarding teenage alcoholism and substance abuse using the disease model of alcoholism. Part ten of a 13 - part series presented by Drs Patrick J Fahey, Lawrence L Gabel, Jeptha Hostetler, John S Monk and Robert E Potts, Ohio State University, Depts of Family Medicine, Preventive Medicine and Biomedical Communications.
Guidance and Counseling; Health and Safety; Psychology; Sociology
Dist - HSCIC

Resolved to be Free 29 MIN
16mm
Color
LC 76-701168
Chronicles Connecticut's role in the American Revolution from 1765 to 1781, includes glimpses of Israel Putnam defending Bunker Hill, Benedict Arnold assaulting Fort Ticonderoga and the sacrifice of Nathan Hale. Features Katharine Hepburn as narrator.
History - United States
Dist - FENWCK **Prod** - FENWCK 1975

Resolving conflict - the art of handling interpersonal tension 16 MIN
VHS
Building better communication at work series
Color (G)
$395.00 purchase, $175.00 rental _ #BBCV3, #BBCV3R
Provides the skills for resolving conflicts. Enables the practice of these skills in real - life situations. Part of a series on enhancing communication in the workplace.
Business and Economics; Psychology; Social Science
Dist - GPERFO

Resolving conflicts 28 MIN
VHS

You can choose series
Color (P I)
$59.95 purchase _ #RB8210
Reveals that Tuggy and Rhonda learn that there are ways to resolve disagreements without fighting. Shows that when a dispute between them puts their class art project in jeopardy, Rhonda and Tuggy learn to work out interpersonal conflicts in a peaceful and positive way. Part of a series hosted by comedian - youth counselor Michael Pritchard which leads children in an unrehearsed problem - solving session where the children explore the issues and arrive at a thoughtful solution.
Guidance and Counseling; Psychology; Sociology
Dist - REVID **Prod** - REVID 1993

Resolving conflicts 22 MIN
16mm / U-matic / VHS
Color (C A)
LC 82-700470
Teaches supervisors and managers how to respond to conflict in the most productive way. Illustrates five conflict resolution strategies - avoidance, giving it back to those involved, imposing a solution, compromise and collaboration.
Business and Economics; Psychology
Dist - CRMP **Prod** - CRMP 1982
MGHT

Resolving Conflicts through Counseling 70 MIN
U-matic
Color (H C A)
LC 77-706017
Shows the integrative approach that can be used by equal employment opportunity counselors in resolving discrimination complaint problems.
Guidance and Counseling; Psychology
Dist - USNAC **Prod** - USIRS 1976

Resolving grief 57 MIN
VHS
Color; PAL; SECAM (G)
$60.00 purchase
Features Connirae Andreas. Shows how to turn personal loss into a positive resource. Guides a man who recently lost an infant son through the procedure to a peaceful resolution. Intermediate level of NLP, neuro - linguistic programming.
Health and Safety; Psychology
Dist - NLPCOM **Prod** - NLPCOM

Resolving Interpersonal Conflicts 11 MIN
U-matic / 35mm strip
Supervising the Disadvantaged Series Module 3
Color
Alerts supervisors to some common conflict situations that may arise when disadvantaged workers are introduced into the work group and describes some actions that can substantially reduce or eliminate these troublesome areas.
Business and Economics; Psychology
Dist - RESEM **Prod** - RESEM

Resolving nurse - physician conflicts 28 MIN
U-matic / VHS
Color (PRO)
$275.00 purchase, $60.00 rental _ #7636S, #7636V
Shows Dr Jacob B Silversin in a workshop on the sources and solutions for friction in the hospital - regulations, policy interpretation, record - keeping accuracy and specific areas of responsbility. Gives specific steps to win - win solutions to conflict resolution. Provides tips on preventing the recurrence of problems in order to create a more harmonious work environment.
Health and Safety
Dist - AJN **Prod** - HOSSN 1988

Resolving personal conflict - Part 3 22 MIN
VHS
Teaching critical thinking about conflict resolution series
Color (C T G)
$185.00 purchase, $60.00 rental
Features teacher Roger Halstead who explores family conflict. Leads from examples of temper and violence to a consideration of more successful ways of resolving conflicts between parents and their children. Shifts the discussion to the international scene and a consensus that the world's rulers can do more toward using peaceful means to resolve conflicts. Part of a three - part series produced by the Educational Film and Video Project.
Civics and Political Systems; Guidance and Counseling; Psychology; Religion and Philosophy; Sociology
Dist - CF

Resolving Power L - 3 3 MIN
16mm
Single - Concept Films in Physics Series
Color (H C)
Shows a pinhold source viewed through a telescope variable aperture. Discusses the rayleigh criterion.
Science - Physical
Dist - OSUMPD **Prod** - OSUMPD 1963

Resolving shame 32 MIN
VHS
Color; PAL; SECAM (G)
$60.00 purchase
Features Steve Andreas. Reveals that shame has been described as a root cause of many difficulties, including alcoholism, drug abuse and codependence. Observes a rapid method for resolving shame and regaining a sense of self - esteem, developed by Steve and Connirae Andreas. Intermediate level of NLP, neuro - linguistic programming.
Health and Safety; Psychology
Dist - NLPCOM **Prod** - NLPCOM

Resonance 30 MIN
U-matic / VHS / 16mm
Mechanical Universe Series
Color (C A)
Explains resonance as the cause of a swaying bridge collapsing in a high wind and a wineglass shattering with a higher octave.
Science - Physical
Dist - FI **Prod** - ANNCPB

Resonance 20 MIN
U-matic / VHS
Basic A C circuits - laboratory sessions series
Color
Industrial and Technical Education
Dist - TXINLC **Prod** - TXINLC

Resonance - waves - Parts 17 and 18 60 MIN
VHS / U-matic
Mechanical universe - and beyond - Part I series
Color (G)
$45.00, $29.95 purchase
Considers why a swaying bridge collapses with a high wind and why a wine glass shatters with a higher octave in Part 17. Looks at how Newton extended mechanics to the propagation of sound with his analysis of simple harmonic motion in Part 18. Parts of a 52 - part series on the mechanics of the universe.
Science; Science - Physical
Dist - ANNCPB **Prod** - SCCON 1985

Resonant Lines 30 MIN
16mm
B&W
LC 74-705529
Explains open and shorted resonant lines. Develops and explains standing waves through use of animation. Shows and explains the phase relationship of the incident and reflected waves of current and voltage. (Kinescope).
Industrial and Technical Education; Science - Physical
Dist - USNAC **Prod** - USAF

Resonant Sections and Matching Devices 25 MIN
16mm
B&W
LC 74-705530
Discusses the uses of resonant sections of transmission lines. Defines and explains the operation of even harmonic filters, metallic insulators, quarter wave matching transformers, half wave transformers, line balance converters and capacitive coupled joints. (Kinescope).
Industrial and Technical Education; Science - Physical
Dist - USNAC **Prod** - USAF

Resorts - paradise reclaimed 58 MIN
16mm / VHS / U-matic
Pride of place series
Color (C)
$40.00, $24.50 rental _ #50824; $89.95 purchase #EX983
Considers the way Americans on vacation have reconnected with values inherent in the American Dream in the places they visit. Notes their escape into nature, the past, or pure fantasy in the bark - and - branch camps of the Adirondacks, in simulations of time travel at Walt Disney World, and in the marble cottages of the wealthy in Newport, Rhode Island. Includes guest Morris Lapidus. Part of an eight - part series hosted by architect Robert Stern.
Fine Arts; Geography - United States; Social Science; Sociology
Dist - PSU **Prod** - FOTH 1986
FOTH

Resource Allocation 30 MIN
U-matic
Medical - Legal Issues Series
(A)
Sets forth the decisions on resource allocation at all levels of the health care system and how they are made in light of legal, ethical and medical considerations.
Civics and Political Systems; Health and Safety; Sociology
Dist - ACCESS **Prod** - ACCESS 1983

Resource Center 28 MIN
16mm
Innovations in Education Series
Color
Dr Dwight Allen, professor of education at Stanford University, presents the functions and uses of resource centers for students in various academic areas, and mentions the operation, staffing and administration of such centers.
Education; Guidance and Counseling; Psychology
Dist - EDUC **Prod** - STNFRD 1966

Resource development for a bright picture
VHS
Color (C PRO G)
$30.00 purchase, $15.00 rental _ #931 - P, #931 - R
Records the 1991 Biennial Convention Keynote Address by nursing leader and scholar Dr Angela Barron McBride. Discusses resource development as a central concern. Dr McBride examines reasons for a collective reluctance to develop resources, considers some of the many forms resource development takes and discusses the attitudes needed for future resource development.
Guidance and Counseling; Health and Safety
Dist - SITHTA **Prod** - SITHTA 1992

Resource Geology 25 MIN
U-matic / VHS / 16mm
Color (H C)
Uses animated graphics to provide a comprehensive overview of the rock cycle, demonstrating the combination of natural forces at work over millions of years which redistributed chemical elements to form deposits of coal, iron and gypsum and other ores. Describes means of extracting these minerals.
Geography - World; Science - Physical
Dist - MEDIAG **Prod** - BBCTV 1985

Resource Geology 25 MIN
VHS / 16mm
Earth's Physical Resources Series
Color (S)
$200.00 purchase _ #236202
Presents a global view of the earth's resource potential. Features footage filmed in Britain, Europe and North America. 'Resource Geology' introduces the wide variety of resources occurring in the earth's crust. Specimens, graphics, maps, stock film and animation are used to discuss global concentrations of selected minerals, their distribution and the forces related to their formation.
Geography - World; Industrial and Technical Education; Science - Physical; Social Science
Dist - ACCESS **Prod** - BBCTV 1984

Resource Recovery 14 MIN
16mm
Screen news digest series; Vol 20; Issue 8
Color (J H C)
Describes the search for ways to recycle raw materials and energy from garbage.
Science - Natural; Social Science
Dist - HEARST **Prod** - HEARST 1978

Resource Recovery 25 MIN
16mm
Color
LC 76-703799
Shows the recovery and remanufacturing of glass, metal, paper and plastics.
Business and Economics; Industrial and Technical Education; Science - Natural
Dist - BCDA **Prod** - BCDA 1974

Resources 10 MIN
U-matic / VHS / 16mm
Economics for Elementary Series
Color (P I)
LC 73-701587
Portrays America as rich in natural resources such as forests, minerals, agricultural land and human potential. Presents conflicting points of view in order to raise questions, stimulate thinking, present alternatives and inspire interest on the part of the student.
Business and Economics; Geography - United States; Social Science
Dist - AIMS **Prod** - OF 1971

Resources and Scarcity - what is Economics all about 30 MIN
U-matic / VHS
Economics USA Series
Color (C)
Business and Economics
Dist - ANNCPB **Prod** - WEFA

Resources and World Trade 14 MIN
U-matic / VHS / 16mm
Color (I J H) (SWEDISH)

LC 78-700920
Explains how resources are used around the world to provide goods for home needs and for trade. Uses maps to show where some of the world's most important resources are located and illustrates the role of rivers and harbors in establishing trade centers.
Business and Economics; Geography - World; Social Science
Dist - PHENIX **Prod** - BEANMN 1978

Resources for congregational planning 20 MIN
VHS
Congregational planning series
Color (G A R)
$39.95 purchase, $10.00 rental _ #35 - 877 - 2076
Focuses on the need for a congregation's members to fully utilize their 'gifts of the Spirit.' Hosted by Dr Margaret Wold. Produced by Seraphim.
Religion and Philosophy
Dist - APH

Resources in its Crust 10 MIN
16mm / U-matic / VHS
Earth Series
Color (I J H)
$255, $180 purchase _ #4152
Shows the different resources of the earth's crust.
Science - Physical; Social Science
Dist - CORF

Resources make it Happen 19 MIN
16mm
Further Education Series
Color (T)
LC 77-702846
Examines effective ways and means of using professional and financial resources in adult education courses.
Education
Dist - CENTWO **Prod** - ADEAV 1976

Respect and You 28 MIN
VHS
(I J)
$189 purchase No. 2516-YZ
Teaches students grades 5-9 to think critically about issues involved in respect for property, authority, other people's ideas, differences, and how giving respect creates self-respect. Presents scenarios and discussion questions. Inclues 28 minute video, teacher's guide.
Education; Psychology
Dist - SUNCOM **Prod** - SUNCOM

Respect for property and authority 15 MIN
VHS
Respect series
CC; Color (I)
$89.95 purchase _ #10418VG
Shows practical ways for giving respect to parents, teachers and other authority figures. Uses live - action, narration, graphics and music to illustrate strategies for respecting property. Comes with a teacher's guide and a set of blackline masters. Part four of a four - part series.
Guidance and Counseling; Home Economics; Psychology; Sociology
Dist - UNL

Respect for the Midland Bank 40 MIN
VHS
Adventurers series
Color (A)
PdS65 purchase
Profiles a self-made millonaire who has an idea that might change the face of an industry. Part of a six-part series on a year in the life of a venture capital house, Grosvenor Venture Managers Ltd, which is approached with up to 600 ideas annually - of which around 20 will receive backing. Explains how the successful ventures are selected, and the drama and conflicts that lie behind the deals.
Business and Economics
Dist - BBCENE

Respect series
Presents children with keys to respecting themselves, others, authority, and property. Uses live - action, narration, music, and graphics to teach courtesy, sensitivity and conflict management. Comes with four 15 - minute videos; four teacher's guides; and four sets of blackline masters.

I was just kidding	15 MIN
Respect for property and authority	15 MIN
Uncommon courtesy	15 MIN
You're right and so am I	15 MIN

Dist - UNL

Respect yourself and others, too 16 MIN
VHS
Color (P I)
$95 purchase No. 2465-YZ
Teaches social sensitivity as a key step in promoting respect and understanding among students. Emphasizes the importance of respecting the rights and needs of others. Includes 16-minute video, eight student worksheets, teacher's guide.
Education; Psychology
Dist - SUNCOM **Prod** - SUNCOM

Respect yourself - say NO to drugs 45 MIN
VHS
Color (H)
$175.00 purchase _ #06831 - 126
Interviews four teenagers from diverse backgrounds and life - styles to show that they have one thing in common - they've said NO to drugs. Discusses the causes and effects of drug abuse and the importance of saying NO and believing it.
Guidance and Counseling; Psychology; Social Science; Sociology
Dist - GA **Prod** - GA

Respect Yourself - Say no to Drugs
U-matic / VHS
(J H C)
$159.00 purchase _ #06831 941
Eamines the tremendous pressures on young people to use drugs. Presents proven techniques to help teenagers resist such pressures and to explore the importance of making their own decisions. In 3 parts.
Guidance and Counseling
Dist - ASPRSS **Prod** - ASPRSS

Respect Yourself - Say no to Drugs
VHS
Learning How to Say no Series
$175.00 purchase _ #IE9100V
Investigates the pressure on people to use drugs and stresses the benefits of teaching people to trust their instincts. Uses dramatization to show how and when to say no.
Health and Safety; Sociology
Dist - CAREER **Prod** - CAREER

A Respectable Lie 30 MIN
VHS / U-matic
Color
Examines the imagery and messages of pornography and its connection to violence against women, stating that in fact one doesn't have to accept this propaganda. Discusses pornography, what it is, how it has affected and continues to affect women.
Sociology
Dist - WMENIF **Prod** - WMENIF

The respectful workplace - Redefining workplace violence 76 MIN
VHS
The respectful workplace - Redefining workplace violence series
Color (PRO IND COR A)
$995,00 purchase, $400.00 rental, $50.00 preview
Redefines workplace violence and helps organizations put an end to the destructive conflicts that occur on a daily basis. Each part of this three-part series includes a facilitator's guide, handouts, and transparencies.
Sociology
Dist - VIDART

The Respectful workplace - redefining workplace violence series
VHS
The Respectful workplace - redefining workplace violence series
Color (IND)
$995.00 purchase, $400.00 rental _ #QMR08A - C
Consists of a three - part series designed to help businesses end hostility, intimidation, harassment and other damaging behaviors. Comes with a facilitator guide, handouts and overhead transparencies. Includes Opening the Right Doors, Diffusing Hostility through Customer Service and Managing Harmony. Produced by Quality Media Resources.
Business and Economics; Guidance and Counseling; Health and Safety; Social Science; Sociology
Dist - EXTR

The respectful workplace - Redefining workplace violence series

Defusing hostility through customer service - Pt 2	25 MIN
Managing harmony - Pt 3	26 MIN
Opening the right doors - Pt 1	25 MIN
The respectful workplace - Redefining workplace violence	76 MIN

Dist - VIDART

Respecting adults and others 27 MIN
VHS
Sunshine factory series
Color (P I R)
$14.99 purchase _ #35 - 83587 - 533
Features P J the repairman and kids in his neighborhood as they travel to the Sunshine Factory, a land populated by puppets, a computer and caring adults. Teaches a Biblically - based lesson on respecting all people, particularly adults.
Religion and Philosophy
Dist - APH **Prod** - WORD

Respecting Differences 11 MIN
16mm
Color
LC 80-700834
Deals with the cultural stresses on the Australian migrant child in the community. Presents the view that if a child is given a bad self - image by his environment, it is difficult, if not impossible, to eradicate it.
Geography - World; Psychology; Sociology
Dist - TASCOR **Prod** - NSWF 1978

Respecting elders - 21 9 MIN
VHS / U-matic
Life's little lessons - self - esteem K - 3 - series
Color (K P)
$129.00, $99.00 _ #V620
Tells about Wilbur Billingsworth, a very old farmer, who teaches some young whippersnappers something about respecting their elders, and wins their friendship. Part of a 30 - part series on self - esteem.
Guidance and Counseling; Health and Safety; Psychology
Dist - BARR **Prod** - CEPRO 1992

Respecting others
VHS
Big changes, big choices series
Color (I J)
$69.95 purchase _ #LVB - 12A
Sensitizes adolescents to the feelings of others. Helps develop an understanding of what it means to treat people with respect. Part of a 12 - part video series designed to help young adolescents work their way though the many anxieties and issues they face. Encourages them to make positive and healthful life choices. Features humorist and youth counselor Michael Pritchard.
Guidance and Counseling; Psychology
Dist - CFKRCM **Prod** - CFKRCM

The Respecting Others Game 11 MIN
U-matic / VHS / 16mm
Learning Responsibility Series
Color (P)
LC 78-700248
Tells of a young boy's realization of the importance of respecting others when his friend shows him how he would feel if his rights were not respected.
Guidance and Counseling; Psychology
Dist - HIGGIN **Prod** - HIGGIN 1978

Respecting privacy - 23 8 MIN
VHS / U-matic
Life's little lessons - self - esteem K - 3 - series
Color (K P)
$129.00, $99.00 _ #V622
Tells about Snoozy Hollow Inn run by Mrs Duart, where famous people come to get away and find peace and total privacy. Reveals that Suzy steps in when Mrs Duart is called away, and almost ruins the reputation of the inn until she learns to respect the privacy of others. Part of a 30 - part series on self - esteem.
Guidance and Counseling; Psychology
Dist - BARR **Prod** - CEPRO 1992

Respecting the law - 22 6 MIN
VHS / U-matic
Life's little lessons - self - esteem K - 3 - series
Color (K P)
$129.00, $99.00 _ #V621
Follows the career of Judge Soy Bean, self - appointed Judge, Sheriff and Justice of the Peace of Scull City, who turns three outlaws into the best deputies ever when they learned to respect the law. Part of a 30 - part series on self - esteem.
Guidance and Counseling; Psychology
Dist - BARR **Prod** - CEPRO 1992

Respighi's The Fountains of Rome
VHS
Music in motion series
Color (J H C G)
$75.00 purchase _ #MUS07V
Expresses visually what is heard in The Fountains of Rome by Respighi. Teaches classical music appreciation, develops interest and enhances listening enjoyment. Includes manual with suggestions for presenting the video, questions for discussion, research projects, correlations with other subject areas and listening and reading lists. Part of an eight - part series.
Fine Arts
Dist - CAMV **Prod** - MUSLOG

Respirando por otros 14 MIN
16mm / U-matic / VHS
Emergency resuscitation - Spanish series
Color (C A) (SPANISH)
A Spanish - language version of the motion picture Breathing For Others. Shows many situations where exhaled air resuscitation may save a life, including asphyxia, drowning, gassing, electric shock and suffocation. Demonstrates the mouth - to - mouth and mouth - to - nose techniques.
Foreign Language; Health and Safety
Dist - IFB **Prod** - UKMD

Respiration 28 MIN
VHS
Human body - the heart and circulation - series
Color (J H G)
$89.95 purchase _ #UW4158
Examines the role of breathing in supplying body cells with oxygen. Explains the breathing mechanism, the function of the diaphragm and ribs, the chemical and neural aspects of breath, the airways to, from and within the lungs, and how the exchange of gases takes place. Looks at the causes and treatment of various breathing disorders. Part of a 39 - part series featuring computer animation, medical photography, electron micrography, full - color drawings and diagrams and three - dimensional working models to cover the workings of the human body from head to toe and inside out.
Science - Natural
Dist - FOTH

Respiration
Software /.Videodisc / Kit
Annenberg - CPB Project Interactive Science Instruction Videodisc
(H)
$495
Enables high school students to conduct simulated biology experiments on respiration without coping with the constraints of time, temperature and luck.
Education; Science
Dist - GPN

Respiration 29 MIN
U-matic
Introducing biology series; Program 14
Color (C A)
Overviews ways in which simpler organisms such as amoebas exchange oxygen and carbon dioxide. Presents various repiratory structures. Focuses on human respiration.
Science - Natural
Dist - CDTEL **Prod** - COAST

Respiration and Circulation 26 MIN
16mm
Color (PRO)
LC FIE61-13
Explains the functions of the circulatory and respiratory systems within the human body and shows how they work together under the direction of the brain through reflex chemoreceptor control. Depicts how these complex systems affect the physiological problems of flight.
Science - Natural
Dist - USNAC **Prod** - USAF 1961

Respiration and transpiration; 2nd ed. 15 MIN
U-matic
Search for science series; Unit VIII - Plants
Color (I)
Shows that respiration is vital to the existence of green plants.
Science - Natural
Dist - GPN **Prod** - WVIZTV

Respiration and waste 6 MIN
VHS
Systems of the human body series
Color (I J)
$24.95 purchase _ #L9626
Uses live and animated sequences to portray respiration. Part of a seven - part series on the human body, using the single - concept format.
Science - Natural
Dist - HUBDSC **Prod** - HUBDSC

Respiration and waste 9 MIN
VHS / 16mm
Systems of the human body series
Color (J H C)
$80.00 purchase _ #194 W 0098, #193 W 2098
Shows oxygen and food taken into the body in relationship to wastes produced. Part of a series on the systems of the human body.
Science - Natural
Dist - WARDS **Prod** - WARDS

Respiration during and After Anesthesia 21 MIN
16mm
Color (PRO)
LC 72-700350
Presents principles of respiratory care during preoperative, intraoperative and postoperative periods. Utilizes dramatizations during which the viewer is asked to interpret findings and decide on a course of action.
Health and Safety; Science
Dist - AYERST **Prod** - AYERST 1973

Respiration - Energy for Life
VHS / U-matic
Color (H)
Explains the related processes of breathing and cell respiration. Reviews the major experiments that have enabled the relationship between bodily activity and cell chemistry to be understood.
Science - Natural
Dist - GA **Prod** - GA

Respiration in Animals 11 MIN
U-matic / VHS / 16mm
Color (J H)
$280, $195 purchase _ #3139
Shows the similaritys between air - breathing and water - breathing animals. Explains the relationship between an animal's size and the complexity of its respiratory system.
Science - Natural
Dist - CORF

Respiration in Man 25 MIN
16mm / U-matic / VHS
Biology - Spanish Series Unit 8 - Human Physiology; Unit 8 - Human physiology
Color (H C) (SPANISH)
Analyzes the structure and function of the respiratory system.
Foreign Language; Science - Natural
Dist - EBEC **Prod** - EBEC

Respiration in Man 26 MIN
U-matic / VHS / 16mm
Biology Series Unit 8 - Human Biology; Unit 8 - Human biology
Color; B&W (H C)
LC 74-702921
Describes the structure and functions of the respiratory system. Provides visual proof of the exchange of carbon dioxide for oxygen. Raises the question of air pollution and how long man will tolerate it.
Science - Natural
Dist - EBEC **Prod** - EBEC 1969

Respiration - the atmosphere and life 23 MIN
16mm / VHS
Color (P)
$465.00, $365.00 purchase, $45.00 rental
Presents three personable students who guide through their class report on the human respiratory system. Uses presentation skills and unique demonstrations for a thorough report, including the latest in medical photography. Includes science vocabulary covering all basic aspects of the repiratory sytem. Encourages care for the health of the delicate respiratory system as well as for the environment which supports all living things.
Science - Natural
Dist - FIESTF **Prod** - FIESTF 1989

Respirator care and maintenance 15 MIN
BETA / VHS / U-matic
Color (IND G)
$395.00 purchase _ #826 - 10
Trains employees on the proper care and maintenance of air purifying respirators. Explains what actions are necessary when a respirator is first assigned to an employee. Discusses proper donning procedures, fit checking the respirator after donning and fit testing. Explains the correct procedures for respirator inspection, replacing worn parts, decontamination procedures, temporary storage of a respirator for transportation to work location, the sanitizing process and storage.
Health and Safety; Industrial and Technical Education; Psychology
Dist - ITSC **Prod** - ITSC 1990

Respirators 13 MIN
16mm / VHS
Safety Gear Series
Color (H C A PRO)
$230.00, $275.00 purchase, $75.00 rental _ #8119
Introduces the different uses of air - purifying and air - supplying respirators.
Health and Safety; Psychology
Dist - AIMS **Prod** - SANDE 1989

Respirators 15 MIN
VHS / U-matic / BETA
Color; PAL (IND G)
$175.00 rental _ #AEB - 102
Takes a close look at respiratory hazards and respiratory safety equipment. Details procedures for selecting a proper respiratory device and explains maintenance procedures. Examines air purifying and air - supplied devices. Includes leader's guide and 10 workbooks.
Business and Economics; Health and Safety; Psychology; Science - Natural
Dist - BNA **Prod** - BNA

Respiratory acidosis and alkalosis 19 MIN
VHS / U-matic
Fluids and electrolytes series
Color (PRO)
Explains causes and identifies acute and chronic diseases associated with respiratory acid - base problems. Shows proper health - team action to be taken.
Health and Safety; Science; Science - Natural
Dist - BRA **Prod** - BRA

Respiratory adaptations of aquatic insects 14 MIN
VHS
Aspects of animal behavior series
Color (J H C G)
$99.00 purchase, $35.00 rental _ #37873
Shows how respiration occurs in two species, the belostomatid bug and the hydrophilid beetle. Part of a series on animal behavior produced by Robert Dickson and Prof George Bartholomew for the Office of Instructional Development, UCLA.
Science - Natural
Dist - UCEMC

Respiratory alkalosis and acidosis 27 MIN
BETA / VHS / U-matic
Acid base balance series
Color (C PRO)
$280.00 purchase _ #605.2
Focuses on the acid - base imbalances that occur as a result of respiratory dysfunction. Stresses identification of patients at risk and recognition of clinical manifestations, including the effects on arterial blood gases. Emphasizes nursing assessments, nursing diagnoses and the importance of initiating appropriate interventions. Produced by Golden West College.
Health and Safety; Science - Natural
Dist - CONMED

Respiratory assessment 30 MIN
VHS
Physical assessment series
Color (PRO C)
$150.00 purchase, $70.00 rental _ #4413
Details a systematic respiratory assessment. Explains normal, abnormal and adventitious breath sounds. Includes guidelines for eliciting a pertinent health history and for performing a thorough respiratory assessment. Part of a seven - part series providing step - by - step guides to physical assessment of various body systems for nursing students and professionals.
Health and Safety; Psychology
Dist - AJN **Prod** - ANSELM 1995

Respiratory Care 60 MIN
U-matic / VHS
Color (PRO)
LC 81-706302
Describes how to formulate a care approach for a patient with chronic obstructive pulmonary disease.
Health and Safety
Dist - USNAC **Prod** - USVA 1980

Respiratory care - 18 19 MIN
VHS
Clinical nursing skills - nursing fundamentals - series
Color (C PRO G)
$395.00 purchase _ #R890 - VI - 054
Introduces the techniques and procedures of basic respiratory care. Describes and demonstrates instrumentation and techniques of oxygen therapy. Presents procedures for the insertion of artificial airways, nasopharyngeal suction and tracheotomy suction and care. Outlines the importance of coughing, deep breathing and incentive spirometry. Part of a 23 - part series on clinical nursing skills.
Health and Safety
Dist - HSCIC **Prod** - CUYAHO 1989

Respiratory, circulatory and digestive systems - Vol 1
Videodisc
STV - human body series
Color; CAV (J H)
$325.00 purchase _ #T81515; $225.00 purchase _ #T81559
Studies the respiratory, circulatory and digestive sytems. Offers medical photography by Lennart Nilsson. Part of a three - part series. Includes videodisc, software diskettes with NGS magazine and book excerpts, glossary and presenter tool, user's guide with directions for interactive

hook - up, barcode directory and activities and library catalog cards. Designed for Macintosh system. Contact distributor for hardware configuration. Basic kit available at lower price.
Science - Natural
Dist - NGS **Prod** - NGS 1992

Respiratory Distress - Auscultation 13 MIN
U-matic / VHS
Color (PRO)
Demonstrates proper auscultatory techniques. Discusses abnormal breath and cardiac sounds and their underlying causes. Notes the limitations of auscultation and the indications for other diagnostic techniques.
Health and Safety; Science - Natural
Dist - UMICHM **Prod** - UMICHM 1983

Respiratory distress - clinical identification 15 MIN
VHS / U-matic
Michigan perinatal education _ Instructional Unit B - respiratory distress series
Color (PRO)
LC 79-707740
Shows how to identify respiratory distress in the newborn infant by demonstrating the observation and identification of abnormalities in respiratory rate, respiratory effort, expiratory effort and skin coloration.
Health and Safety
Dist - UMICH **Prod** - UMICH 1978

Respiratory Distress - Diagnosis by Inspection and Arterial Blood Analysis 18 MIN
16mm
Color (PRO)
Presents case studies of four patients who suffer from respiratory distress and how diagnosis is determined by inspection and arterial blood analysis.
Health and Safety; Science - Natural
Dist - SQUIBB **Prod** - SQUIBB

Respiratory distress - size - maturity factors 13 MIN
U-matic / VHS
Color (PRO)
Covers determining a newborn's gestational age, weight and size, classifying infants by gestational age and size and risk factors related to gestational age and size.
Health and Safety; Psychology; Science - Natural
Dist - UMICHM **Prod** - UMICHM 1983

Respiratory Distress Syndrome 15 MIN
U-matic / VHS
Michigan Perinatal Education, Instructional Unit B - Respiratory Distress Series
Color (PRO)
LC 79-707743
Reviews the clinical factors related to the causes of respiratory distress syndrome, clinical management of the condition in both primary care settings and regional perinatal centers and the clinical course.
Health and Safety
Dist - UMICH **Prod** - UMICH 1978

Respiratory Emergencies 15 MIN
U-matic / VHS
Color (C)
$249.00, $149.00 purchase _ #AD - 1473
Deals with the recognition and emergency treatment of carbon monoxide poisoning, asthma emergencies, chronic obstructive pulmonary disease and hyperventilation. Emphasizes that assuring a victim's breathing takes precedence over all other emergency care.
Health and Safety; Science - Natural
Dist - FOTH **Prod** - FOTH

Respiratory emergencies 50 MIN
VHS
First aid video series
Color (J H T PRO)
$249.00 purchase _ #AH45239
Uses dramatic vignettes and classroom demonstrations to teach current first aid techniques for respiratory emergencies. Includes checkpoint quizzes to test retention of material covered.
Health and Safety
Dist - HTHED **Prod** - HTHED

Respiratory Emergencies 15 MIN
16mm / U-matic / VHS
REACT - Review of Emergency Aid and CPR Training Series
Color (H C A)
Health and Safety
Dist - CORF **Prod** - CORF

Respiratory emergencies 50 MIN
VHS
First aid video series
Color (J H G)
$249.00 purchase _ #60143 - 126
Shows how to deal with respiratory emergencies. Includes vignettes of first aid situations, demonstrations of first aid procedures, dialogue between instructor and students and checkpoint quizzes. Part of a four - part series on first aid.
Health and Safety
Dist - GA **Prod** - HRMC

Respiratory Emergencies and Artificial Respiration 10 MIN
U-matic / VHS / 16mm
Emergency First Aid Training Series
Color (A)
LC 81-700836
Describes first aid procedures to use with a person who has stopped breathing.
Health and Safety
Dist - IFB **Prod** - CRAF 1980

Respiratory Emergencies - Babies and Children 15 MIN
16mm / U-matic / VHS
REACT - Review of Emergency Aid and CPR Training Series
Color (H C A)
Health and Safety
Dist - CORF **Prod** - CORF

Respiratory Exercises for the Parkinson Patient 13 MIN
16mm
Color
LC 74-705531
Demonstrates respiratory exercises designed to enhance the diaphragmatic breathing and lateral costal expansion of the Parkinson patient.
Health and Safety; Psychology
Dist - USNAC **Prod** - USPHS

Respiratory Failure 22 MIN
U-matic
Color (PRO)
LC 76-706102
Discusses factors which may precipitate respiratory failure, symptoms and signs of respiratory acidosis and treatment of respiratory failure.
Health and Safety; Science - Natural
Dist - USNAC **Prod** - WARMP 1970

Respiratory Failure - Etiology and Management 21 MIN
U-matic
Color
Presents lung cancer mortality statistics and describes paraneoplastic syndromes.
Health and Safety
Dist - UTEXSC **Prod** - UTEXSC

Respiratory protection 15 MIN
VHS / U-matic / BETA
Color; PAL (IND G)
$175.00 rental _ #AEB - 111
Illustrates how the lungs work and how they can be damaged by respiratory hazards. Describes types of respirators and motivates workers to use safety precautions to protect themselves from both immediate hazards and the effects of long - term exposure. Includes leader's guide and 10 workbooks.
Business and Economics; Health and Safety; Psychology; Science - Natural
Dist - BNA **Prod** - BNA

Respiratory protection 12 MIN
VHS
Blueprints for safety
Color (IND)
$249.00 purchase _ #CLM45-56
Presents a guideline for safety and compliance requirements, created by certified safety professionals. Includes an instructor's guide, training tips, a learning exercise, five employee handbooks, glossary of terms and template for transparencies.
Health and Safety
Dist - EXTR **Prod** - CLMI

Respiratory Protection 60 MIN
U-matic / VHS
Fire Protection Training Series
Color
Health and Safety
Dist - ITCORP **Prod** - ITCORP

Respiratory Protection 8 MIN
U-matic / VHS
Color (A)
LC 84-707799
Explains the need for respiratory protection when airborne hazardous materials are in excess of safe levels. Shows the use of cartridge and single - use respirators.
Health and Safety; Industrial and Technical Education; Psychology; Science - Natural; Sociology
Dist - IFB **Prod** - KOHLER

Respiratory Protection 60 MIN
VHS
Plant Safety Series
Color (PRO)
$600.00, $1500.00 purchase _ #GMRPR
Describes various types of respiratory hazards - particulates, gases, oxygen deficiency - and respiratory protection gear. Part of a four - part series on plant safety, which is part of a set on general and mechanical maintenance. Includes 10 textbooks and an instructor guide which provide four hours of instruction.
Education; Health and Safety; Industrial and Technical Education; Psychology; Sociology
Dist - NUSTC **Prod** - NUSTC

Respiratory safety - the breath of life 16 MIN
VHS
Color (IND)
$250.00 purchase, $95.00 rental _ #BBP92
Heightens employee awareness of respiratory hazards and gives advice on protection. Includes a leader's guide.
Health and Safety
Dist - EXTR **Prod** - BBP

Respiratory syncytial virus - a seasonal dilemma 16 MIN
VHS
Color (PRO C)
$285.00 purchase, $70.00 rental _ #4382
Covers the signs and symptoms of respiratory synctial virus - RSV, transmission of the infection through viral shedding and self - innoculation and infection control for RSV, the major cause of brochiolitis and pneumonia in infants less than one year old. Describes diagnostic tests and demonstrates treatment with aerosolized ribavirin. Emphasizes the precautions that pediatric medical staff need to take to prevent the spread of RSV to uninfected pediatric patients.
Health and Safety
Dist - AJN **Prod** - AJN

The Respiratory system 26 MIN
VHS
Color (J H)
$99.00 purchase _ #4157 - 026
Shows how the body takes in oxygen and expels carbon dioxide. Looks at how smoking can devastate the respiratory system. Includes teacher's guide.
Education; Health and Safety; Science - Natural
Dist - GA **Prod** - EBEC

Respiratory System 13 MIN
16mm / U-matic / VHS
Human Body Series
Color (J H C)
$315, $220 purchase _ #3960
Shows how air flows through the body, passes through the lungs into the blood, and is carried to the cells to be used.
Science - Natural
Dist - CORF

Respiratory system 40 MIN
VHS / 16mm
Histology review series; Unit X
(C)
$330.00 purchase _ #821VI049
Covers prominent features of the respiratory system and lungs.
Health and Safety
Dist - HSCIC **Prod** - HSCIC 1983

Respiratory system anatomical chart
VHS
(J H C G A)
$36.50 purchase _ #AH70206
Portrays the anatomy of the respiratory system from a variety of angles. Available with mounting rods or framed.
Health and Safety; Science - Natural
Dist - HTHED **Prod** - HTHED

Respiratory system - the review of normal morphology and introduction to pathology 5 MIN
VHS / 16mm
(C)
$385.00 purchase _ #860VI071
REviews the normal morphology of the respiratory system including the trachea, bronchi, and lungs. Presents an introduction to pathology in the respiratory system. Describes characteristic findings in emphysema, bronchopneumonia and squamous carcinoma.
Health and Safety
Dist - HSCIC **Prod** - HSCIC 1986

Respiratory Systems in Animals 14 MIN
U-matic / VHS / 16mm
Animal Systems Series
Color (H C)
LC 70-717742
Compares the respiratory systems of a variety of phyla, examining the intake of oxygen by gills, membranes and lungs.
Science - Natural
Dist - IU **Prod** - IU 1971

Respiratory systems in animals 14 MIN
VHS
Color; PAL (H)
Shows the movement of oxygen and carbon dioxide across a moist permeable membrane in paramecia. Demonstrates the evolution of transport systems for movement of materials in larger animals through the example of an earthworm. Exhibits the spiracles and tracheal system of a grasshopper, the gills of the axolotl, clam, crayfish and fish. Examines the respiratory systems of frogs and mammals.
Science - Natural
Dist - VIEWTH

Respiratory therapy - an introduction for nurses - 3 11 MIN
VHS
Nursing skills series
Color (C PRO G)
$395.00 purchase _ #R930 - VI - 022
Shows how respiratory therapists work in collaboration with nurses to provide quality patient care. Reveals that when a respiratory therapist is not available, nurses must assume the responsibility for administering respiratory treatment and delivering oxygen. Familiarizes nurses with the basic equipment of oxygen delivery and its recommended use. Part of a three - part series on nursing skills produced by Lander Univ Nursing Education, Greenwood, South Carolina.
Health and Safety
Dist - HSCIC

Respiratory Therapy - Basic Principles of Ventilators 12 MIN
VHS / U-matic
Anesthesiology Clerkship Series
Color (PRO)
Describes the classification of the commonly available positive pressure ventilators. Considers the relationship between ventilator characteristics and pulmonary gas exchange.
Health and Safety
Dist - UMICHM **Prod** - UMICHM 1982

Respiratory Therapy - Clinical Applications of Mechanical Ventilators 40 MIN
VHS / U-matic
Anesthesiology Clerkship Series
Color (PRO)
Discusses the clinical use of positive pressure ventilators. Describes the types of patients requiring mechanical ventilation. Discusses both invasive and noninvasive monitoring. Considers methods of weaning from ventilator support.
Health and Safety; Science - Natural
Dist - UMICHM **Prod** - UMICHM 1982

Respiratory Therapy - Humidity Aerosol Treatment 16 MIN
U-matic / VHS
Anesthesiology Clerkship Series
Color (PRO)
Defines both relative and absolute humidity and the calculation of humidity deficit. Indicates the differences between humidifiers and nehulizers, and describes their advantages and disadvantages in clinical use.
Health and Safety
Dist - UMICHM **Prod** - UMICHM 1982

Respiratory therapy in the home 25 MIN
VHS
Color (PRO C G)
$195.00 purchase, $70.00 rental _ #4386
Discusses the important information that nursing professionals need to provide safe care for patients with chronic respiratory problems who are dependent on supplemental oxygen in their home. Covers checking equipment, proper storage and correct rate flow. Compares the benefits and shortcomings of various oxygen delivery systems - compressed oxygen, liquid oxygen and oxygen concentrators. Shows patients using the various systems. Illustrates how to alleviate patient anxiety and stresses the role of the nurse in ensuring the safe use of oxygen in the home.
Health and Safety
Dist - AJN **Prod** - BELHAN

Respiratory Therapy - Oxygen Administration 15 MIN
U-matic / VHS
Anesthesiology Clerkship Series
Color (PRO)
Discusses equipment available for the administration of oxygen therapy. Provides guidelines for the clinical use of this equipment in patients requiring various inspired oxygen concentrations.
Health and Safety
Dist - UMICHM **Prod** - UMICHM 1982

Respiratory Tract 11 MIN
U-matic
Microanatomy Laboratory Orientation Series
Color (C)
Covers the respiratory tract starting at the level of the trachea and continuing downward to the pulmonary alveoli.
Health and Safety; Science - Natural
Dist - UOKLAH **Prod** - UOKLAH 1986

The Respiratory Tract 30 MIN
VHS / U-matic
Color
Presents the respiratory system and how it works. Discusses the problems of pneumonia, puncture, emphysema and air pollution. Looks at how individuals can protect their respiratory system.
Health and Safety; Science - Natural
Dist - AL **Prod** - UILCCC

Respite - because it's right 13 MIN
VHS
Color (G)
$15.00 purchase
Educates the public about the need for and benefits of respite services for families with children who have disabilities.
Health and Safety; Sociology
Dist - TRRN

Respite - taking care 22 MIN
U-matic / VHS
Color (G)
$195.00 purchase, $50.00 rental _ #AB067
Documents four families with diverse situations and needs who have chosen to care for their elderly relatives at home. Shows them managing the burden with the help of community respite services, which include family support groups, adult day - care, in - home respite and institution - based respite service. Produced by Jane Feinberg.
Health and Safety; Sociology
Dist - FANPRO **Prod** - FANPRO

Respond - on - Site Assistance 23 MIN
16mm
Color
LC 74-706390
Designed to motivate local government officials to participate in on - site assistance. Shows how a Federal - State team surveys local government agencies to check their emergency readiness plans and procedures.
Civics and Political Systems; Health and Safety
Dist - USNAC **Prod** - USDCPA 1974

Respondent learning 10 MIN
U-matic / VHS
Protocol materials in teacher education - the process of teaching'- Pt 2 series
Color (T)
Education; Psychology
Dist - MSU **Prod** - MSU

Responding 6 MIN
U-matic / VHS
Color (C A)
Portrays hetorosexual, bisexual, and homosexual lovemaking. Conveys that human lovemaking is essentially the same regardless of sexual orientation.
Health and Safety; Psychology; Sociology
Dist - MMRC **Prod** - MMRC

Responding at appropriate levels 29 MIN
Videoreel / VT2
Interpersonal competence - Unit 02 - communication series; Unit 2 - Communication
Color (C A)
Features a humanistic psychologist who, by analysis and examples, discusses responding at appropriate levels.
Psychology
Dist - TELSTR **Prod** - MVNE 1973

Responding Positively to Change 30 MIN
VHS / U-matic
High Performance Leadership Series
Color
Psychology
Dist - DELTAK **Prod** - VIDAI

Responding to a Baby's Actions 24 MIN
U-matic / VHS
B&W (PRO)
Follows adults interacting with babies, as in imitating the baby's sounds, exploring toys with baby, joining in game baby has started. Presents three un - narrated examples of interaction for group discussions.
Education; Psychology; Sociology
Dist - HSERF **Prod** - HSERF

Responding to Learner's Needs 15 MIN
VHS / 16mm
Focus on Adult Learners Series
Color (C)
$150.00 purchase _ #270602
Combines dramatizations of teaching situations, interviews with exemplary adult instructors, footage of adult education classrooms and voice - over narration. Includes a print support manual which summarizes the key points of each program, recommends further reading and assigns exercises for both individual and group use. 'Responding To Learner's Needs' focuses on the characteristics and special needs of adult learners. Explores the role of adult education and the instructor's role as facilitator. Discusses learning theory, including learner expectations and motivation. Models an eight - stage learning process.
Education; Guidance and Counseling; Mathematics; Psychology
Dist - ACCESS **Prod** - ACCESS 1987

Responding to light 29 MIN
VHS
Photographic vision series
Color (G)
$49.95 purchase _ #RM105V-F
Examines the effects of available light on photography. Presents the technical aspects of photography clearly and simply, including principles of the camera and techniques for controlling exposure, the use of various kinds of lighting, selection of appropriate lenses and film and basic darkroom techniques. Focuses on the world of photographers and photography - its history and evolution, its uses for personal development and expression, and the impact of photography on the world. Part of a 20-part series examining all aspects of the field of photography.
Industrial and Technical Education
Dist - CAMV

Responding to Light 30 MIN
U-matic / VHS
Photographic Vision - all about Photography Series
Color
Industrial and Technical Education
Dist - CDTEL **Prod** - COAST

Responding to New Incentives - the Role of Hospital Managers 20 MIN
VHS / U-matic
Color
Helps hospital managers look at new ways of getting the job done in response to changing financial incentives. Examines examples of hospital - wide changes that have been implemented to achieve increased cost - effectiveness and efficiency.
Business and Economics; Health and Safety
Dist - AHOA **Prod** - AHOA

Responding to the handicapped 26 MIN
VHS
Color (G)
$89.95 purchase _ #UW2361
Shows how handicapped people have to deal both with their handicaps and with people who respond to them with fear, embarrassment or condescension. Opens a path of awareness that can enable viewers to respond more easily to handicapped people.
Health and Safety; Psychology; Social Science
Dist - FOTH

Response 1 20 MIN
U-matic
Challenge to Science Series
Color (J H C)
Reveals the inventions of students who have developed a wind generator, solar heat collectors and storage units and a Minto wheel.
Industrial and Technical Education; Science; Social Science
Dist - TVOTAR **Prod** - TVOTAR 1985

Response 2 20 MIN
U-matic
Challenge to Science Series
Color (J H C)
Reveals the inventions of students who have developed an electric car, a flywheel and two fuel cells.
Industrial and Technical Education; Science; Social Science
Dist - TVOTAR **Prod** - TVOTAR 1985

Response 3 20 MIN
U-matic
Challenge to Science Series
Color (J H C)
Reveals the inventions of students who have developed alternative energy production and conservation items. Inventions include a sawdust burner, a Stirling heat machine and a proposal for standardized bottles.
Industrial and Technical Education; Science; Social Science
Dist - TVOTAR **Prod** - TVOTAR 1985

Response 4 20 MIN
U-matic
Challenge to Science Series
Color (J H C)
Reveals the inventions of students who have developed new ideas for land use, including improving existing farms and designing a highrise solar or methane heated greenhouse complex.
Agriculture; Science
Dist - TVOTAR **Prod** - TVOTAR 1985

Response 5 20 MIN
U-matic
Challenge to Science Series
Color (J H C)
Reveals the inventions of students who have developed underground dwellings and energy efficient homes and living complexes.
Fine Arts; Industrial and Technical Education; Science; Social Science
Dist - TVOTAR **Prod** - TVOTAR 1985

Response 6 20 MIN
U-matic
Challenge to Science Series
Color (J H C)
Reveals the ideas of students for collecting, storing and using solar energy.
Fine Arts; Industrial and Technical Education; Science; Social Science
Dist - TVOTAR **Prod** - TVOTAR 1985

Response 7 20 MIN
U-matic
Challenge to Science Series
Color (J H C)
Reveals the inventions of students who have developed a methane generator, an attempt to make paper from potatoes, an innovative greenhouse design and a garbage separation plant.
Industrial and Technical Education; Science
Dist - TVOTAR **Prod** - TVOTAR 1985

Response 8 20 MIN
U-matic
Challenge to Science Series
Color (J H C)
Reveals the inventions of students who have developed a new use for laser beams, a robot that helps with homework, a model for using sea energy and experiments with garlic.
Science
Dist - TVOTAR **Prod** - TVOTAR 1985

Response of a Resonant System to a Frequency Step 12 MIN
16mm
National Committee for Electrical Engineering Film Series
B&W (C)
LC 70-702545
A computer pantomime motion picture designed to be used as a teaching aid in demonstrating fundamental concepts relevant to linear system theory and frequency modulation. Illustrates the role of transients in providing a smooth transition between initial and final steady - state conditions using rotating phasors to portray the envelope and phase of modulated signals.
Industrial and Technical Education; Science - Physical
Dist - EDC **Prod** - EDS 1968

Response of a Resonant System to a Frequency Step 11 MIN
Videoreel / VHS
B&W
Presents a computer - generated film that visualizes fundamental concepts relevant to linear system theory and frequency modulation.
Science - Physical
Dist - EDC **Prod** - NCEEF

Response of Linear Systems to White Noise Inputs - Continuous Time Case 52 MIN
U-matic / VHS
Modern Control Theory - Stochastic Estimation Series
Color (PRO)
Industrial and Technical Education; Mathematics
Dist - MIOT **Prod** - MIOT

Response of Linear Systems to White Noise Inputs - Discrete Time Case 46 MIN
VHS / U-matic
Modern Control Theory - Stochastic Estimation Series
Color (PRO)
Industrial and Technical Education; Mathematics
Dist - MIOT **Prod** - MIOT

Response to Mechanical Shock 18 MIN
16mm
Color
LC 70-700217
Illustrates several types of mechanical shock, showing the shock signature generated by each. Defines and explains the interdependence of the parameters of mechanical shock - - acceleration, velocity and displacement. Tells how different degrees of damping affect the motion of the spring - mass system during shock response.
Science - Physical
Dist - USNAC **Prod** - USNRC 1968

Response to Misbehavior 9 MIN
U-matic / VHS / 16mm
Moral Decision Making Series
Color (I J)
LC 72-702676
Gives students an opportunity to evaluate and discuss possible choices of action in the area of responsibility.
Guidance and Counseling; Sociology
Dist - AIMS **Prod** - MORLAT 1972

Response to the Challenge 30 MIN
16mm
Color (H C)
Presents a speech by Bob Richards, twice Olympic pole vault champion. Outlines the problems confronting society and gives a description of the ways persons must respond to these problems. Motivates the individual into positive action.
Guidance and Counseling; Physical Education and Recreation; Psychology; Sociology
Dist - NINEFC **Prod** - GEMILL

Response to the environment - cont - Unit 6 and Support, movement and behaviour - Unit 7 - Cassette 8 58 MIN
VHS
Advanced biology - ABAL - series
Color; PAL (J H T)
PdS29.50 purchase
Continues with On seeing and kicking a football. Presents unit 7 with Behavior for survival; The mechanisms of memory; and The display of the Siamese Fighting Fish. Features part eight of a ten - part series focusing on the English biology syllabi and offering support for the teaching of 'A' level biology. Complete set of ABAL worksheets available on request.
Science; Science - Natural
Dist - EMFVL

Responsibile Assertion 28 MIN
16mm / U-matic / VHS
Color (H C A)
Tells that people who are insufficiently assertive find themselves continually manipulated by others, frustrated in their desires and aspirations and even emotionally incapacitated because of their inhibitions. Reveals that effective assertion training demonstrates that although such training is not intended to cure behavioral dysfunction, it can be a potent coping mechanism for most individuals who learn to use it responsibly.
Psychology
Dist - MEDIAG **Prod** - WILEYJ 1978

Responsibilities and Rewards of Parenting 30 MIN
16mm / U-matic / VHS
Look at Me Series
Color (C A)
Summarizes the importance of a parent's role and traces the issues that arise in most parent - child relationships. Narrated by Phil Donahue.
Guidance and Counseling; Home Economics; Psychology; Sociology
Dist - FI **Prod** - WTTWTV 1980

Responsibilities of Configuration Managment 60 MIN
BETA / VHS
Manufacturing Series
(IND)
Explains how configuration managment is implemented.
Business and Economics
Dist - COMSRV **Prod** - COMSRV 1986

Responsibilities of the Contracting Officer 10 MIN
16mm
Color
LC 74-706391
Discusses contracts, purchase orders and unilateral agreements in business.
Business and Economics; Civics and Political Systems
Dist - USNAC **Prod** - USFSS 1966

Responsibility 27 MIN
VHS
Sunshine factory series
Color (P I R)
$14.99 purchase _ #35 - 83554 - 533
Features P J the repairman and kids in his neighborhood as they travel to the Sunshine Factory, a land populated by puppets, a computer and caring adults. Teaches a Biblically - based lesson on responsibility.
Religion and Philosophy
Dist - APH **Prod** - WORD

Responsibility
VHS / U-matic
School Inservice Videotape Series
Color (T)
Presents Dr Ed Frierson lecturing on how to help students develop personal responsibility. Contains three videotapes.
Education; Psychology
Dist - SLOSSF **Prod** - TERRAS

Responsibility 22 MIN
VHS
Fresh talk series
Color (H)
$150.00 purchase, $40.00 rental
Discusses the influence of pornography; pregnancy and parenting; communication; safer sex; sexually transmitted diseases and AIDS. Helps young people develop critical attitudes about the sexual messages in pop culture, learn how to articulate their own sexual feelings and how to communicate them effectively and with respect for others. Part of a four - part series featuring thirty young men and women, ages 15 - 24, who share their reflections on sexuality and growing up. After one or more interviews in any segment, video may be stopped to enable discussion. Directed by Teresa Marshall and Craig Berggold. Study guide available.
Health and Safety; Psychology; Sociology
Dist - CNEMAG

Responsibility 30 MIN
U-matic / VHS
Effective listening series; Tape 2
Color
Discusses the responsibility of both the sender and receiver in personal communication. Looks at the communication circle from the listener's point of view.
English Language
Dist - TELSTR **Prod** - TELSTR

Responsibility and affirmations - 7
VHS
From behind the mask series
Color (J H G)
$129.00 purchase
Presents part seven of a seven - part series filmed in a drug and alcohol rehabilitation center. Discusses the role of taking responsibility for self and the use of positive affirmations in recovery from addictive behavior. Depicts in detail the first steps taken by real people toward recovery from addiction. Produced by Visions Video Productions.
Guidance and Counseling; Health and Safety; Psychology
Dist - MEDIAI

Responsibility for teens 19 MIN
VHS / U-matic
Teen - family life series
Color (J H G)
$179.00, $229.00 purchase, $60.00 rental
Focuses on ways parents can help teenagers take responsibility for all aspects of their life. Includes the rationale for responsibile parenting, different tasks that teenagers are capable of taking on at different ages and strategies to help teens identify and complete their tasks.
Psychology; Sociology
Dist - NDIM **Prod** - FAMLIF 1993

Responsibility for the Future 27 MIN
U-matic / VHS / 16mm
Of Energy, Minerals, and Man Series
Color (J H A)
Examines the consequences of decimating the earth's resources, both mineral and biological.
Science - Natural; Social Science; Sociology
Dist - JOU **Prod** - GAZEL

Responsibility Shared - Autonomous Production Groups 28 MIN
VHS / U-matic
Re - Making of Work Series

Color (C A)
Offers examples of businesses that are being run by their employees. Describes how motivation and profits increase when employees organize and impose their own regulations.
Business and Economics; Sociology
Dist - EBEC

Responsibility - the Gang and I 14 MIN
U-matic / VHS / 16mm
Color (I J)
LC 78-700264
Relates the recollections of David, who tries to convince himself that being part of a gang when he was younger was the only way. Shows David slowly coming to see the irresponsibility and lack of concern for others in the gang's selfish and sometimes dangerous acts.
Guidance and Counseling; Sociology
Dist - AIMS **Prod** - AIMS 1977

Responsibility - the Key to Freedom 30 MIN
U-matic / VHS
Personal Development and Professional Growth - Mike McCaffrey's 'Focus Seminar Series
Color
Psychology
Dist - DELTAK **Prod** - DELTAK

Responsibility to Act 19 MIN
16mm
Color (A)
Uses the story of a tragic school fire to emphasize people's responsibility to spot hazards and eliminate them.
Health and Safety
Dist - VISUCP **Prod** - VISUCP 1981

Responsibility - Work or Home 15 MIN
16mm
Discussion Series
B&W (A)
LC 72-701677
Deals with how far company loyalty should go and where the dividing line between work obligations and home stands. Explains when one's job should take priority over family and when family comes before the job.
Religion and Philosophy
Dist - CPH **Prod** - CPH 1962

Responsible assertion 28 MIN
16mm / VHS
Color (C G PRO)
$495.00 purchase, $22.50 rental _ #32464
Defines assertive behavior and demonstrates procedures that promote the development of assertive skills. Examines nonassertive, assertive and aggressive styles in a confrontation between a student and her advisor, providing a basis for the discussion by Patricia Jakubowski of the cognitive and behavioral aspects of assertiveness. Arthur Lange conducts a training workshop illustrating cognitive restructuring and behavioral rehearsal.
Psychology; Sociology
Dist - PSU **Prod** - BAXMED 1978

Responsible Assertion - a Model for Personal Growth 28 MIN
16mm
Color
Demonstrates the different consequences of nonassertive, aggressive and assertive behaviors by using dramatic scenes of a graduate student confronting her advisor about the demanding requirements of her assistantship.
Psychology
Dist - RESPRC **Prod** - RESPRC

Responsible caring series

Adrianne' man	4 MIN
Boy's Don't do that	6 MIN
Wayne's Decision	6 MIN
What's to Understand	4 MIN

Dist - MEMAPP

The Responsible Consumer 29 MIN
16mm / U-matic / VHS
A Be a Better Shopper Series Program 13; Program 13
Color (H C A)
LC 81-701470
Deals with consumers' responsibilities, both to themselves in terms of getting the best food buy, and to society in terms of dealing fairly and honestly in the marketplace.
Home Economics
Dist - CORNRS **Prod** - CUETV 1978

Responsible Feedback, Pt 1 15 MIN
VHS / U-matic
Protocol Materials in Teacher Education - Interpersonal 'Communication Skills Series
Color (T)
Education; Psychology
Dist - MSU **Prod** - MSU

Responsible Feedback, Pt 2 15 MIN
U-matic / VHS
Protocol Materials in Teacher Education - Interpersonal 'Communication Skills Series
Color (T)
Education; Psychology
Dist - MSU **Prod** - MSU

The Responsible Hunter 23 MIN
VHS / 16mm
(G A)
$250.00 purchase _ #AG - 5540F
Develops responsible hunting attitudes and actions by forcing people to question their behavior and its impact on hunting.
Health and Safety; Physical Education and Recreation
Dist - CORF **Prod** - FILCOM 1984

The Responsible hunter 23 MIN
VHS
Color (H A G)
$120.00 purchase _ #PP104
Promotes responsible, ethical hunting. Examines the issues of posting land, trespassing, and the importance of the hunter - landowner relationship.
Business and Economics; Physical Education and Recreation; Science - Natural; Social Science
Dist - AAVIM **Prod** - AAVIM

The Responsible Level 40 MIN
U-matic / VHS
Management by Responsibility Series
Color
Psychology
Dist - DELTAK **Prod** - TRAINS

Responsible persons 15 MIN
VHS / U-matic / 16mm
Think it through with Winnie the Pooh series
Color (P I)
$400.00, $280.00 purchase _ #JC - 67191
Promotes self - esteem and building interpersonal skills. Uses live action, Puppetronics characters to show how to become 'people you can count on to come through.' Stresses the need to form positive peer groups, accept differences in people and that failing at a task does not mean failing as a person. Part of the Thinking It Through with Winnie the Pooh series.
Fine Arts; Psychology
Dist - CORF **Prod** - DISNEY 1989

Responsible Pricing of Services
VHS / U-matic
Revenues, Rates and Reimbursements Series
Color
Explains pricing health care services with financial survival in mind. Illustrates the five financing requirements basic to all successful pricing structures, direct expenses, indirect expenses, working capital, capital and profit.
Business and Economics; Health and Safety
Dist - TEACHM **Prod** - TEACHM

Responsive Health Care - One Patient's Search 34 MIN
VHS / U-matic
Color (PRO)
Describes a man's positive and negative experiences while seeking diagnosis through a maze of medical specialties and undergoing subsequent treatment for a brain tumor. Views a life - threatening illness from a patient's perspective, covering such topics as pre - surgical fears, postoperative confusion, social support systems, heightened sense of vulnerability and altered body image.
Health and Safety; Psychology
Dist - UMICHM **Prod** - UMICHM 1984

The Responsive Parenting Program 30 MIN
16mm
Color (C A)
LC 78-701609
Focuses on a parent training program in Kansas, in which parents learn to use positive behavior management techniques to improve the management of their children and the general quality of their homelife.
Psychology; Sociology
Dist - UKANS **Prod** - UKANS 1978

Responsive to the amazing grace of God 60 MIN
VHS
Guidelines for growing spiritually mature series
Color (R G)
$49.95 purchase _ #GGSM6
Challenges Christians in today's world to hear anew and respond joyfully to the universal call to holiness. Focuses on one phase of the journey to maturity in the spiritual sense. Offers guidelines according to the teachings of the Roman Catholic Church. Features Dr Susan Muto and the Rev Adrian Van Kaam. Part six of six parts.
Religion and Philosophy
Dist - CTNA **Prod** - CTNA

Rest and Leisure in the USSR 14 MIN
U-matic / VHS / 16mm
Russian Language Series
Color (H C) (RUSSIAN)
A Russian language film. Views the way Soviet citizens enjoy leisure activities.
Foreign Language
Dist - IFB **Prod** - IFB 1963

The Rest of Your Life 28 MIN
16mm / U-matic / VHS
Color (H C A)
LC FIA68-3152
Identifies and examines some of the problems related to retirement. Raises pertinent questions and explains the need for planning for retirement.
Psychology; Sociology
Dist - JOU **Prod** - ALTSUL 1967

Restarts of beads 13 MIN
U-matic / VHS
Electric arc welding series; Chap 8
Color (IND)
Education; Industrial and Technical Education
Dist - TAT **Prod** - TAT

Restaurant 30 MIN
VHS
How do you do - learning English series
Color (H A)
#317710
Shows how CHIPS learns about food, setting a table, cutlery and microwave ovens. Teaches words and expressions associated with restaurant dining. Part of a series that helps newcomers learn English or improve their ability. Includes viewer's guide with grammar explanations and vocabulary drills, worksheets and two audio cassettes.
English Language; Home Economics
Dist - TVOTAR **Prod** - TVOTAR 1990

Resting Metabolic Heart Rate 17 MIN
VHS / 16mm
Nutrition and Dietetics Laboratory Series
Color (H C A)
Provides a thorough understanding of the heart rate and how to conduct this measurement, which is frequently required in health science research and practice.
Health and Safety; Science - Natural
Dist - IOWA **Prod** - IOWA 1987

Restless 12 MIN
16mm
Color (G)
$35.00 rental
Explores Iceland, perpetually in a state of continuing creation which manifests itself in hot springs, steam eruption and geysers. Views the vast expanses, strange rock formations, countless rivers, cascades and glaciers, along with skies laden with moisture and eerie twilights.
Fine Arts; Geography - World
Dist - CANCIN **Prod** - ZDRAVI 1987
FLMKCO

The Restless atmosphere - 4 60 MIN
VHS
Land, location and culture - a geographical synthesis series
Color (J H C)
$89.95 purchase _ #WLU104
Continues the study of the physical earth through the creation of an increasingly complex model of the circulation of the earth's atmosphere. Leads to an examination of weather patterns and, ultimately, climate. Introduces the notion of climate change and human - induced climate change. Examines the more substantial impact of the greenhouse effect following a brief look at the modest changes people have brought about within cities. Considers the sources, consequences and potential strategies for dealing with the greenhouse effect. Part of a 12 - part series.
Geography - World; Science - Physical
Dist - INSTRU

The Restless City Speaks 15 MIN
16mm
B&W (H C A)
Studies complexities of life in a vast urban area, showing their causes and effects.
Psychology; Science - Natural; Social Science; Sociology
Dist - WSUM **Prod** - WSUM 1958

The Restless conscience 113 MIN
VHS
Color (G)
$39.95 purchase _ #10015
Explores the motivating principles and activities of anti - Nazi resistance inside Germany from 1933 to 1945. Highlights the tension between responsibility to personal ethical codes and a tyrannical political system. Produced by Haya Kohav Beller. For home use only.

Civics and Political Systems; History - World
Dist - USHMC

The Restless Earth - Earthquakes 26 MIN
16mm / U-matic / VHS
Restless Earth Series
Color (H C A)
LC 73-701725
Examines theories explaining causes of earthquake and methods of 'Defusing' earthquakes.
Science - Physical
Dist - IU **Prod** - WNETTV 1972

The Restless Earth - Evidence from Ancient Life 11 MIN
16mm / U-matic / VHS
Restless Earth Series
Color (H C A)
LC 73-701724
Presents the relationships between the evolution of plant and animal life and the history of our changing earth. Explains that some species of worms are known to be 600 million years old and some plant life dates back 3,400 million years.
Science - Physical
Dist - IU **Prod** - WNETTV 1972

The Restless Earth - Geology and Man 19 MIN
U-matic / VHS / 16mm
Restless Earth Series
Color (H C A)
LC 73-701726
Explains that life began to evolve more than 100 million years ago, but at man's present rate of consumption and waste production, his effect on future geological history is yet to be determined.
Business and Economics; Science - Natural; Science - Physical; Social Science
Dist - IU **Prod** - WNETTV 1973

The Restless Earth - Plate Tectonics Theory 58 MIN
U-matic / VHS / 16mm
Restless Earth Series
Color (H C A)
LC 73-701723
Explains plate theory through the use of models, examining scientific experiments and visiting geological sites throughout the world.
Science - Physical
Dist - IU **Prod** - WNETTV 1973

The Restless Earth - Plate Tectonics Theory, Pt 1 29 MIN
U-matic / VHS / 16mm
Restless Earth Series
Color (H C A)
LC 73-701723
Explains plate theory through the use of models, examining scientific experiments and visiting geological sites throughout the world.
Science - Physical
Dist - IU **Prod** - WNETTV 1973

The Restless Earth - Plate Tectonics Theory, Pt 2 29 MIN
16mm / U-matic / VHS
Restless Earth Series
Color (H C A)
LC 73-701723
Explains plate theory through the use of models, examining scientific experiments and visiting geological sites throughout the world.
Science - Physical
Dist - IU **Prod** - WNETTV 1973

Restless Earth Series

The Restless Earth - Earthquakes	26 MIN
The Restless Earth - Evidence from Ancient Life	11 MIN
The Restless Earth - Geology and Man	19 MIN
The Restless Earth - Plate Tectonics Theory	58 MIN
The Restless Earth - Plate Tectonics Theory, Pt 1	29 MIN
The Restless Earth - Plate Tectonics Theory, Pt 2	29 MIN

Dist - IU

The Restless Earth - Understanding the Theory of Plate Tectonics 43 MIN
U-matic / VHS
Color
LC 81-706668
Describes the theory of plate tectonics and explains where the material comes from to create a new ocean floor. Explains the source of the force which is able to move continents and change the contours of the ocean floors.
Science - Physical
Dist - GA **Prod** - SCIMAN 1981

The Restless Ocean of Air 20 MIN
16mm
Science Twenty Series
Color (I J T)
LC 73-704162
Shows a student participation film in which students are challenged to form their own answers to the question 'What makes the air so restless.'.
Science - Physical
Dist - SF **Prod** - PRISM 1969

The Restless Ones 105 MIN
16mm
Color
Presents a portrayal of today's teenagers, set to the heartbeat of their trials and triumphs.
Guidance and Counseling; Psychology
Dist - NINEFC **Prod** - WWP

The Restless Sea 36 MIN
16mm / U-matic / VHS
Color (J H)
LC 79-700818
A revised version of the 1964 motion picture The Restless Sea. Uses animation to examine various aspects of the sea, including waves and tides, marine life, erosion of land, the nature of the sea bottom, analysis of sea water and tracing of storms.
Science - Natural; Science - Physical
Dist - CORF **Prod** - DISNEY 1979

The Restless Sky 28 MIN
VHS
Color (S)
$129.00 purchase _ #386 - 9031
Uses the very latest in scientific technology to create stunning visuals and sound to unveil the mysterious inner workings of clouds. Illustrates for the first time a cloud droplet increasing a millionfold to form a single raindrop, and the microscopic processes that create rain, ice, lightning, snow and hail.
Science - Physical
Dist - FI **Prod** - CANBC 1988

The Restless Spirit 35 MIN
BETA / VHS
Color
Contains two of Fred Bear's most famous hunts including his Buffalo hunt in Africa.
Physical Education and Recreation; Science - Natural
Dist - HOMEAF **Prod** - HOMEAF

Restoration 30 MIN
VHS
Tom Keating on painters series
Color (J H C G)
$195.00 purchase
Focuses on restoration art. Features Tom Keating who recreates the style of restoration exactly the way the original work was done and gives biographical information about artists of that era. Part of a six - part series on painters.
Fine Arts
Dist - LANDMK **Prod** - LANDMK 1987

Restoration and Augustan Poetry 28 MIN
U-matic / VHS
Survey of English Verse Series
Color (C)
$249.00, $149.00 purchase _ #AD - 1300
Features the intellectual satire of the Earl of Rochester, the literary and political satire of Dryden, Swift and Pope.
Fine Arts; Literature and Drama
Dist - FOTH **Prod** - FOTH

A Restoration drama 30 MIN
VHS
Human element series
Color; PAL (G)
PdS65 purchase; Not available in the United States or Canada
Presents two factions as they battle over how to conserve an ancient cathedral. Provides a human look at the world of science, showing that there is more to chemistry than meets the eye. Part five of a five - part series.
Fine Arts; Sociology
Dist - BBCENE

Restoration in Bedford Stuyvesant 15 MIN
16mm
Color
LC 77-700025
Focuses on efforts to improve the Bedford Stuyvesant neighborhood of Brooklyn, New York, using community resources and outside help.
Geography - United States; Social Science; Sociology
Dist - BEMPS **Prod** - BUGAS 1976
BUGAS

Restoration man 45 MIN
VHS
Situation vacant series
Color (A)
PdS65 purchase
Features the chief executive of the Royal Albert Hall interviewing candidates to find the right person to turn his restoration dreams into reality. Reveals that he shortlists 13 candidates, but after 20 hours of interviewing, rejects nine on the grounds that he can not work with them. Shows him embarking on reinterviewing the final four. Part of a six-part series looking at selection procedures for a wide range of jobs.
Education; Guidance and Counseling; Psychology
Dist - BBCENE

Restoration of a Class I Facial Pit Cavity Preparation with Amalgam 12 MIN
16mm
Restoration of Cavity Preparations with Amalgam and Tooth - Colored 'Materials Series
Color (PRO)
LC 75-702862
Demonstrates placing copal varnish, condensing, carving, burnishing, finishing and polishing an amalgam restoration in a manikin. Shows in a cross - sectional view, the causes and effects of improper and proper condensing. Presents four - handed procedures.
Health and Safety; Science
Dist - USNAC **Prod** - USBHRD 1974

Restoration of a Class I Occlusal Cavity Preparation with Amalgam 11 MIN
16mm
Restoration of Cavity Preparations with Amalgam and Tooth - Colored 'Materials Series
Color (PRO)
LC 75-702863
Demonstrates placing varnish, condensing, carving, burnishing, occlusal adjustment, finishing and polishing an amalgam restoration in a manikin. Shows four - handed procedures.
Health and Safety; Science
Dist - USNAC **Prod** - USBHRD 1974

Restoration of a Class I Occluso - Lingual Cavity Preparation with Amalgam 9 MIN
16mm
Restoration of Cavity Preparations with Amalgam and Tooth - Colored 'Materials Series
Color
LC 75-702864
Demonstrates placing a secondary metal matrix, condensing, carving, burnishing and polishing in a manikin. Shows four - handed procedures.
Health and Safety; Science
Dist - USNAC **Prod** - USBHRD 1974

Restoration of a Class II Mesio - Occlusal Cavity Preparation with Amalgam 18 MIN
16mm
Restoration of Cavity Preparations with Amalgam and Tooth - Colored 'Materials Series
Color (PRO)
LC 75-702865
Demonstrates condensing, carving, burnishing, occlusal adjustment, finishing and polishing an amalgam restoration in a manikin. Shows four - handed procedures.
Health and Safety; Science
Dist - USNAC **Prod** - USBHRD 1974

Restoration of a Class III Distal Cavity Preparation with Silicate Cement 10 MIN
16mm
Restoration of Cavity Preparations with Amalgam and Tooth - Colored 'Materials Series
Color (PRO)
LC 75-702866
Demonstrates placing a calcium hydroxide liner, adapting a plastic matrix strip, placing silicate cement using the bulk pack technic and finishing in a manikin. Shows four - handed procedures.
Health and Safety; Science
Dist - USNAC **Prod** - USBHRD 1974

Restoration of a Class III Disto - Lingual Cavity Preparation with Amalgam 18 MIN
16mm
Restoration of Cavity Preparations with Amalgam and Tooth - Colored 'Materials Series
Color (PRO)
LC 75-702867
Demonstrates placing varnish, preparing and placing a custom metal matrix strip, condensing, carving, burnishing, finishing and polishing an amalgam restoration in a manikin. Shows four - handed procedures.
Health and Safety; Science
Dist - USNAC **Prod** - USBHRD 1974

Restoration of a Class III Mesial Cavity Preparation with Filled Resin 10 MIN
16mm
Restoration of Cavity Preparations with Amalgam and Tooth - Colored 'Materials Series
Color (PRO)
LC 75-702868
Demonstrates placing calcium hydroxide liner, adapting a plastic matrix strip, placing filled resin with a syringe and finishing in a manikin. Shows four - handed procedures.
Health and Safety; Science
Dist - USNAC **Prod** - USBHRD 1974

Restoration of a Class IV Mesio - Incisal Cavity Preparation with Filled Resin 17 MIN
16mm
Restoration of Cavity Preparations with Amalgam and Tooth - Colored 'Materials Series
Color (PRO)
LC 75-702869
Demonstrates placing a dead soft metal matrix, placing a filled resin with a syringe, finishing and adjustment of occlusion in a manikin. Shows four - handed procedures.
Health and Safety; Science
Dist - USNAC **Prod** - USBHRD 1974

Restoration of a Class V Disto - Facial Cavity Preparation with Amalgam 15 MIN
16mm
Restoration of Cavity Preparations with Amalgam and Tooth - Colored 'Materials Series
Color (PRO)
LC 75-702870
Demonstrates placing a calcium hydroxide base, placing a custom metal matrix, condensing, carving, burnishing, finishing and polishing in a manikin. Shows four - handed procedures.
Health and Safety; Science
Dist - USNAC **Prod** - USBHRD 1974

Restoration of a Class V Facial Cavity Preparation with Amalgam 12 MIN
16mm
Restoration of Cavity Preparations with Amalgam and Tooth - Colored 'Materials Series
Color (PRO)
LC 75-702871
Demonstrates placing varnish, condensing, carving, finishing and polishing in a manikin. Emphasizes the polishing procedure with proper and improper technic. Shows four - handed procedures.
Health and Safety; Science
Dist - USNAC **Prod** - USBHRD 1974

Restoration of a Class V Facial Cavity Preparation with Unfilled Resin 11 MIN
16mm
Restoration of Cavity Preparations with Amalgam and Tooth - Colored 'Materials Series
Color (PRO)
LC 75-702872
Demonstrates placing calcium hydroxide liner, placing unfilled resin with the brush - in technique, finishing and polishing in a manikin. Shows four - handed procedures.
Health and Safety; Science
Dist - USNAC **Prod** - USBHRD 1974

Restoration of Cavity Preparation with Amalgam and Tooth - Colored Materials Series Module 11a
Temporary Restoration of a Class II Mesio - Occlusal Cavity Preparation with Zinc 10 MIN
Dist - USNAC

Restoration of cavity preparations with amalgam and tooth - colored materials series, Module 11b
Assembly of a matrix band and mechanical retainer 4 MIN
Dist - USNAC

Restoration of Cavity Preparations with Amalgam and Tooth - Colored Materials Series
Restoration of a class I facial pit cavity preparation with amalgam 12 MIN
Restoration of a class I occlusal cavity preparation with amalgam 11 MIN
Restoration of a class I occluso - lingual cavity preparation with amalgam 9 MIN
Restoration of a class II mesio - occlusal cavity preparation with amalgam 18 MIN
Restoration of a class III distal cavity preparation with silicate cement 10 MIN
Restoration of a class III disto - lingual cavity preparation with amalgam 18 MIN
Restoration of a class III mesial cavity preparation with filled resin 10 MIN
Restoration of a class IV mesio - incisal cavity preparation with filled resin 17 MIN
Restoration of a class V disto - facial cavity preparation with amalgam 15 MIN
Restoration of a class V facial cavity preparation with amalgam 12 MIN
Restoration of a class V facial cavity preparation with unfilled resin 11 MIN
Dist - USNAC

Restoration of Equestra in Statues at the Memorial Bridge Plaza 16 MIN
16mm
Color (J)
LC 74-701403
Examines the techniques used in the restoration of the equestra in statues at Memorial Bridge Plaza in Washington, DC. Follows the entire restoration process of two statues from the initial cleaning to the final application of gold using the brush electroplating technique.
History - United States; Industrial and Technical Education
Dist - USNBOS **Prod** - USNBOS 1972

Restoration of lost corners by proportionate measurement 90 MIN
U-matic / VHS
Color (A PRO)
$150.00, $245.00 purchase _ #TCA17967, #TCA17966
Covers proportionate measurement as a method for surveyors to restore lost corners. Describes the legal background for using such methods, and points out situations where the method can and can't be used. Student workbooks are available at an extra charge.
Civics and Political Systems; Health and Safety; Industrial and Technical Education; Social Science
Dist - USNAC

The Restoration of the Nightwatch 26 MIN
U-matic / VHS
Color (J A)
Shows the months of effort necessary to restore a famous Rembrandt painting after it was seriously damaged.
Fine Arts
Dist - SUTHRB **Prod** - SUTHRB

Restore breathing - mouth - to - mouth resuscitation 6 MIN
U-matic / VHS
EMT video - group three series
Color (PRO)
Presents methods for determining when mouth - to - mouth resuscitation is required, how it is administered and how to stop the procedure.
Health and Safety
Dist - USNAC **Prod** - USA 1979

Restore breathing - opening the airway 8 MIN
U-matic / VHS
EMT video - group three series
Color (PRO)
LC 84-706484
Describes procedures for positioning the patient, checking for injuries, selecting the method, and properly opening the airway. Illustrates head tilt, thumb jaw lift, two - hand jaw lift, and modified jaw thrust methods. Also describes how to resuscitate an unconscious, nonbreathing patient by first attempting mouth - to - mouth resuscitation, and then by using the oral pharyngeal airway (j - tube).
Health and Safety
Dist - USNAC **Prod** - USA 1983

Restoring Harmony in Marriage 28 MIN
16mm
Christian Home Series no 8; No 8
Color
LC 73-701560
Presents the advice of personal and marriage counselor Henry Brandt that an effective marriage relationship contains no competition. Points out hindrances to cooperation between couples and guidelines for them to follow.
Psychology; Religion and Philosophy; Sociology
Dist - CCFC **Prod** - CCFC 1972

Restoring Profitability to Farming 27 MIN
VHS
(C A)
$16.00 rental
Discusses the importance of farm advisers, the Mediterranean fruit fly, agriculture and the media, newcomers to farming, financing a farm, Federal Crop Insurance program, federal disaster payments, federal tax package and what it means to farmers, increasing productivity, research, Cooperative Extension, conserving farm lands, export, and inflation. Features USDA Secretary John Block.
Agriculture
Dist - CORNRS **Prod** - CORNRS 1981

Restoring Scotland's native trees - episode 2 25 MIN
VHS
Spirit of trees series
Color (G)
$195.00 purchase, $50.00 rental
Visits the Scottish Highlands which serve as a case study of how throughout the world today we are in danger of losing our ancient woodlands of native trees. Explains how deforestation can be reversed and proper forest management can be implemented. Part of an eight - part series on trees and their relationship with the world around them. Hosted by environmentalist Dick Warner, who meets with conservationists, scientists, folklorists, woodsmen, seed collectors, forest rangers, wood turners and more.
Agriculture; Science - Natural; Social Science
Dist - CNEMAG

Restoring the Environment 26 MIN
U-matic / VHS
Color (C)
$249.00, $149.00 purchase _ #AD - 1868
Looks at how technology is being used to correct environmental problems created by technology. Shows the EPA's Oils and Hazardous Materials Spills branch where a mobile incinerator was developed for the destruction of PCBs and a private electroplating business which has developed a pollution control system which may save an entire industry while protecting the environment.
Business and Economics; Psychology; Science - Natural; Sociology
Dist - FOTH **Prod** - FOTH

Restoring the Environment 30 MIN
U-matic / VHS
Innovation Series
Color
Examines how technology can be helpful in alleviating the problems of pollution in the environment.
Science - Natural; Sociology
Dist - PBS **Prod** - WNETTV 1983

Restraining the Adult Patient 10 MIN
VHS / 16mm
(C)
$385.00 purchase _ #861VI056I
Takes a humanistic approach to the use of soft and locked restraints. Identifies and explains unsafe restraint practices.
Health and Safety
Dist - HSCIC **Prod** - HSCIC 1986

Restraint for Survival 8 MIN
16mm
Color
LC 74-705533
Demonstrates the life - saving potential of shoulder harnesses and seat belts. Documents FAA aeromedical research which simulates aircraft accidents using electronically outfitted 'Dummies.'.
Industrial and Technical Education; Social Science
Dist - USFAA **Prod** - FAAFL 1967

Restraints on technology access - employment agreements and protection of trade secrets 22 MIN
U-matic / VHS
Antitrust counseling and the marketing process series
Color (PRO)
Examines the legal opportunities and pitfalls associated with technology access and effective protection of trade secrets.
Business and Economics; Civics and Political Systems
Dist - ABACPE **Prod** - ABACPE

Restraints, Seclusion and a Demonstration of Applying Restraints 30 MIN
U-matic / VHS
Management and Treatment of the Violent Patient Series
Color
Illustrates the need for emergency rooms and psychiatric facilities to have practiced, effective non - assualtive team restraint procedures.
Health and Safety; Psychology
Dist - HEMUL **Prod** - HEMUL

Restricted U S and British Training Films - World War II 110 MIN
U-matic / VHS
B&W
Consists of six short films which are restricted U S and British training films used during World War II. Includes Parachute Training in the German Army, U - Boat Identification and others.
History - United States; Sociology
Dist - IHF **Prod** - IHF

Restriction endonucleases and variable number tandem repeats 84 MIN
VHS
DNA technology in forensic science series
Color (A PRO)
$50.00 purchase _ #TCA17405
Presents two lectures on DNA technology in forensic science. Covers subjects including restriction endonucleases action, nomenclature, difficulties associated with the use of these enzymes, variable number tandem repeats, and more.
Science - Natural; Sociology
Dist - USNAC **Prod** - FBI 1988

Restroom Cleaning Procedures 12 MIN
16mm
Housekeeping Personnel Series
Color (IND)
LC 73-701693
Presents the proper procedures and materials used in cleaning and maintaining a health care facility restroom.
Health and Safety; Home Economics
Dist - COPI **Prod** - COPI 1973

Restructuring America's schools 20 MIN
VHS
Restructuring series
Color (T C PRO)
$278.00 purchase, $120.00 rental _ #614 - 224X01
Visits schools exemplifying ambitious and promising approaches to restructuring. Travels to Littleton, Colorado, an inner - city school in Chicago and a rural school in Kentucky. Shows why school restructuring is necessary to prepare students to take their place in society and maintain a healthy economic and cultural future. Illustrates how restructuring focuses on teaching thinking and problem - solving skills that prepare students for the workplace; integrating curriculums to show connections among subjects; create learning experiences that enable students to be indepedent learners; assess student performance of skills and student ability to learn how to learn. Includes a leader's guide. Part of a series.
Education
Dist - AFSCD **Prod** - AFSCD 1991

Restructuring series
Explores how schools are changing their approaches to teaching and learning. Includes two videos, Restructuring America's Schools and Restructuring the High School - A Case Study, and two leader's guides.

Restructuring America's schools	20 MIN
Restructuring series	45 MIN
Restructuring the high school - a case study	25 MIN

Dist - AFSCD **Prod** - AFSCD 1991

Restructuring the high school - a case study 25 MIN
VHS
Restructuring series
Color (T C PRO)
$278.00 purchase, $120.00 rental _ #614 - 234X01
Focuses on Littleton High School in Colorado to illustrate successful change. Explores six aspects of school restructuring - determining the need for restructuring; ensuring districtwide support; implementing school - based decision making; establishing funding; communicating effectively; setting goals. Shows how to ensure that new initiatives meet student needs and why restructuring programs must vary from school to school. Includes a leader's guide. Part of a series.
Education
Dist - AFSCD **Prod** - AFSCD 1992

The Results of War - are We Making a Good Peace 52 MIN
VHS / 16mm
Europe, the Mighty Continent Series no 6; No 6
Color
LC 77-701561
Analyzes the considerations that affected the formulation of the Treaty of Versailles. Discusses the civil war and the counterrevolution in Russia.
History - World
Dist - TIMLIF **Prod** - BBCTV 1976

The Results of War - are We Making a Good Peace, Pt 1 26 MIN
U-matic
Europe, the Mighty Continent Series no 6; No 6
Color
LC 79-707421
Analyzes the considerations that affected the formulation of the Treaty of Versailles. Discusses the civil war and the counterrevolution in Russia.
Sociology
Dist - TIMLIF **Prod** - BBCTV 1976

The Results of War - are We Making a Good Peace, Pt 2 26 MIN
U-matic
Europe, the Mighty Continent Series no 6; No 6
Color
LC 79-707421
Analyzes the considerations that affected the formulation of the Treaty of Versailles. Discusses the civil war and the counterrevolution in Russia.
Sociology
Dist - TIMLIF **Prod** - BBCTV 1976

The Resume 15 MIN
U-matic
Job Seeking Series
Color (H C A)
Describes the successful resume.
Guidance and Counseling; Psychology
Dist - GPN **Prod** - WCETTV 1979

The Resume Experience 21 MIN
VHS / 16mm
Career Advantage Series
Color (G)
$89.00 purchase _ #PA126V
Presents the necessary elements of an effective resume. Suggests what shouldbe included in or left out of a resume. Examples given.
Guidance and Counseling; Psychology
Dist - JISTW

Resume Preparation 17 MIN
VHS / U-matic
Captioned; Color (S) (AMERICAN SIGN LANGUAGE)
Presents talk with student and placement counselor about how to prepare a resume.
Guidance and Counseling; Psychology
Dist - GALCO **Prod** - GALCO 1980

Resume preparation for displaced workers
VHS
Job search skills for displaced workers series
Color (G A)
$89.00 purchase _ #4216
Discusses the preparation of resumes for displaced workers seeking jobs. Offers a simple and convenient way for the unemployed to acquire the job search skills they need. Part of a three - part series.
Business and Economics; Guidance and Counseling
Dist - NEWCAR

Resume preparation for non - college bound women
VHS
Job search skills for non - college bound women series
Color (J H G)
$89.00 purchase _ #4386
Focuses on resumes for job - hunting women without a college education. Shows how the right attitude and some basic job search skills help. Part of three - part series.
Business and Economics; Guidance and Counseling; Sociology
Dist - NEWCAR

Resume ready 28 MIN
VHS
Color (H C G)
$99.00 purchase _ #JW0530V
Discusses resume format, the importance of choosing the right kind of paper. Teaches step - by - step techniques that can be used to individualize a resume and how to use resume style and appearance to set a resume apart. Includes the book The Resume Solution.
Business and Economics; Guidance and Counseling
Dist - CAMV **Prod** - JISTW 1993

Resume tips for women in non - traditional occupations
VHS
Job search skills for women in non - traditional occupations series
Color (J H G C)
$89.00 purchase _ #4432
Concentrates on preparing resumes for women in non - traditional occupations. Uses footage shot on location at actual women's opportunity centers. Part of a three - part series on breaking into occupations traditionally dominated by men.
Business and Economics; Guidance and Counseling; Sociology
Dist - NEWCAR

Resume Workshop - Pt 1 60 MIN
U-matic / VHS
B&W
Discusses and answers questions concerning resumes. Includes such topics as resume sections on education, field and volunteer experience, interests and references.
Guidance and Counseling; Sociology
Dist - UWISC **Prod** - UWISC 1979

Resume Workshop - Pt 2 12 MIN
U-matic / VHS
B&W
Continues a discussion on resume writing and what an employer looks for in a job application. Tells when to send resumes and where they should be sent and discusses responses to unfair questions and the use of cover letters.
Guidance and Counseling; Sociology
Dist - UWISC **Prod** - UWISC 1979

Resume Writing and Job Interviews 45 MIN
VHS / 16mm
Color (H C)
$125.00 purchase _ #AD1V
Examines all aspects of resume writing and job interviewing, including tracking job leads, arranging interviews and decision making.
Guidance and Counseling; Psychology
Dist - JISTW

Resumes and Interviews 60 MIN
VHS / U-matic
B&W
Discusses the tactics for handling two types of interviews. Demonstrates the difference between ineffectual and successful interviews.
Guidance and Counseling; Sociology
Dist - UWISC **Prod** - UWISC 1979

Resumes and job applications - a practical guide 27 MIN
35mm strip / VHS
Color (J H C)
$145.00, $129.00 purchase _ #2194 - SK, #480 - SK
Teaches teenagers how to create resumes and fill out job applications. Provides techniques for organizing and writing resumes, covering both functional and chronological resumes. Offers step - by - step instructions in filling out typical application forms. Includes teacher's guide.
Guidance and Counseling
Dist - SUNCOM **Prod** - SUNCOM

Resumes - Job Applications
VHS / 35mm strip
$119.00 purchase _ #SB480 for film, $139.00 purchase _ #SB2194V for VHS
Provides techniques for organizing one's work and personal experiences into a resume. Includes a Teacher's guide.
Business and Economics; Guidance and Counseling
Dist - CAREER **Prod** - CAREER

Resumes that Get Interviews - Interviews that Get Jobs
VHS
$219.00 purchase _ #IE6681V
Assists people who have little or no experience break into the job market. Discusses how to organize and write resumes and cover letters.
Business and Economics; Guidance and Counseling
Dist - CAREER **Prod** - CAREER

Resumes that Get Interviews - Interviews that Get Jobs
U-matic / VHS
(J H C)
$219.00 _ #GA200V
Provides instruction, for students with very limited job experience, on writing resumes, creating cover letters and conducting an effective interview. Features live action, and includes a teacher's guide and library kit.
Business and Economics; Education; Guidance and Counseling
Dist - CAMV **Prod** - CAMV

Resumes that get interviews - Interviews that get jobs
VHS
Color (H)
$219.00 purchase _ #06681 - 126
Shows students how to stress their training and potential in resumes and interviews. Gives specific information on how to organize and write effective resumes and cover letters. Presents helpful tips on how to conduct an interview. Covers questions that employers are likely to ask, suggests questions that students can ask about jobs and companies, explains what to avoid doing and saying. Shows how to use grooming and body language to advantage. Stresses the importance of follow - up after the initial interview. In four parts. Includes teacher's guide, library kit, 25 subscriptions to Time magazine for 12 weeks, 12 weekly guides.
Business and Economics; Guidance and Counseling; Psychology
Dist - GA **Prod** - GA 1992

Resurfacing Techniques 60 MIN
VHS
Handtools and Hardware Series

Color (PRO)
$600.00, $1500.00 purchase _ #GMRTE
Demonstrates techniques and materials for resurfacing various surfaces in the plant. Covers selecting the appropriate grade of abrasive, performing hand lapping tasks, checking flat surfaces, grinding in components and checking components for fit with Prussian blue. Part of a seven - part series on handtools and hardware, part of a larger set on general and mechanical maintenance. Includes 10 textbooks and an instructor guide which provide four hours of instruction.
Education; Health and Safety; Industrial and Technical Education; Psychology
Dist - NUSTC **Prod** - NUSTC

Resurgence - the Movement for Equality Vs the KKK 54 MIN
16mm
Color (J)
LC 82-700852
Shows union activists' efforts to improve working conditions at a chicken - packing plant in Laurel, Mississippi, counterpointed with the repressive activities of the United Racist Front, a coalition of the KKK, the American Nazis and the States Rights Party. Reinforces the fact that the following of such groups is on the rise in the United States and offers hope that counter organizations working for civil and economic rights will continue to gain support.
Civics and Political Systems; History - United States; Sociology
Dist - FIRS **Prod** - SKYLIT 1981

Resurgence - the Movement for Equality Vs the Ku Klux Klan 54 MIN
U-matic
Color
Juxtaposes two sides of a political battle now raging in the United States which are efforts of union and civil rights activists to achieve social and economic justice with the upsurge in activity of the Ku Klux Klan and the American Nazi Party. Examines the complex issues of race relations and economic growth.
History - United States; Sociology
Dist - FIRS **Prod** - SKYLN

Resurrecting the Dead Sea scrolls 50 MIN
VHS
Horizon series
Color; PAL (H C A)
PdS99 purchase; Not available in the United States or Canada
Investigates archaeological and scientific evidence that offers insight into the authors of the Dead Sea Scrolls. Explores the controversy surrounding the discovery and how these documents may affect our understanding of Christianity and Judaism.
History - World; Religion and Philosophy
Dist - BBCENE

Resurrection 27 MIN
16mm / U-matic / VHS
Insight Series
Color (H C A)
Presents vignettes which show the temptations Jesus may have undergone between the time he died and the time he was resurrected. Stars James Farentino and Richard Beymer.
Guidance and Counseling; Psychology; Religion and Philosophy
Dist - PAULST **Prod** - PAULST

The Resurrection 30 MIN
16mm
Color
Tells the story of a young black executive who visits his old neighborhood and finds himself having to re - examine his identity. Shows him chased, hunted and shot by the surrealistic figures of THEM. Combines fantasy and realistic situations to tell the story.
Psychology; Sociology
Dist - BLKFMF **Prod** - BLKFMF

Resurrection - Mahler's Symphony no 2 at Masada 120 MIN
VHS
Color (G)
$29.95 purchase _ #1227
Commemmemorates the 40th Anniversary Celebration of Israel. Features the Israel Philharmonic Orchestra conducted by Zubin Mehta performing Mahler's Second Symphony, 'Resurrection,' at the foot of the legendary fortress of Masada. Includes a tribute to 4000 years of Jewish history given by Gregory Peck and Yves Montand.
Fine Arts; Geography - World; History - World; Religion and Philosophy; Sociology
Dist - KULTUR

Resurrection of Bronco Billy 21 MIN
16mm
Color
LC 79-711425
A story of Billy who has his boots, spurs and hat, but no prairie to ride.
Fine Arts
Dist - USC **Prod** - USC 1970

The Resurrection of Jesus 60 MIN
VHS
Who is Jesus series
Color (R G)
$49.95 purchase _ #WJES4
Examines the mysteries and passion of the God - Man, Jesus, according to the teachings of the Roman Catholic Church. Features Donald Goergen, OP, as instructor. Part four of an eight - part series on the life and death and resurrection of Jesus.
Religion and Philosophy
Dist - CTNA **Prod** - CTNA

The Resurrection of Joe Hammond 28 MIN
U-matic / VHS / 16mm
Insight Series
Color; B&W (J)
LC 73-701992
Tells the story of one man's nervous breakdown and recovery to show that accepting love and giving love are what make us emotionally whole.
Guidance and Counseling; Health and Safety
Dist - PAULST **Prod** - KIESER 1973

Resurrection of Turkey 29 MIN
Videoreel / VT2
Course of Our Times I Series
Color
History - World
Dist - PBS **Prod** - WGBHTV

Resuscitation 20 MIN
16mm / VHS / BETA / U-matic
First aid at work training series
Color; PAL (G T)
PdS150, PdS158 purchase
Deals with brief anatomy of the heart and lungs; expired air resuscitation; external chest compressions; heart attack; recovery position; and Holger Neilson. Part of a six - part series produced in the UK by First Aid Training Services Ltd.
Health and Safety; Science - Natural
Dist - EDPAT

Resuscitation 7 MIN
U-matic / VHS / 16mm
First Aid Series
Color (A)
LC 80-701757
Describes the technique of mouth - to - mouth and mouth - to - nose resuscitation of patients who have stopped breathing. Explains how to carry out external cardiac compression on a patient whose heart has stopped beating.
Health and Safety
Dist - IFB **Prod** - HBL 1977

Resuscitation - Bag and Mask Technique 15 MIN
U-matic / VHS
Michigan Perinatal Education, Instructional Unit C - Resuscitation 'Series
Color (PRO)
LC 79-707745
Explains indications for bag and mask ventilation of the newborn, shows appropriate equipment necessary, demonstrates how to perform and evaluate ventilation, and discusses complications and their management.
Health and Safety
Dist - UMICH **Prod** - UMICH 1978

Resuscitation in the Operating Room 22 MIN
16mm
Color (PRO)
LC 72-700349
Dramatizes problems of cardiopulmonary arrest during operations. Stresses the need of teamwork for early detection and remedial action.
Health and Safety; Science
Dist - AYERST **Prod** - AYERST 1973

Resuscitation of Infants and Children 18 MIN
VHS / U-matic
Cardiopulmonary Resuscitation Series
Color (PRO)
Shows how to manage airway obstruction on an infant or child.
Health and Safety
Dist - HSCIC **Prod** - HSCIC 1984

Resuscitation of the Newborn 22 MIN
U-matic / VHS
Color
Demonstrates the principles and practices for resuscitation of the newborn. Emphasizes early recognition of problem babies by appropriate parental history taking and testing.
Health and Safety
Dist - AMCOG **Prod** - AMCOG

Resuscitation of the Newborn 21 MIN
VHS / U-matic
Color (PRO)
Describes and demonstrates routine and emergency treatment for neo - natal depression in new born infants.
Health and Safety
Dist - WFP **Prod** - WFP

Resuscitative Care of the Severely Wounded 24 MIN
16mm
B&W
LC FIE57-79
Describes first aid procedures and corrective surgery to revive severely wounded patients and to counteract injurious results of a wound.
Civics and Political Systems; Health and Safety
Dist - USNAC **Prod** - USA 1957

RET Demonstration with Female Student with Social Anxiety 40 MIN
VHS
Color (G)
$65.00 purchase _ #V003
Features Dr Richard Wessler. Demonstrates how expectations and evaluative cognitions contribute to high levels of anxiety. Shows how to combine cognitive restructuring, imagery techniques and behavior rehearsal into a homework plan. Rational - Emotive Therapy - RET techniques.
Guidance and Counseling; Psychology
Dist - IRL **Prod** - IRL

RET Demonstration with Man with Self - Acceptance and Assertiveness Problems 40 MIN
VHS
Color (G)
$65.00 purchase _ #V002
Features Dr Richard Wessler. Demonstrates cognitive rehearsal, rational - emotive imagery. Rational - Emotive Therapy - RET techniques.
Guidance and Counseling; Psychology
Dist - IRL **Prod** - IRL

RET Group Therapy Demonstration 60 MIN
VHS / 16mm
Color (G)
$65.00 purchase _ #V016
Applies a wide variety of Rational - Emotive Therapy - RET techniques to individual problems within a group therapy setting.
Guidance and Counseling; Psychology
Dist - IRL **Prod** - IRL

Retail and merchandising 15 MIN
VHS
Career success series
Color (H C A)
$29.95 purchase _ #MX218
Presents an introduction to retail and merchandising careers. Covers the necessary skills, and interviews people in these careers on the rewards and stresses involved.
Business and Economics; Education
Dist - CAMV

Retail Cut ID - Beef
VHS
Meat Videos From The University Of Nebraska Series
Color (G)
$89.95 purchase _ #6 - 032 - 100P
Points out identifying characteristics in meat - bones, fat, muscle shape and color. Includes a self - test without narration. Part of a series on meat cutting.
Agriculture; Business and Economics; Social Science
Dist - VEP **Prod** - UNEBR

Retail cut identification series
Pork retail cuts identification 27 MIN
Dist - AAVIM

Retail Cut Identification (Set C) Series
Beef Retail Cuts Identification 41 MIN
Lamb Retail Cuts Identification 17 MIN
Dist - AAVIM

Retail Location 30 MIN
VHS / U-matic
Marketing Perspectives Series
Color
Classifies consumer products based upon purchasing patterns. Covers key criteria in developing a shopping center, advantages and disadvantages of developing a specialty product image.

Business and Economics; Education
Dist - WFVTAE Prod - MATC

Retail management 30 MIN
VHS
Inside Britain 1 series
Color; PAL; NTSC (G) (BULGARIAN CZECH HUNGARIAN SPANISH POLISH ROMANIAN RUSSIAN SLOVAK UKRAINIAN ENGLISH WITH ARABIC SUBTITLES)
PdS65 purchase
Examines department stores which provide the convenience of one - stop shopping, offering everything from food to furniture under one roof. Studies buying, quality control, storage, presentation and marketing in such a store just outside London.
Business and Economics
Dist - CFLVIS Prod - AMAZIN 1991

Retail Marketing Management
VHS
Career Profiles - Business and Office Series
$75.00 purchase _ #KW - 110
Discusses the pros and cons of this occupational field plus the necessary aptitudes and training.
Guidance and Counseling
Dist - CAREER Prod - CAREER

The Retail revolution - Benetton, Esprit and Banana Republic 30 MIN
U-matic
Adam Smith's money world 1986 - 1987 season series; 306
Color (A)
Attempts to demystify the world of money and break it down so that small as well as large businesses and it's people understand and adjust to new social and economic trends. Reports on the major economic stories and discoveries of 1986 and 1987.
Business and Economics
Dist - PBS Prod - WNETTV 1987

Retail Sales
VHS / U-matic
Work - a - Day America
$59.95 purchase _ #VV119V
Helps students achieve career vocational preparation. Stresses the four main points of career awareness and exploration, specific skills intended, employability skills needed, and real people sharing on the job experiences.
Guidance and Counseling
Dist - CAREER Prod - CAREER

Retail Sales Power Series
Improving Customer Relations 22 MIN
Shrink or swim - in - store theft 8 MIN
Dist - PRODEV

Retail Sales - the Supervisor's Role 15 MIN
U-matic / VHS
Customer Focused Selling Series
(PRO A)
$495 Purchase, $150 Rental 5 days, $35 Preview 3 days
Focuses on the supervisor's role in retail, emphasizing such points as establishing communication with employees, and ability to perform effective evaluations.
Business and Economics
Dist - ADVANM Prod - ADVANM

Retail sales training system
VHS
Color (A PRO)
$995.00 purchase, $300.00 rental
Presents a three - part series on retail selling skills. Emphasizes the need to focus on the customer. Also available individually.
Business and Economics; Psychology
Dist - VLEARN

Retail Selling - the Long Cycle 15 MIN
VHS / U-matic
Customer Focused Selling Series
(PRO A)
$495 Purchase, $150 Rental 5 days, $35 Previewed 3 days
Covers the importance of selling skills, greeting customers, presenting merchandise and other skills in the retail world.
Business and Economics
Dist - ADVANM Prod - ADVANM

Retail Selling - the Short Cycle 15 MIN
U-matic / VHS
Customer Focused Selling Series
(PRO A)
$495 Purchase, $150 Rental 5 days, $35 Preview 3 days
Considers basic issues to be faced in the field of retail such as good selling skills, greeting customers properly, and directing customers to merchandise.
Business and Economics
Dist - ADVANM Prod - ADVANM

The Retail store 30 MIN
VHS
Color (C A PRO H)
$69.95 purchase _ #CCP0139V-G
Presents the organization of a retail store and shows how the various parts work to present merchandise. Offers details about planning and buying inventory, retail finance, sales promotion, personnel, operations, and merchandising. Also includes discussion by fashion coordinators, buyers, and sales associates about how they assist customers in buying choices. Appropriate for those involved in retail and those planning or investigating careers in fashion merchandising.
Business and Economics; Guidance and Counseling; Home Economics
Dist - CAMV

Retail Video Series
Retailing
Wholesalers and Distributors
Dist - CAREER

Retailing
VHS
Retail Video Series
$89.95 purchase _ #RPMP11V
Investigates the characteristics of a retail chain and the types of retail chain stores. Discusses the differences between small store operations and large chain store operations.
Business and Economics
Dist - CAREER Prod - CAREER

Retailing 30 MIN
U-matic / VHS
Marketing Perspectives Series
Color
Covers the characteristics of a retail chain, types of retail chain stores, advantages of franchising, advantages, of general merchandising and comparison of advantages of small single store operations to large chain store operations.
Business and Economics; Education
Dist - WFVTAE Prod - MATC

Retailing 25 MIN
VHS
Face to face series
Color (C H A)
$39.95 purchase _ #KARCA02V-G
Offers unrehearsed interviews between actual company representatives and college students seeking employment. Provides strategies for improving an interview style by Dr. Larry Simpson, director of career planning and placement at the University of Virginia. Part of a five-part series.
Business and Economics; Guidance and Counseling
Dist - CAMV

Retailing 24 MIN
VHS / 16mm
Career Builders Video Series
Color
$85.00 purchase _ #V105
Examines a potential career choice by taking the viewer into the working environment and interviewing professionals on the demands, rewards and frustrations on the job.
Business and Economics; Sociology
Dist - EDUCDE Prod - EDUCDE 1987

Retailing
U-matic / VHS
Career Builders Video Series
$95.00 purchase _ #ED105V
Uses actual professionals to talk about the job's demands, rewards, and frustrations. Shows the working environment of the career field.
Guidance and Counseling
Dist - CAREER Prod - CAREER

Retailing - Merchandising 15 MIN
VHS / 16mm
(H C A)
$24.95 purchase _ #CS218
Describes the skills required for a career in retailing and merchandising. Features interviews with professionals in this field.
Guidance and Counseling
Dist - RMIBHF Prod - RMIBHF

Retailing - Sears 20 MIN
U-matic / VHS
Clues to Career Opportunities for Liberal Arts Graduates Series
Color
LC 79-706056
Interviews a representative from Sears, Roebuck and Company in order to describe the jobs available in the retailing field for college graduates with liberal arts degrees. Discusses initial interviews, hiring practices and advancement opportunities.
Business and Economics; Guidance and Counseling
Dist - IU Prod - IU 1978

Retaining your sense of humor - or laugh your way to a healthy classroom - and Adding creativity to your teaching - or try it, you'll like it 30 MIN
VHS
First - year teacher series
Color (T)
$69.95 purchase, $45.00 rental
Discusses the unique challenges and rewards that first - year school teachers face. Serves as the seventh episode of a 12 - part telecourse. Features discussions between first - year teachers and Winthrop College professor Glen Walter on the importance of maintaining one's sense of humor and how to add creativity to teaching.
Education; Psychology
Dist - SCETV Prod - SCETV 1988

Retardation Research 7 MIN
16mm
Color (T)
LC FIA67-5259
Describes a research program to test the Doman - Delacato theory of neuropsychology.
Psychology
Dist - FINLYS Prod - FINLYS 1967

The Retarded Client and His Family 20 MIN
VHS / U-matic
Color
Shows how enlightened family help can shape the future of a retarded person.
Education; Psychology
Dist - PRIMED Prod - PRIMED

Retention 30 MIN
16mm
Aide - Ing in Education Series
Color (T)
Provides a summary of principles of learning that should be present in every student - teacher interaction.
Education; Psychology
Dist - SPF Prod - SPF

Retention Theory for Teachers 28 MIN
16mm
Translating Theory into Classroom Practices Series
B&W (C T)
Features Dr Madeline Hunter discussing the factors that facilitate remembering. Suggests how to incorporate these factors in daily teaching to increase the long term economy and effectiveness of learning.
Education
Dist - SPF Prod - SPF 1967

Rethinking America series
Conservation and the Car 30 MIN
Energy and housing 30 MIN
Energy and industry 30 MIN
Redesigning Appliances 30 MIN
Dist - UMITV

Rethinking Rape 26 MIN
16mm
Color (H)
$900.00 purchase, $60.00, $80.00 rental
Investigates societal and cultural causes of aquaintance rape. Interviews rape victims, social workers and psychologists to describe the problem. Explains why sexual violence has become a widespread, accepted part of society. Produced by Jeanne LePage with the Stanford University Rape Education Project.
Guidance and Counseling; Health and Safety; Psychology; Sociology
Dist - WMENIF

Rethinking Tomorrow 28 MIN
U-matic / VHS / 16mm
Color
Shows growing national concern for energy conservation. Discusses how citizens have adopted comprehensive energy programs in various cities.
Science - Natural; Social Science
Dist - USNAC Prod - USDOE 1980

Retina series
Fluorescein angiography 4 MIN
Dist - AJN

The Retinacular System of the Digits of the Hand 30 MIN
U-matic / VHS
Color (PRO)
Presents an anatomical study of the small ligaments underlying the skin at the level of the finger joints. Attempts to identify and document their relationship to one another by color photographs of dissection of frozen specimens.
Health and Safety
Dist - ASSH Prod - ASSH

Retinal holes, tears and detachment 10 MIN
VHS
5 - part retina series
Color (G)
$75.00 purchase, $40.00 rental _ #5316S, #5316V
Explains the symptoms of trouble and treatments, including cryosurgery, scleral buckling and lasers. Covers risks and complications. Part a five - part series on the retina.
Health and Safety; Science - Natural
Dist - AJN **Prod** - VMED

Retinitis Pigmentosa 12 MIN
16mm
Color
LC 75-703261
Explains in lay language what is known of retinitis pigmentosa and tells of research in progress.
Health and Safety; Science - Natural
Dist - RETIN **Prod** - ITTCMD 1975

Retinoids and Cancer Prevention 48 MIN
U-matic
Color
Discusses the role of retinoids in the prevention and treatment of cancer.
Health and Safety
Dist - UTEXSC **Prod** - UTEXSC

Retire to Life 22 MIN
U-matic / VHS / 16mm
B&W (C A)
Tells the story of an older man facing the problem of retirement when still mentally and physically able.
Psychology; Sociology
Dist - IFB **Prod** - UOKLA 1952

Retirement 29 MIN
U-matic
You and the Law Series Lesson 25
Color (C A)
Discusses the basic workings of recent laws pertaining to retirees and older citizens. Describes retirement plans for savings, selling a business or home and moving.
Civics and Political Systems; Sociology
Dist - CDTEL **Prod** - COAST

Retirement - focus on men - Part 1 31 MIN
VHS / U-matic / BETA
Human development - successful aging series
Color (C PRO)
$150.00 purchase _ #128.6
Presents a video transfer from slide program which explodes the myths surrounding retirement by presenting facts based on research. Delineates factors which incluence the retirement decision and adjustment to it. Presents two real - life stories to show how the experience of retirement has affected the men. Part one of two parts on retirement and part of a series on successful aging.
Guidance and Counseling; Health and Safety; Sociology
Dist - CONMED **Prod** - CONMED

Retirement - focus on women - Part 2 31 MIN
VHS / U-matic / BETA
Human development - successful aging series
Color (C PRO)
$150.00 purchase _ #128.7
Presents a video transfer from slide program which discusses theoretical approaches to retirement as a process of adjustment. Presents the phases of retirement. Presents two real - life stories to show how women have adjusted to retirement and how their experiences relate to the theories. Part two of two parts on retirement and part of a series on successful aging.
Guidance and Counseling; Health and Safety; Sociology
Dist - CONMED **Prod** - CONMED

Retirement Income Security
16mm
Aging in the Future Series
Color
Considers retirement income during the stages of life, social security, the individual's responsibility for maintaining retirement income and the adjustments older people can make for inflation. Urges people in both the pre - retirement and retirement years to consider ways that purchasing power can be maintained.
Health and Safety; Sociology
Dist - UMICH **Prod** - UMICH

Retirement Income Security 14 MIN
U-matic
Aging in the Future Series
Color
Shows young people worrying about whether or not there will be Social Security when they want to retire. Discusses the roles of society and the older citizen.
Health and Safety; Sociology
Dist - UMITV **Prod** - UMITV 1981

Retirement of the Hallam Nuclear Power Facility 35 MIN
16mm
Color (C A)
LC 72-708997
Shows the decommissioning of the 254 MWT sodium cooled graphite - moderated nuclear power reactor located at Nebraska Public Power District's Sheldon station. Stresses the safety procedures necessary for the handling of sodium and radioactive materials.
Health and Safety; Science - Physical
Dist - USERD **Prod** - USNRC 1970

Retirement planning 30 MIN
VHS
Color (A PRO)
$39.95 purchase _ #S01433
Presents the Financial Awareness Institute's educational program on retirement planning.
Business and Economics
Dist - UILL

Retirement planning 30 MIN
U-matic / VHS
Consumer survival series; Personal planning
Color
Presents tips on retirement planning.
Home Economics; Sociology
Dist - MDCPB **Prod** - MDCPB

Retirement Planning - Batteries - Water Filter Systems
VHS / U-matic
Consumer Survival Series
Color
Discusses various aspects of retirement planning, batteries and water filter systems.
Home Economics; Industrial and Technical Education; Sociology
Dist - MDCPB **Prod** - MDCPB

Retirement Planning - Thinking Ahead 13 MIN
U-matic / VHS / 16mm
Color (C A)
$400, $250 purchase _ #83600
Shows how to plan and save money for retirement.
Business and Economics
Dist - CORF

Retirement Plans for Small Business and Professionals - Entering the Top - Heavy and 210 MIN
VHS / U-matic
Color (PRO)
Presents an advanced program focused on the implementation of parity and top - heavy rules enacted by the Tax Equity and Fiscal Responsibility Act of 1982 (TEFRA).
Civics and Political Systems
Dist - ALIABA **Prod** - ALIABA

Retooling the arms industry 29 MIN
VHS
Color (J H C G T A)
$25.00 purchase
Explores the question of whether U S defense contractors will be able to shift to civilian markets as defense spending decreases. Focuses on a conference held in Ohio to explore this and other questions. Includes the perspectives of U S and Soviet experts on the prospects for retooling the defense industry. Produced by Sandy Gottlieb.
Civics and Political Systems; Sociology
Dist - EFVP **Prod** - CDINFO 1990

Retooling the arms industry 30 MIN
VHS
America's defense monitor series; Politics and economics
Color (J H C G)
$29.95 purchase _ #ADM429V
Examines the future of the arms industry in the United States. Part of a five - part series on the politics and economics of American military affairs.
Business and Economics; Civics and Political Systems
Dist - CAMV

Retour a La Terre 10 MIN
16mm
Color (FRENCH)
LC 76-703504
A French language film. Reports on Canada's National Capital Commission's management of gardens in the Ottawa region.
Agriculture; Foreign Language; Geography - World
Dist - MTS **Prod** - NATCAP 1975

Retracing Man's Steps 28 MIN
U-matic / VHS
Origins Series
Color (C)
$249.00, $149.00 purchase _ #AD - 1159
Examines fossils and bones as the records of the family tree of human ancestry. Looks at other records of the past in the cave paintings at Lascaux, France, the development of speech and the use of tools.
English Language; Science - Natural; Science - Physical
Dist - FOTH **Prod** - FOTH

Retracing Steps - American Dance Since Postmodernism 89 MIN
16mm / VHS
Color (H C)
$975.00, $350.00 purchase, $150.00 rental
Features 9 choreographers who eloquently illustrate the eclecticism found in American dance today.
Fine Arts
Dist - BLACKW **Prod** - BLACKW 1988

Retraction cord procedure 10 MIN
U-matic / VHS
Color (C PRO)
$395.00 purchase, $80.00 rental _ #D881 - VI - 021
Introduces dental students to procedures for gum retraction with cotton fibers or cords. Discusses anatomical features of the area and various methods of tissue displacement. Illustrates instruments used in the retraction cord and describes a variety of brand name cords. Demonstrates the procedure on both a model and a patient being prepared for a crown. Presented by Dr Elizabeth Robinson.
Health and Safety
Dist - HSCIC

Retratos 53 MIN
U-matic / VHS / 16mm
Captioned; Color (A) (SPANISH (ENGLISH SUBTITLES))
Portrays the life stories of four New York Puerto Ricans and their attempt to assimilate themselves into American life while maintaining their cultural heritage. Spanish dialog with English subtitles.
Fine Arts; Sociology
Dist - CNEMAG **Prod** - BRSOKS 1980

Retreat 11 MIN
16mm
Revelation Series
Color (H C A)
LC 72-703104
Tells the story of a young man, with backpack and fishing rod, who hikes through the autumn countryside. Points out that everything is pastoral and serene until his war experiences are suddenly awakened in him, turning his retreat into a nightmare.
Guidance and Counseling; Psychology
Dist - FRACOC **Prod** - FRACOC 1970

The Retreat 40 MIN
VHS
Color (G)
$39.95 purchase
Documents a weekend of intensive meditation at a center in Los Angeles, California. Features the director, Shinzen Young, an American who was trained as a Buddhist monk in Japan.
Fine Arts; Religion and Philosophy
Dist - HP

Retreat 39 MIN
U-matic
As We See it Series
Color
Depicts students from Austin, Texas, discovering that rugged outdoor retreats can encourage understanding among people of different races and backgrounds.
Sociology
Dist - PBS **Prod** - WTTWTV

Retreat and Decision 30 MIN
U-matic / VHS / 16mm
Living Christ Series
Color; B&W (G)
Includes the transfiguration of Jesus, followed by more healing miracles.
Literature and Drama; Religion and Philosophy
Dist - CAFM **Prod** - CAFM 1958
ECUFLM

Retriever Training Complete 120 MIN
BETA / VHS
Color
Presents a complete video book on retriever training. Covers obedience, basic and advanced retrieving, force fetch, bank running, water force, handling, and blind retrieving.
Physical Education and Recreation
Dist - HOMEAF **Prod** - HOMEAF

Retrievers at Work 11 MIN
U-matic / VHS / 16mm

Color (P A)
Shows the training of black Labradors, Chesapeakes, goldens and Irish water spaniels.
Physical Education and Recreation; Science - Natural
Dist - IFB **Prod** - IFB 1950

Retrieving the past 29 MIN
VHS / U-matic / BETA
Breaking the mold, breaking the myth - defining the masculine 'identity series
Color (G)
$280.00 purchase _ #804.1
Features psychologist Robert Subby who challenges the stereotypic roles of men in Western culture and confronts the barriers of ignorance that surround them. Stresses the need to examine personal history in order to change the future. Underscores the need for men to work together on solving their problems. Uses personal interviews, group discussion and expert commentary to introduce the many challenges facing men in transition. Part of a three - part series on redefining masculine identity produced by Family Systems, Inc.
Health and Safety; Psychology; Sociology
Dist - CONMED

The Retrograde Amalgam in Endodontics 15 MIN
16mm
Color (PRO)
LC 74-706392
Discusses indications and demonstrates procedures for retrograde root canal filling.
Health and Safety; Science
Dist - USNAC **Prod** - USVA 1970

Retrolabyrinthine Approach to the Cerebellopontine Angle 55 MIN
U-matic / VHS
Color (PRO)
Shows the excellent exposure of the cerebellopontine angle by an approach through the mastoid posterior to the labyrinth. This retrolabyrinthine approach has been used primarily for selective partial section of the trigeminal nerve for tic douloureaux.
Guidance and Counseling; Health and Safety; Science - Natural
Dist - HOUSEI **Prod** - HOUSEI

Retrolabyrinthine Selective Section of the Trigeminal Nerve - Posterior - for Intractable 10 MIN
U-matic / VHS
Color (PRO)
Demonstrates the suboccipital approach to the retrolabyrinthine technique combined with the lower complication rate of the transtemporal approach.
Guidance and Counseling; Health and Safety; Science - Natural
Dist - HOUSEI **Prod** - HOUSEI

Retromandibular Structures and Infratemporal Fossa - Unit 4 15 MIN
VHS / U-matic
Gross Anatomy Prosection Demonstration Series
Color (PRO)
Shows the muscles, nerves, arteries, and other structures that compose the area posterior to the jaw, including the maxillary artery and its branches.
Health and Safety; Science - Natural
Dist - HSCIC **Prod** - HSCIC

Retroperitoneal Ultrasonography 18 MIN
U-matic
Ultrasound in Diagnostic Medicine Series
Color (PRO)
LC 80-706125
Explains how ultrasound can be used to distinguish renal abnormalities such as cysts, abscesses, tumors and hydronephrosis. Presents an evaluation of a renal transplant.
Health and Safety; Science
Dist - USNAC **Prod** - USVA 1979

Retropubic Prostatovesiculectomy 10 MIN
16mm
Color
LC 75-702307
Demonstrates the operative technique of retropubic prostatovesiculectomy. Emphasizes the ideal visualization afforded by the retropubic approach, which assures optimum hemostasis, obviates damage to the lower ureters and rectum and facilitates accurate revisions of the bladder neck and precise vesicourethral anastomosis.
Health and Safety; Science
Dist - EATONL **Prod** - EATONL 1958

Retter Aus Bergnot 5 MIN
U-matic / VHS / 16mm
European Studies - Germany - German Series
Color (H C A) (GERMAN)
A German - language version of the motion picture Mountain Rescue Workers. Shows the operation of a typical German rescue effort following an avalanche.
Foreign Language; Geography - World; Health and Safety
Dist - IFB **Prod** - MFAFRG 1973

The Return 29 MIN
VHS / 16mm
Sonrisas Series
Color (T P) (SPANISH)
$46.00 rental _ #SRSS - 122
Shows how a rift arises between Rafael and his friends after Rafael's brother returns home.
Sociology
Dist - PBS

The Return 27 MIN
U-matic / VHS / 16mm
Color (J) (GERMAN JAPANESE)
Discusses the predictions of the Old Testament prophets, retelling and foretelling the events leading to the final hours in world history. Introduced and narrated by Hal Lindsay, author of The Late Great Planet Earth.
Foreign Language; Religion and Philosophy
Dist - PFP **Prod** - PFP

The Return 27 MIN
16mm / U-matic / VHS
Color
LC 72-702188
A documentary of Biblical prophesies. Filmed in Israel.
Geography - World; Literature and Drama; Religion and Philosophy
Dist - PFP **Prod** - PFP 1972

The Return 23 MIN
16mm
Color
Tells of the struggle of Soviet Jewry for freedom and relates the personal experiences of Soviet Jews as they adjust to their new lives in Israel.
Geography - World; History - World; Sociology
Dist - ALDEN **Prod** - UJA

Return from death - the near death experience 52 MIN
VHS
Color (H C G)
$295.00 purchase, $75.00 rental
Interviews women, men and children who were once declared clinically dead but survived. Reveals that their return to life has often been accompanied with memories of an extraordinary experience while they were seemingly dead. Shows that they described strikingly similar mystical experiences. Produced by Anik Doussau.
Sociology
Dist - FLMLIB

Return from Foster Care through Task Centered Casework 55 MIN
U-matic / VHS
B&W
Explains and demonstrates techniques of the middle phase of 'task centered casework.' Identifies problems and tasks in returning children to mother from foster homes.
Sociology
Dist - UWISC **Prod** - UCHI

Return from Silence - China's Revolutionary Writers 58 MIN
16mm / U-matic / VHS
Color (CHINESE)
Profiles five writers who have dedicated their lives to building an independent China. Interviews are intercut with archival footage, old still photos and scenes of performances of author's major works, including rare footage of the May Fourth Movement, Land Reform and Cultural Revolution. Includes Ai Quing, Ba Jin, Cao Yu, Ding Ling and Mao dun.
History - World; Literature and Drama; Sociology
Dist - GWASHU **Prod** - GWASHU

Return from Witch Mountain 93 MIN
16mm
Color
Tells how two youngsters from outer space arrive in Los Angeles and encounter a fanatical scientific genius. Stars Bette Davis and Christopher Lee.
Fine Arts
Dist - UAE **Prod** - DISNEY 1978

The Return of Count Spirochete 21 MIN
16mm
Color
LC 74-706566
Uses animation to give medical facts about venereal diseases. Describes symptoms, course of infection and the effects of syphilis and gonorrhea on the human body. Emphasizes diagnosis and treatment by a physician as the only means of eradicating the infection.
Health and Safety; Science - Natural
Dist - USNAC **Prod** - USN 1973

The Return of Joe Hill 57 MIN
VHS
Color (J H C)
$350.00 purchase, $95.00 rental
Tells the story of Joe Hill - 1879 - 1915 - a Swedish immigrant to America who became a songwriter, cartoonist and labor organizer for the Industrial Workers of the World - IWW. Looks at his transformation to martyr status for the labor movement and an international hero after being executed by the state of Utah for a crime he did not commit. Directed by Eric Scholl.
Business and Economics; Fine Arts
Dist - CNEMAG

The Return of Milton Whitty 17 MIN
U-matic / VHS / 16mm
Color (IND)
Presents a sequel to the Inner Mind Of Milton Whitty. Shows that prevention of accidents costs less than compensation. Illustrates the steps that should be taken to help eliminate hazards at a construction site.
Business and Economics; Health and Safety; Industrial and Technical Education; Psychology
Dist - IFB **Prod** - CSAO

The Return of Nathan Becker - Nosn Beker fort aheym 80 MIN
35mm
B&W (G) (YIDDISH AND RUSSIAN)
Glorifies Soviet industrial productivity as it denigrates American capitalism and assimilation. Uses the story of bricklayer Nathan Becker who returns home to Russia after 20 years in America to depict the shtetl way of life as primitive and grotesque. Promotes a shift away from traditional Jewish values, reflecting the regime's determined effort to reduce Jewish culture to 'Communist in content and Yiddish in form only.' Neither the author, poet Peretz Markish, the actor Solomon Mikhoels nor the director of the Moscow Yiddish State Theater survived the Stalinist terror. Contact distributor for rental fee. With English subtitles.
History - World; Religion and Philosophy; Sociology
Dist - NCJEWF

Return of Patriotism - 101 30 MIN
U-matic
Currents - 1984 - 85 Season Series
Color (A)
Covers the resurgence of patriotism by some Americans.
Civics and Political Systems; Social Science
Dist - PBS **Prod** - WNETTV 1985

Return of the Allies 27 MIN
U-matic / VHS / 16mm
Victory at Sea Series
B&W (J H)
Recounts the liberation of the Philippines during World War II.
Civics and Political Systems; History - United States; History - World
Dist - LUF **Prod** - NBCTV

The Return of the Child 26 MIN
U-matic / VHS / 16mm
Color
Dramatizes an Algonquin Indian legend about a young man who lost both his wife and his child. Tells of the child freed from the bonds of death by the sap of the fir tree.
Literature and Drama; Social Science
Dist - FOTH **Prod** - FOTH

The Return of the Child - the Effects of El Nino 26 MIN
VHS / 16mm
Blue Revolution Series
Color (J)
$149.00 purchase, $75.00 rental _ #QD - 2287
Follows the development of the weather system El Nino and its place in the ocean waters. Looks at the history of man's study of waves, ocean currents and the interaction of the sea and sky. The seventh of 16 installments of the Blue Revolution Series.
Geography - World; History - World; Science - Physical
Dist - FOTH

Return of the Desert Bighorn 28 MIN
U-matic
Color (J H C)
Follows the efforts of wildlife agencies and conservationists to return the desert bighorn sheep to its former ranges in the Southwestern deserts.
Science - Natural
Dist - CEPRO **Prod** - CEPRO

The Return of the Elephant Seal 29 MIN
16mm / U-matic / VHS
Color (H C A)

LC 82-700287
Discusses elephant seals who were near extinction, but have made a miraculous recovery, doubling their population every ten years and reclaiming most of their original territory on California coastal islands. Traces the nineteenth - century seal hunts through archival footage, records the immense animals' breeding behavior, and traces their annual migration patterns. Ponders and depicts the problems of expanding animal populations.
Science - Natural
Dist - CORF **Prod** - PERSPF 1982

Return of the Great Whales 45 MIN
VHS
Color (S)
$24.95 purchase _ #839 - 9002; $39.95 purchase _ #0062
Documents the return of the humpback and blue whales to the waters of northern California. Features spectacular shots of 125 - foot whales as close as six inches from the filmmaker's camera and of playful dolphins flipping through the water.
Geography - United States; Science - Natural
Dist - FI **Prod** - JONSHA 1986
SEVVID

Return of the Kiteman 30 MIN
U-matic / VHS / 16mm
Color (I)
LC 76-701931
Tells the story of a 45 - year - old man and his efforts trying to fly a kite. Takes place in the future where a large bureaucratic government has declared kiteflying illegal because it is oriented to the self and not to society.
Guidance and Counseling; Sociology
Dist - PHENIX **Prod** - PHENIX 1975

Return of the Nene 9 MIN
16mm
Color (I)
LC FIA67-1764
Tells the story of the nene, Hawaii's state bird. The nene is a nearly extinct goose that inhabits waterless uplands and feeds on berries and vegetation.
Geography - United States; Science - Natural
Dist - SF **Prod** - STUTP 1967

Return of the Raven - the Edison Chiloquin Story 47 MIN
U-matic / VHS
Color (J H C)
Presents, in 1954, a policy which became known as 'Klamath Termination,' the Klamath Tribe of Oregon joined over a hundred tribes throughout the country in loss of federal recognition. Shows the U S government terminate Federal supervision over the property of the Klamath Tribe without their consent. In 1961, the government made individual payments for the reservation land to tribal members. Edison Chiloquin refused payment of over a quarter million dollars for his land and eventually became the first individual Native American to have his land returned by Congress.
Social Science; Sociology
Dist - NAMPBC **Prod** - NAMPBC 1985

Return of the sacred pole 30 MIN
U-matic / VT1 / VHS
Color (G)
$49.95 purchase, $35.00 rental
Tells the story of the Omaha tribe and its reclaiming of the Sacred Pole, a spirit - endowed artifact held for the past 100 years by the Peabody Museum at Harvard University. Recounts the story of the washabagle, 'venerable one,' its importance to the heritage of the Omahas, its stay at the Peabody and its return to its owners.
Social Science
Dist - NAMPBC **Prod** - NETV 1989

The return of the sea elephants 20 MIN
16mm / U-matic / VHS
Undersea world of Jacques Cousteau series
Color (G)
$49.95 purchase _ #Q10609; LC 76-710107
A shortened version of Return Of The Sea Elephant. Utilizes underwater photography to document the life cycle of the sea elephant. Part of a series of 24 programs.
Science - Natural
Dist - CF **Prod** - METROM 1970

Return of the sea otter 28 MIN
16mm / VHS
Color (H C G)
$525.00, $295.00 purchase, $55.00 rental
Shows how the efforts to save a nearly extinct species paid off. Reveals that sea otters, because of their luxurious pelts, were hunted to near extinction in the 1920s. In the 1970s a 'sealift' was organized, transporting a few remaining colonies to to sites in California where they thrive, even though their survival must be vigilantly guarded.
Geography - United States; Science - Natural
Dist - FLMLIB **Prod** - CANBC 1987

Return of the Secaucus 7 106 MIN
35mm / 16mm
Color (G)
Reunites a group of friends whose relationship dates back to the politically active 1960s. Features Mike and Katie, the hosts, who are small - town schoolteachers; Irene and her new lover Chip work for a liberal senator; Francis is in medical school and can't find a satisfying relationship with a man; J T is a singer - songwriter finally getting the courage to try and make it in Los Angeles; and Maura and Jeff have just broken up and are facing painful realities about themselves and each other. A classic of independent filmmaking which served as a model for the blockbuster The Big Chill. Produced by Willima Aydelott and Jeffrey Nelson; written, directed and edited by John Sayles. Contact distributor for price.
Fine Arts; Psychology; Sociology
Dist - OCTOBF

Return of the serve 30 MIN
VHS
Tennis with Van der Meer series
Color (C A)
$95.00 purchase, $55.00 rental
Features tennis player and instructor Dennis Van der Meer in a presentation on returning serves. Uses freeze - frame photography and repetition to stress skill development. Serves as part three of a 10 - part telecourse.
Physical Education and Recreation; Psychology
Dist - SCETV **Prod** - SCETV 1989

The Return of the Serve 29 MIN
U-matic / VHS
Love Tennis Series
Color
Features Lew Gerrard and Don Candy giving tennis instructions, emphasizing the return of the serve.
Physical Education and Recreation
Dist - MDCPB **Prod** - MDCPB

Return of the space shuttle
VHS
Color (G)
$19.95 purchase
Focuses on the flight of the space shuttle 'Discovery,' which marked the United States' return to space flight. Presents exclusive footage of interviews with the 'Discovery' crew, and of the lift - off and flight.
History - United States; History - World
Dist - PBS **Prod** - WNETTV

Return of the wolves 58 MIN
VHS
Color (G)
$19.95 purchase
Chronicles the controversial attempts to reintroduce the wolf into Yellowstone. Contains rare footage and sheds new light on the feared and misunderstood wolf. Produced by John Howe.
Science - Natural
Dist - KUEDTV **Prod** - KUEDTV 1989

The Return of Ulysses to His Homeland
VHS / U-matic
Color (G) (ITALIAN (ENGLISH SUBTITLES))
Presents Dame Janet Baker and Benjamin Luxon in Monteverdi's music drama.
Fine Arts; Foreign Language
Dist - VAI **Prod** - VAI

Return on Investment 20 MIN
VHS / 16mm
Color (A PRO)
$790.00 purchase, $220.00 rental
Dramatizes some principles of capital management. Shows how to accurately determine Return on Capital Employed. Illustrates how to choose between investments using Discounted Cash Flow techniques to ascertain the highest Net Present Value or NPV. Management training.
Business and Economics
Dist - VIDART **Prod** - VIDART 1990

Return to Aguacayo 18 MIN
VHS / U-matic
Color (G)
$65.00 purchase, $35.00 rental
Portrays 450 Salvadorans as they attempt to return to their homes and farms in the Guazapa region of El Salvador. Reveals that the people must face threats of harm from the Salvadoran army, which forced them to leave the first time. Produced by Celeste Greco.
Civics and Political Systems; Geography - World; History - World
Dist - EFVP

Return to Appalachia 28 MIN
16mm
Color
Offers a warm portrait of three sisters in rural America and shows how each has found fulfillment despite differences in temperaments and need.
Geography - United States; Sociology
Dist - FLMLIB **Prod** - MARKSC 1982

Return to Dresden 28 MIN
16mm
Color (G)
Presents an independent production by M Duckworth. Looks at the Dresden Opera House, destroyed by fire bombs in 1945, reopening with a new opera.
Fine Arts; History - United States; History - World
Dist - FIRS

Return to Everest 59 MIN
U-matic / VHS / 16mm
Color
Looks at the efforts of Sir Edmund Hillary, the first man to climb Mount Everest, to help the people who live in the shadow of the mountain by building hospitals, schools and bridges.
Biography; Geography - World
Dist - NGS **Prod** - NGS 1984

Return to glory - Michelangelo revealed 52 MIN
VHS
Color (G)
$39.95 purchase; $39.95 purchase _ #074-9001
Features Edwin Newman who narrates the story of the largest art restoration ever attempted. Looks at the restoration of the Sistine Chapel frescos by Michelangelo, a work still in progress. Shows that 500 years of smoke, soot and varnish have been peeled off, revealing Michelangelo's genius as a colorist.
Fine Arts
Dist - ARTSAM **Prod** - CRVID 1988
FI

Return to Holyoke 15 MIN
16mm
Color
LC 74-705534
Depicts the visit of the director of Women Marines to Mt Holyoke to commemorate the establishment of the Women's Reserve Officer Training School on campus in 1943.
Civics and Political Systems; Sociology
Dist - USNAC **Prod** - USN 1969

A Return to Improvisation 30 MIN
U-matic
Changing Music Series
Color
Fine Arts
Dist - PBS **Prod** - WGBHTV

Return to Isolationism 26 MIN
U-matic / VHS / 16mm
Between the Wars Series
Color (H C)
Points out that President Woodrow Wilson destroyed his health in his desperate struggle for the League of Nations. Explains that his refusal to compromise led to the League's defeat.
Civics and Political Systems; History - United States; History - World
Dist - FI **Prod** - LNDBRG 1978

Return to Iwo Jima 57 MIN
VHS
Color (S)
$19.95 purchase _ #313 - 9003
Chronicles the poignant reunion of the American Marines who fought the bloody battle of Iwo Jima. Shows their meeting, their recollection of fallen comrades and their sharing of the hope that Iwo Jima will always be remembered and never repeated. Ed McMahon is host.
Civics and Political Systems; Geography - World; History - United States; History - World; Sociology
Dist - FI
UILL

Return to life 60 MIN
VHS
Color & B&W (G)
$39.95 purchase _ #642
Reveals that the end of World War II and the collapse of the Nazi regime marked a time of elation for the free world. Focuses on the 1.5 million Jewish refugees in Europe on VE day, for whom the day was not so much a day of celebration as a time to consider the enormity of the disaster which had befallen them. Depicts Jewish efforts to rebuild the shattered fragments of their existence, to reaccustom themselves to freedom and to search for their homes and families as they attempt to return to normal life.
History - World
Dist - ERGOM

Return to Masada 25 MIN
16mm
B&W
Depicts the excavations of Masada, the last Jewish stronghold that resisted the Roman legions in the first millennium.
History - World
Dist - ALDEN **Prod** - ALDEN

Return to my shtetl Delatyn 60 MIN
VHS
Willy Lindwer collection series
Color (G) (DUTCH W/ENGLISH SUBTITLES)
$39.95 purchase _ #654
Joins filmmaker Willy Lindwer and his daughter who accompany Lindwer's father to Galicia - now Poland - Ukraine - in search of his father's shtetl Delatyn. Reveals that, 61 years after he left, Berl Nachim Lindwer wanted to not only find out what happened to his family which perished in the Holocaust, he wanted to see the house where he had grown up and again walk the streets of his shtetl. Juxtaposes historic film of pre - war shtetl life with footage of Lindwer's pilgrimage. English narration. Part of eight documentaries on the Holocaust.
History - World
Dist - ERGOM **Prod** - LINDWE

Return to Nazareth 30 MIN
16mm / VHS / U-matic
Living Christ series
Color; B&W (G)
Contrasts the attitude of Jesus' contemporaries toward Him. Includes the healing of the centurion's servant, the marriage at Cana, the rejection at Nazareth, the midnight visit of Nicodemus and the parable of the Good Samaritan.
Religion and Philosophy
Dist - ECUFLM **Prod** - CAFM 1958
CAFM

Return to nursing 150 MIN
VHS
Color; PAL (C PRO G)
PdS55 purchase
Presents five 30 - minute programs to encourage and attract qualified trained nurses who have left the profession to come back. Reveals that skills already acquired are easily transferred to nursing practice and that non - practicing nurses needn't be apprehensive about have been away from nursing for a time. Contact distributor about availability outside the United Kingdom.
Health and Safety
Dist - ACADEM **Prod** - YORKTV

Return to Oz 57 MIN
16mm
Color
Presents an animated version of L Frank Baum's 'The wizard of Oz.'.
Fine Arts
Dist - TWYMAN **Prod** - UPA 1970

Return to Paradise - Pt 3 50 MIN
VHS
New Pacific Series, the
Color (S)
$79.00 purchase _ #833 - 9111
Explores the cultural, historical, economic and political facets of the Pacific Basin which supports a third of the world's population. No other region contains so great a diversity of race, language and culture. Part 3 of eight parts asks how the Pacific island peoples can maintain their traditional values in the face of technological changes.
Business and Economics; Civics and Political Systems; Geography - World; Guidance and Counseling; History - World; Sociology
Dist - FI **Prod** - BBCTV 1987

Return to Pelican Island 26 MIN
16mm
Audubon wildlife theatre series
Color (I)
Explains that each spring the great white pelicans return from the south to a small island in the Great Salt Lake of Utah, a lake devoid of fish, to breed. Follows the development of the young pelicans from birth, to feather and wing development, and to the time in late summer when the fledglings have at last learned to fly.
Geography - United States; Geography - World; Science - Natural
Dist - AVEXP **Prod** - AVEXP

Return to Reality 35 MIN
16mm
Color
LC 75-702873
Deals with the problems of confusion in one patient, demonstrating the technique of reality orientation as practiced by a team at the Veterans Administration Hospital in Tuscaloosa, Alabama. Shows how this program has helped change the lives of the patient, an elderly stroke victim, and the lives of his family.
Health and Safety; Psychology
Dist - USNAC **Prod** - VAHT 1972

Return to Space 59 MIN
VHS / U-matic
Color
LC 81-707289
Examines the first space shuttle mission factors involved in its heavily military role, and the opportunities to use it for the long - term good of mankind.
Civics and Political Systems; Science - Physical; Sociology
Dist - KTEHTV **Prod** - KTEHTV 1981

Return to the dreaming - Aborigine life 60 MIN
VHS
Australian ark series
Color (G)
$19.95 purchase _ #S02060
Portrays Australia's Aborigine people.
Geography - World; History - World
Dist - UILL

Return to the Jewish ghetto of Venice 28 MIN
VHS
Jewish life around the world series
Color (G)
$34.95 purchase _ #120
Reveals that of the 1300 Jews who lived in Venice, Italy before World War II, only ten families remain.
History - World; Sociology
Dist - ERGOM **Prod** - ERGOM

Return to the magic library series

A Daring rescue 15 MIN
A Different drummer 15 MIN
A Giant tale 15 MIN
Good friends 15 MIN
Grammy May 15 MIN
A Knight - time tale 15 MIN
Mermaids and monsters 15 MIN
Mice in a mystery 15 MIN
Norbert, Snorebert 15 MIN
Voices in verses 15 MIN
Dist - TVOTAR

Return to the Philippines 30 MIN
U-matic / VHS
World War II - GI Diary Series
Color (H C A)
History - United States; History - World
Dist - TIMLIF **Prod** - TIMLIF 1980

Return to the River 29 MIN
16mm
Color
Deals with the Connecticut River. Records the progress against pollution of the river. Shows the varied uses of the river, including the annual Sunfish Race and the Goodspeed Opera House.
Science - Natural; Social Science; Sociology
Dist - FENWCK **Prod** - GRANTE

The Return to the Rocks 17 MIN
16mm
Color
LC 80-700835
Describes the birth of the Australian nation in 1788 and the attempts of early settlers and convicts to survive in the harsh new land.
History - World
Dist - TASCOR **Prod** - IMPACT 1976

Return to the sacred ice 50 MIN
VHS
Legendary trails - everyman special series
Color (A)
PdS99 purchase _ Unavailable in the USA
Explores different expressions of the pilgrim's search. Features Nicholas Shakespeare who visits Peru and witnesses a worship of Christ which overlays a far more ancient belief. Part of a four-part series.
Religion and Philosophy
Dist - BBCENE

Return to the sea series

Presents a 13 - part series on marine life produced by Marine Grafics and University of North Carolina Public TV. Discusses coral reef ecology, sharks, the sensory organs of fish and underwater photography, the night sea and the Sea of Cortez, shipwrecks from World War II, scuba diving, Florida ecology, salt marshes, deep sea diving, submarine medicine, microscopic life on coral reefs and Belize.

A Day on the reef 30 MIN
Deep sea secrets 30 MIN
Fish senses and the art of underwater photography 30 MIN
Graveyards of the Atlantic - graveyards of the Pacific 30 MIN
Life in the salt marsh 30 MIN
The Mystery of the bends 30 MIN
The Ocean at night - The Sea of Cortez 30 MIN
People who make a difference 30 MIN
The Reef and the rainforest 30 MIN
The Reef at the end of the road - Last days of the manatee 30 MIN
Reunion 30 MIN
Secrets of the shark 30 MIN
Small world 30 MIN
Dist - ENVIMC

Returning from the Moon 29 MIN
16mm
Science Reporter Series
B&W (J)
LC 79-708125
Explores the problem of getting the Apollo command module safely back through the atmosphere to earth. Explores the problems of guidance and heating and the manufacturing process for the ablative heat shield.
Industrial and Technical Education; Science - Physical
Dist - USNAC **Prod** - NASA 1966

Returning swallows 48 MIN
VHS
China moon series
Color (I J G)
$295.00 purchase
Reveals that up until the middle of the 19th century, emigration from China was punishable by death. Discloses that those who managed to leave could never return. There are 20 million Chinese living overseas. Returns to China with a Chinese family whose working lives have been spent abroad but who remain loyal to the motherland. Part of a series on China.
Geography - World; History - World
Dist - LANDMK **Prod** - LANDMK 1989

Returning the shadow 23 MIN
16mm
Color (G)
$45.00 rental
Uses five family photographs taken in the 1940s to consider how the meaning of these visual documents changes with life experiences. Allows the viewer to contribute personal memories while exploring the tension between recorded and remembered past and present.
Fine Arts; Sociology
Dist - CANCIN **Prod** - HOLMEK 1985

Returning to Chile 28 MIN
16mm / VHS
Color (G)
$400.00, $250.00 purchase, $50.00 rental; LC 89715549
Investigates the problems of identity and adjustment confronting Chilean youngsters who recently returned to Chile after many years in exile with their parents. Discusses their memories of the 1973 coup and their reactions to the widespread poverty and political repression in Chile today.
Civics and Political Systems; Geography - World; History - World; Sociology
Dist - CNEMAG **Prod** - CNEMAG 1986

Returns to Mexico 18 MIN
16mm
Color; B&W (G)
$35.00 rental
Provides glimpses off the beaten path in Mexico such as the temple of Mexico's Dionysus and inside a prison for women. Documents several trips the filmmaker took to visit his imprisoned sister.
Fine Arts; Geography - World; Sociology
Dist - CANCIN **Prod** - JONESE 1978

Reunion 21 MIN
16mm
B&W
LC 79-700750
Presents an account of the liberation of French prisoners from Nazi concentration camps. Shows the removal of the prisoners to temporary hospitals and pictures joyful reunions with families and friends in Paris.
History - World
Dist - USNAC **Prod** - USOWI 1946

Reunion 28 MIN
16mm
Color
LC 76-703075
Shows how an ex - soldier released from prison for his wife's funeral cannot cope with the situation and tries to retreat to a vanished past.
Fine Arts; Literature and Drama; Sociology
Dist - CANFDC **Prod** - YORKU 1974

Reunion 48 MIN
16mm
B&W (C A)
LC 72-711426
A documentary film in cinema verite style which consists of interviews with alumni of Yale University combined with an impressionistic study of class reunions ranging from the class of 1909 to the class of 1964.
Education; Psychology
Dist - MCQLKN **Prod** - MCQLKN 1970

Reunion 30 MIN
VHS
Color (G)
$59.95 purchase _ #REUN - 000
Views the Holocaust through the memories of an American tank sergeant and a Jewish woman who survived the camps. Features the two people's reunion more than 40 years after the war, a meeting which led to their sharing of their experiences. Interviews Elie Wiesel and other Holocaust survivors, as well as an American judge at the Nuremburg trials.
History - World
Dist - PBS **Prod** - KCTSTV 1985

Reunion 30MIN
VHS
AIDSFILMS series
Color (H C G)
$65.00 purchase
Portrays a family reunion during which two brothers reevaluate their sexual behavior and attitudes when they learn their older brother is HIV positive. Dramatizes the impact and realities of HIV - AIDS on families and heterosexual partners. Provides realistic models for talking about safer sex between partners, and empowers viewers to follow such practices in their own lives.
Health and Safety; Psychology; Social Science; Sociology
Dist - SELMED

Reunion 21 MIN
16mm
B&W (G)
$25.00 rental
Presents emotional, first - hand accounts of the liberation of the Nazi death camps by the Allied armies and their humane efforts to heal the survivors, restore them to their homes and bring the perpetrators to justice. Provides little hard, factual information and no mention is made of Jews or genocide. Directed and photographed by Henri Cartier - Bresson; produced by the US Information Service.
Fine Arts; History - United States; History - World; Religion and Philosophy
Dist - NCJEWF

Reunion 30 MIN
VHS
Return to the sea series
Color (I J H G)
$24.95 purchase _ #RTS204
Reveals that during the early days of World War II, a German submarine, the U - 352, was sunk in a dramatic battle 26 miles off the coast of North Carolina. Visits an emotional reunion 50 years after the sinking of surviving crewmen of the U - boat and of the ship that sank it gathered to honor those who died in the Battle of the Atlantic. Part of a 13 - part series on marine life produced by Marine Grafics and University of North Carolina Public TV.
History - World
Dist - ENVIMC

Reunion and Dark Pony 60 MIN
U-matic / VHS
Color
Fine Arts; Literature and Drama
Dist - ABCLR **Prod** - ABCLR

Reunion as a therapeutic strategy - a teenage adoptee encounters his birth mother 35 MIN
VHS
Wediko series
Color (C G PRO)
$175.00 purchase, $26.50 rental _ #40568
Offers a study of Michael who was about three years old when he was adopted and began to experience problems as a preadolescent. Reveals that his therapist, Dr Hugh Leichtman, found a preoccupation with his birth mother in Michael and an ambivalence with his adoptive family that suggested a reunion with his birth mother might allow him to resolve the conflicting loyalties that were interfering with his development. Part of a series recording spontaneous behavior at Camp Wediko, a pioneer facility for therapeutic camping in Hillsboro, New Hampshire.
Health and Safety; Physical Education and Recreation; Psychology; Sociology
Dist - PSU **Prod** - MASON 1991

Reuse 13 MIN
VHS / Videodisc / 16mm
Protecting our environment series
Color (I J H) (SPANISH)
$395.00, $295.00 purchase, $50.00 rental _ #8254, #8254 - LD
Shows how the utility value of many household items can be extended by modifying them or creating new uses for them. Shows how auto parts can be reconditioned, broken furniture and appliances can be cleaned, repaired and resold by voluntary organizations. Part of a series on the new '3Rs' of environmental protection - Reduce, Reuse and Recycle - produced by Century 21 Video.
Business and Economics; Science - Natural
Dist - AIMS

Revelation 120 MIN
VHS
Standard video Bible study series
Color (G A R)
$54.95 purchase, $10.00 rental _ #35 - 80111 - 2087
Focuses on the apocalyptic New Testament book of Revelation. Attempts to view the book in the context of the Roman Empire. Contains live footage of the cities mentioned in Revelation. Features several noted scholars. Includes leader's guide and study guide. Produced by Kerr Associates.
Literature and Drama; Religion and Philosophy
Dist - APH

Revelation 17 - 22
VHS
The Bible - American Sign Language translation series
Color (S R)
Presents an American Sign Language translation of the New Testament book of Revelation, chapters 17 through 22. Available on a free - loan basis from the Lutheran Church - Missouri Synod's Deaf Ministry.
Guidance and Counseling; Literature and Drama; Religion and Philosophy
Dist - CPH **Prod** - LUMIS

Revelation 8 - 16
VHS
The Bible - American Sign Language translation series
Color (S R)
Presents an American Sign Language translation of the New Testament book of Revelation, chapters 8 through 16. Available on a free - loan basis from the Lutheran Church - Missouri Synod's Deaf Ministry.
Guidance and Counseling; Literature and Drama; Religion and Philosophy
Dist - CPH **Prod** - LUMIS

Revelation 1 - 8
VHS
The Bible - American Sign Language translation series
Color (S R)
Presents an American Sign Language translation of the New Testament book of Revelation, chapters 1 through 8. Available on a free - loan basis from the Lutheran Church - Missouri Synod's Deaf Ministry.
Guidance and Counseling; Literature and Drama; Religion and Philosophy
Dist - CPH **Prod** - LUMIS

Revelation Series
Epiphania - the manifestation 15 MIN
Retreat 11 MIN
Right here, right now 15 MIN
Turned Round to See 11 MIN
Dist - FRACOC

Revelation series
Presents a two - part series describing the history of Christianity. Includes the titles The Beginning of Christianity and The Church in Europe.
The Beginnings of Christianity 25 MIN
The Church in Europe 25 MIN
Revelation series 50 MIN
Dist - LANDMK **Prod** - LANDMK

Revelations - Pt 4 29 MIN
VHS / 16mm
Unorganized Manager Series
Color (A PRO)
$790.00 purchase, $220.00 rental
Summarizes the training on organization, management, communication and supervision given on previous videos in the series. Management training. Part of a series, 'The Unorganized Manager.'
Guidance and Counseling; Psychology
Dist - VIDART **Prod** - VIDART 1990

Revenge - 48 10 MIN
VHS / U-matic
Life's little lessons - self - esteem 4 - 6 series
Color (I)
$129.00, $99.00 purchase _ #V677
Portrays Chester McNabb who was very proud of his prize chickens - and upset when he discovered his neighbors stealing them. Reveals that McNabb was all set for revenge until his wife Mary convinced him to give the stealing neighbors another chicken - which stopped the stealing and made everybody friends. Part of a 65 - part series on self - esteem.
Guidance and Counseling; Psychology; Sociology
Dist - BARR **Prod** - CEPRO 1992

Revenge of Red Chief 24 MIN
U-matic / VHS
Color (K P I)
$335.00 purchase
Fine Arts
Dist - ABCLR **Prod** - ABCLR

Revenge of the Nerd 45 MIN
U-matic / 16mm / VHS
Color (J H)
LC 83-700993; 83-700520
A shortened version of the motion picture Revenge Of The Nerd. Presents the story of high school computer genius Bertram Cummings, who has the reputation of being a 'nerd.' Tells how Bertram seeks revenge against three classmates who try to make a fool out of him. Shows that Bertram's victory is not long - lasting and demonstrates that being yourself is the most important way to behave.
Guidance and Counseling
Dist - LCOA **Prod** - HGATE 1982

Revenge road - Volume 4 45 MIN
VHS
Bubblegum crisis series
Color (A) (JAPANESE WITH ENGLISH SUBTITLES)
$34.95 purchase _ #CPM91004
Presents a Japanese animated film. Viewer discretion is advised as some films contain strong language or violence.
Fine Arts
Dist - CHTSUI

The Revengers 5 MIN
U-matic / VHS
Write on, Set 2 Series
Color (J H)
Deals with the use of 'Could have' and 'Should have' in writing.
English Language
Dist - CTI **Prod** - CTI

Revenues, Rates and Reimbursements Series
Financial Sensibilities and Responsibilities
Responsible Pricing of Services
Toward Price - Based Reimbursement
Validating Pricing Strategies
Dist - TEACHM

Revere the Emperor, Expel the Barbarian 30 MIN
VHS / U-matic
Japan - the Changing Tradition Series
Color (H C A)
History - World
Dist - GPN **Prod** - UMA 1978

Reverence Day 29 MIN
Videoreel / VT2
Our Street Series
Color
Sociology
Dist - PBS **Prod** - MDCPB

Reverend Al Carmines, Carla De Sola and Bill Cordh 30 MIN
U-matic / VHS
Eye on Dance - Dance in Religion and Ritual Series
Color
Discusses dance in the Christian tradition. Hosted by Julinda Lewis.
Fine Arts; Religion and Philosophy
Dist - ARCVID **Prod** - ARCVID

Reversal 28 MIN
VHS
Elephant show series
Color (P I)
$95.00 purchase, $45.00 rental
Presents program 16 in the Sharon, Lois and Bram's Elephant Show series. Teaches reading readiness and social skills while engaging children in making music. Each program explores a new theme through adventure, fantasy, mystery and song with recording artists Sharon, Lois and Bram. Uses traditional materials which stress participation - action songs, sing - along songs, story songs, clapping songs, singing games, playground chants and folk songs from many different traditions. Includes teacher's guide co - authored by a music education specialist.
Fine Arts; Sociology
Dist - BULFRG **Prod** - CAMBFP 1989

Reverse Bevel Flap 19 MIN
8mm cartridge / U-matic
Color (PRO)
LC 74-706396; 77-706187
Shows how a reverse bevel flap is used to remove crevicular epithelium from periodontal pockets and to provide adequate access for subsequent scaling and root planing.
Science
Dist - USNAC **Prod** - USVA 1972

Reverse Dive, Layout Position 4 MIN
16mm
Diving - for Fun and Fame Series
Color
LC 73-702915
Physical Education and Recreation
Dist - PURPOS **Prod** - PART 1972

Reverse Dive, Pike Position 4 MIN
16mm
Diving - for Fun and Fame Series
Color
LC 73-702915
Physical Education and Recreation
Dist - PURPOS **Prod** - PART 1972

Reverse Osmosis 29 MIN
Videoreel / VT2
Interface Series
Color
Business and Economics; Science - Physical
Dist - PBS **Prod** - KCET

The Reverse Side of the Eye 29 MIN
U-matic
Creation of Art Series
Color
Discusses the inner fantasies and visions of artists that are made visible on canvas.
Fine Arts
Dist - UMITV **Prod** - UMITV 1975

Reverse the Charges - How to Save Money on Your Phone Bill 49 MIN
VHS / U-matic
Color (H C A)
Explains how changes in the phone industry are affecting the consumer. Emphasizes how consumers can capitalize on the AT&T breakup and save money on their monthly phone bill. Examines three areas - local calls, equipment selection, and long distance calls.
Industrial and Technical Education; Social Science
Dist - FI **Prod** - TAG 1989

A Reverse Three - Quarter Crown for Non - Parallel Abutments - Jaw Relation 6 MIN
16mm
Reverse Three - Quarter Crown for Non - Parallel Abutments Series 'Part 2
Color (PRO)
LC 77-700820
Demonstrates the procedures for making impressions, jaw relation records and temporary coverage in treating a lingually inclined molar abutment with a reverse three - quarter crown.
Health and Safety; Science
Dist - USNAC **Prod** - VADTC 1977

Reverse Three - Quarter Crown for Non - Parallel Abutments Series Part 1
A Reverse Three - Quarter Crown for Non - Parallel Abutments - Treatment Planning and Tooth 12 MIN
Dist - USNAC

Reverse Three - Quarter Crown for Non - Parallel Abutments Series Part 2
A Reverse Three - Quarter Crown for Non - Parallel Abutments - Jaw Relation Record and 6 MIN
Dist - USNAC

A Reverse Three - Quarter Crown for Non - Parallel Abutments - Treatment Planning and Tooth 12 MIN
16mm
Reverse Three - Quarter Crown for Non - Parallel Abutments Series 'Part 1
Color (PRO)
LC 77-700819
Demonstrates the appropriate instrumentation, procedures and tooth preparation used in treating non - parallel abutments with a reverse three - quarter crown.
Health and Safety; Science
Dist - USNAC **Prod** - VADTC 1977

Reversed Jejunal Segment for Disabling Post - Vagotomy Diarrhea 18 MIN
16mm
Color (PRO)
Explains that a reversed jejunal segment constructed approximately 100 centimeters distal to Treitz's ligament will effectively retard the passage of food stuffs in the proximal small intestine and will serve to correct post - vagotomy diarrhea and intestinal hurry.
Health and Safety; Science
Dist - ACY **Prod** - ACYDGD 1969

Reversible and Irreversible Events 8 MIN
16mm
Color (J)
LC 76-703732
Portrays perceptual events which can proceed in a forward direction as well as in a backward direction and events that are not reversible or do not appear normal when reversed.
Psychology
Dist - PSUPCR **Prod** - GIBSOJ 1973

Reversible and Irreversible Processes 21 MIN
16mm
College Physics Film Program Series
B&W (H C)
LC 74-709338
Shows how a large air - filled cylinder is closed with a heavy piston and when the piston is displaced from equilibrium the system oscillates. Explains two conditions for long oscillations (reversibility) - when the surface area approaches zero, the temperature changes in the gas are high (adiabatic,) and when the surface area becomes very large, there are no measurable temperature changes (isothermal.).
Science - Physical
Dist - MLA **Prod** - ESSOSI 1970

Reversing Paralysis 24 MIN
U-matic / VHS
Color (C)
$249.00, $149.00 purchase _ #AD - 2056
Examines the latest research into reversing at least some of the effects of paralysis, showing how patients can learn to utilize healed or undamaged neurons in the spinal cord and recover some functions in paralyzed extremities. Reveals that between ten and twenty thousand Americans suffer major injuries to their spinal cords each year.
Health and Safety; Science - Natural
Dist - FOTH **Prod** - FOTH

Review 29 MIN
U-matic
Woodcarver's Workshop Series
Color
Industrial and Technical Education
Dist - PBS **Prod** - WOSUTV

Review and Preview 30 MIN
U-matic / VHS
Making it Count Series
Color (H C A)
LC 80-707571
Examines data processing installations. Tours two processing centers to examine the roles of personnel and equipment, security and privacy problems, the selection of computer systems and services, and projections for the future.
Business and Economics; Mathematics
Dist - BCSC **Prod** - BCSC 1980

Review and Rewrite 30 MIN
VHS / U-matic
Effective Writing for Executives Series
Color (C A)
LC 80-707555
Applies the principles of organization, use of language, style and tone in writing a first draft and rewrite. Shows how to frame a negative message. Hosted by Ed Asner.
Business and Economics; English Language
Dist - TIMLIF **Prod** - TIMLIF 1980

Review and Summary 15 MIN
U-matic / VHS
Math Cycle Series
Color (P)
Reviews several ideas, concepts and the four arithmetic operations.
Mathematics
Dist - GPN **Prod** - WDCNTV

Review for the A S V A B
VHS
Standardized video exam review series
Color (H C A)
$39.95 purchase _ #VA410V
Presents a video review for the A S V A B armed forces entry examination. Includes a study guide.
Education
Dist - CAMV

Review for the A C T
VHS
Color (H)
$79.95 purchase _ #VAD003
Offers a review and test tips for the ACT. Includes two videocassettes and a study guide.
Education
Dist - SIV

Review for the Armed Forces Exam
U-matic / VHS
Standardized Video Exam Review Series
(H T)
$39.95 _ #VA410V
Features instructors with experience who council viewers on effective techniques to use in taking the Armed Forces Exam. Includes study guide.
Education
Dist - CAMV **Prod** - CAMV

Review for the G E D
VHS / U-matic
Standardized video exam review series
Color (H C A)
$59.95 purchase _ #VA310V
Presents a video review for the G E D high school equivalency examination. Includes a study guide. Consists of two videocassettes.
Education
Dist - CAMV

Review for the GED
VHS
Color (H)
$79.95 purchase _ #VAD006
Tutors students for the high school diploma equivalency. Includes study guide.
Education
Dist - SIV

Review for the GMAT, math and verbal
VHS
Color (C)
$79.95 purchase _ #VAD001
Presents two videocassettes offering verbal and math reviews in preparation for the GMAT. Includes study guide.
Education
Dist - SIV

Review for the GRE
VHS
Color (C)
$79.95 purchase _ #VAD000
Presents two videocassettes offering verbal and math reviews in preparation for the GRE. Includes study guide.
Education
Dist - SIV

Review for the L S A T
VHS
Standardized video exam review series
Color (H C A)
$69.95 purchase _ #VA910V
Presents a video review for the L S A T law school admissions test. Includes a study guide. Consists of two videocassettes.
Education
Dist - CAMV

Review for the M A T
VHS
Standardized video exam review series
Color (H C A)
$39.95 purchase _ #VA510V
Presents a video review for the M A T, a test used for graduate school admissions. Includes a study guide.
Education
Dist - CAMV

Review for the N T E
VHS
Standardized video exam review series
Color (H C A)
$39.95 purchase _ #VA227V
Presents a video review for the N T E teachers' test. Includes a study guide.
Education
Dist - CAMV

Review for the S A T
VHS
Standardized video exam review series
Color (H C A)
$39.95 purchase _ #VA170V
Presents a video review of mathematics and verbal skills for the S A T college entrance test. Includes a study guide.
Education
Dist - CAMV

Review for the SAT 120 MIN
VHS / 16mm
Test Preparation Video Series
Color (H)
$39.95 _ VAI 108
Reviews the SAT. Testing strategies and problem solving techniques are given.
Education; Psychology
Dist - CADESF **Prod** - CADESF

Review for the T O E F L
VHS
Standardized video exam review series
Color (H C A)
$39.95 purchase _ #VA138V
Presents a video review for the T O E F L test. Includes a study guide.
Education
Dist - CAMV

Review of Combinatorial Logic 30 MIN
U-matic / VHS
Digital Sub - Systems Series
Color
Reviews basic logic elements of NOT, AND, OR, NOR, and NAND. Discusses basic rules of Boolean algebra, and examples of both minimized and non - minimized design.
Industrial and Technical Education; Mathematics; Sociology
Dist - TXINLC **Prod** - TXINLC

Review of electrical fundamentals
U-matic / VHS
Distribution system operation series; Topic 2
Color (IND)
Aims at ensuring the participant has sufficient familiarity with basic electrical theory to understand concepts which will be used throughout the training program. Includes topics such as basic electricity, frequency transformers and current flow in multiple circuits.
Industrial and Technical Education
Dist - LEIKID **Prod** - LEIKID

Review of electrical fundamentals 1
U-matic / VHS
Electric power system operation series; Tape 1
Color (IND)
Covers voltage generation, frequency, current, power, reactive, power factor, three - phase operation, power and energy, watts and vars.
Industrial and Technical Education
Dist - LEIKID **Prod** - LEIKID

Review of electrical fundamentals 2
VHS / U-matic
Electric power system operation series; Tape 2
Color (IND)
Includes inductance, impedance, capacitance, voltage drop, line charging and per unit calculations.
Industrial and Technical Education
Dist - LEIKID **Prod** - LEIKID

Review of Electrical Fundamentals Series
Electrical Fundamentals 1 60 MIN
Electrical Fundamentals 2 60 MIN
Dist - LEIKID

Review of Human Biology - Design for Living 26 MIN
U-matic / VHS / 16mm
Living Body - an Introduction to Human Biology Series
Color
Summarizes the functions and designs of the body's major systems and organs and the methods by which they interact.
Science - Natural
Dist - FOTH **Prod** - FOTH 1985

Review of one rescuer and two rescuer CPR - review of first aid for foreign body obstruction of airway; Revised edition 15 MIN
VHS / U-matic
CPR - yours for life series
Color (H C A)
Provides a review of one rescuer CPR, two rescuer CPR and first aid for foreign body obstruction of the airway. Discusses infant resuscitation and special resuscitation situations.
Health and Safety
Dist - GPN **Prod** - KUONTV 1982

Review of Previews - 31 Lessons 15 MIN
U-matic
Studio M Series
Color (P)
Uses a newscast format to review the Studio M series.
Mathematics
Dist - GPN **Prod** - WCETTV 1979

Review of Probablistic Concepts 50 MIN
U-matic / VHS
Modern Control Theory - Stochastic Estimation Series
Color (PRO)
Industrial and Technical Education; Mathematics
Dist - MIOT **Prod** - MIOT

Review of Safety and Electronic Mathematics 12 MIN
VHS / U-matic
B&W
LC 84-706408
Reviews the safety precautions to be observed when working on electrical equipment. Also reviews the conversion of numbers to powers of 10 and the addition, subtraction, multiplication and division of powers.
Industrial and Technical Education; Mathematics
Dist - USNAC **Prod** - USAF 1983

Review of Sequential Logic 30 MIN
U-matic / VHS
Digital Sub - Systems Series
Color
Gives basic elements required for sequential logic design as well as their truth tables, and follows with development of state diagram, excitation tables, and output tables. Summarizes by reviewing basic sequential design method.
Industrial and Technical Education; Mathematics; Sociology
Dist - TXINLC **Prod** - TXINLC

Review of series parallel circuits
Reviews series - parallel circuit problem solving, including measuring current, voltage and resistance. Discusses practical troubleshooting.
Review of series parallel circuits 24 MIN
Dist - USNAC **Prod** - USAF

Review of the 1987 - 1988 US Supreme Court term 85 MIN
VHS
Color (C PRO A)
$17.40, $75.00 purchase _ #M737, #P242
Presents a review of US Supreme Court decisions in individual rights cases during the second year of Chief Justice Rehnquist's tenure and the year that Justice Anthony Kennedy joined the High Court.
Civics and Political Systems
Dist - ALIABA

Review of the course 28 MIN
U-matic / BETA / VHS
Communication skills 1 - basic series
Color (H C G)
$101.95, $89.95 purchase _ #CA - 52
Reviews the entire series of 26 programs on basic communication skills. Covers written, oral and nonverbal communication, as well as skills in speaking, listening and reading. Part of a series on communication.
English Language; Social Science
Dist - INSTRU

A Review of the Evidence Associating Herpes Type II Virus with Cervical Cancer 40 MIN
U-matic
Color
Discusses the relationship between Herpes II and cervical cancer and the problems that have arisen in this association.
Health and Safety
Dist - UTEXSC **Prod** - UTEXSC

Review of the Report of the National Commission on Marijuana 29 MIN
16mm
Color (H C A)
LC 73-702925
Presents a synopsis of the report of the National Commission on Marijuana. Includes interviews with sociologists, psychiatrists and other professionals who indicate that it is neither physically nor psychologically addictive and may be unfavorable only when used in higher doses.
Health and Safety; Psychology; Sociology
Dist - HAASF **Prod** - NOLAN 1973

Review of the Seventies 44 MIN
U-matic / VHS / 16mm
Color
Provides an overview of the ideas, personalities, historical events and social forces of the 1970's.
History - United States
Dist - CNEMAG **Prod** - DOCUA

Review of the Sixties 44 MIN
U-matic / VHS / 16mm
Color
Chronicles the events and trends of the 1960's.
History - United States
Dist - CNEMAG **Prod** - DOCUA

Review of the Year 1955 15 MIN
16mm
B&W
Gives an account of the first general elections ever held in Malaysia.
Geography - World; History - World
Dist - PMFMUN **Prod** - FILEM 1956

Review of the Year 1959 21 MIN
16mm
B&W
Shows the significant events in the federation of Malaysia and highlights the steady progress made by the government in all fields in 1959.
Geography - World; History - World
Dist - PMFMUN **Prod** - FILEM 1960

Review of the Year 1961 27 MIN
16mm
B&W
Discusses the installation of a new king, rural development, the Association of Southeast Asia, the concept of Malaysia making a resounding impact all over the world and her overseas reputation remaining high in 1961.
Geography - World; History - World
Dist - PMFMUN **Prod** - FILEM 1962

Review of the Year 1962 25 MIN
16mm
B&W
Shows the Malaysian royal visit to India and Pakistan and discusses 1962 as the year where all facets of the National Second Five Year Development Plan were successfully carried out in Malaysia.
Geography - World; History - World
Dist - PMFMUN **Prod** - FILEM 1963

Review of Writing Position and the Last 13 Lower Case Letters Learned 15 MIN
U-matic
Writing Time Series
Color (P)
English Language
Dist - GPN **Prod** - WHROTV

The Review that Builds Commitment 30 MIN
U-matic / VHS
Performance Reviews that Build Commitment Series
Color
Provides an integrated review and basis for continuing growth of managerial skill in the performance appraisal process.
Business and Economics; Guidance and Counseling; Psychology
Dist - DELTAK **Prod** - PRODEV

Reviewing Performance 29 MIN
16mm
Interviewing for Results Series
B&W (IND)
LC 73-703323
Business and Economics; Psychology
Dist - EDSD **Prod** - EDSD 1968

Reviewing the Situation 28 MIN
U-matic / VHS
Please Stand by - a History of Radio Series
(C A)
Fine Arts; History - United States; Psychology; Sociology
Dist - SCCON **Prod** - SCCON 1986

Reviews and Criticisms 6 MIN
VHS / U-matic
Library Skills Tapes Series
Color
Enables students to find reviews and criticisms of plays, poems, short stories and novels through the use of special reference tools.
Education; English Language
Dist - MDCC **Prod** - MDCC

Reviews of series and parallel resistive circuits 23 MIN
U-matic / VHS
B&W
LC 84-706409
Reviews current, voltage and resistance characteristics in series and parallel circuits and reviews balanced and unbalanced bridge circuits.
Industrial and Technical Education; Science - Physical
Dist - USNAC **Prod** - USAF 1983

Revise and Improve 14 MIN
U-matic / VHS / 16mm
Effective Writing Series
Color (J H)
$340, $240 purchase _ #1949
Talks about revision of compositions, focussing on content, structure, and grammar.
English Language
Dist - CORF

Revised Gesell and Amatruda developmental and neurologic examination - with interview - at 18, 24, and 36 Months 75 MIN
U-matic / VHS
Developmental - neurologic approach to assessment in infancy and early childhood series
Color (PRO)
Complete title is Revised Gesell And Amatruda Developmental And Neurologic Examination (With Interview) At 18, 24, And 36 Months. Contains interviews with a mother to get information about the child's current behavior. On 3 tapes.
Guidance and Counseling; Health and Safety; Psychology
Dist - HSCIC **Prod** - HSCIC 1982

Revised Gesell and Amatruda developmental and neurologic examination - with interview - at 18 months 23 MIN
VHS / 16mm
Developmental neurologic approach to assessment in infancy and early childhood - Unit II series
(C)
$330.00 purchase _ #821VI110
Contains an interview with the mother of an 18 month old child. Illustrates techniques for eliciting accurate responses.
Health and Safety
Dist - HSCIC **Prod** - HSCIC 1982

The Revised Gesell and Amatruda developmental and neurologic examination in infancy 29 MIN
U-matic / VHS
Developmental - neurologic approach to assessment in infancy and early childhood series
Color (PRO)
Shows how to present each of the exam materials to the infant, to describe what the infant does, and to give an interpretation of the behaviors observed.
Health and Safety; Psychology
Dist - HSCIC **Prod** - HSCIC 1982

The Revised Gesell and Amatruda developmental and neurologic examination - with interview - at 24 months 24 MIN
VHS / 16mm
Developmental neurologic approach to assessment in infancy and early childhood - Unit II series
(C)
$330.00 purhcase _ #821VI111
Presents an interview with the mother of a 24 month old child. Shows how to present each examination situation and how to move the child from one situation to another without disruption.
Health and Safety
Dist - HSCIC **Prod** - HSCIC 1982

The Revised Gesell and Amatruda developmental and neurologic examination - with interview - at 36 months 28 MIN
VHS / 16mm
Developmental neurologic approach to assessment in infancy and early childhood - Unit II series
(C)
$330.00 purchase _ #821VI112
Shows an interview with the mother of a 36 month old child. Presents the criteria for judging the child's responses to different examination situations.
Health and Safety
Dist - HSCIC **Prod** - HSCIC 1982

Revising and Editing 30 MIN
U-matic / VHS
Writing for Work Series Pt 7
Color (A)
LC 81-706734
Explains how to place oneself in the reader's place when editing a written communication. Describes how to check for errors in grammar and spelling and how to be critical of words, thoughts, order and meaning.
Business and Economics; English Language
Dist - TIMLIF **Prod** - TIMLIF 1981

Revising and proofreading the composition 28 MIN
U-matic / BETA / VHS
Communication skills 1 - basic series
Color (H C G)
$101.95, $89.95 purchase _ #CA - 36
Reveals that revising and proofreading are two skills necessary to every writer so that the final manuscript is as free from error as possible. Shows that revision is a process of rewriting to improve words, sentences and paragraphs, as well as making certain that each thesis point is developed carefully and sufficiently. Organization of material is also examined so that logical order is maintained. Part of a series on communication.
Social Science
Dist - INSTRU

Revision
16mm
B&W
Explores the role of boundary conditions in the subject of partial differential equations and discusses methods available for their solution. Talks about the numerical approach.
Mathematics
Dist - OPENU **Prod** - OPENU

Revision Stapedectomy 55 MIN
U-matic / VHS
Color (PRO)
Shows examples of displaced protheses, incus necrosis, slipped strut, fistulae, idiopathic malleus head fixation and exposed overhanging facial nerve as causes of failure in stapedectomies, and consequently the need for revision stapedectomies. Demonstrates the technique for use of an IRP (wire from the malleus handle) on a case with both incus necrosis and fistula.
Guidance and Counseling; Health and Safety; Science - Natural
Dist - HOUSEI **Prod** - HOUSEI 1982

Revision Strategies 30 MIN
VHS / U-matic
Write Course - an Introduction to College Composition Series
Color (C A)
LC 85-700989
Focuses on the revision stage of writing and goes beyond the concept of revision as merely proofreading and editing.
English Language
Dist - DALCCD **Prod** - DALCCD 1984

Revision strategies - using the writer's tools - Parts 21 and 22 60 MIN
U-matic / VHS
Write course - an introduction to college composition
Color (C)
$45.00, $29.95 purchase
Offers valuable criteria to apply at the revision stage in Part 21. Covers editing, proofreading and instructions in using common reference books in Part 22. Parts of a 30 - part series on college composition.
Education; English Language
Dist - ANNCPB **Prod** - DALCCD 1984

Revitalization movements - dialogue with Paulo Friere 45 MIN
VHS
Color (G)
$225.00 purchase _ #6892
Presents a discussion between Dr Matthew Zachariah, researcher of Gandhi's Sarvodaya approach to social change, and Paulo Friere of Brazil, who participated in the elaboration and popularization of the concept of Conscientization in cultural revitalization movements. Considers the role of class struggle in social change, the validity of violence in the pursuit of justice, and the responsibility of individuals in shaping a more humane world.
Psychology; Sociology
Dist - UCALG **Prod** - UCALG 1983

Revitalize your body 90 MIN
VHS
Color (G)
$29.95 purchase _ #HE - 05
Presents easy exercises to help in the recovery from illness or injury. Features Bob Klein.
Health and Safety; Physical Education and Recreation
Dist - ARVID **Prod** - ARVID

Revival of evil 50 MIN
VHS
Color (H C G A R)
$59.95 purchase, $10.00 rental _ #35 - 87 - 597
Examines witchcraft, psychic revelations, seances, demonic possession and other phenomena.
Religion and Philosophy
Dist - APH **Prod** - NEWLIB

Revival of the desert 50 MIN
U-matic / VHS
Color (H C G)
$250.00 purchase _ #HH - 6392M
Provides a close - up view of a number of seldom seen animals, birds, reptiles, rodents, insects and plants which comprise the desert's hardy ecosystem. Portrays the drama of the Kuwaiti desert through its stark beauty and by the often unseen but abundant life that prospers in its arid environment. Shows how humans can endanger the desert's ecosystem.
Geography - World; Science - Natural
Dist - CORF **Prod** - CORF 1990

The Revival of Victorianism 29 MIN
Videoreel / VT2
University of Chicago Round Table Series
Color
Psychology; Sociology
Dist - PBS **Prod** - WTTWTV

The Revocable Trust 150 MIN
U-matic / VHS
Color (PRO)
Analyzes and explains changes in the Economic Recovery Act of 1981 and the Tax Equity and Fiscal Responsibility Act of 1982. Replaces ABA Video Law Seminar.
Civics and Political Systems; Social Science
Dist - ABACPE **Prod** - ABACPE

The Revolt of Job 98 MIN
35mm / 16mm
Color (G)
Explores the essence of faith. Tells the story of an elderly Jewish couple living in a little Hungarian village in 1943, who adopt a small Catholic boy as their heir in an effort to pass on their wealth and knowledge before Nazi oppression consumes Hungary. Uses humor and social observation as this wild child is tamed through the understanding and patience of the couple he comes to regard as his parents. Produced by Mafilm Tarsulas Studio, Starfilm Macropus and ZDF - MTV Productions. Directed by Imre Gyongyossy and Barna Kabay. Contact distributor for price.
Fine Arts; Religion and Philosophy; Sociology
Dist - OCTOBF **Prod** - MAFIL 1984

The Revolt of Mother 47 MIN
U-matic / VHS / 16mm
Rites of Passage Series
Color (H C A)
$750 purchase - 16 mm, $250 purchase - video _ #5790C
Shows how a woman revolts when her husband breaks a promise to build a better home for the family. Based on the story by Mary E. Wilkins Freeman. Starring Amy Madigan.
Sociology
Dist - CORF

A Revolucao Dos Cravos 3 MIN
16mm
Color (A)
LC 76-703838
Uses animation to reflect on the Portuguese Revolution of 1974.
Fine Arts; History - World
Dist - CONCRU **Prod** - CONCRU 1976

The Revolution 36 MIN
VHS
Color (J H C G)
$89.95 purchase _ #CLE003CV
Traces the emergence of 'Americans' from groups of 'New World Colonists.' Provides a step - by - step report of the major events, campaigns and people of the War for Independence. Includes the actual words of Nathan Hale, Thomas Paine, Washington, Franklin, Adams and other Founders, as well as those of British protagonists.
History - United States; Sociology
Dist - CAMV

Revolution 16 MIN
16mm
Color
LC 74-702508
Traces important events, such as the Boston Massacre and Boston Tea Party, which led to the American Revolution, highlights the significant battles of the Revolutionary War, and examines the American victory in the struggle for independence.
History - United States
Dist - SBS **Prod** - SBS 1974

Revolution 1 MIN
16mm
B&W (G)
$5.00 rental
Presents the closing sequence, 30 seconds long, of Conquest Piece.
Fine Arts
Dist - CANCIN **Prod** - MERRIT 1982

The Revolution 40 MIN
16mm
B&W (C)
$845.00
Experimental film by Martha Haslanger.
Fine Arts
Dist - AFA **Prod** - AFA 1982

Revolution - 1910 - 1940 - Pt 1 57 MIN
VHS
Mexico Series
Color (S)
$49.00 purchase _ #485 - 9001
Traces, through rare archival film and interviews with prominent politicians, writers, historians and other leaders, the history of Mexico, the rise and decline of its one - party political system from its roots in the revolution of 1910 to its transformation in the elections of 1988. Part 1 looks at three decades of revolutionary turmoil which have spawned the institutions and systems that ruled Mexico until to day, and considers the people and events that shaped Mexico's history in the first part of the 20th century. In two parts.
Fine Arts; Geography - World; History - United States; History - World
Dist - FI **Prod** - WGBHTV 1988

Revolution and romantics - the age of the nation - states - Parts 43 and 44 60 MIN
VHS / U-matic
Western tradition - part II series
Color (G)
$45.00, $29.95 purchase
Presents two thirty - minute programs tracing the history of ideas, events and institutions which have shaped modern societies hosted by Eugen Weber. Looks at leaders in the arts, literature and political theory who argued for social justice and national liberation in part 43. Part 44 considers the great powers who cooperated to quell internal revolts, yet competed to acquire colonies. Parts 43 and 44 of a 52 - part series on the Western tradition.
Civics and Political Systems; Fine Arts; Geography - World; History - World; Literature and Drama; Sociology
Dist - ANNCPB **Prod** - WGBH 1989

A Revolution for independence 30 MIN
VHS
American adventure series
Color (G)
$150.00 purchase _ #TAMA - 108
Reviews the events of the Revolutionary War. Focuses on the creation of the Articles of Confederation and on the military battles of the war. Points out the significance of the revolution to various segments in American society.
History - United States
Dist - PBS

Revolution - how it began
Videodisc
Laser learning set 2 series; Set 2
Color; CAV (P I)
$375.00 purchase _ #8L5407
Describes the opening battles of the Revolutionary War at Lexington and Concord on April 19, 1775. Looks at non - fictional history and the purpose of authors. Part of a series of six theme - based interactive videodisc lessons. Requires a Pioneer LD - V2000 or 2200, with barcode reader and adapter, or a Pioneer LD - V4200 or higher. Includes user's guide, two readers.
History - United States; Literature and Drama
Dist - BARR **Prod** - BARR 1992

The Revolution in Mechanical Engineering 24 MIN
U-matic / VHS
Color (C)
$249.00, $149.00 purchase _ #AD - 2164
Chronicles the revolution that resulted from Werner von Siemen's discovery of how to generate electricity and transport it to where it is needed. Shows that even in the age of the supercomputer, von Siemen's discoveries still underlie modern industrial organization and production.
Industrial and Technical Education; Science; Science - Physical; Social Science
Dist - FOTH **Prod** - FOTH

Revolution in Nicaragua 58 MIN
U-matic / VHS
Crisis in Central America Series
Color (A)
Traces the evolution of U S involvement in Nicaragua and the struggle for control of the revolution. Describes the overthrow of the 50 - year - old Somoza dynasty by the Sandinistas in 1979 which the U S tried to prevent, then tried to court and then tried to undermine.
Civics and Political Systems; History - United States; History - World
Dist - FI **Prod** - WGBHTV

Revolution in Russia, 1917 19 MIN
16mm / U-matic / VHS
World War I Series
B&W (H C)
LC FIA67-5251
Shows that the effects of World War I caused the collapse of Imperial Russia, and presents the military, political and economic events that culminated in the first phase of the Russian Revolution. Reviews the efforts of Alexander Kerensky and his administration as it attempted to maintain a democratic government, and the significant events leading to the triumph of the Bolsheviks.
Civics and Political Systems; History - World
Dist - FI **Prod** - CBSTV 1967

Revolution in the Paint Locker 18 MIN
16mm
Color (IND)
LC 77-700078
Shows the impact of paints and coatings on the operation and maintenance of naval ships.
Industrial and Technical Education
Dist - USNAC **Prod** - USN 1975

Revolution in the World of Work 7 MIN
16mm
Color
LC 73-702917
Shows how vocational and career education can provide a saleable skill, as well as give personal security and a sense of relevance and opportunity to the individual.
Guidance and Counseling; Psychology
Dist - PART **Prod** - PART 1973

The Revolution is Advancing 26 MIN
16mm
Color
Deals less with the legacies of the Mozambican past, and more with the outlook for the future. Emphasizes the priority given to educational work, both adult literacy programs and childhood education, and shows some of the steps under way to develop a culture drawing on the strengths of the Mozambican people.
Civics and Political Systems; Geography - World; History - World
Dist - ICARUS **Prod** - ICARUS

The Revolution of necessity 60 MIN
VHS
Out of the fiery furnace series
Color; Captioned (G)
$69.95 purchase _ #OOFF - 104
Focuses on the Industrial Revolution. Shows that a shortage of wood in 17th century England led to the use of coal, which would eventually result in the development of steel. Features examples of ironwork such as the Eiffel Tower. Hosted by Michael Charlton.
History - United States; Social Science
Dist - PBS **Prod** - OPUS 1986

Revolution or Evolution - Music in Progress 30 MIN
U-matic
Changing Music Series
Color
Fine Arts
Dist - PBS **Prod** - WGBHTV

Revolution Until Victory
16mm
B&W
Presents the story of the Palestinian people and the rise of Fateh, the leading guerrilla organization.
Civics and Political Systems; History - World; Sociology
Dist - CANWRL **Prod** - CANWRL 1970

Revolutionaries 54 MIN
VHS
Red empire series
Color (J H C G)
$19.98 purchase _ #FFO9611V
Chronicles the reign of Nicholas and Alexandra over 150 million people of 100 different nationalities. Reveals that life is very hard for the common Russian people and workers are discontented. Siberian goldfield strikes in 1912 ignite the worker's movement and, as the people revolt, Tsar Nicholas takes command of the army while the Tsarina Alexandra consorts with the infamous holy man, Rasputin. Part of a seven - part series tracing Russian history from the fall of the Tsar and rise of Lenin, through World War I, the internal war for communism, the emergence of the brutal and ruthless Stalin, World War II, Krushchev, Brezhnev and Gorbachev.
Civics and Political Systems; History - World; Social Science
Dist - CAMV

The Revolutionary 60 MIN
U-matic / VHS
James Galway's Music in Time Series
Color (J)
Presents flutist James Galway discussing Beethoven, the man who changed the course of music. Provides movements or significant extracts from the 3rd, 6th and 9th Symphonies.
Fine Arts
Dist - FOTH **Prod** - POLTEL 1982

The Revolutionary Age 30 MIN
16mm
How Should We Then Live Series Episode 5; Episode 5
Color (DUTCH)
LC 77-702367
Attributes the tyranny and revolutions of the post - Reformation era to the rejection of the spiritual and religious values embraced during the Reformation. Based on the book How Should We Then Live by Francis A Schaeffer.
History - World; Religion and Philosophy
Dist - GF **Prod** - GF 1977

Revolutionary Regulations 19 MIN
16mm
Color
LC 74-706397
Explains the new Federal regulations for personal flotation devices on recreational boats.
Health and Safety; Physical Education and Recreation
Dist - USNAC **Prod** - USCG 1973

Revolutions Go Backwards I - the South 29 MIN
Videoreel / VT2
Black Experience Series
Color
History - United States
Dist - PBS **Prod** - WTTWTV

Revolutions Go Backwards II - the Nation 29 MIN
Videoreel / VT2
Black Experience Series
Color
History - United States
Dist - PBS **Prod** - WTTWTV

Revolutions Go Backwards III - Redemption 29 MIN
Videoreel / VT2
Black Experience Series
Color
History - United States
Dist - PBS **Prod** - WTTWTV

Revolution's Orphans 28 MIN
U-matic / VHS / 16mm
Color (J)
LC 81-701542
Presents a drama which meshes fact and fiction in a study of the 1956 Hungarian Revolution as seen from the point of view of a young woman, who searches her past to understand those catastrophic days.
History - World; Sociology
Dist - FI **Prod** - NFBC 1981

Revolver 9 MIN
16mm
Color (G)
$30.00 rental
Incorporates diary observations, found and physically manipulated images as well as experiments of shooting through handmade pinhole lenses. Attempts to come to terms with the isolation and displacement that confront the contemporary urban dweller. Produced by David Sherman.
Fine Arts; Sociology
Dist - CANCIN

Revue Des Forces Canadiennes 5 MIN
16mm
Color (FRENCH)
LC 75-701445
A French language version of the film Canadian Forces Year End Review. Shows the major activities of the Canadian Forces in 1973.
History - World
Dist - CDND **Prod** - CDND 1974

Rev.
Treasures of the Earth 15 MIN
Dist - CF

Reward and Punishment 14 MIN
U-matic / VHS / 16mm
Color (J)
LC 74-701923
Discusses principles underlying the two major influences in human development, reward and punishment. Shows guidelines for their use in developing new behaviors of changing existing ones in young children.
Education; Home Economics; Psychology
Dist - CRMP **Prod** - CRMP 1974

Reward of Champions 14 MIN
16mm
Color
Presents the Pan American Turf Handicap, Canadian Turf Handicap and the Florida Derby at Gulfstream Park in Florida.
Geography - United States; Physical Education and Recreation
Dist - FLADC **Prod** - FLADC

Reward, Punishment and Responsibility 25 MIN
U-matic / VHS
Introduction to Philosophy Series
Color (C)
Religion and Philosophy
Dist - UDEL **Prod** - UDEL

Rewards and consequences - supervising safety by positive recognition 24 MIN
BETA / VHS / U-matic
Color (IND G)
$495.00 purchase _ #827 - 20
Trains supervisors about the importance of praise, reward and good communication with their people. Shows how positive recognition influences safe behavior on the job. Discusses why people take risks, how understanding the ABCs of human behavior can improve performance, the role of consequences both positive and negative and the effect of rewarding safe behaviors. Covers ways of improving communication and getting employees mentally and emotionally involved in safety.
Business and Economics; Health and Safety; Industrial and Technical Education; Psychology; Social Science
Dist - ITSC **Prod** - ITSC 1990

Rewards and Reinforcements 26 MIN
16mm
B&W (C T)
LC 76-700843
Points out that economically underprivileged children must often be provided with motives for learning, that the value systems of these children may differ from those of the economically satisfied child, and that behavior may need to be reinforced with rewards such as candy, money, clothes, or other material objects.
Education; Psychology
Dist - IU **Prod** - CINPS 1968

The Rewards of Rewarding 24 MIN
U-matic / VHS / 16mm
Thanks a' Plenty Boss Series
Color; Captioned (SPANISH)
LC 74-700244
Explains to supervisors how to use rewards as a management tool. Tells about a ranch foreman who is out of touch with a worker's real needs. Shows how a wise and experienced ranch cook teaches how and when to show appreciation to subordinates.
Business and Economics; Psychology
Dist - RTBL **Prod** - RTBL 1973

Rewards of Rewarding 24 MIN
VHS / 16mm
(C PRO)
$610.00 purchase, $150.00 rental
Presents a dramatization of how a ranch cook, with the benefit of years of experience in many work situtations, encourages the foreman and the ranch owner to give praise and approval when their ranch hands have performed well.
Education
Dist - VLEARN

Rewriting - Proofreading 29 MIN
VHS / U-matic
Teaching Writing - a Process Approach Series
Color
Emphasizes that the mechanics of writing must be taught within the context of the writing process. Explains that when students understand that the correct punctuation in writing clarifies their message, they refine their writing by using correct mechanical conventions.
Education; English Language
Dist - PBS **Prod** - MSITV 1982

Rewriting - Revising 29 MIN
VHS / U-matic
Teaching Writing - a Process Approach Series
Color
Examines the distinction between revising and proofreading and offers teachers several methods of working with students to revise their initial written work.
Education; English Language
Dist - PBS **Prod** - MSITV 1982

Rex Harrison 29 MIN
Videoreel / VT2
Elliot Norton Reviews II Series
Color
Presents exchanges and arguments between the dean of American theatre critics, Elliot Norton, and Rex Harrison.
Fine Arts
Dist - PBS **Prod** - WGBHTV

Reye's Syndrome 18 MIN
U-matic / VHS
Color (PRO)
Covers the diagnosis, treatment and effects of Reye's syndrome through presentation of a five - year - old patient. Includes presenting symptoms, probable triggering events, four stages of the disease, suggested laboratory work and results that lead to diagnosis and therapy. Emphasizes early detection of the disease.
Health and Safety; Science
Dist - UMICHM **Prod** - UMICHM 1978

Reynolds Aluminum Recycling Pays 10 MIN
16mm
Color
LC 76-702315
Shows the benefits of the Reynolds Metals aluminum recycling program. Demonstrates the program's success in fighting litter, saving energy and conserving natural resources.
Industrial and Technical Education; Science - Natural; Social Science
Dist - REYMC **Prod** - REYMC 1975

Reynolds Price 15 MIN
VHS
Writer's workshop series
Color (C A T)
$69.95 purchase, $45.00 rental
Features Reynolds Price in a lecture and discussion of his work, held as part of a writing workshop series at the University of South Carolina. Hosted by author William Price Fox and introduced by George Plimpton. Part 14 of a 15 - part telecourse.
English Language; Literature and Drama
Dist - SCETV **Prod** - SCETV 1982

Reynolds Price 30 MIN
VHS
Writer's workshop series
Color (G)
$59.95 purchase _ #WRWO - 114
Features author Reynolds Price in a lecture and discussion at the University of South Carolina. Emphasizes his recollections of his native North Carolina as a source for his stories, as well as his belief that writers must work on schedules to be successful. Reveals his disdain for typewriters and belief that style is an overrated concept.
Literature and Drama
Dist - PBS **Prod** - SCETVM 1987

Reynolds Price - a writer's inheritance 29 MIN
VHS
Color (C G)
$140.00 purchase, $16.00 rental _ #36210
Shows the powerful relationship between the work of writer Reynolds Price and his childhood in North Carolina as he reads excerpts from his novels. Addresses the spinal disease that confines him to a wheelchair. Produced by Marcia Rock.
Literature and Drama
Dist - PSU

RF and IF Amplifiers, Pt 1 21 MIN
16mm
B&W
LC 74-705536
Discusses the single tuned RF amplifier using capacitive and transformer coupling. Explains circuit operation with respect to a parallel resonant tank in the plate circuit of the capacitance coupled amplifier and in the grid circuit of the transformer coupled amplifier's second stage. (Kinescope).
Industrial and Technical Education; Science - Physical
Dist - USNAC **Prod** - USAF

RF Glow Discharges 35 MIN
VHS / U-matic
Plasma Sputtering, Deposition and Growth of Microelectronic Films 'for VLSI Series
Color (IND)
Studies and compares RF to DC discharges. Notes that RF includes frequencies from 50 kiloherz to 50 megaherz, and that electron temperature in RF discharge is derived in terms of the applied frequency and voltage as well as gas pressure.
Industrial and Technical Education; Science
Dist - COLOSU **Prod** - COLOSU

RFLP's and multilocus polymorphisms, analysis of forensic material using VNTR probes, and analysis of forensic material using multi and single locus probe 119 MIN
VHS
DNA technology in forensic science series
Color (A PRO)
$50.00 purchase _ #TCA17408
Presents three lectures on DNA technology in forensic science. Covers subjects including the FBI's approach to RFLPs, studies performed, Lifecodes, Cellmark, and more.
Science - Natural; Sociology
Dist - USNAC **Prod** - FBI 1988

Rh - Negative Mother
U-matic / VHS
Color (ARABIC FRENCH SPANISH)
Addresses the natural concern of the Rh - negative mother. Explains how Anti - Rh Globular Serum and 'exchange transfusions' have made it possible for 98% of all Rh incompatible babies to live.
Foreign Language; Health and Safety; Science - Natural; Sociology
Dist - MIFE **Prod** - MIFE

Rhapsody in blue 139 MIN
16mm
Color (G)
$75.00 rental
Presents a biography of George Gershwin. Features his music throughout the film. Starring Robert Alda, Oscar Levant, Charles Coburn and Alexis Smith. Directed by Irving Rapper.
Fine Arts; Religion and Philosophy
Dist - NCJEWF

Rhapsody of a River 12 MIN
16mm
Color
Presents a picture set to music of one day in the life of the countryside and of the city of Cork, Ireland, showing both traditional and modern aspects of life in the region.
Geography - World; Sociology
Dist - CONSUI **Prod** - CONSUI

Rhapsody on a Theme from a House Movie 7 MIN
16mm
B&W
LC 77-702627
Uses experimental techniques to create a world of temporal and spatial relationships that could only exist in dream or memory.
Fine Arts; Industrial and Technical Education
Dist - CANFDC **Prod** - MARINL 1972

Rheinberg, a Small Town on the Outskirts of the Ruhr 5 MIN
U-matic / VHS / 16mm
European Studies - Germany Series
Color (H C) (GERMAN)
Gives a brief history of the Ruhr area and shows how its picturesque tranquility is being threatened by its own economic success.
Geography - World; History - World
Dist - IFB **Prod** - BAYER 1973
MFAFRG

Rheingold 91 MIN
16mm
Color (GERMAN (ENGLISH SUBTITLES))
Travels alongside its namesake, the renowned city train, and relates two love stories, one the legend of beautiful Lorelei, the other a modern melodrama in which the wife of a diplomat loves her former boyfriend, a waiter in the dining car. She is caught by her husband, mortally wounded, and, during the remaining trip through Germany, dies a slow death filled with fragmented memories.
Fine Arts; Foreign Language
Dist - WSTGLC **Prod** - WSTGLC 1977

Rheingold 1 MIN
U-matic / VHS
Color
Shows a classic television commercial with moving bottles, cans and toy trains.
Business and Economics; Psychology; Sociology
Dist - BROOKC **Prod** - BROOKC

Rheostats and Potentiometers 23 MIN
U-matic / VHS / 16mm
B&W
Defines a rheostat and potentiometer. Discusses the characteristics of a rheostat and how it can be used. Gives the characteristics and use of a potentiometer. Concludes with a demonstration of how each of these units are connected in a circuit. (Kinescope).
Industrial and Technical Education; Mathematics; Science - Physical
Dist - USNAC **Prod** - USAF

Rhesus Monkey Births 12 MIN
16mm
Color (C)
LC 75-702187
Features five birth sequences in rhesus monkeys at the California Primate Research Center. Includes normal deliveries by experienced mothers, a breech delivery and a normal delivery by an inexperienced female.
Science; Science - Natural
Dist - PSUPCR **Prod** - MITG 1975

Rhesus Monkey in India 22 MIN
16mm
Color (C T)
Presents a general introduction to the ecology and behavior of the rhesus monkey in northern India - - data on abundance, distribution, habitat preferences, group sizes, sex and age ratios, population trends and interrelationships with humans shows the basic patterns of social behavior of four groups inhabitating a Hindu temple area.
Geography - World; Science - Natural
Dist - PSUPCR **Prod** - JHU 1962

A Rhesus Monkey Infant's First Four Months 32 MIN
16mm
Color (C)
LC 80-701578
Records the social and physical development of a Rhesus monkey from birth through the infant's first 16 weeks.
Psychology; Science - Natural
Dist - PSUPCR **Prod** - HOWES 1980

Rhesus Play 23 MIN
U-matic / VHS / 16mm
Color
LC 78-700110
Studies the question of why animals play by describing and analyzing aggressive play among free - ranging rhesus monkeys on La Cueva Island, Puerto Rico.
Psychology; Science - Natural
Dist - UCEMC **Prod** - HUFSC 1977

Rhetoric of War 29 MIN
U-matic
Color
Gives a reenactment of the verbal battles that preceded the American Revolution. Looks at letters, newspaper accounts and speeches before the Continental Congress.
History - United States; Sociology
Dist - UMITV **Prod** - UMITV 1974

Rheumatic Pain Syndrome 30 MIN
U-matic / VHS
Color
Uses graphic illustrations to describe and explain bursitis, tendinitis and rheumatic diseases which occur outside the joints.
Health and Safety; Science - Natural
Dist - PRIMED **Prod** - PRIMED

Rheumatoid Arthritis 17 MIN
16mm
Doctors at Work Series
B&W (H C A)
LC FIA65-1360
A doctor explains ways to keep joints from deteriorating in a condition of rheumatoid arthritis and exposes quack devices for the cure of arthritis.
Health and Safety
Dist - LAWREN **Prod** - CMA 1962

Rheumatoid Arthritis
U-matic / VHS
Color (SPANISH)
Covers the causes of rheumatoid arthritis and basic elements of a conservative management program. Emphasizes therapy to help prevent damaging changes and help restore function under close medical supervision.
Foreign Language; Health and Safety
Dist - MIFE **Prod** - MIFE

Rheumatoid arthritis 17 MIN
VHS / 16mm
Learning about arthritis series
Color (H C A PRO)
$195.00 purchase, $75.00 rental _ #8084
Discusses rheumatoid arthritis.
Health and Safety; Science - Natural
Dist - AIMS **Prod** - HOSSN 1988

Rheumatoid Arthritis 21 MIN
16mm / U-matic / VHS
Color (J) (SPANISH)
Explores rheumatoid arthritis, discussing how it affects people differently and the various treatments available. Warns against the many 'miracle' cures that promise the impossible and could be harmful.
Foreign Language; Health and Safety
Dist - PRORE **Prod** - JOU 1974

Rheumatoid arthritis in children 19 MIN
VHS / 16mm
Learning about arthritis series
Color (H C A PRO)
$195.00 purchase, $75.00 rental _ #8090
Discusses rheumatoid arthritis in children.
Health and Safety; Science - Natural
Dist - AIMS **Prod** - HOSSN 1988

The Rhine 29 MIN
VHS / 16mm
Color (I J H G)
$495.00, $49.95 purchase
Journeys down one of the world's most beautiful rivers, the Rhine, from the mountains of Switzerland to the flatlands of Holland.
Geography - World
Dist - KAWVAL **Prod** - KAWVAL

The Rhine - a European River 29 MIN
16mm
Color (H C A)
Traces the history of the Rhine River as a vehicle of trade and commerce, an instrument of political change and a stage for drama, literature and art. Shows Rhine landmarks from Switzerland to Holland.
Geography - World; History - World
Dist - WSTGLC **Prod** - WSTGLC

Rhine - Mainz Airport, Frankfurt 5 MIN
16mm / U-matic / VHS
European Studies - Germany Series
Color (H C A)
LC 76-700762
Shows the operations of Germany's largest airport, including air - traffic control.
Geography - World; Social Science
Dist - IFB **Prod** - MFAFRG 1973

The Rhine Valley and the North - Pt 1 40 MIN
16mm
Color (H C A)
Focuses on a variety of scenes, and animates them with commentary. Presents a rounded view of Germans as members of a particular culture.
Geography - World; History - World
Dist - WSTGLC **Prod** - WSTGLC

Rhino 10 MIN
VHS / U-matic
Eye on nature series
Color (I J)
$250.00 purchase _ #HP - 5850C
Looks at the rhino species. Reveals that the menacing appearance of the rhinoceros is used to protect their territory. Shows how male rhinos fend off rivals through bluff or attack, but most of the time rhinos generally cool off in mud, drink at the waterhole and eat enormous amounts of vegetation. Part of the Eye on Nature series.
Science - Natural
Dist - CORF **Prod** - BBCTV 1989

The Rhino - Giant on Land 30 MIN
16mm
Great Plains Trilogy, 1 Series in the Beginning - the Primitive Man; In the beginning - the primitive man
B&W (H C A)
Traces the origin of the rhinoceros forty - five million years ago in the Rocky Mountain areas and its migration to the plains some ten million years ago.
Science - Natural
Dist - UNL **Prod** - KUONTV 1954

Rhino - Part 12 8 MIN
VHS
Safari TV series
Color (P I)
$125.00 purchase
Studies the daily life of the rhinoceros. Part of a 13 - part series on African animals.
Geography - World; Science - Natural
Dist - LANDMK **Prod** - LANDMK 1993

Rhino Rescue 22 MIN
16mm / U-matic / VHS
Color
LC 74-702590
Shows the care of rhinoceros in wildlife preservation.
Science - Natural
Dist - PHENIX **Prod** - IFB 1974

Rhino war 60 MIN
VHS
Color (G)
Portrays the struggle to preserve the African black rhino. Shows the habitats set up for the rhinos, and details the threat they face of extinction.
Geography - World; Science - Natural
Dist - UILL
NGS

Rhinoceroses 10 MIN
VHS
Animal profile series
Color (P I)
$59.95 purchase _ #RB8120
Studies rhinoceroses, massive animals which can reach weights of 5,000 pounds and lengths of 13 feet. Reveals that, despite their size, rhinoceroses are relatively fast runners. They are also in danger of extinction. Part of a series on animals which looks at examples from the mammal, snake and bird classes, filmed in their natural habitat.
Science - Natural
Dist - REVID **Prod** - REVID 1990

Rhinoplasty 15 MIN
16mm / U-matic / VHS
Color (A)
Covers the physical and psychological aspects of rhinoplasty surgery. Features people who have had the surgery and discusses the reasons for having it, reactions to the experience and feelings about the results.
Health and Safety
Dist - PRORE **Prod** - PRORE

Rhinos 8 MIN
16mm / U-matic / VHS
Looking at Animals Series
Color (P I)
Compares the African and Indian varieties of rhinoceros including their physical make up, their native habitats and their methods of caring for the young.
Science - Natural
Dist - IFB **Prod** - IFB 1973

Rhinos and Hippos 6 MIN
U-matic / VHS / 16mm
Zoo Animals in the Wild Series
Color (K P)
Looks at the habits of rhinos and hippos. Shows rhinos rolling in the mud to protect their hairless skin from insects and hippos running gracefully on lake or stream bottoms.
Science - Natural
Dist - CORF **Prod** - CORF 1981

Rhode Island 60 MIN
VHS
Portrait of America series
Color (J H C G)
$99.95 purchase _ #AMB39V
Visits Rhode Island. Offers extensive research into the state's history. Films key locations and presents segments on its history, government, education, folklore, science, journalism, sociology, industry, agriculture and business. Shows what is unique about Rhode Island and what is distinctive about its regional culture and how it got to be that way. Includes teacher study guides. Part of a 50 - part series.
Geography - United States; History - United States
Dist - CAMV

Rhode Island School of Design
VHS
Campus clips series
Color (H C A)
$29.95 purchase _ #CC0098V
Takes a video visit to the campus of the Rhode Island School of Design. Shows many of the distinctive features of the campus, and interviews students about their experiences. Provides information on the composition of the student body, professors, academics, social life, housing, and other subjects.
Education
Dist - CAMV

The Rhone - Saone Lowland 20 MIN
U-matic / VHS / 16mm
Color (I J H)
LC FIA68-2889
Illustrates the physical characteristics of the Rhone - Saone River valleys in France. Shows how the growth of agriculture, industry and modern urban centers is influenced by the continued control of the Rhone, by the development of road, rail and water communications and by the climate of southern France.
Geography - World
Dist - IFB **Prod** - BHA 1967

Rhubarb Power 5 MIN
VHS / U-matic
Write on, Set 1 Series
Color (J H)
Teaches pronoun reference.
English Language
Dist - CTI **Prod** - CTI

Rhyme and Reason 28.23 MIN
U-matic / VHS
Learning through Play Series
(H C A PRO)
$180.00 purchase
Explores the cognitive development of children by watching them explore their environments and building concepts from discoveries in experimental play.
Home Economics; Psychology; Sociology
Dist - AITECH **Prod** - TORMC 1980
UTORMC

The Rhyme and Reason of Politics 30 MIN
VHS / U-matic
Language - Thinking, Writing, Communicating Series
Color

English Language
Dist - MDCPB **Prod** - MDCPB

Rhyme Time 30 MIN
U-matic
Read all about it - One Series
Color (I)
Teaches reading and writing skills as it continues a story in which Chris and his friend Lynn are in Trialviron and meet Doctor Crystal Couplet who helps them reach the Place Of Change.
Education; English Language; Literature and Drama
Dist - TVOTAR **Prod** - TVOTAR 1982

Rhyme Time 15 MIN
VHS / U-matic
Hidden Treasures Series no 11; No 11
Color (T)
LC 82-706551
Uses the adventures of a pirate and his three friends to explore the many facets of language arts. Focuses on poetry writing and encourages the use of this form.
English Language
Dist - GPN **Prod** - WCVETV 1980

Rhymes in Clay 10 MIN
VHS / 16mm / U-matic
Color (K P)
$240, $170, $200 purchase _ #B389
Explains how an old gentleman made of clay likes to read and collect rhymes. Uses animation and encourages viewers to collect rhymes too.
Fine Arts; Literature and Drama
Dist - BARR **Prod** - BARR 1985

Rhymes in Clay 10 MIN
U-matic / 16mm
Color (P)
Uses clay animation to present the rhymes Simple Simon, The Owl And The Pussycat and I Saw A Ship A'Sailing.
Fine Arts; Literature and Drama
Dist - WATTGO **Prod** - WATTGO

A Rhyming Dictionary of Boats 11 MIN
U-matic / VHS / 16mm
Rhyming Dictionary Series
Color (P)
LC 79-700309
Uses songs and rhymes to introduce different types of boats.
Social Science
Dist - JOU **Prod** - ALTSUL 1978

A Rhyming Dictionary of Planes 11 MIN
U-matic / VHS / 16mm
Rhyming Dictionary Series
Color (P)
LC 79-700310
Uses songs and rhymes to introduce different types of airplanes and their functions.
Social Science
Dist - JOU **Prod** - ALTSUL 1978

A Rhyming Dictionary of Shapes and Sizes 11 MIN
16mm / U-matic / VHS
Color (P)
LC 81-700243
Visits playgrounds, food stands and toy rooms to show that geometric shapes are everywhere.
Literature and Drama; Mathematics
Dist - JOU **Prod** - ALTSUL 1981

A Rhyming Dictionary of Trucks 11 MIN
16mm / U-matic / VHS
Rhyming Dictionary Series
Color (P)
LC 79-700311
Uses songs and rhymes to introduce different types of trucks and their functions.
Social Science
Dist - JOU **Prod** - ALTSUL 1978

A Rhyming Dictionary of Zoo Animals 10 MIN
U-matic / VHS / 16mm
Color (K P)
LC 77-703486
Explains scientific facts about animals by using songs and rhymes while taking a tour of a zoo.
Science - Natural
Dist - JOU **Prod** - ALTSUL 1977

Rhyming Dictionary Series
A Rhyming Dictionary of Boats 11 MIN
A Rhyming Dictionary of Planes 11 MIN
A Rhyming Dictionary of Trucks 11 MIN
Dist - JOU

Rhyming Words 15 MIN
VHS / U-matic
Magic Shop Series no 2
Color (P)
LC 83-706147
Employs a magician named Amazing Alexander and his assistants to explore rhyme.
English Language
Dist - GPN **Prod** - CVETVC 1982

Rhythm 10 MIN
VHS
Lessons in visual language series
Color (PRO G C)
$99.00 purchase, $39.00 rental _ #755
Explores the roles of natural and mechanical rhythms in the surrounding world. Shows that rhythm in film or video can be achieved by editing, by rhythmic movement within the frame independent of editing, or by the use of sound. Looks at how rhythmic movement, editing and sound can be combined in imaginative ways. Features Peter Thompson as creator and narrator of a ten - part series on visual language. Produced by the Australian Film, Television and Radio School.
Fine Arts; Industrial and Technical Education; Social Science
Dist - FIRLIT

Rhythm 15 MIN
VHS / U-matic
Arts Express Series
Color (K P I J)
Fine Arts
Dist - KYTV **Prod** - KYTV 1983

Rhythm 1 MIN
16mm
B&W (A)
Presents an experimental film by Lyn Lye which uses jump cuts of the Chrysler assembly line shown over African tribal music.
Fine Arts
Dist - STARRC **Prod** - STARRC 1957
LYEL

Rhythm 15 MIN
U-matic
Music Box Series
Color (K P)
Demonstrates and explains rhythm for the small child.
Fine Arts
Dist - TVOTAR **Prod** - TVOTAR 1971

Rhythm 20 MIN
16mm
All that I Am Series
B&W (C A)
Fine Arts; Guidance and Counseling
Dist - NWUFLM **Prod** - MPATI

Rhythm 21 - Diagonal Symphony 8 MIN
16mm
B&W
Presents pioneer works by two artists, Viking Eggeling and Hans Richter, who first made the transition from abstract painting to abstract film. Includes Eggeling's Diagonal Symphony, which moves hieroglyphic forms along an invisible diagonal, and Richter's Rhythm 21, which orchestrates the squares and rectangles of the film and screen. Produced 1921 - 24.
Fine Arts
Dist - STARRC **Prod** - STARRC

Rhythm 23 3 MIN
16mm
B&W
Presents criss - cross patterns, negative reversals, intercut stringed forms, and further variations of the rectangle and square. By Hans Richter, 1923.
Fine Arts
Dist - STARRC **Prod** - STARRC 1923

Rhythm activities
VHS
Children and movement video series
Color (H A T)
$29.95 purchase _ #MK807
Teaches about rhythm activities appropriate for children ages 3 to 6 years old. Part of a five - part series which guides in conducting physical education programs.
Physical Education and Recreation; Psychology
Dist - AAVIM **Prod** - AAVIM 1992

Rhythm Activities - Our Great Day 11 MIN
U-matic / VHS / 16mm
Color (P I)
Introduces basic concepts of music, including rhythm patterns, notes, rests, melody, words and simple instruments.
Fine Arts
Dist - STANF **Prod** - STANF

Rhythm and Blues 30 MIN
VHS
From Jumpstreet Series
Color (G)
$39.95 purchase _ #FJSG - 112
Tells of the influence black musicians have had on rhythm and blues. Features performances and interviews with several black musicians. Hosted by singer and songwriter Oscar Brown, Jr.
Fine Arts; History - United States
Dist - PBS **Prod** - WETATV 1980

Rhythm and Blues 15 MIN
VHS / U-matic
Strawberry Square II - Take Time Series
Color (P)
Fine Arts
Dist - AITECH **Prod** - NEITV 1984

Rhythm and Blues 30 MIN
VHS / U-matic
From Jumpstreet Series
Color (J H)
Focuses on rhythm and blues artists The Dells and Bo Diddley.
Fine Arts; History - United States; Sociology
Dist - GPN **Prod** - WETATV 1979

Rhythm and Blues Review 90 MIN
16mm
B&W
Presents a musical review starring such greats of the as Lionel Hampton, Count Basie and Duke Ellington.
Fine Arts
Dist - KITPAR **Prod** - STDIOF 1955

Rhythm and Free radicals 5 MIN
16mm
B&W (G)
$22.00 rental
Reveals virtually unknown underground films by the pioneer kinetic artist, sculptor and filmmaker, Len Lye. Displays sense of motion applied to the editing of live footage in which it becomes a kinetic composition, synchronised to the rhythms of African drum music, and a presentation of jump - cutting. Made in 1957. The latter film concentrates on a stark black and white use of the 'direct' method by scratching on black leader. Both films are on one reel.
Fine Arts
Dist - CANCIN **Prod** - LYEL 1979

Rhythm and Movement in Art 19 MIN
U-matic / VHS / 16mm
Color (I J H C)
LC 76-700981
Explains the place of rhythm and movement in art.
Fine Arts
Dist - PHENIX **Prod** - BURN 1969

Rhythm and Rhymes 15 MIN
U-matic / VHS
Mrs Cabobble's Caboose
(P)
Designed to teach primary grade students basic music concepts. Highlights melody, rhythm, harmony and the different families of musical instruments.
Fine Arts
Dist - GPN **Prod** - WDCNTV 1986

Rhythm Around You 4 MIN
U-matic / VHS / 16mm
Most Important Person - Creative Expression Series
Color (K P I)
Portrays the rhythm that's in the rain, in the sea, in the traffic in the street and even inside people.
English Language; Fine Arts; Guidance and Counseling; Psychology
Dist - EBEC **Prod** - EBEC 1972

Rhythm Method - Natural Family Planning 9 MIN
VHS / U-matic
Color
Explains ovulation, menstruation and fertilization. Describes methods of recognizing ovulation.
Science - Natural; Sociology
Dist - MEDFAC **Prod** - MEDFAC 1972

Rhythm of a City 18 MIN
U-matic / VHS / 16mm
B&W (H C A)
Depicts a day in Stockholm, the capital city of Sweden.
Business and Economics; Geography - World
Dist - MGHT **Prod** - SVEN 1972

Rhythm of Africa 17 MIN
16mm
B&W (H C)
Presents traditional ceremonial dances of the Chad. Recorded and photographed in Equatorial Africa.
Fine Arts; Geography - World; History - United States; Sociology
Dist - RADIM **Prod** - VILLIE 1947

Rhythm of Gujarat 17 MIN
16mm
Color (I)
Shows the colorful folk dances of the Gujarat region in India. Presents the story of Radha and Krishna as told in the Raas and Garba dances.
Fine Arts
Dist - NEDINF **Prod** - INDIA

Rhythm on Review 15 MIN
U-matic
It's Mainly Music Series
Color (I)
Teaches children about rhythm in music, two beat marches, three beat waltzes and syncopated rhythm.
Fine Arts
Dist - TVOTAR **Prod** - TVOTAR 1983

Rhythm Pattern 22 MIN
U-matic / VHS
You Can make Music Series
Color (K P I)
$360, $390 purchase _ #V123
Demonstrates the difference between the beat and the rhythm pattern. Introduces the concept of 'ostinato' or repeated patterns.
Fine Arts
Dist - BARR **Prod** - BARR 1987

Rhythm, Rhythm Everywhere 11 MIN
16mm / U-matic / VHS
Color (K P)
LC 74-700653
Shows children jumping rope to rhymes and introduces many lively examples to the rhythms of everyday life. Depicts the youngsters creating rhythms in pantomime to express their inner feelings.
Fine Arts; Physical Education and Recreation
Dist - CORF **Prod** - CORF 1974

Rhythm, Speed and Accuracy in Hand Sending 12 MIN
16mm
Radio Technician Training Series
B&W
LC FIE52-1102
Discusses rhythm and timing and points out that clear, distinct sending is essential in order to assure proper receiving at destination.
Industrial and Technical Education
Dist - USNAC **Prod** - USN 1947

Rythm - strong and weak beats 22 MIN
VHS / U-matic
You can make music series
Color (K P I)
$360.00, $390.00 purchase _ #V122
Teaches that musicians use strong and weak beats as they play a song. Shows how to discern between strong and weak beats. Shows how one can generate many beats just by arranging strong and weak beats in various ways.
Fine Arts
Dist - BARR **Prod** - BARR 1987

Rhythm - the Beat 21 MIN
VHS / U-matic
You Can make Music Series
Color (K P I)
$360, $390 purchase _ #V121
Explains the concept of a beat in music. Teaches that a beat can be fast or slow, but a steady beat goes at the same speed all through the song.
Fine Arts
Dist - BARR **Prod** - BARR 1987

Rhythmetron 40 MIN
16mm / U-matic / VHS
Color (I)
Introduces the basics of ballet in terms of daily activities, sports, and popular dance steps. Features Arthur Mitchell and the Dance Theatre of Harlem.
Fine Arts
Dist - CRMP **Prod** - CAPCBC 1973

Rhythmetron - the Dance Theatre of Harlem with Arthur Mitchell 40 MIN
16mm / U-matic / VHS
Color (J H C)
LC 73-702658
Views a demonstration by the dance theatre of Harlem. Includes a complete ballet barre, accompanied by Arthur Mitchell's explanation of the purpose behind every exercise. Discovers the relationship of classical ballet to everyday life. Explains the application of ballet movement to three styles of dance.
Fine Arts; History - United States; Sociology
Dist - MGHT **Prod** - CAPCBC 1973

Rhythmic Ball Skills for Perceptual - Motor Development 11 MIN
16mm
Color (P I T)
LC 76-714784
Introduces activities using the perceptual - motor approach to learning directional concepts.
Physical Education and Recreation
Dist - MMP **Prod** - MMP 1971

Rhythmic Composition in Yellow Green Minor 9 MIN
16mm
Australian Eye Series
Color
LC 80-700788
Discusses one of the first abstract paintings produced in Australia.
Fine Arts; Geography - World
Dist - TASCOR **Prod** - FLMAUS 1978

Rhythmic Gymnastics - the Perfect New Women's Sport
U-matic / VHS
Color
Demonstrates movements and techniques of beginning rhythmic gymnastics and covers all apparatus. Produced by the coaches of the Penn State University women's gymnastic team.
Physical Education and Recreation
Dist - ATHI **Prod** - ATHI

Rhythmical Gymnastics 22 MIN
16mm
Color
Demonstrates Liss Burmester's modern rhythmic exercises for women.
Physical Education and Recreation
Dist - AUDPLN **Prod** - RDCG

Rhythms and Drives 60 MIN
VHS / U-matic
Brain, Mind and Behavior Series
Color (C A)
Discusses subconscious, instinctive rhythms and drives.
Psychology
Dist - FI **Prod** - WNETTV

Rhythms and drives - Part 3 60 MIN
VHS / U-matic
Brain series
Color (G)
$45.00, $29.95 purchase
Uses vignettes from both the animal world and human society to illustrate the seat of basic instincts, the primitive brain. Looks at its effects on sex, sleep, aggression, depression and euphoria. Part three of an eight - part series on the brain.
Psychology; Science - Natural
Dist - ANNCPB **Prod** - WNETTV 1984

Rhythms of Haiti 25 MIN
16mm
Color (J) (FRENCH SPANISH)
LC 82-700850
Covers the cultural, folklife and tourist aspects of the Caribbean island of Haiti.
Foreign Language; Geography - World; History - World; Sociology
Dist - MOMALA **Prod** - OOAS 1979

Rhythms of light 30 MIN
VHS
Perspectives - natural science - series
Color; PAL; NTSC (G)
PdS90, PdS105 purchase
Examines the influence of day and night upon the productivity of both people and animals.
Science - Natural; Science - Physical
Dist - CFLVIS **Prod** - LONTVS

Rhythms - Pt 1 15 MIN
U-matic / VHS
Song Sampler Series
Color (P)
LC 81-707072
Introduces rhythm and rhythm notations. Presents the songs Bingo, Chicka Hanka and Riding In The Buggy.
Fine Arts
Dist - GPN **Prod** - JCITV 1981

Rhythms - Pt 2 15 MIN
U-matic / VHS
Song Sampler Series
Color (P)
LC 81-707072
Introduces rhythm and rhythm notations. Presents the songs Bingo, Chicka Hanka and Riding In The Buggy.
Fine Arts
Dist - GPN **Prod** - JCITV 1981

Rhythm's the Name of the Game 30 MIN
U-matic / VHS
Third World Dance - Tracing Roots Series
Color
Fine Arts; Industrial and Technical Education; Sociology
Dist - ARCVID **Prod** - ARCVID

Rhythmus 21 - Symphonie Diagonale 8 MIN
16mm
B&W
Presents pioneer works by two artists, Viking Eggeling and Hans Richter, who first made the transition from abstract painting to abstract film. Includes Eggeling's Diagonal Symphony, which moves hieroglyphic forms along an invisible diagonal, and Richter's Rhythm 21, which orchestrates the squares and rectangles of the film and screen. Produced 1921 - 24.
Fine Arts
Dist - STARRC **Prod** - STARRC

Rhythmus 23 3 MIN
16mm
B&W
Presents criss - cross patterns, negative reversals, intercut stringed forms, and further variations of the rectangle and square. By Hans Richter, 1923.
Fine Arts
Dist - STARRC **Prod** - STARRC 1923

Rib - Tickling American Folktales 79 MIN
U-matic / VHS
Rib - Tickling American Folktales Series
Color (P I)
Contains 1 videocassette.
English Language; Literature and Drama
Dist - TROLA **Prod** - TROLA 1987

Rib - Tickling American Folktales Series
Rib - Tickling American Folktales 79 MIN
Dist - TROLA

The Ribbon 50 MIN
VHS / 16mm
Color (C)
$795.00, $480.00 purchase, $95.00 rental
Commemorates a group of mothers, black and white, who assembled a 'Peace Ribbon' to protest the conscription of their sons into the South African army to enforce apartheid. Reveals that these women sewed, drew or painted their visions of peace into the Ribbon, which at the time of filming was 500 meters long and growing. The groups involved in the project were the End Conscription Campaign, the South African Council of Women and the Black Sash.
Civics and Political Systems; Geography - World; History - United States; History - World; Religion and Philosophy; Sociology
Dist - ICARUS

Ribbon Bridge - Launching and Retrieval 17 MIN
U-matic / VHS / 16mm
Color (A)
Discusses two types of bridge bays and connecting hardware. Demonstrates the procedure for launching and retrieving bridge bays.
Civics and Political Systems; Industrial and Technical Education
Dist - USNAC **Prod** - USA 1978

Ribbon of life - one man's reef 48 MIN
VHS
Color (H C G)
$195.00 purchase
Features marine biologist Alastair Birtles who recounts his journeys of discovery through the Great Barrier Reef.
Geography - World; Science - Natural
Dist - LANDMK **Prod** - LANDMK 1993

Ribosomal RNA - the Protein Maker 10 MIN
U-matic
Protein Synthesis Series
Color (H C)
Explains that the mutations that result from the faulty replication of a DNA code are usually harmful, but they are also believed to be the basis of evolution.
Science; Science - Natural; Science - Physical
Dist - TVOTAR **Prod** - TVOTAR 1984

Ricardo Chillida 61 MIN
VHS
Color (H C A)
$39.95
Profiles Spain's sculptor Ricardo Chillida. Displays his abstract sculptures and discusses the inspiration he draws from the culture and landscape of the Basque country.
Fine Arts
Dist - ARTSAM **Prod** - RMART

Ricardo Montalban's South America 28 MIN
VHS
Color (G)
$14.95 purchase
Tours several countries in South America, with narration by actor Ricardo Montalban.
Geography - World
Dist - MARYFA

Rice 26 MIN
U-matic / VHS / 16mm
Color (I)
LC FIA68-1273
Stresses the world - wide importance of rice and describes methods of growing it. Shows measures taken to improve the quantity and quality of rice.
Agriculture; Geography - World; Psychology; Social Science
Dist - MGHT **Prod** - ROCKE 1965

Rice - 5 10 MIN
U-matic / 16mm / VHS
How plants grow series
Color (K P I)
$265.00, $215.00, $185.00 purchase _ #B596
Shows how farmers grow, harvest and process rice. Looks at the growth cycle of the rice plant and explains why it must be grown in fresh water for much of its life. Examines how rice plants are pollinated, the milling process and considers the importance of rice throughout the world. Part of a seven - part series on how plants grow.
Agriculture; English Language; Science - Natural
Dist - BARR **Prod** - GREATT 1990

Rice, America's Food for the World 13 MIN
16mm
Color (I J)
Shows the use of machines in preparing soil, planting and harvesting the crop. Scientific research to improve crops and land conservation are illustrated.
Agriculture; Geography - World
Dist - MLA **Prod** - DAGP 1962

Rice and peas 12 MIN
VHS / 16mm
Color (G)
$160.00, $265.00 purchase, $35.00 rental
Watches Gillian Charles, Gill's Restaurant proprietress and chef, as she prepares her own recipe for the staple of West Indian fare, Rice and Peas. Records her reminiscences of Trinidad and illustrates how she has kept her cultural heritage intact.
Fine Arts; Sociology
Dist - FIRS **Prod** - KRAMRK 1990

Rice and Tea 29 MIN
Videoreel / VT2
Joyce Chen Cooks Series
Color
Features Joyce Chen showing how to adapt Chinese recipes so that they can be prepared in the American kitchen and still retain the authentic flavor. Demonstrates how to prepare rice and tea.
Geography - World; Home Economics
Dist - PBS **Prod** - WGBHTV

Rice - Biggest Small Grain on Earth 12 MIN
16mm / U-matic / VHS
Color (I J)
LC 81-700050
Shows different methods of planting and harvesting rice. Emphasizes the importance of rice as a basic food and source of energy for more than half the world's people.
Agriculture
Dist - CORF **Prod** - CENTRO 1980
VIEWTH

Rice Farmers in Thailand 19 MIN
U-matic / VHS / 16mm
Man and His World Series
Color (P I J H C) (THAI)
LC 74-705493
Contrasts the old and the new way of rice farming in Thailand. Shows ancient ceremonies at the beginning of planting season and when the harvest is in. Depicts rice farmers learning to irrigate land to increase their harvest.
Agriculture; Geography - World; Social Science
Dist - FI **Prod** - FI 1969

Rice Farming in Japan 12 MIN
U-matic / VHS / 16mm
Color (J)
Shows processes involved in rice planting, cultivating, harvesting and cooking.
Geography - World; Social Science
Dist - MCFI **Prod** - UMAVEC 1953

The Rice growers 10 MIN
VHS
Color; PAL (P I J)
PdS29
Shows how a family in southern India grows its main food crop of rice, using methods typical of much of tropical Asia.
Agriculture; Geography - World; Sociology
Dist - BHA

Rice Growing in Nepal 9 MIN
U-matic / VHS / 16mm
Color (P I J)
Shows each major stage in the production of rice in Nepal. Includes views of preparing seed beds, sowing, weeding, harvesting, threshing, winnowing and transporting the rice.
Agriculture; Geography - World
Dist - VIEWTH **Prod** - GATEEF

The Rice Ladle - the Changing Role of Women 28 MIN
16mm
Human Face of Japan Series
Color (H C A)
LC 82-700640
Discusses the status of women in Japan by focusing on Fumiko Sawada, a would - be pop star and Hatsumi Suda, a widow who supports herself as a cook's assistant in a sushi shop.
Geography - World; History - World; Social Science; Sociology
Dist - LCOA **Prod** - FLMAUS 1982

Rich 20 MIN
16mm
B&W
Tells the story of a young man determined to go to college despite his depressed environment and his mother's desire for him to go to work.
Psychology; Sociology
Dist - BLKFMF **Prod** - BLKFMF

Rich 21 MIN
U-matic / VHS / 16mm
Color (I J H)
$50 rental _ #9866
Presents a story of courage and commitment, and a teenager's step into adulthood.
Guidance and Counseling; Sociology
Dist - AIMS **Prod** - AIMS 1987

Rich and Judy 12 MIN
16mm
Color
Opens with a couple riding motor bikes down a country road. Shows them later at home by a swimming pool. Pictures Judy using pelvic thrusting to increase her excitement marked by a sex flush.
Guidance and Counseling; Psychology; Sociology
Dist - MMRC **Prod** - MMRC

Rich and Poor - North - South Dialogue 27 MIN
VHS / U-matic
Color (J H)
Discusses the summit held in Cancun, Mexico in October,1981, where 22 world leaders met to discuss common problems afflicting their nations in light of global interdependence in the world economy. Describes the issues that prompted this meeting and explores the solutions that might be implemented to advance the cause of global and political stability.
Civics and Political Systems; Social Science
Dist - JOU **Prod** - JOU

Rich Cat, Poor Cat 8 MIN
16mm / U-matic / VHS
Bank Street Reading Incentive Film Series
Color (P)
Presents a story read by Bill Cosby about the differences between the way rich cats live and the way Scat, a poor cat, lives.
Literature and Drama; Science - Natural
Dist - MGHT **Prod** - BANKSC 1969

Rich, clever, homeless - Part 5 55 MIN
VHS
Slow boat from Surabaya series
Color (J H C)
$225.00 purchase
Examines 'overseas' Chinese sequestered in Southeast Asia who crackle with dynamism, but the acumen which brings them wealth also brings them trouble. Reveals that they are envied and, because they can't go home to communist China, vulnerable. Focuses on the Chinese situation in Malaysia. Part five of a six - part series on Southeast Asia covering the Philippines, Thailand, Singapore, Indonesia, Malaysia, Vietnam and Kampuchnea.
Geography - World; Sociology
Dist - LANDMK **Prod** - LANDMK 1992

Rich Country, Strong Military 30 MIN
VHS / U-matic
Japan - the Changing Tradition Series
Color (H C A)
History - World
Dist - GPN **Prod** - UMA 1978

The Rich Dummy 28 MIN
VHS / 16mm
Sonrisas Series
Color (T P) (SPANISH)
$46.00 rental _ #SRSS - 127
Shows how greed breaks the children apart. In Spanish and English.
Sociology
Dist - PBS

The Rich get richer - Pt II 52 MIN
VHS
Energy alternatives - a global perspective series
Color (H C G)
$295.00 purchase, $75.00 rental
Focuses on tough, innovative laws and fresh initiatives worldwide helping to contain energy consumption and pollution. Observes a computerized energy - management system in a California home, a high - efficiency building in New York City and a plant converting timber - industry waste into electricity in Sweden. Advocates the 'end - use approach,' stressing energy conservation rather than increasing the supply. Concludes that the West could reduce energy consumption by 50 percent by the year 2030 and retain present standards of living. Part two of a three - part series produced by Grampian Television and INcA based on a five - year study, 'Energy for a Sustainable World.'
Geography - World; Science - Natural; Social Science
Dist - FLMLIB

The Rich, High Desert - Pt 2 57 MIN
VHS / 16mm
Making of a Continent II Series
Color (S)
$750.00, $79.00 purchase _ #568 - 9019
Continues the epic story of the formation of North America, to the heart of the continent. Chronicles its forging by titanic mountain - building processes, its population by an enormous variety of wildlife, the changes in the land as European settlers turned 'The Great American Desert' into the most productive agricultural area on earth. Part 2 of three parts looks at the Great Plains which rest on miles of sediment laid down over millions of years. The last ice age left the Great Lakes and made the area the breadbasket of the world.
Geography - United States; Geography - World; Science - Natural; Science - Physical
Dist - FI **Prod** - BBCTV 1986

Rich man's medicine, poor man's medicine 43 MIN
16mm / VHS
Color (G)
$695.00, $420.00 purchase, $85.00 rental
Focuses on the realities of medical care in developing countries. Ventures to Gabon, Senegal and Kenya. Provides a glimpse into the conflict between 'modern' technological development patterns and traditional, indigenous approaches.
Fine Arts; Health and Safety
Dist - FIRS **Prod** - TRDEPA 1976

Rich Mitch 15 MIN
VHS
Books from cover to cover series
Color (P I G)
$25.00 purchase _ #BFCC - 101
Presents Marjorie Weinman Sharmat's book, 'Rich Mitch.' Features an eleven - year - old boy named Mitch and how his life changes when he wins $250,000 in a contest.
English Language; Fine Arts; Literature and Drama
Dist - PBS **Prod** - WETATV 1988

Rich, Thin, and Beautiful 58 MIN
16mm / U-matic / VHS
Color (H C A)
Takes a look at America's obsession with money and thin, beautiful bodies. Interviews people who make it apparent that in the race for the American Dream, there isn't any finish.
Guidance and Counseling; Psychology
Dist - FI **Prod** - BELLDA 1983

The Rich Young Ruler 27 MIN
16mm
B&W (J)
Portrays the human story of Azor, rich young ruler of Judea. And his search for eternal values.
Religion and Philosophy
Dist - CAFM **Prod** - CAFM

Richard Barnes - 10 - 24 - 74 31 MIN
VHS / Cassette
Poetry Center reading series
Color (G)
#79 - 53
Features the poet reading from his works, including selections from The Complete Poems of Archie Barnes and The Death of Buster Quinine, at the Poetry Center, San Francisco State University, with an introduction by Kathleen Fraser. Available only for listening purposes at the Center; not for sale or rent.
Literature and Drama
Dist - POETRY **Prod** - POETRY 1974

Richard Bradshaw - Australia - Pt 2 56 MIN
VHS
Jim Henson Presents the World of Puppetry Series
Color (I)
$49.00 purchase _ #064 - 9012
Travels the globe to meet some of the finest puppeteers on the planet. Features Muppet creator Jim Henson as host. Part 2 of six parts features Richard Bradshaw of Australia who is best known for his inventive and hilarious shadow puppetry.
Fine Arts; Geography - World; Health and Safety; Literature and Drama; Sociology
Dist - FI **Prod** - HENASS 1988

Richard Branson 47 MIN
VHS
Tycoons series
Color (J H G)
$225.00 purchase
Tells how the founder of Virgin Atlantic Airways expanded his Virgin Group to one of the world's largest entertainment conglomerates that involves over 100 businesses in 30 countries.
Business and Economics; Industrial and Technical Education
Dist - LANDMK

Richard Caddel - 11 - 7 - 85 36 MIN
VHS / Cassette
Poetry Center reading series
Color (G)
$15.00, $45.00 purchase, $15.00 rental _ #670 - 553
Features the poet reading his works at the Poetry Center, San Francisco State University, with an introduction by Frances Phillips.
Literature and Drama
Dist - POETRY **Prod** - POETRY 1975

Richard Cardinal - cry from a diary of a Metis child 30 MIN
U-matic / VHS
Color (PRO C)
$395.00 purchase, $80.00 rental _ #C891 - VI - 033
Shares the diary of Richard Cardinal, a sensitive, articulate young man who finally ran out of hope and committed suicide at the age of 17. Reveals that by the time he died, Cardinal had lived in 28 foster homes, group homes, shelters and lockups throughout Alberta, Canada. He might have been just another statistic if not for his diary and his last foster parents who refused to let his death go unmarked. This resulted in a judicial inquiry that prompted changes in child - welfare administration, acknowledged that native people are quite capable of caring for their own children and created the new Alberta Welfare Act. Presented by Alanis Obomsawin.
Sociology
Dist - HSCIC

Richard Chase - Storyteller - Pt 2 35 MIN
U-matic
Color
Presents Richard Chase telling the stories Jack In The Giant's New Ground and Old Roaney.
English Language; Literature and Drama
Dist - BLUHER **Prod** - BLUHER

Richard E Byrd - Admiral of the Ends of the Earth 24 MIN
VHS
American Lifestyles II - Singular American Series
Color (I)
$70.00 purchase, $50.00 rental _ #9888
Explores the aeronautical brilliance of Richard E Byrd, the first man to fly over both the North and South Poles.
Biography; History - World; Industrial and Technical Education
Dist - AIMS **Prod** - COMCO 1986

Richard Eberhart - writing in the upward years 27 MIN
VHS
Writing in the upward years series
Color (G C)
$195.00 purchase, $55.00 rental
Focuses on the effect of aging on the creative process as demonstrated in the life and writings of poet Richard Eberhart. Features readings by and interviews with the poet.
Fine Arts; Health and Safety; Literature and Drama
Dist - TNF

Richard Grossinger - 5 - 12 - 76 65 MIN
VHS / Cassette
Poetry Center reading series
Color (G)
$15.00, $45.00 purchase, $15.00 rental _ #204 - 161
Features the writer reading selections from his book of essays, The Unfinished Business of Dr Hermes, at the Poetry Center, San Francisco State University, with an introduction by Lewis MacAdams.
Literature and Drama
Dist - POETRY **Prod** - POETRY 1976

Richard Hunt - Outdoor Sculpture 29 MIN
U-matic
Color
Follows the artist from studio to site during the development of an outdoor sculpture. Explores the importance of public art.
Fine Arts
Dist - UMITV **Prod** - UMITV 1975

Richard II 157 MIN
VHS / 16mm
BBC's Shakespeare Series
(H A)
Presents the Shakespearean play Richard II, about an unconventional man and his military adventures in Ireland.
Literature and Drama
Dist - AMBROS **Prod** - AMBROS 1979
BBC
INSIM

Richard II 12 MIN
16mm / U-matic / VHS
Shakespeare Series
Color (H C A)
An excerpt from the play of the same title. Presents Act II, Scene 1 as John of Gaunt speaks to his brother York of 'this sceptered isle' and Act V, Scene 5 as Richard soliloquizes on 'this all - hating world.'.
Fine Arts; Literature and Drama
Dist - IFB **Prod** - IFB 1974

Richard II 157 MIN
U-matic / VHS
Shakespeare Plays Series
Color
LC 79-706937
Presents Shakespeare's play about an uprising to replace an unjust king with a just one. Stars Derek Jacobi, Jon Finch and John Gielgud.
Literature and Drama
Dist - TIMLIF **Prod** - BBCTV 1979

Richard III 228 MIN
VHS / 16mm
BBC's Shakespeare Series
(H A)
$249.95
Tells the story of Richard of Gloucester in the version of Shakespeare's Richard III.
Literature and Drama
Dist - AMBROS **Prod** - AMBROS 1982

Richard III 157 MIN
VHS
BBC Shakespeare series
Color (G C H)
$109.00 purchase _ #DL464
Fine Arts
Dist - INSIM **Prod** - BBC

Richard III 12 MIN
U-matic / VHS / 16mm
Shakespeare Series
Color (H C A)
An excerpt from the play of the same title. Shows Richard's 'winter of our discontent' soliloquy in Act I, Scene 1 and Act I, Scene 2, as Lady Anne scorns Richard who has just declared his love for her.
Fine Arts; Literature and Drama
Dist - IFB **Prod** - IFB 1974

Richard III
U-matic / VHS
Shakespeare Series
B&W (G C J)
$59 purchase _ #04117 - 85
Re - enacts Shakespeare's tragedy about Richard the Third. Stars Sir Laurence Olivier.
Fine Arts; Literature and Drama
Dist - CHUMAN

Richard III 29 MIN
Videoreel / VT2
Feast of Language Series
Color
Features Alan Levitan, associate professor of English at Brandeis University discussing Richard III by Shakespeare.
Literature and Drama
Dist - PBS **Prod** - WGBHTV

Richard III 120 MIN
U-matic / VHS
Shakespeare Plays Series
Color (H C A)
LC 82-707360
Presents William Shakespeare's play about Richard of Gloucester, a self - proclaimed villain, who usurps the crown of King Edward IV.
Literature and Drama
Dist - TIMLIF **Prod** - BBCTV 1982

Richard III 155 MIN
VHS
Color (G)
$39.95 purchase _ #S00541
Features Sir Laurence Olivier as director and star of a film version of Shakespeare's 'Richard III.' Co - stars John Gielgud, Ralph Richardson, and Claire Bloom.
Fine Arts; Literature and Drama
Dist - UILL

Richard III
BETA / VHS
B&W
Presents Sir Lawrence Olivier starring in Shakespeare's tragedy.
Fine Arts; Literature and Drama
Dist - GA **Prod** - GA

Richard Landry - Divided Alto 15 MIN
U-matic / VHS
Color
Presented by Richard Landry.
Fine Arts
Dist - ARTINC **Prod** - ARTINC

Richard Landry - One Two Three Four 8 MIN
U-matic / VHS
B&W
Presents four clapping hands with a strobe light on them.
Fine Arts
Dist - ARTINC **Prod** - ARTINC

Richard Landry - Quad Suite, Six Vibrations for Agnes Martin, Hebes Grande Bois, 4th 35 MIN
VHS / U-matic
B&W
Complete title reads Richard Landry - Quad Suite, Six Vibrations For Agnes Martin, Hebes Grande Bois, 4th Register.
Fine Arts
Dist - ARTINC **Prod** - ARTINC

Richard Leakey - looking ahead to the past 28 MIN
VHS
Eminent scientist series
Color (J H)
$60.00 purchase _ #A2VH 4631
Features archaeologist Richard Leakey. Part of a series on scientists which discusses their childhood, educational backgrounds, decisions affecting their careers and illustrious achievements.
History - World; Science; Science - Physical
Dist - CLRVUE **Prod** - CLRVUE

Richard M Nixon, Gerald Ford 90 MIN
VHS / U-matic
Color
Presents biographies tracing the private and public lives of Nixon and Ford up to the year 1973. Features Nixon's 'Checkers' speech and 1974 resignation speech.
Biography; Civics and Political Systems; History - United States
Dist - IHF **Prod** - IHF

Richard Meier 58 MIN
16mm / VHS
Color (H C)
$875.00, $290.00 purchase, $110.00 rental
Profiles the architect, Richard Meier.
Biography; Fine Arts
Dist - BLACKW **Prod** - BLACKW 1985

Richard Nanes at the United Nations 60 MIN
VHS
Color (G)
$19.95 purchase_#1334
Presents composer and pianist Richard Nanes, a rising star on the international scene, in his video debut performing a recital of his own works. Takes place at the United Nations.
Fine Arts
Dist - KULTUR

Richard Nanes in recital 60 MIN
VHS
Color (G)
$19.95 purchase_#1400
Presents pianist Richard Nanes in performances at the conservatories of Moscow and Kiev. Includes Nanes' Rhapsoday and Fugato No. 2 in D Minor, The Grand Etude No. 2 and Piano Concerto No. 2 A/Solo.
Fine Arts
Dist - KULTUR

Richard Nixon
VHS
Speeches collection series
Color (J H C G)
$29.95 purchase _ #MH1688V
Offers a collection of speeches by Richard Nixon. Part of a ten - part series on the addresses of the 20th - century's most powerful speakers. Witnesses the signing of peace treaties, the inciting of world wars, the making of history with words.
Biography; English Language; History - United States
Dist - CAMV

Richard Nixon 15 MIN
U-matic / VHS
B&W
Portrays Richard Milhous Nixon and his journey to the White House, from his birth in Yorba Linda, California in 1913 to his election as the thirty - seventh President of the United States. Important for understanding the man behind the Watergate affair.
Biography
Dist - KINGFT **Prod** - KINGFT

Richard Nixon - Checkers, Old Glory, Resignation
U-matic / VHS
Color (J C I)
Presents three historic broadcasts spanning the career of Richard M. Nixon.
Biography
Dist - GA **Prod** - GA

Richard Nixon - Crisis in the Presidency 60 MIN
VHS
Modern Presidency Series
Color (G)
$125.00 purchase _ #TMPR - 102
Interviews former President Richard Nixon. Reviews Nixon's foreign policy accomplishments, including arms treaties, the Chinese diplomatic initiative and the winding down of the Vietnam War. Discusses the Watergate scandal and its effect on the Nixon Presidency. Hosted by David Frost.
Biography; Business and Economics; Civics and Political Systems; History - United States; Religion and Philosophy
Dist - PBS **Prod** - ENMED 1989

Richard Prince, Editions 8 MIN
U-matic / VHS
Cross - Overs - Photographers Series
Color
Fine Arts
Dist - ARTINC **Prod** - ARTINC

Richard Scarry's Best ABC Video Ever
VHS / 16mm
Color (K)
$14.44 purchase _ #RH9 - 826736
Presents the alphabet in 26 stories each emphasizing a new letter.
Literature and Drama; Psychology
Dist - EDUCRT **Prod** - RH

Richard Scarry's Best Counting Video Ever
VHS / 16mm
Color (K)
$14.44 purchase _ #RH9 - 826795
Teaches counting from 1 to 10.
Literature and Drama; Psychology
Dist - EDUCRT **Prod** - RH

Richard Serra, an Interview 28 MIN
VHS / U-matic
Color
Interviews Richard Serra. Produced by Liza Bear, Ales Susteric, Michael McClard and C Arcache.
Fine Arts
Dist - ARTINC **Prod** - ARTINC

Richard Serra - Anxious Automation 5 MIN
VHS / U-matic
B&W
Presented by Richard Serra.
Fine Arts
Dist - ARTINC **Prod** - ARTINC

Richard Serra - Boomerang 10 MIN
U-matic / VHS
Color
Presented by Richard Serra.
Fine Arts
Dist - ARTINC **Prod** - ARTINC

Richard Serra - Prisoner's Dilemma 60 MIN
U-matic / VHS
B&W
Criticizes television. Features cops and robbers.
Fine Arts
Dist - ARTINC **Prod** - ARTINC

Richard Serra - Surprise Attack 2 MIN
U-matic / VHS
B&W
Presented by Richard Serra.
Fine Arts
Dist - ARTINC **Prod** - ARTINC

Richard Serra - Television Delivers People 6 MIN
VHS / U-matic
Color
Focuses on broadcasting as corporate czar.
Fine Arts
Dist - ARTINC **Prod** - ARTINC

Richard Simmons slim cooking series
Presents a six - part series which demonstrates step - by - step procedures for low - fat, high - flavor recipes. Features Richard Simmons. Includes Extra Slimous Eggs Benedict, Lightweight Lasagna, Fantabulous Fajitas, Chicken Medallions, Slimmons Scampi and Crepes Slimettes.

Chicken medallions a la slim	30 MIN
Crepes slimettes	30 MIN
Extra slimous Eggs Benedict	30 MIN
Fantabulous fajitas	30 MIN
Lightweight lasagna	30 MIN
Slimmons scampi	30 MIN

Dist - CAMV

Richard T Ely 51 MIN
U-matic / 16mm
Profiles in Courage Series
B&W (I J H)
LC 83-706543; FIA65-1425
Follows the hearings of the case against Professor Ely, an advocate of social Christianity, before the board of regents of the University of Wisconsin that charged him with advocating strikes and boycotts. Examines the implications of the decision in the case by the regents' investigating committee on freedom of speech, knowledge and learning.
Biography; History - United States
Dist - SSSSV **Prod** - SAUDEK 1964

Richard T Ely - Pt 1 25 MIN
16mm
Profiles in Courage Series
B&W (J)
Follows the hearings of the case against Professor Ely, an advocate of social Christianity, before the board of regents of the University of Wisconsin that charged him with advocating strikes and boycotts. Examines the implications of the decision in the case by the regents' investigating committee on freedom of speech, knowledge and learning.
Religion and Philosophy
Dist - SSSSV **Prod** - SAUDEK

Richard T Ely - Pt 2 25 MIN
16mm
Profiles in Courage Series
B&W (J)
Follows the hearings of the case against Professor Ely, an advocate of social Christianity, before the board of regents of the University of Wisconsin that charged him with advocating strikes and boycotts. Examines the implications of the decision in the case by the regents' investigating committee on freedom of speech, knowledge and learning.
Religion and Philosophy
Dist - SSSSV **Prod** - SAUDEK

Richard Tee - contemporary piano 60 MIN
VHS
Color (G)
$49.95 purchase _ #S01831
Interviews pianist Richard Tee. Reveals that Tee has had an extensive career as a session pianist for such contemporary artists as Aretha Franklin, Paul Simon, Quincy Jones and Billy Joel. Tee joins keyboardist and producer Barry Eastmond in a discussion of practicing, chart reading, chord substititions, and more.
Fine Arts
Dist - UILL

Richard Wagner - the Man and His Music 58 MIN
U-matic / VHS
Color
Offers both a biography of Richard Wagner and a guide to his Ring Cycle. Traces his development as a composer and theatrical visionary, his relationship with his patron King Ludwig of Bavaria, the Wagner family and homes and the years in Venice which inspired and solaced Wagner during a tempestuous career.
Fine Arts
Dist - FOTH **Prod** - FOTH 1984

Richard Wentworth 25 MIN
VHS
Five sculptors series
Color (A)
PdS65 purchase
Presents the work of Richard Wentworth, a contemporary British sculptor. Hosted by artist and writer Patrick Hughes.
Fine Arts
Dist - BBCENE

Richard Wilbur - 3 - 8 - 66 38 MIN
VHS / Cassette
NET Outtake series
B&W (G)
$15.00, $125.00 purchase, $15.00 rental _ #214 - 170
Features the writer at his home in Portland, Connecticut where he analyzes and reads his translations of Akhmatova's Lot's Wife and Villon's Ballad for the Ladies of Time Past, and his own poems Seed Leaves; The Lilacs; The Proof; Complaint; Two Voices in a Meadow; Advice to a Prophet; and Shame. Part of a series of films composed of outtakes from the series USA - Poetry, which was produced in 1965 - 66 for National Educational Television, using all retrievable footage to provide rare glimpses of the poets in their own settings. Interviewed by Richard O Moore. Includes insert slide footage courtesy of Dietz - Hamlin Photographers.
Guidance and Counseling; Literature and Drama
Dist - POETRY **Prod** - KQEDTV 1966

Richard Williams 30 MIN
16mm
B&W (H C A)
LC FIA68-3221
Studies the training and work of animator Richard Williams. Shows him in his studio in London performing tasks ranging from preliminary storyboarding to the finishing touches on a nearly completed product.
Fine Arts
Dist - IU **Prod** - NET 1968

Richard's Totem Pole 25 MIN
U-matic / VHS / 16mm
World Cultures and Youth Series
Color (J)
Introduces Richard Harris, a Gitskan Indian living in British Columbia, who helps his father carve a 30 foot totem pole. Shows that while researching symbols to carve on the pole, he gains a new respect for his family's cultural heritage.
Geography - World; Social Science; Sociology
Dist - CORF **Prod** - SUNRIS 1981

Richard's Totem Pole - Canada 25 MIN
U-matic / VHS / 16mm
World Cultures and Youth Series
Color (I J H A)
$520, $250 purchase _ #4266
Discusses the art of totem pole carving and talks about the culture of the Gitskan Indians.
Fine Arts
Dist - CORF

Richardson Goes Five for Five 5 MIN
16mm
Color
Highlights one of baseball's great players, Richardson of the New York Yankees, speaking to the young men at a Fellowship of Christian Athletes huddle about his faith.
Physical Education and Recreation; Religion and Philosophy
Dist - FELLCA **Prod** - FELLCA

A Richer Harvest 22 MIN
16mm
Color
LC FIA67-582
Examines the problems faced by the farmer and demonstrates the scope of an American business company's involvement in world agriculture as exemplified by the world - wide research and distribution of Merck Sharp Dohme.
Agriculture; Business and Economics
Dist - MESHDO **Prod** - MESHDO 1966

Riches from the Earth 23 MIN
U-matic / VHS / 16mm
Color (I)
LC 83-700239
Looks at the earth's resources with scenes of man's first formation of instruments of copper, the industrial revolution, islanders mining their lands in the Pacific Ocean and the clamor of the New York Commodities Exchange.
Science - Natural
Dist - NGS **Prod** - PLATTS 1982

Riches from the Sea 23 MIN
U-matic / VHS / 16mm
Color (J H A)
Depicts the importance of the sea as a source of food, minerals, energy and salt.
Science - Physical
Dist - NGS **Prod** - NGS 1984

Riches of the Earth 17 MIN
16mm
Color (I)
LC FIA66-1341
Depicts with animation the formation of the earth's crust by fire, water, wind and ice. Explains that this crust holds our wealth of minerals, oil, coal, arable land and water power.
Geography - World; Science - Natural; Science - Physical
Dist - SF **Prod** - NFBC 1966

Riches or Happiness 27 MIN
U-matic / VHS / 16mm
Storybook International Series
Color
Presents the Indian story of a young man who offers himself to a goddess. Relates that she in turn offers him riches or enjoyment. Tells how he does not know the difference until she shows him two merchants, one who is rich and not happy and the other who has enjoyment and is very happy.
Guidance and Counseling; Literature and Drama
Dist - JOU **Prod** - JOU 1982

The Richest dog in the world 10 MIN
VHS
Color (R J H)
$17.95 purchase _ #604 - 2
Uses animation to present the challenges of the world's poor. Discusses aid imbalance, interdependence, empowering the poor, limits to growth. Includes discussion guide. Produced by Australian Catholic Aid.
Religion and Philosophy; Sociology
Dist - USCC

The Richest Land 23 MIN
16mm
Color (H C A)
LC 74-700145
Deals with agriculture in California, focusing on Sibu subsidies, politics and battles among small farmers, big farmers, international oil companies and farmworkers. Points out how California agriculture relates to the livelihood, struggles and ideals of many Americans.
Agriculture; Civics and Political Systems; Geography - United States
Dist - BALLIS **Prod** - BALLIS 1973

Richie 31 MIN
16mm / U-matic / VHS
Color (J)
LC 78-701147
Tells the story of a teenage boy who becomes deeply involved with drugs and a series of family conflicts and crises. Shows how the struggle with his family and drugs leads to his death by his father's hand. Based on the book Richie by Thomas Thompson.
Guidance and Counseling; Health and Safety; Sociology
Dist - LCOA **Prod** - JAFFE 1978

Richie 15 MIN
VHS
Color (I J H G)
$69.95 purchase _ #CVT102V
Tells of a middle class high school student who succumbed to peer pressure and tried drugs. Reveals how those drugs destroyed his life. Interviews Richie himself who tells how he started with alcohol and moved on to more dangerous drugs, including marijuana, speed, cocaine and heroin, and spent one - third of his life imprisoned. The story ends with news of the death of Richie, from an overdose, three weeks later.
Guidance and Counseling; Psychology
Dist - CAMV

Richmond remembered 30 MIN
VHS / U-matic / 16mm
Color (G A)
$320.00, $110.00, $45.00 purchase _ #TCA10904, #TCA16790, #TCA16791
Presents a docudrama on Richmond, Virginia during the Civil War. Views matters through the eyes of a Richmond family.
History - United States
Dist - USNAC **Prod** - USNPS 1987

Richness and diversity of nursing 26 MIN
VHS
Color (C PRO G)
$30.00 purchase, $15.00 rental _ #941, #940
Presents a film collage depicting people in numerous roles of the nursing practice and nursing science.
Guidance and Counseling; Health and Safety
Dist - SITHTA **Prod** - SITHTA 1983

The Richness of Activity 17 MIN
U-matic
Color (PRO)
Demonstrates theoretical concepts, activity history, activity analysis and activity process in mental health using case histories as examples.
Health and Safety; Psychology
Dist - AOTA **Prod** - AOTA 1980

Richter on Film 14 MIN
16mm
Color
Presents Hans Richter at age 83, who appears on camera at his Connecticut home and talks about his early experimental films and their relationship to his paintings, scrolls and collages. Includes excerpts from Rhythm 21, Ghosts Before Breakfast and Race Symphony. Produced by Cecile Starr.
Fine Arts
Dist - STARRC **Prod** - STARRC 1972

Rick Amputee - Part I 15 MIN
U-matic / VHS
Color
Shows the training of a 20 - year - old male who has sustained a traumatic right shoulder and left above elbow amputation. Demonstrates the use of numerous adaptive devices and techniques in order to attain maximum independence in daily activities.
Health and Safety; Psychology
Dist - UWASH **Prod** - UWASH

Rick Amputee - Part II 22 MIN
U-matic / VHS
Color
Shows aspects of the comprehensive rehabilitation program for the patient in Part I. Demonstrates measuring and fitting of the protheses, and the occupational therapist is shown performing a functional check - out.
Health and Safety; Psychology
Dist - UWASH **Prod** - UWASH

Rick and Rocky 15 MIN
16mm
Color (G)
$20.00 rental
Documents a surprise wedding shower for Ricky, who is Italian, and Roxann, who is Polish. Looks at the gifts they receive which are held up for the approval of the relatives who, along with the gifts, steal the show from the young couple. Made with Jeff Kreines.
Fine Arts; History - United States; Sociology
Dist - CANCIN **Prod** - PALAZT

Rick Charette
VHS / 16mm
Color (K)
$18.88 purchase _ #PP004
Presents Rick Charette in live concert singing children's songs.
Fine Arts
Dist - EDUCRT

Rick Danko's electric bass techniques 60 MIN
VHS
Color (G)
$39.95 purchase _ #VD - DAN - EB01
Features Rick Danko of The Band who teaches some of the exercises, picking techniques and musical ideas that have formed his style. Demonstrates the use of a flatpick to get a unique percussive sound. Gives several helpful scales and exercises to strengthen the left hand and offers some great bass lines. Describes Danko's musical influences and experiences and he jams with some Woodstock friends.
Fine Arts
Dist - HOMETA **Prod** - HOMETA

Rick, File X - 258375 11 MIN
VHS / U-matic
Professional Drug Films Series
Color
LC 80-707346
Shows how the probation service responds to a youthful narcotics offender. Issued in 1971 as a motion picture.
Health and Safety; Psychology; Sociology
Dist - USNAC **Prod** - NIMH 1980

Rick Johnson - Profile of a Champion 90 MIN
VHS
Motocross Series
Color (G)
$24.98 purchase _ #TT8117
Features Rick Johnson as he works, plays and readies himself for a race.
Industrial and Technical Education; Literature and Drama; Physical Education and Recreation
Dist - TWINTO **Prod** - TWINTO 1990

Rick Johnson's Motivation 60 MIN
VHS
Motocross Series
Color (G)
$19.98 purchase _ #TT8116
Features world champion Rick Johnson demonstrating why he is the winningest rider in Supercross history.
Industrial and Technical Education; Literature and Drama; Physical Education and Recreation
Dist - TWINTO **Prod** - TWINTO 1990

Rick Pitino basketball series
Presents a four - part series on basketball featuring head coach Rick Pitino, U of Kentucky. Includes the titles Offense, Volumes 1 and 2; and Defense, Volumes 1 and 2.
Defense - Volume 1 25 MIN
Defense - Volume 2 25 MIN
Offense - Volume 1 25 MIN
Offense - Volume 2 25 MIN
Dist - CAMV

Rick Ray series
Bali 80 MIN
Iceland 91 MIN
South China Seas 91 MIN
Dist - SVIP

Rick, You're in - a Story about Mainstreaming 20 MIN
U-matic / VHS / 16mm
Color (J H T) (FRENCH)
Depicts the experiences of Rick Rehaut, a handicapped youth who is entering a regular high school for the first time.
Foreign Language; Psychology
Dist - CORF **Prod** - DISNEY

Rickshaw Boy 123 MIN
VHS
Color (G) (MANDARIN CHINESE)
$45.00 purchase _ #1032A
Presents a movie produced in the People's Republic Of China.
Fine Arts; Geography - World; Literature and Drama
Dist - CHTSUI **Prod** - CHTSUI

Ricky 15 MIN
U-matic / VHS
Strawberry Square II - Take Time Series
Color (P)
Fine Arts
Dist - AITECH **Prod** - NEITV 1984

Ricky Goes to Camp 29 MIN
U-matic
A Different Understanding Series
Color (PRO)
Follows a young boy with behavioural problems through a two week session at camp where he acquires some outdoor skills and discovers how to get along better with his peers.
Psychology; Sociology
Dist - TVOTAR **Prod** - TVOTAR 1985

Ricky Goes to Camp 29 MIN
VHS / 16mm
A Different Understanding Series
Color (G)
$90.00 purchase _ #BPN178020
Looks at the Christie Lake Boys Camp, created to help children from low - income, inner - city communities. Follows a young boy with behavioral problems through a two week session. Features a discussion of the camp's history and usefulness by camp director Don Offord. Co - produced with the Mental Health Division, Health and Welfare, Canada.
Sociology
Dist - RMIBHF **Prod** - RMIBHF

Ricky Raccoon Shows the Way 15 MIN
16mm
Color (K P)
LC 80-700122
Teaches safety rules concerning how to drive bicycles in traffic, how to refuse strangers' offers, how to obey signal lights, how to understand street signs and how to wait at bus stops.

Health and Safety
Dist - KLEINW **Prod** - KLEINW 1978

Ricky's Great Adventure 11 MIN
16mm
Color
LC 75-702549
Explains the value of the senses in observing nature. Shows how a six - year - old blind boy employs his highly developed senses of touch and hearing to rescue a bird which has fallen from its nest and to find his way back to his teacher.
Education; Psychology
Dist - ATLAP **Prod** - ATLAP 1969

Rico Carty - an Interview 5 MIN
16mm
Color (H C A)
Features baseball player Rico Carty and his victorious struggle against TB. Explains chemotherapy treatment for the disease.
Health and Safety; Physical Education and Recreation
Dist - AMLUNG **Prod** - NTBA 1971

Rico - Union - Urban Community Development
16mm
Color (A)
LC 72-702860
Highlights PUnc's citizen involvement activities, especially techniques for promoting involvement in urban renewal planning, designing low - income housing, community surveying and the design and building of a west pocket park.
Industrial and Technical Education; Science - Natural; Sociology
Dist - UCLA **Prod** - UCLA 1971

The RIDAC process 8 MIN
16mm
Audio visual research briefs series
Color
LC 75-702425
Deals with the Rehabilitation Initial Diagnosis and Assessment process. Explains program principles and organizational structure for teams which perform the initial assessment of vocational rehabilitation applicants.
Guidance and Counseling; Health and Safety; Psychology
Dist - USNAC **Prod** - USSRS 1974

Riddance 84 MIN
VHS / 16mm
Marta Meszaros series
B&W (G) (HUNGARIAN WITH ENGLISH SUBTITLES)
$175.00 rental
Portrays a young factory worker who falls in love with a student brought up in the 'new bourgeoisie' of Hungary. Reveals that in order to gain his parents' blessing, the student is forced into a succession of lies. Directed by Marta Meszaros.
Fine Arts; Guidance and Counseling
Dist - KINOIC

Riddle of Heredity 29 MIN
16mm / U-matic / VHS
World We Live in Series
Color (I J H)
LC 70-701730
Surveys mankind's efforts to understand and control the processes of reproduction and inheritance.
Science - Natural
Dist - MGHT **Prod** - TIMELI 1968

The Riddle of Lumen 15 MIN
16mm
Color; Silent (C)
$493.00
Experimental film by Stan Brakhage.
Fine Arts
Dist - AFA **Prod** - AFA 1972

The Riddle of Photosynthesis 15 MIN
16mm / U-matic / VHS
Magic of the Atom Series
B&W (J H A)
LC FIA65-1123
Visits the AEC's radiation laboratory at Berkeley. Shows how radioactive carbon is incorporated in algae in order to make it possible to follow the photosynthetic process in plants. Uses chromatography and radioautography to pinpoint compounds.
Science; Science - Natural; Science - Physical
Dist - HANDEL **Prod** - HANDEL 1965

The Riddle of Reality 30 MIN
U-matic
Visions - Artists and the Creative Process Series
Color (H C A)
Shows how three abstract painters explore the philosophical question of what is reality.
Fine Arts; History - World
Dist - TVOTAR **Prod** - TVOTAR 1983

The Riddle of the Dead Sea Scrolls 80 MIN
VHS / 16mm
Color (G)
$395.00 purchase, $110.00 rental
Examines the historial background of the Bible and its portrayal of Jesus. Considers the controversial work of Biblical scholar Dr Barbara Thiering. Thiering has spent 20 years in archeological investigation and analysis of the Dead Sea Scrolls and contends that Jesus was not a deity. Offers new interpretations of miracles and other supernatural events depicted in the Bible.
History - World; Literature and Drama; Religion and Philosophy; Sociology
Dist - CNEMAG **Prod** - CNEMAG 1989

Riddle of the Joints 58 MIN
U-matic / VHS
Nova Series
Color (H C A)
$250 purchase _ #5266C
Discusses the widespread disease of rheumatoid arthritis. Produced by WGBH Boston.
Health and Safety
Dist - CORF

The Riddle of the Rook 25 MIN
16mm / U-matic / VHS
Behavior and Survival Series
Color (H C A)
LC 73-700428
Points out that rooks do great damage to farmlands. Shows what is known about the rook's feeding habits, its annual movements and its behavior. Points out that rooks protect themselves from over - population and make up for their losses, making bullets ineffective as a means for getting rid of them.
Science - Natural
Dist - MGHT **Prod** - MGHT 1973

The Riddle of the sands
VHS
Color (G)
$69.90 purchase _ #0775
Adapts the spy novel 'The Riddle of the Sands' by Erskine Childers. Follows two young Englishmen on a leisurely sailing holiday in the period before World War I. Stars Michael York and Simon MacCorkindale.
Fine Arts; History - World; Literature and Drama
Dist - SEVVID

Riddles of sand and ice 60 MIN
VHS
Miracle planet - the life story of Earth series
Color (I J H)
$100.00 purchase _ #A5VH 1324
Reveals that the Earth has undergone dramatic changes in climate throughout its long history. Discloses that the South Pole was once covered with tropical plants and there is evidence that the Sahara was once agriculturally abundant. Considers changes in the future and asks if there are Ice Ages to come. Part of a six - part series examining the intricate balance of systems known as planet Earth.
Geography - World; Science - Natural; Science - Physical
Dist - CLRVUE

The Ride 7 MIN
16mm
Color (A)
LC FIA64-28
Presents a slapstick comedy in which a portly tycoon takes a wild ride in his Rolls Royce, which becomes a toboggan and escapes from the chauffeur in the snowclad Laurentians.
Fine Arts
Dist - NFBC **Prod** - NFBC 1968

Ride a Mile in My Seat 25 MIN
16mm
Color (C A)
Emphasizes the complexities of driving a school bus safely. Points out that safe transportation is a collective effort involving students and drivers.
Education; Health and Safety; Psychology
Dist - VISUCP **Prod** - VISUCP 1979

Ride a Turquoise Pony 28 MIN
U-matic / VHS / 16mm
Insight Series
Color; B&W (H C A) (SPANISH)
LC 71-713917
A dramatization about the reunion of a Vietnam veteran and his girl who was a Vista volunteer.
Foreign Language; Psychology; Religion and Philosophy
Dist - PAULST **Prod** - PAULST 1971

Ride a Wagon Train 15 MIN
16mm / U-matic / VHS
Color (I J)
Captures a day in the week - long journey of modern adventurers on the Fort Seward Wagon Train in North Dakota. Records the routine along an eleven - mile route as well as the varied wildlife of the countryside.
History - United States
Dist - IFB **Prod** - BERLET 1983

Ride and Tie 22 MIN
VHS / BETA
Color
Combines endurance riding, marathon running, horsemanship, physical conditioning and strategy in 31 miles of trail.
Physical Education and Recreation
Dist - EQVDL **Prod** - LEVI

Ride Lonesome 73 MIN
16mm
Color
Stars Randolph Scott as a man seeking revenge on the man who raped and murdered his wife.
Fine Arts
Dist - KITPAR **Prod** - CPC 1959

The Ride of Your Life Time 23 MIN
VHS
Color (H C G)
Emphasizes the importance of seat belt use in order to save lives in auto accidents.
Health and Safety; Psychology; Social Science
Dist - HUF **Prod** - HUF 1986

Ride on 14 MIN
16mm / U-matic / VHS
Color (I)
LC 73-701804
Provides an amusing look at the world of the bicycle. Concentrates on what safety authorities feel are High Hazard situations. Examines the history of the wheel and the invention of the bicycle.
Health and Safety; History - World; Physical Education and Recreation; Sociology
Dist - MGHT **Prod** - MGHT 1973

Ride Safe 16 MIN
16mm
Color
Describes several riding techniques designed to keep motorcyclists out of accidents. Includes countersteering, combination braking, crossing obstacles and counterweighting.
Health and Safety
Dist - NILLU **Prod** - NILLU 1982

Ride the Roller Coaster
VHS / 16mm
Kidsongs Series
Color (K)
$14.44 purchase _ #WBR3 - 38163
Presents classic songs from the recent and distant past including Let's Twist Again, Whole Lotta Shakin' Goin' On, Here We Go Loopty Loo, Splish Splash, 1812 Overture, and others.
Fine Arts
Dist - EDUCRT

Ride the Sandy River Railroad 30 MIN
VHS
B&W (G)
$24.95 purchase
Takes a look at engines, railbuses and snowplows of the two - foot - gauge Sandy River Railroad Line using early 1930s film made by train enthusiasts. Includes subtitles for the silent film.
Fine Arts; History - United States; Social Science
Dist - NEFILM

Ride the white waves
VHS
Color (G)
$39.80 purchase _ #0276
Reviews three major international offshore powerboat events held off the shore of the United Kingdom in 1985. Includes footage from the helicopters of FM Television.
Physical Education and Recreation
Dist - SEVVID

Ride the Wind - Moods of Hang - Gliding 24 MIN
U-matic
Color (P)
Projects the excitement of the sport of hang - gliding. Shows many of the best hang - glider pilots soaring the beach ridges or flying thousands of feet in the air over rugged mountains.
Physical Education and Recreation
Dist - CRYSP **Prod** - CRYSP

Ride this Way Grey Horse 5 MIN
16mm
Color
LC 79-710436
Shows John Huston at work in Austria directing the motion picture, A Walk With Love and Death. Shows Huston working with his daughter Anjelica and Assaf Dayan, the son of the Israeli defense minister.
Fine Arts
Dist - TWCF **Prod** - KNP 1970

Rider skills
VHS
You and your horse series
Color (G)
$49.95 purchase _ #6 - 027 - 105A
Teaches the basics of using the hands, feet and effectively communicating with a horse for maximum performance. Part of a six - part series on training the western horse featuring B F Yeates, Extension Horse Specialist Emeritus of Texas A&M University.
Physical Education and Recreation
Dist - VEP **Prod** - VEP

The Rider's Aids 21 MIN
U-matic / VHS / 16mm
Riding Training Series
Color (J)
LC 80-701074
Demonstrates how a rider signals a horse to move or change direction using natural and artificial aids. Shows how the aids are first employed in conjunction with voice commands and then used alone. Emphasizes correct application of the aids and shows the use of aids in combination. Introduced by Princess Anne of Great Britain.
Physical Education and Recreation
Dist - IU **Prod** - BHORSE 1979

Riders of the Purple Sage 56 MIN
16mm
B&W
Tells a story of the Old West of a man who sets out to unravel and avenge the kidnapping of his sister. Stars Tom Mix and Marion Nixon. Directed by Lynn Reynolds.
Fine Arts
Dist - KILLIS **Prod** - UNKNWN 1925

Riders of the wind 48 MIN
VHS
Jacques Cousteau II series
Color; CC (G)
$19.95 purchase _ #3048
Reveals that Cousteau unveils a new invention - the cylindrical, high - tech Turbosail system - his revolutionary addition to the sailing ship. Travels with him on a Trans - Atlantic voyage from Tangier to New York. Part of a six - part series by Cousteau.
Geography - World; Physical Education and Recreation
Dist - APRESS

Riders to the Sea 27 MIN
16mm
B&W
LC FI68-648
Presents a tragedy set on one of the Aran Isles off the coast of Ireland concerning an old woman who becomes resigned to death after losing her husband and all her sons to the sea.
Fine Arts
Dist - CBSTV **Prod** - CBSTV 1959

Riders to the Sea 30 MIN
VHS / 16mm
Color (G)
$55.00 rental _ #RTTS - 000
Presents a one - act play by John Millington Synge. Revolves around an old woman waiting for her daughters to learn the fate of her son, who is believed to have drowned.
Fine Arts; Literature and Drama
Dist - PBS **Prod** - WQLN

Riders to the Stars 81 MIN
16mm
B&W (J)
Stars William Lundigan in the science fiction story of three space pilots who attempt to capture a meteor and return it to earth for scientific inspection.
Fine Arts
Dist - UAE **Prod** - UNKNWN

Rides and Escapes 22 MIN
U-matic / VHS / 16mm
Wrestling Series no 3
Color
LC 79-700807
Illustrates rides, breakdowns, escapes and reversals in the sport of wrestling. Focuses on the referee's positions.
Physical Education and Recreation
Dist - ATHI **Prod** - ATHI 1976

Ridin' Cool to School 16 MIN
U-matic / VHS / 16mm
Color (K P)
Uses puppets and live action to delineate safety rules, from bus stop to boarding, riding and getting off the bus.
Health and Safety
Dist - BCNFL **Prod** - BORTF 1983

Riding and pinning
VHS
N C A A instructional video series
Color (H C A)
$39.95 purchase _ #KAR2503V
Presents the third of a three - part series on wrestling. Focuses on riding and pinning techniques.
Physical Education and Recreation
Dist - CAMV **Prod** - NCAAF

Riding for America 60 MIN
U-matic
Color
Illustrates the sport of horseback riding. Features interviews with members of the United States Equestrian team. Focuses on the dedication, teamwork, discipline and effort needed to become an Olympic rider.
Physical Education and Recreation
Dist - MTP **Prod** - USEQT

Riding for America 58 MIN
BETA / VHS
Color
Shows men and women competing in the final selection for the U S Equestrian Team.
Physical Education and Recreation
Dist - EQVDL **Prod** - INSILC

Riding high 14 MIN
VHS
Color (K P I J H)
$195.00 purchase
Offers kids an alternative 'high.' Shows young people performing amazing stunts on roller blades, skateboards and bicycles. Presents a strong and clear message to stay away from alcohol and other drugs. Emphasizes that real fun and excitement in life occurs without alcohol and drugs. Urges kids to undertake the exhilarating journey of setting goals and pushing themselves to reach their true potential, whatever that might be.
Guidance and Counseling; Health and Safety; Psychology
Dist - FMSP **Prod** - ARMFRE

Riding in the sky 8 MIN
VHS
Junior space scientist series
CC; Color (P I)
$55.00 purchase _ #10363VG
Gives a brief history of humans' attempt to fly and space flight. Teaches about gravity, weightlessness, inertia, and orbiting. Covers NASA and the major accomplishments of space programs. Comes with a teacher's guide and blackline masters. Part three of a three - part series.
History - World; Science - Physical
Dist - UNL

Riding Motocross Glover Style 60 MIN
VHS
Motocross Series
Color (G)
$19.98 purchase _ #TT8114
Gives a personal guide to riding successful motocross with six time national champion Broc Glover.
Industrial and Technical Education; Literature and Drama; Physical Education and Recreation
Dist - TWINTO **Prod** - TWINTO 1990

Riding Mowers 26 MIN
VHS
Color (G)
$89.95 purchase _ #6 - 300 - 303P
Looks at the appropriate use for small, medium and heavy duty riding mowers for landscaping. Shows how to select the proper mower. Illustrates safety and maintenance procedures.
Agriculture; Health and Safety
Dist - VEP **Prod** - VEP

The Riding Position 18 MIN
U-matic / VHS / 16mm
Riding Training Series
Color (J)
LC 80-701076
Focuses on the classical riding position, emphasizing its practicality and efficiency. Uses closeups of body movement and position during the application of aids to illustrate the most efficient use of legs, seat and hands while guiding the horse. Concludes with variations of the basic position that are shown during walking, cantering, galloping and jumping. Introduced by Princess Anne of Great Britain.
Physical Education and Recreation
Dist - IU **Prod** - BHORSE 1979

Riding, Scared 10 MIN
U-matic
Readalong Two Series
Color (P)
Provides young viewers with a flexible range of reading experiences through active involvement in reading and writing. Comes with teacher's guide and kit.
Education; English Language; Literature and Drama
Dist - TVOTAR **Prod** - TVOTAR 1976

The Riding solution - magic happens when a horse becomes the personal therapist for a handicapped person 19 MIN
U-matic / VHS / BETA
Color (G PRO)
$29.95, $130.00 purchase _ #LSTF109
Visits the horse schools attended by handicapped people. Shows how horseback riding improves posture, balance, coordination, self esteem, self discipline, strength and overal flexibility for handicapped riders. Helps students to understand their handicapped classmates. Includes teachers' guide. Produced by Nature Episodes.
Health and Safety
Dist - FEDU

Riding the Big Surf 11 MIN
16mm
Color (J H C)
Takes a look at the best surfing areas in Hawaii.
Geography - United States; History - United States; Physical Education and Recreation
Dist - CINEPC **Prod** - TAHARA 1986

Riding the gale 57 MIN
VHS / 16mm
Color (H C G)
$850.00, $495.00 purchase, $85.00 rental
Updates the earlier Pins and Needles which tells about Genni Batterham learning she has multiple sclerosis and its effect upon her marriage and career. Follows Genni and husband Kim eight years later as they continue to battle the degenerative course of her illness. Shows how the challenge has deepened their love and commitment. Although Genni's body has deteriorated, her physical dependency has not crushed her ego and her adventurousness. Shows how she undertakes a journey across the desert.
Health and Safety; Psychology; Sociology
Dist - FLMLIB **Prod** - BTRHAM 1989

Riding the network 9 MIN
VHS
Color (COR)
$195.00 purchase, $95.00 five - day rental, $30.00 three - day preview _ #PRI
Demonstrates that telecommuting, in certain situations, can be beneficial to managers, employees, and the organization. Offers managers an alternative way to using the skills of qualified employees, and helps to avoid having to hire and train new employees. Encourages managers to see telecommuting as an opportunity to select good people from a broad range of resources. Discusses how to monitor projects and due dates, and how to make telecommuters accountable for their time.
Business and Economics; Guidance and Counseling
Dist - ADVANM

Riding the Pulpit 80 MIN
16mm
Color
Tells the story of Jess Moddy, whose persistence, courage, and sense of humor are combined with a deep love for God.
Religion and Philosophy
Dist - GF **Prod** - YOUTH

Riding the Space Range 18 MIN
16mm
Color
Demonstrates how NASA calibrates the equipment in its world - wide net of tracking stations.
Industrial and Technical Education
Dist - NASA **Prod** - NASA 1966

Riding Training Series
Basic paces of the horse 24 MIN
Dressage movements 23 MIN
The Rider's Aids 21 MIN
The Riding Position 18 MIN
Training the Young Horse 27 MIN
Dist - IU

Riding with the King 59 MIN
VHS / 16mm
Color (G)

$350.00 purchase, $95.00 rental; LC 90711291
Captures the legacy of Elvis Presley. Surveys the world of Elvis Presley fans. Documents the pilgrims who travel from around the world to gather at the shrines of Presleydom during the annual Tribute Week in Memphis, Tennessee.
Fine Arts; History - United States; Literature and Drama
Dist - CNEMAG **Prod** - CNEMAG 1989

Riding Your School Bus 9 MIN
16mm
Color (K P I)
LC 72-700614
An elementary teacher discusses school bus safety with her class, and children are shown demonstrating bus safety practices.
Health and Safety
Dist - VADE **Prod** - VADE 1972

Riemann Integration
16mm
B&W
Deals with the definition of the Riemann integral.
Mathematics
Dist - OPENU **Prod** - OPENU

Riff '65 12 MIN
16mm
B&W (J)
LC FIA67-583
A documentary that projects the character of Riff, a resourceful underprivileged youngster who is in conflict with his environment.
Psychology; Sociology
Dist - NYU **Prod** - NYU 1966

Rifle, M16A1, Pt 1 - Care, Cleaning and Lubrication 33 MIN
16mm
B&W
LC 75-702895
Teaches riflemen of the U S Army how to clean, lubricate and care for the M16A1 rifle in the field to prevent weapon failure and keep it in optimum condition ready for use.
Civics and Political Systems; Education
Dist - USNAC **Prod** - USA 1968

Rifle, M16A1, Pt 2 - Field Expedients 17 MIN
16mm
B&W
LC 75-702897
Teaches riflemen of the U S Army how to clean wet and dirty rifles and ammunition. Shows the use of cleaning expedients and of SLA to prevent weapon failures. Stresses the importance of emergency action when weapons fail to fire.
Civics and Political Systems; Education
Dist - USNAC **Prod** - USA 1968

Rifle Platoon in Night Attack 21 MIN
16mm
Color
LC 80-701840
Shows how to lead troops in planning and executing a night attack and how a platoon operates during a surprise assault to seize an assigned objective.
Civics and Political Systems
Dist - USNAC **Prod** - USA 1980

Rifle Shooting Fundamentals - Firing the Shot 13 MIN
U-matic / VHS / 16mm
Rifle Shooting Fundamentals Series
Color (J)
Presents two - time Olympic Rifle Gold Medalist Lones Wigger reviewing the fundamentals of aiming, breath control, hold control, trigger pull and follow through.
Physical Education and Recreation
Dist - ATHI **Prod** - ATHI 1981

Rifle Shooting Fundamentals - Kneeling and Sitting 14 MIN
16mm / U-matic / VHS
Rifle Shooting Fundamentals Series
Color (J)
Presents two - time Olympic Rifle Gold Medalist Gary Anderson and four - time National Rifle Champion Carl Bernosky reviewing the fundamentals necessary for developing the kneeling and sitting shooting positions.
Physical Education and Recreation
Dist - ATHI **Prod** - ATHI 1981

Rifle Shooting Fundamentals Series
Pistol Shooting Fundamentals 15 MIN
Rifle Shooting Fundamentals - Firing the Shot 13 MIN
Rifle Shooting Fundamentals - Kneeling and Sitting 14 MIN
Rifle Shooting Fundamentals - Standing and Prone 13 MIN
Dist - ATHI

Rifle Shooting Fundamentals - Standing and Prone 13 MIN
U-matic / VHS / 16mm
Rifle Shooting Fundamentals Series
Color (J)
Presents World Rifle Champion Sue Ann Sandusky and U S Shooting Team Coach William Krilling reviewing the fundamentals necessary for developing the standing and prone shooting positions.
Physical Education and Recreation
Dist - ATHI **Prod** - ATHI 1981

Rifle Shooting Tips and Techniques 48 MIN
BETA / VHS
Color
Shows techniques for fitting one's rifle, dry firing, sighting in, wind duping, range and bullet drop estimation, and trigger squeeze.
Physical Education and Recreation
Dist - HOMEAF **Prod** - HOMEAF

Rifle shooting tips and techniques
VHS
Color (G)
$29.95 purchase _ #SZ007
Offers tips on dry firing, sighting in, wind doping, range and bullet drop estimation, trigger squeeze, etc. Features marksmen Glen Pearce and Jim Carter.
Physical Education and Recreation
Dist - SIV

The Rifle Squad - Dismounted Movement Techniques 21 MIN
16mm
Color
LC 80-701841
Shows how two fire teams use various techniques to achieve positions of cover and to suppress enemy fire and emplacement.
Civics and Political Systems
Dist - USNAC **Prod** - USA 1980

Rig Floor Safety
U-matic / VHS
Rig Orientation for New Hands Series
Color (IND)
Demonstrates basic safety practices of work on the rig floor while emphasizing what can occur if safe techniques are not used.
Business and Economics; Health and Safety
Dist - GPCV **Prod** - CAODC

Rig Inspections 19 MIN
VHS / Slide / 16mm
Color (A PRO IND)
$160.00 purchase _ #16.1147, $170.00 purchase _ #56.1147
Offers guidelines for creating a rig inspection program to protect employees and equipment from accidents resulting from unsafe conditions.
Industrial and Technical Education; Social Science
Dist - UTEXPE **Prod** - UTEXPE 1979

Rig orientation for new hands series
It ain't easy 33 MIN
Rig Floor Safety
Dist - GPCV

Rigging and forklift operation series
Advanced rigging - 1 60 MIN
Advanced rigging - 2 60 MIN
Basic rigging - 1 60 MIN
Basic rigging - 2 60 MIN
Forklift operation 60 MIN
Dist - NUSTC

Rigging and Lifting 240 MIN
U-matic / VHS
Mechanical Equipment Maintenance Series
Color (IND)
Deals with rigging and lifting. Discusses hand and power operated hoists, forklifts, cranes, ladders and scaffolds.
Industrial and Technical Education
Dist - ITCORP **Prod** - ITCORP

Rigging and lifting 240 MIN
VHS / U-matic
Mechanical equipment maintenance - Spanish series
Color (IND) (SPANISH)
Deals with rigging and lifting. Discusses hand and power operated hoists, forklifts, cranes, ladders and scaffolds.
Industrial and Technical Education
Dist - ITCORP **Prod** - ITCORP

Rigging equipment over the floor 16 MIN
U-matic / VHS
Marshall maintenance training programs series; Tape 41
Color (IND)
Shows common rigging practices of moving equipment using rollers, dollies, roller casters, skids, air jacks and wooden skids.
Industrial and Technical Education; Social Science
Dist - LEIKID **Prod** - LEIKID

Rigging equipment over the floor 16 MIN
BETA / VHS / U-matic
Marshall maintenance programs series
Color (IND G)
$330.00 purchase _ #800 - 56
Demonstrates common rigging practices for moving heavy and light equipment using rollers, dollies, roller casters, skids, air jacks and wooden skids. Emphasizes safety precautions.
Health and Safety; Industrial and Technical Education; Psychology
Dist - ITSC **Prod** - ITSC

Rigging up - the safe way 23 MIN
VHS / Slide / 16mm
Color (A PRO IND)
$160.00 purchase _ #16.1148, $170.00 purchase _ #56.1148
Covers a variety of safety procedures that the rig crew should be familiar with and practice during a rig - up to prevent accidents.
Health and Safety; Industrial and Technical Education
Dist - UTEXPE **Prod** - UTEXPE 1981

Rigging wire rope slings 18 MIN
BETA / VHS / U-matic
Marshall maintenance programs series
Color (IND G)
$385.00 purchase _ #800 - 57
Presents recommended, safe methods for securing maximum use from wire rope slings. Explains procedures to follow for safe and proper rigging conditions and techniques for rigging rope slings without causing dangerous situations.
Health and Safety; Industrial and Technical Education
Dist - ITSC **Prod** - ITSC

Rigging - wire rope slings 18 MIN
16mm
Color (IND)
Presents recommended methods for securing maximum use from wire rope slings. Portrays the skills required to select and properly use slings.
Industrial and Technical Education
Dist - MOKIN **Prod** - MOKIN

Right and Wrong and What's in between 10 MIN
U-matic / VHS / 16mm
Color (P)
$25 rental _ #9737
Stimulates discussion and helps children distinguish between right and wrong.
Guidance and Counseling
Dist - AIMS **Prod** - AIMS 1973

The Right Angle Counter Top 60 MIN
VHS / 16mm
Color (H A)
$229.00 purchase _ W30
Describes component parts of the right angle counter top, including plywood as opposed to particle board base. Details measuring and shows how to use a hand - held laminate trimmer.
Industrial and Technical Education
Dist - BERGL **Prod** - BERGL 1987

The Right Angle Counter Top Project 68 MIN
VHS
(H A IND)
$329.00 purchase, #W30V7
Includes layout and assembly of base, layout and cutting laminate, adhesive application and installation, and trimming and finishing counter top (4 tapes). Includes a Study Guide.
Education; Industrial and Technical Education
Dist - BERGL

Right Angle Radiography with Rinn Circular Positioning Indicating Device - Anterior 9 MIN
16mm
Color (PRO)
LC 77-701398
Demonstrates the use of the Rinn circular positioning indicating device for anterior teeth. Shows how a long, cylindrical tube with instruments positions the film parallel to the long axes of the teeth and how guiding devices direct the x - ray beam at right angles to the film.
Health and Safety; Science
Dist - USNAC **Prod** - USVA 1973

Right Angle Radiography with Rinn Rectangular Positioning Indicating Device - Posterior 11 MIN
16mm
Color (PRO)

LC 75-701266
Demonstrates the use of a rectangular tube to decrease the amount of radiation received by a patient in dental radiography. Shows instruments used to achieve perfect alignment of the posterior teeth.
Health and Safety; Science
Dist - USNAC **Prod** - USVA 1973

Right angle radiography with the versatile intra - oral positioner - a series
Right angle radiography with the versatile intra - oral positioner -'series
Color (PRO)
Discusses various aspects of radiography with the versatile intra - oral positioner. A four - part series.
Health and Safety
Dist - USNAC **Prod** - VADTC 1977

Right Angle Radiography with the Versatile Intra - Oral Positioner, Pt 4 - Bite Wings 12 MIN
16mm
Right Angle Radiography with the Versatile Intra - Oral Positioner 'Series
Color (PRO)
LC 78-700354
Demonstrates a method of bite - wing radiography which positions the film vertically and provides adequate coverage of the height of the crest of the aveolar bone.
Health and Safety
Dist - USNAC **Prod** - VADTC 1977

Right Angle Radiography with the Versatile Intra - Oral Positioner, Pt 1 - Principles 14 MIN
16mm
Right Angle Radiography with the Versatile Intra - Oral Positioner 'Series
Color (PRO)
LC 78-700356
Illustrates how the right - angle parallel plane technique of intra - oral radiography minimizes dimensional distortion. Demonstrates the various components of the versatile intra - oral positioner and explains its assembly and use.
Health and Safety
Dist - USNAC **Prod** - VADTC 1977

Right Angle Radiography with the Versatile Intra - Oral Positioner, Pt 3 - Posterior 16 MIN
16mm
Right Angle Radiography with the Versatile Intra - Oral Positioner 'Series
Color (PRO)
LC 78-700355
Demonstrates the use of the versatile intraoral positioner to record accurate radiographic images of the posterior teeth.
Health and Safety; Science
Dist - USNAC **Prod** - VADTC 1977

Right Angle Radiography with the Versatile Intra - Oral Positioner, Pt 2 - Anterior 11 MIN
16mm
Right Angle Radiography with the Versatile Intra - Oral Positioner 'Series
Color (PRO)
LC 78-700255
Demonstrates the use of the versatile intra - oral positioners (VIP) to radiograph the anterior teeth. Shows how the VIP instrument simplifies placement of the film parallel to the long axes of the anterior teeth and facilitates direction of the X - ray beam at right angles to the film.
Health and Safety
Dist - USNAC **Prod** - VADTC 1977

Right angle radiography with the versatile intra - oral positioner - series
Right angle radiography with the versatile intra - oral positioner - a series
Right Angle Radiography with the Versatile Intra - Oral Positioner, Pt 4 - Bite Wings 12 MIN
Right Angle Radiography with the Versatile Intra - Oral Positioner, Pt 1 - Principles 14 MIN
Right Angle Radiography with the Versatile Intra - Oral Positioner, Pt 3 - Posterior 16 MIN
Right Angle Radiography with the Versatile Intra - Oral Positioner, Pt 2 - Anterior 11 MIN
Dist - USNAC

The Right choice 14 MIN
U-matic / 16mm / VHS
Color (I J)
$150.00, $95.00, $45.00 purchase _ #TCA16821, #TCA16822, #TCA16823
Challenges children to examine their feelings about drugs, peer pressure, and trust. Co - produced with Winn - Dixie stores.
Guidance and Counseling; Health and Safety; Psychology
Dist - USNAC **Prod** - FBI 1987

The Right Choice 6 MIN
8mm cartridge / 16mm
Color
LC 74-706399; 74-706398
Discusses oral hygiene, showing the relationship between the ingestion of sucrose and the conversion of sucrose to dextran and acid by oral bacteria.
Health and Safety
Dist - USNAC **Prod** - USVA 1972

The Right choice 20 MIN
VHS
Color (G)
$395.00 purchase, $140.00 rental _ #91F6010G
Shows the right way and the wrong way to interview people for employment. Uses humor to illustrate the need for an agenda, how not to get sidetracked, using open - ended questions and challenging answers when necessary.
Business and Economics; Guidance and Counseling
Dist - DARTNL **Prod** - DARTNL

The Right choice 20 MIN
VHS / U-matic / BETA
Color (C A G)
$690.00 purchase, $205.00 rental
Explores the four essential stages of interviewing - preparation, organization, exploration and projection. Stars British comics Mel Smith and Griff Rhys as hosts.
Business and Economics; Guidance and Counseling; Psychology
Dist - VIDART **Prod** - VIDART

The Right choice 30 MIN
VHS
Color (P I)
$25.00 rental, $125.00 purchase
Presents an elementary grade level comedy illustrating the importance of healthy food selection. Features a humorous mime clown with several costumes and faces performing in front of a young school assembly audience.
Education; Literature and Drama; Social Science
Dist - SHENFP

The Right choice, with the art of interviewing 24 MIN
VHS
Color (A PRO IND)
$650.00 purchase, $125.00 rental
Stars Mel and Griff in a look at the right and wrong ways to interview people. Presents a four - step system for conducting interviews. Includes role plays of various interview situations.
Business and Economics; Guidance and Counseling; Psychology
Dist - VLEARN **Prod** - CRMF

The Right Container 29 MIN
VHS / U-matic
Flower Show Series
Color
Features Mrs Ascher showing how to choose or make the correct container and using containers to make two arrangements.
Fine Arts; Home Economics; Science - Natural
Dist - MDCPB **Prod** - MDCPB

The Right environment - Bio - remediation 24 MIN
VHS / U-matic
Color (H)
$280.00, $330.00 purchase, $50.00 rental
Investigates how natural bacteria can decontaminate the land and deal with polluted and contaminated soils produced by industrial societies. Reveals how various bacteria can convert household garbage into natural gas and how natural organisms can convert oil pollution and sewage into non - toxic compounds and effluents.
Science - Natural; Sociology
Dist - NDIM **Prod** - LONTVS 1992

The Right Exposure 29 MIN
VHS / U-matic
Photo Show Series
Color
Explains that the most critical factor in getting a technically good photograph is proper exposure. Shows that the first step for proper exposure is choosing the correct film.
Industrial and Technical Education
Dist - PBS **Prod** - WGBHTV 1981

Right eye - left eye 6 MIN
8mm cartridge
Color (G)
$20.00 rental
Explores the narrow and often confounding boundary between the real and the depicted - two - dimensional and three - dimensional components of all photographic processes. Recreates a part of the film installation for a gallery show, namely a World War II Navy training film that described an early three - dimensional photo system called Vectographs.
Fine Arts; Industrial and Technical Education
Dist - CANCIN **Prod** - LIPZIN 1984

Right from day one 10 MIN
BETA / VHS / U-matic
International series
Color (A G)
$395.00 purchase, $125.00 rental
Presents an employee orientation film from Australia geared for the first day on the job. Explains to new hires what they should know about their job and how they can quickly start to contribute. Includes understanding the importance of asking questions, knowing what is expected, and forming independent opinions.
Business and Economics; Psychology
Dist - TELDOC **Prod** - AURORA

Right from Day One 10 MIN
VHS / 16mm
Color (PRO)
$395.00 purchase, $125.00 rental, $35.00 preview
Teaches newly hired employees how to contribute and feel comfortable in their new work environment. Discusses importance of asking questions, knowing what to expect from supervisors and how to perform independently.
Business and Economics; Guidance and Counseling; Psychology
Dist - UTM **Prod** - UTM

Right from the Start 58 MIN
VHS / U-matic
Color
Takes a look at the important relationship between parent and child which begins at birth. Documents the importance of bonding for both the care giver and child, and focuses on some of the practices and institutions in society that can either encourage or hinder this attachment process.
Home Economics; Psychology
Dist - FILAUD **Prod** - CRASCO

Right from the Start 55 MIN
16mm
Color (H C A)
Looks at the important relationship between parent and child that begins at birth. Shows how, moments after a child is born, a parent and child make important connections through touching, responding and eye contact. Illustrates the surprising capabilities and personalites of infants and explains how to interpret a baby's signals.
Home Economics; Sociology
Dist - FILAUD **Prod** - PTST 1983

A Right Good Thing 12 MIN
16mm
Color
LC 80-701173
Focuses on tax problems frequently encountered by older people, such as tax benefits for people over 65, consequences of selling a home after age 55 and treatment of Social Security benefits as taxable income. Discusses the free tax counseling services available to older citizens from the U S Internal Revenue Service.
Business and Economics; Health and Safety; Sociology
Dist - USNAC **Prod** - USIRS 1980

The Right hand of Congress 29 MIN
16mm
Government story series; No 10
Color (H C)
LC 74-707191
Discusses the role of congressional assistants and staff members on Capitol Hill and explains the differences between committee staff members and personal staff members of Senators and Representatives.
Civics and Political Systems
Dist - WBCPRO **Prod** - OGCW 1968

The Right hand of the court 20 MIN
VHS / U-matic
Color
LC 77-715508
Describes the functions and duties of the office of the Court Clerk, while demonstrating the daily workings of a court of law.
Civics and Political Systems; Guidance and Counseling
Dist - IA **Prod** - LACFU LAC 1970

The Right hand of the President 29 MIN
16mm
Government story series; No 25
Color (H C)
LC 78-707192
Describes the creation, growth and duties of the White House staff. Explains the relationship between the White House staff, the Cabinet and the Congress.
Civics and Political Systems
Dist - WBCPRO **Prod** - OGCW 1968

Right Heart Catheterization 13 MIN
U-matic / VHS
Color (PRO)
Includes a review of pertinent intrathoracic anatomy, visualization, and demonstration of pressure wave form transitions.
Health and Safety; Science - Natural
Dist - HSCIC **Prod** - HSCIC 1982

Right hemicolectomy for carcinoma 21 MIN
16mm
Color (PRO)
Presents the procedure of right colectomy for a malignant lesion of the ascending colon. Emphasizes the blood supply and its treatment early in the operation. Demonstrates a palliative prodecure.
Health and Safety
Dist - ACY **Prod** - ACYDGD 1963

Right here, right now 15 MIN
16mm
Revelation series
Color (H C A)
LC 72-700510
Presents a dramatization about a janitor in an apartment house who reaches out to help those around him. Explores the mystery of Christ present today in one's fellowman.
Guidance and Counseling; Psychology; Religion and Philosophy
Dist - FRACOC **Prod** - FRACOC 1970

Right Hose and Fuel Tanks 30 MIN
VHS / BETA
Last Chance Garage Series
Color
Explores picking the right hose. Describes the workings of the fuel tank. Features a 1931 Ford Model A Roadster.
Industrial and Technical Education
Dist - CORF **Prod** - WGBHTV

Right human relations 28 MIN
VHS
Color (J H G)
$75.00 purchase, $35.00 rental
Examines the concept of human rights from ancient times to the present day. Suggests that human rights are inherent in most religious and political traditions. Notes historic landmarks in the progress of human rights, emphasizing the creation of the United Nations in 1945 and the adoption of the Universal Declaration of Human Rights. Includes a copy of the Universal Declaration.
Civics and Political Systems
Dist - EFVP **Prod** - LUCIS 1990

The Right images
CD-ROM
Color (G A)
$158.00 purchase _ #2381
Includes 103 images covering stars, galaxies, the Earth, planets, the moon, shuttle launches and other spacey topics. Presents photos in PICT2 format as 24 and 8 bit color, and 8 bit grey files. For Macintosh Plus, SE and II computers. Requires at least one M of RAM, one floppy disk drive, and an Apple compatible CD - ROM drive.
Computer Science; Fine Arts
Dist - BEP

Right in Der Fuehrer's face 30 MIN
VHS
America in World War II - The home front series
Color (G)
$49.95 purchase _ #AWWH - 106
Scrutinizes the pro - war propaganda created for American air waves. Shows that much of it was comical in form, but reveals that some of the propaganda involved racial attacks on the Japanese, which may have helped make internment of Japanese - Americans more acceptable. Suggests that many of the propaganda techniques used then are still used. Narrated by Eric Sevareid.
History - United States
Dist - PBS

The Right Kind of Toys 17 MIN
VHS / 16mm
Color (H C A)
Focuses on the need to encourage women to enter the fields of engineering, science and technology. Includes brief visits with three women, an extension agronomist, a TV meteorologist and an electronics design engineer.
Guidance and Counseling; Science; Sociology
Dist - IOWA **Prod** - IOWA 1989

The Right Location 16 MIN
16mm
Color
LC 74-702883
Uses the experiences of a small businessman who tries to select a site for his first menswear store to dramatize the relationship of site selection to the success of a business and to identify some of the important factors in selecting a business site.
Business and Economics
Dist - USSBA **Prod** - USSBA 1974

Right Lower Lobectomy 18 MIN
VHS / U-matic
Thoracic Series
Color
Health and Safety; Science - Natural
Dist - SVL **Prod** - SVL

The Right Man 28 MIN
16mm
Color
LC 74-703235
Examines the career of Dr Robert Hayes, black president of Wiley College in Marshall, Texas. Shows how Hayes escaped from the black ghetto, was able to get an education and became a college president.
Education; History - United States
Dist - KPRCTV **Prod** - KPRCTV 1974

The Right Move 15 MIN
16mm
Color
Discusses the problems of moving to a new city. Shows how children should be prepared as well as one's possessions for the important move to a new location. Answers such questions as how to pack and move pets, plants, and valuables, how to sell what you leave behind, when to move, which professional movers to use, what tax advantages, and what troubles to avoid.
Home Economics
Dist - KLEINW **Prod** - KLEINW

The Right moves - ergonomics in the workplace 18 MIN
BETA / VHS / U-matic
Color (IND G)
$495.00 purchase _ #827 - 24
Helps supervisors identify ergonomic deficiencies in the workplace. Discusses the hazards of repetitive motion and other ergonomic disorders. Emphasizes a team approach to controlling hazards. Explains the most common causes of ergonomic disorders and provides step - by - step instructions for identifying problem areas.
Business and Economics; Health and Safety; Industrial and Technical Education; Psychology
Dist - ITSC **Prod** - ITSC 1990

The Right moves II - ergonomics in the workplace 18 MIN
VHS
Color (IND G)
$495.00 purchase _ #152
Trains supervisors in the identification of ergonomic deficiencies in the workplace. Emphasizes a team approach to controlling hazards. Explains the most common causes of ergonomic disorders and provides step - by - step instructions for identifying problem areas. Includes leader guide.
Business and Economics; Health and Safety; Psychology
Dist - GOVINS

The Right not to be a Patient 60 MIN
U-matic
Ethics and Medicine Series
Color
Describes the difference between having a disease and the role of being a patient. Discusses individual freedom and medical care, as well as involuntary confinement in psychiatric hospitals.
Health and Safety; Psychology; Religion and Philosophy
Dist - HRC **Prod** - OHC

Right of privacy 59 MIN
16mm
NET Journal series
B&W (H C A)
LC FIA68-580
Reports on the governmental and business activities which pose a threat to individual privacy today. Discusses the National Data Bank as a collection of statistics and as a potential threat to individual freedom. Documents pre - employment investigations, lie detector tests, credit checks and personality tests. Shows interviews with congressional representatives and other public officials.
Civics and Political Systems; Psychology; Sociology
Dist - IU **Prod** - NET 1968

Right - of - Way for Highways 26 MIN
16mm
Color
LC 74-705540
Shows how a state highway department studies, evaluates and selects the route for a new highway, the various steps in the appraisal of property needed for right - of - way and the negotiation for purchase of the property.
Social Science
Dist - USNAC **Prod** - USDTFH 1961

Right on 78 MIN
16mm
Color (J)
Presents David Nelson, Felipe Luciano and Gylau Kair, black revolutionary and self - professed original last poets, photographed against their ghetto backgrounds, reciting their poetry.
History - United States; Literature and Drama; Sociology
Dist - NLC **Prod** - NLC 1971

Right on 14 MIN
16mm
Color
LC 74-703216
Demonstrates the varied aspects of archery as a competitive and fun sport.
Physical Education and Recreation
Dist - MTP **Prod** - BEARAC 1973

Right on - be Free 15 MIN
U-matic / VHS / 16mm
Color (I)
LC 72-701732
Shows the energy, vitality and strong sense of identity of the black American artist. Portrays experience mood and temperament in music, poetry, painting and dance.
History - United States; Psychology; Sociology
Dist - ALTSUL **Prod** - TAMIMI 1971

Right on - ceremony of us 30 MIN
16mm
B&W (G)
$35.00 rental
Reveals an intense encounter between an all - black group from Watts and the all - white Dancers' Workshop community in a ten - day session conducted by Anna Halprin. Records the group's experience of each other through movement encounter situations and discussions. Filmed by KQED - TV in San Francisco.
Fine Arts; Sociology
Dist - CANCIN

Right on Course 30 MIN
BETA / VHS
Under Sail Series
Color
Describes how to sail a course. Discusses wind direction and knot tying.
Physical Education and Recreation
Dist - CORF **Prod** - WGBHTV

Right on - Poetry on Film 77 MIN
16mm
Color
Features a performance by the Last Poets, three young black men, reciting their poems on rooftops and in the streets of New York City. Presents a poetry based in the vernacular of the black working class, in street language and the rhythms of the ghetto.
History - United States; Literature and Drama; Sociology
Dist - BLKFMF **Prod** - BLKFMF

Right - on Roofer, Pt 1 15 MIN
16mm / U-matic / VHS
Right - On Roofer Safework Series
Color (IND)
LC 81-700863
Deals with such aspects of roofing safety as the correct methods of melting and pouring asphalt, moving filled containers, adjusting temperature and the wearing of a hardhat.
Health and Safety; Industrial and Technical Education
Dist - IFB **Prod** - SAFSEM 1980

Right - on Roofer, Pt 2 12 MIN
U-matic / VHS / 16mm
Right - On Roofer Safework Series
Color (IND)
LC 81-700863
Shows the procedures for working near the edges or openings in a roof, for bringing materials up to the roof and for tearing off and disposing of the old roof.
Health and Safety; Industrial and Technical Education
Dist - IFB **Prod** - SAFSEM 1980

Right - on Roofer, Pt 3 12 MIN
U-matic / VHS / 16mm
Right - On Roofer Safework Series
Color (IND)

LC 81-700863
Describes the proper use of a ladder on roofing jobs, the proper way to lift materials and the proper housekeeping procedures to facilitate finding things.
Health and Safety; Industrial and Technical Education
Dist - IFB **Prod** - SAFSEM 1980

Right - on Roofer, Pt 4 9 MIN
U-matic / VHS / 16mm
Right - On Roofer Safework Series
Color (IND)
LC 81-700863
Provides special safety precautions to be followed when working on steep, shake or tile roofs.
Health and Safety; Industrial and Technical Education
Dist - IFB **Prod** - SAFSEM 1980

Right - on roofer safework - Pt 5 series
Flag warning lines 6 MIN
Dist - IFB

Right - on roofer safework series 48 MIN
16mm / VHS / BETA / U-matic
Right - on roofer safework series
Color; PAL (IND)
PdS250, PdS258 purchase
Provides training in safe work practices, both on the ground and on the roof. Contains five parts which are further divided into specific subject areas which can be viewed and discussed individually. Part 1 titles are Play it Cool with Hot; and Airmail, Hardhats and Barricades. Part 2 titles are Edges, Openings and Warning Guards; Hoists, Forklifts and Conveyors; and Tearoff and Disposal. Part 3 titles are Ladders; Lifting; and Housekeeping. Part 4 titles are Steep Roof Work; Shake Jobs; and Tile Jobs. Part 5, Flag Warning Lines, is for the foreman. Produced by Safety Seminars, Inc.
Health and Safety
Dist - EDPAT

Right - on roofer safework series
Right - on roofer safework series 48 MIN
Dist - EDPAT

Right - On Roofer Safework Series
Right - on Roofer, Pt 1 15 MIN
Right - on Roofer, Pt 2 12 MIN
Right - on Roofer, Pt 3 12 MIN
Right - on Roofer, Pt 4 9 MIN
Dist - IFB

Right on - the original last poets - the roots of rap
VHS
Color (G)
$89.95 purchase
Spans a day in the ghetto, with context, thrust and mood shifting with the change in hour and light. Opens with daily life - street gangs, preachers, hustlers, the junkie, followed by a sequence on the recapturing of identity and manhood. Leads into love poetry with the approach of dusk as the poets - Gylan Kane, Felipe Luciano and David Nelson - call on the brothers and sisters to know themselves and to join together in the fight for change. As the night falls, prophecy and revolution fill the air.
Civics and Political Systems; History - United States; Literature and Drama
Dist - ROLAND **Prod** - NLC

Right or wrong for Lutherans 20 MIN
VHS
Lutherans and their beliefs series
Color (J H C G A R)
$39.95 purchase, $10.00 rental _ #35 - 8112 - 2076
Features Dr Jerry L Schmalenberger in a consideration of the Lutheran perspective of right and wrong. Produced by Seraphim.
Religion and Philosophy
Dist - APH

Right Out of History - the Making of Judy Chicago's Dinner Party, Pt 1 37 MIN
U-matic / VHS / 16mm
Color
LC 80-701260
Follows the creation of the Dinner Party, a monumental artistic tribute to women of achievement throughout history.
Dist - PHENIX **Prod** - PHENIX 1980

Right Out of History - the Making of Judy Chicago's Dinner Party, Pt 2 38 MIN
U-matic / VHS / 16mm
Color
LC 80-701260
Follows the creation of the Dinner Party, a monumental artistic tribute to women of achievement throughout history.
Dist - PHENIX **Prod** - PHENIX 1980

Right Partial Mastectomy 41 MIN
VHS / U-matic
Breast Series
Color
Health and Safety; Science - Natural
Dist - SVL **Prod** - SVL

The Right role 29 MIN
VHS / 16mm
Sonrisas series
Color (T P) (SPANISH AND ENGLISH)
$46.00 rental _ #SRSS - 128
Shows how a group of children are faced with playing roles when a Hollywood producer comes to town. In Spanish and English.
Sociology
Dist - PBS

The Right Start 30 MIN
U-matic / VHS
Training Dogs the Woodhouse Way
Color (H C A)
Home Economics; Science - Natural
Dist - FI **Prod** - BBCTV 1982

The Right start 20 MIN
VHS
Color (A PRO)
$550.00 purchase, $125.00 rental
Presents an orientation plan for new sales associates and other entry - level employees. Stresses follow - up as a critical element.
Business and Economics; Psychology
Dist - VLEARN

The Right stuff 20 MIN
VHS
Textile studies series
Color (A)
PdS65 purchase
Shows how a fashion designer attempts to make protective clothing more attractive so that people will want to wear it. Explores the origins of man-made and natural fiber; the processes of spinning, weaving, printing, dyeing, and finishing; and the uses of different textiles in everyday life. Part of a five-part series.
Home Economics; Industrial and Technical Education
Dist - BBCENE

The Right Stuff
U-matic / VHS
Color (J H C A)
$97.00 purchase _ #05731 94
Dramatizes the American space program. Based on the book The Right Stuff by Tom Wolfe.
Fine Arts; Industrial and Technical Education
Dist - ASPRSS

Right Thumb, Left Thumb 9 MIN
U-matic / VHS / 16mm
Color (P I) (SPANISH)
Tells about a little boy's adventures when he goes to the store alone for the first time.
Foreign Language; Literature and Drama
Dist - AIMS **Prod** - MORLAT 1970

Right Thumb, Left Thumb 9 MIN
U-matic / VHS / 16mm
Reading Short Stories Series
Color (K P I)
LC 73-702457
Presents a story about a little boy's adventures along the road to growing up. Encourages the relating of viewers' own early experiences at accepting responsibility.
English Language; Literature and Drama
Dist - AIMS **Prod** - MORLAT 1970

Right thumb, left thumb 9 MIN
16mm
Color (K P I) (SPANISH)
LC 74-703751
Tells the story of a young boy who is sent to the store on his own for the first time. Shows how he learns the value of being attentive and following directions. Based on the book Right Thumb - Left Thumb by Osmond Molarsky.
Guidance and Counseling; Literature and Drama
Dist - MORLAT **Prod** - MORLAT 1973
AIMS

The Right to be - derecho de estar 29 MIN
VHS / 16mm
Sonrisas series
Color (T P) (SPANISH AND ENGLISH)
$46.00 rental _ #SRSS - 105
Features children helping an illegal alien become a U S citizen.
Sociology
Dist - PBS

The Right to be Desperate 52 MIN
16mm
Color (A)
Observes how Carl Rogers works as a therapist. Comments on what transpires in an initial counseling session, and how to work with clients who are struggling with issues of living and dying. Provides evidence that a clild is open to all experiencing. On two (2) reels.
Psychology
Dist - AACD **Prod** - AACD 1977

Right to Believe, Pt 1 30 MIN
VHS / U-matic
Color (H C A)
Shows how early Americans won religious freedom.
History - United States
Dist - GA **Prod** - ABCTV 1983

Right to Believe, Pt 2 30 MIN
U-matic / VHS
Color (H C A)
Shows how early Americans won religious freedom.
History - United States
Dist - GA **Prod** - ABCTV 1983

Right to Competent Counsel 24 MIN
VHS / U-matic
Color
$335.00 purchase
From the ABC TV Nightline program.
Sociology
Dist - ABCLR **Prod** - ABCLR 1984

The Right to decide 43 MIN
VHS
Color (G)
$195.00 purchase, $100.00 rental _ #CE - 121
Reveals that the Patient Self - Determination Act - PSDA - challenges health - care workers to develop more effective ways to communicate with patients about their preferences. Features actual patient - physician interviews, exploring patient hopes, fears and overall goals with regard to end - of - life care and the use of life - support therapies. Offers a model for discussion about Advance Directives. Produced by Peter Walsh and New World Media Alliance.
Health and Safety
Dist - FANPRO

The Right to die 19 MIN
U-matic / VHS
Color (PRO)
Examines the legal, ethical and emotional issues surrounding a patient's request to have his machines turned off and to be allowed to die.
Health and Safety; Sociology
Dist - BAXMED **Prod** - BAXMED 1986

The Right to Die 28 MIN
U-matic / VHS
Color (C)
$249.00, $149.00 purchase _ #AD - 1577
Presents a Phil Donahue program on the medical, ethical and legal dilemmas posed by the question of the right to die of terminally ill patients. Interviews Governor Richard Lamm of Colorado, a physician attorney, a nurse who unhooked a patient's tubes and is charged with practicing medicine without a license, and a wife who wants doctors to honor her husband's wish to die rather than being tortured by life support machines.
Civics and Political Systems; Health and Safety; Religion and Philosophy; Sociology
Dist - FOTH **Prod** - FOTH

The Right to die 29 MIN
VHS / 16mm
Moral question series
Color (C A G)
$90.00 purchase _ #BPN177909
Discusses the right to die. Presents the cases of Karen and Heather - two young women whose kidney failures caused them severe pain and drove Karen to choose death rather than a life of painful dialysis. Features Heather, a surgeon, a philosophy professor, a medical - ethics expert, and a burn victim discussing this issue.
History - World; Religion and Philosophy; Sociology
Dist - RMIBHF **Prod** - RMIBHF

The Right to Die 30 MIN
U-matic
Color (A)
Provides a documentary examination of the cases of two young women with kidney failure. One choose death over a life of pain. There is a philosophical discussion on the morality of her decision.
Religion and Philosophy; Sociology
Dist - TVOTAR **Prod** - TVOTAR 1985

Right to Die 25 MIN
VHS / U-matic
Color
Examines the right to die controversy. Shows two doctors debating the issue.
Health and Safety; Sociology
Dist - MEDCOM **Prod** - MEDCOM

The Right to Die 56 MIN
16mm
Color (H C A)
LC 74-701428
Touches on such questions as hopeless medical situations, recent technical means for prolonging biological existence, solutions such as mercy killing and suicide and the ability and best means for physicians and clergymen to deal with dying patients.
Health and Safety; Religion and Philosophy; Sociology
Dist - FI **Prod** - ABCMJP 1974

Right to Die - 104 30 MIN
U-matic
Currents - 1984 - 85 Season Series
Color (A)
Focuses on the controversy over living wills and the right of the individual to die in hopeless medical situations.
Social Science; Sociology
Dist - PBS **Prod** - WNETTV 1985

The Right to die - considering the ethical and legal issues 28 MIN
VHS
Color (C PRO)
$250.00 purchase, $70.00 rental _ #6012S, #6012V
Explains the 1991 Patient Self - Determination Act and its implications. Shows medical and non - medical professionals discussing the impact of this federal act on the patient's right to use advance directives, illustrated by a vignette in which a patient determines what medical, nutritional and extraordinary measures to be employed near the end of life. Reviews the role of the ethics committee as a consultant in ethical dilemmas with reference to self - determination, professional mandates, benefits versus burden of treatment and evaluation of the patient's condition. Produced by Health and Sciences Network.
Health and Safety
Dist - AJN

Right to die - decision making and documentation 50 MIN
VHS
Color (A PRO C)
$95.00 purchase _ #Y501
Urges documentation in a specific meaningful writing of a client's 'right to die' to ensure compliance by the agent or surrogate and health care providers. Examines the issues to be raised, the decisions to be made and their conversion to legally sound provisions in living wills, health care proxies or durable power of attorney documents.
Business and Economics; Civics and Political Systems
Dist - ALIABA **Prod** - CLETV 1992

The Right to die - the choice is yours 14 MIN
VHS
Color (G)
$29.95 purchase _ #S02278
Takes a comprehensive look at the 'living will' concept, which allows people to request that no 'heroic measures' be taken to prolong their lives. Considers the legal and ethical implications.
Religion and Philosophy; Sociology
Dist - UILL

A Right to Health 34 MIN
16mm
Color (H C A)
LC 77-700084
Gives an overview of the Office of Economic Opportunity's neighborhood health center. Examines the concept of community medicine and the neighborhood health center function.
Health and Safety; Sociology
Dist - USNAC **Prod** - USOEO 1969

The Right to know 36.5 MIN
U-matic / VHS
Color (C G)
$380, $410 purchase _ #V128
Provides information for people who work with hazardous chemicals and notes that they must receive information about those chemicals. Features hosts, graphics, and instructions on how to help all company employees understand their right to know about working with hazardous chemicals.
Agriculture; Health and Safety
Dist - BARR **Prod** - BARR 1988

The Right to Know 17 MIN
U-matic / VHS / 16mm
Color (J)
LC 73-703394
Documents the hazards of an uninformed citizenry through an historical examination of basic democratic principles and a view of local and national contemporary events. Discusses the personal and institutional obstacles to understanding and points out that unless citizens have access to information, democracy ceases to function.
Civics and Political Systems
Dist - JOU **Prod** - ALTSUL 1973

Right - to - know 29 MIN
VHS / 16mm
Color (G IND)
$5.00 rental
Shows how the Federal Hazard Communication Standard, known as Right - To - Know, really works on the shop floor. Looks at how training is provided and who is covered by the law. Trains shop safety committees.
Civics and Political Systems; Health and Safety; Social Science
Dist - AFLCIO **Prod** - LIPA 1986

Right to Know - Chemical Concerns at Work 30 MIN
U-matic
Color (IND)
Documents the 'right to know' movement featuring case studies and interviews with leading figures such as Ralph Nader, Patrick Tyson, U. S. Representative James Florio, and others as they explore how this legislation will affect business and industry.
Civics and Political Systems; Fine Arts
Dist - BNA **Prod** - BNA 1985

Right - to - know series
MSDS - roadmap to safety
Read the label
Your right - to - know
Dist - AAVIM

Right to know - working around hazardous substances 12 MIN
BETA / VHS / U-matic
Color; PAL (IND G)
$175.00 rental _ #ASF - 151
Stresses the importance of labels on chemical containers. Teaches the proper handling of hazardous chemicals. Shows how to handle and store oxidizers, poisons, corrosives, flammables and water sensitive chemicals, and what to do if a spill occurs. Includes leader's guide and 10 workbooks.
Business and Economics; Health and Safety; Psychology; Science - Physical
Dist - BNA **Prod** - BNA

Right - to - know - working around hazardous substances 12 MIN
BETA / VHS / U-matic
Color (IND G A)
$622.00 purchase, $150.00 rental _ #RIG050
Stresses the importance of employee knowledge about the materials used at work. Suggests what actions employees should take if they suspect some chemical may be causing a problem for them.
Health and Safety; Psychology
Dist - ITF **Prod** - BNA

The Right to legal counsel 14 MIN
16mm / U-matic / VHS
Color (J H C)
LC 70-708049
Tells of the 1963 Supreme Court decision in the Gideon vs Wainright case that ruled that indigent defendants accused of serious crimes must be offered the assignment of counsel. Notes that in making this decision, the Supreme Court overruled the Betts vs Brady decision. Demonstrates a citizen's use of the 5th, 6th and 14th amendments to the Bill of Rights.
Civics and Political Systems
Dist - PHENIX **Prod** - VIGNET 1968

The Right to live and the right to die 60 MIN
U-matic
Ethics and medicine series
Color
Covers three areas of medical ethics - scarcity of life - saving therapies, euthanasia and the definition of death.
Health and Safety; Religion and Philosophy; Sociology
Dist - HRC **Prod** - OHC

Right to live, right to die - Pt 10 60 MIN
U-matic / VHS
Constitution - that delicate balance series
Color (G)
$45.00, $29.95 purchase
Presents a panel with Gloria Steinem, Joseph Califano, Congressman Henry Hyde, Phil Donahue and others discussing the right to make individual decisions about dying, abortion, and other areas of personal freedom and privacy. Part of a thirteen - part series on the United States Constitution created by journalist Fred Friendly.
Civics and Political Systems; Sociology
Dist - ANNCPB **Prod** - WNETTV 1984

The Right to Live - who Decides 17 MIN
U-matic / VHS / 16mm
Searching for Values - a Film Anthology Series
B&W (J)
LC 72-703145
Tells how in the face of general condemnation and at great personal risk, a ship's captain obeys his conscience and makes the agonizing decision to sacrifice some lives in order to save others.
Guidance and Counseling; Psychology; Religion and Philosophy; Sociology
Dist - LCOA **Prod** - LCOA 1972

The Right to lobby 28 MIN
16mm
Government story series; No 14
Color (H C)
LC 71-707193
Traces the history of lobbying and explains the techniques and effects of contemporary lobbyists.
Civics and Political Systems
Dist - WBCPRO **Prod** - OGCW 1968

The Right to Read 28 MIN
16mm
Color
Shows the problem of illiteracy in human terms, what is being done and can be done to improve the reading ability of illiterates from all walks of life in communities everywhere in the nation.
Education
Dist - USOE **Prod** - USOE

The Right to Refuse Treatment 14 MIN
U-matic
Medical - Legal Issues - Observations Series
(A)
Deals with pertinent medical and legal issues in today's complex world of medicine. Co - produced by the Alberta Law Foundation.
Health and Safety; Sociology
Dist - ACCESS **Prod** - ACCESS 1984

The Right to refuse treatment - Tape 3
VHS
Law and persons with mental disability series
Color (C PRO G)
$95.00 purchase
Considers the impact of recent cases on practice in the area of mental illness. Connects these developments with drugging questions that now come up regularly in the involuntary civil commitment process. Considers some unexplored areas of the law where it is likely that right to refuse cases will emerge in the near future. Part of a six - part series featuring Michael I Perlin, JD, on the law and persons with mental disability. Serves as a resource for attorneys practicing mental disability law, advocates working with mentally disabled individuals, mental health professionals, hospital administrators and other care providers subject to legal regulation.
Civics and Political Systems; Psychology
Dist - BAXMED

The Right to treatment, institutional rights, community rights and homelessnes - Tape 2
VHS
Law and persons with mental disability series
Color (C PRO G)
$95.00 purchase
Links together right to treatment, institutional rights, community rights and homelessness trends. Explains their relationships. Offers some predictions as to the ultimate impact of the Americans with Disabilities Act. Discusses myths that have developed around the issue of homelessness. Part of a six - part series featuring Michael I Perlin, JD, on the law and persons with mental disability. Serves as a resource for attorneys practicing mental disability law, advocates working with mentally disabled individuals, mental health professionals, hospital administrators and other care providers subject to legal regulation.
Civics and Political Systems; Psychology
Dist - BAXMED

The Right track 30 MIN
VHS / U-matic
Edit point series; Pt 4
Color (J H)
LC 83-706609
Presents a fictional story of a talented teenager and two friends who are running a television station while the owner is recovering from an illness. Discusses nonrestrictive adjective phrases in a story dealing with an athlete involved in an accident. Shows that good writing skills are necessary in real - life experiences.

English Language
Dist - GPN **Prod** - MAETEL 1983

Right track - middle distance series 45 MIN
VHS / BETA
Right track - middle distance series
Color
Provides workout programs for the middle distance runner. Includes a 75 - page training manual.
Physical Education and Recreation
Dist - HOMEAF **Prod** - HOMEAF

Right track - middle distance series
Right track - middle distance series 45 MIN
Dist - HOMEAF

The Right triangle 23 MIN
Cassette
Color (G)
$95.00, $10.00 purchase
Proposes cooperation in creating programs to promote drug - free living.
Guidance and Counseling; Health and Safety; Psychology
Dist - KELLYP **Prod** - KELLYP

Right triangle applications 30 MIN
VHS
Mathematics series
Color (J)
LC 90713155
Demonstrates right triangle applications. Part of 157 installments in the Mathematics Series.
Mathematics
Dist - GPN

Right triangle applications 30 MIN
VHS
Trigonometry series
Color (H)
$125.00 purchase _ #5012
Explains right triangle applications. Part of a 16 - part series on trigonometry.
Mathematics
Dist - LANDMK **Prod** - LANDMK

Right triangles 30 MIN
VHS
Geometry series
Color (H)
$125.00 purchase _ #7009
Explains right triangles. Part of a 16 - part series on geometry.
Mathematics
Dist - LANDMK **Prod** - LANDMK

Right triangles and trigonometric ratios 29 MIN
16mm
Trigonometry series
B&W (H)
Presents Thales's method for finding the height of a pyramid by using the definitions of sine, cosine and tangent of an angle as ratios of corresponding sides of a right triangle. Derives the values of the sine, cosine and tangent of 30, 45 and 60 degrees.
Mathematics
Dist - MLA **Prod** - CALVIN 1959

Right Upper Lobectomy 39 MIN
U-matic / VHS
Thoracic Series
Color
Health and Safety; Science - Natural
Dist - SVL **Prod** - SVL

Right Ventricular Hypertrophy 49 MIN
U-matic / VHS
Electrocardiogram Series
Color (PRO)
Teaches the criteria for electro - cardiographic diagnosis of right ventricular hypertrophy. Includes a discussion of presumptive evidence of right ventricular hypertrophy and numerous sample ECGs.
Health and Safety; Science; Science - Natural
Dist - HSCIC **Prod** - HSCIC 1982

The Right Way 21 MIN
16mm
Color
LC 74-705539
Highlights the annual Marine Corps physical fitness program for high school students.
Civics and Political Systems; Physical Education and Recreation
Dist - USNAC **Prod** - USN 1972

Right way series
Adverse driving conditions 27 MIN
Alcohol and other drugs 26 MIN
Basic car controls 27 MIN
Basic maneuvers 29 MIN
Buying a new or used car 29 MIN
City and town driving 24 MIN
Collision involvement 26 MIN
Emergency situations 29 MIN
Expressway driving 27 MIN
Highway Driving 22 MIN
Highway Transportation System 28 MIN
Insuring a Car 25 MIN
Licensing and Traffic Laws 29 MIN
Maintenance 26 MIN
Motorcycles 29 MIN
Natural Laws 29 MIN
Parking 24 MIN
Physical Conditions 26 MIN
Psychological Aspects 25 MIN
Vehicle Interaction 21 MIN
Dist - PBS

Right way - wrong way - how to make a sale 9 MIN
VHS / 16mm
Color (PRO)
$295.00 purchase, $85.00 rental, $35.00 preview
Dramatizes humorously the do's and dont's of making a sale. Covers all aspects from initial client contact to contract signature.
Business and Economics; Education; Psychology; Sociology
Dist - UTM **Prod** - UTM

The Right Whale - an Endangered Species 23 MIN
U-matic / VHS / 16mm
Color (J)
LC 76-703409
Studies the southern right whale, the rarest of the ten species of great whales. Describes their feeding and communication habits.
Science - Natural
Dist - NGS **Prod** - NGS 1976

Right Wing Machine 23 MIN
16mm
Color (A)
Identifies the leading right wing organizations, their tactics and goals.
Civics and Political Systems
Dist - AFLCIO **Prod** - AFLCIO 1978

The Righteous enemy 84 MIN
VHS
Color; B&W (G) (ENGLISH SUBTITLES)
$90.00 purchase
Presents an account of the Italian resistance to Hitler's 'final solution.' Shows how Italian officials prevented the deportation of some 40,000 Jews in Italian - occupied zones of France, Greece and Yugoslavia. Explores why these officials subverted Mussolini's orders to comply with German plans and documents how they prevailed with ingenious bureaucratic evasions and literal roadblocks. Includes previously unseen Italian and German newsreel footage, archival photos and excerpts from Eichmann's trial in Jersalem. Produced, directed and written by Joseph Rochlitz for Parstel Ltd Films. Accompanied by study guide.
Civics and Political Systems; Fine Arts; History - World; Religion and Philosophy
Dist - NCJEWF

Rightful discharge 50 MIN
VHS / U-matic / BETA
Color; CC (G IND PRO C)
Offers two parts training supervisors how to handle discharges properly to avoid legal liability and treat employees with dignity and respect. Shows how to properly handle problem employees for increased productivity and higher morale and increase chances of successful defense should a discharge case go to court. Covers the pre - employment interview, public policy violations, statements to and about employees, performance reviews, terminations. Includes two videos, a trainer's manual and ten participant manuals.
Business and Economics; Psychology
Dist - BNA **Prod** - BNA

Rightful discharge series
Minimizing the risk 21 MIN
The Risk 29 MIN
Dist - BNA

Rights and Citizenship Series
Citizenship and voting 30 MIN
Consumer Complaints 15 MIN
Credit cards 15 MIN
Credit ratings 15 MIN
Legal Rights 30 MIN
Dist - CAMB

Rights and remedies after default under UCC Article 9 - Pts 1 and 2 120 MIN
VHS
Color (C PRO A)
$190.00 purchase _ #P227, Y102
Examines the concept of default in commercial transactions where personal property is the collateral. Discusses lender liability under the UCC, application of waiver and estoppal and special state and federal laws to debtor - creditor relations, and more. Part 2 features a discussion of retention and redemption of collateral after default. Highlights various practice problems such as those associated with pursuit of guarantors.
Civics and Political Systems
Dist - ALIABA **Prod** - CLETV 1987

Rights and Responsibilities 15 MIN
16mm
Florida Elementary Social Studies Series
Color (I J)
Examines the dual concept of rights and privileges by using various groups and organizations to demonstrate the privileges gained by memberships in those groups. Describes what is expected of the members in turn for these privileges.
Guidance and Counseling; Sociology
Dist - DADECO **Prod** - DADECO 1973

Rights and Responsibilities 30 MIN
U-matic
Medical - Legal Issues Series
(A)
Analyzes the re - evaluation health care professionals are making about their ethical and legal responsibilities to those in their care.
Civics and Political Systems; Health and Safety; Sociology
Dist - ACCESS **Prod** - ACCESS 1983

Rights and Responsibilities 29 MIN
U-matic
As We See it Series
Color
Recounts the struggle at North Carolina high school to set up a system of school government fair to students, faculty and administrators alike.
Education
Dist - PBS **Prod** - WTTWTV

Rights and Responsibilities Series
At work 19 MIN
Change 20 MIN
Dead Path 20 MIN
I Didn't Care 20 MIN
In - School, Pt 1 20 MIN
In - School, Pt 2 20 MIN
An Interview with Larry 20 MIN
An Open Mind 20 MIN
Police Officer 20 MIN
Sign Here 19 MIN
The Voting Machine 20 MIN
Dist - AITECH

Rights and Responsibilities - Whose is it? 15 MIN
VHS / U-matic
It's a Rainbow World
(P)
Designed to teach social studies to primary grade students. Explains concepts in terms of everyday situations. Focuses on laws and responsibilities.
Psychology; Sociology
Dist - GPN

Rights and rituals 23 MIN
VHS
Meaning of madness series
Color (C G PRO)
$175.00 purchase, $19.00 rental _ #35079
Discusses the management of the insane, control over the process of certification and the advent of voluntary treatment in contrast with the problems of long - term institutionalization. Looks at modern attempts to care for and rehabilitate chronic schizophrenics, including the behavioral and therapeutic community approaches. Part of a four - part series which traces the history of psychiatry in a societal context from the mid - 1800s to modern - day England.
Psychology
Dist - PSU **Prod** - BBC 1982

The Rights of Age 28 MIN
16mm / U-matic / VHS
Emotions of Every - Day Living Series
B&W (C A)
LC FIA67-5282
Describes the many benefits available to the aged who are in need of either physical, psychological or legal assistance, as portrayed in a dramatization about a recluse who becomes physically disabled and discovers the various benefits available to her.
Civics and Political Systems; Guidance and Counseling; Psychology; Sociology
Dist - IFB **Prod** - PASDPW 1967

The Rights of Children 30 MIN
VHS / U-matic
Child Abuse and Neglect Series
Color (H C A)
Home Economics; Sociology
Dist - GPN **Prod** - UMINN 1983

Rights of Reproduction 60 MIN
U-matic
Ethics and Medicine Series
Color
Discusses a couple's reproductive rights in terms of the legal, cultural and medical aspects.
Health and Safety; Religion and Philosophy; Sociology
Dist - HRC **Prod** - OHC

The Rights of Teenagers 30 MIN
VHS
Soapbox With Tom Cottle Series
Color (G)
$59.95 purchase _ #SBOX - 205
Discusses the legal and social rights of teenagers. Shows that many teens are ambivalent about gaining independence from their parents. Hosted by psychologist Tom Cottle.
Civics and Political Systems; Psychology; Sociology
Dist - PBS **Prod** - WGBYTV 1985

Rights of the accused 30 MIN
VHS / 16mm
Government by consent - a national perspective series
Color (I J H C A)
Describes the procedural rights guaranteed by the U S Constitution to persons accused of crimes. Explores the dynamic conflict between the rights of individuals to be safe and secure, and the rights of the accused.
Civics and Political Systems
Dist - DALCCD **Prod** - DALCCD 1990

The Rights of the Accused 30 MIN
VHS / U-matic
American Government 2 Series
Color (C)
Examines the constitutional amendments which protect the rights of those accused of crimes from the time a search warrant is issued through court proceedings.
Civics and Political Systems
Dist - DALCCD **Prod** - DALCCD

Rights of the child 16 MIN
VHS
About the United Nations series
Color (J H)
$150.00 purchase, $30.00 rental
Discusses the United Nations Convention on the Rights of the Child, adopted in 1989, which established the standards that help to guarantee children a right to life, liberty, a name, a nationality, an education and good health. Shows the plight of many children throughout the world and what UN agencies are doing to improve their lives. Part of an eight - part series dealing with international issues and the work of the United Nations. Includes teaching guide.
Civics and Political Systems; Fine Arts; Sociology
Dist - CNEMAG **Prod** - UNDPI 1990

Rights, Wrongs and the First Amendment 28 MIN
16mm
Color
LC 74-702613
Traces the history in the United States of freedom of speech, freedom of the press and freedom of assembly from the Declaration of Independence to the exposure of Watergate. Points out that though personal freedom has often seemed to be in jeopardy, the democratic political process in America has displayed a remarkable resilience.
Civics and Political Systems; History - United States
Dist - SF **Prod** - REPRO

Rigid and Swinging Staging 18 MIN
16mm
B&W
LC FIE52-1203
Shows how to set up rigid staging, use a - frame stage and extension, double boards overlapped and a life line, how to rig swinging staging and how to take down staging and stow it.
Civics and Political Systems; Social Science
Dist - USNAC **Prod** - USN 1948

Rigid bodies
16mm
B&W
Illustrates the principles of mathematical modelling and underlines the significance of the rigid body model.
Mathematics
Dist - OPENU **Prod** - OPENU

The Rigid Heddle Frame 12 MIN
VHS / U-matic
Color (H C)
Describes how the rigid heddle frame provides a simple solution for weaving cloth. Shows an experienced weaver with the complete sequence of threading and getting ready to weave, and the loom in operation, producing an attractive woven jacket.
Fine Arts
Dist - EDMI **Prod** - EDMI 1976

Rigid Heddle Looms and How to Warp Them for Fabric Weaving 29 MIN
U-matic
Your Weekly Weaver Series
Color
Tells how the rigid heddle loom can be used for weaving scarves, shawls, and upholstery or pillow fabric.
Fine Arts
Dist - PBS **Prod** - GAEDTN

Rigid Medullary Fixation of Forearm Fractures 16 MIN
16mm
Color
LC FIE62-2
Describes the principles, technique and advantage of rigid medullary fixation of forearm fractures.
Health and Safety
Dist - USNAC **Prod** - USA 1961

Rigid sigmoidoscopy 13 MIN
U-matic / VHS
Color (PRO C)
$395.00 purchase, $80.00 _ #C880 - VI - 033
Discloses that the diagnosis of diseases of the colon and rectum depends on a careful assessment of information derived from many sources. Reveals that a barium enema enables examination of the colon proximate to the recto - sigmoid junction - however, it is difficult to visualize the rectum and sigmoid due to overlapping shadows and the sigmoidoscope is required. Introduces medical students to procedures for performing a rigid sigmoidoscopy. Presented by Drs Roland Folse and C O Metzmaker and Deborah Buchele, Marsha Prater and James Paul Dow.
Health and Safety; Science - Natural
Dist - HSCIC

Rigid transformations
16mm
B&W
Defines a rigid transformation and investigates its geometric properties in two and three dimensions.
Mathematics
Dist - OPENU **Prod** - OPENU

Rigoberta 13 MIN
16mm
Cuba - a view from inside series
Color (G)
$150.00 purchase, $25.00 rental
Interviews the Nobel Prize - winning Quiche Indian leader who describes the tragic deaths in her family at the hands of Guatemalan authorities and the process which led to her political activism. Features part of a 17 - part series of shorts by and about Cuban women. Directed by Rebecca Chavez. Illustrated catalog available. Contact distributor for programming advice and discount package rental fees.
Civics and Political Systems; Fine Arts; History - World
Dist - CNEMAG

Rigoletto 30 MIN
U-matic / VHS / 16mm
Who's Afraid of Opera Series
Color (J)
LC 73-703433
Presents Joan Sutherland singing the opera Rigoletto. Features puppets in an opera box acting as a reviewing audience conversing with the performers as they enter or leave front stage.
Fine Arts
Dist - PHENIX **Prod** - PHENIX 1973

Rikki - Tikki - Tavi 26 MIN
16mm / U-matic / VHS
Color (P I)
LC 76-702609
Tells the story, as narrated by Orson Welles, of a mongoose who is saved from a storm - tossed drowning by a family and becomes a member of the household and the family's defender against the dreaded cobras that roam the compound.
Literature and Drama
Dist - GA **Prod** - CJE 1976

Rikyu 116 MIN
VHS
Color (G) (JAPANESE WITH ENGLISH SUBTITLES)
$79.95 purchase _ #CAP9201
Illustrates the classic struggle between the impulse to create and the impulse to destroy. Directed by Hiroshi Teshigahara.
Fine Arts
Dist - CHTSUI

Rillettes and Terrines 30 MIN
BETA / VHS
Frugal Gourmet Series
Color
Looks at the differences among pates, terrines and rillettes. Shows how to prepare beef terrine and pork rillette.
Health and Safety; Home Economics; Psychology
Dist - CORF **Prod** - WTTWTV

The Rime of the ancient mariner 42 MIN
16mm
Color (G)
$50.00 rental
Marries the classic engravings of Gustave Dore to the classic poem by Samuel Taylor Coleridge through Orson Welles, a classic narrator. Presents an animated opium dream of the old Mariner who wantonly kills the albatross and suffers the pains of the damned for it.
Literature and Drama
Dist - CANCIN **Prod** - JORDAL 1977

Rime of the ancient mariner 60 MIN
VHS
Color (G)
Presents an adaptation of Samuel Taylor Coleridge's epic poem The Rime Of The Ancient Mariner using both real and animated images. Part 1 deals with Coleridge's life. Part 2 presents a reading of the poem by Sir Michael Redgrave. Directed by Raul da Silva.
Literature and Drama
Dist - KULTUR **Prod** - WNETTV
PBS
UILL

Rimsky - Korsakov's The Golden cockerel
VHS
Music in motion series
Color (J H C G)
$75.00 purchase _ #MUS05V
Expresses visually what is heard in The Golden Cockerel by Rimsky - Korsakov. Teaches classical music appreciation, develops interest and enhances listening enjoyment. Includes manual with suggestions for presenting the video, questions for discussion, research projects, correlations with other subject areas and listening and reading lists. Part of an eight - part series.
Fine Arts
Dist - CAMV **Prod** - MUSLOG

Rin Tin Tin 28 MIN
16mm
History of the motion picture series
B&W (P)
Stars the dog hero of the 1920s, Rin Tin Tin, in scenes from his film Tracked By The Police.
Fine Arts
Dist - KILLIS **Prod** - KILLIS 1927

Ring and Circle Shear Operation 9 MIN
VHS / BETA
Color (IND)
Presents the application of the ring and circle shear for cutting out circles or rings from sheet metal.
Industrial and Technical Education; Psychology
Dist - RMIBHF **Prod** - RMIBHF

A Ring for television 58 MIN
U-matic / VHS
Color
Documents how Richard Wagner's Ring Cycle was filmed offering a fascinating behind - the - facade view of the creation of this epic production.
Fine Arts
Dist - FOTH **Prod** - FOTH 1984

Ring of fire - an Indonesian odyssey series
Dance of the warriors
Dream wanderers of Borneo
East of Krakatoa
Spice island saga
Dist - PBS

The Ring of Gyges 30 MIN
U-matic / VHS
Art of being human series; Module 5
Color (C)
History - World; Literature and Drama; Religion and Philosophy
Dist - MDCC **Prod** - MDCC

Ring of Lakes 24 MIN
16mm
Heading Out Series
Color
LC 76-702049
Shows the lake and parkland region in central Alberta, Canada, around the capital city of Edmonton.

Geography - World
Dist - CENTWO Prod - CENTWO 1975

The Ring of truth series
Uses everyday occurrences to explain concepts of theoretical science. Six - part series is hosted by physics professor Philip Morrison.

Atoms	60 MIN
Change	60 MIN
Clues	60 MIN
Doubt	60 MIN
Looking	60 MIN
Mapping	60 MIN
The Ring of truth series	360 MIN

Dist - PBS Prod - PBA 1975

Ring, ring 15 MIN
VHS / U-matic
Pass it on series
Color (K P)
Discusses the telephone, telephone numbers and using the telephone in an emergency.
Education; Health and Safety
Dist - GPN Prod - WKNOTV 1983

Ring - tailed lemurs 9 MIN
VHS
Animal profile series
Color (P I)
$59.95 purchase _ #RB8104
Studies ring - tailed lemurs, endangered primates from the island of Madagascar. Examines their sunbathing activities and the 'stink - fights' among the males. Shows keepers hand feeding the beasts. Part of a series on animals which looks at examples from the mammal, snake and bird classes, filmed in their natural habitat.
Science - Natural
Dist - REVID Prod - REVID 1990

The Ringer 20 MIN
16mm
Color
LC 72-702334
Shows how drug pushers use high pressure advertising techniques to sell their drugs to young people.
Guidance and Counseling; Health and Safety; Psychology; Sociology
Dist - HEARST Prod - HEARST 1972

The Ringmasters 50 MIN
VHS
Gladio - Timewatch series
Color; PAL (H C A)
PdS99 purchase
Reports on the secret terrorist groups responsible for a series of bombings and murders throughout Europe. Documents the creation of this clandestine organization and its influence in the internal affairs of almost every European country. Part one of a three part series.
History - World; Sociology
Dist - BBCENE

Ringovelser - flying ring exercises 29 MIN
16mm
B&W
Demonstrates a number of flying ring exercises.
Physical Education and Recreation
Dist - STATNS Prod - STATNS 1962

The Rings
VHS
N C A A instructional video series
Color (H C A)
$39.95 purchase _ #KAR2603V
Presents the third of a four - part series on gymnastics. Focuses on the rings.
Physical Education and Recreation
Dist - CAMV Prod - NCAAF

Rings 11 MIN
U-matic / VHS / 16mm
Color (J H C)
LC 71-714074
Introduces the beginning gymnast to the rings in careful progression from beginning to advanced moves.
Physical Education and Recreation
Dist - AIMS Prod - ASSOCF 1971

Rings Around Rabaul 27 MIN
U-matic / VHS / 16mm
Victory at Sea Series
B&W (J H)
Presents highlights of the struggle for the Solomon Islands.
Civics and Political Systems; History - United States; History - World
Dist - LUF Prod - NBCTV

Rings I - the Axiom
16mm
B&W
Examines number systems, polynomials, matrices, and functions. Sets up a formal axiom system which reflects the properties common to all these structures. Explores the internal structure of rings, drawing analogies with group theory.
Mathematics
Dist - OPENU Prod - OPENU

Ringsiders 28 MIN
Videoreel / VT2
Bayou City and thereabouts people show series
Color
Shows people attending Friday night wrestling matches and examines their excitement and the role of the sport in their lives. Features Paul Boesch, a Houston wrestling promoter and former wrestler himself, explaining why wrestling matches attract so many fans.
Physical Education and Recreation
Dist - PBS Prod - KUHTTV

Ringstealer 23 MIN
U-matic / VHS / 16mm
Color (I J)
Presents a mystery story about a boy named Brian, whose experiences point out the importance of values and beliefs, self - esteem and self - image, honesty, truthfulness, friendships and making the right decisions.
Guidance and Counseling
Dist - MCFI Prod - SWAIN 1984

Ringtail 9 MIN
16mm
Color
LC 75-701920
Tells a story about a young boy and his pet raccoon, and their adventures in the wilds of Algonquin Park.
Fine Arts; Geography - World
Dist - EFD Prod - GIB 1973

The Rink 25 MIN
U-matic / VHS / 16mm
Charlie Chaplin comedy theater series
B&W (I)
Features Charlie Chaplin as a somewhat clumsy waiter. Shows how he crashes a society party and demonstrates his skill on roller skates.
Fine Arts
Dist - FI Prod - MUFLM

Rio De Janeiro 3 MIN
16mm
Of all Things Series
Color (P I)
Discusses the city of Rio De Janeiro in Brazil.
Geography - World
Dist - AVED Prod - BAILYL

Rio Escondido - Hidden River 100 MIN
16mm
B&W (SPANISH)
Explores the struggle between a young school teacher and a tyrannical, self - appointed ruler of a village who keeps the villagers in ignorance to enforce his power over them.
Fine Arts
Dist - TRANSW Prod - TRANSW

Rio Grande 40 MIN
16mm
Color
LC 76-702610
Follows the course of the Rio Grande from its headwaters in Colorado to the Texas border. Shows Indian pueblos, Hispanic villages, ranches, the city of Albuquerque and deserts along the route.
Geography - United States; Social Science
Dist - BLUSKY Prod - NMARBC 1976

Rio Grande - ribbon of life 13 MIN
VHS
Color (G)
$19.95 purchase _ #BOR - 9
Describes the 1800 miles of the Rio Grande system, including scenes of work by the Bureau of Reclamation, area farms and cities and scenery.
Geography - United States
Dist - INSTRU Prod - USBR

Rio Grande - Where Four Cultures Meet 16 MIN
U-matic / VHS / 16mm
Color (I J H)
LC 72-700119
Explores the cultural and economic interdependence and interaction of Mexican, Spanish, Indian and Anglo - American peoples of the Rio Grande Valley.
Geography - United States; Sociology
Dist - PHENIX Prod - EVANSA 1972

Riot Control Formations 24 MIN
16mm
Color
LC 74-705541
Shows the composition and application of basic wedge, line and echelon formations in riot control operations. Illustrates commands, hand signals and steps in executing these formations and their variants at the squad, platoon and company level.
Social Science; Sociology
Dist - USNAC Prod - USA 1967

Riot - Control Weapons 6 MIN
16mm
Color
Documents the weapons the government has specifically designed to paralyze mass resistance in the cities.
Civics and Political Systems; Sociology
Dist - CANWRL Prod - CANWRL

Riot of colour 20 MIN
VHS
Textile studies series
Color (A)
PdS65 purchase
Shows different ways of introducing color to fabrics - weaving, dyeing, printing, and embroidery. Explores the origins of man-made and natural fiber; the processes of spinning, weaving, printing, dyeing, and finishing; and the uses of different textiles in everyday life. Part of a five-part series.
Home Economics; Industrial and Technical Education
Dist - BBCENE

RIP 2 MIN
16mm
B&W (G)
$15.00 rental
Shares the result of a conversation with filmmaker Carl Wiedemann on the subject of ripping film in order to vary the size of the projected image.
Fine Arts
Dist - CANCIN Prod - SCHLEM 1989
FLMKCO

Rip - Off 94 MIN
16mm
Color
LC 74-701648
Presents the story of four high - spirited boys in their last year of high school who play very hard at being 'in' and making the groovy scene.
Fine Arts
Dist - CFDEVC Prod - PHENIX

Rip Van Winkle 26 MIN
U-matic / VHS / 16mm
Mr Magoo in Great World Classics Series
Color
Presents Washington Irving's classic story of Rip Van Winkle with Magoo as the lazy ne'er - do - well who sleeps for 20 years, during which time America changes from a colony to an independent republic.
Fine Arts; Literature and Drama
Dist - FI Prod - FLEET 1965

Rip Van Winkle 60 MIN
VHS
Faerie tale theatre series
Color; CC (K P I J)
$19.95 purchase _ #CBS6852
Stars Talia Shire and Harry Dean Stanton.
Literature and Drama
Dist - KNOWUN

Rip Van Winkle 24 MIN
U-matic / VHS / 16mm
Famous Adventures of Mr Magoo Series
Color (P I J)
LC 79-701872
Presents cartoon character Mr Magoo as Rip Van Winkle in an animated version of Washington Irving's story of a man who sleeps for 20 years.
Fine Arts
Dist - MCFI Prod - UPAPOA 1976

Rip Van Winkle 18 MIN
16mm / U-matic / VHS
Color
LC 80-701678
Retells the tale of a man who escaped into the hills, fell into a magical sleep and awoke to find that many years had passed. Based on the story Rip Van Winkle by Washington Irving.
Literature and Drama
Dist - BARR Prod - PHENIX 1980

Rip Van Winkle 15 MIN
16mm / U-matic / VHS
Magic Carpet Series
Color (P)
Presents the American legend of Rip Van Winkle.
Literature and Drama
Dist - GPN Prod - SDCSS 1979

Rip Van Winkle 30 MIN
VHS
American heroes and legends series
Color (P I J)
$12.95 purchase _ #REV10552V
Features Angelica Huston who narrates the American classic tale of Rip Van Winkle and his 20 - year nap in the Catskill Mountains.
Literature and Drama
Dist - KNOWUN

Rip Van Winkle 27 MIN
16mm
Color (SPANISH)
Presents an animated adaptation of Washington Irving's Rip Van Winkle. Tells the story of a free spirit who preferred telling stories to tilling soil.
Fine Arts; Foreign Language
Dist - BBF **Prod** - VINTN

Rip Van Winkle 27 MIN
16mm
Color (J H) (SPANISH)
LC 79-700271
Uses clay animation to present an adaptation of Washington Irving's tale Rip Van Winkle. Includes a dream sequence in which Rip gradually discovers the secret of life. Narrated by Will Geer.
Literature and Drama
Dist - BBF **Prod** - VINTN 1978

Riparian Vegetation 14 MIN
U-matic
Color (J)
Highlights vegetation growing along California's waterways. Discusses management necessary to strike a balance between wildlife habitats controlling floodwater and farming interests.
Agriculture; Geography - United States; Science - Natural; Social Science
Dist - CALDWR **Prod** - CSDWR

The Ripoff 15 MIN
U-matic / VHS / 16mm
Under the law series
Color (J H C)
LC 74-703799
Tells about a young boy who is a habitual thief and his friend whom he persuades to act as decoy while he attempts to steal. Shows how, when the young thief draws a real but unloaded gun and threatens the salesman's life, both boys are arrested and petitions are filed in juvenile court for robbery and burglary.
Civics and Political Systems; Sociology
Dist - CORF **Prod** - USNEI 1974

Ripped down the middle 27 MIN
VHS
Color (G PRO)
$29.95 purchase, $10.00 rental _ #35 - 855892 - 9050
Shows interviews with people who grew up in homes where alcoholism abuse and other traumas occurred. Shares counselors' insights on how they help such people recover from the traumas. Produced by Inter - Varsity Christian Fellowship.
Health and Safety; Religion and Philosophy
Dist - APH

Ripping and crosscutting 19 MIN
16mm
Precision wood machining series
B&W
LC FIE52-60
Shows how each working part of the variety saw functions. Demonstrates how to check saw blades, set the fence, change saw blades, use a cutoff gauge and use a hinged block in crosscutting.
Industrial and Technical Education
Dist - USNAC **Prod** - USOE 1945

The Ripple effect 12 MIN
16mm
Color
LC 74-702865
Presents a poetic essay about some of the qualities required for leadership. Pictures four accomplished individuals and explores the qualities exemplified by each of them that have made it possible for them to become leaders.
Psychology
Dist - GITTFI **Prod** - GITTFI 1974

A Ripple of time 24 MIN
VHS / U-matic
Color (C A)
Alternates interludes of conversation with leisurely and active lovemaking to paint a picture of mature sexuality.
Health and Safety; Psychology
Dist - MMRC **Prod** - NATSF

Ripple tank wave phenomena 5 - Doppler effect and shock waves 8 MIN
16mm
College physics film program series
B&W (C)
LC FIA68-1435
Demonstrates the effects of a wave source in a ripple tank, including the Doppler effect and the formation of shock wave and shock cone.
Science - Physical
Dist - MLA **Prod** - EDS 1962

Ripple tank wave phenomena 4 - Bragg reflection 10 MIN
16mm
College physics film program series
B&W (C)
LC FIA68-1436
Examines the reflection of waves by a lattice of small objects and demonstrates that the reflection changes as the wavelength and angle of incidence are varied.
Science - Physical
Dist - MLA **Prod** - EDS 1962

Ripple tank wave phenomena 3 - barrier penetration 8 MIN
16mm
College physics film program
B&W (C)
LC FIA68-1437
Shows how a wide channel of deep water between two shallow regions in a ripple tank will act to prevent wave movement between the shallow regions. Demonstrates that the narrowing of the channel increases wave transmission.
Science - Physical
Dist - MLA **Prod** - EDS 1962

Ripples 18 MIN
VHS
Color (A PRO IND)
$550.00 purchase, $130.00 rental
Documents the 'ripple' effects of good or bad customer service on all aspects of a company. Uses dramatic vignettes to illustrate the importance of courteous behavior and good customer service skills.
Business and Economics; Guidance and Counseling; Psychology
Dist - VLEARN

Ripples 19 MIN
VHS / 16mm
Color (G) (SPANISH DUTCH NORWEGIAN)
$575.00, $550.00 purchase, $130.00 rental
Shows how good or poor customer service creates a ripple effect that touches employees and customers. Illustrates the results of positive and negative ripples and teaches the importance of courteous behavior and of developing good customer service skills. Includes meeting guide.
Business and Economics
Dist - CCCD **Prod** - ROGGTP

Ripples of change - Japanese women's search for self 57 MIN
16mm / VHS
Color (G)
$90.00, $130.00 rental, $295.00 purchase
Combines political analysis with a personal story in a documentary about the Japanese women's liberation movement in the 1970s and its influence on contemporary Japanese society. Interviews veterans of the movement, features archival footage and the filmmaker's personal impressions. Resource for the study of global feminism, women's roles and Japanese society.
Fine Arts; History - World; Sociology
Dist - WMEN **Prod** - KURIHA 1993

Risa Friedman and Peter Justice 30 MIN
U-matic / VHS
Eye on dance - health and well - being of dancers series
Color
Discusses warm - up and conditioning.
Fine Arts; Physical Education and Recreation
Dist - ARCVID **Prod** - ARCVID

Rischart 3 MIN
16mm
Color (G)
$10.00 rental
Fine Arts
Dist - CANCIN **Prod** - KRENKU 1978

The Rise and Fall of Ben Gizzard, the Parrot and the Thief and the Contests at Cowlick 15 MIN
VHS / U-matic
Readit Series
Color (P I)
Presents three stories in which an old Indian predicts the death of a scoundrel, a thief who steals a parrot finds it to be an awkward eyewitness, and Wally challenges Hogbone and his cutthroats to one contest after another and wins by losing. Based on the books The Rise And Fall Of Ben Gizzard, The Parrot And The Thief and The Contests At Cowlick by Richard Kennedy.
English Language; Literature and Drama
Dist - AITECH **Prod** - POSIMP 1982

The Rise and fall of Cyrus 30 MIN
U-matic
Herodotus - father of history series
Color
Focuses on Persian king Cyrus the Great as seen through the eyes of Herodotus.
History - World
Dist - UMITV **Prod** - UMITV 1980

The Rise and Fall of Money 57 MIN
U-matic / VHS / 16mm
Age of Uncertainty Series
Color (H C A)
LC 77-701493
Focuses on the history and function of money in society. Based on the book The Age Of Uncertainty by John Kenneth Galbraith.
Business and Economics
Dist - FI **Prod** - BBCL 1977

Rise and Fall of Money, the, Pt 1 28 MIN
U-matic / VHS / 16mm
Age of Uncertainty Series
Color (H C A)
LC 77-701493
Focuses on the history and function of money in society. Based on the book The Age Of Uncertainty by John Kenneth Galbraith.
Business and Economics
Dist - FI **Prod** - BBCL 1977

Rise and Fall of Money, the, Pt 2 29 MIN
U-matic / VHS / 16mm
Age of Uncertainty Series
Color (H C A)
LC 77-701493
Focuses on the history and function of money in society. Based on the book The Age Of Uncertainty by John Kenneth Galbraith.
Business and Economics
Dist - FI **Prod** - BBCL 1977

The Rise and fall of prohibition 28 MIN
VHS
This Constitution - a history series
Color (H C G)
$180.00 purchase, $19.00 rental _ #35741
Reveals that one of the most controversial episodes in the history of the American Constitution was the attempt to regulate alcohol consumption through a Constitutional amendment. Looks at the historical tension between social demands and constitutional authority. Offers a case study in constitutional politics and an investigation of how a constitution retains legitimacy in times of massive social change. Part of a five - part series on the philosophical origins, drafting and interpretation of the US Constitution and its effect on American society, produced by the International University Consortium and Project '87.
Civics and Political Systems; History - United States
Dist - PSU

Rise and fall of the Great Lakes 17 MIN
16mm / U-matic / VHS
Color (J)
LC 77-701106
Uses animation, ballad singing, trick photography, and a canoe trip through the Great Lakes in showing how profoundly the last ice age affected the face of the land and how the Great Lakes system which was created continues to change, largely through the intervention of man.
Geography - World; Science - Natural; Sociology
Dist - PFP **Prod** - NFBC 1970

The Rise and fall of the Soviet Union 25 MIN
VHS
Color; CC (H A)
$110.00 purchase - #A51617
Details the political history of the Soviet Union from the beginning of the Bolshevik Revolution through the empire's breakup. Uses archive film and news coverage of the time. Contrasts the political system's military success with its agricultural failure. Includes a teacher's guide.
Civics and Political Systems; Foreign Language; History - World
Dist - NGS **Prod** - NGS 1994

The Rise and fall of the Soviet Union 124 MIN
VHS
Color (J H C G)
$89.95 purchase _ #XE147V
Offers archival footage ranging from 'home movies' of Czar Nicholas with the Royal Family, Stalin's propaganda films - until now severely suppressed behind the Iron Curtain. Clearly sets forth the events which led to the Russian Revolution and takes the viewer through World Wars I and II, the Cold War, Perestroika and the collapse of communism. Features Peter Graves as narrator.
Civics and Political Systems; History - World; Sociology
Dist - CAMV

The Rise and fall of the Third Reich 120 MIN
VHS
Color; B&W (J H G)
Describes the rise of Hitler and his Nazi ideology, focusing on the political and social factors which made it possible. Includes documentary footage, much of it in black - and - white, along with interviews and commentary by William Shirer. Based on the book by Shirer.
Civics and Political Systems; Fine Arts; History - World
Dist - GA **Prod** - GA 1968
ASPRSS
UILL

Rise and fall of the Third Reich series
Presents a four - part series on Hitler. Includes The Rise of Hitler; Nazi Germany - Years of Triumph; Gotterdammerung - Collapse of the Third Reich; Nuremburg Trials.

Gotterdammerung - collapse of the Third Reich - Part III	30 MIN
Nazi Germany - years of triumph - Part II	30 MIN
Nuremberg trials - Part IV	30 MIN
The Rise of Hitler - Pt I	30 MIN

Dist - ADL **Prod** - ADL 1968

Rise and fall of the Third Reich series

Gotterdammerung - the Fall of the Third Reich - Pt 3	28 MIN
Nazi Germany - Years of Triumph	28 MIN
Nazi Germany - Years of Triumph - Pt 2	28 MIN
Rise of Hitler	28 MIN
The Rise of Hitler - Pt 1	28 MIN

Dist - FI

The Rise and rise of Bill Gates 40 MIN
VHS
Business series
Color (A)
PdS65 purchase
Reveals that, in 1992, the market value of the company founded by Harvard University dropout Bill Gates surpassed the value of General Motors. States that Gates amassed a personal fortune which made him one of America's richest men. However, Gates has been accused of unfair business practices by his main competitors and a case has been brought against him before the United States Justice Department. Looks at Gates and his managerial style.
Business and Economics; Computer Science
Dist - BBCENE

The Rise and rise of Daniel Rocket 90 MIN
VHS
American stage play specials series
Color; Captioned (G)
$69.95 purchase _ #PLAH - 411C
Features Tom Hulce as Daniel Rocket, a man who believes he can fly. Shows that Rocket achieves flight. Presents a view of the mores of suburban life. Also stars Timothy Daly and Valerie Mahaffey. Produced by the Program Development Group.
Fine Arts; Literature and Drama
Dist - PBS

The Rise of Adolph Hitler 27 MIN
U-matic / VHS / 16mm
You are There Series
B&W (J H C)
Reconstructs the events of September 9, 1938, at Nuremberg, the climax of Adolph Hitler's rise to power.
Biography; History - World
Dist - MGHT **Prod** - MGHT 1957

The Rise of big business 30 MIN
VHS
America in perspective - US history since 1877 series
Color (H C G)
$99.00 purchase _ #AIP - 2
Examines the reasons for the rapid industrialization of the United States in the late 19th century. Assesses the initial costs and the benefits of that process. Part of a 26 - part series.
History - United States; Social Science
Dist - INSTRU **Prod** - DALCCD 1991

The Rise of big business - Pt 1 30 MIN
VHS / U-matic
America - the second century series
Color (H C)
$34.95 purchase
Supplies a perspective on issues involved in the rapid industrialization of the United States between the Civil War and the Great Crash. Part of a 30-part series focusing on social issues and economic and political problems after 1875.
History - United States
Dist - DALCCD **Prod** - DALCCD
GPN

The rise of big business - Pt 2 30 MIN
U-matic / VHS
America - the second century series
Color (H C)
$34.95 purchase
Contributes historical perspectives on big business after the Great Crash. Part of a 30-part series focusing on economic, political and social issues in the United States after 1875.
History - United States
Dist - DALCCD **Prod** - DALCCD
GPN

The rise of dictatorship - 1920 - 1939 58 MIN
U-matic / VHS
B&W (G) (ENGLISH AND GERMAN)
$249.00, $149.00 purchase _ #AD - 2142
Analyzes in documentary form the conditions which led to the rise of Mussolini in Italy and Hitler in Germany. Looks at the economic, social, political and psychological aspects of society in those countries. Provides a record of the events which led to World War II.
Civics and Political Systems; History - United States; History - World
Dist - FOTH **Prod** - FOTH

The Rise of domesticity 60 MIN
VHS
Europe and America in the modern age - 1776 to the present series
Color (H C PRO)
$95.00 purchase
Presents a lecture by James Sheehan. Focuses on a critical period in European and American history and on leaders of the time. Part of a 20 - part series that looks at the last two centuries in Europe and America. Series presents lectures by David M Kennedy and James Sheehan of Stanford University on such figures as Adam Smith, Marx, Lincoln, Washington, Jefferson, Freud, Margaret Sanger, Susan B Anthony and Jane Adams and their impact on the events of their day. For history resource material and continuing education courses.
Civics and Political Systems; History - United States; History - World
Dist - LANDMK

The Rise of Europe - 1000 - 1500 A D 23 MIN
16mm / U-matic / VHS
Color (J H C) (SPANISH)
LC FIA67-5067
Traces the major social, economic and philosophic developments in Europe between 1000 and 1500 A D. Uses representative art forms to exemplify historical events.
Fine Arts; Foreign Language; History - World; Religion and Philosophy
Dist - MGHT **Prod** - MGHT 1967

The Rise of Europe - 1000 - 1500 a D 23 MIN
U-matic / VHS / 16mm
Color (J H C)
LC FIA67-5067
Traces the major social economic and philosophic developments in Europe between 1000 and 1500 A D. Uses representative art forms to exemplify historical events.
History - World
Dist - MGHT **Prod** - MGHT 1968

The Rise of Greek civilization 30 MIN
VHS
Western tradition series
Color; PAL (J H G)
PdS29.50 purchase
Explores how democracy and philosophy arise in a collection of Greek cities at the end of the civilized world. Presents part of an eight - part series that conveys the excitement of historical inquiry while stimulating critical thinking about the unique events of each major period of history.
Civics and Political Systems; History - World; Religion and Philosophy
Dist - EMFVL **Prod** - CORF

The Rise of Greek civilization - Greek thought 60 MIN
VHS / U-matic
Western tradition - Pt I series; Pts 5 and 6
Color (G)
$45.00, $29.95 purchase
Presents two thirty - minute programs tracing the history of ideas, events and institutions which have shaped modern societies, hosted by Eugen Weber. Looks at the rise of democracy and philosophy in the city states of Ancient Greece in Part 5. Part 6 examines Greek thinkers Socrates, Plato and Aristotle who laid the foundation of Western intellectual thought. Part of a 52 - part series on the Western tradition.
Civics and Political Systems; Geography - World; History - World; Religion and Philosophy; Sociology
Dist - ANNCPB **Prod** - WGBH 1989

The Rise of Greek Tragedy - Sophocles, Oedipus the King 45 MIN
16mm / U-matic / VHS
History of the Drama Series Unit 1; Unit 1
Color (H C A)
LC 75-700102
Presents Sophocles' Oedipus the King, performed in the authentic setting of a fifth - century Greek theater, with the use of masks made after ancient models. Shows how this drama developed from primeval sacrificial ceremonies to Dionysius.
Literature and Drama
Dist - FOTH **Prod** - MANTLH 1975

Rise of Hitler 28 MIN
16mm / U-matic / VHS
Rise and fall of the Third Reich series
B&W (H C A)
LC 74-702559
Discusses Hitler's youth and career.
Biography; History - World
Dist - FI **Prod** - MGMD 1972

The Rise of Hitler - Pt 1 28 MIN
16mm / VHS
Rise and fall of the Third Reich series
B&W (G J H)
$400.00, $79.00 purchase _ #135 - 9007
Addresses why the Germans, supposedly a deeply religious and cultured people, degenerated into savagery in the 20th century. Features Richard Basehart as narrator, based on the book by William L Shirer. Scrutinizes a Germany which in the 1920s had been defeated in war and humiliated in peace. Theorizes that Hitler and his Nazis offered the myth of a new German empire, provoking political crises until democracy crumbled and Hitler was made Chancellor.
Civics and Political Systems; History - United States; History - World
Dist - FI **Prod** - MGM 1972

The Rise of Hitler - Pt I 30 MIN
16mm
Rise and fall of the Third Reich series
B&W (G)
$40.00 rental _ #HRF - 722
Chronicles the rise to power of Adolph Hitler and his associates. Shows how they manipulated events in Germany during that country's crises to achieve power. Part one of a four - part series on Hitler.
Civics and Political Systems; History - World; Sociology
Dist - ADL **Prod** - ADL

Rise of industrial America series

The Farmer in a changing America	27 MIN
The Rise of labor	30 MIN
The Rise of the American City	32 MIN

Dist - EBEC

The Rise of labor 30 MIN
U-matic / VHS / 16mm
Rise of industrial America series
Color; B&W (J H)
LC 79-700632
Traces the history of the American labor movement. Discusses the working conditions from the 1800s to the present, the effects of early strikes in changing governmental attitudes toward labor and the organization of the American Federation of Labor and the Congress of Industrial Organizations.
Business and Economics; History - United States
Dist - EBEC **Prod** - EBEC 1969

The Rise of Mammals 12 MIN
16mm / U-matic / VHS
Evolution of Life Series
Color (I)
LC FIA68-23
Relates how successive evolutionary changes ultimately resulted in the dominance of mammals, gave rise to the great diversity of mammals and enabled mammals to adjust to many different kinds of environmental conditions.

Science - Natural
Dist - MGHT Prod - MGHT 1969

The Rise of mammals 58 MIN
U-matic / VHS
Life on Earth series; Program 9
Color (J)
LC 82-706681
Offers a detailed study of the many marsupial species, paying special attention to the primitive marsupials found in Australia.
Science - Natural
Dist - FI Prod - BBCTV 1981

The Rise of mammals 30 MIN
16mm
Life on Earth series; Pt 18
Color (J)
$495.00 purchase _ #865 - 9039
Blends scientific data with wildlife photography to tell the story of the development of life. Features wildlife expert David Attenborough as host. Part 18 of 27 parts.
Science; Science - Natural; Science - Physical
Dist - FI Prod - BBCTV 1981

The Rise of Minna Nordstrom 30 MIN
U-matic / VHS
Wodehouse playhouse series
Color (C A)
Presents an adaptation of the short story The Rise Of Minna Nordstrom by P G Wodehouse.
Literature and Drama
Dist - TIMLIF Prod - BBCTV 1980

Rise of Modernism in Music Series
Are my ears on wrong - a profile of Charles Ives 24 MIN
Paris - La Belle Epoque 24 MIN
Vienna - Stripping the Facade 25 MIN
Dist - MEDIAG

The Rise of national monarchies - 15th to 16th centuries 30 MIN
VHS
Color (J H C G)
$49.95 purchase _ #SOC7004V
Explains national monarchies in terms of the control exercised by the rulers and the emergence of absolutism as it occurred in France, England and Spain. Explores the implications of centralization of government control and the subjugation of local governments represented by feudal lords. Discusses how patterns of government that evolved 500 years ago affect the present day. Includes teacher's guide.
Civics and Political Systems; History - World
Dist - CAMV

The Rise of nationalism and The legacy 120 MIN
VHS
Africa series
Color (G)
$69.95 purchase _ #S01423
Presents the final two 60 - minute documentaries in a series about Africa Focuses on the independence movements that swept Africa in the post - World War II era, especially those in Ghana, Kenya, Algeria and the Belgian Congo. Discusses the transition to Black rule in Zimbabwe and questions when the same will take place in South Africa. Interviews African political leaders on their vision of Africa's future. Narrated by Basil Davidson.
Civics and Political Systems; History - United States; History - World; Social Science
Dist - UILL

Rise of nations in Europe 13 MIN
U-matic / VHS / 16mm
Color (J H C)
Traces the rise of European nations from feudal beginnings to the highly centralized states of the 17th century.
History - World
Dist - CORF Prod - CORF 1978
INSTRU

Rise of nations in Europe 13 MIN
VHS
Color (J H C G)
$59.00 purchase _ #MF - 3824
Focuses on France from the crowning of Charlemagne through the growth of trade, the rise of the middle class, Joan of Arc, and other elements that led to the concept of nationhood and powerful monarchs in Western Europe.
Civics and Political Systems; History - World
Dist - INSTRU Prod - CORF

The Rise of OPEC 60 MIN
VHS
Oil Series
Color (G)
$59.95 purchase _ #OILO - 104
Documents the creation of the Organization of Petroleum Exporting Countries, or OPEC. Shows that OPEC was created in hopes of counterbalancing the influence of big oil companies, and eventually became the main player. Features an exclusive interview with Libyan dictator Col Moammar Qaddafi.
Business and Economics; Civics and Political Systems
Dist - PBS

The Rise of Rome - 700 BC - 300 BC 15 MIN
VHS
Ancient Rome - the rise and fall of Rome series
Color (J H C G)
$59.95 purchase _ #BU701V
Visits ancient Rome and witnesses the rise of this colorful civilization. Discusses the customs, lifestyles, architecture and religions of the era. Part of a five - part series on Rome.
History - World
Dist - CAMV

The Rise of Rome and The Roman Empire 60 MIN
U-matic / VHS
Western tradition series; Pt I; Pts 9 and 10
Color (G)
$45.00, $29.95 purchase
Presents two thirty - minute programs, hosted by Eugen Weber, tracing the history of ideas, events and institutions which have shaped modern societies. Looks at the empire that shaped the West built with Roman armies in part 9. Part 10 examines the civil engineering of Rome which contributed as much to the Roman Empire as weaponry. Parts 9 and 10 of a 52 - part series on the Western tradition.
Geography - World; History - World; Industrial and Technical Education; Sociology
Dist - ANNCPB Prod - WGBH 1989

The Rise of Soviet power 54 MIN
16mm / U-matic / VHS
B&W (H C A)
LC FIA67-114
Traces the rise of Soviet Russia from revolutionary beginnings to the end of Khrushchev's regime in 1964. Uses footage from the period. Re - narrated from the original version.
Civics and Political Systems; History - World
Dist - MGHT Prod - BBCTV 1966

The Rise of Soviet power - Pt 1 30 MIN
16mm / U-matic / VHS
B&W (H C G)
Traces the rise of Soviet Russia from revolutionary beginnings to the end of Khrushchev's regime in 1964. Uses footage from the period. Re - narrated from the original version.
History - World
Dist - MGHT Prod - BBCTV 1966

The Rise of Soviet power - Pt 2 30 MIN
U-matic / VHS / 16mm
B&W
Traces the rise of Soviet Russia from revolutionary beginnings to the end of Khrushchev's regime in 1964. Uses footage from the period. Re - narrated from the original version.
History - World
Dist - MGHT Prod - BBCTV 1966

The Rise of the American City 32 MIN
U-matic / VHS / 16mm
Rise of Industrial America Series
Color (J)
LC 76-711723
Presents John Lindsay, mayor of New York, and Godfrey Cambridge, well - known black comedian and social observer, commenting on the problems of pollution, poverty, hunger, violence and social change. Searches the heart of the city and of the men and women who are its strength and future.
History - United States; Science - Natural; Social Science; Sociology
Dist - EBEC Prod - EBEC 1970

The Rise of the dictators - form, riflemen, form 52 MIN
16mm / VHS
Europe, the mighty continent series
Color
LC 77-701564
Analyzes conditions in Europe that made Hitler's and Mussolini's rise to power possible. Discusses Stalin's five - year plans in the Soviet Union, the civil war in Spain and the signing of the Nazi - Soviet Pact of 1939.
History - World
Dist - TIMLIF Prod - BBCTV 1976

The Rise of the dictators - form, riflemen, form - Pt 1 26 MIN
U-matic
Europe, the mighty continent series
Color
LC 79-707423
Analyzes conditions in Europe that made Hitler's and Mussolini's rise to power possible. Discusses Stalin's five - year plans in the Soviet Union, the civil war in Spain and the signing of the Nazi - Soviet Pact of 1939.
Civics and Political Systems; History - World
Dist - TIMLIF Prod - BBCTV 1976

The Rise of the dictators - form, riflemen, form - Pt 2 26 MIN
U-matic
Europe, the mighty continent series
Color
LC 79-707423
Analyzes conditions in Europe that made Hitler's and Mussolini's rise to power possible. Discusses Stalin's five - year plans in the Soviet Union, the civil war in Spain and the signing of the Nazi - Soviet Pact of 1939.
Biography; Civics and Political Systems; History - World
Dist - TIMLIF Prod - BBCTV 1976

Rise of the dragon 58 MIN
VHS / U-matic / BETA
Nova - the genius that was China series
Color (H C A)
$250.00 purchase _ #JY - 6181C
Finds that by the end of the 14th century, China was the richest, most powerful and technologically advanced society on Earth. Looks at how China achieved what it did and how Chinese politics, culture and economy kept it from doing more. Part of a four - part series which details the rise, fall and re - emergence of science in China.
Business and Economics; History - World; Sociology
Dist - CORF Prod - WGBHTV 1990

The Rise of the Horsemen 30 MIN
16mm
Great Plains Trilogy, 2 Series Nomad and Indians - Early Man on the 'Plains; Nomad and Indians - early man on the plains
B&W (J)
Describes the new plains life resulting from the spread of Spanish horses. Discusses the change from agriculture to bison hunting (1650 - 1750), the movement of Indian tribes and typical plains Indian culture (1750 - 1850.).
History - United States; Social Science; Sociology
Dist - UNEBR Prod - UNEBR 1954

The Rise of the Industrial Giants 25 MIN
16mm / U-matic / VHS
American History Series
Color (I J H)
LC FIA67-1329
Portrays the rapid industrialization which took place in the United States at the turn of the century and which saw the rise of business combinations and the emergence of trusts.
Business and Economics; History - United States
Dist - MGHT Prod - MGHT 1967

Rise of the Nazis 20 MIN
VHS / U-matic
Witness to the Holocaust Series
B&W (J)
LC 84-706506
Shows how a violent, extralegal group of outsiders and fringe elements rose to power in a democracy and established political and economic institutions of legitimized terror and mass murder in Nazi Germany. Documents the economic, political and attitudinal factors which contributed to the rise of Naziism.
History - World; Religion and Philosophy
Dist - CNEMAG Prod - HORECE 1983

The Rise of the Red Navy 57 MIN
16mm / VHS / U-matic
Color (H C A)
LC 80-706906
States that the Commander - in - Chief of the Russian Navy controls not only powerful warships and nuclear submarines, but also a fishing and oceanographic research fleet larger than that of the rest of the nations put together, a merchant fleet second only to Japan's, and a unique flotilla of over fifty intelligence and surveillance vessels. Traces the history of the Russian Navy from the time of Peter the Great to 1980.
Civics and Political Systems; History - World
Dist - FI Prod - BBCTV 1980

Rise of the Republican Party 30 MIN
VHS
American South Comes of Age Series
Color (J)
$95.00 purchase, $55.00 rental
Considers the rise of the Republican party in the American South. Part of a fourteen - part series on the economic, social and political transformation of the South since World War II.

Civics and Political Systems; Geography - United States; History - United States; Psychology; Sociology
Dist - SCETV **Prod** - SCETV 1985

The Rise of the Soviet Navy 28 MIN
16mm
Color
LC 74-705542
Traces the rise of Soviet seapower from the Imperial Navy of the Czar to the Navy of today. Narrated by Richard Basehart.
Civics and Political Systems; History - World
Dist - USNAC **Prod** - USN 1969

Rise up and walk
U-matic / VHS / 16mm
Color
Explores the beliefs and practices of independent African Christian churches. Shows how they interpret the Christian faith in the context of their own pre - Christian religions and cultural traditions.
Geography - World; Religion and Philosophy
Dist - UCEMC **Prod** - ANKELE

The Risen Lord living forever 30 MIN
VHS
Jesus of Nazareth series; Vol 14
Color (R H C A)
$29.95 purchase, $10.00 rental _ #35-8327-1502
Presents excerpts from the Franco Zeffirelli film on the life and ministry of Jesus. Surveys the events leading up to and including Jesus' resurrection and ascension into heaven.
Literature and Drama; Religion and Philosophy
Dist - APH **Prod** - BOSCO

Rishost Hos Bontoc - Igoroterne - Rice Harvest among the Bontoc Igorots 20 MIN
16mm
Color ((DANISH SUBTITLES))
Portrays a rice harvest among the Bontoc Igorots. Describes the rice being harvested in accordance with the traditional ceremonies.
Agriculture; Foreign Language
Dist - STATNS **Prod** - STATNS 1954

Rishte - relationships 28 MIN
16mm / VHS
Women's lives and choices series
Color (G)
$50.00, $65.00 rental, $195.00 purchase
Follows the story of Lali Devi, a mother who poisoned herself and two of her daughters. Explores the practice of preferring male children in India and how the practice led to Devi's suicide and murder of her two female children. Also looks at the efforts of an activist to establish a community organization dedicated to raising women's awareness about the impact of sex preference on their lives and their legal rights. Part of a three - part series dealing with women's health and the social, cultural and economic factors underlying reproductive choices.
Fine Arts; Sociology
Dist - WMEN **Prod** - RIESEN
MACART

Rising Expectations 28 MIN
16mm
Color
LC 79-701240
Explores the ways in which people with disabilities are making advances in American society in such areas as employment, housing, education, transportation and recreation.
Psychology
Dist - UCPA **Prod** - UCPA 1978

Rising High and Beautiful 14 MIN
16mm
Journal Series
Color
LC 74-703753
Takes a look at the scenic highlights of the Niagara Falls area of southern Ontario.
Geography - World
Dist - CANFDC **Prod** - FIARTS 1973

The Rising of the Moon 81 MIN
16mm
B&W
Presents a trilogy of Irish comedy and drama.
Fine Arts
Dist - TWYMAN **Prod** - WB 1957

The Rising Seas 28 MIN
35mm strip / VHS
Color (J)
$84.00 purchase _ #PE - 512988 - 4, #PE - 512976 - 0
Considers evidence for historical cycles of global warming and cooling, effects of temperature changes on coastlines and environments, and roles played by people, ozone depletion and the Greenhouse Effect in the changes. Filmstrip version includes two filmstrips, two cassettes and teacher's guide.
Science - Physical
Dist - SRA **Prod** - SRA 1989

Rising Star 10 MIN
BETA / VHS / U-matic
(H C A G)
$100.00
Interviews Andre Phillippe Gagnon, an impressionist from Quebec who is achieving international recognition.
Fine Arts
Dist - CTV **Prod** - CTV 1986

Risk 22 MIN
VHS
Color (J H C)
$225.00 purchase
Uses dramatic vignettes featuring young adult performers to provide accurate information about the transmission of AIDS. Focuses on the message - abstain from sexual activity or wear an effective condom or die.
Health and Safety; Sociology
Dist - LANDMK **Prod** - LANDMK 1990

Risk 29 MIN
U-matic
Nuclear Power and You Series
Color
Focuses on the risks and safety factors in nuclear power reactor operations.
Science - Physical; Social Science
Dist - UMITV **Prod** - UMITV 1979

The Risk 29 MIN
U-matic / VHS / BETA
Rightful discharge series
Color; PAL (IND PRO G)
Contact distributor about price
Shows managers the right way to discipline and discharge employees. Trains supervisors to handle discharges properly, to avoid legal liability and treat employees with dignity and respect. Shows how to properly handle problem employees for increased productivity and higher morale. Increases an organization's chance of successful defense should a discharge case go to court. Part of two parts on rightful discharge.
Business and Economics; Guidance and Counseling
Dist - BNA **Prod** - BNA

Risk Analysis and the EDP Security Assurance Review 30 MIN
U-matic / VHS
Auditing EDP Systems Series
Color
Discusses risk analysis and outlines several methods for conducting a risk analysis while stressing that companies must determine the risks which face their computer systems.
Industrial and Technical Education; Psychology
Dist - DELTAK **Prod** - DELTAK

Risk factors 26 MIN
VHS / U-matic / BETA
Handicapped child series
Color (C PRO)
$150.00 purchase _ #125.2
Presents a video transfer from slide program which discusses prevention of childhood handicaps and stresses the importance of early identification of handicapping conditions when they occur so that intervention can occur. Identifies biological and environmental factors frequently associated with childhood handicaps so that professionals can be alerted to the need for close surveillance and assessment of children at risk. Part of a series on handicapped children.
Health and Safety
Dist - CONMED **Prod** - CONMED

Risk Factors in Heart Disease 30 MIN
U-matic / VHS
Here's to Your Health Series
Color (C T)
Discusses hypertension, smoking and high levels of cholesterol in the bloodstream as dangerous health risk factors. Shows how to recognize these dangers and why we should avoid them.
Health and Safety; Science - Natural
Dist - DALCCD **Prod** - DALCCD

Risk factors of coronary disease
VHS / U-matic
Color (SPANISH ARABIC)
Explains how one can reduce the major risk factors that lead to heart disease. Deals with smoking, hypertension, cholesterol as well as such probable factors as diabetes, obesity, stress and inactivity.
Science - Natural
Dist - MIFE **Prod** - MIFE

Risk factors of heart disease 10 MIN
VHS
Color (PRO A)
$250.00 purchase _ #HA - 19
Teaches viewers how to reduce the risk of heart attack or stroke by minimizing or eliminating controllable risks even if they have one or more non - controllable risk factors. Reviews factors such as heredity, age, sex, diabetes, smoking, high cholesterol and high blood pressure. Suggests overall lifestyle changes to help patients reduce risks.
Health and Safety
Dist - MIFE **Prod** - MIFE 1991

Risk Management 11 MIN
16mm
Running Your Own Business Series
Color
Discusses business risks and how to deal with them.
Business and Economics
Dist - EFD **Prod** - EFD

Risk management - reliability approach - a successful combination
16mm / U-matic
Color (A)
Presents two logical tools to help people and equipment perform efficiently and safely. Lists five major causes of breakdowns and suggests ways to avoid them.
Health and Safety
Dist - BNA **Prod** - BNA 1983

Risk, safety and technology 20 MIN
VHS / 16mm
You, me and technology series
Color (J H A)
$150.00 purchase, $30.00 rental
Distinguishes among voluntary, involuntary, perceived, statistical, long - term and short - term risk in a technological society. Demonstrates that to survive the technology society has created, we must learn how to control its advantages and disadvantages.
Business and Economics; Health and Safety; Sociology
Dist - AITECH **Prod** - NJN 1988

Risk stratification of the post - MI patient - a focus on exercise testing - Volume 11
VHS / 8mm cartridge
Cardiology video journal series
Color (PRO)
#FSR - 506
Presents a free - loan program, part of a series on cardiology, which trains medical professionals. Contact distributor for details.
Health and Safety
Dist - WYAYLA **Prod** - WYAYLA

Risk - taking and you 23 MIN
VHS
Color (J H)
$169.00 purchase _ #662-SK; $165.00, $495.00 purchase, $50.00 rental _ #8144
Discusses the tendency among many teenagers toward risk - taking. States that risk - taking is normal, but can lead to disaster. Differentiates between healthy and unhealthy risk - taking. Challenges teenagers to assess the risks they take. Includes teacher's guide.
Psychology; Sociology
Dist - SUNCOM **Prod** - HRMC 1989
AIMS

The Risks of illegal drug use 15 MIN
VHS
Dealing with drugs - teaching kids to say 'no' series
Color; CC (I J H)
$89.95 purchase _ #UW3534
Examines the facts about illegal drugs, their inherent dangers and the risks involved in their use. Part of a six - part series using wit and humor to teach students how to say 'no' to drugs.
Guidance and Counseling; Health and Safety; Psychology
Dist - FOTH

Risks - the price - part II 30 MIN
VHS
Color (A)
$525.00 purchase
Continues the story of Walt Ames as he leaves prison and begins work. Shows how his new company puts itself at risk by revealing its terms of sale, payment schedules and credit agreements to competitors. Notes the need for competent legal advice in business dealings.
Business and Economics; Civics and Political Systems; Education
Dist - COMFLM **Prod** - COMFLM

Risky business 20 MIN
VHS / U-matic / BETA
Color (G)
$595.00 purchase, $125.00 rental _ #RIS009
Exposes potential hazards in an office environment during a routine day.
Business and Economics; Health and Safety; Psychology
Dist - ITF **Prod** - CREMED 1991

Risky Business 30 MIN
BETA / VHS
On the Money Series
Color
Explores the world of bartering. Provides tax tips. Describes how money affects emotions.
Business and Economics; Home Economics
Dist - CORF **Prod** - WGBHTV

Rita Dove - 3 - 5 - 87 31 MIN
VHS / Cassette
Poetry Center reading series
Color (G)
$15.00, $45.00 purchase, $15.00 rental _ #739 - 592
Features the African - American writer reading her works, including selections from Thomas and Beulah, at the Poetry Center, San Francisco State University, with an introduction by Frances Phillips.
Literature and Drama
Dist - POETRY

Rita Moreno - now you can 60 MIN
VHS
Color; CC (A G)
$19.95 purchase _ #MORE
Concentrates on exercise as a means for staying in good health, rather than for reshaping the body. Shows exercisers spanning five decades in age. Features Rita Moreno.
Health and Safety; Physical Education and Recreation
Dist - APRESS

A Rite of Passage 14 MIN
16mm
Color (J H G)
Shows a ceremony called 'marking' which takes place when a !Kung boy kills his first large antelope. Hunting not only provides meat and useful skins, but a young man's successful kill also discharges a social obligation to his potential father in law.
Geography - World; Psychology; Sociology
Dist - DOCEDR **Prod** - DOCEDR 1972

Rite of Renewal
BETA / VHS
Adult Years - Continuity and Change Series
Color
Explores the need for rites of passage to mark important transitions in adult lives. Presents examples of such rituals, including a Bat Mitzvah for adult women, a therapy group and a religious divorce service.
Guidance and Counseling; Psychology; Religion and Philosophy; Sociology
Dist - OHUTC **Prod** - OHUTC

The Rite of spring
CD-ROM
(G A)
$99.00 purchase _ #1923
Contains a digital recording The Rite of Spring by Igor Stravinsky. Features Charles Dutoit conducting the Orchestre Symphonique de Montreal, and supplemental musical excerpts by Robert Winter, members of the UCLA Wind Ensemble and others. Provides a single - screen overview of the entire score enabling the user to hear instantaneously any of the individual sections. Examines Stravinsky's life and times and the inner workings of his music. For Macintosh Plus, SE and II Computers. Requires at least one M of RAM, one floppy disk drive, and an Apple compatible CD - ROM drive.
Computer Science; Fine Arts
Dist - BEP

Rites 52 MIN
VHS
Color (H C G)
$445.00 purchase, $75.00 rental
Explores the custom of female circumcision - clitoridectomy. Shows the efforts of women worldwide to stop the practice. Considers three major contexts within which female genital mutilation occurs - cosmetic, reflecting a cultural hatred of women's physiology; punitive, to chastise women in the late 19th century and early 20th century who stepped out of line; and cultural, as a transition to adulthood and initiation into female life. Directed by Penny Dedman.
Sociology
Dist - FLMLIB **Prod** - CFTV 1991

Rites of passage 60 MIN
VHS
Pastoral bereavement counseling series
Color (R G)
$49.95 purchase _ #PSBC3
Helps participants to understand the dynamics of grief and 'tasks' necessary to journey from grief to healing. Develops the personal, technical and pastoral skills necessary to assist the griever. Shows how to design and lead an effective bereavement ministry team. Features Dr Patrick Del Zoppo. Part of eight parts of a complete training program in ministry to the bereaved. Workbook available separately.
Guidance and Counseling; Health and Safety; Religion and Philosophy; Sociology
Dist - CTNA **Prod** - CTNA

Rites of Passage Series
The Revolt of Mother 47 MIN
Dist - CORF

Ritual 4 MIN
16mm
B&W
LC 75-703226
Presents a visual exploration of the ritual involved in the application of eye make - up and the elaborate materials used.
Fine Arts; Home Economics
Dist - USC **Prod** - USC 1966

Ritual 30 MIN
U-matic / VHS / 16mm
Color (J)
LC 78-700844
A shortened version of the 1977 motion picture Ritual. Portrays various rituals of the Japanese, including those associated with neighborhood life, work, Zen and the samurai.
Geography - World; Religion and Philosophy; Sociology
Dist - WOMBAT **Prod** - PSYMED 1978

The Ritual 75 MIN
VHS
B&W (G)
$39.95 purchase _ #RIT060
Features three actors who are accused of performing an obscene variety show and thus subjected to an intensely personal inquisition by a sadistic judge. Conjures a dark vision of the artist's world, in which art is both a gift and a curse. Ingrid Thulin portrays an alcoholic actress caught up in the nightmare.
Fine Arts; Psychology; Sociology
Dist - HOMVIS **Prod** - JANUS 1969

Ritual child abuse - a professional overview 30 MIN
VHS
Color (A PRO)
$195.00 purchase, $50.00 rental _ #D - 219
Shares the insights of eight clinicians distilled from hundreds of case histories. Discusses mind control techniques, victim credibility, daycare safety, criminal justice system problems, ritual molestation and cult homicides.
Psychology; Religion and Philosophy; Sociology
Dist - CAVLCD **Prod** - CAVLCD

Ritual crime - guidelines for identification 29 MIN
VHS
Color (A PRO)
$195.00 purchase, $50.00 rental _ #D - 218
Provides a comprehensive overview of ritual crime. Prepares law enforcement agencies to deal with ritual crime cases in a thoroughly professional manner.
Civics and Political Systems; Religion and Philosophy; Sociology
Dist - CAVLCD **Prod** - CAVLCD

Ritual crime - guidelines for identification 18 MIN
U-matic / BETA / 16mm / VHS
Color (PRO)
$395.00, $345.00 purchase, $75.00 rental _ #9962
Describes a variety of crimes which may have ritual aspects. Features Sandi Gallant of the San Francisco Police Department Intelligence Division and Jerry Simandl of the Chicago Police Department Gang Crimes Section.
Civics and Political Systems; Religion and Philosophy; Sociology
Dist - AIMS **Prod** - AIMS 1991

Ritual Dance in Three Oriental Cultures 30 MIN
VHS / U-matic
Dance in Religion and Ritual Series
Color
Fine Arts; Industrial and Technical Education; Sociology
Dist - ARCVID **Prod** - ARCVID

Ritual for a split shadow 12 MIN
VHS
Color & B&W (G)
$35.00 purchase
Struggles with issues of internal gods and devils and their effect upon perception, thought and action in the shaping of a personal worldview. Features two layers of 16mm film shot in the mid - 70s - a hand - painted film and a compilation of home movie footage.
Fine Arts; Psychology
Dist - CANCIN **Prod** - ORRJER 1990

A Ritual of life - death 15 MIN
VHS
Color (G)
$30.00 purchase
Looks at how people afflicted with AIDS have chosen to create their own original dramas based on their personal challeges of living with this disease. Shows how they are motivated by a powerful commitment to not only live, but to confront their own life and death issues. Produced by Anna Halprin with the STEPS Theatre Company.
Fine Arts; Health and Safety
Dist - CANCIN

Ritual Vs Social Dance in the Indigenous Lifestyle 30 MIN
VHS / U-matic
Dance in Religion and Ritual Series
Color
Fine Arts; Industrial and Technical Education
Dist - ARCVID **Prod** - ARCVID

Rituals 12 MIN
16mm
B&W (G)
$20.00 rental
Presents a comedy - drama about two young people and their involvement with drugs, sex and death. Reveals their anxieties while on LSD ultimately ending in death. In four parts. Part two pays homage to Lenny Bruce. Produced by JonCutaia. Music by Ysef Latef and Eric Satie.
Fine Arts
Dist - CANCIN

Rituals of man 25 MIN
U-matic / VHS / 16mm
Untamed world series
Color; Mono (J H C A)
$400.00 film, $250.00 video, $50.00 rental
Surveys the variety of man's outward manifestations of his need to communicate with a higher power, the world of spirits, or nature itself.
Religion and Philosophy; Social Science
Dist - CTV **Prod** - CTV 1969

Rituel 30 MIN
16mm
Color
Presents composer Pierre Boulez conducting his own composition Rituel before the New York Philharmonic Orchestra. Uses computer graphics by artist L Schwartz to accompany the musical composition.
Fine Arts; Mathematics
Dist - LILYAN **Prod** - LILYAN

The Ritz 91 MIN
16mm
Color
Stars Jack Weston as a man on the run from the mob who hides out in a gay bathhouse. Directed by Richard Lester.
Fine Arts
Dist - TWYMAN **Prod** - WB 1976

The Ritz - Carlton - quality and training - Horst Schulze 55 MIN
VHS
Color; PAL (C G PRO)
$89.95, $69.95, $16.00 purchase _ #93AST - V - T0, #93AST - T0
Discusses quality and training in the Ritz - Carlton Hotel Company, Atlanta GA. Features President and Chief Operating Officer, Horst Schulze.
Business and Economics; Psychology
Dist - MOBILE **Prod** - ASTD 1993

Ritz Crackers 1 MIN
U-matic / VHS
Color
Shows a classic television commercial with still frame action.
Business and Economics; Psychology; Sociology
Dist - BROOKC **Prod** - BROOKC

The Rivals 12 MIN
16mm
Animatoons Series
Color
LC FIA67-5506
Presents the story of a blacksmith and a tailor who despise each other's job and argue about an accident in which their displays for a fair were destroyed. Explains that a judge makes them settle their argument by exchanging jobs. Shows how they learn to live happily side by side.

Guidance and Counseling; Psychology; Sociology
Dist - RADTV **Prod** - ANTONS 1968

Rivals - the mating game 16 MIN
VHS
Natural history series
Color (I J H)
$80.00 purchase _ #A5VH 1106
Shows why active competition for mates plays a critical role in natural selection. Follows eight different species of insects and demonstrates what role natural selection played in the development of male damselflies with spoon - shaped sex organs and scorpionflies that make edible spitballs. Explains why the male sex is the one which aggressively competes for mates. Part of a series on natural history.
Psychology; Science - Natural
Dist - CLRVUE **Prod** - CLRVUE

The River 29 MIN
U-matic / VHS / 16mm
Color (H C A)
LC 78-701877
Tells how a neglected four - year - old finds his way back to the river where he was baptized in an effort to recapture the self - esteem he felt there. Based on the short story The River by Flannery O'Connor.
Literature and Drama
Dist - PHENIX **Prod** - NOBLEB 1978

The River 32 MIN
16mm / U-matic / VHS
B&W
LC FIE52-584
Traces life in the Mississippi River Valley during the last 150 years. The consequences of sharecropping, soil exhaustion, unchecked erosion and floods are shown. Concludes with scenes of regional planning, T V a development and correlated federal efforts.
Agriculture; Civics and Political Systems; Geography - United States; Science - Natural; Sociology
Dist - USNAC **Prod** - USDA 1939

The River 99 MIN
VHS
Color (G)
$29.95 _ #RIV050
Portrays the river as a mystical symbol for the mystery and magic of India. Celebrates life and love following three girls in postwar India as they wander down the path of first love. Adapts the novel by Rumer Godden. Digitally remastered with original English language soundtrack.
Fine Arts; Geography - World; Psychology
Dist - HOMVIS **Prod** - JANUS 1951

The River 15 MIN
VHS
Color; PAL (P I)
PdS25.00 purchase
Follows Cheshire's River Weaver from its source to the point where it flows into the Manchester Ship Canal, and from there to the Mersey.
Geography - World; Social Science
Dist - EMFVL **Prod** - LOOLEA

River - a first film 10 MIN
U-matic / VHS / 16mm
Color (P I) (FRENCH)
LC 70-700982
Follows the formation of a river from melting snow, which forms streams that join together and flow into the ocean. Explains that cities are often located along river banks to take advantage of the river waters. Shows river ports and ships.
Geography - United States; Science - Natural; Science - Physical
Dist - PHENIX **Prod** - FA 1969

River - an Allegory 11 MIN
U-matic / VHS / 16mm
Color (H C A)
LC 73-707294
Traces the quickening life of a great river and its eventual absorption into the sea. A musical score blends with the movement of the river.
Fine Arts
Dist - IFB **Prod** - HARL 1968

River bank home - Kenya - Part 5 8 MIN
VHS
Natures kingdom series
Color (P I J)
$125.00 purchase
Visits hippopotami on the banks of a river in Kenya. Part of a 26 - part series on animals showing the habitats and traits of various species.
Geography - World; Science - Natural
Dist - LANDMK **Prod** - LANDMK 1992

River Body 8 MIN
16mm
Color
Presents a montage of 87 male and female bodies in continuous dissolve.
Guidance and Counseling; Psychology; Sociology
Dist - MMRC **Prod** - MMRC

A River Called Potomac 29 MIN
16mm
Color
LC 79-700272
Examines the numerous natural resources provided by the Potomac River, such as water for cities and industries, food, and recreational opportunities. Looks at water resource management programs that protect the quality and quantity of water in the river.
Geography - United States; Science - Natural; Social Science
Dist - FINLYS **Prod** - USDENV 1979

River Characteristics 27 MIN
16mm
B&W (C A)
Features a discussion of tributaries and the interrelationship of width, depth, velocity and quantity of various rivers. Explains problems of pools and ripples in streams. Demonstrates meanders and shows flash floods. Utilizes a glass - fronted sand model to visualize maintenance of streams by ground water during the dry season.
Agriculture; Geography - United States; Science - Natural; Science - Physical
Dist - UTEX **Prod** - UTEX 1960

The River - der fluss 4 MIN
U-matic / VHS / 16mm
Color (H C A)
Uses a combination of still photography, rough sketch animation and dissolving images to project a melancholic look not only at young love but also at the other kinds of separation, physical and emotional, that exist in any sphere of human existence.
Fine Arts; Guidance and Counseling
Dist - PHENIX **Prod** - TRICFD

The River farmer 13 MIN
VHS / 16mm
Color (H C G)
$375.00, $195.00 purchase, $50.00 rental
Focuses on 74 - year - old river farmer Ed Myers who grows mussels and oysters on the Damariscotta River in Maine. Produced by Amee Evans.
Geography - United States; Science - Natural
Dist - FLMLIB

River Flows North 15 MIN
16mm
Color
Presents an informative view of Sanford, Florida, which is centrally situated on the St Johns River near numerous attractions.
Geography - United States
Dist - FLADC **Prod** - FLADC

The River horse - Kenya - Part 17 8 MIN
VHS
Natures kingdom series
Color (P I J)
$125.00 purchase
Watches hippopotami who occupy a river bend for their mud baths. Shows that they protect their domain from invading hippos and a crocodile. Part of a 26 - part series on animals showing the habitats and traits of various species.
Geography - World; Science - Natural
Dist - LANDMK **Prod** - LANDMK 1992

River insects 20 MIN
16mm
Color (JAPANESE)
A Japanese language film. Observes the interesting existence and reproduction of various insects in swift mountain streams. Shows the various species of mole crickets living in such surroundings. Points out how the river insects live by adjusting themselves according to their environments.
Foreign Language; Science - Natural
Dist - UNIJAP **Prod** - TOEI 1967

River Journey on the Upper Nile 18 MIN
U-matic / VHS / 16mm
Man and His World Series
Color (P I J H C)
LC 79-705462
Discusses government priority given to education and training in skills for the inhabitants of the Sudan who at present live as primitive farmers.
Geography - World; Social Science; Sociology
Dist - FI **Prod** - FI 1969

River journeys series
Presents a seven - part series on world rivers. Includes The Congo; Lizzie - an Amazon Adventure; The Mekong; The Murray; The Nile; The Sao Francisco and The Wahgi - Eater of Men.

The Congo	57 MIN
River journeys series	399 MIN
The Wahgi - eater of men	57 MIN

Dist - CF **Prod** - BBCTV 1969

River Journeys

Lizzie - an Amazon Adventure	57 MIN
The Mekong	57 MIN
The Murray	57 MIN
The Nile	57 MIN
The Sao Francisco	57 MIN

Dist - CF

The River Kwai expedition 12 MIN
16mm
Color
Presents the finding of prehistoric cave pictures at the River Kwai by the Thai - Danish Expedition. Shows some extensive settlements from the Bronze Age in Bang Khao.
History - World
Dist - AUDPLN **Prod** - RDCG

River Logging 3 MIN
16mm
Of all Things Series
Color (P I)
Discusses river logging.
Business and Economics; Social Science
Dist - AVED **Prod** - BAILYL

A River Museum 15 MIN
U-matic / VHS
Pass it on Series
Color (K P)
Discusses rivers and their uses and takes a trip to a museum to observe river boats.
Education; Geography - United States
Dist - GPN **Prod** - WKNOTV 1983

The River Nile 34 MIN
16mm / U-matic / VHS
Color; B&W (J)
A short version of the film, 'The River Nile.' Pictures the physical characteristics of the river. Discusses its role in history and in the economy of the regions.
Geography - World; History - World
Dist - MGHT **Prod** - NBCTV 1965

River of fire 27 MIN
VHS / U-matic / 16mm
Color (H)
$295.00, $345.00, $475.00 purchase, $50.00 rental
Offers a dramatic production that provides all the reasons not to become sexually active at an early age. Encourages sexual abstinence among teenagers. Produced by the Utah State Board of Education.
Health and Safety
Dist - NDIM

River of grass 26 MIN
16mm
Audubon wildlife theatre series
Color (I)
Examines man's encroachment on the Florida Everglades and his devastating destruction of land, water and wildlife as nature struggles to balance her scales in one of the few tropical wildernesses surviving in North America.
Geography - United States; Science - Natural
Dist - AVEXP **Prod** - AVEXP

River of Ice - Life Cycle of a Glacier 10 MIN
U-matic / VHS / 16mm
Color (I J H)
LC FIA65-1562
Uses scenes of such glaciers as the Knik and Columbian ice field, to show the source, structure and movement of a typical Alpine glacier, the relationship of climate to ice formation and the effect of glaciation upon the land, fauna and flora of the Alpine region.
Science - Natural; Science - Physical
Dist - PHENIX **Prod** - BAILEY 1964

River of Joy 53 MIN
VHS / 16mm
Color (H)
$155.00 purchase
Tells the religious history of Ukrainians in North America and how religion has aided the integration of Ukrainian immigrants into American life.
History - United States; Religion and Philosophy; Sociology
Dist - FLMWST

The River of Life 22 MIN
U-matic / VHS
Phenomenal World Series
Color (J C)
$129.00 purchase _ #3970
Looks at the structure and functions of blood.
Science - Natural
Dist - EBEC

The River of life - the hydrologic cycle and water pollution 120 MIN
VHS
Color (J H)
$89.00 purchase _ #1986VB
Discovers how rare fresh water is created from the vast oceans of salt water which cover the Earth. Follows an imaginary stream from high in the mountains back to the sea to show the many ways that pollution affects freshwater organisms. Examines the effects of acid rain, nutrient pollution, detergents, herbicides and pesticides. Includes teacher's guide and a set of blackline masters.
Science - Natural; Science - Physical; Social Science
Dist - INSTRU

River of Mail 9 MIN
16mm
Color
LC 77-702859
A study of complexities of mail handling. Shows how new methods and new equipment are being used to cope with the constantly increasing flow of mail.
Psychology; Social Science
Dist - USPOST **Prod** - USPOST 1968

River of Power 21 MIN
U-matic / VHS / 16mm
Color (J H)
LC FIA68-3151
Traces the history of the oil well in the United States. Demonstrates the many ways in which oil is used, and describes some of the by - products of petroleum, including plastics, fibers and industrial raw materials.
Business and Economics
Dist - JOU **Prod** - ALTSUL 1968

River of stars 10 MIN
16mm
B&W (G)
$15.00 rental
Presents the viewer with an enormous amount of high energy input. Surges with an intense visualness, pausing only to give brief significance to punctuating images.
Dist - CANCIN **Prod** - WOODBR 1975

River of stone 58 MIN
VHS
Color (G)
$19.95 purchase
Retraces the historic exploration of the Green and Colorado River canyons by Major Powell. Charts the changes which have occurred with the subsequent use and abuse of the river systems he charted. Alternates dramatic footage of the region with some of the first photographs ever taken of the territories Powell explored. Combines interviews with modern experts with excerpts from Powell's writings to bring the history and controversies surrounding the rivers into focus. Produced by John Howe.
Geography - United States; History - United States; History - World
Dist - KUEDTV **Prod** - KUEDTV 1992

River of the future 98 MIN
VHS
Amazon series
Color; CC (G)
$19.95 purchase _ #3082
Examines how humankind is affecting the delicate and vitally important ecosystem of the Amazon River and how the Amazon Valley could be saved. Part of a three - part series on the Amazon River by Jacques Cousteau with narration by actors and actresses who speak American English.
Geography - World; Science - Natural
Dist - APRESS

River of time 8 MIN
16mm
Color (I)
Explains that the Colorado River has carved one of nature's greatest monuments, the Grand Canyon. Reveals life from the past preserved in the rock and life in its constant struggle today.
Geography - United States; Science - Physical
Dist - AVEXP **Prod** - AVEXP

River of Wealth, River of Freedom 24 MIN
16mm
Color
Looks at America's highway system and shows how a mobile population must learn to share the road.
Health and Safety; Social Science
Dist - MTP **Prod** - GM

River Patrol 28 MIN
16mm
Color
LC 74-706227
Presents one aspect of the American Navy's operations in the Mekong Delta, South Vietnam.
Civics and Political Systems; Geography - World; History - United States
Dist - USNAC **Prod** - USN 1968

River patrol - the gamewardens of Vietnam 54 MIN
VHS
Color (G)
$29.95 purchase _ #BWP01V-S
Takes viewers into the heart of the Mekong Delta with firsthand accounts from the sailors of Navy Task Force 116, code named Operation Game Warden, who took their fragile fiberglass patrol boats and aging helicopter gunships in harm's way along South Vietnam's muddy rivers and canals from December 1965 until 1972. Features General Westmoreland recalling the events that gave birth to the Brown Water Navy and Admiral Zumwalt who explains the strategy behind the interdiction efforts. Narrated by Robert Stack.
Civics and Political Systems; Fine Arts; History - World; Sociology
Dist - CAMV

River people 12 MIN
16mm
Places people live series
Color (I)
LC 76-713003
Tells how the river determines the lives of the people living along the Magdelena River in Columbia. Describes how the residenets' houses are built on stilts, how they travel by boat and how the river is their principal source of food. Compares the Mopti living on the Niger River in Mali whose habits vary with the season. Explains that during the wet season they live in their boats and during the dry season they build settlements of thatched huts on the shore.
Geography - World; Psychology; Science - Natural; Social Science; Sociology
Dist - SF **Prod** - SF 1970

River people - behind the case of David Sohappy 50 MIN
VHS
Color (H C G)
$395.00 purchase, $75.00 rental
Portrays a traditional community of fisherman on Che Wana, the Columbia River, at odds with modern ways. Focuses on the story of David Sohappy, an Indian spiritual leader sentenced to a five - year prison term for selling 317 salmon out of season. Reveals that Sohappy claims an ancestral right to fish along the river. American Indians have lived off the great salmon runs of the Columbia River for 10,000 years, but the construction of more than a dozen hydroelectric plants, pollution threats from logging and aluminum factories, and the Hanford Nuclear Reservation - one of the most radioactively polluted areas in the Western hemisphere - have endangered the habitat of the salmon. Produced by Michael Conford and Michele Zaccheo.
Geography - United States; Industrial and Technical Education; Social Science; Sociology
Dist - FLMLIB

River People of Chad 20 MIN
U-matic / VHS / 16mm
Man and His World Series
Color (P I J H C)
LC 76-705464
Contrasts the modern city of Fort Lamy with the villages of Chad where men, women and children use primtive tools for farming, fishing and cooking in a communal effort at existence.
Geography - World; History - United States; Social Science; Sociology
Dist - FI **Prod** - PMI 1969

River - planet earth 27 MIN
U-matic / VHS / 16mm
Color (J)
LC 78-701184
Takes a look at the Saskatchewan - Nelson river in order to examine the impact which a water system has upon the economy, sociology and ecology of a nation.
Geography - World; Science - Natural; Social Science
Dist - MGHT **Prod** - NFBC 1978

River Rain - Gift of Passage 26 MIN
16mm
Color
LC 76-703255
Documents a visit to the Painted Stone at the Echimamish River of northern Manitoba. Recalls how Indian and white traders stopped there for brief celebrations of thanksgiving.
Geography - World; Social Science
Dist - CANFDC **Prod** - CANFDC 1975

The River Rhine 22 MIN
16mm / U-matic / VHS ;
Dist - LCOA **Prod** - LCOA 1969

The River without buoys 95 MIN
VHS
Color (G) (MANDARIN CHINESE (ENGLISH SUBTITLES))
$45.00 purchase _ #1072B
Presents a movie produced in the People's Republic of China.
Fine Arts; Geography - World; Literature and Drama
Dist - CHTSUI **Prod** - CHTSUI

Riverbody 7 MIN
16mm
B&W (A)
$10.00 rental
Creates suspense when a continuous dissolve of 87 male and female nudes produces composite figures, oftentimes hermaphroditic. Produced by Alice Anne Parker aka Anne Severson.
Fine Arts
Dist - CANCIN

Riverplace - Portland, Oregon - Vol 18 - No 3 15 MIN
VHS
Project reference file - PRF - series
Color (G A PRO)
$60.00 purchase _ #R21
Studies the land plan, design and architectural details used to create a new residential neighborhood and rejuvenate the Portland waterfront. Features Larry Dull from the Portland Development Commission, Eric Parsons of the Cornerstone Columbia Development Company and architect Alan Grainger.
Business and Economics; Sociology
Dist - ULI **Prod** - ULI

Rivers 17 MIN
16mm
Color
LC 80-700875
Tells how since the industrial revolution Western man has harnessed rivers to his needs as a producer. Shows that by a historical coincidence, the ravages of industrialization bypass most of the 13,750 miles of rivers in Victoria.
Geography - World
Dist - TASCOR **Prod** - VICCOR 1978

Rivers 12 MIN
16mm
Color (J H C G)
Illustrates the growth of a river from the source to the mouth, using the watershed of the Mississippi system.
Geography - World; Science - Physical
Dist - VIEWTH **Prod** - GATEEF

Rivers 12 MIN
16mm
Color (P I)
LC FIA66-1122
Discusses how rivers develop, their behavior and their importance to man.
Geography - World; Science - Natural; Science - Physical; Social Science
Dist - IU **Prod** - IU 1965

The Rivers 58 MIN
VHS
Conserving America series
Color (J H C G A)
$29.95 purchase
Portrays concerned Americans who are working to conserve U S rivers. Reveals that only one percent of U S rivers are protected by law, with the others subject to dams, channeling, and industrial development. Includes workbook.
Geography - World; Science - Natural; Social Science; Sociology
Dist - EFVP **Prod** - WQED

Rivers and Our History 10 MIN
U-matic / VHS / 16mm
Color; B&W (I)
LC FIA68-1481
Depicts a boy's trip down a river and uses this trip as a basis for an analysis of early trips on rivers during the exploration period in America. Explains how early river settlements grew into vast cities.
Geography - United States; Geography - World; History - United States; Science - Natural
Dist - JOU **Prod** - JOU 1966

Rivers at work 20 MIN
U-matic / VHS / 16mm
Color (J H C)
Introduces the basic concepts of fluvial geomorphology, the science which seeks to understand the ways in which running water contributes to the creation of landforms.
Science - Physical
Dist - LUF **Prod** - LUF 1983
VIEWTH

Rivers, Floods and People 11 MIN
16mm / U-matic / VHS
Color (J H)
LC 74-702024
Shows how fighting the flood has minimized losses and how wise use of the flood plain can let it serve both man and its natural purpose.
Geography - United States; Geography - World; Science - Natural; Science - Physical
Dist - AIMS **Prod** - COUKLA 1973

A River's Legacy 25 MIN
16mm
Color
LC 76-703800
Investigates the agricultural and industrial activities of the Chilliwack area and shows the results from the fertile soil of the Fraser River, British Columbia.
Agriculture; Industrial and Technical Education
Dist - BCDA **Prod** - BCDA 1974

Rivers of fire 30 MIN
VHS
Color (G)
$39.95 purchase
Documents the 1984 eruption of the long - inactive Hawaiian volcano Mauna Loa. Features spectacular footage of the eruption. Narrated by Bob Sevey.
History - United States; Science - Physical
Dist - PBS **Prod** - WNETTV

Rivers of fire 40 MIN
VHS
Color (H C G)
$250.00 purchase
Examines the control of water in the Middle East. Reveals that Turkey is damming the Tigris and Euphrates Rivers which provide water to nearly all of Iraq and much of Syria. The water is being diverted to vast irrigation projects and deprives Iraqi and Syrian projects downstream of the water they need. Turkey now has the power to stop the flow of both rivers.
Geography - World; History - World; Social Science
Dist - LANDMK **Prod** - LANDMK 1991

Rivers of Fire - an eruption of Hawaii's Mauna Loa volcano
U-matic / VHS
Color (P)
Presents 1984 eruption of Mauna Loa volcano, on the Big Island of Hawaii.
Geography - United States; Geography - World; History - United States
Dist - HNHIST **Prod** - HNHIST 1984

Rivers of France 80 MIN
VHS
Color (G)
$19.95 purchase
Takes a luxury cruise on the River Seine. Views picturesque Honfleur, the Bayeux Tapestry, Monet's Giverny, Normandy's D Day beaches, Joan of Arc's Rouen, Mont St Michel. Includes a barge trip visiting Burgundy's vineyards, Dijon, horseracing, the Louvre, the Musee D'Orsay, the new Bastille Opera House and the Grande Arche de la Defense.
Geography - World
Dist - FRANCC **Prod** - FRANCC

Rivers of Kyoto 34 MIN
16mm
Color
Pictures four rivers (Kamo, Uji, Katsura and Kitsu) which run through the city of Kyoto and suggests that culture and history are closely associated with rivers.
Geography - World
Dist - UNIJAP **Prod** - UNIJAP 1971

Rivers of life 10 MIN
VHS
Color; PAL (I J H A)
$19.95 purchase _ #30915
Focuses on the 10,000 miles of rivers and waterways in Bangladesh which bring both life to the land and its people, and wreak havoc during monsoons and seasonal tropical storms. Shows how, despite poverty and tremendous natural obstacles, the people of Bangladesh are struggling to raise their standard of living. Includes teaching notes.
Business and Economics; Geography - World; History - World; Sociology
Dist - WB **Prod** - WB

Rivers of sand 58 MIN
VHS
Color (G)
$390.00 purchase, $75.00 rental
Illustrates the effects of twenty years of drought in Mali, among the world's poorest countries. Looks at one man's efforts to bring relief to at least a part of the barren wastes and his ambitious plan to bring water from the Niger River to counter the effects of this crisis. Filmed over a one year period monitoring the progress of United Nations aid worker Dresser Coulibaly while analyzing reasons for the failure of foreign aid. Produced by Bruno Sorrentino.
Civics and Political Systems; Fine Arts; History - World; Social Science; Sociology
Dist - FIRS

Rivers of Sand 83 MIN
U-matic / VHS / 16mm
Color (H C A)
LC 74-703498
Portrays the people called the Hamar, who live in the scrubland of southwestern Ethiopia. Points out that in this society, the men are the masters and the women are slaves and shows how this sexual inequality affects the mood and behavior of the people.
Social Science; Sociology
Dist - PHENIX **Prod** - GARDNR 1974

Rivers of stone - a visit to Colorado National Monument 30 MIN
VHS
Color (J H)
$29.95 purchase _ #IV108
Visits western Colorado to examine rock formations and their origin. Studies the work of running water and wind and temperature in carving out huge canyons.
Geography - United States; Science - Physical
Dist - INSTRU

Rivers of the Rockies 16 MIN
16mm / U-matic / VHS
Mountain habitat series
Color (I J H)
Shows how high mountain rivers provide attractive habitats for a diverse number of living creatures. Illustrates the dipper bird, harlequin duck and osprey, also known as the sea eagle, and mountain lions and mountain sheep.
Geography - United States; Science - Natural
Dist - BCNFL **Prod** - KARVF 1982

Rivers of the Sea 52 MIN
16mm
Color
LC 81-701096
Joins scientists working at sea and in land - based laboratories who are working on a large - scale oceanographic survey to gain knowledge vital to the prevention of ocean pollution, improved commercial fishing and better understanding of climatic conditions.
Industrial and Technical Education; Science - Natural; Science - Physical
Dist - USNAC **Prod** - NSF 1981

Rivers - the Work of Running Water 22 MIN
16mm / U-matic / VHS
Color (I J H) (SPANISH)
A Spanish language version of the film and videorecording Rivers - The Work Of Running Water.
Foreign Language; Geography - United States
Dist - EBEC **Prod** - EBEC

Rivers to the Sea 46 MIN
16mm / U-matic / VHS
Color (J)
$750.00, $310.00 puchase, $75.00 rental
Explores the life of Atlantic coast rivers through underwater footage shot over two years in all seasons. Promotes the care and management of all rivers. Presented in two parts for schools.
Geography - United States; Geography - World; Science - Natural; Science - Physical
Dist - BULFRG **Prod** - NFBC 1990

Rivet identification - ITP practical project series 17 MIN
U-matic / VHS
Aviation technician training program series
Color (IND)
Treats in entertaining manner the subject of aircraft rivet identification. Gives the subject an interesting and attention - getting twist while providing a wealth of information about the most common aircraft fastener, the rivet.
Industrial and Technical Education
Dist - AVIMA **Prod** - AVIMA 1980

RL Transients 13 MIN
16mm
B&W
LC 74-705543
Determines the values of voltage and current at various time intervals in a series RL circuit with a DC voltage applied. Shows time constant chart. (Kinescope).
Industrial and Technical Education; Science - Physical
Dist - USNAC **Prod** - USAF

RL Transients and Waveshaping 20 MIN
U-matic / VHS / 16mm
B&W
Uses a series RL circuit with a DC voltage applied and a universal time constant chart to determine values of voltage and current at various time intervals. Defines time constants and draws output wave forms for RC and RL circuits. Illustrates integrated and differentiated wave forms.
Industrial and Technical Education; Science - Physical
Dist - USNAC **Prod** - USAF 1983

The RM Connection 24 MIN
16mm
Color
LC 78-700214
Tells how a chemical plant supervisor is annoyed by the extra work required to support a computerized reliability maintenance program until he realizes the system's value when two dangerous failures occur.
Health and Safety; Industrial and Technical Education; Sociology
Dist - UCC **Prod** - UCC 1977

RM Fischer - an industrial 4 MIN
VHS / U-matic
Color
Spotlights R M Fisher's baroque futuristic lamp sculptures. Presented by Carole Ann Klonarides and Michael Owen.
Fine Arts
Dist - ARTINC **Prod** - ARTINC

RMI Stress Management Series
Health and Nutrition Habits
Personal Stress Management
Psychological and Emotional Habits
Stress Relief Techniques
Dist - RMIBHF

RNA Synthesis - the Genetic Messenger 10 MIN
U-matic
Protein Synthesis Series
Color (H C)
Explores the synthesis of a DNA molecule through the use of the messenger RNA which carries the information of the DNA strand to the ribosome, the site of protein manufacture.
Science; Science - Natural; Science - Physical
Dist - TVOTAR **Prod** - TVOTAR 1984

RNA - the messenger of life 21 MIN
VHS
Color (J H)
$165.00 purchase _ #A5VH 1179
Shows how RNA works with DNA to dictate the role each cell will play within an organism. Uses computer graphics to portray the processes of transcription and translation and presents a model of protein synthesis in which students use building blocks to simulate the process.
Science - Natural
Dist - CLRVUE **Prod** - CLRVUE 1992

The Road 28 MIN
16mm / U-matic / VHS
B&W (J)
LC FIA68-809
Documents work of the Frontier Nursing Service, a group of nurses in Appalachia who minister to Appalachians who have no access to modern clinics or hospitals. Shows the service's work with aged, infirm, infants and mothers and outlines its history.
Geography - United States; Health and Safety
Dist - CAROUF **Prod** - FNSI 1968

The Road Ahead 30 MIN
U-matic
China After Mao Series
Color
Speculates about the future paths of Chinese society, politics, science, art and law. Summarizes the China After Mao Series.
Civics and Political Systems; Geography - World
Dist - UMITV **Prod** - UMITV 1980

The Road Ahead 17 MIN
16mm
Working for the United States Series
Color (H A)
LC 77-700710
Presents the new or prospective civil service employee with information on performance requirements, within - grade increases, incentive awards, training and development, upward mobility and merit promotion.
Civics and Political Systems; Guidance and Counseling
Dist - USNAC **Prod** - USCSC 1976

The Road Ahead - Pt 4 50 MIN
16mm / VHS
At the Wheel - Unedited Version - Series
Color (S)
$750.00, $79.00 purchase _ #101 - 9109
Investigates a matter of increasing public concern, death and destruction on our roads and highways. Examines four aspects of the problem of drunk driving. Part 4 of the four part series considers solutions to the problem of drunk driving. Unedited version.
Health and Safety; Industrial and Technical Education; Psychology; Sociology
Dist - FI **Prod** - NFBC 1987

The Road and the Wind - Destination Gold 23 MIN
16mm
Color
LC 80-701375
Depicts a tour through California gold rush country on a motorcycle.
Geography - United States; Physical Education and Recreation
Dist - EJLAD **Prod** - USSUZ 1980

The Road back 49 MIN
U-matic / VHS
B&W
Follows Jim Blattie, boxer, as he struggles to save his life in the midst of drugs, alcohol and high stakes. Takes him through his own treatment and then to counseling youths at a residential drug center.
Health and Safety; Psychology; Sociology
Dist - UCV **Prod** - UCV

Road - Eo 22 MIN
16mm
Color
LC 75-700476
Shows how a truck road - eo, or a demonstration and test of skillful driving of large trucks, is conducted. Shows how road - eos contribute to safe driving attitudes and procedures.
Health and Safety; Social Science
Dist - APATC **Prod** - APATC 1974

The Road home 9 MIN
VHS / 16mm
Color (H C A)
$75.00 purchase, $50.00 rental _ #9957
Tells the true story of Charles Ratcliff - a black Vietnam veteran, a cowboy and a single father. Ratcliff reflects on war and violence, on being black in America, and on the kind of life he wants for his child.
History - United States; Sociology
Dist - AIMS **Prod** - MAURIL 1987

A Road in the Forest 14 MIN
16mm
Color
LC 76-703706
Explores the challenge of building new roads that will have the least impact on the environment. Stresses design criteria which will provide service, safety, beauty, economy and harmony with the landscape.
Industrial and Technical Education; Science - Natural; Social Science
Dist - USNAC **Prod** - USDA 1974

Road kills 16 MIN
VHS / 16mm
Color (G)
$14.95 purchase
Depicts animals killed by traffic. Features dancer Sarah Cook.
Science - Natural; Sociology
Dist - WMMI **Prod** - WMMI 1974

Road map 24 MIN
16mm
B&W (I J)
Pictures the development of California's network of roads and highways from the rutted El Camino Real of mission days to the eight - lane super freeways of the 1960s. Traces the change in vehicles over the years and portrays the role played by Californians in state highway development programs.
Geography - United States; Social Science
Dist - MLA **Prod** - ABCTV 1963

Road repairs 10 MIN
VHS
Stop, look, listen series
Color; PAL (P I J)
Follows the sound of a pneumatic drill to where a road is being repaired. Shows the processes of breaking up the old road bedding, laying rubble, tarmac and asphalt, and the special machinery being used. Part of a series of films which start from some everyday observation and show more of what is happening, how and why. Builds vocabulary and encourages children to be more observant.
English Language; Industrial and Technical Education; Social Science
Dist - VIEWTH

Road running 30 MIN
VHS
Track and field techniques series
Color (H C G)
$29.95 purchase _ #WK1104V
Features road runner Joan Benoit - Samuelson who discusses the skill and improving performance. Part of a series.
Physical Education and Recreation
Dist - CAMV

Road Talk 10 MIN
16mm
Color
Examines road talk, the language drivers use to communicate whenever they're behind the wheel.
Health and Safety; Psychology
Dist - GM **Prod** - GM

The Road to 1984 - a Biography of George Orwell
BETA / VHS
Color
Presents James Fox starring in the story of the true - life experiences that led to Orwell's vision of 'Big Brother'.
Biography; Literature and Drama
Dist - GA **Prod** - GA

Road to Achievement Series
Up the Corporate Ladder 60 MIN
Winning at Work 60 MIN
Winning Entrepreneurial Style 60 MIN
Dist - CAMV

The Road to ancient Egypt 42 MIN
VHS
Color (J H G)
$98.00 purchase _ #TK107
Presents a two - part program that traces the history of ancient Egypt from its earliest settlers. Provides a close - up look at the important people, events and daily life of the civilization. Enhanced video from filmstrip.
History - World
Dist - KNOWUN **Prod** - KNOWUN

The Road to ancient Greece 42 MIN
VHS
Color (J H G)
$98.00 purchase _ #TK109
Presents a two - part program that explores the history of Greek civilization from its roots in Minoan culture to its final fall at the hands of the Romans. Covers philosophers, the rise of city - states, wars, politics, the arts, daily life, as well as the grace and beauty of Athens. Enhanced video from filmstrip.
History - World
Dist - KNOWUN **Prod** - KNOWUN

The Road to ancient Rome 42 MIN
VHS
Color (J H G)
$98.00 purchase _ #TK108
Presents a two - part program revealing that, 3,000 years ago, Rome was more than just a city, it was the center of Western Civilization. Uses colorful images and historical artwork to look at the emperors and politicians, art and architecture, philosophy and popular culture of Rome. Enhanced video from filmstrip.
History - World
Dist - KNOWUN **Prod** - KNOWUN

Road to Appomattox 30 MIN
VHS / U-matic
American story - the beginning to 1877 series
Color (C)
History - United States
Dist - DALCCD **Prod** - DALCCD

Road to Bali 91 MIN
16mm / U-matic / VHS
Color (J)
Stars Bob Hope, Bing Crosby and Dorothy Lamour in one of the six 'road' pictures in which Bob and Bing play song and dance men who flee to the South seas and become deep - sea divers for an evil prince.
Literature and Drama
Dist - FI **Prod** - PAR 1952

Road to Berlin 30 MIN
VHS / 16mm
World War II - G I Diary Series
(J H C)
$99.95 each, $995.00 series _ #21
Depicts the action and emotion that soldiers experienced during World War II, through their eyes and in their words. Narrated by Lloyd Bridges.
History - United States; History - World
Dist - AMBROS **Prod** - AMBROS 1980

The Road to Berlin 20 MIN
16mm / U-matic / VHS
Twentieth Century History Series
Color (H C A)
Presents the story of the final four years of World War II, from Germany's first real defeat at Stalingrad, through the Allied invasion of France, to the eventual invasion of Berlin and the end of the war. Ends with the revelation of the Nazi death camps.
History - United States; History - World
Dist - FI **Prod** - BBCTV 1981

Road to Berlin 30 MIN
VHS / U-matic
World War II - GI Diary Series
Color (H C A)
History - United States; History - World
Dist - TIMLIF **Prod** - TIMLIF 1980

The Road to Berlin - Pt 9 20 MIN
16mm
Twentieth Century History Series - Vol III
Color (S)
$380.00 purchase _ #548 - 9224
Illuminates the events and issues which shaped our modern world. Uses archival footage, maps, drawings, feature film segments, paintings and posters to illustrate historic events. The first thirteen programs are available separately on 16mm. Part 9 of Volume III of thirteen programs, 'The Road To Berlin,' follows the final four years of World War II, from Germany's devastating defeat at Stalingrad, through the Allied Invasion of France, to the capture of Berlin and the end of the war.
Geography - World; History - United States; History - World
Dist - FI **Prod** - BBCTV 1981

The Road to Brown 47 MIN
VHS
Color (G)
$295.00 purchase, $75.00 rental
Recalls the life of Charles Hamilton Houston, black attorney, who launched a number of precedent - setting cases which targeted segregated education in order to undermine the system of racist Jim Crow laws. Reveals that Houston's work launched the Civil Rights movement and that he died in 1950, before the landmark Brown v Board of Education decision. Produced by Wiliam A Elwood and Mykola Kulish.
Biography; Civics and Political Systems; History - United States; Sociology
Dist - CANWRL

The Road to Charlie 11 MIN
16mm / U-matic / VHS
Color (I)
LC 75-700613
Presents an animated film whose main character, Charlie, is shown growing up as the image of his parents' expectations. Deals with his attempts to conform and his realization that his life is too tied to the demands of others.
Fine Arts; Psychology
Dist - WOMBAT **Prod** - FLMAUS 1975

The Road to Disaster 30 MIN
U-matic / VHS
Japan - the Changing Tradition Series
Color (H C A)
History - World
Dist - GPN **Prod** - UMA 1978

The Road to Energy, USA 29 MIN
16mm
Color
Presents the people whose efforts help supply and conserve energy in the United States. Features Bob Hope.
Science - Natural; Social Science
Dist - MTP **Prod** - TEXACO

Road to Happiness 59 MIN
16mm / U-matic / VHS
Color (H C A)
Uses archival footage to explore the life and work of Henry Ford.
Biography; Business and Economics
Dist - FI **Prod** - WGBHTV 1978

Road to independence 14 MIN
VHS
Color (G)
$250.00 purchase, $45.00 rental
Looks at the needs of elders for transportation and independence. Shows how those needs are being met by the Chickasaw Nation and Delaware Tribe of Oklahoma.
Geography - United States; Guidance and Counseling; Health and Safety; Social Science
Dist - SHENFP **Prod** - SHENFP

The Road to independence - Droga do niepodleglosci 112 MIN
VHS
B&W (G A) (POLISH)
$29.95 purchase _ #V117
Presents two historical documentaries from 1937 about the Polish road to independence and a 1935 documentary from Marshal Pilsudski's funeral.
Fine Arts; History - World
Dist - POLART

Road to infamy - the fatal confrontation 50 MIN
VHS
Color (J H C G A)
$39.95 purchase _ #LRP002V
Presents the events and circumstances that led the Japanese to decide to go to war with America and its allies. Explores the impact of the Japanese attack on Pearl Harbor as well as the questions surrounding the

events that led two great nations to the fiercest, no-quarter fighting since the Middle Ages. Uses archival American and Japanese footage and documents to examine both sides of the story of the attack and resulting war.
History - United States; History - World; Sociology
Dist - CAMV

The Road to interdependence 30 MIN
U-matic / VHS / 16mm
History of U S foreign relations series
Color (J H)
Follows the development of U S foreign policy from 1945 up to the mid - 1970s. Describes the onset of the nuclear age and the cold war and underlines the significance of US relations with the Third World. Uses documentary footage.
Civics and Political Systems; History - United States; History - World
Dist - CORF **Prod** - USDS 1976

The Road to Liberty 65 MIN
U-matic / VHS / 16mm
Color (A)
Portrays the new society being created in El Salvador in the third of the country controlled by the Farabundo Marti National Liberation Front.
Civics and Political Systems; History - World
Dist - CNEMAG **Prod** - FIRES 1984

The Road to Mandalay 27 MIN
U-matic / VHS / 16mm
Victory at Sea Series
B&W (J H)
Views highlights of the China, Burma, India and Indian Ocean campaigns during World II.
Civics and Political Systems; History - United States; History - World
Dist - LUF **Prod** - NBCTV

The Road to Mauna Kea 22 MIN
16mm
Color (G)
_ *#106C 0180 505*
Records the construction of one of the world's largest and finest telescopes - a joint project of Canada, France, and Hawaii - on the summit of Mauna Kea, an extinct volcano on the island of Hawaii.
Geography - World; Industrial and Technical Education; Science - Physical
Dist - CFLMDC **Prod** - NFBC 1980

Road to Peace 9 MIN
16mm
B&W
LC FIE52-1937
Explains that the people of the East stand at a crossroads with one of two paths to follow, peace or war, and that the road to peace lies in the program of the United Nations.
Civics and Political Systems; Geography - World
Dist - USNAC **Prod** - USA 1951

The Road to progress 5 MIN
16mm 20 MIN
Color
A combined version of four shorter films, Road To Progress, Food Or Famine, Water Means Life and Medical Aid. Tells the story of people in desperate need of both food and the means to grow their own food. Suggests the need for water that is fit to drink, adequate medical care, education and economic development to increase family incomes that are often less than $200 a year.
Business and Economics; Health and Safety; Social Science; Sociology
Dist - CARE **Prod** - CARE

The Road to Recovery 21 MIN
16mm
Color
LC 78-700382
Shows how C and P Telephone Company repair personnel responded to a flood in West Virginia which wiped out all communications. Points out that lines were restored and a new office established within six days.
Geography - United States; History - World; Industrial and Technical Education; Social Science
Dist - CPTEL **Prod** - CPTEL 1977

The Road to Recovery 50 MIN
U-matic / VHS
Understanding Cancer Series
Color (G)
$150.00
Traces the three main forms of cancer treatment which are surgery, radiotherapy and chemotherapy. Discusses patients' rights and chances for recovery.
Health and Safety
Dist - LANDMK **Prod** - LANDMK 1985

Road to Revolution 30 MIN
U-matic / VHS
American story - the beginning to 1877 series
Color (C)
History - United States
Dist - DALCCD **Prod** - DALCCD

The Road to Ruin - Pt 1 58 MIN
VHS
Only One Earth Series
Color (S)
$129.00 purchase _ #227 - 9001
Explores and demystifies the links between environment and development and illustrates the detrimental clashes between economics and ecology in the first three hour - long programs. Part 1 of eleven tells of great civiliations built around farming systems that overused the soils and forests and then collapsed, creating deserts. Asks if we are today destroying our natural resources and recreating catastrophe.
Agriculture; Science - Natural; Social Science
Dist - FI **Prod** - BBCTV 1987

Road to Santiago 52 MIN
U-matic / VHS / 16mm
Color (H C A)
Describes the journey of three young Britons who walk the ancient symbolic four - week pilgrimage from Jaca in the Pyrenees to Santiago de Composta through the Spanish countryside. In a medieval spirit, they stay at inns or monasteries relying on the Codex Calixtinus, the pilgrim guide from the twelfth century.
Geography - World; History - World
Dist - MEDIAG **Prod** - THAMES 1973

Road to Santiago - France 30 MIN
VHS / U-matic / 16mm
Color (H C A)
LC FIA68-2890
Portrays the road through France and Spain traveled by pilgrims in the 12th century who were journeying to the shrine of St James the greater at Santiago de Compostela. Presents examples of art and architecture along the way.
Fine Arts; Geography - World; History - World
Dist - IFB **Prod** - PILGRM 1968

Road to Santiago - Spain 21 MIN
VHS / U-matic / 16mm
Color (H C A)
LC FIA68-2891
Shows the road through France and Spain traveled by pilgrims in the 17th century who were journeying to the shrine of St James the greater at Santiago de Compostela. Begins at Puente La Reina, documenting a 40-day journey through Spain.
Fine Arts; Geography - World; History - World
Dist - IFB **Prod** - PILGRM 1968

The Road to Success 15 MIN
16mm
Color
LC 76-702050
Shows methods of building wooden roads in Nova Scotia.
Geography - World; Industrial and Technical Education
Dist - NSFPA **Prod** - NSFPA 1975

The Road to Success 30 MIN
VHS / 16mm
Marketing Series
Color (C A)
$130.00, $120.00 purchase _ 15 - 02
Features marketing decisions as practiced by the Mitsubishi company.
Business and Economics
Dist - CDTEL **Prod** - COAST 1989

Road to the Stamping Ground 58 MIN
VHS
Color (S)
$39.95 purchase _ #833 - 9180
Commemorates the largest gathering of Australian tribal dancers ever held, which took place in 1980 on a remote island off the Australian coast. Reveals that one of the few outsiders allowed to witness the event was Danish choreographer Jiri Kylian who subsequently created a modern ballet inspired by what he saw. Stamping is the most important element in the dance and the program includes footage from both the Australian original and the modern adaptation.
Fine Arts; Geography - World; History - World; Physical Education and Recreation
Dist - FI **Prod** - RMART 1987

Road to the Wall 29 MIN
16mm
Big Picture Series
B&W
LC 74-705544
Documents the rise of communism from St Petersburg, Russia, in the early days of Lenin and Trotsky to Berlin and Cuba under the influence of Krushchev.
Biography; Civics and Political Systems; History - World
Dist - USNAC **Prod** - USA 1962

Road to the White House - Pt 1 29 MIN
16mm
Government story series; No 21
Color (H C)
LC 75-707194
Discusses how candidates for the office of President of the United States are created and developed. Explains the role of state primaries and describes the strategies employed by candidates at the national nominating conventions.
Civics and Political Systems
Dist - WBCPRO **Prod** - OGCW 1968

Road to the White House - Pt 2 29 MIN
16mm
Government story series; No 22
Color (H C)
LC 79-707195
Describes the campaign for the presidency from the nominating conventions to the White House. Discusses campaign strategies and the problems of the electoral college system.
Civics and Political Systems
Dist - WBCPRO **Prod** - OGCW 1968

The Road to total war 60 MIN
16mm / U-matic / VHS
War series
Color (C A)
Charts how the major social, economic and technological developments of the last two centuries have changed warfare. Covers 200 year of world military history with anecdotes from past wars.
Civics and Political Systems; Sociology
Dist - FI **Prod** - NFBC

The Road to Wannsee - eleven million sentenced to death 50 MIN
VHS
Willy Lindwer collection series
Color (G) (DUTCH W/ENGLISH SUBTITLES)
$39.95 purchase _ #655
Reveals that 11 million Jews were sentenced to death in a meeting of Nazi civil servants and SS officers, who gathered in utter secrecy for 85 minutes in a villa in the elegant Berlin suburb of Wannsee on January 20, 1942. Discusses the political rise to power of Hitler in 1933, the neutralization of his opponents, his political aims and his obsession with the elimination of Jews. Interviews Professors Yehuda Bauer of the Hebrew University of Jerusalem and Eberhard Jackal of the University of Stuttgart. Contains rare archival footage. Part of eight documentaries on the Holocaust.
History - World
Dist - ERGOM **Prod** - LINDWE

The Road to war 30 MIN
VHS
America in perspective - US history since 1877 series
Color (H C G)
$99.00 purchase _ #AIP - 15
Examines United States foreign policy leading up to the Japanese attack on Pearl Harbor, the reaction to that attack and the effects of wartime mobilization on the American people and their leaders. Part of a 26 - part series.
Civics and Political Systems; History - United States
Dist - INSTRU **Prod** - DALCCD 1991

Road to war series
Presents an eight - part series on the history of World War II using a country - by - country perspective. Looks at France, Germany, Great Britain, Italy, Japan, the USA, and the USSR.

France	50 MIN
Germany	50 MIN
Global war	50 MIN
Great Britain	50 MIN
Italy	50 MIN
Japan	50 MIN
USA	50 MIN
USSR	50 MIN

Dist - CORF **Prod** - BBCTV 1991

The Road to Wigan Pier 52 MIN
16mm / U-matic / VHS
Color (H C A)
Presents a musical documentary about the British working class based on a 1936 book by George Orwell. It opened the eyes of the world to a scene of appalling human suffering and degradation, slum housing and unemployment. Contrasts modern conditions with life in the thirties.
Geography - World; History - World; Literature and Drama; Sociology
Dist - MEDIAG **Prod** - THAMES 1973

The Road to wise money management - planning, credit, and your paycheck 30 MIN
VHS
Living on your own video series
Color (H C A)
$79.00 purchase _ #CCP0020V
Presents the first of a four - part video series dealing with the development of adult responsibilities. Focuses on money management skills, including balancing checkbooks, understanding bank statements, and getting credit. Stresses the importance of developing a sound spending plan. Includes a student guide.
Business and Economics; Home Economics
Dist - CAMV

The Road to wise money mangement - planning, credit and your first paycheck
VHS
Consumer skills series
Color (J H G)
$79.95 purchase _ #CCV580
Discusses money management, balancing checkbooks, bank statements and getting credit. Teaches the importance of financial planning. Shows how to set short and long term goals in spending. Looks at the tax bite in paychecks. Part of a series on consumer skills.
Business and Economics; Home Economics
Dist - CADESF **Prod** - CADESF

The Road to World War I 29 MIN
Videoreel / VT2
Course of Our Times I Series
Color
History - World
Dist - PBS **Prod** - WGBHTV

The Road to World War II 29 MIN
Videoreel / VT2
Course of Our Times I Series
Color
History - World
Dist - PBS **Prod** - WGBHTV

Road to yesterday 27 MIN
16mm
History of the motion picture series
B&W
Presents the 1920 Cecil B Demille film of a strange tale of tangled fortunes and twisted lives spanning two ages -- the fear - ridden days of feudal oppression in the Middle Ages and the pleasure - mad 1920s. Highlights a train - wreck, duel in a castle dungeon and mob scenes. Stars William Boyd and Joseph Schildkraut.
History - World; Literature and Drama
Dist - KILLIS **Prod** - SF 1960

The road you take is yours 19 MIN
VHS
Color (A)
$48.50 purchase
Calls on persons with disabilities to take charge of their lives and community. Presents stories about getting married; finding a new job; learning to live independently; getting married and reuniting with lost family members. Outlines how change begins with a desire for something different, and moves to a planning and action stage. Describes the role non-professional people can play in fully integrating disabled people into society.
Health and Safety
Dist - BRODIE **Prod** - BRODIE

The Roadblock 6 MIN
U-matic / VHS / 16mm
This matter of motivation series
Color (PRO)
LC 75-703853
Discusses the problem of dealing with an elder employee of the company who has lost interest in new ideas, resists changes of any kind, is not performing up to par and is a roadblock to the younger men in the department.
Business and Economics; Psychology; Sociology
Dist - DARTNL **Prod** - CTRACT 1971

Roadblocks to Communication 30 MIN
16mm
Dynamics of Leadership Series
B&W (H C A)
Distinguishes between disagreements and misunderstandings. Explores the concept of 'feedback' as one of the ways to improve communication. Explains the use of watchdog, reaction and audience panels.
English Language; Psychology; Social Science
Dist - IU **Prod** - NET 1963

The Roadbuilders 20 MIN
16mm / U-matic / VHS
Color (H C A)
Reveals the hazards of highway construction work, starting with clearing underbrush and trees, recognizing potential dangers and taking precautions while using equipment and machinery.
Health and Safety
Dist - IFB **Prod** - CSAO

Roadfilm 2 MIN
16mm
Color (G)
$8.00 rental
Entertains with animated outrageousness. Asks the question 'Why not do it in the road?' Music by The Beatles.
Fine Arts
Dist - CANCIN **Prod** - LAWDRS 1970

Roadmap for change II - the Deming legacy 26 MIN
VHS
Color (A PRO IND)
$550.00 purchase, $150.00 rental
Shows how General Motors' Pontiac Fiero plant benefitted from applying the management principles of Dr W Edwards Deming. Interviews plant management and workers. Reveals that quality can be a major focus for any plant.
Business and Economics; Guidance and Counseling; Psychology
Dist - VLEARN **Prod** - EBEC

Roadmap for change III - commitment to quality 30 MIN
VHS
Color (A PRO IND)
$595.00 purchase, $150.00 rental
Shows how Minneapolis' Zytec Corporation benefitted from applying the management principles of Dr W Edwards Deming. Interviews plant management and workers. Reveals that quality can be a major focus for any plant. Includes five pocket guides of Deming's principles.
Business and Economics; Guidance and Counseling; Psychology
Dist - VLEARN **Prod** - EBEC

Roadmap for change - Pt III
VHS
Color (G)
$595.00 purchase, $150.00 rental
Presents part III of 'Roadmap For Change' by Dr W Edwards Deming. Outlines and demonstrates his approach, his legacy and the Commitment to Quality.
Business and Economics; Guidance and Counseling; Psychology
Dist - VLEARN

Roadmap for change - Pts I and II
VHS
Color (G)
$550.00 purchase, $150.00 rental
Presents parts I and II of 'Roadmap For Change' by Dr W Edwards Deming. Outlines and demonstrates his approach, his legacy and the Commitment to Quality.
Business and Economics; Guidance and Counseling; Psychology
Dist - VLEARN

Roadmap for Change - the Deming Approach 29 MIN
16mm / U-matic / VHS
Color (C A)
Uses a case study to examine how Dr W Edwards D Deming's fourteen obligations of management are being implemented at the Pontiac Motor Division of General Motors and shows the reactions of managers and employees to the Deming approach.
Business and Economics; Industrial and Technical Education
Dist - EBEC **Prod** - EBEC 1984

The Roadmap to Control 17 MIN
U-matic / VHS
Understanding Diabetes Series
Color
Tells what diabetes is, how insufficient insulin affects various body functions, and stresses the importance of good general health habits.
Health and Safety
Dist - FAIRGH **Prod** - FAIRGH

Roadmap to Less Effort - the Flow Process Chart 15 MIN
16mm
B&W
LC 74-705545
Illustrates the use, preparation and analysis of the flow process chart, a device for the solution of work efficiency problems. Shows that an analysis of the chart enables actions to be eliminated, combined, changed or reassigned.
Business and Economics
Dist - USNAC **Prod** - USA 1973

Roadrunner - Clown of the Desert 25 MIN
VHS / 16mm
Color (S)
$450.00, $79.00 purchase _ #825 - 9301
Details the unusual habits of the roadrunner. Reveals that the birds cannot fly but can zip around the desert at up to 30 miles per hour in pursuit of mice, insects and reptiles.
Geography - United States; Science - Natural
Dist - FI **Prod** - BBCTV 1987

Roadrunner - clown of the desert - Punk puffins and hard rock 55 MIN
VHS
BBC wildlife specials series
Color (G)
$24.95 purchase _ #ROA02
Takes a look at the real roadrunner, which cannot fly but can zip around the desert at 30 miles per hour in pursuit of mice, insects and reptiles in Roadrunner - Clown of the Desert. Ventures to the island of St Lararia off the coast of Alaska to view the birds which summer there in Punk Puffins and Hard Rock.
Science - Natural
Dist - HOMVIS **Prod** - BBCTV 1990

Roadrunner conquers rattlesnake 10 MIN
16mm / U-matic / VHS
B&W (I J H)
An excerpt from 'Adventures of Chico' that identifies poisonous snakes and their movements. Shows scenes of a fight between a roadrunner and a rattlesnake.
Science - Natural
Dist - IFB **Prod** - IFB 1963

Roads Across the Bay 24 MIN
16mm
B&W (I J)
Traces the history behind the building of the great bridges of San Francisco Bay, showing the need for bridges, proposals made over the years and the actual construction of the Bay Bridge.
Geography - United States; Industrial and Technical Education; Social Science
Dist - MLA **Prod** - ABCTV 1963

Roads and railroads 15 MIN
U-matic / VHS
America past series
(J H)
$125.00 purchase
Considers changes in land transportation and how they affected regional and national development.
History - United States; Social Science
Dist - AITECH **Prod** - KRMATV 1987

Roads from the Ghetto - 1789 to 1917 - Pt 6 60 MIN
VHS / 16mm
Heritage - Civilization and the Jews Series
Color (J)
$800.00, $49.00 purchase _ #405 - 9126
Explores more than 3000 years of the Jewish experience. Uses all available resources to weave a tapestry of the Jewish history and people. Hosted by Abba Eban, Israel's former ambassador to the UN and the US. Part 6 begins with the French and Industrial Revolutions, covers the struggle for Jewish emancipation, and witnesses the rise of modern anti - Semitism and the birth of Zionism.
History - World; Psychology; Religion and Philosophy; Sociology
Dist - FI **Prod** - WNETTV 1984

Roads home - the life and times of A B 'Happy' Chandler 30 MIN
VHS
Color (G)
$250.00 purchase, $50.00 rental
Portrays the life and career of Chandler as a consummate Southern politician during the 'stump speaking' era of American politics. Documents his rise from rural poverty to a long career in public office, including his candidacy as the Democratic nominee for President. Directed by Robby Henson.
Fine Arts; History - United States
Dist - CNEMAG

The Roads less taken 26 MIN
VHS / U-matic
Color (J H G)
$260.00, $310.00 purchase, $60.00 rental
Documents the great migrations in the settling of the American West - the Oregon Trail. Travels back to the mid - 1840s and focuses on the exploration of less traveled routes and the impact on Native American tribes along the way. Produced by OPBS - Dorothy Velasco.
History - United States; Social Science
Dist - NDIM

Roads, Roads, Roads 27 MIN
16mm
Color (H C A)
Provides information on transport policy and strategy in the Federal Republic of Germany, the funding of road construction and maintenance, and the growing understanding of the impact this is having on the environment.
Geography - World; History - World; Social Science
Dist - WSTGLC **Prod** - WSTGLC

Roads without wheels 60 MIN
VHS
Man on the rim - the peopling of the Pacific series
Color (H C)
$295.00 purchase
Shows how South American Indians, isolated from the rest of the world, produced a remarkable range of food plants later introduced to the rest of the world. Reveals that they invented the wheel but used it only in toys, never for transport, and that they exhibited dazzling metalwork in gold, silver and platinum. Part of an 11 - part series on the people of the Pacific rim.
History - World; Social Science; Sociology
Dist - LANDMK **Prod** - LANDMK 1989

Roald Amundsen 52 MIN
U-matic / 16mm / VHS
Ten who Dared Series
Color
LC 77-701580
A shortened version of the 1976 film Roald Amundsen. Dramatizes Amundsen's victory over England's Captain Robert Smith in their 1911 race to the South Pole, the last terrestrial frontier.
Biography; Geography - World; History - World
Dist - TIMLIF **Prod** - BBCTV 1976

Roald Amundsen - South Pole, 1911 - Pt 1 26 MIN
16mm
Ten who Dared Series
Color (I A)
Special classroom version of the film and videorecording Roald Amundsen - South Pole, 1911.
Geography - World; History - World
Dist - TIMLIF **Prod** - BBCTV 1977

Roald Amundsen - South Pole, 1911 - Pt 2 26 MIN
16mm
Ten who Dared Series
Color (I A)
Special classroom version of the film and videorecording Roald Amundsen - South Pole, 1911.
Geography - World; History - World
Dist - TIMLIF **Prod** - BBCTV 1977

Roald Hoffmann
VHS / U-matic
Eminent Chemists - the Interviews Series
Color
Reflects on some of the key accomplishments of Dr Roald Hoffmann, including his work on quantum mechanical studies of chemical reactivity.
Science; Science - Physical
Dist - AMCHEM **Prod** - AMCHEM 1984

Roald Hoffmann, Lecture 1 - the Isolobal Analogy
VHS / U-matic
Eminent Chemists - the Lectures Series
Color
Discusses the bridge between inorganic and organic chemistry by Dr Roald Hoffmann.
Science; Science - Physical
Dist - AMCHEM **Prod** - AMCHEM

Roald Hoffmann, Lecture 2 - Conservation of Orbital Symmetry
U-matic / VHS
Eminent Chemists - the Lectures Series
Color
Features Dr Roald Hoffman in a personal, historical perspective on the development of conservation of orbital symmetry concept and its consequences.
Science; Science - Physical
Dist - AMCHEM **Prod** - AMCHEM

Roamin' Holiday 11 MIN
16mm
B&W
Tells how Spanky and the gang leave home in order to avoid babysitting chores. A Little Rascals film.
Fine Arts
Dist - RMIBHF **Prod** - UNKNWN 1937

Roanaok series
Roanoak series 180 MIN
Dist - NAMPBC

Roanoak 180 MIN
U-matic / VHS
Color (G)
$150.00, $225.00 purchase _ #ROAN - 000
Focuses on the English settlement of Roanoak Island from 1584 to 1590, when all the members of the settlement mysteriously disappeared. Presents both English and Indian views of the settlement, focusing particularly on the lives of settlement governor John White and Indian hunter Wanchese. Stars Victor Garber and Joe Runningfox. Presented in three 60 - minute episodes.
History - United States; History - World; Social Science
Dist - PBS **Prod** - SCETVM 1986

Roanoak series 180 MIN
VHS / U-matic
Roanaok series
Color (G)
$150.00 purchase
Delves into events that took place between 1584 and 1590 on Roanoak Island on the outer banks of the Carolinas, where an entire English settlement disappeared without a trace in 1590. Tells the story of the first prolonged meetings between the English and Indians from both points of view. Part 1 shows the warriors viewing an Elizabethan ship and greeting the colonists with generosity and hospitality. Part 2 views the English settlement gaining strength although food is scarce and the Indians have fallen ill through a bacterial disease from the colonists, resulting in a brutal confrontation. In part 3 John White induces planters to join him in Virginia while the Indians seek revenge after a surprise attack. Sold as a three - part series, 60 minutes each.
History - United States; Social Science
Dist - NAMPBC **Prod** - SCETV 1986

The Roar from within 7 MIN
16mm
B&W (G)
$24.00 rental
Begins with time - motion studies which turn into an abstract depiction of gore and violence. Features music by Caleb Sampson.
Fine Arts
Dist - CANCIN **Prod** - JOHNF 1982

Roar of Power 15 MIN
16mm
Color
Presents the how and why of tractor pulling contests.
Agriculture
Dist - IDEALF **Prod** - ALLISC

The Roar of the gods 20 MIN
16mm
Color (SPANISH)
LC 76-702205
Examines various pre - Columbian stone monoliths found in the area of San Agustin, Colombia and explains their anthropological meaning.
Geography - World; History - World; Sociology
Dist - MOMALA **Prod** - OOAS 1976
MOMALA

The Roaring '20s 15 MIN
VHS
Witness to History Series
Color (J H)
$49.00 purchase _ #60156
Documents the Suffrage Movement and the problems of Prohibition. Looks at the conflict over Darwin's Theory of Evolution, the rise of the Ku Klux Klan, and the advent of automation.
Civics and Political Systems; History - United States
Dist - GA **Prod** - GA 1989

The Roaring 20s - everybody ought to be rich 20 MIN
VHS
Color (I J H)
$99.00 purchase _ #08519 - 026
Presents a fast - paced, entertaining program that captures the exciting sights and sounds of the turbulent decade. Includes teacher's guide and library kit.
History - United States
Dist - INSTRU
GA

Roast turkey 32 MIN
VHS
Cookbook videos series
Color (G)
$19.95 purchase _ #ALW106
Shows how to prepare roast turkey in short, easy - to - learn segments. Lists each ingredient as it is added in subtitles and visually reinforces spoken instructions. Gives recipe background and nutritional facts. Part of the Cookbook Videos series.
Home Economics; Social Science
Dist - CADESF **Prod** - CADESF

Roast turkey 32 MIN
VHS
Cookbook videos series; Vol 4
Color (G)
$19.95 purchase
Shows how to roast a turkey overnight. Demonstrates making turkey gravy and carving. Includes printed abstract of recipes. Part of a series.
Home Economics; Social Science
Dist - ALWHIT **Prod** - ALWHIT

Roast Turkey with 3 Different Stuffings - Lesson 15 30 MIN
VHS
International Cooking School with Chef Rene Series
Color (G)
$69.00 purchase
Presents classic methods of cooking that stress essential flavor. Introduces newer, lighter foods. Lesson 15 shows how to roast turkey and prepare three different stuffings.
Fine Arts; Home Economics; Psychology; Social Science; Sociology
Dist - LUF **Prod** - LUF

Roasting - Lesson 11 10 MIN
8mm cartridge / 16mm
Modern basics of classical cooking series
Color (A)
#MB11
Explains marinating, carving, roasting principles and the degrees of roasting. Demonstrates the effectiveness of heat on meat choice, sauces and gravies, plus the need for a meat thermometer. Part of a series developed in cooperation with the Swiss Association of Restauranteurs and Hoteliers to train food service employees. Includes five instructor's handbooks, a textbook by Eugene Pauli, 20 sets of student tests and 20 sets of student information sheets.
Home Economics; Industrial and Technical Education
Dist - CONPRO **Prod** - CONPRO

The Robber's Guide 5 MIN
U-matic / VHS
Write on, Set 1 Series
Color (J H)
Consists of a lesson on correlative conjunctions.
English Language
Dist - CTI **Prod** - CTI

Robbers, Rooftops and Witches 46 MIN
16mm / U-matic / VHS
LCA Short Story Library Series
Color (I J H)
LC 82-700625
Discusses various aspects of story telling and writing using excerpts from The Chaparral Prince by O Henry, Antaeus by Borden Deal and The Invisible Boy by Ray Bradbury. Includes interviews with an actor portraying writer Washington Irving.
English Language; Literature and Drama
Dist - LCOA **Prod** - HGATE 1982

Robbery and fraud preparedness series
Bank security - kidnap - extortion call - unit 4 15 MIN
Extortion - Unit 3 11 MIN
Importance of Confidentiality - Unit 1 21 MIN
Robbery - Teller and Management Procedures - Unit 2 32 MIN
You Catch a Thief - Unit 5 13 MIN
Dist - UTM

The Robbery of the Diamond Dog Diner - 48
VHS
Reading rainbow series
Color; CC (K P)
$39.95 purchase
Asks if a talkative chicken named Gloria Feather can outwit a couple of Diamond Robber Mutts. Unfolds the story by Eileen Christelow, narrated by Peter Falk. Follows LeVar behind the grill at Rosie's diner and where he gets a quick lesson on short - order cooking. Also shows how pasta is made. Part of a series offering a multicultural approach to generating reading enthusiasm with cross - curricular applications, hosted by LeVar Burton.
English Language; Home Economics; Literature and Drama
Dist - GPN **Prod** - LNMDP

Robbery - Teller and Management Procedures - Unit 2 32 MIN
VHS / 16mm
Robbery and Fraud Preparedness Series
Color (PRO)
$395.00 purchase, $225.00 rental $35.00 preview
Teaches bank staff how to be prepared for robbery and fraud. Shows both what tellers and managers should do during and after an armed robbery. Includes support materials.
Business and Economics; Psychology; Sociology
Dist - UTM **Prod** - UTM

The Robbery transaction 19 MIN
VHS
Color (A) (JAPANESE)
$525.00 purchase
Recreates bank holdups to emphasize ten principles of employee conduct both during and following a holdup.
Business and Economics; Civics and Political Systems
Dist - COMFLM **Prod** - COMFLM

Robbie - a Teenage Quadriplegic 30 MIN
VHS / U-matic
Color
Presents the story of a 17 - year - old quadriplegic. Shares his intimate thoughts, wishes, struggles and hopes. Provides a courageous story of a grave disability.
Health and Safety; Psychology; Science - Natural
Dist - AJN **Prod** - MONTV

The Robe 133 MIN
BETA
Color
Tells the story of a Greek slave and a Roman officer who are affected by Christianity. Stars Richard Burton, Jean Simmons and Victor Mature.
Fine Arts
Dist - RMIBHF **Prod** - UNKNWN 1953

Robert A Taft 51 MIN
16mm
Profiles in courage series
B&W
Tells the story of Senator Robert Taft, who ruined his presidential chances at the time of the Nuremberg Trials because he spoke against trying a man under an ex post facto statute. Based on the book 'Profiles in Courage' by John F Kennedy. Stars Lee Tracy.
Biography; History - World
Dist - SSSSV **Prod** - SAUDEK 1966

Robert A Taft - Mr Republican 15 MIN
VHS / BETA
B&W
Presents Robert A Taft, a leader of the Republican party.
Biography
Dist - STAR **Prod** - STAR

Robert A Taft - Pt 1 25 MIN
16mm
Profiles in courage series
B&W (P)
Tells the story of Senator Taft, who ruined his presidential chances at the time of the Nuremberg Trials, because he spoke against trying a man under an ex post facto statute. Considers justice and genocide.
Dist - SSSSV **Prod** - SAUDEK 1966

Robert A Taft - Pt 2 25 MIN
16mm
Profiles in courage series
B&W (P)
Tells the story of Senator Taft, who ruined his presidential chances at the time of the Nuremberg Trials, because he spoke against trying a man under an ex post facto statute. Considers justice and genocide.
Dist - SSSSV **Prod** - SAUDEK 1966

Robert and Georgette Mosbacher - USA 47 MIN
VHS
Tycoons series
Color (J H G)
$225.00 purchase
Tells how Robert, son of a well - to - do eastern family, developed his own oil business and later served as Secretary of Commerce of the US. Explains how Georgette began her own beauty products company and became a success in her own right.
Business and Economics
Dist - LANDMK

Robert Bateman - Artist and naturalist 57 MIN
VHS
Color (H C A)
$39.95
Profiles wildlife artist Robert Bateman. Shows the artist in his studio and on location in the United States, Canada and Africa.
Fine Arts
Dist - ARTSAM

Robert Bellah 30 MIN
VHS
World of ideas with Bill Moyers - Season I - series
Color (G)
$39.95 purchase _ #BMWI - 112
Interviews sociologist Robert Bellah. Features Bellah's views that values are important not just to the individual, but to society as well. Traces the importance of values through technology, politics, the media and social communities. Hosted by Bill Moyers.
Sociology
Dist - PBS

Robert Bly 29 MIN
U-matic
Poets Talking Series
Color
Literature and Drama
Dist - UMITV **Prod** - UMITV 1975

Robert Bly - 3 - 20 - 84 100 MIN
VHS / Cassette
Poetry Center reading series
Color (G)
$15.00 purchase, rental _ #583 - 493
Features the writer reading from his works including translations of Rumi, Basho, and Antonio Machado at the Poetry Center, San Francisco State University. Contains Bly's comments on Machado, Vietnam, Central America, politics in poetry, the ERA, his book in progress The Wild Man, men's and women's groups, and Spanish vs French surrealism.
Literature and Drama
Dist - POETRY **Prod** - POETRY 1984

Robert Breer - Five and Dime Animator 60 MIN
VHS / 16mm
Color (H A)
$550.00 purchase, $90.00 rental
Looks at the animated films of Robert Breer, discusses many of his innovative techniques.
Fine Arts
Dist - AFA

Robert Browning - His Life and Poetry 21 MIN
U-matic / VHS / 16mm
Color (H C A)
LC 73-702515
Shows things from which Robert Browning drew his inspiration by using paintings, early photographs and scenes of unchanged parts of London and Italy. Illustrates the events of his life and selections from his poetry as read by costumed actors.
Literature and Drama
Dist - IFB **Prod** - IFB 1972

Robert Burns 60 MIN
VHS
Great britons
Color; PAL (C H)
PdS99 purchase
Presents the life of Robert Burns. Describes his poetry and the politically split environment in which he wrote. Fourth in the six - part series Great Britons, which examines the lives of important figures in British culture.
History - World; Literature and Drama
Dist - BBCENE

Robert Burns Cigars 1 MIN
U-matic / VHS
Color
Shows a classic television commercial where memories make a man smoke Burns cigars.
Business and Economics; Psychology; Sociology
Dist - BROOKC **Prod** - BROOKC

Robert Burns - Love and Liberty 38 MIN
U-matic / VHS
Color (C)
$249.00, $149.00 purchase _ #AD - 932
Features Romantic poet Robert Burns who freely used dialect and country subjects. Includes readings of his poetry and performance of his songs. Produced by Scottish Television.
Fine Arts; History - World; Literature and Drama
Dist - FOTH **Prod** - FOTH

Robert Burns - The Ploughman poet 26 MIN
VHS / U-matic
Stamp of greatness series
Color (H C G)
$280.00, $330.00 purchase, $50.00 rental
Pays tribute to the Scottish poet, whose verses are known in nearly every language on Earth, author of some of the finest love poems ever written and whose egalitarian ideals were ahead of his time.
Fine Arts; History - World; Literature and Drama
Dist - NDIM **Prod** - TYNT 1990

Robert Clary - A5174, a Memoir of Liberation 57 MIN
VHS
Color
Provides an autobiographical account of actor Robert Clary's capture, imprisonment and liberation from a German concentration camp.
Biography; Literature and Drama
Dist - HRC **Prod** - OHC

Robert Coles - Teacher 57 MIN
VHS
Color (G)
$390.00 purchase, $75.00 rental
Introduces Robert Coles, Pulitzer Prize winner, who has been listening to children all around the world for over 30 years, recording and absorbing their attitudes toward race relations, poverty, isolation and morality. Records this extraordinary teacher at work, sharing with a class what he has learned from life, such as his encounter with Ruby, the six - year - old black girl who broke the race barrier at an all white New Orleans school in the 1960s. Explains that his course serves not to fulfill a graduation requirement, but is a guide to moral living long after the coursework is forgotten. Produced by Social Media Productions.
Education; Fine Arts; Sociology
Dist - FIRS

Robert Creeley - 11 - 15 - 73 28 MIN
VHS / Cassette
Poetry Center reading series
B&W (G)
$15.00, $45.00 purchase, $15.00 rental _ #22 - 18
Features the poet reading from his works at the Poetry Center, San Francisco State University, with an introduction by Kathleen Fraser.
Literature and Drama
Dist - POETRY

Robert Creeley - 11 - 1 - 78
VHS / Cassette
Poetry Center reading series
Color (G)
$15.00, $45.00 purchase, $15.00 rental _ #370 - 309
Features the experimental poet at the Charles Olson Conference at the University of Iowa. Includes readings, talks and lectures. Co - readers are George Butterick, Edward Dorn, Robert Duncan and Paul Sherman.
Literature and Drama
Dist - POETRY **Prod** - POETRY 1978

Robert Creeley - 5 - 9 - 78 45 MIN
VHS / Cassette
Poetry Center reading series
Color (G)
$15.00, $45.00 purchase, $15.00 rental _ #285 - 239
Features the poet reading from his works at the Poetry Center, San Francisco State University.
Literature and Drama
Dist - POETRY

Robert Creeley - 4 - 13 - 90 58 MIN
VHS / Cassette
Lannan Literary series
Color (G)
$15.00, $19.95 purchase, $15.00 rental _ #960
Features the poet reading from his Collected Poems, 1945 - 1974; Mirrors; Windows; and from works in progress. Includes an interview by Lewis MacAdams. Part of a series of literary videotapes presenting major poets and writers from around the globe reading and talking about their work; readings were sponsored by The Lannan Foundation of Los Angeles, a private contemporary arts organization.
Guidance and Counseling; Literature and Drama
Dist - POETRY **Prod** - METEZT 1990

Robert Creeley - 9 - 24 - 83 34 MIN
VHS / Cassette
Poetry Center reading series
Color (G)
$15.00, $45.00 purchase, $15.00 rental _ #550 - 467
Features the poet reading from his works at the Poetry Center, San Francisco State University.
Literature and Drama
Dist - POETRY

Robert Creeley - 7 - 15 - 65 45 MIN
VHS / Cassette
NET Outtake series
B&W (G)
$15.00, $125.00 purchase, $15.00 rental _ #213 - 169AB
Features an interview with poet Robert Creeley and writer Bobbie Louise Hawkins at their home near Placitas, New Mexico, and readings from his works at the University of California Poetry Conference in Berkeley. Includes an extensive discussion. Part of a series of films composed of outtakes from the series USA - Poetry, which was produced in 1965 - 66 for National Educational Television, using all retrievable footage to provide rare glimpses of the poets in their own settings. Interviewed by Richard O Moore.
Guidance and Counseling; Literature and Drama
Dist - POETRY **Prod** - KQEDTV 1965

Robert Creeley - 3 - 27 - 83 20 MIN
VHS / Cassette
Poetry Center reading series
Color (G)
$15.00, $45.00 purchase, $15.00 rental _ #913 - 464
Features the poet reading from his works at the Poetry Center, San Francisco State University.
Literature and Drama
Dist - POETRY

Robert Duncan - 11 - 1 - 78
VHS / Cassette
Poetry Center reading series
Color (G)

$15.00, $45.00 purchase, $15.00 rental _ #371 - 309
Features the poet at the Charles Olson Conference at the University of Iowa. Includes readings, talks and lectures. Co - readers are George Butterick, Edward Dorn, Robert Creeley and Paul Sherman.
Literature and Drama
Dist - POETRY **Prod** - POETRY 1978

Robert Duncan - 11 - 2 - 65 42 MIN
VHS / Cassette
NET Outtake series
B&W (G)
$15.00, $125.00 purchase, $15.00 rental _ #148 - 115
Features poet Robert Duncan at his home in San Francisco reading sections from his notebook, including The Architecture - Passages 9, and Passages 26. Discusses his process of phrasing and composing, and what he has learned from the Tarot about the human mind's combining of images. Part of a series of films composed of outtakes from the series USA - Poetry, which was produced in 1965 - 66 for National Educational Television, using all retrievable footage to provide rare glimpses of the poets in their own settings. Interviewed by John Wieners.
Guidance and Counseling; Literature and Drama
Dist - POETRY **Prod** - KQEDTV 1965

Robert Duncan - 5 - 17 - 74 120 MIN
VHS / Cassette
Poetry Center reading series
Color (G)
$15.00, $45.00 purchase, $15.00 rental _ #50 - 36A
Presents Poets of the Forties, nine writers in one event, distributed as one tape. Features Duncan reading his works at the Poetry Center, San Francisco State University. Includes James Broughton, William Everson, Madeline Gleason, Robert Horan, Janet Lewis, Richard Moore, Rosalie Moore and Tom Parkinson.
Literature and Drama
Dist - POETRY

Robert Duncan - 5 - 9 - 78 42 MIN
VHS / Cassette
Poetry Center reading series
Color (G)
$15.00, $45.00 purchase, $15.00 rental _ #286 - 240
Features Duncan reading his works, including selections from Dante Etudes, at the Poetry Center, San Francisco State University, with an introduction by Lewis MacAdams.
Literature and Drama
Dist - POETRY

Robert Duncan - 9 - 22 - 84 109 MIN
VHS / Cassette
Poetry Center reading series
Color (G)
$15.00, $45.00 purchase, $15.00 rental _ #597 - 597
Features Duncan reading his works, including selections from Groundwork; In The Dark; and Caeser's Gate, at the Poetry Center, San Francisco State University.
Literature and Drama
Dist - POETRY

Robert Duncan - 10 - 4 - 87 120 MIN
VHS / Cassette
Poetry Center reading series
Color (G)
#925 - 629
Features the writer reading from his works at the Ruth Witt - Diamant Memorial Reading at the Poetry Center, San Francisco State University. Also includes readings by James Broughton, Rosalie Moore, Mark Linenthal, Shirley Taylor, Christy Taylor, Justine Fixel, Lawrence Fixel, Michael McClure, Gail Layton, and Stephen Witt - Diamant. Introduction by Frances Phillips. Slides of Ruth Witt - Diamant courtesy of Caryl Mezey. Available for listening purposes only at the Center; not for sale or rent.
Literature and Drama
Dist - POETRY **Prod** - POETRY 1987

Robert Duncan - 2 - 22 - 73 42 MIN
VHS / Cassette
Poetry Center reading series
B&W (G)
$15.00, $45.00 purchase, $15.00 rental _ #1 - 1
Features the writer reading from his works at the Poetry Center, San Francisco State University.
Literature and Drama
Dist - POETRY

Robert E Lee - Stratford Hall 24 MIN
VHS
Color (H C T A)
$69.95 purchase _ #S01331
Portrays the life and home of Confederate General Robert E Lee. Tours his home, Stratford Hall.
Biography; Civics and Political Systems; History - United States
Dist - UILL

Robert Farber 60 MIN
U-matic / VHS
Famous Photographer Series
Color
Shows top New York photographer, Robert Farber, in behind - the - scenes view of fashion and fine art photography.
Industrial and Technical Education
Dist - SHERVP **Prod** - SHERVP

Robert Frost 60 MIN
VHS / 16mm
Voices and Visions Series
Color (H)
$8.00 rental _ #60733
Profiles Robert Frost (1874 - 1963), focusing on the role of nature in his poetry. Features Frost reading 'After Apple - Picking' and includes clips of interviews with him. Seamus Heaney, Richard Wilbur, Joseph Bradsky, and others read Frost's poetry and discuss his life and work.
Literature and Drama
Dist - PSU

Robert Frost 10 MIN
U-matic / VHS / 16mm
Poetry by Americans series
Color (I J H)
LC 73-701588
Presents a biography of Robert Frost, followed by a reading of his poem 'Mending Wall,' by Leonard Nimoy.
Biography; Literature and Drama
Dist - AIMS **Prod** - EVANSA 1972

Robert Frost - a First Acquaintance 16 MIN
U-matic / VHS / 16mm
Color (I J H)
LC 74-701528
Explores American poet Robert Frost's relationship with children. Shows the poet's daughter, Lesley Frost, at the Frost farm in New Hampshire, where neighboring children interpret the action of Frost's poems at the farm spot which inspired the poet to write them.
Biography; Literature and Drama; Sociology
Dist - FOTH **Prod** - MANTLH 1974

Robert Frost - Part 5 60 MIN
VHS / U-matic
Voices and visions series
Color (G)
$45.00, $29.95 purchase
Contrasts the image of poet Robert Frost as elder statesman with his vigorous, poetic exploration of the darker forces of nature. Part of a thirteen - part series on the lives and works of modern American poets.
Biography; History - United States; Literature and Drama
Dist - ANNCPB **Prod** - NYCVH 1988

Robert Frost's New England 22 MIN
16mm / U-matic / VHS
Color (J)
LC 76-700535
Presents a selection of Frost's poetry relating to New England and its seasons. Describes how he uses the rocks, leaves and snows of Vermont as metaphors to lead the reader into deeper reaches of the mind.
Literature and Drama
Dist - CF **Prod** - JONESD 1976

Robert Fulford - an osteopathic alternative 21 MIN
VHS
Color (A PRO)
$175.00 purchase, $50.00 rental
Surveys osteopathic treatment techniques. Reveals that cranial manipulation, rather than drugs and diagnostic tests, is the main focus of osteopathy. Suggests that osteopathy has the advantages of cost - effectiveness and no side effects. Hosted by osteopathic physician Robert Fulford.
Health and Safety
Dist - UARIZ **Prod** - UARIZ

Robert Fulton 15 MIN
VHS / U-matic
Stories of America Series
Color (P)
Illustrates how Robert Fulton developed his early interest in painting and boats.
History - United States; Social Science
Dist - AITECH **Prod** - OHSDE 1976

Robert Gluck - 11 - 14 - 85 80 MIN
VHS / Cassette
Poetry Center reading series
Color (G)
$15.00, $45.00 purchase, $15.00 rental _ #674 - 555
Features the writer performing from Reader, F O'H and Ovid, and an essay, HTLV3, in a reading to benefit the San Francisco AIDS Foundation at the Poetry Center, San Francisco State University.
Health and Safety; Literature and Drama
Dist - POETRY **Prod** - POETRY 1985

Robert Gluck - 11 - 8 - 84 36 MIN
VHS / Cassette
Poetry Center reading series
Color (G)
$15.00, $45.00 purchase, $15.00 rental _ #604 - 512
Features the writer at the Poetry Center of San Francisco State University, reading selections from Learning To Write - later retitled Reader - and from Jack The Modernist, with an introduction by Jim Hartz.
Literature and Drama
Dist - POETRY **Prod** - POETRY 1984

Robert Gluck - 4 - 3 - 75 37 MIN
VHS / Cassette
Poetry Center reading series
Color (G)
$15.00, $45.00 purchase, $15.00 rental _ #110 - 84
Features the writer reading from his works at the Poetry Center, San Francisco State University.
Literature and Drama
Dist - POETRY **Prod** - POETRY 1975

Robert Grenier - 11 - 27 - 88 30 MIN
VHS / Cassette
Poetry Center reading series
Color (G)
#914
Features the writer at the Poetry Center at San Francisco State University, reading selections from Sentences. Available for listening purposes only at the Center; not for sale or rent.
Literature and Drama
Dist - POETRY **Prod** - POETRY 1988

Robert Grenier - 2 - 21 - 79 53 MIN
VHS / Cassette
Poetry Center reading series
Color (G)
$15.00, $45.00 purchase, $15.00 rental _ #326 - 271
Features the writer reading his works at the Poetry Center, San Francisco State University.
Literature and Drama
Dist - POETRY **Prod** - POETRY 1979

Robert Grenier - 2 - 21 - 85 60 MIN
VHS / Cassette
Poetry Center reading series
Color (G)
$15.00, $45.00 purchase, $15.00 rental _ #618 - 523
Features the writer reading selections from Phantom Anthems and A Day At The Beach at the Poetry Center, San Francisco State University.
Literature and Drama
Dist - POETRY **Prod** - POETRY 1985

Robert Hall Commercial 1 MIN
U-matic / VHS
Color
Shows a classic television commercial with blackbirds singing.
Business and Economics; Psychology; Sociology
Dist - BROOKC **Prod** - BROOKC

Robert Having His Nipple Pierced 33 MIN
16mm
Color (C)
$1120.00
Experimental film by Sandy Daley.
Fine Arts
Dist - AFA **Prod** - AFA 1970

Robert Hayden 29 MIN
U-matic
Poets Talking Series
Color
Literature and Drama
Dist - UMITV **Prod** - UMITV 1975

Robert Kennedy
VHS
Speeches collection series
Color (J H C G)
$29.95 purchase _ #MH1689V
Offers a collection of speeches by Robert Kennedy. Part of a ten - part series on the addresses of the 20th - century's most powerful speakers. Witnesses the signing of peace treaties, the inciting of world wars, the making of history with words.
Biography; English Language; History - United States
Dist - CAMV

Robert Koch 115 MIN
16mm
B&W (GERMAN)
Illustrates the life - long struggle of a small - town general practitioner for acknowledgement of his scientific achievements in discovering the tuberculosis bacillus.
Foreign Language; Health and Safety; Science
Dist - WSTGLC **Prod** - WSTGLC 1939

Robert Krampf's World Of Science Series
Electricity
Minerals
Science with a Microscope
Dist - BEARDW

Robert Leeson 46 MIN
VHS
Color (H C G)
$79.00 purchase
Features the writer discussing with Mary Cadogan his view of writing for children and the relationship of reading to television. Looks at his socialist perspective and its effect on his writing. Talks about his books Grange Hill and Reading and Righting - The Past, Present and Future in Fiction for the Young.
Literature and Drama
Dist - ROLAND **Prod** - INCART

Robert Louis Stevenson
VHS / 35mm strip
Meet the Classic Authors Series
Color (I)
$39.95, $28.00 purchase
Portrays Robert Louis Stevenson. Part of a series on authors.
English Language; Literature and Drama
Dist - PELLER

Robert Lowell 60 MIN
VHS / 16mm
Voices and Visions Series
Color (H)
$8.00 rental _ #60734
Examines the life and poems of Robert Lowell (1917 - 1977), from his birth to his antiwar activism and his bouts of mental illness. Analyzes the roots of his poetry in both Puritan and American romantic traditions, and traces the development of his poetry from the dense formalism of his early work to the open structures and autobiographical subjects of his later work.
Literature and Drama
Dist - PSU

Robert Lowell - Part 7 60 MIN
U-matic / VHS
Voices and visions series
Color (G)
$45.00, $29.95 purchase
Encompasses the political passion of the poetry of Robert Lowell. Presents Lowell reading from his works and discussion of his poetic development and style by Elizabeth Harwick, Robert Hass and others. Part of a thirteen - part series on the lives and works of modern American poets.
Biography; History - United States; Literature and Drama
Dist - ANNCPB **Prod** - NYCVH 1988

Robert MacGregor, PhD, Mary MacGregor , MPsych - Single Parent Struggle 60 MIN
U-matic / VHS
Perceptions, Pt a - Interventions in Family Therapy Series Vol IV, 'Pt A7
Color (PRO)
Demonstrates the multiple impact approach to therapy for a single parent family. Shows the effect of a series of interviews with the whole family and with parent and children separately.
Guidance and Counseling; Psychology; Sociology
Dist - BOSFAM **Prod** - BOSFAM

Robert MacGregor, PhD, Mary MacGregor , 1 MPsych - Private Practice, Chicago 60 MIN
VHS / U-matic
Perceptions, Pt B - Dialogues with Family Therapists Series Vol IV, 'Pt B7
Color (PRO)
Stimulates discussion about working couples and the Multiple Impact Therapy espoused by the MacGregors.
Guidance and Counseling; Psychology; Sociology
Dist - BOSFAM **Prod** - BOSFAM

Robert Mapplethorpe 55 MIN
VHS
Arena series
Color (A)
PdS99 purchase
Charts Mapplethorpe's career from art student to leading figure in the art world. Examines his role in helping to formulate a sense of gay identity in New York City through his photography. Shows how his work has been instrumental in restoring the male nude to mainstream art.
Fine Arts; Industrial and Technical Education
Dist - BBCENE

Robert Maxwell 30 MIN
VHS
Adam Smith's money world series
Color (H C A)
$79.95 purchase
Features host Jerry Goodman, also known as 'Adam Smith,' and his guest, the international publisher Robert Maxwell, as they together look at the world of global finance.
Business and Economics
Dist - PBS **Prod** - WNETTV

Robert Mc Closkey 18 MIN
U-matic / VHS / 16mm
Color; B&W (C A)
LC FIA65-1552
Robert Mc Closkey, who draws picture books, tells how he works, showing not only his craftsmanship but also how he gets his inspiration.
Fine Arts; Literature and Drama
Dist - WWS **Prod** - WWS 1965

The Robert McCloskey Library 58 MIN
VHS
Color (G)
$14.95 purchase
Offers a collection of stories by Maine author Robert McCloskey. Includes Lentil, Make Way for Ducklings, Blueberries for Sal, Time of Wonder, Burt Dow - Deep Water Man and a short documentary on McCloskey.
Fine Arts; History - United States; Literature and Drama
Dist - NEFILM

The Robert McCloskey library 35 MIN
VHS
Children's circle collection series
Color (K P I)
$14.95 purchase _ #WK1180
Offers a collection of stories by children's author Robert McCloskey. Includes Lentil; Make Way for Ducklings; Time of Wonder; Blueberries for Sal; Burt Dow - Deepwater Man; and a conversation with McCloskey.
Fine Arts; Literature and Drama
Dist - KNOWUN

Robert Mondavi - Robert Mondavi Winery, USA 47 MIN
VHS
Tycoons series
Color (J H G)
$225.00 purchase
Tells of Robert Mondavi's beginning his winery with the goal of producing world class wines. Shows how he began a new winery and marketed it to a million - dollar business.
Business and Economics
Dist - LANDMK

Robert Morris - Exchange 32 MIN
VHS / U-matic
B&W
Represents a response to Lynda Benglis' videotape Mumble. Speculates about work, travel and relationships.
Fine Arts
Dist - ARTINC **Prod** - ARTINC

Robert Motherwell 28 MIN
16mm / VHS
Color (H C)
$600.00, $190.00 purchase, $75.00 rental
Depicts Robert Motherwell, one of the last of the original abstract expressionists, painting several large canvases in his studio.
Fine Arts
Dist - BLACKW **Prod** - BLACKW 1973

Robert Oppenheimer 14 MIN
U-matic / VHS
Color (C)
$229.00, $129.00 purchase _ #AD - 1838
Presents a short biography of physicist Robert Oppenheimer, who supervised the Manhatten Project - the pursuit of the ultimate weapon, the atomic bomb. Reveals that after completion of the Project, Oppenheimer realized the moral and human consequences of using such a weapon. He became an outspoken advocate of nuclear restraint and the moral obligations of scientists.
Biography; Business and Economics; Religion and Philosophy; Science; Science - Physical
Dist - FOTH **Prod** - FOTH

Robert P Soup Anderson for Anderson Pea Soup 1 MIN
U-matic / VHS
Color
Shows a classic animated television commercial.
Business and Economics; Psychology; Sociology
Dist - BROOKC **Prod** - BROOKC

Robert Penn Warren 30 MIN
VHS
Writers of today series
B&W (G)
$125.00 purchase, $50.00 rental
Features Warren focusing on the creative process of writing. Discusses the search for Identity which is ubiquitous in his novels and poems as a metaphor for writing itself. Insists that without an innate 'germ,' one cannot simply learn mechanics and become a writer. Part of a series of dialogues between drama and literary critic Walter Kerr and a well - known male writer speaking about contemporary literature and society at the time of his own writing peaks.
Fine Arts; Literature and Drama
Dist - FIRS

Robert Rauschenberg 45 MIN
16mm / VHS
Color (H C)
$790.00, $290.00 purchase, $110.00 rental
Traces artist Robert Rauschenberg's development from his student years to a retrospective of his work at the Museum of Modern Art in New York.
Biography; Fine Arts
Dist - BLACKW **Prod** - BLACKW 1979

Robert Reed and Phyllis Mark 29 MIN
U-matic
Art Show Series
Color
Focuses on painter Robert Reed and sculptor Phyllis Mark who exhibit and describe their work.
Fine Arts
Dist - UMITV **Prod** - UMITV

Robert S Zakanitch 20 MIN
16mm
Color (H A)
$500.00 purchase, $50.00 rental
Traces the career of artist Robert S. Zakanitch from lean minimalism through the lushness of its current efflorescence. Produced by Elliot Caplan.
Fine Arts; Industrial and Technical Education
Dist - AFA

Robert, Suzanne, Et La Boite De Carton 15 MIN
16mm
Creative Writing Skills Series
Color (P I) (FRENCH)
LC 74-703611
A French language version of Tommie, Suzie And The Cardboard Box. Uses three stories about a young boy and girl and their cardboard box to illustrate story structure.
English Language; Foreign Language; Literature and Drama
Dist - MORLAT **Prod** - MORLAT 1973

Robert Taft 26 MIN
16mm
History makers of the 20th Century series
B&W (I)
LC FIA67-15
Uses rare footage to portray the personal life and history - making deeds of Robert Taft.
Biography; History - United States
Dist - SF **Prod** - WOLPER 1966

Robert Taft - January 7, 1951 28 MIN
16mm
Meet the Press series
B&W
LC FI68-561
U S Senator Robert Taft of Ohio, discusses nationalism with Martha Rountree, moderator, Ned Brooks, Marshall Mc Neil, James Reston and Lawrence Spivak.
Civics and Political Systems
Dist - NBCTV **Prod** - NBCTV 1951

Robert Venturi and Denise Scott Brown 58 MIN
16mm / VHS
Color (H C)
$875.00, $290.00 purchase, $110.00 rental
Delves into the philosophy and work of two of America's most controversial architects, Robert Venturi & Denise Scott Brown.
Fine Arts; Religion and Philosophy
Dist - BLACKW **Prod** - BLACKW 1988

Robert Vickrey - lyrical realist 28 MIN
U-matic / 16mm / VHS
Color (H C A)
$39.95, $59.95, $550.00 purchase, $125 rental
Takes a look at artist Robert Vickrey and his use of egg tempera in his art. Shows some of his work, including some of his more than 90 cover portraits for Time Magazine.
Fine Arts
Dist - ARTSAM

Robert W Firestone - a unique perspective , Part I - 10 37 MIN
U-matic / VHS
Glendon programs - a series
Color (C A)
$305.00, $275.00 purchase _ #V596
Presents part one of two - parts which provides insights into Dr Firestone and his ideas, values and unique way of conceptualizing human relationships. Describes the development of his philosophy and his views on a wide variety of social, ethical and philosophical issue. Part of a 12 - part series featuring Dr Robert W Firestone, who is noted for his concept of the 'inner voice' and Voice Therapy.
Biography; Guidance and Counseling; Psychology; Sociology
Dist - BARR **Prod** - CEPRO 1991

Robert W Firestone - a unique perspective - Part II - 11 44 MIN
VHS / U-matic
Glendon programs - a series
Color (C A)
$305.00, $275.00 purchase _ #V597
Presents part two of two - parts which provides insights into Dr Firestone and his ideas, values and unique way of conceptualizing human relationships. Describes the development of his philosophy and his views on a wide variety of social, ethical and philosophical issue. Part of a 12 - part series featuring Dr Robert W Firestone, who is noted for his concept of the 'inner voice' and Voice Therapy.
Biography; Guidance and Counseling; Psychology; Sociology
Dist - BARR **Prod** - CEPRO 1991

Robert Wall - Ex FBI Agent 28 MIN
16mm
B&W (H C A)
Tells how Robert Wall, an idealistic FBI agent, underwent a crisis of conscience as a result of the Vietnamese war and resigned from the bureau. Shows how he was then subject to wiretapping and spying.
Civics and Political Systems; History - World; Sociology
Dist - NYFLMS **Prod** - NYFLMS

Robert Walpole 30 MIN
VHS
Late great britons
Color; PAL (C H)
PdS65 purchase
Covers the life of Robert Walpole. Asks whether he was responsible for a sense of stability during a period of political and religious upheaval. Fifth in the six - part series Late Great Britons, which covers the lives of six important figures in British history.
Civics and Political Systems; History - World
Dist - BBCENE

Roberta 105 MIN
VHS
B&W (G)
$29.95 purchase _ #S01387
Features Fred Astaire and Ginger Rogers in a musical set in Paris. Includes the song 'Smoke Gets in Your Eyes.' Filmed in 1935.
Fine Arts
Dist - UILL

Roberto Bedoya - 10 - 25 - 90 30 MIN
VHS / Cassette
Poetry Center reading series
Color (G)
$15.00, $45.00 purchase _ #950 - 716
Features the Chicano poet reading his works at the Poetry Center, San Francisco State University, with an introduction by Robert Gluck.
Literature and Drama
Dist - POETRY **Prod** - POETRY 1990

Roberto Murolo - a Concert at the Sistine Theatre 40 MIN
U-matic / VHS
Color (G)
Presents the leader of classical Neopolitan music playing guitar at the Sistine Theatre in Rome.
Fine Arts
Dist - RIZACV **Prod** - RIZACV

Robert's Second Chance 30 MIN
U-matic
Khan Du Series
Color
LC 78-706322
Introduces a boy who has a hearing impairment, but wants a career in baseball. Shows how he meets a magical creature who points out the successes of other disabled people.
Education; Guidance and Counseling; Psychology
Dist - USNAC **Prod** - USOE 1978

Robertson Davies 40 MIN
VHS
Color (H C G)
$79.00 purchase
Features the Canadian writer with Edward Blishen discussing viewing life as deceptive and its effect on the writer's works. Talks about his work including The Salterton Trilogy; The Papers of Samuel Marchbanks; and The Lyre of Orpheus.
Literature and Drama
Dist - ROLAND **Prod** - INCART

Robin - a Runaway 32 MIN
U-matic / VHS / 16mm
Color (J H A)
LC 76-701565
Gives both sides of a family communication problem by having a 14 - year - old girl who is arrested as a runaway tell of her parent's pressure on her about school, her dress, her friends and her boyfriend. Presents the parents telling of their daughter's lack of cooperation and communication.
Guidance and Counseling; Psychology; Sociology
Dist - ALTSUL **Prod** - VITASC 1976

Robin and the Seven Hoods 120 MIN
16mm / U-matic / VHS
Color (J)
Stars Frank Sinatra, Dean Martin, Sammy Davis Jr, Peter Falk, Bing Crosby and Edward G Robinson in a songfilled satire of gangster - ridden Chicago in the 1920s. Describes what happens when a would - be payoff is turned over to an orphanage and a mobster is hailed as Chicago's Robin Hood.
Literature and Drama; Sociology
Dist - FI **Prod** - WB 1964

Robin Blaser - 11 - 9 - 83
VHS / Cassette
Poetry Center reading series
Color (G)
$15.00, $45.00 purchase _ #565 - 477 - 8
Features the writer reading from Image - Nations; Syntax; and Mystic East at the Poetry Center, San Francisco State University, with an introduction by Robert Gluck.
Literature and Drama
Dist - POETRY **Prod** - POETRY 1983

Robin Blaser - 9 - 29 - 88 90 MIN
VHS / Cassette
Poetry Center reading series
Color (G)
$15.00, $45.00 purchase _ #825 - 648AB
Features the writer reading from The Pause and Moments; an introduction from Pell Mell; and selections from Useful Triads and The Truth is Laughter at the Poetry Center, San Francisco State University, with an introduction by Robert Gluck. Includes an interview by Michael Palmer.
Guidance and Counseling; Literature and Drama
Dist - POETRY **Prod** - POETRY 1988

Robin Blaser - 2 - 11 - 76 30 MIN
VHS / Cassette
Poetry Center reading series
Color (G)
$15.00, $45.00 purchase _ #164 - 128
Features the writer reading from his works and discussing language, poetics, Marxism, and art at the Poetry Center, San Francisco State University, with an introduction by Lewis MacAdams.
Civics and Political Systems; Literature and Drama
Dist - POETRY **Prod** - POETRY 1976

Robin Hood 26 MIN
16mm / VHS
Children's Classics Series
Color (P)
$195.00 purchase
Recreates the classic tale of Robin Hood. Adapted by William Overgard.
Fine Arts; Literature and Drama
Dist - LUF **Prod** - BROVID

Robin Hood 15 MIN
VHS / 16mm
English Folk Heroes Series
Color (I)
Presents the legend of Robin Hood. The fifth of six installments of the English Folk Heroes Series, which presents figures from English literature in 15 - minute programs.
Literature and Drama
Dist - GPN **Prod** - CTI 1990

Robin Hood Junior 62 MIN
16mm
Color (P I)
Presents what happens when a Norman baron usurps Locksay Castle in 12th century England and the daughter of the rightful heir escapes to the forest. Reveals that the village children will be held hostage by the baron unless she surrenders and shows how Robin saves them all.
Literature and Drama
Dist - LUF **Prod** - LUF 1977

Robin Hood with Mr Magoo 105 MIN
16mm
Color (P I)
Fine Arts
Dist - FI **Prod** - FI

Robin Redbreast 11 MIN
U-matic / VHS / 16mm
Color; B&W (P I)
The story of a robin family from the time the parents build their nest until the baby robins are old enough to take care of themselves.
Science - Natural
Dist - EBEC **Prod** - EBEC 1957

Robinhood of the Plains 15 MIN
16mm
B&W
Features Charles Starrett.
Fine Arts
Dist - FCE **Prod** - FCE

The Robins return 30 MIN
VHS / U-matic
Wild south series
Color (H C T G)
$295.00, $195.00 purchase
Documents the efforts of the New Zealand Wildlife Service and ornithologists to coax the two remaining female Chatham Island black robins to nest several times in one season to increase the population.
Geography - World; Science - Natural
Dist - ALTSUL **Prod** - ALTSUL 1987

Robinson 30 MIN
16mm
Color
Shows the adventures and preparation of Jacky and Hermine who live in southwestern France on the Bay of Biscay, as they experience 'Robinson Crusoe.'
Geography - World; Literature and Drama
Dist - RADIM **Prod** - BEAUVA

Robinson Crusoe 26 MIN
16mm / VHS
Children's classics series
Color (P)
$195.00 purchase
Tells of Robinson Crusoe and his talking parrot Poll shipwrecked on a desert island. Crusoe saves a young man from cannibalism and makes a worthy friend named Friday. Adapted by William Overgard from the novel by Daniel Defoe. Animated.
Fine Arts; Literature and Drama
Dist - LUF **Prod** - BROVID

Robinson Jeffers 30 MIN
16mm
Creative person series
B&W (H C A)
An introduction to the poetry, philosophy and environment of Robinson Jeffers. Novelist Walter Clark and Dame Judith Anderson assess the poet and his works. Dame Anderson presents a passage from Jeffers' 'The Power Beyond Tragedy.' Matches recordings of the poems made by Jeffers in 1941 with scenes illustrating the poems.
Fine Arts; Literature and Drama; Religion and Philosophy
Dist - IU **Prod** - NET 1967

Robinson - Turpin 30 MIN
16mm
IBC Championship Fights, Series 2 Series
B&W
Physical Education and Recreation
Dist - SFI **Prod** - SFI

Robinson, Wilhelmena 29 MIN
U-matic
Like it is Series
Color
Discusses Black female leaders involved in the struggle for equal rights.
History - United States; Sociology
Dist - HRC **Prod** - OHC

Robinson's Place 38 MIN
16mm
B&W (FRENCH)
Features one of two short stories combined in the film, Bad Company. Tells of two petty con - artists who cruise the boulevards of Paris in search of girls.
Foreign Language; Literature and Drama
Dist - NYFLMS **Prod** - NYFLMS 1966

Robot 27 MIN
16mm
Color (JAPANESE)
Explains that about 200 years ago, a Japanese man wrote a book about a mechanical doll. Shows how Professor Tachikawa of Kitazato University made a doll which could serve tea. Points out that an artificial hand called a 'waseda - hand' has been improved at Waseda University, which can grasp a paper glass of water. Emphasizes that improvement in robotizing, leads mechanical engineering and industry towards a highly mechanized civilization.
Foreign Language; Industrial and Technical Education
Dist - UNIJAP **Prod** - IWANMI 1970

The Robot Moles 15 MIN
16mm
Color
Features a girl named Hanaka, who thinks of a mole to cultivate beautiful flowers all over the land. Pictures some laboratory men taking over her project.
Literature and Drama
Dist - UNIJAP **Prod** - GAKKEN 1970

The Robot Revolution 22 MIN
U-matic / VHS
Phenomenal World Series
Color (J C)
$129.00 purchase _ #3973
Looks at the positive and the negative qualities of robots, looking at some of the ways people will think about and use robots in the future.
Industrial and Technical Education
Dist - EBEC

The Robot Revolution 58 MIN
VHS / U-matic
Nova Series
Color (H C A)
Shows how American manufacturers are turning to computers and robots to increase productivity. Explores the workplace of the future and the role of advanced automation in altering the way people work. Originally a NOVA television program.
Business and Economics; Industrial and Technical Education; Sociology
Dist - CORF **Prod** - WGBHTV 1985

The Robot Revolution 19 MIN
16mm / U-matic / VHS
Color (J)
Shows that civilization is fast becoming the driving force behind a new technological revolution.
Sociology
Dist - EBEC **Prod** - EBEC 1984

The Robot revolution 26 MIN
U-matic / VHS
Color
Explores the robot world, how robots are used today, their history, how they might be used tomorrow and how we have come to accept and sometimes love them.
Sociology
Dist - JOU **Prod** - JOU

Robot safety at caterpillar 12 MIN
U-matic / VHS
Color
Demonstrates the hazardous elements present in most robotic systems. Points out safety devices and procedures necessary to protect workers.
Business and Economics; Health and Safety; Industrial and Technical Education
Dist - SME **Prod** - CTRACT

Robot Sub - Systems
VHS / 35mm strip
Robotics Series
Color
$42.00 purchase _ #LX5402 filmstrip, $62.00 purchase _ #LX5402V VHS
Talks about robot drive systems, feedback devices, controllers and control systems, and the PUMA family of high technology robots.
Industrial and Technical Education; Mathematics; Psychology
Dist - CAREER **Prod** - CAREER

Robot Sub - Systems
VHS / 16mm
(A PRO)
$89.00 purchase _ #RB02
Discusses articulation, robot drive systems, feedback devices, controllers and control systems, and the PUMA family of high technology robots.
Computer Science; Education
Dist - RMIBHF **Prod** - RMIBHF

Robotic Revolution 24 MIN
U-matic / VHS
Color (I J H A)
Shows young students learning to program a robot in their classroom. Discusses the importance of robotics, as robots are now used to assemble watches and automobiles, stock supermarket shelves and even assist in surgery.
Computer Science
Dist - NGS **Prod** - NGS

Robotics
VHS
Emerging careers library series
Color (J H G PRO T)
$89.95 purchase _ #ECL1A
Offers the latest in a series of videos describing job duties, working conditions, pay, job outlook, and educational and training requirements for key occupations. Features real workers performing actual job tasks at their place of employment. Ethnic and gender equitability insured. Recommended for use in counseling offices, career centers, libraries, job training and rehabilitation programs.
Business and Economics; Guidance and Counseling
Dist - CFKRCM **Prod** - CFKRCM

Robotics 30 MIN
VHS / U-matic
Innovation Series
Color
Explores the potentials and limitations of artificial intelligence and the more exotic applications of robatic technology.
Science; Sociology
Dist - PBS **Prod** - WNETTV 1983

Robotics 30 MIN
U-matic / VHS
Perspective II Series
Color (J H C A)
$150.00
Explores a variety of science and technology subjects dealing with light and its use as a medium of communication. Shows how they work and discusses the implications of this new knowledge.
Computer Science; Science - Physical
Dist - LANDMK **Prod** - LANDMK 1981

Robotics 29 MIN
VHS / 16mm
Discovery Digest Series
Color (S)
$300.00 purchase _ #707611
Explores a vast array of science - related discoveries, challenges and technological breakthroughs. Profiles and 'demystifies' research and development currently underway in many fields. 'Robotics' examines a robotic leg for amputees, a robot - driven warehouse, robots in the classroom and profiles leading geologist Grant Mossop.
Computer Science; Health and Safety; Psychology; Science; Science - Physical
Dist - ACCESS **Prod** - ACCESS 1989

Robotics Explained 56 MIN
VHS / 35mm strip
(H A)
#880XV7
Includes robotic nomenclature, robots in the workplace, robot classification, and basics of the teachmover robot (4 tapes). Includes a Study Guide.
Computer Science
Dist - BERGL

Robotics Explained
VHS / 35mm strip
$279.00 purchase _ #BX880 filmstrips, $251.00 purchase _ #BX880V VHS
Teaches robot nomenclature and about robots in the workplace. Discusses robot classification and explains the operations of robots in general.
Computer Science
Dist - CAREER **Prod** - CAREER

Robotics in industry
VHS / 16mm
(A PRO)
$89.00 purchase _ #RB01
Defines the term robot. Discusses why robots are needed, the benefits of robotics, current and future robot needs, and robotic possibilities.
Computer Science; Education
Dist - RMIBHF **Prod** - RMIBHF

Robotics - Isaac Asimov's Artificial Man 20 MIN
16mm / VHS / U-matic
Color
Features Isaac Asimov discussing robot technology.
Health and Safety; Mathematics; Science; Science - Natural
Dist - CNEMAG **Prod** - DOCUA

Robotics Series
Applications of Robot Technology
Human Factors in Robotics
Implementation of Robots
Operating Parameters of Robots
Robot Sub - Systems
Robots in Industry
Dist - CAREER

Robotics technician 5 MIN
VHS / 16mm
Good works 5 series
Color (A PRO)
$40.00 purchase _ #BPN238002
Presents the occupation of a robotics technician. Gives a profile of a young person who is either undergoing an apprenticeship or has recently completed training in this field. Takes the viewer on a tour of this person's workplace and explains the practical skills and training offered by employers and schools. Gives a better understanding of the demand for skilled workers today and the potential for personal growth.
Guidance and Counseling
Dist - RMIBHF **Prod** - RMIBHF

Robotics technician 5 MIN
U-matic
Good work series
Color (H)
Provides useful, up to date information on various occupations to aid high school students in career selection. Available in five series of ten jobs each.
Computer Science; Education; Guidance and Counseling
Dist - TVOTAR **Prod** - TVOTAR 1981

Robotics technology - automatic guided vehicle 10 MIN
VHS
Color (H A)
$59.95 purchase _ #SWE592V
Focuses on the Automatic Guided Vehicle, a computer controlled car - like robot which represents advances in robotics. Portrays other high - technology advances. Includes a reproducible printed quiz and answer sheet.
Computer Science
Dist - CAMV

Robotics technology - beyond basics 60 MIN
VHS
Color (H A)
$319.00 purchase _ #VMA31326V
Presents in - depth information on developments in robotics for people who already have some familiarity with the field. Covers subjects including the social and technological history of robotics, safety, classification and components, programming, maintenance, and robot applications. Consists of three videocassettes and a program guide.
Computer Science; Health and Safety
Dist - CAMV **Prod** - CAREER 1987
CAREER

Robotics - the Future is Now 20 MIN
U-matic / VHS / 16mm
Color (I J H C G T A)
$50 rental _ #9778
Describes increasing use of robotics in industry. Narrated by William Shatner.
Science; Science - Physical
Dist - AIMS **Prod** - SAIF 1987

Robots 30 MIN
VHS / 16mm
Interactions Series
Color (H T PRO)
$180.00 purchase, $35.00 rental
Shows that cybernetics - the use of mechanical and electrical systems to replace humans - is a new development dependent upon the computer chip. Demonstrates how early fears that robots would replace workers have not been realized.
Business and Economics; Computer Science; Psychology
Dist - AITECH **Prod** - WHATV 1989

Robots 23 MIN
VHS
Bright sparks series
Color (P I)
$280.00 purchase
Looks at the human brain which is capable of problem - solving and daydreaming, and computers which can do neither without instructions from a human. Shows robots doing tasks which humans find tedious and tiring. Reveals that robots can instruct, entertain, help, and are infinitely capable of precision movement, an ability which may be very important in space exploration. Part of a 12 - part animated series on science and technology.
Computer Science; History - World; Sociology
Dist - LANDMK **Prod** - LANDMK 1989

Robots - 105 29 MIN
VHS
FROG series 1; Series 1; 105
Color (P I J)
$100.00 purchase
Offers the fifth program by Friends of Research and Odd Gadgets. Lifts science off the textbook page into the real world to show how enjoyable and challenging science can be. In this episode, the Froggers compare a chicken claw to a human hand, then decide to build a robot model. Special focus on joint and hinges, industrial uses of robots and robot gadgets. Produced by Greg Rist.
Computer Science; Science - Physical
Dist - BULFRG **Prod** - OWLTV 1993

Robots - 2 29 MIN
VHS
Interactions in Science and Society - Student Programs Series
Color (H T)
$125.00 purchase
Considers cybernetics, the use of mechanical and electrical systems to replace human workers. Reveals that 1973 OSHA legislation requiring worker protection from hazardous working conditions spurred the use of robotics in industry. Part 2 of a 12-part series on interacting technological and societal issues. Includes teacher in-service. Computer component available which enhances decision - making skills.
Computer Science; Psychology; Sociology
Dist - AITECH **Prod** - WHATV 1990

Robots - an important place in American industry
VHS
Understanding robotics video series
Color (G H C VOC)
$79.00 purchase _ #MG5421V-T
Describes the basics of robotics in part of a three videocassette series on robotics. Explains how robots work, their capabilities and limitations, and their potential. Focuses on what robots do in American industry and how they compare to human workers. Illustrates the tasks that robots perform and examines the advantages and disadvantages of their use.
Business and Economics; Computer Science
Dist - CAMV

Robots and Computers 15 MIN
VHS / 16mm
Challenge Series
Color (I)
$125.00 purchase, $25.00 rental
Depicts robots performing various tasks at a Tennessee plant and computers that produce music.
Computer Science; Mathematics; Science
Dist - AITECH **Prod** - WDCNTV 1987

Robots - designed to meet almost any need
VHS
Understanding robotics video series
Color (G H C VOC)
$79.00 purchase _ #MG5422V-T
Describes the basics of robotics in part of a three videocassette series on robotics. Explains how robots work, their capabilities and limitations, and their potential. Focuses on the exact tasks performed by robots and includes close-ups of their work. Compares the work done by two axes robots to ten axes robots, and discusses the work envelope and operation parameters.
Business and Economics; Computer Science
Dist - CAMV

Robots Get Smarter 29 MIN
Videoreel / VT2
Interface Series
Color
Business and Economics; Industrial and Technical Education; Mathematics
Dist - PBS **Prod** - KCET

Robots I - Natural and Artificial Senses 24 MIN
VHS / 16mm
Robots Series
Color (I)
LC 90706235
Covers the history of the development of robots. Shows how robots work, focusing on their ability to imitate the five human senses.
Computer Science; History - World; Science; Science - Natural
Dist - BARR

Robots II - natural and artificial vision 24 MIN
U-matic / VHS
Robots series
Color (I J)
$325.00, $295.00 purchase _ #V189; LC 90-705978
Shows how artificial vision systems work in robots and how they were developed using knowledge gained by studying the human sense of sight. Reveals that while robotic vision is not as complex as human eyesight, robots are capable of recognizing shapes, colors and distances. Part of a four - part series on robots.
Business and Economics; Computer Science; Fine Arts; Psychology; Science - Natural
Dist - BARR **Prod** - GLOBET 1989

Robots III - natural and artificial hearing 24 MIN
VHS / U-matic
Robots series
Color (I J)
$325.00, $295.00 purchase _ #V190; LC 90-705979
Shows that robots are able to recognize sounds and identify words, which is called sound and speech recognition. Part of a four - part series on robots.
Business and Economics; Computer Science; English Language; Fine Arts; Science - Natural
Dist - BARR **Prod** - GLOBET 1989

Robots in assembly and packaging 45 MIN
VHS / 16mm
Manufacturing insights series
Color (A IND)
$200.00, $190.00 purchase _ #VT238, #VT238U
Shows how industrial robots have evolved and are now performing assembly and packaging jobs once thought beyond their capabilities.
Business and Economics; Computer Science; Industrial and Technical Education
Dist - SME **Prod** - SME 1984

Robots in Industry
VHS / 35mm strip
Robotics Series
Color
$42.00 purchase _ #LX5401 filmstrip, $62.00 purchase _ #LX5401V VHS
Explores why we need robots, the benefits of robotics, and future possibilities of using robots.
Industrial and Technical Education; Mathematics; Psychology
Dist - CAREER **Prod** - CAREER

Robots in surface preparation 26 MIN
VHS / 16mm
Manufacturing insights series
Color (A IND)
$200.00, $190.00 purchase _ #VT283, #VT283U
Explains how robots increase productivity and quality while reducing worker stress and fatigue.
Business and Economics; Computer Science; Psychology
Dist - SME **Prod** - SME 1988

Robots in welding and painting 35 MIN
VHS / 16mm
Manufacturing insights series
Color (A IND)
$200.00, $190.00 purchase _ #VT241, #VT241U
Describes the significant developments which have advanced state - of - the - art robotic welding and finishing operations.
Business and Economics; Computer Science; Industrial and Technical Education
Dist - SME **Prod** - SME 1985

Robots IV - natural and artificial touch, taste and smell 24 MIN
VHS / U-matic
Robots series
Color (I J)
$325.00, $295.00 purchase _ #V191; LC 90-705981
Explains the sense of touch in humans and shows how computers can provide robots with a similar sense. Reveals that humans have many sensors and they react to different sensations, while robots don't need all the sensors that humans have. Part of a four - part series on robots.
Business and Economics; Computer Science; Fine Arts; Science - Natural
Dist - BARR **Prod** - GLOBET 1989

Robots - putting them to work
VHS
Understanding robotics video series
Color (G H C VOC)
$79.00 purchase _ #MG5423V-T
Describes the basics of robotics in part of a three videocassette series on robotics. Explains how robots work, their capabilities and limitations, and their potential. Focuses on the exact method to determine whether human workers or robots should be used to perform a task. Includes cost analysis.
Business and Economics; Computer Science
Dist - CAMV

Robots - Selection and Installation 62 MIN
VHS / 35mm strip
(H A G)
#881XV7
Includes robotic design, principles of selection, assembling a robot, and installing and programming (4 tapes). includes a Study Guide.
Computer Science
Dist - BERGL

Robots series
Robots I - Natural and Artificial Senses 24 MIN
Robots II - natural and artificial vision 24 MIN
Robots III - natural and artificial hearing 24 MIN
Robots IV - natural and artificial touch, taste and smell 24 MIN
Dist - BARR

Robots 6 - Tomorrow's Technology on Display 30 MIN
VHS / U-matic
Color
Gives an update on the state - of - the - art industrial robot capabilities, demonstrates laser and video sensing equipment, examines many recently introduced robot systems and explores small robots designed specifically for training and educational purposes.
Business and Economics; Industrial and Technical Education
Dist - SME **Prod** - SME

Robots - the Computer at Work 22 MIN
16mm / VHS
Color (I J H A)
$395.00, $475.00 purchase, $75.00 rental _ #8027
Answers basic questions about robots using examples from Japan which currently uses robots more than anywhere else in the world. Shows robots assisting the handicapped, being used in nursing, firefighting and crime prevention.
Business and Economics; Computer Science; Geography - World; Industrial and Technical Education
Dist - AIMS **Prod** - EDMI 1985

Rocco's Star 27 MIN
U-matic / VHS / 16mm
Color (J H A)
Describes the conflict which ensues when a young man tells his father that he wants to pursue a career as a singer. Shows that out of this tension, both grow to be better men. Stars Billy Hufsey and Al Ruscio.
Guidance and Counseling; Sociology
Dist - PAULST **Prod** - PAULST 1984

Rochester Philharmonic Orchestra - Unlikely Sources of Symphonic Music 60 MIN
Videoreel / VT2
Synergism - Command Performance Series
B&W
Presents the words of Dr Samuel Jones of the Rochester Philharmonic, and uses the music of the orchestra to demonstrate some unlikely sources of symphonic music.
Fine Arts
Dist - PBS **Prod** - WXXITV

The Rock 30 MIN
VHS
Color (H C G)
$49.95 purchase _ #E454; LC 90-712501
Examines the history of Mount Desert Island near Maine. Looks at its role as a resting place for migratory birds, way station for whales and home for a multitude of marine creatures.
Geography - United States; Science - Natural
Dist - GPN **Prod** - MPBN 1985

Rock - a - bye baby 30 MIN
16mm / U-matic / VHS
Life around us series
Color (J) (SPANISH)
LC 73-713395
Presents some of the techniques that psychologists use to measure mothering practices in the human and animal world during the important infant years.
Psychology; Sociology
Dist - TIMLIF **Prod** - TIMLIF 1971

Rock - a - Bye Baby - a Group Projective Test for Children 35 MIN
16mm
B&W (C)
Presents a puppet show designed to elicit projective responses of children from ages five to ten years. Taps the areas of sibling rivalry, aggressions, fears, guilt feelings and attitudes toward parents.
Education; Psychology
Dist - PSUPCR **Prod** - PSUPCR 1956

The Rock and mineral resources of Pennsylvania 16 MIN
VHS
Color (J H C)
$29.95 purchase _ #IVRMRPA
Explores the rich rock and mineral resources of the state of Pennsylvania, including coal mines, iron ore, the gypsum industry, oil wells and natural gas deposits. Shows how the resources are mined and processed. Includes rare footage of mining, detailed diagrams, computer animation and more.
Geography - United States; Science - Physical
Dist - INSTRU

Rock and paper 58 MIN
VHS
Skyscraper series
Color; CC (G)
$89.95 purchase _ #EX2613; Program not available in Canada.
Chronicles the construction of Worldwide Plaza, a 47 - story, 770 - foot tower built on the former site of Madison Square Garden in New York City.
Geography - United States; Industrial and Technical Education
Dist - FOTH **Prod** - WGBH

Rock and Roll 30 MIN
VHS / 16mm
Sesame Street Home Video Series
Color; Captioned (K)
$14.44 purchase _ #RH 9 - 808272T
Features Sesame Street characters singing hit songs.
Fine Arts
Dist - EDUCRT **Prod** - RH

Rock and roll guitar 60 MIN
VHS
Video music lesson series
Color (J H C G)
$29.95 purchase _ #TMV02V
Offers step - by - step rock and roll guitar instruction. Features studio musicians, composers, arrangers and educators who lend hands - on instruction about tuning the instrument, chord progressions, smooth and fluent style, timing and finger exercises, common note combinations, instrument set - up, special sound techniques. Includes examples of chord and scale theory, examples for technical improvement and songs to teach the principles of the instrument. Includes booklet. Part of a 16 - part series on musical instruction.
Fine Arts
Dist - CAMV

Rock and roll rhythm guitar series
Presents a two - part series featuring Amos Garrett, master rhythm guitarist. Illustrates the sounds of Chuck Berry, Bo Diddley, Wilson Pickett and James Nolin in Video One. Looks at Steve Cropper and the Memphis sound - Mustang Sally, the '8th - note hop,' 16th - note 'half - time' feel, arpeggios and ballad accompaniment, doubling the bass line, chord - melody playing and more in Video Two. Includes chords.
Rock and roll rhythm guitar - Video One 90 MIN
Rock and roll rhythm guitar - Video Two 75 MIN
Rock and roll rhythm guitar series 165 MIN
Dist - HOMETA **Prod** - HOMETA

Rock and roll rhythm guitar - Video One 90 MIN
VHS
Rock and roll rhythm guitar series
Color (G)
$39.95 purchase _ #VD - GAR - RH01
Features Amos Garrett, master rhythm guitarist. Illustrates holding the pick, right and left - hand damping techniques, alternate chord shapes, the styles of Chuck Berry, Bo Diddley, Wilson Pickett, James Nolin, shuffle and straight time, two - guitar rhythm drills, half - time stroke, glissando techniques, 'playing air' and more. Includes chords. Part one of a two - part series.
Fine Arts
Dist - HOMETA **Prod** - HOMETA

Rock and roll rhythm guitar - Video Two 75 MIN
VHS
Rock and roll rhythm guitar series
Color (G)
$39.95 purchase _ #VD - GAR - RH02
Features Amos Garrett, master rhythm guitarist. Illustrates Steve Cropper and the Memphis sound - Mustang Sally, the '8th - note hop,' 16th - note 'half - time' feel, arpeggios and ballad accompaniment - When a Man Loves a Woman, doubling the bass line - That's the Way Love Is and Born Under a Bad Sign, chord - melody playing and more. Includes chords. Part two of a two - part series.
Fine Arts
Dist - HOMETA **Prod** - HOMETA

Rock Bolting in Ore Mines 24 MIN
16mm
Color
LC 74-705546
Points up the safe methods of rock bolting practiced in the underground mineral mines of the western part of the United States. Shows various installations and bolting patterns.
Health and Safety; Industrial and Technical Education
Dist - USNAC **Prod** - USBM 1964

Rock Bolting Safety 17 MIN
16mm / U-matic / VHS
Color
Uses live - action photography, animation and working models to explain rock bolting as a means of maintaining mine openings. Traces the history and development of ground support methods, materials and equipment from the earliest timbering practices to today's improved rock bolting techniques.
Health and Safety; Industrial and Technical Education; Social Science
Dist - USNAC **Prod** - USDL 1982

Rock climbing and rappelling 30 MIN
U-matic / VHS
Roughing it series
Color
Discusses rock climbing and rappelling as an outdoor activity that requires 'roughing it.'
Physical Education and Recreation
Dist - KYTV **Prod** - KYTV 1984

Rock Climbing, Rigging, Running 30 MIN
BETA / VHS
Great Outdoors Series
Color
Describes basic rock climbing and rigging. Examines the cause, prevention and treatment of blisters. Discusses trail food.
Physical Education and Recreation
Dist - CORF **Prod** - WGBHTV

Rock Concert Violence 25 MIN
U-matic / VHS
Color (J H C A)
Takes a look at the causes and solutions to violence erupting at rock concerts. Features interviews with behind - the - scenes people.
Psychology; Sociology
Dist - GERBER **Prod** - SIRS

Rock correlation 12 MIN
VHS
History in the rocks series
Color (H C)
$24.95 purchase _ #S9818
Shows how rock strata are matched using a single - concept format. Part of a ten - part series on rocks.
Science - Physical
Dist - HUBDSC **Prod** - HUBDSC

Rock Creek Park 16 MIN
16mm / U-matic / VHS
Color
Visits the recreational facilities, historical points and nature settings of Rock Creek Park in metropolitan Washington, DC.
Geography - United States; Sociology
Dist - USNAC **Prod** - USNPS 1982

The Rock cycle 18 MIN
VHS
Earth science series
Color (J H)
$64.95 purchase _ #ES 8440
Unravels the complex processes that create, change and break down Earth materials. Illustrates clear and concise definitions of the major rock types, using full - motion video and computer graphics. Includes a teachers' guide. Part of a six - part series taking a contemporary look at Planet Earth, its natural resources and the human impact on global environment.
Science - Physical
Dist - INSTRU **Prod** - SCTRES

The Rock cycle 10 MIN
VHS
Earth materials series
Color (H C)
$24.95 purchase _ #S9797
Discusses the geological process of rock formation. Part of a ten - part series on the development of minerals, rocks and soil.
Science - Physical
Dist - HUBDSC **Prod** - HUBDSC

The Rock cycle 22 MIN
VHS
Color (J H)
$99.00 _ #3717 - 026
Examines the importance of the rock cycle as a natural process and a key factor in geological change. Identifies sedimentary, igneous and metamorphic rock classifications. Includes teacher's guide.
Education; Science - Physical
Dist - GA **Prod** - EBEC 1982
EBEC

The Rock Cycle 15 MIN
VHS
Color (J)
$59.95 purchase _ #8440V
Unravels the complex processes which create, change and break down earth materials. Illustrates clear and concise definitions of the major rock types using photography and computer graphics.
Agriculture; Science - Physical
Dist - SCTRES **Prod** - SCTRES

The rock cycle 20 MIN
Videodisc / VHS
Earth science library series
Color (J H)
$99.95, $69.95 purchase _ #Q18442
Utilizes computer graphics and full motion video to illustrate major rock types and explain the processes that create, change and break down earth materials. Features examples of erosion, deposition, metamorphism and volcanism filmed on location in the Rocky Mountains and other areas of North America. Includes teacher's guide.
Agriculture; Science - Physical
Dist - CF

The Rock cycle 18 MIN
VHS
Color (J H)
$70.00 purchase _ #A5VH 1232
Ventures into the Rocky Mountains to unravel the complex processes behind the creation, metamorphosis and break down of Earth's materials. Defines clearly the three major rock types and gives examples of erosion, deposition, metamorphism and volcanism found in the Rocky Mountains and across North America. Illustrates concise definitions using full motion video and computer graphics.
Geography - United States; Geography - World; Science - Physical
Dist - CLRVUE **Prod** - CLRVUE 1992

The rock cycle 20 MIN
Videodisc / VHS
Earth science videolab series
Color (J H)
$179.95, $149.95 purchase _ #Q18447
Presents an interdisciplinary, multi - learning approach to the study of rocks. Demonstrates methods for simulating weathering and erosion, creating rocks, interpreting rock cycle clues and studying the rock cycle on a global scale. Includes teacher's guide and enough materials to teach multiple sections of students. Part of a series of five programs.
Science; Science - Physical
Dist - CF

Rock Gospel 58 MIN
VHS / 16mm
Color (G)
$70.00 rental _ #RGSL - 000
Features the rock band Sons Of Thunder performing rock and gospel music that is simultaneously interpreted into sign language.
Fine Arts; Guidance and Counseling
Dist - PBS **Prod** - WETATV

Rock Hudson suffers from AIDS - Thursday, July 15, 1985 30 MIN
VHS
Nightline series
Color (H C G)
$14.98 purchase _ #MP6149
Focuses on the disclosure that motion picture idol Rock Hudson is homosexual and has been diagnosed as having AIDS.
Fine Arts; Health and Safety; History - United States
Dist - INSTRU **Prod** - ABCNEW 1985

Rock, Ice and Oil 57 MIN
16mm
Color (G)
_ #106C 0184 504
Portrays scientists conducting research in the north as part of the Polar Continental Shelf Project. Includes research in biology, cartography, oceanography, petroleum exploration, climatology, mining and resource development, hydrography, and matters such as cleaning up environmental protection.
Geography - World; Science - Natural; Science - Physical; Social Science
Dist - CFLMDC **Prod** - NFBC 1984

A Rock in the Road 6 MIN
U-matic / VHS / 16mm
Color (P I J)
LC FIA68-390
Uses animation to present a story about a man coming down the road, tripping over a rock and plunging into a hole. Pictures him, in his fury, replacing the rock and hiding as he spots someone else coming down the road. Shows that the second and third men do the same but that the fourth man removes the rock, fills the hole and departs happily.
English Language; Fine Arts; Guidance and Counseling; Psychology
Dist - PHENIX **Prod** - FA 1968

Rock 'n' roll explodes 60 MIN
VHS
History of rock 'n' roll series
Color (G)
$19.99 purchase _ #0 - 7907 - 2425 - 1NK
Features performances by Bruce Springsteen - Born to Run; Elvis Presley; the Rolling Stones; Jimi Hendrix - Wild Thing; Little Richard; Chuck Berry; Bo Diddley. Includes new interviews with enduring superstars. Part of a ten - part series unfolding the history of rock music. May contain mature subject matter and explicit song lyrics.
Fine Arts
Dist - TILIED

Rock n roll girls 75 MIN
16mm
B&W (G)
$120.00 rental
Parodies the Marx Brothers absurdist comedies. Follows the worst girl rock group in New York as they plug along trying to get back - alley jobs in the club circuit. A motley crew of characters helps and hinders their climb to success. Filmed in the Lower East Side of New York and includes local celebrities from the old days of the musical underground circuit. A Jackie Leger production.

Fine Arts
Dist - CANCIN

Rock Paintings of Baja California 25 MIN
16mm / U-matic / VHS
Color
Describes the environmental and cultural setting within which the natives of Baja California developed their rock art work.
Fine Arts
Dist - UCEMC **Prod** - UCEMC

Rock Paintings of Baja California 17 MIN
16mm / U-matic / VHS
Color (H C A)
LC 76-702126
Examines the rock paintings at a recently discovered site in a remote area of Baja California. Provides a brief introduction to prehistoric rock paintings in various parts of the world and compares the style of the Baja paintings to those found elsewhere. Explains their age, how they were painted and their significance to the Indians who painted them.
Fine Arts; Geography - World; History - World; Social Science
Dist - UCEMC **Prod** - MEIC 1975

Rock ptarmigan 25 MIN
VHS
Nature watch series
Color (P I J H C)
$49.00 purchase _ #320205; LC 89-715849
Reveals that rock ptarmigans live in some of the most hostile environments on earth, so they must adapt every aspect of their lives to the elements. Part of a series that explores the curious and uncommon characteristics of a variety of mammals, insects, birds and sea creatures.
Science - Natural
Dist - TVOTAR **Prod** - TVOTAR 1988

Rock, Revere and Revolution 24 MIN
VHS / U-matic
Color (K P I J)
Shows a group of young people reviewing Paul Revere and the American Revolution through a musical presentation.
Fine Arts; History - United States; Sociology
Dist - SUTHRB **Prod** - SUTHRB

Rock roots - journey through jazz 60 MIN
VHS
Color (G)
$99.95 purchase _ #RR01V - F
Provides background information on the development of American jazz, from blues through ragtime and swing to avant garde forms. Points out the emotional expression behind jazz improvisation that distinguishes it from other forms. Talks about the various jazz styles. Includes two 30 - minute videos and teacher's guide.
Fine Arts
Dist - CAMV

Rock roots - the history of American pop music 60 MIN
VHS
Color (G)
$99.95 purchase _ #RR02V - F
Provides background information on the development of American pop music, from ethnic dances, folk, and blues through swing and country to rockabilly, rap and Motown. Presents selections with brief discussions of the historic and social conditions of the time. Talks about the influence of new instruments and new music formats such as records, tapes and videos on styles. Includes two 30 - minute videos and teacher's guide.
Fine Arts
Dist - CAMV

Rock Sonata for Piano and Amplified Cello 29 MIN
VHS / 16mm
Color (G)
35.00 rental _ #RSNT - 000
Features pianist - composer Paul Schoenfield and cellist Peter Howard performing Rock Sonata for piano and amplified cello. Includes four movements of rock, ragtime, blues and hoedown.
Fine Arts
Dist - PBS **Prod** - WGBUTV

Rock Springs 30 MIN
16mm
Color (G)
$50.00 rental
Deals with the filmmaker's visit to his hometown for the first time in 20 years, meeting relatives he had never met. Documents a 'boomtown' built over huge coal deposits. By Richard Beveridge.
Fine Arts; Geography - United States; Literature and Drama
Dist - CANCIN

The Rock that glowed - the importance of recycling 30 MIN
VHS
Color (I J H)
$70.00 purchase _ #A5VH 1385
Presents a science fiction story about school children and a creature from the future. Creates interest in saving natural resources and controlling the ever - growing amounts of waste through recycling.
Literature and Drama; Science - Natural; Sociology
Dist - CLRVUE **Prod** - CLRVUE

Rock - Tilt with a Lilt 29 MIN
U-matic
Music Shop Series
Color
Focuses on the popularity of rock music.
Fine Arts
Dist - UMITV **Prod** - UMITV 1974

Rock weathering - chemical 9 MIN
VHS
Earth materials series
Color (H C)
$24.95 purchase _ #S9799
Discusses chemical decomposition of rocks. Part of a ten - part series on the development of minerals, rocks and soil.
Science - Physical
Dist - HUBDSC **Prod** - HUBDSC

Rock Weathering - Origin of Soils 26 MIN
16mm
B&W (C A)
Discusses mechanical disintegration and chemical decomposition of soil. Describes development of soil and factors in soil formation. Outlines soil zones and illustrates profiles of laterites, podsols, chernozem and sierozem.
Agriculture; Science - Physical
Dist - UTEX **Prod** - UTEX 1960

Rock weathering - physical 9 MIN
VHS
Earth materials series
Color (H C)
$24.95 purchase _ #S9798
Discusses physical weathering of rocks. Part of a ten - part series on the development of minerals, rocks and soil.
Science - Physical
Dist - HUBDSC **Prod** - HUBDSC

Rock Your Baby 12 MIN
16mm
Color
LC 76-703849
Presents a film about filmmakers and the scenes they shoot.
Fine Arts; Industrial and Technical Education
Dist - CONCRU **Prod** - CONCRU 1976

Rockabilly guitar - licks and techniques of the rock pioneers - Video One 90 MIN
VHS
Rockabilly guitar series
Color (G)
$39.95 purchase _ #VD - JIM - RG01
Features Jim Weider. Teaches the country flatpicking - using flatpick and fingers - that Scotty Moore used on the early hits of Elvis Presley. Shows how Duane Eddy got his twangy sound and allows the viewer to see how the single - string lead work of Paul Burlison influenced contemporary guitarists such as Jimmy Page, Jeff Beck and others. Includes music and tablature. Part one of two parts.
Fine Arts
Dist - HOMETA **Prod** - HOMETA

Rockabilly guitar - licks and techniques of the rock pioneers - Video Two 85 MIN
VHS
Rockabilly guitar series
Color (G)
$39.95 purchase _ #VD - JIM - RG02
Features Jim Weider. Teaches the trademark licks and rhythm patterns of Chuck Berry and the innovative solos of Eddie Cochran. Includes music and tablature. Part two of two parts.
Fine Arts
Dist - HOMETA **Prod** - HOMETA

Rockabilly guitar series
Presents a two - part series featuring Jim Weider with special guests Levon Helm, Rick Danko and Chris Zaloom. Focuses on the country of Scotty Moore, shows how Duane Eddy got his twang and how the single - string lead work of Paul Burlison influenced other guitarists in Video One. Teaches the trademark licks and rhythm patterns of Chuck Berry and the innovative solos of Eddie Cochran in Video Two. Includes music and tablature.
Rockabilly guitar - licks and techniques of the rock pioneers - Video One 90 MIN
Rockabilly guitar - licks and techniques of the rock pioneers - Video Two 85 MIN
Dist - HOMETA **Prod** - HOMETA

Rockaby 60 MIN
U-matic / VHS / 16mm
Color
Presents the play Rockaby by Samuel Beckett. Follows the British actress Billie Whitelaw, and American director Alan Schneider as they create, rehearse and premiere Rockaby. By D A Pennebaker and Chris Hegedus.
Fine Arts; Literature and Drama
Dist - PENNAS **Prod** - PENNAS

Rockaby 58 MIN
VHS
Color (G C H)
$139.00 purchase _ #DL252
Presents the world premiere of Samuel Beckett's short play, and also documents the backstage process of dramatic interpretation.
Fine Arts
Dist - INSIM

Rockall 25 MIN
VHS / U-matic
Oceanography series
Color (H C)
$250.00 purchase _ #HP - 5742C
Shows how and why oceanographers use the 10,000 mile Rockall Bank near the British Isles to investigate processes occurring throughout the earth's oceans. Looks at underwater gliders, core samplers, deep water photography, CDT probes, bathythermographs and satellite images to reveal temperature structures and biological productivity. Demonstrates how raw oceanographic data is processed and interpreted and reveals how studying Rockall may affect commercial food and fuel production. Part of a series on oceanography.
Industrial and Technical Education; Science - Physical
Dist - CORF **Prod** - BBCTV 1989

Rocker 9 MIN
VHS / 16mm / U-matic
Color (I J H C A)
LC 77-703398
Presents an experimental film which uses video effects to show kinetic sculptures for dance.
Fine Arts; Industrial and Technical Education
Dist - CHASED **Prod** - CHASED 1977

Rockers 99 MIN
16mm
Color ((ENGLISH SUBTITLES))
Presents a celebration of Jamaica's Rastafarian culture. Directed by Theodoros Bafaloukos. In Rasta patois with English subtitles.
Fine Arts; Foreign Language
Dist - NYFLMS **Prod** - UNKNWN 1978

Rocket Mice on a Record Ride 5 MIN
16mm
Screen news digest series; Vol 3; Issue 4
B&W
Records the story of three mice who traveled higher into the heavens than an creature ever has gone. Shows that the mice have brought man a step closer to his journey into space.
Science - Physical; Social Science
Dist - HEARST **Prod** - HEARST 1960

Rocket Power for Manned Flight 17 MIN
16mm
Color
Presents the X1R99 - RM - 1 Throttlable Rocket Engine which powers the X - 15 and the X - 20. Includes historic flight scenes of early Bell X - 1 and Douglas X - 4 rocket ships to the present X - 15.
Industrial and Technical Education; Science
Dist - THIOKL **Prod** - THIOKL 1960

Rocket Safety 27 MIN
16mm
Color
Demonstrates the safe handling and packaging of rockets and motors. Considers what happens when amateurs work with materials of unknown quality and illustrates several spectacular rocket - test failures. Includes remarks on rocket safety by Dr H W Ritchey.
Industrial and Technical Education
Dist - THIOKL **Prod** - THIOKL 1962

Rocket to Nowhere 79 MIN
16mm
B&W (P I)
Fine Arts
Dist - FI **Prod** - FI

Rocket to the moon 118 MIN
VHS
American stage play specials series

Color; Captioned (G)
$69.95 purchase _ #PLAH - 503C
Presents Clifford Odets' play, 'Rocket to the Moon,' a profile of a 39 - year - old Manhattan dentist who is coming to terms with his life. Stars Judy Davis, John Malkovich and Eli Wallach. Produced by the Program Development Group.
Fine Arts; Literature and Drama
Dist - PBS

RocketKitKongoKit 30 MIN
VHS / 16mm
Color (G)
$60.00 rental
Focuses on South Africa. Uses several narrative voices to expose both neo - colonial military adventurism and its ideological underpinnings in a found footage collage. A Craig Baldwin production. Available for purchase in video format with a group package entitled Three Films.
Civics and Political Systems; Fine Arts; Sociology
Dist - CANCIN

Rockets - how they work 16 MIN
U-matic / VHS / 16mm
Captioned; Color (I J H) (SPANISH)
Discusses the principles of rocket propulsion, construction of a rocket, the need for an internal oxygen supply, fuels and oxidants, the multi - stage rocket and guidance and steering.
Industrial and Technical Education; Science - Physical
Dist - EBEC **Prod** - EBEC 1958

The Rockies 25 MIN
16mm / U-matic / VHS
Untamed World Series
Color; Mono.(J H C A)
$400.00 film, $250.00 video, $50.00 rental
Focuses on the plant and animal life of the Rocky Mountain chain with extensive footage from several locations.
Geography - United States; Geography - World; Science - Natural
Dist - CTV **Prod** - CTV 1971

The Rocking Chair Rebellion 30 MIN
U-matic / VHS / 16mm
Teenage Years Series
Color (P I)
LC 80-700651
An edited version of the motion picture The Rocking Chair Rebellion. Depicts a young girl becoming involved with a group of residents in a home for the elderly and gradually growing in respect for their abilities and needs.
Fine Arts; Health and Safety; Literature and Drama; Sociology
Dist - TIMLIF **Prod** - WILSND 1980

Rocking Horse Cowboy 24 MIN
U-matic / VHS
Color (J C)
$59.00 purchase _ #3498
Studies the true story of a modern - day cowboy growing old and compares it with the romantic image of the American cowboy.
Social Science; Sociology
Dist - EBEC

Rocking Horse Cowboy 24 MIN
16mm / U-matic / VHS
American Character Series
Color (J H C)
LC 77-700618
Presents a character study recording the true story of a modern day cowboy facing the problems of old age. Tells the story in the man's own words and voice, revealing the life of a person who followed his romantic dreams, only to find the life of a real cowboy is bittersweet.
Guidance and Counseling; Health and Safety; History - United States; Literature and Drama; Sociology
Dist - EBEC **Prod** - ALTUSF 1976

The Rocking horse winner 91 MIN
VHS
B&W (G)
$39.95 purchase _ #ROC010
Adapts the short story by D H Lawrence. Dramatizes a sensitive boy's uncanny ability to predict racehorse winners by riding his rocking horse. Determined to make his spendthrift mother happy, he drives himself to death in a desperate attempt to satisfy her desire for luxuries. Directed by Anthony Pelissier.
Fine Arts; Sociology
Dist - HOMVIS **Prod** - JANUS 1949

The Rocking - horse winner 30 MIN
16mm / U-matic / VHS
Classics, dark and dangerous series
Color (H C A) (SPANISH)
LC 76-703936
Presents an adaptation of the novel The Rocking - Horse Winner by D H Lawrence, about a young, sensitive English boy whose rocking horse empowers him to predict winning racehorses at the eventual cost of his life.
Fine Arts; Literature and Drama
Dist - LCOA **Prod** - LCOA 1977

The Rocking - horse winner 30 MIN
U-matic / VHS / 16mm
Classics dark and dangerous - captioned series
Captioned; Color (P)
Tells the story a of young boy who predicts the winners of horseraces by riding on a wooden rocking horse. Based on a story by D H Lawrence.
Literature and Drama; Psychology
Dist - LCOA **Prod** - LCOA 1977

The Rocking Horse Writer 5 MIN
U-matic / VHS
Write on, Set 2 Series
Color (J H)
Demonstrates how to achieve proper emphasis in writing. See also the title Their Finest Paragraph.
English Language
Dist - CTI **Prod** - CTI

Rockingham Castle 30 MIN
VHS
Heirs and graces series
Color (A)
PdS65 purchase
Explores the hidden treasure and a ghostly presence at Rockingham Castle near Corby. The Castle has been a family home for 1000 years. Examines the way the aristocracy lived in the past and live now. Features anecdotes, beautiful architecture, and objects. Lady Victoria Leatham leads the tour. Part three of a five-part series.
Fine Arts; Home Economics; Industrial and Technical Education
Dist - BBCENE

Rocks 10 MIN
U-matic
Take a Look Series
Color (P I)
Identifies three types of rocks as sedimentary, metamorphic, and igneous and their origins.
Science; Science - Physical
Dist - TVOTAR **Prod** - TVOTAR 1986

Rocks and Gems 11 MIN
16mm
Color; B&W (I)
Uses animation to explain the basic principles of the formation of rocks and gems. Describes how to recognize the different types by color, luster, weight, hardness and crystal formations. Shows where to find gems and names many ways rocks and minerals are used.
Science - Physical
Dist - AVED **Prod** - AVED 1960

Rocks and Gems 3 MIN
16mm
Of all Things Series
Color (P I)
Shows rocks and gems.
Physical Education and Recreation; Science - Physical
Dist - AVED **Prod** - BAILYL

Rocks and minerals
VHS
Junior geologist series
CC; Color (P I)
$55.00 purchase_#10026VL
Introduces elementary school students to rocks and minerals. Correlates with a geology and earth sciences curriculum to present mineralogy and the classification of rocks. Part four of a four - part series.
Science - Physical
Dist - UNL

Rocks and Minerals 12 MIN
U-matic / VHS / 16mm
Understanding Our Earth Series
Color (I J)
$295.00, $210.00 purchase _ #3848
Discusses the three main types of rocks and how they are formed.
Science - Physical
Dist - CORF

Rocks and Minerals 28 MIN
VHS / U-matic
Earth Explored Series
Color
Covers the differences in the three basic kinds of rocks, and characteristics for classification. Uses animation, site visits and rock examples.
Science - Physical
Dist - PBS **Prod** - BBCTV

Rocks and Minerals 17 MIN
U-matic / VHS / 16mm
Color (I J)
LC 78-701249
Describes how rocks are formed, what shapes rocks take, and how the form of rocks help in the understanding of their history.
Science - Physical
Dist - PHENIX **Prod** - PHENIX 1978

Rocks and Minerals - Formation 15 MIN
U-matic / VHS
Featherby's Fables Series
Color (P)
Tells a story about a boy who marries a beautiful princess after successfully answering a riddle about how various rocks and minerals are formed.
Science - Physical
Dist - GPN **Prod** - WVUTTV 1983

Rocks and Minerals - How We Identify Them 14 MIN
U-matic / VHS / 16mm
Color (I J)
$340.00, $240.00 purchase _ #3170; LC 75-711491
Shows how common rocks and minerals can be identified by color, texture, hardness, streak and other standard procedures.
Science; Science - Physical
Dist - CORF **Prod** - CORF 1971

The Rocks and minerals of Michigan 30 MIN
VHS
Color (J H C)
$29.95 purchase _ #IVMI04
Reveals that while the native bedrock of Michigan is primarily sedimentary - limestone, sandstone and dolomite - many igneous and metamorphic rocks can be found all over the state because glaciers brought them down from Canada. Discloses that Precambrian and Cambrian rocks abound in the Northern Penninsula, that the copper district of the Keweena Penninsula is world famous. Looks at the principle rock types found across Michigan and where they might be found. Examines the classification, origin and economic importance of these rocks, including gem materials on the Great Lakes shorelines. Introduces the study of mineralogy and supplements Earth science labs.
Geography - United States; History - United States; Science - Physical
Dist - INSTRU

Rocks and minerals of Ohio 40 MIN
VHS
Color (J H C)
$29.95 purchase _ #IVOH04
Reveals that while the native bedrock of Ohio is primarily sedimentary - limestone, sandstone and dolomite - many igneous and metamorphic rocks can be found all over the state because glaciers brought them down from Canada. Looks at the principle rock types found across Ohio and where they might be found. Examines the classification, origin and economic importance of these rocks, including gem materials on the Great Lakes shorelines. Introduces the study of mineralogy and supplements Earth science labs.
Geography - United States; History - United States; Science - Physical
Dist - INSTRU

Rocks and Minerals - Properties 15 MIN
U-matic / VHS
Featherby's Fables Series
Color (P)
Tells a story which reveals the use of simple tests that show the difference between various rocks and minerals.
Science - Physical
Dist - GPN **Prod** - WVUTTV 1983

Rocks and minerals - the hard facts 15 MIN
VHS
Color (P I)
$89.00 purchase _ #RB805
Travels with a geologist to discover what the earth is made of. Investigates a roadcut through which a highway is built and identifies rocks. Performs tests to identify minerals and shows how rocks are formed, and their properties and characteristics. Considers the ongoing processes which create igneous, sedimentary and metamorphic rocks and fossils.
Science - Physical
Dist - REVID **Prod** - REVID

Rocks and Minerals - Uses 15 MIN
VHS / U-matic
Featherby's Fables Series
Color (P)
Tells how certain rocks relate to things like pencils, talcum powder and statues.
Science - Physical
Dist - GPN **Prod** - WVUTTV 1983

Rocks and their Meaning 40 MIN
VHS / U-matic
Basic and Petroleum Geology for Non - geologists - Fundamentals and '- - Series; Fundamentals
Color (IND)
Industrial and Technical Education; Science - Physical
Dist - GPCV **Prod** - PHILLP

Rocks and Time 26 MIN
16mm
B&W (C A)
Considers the relationship of a sequence of formations at an outcrop to similar formations many miles away. Outlines a transgressive cycle to illustrate that as deposition at one place changes from sand to finer materials, the shoreline has moved landward. Shows how this is followed by a regressive cycle, illustrating the entire sequence with a model experiment.
Science - Physical
Dist - UTEX **Prod** - UTEX 1960

Rocks for Beginners 16 MIN
16mm
Color (I J)
LC 70-701209
Presents fundamentals of rock classification. Explains origin and characteristics of different classes of rocks.
Science - Physical
Dist - MLA **Prod** - JHP 1968

Rocks, Fossils and Earth History 17 MIN
16mm / U-matic / VHS
Natural Phenomena Series
Color (J H)
LC 81-701119
Shows several different kinds of fossils and discusses how fossils are formed, the rock cycle and the earth forces that act on them.
Science - Physical
Dist - JOU **Prod** - GLDWER 1981

Rocks, Fossils and Minerals 15 MIN
VHS / 16mm
Challenge Series
Color (I)
$125.00 purchase, $25.00 rental
Identifies various rocks and fossils.
Science - Physical
Dist - AITECH **Prod** - WDCNTV 1987

Rocks in the Heart Surgical Excision of Multifaceted Calcified Right Ventricular Mass 11 MIN
U-matic / VHS / 16mm
Color (PRO)
Discusses the diagnosis and testing (echo and angiograms) of a patient with pulmonary emboli, contracardiac calcifications and obstructive cardiac failure. Demonstrates surgical management.
Health and Safety; Science; Science - Natural
Dist - USNAC **Prod** - USVA

Rocks, mineral and fossils
Videodisc
Color; CAV (P I J)
$189.00 purchase _ #8L396
Introduces the basics of rocks, minerals and fossils. Discusses the chemical compositions and physical properties of minerals, classifications of rocks, and defines fossils and how they are formed. Barcoded for instant random access.
Science - Physical
Dist - BARR **Prod** - BARR 1991

Rocks, Minerals and Fossils 17 MIN
VHS / 16mm / U-matic
Color (I J)
$400.00, $280.00, $310.00 purchase _ #A396
Explains that minerals are natural, inorganic, have definite chemical compositions, and distinguishable physical properties ... color, streak, luster, hardness, density, cleavage, and fracture. Explains that practically everything around him is made from rocks and minerals ... buildings, cars, and the parts in a portable cassette stereo for examples. Explains that rocks are made up of one or more minerals and classified in one of three ways according to how they are made ... igneous rock, sedimentary rock, or metamorphic rock.
Science - Physical
Dist - BARR **Prod** - BARR 1986

Rocks of the plateaulands 24 MIN
VHS
Scenes of the plateaulands and how they came to be series
Color (J H)
$19.95 purchase _ #IVSPL - 1
Offers five parts which examine rocks found on the Colorado Plateau. Discusses how rocks are classified according to hardness, color and other factors. Part of a five - part series which overview the geological forces that formed and are still working on the Colorado Plateau. Includes footage of Colorado, Utah and Arizona, Grand Canyon, Bryce Canyon, Zion National Park, Arches, Bridges, Dinosaur, Petrified Forest and Canyonlands National Parks.
Geography - United States
Dist - INSTRU

Rocks that Form on the Earth's Surface 17 MIN
VHS / 16mm / U-matic
Color (I J H) (SPANISH)
Investigates the nature of sedimentary rocks, asking where they come from, what they are made of and how they are formed.
Science - Physical
Dist - EBEC **Prod** - EBEC

Rocks that Reveal the Past 12 MIN
VHS / 16mm / U-matic
Color (I J H C)
By studying fossils found in layers of sedimentary rocks, scientists reconstruct the plant and animal life of the past. A demonstration to explain how sedimentary rocks are formed and examples of fossils found in certain layers of the Grand Canyon are shown.
Science - Natural; Science - Physical
Dist - PHENIX **Prod** - FA 1962

Rocks to Rings 15 MIN
VHS / 16mm
Challenge Series
Color (I)
$125.00 purchase, $25.00 rental
Shows stones in their natural state and then how they are then cut, polished and made into jewelry.
Science - Physical
Dist - AITECH **Prod** - WDCNTV 1987

Rockschool Series

Basic technique	25 MIN
Blues and rock 'n' roll	25 MIN
Contemporary	25 MIN
Funk	25 MIN
Hardware	25 MIN
Heavy Metal	25 MIN
Reggae	25 MIN
Tuning	25 MIN

Dist - FI

Rocky Mountain adventures 24 MIN
VHS
Wild refuge series
Color (G)
$39.95 purchase
Examines the lifestyles and natural habitat of three groups of animals prevalent in mountainous and bush country. Looks at the wild mustangs and mountain lions in the Rockies and African and Siberian grazing animals successfully transplanted to the hill country in the Southwest. Part of a thirteen - part series on the North American wilderness. Each episode documents a different area and shows how animal species cope with their surroundings to survive.
Geography - United States; Geography - World; Science - Natural
Dist - CNEMAG **Prod** - HOBELP 1976

Rocky Mountain beaver pond 59 MIN
VHS / Videodisc / BETA
Color; CLV; Captioned (G)
$35.20, $24.20 purchase _ #C53332, #C50332
Geography - United States; Science - Natural
Dist - NGS **Prod** - NGS

Rocky Mountain meadow 10 MIN
VHS / U-matic / 16mm
Wild places series
Color (P)
$290.00, $250.00 purchase _ #HP - 6071C
Shows how the warm sunshine and cold wind affect plant life in a high mountain meadow. Studies insects pollinating wildflowers and their role as food for a variety of birds. Looks at how small animals adapt to conditions throughout the year. Part of a series teaching about different kinds of habitats which show how living things adapt to varying environments and how each creature depends upon others for existence. Produced by Partridge Film and Video, Ltd.
Science - Natural
Dist - CORF

Rocky Mountain national park 30 MIN
VHS
Color (G)
$29.95 purchase _ #S01565
Presents a video tour of Rocky Mountain National Park. Portrays the park's peaks, canyons, streams, lakes, wildlife and changing seasons.
Geography - United States
Dist - UILL

Rocky Mountain rainbows and Arctic goose hunt
VHS
Color (G)
$29.90 purchase _ #0394
Presents two features on fishing and hunting in Canada. Travels to the Canadian Rockies to fish for rainbow trout in the first part. Hunts blue geese in the James Bay region of Ontario - Quebec provinces.
Geography - World; Physical Education and Recreation; Science - Natural
Dist - SEVVID

A Rocky Mountain Town - Revelstoke 14 MIN
16mm / U-matic / VHS
This is My Home Series
Color (P I)
Shows how a community changes its environment to provide services to other communities. Accompanies a child and her friends to a dam site where concerned biologists describe minimizing damage to fish populations. Accompanies a train conductor through his duties linking Revelstoke to other communities.
Geography - World; Social Science
Dist - BCNFL **Prod** - BCNFL 1984

The Rocky Mountains 20 MIN
BETA / VHS / U-matic / 16mm
Physical geography of North America series
Color (P I J H)
$315.00, $90.00 purchase _ #C50477, #C51360
Explores the backbone of North America - the Rocky Mountains - geologically young and still changing. Shows how the Rockies are lifted by the same volcanism that fuels the geysers of Yellowstone, and are constantly carved by ice, wind and water. Studies the Continental Divide. Part of a five - part series on the physical geography of North America.
Geography - United States; Geography - World
Dist - NGS **Prod** - NGS 1989

The Rocky Mountains 17 MIN
16mm / U-matic / VHS
Natural Science Series
Color (I J H)
LC 79-701883
Surveys the various types of plants and animals which thrive in the Rocky Mountains, explaining the interrelationships among each. Describes the food chain of the ecosystem and discusses the geological processes which formed the Rockies.
Science - Natural; Science - Physical
Dist - BARR **Prod** - BARR 1980

The Rocky Mountains 25 MIN
U-matic / 16mm
Untamed World Series
Color; Mono (J H C A)
$400.00 film, $250.00 video, $50.00 rental
Looks at the history and current state of the Rocky Mountains, including the animals most indiginous to them such as the North American bison and the brown bear.
Geography - United States; Geography - World
Dist - CTV **Prod** - CTV 1976

The Rocky Mountains - 2 17 MIN
VHS / U-matic / 16mm
Natural science series
Color (P I J)
$370.00, $290.00, $260.00 purchase _ #A291
Overviews the Rocky Mountains which form the continental divide of North America. Shows how the Rockies support a variety of ecosystems, each containing a unique community of plants and animals. Reveals that although the Rockies are situated in a semi - arid climate zone, they provide water to feed some of the continent's largest river systems. Part of a three - part series on natural history.
Geography - United States; Science - Natural
Dist - BARR **Prod** - CASDEN 1980

The Rocky Mountains - the Last Stand 30 MIN
VHS / U-matic
Color
Examines the debate between naturalists, tourists and industry regarding the use of the Rocky Mountain National Parks.
Geography - United States; Geography - World
Dist - JOU **Prod** - CANBC

The Rocky Road to Jupiter 58 MIN
U-matic / VHS
Nova Series
Color (H C A)
$250.00 purchase _ #5138C
Talks about the Galileo probe, which was to have been launched following the Challenger disaster. Produced by WGBH Boston.
Science; Science - Physical
Dist - CORF

Rocky - the American Dream Continues 26 MIN
16mm
Color (I)
Merges film clips from the Rocky trilogy with the real life and screen life stories of Sylvester Stallone and the character he created, Rocky Balboa, to create a personal film record of Stallone's achievements.
Fine Arts
Dist - DIRECT **Prod** - DIRECT 1982

Rod Mill Trimmers 5 MIN
U-matic / VHS
Steel Making Series
Color (IND)
Explains the trimmers' job of cutting scrap and test samples from the hot coils. Emphasizes safety. Covers cleaning reel tangles.
Business and Economics; Health and Safety; Industrial and Technical Education
Dist - LEIKID **Prod** - LEIKID

Rodeo 15 MIN
U-matic / VHS / 16mm
American Scrapbook Series
Color (I)
Explains that a rodeo is not only an entertainment but a testing place for the skills of a working cowboy. Traces the history of rodeos.
Physical Education and Recreation
Dist - GPN **Prod** - WVIZTV 1977

Rodeo 3 MIN
16mm
Of all Things Series
Color (P I)
Discusses the sport of rodeo.
Physical Education and Recreation
Dist - AVED **Prod** - BAILYL

Rodeo 29 MIN
Videoreel / VT2
Bayou City and Thereabouts People Show Series
Color
Explains that small town weekend rodeoing still happens all over the country and is considered a family recreation for many families. Features host Demaret talking to the weekend participants at the Lucky Lady Arena in Spring, Texas.
Physical Education and Recreation
Dist - PBS **Prod** - KUHTTV

Rodeo 20 MIN
U-matic / VHS / 16mm
Color (P I J H)
LC 71-706922
Uses slow motion to emphasize the danger and loneliness that a cowboy experiences as he attempts to win a rodeo event by riding a bull for eight seconds.
Physical Education and Recreation
Dist - PHENIX **Prod** - CUNLIM 1969

Rodeo Boy 28 MIN
16mm
Color (J H)
Introduces Duane Daines, a youth from a small Alberta, Canada town who has wanted to be a professional cowboy ever since he entered his first rodeo at the age of five. Highlights activities at a rodeo school run by Duane's uncle.
Physical Education and Recreation
Dist - FI **Prod** - CANBC

Rodeo Clown - the Daring Breed 25 MIN
U-matic
Color (I)
LC 79-706409
Focuses on rodeo clown Bill Lane, showing him at work in the hazardous rodeo arena and revealing his attitudes toward his job.
Biography; Physical Education and Recreation
Dist - ADAMSF **Prod** - CHPRL 1978

The Rodeo Cowboy 15 MIN
U-matic
Harriet's Magic Hats III Series
(P I J)
Shows a rodeo cowboy in the steer riding competition.
Guidance and Counseling
Dist - ACCESS **Prod** - ACCESS 1985

Rodeo girl 24 MIN
VHS / U-matic
Young people's specials series
Color
Looks at the true story of a 13 - year old girl whose determination and skill made her the youngest world champion barrel racer.
Physical Education and Recreation; Sociology
Dist - MULTPP **Prod** - MULTPP

Rodeo Red and the Runaway 33 MIN
U-matic / 16mm / VHS
Captioned; Color (P I) (FRENCH SPANISH)
A shortened version of the motion picture Rodeo Red And The Runaway. Shows how a young girl refuses to accept her stepmother and runs away from home. Tells how she meets 'Big Red,' a former rodeo horse who becomes her companion. Based on the book Shelter From The Wind by Marion Dane Bauer. An NBC Special Treat.
Fine Arts; Physical Education and Recreation; Sociology
Dist - LCOA **Prod** - LCOA 1979

Rodin and Degas - the final flowering 55 MIN
VHS
Romantic versus Classic art series
Color (G)
PdS19.95 purchase _ #A4-ODY178
Examines the work of Auguste Rodin, whose solid, earthy sensualism makes him the last heir to the great Romantics of the early nineteenth century, and the work of Degas, whose passion for moral truth linked him to the Classicism that aims for the purest representation of reality. One of a series of seven videos about the Romantic Rebellion in art in the second half of the 18th century written and narrated by art historian Kenneth Clark. Produced by Odyssey.
Fine Arts
Dist - AVP

Rodney Fails to Qualify 30 MIN
U-matic / VHS
Wodehouse Playhouse Series
Color (C A)
Presents an adaptation of the short story Rodney Fails To Qualify by P G Wodehouse.
Literature and Drama
Dist - TIMLIF **Prod** - BBCTV 1980

The Rodney King Case - what the jury saw in California v Powell 120 MIN
VHS
Color (J H C G)
$24.98 purchase _ #MH6272V
Views the evidence exactly as it was presented to the jury in Simi Valley hearing evidence on the Rodney King case. Includes the videotaping of the King beating on March 3, 1991, eyewitness accounts and explanations of the laws, rules of evidence and procedural technicalities associated with the case.
Civics and Political Systems; History - United States; Sociology
Dist - CAMV

Rodrigo D - no future 93 MIN
35mm / 16mm / VHS
Color (G) (SPANISH WITH ENGLISH SUBTITLES)
$300.00, $400.00 rental
Portrays the dead - end existence of youths in the murder capital of the world, Medellin, Colombia. Centers around Rodrigo and his reckless friends who are trapped by the violence and drugs which define their lifestyle. The film's actors are Medellin teenagers playing themselves - six of them have been killed since the film's completion. Directed by Victor Gavira.
Fine Arts; Geography - World; Psychology; Sociology
Dist - KINOIC

Rodrigue - Acadiam Artist 24 MIN
U-matic / VHS / 16mm
Color (J H C A)
Follows acadiam artist George Rodrigue throughout south Louisiana as he paints the Cajun people, their humor, music and joic de vivre from ghost stories to Mardi Gras! Rodrigue, called the Louisiana Rousseau, perfectly captures this unique culture as he puts it all on canvas in his own singular style.
Fine Arts; Geography - United States; Social Science; Sociology
Dist - SF **Prod** - SF 1984

Roe v Wade - the debate continues 20 MIN
35mm strip / VHS
Color (J H C T A)
$57.00, $48.00 purchase _ #MB - 002802 - 8, #MB - 002805 - 2
Examines the issue of abortion rights in the US. Considers the arguments of both sides.
Civics and Political Systems; History - United States; Psychology; Sociology
Dist - SRA **Prod** - NYT 1990

Roe vs Wade 20 MIN
VHS
Supreme Court decisions that changed the nation series
Color (J H)
$69.00 _ #60105 - 026
Delves into the controversial case that legalized abortion. Presents part of an eight - part series providing comprehensive history and legal background to landmark rulings and demonstrates their impact on American life. Includes teacher's guide and library kit.
Civics and Political Systems; Education; Sociology
Dist - GA
INSTRU

Roentgen Anatomy of the Normal Alimentary Canal 27 MIN
16mm
Normal Roentgen Anatomy Series
B&W (PRO)
LC FIA67-585
Uses cineflourographic sequences to show functioning anatomy from mouth to bowel, including throat, esophagus, stomach, duodenum, small and large intestine.
Science - Natural
Dist - AMEDA **Prod** - AMCRAD 1966

Roentgen Anatomy of the Normal Bones and Joints 19 MIN
16mm
Normal Roentgen Anatomy Series
B&W (PRO)
LC 78-711430
Uses cineflouroscopy to show the shape, location and movement of the principle joints of the human body as they are seen by radiologists and other physicians. Demonstrates the movements of these joints in normal exercise and then the interior movement of the bones and joints as seen by cinefluoroscopy.
Health and Safety; Science; Science - Natural
Dist - AMEDA **Prod** - GEXRAY 1970

Roentgen Anatomy of the Normal Heart 27 MIN
16mm
Normal Roentgen Anatomy Series
B&W (PRO)
LC FIA66-621
Uses segments of cineflourographic studies plus animation to depict the flow of blood through the heart and the coronary arteries.
Science - Natural
Dist - AMEDA **Prod** - AMCRAD 1965

Roentgen diagnosis series
Cineangiographic diagnosis of coronary artery disease 28 MIN
Dist - NMAC

Roger Baldwin 22 MIN
U-matic / VHS
Color
Presents an intimate biography of Roger Baldwin, founder and former director of the American Civil Liberties Union.
Biography; Civics and Political Systems
Dist - MEDIPR **Prod** - MEDIPR 1978

The Roger Berg Story 15 MIN
U-matic / VHS / 16mm
Focus on Ethics Series
Color (H C A)
LC 77-700213
Illustrates the role values play in the decision - making process. Shows that values also influence the way people deal with the consequences of their decisions.
Business and Economics; Religion and Philosophy
Dist - SALENG **Prod** - SALENG 1977

Roger Corman - Hollywood's Wild Angel 58 MIN
16mm
Introduces Roger Corman, a producer and director. Interviews Corman graduates such as Ron Howard, Jonathan Demme, Peter Fonda, and David Carradine.
Fine Arts
Dist - BLACKW **Prod** - BLACKW

Roger Corman on the Future of Independent Film Production 30 MIN
VHS / 16mm
(PRO G)
$89.95 purchase _ #DGP44
Features Roger Corman discussing the present and future prospects for the independent film business, and what it would take if he were to enter the field today. Hosted by Dick Goldberg.
Business and Economics; Fine Arts
Dist - RMIBHF **Prod** - RMIBHF

Roger Ward 20 MIN
16mm
Sports Legends Series
Color (I J)
Features Roger Ward discussing his career through film clips of some great and harrowing racing moments.
Biography; Physical Education and Recreation
Dist - COUNFI **Prod** - COUNFI

Roger Williams
VHS
Campus clips series
Color (H C A)
$29.95 purchase _ #CC0099V
Takes a video visit to the campus of Roger Williams College in Rhode Island. Shows many of the distinctive features of the campus, and interviews students about their

experiences. Provides information on the composition of the student body, professors, academics, social life, housing, and other subjects.
Education
Dist - CAMV

Roger Williams - Founder of Rhode Island 28 MIN
16mm / U-matic / VHS
B&W (J H C)
Shows the trial of Roger Williams by the magistrate of Massachusetts colony and his banishment for preaching religious freedom. Illustrates the importance of the separation of Church and State.
Biography; Civics and Political Systems; History - United States; Religion and Philosophy
Dist - EBEC **Prod** - EBEC 1956

Roger's story - for Cori 28 MIN
U-matic / VHS
Color (G)
$195.00 purchase, $100.00, $50.00 rental _ #047
Looks at Roger, a 44 - year - old recovering heroin addict who has been diagnosed with AIDS. Reveals that he is devoted to his wife and to his daughter Cori and is dedicated to helping other addicts get clean and avoid drug addiction's most dangerous risk - AIDS. Produced by Howard Shepps.
Health and Safety; Psychology
Dist - FANPRO

RoGoPaG 125 MIN
16mm
B&W (G) (ITALIAN WITH ENGLISH SUBTITLES)
$250.00 rental
Presents a film anthology created by four of Europe's foremost filmmakers - Roberto Rossellini, Jean - Luc Goddard, Pier Paolo Pasolini and Ugo Gregoretti.
Fine Arts
Dist - KINOIC

Roi, Chevalier Et Saint - King, Knight and Saint 52 MIN
16mm
Le Temp Des Cathedrales Series
Color
Visits Europe during the 13th century when Gothic and Art Nouveau developed in Italy, Louis XI tried to bring the knighthood to perfection and La Sainte Chapelle was built. Discusses such events as the papacy moving to Avignon and the publication of Marco Polo's book of wonders.
History - World; Religion and Philosophy
Dist - FACSEA **Prod** - FACSEA 1979

Roland Kirk 30 MIN
Videoreel / VT2
People in Jazz Series
Color (G)
$55.00 rental _ #PEIJ - 108
Presents the jazz music of Roland Kirk. Features host Jim Rockwell interviewing the artist.
Fine Arts
Dist - PBS **Prod** - WTVSTV

The Role and responsibilities of an EEO counselor 12 MIN
U-matic / VHS
Color (A PRO IND)
$95.00 purchase _ #TCA16312, #TCA15084
Covers the role and responsibilities of equal employment opportunity - EEO - counselors in the workplace. Differentiates their functions from those of investigators and EEO officers. Provides guidance on procedural duties and obligations, such as report writing, delivery of notices, and maintaining neutrality.
Civics and Political Systems; Sociology
Dist - USNAC **Prod** - DPVA 1986

Role Enactment in Children's Play - a Developmental Overview 29 MIN
16mm
Training Module on Role Enactment in Children's Play Series One
Color (A)
LC 76-700936
Functions as the main film in a training module of six films on role enactment in children's play. Presents the developmental aspects of role enactment in children 2 to 10 years of age, focusing on four basic concepts, verbal and motoric elements, role perception, age differences in styles of role enactment and thematic content.
Education; Psychology
Dist - CFDC **Prod** - UPITTS 1974

The Role of Coal 17 MIN
16mm / U-matic / VHS
Color (J)
LC 80-700336
Explains the role of coal as an energy source in the past, present and future. Contrasts coal with other energy sources and notes that the scarcity and expense of petroleum necessitates consideration of developing alternative sources.
Social Science
Dist - IU **Prod** - IU 1980

Role of Department Chairpersons 28 MIN
VHS / U-matic
On and about Instruction Series
Color (T)
Examines the rationale for an expanded role of department chairperson as liaison assisting the administration and faculty.
Education
Dist - GPN **Prod** - VADE 1983

Role of Everyday Movement Habits in Chronic Injuries 30 MIN
U-matic / VHS
Care and Feeding of Dancers Series
Color
Fine Arts; Health and Safety; Industrial and Technical Education
Dist - ARCVID **Prod** - ARCVID

Role of Government 20 MIN
16mm
Color
Business and Economics
Dist - CINE **Prod** - CINE

The Role of Government in a Free Society 76 MIN
VHS / U-matic
Milton Friedman Speaking Series Lecture 4
Color (C)
LC 79-708063
Presents economist Milton Friedman examining the role of the U S government in economic and political contexts. Notes that the government's actions have exceeded proper limitations.
Business and Economics; Civics and Political Systems
Dist - HBJ **Prod** - HBJ 1980

The Role of Government in a Free Society - Pt 1 38 MIN
U-matic / VHS
Milton Friedman Speaking Series
Color (C)
LC 79-708063
Presents economist Milton Friedman examining the role of the U S government in economic and political contexts. Notes that the government's actions have exceeded proper limitations.
Business and Economics
Dist - HBJ **Prod** - HBJ 1980

The Role of Government in a Free Society - Pt 2 38 MIN
U-matic / VHS
Milton Friedman Speaking Series
Color (C)
LC 79-708063
Presents economist Milton Friedman examining the role of the U S government in economic and political contexts. Notes that the government's actions have exceeded proper limitations.
Business and Economics
Dist - HBJ **Prod** - HBJ 1980

The Role of government in the economy - fiscal policies, market realities 17 MIN
35mm strip / VHS
Our economy - how it works series
Color (J H C A)
$39.00, $39.00 purchase _ #MB - 510682 - 5, #MB - 508876 - 2
Presents the final segment of a six - part series on basic concepts of economics. Focuses on the role of government in the American economy. Covers the various revenue - raising measures employed by government, as well as the effects of government fiscal policies.
Business and Economics
Dist - SRA **Prod** - SRA

Role of Hemodynamic Monitoring in the Critically Ill 39 MIN
U-matic / VHS
Color (PRO)
Presents a brief look at the history of the Swan - Ganz catheter. Details major issues related to this procedure, such as decision making, indications for monitoring and interpretation of data. Discusses the relationship of cardiac index to performance, pre - load and after - load and the lack of correlation between the wedge pressure and the CVP. Discussion by Dr H J C Swan on complications.
Health and Safety
Dist - AMCARD **Prod** - AMCARD

Role of Hygienist in Dental Care - Pt 1 - History and Examination 11 MIN
VHS / U-matic
Role of the Hygienist in Dental Care Series
Color (PRO)
Demonstrates the procedures involved in recording a patient's medical and dental history, as well as the findings of an extraoral and intraoral examination. Shows positioning and palpation techniques in detail.
Health and Safety; Science - Natural
Dist - USNAC **Prod** - VADTC 1982

Role of Hygienist in Dental Care - Pt 2 - Scaling and Root Planing 15 MIN
VHS / U-matic
Role of the Hygienist in Dental Care Series
Color (PRO)
LC 82-707251
Demonstrates scaling and root planing, the instruments used, and the proper finger placement and instrument grasp. Shows techniques for instrument sharpening.
Health and Safety; Science - Natural
Dist - USNAC **Prod** - VADTC 1982

The Role of Insulin 19 MIN
VHS / 16mm
Learning about Diabetes Series
Color (H A PRO)
$195.00 purchase, $75.00 rental _ #8062
Teaches about the use of insulin when one is a diabetic.
Health and Safety
Dist - AIMS **Prod** - HOSSN 1988

The Role of markets and money 60 MIN
VHS
Macroeconomics series
Color (H C G)
$89.00 purchase _ #GSU - 305
Discusses markets, money and the circular flow of goods and money, as well as domestic and international flows. Interviews Todd Petzel, senior VP and chief economist, Chicago Mercantile Exchange. Part of a 24 - part series instructed by Dr Edward F Stuart, Northwestern University, which focuses on a description of the major economic policy - making bodies in the United States and their interrelationships.
Business and Economics
Dist - INSTRU

The Role of Numerial Analysis in Forest Management 30 MIN
U-matic / VHS
Introduction to Quantitative Analysis of Remote Sensing Data Series
Color
Shows how current accurate information about forest resources can be obtained through analysis of satellite collected data.
Industrial and Technical Education
Dist - PUAVC **Prod** - PUAVC

The Role of Others 29 MIN
VHS / U-matic
Tomorrow's Families Series
Color (H C A)
LC 81-706914
Describes how siblings, members of the extended family, and others in the community affect a child's development.
Home Economics; Psychology; Sociology
Dist - AITECH **Prod** - MDDE 1980

The Role of Pattern Recognition in Remote Sensing 30 MIN
U-matic / VHS
Introduction to Quantitative Analysis of Remote Sensing Data Series
Color
Discusses the role of pattern recognition in remote sensing. Describes how a statistical approach is used to improve decision making in the face of uncertainty.
Industrial and Technical Education
Dist - PUAVC **Prod** - PUAVC

The Role of Phonics 29 MIN
U-matic / VHS / 16mm
Teaching Children to Read Series
Color (C A)
Explores the role of phonics and puts it in perspective in an overall reading program.
Education; English Language
Dist - FI **Prod** - MFFD 1976

Role of play 22 MIN
VHS / U-matic / BETA
Human development - 2.5 to 6 years series
Color (C PRO)
$280.00 purchase _ #620.4
Defines play and discusses some of the functions, including gross and fine motor development, cognitive development, creativity, socialization, self - awareness and therapeutic value. Describes different kinds of play such as physical play, including sensorimotor, mastery or skill play, and rough - and - tumble play, pretend play, dramatic play and games with rules. Discusses the social character of play and gender differences in play. Part of a four - part series on human development, ages 2.5 to 6.

Health and Safety; Physical Education and Recreation; Psychology
Dist - CONMED **Prod** - CONMED

Role of Production Scheduling 60 MIN
VHS / BETA
Manufacturing Series
(IND)
Reviews production scheduling activities and decisions that must be made regarding these activities.
Business and Economics
Dist - COMSRV **Prod** - COMSRV 1986

The Role of Racial Differences in Therapy 70 MIN
VHS / U-matic
B&W
Discusses the often avoided issue of social differences that is avoided by patient and therapist alike. Includes excerpts from therapy sessions with a biracial couple.
Psychology; Sociology
Dist - PSU **Prod** - PSU

The Role of Research 20 MIN
U-matic / VHS / 16mm
Color
Describes research carried on by the U S Fish and Wildlife Service, including environmental contaminant evaluation, endangered species recovery, control of wildlife damage to crops, fish husbandry and genetics, habitat preservation and more.
Agriculture; Civics and Political Systems; Science - Natural
Dist - USNAC **Prod** - USBSFW

Role of Surgery in the Management of Ovarian Cancer 60 MIN
U-matic
Color
Discusses the various treatments for primary carcinoma of the ovary, emphasizing the role of surgery.
Health and Safety
Dist - UTEXSC **Prod** - UTEXSC

Role of Surgical Adjuvant Therapy in the Management of Lung Cancer 45 MIN
U-matic
Color
Demonstrates the expected results of surgery used in conjunction with other modalities in treating lung cancer.
Health and Safety
Dist - UTEXSC **Prod** - UTEXSC

The Role of the assistant editor 45 MIN
VHS
Color (PRO G)
$149.00 purchase, $49.00 rental _ #720
Demonstrates all the basic procedures and housekeeping chores of the film editing room. Begins with edit room design and setup and covers splicing techniques, logging and edge numbers, film leadering and labeling, sound transfer and the syncing of dailies, handling of tail slates, MOS shorts and wild tracks during syncing, the dailies screening and common sync errors, coding and shot breakdown and the preparation of a cut work print for the negative cutter. Includes a separate section on the work of the assistant editor in building sound effects reels, the prepration of cue sheets and the handling of sync loss and other problems arising during the mix. Produced by the Australian Film, Television and Radio School.
Industrial and Technical Education
Dist - FIRLIT

The Role of the Black Inventors 29 MIN
VHS / U-matic
Black Inventors Series
Color
History - United States
Dist - SYLWAT **Prod** - RCOMTV 1982

The Role of the Cello in a String Quartet 15 MIN
U-matic / VHS
Chamber Music - the String Quartet Series
Color (I J H)
Fine Arts
Dist - AITECH **Prod** - NETCHE 1977

The Role of the Chief Executive - a study of federal and state government 30 MIN
VHS
Color (G)
$79.95 purchase _ #CCP0187V-S
Shows students how the Constitution established the Executive Branch and provided for the separation of powers. Look at its relationship to the legislative and judicial branches of the federal and state government. Looks at specific roles of the Chief Executive and its influence and exercise of power since the Constitution was ratified.
Civics and Political Systems; History - United States
Dist - CAMV

The Role of the Clavicle and its Surgical Significance 24 MIN
U-matic / VHS
Color (PRO)
Discusses function of the clavicle and demonstrates excision of the medial two - thirds, tip and entire clavicle.
Health and Safety
Dist - WFP **Prod** - WFP

Role of the Coach 12 MIN
16mm
Coaching Development Programme Series no 2; No 2
Color
LC 76-701042
Outlines the role of the school sports coach.
Physical Education and Recreation
Dist - SARBOO **Prod** - SARBOO 1974

The Role of the Community 28 MIN
U-matic / VHS / 16mm
Justice Series
Color (H C A)
$535.00, $250.00 purchase _ #3882
Shows the different community organizations designed to help people.
Social Science; Sociology
Dist - CORF

The Role of the Covariance Function in Estimation 22 MIN
U-matic / VHS
Probability and Random Processes Introduction to Random Processes 'Series
B&W (PRO)
Returns to the MMSE prediction problem for the case in which the predictor is constrained to be linear.
Mathematics
Dist - MIOT **Prod** - MIOT

The Role of the Crown Prosecutor 29 MIN
U-matic
Criminal Justice System Series
(H C A)
Charts the proceedings followed in a break and enter offense through the Crown Prosecutor's office which represents the interest of society when there are violations.
Civics and Political Systems; History - World
Dist - ACCESS **Prod** - ACCESS 1982

Role of the Engineer Manager 30 MIN
VHS / U-matic
Management for Engineers Series
Color
Business and Economics; Industrial and Technical Education; Psychology
Dist - SME **Prod** - UKY

Role of the Family in Rehabilitation of the Physically Disabled - a Personal Statement 26 MIN
VHS / U-matic
B&W
Describes the personal tragedy of a mother of four children after the deaths of three of her children as a result of Smith - Opitz Syndrome. Describes the lack of support from some medical personnel in attending to parents in crisis.
Health and Safety
Dist - BUSARG **Prod** - BUSARG

The Role of the Father 29 MIN
U-matic / VHS
Tomorrow's Families Series
Color (H C A)
LC 81-706897
Discusses how men can define the economic and nurturing elements of their fathering to suit their personal preferences and their relationships with their partners.
Home Economics; Sociology
Dist - AITECH **Prod** - MDDE 1980

The Role of the Father 7 MIN
U-matic
Take Time Series
(A)
Demonstrates the influence of parents and others caring for pre - schoolers on the physical and emotional development of the child.
Health and Safety; Psychology; Sociology
Dist - ACCESS **Prod** - ACCESS 1976

The Role of the First Violin in a String Quartet 15 MIN
VHS / U-matic
Chamber Music - the String Quartet Series
Color (I J H)
Fine Arts
Dist - AITECH **Prod** - NETCHE 1977

The Role of the Home Visitor 23 MIN
U-matic / VHS
B&W (PRO)
Emphasizes key elements of a successful home visit program. Shows importance of respecting the ideas, suggestions and beliefs of parents, and need for sharing information and experiences. Indicates importance of early stages of screening and training potential home visitors.
Education; Psychology; Sociology
Dist - HSERF **Prod** - HSERF

Role of the Hygienist in Dental Care Series
Role of Hygienist in Dental Care - Pt 1 - History and Examination 11 MIN
Role of Hygienist in Dental Care - Pt 2 - Scaling and Root Planing 15 MIN
Dist - USNAC

Role of the Hypothalamus in Emotion and Behavior - Pt 1 54 MIN
16mm
B&W (C T)
Shows that environmental stimuli associated as many as 480 times with 'sham rage' reactions due to hypothalamic stimulation fail to induce affective states. Points out that, in contrast, recovery animals continue feeding or other adaptative behavior during stimulation and show normal fear and rage despite extensive hypothalamic lesions. Shows that cardiac and vasomotor accompaniments of hypothalamic 'conditioning' are not produced in anesthetized animals.
Science - Natural; Sociology
Dist - PSUPCR **Prod** - PSUPCR 1943

Role of the Instructor 30 MIN
16mm
Teaching Role Series
Color; B&W (C T)
LC 73-703318
Discusses the essential features of the instructor - student relationship.
Education
Dist - TELSTR **Prod** - MVNE 1968

The Role of the Judge 29 MIN
U-matic
Criminal Justice System Series
(H C A)
Examines the role of the judge in the process by which an individual is given a fair trial.
Civics and Political Systems; History - World
Dist - ACCESS **Prod** - ACCESS 1982

Role of the Medical Department in Hearing Conservation 28 MIN
16mm
Color
LC 75-703072
Presents the U S Navy Medical Department's program of hearing conservation with examples of applicable conditions. Explains the use of noise measurement and analysis, engineering control, audiometry, protective devices and education. Emphasizes hearing - loss prevention through periodic audiograms and wearing hearing protection devices.
Health and Safety; Science - Natural; Sociology
Dist - USNAC **Prod** - USN 1973

The Role of the MLR LAB Procedure in Organ Transplantation 20 MIN
U-matic / VHS
Color (PRO)
Presents detailed methods used in the selection of prospective graft donors. Demonstrates the techniques used in obtaining lymphoid cells and performing the MLR procedure. Includes basic immunological concepts as they apply to this laboratory exercise.
Health and Safety
Dist - UMICHM **Prod** - UMICHM 1981

Role of the mosque 65 MIN
VHS
Islamic videos on family and education series
Color (G)
$29.95 purchase _ #110 - 022
Presents a lecture by Imam W Deen Mohammad, who is introduced by former boxer Muhammad Ali, on the role of the mosque. Includes a discussion among Muslim women of Chicago on the education of Islamic children.
Religion and Philosophy
Dist - SOUVIS **Prod** - SOUVIS

The Role of the Mother 29 MIN
U-matic / VHS
Tomorrow's Families Series
Color (H C A)
LC 81-706909
Discusses some aspects of motherhood which are determined biologically and others which vary according to culture and social milieu.

Home Economics; Sociology
Dist - AITECH **Prod** - MDDE 1980

Role of the Natural Parent 30 MIN
VHS / U-matic
Home is Where the Care is Series Module 3; Module 3
Color
Presents a program specialist, foster parents and a natural parent sharing their natural experiences in working together to help children face a changing family structure.
Guidance and Counseling; Sociology
Dist - CORF **Prod** - CORF 1984

The Role of the observer 57 MIN
16mm
Color (G)
$80.00 rental
Asks audiences to examine themselves, who they have been and their 'roles' in the process of change, including sexual and social roles now and in childhood.
Fine Arts; Social Science; Sociology
Dist - CANCIN **Prod** - IRWINJ 1982

The Role of the Occupational Therapist in the Public School - Tape I 25 MIN
U-matic
Color (PRO)
Begins a discussion of the role of the occupational therapist in the public school. Narrated by Virginia Scardina.
Education; Guidance and Counseling; Health and Safety
Dist - AOTA **Prod** - AOTA 1979

The Role of the Occupational Therapist in the Public School - Tape II 20 MIN
U-matic
Color (PRO)
Concludes a discussion of the role of the occupational therapist in the public school. Narrated by Virginia Scardina.
Education; Guidance and Counseling; Health and Safety
Dist - AOTA **Prod** - AOTA 1979

The Role of the Office Worker 9 MIN
U-matic / 35mm strip
Effective Office Worker Series
Color
Shows the office staff where they fit into the overall organization and points out that they are an important part of the team.
Psychology
Dist - RESEM **Prod** - RESEM

The Role of the Operating Room Nurse in Cardiovascular Surgery 19 MIN
16mm
Color (PRO)
Demonstrates the duties and requirements placed upon the nurse from the time the patient enters the operating room until completion of the operative procedure. Emphasizes the necessity for skill, dedication and the ability to work effectively in an active and demanding environment where success depends upon coordinated teamwork.
Health and Safety; Science
Dist - ACY **Prod** - ACYDGD 1968

The Role of the Parents 11 MIN
U-matic / VHS
Color (PRO)
Discusses the impact of preterm delivery on parents, interactions between parents, infant and nursery personnel and ways in which staff can facilitate parents' emotional adjustments.
Health and Safety; Psychology
Dist - UMICHM **Prod** - UMICHM 1983

The Role of the Physician 41 MIN
U-matic / VHS
Terminal Illness Series
Color
Sociology
Dist - UWASHP **Prod** - UWASHP

The Role of the Police 29 MIN
U-matic
Criminal Justice System Series
(H C A)
Follows a typical break and enter offense from the commitment of the crime to the actual laying of charges.
Civics and Political Systems; History - World
Dist - ACCESS **Prod** - ACCESS 1982

The Role of the Police Officer 27 MIN
VHS / U-matic
Cop Talk Series
Color (I J)
Follows a police officer as he performs such duties as telling a father that his son was killed while leaning from a car and warns a car full of young people of that danger.
Social Science
Dist - AITECH **Prod** - UTSBE 1981

The Role of the President's Cabinet 20 MIN
U-matic
Color (H C A)
LC 76-706257
Presents the highlights of a panel discussion concerning the role of the President's cabinet. Discusses the answers to such issues as direct access to the president, role of the office of management and budget and the dilemma of time in managing a government department.
Civics and Political Systems
Dist - USNAC **Prod** - USCSC 1976

The Role of the School Counselor in Career Education 24 MIN
16mm
Color (PRO)
Presents the role of the school counselor in career education within the framework of six possible functions, including teaching, working with teachers, leadership functions, roles with parents, evaluating the career program and direct services to students.
Education; Guidance and Counseling
Dist - AACD **Prod** - AACD 1982

The Role of the script supervisor 28 MIN
VHS
Color (PRO G)
$149.00 purchase, $49.00 rental _ #717
Presents a comprehensive and detailed examination of the duties of the script supervisor and the issues of continuity in film and TV production. Examines continuity of photographic look, sets and makeup, narrative continuity and overlapping action, continuity of screen direction and eyelines, script timing, preparation of 'one liners' and script breakdown, the relationship of the script supervisor and director, the preparation of script notes and the lined script and the completion of notes and reports after the shoot. Produced by the Australian Film, Television and Radio School.
Fine Arts; Industrial and Technical Education
Dist - FIRLIT

The Role of the Second Violin in a String Quartet 15 MIN
U-matic / VHS
Chamber Music - the String Quartet Series
Color (I J H)
Fine Arts
Dist - AITECH **Prod** - NETCHE 1977

The Role of the Supervisor 17 MIN
U-matic / VHS
Leadership Link - Fundamentals of Effective Supervision Series
Color
Business and Economics; Psychology
Dist - DELTAK **Prod** - CHSH

The Role of the Supreme Court 20 MIN
16mm
Government and Public Affairs Films Series
B&W (H A)
Dr David Fellman, professor of political science, University of Wisconsin, analyzes the history, power and judicial procedures of our highest court.
Civics and Political Systems
Dist - MLA **Prod** - RSC 1960

The Role of the Supreme Court - Dr David Fellman 20 MIN
16mm
Building Political Leadership Series
B&W (H C)
Civics and Political Systems
Dist - MLA **Prod** - RSC 1960

The Role of the VA Police Officer 14 MIN
U-matic / VHS
Color (PRO)
Discusses the responsibilities of the Veterans Administration police officer.
Civics and Political Systems; Social Science
Dist - USNAC **Prod** - VAMSLC 1984

The Role of the Viola in a String Quartet 15 MIN
U-matic / VHS
Chamber Music - the String Quartet Series
Color (I J H)
Fine Arts
Dist - AITECH **Prod** - NETCHE 1977

The Role of the Wheel 7 MIN
U-matic / VHS / 16mm
Visual Awareness Series
Color (I J H)
LC FIA63-432
Shows the wheel in its diverse forms and in the various places where it is used in transportation, communication, industry and recreation.
Business and Economics; Fine Arts; Psychology; Social Science
Dist - IFB **Prod** - PAI 1963

Role of the Witness 42 MIN
16mm
Color
LC 75-700695
Offers instruction on being an expert witness in a court action on air pollution.
Civics and Political Systems; Science - Natural
Dist - USNAC **Prod** - USEPA 1969

The Role of Theatre in Ancient Greece 23 MIN
U-matic / VHS
Color (C)
$249.00, $149.00 purchase _ #AD - 1634
Describes the role of theatre as a central aspect of life in ancient Greece.
History - World; Literature and Drama
Dist - FOTH **Prod** - FOTH

The Role of Videotape in the Diagnosis and Management of Laringeal Cancer 11 MIN
VHS / 16mm
Color (C PRO)
$385.00 purchase _ #840VI045
Focuses on the uses of videotape in the outpatient clinic, in the operating room, and for instructional purposes. Illustrates how the coupling of videotape with new developments in endoscopy has produced an objective method for recording laringeal lesions.
Health and Safety
Dist - HSCIC **Prod** - HSCIC 1984

The Role of women 15 MIN
U-matic / VHS
America past series
(J H)
$125.00 purchase
Presents a look at the origin and development of the women's rights movement.
History - United States; History - World
Dist - AITECH **Prod** - KRMATV 1987

The Role of women in the movies 28 MIN
U-matic / VHS / 16mm
Art of film series
Color
Offers a history of cinema's treatment of women from the beginning of movies to the Great Depression. Features sequences from the films of Lillian Gish, Theda Bara, Clara Bow, Gloria Swanson, Jean Harlow, Carole Lombard, Pola Negri, Louise Brooks, Marlene Dietrich, Greta Garbo and Mae West.
Fine Arts; Sociology
Dist - CORF **Prod** - JANUS 1979

Role of women project series
Clorae and Albie 36 MIN
Girls at 12 30 MIN
Dist - EDC

Role - Play, Simulations and Evaluating Classroom Environment 30 MIN
U-matic / VHS
Creating a Learning Environment Series
Color
Education; Guidance and Counseling
Dist - NETCHE **Prod** - NETCHE 1975

Role Playing for Social Values 16 MIN
16mm
B&W (P I)
Presents role - playing as one aspect of the TABA in - service education program.
Education; Guidance and Counseling
Dist - AWPC **Prod** - AWPC 1968

Roles
VHS
Color (A)
$99.95 purchase _ #8131
Examines roles as they relate to children of alcoholics.
Health and Safety; Psychology; Sociology
Dist - HAZELB

Roles and Goals in High School 29 MIN
16mm / U-matic / VHS
Dealing with Classroom Problems Series
Color (T)
Presents Dr William Glasser who extends the application of his Identity Society and Schools Without Failure concepts to the secondary level. Shows how reality therapy can be used to handle discipline problems.
Education
Dist - FI **Prod** - MFFD 1976

Roles and Services 30 MIN
VHS / U-matic
Educational Alternatives for Handicapped Students Series
Color
Covers three major topics, beginning with the need for schools to provide a continuum of educational services for the handicapped, including the various types of programs ranging from mainstreaming to special schools. Illustrates identification and placement procedures for students with special needs, especially those who remain in regular

school programs. Describes the role of classroom teachers and support personnel as they work together on programming for handicapped students and communicate with parents about their programs.
Education; Psychology
Dist - NETCHE **Prod** - NETCHE 1977

Roles in marriage 50 MIN
VHS
God's blueprint for the Christian family series
Color (R G)
$29.95 purchase _ #6139 - 5
Features Dr Tony Evans. Discusses gender - oriented marriage roles from a conservative Christian viewpoint. Part of six parts on marriage, parenting and families.
Guidance and Counseling; Literature and Drama; Religion and Philosophy; Sociology
Dist - MOODY **Prod** - MOODY

The Roles of the President 30 MIN
U-matic / VHS
American Government 2 Series
Color (C)
Presents the parts the President must play, how each role evolved to what it is today and how several Presidents have used these roles to suit their own personalities.
Civics and Political Systems
Dist - DALCCD **Prod** - DALCCD

Roles we play 30 MIN
VHS / U-matic
Art of being human series; Module 10
Color (C)
History - World; Literature and Drama; Religion and Philosophy
Dist - MDCC **Prod** - MDCC

Rolf Harris in Tasmania 27 MIN
16mm
Color
LC 80-700915
Presents Rolf Harris, who takes a look at the wide variety of scenery in Tasmania.
Geography - World
Dist - TASCOR **Prod** - TASCOR 1976

Roll 'Em Lola 5 MIN
16mm
Color
LC 75-700478
Presents an animated film depicting the fantasy of an eternal Hollywood chase which communicates images of psychic unrest.
Fine Arts; Psychology
Dist - USC **Prod** - USC

Roll of Thunder, Hear My Cry 110 MIN
U-matic / VHS / 16mm
Color (J)
LC 80-700026
Tells the story of a Black family in the poverty - stricken South of 1933, who struggle to hold on to the land they have owned for three generations. Based on the book Roll Of Thunder, Hear My Cry by Mildred D Taylor.
Fine Arts; Guidance and Counseling; History - United States; Sociology
Dist - LCOA **Prod** - TOMENT 1979

Roll Out 5 MIN
16mm
Color
LC 75-700479
Shows a group of people who get together to play a game called racquetball. Examines the details of how the game is played and encourages other people to play the game themselves.
Physical Education and Recreation
Dist - AMFVOI **Prod** - AMFVOI 1975

Roll Over 10 MIN
16mm
Color (J)
LC 74-703029
Presents a montage of scenes that expose oppression and celebrate the liberation of women. Includes views of sex role stereotyping and of women working in professions previously restricted to men. Features many feminist businesses and shows scenes about housework, motherhood and working for men, ending with a glance at women in the future.
Sociology
Dist - HERFLM **Prod** - HERFLM 1974

Roll Threading Setup Procedures 14 MIN
VHS / U-matic
Steel Making Series
Color (IND)
Presents a detailed procedure for the setup and change of rolls on a Hartford roll threading machine. Covers feed way assembly timer adjustments.
Business and Economics; Industrial and Technical Education
Dist - LEIKID **Prod** - LEIKID

Roller Bearings 10 MIN
VHS
Power Transmission Series I - PT Products Series
Color (A)
$225.00 purchase, $50.00 rental _ #57968
Describes cylindrical, spherical, tapered and concave roller bearings. Discusses internal clearances, mountings, fixed and floating bearings, housing types. Demonstrates that clearance, type of bore, and presence or absence of grease groove are critical in the selection of bearings.
Industrial and Technical Education
Dist - UILL **Prod** - MAJEC 1986

Roller Chain 22 MIN
U-matic / VHS
Color (IND)
Explains basic components of roller chain, pin link and roller link. Discusses pitch, links and clearances. Includes a section on special chains.
Education; Industrial and Technical Education
Dist - TAT **Prod** - TAT

Roller Chain and Sprockets 18 MIN
VHS
Power Transmission Series I - PT Products Series
Color (A)
$225.00 purchase, $50.00 rental _ #57965
Describes roller chain construction, explaining ANSI standards for numbering and identification. Shows multiple strand, heavy series, double pitch, and self - lubricating chains, including straight lug, bent lug, and extended pin attachments, and bored - to - size and bushed sprockets. Explains how to determine size and type of chain from numbers and also explains the ratio at which adding a chain increases load capacity.
Industrial and Technical Education
Dist - UILL **Prod** - MAJEC 1986

Roller Chain Drive Selection 18 MIN
VHS
Power Transmission Series II - Selection, Application and 'Maintenance Series
Color (A)
$265.00 purchase, $50.00 rental _ #57984
Lists factors relevant to the choice of design in roller chain drives, such as material, sprocket size, center distance, anticipated speeds and loads. Shows how to use service factor tables to determine design (equivalent) horsepower. Recommends the smallest practical pitch choice for the most quiet and economical operation. Discusses multiple strand chains and their service factors. Warns against look - alike chains which are not ANSI standard.
Industrial and Technical Education
Dist - UILL **Prod** - MAJEC 1986

Roller coaster thrills
VHS
Color (G)
$19.95 purchase _ #EK003
Takes a ride on nine of the scariest roller coasters in the US.
Geography - United States; Sociology
Dist - SIV

Roller Cone Bits 27 MIN
U-matic / Slide / VHS / 16mm
Color (IND A PRO) (SPANISH)
$160.00 purchase _ #11.1087, $170.00 purchase _ #51.1087
Discusses the parts, features, and proper techniques for running steel - tooth and carbide - insert bits to bottom.
Business and Economics; Industrial and Technical Education; Social Science
Dist - UTEXPE **Prod** - UTEXPE 1977

Roller Skate Fever 10 MIN
16mm / U-matic / VHS
Color
LC 81-701130
Shows roller skaters in Venice, California, performing dizzying stunts to the accompaniment of rock music.
Fine Arts; Physical Education and Recreation
Dist - PFP **Prod** - SHAPP 1981

Roller Skate Safely 15 MIN
16mm
Color
LC 80-701745
Discusses safety and courtesy while roller skating. Explains the purposes of protective equipment and shows how to lace the boots and adjust the toe stops, wheels and trucks.
Physical Education and Recreation
Dist - FIESTF **Prod** - FIESTF 1980

Roller Skate Safety 15 MIN
U-matic / VHS
Color
LC 80-707492
Illustrates the importance of roller skating safety equipment and stresses the need for routine safety and maintenance checks. Shows a variety of skates and makes recommendations on equipment purchase versus rental. Deals with basic skating safety on sidewalks and streets.
Health and Safety; Physical Education and Recreation
Dist - FIESTF **Prod** - FIESTF 1980

Roller Skating Safety 15 MIN
16mm / U-matic / VHS
Color
LC 81-700740
Discusses safety and etiquette in roller skating.
Physical Education and Recreation
Dist - AIMS **Prod** - CAHILL 1980

Rollerskating Safety 15 MIN
U-matic / VHS / 16mm
Color (P I J H C G T A)
$25.00 rental _ #4641
Shows how to prevent rollerskating accidents that roll into emergency rooms.
Health and Safety; Physical Education and Recreation
Dist - AIMS **Prod** - AIMS 1980

Rolle's Theorem, Mean Value Theorem
U-matic
Calculus Series
Color
Mathematics
Dist - MDCPB **Prod** - MDDE

Rollin' with Love 6 MIN
U-matic / VHS
Color (H C A)
Provides a light side introduction to a discussion on same - sex lifestyles. Uses animation.
Health and Safety; Psychology; Sociology
Dist - MMRC **Prod** - MMRC

Rolling 25 MIN
VHS / U-matic
Technical Studies Series
Color (H C A)
Discusses aspects of industrial rolling.
Industrial and Technical Education
Dist - FI **Prod** - BBCTV 1981

Rolling 11 MIN
U-matic / VHS
Manufacturing Materials and Processes Series
Color
Covers steps in rolling and kinds of rolling processes.
Industrial and Technical Education
Dist - WFVTAE **Prod** - GE

Rolling back the rock - the religious meaning of Holy Week 120 MIN
VHS
Father John Shea series
Color (G R)
$49.95 purchase _ #358
Features Father John Shea who reflects on the true meaning of Holy Thursday, Good Friday and Holy Saturday. Divides into four half - hour segments with questions for discussion and reflection. Appropriate for Lent. Includes 16 - page discussion guide. Part of a series by Father John Shea.
Literature and Drama; Religion and Philosophy
Dist - ACTAF **Prod** - ACTAF

Rolling Contact Bearings 1 60 MIN
VHS
Bearings and Lubrication Series
Color (PRO)
$600.00, $1500.00 purchase _ #GMRC1
Describes various types of rolling contact bearings and their components. Explains mounting methods, fits and tolerances and lubricating methods. Part of a six - part series on bearings and lubrication, part of a larger set on general and mechanical maintenance. Includes 10 textbooks and an instructor guide which provide four hours of instruction.
Education; Industrial and Technical Education; Psychology
Dist - NUSTC **Prod** - NUSTC

Rolling Contact Bearings 2 60 MIN
VHS
Bearings and Lubrication Series
Color (PRO)
$600.00, $1500.00 purchase _ #GMRC2
Focuses on rolling contact bearing maintenance. Includes removal techniques, cleaning and inspection, relubrication and bearing failures. Part of a six - part series on bearings and lubrication, part of a larger set on general and mechanical maintenance. Includes 10 textbooks and an instructor guide which provide four hours of instruction.
Education; Industrial and Technical Education; Psychology
Dist - NUSTC **Prod** - NUSTC

The Rolling Rice Ball 11 MIN
16mm / U-matic / VHS
Color (P)
$280.00, $195.00 purchase _ #1817; LC FIA67-1262
Presents an animated film version of a Japanese fairy tale about a Japanese woodcutter who shares his rice balls with the mice and is rewarded and a grasping hunter who learns the folly of greed when he receives no treasure from the mice.

Guidance and Counseling; Literature and Drama; Psychology
Dist - CORF Prod - GAKKEN 1967

Rolling South 15 MIN
16mm
Color
LC 80-700073
Presents visual imagery with minimum narration to create a picture of a railroad constantly on the move around the clock.
Social Science
Dist - NS Prod - NS 1979

Rolling Steel 14 MIN
U-matic / VHS / 16mm
Color (I J H)
Shows a field trip to a plant where construction steel is manufactured from scrap iron. Reveals giant electric furnaces, searing heat of molten metal and ear piercing din of a steel plant. Explains the elements necessary to produce steel in a variety of shapes for industrial use.
Business and Economics; Science - Physical
Dist - BCNFL Prod - BORTF 1983

Rollo May and Human Encounter - Pt 1 - Self - Self Encounter and Self - Other Encounter 30 MIN
16mm
Color
Features Dr Rollo May who describes man's dilemma as having to see himself as both subject and object in life. Discusses the four elements of human encounter including empathy, eros, friendship and agape. Points out that if any of the four elements is absent, human encounter does not exist.
Psychology; Religion and Philosophy; Sociology
Dist - PSYCHF Prod - PSYCHF

Rollo May and Human Encounter - Pt 2 - Manipulation and Human Encounter, 30 MIN
16mm
Color
Features Dr Rollo May who discusses how man is manipulated when any of the four elements of human encounter is missing. Describes the problems of transference in psychotherapy as a distortion of human encounter. Explains the exploitation of eros, describing modern man's fixation on sexuality and relating this to man's fear of death.
Psychology; Religion and Philosophy; Sociology
Dist - PSYCHF Prod - PSYCHF

Rollo may on Counseling 24 MIN
16mm
Color (C G)
Consists of Rollo May applying his ideas to differing historical periods and outlining the role of the counselor in an age of anxiety.
Guidance and Counseling; Psychology
Dist - AACD Prod - AACD 1975

Rollo may on Creativity and the Tragic 30 MIN
16mm
Color (A)
Discusses Dr Rollo May's early education, theological and graduate training, and onset of tuberculosis. Shows how creativity derives from coming to grips with adversity and death, and rebelling against it.
Psychology
Dist - AACD Prod - AACD 1976

Rollo may on Existential Psychology 30 MIN
16mm
Color (C G)
Presents Rollo May addressing the question of what is existential psychology, and exploring the concepts of will, freedom, being, anxiety, intentionality and meaningfulness of experience. Treats the relationship between loneliness and love, and living in a society whose myths have eroded.
Psychology; Religion and Philosophy
Dist - AACD Prod - AACD 1976

Rollo may on Humanistic Psychology 24 MIN
16mm
Color (C G)
Shows psychologist Rollo May tracing the historical development of humanistic psychology. Discusses its basic principles, which are that psychology deals with the whole person, that a consideration of subjectivity is essential, that no science is value free, and that theory should be based more on normal people.
Psychology
Dist - AACD Prod - AACD 1975

Rollo may, Psychology 29 MIN
VHS / U-matic
Quest for Peace Series
Color (A)
Psychology
Dist - AACD Prod - AACD 1984

Rollo May's Discussion with Richard Evans - Anxiety, Love, will and Dying 28 MIN
U-matic / VHS / 16mm
Notable Contributors to the Psychology of Personality Series
Color (C G T A)
Discusses his notion of existential anxiety. He also deals with how anxiety and depression are related, the relatively new emphasis and concern with dying as a field of psychology, and analyses of love, will, and responsibility.
Biography; Psychology; Sociology
Dist - PSU Prod - PSU 1978

Rollo May's Discussion with Richard Evans - Maturity and Creativity 29 MIN
16mm / U-matic / VHS
Notable Contributors to the Psychology of Personality Series
Color (C G T A)
Discusses his views of maturity and his own recent work on the process of creativity. He also evaluates his most significant contributions, reacts to his critics, and discusses his future plans.
Biography; Psychology
Dist - PSU Prod - PSU 1978

Rollo Mays Discussion with Richard Evans - Reactions to Psychoanalytic Concepts 29 MIN
U-matic / VHS / 16mm
Notable Contributors to the Psychology of Personality Series
Color (C G T A)
Discusses his reactions to the ideas of Freud, Rank, Sullivan, Adler, and Jung.
Biography; Psychology
Dist - PSUPCR Prod - PSUPCR 1978

Rollos / roles 30 MIN
U-matic / VHS
La Esquina series
Color (H C A)
Uses a story to try to reduce the minority isolation of Mexican - American students by showing the teenager as an individual, as a member of a unique cultural group and as a member of a larger complex society.
Sociology
Dist - GPN Prod - SWEDL 1976

Roly Poly Blues 42 MIN
U-matic / VHS / 16mm
Color
Gives information and personal testimonial on obesity and excess weight.
Health and Safety
Dist - PEREN Prod - PEREN

Roma Barocca 10 MIN
16mm
Color (I J H C)
LC 76-703637
Depicts Roman fountains to present an exercise in how to isolate a single concept from a conglomeration of materials. Shows the importance of being able to discern and to separate what one sees from its surroundings.
Psychology; Sociology
Dist - MALIBU Prod - GREGGB 1974

The Roman Age 30 MIN
16mm
How Should We Then Live Series
Color
LC 77-702363
Interprets the collapse of Rome as being the result of the Romans' failure to embrace Christianity. Attributes the survival of the early Christians to their belief in God's existence. Based on the book How Should We Then Live by Francis A Schaeffer.
History - World; Religion and Philosophy
Dist - GF Prod - GF 1977

The Roman Army 30 MIN
VHS
Saints and legions series
Color (H)
$69.95 purchase
Considers the Roman army. Part 3 of a twenty - six part series which introduces personalities, movements and events in ancient history responsible for the beginnings of Western Civilization.
Civics and Political Systems; Geography - World; Guidance and Counseling; History - World
Dist - SCETV Prod - SCETV 1982

Roman awnings 50 MIN
VHS
Secrets of lost empires series
Color; PAL (G)
PdS99 purchase; Not availble in the United States or Canada
Observes engineer Ove Arup as he attempts to recreate the awnings that covered Roman ampitheatres using only timber, canvas and rope. Interweaves practical demonstrations and debate with location sequences at ancient Roman sites and explorations of the culture of the Roman empire. Part three of a four - part series.
History - United States; History - World; Industrial and Technical Education
Dist - BBCENE

Roman Banquet Stretch 10 MIN
Videoreel / VT2
Janaki Series
Color
Physical Education and Recreation
Dist - PBS Prod - WGBHTV

Roman Britain - fortifications 14 MIN
U-matic / VHS / BETA
Color; NTSC; PAL; SECAM (I J)
PdS58
Examines the conquest and occupation of Britain by ancient Rome. Discusses fortifications in three sections - typical early forts; Hadrian's Wall, its construction and manner of defense; the forts of the Saxon shore. Uses animated maps and pictorial reconstructions to suggest the appearance of military structures at the time, as well as models to show details of forts and the buildings on Hadrian's Wall. Advised by Dr D J Smith, JSA, Kepper of the Museum of Antiquities, University of Newcastle - Upon - Tyne.
History - World
Dist - VIEWTH

Roman Britain - the towns 15 MIN
U-matic / VHS / BETA
Color; NTSC; PAL; SECAM (I J)
PdS58
Shows the manner in which archeological excavation, followed by a careful examination of the objects discovered, has gradually built up knowledge of life in Roman Britain. Shows Roman sites in Verulamium, Bath, Carleon, Vindolanda, and a wide range of the objects discovered. Reconstructs a Roman family scene, using actors in costume, advised by D Gareth Davies, Director of Verulamium Museum.
History - World
Dist - VIEWTH

Roman comedy - Part I 22 MIN
VHS
Color (H C)
$159.00 purchase _ #DF297
Compares scenes from Amphitryon by Plautus with A Comedy of Errors by Shakespeare to show how Roman comedy inspired Shakespeare and later playwrights. Looks at Rome in the time of Plautus and illustrates the art, architecture and locations which inspired him. Uses authentic oversized masks to show how exaggerated gestures and vocal techniques were used in ancient theater. Part one of two parts on Roman comedy.
Fine Arts; History - World; Literature and Drama
Dist - INSIM

Roman comedy - Part II 24 MIN
VHS
Color (H C)
$159.00 purchase _ #DF298
Uses scenes from Phormio by Terence juxtaposed with scenes from Scalpin by Moliere to illustrate Moliere's admiration for the sophisticated plots of Terence. Illustrates authentic oversized masks to show how exaggerated gestures and vocal techniques were used in ancient theater. Part two of two parts on Roman comedy.
Fine Arts; History - World; Literature and Drama
Dist - INSIM

The Roman empire 30 MIN
VHS
Western tradition series
Color; PAL (J H G)
PdS29.50 purchase
Relates how Rome began to destroy its own greatness by building an empire. Presents part of an eight - part series that conveys the excitement of historical inquiry while stimulating critical thinking about the unique events of each major period of history.
History - World
Dist - EMFVL Prod - CORF

The Roman Empire - 300 BC - 200 AD 15 MIN
VHS
Ancient Rome - the rise and fall of Rome series
Color (J H C G)
$59.95 purchase _ #BU702V
Visits the Roman Empire and witnesses its development. Discusses the customs, lifestyles, architecture and religions of the era. Part of a five - part series on Rome.

History - World
Dist - CAMV

Roman Holiday 118 MIN
16mm / U-matic / VHS
Color
Describes the romance which blooms between a newspaper man and a princess yearning to escape the dull life of diplomatic duties. Stars Audrey Hepburn and Gregory Peck.
Fine Arts
Dist - FI **Prod** - PAR 1953

Roman Life in Ancient Pompeii 16 MIN
16mm
Color (I J)
The voice of a young girl recounts the story of her life in Pompeii before the eruption of Vesuvius. The camera retraces her steps through the silent ruins as she helps with family tasks, shops, visits friends and goes to the amphitheater.
History - World
Dist - SUTHLA **Prod** - SUTHLA 1962

The Roman numeral series
I 6 MIN
II 9 MIN
IV2 MIN
V 3 MIN
VI13 MIN
VII 5 MIN
VIII 4 MIN
IX2 MIN
Dist - CANCIN

Roman Provincial Society 25 MIN
16mm / U-matic / VHS
Color (J H)
Explains the significance of excavated Roman archaeological sites in Britain, France and Africa. Uses artists' reconstructions where archeological remains are too fragmentary for immediate understanding.
History - World
Dist - VIEWTH **Prod** - GATEEF

Roman Renaissance 27 MIN
U-matic / VHS / 16mm
Victory at Sea Series
B&W (J H)
Views the Sicilian and Italian campaigns during World War II.
Civics and Political Systems; History - United States; History - World
Dist - LUF **Prod** - NBCTV

The Roman renaissance 15 MIN
VHS
Ancient Rome - the rise and fall of Rome series
Color (J H C G)
$59.95 purchase _ #BU705V
Examines the historical legacy of Rome. Part of a five - part series on Rome.
History - World
Dist - CAMV

The Roman tragedies - Shakespeare workshop 3 60 MIN
VHS
Shakespeare workshop series
Color; PAL (J H C G)
PdS29.50 purchase
Imparts something of the original excitement of the theatrical experience and serves as a stimulating complement to textual analysis. Provides a useful introduction to Shakespeare's Roman tragedies for GCSE and A level students, although those in further education will benefit also. Part of a three - part series.
Fine Arts; Literature and Drama
Dist - EMFVL

The Roman Wall 16 MIN
16mm
Color (I J H C G)
Deals with the Roman occupation of Britain beginning with the expansion of the Roman Empire. Focuses on the defenses built across the North of Britain by Hadrian. Examines remains of these walls and describes layout, construction, uses and defense.
History - World; Sociology
Dist - VIEWTH **Prod** - GATEEF

The Roman World 23 MIN
U-matic / VHS / 16mm
Color (J H C)
LC FIA65-928
Gives a general picture of life in the Roman Empire at its greatest extent. Shows many aspects of Roman practical achievements.
History - World
Dist - IFB **Prod** - IFB 1963

Romance 134 MIN
U-matic / VHS
B&W
Conjoins sexual ambiguity with narrative breakdown.
Fine Arts
Dist - KITCHN **Prod** - KITCHN

Romance and Reality 52 MIN
16mm / U-matic / VHS
Civilisation Series no 3; No 3
Color (J)
LC 76-708458
Surveys the development of Western civilization during the 13th century. Depicts a world of chivalry, courtesy and romance as evidenced in the emergence of courtly love as the ultimate in aesthetic and ascetic devotion, and as reflected in the poetry of Dante and the Anjou tapestries. Points out the spiritual happiness of the period as seen in the life of St Francis and in the work, 'the little flowers.'.
Fine Arts; History - World; Literature and Drama; Psychology; Religion and Philosophy; Sociology
Dist - FI **Prod** - BBCTV 1970

Romance and Reality - Pt 1 24 MIN
U-matic / VHS / 16mm
Civilisation Series no 3; No 3
Color (J)
LC 76-708458
Surveys the development of Western civilization during the 13th century. Depicts a world of chivalry, courtesy and romance as evidenced in the emergence of courtly love as the ultimate in aesthetic and ascetic devotion, and as reflected in the poetry of Dante and the Anjou tapestries. Points out the spiritual happiness of the period as seen in the life of St Francis and in the work, 'The little flowers.'.
Fine Arts; Literature and Drama
Dist - FI **Prod** - BBCTV 1970

Romance and Reality - Pt 2 28 MIN
U-matic / VHS / 16mm
Civilisation Series no 3; No 3
Color (J)
LC 76-708458
Surveys the development of Western civilization during the 13th century. Depicts a world of chivalry, courtesy and romance as evidenced in the emergence of courtly love as the ultimate in aesthetic and ascetic devotion, and as reflected in the poetry of Dante and the Anjou tapestries. Points out the spiritual happiness of the period as seen in the life of St Francis and in the work, 'The little flowers.'.
Fine Arts; Literature and Drama
Dist - FI **Prod** - BBCTV 1970

Romance at Droitwich Spa 30 MIN
U-matic / VHS
Wodehouse Playhouse Series
Color (C A)
Presents an adaptation of the short story Romance At Droitwich Spa by P G Wodehouse.
Literature and Drama
Dist - TIMLIF **Prod** - BBCTV 1980

Romance in Snow Country 25 MIN
16mm
Color (C A)
Tells the true story of Shoshin, who lived in northern Japan's snowladen mountains. Explains that he was destined to become a Shinto priest like his father until a Christian radio program changed the course of his life.
Guidance and Counseling; Religion and Philosophy
Dist - CBFMS **Prod** - CBFMS

Romance in solitude 29 MIN
16mm
Color (G)
$50.00 rental
Follows a hero's journey in four parts. Begins in the zone between man and nature desiring love. Encounters war, philosophy and religion. Produced by Bruce Cooper.
Fine Arts; Religion and Philosophy; Sociology
Dist - CANCIN

Romance of a Horsethief 101 MIN
16mm
Color (H C A)
Presents a folk tale set in a small Polish border town in 1904 as a young revolutionary woman is torn between her love for her fiance and fellow revolutionary and her handsome childhood sweetheart. Stars Yul Brynner and Eli Wallach.
Fine Arts
Dist - CINEWO **Prod** - CINEWO 1971

Romance of a Jewess 10 MIN
VHS
Silent; B&W (G) (SILENT WITH ENGLISH INTERTITLES)
$50.00 purchase
Portrays the generational conflict between Jewish family members in the Lower East Side of New York City. Tells the story of Ruth, who is disowned by her father for defying his wish to marry a rich man - instead she is happily married to a poor bookseller. Eventually her father makes amends and the family is reunited after certain tragic events. Directed by D W Griffith. Silent with English intertitles.
Religion and Philosophy; Sociology
Dist - NCJEWF

Romance of the lumberjack 16 MIN
VHS
Color (I J H C)
$59.00 purchase _ #866
Recalls 19th - century lumbering. Shows how one of the United States' most important natural resources was exploited a hundred years ago. Includes music by authentic lumberjack folksingers.
Agriculture; Industrial and Technical Education
Dist - HAWHIL **Prod** - HAWHIL

The Romance of Transportation 11 MIN
U-matic / VHS / 16mm
Color
Uses animation to show the growth of transportation in North America. Comments on the development of the canoe, oxcart, barge, steamboat, railroad, automobile, and airplane.
Social Science
Dist - IFB **Prod** - NFBC 1954

The Romance of Transportation in Canada 11 MIN
U-matic / VHS / 16mm
Color (I)
Uses animated figures to portray, with humorous effect, stages in the developmnet of transportation in Canada, from the first footpaths, canoe, barge and steamboat, oxcart, railway and automobile to the aircraft. Commentator delivers historical narrative.
Geography - World; Social Science
Dist - IFB **Prod** - NFBC 1952

The Romance of Vienna 60 MIN
VHS
Traveloguer collection series
Color (G)
$29.95 purchase _ #QU000
Visits Vienna, Austria. Offers historical and geographic highlights.
Geography - World
Dist - SIV

The Romance of wood 13 MIN
VHS
Color (G)
$14.95 purchase
Portrays the 'love affair' of living with wood stoves.
Home Economics; Social Science
Dist - WMMI **Prod** - WMMI 1981

Romance, Sex, and Marriage - all the Guys Ever Want is S - E - X 26 MIN
U-matic / VHS / 16mm
Color
Records the conversations of high school students as they describe their feelings about sex. Covers birth control, virginity, physical appearance, emotional involvement, acceptance, sexual abuse, masturbation and self - confidence.
Health and Safety; Psychology
Dist - CNEMAG **Prod** - DOCUA

Romance, Sex and Marriage - all the Guys Ever Want is Sex 26 MIN
U-matic / VHS / 16mm
Color (H C A)
LC 76-701180
Presents groups and individuals from different environments describing some of their experiences and expressing opinions about the meaning and value of sexual relationships. Includes discussion of virginity, birth control, physical appearance, emotional involvement, acceptance, sexual abuse, masturbation and self - confidence.
Guidance and Counseling; Health and Safety; Psychology; Sociology
Dist - CNEMAG **Prod** - HOBLEI 1976

Romance to Recovery 34 MIN
16mm
Color (H C A)
LC 79-700995
Uses the story of a typical family's problems with alcoholism to explain how alcohol can lead to the disintegration of the family unit. Emphasizes the importance of rehabilitation for the 'co - alcoholic' as well as the alcoholic.
Guidance and Counseling; Health and Safety; Psychology; Sociology
Dist - FMSP **Prod** - FMSP 1979

Romance to Recovery
U-matic / VHS / 16mm
(H C A)
$450.00 purchase _ #81380 3/4 INCH and #81372 VHS and #81364 FILM,
Discusses the lives and lifestyles of a typical alcoholic family.
Guidance and Counseling; Psychology; Sociology
Dist - CMPCAR

Romance with a double base 40 MIN
VHS
Color (G)
$19.95 purchase _ #1664
Stars John Cleese and Connie Booth in a comic adaptation of the short story by Anton Chekhov. Tells of Smychkov, a double - bass player on his way to perform at the betrothal ball of a princess. On the way, he skinny - dips in the royal lake while, unknown to him, the princess has decided to do the same. A thief steals their clothing, Smychkov chivalrously carries the naked princess to the palace in his double - bass case and romance ensues.
Literature and Drama
Dist - KULTUR **Prod** - KULTUR 1993

Romancing the seed 55 MIN
VHS
Color (G)
$49.95 purchase _ #6 - 072 - 101N
Covers production, care and planting of seeds. Features interviews with professional seed growers and breeders in gardens, fields and greenhouses. Shows how to start plants from seed. Discusses seed beds, soil mix, use of heat and water, successive plantings, planting depths, thinning and transplanting.
Agriculture; Science - Natural
Dist - VEP **Prod** - VEP

Romancing the seed 55 MIN
VHS
Color (H C G)
$19.95 purchase
Views the commercial seed industry behind - the - scenes. Explores basic botanical aspects of seed production. Covers controlled pollination techniques in the production of hybrid seed, breeding strategies for both flower and seed crop plants, anther culture, seed harvesting, cleaning, packaging and marketing techniques.
Agriculture; Science - Natural
Dist - BBG **Prod** - BBG 1988

Romanesque art 29 MIN
35mm strip / VHS
Color (J H C T A)
$93.00 purchase _ #MB - 540613 - 6, #MB - 540614 - 4
Traces the historic and artistic development of Romanesque art. Shows how Romanseque art borrowed from Roman, Byzantine, Spanish, Islamic and Nordic sources.
Fine Arts; History - World
Dist - SRA **Prod** - SRA 1988

Romanesque Painters (1000 - 1200 a D) 11 MIN
16mm
Color
Discusses Romanesque painters from 1000 to 1200 A D. Shows 12th century church murals that use color and design to create a universe of pure symbols around the figure of a tender and mystical Jesus which are startlingly modern in their stylized, almost abstract imagery.
Fine Arts; History - World
Dist - ROLAND **Prod** - ROLAND

Romania 20 MIN
16mm
Color (I)
Describes the character of the people of Romania and the strength and dignity of their culture. Emphasizes the historical importance of both the land and its major waterway, the Danube. Discusses the political turmoil resulting from today's communist domination.
Civics and Political Systems; Geography - World
Dist - AVED **Prod** - WIANCK 1962

Romania 25 MIN
16mm
Eye of the Beholder Series
Color
LC 75-701922
Presents a view of Romania, the ancient land of Eastern Europe whose traditions and name stem from a time before the ancient Romans.
Geography - World; Sociology
Dist - VIACOM **Prod** - RCPDF 1974

Romania 18 MIN
16mm / U-matic / VHS
Man and His World Series
Color (I J)
LC 74-702564
Describes the way of life of the Romaian people, the basis of the agricultural economy and the geographical location of Romania. Shows the home of one of the workers and discusses the change from a rural - agricultural society to an urban - industrial society.
Agriculture; Geography - World; History - World; Industrial and Technical Education; Sociology
Dist - FI **Prod** - IFFB 1970

Romanian Village Life - on the Danube Delta 15 MIN
16mm
Color (J)
LC 73-700011
Portrays the daily life of a family in a small Romanian village. Notes the ways in which the men repair their boats and nets and gather fish and frogs while the women wash clothes and prepare food and the children do various chores and play. Details the slow painstaking methods by which all these essential tasks are performed and accomplished.
Geography - World; Social Science; Sociology
Dist - IFF **Prod** - IFF 1972

The Romans 24 MIN
U-matic / VHS / 16mm
Color (H C A) (FRENCH GREEK SWEDISH)
Describes how the Romans imitated the Greek ideal of the city - state and how they emerged as the ruling force of the ancient world. Uses models of Rome and photographs of amphitheaters, aqueducts and roads to demonstrate the brilliance of Roman architecture and indicate the relationship between engineering and military accomplishments.
Foreign Language; History - World
Dist - IFB **Prod** - IFB

The Romans in Britain 21 MIN
VHS
Color; PAL (J H)
PdS29
Surveys principle Roman ruins in Britain, as well as excavated material and reconstructed models and diagrams. Tells the story of the Roman Conquest of Britain and of life during the period of occupation. Outlines the relationship of Roman Britain with the rest of the Roman Empire. Closes with a discussion of the techniques of modern archaeology to show how knowledge of the period has been obtained.
History - World
Dist - BHA

The Romans - Life, Laughter and Law 22 MIN
U-matic / VHS / 16mm
Captioned; Color (J) (SPANISH)
Brings Rome's Golden Age to life through writings of the time.
History - World; Sociology
Dist - LCOA **Prod** - SCNDRI 1971

The Romans - Life, Laughter and Law 22 MIN
U-matic / VHS / 16mm
Western Civilization - Majesty and Madness Series
Color (J)
LC 79-710042
Recreates the human side of the Roman empire by showing excerpts from Roman writings.
Civics and Political Systems; History - World; Literature and Drama
Dist - LCOA **Prod** - SCNDRI 1971

The Romantic Age in English Literature
VHS / U-matic
Color (H)
Explores the literary themes and social currents of the Romantic Age through the works of Wordsworth, Shelley, Byron and Keats. Gives biographical notes on each poet with an analysis of their works. Includes original illustrations and paintings from the period.
Literature and Drama
Dist - GA **Prod** - GA

The Romantic Age - Wordsworth, Byron, Shelly, and Keats
VHS / Slide / 35mm strip / U-matic
English Literature Series
(G C J)
$109.00, $139.00, $189.00 purchase _ #06208 - 85
Explores the period's literary themes and social currents through readings and excerpts. Discusses the traditions preceding Romanticism, and the effect of this movement on subsequent literature.
Literature and Drama
Dist - CHUMAN **Prod** - GA

The Romantic Ballet 52 MIN
U-matic / VHS / 16mm
Magic of Dance Series
Color (J)
Traces the story of the Romantic Ballet and its greatest exponents.
Fine Arts
Dist - TIMLIF **Prod** - BBCTV 1980

Romantic Caribbean Islands
VHS
Color (G)
$49.90 purchase _ #0747
Shares a romantic voyage with husband and wife Herb and Doris and five fellow adventurers as they discover jungle waterfalls, seething volcanoes, anchor in secluded coves, dive on a shipwreck, harvest coconuts and bananas. Explores the lifestyle of the Caribbean islands.
Geography - World; Physical Education and Recreation; Science - Natural
Dist - SEVVID

The Romantic Days of Fire Horses 10 MIN
16mm
B&W
LC 72-700770
Presents edited biograph and Edison footage from the paperprint collection and from the George Kleine collection, in the library of Congress. Shows an exhibition drill of New York firemen in Union Square, which was photographed in 1904, a run of the New York Fire Department in 1903 and exhibitions of efficiency by the fire departments of Schennectady, New York and Chelsea, Massachusetts.
Fine Arts; Health and Safety; History - United States; Industrial and Technical Education; Sociology
Dist - RMIBHF **Prod** - RMIBHF 1972

The Romantic Era 88 MIN
VHS / U-matic
Color
Fine Arts
Dist - ABCLR **Prod** - ABCLR

The Romantic era 89 MIN
VHS
Color; Hi-fi; Dolby stereo (G)
$39.95 purchase _ #1145
Presents four world - reknown prima ballerinas in performances and conversations illustrating the romantic style in ballet. Features Alicia Alonso of the Ballet Nacional de Cuba, Carla Fracci of La Scala, Ghislaine Thesmar of the Paris Opera Ballet, and Eva Evdokimova of the Berlin Opera. Each performs a pas de duex from ballets of the Romantic Era and all four collaborate in a piece, Le Grand Pas De Quatre, choreographed by Sir Anton Dolin.
Fine Arts
Dist - KULTUR **Prod** - KULTUR

Romantic Germany 60 MIN
VHS
Traveloguer collection series
Color (G)
$29.95 purchase _ #QU003
Visits Germany. Offers historical and geographic highlights.
Geography - World; History - World
Dist - SIV

The Romantic Horizon 52 MIN
U-matic / VHS
West of the Imagination Series
Color (G)
$279.00, $179.00 purchase _ #AD - 1102
Follows the path of explorers Lewis and Clark. Sees the new lands through the eyes of artists George Catlin, Karl Bodmer and Alfred Jacob Miller. Part of a six - part series on the West of imagination, as reported by artists, writers and photographers who went to the frontiers and reported what they saw - or wished they had seen.
Fine Arts; Geography - United States; Industrial and Technical Education; Literature and Drama
Dist - FOTH **Prod** - FOTH

Romantic Mexico, Acapulco and Puerto Vallarta
VHS
Color (G)
$19.80 purchase _ #0876
Visits the Mexican resorts of Acapulco and Puerto Vallarta, explores Fort San Diego, and features cliff diving, snorkeling and scuba cruises.
Geography - World; Physical Education and Recreation
Dist - SEVVID

Romantic Pioneers 28 MIN
U-matic / VHS
Survey of English Verse Series
Color (C)
$249.00, $149.00 purchase _ #AD - 1301
Focuses on the pioneers of British Romanticism with poetry by Christopher Smart, William Blake, Coleridge and Wordsworth.
Fine Arts; Literature and Drama
Dist - FOTH **Prod** - FOTH

The Romantic Rebellion 50 MIN
U-matic / VHS / 16mm
Romantic Vs Classic Art (Spanish Series
Color (H C A) (SPANISH)
Outlines the historic background of the Romantic movement and illustrates the general principles of Romantic and Classic art with illustrations from the work of individual artists.
Fine Arts; Foreign Language
Dist - PFP **Prod** - VPSL

Romantic Versus Classic Art - Auguste Rodin 26 MIN
16mm / U-matic / VHS
Romantic Versus Classic Art Series
Color (J)
LC 75-700648
Presents the works of sculptor Auguste Rodin (1840 - 1917.) Includes the statue of Balzac.
Fine Arts
Dist - PFP **Prod** - VPSL 1974

Romantic Versus Classic Art - Edgar Degas 26 MIN
16mm / U-matic / VHS
Romantic Versus Classic Art Series
Color (J)
LC 75-700642
Features Kenneth Clark discussing the classical paintings of French artist Edgar Degas. Televised in the series The romantic rebellion.
Fine Arts
Dist - PFP **Prod** - VPSL 1974

Romantic Versus Classic Art - Eugene Delacroix 26 MIN
16mm / U-matic / VHS
Romantic Versus Classic Art Series
Color (J)
LC 74-703826
Features Kenneth Clark discussing the underlying themes in the paintings of French artist Eugene Delacroix. Televised in the series The romantic rebellion.
Fine Arts
Dist - PFP **Prod** - VPSL 1974

Romantic Versus Classic Art - Francisco Goya Y Lucientes 26 MIN
U-matic / VHS / 16mm
Romantic Versus Classic Art Series
Color (J)
LC 75-700644
Features Kenneth Clark discussing Goya's transition from the classic tradition in painting to that of Romanticism. Televised in the series The romantic rebellion.
Fine Arts
Dist - PFP **Prod** - VPSL 1974

Romantic Versus Classic Art - Gian - Battista Piranesi - Henry Fuseli 26 MIN
16mm
Romantic Versus Classic Art Series
Color (J)
LC 75-700647
Features Kenneth Clark discussing the art works of Gian - Battista and Henry Fuseli. Televised in the series The romantic rebellion.
Fine Arts
Dist - PFP **Prod** - VPSL 1974

Romantic Versus Classic Art - Jacques Louis David 26 MIN
U-matic / VHS / 16mm
Romantic Versus Classic Art Series
Color (J)
LC 75-700641
Features Kenneth Clark discussing the classical paintings of French artist Jacques Louis David. Televised in the series The romantic rebellion.
Fine Arts
Dist - PFP **Prod** - VPSL 1974

Romantic Versus Classic Art - James William Mallord Turner - Pt 1 26 MIN
16mm / U-matic / VHS
Romantic Versus Classic Art Series
Color (J)
LC 75-700649
Features Kenneth Clark tracing Turner's development from traditional Romantic paintings to works composed of swirling color forms. Televised in the series The romantic rebellion.
Fine Arts
Dist - PFP **Prod** - VPSL 1974

Romantic Versus Classic Art - James William Mallord Turner - Pt 2 26 MIN
U-matic / VHS / 16mm
Romantic Versus Classic Art Series
Color (J)
LC 75-700649
Features Kenneth Clark tracing Turner's development from traditional Romantic paintings to works composed of swirling color forms. Televised in the series The romantic rebellion.
Fine Arts
Dist - PFP **Prod** - VPSL 1974

Romantic Versus Classic Art - Jean Auguste Dominique Ingres - Pt 1 26 MIN
U-matic / VHS / 16mm
Romantic Versus Classic Art Series
Color (J)
LC 75-700645
Features Kenneth Clark discussing the classic tradition of the paintings of French artist Jean Auguste Dominique Ingres. Televised in the series The romantic rebellion.
Fine Arts
Dist - PFP **Prod** - VPSL 1974

Romantic Versus Classic Art - Jean Auguste Dominique Ingres - Pt 2 26 MIN
16mm / U-matic / VHS
Romantic Versus Classic Art Series
Color (J)
LC 75-700645
Features Kenneth Clark discussing the classic tradition of the paintings of French artist Jean Auguste Dominique Ingres. Televised in the series The romantic rebellion.
Fine Arts
Dist - PFP **Prod** - VPSL 1974

Romantic Versus Classic Art - Jean Francois Millet 26 MIN
16mm / U-matic / VHS
Romantic Versus Classic Art Series
Color (J)
LC 75-700646
Features Kenneth Clark discussing the paintings of French artist Jean Francois Millet. Televised in the series The romantic rebellion.
Fine Arts
Dist - PFP **Prod** - VPSL 1974

Romantic Versus Classic Art - John Constable 26 MIN
16mm / U-matic / VHS
Romantic Versus Classic Art Series
Color (J)
LC 75-700640
Features Kenneth Clark discussing the paintings of English artist John Constable. Televised in the series The romantic rebellion.
Fine Arts
Dist - PFP **Prod** - VPSL 1974

Romantic versus Classic art series
Presents a series of seven videos investigating and discussing the art of the last half of the 18th century. Includes Romantic and Classic artists such as David, Piranesi, Fuseli, Turner, Ingres, Blake, Goya, Delacroix, Millet, Gericault, Constable, Rodin, and Degas. Features art historian Kenneth Clark, who illuminates the interplay between Classical restraint and the freedom of Romanticism. Videos available individually. Produced by Odyssey.
The Art of Blake and Goya - visions and nightmares 55 MIN
David, Piranesi, and Fuseli - morality and fear 55 MIN
Delacroix and Millet - earthly owners 55 MIN
Gericault and Constable - destruction and creation 55 MIN
Ingres - the high priest of purity 55 MIN
Rodin and Degas - the final flowering 55 MIN
Turner - master of the sublime 55 MIN
Dist - AVP

Romantic Versus Classic Art Series
Romantic Versus Classic Art - Auguste Rodin 26 MIN
Romantic Versus Classic Art - Edgar Degas 26 MIN
Romantic Versus Classic Art - Eugene Delacroix 26 MIN
Romantic Versus Classic Art - Francisco Goya Y Lucientes 26 MIN
Romantic Versus Classic Art - Gian - Battista Piranesi - Henry Fuseli 26 MIN
Romantic Versus Classic Art - Jacques Louis David 26 MIN
Romantic Versus Classic Art - James William Mallord Turner - Pt 1 26 MIN
Romantic Versus Classic Art - James William Mallord Turner - Pt 2 26 MIN
Romantic Versus Classic Art - Jean Auguste Dominique Ingres - Pt 1 26 MIN
Romantic Versus Classic Art - Jean Auguste Dominique Ingres - Pt 2 26 MIN
Romantic Versus Classic Art - Jean Francois Millet 26 MIN
Romantic Versus Classic Art - John Constable 26 MIN
Romantic Versus Classic Art - the Romantic Rebellion 50 MIN
Romantic Versus Classic Art - Theodore Gericault 26 MIN
Romantic Versus Classic Art - William Blake 26 MIN
Dist - PFP

Romantic Versus Classic Art - the Romantic Rebellion 50 MIN
U-matic / VHS / 16mm
Romantic Versus Classic Art Series
Color (J)
LC 75-700639
Features Kenneth Clark discussing the basic principles of classic and Romantic art and demonstrates how they have been in conflict. Televised in the series The romantic rebellion.
Fine Arts
Dist - PFP **Prod** - VPSL 1974

Romantic Versus Classic Art - Theodore Gericault 26 MIN
U-matic / VHS / 16mm
Romantic Versus Classic Art Series
Color (J)
LC 75-700643
Features Kenneth Clark discussing the paintings of French artist Theodore Gericault. Televised in the series The romantic rebellion.
Fine Arts
Dist - PFP **Prod** - VPSL 1974

Romantic Versus Classic Art - William Blake 26 MIN
16mm / U-matic / VHS
Romantic Versus Classic Art Series
Color (J)
LC 74-703085
Features Kenneth Clark discussing the art of William Blake, focusing on the drawings and engravings which expressed the need for a new religion in the Romantic period. Televised in the series The romantic rebellion.
Fine Arts
Dist - PFP **Prod** - VPSL 1974

Romantic vs classic art series
Edgar Degas 26 MIN
Gian - Battista Piranesi - Henry Fuseli 26 MIN
Jean - Auguste Dominique Ingres, Pt I 26 MIN
Jean - Francois Millet 26 MIN
Dist - PFP

Romantic Vs Classic Art (Spanish Series
Auguste Rodin 26 MIN
Eugene Delacroix 26 MIN
Francisco Goya 26 MIN
Jacques Louis David 26 MIN
Joseph Mallord - William Turner, Pt I 26 MIN
Joseph Mallord - William Turner, Pt II 26 MIN
The Romantic Rebellion 50 MIN
Theodore Gericault 26 MIN
William Blake 26 MIN
Dist - PFP

Romantic vs classic art-spanish series
Auguste Rodin 26 MIN
Dist - PFP

Romantic Vs Classic Art
Jean - Auguste Dominique Ingres, Pt II 26 MIN
Dist - PFP

Romanticism - the revolt of the spirit 24 MIN
BETA / VHS / U-matic
Western civilization - majesty and madness series
Color (J H C A)
$89.00 purchase _ #JY - LEG505
Examines the romantic heritage of the 18th and 19th centuries.
Fine Arts; History - World; Literature and Drama; Sociology
Dist - CORF **Prod** - LCOA 1971

Romanticism - the Revolt of the Spirit 24 MIN
U-matic / 16mm / VHS
Color (J) (SPANISH)
LC 76-710044
Presents the romantic movement as an era much like our own, an era of spiraling technology and bewildering change. Dramatizes excerpts from the works of Hugo, Shelley, Byron, Emily Bronte and others who spoke out for individuality, freedom, sentiment and revolt.
Foreign Language; Literature and Drama
Dist - LCOA **Prod** - SCNDRI 1971

The Romantics 60 MIN
U-matic / VHS
James Galway's Music in Time Series
Color (J)
Presents flutist James Galway discussing the Romantic movement in music that strove for music and self - expression. Includes music from Chopin's Polonaise in A - Flat, Mendelssohn's Elijah and Brahms' German Requiem.
Fine Arts
Dist - FOTH **Prod** - POLTEL 1982

Romantics and Realists 28 MIN
U-matic / VHS
Survey of English Verse Series
Color (C)
$249.00, $149.00 purchase _ #AD - 1306
Considers the foundations of modern English poetry. Features Hardy, Hopkins, Housman and Kipling.
Fine Arts; Literature and Drama
Dist - FOTH **Prod** - FOTH

Romantische Stadte 13 MIN
U-matic / VHS / 16mm
Color (H C) (GERMAN)
LC 75-710017
Shows the cities of Munich, Dinkelsbuhl and Rothenburg. A German language film.
Foreign Language
Dist - IFB **Prod** - IFB 1961

Rome 30 MIN
VHS
Color (G)
$29.95 purchase _ #S02029
Tours Rome. Features the Coliseum, St Peter's, the Forum, Trevi Fountain, and a side trip to nearby beach resorts.
Geography - World
Dist - UILL

Rome 3 MIN
16mm
Of all Things Series
Color (P I)
Discusses the city of Rome in Italy.
Geography - World
Dist - AVED **Prod** - BAILYL

Rome 13 MIN
16mm / U-matic / VHS
Color (I)
Capsulizes the early growth of the city of Rome, which became a metropolis of the ancient world and describes the life and times of the Caesars.
History - World
Dist - LUF **Prod** - LUF 1981

Rome 52 MIN
BETA / VHS
Color (G)
$24.95 purchase
Tours Rome and the Alban Hills. Shows how Napolean copied monuments in the Roman Forum for the city of Paris. Highlights the Campidoglio, Piazza Navonna, the Appian Way, the Vatican and treasures of the Sistine Chapel. Produced by Robin Willams Films.
Fine Arts; Geography - World; History - World
Dist - ARTSAM

Rome 45 MIN
35mm strip / VHS
Western man and the modern world series - Unit I
Color (J H C T A)
$102.00, $102.00 purchase _ #MB - 510430 - X, #MB - 510215 - 3
Covers the rise and fall of the Roman Empire. Features numerous examples of the artwork and architectural ruins.
Fine Arts; History - World
Dist - SRA

Rome 11 MIN
U-matic / VHS / BETA
Color; PAL (G H C)
PdS40, PdS48 purchase
Features Roman history from its founding on the banks of the Tiber to the fall of the Roman republic.
Fine Arts; Geography - World; History - World
Dist - EDPAT

Rome 45 MIN
U-matic / Kit / VHS
Western Man and the Modern World in Video
Color (J H)
$1378.12 the 25 part series _ #C6756 - 27347 - 5, $89.95 each
Follows the rise and fall of Rome as the center of the world's largest empire. Highlights Roman art, roads, temples, aqueducts and amphitheatres.
History - World
Dist - RH

Rome and Pompeii 60 MIN
VHS
Great cities of the ancient world series
Color (G)
$29.95 purchase _ #QV2321V-S
Journeys back to the glory that was Rome and witnesses Pompeii at the height of its ancient civilization. Reconstructs buildings, baths, temples and palaces with computer-generated graphics. Visits the Colosseum, the Roman Forum, Circus Maximus, Nero's Rome ablaze and Vesuvius' devastation of Pompeii. Part of a three-part series.
History - World; Sociology
Dist - CAMV

Rome and the Vatican - Pope John Paul II 26 MIN
16mm / U-matic / VHS
Color (I J A)
Follows the visit of six British school children to Rome and films their meeting with Pope John Paul II.
Religion and Philosophy
Dist - MEDIAG **Prod** - THAMES 1984

Rome - art and architecture - Part I 39 MIN
VHS
Color (G)
$34.95 purchase _ #ACE01V - F
Visits fountains in Rome to follow its history from classical times to the Renaissance period. Views the Forum, Castle Sant'Angelo, the Basilicas, Saint Peter and the Pantheon. Part one of two parts.
Fine Arts
Dist - CAMV

Rome - art and architecture - Part II 33 MIN
VHS
Color (G)
$34.95 purchase _ #ACE02V - F
Visits fountains in Rome to follow its history from classical times to the Renaissance period. Views the Forum, Castle Sant'Angelo, the Basilicas, Saint Peter and the Pantheon. Part two of two parts.
Fine Arts
Dist - CAMV

Rome - City Eternal 11 MIN
16mm / U-matic / VHS
Color (I J H) (SPANISH)
Portrays the glories of Rome, including the Colosseum, St Peter's Square, the art treasures of the Basilica of St Peter, the fountains of the Villa d'Este and the Piazza Navona, the ruins of the Forum and Hadrian's villa.
Foreign Language; Geography - World
Dist - EBEC **Prod** - EBEC

Rome, City of Fountains 3 MIN
16mm
Of all Things Series
Color (P I)
Discusses the city of Rome in Italy.
Geography - World
Dist - AVED **Prod** - BAILYL

Rome - Impact of an Idea 27 MIN
16mm / U-matic / VHS
Understanding Cities Series
Color (H C A)
Examines the design of Rome by Pope Sixtus V. Shows that Sixtus was the first to see the city as a system.
Geography - World; Sociology
Dist - FI **Prod** - FI 1983

Rome - Sacred City 13 MIN
16mm
Color
Takes a reverent look at the eternal city as the camera spans the centuries.
Geography - World; History - World
Dist - PANWA **Prod** - PANWA

Rome - the eternal city 55 MIN
VHS
Color (G)
PdS17.50 purchase _ #ML-IVN112
Introduces viewers to some of the glories of Rome, one of the most famous cities in Western history. Begins with a video visit to the Palatine Hill. Takes viewers into the Colosseum and the ruins of the Roman Forum. Introduces viewers to Romans in such places as Piazza Navona, Campo dei Fiori, and the Trevi Fountain. Includes trips through St Peter's Basilica, the Sistine Chapel, and the Vatican museums.
Geography - World
Dist - AVP **Prod** - IVNET

Rome - the Eternal City 21 MIN
U-matic / VHS / 16mm
Color (I)
LC 79-701764
Presents information on the history of Rome from the time it was founded to the 1970's.
Geography - World; History - World
Dist - MCFI **Prod** - HOE 1977

Rome - the eternal city 60 MIN
VHS
European collection series
Color (J H C G)
$29.95 purchase _ #IVN112V-S
Tours the city of Rome. Visits Palatine Hill, the Forum, the Colosseum, the Via Condotti, the Spanish Steps, and the city's museums. Part of a 16-part series on European countries and cities. Also part of a larger series entitled Video Visits that travels to six continents.
Geography - World
Dist - CAMV **Prod** - WNETTV

Rome - the Fading Glory 12 MIN
VHS / U-matic
Color
Shows how the ancient city of Rome has begun to show the effects of modern pollution.
Geography - World; Sociology
Dist - JOU **Prod** - UPI

Rome - the ultimate empire 50 MIN
VHS
Lost civilizations video series
Color (G)
$19.99 purchase _ #0 - 7835 - 8275 - 7NK
Recreates the blood games of the Coloseum, Pompeii's last hours and the assassination of Julius Caesar. Explores Rome at its zenith of power. Shows how the Romans conquered the Western world and why their empire eventually declined and fell. Part of a ten - part series incorporating the newest research, evidence and discoveries; orginal cinematography in 25 countries on 5 continents; dramatized recreations of scenes from the past; three - dimensional computer graphics to reconstruct ancient cities and monumental feats of engineering; historic footage; and computer - animated maps.
History - World
Dist - TILIED **Prod** - TILIED 1995

Romeo and Juliet 45 MIN
16mm / U-matic / VHS
Color (H C A)
A shortened version of the 1968 Franco Zeffirelli film Romeo And Juliet, based on the play by Shakespeare. Traces Romeo and Juliet's love from their first meeting to their self - inflicted deaths.
Fine Arts; Literature and Drama
Dist - AIMS **Prod** - ZEFFIF 1968

Romeo and Juliet 40 MIN
16mm
B&W
LC FIA52-4977
An excerpt from the feature film of the same title. Includes the duel scene, the death scene, Friar Lawrence's cell and flashes of the Capulet - Montague feud. Stars John Barrymore, Leslie Howard and Norma Shearer.
Literature and Drama
Dist - FI **Prod** - PMI 1936

Romeo and Juliet 30 MIN
VHS / U-matic
Shakespeare in Perspective Series
Color (J)
Presents an adaptation of Shakespeare's play Romeo And Juliet, a tragedy of circumstance where love chooses as its object its own hated enemy. Includes the plays Macbeth, Julius Caesar and Hamlet on the same tape.
Literature and Drama
Dist - FI **Prod** - FI 1984

Romeo and Juliet
Videodisc
Laserdisc learning series
Color; CAV (J H)
$40.00 purchase _ #8L205
Adapts the play 'Romeo and Juliet' by William Shakespeare. A teacher's guide is available separately.
Literature and Drama
Dist - BARR **Prod** - BARR 1992

Romeo and Juliet 8 MIN
16mm / U-matic / VHS
Shakespeare Series
Color (H C)
Presents the prologue and an excerpt from Act V, Scene III of William Shakespeare's play Romeo And Juliet.
Literature and Drama
Dist - IFB **Prod** - IFB 1974

Romeo and Juliet
VHS / U-matic
Classic Films - on - Video Series
Color (G C J)
$89 purchase _ #05638 - 85
Screens Shakespeare's tragedy concerning two warring families, and the doomed affair between two youths of the opposing households. Directed by Franco Zeffirelli and starring Olivia Hussey.
Fine Arts
Dist - CHUMAN

Romeo and Juliet 167 MIN
VHS / 16mm
BBC's Shakespeare Series
(H A)
$249.95
Presents the popular, dramatic, and tragic romance of Romeo And Juliet, by William Shakespeare.
Literature and Drama
Dist - AMBROS **Prod** - AMBROS 1979

Romeo and Juliet 139 MIN
VHS
Color (G J C I)
$39.95 purchase _ #S00541
Presents director Franco Zeffirelli's version of Shakespeare's 'Romeo and Juliet.' Stars Olivia Hussey, Leonard Whitting, Michael York and John McEnery. Noted for its use of teenage actors to play the lead roles. Narrated by Sir Laurence Olivier.
Literature and Drama
Dist - UILL **Prod** - GA 1968
PA

Romeo and Juliet 165 MIN
U-matic / VHS
Shakespeare Plays Series
Color
LC 79-706938
Presents Shakespeare's play of young love and death in medieval Italy. Stars Sir John Gielgud, Rebecca Saire and Patrick Ryecart.
Literature and Drama
Dist - TIMLIF **Prod** - BBCTV 1979

Romeo and Juliet 142 MIN
16mm
Color
Presents a version of Romeo and Juliet, William Shakespeare's Mediterranean tragedy of blood feuds and star - crossed lovers. Stars Laurence Harvey, Susan Shentall and Flora Robson.
Fine Arts; Literature and Drama
Dist - LCOA **Prod** - UNKNWN 1954

Romeo and Juliet 45 MIN
VHS
Color
$69.95 purchase _ #4003
Brings Renaissance Verona to life, and follows the star crossed lovers from their first meeting to their tragic end.
Literature and Drama
Dist - AIMS **Prod** - AIMS

Romeo and Juliet 124 MIN
16mm / U-matic / VHS
Color (J)
Stars the Royal Ballet with Margot Fonteyn and Rudolf Nureyev in the ballet with musical score provided by Serge Prokofiev.
Fine Arts
Dist - FI **Prod** - IDEAL 1966

Romeo and Juliet 234 MIN
Cassette / U-matic / VHS
Color; B&W; Stereo; Color; PAL (J H G)
PdS65 purchase; LC FI68-231
Presents a production of Romeo and Juliet set in the first half of the Italian Renaissance. Stars Ann Hasson and Christopher Neame in the title roles. In nine parts of 26 minutes each. Includes footnotes to studio discussion. Contact distributor about availability outside the United Kingdom.
Literature and Drama
Dist - VAI **Prod** - VAI

Romeo and Juliet 25 MIN
VHS / U-matic / 16mm
Shakespeare in rehearsal series
Color (H C)
$495.00, $250.00 purchase _ #HP - 5793C
Introduces the play 'Romeo and Juliet' by Shakespeare. Portrays a rehearsal of the play in 16th century England by Shakespeare himself. Gains insight into how actors interpret characters and the key issues of the production. Part of a series on Shakespeare in rehearsal.
Fine Arts; Literature and Drama
Dist - CORF **Prod** - BBCTV 1989

Romeo and Juliet 90 MIN
VHS
Understanding Shakespeare - The Tragedies series
Color; CC (I J H C)
$49.95 purchase _ #US04
Features key scenes, along with commentary by Shakespearean scholars. Cuts through the 16th - century language barrier to provide a way for students to increase their comprehension of these classics. Includes a teacher's guide.
Literature and Drama
Dist - SVIP

Romeo and Juliet 167 MIN
VHS
BBC Shakespeare series
Color (G C H)
$109.00 purchase _ #DL465
Fine Arts
Dist - INSIM **Prod** - BBC

Romeo and Juliet 165 MIN
VHS
Shakespearean drama series
Color (I J H C)
$59.95 purchase _ #US26
Presents one of a series in which the Bard's works are staged almost exactly as seen in the 16th century, but without unfamiliar English accents. Stars Alex Hyde - White and Blanche Baker.
Literature and Drama
Dist - SVIP

Romeo and Juliet 95 MIN
VHS
Color (G)
$29.95 purchase _ #1202
Presents the Bolshoi Ballet production of 'Romeo And Juliet' choreographed by Leonid Lavrovsky and starring Galina Ulanova. Costars Yuri Zhdanov as Romeo. Genadi Rozhdestvensky conducts.
Fine Arts; Foreign Language; Geography - World; Physical Education and Recreation
Dist - KULTUR

Romeo and Juliet 30 MIN
VHS / 16mm / BETA
Shakespeare - from Page to Stage Series
Color (J H A)
Presents key scenes from Shakespeare's plays bridged with on - camera commentary by one of the actors to reinforce the literary amd thematic aspects of the play. Includes written editions of the complete plays and study guides.
Literature and Drama
Dist - BCNFL **Prod** - CBCEN 1987

Romeo and Juliet 36 MIN
U-matic / VHS / 16mm
World of William Shakespeare Series
Color (H C A)
LC 78-700747
Presents an abridged version of William Shakespeare's play Romeo And Juliet.
Literature and Drama
Dist - NGS **Prod** - NGS 1978

Romeo and Juliet 140 MIN
VHS
Color (S)
$39.95 purchase _ #623 - 9386
Reinterprets 'Romeo And Juliet' by Prokofiev. Stars Wayne Eagling and Alessandra Ferri. Choreography by Kenneth MacMillan.
Fine Arts; Physical Education and Recreation
Dist - FI **Prod** - NVIDC 1986

Romeo and Juliet 8 MIN
U-matic / VHS / 16mm
Color; Captioned (H C A)
Presents excerpts from Romeo and Juliet. The chorus emerges from the inner stage and speaks to the audience in the prologue. Romeo, beside Juliet's body, drinks poison and dies. Juliet awakens and kills herself, Act V scene iii.
Literature and Drama
Dist - IFB

Romeo and Juliet (1595) 45 MIN
16mm
B&W (J)
Presents Otto Krejca's production of William Shakespeare's tragedy performed in Prague's National Theatre and shows actors in rehearsal.
Literature and Drama
Dist - ROLAND **Prod** - ROLAND

Romeo and Juliet - Act II, Scene II 9 MIN
U-matic / VHS / 16mm
Great Scenes from Shakespeare Series
Color (J)
LC 76-714374
Presents a dramatization of Act II, Scene II of Shakespeare's play Romeo And Juliet.
Literature and Drama
Dist - PHENIX **Prod** - SEABEN 1971

Romeo and Juliet Ballet
VHS / BETA
Color
Presents Prokofiev's Romeo And Juliet danced by the Bolshoi Ballet Company.
Fine Arts
Dist - GA **Prod** - GA

Romeo and Juliet - Bessmertnova 108 MIN
VHS
Color (G)
$39.95 purchase _ #1173
Presents the Bolshoi Ballet production of 'Romeo And Juliet' filmed in 1976 on the Bicentennial Anniversary of the Bolshoi Theatre in Moscow. Stars Natalia Bessmertnova and Mikhail Lavrovsky.
Fine Arts; Foreign Language; Geography - World; Physical Education and Recreation
Dist - KULTUR

Romeo and Juliet in Kansas City 28 MIN
VHS / 16mm / U-matic
Color (I A)
LC 76-700076
Features Tchaikovsky's Romeo and Juliet Overture, played by the Kansas City Philharmonic, interspersed with quotations from Shakespeare's play Romeo and Juliet.
Fine Arts; Literature and Drama
Dist - PFP **Prod** - MUSICP 1975

Romeo and Juliet - Nureyev and Fonteyn 124 MIN
VHS
Color (G)
$24.95 purchase_#1183
Stars dance partners Nureyev and Fonteyn in performance of the ballet Romeo and Juliet. Features Sir Kenneth MacMillan's choreography. Music by Sergei Prokofiev.
Fine Arts
Dist - KULTUR

Romeo and Juliet - Nureyev and Fracci 129 MIN
VHS
Color (G)
$39.95 purchase _ #1123
Presents Rudolf Nureyev, Carla Fracci and Dame Margot Fonteyn together in 'Romeo And Juliet,' on the stage of Milan's Teatro alla Scala. Features the Prokofiev score.
Fine Arts; Physical Education and Recreation
Dist - KULTUR

Romeo and Juliet - West Side story
Videodisc
Color; CLV (J H C G)
$299.00 purchase _ #6485 - HH
Juxtaposes two classics of literature. Uses the California literature structure of venturing in, passing through and going beyond to explore the topics of characterization, literary technique, structure and theme. A variety of lessons access clips of the novels to reinforce topics. Includes two disks and a teacher's guide. Requires 2MB Macintosh.
Literature and Drama
Dist - SUNCOM **Prod** - INTMUL

Romeria - day of the Virgin 54 MIN
VHS / 16mm
Films from Andalusia, Spain series
Color (G) (SPANISH WITH ENGLISH SUBTITLES)
$850.00, $400.00 purchase, $85.00, $50.00 rental
Portrays a religious pilgrimage to a local shirine of the Virgin near the town of Alcala de los Gazules, Cadiz, Spain. Shows families making elaborate preparations for the day long event. Pilgrimage organizers and worshippers discuss the ambiguities of their beliefs and affiliations. Part of a series.
Geography - World; History - World; Religion and Philosophy; Sociology
Dist - DOCEDR **Prod** - MINTZJ 1986

Romero 105 MIN
35mm / 16mm
Color (G)
Tells the real - life story of Salvadoran Archbishop Oscar Romero and his assassination in 1980 while he celebrated the Eucharist Mass. Features Raul Julia who eloquently expresses Romero's initial self - doubt on breaking his silence regarding politics and the confidence he gained as he realized that he had a moral duty to speak out against the poverty and murder destroying the peole of El Salvador. Directed by John Duigan. Contact distributor for price.
Civics and Political Systems; Fine Arts; History - World; Religion and Philosophy; Sociology
Dist - OCTOBF **Prod** - KIESER 1989

Romie - O and Julie - 8 25 MIN
16mm / U-matic / VHS
Color
Shows two robots falling in love, though supposedly without feelings. Teaches their human creators about feeling and caring for one another. Animated.
Literature and Drama
Dist - BCNFL **Prod** - NELVNA 1980

Rommel - the desert fox
VHS
Nazis series
Color (J H C G)
$29.95 purchase _ #MH1875V
Tells the complete story of Rommel, the Nazi Field Marshal who masterminded a 'lightning war' in Europe and North Africa. Part of a five - part series on the Nazis.
Civics and Political Systems; History - World; Sociology
Dist - CAMV

Romper stomper 92 MIN
35mm / 16mm
Color (G)
Depicts the last days of a neo - Nazi skinhead gang as it fights to protects its turf from being taken over by Asian immigrants. Focuses on Hando, the charismatic leader of the gang, who has a strong loyalty to his friend Davey but

is consumed by a blind belief in Hitler's doctrine of racial purity. Davey falls in love and begins to crave a domestic stability impossible to have if he keeps hanging out with Hando and the rest of the gang. A disturbing, brutally realistic production by Daniel Scharf and Ian Pringle. Written and directed by Geoffrey Wright. Contact distributor for price.
Fine Arts; Psychology; Sociology
Dist - OCTOBF

Romulus, Remus and Rome 12 MIN
VHS / 16mm
Greek and Roman Mythology in Ancient Art Series
Color (I)
LC 90708207
Examines the myth of Romulus and Remus, twins raised by a she - wolf.
Fine Arts; History - World; Religion and Philosophy
Dist - BARR

Ron amok - dog party 4 MIN
16mm
Trildogy series
Color (G)
$8.00 rental
Records six pooches interacting at an all - dog birthday party. Features part of the Trildogy with music by Clyde McCoy.
Fine Arts
Dist - CANCIN **Prod** - WENDTD 1977

Ron Brooks and Group 29 MIN
Videoreel / VT2
People in Jazz Series
Color (G)
$55.00 rental _ #PIEJ-109
Presents the jazz music of Ron Brooks and group. Features host Jim Rockwell interviewing these artists.
Biography; Fine Arts
Dist - PBS **Prod** - WTVSTV

Ron Palelek - Feeding Your Horse 28 MIN
VHS / BETA
Ron Palelek Training Series
Color
Addresses the proper use of roughage and concentrates in feeding horses. Points out differences between feeding young and older horses.
Physical Education and Recreation
Dist - EQVDL **Prod** - VDTECH

Ron Palelek - Grooming Your Horse 61 MIN
BETA / VHS
Ron Palelek Training Series
Color
Discusses horse grooming. Describes equipment, brushing techniques, bathing and hoof care, among other things.
Physical Education and Recreation
Dist - EQVDL **Prod** - VDTECH

Ron Palelek - Leading Your Horse 62 MIN
BETA / VHS
Ron Palelek Training Series
Color
Shows how to lead a horse. Involves halterbreaking.
Physical Education and Recreation
Dist - EQVDL **Prod** - VDTECH

Ron Palelek - Preparing the Halter Horse for Show 61 MIN
VHS / BETA
Ron Palelek Training Series
Color
Discusses preparing the halter horse for show, including hoof care, feeding and exercising.
Physical Education and Recreation
Dist - EQVDL **Prod** - VDTECH

Ron Palelek Training Series
Ron Palelek - Feeding Your Horse 28 MIN
Ron Palelek - Grooming Your Horse 61 MIN
Ron Palelek - Leading Your Horse 62 MIN
Ron Palelek - Preparing the Halter Horse for Show 61 MIN
Dist - EQVDL

Ronald Dworkin - the changing story 60 MIN
VHS / U-matic
In search of the Constitution series
Color (A G)
$59.95, $79.95 purchase _ #MOYR - 105
Visits with Ronald Dworkin, legal philosopher, professor of law at New York University, and professor of jurisprudence at Oxford University. Part of an 11 - part series in which Bill Moyers examines the vitality of our nation's most important document by listening to people who interpret and teach it and people whose lives have been changed by it.
Civics and Political Systems
Dist - PBS

Ronald Neame 105 MIN
VHS
Color (PRO G C)
$179.00 purchase, $49.00 rental _ #602
Condenses a week - long seminar with film director Ronald Neame at the Tahoe Film and Video Workshop. Focuses on The Director - Producer Relationship in Part One, in particular on writer - director Noel Coward. Parts Two and Three consider The Director - Writer Relationship and The Director - Actor Relationship, discussing Alec Guinness and Judy Garland. Produced by Frank Beacham Productions.
Fine Arts; Industrial and Technical Education
Dist - FIRLIT

Ronald Reagan
VHS / U-matic
Color (H C A)
$29.95 purchase _ #501875
Follows Ronald Reagan's career from its Hollywood beginnings to his candidacy in the 1980 elections.
Biography; History - United States
Dist - JOU **Prod** - UPI
UILL

Ronald Reagan elected President - Wednesday, November 5, 1980 120 MIN
VHS
Nightline series
Color (H C G)
$14.98 purchase _ #MP6131
Covers the electoral victory of Ronald Reagan.
Biography; Fine Arts
Dist - INSTRU **Prod** - ABCNEW 1980

Ronald Reagan - Identification of the Japanese Zero 24 MIN
U-matic / VHS
B&W
Focuses on the necessity of American pilots' recognizing the difference between a P - 40 and a Japanese Zero. Made by young Ronald Reagan.
History - United States; Sociology
Dist - IHF **Prod** - IHF

Ronald Reagan - the Presidency of Affirmation 60 MIN
VHS
Modern Presidency Series
Color (G)
$125.00 purchase _ #TMPR - 105
Interviews former President Ronald Reagan. Discusses his domestic policies in depth, while also giving attention to the role of the president as commander - in - chief of the armed forces. The program also considers the role of First Ladies Ford, Carter, Reagan and Bush. Hosted by David Frost.
Biography; Civics and Political Systems; History - United States
Dist - PBS **Prod** - ENMED 1989

Ronald W Estabrook 50 MIN
VHS / U-matic
Eminent Chemists - the Interviev s Series
Color
Reviews the research events of the 60s leading to the discovery of the significance of cytochrome P - 450 to chemical carcinogenesis, featuring Dr Ronald W Estabrook.
Science; Science - Physical
Dist - AMCHEM **Prod** - AMCHEM 1982

Rondo 25 MIN
16mm
Color (G)
$40.00 rental
Portrays Huntington Square in Nob Hill, San Francisco which is a playground for pigeons, children and fountain statuary. Features Lou Harrison's Suite for Violin, Piano and Small Orchestra. Produced by Chester Kessler.
Fine Arts; Geography - United States
Dist - CANCIN

Ronnie 7 MIN
16mm
B&W (A)
$20.00 rental
Portrays a naked hustler who tells his story nonstop.
Fine Arts; Sociology
Dist - CANCIN **Prod** - MCDOWE 1972

Ronnie's Tune 18 MIN
U-matic / VHS / 16mm
Color
LC 78-700152
Presents a story about an 11 - year - old girl who, through her love for her dead cousin, helps the grieving mother overcome her sorrows.
Fine Arts; Sociology
Dist - WOMBAT **Prod** - WOMBAT 1978

Roof Bolting in Coal Mines 19 MIN
U-matic / VHS / 16mm
Color
Explains the principles and purposes of roof bolting in coal mining. Coordinates mining operations and bolting methods, and stresses safety throughout the roof control process.
Health and Safety; Industrial and Technical Education; Social Science
Dist - USNAC **Prod** - USDL

Roof Check 30 MIN
VHS / BETA
This Old House, Pt 2 - Suburban '50s Series
Color
Checks the condition of a house's roof. Considers installing a wood burning stove and a new bathroom.
Industrial and Technical Education; Sociology
Dist - CORF **Prod** - WGBHTV

Roof Framing and Sheathing 25 MIN
U-matic / VHS
Garages Series
$39.95 purchase _ #DI - 132
Discusses how to frame the roof, install the roof and wall sheathing, install windows and doors.
Industrial and Technical Education
Dist - CAREER **Prod** - CAREER

Roof tiling using man made slates - Part one of Unit G - Cassette 13 42 MIN
VHS
Building crafts - the teaching and learning process series
Color; PAL (J H IND)
PdS29.50 purchase
Features part of an 18 - part series which observes teaching and learning in a variety of workshop situations. Includes such skills as plumbing, brickwork, carpentry, painting and decorating.
Industrial and Technical Education
Dist - EMFVL

Roof tiling using man made slates - the students' attempts - Part two of Unit G - Cassette 14 48 MIN
VHS
Building crafts - the teaching and learning process series
Color; PAL (J H IND)
PdS29.50 purchase
Features part of an 18 - part series which observes teaching and learning in a variety of workshop situations. Includes such skills as plumbing, brickwork, carpentry, painting and decorating.
Industrial and Technical Education
Dist - EMFVL

Roofer's Pitch - Safety in Roofing 21 MIN
16mm / U-matic / VHS
Color (IND)
Covers all facets of safety for roofers.
Health and Safety; Industrial and Technical Education; Psychology
Dist - IFB **Prod** - CSAO

Roofing 37 MIN
VHS
Building construction video series
Color (G H VOC)
$49.95 purchase _ #CEV00809V-T
Describes the correct method, through a step-by-step process, to install the roof of a building. Explains the proper procedures for installing decking materials, flashing, marking the roof, laying felt, and applying shingles.
Industrial and Technical Education
Dist - CAMV

Roofing
VHS / 35mm strip
Basic carpentry and building construction series
$287.00 purchase _ #PX974 filmstrips, $287.00 purchase _ #PX974V VHS
Shows the key steps of construction from initial framing to final shingle.
Education; Industrial and Technical Education
Dist - CAREER **Prod** - CAREER

Roofing, Siding, and Finishing 30 MIN
U-matic / VHS
Garages Series
$39.95 purchase _ #DI - 133
Discusses how to shingle the roof, install siding, finish trim, install garage door, and a garage door opener.
Industrial and Technical Education
Dist - CAREER **Prod** - CAREER

Rooftop Road 8 MIN
U-matic / VHS / 16mm
Color (H C A)
Presents a survey of Chicago's major transportation system, the elevated CTA. Captures the changing scenes from the train's windows, from the pastoral suburbs to the bustling city.
Geography - United States; Social Science; Sociology
Dist - IFB **Prod** - IFB 1974

Rooftopics 11 MIN
16mm
Color (J A)
LC 72-702256
Provides a different perspective on Australia's largest city with views of rooftops in Sydney.
Geography - World; Social Science
Dist - AUIS **Prod** - ANAIB 1971

Rookie of the Year 47 MIN
16mm / U-matic / VHS
Teenage Years Series
Color
LC 75-703036
Deals with the problems of identity and sex discrimination among adolescents, examining the controversy which is triggered when a girl plays on her brother's baseball team.
Guidance and Counseling; Physical Education and Recreation; Sociology
Dist - TIMLIF **Prod** - WILSND 1975

Rookie of the Year - Pt 1 23 MIN
16mm
Teenage Years Series
Color
LC 75-703036
Deals with the problems of identity and sex discrimination among adolescents. Examines the controversy which is triggered when a girl plays on her brother's baseball team.
Psychology; Sociology
Dist - TIMLIF **Prod** - WILSND 1975

Rookie of the Year - Pt 2 24 MIN
16mm
Teenage Years Series
Color
LC 75-703036
Deals with the problems of identity and sex discrimination among adolescents. Examines the controversy which is triggered when a girl plays on her brother's baseball team.
Psychology; Sociology
Dist - TIMLIF **Prod** - WILSND 1975

The Rookies 1 MIN
16mm
Color
LC 78-700377
Provides a lead - in without narration to the television show The Rookies.
Fine Arts
Dist - VIACOM **Prod** - VIACOM 1978

The Room 10 MIN
U-matic / VHS / 16mm
Color (C A)
Presents a room located in dada space in which everything is reduced to basic forms in the simple, bare room with lines forming shapes, penetrating the artist's subconscious.
Fine Arts
Dist - TEXFLM **Prod** - UWFKD

Room 309 - Classroom Management for Secondary Classrooms - Part 1 14 MIN
U-matic / VHS
(T C)
$98.00 _ #MS001
Uses scenarios to depict problems that teachers might encounter in the secondary classroom, and offers solutions for handling these problems. Covers such areas as roll call, note passing, napping, talking, and much more. Includes study guide, reaction forms, annotated ideas, references and bibliographicl information.
Education
Dist - AAVIM **Prod** - AAVIM

Room 309 - Classroom Management for Secondary Classrooms - Part 2 14 MIN
U-matic / VHS
(T C)
$98.00 _ #MS002
Uses scenarios to depict some problems that a teacher might encounter in a secondary classroom, and offers solutions to these problems. Looks at assigning homework, students' paying attention, late quizzes, romance in the classroom, and much more. Includes teacher's study guide, reaction forms, annotated ideas, references and bibliographical information.
Education
Dist - AAVIM **Prod** - AAVIM

Room and Board 5 MIN
16mm
Color (H C)
LC 76-703638
Presents an animated film depicting man's quest for the unattainable. Shows a cartoon character placed in an empty room with a single golden door knob. Shows how he grows, matures, withers and dies as all the while he tries to open the door with the golden knob.
Guidance and Counseling; Psychology; Sociology
Dist - MALIBU **Prod** - CARTR 1976

Room arrangement and scheduling - getting it all together 30 MIN
VHS
Calico pie series
Color (C A T)
$69.95 purchase
Presents part 15 of a 16 - part telecourse for teachers who work with children ages three to five. Discusses strategies for room arrangement and scheduling in the classroom. Hosted by Dr Carolyn Dorrell, an early childhood specialist.
Education; Psychology
Dist - SCETV **Prod** - SCETV 1983

Room arranging do's and don'ts 25 MIN
VHS
Better homes and gardens video library series
Color (H VOC A)
Provides basic information for the interior design student in a format that lets him see the effect even small changes can make in a room's atmosphere. Demonstrates how to use simple furnishings to create attractive and inviting rooms. Teaches how to best use focal points and unmatched pieces and what to do with small rooms and large awkward spaces. Includes planning guide.
Home Economics
Dist - PBS **Prod** - WNETTV
CAMV

Room Arranging Do's and Don'ts 25 MIN
VHS
Color (G)
$19.95 purchase _ #6117
Home Economics; Sociology
Dist - SYBVIS **Prod** - HOMES

Room at the Top 115 MIN
16mm
B&W
Focuses on a factory worker who tries to court the boss's daughter but ends up with another woman. Stars Laurence Harvey and Simone Signoret.
Fine Arts
Dist - KITPAR **Prod** - UNKNWN 1958

Room at the Top 28 MIN
16mm
B&W (I J H)
LC 71-708123
Explains that at the top of the Saturn - Apollo is the command module, the crew quarters, flight center and command post for the flight to the moon.
Industrial and Technical Education; Science - Physical
Dist - USNAC **Prod** - NASA 1966

A Room check 30 MIN
Videoreel / VT2
Designing home interiors series; Unit 26
Color (C A)
Explains how all the small, individual plans discussed throughout the telecourse work together to create a complete design plan. Details importance of utilizing extended living spaces in a home.
Home Economics
Dist - CDTEL **Prod** - COAST

Room Film 52 MIN
16mm
Color; Silent (C)
$2400.00
Experimental film by Peter Gidal.
Fine Arts
Dist - AFA **Prod** - AFA 1973

Room for Heroes 14 MIN
U-matic / VHS / 16mm
Color
LC 72-700148
Explains that legendary heroes have traditionally grown out of the needs of the people, and have represented the ideals and distinguishing characteristics of particular groups or nations. Describes the exploits of such heroes as Johnny Appleseed, Pecos Bill, Casey Jones, Davy Crockett and others who became legends in their own time.
Biography; Religion and Philosophy; Social Science; Sociology
Dist - CORF **Prod** - DISNEY 1971

Room for Us 28 MIN
VHS / 16mm
Sonrisas Series
Color (T P) (SPANISH)
$46.00 rental _ #SRSS - 103
Shows the Carriage House community expanding to include Puerto Rican and Cuban children. In Spanish and English.
Sociology
Dist - PBS

A Room full of men - therapy for abusive men 48 MIN
VHS
Color (H C G)
$350.00 purchase, $65.00 rental
Asks why men are abusive to women and how they can change. Examines a group of men with a history of abuse towards women and their efforts to change. Follows three men who have joined a program to help them change their lives and learn that violence involves more than bruises and beatings. As long as men believe they have authority and control over women physically and mentally, there is a potential for violence to maintain that authority and control. Produced by Heartland Motion Pictures.
Sociology
Dist - FLMLIB

The Room in the Tower 17 MIN
VHS / U-matic
Color (J H A)
Shows a young woman who has been haunted by the same dream for years. In the dream she visits a family in an old mansion and they always invite her to stay in the room in the tower. She is suddenly put into the real life situation when she visits the home of some friends. The images from her dreams suddenly become quite real and she is unable to no longer distinguish reality from dreams as she enters the room in the tower.
English Language; Social Science
Dist - MTOLP **Prod** - MTOLP 1986

Room list 20 MIN
16mm
B&W (G)
$30.00 rental
Takes the viewer on a tour of the filmmaker's room and the objects in it while the narrator tells about his personal belongings, their origins and uses, and the systems of organization governing their placement. Draws attention to details and demonstrates how one person structures his living space on functional as well as sentimental grounds. Produced by Andy Moore.
Fine Arts; Literature and Drama; Sociology
Dist - CANCIN

A Room of one's own 55 MIN
VHS
Color (G C H)
$129.00 purchase _ #DL352
Presents the Broadway adaptation of the essay by Virginia Woolf. Stars Eileen Atkins.
Fine Arts
Dist - INSIM

Room Service 78 MIN
U-matic / VHS / 16mm
B&W (J)
Stars Groucho, Harpo and Chico Marx with Ann Miller and Lucille Ball in the comedy story of a show manager's unscrupulous efforts to get backing for a new show and to keep his theatrical company fed while living in a hotel without paying bills.
Fine Arts
Dist - FI **Prod** - RKOP 1938

Room Service 15 MIN
16mm
Color
Presents a filmed version of the dance piece by Yvonne Rainer, as performed at the 81st St Theatre Rally.
Fine Arts
Dist - VANBKS **Prod** - VANBKS 1965

Room Service 10 MIN
U-matic / VHS / 16mm
Professional Hotel and Tourism Programs Series
Color (J)
LC 74-700224
Deals with special problems of room service, including duties of waiter or waitress and order taker. Stresses the importance of getting the order complete and having exact identification of the guest and room. Explains that servers must check trays, make sure the order is complete, give instruction for entering a room, serve guests and observe discretion and courtesy throughout.
Guidance and Counseling; Psychology
Dist - NEM **Prod** - NEM 1973

Room 10 - Ramsey Hospital Emergency 24 MIN
U-matic / VHS
Color
Shows the dramatic efforts of an emergency team to save the life of an auto accident victim. Reveals the thoughts and attitudes of people who work daily with death.
Health and Safety
Dist - WCCOTV **Prod** - WCCOTV 1972

Room to Learn 22 MIN
16mm
Color
Shows a preschool facility based on the Montessori methods, with children playing and learning in an environment that encourages participation in the learning process.
Education; Psychology
Dist - NYU **Prod** - NYU

Room to Let 20 MIN
16mm
Color (P I)
Shows what happens when the Chiffy Kids befriend a friendly but crafty hobo by allowing him to use their den for temporary shelter. Relates how the old man then refuses to leave.
Literature and Drama
Dist - LUF **Prod** - LUF 1979

Room to Live 27 MIN
16mm
Color
LC 80-701376
Deals with the importance of wearing seatbelt safety restraints when riding in an automobile.
Health and Safety
Dist - MEGROU **Prod** - MEGROU 1979

Room to live III 27 MIN
VHS / U-matic / BETA
Color (G)
$980.00 purchase, $125.00 rental _ #ROO031
Reveals that even with mandatory seat belt laws, the actual number of people using seatbelts religiously is unacceptably low. Features Sgt Jack Ware who teaches why seat belts are the best protection in an auto crash.
Health and Safety; Industrial and Technical Education
Dist - ITF **Prod** - MEGROU 1991

Room to manoeuvre - driving 10 MIN
VHS
Color; PAL; NTSC (G)
PdS 57, PdS67 purchase
Discusses the importance of leaving sufficient room to maneuver on the crowded highways - an important factor in avoiding automobile accidents. Produced for the British Department of Transport.
Health and Safety
Dist - CFLVIS **Prod** - BRCOI 1980

Room to Move 52 MIN
U-matic / VHS
Winners from Down Under Series
Color (K)
$349.00, $249.00 purchase _ #AD - 1358
Contrasts parental pressure on Carol to succeed as an athlete with the lack of concern shown by Angie's parents. Reveals that this contrast and the mutual love of Carol and Angie for physical fitness brings the girls together. Part of an eight - part series on children's winning over their circumstances produced by the Australian Children's Television Foundation.
Literature and Drama; Physical Education and Recreation; Sociology
Dist - FOTH **Prod** - FOTH

A Room with a view 15 MIN
VHS
Not Another Science Show
Color (T G)
$50.00 purchase
Reveals that distance education offers significant new opportunities to learners of all ages. Shows that, with the construction of the Iowa Communications Network linking more than 100 educational sites, Iowa has demonstrated its commitment to a high - quality, innovative educational system. Discusses the opportunities offered by this new technology and offers vignettes from actual distance education classrooms.
Education
Dist - AECT **Prod** - IODIED 1995

A Room with a view 115 MIN
35mm / 16mm
Color (G)
Adapts the novel, Howard's End, by E M Forster - set partly in picturesque turn - of - the - century Florence, Italy and partly in the English countryside. Tells the story of Lucy Honeychurch, a young Englishwoman who travels to Italy in 1907, falls in love and is eventually liberated from the mores and conventions of Victorian England. Features music by Puccini. Produced by Ismail Merchant; screenplay by Ruth Prawler Jhabvala; stars Maggie Smith, Helena Bonham Carter, Denholm Elliot, Julian Sands, Daniel Day Lewis and Simon Callow.
Fine Arts; Psychology; Sociology
Dist - OCTOBF

Roommates on a Rainy Day 26 MIN
16mm / U-matic / VHS
Insight Series
Color; B&W (H C A) (SPANISH)
Looks at the relationship between a woman who wants a deeper commitment and a man who is afraid of marriage. Tells how the man's encounter with a jaded swinger forces him to reexamine his priorities. Stars Martin Sheen.
Fine Arts; Foreign Language; Sociology
Dist - PAULST **Prod** - PAULST

Roommates on a Rainy Day 28 MIN
U-matic / VHS / 16mm
Insight Series
Color; B&W (J) (SPANISH)
LC 73-701994
Explains that Jenny and Vince are roommates and that he likes the arrangement but that she wants more. Shows that marriage is the relationship in which men and women can grow to fullfillment.
Foreign Language; Psychology; Religion and Philosophy
Dist - PAULST **Prod** - KIESER 1973

Roommates on a Rainy Day 28 MIN
16mm / U-matic / VHS
Color (J)
LC 73-701994
Explains that Jenny and Vince are roommates and that he likes the arrangement but that she wants more. Shows that marriage is the relationship in which men and women can grow to fulfillment.
Psychology; Religion and Philosophy
Dist - MEDIAG **Prod** - PAULST 1973

Roommates on a Rainy Day 26 MIN
U-matic / VHS / 16mm
Color; B&W (H C A)
Looks at the relationship between a woman who wants a deeper commitment and a man who is afraid of marriage. Tells how the man's encounter with a jaded swinger forces him to reexamine his priorities. Stars Martin Sheen.
Fine Arts; Sociology
Dist - MEDIAG **Prod** - PAULST

Roomnastics series

Arm circles - back stretcher - hopping	15 MIN
Arm pull - bend and twist - side straddle jump	15 MIN
Arm stretcher - forward and backward bending - elevator	15 MIN
Arm twister - alternate toe touching - sprinter	15 MIN
Backward stretcher - toe touching - strider	15 MIN
Breast stroke and double arm lift - swing and twist - single heel lifts	15 MIN
Chain Breaker - Forward Lunge and Turn - Half - Squat Jumps	15 MIN
Crawl stroke - body bend and reverse arm swing - squat straddle jumps	15 MIN
Cross chest arm swing - trunk circles - alternate lunges	15 MIN
Double arm coordinators - toe touch and leg crosses - forward leg lifts	15 MIN
Double armlifts forward - front and back bend with trunk rotation - leg bend and twist	15 MIN
Double armlifts sideward - sideward bend with trunk twist - toe - heel, lift	15 MIN
Double armstretchers - sideward bend and trunk rotation - leg crosses	15 MIN
Elbow Bender / Sideward Bending / Blast - Off	15 MIN
Forward stretcher - trunk rotation / knee bend, heat up	15 MIN
Giant Circles - Trunk Twister - Knee Lifts	15 MIN
Overarm Sweep and Shoulder Shrug / Trunk Stretcher / Forward and Backward Leg Lifts	15 MIN
Rope Pull / Swing and Bend / Double Heel Lifts	15 MIN
Rower / Sideward Lunge and Bend / Lower Leg Stretcher	15 MIN
Signaler - forward lunge and bend - Siam squat	15 MIN
Single Arm Coordinators / Front and Back Knee Touch / Jumping Leg Crossovers	15 MIN
Single Armlifts Forward / Sideward Bend with Front and Back Bend / Leg Bend and Crossover	15 MIN
Single Armlifts Sideward / Trunk Twist with Front and Back Bend / Leg Coordinator	15 MIN
Single Armstretchers / Trunk Twist and Rotation / Leg Circles	15 MIN

Dist - GPN

Rooms with a view - women's art in Norway 1880 - 1890 16 MIN
VHS
Color (G)
Free loan
Illustrates the artistic work of four generations of women artists in an art exhibition of women's art in Norway from 1880 - 1890.
Fine Arts
Dist - NIS

Roo's eye view 29 MIN
VHS / U-matic
Survivors series
Color (H C)
$250.00 purchase _ #HP - 6104C
Enters the world of a baby red kangaroo as he leaves his mother's pouch to explore new surroundings in a national park in New South Wales, Australia. Shows why the kangaroo is struggling for survival despite its unique adaptation to harsh conditions, due to the hatred of farmers and extensive culling by hunters. Part of a series on the issue of wildlife conservation and the enormity of the task of protecting wildlife and wilderness.
Geography - World; Physical Education and Recreation; Science - Natural
Dist - CORF **Prod** - BBCTV 1990

Roosevelt and the New Deal 20 MIN
U-matic / VHS / 16mm
Twentieth Century History Series
Color (H C A)
Examines Franklin Roosevelt's New Deal, a set of programs designed to end the Great Depression. Describes the process and the main aims of the programs which brought about profound changes in the United States.
History - United States
Dist - FI **Prod** - BBCTV 1981

Roosevelt and the New Deal - Pt 4 20 MIN
16mm
Twentieth Century History Series - Vol I
Color (S)
$380.00 purchase _ #548 - 9233
Illuminates the events and issues which shaped our modern world. Uses archival footage, maps, drawings, feature film segments, paintings and posters to illustrate historic events. The first thirteen programs are available separately on 16mm. Part 4 of Volume I of thirteen programs, 'Roosevelt And The New Deal,' considers Franklin Delano Roosevelt who became US president in 1933 and began a vast number of programs, called the New Deal, to battle the Great Depression.
History - United States; History - World
Dist - FI **Prod** - BBCTV 1981

Roosevelt and U S History - 1882 - 1929 28 MIN
U-matic / VHS / 16mm
World Leaders Series
B&W (H C A)
$485.00, $250.00 purchase _ #76563
Discusses the early family life and political career of Franklin Roosevelt and his role in the World War I war effort.
Biography; History - United States
Dist - CORF

Roosevelt and U S History - 1930 - 1945 32 MIN
U-matic / VHS / 16mm
World Leaders Series
B&W (H C A)
$535, $250 purchase _ #76566
Discusses the Depression, World War II and Franklin Roosevelt's influence during it, the Yalta Conference, and Roosevelt's relations with Hitler and Stalin.
Biography; History - United States
Dist - CORF

Roosevelt - Hail to the Chief 24 MIN
U-matic / VHS / 16mm
Leaders of the 20th century - portraits of power series
Color (H C A)
Shows President Franklin Roosevelt as he offered leadership and a New Deal during the depths of the Depression.
Biography; Guidance and Counseling; History - United States; Psychology
Dist - LCOA **Prod** - NIELSE 1979

Roosevelt - Hail to the Chief 24 MIN
16mm / U-matic / VHS

Color (H C A) (SPANISH)
Features Roosevelt's leadership, vigor and courage that helped restore a sense of purpose to a whole nation.
Biography; Business and Economics; Foreign Language; History - United States
Dist - LCOA **Prod** - NIELSE 1979

Roosevelt - Manipulator - in - Chief 24 MIN
16mm / U-matic / VHS
Leaders of the 20th century - portraits of power series
Color (H C A)
Shows how Franklin Roosevelt dealt with the problems of leading America into another world war.
Biography; Guidance and Counseling; History - United States; Psychology
Dist - LCOA **Prod** - NIELSE 1979

Roosevelt - Manipulator - in - Chief 24 MIN
U-matic / VHS / 16mm
Color (H C A) (SPANISH)
Shows how Roosevelt took a united nation into a foreign land.
Biography; Foreign Language; History - United States
Dist - LCOA **Prod** - NIELSE 1979

Roosevelt, New Jersey - Visions of Utopia 52 MIN
U-matic / VHS / 16mm
Color (J)
Tells the history of Roosevelt, New Jersey, an experimental project set up by the Theodore Roosevelt administration which resettled Jewish immigrants from the Lower East Side of New York into a cooperative in the Jersey countryside.
Geography - United States; Sociology
Dist - CNEMAG **Prod** - LUMEN 1984

Roosevelt Vs Isolation 25 MIN
U-matic / VHS / 16mm
Men in Crisis Series
B&W (J H C)
LC 75-706749
Describes the conflict in America between pacifist isolationists and President F D Roosevelt, who favored lend - lease and military aid to Britain and France. Discusses the first peace - time draft in U S history, and the 50 destroyers sent to England. Shows Roosevelt's war plant tours.
Biography; History - United States; History - World
Dist - FI **Prod** - WOLPER 1965

The Roosevelt years to American entry into World War II 57 MIN
VHS
History machine series
B&W (H C G)
Documents the early years of Franklin D Roosevelt in 1882 - 1932, Roosevelt's fireside chats in 1933, Roosevelt's critics in the election of 1936, Third party and minority party challenges in the 1936 Presidential election, the move of Roosevelt toward World War II involvement in 1939 - 1940, the expansion of World War II in 1941, and the entry of the United States into the war in 1941, after Pearl Harbor. Part of a seven - part historical series on American history produced by Arthur M Schlesinger, Jr, and a team of historians and film editors.
Biography; Civics and Political Systems; History - United States
Dist - VIEWTH **Prod** - VIEWTH

Rooster 20 MIN
16mm
Color
LC 79-701294
Tells about a boy who finds his father's expectations to be too much too soon when he is taken to a brothel.
Fine Arts
Dist - USC **Prod** - USC 1979

The Rooster and Mice have a Race 8 MIN
16mm
Color (P I)
LC 75-706879
Tells the story of a race between a rooster and some mice to stimulate oral language skills.
English Language; Literature and Drama
Dist - MLA **Prod** - DBA 1969

The Rooster and Mice make Pretzels 10 MIN
16mm
Color (P I)
LC 70-706880
Shows all the steps necessary in order to bake pretzels or bread. Stimulates oral language skills.
English Language; Literature and Drama
Dist - MLA **Prod** - DBA 1969

Root Amputation of First Maxillary Molar Mesial Buccal Root 9 MIN
8mm cartridge / 16mm
Color (PRO)
LC 75-702482; 75-702481
Presents a demonstration by Robert A Uchin of the treatment of a patient with localized periodontal disease of a maxillary first molar by removal of the mesial buccal root. Describes the access, separation of the root from the remaining tooth structure and the contouring of the crown.
Health and Safety; Science
Dist - USNAC **Prod** - USVA 1974

Root Canal Therapy on an Extracted Lower Molar - Access and Length Determination 10 MIN
U-matic
Color
LC 79-706767
Describes the armamentarium needed to perform root canal therapy, explains the three stages of access preparation and demonstrates the procedures for determining the length of roots.
Health and Safety
Dist - USNAC **Prod** - MUSC 1978

Root Canal Therapy on an Extracted Lower Molar - Instrumentation 14 MIN
U-matic
Color
LC 79-706768
Describes the armamentarium needed for root canal therapy and demonstrates the cleaning and instrumentation of a root canal.
Health and Safety
Dist - USNAC **Prod** - MUSC 1978

Root Canal Therapy on an Extracted Lower Molar - Obturation 10 MIN
U-matic
Color
LC 79-706769
Demonstrates obturation of the root canal using the softened gutta - percha techniques. Describes the rationale for recapitulation and the procedure for filling the canal.
Health and Safety
Dist - USNAC **Prod** - MUSC 1978

The Root cellar 15 MIN
VHS
More books from cover to cover series
Color (I G)
$25.00 purchase _ #MBCC - 114
Tells the story of Rose, a twelve - year - old orphan who goes to live with farming relatives in Canada. Describes how she meets people, in her aunt's root cellar, who lived on the farm more than 100 years ago. Based on the book 'The Root Cellar' by Janet Lunn.
Education; English Language; Literature and Drama
Dist - PBS **Prod** - WETATV 1987

Root hog or die - Pt 2 29 MIN
16mm
B&W
LC 80-700219
Chronicles the lives of western Massachusetts farmers.
Social Science
Dist - DOCEDR **Prod** - WGBYTV 1978

Root of the Neck and the Thorax - Unit 14 23 MIN
VHS / U-matic
Gross Anatomy Prosection Demonstration Series
Color (PRO)
Introduces the anterior chest wall, the organs and vessels of the thorax, and the structures in the posterior mediastinum.
Health and Safety; Science - Natural
Dist - HSCIC **Prod** - HSCIC

Root planing and gingival curettage - Pt 1 - rationale and instrumentation 16 MIN
U-matic / VHS
Root planing and gingival curettage series
Color (PRO)
LC 83-706069
Describes the histopathologic changes which occur in diseased gingiva following root planing and curettage. Describes the recommended instrumentation and demonstrates techniques on typodont models.
Health and Safety; Science - Natural
Dist - USNAC **Prod** - VADTC 1982

Root planing and gingival curettage - Pt 2 - clinical demonstrations 14 MIN
U-matic / VHS
Root planing and gingival curettage series
Color (PRO)
LC 83-706069
Demonstrates scaling, root planing and gingival curettage on a patient with gingival inflammation associated with heavy hard and soft deposits on his teeth. Shows a prearranged sterile tray setup and demonstrates instrumentation of one quadrant. Shows postoperative results.
Health and Safety; Science - Natural
Dist - USNAC **Prod** - VADTC 1982

Root planing and gingival curettage series
Root planing and gingival curettage - Pt 1 - rationale and instrumentation 16 MIN
Root planing and gingival curettage - Pt 2 - clinical demonstrations 14 MIN
Dist - USNAC

Rooted in the Past 13 MIN
U-matic / VHS / 16mm
Zoom Series
Color
LC 78-700145
Depicts the lifestyles of two young people living in New Mexico, one in an Indian village and the other on a cattle ranch.
Social Science; Sociology
Dist - FI **Prod** - WGBH 1977

Roots 105 MIN
VHS
Performance series
Color (A)
PdS99 purchase
Features Jane Harrocks as Beatie in this play dealing with the liberating power of education and the awakening of self-identity. Set in the feudal farming community of 1950s Norfolk, it pictures Beatie, back from sophisticated London, dealing with her family who is too busy scratching a living to be bothered with culture and politics. Written by Arnold Wesker.
Fine Arts; Literature and Drama; Sociology
Dist - BBCENE

Roots 720 MIN
16mm / VHS / U-matic
Color (G)
Traces the American family of Alex Haley for over 100 years, beginning with the birth of a boy, Kunta Kinte, in a West African village in 1750. Depicts the boy's abduction to America as a slave which leads to a fight for freedom of body and soul that continues throughout his life and the lives of the generations that followed.
History - United States; Sociology
Dist - FI **Prod** - WOLPER 1977
UILL
GA

Roots - a Pennsylvania story 60 MIN
VHS
Americans, too - black experiences in rural America series
Color (J H C G)
$70.00 purchase, $12.50 rental _ #61558
Traces the history of the Norris - Richardson - Harris family of Huntington, Pennsylvania, from their oldest known ancestor Jeremiah Norris - died 1860 - to the family's 51st reunion in 1990. Reveals that the family history covers a wide variety of American experiences. Part of a six - part series visiting widely scattered geographic areas of Pennsylvania to interview and understand the rural black community.
Geography - United States; History - United States; Sociology
Dist - PSU **Prod** - OCONEL 1992

Roots and radicals - Pt I
VHS
Algebra 1 series
Color (J H)
$125.00 purchase _ #A14
Teaches the concepts involved in using roots and radicals in algebraic expressions. Part of a series of 16 videos, each between 25 and 30 minutes long, that explain and reinforce 89 basic concepts of algebra. Includes a stated objective for each segment. Tutors the student through definitions, theorems, step - by - step solutions and examples. Videos are also available in a set.
Mathematics
Dist - LANDMK
GPN

Roots and radicals - Pt II
VHS
Algebra 1 series
Color (J H)
$125.00 purchase _ #A15
Teaches the concepts involved in using roots and radicals in algebraic expressions. Part of a series of 16 videos, each between 25 and 30 minutes long, that explain and reinforce 89 basic concepts of algebra. Includes a stated objective for each segment. Tutors the student through definitions, theorems, step - by - step solutions and examples. Videos are also available in a set.
Mathematics
Dist - LANDMK
GPN

Roots and wings - a Jewish congregation 28 MIN
VHS
Color (G)
$14.95 purchase _ #101
Introduces a Jewish congregation. Presents the ways in which Judaism is passed on from generation to generation in a predominantly Christian society.
Religion and Philosophy; Sociology
Dist - MARYFA **Prod** - MARYFA 1994

The Roots of Aggression - 1929 - 1939 14 MIN
U-matic / VHS / 16mm
World War II Series
Color (J H C A)
$350.00, $245.00 purchase _ #4472
Discusses the worldwide economic depression preceding World War II, and Adolph Hitler's rise to power.
History - World
Dist - CORF

The Roots of Black Resistance 30 MIN
16mm
Black History, Section 11 - W E B Dubois and the New Century Series; Section 11 - W E B Dubois and the new century
B&W (H C A)
LC 72-704072
Dr earl E Thorpe describes the efforts of Dubois and other blacks to form progressive movements and work for their rights as Americans during the early years of the century, as evidenced by the formation of such groups as the N A A C P, the National Negro Business League and the Niagara movement. He describes the conflict between W E B Dubois and Booker T Washington.
Civics and Political Systems; History - United States
Dist - HRAW **Prod** - WCBSTV 1969

The Roots of Change 30 MIN
16mm
Color
Concentrates on Ghana and records the changes occurring there, especially in the cities. Deals with the Christian self - help projects in Accra and Kumasi where the Ashanti culture is being threatened by the break - up of tribal and family customs.
Geography - World; Religion and Philosophy; Sociology
Dist - CCNCC **Prod** - CBSTV

The Roots of consciousness quartet 120 MIN
BETA / VHS
Color (G)
$69.95 purchase _ #Q154
Presents a four - part discussion of the roots of consciousness. Includes 'Understanding Mythology' with Joseph Campbell, 'Psychology of Religious Experience' with Dr Huston Smith, 'Determinism, Free Will and Fate' with Arthur M Young, and 'Toward a New Paradigm of the Unconscious' with Dr Stanislav Grof.
History - World; Psychology; Religion and Philosophy; Science - Natural; Science - Physical
Dist - THINKA **Prod** - THINKA

Roots of consciousness series
Determinism, free will and fate 30 MIN
Psychology of religious experience 30 MIN
Toward a new paradigm of the unconscious 30 MIN
Understanding mythology 30 MIN
Dist - THINKA

The Roots of Dance on Television and Film 30 MIN
U-matic / VHS
Dance on Television - Ipiotis Series
Color
Fine Arts; Industrial and Technical Education
Dist - ARCVID **Prod** - ARCVID

The Roots of Democracy
U-matic / VHS
Color
Civics and Political Systems; History - United States
Dist - MSTVIS **Prod** - MSTVIS

The Roots of Disbelief 37 MIN
16mm / U-matic / VHS
Christians Series Episode 12; Episode 12
Color (H C A)
LC 78-701662
Looks at the causes for indifference to Christianity, citing the advance of science typified by the work of Charles Darwin as the main reason.
History - World; Religion and Philosophy
Dist - MGHT **Prod** - GRATV 1978

Roots of excellence
VHS / BETA / U-matic
Color (C G PRO)
$135.00 purchase _ #DI 46100
Features Dr J Clayton Lafferty in a keynote address to a group of executives. Describes achievement thinking and motivation as related to the LSI - Life Styles Inventory.
Business and Economics; Guidance and Counseling; Psychology
Dist - HUMSYN **Prod** - HUMSYN

The Roots of gospel - gospel in the Holy Land - Volume 1 60 MIN
VHS
Color (G R)
$29.95 purchase _ #35 - 88 - 94
Features the New World Gospel Choir in performances throughout the Holy Land. Produced by Mercury Films.
Fine Arts; Religion and Philosophy
Dist - APH

The Roots of gospel - gospel in the Holy Land - Volume 2 45 MIN
VHS
Color (G R)
$29.95 purchase _ #35 - 89 - 94
Features the New World Gospel Choir in performances throughout the Holy Land. Produced by Mercury Films.
Fine Arts; Religion and Philosophy
Dist - APH

Roots of Happiness 21 MIN
16mm / U-matic / VHS
Color (I J H)
Uses the character of Phil the philodendron to explain plant care. Emphasizes that water, air and light are the three basic necessities in producing healthy plants.
Agriculture; Science - Natural
Dist - LUF **Prod** - LUF 1977

Roots of Happiness 25 MIN
U-matic / VHS / 16mm
Emotions of Everyday Living Series
B&W (C A)
The story of a family living in a poor rural area of Puerto Rico. Points out the recognizable elements that make a happy atmosphere for family living, particularly the role of the father.
Psychology; Sociology
Dist - IFB **Prod** - MHFB 1953

Roots of healing - the new medicine 180 MIN
VHS
Color (G)
$18.95 _ #ARO - N001
Explores the important relationship between doctors and their patients, the challenges of life - threatening illnesses from the perspective of the whole person. Looks at how the Western medical system can benefit from complementary medical practices, such as Asian medicine. Features Michael Toms and Andrew Weil.
Health and Safety; Psychology
Dist - NOETIC **Prod** - NEWDIF 1994

Roots of High Order 28 MIN
16mm
Intermediate Algebra Series
B&W (H)
Discusses radicals of higher order than two, explaining that odd roots, not even roots, of negative numbers are real numbers. Describes the complex number system, which includes all real and imaginary numbers, and illustrates the use of these numbers.
Mathematics
Dist - MLA **Prod** - CALVIN 1959

Roots of hunger, roots of change 27 MIN
VHS / 16mm
Color (H C G)
Looks at the lingering impact of colonialism and the root causes of hunger in part of the Sahel, northern Senegal.
Geography - World; History - World; Social Science
Dist - ASTRSK **Prod** - ASTRSK 1985

Roots of narcotics supply - Part 2
VHS
Roundtables discussions series
Color (G A)
$20.00 purchase
Presents a roundtable discussion of the routes used to supply illicit drugs in the US and abroad by religious leaders, treatment specialists, former DEA agents, former gang members, physicians and policy makers. Features Harvard Law Professors Charles Nesson and Charles Ogletree as moderators. Part two of three parts produced by 'Causes and Cures,' a national campaign on the narcotics epidemic.
Civics and Political Systems; Guidance and Counseling; Health and Safety; Sociology
Dist - CRINST **Prod** - CRINST

Roots of plants 11 MIN
U-matic / 16mm / VHS
Color; B&W (I J H C) (SPANISH)
Shows the structure and growth patterns of various forms of plant roots, and explains the functions of root - caps and hair - roots. Illustrates osmosis.
Science - Natural
Dist - EBEC **Prod** - EBEC 1957

Roots of Resistance - a Story of the Underground Railroad 60 MIN
VHS / 16mm
American Experience Series
Color; Captioned (G)
$59.95 purchase _ #AMEX - 216
Retells the story of black America's secret railroad to freedom through the narratives of escaped slaves. Interviews descendents of slaves and slaveholders who describe the personal danger and terrible risk involved in each slave's escape. Part of an ongoing series which highlights personal stories behind the historic events of America. Produced by WGBHTV, WNETTV and KCETTV.
Biography; History - United States; Sociology
Dist - PBS

Roots of the Nation 29 MIN
16mm
Color
LC 76-702716
Shows how forests have influenced the development of America.
Agriculture; Geography - United States; Science - Natural
Dist - USNAC **Prod** - USFS 1976

Roots of the Tree 32 MIN
16mm
B&W (J)
Portrays three centuries of the history of the Oregon country and shows the period of exploration of the Northwest coast by sea, the charting of the land by fur traders and explorers, the arrival of the settlers and typical scenes of life in the area during the early years of the 20th century.
Geography - United States; History - United States
Dist - OREGHS **Prod** - OREGHS 1959

The Roots of War 60 MIN
U-matic / VHS / 16mm
Vietnam - a television history series; Episode 1
Color (H C A)
Offers a short history of the century during which France dominated Vietnam under the colonial tradition leading up to the rise of Ho Chi Minh. Shows that at the end of World War II Ho, flanked by U S officers, declared independence in Hanoi, but that the British helped the French regain control of Saigon.
History - United States; History - World
Dist - FI **Prod** - WGBHTV 1983

The Roots of war and the first Vietnam war, 1946 - 1954 - Volume 1 120 MIN
VHS
Vietnam - a television history series
Color (H C A)
$14.95 purchase
Presents the first two episodes of a 13 - part series covering the history of the Vietnam War. Includes the episodes 'The Roots Of War' and 'The First Vietnam War, 1946 - 1954.'
History - United States
Dist - PBS **Prod** - WNETTV

The Roots of war - Volume 1 120 MIN
VHS
Vietnam - a television history series
Color (G)
$29.95 purchase _ #S01527
Consists of two 60 - minute episodes examining the US involvement in Vietnam - 'The Roots of War' and 'The First Vietnam War.' Covers the years from 1946 to 1954.
History - United States
Dist - UILL **Prod** - PBS

Roots / races 30 MIN
VHS / U-matic
La Esquina series
Color (H C A)
Presents a story centering on a real Mexican celebration. Uses the story to try to reduce the minority isolation of Mexican - American students by showing the teenager as an individual, as a member of a unique cultural group and as a member of a larger complex society.
Sociology
Dist - GPN **Prod** - SWEDL 1976

Roots series
The African - Pt 1 47 MIN
The African - Pt 2 50 MIN
Chicken George - Pt 1 48 MIN
Chicken George - Pt 2 48 MIN
The Choice 49 MIN
The Escape 48 MIN
Freedom - Pt 1 52 MIN
Freedom - Pt 2 44 MIN
The Slave - Pt 1 53 MIN
The Slave - Pt 2 48 MIN
The Uprooted 48 MIN
The War 52 MIN
Dist - FI

Roots to Cherish 30 MIN
16mm / U-matic / VHS
Color
Identifies and illustrates the consequences of cultural differences on school performance, ways to conduct a more appropriate evaluation and suggestions for program modifications to improve individual pupil achievement.
Social Science
Dist - SHENFP **Prod** - SHENFP

Rooty Toot Toot 8 MIN
16mm
Color
Presents an animated story based on the song Frankie And Johnny.
Fine Arts
Dist - TIMLIF **Prod** - TIMLIF 1982

The Rope 81 MIN
16mm
Color (G)
$75.00 rental
Features a frightening classic which concerns two college boys who kill for thrills. Presents a story full of suspense and ingenious camera work from director Alfred Hitchcock - his first film in color. Based on the Leopold - Loeb case. Stars James Stewart, John Dall, Farley Granger, Cedric Hardwicke.
Fine Arts; Literature and Drama; Sociology
Dist - NCJEWF

Rope Jumping 15 MIN
U-matic / VHS
Leaps and Bounds Series no 11
Color (T)
Explains how to teach primary students to turn a long rope, jump inside a long rope, jump in rhythm, turn a short rope, jump a short rope turning forward and backward, and jump to a rhyme.
Physical Education and Recreation
Dist - AITECH

Rope Pull / Swing and Bend / Double Heel Lifts 15 MIN
U-matic / VHS
Roomnastics Series
Color (P)
Presents several exercises which can be performed in a classroom setting.
Physical Education and Recreation
Dist - GPN **Prod** - WVIZTV 1979

Rope Skipping - Basic Steps 16 MIN
16mm
Color (I J H)
LC FIA66-1088
Describes the purposes of rope skipping in maintaining physical fitness. Demonstrates eleven basic steps of jump roping, done in various tempos.
Physical Education and Recreation
Dist - MMP **Prod** - MMP 1965

Ropes and Knots 20 MIN
VHS
Firefighter I Video Series
Color (PRO G)
$115.00 purchase _ #35098
Shows how a firefighter uses ropes and knots to secure and hoist personnel and equipment. Demonstrates all knots clearly. Includes an instruction guide for review. Part of a video series on Firefighter I training codes to be used with complementing IFSTA manuals.
Health and Safety; Psychology; Social Science
Dist - OKSU **Prod** - OKSU

Ropes and knots 18 MIN
VHS
Firefighter I series
Color (IND)
$130.00 purchase _ #35637
Presents one part of a 19 - part series that is the teaching companion for IFSTA's Essentials of Fire Fighting manual. Looks at the types of ropes and explains how to identify them; procedures for maintaining, inspecting and storing rope; and how to tie a variety of knots. Based on Chapter 4.
Health and Safety; Science - Physical; Social Science
Dist - OKSU **Prod** - ACCTRA

Ropics level 2 for experienced jumpers 60 MIN
VHS
Color (J H C G)
$29.95 purchase _ #ROP200V
Presents more advanced step - by - step instruction on over 20 basic to advanced intermediate level techniques in rope jumping. Shows how to measure a jump rope and discusses surface, shoes and age - specific programs.
Physical Education and Recreation
Dist - CAMV

Ropics - rope jumping redefined 55 MIN
VHS
Color (H C A)
$29.95 purchase _ #ROP100V
Takes a comprehensive look at Ropics, a rope - based exercise program that avoids the problems usually associated with rope jumping - such as early exhaustion, shin splints, and sore calves. Explains and demonstrates 15 exercise techniques, many of which require no jumping at all. Includes a booklet.
Physical Education and Recreation
Dist - CAMV

The Ropin' Fool 20 MIN
16mm
B&W
Features Will Rogers as Ropes Reilly, a cowhand who gets fired because he likes roping more than eating and even ropes in his sleep.
Fine Arts
Dist - REELIM **Prod** - UNKNWN 1921

Rordrum - Botaurus Stellaris (Bittern) 10 MIN
16mm
Color
Describes the bittern in its natural surroundings, accompanied by sound effects.
Science - Natural
Dist - STATNS **Prod** - STATNS 1969

Rorskoven (Forest of Reeds) 18 MIN
16mm
Color
Describes animal life among the reeds of a woodland lake. Includes music and sound effects.
Science - Natural
Dist - STATNS **Prod** - STATNS 1964

Rosa - an Editing Exercise 33 MIN
16mm
Color (H C A)
LC 78-701186
Presents an editing exercise which consists of unedited scenes that are designed to be edited into various narrative and non - narrative works.
Education; English Language
Dist - TEMPLU **Prod** - MARBLO 1978

Rosabeth Moss Kanter on synergies, alliances and new ventures 93 MIN
VHS / BETA
Proven strategies for competitive success series
Color; PAL (G)
$2000.00 purchase
Considers internal and external corporate collaborations which have potential for profit in times of cutbacks. Features Rosabeth Moss Kanter.
Business and Economics; Psychology
Dist - NATTYL **Prod** - HBS 1990

Rosalie goes shopping 94 MIN
35mm / 16mm
Color (G)
Features the saga of Rosalie Greenspace - played by Marianne Saegebrecht - a queen - sized woman with a heart to match, who wants only the best for her crop - duster husband and seven children. Portrays Rosalie's resolve not to let a little thing like money get in the way and so charges her 37 credit cards to the limit, juggles a dozen false identites and writes bad checks all over town. Her philosophy includes the realization that when you're $100,000 in debt, it's your problem, but when you're $1,000,000 in debt, it's the bank's problem. A whimsical social satire about American consumer madness. Produced by Percy Adlon and Eleonore Adlon; directed by Percy Adlon. Stars Brad Davis and Judge Reinhold. Contact distributor for price.
Fine Arts; Literature and Drama; Psychology; Sociology
Dist - OCTOBF

Rosalie Moore - 10 - 4 - 87 120 MIN
VHS / Cassette
Poetry Center reading series
Color (G)
#927 - 629
Features the writer reading from her works at the Ruth Witt - Diamant Memorial Reading at the Poetry Center, San Francisco State University. Also includes readings by James Broughton, Robert Duncan, Mark Linenthal, Shirley Taylor, Christy Taylor, Justine Fixel, Lawrence Fixel, Michael McClure, Gail Layton, and Stephen Witt - Diamant. Introduction by Frances Phillips. Slides of Ruth Witt - Diamant courtesy of Caryl Mezey. Available for listening purposes only at the Center; not for sale or rent.
Literature and Drama
Dist - POETRY **Prod** - POETRY 1987

Rosalina 23 MIN
16mm / VHS
Color (G)
$475.00, $190.00 purchase, $50.00 rental
Spends a day in the life of Rosalina, a 12 - year - old Salvadoran girl whose family has fled to a refugee camp in Honduras after their house was set on fire during the civil war in El Salvador. Follows her as she goes to school, helps her mother, plays games with her friends.
Fine Arts; Sociology
Dist - FIRS **Prod** - JENKIN 1987

Rosalyn S Yalow 30 MIN
VHS
Eminent chemists videotapes series
Color (H C G)
$60.00 purchase _ #VT - 026
Meets chemist Rosalyn S Yalow. Part of a series glimpsing into the history of chemistry and offering insights into the successes, trials and tribulations of some of the most distinguished names in the world of chemistry.
Science
Dist - AMCHEM

Roscoe Holcomb and Jean Redpath 52 MIN
U-matic / VHS
Rainbow quest series
Color
Shows Pete Seeger and Roscoe Holcomb trading traditional American songs. Features Jean Redpath singing several songs from her native Scotland.
Fine Arts
Dist - NORROS **Prod** - SEEGER

Roscoe's Rules 10 MIN
16mm / U-matic / VHS
Color (K P)
LC 76-702171
Presents Roscoe the Drumming Bear as the symbol for the four basic safety rules for avoiding molestation. Depicts a police officer talking to a class of second graders and introducing them to Roscoe's four special safety rules. Shows that during the next few days, some of the children are tempted to forget one of Roscoe's rules until the little drumming bear pops into their minds and triggers a recollection of the rule.
Guidance and Counseling; Health and Safety; Social Science
Dist - AIMS **Prod** - DAVP 1973

Rose 13 MIN
VHS / U-matic
En Francais series
Color (H C A)
Takes place in a small country restaurant and in an elegant restaurant along the Seine.
Foreign Language; Geography - World
Dist - AITECH **Prod** - MOFAFR 1970

Rose and daisy 30 MIN
VHS / 16mm
Art of decorating cakes series
(G)
$49.00 purchase _ #BCD3
Instructs in the art of cake decorating. Shows how to make the rose on the flower nail, using the rose tip. Illustrates construction of the daisy directly applied to the cake, using the rose tip. Taught by Leon Simmons, master cake decorator.
Home Economics; Industrial and Technical Education
Dist - RMIBHF **Prod** - RMIBHF

Rose and Rose Elaine 11 MIN
16mm
B&W (G)
$17.00 rental
Tries to bridge the pain of a broken family reunion. Consists of the grains of memory, an unconscious faith and terror. A David Sherman production.
Fine Arts; Psychology
Dist - CANCIN

The Rose and the Mignonette 8 MIN
16mm
B&W
Interprets a poem by Louis Aragon, a noted French poet. Illustrates the thesis that unified faith, regardless of individual beliefs, forms a bond against invading forces.
Literature and Drama
Dist - RADIM **Prod** - FILIM

Rose Argoff 9 MIN
U-matic / VHS / 16mm
Bitter Vintage Series
Color (H C A)
LC 73-703136
Presents a courageous old lady who tells about her life in America, after emigrating to this country from Russia.
Sociology
Dist - CAROUF **Prod** - WNETTV 1973

The Rose Bowl - Granddaddy of Them all - History of the Rose Bowl 'Til 1969 54 MIN
16mm

Color (H C A)
LC 73-702565
Presents the complete history of the Rose Bowl through 1969. Includes capsule interviews of famous coaches and their teams through the years. Shows many of the famous plays and older uniforms.
Physical Education and Recreation
Dist - TRA **Prod** - TRA 1969

Rose by Any Other Name 15 MIN
16mm
Color (H C A)
LC 80-700446
Presents a dramatization about a 79 - year - old woman resident of a nursing home who is found in the bed of a male resident. Shows how their warm, intimate and fulfilling relationship is threatened by the administration, the staff, the residents and her family.
Health and Safety; Sociology
Dist - ADELPH **Prod** - ADELPH 1979

A Rose for Emily 27 MIN
U-matic / VHS / 16mm
Color
Presents the tale of an indomitable Southern woman who clutched the past so resolutely that life itself was denied. Based on the short story A Rose For Emily by William Faulkner.
Literature and Drama
Dist - PFP **Prod** - CHBDYL 1982

Rose gumpaste 30 MIN
VHS / 16mm
Art of decorating cakes series
(G)
$49.00 purchase _ #BCD7
Instructs in the art of cake decorating. Shows how to hand shape a rose out of gumpaste, using small cutters and molding in the hand. Taught by master cake decorator Leon Simmons.
Home Economics; Industrial and Technical Education
Dist - RMIBHF **Prod** - RMIBHF

Rose Kennedy - a Mother's Story 46 MIN
U-matic / VHS
Color (G)
$249.00, $149.00 purchase _ #AD - 1631
Presents the story of the Kennedys as told by 96 - year - old Rose Kennedy and through Kennedy family home movies, rare documentary footage and interviews with major participants.
Biography; Sociology
Dist - FOTH **Prod** - FOTH

Rose of the night 8 MIN
16mm
Color (G)
$15.00 purchase
Relies entirely on abstract vision, digging into emotions in a production by Zack Stiglicz.
Fine Arts; Psychology
Dist - CANCIN

Rose parade - Pasadena 3 MIN
16mm
Of all things series
Color (P I)
Discusses the Rose Parade in the city of Pasadena, California.
Geography - United States; Physical Education and Recreation
Dist - AVED **Prod** - BAILYL

Roseblood 8 MIN
16mm
Color (G)
$15.00 rental
Unveils images of a woman in dance, in flora, in architecture, in space, in confusion, in birth, in the Valley of Sorrow and so on. Features the dance of Carolyn Chave Kaplan with music by Stockhausen and Enesco.
Fine Arts
Dist - CANCIN **Prod** - COUZS 1974

Rosebud 14 MIN
VHS / 16mm
Color (G)
$75.00 rental, $275.00 purchase
Dramatizes the story about a young artist who moves into a new apartment and finds herself unexpectedly drawn to the open sexuality of the lesbian couple who live next door. Looks at how images of women begin appearing in her paintings as her imagination runs wild and she eventually sets out to make her fantasies a reality. A film by Cheryl Farthing; produced by the British Film Institute.
Fine Arts
Dist - WMEN

Rosedale - the Way it is 57 MIN
U-matic / VHS / 16mm
Color (H C A)
LC 77-700771
Captures the sights, sounds and tensions of Rosedale, a New York community fighting to keep from becoming a slum area.
Geography - United States; Social Science; Sociology
Dist - IU **Prod** - WNETTV 1976

Rosemary Ann Sisson on Richard III 25 MIN
VHS
Shakespeare in perspective series
Color (A)
PdS45 purchase _ Unavailable in USA
Films Rosemary Ann Sisson and her commentary on location and includes extracts of the Shakespeare play Richard III. Challenges many of the more traditional interpretations of Shakespeare's works. Part of a series produced between 1978 and 1985.
Literature and Drama
Dist - BBCENE

Rosemary Dunleavy, Mary Barr ett and Alan Lewis 30 MIN
U-matic / VHS
Eye on Dance - Behind the Scenes Series
Color
Focuses on rehearsing a dance company. Looks at excerpts of 'Esoterica' with Christine Spizzo. Hosted by Celia Ipiotis.
Fine Arts
Dist - ARCVID **Prod** - ARCVID

The Rosen Incontinence Procedure 10 MIN
U-matic / VHS
Color (PRO)
Shows silicone prothesis implantaion to allow patients to control incontinence.
Health and Safety
Dist - WFP **Prod** - WFP

Roses 29 MIN
Videoreel / VT2
Dig it Series
Color
Features Tom Lied explaining the types of roses and where they will grow best. Gives tips on the handling, planting, pruning, fertilizing and watering of roses.
Agriculture; Science - Natural
Dist - PBS **Prod** - WMVSTV

Roses 30 MIN
VHS / U-matic
Home Gardener with John Lenanton Series Lesson 18; Lesson 18
Color (C A)
Tells how and when to select healthy roses. Recommends nine step - by - step pruning procedures. Explains rose grading and selection processes.
Agriculture
Dist - CDTEL **Prod** - COAST

Roses 47 MIN
VHS / BETA / 16mm
Color (G)
$39.95 purchase _ #VT1029
Tells all about roses. Covers hybrids and miniatures and tells how to grow climbing and tree roses. Includes information on fertilization and insect control. Taught by Ed Hume.
Science - Natural
Dist - RMIBHF **Prod** - RMIBHF

Roses and garbage - meditation and peace 120 MIN
VHS / BETA
Color; PAL (G)
PdS27, $54.00 purchase
Features a speech by Thich Nhat Hanh in London, January 1988.
Fine Arts; Religion and Philosophy
Dist - MERIDT

Roses and rose gardens
VHS
Gardens of the world series
Color (H C G)
$24.95 purchase _ #GW01
Focuses on roses. Features host Audrey Hepburn and narrator Michael York. Part of a six - part series on gardens.
Agriculture; Science - Natural
Dist - SVIP **Prod** - AUVICA 1993

Roses are red - six versions 30 MIN
VHS
Called - the ministry of teaching series
Color (G A R)
$39.95 purchase, $10.00 rental _ #35 - 858 - 2076
Offers tips in classroom instruction for teachers. Includes study guide. Hosted by Sharon Lee. Produced by Seraphim.
Education; Religion and Philosophy
Dist - APH

Roses in December - the Story of Jean Donovan 55 MIN
16mm
Color
Chronicles the life of Jean Donovan, a lay missioner who was murdered by members of the government security forces in El Salvador. Raises questions about the relationship that exists between the U S government and the military leaders of El Salvador.
Civics and Political Systems; Geography - World
Dist - FIRS **Prod** - FIRS

Roses - Planting and Care 60 MIN
VHS / U-matic
Ortho's Video Series
Color (A)
$24.95 _ #OR102
Gives the viewer tips on planting and maintaining healthy rose plants. Covers storing, pest control, pruning and more.
Agriculture; Science - Natural
Dist - AAVIM **Prod** - AAVIM

Rosey Grier - the Courage to be Me 23 MIN
U-matic / VHS / 16mm
Color (J H C)
Presents a profile of Rosey Grier and details how he overcame shyness, rejection and failures and achieved success in sports, politics, entertainment and service to young people.
Biography; Physical Education and Recreation
Dist - CF **Prod** - CF 1978

Rosh Hashana / Yom Kippur 15 MIN
U-matic
Celebrate Series
Color (P)
Religion and Philosophy; Social Science
Dist - GPN **Prod** - KUONTV 1978

Rosie 24 MIN
16mm / U-matic / VHS
Color (K)
$495.00, $349.00, $249.00 purchase _ #AD - 1498
Tells the story of Rosie and her family. Provides a touching story of life with a terminally ill child.
Literature and Drama; Psychology; Sociology
Dist - FOTH **Prod** - FOTH

Rosie's walk 5 MIN
16mm / U-matic / VHS
Color (K P)
Tells the story about Rosie, a hen, who went for a walk across the yard, around the pond, over the haystack, past the mill, through the fence, under the beehives and got back in time for dinner. A fox stalks close behind the proud little hen. Rosie struts across the barnyard, to the tune of 'Turkey in the Straw,' keeping her country - cool and unwittingly leading the fox into one disaster after another.
Literature and Drama
Dist - WWS **Prod** - WWS

Rosie's walk 42 MIN
16mm / VHS
Color (K P T)
$550.00, $29.95 purchase
Features storyteller Lynn Rubright who tells the story Rosie's Walk by Pat Hutchins using chant, traditional storytelling and movement activity. Follows with a training session for educators. Tells how to select a story and practice storytelling. Discusses how to use storytelling to extend language development and vocabulary, how storytelling works with disabled and gifted children.
Education; English Language; Literature and Drama
Dist - KAWVAL **Prod** - KAWVAL

The Roslyn Migration 30 MIN
U-matic
South by Northwest Series
Color
Focuses on the tough coal mining town of Roslyn, Washington, established by the Northern Pacific Railroad around 1886. Tells about the Black strike breakers who were brought in to mine after the 1888 miner's strike. Focuses on the role of James E Sheppardson.
Biography; History - United States
Dist - GPN **Prod** - KWSU

Roslyn Romance - is it really true - Intro I and II 18 MIN
16mm
Color (C)
$548.00
Experimental film by Bruce Bailliem.
Fine Arts
Dist - AFA **Prod** - AFA 1977

Ross 200 60 MIN
VHS
Using Loran series

Color (G A)
$29.90 purchase _ #0764
Shows how to operate the Ross 200 Loran model. Includes installation tips, initialization, calibration, chain selection, notch filters, signal - to - noise ratio, time differentials, Lat - Lon functions, selecting and programming waypoints, setting anchor and waypoint alarm, cross - track error, determining course to steer and distance to go. Part of a series on the most popular Loran models.
Physical Education and Recreation; Social Science
Dist - SEVVID

Ross Bridge 18 MIN
16mm
Color
LC 80-700919
Takes a close look at the intricate symbolic carving on both sides of the Ross Bridge in Tasmania, with an explanation of the possible reasons for the work behind this Australian landmark.
Fine Arts; Geography - World
Dist - TASCOR **Prod** - TASCOR 1977

Ross MacDonald 29 MIN
U-matic / VHS / 16mm
Writer in America Series
Color
Presents an interview with author Ross MacDonald, whose stories tend to deal with the effects of the long - buried past on the present. Shows how he weaves common Southern California locales and the common fears on the 1980s into his mystery stories.
Literature and Drama
Dist - CORF **Prod** - MOORER 1978

Ross Perot - straight talk 60 MIN
VHS
Color (J H C G)
$19.98 purchase _ #FF0076V
Portrays H Ross Perot, the Texas billionaire who mounted a challenge to the campaigns of traditional presidential candidates in the election of 1992. Traces his meteoric rise in the business world, his personally directed campaign to free his company's imprisoned employees in Iran, his notorious battle with the management of General Motors. Features David Frost.
Biography; Business and Economics; Civics and Political Systems
Dist - CAMV

Ross Taylor
U-matic / VHS
Third R - Teaching Basic Mathematics Skills Series
Color
Emphasizes that specialized skills for a technology - centered society are becoming increasingly important. Emphasizes the use of calculators and computers in the mathematics classroom.
Education; Mathematics
Dist - EDCPUB **Prod** - EDCPUB

Rossini - La Cenerentola 94 MIN
VHS
Color (G)
$39.95 purchase _ #VU1404V - F
Presents Rossini's operatic version of the story of Cinderella as filmed in Italy and sung in Italian with narratives in English. Stars Fedora Barbieri and Afro Poli and the Rome Opera as directed by Oliviero de Fabritiis.
Fine Arts
Dist - CAMV

Rostropovich - Dvorak Cello Concerto and Saint - Saens Cello Concerto no 1 65 MIN
VHS
Color (G)
$29.95 purchase _ #1160
Presents cellist Mstislav Rostropovich performing a 'Cello Concerto' by Dvorak and 'Cello Concerto No 1' by Saint - Saens. Features the accompaniment of the London Philharmonic Orchestra conducted by Carlo Maria Guilini.
Fine Arts; Geography - World
Dist - KULTUR

Rotameter Equipment 10 MIN
U-matic / VHS
Color (A)
LC 84-706453
Illustrates the calibration of a rotameter by the assignment of flow rate values to the rotameter's scale markings. Includes information on primary, secondary and intermediate standards and a listing of equipment set - up interconnection and operation, as well as how to pilot the flow chart for the rotameter.
Health and Safety; Mathematics
Dist - USNAC **Prod** - USNAC 1978

Rotaries, blocks and swivels - Pt 1 - the swivel 19 MIN
Slide / VHS / U-matic / 16mm
(A PRO)
$160.00 purchase _ #11.1070, $170.00 purchase _ #51.1070
Explains the function, workings, and maintenance of the swivel with emphasis on longer equipment life and increased personnel safety on the rig.
Industrial and Technical Education; Social Science
Dist - UTEXPE **Prod** - UTEXPE 1980

Rotaries, blocks, and swivels - Pt 2 - the rotary table 20 MIN
Slide / VHS / U-matic / 16mm
(A PRO)
$160.00 purchase _ #11.1071, $170.00 purchase _ #51.1071
Shows the rotary table broken down into its component parts and gives the table construction, workings, and basic maintenance, stressing a well - planned preventive maintenance program.
Industrial and Technical Education; Social Science
Dist - UTEXPE **Prod** - UTEXPE 1981

Rotary Compressors 60 MIN
VHS / U-matic
Mechanical Equipment Maintenance, Module 9 - Air Compressors Series
Color (IND)
Industrial and Technical Education
Dist - LEIKID **Prod** - LEIKID

Rotary Drilling Fluids 24 MIN
16mm
Color (IND)
LC 76-700853
Considers the use, testing and treatment of water base drilling fluids and the role they play in the prevention of blowouts.
Business and Economics; Industrial and Technical Education
Dist - UTEXPE **Prod** - UTEXPE 1975

Rotary drilling fluids series
Field testing 21 MIN
Functions 19 MIN
Hole problems 22 MIN
Oil muds 24 MIN
Water - base muds 29 MIN
Dist - UTEXPE

Rotary Edger - Trimmer
VHS
Landscape Equipment Maintenance Series
Color (G) (SPANISH)
$65.00 purchase _ #6 - 074 - 100P, #6 - 074 - 200P - Spanish
Presents proper procedures on maintenance, safety and operation of the rotary edger - trimmer for landscaping. Part of a five - part series on landscaping.
Agriculture; Health and Safety
Dist - VEP **Prod** - VEP

Rotary - Engine of the Future 11 MIN
U-matic / VHS / 16mm
Color (J)
LC 74-702565
Uses live action and animation to illustrate the workings of the rotary engine, pointing out the advantages of only seven moving parts, lightness, greater efficiency and less polluting emissions than the piston engine.
Industrial and Technical Education; Sociology
Dist - FI **Prod** - IFFB 1973

Rotary gear pumps - Pt 1 14 MIN
VHS / U-matic
Marshall maintenance training programs series; Tape 45
Color (IND)
Outlines installation and maintenance procedures showing the importance of installing base plate on a solid foundation. Discusses recommended piping methods, the necessity of safety relief valves on positive displacement pumps, start - up procedures and preventive maintenance procedures using vacuum and pressure gauges.
Industrial and Technical Education
Dist - LEIKID **Prod** - LEIKID

Rotary gear pumps - Pt 2 14 MIN
VHS / U-matic
Marshall maintenance training programs series; Tape 46
Color (IND)
Covers inspection and repair of rotary gear pumps. Emphasizes importance of locking out the main disconnect and venting the pump chamber.
Industrial and Technical Education
Dist - LEIKID **Prod** - LEIKID

Rotary joints - installation and maintenance 13 MIN
VHS / U-matic
Marshall maintenance training programs series; Tape 43
Color (IND)
Shows the function of the joint that connect a stationary supply pipe to a rotating machine part to cool or heat the unit. Demonstrates how the joint is repaired and installed.
Industrial and Technical Education
Dist - LEIKID **Prod** - LEIKID

Rotating Flows 29 MIN
U-matic / VHS / 16mm
Fluid Mechanics Films Series
Color (H C)
LC 76-705657
Illustrates the phenomena associated with rotation of homogenous fluids, including horizontal trajectories in surface gravity waves, low and high - Rossby - number flows around spheres, Taylor walls, normal modes of inertia oscillation and rossby waves in a cylindrical annulus.
Science - Physical
Dist - EBEC **Prod** - EDS 1968

Rotating Machinery Explained - DC Motors 75 MIN
VHS / 35mm strip
(H A IND)
#810XV7
Explains the parts, principles and operations of direct current motors. Includes principles of operation part one, principles of operation part two, identify the armature and filds, measuring motor resistance voltmeter ammeter method, and counter electromotive force (5 tapes). Prerequisite required. Includes a Study Guide.
Education; Industrial and Technical Education
Dist - BERGL

Rotating Machinery Explained - Motor Control Fundamentals 62 MIN
VHS / 35mm strip
(H A IND)
#814XV7
Explains the principles of motor controls and how to read and understand line diagrams. Includes line diagrams and electrical symbols, interpreting complex line diagrams, reduced voltage starters, part winding and Wye Delta starter, and jogging, braking and plugging (5 tapes). Prerequisites required. Includes a Study Guide.
Education; Industrial and Technical Education
Dist - BERGL

Rotating Machinery Explained - Single Phase AC Motors 64 MIN
VHS / 35mm strip
(H A IND)
#812XV7
Introduces the parts, operations and application of various single phase AC motors. Includes split phase induction motor, capacitor induction motors, repulsion type motors, and universal motor (4 tapes). Prerequisite required. Includes a Study Guide.
Education; Industrial and Technical Education
Dist - BERGL

Rotating Machinery Explained - Three Phase AC Motors 60 MIN
VHS / 35mm strip
(H A IND)
#813XV7
Provides an explanation of the operating principles and characteristics of various three phase AC motors. Includes squirrel cage induction motors part one, squirrel cage induction motors part two, across the line starter, and reversing magnetic starters (4 tapes). Prerequisites required. Includes a Study Guide.
Education; Industrial and Technical Education
Dist - BERGL

Rotating magnetic fields 13 MIN
U-matic
Electrical work - electrical machinery series
B&W (IND)
LC 78-706141
Discusses the rotating magnetic field pattern, three - phase winding in a demonstration stator, factors that cause rotation of the magnetic field, and the construction of polyphase motors. Issued in 1945 as a motion picture.
Industrial and Technical Education
Dist - USNAC **Prod** - USOE 1978

Rotating magnetic fields 10 MIN
16mm
Electrical work - electrical machinery series; No 2
B&W
LC FIE52-349
Explains a rotating magnetic field pattern, threephase winding in a demonstration stator, factors that cause rotation of the magnetic field, and the construction of polyphase motors.
Industrial and Technical Education
Dist - USNAC **Prod** - USOE 1945

Rotation 30 MIN
U-matic / VHS
Kinetic Karnival of Jearl Walker Pt 2
Color (H)

LC 83-706116
Presents physics professor Jearl Walker offering graphic and unusual demonstrations exemplifying the principles of the rotation of solids.
Science - Physical
Dist - GPN **Prod** - WVIZTV 1982

Rotation 18 MIN
U-matic / VHS
Numerical Control/Computerized Numerical Control - Advanced 'Programming Series Module 2
Color (IND)
Includes rotation and its rules, rotating a program and terminating rotation.
Business and Economics; Industrial and Technical Education
Dist - LEIKID **Prod** - LEIKID

Rotation - 11 46 MIN
VHS
Conceptual physics alive series
Color (H C)
$45.00 purchase
Develops and illustrates the concept of rotational inertia with a variety of examples. Includes demonstrations such as rolling cans filled with liquids and solids - and Prof Hewitt on a rotating roundtable demonstrating the conservation of angular momentum. Part 11 of a 35 - part series adapted from the college and high school textbook Conceptual Physics by Professor Paul Hewitt.
Science - Physical
Dist - MMENTE **Prod** - HEWITP 1992

Rotation and motivation exercise series
Presents a three - part series of exercise programs. Includes aerobics, waistline and muscle toning workouts.
Calorie burner workout
No flab workout
Tighten up workout
Dist - CAMV

Rotational path concept in removable partial denture design - a series
VHS / U-matic
Rotational path concept in removable partial denture design - a'series
Color (PRO)
Describes the use of the rotational path in maxillary Class IV partially edentulous arches and maxillary and mandibular Class III bilateral partially edentulous arches. Rotational Path Concept In Removable Partial - - ; Rotational Path Concept In Removable Partial - - .
Health and Safety; Science; Science - Natural
Dist - USNAC **Prod** - VADTC

Rotational path concept in removable partial denture design - a series
Rotational path concept in removable partial denture design - a series
Dist - USNAC

Rotational path concept in removable partial denture design - Pt 1 12 MIN
VHS / U-matic
Rotational path concept in removable partial denture design series
Color (PRO)
Describes the use of the rotational path of insertion in designing removable partial dentures for maxillary class IV partially edentulous arches. Eliminates clasps to improve aesthetics and minimize plaque accumulation.
Health and Safety; Science; Science - Natural
Dist - USNAC **Prod** - VADTC

Rotational path concept in removable partial denture design - Pt 2 12 MIN
U-matic
Rotational path concept in removable partial denture design series
Color (PRO)
Describes the use of the rotational path concept in the maxillary and mandibular Class III bilateral partially edentulous arches. Eliminates clasps to improve aesthetics and minimize plaque accumulation.
Health and Safety; Science; Science - Natural
Dist - USNAC **Prod** - VADTC

Rotational path concept in removable partial denture design series
Rotational path concept in removable partial denture design - Pt 1 12 MIN
Rotational path concept in removable partial denture design - Pt 2 12 MIN
Dist - USNAC

ROTC 20 MIN
16mm
B&W
Explains that ROTC is a primary issue on many college campuses and is a major focus of anti - war activity. Shows the university's ties to the military - industrial complex and shows how ROTC serves this relationship.
Civics and Political Systems; Education; Sociology
Dist - CANWRL **Prod** - CANWRL

The Rothko Conspiracy 90 MIN
U-matic / VHS
Color (H C A)
Recounts the tragedy of artist Mark Rothko, who became insane and committed suicide at the age of 66. Tells that when he died, the people he had depended on to handle his legacy unscrupulously emptied his estate of most of his assets including over 1,000 paintings.
Fine Arts
Dist - FI **Prod** - FI

Rotor Assembly 60 MIN
VHS / U-matic
Mechanical Equipment Maintenance, Module 5 - Centrifugal Pumps 'Series
Color (IND)
Industrial and Technical Education
Dist - LEIKID **Prod** - LEIKID

Rotor Repair 60 MIN
VHS / U-matic
Mechanical Equipment Maintenance, Module 5 - Centrifugal Pumps 'Series
Color (IND)
Industrial and Technical Education
Dist - LEIKID **Prod** - LEIKID

The Rotten truth 30 MIN
VHS
Color (K P I J H C G T A)
$19.95 purchase
Uses animation, music and innovative graphics to describe the growing problem with waste disposal. Visits landfills and the "Museum of Modern Garbage" to further illustrate the problem. Features the "Rappin' Wrapper." From the PBS "3 - 2 - 1 Contact" series.
Science; Science - Natural
Dist - EFVP **Prod** - CTELWO 1990

The Rotten World about Us 50 MIN
U-matic / VHS / 16mm
Color (H C A)
Unravels the mysteries of mushrooms and molds and shows how fungi feed, grow and multiply. Depicts fungi that lay traps for worms and others that can kill flies.
Science - Natural
Dist - FI **Prod** - BBCTV 1981

Rotterdam - a Port Story 20 MIN
16mm / VHS
Color (J H A)
$350.00, $440.00 purchase, $50.00 rental _ #8028
Surveys the river port of Rotterdam on the north branch of the Rhine River in the Netherlands. Considers shipping and commerce.
Geography - World; Social Science
Dist - AIMS **Prod** - EDMI 1987

Rotterdam - a port study 20 MIN
VHS
Color (J H G)
$69.95 purchase _ #8028D
Studies the port of Rotterdam, in the Netherlands, a vast, interlocking network of waterways, railroads, pipelines and highways, connecting Europe with the rest of the world.
Business and Economics
Dist - INSTRU

Rotterdam - Europort Gateway to Europe 20 MIN
U-matic / VHS / 16mm
Color (I J H)
LC 70-712992
Studies life in Rotterdam. Includes views of the city and its people.
Geography - World; Social Science
Dist - EBEC **Prod** - EBEC 1971

Rouad - Island of the Crusaders 10 MIN
16mm
B&W
Examines the anachronistic life of the fishermen on Rouad, a tiny Mediterranean island. Shows the simplicity of life that takes place in this 20th century community which still works and lives under conditions which prevailed during the Crusades.
Geography - World; Social Science; Sociology
Dist - RADIM **Prod** - FILIM 1945

Rouge baiser 100 MIN
16mm
Color (G) (FRENCH WITH ENGLISH SUBTITLES)
Portrays the 1950s Yankee - hating, Stalin - loving young daughter of Jewish refugees from Eastern Europe who falls madly in love with a bourgeois freelance photographer and finds her idealism colliding with real life. Directed by Vera Belmont.
Civics and Political Systems; Fine Arts
Dist - KINOIC

Rough Country 17 MIN
16mm / U-matic / VHS
Color (I J H)
Stresses that the need for education and the development of new skills are of utmost importance so that machine power now available can be properly and prudently used.
Guidance and Counseling; Industrial and Technical Education; Psychology; Sociology
Dist - IFB **Prod** - IFB 1963

Rough - Facing, Boring and Turning a Shoulder 22 MIN
16mm
Machine Shop Work Series
B&W
LC FIE51-518
Demonstrates how to set up a rough casting on a vertical turret lathe, face a flange and turn a shoulder with the sidehead turret, and face a flange and bore a hole with the vertical turret.
Industrial and Technical Education
Dist - USNAC **Prod** - USOE 1942

Rough - Facing, Turning and Drilling 31 MIN
16mm
Machine Shop Work Series Operations on the Vertical Boring Mill, no '1
B&W
LC FIE51-517
Tells how to operate the controls of a vertical turret lathe, set up tools in the main turret head, rough - face and rough - turn an aluminum casting and drill the center hole.
Industrial and Technical Education
Dist - USNAC **Prod** - USOE 1942

Rough Grinding by Pin - Bar 19 MIN
16mm
Optical Craftsmanship Series Spherical Surfaces
B&W
LC FIE52-350
Demonstrates how to use the job card, select and adjust the grinding tool, use abrasive, perform the grinding operation, clean the grinding tool and correct worn grinding tools.
Industrial and Technical Education
Dist - USNAC **Prod** - USOE

Rough Grinding with Vertical Surface Grinder Flat Surfaces 26 MIN
16mm
B&W
LC FIE52-1106
Describes machine grinding flat surfaces and methods of blocking to grind all surface with a minimum of changes in position.
Industrial and Technical Education
Dist - USNAC **Prod** - USN 1944

Rough Line - Boring 19 MIN
16mm
B&W
LC FIE51-588
Shows how to install the boring bar and cutters, bore, counterbore and spot - face holes and reposition from one hole to another.
Industrial and Technical Education
Dist - USNAC **Prod** - USOE 1945

Rough plumbing and heating
VHS / 35mm strip
Basic carpentry and building construction series
$185.00 purchase _ #PX976 filmstrips, $185.00 purchase _ #PX976V VHS
Portrays how to install waste and drainage lines and heating and hot water systems.
Education; Industrial and Technical Education
Dist - CAREER **Prod** - CAREER

Rough Turning between Centers 15 MIN
16mm
Machine Work Series Operations on the Engine Lathe
B&W
LC FIE51-516
Explains how to set up an engine lathe, operate the controls, grind clearances on cutting tools and roughturn round bar stock to a specified diameter.
Industrial and Technical Education
Dist - USNAC **Prod** - USOE 1941

Roughhousing 30 MIN
VHS
Color (G)
$39.95 purchase _ #AF100V
Guides on safe, fun, physical play for children. Features child care expert Rick Porter.
Health and Safety; Sociology
Dist - CAMV

Roughing and Finishing External Threads on the Lathe 15 MIN
U-matic / VHS
Machining and the Operation of Machine Tools, Module 3 - 'Intermediate Engine Lathe Series
Color (IND)
Industrial and Technical Education
Dist - LEIKID **Prod** - LEIKID

Roughing and finishing external threads on the lathe
U-matic / VHS
Intermediate engine lathe operation series
Color (SPANISH)
Industrial and Technical Education
Dist - VTRI **Prod** - VTRI

Roughing - in Nonmetallic Sheathed Cable 24 MIN
16mm
B&W
LC FIE52-103
Shows how to determine the location of required runs, install an offset bar hanger and ceiling outlet box, rough - in a circuit run and make up connections for switches, receptacles and fixtures.
Industrial and Technical Education
Dist - USNAC **Prod** - USOE

Roughing it Series

Bicycle touring	30 MIN
Canoeing	30 MIN
Cave exploration	30 MIN
Day Hiking	30 MIN
Family Camping	30 MIN
Kayaking and Rafting	30 MIN
Nature Photography	30 MIN
Outdoor Cooking	30 MIN
Outdoor Gear	30 MIN
Overnight Camping	30 MIN
Preparation for Overnight Camping	30 MIN
Rock climbing and rappelling	30 MIN
Wildflowers	30 MIN

Dist - KYTV

Roughneck Training Series

Care and Use of Tongs	12 MIN
Laying Down Pipe	11 MIN
Making a Connection	12 MIN
Making a Trip	18 MIN
What are Slips	12 MIN

Dist - UTEXPE

Roulement, rouerie, aubage 15 MIN
16mm
B&W; Color (G)
$30.00 rental
Consists of three short films dealing with a water wheel on the Sorgue. Reflects the process involved through the title which means 'rotation, wiliness and paddle wheel unit.'
Fine Arts; Geography - World
Dist - CANCIN **Prod** - LOWDER 1978

Round and Round 15 MIN
U-matic / VHS
Mrs Cabobble's Caboose
(P)
Designed to teach primary grade students basic music concepts. Highlights melody, rhythm, harmony and the different families of instruments. Features Mrs. Fran Powell.
Fine Arts
Dist - GPN **Prod** - WDCNTV 1986

A Round Around 9 MIN
16mm
Color
Presents a turn dance on the streets of New York with different voices in different languages counting the turns. Emphasizes the disinterest of the people on the streets to the dance.
Social Science; Sociology
Dist - FINLYS **Prod** - FINLYS

Round Dance 3 MIN
VHS / 16mm
Color (G)
$110.00 purchase, $10.00 rental
Presents a group of dancers performing the round dance.
Social Science
Dist - BIECC **Prod** - BIECC

Round Elbow Pattern Layout using End Gore Template 17 MIN
BETA / VHS
Metal Fabrication - Parallel Line Development Series
Color (IND)
Industrial and Technical Education; Psychology
Dist - RMIBHF **Prod** - RMIBHF

Round our way - Cassette 2 73 MIN
VHS
Exploring your neighbourhood series
Color; PAL (P I)
PdS29.50 purchase
Provides a framework within which children can investigate their neighborhood. Helps them develop skills and techniques which enable them to satisfy their curiosity. Part two of a four - part series.
Social Science; Sociology
Dist - EMFVL

Round Pipe Different Diameters 45 Degree Intersection Offset 21 MIN
BETA / VHS
Metal Fabrication - Parallel Line Development Series
Color (IND)
Industrial and Technical Education; Psychology
Dist - RMIBHF **Prod** - RMIBHF

Round Pipe Different Diameters 90 Degree Intersection Offset 22 MIN
BETA / VHS
Metal Fabrication - Parallel Line Development Series
Color (IND)
Industrial and Technical Education; Psychology
Dist - RMIBHF **Prod** - RMIBHF

Round Pipe Fabrication - Grooved Lock Seam 19 MIN
BETA / VHS
Metal Fabrication - Round Pipe Fabrication Series
Color (IND)
Industrial and Technical Education; Psychology
Dist - RMIBHF **Prod** - RMIBHF

Round Pipe Fabrication - Machine Formed Seam 9 MIN
BETA / VHS
Metal Fabrication - Round Pipe Fabrication Series
Color (IND)
Industrial and Technical Education; Psychology
Dist - RMIBHF **Prod** - RMIBHF

Round Pipe Intersected by Rectangular Pipe Centered at 45 Degree 20 MIN
VHS / BETA
Metal Fabrication - Parallel Line Development Series
Color (IND)
Industrial and Technical Education; Psychology
Dist - RMIBHF **Prod** - RMIBHF

Round Pipe Intersecting a Round Taper at 45 Degrees 13 MIN
VHS / BETA
Metal Fabrication - Parallel Line Development Series
Color (IND)
Industrial and Technical Education; Psychology
Dist - RMIBHF **Prod** - RMIBHF

Round Pipe Intersecting a Round Taper at 90 Degrees 18 MIN
BETA / VHS
Metal Fabrication - Parallel Line Development Series
Color (IND)
Industrial and Technical Education; Psychology
Dist - RMIBHF **Prod** - RMIBHF

Round Pipe Mitered End 32 MIN
BETA / VHS
Metal Fabrication - Parallel Line Development Series
Color (IND)
Industrial and Technical Education; Psychology
Dist - RMIBHF **Prod** - RMIBHF

Round Pipe same Diameter 45 Degree Intersection 24 MIN
BETA / VHS
Metal Fabrication - Parallel Line Development Series
Color (IND)
Industrial and Technical Education; Psychology
Dist - RMIBHF **Prod** - RMIBHF

Round Pipe same Diameter 90 Degree Intersection 40 MIN
VHS / BETA
Metal Fabrication - Parallel Line Development Series
Color (IND)
Industrial and Technical Education; Psychology
Dist - RMIBHF **Prod** - RMIBHF

Round Robin 15 MIN
U-matic / VHS / 16mm
Color (J)
LC 80-701155
Presents the natural history of the British robin through the activities of one particular bird who establishes his territory in a suburban neighborhood, finds a mate, raises a brood and stays through the winter.
Geography - World; Science - Natural
Dist - BCNFL **Prod** - RSFPB 1980

Round Robin 14 MIN
U-matic / VHS
Color (I J)
Features a robin presenting an account of its own life.
Science - Natural
Dist - VIEWTH **Prod** - VIEWTH

A Round Seven Months 29 MIN
Videoreel / VT2
Maggie and the Beautiful Machine - Pregnancy Series
Color
Health and Safety; Physical Education and Recreation
Dist - PBS **Prod** - WGBHTV

Round Shapes 15 MIN
U-matic / VHS
Pass it on Series
Color (K P)
Identifies round shapes and discusses alike and different in shapes.
Education
Dist - GPN **Prod** - WKNOTV 1983

Round Tap Collar Formed with Beader and Notcher 8 MIN
VHS / BETA
Color (IND)
Explains the application of a tap collar, and use of the beading machine and a hand notcher.
Industrial and Technical Education; Psychology
Dist - RMIBHF **Prod** - RMIBHF

Round Tap Collar Formed with Dovetail Hand Tool 5 MIN
BETA / VHS
Color (IND)
Illustrates the use of the dovetail hand tool for forming the tap collar connection.
Industrial and Technical Education; Psychology
Dist - RMIBHF **Prod** - RMIBHF

Round Tap Collar Formed with Elbow Edge 9 MIN
BETA / VHS
Color (IND)
Illustrates the use of the elbow edge wheels for forming a screw in the round tap collar.
Industrial and Technical Education; Psychology
Dist - RMIBHF **Prod** - RMIBHF

Round Tap Collar Formed with Hand Tap - in Tool 6 MIN
BETA / VHS
Color (IND)
Discusses the use of a hand tap - in tool for forming the tap collar connection.
Industrial and Technical Education; Psychology
Dist - RMIBHF **Prod** - RMIBHF

Round Taper Intersecting a Round Pipe at 45 Degrees 32 MIN
VHS / BETA
Metal Fabrication - Round Tapers Series
Color (IND)
Industrial and Technical Education; Psychology
Dist - RMIBHF **Prod** - RMIBHF

Round Taper Intersecting a Round Pipe at 90 Degrees 14 MIN
BETA / VHS
Metal Fabrication - Round Tapers Series
Color (IND)
Industrial and Technical Education; Psychology
Dist - RMIBHF **Prod** - RMIBHF

Round Tapers - Internal or External Offset 19 MIN
BETA / VHS
Metal Fabrication - Round Tapers Series
Color (IND)
Industrial and Technical Education; Psychology
Dist - RMIBHF **Prod** - RMIBHF

Round the Bend 50 MIN
16mm
Color (PRO)
LC 81-700712
Dramatizes the case history of a schizophrenic patient in a psychiatric hospital.
Psychology
Dist - TASCOR **Prod** - TASCOR 1981

Round Trip 8 MIN
16mm / U-matic / VHS
Color (P I)
LC 77-701533
Presents a children's story about human kindness and equality, which involves three snowmen who, at various stages, get covered with soot and realize that color is unimportant.
Guidance and Counseling; Literature and Drama
Dist - FI **Prod** - WHTF 1977

Round Y - Branch Layout 57 MIN
BETA / VHS
Metal Fabrication - Round Tapers Series
Color (IND)
Industrial and Technical Education; Psychology
Dist - RMIBHF **Prod** - RMIBHF

Roundabout 19 MIN
U-matic / VHS / 16mm
Color (K P I)
$49.95 purchase _ #L10253; LC 78-700286
Presents a story about a young boy's experience with an old man who owns a magical toy merry - go - round. Narrates what happens when it is stolen by the boy's friends. Focuses on responsibility and consideration for others.
Guidance and Counseling; Literature and Drama; Sociology
Dist - CF **Prod** - CF 1977

Rounded Vowels and Labio - Dentals 10 MIN
BETA / VHS
Speech Reading Materials Series
Color (A)
English Language
Dist - RMIBHF **Prod** - RMIBHF

The Rounders 8 MIN
16mm
B&W (J)
Charlie Chaplin, Fatty Arbuckle and Minta Durfee star in a slapstick comedy. The story revolves around two men who arrive home 'tipsy' and are met by irate wives.
Fine Arts; Literature and Drama
Dist - RMIBHF **Prod** - SENN 1914

Rounding 11 MIN
VHS
Children's encyclopedia of mathematics - decimals series
Color (I)
$49.95 purchase _ #8366
Discusses the process of rounding off when using decimals. Part of a five - part series on decimals.
Mathematics
Dist - AIMS **Prod** - DAVFMS 1991

Rounds - Pt 1 15 MIN
U-matic / VHS
Song sampler series
Color (P)
LC 81-707073
Demonstrates how to sing a round and play an instrumental ostinato accompaniment. Presents the songs The Donkey and Scotland's Burning.
Fine Arts
Dist - GPN **Prod** - JCITV 1981

Rounds - Pt 2 15 MIN
VHS / U-matic
Song sampler series
Color (P)
LC 81-707073
Demonstrates how to sing a round and play an instrumental ostinato accompaniment. Presents the songs The Donkey and Scotland's Burning.
Fine Arts
Dist - GPN **Prod** - JCITV 1981

Roundtable discussions series
Presents a three - part roundtable discussion of narcotics trafficking, supply and demand in the US and abroad, with expert opinion by religious leaders, treatment specialists, former DEA agents, former gang members, physicians and policy makers. Features Harvard Law Professors Charles Nesson and Charles Ogletree as moderators.
Roundtable discussions series
Dist - CRINST **Prod** - CRINST 1981

Roundtables discussions series
Dynamics of narcotics demands - Part 3
Narcotics trafficking - Part 1
Roots of narcotics supply - Part 2
Dist - CRINST

Rousing home renovations 30 MIN
VHS
A House for all seasons series
Color (G)
$49.95 purchase _ #AHFS - 301
Teaches techniques for adding space and energy - efficient improvements in unusual situations. Applies these techniques to Victorian homes, carports and houses built in the 1950s. Shows how solar energy can be used in cloudy locations such as Seattle.
Home Economics; Industrial and Technical Education; Science - Natural; Social Science; Sociology
Dist - PBS **Prod** - KRMATV 1986

Route 1 15 MIN
VHS / U-matic
Jackson Junior High Series
Color (I J)
Shows an eighth grade science class studying alcohol. Includes an animated segment showing the route alcohol takes through the body.
Health and Safety
Dist - GPN **Prod** - EFLMC

Route Du Champagne
VHS / U-matic
Tableside Series
Color
Home Economics; Industrial and Technical Education
Dist - CULINA **Prod** - CULINA

The Route into the Cosmos 30 MIN
VHS / 16mm
Conquest of Space Series
Color (G)
Describes the contributions of the Voyager and Pioneer missions to knowledge about the solar system. Discusses the prospects of exploring Mars and Venus.
History - World; Industrial and Technical Education; Science - Physical
Dist - FLMWST

Route One 15 MIN
16mm
Jackson Junior High Series
Color (J)
LC 76-704032
Shows an eighth grade science class and its study of different kinds of alcohol. Presents factual information on alcohol and discusses hangover cures. Uses animation to show how alcohol travels through the body and how it effects the brain and other systems.
Health and Safety; Psychology; Sociology
Dist - USNAC **Prod** - USOLLR 1976

The Router 39 MIN
VHS / 35mm strip
(H A IND)
#706XV7
Explains the safe use and operating procedures of the router in various applications. Includes operating the router, advanced cuts, and plastic laminates (3 tapes). Prerequisites required. Includes a Study Guide.
Education; Industrial and Technical Education
Dist - BERGL

Router and Shaper 14 MIN
VHS / BETA
Woodworking Power Tools Series
Color (IND)
Industrial and Technical Education; Psychology
Dist - RMIBHF **Prod** - RMIBHF

Router and Shaper
VHS
Woodworking Power Tools Series
(C G)
$59.00 _ CA183
Demonstrates the handling and operation of the router and shaper.
Industrial and Technical Education
Dist - AAVIM **Prod** - AAVIM 1989

Router Jigs and Techniques
VHS
Video Workshops Series
$29.95 purchase _ #FW600
Shows a master craftsman demonstrating his technique for using router jigs.
Education; Industrial and Technical Education
Dist - CAREER **Prod** - CAREER

Router Jigs and Techniques with Bernie Maas and Michael Fortune 60 MIN
VHS / BETA
Color (H C A)
Focuses on teaching basic router joinery, demonstrating how to make the spline joint, the mortise and tenon and sliding dovetail. Also shows how the router can work with a series of jigs to create a hand mirror. Comes with booklet.
Industrial and Technical Education
Dist - TANTON **Prod** - TANTON

Routes of Exile - a Moroccan Jewish Odyssey 90 MIN
16mm
Color (H C A)
Examines the ancient origins of the Jews of Morocco, covering their Berber roots, illustrious Spanish heritage, and long co - existence with Arabs in a Moslem country. Investigates the impact of colonialism on Arab - Jewish relations and follows the Moroccan exodus to Europe, the New World and Israel where Jews of Moroccan origin are waging a fierce struggle for equality in Israeli society.
Geography - World; History - World
Dist - FIRS **Prod** - FIRS 1982

Routes of rhythm with Harry Belafonte - Program 1 58 MIN
VHS
Routes of rhythm with Harry Belafonte series
Color (G)
$150.00 purchase, $95.00 rental
Follows the flow of Afro - Cuban music from its origins five centuries ago in Africa and Spain in the first part of three parts on Latin American music. Features Harry Belafonte as host. Produced and directed by Howard Dratch and Eugene Rostow.
Fine Arts; History - United States
Dist - CNEMAG

Routes of rhythm with Harry Belafonte - Program 2 58 MIN
VHS
Routes of rhythm with Harry Belafonte series
Color (G)
$150.00 purchase, $95.00 rental
Follows the flow of Afro - Cuban music from its origins five centuries ago in Africa and Spain through its cultural blending in the Caribbean in the second part of three parts on Latin American music. Features Harry Belafonte as host. Produced and directed by Howard Dratch and Eugene Rostow.
Fine Arts; History - United States
Dist - CNEMAG

Routes of rhythm with Harry Belafonte - Program 3 58 MIN
VHS
Routes of rhythm with Harry Belafonte series
Color (G)
$150.00 purchase, $95.00 rental
Follows the flow of Afro - Cuban music from its origins five centuries ago in Africa and Spain to its popularity in the United States and throughout the entire world in the third part of three parts on Latin American music. Features Harry Belafonte as host. Produced and directed by Howard Dratch and Eugene Rostow.
Fine Arts; History - United States
Dist - CNEMAG

Routes of rhythm with Harry Belafonte series
Follows the flow of Afro - Cuban music from its origins five centuries ago in Africa and Spain through its cultural blending in the Caribbean to its popularity in the United States and throughout the entire world in three parts. Features Harry Belafonte as host. Produced and directed by Howard Dratch and Eugene Rostow.
Routes of rhythm with Harry Belafonte - Program 1 58 MIN
Routes of rhythm with Harry Belafonte - Program 2 58 MIN
Routes of rhythm with Harry Belafonte - Program 3 58 MIN
Dist - CNEMAG

Routine abdominal skin prep - gel 10 MIN
U-matic / VHS
Color (PRO)
Demonstrates a step - by - step procedure for performing an abdominal skin prep using a gel prepping agent. Emphasizes maintenance of aseptic technique and careful handling of supplies to prevent contamination.
Health and Safety
Dist - UMICHM **Prod** - UMICHM 1983

Routine abdominal skin prep - wet 10 MIN
U-matic / VHS
Color (PRO)
Demonstrates a step - by - step procedure for performing an abdominal skin prep using a wet prepping agent. Emphasizes maintenance of aseptic technique and careful handling of supplies to prevent contamination.
Health and Safety
Dist - UMICHM **Prod** - UMICHM 1983

Routine Admissions 11 MIN
VHS / 16mm
Licensed Practical Nursing Assistant Refresher Series
Color (C)
$75.00 purchase _ #270508
Helps nursing assistants make the transition back to their chosen career after an extended absence. Updates nursing techniques and procedures which have changed substantially in the last decade. Provides a practical demonstration of step - by - step nursing procedures. 'Routine Admissions' serves as a general guide to the admission of new patients. Concentrates on two main objectives, collecting all pertinent information and making the patient feel comfortable in new surroundings.
Health and Safety; Science
Dist - ACCESS **Prod** - ACCESS 1989

Routine Anorectal and Signoidoscopic Examination with Differential Diagnosis 30 MIN
16mm
Color (PRO)
Stresses the value of routine anorectal and sigmoidoscopic examination in general practice by the internist, pediatrician and general surgeon, as well as the proctologist. Shows various aspects of this examination.
Health and Safety
Dist - LOMAM **Prod** - LOMAM

Routine compliance testing for diagnostic x - ray machines - abovetable x - ray source 30 MIN
U-matic / VHS
Routine compliance testing for diagnostic x - ray machines series
Color
Complete title is Routine Compliance Testing For Diagnostic X - Ray Machines - Abovetable X - Ray Source Radiographic Systems. Shows the test steps to be performed on stationary, mobile, abovetable, fluoroscopic, mammographic and dental X - ray equipment, and how to determine peak kilovoltage for compliance with PL 90 - 602.
Health and Safety; Industrial and Technical Education; Science - Physical
Dist - USNAC **Prod** - USHHS

Routine Compliance Testing for Diagnostic X - Ray Machines - Abovetable X - Ray Source 14 MIN
VHS / U-matic
Routine Compliance Testing for Diagnostic X - Ray Machines Series
Color
Complete title is Routine Compliance Testing For Diagnostic X - Ray Machines - Abovetable X - Ray Source Fluoroscopic And Spot Film Systems. Shows the test steps to be performed in determining the compliance of abovetable source fluoroscopic X - ray systems to federal performance standards. Shows a remote controlled system with automatic and manual technique factor selection.
Health and Safety; Industrial and Technical Education; Science - Physical
Dist - USNAC **Prod** - USHHS

Routine compliance testing for diagnostic x - ray machines - dental radiographic systems 12 MIN
U-matic / VHS
Routine compliance testing for diagnostic x - ray machines series
Color
Shows test steps to be performed to determine the compliance of intraoral dental X - ray systems to the federal performance standards. Shows testing of a system with both fixed KVP and MA.
Health and Safety; Industrial and Technical Education; Science - Physical
Dist - USNAC **Prod** - USHHS

Routine compliance testing for diagnostic x - ray machines - mammographic systems 13 MIN
U-matic / VHS
Routine compliance testing for diagnostic x - ray machines series
Color
Shows the test steps to be performed in determining the compliance of mobile or stationary special - purpose mammographic X - ray systems to federal performance standards. Shows testing of a stationary system with fixed SID and variable KVP.
Health and Safety; Industrial and Technical Education; Science - Physical
Dist - USNAC **Prod** - USHHS

Routine compliance testing for diagnostic x - ray machines - mobile radiographic system 16 MIN
VHS / U-matic
Routine compliance testing for diagnostic x - ray machines series
Color
Shows the test steps to be performed to determine the compliance of mobile and/or portable X - ray systems to the federal performance standards. Shows tests on a battery powered mobile system with various KVP and 'MA's only' selection.
Health and Safety; Industrial and Technical Education; Science - Physical
Dist - USNAC **Prod** - USHHS

Routine compliance testing for diagnostic x - ray machines - peak kilovoltage determination 10 MIN
VHS / U-matic
Routine compliance testing for diagnostic x - ray machines series
Color
Shows the test steps to be performed to determine the compliance of the tube potential (KVP) for stationary and mobile radiographic systems to the federal performance standards. This test method is to be employed routinely by both state and federal investigators.
Health and Safety; Industrial and Technical Education; Science - Physical
Dist - USNAC **Prod** - USHHS

Routine compliance testing for diagnostic x - ray machines series

Routine compliance testing for diagnostic x - ray machines - abovetable x - ray source 30 MIN
Routine compliance testing for diagnostic x - ray machines - dental radiographic systems 12 MIN
Routine compliance testing for diagnostic x - ray machines - mammographic systems 13 MIN
Routine compliance testing for diagnostic x - ray machines - mobile radiographic system 16 MIN
Routine compliance testing for diagnostic x - ray machines - peak kilovoltage determination 10 MIN
Routine compliance testing for diagnostic x - ray machines - undertable source 28 MIN
Dist - USNAC

Routine compliance testing for diagnostic x - ray machines - undertable source 28 MIN
VHS / U-matic
Routine compliance testing for diagnostic x - ray machines series
Color
Complete title is Routine Compliance Testing For Diagnostic X - Ray Machines - Undertable Source Fluoroscopic And Spot Film Systems. Shows the test steps to be performed to determine the compliance of conventional undertable source fluoroscopic X - ray systems. Shows tests on a combination radioscopic/fluoroscopic system with a spot film capability and automatic technique factor selection.
Health and Safety; Industrial and Technical Education; Science - Physical
Dist - USNAC **Prod** - USHHS

Routine Dental Care of the Equine 90401 33 MIN
VHS / BETA
Color
Provides an overview of dental needs and problems of the horse.
Health and Safety; Physical Education and Recreation
Dist - EQVDL **Prod** - MSU

The Routine Female Physical Examination 26 MIN
U-matic / VHS
Color (PRO)
Covers instruments and techniques used in the general physical exam of a female patient.
Health and Safety
Dist - HSCIC **Prod** - HSCIC 1982

The Routine General Physical Examination 22 MIN
U-matic / VHS
Color (PRO)
Demonstrates the general physical examination, which is aimed at detecting conditions that are not producing symptoms.
Health and Safety
Dist - HSCIC **Prod** - HSCIC 1977

Routine Maintenance
VHS / 35mm strip
Small Engine Know - How Series
$85.00 purchase _ #DXSEK030 filmstrip, $85.00 purchase _ #DXSEK030V
Teaches how to perform preventive maintenance, tune - up the ignition, and tune - up the fuel system.
Industrial and Technical Education
Dist - CAREER **Prod** - CAREER

Routine Maintenance of Hypodermic Jet Injection Apparatus 27 MIN
16mm
Color (PRO)
LC 74-706228
Demonstrates maintenance procedures for the hypodermic jet injection apparatus. Discusses the components and the functioning of the injector.
Science
Dist - USNAC **Prod** - USA 1972

Routine Pelvic Examination and the Cytologic Method 15 MIN
16mm
Color (PRO)
Illustrates the technique of bimanual physical examination of the pelvis, using both a live model and a rubber model. Shows the technique of obtaining cellular material from the vagina, cervix and endocervix for use in cytologic testing. Demonstrates how specimen material may be obtained with various standard sampling tools and how specimens may be transferred to slides.
Health and Safety; Science
Dist - AMCS **Prod** - AMCS 1958

The Routine Physical Examination - the Adult Male 26 MIN
U-matic / VHS
Color (PRO)
Illustrates correct techniques to use in the general physical exam of an adult male.
Health and Safety
Dist - HSCIC **Prod** - HSCIC 1982

Routine Stops 18 MIN
16mm / U-matic / VHS
Color (PRO)
Demonstrates safe, proper procedures for police officers conducting so - called routine stops. Gives a basic approach and variations for the one - officer patrol car and a two - officer patrol car. Covers drunk - drugged stops and the different tactics that must be used for stopping vans and campers. Deals with felony van stops and outlaw biker stops.
Civics and Political Systems; Social Science
Dist - AIMS **Prod** - AIMS 1980

Routine Work 26 MIN
U-matic / VHS
Color
Chronicles the filming of a modern dance routine. Shows that while the production team is working on the studio's sound stage, a second unit is filming them.
Fine Arts
Dist - FI **Prod** - BBCTV

The Rowe String Quartet 60 MIN
VHS / U-matic
Color
Presents members of the Rowe String Quartet discussing their individual musical backgrounds, their instruments and their positions in the group.
Fine Arts
Dist - MDCPB **Prod** - WTVITV

Rower / Sideward Lunge and Bend / Lower Leg Stretcher 15 MIN
U-matic / VHS
Roomnastics Series
Color (P)
Presents several exercises which can be performed in a classroom setting.
Physical Education and Recreation
Dist - GPN **Prod** - WVIZTV 1979

Rowing - a Symphony in Motion 26 MIN
U-matic / VHS / 16mm
Color (J)
LC 74-701141
Surveys the different varieties of rowing, from sport with a single oarsman to competition with an eight - oar crew.
Physical Education and Recreation
Dist - PHENIX **Prod** - DOCU 1974

Roy Campanella 20 MIN
16mm
Sports Legends Series
Color (I J)
Interviews Roy Campanella, one of the greatest catchers in baseball history. Includes film footage of Campy, Jackie Robinson, Gil Hodges and other Brooklyn Dodger players. Covers the career of this Hall Of Fame member during the Dodgers' great years in New York.
Biography; Physical Education and Recreation
Dist - COUNFI **Prod** - COUNFI

Roy Harris 30 MIN
16mm
Sum and Substance Series
B&W (R)
LC FIA67-5267
Roy Harris, music composer and teacher, relates his creative capacity to the larger values he finds in human life - - the moral laws of the universe and the renewal he sees in nature and in each successive generation of students. (Kinescope).

Biography; Fine Arts; Religion and Philosophy
Dist - MLA **Prod** - USC 1964

Roy Lichtenstein 30 MIN
VHS
Seven artists series
Color (A)
PdS65 purchase _ Unavailable in Europe
Focuses on some of the main features of 20th-century art by exploring the work of Roy Lichtenstein. The development of art in this century has resulted in a multiplicity and profusion of styles. Lichtenstein is placed in his own social and geographical environment. Follows the creation of an art object begun and completed under the camera's eye.
Fine Arts
Dist - BBCENE

Roy Lichtenstein 52 MIN
16mm
Color
LC 76-703156
Features Roy Lichtenstein working on a series of paintings in his Long Island, New York, studio. Records his view on color and abstraction and his position in the Pop Art movement. Includes appearances and comments by art critics Lawrence Alloway and John Coplans as well as fellow artists Rivers, Rauschenberg, Odenburg and Rosenquist.
Fine Arts
Dist - BLACKW **Prod** - BLACKW 1976

Roy Lichtenstein - Pt 1 26 MIN
16mm
Color
LC 76-703156
Features Roy Lichtenstein working on a series of paintings in his Long Island, New York, studio. Records his view on color and abstraction and his position in the Pop Art movement. Includes appearances and comments by art critics Lawrence Alloway and John Coplans as well as fellow artists Rivers, Rauschenberg, Odenburg and Rosenquist.
Fine Arts
Dist - BLACKW **Prod** - BLACKW 1976

Roy Lichtenstein - Pt 2 26 MIN
16mm
Color
LC 76-703156
Features Roy Lichtenstein working on a series of paintings in his Long Island, New York, studio. Records his view on color and abstraction and his position in the Pop Art movement. Includes appearances and comments by art critics Lawrence Alloway and John Coplans as well as fellow artists Rivers, Rauschenberg, Odenburg and Rosenquist.
Fine Arts
Dist - BLACKW **Prod** - BLACKW 1976

Roy Lichtenstein - reflections 30 MIN
VHS
Color (G)
$39.95 purchase _ #LIC - 03
Portrays Roy Lichtenstein, discussing his work, his artistic process and the sources of his inspiration. Features several leading authorities on contemporary art, and an interview with the artist's dealer by Isabella Rosselini. Features Lichtenstein's large scale murals, reflections series and his recent interior series.
Fine Arts
Dist - ARTSAM **Prod** - CHCFND 1993

Roy Marsden 30 MIN
VHS
Making their mark series
Color (A)
PdS65 purchase _ Unavailable in South Africa
Profiles Roy Marsden, who has a unique drawing style and way of working. Introduces the viewer to practical and aesthetic aspects of the skill of drawing. Part of a six-part series.
Fine Arts
Dist - BBCENE

Roy Obi 13 MIN
16mm
B&W
LC 79-700849
Tells the story of a factory worker who seems to go insane, locking himself in his room and refusing to come out for anyone or anything.
Psychology
Dist - KRUSNK **Prod** - KRUSNK 1977

Roy Wilkins - the Right to Dignity 20 MIN
16mm
Color (J H C)
LC 79-700827
Reviews the career of Black activist Roy Wilkins with the National Association for the Advancement of Colored People (NAACP). Outlines the impact and growth of the organization, including its role in the 1954 Supreme Court ruling on school desegregation and the landmark civil rights legislation of the 1960's.
Biography; Civics and Political Systems; History - United States
Dist - USNAC **Prod** - USINCA 1978

The Royal Archives of Ebla 58 MIN
U-matic / VHS / 16mm
Color (H C A)
LC 81-700474
Examines the archeological finds at Ebla in Syria, where 17,000 clay tablets covered in cuneiform writing were unearthed.
History - World; Sociology
Dist - FI **Prod** - FI 1980

The Royal Ballet 132 MIN
VHS
Color (S)
$29.95 purchase _ #384 - 9576
Showcases the talents of world - acclaimed prima ballerina Margot Fonteyn and Britain's Royal Ballet company. Presents three dance segments filmed at London's Covent Garden - 'Swan Lake,' Act II, by Tchaikovsky, 'The Firebird' by Stravinsky, and 'Ondine' by Henze, the latter created expressly for Fonteyn.
Fine Arts; Physical Education and Recreation
Dist - FI **Prod** - PAR 1988

Royal ballet 132 MIN
VHS
Color (G A)
$29.95 purchase
Features ballet star Margot Fonteyn in a performance of three ballets - 'Swan Lake (Act II),' 'The Firebird,' and 'Ondine.' Also includes Michael Somes and England's Royal Ballet.
Fine Arts
Dist - PBS **Prod** - WNETTV

The Royal Bed 73 MIN
BETA
B&W
Offers a comedy - drama about the foibles of royalty.
Fine Arts
Dist - VIDIM **Prod** - UNKNWN 1930

Royal Boy of Samoa 30 MIN
16mm
Color
Recounts the life of a Samoan boy, including his birth, boyhood, manhood and marriage.
Geography - World; Literature and Drama; Social Science
Dist - CINEPC **Prod** - CINEPC 1975

The Royal Dancers and Musicians from the Kingdom of Bhutan 29 MIN
16mm
Color
LC 80-701261
Documents an important Bhutanese festival in which masked dancers are the central feature. Shows preparations for the festival and provides a brief overview of daily life in Bhutan.
Geography - World
Dist - AS **Prod** - AS 1979

Royal federal blues - the story of the African - American Civil War soldier 45 MIN
VHS
Color (J H C G)
$39.95 purchase _ #PE791V
Documents the inception of African - Americans into the Union Army. Quotes Abraham Lincoln, 'The sight of 50,000 armed and drilled black soldiers upon the banks of the Mississippi would end the rebellion at once,' and with these words, the Union made a bold move that changed the tide of the Civil War.
History - United States
Dist - CAMV

Royal heritage series

Charles I	60 MIN
Edward VII and the House of Windsor	60 MIN
The First three Georges	52 MIN
George IV	52 MIN
The Medieval Kings	60 MIN
The Queen and Prince Philip	60 MIN
The Stuarts Restored	60 MIN
The Tudors	60 MIN
Victoria and Albert	60 MIN
Victoria, Queen and Empress	60 MIN

Dist - FI

Royal houses of the world series
Royalty - an uncommon working family
Dist - IHF

Royal Institution Crystals & Lasers Lectures for Young People Series

Applications of lasers	58 MIN
The Architecture of crystals	58 MIN
Constructing a Laser	58 MIN
Crystals, Lasers, and the Human Body	58 MIN
Introducing Crystals and Lasers	58 MIN
Semiconductors, Superconductors, and Catalysts	58 MIN

Dist - FOTH

Royal Jordan 30 MIN
U-matic / VHS / BETA
Color; PAL (G H C)
PdS60, PdS68 purchase
Looks at the Hashemite Kingdom of Jordan, along with Amman, the amazing city of Petra, the Dead Sea and Aqaba.
Fine Arts; Geography - World
Dist - EDPAT

Royal London
VHS
International travel films from Doug Jones series
Color (G H)
$19.95 purchase _ #IT10
Explores London.
Geography - World
Dist - SVIP

The Royal Marine's office 45 MIN
VHS
Situation vacant series
Color (A)
PdS65 purchase
Follows four young men, their hearts set on becoming officers of the Royal Marine Regiment, as they put themselves through the punishing commando selection, one of the world's toughest entry procedures. Part of a six-part series looking at selection procedures for a wide range of jobs.
Education; Psychology
Dist - BBCENE

Royal Ontario Museum 11 MIN
16mm
B&W
LC 77-702630
Focuses on the contents of the Royal Ontario Museum.
Fine Arts; Geography - World
Dist - CANFDC **Prod** - CANFDC 1972

The Royal Palace, Stockholm 26 MIN
16mm / U-matic / VHS
Place in Europe Series
Color (H C A)
Features Swedish history and culture as represented in the imposing Royal Palace in Stockholm, a seven - hundred - room edifice whose small royal apartment houses the world's youngest monarch, Karl XVI Gustav, descendant of one of Napoleon's marshalls who became king of Sweden.
Geography - World
Dist - MEDIAG **Prod** - THAMES 1975

Royal Road 28 MIN
U-matic / VHS / 16mm
Understanding Space and Time Series
Color
Retraces Einstein's logic to demonstrate that space and time are curved or warped by the distribution of matter in the universe and that matter and energy move along this curvature of space/time.
Science - Physical
Dist - UCEMC **Prod** - BBCTV 1980

Royal Rococo (1725 - 1750) 12 MIN
16mm
Color
Shows an Archbiship's palace that is an example of the gaiety and elegance of the 18th century churchmen who decorated their splendid homes with pagan scenes in glowing shell - like polychrome.
Fine Arts
Dist - ROLAND **Prod** - ROLAND

Royal Shakespeare Company Series

Exploring a Character	51 MIN
Irony and Ambiguity	51 MIN
Language and Character	51 MIN
Passion and Coolness	52 MIN
Poetry and Hidden Poetry	53 MIN
Rehearsing the Text	53 MIN
Set speeches and soliloquies	52 MIN
The Two Traditions	50 MIN
Using the Verse	50 MIN

Dist - FOTH

The Royal Silk of Thailand 14 MIN
16mm
Color (C A)
LC 75-702557
A study of hand - woven Thai silk, Thailand's fastest growing export commodity. Follows the process of the creation of silk from the tiny bombyx - mori moth to the finished product. Includes scenes of temples, waterways, the villages and the inhabitants of Thailand.
Geography - World; Psychology; Social Science
Dist - MCDO **Prod** - THAI 1968

Royal Silver Jubilee 26 MIN
U-matic / VHS
Color
Presents an overview of Queen Elizabeth II's first twenty - five years of rule in Britain. Documents the many changes made not only in the Monarchy but also in the British Empire.
Biography; Civics and Political Systems; History - World
Dist - JOU **Prod** - JOU

Royal Tour of South Africa 30 MIN
VHS / U-matic
B&W
Documents the historic Royal Family tour of South Africa. Show Zulu tribesmen performing dances in their honor.
History - World
Dist - IHF **Prod** - IHF

The Royal Visit 28 MIN
16mm
Color
Looks at the 1976 visit of Queen Elizabeth II and Prince Philip to the Washington Cathedral on the occasion of the dedication of the nave for the reconciliation of the people's of the earth.
Geography - United States; History - United States; Religion and Philosophy
Dist - NCATHA **Prod** - NCATHA

Royal Wedding - HRH the Prince Andrew and Miss Sarah Ferguson 100 MIN
VHS
Color (S)
$29.95 purchase _ #781 - 9001
Presents an exclusive commemorative program of the wedding of Andrew and Sarah. Includes the procession through London, the return to Buckingham Palace, and the entire wedding service which took place in historic Westminster Abbey.
Civics and Political Systems; Geography - World; History - World; Sociology
Dist - FI **Prod** - BBCTV 1986

Royal Westminster 50 MIN
VHS
The great palace: the story of parliament
Color; PAL (C H)
PdS99 purchase
Presents the history of royal Westminster. Includes the historic events which have transpired in Westminster Hall. First in the eight - part series The Great Palace: The Story of Parliament, which documents the significance of the institution.
Civics and Political Systems; History - World
Dist - BBCENE

Royalty - an uncommon working family
VHS
Royal houses of the world series
Color (G)
$59.95 purchase _ #392
Follows the activities of the British royal family throughout an entire year. Shows many of the hundreds of additional private and public activities in which family members participate every year, while in - depth interviews provide insights into their characters and interests. Produced by Norddeutsche Rundfunk, NDR.
Civics and Political Systems; Fine Arts; Geography - World; History - World; Sociology
Dist - IHF

The RPI clasp assembly 9 MIN
U-matic / VHS
Color (C PRO)
$395.00 purchase, $80.00 rental _ #D880 - VI - 010
Focuses on the design concept of the Rest - Plate - I - bar clasp assembly - RPI - in relation to removable partial dentures. Uses a plaster model to augment the description of the mechanics of the RPI clasp assembly on the abutment tooth. Addresses the advantages, disadvantages, indications and contraindications of the RPI clasp assembly. Presented by Dr Barry C Ries.
Health and Safety
Dist - HSCIC

RR 8 MIN
16mm
Color (G)
$322.00 purchase, $18.00 rental
Mixes landscape images seen from train windows and the patterned shapes and shifting tones of moving - visual - thought thus prompted, inspired by Robert Breer's Fuji.
Fine Arts
Dist - CANCIN **Prod** - BRAKS 1981

RSPB Collection Series

A Heron Named Bill	25 MIN
Kingfisher	20 MIN
The Masterbuilders	15 MIN
Osprey	35 MIN
Pinkfoot	19 MIN
Seabirds	16 MIN
Short Eared Owl	17 MIN
Talons	22 MIN

Dist - BCNFL

RTDs and Thermistors
Software / BETA
Temperature and Temperature Measurement Series
Color (PRO)
$600.00 - $1500.00 purchase _ #IDRTD
Identifies the principle parts of an RTD. Describes how an RTD works and similarities and differences between RTDs and thermistors. Part of a four - part series on temperature and temperature measurement. Interactive training system includes course administrator guide, videodisc and computer software.
Industrial and Technical Education; Mathematics; Psychology
Dist - NUSTC **Prod** - NUSTC

RU - 486 - banned in America 29 MIN
VHS
America's drug forum second season series
Color (G)
$19.95 purchase _ #219
Explores the conflict behind Food and Drug Admnistration restrictions on RU - 486, a drug used in some countries to terminate pregnancy. Cites studies showing that RU - 486 could treat many serious illnesses such as breast cancer and Cushing's Syndrome. Reveals medical researcher contention that anti - abortion groups' objections to RU - 486 as an abortifacient have hampered testing of the drug. Asks if the use of the drug as an abortion agent should supercede its importance as a potentially life - saving drug. Features Dr William Regelson, oncologist, Medical College of Virginia, Dr Janice Raymond, medical ethicist, U of Massachussetts, Richard Glascow, National Right to Life, Lois Murphy, attorney, National Abortion Rights Action League.
Civics and Political Systems; Health and Safety; Sociology
Dist - DRUGPF **Prod** - DRUGPF 1992

Rub - a - Dub - Dub 10 MIN
U-matic / VHS
Book, Look and Listen Series
Color (K P)
Points out that one story may be illustrated in many ways.
English Language; Literature and Drama
Dist - AITECH **Prod** - MDDE 1977

Rub a dub dub - 25 title series 25 MIN
16mm / U-matic / VHS
Rub a dub dub - 25 title series
Color (K P)
Prsents favorite nursery rhymes in animation. Produced by Joe Wolf David Yates, Alan Rogers, and David Yates.
Fine Arts
Dist - DIRECT **Prod** - DIERNG 1985

Rub a dub dub - 25 title series
Rub a dub dub - 25 title series 25 MIN
Dist - DIRECT

Rubber band - instructions for the hearing impaired child series
Children's stories 20 MIN
Dist - IU

Rubber Boots 5 MIN
16mm
Adventures in the High Grass Series
Color (K P I)
LC 74-702125
Portrays an insect community in puppet animation.
Guidance and Counseling; Literature and Drama; Science - Natural
Dist - MMA **Prod** - MMA 1972

Rubber Cement 10 MIN
U-matic
Color (C)
$325.00
Experimental film by Robert Breer.
Fine Arts
Dist - AFA **Prod** - AFA 1975

Rubber Dam Application 35 MIN
U-matic / VHS
Color (PRO)
Introduces the use of the rubber dam as a means of operative field isolation. Includes specific instruction for those restorative procedures requiring gingival tissue retraction and tooth separation. Includes the working field preparation, dam application to maxillary anterior teeth using a wizard rubber dam holder or a Young's frame, the application of a Ferrier separator interproximally on anterior teeth, dam application to posterior areas and demonstration of the use of the Ferrier 212 gingival clamp.
Health and Safety; Science - Natural
Dist - UWASH **Prod** - UWASH

Rubber Dam Application and Removal 7 MIN
16mm
Four - Handed Dentistry Series
Color (PRO)
LC 75-704335
Demonstrates a method of assisting the application and removal of a rubber dam in dentistry.
Health and Safety
Dist - SAIT **Prod** - SAIT 1973

The Rubber Dam in Dentistry 19 MIN
16mm
Color
LC FIE56-126
Illustrates the use of the rubber dam in restorative dentistry and shows techniques of its application.
Science
Dist - USNAC **Prod** - USN 1955

Rubber Dam Ligation 27 MIN
U-matic
Color (C)
Demonstrates a tooth ligation method of inverting the rubber dam about the teeth, therby exposing maximum crown length while depressing the interdental papilla to gain an improved operating field.
Health and Safety; Science - Natural
Dist - UOKLAH **Prod** - UOKLAH 1986

Rubber Elasticity 39 MIN
VHS / U-matic
Colloid and Surface Chemistry - Lyophilic Colloids Series
Color
Science; Science - Physical
Dist - KALMIA **Prod** - KALMIA

Rubber plantation - southeast Asia 10 MIN
U-matic / VHS / 16mm
Color (J)
LC 80-700967
Shows that natural rubber production is a time - consuming process. Explains that it has become a major factor in the national economy of Malaysia due to the scarcity of petroleum.
Agriculture; Geography - World
Dist - LUF **Prod** - ASIABU 1979

The Rubber tappers 11 MIN
VHS
Decade of destruction - classroom version series
Color (J H)
$150.00 purchase, $25.00 rental
Looks at the relationship between the Indians and the rubber tappers, who had made peace with the Indians and learned the nesessary skills for survival 70 years ago. Contrasts their lifestyle, which can be sustained indefinitely, to that of colonists who invaded their land. Remembers Chico Mendes, one of the leaders of the rubber tappers who campaigned for the defense of all Amazonia, who was assassinated by local ranchers.
Fine Arts; Science - Natural; Sociology
Dist - BULFRG **Prod** - COWELL 1991

Rubber - Tired Haulage in Underground Coal Mining 14 MIN
16mm
Color
LC 75-702460
Shows six of the most frequently occuring haulage accidents, explaining why they happened and what could have been done to prevent them. Points out the need for closer supervision and more adequate employee job and safety training.
Health and Safety; Social Science; Sociology
Dist - USNAC **Prod** - USMESA 1974

Rubbish to Riches 11 MIN
U-matic / VHS / 16mm
Color (J)
LC 81-700719
Shows how refuse can be processed to extract usable by - products.
Science - Natural
Dist - AIMS **Prod** - LINDH 1979

Rubble Trouble 11 MIN
16mm
Color (I)
LC 76-702630
Uses live action and animation to show how to prevent fires by using the most efficient methods of collecting, storing and removing industrial wastes.
Health and Safety
Dist - FILCOM **Prod** - FACTMS 1972

Rubblewomen - Trummerfrauen 16 MIN
16mm
Color (G)
$25.00 rental
Documents how the women of Berlin, Germany cleaned up one of the largest manmade messes in our history during 1945 - 1946 and today they are forgotten to the point of negation. Takes a subjective approach and relies completely on eyewitness reports of the time, use of archival footage and remembrances of a woman who lived in Berlin at that time. Voiceover composed of both English and German commentary. Produced by Gamma Bak with Bryan Sutton and Ian Doncaster.
Fine Arts; History - World; Sociology
Dist - CANCIN

Rubens 6 MIN
16mm
Color
Reflects the richness and exuberance of both the art and the life reflected in Ruben's portraits, classical themes and religious paintings.
Fine Arts
Dist - USNGA **Prod** - USNGA

Rubens 26 MIN
16mm / U-matic / VHS
Color (H C A)
Documents the life and artistic philosophy of Flemish artist, Rubens. Shows examples of the portraits and baroque works commissioned while he was a court painter and diplomat. Emphasizes Rubens' message of personal and artistic freedom.
Biography; Fine Arts; History - World
Dist - IFB **Prod** - IFB 1974

Rubinesque make - up techniques 60 MIN
VHS
Make - up techniques with David Nicholas series
Color (H C G)
$48.00 purchase _ #BY203V
Helps heavyset women develop their full beautfy potential. Teaches about skin care, how to minimize imperfections and accentuate postives. Part of a series featuring makeup artist David Nicholas.
Home Economics
Dist - CAMV

Rubinstein Remembered 58 MIN
VHS
Color (S)
$49.95 purchase _ #055 - 9003
Traces the remarkable career of pianist Artur Rubinstein with excerpts from his performances, Rubinstein's reminiscences and interviews with his family, friends, and colleagues.
Fine Arts
Dist - FI **Prod** - VAI 1988

Ruby in paradise 115 MIN
35mm / 16mm
Color (G)
$200.00 rental
Portrays a young woman's inner life after she escapes from a small town in Tennessee and goes to Panama City Beach, a tourist town on Florida's Redneck Riviera. Follows Ruby, played by Ashley Judd, as she struggles to understand her impulses and actions through winter and into the beginning of the frantic madness of spring break. Produced by Keith Crofford; written, directed and edited by Victor Nunez.
Fine Arts; Psychology; Sociology
Dist - OCTOBF

Ruby Red 14 MIN
16mm
Color (G)
$20.00 rental
Documents an amateur country - western talent search in Iowa City, Iowa.
Fine Arts
Dist - CANCIN **Prod** - HUDINA 1975

Ruby Shang and Mel Wong 30 MIN
VHS / U-matic
Eye on Dance - Dance and the Plastic Arts Series
Color
Draws parallels between dance, the visual arts and environments. Features 'Esoterica' with Ohad Naharin. Hosted by Celia Ipiotis.
Fine Arts
Dist - ARCVID **Prod** - ARCVID

Ruddy kingfisher 25 MIN
VHS
Nature watch series
Color (P I J H C)
$49.00 purchase _ #320201; LC 89-715845
Profiles the kingfisher, one of nature's most versatile and successful hunters on land and water. Part of a series that explores the curious and uncommon characteristics of a variety of mammals, insects, birds and sea creatures.
Science - Natural
Dist - TVOTAR **Prod** - TVOTAR 1988

Rudolf 13 MIN
VHS
Wreck of a Marriage
Color (P)
Examines Rudolf's adjustment to life after divorcing his wife. Shows how Rudolf and his daughter Rikki cope with problems associated with divorce and Rudolf's new relationship with a woman named Emma.
Sociology
Dist - CEPRO **Prod** - CEPRO 1989

Rudolf Nureyev's Film of Don Quixote 109 MIN
VHS
Color (G)
$39.95 purchase _ #1175
Stars Rudolf Nureyev, Sir Robert Helpmann and Lucette Aldous in an innovative dance film production of 'Don Quixote.' Features spectacular sets and perfect lighting for a film version and Nureyev at his best.
Fine Arts; Physical Education and Recreation
Dist - KULTUR

Rudolf Nureyev's Film of Don Quixote Series
Basilio and Kitri, the lovers 15 MIN
The Marketplace in the Port of Barcelona 15 MIN
A Tavern Celebration 15 MIN
The Wedding Reception - the Grand Pas De Deux 15 MIN
Dist - SF

Rudolf Valentino 14 MIN
U-matic / VHS
Color (C)
$69.95 purchase _ #EX1858
Chronicles the life of Rudolf Valentino who came to America without money, skills or friends. Reveals that he learned a new language, changed his name, and in making his mark in Hollywood, changed America's vision of manliness, romance and love.
Fine Arts
Dist - FOTH **Prod** - FOTH

Rudolph and Frosty's Christmas in July 97 MIN
VHS / U-matic
Color
Recounts the story of how Rudolph the Red - Nosed Reindeer and his pal Frosty The Snowman try to save an impoverished circus by making guest appearances on the Fourth of July weekend. Features the voices of Mickey Rooney, Ethel Merman and Jackie Vernon.
Fine Arts
Dist - TIMLIF **Prod** - TIMLIF 1982

Rudolph, the Red - Nosed Reindeer 50 MIN
16mm
Color (P I J H A)
$895.00 purchase _ #4444
Tells the story of the reindeer who saves the day for Santa. Narrated by Burl Ives. A Perspective film.
Literature and Drama; Social Science
Dist - CORF

Rudolph the red nosed reindeer 57 MIN
U-matic / VHS / 16mm
Color (I J H C)
Features Burl Ives as the singing snowman in an animated puppet version of the Christmas story, 'Rudolph the Red Nosed Reindeer.'
Literature and Drama; Religion and Philosophy
Dist - FI **Prod** - UPA 1969

Rudolph the red nosed reindeer - Pt 1 28 MIN
16mm / U-matic / VHS
Color (I J H C)
Features the voice of Burl Ives as the singing snowman in an animated puppet version of the Christmas story Rudolph The Red Nosed Reindeer.
Literature and Drama
Dist - FI **Prod** - UPA 1969

Rudolph the red nosed reindeer - Pt 2 29 MIN
16mm / U-matic / VHS
Color (I J H C)
Features the voice of Burl Ives as the singing snowman in an animated puppet version of the Christmas story Rudolph The Red Nosed Reindeer.
Literature and Drama
Dist - FI **Prod** - UPA 1969

Rudyard Kipling
VHS / 35mm strip
Meet the Classic Authors Series
Color (I)
$39.95, $28.00 purchase
Portrays Rudyard Kipling. Part of a series on authors.
English Language; Literature and Drama
Dist - PELLER

Rudyard Kipling - the road from Mandalay 30 MIN
U-matic / VHS / 16mm
Biographies series
Color (J H C A)
$660.00, $250.00 purchase _ #77532
Shows a day in the life of Rudyard Kipling, focussing on his career as a newspaper writer.
Literature and Drama
Dist - CORF

Rue des Teinturiers 31 MIN
16mm
Color (G)
$60.00 rental
Records frame by frame in the camera with focus adjusted so certain graphic features of the street in title are inscribed onto the film strip. Consists of twelve 2.75 - minute reels, each filmed on a different day during a six - month period. No editing was undertaken other than joining the reels together.
Fine Arts; Geography - World
Dist - CANCIN **Prod** - LOWDER 1979

Ruffled grouse 35 MIN
VHS
Color (H A G)
$69.95 purchase _ #CV908
Looks at hunting techniques for ruffled grouse. Considers the most productive hunting habitat, color phases, sexing and field care. Features research biologist John Kubisak. Nancy Frank joins Dan Small to create two recipes for the bird.
Home Economics; Physical Education and Recreation; Science - Natural; Social Science
Dist - AAVIM **Prod** - AAVIM

Rufino Tamayo 56 MIN
U-matic / VHS
Color (C) (SPANISH)
$279.00, $179.00 purchase _ #AD - 2187
Covers a broad range of the work of Mexican artist Rufino Tamayo, born in Oaxaca. In Spanish.
Biography; Civics and Political Systems; Fine Arts; Foreign Language; Geography - World; History - World; Social Science
Dist - FOTH **Prod** - FOTH

Rufino Tamayo - The Sources of his art 28 MIN
VHS
Color (H C A)
$50.00
Presents Mexican artist Rufino Tamayo, a Zapotecan Indian, and his art. Brings out the relationship between his surroundings and his work. Narrated by John Huston.
Fine Arts
Dist - ARTSAM **Prod** - MFV

Rufus M, Try Again 13 MIN
16mm / U-matic / VHS
Color (P)
LC 78-700921
Dramatizes chapter one of the book Rufus M by Eleanor Estes, where Rufus Moffat learns about the library. Tells how his older brother and sister taunt him because he can't read, so he goes to the library to check out a book, only to run into difficulties.
Guidance and Counseling; Social Science
Dist - PHENIX **Prod** - PHENIX 1977

Rufus M, try again and Ira sleeps over 30 MIN
VHS
Color (K P I J)
$89.00 purchase _ #S01097
Presents two stories about little boys. 'Rufus M, Try Again,' from the book by Eleanor Estes, is the story of a little boy who can't get a library card because he hasn't learned how to write his name. Bernard Waber's story 'Ira Sleeps Over' tells how Ira, a boy who has never slept away from home before, decides whether to bring his teddy bear along.
Literature and Drama; Sociology
Dist - UILL

Rufus M, try again - Ira sleeps over 20 MIN
BETA / VHS
Color
Tells about Rufus M, a little boy who can't get a library card because he can't write his name. Based on the book by Eleanor Estes. Tells the story of Ira's first night away from home, based on the book by Bernard Waber.
Literature and Drama
Dist - PHENIX **Prod** - PHENIX

Rufus Xavier Sarsaparilla 3 MIN
U-matic / VHS
Grammar Rock Series
Color (P I)
Illustrates the need for pronouns.
English Language
Dist - GA **Prod** - ABCTV 1978

The Rug maker - a folktale of Africa 10 MIN
16mm / U-matic / VHS
Color (P I A) (SPANISH)
LC 78-705959
An animated East African folktale which shows the benefits, even for a chief's son, of knowing a trade.
Literature and Drama
Dist - LCOA **Prod** - LCOA 1970

Rug Spots 15 MIN
Videoreel / VT2
Making Things Work Series
Color
Home Economics
Dist - PBS **Prod** - WGBHTV

Ruggero Raimondi 50 MIN
VHS
B&W (G)
$19.95 purchase_#1426
Highlights the career of opera star Ruggero Raimondi, known for his powerful voice and stage presence. Uses a documentary format to provide a look into the international world of opera. Includes selections from some of Raimondi's major roles in grand opera, including Moses in Egypt, Don Quixote, Boris Godunov and his most famous role, Don Giovanni.
Fine Arts
Dist - KULTUR

Ruggie and the Momma Junkie 10 MIN
16mm
B&W
Tells the story of a young man who wanders into an auto junkyard and encounters its lone female resident.
Fine Arts; Sociology
Dist - NYU **Prod** - NYU

Ruggles of Red Gap 90 MIN
16mm
B&W
Tells the story of a gentleman butler thrown out of his element into the American wild west. Stars Charles Laughton, Charlie Ruggles, Zasu Pitts and Mary Boland. Directed by Leo Mc Carey.
Fine Arts
Dist - TWYMAN **Prod** - UPCI

Rugs 25 MIN
VHS / U-matic
Craft of the Weaver Series
Color (J)
Portrays the making of plain weave rag rugs and demonstrates twill weave. Discusses woolen rugs and the considerations when weaving for the floor. Explains the operation of the Dobby loom in making patterned weaves. Illustrates the variety of design, color and texture of rugs from around the world.
Fine Arts
Dist - FI **Prod** - BBCTV 1983

The Ruins 19 MIN
16mm
Color (H C)
Describes the creative processes involved in creating a breakthrough style of painting. Follows the artist as he searches for the right subjects which will reflect his present passion for the visual aspects and evocations of ruins.
Fine Arts
Dist - SF **Prod** - SF 1972

Ruins of Athens 20 MIN
U-matic / VHS
Color (J)
LC 82-706784
Visits Athens, showing the Parthenon, the acropolis and other ancient ruins.
Geography - World; History - World
Dist - AWSS **Prod** - AWSS 1981

Rule Bound Behavior 42 MIN
U-matic
Color (PRO)
Presents a theoretical discussion of rule bound behavior and defines rules as one classification of symbol. Suggests implications for treatment, specifically the teaching - learning process. Narrated by Ann Robinson Popper.
Health and Safety; Psychology
Dist - AOTA **Prod** - AOTA 1977

Rule by Consent 22 MIN
16mm
B&W (I)
Depicts the recent electioneering spirit in India and includes a few striking events which have occurred during the last 20 years.
Civics and Political Systems; History - World
Dist - NEDINF **Prod** - INDIA

The Rule of Law - Pt 5 58 MIN
VHS
Struggle for Democracy Series
Color (S)
$49.00 purchase _ #039 - 9005
Explores the concept of democracy and how it works. Features Patrick Watson, author with Benjamin Barber of 'The Struggle For Democracy,' as host who travels to more than 30 countries around the world, examining issues such as rule of law, freedom of information, the tyranny of the majority and the relationship of economic prosperity to democracy. Part 5 explores whether the law should uphold the rights of the individual or the interests of the community, through an examination of societies around the world and throughout history.
Civics and Political Systems; History - World
Dist - FI **Prod** - DFL 1989

Rule of Thumb 16 MIN
U-matic / VHS / 16mm
Color (J)
LC 76-702176
Treats the dangerous side of hitchhiking, depicting the robber, the junkie and the rapist. Stresses the importance of thinking hard before picking up a hitchhiker or thumbing a ride.
Health and Safety; Social Science; Sociology
Dist - AIMS **Prod** - DAVP 1972

Rule of thumb - order of protection 22 MIN
VHS
Color (G)
$225.00 purchase, $60.00 rental
Explores domestic violence through the perspective of women who have left abusive relationships. Interviews five women from different backgrounds who discuss their ordeals and the steps they have taken to eradicate fear and violence from their lives. Includes testimonies from a woman judge, a police officer and a former abuser. Shows how to obtain an order of protection and support services. Produced by the National Council of Jewish Women, St Louis Section.
Sociology
Dist - WMEN

Rulebound Reggie 12 MIN
VHS / 16mm
Managing Problem People Series
Color (A PRO)
$415.00 purchase, $195.00 rental
Features comedian John Cleese as a supervisor who controls both supplies and staff. Part of a series on managing 'problem' employees.
Business and Economics; Guidance and Counseling
Dist - VIDART **Prod** - VIDART 1990

Rulers with an iron hand 14 MIN
VHS
Color (H C G)
$49.95 purchase _ #3036D
Offers biographies of 20th century dictators - Zaldivar Batista, Juan Peron, Francisco Franco and Marshall Josif Tito. Features Bob Considine as host.
Civics and Political Systems
Dist - INSTRU

Rules 24 MIN
16mm
Good Time Growing Show Series Show 5; Show 5
Color (K P I)
Reveals how Josh is worried because he has gotten in trouble in school. Tells how Mickey explains to him that all people have broken God's rules and that all can be forgiven. Looks at how Boaz decides to make up his own rules because everyone else seems to have rules. Shows him God's rules are for the good of humanity.
Psychology; Religion and Philosophy
Dist - WHLION **Prod** - WHLION

Rules and faithfulness - Volume 3 60 MIN
VHS
Families - quality relationships in changing times series
Color (G R)
$29.95 purchase, $10.00 rental _ #35 - 83727 - 1
Consists of two 30 - minute sessions. Covers the importance of spoken and unspoken rules, as well as the need to determine necessary rules and commitments. Hosted by seminary professor Dr Roland Martinson.
Religion and Philosophy; Sociology
Dist - APH

Rules and Laws 15 MIN
U-matic
We Live Next Door Series
Color (K)
Continues the story of Nutdale with a big grey blob knocking down things until Officer Tuff discovers that the vandal has lost his glasses and cannot see where he is going.
Psychology; Social Science
Dist - TVOTAR **Prod** - TVOTAR 1981

Rules are for Everyone 30 MIN
VHS / U-matic
Coping with Kids Series
Color
Presents the principles of allowing children to learn by the consequences of their actions and how to help children experience the logic of social living.
Guidance and Counseling; Sociology
Dist - OHUTC **Prod** - OHUTC

Rules are for Everyone 29 MIN
VHS / U-matic
Coping with Kids Series
Color (T)
Education
Dist - FI **Prod** - MFFD

Rules are for gorillas, too 11 MIN
U-matic / VHS / 16mm
Beginning responsibility series
Color (P)
$275.00, $195.00 purchase _ #4294
Shows the importance of rules and why people follow them.
Guidance and Counseling
Dist - CORF

Rules are Good Directions 13 MIN
U-matic / VHS / 16mm
Color (P I)
LC 83-700644
Presents the reasons behind various safety rules.
Health and Safety
Dist - BARR **Prod** - SAIF 1983

Rules in Fog 17 MIN
16mm
B&W
LC 74-705550
Explains when to use fog and danger signals, the meaning of fog signals under inland and international rules and how to determine safe speed in fog.
Civics and Political Systems; Health and Safety; Social Science
Dist - USNAC **Prod** - USN 1943

Rules of danger series
Presents a two - part series on workings safely around electric power. Includes the titles Basic Principles of Electricity and Working Safely With Electricity. A leader's guide and ten participant workbooks accompany each video.
Basic principles of electricity - I 12 MIN
Working safely with electricity - II 10 MIN
Dist - BNA

Rules of golf 24 MIN
VHS
Color (G)
$29.95 purchase
Features Tom Watson, Juli Inkster, and Peter Alliss in an examination of the official rules of golf. Includes an official United States Golf Association rule book.
Physical Education and Recreation
Dist - PBS **Prod** - WNETTV

Rules of the game 108 MIN
16mm
B&W (A) (FRENCH (ENGLISH SUBTITLES))
A French language motion picture. Presents Jean Renoir's strange, subtle and dreamlike study of a society in collapse on the eve of a war. Tells the story of an aviator who lands in Paris after a kind of Lindbergian solo flight.
Fine Arts; Foreign Language
Dist - KITPAR **Prod** - IHF 1939
IHF

Rules of the game 110 MIN
VHS
B&W (G)
$29.95 _ #RUL010
Satirizes the erotic charades of the French leisure class as it teeters near collapse on the brink of World War II. Forsakes the humanism of Renoir's earlier films. Forced off the screen by angry Parisians and later banned by the Nazis, it stands as one of his greatest artistic achievements. Remastered with new subtitles.
Fine Arts; Guidance and Counseling; Literature and Drama; Sociology
Dist - HOMVIS **Prod** - JANUS 1939

Rules of the Game 19 MIN
16mm / U-matic / VHS
Working Series
Color (H C A)
LC 81-700247
Dramatizes aspects of work habits, deadlines, loyalty and business etiquette and examines the power structure.
Guidance and Counseling; Psychology
Dist - JOU **Prod** - JOU 1980

The Rules of the Game - WP - 6 11 MIN
U-matic
Word Processing Series
(PRO)

$235.00 purchase
Offers a process description of how to implement word processing into an organization.
Business and Economics
Dist - MONAD **Prod** - MONAD

Rules of the Nautical Road - Introduction 22 MIN
16mm
B&W
LC FIE52-932
Describes international rules of navigation, the importance of taking bearings and selected nautical terms.
Civics and Political Systems; Health and Safety; Social Science
Dist - USNAC **Prod** - USN

Rules of the Road 24 MIN
16mm
Color
Shows how the Honolulu Marathon Clinic teaches individuals to prepare for, and finish, a running marathon. Presents the rules for healthy running.
Physical Education and Recreation
Dist - MTP **Prod** - MTP

Rules of the road 31 MIN
VHS / 16mm
Color (G)
$100.00 rental, $275.00 purchase
Tells the story of a lesbian love affair and its demise. Focuses on one of the primary objects shared by the couple - a beige station wagon with fake wood paneling along the sides - the typical American family car for an atypical couple. Takes a whimsical and somewhat caustic look at how dreams of freedom, pleasure, security and family are so often symbolized by the automobile.
Religion and Philosophy
Dist - WMEN **Prod** - SUFR 1993

Rules of the Road for Boatmen 16 MIN
16mm
Color
LC FIE63-237
Interprets inland rules for boatmen. Uses animation and live action photography to demonstrate meeting, passing and overtaking situations, including proper procedure in fog.
Health and Safety; Physical Education and Recreation; Social Science
Dist - USNAC **Prod** - USGEOS 1959

The Rules of the Road for Boatmen 16 MIN
U-matic
Color
LC 79-706676
Presents the inland rules applicable to all vessels, including small craft regulations (except those under international rules), Western rivers rules and the Great Lakes rules. Presents meeting, passing and overtaking situations, small craft versus large vessels and proper procedures for boating in fog.
Health and Safety; Social Science; Sociology
Dist - USNAC **Prod** - USCG 1979

Rules of the Road, International - Restricted Visibility Situations 10 MIN
16mm
B&W
LC FIE56-256
Shows what to do in situations when visibility is restricted.
Civics and Political Systems; Health and Safety; Social Science
Dist - USNAC **Prod** - USN 1955

Rules of the Road, International - Special Daytime Situations 11 MIN
16mm
Color
LC FIE56-257
Shows how to tell the status, occupation or degree of maneuverability of vessels not in independent operation in daylight.
Civics and Political Systems; Health and Safety; Social Science
Dist - USNAC **Prod** - USN 1955

Rules of the Road, International - Vessel Crossing, Daytime 21 MIN
16mm
B&W
LC 74-705551
Shows what should be done when vessels cross in the daytime.
Civics and Political Systems; Health and Safety; Social Science
Dist - USNAC **Prod** - USN 1956

Rules of the road, international - vessels overtaking, daytime 19 MIN
16mm
B&W
LC FIE56-214
Shows what should be done when vessels are overtaken in daytime and stresses the obligation of all vessels in obeying the rule that the overtaking vessel must keep out of the way of the overtaken vessel.
Civics and Political Systems; Health and Safety; Social Science
Dist - USNAC **Prod** - USN 1956

Rules of the sea
VHS
Under sail with Robbie Doyle series
Color (G A)
$19.90 purchase _ #0471
Looks at the rules of the road at sea. Explores the shape of sails and how they affect the balance of forces on the water. Features Robbie Doyle.
Physical Education and Recreation
Dist - SEVVID

Rules protect freedom with a fourth - year GCSE group in a Jewish school - Unit F 33 MIN
VHS
Religious education in secondary schools series
Color; PAL (T)
PdS35.00 purchase
Presents religious education in ways which are relevant to pupils in mixed - ability classes. Demonstrates a variety of approaches used by four teachers in very different situations. Part of an eight - part series.
Education; Religion and Philosophy
Dist - EMFVL

Rules Rules Rules 10 MIN
U-matic
Color (I J H)
Explains how the children in Ms Krumsky's class decide to set up their own system of 'backwards' rules and then determine to abolish them when they become too confusing. Tells how they come to appreciate the importance of rational rules.
Civics and Political Systems; Fine Arts; Guidance and Counseling
Dist - GA **Prod** - GA

Rules to the Rescue
U-matic / VHS / 16mm
Color
Shows the advantages of following rules, as well as the natural consequences of not following them.
Guidance and Counseling
Dist - HIGGIN **Prod** - HIGGIN

Rules - who needs them
VHS
Bippity boppity bunch series
Color (K P I R)
$14.95 purchase _ #35 - 817 - 8579
Uses an incident where Maxine is hit by Freddy's bicycle to teach the importance of rules.
Literature and Drama; Religion and Philosophy
Dist - APH **Prod** - FAMF

The Ruling Houses, 1900 - the Day of Empires has Arrived 52 MIN
16mm
Europe, the Mighty Continent Series no 2; No 2
Color
LC 77-701557
Discusses the forces of unrest threatening the European empires at the turn of the century, including revolutionaries in Russia, the theories of Marx and Engels and the weakening of the Austro - Hungarian and Ottoman empires.
History - World
Dist - TIMLIF **Prod** - BBCTV 1976

The Ruling houses - 1900 - the day of empires has arrived - Pt 1 26 MIN
VHS / U-matic
Europe - the mighty continent series
Color (H C A)
Special two - part version of the film and videorecording The Ruling Houses - 1900 - The Day Of Empires Has Arrived.
History - World
Dist - TIMLIF **Prod** - BBCTV 1976

The Ruling houses - 1900 - the day of empires has arrived - Pt 2 26 MIN
U-matic / VHS
Europe - the mighty continent series
Color (H C A)
Special two - part version of the film and videorecording The Ruling Houses - 1900 - The Day Of Empires Has Arrived.
History - World
Dist - TIMLIF **Prod** - BBCTV 1976

Rum Paradise 25 MIN
U-matic / 16mm
Maclear Series
Color; Mono (J H C A)
MV $250.00, MP $350.00 purchase, $50.00 rental
Studies the Grand Cayman island in the Caribbean from an economic and political standpoint. Millions of Canadian dollars are tied up in this tax haven and the Canadian government is suffering for it.
Geography - World
Dist - CTV **Prod** - CTV 1976

Rumania on the Tightrope 29 MIN
Videoreel / VT2
Course of Our Times III Series
Color
Biography; Civics and Political Systems; History - United States
Dist - PBS **Prod** - WGBHTV

Rumba
VHS
Arthur Murray dance lessons series
Color (G)
$19.95 purchase _ #MC048
Offers lessons in classic ballroom dancing from instructors in Arthur Murray studios, focusing on the rumba. Part of a 12 - part series on various ballroom dancing styles.
Fine Arts; Physical Education and Recreation; Sociology
Dist - SIV

Rumba 60 MIN
VHS
Kathy Blake dance studios - let's learn how to dance series
Color (G A)
$39.95 purchase
Features dance instructors Kathy Blake and Gene Russo, who instruct viewers on the basics of the Rumba. First of three parts.
Fine Arts
Dist - PBS **Prod** - WNETTV

Rumba II 60 MIN
VHS
Kathy Blake dance studios - let's learn how to dance series
Color (G A)
$39.95 purchase
Features dance instructors Kathy Blake and Gene Russo, who instruct viewers on the basics of the Rumba. Second of three parts.
Fine Arts
Dist - PBS **Prod** - WNETTV

Rumba III 60 MIN
VHS
Kathy Blake dance studios - let's learn how to dance series
Color (G A)
$39.95 purchase
Features dance instructors Kathy Blake and Gene Russo, who instruct viewers on the basics of the Rumba. Third of three parts.
Fine Arts
Dist - PBS **Prod** - WNETTV

The Rumble of wheels, the jingle of chain 14 MIN
16mm
Color
LC 78-700303
Tells the story of a Clydesdale horse from birth, its training and how it becomes a member of the famous team which pulls the Budweiser wagon.
Physical Education and Recreation; Science - Natural
Dist - MTP **Prod** - ANHBUS 1978

Rumblefish 94 MIN
VHS / BETA
Color
$89.00 purchase _ #05926 - 85; $79.00 purchase _ 05926 - 126
Presents S E Hinton's story of a young tough's adoration of his even tougher older brother, starring Matt Dillon and Mickey Rourke.
Fine Arts; Literature and Drama
Dist - GA **Prod** - GA
CHUMAN

Rummage 25 MIN
VHS
B&W (G)
$100.00 purchase
Intends to be an experimental documentary of the legendary Visiting Nurse Association of Somerset Hills Rummage Sale that takes place in Far Hills, New Jersey every first weekend in May and October. Captures the full range of emotions and gestures at the sale over a three - year period. Soundtrack consists of an interview with a venerable member of the Rummage Sale staff and of ambient sounds such as hamburger orders, haggling, etc.
Fine Arts
Dist - CANCIN **Prod** - NIGRIN 1989

Rumor 6 MIN
16mm
Challenge Series
B&W (H C A)
Traces the course of a rumor, how it starts, spreads and its results. Discusses ways of dealing with rumors.

English Language; Guidance and Counseling; Psychology; Social Science; Sociology
Dist - ADL

Rumor clinic 2 MIN
16mm
B&W (J H C A)
Presents an entertainment show with a message stating the necessity of getting facts rather than rumors.
Guidance and Counseling; Psychology; Sociology
Dist - ADL **Prod** - NBCTV

Rumors - Black history - sex discrimination 29 MIN
U-matic
As we see it series
Color
Presents Portland, Oregon, students showing how the old game of 'telephone' illustrates the realities of their desegregated high school. Asks whether a high school in Harrisburg, Pennsylvania, should give special emphasis to black history. Focuses on Latino girls in Chicago for whom old - world standards suddenly seem oppressive.
Education; Sociology
Dist - PBS **Prod** - WTTWTV

Rumors run deep 102 MIN
VHS
Color (G) (CHINESE WITH ENGLISH SUBTITLES)
$45.00 purchase _ #6064C
Presents a film from the People's Republic of China.
Geography - World; Literature and Drama
Dist - CHTSUI

Rumpelstiltskin
VHS / 35mm strip
Caldecotts on Filmstrip Series
Color (K)
$35.00 purchase
Presents a children's story. Part of the Caldecott Series.
English Language; Literature and Drama
Dist - PELLER

Rumpelstiltskin 8 MIN
U-matic / VHS / 16mm
Halas and Batchelor Fairy Tale Films Series
Color (P)
LC 70-704563
An adaptation of the fairy tale by the Brothers Grimm about the strange little man who agreed to teach the miller's daughter how to spin straw into gold.
Literature and Drama
Dist - EBEC **Prod** - HALAS 1969

Rumpelstiltskin 12 MIN
VHS
Color (P)
Presents an animated version of 'Rumpelstiltskin.'
Fine Arts; Literature and Drama
Dist - VIEWTH **Prod** - VIEWTH

Rumpelstiltskin 30 MIN
VHS
Rabbit ears collection series
Color (K P I J)
$12.95 purchase _ #490201
Features Kathleen Turner who narrates the story of a mysterious little man who underestimates the power of a mother's love.
Literature and Drama
Dist - KNOWUN **Prod** - RABBIT

Rumpelstiltskin 12 MIN
U-matic / VHS / 16mm
Color (K P I)
$295.00, $210.00 purchase _ #4084; LC 81-701121
Relates the story of a queen who has promised her first born child to a little man who has spun her straw into gold. Describes how the queen gets out of the bargain by guessing the little man's name.
Fine Arts; Literature and Drama
Dist - CORF **Prod** - PERSPF 1981

Rumpelstiltskin 17 MIN
16mm / U-matic / VHS
Children's Classics Story Series
Color (K P I)
LC FIA67-588
Dramatizes Grimm's fairy tale about the dwarf with magic powers and a funny name and a queen who has to guess his name or lose her infant son.
English Language; Literature and Drama
Dist - MGHT **Prod** - SCHWAR 1966

Rumpelstiltskin 7 MIN
U-matic / VHS / BETA
Classic fairy tales series
Color; PAL (P I)
PdS30, PdS38 purchase
Tells the story of a strange little man who helps the miller's daughter spin straw into gold and to marry the king, demanding something from her in return. Features part of a six - part series containing the essence of the Brothers Grimm, Charles Perrault and Hans Anderson.
Literature and Drama
Dist - EDPAT **Prod** - HALAS 1992

Rumpelstiltskin 10 MIN
16mm
Color (K P I)
A group of Connecticut school children play all the roles in a live version of the fairy tale.
English Language; Literature and Drama
Dist - SF **Prod** - SF 1963

Rumpelstiltskin - 42
VHS
Reading rainbow series
Color; CC (K P)
$39.95 purchase
Shows how the classic fairy tale, retold and illustrated by Paul O Zelinsky, comes to life when LeVar visits a Renaissance festival in Agoura Hills, California. Allows viewers to experience what it was like to live in the days of lords, kings and queens and knights in shining armor. LeVar explores the festival where daily Renaissance life is reenacted and traveling performers such as minstrels and jesters all take part in the fanfare. Part of a series offering a multicultural approach to generating reading enthusiasm with cross - curricular applications, hosted by LeVar Burton.
English Language; History - World; Literature and Drama
Dist - GPN **Prod** - LNMDP

Rumpelstiltskin - presents a group of Connecticut school children who play 10 MIN
VHS / U-matic
Color (K P I)
all roles in a live version of the fairy tale Rumpelstiltskin.
English Language; Literature and Drama
Dist - SF **Prod** - SF 1963

Rumpelstiltskin - Snowy day stories and poems
VHS
Reading rainbow treasury series
Color (K P)
$12.95 purchase _ #PBS440
Presents two animated stories. Features Levar Burton as host. Part of a six - part series.
English Language; Fine Arts; Literature and Drama
Dist - KNOWUN **Prod** - PBS

Rumpelstilzchen 88 MIN
16mm
Color
Presents Grimm's fairy tale of the poor miller whose daughter could presumably spin straw into gold.
Fine Arts; Literature and Drama
Dist - WSTGLC **Prod** - WSTGLC 1955

Rumplestiltskin 15 MIN
16mm / U-matic / VHS
Timeless Tales Series
Color (P I)
Tells about a queen who outsmarts a little man and guesses his name - Rumplestiltskin.
Literature and Drama
Dist - LUF **Prod** - WESFAL

Rumplestiltskin
U-matic / VHS
Color (P I)
Presents an enactment of the classic fairy tale Rumplestiltskin.
Literature and Drama
Dist - GA **Prod** - GA

Rumplestiltzkin 28 MIN
16mm
Color
Presents the Cosmic Box Players of Kenyon College, Gambier, Ohio, in their stage production of the Grimm Brothers' classic, Rumpelstiltzkin. Features characters who are neither hero nor villain, allowing each child to make his own judgments and react in his own individual way.
Literature and Drama
Dist - ASPTEF **Prod** - ASPTEF

Rums Paradise 25 MIN
BETA / 16mm / VHS
Color
LC 77-702522
Takes a close look at Grand Cayman, a Caribbean tax haven for both individuals and multinational corporations. Notes that these tax havens provide a tax dodge that creates financial hardship for the rest of the taxpaying population.
Business and Economics; Geography - World
Dist - CTV **Prod** - CTV 1976

Rumtek Monastery 30 MIN
U-matic / VHS
Journey into the Himalayas series
Color (J S C A)
$195.00 purchase
Concentrates on the Buddhist monastery at Rumtek which was founded by the Gyalwa Karmapa, a high lama who fled Tibet just ahead of Mao's Chinese army.
Geography - World; History - World; Religion and Philosophy
Dist - LANDMK **Prod** - LANDMK 1986

Run - a - Ways 10 MIN
16mm
Color (J)
LC 76-709317
Endeavors to show teenagers the folly of the immature act of running away from home.
Guidance and Counseling; Psychology; Sociology
Dist - DAVP **Prod** - DAVP 1969

Run, appaloosa, run 48 MIN
U-matic / VHS / 16mm
Animal featurettes series; Set 2
Color
Presents a story about an Indian girl and her love for an Appaloosa colt. Shows how together they bring honor and glory to the Nez Perce Indian nation.
Literature and Drama
Dist - CORF **Prod** - DISNEY

Run, appaloosa, run - pt 1 24 MIN
U-matic / VHS / 16mm
Animal featurettes series; Set 2
Color
LC 76-701288
Presents a story about an Indian girl and her love for an Appaloosa colt. Shows how they bring honor and glory to the Nez Perce Indian nation.
Literature and Drama
Dist - CORF **Prod** - DISNEY 1976

Run, appaloosa, run - Pt 2 24 MIN
16mm / U-matic / VHS
Animal featurettes series; Set 2
Color
LC 76-701288
Presents a story about an Indian girl and her love for an Appaloosa colt. Shows how they bring honor and glory to the Nez Perce Indian nation.
Literature and Drama
Dist - CORF **Prod** - DISNEY 1976

Run Dick, Run Jane 20 MIN
16mm
Color
LC 72-700176
Illustrates through laboratory statistics and case studies, the benefits of a personal fitness program. Includes views of Larry Lewis, a 104 - year - old runner, and of Peter Strudwick, who jogs with no feet.
Health and Safety; Physical Education and Recreation
Dist - BYU **Prod** - BYU 1971

Run for life 24 MIN
16mm
Color
LC 79-701117
Depicts a young married couple who begin the Run for Life educational fitness program under the guidance of marathon runner Frank Shorter and Dr Lenore R Zohman. Emphasizes guidelines for graduated exercise and offers motivational advice to help new runners stay with running.
Physical Education and Recreation
Dist - CONML **Prod** - CONML 1978

Run for the Trees 7 MIN
16mm
Color
LC 80-700409
Documents a ten kilometer race in Los Angeles in which every runner received a smog - tolerant tree.
Physical Education and Recreation; Science - Natural
Dist - LOUPAC **Prod** - LOUPAC 1979

Run for Your Life 15 MIN
16mm
World of Health Series
Color (J)
LC 76-703424
Shows a group of high school students as they participate in a three month training program including running and other endurance sports. Emphasizes the role of exercise in the prevention of cardiovascular disease.
Health and Safety; Physical Education and Recreation
Dist - SF **Prod** - INFORP 1975

A Run for Your Money 30 MIN
VHS / U-matic
Money Puzzle - the World of Macroeconomics Series Module 11

Color
Presents the workings of the banking system, showing the importance of loans and pointing out how one loan can create billions of dollars.
Business and Economics; Sociology
Dist - MDCC **Prod** - MDCC

Run for Yourself 26 MIN
16mm
Color
Follows doctors as they prepare for the grueling, 26 - mile City Of Lakes Big Green Team Marathon. Scans the training regimen, pros and cons of running and the actual performance of the doctors in the race, one of whom was himself a heart attack victim. Contains a note of optimism for those who think they're beyond the athletic age.
Health and Safety; Physical Education and Recreation
Dist - MTP **Prod** - NCRENT

Run, Sister, Run 39 MIN
16mm / VHS
Color (G)
$500.00, $225.00 purchase, $65.00 rental
Looks at a collaboration between Denver - based choreographer Cleo Robinson, often called the Alvin Ailey of the West, and socially concerned photographer - composer Gordon Parks, Sr. Presents an urban dance piece based on the fugitive flight of black activist, Angela Davis.
Fine Arts; History - United States
Dist - WMEN **Prod** - MSHL 1986

Run the Team 10 MIN
16mm
Safety Management Series
Color
Business and Economics; Health and Safety
Dist - NSC **Prod** - NSC

Run to live 22 MIN
U-matic / VHS / 16mm
Color (J A)
LC 81-700441;
Presents a documentary which studies Dr Dorothy Brow, surgeon, educator and civic leader, whose life reflects the promise of the American dream. Shows her as she reflects on her past and accepts the challenges of the present. Follows her through her professional day.
Biography; Health and Safety; History - United States
Dist - ECUFLM **Prod** - UMCOM 1980

Run Wild, Run Free 100 MIN
16mm
Color
Tells what happens when a mute boy befriends a white colt.
Fine Arts
Dist - TIMLIF **Prod** - CPC 1969

Runa - guardians of the forest 28 MIN
16mm / VHS
Color (H C G)
$575.00, $250.00 purchase, $45.00 rental _ #11397, #37975
Explores the profound ecological knowledge of the Runa, an Indian community in Amazonian Ecuador. Includes commentary by the Runa, who discuss their adaptation to life in the rainforest and their reactions to outside forces which are increasingly encroaching upon their environment, traditional lands and way of life. Produced by Ellen Speiser and Dominique Irvine.
Science - Natural; Social Science
Dist - UCEMC

The Runaround 12 MIN
16mm
Color (J)
Searches for those responsible for air pollution.
Science - Natural; Sociology
Dist - AMLUNG **Prod** - NTBA 1969

Runaway 33 MIN
U-matic / VHS
Cop Talk Series
Color (I J)
Relates the story of 15 - year - old Karen who runs away from the problems she faces with an alcoholic mother and finds herself having to cope with hunger, cold, disorientation and danger. Shows that when the police pick her up for a curfew violation, she and her mother receive joint counseling.
Social Science; Sociology
Dist - AITECH **Prod** - UTSBE 1981

Runaway 6 MIN
16mm
B&W (C)
$157.00
Experimental film by Standish D Lawder.
Fine Arts
Dist - AFA **Prod** - AFA 1969

Runaway 54 MIN
U-matic / VHS / 16mm
Color (A)
Tells what happens to the nearly one million children who run away from home each year. Looks at the runaway shelters which have sprung up since the passage of the Runaway and Homeless Youth Act of 1974. Includes interviews with runaways, parents, police and counselors.
Sociology
Dist - MEDIAG **Prod** - MEDIAG 1981

The Runaway 30 MIN
U-matic / VHS
Gettin' to Know Me Series
Color (I J H)
History - United States; Sociology
Dist - MDCPB **Prod** - CTI 1979

The Runaway 30 MIN
U-matic / VT1 / VHS
Color (G)
$49.95 purchase, $30.00 rental
Portrays 14 - year - old Darlene Horse who runs away from a difficult home situation - her mother and stepfather drink too much and Darlene is caught in the middle of a pattern of violence. Reveals that although Darlene's Aunt Linda is a caring, positive role model, Alice, the social worker, is concerned that Linda's house is too crowded for Darlene to stay. Alice's supervisor and a Native American alcholism counselor guide Alice in helping the family through appreciation of their culture and use of counseling groups. Not every problem is solved but things do get better. Coproduced with Nebraska ETV, Nebraska Dept of Education, Lincoln Multi - Cultural Center.
Guidance and Counseling; Health and Safety; Social Science; Sociology
Dist - NAMPBC **Prod** - NAMPBC

Runaway 59 MIN
VHS
Wonderworks collection series
Color (I J H)
$29.95 purchase _ #RUN01
Portrays a young boy who runs away to live in the subway tunnels because he blames himself for the death of his friend.
Guidance and Counseling; Literature and Drama
Dist - KNOWUN **Prod** - PBS

The Runaway and Officer Bob 30 MIN
VHS
Davey and Goliath series
Color (P I R)
$19.95 purchase, $10.00 rental _ #4 - 8828
Presents two 15 - minute 'Davey and Goliath' episodes. 'The Runaway' takes a modern view of the Prodigal Son parable, as Davey runs away to join the circus, only to find his circus life to be less than glamorous. 'Officer Bob' finds Davey fearing that he has lost Officer Bob's friendship after breaking a safety rule. Produced by the Evangelical Lutheran Church in America.
Literature and Drama; Religion and Philosophy
Dist - APH

The Runaway and the neighbor - Volume 7 45 MIN
VHS
Flying house series
Color (K P I R)
$11.99 purchase _ #35 - 8956 - 979
Uses an animated format to present events from the New Testament era, as three children, a professor and a robot travel in the 'Flying House' back to that time. 'The Runaway' tells the story of Jesus' feeding of the 5,000, while 'The Neighbor' reviews the story of the Good Samaritan.
Literature and Drama; Religion and Philosophy
Dist - APH **Prod** - TYHP

The Runaway brain 52 MIN
VHS
Planet for the taking series
Color (H C T G)
$198.00 purchase
Presents the world as a pyramid of life with humans at the very top. Asks if humans can integrate themselves into the complex pattern of life rather than trying to dominate life. Features David Suzuki who explores the concept that if humans create a problem with their technology, they must be able to solve it with technology. Part of an eight - part series.
Science - Natural; Sociology
Dist - FI **Prod** - CANBC 1988

Runaway Camel 15 MIN
U-matic / VHS
Encounter in the Desert Series
Color (I)
Shows the life of Bedouin nomads. Tells of recapturing an escaped camel.
Geography - World; Social Science; Sociology
Dist - CTI **Prod** - CTI

The Runaway duck - 40
VHS
Reading rainbow series
Color; CC (K P)
$39.95 purchase
Tells about Egbert, a carved wooden duck, who doesn't mean to take a trip around the world, but that's what happens in a story by David Lyon. Chronicles Egbert's travels in air, on land and at sea. LeVar takes his own trip to Maryland's Chesapeake Bay to learn about waterfowl. Glimpses at the artistry of duck carving and observes, visually and aurally, how expert duck callers 'call' a duck. Part of a series offering a multicultural approach to generating reading enthusiasm with cross - curricular applications, hosted by LeVar Burton.
English Language; Literature and Drama; Science - Natural
Dist - GPN **Prod** - LNMDP

Runaway - Freedom or Fright 10 MIN
16mm / U-matic / VHS
Color (J)
LC 81-700730
Explores the problems and dangers connected with running away from home. Suggests that family problems aren't solved by running away.
Sociology
Dist - AIMS **Prod** - CAHILL 1980

The Runaway problem 13 MIN
16mm / U-matic / VHS
Color (I)
LC 81-700055
Offers information on teenage runaways and tells how the Runaway Hotline serves to comfort and inform families.
Sociology
Dist - CORF **Prod** - MILPRO 1980

The Runaway problem 13 MIN
16mm / U-matic / VHS
Color (I J H C A)
$315.00, $220.00 purchase _ #80539
Explains the problems of teenage runaways and the emotional disturbances experienced by their parents.
Psychology; Sociology
Dist - CORF

Runaway railway 55 MIN
U-matic / VHS / 16mm
B&W
A sad group of children are waiting at Barming Station in England for the station to be closed and their favorite engine 'Matilda' to be demolished. Deciding to borrow time by a minor act of sabotage, the children and 'Matilda' run amok in some wild, wooly adventures.
Literature and Drama; Social Science
Dist - LUF **Prod** - CHILDF 1967

Runaway Ralph 40 MIN
16mm / VHS
Color (P I)
$495.00, $225.00 purchase, $75.00 rental
Finds Ralph S Mouse running away from his home at the Mountain View Inn to avoid sharing his motorcycle. Reveals that Ralph roars off to a summer camp where he befriends a boy named Garfield and becomes the nemesis of Catso, the camp cat. Stars Fred Savage. From the book by Beverly Cleary.
Literature and Drama
Dist - CF **Prod** - MATTHE 1988

Runaway Slave 15 MIN
U-matic / VHS
Stories of America Series
Color (P)
Tells the story of the life of Harriet Tubman.
History - United States
Dist - AITECH **Prod** - OHSDE 1976

Runaway to Glory 24 MIN
16mm / U-matic / VHS
Color (K)
$495.00, $349.00, $249.00 purchase _ #AD - 1126
Discloses that when a heavy storm causes serious damage to the family farm, Milly and Grandpa set out on a routine errand which proves courage and quick thinking know no age.
Literature and Drama; Social Science; Sociology
Dist - FOTH **Prod** - FOTH

Runaways 24 MIN
VHS / 16mm
Color (J)
LC 76-700418
Presents the story of a girl who ran away from home after a breakdown in family communications. Shows what it is like to be a runaway trying to survive on the streets. Examines the very limited facilities available to help these children.
Social Science; Sociology
Dist - LRF **Prod** - LRF 1975

Runaways 10 MIN
U-matic / VHS / 16mm
Color (J)
Follows the separate cases of two teenage runaways, Danny and Alice.
Guidance and Counseling; Sociology
Dist - AIMS **Prod** - DAVP

Rund Um Den Munchner Marienplatz 5 MIN
U-matic / VHS / 16mm
European Studies - Germany (German Series
Color (H C A) (GERMAN)
A German - language version of the motion picture Around And About The Marienplatz In Munich. Explores the history and economy of Munich, the most famous of Germany's state capitals.
Foreign Language; Geography - World; History - World
Dist - IFB **Prod** - MFAFRG 1973

Running a Dance Company 30 MIN
VHS / U-matic
Update - Topics of Current Concern Series
Color
Business and Economics; Fine Arts
Dist - ARCVID **Prod** - ARCVID

Running a Movie Theatre 30 MIN
VHS / 16mm
(PRO G)
$89.95 purchase _ #DGP13
Discusses how easy it is to start a movie theatre, but how difficult it is to make a profit. Hosted by Dick Goldberg.
Business and Economics
Dist - RMIBHF **Prod** - RMIBHF

Running a river - the Wisconsin 29 MIN
U-matic / VHS
Color (J A)
Explores the diverse activities along one of Wisconsin's great natural resources. The Wisconsin River flows 430 miles, from the state's northern border to the Mississippi River.
Geography - United States; Geography - World; Industrial and Technical Education; Physical Education and Recreation; Social Science
Dist - UWISCA **Prod** - UWISCA 1986

Running a Small Business Series
Basic records for a small business 18 MIN
Credit and collections for a small business 15 MIN
Evaluating a small business 17 MIN
Financing a Small Business 18 MIN
Insurance Needs for a Small Business 17 MIN
Inventory Control for Manufacturers 12 MIN
Merchandise Control for Retailers 14 MIN
Dist - BCNFL

Running a steam locomotive
VHS
Running a steam locomotive series
Color (G)
$34.95 purchase _ #HDS000
Presents the first of a 3 - part series covering the ins and outs of running a steam locomotive.
Social Science
Dist - SIV

Running a steam locomotive series
Running a steam locomotive
Dist - SIV

Running a stringer bead in flat position - running weave beads in flat position - padding 28 MIN
U-matic / VHS / 16mm
Arc welding series
Color (H C A)
Industrial and Technical Education
Dist - CORNRS **Prod** - CUETV 1981

Running and handling of tubular goods 18 MIN
16mm / VHS
Color (A IND)
$360.00, $335.00 purchase _ #30.0129, #50.0129
Tells how to run and handle tubular goods successfully in the oil field.
Industrial and Technical Education; Social Science
Dist - UTEXPE **Prod** - HYDRIL 1982

Running and Riding Smooth - Tune - Up and Shocks 60 MIN
VHS / BETA
Car Care Series
Color
Shows how to perform an engine tune - up. Demonstrates changing spark plugs, points and condensers. Covers servicing a car's PCV System and timing an engine.
Industrial and Technical Education
Dist - MOHOMV **Prod** - MOHOMV

Running away, dropping out - voices from Nightmare Street series
VHS
Running away, dropping out - voices from Nightmare Street series
Color (I J H)
$149.00 purchase _ #CCP0171SV - K
Presents two parts on the reality of teenagers struggling to survive on the streets. Includes Children of the Night - the Lost Ones and Starting Over - the Long Road Back.
Guidance and Counseling; History - United States; Sociology
Dist - CAMV **Prod** - CAMV 1993

Running away, dropping out - voices from the nightmare street 35 MIN
VHS
Running away series
Color (H)
$79.95 purchase _ #CCP0170V-D
Presents a two-part series that graphically describes the struggles of teen-agers who live on the streets. Offers information designed for several different types of kids, including those who are thinking about running away, those who have done so, and those who have been thrown out of their homes. Informs kids that there are people who care about them and want to help them.
Guidance and Counseling; Sociology
Dist - CAMV

Running away series
Running away, dropping out - voices from the nightmare street 35 MIN
Dist - CAMV

The Running back 11 MIN
16mm
B&W (J H)
Presents instruction on stance, runniing forward, right and left receiving the hand-off, flanking on receiving the ball, following the blocker and changing pace and direction while running with the ball.
Physical Education and Recreation
Dist - COCA **Prod** - BORDEN

Running back techniques
VHS
NCAA football videos - offensive series
Color (A G T)
$39.95 purchase _ #KAR1301V-P
Presents instruction on skills and drills given by NCAA coaches. Features Earle Bruce explaining running back techniques. One of a series of videos that provide coaching tips to offensive and defensive players and coaches. Series is available as a set of offensive series, defensive series, or both combined.
Physical Education and Recreation
Dist - CAMV

Running back techniques
VHS
NCAA football instructional videos series
Color (H C A)
$39.95 purchase _ #KAR1301V
Features Colorado State head football coach Earle Bruce teaching various skills and drills for running backs. Produced by the National Collegiate Athletic Association.
Physical Education and Recreation
Dist - CAMV **Prod** - NCAAF

Running continuous bead in horizontal and vertical down position
U-matic / VHS
Shielded metal arc welding - Spanish series
Color (SPANISH)
Foreign Language; Industrial and Technical Education
Dist - VTRI **Prod** - VTRI

Running continuous beads in vertical up and overhead position
VHS / U-matic
Shielded metal arc welding - Spanish series
Color (SPANISH)
Foreign Language; Industrial and Technical Education
Dist - VTRI **Prod** - VTRI

Running dogs and other fables 25 MIN
16mm / U-matic / VHS
Maclear Series
Color; Mono (J H C A)
$300.00 film, $250.00 video, $50.00 rental
Serves as an expose of casinos, big businesses, unions, and Ho Ying, the man who controls the action in Macau, a Portuguese colony which is tied to China by a peninsula.
Business and Economics; Civics and Political Systems; Geography - World
Dist - CTV **Prod** - CTV 1975

The Running Events - Men 21 MIN
U-matic / VHS / 16mm
LeRoy Walker Track and Field - Men Series
Color (J H C)
Examines the running events at all distances plus hurdling and sprint relay techniques.
Physical Education and Recreation
Dist - ATHI **Prod** - ATHI 1976

The Running events - women 21 MIN
U-matic / VHS / 16mm
LeRoy walker track and field - women series
Color (J H C)
Studies sprints, middle distance, hurdling and sprint relays.
Physical Education and Recreation
Dist - ATHI **Prod** - ATHI 1976

Running for Life 28 MIN
U-matic / VHS / 16mm
Color (H C)
LC 70-706185
Discusses the U S Office of Public Health's two - year experiment to determine the effects of exercise on middle - aged persons and whether such exercising can reduce the chances of heart disease. Shows faculty members of the University of Wiscosin exercising and reporting on their experiences.
Health and Safety; Physical Education and Recreation; Psychology; Science - Natural
Dist - IU **Prod** - NET 1970

Running free of injury 60 MIN
VHS
Color (G)
$34.95 purchase
Shows runners how to avoid injuries. Discusses what causes running injuries and steps to take to eliminate the possibility of injury. Features Dr Janet Keeney - Valenza, specialist in sports medicine, as host. Contains graphics, animation and freeze frames.
Physical Education and Recreation
Dist - WONYEA **Prod** - WONYEA 1994

Running from the ghost - pt 2 48 MIN
VHS
Human face of Hong Kong series
Color (S)
$99.00 purchase _ #118 - 9032
Shows the different life - styles of Hong Kong society - the world of the wealthy and powerful and the world of the working class. Hong Kong is known as a successful manufacturing and trading center and an exotic international stopover, but it is still a British colony. China will regain sovereignty over the area in 1997. Part 2 of two parts considers ordinary, hardworking families who have no access to the law nor to the government bureaucracy, which exist to maintain the laissez - faire, low - tax 'economic miracle' that is Hong Kong.
Business and Economics; Geography - World; History - World; Social Science; Sociology
Dist - FI **Prod** - FLMAUS 1987

Running gay 20 MIN
VHS
Color (H G)
$195.00 purchase, $50.00 rental
Examines the participation of lesbians and gay men in sports. Focuses on the homophobia they confront in mainstream sporting events and their recent efforts to organize gay teams, organizations and events. Directed by Maya Chowdhry.
Physical Education and Recreation; Sociology
Dist - CNEMAG

Running Gear 14 MIN
16mm
Color (H)
Uses a specially prepared chassis to demonstrate the qualities of frame design and development. Shows integral body and frame construction and emphasizes the types and functions of springs, shackles and shock absorbers. Examines independent suspension systems and demonstrates mechanical and hydraulic braking systems.
Industrial and Technical Education
Dist - SF **Prod** - SF 1969

Running Great with Grete Waitz 60 MIN
VHS
(H C A)
$29.95 puchase _ #CH900V
Presents olympic champion Grete Waitz who offers a comprehensive running program. Explains methods for improving and maintaining form and increasing speed and endurance while running. Discusses interval training, climbing exercises, training schedules and more.
Physical Education and Recreation
Dist - CAMV

Running Ground 29 MIN
U-matic
Color (H)
LC 80-707476
Dramatizes one high school student's choices as he examines the directionless lives of his friends, many of

whom are involved in drugs and alcohol. Shows how he is able to set a clearer direction in his own life by running and writing.
Sociology
Dist - MESJ **Prod** - MESJ 1980

Running Hard, Breathing Easy - the Jeanette Bolden Story 13 MIN
U-matic
Color
Tells the story of Jeanette Bolden, a young woman who overcame asthma to become a world - class sprinter and a member of the 1980 U.S. Olympic team. Stresses how she was helped by good medical treatment.
Health and Safety; Physical Education and Recreation
Dist - MTP **Prod** - SCHPLO

Running home 58 MIN
VHS
Color (J H G)
$250.00 purchase, $65.00 rental
Tells of four teenage friends and their troubled family relationships. Shows how they draw strength from each other as they search for individual solutions to their unhappy situations. Evokes discussion from teenage audiences who relate to the problems of the culturally and socioeconomically diverse characters.
Guidance and Counseling; Psychology; Sociology
Dist - BAXMED

Running, jumping and standing still film 10 MIN
16mm
B&W (J)
LC 77-709667
Presents, in the style of silent comedy, Peter Sellers and his 'Goon Show' troupe as they pursue their eccentric courses across the British countryside.
Fine Arts
Dist - VIEWFI **Prod** - PFP 1970

The Running Man 103 MIN
U-matic / VHS / 16mm
Color (H C A)
Stars Laurence Harvey, Lee Remick and Allan Bates. Tells of a likeable young adventurer who perpetrates a successful insurance fraud and then gradually becomes obsessed both by suspicion that he is being pursued and a desire to work the stunt again.
Fine Arts
Dist - FI **Prod** - CPC 1963

Running MS DOS learning system 180 MIN
U-matic / VHS
(A PRO)
$495.00 purchase, $595.00 purchase
Aids users with theory and operation of DOS, external DOS commands and hard disk management. Developed and endorsed by MicroSoft Press.
Computer Science
Dist - VIDEOT **Prod** - VIDEOT 1988

Running My Way 28 MIN
16mm
Color (I J A)
LC 82 - 700197
Depicts various ways teenagers struggle with their maturing sexuality.
Guidance and Counseling; Health and Safety; Sociology
Dist - CHSCA **Prod** - LITMAN 1981

Running My Way 28 MIN
16mm
Color (I J A)
LC 82-700197
Depicts various ways teenagers struggle with their maturing sexuality.
Guidance and Counseling; Health and Safety; Sociology
Dist - CHSCA **Prod** - CHSCA 1981

Running on Empty - the Fuel Economy Challenge 27 MIN
16mm
Color
LC 78-701241
Illustrates various driving and fuel economy techniques practiced on a 90 - mile rally. Shows how average drivers can practice ways to achieve maximum savings in gasoline and money while traveling city streets, country roads and major highways.
Health and Safety; Industrial and Technical Education; Social Science
Dist - USNAC **Prod** - USDOE 1978

Running on the edge of the rainbow - Laguna stories and poems 28 MIN
VHS / U-matic
Words and place series
Color
Reflects on the nature of Laguna storytelling, its functions and the problems an Indian poet faces. Discusses how these stories are current versions of traditional tales.
Literature and Drama; Social Science
Dist - NORROS **Prod** - NORROS

Running Out of Steam 26 MIN
U-matic / VHS / 16mm
Turning the Tide Series
Color (J)
$275.00, $250.00 purchase, $50.00 rental
Proposes that more efficient use of energy, combined with a commitment to renewable resources, would lead to more jobs and better homes than would the building of more power plants.
Business and Economics; Home Economics; Social Science; Sociology
Dist - BULFRG **Prod** - TYNT 1988

Running Out of Water 30 MIN
U-matic / VHS
Time's Harvest - Exploring the Future Series
Color (C)
Sociology
Dist - MDCPB **Prod** - MDCPB

Running Programs, Mathematical Expressions 60 MIN
U-matic / VHS
Introduction to BASIC Series Lecture 2; Lecture 2
Color
Industrial and Technical Education; Mathematics
Dist - UIDEEO **Prod** - UIDEEO

Running shadow - part one 20 MIN
VHS
Color (G)
$30.00 purchase
Features overflowing screen with rapid frames and superimpositions of rushing streams, crashing waves, butterfly flutters and assorted arcs and rotations. Includes a soundtrack full of altered natural sounds, and bird and insect sounds.
Fine Arts; Industrial and Technical Education; Science - Physical
Dist - CANCIN **Prod** - FULTON 1987

Running shadow - part two 20 MIN
VHS
Color (G)
$30.00 purchase
Records Carribean people and Peruvian natives going about their daily tasks, which the camera fills with meaning by intense focus and slow motion. Shows camera angles full of curves, cartwheels, rolling barrel loops - without gravity and straight lines.
Fine Arts; Geography - World; Science - Physical; Social Science
Dist - CANCIN **Prod** - FULTON 1987

Running - Short Course on the Long Run 18 MIN
U-matic / VHS / 16mm
Color (H C A)
Explains how to begin a running program, from first introduction to the point of running 30 minutes at a time, every other day.
Physical Education and Recreation
Dist - ATHI **Prod** - ATHI 1982

Running Smooth 60 MIN
VHS
Color (H C A PRO)
$20.00 purchase _ #TA227
Shows step by step how to change spark plugs, points and condensers in doing a car tune up.
Industrial and Technical Education
Dist - AAVIM **Prod** - AAVIM 1990

Running software and keyboarding skills 30 MIN
U-matic / VHS
On and on about instruction - microcomputers series
Color (C T A PRO)
Demonstrates setting up the computer and loading packaged software of various brands and configurations of microcomputers. Discusses keyboarding skills.
Industrial and Technical Education; Mathematics; Psychology
Dist - GPN **Prod** - VADE 1984-1985

A Running Start 28 MIN
VHS / BETA
Color
Highlights 30 years of California's history in horse racing and breeding.
Physical Education and Recreation
Dist - EQVDL **Prod** - CTBRDA

A Running Start - Preparing for Participation 12 MIN
16mm / U-matic / VHS
Football Injury Prevention Series
Color (I J H)
Stresses the importance of pre - season football conditioning and the need for emphasizing building endurance and weight training.
Physical Education and Recreation
Dist - ATHI **Prod** - ATHI

Running the numbers with the Si - Tex 790
VHS
Color (G A)
$29.90 purchase _ #0731
Shows how to install, set up and use the Loran C, Si - Tex 790 model.
Physical Education and Recreation; Social Science
Dist - SEVVID

Running the numbers with the Si - Tex EZ - 97
VHS
Color (G A)
$29.90 purchase _ #0285
Shows how to install, set up and use the Loran C, Si - Tex EZ - 97 model.
Physical Education and Recreation; Social Science
Dist - SEVVID

Running the Show 30 MIN
U-matic / VHS / 16mm
Case Studies in Small Business Series
Color (C A)
Business and Economics
Dist - GPN **Prod** - UMA 1979

Running the show - the conductor 15 MIN
U-matic / VHS
Arts - a - bound
(I)
$130.00 purchase, $25.00 rental
Explores the process and performance of the conductor's art. Uses a documentary format featuring interviews with artists and performers on location, from rehearsal to finished performance.
Fine Arts
Dist - GPN **Prod** - NCGE 1985

Running the show - the curator 15 MIN
VHS / U-matic
Arts - a - bound
(I)
$130.00 purchase, $25.00 rental
Explores the curator's art. Uses a documentary format featuring interviews with artists and curators on location, from a project's inception to the finished exhibit.
Fine Arts
Dist - GPN **Prod** - NCGE 1985

Running the show - the director 15 MIN
U-matic / VHS
Arts - a - bound
(I)
$130.00 purchase, $25.00 rental
Explores the process and execution of the director's art. Uses a documentary format featuring interviews with artists and performers on location, from rehearsal to finished performance.
Fine Arts
Dist - GPN **Prod** - NCGE 1985

Running water - erosion, deposition and transportation 20 MIN
VHS
Basic concepts in physical geology video series
Color (J H)
$53.95 purchase _ #193 Y 0185
Looks at the impact of running water on the land. Investigates the concepts of suspension, solution, load, rapids, meanders and deltas. Illustrates the characteristics of youthful, mature and old streams. Part of a ten - part series on physical geology.
Science - Physical
Dist - WARDS **Prod** - WARDS 1990

Running Water - Erosion, Deposition and Transportation 20 MIN
VHS
Color (J)
$56.50 purchase _ #ES 8180
Explores the relationship of running water to land. Includes the concepts of suspension, solution, load, rapids, meanders and deltas. Illustrates the characteristics of youthful, mature and old streams.
Agriculture; Science; Science - Physical
Dist - SCTRES **Prod** - SCTRES

Running Water - from Rain to River to Ocean 20 MIN
VHS
Color (J)
$56.50 purchase _ #ES 8170
Introduces the hydrologic process. Includes laminar, turbulent and shooting flow, waterfalls and floods. Considers the relationship between velocity, gradient, discharge and the type of stream which occurs. Includes teacher's guide.
Science; Science - Physical; Social Science
Dist - SCTRES **Prod** - SCTRES

Running water - rain to river to ocean 20 MIN
VHS
Basic concepts in physical geology video series
Color (J H)
$53.95 purchase _ #193 Y 0182
Introduces the hydrologic process. Includes laminar, turbulent and shooting flow, waterfalls and floods. Covers velocity, gradient, discharge and the types of streams. Part of a ten - part series on physical geology.
Science - Physical
Dist - WARDS **Prod** - WARDS 1990

Running Wild 50 MIN
VHS / U-matic
Color (H C A)
Features a scheme devised by the organization Visionquest for rehabilitating tough young offenders in which they face the challenge of breaking a wild mustang. Tells the history of the wild mustang in America, brought over from Spain. Portrays the respect that develops between the youth and the horse resulting in taming them both.
Education; Guidance and Counseling; Psychology; Sociology
Dist - FI **Prod** - BBCTV

Running with Jesse 60 MIN
VHS
Frontline Series
Color; Captioned (G)
$200.00 purchase, $95.00 rental _ #FRON - 704K
Reviews the 1988 presidential campaign of Jesse Jackson. Interviews members of the media, Jackson supporters and critics. Shows how Jackson, despite losing the nomination, nevertheless had a strong impact on the Democratic convention.
Civics and Political Systems; History - United States
Dist - PBS **Prod** - DOCCON 1989

Running Your Own Business Series

Accounting - the language of business	11 MIN
Bankruptcy	11 MIN
Capital Gains	11 MIN
Capital Investments	11 MIN
Inventory Management	11 MIN
Management Controls	11 MIN
Planning for Profit	11 MIN
Risk Management	11 MIN
Sources of Capital	11 MIN
Taxation	11 MIN

Dist - EFD

Running your own home-based sewing business - Pt 1 18 MIN
VHS
Running your own home-based sewing business series
Color (A)
$39.95 purchase _ #SWE774V-H
Discusses how and why to start a home-based sewing business. Viewers learn what to do to get a business off the ground, how to keep books and records and the importance of advertising and promotions. Viewers learn how they can put their sewing skills to work and make money.
Business and Economics; Home Economics
Dist - CAMV

Running your own home-based sewing business - Pt 2 13 MIN
VHS
Running your own home-based sewing business series
Color (A)
$39.95 purchase _ #SWE775V-H
Stresses how to work with clients of a home-based sewing business. Covers the first conversations with clients and the importance of telephone screening. Viewers learn about setting their own policies and procedures and will find many organizational tips.
Business and Economics; Home Economics
Dist - CAMV

Running your own home-based sewing business series
Presents the hows and whys of starting a home-based sewing business, including how to get the business off the ground, keep books and records, work with clients, establishing policies and procedures and many other organizational tips.

Running your own home-based sewing business - Pt 1	18 MIN
Running your own home-based sewing business - Pt 2	13 MIN

Dist - CAMV

Runoff, Land Use and Water Quality 21 MIN
16mm / U-matic / VHS
Color
LC 79-701190
Explores the ways in which land use affects water quality.
Science - Natural; Social Science
Dist - MCFI **Prod** - UWISCA 1978

Runs Good 1970
16mm
Color (C)
$258.00
Experimental film by Pat O'Neill.
Fine Arts
Dist - AFA **Prod** - AFA 1970

Runs test
VHS
Probability and statistics series
Color (H C)
$125.00 purchase _ #8058
Provides resource material about runs testing for help in the study of probability and statistics. Presents a 60 - video series, each part 25 to 30 minutes long, that explains and reinforces concepts using definitions, theorems, examples and step - by - step solutions to tutor the student. Videos are also available in a set.
Mathematics
Dist - LANDMK

The Runt 14 MIN
U-matic / VHS / 16mm
Learning Values with Fat Albert and the Cosby Kids, Set I Series
Color (K P I)
Tells how Bill and the rest of the kids help Pee Wee accept himself for himself and not his size. Relates how Pee Wee joins the others in a game of football. Explains that the football gets stuck in a tiny place and Cluck, the pet duck, gets stuck going after the football. Concludes with Pee Wee getting into the crevice and retrieving them both.
Guidance and Counseling
Dist - MGHT **Prod** - FLMTON 1975

Runt of the Litter 13 MIN
16mm
Peppermint Stick Selection Series
Color (P I)
LC 77-701720
An excerpt from the motion picture Charlotte's Web. Tells how a pig named Wilbur is desolate when he discovers he is destined to be the farmer's Christmas dinner, until his spider friend, Charlotte, decides to help him. Based on the book Charlotte's Web by E B White.
English Language; Fine Arts; Literature and Drama
Dist - FI **Prod** - FI 1976

Runway 50 MIN
VHS
Look series
Color (A)
PdS99 purchase _ Unavailable in the USA
Features catwalk smalltalk from models and designers. Strips away the glitz and glamor of the fashion business to look behind the scenes. Explores the mystique of the designer label and debates the meaning of style. Reveals the mysteries of material and unveils the interdependence between the fashion industry, the media, financiers, and the consumer. Part of a six-part series.
Home Economics
Dist - BBCENE

Rupert Murdoch - the Press baron who would be king 60 MIN
VHS
Inside story series
Color (G)
$50.00 purchase _ #INST - 414
Profiles Australian newspaper publisher Rupert Murdoch. Interviews Murdoch on his views of journalism, his political agenda and his aspirations for U S journalism. Reveals that Murdoch controls more than 80 newspapers worldwide, including the Chicago Sun - Times and the New York Post in the U S. Hosted by Hodding Carter.
Literature and Drama; Social Science
Dist - PBS

Ruptured Lumbar Discs - Treatment by Vertebral Body Fusion 20 MIN
16mm
Color (PRO)
Examines the steps of discography employed to demonstrate the etiology of low back pain and its relation to the intervertebral discs. Shows the entire surgical procedure for the removal of a pathological lumbar disc and replacement with bone grafts.
Health and Safety; Science - Natural
Dist - SQUIBB **Prod** - SQUIBB

Rural America 18 MIN
U-matic / VHS / 16mm
American Condition Series
Color (H C A)
LC 77-700632
Presents a documentary on the effects of a recession on the people of Pecatonica, Illinois. Shows how the economic survival of the city depends on the surrounding farm community and the availability of jobs in two industrial centers that are 15 miles away. Records what people can and cannot afford in a recession and what they think about America's promise for the future.
Agriculture; Business and Economics; Sociology
Dist - MGHT **Prod** - ABCTV 1976

Rural America - Coming of Age 29 MIN
U-matic / VHS
Color (H C G T A)
Focuses on innovative programs already in place that are helping to solve problems facing the rural elderly - transportation, employment, health, energy, housing, and loneliness. Narrated by Lorne Greene. Examines the involvement of an older workers' organization known as Green Thumb in finding employment for elderly citizens, the role played by Inter Faith Friends in arranging visits to shut ins, and the way in which a transportation authority in north central Pennsylvania increases the mobility of the elderly in isolated rural areas.
Health and Safety; Sociology
Dist - PSU **Prod** - PSU 1981

The Rural cooperative 15 MIN
16mm
Faces of change - Taiwan series
Color
Presents a portrait of the Tsao Tun Farmers' Association, which typifies rural cooperatives in Taiwan. Shows it as being the center of social, leisure and economic activities for the 9,600 families who own the cooperative and rely on it for services ranging from irrigation, provision of seeds, farm implements and fertilizers to crop storage and marketing.
Agriculture; Geography - World; Sociology
Dist - WHEELK **Prod** - AUFS

Rural Crime Prevention 16 MIN
U-matic / VHS / 16mm
Color
Points out the special vulnerability of rural property to crime and the steps people who live and work in sparsely populated areas can take to minimize opportunity for crime.
Sociology
Dist - CORF **Prod** - HAR 1984

Rural Crime - They're Stealin' the Farm 18 MIN
U-matic / VHS / 16mm
Color (H C A)
LC 83-701067
Explains how to protect equipment, animals and crops on the farm.
Agriculture; Sociology
Dist - AIMS **Prod** - CAGO 1982

Rural Driving 35 MIN
16mm
To Get from Here to There Series
Color (H)
Depicts country and mountain road conditions as they affect the driver. Illustrates crash - producing situations and how to avoid them.
Health and Safety; Psychology
Dist - PROART **Prod** - PROART

Rural Driving 10 MIN
16mm / U-matic / VHS
Driver Education Series
Color
Discusses speed relationships with other vehicles and roadway elements.
Health and Safety; Psychology
Dist - FORDFL **Prod** - FMCMP 1969

Rural Mental Health Practice 23 MIN
U-matic
Color
Interviews four mental health professionals who have made the transition from urban to rural practice. Discusses their transition in terms of an impractical romanticizing about rural life.
Psychology
Dist - UWASHP **Prod** - UWASHP

Rural Migrants - no Place to Live 20 MIN
U-matic / VHS / 16mm
Color (J H C)
LC 77-703321
Revised version of the 1975 motion picture No Place To Go. Explores the problems in Africa, Latin America and Asia caused by the influx of rural migrants into the cities.
Geography - World; Social Science; Sociology
Dist - BARR **Prod** - UN 1977

Rural Neighborhood - a Beautiful Place 15 MIN
U-matic / VHS
Neighborhoods Series
Color (P)
Explains how beautiful a rural neighborhood can be.
Sociology
Dist - GPN **Prod** - NEITV 1981

Rural Neighborhood - a General Description 15 MIN
VHS / U-matic
Neighborhoods Series
Color (P)
Provides a general description of rural neighborhoods.
Sociology
Dist - GPN **Prod** - NEITV 1981

Rural Neighborhood - Good Neighbors Help each Other 15 MIN
U-matic / VHS
Neighborhoods Series
Color (P)
Shows good neighbors help each other in a rural environment.
Sociology
Dist - GPN **Prod** - NEITV 1981

Rural Politics 30 MIN
U-matic / VHS
American Government Series; 1
Color (C)
Details some of the political problems faced by rural Americans, a new minority group lacking the political clout farmers once enjoyed.
Civics and Political Systems
Dist - DALCCD **Prod** - DALCCD

Rural rat control 16 MIN
16mm
B&W (SPANISH)
LC FIE53-204
Explains how a farmer who understands rat habits can free his farm of rats through ratproofing buildings and food sources, burying garbage in a one - man land fill and using approved poisons.
Agriculture; Health and Safety; Home Economics
Dist - USNAC **Prod** - USPHS NMAC 1951

Rural Recreations 23 MIN
16mm
B&W (I)
Presents simple pastimes of rural Indian folk and highlights festivals like Gokul Astami and Diwali and Kerala's boat races.
Physical Education and Recreation
Dist - NEDINF **Prod** - INDIA

The Rural republic 30 MIN
VHS
American adventure series
Color (G)
$150.00 purchase _ #TAMA - 112
Stresses the impact of the Industrial Revolution on the largely agrarian American society. Discusses the resulting social changes.
History - United States
Dist - PBS

Rural Tanker Evolutions 30 MIN
VHS
Tanker Operations Series
Color (G PRO)
$125.00 purchase _ #35372
Ties together planning and resources to develop adequate fireground water supplies for rural areas and tanker management. Trains firefighting personnel.
Health and Safety; Psychology; Social Science
Dist - OKSU **Prod** - OKSU

Rusalka 159 MIN
VHS
Color (S)
$39.95 purchase _ #623 - 9292
Stars Eilene Hannan, Ann Howard, Rodney Macann and John Treleaven in the English National Opera production of 'Rusalka.' Uses David Pountney's English version of the Dvorak fairy tale. Mark Elder conducts.
Fine Arts; Geography - World
Dist - FI **Prod** - RMART 1987

Rush 3 MIN
16mm
Color (J H C)
Presents a rapid fire, humorous comment on the pace of our lives today.
Literature and Drama; Sociology
Dist - SLFP **Prod** - NWSWGR 1968

Rush hour service 10 MIN
U-matic / 16mm / VHS
Professional food preparation and service program series
Color (J) (POLISH)
LC 74-700218
Illustrates techniques for properly confronting the rush hour in dining rooms and coffee shops stressing that this is the time for the greatest profits and the greatest losses.
Industrial and Technical Education
Dist - NEM **Prod** - NEM 1971

The Rush to burn 35 MIN
VHS
Color (J H C G T A)
$55.00 purchase, $30.00 rental
Examines the growing use of hazardous waste incinerators in the U S. Reveals that most of the 525 billion pounds of hazardous waste produced yearly is burned. Questions the safety of incineration, examines government regulation, and suggests alternatives. Produced by Chris Bedford and Foongy Kyu Lee.
Health and Safety; Science - Natural; Sociology
Dist - EFVP **Prod** - GRNPCE 1989

Rush to Judgment 110 MIN
16mm
B&W
Disputes the findings and conclusions of the Warren Commission's report on the assassination of President John F Kennedy. Directed by Emile de Antonio.
Fine Arts; History - United States; Sociology
Dist - NYFLMS **Prod** - NYFLMS 1967

Rushes 56 MIN
16mm
B&W
Presents a self - destructive filmmaker who proposes to film the last 24 hours of his life. Reveals his relationships through telephone conversations, confrontations and interviews. Shows that despite the threats and pleading of those who care, he poisons himself.
Fine Arts; Sociology
Dist - DIRECT **Prod** - SPINLB 1979

Rushlight 42 MIN
16mm
Color
Presents Holly Fisher's film entry selected from the 1985 Whitney Biennial Film and Video Exhibition.
Fine Arts
Dist - AFA **Prod** - AFA 1986

Russell Hoban 36 MIN
VHS
Color (H C G)
$79.00 purchase
Features the writer discussing with Dee Palmer writing in the first person and how to begin and complete a novel. Talks about his works including Pilgermann; Turtle Diary; Kleinzeit; and The Medusa Frequency, as well as books for children.
Literature and Drama
Dist - ROLAND **Prod** - INCART

Russell L Ackoff - Organizational learning and beyond 100 MIN
Cassette
1992 conference collection series
Color; PAL (C G PRO)
$150.00, $25.00 purchase _ #V9202, #T9202
Describes three conditions that must exist for significant organizational learning to occur - corporate democracy, an internal decision - making structure; an internal market economy in which each unit can buy or sell services or products from or to whatever source it wants; and decision support systems in which errors can be anticipated or identified, then diagnosed or corrected. Features Prof Ackoff, chair of the board at INTERACT and author of Creating the Corporate Future and The Art of Problems Solving. Part of a three - part series on the 1992 Systems Thinking in Action Conference.
Business and Economics; Education; Psychology
Dist - PEGASU **Prod** - PEGASU 1992

Russi Mody - India's man of steel - Pt 10 30 MIN
U-matic / VHS
Profiles in progress series
Color (H C)
$325.00, $295.00 purchase _ #V555
Looks at Russi Mody, a key contributor to India's economic growth. Shows how he transformed a small steel company into India's biggest private - sector company. Emphasizes that private enterprise is often the best way to promote development, especially in countries with a large work force and natural resources. Part of a 13 - part series on people who are moving their tradition - bound countries into modern times.
Business and Economics; Geography - World; Social Science
Dist - BARR **Prod** - CEPRO 1991

Russia
VHS
Dances of the world series
Color (G)
$39.95 purchase _ #FD400V
Presents performances of dances from Russia. Interviews the dancers.
Fine Arts; Geography - World; Physical Education and Recreation
Dist - CAMV **Prod** - CAMV

Russia 21 MIN
VHS / 16mm
Paradise Steamship Co Series
Color (I H C A)
$300.00, $225.00 purchase
Tours the land of Russia with sightseeing stops at Red Square and Gorky Park, looking in on a rehearsal session of the Moscow Classical Ballet Company.
Geography - World
Dist - CAROUF **Prod** - KCBS 1989

Russia 60 MIN
VHS
Traveloguer collection series
Color (I J H A)
$29.95 purchase _ #QC106V-S
Presents information about the historic past and the current status of Russia, including information about the cities and the countryside. Shows famous landmarks, out-of-the way sites, struggles and hardships, victories and championships, and the legends of the region. Uses live-action footage and historical clips to show the geography, history, and culture. Includes 16 60-minute programs on northern, western, eastern, and southern Europe.
Geography - World
Dist - CAMV

Russia 18 MIN
U-matic / VHS / 16mm
Color (J)
Provides an overview of the Soviet Union from the last of the czars to Lenin. Shows today's Russians at work and play.
History - World
Dist - LUF **Prod** - LUF

Russia 60 MIN
VHS
Traveloguer Eastern Europe series
Color (J H C G)
$29.95 purchase _ #QC106V
Visits Russia and its cities. Illustrates notable landmarks, special events in history and the legends that are part of Russian culture. Part of a four part series on Eastern Europe.
Geography - World; History - World
Dist - CAMV

Russia - a cultural revolution 27 MIN
16mm
Color (J H A)
LC 79-701203
Tells the effect of the Russian Revolution in 1917 on Russian culture. Explains that the revolution ended a period of brilliant creativity in the Russian arts by using these arts solely to sell the dream of a worker's paradise to the people in order to inspire them to work harder toward communist goals. Relates the Russian definition of the word 'culture.'
Civics and Political Systems; Fine Arts; Geography - World; History - World; Sociology
Dist - AVED **Prod** - AVED 1967

Russia - after the USSR 25 MIN
VHS
Color; CC (J H A)
$110.00 purchase - #A51637
Focuses on the political and economic position of Russia after the breakup of the Soviet Union through interviews with a journalist, an auto worker, a police officer and a priest. Points out Russia's governmental and environmental crises. Includes a teacher's guide.
Civics and Political Systems; Foreign Language; History - World
Dist - NGS **Prod** - NGS 1994

Russia - an introduction 21 MIN
U-matic / VHS / BETA
Color; NTSC; PAL; SECAM (I J)
PdS43
Follows a brief history of Russia from Peter the Great to the October Revolution in 1917 with a social study of Russia. Examines town life, housing, transportation, industry, shopping and leisure time activities, including holidays and holiday resorts. Illustrates large numbers of Russian people in everyday situations before Glasnost.
Geography - World; History - World
Dist - VIEWTH

Russia - an Introduction 21 MIN
16mm
Color (J H C G)
Covers a brief history of prerevolution Russia and a social study of the Societ Union.
History - World; Social Science; Sociology
Dist - VIEWTH **Prod** - GATEEF

Russia - Czar to Lenin 29 MIN
U-matic / VHS / 16mm
B&W (J H C)
LC FIA67-1334
Uses actual footage to document the causes and outbreak of the Russian Revolution.

Civics and Political Systems; History - World
Dist - MGHT **Prod** - MGHT 1966

Russia for sale - the rough road to capitalism 58 MIN
VHS
Color (G)
$295.00 purchase, $95.00 rental
Tells the compelling stories of three Russians against the backdrop of the former Soviet Union's breakup and historic transition from communism to capitalism. Shows how the psychology and historical roots of decades of communism influence daily life and economic and democratic reform today. Interweaves archival footage from 1917 - 1935 with gripping contemporary images of a nation in crisis. Directed by Natasha Lance. English voiceover narration.
Business and Economics; Civics and Political Systems; Fine Arts; Geography - World; History - World
Dist - CNEMAG

Russia in Europe 19 MIN
U-matic / VHS / 16mm
Color (H C A)
LC FIA65-1540
Depicts and discusses the geographical characteristics, natural forestation, agriculture, the inland waterways system and the chief cities of white Russia, the Ukraine and the Crimea. Explains Russia's one party system.
Civics and Political Systems; Geography - World
Dist - IFB **Prod** - IFB 1961

Russia in World War I 20 MIN
U-matic / VHS / 16mm
Russian revolution series
B&W
LC 76-712755
Covers the Russian declaration of war on Germany in the first World War, a major defeat of Russia in its first battle, and the 'No Surrender' policy of the Tsar which contributed to the overthrow of the Tsar and his government.
History - World
Dist - FI **Prod** - GRATV 1971

Russia - off the record ; 1987 58 MIN
VHS / U-matic
Other countries, other views series
Color (J H C)
LC 87-707226
Provides a candid view of life in the Soviet Union while examining common myths and stereotypes.
History - World; Sociology
Dist - JOU

Russia, Siberia - the Way it is 16 MIN
16mm
Color (I)
LC 73-702808
Shows the people, cities, country, art and architecture of russia, giving a feeling for the present as well as a sense of history.
Fine Arts; Geography - World; History - World; Sociology
Dist - SCREEI **Prod** - PORTIN 1973

Russia - The People speak 22 MIN
VHS / U-matic / 16mm
Color (J H G)
$280.00, $330.00, $495.00 purchase, $50.00 rental
Gives a glimpse into the lives of Russians of all ages with interests and concerns similar to citizens of the United States. Features an American documentary crew who ask Russians from all walks of life - workers, housewives, students and peasants - 'What would you like to say to America.'
Civics and Political Systems; Fine Arts; Geography - World
Dist - NDIM **Prod** - DEVYAT 1986

Russia - the Unfinished Revolution 60 MIN
16mm
New Journal Series
B&W (J)
LC FIA68-579
Discusses the thesis that Russia's Revolution is unfinished, since it has not yet come into harmony with the talents of the Russian people. Shows scenes of life in Russia today and presents interviews with leading persons in economics, medicine, science, children's literature and poetry.
Geography - World; History - World
Dist - IU **Prod** - NET 1968

Russia then and now 80 MIN
VHS
Color (G)
$19.95 purchase
Views contrasts of the past and present seen in a journey through the new Commonwealth of Russia, as well as the newly independent republics of the old Soviet Union. Visits the Summer Palace in St Petersburg, the art treasures of the Hermitage. Recalls the past in an exploration of Red Square, the Bolshoi Ballet, the Moscow Circus. Travels to independent Ukraine to visit Kiev, recalls World War II at Yalta and relaxes at a Black Sea resort. Ventures aboard the Trans - Siberian Railroad to Lake Baikal and to meet the reindeer people.
Geography - World; History - World
Dist - FRANCC **Prod** - FRANCC

Russia today - daily life
VHS
CC; Color (I J)
$89.95_#10331VL
Features on - location footage of Russia and its people. Presents discussions with teens from Moscow, St Petersburg and Kiev as they talk about their daily lives.
Geography - World; Psychology; Social Science
Dist - UNL

Russia Today Series

Leisure Time - USSR	12 MIN
Religion in Russia	20 MIN
The Russian Consumer	14 MIN
The Russian Consumer - Rubles and Kopecks	13 MIN
The Russian peasant - the story of Russian agriculture	20 MIN
Women of Russia	12 MIN

Dist - IFF

Russia Under Stalin 29 MIN
Videoreel / VT2
Course of Our Times I Series
Color
History - World
Dist - PBS **Prod** - WGBHTV

The Russian and the Tartar 27 MIN
U-matic / VHS / 16mm
Storybook International Series
Color
Presents the Russian story of a Russian and a Tartar who are traveling together and argue over who will watch the horses. Shows them trying to trick each other throughout the night.
Guidance and Counseling; Literature and Drama
Dist - JOU **Prod** - JOU 1982

The Russian Athlete 50 MIN
BETA / 16mm / VHS
Color
LC 77-702543
Presents a television special from the CTV program Olympiad, which examines the performances of Soviet athletes in Olympic competition.
Physical Education and Recreation
Dist - CTV **Prod** - CTV 1976

The Russian Athlete 50 MIN
16mm / U-matic
Olympiad Series
Color; Mono (J H C A)
$650.00 film, $350.00 video, $50.00 rental
Examines the contributions of the Russians through modern Olympic history. Focuses on their strongest events and the athletes that are recognized as the best.
Geography - World; Physical Education and Recreation
Dist - CTV **Prod** - CTV 1976

The Russian Athlete - Pt 1 25 MIN
16mm / VHS / BETA
Color
LC 77-702543
Presents a television special from the CTV program Olympiad, which examines the performances of Soviet athletes in Olympic competition.
Physical Education and Recreation
Dist - CTV **Prod** - CTV 1976

The Russian Athlete - Pt 2 25 MIN
BETA / 16mm / VHS
Color
LC 77-702543
Presents a television special from the CTV program Olympiad, which examines the performances of Soviet athletes in Olympic competition.
Physical Education and Recreation
Dist - CTV **Prod** - CTV 1976

The Russian Chinese Rupture 29 MIN
Videoreel / VT2
Course of Our Times II Series
Color
History - World
Dist - PBS **Prod** - WGBHTV

The Russian Connection 50 MIN
U-matic / VHS / 16mm
Color (H C A)
LC 81-701009
Tells about the backing of terrorist organizations by the USSR and includes interviews with two members of the PLO. Explains that once the Soviets have trained and aided such groups, they can then require them to carry out actions on their behalf in trouble spots throughout the world without being directly linked to their activities.
Civics and Political Systems; History - World; Sociology
Dist - PHENIX **Prod** - CANBC 1980

The Russian connection - Pt 1 25 MIN
16mm / U-matic / VHS
Color (H C A)
LC 81-701009
Tells about the backing of terrorist organizations by the USSR and includes interviews with two members of the PLO. Explains that once the Soviets have trained and aided such groups, they can then require them to carry out actions on their behalf in trouble spots throughout the world without being directly linked to their activities.
Sociology
Dist - PHENIX **Prod** - CANBC 1980

The Russian connection - Pt 2 25 MIN
16mm / U-matic / VHS
Color (H C A)
LC 81-701009
Tells about the backing of terrorist organizations by the USSR and includes interviews with two members of the PLO. Explains that once the Soviets have trained and aided such groups, they can then require them to carry out actions on their behalf in trouble spots throughout the world without being directly linked to their activities.
Sociology
Dist - PHENIX **Prod** - CANBC 1980

The Russian Consumer 14 MIN
U-matic / VHS
Russia Today Series
Color (J)
Geography - World; History - World
Dist - IFF **Prod** - IFF

The Russian Consumer - Rubles and Kopecks 13 MIN
16mm
Russia Today Series
Color (J H)
LC 70-701844
Shows the progress which has been made over the last twenty years in furnishing better consumer goods to the Russian city dweller, but not to the peasant.
Business and Economics; Geography - World
Dist - IFF **Prod** - IFF 1968

Russian folk song and dance 78 MIN
VHS
Color (G)
$39.95 purchase _ #1107; $59.95 purchase _ #S00129
Presents the performances of four great Russian folk dance troupes. Shows dance from the Ukraine, song, dance and musicians from Siberia, dance from Samarkand, and melodies and dance from northwestern Russia. Tony Randall narrates.
Fine Arts; Foreign Language; Geography - World; Physical Education and Recreation
Dist - KULTUR

Russian folk song and dance 70 MIN
VHS
Color (H C A)
$59.95 purchase
Presents four performances of folk song and dance from the Soviet Union. Includes performances from the Ukraine, Siberia, Samarkind, and northern Russia. Narrated by Tony Randall.
Fine Arts
Dist - PBS **Prod** - WNETTV

Russian - German War Series

Breakout to Berlin	48.30 MIN
The Killing Ground	47.30 MIN
The Politics of fear	48.30 MIN

Dist - CTV

A Russian journey 60 MIN
VHS
Traveloguer collection series
Color (G)
$29.95 purchase _ #QU013
Visits the Soviet Union. Offers historical and geographic highlights.
Geography - World; History - World
Dist - SIV

Russian Language and People 540 MIN
VHS
Color (S) (RUSSIAN)
$980.00 purchase _ #548 - 9555
Meets the needs of the beginning Russian student by combining an introduction to the language with a fascinating journey into Russian daily life. Incorporates footage of Moscow and Leningrad, Soviet films and television programs, and a 15 - part BBC dramatic serial written and filmed in the USSR. Emphasizes 'understanding' Russian, both written and spoken. Each program presents key language structures in everyday situations as it explores the lives and culture of the Russian people. Twenty 25 - minute programs.

Foreign Language; Geography - World; History - World
Dist - FI **Prod** - BBCTV 1983

Russian language and people - good - bye summer - the story
VHS
Color (S) (RUSSIAN)
$499.00 purchase
Follows a group of young Russians as they struggle to fulfill their dreams, ambitions and desires. Stimulates the study of Russian with language that is natural but not too complicated, and a musical accompaniment. Edited from the complete 'Russian Language And People.'
Foreign Language; Geography - World; History - World
Dist - FI **Prod** - BBCTV 1989

Russian Language Series
From Moscow to the Baykal 14 MIN
Moscow and Leningrad 14 MIN
Rest and Leisure in the USSR 14 MIN
Science, technology and art in the USSR 13 MIN
Dist - IFB

Russian Lubok 10 MIN
U-matic / VHS / 16mm
Color (J)
LC 75-713871
Portrays eighteenth century Russian folk art, emphasizing icon and pagan painting. Provides examples of contemporary wood carving and sculpture.
Fine Arts; Geography - World; History - World; Industrial and Technical Education
Dist - CAROUF **Prod** - FMPORT 1971

The Russian peasant - the story of Russian agriculture 20 MIN
16mm
Russia today series
Color (J H)
LC 74-701845
Presents the story of Russian agriculture and the dilemma of her peasants in historical perspective. Uses rare old engravings to show the harsh life under the Tsar. Includes sequences on the revolution, the drive toward collectivization, and the devastation of World War II which show the successes and shortcomings of Soviet agricultural policy.
Agriculture; Geography - World; History - World; Sociology
Dist - IFF **Prod** - IFF 1968

The Russian prison - A separate life 10 MIN
VHS
Magnum eye series
Color (G)
$125.00 purchase, $30.00 rental
Gains rare entry into one of Russia's normally impenetrable prisons. Records prisoners telling their stories - why they are incarcerated, their loved ones who visit too infrequently and the significance of the tatoos which adorn their bodies. Looks at their monotonous daily routine of mining iron which is fiercely regulated by guards, vicious German Shepards and barbed wire. Directed by Gueorgui Pinkhassov. Part of a series by photographers from the Magnum Photo Agency.
Fine Arts; Geography - World; Sociology
Dist - FIRS **Prod** - MIYAKE 1993

Russian Revolution 30 MIN
U-matic / VHS
Historically Speaking Series Part 20; Pt 20
Color (H)
Recounts the tzar's attempts at reform, Russia's 1905 defeat by Japan and the causes of the February Revolution of 1917. Describes the radical demands of the Soviets and Lenin's return.
History - World
Dist - AITECH **Prod** - KRMATV 1983

The Russian Revolution 15 MIN
VHS
Witness to history II series
Color (J H)
$49.00 purchase _ #60104 - 026
Provides an eyewitness view of the downfall of Russia's ancient autocracy and the rise of a Communist state. Shows rare scenes of Lenin from 1918 to 1924, the despair of the famine - stricken peasants in Samara as they pack the local square for cholera vaccinations and handouts of grain. Part of a four part - series. Includes teacher's guide and library kit.
Civics and Political Systems; Education; Fine Arts; History - World
Dist - GA

The Russian Revolution 15 MIN
VHS
Color (I J H)
$49.00 purchase _ #60104 - 026
Witnesses the downfall of the ancient aristocracy of Russia and the rise of the communist state. Includes rare scenes of Lenin from 1918 - 1924. Shows the despair of the famine - stricken peasants in Samara as they pack the local square for cholera vaccinations and handouts of grain. Includes a teachers' guide and library kit.
Civics and Political Systems; History - World
Dist - INSTRU

The Russian Revolution 1917 - 1967 20 MIN
16mm
Screen news digest series; Vol 10; Issue 4
B&W
Presents a timely and penetrating analysis of the origins and objectives, strengths and weaknesses of international communism.
Civics and Political Systems; Geography - World; History - World
Dist - HEARST **Prod** - HEARST 1967

The Russian Revolution and the 50 Years that Followed 16 MIN
16mm
Screen news digest series; Vol 10; Issue 4
B&W
LC FIA68-1665
Analyzes the origins, objectives, strengths and weaknesses of international communism.
Civics and Political Systems; History - World
Dist - HEARST **Prod** - HEARST 1967

Russian Revolution Series
The Bolshevik victory 20 MIN
Last Years of the Tsars 19 MIN
Lenin Prepares for Revolution 22 MIN
Russia in World War I 20 MIN
Dist - FI

Russian right stuff - the mission 60 MIN
Videodisc / VHS
Color (G)
$39.95, $29.98 purchase _ #9988
Covers the arduous training of cosmonauts involved in the space station MIR.
History - World; Industrial and Technical Education
Dist - INSTRU **Prod** - NOVA

RussianAlive series
The General's daughter 65 MIN
RussianAlive videos
Dist - CIORAN

RussianAlive videos
VHS
RussianAlive series
Color (C G)
$300.00 purchase
Presents nine videos supporting the Russian Alive series published by ARDIS, Ann Arbor, Michigan. Covers the Russian alphabet and cases of nouns and adjectives.
Foreign Language
Dist - CIORAN **Prod** - CIORAN 1993

Russians Series
People of Influence 30 MIN
People of the Cities 30 MIN
People of the Country 30 MIN
Dist - LCOA

Russia's deep secrets 50 MIN
VHS
Horizon series
Color; PAL (G)
PdS99 purchase
Accompanies Russian scientists as they attempt to decommission one of 60 nuclear submarines along the coast of arctic Russia. Explores the scientific and logistical challenges of post Cold War submarines. Focusses on the complexity of the technical problems posed by the rest of Russia's submarines.
Industrial and Technical Education; Physical Education and Recreation; Science - Physical
Dist - BBCENE

Rust Repair
VHS
Color (H C A PRO)
$20.00 purchase _ #TP104
Covers surface rust removal and small patchwork as well as installation of steel replacement panels on car bodies.
Industrial and Technical Education
Dist - AAVIM **Prod** - AAVIM 1990

Rustic delights 9 MIN
16mm
B&W (I)
Describes how puppet shows have delighted rural Indian audiences for centuries, especially in Rajasthan and South India. Shows select scenes from the puppet play 'Harischandra' and provides glimpses of behind - the - scene activities of puppeteers.
Fine Arts; Physical Education and Recreation
Dist - NEDINF **Prod** - INDIA

Rutabagas - the Root of Good Eating 14 MIN
U-matic / VHS / 16mm
Color (H C A)
Shows a girl visiting her uncle on a farm and learning how the rutabaga travels from the planting and harvesting in the fields to the processing plant and then to the table.
Agriculture
Dist - MCFI **Prod** - LOCKF 1984

Rutgers
VHS
Campus clips series
Color (H C A)
$29.95 purchase _ #CC0070V
Takes a video visit to the campus of Rutgers University in New Jersey. Shows many of the distinctive features of the campus, and interviews students about their experiences. Provides information on the composition of the student body, professors, academics, social life, housing, and other subjects.
Education
Dist - CAMV

Ruth 14 MIN
VHS / 16mm
Recovery series
(G)
$50.00 rental
Presents Ruth, an 18 - year drug and alcohol addict and frequent prostitute who has finally decided to take responsibility for her own life. Shows how after one relapse, she now has a more realistic understanding of what her recovery will take.
Health and Safety; Sociology
Dist - BAXMED **Prod** - NFBC 1989

Ruth and Jonah
VHS
The Bible - American Sign Language translation series
Color (S R)
Presents an American Sign Language translation of the Old Testament books of Ruth and Jonah. Available on a free - loan basis from the Lutheran Church - Missouri Synod's Deaf Ministry.
Guidance and Counseling; Literature and Drama; Religion and Philosophy
Dist - CPH **Prod** - LUMIS

Ruth Heller language stories series
Presents a four - part series which adapts picture books teaching grammar by Ruth Heller. Includes A Cache of Jewels, Kites Sail High, Many Luscious Lollipops and Merry Go Round.
A Cache of jewels 11 MIN
Kites sail high 11 MIN
Many luscious lollipops 11 MIN
Merry go round 11 MIN
Ruth Heller language stories series 44 MIN
Dist - KNOWUN

Ruth Page - an American Original 58 MIN
U-matic / VHS / 16mm
Color (H C A)
LC 80-701331
Presents choreographer Ruth Page reminiscing about her life. Includes dance sequences.
Biography; Fine Arts
Dist - TEXFLM **Prod** - OTTERP 1979

Ruth Rendell 40 MIN
VHS
Color (H C G)
$79.00 purchase
Features the writer talking with P D James about writing mysteries that involve death and madness. Discusses her work including A Fatal Inversion and A Dark - Adapted Eye.
Literature and Drama; Psychology; Sociology
Dist - ROLAND **Prod** - INCART

Ruth Rubin 52 MIN
U-matic / VHS
Rainbow quest series
Color
Presents Ruth Rubin performing several well - known Yiddish songs.
Fine Arts
Dist - NORROS **Prod** - SEEGER

Ruth St Denis by Baribault 24 MIN
16mm
Color (J)
LC 78-701822
Presents five dances performed by Ruth St Denis filmed in the 1940s and early 1950s by her friend and photographer, Phillip Baribault. Includes White Jade, Dance Of The Red And Gold Saree, Gregorian Chant, Tillers Of The Soil and Incense.
Fine Arts
Dist - UR **Prod** - UR 1978

Ruth Stout's Garden 23 MIN
16mm
Color (A)
LC 76-700419
Journeys into the life of a woman who, from a perspective of more than 90 years, has a great deal to offer young and old on subjects ranging from growing vegetables to growing old.
Health and Safety; Sociology
Dist - MOKIN **Prod** - MOKIN 1976

Ruth Witt - Diamant Memorial Reading - 10 - 4 - 87 120 MIN
VHS / Cassette
Poetry Center reading series
Color (G)
#799 - 629
Features various writers at the Ruth Witt - Diamant Memorial Reading at the Poetry Center, San Francisco State University. Includes readings by Robert Duncan, James Broughton, Rosalie Moore, Mark Linenthal, Shirley Taylor, Christy Taylor, Justine Fixel, Lawrence Fixel, Michael McClure, Gail Layton, and Stephen Witt - Diamant. Introduction by Frances Phillips. Slides of Ruth Witt - Diamant courtesy of Caryl Mezey. Available for listening purposes only at the Center; not for sale or rent.
Literature and Drama
Dist - POETRY **Prod** - POETRY 1987

Rutherford Atom 40 MIN
16mm
PSSC Physics Films Series
B&W (H C)
Uses a cloud chamber and gold foil in a simple alphaparticle scattering experiment to illustrate the historic Rutherford experiment which led to the nuclear model of the atom. Uses scale models to illustrate the nuclear atom and coulomb scattering.
Science; Science - Physical
Dist - MLA **Prod** - PSSC 1961

The Rutherford - Bohr Atom 10 MIN
U-matic
Electron Arrangement and Bonding Series
Color (H C)
Explores Bohr's hypothesis that electrons can occupy only definite energy levels. Discusses the transfer of electrons between energy levels and the relationship between the properties of an atom and its electron arrangement.
Science; Science - Physical
Dist - TVOTAR **Prod** - TVOTAR 1984

The Rutherford Model 10 MIN
U-matic
Structure of the Atom Series
Color (H C)
Examines Rutherford's contributions to atomic theory.
Science; Science - Physical
Dist - TVOTAR **Prod** - TVOTAR 1984

The Rutherford Model of the Atom 16 MIN
U-matic / VHS / 16mm
Color (H C)
Deals with the Geiger and Marsden's experiment on the scattering of alpha particles by a metal foil. Shows that the relationship between the angle of deflection of the deflecting force is a square law.
Science - Physical
Dist - VIEWTH **Prod** - MULLRD

The Rutherford Scattering of Alpha Particles 15 MIN
U-matic / VHS
Experiment - Physics Level 2 Series
Color (C)
$249.00, $149.00 purchase _ #AD - 1079
Reproduces the experimental observations which led to the development of the Rutherford model of the atom. Part of a series of videos demonstrating physics experiments impractical to perform in a classroom laboratory.
Education; Psychology; Science - Physical
Dist - FOTH **Prod** - FOTH

Ruthie Gordon - folk singer 30 MIN
U-matic
Color
Features feminist folk singer Ruthie Gordon singing a selection of folk songs concerning the struggles of women, third world people and workers to change their situations. Gives background history of the songs and talks about how the songs reflect her experience and feelings as a woman and as a singer.
Fine Arts; Sociology
Dist - WMENIF **Prod** - WMENIF

Ruthmarie Arguello - Sheehan Video 30 MIN
VHS
Tell Me a Story Series
Color (K)
$19.95 purchase _ #W181 - 050
Features Ruthmarie Arguello - Sheehan as storyteller. Includes 'Tommy Knocker And The Magic Fan,' 'The Extraordinary Cat,' 'The Indian Chief And The Baby' and 'Calymba Story - The Lion In The Path.' Part of an eight - unit series.
Literature and Drama
Dist - UPSTRT **Prod** - UPSTRT

Rwandan nightmare 41 MIN
VHS
Color (G)
$325.00 purchase, $65.00 rental
Presents eye - witness accounts of the slaughter in Rwanda. Raises the chilling possibility that the massacre of tens of thousands could have been premeditated. Features correspondent Catherine Bond, who provides historical roots of the conflict between the majority Hutu and minority Tutsi. Interviews key political figures. Produced by Simon Gallimore.
Fine Arts; History - World; Social Science; Sociology
Dist - FIRS

RX for Absenteeitis 15 MIN
U-matic / VHS / 16mm
Color
Presents five techniques for conquering absenteeism.
Business and Economics; Psychology
Dist - DARTNL **Prod** - DARTNL

Rx for attorneys - Choosing and using expert witnesses in medical malpractice cases 50 MIN
VHS
Color (C PRO A)
$95.00 purchase _ #Y104
Illustrates the types of medical malpractice cases in which expert witness testimony must be presented. Explains how plaintiff and defense counsel should select expert medical witnesses and prepare them for giving depositions and testifying at trial.
Civics and Political Systems
Dist - ALIABA **Prod** - CLETV 1989

Rx for Hope 15 MIN
16mm
Color
Explains how non - addictive, anti - depressant drug therapy can be used to treat depression.
Health and Safety; Psychology
Dist - MTP **Prod** - CIBA

Rx Understanding 16 MIN
16mm
Color (H C)
LC FIA66-20
Shows a skillful pediatrician as he works with three children and their mothers. Discusses clinical aspects, such as interview techniques and routines for physical examinations. Also emphasizes the art of dealing with people, especially when offering advice.
Psychology
Dist - OSUMPD **Prod** - OSUMPD 1958

Ryan 26 MIN
16mm
Color
LC 76-701541
Uses the subjective camera technique to portray the systems approach to apprehending, identifying and rehabilitating problem drinking drivers. Follows a problem drinker from the time of arrest through jail and court and eventually to a rehabilitation program.
Health and Safety; Psychology; Sociology
Dist - USNAC **Prod** - SEKCAS 1973

Ryan White Talks to Kids about AIDS 28 MIN
VHS / 16mm
Color (PRO G I J H)
$149.00, $249.00, purchase _ #AD - 1998
Features Ryan White, a 16 year old hemophiliac who contracted AIDS from contaminated blood products he was given to control his hemophilia. Shows how, supported by his mother, he had to contend with schools which did not want him and schoolmates who were coached by their parents shun him. Allows Ryan to share, in an articulate and informative way, his first hand knowledge of AIDS with an audience of teens and pre - teens. Ryan White died in 1990.
Health and Safety; Psychology; Sociology
Dist - FOTH **Prod** - FOTH 1990

Ryan White - Wednesday, March 2, 1988 and Wednesday, April 11, 1990 60 MIN
VHS
Nightline series
Color (H C G)
$14.98 purchase _ #MP6165
Focuses on the plight of young hemophiliac Ryan White, who contracted AIDS from contaminated blood.
Fine Arts; Health and Safety
Dist - INSTRU **Prod** - ABCNEW 1988

Ryoanji 20 MIN
16mm / VHS
Films for music for film series
Color (G)
$75.00 rental, $60.00 purchase
Presents one of a series of films by Lawrence Brose that reconsider the interactive dynamic of sound and image in film. Offers a hand - painted film that creates a visual image of musical glissandi. Features music by John Cage.
Fine Arts
Dist - CANCIN

Ryszard Kapuscinski 45 MIN
VHS
Color (H C G)
$79.00 purchase
Features the writer discussing with Fred Halliday writing about overwhelming change and revolution in the lives of characters. Talks about his works including Shah of Shahs; The Emperor and books based on Poland's history and geography.
History - World; Literature and Drama; Social Science
Dist - ROLAND **Prod** - INCART

Rythmetic 9 MIN
16mm / U-matic / VHS
Color
Shows how animation artist Norman Mc Laren turns the screen into a numerical free - for - all as digits meet in playful encounter, jostling, attacking and eluding one another.
Fine Arts; Mathematics
Dist - IFB **Prod** - NFBC 1956

Rytmisk pigegymnastik - rhythmic gymnastics for girls 16 MIN
16mm
B&W ((DANISH SUBTITLES))
Describes various rhythmic exercises for girls. Includes Danish subtitles.
Foreign Language; Health and Safety; Physical Education and Recreation
Dist - STATNS **Prod** - STATNS 1961

S

S-8 diaries - 1987 - 89 11 MIN
VHS / 8mm cartridge
Color (G)
$25.00 rental
Records a sync sound memento of a 1987 West Coast visit with Buddy K, the desert, Filmforum, Hollywood. Continues with Wildwood 1988, a Sunday winter drive to the Jersey shore and back. Two films on one reel.
Fine Arts; Geography - United States; Geography - World
Dist - CANCIN **Prod** - ADLEST
FLMKCO

S - 8 Logger 8 MIN
16mm
Color
LC 75-703533
Describes the International Harvester S - 8 logger.
Agriculture
Dist - IH **Prod** - IH 1974

S A T Exam Preparation Series
S A T Overview and Test Taking Strategy 120 MIN
Dist - KRLSOF

S A T Overview and Test Taking Strategy 120 MIN
U-matic / VHS
S A T Exam Preparation Series
Color
Education
Dist - KRLSOF **Prod** - KRLSOF 1985

S A T - P S A T math review 120 MIN
VHS
Color (H)
$29.95 purchase
Presents a program for students to review mathematics skills for the Preliminary Scholastic and the Scholastic Aptitude Tests. Offers test - taking techniques, time - saving hints, multiple - choice strategies, and more. Includes study guide.
Education
Dist - PBS **Prod** - WNETTV

S A T - P S A T verbal review 105 MIN
VHS
Color (H)
$29.95 purchase
Presents a program for students to review verbal skills for the Preliminary Scholastic and the Scholastic Aptitude Tests. Offers test - taking techniques, time - saving hints, multiple - choice strategies, and more. Includes study guide.
Education
Dist - PBS **Prod** - WNETTV

S A T prep video - math edition 60 MIN
VHS
Color (H)
$19.95 purchase
Uses an interactive format to help students prepare for the mathematics portion of the Scholastic Aptitude Test. Discusses strategies for specific questions, test - taking techniques, reviews appropriate areas of knowledge, and more. Hosted by Fran Levin.
Education
Dist - PBS **Prod** - WNETTV

S A T prep video - verbal edition 60 MIN
VHS
Color (H)
$19.95 purchase
Uses an interactive format to help students prepare for the verbal portion of the Scholastic Aptitude Test. Discusses strategies for specific questions, test - taking techniques, reviews appropriate areas of knowledge, and more. Hosted by Fran Levin.
Education
Dist - PBS **Prod** - WNETTV

S A T - T V review 120 MIN
VHS
Color (H C A)
$79.95 purchase _ #CPS100V
Presents a video review course for students preparing to take or retake the Scholastic Aptitude Test - S A T. Reviews relevant math and verbal skills, including arithmetic reasoning, fractions, decimals, whole numbers, vocabulary, synonyms, and more. Includes a workbook. Additional copies of the workbook are available at extra charge.
Education
Dist - CAMV

S - E - X 30 MIN
VHS
Color (J H)
$59.95 purchase _ #AH45178
Examines the choices young men and women must make regarding sexual activity. Emphasizes the risk of AIDS as a major issue.
Guidance and Counseling; Health and Safety
Dist - HTHED **Prod** - PBS

S - E - X 30 MIN
VHS
Soapbox With Tom Cottle Series
Color (G)
$59.95 purchase _ #SBOX - 402
Provides teenagers' views about sexuality. Shows that virginity and readiness for sex are their main concerns. Suggests that many teenagers are uncomfortable about discussing sexual matters with their parents. Hosted by psychologist Tom Cottle.
Guidance and Counseling; Health and Safety; Psychology; Sociology
Dist - PBS **Prod** - WGBYTV 1985

S - expressions 50 MIN
U-matic / VHS
Computer languages series; Pt 1
Color
Discusses S - expressions and the functions which operate on them in computer languages.
Computer Science; Industrial and Technical Education; Mathematics
Dist - MIOT **Prod** - MIOT

S is for Science 26 MIN
U-matic / VHS
Color (G)
$249.00, $149.00 purchase _ #AD - 1830
Looks at methods being used to reverse the decline in science education. Considers high - tech museums, new technologies like interactive videodiscs and laser scanners, and the Network for Excellence in Teaching Science, which shows teachers how to teach science.
Computer Science; Education; Psychology; Science
Dist - FOTH **Prod** - FOTH

S is for Single Parent 8 MIN
16mm
ABC's of Canadian Life Series
Color
Looks at the men and women who raise their children alone and the many difficulties they face in terms of finances, finding adequate housing and daycare, and coping with loneliness.
Geography - World; Sociology
Dist - UTORMC **Prod** - UTORMC

S is for soybean 14 MIN
U-matic / 16mm / VHS
Food from A to Z series
Color (P I)
$325.00 purchase
Examines the economic value of soybeans and their wide variety of uses as a human and animal food, and in producing industrial products such as plastics.
Agriculture; Social Science
Dist - HANDEL **Prod** - HANDEL 1989

S, L, R
U-matic / VHS
Educational Video Concepts for Early Childhood Language Development 'Series
Color
English Language
Dist - ECCOAZ **Prod** - ECCOAZ

S - M 50 MIN
16mm
B&W (C A)
Presents a documentary about a real world of deviant sex hidden behind artificial taboos.
Psychology; Sociology
Dist - GROVE **Prod** - GROVE

The S M E D system 40 MIN
Slide / VHS
Color (A PRO IND)
$749.00 purchase _ #V5 - 721, #S5 - 721
Explains the Single - Minute Exchange of Die, or SMED, concept as created by Shigeo Shingo. Covers the background, theory, and four conceptual stages of SMED, and applies it to various situations. Includes facilitators' guides.
Business and Economics
Dist - PRODUC **Prod** - PRODUC

'S no dance 20 MIN
16mm
Color (G)
$45.00 rental
Looks at how a single instant can hold all time within it by evoking a timeless quality through gentle movements. Presents mysterious plays of light and wind in still scenes. Made between 1976 and 1981.
Fine Arts
Dist - CANCIN **Prod** - WHITDL

S - Offset Change Cheeks - same Depth 22 MIN
BETA / VHS
Color (IND)
Presents a mechanical layout method of drawing an S - offset when the cheek dimensions change size.
Industrial and Technical Education; Psychology
Dist - RMIBHF **Prod** - RMIBHF

S - Offset same Size Cheeks - same Size Openings 16 MIN
VHS / BETA
Color (IND)
Presents a mechanical layout method of drawing an accurate O gee curve for an S - offset.
Industrial and Technical Education; Psychology
Dist - RMIBHF **Prod** - RMIBHF

S Sound 14 MIN
VHS / U-matic
I - Land Treasure Series
Color (K)
English Language
Dist - AITECH **Prod** - NETCHE 1980

S - TREAM - SS - SS - ECTION - S - ECTIONED 42 MIN
16mm
Color (C)
$975.00
Experimental film by Paul Sharits.
Fine Arts
Dist - AFA **Prod** - AFA 1970

S W L A 8 MIN
16mm
Color (H C A)
LC 70-713816
Presents an abstract interpretation of the Industrial area of Southwest Los Angeles. Includes music which emphasizes the continual activity and the ceaseless pulsation of modern machinery.
Business and Economics; Geography - United States; Social Science; Sociology
Dist - CFS **Prod** - THOMPR CFS 1971

Sa - I - Gu - from Korean women's perspectives 39 MIN
VHS
Color (G)
$150.00 purchase, $75.00 rental
Explores the embittering effect of the Rodney King verdict rebellion on a group of Korean American women shopkeepers. Underscores the shattering of the American Dream while taking the media to task for playing up the 'Korean - Black' aspect of the rioting. Reveals that these women, rendered voiceless and invisible by mainstream media, suffered more than half of the material losses in the conflict. Written and directed by Dai Sil Kim - Gibson and co - directed by Christine Choy. Produced by Christine Choy, Elaine Kim and Dai Sil Kim - Gibson.
Sociology
Dist - CROCUR

Sa Sa Di 29 MIN
Videoreel / VT2
Changing rhythms series
Color
Presents Sa Sa Di, a group of nine instrumentalists, ranging from flugelhorn to electric piano, performing the instrumental piece, 200, Freddie's Dead and other selections.
Fine Arts; History - United States
Dist - PBS **Prod** - KRMATV

Saar 28 MIN
16mm / VHS
Color (G)
$60.00, $75.00 rental, $250.00 purchase
Entertains with a dinner party of food, music and memories when six women of diverse African - Canadian ancestry gather for a night with the girls. Evolves into a ritual celebration, somewhat related to 'saar', an East African women's cleansing ritual.
Sociology
Dist - WMEN **Prod** - WSELIN 1994

Sabato Fiorello 9 MIN
16mm
Color (C A)
LC 72-702044
Features a surrealist who use the underpinnings of the old art movement to rationalize his compulsion for collecting thousands of unwanted objects to furnish his house. Roams about the rooms of a cluttered mansion, while its artist - owner engages in a one - way conversation with the viewer, asking him if he believes in his own reality.
Fine Arts; Psychology
Dist - CFS **Prod** - CFS 1971

The Sabbath 18 MIN
VHS
Color (K P I)
$29.95 purchase _ #832
Presents four animated and live action shorts to raise questions and stimulate discussion on a variety of topics related to the Jewish Sabbath.
Religion and Philosophy; Sociology
Dist - ERGOM **Prod** - ERGOM

The Sabbath bride 52 MIN
VHS
Color (G)
$90.00 purchase
Defines Shabbat as a cherished observance that provides a sanctuary from the stresses and strains of the work week; a legacy passed from one generation to the next; and a symbol of the enduring strength of Judaism. Follows the order of a traditional Shabbat in London. Produced and directed by Naomi Gryn.
Religion and Philosophy; Sociology
Dist - NCJEWF

Sabda 15 MIN
VHS
Color
Presents Dan Reeves' video entry selected from the 1985 Whitney Biennial Film and Video Exhibition.
Fine Arts
Dist - AFA **Prod** - AFA 1986

Sabertooth 9 MIN
16mm
Color
LC 80-701377
Describes the ancient sabertooth tigers' weaponry as evidenced by remains found in tar pits. Discusses the weaponry of today's cats and raises the question of man's aberrant use of weapons.
Science - Natural
Dist - HARTK **Prod** - HARTK 1980

Sabina Lietzmann 29 MIN
U-matic
Foreign Assignment - U S a Series
Color
Interviews a West German correspondent who covers the United States for Frankfurter Allgemeine Zeitung.
Literature and Drama; Social Science; Sociology
Dist - UMITV **Prod** - UMITV 1978

Sable Island 20 MIN
16mm
Color
LC 74-702419
Tells the story of the animals and people of Sable Island, an area off Nova Scotia composed of nothing but sand and grass.
Geography - World
Dist - FI **Prod** - DALHSU 1973

Sabotage 77 MIN
BETA / VHS
B&W
Tells how the manager of a small British cinema is suspected of disrupting the supply of electricity to the city and setting off a time bomb. Directed by Alfred Hitchcock.
Fine Arts
Dist - VIDIM **Prod** - UNKNWN 1936

Sabu and the Magic Ring 62 MIN
16mm
Color (I J)
Tells of Sabu, the Caliph's elephant boy, who finds a ring which he need only rub to summon a huge genie ready to answer his every wish.
Literature and Drama
Dist - CINEWO **Prod** - CINEWO 1957

SAC Command Post 20 MIN
16mm
Color
LC 74-706229
Presents physical characteristics of the Strategic Air Command's air defense and communications network. Points out the command post's control over SAC operations during peacetime and in event of enemy air attack.
Civics and Political Systems; Social Science
Dist - USNAC **Prod** - USAF 1966

SAC Numbered Air Forces - this is the 8th Air Force 13 MIN
16mm
Color
LC 74-706231
Explains the mission of the 8th Air Force, a major arm of the Strategic Air Command. Reviews its missile and aircraft inventory and shows the readiness of its personnel and equipment.
Civics and Political Systems
Dist - USNAC **Prod** - USAF 1967

Sacajawea 24 MIN
U-matic / VHS
Young people's specials series
Color
Tells the true story of the young Indian girl who guided the Lewis and Clark Expedition.
Fine Arts; History - United States; Social Science
Dist - MULTPP **Prod** - MULTPP

Sacajawea 18 MIN
16mm / VHS
Color (I J)
$425.00, $385.00 purchase, $45.00 rental _ #C - 532
Tells the story of Sacajawea, an explorer who served as a guide, provider, translator, chef and ambassador for the Lewis and Clark Expedition. Uses the voice of a childhood friend with whom Sacajawea was captured at the age of 12. Traces Sacajawea's journey from the eastern United States, over the plains and mountains of middle and western America to the Pacific. Produced by Neil Affleck.
Geography - United States; History - United States; History - World; Social Science
Dist - ALTSUL

Sacco and Vanzetti
U-matic / VHS
Color (J C I)
Presents an account of the controversial arrest, trial and eventual execution of two anarchists in the 1920's.
Civics and Political Systems
Dist - GA **Prod** - GA

Sachiyo Ito, Ritha Devi and Sun Ock Lee 30 MIN
U-matic / VHS
Eye on dance - third world dance, beyond the white stream series
Color
Looks at ethnic dance. Discusses how members of other cultures see ethnic dances.
Fine Arts
Dist - ARCVID **Prod** - ARCVID

The Sacrament of baptism - Tape 3 20 MIN
VHS
Journeys in faith - Volume II
Color (J H C G A R)
$29.95 purchase, $10.00 rental _ #35 - 8120 - 2076
Examines the Lutheran doctrine behind the sacrament of baptism. Produced by Seraphim.
Religion and Philosophy
Dist - APH

Sacrament Series
Baptism - sacrament of belonging 10 MIN
Penance - Sacrament of Peace 11 MIN
Dist - FRACOC

The Sacraments of the altar - Tape 2 20 MIN
VHS
Journeys in faith - Volume II
Color (J H C G A R)
$29.95 purchase, $10.00 rental _ #35 - 8119 - 2076
Examines the Lutheran concept of the sacraments of the altar. Produced by Seraphim.
Religion and Philosophy
Dist - APH

Sacraments Series
Eucharist, Sacrament of Life 10 MIN
Dist - FRACOC

Sacraments - Signs of faith and grace series
Anointing of the sick - Part 8 30 MIN
Baptism - Part 5 30 MIN
Confirmation - Part 6 30 MIN
The Eucharist - Part 2 30 MIN
Holy orders - Part 4 30 MIN
A Look at the sacraments - Part 1 30 MIN
Marriage - Part 3 30 MIN
Penance - Part 7 30 MIN
Dist - CTNA

Sacred again - Jews in Berlin 10 MIN
VHS
Magnum eye series
Color (G)
$125.00 purchase, $30.00 rental
Interviews five Jews who are seeking their place in post - Wall Berlin, the fall of which gave rise not only to a unified German national pride, but to a resurgence of neo - Nazism and intolerance. Tells the stories of two survivors of the concentration camps, assaults by neo - Nazis and of finding Jewish gravemarkers vandalized. Three younger Jews descibe the new prejudice; their efforts to enlighten and change the future of the united Germany; and the new sense of Jewish identity, solidarity and strength emerging. Directed by Thomas Hoepker. Part of a series by photographers from the Magnum Photo Agency.
Fine Arts; History - World; Sociology
Dist - FIRS **Prod** - MIYAKE 1993

The Sacred art of Tibet 28 MIN
16mm
Color (G)
$40.00 rental
Reflects the basic tenets of northern Mahayana Buddhism. Consists of a living or 'experiential' form merging with mantras and ritual music on the soundtrack. Tarthang Tulku, a Tibetan Lama, was the advisor.
Fine Arts; Religion and Philosophy
Dist - CANCIN **Prod** - JORDAL 1972

Sacred buffalo people 60 MIN
VHS / U-matic
Color (G)
$59.95 purchase, $35.00 rental
Looks at the relationship between the Indian of the Northern Plains and the buffalo. Weaves together traditional beliefs, history, and modern reservation humor. Features Indian park rangers, wildlife managers, traditional storytellers and dancers.
Social Science
Dist - NAMPBC

The Sacred Circle 30 MIN
U-matic
Native Religious Traditions Series
(H C A)
Shows that a sense of cycles underlies the attitudes of Plains Indians regarding creation of the earth and the role of mankind in creation and that this is the spiritual basis for religious practice.
Social Science
Dist - ACCESS **Prod** - ACCESS 1980

The Sacred Circle - Recovery 30 MIN
U-matic
Native Religious Traditions Series
(H C A)
Describes how Native religious practice and thought was suppressed with the movement of Christian society into the West. However, Native people have continued to make a variety of efforts to recover and preserve their religious traditions.
Social Science
Dist - ACCESS **Prod** - ACCESS 1980

Sacred games 59 MIN
VHS / 16mm
Color (C G)
$995.00, $410.00 purchase, $70.00 rental _ #11378, #37901
Reveals that every year, in a small village in the highlands of Chiapas in Southern Mexico, thousands of Maya Indians gather to celebrate Carnival. Discloses that the Chamula people call their Carnival the 'festival of games,' the most spectacular, popular and costly festival of their ritual calendar. The pageant merges Roman Catholicism with ancient Mayan rites. Documents the complex, week - long activities, focusing on one man's experiences as a ritual leader during the nonstop parading, dancing and feasting. Produced by Thor Anderson.
Geography - World; History - World; Religion and Philosophy; Social Science; Sociology
Dist - UCEMC

Sacred grounds
VHS
Color (G)
$19.95 purchase _ #EK066
Visits mystic lands and sacred temples where Indian spirits and gods dwell. Looks at the spiritual secrets of ancient Native Americans.
Social Science
Dist - SIV

Sacred music and sacred dance 75 MIN
VHS / BETA
Color; PAL (G)
PdS18, $36.00 purchase
Features monks from Drepung Loseling Monastery, India, in Barnstaple, England, June 1989.
Fine Arts; Religion and Philosophy
Dist - MERIDT

Sacred symmetry video - a relaxing journey to an inner world 60 MIN
VHS
Color (G)
$24.95 purchase _ #V - SSY
Records the geometric mathematical unfolding through color of a spiritual experience. Includes Alpha - Theta - Delta brain wave tones to enhance deep states of relaxation, inner peace and a feeling of well being.
Religion and Philosophy
Dist - WHOLEL

Sacred Trances in Bali and Java 30 MIN
VHS / U-matic
Color
Shows sacred rituals of Bali and Java in which invisible spirits are brought down to enter the bodies of trancers, who perform supernormal feats such as walking on fire, piercing cheeks with pins and palling on broken glass.
Religion and Philosophy
Dist - HP **Prod** - HP

Sacred Trances of Java and Bali 30 MIN
16mm
Color (A)
LC 75-704182
Focuses on the religious practices of people living in Java and Bali. Describes the function of a horse - trance ritual that combines the basic tenets of Islam with an ancient belief in animism.
Geography - World; Religion and Philosophy; Sociology
Dist - HP **Prod** - HP 1975

Sacrifice and Bliss 58 MIN
Cassette / VHS
Power of Myth Series
Color (G)
$29.95, $9.95 purchase _ #XVSB, XASB
Focuses on the sacrifices women make to society on behalf of their children. Part of the Power Of Myth series featuring Joseph Campbell.
Literature and Drama; Religion and Philosophy; Sociology
Dist - GAINST **Prod** - PBS

Sacrifice and bliss 60 MIN
VHS
Moyers - Joseph Campbell and the power of myth series
Color (G)
$39.95 purchase _ #TWOM - 104
Interviews the late mythological scholar Joseph Campbell on the concepts of sacrifice and bliss. Reveals Campbell's views that sacrifice symbolizes the necessity for rebirth. Emphasizes his view that all people need to find their 'bliss,' or their true place in the world.
Religion and Philosophy; Sociology
Dist - PBS

Sacrifice and Bliss
VHS / Cassette
Power of Myth Series
(G)
$29.95, $9.95 purchase
Features Joseph Campbell and Bill Moyers.
Literature and Drama; Religion and Philosophy
Dist - BKPEOP **Prod** - MFV

Sacrifice and bliss
VHS
Power of myth series
Color (G)
$29.95 purchase
Presents 'Sacrifice And Bliss,' the fourth part of the 'Power Of Myth' series with the late Joseph Campbell and Bill Moyers.

Religion and Philosophy
Dist - PBS **Prod** - WNETTV

Sacrifice and bliss, vol 4 60 MIN
VHS
Power of Myth series
Color (G)
$29.95 purchase _ #685
Features storyteller Joseph Campbell who describes the role of sacrifice in myth, which symbolizes rebirth, and the significance of sacrifice in relationships. Part of a six - part series on Joseph Campbell with introductions by Bill Moyers.
Literature and Drama; Religion and Philosophy
Dist - YELMON **Prod** - PBS

Sacrifice and shortages 30 MIN
VHS
America in World War II - The home front series
Color (G)
$49.95 purchase _ #AWWH - 103
Documents the successes of the U S Navy in its Pacific battles, as well as the Soviets' defense against Hitler's assaults. Relates how rationing and even recycling became necessary in the U S as stepped - up military production created shortages of some basic items. Shows that Americans took it all in good spirits. Narrated by Eric Severeid.
History - United States
Dist - PBS

Sacrificial Burnings 40 MIN
U-matic
Color
Explores how patriarchal authority vested in the institutions of Church, State and Marriage has suppressed dissident female voices.
Sociology
Dist - WMENIF **Prod** - WMENIF

Sacrified Youth 95 MIN
VHS
Color (G) (MANDARIN CHINESE (ENGLISH SUBTITLES) (CHINESE SUBTITLES))
$45.00 purchase _ #1109A
Presents a Mandarin Chinese language movie produced in the People's Republic of China.
Fine Arts; Geography - World; Literature and Drama
Dist - CHTSUI **Prod** - CHTSUI

The Sacroiliac, Buttock and Hip 30 MIN
VHS / U-matic
Cyriax on Orthopaedic Medicine Series
Color
Examines the sacroiliac, buttock and hip, covering the sign of the buttock, gluteal bursitis, psoas bursitis, osteoarthrosis, rheumatoid arthritis, loose body, hamstrings and rectus femoris.
Health and Safety; Science - Natural
Dist - VTRI **Prod** - VTRI

Sad, bad and mad 50 MIN
VHS
Trial series
Color; PAL (H C A)
PdS99 purchase; Available in the United Kingdom or Ireland only
Documents the multifarious duties of Neil Allan, a procurator fiscal for the Scottish courts. Presents Allan opposing bail in Edinburgh's Sheriff Court one day, and then prosecuting in the Summary Trial Court the next. Fifth in a series of five programs filmed by the BBC in the Scottish courts.
Civics and Political Systems
Dist - BBCENE

Sad Clowns 27 MIN
16mm
History of the Motion Picture Series
B&W
Pictures styles and techniques that made Charlie Chaplin, Buster Keaton and Harry Langdon great comedians.
Fine Arts
Dist - KILLIS **Prod** - SF 1960

Sad Song of Touha 12 MIN
16mm
B&W
Comments on the poverty and desperation of street performers, jugglers, contortionists and fire eaters. Filmed in one of the poorest sections of Cairo.
Geography - World; Sociology
Dist - ICARUS **Prod** - ICARUS 1971

Sad Song of Yellow Skin 58 MIN
16mm / U-matic / VHS
Color
LC 76-710935
Presents a different view of Saigon, as seen by three young Americans working for peace in a city where bombs seldom fall, but all of life is shaped by decades of war. Includes nostalgic Vietnamese street ballads and close - up views of the people of Saigon, emphasizing the children.
Geography - World; Psychology; Sociology
Dist - FI **Prod** - NFBC 1970

Sadako and the thousand paper cranes 30 MIN
16mm / VHS
Color (P I J G) (FRENCH)
$595.00, $195.00 purchase
Adapts the classic children's story published by Canadian author Eleanor Coerr in 1977. Tells the true story of Sadako Sasaki, a young Japanese girl on the threshold of adolescence, who developed leukeumia in 1955, the effects of radiation from the bombing of Hiroshima. While hospitalized, her closest friend reminded her of the Japanese legend that if she folded a thousand paper cranes, the gods might grant her wish to be well again. Features Liv Ullmann as narrater, solo guitar music performed by George Winston, artwork by Ed Young, produced and directed by George Levenson.
History - World; Literature and Drama; Sociology
Dist - INDEMO **Prod** - INDEMO 1990

Sadat - the presidency and the legacy 26 MIN
VHS
Color (H C T A)
$49.95 purchase _ #S01061
Profiles the life of the late Egyptian president Anwar Sadat. Focuses on his presidency and key role in world events such as the Camp David accords.
Geography - World; History - World
Dist - UILL **Prod** - JOU
JOU

Sadat's Eternal Egypt 45 MIN
U-matic / VHS / 16mm
Color (H C)
LC 80-701931
Examines the treasures that remain from the reign of the Pharoahs. Presents Egyptian president Anwar Sadat reflecting on the society and people who produced these works of art. Narrated by Walter Cronkite.
Geography - World; History - World
Dist - CAROUF **Prod** - CBSTV 1980

Saddam Hussein - defying the world 58 MIN
VHS
Color (J H C)
$250.00 purchase
Shows how every picture of Saddam Hussein on television or in portraits has a special meaning designed to enhance his image as the all - powerful cornerstone of his country. Details his violent family history and the way he murdered his way to power. Illustrates how the violent history of Iraq made that rise inevitable, as well as his subsequent attempts to murder potential rivals. Examines the wars he has conducted, his use of chemical weapons, his genocidal attacks on the Kurds, and his efforts to develop nuclear warheads. Subdivided into five parts.
History - World; Sociology
Dist - LANDMK **Prod** - LANDMK 1993

Saddam's killing fields 52 MIN
VHS
Color (J H G)
$250.00 purchase
Focuses on the Shia Marsh Arabs of southern Iraq, who rose up in vain against Saddam Hussein at the end of the Gulf War. Reveals that more than 300,000 Shia are believed to have been killed and their ancient culture, which goes back 5,000 years, is being systematically wiped out. Features historian Michael Wood who explains the evidence of the decimation.
History - World; Sociology
Dist - LANDMK

Saddle Bronc Clinic 30 MIN
BETA / VHS
Western Training Series
Color
Presents a saddle bronc clinic. Ranges from chute to whistle.
Physical Education and Recreation
Dist - EQVDL **Prod** - EQVDL

Saddle Up 15 MIN
16mm
Color (P I J H)
Reveals the past and present importance of the horse. Illustrates the different kinds of horses and the purposes to which each is best suited. Shows how and why a well - handled horse responds to command.
Agriculture; Physical Education and Recreation; Science - Natural
Dist - MALIBU **Prod** - MALIBU

Saddleback 25 MIN
U-matic / VHS / 16mm
Color (J)
LC 80-700717
Discusses the rescue mission which saved the Saddleback bird from extinction in New Zealand.
Geography - World; Science - Natural
Dist - JOU **Prod** - SPRKTF 1980

Saddling the Finest
BETA / VHS
Color
Demonstrates what to look for in a dressage saddle and how to fit it. Shows how to saddle up.
Physical Education and Recreation
Dist - EQVDL **Prod** - ELCMR

Sadhana - the path to enlightenment 60 MIN
VHS 80 MIN
Color (G)
$39.95 purchase _ #P12
Travels through India to visit extraordinary holy men Bede Griffiths, Bhairav Muni, Swami Shyam and Swami Premananda, who discuss the meaning of life.
Fine Arts; Geography - World; Religion and Philosophy
Dist - HP

Sadie Thompson 97 MIN
35mm / VHS
B&W (G)
$300.00 rental
Adapts the short story by W S Maugham about a prostitute who shares an island with a company of marines and a fanatical minister. Stars Gloria Swanson. Directed by Raoul Walsh. Silent production with orchestral soundtrack.
Fine Arts; Literature and Drama
Dist - KINOIC

Sadler Wells ballerina 18 MIN
U-matic / VHS / BETA
Life in Britain in the forties series
Color; PAL (G H C)
PdS30, PdS38 purchase
Visits a close - knit community of artists. Sits in on dance rehearsals and part of an actual performance. Centers on Patricia Miller, ballerina. Without narration. Part of a five - part series.
Fine Arts; History - World; Social Science
Dist - EDPAT **Prod** - IFF

The Sadrina Project
U-matic / VHS / 16mm
Color
Presents an intermediate level series aimed at those who need to use English when they travel.
English Language
Dist - NORTNJ **Prod** - NORTNJ

Saenghwal toye
VHS
Color (G)
$80.00 _ #42088
Features a video on graphic design.
Industrial and Technical Education
Dist - PANASI

Safari 25 MIN
U-matic / VHS / 16mm
Untamed World Series
Color; Mono (J H C A)
$400.00 film, $250.00 video, $50.00 rental
Explores the people and history of the largest desert in the world.
Geography - World
Dist - CTV **Prod** - CTV 1971

Safari Drums 71 MIN
16mm
Bomba, the Jungle Boy Series
B&W (I)
Fine Arts; Literature and Drama
Dist - CINEWO **Prod** - CINEWO 1953

Safari park 10 MIN
VHS
Stop, look, listen series
Color; PAL (P I J)
Visits a safari park to see rhinoceros, elephants, ostrich, zebras, giraffe, camels, wildebeeste, baboons, lions, tigers, bears and wolves. Part of a series of films which start from some everyday observation and show more of what is happening, how and why. Builds vocabulary and encourages children to be more observant.
English Language; Science - Natural; Social Science
Dist - VIEWTH

Safari Rally 12 MIN
U-matic / VHS
Color
Views an auto rally set in the heart of Africa. Shows how the rough roads and trails test the skill of the most accomplished drivers.
Geography - World; Physical Education and Recreation
Dist - JOU **Prod** - UPI

Safari to Tsavo 28 MIN
16mm
Color
LC 76-702467
Presents a documentary on Tsavo, the largest game reserve in Kenya.
Geography - World; Science - Natural
Dist - RUDDEL **Prod** - RUDDEL 1975

Safari TV series
Presents a 13 - part series on African animals. Looks at the lion, elephant, flamingo, warthog, leopard, hippotamus, zebra, antelope, ostrich, cheetah, rhinoceros and elephants bathing.

Antelope - oryx and waterbuck - Part 9	8 MIN
Cheetah - Part 11	8 MIN
Elephant - Part 2	8 MIN
The Elephant's bath - Part 13	8 MIN
Flamingo - Part 3	8 MIN
Giraffe - Part 4	8 MIN
Hippopotamus - Part 7	8 MIN
Leopard - Part 6	8 MIN
Lion - Part 1	8 MIN
Ostrich - Part 10	8 MIN
Rhino - Part 12	8 MIN
Warthog - Part 5	8 MIN
Zebra - Part 8	8 MIN

Dist - LANDMK **Prod** - LANDMK 1975

Safe Altitude Warning 8 MIN
U-matic / VHS
Color (A)
Explains the safe altitude warning system. Covers Arch 3 and the air traffic controller, MSAW features and functions, including various types of terrain monitoring and system responses to differing circumstances.
Industrial and Technical Education
Dist - AVIMA **Prod** - FAAFL

Safe and Conservative Treatment of Lesions of the Female Breast 32 MIN
16mm
Color
Demonstrates the safe substitution of aspiration for biopsy in fibrocystic mastitis. Includes the ease and simplicity of this maneuver, cosmetic incisions for biopsy of clinically benign solid masses and avoidance of recurrence in scar of radical mastectomy.
Health and Safety; Science
Dist - ACY **Prod** - ACYDGD 1957

Safe and Effective Pest Management 19 MIN
U-matic
Color (J H)
Shows how safe and effective pest management can be provided while still protecting and enhancing the environment. Focuses on controlling the damage plants and animals can cause to dams, aqueducts and levees.
Agriculture; Science - Natural; Social Science
Dist - CALDWR **Prod** - CSDWR

Safe and effective use of low - energy X - rays for the treatment of skin cancer 29 MIN
U-matic / VHS
Color (PRO C)
$395.00 purchase, $80.00 rental _ #C870 - VI - 019
Introduces radiation treatment personnel to the equipment and procedures used for treating skin cancer with low - energy X - rays, with a special emphasis on safety. Outlines the risks involved in using low - energy X - rays and provides an overview of the important principles of radiation physics. Presented by Marcia Shane, Dr Frank Kearly and Robert Morton.
Health and Safety; Science - Natural
Dist - HSCIC

Safe and Sound 17 MIN
VHS
Baby Care Workshop Series
Color (I J H A) (SPANISH)
$175.00 purchase
Helps parents understand how to create a safe environment for an infant. Considers home environment, transportation and accident prevention in daily activities. Spanish version available.
Guidance and Counseling; Health and Safety; Home Economics; Sociology
Dist - PROPAR **Prod** - PROPAR 1988

Safe and sound - choosing quality child care 56 MIN
U-matic / VHS
Color (G)
$250.00, $195.00 purchase, $120.00, $100.00 rental
Shows how to choose child care facilities. Discusses the types of child care and interviews parents who explain how they located a program and why they chose a particular type. Stresses the importance of observing the interaction between children and adults and illustrates positive examples. Addresses the relationship between self - esteem and learning and emphasizes placing a child in a developmentally appropriate program. Provides guidelines for assessing the quality of health and safety practices. Makes the point that high quality day care programs welcome parental questions and involvement. Looks at different in - home care providers and cost for low income parents. Produced by Eyemedia. Available in a shorter version.
Business and Economics; Health and Safety; Home Economics
Dist - BAXMED

Safe and sound in Japan cultural video series - Video 1
VHS
Safe and sound in Japan cultural video series
Color (G) (JAPANESE)
$99.95 purchase _ #CVS - 01
Presents the skits, 'We Don't Have Much to Offer You But Help Yourself' and 'Where Are the Bathroom Slips,' in Part 1 of a five - part series. Highlights the differences between Japanese and American culture, lifestyles and customs in everyday life. Uses simple grammar to show the subtle, non - verbal aspects of Japanese communication. Illustrates differences in levels of speech through conversations between men and women, parents and children, superiors and their staff.
Foreign Language; History - World; Social Science; Sociology
Dist - CHTSUI

Safe and sound in Japan cultural video series - Video 2
VHS
Safe and sound in Japan cultural video series
Color (G) (JAPANESE)
$99.95 purchase _ #CVS - 02
Presents the skits, 'This Is Only a Small Gift but Please Accept It' and 'Would You Like to Go for a Ride,' in Part 2 of a five - part series. Highlights the differences between Japanese and American culture, lifestyles and customs in everyday life. Uses simple grammar to show the subtle, non - verbal aspects of Japanese communication. Illustrates differences in levels of speech through conversations between men and women, parents and children, superiors and their staff.
Foreign Language; History - World; Social Science; Sociology
Dist - CHTSUI

Safe and sound in Japan cultural video series - Video 3
VHS
Safe and sound in Japan cultural video series
Color (G) (JAPANESE)
$99.95 purchase _ #CVS - 03
Presents the skits, 'How Are You Suzuki - Sensei' and 'You Speak Japanese so Well,' in Part 3 of a five - part series. Highlights the differences between Japanese and American culture, lifestyles and customs in everyday life. Uses simple grammar to show the subtle, non - verbal aspects of Japanese communication. Illustrates differences in levels of speech through conversations between men and women, parents and children, superiors and their staff.
Foreign Language; History - World; Social Science; Sociology
Dist - CHTSUI

Safe and sound in Japan cultural video series - Video 4
VHS
Safe and sound in Japan cultural video series
Color (G) (JAPANESE)
$99.95 purchase _ #CVS - 04
Presents the skits, 'Hello, I'm Jane. It's Nice to Meet You' and 'Japanese People Drink a Lot, Don't They,' in Part 4 of a five - part series. Highlights the differences between Japanese and American culture, lifestyles and customs in everyday life. Uses simple grammar to show the subtle, non - verbal aspects of Japanese communication. Illustrates differences in levels of speech through conversations between men and women, parents and children, superiors and their staff.
Foreign Language; History - World; Social Science; Sociology
Dist - CHTSUI

Safe and sound in Japan cultural video series - Video 5
VHS
Safe and sound in Japan cultural video series
Color (G) (JAPANESE)
$99.95 purchase _ #CVS - 05
Presents the skits, 'This Is Yesterday's Homework. Here You Are' and 'Japan Is Interesting, Isn't It,' in Part 5 of a five - part series. Highlights the differences between Japanese and American culture, lifestyles and customs in everyday life. Uses simple grammar to show the subtle, non - verbal aspects of Japanese communication. Illustrates differences in levels of speech through conversations between men and women, parents and children, superiors and their staff.
Foreign Language; History - World; Social Science; Sociology
Dist - CHTSUI

Safe and sound in Japan cultural video series
Safe and sound in Japan cultural video series - Video 1
Safe and sound in Japan cultural video series - Video 2
Safe and sound in Japan cultural video series - Video 3
Safe and sound in Japan cultural video series - Video 4
Safe and sound in Japan cultural video series - Video 5
Dist - CHTSUI

Safe Area Operating Limits for Power Transistors 28 MIN
U-matic
Color
Suggests improvements in methods for measuring and specifying transistor power limits for forward bias operation.
Industrial and Technical Education; Science - Physical
Dist - MTP **Prod** - USNBOS

Safe as houses 30 MIN
VHS
Wall to wall series
Color (A)
PdS65 purchase
Explores brick and the architectural implication of its wide use as the prominent building material for the Georgian age. Examines the vast range of dwelling places and buildings which can be found in the United Kingdom and abroad, and charts their history and evolution. Looks at the different building materials used through the centuries and compares and contrasts British buildings with similar structures found abroad.
Fine Arts; Industrial and Technical Education
Dist - BBCENE

Safe as You Know How 10 MIN
16mm
B&W
Shows unsafe acts and conditions and how they cause accidents. Urges action towards safety.
Guidance and Counseling; Health and Safety
Dist - NSC **Prod** - DUNN 1960

Safe as You make it
16mm / 8mm cartridge
B&W
Contrasts the safety of the high rides at amusement parks with the hazards of the seemingly safe things people encounter daily.
Health and Safety
Dist - NSC **Prod** - NSC

Safe at Home 10 MIN
U-matic / VHS
Color
Shows Bill Kunkel, American League Umpire, who is back in the game after an operation for colorectal cancer. Tells story in his own words and those of his peers, including Reggie Jackson, George Steinbrenner, Carlton Fisk, and Bucky Dent and his wife and children.
Health and Safety; Physical Education and Recreation
Dist - AMCS **Prod** - AMCS 1982

Safe at Home Series

Clowning Around	13 MIN
Late for Supper	13 MIN
What on Earth	14 MIN

Dist - LANDMK

Safe Bicycling 13 MIN
16mm / U-matic / VHS
Color (P I J) (HEBREW)
Illustrates the basic instructions in bicycle safety. Stresses the need for parents to see that children have a properly equipped bicycle in good mechanical working condition.
Foreign Language; Guidance and Counseling; Health and Safety
Dist - IFB **Prod** - CRAF 1959

Safe bicycling in traffic 19 MIN
U-matic / VHS / 16mm
Color (J H C A)
$435.00, $250.00 purchase _ #81522; LC 81-701530
Shows experienced bicyclists how to become a predictable part of the normal traffic flow. Gives examples of anticipating motorists' errors, performing basic traffic manuevers, approaching intersections, riding safely with cars, and riding in a group.
Health and Safety
Dist - CORF **Prod** - IOWA 1981

Safe breaking into closed equipment 7 MIN
VHS / U-matic / BETA
Hazard management safety series
Color (IND G A)
$589.00 purchase, $125.00 rental _ #SAF043
Discusses practical, safe procedures for breaking into process machines or equipment after they have been shut down, isolated and cleared. Reveals that hazards such as corrosive or toxic chemicals, high temperatures, excessive pressures or a combination of all three can occur during such processes. Part of a four - part series on hazard management safety.
Health and Safety; Industrial and Technical Education; Psychology
Dist - ITF **Prod** - GPCV

Safe Child Program - K - 3 - Series
Being your own best friend 35 MIN
The Choice is yours 34 MIN
It's Your Body 29 MIN
Preventing Child Abuse 31 MIN
Speak Up for Yourself 45 MIN
Strangers and Self - Care 27 MIN
Strangers Aren't Bad, They're Just Strangers 27 MIN
Dist - LUF

Safe Child Program - Preschool - Series
All about strangers 28 MIN
Your Body Belongs to You 30 MIN
Dist - LUF

Safe child series
Burns 7 MIN
Fire 8 MIN
Smoke 8 MIN
Dist - FPF

Safe Diving 22 MIN
VHS / U-matic
Offshore Safety Series
Color
Stresses numerous safety measures for diving in offshore oil operations.
Health and Safety
Dist - FLMWST **Prod** - FLMWST

Safe driving in hazardous conditions 17 MIN
VHS
Color (IND)
$295.00 purchase, $125.00 rental _ #TAT10
Demonstrates techniques for preparing for and driving during bad weather. Includes a multiple choice quiz.
Health and Safety
Dist - EXTR **Prod** - TAT

Safe food handling 12 MIN
16mm / VHS / BETA / U-matic
Color; PAL (PRO IND)
PdS115, PdS123 purchase
Discusses the importance of hygiene and cleanliness in the preparation of food for sale to the public.
Industrial and Technical Education; Social Science
Dist - EDPAT

Safe food storage - I thought it would last forever 10 MIN
VHS
Video basics of kitchen safety and organization
Color (H A)
$39.95 purchase _ #CDKIT104V-H
Describes the proper storage of baked goods, dairy - eggs, meats, seafood and produce. Stresses details - holding temperatures, shelf life, optimum storage conditions and how to tell if a food is spoiled.
Health and Safety
Dist - CAMV

Safe for life 18 MIN
VHS
Color (J H C)
$180.00 purchase _ #BO51 - V8
Combines upbeat music and an irreverent, animated talking condom which convinces a reluctant teenage boy to always wear a condom during sex to protect against STDs and AIDS. Stresses that sexual pleasure and responsibility must go together, and refutes the most common excuses for not wearing condoms.
Guidance and Counseling; Health and Safety; Sociology
Dist - ETRASS **Prod** - ETRASS

Safe Handling and Storage of Flammables and Combustibles on Drilling Rigs 25 MIN
Slide / VHS / 16mm
(A PRO)
$150.00 purchase _ #16.1144, $160.00 purchase _ #56.1144
Defines flammables and combustibles and details the procedures needed for proper use and care of such materials on the rig.
Industrial and Technical Education; Social Science
Dist - UTEXPE **Prod** - UTEXPE 1977

Safe Handling of Compressed Gas Cylinders 32 MIN
VHS / U-matic
Color (IND)
Covers safe storage, inspection, transportation and use of metal cylinders that contain various gases under pressure.
Health and Safety; Social Science
Dist - UTEXPE **Prod** - UTEXPE 1978

Safe Handling of Diving Injuries 20 MIN
U-matic / VHS
Color
Depicts the critical aspects of a spinal cord injury. Shows how it should be handled after the diving accident.
Health and Safety; Physical Education and Recreation
Dist - PRIMED **Prod** - PRIMED

The Safe Handling of Enriched Uranium 22 MIN
16mm
Color (H C A)
LC 71-703797
Introduces the concept of nuclear fission and criticality, and explains the reasons for safety procedures that are observed in the handling of enriched uranium and other fissionalbe materials.
Industrial and Technical Education; Science - Physical
Dist - USERD **Prod** - USNRC 1969

Safe Handling of Foals and Yearlings 51 MIN
VHS / BETA
Color
Shows methods of working with new foals to accustom them to haltering, handling, loading, trailering and training.
Physical Education and Recreation
Dist - EQVDL **Prod** - CSPC

Safe Handling of Foods in Quantity 17 MIN
16mm / U-matic / VHS
Color (IND)
LC FIA66-1428
A dietician discussing with her food - service personnel the precautions to take in order to prevent contaminations of cooked foods by staphylococci and salmonells. Shows positive methods used to avoid intestinal illnesses.
Health and Safety
Dist - CORNRS **Prod** - NYSCHE 1964

Safe handling of kitchen tools and machinery 10 MIN
U-matic / VHS / 16mm
It's your responsibility series
Color (PRO A)
$395.00 purchase, $150.00 rental
Outlines sanitation and safety needs to be utilized in the kitchen when hankling tools and machines.
Business and Economics
Dist - ADVANM **Prod** - ADVANM

Safe Handling of Laboratory Animals 14 MIN
16mm
Color
LC FIE67-62
Demonstrates techniques for caretakers in handling laboratory animals. Emphasizes methods of avoiding injury and infection for both caretaker and animals.
Science
Dist - USNAC **Prod** - USPHS 1964

Safe Handling of Lumber and Building Supplies 20 MIN
VHS / 16mm
Color (A IND)
LC 91705374
Outlines safe work practices for handling lumber and building supplies; covers lifting, driving fork lift trucks, housekeeping, and safe use of power tools.
Education; Health and Safety; Industrial and Technical Education
Dist - IFB

Safe Handling of Medical Gases 19 MIN
VHS / U-matic
Color
LC 82-707080
Explains fire hazards associated with storage and handling of oxygen, nitrous oxide and other gases that are commonly used in health care facilities. Discusses safety features of gas dispensing equipment, as well as proper maintenance and testing procedures. Also provides information on correct procedures for the safety of patients in the event of fire in areas where medical gases are used.
Health and Safety
Dist - NFPA **Prod** - NFPA 1982

The Safe Handling of Oxy Fuel Gas Heating Equipment 14 MIN
VHS / U-matic
Steel Making Series
Color (IND)
Includes details on protective clothing, procedures for the safe handling of propane and oxygen cylinders, regulators, hoses and torches. Covers proper start - up and shutdown techniques as well as the procedure to follow in the event of a blow back.
Business and Economics; Health and Safety; Industrial and Technical Education
Dist - LEIKID **Prod** - LEIKID

Safe Harbor 25 MIN
U-matic / VHS / 16mm
Color (H A)
Discusses the effect of fear of nuclear war on teenage depression, leading to drug and alcohol abuse and even suicide. Presents the story of three unemployed school dropouts.
Sociology
Dist - MEDIAG **Prod** - PAULST 1985

Safe Haven 60 MIN
VHS
Color (G)
$59.95 purchase _ #SAHA - 000
Reveals that nearly a thousand Holocaust refugees were able to stay in Oswego, New York during World War II. Tells how the refugees were confined while the Roosevelt Administration tried to decide whether they would be allowed to stay. Uses interviews and archival film footage to tell the story.
History - World
Dist - PBS **Prod** - WXXITV 1988

Safe Home Maintenance 17 MIN
VHS / U-matic
Home Safety and Security Series
Color (A)
Provides tips on home maintenance and a checklist for preparing and fixing equipment and doing large and small jobs. Suggestions include spot checks of tools, equipment, and supplies.
Health and Safety
Dist - IFB **Prod** - ALLAMI 1986

Safe Housekeeping 10 MIN
VHS / 16mm
Color (A IND)
LC 91705447
Promotes safety awareness in hotel housekeepers by showing an experienced housekeeper in a large hotel training a new worker in safe housekeeping practices.
Education; Health and Safety; Psychology
Dist - IFB

Safe in Nature 20 MIN
U-matic / VHS / 16mm
Color (I J)
LC 75-701084
Uses examples of persons lost in the desert and in the mountains in order to show basic techniques of survival when lost in wilderness areas. Emphasizes that three basic principles are staying in one place, making shelter and giving distress signals.
Health and Safety; Science - Natural; Social Science; Sociology
Dist - ALTSUL **Prod** - ALTSUL 1975

Safe in Recreation 15 MIN
U-matic / VHS / 16mm
Color (K P I)
LC 74-703654
Shows typical accidents that can occur during recreation activities in the home, on the playground and out - of - doors. Illustrates precautions and behaviors that could prevent these accidents.
Health and Safety; Physical Education and Recreation
Dist - ALTSUL **Prod** - ALTSUL 1974

Safe in the Water 15 MIN
U-matic / VHS / 16mm
Color (P I J H)
LC 72-701080
Teaches good safety practices in the water, including personal safety, helping others in an emergency and helping yourself in an emergency. Describes safety at beaches, lakes, rivers and pools.
Health and Safety; Physical Education and Recreation
Dist - ALTSUL **Prod** - ALTSUL 1972

Safe journey 13 MIN
VHS
Color; PAL; NTSC (G)
PdS57, PdS67 purchase
Examines the history of commercial airlines from the first scheduled flight in 1919. Follows with a look at the role of Britain's Civil Aviation Authority from its inception in 1972 to present day. Reveals that the Authority's responsibilities include providing National Air Traffic Services jointly with the Ministry of Defense, economic regulation of the civil aviation industry and air safety. Produced by the British Civil Aviation Authority.

Industrial and Technical Education
Dist - CFLVIS

Safe laboratory procedures - Video III 32 MIN
VHS
Introduction to chemical laboratory safety series
Color; PAL (C PRO)
$695.00 purchase _ #V - 4803 - 18110
Shows accident minimization through practical, proven techniques in daily routine. Offers instruction on safely handling everything from waste disposal to glassware breakage. Discusses glassware under general conditions and vacuum and pressure, why it breaks, how to prevent flying shards of glass; safe methods for pouring, pipetting and other chemical transfers; heating methods used with water, steam, oil and metal; overtemperature protection techniques; the use of cryogenics and cold traps; compressed gas safety; emergency equipment and procedures - why and when needed; minimizing waste through stoichiometry and reagent reuse and exchange; conservation efforts. Part three of four parts on chemical lab safety. Technical advisor, George D Heindel.
Health and Safety; Science; Science - Physical
Dist - AMCHEM

Safe lifting 10 MIN
VHS
Color (IND)
$295.00 purchase, $85.00 rental _ #AUR11
Instructs on proper lifting techniques to protect from back injury. Includes a leader's guide. Produced by Aurora.
Health and Safety; Science - Natural
Dist - EXTR

Safe Methods for Canning 25 MIN
U-matic / VHS
Consumer Education for the Deaf Adult Series
Captioned; Color (S)
Discusses methods of home food canning, equipment, and precautions.
Guidance and Counseling; Home Economics; Psychology
Dist - GALCO **Prod** - GALCO 1975

Safe mobility and patient transfer 25 MIN
VHS
Home care training videos - HCTV - series
Color (C PRO)
$125.00 purchase, $60.00 rental _ #42 - 2377, #42 - 2377R
Covers positioning bed - confined patients, transfer of patients to wheelchair, toilet or bathtub. Shows how to use body mechanics to properly lift patients. Discusses the use of mobility to improve circulation and avoid pressure sores and the appropriate use of simple motion exercises. Includes instructional guide for review and testing and meets OBRA federal regulations. Part of a five - part series training home health aides in essential skills and teaching basic skills to nursing students.
Health and Safety; Physical Education and Recreation; Science - Natural
Dist - NLFN **Prod** - NLFN

Safe Operation of a Battery Charger 13 MIN
VHS / 16mm
Kirkwood Community College Auto Mechanics Series
(G PRO)
$68.50 purchase _ #KTI49
Shows how to safely operate a battery charger.
Industrial and Technical Education
Dist - RMIBHF **Prod** - RMIBHF

Safe Operation of Farm Tractors 14 MIN
16mm / U-matic / VHS
Color (J)
LC 73-701077
Outlines a daily service routine which helps to insure a safe tractor. Shows the use of protective equipment, road and field hazards, hydraulics and necessary skills to become a certified operator.
Agriculture
Dist - CORNRS **Prod** - CORNRS 1973

Safe Operation of the Backhoe and Bulldozer 14 MIN
U-matic / VHS / 16mm
Color (H C A)
LC 81-700684
Emphasizes service checks and operative procedures for the backhoe and bulldozer.
Health and Safety; Industrial and Technical Education
Dist - CORNRS **Prod** - CUETV 1977

Safe operation of the forklift truck 30 MIN
VHS / U-matic / BETA
Color (IND G A)
$622.00 purchase, $150.00 rental _ #SAF015
Teaches forklift safety. Includes pre - trip examination, operating forklifts in warehouses, trucks and box cars, on loading docks, ramps and on the ground. Illustrates proper lifting procedures and discusses visual, written and weekly checks.
Health and Safety; Psychology
Dist - ITF **Prod** - BNA

Safe operations 20 MIN
VHS
Hazmat emergency series
Color (IND PRO)
$265.00 purchase
Presents one of three videos in the Hazmat Emergency series. Teaches safe procedures during on - site operations and the importance of pre - incident planning and continuous size - up. Shows how an effective command system operates at the incident scene and how control zones are established. Also reveals the dangers involved in search and rescue operations, safety concerns at a hazmat incident and the importance of good communications while using protective equipment.
Health and Safety; Social Science
Dist - JEWELR

A Safe place for children 10 MIN
VHS / 16mm
Emotional factors affecting children and parents in the hospital series
Color (C A)
LC 81-701487
Presents a psychologist who looks at the activities on orthopedic day in a clinic waiting room and helps the children there explore their fantasies about the plaster casts they've placed on dolls. Shows the children learning how the noisy cast - cutting machine operates as a doctor saws the casts off their dolls.
Health and Safety; Sociology
Dist - LRF **Prod** - LRF 1979

Safe Practices in Marine and Offshore Drilling and Workover 27 MIN
VHS / U-matic
Color (IND) (SPANISH)
A Spanish language version of Safe Practices In Marine And Offshore Drilling And Workover.
Business and Economics; Health and Safety; Industrial and Technical Education; Social Science
Dist - UTEXPE **Prod** - UTEXPE

Safe Practices in Well Drilling and Workover 30 MIN
U-matic / VHS
Color (IND A PRO) (SPANISH)
$150.00 purchase _ #16.1132, $160.00 purchase _ #56.1132
Introduces new personnel to many of the techniques and components of land rotary drilling and workover rigs. Explains safe procedures to be used.
Health and Safety; Industrial and Technical Education; Social Science
Dist - UTEXPE **Prod** - UTEXPE 1977

Safe rescues in confined spaces 13 MIN
VHS
Color (G A PRO)
$59.99 purchase _ #V2400GA
Emphasizes the importance of planning for possible accidents and providing written procedural policies in case of confined - space mishaps. Demonstrates a suggested four - part procedure that includes assessing the site, planning the procedure to be followed, preparing for the procedure and carrying out the procedure, following policy as written.
Health and Safety
Dist - WAENFE

A Safe ride on your school bus 14 MIN
16mm
Color (K P I)
LC 79-714782
Reviews safety and courtesy standards for school bus use. Suggests practices for safe walking to the bus stop, waiting for the bus, boarding, riding and leaving the bus. Shows driver training and bus maintenance.
Health and Safety
Dist - MMP **Prod** - MMP 1970

Safe science - lab safety awareness 40 MIN
VHS
CC; Color (J H)
$135 purchase_#10106VL
Teaches methods of safe science laboratory behavior and prevention of accidents. Includes lessons on recognizing hazards; coping with emergencies; putting out a fire; and the effects of acid and electricity on people. Comes with interactive video quizzes; a teacher's guide with lesson plans; student activities; discussion questions; quizzes; a set of blackline masters; and a supplementary maintenance guide for teachers.
Science
Dist - UNL

Safe sex 28 MIN
VHS / 16mm
Color (PRO G)
$149.00, $249.00, purchase _ #AD - 1260
Explains that AIDS is not just a plague that affects gay men but thatone million heterosexuals will fall victim to the virus by 1991. Concludes that it is better to discuss safe sex frankly with teenagers, and even children, rather than risk them becoming infected with AIDS through ignorance. Features Safe Sex Educator Paula Van Ness of the Los Angeles AIDS Project, a brothel owner who requires the use of condoms, and several heterosexual AIDS patients.
Health and Safety; Sociology
Dist - FOTH **Prod** - FOTH 1990

Safe sex - don't buy the lie 39 MIN
VHS
Color (J H R)
$24.95 purchase, $10.00 rental _ #35 - 8594 - 1518
Challenges the concept of 'safe sex.' Suggests that a casual attitude toward sex has led to many teenagers developing poor self - images and to many unwanted pregnancies.
Health and Safety
Dist - APH **Prod** - GF

Safe sex slut 30 MIN
VHS
Color (G)
$30.00 purchase
Contains a collection of music videos and comedy spots. Includes the title song Safe Sex Slut, as well as Pope, Don't Preach, I'm terminating my Pregnancy; Bad Laws; and The Star Spangled Banner with Scarlot Harlot and the Sisters of Perpetual Indulgence Unincorporated. Shows clips of talk show appearances. Distributed as part of Video Against AIDS by Video Databank.
Fine Arts; Health and Safety; Literature and Drama
Dist - CANCIN **Prod** - LEIGHC 1987

Safe skateboarding 15 MIN
16mm
Color
LC 77-702137
Outlines safety procedures and regulations regarding skateboard use. Includes information on maintenance of the board, riding techniques and protective clothing.
Health and Safety; Physical Education and Recreation
Dist - AMEDFL **Prod** - AMEDFL 1977

Safe skateboarding 15 MIN
U-matic / VHS / BETA
Color; PAL (J H C G)
PdS40, PdS48 purchase
Gives skateboarders advice on maintenance, riding techniques, protective clothing and helmets. Features doctors discussing physical dangers and looks at talented skateboarders.
Physical Education and Recreation
Dist - EDPAT

Safe spaces - drug and alcohol prevention for special needs and drug exposed K - 2 children 27 MIN
VHS
Color (PRO T C)
$95.00 purchase
Presents a two - part staff development video produced by Project Healthy Choice at Bank Street College of Education for educators and trainers working with young special needs and drug exposed children. Examines the impact of alcohol and other drugs on these children, why prevention education is important, explores what 'drug exposed' means, demonstrates skills and strategies for working with these at - risk children and creating classrooms with 'safe spaces' environments for them in Part 1 - Awareness, Skills and Practices. Part 2 - Early Intervention and Family - School Collaboration explores the vital roles of early intervention and collaboration between school and family in drug prevention education for young children.
Education; Guidance and Counseling
Dist - SELMED

Safe stations 18 MIN
VHS
Visual display units series
Color; PAL (IND G)
PdS95 purchase
Instructs supervisors and other managerial professionals on overseeing the implementation of the regulations outlined in new EC legislation. Provides help with putting the requirements into practice. Describes key areas and offers examples for reducing risk. Part of a two - part series to assist businesses in conforming with new EC directives. Includes a booklet and checklist.
Business and Economics; Health and Safety; Psychology
Dist - CFLVIS **Prod** - SCHWOP 1994

Safe summer fun 15 MIN
VHS / U-matic
Pass it on series
Color (K P)
Discusses the summer season, focusing on safety rules and things to do in summer.
Education; Health and Safety; Science - Natural
Dist - GPN **Prod** - WKNOTV 1983

Safe Transport of Radioactive Materials 20 MIN
16mm
Color
Describes radioactivity and shows the comparatively simple transport of unused fuel elements compared to the special means needed for transporting fuel elements under special supervision after they have been used in a reactor. Illustrates the transport of radioisotopes, starting with their preparation and shows some of the many ways in which they are used.
Industrial and Technical Education; Science - Physical; Social Science
Dist - UKAEA **Prod** - UKAEA 1964

Safe use of catheads and air hoists 20 MIN
U-matic / VHS
Color (IND) (SPANISH)
Explains the proper procedures for making a safe lift using a cathead or an air hoist on the drilling or workover rig.
Health and Safety; Industrial and Technical Education
Dist - UTEXPE **Prod** - UTEXPE 1979

Safe Use of Drill Pipe Tongs
U-matic / VHS
Working Offshore Series
Color (IND)
Looks at various roughneck duties associated with drill pipe tongs and emphasizing safety. Covers installation of tongs, safe procedures for work when using wire rope, cleaning and maintenance and inserting tong dies.
Business and Economics; Industrial and Technical Education; Social Science
Dist - GPCV **Prod** - GPCV

Safe use of drill pipe tongs 17 MIN
U-matic / Slide / VHS / 16mm
Color (IND A PRO) (SPANISH)
$150.00 purchase _ #16.1081, $160.00 purchase _ #56.1081
Covers the correct and safe installation, maintenance, and use of drill pipe tongs.
Health and Safety; Industrial and Technical Education; Social Science
Dist - UTEXPE **Prod** - UTEXPE 1978

Safe use of hand tools 18 MIN
VHS / U-matic
Industrial safety series
Color (IND)
Focuses on several aspects of safety in the use of hand tools. Includes need for prior inspection before using any tools, proper use, power tool safety and techniques to avoid electrical shock. Discusses what to do if a fellow worker receives an electric shock.
Health and Safety; Industrial and Technical Education
Dist - LEIKID **Prod** - LEIKID

The Safe use of hydrofluoric acid in the solid - state devices lab 11 MIN
VHS
Color (C G)
$195.00 purchase, $45.00 rental _ #38068
Illustrates in detail the safe handling of hydrofluoric acid - HF. Demonstrates safe practices to prevent exposure. Describes the physiological effects of exposure to HF and shows the necessary materials and procedures for the prompt neutralization of HF in emergency situations. Produced by the University of California - Davis - Instructional Media.
Health and Safety; Science
Dist - UCEMC

Safe Use of Low Energy X - Rays for the Treatment of Skin Cancer 29 MIN
VHS / U-matic
Color (PRO)
Presents advantages and disadvantages of low energy X - rays for the treatment of skin cancer. Gives indications and methods for treatment, and safety procedures. Creates an understanding of the applicability of physics for therapy.
Health and Safety; Industrial and Technical Education; Science; Science - Natural; Science - Physical
Dist - USNAC **Prod** - USNAC

Safe Use of Non - Prescription Drugs 4 MIN
VHS / U-matic
Color
Describes how non - prescription drugs can be useful in relieving ailments.
Health and Safety
Dist - MEDCOM **Prod** - MEDCOM

The Safe Use of Pesticides 21 MIN
16mm
Color
LC FIE64-105
Explains the proper use of pesticides, emphasizing the importance of following instructions on the labels to avoid seizure of crops because of harmful residue.
Agriculture; Health and Safety
Dist - USNAC **Prod** - USDA 1964

Safe work permits 11 MIN
BETA / VHS / U-matic
Hazard management safety series
Color (IND G A)
$589.00 purchase, $125.00 rental _ #SAF044
Looks at generally accepted procedures for issuing safe work permits. Reveals that a safe work permit should guarantee that all safety procedures have been met. Part of a four - part series on hazard management safety.
Health and Safety; Psychology
Dist - ITF **Prod** - GPCV

Safeguard 22 MIN
U-matic / VHS / 16mm
Color
Views the variety of attitudes that workers and management have toward safety matters. Shows the necessity for machine guards and their benefits. Points out that innocent bystanders may be hurt by non - compliance with safety regulations.
Business and Economics; Health and Safety
Dist - IFB **Prod** - MILLBK

Safeguard 22 MIN
16mm / U-matic / VHS
Color (IND A)
$525.00 purchase, $75.00 rental
Compares the attitudes of labor and management regarding the use of machine guards. Does not explain the different machine guards, but dramatizes the importance of using them.
Health and Safety
Dist - IFB

Safeguarding 11 MIN
VHS / 16mm / U-matic
Information Security Briefing Series
Color (A)
Discusses the storage, control, access, reproduction, disposal and transmission of National Security Information. Discusses leaks and precautions to minimize compromise.
Civics and Political Systems
Dist - USNAC **Prod** - USISOO 1982

Safeguarding Military Information 16 MIN
16mm
B&W
LC FIE62-2091
Stresses the importance of safeguarding military information for both military and civilian personnel.
Civics and Political Systems
Dist - USNAC **Prod** - USA 1952

Safeguarding of Machine Tools 17 MIN
16mm / U-matic / VHS
Machine Tool Safety Series
Color (IND)
Health and Safety; Industrial and Technical Education
Dist - NATMTB **Prod** - NATMTB

Safeguarding Our Highways 15 MIN
16mm
Color (H C A)
Describes how steel median guard rail increases highway safety and the role local groups can play in improving area road safety.
Health and Safety; Industrial and Technical Education; Science - Physical
Dist - AIAS **Prod** - AIAS

Safeguarding Your Health 15 MIN
U-matic
Color (A)
Tells employees about precertification of medical treatment and second surgical opinions. Comes with a booklet.
Health and Safety
Dist - VLEARN **Prod** - VLEARN 1986

Safeguarding Your Patient 15 MIN
U-matic / VHS
Color
Reviews basic safety concepts for health care personnel so injuries and accidents to patients can be prevented. Emphasizes the prevention of burns, decubiti, treatment errors and property loss or damage.
Health and Safety
Dist - FAIRGH **Prod** - FAIRGH

Safely Walk to School 12 MIN
16mm / U-matic / VHS
Color (P)
LC 83-700106
Presents guidelines for walking to school safely. Stresses the importance of remembering to look both ways before going into the street and crossing streets and driveways.
Health and Safety
Dist - AIMS **Prod** - AIMS 1983

A Safer Game - a Better Game 12 MIN
U-matic / VHS / 16mm
Football Injury Prevention Series
Color (I J H)
Explains the importance of many different elements of football safety practice and procedure, proper conditioning, good coaching, competent officiating, improved equipment and facilities, and adequate medical precautions and supervision.
Physical Education and Recreation
Dist - ATHI **Prod** - ATHI

A Safer place 20 MIN
VHS
Color (G C)
$89.95 purchase, $35.00 rental
Looks at abuse of the elderly through the experiences of a former abuser and two abuse victims, discussing the emotions involved in finding solutions to the abusive situations.
Guidance and Counseling; Health and Safety
Dist - TNF

A Safer Place to Eat 15 MIN
16mm
Color (A)
LC 77-703415
Points out the dangers of food contamination from several types of bacteria and shows how to prevent contamination by keeping food stored in a cold environment.
Health and Safety; Home Economics
Dist - USNAC **Prod** - USFDA 1976

Safer sex 19 MIN
VHS / 16mm
Color (PRO G)
$149.00, $249.00, purchase _ #AD - 2014
Examines the prevention of STD's, especially AIDS. Features a mother of two, a group of college students, and the director of the STD section of the Center for Disease Control advocating greater awareness of the dangers of unprotected sex, and the advantages of monogamous sex. Discusses the use of condoms and spermicide. Investigates a dating club which offers an AIDS test for screening prospective sex partners. Examines how AIDS has changed social and sexual habits.
Health and Safety; Sociology
Dist - FOTH **Prod** - FOTH 1990

Safer Way Down - Sky Genie 23 MIN
16mm
Color (H C A)
LC 76-701749
Describes the characteristics of the sky genie, a safety device for the controlled safe descent of personnel. Illustrates some of its uses in rescue operations.
Health and Safety; Industrial and Technical Education
Dist - FILCOM **Prod** - USFC 1976

Safer You Series

Bicycle safety	15 MIN
Consumer Decisions	15 MIN
Fire safety	15 MIN
Fitness for everybody	15 MIN
Home Play	15 MIN
How Can I Help	15 MIN
Moving	15 MIN
Pedestrian Safety	15 MIN
Playground Safety	15 MIN
The Real You	15 MIN
Traveling	15 MIN

Dist - GPN

The Safest Way 15 MIN
VHS / U-matic
It's Your Move Series
Color (P)
Shows how David walks to the theater and encounters some hazards at an intersection and a railroad crossing.
Health and Safety
Dist - AITECH **Prod** - WETN 1977

Safetalk - parents and teachers discuss AIDS
VHS
Color (T G)
$195.00 purchase, $50.00 rental
Gathers experts on HIV infection and human sexuality, persons with AIDS and parents of children with AIDs from across the US to assist parents and teachers with the important task of teaching youth to protect themselves from the deadly AIDS virus.
Education; Health and Safety
Dist - NEWIST **Prod** - NEWIST

Safetitudes
VHS / 35mm strip
Color
$96.00 purchase _ #TXSF filmstrips, $186.00 purchase _ #TXSFV VHS
Talks about safety attitudes and deals with listening, asking questions, accident - prone personalities, and common sense. Features action - oriented cartoons.

Health and Safety
Dist - CAREER **Prod** - CAREER

Safety 10 MIN
U-matic
Calling Captain Consumer Series
Color (P I J)
Demonstrates the need to check that products have passed safety standards and to inform the proper agencies or manufacturer if a product is not safe.
Business and Economics; Home Economics
Dist - TVOTAR **Prod** - TVOTAR 1985

Safety 6 MIN
VHS
Color (K P S)
$45 purchase _ #2096VG
Provides a basic introduction to safety and survival for children. Uses an animated story to present information concerning the language and functions of safety signs. Includes a teacher's guide and blackline masters.
Health and Safety; Physical Education and Recreation
Dist - UNL

Safety 20 MIN
VHS / U-matic
Engineering Crafts Series
Color (H C A)
Industrial and Technical Education
Dist - FI **Prod** - BBCTV 1981

Safety
VHS
Color (K)
$14.95 purchase _ #V2914 - 10
Instructs students about safety at home, at school, in the streets and in the water. Includes information about safety on bicycles, in automobiles and with animals.
Health and Safety; Industrial and Technical Education
Dist - SCHSCI

Safety 15 MIN
VHS
Zardips search for healthy wellness series
Color (P I)
LC 90-707999
Presents an episode in a series which helps young children understand basic health issues and the value of taking good care of their bodies. Helps children understand the importance of safety. Includes a teacher's guide.
Education; Health and Safety
Dist - TVOTAR **Prod** - TVOTAR 1989

Safety 6 MIN
U-matic / VHS
Steel Making Series
Color (IND)
Emphasizes the fact that safety on the job is a matter of professional attitude, communications, paying attention and good housekeeping.
Business and Economics; Health and Safety; Industrial and Technical Education
Dist - LEIKID **Prod** - LEIKID

Safety 9 MIN
U-matic / VHS / 16mm
B&W
Depicts the dangers of the electronic environment, showing the causes of electrical shock, how to avoid shock and what to do for a shock victim. Describes how to fight an electrical fire.
Health and Safety; Industrial and Technical Education
Dist - USNAC **Prod** - USAF 1983

Safety 13 MIN
VHS / U-matic / BETA
Pediatrics - physical care series
Color (C PRO)
$150.00 purchase _ #147.2
Presents a video transfer of a slide program which describes factors in growth and development that makes infants, toddlers and preschoolers prone to accidents. Discusses measures to protect them, with emphasis on prevention of strangulation, aspiration and falls. Part of a series on physical care in pediatric nursing.
Health and Safety
Dist - CONMED **Prod** - CONMED

Safety action for employees series

Cleaning with hot water and steam	15 MIN
Fire Protection Awareness	17 MIN
Guide to Industrial Housekeeping	
Handling Compressed Gas Cylinders	24 MIN
Machine Shop Safety	17 MIN
Manual Lifting	19 MIN
Personal Protective Equipment	
Preventing electrical injuries - Part 1	22 MIN
Preventing electrical injuries - Part 2	21 MIN
Working Safely with Scaffolds	19 MIN

Dist - GPCV

Safety Ajction for Employees Series
Handling Flammables and Combustibles 29 MIN
Dist - GPCV

Safety Aloft 20 MIN
U-matic / VHS / 16mm
Color (A)
Highlights the proper use of safety equipment in tower erection. Describes two key components of safety - the Fall Arrester and Life Line.
Health and Safety
Dist - BCNFL **Prod** - OHMPS 1984

Safety and accident prevention - everyone's responsibility 40 MIN
U-matic / Slide / VHS
Color (PRO)
$320.00, $300.00 purchase, $60.00 rental _ #AT17, #4253S, #4253V
Presents a rich array of methods and devices for creating safe environments for geriatric patients. Interweaves real situations with cartoons. Divides into four modules - The Patient Room, The Bathroom, Patient Transport, and Ambulatory Aids.
Health and Safety
Dist - AJN **Prod** - LUMIEL 1981

Safety and basic fundamentals of the engine lathe - Pt I 11 MIN
VHS
Color (J H A G)
$49.95 purchase _ #AM1426
Describes the function of an engine lathe and the operations of which it is capable. Names the main parts and outlines procedures for changing power and spindle speed, adjusting for desired feed and reversing feed. Emphasizes safety throughout. Part one of a two - part series on engine lathes.
Health and Safety; Industrial and Technical Education
Dist - AAVIM **Prod** - AAVIM 1992

Safety and basic fundamentals of the engine lathe - Pt II 13 MIN
VHS
Color (J H A G)
$49.95 purchase _ #AM1427
Looks at the characteristics of various kinds of chucks and tool bits, locating and drilling center holes and mounting stock. Demonstrates procedures for fixing a tool in the holder, locking the holder in position, adjusting the position and running the lathe. Part two of a two - part series on engine lathes.
Health and Safety; Industrial and Technical Education
Dist - AAVIM **Prod** - AAVIM 1992

Safety and basic fundamentals on the engine lathe - Pt 1 11 MIN
U-matic / VHS / 16mm
Metal shop - safety and operations series
Color (J A) (ARABIC SPANISH)
LC 78-704769
Demonstrates the basic safety points and basic processes in engine lathe operation.
Foreign Language; Industrial and Technical Education
Dist - AIMS **Prod** - EPRI 1970

Safety and basic fundamentals on the engine lathe - Pt 2 13 MIN
U-matic / VHS / 16mm
Metal shop - safety and operations series
Color (J A) (ARABIC SPANISH)
LC 72-704770
Demonstrates the basic safety points and processes in engine lathe operation.
Industrial and Technical Education
Dist - AIMS **Prod** - EPRI 1970

Safety and economics 55 MIN
BETA / VHS / U-matic
Color
$400 purchase
Gives advantages over competitive equipments and techniques.
Health and Safety; Industrial and Technical Education
Dist - ASM **Prod** - ASM

Safety and equipment for gas shielded arc welding
VHS / U-matic
MIG and tig welding - spanish series
Color (SPANISH)
Health and Safety; Industrial and Technical Education
Dist - VTRI **Prod** - VTRI

Safety and Familiarization on Radial Arm Drill Press 26 MIN
BETA / VHS
Machine Shop - Drill Press, Radial Drill, Drill Grinder Series
Color (IND)
Industrial and Technical Education; Psychology
Dist - RMIBHF **Prod** - RMIBHF

Safety and Familiarization on the Bridgeport Series I Milling Machine 23 MIN
BETA / VHS
Machine Shop - Milling Machine Series
Color (IND)
Industrial and Technical Education; Psychology
Dist - RMIBHF **Prod** - RMIBHF

Safety and Familiarization on the Bridgeport Series II Milling Machine 21 MIN
BETA / VHS
Machine Shop - Milling Machine Series
Color (IND)
Industrial and Technical Education; Psychology
Dist - RMIBHF **Prod** - RMIBHF

Safety and familiarization on the Clausing Colchester engine lathe 25 MIN
VHS / BETA
Machine shop - engine lathe series
Color (IND)
Industrial and Technical Education; Psychology
Dist - RMIBHF **Prod** - RMIBHF

Safety and familiarization on the horizontal bandsaw 18 MIN
VHS / BETA / 16mm
Machine shop - bandsaw series
(IND)
$100.00 purchase _ #MS12
Familiarizes the student to safety and use of the horizontal bandsaw.
Industrial and Technical Education
Dist - RMIBHF **Prod** - RMIBHF

Safety and Familiarization on the Horizontal Boring Mill 24 MIN
BETA / VHS
Machine Shop - Milling Machine Series
Color (IND)
Industrial and Technical Education; Psychology
Dist - RMIBHF **Prod** - RMIBHF

Safety and familiarization on the kearney and trecher milling machine - Pt 1 22 MIN
VHS / BETA
Machine shop - milling machine series
Color (IND)
Industrial and Technical Education; Psychology
Dist - RMIBHF **Prod** - RMIBHF

Safety and familiarization on the kearney and trecher milling machine - Pt 2 17 MIN
VHS / BETA
Machine shop - milling machine series
Color (IND)
Industrial and Technical Education; Psychology
Dist - RMIBHF **Prod** - RMIBHF

Safety and familiarization on the LeBlond engine lathe 22 MIN
BETA / VHS
Machine shop - engine lathe series
Color (IND)
Industrial and Technical Education; Psychology
Dist - RMIBHF **Prod** - RMIBHF

Safety and familiarization on the South Bend engine lathe 30 MIN
BETA / VHS
Machine shop - engine lathe series
Color (IND)
Industrial and Technical Education; Psychology
Dist - RMIBHF **Prod** - RMIBHF

Safety and Familiarization on the Surface Grinder 33 MIN
BETA / VHS
Machine Shop - Surface Grinder Series
Color (IND)
Industrial and Technical Education; Psychology
Dist - RMIBHF **Prod** - RMIBHF

Safety and familiarization on the vertical bandsaw 25 MIN
BETA / VHS / 16mm
Machine shop - bandsaw series
(IND)
$99.00 purchase _ #MS13
Familiarizes the viewer with safety and use of the vertical bandsaw.
Industrial and Technical Education
Dist - RMIBHF **Prod** - RMIBHF

Safety and instrumentation grounding problems 60 MIN
U-matic / VHS

Instrumentation basics - instrumentation electrical and mechanical ·connections series; Instrumentation electrical and mechanical connections
Color (IND)
Industrial and Technical Education; Mathematics
Dist - ISA **Prod** - ISA

Safety and operation of faceplate turning - Pt 1 8 MIN
U-matic / VHS / 16mm
Wood shop - safety and operations series
Color (J H C A) (SPANISH ARABIC)
LC 70-714079
Covers the basic techniques and safety points to follow in the operation of faceplate turning.
Industrial and Technical Education
Dist - AIMS **Prod** - EPRI 1971

Safety and operation of faceplate turning - Pt 2 12 MIN
VHS / 16mm / U-matic
Wood shop - safety and operations series
Color (J H C A) (SPANISH ARABIC)
LC 74-714080
Covers the basic techniques and safety points to follow in the operation of faceplate turning.
Industrial and Technical Education
Dist - AIMS **Prod** - EPRI 1971

Safety and operation of faceplate turning - Pt I 8 MIN
VHS
Color (J H A T)
$49.95 purchase _ #AM1442
Defines faceplate turning and bowl or dish turning and shows that bowl stock must usually be fastened to a backing block. Shows how to mount the block to the faceplate, locate the center of the stock, fasten stock to the block with glue and paper, mark the stock and cut off excess on the bandsaw.
Industrial and Technical Education
Dist - AAVIM **Prod** - AAVIM 1992

Safety and operation of faceplate turning - Pt II 11 MIN
VHS
Color (J H A T)
$49.95 purchase _ #AM1443
Demonstrates how to mount the faceplate to the spindle and support the assembly with a center. Shows how to install and adjust the tool rest, select proper spindle speed and adjust speed as work progresses. Illustrates holding the tools, working the stock, sanding and finishing a bowl.
Industrial and Technical Education
Dist - AAVIM **Prod** - AAVIM 1992

Safety and operation series

Electrical safety	33 MIN
Large metal power tools	45 MIN
Large wood power tools - I	35 MIN
Large wood power tools - II	35 MIN
Portable wood power tools	35 MIN

Dist - AAVIM

Safety & slaughter 14 MIN
16mm / VHS / BETA / U-matic
Color; PAL (G)
Lists the common factors that cause accidents. Analyzes speeding, driver irritation, driver fatigue, poor road conditions.
Health and Safety
Dist - EDPAT

Safety and substance abuse 11 MIN
BETA / VHS / U-matic
Safety meetings series
Color (G IND)
$495.00 purchase, $95.00 rental _ #WHM1
Discloses confessions about drugs in the workplace, the danger of drugs, and how safety is severely hampered when drugs are present and being used.
Business and Economics; Guidance and Counseling; Health and Safety; Psychology
Dist - BBP **Prod** - BBP 1990

Safety and the Foreman Series

Fact Finding, not Fault Finding	13 MIN
Foresight - not hindsight	10 MIN
What they Don't Know Can Hurt	13 MIN

Dist - NSC

Safety and You Series

Communications	9 MIN
Motivation	9 MIN
Physical Limitations	10 MIN
Physiological Limitations	11 MIN
Psychological Limitations	11 MIN
Supervision	8 MIN
Tools	6 MIN

Dist - FILCOM

Safety and Your Car 20 MIN
U-matic / VHS / 16mm
Color (H C A)
LC 76-700811
Presents race driver Mark Donohue and other noted personalities discussing the differences among street automobiles and demonstrating how these differences affect safe driving. Shows how improper alterations to tires and chassis can have serious results.
Health and Safety
Dist - AIMS **Prod** - SCCA 1976

Safety as We Play 7 MIN
16mm / U-matic / VHS
Starting to Read Series
Color (K P)
No descriptive information available.
Health and Safety
Dist - AIMS **Prod** - ACI 1971

Safety at home 15 MIN
U-matic
Calling all safety scouts series
Color (K P)
Teaches young children how to avoid falls, burns and electrical hazards and how to recognize warning labels.
Health and Safety
Dist - TVOTAR **Prod** - TVOTAR 1983

Safety at home - electricity 20 MIN
16mm / VHS
Color (J H A)
$395.00, $480.00 purchase, $75.00 rental _ #9837
Teaches the safe use of electricity in the home through a series of vignettes.
Health and Safety
Dist - AIMS **Prod** - SANDE 1987

Safety at Play 15 MIN
U-matic
Calling all Safety Scouts Series
Color (K P)
Teaches children about finding a safe place to play, wearing the correct sports equipment, tobogganing safely and being wary of thin ice. Also includes the dangers of retrieving a kite from electrical wires and of chasing a ball into the street.
Health and Safety
Dist - TVOTAR **Prod** - TVOTAR 1983

Safety at School 9 MIN
U-matic / VHS / 16mm
Color (K P I) (SPANISH)
LC 74-702689
Depicts children following practices of safety and courtesy for hall and stairway travel, for lunchtime eating habits, for play in the yard and for drinking fountain use. Illustrates what can occur when students 'forget' their manners.
Health and Safety; Social Science
Dist - AIMS **Prod** - TFBCH 1974

Safety at school 15 MIN
U-matic
Calling all safety scouts series
Color (K P)
Teaches children how to behave safely on the school bus, on the playground and at school. Also gives a warning about the dangers of pushing and shoving on the stairs.
Health and Safety
Dist - TVOTAR **Prod** - TVOTAR 1983

Safety at sea - Vol 3 94 MIN
VHS
Annapolis book of seamanship with John Rousmaniere series
Color (G)
LC 90-712263
Gives instructions on sailing safety. Part of a five - part series on seamanship by John Rousmaniere.
Health and Safety; Physical Education and Recreation
Dist - CREPRI **Prod** - CREPRI 1987
CPI

Safety at wheels 15 MIN
U-matic
Calling all safety scouts series
Color (K P)
Teaches children safety measures in cars, on bicycles and near trains.
Health and Safety
Dist - TVOTAR **Prod** - TVOTAR 1983

Safety at Work 19 MIN
16mm
Color (C A)
Shows the precautions that should be taken in industry to prevent industrial accidents that cost Americans four billion dollars a year.
Business and Economics; Health and Safety
Dist - AETNA **Prod** - AETNA

Safety at Work
VHS
$397 purchase _ #PX3370V
Uses a video series to teach the most important aspects of safety. Outlines individual responsibility in given situations, correct handling of equipment, protective measures that should be used and first aid techniques. Three videos from filmstrip.
Health and Safety
Dist - CAREER **Prod** - CAREER

Safety at work 20 MIN
16mm / VHS / BETA / U-matic
Common sense guide series
Color; PAL (G IND PRO)
PdS250, PdS258 purchase
Explores the United Kingdom's Health/Safety at Work Act in human terms in part of a ten - part series.
Health and Safety
Dist - EDPAT

Safety belt for Susie 11 MIN
16mm / U-matic / VHS
Automobile safety series
Color (P I A) (SPANISH)
Uses anthropometric dummies and dolls to show what could happen to children not wearing safety belts in collisons. Emphasizes that children, one - year - old and older, should wear safety belts.
Guidance and Counseling; Health and Safety
Dist - AIMS **Prod** - CAHILL 1963

Safety Belts 24 MIN
U-matic / VHS / 16mm
Color (IND)
Presents falls using safety belts and lanyards to convince workers of the importance of wearing safety belts for high construction site work. Shows how to choose and wear a belt correctly and demonstrates the triple rolling hitch knot.
Health and Safety; Industrial and Technical Education; Psychology
Dist - IFB **Prod** - CSAO

Safety belts - a smashing success 14 MIN
16mm / U-matic / VHS
Color (J) (SPANISH)
LC 75-700963
Presents data from tests and statistics and shows automobile collision experiments at UCLA in order to solidify the arguments for the use of safety belts and harnesses.
Health and Safety; Science
Dist - AIMS **Prod** - CAHILL 1975

Safety Belts and You 9 MIN
U-matic / VHS / 16mm
Color
Shows what happens to belted and unbelted drivers and passengers in fast - moving automobile crashes.
Health and Safety; Industrial and Technical Education
Dist - FORDFL **Prod** - FORDFL

Safety Belts - Short Version 9 MIN
U-matic / VHS / 16mm
Color (IND)
Demonstrates the correct use of nylon webbing safety belts and lanyard. A shortened version of the film Safety Belts.
Health and Safety; Industrial and Technical Education; Psychology
Dist - IFB **Prod** - CSAO

Safety bound 24 MIN
8mm cartridge / VHS / BETA / U-matic
Color; PAL (IND G)
$295.00 purchase, $175.00 rental _ #MOB - 003
Follows the adventures of ten employees as they take the Outward Bound challenge in the Colorado mountains. Reveals that their mountain climbing experience in the wilderness relate to the safety skills and awareness needed on the job. Shows how the workers learn important lessons in safety - no work is as important as teamwork, to stay calm during a crisis, to know limits, to use proper equipment, to develop an attitude of safety, to understand that safety is everyone's duty. Includes leader's guide.
Health and Safety; Psychology
Dist - BNA

Safety - breathing 10 MIN
16mm / VHS / BETA / U-matic
Color; PAL (PRO IND)
PdS125, PdS133 purchase
Shows how fumes and dust can cause respiratory diseases resulting in death. Explains how respiratory illness can be prevented.
Health and Safety
Dist - EDPAT

Safety by design 17 MIN
VHS / U-matic / BETA

Color (G)
$595.00 purchase, $125.00 rental _ #SAF031
Explains the impact of system and environment design on daily work tasks in the office. Looks at ergonomic aspects and conducts interviews.
Business and Economics; Health and Safety; Psychology
Dist - ITF **Prod** - CREMED 1991

Safety by the Numbers 32 MIN
16mm
Color (P I J)
LC 71-702860
A safety - education film for pilots and aviation groups. A lumberman searching for a lost barge is introduced to safety by the numbers in a twin engine aircraft.
Industrial and Technical Education
Dist - USFAA **Prod** - FAAFL 1969

Safety Can't Wait - the Safety Responsibilities of Middle Managers 14 MIN
U-matic
Color (IND)
Reinforces the principle that middle managers have an important role in safety programs and demonstrates how the responsibility can be managed to improve performance.
Business and Economics; Health and Safety
Dist - BNA **Prod** - ALLIED 1986

The Safety catch - the quality of safety 35 MIN
VHS / 16mm
Color (A PRO)
$790.00 purchase, $220.00 rental
Uses a dramatization to illustrate the efficiency and cost effectiveness of a safe workplace. Management training.
Health and Safety
Dist - VIDART **Prod** - VIDART 1990

Safety check 10 MIN
U-matic
Calling Captain Consumer series
Color (P I J)
Shows a boy who is building a go kart who is intrigued by his neighbor's safety inspection project.
Health and Safety; Home Economics
Dist - TVOTAR **Prod** - TVOTAR 1985

Safety Check Your Car 16 MIN
VHS / 16mm / U-matic
Color (H C A)
LC 77-701108
Explains how to safety check a car. Points out potential problem areas and shows how to recognize signs of potential trouble for brakes, mufflers, shock absorbers, tires and other automobile systems.
Health and Safety; Industrial and Technical Education
Dist - PFP **Prod** - STNLYL 1976

Safety Check Your Driving 13 MIN
U-matic / VHS
Color (H C G)
Tells how to avoid potentially dangerous situations on the road and while performing emergency repairs.
Health and Safety; Psychology; Social Science
Dist - HUF **Prod** - HUF

Safety consciousness 10 MIN
16mm
Foremanship training series
Color
LC 74-705565
Demonstrates how to develop safe attitudes in daily activities by clarity in thinking, acting and outlook on life.
Health and Safety
Dist - USNAC **Prod** - USBM 1969

Safety Considerations in Die Design 14 MIN
16mm / U-matic / VHS
Machine Tool Safety Series
Color (IND)
Health and Safety; Industrial and Technical Education
Dist - NATMTB **Prod** - NATMTB

The Safety deck 26 MIN
8mm cartridge / VHS / BETA / U-matic
Color; CC; PAL (IND G)
$495.00 purchase, $175.00 rental _ #TSD - 100
Features a master 'cardshark' who cuts his way through a specially designed deck, turning up 13 individual safety issues as he deals from deuce to ace. Covers chemical spills; fire protection; confined spaces; emergency plans; personal protective equipment; hazardous waste; lockout and tagout; safe lifting; housekeeping; signs, tags and labels; chemical handing; hearing protectors and respirators. Includes an instructor's manual and ten decks of Safety Deck Playing Cards.
Health and Safety; Psychology
Dist - BNA **Prod** - BNA 1994

Safety demonstration on the band saw 14 MIN
U-matic / VHS / 16mm
Wood shop - safety and operations series
Color (J H A) (ARABIC SPANISH)
LC 77-705459
Demonstrates close - up photography of basic safety procedures and operational points on the table saw.
Health and Safety; Industrial and Technical Education
Dist - AIMS **Prod** - EPRI 1970

Safety demonstration on the band saw 14 MIN
VHS
Color (J H A T)
$49.95 purchase _ #AM1444
Teaches how to adjust the table angle and the height of the upper guard and guide assembly. Shows the operation of the brake and explains pre - visualization of cutting moves, the need for a maximum of forward cuts and how to use relief cuts. Demonstrates how to feed stock and how to avoid pulling the blades of the drive wheels.
Industrial and Technical Education
Dist - AAVIM **Prod** - AAVIM 1992

Safety demonstration on the jointer 12 MIN
VHS
Color (J H A T)
$49.95 purchase _ #AM1445
Teaches the uses of the wood joint and identifies its parts. Tells how to determine minimum length and thickness of stock, how to feed stock with regard to grain and how to joint an edge, a face and an end. Demonstrates bevel cuts, how to feed stock with the hands and with a push stick.
Industrial and Technical Education
Dist - AAVIM **Prod** - AAVIM 1992

Safety demonstration on the jointer 12 MIN
16mm / U-matic / VHS
Wood shop - safety and operations series
Color (J A) (ARABIC SPANISH)
LC 76-704771
Demonstrates the basic safety points and processes of operating the jointer.
Health and Safety; Industrial and Technical Education
Dist - AIMS **Prod** - EPRI 1970

Safety demonstration on the radial saw 12 MIN
VHS
Color (J H A T)
$49.95 purchase _ #AM1446
Shows how to adjust the motor yoke on the radial saw for crosscutting and ripping, how to change the cutting angle and adjust for depth of cut, how to raise and lower the blades and how to change blades. Illustrates how to use the friction brake and the procedures for ripping and crosscutting, including adjust of the blade guard and anti - kickback bar.
Industrial and Technical Education
Dist - AAVIM **Prod** - AAVIM 1992

Safety demonstration on the radial saw 12 MIN
16mm / U-matic / 8mm cartridge / VHS
Wood shop - safety and operations series
Color (IND) (ARABIC SPANISH)
Shows close - up photography of basic safety procedures and operational points in using the radial saw.
Health and Safety; Industrial and Technical Education
Dist - AIMS **Prod** - EPRI 1971

Safety demonstration on the single - surface planer 16 MIN
VHS
Color (J H A T)
$49.95 purchase _ #AM1449
Describes the uses of the single - surface planer and the details of its operation. Demonstrates how to determine the setting for depth of cut, select correct feedroll speed, determine maximum width and minimum length of stock and how to feed stock with regard to grain. Looks at the procedures for dealing with 'stuck' stock and discourages the planing of plywood.
Industrial and Technical Education
Dist - AAVIM **Prod** - AAVIM 1992

Safety demonstration on the single surface planer 15 MIN
16mm / U-matic / 8mm cartridge / VHS
Wood shop - safety and operations series
Color (J H C A) (ARABIC SPANISH)
LC 70-704722; 70-704772
Demonstrates the basic safety points and the basic operations on the single - surface planer.
Health and Safety; Industrial and Technical Education
Dist - AIMS **Prod** - EPRI 1970

Safety demonstration on the table saw 20 MIN
U-matic / VHS / 16mm
Wood shop - safety and operations series
Color (J)
LC 71-705460
Demonstrates basic safety procedures and operational points on the table saw.
Health and Safety; Industrial and Technical Education
Dist - AIMS **Prod** - EPRI 1970

Safety demonstration on the table saw - Pt 1 11 MIN
VHS / 16mm / U-matic
Wood shop - safety and operations series
Color (J) (SPANISH ARABIC)
LC 71-705460
Demonstrates close - up photography of basic safety procedures and operational points on the table saw.
Health and Safety; Industrial and Technical Education
Dist - AIMS **Prod** - EPRI 1970

Safety demonstration on the table saw - Pt I 11 MIN
VHS
Color (J H A T)
$49.95 purchase _ #AM1450
Describes the functions of rip fence, blade guard and miter gauge. Shows how to change blades and adjust the blade for depth and angle of cut. Illustrates safe procedures for feeding wide stock past the blade during cutting and protecting against kickback. Part one of two parts.
Industrial and Technical Education
Dist - AAVIM **Prod** - AAVIM 1992

Safety demonstration on the table saw - Pt II 9 MIN
VHS
Color (J H A T)
$49.95 purchase _ #AM1451
Elaborates on the use of the rip fence and miter gauge for ripping and crosscutting. Shows correct positioning of hands and fingers on stock, how to rip narrow or irregularly shaped stock. Cautions against backing stock out of a cut or removing it halfway through a cut. Part two of two parts.
Industrial and Technical Education
Dist - AAVIM **Prod** - AAVIM 1992

Safety demonstration on the wood lathe 11 MIN
U-matic / 8mm cartridge / VHS / 16mm
Wood shop - safety and operations series
Color (J IND) (SPANISH)
Shows close - up photography of basic safety points and operational procedures in using the wood lathe.
Industrial and Technical Education
Dist - AIMS **Prod** - EPRI 1971

Safety demonstration on the wood lathe 11 MIN
VHS
Color (J H A T)
$49.95 purchase _ #AM1452
Identifies the main parts of the wood lathe and their functions. Shows how the wood lathe is used to shape a project, cut it to size, sand it and finish. Describes the uses of gouges, skews, parting tools and various scrapers. Stresses safety and care of tools while showing how to mount stock, adjust the tool rest, hold the turning tools and determine correct spindle speed.
Industrial and Technical Education
Dist - AAVIM **Prod** - AAVIM 1992

Safety demonstration on the wood shaper - Pt 1 11 MIN
U-matic / VHS / 16mm
Wood shop - safety and operations series
Color (J) (ARABIC SPANISH)
Describes the uses of the wood shaper, showing a variety of spindles and cutter shapes and sizes. Tells how to install and align the fence and discusses how to select correct cutter rotation and how to reverse direction.
Health and Safety; Industrial and Technical Education
Dist - AIMS **Prod** - AIMS 1970

Safety demonstration on the wood shaper - Pt 2 10 MIN
16mm / U-matic / VHS
Wood shop - safety and operations series
Color (J) (ARABIC SPANISH)
Discusses the use of the wood shaper, explaining that steady feed is best and that stopping and backing up are dangerous. Shows how to feed for straight facing, how to use rub collar for irregular shaping, and how to feed stock using a starting pin and rub collar. Illustrates use of spring ring guard, pressure bar, tall fence, and bevel fence. Explains how to minimize end - grain chipping and how to shape short ends. Describes the procedure for internal shaping.
Health and Safety; Industrial and Technical Education
Dist - AIMS **Prod** - AIMS 1970

Safety demonstration on the wood shaper - Pt I 11 MIN
VHS
Color (J H A T)
$49.95 purchase _ #AM1447
Demonstrates the uses of the wood shaper. Shows a variety of spindles and cutter shapes and sizes. Illustrates changing spindles and cutters, installing and aligning the fence, selecting correct cutter rotation and reversing directions. Teaches how to test a set up.
Industrial and Technical Education
Dist - AAVIM **Prod** - AAVIM 1992

Safety demonstration on the wood shaper - Pt II 10 MIN
VHS
Color (J H A T)
$49.95 purchase _ #AM1448
Explains that steadily feeding stock into the shaper is best, that stopping and backing up is dangerous. Demonstrates how to feed for straight facing, use a rub collar for irregular shaping and feed stock using a starting pin and rub collar. Illustrates the use of the spring ring guard, pressure bar, tall fence and bevel fence.
Industrial and Technical Education
Dist - AAVIM **Prod** - AAVIM 1992

Safety Depends on You 9 MIN
16mm
Color (H C A)
Demonstrates the safe and proper use of tools in firefighting and other work.
Health and Safety
Dist - FILCOM **Prod** - PUBSF

Safety - dermatitis 10 MIN
16mm / VHS / BETA / U-matic
Color; PAL (PRO IND)
PdS125, PdS133 purchase
Explains how dermatitis is caused and how it can be avoided.
Health and Safety
Dist - EDPAT

Safety doesn't happen
8mm cartridge / 16mm
B&W
Shows how accidents result in production lags, slowing up shipments and disrupting employee efficiency.
Health and Safety
Dist - NSC **Prod** - NSC

Safety Elements in Laboratory Practice 20 MIN
U-matic / VHS
Color
Illustrates eye protection, protective clothing, toxicity, flammability and other safety elements in laboratory practice.
Health and Safety; Science
Dist - FPF **Prod** - FPF

The Safety Factor 60 MIN
16mm
Nova Series
Color
Looks at the realities of airline safety, using a flight from London to Los Angeles as a case study. Examines crew training and responsibilities, equipment maintenance and air traffic control systems. Explores the role of the aircraft builder in design, construction and updating to ensure safety. Studies remedies inherent in flying and shows prototypes of flight and control systems operated by computers.
Health and Safety; Industrial and Technical Education; Social Science
Dist - KINGFT **Prod** - WGBHTV 1979

Safety First 29 MIN
Videoreel / VT2
Discover Flying - Just Like a Bird Series
Color
Industrial and Technical Education; Social Science
Dist - PBS **Prod** - WKYCTV

Safety first 30 MIN
VHS
Join in series
Color (K P)
#362303
Shows a police constable who checks the workshop where Jacob is working late and ends up singing songs and playing a game about safety. Tells a story about a young rabbit who gets in trouble when he disobeys his mother's rule about staying inside at night. Part of a series about three artist - performers who share studio space in a converted warehouse.
Health and Safety; Literature and Drama
Dist - TVOTAR **Prod** - TVOTAR 1989

Safety first
VHS / U-matic
Color
Makes use of humor in a review of safety rules for a business organization.
Business and Economics; Health and Safety; Literature and Drama
Dist - MEETS **Prod** - BBB

Safety first - auto shop safety 30 MIN
VHS
Color (G H)
$79.95 purchase _ #CCP0212V-T
Describes a video tape that explains the basics of safety in the auto shop. Provides information on proper attire, operation of heavy equipment, hydraulic jacks, chain falls, procedures for handling batteries (disposal, recharging, acid and cleaning), cleaning spills, bringing autos into the shop, ventilation, removing radiator caps, and more. Includes a video cassette.
Education; Industrial and Technical Education
Dist - CAMV

Safety first - electrical safety 30 MIN
VHS
Color (G H)
$79.95 purchase _ #CCP0215V-T
Describes correct electrical shop safety; proper clothing and eyewear, boots, and mental state. Explains the safety in understanding what different color wires mean, how to handle rolls or circuit wire and breaker boxes, insulation, wire guage for different tasks. Includes information on treating electirical shock, and prevention.
Education; Health and Safety; Industrial and Technical Education
Dist - CAMV

Safety first in campus labs 20 MIN
VHS
Color (H C)
$295.00 purchase
Presents general principles of laboratory safety that are important in all scientific investigations. Produced by SIO Video Productions - UCSD.
Health and Safety; Science
Dist - PFP

Safety first - welding shop safety 30 MIN
VHS
Color (G H VOC IND)
$79.95 purchase _ #CCP0213V-T
Describes the proper methods of shop safety when welding. Explains the correct clothing, goggles, gloves, ear protection, boots, as well as the specific gear for welders. Discusses the importance of a clear mental state when working with dangerous equipment. Provides information on storage, testing equipment, grounding machines and more.
Education; Industrial and Technical Education
Dist - CAMV

Safety for elementary series
Safety in the home 9 MIN
Safety in the street 10 MIN
Safety in transit 8 MIN
School safety 9 MIN
Dist - AIMS

Safety for Oilfield Contractors Series
Breakout 15 MIN
Professional attitudes 15 MIN
Trenching - a Grave Affair 15 MIN
Dist - FLMWST

Safety for Oilfield Contractors Series
Wide World of Records 17 MIN
Dist - FLMWST
UTEXPE

Safety for seniors series
Presents a three - part series on safety for the elderly. Covers home safety, prevention of burglary and assault in the home and prevention of fraud.
Defense against fraud - Part 3 18 MIN
Defense against theft and attack - Part 2 20 MIN
Prevention of accidents at home - Part 1 23 MIN
Dist - HANDEL **Prod** - HANDEL 1995

Safety for special needs children 14 MIN
Videoreel / VHS
Color
Shows special considerations for children who are disabled with visual, lower extremity and developmental impairments.
Education; Health and Safety; Home Economics; Psychology
Dist - UNDMC **Prod** - UNDMC

Safety for the New Employee 20 MIN
16mm
Color (IND)
Shows major safety hazards a new employee will be exposed to in an industrial plant or maintenance shop. Covers housekeeping, ladders, welding flashes and improperly grounded electrical tools. Stresses the importance of safety glasses, hard hats and safety shoes.
Health and Safety; Psychology
Dist - MOKIN **Prod** - MOKIN

Safety Gear Series
Eye and face protection 13 MIN
Foot protection 11 MIN
Hand and Arm Protection 11 MIN
Head Protection 10 MIN
Hearing Protection 13 MIN
Respirators 13 MIN
Dist - AIMS

Safety - Harm Hides at Home 16 MIN
U-matic / VHS / 16mm
Safety Series
Color (P I)
LC 77-703328
Uses a story about children who are rescued from accidents at home to create an awareness of home safety and provides examples for accident prevention.
Guidance and Counseling; Health and Safety
Dist - BARR **Prod** - FILMCO 1977

Safety, health, and loss control - managing effective programs - a series
Managing effective programs series
Color (IND)
LC 81-706200
Discusses all main aspects of the OSHA Act, new regulations by the Occupational Safety and Health Administration and industry's reaction to them, safety and cost considerations, and security measures. Addresses behavior management, executive security, health compliance for small industries, new government regulations, industry's reaction to OSHA changes, loss control, management, management's safety mirror, monitoring the work environment, occupational safety, responsibility, and prevention of occupational injury.
Health and Safety
Dist - AMCEE **Prod** - AMCEE 1979

Safety, health, and loss control - managing effective programs series
Behavior management for safety 40 MIN
Prevention of occupational injury and disease through control technology 40 MIN
Dist - AMCEE

Safety - hearing 10 MIN
16mm / VHS / BETA / U-matic
Color; PAL (G T)
PdS125, PdS133 purchase
Reveals how deafness is caused and how objectionable noise can be controlled.
Guidance and Counseling; Health and Safety; Science - Natural
Dist - EDPAT

Safety - home, safe home 14 MIN
U-matic / VHS / 16mm
Color (P I)
LC 72-701042
Utilizes 'inquiry' mode of stop - projector technique for teaching basic concepts of home safety. Presents typical household hazards and situations for student discussion.
Guidance and Counseling; Health and Safety
Dist - AIMS **Prod** - CAHILL 1972

Safety housekeeping and accident prevention 15 MIN
VHS
Basic safety series
Color (IND G)
$395.00 purchase, $75.00 rental _ #8302
Shows employees how to prevent workplace accidents by paying special attention to safety housekeeping considerations. Encourages employees to become very familiar with their work environment and its risks. Complies with the mandates of OSHA regulations.
Health and Safety
Dist - AIMS **Prod** - MARCOM 1991

Safety in Construction Series
Cost of Chaos 11 MIN
Excavations 9 MIN
Lifting Equipment 10 MIN
Mechanical Aids 10 MIN
Scaffolding 11 MIN
Dist - IFB

Safety - in Danger Out of Doors 15 MIN
16mm / U-matic / VHS
Safety Series
Color (P I)
LC 77-703329
Shows how Safety Woman comes to the rescue of children in hazardous situations. Presents basic rules of water safety and other basic safety rules.
Health and Safety
Dist - BARR **Prod** - FILMCO 1977

Safety in drilling, milling and boring machines 17 MIN
VHS
Metal cutting machines series
Color (IND G)
$300.00 purchase, $150.00 rental
Details safety requirements for construction, care and use of drilling, milling and boring machines as referenced in ANSI - approved B11.8 - 1983.
Health and Safety; Industrial and Technical Education; Psychology
Dist - ASMATE

Safety in Drilling, Milling and Boring Operations 17 MIN
16mm / U-matic / VHS
Machine Tool Safety Series
Color (IND)
Health and Safety; Industrial and Technical Education
Dist - NATMTB **Prod** - NATMTB

Safety in electric - arc welding and terms
U-matic / VHS
Shielded metal arc welding - Spanish series
Color (SPANISH)
Health and Safety; Industrial and Technical Education
Dist - VTRI **Prod** - VTRI

Safety in Electrical Maintenance 60 MIN
VHS
Electrical Maintenance Practices Series
Color (PRO)
$600.00, $1500.00 purchase _ #EMSEM
Describes electrical shock hazards that exist in electrical facilities and ways in which electrical maintenance work can be made safe. Examines the effects of current on the human body, protective clothing and equipment, proper grounding of electrical tools and motors, safe procedures for working on or around batteries, transformers and capacitors and high voltage hazards. Part of a six - part series on electrical maintenance practices, which is part of a 29 unit set on electrical maintenance. Includes 10 textbooks and an instructor guide which provide four hours of instruction.
Education; Health and Safety; Industrial and Technical Education; Psychology; Science - Physical
Dist - NUSTC **Prod** - NUSTC

Safety in gas tungsten arc welding
U-matic / VHS
MIG and TIG Welding - Spanish Series
Color (SPANISH)
Health and Safety; Industrial and Technical Education
Dist - VTRI **Prod** - VTRI

Safety in home care 25 MIN
VHS
Color (C PRO)
$195.00 purchase, $70.00 rental _ #4348S, #4348V
Shows a home health nurse on an initial visit to a patient. Follows the nurse as she assesses, identifies and helps eliminate safety risks in the patient's environment. Includes a checklist of safety information on outdoor risks for one - level and multi - level homes and demonstrations of safety equipment, such as the trapeze, tub safety rail, toilet safety frame and commode chair.
Health and Safety
Dist - AJN **Prod** - BELHAN 1993

Safety in Hospitals 27 MIN
16mm
B&W
LC 74-706232
Discusses major aspects of the safety program required in Army hospitals.
Civics and Political Systems; Health and Safety
Dist - USNAC **Prod** - USA 1967

Safety in Instrumentation Maintenance 60 MIN
VHS
Fundamentals of Instrumentation and Control Series
Color (PRO)
$600.00 - $1500.00 purchase _ #ICSIM
Focuses on the hazards associated with plant environment and typical plant instrumentation systems. Shows how to select and use the proper protective equipment for various types of hazards and potentially hazardous situations and follow applicable safety procedures. Part of a nineteen - part series on the fundamentals of instrumentation and control, which is part of a 49 - unit set on instrumentation and control. Includes five textbooks and an instructor guide to support four hours of instruction.
Health and Safety; Industrial and Technical Education; Psychology
Dist - NUSTC **Prod** - NUSTC

Safety in Metal Turning Operations 17 MIN
16mm / U-matic / VHS
Machine Tool Safety Series
Color (IND)
Health and Safety; Industrial and Technical Education
Dist - NATMTB **Prod** - NATMTB

Safety in mountain surveying 27 MIN
16mm
Color
LC 74-705567
Introduces some of the basic techniques of safe mountain climbing to Federal Highway Administration personnel. Covers knot tying, rope testing, proper equipment and basic safe methods of moving on rock.
Health and Safety; Physical Education and Recreation
Dist - USNAC **Prod** - USDTFH 1969

Safety in Plywood Operations 10 MIN
16mm
Color (J)
Points out specific things to watch for in plywood manufacturing for both new and experienced plywood employees. Illustrates principles of individual and managerial responsibility.
Business and Economics; Health and Safety; Industrial and Technical Education
Dist - RARIG **Prod** - RARIG 1970

Safety in rigging series
Cranes - types and components, case histories 19 MIN
Hazard awareness in crane operating areas 14.5 MIN
Hoists, Winches and Related Devices 20 MIN
International Hand Signals 7 MIN
Wire Rope 19 MIN
Dist - IFB

Safety in Rigging
Hardware 20 MIN
Reeving 15 MIN
Slings 21 MIN
Dist - IFB

Safety in shipbuilding 20 MIN
16mm / VHS / BETA / U-matic
Color; PAL (IND)
PdS150, PdS158 purchase
Makes everyone employed in the industry more aware of the hazards that exist and the consequences of carelessness.
Health and Safety; Industrial and Technical Education
Dist - EDPAT

Safety in strip mining 24 MIN
16mm
Color
LC 74-705568
Presents a general treatment of surface mining operations and the hazards connected with truck haulage, blasting, falling material, power cables, and other aspects of mining.
Health and Safety; Industrial and Technical Education
Dist - USNAC **Prod** - USBM 1961

Safety in Surface Coal Mining 22 MIN
16mm
Color
LC 82-700675
Presents a history and overall view of surface coal mining operations with a close look at some of most common hazards connected with specific jobs and working environments. Points out dangers in the use of bulldozers, power shovels, dump trucks and other mining equipment. Demonstrates appropriate safety practices and operating procedures to eliminate or reduce possible accidents.
Health and Safety; Social Science
Dist - USNAC **Prod** - USDL 1982

Safety in the auto body shop 9 MIN
VHS / 35mm strip
(J H A IND)
#431XV7
Describes the hazards of working in an auto body shop and provides tips on safe working habits. Includes a Study Guide.
Education; Health and Safety; Industrial and Technical Education
Dist - BERGL

Safety in the auto shop
VHS
Shop safety series
(H C G)
$59.00 _ CA204
Discusses auto shop safety including proper use of lifts, jacks, hoists and overhead cranes. Points out out precautions to be taken while spray painting and working with batteries.
Health and Safety; Industrial and Technical Education
Dist - AAVIM **Prod** - AAVIM 1989

Safety in the Balance 23 MIN
U-matic / VHS / 16mm
Color (IND)
Crane safety is highlighted by showing various hazards encountered on the job. Warns crane operators about the many factors that must be taken into account to insure safe operation of the equipment and successful completion of the job.
Health and Safety; Industrial and Technical Education; Psychology
Dist - IFB **Prod** - CSAO

Safety in the country 15 MIN
U-matic
Calling all safety scouts series
Color (K P)
Teaches children about keeping clear of farm machinery and bulls, avoiding wild animals and poison ivy and being careful around lawnmowers.
Health and Safety; Social Science
Dist - TVOTAR **Prod** - TVOTAR 1983

Safety in the Electronics Shop
VHS / U-matic
Color (J H)
Explores the major causes of injuries and accidents in the electronics field.
Health and Safety; Industrial and Technical Education
Dist - CAREER **Prod** - CAREER 1972

Safety in the electronics shop
VHS
Shop safety series
(H C G)
$59.00 _ CA205
Focuses on safety procedures when working with hand tools, electrical equipment, high voltage electricity, T V batteries, and radio transmitters.
Health and Safety; Industrial and Technical Education
Dist - AAVIM **Prod** - AAVIM 1989

Safety in the Health Care Environment 15 MIN
U-matic / VHS
Health Care Security Training Series
Color
Covers the health care facility's moral, legal and economic responsibility to maintain safety standards.
Health and Safety
Dist - CORF **Prod** - GREESM

Safety in the Home 12 MIN
U-matic / VHS / 16mm
Captioned; Color (I)
Demonstrates the need for making common sense decisions for safety in the home. Depicts causes of accidents.
Guidance and Counseling; Health and Safety
Dist - EBEC **Prod** - EBEC 1965

Safety in the home 9 MIN
U-matic / VHS / 16mm
Safety for elementary series
Color (K P I) (SPANISH)
LC 74-702960
Identifies home safety hzards and shows how to correct them.
Health and Safety
Dist - AIMS **Prod** - MORLAT 1974

Safety in the Kitchen 14 MIN
16mm
Color
LC 79-700444
Covers 18 major hazard areas in the kitchen. Discusses knives and utensils, matches, gas and electric ranges, electric appliances, hot objects, deep fat frying, fire and escaping gas, glassware, food storage and kitchen cleanliness.
Health and Safety; Home Economics
Dist - FILCOM **Prod** - GRDNHN 1969

Safety in the kitchen 9 MIN
VHS / 16mm
Color (A IND)
LC 91705450
Trains workers in safety hazards by providing a tour of a commercial kitchen which illustrates how to avoid falls, injuries, cuts, burns, and sprains from lifting.
Health and Safety; Industrial and Technical Education; Psychology
Dist - IFB

Safety in the Kitchen
VHS
$59 purchase _ #FY550V
Discusses the leading causes of accidents in the kitchen which are falls, fires, burns, poisonings, and electric shock. Features accident scenarios involving teens and animation sequences to show how to act in the event an accident does occur.
Health and Safety; Home Economics
Dist - CAREER **Prod** - CAREER

Safety in the Laboratory 8 MIN
U-matic
Chemistry 101 Series
Color (C)
Demonstrates the importance of following safety regulations in a chemistry laboratory.
Science
Dist - UILL **Prod** - UILL 1976

Safety in the Laboratory Series
Chemical Hazards 4 MIN
Fire in the Laboratory 4 MIN
Personal Safety 3 MIN
Dist - KALMIA

Safety in the Metal Shop
VHS
Shop Safety Series

(H C G)
$59.00 _ CA202
Gives students instruction on safe use of the lathe, milling machine, shaper, drill press, and grinder.
Industrial and Technical Education
Dist - AAVIM **Prod** - AAVIM 1989

Safety in the Metal Shop
U-matic / VHS
Color (J H)
Illustrates the ways to avoid injury in the metal shop by informing students of potential dangers.
Health and Safety; Industrial and Technical Education
Dist - CAREER **Prod** - CAREER

Safety in the Office 13 MIN
VHS / 16mm
Color (C A PRO)
$295.00 purchase, $75.00 rental _ #8195
Stresses the role of employees in office safety.
Health and Safety; Psychology
Dist - AIMS **Prod** - AIMS 1990

Safety in the plowshare program 22 MIN
16mm
Color
LC FIE66-13
Documents the safety precautions which are taken during experiments or projects in the U S program to develop peaceful uses of nuclear explosives. Shows how radioactivity and other effects of nuclear explosions are controlled in order to insure the public safety.
Health and Safety; Science - Physical; Sociology
Dist - USNAC **Prod** - USNRC 1966

Safety in the science lab 30 MIN
U-matic / VHS
Color
Clarifies safety procedures for fire emergencies and other lab activities. Emphasizes dangerous lab practices. Includes ten follow - up questions.
Education; Health and Safety; Science
Dist - EDMEC **Prod** - EDMEC

Safety in the science laboratory 30 MIN
U-matic / VHS / BETA
Color (T)
$39.95 purchase _ #5401
Discusses potentially dangerous everyday situations involving chemicals, fire and glass breakage. Demonstrates clear - cut safety rule in a lab setting. Part of a series teaching teachers of junior high students and up how to teach chemistry. Covers important concepts, assists substitute teachers. Shows how to deal with student absenteeism, compensate for differences in learning rates, improve preparation time and review lessons.
Education; Health and Safety; Science - Physical
Dist - INSTRU

Safety in the shop 12 MIN
16mm
B&W (SPANISH)
LC FIE62-81
Dramatizes three typical shop accidents and shows how poor supervision or inadequate training may have been the real cause behind these accidents.
Health and Safety
Dist - USNAC **Prod** - USOE 1944

Safety in the Shop - Basic Practices 13 MIN
16mm / U-matic / VHS
Safety in the Shop Series
Color (H C A)
Emphasizes the worker's responsibility for safety in using hand and power tools in both wood and metal shops. Shows the importance of proper clothing, the safe way to lift and carry, the value of tidiness in a shop and ways to guard against possible fires.
Health and Safety; Industrial and Technical Education
Dist - CORF **Prod** - CORF 1970

Safety in the Shop - General
VHS
Shop Safety Series
(H C G)
$59.00 _ CA200
Illustrates basic shop safety conditions such as proper dress, correct tool useage, and the like.
Industrial and Technical Education
Dist - AAVIM **Prod** - AAVIM 1989

Safety in the Shop - Hand Tools 13 MIN
U-matic / VHS / 16mm
Safety in the Shop Series
Color (H C A)
LC 79-709429
Shows the value of keeping hand tools in good condition. Emphasizes the importance of protective clothing and demonstrates safe use of the forge and welding equipment.
Health and Safety; Industrial and Technical Education
Dist - CORF **Prod** - CORF 1970

Safety in the Shop - Power Tools 13 MIN
U-matic / VHS / 16mm
Safety in the Shop Series
Color (H C A)
LC 75-709428
Stresses common sense practices with power saws, lathes and other woodworking and metalworking machine tools, proper clothing, adjusting machine before starting, and dealing with broken blades.
Health and Safety; Industrial and Technical Education
Dist - CORF **Prod** - CORF 1970

Safety in the Shop Series
Basic practices 13 MIN
Hand Tools 12 MIN
Power Tools 13 MIN
Safety in the Shop - Basic Practices 13 MIN
Safety in the Shop - Hand Tools 13 MIN
Safety in the Shop - Power Tools 13 MIN
Dist - CORF

Safety in the street 10 MIN
16mm / U-matic / VHS
Safety for elementary series
Color (K P I) (ENGLISH, SPANISH)
LC 74-702961
Explains how accidents can happen to pedestrians and stresses how alertness and patience are essential for safety in the street.
Health and Safety
Dist - AIMS **Prod** - MORLAT 1974

Safety in the Wood Shop
VHS / U-matic
Color (J H)
Focuses on the hazards that can happen in the wood shop when students fail to follow safety precautions.
Health and Safety; Industrial and Technical Education
Dist - CAREER **Prod** - CAREER

Safety in the Wood Shop
VHS
(H C G)
$59.00 _ CA178
Focuses on woodshop hazards and teaches the importance of following woodshop procedures.
Industrial and Technical Education
Dist - AAVIM **Prod** - AAVIM 1989

Safety in the Wood Shop
VHS
Shop Safety Series
(H C G)
$59.00 _ CA201
Focuses on safety hazards found in the wood shop and includes the safe use and care of hand and power tools as well as tips for proper dress, neatness, and personal attitude toward safety.
Industrial and Technical Education
Dist - AAVIM **Prod** - AAVIM 1989

Safety in transit 8 MIN
16mm / U-matic / VHS
Safety for elementary series
Color (K P I) (ENGLISH, SPANISH)
Depicts accidents which occur in business, commuter stations and subways.
Health and Safety
Dist - AIMS **Prod** - MORLAT 1974

Safety in Your Home 14 MIN
16mm / U-matic / VHS
Color (I J)
LC 80-700039
Features a house that talks back as it instructs a family on ways to prevent accidents involving falls, fires, misplaced tools, electric shock and poisons.
Health and Safety
Dist - PHENIX **Prod** - GREENF 1979

Safety inspection and maintenance of playgrounds
VHS
Color (G)
$114.00 purchase _ #6 - 202 - 105A
Uses demonstrations by professional maintenance workers to show how to inspect and maintain a wide variety of common playground equipment such swings, slides, clatter bridges, decks, rings and balance beams. Shows how to keep landing areas clean and safe and how to use a written daily inspection chart to make sure that nothing is overlooked.
Health and Safety
Dist - VEP **Prod** - VEP

Safety inspections 10 MIN
VHS
Supervisors' development program series
Color (IND)
$280.00 purchase _ #15485 - 2222
Shows how to conduct a safety inspection in the work environment. Features William Shatner as host. Part of a 13 - part series on employee safety which stresses the four - step SAFE model - Search for hazards, Assess risks, Find solutions, Enforce solutions.
Business and Economics; Health and Safety; Industrial and Technical Education; Psychology
Dist - NSC **Prod** - NSC

Safety instruction series
Application and use of breathing apparatus
CPR
Emergency Handling of External Bleeding and Bandaging 13 MIN
Fire Protection Training
First Aid to Industry
How to handle a heart attack 15 MIN
Hydrogen Sulphide Alert
Dist - VTRI

Safety is a Full Time Job - Rules for Tools
U-matic / VHS
Color
Tackles the problem of safety awareness and accident prevention on the job and in educational programs using tools. Includes humorous dialogue and step - by - step demonstrations.
Health and Safety
Dist - EDUACT **Prod** - EDUACT

Safety is caring about identifying hazards 12 MIN
BETA / VHS / U-matic
Color; PAL (IND G)
$175.00 rental _ #ASF - 154; $620.00 purchase, $150.00 rental _ #SAF023
Tours a typical shop to view and identify hazards to workers. Reviews each of the workplace hazards, illustrates its potential consequences and shows how proper equipment or procedures can prevent or eliminate it. Includes leader's guide and 10 workbooks.
Business and Economics; Health and Safety; Psychology
Dist - BNA **Prod** - BNA
ITF

Safety is everyone's business 21 MIN
VHS
Color (PRO C G)
#24777, call for price
Uses humor to portray a health care administrator attempting to pinpoint the cause of an epidemic of accidents. Discusses steps all employees can take to reduce common safety hazards in health care institutions. Examines dangerous conditions from the point of view of workers, clients and visitors. Covers falls, fires, electrical hazards, burns and cuts and stresses the importance of incident reports. Produced by the Coordinating Council for Continuing Education in Health Care at Penn State.
Health and Safety
Dist - PSU

Safety is in Order 10 MIN
16mm
Safety Management Series
Color
Business and Economics; Health and Safety
Dist - NSC **Prod** - NSC

Safety - Isn't it Worth it 15 MIN
16mm
Color (A)
LC 81-701373
Stresses the importance of safety in biological labs. Demonstrates the consequences of negligence. Narrated by Jack Klugman.
Health and Safety; Science
Dist - FILCOM **Prod** - FISHSC 1981

Safety issues in handling - 8 30 MIN
VHS / U-matic
Chemotherapy series
Color (PRO)
$275.00 purchase, $60.00 rental _ #7121S, #7121V
Presents a program on safety issues in handling agents used in cancer chemotherapy. Includes a 50 - question post - test. Part of a twelve - part series on chemotherapy.
Health and Safety; Science
Dist - AJN **Prod** - HOSSN 1988

Safety - it's your responsibility 19 MIN
16mm / VHS
Color (A IND G)
$95.00, $200.00 purchase _ #SHA11950, #SHA11947
Shows that it is the supervisor's responsibility to set a good safety example for employees, because accidents can happen in a split second when exceptions to safety rules are made.
Health and Safety
Dist - USNAC **Prod** - USPS 1983

Safety - It's Your Responsibility Series
The High Cost of Falls and Strains 10 MIN
How to Avoid Kitchen Burns 10 MIN
Dist - ADVANM

Safety - live action video series
Confined space entry - do it right.. .stay alive — 24 MIN
Contractor safety orientation — 20 MIN
Don't fall for it - preventing slips, trips and falls — 18 MIN
Drum handling — 16 MIN
Fire extinguishers - first line of defense — 26 MIN
Forklift safety inspection — 18 MIN
Forklift safety inspection - forklift safety operation — 28 MIN
Forklift safety operation — 20 MIN
Industrial fire prevention — 16 MIN
It won't happen to me - behavior modification — 15 MIN
LOTO - lockout tagout, your ticket to safety - Loteria - cierre y etiquette - su billete para la seguridad — 15 MIN
Me and my back - back safety — 22 MIN
The Newcomers - safety motivation — 20 MIN
Safety - take it home — 12 MIN
With safety everybody wins - Con la seguridad todos ganamos — 18 MIN
Dist - ITSC

Safety, Look, Rock — 10 MIN
U-matic
Readalong One Series
Color (K P)
Introduces reading and spelling for preschoolers and children in grades 1 to 3 with animation, puppets, humor and music. Comes with teacher's guide and kit.
Education; English Language; Literature and Drama
Dist - TVOTAR **Prod** - TVOTAR 1975

Safety management — 10 MIN
VHS
Supervisors' development program series
Color (IND)
$280.00 purchase _ #15482 - 2222
Shows how to motivate employee observance of health and safety principles while on the job. Features William Shatner as host. Part of a 13 - part series on employee safety which stresses the four - step SAFE model - Search for hazards, Assess risks, Find solutions, Enforce solutions.
Business and Economics; Health and Safety; Industrial and Technical Education; Psychology
Dist - NSC **Prod** - NSC

Safety Management Course Series
Chemicals Under Control — 17 MIN
Shape up — 17 MIN
Dist - EDRF

Safety Management Series
Guard Duty — 10 MIN
Let Them Know — 10 MIN
Mind Over Matter — 10 MIN
Plan for Prevention — 10 MIN
Run the Team — 10 MIN
Safety is in Order — 10 MIN
Sell Safety — 10 MIN
Dist - NSC

Safety matters — 20 MIN
VHS
Color; PAL; NTSC (IND G)
PdS60, PdS70 purchase
Demonstrates that health and safety is a very important matter, even for small businesses. Portrays a small company where an accident puts a key employee out of action and the organization nearly goes bankrupt as a result. Available in Europe only.
Business and Economics; Health and Safety
Dist - CFLVIS

Safety meetings series
Drive safely
Lockout - tagout — 11 MIN
Safety and substance abuse — 11 MIN
Work zone safety
Dist - BBP

Safety - Mrs Andrews - Attending to tasks - Miss George — 35 MIN
U-matic
Color (PRO)
Assists nurses in developing awareness of the specific subtleties related to assessment and clinical management of right and left stroke patients. Discusses the issues of safety and attending to the daily task of eating.
Health and Safety
Dist - RICHGO **Prod** - RICHGO

A Safety net — 29 MIN
16mm / VHS
Color (C A)
$550.00, $160.00 purchase, $30.00 rental _ #CC4137
Features Dr. Edward Anyensu of Ghana discussing how food aid from Western nations may hinder the ability of Africa to become self - suffient in food production.
Agriculture; Civics and Political Systems; Geography - World
Dist - IU **Prod** - NFBC 1990

The Safety net
16mm / VHS
Color (IND) (SPANISH)
$795.00, $690.00 purchase
Tells the story of an accident caused by carelessness at an oil refinery. Suggests that each time a worker in the refinery breaks a rule or overlooks a detail, it is analogous to the image of a fraying rope on a circus act's safety net.
Business and Economics; Health and Safety; Psychology
Dist - FLMWST

The Safety Net — 28 MIN
VHS / 16mm
Color (A IND)
$690.00 purchase _ #40.0152
Uses an oil refinery setting to demonstrate that accidents are usually the result of a series of small events as opposed to one act.
Health and Safety; Industrial and Technical Education
Dist - UTEXPE

Safety - not by accident — 11 MIN
8mm cartridge / VHS / BETA / U-matic
Color; PAL (IND G PRO)
$295.00 purchase, $175.00 rental _ #SOU - 108
Helps employees to become more alert to safety concerns by showing them how to tune into 'safety prompters' both on and off the job. Reveals that safety prompters serve as visual triggers to remind workers of safety principles they have learned and to keep them focused on doing the job safely. Discusses prompters such as safety equipment and clothing, warning signs, labels, supervisors and close calls. Points out that what may get in the way of safety include over familiarity, haste, taking chances, unsafe acts by co - workers, distractions, fatigue and more. Includes leader's guide and ten participant workbooks.
Health and Safety
Dist - BNA

Safety, Nurturance, and Expectations — 30 MIN
16mm
Middle Road Traveler Series
Color (J H)
LC 80-701710
Explains the importance of nurturance, expectations and safety in child - rearing.
Guidance and Counseling; Sociology
Dist - GPN **Prod** - GRETVO 1978

The Safety of Being Understood
U-matic / 16mm
Color (A)
Demonstrates how to give clear orders and make certain they are understood so there is no room for assumptions or misunderstandings which so often lead to accidents.
Business and Economics; Health and Safety
Dist - BNA **Prod** - BNA 1983

Safety of meats — 15 MIN
U-matic
Meats in Canada series
(A)
Explains that the most obvious food poisoning agent in meat is bacteria. Discusses means of protection, methods of preparation, shelf life, forms of retail packaging and signs of contamination.
Agriculture; Home Economics; Social Science
Dist - ACCESS **Prod** - ACCESS 1983

Safety on Our School Bus — 13 MIN
16mm / U-matic / VHS
Color (P I)
LC 80-701809
Illustrates proper conduct for riding in a school bus.
Health and Safety
Dist - EBEC **Prod** - EBEC 1980

Safety on street and sidewalk — 11 MIN
U-matic / VHS / 16mm
Color (P I) (ENGLISH, SPANISH)
Provides basic pedestrian safety techniques, including planning and mapping the safest route to and from school, crossing streets under a variety of conditions and the proper method of walking along the roadway where there are no sidewalks.
Health and Safety
Dist - CORF **Prod** - CENTRO 1976

Safety on the Farm — 8 MIN
16mm
Color
Cites possible dangers around the farm and discusses common causes of accidents.
Agriculture; Health and Safety
Dist - TASCOR **Prod** - TASCOR 1976

Safety on the Job - Accident Causes and Prevention — 17 MIN
U-matic / VHS / 16mm
Color (H A)
Looks at the behaviors that cause accidents. Examines stress, negligence, recklessness, over - exertion and fatigue as causes of accidents on the job. Offers techniques for preventing potentially dangerous situations.
Health and Safety
Dist - AIMS **Prod** - AIMS 1984

Safety on - the - Job at Sea — 17 MIN
16mm
B&W
LC FIE58-11
Describes the organization for shipboard safety, how shipboard accidents can occur, accident prevention measures and the importance of crew safety consciousness.
Health and Safety; Social Science
Dist - USNAC **Prod** - USN

Safety on the Job - First Aid for Accidents — 20 MIN
U-matic / VHS / 16mm
Color (C G T A)
$75 rental _ #9791
Describes first aid procedures to be used when treating industrial accidents.
Health and Safety
Dist - AIMS **Prod** - AIMS 1985

Safety on the job series
Accident causes and prevention — 16 MIN
The Air - purifying respirator — 13 MIN
The Air - supplied respirator — 12 MIN
Forklift operation — 19 MIN
Manual Load Handling in the Warehouse — 12 MIN
Powered equipment in the warehouse — 12 MIN
Preventing Back Injuries — 24 MIN
Working on Aerial Lifts, Cranes and Swing Stages — 15 MIN
Working on Ladders, Poles and Scaffolds — 15 MIN
Working with Electricity — 16 MIN
Dist - AIMS

Safety on the job series
The Hazards of substance abuse — 17 MIN
Dist - AIMS
VEP

Safety on the job series
Accident cause and prevention — 16 MIN
Air - purifying respirator — 13 MIN
Air - supplied respirator — 12 MIN
Fire extinguishers — 23 MIN
First aid for accidents
Forklift operation — 19 MIN
Manual load handling in the warehouse — 12 MIN
Powered equipment in the warehouse — 12 MIN
Preventing back injuries — 24 MIN
Slips, trips and falls — 17 MIN
Working with electricity — 16 MIN
Working with machinery — 17 MIN
Dist - VEP

Safety on the Job - Slips, Trips, and Falls — 16 MIN
U-matic / VHS / 16mm
Color (H C A)
$75 rental _ #9798
Makes viewers aware of the safety hazards to which employees are exposed.
Health and Safety
Dist - AIMS **Prod** - SAIF 1985

Safety on the Job - the Hazards of Substance Abuse — 18 MIN
16mm / U-matic / VHS
Color (H C A)
LC 83-701068
Discusses and demonstrates the safety hazards caused by misuse of drugs in the workplace.
Health and Safety; Psychology; Sociology
Dist - AIMS **Prod** - AIMS 1983

Safety on the job - van and truck driving — 23 MIN
16mm / U-matic / VHS
Color (H C A)
$75 rental _ #9850
Provides drivers with the information they need to develop a safe, professional attitude.
Health and Safety; Social Science
Dist - AIMS **Prod** - BROFLM 1985

Safety on the Job - Working with Machinery — 17 MIN
U-matic / VHS / 16mm
Color (H A)
$75 rental _ #9831
Provides operators of machinery with safety precautions - what safety equipment to use, how to use it, and when to use it. Importance of safe attitude stressed.

Health and Safety
Dist - AIMS **Prod** - AIMS 1985

Safety on the Move - Truck Haulage Safety 16 MIN
16mm / U-matic / VHS
Color (IND)
Focuses on an open - pit mining operation. Shows huge haulage trucks, pointing out existing and potential hazards involved in their operation. Reenacts common accidents, explains their causes and outlines the steps necessary to prevent their reoccurrence.
Health and Safety; Psychology; Social Science
Dist - USNAC **Prod** - USDL 1982

Safety on the Playground 13 MIN
U-matic / VHS / 16mm
Color; B&W (I)
LC FIA67-1246
Points up safe practices in catching and batting softballs, and playing on see - saws, slides and swings. Emphasizes that consideration for others on the playground results in a good time for all.
Health and Safety; Physical Education and Recreation
Dist - EBEC **Prod** - EBEC 1966

Safety on the Street 11 MIN
U-matic / VHS / 16mm
Color; B&W (I)
LC FIA66-606
Places the responsibility for safety on children. Explains why they must be alert and why safety is their own decision.
Health and Safety
Dist - EBEC **Prod** - EBEC 1965

Safety on the Way to School 7 MIN
U-matic / VHS / 16mm
Color (P I)
Emphasizes the importance of following safety rules while crossing streets and obeying traffic signals on the way to school. Reinforces the idea that it takes time for vehicles to stop.
Health and Safety
Dist - LUF **Prod** - LUF 1983

Safety or Slaughter 14 MIN
U-matic / VHS / 16mm
Color (P)
Presents the reasons why industry should be concerned with traffic accidents. Illustrates safe driving techniques and stresses courtesy.
Health and Safety
Dist - IFB **Prod** - CRAF 1958

Safety orientation - healthcare edition 16 MIN
VHS
Color (IND PRO)
$495.00 purchase, $95.00 rental _ #BBP53
Illustrates simple safety habits for workers at every level in a healthcare facility. Includes a companion leader's guide.
Health and Safety
Dist - EXTR

Safety - Oriented First Aid Multimedia Course Series
Safety - oriented first aid multimedia course - Unit 1 290 MIN
Safety - oriented first aid multimedia course - Unit 2 22 MIN
Safety - Oriented First Aid Multimedia Course, Unit 3 28 MIN
Safety - Oriented First Aid Multimedia Course, Unit 4 10 MIN
Dist - IFB

Safety - oriented first aid multimedia course - Unit 1 290 MIN
29 MIN
16mm / VHS / U-matic
Safety - oriented first aid multimedia course series
Color (C A)
Deals with such first aid topics as respiratory emergencies and artificial respiration, indirect methods of artificial respiration, bleeding, embedded foreign objects, dressings and bandages.
Health and Safety
Dist - IFB **Prod** - CRAF

Safety - oriented first aid multimedia course - Unit 2 22 MIN
U-matic / VHS / 16mm
Safety - oriented first aid multimedia course series
Color (C A)
Deals with such first aid topics as shock, fractures and dislocations of the upper and lower limbs, and chest injuries.
Health and Safety
Dist - IFB **Prod** - CRAF

Safety - Oriented First Aid Multimedia Course, Unit 3 28 MIN
16mm / U-matic / VHS
Safety - Oriented First Aid Multimedia Course Series
Color (C A)
Deals with such first aid topics as head, neck and back injuries, burns and scalds, eye injuries, handling and moving casualties, and poisoning.
Health and Safety
Dist - IFB **Prod** - CRAF

Safety - Oriented First Aid Multimedia Course, Unit 4 10 MIN
16mm / U-matic / VHS
Safety - Oriented First Aid Multimedia Course Series
Color (C A)
Deals with casualty management.
Health and Safety
Dist - IFB **Prod** - CRAF

Safety partners series
Bulk liquid safety concerns
Handling bulk liquids in barges
Handling bulk liquids in tank cars
Handling bulk liquids in tank trucks
Dist - NUSTC

Safety - Peril Rides the Roads 15 MIN
16mm / U-matic / VHS
Safety Series
Color (P I)
LC 77-703330
Presents Safety Woman who rescues children from perilous situations. Provides examples of street, bicycle and traffic safety rules.
Health and Safety
Dist - BARR **Prod** - FILMCO 1977

Safety Pipetting 5 MIN
16mm
Color
LC 74-705569
Presents three commonly used instruments that are employed in the laboratory for safety pipetting. Demonstrates the operation of these instruments in detail.
Science; Science - Physical
Dist - USNAC **Prod** - USPHS 1965

Safety - Playground Spirits 9 MIN
U-matic / VHS / 16mm
Joy of Growing Series
Color (P I)
LC 72-700985
Presents good and bad playground spirits to show social problems and safety hazards that exist in recreational areas. Stresses the importance of safety, consideration of others and the right to privacy.
Health and Safety; Physical Education and Recreation; Psychology
Dist - EBEC **Prod** - EBEC 1971

Safety Plays and End Plays 30 MIN
U-matic / VHS
Play Bridge Series
Color (A)
Physical Education and Recreation
Dist - KYTV **Prod** - KYTV 1983

Safety Practices in Dredging Operations 16 MIN
U-matic / VHS / 16mm
Color (IND)
Shows that underwater mining for sand and gravel presents safety problems. Shows the tasks performed on a modern dredge and the hazards involved, and stresses the need for employees to be alert to the dangers and to work safely.
Health and Safety; Social Science
Dist - USNAC **Prod** - USDL 1982

Safety Practices in Low - Coal Mining 15 MIN
16mm
Color
LC 74-705570
Shows the special hazards workmen must guard against in thin - seam mines. Illustrates how restricted work space, curtailed field of vision and cramped body position can intensify the dangers involved in working with fast - moving, high - powered machines.
Health and Safety; Industrial and Technical Education
Dist - USNAC **Prod** - USBM 1971

Safety practices - tag out - personnel protective gear - voltage limitations 60 MIN
VHS / U-matic
Electrical maintenance basics series; Pt 1
Color (IND) (ENGLISH, SPANISH)
Health and Safety; Industrial and Technical Education
Dist - ITCORP **Prod** - ITCORP

Safety Precautions and Work Habits 30 MIN
U-matic / VHS
Keep it Running Series
Color
Teaches the student to recognize safety hazards and describes precautions to take to minimize the possibility of injury. Describes basic safety equipment available to the weekend mechanic.
Industrial and Technical Education
Dist - NETCHE **Prod** - NETCHE 1982

Safety Precautions for Electronics Personnel 18 MIN
16mm
B&W
LC FIE52-1291
Shows electrical and mechanical hazards which technicians encounter in their normal work and stresses precautions which should be used to prevent accidents.
Industrial and Technical Education
Dist - USNAC **Prod** - USN 1952

Safety programs 72 MIN
VHS
Color (G)
$15.00 purchase _ #DKVH U89580EN
Combines seven John Deere safety programs. Presents safety tips and discusses safe work habits in working with agricultural machinery.
Agriculture; Health and Safety
Dist - DEERE **Prod** - DEERE

Safety Record 10 MIN
16mm
Personal Side of Safety Series
B&W
Shows how each employee has a role in achieving a good safety record.
Business and Economics; Health and Safety
Dist - NSC **Prod** - NSC

Safety restoration during snow removal - guidelines 26 MIN
U-matic / VHS
Color (IND)
$80.00, $110.00 purchase _ #TCA18047, #TCA18046
Covers the correct procedures for plowing during snow removal operations.
Civics and Political Systems; Health and Safety; Industrial and Technical Education; Social Science
Dist - USNAC **Prod** - USDTFH 1989

Safety rules and you 15 MIN
VHS / 16mm
Color (P I)
$395.00, $345.00 purchase, $50.00 rental _ #8233
Shows children how important it is to think before they act. Gives tips on pedestrian behavior and actions at home to prevent accidents. Stresses self - protection.
Health and Safety
Dist - AIMS **Prod** - SANDE 1990

Safety Rules for School 11 MIN
U-matic / VHS / 16mm
Color (P)
$35 rental _ #9805
Teaches students through safety rules they should observe on the way to school, inside school, and on the playground.
Health and Safety
Dist - AIMS **Prod** - AIMS 1985

Safety - second to none 15 MIN
16mm / U-matic
Color
LC 74-703764
A number of experts in atomic safety point out the elaborate safety precautions and procedures required by the AEC for the nuclear power industry.
Health and Safety; Industrial and Technical Education; Social Science
Dist - USNAC **Prod** - USNRC 1974

The Safety secret 25 MIN
U-matic / VHS
(PRO)
$475.00 purchase, $110.00 rental
Discusses work safety, presents safety techniques for various settings.
Health and Safety
Dist - CREMED VLEARN **Prod** - CREMED 1987

Safety - seeing 10 MIN
16mm / VHS / BETA / U-matic
Color; PAL (G T)
PdS125, PdS133 purchase
Talks about eye protection to encourage people to take sensible precautions when working in hazardous areas.
Health and Safety
Dist - EDPAT

Safety Sense Series Pt 10
School Safety 20 MIN
Dist - GPN

Safety Sense Series Pt 11
Consumer Safety 20 MIN
Dist - GPN

Safety Sense Series Pt 13
Drug Effects 20 MIN
Dist - GPN

Safety Sense Series Pt 15
In - Service Program for Teachers 20 MIN
Dist - GPN

Safety Sense Series Pt 1
Jogging Safety 20 MIN
Dist - GPN

Safety Sense Series Pt 8
Self - Protection 20 MIN
Dist - GPN

Safety Sense Series Pt 9
Home Safety 20 MIN
Dist - GPN

Safety sense series
Babysitting safety 20 MIN
Bicycle Safety 20 MIN
Boating safety 20 MIN
Camping safety 20 MIN
Survival 20 MIN
Dist - GPN

Safety Series
Safety - Harm Hides at Home 16 MIN
Safety - in Danger Out of Doors 15 MIN
Safety - Peril Rides the Roads 15 MIN
Dist - BARR

Safety standards for the fire service 13 MIN
VHS
Firefighter I series
Color (IND)
$100.00 purchase _ #35638
Presents one part of a 19 - part series that is the teaching companion for IFSTA's Essentials of Fire Fighting manual. Provides an overview of a firefighter's safety responsibilities required by NFPA 1500. Demonstrates safety procedures and equipment used in the line of duty. Based on Chapter 19.
Health and Safety; Science - Physical; Social Science
Dist - OKSU **Prod** - ACCTRA

Safety - take it home 12 MIN
BETA / VHS / U-matic
Safety - live action video series
Color (IND G)
$495.00 purchase _ #600 - 15
Describes and stresses basic home safety techniques. Part of a series on safety.
Health and Safety
Dist - ITSC **Prod** - ITSC

Safety - the big picture - Seguridad - el cuadro completo 12 MIN
U-matic / BETA / VHS
Color (IND G) (SPANISH)
$495.00 purchase _ #825 - 01, #825 - 04
Motivates and encourages supervisors to promote safety within their operations. Identifies the supervisors' responsibilities to ensure the safety of their employees and discusses how the incidence of accidents can be lowered by reducing unsafe behavior.
Business and Economics; Health and Safety; Industrial and Technical Education; Psychology
Dist - ITSC **Prod** - ITSC

Safety - the Helpful Burglars 11 MIN
U-matic / VHS / 16mm
Joy of Growing Series
Color (P)
LC 72-701035
Points out the important lesson that household hazards are a threat to everyone.
Health and Safety
Dist - EBEC **Prod** - EBEC 1971

Safety - the science laboratory
VHS
Science laboratory technique series
Color (J H)
$79.95 purchase _ #193 W 2204
Focuses on the three most frequent sources of injuries in the laboratory - glassware, chemicals and heat. Part of a series on laboratory technique, including proper use and handling of equipment, preparation of materials and recording observations. Includes a supplementary teaching guide.
Science
Dist - WARDS **Prod** - WARDS

Safety - the traffic jungle 7 MIN
U-matic / VHS / 16mm
Color (P)
Teaches children how to avoid injury in the urban 'traffic jungle' by learning and observing traffic safety rules.
Health and Safety
Dist - EBEC **Prod** - EBEC 1971

Safety Times Three 16 MIN
16mm
Color (J H C)
LC 74-703048
Explains that the three elements which make up safe driving are the driver, the car and the road. Discusses the need for courtesy and attentiveness on the part of the driver and details the skills and knowledge needed to be a good defensive driver.
Health and Safety; Psychology
Dist - GM **Prod** - GM 1972

Safety tips 30 MIN
VHS
Parents' point of view series
Color (T A PRO)
$69.95 purchase
Presents advice on caring for children under five years old. Targeted to both parents and care providers. Covers safety tips for the family home. Hosted by Nancy Thurmond, ex - wife of Senator Strom Thurmond.
Education; Guidance and Counseling; Health and Safety
Dist - SCETV **Prod** - SCETV 1988

Safety - total loss control 10 MIN
16mm / U-matic / VHS
Color (IND)
LC 72-702121
Points out that industry must direct its accident prevention efforts toward all incidents which might eventually lead to injury of employees. Notes that fire prevention, theft prevention, reduction in pollution and improvement of industrial health and hygiene are of particular importance to loss control.
Business and Economics; Health and Safety
Dist - IFB **Prod** - IAPA 1972
CRAF

Safety training series
Application and use of breathing apparatus 30 MIN
Cardio - pulmonary resuscitation 45 MIN
Hydrogen Sulphide Alert 60 MIN
Dist - LEIKID

Safety, Use, and Maintenance of Air - Powered Bumper Jacks 7 MIN
VHS / 16mm
Kirkwood Community College Auto Mechanics Series
(G PRO)
$53.50 purchase _ #KTI51
Instructs on the safety, use and maintenance of air - powered bumper jacks.
Industrial and Technical Education
Dist - RMIBHF **Prod** - RMIBHF

Safety, Use, and Maintenance of Hydraulic Floor Jacks 10 MIN
VHS / 16mm
Kirkwood Community College Auto Mechanics Series
(G PRO)
$61.00 purchase _ #KTI53
Instructs on the safety, use, and maintenance of an hydraulic floor jack. Includes checking and filling.
Industrial and Technical Education
Dist - RMIBHF **Prod** - RMIBHF

Safety Valves - 1 60 MIN
VHS
Piping and Valves Series
Color (PRO)
$600.00, $1500.00 purchase _ #GMSV1
Addresses the function and importance of safety and relief valves. Part of a six - part series on piping and valves, which is part of a set on general and mechanical maintenance. Includes 10 textbooks and an instructor guide which provide four hours of instruction.
Education; Health and Safety; Industrial and Technical Education; Psychology
Dist - NUSTC **Prod** - NUSTC

Safety Valves - 2 60 MIN
VHS
Piping and Valves Series
Color (PRO)
$600.00, $1500.00 purchase _ #GMSV2
Expands on the concepts in Part 1. Emphasizes safety and maintenance. Part of a six - part series on piping and valves, which is part of a set on general and mechanical maintenance. Includes 10 textbooks and an instructor guide which provide four hours of instruction.
Education; Health and Safety; Industrial and Technical Education; Psychology
Dist - NUSTC **Prod** - NUSTC

Safety wear for construction electricians 10 MIN
VHS
Color (H A T)
$49.00 purchase _ #VC306
Overviews basic clothing and protective equipment for work on commercial construction projects. Discusses protection for head, hands, feet, eyes, ears and airway.
Industrial and Technical Education
Dist - AAVIM **Prod** - AAVIM 1992

Safety Wise Series
Help yourself to safety 10 MIN
Not Even One Chance 10 MIN
Dist - NSC

Safety with Electricity 10 MIN
U-matic / VHS / 16mm
Color; B&W (P)
Demonstrates that electricity can be dangerous, shows how these dangers can be minimized by simple safety precautions and illustrates some of the uses of electricity. Shows the nature and sources of electicity.
Guidance and Counseling; Health and Safety; Science - Physical
Dist - EBEC **Prod** - EBEC 1963

Saffron - Autumn Gold 26 MIN
VHS / U-matic
Spice of Life Series
Color (J A)
Discloses the secrets of saffron in the preparation of select dishes from bouillabaisse to saffron buns.
Health and Safety; Home Economics
Dist - BCNFL **Prod** - BLCKRD 1985

Saga of progress 15 MIN
16mm
B&W (I)
Presents the achievements of the five - year plans in the urban areas of India. Shows the major projects set up according to the plans and the progress made by them.
History - World; Sociology
Dist - NEDINF **Prod** - INDIA

Saga of Safety Sam 15 MIN
16mm / U-matic / VHS
B&W (J H C)
Employs a folk song to stress the importance of using safety shoes, non - slip gloves, goggles, a non - sinkable jacket and a safety hat in situations where necessary.
Health and Safety
Dist - IFB **Prod** - CRAF 1959

Saga of the Semis 25 MIN
16mm
Color
LC 77-702138
Focuses on the capabilities of the Rowan Companies' semi - submersible oil drilling platforms.
Industrial and Technical Education; Social Science
Dist - ROWAN **Prod** - ROWAN 1977

Saga of the whale - Too many elephants 46 MIN
U-matic / VHS
Color
Traces the annual migration of the gray whale from Alaska to Baja California where they court and calve in the warm winter waters. Examines the elephant's family and herd structures and the life cycle of this long - living animal with particular attention to the consequences a herd has on its environment.
Science - Natural
Dist - TIMLIF **Prod** - TIMLIF 1979

Saga of Western Man Series
Beethoven - Ordeal and Triumph, Pt 1 26 MIN
Beethoven - Ordeal and Triumph, Pt 2 26 MIN
Dist - CRMP

Saga of Western Man Series
Beethoven - Ordeal and Triumph 52 MIN
Cortez and the Legend 52 MIN
Cortez and the Legend, Pt 1 26 MIN
Cortez and the Legend, Pt 2 26 MIN
Custer - the American surge westward 33 MIN
Eighteen ninety - eight 54 MIN
Eighteen ninety - eight - Pt 1 27 MIN
Eighteen ninety - eight - Pt 2 27 MIN
Fourteen Ninety - Two 54 MIN
Fourteen Ninety - Two, Pt 1 - the Renaissance 14 MIN
Fourteen Ninety - Two, Pt 2 - Christopher Columbus 40 MIN
I Am a Soldier 51 MIN
I Am a Soldier, Pt 1 25 MIN
I Am a Soldier, Pt 2 26 MIN
I, Leonardo Da Vinci 54 MIN
I, Leonardo Da Vinci, Pt 1 27 MIN
I, Leonardo Da Vinci, Pt 2 27 MIN
The Legacy of Rome 52 MIN
Legacy of Rome, the, Pt 1 22 MIN
Legacy of Rome, the, Pt 2 30 MIN
Nineteen Sixty - Four 54 MIN
Nineteen Sixty - Four, Pt 1 27 MIN
Nineteen Sixty - Four, Pt 2 27 MIN
The Pilgrim Adventure 54 MIN
The Pilgrim Adventure - Pt 1 27 MIN
The Pilgrim Adventure - Pt 2 27 MIN
Seventeen seventy - six 54 MIN

Seventeen seventy - six - Pt 1 27 MIN
Seventeen seventy - six - Pt 2 27 MIN
Dist - MGHT

Saga of Windwagon Smith 13 MIN
16mm / U-matic / VHS
Color (I J)
LC 72-714976
Presents a tale about Captain Windwagon Smith, who blew into a Kansas town in a prairie schooner, outfitted with mast, sails, and other seagoing equipment. The townspeople helped build a super windwagon to haul freight, but it was blown away by a Kansas twister.
Literature and Drama
Dist - CORF Prod - DISNEY 1971

The Sage and the Sayer - Ralph Waldo Emerson and Henry David Thoreau 20 MIN
VHS / U-matic
American Literature Series
Color (H C A)
LC 83-706252
Presents conversations and soliloquies excerpted from Ralph Waldo Emerson's and Henry David Thoreau's essays and other writings.
Literature and Drama
Dist - AITECH Prod - AUBU 1983

The Sage of Monticello and Old Hickory 20 MIN
U-matic
Truly American Series
Color (I)
Offers information on Thomas Jefferson and Andrew Jackson.
Biography
Dist - GPN Prod - WVIZTV 1979

SAGE - Semi - Automatic Ground Environment System 19 MIN
16mm
Color
LC 74-706233
Describes the mission, operations, capabilities and military importance of the SAGE system. Shows how SAGE sectors electronically compute aircraft movement information which is received from the observer agencies.
Civics and Political Systems; Industrial and Technical Education
Dist - USNAC Prod - USAF 1964

Sagebrush country 28 MIN
VHS / U-matic / 16mm
Color (J H G)
$280.00, $330.00, $535.00 purchase, $50.00 rental
Documents the ecology of the high desert country of the American West. Traces the history of one area in this environmental niche and how current land practices may assure the preservation of this potentially fragile ecosystem.
Fine Arts; Geography - United States; Science - Natural
Dist - NDIM Prod - OSU 1987

Sagebrush sailors 27 MIN
VHS / U-matic
Color (I J H G)
$280.00, $330.00 purchase, $50.00 rental
Features a historical documentary on the Columbia River, before the great dams were built, about the captains and crews who ran the river boats and who vied for commerce by running the mighty rapids of the Columbia. Shows the 100 rapids between Lewiston, Idaho and The Dalles, Oregon. Produced by Tryon Productions.
Geography - United States; History - United States
Dist - NDIM

Saguaroland 15 MIN
16mm
Color
Karl Maslowski tells amusing story of Chipmunk and an egg, including many birds in natural Arizona habitat.
Geography - United States; Science - Natural
Dist - SFI Prod - SFI

Sahara 97 MIN
16mm / U-matic / VHS
B&W (J)
Stars Humphrey Bogart as Sergeant Gunn who is in charge of an army tank, 'Lulubelle,' lumbering across the desert after the fall of Tobruk. Tells the story of her crew and of an assortment of allies which she picks up on her determined dash to avoid the enemy.
Fine Arts
Dist - FI Prod - CPC 1943

Sahara fantasia - a desert festival of Morocco 9 MIN
VHS / U-matic
Color
Features nomadic desert tribes coming together in Southern Morocco to celebrate their Moussem, a unique Saharan festival. Covers music and dancing, colorful tents of trade, highlighted by the celebration of 'fantasia', a traditional event combining ancient musketry and skilled horsemanship. Unnarrated.
Geography - World; Religion and Philosophy
Dist - IFF Prod - IFF

Sahel - struggle for survival 18 MIN
16mm
Color
Shows the Catholic Relief Services teaching Africans how to combat the long - term effects of drought.
Geography - World; History - World; Religion and Philosophy; Sociology
Dist - MTP Prod - CATHRS

Said, Asked 10 MIN
U-matic
Readalong Two Series
Color (P)
Provides young viewers with a flexible range of reading experiences through active involvement in reading and writing. Comes with teacher's guide and kit.
Education; English Language; Literature and Drama
Dist - TVOTAR Prod - TVOTAR 1976

Said the whiting to the snail 15 MIN
U-matic / VHS
Other families, other friends series
Color (P)
Explains the process of commercial fishing in Maine. Blue module of the series.
Geography - United States; Geography - World; Social Science
Dist - AITECH Prod - WVIZTV 1971

Sail Away 18 MIN
16mm
Color (I J)
Documents the adventures of a young boy who goes sailing in a trimaran with a friend and encounters different forms of marine life and a dramatic storm.
Fine Arts; Literature and Drama
Dist - MOKIN Prod - NFBC 1978

Sail away 14 MIN
16mm
Journal series
Color
LC 74-703754
Takes a look at the sport of sailboat racing.
Physical Education and Recreation
Dist - CANFDC Prod - FIARTS 1973

Sail Belize, Central America 30 MIN
VHS
Scuba World series
Color (G)
$24.90 purchase _ #0435
Visits the 176 mile long barrier reef near Belize, Central America.
Geography - World; Physical Education and Recreation
Dist - SEVVID

Sail on 22 MIN
VHS
Color (PRO IND A)
$595.00 purchase, $175.00 rental _ #DET10
Tells the story of Captain William Pinkney, first African - American of the three Americans to circumnavigate the world alone. Motivates the viewer to commitment, action and courage. Short version also available.
Business and Economics; History - United States; Physical Education and Recreation; Psychology
Dist - EXTR Prod - DETERM

Sail on Voyager - physical science 60 MIN
VHS
Infinite voyage series
Color (H C A)
Shares the discoveries of Voyager as it travels over four billion miles, gathering previously unknown facts about the solar system. Combines film footage, special effects, computer graphics and soundtracks to bring complex scientific concepts to life for students. Includes instructor's guide with terms and definitions, learning objectives and follow-up activities. Part of a 20-part series.
History - World; Science - Physical
Dist - INSTRU Prod - WQED
INTM

Sail the ocean blue 8 MIN
U-matic / VHS / 16mm
Color (I J)
LC 73-702735
Points out that few sports offer such a unique sense of individual satisfaction as does sailing. Captures a succession of striking images which transmits some of the feeling encountered by the crew of a racing sail boat. Serves as a springboard to both written and oral expression.
Physical Education and Recreation
Dist - AIMS Prod - EVANSA 1973

Sail to glory
VHS
Color (G)
$29.80 purchase _ #0063
Recreates the first America's Cup of 1851. Uses the exact replica of the original schooner America. Features Robert Stack and music by Doc Severinson.
Physical Education and Recreation
Dist - SEVVID

Sail to Glory 56 MIN
VHS
Color (G)
$29.95 purchase _ #YS - 9
Dramatizes the 1851 victory of the yacht America over a fleet of English yachts off Cowes, England. Reveals that America won the coveted trophy that became the America's Cup.
Geography - World; Literature and Drama; Physical Education and Recreation
Dist - MYSTIC Prod - MYSTIC 1967

Sail to glory 50 MIN
16mm
Color
Dramatizes the first America's Cup Race and traces the history of the winning sailing vessel, the America.
Physical Education and Recreation
Dist - COUNFI Prod - COUNFI 1977

Sail to win
VHS
Color (G)
$24.95 purchase; $24.95 purchase _ #0936
Presents three boating sequences. Focuses on the history, salvage and restoration of Ibis, one of the famous 1904 New York Yacht Club 30 foot racing sloops, in part one. Boards 73 foot Windward Passage for a record breaking run in the 1971 Miami to Montego Bay race in part two. Concludes with ARC '87, featuring the Atlantic Rally for Cruisers race from the Canary Islands to Barbados.
Physical Education and Recreation
Dist - MYSTIC Prod - MYSTIC
SEVVID

Sail wars 58 MIN
U-matic / VHS
Nova series
Color (H C A)
$250 purchase _ #5128C
Shows engineering efforts to design the sailboat that defeated the Australians. Produced by WGBH Boston.
Industrial and Technical Education; Physical Education and Recreation
Dist - CORF

Sail west to Desolation Sound
VHS
Color (G)
$39.90 purchase _ #0749
Travels through the waters of the Pacific Northwest from Princess Louisa inlet to Savary Island aboard Helena IV and Scaup. Photographs marine facilities from sea and air.
Geography - United States; Geography - World; Physical Education and Recreation
Dist - SEVVID

Sailboat 3 MIN
16mm
Color (G)
$6.00 rental
Presents an image of a toy - like sailboat floating on the water to the sound of roaring waves. Evokes a sense of sadness and nostalgia.
Fine Arts
Dist - CANCIN Prod - WIELNJ 1967

Sailboat navigation - Vol 4 75 MIN
VHS
Annapolis book of seamanship with John Rousmaniere series
Color (G)
LC 90-712265
Gives instructions on navigation at sea. Part of a five - part series on seamanship by John Rousmaniere.
Health and Safety; Physical Education and Recreation
Dist - CREPRI Prod - CREPRI 1987
CPI

Sailfish ho 15 MIN
16mm
Color
Shows champions George and Phyllis Bass catch sailfish off Florida and the Gulf Stream.
Geography - United States; Physical Education and Recreation
Dist - SFI Prod - SFI

Sailfishing with Roland Martin
VHS
Color (G)
$29.80 purchase _ #0140
Travels with Roland Martin and his friend James to fish for sailfish in the Atlantic Ocean off West Palm Beach, Florida.
Geography - United States; Geography - World; Physical Education and Recreation; Science - Natural
Dist - SEVVID

Sailing 3 MIN
16mm
Of all things series
Color (P I)
Discusses the sport of sailing.
Physical Education and Recreation
Dist - AVED **Prod** - BAILYL

Sailing Above the Alps 28 MIN
16mm / U-matic / VHS
Color (H C A)
LC 83-700661
Shows a group of hang - gliding enthusiasts on the Alpine peaks of Switzerland. Features photographer Eric Jones receiving elementary hang - gliding lessons.
Geography - World; Physical Education and Recreation
Dist - IU **Prod** - GSAVL 1981

Sailing all seas 60 MIN
VHS
Color (G)
$29.95 purchase
Sails around the world with Dwight Long on a 32 - foot ketch, the Idle Hour, a voyage that started in 1934.
Geography - World; Physical Education and Recreation
Dist - MYSTIC **Prod** - MYSTIC

Sailing and racing - Volume 5 60 MIN
VHS
Annapolis book of seamanship with John Rousmaniere series
Color (G)
LC 90-712268
Gives instructions on racing sailing boats. Part of a five - part series on seamanship by John Rousmaniere.
Health and Safety; Physical Education and Recreation
Dist - CREPRI **Prod** - CREPRI 1987

Sailing - do it right, keep it safe 28 MIN
16mm
Color
Reviews the terms, techniques and equipment used in sailing. Highlights the camaraderie and teamwork that can be developed in the sport.
Physical Education and Recreation
Dist - MTP **Prod** - MICLOB

Sailing film festival
VHS
Color (G)
$29.80 purchase _ #0054
Illustrates an S - 2 in action, as well as the Grand Slam Nationals in Holland, Michigan. Views the tall ships sailing out of Newport and sailing near Santa Barbara.
Physical Education and Recreation
Dist - SEVVID

Sailing for new sailors
VHS
Under sail with Robbie Doyle series
Color (G A)
$19.90 purchase _ #0475
Teaches some of the language of the sea, as well as the basics of sailing and seamanship. Features Robbie Doyle.
Physical Education and Recreation
Dist - SEVVID

Sailing for paradise
VHS
Under sail with Robbie Doyle series
Color (G A)
$19.90 purchase _ #0474
Looks at ways to get into sailing. Travels to a boat show, shows what to look for when buying a boat. Examines sailing schools and the charter industry. Features Robbie Doyle.
Physical Education and Recreation
Dist - SEVVID

Sailing fundamentals 58 MIN
VHS
Color (G A)
$100.00 rental _ #0110
Teaches seamanship to keel boat daysailors and operators of 20 - 40 foot cruising sailboats. Covers wind awareness, helmsmanship, points of sail, tacking and jibing, docking, mooring, anchoring, navigation, sail trim, spinnaker, rights of way rules, knots. For beginning and intermediate sailors.
Physical Education and Recreation
Dist - SEVVID

Sailing - Pt 1 28 MIN
16mm
B&W (I)
LC 78-704655
Explains and demonstrates the principles and terminology of sailing. Emphasizes that each person on a sailboat must know how to swim and the correct way to use a life preserver. Explains the major parts of a sailboat, the mast, boom and centerboard housing. Shows how responses to wind should be made before going out in a sailboat, and demonstrates the effects of wind upon the sail.
Physical Education and Recreation
Dist - IU **Prod** - NET 1969

Sailing - Pt 2 27 MIN
16mm
B&W (I)
LC 71-704656
Investigates the effects of weight placement, wind and sail adjustment to gain smooth and efficient sailing. Shows that the sail must be let in and out and the tension changed for different kinds of wind. Demonstrates the rules of navigation using sailboat models to show which boat would have the right of way under certain conditions. Compares these demonstrations with live scenes of the same maneuvers using real sailboats.
Physical Education and Recreation
Dist - IU **Prod** - NET 1969

Sailing quarterly - Vol 1, No 1 - premiere issue 60 MIN
VHS
Color (G)
$29.95 purchase _ #0550
Contains segments on Tristan Jones in Thailand, racing tips from John Kolius, Spice Island with Don Street, and photography tips from Sharon Green. Also presents an interview with Loon yacht designer Robert Perry and discusses equipment. Represents the premiere issue of Sailing Quarterly which offers sailing action, cruising information, interviews and charter destinations.
Physical Education and Recreation
Dist - SEVVID

Sailing with the Clouds 9 MIN
16mm / U-matic / VHS
Color (P I J H C)
LC 75-700158
Depicts the experience of soaring through the sky in a sailplane. Portrays the visual and emotional experience from the point of view of the pilot.
Guidance and Counseling; Physical Education and Recreation
Dist - JOU **Prod** - GLDWER 1974

A Sailor - made man - Grandma's boy 83 MIN
16mm / U-matic / VHS
Harold Lloyd series
Color
LC 77-701702
Reissue of the 1921 silent Harold LLoyd comedy A Sailor - Made Man. Tells the story of a young man who joins the Navy in order to impress his girlfriend's father. Includes the 1922 Harold Lloyd comedy about a timid young man who, with the help of a lucky charm, manages to capture the local bandit, thrash his bullying rival and win the affection of his girlfriend.
Fine Arts; Literature and Drama
Dist - TIMLIF **Prod** - ROACH 1976

Sailor with a Future 21 MIN
16mm
Color
LC 74-706567
Deals with the naval nuclear propulsion program. Shows a young nuclear propulsion plant operator aboard the USS Long Beach as he looks back at the training that prepared him for a career in the Navy.
Civics and Political Systems; Guidance and Counseling; Psychology; Science - Physical
Dist - USNAC **Prod** - USN 1968

A Sailor's dream 47 MIN
VHS
Color (G)
$49.90 purchase _ #0493
Romances the sea. Tells of sailors' love for the sea and the ships in which they sail. Looks at classic yachts and 12 meter racers. Gary Jobson narrates.
Physical Education and Recreation
Dist - SEVVID

Sailors in Green 28 MIN
16mm
Color
LC 74-706568
Describes the founding of the Navy Seabees and highlights their participation in the Pacific and European theaters during World War II, Korea and Vietnam. Shows Seabee assistance as disaster teams during Hurricane Camille and taking part in civic action in Micronesia and in underwater construction in naval research projects.
Civics and Political Systems; Industrial and Technical Education
Dist - USNAC **Prod** - USN 1972

Sailors' knots and splices
VHS
Color (G A)
$39.80 purchase _ #0203
Features Brian Toss who guides step - by - step through 18 knots, whippings and splices in three - strand and double - braid rope. Uses close - up detail from the viewer's perspective.
Physical Education and Recreation
Dist - SEVVID

Sails and Sailors - J Boats '37
BETA / VHS
B&W
Shows a glimpse of Newport and the Cup race of 1937 between J's Ranger and Endeavor II.
Geography - United States; Geography - World; Physical Education and Recreation; Social Science
Dist - MYSTIC **Prod** - MYSTIC 1983

Sails of Doom 60 MIN
VHS
Triumph Of The Nomads Series
Color (G)
$49.95 purchase _ #TRON - 103
Shows how the Aboriginal culture changed after 1770, when the British first came to Australia. Reviews the accomplishments of Aborigines in areas of food, medicine, manufacturing and development of natural resources.
History - World; Sociology
Dist - PBS **Prod** - NOMDFI 1989

Saint Augustine 57 MIN
U-matic / VHS / 16mm
Third testament series
Color
LC 75-703365
Presents the life and thought of St Augustine.
Biography; Literature and Drama; Religion and Philosophy
Dist - TIMLIF **Prod** - NIELSE 1974

Saint Flournoy Lobos - Logos and the eastern Europe fetus taxing Japan brides in west coast places sucking rides in west coast places sucking ng Alabama air 12 MIN
16mm
Color (G)
$25.00 rental
Presages details and intent of the Charles Manson family's cult and actions as it was filmed uncannily months before the facts were known. Features Death Valley location in a film by Will Hindle.
Fine Arts; Religion and Philosophy; Sociology
Dist - CANCIN

The Saint from North Battleford 23 MIN
16mm / VHS
Color (J)
$495.00, $445.00 purhcase
Profiles Reuben Mayes, a successful NFL running back from Saskatchewan. Reveals that the Mayes family, blacks from Oklahoma, moved to Candada in 1910. Examines Mayes' return to the Southern United States and his success with New Orleans' football team.
Biography; Physical Education and Recreation; Sociology
Dist - FLMWST

The Saint - Galy Tiles of Williamsburg 29 MIN
VHS / 16mm
Color (G)
$55.00 rental _ #STGT - 000
Studies the art of tile - making and the history of colonial Williamsburg and the Virginia colony. Follows artist Gaza St Galy as he sketches and prepares tiles for a mosaic.
Fine Arts
Dist - PBS **Prod** - WCVETV

Saint - Gaudens - masque of the golden bowl 59 MIN
VHS / U-matic
Color (G)
$39.95 purchase _ #412 - 9054; $39.95 purchase
Dramatizes the life and work of Augustus Saint - Gaudens, preeminent sculptor of the American Renaissance. Recreates one day in the summer of 1905 when Saint - Gaudens, played by James Hurdle, celebrated the 20th anniversary of the founding of the Cornish colony. At a masque and pageant on the grounds of his home, friends and fellow artists such as Stanford White, played by Kevin Conway, reflect on Saint - Gaudens' life and career.
Fine Arts
Dist - FI **Prod** - MMOA 1987
ARTSAM

Saint George and the Dragon
VHS / 35mm strip
Caldecotts on Filmstrip Series
Color (K)
$35.00 purchase
Presents a children's story. Part of the Caldecott series.
English Language; Literature and Drama
Dist - PELLER

Saint John Neumann 28 MIN
BETA / VHS
Color
Covers the life of John Neumann who became Bishop of Philadelphia.
Biography; Religion and Philosophy
Dist - DSP **Prod** - DSP

The Saint Lawrence 50 MIN
U-matic / 16mm / VHS
Canada - five portraits series
Color; Mono (G) (FRENCH)
MV $350.00 _ MP $475.00 purchase, $50.00 rental
Documents a journey from the mouth of the Saint Lawrence to the farm - lined shores near Quebec to its narrowest point at Montreal. This is a river of dramatic differences. French - Canadian actress Patricia Dumas talks about her personal experiences, tells stories of her childhood and discusses her theatrical career in Montreal. Ms. Dumas reveals an unusual bond of devotion between the river and its people.
Geography - World
Dist - CTV **Prod** - CTV 1973

Saint Louis - Gateway to the West 25 MIN
16mm
Color (I)
LC Fl68-235
Describes the results of the bicentennial celebration of Saint Louis, which led to the rebuilding of much of the city, beginning in 1955. Includes views of the city's industries, universities, hospitals, museums, zoo and attractive living areas.
Geography - United States; Psychology; Science - Natural; Sociology
Dist - SWBELL **Prod** - SWBELL 1966

Saint Maria Goretti 18 MIN
BETA / VHS
Color
Tells the story of the martyred child Maria Goretti.
Biography; Religion and Philosophy
Dist - DSP **Prod** - DSP

Saint - Urbain in Troyes 28 MIN
16mm / U-matic / VHS
Color (H C A)
Explores the history of the cathedral of Saint - Urbain de Troyes in France. Details its Gothic architecture and looks at other French cathedrals in comparison.
Fine Arts; History - World
Dist - IFB **Prod** - NFBC 1973

Saints and legions series

Alexander the Great	30 MIN
Augustine	30 MIN
The Barbarians	30 MIN
Battle of Chalons	30 MIN
The Byzantine army	30 MIN
The Byzantine navy	30 MIN
The Celtic Church	30 MIN
Charlemagne and the Vikings	30 MIN
Constantine	30 MIN
The Crusaders	30 MIN
Early Christianity	30 MIN
Eastern Europe	30 MIN
Great church council	30 MIN
Great heresies	30 MIN
The Great schism	30 MIN
Heraclius	30 MIN
Islam	30 MIN
Julian the Apostate	30 MIN
Justinian	30 MIN
Justinian and Theodora	30 MIN
Leo the Iconoclast	30 MIN
Monasticism	30 MIN
Mystery religions	30 MIN
Pope Gregory	30 MIN
The Roman Army	30 MIN
Theodoric - Ostrogoth	30 MIN

Dist - SCETV

Saints and spirits 25 MIN
VHS
Disappearing world series
Color (G C)
$99.00 purchase, $19.00 rental _ #36284
Reveals that Islamic women in the Moroccan city of Marrakech rarely attend mosque and hold their rituals and celebrations at home. Discloses that female pilgrims often make the arduous journey to the mountain shrine of Saint Sidhi Chamharou, and a Shawapa, or seer, performs the annual rite of sacrifice that binds them to the spirit Sidhi Mahmoun. Features anthropologist Elizabeth Fernea. Part of a series working closely with anthropologists who lived for a year or more in societies whose social structures, beliefs and practices are threatened by the expansion of technocratic civilization.
Religion and Philosophy; Sociology
Dist - PSU **Prod** - GRANDA 1978

Saints and Spirits 26 MIN
U-matic / VHS / 16mm
Color (H C A)
LC 80-701149
Looks at one group of Moroccan Muslims, telling how they view their worship of saints and spirits as part of the wider Islamic tradition. Shows them visiting shrines in Marrakech and in the Atlas Mountains.
Geography - World; Religion and Philosophy
Dist - ICARUS **Prod** - UTEX 1980

Sakharov 120 MIN
U-matic / VHS
Color (G)
$299.00, $149.00 purchase _ #AD - 847
Dramatizes the life of Sakharov, a Russian physicist who won the Stalin Prize and the Order of Lenin. Reveals that he became a social outcast for demonstrating honesty, compassion and resistance to injustice. Features Jason Robards, Jr, and Glenda Jackson.
Biography; Geography - World; History - World; Science
Dist - FOTH **Prod** - FOTH

The Sakuddei of Indonesia 52 MIN
VHS
Disappearing world series
Color (H C G)
$445.00 purchase, $75.00 rental
Reveals that off the coast of Indonesia live the Sakuddei, completely cut off from the outside world. Shows an egalitarian society, in near perfect harmony with the environment, with no leaders, equality of women and men, the cherishing of peace. Unfortunately, this Utopian way of life is threatened by encroaching 'civilization.'
Civics and Political Systems; Geography - World; Sociology
Dist - FLMLIB **Prod** - GRATV 1987

Salaam Bombay 113 MIN
35mm
Color; PAL (G)
Shows children caught in the inescapable poverty trap in India, scavenging and trying to evade the worst fate - the institutions and children's homes. Affirms the strength and spirit of hope. Shot in the streets and brothels of Bombay with a cast of street kids. Produced by Mirabai Films, New York; National Film Development Corporation, India; Channel Four Television, UK; and Cadrage SA, Paris, India, France and UK. Contact distributor about price and availability outside the United Kingdom.
Fine Arts; Geography - World; Sociology
Dist - BALFOR

Salad dressings 43 MIN
VHS
Cookbook videos series
Color (G)
$19.95 purchase _ #ALW130; $19.95 purchase
Shows how to prepare salad dressings in short, easy - to - learn segments. Lists each ingredient as it is added in subtitles and visually reinforces spoken instructions. Gives recipe background and nutritional facts. Part of the Cookbook Videos series.
Home Economics; Social Science
Dist - CADESF **Prod** - CADESF
ALWHIT

Salad preparation 16 MIN
8mm cartridge / 16mm
Food service employee series
Color (IND A)
LC 72-707354
Stresses the importance of salads in the diet, and shows the correct procedures to follow in their preparation and serving.
Home Economics; Industrial and Technical Education
Dist - COPI **Prod** - COPI 1969

Salad Presentation
VHS / U-matic
Color
Home Economics; Industrial and Technical Education
Dist - CULINA **Prod** - CULINA

Salads
U-matic
Matter of taste series
Color (H A)
Suggests that salads have potential for greater variety than many other foods because many kinds of foods can be combined. Demonstrates how to make a basic salad which can be made into a main dish. Lesson six in the series.
Home Economics
Dist - CDTEL **Prod** - COAST

Salads
VHS / 35mm strip
Food preparation series
$119.00 purchase _ #PX1143 filmstrip, $119.00 purchase _ #PX1143V
Presents the main types of salads and salad dressings. Demonstrates techniques for making an appetizer, accompaniment, entree and dessert. Shows French dressings, mayonnaise and cooked dressings.
Health and Safety; Home Economics; Industrial and Technical Education; Social Science
Dist - CAREER **Prod** - CAREER

Salads 45 MIN
VHS
Le Cordon Bleu cooking series
Color (H C G)
$24.95 purchase _ #LCB004V
Details, with close - up footage, techniques and practical methods needed to prepare a fabulous assortment of salads. Features the world - renowned chefs of Le Cordon Bleu's teaching staff. Part of an eight - part series.
Home Economics
Dist - CAMV

Salads - from Spinach to Hot Steak 30 MIN
Salad - Lesson 2
VHS
International Cooking School with Chef Rene Series
Color (G)
$69.00 purchase
Presents classic methods of cooking that stress essential flavor. Introduces newer, lighter foods. Lesson 2 deals with salads.
Fine Arts; Home Economics; Psychology; Social Science; Sociology
Dist - LUF **Prod** - LUF

Salads supreme
VHS
Video cooking library series
Color (J H G)
$19.95 purchase _ #KVC943V
Illustrates the preparation of salads through step - by - step demonstrations. Covers everything needed from ingredients to equipment, with clear explanations of cooking techniques. Includes recipes. Part of a 22 - part series.
Home Economics
Dist - CAMV

Salamander 25 MIN
VHS
Nature watch series
Color (P I J H C)
$49.00 purchase _ #320216; LC 89-715859
Studies the salamander. Part of a series that explores the curious and uncommon characteristics of a variety of mammals, insects, birds and sea creatures.
Science - Natural
Dist - TVOTAR **Prod** - TVOTAR 1988

The Salamander room - 94
VHS
Reading rainbow series
Color; CC (K P)
$39.95 purchase
Shows that there's more to creating an animal habitat than meets the eye in a story by Anne Mazer, illustrated by Steve Johnson and narrated by Lynn Thigpin. Visits Jungle World, a simulated rainforest at the Bronx Zoo, with LeVar. Demonstrates how the rainforest environment was created. Part of a series offering a multicultural approach to generating reading enthusiasm with cross - curricular applications, hosted by LeVar Burton.
English Language; Literature and Drama; Science; Science - Natural
Dist - GPN **Prod** - LNMDP 1993

Salamanders - a night at the Phi Delt House 14 MIN
U-matic / VHS
Color
Looks at a fraternity at a major state university which celebrates the end of the school year by ritually capturing and eating live salamanders.
Education; Sociology
Dist - FLMLIB **Prod** - HRNBIG 1984

Salamanders and Lizards 11 MIN
U-matic
Color (P)
Depicts salamanders and chameleons in a tank. Explains how life evolved from water to land and emphasizes the similarity between lizards and the dinosaurs.
Science - Natural
Dist - GA **Prod** - BOBWIN

Salavdor Dali - a soft self - portrait 60 MIN
VHS
Color (H C G T A)
$39.95 purchase _ #S01447
Profiles Spanish painter Salvador Dali. Filmed at Dali's home at Port Ligat, Spain. Narrated by Orson Welles.
Fine Arts
Dist - UILL **Prod** - UILL

The Sale and purchase of financially troubled businesses 50 MIN
VHS
Color (C PRO A)
$95.00 purchase _ #Y601
Covers the procedures and problems associated with sales and purchases of companies and their assets in bankruptcy. Features a panel of lawyers who represent both sides that flag areas of concern and offer sensible tips on ensuring a smooth transaction.
Business and Economics; Civics and Political Systems
Dist - ALIABA **Prod** - CLETV 1992

Sale - O - Robics 3 MIN
VHS / 16mm
Color (PRO)
$245.00 purhcase, $125.00 rental, $30.00 preview
Uses puppets to humorously comment on aspects of sales. Intended for use during sales meetings to introduce a break.
Business and Economics; Psychology
Dist - UTM **Prod** - UTM

Salem Witch Trials 28 MIN
U-matic / VHS / 16mm
You are There Series
B&W (J H C)
Reconstructs two witch trials and depicts hysterical young girls accusing innocent people of being witches.
History - United States; Psychology; Sociology
Dist - MGHT **Prod** - CBSTV 1957

Sales 20 TO 30 MIN
U-matic
Opportunity Profile Series
(H C A)
$99.95 _ #AI208
Illustrates the daily activities involved in a career in sales. Working professionals in related occupations present the negative and positive aspects of such jobs.
Business and Economics; Guidance and Counseling
Dist - CAMV **Prod** - CAMV

Sales
U-matic / VHS
Opportunity Profile Series
$99.95 purchase _ #AJ107V
Provides advice on the skills and educational background desired by companies, the day to day activities of various careers, and the positive and negative aspects of various careers from corporate vice presidents, managers, and other working professionals.
Guidance and Counseling
Dist - CAREER **Prod** - CAREER

Sales 30 MIN
U-matic / VHS
How to be more successful in your own business series
Color (G)
$279.00, $179.00 purchase _ #AD - 2005
Covers the elements of successful sales. Looks at people skills, keeping good records, researching the competition, understanding the customer, establishing compensation packages that motivate sales. Part of an eight - part series on successful business management moderated by David Susskind.
Business and Economics
Dist - FOTH **Prod** - FOTH

Sales 21 MIN
VHS / U-matic
Clues to Career Opportunities for Liberal Arts Graduates Series
Color (C A)
LC 80-706236
Presents a representative from a major corporation who defines sales and outlines some of the advantages of a career in sales. Discusses salaries, working conditions, and opportunities for advancement.
Business and Economics; Psychology
Dist - IU **Prod** - IU 1979

Sales and income tax 15 MIN
U-matic / VHS
Consumer education series
Color
Business and Economics; Home Economics
Dist - CAMB **Prod** - MAETEL

Sales and morale - G rated 5 MIN
VHS / 16mm
Spirit of Patton series
Color (G)
$150.00 purchase, $100.00 rental
Spoofs General George Patton. Motivates team spirit in sales personnel. Suitable for a general audience.
Business and Economics
Dist - PROSOR
UTM

Sales and morale - R rated 5 MIN
VHS / 16mm
Spirit of Patton series
Color (A)
$150.00 purchase, $100.00 rental
Spoofs General George Patton. Motivates team spirit in sales personnel. Not suitable for a general audience.
Business and Economics
Dist - PROSOR
UTM

Sales and the competition 6 MIN
VHS / 16mm
Spirit of Patton series
Color (G)
$150.00 purchase, $100.00 rental
Spoofs General George Patton. Motivates sales personnel.
Business and Economics; Literature and Drama
Dist - PROSOR
UTM

The Sales Building Role 7 MIN
16mm
People Sell People Series
Color (H A)
LC FI68-236
Depicts how to satisfy the customer's wants in both quantity and quality. Shows how sales and service can be increased through intelligent and appropriate suggestions of additional or higher priced merchandise.
Business and Economics
Dist - MLA **Prod** - SAUM 1965

Sales Communications Series
In Two Minds 19 MIN
The Meeting of Minds 14 MIN
Dist - VISUCP

The Sales Film 27 MIN
U-matic / VHS
Color (A)
Focuses on sales training. Includes customer relations, overcoming objections and other sales techniques. Uses story format.
Business and Economics
Dist - AMEDIA **Prod** - AMEDIA

Sales force sizing and deployment using a decision calculus model
VHS
Color (C PRO G)
$150.00 purchase _ #87.01
Shows how a decision calculus model for sales force size and deployment was devised by Syntex managers, with a time horizon of three years. Reveals that the model recommended large increases in sales force size, changes in sales force allocation of time to some products and market services and away from others. Model predictions proved to be more accurate than standard forecast and in financial terms resulted in increases of $25 million. Syntex Laboratories Inc. Leonard M Lodish, Ellen Curtis, Michael Ness.
Business and Economics; Sociology
Dist - INMASC

Sales - marketing 30 MIN
U-matic / VHS
Videosearch performance appraisal - case studies series
Color
Business and Economics; Fine Arts; Psychology
Dist - DELTAK **Prod** - DELTAK

Sales meeting breaks 10 MIN
BETA / VHS / U-matic
Humatoons meeting breaks series
Color (C A G)
$495.00 purchase, $250.00 rental
Presents a series of short, comic vignettes for sales meeting breaks featuring a repertory cast of actors as real business people in cartoon - like situations. Includes Your Future in Sales, Product Introduction, Beverage Flight, Good Help Is Hard to Fire.
Business and Economics; Literature and Drama
Dist - VIDART **Prod** - VIDART

Sales Meeting Films Series
Building for success 2 MIN
Demonstration - a selling technique 3 MIN
Efficiency in the field 3 MIN
Selling as a Profession 2 MIN
Dist - CORF

The Sales professionals - building your clients' confidence 23 MIN
VHS / 16mm
Color (A PRO)
$790.00 purchase, $220.00 rental
Examines case histories of three professionals - a computer salesperson, an insurance broker and an accountant. Stresses functioning as a consultant, a problem solver and a professional partner to build a long - term relationship with customers. Focuses on sales training.
Business and Economics; Psychology
Dist - VIDART **Prod** - VIDART 1990

Sales series
The Complete telesales training kit
A Good person to do business with
Dist - VLEARN

Sales Talk 25 MIN
U-matic / VHS / 16mm
Color (A)
Dramatizes a true - life case involving two salespeople and their unintentional misrepresentation of their products and services. Shows the result of these misrepresentations in the loss of business and goodwill.
Business and Economics
Dist - RTBL **Prod** - RTBL

Sales Tax - Yes or no 15 MIN
16mm
Color; B&W (C G T A S R PRO IND)
Deals with a 1965 tax issue in the election in Idaho. Voters decided to implement a state sales tax due to the lack of adequate school funding in the state.
Civics and Political Systems; Education; History - United States
Dist - FO **Prod** - FO 1966

Sales training I 75 MIN
VHS
Color (H C)
$79.95 purchase _ #SE - 15
Features Shelley Archer. Guides clients to sales knowledge and ability through understanding the dynamics of client - customer relationships, gaining a sense of purpose and esteem in sales - marketing, identifying and enhancing capabilities and talents, establishing goals and superior techniques to reach goals, creating lasting, repeatable quality successes, savoring the joy of accomplishment. Focuses on individual characteristics of companies, situations and people using a fundamental balance of honesty, openness and desire 'to have fun making money.'
Business and Economics
Dist - INSTRU

Salesline 3 MIN
VHS / 16mm
Color (PRO)
$245.00 purchase, $125.00 rental, $30.00 preview
Uses puppets to humorously comment on aspects of sales. Intended for use during sales meetings to introduce a break.
Business and Economics; Psychology
Dist - UTM **Prod** - UTM

Salesman 90 MIN
16mm
B&W
LC 72-710820
Uses cinema verite style to follow the activities of four door - to - door Bible salesmen on their routes.
Business and Economics; Religion and Philosophy
Dist - MAYSLS **Prod** - MAYSLS 1969

Salesman 29 MIN
16mm / U-matic / VHS
Color
Features a salesman who likes his job, telling why he likes it. Reveals the challenge of selling, the satisfaction of doing the job right and the rewards that the dedicated salesman receives.
Business and Economics; Guidance and Counseling
Dist - DARTNL **Prod** - DARTNL

Salesmanship - career opportunities 15 MIN
16mm / U-matic / VHS
Color (H C) (SPANISH)
LC FIA68-3154
Presents vocational opportunities available in a sales career. Discusses qualifications, techniques, compensation methods, training and sales tools needed in this career. Shows the importance of the salesman in the marketing and industrial complex.
Business and Economics; Guidance and Counseling; Psychology
Dist - JOU **Prod** - ALTSUL 1968

Salesmanship on the line 20 MIN
VHS
Color (A PRO)

$495.00 purchase, $150.00 rental
Presents a 1950s fable about a young salesman learning consultative sales. Emphasizes the concept that selling is simply solving customer problems. Narrated by Dirk and Don Beveridge.
Business and Economics; Psychology
Dist - VLEARN **Prod** - DARTNL

Salifu's harvest 20 MIN
VHS
Color; Captioned (G R S)
$12.50 purchase _ #S12364 ; #87047
Presents a captioned account of the mission work of Nicolas Salifu in West Africa. Available on a free - loan basis from the Lutheran Church - Missouri Synod's Deaf Ministry.
Literature and Drama; Religion and Philosophy
Dist - CPH **Prod** - LUMIS

Salisbury's Report on China - the Revolution and Beyond Series
From liberalization to crackdown - Pt 3 45 MIN
The Leaders of the Revolution, Pt 1 45 MIN
Slogans and policies - Pt 2 45 MIN
Dist - FOTH

Salivary Glands 19 MIN
U-matic
Microanatomy Laboratory Orientation Series
Color (C)
Describes glands and their ducts with special consideration given to the organization of the serous, mucous and mixed forms of salivary alveoli.
Health and Safety; Science - Natural
Dist - UOKLAH **Prod** - UOKLAH 1986

Salivation of Professor Bizarrov 70 MIN
16mm
Color (A)
$200.00 rental
Follows an insidious professor as he sets out to conquer the world and instead is psychotechnologically manipulated into becoming a guru's disciple. Reveals his neverending dreams of a sexy siren who lures him until he drools. The ending is totally ridiculous. Featuring a cast of thousands, including the masses of India.
Fine Arts
Dist - CANCIN **Prod** - DEGRAS 1978

Sallah 105 MIN
VHS
B&W (G) (HEBREW WITH ENGLISH SUBTITLES)
$79.95 purchase _ #533
Portrays Sallah, a new immigrant to Israel who arrives with his large family from the Orient with great expectations. Reveals that he lands in a ramshackle transit camp that arouses his disgust. Stars Topol, Gila Almagor, Arik Einstein and Geula Nona. Written and directed by Ephraim Kishon.
Fine Arts; History - World; Literature and Drama; Sociology
Dist - ERGOM **Prod** - ERGOM 1965

Sallah Shabbati 105 MIN
VHS / 16mm
Sephardic Jewry series
B&W (G) (HEBREW WITH ENGLISH SUBTITLES)
Tells the story of Sallah, North African Jew who finds himself in a transit camp after immigrating to Israel in 1949 and confronts the bureaucracy standing in the way of his family's need for permanent housing. Part two of program four of the Sephardic Jewry series which illuminates the histories of the Sephardic Diaspora communities and addresses the social and political issues confronting the Sephardim in the 20th century.
Fine Arts; History - World; Religion and Philosophy; Sociology
Dist - NCJEWF

Sally 8 MIN
U-matic / VHS / 16mm
Color (K P)
LC 78-700075
Tells how a local wizard teaches a little girl the importance of telling the truth.
Guidance and Counseling; Literature and Drama
Dist - LCOA **Prod** - KRATKY 1978

Sally at 13 18 MIN
U-matic / VHS / 16mm
Color (J)
Deals with the concerns most girls face as they enter puberty.
Health and Safety; Psychology
Dist - PEREN **Prod** - RUSELP

Sally Garcia and Family 35 MIN
16mm
Color
LC 78-700304
Presents a profile of Sally Garcia, a 40 - year - old wife and mother of five children, who counsels women and adolescents in career planning while attending school in the evenings to obtain her BA. Deals with the issues that surround the separate demands of children, a husband, work and continuing education.
Education; Guidance and Counseling; Sociology
Dist - EDC **Prod** - EDC 1977

Sally of the Sawdust 92 MIN
16mm
B&W
Introduces Eustace McGargle, a carnival barker who has adopted Sally and enjoys an occasional nip or two, yet is on record as being none too fond of children or dogs. Stars W C Fields. Directed by D W Griffith.
Fine Arts
Dist - KILLIS **Prod** - GFITH 1925

Sally Osborne - Mechanical Engineer 10 MIN
16mm
Color
Follows a mechanical engineer through her day's work and examines the diversity of her job. Shows how this mechanical engineer manages both home and career.
Guidance and Counseling; Industrial and Technical Education; Sociology
Dist - MTP **Prod** - POLARD

Sally Ride - Lady Astronaut 14 MIN
U-matic / VHS
Color
Profiles Sally Ride, a 30 - year - old astro - physicist who became the first American woman in space when she flew in the space shuttle Challenger in 1983.
Biography; History - World; Sociology
Dist - KINGFT **Prod** - KINGFT 1983

Sally Sommer and Beate Gordon 30 MIN
U-matic / VHS
Eye on Dance - Third World Dance, Beyond the White Stream Series
Color
Focuses on obtaining a broader understanding of ethnic dance.
Fine Arts
Dist - ARCVID **Prod** - ARCVID

Sally's beauty spot 12 MIN
VHS / 16mm
Color (G)
$350.00, $225.00 purchase, $50.00 rental
Uses a large black mole above an Asian woman's breast as a metaphor for cultural and racial difference. Includes women's voices offscreen and scenes from the film, The World of Suzie Wong, to comment on Asian femininity.
Sociology
Dist - WMEN

Sally's Ride 30 MIN
U-matic
Color (A)
Gives an account of the training and flights of astronaut Sally Ride, the first American woman to go into space.
History - World; Industrial and Technical Education; Social Science
Dist - ASVS **Prod** - RICON 1986

Salman Rushdie with Charlotte Cornwall 40 MIN
VHS
Color (H C G)
$79.00 purchase
Features the writer talking with Charlotte Cornwall about writing cultural history from a political view. Discusses his portrait of Nicaragua in The Jaguar Smile. His book The Satanic Verses is discussed in a separate video, Salman Rushdie with W L Webb.
Geography - World; Literature and Drama
Dist - ROLAND **Prod** - INCART

Salman Rushdie with W L Webb 40 MIN
VHS
Color (H C G)
$79.00 purchase
Features the writer talking about his work The Satanic Verses. Discusses its background and his experiences as a native of India writing about other countries and other cultures. Looks at his television films The Riddle of Midnight and The Painter and the Pest. His novels are discussed in the video Salman Rushdie with Charlotte Cornwall which is available separately.
Literature and Drama; Religion and Philosophy
Dist - ROLAND **Prod** - INCART

Salmon and Trout 60 MIN
BETA / VHS
Color
Teaches the early season secrets of lake trout. Views a segment on the fall run of pink salmon. Shows a method for taking fish on plankboard, and skiing for steel head and lake trout.
Physical Education and Recreation; Science - Natural
Dist - HOMEAF **Prod** - HOMEAF

Salmon for all Seasons 23 MIN
16mm
Color
LC 78-701568
Discusses the problem of declining natural salmon runs and explains how ocean ranching can benefit both man and nature.
Industrial and Technical Education; Science - Natural
Dist - ODS **Prod** - WEYCO 1978

Salmon - Life Cycle 3 MIN
16mm
Of all Things Series
Color (P I)
Discusses the life cycle of the salmon fish.
Science - Natural
Dist - AVED **Prod** - BAILYL

Salmon - Life Cycle of the Sockeye 11 MIN
U-matic / VHS / 16mm
Color (I)
LC 79-701765
Presents the complete life cycle of the sockeye salmon from laying and fertilization of the eggs, through the development of the sac fry and the growth of the young fish. Continues with the long journey of the fingerlings to the sea and the final return of the mature salmon to their birthplace, where they spawn and die.
Science - Natural
Dist - MCFI **Prod** - HOE 1971

Salmon on the Run 57 MIN
16mm / VHS
Nova Series
(J H C)
$99.95 each
Looks at new innovations in the salmon fishing industry.
Industrial and Technical Education; Science; Sociology
Dist - AMBROS **Prod** - AMBROS 1983

Salmon on the run 57 MIN
U-matic / VHS / 16mm
Nova series
Color (H C A)
Shows how business and technology are changing the future of the fishing industry, with salmon now 'farmed' on 'ranches.' Presents an argument to let salmon remain as wild as possible.
Industrial and Technical Education; Science
Dist - TIMLIF **Prod** - WGBHTV 1982
AMBROS

The Salmon people 25 MIN
16mm
Color
#106C 0177 016N
Geography - World
Dist - CFLMDC **Prod** - NFBC 1977

Salmon story 27 MIN
VHS / 16mm
Color (G)
$55.00 rental _ #SLMN - 000
Follows a team of scientists studying the habits of salmon. Probes humankind's relationship with the salmon from prehistoric.
Science - Natural
Dist - PBS **Prod** - UWISCA

Salome 3 MIN
16mm
Color (G)
$127.00 purchase, $10.00 rental
Portrays the chess master, aesthetician, human being, Eugene Salome.
Fine Arts
Dist - CANCIN **Prod** - BRAKS 1980

Salomon 727 6 MIN
16mm
Color (FRENCH GERMAN ITALIAN)
LC 78-701483
Discusses the technical features of the Salomon 727 ski binding.
Physical Education and Recreation
Dist - SALNA **Prod** - SALNA 1978

Salon Esso De Artistas Jovenes 16 MIN
16mm
Color
LC 75-700282
Discusses a selection of works by prize - winning Latin American artists at the 1964 Esso Salon of Young Artists.
Fine Arts
Dist - PAN **Prod** - OOAS 1970

Salp'uri - Korean improvisational dance 15 MIN
16mm / VHS / U-matic
Ethnic music and dance series
B&W (G)
LC 72-700241
Demonstrates one of the dance forms from the southwestern Korean province of Cholla, an improvisational dance called Salp'uri.

Fine Arts; Geography - World
Dist - UWASHP Prod - UWASH 1971

Salsa
VHS
Arthur Murray dance lessons series
Color (G)
$19.95 purchase _ #MC049
Offers lessons in classic ballroom dancing from instructors in Arthur Murray studios, focusing on salsa. Part of a 12 - part series on various ballroom dancing styles.
Fine Arts; Physical Education and Recreation; Sociology
Dist - SIV

Salsa 60 MIN
VHS
Kathy Blake dance studios - let's learn how to dance series
Color (G A)
$39.95 purchase
Features dance instructors Kathy Blake and Gene Russo, who instruct viewers on the basics of salsa dancing.
Fine Arts
Dist - PBS **Prod** - WNETTV

Salt and hypertension - how to save your own life 26 MIN
U-matic / VHS / 16mm
Color (J)
LC 82-700120
Discusses the causes and effects of hypertension, pointing out that high blood pressure can be controlled by reducing the intake of salt. Shows how to limit salt intake by revealing the often surprising salt content of many foods. Presents strategies for shopping and food preparation.
Health and Safety; Home Economics
Dist - PFP **Prod** - IA 1982

Salt babies - an exercise in teen parenting 13 MIN
VHS
Color (J H C)
$119.00 purchase _ #CG - 902 - VS
Reveals that by age 20, seven out of every ten girls will have become pregnant, and documents an exercise in which high school students play parent, treating a 5 pound bag of salt as though it were an actual infant. Presents a very real problem as a 'hypothetical situation,' giving students and their parents an opportunity to talk about teenage pregnancy before it happens.
Health and Safety; Sociology
Dist - HRMC **Prod** - HRMC

The Salt Marsh - a Question of Values 22 MIN
U-matic / VHS / 16mm
Environmental Studies Series
Color (J)
LC 75-701426
Shows researchers from the University of Georgia as they examine the complex ecological system of a salt marsh. Shows how marshland provides an important link in the ecological system of the neighboring ocean.
Science - Natural
Dist - EBEC **Prod** - EBEC 1975

Salt of the earth 94 MIN
16mm / U-matic / VHS
B&W
Highlights the Mexican - American miners' struggle for organization and equality and the women's struggle for dignity and humanity.
Social Science; Sociology
Dist - FI **Prod** - AMDOC 1954

Salt of the Earth 46 MIN
VHS
Color (H C G)
$395.00 purchase, $65.00 rental
Looks at the history, uses and technology of sodium chloride - salt. Reveals that salt was once thought to be so rare that traders went to the ends of the known Earth to find it. Ancient Egyptians used it in the mummification process and salt was crucial to the preservation of food in the Middle Ages. Examines dietary habits throughout the world and their relationship to hypertension. Shows the function of kidneys in regulating salt balance in the human body. Explores how animals satisfy their need for salt, such as elephant herds in Kenya who have carved caves from solid rock while seeking the sodium deposits they need. Features David Suzuki and Craig Claiborne.
Geography - World; Social Science
Dist - FLMLIB **Prod** - CANBC 1992

Salt of the Earth 15 MIN
U-matic / VHS
Explorers Unlimited Series
Color (P I)
Visits a salt mine in Cleveland to examine methods of extracting salt.
Social Science
Dist - AITECH **Prod** - WVIZTV 1971

Salt of the sea 4 MIN
16mm
Color (G)
$10.00 rental
Describes itself as 'founded under water, all at sea, made at land.'
Fine Arts; Geography - World
Dist - CANCIN **Prod** - LEVINE 1965

Salt or Sugar 20 MIN
16mm
Science Twenty Series
Color (P)
LC 77-704163
Presents a student participation film in which students observe and record the physical and chemical properties of two common materials, salt and sugar.
Science - Physical
Dist - SF **Prod** - PRISM 1969

Salt - the Essence of Life 28 MIN
16mm
Color
Tells the story of salt and its importance to man and animals. Demonstrates its production through the mining of rocksalt and the evaporation of brine either mechanically or by the sun. Explores the principal and varied uses of salt and how salt affects every aspect of human life.
Health and Safety; Home Economics; Social Science
Dist - MTP **Prod** - SALTI 1982

Salt - the hidden threat 21 MIN
16mm / U-matic / VHS
Color (J)
LC 82-701125
Explores the problems caused by people's eating too much salt. Provides examples of sodium contents of certain foods and shows ways in which salt intake can be reduced.
Health and Safety; Home Economics
Dist - HIGGIN **Prod** - HIGGIN 1983

Salts and Oxidizers 30 MIN
U-matic / VHS
HTM - Hazardous Toxic Materials Series Unit II; Unit II
Color (PRO)
Health and Safety; Social Science
Dist - FILCOM **Prod** - FILCOM

Saltwater fishing
VHS
Color (G)
$29.80 purchase _ #0134
Films a 17 - day saltwater fishing trip. Shows how to plan a trip, the actual fishing and how to get the catch back home.
Geography - World; Physical Education and Recreation; Science - Natural
Dist - SEVVID

Salty 93 MIN
U-matic / VHS
Color
Reveals that when a lovable but mischievous sea lion, formerly with a circus, becomes the pet of two brothers, its escapades manage to complicate the boys' lives when they volunteer to help a friend renovate a Florida marina.
Fine Arts
Dist - TIMLIF **Prod** - TIMLIF 1982

Saludos series
Como te llamas - what is your name 15 MIN
Entra a mi casa - enter in my house 15 MIN
Dist - GPN

Saludos
Como esta el tiempo - how is the weather 15 MIN
Cuantos Anos Tienes? - How Old are You? 15 MIN
El Supermercado - the Supermarket 15 MIN
Hola, Como Estas - Hello, How are You 15 MIN
La Biblioteca - the Library 15 MIN
La Carta - the Letter 15 MIN
La Clase - the Classroom 15 MIN
La Fiesta Mejicana - the Mexican Party 15 MIN
La Ropa De Ninas - Clothing for Girls 15 MIN
La Vista De La Abuelita - Grandmother's Visit 15 MIN
Las Partes Del Cuerpo, Pt 1 - the Parts of the Body, Pt 1 15 MIN
Las Partes Del Cuerpo, Pt 2 - the Parts of the Body, PT 2 15 MIN
Los Animales - the Animals 15 MIN
Los Dias De La Semana - the Days of the Week 15 MIN
Los Regalos - the Presents 15 MIN
Mas Numeros - more Numbers 15 MIN
Mi Familia 15 MIN
Vamos a Comer - Let's Eat 15 MIN
Vamos a Dibujar - Let's Draw 15 MIN
Vamos a Repasar - Let's Review 15 MIN
Vamos a Repasar II - Let's Review II 15 MIN
Vamos a Repasar III - Let's Review III 15 MIN
Vamos Al Campo - Let's Go to the Country 15 MIN
Dist - GPN

Salut - French Language Lessons Series
Bonjour 10 MIN
C'est Le Premier Juillet 10 MIN
C'est Un Sac D'ecole 10 MIN
De la creme glacee 10 MIN
Est - Ce Que Vous Etes Bucheron 10 MIN
Il Fait Beau 10 MIN
Il Frappe La Balle 10 MIN
Il Y a Trois Chiens 10 MIN
J'ai hate 10 MIN
J'ai vingt robes 10 MIN
J'aime la campagne 10 MIN
Je Fais Mes Devoirs 10 MIN
Je Me Leve a Sept Heures 10 MIN
Je Parle, Tu Ecoutes 10 MIN
Je Peux Vous Aider 10 MIN
Je Vais En Auto 10 MIN
A La Ville 10 MIN
Lancez 10 MIN
Les Belles Couleurs 10 MIN
Mon Bras, Ton Nez 10 MIN
Nous Jouons 10 MIN
Pas De Moutarde 10 MIN
Que Fais - Tu Aujourd'hui 10 MIN
Son Pantalon 10 MIN
Tu Es Dans La Maison 10 MIN
Dist - BCNFL

Salut, Montreal 12 MIN
U-matic / VHS / 16mm
Connaissons - nous series
Color (H C A) (FRENCH)
Shows two Quebec students taking two exchange students on a tour of Montreal to see sights, sounds and atmosphere of the city.
Geography - World; Sociology
Dist - BCNFL **Prod** - INCC 1982

Salute to a Crusader - Dwight Eisenhower Portrait of a Patriot 14 MIN
16mm
Screen news digest series; Vol 11; Issue 9
B&W (J H)
LC 70-703471
Traces the career of a Kansas farm boy, Dwight David Eisenhower, who served his country in war as a great military commander and in peace as its 34th President.
Biography; Civics and Political Systems; History - United States
Dist - HEARST **Prod** - HEARST 1969

Salute to the Edinburgh Tattoo 108 MIN
VHS
Color (G)
$29.95 purchase _ #781 - 9032
Documents the Edinburgh Military Tattoo which features troops marching and countermarching with precision to the music of massed military bands. Includes moments from five Tattoos between 1975 and 1980.
Fine Arts; Geography - World; History - World
Dist - FI **Prod** - BBCTV 1989

Salvador 123 MIN
35mm / 16mm
Color (G)
Tells the story of outspoken American photojournalist Richard Boyle and the events he witnessed during the 1980 civil war in El Salvador. Travels with Boyle, played by James Woods, and his space - cadet buddy, Jim Belushi, in search of a hot story that will put him out of debt. Exposes the vital truth of a combat photographer's existence. Produced by Gerald Green and Oliver Stone; screenplay by Stone and Richard Boyle. Contact distributor for price.
Fine Arts; History - World; Industrial and Technical Education; Sociology
Dist - OCTOBF **Prod** - STONEO 1986

Salvador Dali - a soft self - portrait 60 MIN
VHS
Color (H C A)
$39.95 purchase; $39.95 purchase
Explores the world of Salvador Dali through his art and his philosophies. Uses location footage of his villa in Spain. Displays the acting talents of the artist himself. Narrated by Orson Welles.
Fine Arts
Dist - PBS **Prod** - WNETTV
ARTSAM

Salvador Minuchin, MD, Director, Philadelphia Child Guidance Clinic 60 MIN
U-matic / VHS
Perceptions, Pt B - dialogues with family therapists series Vol VIII, Pt B16
Color (PRO)
Features Frederick J Duhl interviewing Salvador Minuchin concerning his background in Argentina, Israel and New York as it affects his approach to family therapy.
Guidance and Counseling; Psychology; Sociology
Dist - BOSFAM **Prod** - BOSFAM

Salvage 15 MIN
VHS / U-matic
Firefighter I video series
Color (PRO G)
$115.00 purchase _ #35201
Shows how buildings and contents are salvaged, including the folding and throwing of covers. Emphasizes protection of public and private property. Includes an instruction guide for review. Part of a video series on Firefighter I training codes to be used with complementing IFSTA manuals.
Health and Safety; Psychology; Social Science
Dist - OKSU **Prod** - OKSU

Salvage and Overhaul Operations 30 MIN
VHS
Firefighter II - III Video Series
Color (G PRO)
$145.00 purchase _ #35254
Shows effective, practical procedures for evacuating water and debris from structures using water chutes, catch - alls and other salvage tools. Demonstrates methods of detecting and extinguishing hidden fires and performing general overhaul.
Agriculture; Health and Safety; Industrial and Technical Education; Psychology; Science - Physical; Social Science
Dist - OKSU **Prod** - OKSU

The Salvage gang 52 MIN
U-matic / VHS / 16mm
B&W (K P I)
LC FIA67-5306
Tells of Kim, who breaks a saw belonging to a friend's father and, with the help of his gang, tries to earn enough money to replace it. After failing, they turn to salvage collecting and encounter more problems because of a brass bed they find.
Literature and Drama
Dist - LUF **Prod** - CHILDF 1963

Salvage of the Gunboat Cairo 26 MIN
16mm
Color (A)
LC 77-703129
Documents the raising of the Union gunboat USS Cairo from the riverbed of the Mississippi River.
History - United States; Social Science
Dist - USNAC **Prod** - USNPS 1969

Salvage of the Sub Squalus 45 MIN
16mm
B&W
LC 74-706569
Shows the salvage of the submarine USS Squalus.
Civics and Political Systems; Industrial and Technical Education
Dist - USNAC **Prod** - USN 1968

Salvage of the USS Lafayette 35 MIN
16mm
B&W
LC 74-706570
Shows salvage operations from time of fire to drydocking of the ship USS Lafayette. Demonstrates the work of salvage engineers and divers, shows the design and placement of patches, demonstrates how to shore up decks and bulkheads, how to place pumps, how to stop leaks with concrete and how to moor the ship during pumping.
Civics and Political Systems; Industrial and Technical Education
Dist - USNAC **Prod** - USN 1944

Salvage operations 19 MIN
VHS
Firefighter I series
Color (IND)
$130.00 purchase _ #35639
Presents one part of a 19 - part series that is the teaching companion for IFSTA's Essentials of Fire Fighting manual. Presents the benefits of salvage to the public and the fire department. Demonstrates the use of salvage covers and the care and maintenance of salvage equipment. Based on Chapter 14.
Health and Safety; Science - Physical; Social Science
Dist - OKSU **Prod** - ACCTRA

A Salvage picture 15 MIN
Videoreel / VT2
Art corner series
B&W (P)
Details creating designs or pictures using feathers, cloth, yarn, buttons, seeds, bark and other salvage or nature materials.
Fine Arts
Dist - GPN **Prod** - CVETVC

Salvaging American Prehistory, Pt 1 28 MIN
16mm
Spadework for History Series
Color (C A)
Treats the general subject of archeology and reservoir salvage and travels over the whole United States.
History - United States; History - World; Science - Physical
Dist - UTEX **Prod** - UTEX 1964

Salvaging Texas prehistory 28 MIN
16mm
Spadework for history series
Color (C A)
Tells of the problems faced in a site in central Texas as seen against the varied background of archeological effort in Texas as a whole. Shows how the scientific process takes place - how the information from one project serves to check the hypotheses formed from the earlier ones, resulting in further hypotheses to be checked by further work.
Geography - United States; History - United States; History - World; Science - Physical
Dist - UTEX **Prod** - UTEX 1964

Salvation and Christian fellowship 17 MIN
16mm
Book of Acts series
Color; B&W (J H T R)
Explains that many of the early Jewish Christians found it difficult to accept Gentiles into the fellowship. Shows Paul and Barnabas called to Jerusalem to report on the work in Antioch. Stresses salvation by grace through faith.
Religion and Philosophy
Dist - FAMF **Prod** - BROADM 1957

Salvation is open to all - Tape 5 30 MIN
VHS
Acts of the Apostles series
Color (I J H C G A R)
$29.95 purchase, $10.00 rental _ #35 - 8366 - 1502
Presents stories of the early Christian church as described in the New Testament book of Acts. Covers the events of Rome's rule by Caligula, Peter's ministry in Joppa and Jerusalem, discussion of baptism among Gentiles, and Barnabas' presentation of Paul.
Literature and Drama; Religion and Philosophy
Dist - APH **Prod** - BOSCO

Salvation, Pt II 26 MIN
VHS / U-matic
Unorganized Manager Series
Color
Offers plans for organizing, delegating, setting priorities, scheduling time for active tasks and allocating time for reactive tasks.
Psychology
Dist - VISUCP **Prod** - VIDART

Salve 14 MIN
16mm
Color (G)
$30.00 rental
Plays with language and history. Weaves, in the words of a child, a disappearing landscape into the fabric of a film of numbers, sounds and textures. Features Gradiva Couzin.
Fine Arts
Dist - CANCIN **Prod** - COUZS 1981

Sam 25 MIN
VHS
Color (G)
$34.95 purchase, $10.00 rental _ #35 - 87400 - 460
Profiles Sam, a child with cerebral palsy. Demonstrates the frustrations, love and responses Sam goes through every day.
Health and Safety; Religion and Philosophy
Dist - APH **Prod** - FRACOC

Sam 25 MIN
U-matic / 16mm / VHS
Color; Captioned (I J)
$560.00, $420.00, $390.00 purchase _ #C319
Adapts from the book 'Sam and His Cart' by Arthur Honeyman. Tells about Sam who has cerebral palsy. Sam can't walk or talk like the others and he just shakes and shakes. Inside, however, Sam is just like the other kids. Shows Sam's frustrations and people's kind and cruel responses to him.
Health and Safety; Literature and Drama
Dist - BARR **Prod** - HOFD 1981

Sam 25 MIN
VHS
Lowdown series
Color; PAL (G F)
PdS45 purchase
Profiles Sameer Pimpalkhare, a ten year old boy born with cerebral palsy who is unable to speak. Observes as he is able to speak for the first time with the use of an artificial voice box. Follows the boy's progress as he adjusts to his new life and ability to vocalize his thoughts.
Health and Safety; Psychology
Dist - BBCENE

Sam 28 MIN
16mm / U-matic / VHS
Insight series
Color; B&W (H C A) (SPANISH)
LC 72-705439
Presents a dramatization in which a vaudeville comedian, the last human being left after computers have taken over the world, who becomes disillusioned when he discovers that a little boy who has befriended him is also a computer.
Psychology; Religion and Philosophy; Sociology
Dist - PAULST **Prod** - PAULST 1969

Sam 14 MIN
16mm
Color (P I)
LC 81-701248
Uses the dialogue of the television show Dragnet to show a case officer introducing and investigating the circumstances surrounding the abandonment and abuse of a dog named Sam. Emphasizes the responsibilities involved in pet ownership.
Science - Natural
Dist - ADELPH **Prod** - ASPCA 1981

Sam, bangs and moonshine
VHS / 35mm strip
Caldecotts on filmstrip series
Color (K)
$35.00 purchase
Presents a children's story. Part of the Caldecott series.
English Language; Literature and Drama
Dist - PELLER

Sam, Bangs and Moonshine 15 MIN
16mm / U-matic / VHS
Color (P I)
LC 77-700101
Presents an adaptation of the children's story Sam, Bangs And Moonshine by Evaline Ness, about a young girl whose habit of pretending causes unexpected troubles.
English Language; Literature and Drama
Dist - PHENIX **Prod** - JOHR 1976

Sam Daggett's house 28 MIN
U-matic / VHS / 16mm
Color (H C A)
Looks at the history of an 18th - century house, and at the life of the man who built it.
Biography; Fine Arts; History - United States; Sociology
Dist - JOU **Prod** - JOU

Sam Francis 52 MIN
16mm
Color
LC 76-703157
Features Sam Francis, an American artist, in Paris, Tokyo and Los Angeles, where he lives and works. Shows him talking about his career, the importance of dreams in his paintings and his relationship with color.
Biography; Fine Arts
Dist - BLACKW **Prod** - BLACKW 1976

Sam Houston 51 MIN
VHS / U-matic
Profiles in courage series
B&W (J H)
LC 83-706545
Describes the military and political career of Sam Houston. Emphasizes his life as governor and his fight to keep Texas in the Union. Based on the book Profiles In Courage by John F Kennedy.
Biography; Civics and Political Systems; History - United States
Dist - SSSSV **Prod** - SAUDEK 1964

Sam Houston - a giant man for a giant land 24 MIN
VHS
Color (H C T A)
$69.95 purchase _ #S01332
Profiles Sam Houston, a military hero who led Texas to independence from Mexico and became the first president of the Republic of Texas. Focuses on Houston's military career.
Biography; Civics and Political Systems; History - United States
Dist - UILL

Sam Houston and Texas - a giant man for a giant land 24 MIN
VHS / Videodisc / 16mm
American lifestyle series; Politics and the military
Color (J H C A)
#9881, #9880
Profiles Sam Houston, general and first president of the Republic of Texas. Emphasizes Houston's military career. Hosted and narrated by E G Marshall.
Biography; History - United States
Dist - AIMS **Prod** - COMCO 1986

Sam Houston - Pt 1 25 MIN
16mm
Profiles in courage series
B&W (J H)
Depicts how Sam Houston relinquished the governorship rather than preside over Texas as she left the Union.
Dist - SSSSV **Prod** - SAUDEK 1966

Sam Houston - Pt 2 25 MIN
16mm
Profiles in courage series
B&W (J H)
Depicts how Sam Houston relinquished the governorship rather than preside over Texas as she left the Union.
Dist - SSSSV **Prod** - SAUDEK 1966

Sam Maloof - Woodworker 17 MIN
16mm / U-matic / VHS
Color
LC 74-700521
Observes Sam Maloof making furniture and commenting on his work and philosophy.
Industrial and Technical Education
Dist - AIMS **Prod** - ORMEN 1973

Sam Maloof - woodworking profile 60 MIN
VHS / BETA
Color (G A)
$29.95 _ #060045
Displays the woodworking skills of Sam Maloof. Shows how he builds tables and chairs and rockers.
Fine Arts; Industrial and Technical Education
Dist - TANTON **Prod** - TANTON

Sam on the Busses 15 MIN
16mm
Color (I J H)
LC 82-700352
Introduces Sam The Safety Duck who shows what can happen to children as the result of inconsiderate or wrongful behavior on the school bus and illustrates rules to prevent injuries while riding the school bus.
Health and Safety
Dist - FIESTF **Prod** - OMTC 1982

Sam on Winter Safety 18 MIN
16mm
Color (P I J)
LC 82-700353
Shows the animated character Sam the Safety Duck taking a helicopter ride to spot the dangers of winter for winter sports enthusiasts. Discusses preventive measures and emergency care directions for winter accidents.
Health and Safety; Physical Education and Recreation
Dist - FIESTF **Prod** - OMTC 1982

Sam Seagull Presents Cape Cod 28 MIN
16mm
Color
Explores the countryside, culture and recreation available in Cape Cod, Massachusetts.
Geography - United States; History - United States; Physical Education and Recreation
Dist - MTP **Prod** - CCCOC

Sam Shepard - 6 - 1 - 78 40 MIN
VHS / Cassette
Poetry Center reading series
B&W (G)
$15.00 purchase, rental _ #320 - 268
Features the playwrights Joseph Chaikin and Sam Shepard reading Tongues, a play and collaboration between Chaikin and Shepard, at the Poetry Center, San Francisco State University.
Literature and Drama
Dist - POETRY **Prod** - POETRY 1978

Sam Snead 20 MIN
16mm
Sports Legends Series
Color (I J)
Tells how Sam Snead was a hillbilly from Hot Springs, Virginia, who came to the game a barefoot caddy, and now over 60, is still playing golf competitively on the pro circuit. Features Snead reviewing more than half a century of golf.
Biography; Physical Education and Recreation
Dist - COUNFI **Prod** - COUNFI

Sam the Safety Duck Learns to Drive a Bicycle 6 MIN
16mm
Color (P)
LC 82-700354
Presents Sam the Safety Duck, an animated character, who discusses the concerns of new bicycle drivers. Deals with learning the rules of traffic, choosing the bicycle, and equipping the bicycle with the proper safety equipment.
Health and Safety; Physical Education and Recreation
Dist - FIESTF **Prod** - OMTC 1982

Sam the Safety Duck Learns to Drive a Bicycle 5 MIN
U-matic / VHS
Color (P)
Presents Sam the Safety Duck in an animated sequence illustrating basic techniques of bicycling safety. Compares cycling with automobile driving. Lists necessary safety equipment.
Education; Health and Safety
Dist - FIESTF **Prod** - CMT 1984

Sam the sea cow - 82
VHS
Reading rainbow series
Color; CC (K P)
$39.95 purchase
Tells the true story of Sam the sea cow in a story by Francine Jacobs, illustrated by Laura Kelly and narrated by Jason Robards. Travels with LeVar to Sea World of Florida for an up - close look at manatees. Part of a series offering a multicultural approach to generating reading enthusiasm with cross - curricular applications, hosted by LeVar Burton.
English Language; Literature and Drama; Science; Science - Natural
Dist - GPN **Prod** - LNMDP

Samal dances from Taluksangay 12 MIN
16mm
Ethnic music and dance series
Color (J)
LC 72-700240
Shows a group of Samal people performing three major dances of the type known as Umaral. Presents these people of the village of Taluksangay in the Sulu Archipelago who demonstrate a special stylized form of dance called Kuntaw.
Fine Arts
Dist - UWASHP **Prod** - UWASH 1971

Samantha gets a visitor 26 MIN
16mm / U-matic / VHS
Color (I J)
Tells how country girl Samantha learns to like camping after she, her younger brother and her city cousin lose their way in the woods.
Health and Safety; Literature and Drama; Physical Education and Recreation; Psychology; Sociology
Dist - BCNFL **Prod** - PLAYTM 1985

Samantha rastles the woman question 50 MIN
VHS / U-matic
Color (G)
LC 83-707104
Presents a one - woman performance in which Jane Curry portrays Samantha Smith Allen, a character created by author Marietta Holley. Deals with questions concerning women, such as rights denied them by the church, powerlessness before the law, their social status and role assumptions in the 19th century.
Sociology
Dist - CORNRS **Prod** - CUETV 1983

Samantha rastles the woman question - questions and answers with Jane Curry 45 MIN
U-matic / VHS
Color (G)
LC 83-707105
Presents Jane Curry, and the nineteenth - century Marietta Holley character she portrays, responding to audience questions dealing with how Samantha would deal with concerns of women in the 1980's.
Sociology
Dist - CORNRS **Prod** - CUETV 1983

The Samaritans 30 MIN
16mm
Color (J)
Looks at the Samaritans, people who separated themselves from the Jewish people 2,500 years ago and consider themselves Hebrew, not Jewish. Reveals how their ritual practices are derived from the Samaritan Pentateuch, not the Torah.
Religion and Philosophy
Dist - NJWB **Prod** - SPECJO 1971

Samba
VHS
Arthur Murray dance lessons series
Color (G)
$19.95 purchase _ #MC054
Offers lessons in classic ballroom dancing from instructors in Arthur Murray studios, focusing on the samba. Part of a 12 - part series on various ballroom dancing styles.
Fine Arts; Physical Education and Recreation; Sociology
Dist - SIV

Samba 60 MIN
VHS
Kathy Blake dance studios - let's learn how to dance series
Color (G A)
$39.95 purchase
Features dance instructors Kathy Blake and Gene Russo, who instruct viewers on the basics of the Samba. First of two parts.
Fine Arts; Physical Education and Recreation; Sociology
Dist - PBS **Prod** - WNETTV

Samba II - cha cha II 60 MIN
VHS
Kathy Blake dance studios - let's learn how to dance series
Color (G A)
$39.95 purchase
Features dance instructors Kathy Blake and Gene Russo, who instruct viewers on the basics of the Samba and the Cha Cha. Second of two parts.
Fine Arts; Sociology
Dist - PBS **Prod** - WNETTV

Sambhoga - Kaya 6 MIN
16mm
B&W (G)
$20.00 rental
Refers to the Tibetan Buddhist term meaning enjoying the wealth of the Five Certainties. Translates the filmmaker's awareness of this state of enlightenment.
Fine Arts; Religion and Philosophy
Dist - CANCIN FLMKCO **Prod** - ANGERA 1982

Sambizanga 102 MIN
16mm
Color (PORTUGUESE (ENGLISH SUBTITLES))
Focuses on a young black couple who bask in each other's presence until the husband, a tractor driver, is suddenly arrested as a political prisoner in Angola. Portrays the relationship between white and black Africans.
Fine Arts; History - World; Sociology
Dist - NYFLMS **Prod** - NYFLMS 1972

Same and Different 15 MIN
U-matic / VHS
Hidden Treasures Series no 4; No 4
Color (T)
LC 82-706528
Uses the adventures of a pirate and his three friends to explore the many facets of language arts. Focuses on synonyms and antonyms, shows what they are, and how they are used in oral and written expression.
English Language
Dist - GPN **Prod** - WCVETV 1980

Same and Different 30 MIN
U-matic
Polka Dot Door Series
Color (K)
Presents a variety show for pre - school children. Includes songs, mime, stories, film sequences, talk, dance and fantasy figures. Each show emphasizes a particular theme such as numbers, feelings, exploring, music or time. Comes with parent teacher guide.
Fine Arts; Literature and Drama
Dist - TVOTAR **Prod** - TVOTAR 1985

Same and different
VHS
Lola May's fundamental math series
Color (K)
$45.00 purchase _ #10251VG
Teaches the selection of same and different objects. Challenges young children to logically group objects to emphasize differentiation of attributes. Comes with a teacher's guide and blackline masters. Part one of a 30 - part series.
Mathematics
Dist - UNL

The Same - but different 15 MIN
VHS / Software / U-matic
Genetics series
Color (J H)
$125.00 purchase,$95.00 software purchase
Explores gene pools and genetics through study of inherited traits.
Science - Natural
Dist - AITECH **Prod** - WETN 1985

Same but different 4 MIN
16mm
Color (I)
LC 72-700407
Uses cartoon characters to tell the story of Percy, a conformist, and his friend Sidney, a nonconformist. Describes the resulting frustration as Percy copies Sidney until Sidney cannot succeed in being different.
Psychology
Dist - MMA **Prod** - PHID 1970

The Same but different 15 MIN
VHS / U-matic
Dragons, wagons and wax - Set 2 series
Color (K P)
Shows how each human being is a unique individual.
Science; Science - Natural
Dist - CTI **Prod** - CTI

Same difference 18 MIN
16mm
Color (G)
$50.00 rental
Involves different kinds of time lapses and juxtapositions of movements such as the uninterrupted action of drinking a glass of water over the changing skies. Takes place around two windows overlooking the San Francisco skyline.
Fine Arts
Dist - CANCIN **Prod** - WONGAL 1975

The Same Gospel - different disciples 15 MIN
VHS
Mission videos series
Color (G R)
$12.50 purchase _ #S12363
Focuses on the mission work of the India Evangelical Lutheran Church, a partner church to the Lutheran Church - Missouri Synod, as it evangelizes among Hindus and Moslems in the cities of India.
Guidance and Counseling; Religion and Philosophy
Dist - CPH **Prod** - LUMIS

Same inside 13 MIN
16mm / U-matic / VHS
Color (K P I)
Presents four children with birth defects who talk about what they like to do and how they cope with their handicaps. Demonstrates that feelings can transcend external differences.
Psychology
Dist - NFMD **Prod** - NFMD 1982

Same Subject, Different Treatment 11 MIN
U-matic / VHS / 16mm
Art of Seeing Series
Color (J)
LC 72-714330
Explains that in nature and in art the same objects are seen in many different ways. Uses the example of the sun at dawn to show these differences and to demonstrate that each artist has his own way of portraying it.
Fine Arts; Psychology
Dist - FI **Prod** - AFA 1972

Same Time, Next Year 119 MIN
16mm
Color
Tells how a man and a woman, both married to other people, meet every year for 26 years. Stars Ellen Burstyn and Alan Alda.
Fine Arts
Dist - TWYMAN **Prod** - UPCI 1978

The Sami - Four Lands, One People 24 MIN
16mm
Color (J)
LC 79-701748
Focuses on the life styles of four Sami families at the crossroads of modernity and tradition.
Sociology
Dist - BNCHMK **Prod** - NFBC 1979

Sami Herders 28 MIN
16mm
Color (I J H)
LC 79-701749
Traces the life, over a 12 - month period, of a family of Laplanders traveling from Norway up the Arctic coast with their herd of reindeer.
Sociology
Dist - BNCHMK **Prod** - NFBC 1979

Sammy and Rosie get laid 97 MIN
35mm / 16mm
Color (G)
Features a black comedy of Thatcher England. Tells the story of Rafi Rahman who returns to the London of his youth only to find the streets on fire with race riots. When he renews relationships with his son and Alice, a white married woman he had been in love with in his youth, he confronts the consequences of his life as a tyrannic violator of human rights. Produced by Tim Bevan and Sarah Radclyffe; directed by Stephan Frears; written by Hanif Kureishi. Contact distributor for price.
Civics and Political Systems; Fine Arts; Sociology
Dist - OCTOBF

Sammy Davis, Jr 28 MIN
U-matic / VHS
Color (G)
$249.00, $149.00 purchase _ #AD - 2168
Interviews Sammy Davis, Jr, dancer, singer, entertainer, in a Phil Donahue program. Tells of the ups and downs of his career and what it took beyond talent to achieve success.
Biography; Fine Arts; History - United States
Dist - FOTH **Prod** - FOTH

Sammy Mayfield and the Outcasts 29 MIN
Videoreel / VT2
Changing rhythms series
Color
Features Sammy and the Outcasts playing some hard - driving blues that contrasts with the easy sounds of vocalist Dee Dee Walker and Howard Bomar.
Fine Arts; History - United States
Dist - PBS **Prod** - KRMATV

Sammy, Sammy 20 MIN
16mm
Color
LC 76-701362
Presents the meaningless and pointless existence of a young man named Sammy.
Fine Arts; Psychology; Religion and Philosophy; Sociology
Dist - SFRASU **Prod** - SFRASU 1975

Sammy Williams, Bill Bradley and Gloria Rosenthal 30 MIN
U-matic / VHS
Eye on Dance - Broadway Series
Color
Presents the tale of the gypsy robe. Looks at 'Esoterica' with Helen Guditis. Hosted by Celia Ipiotis.
Fine Arts
Dist - ARCVID **Prod** - ARCVID

Sammy's Super T - Shirt 58 MIN
16mm
Color (P I)
Tells the story of pint - sized Sammy who possesses a T - shirt which endows him with great physical strength. Shows what happens when a friend convinces him to run a race without it.
Fine Arts
Dist - LUF **Prod** - CHILDF 1979

Samoa - culture in crisis 28 MIN
VHS
Color (G)
$14.95 purchase _ #69
Shows how a traditionally peaceful culture, despite the richness of its heritage, is forced to face modern - day violence. Reveals that, when a killing occurs in a village, the power of tradition is put to the test.
Guidance and Counseling; Sociology
Dist - MARYFA **Prod** - MARYFA 1982

Samoa I Sisifo (Western Samoa) 26 MIN
U-matic / VHS / 16mm
Village Life Series
Color
Demonstrates how traditional values and progressive development are interwoven in Western Samoa. Shows how limited resources have brought about new methods of poultry raising, food gathering and fishing.
Geography - World; Sociology
Dist - JOU **Prod** - IFF

Samora Machel, son of Africa 28 MIN
VHS
Color (C)
$190.00 purchase, $50.00 rental
Interweaves documentary footage of President of Mozambique Samora Machel leading a political rally in Zimbabwe, a musical tribute to FRELIMO performed by peasants and the reflections of John Saul, a former teacher at the FRELIMO party school who was a personal friend to Machel. Includes an interview with Machel given before his death in a 1986 plane crash, which many suspect was caused by South African sabotage. Machel defends Mozambique's policies after independence and condemns South African efforts to destabilize his government.
Civics and Political Systems; Geography - World; History - United States; Sociology
Dist - ICARUS

Sampan family 16 MIN
16mm
B&W (P I J H C)
Tells the stories of families who live and make their living aboard the small Chinese river boats known as sampans.
Geography - World; Sociology
Dist - IFF **Prod** - IFF 1949

Sample bus transactions 30 MIN
U-matic / VHS
IEEE 488 bus series
Color (IND)
Shows how addresses and command messages are differentiated from data, and how this information is used by all participants on the Bus. Uses block diagrams and byte - by - byte examples and timing diagrams to show actual data sent in Bus transactions. Explains ASCH table and IEEE commands.
Industrial and Technical Education; Mathematics; Sociology
Dist - COLOSU **Prod** - COLOSU

Sample Means and the Weak Law of Large Numbers 30 MIN
VHS / U-matic
Probability and Random Processes - Limit Theorems and Statistics 'Series
B&W (PRO)
Presents the sample mean as an estimator of expectation. Discusses different types of convergence.
Mathematics
Dist - MIOT **Prod** - MIOT

Sample mounting techniques - evaporation 6 MIN
16mm
Color (PRO)
LC 74-705571
Demonstrates three methods for mounting solid samples by evaporation - pouring a slurry, pipetting a slurry and pouring a dissolved solution.
Science; Science - Natural
Dist - USNAC **Prod** - USPHS 1966

Sample mounting techniques - filtration 7 MIN
16mm
Color (PRO)
LC 74-705573
Illustrates that filtration is a common technique used to mount precipitated samples by the use of a vacuum, suction flash, filter paper and filter tower. Depicts 3 types of filter towers - glass, teflon and stainless steel. Shows filter paper placed in a counting dish and dried under a heat lamp and more permanently mounted with a ring and disk.
Science; Science - Natural
Dist - USNAC **Prod** - USPHS 1966

Sample Skemp mathematics learning activities 88 MIN
VHS
Color (T)
$325.00 purchase _ #6806
Demonstrates thirteen structured mathematics learning activities developed by professor Richard Skemp. Shows in two parts Skemp and teacher Marilyn Harrison interacting with small groups of elementary children to teach concepts in numeration, addition, subtraction, multiplication, division and fractions.
Education; Mathematics
Dist - UCALG **Prod** - UCALG 1990

Sample spaces and events
VHS
Probability and statistics series
Color (H C)
$125.00 purchase _ #8008
Provides resource material about the meaning of sample spaces and events and how to represent data to help in the study of probability and statistics. Part of a 60 - video series, each part 25 to 30 minutes long, that explains and reinforces concepts using definitions, theorems, examples and step - by - step solutions to tutor the student. Videos are also available in a set.
Mathematics
Dist - LANDMK

A Sampler of Selections from Favorite Authors 29 MIN
Videoreel / VT2
One to One Series
Color
Literature and Drama
Dist - PBS **Prod** - WETATV

Sampling 10 MIN
U-matic
Geography Skills Series
Color (J H)
Introduces three fundamental concepts employed by geographers when sampling - average, percent and density.
Computer Science; Education; Geography - World
Dist - TVOTAR **Prod** - TVOTAR 1985

Sampling, Aliasing, and Frequency Response 28 MIN
U-matic / VHS

Digital Signal Processing - an Introduction Series
Color
Demonstrates sampling and aliasing with a sinusoidal signal, sinusoidal response of a digital filter and dependence of frequency response on sampling period.
Industrial and Technical Education; Mathematics
Dist - MIOT **Prod** - MIOT

Sampling, Aliasing and Frequency Response 28 MIN
VHS / U-matic
Digital Signal Processing Series
Color (PRO)
Industrial and Technical Education; Mathematics
Dist - GPCV **Prod** - GPCV

Sampling and Descriptive Statistics 30 MIN
U-matic / VHS
Engineering Statistics Series
Color (IND)
Begins by discussing first step in a practical situation, that of taking a sample from a population. Cites examples relating to particular problems on a production line. Describes graphical display techniques.
Industrial and Technical Education; Mathematics; Psychology
Dist - COLOSU **Prod** - COLOSU

Sampling and Estimation 23 MIN
U-matic / VHS / 16mm
Inferential Statistics Series
Color (C)
LC 77-700926
Introduces basic concepts in statistics such as sample, random sample, sample bias, point estimation and confidence intervals.
Education; Mathematics; Psychology
Dist - MEDIAG **Prod** - WILEYJ 1977

Sampling distribution to mean
VHS
Probability and statistics series
Color (H C)
$125.00 purchase _ #8028
Provides resource material about sampling distributions and the mean to help in the study of probability and statistics. Part of a 60 - video series, each part 25 to 30 minutes long, that explains and reinforces concepts using definitions, theorems, examples and step - by - step solutions to tutor the student. Videos are also available in a set.
Mathematics
Dist - LANDMK

Sampling Respirable Dusts - Key Words 7 MIN
BETA / VHS
Color
Discusses dust control, dust measurement and environmental health.
Health and Safety; Sociology
Dist - RMIBHF **Prod** - RMIBHF

Sampling Respirable Dusts - Sample Records 14 MIN
BETA / VHS
Color
Discusses dust control, dust measurement and environmental health.
Health and Safety; Sociology
Dist - RMIBHF **Prod** - RMIBHF

Sampling theorem 28 MIN
U-matic / VHS
Probability and random processes - linear systems series
B&W (PRO)
Discusses the presentation of a bandlimited waveform by its time samples.
Mathematics
Dist - MIOT **Prod** - MIOT

Sampuran Singh - a farmer from Punjab 29 MIN
VHS
Color; PAL (P I J H)
Tells the story of Sampuran Singh, a 60 - year - old Sikh farmer who was one of the thousands of refugees who fled their homeland at the partition of India and Pakistan in 1947. Shows Singh to be highly successful and prosperous. Looks at the Sikh culture, their history, their religion, character and customs.
Geography - World; History - World
Dist - VIEWTH **Prod** - VIEWTH

Sam's secret 10 MIN
16mm / U-matic / VHS
Color (G PRO) (DUTCH SPANISH SWEDISH NORWEGIAN PORTUGUESE)
LC FIA67-171
Presents a successful salesman who reveals the secret of his success to his colleagues at a sales meeting.
Business and Economics
Dist - RTBL **Prod** - PORTA 1965

Sam's song - the legacy of a free economy - Business money - where it comes from and where it goes 27 MIN
16mm
Color (C H G)
Presents the films Sam's Song - The Legacy Of A Free Economy and Business Money - Where It Comes From And Where It Goes. Introduces in Sam's Song the role of supply and demand and tells about capital and profit in Business Money.
Business and Economics
Dist - KAROL **Prod** - SUNCO

Sam's speech 30 MIN
U-matic
Today's special series
Color (K P)
Develops language arts skills in children. Programs are thematically designed around subjects of interest to youngsters. Action takes place in a department store where people, mannequins, puppets, comic characters and special guests present a lighthearted approach to language arts.
Fine Arts; Literature and Drama; Psychology
Dist - TVOTAR **Prod** - TVOTAR 1985

Samsara 29 MIN
16mm / VHS
Color (G)
$495.00, $195.00 purchase, $65.00, $45.00 rental
Documents the struggle of the people of Cambodia to rebuild a shattered society in a climate of war and with limited resources. Uses ancient prophecy, Buddhist teachings and folklore to provide a context for understanding the Cambodian tragedy. Examines the spiritual and philosophical beliefs of the Khmer people.
Geography - World; History - World; Religion and Philosophy; Sociology
Dist - ROLAND

Samsara - death and rebirth in Cambodia 29 MIN
U-matic / 16mm / VHS
Color (G)
$535.00, $295.00 purchase, $75.00, $45.00 rental
Documents the lives of the people of Cambodia who persevere through the trauma of perpetual warfare. Uses the Buddhist metaphor of Samsara - the repetitive journey through the six illusory realms of hell, hungry ghosts, animals, angry gods, man and heaven - to describe the experience of the Khmer people of Cambodia.
Civics and Political Systems; History - World; Religion and Philosophy; Sociology
Dist - CMSMS **Prod** - EBRUNO 1989

Samson and Delilah 52 MIN
U-matic / VHS / 16mm
Greatest heroes of the Bible series
Color (I)
Accounts for Samson's great strength by showing that God gave it to him with the condition that he never touch unclean food, never take wine or drink, and never let a razor touch his hair. Re - enacts how Samson meets his downfall when Delilah seduces him and cuts off his hair, rendering him powerless. Stars John Beck and Victor Jory.
Literature and Drama; Religion and Philosophy
Dist - LUF **Prod** - LUF 1979

Samson and Delilah 30 MIN
VHS
Greatest adventure series
Color (P I R)
$14.95 purchase _ #35 - 830007 - 1518
Uses animation format to present the Biblical story of Samson and Delilah. Features the voice of Linda Purl as Delilah and Perry King as Samson.
Literature and Drama; Religion and Philosophy
Dist - APH **Prod** - HANBAR

Samson Et Dalila 140 MIN
VHS
Color (S) (FRENCH)
$39.95 purchase _ #623 - 9351
Stars Jon Vickers and Shirley Verrett in the Royal Opera production of 'Samson Et Dalia' by Saint - Saens. Features Colin Davis as conductor.
Fine Arts; Foreign Language; Geography - World
Dist - FI **Prod** - NVIDC 1986

Samson Et Dalila 118 MIN
VHS
Color (S) (FRENCH)
$39.95 purchase _ #833 - 9518
Stars Placido Domingo, Shirley Verrett and Wolfgang Brendel in the San Francisco Opera production of 'Samson Et Dalila' by Saint - Saens. Features Julius Rudel as conductor.
Fine Arts; Foreign Language
Dist - FI **Prod** - RMART 1989

Samuel Adams 10 MIN
U-matic / VHS
Color (G)
$229.00, $129.00 purchase _ #AD - 1761
Profiles Samuel Adams, American patriot and pamphleteer. Reveals that he was instrumental in arousing public opinion against England before the American Revolution and the leading spirit behind the Boston Tea Party.
Biography; History - United States; History - World
Dist - FOTH **Prod** - FOTH

Samuel Beckett 80 MIN
U-matic / VHS
Color (C)
$299.00, $199.00 purchase _ #AD - 896
Portrays Samuel Beckett. Traces his artistic life through his prose, plays and poetry.
History - World; Literature and Drama
Dist - FOTH **Prod** - FOTH

Samuel De Champlain 15 MIN
16mm
Color
3106C 0164 130
Geography - World; History - World
Dist - CFLMDC **Prod** - NFBC 1964

Samuel Johnson 30 MIN
VHS
Famous authors series
Color (J H G)
$225.00 purchase
Looks at the life and career of the British writer through selections from his diary and letters. Uses the music and events of his time, including his work on the Dictionary of 1755. Part of a series of videos about 24 major American and British authors. Videos are also available in a set.
History - World; Literature and Drama
Dist - LANDMK

Samuel Morse - the telegraph 24 MIN
VHS / 16mm
Color (I)
LC 90706271
Re - enacts Samuel Morse's research leading to the development of the telegraph. Examines other historical developments in communications.
Business and Economics; Computer Science; Industrial and Technical Education
Dist - BARR

Samuel Ruiz Garcia - Mexico's Bishop to the Indians 24 MIN
U-matic / VHS
Color
$335.00 purchase
Presents a program about Samuel Ruiz Garcia, from the ABC TV program, Directions.
Religion and Philosophy
Dist - ABCLR **Prod** - ABCLR 1979

Samuel Slater and the Industrial Revolution 30 MIN
VHS / U-matic
American Business History Series
Color (C A)
Business and Economics; History - United States
Dist - GPN **Prod** - UMINN 1981

Samuel Taylor Coleridge - 'the Rime of the Ancient Mariner' 52 MIN
U-matic / VHS
Color (C)
$299.00, $199.00 purchase _ #AD - 930
Draws a parallel between 'The Rime Of The Ancient Mariner' and the life of its author, Samuel Taylor Coleridge. Reveals his addiction to opium, his time and friends, focusing on his relationship with William Wordsworth. Features David Hemmings as Coleridge. Produced by Ken Russell.
Fine Arts; Literature and Drama
Dist - FOTH **Prod** - FOTH

The Samurai 30 MIN
VHS / U-matic
Journey into Japan Series
Color (J S C G)
MV=$195.00
Shows that the spirit of the Samurai lives on and permeates business and industrial life in Japan. Views the making of a Samurai movie.
Geography - World; History - World
Dist - LANDMK **Prod** - LANDMK 1986

Samurai I - Musashi Miyamoto 97 MIN
VHS
Samurai trilogy series
Color (G)
$29.95 _ #SAM040
Follows the formative years of Musashi Miyamoto, the most famed of all Japanese swordsmen, as he goes off to a civil war in search of glory but finds defeat instead.

Unlocks the beautiful and savage world of the samurai. Part one of a three - part series. Digitally remastered.
Fine Arts; History - World; Sociology
Dist - HOMVIS **Prod** - JANUS 1955

Samurai II - Duel at Ichijoji Temple 107 MIN
VHS
Samurai trilogy series
Color (G)
$29.95 _ #SAM050
Depicts the wanderings of Musashi Miyamoto, the most famed of all Japanese swordsmen. Ventures through the turmoil of 17th - century Japan with Miyamoto in search of both the skill and temperament worthy of a great warrior. Part two of a three - part series. Digitally remastered.
Fine Arts; History - World; Sociology
Dist - HOMVIS **Prod** - JANUS 1956

Samurai III - Duel at Ganryu Island 108 MIN
VHS
Samurai trilogy series
Color (G)
$29.95 _ #SAM060
Depicts the final showdown for Japanese swordsman Musashi Miyamoto and his arch - rival Kojiro Sasaki. Part three of a three - part series. Digitally remastered.
Fine Arts; History - World; Sociology
Dist - HOMVIS **Prod** - JANUS 1956

Samurai - Part 1 92 MIN
VHS
Color (G) (JAPANESE WITH ENGLISH SUBTITLES)
$22.95 purchase _ #NEL6139
Presents the first part of the three - part Japanese movie Samurai.
Fine Arts
Dist - CHTSUI

Samurai - Part 2 104 MIN
VHS
Color (G) (JAPANESE WITH ENGLISH SUBTITLES)
$22.95 purchase _ #NEL6140
Presents the second part of the three - part Japanese movie Samurai.
Fine Arts
Dist - CHTSUI

Samurai - Part 3 105 MIN
VHS
Color (G) (JAPANESE WITH ENGLISH SUBTITLES)
$22.95 purchase _ #NEL6141
Presents the third part of the three - part Japanese movie Samurai.
Fine Arts
Dist - CHTSUI

Samurai toys 3 MIN
VHS / U-matic
Color
Presents a music video guide to psychic self - defense. Features music by the Ballistic Kisses.
Fine Arts
Dist - KITCHN **Prod** - KITCHN

The Samurai trilogy 312 MIN
VHS
Samurai trilogy series
Color (G)
$69.95 _ #SAM030
Features an epic relating the exploits of Musashi Miyamoto, the most famed of all Japanese swordsmen. Includes three tapes - Samurai I - Musashi Miyamoto; Samurai II - Duel at Ichijoji Temple; Samurai III - Duel at Ganryu Island. See individual titles for descriptions.
Fine Arts; History - World; Sociology
Dist - HOMVIS **Prod** - JANUS

Samurai trilogy series
Samurai I - Musashi Miyamoto 97 MIN
Samurai II - Duel at Ichijoji Temple 107 MIN
Samurai III - Duel at Ganryu Island 108 MIN
The Samurai trilogy 312 MIN
Dist - HOMVIS

The San Andreas Fault 21 MIN
U-matic / VHS / 16mm
Earth science program series
Color (J H)
LC 74-700656
Shows the mapping of the geologic history of the California fault region and talks to scientists engaged in monitoring current conditions. Explains that elaborate sensing equipment has been distributed along the faultline of San Andreas in an effort to coordinate data about the forces at work in the fault system.
Geography - United States; Science - Physical
Dist - EBEC **Prod** - EBEC 1974

San Antonio Talk, Pt 1 60 MIN
VHS / U-matic
Color
Covers true happiness, unchanging One in the changing Universe, selfless living, endless nature of desires and coming into life and leaving with nothing.
Religion and Philosophy
Dist - IYOGA **Prod** - IYOGA

San Antonio Talk, Pt 2 60 MIN
VHS / U-matic
Color
Covers the function of pain, how man has created his own health problems, and the purpose and benefit of yoga communities in correcting health problems and in strengthening the mind.
Religion and Philosophy
Dist - IYOGA **Prod** - IYOGA

San Antonio, the Heart of Texas 28 MIN
16mm
Color
LC 79-701192
Presents a look at the historic past and colorful present of San Antonio, Texas.
Geography - United States; History - United States
Dist - MFCFP **Prod** - MFCFP 1979

San Diego Children's Center 20 MIN
U-matic / VHS
B&W
Shows how the San Diego Children's Center helps the parent adjust to the child being at the center. Includes such children's problems as introversion, mild retardation, hyperactivity and being 'uncontrollable.'.
Psychology; Sociology
Dist - UWISC **Prod** - SDCC 1977

San Diego Model Railroad Museum
VHS
Color (G)
$19.95 purchase _ #PX030
Presents a visit to America's largest model railroad exhibit and examines closely the craftsmanship.
Social Science
Dist - SIV

San Diego wild animal park 30 MIN
VHS
Color (G)
$24.95 purchase _ #S02284
Tells the story of San Diego's Wild Animal Park, whose mission is to preserve various animals and plants from extinction. Interviews the director, fieldkeepers and a veterinarian on their roles at the park.
Science - Natural
Dist - UILL

San Diego Zoo 17 MIN
16mm / U-matic / VHS
Color (P I A)
Visits the San Diego Zoo which covers 100 acres with large outdoor enclosures that simulate natural environments. Shows that the park allows the animals to live as they would in their natural environments.
Geography - United States; Science - Natural
Dist - LUF **Prod** - LUF 1970

San Diego Zoo 30 MIN
VHS
VideoTours history series
Color (G I J H)
$19.95 purchase _ #ZA05
Visits the San Diego Zoo.
Geography - United States; Science - Natural
Dist - SVIP

San Diego zoo - it's a wild life 30 MIN
VHS
Color (G)
$24.95 purchase _ #S02283
Portrays one day in the life of the animals at the San Diego zoo. Presents historical background on the zoo, as well as focusing on how the zoo has changed to become a more 'animal - friendly' environment.
Science - Natural
Dist - UILL

San Francisco 26 MIN
VHS / 16mm
Color (I J H G)
$460.00, $39.95 purchase
Presents the history of San Francisco from its small beginning to its status as a beautiful and exciting city in North America.
Geography - United States; History - United States
Dist - KAWVAL **Prod** - KAWVAL

San Francisco 13 MIN
U-matic / VHS / 16mm
Color (I)
Views San Francisco which has cable cars, hills and unmatched beauty at every turn.
Geography - United States
Dist - LUF **Prod** - LUF 1980

San Francisco and Southern California
VHS
Color (G)
$19.80 purchase _ #0885
Explores the Barbary Coast founded by pirates and forty - niners. Visits museums, operas, symphonies, Chinatown and Fisherman's Wharf in San Francisco. Tours Hollywood and Beverly Hills. Looks at the Spanish heritage of California.
Geography - United States; History - United States; Physical Education and Recreation; Sociology
Dist - SEVVID

San Francisco Bay 53 MIN
VHS / BETA
Color
Presents sailing and racing in San Francisco Bay. Combines the shorter titles 'Big Boats,' 'Eyedeen (18) Footers' and 'Heavy Weather Slalom.'.
Geography - United States; Physical Education and Recreation
Dist - OFFSHR **Prod** - OFFSHR

San Francisco Bay Area Filmmakers Series
Diane Li 30 MIN
Fred Padula 30 MIN
Seth Hill 28 MIN
Dist - DANKAR

San Francisco Bay area - land and water series 56 MIN
VHS
San Francisco Bay area - land and water series
Color (I J H C G)
$350.00 purchase
Presents a two - part series on the San Francisco Bay Area produced by Chris Beaver and Judy Irving. Includes the titles Treasures of the Greenbelt and Secrets of the Bay.
Geography - United States; Science - Natural
Dist - UCEMC

San Francisco Bay area - land and water series
San Francisco Bay area - land and water series 56 MIN
Secrets of the Bay 28 MIN
Treasures of the greenbelt 28 MIN
Dist - UCEMC

San Francisco Bay racing
VHS
Color (G)
$49.90 purchase _ #0229
Records 40 laser sailors in 20 - 40 knots of wind, as well as the importation of Sydney Harbor 18s to the Bay. Shows boat speeds up to 30 knots. Five world races compete in the St Francis Perpetual Series.
Physical Education and Recreation
Dist - SEVVID

San Francisco - city at the end of the rainbow
VHS
International travel films from Doug Jones series
Color (G H)
$19.95 purchase _ #IT11
Explores San Francisco.
Geography - United States; Geography - World
Dist - SVIP

San Francisco - City of Bridges 3 MIN
16mm
Of all Things Series
Color (P I)
Discusses the city of San Francisco, California.
Geography - United States
Dist - AVED **Prod** - BAILYL

San Francisco - City of Hills 3 MIN
16mm
Of all Things Series
Color (P I)
Discusses the city of San Francisco, California.
Geography - United States
Dist - AVED **Prod** - BAILYL

San Francisco diary '79 - shadow trail 9 MIN
16mm
Color (G)
$25.00 rental
Journeys into filmmaker Howard Guttenplan's mind's eye. Features a week in November 1979 partly spent in the house of Carmen Vigil.
Fine Arts
Dist - CANCIN

San Francisco foundlings 63 MIN
16mm
Color & B&W (G)
$190.00 rental
Features a sampler of seven works ranging from deconstructivist slapstick to surgical introspection. Notes that a foundling is defined as an infant of unknown parentage found abandoned and so hints at the orphanage that San Francisco has become for found footage filmmaking. Titles and production dates are - Short of Breath - 1990 - by Jay Rosenblatt; A Different

Kind of Green - 1989 - by Thad Povey; Step Off a Ten Foot Platform with Your Clothes On - 1990 - by Scott Miller; Cowboys were not Nice People - 1990 - by Larry Kless; Film For ... - 1989 - by Alfonso Alvarez; Futility - 1989 - by Greta Snider; and Decodings - 1988 - by Michael Wallin. Films also available separately. Listed in order of suggested sequence.
Fine Arts
Dist - CANCIN

San Francisco Good Times 60 MIN
U-matic / VHS / 16mm
B&W
Chronicles life in San Francisco between the years 1968 and 1972 as seen in the pages of Good Times, San Francisco's underground newspaper. Provides a colorful portrait of the culture and lifestyles of the era, including rock music, brown rice, organic gardens, astrology, communes and collectives, and assorted chemical contraband.
Geography - United States; History - United States; Sociology
Dist - CNEMAG **Prod** - FARE

San Francisco State Sit - in 22 MIN
16mm
B&W
Presents a critical account of the spring 1968 student take - over of the Administration Building at San Francisco State College.
Education; Psychology; Sociology
Dist - CANWRL **Prod** - CANWRL 1968

San Francisco - Story of a City 21 MIN
U-matic / VHS / 16mm
Color
Portrays the history of San Francisco pointing out that sailing ships brought the gold miners of 1848, the workers who built the transcontinental railroads, and the farmers, merchants, loggers and cattlemen. Depicts the city today as a center of wealth, culture and beauty.
Geography - United States; History - United States; Social Science
Dist - MCFI **Prod** - HOE 1963

San Francisco, the city by the bay 20 MIN
VHS / U-matic
Color (G)
LC 82-706785
Takes viewers to San Francisco. Discusses the gold rush and the 1906 earthquake and shows the cable cars, Chinatown and Alcatraz.
Geography - United States; History - United States
Dist - AWSS **Prod** - AWSS 1980

San Francisco - the Golden Gate 28 MIN
U-matic / VHS / 16mm
See America series
Color (G)
Reviews San Francisco, the Fire, Alcatraz, Chinatown, trolley cars, sourdough bread, the chocolate factory, pasta, and the Golden Gate, with historical footage of its construction and a bizarre accident.
Geography - United States; Social Science
Dist - MTOLP **Prod** - MTOLP 1986

San Jose Dance Theatre - Sam Richardson profile 30 MIN
U-matic / VHS
Kaleidoscope series
Color
Fine Arts
Dist - SCCOE **Prod** - KTEHTV

San - Ju - Wasi series

An Argument about a marriage	18 MIN
Baobab play	8 MIN
Bitter melons	30 MIN
Children throw toy assegais	4 MIN
A Curing ceremony	8 MIN
A Group of women	5 MIN
A Joking relationship	13 MIN
Kung Bushmen hunting equipment	37 MIN
The Kung San - resettlement	28 MIN
Lion game	4 MIN
The Meat fight	14 MIN
The Melon tossing game	15 MIN
Men bathing	14 MIN
Playing with scorpions	4 MIN
Pull ourselves up or die out	26 MIN
Tug - of - war - Bushmen	6 MIN
The Wasp nest	20 MIN

Dist - DOCEDR

The San Juan Islands 26 MIN
16mm
Color (I J)
LC 77-709387
Presents a family which discovers sites of historical interest and observes the natural beauty of the San Juan islands and waterways of Northwest Washington.
Geography - United States; Geography - World; Psychology; Sociology
Dist - SOUND **Prod** - SOUND 1970

San Juan Islands
VHS
Color (G)
$24.80 purchase _ #0295
Travels to the San Juan Islands between Washington state and Vancouver Island.
Geography - United States; Geography - World; Physical Education and Recreation
Dist - SEVVID

San Juan River tarpon and a world record marlin 30 MIN
VHS
Color (G)
$29.90 purchase _ #0386
Rides in a dugout canoe on the San Juan River, surrounded by jungle, to catch a tarpon on a fly. Features Lee Wulff who catches a world record marlin on a fly in the Humboldt Current at Salinas, Ecuador.
Geography - World; Physical Education and Recreation; Science - Natural
Dist - SEVVID

San Remo - '85 90 MIN
U-matic / VHS
Color (G)
Presents Italian music live from San Remo; features Gigliola Cinquetti, Anna Oxa, Peppino di Capri, and others.
Fine Arts
Dist - RIZACV **Prod** - RIZACV 1985

Sanaguagat - Inuit masterworks of 1000 years 25 MIN
16mm
Color (J)
Explains that the Inuit are inhabitants of the Arctic. Discusses their philosophy and lifestyle.
Fine Arts; Geography - World; Social Science; Sociology
Dist - NFBC **Prod** - CDIAND 1975

Sananguagat - Inuit Masterworks 25 MIN
16mm
Color (G)
_ #106C 0174 525
Shows the art of the Inuit Eskimo, the expression in stone, ivory and bone, of their life and the animal co dwellers of their Arctic domain.
Fine Arts; Social Science
Dist - CFLMDC **Prod** - NFBC 1974

Sanasuagat - Inuit Masterworks of 1000 Years 25 MIN
16mm
Color
LC 75-701923
Presents an exhibition of Eskimo carvings from a collection of the Canadian Eskimo Arts Council.
Fine Arts; Social Science
Dist - CDIAND **Prod** - CDIAND 1974

Sanctions and Protective Orders in Civil Discovery Practice 120 MIN
U-matic / VHS / Cassette
Color; Mono (PRO)
Focuses on when to request a protective order, what type order is appropriate, how to argue and defend this type of motion in court and the tactical decisions to make before seeking sanctions. Discusses sanctions in arbitration and the content, form and enforcement of orders.
Civics and Political Systems
Dist - CCEB **Prod** - CCEB

Sanctions and South Africa 16 MIN
VHS
Color (H)
Examines economic interdependency among South Africa and neighboring countries in the face of economic sanctions. Available for free loan from the distributor.
Business and Economics; Geography - World
Dist - AUDPLN

Sanctuary 58 MIN
VHS / U-matic
Frontline Series
Color
Observes the new 'underground system' in the United States. This is a network of individuals and organizations providing shelter, food and hope for illegal aliens fleeing oppression.
Civics and Political Systems; Sociology
Dist - PBS **Prod** - DOCCON

Sanctuary - a question of conscience 26 MIN
16mm / U-matic / VHS
Color (H C A)
$425 purchase - 16 mm, $295 purchase - video, $55 rental
Examines the Sanctuary movement which involves a group of people who illegally provide shelter for refugees from Latin America. Examines beliefs of Sanctuary activists. Directed by Wynn Hausser.
Civics and Political Systems; Sociology
Dist - CNEMAG

Sanctuary of the sea 25 MIN
VHS / U-matic / 16mm
Color; Mono (G) (FRENCH)
MV $185.00 _ MP $530.00 purchase, $50.00 rental
Presents a view of the day to day workings of one of the world's leading marine aquaria. Features live performances, research and care of the marine animals residing at the aquaria.
Science - Natural
Dist - CTV **Prod** - MAKOF 1981

Sanctuary of the Sea 22 MIN
16mm
Color
Describes in depth the behind the scenes action at Miami Seaquarium, from the capture of certain sea animals to the return of others to the sea.
Science - Natural
Dist - MIAMIS **Prod** - MIAMIS

Sanctuary - the Great Smokey Mountains 10 MIN
16mm
Color
LC 79-701512
Examines the landscape, foliage and wildlife of the Great Smokey Mountains National Park. Follows the seasonal changes of the Smokies.
Geography - United States
Dist - USNAC **Prod** - USNPS 1979

Sanctus 19 MIN
VHS
B&W; Color (G)
$60.00 rental, $50.00 purchase
Addresses the co - fragility of both human existence and the film emulsion, onto which the artist creates images. Transforms found footage of scientific X - ray films from the 1950s into a celebration of the body as temple.
Fine Arts
Dist - CANCIN **Prod** - BARHAM 1990

Sand 10 MIN
16mm
Color
LC 77-701109
Features, without narration, sculptor Saul Leyton creating a sand sculpture at the beach. Shows an assembling crowd which aids in the construction of reclining human figures. Views the impermanence of the creation when an afternoon tide begins to destroy the completed work.
Fine Arts; Guidance and Counseling
Dist - VIEWFI **Prod** - LEYTNS 1973

Sand 12 MIN
U-matic / VHS / 16mm
Early Childhood Education Series
Color (C)
Demonstrates how play with sand provides children with new sensory and perceptual experiences including those involving weight, texture and quantity.
Education; Psychology
Dist - MEDIAG **Prod** - MEDIAG 1976

Sand 10 MIN
16mm
B&W (C)
$195.00
Presents an experimental film by Caroline Leaf.
Fine Arts
Dist - AFA **Prod** - AFA 1969

Sand and gravel is for the birds - a mining reclamation success story 8 MIN
U-matic / VHS
Color (I J H C A)
Shows how land restoration following mining can be effective to preserve environmental diversity.
Science - Natural; Social Science
Dist - CEPRO **Prod** - CEPRO 1986

Sand and snow 26 MIN
16mm
Winston Churchill - the Valiant Years Series no 12
B&W
LC FI67-2112
Presents documentary footage of the establishment of the free French government, the successful conclusion of the North African campaign, the Roosevelt - Churchill meeting at Casablanca in 1943 and the Battle of Stalingrad.
History - World
Dist - SG **Prod** - ABCTV 1961

Sand and Steel 16 MIN
16mm
B&W
LC 74-706234
Describes the construction of the Marine airfield at Chu Lai in Vietnam.
Civics and Political Systems; Industrial and Technical Education
Dist - USNAC **Prod** - USMC 1966

The Sand barrier 25 MIN
16mm
Color (G)
#106C 0179 383
Presents the Syncrude project of producing crude oil from oil sands.
Social Science
Dist - CFLMDC **Prod** - NFBC 1979

Sand casting 25 MIN
U-matic / VHS
Technical studies series
Color (H C A)
Discusses aspects of sand casting.
Industrial and Technical Education
Dist - FI **Prod** - BBCTV 1981

The Sand Castle 14 MIN
16mm
Color (K P I)
Uses animation to show fantasy creatures transforming sand into a community of sand structures only to have the wind destroy them.
Fine Arts
Dist - NFBC **Prod** - NFBC 1978

Sand County Almanac 16 MIN
U-matic / VHS / 16mm
Color (J)
LC 79-700506
Presents the writings of Aldo Leopold, a professor of biology who wrote about the natural environment throughout America, but especially his Sand County farm in Wisconsin. Explores Leopold's ideas on ecology and his concept for land use called 'land ethic.'.
Literature and Drama; Science - Natural; Sociology
Dist - PHENIX **Prod** - JANOFF 1979

Sand drains 24 MIN
16mm
Color
LC 72-701967
Explains the sand drain method of consolidating swampy areas for the construction of highways. Uses animation and scenes of an actual project to show preparation of the site, driving the sand drains, placing the control devices and overload, final preparation of the roadway and paving.
Industrial and Technical Education; Social Science
Dist - USNAC **Prod** - USDTFH 1965

Sand Dune Erosion Project 14 MIN
VHS / U-matic
Color (H A)
Points out the value of sand dunes to the environment and to people. Describes the growth pattern of beach grass which helps to control sand dune erosion.
Agriculture; Science - Natural
Dist - CORNRS **Prod** - CUETV

Sand dunes 27 MIN
16mm
B&W (C A)
Outlines Stoke's law and visualizes transportation by suspension, saltation and traction as being size controlled. Pictures actual sand transport and illustrates development of transverse, barchan and longitudinal dunes and sand avalanches. Summarizes the inter - relationship of wind and sand, as well as water and vegetation.
Science - Physical
Dist - UTEX **Prod** - UTEX 1960

Sand fishermen 9 MIN
U-matic / VHS
Color
Illustrates the gathering of sand near Bogota, Columbia with which to make cement by 'fishing' river bottoms. Shows how required sand is necessary for Colombia's skyscrapers and modern roads. No narration.
Geography - World; History - World; Industrial and Technical Education
Dist - IFF **Prod** - IFF

Sand in Art 12 MIN
U-matic / VHS / 16mm
Color (FRENCH)
LC 81-701109;
Shows how sand can be molded and combined with different tools and substances to create permanent works of art.
Fine Arts
Dist - ALTSUL **Prod** - AMBELH 1981

Sand or Peter and the Wolf 10 MIN
U-matic / VHS / 16mm
B&W (K P)
LC 78-706101
Retells the story of Peter And The Wolf using the medium of animated sand. Follows the story line of the fable, but takes musical and pictorial liberties.
Fine Arts; Literature and Drama
Dist - PHENIX **Prod** - CCVISA 1969

Sand painting - sacred art of Tibetan Buddhism 30 MIN
VHS
Color (G R)
$34.95 purchase _ #SAPAVI
Records the creation of the Kalachakra mandala by monks of the Nambyal Monastery led by Lobsang Samten during the 1991 Asian Art Museum exhibit of Tibetan Art. Explores the meaning of the symbols within the mandala with its five levels and hundreds of deities.
Religion and Philosophy
Dist - SNOWLI

The Sand Pebbles 195 MIN
BETA
Color
Involves the crew of an American gunboat caught between Chinese war lords and foreign powers. Stars Steve McQueen, Richard Crenna and Candice Bergen.
Fine Arts
Dist - RMIBHF **Prod** - UNKNWN 1966

Sand - the desert in motion 11 MIN
U-matic / VHS / 16mm
Color (I J H)
LC 73-706585
Examines the origin and distribution of desert sands. Pictures deserts of many regions and explains the effects of water, wind and the sharp edges of the grains of sand on rocky surfaces. Concludes that in some areas man has been able to bring water to the desert and convert sandy wasteland to productive crop - growing soil.
Agriculture; Geography - World; Science - Natural; Science - Physical
Dist - PHENIX **Prod** - BYE 1969

The Sandalmaker 27 MIN
16mm / U-matic / VHS
Insight series
Color; B&W (H C A)
LC 77-705440
Tells about a College dropout who, after being charged with the murder of his hippie girl friend, chooses to admit being on LSD and not remembering what happened rather than accept a contrived acquittal arranged by his prominent attorney father.
Guidance and Counseling; Psychology; Sociology
Dist - PAULST **Prod** - PAULST 1968

Sandbox 10 MIN
16mm
B&W
LC 75-703228
Presents a screen adaptation of the play of the same name by Edward Albee. Uses abstract dialogue and setting to comment on contemporary American family relationships and particularly attitudes towards the elderly.
Guidance and Counseling; Literature and Drama; Psychology; Sociology
Dist - USC **Prod** - USC 1965

The Sandbox 25 MIN
U-matic / VHS
Blizzard's Wonderful Wooden Toys Series
Color (H C A)
Demonstrates how to make a sandbox and toys that can be used in and around it - a crane, a sand hopper and a dump truck. Shows how to design a model from the original.
Fine Arts
Dist - FI **Prod** - BBCTV

Sandcastle - a film about teamwork 14 MIN
16mm / VHS
Color (G)
$535.00 purchase, $150.00 rental _ #165
Shows sand creatures creating shapes from sand. Illustrates the relationship between teamwork and productivity, especially with a diverse group. No narrative. Includes Leader's Guide.
Business and Economics; Psychology
Dist - SALENG **Prod** - NFBC 1977

Sandcastles 30 MIN
16mm
Color (R)
Presents psychologist Dr Bruce Narramore explaining the role of Christ in family relationships and communication.
Guidance and Counseling; Religion and Philosophy; Sociology
Dist - GF **Prod** - GF

Sandefjord
VHS
Color (G)
$100.00 rental _ #0811
Shows how six adventurers refitted a battered 50 - year - old wooden ketch and sailed it westward around the world.
Geography - World; Physical Education and Recreation
Dist - SEVVID

Sanders of the River 80 MIN
16mm
B&W
Depicts the adventures of a black chief who comes to the aid of a British district head in Africa. Stars Paul Robeson and Leslie Banks.
Fine Arts
Dist - REELIM **Prod** - UNKNWN 1935

Sandfly Control 32 MIN
16mm
Color
LC FIE52-1723
Explains the symptoms and treatment of diseases transmitted by the sandfly. Describes the principles and methods of sanitation essential to control.
Health and Safety; Home Economics
Dist - USNAC **Prod** - USA 1950

Sandhills Album 60 MIN
VHS / U-matic
(G)
Uses vintage and contemporary photographs to evoke the daily life of ordinary Nebraskans from pioneer times through the present. Activities include a rodeo and a local saloon's Independence Day festivities.
History - United States
Dist - GPN **Prod** - NETV 1982

Sandi Mehring - a Special Kind of Drive 6 MIN
16mm
Color
Introduces Sandi Mehring, a bright young woman who found a career as a truckdriver.
Guidance and Counseling; Social Science; Sociology
Dist - MTP **Prod** - ATA

Sandi Patti - let there be praise 95 MIN
VHS
Color (G R)
$19.95 purchase _ #35 - 85029 - 533
Presents Christian vocalist Sandi Patti in a performance of many of her songs, including 'Let There Be Praise,' 'Hosanna,' 'Via Dolorosa,' 'Was It a Morning Like This?' and more.
Fine Arts; Religion and Philosophy
Dist - APH **Prod** - WORD

Sandi Patti...live 56 MIN
VHS
Color (G R)
$19.95 purchase, $10.00 rental _ #35 - 81 - 92
Features Christian vocalist Sandi Patti in a live performance of many of her songs.
Fine Arts; Religion and Philosophy
Dist - APH

Sandia spinoff 11 MIN
16mm
Color (H C)
LC FIA67-592
Illustrates the Sandia Laminar flow cleanroom principle with live action and animation. Indicates its industrial and medical applications. Describes an iron plating process and an automated method of producing printed circuits.
Industrial and Technical Education
Dist - SANDIA **Prod** - SANDIA 1966

Sanding and finishing hardwood floors with Don Bollinger 40 MIN
BETA / VHS
Color (G A)
$19.95 _ #060059
Shows how to preserve and finish strip, plank or parquet hardwood floors. Features carpenter Don Bollinger. Also available in book format.
Fine Arts; Home Economics; Industrial and Technical Education
Dist - TANTON **Prod** - TANTON

Sanding Machines
VHS
Woodworking Power Tools Series
(C G)
$59.00 _ CA186
Demonstrates the safe handling and operation of sanding machines.
Industrial and Technical Education
Dist - AAVIM **Prod** - AAVIM 1989

Sanding Machines 13 MIN
VHS / BETA

Woodworking Power Tools Series
Color (IND)
Industrial and Technical Education; Psychology
Dist - RMIBHF **Prod** - RMIBHF

Sanding Methods 8 MIN
VHS / BETA / 16mm
Color (A PRO)
$56.00 purchase _ #AB155
Illustrates the sanding method of feathering a repair to eliminate bullseyes.
Industrial and Technical Education
Dist - RMIBHF **Prod** - RMIBHF

Sanding Techniques 14 MIN
BETA / VHS / 16mm
Color (A PRO)
$69.75 purchase _ #AB154
Explains various techniques of sanding a surface for refinishing.
Industrial and Technical Education
Dist - RMIBHF **Prod** - RMIBHF

Sandino, Today and Forever 55 MIN
U-matic / VHS / 16mm
Color
Studies the tremendous social changes which have taken place in Nicaragua since the overthrow of Somoza as seen through the life of Pedro Pablo, a small farmer and member of a recently founded agricultural cooperative.
History - World
Dist - ICARUS **Prod** - TERCIN 1981

Sandpipers, Pt 1 3 MIN
16mm
Of all Things Series
Color (P I)
Discusses the birds known as sandpipers.
Science - Natural
Dist - AVED **Prod** - BAILYL

Sandpipers, Pt 2 3 MIN
16mm
Of all Things Series
Color (P I)
Discusses the birds known as sandpipers.
Science - Natural
Dist - AVED **Prod** - BAILYL

Sandra and Her Kids 28 MIN
16mm
Color
Tells of a dynamic woman who has adopted 20 handicapped children from around the world. Reveals how she organized Families For Children, an agency which has handled over 2,000 adoptions.
Education; Sociology
Dist - FLMLIB **Prod** - CANBC 1982

Sandra Gilbert - 5 - 6 - 82 50 MIN
VHS / Cassette
Poetry Center reading series
Color (G)
$15.00, $45.00 purchase, $15.00 rental _ #493 - 416
Features the writer at the Poetry Center of San Francisco State University, reading Rewriting the Myth, a paper on confessional mythology. Discusses the impulse in women's poetry toward 'visioning and revisioning' conventional notions and definitions of mythology.
Literature and Drama; Religion and Philosophy; Sociology
Dist - POETRY **Prod** - POETRY 1982

Sandra Gilbert - 4 - 13 - 85 90 MIN
VHS / Cassette
Poetry Center reading series
Color (G)
$15.00, $45.00 purchase, $15.00 rental _ #638 - 534
Features the writer participating in the Women Working in Literature conference. Presents a panel discussion on The Impact of Feminist Criticism on Contemporary Women's Writing held at the Poetry Center, San Francisco State University, with Deborah Rosenfelt, moderator.
Literature and Drama; Sociology
Dist - POETRY **Prod** - POETRY 1985

Sandra Jamrog, Dr Hans Kraus and Priscilla Tablante 30 MIN
U-matic / VHS
Eye on Dance - Health and Well - Being of Dancers Series
Color
Focuses on exercise for pregnant women. Includes demonstrations.
Fine Arts
Dist - ARCVID **Prod** - ARCVID

Sandra's garden - Women and incest 34 MIN
VHS
Color (G)
$60.00 rental, $275.00 purchase
Tells the story of one woman who, in finding the courage to speak about her experience of incest, began to overcome the fear, guilt and denial that had shaped her life. Conveys the sense of wholeness that Sandra finds through the land on which she lives; her loving relationship with a woman; and the support of women in her community. A film by Bonnie Dickie.
Fine Arts; Psychology; Sociology
Dist - WMEN **Prod** - NFBC 1991

Sandringham - a royal retreat 25 MIN
VHS
Color (G)
$19.95 purchase _ #S01466
Visits the British royal family's retreat home, Sandringham, located 100 miles north of London. Presents relevant historical events. Reveals that although Sandringham is still used by the royal family, it is open to visitors.
Civics and Political Systems; Geography - World; History - World
Dist - UILL

Sands of Time 14 MIN
16mm
Color
LC 76-702882
Uses extreme closeup and microphotography to provide a view of the manufacturing techniques and skills required in the production of solid state devices and integrated circuits that are revolutionizing many products.
Business and Economics; Industrial and Technical Education
Dist - HONEYW **Prod** - HONEYW 1976

Sandsong 18 MIN
U-matic / VHS / 16mm
Color (J)
LC 81-700065
Introduces Gerry Lynas, an artist who sculpts in sand at the edge of the sea. Shows him creating a sculpture which is eventually reclaimed by the ocean.
Fine Arts
Dist - WOMBAT **Prod** - MMMAST 1981

Sandsong 18 MIN
VHS
Color (H C G T A)
$49.95 purchase _ #S01062
Presents the unique art form known as sand sculpture. Reveals that sand sculptures reflect both art and life, as well as the permanent and the ephemeral.
Fine Arts
Dist - UILL **Prod** - UILL

Sandstone deposition - dunes, beaches, and submarine fans 43 MIN
U-matic / VHS
Basic geology series
Color (IND)
Industrial and Technical Education; Science - Physical
Dist - GPCV **Prod** - GPCV

Sandstone Deposition - Rivers and Deltas 53 MIN
U-matic / VHS
Basic Geology Series
Color (IND)
Industrial and Technical Education; Science - Physical
Dist - GPCV **Prod** - GPCV

Sandstone secrets 28 MIN
VHS / U-matic
Earth explored series
Color
Covers the various sampling and observation techniques used for the interpretation of sediments.
Science - Physical
Dist - PBS **Prod** - BBCTV

Sandstorm in the Gulf - digging out 30 MIN
VHS
America's defense monitor series; War with Iraq
Color (J H C G)
$29.95 purchase _ #ADM426V
Examines the aftermath of the war with Iraq. Part of a six - part series examining the United States' war with Iraq, 1990 - 1991.
Civics and Political Systems; History - United States; History - World; Sociology
Dist - CAMV

Sandwich preparation and presentation 8 MIN
U-matic / VHS / 16mm
Professional food preparation and service program series
Color (J) (SPANISH GERMAN)
LC 74-703054
Discusses how to achieve variety in sandwiches. Shows the actual preparation of distinctive open and closed sandwiches by a professional. Demonstrates how a clean, efficient sandwich area is organized.
Home Economics; Industrial and Technical Education
Dist - NEM **Prod** - NEM 1969

Sandwich Savvy 11 MIN
VHS / U-matic
Color (PRO)
Examines the basic elements of any sandwich and shows how to build upon these to make a variety, including hearty closed sandwiches, canapes, and Scandinavian - style open - faced sandwiches.
Home Economics; Industrial and Technical Education
Dist - CULINA **Prod** - CULINA

Sandwich stuff 15 MIN
U-matic / VHS / 16mm
Let's visit series
Color (P I)
Covers the manufacture of each ingredient of a peanut butter and jam sandwich. Children's observations inform the viewer about each stage in process.
Home Economics; Social Science
Dist - BCNFL **Prod** - BCNFL 1984

Sandwich Supreme 6 MIN
U-matic / VHS
Cooking with Jack and Jill Series
Color (P I)
$95.00
Portrays the skills of twins Jack and Jill as they cook nutritious and delicious snacks that are easy to prepare. Kitchen safety is emphasized. Animated.
Home Economics
Dist - LANDMK **Prod** - LANDMK 1986

Sandwiches
VHS / 35mm strip
Food preparation series
$119.00 purchase _ #PX1144 filmstrip, $119.00 purchase _ #PX1144V
Shows a variety of hot and cold sandwiches, canapes and hors d'oeuvres. Gives a description of club, tea, hot, open faced and closed face sandwiches. Shows techniques for making, decorating and presenting sandwiches.
Health and Safety; Home Economics; Industrial and Technical Education; Social Science
Dist - CAREER **Prod** - CAREER

Sandwiches - Dinner, Tea and Canape, Scandinavian 26 MIN
U-matic / VHS
Color (PRO)
Shows how to make ham on rye, turkey club, grilled cheese and Reuben sandwiches, also tunafish concolaise canapes, salami canapes twisted into cornucopias and tea sandwiches. Emphasizes Scandinavian - style sandwiches.
Home Economics; Industrial and Technical Education
Dist - CULINA **Prod** - CULINA

Sandwoman's moon 7 MIN
16mm
Color (G)
$20.00 rental
Presents an experimental film.
Fine Arts
Dist - CANCIN **Prod** - DOBERG 1976

Sandy and Madeleine's family 30 MIN
VHS / U-matic / 16mm
Color (C A)
Documents a child custody case where children were awarded to mothers even though they openly admitted their homosexual relationship. Anthropologist Margaret Mead expresses her view that the welfare of the children will depend on the love and warmth of their family environment and not on the sexual orientation of the parents.
Health and Safety; Psychology; Sociology
Dist - MMRC **Prod** - FARELS 1973

Sandy and Rick - Birth 7
U-matic
Video birth library series
Color (J H G)
$100.00 purchase
Follows the childbirth experiences of Sandy and Rick, a young married couple having their first baby after a miscarriage two years before. Reveals that during this pregnancy Sandy was briefly hospitalized at 8 weeks because of bleeding. Now at term, she is 5 cm dilated when admitted. Rick helps her to use the Jacuzzi and she rapidly dilates to 10 cm. Part of a 15 - part series on childbirth education.
Health and Safety
Dist - POLYMR **Prod** - POLYMR

Sandy's Hospital Story 14 MIN
VHS / 16mm
Color (K)
$95.00 purchase
Attempts to familiarize children with hospital procedures. Includes explanations of technical terms and procedures that can be understood by children.
Health and Safety; Sociology
Dist - FLMWST

Sanford Meisner - The theater's best - kept secret 56 MIN
U-matic / VHS
Color (H C)
$89.95 purchase _ #EX819
Portrays acting teacher Sanford Meisner at work. Interviews Meisner students such as Robert Duvall, Tony Randall and Joanne Woodward.
Fine Arts; Literature and Drama
Dist - FOTH **Prod** - FOTH

Sanguine memories 7 MIN
16mm / VHS
Color; B&W (G)
$10.00 rental
Narrates the state of mind of the male protagonist and his fleeting memories of an ambiguously depicted female while he attempts to escape his own self. Explores the 'color' of memory and uses the flashback as a mirroring device to reflect the protagonist's thoughts. Produced by Jerome Carolfi.
Fine Arts
Dist - CANCIN

Sanitary landfill - you're the operator 22 MIN
16mm
Color (PRO G) (SPANISH)
LC 75-701731
Demonstrates that a sanitary landfill can be a good neighbor and a community asset. Illustrates the careful planning and precise techniques required to achieve maximum standards.
Health and Safety; Industrial and Technical Education; Science - Natural; Sociology
Dist - USNAC **Prod** - USEPA 1973

Sanitation and Food Safety - K J Baker, MS 32 MIN
U-matic
Food and Nutrition Seminars for Health Professionals Series
Color (PRO)
LC 78-706166
Discusses the extent of the foodborne illness program, covering the causes as well as the preventive measures that can be taken to reduce contamination of food.
Health and Safety; Social Science
Dist - USNAC **Prod** - USFDA 1976

Sanitation and hygiene - basic rules
U-matic / VHS / 16mm
Professional food preparation and service program series
Color
Emphasizes basic rules of kitchen sanitation and hygiene including how to handle potentially hazardous foods including fowl, seafood and custards. Illustrates control of pests, personal cleanliness and proper techniques for cooling, storage and refrigeration. Emphasizes the importance of clean hands and proper washing methods.
Health and Safety; Home Economics; Industrial and Technical Education
Dist - NEM **Prod** - NEM 1983

Sanitation and hygiene for dining room personnel
16mm / U-matic / VHS
Professional food preparation and service program series
Color
Demonstrates techniques of sanitary food handling for dining room personnel. Emphasizes the importance of the servers' personal cleanliness, hygiene and grooming. Includes sanitary practices necessary before reporting for work, as well as dining practices that inhibit growth of germs.
Health and Safety; Industrial and Technical Education
Dist - NEM **Prod** - NEM 1983

Sanitation and hygiene - why the importance
16mm / U-matic / VHS
Professional food preparation and service program series
Color
Introduces kitchen sanitation and hygiene. Shows biological reasons for sanitation and hygiene and the conditions for controlling bacterial growth. Explains the danger of bacteria, how bacteria spread from place to place and how their growth can be accelerated or retarded. Demonstrates how hands, clothing, kitchen tools, unclean surfaces, rats, roaches and flies can carry germs.
Health and Safety; Industrial and Technical Education
Dist - NEM **Prod** - NEM 1983

Sanitation and safety
VHS / 35mm strip
Food service - skills and equipment series
$109.00 purchase _ #PX1131 filmstrip, $109.00 purchase _ #PX1131V
Provides a knowledge of hygiene in the food service environment. Portrays common accidents and prevention of kitchen fires.
Health and Safety; Industrial and Technical Education
Dist - CAREER **Prod** - CAREER

Sanitation - conquering kitchen germs 17 MIN
VHS
Color (H C A IND)
LC 90-716357
Trains kitchen employees about sanitation. Produced by Media Magic.
Health and Safety; Industrial and Technical Education; Psychology; Social Science
Dist - EIAHM

Sanitation for food service workers - housekeeping and safety in the - Pt 7
VHS / U-matic
We care series
Color
Describes germs that can cause foodborne disease, shows how to keep the kitchen and equipment clean and suggests practical assembly - line methods that function best for preparing patient trays and/or table service.
Health and Safety; Home Economics
Dist - VTRI **Prod** - VTRI

Sanitation - rodent and insect control 10 MIN
VHS / 16mm / U-matic
Professional food preparation and service program series
Color (SPANISH)
LC 73-702055
Discusses the ways in which food service workers can control and eliminate rodent and insect infestation of food preparation areas.
Agriculture; Health and Safety; Industrial and Technical Education
Dist - NEM **Prod** - NEM 1972

Sanitation safety 15 MIN
16mm / VHS / BETA / U-matic
Color; PAL (IND)
PdS125, PdS133 purchase
Offers a training program for sanitation workers. Discusses avoiding hazards.
Health and Safety; Industrial and Technical Education
Dist - EDPAT

Sanitation Safety 8 MIN
VHS / 16mm
Color (A IND)
LC 91705377
Outlines the hazards involved in sanitation work, the materials to be picked up, and the methods used. Shows personal protection clothing needed and safety checks necessary for vehicles.
Education; Health and Safety; Industrial and Technical Education
Dist - IFB

Sanjo - Korean improvisational music 31 MIN
16mm / VHS / U-matic
Ethnic music and dance series
B&W (J)
LC 72-700239
Presents a performance of sanjo, an improvisational music from Cholla province in Southwestern Korea. Includes two performances on the 12 - stringed zither, kayagum, and shows one performance on an instrument that is a seven - stringed, bowed zither called ajaeng.
Fine Arts; Geography - World
Dist - UWASHP **Prod** - UWASH 1971

Sanjuro 96 MIN
VHS
B&W (G) (JAPANESE WITH ENGLISH SUBTITLES)
$22.95 purchase _ #NEL6063
Presents a sequel to Yojimbo starring Toshiro Mifune and directed by Akira Kurosawa.
Fine Arts
Dist - CHTSUI

Sans titre 84 14 MIN
16mm
Color (G)
$40.00 rental
Rearranges photos of the Arc de Triomphe into vertical, horizontal, and diagonal strips, transforming and reforming the Arc. Requires two projectors. By Yann Beauvais.
Fine Arts
Dist - CANCIN

Sanshiro Sugata 82 MIN
VHS
Japan Film Collection from SVS Series
B&W (G) (JAPANESE (ENGLISH SUBTITLES))
$59.95 purchase _ #K0690
Features Akira Kurosawa as director. Stars Susumu Fujita.
Fine Arts; Geography - World
Dist - CHTSUI **Prod** - SONY

Sansho the Bailiff 132 MIN
VHS
Japan Film Collection from SVS Series
B&W (G) (JAPANESE (ENGLISH SUBTITLES))
$59.95 purchase _ #K0689
Presents a movie produced in Japan. Features Kenji Mizoguchi as director. Stars Kinuyo Tanaka, Yoshiaki Hanayagi and Kyoko Kagawa.
Fine Arts; Geography - World
Dist - CHTSUI **Prod** - SONY

Sanskrit drama 14 MIN
VHS
Color (G C H)
$129.00 purchase _ #DL317
Features Mrinalini Sarabhai, founder of the Darpana Academy of Performing Arts in Ahmedabad, India. Introduces Indian costuming, mannerisms, movement, and makeup.
Fine Arts; History - World
Dist - INSIM

Santa Barbara - Everybody's Mistake 30 MIN
16mm / U-matic / VHS
Our Vanishing Wilderness Series no 6
Color (H C A)
LC 73-710657
Examines the controversies behind the two - million gallon oil leak off the shore of California in 1969. Points out that the smog created by the oil is killing pine trees 6,000 feet above sea level.
Science - Natural
Dist - IU **Prod** - NET 1970

Santa Claus 15 MIN
VHS / U-matic
Draw Along Series
(K P)
$125.00 purchase
Shows how to draw Santa's head first and then adds his body.
Fine Arts
Dist - AITECH **Prod** - AITECH 1983

Santa Claus has Blue Eyes 45 MIN
16mm
B&W (FRENCH)
Features one of two short stories combined in the film, Bad Company. Tells of a youth in a provincial French town who finally lands a job posing as Santa Claus at Christmas time.
Foreign Language; Literature and Drama
Dist - NYFLMS **Prod** - NYFLMS 1966

Santa Fe 16 MIN
16mm
Color
LC 76-704009
Discusses the Indian, Spanish and Mexican heritage of Santa Fe, New Mexico.
Geography - United States; History - United States
Dist - USNAC **Prod** - USIA 1974

Santa Fe Chamber Music Festival 90 MIN
VHS / U-matic
Color
Fine Arts
Dist - ABCLR **Prod** - ABCLR

Santa Fe Trail 16 MIN
16mm / U-matic / VHS
Color (I)
LC 79-700006
Traces the history of the Santa Fe Trail.
History - United States; Social Science
Dist - PHENIX **Prod** - CALVIN 1978

Santa Fe's Mojave Mainline
VHS
Color (G)
$39.95 purchase _ #PX031
Explores the Mojave desert along the tracks of the Santa Fe railroad.
Geography - United States; Social Science
Dist - SIV

Santa Marta - Two Weeks in the Slums 54 MIN
U-matic / VHS
Color (H C A) (PORTUGUESE (ENGLISH SUBTITLES))
$395 purchase, $90 rental
Looks at daily life in a slum in Rio de Janeiro. Talks about police harassment, lack of educational and employment opportunities, problems of sanitation, violence, drugs and alcohol in the community, and social and racial discrimination. Directed by Eduardo Coutinho.
Sociology
Dist - CNEMAG

The Santa Monica project 30 MIN
16mm
Color (T)
Depicts the engineered classroom for educationally handicapped children as described in Dr Frank W Hewett's book, 'The Emotionally Disturbed Child in the Classroom.'
Education; Psychology
Dist - NYSED **Prod** - NYSED

The Santa Monica Project 28 MIN
U-matic / VHS / 16mm
Color (C T)
LC 70-714324
Describes educational procedures in a public school class for emotionally disturbed children, ages six to 15. Describes the hierarchy of educational goals and means of promoting attention and response. Emphasizes routine, learning to understand environment, mastering academic skills and utilizing commercially available materials.
Education; Psychology
Dist - AIMS **Prod** - SMUSD 1972

Santa's Christmas stories 29 MIN
VHS
Color (P)
$49.95 purchase _ #8338
Features Santa Claus who presents three animated Christmas stories, including The Night Before Christmas by Clement C Moore.
Literature and Drama; Social Science
Dist - AIMS **Prod** - APOLF 1991

Santa's Toys 8 MIN
16mm / U-matic / VHS
Color (K P I)
LC 74-703792
Presents an animated film which tells the story of Christmas Eve. Shows how the toys that Santa Claus has left come to life, decorate the tree, fill the stockings and make everything ready for Christmas day.
Fine Arts; Social Science
Dist - CORF **Prod** - DISNEY 1974

Santeros - Saintmakers 33 MIN
VHS / 16mm
Color (H C A)
$150.00 purchase, $25.00 rental _ #RC1281
Documents the work of Hispanic wood sculptors, santeros, who carry on a 300 - year - old tradition of "saintmaking". Focuses on five artisans in New Mexico. Features scenic shots of the New Mexican landscape.
Fine Arts
Dist - IU **Prod** - NENDOW 1986

Santiago's ark 47 MIN
U-matic / VHS / 16mm
Color; Captioned (P I J)
LC 73-700911
Shows that dreams, even in a ghetto, can become reality with encouragement and persistence. Tells the story of a Puerto Rican boy who inspires a Spanish Harlem neighborhood by building a boat on a tenement rooftop. Follows the boy, Santiago, as he gathers materials from the street and alleys and pursues his project with fervor.
Guidance and Counseling; Sociology
Dist - CAROUF **Prod** - ACW 1972

The Sao Francisco 57 MIN
VHS / U-matic
River Journeys
Color (H C A)
$1225 purchase (entire series), $285 purchase (each)
Discusses Germaine Greer's journey down the Sao Francisco River. Produced by BBC - TV and RKO pictures for public television.
Geography - World
Dist - CF

Sapmi, the Sami people in Norway 34 MIN
VHS
Color (G)
Free loan
Looks at Norway's Lapland and presents the contemporary Sami way of life. Defines the challenges faced by the Sami people.
Geography - World; Sociology
Dist - NIS

Sappho 50 MIN
16mm
Color (G)
$89.00 rental
Presents a biography of Sappho. Centers on her poetry but also extends beyond her life to her legacy as one of the most remembered names of Western Civilization. Conveys filmmaker Walter Gutman's belief that history is the womb of humanity, in particular the history of the Hellenes and Greeks.
History - World
Dist - CANCIN

Sappho 7 MIN
16mm
Color (G)
$20.00 rental
Watches a group of women unwrapping papyrus gauze and bringing the lesbian goddess, Sappho, to life. Uses her 6th - century BC poetry.
Literature and Drama; Sociology
Dist - CANCIN **Prod** - BARHAM 1978

Saps at Sea 61 MIN
16mm
B&W
Presents the story of two hard - working horntesters who decide they need a vacation and buy a leaky sail boat for a cruise.
Fine Arts
Dist - RMIBHF **Prod** - ROACH 1940

SAR mission coordinator - search and rescue 27 MIN
16mm
Color
LC 74-706235
Describes how a mission coordinator in the Air Force organizes and conducts an inland search and rescue mission. Shows how search crews are instructed on the types of flight patterns and the areas to be covered and demonstrates a successful rescue.
Civics and Political Systems; Industrial and Technical Education
Dist - USNAC **Prod** - USAF 1966

Sara and Maybelle 10 MIN
U-matic / VHS / 16mm
B&W (A)
Presents two members from the original Carter family singing 'Sweet Fern' and 'Solid Gone,' two songs which demonstrate their famous guitar picking style and harmony singing.
Fine Arts
Dist - CNEMAG **Prod** - CNEMAG 1981

Sara has Down's Syndrome 17 MIN
16mm
Exploring Childhood Series
B&W
LC 74-702512
Shows a six - year - old child suffering from Down's syndrome as she interacts with her family and works in school. Shows how her family copes with this form of mongoloidism.
Education; Psychology; Sociology
Dist - EDC **Prod** - USOCHD 1974

Sara Lightfoot 30 MIN
VHS
World of ideas with Bill Moyers - Season I - series
Color (G)
$39.95 purchase _ #BMWI - 123
Interviews Harvard education professor Sara Lightfoot, who shares her ideas on what makes schools and teachers good. Stresses both the problems and accomplishments of American schools. Hosted by Bill Moyers.
Education
Dist - PBS

Sarah 10 MIN
16mm
One to Grow on Series
Color (T)
LC 73-701941
Portrays a critical incident which revolves around confidential information between a student and a teacher. Shows how the incident leads to a triangular conflict among student, teacher and counselor with important decisions and consequences confronting each.
Education
Dist - USNAC **Prod** - NIMH 1973

Sarah 27 MIN
16mm
Color
Tells the story of a woman in her forties who invites a man to her home, along with her family, for Thanksgiving. Shows her family being scornful and abusive and her turning to a friend for understanding. Tells of a woman seeking affirmation in mid - life.
Psychology; Sociology
Dist - BLKFMF **Prod** - BLKFMF

Sarah at 2 - 1/2 17 MIN
16mm
Color
Portrays the talents and interests of a child at age two and a half years.
Psychology
Dist - URBNIM **Prod** - URBNIM 1978

Sarah Bailey 29 MIN
VHS / 16mm
Color (G)
$100.00 purchase _ #SARAHVH
Views folk artist Sarah Bailey at work and teaching in an elder hostel. Features her corn shuck dolls, flower art work and weaving.
Fine Arts; Geography - United States
Dist - APPAL

Sarah Bernhardt 14 MIN
VHS
Color (C)
$69.95 purchase _ #EX1840
Portrays the legendary French actress. Reveals her spectacular performing style and the tragedies and triumphs of her personal life.
Fine Arts; History - World; Literature and Drama
Dist - FOTH **Prod** - FOTH

Sarah, Plain and Tall
35mm strip / VHS / Cassette
Newbery Award - Winners Series
Color (I)
$66.00, $14.00 purchase
English Language; Literature and Drama
Dist - PELLER

Sarah, plain and tall 98 MIN
VHS
Color (I J H)
$17.98 purchase _ #473549
Stars Glenn Close as an uncompromising New England woman who shows a lonely family that anything is possible. Adapts a story by Patricia MacLachan.
Literature and Drama
Dist - KNOWUN

Sarah Rudner 30 MIN
U-matic / VHS
Doris Chase Dance Series
Color
Features dancer/choreographer Sarah Rudner in three video variations.
Fine Arts; Physical Education and Recreation
Dist - CHASED **Prod** - CHASED

Sarah Wilson 8 MIN
16mm
Color
LC 74-705575
Discusses an 'open end' situation aimed at promotion. Presents and describes how at a meeting of health office personnel, a proposal by one member encounters opposition from the majority of the group.
Health and Safety; Sociology
Dist - USNAC **Prod** - USPHS

Sarah's War 30 MIN
16mm
Color
LC 74-703439
Presents the story of a young woman who is separated from her husband. Shows that when obliged to make money to support herself and her child, she becomes involved in crime and ends up in prison.
Sociology
Dist - CFDEVC **Prod** - JUNGR 1973

Sara's summer of the swans 33 MIN
U-matic / VHS / 16mm
Teenage years series
Color
LC 77-702490
Shows how a teenage girl gains new insight into herself and her family when her five - year - old brother gets lost. Based on the book The Summer Of The Swans by Betsy Byars.
Guidance and Counseling; Sociology
Dist - TIMLIF **Prod** - TAHSEM 1976

Sarawak Story 26 MIN
16mm
Color (J H C G)
Shows the homes and domestic lives of the three principal races in Malapia, the Malays, Chinese and Ibans. Covers town and country life.
Geography - World; Social Science; Sociology
Dist - VIEWTH **Prod** - GATEEF

Sarcoma 55 MIN
U-matic
Color
Describes the different ways soft - tissue sarcomas are treated. Shows how they were previously managed with radical surgery and how physicians are now combining radiotherapy with more conservative surgery.
Health and Safety
Dist - UTEXSC **Prod** - UTEXSC

Sargent Swell 16 MIN
16mm
Color (P I J H C)
Presents a satire involving a Canadian mountie, a gay Indian chief, an alcoholic father and tomboy daughter all living up to their expected roles in the Wild West.

Literature and Drama
Dist - CFS **Prod** - JANMEN 1973

Sari red 12 MIN
VHS / U-matic
Pratibha Parmar series
Color (G)
$250.00, $200.00 purchase, $50.00 rental
Remembers Kalbinder Kaur Hayne, a young Indian woman killed in England in 1985 by fascists. Examines the effect of the ever - present threat of violence upon the lives of Asian women in both private and public.
Civics and Political Systems; Geography - World; Sociology
Dist - WMEN **Prod** - PARMAR 1988

Sartre by Sartre - Sartre par lui - meme 190 MIN
VHS
Color (G) (FRENCH (ENGLISH SUBTITLES))
$200.00 purchase _ #S02212
Documents the life and work of French existentialist philosopher and writer Jean - Paul Sartre. Interviews Sartre on his writing, his work with the French Resistance in World War II, his philosophy, his relationship with Simone De Beauvoir, and many other subjects.
Literature and Drama; Religion and Philosophy
Dist - UILL

Sartre, Pt 4 - Masochism and Sadism, Extremities of Hatred 30 MIN
U-matic
From Socrates to Sartre Series
Color
Describes the concepts of masochism and sadism in the philosophy of Sartre.
Religion and Philosophy
Dist - MDCPB **Prod** - MDCPB

Sartre, Pt 1 - Existentialism, Development from Kierkegaard and Nietzsche 30 MIN
U-matic
From Socrates to Sartre Series
Color
Discusses the existentialist theory and its development from Kierkegaard and Nietzsche.
Religion and Philosophy
Dist - MDCPB **Prod** - MDCPB

Sartre, Pt 3 - Metaphysics, Influence of Descartes, Hegel, Husserle 30 MIN
U-matic
From Socrates to Sartre Series
Color
Discusses metaphysics in the philosophy of Sartre. Considers the influence of Hegel, Descartes and Husserle.
Religion and Philosophy
Dist - MDCPB **Prod** - MDCPB

Sartre, Pt 2 - Bad Faith, Ethics, Freedom Dread and Nothingness 30 MIN
U-matic
From Socrates to Sartre Series
Color
Examines the concepts of bad faith, ethics, freedom, dread and nothingness in the work of Sartre.
Religion and Philosophy
Dist - MDCPB **Prod** - MDCPB

Sarvapalli Radhakrishnan - President of India 94 MIN
16mm
Color (I)
Presents a biographical documentary on ex - President Sarvapalli Radhakrishnan. Portrays his earlier life as a Professor of philosophy, educationist, writer, lecturer and diplomat. Includes passages spoken by the President himself on various occasions.
Biography
Dist - NEDINF **Prod** - INDIA

SAS - understanding its capabilities 20 MIN
VHS / U-matic
Color
Provides potential SAS (statistical analysis system) users with an understanding of what SAS is and what SAS can do for them and gives a unique way of thinking about the language of SAS as an introduction to further training needed to become effective users.
Industrial and Technical Education; Mathematics; Psychology
Dist - DELTAK **Prod** - DELTAK

Sasha, Yasha, Yakov and the Wolf 11 MIN
U-matic / VHS / 16mm
Color (K P)
LC 71-713870
A three - dimensional animated puppet film which explores concepts of friendship, sharing and helping by presenting an up - dated version of the Three Little Pigs.
Literature and Drama; Psychology; Sociology
Dist - CAROUF **Prod** - PSFS 1971

Saskatchewan, land alive 28 MIN
16mm
Color (G)
#106C 0180 223
Shows Saskatchewan's past and the vitality of its present. It joined the Canadian federation in 1905.
Geography - World; History - World
Dist - CFLMDC **Prod** - NFBC 1980

Sasquatch amongst us 48 MIN
16mm
B&W (G)
$50.00 rental
Takes a close and intensive look at the strange phenomenon of the Bigfoot - Sasquatch monsters. Interviews alleged eyewitnesses and provides detailed analysis of the evidence by scientific experts. Includes previously unseen 'actual footage of a Sasquatch.'
Fine Arts
Dist - CANCIN **Prod** - WENDTD 1973

Sassy Wantalot's amazing journey to Bible times video 50 MIN
VHS
Color (P I J R)
$14.99 purchase _ #SPCN 85116.00426
Presents 10 skits introducing important Bible stories to children. Features adventurer Sassy Wantalot who searches for the Fountain of Youth, meets Bible characters and finally finds eternal life in the person of Jesus Christ.
Religion and Philosophy
Dist - GOSPEL **Prod** - GOSPEL

S A T - analogies
VHS
Color (H)
$39.95 purchase _ #VAD033
Covers 9 types of questions on analogies, plus a simple technique to eliminate wrong answers in preparation for the SAT. Includes study guide.
Education; English Language
Dist - SIV

SAT exam preparation series

Math - all Skill Areas and Problem Types	120 MIN
Math - Quantitative Comparison	120 MIN
Model Examination I with Explanations	120 MIN
Model Examination II with Explanations	120 MIN
Model Examination III with Explanations	120 MIN
Preparing Your Students for the S A T	120 MIN
Reading comprehension	120 MIN
S A T overview and test taking strategy	120 MIN
Test of Standard Written English	120 MIN
Vocabulary and Word Analogies	120 MIN

Dist - KRLSOF

S A T Overview and Test Taking Strategy 120 MIN
U-matic / VHS
SAT Exam Preparation Series
Color
Education
Dist - KRLSOF **Prod** - KRLSOF 1985

The SAT Prep Video
VHS
(G)
$99 purchase _ #BK30V
Provides a review of the SAT from test taking strategies to practice tests.
Education
Dist - CAREER **Prod** - CAREER

SAT - PSAT math review
VHS
Color (H)
$39.95 purchase _ #VAD027
Covers problem - solving techniques, time - saving tips and test strategies for the SAT and PSAT. Includes study guide.
Education; Mathematics
Dist - SIV

SAT - PSAT verbal review
VHS
Color (H)
$39.95 purchase _ #VAD030
Covers every verbal skill tested on the SAT and PSAT. Includes study guide.
Education; English Language
Dist - SIV

SAT - reading comprehension
VHS
Color (H)
$39.95 purchase _ #VAD032
Teaches a proven three - step method for quicker and better reading comprehension in preparation for the SAT. Includes study guide.
Education; English Language
Dist - SIV

S A T Review - Math
BETA / VHS
Color (H)
Reviews the math skills tested on SAT and PSAT exams. Offers creative problem - solving and test - taking techniques, time - saving hints and multiple - choice strategies.
Education; Mathematics
Dist - GA **Prod** - GA

S A T Review - Verbal
BETA / VHS
Color (H)
Reviews the verbal skills tested on SAT and PSAT exams. Offers creative problem - solving and test - taking techniques, time - saving hints and multiple - choice strategies.
English Language
Dist - GA **Prod** - GA

SAT TV review 120 MIN
VHS
Color (J H)
$79.95 purchase _ #CPS100V
Helps college - bound students preparing for the Scholastic Aptitude Test - SAT by reviewing academic content, developing test - taking techniques and study skills and building confidence. Includes workbook.
Education
Dist - CAMV

SAT TV review 120 MIN
VHS
Color (J H)
$69.95 purchase _ #GW - 5060 - VS
Builds confidence in students who have an aversion to taking standardized exams - they know the material but they don't do well when faced with the stressful reality of a test; and in others who are unsure about the material to be covered and apprehensive about the knowledge and skills they think may be required. Reviews academic content, develops test - taking techniques and study skills and builds confidence in college - bound students preparing for the Scholastic Aptitude Test - SAT. Once mastered, these skills are useful in college and beyond.
Education
Dist - HRMC **Prod** - COPREP

SAT verbal preparation series
Presents a three - part series on preparing for the SAT - Scholastic Aptitude Test. Covers the three - step method for reading passages efficiently, approaching each type of question and common types of wrong answers to recognize and avoid in SAT - Reading Comprehension. Shows how to understand the logic behind analogy questions, analogy relationships and patterns, build and use bridges as tools for analysis and deal with obscure words and complex analogy relationships in SAT - Analogies. Gives techniques for expanding and refining vocabulary, understanding and using word roots, etymologies, connotations and context clues as vocabulary keys, understanding antonym questions and saving time when taking tests. Includes study guide.

SAT verbal preparation series	360 MIN

Dist - CAMV

SAT - vocabulary
VHS
Color (H)
$39.95 purchase _ #VAD028
Shows how to sharpen word skills and learn simple techniques to score higher on the SAT. Includes study guide.
Education; English Language
Dist - SIV

SAT/ACT Examination Video Review Series

Mathematics Review, Tape 1	45 MIN
Mathematics Review, Tape 2	45 MIN
Mathematics Review, Tape 3	45 MIN
Mathematics Review, Tape 4	45 MIN
Mathematics Review, Tape 5	45 MIN
Mathematics Review, Tape 6	45 MIN
Mathematics Review, Tape 7	45 MIN
Mathematics Review, Tape 8	45 MIN
Verbal Review, Tape 1	45 MIN
Verbal Review, Tape 2	45 MIN
Verbal Review, Tape 3	45 MIN
Verbal Review, Tape 4	45 MIN
Verbal Review, Tape 5	45 MIN
Verbal Review, Tape 6	45 MIN

Verbal Review, Tape 7 45 MIN
Verbal Review, Tape 8 45 MIN
Dist - COMEX

Satan in the Church 9 MIN
16mm
Color (C A R)
LC 72-700406
Uses animation to show a battle of good and evil, as the Devil disrupts a group of monks who are worshipping in a church sanctuary. Shows how the mass becomes an orgiastic affair with Satan emerging victorious.
Religion and Philosophy
Dist - MMA **Prod** - IVANOV 1971

Satan on the Loose 30 MIN
16mm
Color (R)
Tells of the early life of former New York hoodlum, Nicky Cruz. Traces his upbringing in Puerto Rico where his parents were Satan worshippers.
Guidance and Counseling; Religion and Philosophy
Dist - GF **Prod** - GF

Satanic Crimes 40 MIN
VHS
Crime to Court Procedural Specials Series
Color (PRO)
$99.00 purchase
Explores illegal activities associated with Satanism. Trains law enforcement personnel. Part of an ongoing series to look in depth at topics presented in 'Crime To Court.' Produced in cooperation with the South Carolina Criminal Justice Academy and the National Sheriff's Association.
Civics and Political Systems; Religion and Philosophy; Sociology
Dist - SCETV **Prod** - SCETV

Satanism and Pre - Teens 28 MIN
U-matic / VHS
Color (G)
$249.00, $149.00 purchase _ #AD - 2167
Interviews parents whose children were recruited into satanic cults. Asks why the children were so easily enticed into satanic servitude and tells how the parents rescued their children. Adapts a Phil Donahue program.
Religion and Philosophy; Sociology
Dist - FOTH **Prod** - FOTH

Satan's brew 110 MIN
16mm
Color (GERMAN (ENGLISH SUBTITLES))
Presents a comedy centering around a so - called revolutionary poet who hasn't written a word in two years. Explains that he will do anything to get money or to write again. Directed by Rainer Werner Fassbinder. With English subtitles.
Fine Arts
Dist - NYFLMS **Prod** - UNKNWN 1976

Satan's guru 9 MIN
16mm
Color (G)
$22.00 rental
Presents a passion play twentieth century style where Ego is a false guru and has an assistant named Dogma. Depicts a black mass to call up Satan.
Fine Arts; Religion and Philosophy
Dist - CANCIN **Prod** - DEGRAS 1970

Satchmo and all that Jazz 12 MIN
VHS / U-matic
Screen news digest series; Vol 15; Issue 3
Color
Present a look at the life and times of musician Louis Armstrong.
Biography; Fine Arts
Dist - AFA **Prod** - AFA 1972

Satellite and earth station technology 30 MIN
U-matic / VHS
Communications satellite systems series
Color
Introduces the components of the satellite and earth station and explores the impact of future technology on communications satellite systems.
Industrial and Technical Education; Science - Physical; Social Science
Dist - DELTAK **Prod** - DELTAK

Satellite applications and demand assignment for data - Pt 1 53 MIN
VHS / U-matic
Packet switching series
Color
Industrial and Technical Education; Mathematics; Sociology
Dist - MIOT **Prod** - MIOT

Satellite applications and demand assignment for data - Pt 2 55 MIN
U-matic / VHS
Packet switching series
Color
Industrial and Technical Education; Mathematics; Sociology
Dist - MIOT **Prod** - MIOT

Satellite communications 22 MIN
VHS / BETA / U-matic
Color; PAL (J H)
PdS15.00 purchase
Looks at the science and technology behind satellite communications. Covers everything from Marconi's pioneering work with radio waves to the launch of Intelsat VI in 1989, including microwaves, aerials and Earth station control. Shows how schools can set up their own educational Satellite receiving system. Includes teachers' and students' notes. Contact distributor for free loan information.
Education; Industrial and Technical Education; Science - Physical; Sociology
Dist - BTEDSE

Satellite links - problems and solutions 30 MIN
VHS / U-matic
Communications satellite systems series
Color
Discusses the problems of delay, outages, noise, satellite failures and security risks in satellite links. Points out that good design can overcome all of them.
Industrial and Technical Education; Science - Physical; Social Science
Dist - DELTAK **Prod** - DELTAK

Satellite motion - 14 40 MIN
VHS
Conceptual physics alive series
Color (H C)
$45.00 purchase
Extends the concept of projectile motion to satellite motion - first circular, then elliptical. Discusses escape speed and concludes with a summary of previously learned concepts in mechanics. Part 14 of a 35 - part series adapted from the college and high school textbook Conceptual Physics by Professor Paul Hewitt.
Science - Physical
Dist - MMENTE **Prod** - HEWITP 1992

Satellite rescue in space
U-matic / VHS
Color (P I J)
Introduces children to the marvels of the world.
Industrial and Technical Education
Dist - KTVID **Prod** - CNVID

Satellite rescue in space - shuttle flights 41C and 51A 42 MIN
VHS
Color (G)
$29.95 purchase _ #V41
Joins the shuttle crew as they narrate the most interesting and spectacular scenes to date, depicting life aboard the space shuttle. Offers footage shot at their sides, floating above Earth, rescuing satellites and performing experiments. Includes a free - floating tour inside the shuttle.
History - World; Industrial and Technical Education
Dist - INSTRU

Satellite TV - birth of an industry - Pts 1 and 2 56 MIN
VHS / U-matic
Color
Presents satellite information as produced by Liza Bear and Michael McClard in conjunction with Willoughby Sharp.
Fine Arts
Dist - ARTINC **Prod** - ARTINC

Satellites 30 MIN
VHS / U-matic
Perspective II series
Color (J H C A)
$150.00
Explores a variety of science and technology subjects dealing with light and its use as a medium of communication. Shows how satellites work and discusses the implications of this new knowledge.
Industrial and Technical Education; Science - Physical
Dist - LANDMK **Prod** - LANDMK 1981

Satellites and Men in Orbit 24 MIN
U-matic / VHS / 16mm
Man into Space - the Story of Rockets and Space Science Series
Color (I)
Discusses 'near space,' including atmosphere, the effects of gravity and the physics of achieving orbit. Describes the operation, discoveries and types of satellites and depicts man in orbit.
Science - Physical
Dist - AIMS **Prod** - ACI 1974

Satellites in education - INSET 19 MIN
VHS / BETA / U-matic
Color; PAL (T)
PdS7.50 purchase
Offers an introduction for teachers to the uses of Satellite data and images for secondary and primary school curriculum. Incorporates material relevant to a wide variety of courses, such as geography, technology, science, math, electronics, modern languages and media studies. Designed as an INSET resource. Contact distributor for free loan information.
Education; Science; Sociology
Dist - BTEDSE

Satellites in the sky 26 MIN
VHS / U-matic
Color (J H G)
$240.00, $290.00 purchase, $60.00 rental
Traces the history of news - gathering from the 1890s through modern satellite news. Takes the viewer through the development of a satellite news story, the equipment and the logistics that allow instantaneous news reporting.
Business and Economics; Fine Arts
Dist - NDIM **Prod** - LONTVS 1993

Satellites of Hughes 14 MIN
VHS
Color (G)
Presents a history of Hughes Aircraft synchronous satellites from SYNCOM to INTELSAT IV and IVa. Includes a discussion about the company's business satellites such as COMSTAR, SBS and LEASAT. Available for free loan from the distributor.
Industrial and Technical Education; Science - Natural
Dist - AUDPLN

Satellites of the Sun 12 MIN
16mm / U-matic / VHS
Color (I)
LC 76-702496
Uses animation in order to explore the characteristics of the solar system.
Science - Physical
Dist - PHENIX **Prod** - NFBC 1975

Satiemania 15 MIN
16mm / U-matic / VHS
Color (H C A)
LC 81-701572
Presents complex animated images set to the music of Erik Satie and which change in mood from satirical to abrasive to introspective to lyrical. Uses cel animation to present the themes art movements, morality and values in Western civilization, and the divergence between men and women.
Fine Arts; Guidance and Counseling
Dist - IFB **Prod** - ZAGREB 1981

Satisfaction - a job well done 9 MIN
U-matic / VHS / 16mm
Color (C A)
LC 84-700176
Interviews a master shipbuilder and illustrates how a master craftsman motivates his employees by setting high standards, giving continuous honest feedback and providing encouragement and praise. Originally shown on the CBS program On The Road With Charles Kuralt.
Psychology
Dist - SALENG **Prod** - CBSTV 1984
VLEARN

Satori and Japanese philosophy 30 MIN
VHS
Color (G)
$24.95 purchase _ #P31
Provides an intimate look at Japanese Buddhist spirituality and its impact on everyday life. Explores Buddhists' approach to life and views students struggling to empty their minds to attain satori. Visits street festivals, a Zen business school and a Shinto ceremony.
Fine Arts; Geography - World
Dist - HP

Satrapy 13 MIN
16mm
Color (G)
$40.00 rental
Looks at the threatening power of female sexuality. Presents a collage of fragments of larger still images which actually generate their own sounds, since they overlap onto the optical soundtrack area. Creates crude musical rhythms and tonalities based on visual rather than aural cues. Produced by Scott Stark.
Fine Arts; Sociology
Dist - CANCIN

Satsang with Sri Gurudev Satchidananda Ashram Yogaville East 60 MIN
VHS / U-matic

Color
Addresses vegetarian cats and dogs, value of abstaining from meat, alcohol and cigarettes, growing spiritually at one's own speed and dangers of acquiring supernatural powers with an impure attitude.
Religion and Philosophy
Dist - IYOGA **Prod** - IYOGA

Satsang with Sri Gurudev Satchidananda Ashram Yogaville Virginia 60 MIN
U-matic / VHS
Color
Presents Sri Gurudev speaking on prostrating to the Guru and rising above the pleasure and pain of worldly happiness.
Religion and Philosophy
Dist - IYOGA **Prod** - IYOGA

Satsang with Sri Gurudev SAY VA 60 MIN
VHS / U-matic
Color
Presents Sri Gurudev speaking on work and play and the story of the pariah farm worker going to a festival.
Religion and Philosophy
Dist - IYOGA **Prod** - IYOGA

Satsang with Sri Gurudev SAYE 30 MIN
VHS / U-matic
Color
Presents Sri Gurudev speaking on Lord Jesus, the crucifixion and ahimsa, simplicity, control of the mind and death of John Lennon.
Religion and Philosophy
Dist - IYOGA **Prod** - IYOGA

Satsang with Sri Swami Satchidanada, Washington DC 50 MIN
U-matic / VHS
Color
Explains we are essentially one in spirit and variety is for our fun. Tells about our first and foremost duty in life.
Religion and Philosophy
Dist - IYOGA **Prod** - IYOGA

Satsang with Sri Swami Satchidananda 30 MIN
U-matic / VHS
Color
Answers questions regarding deities existing on this plane or just in the mind. Explains how God is superior, unconditional love.
Religion and Philosophy
Dist - IYOGA **Prod** - IYOGA

Satsang with Sri Swami Satchidananda at SAYE 50 MIN
U-matic / VHS
Color
Answers questions about God's will and ours, and how does one function on the earthly plane having reached the highest level of samadhi.
Religion and Philosophy
Dist - IYOGA **Prod** - IYOGA

Satsang with Sri Swami Satchidananda SAY VA 30 MIN
60 MIN
U-matic / VHS
Color
Presents Sri Gurudev giving his first satsang after returning from 1981 India trip.
Religion and Philosophy
Dist - IYOGA **Prod** - IYOGA

Satsang with Sri Swami Satchidananda SAY VA 100 MIN
U-matic / VHS
Color
Presents Sri Gurudev speaking on the purpose of human endeavor, renunciation and attachment and the importance of knowing the goal of one's path.
Religion and Philosophy
Dist - IYOGA **Prod** - IYOGA

Satsang with Sri Swami Satchidananda SAYE 40 MIN
U-matic / VHS
Color
Answers questions about the soul and the mind. Talks about detachment and renunciation and making yourself strong.
Religion and Philosophy
Dist - IYOGA **Prod** - IYOGA

Satsang with Sri Swami Satchidananda SAYE
U-matic / VHS
Color
Answers questions about hell and the cause of excessive worry. Explains how picking flowers is not a violent act.
Religion and Philosophy
Dist - IYOGA **Prod** - IYOGA

Satsang with Sri Swami Satchidananda, SAYVA 52 MIN
U-matic / VHS
Color
Explains that both pleasure and pain are one's own creation. Speaks on reincarnation and the three rare qualities.
Religion and Philosophy
Dist - IYOGA **Prod** - IYOGA

Satsang with Sri Swami Satchidananda, SAYVA 55 MIN
VHS / U-matic
Color
Tells how we all must renounce to know permanent peace. Speaks on free will vs God's will. Tells how work is worship.
Religion and Philosophy
Dist - IYOGA **Prod** - IYOGA

Satsang with Sri Swami Satchidananda SAYVA 45 MIN
VHS / U-matic
Color
Answers questions regarding the difference between deep sleep and samadhi. Talks about training the mind.
Religion and Philosophy
Dist - IYOGA **Prod** - IYOGA

Satsang with Sri Swami Satchidananda SAYVA 46 MIN
U-matic / VHS
Color
Presents Sri Gurudev answering questions on how far into pregnancy can one do the shoulder stand and how to teach beginning students.
Religion and Philosophy
Dist - IYOGA **Prod** - IYOGA

Satsang with Sri Swami Satchidananda, SAYVA 50 MIN
U-matic / VHS
Color
Answers questions on how to lose attachment to the body and how to increase faith.
Religion and Philosophy
Dist - IYOGA **Prod** - IYOGA

Satsang with Sri Swami Satchindananda SAYVA 50 MIN
VHS / U-matic
Color
Explains the unifying aspect of diversity. Explains all religions have the same essence and goal.
Religion and Philosophy
Dist - IYOGA **Prod** - IYOGA

Satsang with Swami Chidananda and Sri Gurudev at SAYE 60 MIN
VHS / U-matic
Color
Presents Swami Chidananda giving a talk on our divine path and the four qualities of the spiritual aspirant according to Master Sivananda.
Religion and Philosophy
Dist - IYOGA **Prod** - IYOGA

Saturable Reactors 23 MIN
16mm
B&W
LC 74-705576
Develops a hysteresis loop through the use of an applied AC sine wave to a coil containing a core material. Includes the core's control on the loop shape, the effect on switching action and how the loop is associated with the operation of a saturable reactor. (Kinescope).
Industrial and Technical Education; Science - Physical
Dist - USNAC **Prod** - USAF

Saturation Diving 20 MIN
VHS / U-matic
Color
Explains that, under pressure, gas dissolves in the bloodstream, something all divers should know. Illustrates diving equipment.
Health and Safety
Dist - FLMWST **Prod** - FLMWST

Saturation diving 20 MIN
16mm / VHS / U-matic
Color (IND)
$695.00, $645.00 purchase
Explains hypothermia, saturation diving and the process of gas dissolution in the bloodstream. Presents precautionary measures for each stage of an entire operation. Includes a demonstration of equipment used in diving at great depths.
Health and Safety; Industrial and Technical Education
Dist - FLMWST

Saturday 5 MIN
16mm
Color (I)
LC 74-701546
Shows the art of the dance as executed at the Lexington School of Modern Dance. Emphasizes the grace of movement in the performance of the dancers.
Fine Arts
Dist - CELLAR **Prod** - CELLAR 1970

Saturday Afternoon 27 MIN
16mm
B&W (I J H C)
Stars Harry Langdon as a hen - pecked foundry worker whose every move must be reported to his domineering wife.
Fine Arts
Dist - TWYMAN **Prod** - UNKNWN 1926

Saturday Afternoon 11 MIN
16mm
Contemporary Family Series
Color
LC 75-700480
Demonstrates, through pantomime, a young couple depicting what happens when husband and wife develop roles that block real communication and personal growth.
Guidance and Counseling; Psychology; Sociology
Dist - FRACOC **Prod** - FRACOC 1975

The Saturday club - James Russell Lowell, Henry Wadsworth Longfellow, John Greenleaf Whittier 20 MIN
VHS / U-matic
American literature series
Color (H C A)
LC 83-706253
Offers a dramatic re - creation of a meeting in which members of the Saturday Club including James Russell Lowell, Henry Wadsworth Longfellow, John Greenleaf Whittier and Oliver Wendell Holmes discuss an early edition of The Atlantic Monthly in a posh Boston eating club and recite from their works.
Literature and Drama
Dist - AITECH **Prod** - AUBU 1983

Saturday Morning 88 MIN
16mm / U-matic / VHS
Color (J)
LC 73-701449
Discusses adolescent issues which young people find most urgent - their feelings about parents, sex, morality and their search for identity and love.
Guidance and Counseling; Psychology; Social Science
Dist - CF **Prod** - DF 1972

Saturday night again 10 MIN
16mm / VHS / BETA / U-matic
Color; PAL (G)
PdS110, PdS118 purchase
Deals with attitudes of young people who believe they can drink and drive and looks at how boredom is a definite reality with this group.
Health and Safety; Sociology
Dist - EDPAT

Saturday's Children 36 MIN
VHS / 16mm / U-matic
Color (H C A)
LC 83-700003
Documents four prepared, unmedicated births that took place in one day in a traditional, but progressive, hospital delivery room. Follows mothers through labor and delivery with examples of labor coaching and support by fathers and staff.
Health and Safety
Dist - COURTR

Saturn 29 MIN
U-matic
Project universe - astronomy series lesson 11
Color (C A)
Describes characteristics of Saturn and its ring system. Discusses the nature of the atmospheres of Jovian planets. Shows excerpts from two NASA films of Saturn.
Science - Physical
Dist - CDTEL **Prod** - COAST

Saturn 3 95 MIN
16mm
Color
Stars Kirk Douglas and Farrah Fawcett as scientists living on a research station in space, 400 years in the future.
Fine Arts
Dist - SWANK **Prod** - UNKNWN

Saturn first stage 5 MIN
16mm
Apollo digest series
Color
LC 74-705577
Looks at the first stage of the Saturn 5. Explains the role of the first stage and its various components.

Industrial and Technical Education; Science - Physical
Dist - USNAC **Prod** - NASA 1969

Saturn second stage 5 MIN
16mm
Apollo digest series
Color
LC 74-705578
Presents a close - up view of the Saturn second stage. Includes scenes of manufacturing and testing.
Industrial and Technical Education; Science; Science - Physical
Dist - USNAC **Prod** - NASA 1969

Saturn third stage 5 MIN
16mm
Apollo digest series
Color
LC 74-705579
Reports on the final stage of the Saturn. Includes scenes of test firings and examines the precise role of the stage during flight.
Industrial and Technical Education; Science; Science - Physical
Dist - USNAC **Prod** - NASA 1969

Saturnus Alchimia 18 MIN
U-matic / VHS
Color
Uses color, shape, texture and rhythm to form visual music compositions.
Fine Arts
Dist - KITCHN **Prod** - KITCHN

Satyajit Ray 28 MIN
16mm
B&W (H C A)
LC 74-705974
Shows Satyajit Ray, noted Indian film maker, explaining the underlying philosophy guiding him in the production of his films, which he sees as a confluence of Eastern and Western cultures. Ray's main objective is to make his audiences see and think about issues such as poverty and politics.
Fine Arts; Religion and Philosophy; Sociology
Dist - IU **Prod** - NET 1970

Sauce for the Gander 22 MIN
16mm
Color
LC 74-705581
Examines attitudes of a man who expects perfection from others. Shows importance of a right - the - first - time attitude, which also applies to him.
Business and Economics; Guidance and Counseling; Psychology; Sociology
Dist - USNAC **Prod** - USN 1963

Sauce Preparation - Veloute 20 MIN
VHS / BETA
Color (G PRO)
$59.00 purchase _ #QF27
Describes the important steps involved in the incorporation of roux into a liquid. Discusses the four basic mother sauces. Features Chef Paul, who uses a blonde roux and light stock to show how a veloute sauce is created.
Home Economics
Dist - RMIBHF **Prod** - RMIBHF

Sauces
VHS
Frugal gourmet - ancient cuisines from China, Greece and Rome series
Color (G)
$19.95 purchase _ #CCP851
Shows how to prepare sauces from the cultures of ancient China, Greece and Rome. Features Jeff Smith, the Frugal Gourmet. Part of a five - part series on ancient cuisines.
History - World; Home Economics; Physical Education and Recreation
Dist - CADESF **Prod** - CADESF

Sauces - creamy, dreamy, easy 23 MIN
35mm strip / VHS
Color (J H C A)
$93.00, $93.00 purchase _ #MB - 540640 - 3, #MB - 540619 - 5
Presents an introductory course in sauce preparation. Focuses on the most popular basic sauces. Explains food chemistry as it impacts on recipes.
Health and Safety; Home Economics; Industrial and Technical Education
Dist - SRA **Prod** - SRA 1988

Saudade - Nostalgia 57 MIN
VHS
Color (G)
$200.00 purchase, $40.00 rental
Documents the experience and culture of Portuguese in the United States. Focuses on the experiences of seven Portuguese women and men in New Bedford, Massachussetts - six immigrants from the Azores, Madeira, the mainland, one second generation Portuguese - American. Produced by Brazilian anthropologist Bela Feldman - Bianco.
Geography - United States; History - United States; Sociology
Dist - DOCEDR **Prod** - DOCEDR 1991

Saudi Arabia 25 MIN
U-matic / VHS
Color (H C A)
Focuses on the cultural clash which has occurred as Saudi Arabia emerges as a major power of the 20th century. Contrasts the country's wealth with its traditional culture.
Geography - World
Dist - JOU **Prod** - UPI

Saudi Arabia 28 MIN
Videoreel / VHS
Marilyn's Manhattan series
Color
Features an interview with Mr Saud Shawwaf, Special Representative on a people to people tour of the United States from Saudi Arabia. Hosted by Marilyn Perry.
Business and Economics; Civics and Political Systems; Geography - World
Dist - PERRYM **Prod** - PERRYM

Saudi Arabia 18 MIN
U-matic / VHS / 16mm
Oil and American Power Series
Color (H C A)
Discusses the traditions and politics of Saudi Arabia and points out that its concentration of crude oil makes it a world power and a key factor in America's economic well - being. Extracted from the NBC television show No More Vietnams, But.
Civics and Political Systems; Geography - World; Social Science
Dist - FI **Prod** - NBCTV 1979

Saudi Arabia - International Byline 28 MIN
Videoreel / VHS
International Byline Series
Color
Interviews His Royal Highness Prince Mohamed Al - Faisal, son of the late King Faisal, on Islam, oil, women, economic development and the Middle East. Hosted by Marilyn Perry.
Business and Economics; Civics and Political Systems; Geography - World
Dist - PERRYM **Prod** - PERRYM

Saudi Arabia - Kingdom of Black Gold 29 MIN
VHS / 16mm
Countries and Peoples Series
Color (H C G)
$90.00 purchase _ #BPN213303
Gives a history of Saudi Arabia and how it became the world's largest exporter of oil.
Geography - World; History - World
Dist - RMIBHF **Prod** - RMIBHF

Saudi Arabia - Kingdom of Black Gold 30 MIN
U-matic
Countries and Peoples Series
Color (H C)
Gives a history of the development of Saudi Arabia and tells how it became the world's largest exporter of oil.
Geography - World; History - World
Dist - TVOTAR **Prod** - TVOTAR 1982

Saudi Arabia Series
The Kingdom - Pt 1 59 MIN
Oil, Money and Politics - Pt 3 59 MIN
Race with Time - Pt 2 59 MIN
Dist - FI

Saudi Arabia - the oil revolution 25 MIN
U-matic / VHS / 16mm
Arab experience series
Color (H C A) (SPANISH)
LC 76-700281;
Looks at the world's richest oil - producing country and its diverseculture, ranging from extreme orthodoxy to influences of Western modernization.
Geography - World; History - World; Religion and Philosophy; Sociology
Dist - LCOA **Prod** - LCOA 1976

Saudi Arabia today 28 MIN
U-matic
Color
Depicts the scenic and cultural variety of modern Saudi Arabia, including mountains, deserts, farms, construction sights, villages and suburbs. Treats concerns of individual Saudis.
Geography - World; Sociology
Dist - MTP **Prod** - EXXON 1981

The Saudis 49 MIN
16mm / U-matic / VHS
Color (J)
Presents a documentary report on America's largest oil supplier and tenuous ally, Saudi Arabia. Discusses government, customs, business methods, law, religion, modernization and the relationship of the sexes in that country.
Geography - World; Sociology
Dist - PHENIX **Prod** - CBSTV 1980

Sauerkraut 4 MIN
16mm
Beatrice Trum Hunter's Natural Foods Series
Color
Home Economics
Dist - PBS **Prod** - PBS 1974

Sauerkraut 3 MIN
Videoreel / VT2
Beatrice Trum Hunter's Natural Foods Series
Color
Suggests making sauerkraut from red cabbage. Demonstrates the steps in the process and gives instructions on the preparation of the cabbage, storing of the mixture for fermentation to take place and caring for it during fermentation. Shows how it looks when it is ready to eat.
Home Economics; Social Science
Dist - PBS **Prod** - WGBH

Saugus series
Experimental film by Pat O'Neill.
Saugus series 18 MIN
Dist - AFA **Prod** - AFA

A Sauk County almanac 29 MIN
U-matic / VHS
Color (H C G)
$385.00, $355.00 purchase _ #V483
Returns to Sauk County, celebrated in the writings of Aldo Leopold, a pioneer in the environmental conservation movement. Contrasts information about Sauk County's bald eagles and geologic formations with the native prairies and turkey vultures.
Geography - United States; Literature and Drama; Science - Natural
Dist - BARR **Prod** - CEPRO 1989
CEPRO

Saul Alinsky Went to War 57 MIN
16mm
B&W (H C A)
LC 76-706382
Presents a documentary on Saul Alinsky and his work with minority groups. Shows how he hires himself out to the poor and oppressed, instructs them in the art of protest and sends them to do battle against the establishment.
Psychology; Sociology
Dist - NFBC **Prod** - NFBC 1969

Saul Alinsky went to war - Pt 1 25 MIN
16mm
B&W (H C A)
LC 76-706382
Presents Saul Alinsky, executive director of the Industrial Areas Foundation, who explains his approach in organizing communities to fight poverty and injustice.
Sociology
Dist - NFBC **Prod** - NFBC 1969

Saul Alinsky went to war - Pt 2 32 MIN
16mm
B&W (H C A)
LC 76-706382
Presents Saul Alinsky, executive director of the Industrial Areas Foundation, who explains his approach in organizing communities to fight poverty and injustice.
Sociology
Dist - NFBC **Prod** - NFBC 1969

Saul and David 110 MIN
BETA / VHS
Color
Tells the Bible story of King Saul and David, the young shepherd boy who killed Goliath.
Religion and Philosophy
Dist - DSP **Prod** - DSP

Sausage city 6 MIN
16mm
Color (G)
$10.00 rental
Starts with animated interlocking boxes evolving and changing perspective which become carefully rendered sausages that grow to fill the screen. By Adam Beckett.
Fine Arts
Dist - CANCIN

Sausalito 9 MIN
16mm
B&W
Presents an intimate, personal sketchbook of a small village on the shore of San Francisco bay. Combines lectures, sounds and pieces of visual experience arising from contact with this village to create a poetic fabric of Sausalito's odd atmosphere.

Geography - United States
Dist - RADIM **Prod** - STAHER

Sauteeing and White Searing 20 MIN
BETA / VHS / 16mm
Color (G PRO)
$59.00 purchase _ #QF18
Demonstrates the techniques of white searing and sauteeing. Uses a liver saute and a chicken supreme as examples. Features Chef Paul Gillette.
Home Economics; Industrial and Technical Education
Dist - RMIBHF **Prod** - RMIBHF

Sauteing 30 MIN
VHS
Gourmet techniques series
Color (H C G)
$19.95 purchase _ #IVN041V
Features expert chef instructors from the California Culinary Academy in San Francisco who share their secrets on sauteing. Part of a three - part series on gourmet techniques.
Home Economics
Dist - CAMV

Sauteing and pan frying 12 MIN
U-matic / VHS / 16mm
Professional food preparation and service program series
Color (A)
Presents the subtleties of two classic cooking techniques, sauteing and pan frying. Describes skillets, frying pans and saute pans and when the different types should be used. Demonstrates correct procedures with thin, tender foods as well as thicker, slower cooking items.
Industrial and Technical Education
Dist - NEM **Prod** - NEM

Sauteing - pan frying - Lesson 7 8 MIN
8mm cartridge / 16mm
Modern basics of classical cooking series
Color (A)
#MB07
Discusses the three basic cooking utensils - straight - sided pan, slope - sided pan and the frying or omelet pan. Demonstrates the proceedures of sauteing, including field application techniques for home use. Part of a series developed in cooperation with the Swiss Association of Restauranteurs and Hoteliers to train foodservice employees. Includes five instructor's handbooks, a textbook by Eugene Pauli, 20 sets of student tests and 20 sets of student information sheets.
Home Economics; Industrial and Technical Education
Dist - CONPRO **Prod** - CONPRO

Savage 25 MIN
U-matic / VHS
Color
Portrays the world of live professional wrestling. Focuses on the ritualistic acting aspect of the phenomenon.
Fine Arts; Physical Education and Recreation; Religion and Philosophy
Dist - MEDIPR **Prod** - MEDIPR 1978

Savage and beautiful 60 MIN
VHS
Color (G)
$19.95 purchase _ #S02087
Presents a worldwide view of the earth's animal kingdom in their natural habitats. Musical score by Vangelis. Narrated by Donald Sutherland.
Fine Arts; Science - Natural
Dist - UILL

Savage Iron 21 MIN
16mm
Color
LC 80-700920
Shows development of the iron ore mine at Savage River in Australia, including construction of a complete township, mill, ore slurry, pipeline pelletising plant at Port Latta and offshore loading facilities for bulk ore carriers of up to 100,000 tons.
Geography - World; Industrial and Technical Education; Social Science
Dist - TASCOR **Prod** - TASCOR 1968

Savage River Iron 22 MIN
16mm
Color (H C A)
Tells the story of Savage River Mines, the only iron ore mining operation in Australia's island state of Tasmania. Explains in detail the development of the modern mining and processing facilities as well as the world's longest iron slurry pipeline and unique offshore loading system extending a mile out to sea.
Geography - World; Industrial and Technical Education; Social Science
Dist - PICMAT **Prod** - PICMAT

Savage Road to China 30 MIN
VHS / 16mm
World War II - G I Diary Series
(J H C)
$99.95 each, $995.00 series _ #17
Depicts the action and emotion that soldiers experienced during World War II, through their eyes and in their words. Narrated by Lloyd Bridges.
History - United States; History - World
Dist - AMBROS **Prod** - AMBROS 1980

Savage Road to China 30 MIN
VHS / U-matic
World War II - GI Diary Series
Color (H C A)
History - United States; History - World
Dist - TIMLIF **Prod** - TIMLIF 1980

Savannah 30 MIN
VHS
John Stobart's WorldScape series
Color (A G)
$19.95 purchase _ #STO - 07
Takes a look at a famous and historical Southern town. Follows artist John Stobart as he travels the globe, painting directly from life, and demonstrates the simplicity of the method that has made him the foremost living maritime artist. Demonstrates Stobart's classical maritime style in numerous evocative settings around the world. Part of a series on painting outdoors.
Fine Arts
Dist - ARTSAM **Prod** - WORLDS

The Save a Bit Hop 30 MIN
16mm
Color (J H)
Shows how Tommy and his classmates use ridesharing and other energy - conservation techniques to raise money for the big senior class dance.
Social Science
Dist - SUNCO **Prod** - GRAVAR

The Save - a - Life Test - with Frank Field
VHS
Color
Tests students' knowledge of First Aid techniques through the lively format of live action situations. Illustrates many life saving procedures.
Health and Safety
Dist - HRMC **Prod** - HRMC 1986

Save it, Food, Fiber and Environment 28 MIN
16mm
Color (J)
LC 75-701973
Tells how men in the sheep industry in the United States work to conserve water, soil and wildlife, the elements upon which they rely upon for their existence.
Business and Economics; Science - Natural; Social Science
Dist - AUDPLN **Prod** - ASPC 1972

Save our planet 30 MIN
VHS
Color (P I J H)
LC 91-705729
Focuses on a young student who learns what can be done to help the environment.
Science - Natural; Sociology
Dist - BENNUP **Prod** - BENNUP 1990

Save Our Soil - Save Our Streams 20 MIN
16mm / U-matic / VHS
Color (H A)
Discusses soil erosion from cropland and construction sites and how this relates to the nation's clean water goals. Shows how local government, cooperating with landowners and conservation groups, can stop almost all erosion problems, saving both soil and streams.
Agriculture; Civics and Political Systems; Science - Natural
Dist - USNAC **Prod** - UWISC 1983

Save the earth 60 MIN
VHS
Color (G)
$19.95 purchase _ #XVSTE: $39.95 purchase _ #TC100V-S
Shows how anyone can make a difference in combating serious environmental problems. Covers acid rain, ozone depletion, rain forests, water conservation, recycling, toxic waste and the greenhouse effect.
Science - Natural
Dist - GAINST
CAMV

Save the earth - a how - to video 60 MIN
VHS
Color (P I J H C G A)
$19.95 purchase
Depicts many of the environmental hazards, including global warming, acid rain, toxic waste, and others. Advocates a combination of individual and collective action to change destructive policies and practices. Features cameo appearances by stars Jeff Bridges, Chevy Chase, Whitney Kershaw, and Charlton Heston, as well as the music of Randy Newman and Don Henley. Hosted by Jere Burns of the NBC TV show 'Dear John.' Produced by International Video Publications, Inc.
Geography - World; Social Science; Sociology
Dist - EFVP

Save the panda 60 MIN
VHS
National Geographic video series
Color (G)
$29.95 purchase
Profiles the efforts of scientists to save the Chinese panda bear from extinction. Shows how scientists have tracked the pandas into the mountains of central China, to learn more about them.
Science - Natural
Dist - PBS **Prod** - WNETTV

Save the panda 60 MIN
VHS
Color; Captioned (G)
$29.95 purchase _ #S00866
Documents the struggle to save China's Giant Pandas from extinction. Features footage of the pandas in their native setting in the bamboo forests of China.
Geography - World; Science - Natural
Dist - UILL **Prod** - NGS

Save the Planet 18 MIN
VHS / U-matic
Color
Presents the origins and key pressure points of the nuclear debate.
Social Science
Dist - GMPF **Prod** - MUSEI

Save the Wetlands 10 MIN
VHS / U-matic
Color (H C A)
Provides a look at New Orleans, Louisiana and stresses the need to protect river and wetland environments.
Science - Natural
Dist - CEPRO **Prod** - CEPRO 1986

Save Water 5 MIN
U-matic
Color (K P I)
Shows how children, their families and friends and neighbors can avoid wasting water.
Geography - United States; Science - Natural; Social Science
Dist - CALDWR **Prod** - CSDWR

Save your child's life 45 MIN
VHS
Color (H A)
$29.95 purchase _ #XE100V
Demonstrates what to do in the case of an infant or child respiratory emergency. Covers choking, unconscious choking, mouth - to - mouth breathing, and cardiopulmonary resuscitation. Also considers various household safety tips, preventive measures, and more.
Health and Safety
Dist - CAMV **Prod** - CAMV 1986

Save your kids, save yourself 30 MIN
VHS
Color (H C A)
$34.95 purchase _ #GOF300V
Dramatizes four common situations in which an attack can occur - a child walking home from school, a woman jogging in a park, a woman on a date, and a man opening an outside door. Demonstrates appropriate and effective techniques for dealing with such situations.
Health and Safety; Physical Education and Recreation
Dist - CAMV

Saved by the Bell 10 MIN
U-matic / VHS
Color
LC 81-707124
Explains how many home fires can be avoided by using common sense.
Health and Safety
Dist - USNAC **Prod** - USCPSD 1981

Saved from the Pound 30 MIN
U-matic / VHS
High Feather Series; Pt 9
Color (I J)
LC 83-706055
Focuses on the parallel between one's responsibility to take care of a pet and one's responsibility to eat properly.
Health and Safety; Social Science
Dist - GPN **Prod** - NYSED 1982

Saving a generation 28 MIN
VHS
Color; CC (T PRO)
$190.00 purchase
Demonstrates successful HIV prevention strategies that teachers can adapt for classroom use.
Health and Safety
Dist - SELMED **Prod** - SACVP 1990

Saving a generation I and II series
Overcoming the obstacles - Program 1 28 MIN
Techniques that work - Program 2 28 MIN
Dist - SELMED

Saving a species 26 MIN
U-matic / VHS
Color (C)
$249.00, $149.00 purchase _ #AD - 1981
Reveals that many animals now face extinction because their habitats have been tampered with or destroyed, or their food supplies polluted. Shows that many species can be found only in zoos, while others have disappeared completely.
Science - Natural
Dist - FOTH **Prod** - FOTH

Saving Energy at Home 13 MIN
16mm
Color (J)
LC 75-700919
Identifies the major sources of energy waste in the home and offers tips on how to cut down on home energy consumption.
Home Economics; Science - Natural; Science - Physical; Social Science
Dist - SUTHRB **Prod** - RAMFLM 1975

Saving Energy on the Road 15 MIN
U-matic / VHS
Color (I A)
Presents an entertaining but practical guide to better gas mileage. Presents facts that can save drivers money.
Science - Natural; Social Science
Dist - SUTHRB **Prod** - SUTHRB

Saving Face - American Obsession with Looking Young 20 MIN
U-matic / VHS
Color
$335.00 purchase
From the ABC TV program, 20 20.
Health and Safety; Sociology
Dist - ABCLR **Prod** - ABCLR 1983

Saving lives - that's what it's all about 11 MIN
VHS
Color (C PRO G)
$395.00 purchase _ #R851 - VI - 046
Addresses procedures for assuring patient safety, extinguishing and - or containing fire, and patient - employee evacuation in healthcare facilities. Discusses patient carry techniques and fire extinguisher classifications and uses. Produced at Robinson Memorial Hospital, Ravenna, Ohio.
Health and Safety
Dist - HSCIC

The Saving of the President 31 MIN
16mm
Color
LC 82-700378
Presents a documentary drama covering the events immediately following the assassination attempt on President Ronald Reagan's life in Washington, DC, on March 30, 1981. Recreates the events with the actual doctors and nurses and others who were part of the effort to save President Reagan's life on that day and into the night. Shares the events and feelings of those involved through the unscripted recollections of the President, the U S Secret Service and staff of the George Washington University Medical Center.
Biography; Health and Safety
Dist - GWASHU **Prod** - GWASHU 1982

Saving our children in America
VHS
Video lectures of Khurram Murad series
Color (G)
$15.00 purchase _ #110 - 032
Features Islamic lecturer Khurram Murad who urges his listeners to think of all children as their children, of America as their land. Argues that only by trying to save everyone will families be saved; otherwise, saving only the children of Muslims will remain an elusive, selfish and defensive strategy.
Religion and Philosophy
Dist - SOUVIS **Prod** - SOUVIS

Saving Premature Infants 19 MIN
VHS / 16mm
Color (G)
$149.00, $249.00, purchase _ #AD - 1463
Highlights revolutionary technologies in perinatology and neonatology which save thousands of babies each year. Profiles a mother who lost her first premature child more than a decade earlier, the second survived and is now a healthy toddler. Looks at the long term effects of prematurity through a Stanford University follow - up report on teenagers who were born prematurely.
Health and Safety
Dist - FOTH **Prod** - FOTH 1990

Saving Sight 19 MIN
U-matic / VHS
Color (C)
$249.00, $149.00 purchase _ #AD - 1464
Focuses on the latest advancements in eye surgery. Includes laser surgery and vitrectomy. Profiles the victim of a gunshot wound to the eye which would have condemned him to blindness years ago.
Guidance and Counseling; Health and Safety; Science - Natural
Dist - FOTH **Prod** - FOTH

Saving Teeth for Lifetime Service, Conservative Class I and II Amalgam Restoration 263 MIN
VHS / U-matic
Saving Teeth for Lifetime Service Series
Color (PRO)
LC 84-706519
Presents Dr Miles Markley's philosophy of restorative dentistry, discussing the purposes and techniques of conservative dentistry.
Health and Safety; Science - Natural
Dist - USNAC **Prod** - USAF 1983

Saving Teeth for Lifetime Service, Foundations for Restorations and Cavity Liners 58 MIN
U-matic / VHS
Saving Teeth for Lifetime Service Series
Color (PRO)
LC 84-706520
Discusses Dr Miles Markley's philosophy of restorative dentistry, with information on intermediary bases and cavity liners.
Health and Safety; Science - Natural
Dist - USNAC **Prod** - USAF 1983

Saving Teeth for Lifetime Service, Pin Retention of Amalgam Foundations and 107 MIN
U-matic / VHS
Saving Teeth for Lifetime Service Series
Color (PRO)
LC 84-706521
Complete title is Saving Teeth For Lifetime Service, Pin Retention Of Amalgam Foundations And Restorations - Pin Reinforcement Of Weakened Teeth. Shows advantages of and techniques for using cemented pins in restorative dentistry.
Health and Safety; Science - Natural
Dist - USNAC **Prod** - USAF 1983

Saving Teeth for Lifetime Service, Prevention is a Prerequisite to Dental Health 59 MIN
U-matic / VHS
Saving Teeth for Lifetime Service Series
Color (PRO)
LC 84-706522
Presents Dr Miles Markley's philosophy of restorative dentistry. Promotes an awareness of the need and method for educating patients in oral hygiene.
Health and Safety; Science - Natural
Dist - USNAC **Prod** - USAF 1983

Saving teeth for lifetime service, restoration and maintenance of class v or gingivil third areas 101 MIN
VHS / U-matic
Saving teeth for lifetime service series
Color (PRO)
LC 84-706523
Complete title is Saving Teeth For Lifetime Service, Restoration And Maintenance Of Class V Or Gingival Third Areas. Discusses Dr Miles Markley's philosophy of restorative dentistry and presents techniques of class V restorations.
Health and Safety; Science - Natural
Dist - USNAC **Prod** - USAF 1983

Saving Teeth for Lifetime Service, Restoring the Distal of Cuspids 14 MIN
U-matic / VHS
Saving Teeth for Lifetime Service Series
Color (PRO)
LC 84-706524
Discusses Dr Miles Markley's philosophy of restorative dentistry. Presents a technique for conservative restoration of cuspids.
Health and Safety; Science - Natural
Dist - USNAC **Prod** - USAF 1983

Saving Teeth for Lifetime Service Series
Saving Teeth for Lifetime Service, Conservative Class I and II Amalgam Restoration 263 MIN
Saving Teeth for Lifetime Service, Foundations for Restorations and Cavity Liners 58 MIN
Saving Teeth for Lifetime Service, Pin Retention of Amalgam Foundations and 107 MIN
Saving Teeth for Lifetime Service, Prevention is a Prerequisite to Dental Health 59 MIN
Saving teeth for lifetime service, restoration and maintenance of class v or gingivil third areas 101 MIN
Saving Teeth for Lifetime Service, Restoring the Distal of Cuspids 14 MIN
Dist - USNAC

Saving the gorilla 23 MIN
U-matic / VHS / 16mm
Color (J)
Documents the work of Dr Dian Fossey with the endangered mountain gorillas in Rwanda, Africa.
Science; Science - Natural
Dist - NGS **Prod** - NGS 1982

Saving the largest bird in the world 24 MIN
VHS
Wild refuge series
Color (G)
$39.95 purchase
Journeys to the High Sierras, last refuge of the California Condors, which number fewer than 100. Visits the woods of British Columbia where a researcher is working on preservation of another sort - nature's disappearing soundscape. Part of a thirteen - part series on the North American wilderness. Each episode documents a different area and shows how animal species cope with their surroundings to survive.
Geography - United States; Geography - World; Science - Natural
Dist - CNEMAG **Prod** - HOBELP 1976

Saving the proof 11 MIN
16mm
Color (G)
$25.00 rental
Transforms the ordinary action of a woman walking into a complex process by focusing on the rhythm of her gait and repetitive sounds as she transverses city streets, passes windows and descends stairs. Illuminates a complex system of dichotomies both in form and content.
Fine Arts
Dist - CANCIN **Prod** - HOLMEK 1979

Saving the Sistine Chapel 60 MIN
VHS
Nova video library
Color (G)
$29.95 purchase
Documents the restoration efforts at the Sistine Chapel, the location of Michelangelo's masterpiece. From the PBS series 'NOVA.'
Fine Arts
Dist - PBS **Prod** - WNETTV

Saving through Automation 13 MIN
VHS
(PRO)
Presents results of a consultation with Yamatake Honeywell in Japan. Describes labor relations and problems at Yamatake Honeywell and how they were solved.
Business and Economics
Dist - TOYOVS **Prod** - JPC 1987

Saving water - the conservation unit
VHS
Color (I J H)
$59.00 purchase _ #Z1295GA
Examines the possible consequences of continued pollution of water resources. Features Dino Sorrus, an animated character, with computer graphics emphasizing ways students can help clean up and conserve water. Package includes one videocassette, one teacher's guide and 20 student workbooks. Additional materials are also available.
Science - Natural; Social Science
Dist - WAENFE

Saving Your Own Life 1 MIN
U-matic / VHS
Color
Features a fireman and his concerned wife regarding fears about checkups for colorectal cancer. Quotes wife who says 'he risks his life for strangers' but was afraid of a checkup for colorectal cancer. Carries message aimed at over - 50 viewers. Uses TV spot format.
Health and Safety
Dist - AMCS **Prod** - AMCS 1984

Saving yourself a lot of grief - or how to complete form 5074 11 MIN
U-matic / VHS
Color
Offers instructions on how to fill out the activities report Form 5074 for nursing and health services.

Civics and Political Systems; Health and Safety; Sociology
Dist - AMRC **Prod** - AMRC 1977

Savings Plans
VHS
Financial Planning and Management Series
(C G)
$59.00_CA272
Covers savings plans for personal finance goals.
Business and Economics
Dist - AAVIM **Prod** - AAVIM 1989

Savory veal dishes 48 MIN
VHS
Cookbook videos series
Color (G)
$19.95 purchase _ #ALW140
Shows how to prepare veal dishes in short, easy - to - learn segments. Lists each ingredient as it is added in subtitles and visually reinforces spoken instructions. Gives recipe background and nutritional facts. Part of the Cookbook Videos series.
Home Economics; Social Science
Dist - CADESF **Prod** - CADESF

Savory veal dishes 48 MIN
VHS
Cookbook videos series; Vol 21
Color (G)
$19.95 purchase
Shows how to make veal dishes. Offers veal picatta, pomo, marsala, parmegiana and cordon - bleu. Includes an abstract of recipes. Part of a series.
Home Economics; Social Science
Dist - ALWHIT **Prod** - ALWHIT

Saw timber 25 MIN
16mm
Color; B&W (I J H C G T A)
Analyzes conservation practices and methods of logging which ensure tree growth and reproduction. Shows how the trees are guarded from fire, inspected for insects, pruned, thinned and studied.
Agriculture; Geography - United States; Guidance and Counseling; Social Science
Dist - FO **Prod** - FO 1966

Sawdust and tinsel - The Naked night 87 MIN
VHS
B&W (G)
$29.95 purchase _ #SAW020
Presents an essay on passion, jealousy and betrayal against the backdrop of an impoverished traveling circus in turn - of - the - century Sweden. Revolves around the aging circus owner, who suffers heartbreak and humiliation at the hands of his young mistress and her brutal lovor. Uoco ctark black and white photography and editing of sound and visuals to construct an allegory of human weakness and spiritual despair.
Fine Arts; Literature and Drama; Psychology
Dist - HOMVIS **Prod** - JANUS 1953

Sawing a reverse curve and a bevel reverse curve 18 MIN
16mm
Precision wood machining series operations on the band saw, no 2
B&W
LC FIE52-49
Shows how to select and lay out stock to avoid waste, reverse curves to contour lines, use the table tilting gauge, saw a beveled reverse curve, prepare a template for a newel post and saw a newel post.
Industrial and Technical Education
Dist - USNAC **Prod** - USOE 1945

Sawing an Internal Irregular Shape 32 MIN
16mm
Machine Shop Work Series Operations on the Metal Cutting Band Saw, 'no 1
B&W
LC FIE51-585
Shows how to drill the saw - starting hole, make the saw selection, set up a band saw machine, weld saw bands, saw an internal contour shape and store a band saw.
Industrial and Technical Education
Dist - USNAC **Prod** - USOE 1944

Sawing Template Metal 17 MIN
16mm
B&W
LC FIE52-33
Demonstrates the mounting of the saw blade on a band saw, selecting the adjusting blade guides, sawing to a layout line, 'CHEWING OUT' metal from a notch and removing burrs.
Industrial and Technical Education
Dist - USNAC **Prod** - USOE 1943

Sawing with Jig and Changing Band 20 MIN
16mm
Precision Wood Machining Series
B&W
LC FIE52-48
Shows how to select proper band saw blades for the job, adjust saw guides, mark stock and cut to the mark, prepare a jig, and cut discs using a jig.
Industrial and Technical Education
Dist - USNAC **Prod** - USOE 1945

Sawmill operations 10 MIN
VHS
Skills - occupational programs series
Color (H C)
$49.00 purchase, $15.00 rental _ #316612; LC 91-712387
Features Ontarios sawmill employees describing their jobs and the skills needed to do them. Shows logs progressing from rough timber to finished lumber. Part of a series that features occupations in the skilled trades, in service industries and in business leading to careers in areas of demand and future growth. Includes teacher's guide with reproducible worksheets.
Guidance and Counseling; Industrial and Technical Education; Psychology
Dist - TVOTAR **Prod** - TVOTAR 1990

Saxophone for beginners 50 MIN
VHS
Maestro instructional series
Color (J H C G)
$29.95 purchase _ #BSPX26V
Supplements class lessons and reinforces private lessons on the saxophone. Offers clear - cut examples and demonstrations on how to unpack and assemble the instrument, proper hand position and instrumental nomenclature. Discusses notes, breathing, posture, reading music and care and maintenance of the instrument. Includes booklet. Part of a ten - part series on musical instruments.
Fine Arts
Dist - CAMV

Saxophones 20 MIN
VHS / 16mm
Junior High Music - Instrumental Series
Color (I)
$175.00, $200.00 purchase _ #288106
Features a host who introduces each program and offers a brief history of the instrument to be studied. Presents a master teacher, a professional musician with a symphony philharmonic, who demonstrates proper assembly, breathing and tone production, hand position, embouchure and articulation. A performance rounds out the program. 'Saxophone' demonstrates the youngest of the woodwind family. The importance of body position is explained, as well as the need for a good quality mouthpiece, hand and finger positions and proper placement of the mouthpiece and tongue to avoid the tendency to slur notes.
Fine Arts
Dist - ACCESS **Prod** - ACCESS 1988

Say amen, somebody 100 MIN
35mm / 16mm
Color (G)
Explores gospel, the music of the soul. Looks at this manifestation of religious calling by portraying both the Mother - Willie Mae Ford Smith - and the Father - Thomas A Dorsey - of gospel music. Celebrates their personal lives as they travel around spreading the word with an infectious enthusiasm. Contact distributor for price.
Fine Arts; Religion and Philosophy
Dist - OCTOBF **Prod** - NIERNG 1983

Say Amen, Somebody
VHS / BETA
Color
Presents a documentary about gospel music, featuring performances and interviews with gospel greats.
Fine Arts
Dist - GA **Prod** - GA

Say Brother National Edition Series

Aborigine	30 MIN
African liberation	30 MIN
Ancient African Kingdoms	30 MIN
Attica	30 MIN
The Black College	30 MIN
Caribbean	30 MIN
Desegregation	30 MIN
Islam	30 MIN
Middle Passage	30 MIN
New Music	30 MIN
Old, Black and Alive	30 MIN
Poetry and Arts	30 MIN
Vietnam	30 MIN

Dist - PBS

Say brother special - the nation of Islam 60 MIN
VHS / 16mm
Color (G)
$70.00 rental _ #SBRS - 000
Portrays the Nation of Islam in the words of the followers of Elijah Muhammad practicing in the United States.
Religion and Philosophy; Sociology
Dist - PBS **Prod** - WGBHTV

Say Cheese 25 MIN
U-matic
Not Another Science Show Series
Color (H C)
Looks at how cameras work and how film is developed.
Science
Dist - TVOTAR **Prod** - TVOTAR 1986

Say goodbye 51 MIN
16mm
Color (K P A)
LC 76-711435
Examines man's careless arrogance toward the delicate balance of nature and shows the necessity of sharing the earth with the wild creatures.
Science - Natural; Sociology
Dist - WOLPER **Prod** - QUO 1971

Say Goodbye Again - Children of Divorce 26 MIN
U-matic / VHS / 16mm
Color (C A)
Analyzes the impact of divorce on the young people involved. Focuses on three families over a two - year period illustrating how children from different age groups deal with the social and psychological effects of each phase of the divorce process. Interviews various experts to examine several programs designed to help both parents and children cope with the feelings, attitudes and concerns arising from a divorce.
Psychology; Sociology
Dist - CORF **Prod** - CINSF 1981

Say Goodbye - America's Endangered Species 50 MIN
16mm
Color (J H)
Shows how humans are damaging the delicate balance of nature in North America.
Science - Natural
Dist - FI **Prod** - WOLPER 1973

Say goodbye - Pt 1 26 MIN
16mm
Color (K P A)
LC 76-711435
Examines man's careless arrogance toward the delicate balance of nature and shows the necessity of sharing the earth with the wild creatures.
Science - Natural
Dist - WOLPER **Prod** - QUO 1971

Say goodbye - Pt 2 26 MIN
16mm
Color (K P A)
LC 76-711435
Examines man's careless arrogance toward the delicate balance of nature and shows the necessity of sharing the earth with the wild creatures.
Science - Natural
Dist - WOLPER **Prod** - QUO 1971

Say goodbye to back pain 96 MIN
VHS
Color (G)
$39.95 purchase
Presents a six - week program for eliminating, reducing, and preventing back pain. Reveals the two main causes of back pain, six tests to find problem areas, seven tips on pain prevention, and ways to reduce stress and tension.
Health and Safety
Dist - PBS **Prod** - WNETTV

Say Goodbye to Back Pain 96 MIN
VHS
Color (G)
$29.95 purchase _ #6028
Presents a six - week program to alleviate back pain developed by Dr Hans Kraus, President John F Kennedy's back doctor.
Health and Safety; Physical Education and Recreation; Science - Natural
Dist - SYBVIS **Prod** - SYBVIS

Say goodbye to back pain 45 MIN
VHS
(G)
$44.00 purchase _ #NS300V
Discusses ways to eleviate common back pain through muscle relaxation and flexibility. Presents simple exercises.
Health and Safety
Dist - CAMV

Say goodbye to high blood pressure 45 MIN
VHS
Color (G)
$24.95 purchase _ #6317
Features Dr Alan Xenakis. Shows how simple exercise, proper diet and nutrition and relaxing programs can control the risk factors for high blood pressure.
Health and Safety; Physical Education and Recreation; Science - Natural
Dist - SYBVIS **Prod** - SYBVIS

Say I'm a Jew 28 MIN
U-matic / BETA / VHS
Color; Stereo (J S C A G)
Reveals the Jewish experience since World War II through the faces and voices of European Jews who were transplanted to America. Shares their ambivalence to their Jewish identity, and their efforts to resolve their conflicts and accept their heritage.
Religion and Philosophy; Sociology
Dist - UCV

A Say in Your Community with the Australian Assistance Plan 31 MIN
16mm
Color
LC 76-701870
Profiles a large, complex Australian community in terms of its social and welfare needs and illustrates the benefits available to community groups throughout the country under the Australian Assistance Plan.
Geography - World; Sociology
Dist - AUIS **Prod** - FLMAUS 1975

Say it Again, Sam 15 MIN
U-matic / VHS
Movies, Movies Series
Color (J H)
Examines the manipulation of picture and sound to create mood in motion pictures.
Fine Arts; Industrial and Technical Education
Dist - CTI **Prod** - CTI

Say it by signing 60 MIN
VHS
Color (G)
$29.95 purchase _ #X015
Offers four complete lessons in sign language which include the most commonly used sign expressions and a comprehensive manual vocabulary. Features Dr Elaine Costello, director of Gallaudet College Press.
Education; English Language; Social Science
Dist - STRUE **Prod** - CRVID 1993

Say it by signing 60 MIN
VHS
Color (G)
$29.95 purchase _ #S00469
Teaches the basics of sign language, stressing commonly used words and phrases.
Education; Guidance and Counseling; Social Science
Dist - UILL

Say it by signing 60 MIN
VHS
Color (G)
$29.95 purchase
Teaches the basics of sign language, focusing on everyday words and phrases.
Education
Dist - PBS **Prod** - WNETTV

Say it by Signing 60 MIN
BETA / VHS
Color
Provides instruction in basic sign language.
Education
Dist - CROWNP **Prod** - CROWNP

Say it right 14 MIN
U-matic / VHS
Emergency medical training series; Lesson 7
Color (IND)
Helps standardize radio procedure for communicating patient information to the emergency department of a hospital or to a doctor.
Health and Safety; Industrial and Technical Education
Dist - LEIKID **Prod** - LEIKID

Say it with sign - review - Parts 11 - 14 30 MIN
U-matic / VHS
Say it with sign series; Pt 15
Color (H C A) (AMERICAN SIGN)
Presents Lawrence Solow and Sharon Neumann Solow introducing American Sign Language used by the hearing - impaired. Reviews the contents of parts 11 through 14 of the Say It With Sign Series.
Education
Dist - FI **Prod** - KNBCTV 1982

Say it with sign - review - Parts 16 - 19 30 MIN
U-matic / VHS
Say it with sign series; Pt 20
Color (H C A) (AMERICAN SIGN)
Presents Lawrence Solow and Sharon Neumann Solow introducing American Sign Language used by the hearing - impaired. Reviews the contents of parts 16 through 19 of the Say It With Sign Series.
Education
Dist - FI **Prod** - KNBCTV 1982

Say it with sign - review - Parts 21 - 24 30 MIN
U-matic / VHS
Say it with sign series; Pt 25
Color (H C A) (AMERICAN SIGN)
Presents Lawrence Solow and Sharon Neumann Solow introducing American Sign Language used by the hearing - impaired. Reviews the contents of parts 21 through 24 of the Say It With Sign Series.
Education
Dist - FI **Prod** - KNBCTV 1982

Say it with sign - review - Parts 26 - 29 30 MIN
U-matic / VHS
Say it with sign series; Pt 30
Color (H C A) (AMERICAN SIGN)
Presents Lawrence Solow and Sharon Neumann Solow introducing American Sign Language used by the hearing - impaired. Reviews the contents of parts 26 through 29 of the Say It With Sign Series.
Education
Dist - FI **Prod** - KNBCTV 1982

Say it with sign - review - Parts 31 - 34 30 MIN
VHS / U-matic
Say it with sign series; Pt 35
Color (H C A) (AMERICAN SIGN)
Presents Lawrence Solow and Sharon Neumann Solow introducing American Sign Language used by the hearing - impaired. Reviews the contents of parts 31 through 34 of the Say It With Sign Series.
Education
Dist - FI **Prod** - KNBCTV 1982

Say it with sign - review - Parts 36 - 39 30 MIN
U-matic / VHS
Say it with sign series; Pt 40
Color (H C A) (AMERICAN SIGN)
Presents Lawrence Solow and Sharon Neumann Solow introducing American Sign Language used by the hearing - impaired. Reviews the contents of parts 36 through 39 of the Say It With Sign Series.
Education
Dist - FI **Prod** - KNBCTV 1982

Say it with sign - review - Parts 1 - 4 30 MIN
VHS / U-matic
Say it with sign series; Pt 5
Color (H C A) (AMERICAN SIGN)
Presents Lawrence Solow and Sharon Neumann Solow introducing American Sign Language used by the hearing - impaired. Reviews the contents of parts 1 through 4 of the Say It With Sign Series.
Education
Dist - FI **Prod** - KNBCTV 1982

Say it with sign - review - Parts 6 - 9 30 MIN
U-matic / VHS
Say it with sign series; Pt 10
Color (H C A) (AMERICAN SIGN)
Presents Lawrence Solow and Sharon Neumann Solow introducing American Sign Language used by the hearing - impaired. Reviews the contents of parts 6 through 9 of the Say It With Sign Series.
Education
Dist - FI **Prod** - KNBCTV 1982

Say it with sign series
Around the house 30 MIN
Basic conversation 30 MIN
Beauty parlor - occupations 30 MIN
Colors 30 MIN
Decoder 30 MIN
Emergency signs 30 MIN
Emotions 30 MIN
Family II 30 MIN
Family III 30 MIN
Family vacation 30 MIN
Food 30 MIN
Fruits and colors 30 MIN
Furniture 30 MIN
General health 30 MIN
Golf 30 MIN
Holidays and seasons 30 MIN
Megan at 2 30 MIN
More signs you already know 30 MIN
Numbers 30 MIN
Say it with sign - review - Parts 1 - 4 30 MIN
Say it with sign - review - Parts 6 - 9 30 MIN
Say it with sign - review - Parts 11 -14 30 MIN
Say it with sign - review - Parts 16 -19 30 MIN
Say it with sign - review - Parts 21 - 24 30 MIN
Say it with sign - review - Parts 26 29- 30 MIN
Say it with sign - review - Parts 31 - 34 30 MIN
Say it with sign - review - Parts 36 - 39 30 MIN
Signs you already know 30 MIN
Sports 30 MIN
Still more signs you already know 30 MIN
Time I 30 MIN
Time II 30 MIN
Time III 30 MIN
TTY - Telephone 30 MIN
Vacationing 30 MIN
Vehicles 30 MIN
Weather I 30 MIN
Weather II 30 MIN
Wonderful baby 30 MIN
Dist - FI

Say it with spills 11 MIN
16mm
Warner - Pathe newsreel series
B&W (G)
$15.00 rental
Focuses on folks who risk their necks at rodeos, in the boxing ring and on the auto track. Presents part of a series by Robert Youngson for Warner - Pathe Newsreels.
Fine Arts; Literature and Drama; Physical Education and Recreation
Dist - KITPAR **Prod** - WARPAN 1953

Say it with words 10 MIN
VHS / U-matic / BETA
Student know - how series
Color; Stereo (H)
Explains the important differences between private writing and public speaking and skills developed. Includes use of visual aids.
Education; English Language
Dist - SEVDIM **Prod** - SEVDIM 1985

Say it without words - 10 30 MIN
VHS
English 101 - Ingles 101 series
Color (H)
$125.00 purchase
Focuses on a specific topic in order to emphasize a particular grammatical point or set of idioms. English is used from the beginning as the primary language of instruction but Spanish translations are included to ensure understanding. Part 10 looks at subject pronouns, review of parts of a sentence, using subject pronouns correctly, review of pronoun - verb contractions, subject pronouns in short answers. Part of a series ofo 30 programs.
English Language; Foreign Language
Dist - AITECH **Prod** - UPRICO 1988

Say no elementary 50 MIN
VHS
Color (P I)
$85.00 purchase _ #CG - 978 - VS
Features rock musician and former drug abuser Jevon Thompson. Highlights decision making and helps to form a basic awareness of the gateway drugs, advertising influences, peer pressure and self esteem. Includes workbook and discussion guide.
Guidance and Counseling; Psychology
Dist - HRMC **Prod** - HRMC 1992

Say no films series
Deciso 3003 8 MIN
Doin' what the crowd does 5 MIN
Jojo's Blues 6 MIN
Dist - CF

Say no series
Deciso 3003 8 MIN
Doin' what the crowd does 5 MIN
Jojo's Blues 6 MIN
Dist - CF

Say no to Drugs 45 MIN
VHS
Color (K)
$19.95 purchase _ #V2652 - 10
Teaches parents how to prevent drug and alcohol abuse by their children.
Health and Safety; Psychology
Dist - SCHSCI

Say no to drugs 45 MIN
VHS
(C A)
$29.95 purchase _ #TT100V
Provides parents with an understanding of the issues concerning teen drug abuse, including young people's motivations, moods and problems and how these can lead to drug involvement.
Guidance and Counseling; Psychology; Sociology
Dist - CAMV **Prod** - CAMV

Say no to drugs 45 MIN
VHS
Color (G A)

$39.95 purchase _ #SNV100
Helps parents to understand the issues of drug and alcohol use in young adults. Discusses the motivation, moods and problems of young people and how these can lead to drug use. Offers parenting guidelines for preventing drug use and coping with it if it occurs.
Guidance and Counseling; Health and Safety; Psychology; Sociology
Dist - CADESF **Prod** - CADESF 1986

Say no to Drugs 45 MIN
VHS
Color; Stereo (J A)
$14.98 purchase _ #TT8035
Provides a practical guide for parents who want to keep their children off drugs.
Guidance and Counseling; Psychology
Dist - TWINTO **Prod** - TWINTO 1990

Say no to drugs - it's your decision 17 MIN
VHS / U-matic
Color; Captioned (I J H)
$55.00, $95.00 purchase _ #TCA16172, #TCA16171
Presents information about the use and abuse of both legal and illegal drugs. Features the testimony of teenagers and professionals. Stresses the importance of having a well - established value system and strong self - image, both of which can help teens say no to drugs. Narrated by baseball star Dave Winfield.
Guidance and Counseling; Health and Safety; Psychology
Dist - USNAC

Say no to Strangers 27 MIN
VHS / 16mm
Color (K)
LC 90713679
Utilizes three scenarios to teach children how to avoid being abducted. Stresses the importance of refusing strangers' offers.
Health and Safety; Psychology; Sociology
Dist - BENNUP

Say Old Man, Can You Play the Fiddle 20 MIN
U-matic / VHS / 16mm
B&W
Portrays an old man in Downey, California, who plays a fiddle made by his blind father.
Fine Arts
Dist - UCEMC **Prod** - HAWESB 1974

Say that One more Time 14 MIN
VHS / U-matic
Making it Work Series
Color (H A)
Presents two versions of Jane's first day showing that when Jane asks and answers questions, pays attention and takes notes, she learns. Shows Paula demonstrating poor and good telephone communication skills.
Guidance and Counseling; Psychology
Dist - AITECH **Prod** - ERF 1983

Say what you want 30 MIN
VHS
Color (A PRO IND)
$795.00 purchase, $185.00 rental
Outlines a six - point strategy for managers to get their messages across - decide what is wanted, speaking clearly and specifically, paying attention to how something is said, avoiding being manipulated or sidetracked, listening, and aiming for an 'everybody wins' result.
Business and Economics; English Language; Guidance and Counseling; Psychology; Social Science
Dist - VLEARN **Prod** - MELROS

Say what You Want
VHS
Management Development Series
Color (G)
$795.00 purchase, $185.00 rental
Dramatizes effective assertiveness skills. Part of a five - part series on management development.
Business and Economics; Guidance and Counseling; Psychology; Social Science
Dist - VLEARN **Prod** - MELROS

Say what You Want 30 MIN
VHS / 16mm
Color (PRO)
$695.00 purchase each, $150.00 rental, $45.00 preview
Teaches employees and supervisors how to be properly assertive. Based on the assertiveness training work of Kate and Ken Black.
Business and Economics; Guidance and Counseling; Psychology
Dist - UTM **Prod** - UTM

Say yes 17 MIN
16mm
Color (H C A)
LC 79-700538
Emphasizes the importance of immunizing children against measles, polio, rubella, mumps, diphtheria, whooping cough and tetanus.
Health and Safety; Home Economics
Dist - BLONDL **Prod** - BLONDL 1978

Say yes 35 MIN
VHS
Color (A IND)
$275.00 purchase _ #AH45234
Contrasts healthy lifestyles with those involving drug and alcohol abuse. Encourages employees to choose healthier ways of feeling good and relieving stress.
Health and Safety; Psychology
Dist - HTHED **Prod** - HTHED

Say Yes - healthy choices for feeling good 35 MIN
U-matic / VHS
Color (G)
$495.00 purchase, $150.00 rental
Presents a multi - component training package designed to be an employee drug and alcohol abuse prevention program. Encourages employees to adopt a healthier lifestyle by giving essential tools for behavior change that will make them feel better. Includes videocassette, employee handbook, guide, T - shirt with Say Yes logo and 10 drug information handouts for employees. Features Willard Scott. Produced by ISA Associates.
Guidance and Counseling; Psychology
Dist - BAXMED

Say Yes to Seat Belts 13 MIN
VHS / U-matic
Color (H C G)
Explains why mandatory seat belt use laws in every state can work to save more than eight thousand lives a year.
Health and Safety; Psychology; Social Science
Dist - HUF **Prod** - HUF

Say you're sorry when you're wrong, the importance of saying thank you - Volume 5 60 MIN
VHS
Our friends on Wooster Square series
Color (K P I R)
$34.95 purchase, $10.00 rental _ #35 - 87171 - 460
Presents religious concepts through storylines, songs and Scripture. Features puppet characters including Smedly, Troll and Sizzle.
Fine Arts; Literature and Drama; Religion and Philosophy
Dist - APH **Prod** - FRACOC

Saybrook - the colony 1635 - 1985 23 MIN
16mm
Color
Shows how Saybrook Colony, the third oldest settlement in Connecticut, and the seven towns that developed from it represent a microcosm of American society in a river - oriented environment. Begins with the Mehantics, the river Indians who first occupied Pashbeshauke, 'the place at the river's mouth.'
History - United States
Dist - FENWCK **Prod** - GRANTE

Saydu - Conflict of Commitment 28 MIN
16mm
Color (J H)
Tells the story of Saydu, a teenager who is caught in changing Africa and finds his allegiance divided between the traditional ways of his father's village and life in the bustling city of Abidjan.
Geography - World; Social Science; Sociology
Dist - CBFMS **Prod** - CBFMS

Saying good - bye 26 MIN
VHS
Color (G)
$149.00 purchase, $75.00 rental _ #UW2373
Talks to people to find out how they dealt with their grief - a support group for widows, a woman whose parents died within a year of each other, and a woman whose husband died of cancer. Interviews a hospital chaplain and the director of a hospice.
Sociology
Dist - FOTH

Saying Goodbye 22 MIN
VHS / 16mm
Color (G)
$350.00 purchase, $50.00, $60.00 rental
Presents, through children's eyes, the intense emotions that accompany the process of learning to accept death as a reality. Depicts the experiences of a group of children when one of their classmates dies. Allows the viewer to understand the often underestimated capacity for children to contemplate and grasp complex and painful issues. Produced by Kate White.
Health and Safety; Psychology; Sociology
Dist - WMENIF

Saying goodbye - grief counseling program 15 MIN
VHS
Color (G)
$195.00 purchase, $100.00 rental _ #CN-102
Reveals that, until recently, there was little acknowledgement of the intensity and depth of grief that may be suffered by parents who experience a perinatal loss. Shows the grief counseling program of Bethesda Hospital, Cincinnati, which works with physicians to treat the emotional as well as the physiological aftermath. Interviews an obstetrician, a staff development instructor, a nurse who is the perinatal grief director and a family to outline the components of a comprehensive care program, including individual counseling, support groups, memorial services and encouragement for the entire family to spend time with their baby. Produced by Bethesda Hospital.
Sociology
Dist - FANPRO

Saying goodbye - on bereavement series 150 MIN
VHS
Saying goodbye - on bereavement series
Color (H C G)
$995.00 purchase, $150.00 rental
Presents a five - part series on bereavement produced in cooperation with Insight Production. Includes the titles A Grief Shared, Thunder in My Head, A Home Alone, A Promise Broken, The First Snowfall, which discuss the death of infants, sudden widowhood, men's experience of bereavement, teen suicide and terminal illness of a parent.
Guidance and Counseling; Sociology
Dist - FLMLIB **Prod** - TVOTAR 1990

Saying no 28 MIN
VHS
You can choose series
Color (P I)
$59.95 purchase _ #RB8204
Focuses on Missie Mouse who has to choose whether to say 'no' to a friend or to do something she knows is wrong. Reveals that when her best friend Rhonda tries to pressure her into smoking, Missie agonizes over her options before discovering that there are ways to say 'no' without ruffling Rhonda's feathers. Part of a series hosted by comedian - youth counselor Michael Pritchard which leads children in an unrehearsed problem - solving session where the children explore the issues and arrive at a thoughtful solution.
Guidance and Counseling; Sociology
Dist - REVID **Prod** - REVID 1993

Saying no 17 MIN
U-matic / VHS / 16mm
Color
Presents young women talking about their personal decisions regarding sexuality, how they have been affected by their decisions, and how they respect themselves for having the courage and will - power to abstain from sex.
Guidance and Counseling; Health and Safety
Dist - PEREN **Prod** - PEREN

Saying no - a Few Words to Young Women about Sex 17 MIN
16mm
Color (J H A)
Presents young women talking about their personal decisions regarding sexuality, how they have been affected by their decisions, how they feel about themselves and how much they respect themselves for having the courage and willpower to abstain from sex.
Health and Safety; Psychology; Sociology
Dist - CROMIE **Prod** - CROMIE 1983

Saying no to Alcohol and Drugs - Peer Pressure 13 MIN
16mm / VHS
Color (P) (ENGLISH (SPANISH SUBTITLES))
$275.00, $250.00 purchase, $30.00 rental _ #C - 489; LC 85702653
Presents ways to say 'No' to peers when one is offered dangerous substances. Seeks to build self - esteem, assertiveness and establish awareness of positive alternatives to drug use. Features Valerie Brisco - Hooks, winner of three gold medals in the 1984 Olympics. Produced by North Window Productions.
Guidance and Counseling; Health and Safety; Psychology; Sociology
Dist - ALTSUL

Saying 'no' to alcohol and other drugs
VHS
Big changes, big choices series
Color (I J)
$69.95 purchase _ #LVB - 8A
Presents and reinforces anti - drug attitudes. Teaches practical techniques for saying 'no' to friends without being uncool. Part of a 12 - part video series designed to help young adolescents work their way though the many anxieties and issues they face. Encourages them to make positive and healthful life choices. Features humorist and youth counselor Michael Pritchard.

Guidance and Counseling; Psychology
Dist - CFKRCM Prod - CFKRCM

Saying no to danger 11 MIN
VHS
Taking responsibility series
Color (P)
Reveals that natural curiosity and negative peer pressure can cause children to explore unsafe areas. Uses the animated adventures of three pigs to show that saying 'No' to danger is a smart thing to do. Shows how to recognize and avoid dangerous places, objects and behavior. Part of a series teaching health, safety and responsibility to youngsters.
Health and Safety; Sociology
Dist - VIEWTH Prod - VIEWTH

Saying no to danger 11 MIN
U-matic / VHS / 16mm
Taking responsibility series
Color (P I)
$320.00, $250.00 purchase _ #4644C
Shows how to avoid dangerous places and behavior.
Health and Safety
Dist - CORF

Saying no to drinking drivers 23 MIN
VHS
Color (J H C)
$455.00, $340.00 purchase, $60.00 rental
Reveals that one key to the teen drunk driving problem is the crucial moment when a teen decides whether to step into the car, as passenger or driver. Provides essential tools students need to cope with peer pressure. Dramatizes typical situations with optional stops in the program for discussion. Uses positive modeling by peers to reveal options and solutions, including the most effective one - planning ahead.
Guidance and Counseling; Health and Safety; Psychology; Social Science
Dist - CF

The Sayings of the fathers 30 MIN
16mm
B&W
LC FIA64-1140
Uses dramatic readings from a collection of Rabbinical sayings, Pirke Avot, to explain the meaning of life to a disillusioned businessman.
Guidance and Counseling; Psychology; Religion and Philosophy
Dist - NAAJS Prod - JTS 1955

Scabies 5 MIN
16mm
Color
Explores problems associated with the affliction of scabies.
Health and Safety
Dist - TASCOR Prod - VICCOR 1978

Scabies - the itch 7 MIN
16mm
Color (J)
LC 72-700405
A commentary on the composition of society and the irritants of life as revealed by a story about a man whose composure is interrupted by itching sensations and a cough, which he traces to little men inside his clothing.
Literature and Drama; Sociology
Dist - MMA Prod - ZAGREB 1971

Scaffold instruction of listening comprehension with first graders
VHS
Cognition and learning series
Color (T)
$49.95 purchase
Investigates reciprocal teaching in which first grade teachers engage students in discussion about expository text read aloud to them. Shares the results of a longitudinal, three year study in terms of changes in student - teacher interactions over time, on measures of listening, reading comprehension and strategy knowledge. Presented by Dr Annemarie Sullivan Palincsar of Michigan State University. Part of a six - part series on recent theoretical and empirical work done on cognition and learning.
Education; English Language; Psychology
Dist - UCALG Prod - UCALG 1991

Scaffolding 11 MIN
U-matic / VHS / 16mm
Safety in Construction Series
Color
Covers setting out and erecting scaffolds safely, including mobile scaffolds. Explains the main causes of scaffold collapse.
Health and Safety; Industrial and Technical Education
Dist - IFB Prod - NFBTE

Scaffolds 16 MIN
U-matic / VHS
Color (IND A)
Demonstrates safe construction and use of scaffolds. Briefly surveys the causes of scaffold accidents and discusses safe set up, use, and dismantling of scaffolds.
Health and Safety
Dist - IFB Prod - CSAO 1987

Scag - the Story of Heroin 21 MIN
U-matic / VHS / 16mm
Drug Abuse Education Series
Color (I J H)
LC 70-711436
Examines the physical, emotional and social consequences of shooting heroin.
Health and Safety; Sociology
Dist - EBEC Prod - CONCPT 1970

Scale 12 MIN
16mm / U-matic / VHS
Map skills series
Color (I J)
$350.00, $250.00 purchase _ #5191C
Shows the importance of understanding scale on maps, unit comparison, and bar scale. Produced by Christianson Productions, Inc.
Social Science
Dist - CORF

Scale Factor 20 MIN
U-matic / VHS
Math Topics - Trigonometry Series
Color (J H C)
Mathematics
Dist - FI Prod - BBCTV

Scales and Scale Bowings 30 MIN
VHS / U-matic
Cello Sounds of Today Series
Color (J H A)
Fine Arts
Dist - IU Prod - IU 1984

Scales, modes and other essentials - Video One 82 MIN
VHS
You can play jazz guitar series
Color (G)
$49.95 purchase _ #VD - DEM - GT01
Features jazz guitarist Mike DeMicco. Teaches scales, modes and voicings. Shows the viewer how to use them in DeMicco's easy - to - play melodic tune, Just Too Many. Includes music and diagrams. Part one of a three - part series.
Fine Arts
Dist - HOMETA Prod - HOMETA

The Scales of justice - our court system
U-matic / VHS / 35mm strip
(J H C)
$109.00, $139.00 purchase _ #06280 94
Examines each level of jurisdiction in the American court system. Traces trial procedures and considers major problems facing the court system today. Explains how the Supreme Court relates to the legislative and executive branches of the government. In 2 parts.
Civics and Political Systems
Dist - ASPRSS Prod - GA
GA

Scaling 5 MIN
16mm
B&W (G)
$10.00 rental
Envisions the center of an empty horizon and the place of doubles in a Michael Hoolboom production.
Fine Arts
Dist - CANCIN

Scaling 16 MIN
U-matic / VHS
Numerical Control/Computerized Numerical Control - Advanced 'Programming Series Module 2
Color (IND)
Includes scaling limits and rules, how to write a scaling statement and terminating a scaling statement.
Business and Economics; Industrial and Technical Education
Dist - LEIKID Prod - LEIKID

Scaling - 18 39 MIN
VHS
Conceptual physics alive series
Color (H C)
$45.00 purchase
Distinguishes surface area and volume with simple demonstrations. Uses several examples to illustrate the proportional changes in area and volume when objects are scaled up or down in size. Part 18 of a 35 - part series adapted from the college and high school textbook Conceptual Physics by Professor Paul Hewitt.
Mathematics; Science - Physical
Dist - MMENTE Prod - HEWITP 1992

Scaling and root planing - Pt 1 - maxillary teeth 13 MIN
8mm cartridge / 16mm
Color (PRO)
LC 75-702487; 75-702485
Presents a demonstration by Robert R Nissle and Sigurd P Ramfjord of an effective method of scaling and root planing. Uses one representative tooth from each segment of the dental arch. Stresses the necessity for removal of supra - and subgingival calculus deposits and subsequent smoothing of these tooth surfaces.
Health and Safety
Dist - USNAC Prod - USVA 1974

Scaling Techniques Series

Fulcrums and Vision	27 MIN
Introduction to Basic Skills	21 MIN
Operator - Patient and Light Positions	9 MIN
Polishing	15 MIN
Use of Sickle Scalers	21 MIN
Use of the Explorer	15 MIN
Use of the Gracey Curet no 07 - 08	21 MIN
Use of the Gracey Curet no 11 - 12	13 MIN
Use of the Gracey Curet no 13 - 14	12 MIN
Use of the Periodontal Probe	11 MIN

Dist - USNAC

The Scalp as a Skin Donar Site 10 MIN
U-matic / VHS
Color (PRO)
Presents transparent dressings as a means of promoting rapid healing of skin graft donor sites with virtually no pain.
Health and Safety
Dist - MMAMC Prod - MMAMC

Scandal Sheet 82 MIN
16mm
B&W
Tells how a new editor turns a conservative newspaper into a yellow journal until the circulation quadruples. Shows how a reporter and his photographer unravel the murder of a woman. Stars Broderick Crawford, Donna Reed and John Derek.
Fine Arts
Dist - KITPAR Prod - CPC 1952

Scandals at the Check - Out Counter 29 MIN
VHS / U-matic
Inside Story Series
Color
LC 83-706853
Examines the journalistic practices and philosophy behind supermarket tabloids. Looks at how one company, Globe Communications, develops its stories and the impact such tabloids have had on other forms of popular communication.
Literature and Drama; Social Science
Dist - PBS Prod - PBS 1981

Scandinavia 57 MIN
VHS
Color (G)
$29.95 purchase _ #ST - IV0152
Visits Denmark and its medieval architecture and the ancient seat of Viking kings.
Geography - World
Dist - INSTRU

Scandinavia 24 MIN
16mm
Color (I)
LC 76-702867
Introduces the geography, people and industry of Denmark, Sweden, Norway, Finland and Iceland.
Geography - World; Social Science
Dist - IFF Prod - IFF 1976

Scandinavia 25 MIN
16mm / U-matic
Untamed World Series
Color; Mono (J H C A)
$400.00 film, $250.00 video, $50.00 rental
Examines the geography, animal life and the way of life for the people of Scandinavia.
Geography - World
Dist - CTV Prod - CTV 1972

Scandinavia 1 15 MIN
U-matic
It's Your World Series
Color (I)
Introduces students to the world around them. Segment titles are; The Countries, Exercise And Sport, Things Scandinavian, Architecture And Crafts.
Education; Geography - World
Dist - TVOTAR Prod - TVOTAR 1984

Scandinavia 2 15 MIN
U-matic
It's Your World Series

Color (I)
Introduces students to the world around them. Segment titles are; Norway, Sweden, Finland.
Education; Geography - World
Dist - TVOTAR **Prod** - TVOTAR 1984

Scandinavia 3 15 MIN
U-matic
It's Your World Series
Color (I)
Introduces students to the world around them. Segment titles are; Denmark, Iceland, Lapland, Living Near Water.
Education; Geography - World
Dist - TVOTAR **Prod** - TVOTAR 1984

Scandinavia - a Place Apart 28 MIN
16mm
Color (C A)
Explains how the people and scenery of Scandinavia separate those Nordic nations from other parts of the world, and focuses on the specific differences among the five countries. A new film by Fritz and Ingaborg Kahlenberg.
Geography - World; History - World
Dist - WSTGLC **Prod** - WSTGLC

Scandinavia, in Short 15 MIN
16mm
Color (C A)
Highlights five Scandinavian countries. Discusses the architecture of Finland, the hot tubs of Iceland, the Denmark home of Hans Christian Andersen, the elegance of Sweden and the castles of Norway.
Geography - World; History - World
Dist - WSTGLC **Prod** - WSTGLC

Scandinavia - land of the midnight sun 60 MIN
VHS
European collection series
Color (J H C G)
$29.95 purchase _ #IVN152V-S
Teaches about the people, culture and history of Scandinavia. Visits historic buildings, monuments and landmarks. Examines the physical topography of the country. Part of a 16-part series on European countries. Also part of a larger series entitled Video Visits that travels to six continents.
Geography - World; History - World
Dist - CAMV **Prod** - WNETTV

Scandinavia - Nations of the North 21 MIN
16mm / U-matic / VHS
Color (I J H)
LC 81-701065
Focuses on Denmark, Sweden and Norway, providing information on their systems of social service.
Geography - World; History - World; Sociology
Dist - PHENIX **Prod** - SVEK 1981

Scandinavia - unique northern societies 25 MIN
U-matic / VHS / BETA
Color; PAL (G H C)
PdS50, PdS58 purchase
Surveys the five Northern European nations called Scandinavia. Opens with lively animation, locates Scandinavia, traces the routes of the Vikings, then, using live action photography, shows Denmark, Sweden, Norway, Finland and Iceland at different times of the year.
Fine Arts; Geography - World; History - World
Dist - EDPAT **Prod** - IFF

Scandinavia - unique northern societies 24 MIN
VHS / U-matic
Color (J)
Surveys Scandinavia as a whole, with emphasis on industry. presents information on geography and climate, lifestyle of the Lapps, education, art, and government. Points out the problems that may arise in such a system, even though living standards are high.
Business and Economics; Geography - World; History - World
Dist - IFF **Prod** - IFF

Scandinavian Saga 27 MIN
16mm
Color
Features more than 50 species of Scandinavian birds and other animals. Depicts other colorful aspects of life in Denmark, Finland, Norway and Sweden.
Geography - World; Science - Natural
Dist - SWNTO **Prod** - SWNTO 1968

Scandinavian Sketchbook 20 MIN
16mm
Color
LC FIA66-1391
Follows a family which is interested in tracing its ancestry in Sweden as it travels by car through Denmark, Sweden and Norway.
Geography - World; Guidance and Counseling; Physical Education and Recreation
Dist - SWNTO **Prod** - GOFFD 1965

Scanners and colory theory 60 MIN
VHS
Color (H C)
$79.95 purchase _ #SE - 18
Looks at a scanner operator's evaluation of original copy to determine where to place tone values in printing density. Covers gray balance, highight, shadow gradation, color correction, under color removal, integrated color removal and unsharp maskings. Proofs are made to show enhancement between reproductions. Shows several models of scanners and step - by - step setup procedures for the D S America 608 and the Hell 399 ER scanners.
Industrial and Technical Education
Dist - INSTRU

Scanners explained 30 MIN
VHS
Color (H A)
$169.00 purchase _ #BXA25XSV; $149.00 purchase _ A25
Describes scanners and how they are used in automotive repair. Consists of two videocassettes and a study guide.
Industrial and Technical Education
Dist - CAMV **Prod** - BERGL 1989
BERGL

Scanning 3 MIN
16mm
Color (G)
$20.00 rental
Juxtaposes religious drama, murder mystery, musicals, horse races and horror films recorded and photographed directly from a television set. Features optically reprinted imagery that was also color tinted by hand. Produced by Paul Glabicki.
Fine Arts; History - United States
Dist - CANCIN

Scanning automotive computer problems 25 MIN
VHS
Color (G H)
$95.00 purchase _ #MG5131V-T
Explains that this sequel to automobile self-diagnosis helps students learn about various `scanning tools to analyze difficult to locate computer system problems.' Provides information on general scanner use, electrical values, modern type analysis, and other tools. Includes information that many advanced automotive repair students might find helpful.
Education; Industrial and Technical Education
Dist - CAMV

Scapegoat 50 MIN
VHS
Watergate series
Color; PAL (H C A)
PdS99 purchase; Not available in the United States or Canada
Investigates the events of the Watergate Affair that led to Richard Nixon's resignation in 1974. Follows the story of John Dean, a targeted scapegoat in the affair who refused to accept the blame for the burglary at the Democratic headquarters. Features both the Watergate investigators and those who were convicted of Watergate crimes. Third in a five - part series.
Civics and Political Systems; History - United States
Dist - BBCENE

Scapular and Deltoid Regions - Unit 9 16 MIN
U-matic / VHS
Gross Anatomy Prosection Demonstration Series
Color (PRO)
Describes the musculature of the scapular and deltoid regions, the boundries and contents of the subdivisions of those regions, and the dorsal scapular region and its muscles, arteries, nerves, and other related structures.
Health and Safety; Science - Natural
Dist - HSCIC **Prod** - HSCIC

The Scar Beneath 28 MIN
16mm
B&W (PRO)
LC FIE65-94
Explores vocational rehabilitation of prison inmates through the story of the successful rehabilitation of a youthful and disfigured first offender.
Health and Safety; Psychology; Sociology
Dist - USNAC **Prod** - USOVR 1964

The Scar Beneath 32 MIN
U-matic
B&W
Describes the vocational rehabilitation of a prison inmate arrested for his first offense.
Guidance and Counseling; Health and Safety; Sociology
Dist - USNAC **Prod** - USNAC 1972

The Scar of Shame 69 MIN
16mm
B&W
Presents a noted production made by blacks, considered to be the equivalent of Hollywood productions made during the same period.
Fine Arts; History - United States
Dist - KITPAR **Prod** - UNKNWN 1927

Scar tissue 7 MIN
16mm
B&W (G)
$18.00 rental
Notes the essential rhythms and emotions of downtown Manhattan while simultaneously undermining them. Concerns the chaste being chased and the captor being captive.
Fine Arts
Dist - CANCIN **Prod** - SUFR 1979

Scarborough - Ontario, Canada 13 MIN
16mm
Color
LC 77-702634
Describes daily life in Scarborough, Ontario. Includes topics such as housing, recreation, business and industry, municipal government and education. Presents the Scarborough Civic Centre.
Geography - World; Sociology
Dist - SCARCC **Prod** - SCARCC 1975

Scarcity 15 MIN
VHS / 16mm
Econ and Me Series
Color (P)
$95.00 purchase, $25.00 rental
Defines scarcity as when people can't have everything they want and must set priorities. Shows children dealing with space as the scarcity and making choices that affect all involved.
Business and Economics
Dist - AITECH **Prod** - AITECH 1989

Scarcity 30 MIN
VHS / U-matic
Economics exchange series; Program 1
Color (T)
LC 82-706413
Presents Dr Willard M Kniep of Arizona State University instructing teachers in the strategies and skills of teaching children economics and consumer education concepts. Focuses on the topic of scarcity by explaining it and then demonstrating specific approaches that teachers can use in their classrooms.
Business and Economics; Education; Home Economics
Dist - GPN **Prod** - KAETTV 1981

Scarcity and planning 16 MIN
16mm / U-matic / VHS
People on market street series
Color (H A)
LC 77-702411
Introduces the concept of scarcity, explaining that people want more and better goods than are available. Relates the economic problem of organizing and coordinating the work of many people to produce desired goods.
Business and Economics; Social Science
Dist - CORF **Prod** - FNDREE 1977

Scare Me 20 MIN
U-matic / VHS
Once upon a Town Series
Color (P I)
Presents literary selections that deal with the excitement of fantasy and the supernatural.
English Language; Literature and Drama
Dist - AITECH **Prod** - MDDE 1977

Scarecrow 115 MIN
16mm
Color
Stars Gene Hackman and Al Pacino as a couple of drifters who team up.
Fine Arts
Dist - TWYMAN **Prod** - WB 1973

The Scarecrow 17 MIN
16mm
B&W (J)
Stars Buster Keaton.
Fine Arts
Dist - TWYMAN **Prod** - MGM 1920

Scarecrow 127 MIN
35mm / 16mm
Color (G) (RUSSIAN WITH ENGLISH SUBTITLES)
$250.00, $300.00 rental
Portrays Nikolai Nikoleyich and his 12 - year - old granddaughter Lena who move into a new town and are scorned by its villagers. Shows how they display the fortitude and courage to persevere and how they depart the town, leaving a permanent imprint upon its inhabitants. Directed by Rolan Bykov.
Fine Arts; Sociology
Dist - KINOIC **Prod** - IFEX 1985

Scarecrow Man 8 MIN
16mm
Color
Explains that Scarecrow Man is a person who has taken it upon himself to expose a person's worst character trait to the community in an attempt to help that person see what he really looks like to his friends and neighbors. Demonstrates that if everyone could see themselves as others do, then they would probably not continue their bad behavioral habits.
Guidance and Counseling
Dist - ECI **Prod** - ECI

Scared, sad and mad 17 MIN
U-matic / BETA / 16mm / VHS
Color (P)
$480.00, $380.00 purchase _ #JR - 5888M
Reveals that the actions of an alcoholic parent can have subtle, yet devastating effects on children. Combines live action and puppetry starring Fergus Bunny to teach youngsters that no child is ever to blame for the problems of alcoholism, that alcoholism is a disease, that hiding a problem won't make it go away or get better, and that steps can be taken to find help.
Health and Safety; Psychology; Sociology
Dist - CORF **Prod** - MITCHG 1989

Scared straight 54 MIN
U-matic / VHS / 16mm
Color (H C A)
$59.95 purchase _ #S01455; LC 79-700008
Presents a documentary about a program in which adolescent offenders visit Rahway Prison in New Jersey and experience the realities of life in a maximum security prison. Shows how a group of criminals serving life sentences convince young delinquents to obey the law. Narrated by actor Peter Falk.
Guidance and Counseling; Sociology
Dist - PFP **Prod** - GWB 1978
UILL

Scared straight - 10 years later 45 MIN
VHS
Color (J H A C)
$295.00 purchase
Updates the results of a meeting between convicts and youth at risk at Rahway State Prison, showing the lives of members of both groups ten years after the initial meeting. Contrasts interviews from past and present, emphasizing that convict - youth programs help deter some from crime. Hosted by Whoopi Goldberg. A television version including the original Scared Straight is also available. Package includes discussion guide.
Social Science; Sociology
Dist - PFP **Prod** - ASHAP

Scaredy - cat
VHS
Bippity boppity bunch series
Color (K P I R)
$14.95 purchase _ #35 - 818 - 8579
Describes how the Bippity Boppity bunch is scared by a 'monster' during a camping trip. Teaches that because God is always present, there is no need to be afraid.
Literature and Drama; Religion and Philosophy
Dist - APH **Prod** - FAMF

Scarf sensations 30 MIN
VHS
Color (J H C G)
$29.95 purchase _ #CCV808
Demonstrates how to add color accents to casual, evening or career wardrobes using scarves. Demonstrates the use of three scarf shapes - bias, oblong and square and how to tie various knots.
Home Economics; Sociology
Dist - CADESF **Prod** - CADESF 1987

Scarf Sensations 30 MIN
VHS
(J H C A)
$29.95 _ #PE300V
Explains how to add color accents to casual evening, or career wardrobes using scarves. Discusses scarf shapes and styles, as well as how to knot scarves in different ways.
Home Economics
Dist - CAMV **Prod** - CAMV

Scarface - Story of the Sundance 15 MIN
VHS / 16mm
Ukrainian Shadow Puppets Series
Color (I) (ENGLISH AND UKRAINIAN)
$175.00 purchase _ #277103
Introduces some of the cultural heritage of the Cree and Blackfoot people of Alberta, Canada, through a Ukrainian bilingual program to reach the Ukrainian commmunity. Contains a unique blend of myths and legends and original music and artwork commissioned from Cree and Blackfoot artists with Ukrainian silhouette puppets. 'Scarface - Story Of The Sundance' presents a mythical hero who undergoes severe trials on earth before he triumphs. Scarface travels to the sun to remove a scar from his face so he can marry the beautiful Sun Maiden. He returns, marries the maiden, and together they create the rituals of the Sundance. Includes a booklet with Ukrainian language transcripts.
Geography - World; History - World; Literature and Drama; Religion and Philosophy; Social Science; Sociology
Dist - ACCESS **Prod** - ACCESS 1987

Scarfing Safely 7 MIN
U-matic / VHS
Steel Making Series
Color (IND)
Discusses necessity of understanding the job and procedures of scarfing in order to know how to react to a problem in scarfing.
Business and Economics; Industrial and Technical Education
Dist - LEIKID **Prod** - LEIKID

The Scariest Place on Earth 23 MIN
U-matic / VHS
Color (K)
Visits the deep Columbian rainforest where a variety of animals reside, including the anaconda, cayman crocodile and piranha.
Geography - World; Science - Natural
Dist - NWLDPR **Prod** - NWLDPR 1982

Scarlatti, Debussy and Ravel 52 MIN
VHS
Color (G)
$19.95 purchase _ #1250
Presents a concert of Scarlatti, Debussy And Ravel produced in the Chateau de Sceaux. Features Argerich, Maisky and Freire performing.
Fine Arts
Dist - KULTUR

Scarlet and Gold 14 MIN
16mm
Journal Series
Color
LC 76-702093
Traces the early history of the North - West Mounted Police of Canada.
Civics and Political Systems; History - World
Dist - FIARTS **Prod** - FIARTS 1975

The Scarlet letter 232 MIN
VHS / U-matic
Color (G)
$200.00, $350.00 purchase _ #SCAR - 000L
Presents Nathaniel Hawthorne's 'The Scarlet Letter,' a tale set in Puritan America. Tells the story of Hester Prynne, a woman accused of adultery, and her secret lover, Rev Arthur Dimmesdale, the father of her child. Stars Meg Foster and John Heard. Presented in four 58 - minute episodes.
Literature and Drama
Dist - PBS **Prod** - WGBHTV 1980

The Scarlet Letter
Cassette / 16mm
Now Age Reading Programs, Set 2 Series
Color (I J)
$9.95 purchase _ #8F - PN681948
Brings a classic tale to young readers. Filmstrip set includes filmstrip, cassette, corresponding book, classroom exercise materials and a poster. The read - along set includes student activity book, cassette, and paperback.
English Language; Literature and Drama
Dist - MAFEX

The Scarlet letter 69 MIN
VHS
B&W (J H)
$39.00 purchase _ #04518 - 126; $29.00 purchase _ #04518 - 85
Presents a 1934 film version of The Scarlet Letter by Nathaniel Hawthorne.
Literature and Drama; Sociology
Dist - GA **Prod** - GA
CHUMAN

The Scarlet Pen Pal 5 MIN
VHS / U-matic
Write on, Set 2 Series
Color (J H)
Shows how to develop paragraphs through the use of contrast.
English Language
Dist - CTI **Prod** - CTI

The Scarlet pimpernel 98 MIN
VHS
B&W (H C)
$49.00 purchase _ #04519 - 126
Stars Leslie Howard and Merle Oberon in a swashbuckling classic with richly detailed sets and costumes. Adapts the novel by Baroness Orczy.
Fine Arts; Literature and Drama
Dist - GA **Prod** - GA

Scarlet Street 103 MIN
16mm
B&W
Tells the tragic story of a middle - aged cashier who falls in love with a golddigger. Stars Edward G Robinson and Joan Bennett.
Fine Arts
Dist - REELIM **Prod** - UPCI 1945

Scars 12 MIN
U-matic
Color (C)
$250.00 purchase, $35.00, $45.00 rental
Presents interviews with four women who experienced self - mutilation of their bodies. Deals with the issues of emotional release, guilt, disapproval, and suicide. Produced by Lorna Boschman.
Sociology
Dist - WMENIF

Scarves - tie into a great look 25 MIN
VHS
Color (H C G)
$29.95 purchase _ #LK100V
Shows how to use scarves as fashion accessories 25 different ways.
Home Economics
Dist - CAMV

The Scary movie 9 MIN
16mm
B&W (H C A)
$30.00 rental
Explores feminism, psychoanalytic theory, home movie aesthetics, film genre conventions, and the notion of self-reflexivity in film. Plays with Freudian psychoanalytic thinking by conspicuously lacking men even when the narrative calls for male roles. Combines seriousness and gravity with wit and frankness. Directed by Peggy Ahwesh.
Psychology; Sociology
Dist - CANCIN

Scary poems for rotten kids
CD-ROM
Discis Books on CD - ROM
(P I) (SPANISH)
$84.00 purchase _ #2558
Contains the original text and illustrations of Scary Poems for Rotten Kids by Sean O'Huigin. Enhances understanding with real voices, music, and sound effects. Every word in the text has an in - context explanation, pronunciation and syllables, available through a click of the mouse. Spanish - English version available for an extra $5 per disc. For Macintosh Classics, Plus, II and SE computers, requires 1MB of RAM, one floppy disk drive, and an Apple compatible CD - ROM drive.
English Language; Literature and Drama
Dist - BEP

Scary stories 35 MIN
VHS
Storytellers collection series
Color (K P I)
$14.95 purchase _ #ATL421
Offers four scary stories. Features four of the United States' most accomplished storytellers. Part of a four - part series.
Literature and Drama
Dist - KNOWUN

Scattered remains 14 MIN
16mm
Color (G)
$30.00 rental
Creates a multifaceted portrait of poet and filmmaker James Broughton acting out his verses in unlikely situations and photographed by Joel Singer.
Fine Arts; Literature and Drama
Dist - CANCIN **Prod** - BROUGH 1988

Scattering and Absorption Loses 40 MIN
U-matic / VHS
Integrated Optics Series
Color (C)
Discusses the scattering and absorption losses experienced by waves propagating in various waveguides. Deals with theoretical expressions for loss derived and illustrated with experimentally measured data.
Science - Physical
Dist - UDEL **Prod** - UDEL

Scattering Demonstrations using Microwaves 14 MIN
16mm
College Physics Film Series
B&W (C)
LC 78-709339
Demonstrates the polarization and intensity of 12mm microwaves scattered by various metallic objects, some much larger, others much smaller, than the microwavelength. Uses flat surfaces, wire grating, wires

and small beads. Shows radiation scattered from the small beads to be linearly polarized, even when the incident radiation is circularly polarized. Also shows how light is polarized as it is scattered by the air molecules in the atmosphere.
Science - Physical
Dist - MLA **Prod** - EDS 1970

Scattering stars 2 MIN
16mm
B&W (H C A)
$20.00 rental
Features a night-time sky exploding with stars while gleaming male body parts light up. Uses solarisation to make the fireworks seem to emerge from the very center of the human bodies. Alludes to the after-glow of a physical encounter. Produced by Matthias Muller.
Science - Natural; Science - Physical
Dist - CANCIN

Scavengers 49 MIN
VHS
Color (G)
$375.00 purchase, $75.00 rental
Follows the group of poor in Brazilian cities who earn their livings scavenging in the immense urban garbage dumps, searching for whatever they can find to sell - paper, plastic, scrap metal, tin cans - as well as whatever they can find to eat. Records, without judgment or narration, five scavengers who work at the Itaoca garbage dump in Sao Goncalo, Rio de Janeiro, as they go about their daily routines with friends and families. Produced by Eduardo Coutinho.
Business and Economics; Fine Arts; Sociology
Dist - FIRS

SCBA 1 - introduction and overview 21 MIN
VHS
Firefighter I series
Color (IND)
$130.00 purchase _ #35640
Presents one part of a 19 - part series that is the teaching companion for IFSTA's Essentials of Fire Fighting manual. Features the components, functions and safety features of various SCBA. Explains the limitations of the equipment. Gives an overview of the hazardous environments that require SCBA use. Based on Chapter 3.
Health and Safety; Science - Physical; Social Science
Dist - OKSU **Prod** - ACCTRA

SCBA 2 - use and maintenance 18 MIN
VHS
Firefighter I series
Color (IND)
$130.00 purchase _ #35641
Presents one part of a 19 - part series that is the teaching companion for IFSTA's Essentials of Fire Fighting manual. Demonstrates correct procedures for donning and doffing. Shows how to change cylinders at an emergency scene. Presents inspection and maintenance tasks. Explains safety precautions for using SCBA in emergency situations. Based on Chapter 3.
Health and Safety; Science - Physical; Social Science
Dist - OKSU **Prod** - ACCTRA

Scenario Du Film 'Passion' 53 MIN
U-matic / VHS
Color (FRENCH AND ENGLISH)
A French language version of the videotape Scenario of the Film 'Passion.' Subtitles in English. Provides a tour of Jean - Luc Godard's production facility. Describes his methods.
Fine Arts; Foreign Language
Dist - KITCHN **Prod** - KITCHN

Scenarios for Discussion 16 MIN
U-matic
Nursing Preceptorship Series
(PRO)
Covers six dramatized versions of problems a recent graduate nurse is liable to face.
Health and Safety
Dist - ACCESS **Prod** - ACCESS 1983

Scene building 30 MIN
VHS / 16mm
Art of decorating cakes series
(G)
$49.00 purchase _ #BCD12
Instructs in the art of cake decorating. Shows how to build a scene around plastic items to better emphasize the item and make an attractive cake. Shows how to use parts of the cake to build mountains and roads. Taught by master cake decorator Leon Simmons.
Home Economics; Industrial and Technical Education
Dist - RMIBHF **Prod** - RMIBHF

The Scene changes 52 MIN
U-matic / VHS / 16mm
Magic of dance series
Color (J)
Presents Margot Fonteyn exploring her own world of dance, from the dominance of the ballerina in the 1930s to the great male dancers of the '60s and '70s.
Fine Arts
Dist - TIMLIF **Prod** - BBCTV 1980

The Scene is set
16mm
Color
Introduces set theory, algebra, topology, and finite machine computations. Highlights the relationship between set theory and the rest of mathematics.
Mathematics
Dist - OPENU **Prod** - OPENU

Scene of the Crime 30 MIN
U-matic / VHS
Burglar - Proofing Series
Color
Health and Safety; Sociology
Dist - MDCPB **Prod** - MDCPB

Scene of the crime 90 MIN
35mm / 16mm / VHS
Color (G) (FRENCH WITH ENGLISH SUBTITLES)
$200.00, $250.00 rental
Stars Catherine Deneuve and Danielle Darrieux in a thriller about a woman and her 14 - year - old son who become involved with an escaped convict. Directed by Andre Techine.
Fine Arts; Literature and Drama
Dist - KINOIC

Scene Playing 15 MIN
U-matic / VHS
Word Shop Series
Color (P)
Literature and Drama
Dist - WETATV **Prod** - WETATV

Scene - politic 68, an artist's report 59 MIN
16mm
Artist as a reporter series
Color (J)
LC 71-701733
Artist - reporter Franklin Mc Mahon presents a review of the presidential campaign of 1968. Follows the candidates from the primary campaigns in New Hampshire, Wisconsin, Indiana, Oregon, California and to both political conventions, and through the final campaigns to the election.
Civics and Political Systems
Dist - ROCSS **Prod** - ROCSS 1968

Scenery 30 MIN
Videoreel / VT2
Trains, Tracks and Trestles Series
Color
Physical Education and Recreation
Dist - PBS **Prod** - WMVSTV

Scenes at a fountain and the limit 43 MIN
VHS
Glasnost film festival series
Color (H C G T A) (RUSSIAN (ENGLISH SUBTITLES))
$59.95 purchase, $35.00 rental
Presents two of the Soviet films shown at the Glasnost Film Festival. 'Scenes At A Fountain' documents the struggle of Soviet firefighters against a natural gas fire which burned for one year on the shore of the Caspian Sea. Reveals that the firefighters had to battle a 600 - foot high blaze, and that one man died from coming too close. 'The Limit' scrutinizes the negative social consequences of alcoholism in Soviet families.
Business and Economics; Civics and Political Systems; History - World; Sociology
Dist - EFVP

Scenes de la vie Francaise series

Avignon	11 MIN
La Ciotat	31 MIN
Paris	26 MIN

Dist - CANCIN

Scenes from a Divorce 20 MIN
U-matic / VHS
B&W
Follows a couple working through stages encountered during the course of a divorce, including a typical argument and early realization of questions about custody.
Sociology
Dist - UWISC **Prod** - UWISC 1978

Scenes from a marriage 168 MIN
VHS
Color (G)
$39.95 purchase _ #SCE020
Portrays the disintegration of a marriage. Features Liv Ullman as a happily married lawyer whose husband suddenly leaves her for another woman. Ingmar Bergman skillfully edited the story's original six television episodes into this feature - length production.
Fine Arts; Psychology; Sociology
Dist - HOMVIS **Prod** - JANUS 1974

Scenes from Great Expectations by Charles Dickens 30 MIN
U-matic / VHS
Color (H C)
$250.00 purchase _ #HP - 6089C
Dramatizes scenes from the novel 'Great Expectations' by Charles Dickens which feature its more memorable characters. Includes Pip, Magwitch, Miss Havisham, Estella, Jaegers and others.
Literature and Drama
Dist - CORF **Prod** - BBCTV 1990

Scenes from New York City Transit 17 MIN
16mm
Color (G)
Portrays the loneliness and alienation that subway riders experience in the New York City Subway system.
Fine Arts; Geography - United States; Social Science; Sociology
Dist - CRAR **Prod** - CRAR 1972

Scenes from the Holocaust 10 MIN
16mm
Color (G)
$115.00 purchase, $20.00 rental _ #HPF - 728, #HRF - 728
Uses pen, pencil and charcoal sketches by Jewish artists who were among the millions sent to the death camps of Nazi Germany during World War II. Offers minimal narration and a musical soundtrack.
Fine Arts; History - World; Sociology
Dist - ADL **Prod** - ADL

Scenes from the life of Andy Warhol 36 MIN
16mm
Color (G)
$100.00 rental
Features Jonas Mekas' film diaries related to Andy Warhol from the years 1965 - 1982. Captures the Velvet Underground starring Nico at the Dom in the opening segment and ends with the Mass for Warhol at St. Patrick's Cathedral. The list of musicians, artists, performers, writers and various glitterati appearing in this film is seemingly endless. Completed in June 1990.
Fine Arts
Dist - CANCIN

Scenes from the Microwar 24 MIN
U-matic / VHS
Sherry Millner Series
Color (G)
$250.00, $200.00 purchase, $50.00 rental
Follows the olive drab misadventures of a family hypnotized by the Space Wars of Ronald Reagan and Rambo - Commando fashions. Reveals that everything they own, including the car and shower curtains, is in camouflage, and a typical day is spent eating C - rations with their 2 - year - old and training with Uzi machine guns.
Civics and Political Systems; Sociology
Dist - WMEN **Prod** - SHEMIL 1985

Scenes from the workplace 29 MIN
16mm
Color (A)
Presents eight different confrontational situations between a worker and a supervisor. Discusses contract language and what does and does not constitute a union grievance.
Business and Economics; Psychology; Sociology
Dist - AFLCIO USNAC **Prod** - USDL USDELR 1975

Scenes from Travel in Colombia 26 MIN
16mm / U-matic / VHS
Color (J)
LC 81-700931
Presents a sampler of the lives, places and events which make up Colombia, South America. Provides insights into the look and feel of Colombia, as well as Latin America as a whole.
Geography - World
Dist - PHENIX **Prod** - SMITD 1978

Scenes from under childhood section no 1 25 MIN
16mm
Color (G)
$69.00 rental, $1087.00 purchase
Says filmmaker Brakhage, '...a shattering of the myths of childhood through revelation of the extremes of violent terror and overwhelming joy of that world darkened to most adults by their sentimental remembering of it...'
Fine Arts; Psychology
Dist - CANCIN **Prod** - BRAKS 1967

Scenes from under childhood section no 2 40 MIN
16mm
Color (G)
$104.00 rental, $1639.00 purchase
Says filmmaker Brakhage, '...a shattering of the myths of childhood through revelation of the extremes of violent terror and overwhelming joy of that world darkened to most adults by their sentimental remembering of it...'

Fine Arts; Psychology
Dist - CANCIN **Prod** - BRAKS 1969

Scenes from under childhood section no 3 25 MIN
16mm
Color (G)
$69.00 rental, $1087.00 purchase
Says filmmaker Brakhage, '...a shattering of the myths of childhood through revelation of the extremes of violent terror and overwhelming joy of that world darkened to most adults by their sentimental remembering of it...'
Fine Arts; Psychology
Dist - CANCIN **Prod** - BRAKS 1969

Scenes from under childhood section no 4 45 MIN
16mm
Color (G)
$104.00 rental, $1639.00 purchase
Says filmmaker Brakhage, '...a shattering of the myths of childhood through revelation of the extremes of violent terror and overwhelming joy of that world darkened to most adults by their sentimental remembering of it...'
Fine Arts; Psychology
Dist - CANCIN **Prod** - BRAKS 1970

Scenes of Natural Reserve 13 MIN
16mm
Color
Shows rare animal and bird species roaming freely in Israel's natural reserves.
Geography - World; Science - Natural
Dist - ALDEN **Prod** - ALDEN

Scenes of the plateaulands and how they came to be series
Presents five parts which overview the geological forces that formed the Colorado Plateau. Includes footage of Colorado, Utah and Arizona, Grand Canyon, Bryce Canyon, Zion National Park, Arches, Bridges, Dinosaur, Petrified Forest and Canyonlands National Parks. Titles include Rocks of the Plateaulands; The Work of Running Water; Erosion in the Plateaulands; Geology in the Plateaulands; and Meteor Craters and Cliff Dwellers. Available on five separate cassettes or on a single cassette.
Erosion in the plateaulands 13 MIN
Geology in the plateaulands 16 MIN
Meteor craters and cliff dwellings 12 MIN
Rocks of the plateaulands 24 MIN
The Work of running water 27 MIN
Dist - INSTRU

Scenes with Allen Jones 28 MIN
16mm
Color (H C)
$600.00 purchase, $75.00 rental
Features Allen Jones, one of the most important early figures of the Pop Art movement in Britain, at work in his London studio.
Fine Arts
Dist - BLACKW **Prod** - BLACKW 1973

Scenic photography 30 MIN
VHS
Color (G)
$24.95 purchase _ #S00940
Presents techniques for improving the quality of scenic photography.
Fine Arts; Industrial and Technical Education
Dist - UILL **Prod** - EKC

The Scenic Route 76 MIN
16mm
Color (G)
Presents an independent production by Mark Rappaport. Offers an incestuous triangle formed by two sisters and a man.
Fine Arts; Psychology; Sociology
Dist - FIRS

Scenic Seattle 30 MIN
VHS
Color (G)
$29.95 purchase _ #S01622
Tours Seattle, a city of lakes, rivers and streams. Shows the many scenic, cultural and tourist attractions of the area.
Geography - United States
Dist - UILL

Scenic wonders of America 180 MIN
VHS
Color (G)
$56.96 purchase
Presents a three videocassette scenic tour of America. Includes Atlantic Vistas, American West and Pacific Frontiers.
Geography - United States
Dist - READER **Prod** - READER 1991

Scenic wonders of America series
Presents three videos on the scenic wonders of America. Includes American West, Atlantic Vistas and Pacific Frontiers.
American West 60 MIN
Atlantic vistas 60 MIN
Pacific frontiers 60 MIN
Dist - APRESS **Prod** - READ 1991

Scenting the money 50 MIN
VHS
Look series
Color (A)
PdS99 purchase _ Unavailable in the USA
Reveals that fashion is one of the largest industries in the world, but haute couture alone does not pay. Shows how a designer may make a name through the publicity given by the international media and that, following such media success and glamour, it can be licensed as a valuable commodity. Features interviews with top designers - Donna Karan, Calvin Klein, and Christian Lacroix. Part of a six-part series.
Home Economics
Dist - BBCENE

Schatzi 3 MIN
16mm
B&W (G)
$10.00 rental
Explores the irony of a formal image device and interacts with the viewer only to reveal that the picture is of an army officer surveying a field of corpses.
Fine Arts; Industrial and Technical Education
Dist - CANCIN **Prod** - KRENKU 1968

Schechter Revisited at Cambridge University 30 MIN
16mm
Eternal Light Series
B&W (H C A)
LC 71-700953
Presents a panel discussion of Solomon Schechter and his discovery of the Cairo Genizah manuscripts. (Kinescope).
Religion and Philosophy
Dist - NAAJS **Prod** - JTS 1966

The Schedule masters 25 MIN
16mm
Color (GERMAN DUTCH FRENCH ITALIAN NORWEGIAN)
LC 80-700412; 80 - 700412
Traces the development of the 40 series tractors and introduces each model. Emphasizes Deere and Company's commitment to its European farming customers.
Agriculture; Business and Economics; Foreign Language
Dist - DEERE **Prod** - DEERE 1979

Scheduling 30 MIN
VHS / U-matic
Maintenance Management Series
Color
Delineates principles of scheduling. Explores scheduling techniques. Covers emergency maintenance.
Business and Economics; Psychology
Dist - ITCORP **Prod** - ITCORP

Scheduling Operation Sequence 60 MIN
BETA / VHS
Manufacturing Series
(IND)
Describes how to control the sequence of operation starts in the work centers. Defines dispatch list, work in process status records and how to verify the contents of records.
Business and Economics
Dist - COMSRV **Prod** - COMSRV 1986

Scheduling the Operation Desert Storm airlift - An Advanced automated scheduling support system
VHS
Color (C PRO G)
$150.00 purchase _ #91.07
Focuses on an airlift deployment analysis system planned for the summer of 1991 and accelerated on the shortest of notice for Operation Desert Storm. Reveals that a dynamic programming algorithm is embedded within a rule - based heuristic, within constraints, for the most efficient delivery of cargo with a minimum of flying hours. An additional benefit is the ability to schedule hundreds of missions in minutes, instead of hours, as required by traditional approaches. Military Airlift Command. Michael R Hilliard, Rajendra S Solanki, Ingrid K Busch, Cheng Liu, Ronald D Kraemer, Glen Harrison.
Business and Economics; Social Science
Dist - INMASC

Scheduling Your Time 29 MIN
VHS / U-matic
Personal Time Management Series
Color
Business and Economics
Dist - DELTAK **Prod** - TELSTR

Scheduling Your Time and Others' Time 30 MIN
U-matic / VHS
Personal Time Management Series
Color
Helps the viewer examine a personal time schedule. Gives consideration to the scheduling time of others.
Business and Economics; Psychology
Dist - TELSTR **Prod** - TELSTR

Schematic diagrams 60 MIN
U-matic / VHS
Electrical maintenance training series; Module C - Electrical print reading
Color (IND)
Industrial and Technical Education
Dist - LEIKID **Prod** - LEIKID

Scherben 48 MIN
16mm
B&W ((GERMAN SUBTITLES))
A silent motion picture with German subtitles. Tells the story of a railway inspector, who arrives at a lonely block station and seduces the signalmaster's daughter. Relates how they are discovered by the suspicious mother who, brokenhearted, walks into the snow to pray and freezes to death. Continues as the daughter implores the inspector to take her to town but is rejected, and ends with the daughter taking revenge by asking her father to demand satisfaction.
Fine Arts; Foreign Language
Dist - WSTGLC **Prod** - WSTGLC 1921

Schindler 79 MIN
VHS
Color; PAL (H)
PdS40 purchase
Examines the life of Oskar Schindler, who was a German spy. Reveals that he saved thousands of Jews from Hitler's extermination camps during World War II. Uses archival footage and interviews with Schindler's wife and mistress. Contact distributor about availability outside the United Kingdom.
Civics and Political Systems; Fine Arts; History - World
Dist - ACADEM

Schistosomes in the Primary Host 7 MIN
16mm
Schistosomiasis Mansoni Study Films Series
B&W
LC FIE53-186
Shows through photomicrography the development of male and female schistosomes in various stages of growth in rabbit and mouse. For professional use.
Health and Safety
Dist - USNAC **Prod** - USPHS 1948

Schistosomiasis Mansoni Study Films Series
Schistosomes in the Primary Host 7 MIN
Dist - USNAC

Schizophrenia 28 MIN
U-matic / VHS
Color (G)
$249.00, $149.00 purchase _ #AD - 1100
Offers basic information about schizophrenia. Features Dr E Fuller Torrey, author of 'Surviving Schizophrenia - A Family Manual,' who reviews the suspected causes, symptoms, prognosis and the steps to be taken by family members.
Health and Safety; Psychology; Sociology
Dist - FOTH **Prod** - FOTH

Schizophrenia - acute care 23 MIN
BETA / VHS / U-matic
Psychopathologies - descriptions and interventions series
Color (C PRO)
$150.00 purchase _ #134.8
Presents a video transfer from slide program which discusses the role of the health professional caring for a patient with an acute psychotic episode. Examines measures such as reducing anxiety, establishing control and monitoring the patient's physical health. Highlights therapeutic intervention techniques. Part of a series on psychopathologies.
Health and Safety; Psychology
Dist - CONMED **Prod** - CONMED

Schizophrenia - causation 20 MIN
VHS / U-matic / BETA
Psychopathologies - descriptions and interventions series
Color (C PRO)
$150.00 purchase _ #134.6
Presents a video transfer from slide program which discusses several theories regarding the etiology of schizophrenia - the biological theories - genetic and biochemical; the family theories, the sociological theories; and the psychoanalytic theories. Discusses the premorbid personality of the individual prone to schizophrenia. Part of a series on psychopathologies.
Health and Safety; Psychology
Dist - CONMED **Prod** - CONMED

Schizophrenia of working for the war 27 MIN
16mm
Color (G)
$40.00 rental
Illuminates the dilemma of engineers who produced weapons for the Vietnam war, despite their opposition to it. Portrays the actual men, and their stories, employed at some of the most prestigious California institutes. Three types of responses are distinguished - the rationalizer, who reasons that he makes weapons as protective devices; the drop - out, who actually quits his job; and the organizer, who opposes the war openly and is fired from his job only to spearhead a major non - profit group which helps defense engineers segue into peace - oriented employment. Produced by Leonard Henny.
Civics and Political Systems; Sociology
Dist - CANCIN

Schizophrenia - Out of Mind 52 MIN
VHS / 16mm
Color (A)
$179.00 purchase, $75.00 rental _ #OD - 2213
Depicts the lives of schizophrenics and the efforts of family and mental health care professionals to deal with their illness. Originally shown on the CBS television program 48 Hours.
Health and Safety; Psychology
Dist - FOTH

Schizophrenia - rehabilitation 17 MIN
BETA / VHS / U-matic
Psychopathologies - descriptions and interventions series
Color (C PRO)
$150.00 purchase _ #134.9
Presents a video transfer from slide program which discusses some of the problems faced by a person recovering from a psychotic episode. Discusses discharge planning for patients vulnerable to psychosis. Details reentry problems a patient encounters upon leaving the hospital. Part of a series on psychopathologies.
Health and Safety; Psychology
Dist - CONMED **Prod** - CONMED

Schizophrenia - Removing the Veil 30 MIN
VHS
Color (J)
LC 85-703934
Explores the symptoms, causes and treatment of schizophrenia. Defines the term, dispels misconceptions and provides examples of the major types.
Psychology
Dist - HRMC **Prod** - HRMC

Schizophrenia - Removing the Veil Series
Causes and treatment
What is Schizophrenia
Dist - IBIS

Schizophrenia Series
Interview with a Patient Discussing Her Schizophrenic Episode 60 MIN
Psychotherapy of the Schizophrenic 60 MIN
Dist - HEMUL

Schizophrenia - symptomology 22 MIN
BETA / VHS / U-matic
Psychopathologies - descriptions and interventions series
Color (C PRO)
$150.00 purchase _ #134.7
Presents a video transfer from slide program which describes Bleuler's '4 - D' classification of schizophrenia. Discusses the cognitive and sensory aberrations found in some patients with the disorder. Defines illusions, hallucinations and delusions and discusses them as symptoms of schizophrenia. Part of a series on psychopathologies.
Health and Safety; Psychology
Dist - CONMED **Prod** - CONMED

Schizophrenia - the Shattered Mirror 60 MIN
U-matic / VHS / 16mm
B&W (C A)
LC FIA67-593
Examines some experiences of victims of schizophrenia. Reviews the research being conducted toward developing a better knowledge of the disease.
Psychology
Dist - IU **Prod** - NET 1967

Schizophrenic disorders - case numbers 9 - 12 35 MIN
VHS / U-matic
Psychopathology - diagnostic vignettes series
Color (C A)
Represents classic patterns of schizophrenia, emphasizing the heterogeneity of this category. Shows patients exhibiting various signs of formal thought disorder, including derailment, tangentiality, neologisms, poverty of content of speech, and illogicality.
Health and Safety; Psychology
Dist - IU **Prod** - IU 1984

Schizophrenic Disorders, Psychoses not Elsewhere Classified, and Paranoid Disorders 66 MIN
U-matic / VHS
Psychiatry Learning System Pt 2 - Disorders Series
Color (PRO)
Teaches how to diagnose schizophrenia, paranoid disorders, and some psychoses.
Health and Safety; Psychology
Dist - HSCIC **Prod** - HSCIC 1982

The Schizophrenic patient - Part 3 15 MIN
U-matic / VHS
Caring for the psychiatric patient series
Color (PRO)
$200.00 purchase, $40.00 rental _ #4263S, #4263V
Outlines the major steps in coping with the schizophrenic patient - immediate recognition of the patient's distorted perception, removal of harmful objects, including shoelaces, formal and careful communications with the patient to avoid words or actions that could be misinterpreted, and physical restraint, if necessary. Part of a four - part series on psychiatric nursing care which stresses the integration of physical and psychological care.
Health and Safety
Dist - AJN **Prod** - SEH 1985

Schizophrenic Superman 5 MIN
16mm
Color
LC 77-702636
Discusses sex and violence in comic books.
Literature and Drama; Psychology; Sociology
Dist - CANFDC **Prod** - PSYMED 1973

Schizophrenics in the Streets 28 MIN
U-matic / VHS
Color (G)
$249.00, $149.00 purchase _ #AD - 2030
Features Dr E Fuller Torrey, author of 'Surviving Schizophrenia - A Family Manual,' who examines the results of emptying psychiatric facilities and putting patients back into society with a bottle of pills in their pocket and the hope that their families can or will provide the sheltered environment they need. Views the resulting phenomenon of tens of thousands of mentally ill living on the streets - or dying in them, an urban danger and an economic disaster.
Health and Safety; Psychology; Sociology
Dist - FOTH **Prod** - FOTH

Schlact Um Berline 85 MIN
16mm
B&W
Portrays Stalin, Hitler, Rossevelt and Churchill during decisive phases of World War II.
History - World
Dist - WSTGLC **Prod** - WSTGLC 1969

Schlock it to 'Em 25 MIN
16mm / VHS / BETA
Color
LC 77-702524
Shows correspondent Michael Maclear in Hollywood, California, where he reports on the film and television industry. Notes what he considers to be the increasing cultural mindlessness of an industry where mediocrity abounds with violence and sadistic sex and with exploitaton films which seem to reflect the general malaise of North America.
Business and Economics; Fine Arts; Guidance and Counseling; Sociology
Dist - CTV **Prod** - CTV 1976

Schloss Johannisberg, Germany 26 MIN
U-matic / VHS / 16mm
Place in Europe Series
Color (H C A) (GERMAN)
Presents Schloss Johannisberg in Germany, which was built as a small monastery in the year 860. It was destroyed by Royal Air Force bombers during the second World War and reconstructed on the original foundations by the castle's present - day owners, descendants of Prince Metternich.
Geography - World
Dist - MEDIAG **Prod** - THAMES 1975

Schloss Valduz - Liechtenstein 26 MIN
U-matic / VHS / 16mm
Place in Europe Series
Color (H C A)
Shows the descendants of Liechtenstein's ruling family living in a small apartment within their huge thirteenth - century castle, which houses the world's largest private art collection. The income of this smallest country in the world is from forestry, agriculture and banking.
Geography - World
Dist - MEDIAG **Prod** - THAMES 1975

Schloss Vogeloed 60 MIN
16mm
B&W ((GERMAN SUBTITLES))
A silent motion picture with German subtitles. Tells the story Of Count Oetsch, who is suspected of having murdered his brother, and in the disguise of a priest is able to expose the real murderer.
Fine Arts; Foreign Language
Dist - WSTGLC **Prod** - WSTGLC 1921

Schmeerguntz 15 MIN
16mm
B&W (G)
$40.00 rental
Satirizes the American home which hides its animal functions beneath a shiny public surface.
Fine Arts; Literature and Drama
Dist - CANCIN **Prod** - NELSOG 1966

Schmid Membrane Model - Non - Equilibrium Thermodynamics of Electrophoresis and 30 MIN
U-matic / VHS
Colloids and Surface Chemistry Electrokinetics and Membrane - - 'Series
B&W
Shows Schmid membrane model. Teaches non - equilibrium thermodynamics of electrophoresis and sedimentation potential.
Science - Physical
Dist - MIOT **Prod** - MIOT

Schmid Membrane Model, Non - Equilibrium Thermodynamics of Electrophoresis and 30 MIN
U-matic / VHS
Colloid and Surface Chemistry - Electrokinetics and Membrane Series
Color
Discusses the Schmid membrane model, non - equilibrium thermodynamics of electrophoresis and sedimentation potential.
Science; Science - Physical
Dist - KALMIA **Prod** - KALMIA

Schneegloeckchen Bluehen Im September 109 MIN
16mm
Color (GERMAN (ENGLISH SUBTITLES))
Tells the story of two blue - collar workers employed by a large corporation. Focuses on some of the union battles in 1971 and 1972, and the negotiations to obtain a cost of living increase for the workers in 1973. Brings to light the general fear of all workers that they will lose their jobs, and thus their general reluctance to participate actively in union conflicts.
Business and Economics; Foreign Language; Sociology
Dist - WSTGLC **Prod** - WSTGLC 1974

Schneeweisschen Und Rosenrot 62 MIN
16mm
Color
Relates the fairytale by the Grimm brothers called Snow White And Rose Red.
Fine Arts; Literature and Drama
Dist - WSTGLC **Prod** - WSTGLC 1955

The Scholar in Society - Northrop Frye in Conversation 28 MIN
16mm
Color (G)
_ #106C 0184 052
Interviews Canada's foremost literary critic Northrop Frye who talks on social issues, language, democracy and the role of the modern university. Claims that the university is a place where individual liberty becomes possible.
Civics and Political Systems; Education; History - World; Literature and Drama
Dist - CFLMDC **Prod** - NFBC 1984

Schonzeit Fuer Fuechse 92 MIN
16mm
B&W (GERMAN (ENGLISH SUBTITLES))
Traces the reactions of two young men in their late twenties who suddenly realize that they have reached the peak of their lives.
Foreign Language; Sociology
Dist - WSTGLC **Prod** - WSTGLC 1965

School 30 MIN
U-matic
Today's Special Series
Color (K P)
Develops language arts skills in children. Programs are thematically designed around subjects of interest to youngsters. Action takes place in a department store where people, mannequins, puppets, comic characters and special guests present a light hearted approach to language arts.
Fine Arts; Literature and Drama; Psychology
Dist - TVOTAR **Prod** - TVOTAR 1985

School 15 MIN
16mm
Off to Adventure Series
Color (P I J)
Geography - World; Social Science
Dist - YALEDV **Prod** - YALEDV

School 29 MIN
VHS / 16mm
Villa Alegre Series
Color (P T)
$46.00 rental _ #VILA - 126
Presents educational material in both Spanish and English.
Education; Social Science
Dist - PBS

School 25 MIN
VHS
Dragon's tongue series
Color (J H G)
$195.00 purchase
Teaches basics of Putonghua, China's official language. Presents one video in a series of nineteen that help students develop comprehension skills by using only Chinese - no subtitles. Shows authentic scenes of Chinese homes, cities and the countryside. Features Colin Mackerras of Griffith University.
Foreign Language
Dist - LANDMK

School - Age Child 41 MIN
U-matic / VHS
Infancy through Adolescence Series
Color
Shows the refinement of motor skills and continuous activity of the child aged six to 12. Demonstrates continual socialization activities via play activities.
Psychology
Dist - AJN **Prod** - WSUN

School age children - Vol 2 52 MIN
VHS / 16mm
Art of parenting video series
Color (G)
$69.95 purchase
Offers tips, suggestions and solutions to parenting problems. Focuses on school age children. Considers homework, no friends, self - esteem, divorce, latch key kids, talking about sex, alternatives to spanking, and more. Part of a three - part series on the art of parenting which features Evelyn Peterson, family life education expert.
Social Science; Sociology
Dist - PROSOR

The School - age connection 20 MIN
VHS
Training for child care providers series
Color (H A)
$89.95 purchase _ #CEVK20366V
Discusses how to provide care for elementary school children. Provides examples of activities that can be used to promote self - awareness, appreciation from others, and the importance of goal - setting. Includes a leader's guide and reproducible study materials.
Health and Safety; Psychology
Dist - CAMV

The School - age connection 19 MIN
VHS
Color (H A T G)
$59.95 purchase _ #CV970
Focuses on after school care for elementary school children. Stresses the importance of continuing to build and promote self - esteem once a child has entered school. Presents over 20 examples of activities which promote self - awareness, appreciation of others and the importance of goal setting. Guide available separately.
Fine Arts; Health and Safety; Home Economics; Psychology; Social Science
Dist - AAVIM **Prod** - AAVIM

School and Classrooms 29 MIN
U-matic / VHS
Mainstreaming the Exceptional Child Series
Color (T)
Education; Psychology
Dist - FI **Prod** - MFFD

School and community 25 MIN
VHS
Discover Korea series
Color (I J H)
$27.95 purchase _ #1102 - 02
Explores school and community life in Korea. Presents part of a three - part series which examines Korean culture and society as seen through the eyes of children. Includes a poster and a teacher's guide.
Geography - World
Dist - KNOWUN

School and School Bus Safety 25 MIN
VHS
Color (P)
$18.95 purchase _ #VS101 - 10
Emphasizes safety awareness for students while on the school bus or on the campus. Lists specific safety concerns related to getting on and off the bus and riding the bus. Safety in the classroom, on the stairways, in the hallways and on campus surroundings is also discussed. Stresses importance of behavior, discipline and authority in matters of safety.
Education; Health and Safety
Dist - SCHSCI

The School blues - overcoming school - related problems 30 MIN
VHS
Color (J H)
Addresses major questions concerning the state of education. Helps students confront and cope with test anxiety, the failure syndrome, procrastination and boredom, and to realize the consequences of being poorly educated.
Education; Guidance and Counseling; Health and Safety; Psychology
Dist - HRMC **Prod** - HRMC 1981

School Board Debates - Career Education Series

Career education	37 MIN
Ken Hoyt Comments - Pt 1	20 MIN
Ken Hoyt Comments - Pt 2	20 MIN
Ken Hoyt Comments I	20 MIN
Ken Hoyt Comments II	20 MIN
Questions and Answers	33 MIN

Dist - SWRLFF

The School Bus Driver 15 MIN
16mm
Color (H A)
LC 72-700613
Describes the school bus drivers's duties and responsibilities. Demonstrates driving skills and safety practices in city traffic and in rural areas.
Education; Guidance and Counseling; Health and Safety; Social Science
Dist - VADE **Prod** - VADE 1972

School bus driving - controlling skids 15 MIN
VHS
Color (H G)
$295.00 purchase, $75.00 rental _ #8314
Shows how to handle skids when driving school buses.
Health and Safety; Psychology
Dist - AIMS **Prod** - GND 1991

School bus driving - Pt 1 10 MIN
U-matic / VHS / 16mm
Color (A) (SPANISH)
LC 76-703739
Introduces techniques of safe school bus driving. Stresses defensive driving techniques. Shows proper multiple mirror usage, stop light measures and procedures for determining correct following distance, reaction time and stopping distances along with methods for turning and evaluating turns.
Foreign Language; Health and Safety; Industrial and Technical Education; Psychology
Dist - AIMS **Prod** - CAHILL 1976

School bus driving - Pt 2 10 MIN
U-matic / VHS / 16mm
Color (A) (SPANISH)
LC 76-703739
Introduces techniques of safe school bus driving. Stresses safety, not schedules as the first priority. Demonstrates left turn situations, backing and downhill parking and stopping.
Health and Safety; Industrial and Technical Education; Psychology
Dist - AIMS **Prod** - CAHILL 1976

School Bus Driving - Special Education Transportation 14 MIN
U-matic / VHS / 16mm
Color (A)
LC 78-700625
Discusses the talents and attitudes helpful in transporting handicapped school children. Describes the techniques and equipment used in driving children who are blind, orthopedically handicapped, retarded or those with epilepsy or cerebral palsy.
Education; Guidance and Counseling; Health and Safety; Psychology; Social Science
Dist - AIMS **Prod** - CAHILL 1977

School Bus Driving Tactics 22 MIN
16mm / U-matic / VHS
Color (A) (SPANISH)
LC 76-703741
Shows, through the solo trip of a new driver, basic duties and responsibilities of driving a school bus. Includes pre - trip bus inspection, safety practices during loading and unloading, actual driving techniques and simulated incidents. Dramatizes the need for safe driving practices with a staged crash of a school bus and automobile, filmed in slow motion.
Health and Safety; Industrial and Technical Education; Psychology
Dist - AIMS **Prod** - CAHILL 1976

School Bus Emergencies and Evacuation Procedures 13 MIN
U-matic / VHS / 16mm
Color (A) (SPANISH)
LC 76-703742
Builds on the theme of safety, not speed, in school bus emergencies and evacuation procedures. Demonstrates skids and skid control and the use of flares and reflectors. Shows evacuation procedures and the importance of choosing student assistants.
Health and Safety; Industrial and Technical Education; Psychology
Dist - AIMS **Prod** - CAHILL 1976

School Bus Evacuation for Students 9 MIN
16mm / U-matic / VHS
Color; Captioned (I) (SPANISH)
LC 76-703746
Shows students how to deal with school bus evacuation during an emergency. Demonstrates how to shut off the engine, set brakes and open the front door, emergency doors and exits. Emphasizes quick access to emergency phone numbers, along with orderliness and cooperation with student bus leaders.
Health and Safety
Dist - AIMS **Prod** - CAHILL 1976

School Bus Loading and Unloading 11 MIN
U-matic / VHS / 16mm
Color (A)
LC 76-703740
Shows the need for cooperation between bus drivers and passengers during loading and unloading of buses. Demonstrates how to stop for loading, maintain order prior to boarding and use red flashers. Stresses the importance of counting and controlling passengers and shows the correct way for children to cross the street after unloading.
Guidance and Counseling; Health and Safety
Dist - AIMS **Prod** - CAHILL 1976

The School bus pre - trip inspection 14 MIN
U-matic / VHS / 16mm
Color (A)
LC 76-703743
Shows bus drivers how to inspect a school bus for safe driving. Covers dashboard instruments, air brakes, lights and emergency equipment plus under-the-hood items. Teaches a driver, in a circle tour of a bus, how to check mirrors, wheels, tires, brake lights, flashers and turn signals. Presents a condensed version of a complete brake system check.
Health and Safety
Dist - AIMS **Prod** - CAHILL 1976

School Bus Rescue 45 MIN
VHS
Extrication Video from Carbusters Series
Color (G PRO)
$149.95 purchase _ #35400
Presents blueprint of organization and solutions with a set of goals and priorities. Demonstrates step - by - step how to make openings in a large vehicle. Illustrates the physical and psychological difficulties encountered at a large vehicle, multi - passenger incident.
Business and Economics; Health and Safety; Psychology; Social Science
Dist - OKSU

School Bus Safety - a Schmoadle Nightmare 9 MIN
U-matic / VHS / 16mm
Color (P)
Shows how to behave on a school bus.
Health and Safety
Dist - CRMP **Prod** - CROCUS 1975

School Bus Safety and Courtesy 15 MIN
U-matic / VHS / 16mm
Color (P I J)
$350.00, $245.00 purchase _ #81516
Covers safety rules such as proper conduct to and from the bus stop, proper behavior while riding the bus, respect for the bus driver and orderly boarding and leaving of the bus. Includes a demonstration of emergency evacuation procedures.
Health and Safety
Dist - CENTEF **Prod** - CENTRO 1983
CORF

School Bus Safety and Courtesy 15 MIN
U-matic / VHS / 16mm
Color (P I J) (SPANISH)
Deals with safety to and from the bus stop in both rural and urban settings, proper deportment on the bus and emergency evacuation procedures.

Foreign Language; Health and Safety
Dist - CORF **Prod** - CENTRO 1974

School bus safety assistants training tape 12 MIN
VHS
Color (J H A)
$30.00 purchase _ #464
Teaches mature students and adults to assist school bus drivers in specific areas of operation. Shows how to assist in loading and unloading phases, front bus crossings and emergency situations.
Health and Safety
Dist - AAAFTS **Prod** - AAAFTS 1976

School Bus Safety - Schmoadle Nightmare 9 MIN
U-matic / VHS / 16mm
Color (P I)
Presents the most important rule for riding the school bus safely. Stresses the importance of using common sense in waiting for, entering, riding and exiting from the school bus.
Health and Safety; Social Science
Dist - MGHT **Prod** - NSC 1975

School bus safety - with strings attached 28 MIN
16mm / U-matic / VHS
B&W (I)
LC FIA65-1162
Re - creates a bus hootenanny assembly program, showing student volunteers in an unrehearsed demonstration the basic principles of school bus safety. Made in collaboration with the National Safety Council.
Guidance and Counseling; Health and Safety
Dist - JOU **Prod** - JOU 1964

School citizenship series
School lunchroom manners 10 MIN
Taking care of your school building 15 MIN
Use and Care of Books 13 MIN
Using and Caring for Art Materials 11 MIN
Dist - CORF

A School Day 24 MIN
16mm
Color
Follows a bright, well - adjusted nine - year - old girl, who is congenitally blind, during her usual day. Portrays her as she arrives at her neighborhood school, goes to special instruction for the visually handicapped and participates in class with sighted peers.
Education; Guidance and Counseling; Psychology
Dist - NYU **Prod** - VASSAR

School Day in Japan 10 MIN
U-matic / VHS / 16mm
Color (P I)
LC 71-709041
Illustrates the typical school day in the life of a young Japanese boy and his sister. Presents the children's attitudes as an interesing contrast from the American school system.
Education; Geography - World
Dist - FI **Prod** - FI 1970

School Days
16mm
Color
Documents the radical high school students organizing in New York City. Shows how they begin to use newspapers an an organizing tool, struggle to develop ways to protect themselves against repression and attempt to counteract tendencies toward insignificant reform.
Geography - United States; Social Science; Sociology
Dist - CANWRL **Prod** - SBARGE

School Days
VHS
Practical Parenting Series
$89.95 purchase _ #014 - 149
Portrays the process of preparing children for preschool to teach viewers about their roles in the education of children.
Health and Safety; Sociology
Dist - CAREER **Prod** - CAREER

School days 15 MIN
U-matic / VHS
Other families, other friends series; Quebec
Color (P)
Presents a tour of carpenter, guide and cooking schools established by the Canadian government.
Geography - World; Social Science
Dist - AITECH **Prod** - WVIZTV 1971

School days 25 MIN
VHS
Dragon's tongue series
Color (C G) (CHINESE)
$195.00 purchase
Visits schools in the People's Republic of China, using Putonghua - the, official language of China based on the dialect of Beijing. Part of a 10 - part series hosted by Prof Colin Mackerras, Co - Director of the Key Center for Asian Languages and Studies at Griffith University.
Education; Foreign Language; Geography - World
Dist - LANDMK **Prod** - LANDMK 1990

School Daze - the Teacher Talks to OTs 17 MIN
VHS / U-matic
Color (PRO)
Presents personal accounts of teachers who have worked with occupational therapists (OTs) in public schools.
Education; Health and Safety
Dist - BUSARG **Prod** - BUSARG

The School Desegregation Missed 29 MIN
U-matic
As We See it Series
Color
Describes an all - black school in Memphis, Tennessee, which was not desegregated by court order. Shows how students from a low income area lack the same opportunities as students in desegregated schools.
Education; Geography - United States; Sociology
Dist - PBS **Prod** - WTTWTV

School Discipline 48 MIN
VHS / U-matic
Color
$455.00 purchase
Education
Dist - ABCLR **Prod** - ABCLR 1984

School District Experiences in Implementing Technology 65 MIN
U-matic / VHS
New Technology in Education Series
Color (J)
Presents a panel of representatives from five school districts discussing the experiences of their districts in implementing technology and identifying some of the issues which emerged.
Education; Industrial and Technical Education
Dist - USNAC **Prod** - USDOE 1983

School dropout - who cares 17 MIN
VHS
Color (J H P I)
$45.00 purchase _ #DPS316V - B
Focuses on the problem of non - completers and the factors influencing them. Examines dropouts, step - outs and let - outs. Appropriate for both school and community audiences. Includes user's guide.
Business and Economics; Education; Guidance and Counseling
Dist - CENTER **Prod** - CENTER

School Excursion 8 MIN
U-matic / VHS / 16mm
Color
LC 81-700930
Tells the animated story of two children who, fearing that their teacher won't allow them to bring their neighbor's dog on a school trip, use a magic earphone to turn him into a boy who walks on all fours.
Fine Arts; Literature and Drama
Dist - PHENIX **Prod** - KRATKY 1978

School Experiences 10 MIN
U-matic / VHS
You (Parents are Special Series
Color
Features Fred Rogers discussing experiences children have at school.
Psychology; Sociology
Dist - FAMCOM **Prod** - FAMCOM

School for Clowns 11 MIN
16mm
Color
LC 77-706882
A story about a boy who runs away from school to be a clown is used to stimulate oral language skills.
English Language; Fine Arts
Dist - MLA **Prod** - DBA 1969

School for Fours 27 MIN
16mm
B&W (C T)
LC FIA68-2412
Shows how play can become a learning experience for a four - year - old. Illustrates seven typical play activities, for both indoor and outdoor learning. Discusses the effects of teaching and discipline on the child's behavior.
Education; Psychology
Dist - OSUMPD **Prod** - OHIOSU 1967

A School for Me 30 MIN
16mm
Color (C A)
LC 75-702928
Shows the techniques and methods employed by special education teachers in the field of teaching mentally retarded children, using the example of children from Navajo Indian reservations.
Education; Psychology
Dist - AVED **Prod** - USBIA 1975

School for Playing 25 MIN
16mm / U-matic / VHS
Color (H C A)
Features the school for gifted young musicians, run by world - renowned violinist Yehudi Menuhin. Shows how he views music as relaxation with a purpose and attempts to impart this philosophy to beginners on the violin, cello and piano. Discusses the importance of practice and music's role in life.
Fine Arts
Dist - MEDIAG **Prod** - THAMES 1975

The School for scandal 100 MIN
VHS
Color (H C G)
$89.00 purchase _ #DL115
Presents an 18th - century satire of morals and manners by Richard Sheridan filmed before a live audience. Stars Joan Plowright and Felix Aylmer.
Fine Arts; History - World; Literature and Drama
Dist - INSIM

School for Wives 30 MIN
VHS / 16mm
Color (G)
$55.00 rental _ #SCHW - 000
Shows the Cullberg Balleten performing School For Wives, Moliere's classic comic - tragedy.
Fine Arts
Dist - PBS **Prod** - WHATV

School hazard commuication - your class is waiting 15 MIN
U-matic / BETA / VHS
Hazard communication series
Color (IND G)
$395.00 purchase _ #860 - 01
Trains school and college employees and department heads required to work with hazardous or potentially hazardous chemicals. Discusses the legal and regulatory aspects of OSHA Hazard Communication Standard. Part of a series on hazard communication.
Education; Health and Safety; Psychology
Dist - ITSC **Prod** - ITSC

School hazard communication - your class is waiting 15 MIN
VHS
Color (IND)
$395.00 purchase, $95.00 rental _ #860 - 01
Offers OSHA Hazard Communication Standard information for school or college employees required to work with hazardous or potentially hazardous chemicals. Includes leader's guide.
Health and Safety; Psychology
Dist - ITSC **Prod** - ITSC

School Health in Action 23 MIN
U-matic / VHS / 16mm
Color (A)
LC FIA58-1119
Tells how a health council of parents and professional people was formed in a small Oklahoma town to work for a healthful environment, improved health services and better health teaching methods.
Education; Health and Safety; Sociology
Dist - IFB **Prod** - OFP 1952

School health services - separating medicine from education - Tape 5 62 MIN
VHS
Legal challenges in special education series
Color (G)
$90.00 purchase
Explains the congressional requirements that govern school health services, legal issues in providing services to students with communicable diseases, the Supreme Court decision in Tatro, and the questions raised by later interpretations. Features Reed Martin, JD. Includes resource materials. Part of a 12 - part series on Public Law 94 - 142.
Civics and Political Systems; Education
Dist - BAXMED

School Helpers 9 MIN
16mm
Color (K P)
LC FIA68-637
Shows the teacher, the principal, school nurse and other helpful people. Suggests the ways in which boys and girls can help the school to run more smoothly and safely.
Guidance and Counseling; Health and Safety; Social Science
Dist - FILCOM **Prod** - SIGMA 1967

School hero - a story about staying in school 20 MIN
U-matic / BETA / 16mm / VHS

Color (I)
$450.00, $325.00 purchase _ #JR - 67172
Tells about Mike who is having a tough time in sixth grade and succumbs to peer pressure to cut school. Reveals that he is befriended by Joe, the school custodian, who never learned to read or write and had a promising baseball career cut short by injury. Joe agrees to coach Mike in baseball if Mike promises to work harder in school - and Mike helps Joe with his reading.
Psychology
Dist - CORF **Prod** - EPCOT 1988

School housekeeping series
Basics of carpet care 22 MIN
Basics of floor care - Part 2 16 MIN
Basics of floor care - Part one 18 MIN
Classroom cleaning 17.5 MIN
Custodial safety 15 MIN
Institutional Restroom Cleaning 20.5 MIN
Introduction to housekeeping 13.5 MIN
Kitchen Sanitation 16 MIN
Lawn Care 4.25 MIN
Lawn Care (Pt 2) 19.25 MIN
Shower and locker room 14 MIN
Dist - CTT

School Improvement through Staff Development 33 MIN
U-matic
Color (T)
Explains systematic school improvement. Tells how to plan for long term change, training, implementation and maintenance. Emphasizes the need for staff involvement and supportive leadership.
Education
Dist - AFSCD **Prod** - AFSCD 1986

School Inservice Videotape Series
Discipline
The Effective principal
Evaluation of Teacher Performance
The Gifted and the Talented
Microcomputers in Your School
Responsibility
Success Oriented Schools
Dist - SLOSSF

School is for Children 17 MIN
16mm
Color
LC 75-701322
Shows the exceptional child being prepared for his first trip to school. Shows children participating in school activities designed to help them achieve self - confidence, social and motor skills and enthusiasm for learning.
Education; Psychology
Dist - USNAC **Prod** - USBEH

School is out 20 MIN
VHS
First Tuesday series
Color; PAL (H C G)
PdS20 purchase
Studies two dyslexic youngsters in Great Britain as they struggle to glean an education from a system that seems stacked against them. Shows that help from the state is limited in most areas and some parents send their children to private schools in order to get special help. Others youngsters are simply left to suffer the taunts of classmates. Contact distributor about availability outside the United Kingdom.
Education; History - World; Psychology
Dist - ACADEM **Prod** - YORKTV

School Lab Safety 20 MIN
U-matic / VHS / 16mm
Color; Captioned
Points out the potential hazards in school labs and shows ways to prevent accidents.
Health and Safety
Dist - HANDEL **Prod** - HANDEL 1980

School Law 29 MIN
Videoreel / VT2
Just Generation Series
Color (H C A)
Discusses laws that directly affect young people, the laws that govern education. Shows the Ace Trucking Company satirizing dress codes and discussion progresses from dress codes to students' rights.
Civics and Political Systems; Social Science
Dist - PBS **Prod** - WITFTV 1972

School lunchroom manners 10 MIN
U-matic / VHS / 16mm
School citizenship series
Color (P I)
$265.00, $185.00 purchase _ #78505
Shows the importance of good manners in the school lunchroom.
Guidance and Counseling; Psychology
Dist - CORF **Prod** - CENTRO 1979

School meals 10 MIN
VHS
Stop, look, listen series
Color; PAL (P I J)
Finds the teacher helping the cook make school dinners. Observes them separating eggs for a meringue, beating the whites and stirring the custard. Shows how the cook and her helpers plan to make sure that everything is ready in time for dinner including the time necessary for cooking certain foods. Part of a series of films which start from some everyday observation and show more of what is happening, how and why. Builds vocabulary and encourages children to be more observant.
English Language; Home Economics; Industrial and Technical Education; Social Science
Dist - VIEWTH

School, money, management, television - social responsibility - career planning 60 MIN
BETA / VHS
Successful parenting series
Color (G)
Guidance and Counseling; Religion and Philosophy; Sociology
Dist - DSP **Prod** - DSP

School of assassins 18 MIN
VHS
Color (G)
$14.95 purchase _ #103
Examines the United States Army School of the Americas, established in 1946, which has trained over 57,000 troops, nearly 2,000 a year, from Latin American and Caribbean countries. Shows that some of these students are the former dictators of Argentina, Bolivia, Honduras and Panama, and that some have been guilty of the deaths of tens of thousands of people - including Archbishop Romero of El Salvador. Information from the United Nations indicates that the majority of officers responsible for human rights crimes in El Salvador studied at the school. Narrated by Susan Sarandon.
Civics and Political Systems
Dist - MARYFA **Prod** - MARYFA 1994

School of Physic 18 MIN
16mm
Color (J)
LC 81-700713
Demonstrates research in such areas as solar energy, plasma physics, astronomy, astrophysics, and environmental physics.
Science - Physical
Dist - TASCOR **Prod** - SYDUN 1977

School of the Sky - Parachuting at the U S Air Force Academy 12 MIN
16mm
Color
LC 74-706238
Discusses the basic parachute training program used by the military forces, focusing on the program of the U S Air Force Academy.
Civics and Political Systems; Industrial and Technical Education
Dist - USNAC **Prod** - USAF 1969

School of Visual Arts in New York City 15 MIN
16mm
Color (H)
Highlights different cinematic techniques at The School of Visual Arts in New York City as it portrays such areas as photography, media arts, film and video, art therapy and education, journalism and fine arts.
Education; Industrial and Technical Education
Dist - MTP **Prod** - SVA

School Otological - Audiological Follow - Up 10 MIN
16mm
International Education of the Nearing Impaired Child Series
Color
LC 74-705584
Presents otological and audiological assessment within the School for the Partially Hearing and hearing aid check at the School for the Deaf, Stockholm.
Education; Guidance and Counseling
Dist - USNAC **Prod** - USBEH 1970

School Prayer 24 MIN
VHS / U-matic
Color
$335.00 purchase
Religion and Philosophy
Dist - ABCLR **Prod** - ABCLR 1984

School Prayer, Gun Control and the Right to Assemble 60 MIN
U-matic / VHS
Constitution - that Delicate Balance Series
Color
Debates what the courts' role is in determining policy on school prayer, gun control and the right to assemble. Visits a hypothetical town beset by First and Second Amendment controversies.
Civics and Political Systems
Dist - FI **Prod** - WTTWTV 1984

School prayer, gun control and the right to assemble - Part 9 60 MIN
U-matic / VHS
Constitution - that delicate balance series
Color (G)
$45.00, $29.95 purchase
Presents a panel with former Attorney General Griffin Bell, former Secretary of Education Shirley Hufstedler and civil liberties counsel Jeanne Baker. Debates school prayer, gun control and the right to assemble - First and Second Amendment controversies. Part of a thirteen - part series on the United States Constitution created by journalist Fred Friendly.
Civics and Political Systems
Dist - ANNCPB **Prod** - WNETTV 1984

School Professionals and Parents 22 MIN
16mm / U-matic / VHS
Color (A)
Presents 12 vignettes which demonstrate typical situations parents might encounter when dealing with school professionals such as parents who need but reject the assistance of a psychologist or social worker, parents who reject advice about their child or request inappropriate placement, parents who ask the school to be responsible for something outside its domain and parents who object to the presence of the teacher or the child in discussions about the child's problem.
Psychology; Sociology
Dist - CORF **Prod** - CORF

School Readiness 25 MIN
U-matic / VHS
Color (PRO)
Shows a variety of tests administered to children by a pediatrician to determine their psychological as well as physical readiness to enter the school world.
Health and Safety; Psychology
Dist - WFP **Prod** - WFP

School safety 9 MIN
U-matic / VHS / 16mm
Safety for elementary series
Color (K P I) (SPANISH)
LC 74-702967
Presents ways to help ensure safety when playing in the schoolyard, when using supplies in the classroom and when responding to emergency drills at school.
Health and Safety
Dist - AIMS **Prod** - MORLAT 1974

School Safety 20 MIN
VHS / U-matic
Safety Sense Series Pt 10
Color (J)
Discusses various aspects of school safety.
Health and Safety
Dist - GPN **Prod** - WCVETV 1981

School shop safety 15 MIN
U-matic / VHS / 16mm
Color; B&W (J H) (SPANISH)
LC FIA68-1840
Emphasizes basic safety practices to be observed when handling various materials, hand tools, and machine tools and electricity. Points out that paying careful attention to safety rules is the first good habit of safety in any school shop.
Guidance and Counseling; Health and Safety; Industrial and Technical Education
Dist - PHENIX **Prod** - FA 1968

School solutions video series
Presents a ten - part series to build student success. Includes the titles Basic Study Skills; Why Use Computers; Writing Papers Without Them Riding You; Why Schools Have Rules - the School - Work Connection; Taking Multiple Choice, True - False and Essay Tests; Peer Pressure Cooker - Developing Self Discipline; Taking Notes Without Falling Asleep - Critical Listening Skills; Getting Along with Teachers without Going Bananas; How to Problem Solve - Critical Thinking Skills; Why Stay in School - Building Self - Esteem for At - Risk Students.
Basic study skills
Getting along with teachers without going bananas
How to solve problems - critical thinking skills
Peer pressure cooker - developing self discipline
Taking multiple choice - true - false

and essay tests
Taking notes without falling asleep - critical listening skills
Why schools have rules - the school - work connection
Why stay in school - building self - esteem for at - risk students
Why use computers
Writing papers without them riding you
Dist - CAMV

School story - Pt 11 30 MIN
VHS / U-matic
Profiles in progress series
Color (H C)
$325.00, $295.00 purchase _ #V556
Tells a story of two schools, one in the backwaters area of India's Haryana State and the other in Amman, Jordan. Shows the role of education in the economic development and social progress of Third World societies. Part of a 13 - part series on people who are moving their tradition - bound countries into modern times.
Education; Geography - World
Dist - BARR **Prod** - CEPRO 1991

School Survival Skills - How to Study Effectively 57 MIN
U-matic / VHS
Color
LC 81-706694
Shows how students can budget their time and study effectively.
Education
Dist - GA **Prod** - CHUMAN 1981

The School survival video game
VHS
Color (I J H)
$299.00 purchase _ #SVB100
Teaches the basics of surviving and succeeding in school. Looks at the eight major school tasks - time management, self awareness, study skills, learning styles, self esteem, stress management, getting along with others, and goal setting. Includes two videos - Values Video and School Survival Video, a game kit and reproducible worksheets. Can also be used in combination with School Survival Software Challenge, which is available separately.
Education; Psychology
Dist - CADESF **Prod** - CADESF 1989
CAMV

The School Survival Video Game
Software / VHS / 16mm
Color (J)
$98.00, $103.00, $299.00 _ SVS 101,SVS 100,SVS 200,SVB 100
Introduces eight major school tasks in a game format.
Education; Psychology
Dist - CADESF **Prod** - CADESF

School teacher 30 MIN
VHS
Effective teacher telecourse series
Color (T)
$69.95 purchase, $50.00 rental
Discusses the characteristics of a teacher. Hosted by Dr Loren Anderson.
Education; Psychology
Dist - SCETV **Prod** - SCETV 1987

The School that Went to Town 15 MIN
16mm
B&W
Records health - related activities in an elementary school classroom over the course of a year.
Education; Health and Safety; Home Economics; Social Science
Dist - VTDH **Prod** - VTDH

School - the Child's Community 15 MIN
16mm
B&W (C T)
Compares the adult - dominated world where the child has no opportunity to help make decisions with the classroom situation where the child is encouraged to share in the decisions.
Education; Psychology; Social Science; Sociology
Dist - WSUM **Prod** - WSUM 1959

School to work - communication connections for the real world series
VHS
School to work - communications connections for the real world 'series
Color (J H C G)
$1339.00 purchase _ #CDCOM100SV
Presents a ten - part series which discusses why communications skills are a vital part of careers in the vocational work world. Meets the requirements for integrating academic communication skills with the vocational work world of the Carl Perkins Applied Technology Act. Includes Accounting and Office Systems, Marketing and Customer Service, Electronics, Health Occupations, Home Economics, Automotive Repair, Agribusiness, Construction, Food Service and Hospitality, and Production Technology.
Business and Economics; Education; Guidance and Counseling; Industrial and Technical Education; Social Science
Dist - CAMV

School to work - communications connections for the real world series
Accounting and office systems
Agribusiness
Automotive repair
Construction
Electronics
Food service and hospitality
Health occupations
Home economics
Marketing and customer service
Production technology
School to work - communication connections for the real world series
Dist - CAMV

School - to - work transition series
Career cluster decisions
Career plan
Developing partnerships
Dist - CAMV
CENTER

School Vandalism 9 MIN
U-matic / VHS / 16mm
Color (I J)
LC 72-701724
Explores school vandalism through the actions and laments of four trouble - making youths. Uses flashback techniques to unfold the story of breaking in and accidental fire.
Education; Guidance and Counseling; Sociology
Dist - AIMS **Prod** - EVANSA 1972

School Volunteers - a New Dimension for Learning 9 MIN
16mm
Color
LC 76-702139
Shows how four people became interested in school volunteer work and how their services contribute to the quality of children's education.
Education; Social Science; Sociology
Dist - FSDOE **Prod** - FSDOE 1977

School - who needs it 30 MIN
VHS
Davey and Goliath series
Color (P I R)
$19.95 purchase, $10.00 rental _ #4 - 8829
Shows how unexpected events serve to change the anti - school attitudes of Davey and his friends. Emphasizes the importance of school. Produced by the Evangelical Lutheran Church in America.
Literature and Drama; Religion and Philosophy
Dist - APH

School workers 12 MIN
16mm / U-matic / VHS
Community helpers series
Color (P I)
$315.00, $215.00 purchase _ #79526
Shows the different people who help the children at a school and their different responsibilities.
Social Science
Dist - CORF

Schoolboy Father 30 MIN
U-matic / VHS / 16mm
Color (J H)
LC 81-700957
Tells a story about an unplanned, teenage pregnancy and the father's attempt to raise the child. Shows him finally realizing that he should give the child up for adoption. Originally shown as an ABC Afterschool Special.
Guidance and Counseling; Health and Safety; Sociology
Dist - LCOA **Prod** - TAHSEM 1980

The Schoolboys who cracked the Soviet secret 58 MIN
VHS / U-matic
Nova series
Color (H C A)
$250.00 purchase _ #HP - 6176C
Dramatizes the exploits of the Kettering Group, a group of English schoolboys and their teacher, Geoffrey Perry, who began monitoring transmissions from Russian satellites as part of an 'individual teaching method.' The project maintained high interest for eight years and led to the discovery of a hidden launch site for Russian reconnaissance satellites during the early 1960s. Part of the NOVA series.
History - World; Industrial and Technical Education; Sociology
Dist - CORF **Prod** - WGBHTV 1989

Schooled in safety series
Forces and laws 5 MIN
Dist - AMROIL

Schools 29 MIN
VHS / U-matic
Feelings Series
Color (A)
Discusses whether children are learning what they are being taught in schools or if they are getting different messages.
Guidance and Counseling
Dist - PBS **Prod** - SCETV 1979

Schools 15 MIN
VHS / U-matic / 16mm / BETA
Your town II series
Color (K P)
$245.00, $68.00 purchase _ #C50732, #C51490
Looks at hands - on science classes, gym, a field trip, a parent - teacher conference. Focuses on elementary schools, but visits classes in middle schools, high schools, universities and adult education facilities. Observes school faculty and administrative staff, student helpers, to show the purpose of a school and its role within the community. Part of a five - part series on community services.
Education; Social Science; Sociology
Dist - NGS **Prod** - NGS 1992

Schools 29 MIN
VHS
Feelings series
Color (C T A)
$69.95 purchase; $55.00 rental _ #FEES - 113
Features child psychologist Dr Lee Salk in an exploration of children's feelings toward themselves and their problems. Combines dramatized situations with discussion sessions in a focus on schools. Final episode of 13 episodes in a telecourse series.
Education; Guidance and Counseling; Sociology
Dist - SCETV **Prod** - SCETV 1979
PBS

The School's Environment 30 MIN
16mm
Starting Tomorrow Series Unit 2 - Understanding the School's 'Neighborhood
Color (T)
Provides lesson ideas dealing with the investigation of the school's environment.
Education
Dist - WALKED **Prod** - EALING 1968

School's in - Soviet Style 27 MIN
16mm / U-matic / VHS
Soviet Style Series
Color (J)
Follows the progress of Soviet students in a rural and urban school. Examines student - teacher attitudes, the curricula and aspirations.
Education; Geography - World; History - World; Sociology
Dist - JOU **Prod** - JOU 1982

Schools of quality 30 MIN
VHS
Color (A C PRO)
$398.00 purchase, $125.00 rental _ #614 - 252X01
Promotes use of the total quality management approach in managing school systems. Shows how a school district in Michigan used the approach to analyze the management system then in use, determine necessary improvements and implement them to better meet student needs. Includes one 30 - minute videotape, a discussion and workshop guide and book by John Jay Bonstingl.
Education; Psychology
Dist - AFSCD

Schools of quality 30 MIN
VHS
Color (T C PRO)
$398.00 purchase, $125.00 rental _ #614 - 252X01
Presents the four pillars of the Quality philosophy - focus on customers and suppliers; maintain a constant dedication to continuous improvement; apply a process - systems approach; have strong and consistent quality leadership from top management. Shows how to establish a direction for change which is focused on increased student success, guide problem solving so that weaknesses in the educational system are addressed and develop commitments to long - term improvement. Includes a video, a facilitator's guide, and the book Schools of Quality by John Jay Bonstingl.
Business and Economics; Education
Dist - AFSCD **Prod** - AFSCD 1993

Schools on Trial 52 MIN
U-matic / VHS
Color (G)
$249.00, $149.00 purchase _ #AD - 1509
Examines the case of a PTA which demanded the firing of an 'incompetent teacher.' Features Charles Nesson of Harvard Law School as host.
Civics and Political Systems; Education; Social Science
Dist - FOTH **Prod** - FOTH

School's out 260 MIN
VHS
Color; PAL (H)
PdS40 purchase
Presents ten 26 - minute programs which help students to prepare for life after school - even the possibility of unemployment. Includes case studies, group discussion and interviews with celebrities. Two programs are directly linked to the Youth Training Scheme. Contact distributor about availability outside the United Kingdom.
Business and Economics; Guidance and Counseling
Dist - ACADEM

School's out - lesbian and gay youth 30 MIN
VHS
Color (H)
$250.00 purchase, $50.00 rental
Examines the difficulties facing gay and lesbian teenagers and the emergence of new special educational programs designed for them. Interviews administrators at NYC's Hetrick - Martin Institute who discuss the physical and verbal abuse directed at these youth by other students and the new counseling and recreational programs available to them such as the historic Harvey Milk School. Includes interviews. Directed by Ron Spalding.
Sociology
Dist - CNEMAG

Schools that Care
16mm / U-matic / VHS
Dealing with Social Problems in the Classroom Series
Color (T)
Education
Dist - FI **Prod** - MFFD 1983

Schoolyard 28 MIN
VHS
Elephant show series
Color (P I)
$95.00 purchase, $45.00 rental
Presents program 1 in the Sharon, Lois and Bram's Elephant Show series. Teaches reading readiness and social skills while engaging children in making music. Each program explores a new theme through adventure, fantasy, mystery and song with recording artists Sharon, Lois and Bram. Uses traditional materials which stress participation - action songs, sing - along songs, story songs, clapping songs, singing games, playground chants and folk songs from many different traditions. Includes teacher's guide co - authored by a music education specialist.
Fine Arts; Sociology
Dist - BULFRG **Prod** - CAMBFP 1988

Schopenhauer 45 MIN
VHS
Great philosphers series
Color; PAL (H C A)
PdS99 purchase
Introduces the concepts of Western philosophy and one of its greatest thinkers. Features a contemporary philosopher who, in conversation with Bryan Magee, discusses Schopenhauer and his ideas. Part ten of a fifteen part series.
Education; Religion and Philosophy
Dist - BBCENE

Schubert 27 MIN
16mm / U-matic / VHS
Color (H C A)
LC 75-700391
Describes the composer, Franz Schubert, as a quiet, unassuming man who lived in the classical era, but whose orchestral and piano works had a romantic strain that anticipated the lighthearted spirit of the 19th century. Focuses on some of his most famous compositions.
Fine Arts
Dist - IFB **Prod** - SEABEN 1974

Schubert, the Piano Trio, and Peter Frankl, Gyorgy Pauk and Ralph Kirshbaum 26 MIN
U-matic / VHS / 16mm
Musical Triangle Series
Color (J)
States that Austrian composer Franz Schubert (1797 - 1828) is noted for chamber works, symphonies, overtures, masses and piano music in the romantic style. Presents a trio composed of Peter Frankl playing the piano, Gyorgy Paul playing the violin and Ralph Kirshbaum playing the cello performing some of Schubert's music.
Fine Arts
Dist - MEDIAG **Prod** - THAMES 1975

Schubert - the Young Romantic 53 MIN
U-matic / VHS
Man and Music Series
Color (C)
$279.00, $179.00 purchase _ #AD - 1778
Focuses on Classical Vienna. Looks at Schubert who composed in the shadow of Beethoven. Considers him as the first and greatest composer of German lieder and of some of the best chamber music. Part of a 22 - part series that sets Western music into the historial and cultural context of its time.
Fine Arts; Geography - World; History - World
Dist - FOTH **Prod** - FOTH

Schubert's lantern 3 MIN
16mm
B&W (G)
$10.00 rental
Pays homage to Schubert the composer, and Schubert the filmmaker's dog, inspired by the magic of Melies.
Fine Arts
Dist - CANCIN **Prod** - WEISMA 1974

The Schuster / Issacson Family 9 MIN
U-matic / VHS / 16mm
American Family - an Endangered Species Series
Color (H C A)
Introduces a lesbian couple who have kept their children.
Sociology
Dist - FI **Prod** - NBCTV 1979

Schwarzhuhnbraunhuhnschwartz-huhnweisshuhnrothhuhnweiss Oder Put - Putt 10 MIN
16mm
Color (G)
$15.00 rental
Features an independent film from Hamburg by Werner Nekes, who founded the Hamburg Cooperative in 1967 and has run the Hamburger Filmschau since then. Describes itself as 'being used at the expression of movement - a chicken - and a collage of music out of 200 different beginnings and ends of compositions.' Title translates as blackchickenbrownchickenblack-chickenwhitechicken-redchicken white or put - putt.
Fine Arts
Dist - CANCIN

Schwechater 1 MIN
16mm
Color (G)
$20.00 rental
Features a reel of two prints. Moves with precision in a Peter Kubelka production.
Fine Arts; Industrial and Technical Education
Dist - CANCIN

Schweinfurt and Regensburg 14 MIN
U-matic / VHS
Color
Records the famous bombing mission over Germany's ball - bearing plants, August 17, 1943.
History - World
Dist - IHF **Prod** - IHF

Schwepps Tonic Water 1 MIN
U-matic / VHS
Color
Shows a classic television commercial with a dignified woman and man trying to find out where they met each other.
Business and Economics; Psychology; Sociology
Dist - BROOKC **Prod** - BROOKC

Sci - Fair Series

Application	15 MIN
Conducting Research	15 MIN
Selecting an Investigation	15 MIN
The Teacher - inservice	15 MIN

Dist - GPN

Sciatic Pain and the Intervertebral Disk 33 MIN
16mm
Color (PRO)
LC FIE52-1072
Explains symptoms and treatment of functional and organic rupturing of the spine in the lower lunbar region, especially at the intervertebral disk.
Health and Safety; Science - Natural
Dist - USNAC **Prod** - USN

Science Abled - Good Minds at Work 40 MIN
VHS / 16mm
Science Abled Series
Color (I H A)
$150.00 purchase, $25.00 rental
Features scientists of varying occupations, degrees, disabilities, ethnic backgrounds and lifestyles.
Guidance and Counseling; Psychology; Science
Dist - AITECH **Prod** - UNMICH 1987

Science Abled - Good Minds at Work - 1 40 MIN
VHS
Science Abled Series
Color (J)
$150.00 purchase
Features scientists of both sexes in varying occupations, and having a diversity of degrees, disabilities, ethnic backgrounds and lifestyles. Includes a science teacher, a computer programmer, a psychiatrist, a physicist, a medical technologist, a systems engineer and a chemistry professor. Part of the Science Abled Series which encourages talented young people with physical and - or sensory disabilities to pursue coursework and careers in science or technology.
Business and Economics; Guidance and Counseling; Health and Safety; Psychology; Science
Dist - AITECH **Prod** - UMICH 1987

Science Abled - Return on Equity 40 MIN
VHS / 16mm
Science Abled Series
Color (I H A)
$150.00 purchase, $25.00 rental
Includes the opinions of supervisors, co - workers and other employees about the contributions of and working with disabled scientists. Addresses general concerns about employing people with disabilities.
Guidance and Counseling; Health and Safety; Psychology; Science
Dist - AITECH **Prod** - UNMICH 1987

Science Abled - Return on Equity - 2 34 MIN
VHS
Science Abled Series
Color (J)
$150.00 purchase
Aims at potential employers of disabled scientists. Includes the opinions of supervisors, co - workers and other employees about the contributions of and working with disabled scientists in general, and those role models featured in Part 1 in particular. Addresses other general concerns about employing people with disabilities. Part of the Science Abled Series which encourages talented young people with physical and - or sensory disabilities to pursue coursework and careers in science or technology.
Business and Economics; Guidance and Counseling; Health and Safety; Psychology; Science
Dist - AITECH **Prod** - UMICH 1987

Science Abled Series

Science Abled - Good Minds at Work	40 MIN
Science Abled - Good Minds at Work - 1	40 MIN
Science Abled - Return on Equity	40 MIN
Science Abled - Return on Equity - 2	34 MIN

Dist - AITECH

Science alliance series

Air	15 MIN
Electricity	15 MIN
Energy	15 MIN
Heat	15 MIN
Light	15 MIN
Machines	15 MIN
Magnets	15 MIN
Matter	15 MIN
Sound	15 MIN

Dist - TVOTAR

Science and archeology 145 MIN
U-matic
University of the air series
Color (J H C A)
$750.00 purchase, $250.00 rental
Illustrates the new methods of science developed for the archeologist. Contains a series of five cassettes 29 minutes each.
History - World; Sociology
Dist - CTV **Prod** - CTV 1978

Science and art of football series

Defensive line play	26 MIN

Dist - PHENIX

Science and cooking with young children - Part I 30 MIN
VHS
Calico pie series
Color (C A T)
$69.95 purchase
Presents part nine of a 16 - part telecourse for teachers who work with children ages three to five. Discusses how science and cooking can be taught in the classroom. Hosted by Dr Carolyn Dorrell, an early childhood specialist.
Education; Psychology
Dist - SCETV **Prod** - SCETV 1983

Science and cooking with young children - Part II 30 MIN
VHS
Calico pie series
Color (C A T)
$69.95 purchase
Presents part 10 of a 16 - part telecourse for teachers who work with children ages three to five. Discusses how science and cooking can be taught in the classroom. Hosted by Dr Carolyn Dorrell, an early childhood specialist.
Education; Psychology
Dist - SCETV **Prod** - SCETV 1983

Science and culture in the Western tradition series
Features BBC writer and producer James Burke in a telecourse covering the history of science and culture in Western society. Portrays many of the most influential thinkers, including Galileo, Newton, Copernicus, Marx, Darwin, and others. Examines how social changes were important. Based on the PBS series "The Day The Universe Changed." Also features Dr Benjamin Dunlap and other University of South Carolina faculty. Consists of 30 half - hour programs.
Science and culture in the Western tradition series 900 MIN
Dist - SCETV **Prod** - SCETV 1983

Science and gender with Evelyn Fox Keller 30 MIN
VHS / U-matic
World of ideas with Bill Moyers - Season 2 series
Color; Captioned (A G)
$39.95, $59.95 purchase _ #WIWM - 215
Reveals that when theoretical physicist Evelyn Fox Keller set out in the 1950s to be a scientist, she discovered it was a man's world. Discusses how gender plays a significant role in the language that scientists use to describe their work. Part of a series of interviews with Bill Moyers featuring scientists, writers, artists, philosophers and historians. Produced by Public Affairs Television, New York.
Sociology
Dist - PBS

Science and human values 24 MIN
VHS
Color (I J H)
$80.00 purchase _ #A5VH 1379
Combines environmental studies with learning about the scientific method in two parts. Explores the mushrooming ecological, social, economic and aesthetic problems of solid waste disposal and describes how scientific studies are changing societal views on how to dispose of waste. Part 2 shows how new technologies derive energy and resources from garbage. Focuses on environmental goals - recycling, eliminating excessive packaging, community involvement and the interaction of science and personal values.
Guidance and Counseling; Science - Natural; Sociology
Dist - CLRVUE **Prod** - CLRVUE

Science and nature series
Death trap - a study of carnivorous plants
Dist - BARR
CHUMAN

Science and Nature Series
Birth of the bees
Death Trap - a Study of Carnivorous Plants
Enemies of the Oak
Face of the deep - a study of underwater independence
Flights of fancy - insect courtship
Home Sweet Hole - Animal Dwellings
An Inordinate Fondness for Beetles
It's a Frog's Life
Sexual Encounters of the Floral Kind
A Thousand Million Ants - a Study of Social Organization
To be a Butterfly - a Study of Protective Strategies
Webs and Other Wonders
Within the Coral Wall - Australia's Great Barrier Reef
Dist - CHUMAN

Science and our universe - the solar system - a new look 20 MIN
VHS
Color (J H)
$39.00 purchase _ #60484 - 026
Uses NASA research to highlight the most important aspects of the universe and its components.
Science; Science - Physical
Dist - GA

Science and religion 30 MIN
BETA / VHS
Science and the spirit series
Color (G)
$29.95 purchase _ #S114
Reveals that while conventional religion and science are often in conflict, there is a growing convergence between non - reductionist science and internally oriented religious traditions. Features Dr Willis Harman, Institute of Noetic Sciences and author of Higher Creativity and An Incomplete Guide To The Future. Part of a four - part series on science and the spirit.
Religion and Philosophy
Dist - THINKA **Prod** - THINKA

Science and Society 18 MIN
U-matic / VHS / 16mm
Humanities Series
Color (J H C)
LC 70-714123
Presents an introduction to science and its role in society.
History - World; Science; Social Science; Sociology
Dist - MGHT **Prod** - MGHT 1971

Science and Society - a Race Against Time 30 MIN
16mm
Spectrum Series
B&W (H C A)
LC FIA68-414
Discusses the social problems created by technology and the probability of correction in the near future. Points out that social problems have resulted not from knowledge but from the application of that knowledge. Predicts that problems will be solved but that they will first become worse.
Psychology; Sociology
Dist - IU **Prod** - NET 1968

Science and society - future quest 46 MIN
VHS
Future quest series
Color; CC (J H C)
$79.00 purchase _ #315
Introduces issues in science, technology and society. Asks how science and technology can help save the Earth and the humans who inhabit it. Examines whether or not natural resources are unlimited and the seriousness of overpopulation. Looks at toxic wastes, acid rain and the greenhouse effect. Interviews scientists and environmentalists. Includes a guide. Part of ten parts.
Science; Science - Natural; Science - Physical; Sociology
Dist - HAWHIL **Prod** - HAWHIL

Science and society - the good news 16 MIN
VHS
Color; CC (G)
$79.00 purchase _ #350
Presents a science fiction fantasy proposing that, although science and technology have brought about new problems, they have also led humans to new levels of health and success on spaceship Earth.
Literature and Drama; Sociology
Dist - HAWHIL **Prod** - HAWHIL 1994

Science and spiritual traditions 30 MIN
BETA / VHS
Science and the spirit series
Color (G)
$29.95 purchase _ #S111
Suggests that individuals may someday be able to specify which types of spiritual discipline would be the most beneficial to them. Features Dr Charles Tart, author of States Of Consciousness and Transpersonal Psychology, who reveals that western science and traditional spiritual practices are both dedicated to the search for truth. Part of a four - part series on science and the spirit.
Psychology; Religion and Philosophy; Science
Dist - THINKA **Prod** - THINKA

Science and technology 30 MIN
VHS
Color (H C)
$89.95 purchase _ #TSI - 124
Examines the institution of science, how it exists in a social context, how it is influenced by government and forces within the community. Illustrates these points, using research on AIDS, showing the effects of research and treatment on individuals.
Business and Economics; Health and Safety; Science; Sociology
Dist - INSTRU

Science and technology 25 MIN
VHS
Career encounters series
Color (J H C A)
$95.00 purchase _ #MG3403V-J
Presents a documentary-style program that explores a career in science and technology. Features professionals at work, explaining what they do and how they got where they are. Emphasizes diversity of occupational opportunities and of men and women in the field. Offers information about new developments and technologies and about educational and certification requirements for entering the profession. One of a series of videos about professions available individually or as a set.
Business and Economics; Guidance and Counseling; Science
Dist - CAMV

Science and technology 30 MIN
U-matic
China after Mao series
Color
Discusses the effect of the Cultural Revolution on Chinese science and technology.
Civics and Political Systems; History - World
Dist - UMITV **Prod** - UMITV 1980

Science and Technology Advisory Committee - the Future in Focus 20 MIN
16mm
Color
Depicts the story of the Science And Technology Advisory Committee from its inception by James Webb in 1964 to its climactic meeting in September 1969.
Industrial and Technical Education; Science - Physical
Dist - NASA **Prod** - NASA

Science and the Free Mind 30 MIN
U-matic / VHS
Moral Values in Contemporary Society Series
Color (J)
Presents Nobel Laureate Sir John Eccles discussing science and the free mind.
Religion and Philosophy; Science - Natural; Science - Physical; Sociology
Dist - AMHUMA **Prod** - AMHUMA

Science and the Metric System 20 MIN
U-matic
Metric System Series
Color (J)
Presents the seven base units of the metric system. Includes a segment on scientific notation.
Mathematics
Dist - GPN **Prod** - MAETEL 1975

Science and the sea - Pt 2 30 MIN
U-matic
What on earth series
Color (J)
Follows the cruise of the research vessel Eastward, showing how scientists study plankton and bottom communities and sample water and air pollution.
Science; Science - Physical; Sociology
Dist - GPN **Prod** - NCSDPI 1979

Science and the spirit quartet 120 MIN
BETA / VHS
Color (G)
$69.95 purchase _ #Q114
Presents a four - part series on science and the spirit. Includes Science And Spiritual Traditions with Dr Charles Tart, Science And Religion with Dr Willis Harman, Value And Purpose In Science with Arthur M Young and Beyond The Post - Modern Mind with Dr Huston Smith.
Guidance and Counseling; Psychology; Religion and Philosophy
Dist - THINKA **Prod** - THINKA

Science and the spirit series
Beyond the post - modern mind 30 MIN
Science and religion 30 MIN
Science and spiritual traditions 30 MIN
Value and purpose in science 30 MIN
Dist - THINKA

Science animal life series
Buffalo 10 MIN
Cattle 10 MIN
Dist - MORLAT

Science at Kew Gardens 27 MIN
U-matic / VHS / 16mm
Perspective series
Color (J)
Explores the behind - the - scenes scientific work and research at Kew Gardens in London.
Agriculture; History - World; Science; Science - Natural
Dist - STNFLD **Prod** - LONTVS

Science Close - Up Series
The Bottled candle mystery 7 MIN
The Ghost 8 MIN
Inside a Laser 10 MIN
Mystery of Plant Movement 11 MIN
Secret in the White Cell 11 MIN
Snake Hunt 10 MIN
Dist - SF

Science corner I series
Science corner I, Unit VIII - communication - a series
Dist - GPN

Science corner I, Unit VII - obtaining and preserving foods - a series
Obtaining and preserving foods series
Color (P)
Illustrates the story of how the foods we eat are secured, prepared and preserved. How Do Canning And Cooling Preserve Foods; How Do We Make Bread; How Do We Preserve Foods; What Foods Do We Get From The Sea; Where Does Your Breakfast Come From.
Home Economics; Science - Natural; Social Science
Dist - GPN **Prod** - MPATI

Science corner I, Unit VIII - communication - a series
Science corner I series
Color (P)
Introduces children to the many different kinds of sound impressions. Experiments with sound interpretation that can extend a child's acquaintance with the world. How Can We Make High And Low Sounds; How Can We Make Rhythm Instruments; How Do We Make Sounds; How Do We Make Sounds Louder; How Do We Make Sounds Softer; How Do We Record Sounds; How Does Sound Travel; Why Do We Use Mirrors.
Fine Arts; Science - Physical; Social Science
Dist - GPN **Prod** - MPATI

Science corner II, Unit V - school science fair series
Science corner series
Color (I)
Discusses the effectiveness found in the organization of a school fair on one or more grade levels. How Can We Plan A School Science Fair.
Science; Science - Natural; Science - Physical
Dist - GPN **Prod** - MPATI

Science corner series
Science corner II, Unit V - school science fair series
Dist - GPN

Science discovery for children
VHS
Children's discovery series
Color (P I J)
$29.95 purchase _ #IV - 041
Presents simple science projects that can be done at home. Uses materials easily available.
Physical Education and Recreation; Science - Physical
Dist - INCRSE **Prod** - INCRSE

Science - ecology series
Energy - harnessing the sun 19 MIN
Dist - SF

Science Fair 14 MIN
U-matic / VHS / 16mm
Color (J)
LC 78-706893
Depicts the carrying out of science fair projects, common difficulties, final papers and displays. Indicates the organizational details encountered by sponsors, chairmen and assistants.
Guidance and Counseling; Psychology; Science
Dist - IFB **Prod** - VEF 1960

Science Fairs 20 MIN
U-matic / VHS / 16mm
Color
Shows how science fairs can be set up within a school district and how some projects can gain wider recognition. Provides examples of student - built science experiments.
Education; Science
Dist - HANDEL **Prod** - HANDEL 1984

Science fiction 50 MIN
VHS / U-matic
Color (H C G T A)
Calls into question some of our basic scientific assumptions. Notes that the observations and facts that modern science are based on are actually open to interpretation.
Science
Dist - PSU **Prod** - PSU 1987

Science fiction 5 MIN
16mm
Color (G)
$15.00 rental
Explores the space - time continuum as it applies to narrative structure. Experiments with fantasy using technical trickery. Made from a high school - level film on the effects of relativity. Produced by J J Murphy.
Fine Arts
Dist - CANCIN

Science fiction films 30 MIN
16mm
Literature of science fiction series
Color (H C T)
LC 72-700534
Features Forrest Ackerman, major historian of science fiction and horror films, discussing the development of science fiction films according to the subject or themes.
Fine Arts; Literature and Drama
Dist - UKANS **Prod** - UKANS 1971

Science fiction highlights - No 2 30 MIN
16mm
B&W
Presents excerpts from science fiction films.
Fine Arts; Literature and Drama
Dist - CFS **Prod** - CFS 1975

Science Fiction - Jules Verne to Ray Bradbury 51 MIN
VHS / U-matic
Color
LC 81-706689
Tells how science fiction continues to frighten and entertain readers but is being taken more seriously. Distinguishes between science fiction and fantasy.
Literature and Drama
Dist - GA **Prod** - CHUMAN 1981

Science fiction - Jules Verne to Ray Bradbury and beyond 30 MIN
VHS
Color (J H)
$249.00 purchase _ #00365 - 126
Illustrates some major themes in science fiction through screen adaptations of Frankenstein, 20,000 Leagues Under the Sea, The Time Machine, War of the Worlds, 1984, The Martian Chronicles, 2001 - A Space Odessey. Uses these and other examples from the writings of Mary Shelley, Jules Verne, H G Wells, George Orwell, Ray Bradbury and Arthur C Clarke to examine the development of science fiction in the 20th century and why it continues to be popular.
Literature and Drama
Dist - GA **Prod** - GA

Science fiction - the Promethean imagination 145 MIN
U-matic
University of the air series
Color (J H C A)
$750.00 purchase, $250.00 rental
Explores the Promethean imagination of science as it is depicted in five famous science fiction works. Program contains a series of five cassettes of 29 minutes each.
Fine Arts; Literature and Drama
Dist - CTV **Prod** - CTV 1977

Science friction 9 MIN
16mm
Color (C A)
Presents an experimental film by Stan Vanderbeek, satirizing mass society, conformism, and infatuation with rockets.
Fine Arts; Social Science
Dist - VANBKS AFA **Prod** - VANBKS 1959

Science Goes Underground - Japan's Road - Builders Beat the Swampland 15 MIN
16mm
Color
Explains that the Sendai By - pass was constructed to relieve traffic congestion on the national road, route number four, which passes through Sendai City. Introduces the sand and paper drain methods and various types of experiments to improve the foundation of the road to be constructed on marsh land. Documents construction progress from start to completion.
Geography - World; Industrial and Technical Education; Social Science
Dist - UNIJAP **Prod** - UNIJAP 1967

Science, Health and Math Series

Basketball and touch - flag football for kids	30 MIN
Computers for Kids	30 MIN
Defeat of the bacteria monsters	30 MIN
Dinosaurs and other prehistoric animals	30 MIN
Nutrition Trio's Fantastic Voyage through Your Body	30 MIN
People who Help You	30 MIN
Secrets of the Solar System	30 MIN
Up and Down, in and Out, Big and Little	30 MIN
What Should I be When I Grow Up	30 MIN
What's Inside Your Body, Volume 2	30 MIN
What's Inside Your Body, Volume I	30 MIN

Dist - EDUCRT

Science helper K - 8
CD-ROM
(T)
$195.00 purchase _ #1522
Offers over 1,000 science and mathematics lesson plans for kindergarten through eighth grade developed over a 15 year period by the National Science Foundation. For IBM PCs and compatibles. Requires 640K RAM, DOS Version 3.1 or greater, one floppy disk drive - a hard drive is recommended, one empty expansion slot, and an IBM compatible CD - ROM drive.
Science
Dist - BEP

Science in Action Series

Advances in Bio - Medical engineering	15 MIN
Agricultural genetics improves yields	15 MIN
Environmental impact study safeguards northlands	15 MIN
Glacier research	14 MIN
Manmade Extinction	15 MIN
Mars - the Search for Life Begins	15 MIN
The New Solar System	15 MIN
New Ways to Disseminate Scientific Knowledge	15 MIN
Probing planetary processes	15 MIN
Radio Astronomers Probe the Universe	15 MIN
Research into High Blood Pressure	15 MIN
Reshaping Aquatic Environments	15 MIN
The Search for new energy - Pt 1	15 MIN
The Search for new energy - Pt 2	15 MIN
Secrets of the Brain	15 MIN
Shark - ancient mystery of the sea	15 MIN
Studies in Meteorology	15 MIN
Studying the Big Cats of Africa	15 MIN
To Save a Species	15 MIN
Towers Without Infernos	15 MIN
The Upwelling Phenomenon	15 MIN
Water for a Thirsty World	15 MIN

Dist - COUNFI

Science in Museums 27 MIN
U-matic / VHS / 16mm
Perspective Series
Color (J)
Explores the role of Britain's museums in scientific research.
Fine Arts; History - World; Science
Dist - STNFLD **Prod** - LONTVS

Science in Our National Parks

Bryce Canyon National Park	9.5 MIN
Grand Canyon National Park	12 MIN
Lassen Volcanic National Park	13 MIN
Yosemite National Park	14 MIN

Dist - IFB

Science in the saddle 30 MIN
VHS
Perspectives - health and medicine - series
Color; PAL; NTSC (G)
PdS90, PdS105 purchase
Discloses that big money in racing horses means that veterinary surgery is of paramount importance.
Health and Safety; Physical Education and Recreation
Dist - CFLVIS **Prod** - LONTVS

Science is Discovery Series
How are Non - Green Plants Alike 15 MIN
Dist - GPN

Science is Everywhere Series no 4
Molecules at Work, Pt 1 15 MIN
Dist - GPN

Science is Everywhere Series no 5
Molecules at Work, Pt 2 15 MIN
Dist - GPN

Science is Everywhere Series no 6
Molecules at Work, Pt 3 15 MIN
Dist - GPN

Science Island 5 MIN
16mm
Screen news digest series
B&W
Portrays a unique natural science school on Toronto Island in Canada where children can learn science through first hand experience with nature. Volume four, issue seven of the series.
Education; Geography - World; Science; Science - Natural
Dist - HEARST **Prod** - HEARST 1962

Science laboratory safety - Pt 1 18 MIN
16mm
Color (J H)
LC 79-709019
Emphasizes the importance of safety measures in using lab equipment and performing experiments in the school science lab.
Health and Safety
Dist - VADE **Prod** - VADE 1970

Science laboratory safety - Pt 2 15 MIN
16mm
Color (J H C)
Discusses the importance of using proper safety measures while performing experiments or using equipment in the biology laboratory.

Health and Safety; Science
Dist - VADE **Prod** - VADE 1975

Science laboratory technique series
Microbiological techniques
Preparing and using microscope slides
Safety - the science laboratory
Using a compound microscope
Dist - WARDS

Science live - Earth science lab sessions video
VHS
Color (I J H)
$19.95 purchase _ #S3028
Illustrates eight Earth science investigations with detailed instructions and materials lists given in accompanying teacher's guide. Covers dew point, stream erosion, molecular structure, porosity and permeability, heat transfer, sun's path, density and contour lines. Kits which support activities available separately.
Science - Physical
Dist - HUBDSC **Prod** - HUBDSC

Science - New Frontiers Series
Exploring the Human Brain 18 MIN
Extending life 15 MIN
Hungry World 13 MIN
Is the weather changing 16 MIN
No Easy Answers 14 MIN
PSI - Boundaries of the Mind 17 MIN
Dist - PHENIX

The Science of biological decomposition - effective composting methods 22 MIN
VHS
Color (G)
$89.95 purchase _ #6 - 070 - 108A
Teaches what compost is and how it can be effectively produced. Starts at the microscopic level to teach the science of aerobic hot composting. Shows how to construct bins, create a good C to N - brown to green - ratio, ratio when layering, proper watering and how to use a thermometer to determine the pile's mesophilic - thermophilic cycle. Discusses sheet composting, pit composting and worm composting.
Agriculture; Science - Natural
Dist - VEP **Prod** - VEP 1993

The Science of Chemistry 10 MIN
16mm
Color (J H)
LC FIA61-806
Helps take the mystery out of chemistry for the beginning student. Uses diagrammatic animation to explain simple atomic and molecular processes in the formation of compounds.
Science - Physical
Dist - CLI **Prod** - CLI 1960

The Science of Cooking 30 MIN
U-matic / VHS
Kinetic Karnival of Jearl Walker Pt 6
Color (H)
LC 83-706120
Presents physics professor Jearl Walker offering graphic and unusual demonstrations exemplifying the principles of heat through the science of cooking.
Science - Physical
Dist - GPN **Prod** - WVIZTV 1982

The Science of cross examination with Terence MacCarthy 140 MIN
Cassette
Color (PRO)
$195.00, $50.00 purchase, $100.00 rental _ #XEX1-000, #AXEX-000
Features Terry MacCarthy, who explains and demonstrates his innovative system of cross examination. Gives straightforward methods to control the intractable witness, enhance jurors' receptiveness to one's themes, structure cross examination with transitions, respond to objections, and give one's side of the case an aura of power and infallibility. Includes study guide.
Civics and Political Systems
Dist - AMBAR **Prod** - AMBAR 1992

The Science of energy 28 MIN
VHS
Color (J H C)
$189.00 purchase _ #GW - 138 - VS
Explores core curriculum material on the biology and physics of energy. Uses animation, historic footage and original songs which encapsulate scientific concepts in a music - video style that will appeal to learners of all ages. Covers the scientific history of energy from Galileo to Einstein; the first and second laws of thermodynamics; the sun as the ultimate energy source for Earth; photosynthesis and respiration. Includes teacher's resource book.
Science - Physical; Social Science
Dist - HRMC **Prod** - MEDCIN

The Science of energy - from fossil fuels to nuclear reactors 40 MIN
VHS
Color (H)
$139.00 purchase _ #60404 - 025
Studies fossil fuels at a nature center and nuclear energy at a generating plant. Shows how to read electric meters, calculate the cost of electricity and the cost of operating various appliances. Explores ways of using electricity more efficiently in order to protect natural resources, reduce environmental pollution and cut down on utility bills. Includes teacher's guide and library kit.
Science - Natural; Social Science; Sociology
Dist - GA **Prod** - GA 1992

Science of energy series
The Breeder 23 MIN
Energy consequences 21 MIN
The Solar Generation 21 MIN
Which Energy 23 MIN
Dist - FINLYS

The Science of Genetics - Feeding a Growing World 27 MIN
16mm
Color
Examines applied genetics in agriculture. Provides an overview of Pioneer research programs in six major U S crops, including corn, soybeans, wheat, alfalfa, sorghum and cotton.
Agriculture
Dist - MTP

The Science of Hitting 28 MIN
16mm
Color
Reveals baseball super - star Ted Williams' secrets of being a good hitter.
Physical Education and Recreation
Dist - MTP **Prod** - SEARS

The Science of hope with Jonas Salk 30 MIN
VHS
World of ideas with Bill Moyers - season II - series
Color; Captioned (G)
$39.95 purchase _ #WIWM - 204
Interviews famed medical researcher Dr. Jonas Salk, who developed the polio vaccine. Explores Salk's views that AIDS has changed the way medical research will be conducted in the future. Hosted by Bill Moyers.
Health and Safety
Dist - PBS

The Science of immuno - imagery - Imaging with immuno - imagery 40 MIN
VHS
Immuno - imagery series
Color (H G)
$149.00 purchase
Presents a two - part series which illustrates in detail a healthy immune system and offers a guided imagery session. Uses microcinematography of actual immune system cells coupled with animation to illustrate the immune system in the first part. Part two offers visualization techniques.
Health and Safety
Dist - SIEPRO **Prod** - BIOIMA 1993

Science of Life Series
Energy and Life 20 MIN
Dist - MLA

Science of Life Series
The Animal worldsense 25 MIN
The Ascent of man 24 MIN
Check and balance in nature 22 MIN
Death - an invention of life 23 MIN
Energy in life 22 MIN
Man, the Symbol Maker 25 MIN
Man's Impact on the Environment 20 MIN
Technological Man 25 MIN
Dist - WARDS

Science of murder 60 MIN
VHS
NOVA video library
Color (G)
$29.95 purchase
Reveals the work of medical detectives, and advances that have allowed them to be able to use hair, skin, and teeth to track down murderers. Discusses why people kill. From the PBS series 'NOVA.'
Health and Safety; Sociology
Dist - PBS **Prod** - WNETTV

The Science of Murder 57 MIN
16mm / U-matic / VHS
Nova Series
Color (H C A)
LC 83-700016
Examines the reality of murder, including the social distress it causes and the clinical expertise needed to determine responsibillity. Studies the work of a medical examiner, the police, a pathologist and laboratory technicians. Includes discussions by forensic psychiatrists, convicted murderers and former U S Attorney - General Ramsey Clark as to the motives which lead people to mortal violence.
Civics and Political Systems; Social Science; Sociology
Dist - TIMLIF **Prod** - WGBHTV 1981

Science of Orbiting 28 MIN
16mm
Mr Wizard Series
B&W (I J)
Uses a tub, a swing and a carbon dioxide fire extinguisher to explain such things as weightlessness, telemetry, heat shield and retro rockets.
Science - Physical
Dist - MLA **Prod** - PRISM 1963

The Science of Pitching 60 MIN
VHS / BETA
Color
Demonstrates pitching technique in baseball. Features slow motion and stop action photography.
Physical Education and Recreation
Dist - MOHOMV **Prod** - MOHOMV

Science of pitching 60 MIN
VHS
Baseball series
(J H C)
$39.95 _ #MXS330V
Explains the fundamentals of pitching, position, wind up, and follow through in baseball. Demonstrates drills and discusses causes of throwing problems.
Physical Education and Recreation
Dist - CAMV

Science of salmon industry
U-matic / VHS / BETA
Search encounters in science series
Color; PAL (G H C)
PdS25, PdS33 purchase
Brings modern research efforts of the world's leading scientists into the classroom. Features one of a series of 24 mini - documentaries. Each film is 5 - 7 minutes in length.
Industrial and Technical Education; Science; Science - Natural
Dist - EDPAT **Prod** - NSF

The Science of skin care 24 MIN
U-matic / VHS
Color (C)
$249.00, $149.00 purchase _ #AD - 2025
Considers the two primary criteria for evaluating skin care products - safety and effectiveness. Visits the Skin Care Study Center in Philadelphia where researchers test for product safety and effectiveness. Examines skin care equipment and the role of Vitamin A in skin care.
Health and Safety; Psychology; Science - Natural; Social Science
Dist - FOTH **Prod** - FOTH

Science of Sport 30 MIN
VHS / U-matic
Innovation Series
Color
Discusses sports medicine, pointing out that a team physician can be as important to its players as the coach.
Health and Safety; Physical Education and Recreation
Dist - PBS **Prod** - WNETTV 1983

Science of the Sea 19 MIN
U-matic / VHS / 16mm
Color (H C A)
Describes the efforts of oceanographers as they study the physical, geological, meteorological, chemical and biological aspects of the ocean.
Science - Natural; Science - Physical
Dist - IFB **Prod** - IFB 1958

The Science of Wellness 26 MIN
VHS / 16mm
Color (A)
$149.00 purchase, $75.00 rental _ #OD - 2234
Discusses the effects of preventive medicine, which involves changes in diet and lifestyle.
Health and Safety
Dist - FOTH

The Science of wellness 30 MIN
U-matic / VHS
Innovation series
Color
Points out that a great deal of attention is being placed on preventive medicine, instead of treating diseases after they occur.
Health and Safety
Dist - PBS **Prod** - WNETTV 1983

Science on the light 29 MIN
Videoreel / VT2
Observing eye series
Color
Science; Science - Physical
Dist - PBS **Prod** - WGBHTV

Science Processes Series

Classifying	14 MIN
Experimenting	10 MIN
Measuring	13 MIN
Observing and Describing	10 MIN
Time	14 MIN

Dist - MGHT

Science project 14 MIN
U-matic / VHS / 16mm
Color (J)
LC FIA65-372
Records a student's adventure preparing his first science project - - the search for a project idea, research, planning and building, and the exhibition.
Science
Dist - IFB **Prod** - VEF 1960

Science projects for junior high 28 MIN
VHS
Color (I J H)
$140.00 purchase _ #A1VH 9435
Focuses on experiments conducted exclusively by middle school students. Presents over 40 experiments at various levels of difficulty, accompanied by student interviews. Includes booklet for teachers and students.
Science
Dist - CLRVUE **Prod** - CLRVUE

Science questions sometimes are issue questions 20 MIN
U-matic
Access series
Color (T)
LC 76-706258
Points out that what may appear to be a science question may really be a question about a current issue.
Education; Science
Dist - USNAC **Prod** - UDEN 1976

Science Reporter Series

Man as He Behaves	30 MIN

Dist - IU

Science Reporter Series

Landing on the Moon	28 MIN
Returning from the Moon	29 MIN

Dist - USNAC

Science revises the heavens - Program 5 52 MIN
VHS
Day the universe changed series
Color (H C G)
$695.00, $300.00 purchase, $75.00 rental
Discusses the Scientific Revolution which finally demolished the physics of Aristotle and caused bitter conflict with the Roman Catholic Church. Explores advances beginning with Copernicus' explanation that the heavens do not revolve around the Earth, Galileo's exploration of the acceleration of falling objects, and ends with the theories of Newton and his synthesis of the ideas of his predecessors. Part of a ten - part series on Western thought hosted by James Burke.
Religion and Philosophy; Science; Sociology
Dist - CF **Prod** - BBCTV 1986

Science rock
VHS / 16mm
ABC schoolhouse rock series
Color (K)
$11.88 purchase _ #GLD13833
Uses songs and humor to teach science. Narrated by Cloris Leachman.
Psychology; Science
Dist - EDUCRT

Science rock series

The Body machine	3 MIN
Do the circulation	3 MIN
Electricity, Electricity	3 MIN
The Energy blues	3 MIN
Interplanet Janet	3 MIN
Telegraph Line	3 MIN
Them not - So - Dry Bones	3 MIN
A Victim of Gravity	3 MIN
Weather	3 MIN

Dist - GA

Science Room Series

Vertebrates and Invertebrates in the Sea	20 MIN

Dist - GPN

Science safety 29 MIN
VHS
Color (I J H)
$110.00 purchase _ #A1VH 9434
Shows a broad range of proper laboratory safety techniques. Illustrates numerous safe science practices, including the way to smell unknown chemicals, the use of a water bath, methods of working with acids and bases, safeguards to use when conducting experiments with electricity or machines. Identifies many laboratory hardware items and glassware. Stresses proper measure - checking techniques. Includes teacher's guide with outlines for safety procedures, first aid instructions and reproducible worksheets.
Health and Safety; Science
Dist - CLRVUE **Prod** - CLRVUE

Science, salvage or scrap 50 MIN
VHS
Discoveries underwater series
Color; PAL (G)
PdS99 purchase
Outlines the dilemma of what to do with new discoveries found underwater. Interviews marine archaeologists as they debate over the proper usage for underwater findings. Looks at the growing science of underwater archaeology. Part eight of an eight - part series.
History - World; Social Science
Dist - BBCENE

Science screen report - No 02 17 MIN
16mm
Science screen report series
Color
Illustrates the importance of science in protecting man from the menace of shark attacks. Depicts scientific efforts to find ecologically sound disposal methods for waste. Shows scientists' efforts in striving to conquer the problem of insect control without polluting the atmosphere with poisons. Reports on a new method used by engineers to determine and solve problems connected with automobile safety. Demonstrates the versatility and capability of space technologists in developing the Lunar Rover, which can perform all tasks necessary to the moon mission.
Health and Safety; Industrial and Technical Education; Science; Science - Natural; Science - Physical
Dist - SF **Prod** - ALLFP

Science screen report - No 03 14 MIN
16mm
Science screen report series
Color
Reports on sulfur mining off the Louisiana coast and the removal of sulfur from fuel oils. Shows two instruments which aid man in extending his senses into the realm of the large and small, the macrocosm and microcosm. Presents a report on a systematic data collection and flood warning system. Describes the selection and breeding of tomatoes for easier machine harvesting. Tests the effects of impact, using a live human subject.
Agriculture; Geography - United States; Science; Science - Natural
Dist - SF **Prod** - ALLFP

Science screen report - No 04 17 MIN
16mm
Science screen report series
Color
Investigates the web of life in arid lands. Presents a new temperature - controlled method to grow near perfect crystals. Features researchers who have created an automated wheel chair and voice - dial telephone to aid the handicapped. Introduces a new triple - control autopilot which can land a jetliner perfectly in the case of an emergency.
Industrial and Technical Education; Psychology; Science; Science - Natural
Dist - SF **Prod** - ALLFP

Science screen report - No 05 17 MIN
16mm
Science screen report series
Color
Theorizes new answers to noise pollution. Analyzes the atmosphere of the different planets through the use of spectroscopy. Describes an astronaut's wardrobe where each spacesuit is individually designed and precision - built to provide protection in an airless, hostile environment. Features sea lions which have been taught underwater recovery.
Science; Science - Natural; Science - Physical
Dist - SF **Prod** - ALLFP

Science screen report - No 06 18 MIN
16mm
Science screen report series
Color
Investigates research into the relationship between trace elements and heart disease and the development of two new heart pacers. Features a tornado watch of the severe storms forecasting program and weather phenomena viewed from orbit. Explains that a laser's energy can be measured by means of torsion pendulum. Describes tests made on a new twin - hulled, semi - submerged, high - speed ship.
Health and Safety; Science; Science - Natural; Science - Physical
Dist - SF **Prod** - ALLFP

Science screen report - No 07 16 MIN
16mm
Science screen report series
Color
Explains that chemicals provide one way to check crop destruction. Describes stimulation by computers that help study complex effects of fluid flow.
Agriculture; Mathematics; Science; Science - Physical
Dist - SF **Prod** - ALLFP

Science screen report - No 08 16 MIN
16mm
Science screen report series
Color
Investigates the structure and function of the cell. Describes new 'vocoders' that help the deaf by converting sound to other forms of energy. Features a tiny new laser, lasers to aid the ecologist and lasers to aid the blind. Introduces a three - dimensional lunar relief map to help simulate moon landings. Reveals a spacecraft that is investigating Jupiter, the largest planet. Includes scenes of a school for chimpanzees that prepares them to be subjects in scientific research.
Guidance and Counseling; Science; Science - Natural; Science - Physical
Dist - SF **Prod** - ALLFP

Science screen report - No 09 20 MIN
16mm
Science screen report series
Color
Views researchers who study arid expanses of sargassum weed in the Atlantic. Presents Mariner orbiters and Viking landers who investigated Mars in the 1970's. Features a magnetic separation which may extract resources and decontaminate oil and water. Analyzes a new national astronomical observatory which is studying the universe.
History - World; Industrial and Technical Education; Science; Science - Natural; Science - Physical
Dist - SF **Prod** - ALLFP

Science screen report - No 10 17 MIN
16mm
Science screen report series
Color
Explains that Skylab, the first U S space station, will probe earth resources, materials processing, biomedical reactions and stellar phenomena. Describes a new way to obtain germfree animals for medical research. Reports on leukemia study with cattle. Reveals steel crash cushions which promise to improve automobile safety and new experimental safety vehicles.
Agriculture; Health and Safety; Industrial and Technical Education; Psychology; Science; Science - Physical
Dist - SF **Prod** - ALLFP

Science screen report - No 11 18 MIN
16mm
Science screen report series
Color
Examines Antarctic research to study world environmental history, continental drift, polar life forms and weather origins. Focuses on grooving as an answer to hydroplaning accidents. Explains how space technology is applied to keep operating rooms sterile, help the handicapped get around, enhance x - rays and remove a bullet from a person's brain.
Health and Safety; Science; Science - Natural; Science - Physical; Sociology
Dist - SF **Prod** - ALLFP

Science screen report - No 12 17 MIN
16mm
Science screen report series
Color
Examines recycling research in progress on garbage, paper, glass and water. Features the first laser lighthouse, which has a beam visible for 22 miles. Describes ERTS, Earth Resources Technology Satellite, designed to inventory this planet's natural resources.
Geography - World; Science; Science - Natural; Social Science
Dist - SF **Prod** - ALLFP

Science screen report - No 13 16 MIN
16mm
Science screen report series
Color
Probes noise pollution, unwanted sound that is a growing national problem. Presents new facts about metal crystal structures that lead to better bearings. Features researchers who study photos and simulate whirlwinds to learn about tornados.
Science; Science - Natural; Science - Physical
Dist - SF **Prod** - ALLFP

Science screen report - No 14 14 MIN
16mm
Science screen report series
Color
Presents researchers who investigate possible medicines that can be derived from sea life. Establishes different life surrounding off - shore drilling platforms. Features a pilot whale who was taught to recover objects 1500 feet down.
Health and Safety; Science; Science - Natural; Science - Physical
Dist - SF **Prod** - ALLFP

Science screen report - No 15 15 MIN
16mm
Science screen report series
Color
Establishes the clean air cycle and describes how man - made pollution has overloaded this cycle. Views chick embryos which are X - rayed to study the effects on the vascular system.
Science; Science - Natural; Sociology
Dist - SF **Prod** - ALLFP

Science screen report - No 16 15 MIN
16mm
Science screen report series
Color
Features a deep sea drilling vessel that finds evidence of continental drift. Describes studies using anthropometric dummies and computers that promote auto safety.
Health and Safety; Industrial and Technical Education; Science; Science - Physical
Dist - SF **Prod** - ALLFP

Science screen report - No 17 15 MIN
16mm
Science screen report series
Color
Evaluates a new approach to ocean research, FLARE, which investigates reefs using mobile habitat. Features unmanned space probes which study Venus, Mercury, the asteroids and Jupiter.
Industrial and Technical Education; Science; Science - Physical
Dist - SF **Prod** - ALLFP

Science screen report - No 18 15 MIN
16mm
Science screen report series
Color
Explores the scientific uses of photography exemplified in space exploration. Features telephoned drawings of liquid crystals. Analyzes a new approach to diagnosing deafness in children using computer - recorded brainwaves.
Health and Safety; Industrial and Technical Education; Science; Science - Physical
Dist - SF **Prod** - ALLFP

Science screen report series
Science screen report - No 02 17 MIN
Science screen report - No 03 14 MIN
Science screen report - No 04 17 MIN
Science screen report - No 05 17 MIN
Science screen report - No 06 18 MIN
Science screen report - No 07 16 MIN
Science screen report - No 08 16 MIN
Science screen report - No 09 20 MIN
Science screen report - No 10 17 MIN
Science screen report - No 11 18 MIN
Science screen report - No 12 17 MIN
Science screen report - No 13 16 MIN
Science screen report - No 14 14 MIN
Science screen report - No 15 15 MIN
Science screen report - No 16 15 MIN
Science screen report - No 17 15 MIN
Science screen report - No 18 15 MIN
Dist - SF

Science Series
Exploring the Moon 9 MIN
Heat and Hemispheres 8 MIN
Light and Shadow 7 MIN
The Size of the Moon 8 MIN
The Sun 9 MIN
Time and Direction 7 MIN
What is Autumn 7 MIN
What is Spring 7 MIN
What is Summer 7 MIN
What is Winter 8 MIN
Dist - SF

The Science Show 25 MIN
U-matic
Not Another Science Show Series
Color (H C)
Presents scientists attending a conference of the American Association for the Advancement of Science giving their answers to what science is and what scientists do.
Science
Dist - TVOTAR **Prod** - TVOTAR 1986

Science skills film - No 5 - conducting an experiment in cleaning our air 15 MIN
U-matic / VHS / 16mm
Science skills series
Color (I J)
LC 75-704275
Shows how the basic science skills are used in a scientific investigation. Uses an experiment on particles in the air to show how these skills are employed in scientific experimentation.
Science; Science - Natural
Dist - JOU **Prod** - GLDWER 1975

Science skills film - No 4 - interpreting data, testing hypotheses 16 MIN
U-matic / VHS / 16mm
Science skills - Spanish series
Color (I J) (SPANISH)
Introduces basic skills needed to conduct a scientific investigation by studying data on the pollution of a pond to determine if there are any fish in it.
Science; Science - Natural
Dist - JOU **Prod** - GLDWER 1975

Science skills film - No 1 - observing, recording, mapping and graphing 16 MIN
16mm / U-matic / VHS
Science skills series
Color (I J H)
LC 75-702168
Introduces basic skills needed to conduct a scientific investigation by studying a swarm of honeybees being handled by a beekeeper. Emphasizes the proper way to observe the action of bees and the way to record these observations.
Science; Science - Natural
Dist - JOU **Prod** - GLDWER 1975

Science skills film - No 3 - defining, classifying and identifying 16 MIN
U-matic / VHS / 16mm
Science skills series
Color (I J H)
LC 75-702170
Introduces basic skills needed to conduct a scientific investigation by conducting tests on three unknown materials. Explains the process of defining the properties of the minerals and shows how classifying and identifying are important to the scientific inquiry.
Science; Science - Physical
Dist - JOU **Prod** - GLDWER 1975

Science skills film - No 2 - controlling variables, making measurements 15 MIN
16mm / U-matic / VHS
Science skills series
Color (I J H)
LC 75-702169
Introduces basic skills needed to conduct a scientific investigation by observing an experiment in which sunflower seeds are grown under controlled conditions. Demonstrates that by controlling the variables and making measurements of the plants as they grow, the effect of chemical nutrients can be learned.
Mathematics; Science; Science - Natural
Dist - JOU **Prod** - GLDWER 1975

Science skills series
Science skills film - No 5 - conducting an experiment in cleaning our air 15 MIN
Science skills film - No 1 - observing , recording, mapping and graphing 16 MIN
Science skills film - No 3 - defining, classifying and identifying 16 MIN
Science skills film - No 2 - controlling variables, making measurements 15 MIN
Dist - JOU

Science skills - Spanish series
Science skills film - No 4 - interpreting data, testing hypotheses 16 MIN
Dist - JOU

Science, sound and energy 30 MIN
VHS
Tell me why video series
Color (P I)
$19.95 purchase _ #51439
Answers approximately 50 questions about science, sound and energy. Uses colorful graphics and attention - grabbing film footage. Part of a series.
Science; Science - Physical
Dist - KNOWUN

Science stalks the criminal 25 MIN
VHS
Color (G A)
$19.95 purchase _ #TCO116CE
Reveals the high - technology advances that have made collection of criminal evidence easier. Shows that genetic, dental, fingerprint, and other forms of evidence can be analyzed more efficiently. Hosted by CNN correspondent Charles Crawford.
Civics and Political Systems; Sociology
Dist - TMM **Prod** - TMM

Science story
U-matic / VHS
Color (H C A)
Presents 1) The quest For Fusion. After thirty years of fusion research, physicists and engineers grow closer to harnessing the source of energy that sparked the hydrogen bomb. 2) Fusion Power, The Technical Challenge. Describes some of the obstacles to developing fusion as an alternative source of energy. 3) Fusion Economics. Looks at the cost factors involved in creating energy from fusion.
History - World; Science - Physical; Social Science
Dist - UEUWIS **Prod** - UEUWIS 1982

Science, technology and art in the USSR 13 MIN
16mm / U-matic / VHS
Russian language series
Color (H C) (RUSSIAN)
A Russian language film. Depicts the uses of atomic energy in power stations, steel mills and cultural activities of Russians. Shows how young people study.
Foreign Language; Geography - World
Dist - IFB **Prod** - IFB 1963

Science, technology and man 30 MIN
U-matic / Kit / VHS
Western man and the modern world in video
Color (J H)
$1378.12 the 25 part series _ #C676 - 27347 - 5, $69.95 the individual
Discusses the influence of technology on industrial and developing nations. Covers urban planning, agriculture, biology and nutrition. Addresses such questions as energy shortages, population growth and genetic engineering.
Agriculture; History - World; Social Science
Dist - RH

Science, technology and man 30 MIN
35mm strip / VHS
Western man and the modern world series
Color (J H C T A)
$72.00, $72.00 purchase _ #MB - 510382 - 6, #MB - 510287 - 0
Examines current issues of science and technology as they affect humans. Includes assessments of experts in various fields. Considers issues including energy shortages, population growth, and genetic manipulation. Unit VII of the series.
History - World; Social Science; Sociology
Dist - SRA

Science through Discovery 28 MIN
16mm
B&W (T)
LC FIE63-28
Demonstrates the use of modern teaching techniques in science teaching, including audio - visual illustration. Considers the parts played by outside specialists as consultants, the committee project and report system, and individual student - teacher conferences.
Education; Science
Dist - USNAC **Prod** - USOE 1972

Science topics series
Periodic table 20 MIN
Dist - BBCENE

Science Twenty Series
The Falling Barometer 20 MIN
Homemade electricity 20 MIN
How Much is Enough 20 MIN
Measuring Molecules 20 MIN
The Restless Ocean of Air 20 MIN
Salt or Sugar 20 MIN
Water - Coming and Going 20 MIN
Dist - SF

Science with a Microscope
VHS
Robert Krampf's World Of Science Series
Color (J H T)
$79.95 purchase
Presents science educator Robert Krampf discussing the history of the microscope, how to prepare slides, and how to use a compound microscope. Offers a camera's eye view deep into the microscopic world of plant and animal cells, focusing on living creatures. Includes teacher guide, worksheets and quizzes.
Science - Natural
Dist - BEARDW **Prod** - BEARDW 1991

Science - Woman's Work 27 MIN
16mm
Color
Looks at the various science careers available to women. Emphasizes the need for a strong science and math background in high school coursework.
Science; Sociology
Dist - USNAC **Prod** - NSF 1982

Science world 6 MIN
VHS / U-matic
Kidzone series
Color (I J)
$60.00, $110.00 purchase, $40.00 rental
Looks at the design and functions of an aquarium. Pays special attention to the Beluga whale exhibit and the habits of that mammal.
Science; Science - Natural
Dist - NDIM **Prod** - KNONET 1992

Scientific 45 MIN
VHS
Video guide to occupational exploration - the video GOE series
Color (J H C G)
$69.95 purchase _ #CCP1002V
Explores various occupations in the sciences, including physical science, life science, medicine, and laboratory technology. Includes interviews with a meteorologist, astronomer, computer engineer, food technician, ophthalmologist, veterinarian, radiologist, pharmacist, lab technician and polygraphyer. Part of a 14 - part series exploring occupational clusters.
Business and Economics; Guidance and Counseling; Science
Dist - CAMV **Prod** - CAMV 1991

The Scientific age 30 MIN
16mm
How should we then live series
Color (DUTCH, ENGLISH)
LC 77-702368
Contends that the theories of Galileo, Bacon and Copernicus have a Biblical interpretation of the universe as their foundation. Warns that a departure from such a Biblical framework can make science a threat to man. Based on the book How Should We Then Live by Francis A Schaeffer. Number six in the series.
Religion and Philosophy; Science
Dist - GF **Prod** - GF 1977

Scientific Bases for Conditioning and Training 29 MIN
U-matic
Sports Medicine in the 80's Series
Color
Teaches the role of sports medicine as it relates to athlete, coach, trainer, team and school. Covers most kinds of injuries encountered in sports.
Health and Safety; Physical Education and Recreation
Dist - CEPRO **Prod** - CEPRO

Scientific careers for women - doors to the future 30 MIN
VHS / 16mm
Women in science series
Color (I H A)
$150.00 purchase, $35.00 rental
Relates comments from role models seen in other programs in the series, addressing barriers that discourage young women from pursuing science careers.
Business and Economics; Psychology; Sociology
Dist - AITECH **Prod** - UNMICH 1984

Scientific Evidence - the Polygraph Series
The Polygraph - Demonstration and Discussion 43 MIN
The Polygraph - Useful Tool or Dangerous Weapon 58 MIN
Dist - ABACPE

Scientific eye - series 1 200 MIN
VHS
Scientific eye series
Color; PAL (J H)
PdS45 purchase
Presents a ten - part series which encourages students to think and react like scientists - testing theories, solving problems and conducting experiments to explain how and why things work. Uses drama, documentary and graphics, as well as film of pupils involved in scientific investigations both inside and outside the science laboratory. Includes the titles Keeping Warm; Acids; Fire and Flame; Force and Friction; Gravity; Keeping Cool; Drying Out; Lighter Than Air; Microbeasts and Disease; River of Rock. Contact distributor about availability outside the United Kingdom.
Science; Science - Physical
Dist - ACADEM **Prod** - YORKTV

Scientific eye - series 2 200 MIN
VHS
Scientific eye series
Color; PAL (J H)
PdS45 purchase
Presents a ten - part series which encourages students to think and react like scientists - testing theories, solving problems and conducting experiments to explain how and why things work. Uses drama, documentary and graphics, as well as film of pupils involved in scientific investigations both inside and outside the science laboratory. Includes the titles Floating and Sinking; Hearing and Sound; Seeing and Believing; Plants for Food; Earth Ltd; Fitness and Sport; Getting Things Clean; Shape and Strength; Crimebusters; What is Life. Contact distributor about availability outside the United Kingdom.
Science; Science - Physical
Dist - ACADEM **Prod** - YORKTV

Scientific eye - series 3 100 MIN
VHS
Scientific eye series
Color; PAL (J H)
PdS35 purchase
Presents a five - part series which encourages students to think and react like scientists - testing theories, solving problems and conducting experiments to explain how and why things work. Uses drama, documentary and graphics, as well as film of pupils involved in scientific investigations both inside and outside the science laboratory. Includes the titles Habitat and Dependence; Cells and Systems; Stars and Planets; Weather and Rocks; Electronics and Control. Contact distributor about availability outside the United Kingdom.
Industrial and Technical Education; Science; Science - Natural; Science - Physical
Dist - ACADEM **Prod** - YORKTV

Scientific eye - series 4 100 MIN
VHS
Scientific eye series
Color; PAL (J H)
PdS35 purchase
Presents a five - part series which encourages students to think and react like scientists - testing theories, solving problems and conducting experiments to explain how and why things work. Uses drama, documentary and graphics, as well as film of pupils involved in scientific investigations both inside and outside the science laboratory. Includes the titles The Greenhouse Effect; Variety and Survival; Solids, Liquids and Gases; Variables; Machines. Contact distributor about availability outside the United Kingdom.
Mathematics; Science; Science - Natural; Science - Physical
Dist - ACADEM **Prod** - YORKTV

Scientific eye - series 5 80 MIN
VHS
Scientific eye series
Color; PAL (J H)
PdS35 purchase
Presents a four - part series which encourages students to think and react like scientists - testing theories, solving problems and conducting experiments to explain how and why things work. Uses drama, documentary and graphics, as well as film of pupils involved in scientific investigations both inside and outside the science laboratory. Includes the titles Electricity and Magnetism; Energy; Metals; and Pressure. Contact distributor about availability outside the United Kingdom.
Science; Science - Physical
Dist - ACADEM **Prod** - YORKTV

Scientific eye - series 6 80 MIN
VHS
Scientific eye series
Color; PAL (J H)
PdS35 purchase
Presents a four - part series which encourages students to think and react like scientists - testing theories, solving problems and conducting experiments to explain how and why things work. Uses drama, documentary and graphics, as well as film of pupils involved in scientific investigations both inside and outside the science laboratory. Includes the titles Growth; Chemical Reactions; Plastics and Polymers; and Speed and Safety. Contact distributor about availability outside the United Kingdom.
Health and Safety; Industrial and Technical Education; Science; Science - Physical
Dist - ACADEM **Prod** - YORKTV

Scientific eye - series 7 80 MIN
VHS
Scientific eye series
Color; PAL (J H)
PdS35 purchase
Presents a four - part series which encourages students to think and react like scientists - testing theories, solving problems and conducting experiments to explain how and why things work. Uses drama, documentary and graphics, as well as film of pupils involved in scientific investigations both inside and outside the science laboratory. Includes the titles Seeing the Light; Atoms and Molecules; Design a Clock; and Reproductions and Genetics. Contact distributor about availability outside the United Kingdom.
Mathematics; Science; Science - Natural; Science - Physical
Dist - ACADEM **Prod** - YORKTV

Scientific eye - series 1 - acids 20 MIN
VHS
Scientific eye series
Color; PAL (J H)
PdS15 purchase
Investigates the chemical actions of acid. Encourages students to think and react like scientists - testing theories, solving problems and conducting experiments to explain how and why things work. Uses drama, documentary and graphics, as well as film of pupils involved in scientific investigations both inside and outside the science laboratory. Part of a ten - part series. Contact distributor about availability outside the United Kingdom.
Science; Science - Physical
Dist - ACADEM **Prod** - YORKTV

Scientific eye - series 1 - drying out 20 MIN
VHS
Scientific eye series
Color; PAL (J H)
PdS15 purchase
Investigates the physics of drying. Encourages students to think and react like scientists - testing theories, solving problems and conducting experiments to explain how and why things work. Uses drama, documentary and graphics, as well as film of pupils involved in scientific investigations both inside and outside the science laboratory. Part of a ten - part series. Contact distributor about availability outside the United Kingdom.
Science; Science - Physical
Dist - ACADEM **Prod** - YORKTV

Scientific eye - series 1 - fire and flame 20 MIN
VHS
Scientific eye series
Color; PAL (J H)
PdS15 purchase
Investigates the chemical action of fire and flame. Encourages students to think and react like scientists - testing theories, solving problems and conducting experiments to explain how and why things work. Uses drama, documentary and graphics, as well as film of pupils involved in scientific investigations both inside and outside the science laboratory. Part of a ten - part series. Contact distributor about availability outside the United Kingdom.
Science; Science - Physical
Dist - ACADEM **Prod** - YORKTV

Scientific eye - series 1 - force and friction 20 MIN
VHS
Scientific eye series
Color; PAL (J H)
PdS15 purchase
Investigates the physical properties of force and friction. Encourages students to think and react like scientists - testing theories, solving problems and conducting experiments to explain how and why things work. Uses drama, documentary and graphics, as well as film of pupils involved in scientific investigations both inside and outside the science laboratory. Part of a ten - part series. Contact distributor about availability outside the United Kingdom.
Science; Science - Physical
Dist - ACADEM **Prod** - YORKTV

Scientific eye - series 1 - gravity 20 MIN
VHS
Scientific eye series
Color; PAL (J H)
PdS15 purchase
Investigates the physical properties of gravity. Encourages students to think and react like scientists - testing theories, solving problems and conducting experiments to explain how and why things work. Uses drama, documentary and graphics, as well as film of pupils involved in scientific investigations both inside and outside the science laboratory. Part of a ten - part series. Contact distributor about availability outside the United Kingdom.
Science; Science - Physical
Dist - ACADEM **Prod** - YORKTV

Scientific eye - series 1 - keeping cool 20 MIN
VHS
Scientific eye series
Color; PAL (J H)
PdS15 purchase
Investigates the physics of cooling. Encourages students to think and react like scientists - testing theories, solving problems and conducting experiments to explain how and why things work. Uses drama, documentary and graphics, as well as film of pupils involved in scientific investigations

both inside and outside the science laboratory. Part of a ten - part series. Contact distributor about availability outside the United Kingdom.
Science; Science - Physical
Dist - ACADEM **Prod** - YORKTV

Scientific eye - series 1 - keeping warm 20 MIN
VHS
Scientific eye series
Color; PAL (J H)
PdS15 purchase
Examines the dynamics of heat. Encourages students to think and react like scientists - testing theories, solving problems and conducting experiments to explain how and why things work. Uses drama, documentary and graphics, as well as film of pupils involved in scientific investigations both inside and outside the science laboratory. Part of a ten - part series. Contact distributor about availability outside the United Kingdom.
Science; Science - Physical
Dist - ACADEM **Prod** - YORKTV

Scientific eye - series 1 - lighter than air 20 MIN
VHS
Scientific eye series
Color; PAL (J H)
PdS15 purchase
Investigates the properties of lighter than air mechanics. Encourages students to think and react like scientists - testing theories, solving problems and conducting experiments to explain how and why things work. Uses drama, documentary and graphics, as well as films of pupil involved in scientific investigations both inside and outside the science laboratory. Part of a ten - part series. Contact distributor about availability outside the United Kingdom.
Science; Science - Physical
Dist - ACADEM **Prod** - YORKTV

Scientific eye - series 1 - microbeasts and disease 20 MIN
VHS
Scientific eye series
Color; PAL (J H)
PdS15 purchase
Examines the role of microorganisms in the cause of disease. Encourages students to think and react like scientists - testing theories, solving problems and conducting experiments to explain how and why things work. Uses drama, documentary and graphics, as well as film of pupils involved in scientific investigations both inside and outside the science laboratory. Part of a ten - part series. Contact distributor about availability outside the United Kingdom.
Health and Safety; Science; Science - Natural
Dist - ACADEM **Prod** - YORKTV

Scientific eye - series 1 - river of rock 20 MIN
VHS
Scientific eye series
Color; PAL (J H)
PdS15 purchase
Focuses on geology. Encourages students to think and react like scientists - testing theories, solving problems and conducting experiments to explain how and why things work. Uses drama, documentary and graphics, as well as film of pupils involved in scientific investigations both inside and outside the science laboratory. Part of a ten - part series. Contact distributor about availability outside the United Kingdom.
Science; Science - Physical
Dist - ACADEM **Prod** - YORKTV

Scientific eye - series 2 - crimebusters 20 MIN
VHS
Scientific eye series
Color; PAL (J H)
PdS15 purchase
Looks at the use of science in solving crime. Encourages students to think and react like scientists - testing theories, solving problems and conducting experiments to explain how and why things work. Uses drama, documentary and graphics, as well as film of pupils involved in scientific investigations both inside and outside the science laboratory. Part of a ten - part series. Contact distributor about availability outside the United Kingdom.
Science; Sociology
Dist - ACADEM **Prod** - YORKTV

Scientific eye - series 2 - earth ltd 20 MIN
VHS
Scientific eye series
Color; PAL (J H)
PdS15 purchase
Examines the challenge to planet Earth presented by the uncontrolled increase in human population and the increasing concerns over environmental protection. Encourages students to think and react like scientists - testing theories, solving problems and conducting experiments to explain how and why things work. Uses drama, documentary and graphics, as well as film of pupils involved in scientific investigations both inside and outside the science laboratory. Part of a ten - part series. Contact distributor about availability outside the United Kingdom.
Science; Science - Physical; Sociology
Dist - ACADEM **Prod** - YORKTV

Scientific eye - series 2 - fitness and sport 20 MIN
VHS
Scientific eye series
Color; PAL (J H)
PdS15 purchase
Looks at the role of sports in fitness. Encourages students to think and react like scientists - testing theories, solving problems and conducting experiments to explain how and why things work. Uses drama, documentary and graphics, as well as film of pupils involved in scientific investigations both inside and outside the science laboratory. Part of a ten - part series. Contact distributor about availability outside the United Kingdom.
Physical Education and Recreation; Science
Dist - ACADEM **Prod** - YORKTV

Scientific eye - series 2 - floating and sinking 20 MIN
VHS
Scientific eye series
Color; PAL (J H)
PdS15 purchase
Examines the mechanics of buoyancy. Encourages students to think and react like scientists - testing theories, solving problems and conducting experiments to explain how and why things work. Uses drama, documentary and graphics, as well as film of pupils involved in scientific investigations both inside and outside the science laboratory. Part of a ten - part series. Contact distributor about availability outside the United Kingdom.
Science; Science - Physical
Dist - ACADEM **Prod** - YORKTV

Scientific eye - series 2 - getting things clean 20 MIN
VHS
Scientific eye series
Color; PAL (J H)
PdS15 purchase
Looks at soap and other means of cleanliness. Encourages students to think and react like scientists - testing theories, solving problems and conducting experiments to explain how and why things work. Uses drama, documentary and graphics, as well as film of pupils involved in scientific investigations both inside and outside the science laboratory. Part of a ten - part series. Contact distributor about availability outside the United Kingdom.
Home Economics; Science
Dist - ACADEM **Prod** - YORKTV

Scientific eye - series 2 - hearing and sound 20 MIN
VHS
Scientific eye series
Color; PAL (J H)
PdS15 purchase
Examines the sense of hearing and the perception of sound. Encourages students to think and react like scientists - testing theories, solving problems and conducting experiments to explain how and why things work. Uses drama, documentary and graphics, as well as film of pupils involved in scientific investigations both inside and outside the science laboratory. Part of a ten - part series. Contact distributor about availability outside the United Kingdom.
Psychology; Science; Science - Natural; Science - Physical
Dist - ACADEM **Prod** - YORKTV

Scientific eye - series 2 - plants for food 20 MIN
VHS
Scientific eye series
Color; PAL (J H)
PdS15 purchase
Looks at the use of plants as food. Encourages students to think and react like scientists - testing theories, solving problems and conducting experiments to explain how and why things work. Uses drama, documentary and graphics, as well as film of pupils involved in scientific investigations both inside and outside the science laboratory. Part of a ten - part series. Contact distributor about availability outside the United Kingdom.
Home Economics; Science; Science - Natural
Dist - ACADEM **Prod** - YORKTV

Scientific eye - series 2 - seeing and believing 20 MIN
VHS
Scientific eye series
Color; PAL (J H)
PdS15 purchase
Examines the use of sensory data in empirical evidence. Encourages students to think and react like scientists - testing theories, solving problems and conducting experiments to explain how and why things work. Uses drama, documentary and graphics, as well as film of pupils involved in scientific investigations both inside and outside the science laboratory. Part of a ten - part series. Contact distributor about availability outside the United Kingdom.
Psychology; Science
Dist - ACADEM **Prod** - YORKTV

Scientific eye - series 2 - shape and strength 20 MIN
VHS
Scientific eye series
Color; PAL (J H)
PdS15 purchase
Looks at the physical properties of shapes and weight distribution that create their sometimes surprising strengths. Encourages students to think and react like scientists - testing theories, solving problems and conducting experiments to explain how and why things work. Uses drama, documentary and graphics, as well as film of pupils involved in scientific investigations both inside and outside the science laboratory. Part of a ten - part series. Contact distributor about availability outside the United Kingdom.
Science
Dist - ACADEM **Prod** - YORKTV

Scientific eye - series 2 - what is life 20 MIN
VHS
Scientific eye series
Color; PAL (J H)
PdS15 purchase
Considers the meaning of life in scientific terms. Encourages students to think and react like scientists - testing theories, solving problems and conducting experiments to explain how and why things work. Uses drama, documentary and graphics, as well as film of pupils involved in scientific investigations both inside and outside the science laboratory. Part of a ten - part series. Contact distributor about availability outside the United Kingdom.
Science; Science - Natural
Dist - ACADEM **Prod** - YORKTV

Scientific eye - series 3 - cells and systems 20 MIN
VHS
Scientific eye series
Color; PAL (J H)
PdS15 purchase
Examines the biological role of cells both as independent entities and as parts of systems. Encourages students to think and react like scientists - testing theories, solving problems and conducting experiments to explain how and why things work. Uses drama, documentary and graphics, as well as film of pupils involved in scientific investigations both inside and outside the science laboratory. Part of a five - part series. Contact distributor about availability outside the United Kingdom.
Science; Science - Natural
Dist - ACADEM **Prod** - YORKTV

Scientific eye - series 3 - electronics and control 20 MIN
VHS
Scientific eye series
Color; PAL (J H)
PdS15 purchase
Considers the use of electronics in control systems. Encourages students to think and react like scientists - testing theories, solving problems and conducting experiments to explain how and why things work. Uses drama, documentary and graphics, as well as film of pupils involved in scientific investigations both inside and outside the science laboratory. Part of a five - part series. Contact distributor about availability outside the United Kingdom.
Industrial and Technical Education; Science
Dist - ACADEM **Prod** - YORKTV

Scientific eye - series 3 - habitat and dependence 20 MIN
VHS
Scientific eye series
Color; PAL (J H)
PdS15 purchase
Looks at the biological role of habitat. Encourages students to think and react like scientists - testing theories, solving problems and conducting experiments to explain how and why things work. Uses drama, documentary and graphics, as well as film of pupils involved in scientific investigations both inside and outside the science laboratory. Part of a five - part series. Contact distributor about availability outside the United Kingdom.
Science; Science - Natural
Dist - ACADEM **Prod** - YORKTV

Scientific eye - series 3 - stars and planets 20 MIN
VHS
Scientific eye series
Color; PAL (J H)

PdS15 purchase
Considers outer space, stars and planets. Encourages students to think and react like scientists - testing theories, solving problems and conducting experiments to explain how and why things work. Uses drama, documentary and graphics, as well as film of pupils involved in scientific investigations both inside and outside the science laboratory. Part of a five - part series. Contact distributor about availability outside the United Kingdom.
Science; Science - Physical
Dist - ACADEM **Prod** - YORKTV

Scientific eye - series 3 - weather and rocks 20 MIN
VHS
Scientific eye series
Color; PAL (J H)
PdS15 purchase
Looks at weather and its effects upon the Earth's surface. Encourages students to think and react like scientists - testing theories, solving problems and conducting experiments to explain how and why things work. Uses drama, documentary and graphics, as well as film of pupils involved in scientific investigations both inside and outside the science laboratory. Part of a five - part series. Contact distributor about availability outside the United Kingdom.
Science; Science - Physical
Dist - ACADEM **Prod** - YORKTV

Scientific eye - series 4 - machines 20 MIN
VHS
Scientific eye series
Color; PAL (J H)
PdS15 purchase
Looks at machines. Encourages students to think and react like scientists - testing theories, solving problems and conducting experiments to explain how and why things work. Uses drama, documentary and graphics, as well as film of pupils involved in scientific investigations both inside and outside the science laboratory. Part of a five - part series. Contact distributor about availability outside the United Kingdom.
Science; Science - Physical
Dist - ACADEM **Prod** - YORKTV

Scientific eye - series 4 - solids, liquids and gases 20 MIN
VHS
Scientific eye series
Color; PAL (J H)
PdS15 purchase
Examines the physical states of matter. Encourages students to think and react like scientists - testing theories, solving problems and conducting experiments to explain how and why things work. Uses drama, documentary and graphics, as well as film of pupils involved in scientific investigations both inside and outside the science laboratory. Part of a five - part series. Contact distributor about availability outside the United Kingdom.
Science; Science - Physical
Dist - ACADEM **Prod** - YORKTV

Scientific eye - series 4 - the greenhouse effect 20 MIN
VHS
Scientific eye series
Color; PAL (J H)
PdS15 purchase
Looks at industrialization and the greenhouse effect. Encourages students to think and react like scientists - testing theories, solving problems and conducting experiments to explain how and why things work. Uses drama, documentary and graphics, as well as film of pupils involved in scientific investigations both inside and outside the science laboratory. Part of a five - part series. Contact distributor about availability outside the United Kingdom.
Science; Science - Natural; Science - Physical; Social Science
Dist - ACADEM **Prod** - YORKTV

Scientific eye - series 4 - variables 20 MIN
VHS
Scientific eye series
Color; PAL (J H)
PdS15 purchase
Looks at use of variables in scientific investigation. Encourages students to think and react like scientists - testing theories, solving problems and conducting experiments to explain how and why things work. Uses drama, documentary and graphics, as well as film of pupils involved in scientific investigations both inside and outside the science laboratory. Part of a five - part series. Contact distributor about availability outside the United Kingdom.
Science
Dist - ACADEM **Prod** - YORKTV

Scientific eye - series 4 - variety and survival 20 MIN
VHS
Scientific eye series
Color; PAL (J H)
PdS15 purchase
Examines the biological use of diversity and variety as a survival tactic. Encourages students to think and react like scientists - testing theories, solving problems and conducting experiments to explain how and why things work. Uses drama, documentary and graphics, as well as film of pupils involved in scientific investigations both inside and outside the science laboratory. Part of a five - part series. Contact distributor about availability outside the United Kingdom.
Science; Science - Natural
Dist - ACADEM **Prod** - YORKTV

Scientific eye - series 5 - electricity and magnetism 20 MIN
VHS
Scientific eye series
Color; PAL (J H)
PdS15 purchase
Looks at electricity and magnetism and their relationship. Encourages students to think and react like scientists - testing theories, solving problems and conducting experiments to explain how and why things work. Uses drama, documentary and graphics, as well as film of pupils involved in scientific investigations both inside and outside the science laboratory. Part of a four - part series. Contact distributor about availability outside the United Kingdom.
Science; Science - Physical
Dist - ACADEM **Prod** - YORKTV

Scientific eye - series 5 - energy 20 MIN
VHS
Scientific eye series
Color; PAL (J H)
PdS15 purchase
Looks at energy. Encourages students to think and react like scientists - testing theories, solving problems and conducting experiments to explain how and why things work. Uses drama, documentary and graphics, as well as film of pupils involved in scientific investigations both inside and outside the science laboratory. Part of a four - part series. Contact distributor about availability outside the United Kingdom.
Science; Science - Physical
Dist - ACADEM **Prod** - YORKTV

Scientific eye - series 5 - metals 20 MIN
VHS
Scientific eye series
Color; PAL (J H)
PdS15 purchase
Examines metals and their properties. Encourages students to think and react like scientists - testing theories, solving problems and conducting experiments to explain how and why things work. Uses drama, documentary and graphics, as well as film of pupils involved in scientific investigations both inside and outside the science laboratory. Part of a four - part series. Contact distributor about availability outside the United Kingdom.
Science; Science - Physical
Dist - ACADEM **Prod** - YORKTV

Scientific eye - series 5 - pressure 20 MIN
VHS
Scientific eye series
Color; PAL (J H)
PdS15 purchase
Considers pressure, how it is measured and other physical aspects of the phenomena. Encourages students to think and react like scientists - testing theories, solving problems and conducting experiments to explain how and why things work. Uses drama, documentary and graphics, as well as film of pupils involved in scientific investigations both inside and outside the science laboratory. Part of a four - part series. Contact distributor about availability outside the United Kingdom.
Science; Science - Physical
Dist - ACADEM **Prod** - YORKTV

Scientific eye - series 6 - chemical reactions 20 MIN
VHS
Scientific eye series
Color; PAL (J H)
PdS15 purchase
Examines chemical reactions. Encourages students to think and react like scientists - testing theories, solving problems and conducting experiments to explain how and why things work. Uses drama, documentary and graphics, as well as film of pupils involved in scientific investigations both inside and outside the science laboratory. Part of a four - part series. Contact distributor about availability outside the United Kingdom.
Science; Science - Physical
Dist - ACADEM **Prod** - YORKTV

Scientific eye - series 6 - growth 20 MIN
VHS
Scientific eye series
Color; PAL (J H)
PdS15 purchase
Looks at the biological aspects of growth. Encourages students to think and react like scientists - testing theories, solving problems and conducting experiments to explain how and why things work. Uses drama, documentary and graphics, as well as film of pupils involved in scientific investigations both inside and outside the science laboratory. Part of a four - part series. Contact distributor about availability outside the United Kingdom.
Science; Science - Natural
Dist - ACADEM **Prod** - YORKTV

Scientific eye - series 6 - plastics and polymers 20 MIN
VHS
Scientific eye series
Color; PAL (J H)
PdS15 purchase
Looks at plastics and polymers. Encourages students to think and react like scientists - testing theories, solving problems and conducting experiments to explain how and why things work. Uses drama, documentary and graphics, as well as film of pupils involved in scientific investigations both inside and outside the science laboratory. Part of a four - part series. Contact distributor about availability outside the United Kingdom.
Industrial and Technical Education; Science; Science - Physical
Dist - ACADEM **Prod** - YORKTV

Scientific eye - series 6 - speed and safety 20 MIN
VHS
Scientific eye series
Color; PAL (J H)
PdS15 purchase
Examines speed and safety. Encourages students to think and react like scientists - testing theories, solving problems and conducting experiments to explain how and why things work. Uses drama, documentary and graphics, as well as film of pupils involved in scientific investigations both inside and outside the science laboratory. Part of a four - part series. Contact distributor about availability outside the United Kingdom.
Health and Safety; Science; Science - Physical
Dist - ACADEM **Prod** - YORKTV

Scientific eye - series 7 - atoms and molecules 20 MIN
VHS
Scientific eye series
Color; PAL (J H)
PdS15 purchase
Examines atoms and molecules. Encourages students to think and react like scientists - testing theories, solving problems and conducting experiments to explain how and why things work. Uses drama, documentary and graphics, as well as film of pupils involved in scientific investigations both inside and outside the science laboratory. Part of a four - part series. Contact distributor about availability outside the United Kingdom.
Science; Science - Physical
Dist - ACADEM **Prod** - YORKTV

Scientific eye - series 7 - design a clock 20 MIN
VHS
Scientific eye series
Color; PAL (J H)
PdS15 purchase
Shows how to design a clock and discusses the measurement of time. Encourages students to think and react like scientists - testing theories, solving problems and conducting experiments to explain how and why things work. Uses drama, documentary and graphics, as well as film of pupils involved in scientific investigations both inside and outside the science laboratory. Part of a four - part series. Contact distributor about availability outside the United Kingdom.
Mathematics; Science
Dist - ACADEM **Prod** - YORKTV

Scientific eye - series 7 - reproductions and genetics 20 MIN
VHS
Scientific eye series
Color; PAL (J H)
PdS15 purchase
Considers reproduction of species, replication of chromosomes and genetics. Encourages students to think and react like scientists - testing theories, solving problems and conducting experiments to explain how and why things work. Uses drama, documentary and graphics, as well as film of pupils involved in scientific investigations both inside and outside the science laboratory. Part of a four - part series. Contact distributor about availability outside the United Kingdom.

Science; Science - Natural
Dist - ACADEM **Prod** - YORKTV

Scientific eye - series 7 - seeing the light 20 MIN
VHS
Scientific eye series
Color; PAL (J H)
PdS15 purchase
Looks at the visual perception of light, as well as the nature of light. Encourages students to think and react like scientists - testing theories, solving problems and conducting experiments to explain how and why things work. Uses drama, documentary and graphics, as well as film of pupils involved in scientific investigations both inside and outside the science laboratory. Part of a four - part series. Contact distributor about availability outside the United Kingdom.
Psychology; Science; Science - Physical
Dist - ACADEM **Prod** - YORKTV

Scientific eye series

Scientific eye - series 1	200 MIN
Scientific eye - series 2	200 MIN
Scientific eye - series 3	100 MIN
Scientific eye - series 4	100 MIN
Scientific eye - series 5	80 MIN
Scientific eye - series 6	80 MIN
Scientific eye - series 7	80 MIN
Scientific eye - series 5 - electricity and magnetism	20 MIN
Scientific eye - series 5 - energy	20 MIN
Scientific eye - series 5 - metals	20 MIN
Scientific eye - series 5 - pressure	20 MIN
Scientific eye - series 4 - machines	20 MIN
Scientific eye - series 4 - solids, liquids and gases	20 MIN
Scientific eye - series 4 - the greenhouse effect	20 MIN
Scientific eye - series 4 - variables	20 MIN
Scientific eye - series 4 - variety and survival	20 MIN
Scientific eye - series 1 - acids	20 MIN
Scientific eye - series 1 - drying out	20 MIN
Scientific eye - series 1 - fire and flame	20 MIN
Scientific eye - series 1 - force and friction	20 MIN
Scientific eye - series 1 - gravity	20 MIN
Scientific eye - series 1 - keeping cool	20 MIN
Scientific eye - series 1 - keeping warm	20 MIN
Scientific eye - series 1 - lighter than air	20 MIN
Scientific eye - series 1 - microbeasts and disease	20 MIN
Scientific eye - series 1 - river of rock	20 MIN
Scientific eye - series 7 - atoms and molecules	20 MIN
Scientific eye - series 7 - design a clock	20 MIN
Scientific eye - series 7 - reproductions and genetics	20 MIN
Scientific eye - series 7 - seeing the light	20 MIN
Scientific eye - series 6 - chemical reactions	20 MIN
Scientific eye - series 6 - growth	20 MIN
Scientific eye - series 6 - plastics and polymers	20 MIN
Scientific eye - series 6 - speed and safety	20 MIN
Scientific eye - series 3 - cells and systems	20 MIN
Scientific eye - series 3 - electronics and control	20 MIN
Scientific eye - series 3 - habitat and dependence	20 MIN
Scientific eye - series 3 - stars and planets	20 MIN
Scientific eye - series 3 - weather and rocks	20 MIN
Scientific eye - series 2 - crimebusters	20 MIN
Scientific eye - series 2 - earth ltd	20 MIN
Scientific eye - series 2 - fitness and sport	20 MIN
Scientific eye - series 2 - floating and sinking	20 MIN
Scientific eye - series 2 - getting things clean	20 MIN
Scientific eye - series 2 - hearing and sound	20 MIN
Scientific eye - series 2 - plants for food	20 MIN
Scientific eye - series 2 - seeing and believing	20 MIN
Scientific eye - series 2 - shape and strength	20 MIN
Scientific eye - series 2 - what is life	20 MIN

Dist - ACADEM

Scientific Fact and Fun Series

Arcs and sparks	13 MIN
Everything is Something	13 MIN
How Much Does the Earth Weigh	13 MIN
Looking into Things	13 MIN
Machines, Engines and Motors	13 MIN
Making Sense of it	13 MIN
Seeds and Weeds	13 MIN
Water Runs Downhill	13 MIN
What's in a Rainbow	13 MIN
What's in a Shadow	13 MIN
What's in a Spider Web	13 MIN
What's in an Egg	13 MIN

Dist - JOU

The Scientific girl 18 MIN
VHS / 16mm
Color (G)
$375.00 purchase, $75.00, $60.00 rental
Looks at the relationship between the development of psychoanalytic theory and the birth of early cinema. Compares the women diagnosed as 'madwomen' in France of the 1890s with American movie stars of the 1940s 'women's films.' Doctors, lawyers and private eyes depicted in these films interpret 'women's problems' as did Dr Charcot in Paris 50 years earlier. Presented by Kim Derko.
Fine Arts; Psychology; Sociology
Dist - WMENIF **Prod** - WMENIF 1988

Scientific graphs 45 MIN
VHS
(PRO A C H)
$179.00 purchase
Shows how to gather data from experiments and create bar, line, and pie graphs. Explains how to plot graphs as well as how to interpret them. Explains the standard distribution curve.
Mathematics; Science
Dist - EAV **Prod** - EAV 1987

Scientific graphs - how to make them and make sense of them
VHS / U-matic
Color (H)
Uses video segments and computer graphics to explain bar, line and pie graphs. Teaches how to construct an appropriate graph form, plot data and interpret finished graphs correctly.
Mathematics
Dist - GA **Prod** - GA

Scientific imagination in the Renaissance - Program 3 52 MIN
16mm / VHS
Day the universe changed series
Color (H C G)
$695.00, $300.00 purchase, $75.00 rental
Examines the role of Arab civilization in the Renaissance of Europe. Reveals that the study of Arab optics led to the discovery of perspective geometry and new painting and architecture, the ability to measure at a distance and to map the world, and the confidence to cross the Atlantic. The new knowledge led also to a new concept of the individual. Part of a ten - part series on Western thought hosted by James Burke.
History - World; Sociology
Dist - CF **Prod** - BBCTV 1986

Scientific Investigation Series

Studying Chemical Interactions	17 MIN
Studying electricity	16 MIN
Studying Fluid Behavior	17 MIN
Studying Gravitation and Mass	16 MIN
Studying Heat and its Behavior	17 MIN
Studying the Behavior of Light	16 MIN

Dist - JOU

Scientific Literacy 30 MIN
VHS / U-matic
Innovation Series
Color
Looks at the role of computers and how this role conflicts with the traditional notions of a 'good' education.
Education; Mathematics; Sociology
Dist - PBS **Prod** - WNETTV 1983

Scientific measurement
Videodisc
Color; CAV (J H)
$189.00 purchase _ #8L433
Examines a variety of measurements, including time, distance, speed, volume, mass weight, density, temperature and exponents. Shows the importance of measurement in science and research. Barcoded for instant random access.
Mathematics; Science
Dist - BARR **Prod** - BARR 1991

Scientific Measurement 18.5 MIN
VHS / 16mm / U-matic
Color (I J H)
$405, $305, $335 purchase _ #A433
Discusses all forms of measurement which include time, dimension, speed, temperature, energy output and so on which were created by man to better understand and chronicle the world around him. Examines a variety of measurements, including time, distance, speed, volume, mass, weight, density, temperature and exponents.
Science
Dist - BARR **Prod** - BARR 1987

Scientific method
Videodisc
Color; CAV (J H)
$189.00 purchase _ #8L541
Demonstrates the scientifiic method's systematic three - part process - observation, theorizing or hypothesizing, and testing the hypothesis through experimentation. Shows several examples of the scientific method at work in the classroom as well as in professional research and development. Barcoded for instant random access.
Psychology; Science
Dist - BARR **Prod** - BARR 1991

The Scientific Method 23 MIN
U-matic / VHS / 16mm
Color (J H)
$510, $360, $390 purchase _ #A541
Observes that the word science comes from the Latin word for knowledge. Traces the evolution of knowledge gained from the scientific method. Demonstrates the scientific method's systematic, three part process of observation, theorizing or hypothesizing, and testing the hypothesis through experimentation. Points out that the process is never ending.
Psychology; Science
Dist - BARR **Prod** - BARR 1988

The Scientific method 12 MIN
16mm / U-matic / VHS
Color; B&W (J H)
Explains the steps of the scientific method, demonstrates the way this method of problem solving is applied by scientists and discusses the value of scientific thinking in dealing with problems of everyday life. Features the discovery of penicillin by Sir Alexander Fleming.
Psychology; Science
Dist - EBEC **Prod** - EBEC 1954

Scientific method and measurement 38 MIN
VHS
CC; Color (I J)
$125 purchase_#10220VL
Presents and demonstrates the scientific method of hypothesis, experimentation, observation, and conclusion. Shows the use of measurements and the metric system in scientific investigation. Teaches about common laboratory equipment and how to conduct experiments. The two videos come with a teacher's guide; student activities; projects; discussion questions; and 11 blackline masters.
Mathematics; Science
Dist - UNL

Scientific method in action 19 MIN
U-matic / VHS / 16mm
Captioned; Color (J H)
Shows how the scientific method has contributed to the advancement of scientific knowledge and to a better understanding of the world. Re - creates Galileo's experiments with gravity and Salk's conquest of polio. Analyzes the six formal steps of the scientific method. Captioned for the hearing impaired.
Psychology; Science
Dist - IFB **Prod** - VEF 1960

Scientific methods and values 34 MIN
VHS
Color (J H)
$130.00 purchase _ #A5VH 1003
Presents a two - part introduction to science. Describes the history of how scientific methods and values came to be, in Part One. Part Two discusses methods and values in science today. Includes a supplemental book.
Science
Dist - CLRVUE **Prod** - CLRVUE

Scientific methods in values 34 MIN
VHS
Color; CC (H C)
$129.00 purchase _ #115
Introduces science at high school or junior college level. Presents two parts which examine the history of science and modern methods and values in science. The Growth of Science, Part 1, looks at how scientific methods and values came to be. Visits the homes and laboratories of Isaac Newton, Charles Darwin, Marie Curie and other famous scientists. Part 2 is entitled Methods and Values in Science Today. Includes a book of the same title from the Learning Power series.
Guidance and Counseling; Science
Dist - HAWHIL **Prod** - HAWHIL 1994

Scientific noise 28 MIN
16mm
Mr Wizard series
B&W (I J)
Explains that sound changed in volume and frequency becomes noise. Shows how scrambled letters may be unscrambled with a filter and how a screened photograph with 'interference' removed may be identified.
Science - Physical
Dist - MLA **Prod** - PRISM 1964

Scientific notation 20 MIN
U-matic
Mainly math series
Color (H C)
Emphasizes the importance of scientific notation in astronomy, physics and economics.
Business and Economics; Mathematics; Science - Physical
Dist - GPN **Prod** - WCVETV 1977

Scientific notation and metric prefixes 30 MIN
VHS / U-matic
Basic electricity and D C circuits series
Color
Introduces simple 'metric chart' to help master number conversions from decimal form to scientific notation and metric prefixed format or vice versa. Discusses addition, subtraction, multiplication and division of numbers written in scientific notation.
Industrial and Technical Education; Mathematics; Science - Physical; Social Science
Dist - TXINLC **Prod** - TXINLC

Scientific problem solving 22 MIN
VHS
Understanding science video series
Color (I J H)
$39.95 purchase _ #KUS201
Covers the correct steps for solving a problems scientifically, as well as lab safety procedures. Presents part of a six - part series on science.
Science
Dist - KNOWUN

Scientific problem solving 15 MIN
VHS
Understanding science series
Color (J H)
$39.00 purchase _ #60486 - 026
Features part of a six - part series that features difficult scientific concepts in an easy - to - understand format, designed with natural stopping points so the instructor can choose when to stop for classroom discussion.
Psychology; Science
Dist - GA

Scientific problem solving 15 MIN
VHS
Understanding science series
Color (J H)
$39.00 purchase _ #60486 - 026
Part of a series that presents difficult scientific concepts in an easy - to - understand format designed with natural stopping points so the instructor can choose when to stop for classroom discussion.
Science
Dist - GA **Prod** - GA 1993

Scientific problem solving - Volume 1 18 MIN
VHS
Understanding science series
Color (I J)
$39.95 purchase _ #SC01
Presents experiments and demonstrations that can be easily repeated in the classroom. Explains how to solve problems using the scientific method. Includes teacher's guide. Part of a six - part series explaining difficult scientific ideas in an informal way.
Science
Dist - SVIP

Scientific revolution 30 MIN
U-matic / VHS
Historically speaking series
Color (H)
Discusses Ptolemy's view of the universe and how it was challenged by Copernicus and Galileo. Shows that mathematics is the language of science and deals with Newton's contributions, the beginnings of scientific medicine and the concept of natural laws. Part four of the series.
History - World; Science
Dist - AITECH **Prod** - KRMATV 1983

The Scientific revolution 48
VHS / 35mm strip
Color (J H)
$150.00 purchase _ #A7VH 0230, #A9K 0002
Presents three parts on the Scientific Revolution, 1540 - 1700, within its historical context. Defines its relationship to the Enlightenment and Industrial Revolution. Combines original and documentary visuals with treatment of the key ideas, discoveries and inventions that formed the basis of one of the most fruitful periods in the history of science. Includes Science Before the Revolution - Aristotelianism, The Rise of Modern Science - from Copernicus to Galileo, The Triumph of the New Science - Newton's Synthesis.
History - World; Science
Dist - CLRVUE **Prod** - CLRVUE

The Scientific revolution 41 MIN
VHS / 16mm
Color (I)
LC 90700043
Discusses the overturning of the European world view based primarily on tradition and authority. Describes the political and social conditions which spawned the scientific revolution and the challenges to Aristotelian science. Examines Newton's synthesis of components of the new science and the influence of Newtonian physics.
History - World; Science
Dist - EAV **Prod** - EAV 1974

Scientific Super Sleuths 10 MIN
16mm
Color
LC 79-701539
Shows different scientific methods used in identifying criminals, including handwriting analysis, voice print identification, gunshot residue identification, ballistic testing, fingerprinting and identification of moonshine samples.
Civics and Political Systems; Social Science; Sociology
Dist - USNAC **Prod** - USBATF 1975

Scientific uses, international cooperation 20 MIN
VHS / U-matic
Space stations series
Color (I J H G)
$245.00, $295.00 purchase, $50.00 rental
Covers all the potential uses of the space station, including fundamental research on space processes, commercially viable techniques for the use of space, micro - gravity processing and telescopic observation. Theorizes on the use of the space station as a stepping stone to further planetary exploration as well as a potential bridge to international cooperation. Part of a three - part series. Produced by Media Craft Communications.
Industrial and Technical Education; Science
Dist - NDIM

Scientific visualization 26 MIN
U-matic / VHS
Color (C)
$249.00, $149.00 purchase _ #AD - 2136
Shows how the increasing crush of numerical data from space probes, satellites and supercomputers is being translated into computer graphics to reduce huge masses of information into accessible and manipulative media. Looks at the tools used, many derived from film industry special - effects techniques. Shows how Einstein's theory of relativity is described as a picture, and how gas jet simulations are translated into images.
Computer Science; Mathematics
Dist - FOTH **Prod** - FOTH

Scientist in the sea 16 MIN
16mm
Color
LC FIE68-28
Tells how an oceanographer, skilled in the use of SCUBA gear, utilizes scientific knowledge to aid in the study of the ocean.
Science; Science - Physical
Dist - USNAC **Prod** - USN 1967

Scientists at Work
Biologists at work 45 MIN
Chemists at Work 45 MIN
Earth scientists at work
Physicists at Work 45 MIN
Dist - RH

Scientists in blue jeans 5 MIN
16mm
Screen news digest series
B&W
Surveys the work being done by the Future Engineers of America, an organization sponsoring scientific talent at the pre - college level. Presents some of the projects underway at an experimental E center in California. Volume three, issue two of the series.
Education; Industrial and Technical Education
Dist - HEARST **Prod** - HEARST 1960

Scintillation Spectrometry a - 2 3 MIN
16mm
Single - Concept Films in Physics Series
Color (H C)
Pictures the assembly of a detector. Identifies the single gamma - ray displayed with various statistics, photo - peak, Compton edge and backscatter.
Science; Science - Physical
Dist - OSUMPD **Prod** - OSUMPD 1963

Scissors 5 MIN
16mm
B&W (G)
$5.00 rental
Presents the life cycle of a pair of scissors in this hand - animated film. Tells the story of a litter of scissors in which one is abandoned and grows up, passes through puberty, marries and eventually gets eaten by a scissor - eating monster. Produced by Keewatin Dewdney.
Fine Arts
Dist - CANCIN

The Scoffer 8 MIN
16mm / U-matic / VHS
Dealing with problem people series
Color (H A)
LC 74-715420
Shows that the scoffer is acting out an inferiority complex (he tries to make himself bigger by belittling the rules) or a superiority complex (he usually thinks he is above such childish nonsense as regulations.) Indicates that either way he is a problem.
Psychology
Dist - JOU **Prod** - JOU 1969

Scoliosis 8 MIN
16mm
Color (I)
LC 82-700300
Defines scoliosis and kyphosis and describes how these conditions are treated.
Health and Safety; Science - Natural
Dist - HFHSC **Prod** - HFHSC 1981

Scoliosis 30 MIN
U-matic / VHS
Color (C PRO)
$330.00 purchase _ #800VI004
Focuses on diagnostic and therapeutic aspects of scoliosis and presents case studies to highlight discussions by specialists in the field.
Health and Safety; Science - Natural
Dist - HSCIC **Prod** - HSCIC 1980

Scoliosis 15 MIN
U-matic
Color (C)
Emphasizes certain points about scoliosis. Discusses history and treatment using various devices.
Health and Safety; Science - Natural
Dist - UOKLAH **Prod** - UOKLAH 1984

Scoliosis screening 9 MIN
U-matic
(A)
Corrects misconceptions and alleviates fears about the long and short term effects of scoliosis as well as giving information on diagnosis and treatment.
Health and Safety; Science - Natural
Dist - ACCESS **Prod** - ACCESS 1980

Scoliosis screening for early detection 14 MIN
16mm
Color (PRO)
LC 75-703774
Demonstrates step - by - step techniques for scoliosis screening, focusing on when and who to screen, what to look for, what to do if scoliosis is found and why early detection is crucial. Describes the establishment and evaluation of community screening programs, their facilities and staff.
Health and Safety; Science - Natural
Dist - EMCOM **Prod** - MVI 1974

Scoop chase - Volume 8 45 MIN
VHS
Bubblegum crisis series
Color (A) (JAPANESE WITH ENGLISH SUBTITLES)
$34.95 purchase _ #CPM91008
Presents a Japanese animated film. Viewer discretion is advised as some films contain strong language or violence.
Fine Arts
Dist - CHTSUI

Scope of Systems Engineering Problem 53 MIN
U-matic / VHS
Systems Engineering and Systems Management Series
Color
Provides a picture of the overall systems engineering problem, its common characteristics and procedures for engineering a system.
Industrial and Technical Education
Dist - MIOT **Prod** - MIOT

Scope of the Problem 28 MIN
U-matic / VHS
Color (J A)
Presents a discussion of alcohol abuse and alcoholism. Features former United States Senator Harold Hughes.
Health and Safety; Psychology; Sociology
Dist - SUTHRB **Prod** - SUTHRB

Scope two 3 MIN
16mm
Color (J H C)
Presents an audio - visual performance which exemplifies the modern age - an age in which both the painter and composer use the tools of the scientist to create their artistry.
Fine Arts; History - United States
Dist - CFS **Prod** - STOCH

Scoraform 10 MIN
16mm / U-matic / VHS
Color (J)
LC 72-702678
Follows the design and construction processes of scoraform sculpture, showing a variety of an artist's works. Explains that scoraform sculpture is created by scoring the surface of paper, cardboard or plastic and then bending the material into an original design.
Fine Arts
Dist - AIMS **Prod** - MCCBUR

The Score offshore 20 MIN
16mm
Color
LC 75-702461
Provides current Federal legal requirements for boat operators. Informs new boat owners about the requirements which all boat operators must fulfill before they are allowed to leave the dock.
Civics and Political Systems; Physical Education and Recreation; Social Science
Dist - USNAC **Prod** - USCG 1974

Score yourself 30 MIN
U-matic / VHS
CHD and you series
Color
Discusses nine traits or habits which characterize an individual who may develop CHD.
Health and Safety
Dist - NETCHE **Prod** - NETCHE 1976

The Scorn of women 52 MIN
U-matic / VHS / 16mm
Jack London's tales of the Klondike series
Color (H C A)
Introduces Floyd Vanderlipp, a manly hero much admired for his prowess in overcoming the perils of the frozen North. Shows how a comedy of errors leads Floyd to meet his match as three ladies from one of the Yukon's more civilized outposts attempt to ensnare him in a web of feminine intrigue. Based on the short story The Scorn Of Women by Jack London.
Literature and Drama
Dist - EBEC **Prod** - NORWK 1982

Scorpio rising 29 MIN
16mm
Color (G)
$60.00 rental
Portrays the myth of the American motorcyclist. Looks at the machine as totem, from toy to terror, or Thanatos in chrome and leather.
Fine Arts; Industrial and Technical Education
Dist - CANCIN **Prod** - ANGERK 1963

Scorpion 25 MIN
16mm / U-matic / VHS
Color (H C A)
Observes the private world of the scorpion, its habits and its life cycle.
Science - Natural
Dist - FI **Prod** - BBCTV 1981

Scorpion 10 MIN
VHS / U-matic
Eye on nature series
Color (I J)
$250.00 purchase _ #HP - 5855C
Looks at the scorpion species. Reveals that scorpions are closely related to spiders. Shows how they feed, mate, reproduce and raise their young. Discusses their ability to live in harsh environments and their ranges in size and their venom.
Science - Natural
Dist - CORF **Prod** - BBCTV 1989

Scorpions
35mm strip / VHS / Cassette
Newbery Award - Winners Series
Color (I)
$99.00, $66.00, $14.00 purchase
English Language; Literature and Drama
Dist - PELLER

The Scotch - Irish - the diffusion of American culture 9 MIN
VHS
Columbus legacy series
Color (J H C G)
$40.00 purchase, $11.00 rental _ #12334
Features historian Bruce Weston who looks at the tendency of the Scotch - Irish to be pioneers, and their contributions to American culture - blue grass music, the McGuffey Reader, the McCormack Reaper, Morse code, the log cabin and several famous pioneers and presidents. Part of a 15 - part series commemorating the 500th anniversary of Columbus' journeys to the Americas - journeys that brought together a constantly evolving collection of different ethnic groups and examining the contributions of 15 distinct groups who imprinted their heritage on the day - to - day life of Pennsylvania.
History - United States; Sociology
Dist - PSU **Prod** - WPSXTV 1992

Scotchcast Casting Tape Techniques 10 MIN
U-matic
Color (PRO)
Presents step - by - step instructions on how to apply a cast using water - activated fiberglass casting tape.
Health and Safety
Dist - MMAMC **Prod** - MMAMC

Scotland 60 MIN
VHS
Traveloguer Western Europe series
Color (J H C G)
$29.95 purchase _ #QC109V
Visits Scotland and its cities. Illustrates notable landmarks, special events in history and the legends that are part of Scottish culture. Part of a four part series on Western Europe.
Geography - World; History - World
Dist - CAMV

Scotland; 1986 21 MIN
16mm
Modern Europe series
Color (P I J)
LC 88-712601; 88-712602
Illustrates the geography, history and culture of Scotland.
Geography - World; History - World
Dist - JOU **Prod** - INTERF 1986

Scotland 60 MIN
VHS
Traveloguer collection series
Color (I J H A)
$29.95 purchase _ #QC109V-S
Presents information about the historic past and the current status of Scotland, including information about the cities and the countryside. Shows famous landmarks, out-of-the way sites, struggles and hardships, victories and championships, and the legends of the region. Uses live-action footage and historical clips to show the geography, history, and culture. Includes 16 60-minute programs on northern, western, eastern, and southern Europe.
Geography - World
Dist - CAMV

Scotland and the North - Pt 1 87 MIN
VHS
Great Houses of Britain series
Color (S)
$29.95 purchase _ #057 - 9001
Joins art historian Viscount Norwich for a tour of twelve of Britain's great houses and castles. Teaches about British architecture, views the exquisite contents of the houses and surveys the magnificent grounds from a helicopter. Interviews the owners and caretakes - a fascinating cast of characters which includes a water - skiing marquis and an especially articulate kitchen maid. Part 1 takes the viewer to Traquair Castle, the oldest inhabited house in Scotland, Alnwick Castle, where four - story battlements overlook some of the finest views in Northern England, and Beningborough Hall, known for its exquisite woodwork and carving.
Fine Arts; Geography - World; History - World; Sociology
Dist - FI

Scotland - land of contrasts 45 MIN
VHS
Color (G)
$19.95 purchase _ #S01467
Presents scenic views of Scotland. Includes historical information.
Geography - World; History - World
Dist - UILL

Scotland Oil Report 11 MIN
U-matic / VHS
Color (H C A)
Examines the development of Scottish off - shore oil fields and describes the methods being implemented to ensure safe delivery.
Geography - World; Social Science
Dist - JOU **Prod** - UPI

Scotland - the Highlands 18 MIN
U-matic / VHS / 16mm
Color (I J H)
LC 75-707281
Shows the physical character of this region and the rapidly changing pattern of its economic development and focuses attention on the crofter settlements and the fishing ports along the coast. Emphasizes the developments which have most affected the growing economy of the region, such as tourism, hydro - electric power and the consequent attraction of certain industries.
Geography - World; History - World
Dist - IFB **Prod** - BHA 1970

Scotland - the southern uplands and central lowlands 16 MIN
U-matic / VHS / 16mm
Color (I J H)
LC 79-707282
Presents the physical, agricultural, industrial and human geography of the two southern regions of Scotland. Focuses on the woolen industry, specialized farming, the heavy industries of the Clyde Basin and the lighter engineering industries of the new towns.
Agriculture; Business and Economics; Geography - World
Dist - IFB **Prod** - BHA 1970

Scotland - world of a difference 25 MIN
VHS
Color (S)
$19.95 purchase _ #423 - 9002
Views the superb landscapes of the Highlands, the islands, the beautiful Border Country, as well as Scotland's cities and castles. Includes the unique architectural and cultural treasures of Scotland.
Geography - World; History - World
Dist - FI

Scotland yard 60 MIN
VHS
Color (G)
$24.95 purchase _ #S02204
Presents filmmaker Lucy Jarvis' behind - the - scenes look at Scotland Yard, as well as a historical review of British crime and those who fought it. Hosted by David Niven.
Civics and Political Systems; Geography - World; Sociology
Dist - UILL

The Scots 51 MIN
U-matic / 16mm / VHS
Heritage Series
Color; Mono (G)
MV $350.00 _ MP $600.00 purchase, $50.00 rental
Features the hale and hearty Scots and their cultural traditions. Describes the persercution and oppression the Scottish have suffered over their long and arduous history. Through it all, they have clung strongly to their traditions that are such familiar sights today, including bagpipes and tartan kilts, once banned in Scotland. The Heritage profile of The Scots also outlines the many contributions of Canadian Scottish.
History - World
Dist - CTV **Prod** - CTV

The Scots - Pt 1 25 MIN
BETA / 16mm / VHS
Heritage series
Color
LC 77-702837
Explores Scotland's contributions to Canada. Traces the history of the Scottish people in Canada. Points out that the people of Scottish descent in Canada have a strong identity and are a proud, hard - working, cultural group.
History - World; Sociology
Dist - CTV **Prod** - CTV 1976

The Scots - Pt 2 25 MIN
BETA / 16mm / VHS
Heritage Series
Color
LC 77-702837
Explores Scotland's contributions to Canada. Traces the history of the Scottish people in Canada. Points out that the people of Scottish descent in Canada have a strong identity and are a proud, hard - working, cultural group.
History - World; Sociology
Dist - CTV **Prod** - CTV 1976

Scots, the, Pt 2 25 MIN
16mm
Heritage Series
Color
LC 77-702837
Explores Scotland's contributions to Canada. Traces the history of the Scottish people in Canada. Points out that the people of Scottish descent in Canada have a strong identity and are a proud, hard - working, cultural group.
Sociology
Dist - CTV **Prod** - CTV 1976

Scott Cramer's in - line skating dances 90 MIN
VHS
Color (G)

$29.95 purchase _ #SF10
Shows how this former world champion ice skater stays fit off the ice with in - line roller skates. Presents 16 original dances, with and without a partner, useful as an aerobic workout.
Fine Arts; Physical Education and Recreation
Dist - SVIP

Scott Goes to the Hospital 11 MIN
U-matic / VHS / 16mm
Color (P)
Follows Scott, who requires a tonsillectomy, through a typical day in the hospital. Depicts the friendly nurses, doctors and assistants and shows how his room, equipped with television, night - lights and call - button helps to reassure him.
Guidance and Counseling; Health and Safety; Social Science
Dist - HIGGIN **Prod** - HIGGIN 1973

Scott Joplin 15 MIN
U-matic / VHS / 16mm
Color (I)
LC 77-701111
Presents the life and music of ragtime musician Scott Joplin, narrated by Eartha Kitt. Follows his discovery and initial success to the failure of his opera Treemonisha and his early death in poverty and obscurity. Includes examples of his music and excerpts from the posthumous performance of Treemonisha.
Biography; Fine Arts; History - United States
Dist - PFP **Prod** - ANDSNA 1977

Scott O'Dell in His Home 15 MIN
U-matic / VHS
Color
LC 83-707202
Features children's author Scott O'Dell talking about his writing and his books for children and young adults,.
Literature and Drama
Dist - CLRFLM **Prod** - HMC 1983

Scottish symphony 30 MIN
16mm
Color (P I)
LC 72-700768
Traces the journey of the young German composer, Felix Mendelssohn, as he traveled throughout Scotland in 1829. Includes movements of the 'Scottish Symphony' and accompanying scenes of the sights that moved him to compose the symphony. Features the London Philharmonic, conducted by Otto Klemperer.
Biography; Fine Arts
Dist - BNCHMK **Prod** - DKMNH 1972

The Scottish Tragedy 30 MIN
U-matic / VHS
Color
Highlights the problems which can so easily overwhelm a badly organized film unit on location. Reveals that the efforts of the long - suffering production manager to run an efficient unit are continually thwarted by the determined, but inexperienced, young director.
Fine Arts
Dist - FI **Prod** - BBCTV

Scott's old new friend 22 MIN
U-matic / VHS / 16mm
If you know how I feel series
Color (I)
Presents Scott, who stops off at the park to play ball with classmates every day after school. Tells how he meets an old lady in the park and although his classmates ignore her, Scott makes friends with her and learns that a difference in age is no reason not to make friends.
Guidance and Counseling; Psychology; Sociology
Dist - CENTEF **Prod** - CENTRO 1983
CORF

Scouring, bleaching, dyeing, printing, finishing
U-matic / VHS
ITMA 1983 review series
Color
Industrial and Technical Education
Dist - NCSU **Prod** - NCSU

The Scout 10 MIN
U-matic / VHS / 16mm
Color
LC 76-702884
Presents an adaptation of Jack London's short story entitled War, in which a cavalry scout chances upon an enemy soldier in the woods and, unseen, hesitates to shoot. Shows how the scout is later killed by the man he had spared.
Literature and Drama; Sociology
Dist - WOMBAT **Prod** - UONEFP 1976

Scout Squad Operations 26 MIN
16mm
Color
LC 80-701842
Shows how a scout squad prepares for and conducts patrols while the parent platoon performs reconnaissance and security operations in support of a task force tank battalion.
Civics and Political Systems
Dist - USNAC **Prod** - USA 1980

Scouting and match plans
VHS
Coaching boys' volleyball III series
Color (J H C G)
$49.95 purchase _ #TRS583V
Features Bill Neville, USA National Team coach. Focuses on scouting and match plans in volleyball. Part of a two - part series on volleyball coaching tactics and an eight - part series on boys' volleyball.
Physical Education and Recreation
Dist - CAMV

Scouting for common alfalfa diseases 15 MIN
VHS
Color (C A)
$50.00 purchase, $18.00 rental
Describes the symptoms to look for when scouting a field for vascular wilts - root, crown and stem roots - and foliar leaf and stem blights.
Agriculture
Dist - CORNRS **Prod** - CORNRS 1988

Scouting for giant bass 22 MIN
16mm
Color
LC 79-701446
Follows outdoor sports writer Homer Circle on a fishing expedition deep in Ocala National Forest.
Physical Education and Recreation
Dist - IPHC **Prod** - IH 1979

Scouting of Old Sandy 22 MIN
16mm
Color
LC 79-701448
Shows how champion skier Billy Kidd and a friend take a four - wheel - drive Scout to the top of Sand Mountain to ski.
Physical Education and Recreation
Dist - IPHC **Prod** - IH 1979

Scouts - the rise of the world scouting movement 57 MIN
VHS
Color (J H C G)
$695.00, $195.00 purchase, $75.00 rental
Traces the life of Lord Robert Baden - Powell, founder of the Boy Scouts, and the development of the World Scouting Movement during his life time and after. Includes archival footage.
Sociology
Dist - CF **Prod** - CLEHOR 1986

Scram 20 MIN
35mm
B&W (G)
Features Laurel and Hardy meeting a vagrant who offers them the home of a sourpuss judge for the night. Contact distributor for rental price.
Fine Arts; Psychology
Dist - KITPAR **Prod** - ROACH 1932

Scram 20 MIN
16mm
Cellar door cine mites series
Color (I)
LC 74-701552
Fine Arts; Literature and Drama
Dist - CELLAR **Prod** - CELLAR 1972

Scramble 43 MIN
16mm
Color (P I J)
Tells about Jimmy, who has been in trouble with the police, trying to start a new life.
Literature and Drama
Dist - LUF **Prod** - LUF

The Scramble 22 MIN
16mm
Color
Features former football quarterback Fran Tarkenton, who presents a plan for achieving top individual performance. Stresses the importance of defining and developing one's own strengths through a five - point program.
Psychology
Dist - PROTC **Prod** - PROTC 1979

Scrambled Eggs and Canned Meat 14 MIN
Videoreel / VT2
Living Better II Series
Color
Prepares a dish made with the commodity foods, dried eggs and canned meats. Discusses tips for using eggs and what can be used if not on the commodity program. Emphasizes eggs as a source of protein and shows many ways eggs can be prepared.
Health and Safety; Home Economics; Social Science
Dist - PBS **Prod** - MAETEL

Scrambling for dollars 30 MIN
VHS
America's defense monitor series; Politics and economics
Color (J H C G)
$29.95 purchase _ #ADM348V
Examines the future of defense industries in the United States. Part of a five - part series on the politics and economics of American military affairs.
Business and Economics; Civics and Political Systems
Dist - CAMV

Scranton fire test 30 MIN
U-matic / VHS
Color
Shows a full - scale fire test which was conducted in a modern, operating, multi - story open - air parking structure in order to study the effects of an uncontrolled fire in an automobile on the integrity of the exposed steel frame.
Health and Safety; Industrial and Technical Education
Dist - MPS **Prod** - ALSC

A Scrap of Paper and a Piece of String 6 MIN
16mm / U-matic / VHS
Color (P I)
Uses animation to tell of the friendship between a scrap of paper and a piece of string. Points out the significance of paper and string to the economy.
English Language; Literature and Drama; Psychology; Social Science; Sociology
Dist - MGHT **Prod** - NBCTV 1964

The Scrapbook Experience 17 MIN
U-matic / VHS
Color (J A)
Shows one way a foster child develops a sense of identity by writing his own biographical scrapbook under the guidance of a social worker.
Sociology
Dist - SUTHRB **Prod** - SUTHRB

The Scrapbook Experience - Building a Child's Identity 16 MIN
16mm
Color (PRO)
LC 79-700700
Introduces the use of the scrapbook technique to aid young people in gaining a sense of personal history and self - identity.
Education; Psychology; Sociology
Dist - IA **Prod** - LAC 1975

The Scrapbook experience - building a child's identity 16 MIN
U-matic / VHS
Color
Shows a social worker and a child gathering photos, documents, remembrances and souvenirs into a scrapbook of a foster child's life in order to create a self - identity and personal history.
Sociology
Dist - IA **Prod** - LACFU
SUTHRB

Scrapers and Abrasives 13 MIN
16mm
Hand Tools for Wood Working Series
Color (H C A)
LC FIA67-965
Describes concepts in scrapers and abrasives for woodwork, such as using cabinet and hand scrapers, sharpening scrapers, preparing wood surfaces and sandpapers and sanding.
Industrial and Technical Education
Dist - SF **Prod** - MORLAT 1967

Scraping flat surfaces 14 MIN
16mm
Machine shop work series
B&W
Shows how surface plates are used to check the flatness of surfaces. Discusses the types of scrapers and shows how to remove high spots and to determine when a surface is scraped flat. Number two in the series focuses on bench work.
Industrial and Technical Education
Dist - USNAC **Prod** - USOE 1942

Scrapping nuclear weapons 28 MIN
VHS
Color (J H C G)

$34.95 purchase _ #ADM538V
Reveals that the possible dismantling of thousands of nuclear warheads creates a new problem - how to dispose of their radioactive contents.
Civics and Political Systems; Sociology
Dist - CAMV

Scraps 5 MIN
U-matic
Color (K P)
Documents how poor women in Amedabad, India, recylce scraps of trash into toy birds. Features Bangali flute music instead of narration.
Geography - World; Science - Natural
Dist - HANMNY **Prod** - HANMNY 1971

Scraps of life 28 MIN
VHS
Color (H C G)
$295.00 purchase, $55.00 rental
Reveals that 2000 people were murdered in Chile during the Pinochet years. Shows that their survivors - mothers, sisters and wives - have come together to express their sorrow and to demand truth and justice from the new government, sewing murals out of scraps of fabrics, arpilleras, to record Chile's bloody history. Produced by Gayla Jamison.
Civics and Political Systems; Geography - World
Dist - FLMLIB

Scratch 4 MIN
16mm
B&W (G)
$10.00 purchase
Stimulates with a visually chaotic manipulation of film emulsion.
Fine Arts
Dist - CANCIN **Prod** - STREEM 1983

Scratch Pad 7 MIN
16mm
Color (J)
Presents a collage film.
Fine Arts
Dist - CFS **Prod** - CFS 1960

Scratches, Inc 4 MIN
16mm
B&W (G)
$20.00 rental
Features a light comical production employing the technique of scratching emulsion off the film. Creates illusions of color and texture.
Fine Arts
Dist - CANCIN **Prod** - ANGERA 1975
FLMKCO

The Scratching Pole 30 MIN
16mm
Footsteps Series
Color
LC 79-701552
Discusses the concept of developmental tasks and explains how parents can interpret their child's behavior in terms of developmental tasks. Shows that parents can be more tolerant and helpful if they can determine what their children are trying to accomplish by behaving in a certain manner.
Home Economics; Psychology; Sociology
Dist - USNAC **Prod** - USOE 1978

Scratching the surface 30 MIN
VHS
Open space series
Color (H C A)
PdS50 purchase _ Available only in UK and Eire
Reveals that approximately 7.5 million British people have some type of disfigurement or skin disease, with accompanying discrimination and stigma. Features Ashley Medicks, a 24-year sufferer, attempting to raise public awareness of skin disease in the UK, where only one in ten GPs has had any formal dermatology training.
Health and Safety; Science - Natural
Dist - BBCENE

Scratching where it itches 28 MIN
16mm
Color
Explains how to minimize the symptoms and explore the cause of scratching where it itches.
Guidance and Counseling; Sociology
Dist - ECUFLM **Prod** - UMCOM 1982

A Scream from Silence 96 MIN
16mm
Color (C A)
Documents the rape and eventual suicide of Suzanne, a nurse whose physical and emotional health deteriorates beyond repair as a result of the violence inflicted on her. Explores society's attitudes which cause women to feel guilty for being raped. Touches upon the physical, emotional, spiritual and legal aspects of this crime.
Sociology
Dist - NFBC **Prod** - NFBC 1979

Screaming Eagles in Vietnam 29 MIN
16mm / VHS / U-matic
Big picture series
Color
LC 74-706239
Shows some of the activities of the Screaming Eagles, the 101st Division of the Army, in Vietnam.
Civics and Political Systems; History - World; Industrial and Technical Education
Dist - USNAC **Prod** - USA 1967
IHF

Screen digest series
Focus on South Korea - fifteen years after the armistice 15 MIN
Dist - HEARST

Screen new digest series
Remember Pearl Harbor - America at War, 1941 - 45 17 MIN
Dist - HEARST

Screen news digest series
America - 1970 14 MIN
America - the melting pot 14 MIN
America becomes a world power 12 MIN
An american farmer 12 MIN
The American presidency - from Washington to Carter 12 MIN
An American tragedy - the assassination of John F Kennedy 20 MIN
America's first women astronauts 14 MIN
The Art of Diplomacy 12 MIN
The Automobile in America 12 MIN
The Bully pulpit - Roosevelt and Reagan 13 MIN
The Business of America 15 MIN
The Chancellor - Konrad Adenauer 10 MIN
The Changing Face of Eastern Europe 13 MIN
The Changing Face of Franco Spain 12 MIN
Charles De Gaulle - France is a Widow 14 MIN
China today 20 MIN
Choosing the candidates 12 MIN
Cleantown, USA 13 MIN
Conquest of the Skies 10 MIN
The Crucial Arean 14 MIN
Der Fuehrer - Adolf Hitler 13 MIN
Destination Moon 13 MIN
Down on the farm 15 MIN
The Dragon and the Bear 13 MIN
Earning and Learning 13 MIN
The Energy challenge 23 MIN
Fabled land - troubled land 13 MIN
Father of the Space Age - Dr Robert Goddard 18 MIN
Feeding the world 13 MIN
The Flight of Apollo 15 12 MIN
Focus on 1945 - victory in Europe and victory in the Pacific 21 MIN
Focus on 1958 13 MIN
A Fortnight at nine fathoms 13 MIN
The Genius of Japan 14 MIN
The Information Revolution 13 MIN
The Jackie Robinson Story 14 MIN
John F Kennedy Remembered 14 MIN
Money, Money, Money 14 MIN
Platform to the stars 11 MIN
Poland - a new nightmare 13 MIN
Pushbuttons and People 10 MIN
Satchmo and all that Jazz 12 MIN
Space Medicine - Serving Manking 13 MIN
Thunder out of Asia 12 MIN
The Truman legacy 14 MIN
United States and China Relations 13 MIN
Dist - AFA

Screen news digest series
Communism in conflict 17 MIN
Energy - choices, options, decisions 14 MIN
The First Tuesday after the first Monday - election of a president 15 MIN
Dist - AFA
HEARST

Screen news digest series
America - the melting pot 15 MIN
America becomes a world power 14 MIN
America votes 3 MIN
An american farmer 14 MIN
An American tragedy - the death of President Kennedy 21 MIN
The American Vice Presidency 15 MIN
America's new weather eye 4 MIN
Ancient land, troubled land 14 MIN
The Apollo project - a progress report 13 MIN
Asia, the crucial arena - the quest for peace 16 MIN
At sea with the Kitty Hawk 5 MIN
The Atomic dilemma - challenge of our age 21 MIN
The Automobile in America 14 MIN
Bravest of the brave - focus on the congo 20 MIN
Bravest of the Brave - the Congressional Medal of Honor 6 MIN
Caribbean powdorkeg 12 MIN
The Chancellor - a Portrait of Konrad Adenauer 11 MIN
The Changing Face of Eastern Europe 14 MIN
The Changing Face of Franco Spain 13 MIN
Changing of the Guard 5 MIN
Charles De Gaulle - 1890 - 1970 14 MIN
China in the 20th century - the two - headed dragon 17 MIN
Choosing the candidates 15 MIN
Chopin anniversary 5 MIN
Churchill biography - Johnson inauguration 20 MIN
Clean town, usa 15 MIN
Convention time in the U S A 5 MIN
A Country to Watch 7 MIN
A Crack in the Wall - an Historical Agreement 15 MIN
Crises and powder kegs 9 MIN
Czechoslovakia in chains - the death of a dream 14 MIN
Death of President Kennedy 20 MIN
The Degaulle dilemma - a timely report on NATO 18 MIN
Democracy in action - presidential election 1960 17 MIN
Democracy in action - the candidates are chosen 17 MIN
Democracy in action - the oath is taken 7 MIN
Der Fuehrer - the rise and fall of Adolph Hitler 14 MIN
Destination Moon - America's first spaceport 15 MIN
Detente - with a question 25 MIN
Dragon and the Bear - who is Number 1 14 MIN
Duce 14 MIN
Dwight D Eisenhower - Portrait of a Patriot 16 MIN
Education in the Andes 5 MIN
The Energy challenge 26 MIN
Europe Goes to War, 1939 12 MIN
The Executive power 15 MIN
Fabled land, troubled land - the crisis over Kashmir 15 MIN
Faith in Ourselves 22 MIN
Father of the space age 15 MIN
First man in space 10 MIN
The Flight of Apollo 15 14 MIN
Flight of Apollo 7 14 MIN
The Flight of the Friendship 7 22 MIN
Focus on - Alexander Graham Bell 7 MIN
Focus on 1932 - the year of change 19 MIN
Focus on 1939 - Europe goes to war 18 MIN
Focus on 1941 - America goes to war 16 MIN
Focus on 1954 14 MIN
Focus on a model rocket society - junior missile men in action 15 MIN
Focus on a nuclear submarine, at sea with the USSR skate 9 MIN
Focus on Algeria 10 MIN
Focus on Antarctica - the last frontier 11 MIN
Focus on Argentina - a country at the crossroads 9 MIN
Focus on Berlin - frontier of freedom 10 MIN
Focus on Cambodia - ancient land, troubled land 20 MIN
Focus on Camp Century - a city under the ice 11 MIN
Focus on Cuba 7 MIN
Focus on Cuba - the years under Castro 16 MIN
Focus on desalinization - fresh water from the sea 10 MIN
Focus on Dr Harley - 'the healer' and his works 8 MIN
Focus on Indonesia - words and deeds 11 MIN
Focus on Interpol - International Police Commission 9 MIN
Focus on junior achievement - learning by doing 5 MIN
Focus on Khrushchev, successor to Stalin 9 MIN
Focus on Korea 20 MIN
Focus on Kwame Nkrumah - the fallen idol 15 MIN
Focus on Laos 13 MIN
Focus on Latin America - past, present, future - operation amigo 15 MIN
Focus on NATO - the De Gaulle dilemma 20 MIN

Focus on Nikita Khrushchev - shakeup in the Kremlin 10 MIN
Focus on Pooch Harrington, America's youngest Olympian 21 MIN
Focus on Sir Winston Churchill - four score years and ten 10 MIN
Focus on South Viet Nam 20 MIN
Focus on the Aswan Dam - harnessing the Nile 9 MIN
Focus on the candidates - showdown at San Francisco 10 MIN
Focus on the capitol - the heart of America 15 MIN
Focus on the common market - union in Europe 10 MIN
Focus on the Congo - a troubled land 9 MIN
Focus on the decline and fall of Josef Stalin - the fallen idol 10 MIN
Focus on the flight of the Apollo 7 - a step toward the moon 20 MIN
Focus on the Middle East 14 MIN
Focus on the Peace Corps - Americans who serve 8 MIN
Focus on the United Nations - a look at the record 18 MIN
Focus on the United Nations - in pursuit of peace 11 MIN
Focus on the United Nations - mankind at the crossroads 18 MIN
Focus on the United Nations - the first twenty - five years 20 MIN
Focus on the United Nations - the problem of micro - states 14 MIN
Focus on the X - 15, man into space 29 MIN
Focus on United Nations - a successor for U Thant 20 MIN
Focus on Winston Churchill 10 MIN
A Former president is mourned - Herbert Hoover - 1874 - 1964 5 MIN
Forward together - Vol 17, Issue 01 14 MIN
Free China on Alert 5 MIN
From enemy to ally 13 MIN
From Kitty Hawk to jumbo jet 14 MIN
Frontiers, 1965 - the Sky Above, the Sea Below 18 MIN
Gold and you - drain on the dollar 14 MIN
Golden door 15 MIN
The Great Depression 15 MIN
The Great gold rush 5 MIN
The Growing Common Market
Growing Pains for the Common Market 13 MIN
Guantanamo Exclusive 5 MIN
Horizons in science - in and out of this world 16 MIN
I have a Dream 14 MIN
Indonesia - Words and Deeds 10 MIN
Inside Cuba Today 18 MIN
Jamboree City, 1960 5 MIN
Kwame Nkrumah - the Fallen Idol 15 MIN
A Land Divided - India and Pakistan at War 15 MIN
The Land of the Peacock Throne 14 MIN
Laos - Outpost in Peril 5 MIN
Lightning War in the Middle East 14 MIN
The Magic Lantern Show - and How it Grew - a History of Movies 14 MIN
The Man and the Rocket
Man Called 'Duce,' a - Benito Mussolini in Perspective 15 MIN
Mankind and the Atom 20 MIN
Mariner Mars Space Probe - President Kennedy Remembered - Focus on the Aswan Dam 20 MIN
Milestones in Space 5 MIN
Mission to the Moon - Report on Project Apollo 16 MIN
Ms - the Struggle for Women's Rights 14 MIN
A Nation within a Nation 14 MIN
NATO - Past, Present, Future 20 MIN
A New Job for U Thant 5 MIN
The New York World's Fair - Peace through Understanding 9 MIN
Nigeria and Biafra - the Story Behind the Struggle 14 MIN
The Nineteen Sixty - Four Conventions - Goldwater, Johnson Nominated 20 MIN
Nineteen Sixty - Four Presidential Election - Death of Herbert Hoover - Downfall of Krushchev 20 MIN
Nuclear Fallout - Fiction and Fact 10 MIN
The Oath is Taken 8 MIN
The Old Soldier - a Biography of Douglas Mac Arthur 15 MIN
One Small Step 17 MIN
Operation Big Lift 6 MIN
Painting on Copper 5 MIN
Pilgrimage to a Mountain Peak 4 MIN
A Porpoise with a purpose 5 MIN
Portrait of a President - Lyndon Baines Johnson 17 MIN
Powder keg in the Congo - a special report 5 MIN
Power from the Sun 5 MIN
A President remembered 5 MIN
Profile of a President - Richard Milhous Nixon 15 MIN
Project apollo - mission to the moon 18 MIN
Project Gemini - the Next Step in Space 9 MIN
Promised land, troubled land 14 MIN
Resource Recovery 14 MIN
Rocket Mice on a Record Ride 5 MIN
The Russian Revolution 1917 - 1967 20 MIN
The Russian Revolution and the 50 Years that Followed 16 MIN
Salute to a Crusader - Dwight Eisenhower Portrait of a Patriot 14 MIN
Science Island 5 MIN
Scientists in blue jeans 5 MIN
Shooting for mars 3 MIN
Sitting on Top of the World 5 MIN
South Viet Nam - Tinderbox in Asia 5 MIN
Space Age - Dr Goddard to Project Gemini 18 MIN
Staking Out the Oceans, a New Age in Marine Explorations 14 MIN
State of the Union 5 MIN
The State of the Union - Viet Nam Report 1966 14 MIN
Stepping Stones in Space 14 MIN
The Story of a violin 5 MIN
The Story of the space age - a special report 19 MIN
Students track the space age 6 MIN
Summer - 1966 20 MIN
Summer, 1966 - a nation builds under fire 4 MIN
Summer, 1966 - conquest in space 4 MIN
Summer, 1966 - Mission to Moscow 5 MIN
Summer, 1966 - pilgrimage into the past 4 MIN
Thailand - Ally Under Fire 20 MIN
This way to the White House 13 MIN
A Town that Washes its Water 13 MIN
The Treasures of Abu Simbel 3 MIN
Troubled Neighbors - Cuba and the United States 15 MIN
Turmoil in Communist China - the Troubles of Mao - Tse - Tung 16 MIN
The Two - Headed Dragon 16 MIN
U N in Crisis - a Successor for U Thant 17 MIN
Viet Nam - Why - a Timely Report 15 MIN
Viet Nam Report - Focus on Indonesia 20 MIN
Vietnam Epilogue - the End of the Tunnel 15 MIN
Vietnam Report - Guardians at the Gate 12 MIN
Visit to a Russian School 5 MIN
A Visit to Fra Mauro 14 MIN
Vital Waterway - the Suez Canal 14 MIN
Walk on the Moon 15 MIN
We Seek no Wider War 6 MIN
We, the People - Story of Our Federal Government 20 MIN
West Berlin - a Show of Faith 5 MIN
Worst Winter of the Century 5 MIN
Zero Draft 14 MIN
Dist - HEARST

The Screen Play 13 MIN
16mm / U-matic / VHS
Color (J)
LC 73-700755
Presents the fundamentals of writing for the screen. Encourages people of all ages and backgrounds to try their hand at script writing.
English Language; Fine Arts
Dist - PFP **Prod** - PFP 1972

Screen printing 25 MIN
VHS
Artists in print series
Color (A)
PdS65 purchase
Introduces the art of printmaking and illustrates basic printmaking techniques. Artists talk about their approach to the medium and are seen at all stages of making a print. Asks what a print is and explains the difference between an original and a reproduction. Part of a five-part series.
Fine Arts; Industrial and Technical Education
Dist - BBCENE

Screen, projector and film 14 MIN
16mm
Color (G)
$56.00 rental
Deals with the filming and projecting - taking and giving - into the same space of present and past. Requires a freestanding screen three feet by three feet for viewing.
Fine Arts
Dist - CANCIN **Prod** - WONGAL 1978

Screen Test 25 MIN
16mm
Screen Test Series
Color; Silent (J H C G T A)
Presents a series of short animated films packed with message in a humorous manner. A little 'Everyman' is caught inside the screen of the world. The door to salvation beckons and no matter how he reacts to it, ignores it, or tries to avoid it, he cannot escape the persistence of God's love.
Fine Arts; Religion and Philosophy
Dist - WHLION **Prod** - WHLION

Screen Test Series
The Hand 25 MIN
The Key 25 MIN
The Line 25 MIN
Screen Test 25 MIN
The Shadow 25 MIN
The Trap 25 MIN
Dist - WHLION

Screening and management of plasma lipids 21 MIN
U-matic / VHS
Color (PRO)
Discusses questions that the physician must consider in developing a rational approach to the prevention of arteriosclertic disease.
Health and Safety
Dist - UMICHM **Prod** - UMICHM 1977

Screening for colorectal cancer 11 MIN
VHS
Color (PRO A G) (SPANISH)
$200.00 purchase _ #GI - 11
Reinforces physician's recommendations that patients have regular exams for early detection of colorectal cancer. Provides an overview of how the colon works, relationship between polyps and cancer development, and symptoms of colon cancer. Also discusses diet, high risk groups and cure rate with early detection. Describes the complete range of possible testing from occult blood tests to colonoscopy.
Health and Safety; Science - Natural
Dist - MIFE **Prod** - MIFE

Screening for Driver Limitations - Aging 19 MIN
16mm
Color (A)
LC 77-703250
Presents adverse medical conditions which may be more common in older drivers and offers general recommendations to driver examiners screening these individuals.
Health and Safety; Psychology
Dist - USNAC **Prod** - USHTSA 1976

Screening for Driver Limitations - Cardiovascular 18 MIN
16mm
Color (A)
LC 77-703251
Presents information on such cardiovascular conditions as coronary disease, hypertension, arterial disorders, coronary bypass surgery and pacemakers. Gives clues to help driver examiners identify drivers whose degree of impairment should be medically evaluated before they are licensed.
Health and Safety; Psychology
Dist - USNAC **Prod** - USHTSA 1976

Screening for driver limitations - general medicine 16 MIN
16mm
Color (A)
LC 77-703254
Presents a wide variety of medical conditions, such as metabolic disorders, diabetes, orthopedic problems, hearing and respiratory disorders, and the impact these conditions may have on driving ability. Shows the signs of these disorders, which will help driver examiners identify those drivers whose impairment should be medically evaluated before they are licensed.
Health and Safety; Psychology
Dist - USNAC **Prod** - USHTSA 1976

Screening for Driver Limitations - Introduction 8 MIN
16mm
Color (A)
LC 77-703252
Presents signs and symptoms of conditions which may impair a driver's ability to safely operate a motor vehicle.

Health and Safety; Psychology
Dist - USNAC **Prod** - USHTSA 1976

Screening for Driver Limitations - Mental and Emotional 21 MIN
16mm
Color (A)
LC 77-703255
Presents a wide range of mental and emotional disorders, including alcoholism, drug abuse and suicide, which driver examiners need to identify in order that medical evaluation can be made before the individual is licensed.
Health and Safety; Psychology
Dist - USNAC **Prod** - USHTSA 1976

Screening for driver limitations - neurological 16 MIN
16mm
Color (A)
LC 77-703256
Presents information on such neurological diseases as epilepsy and other central nervous system and neuromuscular disorders, which may have an impact on driving ability. Gives clues to help driver examiners identify drivers whose degree of impairment should be medically evaluated before they are licensed.
Health and Safety; Psychology
Dist - USNAC **Prod** - USHTSA 1976

Screening for Driver Limitations - Vision 21 MIN
16mm
Color (A)
LC 77-703257
Shows the importance of good vision to the ability to drive safely and describes visual diseases and disorders which should be evaluated by a specialist.
Health and Safety; Psychology
Dist - USNAC **Prod** - USHTSA 1976

Screening for glaucoma in your office - tonometry 15 MIN
U-matic / VHS
Color (PRO)
Gives a brief overview of intraocular pressure. Presents standards for normal and elevated pressure and a step - by - step description of how to perform tonometry.
Health and Safety; Science - Natural
Dist - UMICHM **Prod** - UMICHM 1973

Screening for Strabismus - the Hirschberg Corneal Light Reflex Test 9 MIN
U-matic / VHS / 16mm
Color (PRO)
LC FIA68-2884
Demonstrates the Hirschberg Corneal Light Reflex Test on normal estropic and extropic children. Shows the importance of detecting strabismus at different ages.
Health and Safety; Science - Natural
Dist - IFB **Prod** - ODOH 1967

The Screening Physical Examination 43 MIN
VHS / 16mm
Branched and Screening Examination Series
(C)
$385.00 purchase _ #850VI036
Introduces the procedures for a screening physical examination. Features techniques for palpation, percussion, auscultation, and inspection.
Health and Safety
Dist - HSCIC **Prod** - HSCIC 1985

A Screening technique for colon cancer 9 MIN
VHS / U-matic
Color
LC 81-706285
Discusses the prevalence of colon cancer, explains what it is, and demonstrates a self - administered test for its early detection.
Health and Safety
Dist - USNAC **Prod** - VAHSL 1980

A Screening test for sensory integrative dysfunction 27 MIN
U-matic / VHS
B&W
Demonstrates ways of screening children for sensory - integrative problems, using performances by children to illustrate these problems.
Health and Safety; Science - Natural
Dist - BUSARG **Prod** - BUSARG

Screening's logo 3 MIN
16mm
B&W (G)
$5.00 rental
Conveys a visual 'welcome to the movies' message. Suggests using film to begin any film showing. Produced by Focus Pocus Film Squad.
Fine Arts
Dist - CANCIN

Screenprinting 25 MIN
VHS / U-matic
Artist in print series
Color (H C A)
Shows an artist in her studio using hand - cut stencils and photographic techniques to make a print of Al Capone. Shows a German artist, a student of master printer, Chris Prater, making a screenprint of an Arabian wall.
Industrial and Technical Education
Dist - FI **Prod** - BBCTV

Screentest 20 MIN
U-matic / VHS / 16mm
Color (H A G)
Presents a kaleidoscopic portrait of nine people indulging in their favorite fantasies.
Sociology
Dist - DIRECT **Prod** - MOURIS 1975

Screentest 20 MIN
U-matic / VHS / 16mm
Color (J)
LC 76-701932
Represents the first 16mm screen test of a group of amateur actor/mimes who made more than 50 8mm films themselves. Shows how then, as now, they did all the costumes, sets and make - up and created and acted all the roles.
Education; Fine Arts
Dist - PHENIX **Prod** - PHENIX 1976

The Screenwriter 29 MIN
U-matic
Directions - the Cinema Series
Color
Interviews screenwriter Rob Thompson. Focuses on the role of the screenwriter today in the development and production of a major motion picture.
Fine Arts
Dist - UMITV **Prod** - UMITV 1976

Screenwriting 24 MIN
U-matic / VHS / 16mm
Art of film series
Color
LC 75-703761
Uses sections from the motion pictures Oliver Twist, The 400 Blows, Metropolis, Pygmalion, and Caesar And Cleopatra to illustrate the importance of the screenplay.
Fine Arts
Dist - CORF **Prod** - JANUS 1975

The Screw and the Wheel 5 MIN
U-matic
Eureka Series
Color (J)
Defines a screw as a twisted inclined plane and a wheel as a circular lever whose fulcrum has become an axis.
Science; Science - Physical
Dist - TVOTAR **Prod** - TVOTAR 1980

Screws and Screwdrivers 13 MIN
16mm
Hand Tools for Wood Working Series
Color (H C A)
LC FIA67-967
Discusses the woodscrew and screwdrivers. Demonstrates the use of flat blade, phillips, socket and special purpose screwdrivers.
Industrial and Technical Education
Dist - SF **Prod** - MORLAT 1967

Scribbling Beauty - Pt 1 5 MIN
VHS / U-matic
Write on - Set 2 series
Color (J H)
Deals with coherence in writing.
English Language
Dist - CTI **Prod** - CTI

Scribbling Beauty - Pt 2 5 MIN
U-matic / VHS
Write on - Set 2 series
Color (J H)
Continues the lesson on coherence in writing.
English Language
Dist - CTI **Prod** - CTI

The Scribe 30 MIN
U-matic / VHS / 16mm
Color (J)
LC 72-700520
Uses the comic style of Buster Keaton to drive home a serious construction safety message. Presents Keaton wearing his famous flat fedora, who visits a large construction site as a newspaper reporter out to do a story on safety construction.
Health and Safety
Dist - IFB **Prod** - CSAO

A Script for Scandinavia 27 MIN
16mm
Color (C A)
LC FIAL7-597
An air - travel film about Denmark, Sweden, Finland and Norway. Includes scenes of the beauty and exhilaration of Nordic winter life as contrasted with the pastoral loveliness of summer. Shows cosmopolitan centers such as Copenhagen, Gothenburg, Stockholm, Helsinki and Bergen.
Geography - World; Social Science
Dist - MCDO **Prod** - DAC 1966

Script to screen 30 MIN
VHS
Color (PRO G)
$149.00 purchase, $49.00 rental _ #702
Follows director Brian Bell as he prepares a stage play for television production. Shows how information and emotions communicated on stage through lengthy dialog can be communicated on screen through purely visual means. Produced by the Australian Film, Television and Radio School.
Fine Arts; Industrial and Technical Education
Dist - FIRLIT

Script to Screen 39 MIN
U-matic / VHS
BBC TV Production Training Course Series
Color (C)
$279.00, $179.00 purchase _ #AD - 2075
Follows the entire process of producing a sitcom. Part of a twelve - part series on TV production by the BBC.
Fine Arts; Geography - World; Industrial and Technical Education
Dist - FOTH **Prod** - FOTH

Script Writing 15 MIN
U-matic / VHS
Zebra Wings Series
Color (I)
Provides an introduction to a study unit on filming and videotaping. Explains and illustrates camera movements, sound and picture alignment, and the addition of music and sound effects.
English Language; Literature and Drama
Dist - AITECH **Prod** - NITC 1975

Scripting 9.24 MIN
VHS
On Location
(J)
$180 series purchase, $50 rental, $110 self dub
Demonstrates video production skills for small format student video productions. Focuses on the elements of scriptwriting, highlighting outlining, writing style, interviewing and development. Fourth in an eight part series.
Fine Arts
Dist - GPN **Prod** - NCGE

Scripting and how it affects your classroom - or how a twig is bent so grows the teacher 30 MIN
VHS
First - year teacher series
Color (T)
$69.95 purchase, $45.00 rental
Discusses the unique challenges and rewards that first - year school teachers face. Serves as the tenth episode of a 12 - part telecourse. Features discussions between first - year teachers and Winthrop College professor Glen Walter on scripting.
Education; Psychology
Dist - SCETV **Prod** - SCETV 1988

The Scriptures 20 MIN
VHS
Lutherans and their beliefs series
Color (J H C G A R)
$39.95 purchase, $10.00 rental _ #35 - 8106 - 2076
Features Dr Jerry L Schmalenberger in a consideration of Lutheran views on the Bible. Produced by Seraphim.
Religion and Philosophy
Dist - APH

The Scroll saw 13 MIN
16mm
Woodwork - machine tools series
Color (H C A)
LC 70-712772
Presents instruction in the properties and use of a scroll saw. Illustrates parts of the saw, the blades to be selected and inserted and the tension and machine speed when the saw is in use. Shows the type of table, hold - down and operation.
Industrial and Technical Education
Dist - SF **Prod** - MORLAT 1967

Scrooge McDuck and Money 15 MIN
U-matic / VHS / 16mm

Color (I J)
LC 75-700668
Features cartoon character Scrooge McDuck and a variety of songs, dances and choruses to help young people understand the concept of money, money flow, inflation and deflation. Outlines the uses of money throughout history and relates some of the money words and phrases in use today.
Business and Economics; Social Science
Dist - CORF **Prod** - DISNEY 1974

Scrotal Hydrocele 15 MIN
VHS / U-matic
Pediatric Series
Color
Health and Safety
Dist - SVL **Prod** - SVL

SCR's 16 MIN
VHS / 16mm
Electronics series
(C A IND)
$99.00 purchase _ #VCI8
Gives the learner practice in identification of silicon controlled rectifiers - SCRs, their functions and applications. Describes the avalanche effect and how SCRs function in AC and DC circuits. Utilizes an additional workbook.
Industrial and Technical Education
Dist - RMIBHF **Prod** - RMIBHF

Scrubbing, Gowning, and Gloving 21 MIN
VHS / U-matic
Color (PRO)
Demonstrates and explains an anatomical stroke count scrub, hand drying, gowning and gloving unassisted and assisted, as well as proper techniques for removing gown and gloves.
Health and Safety
Dist - PRIMED **Prod** - PRIMED

Scrubbing, Gowning and Gloving 20 MIN
U-matic / VHS
Basic Clinical Skills Series
Color (PRO)
Demonstrates in detail, basic surgical scrubbing techniques and illustrates assisted and unassisted methods of gowning and gloving.
Health and Safety; Science
Dist - HSCIC **Prod** - HSCIC 1984

Scrubbing, gowning and gloving 20 MIN
VHS / U-matic
Color (PRO)
$250.00 purchase, $60.00 rental _ #4266S, #4266V
Presents a step - by - step review of the one - minute hand wash, the five - minute surgical scrub, drying and double septisol application. Offers methods of gowning and gloving with the help of others as well as on one's own. Illustrates proper operating room dress and precautions for remaining sterile.
Health and Safety
Dist - AJN **Prod** - IRVINC 1986

Scruffy 7 MIN
16mm
Color (K P F)
Scruffy Kitten runs away from home to find a sunbeam and is joined by other small animals of the woods. Grandfather Hare saves them when their boat is carried over a water fall, and they return home much wiser.
Literature and Drama
Dist - SF **Prod** - SF 1959

SCUBA
VHS
Color (G)
$59.90 purchase _ #0194
Explores the Caribbean underwater. Examines exotic flora and fauna.
Geography - World; Industrial and Technical Education; Physical Education and Recreation
Dist - SEVVID

SCUBA 22 MIN
U-matic / VHS / 16mm
Color (A)
LC 75-704200
Provides an introduction to the sport of SCUBA diving. Observes a SCUBA class in which basic diving is learned.
Physical Education and Recreation
Dist - MCFI **Prod** - KROWN 1975

Scuba diving across the USA - ice diving 30 MIN
VHS
Scuba World series
Color (G)
$24.90 purchase _ #0438
Joins Scuba World to experience some contrasts in diving. Dives in a frozen lake and in the ever warm water of the San Marcos River.
Physical Education and Recreation
Dist - SEVVID

Scuba gear maintenance
VHS
Color (G)
$19.95 purchase _ #0858
Covers the fundamentals of scuba gear maintenance. Includes cleaning, the basics of maintenance, wet and dry suits, masks, camera quipment, dive knives, gauges and computers, storage, minor repairs, regulators, buoyancy compensators, tanks, spear guns.
Physical Education and Recreation
Dist - SEVVID

Scuba - how to use dive tables 30 MIN
VHS
(H C A)
$39.95 purchase _ #BM342V
Teaches scuba divers how to correctly use the United States Naval Dive Tables. Explains how to prevent decompression sickness, using planning guides, and more.
Physical Education and Recreation
Dist - CAMV

Scuba video refresher course 40 MIN
VHS
Color (G)
$29.90 purchase _ #0284; $39.95 purchase _ #BM341V
Presents a complete review of basic scuba diving techniques and safe practices for certified divers.
Physical Education and Recreation
Dist - SEVVID
CAMV

Scuba world series

Adventures in Baja California - MV Rio Rita	30 MIN
Bahamas	30 MIN
Bahamas - Treasure Cay	30 MIN
Cayman alternative - hospitality world	30 MIN
Cayman trilogy - Cayman paradise found	30 MIN
Costa Rica - Island of Kings - Bruce Penhall	30 MIN
Cozumel, Mexico - Palancar Reef	30 MIN
Culebra, Puerto Rico - Gil Gerard	30 MIN
Fishwatcher's primer	30 MIN
The Habitat - Key Largo, Florida	30 MIN
Jamaica jamboree - come back to Jamaica	30 MIN
Kirk Pride - Gil Gerard - PM Magazine	30 MIN
Lahaina divers, Maui, Hawaii - fish show off	30 MIN
MV Cayman Aggressors I and II - the dynamic duo	30 MIN
Pirate's week - Cayman, October	30 MIN
Plantation Beach, Honduras	30 MIN
Ports of Call motor vessel - Cayman Brac	30 MIN
Puerto Rico - south coast diving - Gil Gerard	30 MIN
Sail Belize, Central America	30 MIN
Scuba diving across the USA - ice diving	30 MIN
Sea of Cortez, Mexico	30 MIN
St Croix, US Virgin Islands - pier diving	30 MIN
St George's Cay Belize - underwater wedding and more	30 MIN
Treasure cay, the place to be	30 MIN
Treasure hunting	30 MIN
Upon a coral reef - Belize, Hawaii, Sea of Cortez	30 MIN
Venezuela - South American diving	30 MIN
Wrecks of the Caribbean	30 MIN

Dist - SEVVID

Sculpting on the Square 15 MIN
U-matic / VHS
Strawberry Square II - Take Time Series
Color (P)
Fine Arts
Dist - AITECH **Prod** - NEITV 1984

The Sculptor 15 MIN
16mm
Color (J)
LC 74-705585
Shows the sources of the sculptor's inspiration in the world around him and describes how he adapts materials and equipment to the medium at hand. Covers the process whereby a group of birds in flight is sculptured in welded brass.
Fine Arts
Dist - AVED **Prod** - AVED 1963

Sculpture 15 MIN
U-matic / VHS
Expressions
(I J)
$130 purchase, $25 rental, $75 self dub
Designed to interest fifth through ninth graders in art. Emphasizes creativity and experimentation. Features Bruce Stanford and Sean Browne sculpting. Fifteenth in an 18 part series.
Fine Arts
Dist - GPN

Sculpture 7 MIN
U-matic
Take Time Series
Demonstrates the influence of parents and others caring for pre - schoolers on the physical and emotional development of the child.
Health and Safety; Psychology; Sociology
Dist - ACCESS **Prod** - ACCESS 1976

Sculpture 17 MIN
U-matic / VHS / 16mm
B&W (J H C)
LC 72-707283
A basic introduction to the materials and techniques used in sculpting. Shows sculptors George Grard and Rik Poot at work on various materials such as clay, stone, wood and plaster. Compares the sculpted forms of ancient civilization and the emerging shapes of today, with Rodin as a kind of link between the two. Uses time - lapse photography of clay forms to demonstrate the transition from realism to cubism.
Education; Fine Arts
Dist - IFB **Prod** - BELMNE 1969

Sculpture 1 30 MIN
U-matic
Media and methods of the artist series
Color (H C A)
Demonstrates methods of clay modelling and building plus work done directly in plaster, wood carving, stone carving and metal casting.
Fine Arts
Dist - TVOTAR **Prod** - TVOTAR 1971

Sculpture 2 30 MIN
U-matic
Media and methods of the artist series
Color (H C A)
Explores contemporary materials used by sculptors including plastics, fiberglass resin and liquids.
Fine Arts
Dist - TVOTAR **Prod** - TVOTAR 1971

Sculpture 58 - the story of a creation 12 MIN
16mm
Color
Follows a sculptor struggling with his material and inspiration to create a large sculptural group. Watches him from earliest drawings through models to the final triumph of full - scale bronze.
Fine Arts
Dist - ROLAND **Prod** - ROLAND

Sculpture and the creative process 29 MIN
VHS
Color (J H C G)
$39.95 purchase _ #CPC838V
Explores the works of sculptor Dale Lamphere. Observes the artist in his studio as he converts his ideas into three - dimensional forms. Shows how Lamphere makes thumb - nail sketches in clay, makes maquette and the armature, and then sculpts the finished work. Discusses ideas important for anyone considering a career as a sculptor. Overviews the lost wax casting process by following each step from coating the sculpture with latex to pouring the bronze and finishing with patina.
Fine Arts; Guidance and Counseling
Dist - CAMV

Sculpture at the Middelheim 11 MIN
16mm / U-matic / VHS
Color (H C)
LC 79-710018
Presents the works of outstanding twentieth century sculptors on display at the Middelheim Park in Antwerp, Belgium. Includes the work of Henry Moore, Giacometti, Manzu, Maillol and Gargallo.
Fine Arts
Dist - IFB **Prod** - BELMNE 1969

Sculpture Australia 30 MIN
16mm
Color (H C A)
LC 75-709227
A survey of contemporary Australian sculpture in which some sculptors, working in Australia and overseas, discuss and show some of their work.
Fine Arts
Dist - AUIS **Prod** - ANAIB 1969

Sculpture by Isaac Witkin 22 MIN
16mm
Color

LC 76-702668
Explores the philosophy, artistic methods and abstract sculpture of Isaac Witkin.
Fine Arts
Dist - CINETU **Prod** - CINETU 1976

Sculpture - Elements of Dimension 30 MIN
U-matic
Humanities through the Arts with Maya Angelou Series Lesson 23; Lesson 23
Color (C A)
Studies elements of sculpture as an art form. Explores relief and monolith forms of sculpture that preceded modern sculpture.
Fine Arts
Dist - CDTEL **Prod** - COAST

Sculpture from Life 11 MIN
16mm
Color; B&W (J)
Grant Beach of the Grant Beach Arts and Crafts School creates a life - sized head, working from a posed model. Starting with the armature, he adds clay, constructs the head and details of the face and forms the hair.
Fine Arts
Dist - AVED **Prod** - AVED 1957

Sculpture in the City - Spoleto (1960's) 11 MIN
16mm
Color
Presents the anguished imagery of modern sculpture that invades the serene old Lombard town of Spoleto each year, disturbing the piazzas with metal monsters.
Fine Arts; History - World
Dist - ROLAND **Prod** - ROLAND

Sculpture in the open 30 MIN
VHS / 16mm
Color (G)
$55.00 rental _ #SITO - 000
Views and discusses the many famous sculptures on Princeton's grounds.
Education; Fine Arts
Dist - PBS **Prod** - NJPBA

Sculpture in the round 28 MIN
U-matic
Woodcarver's workshop series
Color
Fine Arts; Industrial and Technical Education
Dist - PBS **Prod** - WOSUTV

Sculpture - Kitsch Catch or Creative Space? 19 MIN
16mm
Color (H C A)
$350 purchase, $45 rental
Examines the experiments of contemporary sculpture with a variety of images and abstractions in order to introduce new ideas about sculpture as an art form. Examines the work of Javacheff Christo and shows new materials available to artists.
Fine Arts
Dist - CNEMAG **Prod** - DOCUA 1988

Sculpture - meaning through the body's form 30 MIN
U-matic
Humanities through the arts with Maya Angelou series
Color (C A)
Explores unique ways in which sculpture conveys meaning through three - dimensional form. Focuses on life and works of August Rodin. Lesson 24 of the series.
Fine Arts
Dist - CDTEL **Prod** - COAST

Sculpture - mirror of man's being 30 MIN
U-matic
Humanities through the arts with Maya Angelou series
Color (C A)
Outlines the history of sculpture. Offers understanding of diverse ways humans have expressed their perception through three - dimensional forms. Shows representative works of sculpture. Lesson 22 of the series.
Fine Arts
Dist - CDTEL **Prod** - COAST

Sculpture - most difficult of arts 30 MIN
U-matic
Humanities through the arts with Maya Angelou series
Color (C A)
Discusses personal reactions to minimal sculpture, the roles of the critic in sculpture and the responsibility of the critic for informing and encouraging the sculptor. Features Maya Angelou, curator Donna Stein, and sculptor Oliver Andrews. Lesson 25 of the series.
Fine Arts
Dist - CDTEL **Prod** - COAST

The Sculpture of Ron Boise 9 MIN
VHS / 16mm
Color (G)
$30.00 rental, $45.00 purchase
Documents the contemporary metal sculptor, showing him at work on one of the last pieces completed before his untimely death. Records the step - by - step process of creation as the artist collects, cuts, shapes and welds cast - off materials into a sensitive human figure. Boise was a pioneer in the use of 'available' materials.
Fine Arts
Dist - CANCIN **Prod** - AUSLDR

The Sculpture of the Parthenon 15 MIN
U-matic / VHS / BETA
Color; NTSC; PAL; SECAM (J H C G)
PdS58
Presents a comprehensive coverage of the Parthenon on film. Uses, in addition to the ruins in Athens, the full - scale replica of the Parthenon at Nashville, Tennessee, the model and exhibits in the Royal Ontario Museum of Toronto, Canada, and the Elgin Marbles in the British Museum.
Fine Arts; History - World
Dist - VIEWTH

Sculpture - Process of Discovery 11 MIN
U-matic / VHS / 16mm
Color (J)
LC 75-704366
Presents sculptor Norm Hines discussing his approach to creativity, explaining how he works with no preconceived form but follows the shape which is indicated by the rock itself.
Fine Arts
Dist - BARR **Prod** - BARR 1975

Sculpture - the Forms of Life 18 MIN
U-matic / VHS / 16mm
Humanities Series
Color (J H)
Shows the materials of the sculptor, the wide range of techniques and many examples of works from around the the world.
Fine Arts
Dist - MGHT **Prod** - MGHT 1971

Sculpture Today 19 MIN
U-matic / VHS / 16mm
B&W (J H C)
LC 76-707284
Illustrates the many styles of modern sculpture, with emphasis on the expressive potential of the material. Includes examples of the work of Adam, Arp, Calder, Gabo, Giacometti, Hepworth, Laurens, Manzu, Moore, Walrauens and Zadkine.
Fine Arts
Dist - IFB **Prod** - BELMNE 1967

Sculpturing Copper with a Torch 14 MIN
U-matic / VHS / 16mm
Color (H C A S)
Shows the use of copper tube, wire, sheets and pipes. Explains the processes of forming, patching, enameling, brazing, cleaning and oxidation.
Fine Arts
Dist - IFB **Prod** - MOTIVF 1965

Scylla and Charybdis 15 MIN
U-matic / VHS
Homer's Odyssey Series
Color (C)
$239.00, $139.00 purchase _ #AD - 2044
Shows Odysseus warning his crew to plug their ears with wax so they will not hear the Sirens' song. Tells of the navigation between the monstrous man - devouring Scylla and the wandering ship - wrecking rocks of Charybdis. Part of a six - part series.
History - World; Literature and Drama
Dist - FOTH **Prod** - FOTH

SDC 14 MIN
16mm
Color
LC 80-700443
Shows a taxpayer questioning the role of the Social Development Commission. Uses interviews with SDC clients to explain the way it deals with various social and economic problems in Milwaukee County.
Civics and Political Systems; Sociology
Dist - MOYA **Prod** - CRSDC 1980

Se Empieza Desde Arriba 18 MIN
U-matic / VHS / 16mm
Color (IND A) (SPANISH)
Highlights the gravity of slip and fall accidents and explains how to deal with hazards that cause them. Emphasizes the need for shared responsibility between labor and management to make safety policies work.
Health and Safety
Dist - IFB **Prod** - CSAO 1986

The Sea 27 MIN
U-matic / VHS / 16mm
Biology series
Color (H) (SPANISH)
Describes the interrelationships between living things in the sea, pointing out their dependence on each other and on the conditions of the marine environment. Illustrates basic concepts of marine ecology. Unit two of the series focuses on ecosystems.
Science - Natural; Science - Physical
Dist - EBEC **Prod** - EBEC

The Sea 60 MIN
VHS
Color (G)
$29.95 purchase _ #0959
Combines undersea photography and classical music.
Fine Arts; Industrial and Technical Education; Science - Natural
Dist - SEVVID

The Sea 29 MIN
16mm
Color (G)
_ #106C 0171 538
Explains the dominant force of this planet is the sea, not the continents. Shows scientists aboard a Canadian oceanographic vessel exploring the secrets of the oceans.
Science - Physical
Dist - CFLMDC **Prod** - NFBC 1971

The Sea 30 MIN
U-matic
Today's Special Series
Color (K P)
Develops language arts skills in children. Programs are thematically designed around subjects of interest to youngsters. Action takes place in a department store where people, mannequins, puppets, comic characters and special guests present a light hearted approach to language arts.
English Language; Literature and Drama; Psychology
Dist - TVOTAR **Prod** - TVOTAR 1985

Sea Adventures of Sandy the Snail - a Lesson in Finger Painting 16 MIN
16mm / U-matic / VHS
Color; B&W (P I)
Artist and teacher, Betty Ohlrogge, uses a series of finger paintings to tell the story of a little snail's adventures with several marine animals.
Fine Arts; Literature and Drama
Dist - EBEC **Prod** - EBEC 1957

The Sea and Me 15 MIN
VHS / 16mm
Color (P)
$350.00, $205.00 purchase
Discusses the physical properties of the ocean, its wide - ranging depths, mountain ranges, tides and currents. Shows how the wind causes waves and goes underwater for a review of the dazzling array of living things in the water.
Health and Safety; Science - Natural; Science - Physical
Dist - LUF **Prod** - LUF

Sea and Sand 27 MIN
U-matic / VHS / 16mm
Victory at Sea Series
B&W (J H)
Depicts the Invasion of North Africa from 1942 - 1943.
Civics and Political Systems; History - United States; History - World
Dist - LUF **Prod** - NBCTV

Sea and sand - Beneath the Southern Cross - Magnetic north - Conquest of Micronesia 108 MIN
VHS
Victory at sea series
B&W (G)
$24.95 purchase _ #S01156
Contains four episodes from the Victory at Sea series, documenting the US Navy battles of World War II. 'Sea and Sand' covers the Allied support of the Soviet Union in 1942, while 'Beneath the Southern Cross' focuses on the Allied defense of the South Atlantic, which was important to the African military campaigns. 'Magnetic North' covers the Allied supply efforts which involved crossing the Arctic, and 'Conquest of Micronesia' documents the struggle for control of the Gilbert and Marshall Islands.
Civics and Political Systems; History - United States
Dist - UILL

Sea Area Forties 29 MIN
16mm
Color
Provides a look at undersea oil gathering operations in Great Britain's North Sea. Focuses on all aspects of bringing the oil ashore, from locating the oil in 400 feet of treacherous water to respecting the fragility of nature.
History - World; Industrial and Technical Education; Social Science
Dist - MTP **Prod** - BPNA

The Sea Behind the Dunes 57 MIN
16mm / U-matic / VHS
Nova Series
Color (H C A)
LC 81-700873
Looks at the ecology of an ocean inlet. Describes the interrelationship of the ocean, bay, barrier beach and salt marsh and shows the animals that inhabit this ecosystem.
Science - Natural
Dist - TIMLIF **Prod** - WGBHTV 1981

The sea birds of Isabela 23 MIN
U-matic / VHS / 16mm
Undersea world of Jacques Cousteau series
Color (G)
$49.95 purchase _ #Q10626; LC 77-703384
A shortened version of Sea Birds Of Isabela. Presents a study of the habits and interrelationships of various species of birds on the island of Isabela in the Galapagos Islands as seen by Jacques Cousteau and his expedition. Part of a series of 24 programs.
Psychology; Science - Natural
Dist - CF **Prod** - METROM 1977

The Sea can kill 27 MIN
U-matic / VHS / 16mm
Color (A)
LC 79-701686
Presents a dramatization of a crew being forced to abandon ship during a storm and the procedures which they follow afterward. Shows how to abandon ship and board a raft, how to search for survivors, care for injured, avoid hypothermia, apportion rations and post lookouts.
Health and Safety
Dist - IFB **Prod** - UKMD 1978

The Sea - Career Day 15 MIN
16mm
Color
LC 74-706573
Shows Navy occupations and scenes of life at sea.
Civics and Political Systems; Guidance and Counseling; Psychology
Dist - USNAC **Prod** - USN 1971

Sea Creatures 12 MIN
U-matic / VHS / 16mm
Color (P I J H C)
LC 74-703507
Features lower - depth sea life including crabs, jellyfish, spiny urchins, zebra - striped fish, snakes and the giant manta ray.
Science - Natural
Dist - PHENIX **Prod** - PHENIX 1974

Sea Dream 6 MIN
U-matic / VHS / 16mm
Color (P)
LC 81-700793
Presents an animated story about a little girl, who after suffering through a bad day, escapes into an underwater fantasy featuring a lady octopus who comforts her. Shows how, after they do many things together, the girl awakens, ready to start a new day.
Fine Arts; Literature and Drama
Dist - PHENIX **Prod** - NFBC 1980

Sea dweller 5 MIN
U-matic / 16mm / VHS
Color; Mono (G)
MV $85.00 _ MP $170.00
Reveals the important work of Norine Rouse, an acknowledged leader in the world of marine conservation. Discusses her important contribution towards better understanding of the giant sea turtles that visit the waters off the coast of Florida.
Science - Natural
Dist - CTV **Prod** - MAKOF 1982

The Sea Egg 15 MIN
VHS / U-matic
Best of Cover to Cover 1 Series
Color (P)
Literature and Drama
Dist - WETATV **Prod** - WETATV

Sea fans - fall 1987 90 MIN
VHS
Sea fans video magazine series
Color (G)
$19.95 purchase _ #0604
Tours Cozumel, Andros, Bahamas. Conducts an underwater photography clinic with Carl Roessler. Looks at alternative air sources. Discusses blue sharks, the Cayman Submersible and Mountain Lake. Part of a quarterly video magazine, Sea Fans, which travels to underwater diving spots all over the world. Hosts include Jimmy Ibbotson and Lynne Eisaquirre, soundtrack by Jerome Gilmer, photography by Scott Ogle.
Industrial and Technical Education; Physical Education and Recreation
Dist - SEVVID

Sea fans - spring 1987 90 MIN
VHS
Sea fans video magazine series
Color (G)
$19.95 purchase _ #0602
Sails to Little Cayman Plunge. Tells about wide - angle photography with Howard Hall. Travels to Micronesia and Palau. Reviews DEMA equiment. Experiences seaplane diving and diving at Trunk Lagoon. Part of a quarterly video magazine, Sea Fans, which travels to underwater diving spots all over the world. Hosts include Jimmy Ibbotson and Lynne Eisaquirre, soundtrack by Jerome Gilmer, photography by Scott Ogle.
Industrial and Technical Education; Physical Education and Recreation
Dist - SEVVID

Sea fans - summer 1987 90 MIN
VHS
Sea fans video magazine series
Color (G)
$19.95 purchase _ #0603
Dives freshwater in Florida. Visits Micronesia and the Barrier Reef of Southern Belize. Conducts a photography clinic with Stephen Frink. Looks at angel fish around the world. Part of a quarterly video magazine, Sea Fans, which travels to underwater diving spots all over the world. Hosts include Jimmy Ibbotson and Lynne Eisaquirre, soundtrack by Jerome Gilmer, photography by Scott Ogle.
Industrial and Technical Education; Physical Education and Recreation
Dist - SEVVID

Sea fans video magazine series

Sea fans - fall 1987	90 MIN
Sea fans - spring 1987	90 MIN
Sea fans - summer 1987	90 MIN
Sea fans - Vol 2, Number 2	90 MIN
Sea fans - Vol 2, Number 3	90 MIN
Sea fans - Vol 2, Number 4	90 MIN
Sea fans - Vol 3, Number 1	90 MIN
Sea fans - Vol 3, Number 2	90 MIN
Sea fans - winter 1986	90 MIN

Dist - SEVVID

Sea fans - Vol 2, Number 2 90 MIN
VHS
Sea fans video magazine series
Color (G)
$19.95 purchase _ #0605
Visits Saba. Conducts a photography clinic on multiple light sources. Looks at a liveaboard dive boat, dive knives and other equipment, and visits Maui, Key Largo, and Yap Island. Hosts include Jimmy Ibbotson and Lynne Eisaquirre, soundtrack by Jerome Gilmer, photography by Scott Ogle.
Industrial and Technical Education; Physical Education and Recreation
Dist - SEVVID

Sea fans - Vol 2, Number 3 90 MIN
VHS
Sea fans video magazine series
Color (G)
$19.95 purchase _ #0608
Visits Monterey Peninsula, Eastern Caribbean, and Roatan, Honduras. Conducts a photography clinic on underwater modeling and video photography. Investigates barracudas. Features Puerto Rico. Hosts include Jimmy Ibbotson and Lynne Eisaquirre, soundtrack by Jerome Gilmer, photography by Scott Ogle.
Industrial and Technical Education; Physical Education and Recreation
Dist - SEVVID

Sea fans - Vol 2, Number 4 90 MIN
VHS
Sea fans video magazine series
Color (G)
$19.95 purchase _ #0609
Visits St. Vincent, Roatan, the second largest barrier reef at Belize, Michigan, Guam and the Northern Marianas. Discusses underwater video photography and equipment. Hosts include Jimmy Ibbotson and Lynne Eisaquirre, soundtrack by Jerome Gilmer, photography by Scott Ogle.
Industrial and Technical Education; Physical Education and Recreation
Dist - SEVVID

Sea fans - Vol 3, Number 1 90 MIN
VHS
Sea fans video magazine series
Color (G)
$19.95 purchase _ #0610
Visits the Red Sea, the island of Bequia in the Grenadies, the US Virgin Islands. Looks at equipment for multilevel diving and underwater video photography. Hosts include Jimmy Ibbotson and Lynne Eisaquirre, soundtrack by Jerome Gilmer, photography by Scott Ogle.
Industrial and Technical Education; Physical Education and Recreation
Dist - SEVVID

Sea fans - Vol 3, Number 2 90 MIN
VHS
Sea fans video magazine series
Color (G)
$19.95 purchase _ #0611
Visits Cozumel, the Red Sea. Investigates octupus dofleni. Features Goombay in Nassau. Includes dive news. Hosts include Jimmy Ibbotson and Lynne Eisaquirre, soundtrack by Jerome Gilmer, photography by Scott Ogle.
Industrial and Technical Education; Physical Education and Recreation
Dist - SEVVID

Sea fans - Vol 3, Number 4 90 MIN
VHS
Color (G)
$19.95 purchase _ #0612
Visits Truk Lagoon. Investigates liveaboard dive boats, dive bags. Features Curacoa. Hosts include Jimmy Ibbotson and Lynne Eisaquirre, soundtrack by Jerome Gilmer, photography by Scott Ogle.
Industrial and Technical Education; Physical Education and Recreation
Dist - SEVVID

Sea fans - winter 1986 90 MIN
VHS
Sea fans video magazine series
Color (G)
$19.95 purchase _ #0601
Looks at diving expeditions to the Sea of Cortez, Bonaire, Kauai. Features Chris Newbert who explains Macro photography. Informs on the new regular G250. Ian Koblick discusses a Certified Aquanaut Program. Part of a quarterly video magazine, Sea Fans, which travels to underwater diving spots all over the world. Hosts include Jimmy Ibbotson and Lynne Eisaquirre, soundtrack by Jerome Gilmer, photography by Scott Ogle.
Industrial and Technical Education; Physical Education and Recreation
Dist - SEVVID

Sea fever 6 MIN
U-matic / VHS / 16mm
Color (I) (JAPANESE SPANISH)
LC FIA67-5023
Presents a visual interpretation of John Masefield's poem 'Sea Fever,' which expresses his feeling about salt air, clear skies and the freedom of the sea. Narrated by Lorne Greene.
Geography - World; Literature and Drama; Social Science
Dist - AIMS **Prod** - CAHILL 1966

Sea - floor spreading 15 MIN
VHS
Color (J H)
$95.00 purchase _ #A2VH 4683
Shows how and why the 'Permanence' theory was replaced by sea - floor spreading to explain the origin of ocean basins. Covers the role of magnetic anomalies and paleomagnetism sediment studies and heat flow along the mid - ocean ridge in verifying the new theory.
Science - Physical
Dist - CLRVUE **Prod** - CLRVUE

Sea Gulls 3 MIN
16mm
Of all Things Series
Color (P I)
Discusses the birds known as sea gulls.
Science - Natural
Dist - AVED **Prod** - BAILYL

The Sea gulls 10 MIN
U-matic / VHS / 16mm
Color (K P I)
LC 77-710544
Teaches the importance of observing things more closely and shows close - up details of the sea gull which are revealed to a boy exploring on the beach.
Psychology; Science - Natural
Dist - AIMS **Prod** - ASSOCF 1969

Sea Ice 28 MIN
16mm
Color
Points out that every winter, the Sea of Okhotsk becomes the scene of a dynamic development of sea ice but that the causes of its formation, its movement and its characteristics have remained a mystery. Presents the account of scientific research conducted by Hokkaido University's Institute of Low Temperature Science with cooperation from the Maritime Safety Agency to probe into this mystery.
Geography - World; Science - Physical
Dist - UNIJAP **Prod** - KAJIMA 1970

Sea, ice and fire 26 MIN
16mm
Audubon wildlife theatre series
Color (P)

LC 77-709407
A study of Iceland and its people, describing their way of life within their natural heritage of glaciers, hot springs and wildlife. Includes scenes of murres, gannets, puffins and kittiwakes.
Geography - World; Science - Natural
Dist - AVEXP **Prod** - KEGPL 1969

The Sea in miniature 60 MIN
VHS / U-matic / 16mm
Last frontier series
Color; Mono (G)
MV $225.00 _ MP $550.00
Focuses on the tiny creatures of the reef. Several sequences devoted to small marine animals just as ferocious as the sharks.
Science - Natural
Dist - CTV **Prod** - MAKOF 1985

A Sea in the Clouds 22 MIN
16mm / U-matic / VHS
Color
LC 77-702286
Traces the history of Lake Tahoe from its discovery and initial period of development in the mid - 1800's. Examines how the lake was polluted by huge logging operations in the 19th century, cleansed itself in the absence of that industry and is now being destroyed again by commercial development.
Geography - United States; History - United States; Science - Natural; Sociology
Dist - ALTSUL **Prod** - PNDRGN 1977

The Sea in Watercolors 50 MIN
U-matic
E John Robinson Fine Art Instruction Series
Color (A)
Teaches watercolor techniques for painting seascapes.
Fine Arts
Dist - CANSTU **Prod** - CANSTU

Sea Islands 25 MIN
16mm / U-matic / VHS
Untamed World Series
Color; Mono (J H C A)
$400.00 film, $250.00 video, $50.00 rental
Reveals the rocky islands of the North Atlantic focusing on the abundant animal, mammal and bird life thriving there.
Geography - World; Science - Natural
Dist - CTV **Prod** - CTV 1973

Sea Life that Doesn't Crawl 15 MIN
Videoreel / VT2
Tell Me what You See Series
Color (P)
Observes the peculiar and adaptive qualities of the starfish, sea anemone, sea urchin, hermit crab, shark, lung fish, grouper and scavenger. Studies a large goldfish.
Science - Natural
Dist - GPN **Prod** - GPN

The Sea Lion 22 MIN
U-matic / VHS / 16mm
Last of the Wild Series
Color
Offers information on sea lions, showing how these animals help man. Narrated by Lorne Greene.
Science - Natural
Dist - FI **Prod** - MACM

Sea lion figure piping 30 MIN
VHS / 16mm
Art of decorating cakes series
(G)
$49.00 purchase _ #BCD11
Instructs in the art of cake decorating. Shows how to figure pipe a sea lion directly on the cake. Illustrates how to use piping gel around the sea lions to give water effect. Taught by Leon Simmons, master cake decorator.
Home Economics; Industrial and Technical Education
Dist - RMIBHF **Prod** - RMIBHF

Sea of conflict - Pt 3 59 MIN
VHS
The Oil kingdoms series
Color (S)
$49.00 purchase _ #315 - 9007
Offers a look at the history of five small countries - Kuwait, Qatar, Bahrain, the United Arab Emirates, and Oman - and their transformation from Biblical times to today's extremely wealthy societies. Reveals that the discovery of oil is the latest chapter in the colorful story of the Persian Gulf. Part 3 of three parts examines the position Persian Gulf countries occupy in world politics, economics, and miltary strategy. Provides some of the background needed to understand current Mideast events.
Foreign Language; Geography - World; History - World; Religion and Philosophy; Social Science; Sociology
Dist - FI **Prod** - PP 1986

The Sea of Cortez 60 MIN
U-matic / 16mm / VHS
Last frontier series
Color; Mono (G)
MV $225.00 _ MP $550.00
Surveys the fish and marine life that exists in the Sea of Cortez. Emphasizes the manta ray - long thought of as a devil fish by early mariners.
Science - Natural
Dist - CTV **Prod** - MAKOF 1985

Sea of Cortez, Mexico 30 MIN
VHS
Scuba World series
Color (G)
$24.90 purchase _ #0439
Cruises the Sea of Cortez aboard the 87 foot Don Jose. Visits remote diving sites and uninhabited islands. Views the sea creatures who use the sea as a breeding ground.
Geography - World; Physical Education and Recreation
Dist - SEVVID

Sea of Galilee 25 MIN
VHS
Archaeology series
Color (G)
$29.95 purchase _ #222
Travels along the shores of the harp - shaped Sea of Galilee. Reveals ancient sites and modern activity of the area. Features Walter Zanger as host.
History - World; Religion and Philosophy; Sociology
Dist - ERGOM **Prod** - ERGOM

Sea of oil 29 MIN
16mm / VHS
Color (H C G)
$525.00, $295.00 purchase, $100.00, $55.00 rental
Shows the profound effect of the Exxon oil spill on life in the community of Valdez, Alaska. Captures the crisis faced by the residents not only in the environment but because of the crowding in of job seekers from all over North America to the once quiet coast community. Questions not only the responbility of Exxon for the spill, but the responsibility of everyone who participates in heavy dependence upon oil necessitating the risks of transporting it. Produced by M R Katzke, Director - Affinity Films. Features music by Philip Glass.
Science - Natural
Dist - FLMLIB

Sea of slaughter 96 MIN
VHS
Color (H C G)
$350.00 purchase, $85.00 rental
Tells a devastating history of the decimation of marine wildlife along the North Atlantic Coast, particularly the whaling and sealing industries. Shows how this natural world was ruthlessly plundered to meet consumers' demands. Based on the book of the same name by author and environmentalist, Farley Mowat. Available in 4 parts for schools.
Fine Arts; Geography - World; Science - Natural
Dist - BULFRG **Prod** - CANBC 1990

The Sea of whales 26 MIN
VHS
Challenge of the seas series
Color (I J H)
$225.00 purchase
Reveals that whales were nearly hunted to extinction off the coast of California during the 1960s. Discloses that under protection they began a comeback and by the mid 1980s several hundred whales were swimming off San Francisco. The old threat to whales of harpoons is being replaced by the new menace of pollution. Part of a 26 - part series on the oceans.
Science - Natural; Science - Physical
Dist - LANDMK **Prod** - LANDMK 1991

The Sea Otter 3 MIN
16mm
Of all Things Series
Color (P I)
Discusses the mammal known as the sea otter.
Science - Natural
Dist - AVED **Prod** - BAILYL

Sea Otters - the California Rough Riders 23 MIN
VHS / U-matic
Color
Goes to the coast of California where a sea otter mother and pup evade great white sharks and ride the rough waves of the storm - tossed Pacific.
Science - Natural
Dist - NWLDPR **Prod** - NWLDPR

Sea Power - a Destiny upon the Waters 28 MIN
16mm
Color
LC 74-705586
Shows the evolution of naval power and its impact on the development of empires and the age of exploration from the Phoenicians to the mid - 18th century.
Civics and Political Systems; History - United States; History - World
Dist - USNAC **Prod** - USN 1968

Sea power in the Pacific 30 MIN
16mm
B&W
LC 74-705589
Traces the history and depicts the role of American sea power in the Pacific during World War II.
Civics and Political Systems; History - United States
Dist - USNAC **Prod** - USN 1946

Sea Power on the Move 28 MIN
16mm
Color
LC 74-706572
Describes the mobility, versatility and flexibility of naval forces. Explains the overall naval purpose, mission and philosophies of the use of sea power.
Civics and Political Systems
Dist - USNAC **Prod** - USN 1969

Sea Power - Seas of Liberty 28 MIN
16mm
Color
LC 74-705587
Illustrates the impact of sea power on the national economy, geopolitical aspects of the seas from the mid - 18th century and the necessity for freedom of the seas.
Business and Economics; Civics and Political Systems; History - United States; Social Science
Dist - USNAC **Prod** - USN 1968

Sea power - the sea is a special place 28 MIN
16mm
Color
LC 74-705588
Shows the responsibilities of command and the demands and rewards for the people who make the complex and sophisticated naval machinery work.
Civics and Political Systems; Industrial and Technical Education
Dist - USNAC **Prod** - USN 1968

The Sea river 14 MIN
VHS
Color (H C)
$18.95 purchase _ #IV186
Documents the first scientific measurement of the Amazon River conducted by a Geological Survey team of hydrologists working in cooperation with the Brazilian Navy and the University of Brazil. Includes scenes of the river and its rain forests and the town of Obidos, the site selected for measurements. Uses animated sequences to illustrate how the flow of a large river is scientifically measured.
Geography - World
Dist - INSTRU **Prod** - USGEOS

Sea scapes 30 MIN
VHS / 16mm
Art of decorating cakes series
(G)
$49.00 purchase _ #BCD10
Instructs in the art of cake decoration. Shows how to pipe a sail boat in a sunset. Illustrates coloring the sky, using piping gel as water effect.
Home Economics; Industrial and Technical Education
Dist - RMIBHF **Prod** - RMIBHF

Sea shell animals 10 MIN
16mm / U-matic / VHS
Color (I J H) (SPANISH)
Presents a Survey of mollusks photographed at Marineland of the Pacific, under the direction of the curator of the oceanarium.
Science - Natural
Dist - PHENIX **Prod** - FA 1955

Sea Snakes - Friend or Foe 25 MIN
VHS / 16mm
Color (S)
$450.00, $79.00 purchase _ #825 - 9302
Scrutinizes yellow - bellied sea snakes which are believed to be the deadliest of all reptiles. Reveals that they have already colonized the Indian and Pacific Oceans and seem poised to invade the Atlantic Ocean as well. Narrated by David Attenborough.
Geography - World; Science - Natural
Dist - FI **Prod** - BBCTV 1987

Sea space 8 MIN
16mm
B&W (G)
$20.00 rental
Revolves around a confessional conversation by a fellow crew member with the filmmaker on a ship in the South China Sea. Uses formal static images within the ship's harsh interior. The ship becomes the silent witness to a man's realization of his sin and subsequent remorse.

Fine Arts
Dist - CANCIN **Prod** - FARWIL 1973

The Sea Squawk 18 MIN
16mm
B&W (J)
Stars Harry Langdon as a kilted bagpipe carrying Scotsman aboard a ship enroute to the United States.
Fine Arts
Dist - TWYMAN **Prod** - MGM 1924

Sea star
VHS
Pieper - zoology prelab dissections - series
Color (J H C)
$95.00 purchase _ #CG - 894 - VS
Presents dissection instruction and an anatomy review of the sea star. Includes a brief post test to gauge student retention. Part of a 15 - part series on zoological lab dissection, including a lab safety review, produced by Bill Pieper.
Science; Science - Natural
Dist - HRMC

Sea Survival 21 MIN
U-matic / VHS
Fisheries Safety and Survival Series
Color (PRO)
Demonstrates the most important points of surviving a mishap at sea. Includes information about life rafts and survival suits, and interviews with survivors at accidents at sea.
Health and Safety
Dist - USNAC **Prod** - USCG 1983

Sea Survival - the Physical and Mental Challenge 22 MIN
U-matic / VHS / 16mm
Color
Deals with the psychological and physical problems of long - term survival at sea encountered by aircrew members after ditching or ejection over water. Illustrates actual living conditions and a variety of problems.
Health and Safety; Industrial and Technical Education; Social Science
Dist - USNAC **Prod** - USAF

Sea to sea 25 MIN
16mm
Color
LC 76-701478
Views the Canadian fishing industry on both the east and west coasts of Canada and the way of life of those who work in the fishing industry.
Business and Economics; Geography - World; Social Science; Sociology
Dist - WILFGP **Prod** - WILFGP 1975

Sea Turtles 13 MIN
U-matic / VHS / 16mm
Wild, Wild World of Animals Series
Color
LC 77-701749
Shows the birth of sea turtles and their race for survival into the sea to escape attacking predators. Edited from the television program Wild, Wild World Of Animals.
Science - Natural
Dist - TIMLIF **Prod** - TIMLIF 1976

Sea turtles 60 MIN
VHS
Color (G)
$29.98 purchase _ #0803
Takes an intimate look at the behavior of wild sea turtles and their fight for survival.
Science - Natural
Dist - SEVVID

Sea turtles - Ancient nomads 60 MIN
VHS
National Audubon Society specials series
Color; Captioned (G)
$49.95 purchase _ #NTAS - 402
Features the sea turtle, which has not changed for more than 100 million years. Reveals that they could soon become extinct if action is not taken. Focuses on the efforts of the late Dr Archie Carr to preserve the sea turtle. Also produced by Turner Broadcasting and WETA - TV. Narrated by Jane Alexander.
Science - Natural
Dist - PBS **Prod** - NAS 1988

Sea turtles' last dance 30 MIN
VHS
Color (G)
$39.95 purchase _ #STRT - 000C
Tells how all seven species of sea turtle are in threatened or endangered status, with the Kemp's Ridley species near extinction. Includes extensive footage of sea turtles. Shows that shrimp trawlers and coastal development are largely responsible for the decline in sea turtle populations. Produced by WEDU - TV, Tampa.
Science - Natural; Science - Physical
Dist - PBS

Sea Un Profesional 14 MIN
U-matic / VHS / 16mm
Color (J H A) (SPANISH)
Explains that professional players use the best equipment to protect themselves from injury when playing. Discusses such techniques as applied to automobile driving and machine work. A Spanish - language version of the motion picture Be A Pro.
Health and Safety; Physical Education and Recreation
Dist - IFB **Prod** - CHET 1966

Sea war - war in the Mediterranean 1941 - 43 52 MIN
VHS
Century of warfare series
Color (G)
$19.99 purchase _ #0 - 7835 - 8419 - 9NK
Looks at sea warfare in the Mediterranean region during World War II, 1941 - 1943. Covers strategy, tactics, weapons, personalities, battles and campaigns, victories and defeats. Part of a 20 - part series on 20th - century warfare.
Civics and Political Systems; History - World; Sociology
Dist - TILIED

Sea Water and the Floor 17 MIN
U-matic / VHS / 16mm
Earth Science Series
Color (J H)
LC 75-706765
Describes the composition of sea water, the variations in temperature of sea water, the substances dissolved in sea water, the sediments that cover the sea floor and the topograhy of the sea floor.
Science - Natural; Science - Physical
Dist - MEDIAG **Prod** - WILEYJ 1970

A Sea we cannot sense 28 MIN
16mm
Color
LC 74-700712
Shows how radiation made by both humans and nature are measured in order to determine their prevalence and their possible effects on human life.
Health and Safety; Science - Physical; Sociology
Dist - USNAC **Prod** - ANL 1973

Sea Witch - Esso Brussels collision and fire 26 MIN
16mm
Color
LC 76-702717
Documents the collision and resulting fire of the container vessel Sea Witch and the anchored Belgian tanker Esso Brussels in 1973. Depicts the events following steering control failure aboard the Sea Witch, which was leaving New York Harbor. Describes the rescue efforts, structural damage to the vessels and effects of the fire on various types of containers.
Health and Safety; Social Science
Dist - USNAC **Prod** - USCG 1976

The Sea within 10 MIN
U-matic
Homeostasis Series
Color (H C)
Describes the five basic mechanisms of homeostasis that control the exchange of intracellular and extracellular fluids.
Science; Science - Natural; Science - Physical
Dist - TVOTAR **Prod** - TVOTAR 1984

Seabee Teams 30 MIN
16mm
Color
LC 74-706240
Shows the navy 'STAT' teams training Vietnamese to build roads, homes and schools in South Vietnam.
Civics and Political Systems; Geography - World; Industrial and Technical Education
Dist - USNAC **Prod** - USN 1966

Seabirds 16 MIN
U-matic / VHS / 16mm
RSPB Collection Series
Color (K P I J H)
LC 83-707194
Observes the seabirds along the shores of the British Isles, where twenty - four species nest and raise their young. Looks at their various fishing styles and techniques of cleaning and preening.
Science - Natural
Dist - BCNFL **Prod** - RSFPB 1983

Seabrook 1977 87 MIN
VHS
Color (J H C G)
$89.95 purchase, $45.00 rental _ #TTP134
Tells the story of how the small coastal town of Seabrook, New Hampshire became an international symbol in 1977 in the battle over atomic energy. Documents how over 2000 members of the Clamshell Alliance, a coalition of environmental groups, attempted to block construction of a nuclear power plant in Seabrook. Over 1400 people were arrested and jailed en masse. Filmed in a video - verite style to chronicle the events which sparked the creation of grassroots antinuclear power movement across the United States.
Fine Arts; History - United States; Social Science; Sociology
Dist - TURTID

Seabrook - do we need it 29 MIN
VHS / 16mm
Color (G)
$55.00 rental _ #SDWN - 000
Documents the four year history of the partially - completed nuclear power plant in Seabrook, New Hampshire and examines the larger question of who decides how much power people need and how to get it. Explores the issues of nuclear safety, waste disposal and possible alternative energy sources.
Sociology
Dist - PBS **Prod** - WGBHTV

Seacoal 82 MIN
16mm / U-matic / VHS
Color (H C A) (ENGLISH (ENGLISH SUBTITLES))
$175 rental
Dramatizes the lives of 'seacoalers,' who gather coal spilled from local pits and washed ashore by the tide. Northumberland dialect.
History - World; Sociology
Dist - CNEMAG

Seacoast people 14 MIN
16mm
Places people live series
Color (I)
Depicts a day in the life of a lobster fisherman in York Harbor, Maine. Shows how he picks up the bait early in the morning, checks and baits half of his traps, gathers his catch and returns at the end of the day to sell it to a wholesaler. Tells of the similar methods of the Norwegian crab fisherman who sells his catch directly to the people at the dock.
Science - Natural; Social Science
Dist - SF **Prod** - SF

A Seacoast port city - Port of Vancouver 14 MIN
16mm / U-matic / VHS
This is my home series
Color (P I)
Develops an understanding of how communities interact by means of resources and transportation through the experiences of a young boy who learns the origin of some of the products his family buys.
Geography - World; Social Science
Dist - BCNFL **Prod** - BCNFL 1984

Seacoast Villages of Japan 19 MIN
16mm
Color (I)
Pictures life in a small fishing village, an important part of the Japanese economy. Shows the co - operation of the old with the young in performing daily tasks.
Geography - World
Dist - ATLAP **Prod** - ATLAP 1962

Seacoasts - a First Film 10 MIN
U-matic / VHS / 16mm
B&W (I J)
LC 73-701287
Describes the various kinds of seacoasts and the variety of animals that live in the intertidal zone.
Science - Natural
Dist - PHENIX **Prod** - NELLES 1973

Seaflight 12 MIN
16mm / U-matic / VHS
Color (I)
LC 82-700684
Presents the state of the art of surfing as well as exhibiting a new quality level of surfing film photography. Looks at wind surfing. Without narration.
Fine Arts; Industrial and Technical Education; Physical Education and Recreation
Dist - PFP **Prod** - PFP 1982

Seafood 29 MIN
Videoreel / VT2
Cookin' Cajun Series
Color
Features gourmet - humorist Justin Wilson showing ways to cook seafood with various ingredients.
Geography - United States; Home Economics
Dist - PBS **Prod** - MAETEL

Seafood and the Microwave Oven - a Perfect Match 22 MIN
VHS
Color (C A)
$45.00 purchase, $18.00 rental
Explains why cooking seafood in a microwave is desirable. Shows cooking utensils, explains cooking time, and then shows the final product.
Home Economics
Dist - CORNRS **Prod** - CORNRS 1986

Seafood Cookery 21 MIN
16mm
Color
LC 74-706574
Shows various methods of cooking seafood.
Home Economics
Dist - USNAC **Prod** - USN 1966

Seafood Cookery 57 MIN
BETA / VHS
Color
Demonstrates the preparation of a variety of fish and shellfish.
Home Economics
Dist - MOHOMV **Prod** - MOHOMV

Seafood Cookery 57 MIN
VHS / 16mm
Color (G)
$39.95 purchase _ #VT1080; $39.95 purchase _ #MX502V
Teaches how to select fresh seafood, how to store it, and how to avoid overcooking it. Shows how to saute, poach, bake, broil, steam, grill, and stew seafood. Features a demonstration by a Northwest Indian preparing salmon in traditional tribal fashion. Taught by Sharon Kramis.
Home Economics
Dist - RMIBHF **Prod** - RMIBHF
CAMV

Seafood Specialties 12 MIN
16mm
Eat Right to Your Heart's Delight Series
Color (J H)
Examines the advantages of fish and seafood for low - fat meals, encouraging the use of more seafood with beautifully presented dishes and easy, tasty recipes. Shows the selection and preparation of many kinds of fish, including fresh and frozen, fillets and whole. Provides a special section, showing how to tell the freshness of fish and how to slice bone - free fillets from whole fish.
Health and Safety; Home Economics; Psychology
Dist - IPS **Prod** - IPS 1976

Seagull story 29 MIN
VHS / U-matic
Survivors series
Color (H C)
$250.00 purchase _ #HP - 6108C
Uses footage of black - backed seagulls taken in Britain, Portugal and north Africa to examine the life and migration of the birds. Shows how they interact with various environments, breed, raise their young, what they eat and why they can live in a wide range of habitats - and the extent to which humans have encrouched upon, or damaged areas where seagulls dwell. Part of a series on the issue of wildlife conservation and the enormity of the task of protecting wildlife and wilderness.
Science - Natural
Dist - CORF **Prod** - BBCTV 1990

The Seahorse - a most Exceptional Fish 12 MIN
16mm
Color (J)
Reviews external anatomy, feeding and birth of the young through the use of time - lapse microscopic scenes of developing embryos and microscopic scenes of newborn sea horses. Shows the function of the air bladder and relates this apparatus to the countercurrent exchange system.
Science - Natural
Dist - MIAMIS **Prod** - REELA 1968

Seahouse series
Presents a complete series of ten parts on marine animals. Includes the titles 'Breakfast, Lunch and Dinner', 'The Nursery', 'Reefs', 'First Star', 'Something Fishy', 'Where Did They Go', 'Partners', 'The Cleaning Station', 'Breathing Underwater', 'Is It Safe'.

Breakfast, lunch and dinner	5 MIN
Breathing underwater	5 MIN
The Cleaning station	5 MIN
First star	5 MIN
Is it safe	5 MIN
The Nursery	5 MIN
Partners	5 MIN
Reefs	5 MIN
Something fishy	5 MIN
Where did they go	5 MIN

Dist - REVID **Prod** - REVID 1968

Seal beach - Argentina - Part 10 8 MIN
VHS
Natures kingdom series
Color (P I J)
$125.00 purchase
Shows how carnivorous 3.5 ton elephant seals adapted to aquatic life. Reveals that baby seals gain 25 pounds a day and spend their time on beaches. Part of a 26 - part series on animals showing the habitats and traits of various species.
Geography - World; Science - Natural
Dist - LANDMK **Prod** - LANDMK 1992

Seal country 26 MIN
VHS
Challenge of the seas series
Color (I J H)
$225.00 purchase
Reveals that elephant seals are becoming so numerous in some parts of northern California that they may begin to push people off a few beaches. Discloses that each spring the huge marine mammals come to Ano Nuevo State Park to breed and have pups. Examines the dilemma of conflict between humans and the seals. Part of a 26 - part series on the oceans.
Geography - United States; Science - Natural; Science - Physical
Dist - LANDMK **Prod** - LANDMK 1991

Seal Island 27 MIN
16mm / U-matic / VHS
Color (I J H) (DANISH FRENCH GERMAN SPANISH AFRIKAANS)
Tells the story of the fur - bearing seals of the Pribilof Islands. Teaches respect for nature's balance.
Geography - United States; Science - Natural
Dist - CORF **Prod** - DISNEY 1953

Seal Island 55 MIN
16mm
Color (P I)
Reveals what happens when two children discover that although an island has been sold to conservationists, permission has been granted for two killers to shoot seals on the island until the sale is completed.
Literature and Drama
Dist - LUF **Prod** - LUF 1979

The Seal Mother
VHS / 35mm strip
Favorite Filmstrips from Children's Books Series
Color (K)
$33.00 purchase
Recreates a folktale about a seal transformed into a beautiful woman. Part of a series.
English Language; Literature and Drama
Dist - PELLER

Seal upon thy heart - marriage 30 MIN
VHS
Color (G)
$39.95 purchase _ #854
Portrays a young Jewish couple's approaching marriage. Documents a modern Orthodox wedding, placing special emphasis on the Biblical and Talmudic sources of the wedding ceremony. Explores the couple's engagement, preparations for marriage and the wedding, as well as the couple's reflections several months after their marriage.
Religion and Philosophy; Sociology
Dist - ERGOM **Prod** - ERGOM

Sealab 1 28 MIN
16mm
Color
LC 74-705590
Shows the navy's exploratory attempt to apply laboratory studies of man's ability to live and work in an artificial atmosphere at a depth of 200 feet for prolonged periods.
Civics and Political Systems; Science; Science - Natural; Science - Physical
Dist - USNAC **Prod** - USN 1965

Sealed in Glass 11 MIN
16mm
Color (PRO)
Explains the manufacture of glass containers.
Health and Safety; Home Economics; Social Science
Dist - FPI **Prod** - FPI

Sealegs 15 MIN
U-matic / 16mm
Color
Discusses the carrier environment and the special aircraft on board.
Civics and Political Systems
Dist - WSTGLC **Prod** - WSTGLC

Sealing the Breach 27 MIN
16mm / U-matic / VHS
Victory at Sea Series
B&W (J H)
Documents anti - submarine warfare between 1941 - 1943.
Civics and Political Systems; History - United States; History - World
Dist - LUF **Prod** - NBCTV

Seals 22 MIN
16mm / U-matic / VHS
Undersea world of Jacques Cousteau series
Color (G)
$49.95 purchase _ #Q10610; LC 78-710110
Presents Pepito and Cristabal, two young sea lion pups taken aboard the Calypso off the coast of Africa. Records the behavior of the sea lions and the relationship that develops between the crew and the sea lions. Part of a series of 24 programs. A shortened version of Seals.
Science - Natural; Science - Physical; Sociology
Dist - CF **Prod** - METROM

Seamless modern - general pipe making 13 MIN
16mm
Pipe and tubing series
Color
Explains how seamless steel pipes are made.
Business and Economics; Industrial and Technical Education
Dist - USSC **Prod** - USSC 1968

The Seamless web 30 MIN
16mm
Man builds - man destroys series
Color (J)
LC 75-704153
Examines humanity's relationship to the environment and the choices we must make to preserve it.
Science - Natural; Sociology
Dist - GPN **Prod** - UN 1974

Seams and Edges 41 MIN
BETA / VHS
Color (IND)
Deals with the application of the various seams and edges used in light gauge sheet metal fabricating. Gives seam allowances.
Industrial and Technical Education; Psychology
Dist - RMIBHF **Prod** - RMIBHF

Seams and Hems 26 MIN
U-matic / VHS
Clothing Construction Techniques Series
Color (C A)
Covers making French and flat fell seams, making square or V - shaped corners, sewing unlike curved seams, sewing crotch seams, preparing a hem, finishing a hem.
Home Economics
Dist - IOWASP **Prod** - IOWASP

Seams and Hems - Basting 10 MIN
16mm
Sewing Series
Color (H C A)
Presents concepts in sewing, such as machine basting, pressing and pinning the hem and machine and hand hem stitches.
Home Economics
Dist - SF **Prod** - MORLAT 1967

The Seamstress of Salzburg 15 MIN
VHS / U-matic
Magic Pages Series
Color (P)
Literature and Drama
Dist - AITECH **Prod** - KLVXTV 1976

Seamus Heaney - Poet in Limboland 29 MIN
16mm / U-matic / VHS
Color (H C A)
LC 72-702965
Traces the life and development of the Belfast poet who is considered the most promising young talent in Ireland today, Seamus Heaney. Explains that his poems arise from the involvement with his people.
Geography - World; Literature and Drama
Dist - FOTH **Prod** - MANTLH 1972

Sean 15 MIN
16mm
B&W
LC 70-705007
A four - year - old boy who lives in the Haight Ashbury district of San Francisco describes his world and the adult world as he sees it.
Psychology; Social Science; Sociology
Dist - ARRA **Prod** - ARRA 1969

Sean Lavery and Merrill Ashley 30 MIN
VHS / U-matic
Eye on Dance - Partners in Dance Series
Color
Fine Arts
Dist - ARCVID **Prod** - ARCVID

Seance on a wet afternoon 115 MIN
VHS

B&W (G)
$29.95 _ #SEA030
Creates an atmosphere of unrelenting suspense in the eerie tale of a professional medium and her weak - willed husband who execute a kidnapping plot in a production directed by Bryan Forbes.
Fine Arts; Sociology
Dist - HOMVIS **Prod** - JANUS 1964

Sean's Story 12 MIN
16mm / U-matic / VHS
American Family - an Endangered Species Series
Color (H C A)
Shows 12 - year - old Sean who divides his time between his divorced parents.
Sociology
Dist - FI **Prod** - NBCNEW 1979

Seaport at sunset 30 MIN
VHS
Palette series
Color (G C)
$70.00 purchase, $12.50, rental _ #36405
Examines Claude Lorrain's Seaport at Sunset (1639), which depicts ships at anchor, receding buildings and strolling people under a setting sun. Part of a 13 - part series that examines famous paintings. Uses video effects to investigate artistic enigmas and to study material, technique, style and significance. Narrated by Marcel Cuvelier, directed by Alain Jaubert.
Fine Arts
Dist - PSU **Prod** - LOUVRE 1992

Seaports and ships 15 MIN
16mm / U-matic / VHS
American legacy series
Color (I)
Shows fishermen along the New England coast and in the Atlantic catching lobster.
Geography - United States; History - United States; Physical Education and Recreation
Dist - AITECH **Prod** - KRMATV 1983

Seapower 28 MIN
16mm
Color
Illustrates the tasks and mission of the navy in protecting the sea lanes and the security of the free world. Shows how a strong navy should stress our nation's reliance on maritime trade and the necessity for development of the wealth of undersea resources. Portrays the practical applications of versatile naval strength in contributing to the solution of the 1962 Cuban crisis. Narrated by Glenn Ford.
Civics and Political Systems; Social Science
Dist - WB **Prod** - WB 1964

Seapower 107 MIN
VHS
Color (G)
$29.95 purchase _ #781 - 9005; $37.80 purchase _ #0058; $39.95 purchase _ #S01504
Traces the development of navies from the early years of the 20th century to the present. Uses footage of the British Royal Navy and the US Navy, as well as previously unseen archival materials. Provides a history of seapower.
Civics and Political Systems; History - World
Dist - FI **Prod** - BBCTV 1987
SEVVID BBC
UILL BBCL

Seapower - Plymouth Rock to Polaris 28 MIN
16mm
Color
LC 74-705591
Shows the history, growth and importance of American naval power.
Civics and Political Systems; History - United States; Social Science
Dist - USNAC **Prod** - USN 1965

Seaquarium 5 MIN
VHS / U-matic / 16mm
Color; Mono (G)
MV $85.00 _ MP $170.00 purchase, $50.00 rental
Features creatures that live at one of the worlds leading marine aquaria. Footage devoted to dolphins, sea lions, manatee's, and killer whales. Program is set to music.
Science - Natural
Dist - CTV **Prod** - MAKOF 1982

Searanger
VHS
Loran operation guide series
Color (G A)
$29.90 purchase _ #0915
Teaches Loran C programming for the Searanger in nautical navigation. Shows how to enter the correct Loran chain for specific positions, how to program positions, determine the accuracy of a Loran C 'fix' and how to deal with the intricacies of specific machines.
Physical Education and Recreation; Social Science
Dist - SEVVID

Searanger - ASB 2001, LCN 100, ALN 200 60 MIN
VHS
Using Loran series
Color (G A)
$29.90 purchase _ #0744
Shows how to operate the Searanger - ASB 2001, LCN 200 and ALN 200 Loran models. Includes installation tips, initialization, calibration, chain selection, notch filters, signal - to - noise ratio, time differentials, Lat - Lon functions, selecting and programming waypoints, setting anchor and waypoint alarm, cross - track error, determining course to steer and distance to go. Part of a series on the most popular Loran models.
Physical Education and Recreation; Social Science
Dist - SEVVID

The Search 29 MIN
16mm
Government story series; No 15
Color
LC 70-707198
Explains the difference between Congressional hearings and investigations, pointing out that hearings become investigations when a committee uses its power to subpoena witnesses and demand testimony.
Civics and Political Systems
Dist - WBCPRO **Prod** - OGCW 1968

Search 13 MIN
16mm
Color
LC 80-701627
Shows the wide range and diversity of ongoing scientific research, and examines the curiosity and motivation of scientists, who attempt to know what no one knew before.
Science
Dist - USNAC **Prod** - NSF 1980

Search 6 MIN
16mm
Christian encounter series
Color (J)
LC 72-700558
Shows how to discover God in human experience.
Guidance and Counseling; Religion and Philosophy
Dist - FRACOC **Prod** - FRACOC 1969

The Search 13 MIN
16mm
Color
LC FIA68-1777
Blends poetry, sculpture and music with the sounds and the beauty of a far north river bank in the spring.
Fine Arts; Geography - United States; Literature and Drama; Science - Natural
Dist - RADIM **Prod** - CALCAG 1968

Search 6 MIN
16mm
Christian Encounter Series,
Color (J)
LC 72-700558
Shows how to discover God in human experience.
Guidance and Counseling; Religion and Philosophy
Dist - FRACOC **Prod** - FRACOC 1969

The Search 15 MIN
VHS / 16mm
First Americans Series
Color (I)
Tells the story of a young Navajo who searches to understand what it means to be an American Indian. The first of six installments of The First Americans Series, which attempts to present a more accurate portrait of American Indians than has been presented in the media.
Psychology; Social Science
Dist - GPN **Prod** - CTI 1990

The Search 15 MIN
U-matic
Success in the Job Market Series
Color (H)
Shows ways of locating jobs. Examines the letter of application and the process of making telephone contact. Offers advice on self - preparation for a personal interview.
Guidance and Counseling; Psychology
Dist - GPN **Prod** - KUONTV 1980

Search 22 MIN
16mm
Color (H C)
LC FIA66-762
Shows the operation of the General Motors Research Laboratories, part of Saarinen's Technical Center.
Business and Economics; Industrial and Technical Education
Dist - GM **Prod** - GM 1965

The Search 19 MIN
16mm
Aventuras de Joselito y Pulgarcito series; No 4
Color (H C) (SPANISH)
Depicts scenes of Mexico as Joselito and Pulgarcito search for Joselito's father. Follows the boys as they visit the bullring, the Church of the Virgin of Guadalupe and the newspaper office.
Foreign Language
Dist - TRANSW **Prod** - IFB 1961

Search and destroy 91 MIN
35mm / 16mm
Color (G)
$200.00 rental
Tells the story of a bankrupt promoter dumped by his wife, tossed from his condo and determined to succeed in the movies. Mixes realism and excess, theater and cinema to produce a sharp commentary on modern life, and a darkly comic tale about the dangers of acting on all of one's impulses. Adapts the play by Pulitzer Prize - nominee Howard Korder. Produced by Ruth Charny, Dan Lupovitz and Elie Cohn; directed by David Salle; screenplay by Michael Almereyda.
Fine Arts; Psychology
Dist - OCTOBF

Search and Identification 15 MIN
U-matic / VHS / 16mm
Physical Evidence Series
Color
Discusses how police officers should go about searching for and identifying physical evidence.
Civics and Political Systems; Social Science
Dist - CORF **Prod** - WORON

Search and Rescue
VHS / U-matic
Color (PRO)
Shows techniques for searching for victims in all types of occupancies, such as hotels, apartments, homes and large industrial complexes. Demonstrates tips for maintaining good communications via the buddy system and larger teams and techniques for covering all areas.
Health and Safety; Social Science
Dist - FILCOM **Prod** - LACFD

Search and rescue 20 MIN
U-matic / VHS
Color
$335.00 purchase
Presents a program on the Coast Guard. From the ABC TV program, 20/20.
Civics and Political Systems
Dist - ABCLR **Prod** - ABCLR 1983

Search and Rescue - Pleasure Craft 26 MIN
16mm
Color
LC FIE63-240
Explains the operation of the search and rescue network as it applies to surface craft. Discusses the procedures to be followed by vessels in distress in order to obtain search and rescue assistance.
Health and Safety; Social Science
Dist - USNAC **Prod** - USGEOS 1960

Search and rescue scanning and sighting techniques 7 MIN
16mm
Color
LC FIE62-76
Shows the proper method for systematic scanning and sighting during search operations. Describes fixation points, clock systems and reference points.
Civics and Political Systems; Industrial and Technical Education
Dist - USNAC **Prod** - USAF 1960

Search and rescue - visual aspects of search and signalling 19 MIN
16mm
Color
LC 74-705592
Shows relative merits of dye markers, various pistols, flares, smokes and mirrors. Describes air search patterns.
Health and Safety; Social Science
Dist - USNAC **Prod** - USN 1947

Search and Research - Hunting Animals of the Past 30 MIN
16mm
Great Plains Trilogy, 1 Series in the Beginning - the Primitive Man; In the beginning - the primitive man
B&W (H C A)
Describes the methods for finding the remains of prehistoric animals, uncovering and collecting them, preparing specimens and mounting skeletons. Features a field - trip.
Science - Natural
Dist - UNL **Prod** - KUONTV 1954

Search and research - psychology in perspective 30 MIN
16mm
B&W (H C T)
LC FIA66-1378
Describes through a story about a young lady who seeks psychotherapy, the three forces of psychology - experimental, psychoanalytic and existential or humanistic. Includes interviews with psychologists Harry Harlow, Rollo May and Carl Rogers.
Psychology
Dist - PSYCHF **Prod** - PSYCHF 1963

Search and Seizure 19 MIN
U-matic / VHS
Cop Talk Series
Color (I J)
Uses three very different incidents to show how police handle search and seizure differently but always legally. Tackles the tricky questions of probable cause and privacy from the viewpoints of teens and the police.
Civics and Political Systems; Social Science; Sociology
Dist - AITECH **Prod** - UTSBE 1981

Search and seizure law revisited 210 MIN
VHS
Color (C PRO A)
$52.20, $150.00 purchase _ #M654, #P177
Covers doctrinal developments, determining Fourth Amendment coverage, exceptions to the warrant requirement and review of holdings in recent 'stop and frisk' cases.
Civics and Political Systems
Dist - ALIABA **Prod** - ALIABA 1985

The Search Begins 15 MIN
U-matic / VHS
Writer's Realm Series
Color (I)
$125.00 purchase
Examines the process of researching creative writing. Includes sources and methods of reference.
English Language; Literature and Drama; Social Science
Dist - AITECH **Prod** - MDINTV 1987

Search - Communication series 75 MIN
VHS
Search series
Color; PAL (I J)
PdS25 purchase
Focuses on the social importance of communication. Introduces a range of study skills which, when mastered, will help student - learning processes through school life and long afterward. Teaches by example to motivate children to learn about the world around them, focusing on parts of their everyday lives and representing areas which are sometimes neglected in education. Aims to create more aware, tolerant, concerned and caring individuals. Five programs, 15 minutes each. Contact distributor about availability outside the United Kingdom.
Civics and Political Systems; Psychology; Social Science
Dist - ACADEM

Search - Conservation series 60 MIN
VHS
Search series
Color; PAL (I J)
PdS25 purchase
Focuses on the social importance of conservation. Introduces a range of study skills which, when mastered, will help student - learning processes through school life and long afterward. Teaches by example to motivate children to learn about the world around them, focusing on parts of their everyday lives and representing areas which are sometimes neglected in education. Aims to create more aware, tolerant, concerned and caring individuals. Four programs, 15 minutes each. Contact distributor about availability outside the United Kingdom.
Civics and Political Systems; Science - Natural; Social Science
Dist - ACADEM

Search - Design and manufacture series 60 MIN
VHS
Search series
Color; PAL (I J)
PdS25 purchase
Focuses on the industrial skills of design and manufacture. Introduces a range of study skills which, when mastered, will help student - learning processes through school life and long afterward. Teaches by example to motivate children to learn about the world around them, focusing on parts of their everyday lives and representing areas which are sometimes neglected in education. Aims to create more aware, tolerant, concerned and caring individuals. Four programs, 15 minutes each. Contact distributor about availability outside the United Kingdom.
Business and Economics; Civics and Political Systems; Social Science
Dist - ACADEM

Search encounters in science series
Outlasting the quakes 4 MIN
Dist - AMEDFL
EDPAT

Search encounters in science series
Desert in the deep
Discovery in the deep - 9
Earth resources technology
Enzymes for industry - 7
Help for Hail Alley
Holography - 2
Land that will not heal
Lead - a four letter word
Math minus mystery
Measuring brain gain - 1
Pastures of sea
Power from the Earth
Promises of Pluto - 8
Pyramid probe - cosmic radiation - 4
Science of salmon industry
Seeing with sound - acoustical holography - 10
Solar eclipse
South of nearly everywhere - Antarctic
Star clusters - 6
Tall buildings - psychological problems
Test tubes for the sea
To bottle the Sun - 3
Dist - EDPAT

Search encounters with science series
Building in the wind 6 MIN
Putting the sun to work 5 MIN
Dist - AMEDFL

The Search for a Cause 50 MIN
U-matic / VHS
Understanding Cancer Series
Color (G)
$150.00
Looks at how an alteration to the genetic information in a cell can cause a malignant change and result in a particular cancer.
Health and Safety
Dist - LANDMK **Prod** - LANDMK 1985

Search for a Century 59 MIN
16mm / U-matic / VHS
Color (J H C A)
Conveys the excitement of rediscovering Wolstenholme Towne, a 17th - century settlement which was left in ruins by an Indian uprising in 1622. Shows archeologists from Colonial Williamsburg uncovering artifacts in trash pits, wells and the remains of the people's homes.
History - United States; Sociology
Dist - CWMS **Prod** - CWMS 1980

The Search for a new architecture - 1920 - 1950 12 MIN
16mm
Twelve decades of concrete in American architecture series
Color
Industrial and Technical Education
Dist - PRTLND **Prod** - PRTLND 1965

Search for a tropical Arctic 28 MIN
VHS
Color (H C G)
$295.00 purchase, $55.00 rental
Follows a team of international experts to sites within 600 miles of the North Pole. Shows that they discover the remains of alligators, turtles, rare mammals and giant redwood trees. Reveals that not only was the ancient Arctic lush and warm, it was also a cradle of evolution. Produced by Breakthrough Films.
Science - Natural
Dist - FLMLIB

The Search for a usable past 58 MIN
16mm / VHS / U-matic
Pride of place series
Color (C)
$40.00, $24.50 rental _ #50829; $89.95 purchase _ #EX979
Presents architect Robert Stern's thesis that American architecture represents the immigrant's dream of a better world. Surveys American architecture and searches for continuity and the need for innovation in such places as Plimouth Plantation, Monticello and Hill - Stead. Features architect Philip Johnson. Eighth of eight installments of the Pride Of Place - Building The American Dream Series, hosted by architect Robert Stern.
Fine Arts; Geography - United States; Sociology
Dist - PSU **Prod** - FOTH 1986
FOTH

The Search for a Voice 53 MIN
U-matic / VHS
Man and Music Series
Color (C)
$279.00, $179.00 purchase _ #AD - 2066
Focuses on Tsarist Russia. Traces its cultural history from the 17th century, covering the romance with France which ended with Napoleon's invasion, to Pushkin and Glinka. Part of a 22 - part series that sets Western music into the historial and cultural context of its time.
Civics and Political Systems; Fine Arts; Foreign Language; History - World
Dist - FOTH **Prod** - FOTH

The Search for Acadia 15 MIN
16mm
Color
LC 80-701628
Shows the diverse aspects of the terrain at Acadia National Park in Maine, along with a brief review of the history of Mt Desert Island. Includes scenes of the pounding of the Maine coast surf and the muted colors in a fog to convey the many moods of Acadia.
Geography - United States
Dist - USNAC **Prod** - USNPS 1980

Search for Achievement 27 MIN
16mm
Color (C A)
LC 77-702216
Presents Dr Jay Hall discussing the relationship between managerial behavior and managerial achievement, illustrating types of behavior that cause managers to become high achievers, moderate achievers or low achievers.
Business and Economics; Guidance and Counseling; Psychology
Dist - TELEO **Prod** - TELEO 1976

Search for Alexander the Great Series Pt 1
The Young Lion 60 MIN
Dist - TIMLIF

Search for Alexander the Great Series Pt 2
The Young Conqueror 60 MIN
Dist - TIMLIF

Search for Alexander the Great Series Pt 3
Lord of Asia 60 MIN
Dist - TIMLIF

Search for Alexander the Great Series
The Last March 60 MIN
Dist - TIMLIF

The Search for alternate life - styles and philosophies 20 MIN
U-matic / VHS / 16mm
Color (J)
LC 73-701224
Explores some of the efforts being made today to find personal harmony and a fulfilling life - style. Visits a cooperative village in the Sierras with a life - style based on a yoga philosophy.
Guidance and Counseling; Psychology; Religion and Philosophy; Sociology
Dist - ALTSUL **Prod** - MITCHG 1973

A Search for Antiworlds 25 MIN
16mm / U-matic / VHS
Color
LC 77-700575
Documents a physics research experiment at the Lawrence Berkeley Laboratory of the University of California, which seeks to determine the existence of large amounts of antimatter in the universe.
Science; Science - Physical
Dist - PFP **Prod** - BERKFA 1977

Search for balance 48 MIN
VHS
China moon series
Color (I J G)
$295.00 purchase
Studies Chinese healers who seek to find balance between body and spirit through traditional Chinese methods. Shows how a balance is sought between the competing claims of Eastern and Western medicine. Part of a series on China.
Geography - World; Health and Safety
Dist - LANDMK **Prod** - LANDMK 1989

Search for Battleship Bismarck 59 MIN
VHS / BETA
Color (G)
$24.20 purchase _ #C51389
History - World; Sociology
Dist - NGS **Prod** - NGS

Search for Coal 18 MIN
16mm
Color
LC 80-700839
Tells how coal was formed, its geological characteristics, where coal is mined and likely locations of reserves as well as exploration techiques. Stresses the continuous

need for an intensive proving program in order to ensure adequate reserves of energy to sustain future natural growth.
Industrial and Technical Education; Science - Physical; Social Science
Dist - TASCOR **Prod** - IMPACT 1978

The Search for common ground 40 MIN
VHS
Color (G)
$40.00 purchase, $30.00 rental
Demonstrates a new method of dispute resolution known as the 'Common Ground Approach,' in which participants with differing views actively seek points of agreement. Presents two episodes which demonstrate the techniques involved. Moderated by William Ury.
Guidance and Counseling; Psychology
Dist - EFVP

Search for Common Ground Series
Common ground approach to conflict resolution 40 MIN
Preventing the Final Mistake 15 MIN
Dist - EFVP

The Search for Deliverance - 1492 to 1789 - Pt 5 60 MIN
VHS / 16mm
Heritage - Civilization and the Jews Series
Color (J)
$800.00, $49.00 purchase _ #405 - 9125
Explores more than 3000 years of the Jewish experience and its intimate connections with the civilizations of the world. Uses all available resources to weave an extraordinary tapestry of the Jewish history and people. Hosted by Abba Eban, Israel's former ambassador to the UN and the US. Part 5 focuses on the bustle of Jewish life in Amsterdam, Constantinople, Safed and Venice after expulsion from Spain. Explores the flourishing of Polish Jewry.
History - World; Psychology; Religion and Philosophy; Sociology
Dist - FI **Prod** - WNETTV 1984

The Search for Electromagnetic Induction 43 MIN
16mm
Color
LC 81-700393
Recounts the story of research into methods of producing electricity with magnetism, emphasizing Oersted's chance discovery of electromagnetism in 1820.
Science; Science - Physical
Dist - PURDEV **Prod** - PURDEV 1980

The Search for electromagnetic induction - Pt 1 22 MIN
16mm
Color (C IND VOC)
LC 81-700393
Recounts the story of research into methods of producing electricity with magnetism, emphasizing Oersted's chance discovery of electromagnetism in 1820.
Science - Physical
Dist - PURDEV **Prod** - PURDEV 1980

The Search for electromagnetic induction - Pt 2 21 MIN
16mm
Color (C IND VOC)
LC 81-700393
Recounts the story of research into methods of producing electricity with magnetism, emphasizing Oersted's chance discovery of electromagnetism in 1820.
Science - Physical
Dist - PURDEV **Prod** - PURDEV 1980

The Search for extra terrestrial life 30 MIN
U-matic / VHS / 16mm
Cosmos series; Edited version
Color (J H C)
Presents Dr Carl Sagan who examines the evidence for UFO's and discusses the attempts to establish contact with civilizations that may exist elsewhere in the galaxy. Discusses radio astronomy which is the chosen code and visits the radio telescope at Arecibo, Puerto Rico. Uses the Drake Equation to estimate the statistical chance that intelligent life exists elsewhere in the universe. Edited from an episode of the Cosmos series.
Science - Natural; Science - Physical
Dist - FI **Prod** - SAGANC 1980

The Search for faith 12 MIN
U-matic / VHS / 16mm
Vignettes series
Color (J)
LC 73-701995
Probes the faith experience in three vignettes in which a teenage girl discovers God through the wisdom of an old Navajo, a disillusioned advertising executive finds God through the practice of meditation and a jaded rock star meets God by writing a song about Jesus.
Religion and Philosophy
Dist - PAULST **Prod** - PAULST 1973

Search for Fossil Man 24 MIN
16mm / U-matic / VHS
Color (H C A)
Presents Dr Phillip Tobias as he takes a team of amateur anthropologists to the famous Makapansgat fossil - hominid site in Africa. Shows how the team members continue a search for early hominid remains and how they excavate and develop the finesse necessary for chipping fossils from the rock in which they are encased.
Geography - World; Sociology
Dist - NGS **Prod** - NGS 1974

The Search for Gertie 25 MIN
16mm / U-matic
Untamed World Series
Color; Mono (J H C A)
$400.00 film, $250.00 video, $50.00 rental
Profiles two devoted naturalists and follows their search for a long haired rhino named 'Gertie in an African game preserve.
Science; Science - Natural
Dist - CTV **Prod** - CTV 1969

The Search for gravity waves 30 MIN
VHS
Color (H C G)
$250.00 purchase
Illustrates in lay terms complex ideas in astrophysics and discusses the awesome task of detecting movement caused by a passing gravity wave.
Science - Physical
Dist - LANDMK **Prod** - LANDMK 1990

The Search for Grissi 15 MIN
VHS
Books from cover to cover series
Color (P I G)
$25.00 purchase _ #BFCC - 114
Tells the story of Peter, an eleven - year - old boy who is unhappy after his family moves to Brooklyn. Shows how Peter's experience of searching for his sister's lost cat opens his life to new experiences. Hosted by John Robbins. Based on the book 'The Search for Grissi' by Mary Francis Shura.
Fine Arts; Literature and Drama
Dist - PBS **Prod** - WETATV 1988

The Search for Life 30 MIN
U-matic / VHS / 16mm
Nova Series
Color (H C A)
LC 78-700567
Describes experiments that have been conducted in an attempt to understand the origins of life.
Science; Science - Natural; Science - Physical
Dist - TIMLIF **Prod** - WGBHTV 1976

The Search for mind - Part 1 60 MIN
VHS
Mind series
Color; Captioned (G)
$59.95 purchase _ #MIND - 101
Explores historical and contemporary concepts of the human mind. Interviews ethnologist Jane Goodall, who shares her theory of how the human mind evolved from the primate brain. Considers the nature and evolution of consciousness, the unconscious, brain deficits, and psychological theories of the mind. Presents the first program of a nine - part series exploring the human mind.
Psychology; Sociology
Dist - PBS **Prod** - WNETTV 1988
PSU

The Search for Moyaone 5 MIN
16mm
Color (C H G)
LC 72-701789
Demonstrates the basic techniques of archaeology. Shows University of Maryland students as they excavate a site on the Potomac River believed to be the remains of the chief village of the Piscataway Indians, last seen by Captain John Smith.
Geography - United States; History - United States; History - World; Science - Physical; Sociology
Dist - UMD **Prod** - UMD 1972

The Search for new energy - Pt 1 15 MIN
16mm
Science in action series
Color (C)
Examines the efforts of scientists and engineers to discover and develop new sources of fuel in order to solve the problems created by the energy crisis. Examines new power sources, such as the magnetohydrodynamic generator and geothermal energy.
Home Economics; Industrial and Technical Education; Science; Science - Natural
Dist - COUNFI **Prod** - ALLFP

The Search for new energy - Pt 2 15 MIN
16mm
Science in action series
Color (C)
Examines the new, sophisticated sources of power being developed for long - range usage and supply. Explains that some of these include the breeder reactor, fusion, solar power systems, windmills, tidal power and atmospheric electricity.
Industrial and Technical Education; Science; Science - Natural
Dist - COUNFI **Prod** - ALLFP

The Search for Opportunity 30 MIN
U-matic / VHS
Japan - the Changing Tradition Series
Color (H C A)
History - World
Dist - GPN **Prod** - UMA 1978

The Search for Planet X 26 MIN
U-matic / VHS
Planets Series
Color (C)
$249.00, $149.00 purchase _ #AD - 1147
Introduces the only man alive who has discovered a planet. Tells about the earlier discoveries of planets in the Solar System. Bob Harrington of the US Naval Observatory is certain that a tenth planet exists, though he has not yet located it. Part of a seven - part series on planets.
History - World; Industrial and Technical Education; Psychology; Science - Physical
Dist - FOTH **Prod** - FOTH

The Search for Power 15 MIN
U-matic
North America - Growth of a Continent Series
Color (J H)
Discusses common sources of electrical power including water, thermal heat and nuclear energy. Also discusses alternative sources such as solar heat collectors, wind generators, satellites, geysers and hydrogen fusion.
Geography - United States; Geography - World
Dist - TVOTAR **Prod** - TVOTAR 1980

Search for Safety 15 MIN
U-matic
Color (IND)
Illustrates the procedures of conducting a Job Safety Analysis explaining its benefits to the operation. Shows how to write standard job procedures and work safety guidelines for the improvement of safety and productivity.
Business and Economics; Guidance and Counseling; Health and Safety
Dist - BNA **Prod** - ERESI 1983

Search for Safety 42 MIN
U-matic
Supervisory Safety Course Series
Color (IND)
Emphasizes the understanding and practice of specific supervisory skills by providing training in some of the basic management responsibilities. Contains three tapes and a 75 page leader's guide for group training.
Health and Safety
Dist - BNA **Prod** - ERESI 1984

The Search for Sandra Laing
16mm
World Series
Color (H C A)
Tells the story of a 'colored' child born to white parents in South Africa and her rejection by a small town.
History - World; Sociology
Dist - INTENC **Prod** - INTENC 1977

Search for Science - Search for Science 15 MIN
U-matic
Color (P)
Demonstrates that the greater the degree of organization in scientific work, the better or more tangible the results.
Science
Dist - GPN **Prod** - WVIZTV

Search for science series
Balanced flight - Pt 1 15 MIN
Balanced flight - Pt 2 15 MIN
The Bird - adaptation 15 MIN
The Bird - how we change the numbers 15 MIN
Chemical electricity 15 MIN
The Earth and the moon 15 MIN
The Fish and its survival 15 MIN
Fish and water in the biosphere 15 MIN
The Food web and how animals fit into it 15 MIN
Jet engines 15 MIN
Magnetism - Pt 1 15 MIN
Magnetism - Pt 2 15 MIN
Mechanical electricity 15 MIN
The Ocean - always the weak and the strong 15 MIN
The Ocean - animal relationships 15 MIN

The Ocean - animals of a different kind 15 MIN
Photosynthesis - Pt 1 8 MIN
Photosynthesis - Pt 2 7 MIN
Properties of air 15 MIN
Respiration and transpiration 15 MIN
Series and parallel circuits 15 MIN
The Solar system 15 MIN
Space exploration 15 MIN
Tropism - Pt 1 15 MIN
Tropism - Pt 2 15 MIN
Weather - the water cycle 15 MIN
Dist - GPN

Search for silence 15 MIN
16mm
B&W
LC FIE61-118
Explains what the navy is doing to curb the noise of jet aircraft around naval air stations and follows a naval aviator as he points out the salient features of the navy's noise abatement program.
Industrial and Technical Education; Science - Natural; Social Science; Sociology
Dist - USNAC **Prod** - USN 1960

The Search for Solid Ground 62 MIN
16mm
MAA Individual Lecturers Series
B&W (H C T)
Presents a panel discussion on various developments in logic and their implications for mathematics.
Mathematics; Religion and Philosophy
Dist - MLA **Prod** - MAA 1966

The Search for Solid Ground 45 MIN
16mm
Mathematics Today Series
B&W (C H)
LC FIA66-1278
Presents a panel discussion in which Mark Kac, John Kemeny, Harley Rogers and Raymond Smullyan discuss recent developments in logic and their implications for modern mathematics.
Mathematics
Dist - MLA **Prod** - WNETTV 1963

Search for Solutions Series
Adaptation 18 MIN
Context 18 MIN
Evidence 18 MIN
Investigation 18 MIN
Modeling 18 MIN
Patterns 18 MIN
Prediction 18 MIN
Theory 18 MIN
Trial and Error 18 MIN
Dist - KAROL

Search for Sounds 29 MIN
U-matic
Music Shop Series
Color
Focuses on how to look for the right combination of instruments to play a song.
Fine Arts
Dist - UMITV **Prod** - UMITV 1974

The Search for the Disappeared 58 MIN
VHS / U-matic
Nova Series
Color (H C A)
$250 purchase _ #5121C
Shows scientists in Argentina locating kidnapped children and using forensic medicine to identify the dead. Produced by WGBH Boston.
Sociology
Dist - CORF

Search for the great apes 52 MIN
U-matic / VHS / 16mm / Videodisc / BETA
Color (H C)
Shows women scientists studying the wild orangutans of Borneo and mountain gorillas of central Africa.
Science - Natural; Sociology
Dist - NGS **Prod** - NGS 1975

Search for the great apes 60 MIN
VHS
National Geographic video series
Color (G)
$29.95 purchase
Features Dian Fossey and her pioneering but sometimes controversial fieldwork with the mountain gorillas of Africa.
Science - Natural; Sociology
Dist - PBS **Prod** - WNETTV

Search for the magic bullet 55 MIN
VHS
Microbes and men
Color; PAL (C PRO H)
PdS99 purchase; Not available in the United States
Covers the development of salvarsan by Paul Ehrlich. Explains the significance of this as the beginning of the 'miracle drugs.' Sixth in the six - part series Microbes and Men, which covers the history and development of modern medicine.
Health and Safety; Science
Dist - BBCENE

The Search for the Mary Rose - Pt 6 20 MIN
VHS
Tudors Series
Color (I)
$79.00 purchase _ #825 - 9426
Paints a detailed and historically accurate picture of the Tudor period, 1485 - 1603, in British history. Examines historical trends over a broad time period or concentrates on one aspect of the era. The dramatizations are based on source material and the locations are authentic. Part 6 of seven parts explores the historical background of the famous Tudor flagship.
Civics and Political Systems; History - World; Social Science
Dist - FI **Prod** - BBCTV 1987

Search for the Mind 60 MIN
VHS / U-matic
Discovery of Animal Behavior Series
Color (H C A)
Reveals that Darwin's theory of natural selection was followed by Lewis Henry Morgan who discovered evidence of cogitation in beavers, George Romanes experimenting with fish, cats and dogs, Douglas Spalding working with newborn chicks and Jacques Loeb attempting to prove animals mindless.
Science; Science - Natural
Dist - FI **Prod** - WNETTV 1982

Search for the Nile Series no 1
The Dream of the Wanderer 60 MIN
Dist - TIMLIF

Search for the Nile Series no 2
Discovery and Betrayal 60 MIN
Dist - TIMLIF

Search for the Nile Series no 4
The Great Debate 52 MIN
Dist - TIMLIF

Search for the Nile Series no 5
Find Livingstone 60 MIN
Dist - TIMLIF

Search for the Nile Series no 6
Conquest and Death 60 MIN
Dist - TIMLIF

Search for the Nile (Spanish Series no 1
The Dream of the Wanderer 52 MIN
Dist - TIMLIF

Search for the Nile (Spanish Series no 5
Find Livingstone 52 MIN
Dist - TIMLIF

Search for the nile - Spanish series
The Great debate 52 MIN
Dist - TIMLIF

Search for the Nile
The Secret fountains 60 MIN
Dist - TIMLIF

Search for the past - Pt 1 30 MIN
U-matic
Africa file series
Color (J H)
Gives west African history up to the time of the slave trade.
Business and Economics; Geography - World; History - World
Dist - TVOTAR **Prod** - TVOTAR 1985

Search for the past - Pt 2 30 MIN
U-matic
Africa file series
Color (J H)
Gives west African history from the days of the slave trade to the independence movements of the 1950s.
Business and Economics; Geography - World; History - World
Dist - TVOTAR **Prod** - TVOTAR 1985

Search for the Silver Fleet - Part One 60 MIN
VHS / U-matic / 16mm
Last Frontier Series
Color; Mono (J H C A G)
MV $225.00 _ MP $550.00
Explores the site of an old shipwreck off the coast of Central America. Members of the Foundation for Ocean Research excavate the site and find a silver ingot from the Spanish Fleet of 1726.
History - World
Dist - CTV **Prod** - MAKOF 1985

Search for the Silver Fleet - Part Two 60 MIN
VHS / U-matic / 16mm
Last Frontier Series
Color; Mono (G)
MV $225.00 _ MP $550.00
Pursues the continuing excavation of the wreck sight featured in Part One of this title. Sharks begin to harass the divers and a hurricane drives the search team from the sea, but not before numerous treasures have been excavated.
History - World
Dist - CTV **Prod** - MAKOF 1985

Search for the Western Sea 29 MIN
U-matic / VHS / 16mm
Color (J H)
LC 78-701263
Tells the story of Alexander Mackenzie's overland expedition from Fort Chippewyan to the Pacific coast during the 18th century.
Biography; Geography - World; History - World
Dist - MGHT **Prod** - DEVGCF 1978

Search for the Whale 20 MIN
16mm
Color (PRO)
LC 77-701400
Explains the U S Navy's continuing research into the sounds of ocean mammals, their effects on sonar and the benefits of new knowledge for fleet operations.
Civics and Political Systems; Science - Natural
Dist - USNAC **Prod** - USN 1976

Search for Ulysses 56 MIN
U-matic / VHS / 16mm
Color (J)
LC 76-709786
British sailor and scholar Ernle Bradford explains his theory that Homer's Ulysses really lived and that his adventures took place on islands which still exist.
Geography - World; History - World; Literature and Drama
Dist - CAROUF **Prod** - CBSTV 1965

Search for Ulysses - Pt 1 26 MIN
U-matic / VHS / 16mm
Color (J)
British sailor and scholar Ernle Bradford explains his theory that Homer's Ulysses really lived and that his adventures took place on islands which still exist.
Geography - World; History - World
Dist - CAROUF **Prod** - CBSTV 1965

Search for Ulysses - Pt 2 26 MIN
16mm / U-matic / VHS
Color (J)
British sailor and scholar Ernle Bradford explains his theory that Homer's Ulysses really lived and that his adventures took place on islands which still exist.
Geography - World; History - World
Dist - CAROUF **Prod** - CBSTV 1965

The Search for Understanding 18 MIN
16mm
Color
LC 79-700053
Explains the operation of the Clinton P Anderson Meson Physics Facility in Los Alamos, New Mexico.
Science
Dist - LASL **Prod** - LASL 1978

A Search for unity - a European idea 52 MIN
VHS / 16mm
Europe, the mighty continent series no 13; No 13
Color
LC 77-701569
Analyzes developments in Europe during the 1960's and 1970's. Describes the Soviet invasion of Czechoslovakia, the weakening of the European Economic Community by the Middle East War and the subsequent oil crisis, and the evolution of detente relations between East and West. Discusses prospects for Europe's future.
Business and Economics; History - World
Dist - TIMLIF **Prod** - BBCTV 1976

A Search for unity - a European idea - Pt 1 26 MIN
U-matic
Europe, the mighty continent series no 13; No 13
Color
Analyzes developments in Europe during the 1960's and 1970's. Describes the Soviet invasion of Czechoslovakia, the weakening of the European Economic Community by the Middle East War and the subsequent oil crisis, and the evolution of detente relations between East and West. Discusses prospects for Europe's future.
History - World; Sociology
Dist - TIMLIF **Prod** - BBCTV 1976

A Search for unity - a European idea - Pt 2 26 MIN
U-matic
Europe, the mighty continent series no 13; No 13
Color
Analyzes developments in Europe during the 1960's and 1970's. Describes the Soviet invasion of Czechoslovakia,

the weakening of the European Economic Community by the Middle East War and the subsequent oil crisis, and the evolution of detente relations between East and West. Discusses prospects for Europe's future.
History - World; Sociology
Dist - TIMLIF **Prod** - BBCTV 1976

The Search for Water 20 MIN
16mm
Color
Examines the possible consequences of diversion of Connecticut River water to the Boston metropolitan area. Suggests alternative solutions. Uses interviews with scientists and planners, animation and wildlife footage.
Science - Natural; Social Science
Dist - FENWCK **Prod** - HANOVF

The Search for Water 21 MIN
16mm
Color (J)
LC 76-700244
Uses the city of Boston as a model to explain ways in which cities secure suitable water supplies. Shows that environmental disruption associated with the process may be minimized by water recycling.
Science - Natural; Social Science; Sociology
Dist - HANOVC **Prod** - HANOVC 1975

The Search for zest 25 MIN
16mm / U-matic / VHS
Boredom at work series
B&W (C A)
A man's subconscious associations with his past are wrecking his family life and job. Clinical treatment creates a normal pattern of life for him.
Guidance and Counseling; Health and Safety; Psychology; Sociology
Dist - IFB **Prod** - ODOH 1963

Search in the Deep 52 MIN
U-matic / VHS / 16mm
Undersea World of Jacques Cousteau Series
Color
Presents Jacques Cousteau and his scientists recording the 400 - pound green sea turtles' 1,000 - mile migration to lay eggs. Shows the green turtles' emergence at birth and the unending struggle for survival.
Science - Natural
Dist - CF **Prod** - METROM 1970

A Search in the sun - Pt 12 30 MIN
VHS / U-matic
Profiles in progress series
Color (H C)
$325.00, $295.00 purchase _ #V557
Looks at Belize, formerly British Honduras, which is modernizing. Shows how Belize is discovering the value of its natural and cultural resources with the world's second largest barrier reef and its Mayan ruins. Shows how Belize is emphasizing 'eco - tourism' in an effort to prevent reckless tourism promotion which could result in great social and cultural trauma. Part of a 13 - part series on people who are moving their tradition - bound countries into modern times.
Geography - World; History - World
Dist - BARR **Prod** - CEPRO 1991

Search into White Space 16 MIN
16mm
Color (G)
_ #106C 0170 562
Considers the possibility of oil under the high Arctic. Shows pinpointing a drilling location, the prospectors, the drills, back up equipment, and helicopters needed.
Geography - World; Industrial and Technical Education; Social Science
Dist - CFLMDC **Prod** - NFBC 1970

Search of Zubin Mehta Series

Education of Zubin Mehta in the Eastern and Western worlds	25 MIN
Zubin Mehta - Commitment and Fulfillment as a Way of Life	22 MIN
Zubin Mehta - if You are Going to Lead, Lead	36 MIN
Zubin Mehta and His Masters - Piatigorsky and Rubinstein	29 MIN
Zubin Mehta Rocks the Gospel	21 MIN

Dist - ESMRDA

Search Operations 29 MIN
16mm
B&W
LC FIE63-271
Demonstrates the systematic search and rescue operations conducted according to the National Search and Rescue Plan and the National Search and Rescue Agreement. Depicts areas of responsibility delegated to the armed forces, Civil Air Patrol and local authorities.
Civics and Political Systems; Health and Safety
Dist - USNAC **Prod** - USDD 1961

Search - Our world - our community series 75 MIN
VHS
Search series
Color; PAL (I J)
PdS25 purchase
Introduces a range of study skills which, when mastered, will help student - learning processes through school life and long afterward. Teaches by example to motivate children to learn about the world around them, focusing on parts of their everyday lives and representing areas which are sometimes neglected in education. Aims to create more aware, tolerant, concerned and caring individuals. Five programs, 15 minutes each. Contact distributor about availability outside the United Kingdom.
Civics and Political Systems; Social Science
Dist - ACADEM

Search series
Presents four series introducing a range of study skills which, when mastered, will help student - learning processes through school life and long afterward. Teaches by example to motivate children to learn about the world around them, focusing on parts of their everyday lives and representing areas which are sometimes neglected in education. Aims to create more aware, tolerant, concerned and caring individuals. Includes Our World - Our Community; Conservation; Communication; Design and Manufacture. Contact distributor about availability outside the United Kingdom.

Search - Communication series	75 MIN
Search - Conservation series	60 MIN
Search - Design and manufacture series	60 MIN
Search - Our world - our community series	75 MIN

Dist - ACADEM

SEARCH - the art of observation in pediatrics 16 MIN
U-matic / VHS
Color (PRO C)
$395.00 purchase, $80.00 _ #C871 - VI - 038
Presents medical students and pediatric nursing personnel with a quick sytematic method of assessing illness in an infant, using only one's eyes and brain. Uses the mnemonic SEARCH representing the six areas of observation - Social stimulation, Energy, Appearance, Reaction to parent, Cry and Hydration. Offers a thorough explanation of what to look for in each of these areas and representative cases to observe. Presented by Ross Dehovitz.
Health and Safety
Dist - HSCIC

Searches Incident to Lawful Arrests 50 MIN
U-matic / VHS
Criminal Procedure and the Trial Advocate Series
Color (PRO)
Examines the search incident to lawful arrest. Raises questions on how far the search can extend, what is necessary to protect the arresting officer, what is meant by wingspan and how far the search of an automobile may extend.
Civics and Political Systems
Dist - ABACPE **Prod** - ABACPE

Searching - Adoption Stories 60 MIN
U-matic
A Different Understanding Series
Color (PRO)
Examines the thoughts and feelings of people whose lives have been complicated and enriched by adoption.
Psychology; Sociology
Dist - TVOTAR **Prod** - TVOTAR 1985

The Searching eye 18 MIN
16mm / U-matic / VHS
Color (P I) (FRENCH GERMAN)
LC FIA65-530
Explores the art of seeing and the power of observation. Describes the actions of a young boy at the beach, with the camera showing what the boy cannot see. Views the world under the sea, the world of past geological formations, the inner world of microscopic creatures, the process of growth and fruition, the world of outer space and the world of imagination. Provides a visual metaphor for the normally unseen world.
Psychology
Dist - PFP **Prod** - BASSS 1964

Searching for fish 29 MIN
16mm
Color (JAPANESE)
Emphasizes the significance of marine resources by depicting the relationship between seaweed and fish.
Science - Natural
Dist - UNIJAP **Prod** - UNIJAP 1968

Searching for My Picture 29 MIN
U-matic
Artist at Work Series
Color
Demonstrates posing and re - posing a model.
Fine Arts
Dist - UMITV **Prod** - UMITV 1973

Searching for Solutions 30 MIN
VHS / U-matic
Eager to Learn Series
Color (T)
Education; Psychology
Dist - KTEHTV **Prod** - KTEHTV

Searching for some love and care 11 MIN
16mm / U-matic / VHS
Growing up with Sandy Offenheim series
Color (K P)
LC 82-707059
Explores emotions and feelings toward one's parents and reflections on what parents expect of children.
Psychology; Sociology
Dist - BCNFL **Prod** - PLAYTM 1982

Searching for Values - a Film Anthology Series
My Country Right or Wrong 14 MIN^16 MIN
Dist - CORF

Searching for Values - a Film Anthology Series

The Dehumanizing city and Hymie Schultz	15 MIN
The Fine Art of Aggression	16 MIN
I who am, who am I	17 MIN
Loneliness - and Loving	17 MIN
Love to Kill	15 MIN
My Country Right or Wrong	15 MIN
Politics, power and the public good	20 MIN
Pride and principle	17 MIN
The Right to Live - who Decides	17 MIN
A Sense of Purpose	14 MIN
Spaces between People	18 MIN
Trouble with the Law	16 MIN
Violence - Just for Fun	15 MIN
When Parents Grow Old	15 MIN
Whether to Tell the Truth	18 MIN

Dist - LCOA

The Searching heart - a medieval legend 20 MIN
16mm
B&W
Describes the early Renaissance conception of life. Suggests the later Pilgrim's Progress and tells the travels of a human heart in its search for maturity and a place for the traditional 'Girl with Yelloy Hair.'
History - World; Literature and Drama
Dist - RADIM **Prod** - FILIM

Seas of Grass 55 MIN
16mm / VHS
Living Planet Series
(J H C)
$99.95 each, $595.00 series
Visits the African grasslands for a look at the beauty and uniqueness of natural life there. Hosted by David Attenborough.
Science; Science - Natural; Science - Physical
Dist - AMBROS **Prod** - AMBROS 1984

Seas of Grass 55 MIN
16mm / U-matic / VHS
Living Planet Series Pt 5
Color (H C A)
Visits the African grasslands which are home to the greatest collections of savannah animals. Shows how the antelope, zebra and wildebeest reside with their predators, lions and cheetahs.
Science - Natural
Dist - TIMLIF **Prod** - BBCTV 1984

Seas of Infinity 15 MIN
16mm
Color (H C A)
LC 72-701239
Reviews the planning, development, launching and function of the orbiting astronomical observatory, a series of orbiting telescopes which are being used to study the solar system and the stars. Features comments by leading scientists on the potential of this advancement in astronomy.
Science - Physical
Dist - NASA **Prod** - NASA 1969

Seas of Tomorrow 14 MIN
16mm
Color
LC 75-700577
Shows a young man as he decides on a career in the Navy. Mixes scenes of Navy life and training with sailing scenes in order to convey the theme of man's ageless identity with the sea.
Civics and Political Systems; Guidance and Counseling; Psychology
Dist - USNAC **Prod** - USN 1972

Seas Under Siege 56 MIN
U-matic / VHS
Color (C)
$279.00, $179.00 purchase _ #AD - 2131
Looks at some of the sources of toxic contamination which is found off all coastlines throughout the industrialized world. Considers the consequences of this pollution, polluted beaches, animal - kills, inedible fish and other food sources. Warns that opportunities for remedial action are rapidly growing slimmer.
Science - Natural; Sociology
Dist - FOTH **Prod** - FOTH

Seascape 29 MIN
U-matic
Magic of Oil Painting Series
Color
Fine Arts
Dist - PBS **Prod** - KOCETV

Seashells 14 MIN
16mm
B&W (P I J)
Shows how shelled sea animals move and feed. Discusses their enemies, sea birds and stormy weather.
Science - Natural
Dist - VIEWTH **Prod** - GATEEF

Seashore 11 MIN
16mm
B&W (G)
$20.00 rental
Sets up a series of rhythmical patterns with the basic image derived from a shot of an old movie depicting women in long dresses standing along the edge of the ocean. Stylizes the images repeating certain motions over and over within an eight - second loop.
Fine Arts; Geography - World
Dist - CANCIN **Prod** - RIMMER 1971

Seashore 7 MIN
U-matic / VHS / 16mm
Color
LC 78-715456
Views the beauties of the ocean and its wildlife. Includes super - slow motion sequences of pelicans diving for fish.
Geography - World; Science - Natural
Dist - PFP **Prod** - PFP 1971

The Seashore - Atlantic coast 15 MIN
VHS / U-matic / 16mm
Color; Captioned (I J H G)
$260, $180, $210 purchase _ #A167; LC 73-702935
Explores the variety of shorelines that stretch from Nova Scotia south to Florida and reveals the variety of animal life that lives along the rocky coasts, the sandy beaches, and salt marshes of the Atlantic coastline.
Geography - World; Science - Natural
Dist - BARR **Prod** - BARR 1973

A Seashore Community 15 MIN
VHS / U-matic
Why Series
Color (P I)
Discusses the living things found at the seashore.
Science - Natural
Dist - AITECH **Prod** - WDCNTV 1976

Seashore Ecology 16 MIN
16mm / U-matic / VHS
Color (I)
Analyzes some of the flora and fauna to be found in various types of shorelines. Identifies each species and indicates the characteristic features of each.
Science - Natural
Dist - LUF **Prod** - LUF 1983

Seashore Ecology 16 MIN
16mm
Color (J H C G)
Presents some of the typical flora and fauna found on various types of shorelines. Shows the seashore providing numerous habitats for different types of plants and animals which have adapted themselves during the evolutionary process to rocky shores, sandy bays or mud banks. Shows students how to discover and examine seashore wildlife.
Science - Natural
Dist - VIEWTH **Prod** - GATEEF

Seashore life 10 MIN
16mm / U-matic / VHS
Color (P I J)
Portrays life on three kinds of seashores - the sandy beach, the rock pool and the mud flat. Shows the adaptations seashore animals make to their special environments.
Science - Natural
Dist - EBEC **Prod** - EBEC 1950

Seashore life 29 MIN
Videoreel / VT2
Observing eye series
Color
Science - Natural; Sociology
Dist - PBS **Prod** - WGBHTV

The Seashore - Pacific coast 10 MIN
16mm / U-matic / VHS
Color (I J)
LC FIA68-2978
Explores beaches and coastlines of the Pacific shore. Examines plants, birds, shells, and animals along beaches and in tide pools.
Geography - United States; Geography - World; Science - Natural
Dist - BARR **Prod** - BARR 1968

Seashore surprises - 88
VHS
Reading rainbow series
Color; CC (K P)
$39.95 purchase
Shows that there's more to the beach than meets the eye in a book by Rose Wyler, illustrated by Steven James Petruccio. Goes beachcombing in southwestern Florida. Meets two local naturalists and explores plant and animal life at the edge of the sea, including shells, mangroves and more. Part of a series offering a multicultural approach to generating reading enthusiasm with cross - curricular applications, hosted by LeVar Burton.
English Language; Literature and Drama; Science; Science - Natural
Dist - GPN **Prod** - LNMDP

Seashores 30 MIN
VHS / 16mm
Our natural heritage series
Color (G)
$14.44 purchase _ #HSV4027
Explores the U.S. shorelines of the Atlantic and Pacific Oceans.
Geography - World; Science - Natural
Dist - EDUCRT

Seashores 25 MIN
VHS
Color (G)
$19.90 purchase _ #0723
Describes the Atlantic Coast of North America from the Bay of Fundy to the Florida Keys, as well as parts of the Pacific Coast. Looks in detail at shoreline flowers and birds.
Geography - United States; Science - Natural
Dist - SEVVID

Seaside 10 MIN
VHS
Stop, look, listen series
Color; PAL (P I J)
Looks at family seaside holiday to show activities on the beach, marine life and boats in the harbor. Part of a series of films which start from some everyday observation and show more of what is happening, how and why. Builds vocabulary and encourages children to be more observant.
English Language; Physical Education and Recreation; Social Science; Sociology
Dist - VIEWTH

Seaside - Walton County, Florida - Vol 16, No 16 15 MIN
VHS
Project reference file - PRF - series
Color (G A PRO)
$60.00 purchase _ #S40
Looks at a community in a small resort town on the Gulf of Mexico in northwest Florida. Examines a land use plan with an emphasis on pedestrian convenience. Features developer Robert Davis and planners Andres Duany and Elizabeth Plater - Zyberk.
Business and Economics; Geography - United States; Sociology
Dist - ULI **Prod** - ULI

The Season 15 MIN
VHS / 16mm
Color (J)
LC 79-700706
Uses a serio - comic technique to contemplate certain aspects of Christmas in Los Angeles. Uses an interview with Sunday schoolers and shows scenes of stinging crassness with the relentless exploitation of innocence for a fast buck.
Psychology; Religion and Philosophy; Sociology
Dist - LRF **Prod** - DONMAC 1968

A Season in the sun 55 MIN
16mm / VHS
Life science - ecosystems series
Color (I J H C)
$795.00, $545.00 purchase, $80.00, $55.00 rental
Visits East Africa which has only two seasons, wet and dry. Reveals that after the rainy season, as the land dries out, animals from elephants to snails must find ways to survive. Observes the different adaptations. Covers the concepts of survival adaptations, population control, courtship and competition, rearing young, aestivation - summer hibernation and niches. Produced by Alan Root. Part of a series. Also available in 30 - minute version.
Geography - World; Science - Natural
Dist - BNCHMK

Season of Fire 15 MIN
16mm
Color (J)
LC 74-702155
Shows the January 23, 1973, eruption of Helgafell Volcano on Heimaey Island, Iceland. Reports the evacuation of the area and the efforts to save the fishing port on the island from destruction.
Geography - World; Health and Safety; Science - Physical
Dist - FI **Prod** - NINESP 1974

A Season of grandmothers 29 MIN
VHS / U-matic
Real people series
Color (G)
Shows how long, snow covered months have always been the Indian time for remembering a childhood, recalling a song or telling old stories. Emphasizes the revival of traditional Indian education, reverence for elders, and a yearning for the old ways by using the traditional teachers, the Grandmothers, to reminisce and teach the ways of old.
Social Science; Sociology
Dist - NAMPBC GPN **Prod** - NAMPBC KSPSTV 1976

Season of hope 28 MIN
VHS
Color (H C)
$295.00 purchase
Shows interviews with mothers who are recovering from addictions, emphasizing that such women care for their children as all mothers do. Provides hope for recovery for substance abusers who are mothers. Serves as a resource for guidance counselors and for substance abuse education programs. Produced by Ashley James.
Guidance and Counseling; Health and Safety; Psychology
Dist - PFP

Season on the water 26 MIN
16mm / VHS
Color (I J A)
$395.00, $495.00 purchase, $75.00 rental _ #8124
Focuses on a family where the tradition of fisherman bequeathing their skills to their progeny is broken.
Industrial and Technical Education; Sociology
Dist - AIMS **Prod** - ITFE 1989

Seasonal Differences - Constitutional Rights 47 MIN
U-matic / VHS
Color (J H G)
$395, $425 _ #V134
Tells a story of religious conflicts and anti Semitism at an American high school.
Literature and Drama; Psychology
Dist - BARR **Prod** - BARR 1988

Seasonal Farm Workers Series
A Healthier Place to Live 11 MIN
Dist - USNAC

Seasons 9 MIN
VHS / 16mm
Color (C)
$80.00, $34.95 purchase _ #194 E 0083, 193 E 2083
Examines summer solstice, winter solstice, spring equinox and fall equinox, and explores the basis for the equator, the Antarctic and Arctic circles, and the Tropics of Capricorn and Cancer.
Geography - World; Science; Science - Physical
Dist - WARDS **Prod** - AAS

Seasons 10 MIN
U-matic
Take a look series
Color (P I)
Visits a marsh in the summer and winter to show the changes that the seasons bring.
Science; Science - Physical
Dist - TVOTAR **Prod** - TVOTAR 1986

Seasons 15 MIN
U-matic / VHS / 16mm
Color (J)
Explores the underlying reasons for marked seasonal changes during the year.
Science - Natural
Dist - LUF **Prod** - LUF 1983

Seasons 16 MIN
16mm
Color

LC 74-705594
Deals with the health and rehabilitation of older people, including nursing and rest home conditions and effective programs in geriatric therapy.
Health and Safety; Sociology
Dist - USNAC **Prod** - USSRS 1971

The Seasons 15 MIN
16mm
Color (I J A)
Examines the seasonal climates in the Western hemisphere, emphasizing that seasonal changes are due in part to the tilt of the earth on its axis and the earth's rotation around the sun. Uses animation and live photography to show examples and conditions of seasonal changes.
Science - Natural; Science - Physical
Dist - AVED **Prod** - AVED 1962

Seasons 9 MIN
VHS
Astronomy series
Color (J H)
$34.95 purchase _ #193 W 0051; $24.95 purchase _ #S9104
Examines the dynamics of the changing seasons in detail. Uses close - up side and overhead views of the Earth at each seasonal position. Part of a six - part series presenting a single concept about astronomy.
Geography - World; Mathematics; Science - Physical
Dist - WARDS HUBDSC **Prod** - WARDS HUBDSC

The Seasons 17 MIN
U-matic / VHS / 16mm
Captioned; Color (P I J)
LC 70-713788
Records the cycle of the seasons on a dairy farm in the Pennsylvania Dutch country.
Agriculture; Science - Natural
Dist - MOKIN **Prod** - MOKIN 1971

Seasons (2nd Ed Series
Fall is Here 10 MIN
Spring is Here 11 MIN
Winter is Here 11 MIN
Dist - IFB

Seasons - a Year of Change 15 MIN
U-matic / VHS / 16mm
Color (J)
LC 81-700731
Shows the life cycles of flora and fauna during a year in a North American forest.
Science - Natural
Dist - AIMS **Prod** - CAHILL 1980

Seasons - an Introductory Series
Fall is Here
Summer is Here
Winter is Here
Dist - IFB

Seasons and Days 13 MIN
U-matic / Videodisc / VHS / 16mm
Color (I J H)
$49.95 purchase _ #Q10908
Utilizes extensive animation to illustrate how changes in seasons and the length of daylight result from the earth revolving around the sun on an inclined axis. Explains polar circles and the tropics.
Science - Physical
Dist - CF

Seasons and Days 13 MIN
U-matic / VHS / 16mm
Color (I J H)
Shows how changes in seasons and the length of daylight result from the earth revolving around the sun on an inclined axis. Explains polar circles and the tropics.
Science - Natural
Dist - CF **Prod** - IFFB 1984

The Seasons and the symphony 60 MIN
U-matic / VHS
James Galway's music in time series
Color (J)
LC 83-706230
Presents flutist James Galway studying the operatic developments wrought by Gluck and discussing Vivaldi and Haydn. Talks about new ideas for symphonic compositions developed at Mannheim.
Fine Arts
Dist - FOTH **Prod** - POLTEL 1982

The Seasons - autumn 25 MIN
16mm / U-matic / VHS
Untamed frontier series
Color; Mono (J H C A)
$400.00 film, $250.00 video, $50.00 rental
Examines the season, autumn, and the changes it brings about in the environment. Illustrates these changes through a photographic study of the abundant fields and woods of central Europe.
Geography - World; History - World; Science - Natural
Dist - CTV **Prod** - CTV 1975

Seasons change 10 MIN
16mm
Color (P I)
LC 83-700152
Shows children and adults involved in various seasonal activities such as gardening, going to a country fair and savoring winter weather.
Science - Natural
Dist - MOKIN **Prod** - MOKIN 1983

The Seasons - Fall and Winter 15 MIN
U-matic / VHS
Featherby's Fables Series
Color (P)
Tells why fall is the harvest and leaf - dropping season and why animals either hibernate or move to warmer climes during the winter.
Science - Natural
Dist - GPN **Prod** - WVUTTV 1983

Seasons in nature series
Autumn in nature 14 MIN
Spring in Nature 17 MIN
Summer in Nature 14 MIN
Winter in Nature 12 MIN
Dist - ALTSUL

Seasons in the City Series
Spring Comes to the City 11 MIN
Winter Comes to the City 10 MIN
Dist - CORF

Seasons of a Navajo 60 MIN
U-matic / VHS
Color
Presents an intimate portrait of a traditional Navajo Indian family, whose heritage of sacred songs, ceremonies and oral tradition comes alive through the grandparents, Chauncey and Dorothy Nehoyia, who farm, weave and tend sheep in a traditional hogan dwelling without water or electricity, while their children live in tract homes and their grandchildren attend modern public schools.
Social Science; Sociology
Dist - PBS NAMPBC **Prod** - NAMPBC 1984

Seasons of sexuality 14 MIN
U-matic / VHS / 16mm
Color; Captioned (J H C)
LC 81-700041
Demonstrates the manifestations of sexuality at different stages of human development. Shows a toddler's unconcern for physical distinctions, children's dislike for members of the opposite sex, adolescents experiencing first romantic love, and an older married couple.
Health and Safety; Psychology
Dist - PEREN **Prod** - PPSY 1980

Seasons of Survival 21 MIN
VHS / U-matic
Phenomenal World Series
Color (J C)
$129.00 purchase _ #3962
Follows the animals who inhabit the Rocky Mountains, one of the most demanding environments on earth, as they struggle to endure the harsh climate and to evade hungry predators.
Science - Natural
Dist - EBEC

Seasons of the Basque 29 MIN
U-matic / VHS
Color
Traces the movements of the Basque sheepherders in Nevada throughout the seasons' changes. Records their skills and way of life.
Geography - United States; History - United States; Sociology
Dist - MEDIPR **Prod** - MEDIPR 1978

Seasons of the Elk 20 MIN
16mm
Color
Follows the elks through the four seasons of the year and witnesses the winter migration of thousands of elk to the National Elk Refuge at Jackson, Wyoming. Discusses the problem of poaching and the place of legitimate hunting in thinning the herds of elk.
Science - Natural
Dist - BERLET **Prod** - BERLET 1981

Seasons of the Navajo
VHS
American Indian collection series
Color (J H C G)
$29.95 purchase _ #PAV275V
Portrays a traditional Navajo family living a life far removed from the stress of the 20th century. Teaches that the Navajo prayer, Today I Live Well, means working hard and maintaining a kinship with the Earth, the animals, Navajo crafts and traditions. Part of a five - part series on American Indians.
Social Science
Dist - CAMV

The Seasons of the year 11 MIN
U-matic / VHS / 16mm
Color (P I)
$270, $190 purchase _ #504
Highlights the different changes in nature and in human activities that occur in each season.
Science - Natural
Dist - CORF

The Seasons - Pt 1 - the round earth and the sun's rays 5 MIN
16mm
Color (J H C G)
Explains the Earth's movements in relation to the sun. Shows how the earth spins on its axis and revolves around the sun. Shows how the sun's rays affect the earth.
Science - Natural; Science - Physical
Dist - VIEWTH **Prod** - GBI

The Seasons - Pt 3 - seasonal changes in the temperate regions 9 MIN
16mm
Color (J H C G)
Completes the series on the seasons by looking in detail at the temperature regions of the Earth and the changes of temperature in them at different seasons.
Geography - World; Science - Natural
Dist - VIEWTH **Prod** - GBI

The Seasons - Pt 2 - the earth and its seasonal movement round the sun, 12 MIN
16mm
Color (J H C G)
Explains how the earth's movement around the sun causes the four seasons.
Science - Natural; Science - Physical
Dist - VIEWTH **Prod** - GBI

Seasons Series
Spring 11 MIN
Dist - CENTRO CORF

Seasons series
Autumn 11 MIN
Autumn comes to the forest 11 MIN
Spring Comes to the Forest 11 MIN
Spring Comes to the Pond 10 MIN
Summer 11 MIN
Winter 11 MIN
Winter Comes to the Forest 11 MIN
Dist - CORF

Seasons series
Summer is here 11 MIN
Dist - IFB

The Seasons - Spring 15 MIN
VHS / U-matic
Featherby's Fables Series
Color (P)
Tells about spring rains, growth and new life. Describes how the tilting earth brings warmer weather.
Science - Natural
Dist - GPN **Prod** - WVUTTV 1983

The Seasons - Spring 25 MIN
U-matic / VHS / 16mm
Untamed Frontier Series
Color; Mono (J H C A)
$400.00 film, $250.00 video, $50.00 rental
Studies nature's return to longer days and increased activity in the spring by looking at the wildlife of the northern European countryside.
Geography - World; Science - Natural
Dist - CTV **Prod** - CTV 1975

The Seasons - summer 25 MIN
U-matic / VHS / 16mm
Untamed frontier series
Color; Mono (J H C A)
$400.00 film, $250.00 video, $50.00 rental
Explores nature by examining the activity in a forest of central Europe during summer.
Geography - World; Science - Natural
Dist - CTV **Prod** - CTV 1975

The Seasons - Summer 15 MIN
VHS / U-matic
Featherby's Fables Series
Color (P)
Describes how people and animals keep cool in the summer and why plants grow bigger and stronger.
Science - Natural
Dist - GPN **Prod** - WVUTTV 1983

The Seasons - Winter 25 MIN
16mm / U-matic / VHS
Untamed Frontier Series
Color; Mono (J H C A)
$400.00 film, $250.00 video, $50.00 rental
Plots the patterns of nature's creatures in a central European forest during winter to demonstrate adaptation to the seasons.
Geography - World; History - World; Science - Natural
Dist - CTV **Prod** - CTV 1975

Seasound 8 MIN
16mm
Color (G)
$20.00 rental
Engages in a study of the rhythmic unending motion of waves on the ocean. Realizes the connection between the eyes and ears by presenting the film without sound. Audiences claim to hear the sound of the sea. Produced by R Raffaello Dvorak.
Fine Arts; Geography - World
Dist - CANCIN

Seat Belt Hernia - Price for Survival 8 MIN
16mm
Color
LC FIA66-638
Presents a kaleidoscopic view of the 1962 Seattle World's Fair including brief glimpses of the architecture, art, science exhibits, shops, dancers from foreign countries and midway. Natural sound and modern jazz music take the place of narration.
Health and Safety
Dist - AMCSUR **Prod** - MFIORH 1965

Seat Belt Safety 30 MIN
U-matic / VHS
Color (PRO)
Presents information on seat belt safety. Tells why people don't wear them and survival statistics that support wearing them. Focuses on the use of seat belts by firefighters and emergency personnel.
Health and Safety; Industrial and Technical Education; Social Science
Dist - FILCOM **Prod** - LACFD

Seat belt safety 22 MIN
VHS / 16mm
Color (J)
$465.00, $225.00 purchase
Explains momentum clearly, logically. Explores how momentum affects driver and passengers in front and rear seats. Deals with common excuses for not buckling up, shows how unreasonable and dangerous these 'reasons' are.
Education; Health and Safety; Industrial and Technical Education
Dist - LUF **Prod** - LUF 1986

Seat Belts are for Kids Too 10 MIN
16mm / VHS
Adventures of Safety Frog Series
Color (K P I)
$195.00, $240.00 purchase, $30.00 rental _ #9921
Teaches children how to wear seat belts correctly and why the shoulder and lap belts give greater protection than lap belts alone.
Health and Safety; Industrial and Technical Education
Dist - AIMS **Prod** - AIMS 1987

Seat Belts - the Lifesaving Habit 20 MIN
U-matic / VHS / 16mm
Color (H C G T A)
$75 rental _ #9838
Refutes the common excuses for not wearing seat belts. Explains that seat belts are the best protection we have against injury.
Health and Safety; Industrial and Technical Education
Dist - AIMS **Prod** - AIMS 1986

Seat Removal from an Automobile 8 MIN
VHS / BETA / 16mm
Color (A PRO)
$56.00 purchase _ #KTI56
Shows procedures for removing a seat from an automobile. Includes consideration of the necessary electrical interlocks.
Industrial and Technical Education
Dist - RMIBHF **Prod** - RMIBHF

Seatbelts and birthdays 10 MIN
VHS / U-matic / BETA
Color (G)
$667.00 purchase, $125.00 rental _ #SEA017
Stresses the reason for always wearing seatbelts. Features dramatic footage of an auto accident and the subsequent accident scene attended by police, fire and other emergency service personnel.
Health and Safety; Industrial and Technical Education
Dist - ITF **Prod** - ERF 1991

Seatbelts and passenger restraints - 4 17 MIN
U-matic / VHS
Driver safety series
Color (H C G)
$255.00, $225.00 _ #V154
Discusses how properly used seatbelts are an excellent safety precaution when driving. Looks at the technology of air bags, safety glass, prevention of impact into the windshield and the use of proper restraints for children. Features Mike Muffins as host. Part four of a five - part series on driver safety.
Health and Safety; Industrial and Technical Education
Dist - BARR **Prod** - PAWPAW 1989

Seatbelts, Your Life Insurance 9 MIN
16mm
Color
LC FIE64-54
Emphasizes the benefits of seat belts in preventing fatalities and reducing injuries. Shows methods of installation.
Health and Safety
Dist - USNAC **Prod** - USAF 1962

Seated figures 50 MIN
16mm
Color (G)
$70.00 rental
Considers a landscape from the perspective of an exhaust pipe. Juxtaposes the audience's seated, static figures against a constantly moving ground. Filmmaker bolted his camera down onto a metal arm extending over the back of his truck then drove over asphalt, dirt roads, out to the beach, along a riverbed, and through a field of daisies, the movement punctuated by the truck's stops, reverses, acceleration.
Fine Arts; Science - Physical
Dist - CANCIN **Prod** - SNOWM 1988

Seattle 32 MIN
VHS / 16mm
Color (I J H G)
$550.00, $39.95 purchase
Chronicles the history of Seattle from its settlement in 1852 to the Klondike Gold Rush to its present day position as the world's largest producer of commercial aircraft. Visits Seattle Center, the Space Needle, Boeing and other major industries, the Washington State Ferries and nearby Victoria, British Columbia in Canada.
Geography - United States; Geography - World; History - United States
Dist - KAWVAL **Prod** - KAWVAL

Seawards the Great Ships 29 MIN
16mm
Color
Presents shipbuilding on the Clyde River in Scotland. Shows how the flat plates of steel are molded and shaped into various kinds of sailing vessels.
Geography - World; Industrial and Technical Education; Social Science
Dist - SF **Prod** - BIS 1961

The Seaway 15 MIN
U-matic
It's your world series
Color (I)
Introduces students to the world around them. Segment titles are; Thunder Bay, The Welland Canal, How Locks Work, Enlarging The Seaway.
Geography - World; Social Science
Dist - TVOTAR **Prod** - TVOTAR 1984

Seaway - Patronage and Paydirt 46 MIN
U-matic / 16mm / VHS
Inquiry Series
Color; Mono (H C A)
MV $350.00 _ MP $600.00 purchase, $50.00 rental
Probes management and operation practices of the St. Lawrence Seaway. Allegations of political favoritism, bid rigging, and corrupt management were aimed at politicians and businessmen in a scandal that became known as `Harbourgate.' Canadians were asked to rate politicians on matters of trust, honesty and integrity, this film.
Civics and Political Systems; History - World
Dist - CTV **Prod** - CTV

Seaway to the heartland 28 MIN
16mm
Color (G)
_ *#106C 0175 700*
Shows the construction, operation and impact on the economy of the St Lawrence Seaway. Gives a brief historical review of the earlier canals which were built as long as 200 years ago.
Geography - World; History - World; Industrial and Technical Education; Social Science
Dist - CFLMDC **Prod** - NFBC 1975

Sebastian Coe - born to run 50 MIN
U-matic / VHS
Color (J H C A)
Traces the running career of Olympic champion and world record holder Sebastian Coe. Features interviews with Sebastian, his father and other family and friends, as well as footage from Coe's record races and Olympic victories.
Biography; Physical Education and Recreation
Dist - TRACKN **Prod** - TRACKN 1984

Sebokeng by night 26 MIN
VHS
Ordinary people series
Color (G)
$190.00 purchase, $50.00 rental
Shares the experience of one night in Sebokeng, a township outside Johannesburg. Portrays the violence of Zone 12, the scene of many recent massacres by 'invisible' gunmen. Three camera crews capture different locations, events and people for a variety of perspectives. Part of a series which chronicles an event in South Africa through the eyes of three or four 'ordinary' people, chosen to represent diverse backgrounds or dissimilar points of view. This series seeks to provide insight into the collective South African conscience.
Fine Arts; History - World; Sociology
Dist - FIRS **Prod** - GAVSHO 1993

Sebring '66 30 MIN
16mm
Color
Fords sweep 12 hours of endurance.
Physical Education and Recreation
Dist - SFI **Prod** - SFI

Seclusion 12 MIN
VHS / U-matic
Color (PRO)
Provides basic information on seclusion. Defines seclusion and the kinds of situations that call for its use.
Health and Safety
Dist - HSCIC **Prod** - HSCIC 1985

The Second American Revolution - Pt 1 58 MIN
VHS / U-matic
Walk through the 20th century with Bill Moyers series
Color
LC 84-707295
Presents Ossie Davis and Ruby Dee who re - create and dramatize the world of blacks whose lives and ideas marked the struggle for equality in the 1900's to 1920. Looks at the lives of Booker T Washington, W E B DuBois, Marcus Garvey, Jack Johnson and Langston Hughes.
History - United States
Dist - PBS **Prod** - CORPEL 1983

The Second American Revolution - Pt 2 58 MIN
U-matic / VHS
Walk through the 20th century with Bill Moyers series
Color
LC 84-707295
Tells how the New Deal, World War II and postwar social changes set the stage for the 1954 Supreme Court decision to outlaw racial segregation in schools. Shows how the decision sparked a decade of continuing nonviolent revolution, leading to the Voting Rights Act of 1965. Depicts Thurgood Marshall, Rosa Parks, Martin Luther King, Malcolm X, Kenneth Clark, Daisy Bates and others. Features Ossie Davis, Ruby Dee and Bill Moyers.
History - United States
Dist - PBS **Prod** - CORPEL 1983

Second and Third Witnesses 44 MIN
VHS / U-matic
Remedies Phase of an EEO Case - Individual Determinations Series Pt '2
Color (PRO)
Demonstrates the testimony of two defense witnesses. Focuses on promotion policy of the hypothetical defendant.
Civics and Political Systems
Dist - ABACPE **Prod** - ALIABA

A Second Breath - a Guide for Home Tracheostomy Care 12 MIN
U-matic / VHS
Color (PRO)
Provides nurses with information to convey to tracheostomy patients and their families concerning basic home care procedures.
Health and Safety
Dist - HSCIC **Prod** - HSCIC 1982

A Second Career - Dentistry in the U S Army Reserve 16 MIN
16mm
Color
LC 80-701967
Describes the role of reserve and active Army dental personnel in implementing the dental care system.
Civics and Political Systems; Health and Safety
Dist - USNAC **Prod** - USA 1979

A Second chance 27 MIN
16mm / U-matic / VHS
Color (J H C A)
$50 rental _ #9801
Shows friendship, loyalty, guilt, and regret come under scrutiny as events lead up to an accidental shooting of a boy's best friend.
Health and Safety; Sociology
Dist - AIMS **Prod** - AIMS 1985

Second Chance 13 MIN
16mm
We Can Help Series
Color
LC 78-702032
Presents the case of a child admitted to the hospital with a diagnosis of maternal deprivation and emotional maltreatment. Shows the 6 - week treatment course provided by the hospital involving staff members and a volunteer foster grandparent.
Health and Safety; Sociology
Dist - USNAC **Prod** - NCCAN 1978

Second Chance 12 MIN
16mm
Color
LC FIA68-161
Shows how a twenty - two - month - old child who is severely retarded mentally, physically and emotionally was helped through the Mother Bank Volunteer Program.
Education; Psychology; Sociology
Dist - CMHOSP **Prod** - CMHOSP 1967

A Second Chance 25 MIN
16mm
Color
LC 75-700578
Illustrates the problems encountered between court volunteers and their wards. Dramatizes an actual case study which provides an overall view of the many phases of the problem.
Civics and Political Systems; Sociology
Dist - USNAC **Prod** - USSRS 1970

Second Chance 10 MIN
8mm cartridge / 16mm
Heart Series no 1; No 1
Color (H C A)
LC 75-700038
Shows the actual experiences of a heart attack victim, describing the recovery period after the attack, the modification of the life - style upon returning home from the hospital and the proper care that will help the victim lead a long and full life.
Health and Safety
Dist - MIFE **Prod** - MIFE 1974

A Second Chance - Consumers Guide to Fire Extinguishers 15 MIN
16mm
Color
Discusses fire safety, covering escape planning, fire protection and control, kitchen discipline, electrical responsibility, what extinguishers to buy, where to place them, how to operate them, and how to maintain them.
Health and Safety; Home Economics
Dist - KLEINW **Prod** - KLEINW

A Second chance - getting straight 15 MIN
U-matic / VHS
Drug wise series; Module 4
Color (J)
Tells stories of four recovering young people in aftercare, from thee stage of harmful involvement through treatment in aftercare.
Health and Safety; Psychology
Dist - GPN **Prod** - WDCNTV

A Second chance - getting straight 15 MIN
U-matic / VHS
Drug wise series
(J)
$40 purchase, $25 rental, $75 self dub
Explains the harmful effects of drug abuse and explores recovery. Presents the case histories of four young people in aftercare.
Health and Safety; Psychology; Sociology
Dist - GPN **Prod** - NCGE 1984 - 1985

Second chance - organ transplants 52 MIN
VHS
Color (G)
$149.00 purchase, $75.00 rental _ #UW2483
Tells about the medical miracle and human drama of organ transplants and about the dying patient's dependence on the kindness of others to donate organs. Shows a heart transplant operation and explains how viewers can give others a second chance.
Health and Safety
Dist - FOTH

A Second Chance - Protecting Endangered Species 27 MIN
16mm
Color
Describes how some wildlife, including some endangered species, are attracted to and benefited by electrical operations.
Science - Natural; Social Science
Dist - MTP **Prod** - EEI

Second chance - sea 11 MIN
U-matic / VHS / 16mm
Color
LC 76-702885
Presents, without narration, an animated film which examines many aspects and meanings of the sea and humanity's relationship with it.
Science - Natural; Social Science; Sociology
Dist - PFP **Prod** - HUBLEY 1976

Second Childhood 19 MIN
16mm
B&W
Describes grouchy Zeffie Tilbury's disgust at turning 66 and shows what happens when Alfalfa, Porky, Darla, Spanky and Buckwheat pitch in to cheer her up. A Little Rascals film.
Fine Arts
Dist - RMIBHF **Prod** - ROACH 1936

Second chorus 84 MIN
VHS / BETA / 16mm
B&W
Describes how two trumpet players compete for the same girl and a job with the Artie Shaw orchestra. Stars Fred Astaire and Paulette Goddard.
Fine Arts
Dist - VIDIM **Prod** - PAR 1940
REELIM

Second Chorus 25 MIN
U-matic / VHS / 16mm
Color (J)
LC 79-700757
Shows a divorced couple meeting on the occasion of their son's marriage. Relates that the son backs out at the last moment, explaining that even when his parents fought, they showed honesty and caring which he had not found with his fiance. Describes how this leads the couple to reflect on the nature of their marriage and their fighting and, ultimately, to reconciliation.
Fine Arts; Sociology
Dist - MEDIAG **Prod** - PAULST 1978

Second Class Passenger 11 MIN
16mm / U-matic / VHS
Color (J H)
LC 74-701713
Presents a metaphor for life by showing a man on a train who encounters a progression of strange characters. Shows how he remains optimistic in spite of the fact that things get worse.
Psychology; Social Science
Dist - MGHT **Prod** - ZAGREB 1974

The Second Collision 30 MIN
U-matic / VHS
Behind the Wheel Series
Color (H)
Demonstrates the results of the 'second collision' within a vehicle in an accident when safety belts are not used. Stresses the importance of using safety restraints.
Health and Safety; Industrial and Technical Education; Psychology
Dist - GPN **Prod** - WCVETV 1983

The Second Commandment 30 MIN
16mm
B&W
Explains the meaning of the commandment against idolatry, a frequently misunderstood passage in the Bible. (Kinescope).
Religion and Philosophy
Dist - NAAJS **Prod** - JTS 1955

Second derivative, inflection points and concavity 30 MIN
VHS
Calculus series
Color (C)
$125.00 purchase _ #6012
Explains second derivative, inflection points and concavity. Part of a 56 - part series on calculus.
Mathematics
Dist - LANDMK **Prod** - LANDMK

Second derivative, inflection points and concavity 30 MIN
VHS
Mathematics series
Color (J)
LC 95713155
Discusses second derivative and its inflection points and concavity. The 121 of 157 installments of the Mathematics Series.
Mathematics
Dist - GPN

Second edition 20 MIN
VHS / U-matic
Color
Covers such stories as housing renovation in Manhattan, the subway rate hike, the Guardian Angels, the New York Mets' batboys, an interview with Dick Cavett and a look at the teenagers in the summer youth employment program who made this videotape.
Guidance and Counseling; Industrial and Technical Education; Social Science
Dist - DCTVC **Prod** - DCTVC

Second Effort 28 MIN
16mm / U-matic / VHS
Color (PRO)
LC 72-709367
Vince Lombardi, the former Green Bay Packer coach, shows how the five motivational principles he used so successfully to build great football teams, can be used with equal success in improving the performance of any salesman.
Business and Economics
Dist - DARTNL **Prod** - DARTNL 1968

Second effort II 30 MIN
VHS
Color (G)
$565.00 purchase, $150.00 rental _ #91F6023
Combines the 'how to win' philosophy of Vince Lombardi with a story line for sales motivation.
Business and Economics; Psychology
Dist - DARTNL **Prod** - DARTNL

The Second Front 20 MIN
U-matic / VHS
Color
$335.00 purchase
Presents a story on drug smuggling as shown on ABC TV's 20/20.
Psychology; Sociology
Dist - ABCLR **Prod** - ABCLR 1983

Second Generation Microelectronics 25 MIN
16mm
Color (J)
Depicts the research, development and systems applications of advanced microelectronics. Describes the evolution of integrated circuits, thin films, ceramic printed circuits to multi - functional Ic's, metal oxide semiconductors and silicon - on - sapphire devices and their applications. Discusses the future use of epitaxial ferrite micro - memory, silicon - on - sapphire stripline waveguides and Gunn - effect oscillators.
Industrial and Technical Education
Dist - RCKWL **Prod** - NAA

The Second Golden Age 25 MIN
16mm
Color
Shows the world of wine tasting throughout the country in preparation for an annual wine auction.
Home Economics
Dist - MTP **Prod** - MTP

Second Grade Embarassment 5 MIN
16mm
Color (I) (AMERICAN SIGN)
LC 76-701701
Presents Willard Madsen relating in American sign language a personal experience of what it was like to be a deaf boy in second grade attending a public school for the deaf where the teacher did not know enough sign language to understand an urgent request.
Education; Guidance and Counseling; Psychology
Dist - JOYCE **Prod** - JOYCE 1976

Second half - the Thomas Henderson story 29 MIN
VHS
Color (I J H G) (SPANISH)
$325.00 purchase
Focuses on Thomas 'Hollywood' Henderson who was the National Football League's first cocaine casualty. Reveals that the use of cocaine cost Henderson his career and, for a few years, his freedom. More importantly, Henderson has been clean and sober since 1983 and he has a message for young and old - 'Life can be better. It can be different. You don't have to live this way anymore.'
Guidance and Counseling; Health and Safety; Psychology
Dist - FMSP **Prod** - FMSP

Second homes - calculators - medical insurance
U-matic / VHS

Consumer survival series
Color
Presents tips on buying second homes, calculators and medical insurance.
Business and Economics; Home Economics
Dist - MDCPB **Prod** - MDCPB

The Second Hundred Years 20 MIN
U-matic / VHS / 16mm
B&W (J)
Stars Laurel and Hardy as prison cellmates, encountering a series of misadventures in trying to escape.
Fine Arts
Dist - FI **Prod** - ROACH 1927

Second - Moment Characterizations 38 MIN
U-matic / VHS
Probability and Random Processes Introduction to Random Processes 'Series
B&W (PRO)
Relaxes the constraint of complete characterization by introducing the concept of partial characterization by the mean function and correlation function.
Mathematics
Dist - MIOT **Prod** - MIOT

The Second national driving test - one for the road 30 MIN
U-matic / 16mm / VHS
Color; Mono (H C A G) (FRENCH)
MV $185.00 _ MP $530.00 purchase, $50.00 rental
Illustrates the various human functions that are impaired by alcohol. Program includes party games and a driving simulator which are used to demonstrate the effects of drinking on driving ability.
Health and Safety; Sociology
Dist - CTV **Prod** - CTV 1980

The Second Pollution 22 MIN
16mm
Color
LC 73-702056
Discusses air pollution. Examines the problem which exists in Los Angeles and Chicago.
Science - Natural
Dist - FINLYS **Prod** - FINLYS 1973

Second review week 1 10 MIN
U-matic
Readalong two series
Color (P)
Provides young viewers with a flexible range of reading experiences through active involvement in reading and writing. Comes with teacher's guide and kit.
Education; English Language; Literature and Drama
Dist - TVOTAR **Prod** - TVOTAR 1976

Second review week 2 10 MIN
U-matic
Readalong two series
Color (P)
Provides young viewers with a flexible range of reading experiences through active involvement in reading and writing. Comes with teacher's guide and kit.
Education; English Language; Literature and Drama
Dist - TVOTAR **Prod** - TVOTAR 1976

Second review week 3 10 MIN
U-matic
Readalong two series
Color (P)
Provides young viewers with a flexible range of reading experiences through active involvement in reading and writing. Comes with teacher's guide and kit.
Education; English Language; Literature and Drama
Dist - TVOTAR **Prod** - TVOTAR 1976

Second Sitting 29 MIN
U-matic
Artist at Work Series
Color
Discusses reappraising the painting and making changes.
Fine Arts
Dist - UMITV **Prod** - UMITV 1973

Second skin 16 MIN
16mm
Color (G)
$40.00 rental
Explores the struggle to establish and maintain identity amidst the ambivalence of the exterior world. Explores the struggle between security and insecurity, confidence and doubt, and the fluctuating perceptions of physical boundaries vs personal space through an intimate look at a woman's struggle with her agoraphobia. Produced by Paula Froehle.
Fine Arts; Psychology
Dist - CANCIN

Second skin and Spitting image 19 MIN
16mm
Color (G)
$50.00 rental
Features Second Skin, an exploration of the struggle to establish and maintain identity amidst the exterior world, and Spitting Image, a personal narrative about the struggle to free oneself of the haunting memories of one's past. A Paula Froehle production. Titles available for separate rental.
Fine Arts; Psychology
Dist - CANCIN

Second step - grades 4 - 5
VHS
Color (I)
$215.00 purchase _ #230L
Presents a curriculum for improving social skills in grades 4-5 in 45 lessons. Teaches children how to identify feelings, solve problems with peers and reduce anger in frustrating situations. Includes 11x17 laminated photos and parent activity sheets.
Guidance and Counseling; Psychology; Social Science
Dist - SICACC **Prod** - SICACC

Second step - grades 1 - 3
VHS
Color (P)
$235.00 purchase _ #130L
Presents a curriculum for improving social skills in grades 1-3 in 49 lessons. Teaches children how to identify feelings, solve problems with peers and reduce anger in frustrating situations. Includes 11x17 laminated photos and parent activity sheets.
Guidance and Counseling; Psychology; Social Science
Dist - SICACC **Prod** - SICACC

Second step - grades 6 - 8
VHS
Color (I J)
$275.00 purchase _ #330L
Presents curriculum for improving social skills in grades 6 - 8 in 15 lessons. Teaches adolescents about interpersonal violence, empathy, options for problem solving and anger management. Uses group discussion, role playing and the analysis of story scenarios. Includes 8.5x11 laminated photos, overhead transparencies and five live action lessons - in - video.
Guidance and Counseling; Psychology; Social Science; Sociology
Dist - SICACC **Prod** - SICACC

Second Thoughts on Being Single 52 MIN
U-matic / VHS
Color (A)
LC 84-707302
Reveals that women who formerly shunned monogamous relationships for sexual liberation or who postponed marriage to further careers are adopting more conservative sexual values and seeking marriage. Considers reasons for this change of heart and for the frustrating elusiveness of husband and family.
Sociology
Dist - FI **Prod** - NBCNEW 1984

Second Time Around 60 MIN
U-matic / VHS
Middletown Series
Color (J)
Presents a picture of the issues and complexities of contemporary marriage by focusing on a couple in which the man is getting married because everyone is doing it yet wants a church wedding.
Geography - United States; History - United States; Sociology
Dist - FI **Prod** - WQED 1982

Second Time Around - Career Options for Dancers Series
Deborah Jowitt, Sally Brayley - Bliss and Helen Heineman 30 MIN
Ellen Jacob, Jo Ellen Grzyb and Mara Greenberg 30 MIN
Dist - ARCVID

Second to Nobody 25 MIN
16mm
Color
Analyzes the role of management, union and public opinion in the daily life of New York City sanitation workers.
Business and Economics; Geography - United States
Dist - MRMKF **Prod** - SCHLP 1983

A Second transcontinental nation - 1872 57 MIN
16mm
Struggle for a border
B&W (G H C)
_ #106B 0169 014
Shows that for Canada the struggle to preserve the Canadian American border continued. Shows, emerging from the long historical background, Canada's survival as a nation independent of the United States.
History - United States; History - World
Dist - CFLMDC **Prod** - NFBC 1969

The Second Trimester 29 MIN
U-matic / VHS
Tomorrow's Families Series
Color (H C A)
LC 81-706900
Discusses the development of the fetus during the second trimester of pregnancy. States that the parents must now make decisions about delivery.
Health and Safety
Dist - AITECH **Prod** - MDDE 1980

A Second voice 13 MIN
16mm
Color (H C A)
Portrays the services of the International Association of Laryngectomies (IAL) beginning with surgery on a patient and ending with his participation in the national convention in Chicago.
Health and Safety
Dist - AMCS **Prod** - AMCS

Second World Conference 28 MIN
16mm
Color (A)
LC 77-703130
Presents a documentary on the Second World Conference on National Parks, held at Yellowstone and Grand Teton National Parks in October, 1972. Shows representatives from over 90 countries in the process of developing an international philosophy on conservation and park management. Includes discussions on the world environmental crisis.
Geography - United States; Science - Natural
Dist - USNAC **Prod** - USNPS 1973

The Second World War 30 MIN
VHS
Western tradition series
Color; PAL (J H G)
PdS29.50 purchase
Records how the war leaves Europe balanced between the first two superpowers, the Soviet Union and the United States. Presents part of an eight - part series about key events of each major period of history.
History - United States; History - World
Dist - EMFVL **Prod** - CORF

The Second World War 30 MIN
U-matic / VHS
How Wars End Series
Color (G)
$249.00, $149.00 purchase _ #AD - 914
Reveals that World War II ended in different places at different times - France bowed out in 1940, Italy in 1943, Japan only after the atomic bombing of Hiroshima and Nagasaki. Stresses that the Allied insistence on unconditional surrender lengthened the war by giving the Axis powers nothing to bargain for. Part of a six - part series on how wars end, hosted by historian A J P Taylor.
History - United States; History - World; Sociology
Dist - FOTH **Prod** - FOTH

The Second World War - Allied Victory 28 MIN
16mm / U-matic / VHS
B&W (J H) (SPANISH)
Uses newsreels, captured Axis films and armed forces' footage to document key events of World War II from 1944 to Japan's surrender in 1945. Explains how total mobilization of manpower and resources was achieved.
History - World
Dist - EBEC **Prod** - EBEC 1963

The Second World War - D - Day 26 MIN
U-matic / VHS / 16mm
B&W (H C)
LC FIA67-1961
Shows the invasion of Europe on June 6, 1944. Examines the anxiety of two million soldiers as they prepare for D - Day. Pictures both the leaders of the invasion - Eisenhower, Patton and Bradley and the German High Command. Edited version of the 52 minute film D - Day.
Civics and Political Systems; History - World
Dist - FI **Prod** - WOLPER 1967

The Second World War - Prelude to Conflict 29 MIN
U-matic / VHS / 16mm
B&W (J H) (GERMAN)
Uses newsreels, captured Axis films and armed forces' footage to document causes of World War II. Depicts the failure of the Versailles Peace Treaty, the political crisis which resulted from economic chaos in Germany and the isolationism of the United States.
History - United States; History - World
Dist - EBEC **Prod** - EBEC 1964

The Second World War - Triumph of the Axis 25 MIN
U-matic / VHS / 16mm

B&W (J H)
Shows how Germany and Japan conceived and nearly carried out their bold plan for world conquest. Explains how Allied indecision and military unpreparedness resulted in Axis aggression.
History - World
Dist - EBEC **Prod** - EBEC 1963

Second year in the life of a child series
Presents a 4 - part series, each part 18 to 24 minutes long, that follows the normal development of a child during the second year of life. Focuses on the child at 15, 18, 21 and 24 months.
The Child at eighteen months
The Child at fifteen months
The Child at twenty - four months
The Child at twenty - one months
Dist - FOTH **Prod** - SPCMUM 1963

The Second Year - the Birth of the Individual 29 MIN
U-matic / VHS / 16mm
All about Babies - a Guide to the First Two Years of Life Series
Color (H C A)
$495 purchase - 16 mm, $355 purchase - video
Discusses the baby's growing awareness of himself as an individual during the second year of life. A Signs of Life film. Directed by Deborah Koons.
Psychology; Sociology
Dist - CF

Secondary currents 18 MIN
16mm
B&W (G)
$30.00 rental
Delves into the relationships between the mind and language. Presents a narrator who speaks an assortment of nonsense, while the 'imageless' film shifts between voice - over commentary and subtitled narration. A dark metaphor for the order and entropy of language by Peter Rose.
Fine Arts; Foreign Language; Literature and Drama; Psychology
Dist - CANCIN

Secondary distribution systems
VHS / U-matic
Distribution system operation series; Topic 5
Color (IND)
Aquaints participants with the features and operating characteristics of various types of secondary distribution. Includes spot and distributed loads in overhead secondary and underground secondary.
Industrial and Technical Education
Dist - LEIKID **Prod** - LEIKID

Secondary, first year - Unit D 36 MIN
VHS
Looking at size and shape series
Color; PAL (H C T)
PdS35 purchase
Shows children experiencing and developing notions of size and shape and documents how the development of children's perception of space is a continuous process. Presents part of a six - part series of observation material.
Psychology
Dist - EMFVL

Secondary, fourth year - Unit E 41 MIN
VHS
Looking at size and shape series
Color; PAL (H C T)
PdS35 purchase
Shows children experiencing and developing notions of size and shape and documents how the development of children's perception of space is a continuous process. Presents part of a six - part series of observation material.
Psychology
Dist - EMFVL

Secondary gymnastics series
Year one, boys and girls inversion with body shape - Unit D 57 MIN
Year one, traveling with changes of body shape - Unit A 40 MIN
Year three, partner work with twisting and turning - Unit C 50 MIN
Year two, twisting and turning - Unit B 41 MIN
Dist - EMFVL

Secondary Impressions for the Distal Extension Base, Removable Partial Denture 15 MIN
VHS / U-matic
Color
Demonstrates the procedures incident to obtaining impressions of edentulous areas made on bases attached to the removable partial denture framework.
Health and Safety; Science
Dist - AMDA **Prod** - VADTC 1970

Secondary Lens Implantation 17 MIN
U-matic / VHS
Color (PRO)
Demonstrates implantation procedure using a newly developed intraocular lens called Stable Flex.
Health and Safety; Science - Natural
Dist - HSCIC **Prod** - HSCIC 1984

Secondary lens implantation 11 MIN
VHS
Color (G PRO C)
$150.00 purchase _ #EY - 20
Helps former cataract patients to understand that an IOL implant may be appropriate when aphakic spectacles or contact lenses are no longer satisfactory. Uses animation to illustrate the insertion of the IOL. Discusses patient preparation and post - op recovery and care. Includes risks and complications.
Health and Safety; Science - Natural
Dist - MIFE **Prod** - MIFE

Secondary Particle Emissions from Surfaces, I 35 MIN
U-matic / VHS
Plasma Sputtering, Deposition and Growth of Microelectronic Films 'for VLSI Series
Color (IND)
Notes how secondary particle emission from surfaces after bombardment may be used for both qualitative and quantitative surface analysis. Points out that the bombardment/emission sequence is basis for various surface analysis techniques that allow categorization and measurement of atomic and compound species concentrations in a solid sample.
Industrial and Technical Education; Science
Dist - COLOSU **Prod** - COLOSU

Secondary Particle Emissions from Surfaces, II 35 MIN
VHS / U-matic
Plasma Sputtering, Deposition and Growth of Microelectronic Films for VLSI Series
Color (IND)
Discusses specific examples of Auger analysis, energy dispersive x - ray analysis, ESCA or XPS analysis and SIMS probing of surfaces. Describes and compares various surface analytical techniques.
Industrial and Technical Education; Science
Dist - COLOSU **Prod** - COLOSU

Secondary physical education series
Action planning 10 MIN
Dance 10 MIN
Dimensions of success 10 MIN
Evaluation 10 MIN
Fitness 10 MIN
Games 10 MIN
Gymnastics 10 MIN
Management and Organization 10 MIN
Teaching Methods 10 MIN
Dist - ACCESS

The Secondary plant body - Part 2 20 MIN
VHS
Plant anatomy collection series
Color (J H)
$60.00 purchase _ #A5VH 1034
Gives detailed coverage of the secondary meristems and the development of secondary xylem and cork. Illustrates the cellular nature of wood and its effects on the qualities of wood. Part two of a three - part series introducing the structures and functions of plant anatomy.
Science - Natural
Dist - CLRVUE **Prod** - CLRVUE

Secondary School Safety Series
Noontime Nonsense 13 MIN
You're in Charge 12 MIN
Dist - NSC

Secondary science teaching with television 40 MIN
VHS
Inset series
Color; PAL (C T)
PdS30 purchase
Presents two 20 - minute programs designed to help science teachers get the best from television curriculum. Uses examples from the Scientific Eye Series to advise on how to use TV as a springboard for other activities and how to plan for active classroom viewing. Includes case studies from teachers who are using TV as an essential part of science curriculum and a set of discussion notes. Contact distributor about availability outside the United Kingdom.
Education; Science
Dist - ACADEM

Secondary storage
U-matic / VHS
Audio visual library of computer education series
Color
Discusses information storage, introducing such terms as random access, parity and byte, which provides a sound basis for evaluating the magnetic storage media with reference to an ideal device. Uses a combination of diagrams which explain how information is stored on the various media, and photographs which illustrate the full range of equipment within a typical computer system.
Business and Economics; Mathematics
Dist - PRISPR **Prod** - PRISPR

Secondary storage - processors - Parts 9 and 10 60 MIN
U-matic / VHS
New literacy - an introduction to computers
Color (G)
$45.00, $29.95 purchase
Covers the relationship between batch input and magnetic - tape files and the variety of tape and disc options in Part 9. Examines the internal workings of a computer as well as the relationship between microprocessors and other processors in Part 10. Parts of a 26 - part series on computing machines.
Computer Science; Industrial and Technical Education; Mathematics; Psychology
Dist - ANNCPB **Prod** - SCCON 1988

Secondary Surgery for Recurrent Ulcer 28 MIN
16mm
Color (PRO)
Outlines the major physiological patterns responsible for recurrent ulcer. Includes examples of secondary pyloric obstruction, continued vagal activity after simple gastric resection and hypersecretion due to the activity of a portion of retained antrum.
Health and Safety; Science
Dist - ACY **Prod** - ACYDGD 1966

Secondary Survey, Control Points and Hydrographic Developments 18 MIN
16mm
Color
LC FIE52-1268
Describes secondary signals building, sounding and wire dragging operations and other miscellaneous survey work.
Industrial and Technical Education; Science - Physical
Dist - USNAC **Prod** - USN 1950

Secondhand smoke 16 MIN
VHS
Color (I J H A) (SPANISH)
$295.00 purchase
Features animation and humor in discussion of the dangers to non - smokers caused by 'passive' smoking. Presents evidence of the ill effects and urges non - smokers to defend their right to clear air. Features Jack Klugman as narrator. Includes a guide written by Americans for Nonsmokers' Rights and the Lawrence Hall of Science at the University of California at Berkeley.
Guidance and Counseling; Health and Safety; Psychology
Dist - PFP **Prod** - PFP

Seconds count 15 MIN
U-matic / VHS / 16mm
Emergency resuscitation series
Color (C A)
Emphasizes the need for speed in applying emergency resuscitation by the mouth - to - mouth method using incidents stemming from drowning and asphyxia.
Health and Safety
Dist - IFB **Prod** - UKMD

Seconds to live 30 MIN
VHS / U-matic / BETA
Color (G)
$899.00 purchase, $125.00 rental _ #SEC060
Reveals that defensive driving is common sense and good judgment. Features Sgt Jack Ware who describes deadly driving habits which could cost more than lost seconds.
Health and Safety; Industrial and Technical Education
Dist - ITF **Prod** - MEGROU

Seconds to play 28 MIN
16mm / U-matic / VHS
Color (J H C)
LC 76-703613
Examines technical and human factors involved in the production of a major television sports event. Shows the broadcast of a football game to demonstrate the electronic equipment, advance planning, tensions and split - second decisions involved in televising the event.
Fine Arts; Industrial and Technical Education; Physical Education and Recreation
Dist - FI **Prod** - CROWLP 1976

The Secret 15 MIN
U-matic / VHS / 16mm
Bloomin' Human Series
Color

LC 78-701485

Tells how a group of children accidentally chase a stray dog off a cliff and agree not to tell anyone. Explains how one boy goes back, discovers the dog alive and nurses it back to health.

Fine Arts

Dist - MEDIAG **Prod** - PAULST 1977

Secret addictions series

Presents a two - part series on women and addiction hosted by Collin Siedor. Looks at women in the socioeconomic and racial groups most likely to abuse alcohol and drugs and the treatment of addiction. Produced by Dystar Television, Inc.

Secret addictions - women, drugs and alcohol 35 MIN
Secret addictions - women in treatment 32 MIN
Secret addictions series 67 MIN

Dist - CORF

Secret addictions - women, drugs and alcohol 35 MIN
BETA / VHS / U-matic
Secret addictions series
Color (G)
$495.00 purchase _ #KC - 6253M

Looks at women with drug and alcohol addictions. Examines the socioeconomic and racial groups which are most likely to abuse alcohol and drugs, and the difference in addiction patterns between younger and older women. Interviews recovering substance abusers who describe their addictions and the steps they have taken toward recovery. Part of a two - part series on women and addiction hosted by Collin Siedor and produced by Dystar Television, Inc.

Guidance and Counseling; Health and Safety; Psychology; Sociology

Dist - CORF

Secret addictions - women in treatment 32 MIN
VHS / U-matic / BETA
Secret addictions series
Color (G)
$495.00 purchase _ #KC - 6254M

Explores the difficulties faced by single and married women, mothers, and their children, as they struggle to recover from their addictions. Discusses personal turning points which made abusers seek help, child custody fears which keep women from seeking help, group therapy sessions and their role in treatment programs. Part of a two - part series on women and addiction hosted by Collin Siedor and produced by Dystar Television, Inc.

Guidance and Counseling; Health and Safety; Psychology; Sociology

Dist - CORF

The Secret agent 86 MIN
VHS
B&W (G)
$24.95 purchase _ #SEC120

Features an offbeat mystery in which an innocent man appears guilty. Builds to a shattering climax as a novice British agent, a lovely spy apprentice, and an eccentric assassin unmask their enemy.

Fine Arts

Dist - HOMVIS **Prod** - HITCH 1936

The Secret agent 84 MIN
16mm
B&W

Presents a mystery story involving fake funerals, a one - armed man and the inadvertent conviction of the wrong man. Stars John Geilgud, Peter Lorre and Robert Young. Directed by Alfred Hitchcock.

Fine Arts

Dist - REELIM **Prod** - GBIF 1936

Secret diaries
VHS
Color; PAL (J)
PdS30 purchase

Presents four programs about diaries. Asks why diaries are written in the introductory program. The following three programs focus on three diaries written at different times under very different circumstances over the last two centuries. Presents history, written at the end of each day, as it was lived by three young boys. Frances Middlebrook traces the farming calendar in a Yorkshire village in the mid 19th century; Kenneth Holmes records the spirit of the blitz in wartime London; and William Treadwell describes country life of a prosperous family in the 1830s. Contact distributor about availability outside the United Kingdom.

History - World; Literature and Drama

Dist - ACADEM

The Secret discovered 15 MIN
VHS
Zardips search for healthy wellness series
Color (P I)
LC 90-708001

Presents an episode in a series which helps young children understand basic health issues and the value of taking good care of their bodies. Includes a teacher's guide.

Education; Health and Safety

Dist - TVOTAR **Prod** - TVOTAR 1989

The Secret File 58 MIN
VHS
Color (S)
$79.00 purchase _ #083 - 9002

Considers Penn Kimball, an ordinary citizen, a university professor, a former 'New York Times' editor, Rhodes Scholar, Eagle Scout. Discloses the stunning discovery that for 30 years the US Government had files on him declaring him a disloyal American. Looks at Kimball's fight to clear his name and considers whether the government has the right to gather and classify information on American citizens.

Civics and Political Systems

Dist - FI **Prod** - WGBHTV 1987

The Secret files of J Edgar Hoover 120 MIN
VHS
Color (J H C G)
$24.95 purchase _ #HGE626V

Opens some of the files maintained by J Edgar Hoover on such public figures as Martin Luther King, Jr; John Lennon; Rock Hudson; and one of Hoover's favorite targets, John F Kennedy. Offers three segments - Hoover and the FBI; Presidential Indiscretions and Political Payoffs; and Hoover, Hollywood and Spycraft.

Biography; Civics and Political Systems; History - United States

Dist - CAMV

The Secret fountains 60 MIN
VHS / U-matic / 16mm
Search for the Nile; 3
Color (H C A) (SPANISH)
LC 73-701098; 77-701628

Follow Speke as he is appointed leader of a second journey into the jungles to reaffirm his Lake Victoria theory about the Nile's source. Describes how he makes another discovery, the Ripon Falls, where the Nile leaves the lake.

Foreign Language; Geography - World; History - World

Dist - TIMLIF **Prod** - BBCTV 1972

The Secret garden 23 MIN
16mm
Color; Silent (G A)
$75.00 rental

Presents the work of filmmaker Phil Solomon. Creates a metaphor of being lost within the dark walls of a nuclear family. Incorporates found footage and original images to examine the myth of the Great Father.

Fine Arts; History - United States; Industrial and Technical Education

Dist - PARART **Prod** - CANCIN 1986

The Secret garden 107 MIN
VHS
Color (I J H)
$19.95 purchase _ #CBS3766

Adapts the Frances Hodgson Burnett story about an orphan who finds strength in a special garden.

Literature and Drama

Dist - KNOWUN **Prod** - BBCTV 1984

The Secret Horror 14 MIN
U-matic / VHS
Color

Features a surrealistic comedy involving the kidnapping of Mike. Presents a thematic journey to a place somewhere between initiation and renovation.

Fine Arts

Dist - KITCHN **Prod** - KITCHN

The Secret in Bubbie's attic 43 MIN
VHS
Color (K P I)
$24.95 purchase _ #825

Finds a Torah, a shofar, a Hanukah menorah and a very special piece of cloth in Grandmother's attic. Explains the High Holidays, the Festival of Sukkot and the story of Hanukah. Features Eva Grayzel and Suri Levow - Krieger.

Religion and Philosophy; Sociology

Dist - ERGOM **Prod** - ERGOM

Secret in the White Cell 11 MIN
16mm
Science Close - Up Series
B&W (J H)
LC FIA67-5013

Pictures how the enzymes in the granules within white cells are released to kill and digest microbes.

Science - Natural

Dist - SF **Prod** - PRISM 1967

Secret intelligence series

Uses the Iran - Contra affair to illustrate the frequent conflict between national security and democratic principles. Traces the history of American intelligence from the Revolutionary War to the present day. The four - part series features interviews with intelligence experts, including former CIA director William Casey in his last television interview.

The Enterprise 60 MIN
Intervention 60 MIN
Learning to Say no 60 MIN
The Only Rule is Win 60 MIN

Dist - PBS **Prod** - KCET 1967

Secret Lake 30 MIN
U-matic
Sport Fishing Series
Color (G)

Shows the intricacies of pike fishing and of humane handling of fish and cautions that no one should take more fish than he can use.

Physical Education and Recreation

Dist - TVOTAR **Prod** - TVOTAR 1985

Secret Life of a Trout River 10 MIN
U-matic / VHS / 16mm
Bio - Science Series
Color (J H)

Shows a trout river to be a complex, delicately balanced ecological system.

Science - Natural

Dist - NGS **Prod** - NGS 1974

The Secret Life of an Orchestra 28 MIN
16mm / U-matic / VHS
Color
LC 75-703612

Shows the Denver Symphony as they rehearse and perform the overture from Wagner's Die Meistersinger. Includes film images which take the viewer into the minds of the musicians, in their conscious and unconscious focus upon performance.

Fine Arts

Dist - PFP **Prod** - MUSICP 1975

The Secret Life of T K Dearing 47 MIN
16mm / U-matic / VHS
Teenage Years Series
Color
LC 78-701271

Presents the story of a teenage girl's relationship with her grandfather and the lessons which she learns as a result. Based on the book The Secret Life Of T K Dearing by Jean Robinson.

Fine Arts; Guidance and Counseling; Literature and Drama; Sociology

Dist - TIMLIF **Prod** - WILSND 1978

The Secret Life of the Underwear Champ
VHS / 35mm strip
Sound Filmstrips - Young Adult Series
Color (P)
$63.00 purchase

Reveals that Larry Pryor discovers that starring in TV commercials isn't what it's cracked up to be, especially if you have to model underwear. Part of a series.

English Language; Literature and Drama; Sociology

Dist - PELLER

The Secret Love of Sandra Blain 28 MIN
VHS / U-matic
Color (J A) (SPANISH)

Dramatizes the story of a suburban housewife who becomes an alcoholic.

Fine Arts; Foreign Language; Psychology; Sociology

Dist - SUTHRB **Prod** - SUTHRB

The Secret Love of Sandra Blain 22 MIN
VHS / U-matic
Color

Tells the story of a wife and mother who finds a seductive but treacherous solution for frustration and loneliness in alcohol. Reveals the facilities and treatment centers available to the woman alcoholic.

Psychology; Sociology

Dist - IA **Prod** - LACFU

The Secret Love of Sandra Blain 28 MIN
U-matic / VHS / 16mm
Color (H C A)
LC 70-712330

Shows the progression into alcoholism of a wife and mother. Focuses on facilities for rehabilitation and treatments available for complete recovery.

Guidance and Counseling; Health and Safety; Psychology; Sociology

Dist - AIMS **Prod** - AIMS 1971

The Secret Love of Sandra Blain 27 MIN
U-matic / VHS / 16mm
Color (H C A) (SPANISH)
LC 70-712339

Presents the experiences of a wife and mother who turns to alcohol to escape frustration, boredom, anxiety and loneliness.

Health and Safety; Psychology; Sociology

Dist - AIMS **Prod** - LAC 1971

The Secret Message 15 MIN
U-matic
Two Plus You - Math Patrol One Series
Color (K P)
Presents the mathematical concepts of symbolism and terminology for place holders and the construction of a simple alphabet code, setting up a one to one matching of letters and numbers.
Education; Mathematics
Dist - TVOTAR **Prod** - TVOTAR 1976

The Secret of Castle Hill 50 MIN
VHS
First Tuesday series
Color; PAL (H C G)
PdS30 purchase
Examines one of the worst cases of institutional abuse ever seen on British television. Reveals that 44 young boys sent to a British special school suffered sexual and physical assaults, including buggery and vicious beatings, for eight years. School principal Ralph Morris was jailed for 12 years for his part in the abuse. Contact distributor about availability outside the United Kingdom.
History - World; Sociology
Dist - ACADEM **Prod** - YORKTV

The Secret of Danish agriculture 26 MIN
VHS
Color (G)
Uses the character of a secret agent to explore Danish agricultural methods. Portrays the skill, efficiency and care involved in Danish agriculture. Available for free loan from the distributor.
Agriculture; Geography - World
Dist - AUDPLN

Secret of guest relations 23 MIN
VHS
Color (A PRO IND)
$475.00 purchase, $110.00 rental
Stresses the importance of cultivating good guest or patient relations. Reveals that a bad reputation in this area travels much faster than a good one.
Business and Economics; Guidance and Counseling; Psychology
Dist - VLEARN **Prod** - AIMS

The Secret of Guest Relations 22 MIN
VHS / 16mm
Color (PRO)
$475.00 purchase, $110.00 rental, $35.00 preview
Explains how unhappy hospital guests can contribute to economic failure of a hospital. Trains hospital staff how to establish good patient relations, show concern for patients and how to handle the irate patient.
Health and Safety; Home Economics; Psychology
Dist - UTM **Prod** - UTM

The Secret of Job Success - Self - Management Skills 25 MIN
VHS / 16mm
Color (PRO)
$425.00 purchase, $110.00 rental, $35.00 preview
Explains the importance of self - management skills to employees. Discusses reliability, promptness, willingness to learn, and cooperativeness. Shows young employees how these skills affect the way they are perceived by their employers.
Business and Economics; Guidance and Counseling; Psychology; Sociology
Dist - UTM **Prod** - UTM

Secret of life series
Cell wars 60 MIN
Children by design 60 MIN
Conquering cancer 60 MIN
Dist - FOTH

The Secret of Little Ned 30 MIN
16mm
Footsteps Series
Color
LC 79-701553
Discusses the different types of ideas, feelings and concerns which children may express in ways other than speaking, and shows how parents can determine and respond to what is being expressed.
Guidance and Counseling; Home Economics; Psychology; Sociology
Dist - USNAC **Prod** - USOE 1978

The Secret of Michelangelo - Every Man's Dream 60 MIN
16mm
Color
LC 73-702673
Shows details of the Sistine Chapel fresco by Michelangelo.
Fine Arts
Dist - CAPCBC **Prod** - MMAMC 1968

The Secret of pushbuttons 4 MIN
16mm
Otto the auto - pedestrian safety - D series
Color (K P)
$30.00 purchase _ #205
Features Otto the Auto who shows how to use pedestrian crosswalk pushbuttons on traffic signals. Part of a series on pedestrian safety. Complete series available on 0.5 inch VHS.
Health and Safety
Dist - AAAFTS **Prod** - AAAFTS 1971

Secret of Quetzalcoatl 3 MIN
16mm
Color (G)
$15.00 rental
Presents the history of civilization as seen through the eyes of the Aztec Indians. Delves into Aztec legend, the invasion of Western culture and its effect upon Mexico.
Fine Arts; Social Science; Sociology
Dist - CANCIN **Prod** - PEARLY

The Secret of Success 10 MIN
16mm
Dr Bob Jones Says Series
Color (R)
Dr. Bob Jones, Sr. speaks about basic life truths.
Religion and Philosophy
Dist - UF **Prod** - UF

The Secret of the second basement 30 MIN
VHS
Nanny and Isaiah adventure series
Color (K P I R)
$14.95 purchase _ #87EE0136
Introduces Nanny Feather, an unwanted child who becomes part of a family of 'street people.' Shows how the other family members teach her about Christmas and Jesus' love for all people.
Fine Arts; Guidance and Counseling; Literature and Drama; Religion and Philosophy
Dist - CPH **Prod** - CPH

The Secret of the second basement 12 MIN
VHS
Color (K P I R)
$14.95 purchase, $10.00 rental _ #35 - 8131 - 19
Features Nanny and Isaiah as they learn about homelessness and the true meaning of charity.
Literature and Drama; Religion and Philosophy
Dist - APH **Prod** - CPH

Secret of the sexes 60 MIN
VHS
Nova video library
Color (G)
$29.95 purchase
Investigates how girls and boys are typecast. Features the perspectives of psychologists, sociologists, and families. From the PBS series 'Nova.'
Sociology
Dist - PBS **Prod** - WNETTV

Secret of the Sunken Caves 52 MIN
U-matic / VHS / 16mm
Undersea World of Jacques Cousteau Series
Color (I)
Science - Natural; Science - Physical
Dist - CF **Prod** - METROM 1970

The Secret of the Universe 2 MIN
16mm
Color
LC 73-702202
Attempts to explain allegorically how a basketball player shoots an impossible shot.
Physical Education and Recreation
Dist - GROENG **Prod** - GROENG 1973

Secret of the Waterfall 29 MIN
VHS / U-matic
Color
Presents a dancing weekend at Martha's Vineyard, in a garden, street, living room, patio, chapel, bedroom and at the beach. Involves two poets.
Fine Arts; Literature and Drama
Dist - KITCHN **Prod** - WGBH

Secret of the White Cell 30 MIN
16mm
Experiment Series
B&W (J)
Reports on the successful search for the way in which white cells kill germs in the body. Depicts a method of separating and analyzing subcellular components of the white cell, cinephotomicrography of white cells ingesting germs, and electron microscope photos of internal structures which release germicidal materials.
Science; Science - Natural
Dist - IU **Prod** - PRISM 1966

The Secret of Wendel Samson 31 MIN
16mm
Color (H C)
Presents a Freudian psychodrama dealing with homosexuality.
Psychology; Sociology
Dist - CFS **Prod** - CFS

A Secret Order - the Druzes 27 MIN
U-matic / VHS / 16mm
In the Footsteps of Abraham - a series
Color (J H C A)
$475.00 purchase
Focuses on the Druzes, a secret group who have a strict prohibition on divulging the doctrine and the practice of their religion. This has always contributed to the misunderstanding of the sect which seems to stem from Islam.
Religion and Philosophy
Dist - LANDMK **Prod** - LANDMK 1984

The Secret Return 10 MIN
16mm
Color
Looks at the nesting habits of the sea turtle which sometimes travels hundreds of miles to reach a particular beach where ancestors hatched eons earlier.
Science - Natural
Dist - UGAIA **Prod** - UGAIA

Secret sounds screaming 30 MIN
VHS / 16mm
Color (G)
$225.00 purchase, $30.00 rental
Explores the sexual abuse of young people as a power issue. Uses voices of survivors, parents, social workers, community activists and abusers to focus on societal attitudes, the impact of race and class, the legal system, media's role in eroticizing children and offers suggestions on educating young people to protect them. Produced by Ayoka Chenzira.
Civics and Political Systems; Health and Safety; Psychology; Sociology
Dist - WMEN **Prod** - AYCH 1986

A Secret space 80 MIN
VHS
Color (G)
$79.95 purchase _ #411
Portrays David Goodman, the son of liberal, determinedly secular parents, who stumbles into an abandoned Lower East Side synagogue being reclaimed by a group searching for Jewish meaning in their lives. Reveals that, to the dismay of his parents, Goodman becomes increasingly interested in his Jewish roots as he is welcomed into the 'havurah,' community of persons from diverse backgrounds who worship together. As he approaches his Bar Mitzvah, Goodman finally seems to feel comfortable as a Jew. Features Phyllis Newman, Robert Klein, Jon Matthews, Sam Schacht and Virginia Graham.
Guidance and Counseling; Religion and Philosophy; Sociology
Dist - ERGOM **Prod** - ERGOM

Secret survivors
VHS
Color (G PRO)
$39.95 purchase _ #91010
Educates health care workers on the needs of illiterate patients. Offers vignettes which show how to identify signs of illiteracy in patients, how to be sensitive to these patients' needs and how to increase communication so that the patient is served, frustration is limited and danger is avoided. Inclues a packet of worksheets and laminated Patient Communication Card. Communication card available separately.
English Language; Health and Safety; Social Science
Dist - LITERA

The Secret to a satisfied life 50 MIN
VHS
Color (G)
$29.95 purchase _ #5855H
Helps persons in recovery to focus on their attitudes and perceptions of people and the events of life. Uses dramatic vignettes to demonstrate the 'whys' of actions and attitudes. Features Earnie Larsen.
Guidance and Counseling; Health and Safety; Psychology
Dist - HAZELB **Prod** - HAZELB

The Secret to it all - Believe in yourself - Vol 8 22 MIN
VHS / 16mm
Friend Like Patty Series
Color (G)
$95.00 purchase
Focuses upon positive messages to teenage girls. Emphasizes self - esteem. Part of an eight - part series, 'A Friend Like Patty,' featuring Patty Ellis.
Guidance and Counseling; Health and Safety; Psychology; Sociology
Dist - PROSOR

The Secret War - Vol I 101 MIN
VHS
Color (S)
$29.95 purchase _ #781 - 9014
Uncovers clandestine operations that led to the development of some of the most effective Axis and Allied weaponry. Uses rare B&W and color footage to take viewer to laboratories and testing grounds where struggles to devise or counteract new technology were as crucial to the war effort as battlefield combat. Volume I of this three - part series is divided into 'The Battle Of The Beams' which focuses on the German use of radio beams to guide night bombers to pinpoint targets anywhere on the British Isles and British attempts to thwart the technology, and 'To See For A Hundred Miles,' which discusses the war for supremacy in radar technology.
Business and Economics; Civics and Political Systems; Geography - World; History - United States; History - World; Industrial and Technical Education; Sociology
Dist - FI **Prod** - BBCTV 1988

The Secret war - Vol II 99 MIN
VHS
Color (S)
$29.95 purchase _ #781 - 9014
Uncovers clandestine operations that led to the development of some of the most effective Axis and Allied weaponry. Uses rare B&W and color footage to take viewer to laboratories and testing grounds where struggles to devise or counteract new technology were as crucial to the war effort as battlefield combat. Volume II of this three - part series is divided into 'Terror Weapons' which focuses on the crash of June, 1944 in Britain, of a German plane with no pilot or crew and British research to discover how it worked, and 'If' which discusses some weapons which didn't get past the drawing board. Gigant, a glider almost as large as today's jumbo jet and the Komet, a rocket powered fighter are examples of these weapons.
Business and Economics; Civics and Political Systems; Computer Science; Geography - World; Industrial and Technical Education; Sociology
Dist - FI **Prod** - BBCTV 1988

The Secret War - Vol III 100 MIN
VHS
Color (S)
$29.95 purchase _ #781 - 9014
Uncovers clandestine operations that led to the development of some of the most effective Axis and Allied weaponry. Uses rare B&W and color footage to take viewer to laboratories and testing grounds where struggles to devise or counteract new technology were as crucial to the war effort as battlefield combat. Volume III of this three - part series is divided into 'The Deadly Waves,' which focuses on the magnetic mine, invented by the British in 1917, and adapted by the Germans in WWII into new levels of deadly effectiveness, and 'Still Secret,' the penetration of the German codes known as Enigma by British intelligence.
Business and Economics; Civics and Political Systems; Computer Science; Geography - World; History - United States; Science - Physical
Dist - FI **Prod** - BBCTV 1988

Secret Weapons of WW II 30 MIN
VHS
Color (G)
$14.98 purchase _ #TT8124
Shows the extraordinary breakthroughs in aviation and rocket experimentation that almost turned World War II into a futuristic nightmare. Produced by Midwich Entertainment, Inc.
Civics and Political Systems; History - United States; History - World
Dist - TWINTO **Prod** - TWINTO 1990

The Secret world 28 MIN
VHS
Color (P I J H)
Looks at the wildlife which flourishes within the confines of Greater London. Watches sparrows rear their young in Charing Cross, a hedgehog roaming a Power Station at Bow, a kestral hawk nesting on the BBC building.
Geography - World; Science - Natural
Dist - VIEWTH **Prod** - VIEWTH

The Secret World of Odilon Redon 30 MIN
U-matic / VHS / 16mm
Color (H C A)
LC 77-701028
Examines the life, work and techniques of 19th century artist Odilon Redon. Includes Redon's own comments on his work.
Fine Arts
Dist - FI **Prod** - ACOGRB 1973

The Secret world of the CIA 35 MIN
VHS
Color (J H C G T A)
$122.00 purchase, $45.00 rental
Features ex - CIA agent John Stockwell in an inside look at the agency's covert operations overseas. Emphasizes his view that the CIA should radically alter its covert policies. Includes teacher's guide.
Civics and Political Systems; Sociology
Dist - EFVP **Prod** - INST 1988

Secretarial 20 TO 30 MIN
U-matic
Opportunity Profile Series
(H C A)
$99.95 _ #AI209
Illustrates the daily activities involved in secretarial careers. Working professionals in related occupations present the negative and positive aspects of such jobs.
Business and Economics; Guidance and Counseling
Dist - CAMV **Prod** - CAMV

Secretarial
U-matic / VHS
Work - a - Day America
$59.95 purchase _ #VV120V
Helps students achieve career vocational preparation. Stresses the four main points of career awareness and exploration, specific skills intended, employability skills needed, and real people sharing on the job experiences.
Guidance and Counseling
Dist - CAREER **Prod** - CAREER

Secretarial
U-matic / VHS
Opportunity Profile Series
$99.95 purchase _ #AJ108V
Provides advice on the skills and educational background desired by companies, the day to day activities of various careers, and the positive and negative aspects of various careers from corporate vice presidents, managers, and other working professionals.
Guidance and Counseling
Dist - CAREER **Prod** - CAREER

Secretarial Services 15 MIN
VHS / U-matic / BETA
Career Success Series
(H C A)
$29.95 _ #MX204
Portrays occupations in secretarial services by reviewing required abilities and interviewing people employed in this field. Tells of the anxieties and rewards involved in pursuing a career as a secretary.
Business and Economics; Education; Guidance and Counseling
Dist - CAMV **Prod** - CAMV

Secretarial Services 15 MIN
VHS / 16mm
(H C A)
$24.95 purchase _ #CS204
Describes the skills necessary for a career in secretarial services. Features interviews with professionals in this field.
Guidance and Counseling
Dist - RMIBHF **Prod** - RMIBHF

Secretarial Work Sampling 18 MIN
16mm
Color
LC 72-701955
Introduces methods of work observation to management. Explains that each member of the audience keeps an account of the work done by a secretary each day of the week. Measures these samplings against the actual record of her achievements to increase efficiency in observation.
Business and Economics; Guidance and Counseling; Psychology
Dist - VOAERO **Prod** - VOAERO 1971

Secretariat - Big Red's Last Race 24 MIN
16mm / U-matic / VHS
Color (I)
LC 76-701839
Takes a look at the last racing achievements of Secretariat, the championship race horse, running at the Canadian International Championship in October 1973.
Physical Education and Recreation; Sociology
Dist - WOMBAT **Prod** - INST 1976

The Secretary and her boss - Try to see it my way - Pt 1 28 MIN
U-matic / VHS
Color (A)
Employs humor to show the quirks, mannerisms, demands and actions that destroy the mutual respect of a secretary and her boss and bring productivity to a halt. Focuses on routines, mail, appointments and filing.
Business and Economics; Psychology; Sociology
Dist - XICOM **Prod** - XICOM

The Secretary and her boss - We can work it out - Pt 2 28 MIN
U-matic / VHS
Color (A)
Uses the somewhat humorous characters of John and Adrienne to illustrate good techniques for interaction between bosses and secretaries. Focuses on three main areas - visitors, telephone callers and dictation.
Business and Economics; Psychology; Sociology
Dist - XICOM **Prod** - XICOM

Secretary and Management Relationship Series no 1
Try to See it My Way 27 MIN
Dist - VISUCP

Secretary and Management Relationship Series no 2
We Can Work it Out 29 MIN
Dist - VISUCP

Secretary General of the United Nations 28 MIN
Videoreel / VHS
International Byline Series
Color
Interviews Kurt Waldheim, Secretary General of the United Nations. Discusses his varied and unique responsibilities. Hosted by Marilyn Perry.
Business and Economics; Civics and Political Systems; Geography - World
Dist - PERRYM **Prod** - PERRYM

Secretary to Hitler 26 MIN
U-matic / VHS
World at War Specials Series
Color (H C A)
Relates that Hitler's private secretary, Traudi Junge, was with Hitler at his death in his private bunker. Her extensive information about Hitler during the war years and in defeat illuminate what he was like as a man and how he reacted to adversity.
Biography; History - World
Dist - MEDIAG **Prod** - THAMES 1974

The Secrete of Life 15 MIN
16mm
Color (C)
$392.00
Experimental film by Victor Faccinto.
Fine Arts
Dist - AFA **Prod** - AFA

The Secretion of Insulin 23 MIN
U-matic / VHS
Color (PRO)
Describes a pioneer research project which seeks to determine how insulin is secreted from the pancreas into the blood stream.
Health and Safety
Dist - WFP **Prod** - WFP

Secretory Otitis Media
U-matic / VHS
Color
Shows how the ear works, why the middle ear needs air furnished by the Eustachian tubes, and the various way blockage occurs. Explains various diagnostic procedures and treatment.
Science - Natural
Dist - MIFE **Prod** - MIFE

Secrets 8 MIN
16mm
Color
Presents an elegant 80 - year - old man whose daily life consists of work in a well - furnished office, attention by a chauffeur and secretary and lunch with a lovely lady. Demonstrates that there are no stereotypes in considering the lifestyles of the aged.
Fine Arts; Sociology
Dist - FLMLIB **Prod** - THOMAC 1980

Secrets 13 MIN
16mm
Color (H C A)
LC 73-700756
Presents artist Phillip Jones' character study of a girl combining paintings, sketches, anatomical cross sections, photographs and colored washes of a pretty girl's face with ominous orchestral background music and sounds of the night to invoke his subject's hidden identity.
Fine Arts; Guidance and Counseling
Dist - VIEWFI **Prod** - PFP 1973

Secrets and timesavers
VHS
WordPerfect 5.1 series
Color (G)
$39.95 purchase _ #VIA017
Teaches shortcuts in WordPerfect, version 5.1.
Computer Science
Dist - SIV

Secrets and timesavers
VHS
PageMaker 4.0 series
Color (G)
$39.95 purchase _ #VIA009
Teaches PageMaker 4.0 desktop publishing secrets and timesavers.
Computer Science
Dist - SIV

Secrets for a Happy Hostess 13 MIN
16mm
Color
Presents Patty and Susie planning the menu, shopping, preparing and serving the 20th anniversary dinner for their parents and family. Illustrates time and appliance - use management, highlighting the dishwasher and the food waste disposer.
Guidance and Counseling; Home Economics
Dist - MAY **Prod** - MAY

Secrets for Catching Walleye 30 MIN
VHS
Sportsmans Workshop Video Library Series
Color (K IND)
Presents tips and techniques used for walleye fishing.
Physical Education and Recreation
Dist - WRBPRO **Prod** - WRBPRO 1984

Secrets in the Desert 20 MIN
U-matic / VHS
Color
$335.00 purchase
From the ABC TV program, 20 20.
Agriculture; Sociology
Dist - ABCLR **Prod** - ABCLR 1983

Secrets in your cells 15 MIN
U-matic / VHS
All about you series
Color (P)
Introduces the idea of genetic inheritance.
Science - Natural
Dist - AITECH **Prod** - WGBHTV 1975

Secrets of a Brook 30 MIN
16mm
Synergism - Gallimaufry series
B&W (P I J)
LC 79-700344
Presents a view of the travels of a brook as seen through the eyes of a ten - year - old girl. 1967 award series.
Fine Arts
Dist - IU **Prod** - KVIETV 1967
PBS

Secrets of a Desert Sea 52 MIN
VHS
Color (S)
$24.95 purchase _ #839 - 9006
Tells the story of Mexico's Sea of Cortez, an isolated body of water that is home to many indigenous species. Shows filmmaker Hardy Jones climbing on the back of a giant manta ray for a ride.
Geography - World; Science - Natural
Dist - FI **Prod** - JONSHA 1988

Secrets of a volcano 26 MIN
U-matic / VHS / 16mm
Conquest series
B&W (J)
Pictures the active Kilauea volcano and the Hawaiian volcano observatory. Presents new discoveries about the earth's composition - that the crust is no more than ten miles thick in Hawaii and that earthquakes do not start in the crust but in the mantle between the crust and core of the earth.
Geography - United States; Science - Physical
Dist - CAROUF **Prod** - CBSTV 1960

Secrets of an Alien World 52 MIN
U-matic / VHS
Color (J H A)
Reveals the physiology and behavior of insects that gives them the potential to be both allies and competitors of people.
Science - Natural
Dist - BRAVFI **Prod** - BRAVFI 1980

Secrets of animal survial 15 MIN
BETA / VHS / U-matic / 16mm
Exploring the animal kingdom series
Color (K P)
$245.00, $68.00 purchase _ #C50498, #C51367
Shows how animals are equipped with acute senses, or use camouflage, threats and other defensive behavior for survival. Part of a five - part series on the animal kingdom.
Science - Natural
Dist - NGS **Prod** - NGS 1989

The Secrets of Cancer 26 MIN
16mm / U-matic
Color
Explains how cancer develops and how it could possibly be prevented. Describes a preventive technique called chemo - prevention.
Health and Safety
Dist - MTP **Prod** - NFCR

Secrets of Chinese love making - Part 1
VHS
Color (A)
$39.95 purchase _ #V - SCLM
Teaches awareness techniques in the art of lovemaking based on the sexual teachings of Chinese Taoism. Features James McNeil, student of Master Chiao Chang Huang. Takes the viewer through several different sets of exercises designed to enhance the flow of chi to the sexual organs. Demonstrates proper breathing along with simulated demonstrations of Taoist sexual practices. Focuses on showing men how to bring sexual pleasure to women. Part one of two parts.
Fine Arts; Health and Safety; Religion and Philosophy
Dist - PACSPI

Secrets of Chinese love making - Part 2
VHS
Color (A)
$39.95 purchase _ #V - 2SCLM
Shows specific ways for sexual partners to take each other to higher levels of sexual pleasure. Features James McNeil, student of Master Chiao Chang Huang. Teaches advanced sexual techniques, including meditation, foreplay and pleasure enhancing exercises for partners drawn from Taoist sexual practices. Part two of two parts.
Fine Arts; Health and Safety; Physical Education and Recreation; Religion and Philosophy
Dist - PACSPI

Secrets of Chinese love making - Parts 1 and 2
VHS
Color (A)
$69.00 purchase
Presents two programs which teach awareness techniques in the art of lovemaking based on the sexual teachings of Chinese Taoism. Features James McNeil, student of Master Chiao Chang Huang. Part 1 takes the viewer through several different sets of exercises designed to enhance the flow of chi to the sexual organs. Demonstrates proper breathing along with simulated demonstrations of Taoist sexual practices. Focuses on showing men how to bring sexual pleasure to women. Part two teaches advanced sexual techniques and shows both men and women how to pleasure each other.
Fine Arts; Health and Safety; Physical Education and Recreation; Religion and Philosophy
Dist - PACSPI

Secrets of Easter Island 58 MIN
U-matic / VHS
Nova series
Color (H C A)
$250.00 purchase _ #HP - 5921C
Probes the mysteries of Easter Island. Presents some theories on the origin of its people and questions why none of the island's 2,000 present inhabitants know how, why and by whom the giant stone statues were created. Part of a two - part series on Easter Island and part of the Nova series.
Fine Arts; History - World
Dist - CORF **Prod** - WGBHTV 1989

Secrets of Effective Radio Advertising 75 MIN
U-matic / VHS
Media Studies Series
Color (C)
$349.00, $249.00 purchase _ #AD - 2060
Features Tony Schwartz who demonstrates the effectiveness of radio in advertising, politics and promoting public interest groups.
Business and Economics; Computer Science; Fine Arts; Psychology; Sociology
Dist - FOTH **Prod** - FOTH

The Secrets of interview success 40 MIN
VHS
Get the job you want series
Color (H G)
$69.00 purchase _ #BC13A
Conveys the skills job applicants need to make the first impression the best it can be. Includes Job Search Journal. Third in a 3 - part series.
Business and Economics; Guidance and Counseling
Dist - CFKRCM **Prod** - CFKRCM

Secrets of Life Series

Secrets of the ant and insect world	13 MIN
Secrets of the bee world	13 MIN
Secrets of the Plant World	15 MIN
Secrets of the underwater world	16 MIN

Dist - CORF

Secrets of Limestone Groundwater 14 MIN
U-matic / VHS / 16mm
Color (H C)
LC 80-701640
Shows how groundwater from springs, wells, and underground rivers in limestone country may well be polluted by human sewage and garbage that was unintentionally allowed to filter down into the water table.
Science - Natural; Sociology
Dist - IU **Prod** - INERTH 1980

Secrets of lost empires series
Challenges modern engineers to reproduce some of the greatest monuments of ancient civilizations. Interweaves practical demonstrations and debates with location sequences and explorations of the various cultures. Covers such monuments as Stonehenge; Incan grass bridges; Roman awnings; and the obelisks of ancient Egypt. Four videos constitute this series.

Obelisks of ancient Egypt	50 MIN
Peru	50 MIN
Roman awnings	50 MIN
Secrets of lost empires series	200 MIN
Stonehenge	50 MIN

Dist - BBCENE

The Secrets of making good grades 15 MIN
16mm / U-matic / VHS
Color (J H C)
$350.00, $245.00 purchase _ #4369; LC 83-701076
Tells the secrets six successful students have used to achieve good grades. Offers tips on lecture note taking, reviewing, reading textbooks and test - taking.
Education; Guidance and Counseling
Dist - CORF **Prod** - CROMIE 1983

The Secrets of Nikola Tesla 120 MIN
VHS / U-matic
Color
Features Orson Welles, Strother Martin and Dennis Patrick in a film about clean energy.
Fine Arts; Social Science
Dist - PLACE **Prod** - ZAGREB

Secrets of reconstructive and corrective make - up 60 MIN
VHS
Make - up techniques with David Nicholas series
Color (H C G)
$48.00 purchase _ #BY204V
Shows how to apply corrective makeup to hide birth marks and scars, whether from acne, burns or other accidents. Offers step - by - step demonstrations that show more complex corrective applications that are waterproof and last for hours. Part of a series featuring makeup artist David Nicholas.
Home Economics
Dist - CAMV

Secrets of science - life science series - Set One 188 MIN
VHS
Secrets of science series
Color (I J H C)
$159.00 purchase
Presents four videos on life science. Includes From the Beginning; Life's Building Blocks; Brain Power and The Life Around Us. Hosted by Discover Magazine Editor in Chief Paul Hoffman. Part One of three parts on science.
Science - Natural
Dist - EFVP **Prod** - DSCOVM 1994

Secrets of science series
Presents 13 videos on science divided into 53 segments on life, Earth and space and physical science. Includes From the Beginning; Life's Building Blocks; Brain Power; and The Life Around Us in Set One - Life Science; Planet Earth, Our Home; Earth's Extremes; Our Sea and Sky; Into Outer Space; and Our Sun and Solar System in Set Two - Earth and space science; and The Mysteries of Motion and Power; Exploring Energy; Of Wheels and Wings; and Through the Looking Glass in Set Three - physical science. Hosted by Discover Magazine Editor in Chief Paul Hoffman.

Earth and space science - secrets of science series - Set Two	235 MIN
Physical science - secrets of science series - Set Three	188 MIN
Secrets of science - life science series - Set One	188 MIN
Through the looking glass and Video 13	47 MIN

Dist - EFVP **Prod** - DSCOVM 1994

Secrets of Sleep 52 MIN
U-matic / VHS / 16mm
Nova Series
Color (H C A)
LC 78-700616
Uses animation and documentary footage of experiments conducted to study the effects of sleep. Considers what happens during sleep, how much the average person

needs, the the quality of sleep induced by pills and the importance of dreaming and interpreting dreams.
Health and Safety; Psychology; Science; Science - Natural
Dist - TIMLIF **Prod** - WGBHTV 1976

The Secrets of Sleep 60 MIN
U-matic
Color
Examines some of the theories of sleep and the reason for dreams. Shows the kinds of sleep research being conducted and looks at a group session in which the hidden meanings that dreams may have are unravelled.
Psychology
Dist - PBS **Prod** - WGBH 1974

Secrets of Spinner Bait 30 MIN
VHS / BETA
Color
Presents all aspects of fishing spinner baits, including the size and color of blade, and casting and retrieving spinner baits.
Physical Education and Recreation; Science - Natural
Dist - HOMEAF **Prod** - HOMEAF

Secrets of Super Salespeople 20 MIN
16mm / VHS
Color (H C A)
$575.00 purchase, $150.00 rental _ #175
Includes Leader's Guide. Presents attitudes and skills necessary for a successful career in sales.
Business and Economics; Psychology
Dist - SALENG **Prod** - SALENG 1985

Secrets of the ant and insect world 13 MIN
U-matic / VHS / 16mm
Secrets of life series
Color (I J H) (GERMAN AFRIKAANS NORWEGIAN SWEDISH)
Presents facts about the subterranean world of the ant, including a description of the warfare that persist between rival tribes of ants and their desparate struggle to protect their nests from invasion. Discusses in detail the honeycast, hunting and leafcutter ants.
Foreign Language; Science - Natural
Dist - CORF **Prod** - DISNEY 1961

Secrets of the Bay 28 MIN
VHS
San Francisco Bay area - land and water series
Color (I J H C G)
$195.00 purchase, $40.00 rental _ #37990
Takes a look at the wildlife hidden in, on and by San Francisco Bay among the region's six million human inhabitants. Includes an endangered peregrine falcon nesting on the bay bridge, baby harbor seals learning to crawl in their marshland napping areas, a lovesick bird on a most unlikely 'lover's lane,' and a shorebird ballet featuring slow - motion photography of pelicans, avocets and a supporting cast of thousands. Demonstrates the fragility of the Bay environment under the encroachment of urbanization. Urges that this national treasure be protected and preserved for future generations. Hosted by San Francisco TV personality Jan Yanehiro. Produced by Chris Beaver and Judy Irving. Part of a two - part series.
Geography - United States; Science - Natural
Dist - UCEMC

Secrets of the bee world 13 MIN
16mm / U-matic / VHS
Secrets of life series
Color (I J H) (SPANISH AFRIKAANS GERMAN NORWEGIAN DUTCH SWEDISH)
Shows the many facets of life in a highly organized bee colony. Describes the construction of the comb, discusses the importance of the queen bee and explains about the work of bees in the pollination process.
Science - Natural
Dist - CORF **Prod** - DISNEY 1961

Secrets of the Brain 15 MIN
16mm
Science in Action Series
Color (C)
Explains that the prevention, treatment and cure of cerebral palsy are the goals of intensive research into the subtle and delicate processes of the brain. Shows methods being researched for curing such problems as headaches, muscular spasms and learning difficulties.
Health and Safety; Science; Science - Natural
Dist - COUNFI **Prod** - ALLFP

Secrets of the desert sea 57 MIN
VHS
Color (G)
$39.95 purchase _ #S01963
Describes the ecosystem of Mexico's Sea of Cortez.
Science - Natural
Dist - UILL

Secrets of the Greenland Ice 30 MIN
U-matic / VHS
(G)
Describes the activities of Swiss, Danish and American scientists who are exploring Greenland's glacial ice for archaeological climatic information. Highlights the Greenland Ice Sheet Program and the University of Nebraska's Polar Ice Coring Office. Shows how ice core samples are collected, examined, and interpreted and how the information is used. Narrated by E G Marshall.
Science - Physical
Dist - GPN **Prod** - NETV 1983

The Secrets of the Mary Rose - Pt 7 20 MIN
VHS
Tudors Series
Color (I)
$79.00 purchase _ #825 - 9427
Paints a detailed and historically accurate picture of the Tudor period, 1485 - 1603, in British history. Examines historical trends over a broad time period or concentrates on one aspect of the era. The dramatizations are based on source material and the locations are authentic. Part 7 of seven parts examines the artifacts discovered on the 'Mary Rose' which reveal details of seafaring under the Tudors.
Civics and Political Systems; History - World; Social Science
Dist - FI **Prod** - BBCTV 1987

Secrets of the Plant World 15 MIN
U-matic / VHS / 16mm
Secrets of Life Series
Color (I J H) (GREEK SWEDISH NORWEGIAN PORTUGUESE SPANISH)
Describes the various ways in which seeds are planted without the help of man. Uses time - lapse photography to show the growing, budding and flowering of many plants.
Science - Natural
Dist - CORF **Prod** - DISNEY 1961

Secrets of the Pond 30 MIN
U-matic / VHS / 16mm
KnowZone Series
Color (I J H)
$550 purchase - 16 mm, $250 purchase - video _ #5070C
Talks about the animals who live around a pond and how they adapt. Adapted from the Nova series. Hosted by David Morse.
Science - Natural
Dist - CORF

Secrets of the salt marsh 20 MIN
VHS
Color (G T)
$150.00 purchase, $20.00 rental
Presents an overview of salt marsh ecology with aerial, underwater and time lapse photography. Looks at the ecosystems, how marshes protect the mainland from flooding, migrating birds, the food chain, terrapin turtles, and more. Produced by Natural Arts Films for The Wetlands Institute. Includes study guide.
Science - Natural
Dist - BULFRG

Secrets of the Sea 15 MIN
16mm / U-matic / VHS
Color (J)
LC 74-702620
Pictures two scuba divers as they explore a coral reef and observe its inhabitants. Shows views of colored fish and other sea animals, a wrecked ship, a shark and a barracuda.
Geography - World; Science - Natural
Dist - AIMS **Prod** - DUTCHE 1974

Secrets of the Selva - of Plants and People 58 MIN
VHS
Color (G)
$49.00 purchase _ #6 - 300 - 305P
Overviews the urban horticulture industry from Florida to California. Shows how to decorate with plants in homes, offices and shopping centers. Illustrates how tissue culture propagation is used to meet industry demands.
Fine Arts; Home Economics; Science - Natural
Dist - VEP **Prod** - VEP

Secrets of the shark 30 MIN
VHS
Return to the sea series
Color (I J H G)
$24.95 purchase _ #RTS102
Explores the physiology of sharks and shows what makes them different from other fish. Reveals how filmmakers get close - up footage of sharks to give viewers a distorted and fearsome image of the beasts. Discloses that human fear of sharks threatens their survival. Part of a 13 - part series on marine life produced by Marine Grafics and University of North Carolina Public TV.
Science - Natural; Science - Physical
Dist - ENVIMC

Secrets of the Solar System 30 MIN
VHS / 16mm
Science, Health and Math Series
Color (P)
$39.95 purchase _ #CL7904
Introduces basic concepts concerning the solar system.
Science; Science - Physical
Dist - EDUCRT

Secrets of the stars series
Beverly Sassoon - a video guide to total beauty and fashion with special stars Cathy Lee Crosby, Eva Gabor and Marla Gibbs
The Fifth Avenue doctor's consultation on dermatology and cosmetic surgery
Shirley Jones' and Sheila Cluff's complete fitness and beauty program
Dist - INCRSE

Secrets of the sun 26 MIN
VHS
Stars series
Color (I J H)
$195.00 purchase
Discusses the relationship of the sun and its effect on the Earth. Explores the dependency of Earth on the sun and how the sun is fueled. Looks at sun spots and their effect upon Earth's weather. Uses film of sun flares to observe the effects of the Aurora Borealis through a solar telescope. Observes a solar eclipse and visits an underground laboratory to learn about neutrinos. Part of a six - part series on astronomy.
Science - Physical
Dist - LANDMK **Prod** - LANDMK 1988

Secrets of the tarot revealed - beginning 120 MIN
VHS
Color (G)
$39.95 purchase _ #V312
Features Laura Clarson who discusses the origin and nature of tarot and how to interpret the cards to reveal mysteries and offer guidance.
Religion and Philosophy
Dist - LIBSOR

Secrets of the Titanic 60 MIN
VHS / BETA
National Geographic video series
Color (G)
$35.20, $24.20, $29.90, $29.95 purchase _ #C51287, #0309, #S00999
Highlights the underwater expedition of the century to the remains of the Titanic, which sank in 1912, 2.5 miles beneath the surface of the Atlantic.
History - United States; History - World; Physical Education and Recreation; Science - Physical
Dist - NGS **Prod** - NGS
PBS WNETTV
SEVVID
UILL

Secrets of the underwater world 16 MIN
16mm / U-matic / VHS
Secrets of life series
Color (I J H) (GERMAN NORWEGIAN AFRIKAANS ARABIC SPANISH PORTUGUESE SWEDISH)
Introduces life beneath the water's surface. Examines the habits of those animals who inhabit tidal fringes, fresh water and shallow seas.
Science - Natural
Dist - CORF **Prod** - DISNEY 1961

Secrets of the Wicker Bay - Talemnice wiklinowej zatoki 73 MIN
VHS
Color (P I J) (POLISH)
$17.95 purchase _ #V166
Presents a full length animated story of a young muskrat starting his adult life in Wicker Bay.
Fine Arts; Literature and Drama; Science - Natural
Dist - POLART

The Secrets of writing the college admission essay
VHS
Color (H)
$39.95 purchase _ #VAI124, VAI 124
Covers tips and strategies for writing a college admission essay.
Business and Economics; Education; English Language; Psychology; Social Science
Dist - CADESF **Prod** - CADESF

The Secrets to college success 77 MIN
VHS
Color (C H)
$59.95 purchase _ #SFI333V-G
Contains information about college life and offers ideas for achieving success in higher education. Includes topics such as setting goals for classroom learning and study

techniques, test-taking skills, organizing time, the social environment, dorm life, the first semester, and more. Also delivers advice on choosing a college, admissions tests, financial aid, and other related subjects.
Education; Psychology
Dist - CAMV

Section 1983 and public schools - Tape 17 40 MIN
VHS
Legal Challenges in special education series
Color (G PRO A)
$90.00 purchase
Features Reed Martin, attorney, in the 17th part of a 17 - part series on legal challenges in special education. Discusses Section 1983 and public schools. Includes print resource materials.
Civics and Political Systems; Education
Dist - BAXMED

Section 504 - expanding school's duties to handicapped students - Tape 12 60 MIN
VHS
Legal challenges in special education series
Color (G)
$90.00 purchase
Addresses eligibility criteria, procedures which differ from the requirements of the EHA, remedies which exceed the EHA and make claims for compensatory education more likely. Discusses enforcement by the Office for Civil Rights, which has broad powers to investigate complaints and order compliance, even to the point of withholding federal funds. Provides examples of some recent remedies ordered by OCR with regard to reimbursement of parents, new IEPs and illegal segregation of handicapped students. Features Reed Martin, JD. Includes resource materials. Part of a 12 - part series on Public Law 94 - 142.
Education; Health and Safety
Dist - BAXMED

Section Four 20 MIN
U-matic
Final Chapter Series
Color (H C)
Explains the inevitable nuclear winter in both the Northern and Southern hemispheres if nuclear weapons are ever used. Has concluding statements by prominent scientists.
Civics and Political Systems; Science
Dist - TVOTAR **Prod** - TVOTAR 1985

Section One 18 MIN
U-matic
Final Chapter Series
Color (H C)
Gives statements from scientists and a history of the development and testing of atomic weaponry.
Civics and Political Systems; Science
Dist - TVOTAR **Prod** - TVOTAR 1985

Section Three 21 MIN
U-matic
Final Chapter Series
Color (H C)
Examines the awesome force of a nuclear blast and the effects of radiation on human, plant and animal life and the long term effects of the bomb on the people of Hiroshima.
Civics and Political Systems; Science
Dist - TVOTAR **Prod** - TVOTAR 1985

Section Two 18 MIN
U-matic
Final Chapter Series
Color (H C)
Simulates the effects of a one megaton nuclear bomb dropped on a large city. Discusses worldwide deployment of nuclear weapons and has comments from Soviet and American scientists.
Civics and Political Systems; Science
Dist - TVOTAR **Prod** - TVOTAR 1985

Section Views
VHS
Engineering Drawing Videos Series
$69.95 purchase _ #017 - 091
Talks about full, half, broken - out, offset, removed, and revolved sections.
Industrial and Technical Education
Dist - CAREER **Prod** - CAREER

Section views
VHS
Engineering drawing series
Color (H A)
$59.95 purchase _ #HHED6V
Discusses the subject of section views. Uses manual and computer graphic techniques to show a variety of views. Includes an Engineering Drawing 100 workbook and an instructor's guide.
Computer Science; Industrial and Technical Education
Dist - CAMV

Sectional Views and Projections - Finish Marks 15 MIN
U-matic
Machine Shop Work - Fundamentals of Blueprint Reading Series
B&W
LC 79-707981
Defines technical drawing terms such as dimension, center, cross section, and object lines. Discusses the projection of a section view, the uses of finish marks, and the significance of standard cross section lines. Issued in 1944 as a motion picture.
Fine Arts; Industrial and Technical Education
Dist - USNAC **Prod** - USOE 1979

Sectional Views and Projections, Finish Marks 15 MIN
16mm
Machine Work Series Fundamentals of Blueprint Reading
B&W
LC FIE51-504
Shows dimension, center, cross - section and object lines. Discusses the uses of finish marks and the meanings of standard cross - section lines.
Industrial and Technical Education
Dist - USNAC **Prod** - USOE 1944

Sections
VHS
Drafting I series
(H C)
$59.00 _ CA138
Explains the cutting plane, the purpose of crosshatching, and examples of the frontal section, cross section, and the top section.
Education; Industrial and Technical Education
Dist - AAVIM **Prod** - AAVIM 1989

Secto and the seconaut 9 MIN
16mm
B&W (G)
$13.50 rental
Illustrates the problems of life when one's consciousness is eating a banana, compounded with technical difficulties. Uses clay animation. Produced by Nichael Connor.
Fine Arts
Dist - CANCIN

Sector Boss 21 MIN
16mm
Color
LC 74-705596
Identifies the specific sector boss responsibilities and their critical relationship to successful and economical fire management.
Business and Economics; Guidance and Counseling; Health and Safety
Dist - USNAC **Prod** - USDA 1970

Secular humanism, evolution and the decline of America
VHS
Counterfeits series
Color (H C G A R)
$10.00 rental _ #36 - 85 - 2024
Examines the underlying concepts of evolution and secular humanism. Suggests that both are fallacious and responsible for moral decline. Offers strategies for evangelism. Hosted by Ron Carlson. Produced by Cinema Associates and Film Educators.
Religion and Philosophy
Dist - APH

Secular Music of the Renaissance - Josquin Des Pres 30 MIN
16mm
World of Music Series
B&W (J)
Discusses the primacy of Josquin des Pres in Renaissance music and presents several examples of his works which are played and sung by the New York Pro Musica.
Fine Arts; History - World
Dist - IU **Prod** - NET 1965

The Secure Society 30 MIN
16mm
Face of Sweden Series
B&W
Describes the Swedish welfare program.
Sociology
Dist - SIS **Prod** - SIS 1963

Secure Your Child's Future 14 MIN
U-matic / VHS / 16mm
Color (H C A)
LC 81-700776
Explains the consequences of neglecting to use car safety restraints when children are passengers in a car. Discusses how to choose and install safety restraints.
Health and Safety; Home Economics
Dist - IFB **Prod** - IFB 1980

Secure Your Child's Future
U-matic / VHS / 16mm
Color (H C A)
Explains that a child's size determines which type of car safety restraint to use to prevent injury or death. Uses dramatizations and humor to show the importance of proper installation and consistent use.
Health and Safety; Science - Natural
Dist - IFB **Prod** - CRAF 1985

Securities 19 MIN
16mm
Money Management and Family Financial Planning Series
Color (H C A)
Explains various types of security investments, including stocks, bonds and mutual funds. Follows Jeff and a friend who meet a stockbroker at his office where they listen to an explanation of stock exchanges, tour the office and learn to read stock quotations on the financial page.
Business and Economics; Guidance and Counseling; Home Economics; Social Science; Sociology
Dist - AETNA **Prod** - AETNA

Securities arbitrator training 52 MIN
VHS / U-matic / BETA
Color (PRO)
$150.00 purchase
Teaches securities arbitrators effective case handling skills. Introduces the arbitration process to securities personnel. Addresses 17 procedural issues that an arbitrator might encounter at a securities hearing. Portrays the more difficult and complex issues. Includes a discussion guide.
Business and Economics; Psychology
Dist - AARA **Prod** - AARA

Security 30 MIN
U-matic
Fast Forward Series
Color (H C)
Looks at the powerful new tools the microelectronic revolution has provided for securing persons, property and information.
Computer Science; Science
Dist - TVOTAR **Prod** - TVOTAR 1979

Security and 'C' Language
U-matic / VHS
UNIX Overview Series Unit 6
Color
Describes the three major areas of concern regarding security and how UNIX handles them, the four characteristics of 'C' language and identifies why 'C' language is popular.
Business and Economics; Computer Science; Industrial and Technical Education; Mathematics; Sociology
Dist - COMTEG **Prod** - COMTEG

Security and emergency preparedness
Videodisc
Financial FLASHFAX security series
(H A)
$1995.00
Explains strategies for handling security and other emergency situations including robberies, bomb threats and fires with discussion of records and property protection. Helps financial institutions meet security training requirements. Can be customized for a particular institution. Includes practice material, quizzes and tests.
Business and Economics
Dist - CMSL **Prod** - CMSL

Security and Integrity 25 MIN
U-matic / VHS / 16mm
Color
Offers an overview of insurance database procedures at Blue Cross/Blue Shield in Boston, demonstrating ways the system guards against unauthorized disclosure of sensitive information. Shows controls at each of three system software levels that govern access - terminal restrictions, codes and passwords, and handling flags for specific classification of information.
Business and Economics; Mathematics
Dist - MEDIAG **Prod** - OPENU 1980

Security and Loss Prevention Control 15 MIN
VHS / U-matic
Health Care Security Training Series
Color
Teaches ways to prevent, detect and investigate losses at health care facilities by means of patrol, consistent systems enforcement and parcel inspection.
Civics and Political Systems; Health and Safety; Sociology
Dist - CORF **Prod** - GREESM

Security and the Law 14 MIN
U-matic / VHS
Professional Security Training Series Module 4
Color
Examines the extent and types of authority legally held by private security officers. Covers such topics as probable cause, laws of arrest, discretionary authority and law enforcement coordination.

Civics and Political Systems; Sociology
Dist - CORF **Prod** - CORF

Security and Weatherproofing - Door Locks, Burglar Alarms, Wall Safe, Garage Door 90 MIN
BETA / VHS
Best of Wally's Workshop Series
Color
Explains do - it - yourself procedures for the homeowner. Title continues ...Openers, Fiberglass Insulation, Weatherstripping.
Industrial and Technical Education
Dist - KARTES **Prod** - KARTES

Security Control - You Never Can Tell 36 MIN
16mm
B&W
Explains the elements of security by following a Naval Security Officer through the offices, laboratory and production plant of a manufacturer producing a classified device for the U S Navy.
Business and Economics; Civics and Political Systems
Dist - USNAC **Prod** - USN 1951

Security Council 18 MIN
16mm / U-matic / VHS
Color
Describes the role, functions, composition and activities of the Security Council within the context of the overall UN structure.
Civics and Political Systems
Dist - ICARUS **Prod** - UN 1982

Security, Custody and Control
16mm
View and do Series
B&W (PRO)
LC 73-700192
Provides information on security, custody and control.
Sociology
Dist - SCETV **Prod** - SCETV 1971

Security - employee awareness and problem prevention 19 MIN
VHS
Security series
Color (H C A IND)
LC 90-716416
Trains hotel employees about security procedures. Produced by Media Magic.
Business and Economics; Psychology; Sociology
Dist - EIAHM

Security - handling disturbances 18 MIN
VHS
Security series
Color (H C A IND)
LC 90-716387
Trains hotel employees about security procedures in handling disturbances. Produced by Media Magic.
Business and Economics; Psychology; Sociology
Dist - EIAHM

Security in Data Communications 46 MIN
VHS / U-matic
Telecommunications and the Computer Series
Color
Industrial and Technical Education; Mathematics
Dist - MIOT **Prod** - MIOT

Security is Everybody's Business 22 MIN
16mm / U-matic / VHS
Color
$75 rental _ #9807
Identifies security and safety problems that include substance abuse and theft of drugs for resale, accidental injury, mugging, kidnapping, theft of records in hospitals.
Health and Safety; Sociology
Dist - AIMS **Prod** - AIMS 1985

Security - key control and guest privacy 18 MIN
VHS
Security series
Color (H C A IND)
LC 90-716392
Trains hotel employees about security procedures. Produced by Media Magic.
Business and Economics; Psychology; Sociology
Dist - EIAHM

Security Man 17 MIN
16mm
B&W
Follows a government security man as he visits an industrial facility and points out some of the problems encountered.
Business and Economics; Civics and Political Systems; Guidance and Counseling
Dist - USNAC **Prod** - USA 1961

Security Markets 30 MIN
U-matic
It's Everybody's Business Series Unit 3, Financing a Business
Color
Business and Economics
Dist - DALCCD **Prod** - DALCCD

Security Officer Series
Pilferage, Cargo Theft and Shoplifting 13 MIN
Dist - AIMS

Security - protecting your property and guests 23 MIN
VHS
Security series
Color (H C A IND)
LC 90-716401
Trains hotel employees about security procedures. Produced by Media Magic.
Business and Economics; Psychology; Sociology
Dist - EIAHM

Security series
Security - employee awareness and problem prevention 19 MIN
Security - handling disturbances 18 MIN
Security - key control and guest privacy 18 MIN
Security - protecting your property and guests 23 MIN
Dist - EIAHM

Security services 10 MIN
VHS
Skills - occupational programs series
Color (H A)
$49.00 purchase, $15.00 rental _ #316608; LC 91-709478
Features a security staff demonstrating the skills involved in access control, crowd control, surveillance, armed protection and canine patrol. Explains why self - confidence and maturity are assets. Part of a series featuring occupations in the skilled trades, in service industries and in business leading to careers in areas of demand and future growth. Includes teacher's guide with reproducible wooksheets.
Guidance and Counseling; Psychology
Dist - TVOTAR **Prod** - TVOTAR 1990

The Security Story 12 MIN
U-matic / VHS
Professional Security Training Series Module 1
Color
Presents a brief history of private security in America. Explores the role of the security professional as a protector of assets. Shows modern security tools and emphasizes the need for training in their proper usage.
Health and Safety; Sociology
Dist - CORF **Prod** - CORF

Security Surveys in Manufacturing 11 MIN
U-matic / VHS / 16mm
Color
Deals with a clothing manufacturer's security - crime prevention plan. Uncovers weaknesses in windows, alarms and internal procedures.
Business and Economics; Civics and Political Systems; Sociology
Dist - CORF **Prod** - WORON

Sedatives, Hypnotics and Alcohol 30 MIN
16mm
Pharmacology Series
B&W (C)
LC 73-703334
Health and Safety; Psychology
Dist - TELSTR **Prod** - MVNE 1971

Sedimentary Processes and Basin Analysis Series
Barrier Islands 23 MIN
Before the Mountains 30 MIN
Birth of the Rockies 29 MIN
A Carbonate shelf 21 MIN
Deep sea sands 44 MIN
Deltaic environments 23 MIN
Extensional tectonics 23 MIN
Fluvial environments 23 MIN
The Foreland Basin 30 MIN
Modern Carbonates 17 MIN
North Sea 1 - the Tectonic Framework 58 MIN
North Sea 3 - Reservoirs 59 MIN
North Sea 2 - the Origin and Migration of Hydrocarbons 58 MIN
Seismic Reflection Processing 35 MIN
Seismic Stratigraphy 49 MIN
Shelf Sediments - Storms and Tides 17 MIN
Shelf Sediments - Upper Jurassic of Dorset 17 MIN
Dist - ACCESS

Sedimentary Rock 10 MIN
U-matic / VHS / 16mm
Color (J H)
$290 purchase - 16 mm, $250 purchase - video _ #5796C
Discusses sedimentary rock and its many forms. Discusses how strata becomes sedimentary rock. A BBC Television production for the Open University.
Science - Physical
Dist - CORF

Sedimentary Rock Depositional Patterns 30 MIN
U-matic / VHS
Basic Geology Series
Color (IND)
Industrial and Technical Education; Science - Physical
Dist - GPCV **Prod** - GPCV

Sedimentary Rock Lithologies 51 MIN
U-matic / VHS
Basic and Petroleum Geology for Non - Geologists - Sedimentary Rocks'Series; Sedimentary rocks
Color (IND)
Industrial and Technical Education; Science - Physical
Dist - GPCV **Prod** - PHILLP

Sedimentary Rock Structures 47 MIN
VHS / U-matic
Basic and Petroleum Geology for Non - Geologists - Sedimentary Rocks'Series; Sedimentary rocks
Color (IND)
Industrial and Technical Education; Science - Physical
Dist - GPCV **Prod** - PHILLP

Sedimentary Rock Textures 36 MIN
U-matic / VHS
Basic and Petroleum Geology for Non - Geologists - Sedimentary Rocks'Series; Sedimentary rocks
Color (IND)
Industrial and Technical Education; Science - Physical
Dist - GPCV **Prod** - PHILLP

Sedimentary rocks 15 MIN
U-matic / VHS
Discovering series; Unit 6 - Rocks and minerals
Color (I)
Science - Physical
Dist - AITECH **Prod** - WDCNTV 1978

Sedimentary rocks 12 MIN
VHS
Earth materials series
Color (H C)
$24.95 purchase _ #S9794
Discusses sedimentary rocks. Part of a ten - part series on the development of minerals, rocks and soil.
Science - Physical
Dist - HUBDSC **Prod** - HUBDSC

The Sedimentary solution 21 MIN
VHS
Color (G)
$275.00 purchase _ #8032
Visits Calgary and southern Alberta with Sherlock Holmes and Dr Watson to investigate the mysteries and origins of modern day landforms. Considers the birth of the Rockies, the end of the Ice Age and the development of modern day rivers.
Geography - World; Science - Physical
Dist - UCALG **Prod** - UCALG 1990

Sedimentation - settling rates 10 MIN
VHS
Geology stream table series
Color (H C)
$24.95 purchase _ #S9007, #193E2074
Treats sediment settling in a single - concept format, using models and NASA footage. Part of a 12 - part series on stream tables. Demonstrates effect of size, shape and density on rate at which particles settel in a water medium. Teacher's guide provided.
Agriculture; Geography - World; Science - Physical
Dist - HUBDSC **Prod** - HUBDSC 1990
WARDS

Sedimentation - Settling Rates 9 MIN
VHS
Color (C)
$34.95 purchase _ #193 E 2074
Demonstrates effect of size, shape and density on rate at which particles settle in a water medium. Teacher's guide provided.
Science - Physical
Dist - WARDS

Sedimentation - turbidity currents 9 MIN
VHS
Geology stream table series
Color (H C)
$24.95 purchase _ #S9006
Treats sedimentation and turbidity currents in a single - concept format, using models and NASA footage. Depicts sediments released in a large flume under varying conditions with close - ups of particle sorting. Teacher's guide provided. Part of a 12 - part series on stream tables.
Agriculture; Geography - World; Science - Physical
Dist - HUBDSC **Prod** - HUBDSC
WARDS

Sedimentation - Turbidity Currents 9 MIN
VHS
Color (C)
$34.95 purchase _ #193 E 2073
Depicts sediments released in a large flume under varying conditions with close - ups of particle sorting. Teacher's guide provided.
Science - Physical
Dist - WARDS

Sedona - Psychic Vortex Experience 65 MIN
VHS
Color (G)
$39.95 purchase _ #VHS102, BTA202
Tours four Sedona, Arizona, psychic energy vortexes. Includes Bell Rock, Courthouse Rock, Airport Mesa and Boynton Canyon. Intercuts to a seminar with Dick Sutphen where he is preparing participants for their encounter with the vortexes.
Geography - United States; Religion and Philosophy
Dist - VSPU **Prod** - VSPU

The Seduction of Joe Tynan 107 MIN
16mm
Color
Stars Alan Alda as a married senator who becomes involved with another woman (Meryl Streep).
Fine Arts
Dist - SWANK **Prod** - UPCI

Seduction - the cruel woman 84 MIN
16mm
Color (C)
Presents an independent production by Elfi Mikesch and Monika Treut. Portrays Wanda, a dominatrix who runs a 'gallery' on the Hamburg waterfront where audiences pay to watch her humiliate her slaves. Features dancer Mechthild Grossmann as Wanda. Also available in 35mm film format.
Fine Arts; Psychology; Sociology
Dist - FIRS

Seductive behavior - communication between foster parents 4 MIN
VHS
Sexually abused children in foster care training videotapes series
Color (PRO A C G)
$5.95 purchase _ #V517
Models a foster mother speaking to a foster father about one of the many problems that may occur when caring for a sexually abused child - seductive behavior. Reveals that the issue can be very sensitive and the tape gives foster parents an example of how to approach this kind of discussion. Part of an eight - part series training foster parents on the care of sexually abused children.
Social Science; Sociology
Dist - FFBH **Prod** - FFBH 1993

See 13 MIN
16mm / U-matic / VHS
Color (I)
LC 75-703004
Reveals the beauty and wonders of the sea.
Geography - World; Science - Natural; Science - Physical
Dist - PHENIX **Prod** - OPUS 1975

See America Series

California drive	28 MIN
New England, an Independence of Spirit	30 MIN
New Orleans, the Big Easy	27 MIN
San Francisco - the Golden Gate	28 MIN

Dist - MTOLP

See and be seen 9 MIN
VHS / 16mm
Color (K P)
$55.00, $30.00 purchase _ #248, #462
Teaches safe street crossing techniques for young children. Tells the story of two boys involved in a traffic mishap while playing. A friendly talking car teaches safe crossing rules.
Health and Safety
Dist - AAAFTS **Prod** - AAAFTS 1985

See Andy Run 20 MIN
16mm
Color
LC 77-702640
Features a satirical look at the pros and cons surrounding higher education.
Education; Sociology
Dist - CANFDC **Prod** - CANFDC 1975

See Dick and Jane lie, cheat and steal - teaching morality to kids 47 MIN
VHS
Raising good kids in bad times series
Color (H C A)
$95.00 purchase
Illustrates problems among people and possible solutions, focusing on child - rearing methods. Provides material for educators and community leaders as well as young people. Written, produced and directed by Carol Fleisher.
Guidance and Counseling; Health and Safety; Sociology
Dist - PFP **Prod** - ASHAP

See for yourself 15 MIN
U-matic
Color (H A IND)
$125.00 purchase
Shows the industrial worker how to identify jobs or operations where eye injuries are most frequent. Illustrates ways to prevent eye injuries and select eye protection.
Health and Safety
Dist - BNA **Prod** - ERESI 1982
AITECH

See Hear 15 MIN
16mm
Color (PRO)
LC FIA68-1198
Briefly describes the hearing difficulties encountered by individuals with conductive and sensori - neural hearing impairments. Demonstrates the importance of speech by simulating these losses on the sound track of the film.
English Language; Health and Safety; Science - Natural
Dist - EAR **Prod** - EAR 1964

See, Hear and Identify the Bird of North America, Vol I 94 MIN
VHS
Audubon Society's Video Guide Series
Color (G)
$29.95 purchase _ #VHX075
Identifies 116 species of loons, grebes, pelicans and their allies, swans, geese and ducks, hawks, vultures and falcons, and the chicken - like birds - pheasants, grouse, quail, ptarmigans. Part of a series produced by the Audubon Society which combines bird sights and sounds for accurate identification of 505 species. Includes computer - animated range maps which show the breeding and wintering areas for each species, and bird calls and sounds from the Cornell Laboratory of Ornithology.
Science - Natural
Dist - AUDIOE

See, Hear and Identify the Bird of North America, Vol II 78 MIN
VHS
Audubon Society's Video Guide Series
Color (G)
$29.95 purchase _ #VHX076
Identifies 105 species of water birds, including herons and egrets, cranes, shorebirds, gulls, terns and alcids. Part of a series produced by the Audubon Society which combines bird sights and sounds for accurate identification of 505 species. Includes computer - animated range maps which show the breeding and wintering areas for each species, and bird calls and sounds from the Cornell Laboratory of Ornithology.
Science - Natural
Dist - AUDIOE

See, Hear and Identify the Bird of North America, Vol III 61 MIN
VHS
Audubon Society's Video Guide Series
Color (G)
$29.95 purchase _ #VHX077
Identifies 77 species of pigeons and doves, cuckoos, owls, nighthawks, hummingbirds and swifts, trogons, kingfishers and woodpeckers. Part of a series produced by the Audubon Society which combines bird sights and sounds for accurate identification of 505 species. Includes computer - animated range maps which show the breeding and wintering areas for each species, and bird calls and sounds from the Cornell Laboratory of Ornithology.
Science - Natural
Dist - AUDIOE

See, Hear and Identify the Bird of North America, Vol IV - Songbirds I 75 MIN
VHS
Audubon Society's Video Guide Series
Color (G)
$29.95 purchase _ #VHX078
Identifies 98 species of flycatchers, larks, swallows, crows and jays, titmice and chickadees, nuthatches, creepers, wrens, thrushes, waxwings, shrikes, thrashers and vireos. Part of a series produced by the Audubon Society which combines bird sights and sounds for accurate identification of 505 species. Includes computer - animated range maps which show the breeding and wintering areas for each species, and bird calls and sounds from the Cornell Laboratory of Ornithology.
Science - Natural
Dist - AUDIOE

See, Hear and Identify the Bird of North America, Vol V - Songbirds II 80 MIN
VHS
Audubon Society's Video Guide Series
Color (G)
$29.95 purchase _ #VHX079
Identifies 109 species of warblers, orioles and blackbirds, tanagers, grosbeaks, finches, buntings and sparrows. Part of a series produced by the Audubon Society which combines bird sights and sounds for accurate identification of 505 species. Includes computer - animated range maps which show the breeding and wintering areas for each species, and bird calls and sounds from the Cornell Laboratory of Ornithology.
Science - Natural
Dist - AUDIOE

See, Hear - Canada's North Series

Package Four	50 MIN
Package One	50 MIN
Package Three	50 MIN
Package Two	50 MIN

Dist - TVOTAR

See, Hear - the Middle East Series

Architecture	5 MIN
The Bosporus	5 MIN
Istanbul	5 MIN
Jerusalem	5 MIN
A Jewish Identity	5 MIN
Kibbutz	5 MIN
Kurban Bayram	5 MIN
Legacy of the Crusaders	5 MIN
Life in the Desert	5 MIN
Modernization	5 MIN
The Muslim Family	5 MIN
Pearl Diving in the Persian Gulf	5 MIN
Petra	5 MIN
Turkey in Transition	5 MIN

Dist - TVOTAR

See How the Cat Walks 10 MIN
16mm
Color
LC 76-703801
Presents one man's passion for life expressed through his zest for the ancient game of chess.
Guidance and Counseling; Physical Education and Recreation; Sociology
Dist - RYERI **Prod** - RYERI 1975

See how they fit 15 MIN
U-matic / VHS
Dragons, wagons and wax - Set 1 series
Color (K P)
Shows how living things survive in their environment.
Science; Science - Natural
Dist - CTI **Prod** - CTI

See How they Grow
16mm
B&W
Introduces the concept of differential equations. Discusses three methods of solving differential equations.
Mathematics
Dist - OPENU **Prod** - OPENU

See how they grow 15 MIN
VHS / U-matic
Dragons, wagons and wax - Set 1 series
Color (K P)
Shows that all living things undergo developmental changes.
Science; Science - Natural
Dist - CTI **Prod** - CTI

See How they Ran, Pt 1 24 MIN
16mm
Color
Reviews William McKinley's campaign and election in 1896, through the campaigns of Theodore Roosevelt, William Howard Taft, Woodrow Wilson, Warren G Harding, Calvin Coolidge and Herbert Hoover, to the 1932 election of Franklin Delano Roosevelt.
Biography; Civics and Political Systems; History - United States
Dist - REAF **Prod** - INTEXT

See How they Ran, Pt 2 24 MIN
16mm
Color
Highlights the re - election of Franklin Delano Roosevelt in 1936, 1940 and 1944, Harry Truman's surprise win over Thomas E Dewey in 1948, the election of the late war hero Dwight D Eisenhower in 1952 and his landslide re - election in 1956.
Biography; Civics and Political Systems; History - United States
Dist - REAF **Prod** - INTEXT

See How they Ran, Pt 3 24 MIN
16mm
Color
Shows the shifting trends of U S public opinion concerning the United States as a world power, the fears of an atomic holocaust and the growing impact of the electronic communications media on the U S political scene.
Civics and Political Systems; History - United States; Social Science
Dist - REAF **Prod** - INTEXT

See How they Run 30 MIN
VHS
Inside Story Series
Color (G)
$50.00 purchase _ #INST - 406
Documents the activities of press and party officials at an Iowa Democratic Party caucus. Provides a view of the history of the Iowa Democrats. Suggests that an interdependency exists between journalists and politicians. Hosted by Hodding Carter.
Civics and Political Systems; Literature and Drama; Sociology
Dist - PBS

See How We Run 31 MIN
U-matic / VHS / 16mm
Color (J)
Explains ways to prevent common running accidents and injuries to the feet, knees, bones, tendons and ligaments. Outlines methods of diagnosis and treatment.
Physical Education and Recreation
Dist - LUF **Prod** - LUF

See it and Believe it 10 MIN
16mm
Color (P I A)
LC FIA66-1690
Hollywood's jungle compound beasts are put through their paces, apparently for their own amusement. All of the animals want to be king of the beasts and they put on their act for the approval of admiring chimps.
Science - Natural
Dist - AVED **Prod** - AVED 1961

See it My Way 15 MIN
VHS / U-matic
It's Your Move Series
Color (I)
Describes an accident involving a pedestrian, a truck driver and a bike rider. Replays the incident so that each person can see how things look from another person's perspective.
Health and Safety
Dist - AITECH **Prod** - WETN 1977

See 'N Tell Series
Lizard 11 MIN
Silk Moth 7 MIN
Dist - FI

See no Evil 15 MIN
16mm
B&W
LC 77-700029
Documents the difficulties an elderly couple have in working out their relationship. Explores their lifestyle and offers their comments on themselves, their contemporaries, aging, love, life and death.
Health and Safety; Psychology; Religion and Philosophy; Sociology
Dist - FLMLIB **Prod** - CREVAS 1976

See Other Americans Series
Ginger Bread Town 7 MIN
Dist - WEBC

See, Saw, Seems 12 MIN
16mm
Color
Presents an experiment in animation in which the eye of the viewer travels deeper and deeper into each scene, finding new relationships and visual metaphors in what appears at first sight to be a simple scene.
Fine Arts; Industrial and Technical Education; Psychology
Dist - VANBKS **Prod** - VANBKS 1967

See Saw Seems 10 MIN
16mm
B&W (H C A)
Views a writer's portrait microscopically and slowly transforms it into other images through variances in texture and form.
Fine Arts; Industrial and Technical Education
Dist - UWFKD **Prod** - UWFKD 1972

See the cites with CINAHL 12 MIN
VHS
Color (G)
$85.00 purchase
Teaches basic ways to plan and execute a search on the Nursing and Allied Health - CINAHL - database. Includes using the thesaurus, finding and understanding CINAHL citations and building a search strategy for print, CD - ROM, or online.
Education; Health and Safety
Dist - CUMLIN **Prod** - CUMLIN

See the life of Jesus...come alive - Part 1 35 MIN
VHS
Bible walk series
Color (K P I R)
$30.00 rental _ #36 - 83 - 2078
Features Dr Tuell in an introduction to the New Testament. Uses spray paints, learning games and a unique teaching style to present a chronological overview of key Biblical events and to encourage an appreciation for Biblical insights. Utilizes the 26 letters of the alphabet as memory pegs to help children through the New Testament. Produced by Educational Evangelism.
Literature and Drama; Religion and Philosophy
Dist - APH

See the life of Jesus...come alive - Part 2 35 MIN
VHS
Bible walk series
Color (K P I R)
$30.00 rental _ #36 - 84 - 2078
Features Dr Tuell in an introduction to the New Testament. Uses spray paints, learning games and a unique teaching style to present a chronological overview of key Biblical events and to encourage an appreciation for Biblical insights. Features the use of cartoons, spray - painted creations, maps and games in teaching about Jesus. Produced by Educational Evangelism.
Literature and Drama; Religion and Philosophy
Dist - APH

See the life of Paul...come alive 35 MIN
VHS
Bible walk series
Color (K P I R)
$30.00 rental _ #36 - 85 - 2078
Features Dr Tuell in an introduction to the New Testament. Uses spray paints, learning games and a unique teaching style to present a chronological overview of key Biblical events and to encourage an appreciation for Biblical insights. Focuses on the life and travels of the Apostle Paul, who is portrayed by Dr Tuell in full costume. Produced by Educational Evangelism.
Literature and Drama; Religion and Philosophy
Dist - APH

See the Old Testament...come alive - Part 1 35 MIN
VHS
Bible walk series
Color (K P I R)
$30.00 rental _ #36 - 81 - 2078
Features Dr Tuell in an introduction to the Old Testament. Uses spray paints, learning games and a unique teaching style to present a chronological overview of key Biblical events and to encourage an appreciation for Biblical insights. Produced by Educational Evangelism.
Literature and Drama; Religion and Philosophy
Dist - APH

See the Old Testament...come alive - Part 2 35 MIN
VHS
Bible walk series
Color (K P I R)
$30.00 rental _ #36 - 82 - 2078
Features Dr Tuell in an introduction to the Old Testament. Uses spray paints, learning games and a unique teaching style to present a chronological overview of key Biblical events and to encourage an appreciation for Biblical insights. Teaches 27 words which serve as memory pegs to help children through the Old Testament. Produced by Educational Evangelism.
Literature and Drama; Religion and Philosophy
Dist - APH

See - Touch - Feel 29 MIN
16mm
Color
LC 75-702426
Shows how adults and young students learn from professional visual artists to see, touch and feel through prismatic two - dimensional forms and sculpture created from the obsolescent products of junk yards.
Education; Fine Arts
Dist - USNAC **Prod** - NENDOW 1971

See - Touch - Feel 31 MIN
16mm / U-matic / VHS
Color (J)
LC 76-701513
Features artists - in - residence at high schools in Pennsylvania, Minnesota and Colorado demonstrating and discussing their methods of teaching young people. Includes artists Mac Fisher, a watercolorist, Charles Huntington, a Chippewa Indian who creates metal sculpture, and Don Coel, a painter.
Education; Fine Arts
Dist - AIMS **Prod** - CEMREL 1971

See what I Feel - a Blind Child 6 MIN
16mm / U-matic / VHS
Like You, Like Me Series
Color (K P)
Describes the adventures of Laura, a blind girl, as she visits the zoo.
Education; Guidance and Counseling
Dist - EBEC **Prod** - EBEC 1977

See what I mean 28 MIN
VHS
Color (A PRO)
$495.00 purchase, $140.00 rental
Documents the increasingly important role of visual aids in a presentation. Covers all of the most popular visual aids, describing their advantages and disadvantages.
Business and Economics; English Language; Psychology
Dist - VLEARN **Prod** - DARTNL

See what I Say 24 MIN
16mm
Color (J)
LC 81-701376
Presents interviews with hearing - impaired people who reveal the frustration they feel about having limited access to cultural events.
Education; Guidance and Counseling
Dist - FLMLIB **Prod** - FLMLIB 1981

See what I'm saying 31 MIN
VHS
Color; CC (G)
$195.00 purchase, $100.00 rental _ #CN - 090
Follows Patricia, a deaf child from a hearing, Spanish - speaking family, through her first year at the Kendall Demonstration Elementary School of Galluadet University. Illustrates how the acquisition of communication skills, particularly sign language, enhances a child's self - esteem, confidence and family relationships. Reassures parents and teachers that deaf children can become successful communication and active learners whether or not they learn to speak. Produced by Thomas Kaufman.
Education; Guidance and Counseling; Health and Safety; Psychology; Social Science
Dist - FANPRO

See what I'm Saying 15 MIN
U-matic / VHS
Writer's Realm Series
Color (I)
$125.00 purchase
Explores the combining of visual and verbal elements to improve the quality of writing.
English Language; Literature and Drama; Social Science
Dist - AITECH **Prod** - MDINTV 1987

See you again soon - Pt 2 24 MIN
VHS / U-matic
Hotel and restaurant selling - Welcome customer series
Color (A PRO)
$695.00 purchase, $205.00 rental
Focuses on food service and waitstaff. Demonstrates the wrong and right ways to meet and exceed customer expectations. Part 2 of a two - part series on customer service in the hospitality industry.
Business and Economics; Industrial and Technical Education
Dist - VIDART **Prod** - VIDART 1990
VISUCP XICOM
XICOM

See you in court 26 MIN
U-matic / VHS
Color (G)
$249.00, $149.00 purchase _ #AD - 1944
Reveals that Americans in record numbers are turning to courts to solve disagreements. Examines whether the United States is an adversarial society and why people go to court so readily. Considers how mediation can intervene between conflicting parties to promote reconciliation, settlement or compromise.
Civics and Political Systems; Psychology
Dist - FOTH **Prod** - FOTH

See you later - Au revoir 18 MIN
16mm
Color (G)
$50.00 rental
Shows a staged, formally complete, common event - a man leaves an office. Extends the real - time action of 30 seconds to 17.5 minutes on the screen. The sync sound of the typewriter and two voices was slowed down the same amount of time.
Fine Arts
Dist - CANCIN **Prod** - SNOWM 1990

The Seed bank - genes in hibernation 15 MIN
VHS
Fruits of the earth series
Color (G)
$175.00 purchase
Looks at efforts to preserve plant gene pools by seed banks. Considers the threat of stressful conditions such as temperature variations and decreasing water resources

on plant varieties. Part of a series of 15 videos that describe everyday conditions in regions throughout the earth and look at plants available for environmentally sound, economically productive development.
Science - Natural
Dist - LANDMK

Seed Cake Making and General Camp Activity 21 MIN
16mm / U-matic / VHS
People of the Australian Western Desert Series
B&W (H C G T A)
Shows aboriginal women gather woollybutt grass seed near surface pools and return to camp to thresh and pan the seed, grind it into a flour on stones, mix the flour in water, and bake it in hot ashes.
Geography - World; Social Science; Sociology
Dist - PSU **Prod** - PSU 1965

Seed cones and reforestation 23 MIN
16mm
Man and the forest series
Color (J)
LC 76-702995
Illustrates the need for reforestation and shows methods used today to speed the development of new forests, including how seed cones are collected and stored, how seedlings are started, various planting techniques, selective cross - breeding and storing and grafting.
Agriculture; Science - Natural
Dist - MMP **Prod** - MMP 1976

Seed dispersal 11 MIN
16mm / U-matic / VHS
Color (P I) (SPANISH)
Presents a visual report on different types of seedcoats and shows how external agents help each kind become dispersed.
Foreign Language; Science - Natural
Dist - EBEC **Prod** - EBEC 1971

Seed Dispersal 15 MIN
VHS / 16mm
Color (I J)
Discusses such topics as why flowers exist, why there are so many flowers on one plant, what grapes and milkweed have in common, what fruit really is, the complexity of design in nature, different ways seeds are dispersed and what a symbiotic relationship is.
Science - Natural
Dist - MIS **Prod** - MIS 1981

Seed Dispersal 12 MIN
16mm / U-matic / VHS
Many Worlds of Nature Series
Color (I)
Shows the various methods plants use to get their seeds dispersed to continue and spread their species.
Science - Natural
Dist - CORF **Prod** - SCRESC

Seed germination 15 MIN
U-matic / VHS / 16mm
Biology Series Unit 6 - Plant Classification and Physiology; Unit 6 - Plant classification and physiology
Color; B&W (H)
Explains how seeds serve plants in reproduction, distribution and as a device to survive unfavorable climatic periods. Shows how seed germination studies aid biologists in understanding growth, development and metabolism. Time - lapse photography shows germination process.
Foreign Language; Science - Natural
Dist - EBEC **Prod** - EBEC 1960

Seed of Dissent 28 MIN
U-matic / VHS / 16mm
Insight Series
B&W (H C A)
LC 78-705443
Tells of a successful businessman who thinks that he believes in God until his teenage daughter is raped and made pregnant.
Guidance and Counseling; Psychology
Dist - PAULST **Prod** - PAULST 1967

Seeding and Sodding 29 MIN
U-matic
Grounds Maintenance Training Series
Color
Explains turf construction, grading, soil types, fertilizing, sodding and moving. Instructs in proper equipment needed.
Agriculture
Dist - UMITV **Prod** - UMITV 1978

Seedless plants 15 MIN
VHS
Color (J H)
$130.00 purchase _ #A5VH 1042
Journeys through the world of seedless plants. Features biology teacher Jan Mongoven who starts the program by exploring the role that plants play as producers as well as their contribution to the creation of fossil fuels. Examines the evolution of plants from green algae and their adjustment to life on land. Covers the structures and functions of common seedless plants such as bryophyte, mosses, liverworts, horsetails and ferns.
Science - Natural
Dist - CLRVUE **Prod** - CLRVUE 1992

Seeds 10 MIN
VHS
Color (J H)
$60.00 purchase _ #A5VH 1039
Introduces one of the most important and basic elements of botany - seeds and their method of reproduction. Explores seed structure, dormancy, dispersal and germination.
Science - Natural
Dist - CLRVUE **Prod** - CLRVUE

The Seeds 60 MIN
16mm
Color (R)
Follows Hugh Downs as he visits sites which recall the first 600 years of the Christian church. Includes scenes from Rome, Pompeii, Carthage and Istanbul. Compares the similarities between issues facing Christians then and now.
History - World; Religion and Philosophy
Dist - CCNCC **Prod** - NBCTV

Seeds
16mm / U-matic
Color (J)
$550.00, $420.00 purchase, $60 rental
Explains the importance of genetic diversity to the world food supply.
Agriculture; Business and Economics; Health and Safety; Religion and Philosophy; Science - Natural; Social Science
Dist - BULFRG **Prod** - KENCOM 1987

Seeds 29 MIN
Videoreel / VT2
Making Things Grow III Series
Color
Agriculture; Science - Natural
Dist - PBS **Prod** - WGBHTV

Seeds 15 MIN
VHS
Color (H C)
$39.95 purchase _ #49 - 8503 - V
Introduces the seed method of reproduction. Discusses seed structure, dispersal, dormancy and germination. Examines the nature of seed plants and the significance of the seed in the success of plants as terrestrial organisms. Still frame.
Science - Natural
Dist - INSTRU **Prod** - CBSC

Seeds and Nonseeds 15 MIN
U-matic / VHS
Hands on, Grade 1 Series Unit 3 - Classifying; Unit 3 - Classifying
Color (P)
Science; Science - Natural
Dist - AITECH **Prod** - VAOG 1975

Seeds and Seasons 10 MIN
16mm / U-matic / VHS
Color (P I)
$49.95 purchase _ #Q10977
Illustrates the reproductive cycles of plants utilizing stop - motion photography and sunflowers. Features the dropping of seeds in winter; growth with warm weather; function of roots, stems, leaves, and flowers; and the fertilization and growth of new seeds.
Science - Natural
Dist - CF

Seeds and Weeds 13 MIN
U-matic / VHS / 16mm
Scientific Fact and Fun Series
Color (P I)
LC 82-700385
Shows the characteristics of a weed, showing how they spread their seeds and grow.
Science - Natural
Dist - JOU **Prod** - GLDWER 1981

Seeds grow 6 MIN
VHS
Color; PAL (K P)
PdS29
Shows very young children the wonder of the growth of plants from seeds. Portrays two young children, one unable to go out because of a cold, who plant broad beans and cress seeds. Uses time - lapse photography to add an element of magic to the real business of planting seeds against wet blotting paper and in earth. Later the children plant seeds in a country school garden and the resulting flowers are shown.
Science - Natural
Dist - BHA

Seeds Grow into Plants 7 MIN
U-matic / VHS / 16mm
Color (P I)
$190.00 purchase - 16mm, $135.00 purchase - video _ #3941; LC 78-700512
Uses time - lapse photography in tracing the life cycle of a plant. Observes seed types, methods of dispersal and stages of development to explain the basic concepts involved in plant reproduction and growth.
Science - Natural
Dist - CORF **Prod** - CORF 1978

Seeds - How they Germinate 11 MIN
U-matic / VHS / 16mm
Color (I J)
$270.00 purchase - 16 mm, $190.00 purchase - video _ #3111; LC 73-713537
Shows the structure of a seed embryo, seed dispersal, differences between a monocotyledon and a dicotyledon, and the stages in the growth of the seed embryo.
Science - Natural
Dist - CORF **Prod** - CORF 1971

Seeds, Indeed 15 MIN
16mm
Fingermouse, Yoffy and Friends Series
Color (K P I)
LC 73-700445
Shows Yoffy illustrating an animated story about Ivan the impatient gardener with several different types of seeds.
Guidance and Counseling; Literature and Drama
Dist - VEDO **Prod** - BBCTV 1972

The Seeds of Cure 25 MIN
VHS / U-matic
Color
Shows polio vaccine pioneer Dr Jonas Salk and six UC San Diego medical students discussing views on man, medicine and medical research. Presents a look at Salk's cancer research at the Salk Institute in La Jolla, who also notes that 'Although historically mankind has sown the seeds of his own destruction, we also possess the potential for sowing the seeds of cure.'.
Health and Safety
Dist - MEDCOM **Prod** - MEDCOM

Seeds of Destiny 21 MIN
U-matic / VHS / 16mm
B&W
Documents the plight of victims of Nazi Germany's plan to subjugate the populations of adjacent countries by starvation. By the end of the war, millions of children were left without food, clothing or medical attention.
Civics and Political Systems; Geography - World; History - World
Dist - USNAC **Prod** - USAPS

Seeds of Destruction 25 MIN
U-matic / 16mm
CTV Reports Series
Color; Mono (J H C A)
$300.00 film, $250.00 video, $50.00 rental
Examines the effort to slow the drug trade from Mexico by hitting the poppy field within Mexico itself. This program also looks at the problem of synthetic narcotics and how their market is increased as the naturally grown poppy is destroyed.
Sociology
Dist - CTV **Prod** - CTV 1978

Seeds of Discord (1933 to 1936) 24 MIN
16mm / U-matic / VHS
American Chronicles Series
Color (J H C G T A)
$75 rental _ #9814
Shows workers unite behind John L Lewis. Hitler and Mussolini display intentions of conquering the world.
Civics and Political Systems; History - United States; History - World; Social Science
Dist - AIMS **Prod** - AIMS 1986

Seeds of Hate 20 MIN
U-matic / VHS / 16mm
Color (H C A)
Documents how religious fanatics are feeding on the farmers' financial despair and advocating white Christian supremacy.
Religion and Philosophy; Sociology
Dist - CORF **Prod** - ABCTV

Seeds of Health - Resurrection in Guatemala 27 MIN
U-matic / VHS / 16mm
(H A)
Focuses on a rural health project in the mountains of Guatemala which features grassroots para medical workers, women's groups, and low input agricultural development. Highlights the people's desires for self sufficiency.
Geography - World; Health and Safety
Dist - RTVA **Prod** - RTVA 1978

Seeds of life 30 MIN
VHS
Lifesense series
Color; PAL (H C A)
PdS65 purchase; Not available in the United States
Examines human evolution from the point of view of other species. Describes how plants ensure that humans will cultivate them for food crops. Part of the Lifesense series.
Science - Natural
Dist - BBCENE

Seeds of plenty, seeds of sorrow - 5 52 MIN
VHS
Developing stories series
Color (H C G)
$150.00 purchase, $75.00 rental
Documents the effects in India of the highly touted Green Revolution, which is widely regarded as one of the most successful development strategies of the 20th century. Reveals, however, that it has helped to create a new serf class and the dramatic yields of the early years have fallen away in the wake of pesticide poisoning and the short - lived miracle wheat strains. A film by Manjira Datta for Media Workshop - BBC. Part of a six - part series highlighting debates of the Earth Summit.
Agriculture; Civics and Political Systems; Fine Arts; Geography - World; Sociology
Dist - CANCIN **Prod** - BBCTV 1994

Seeds of progress 28 MIN
VHS
Color; PAL (I J H A)
$39.95 purchase _ #30919
Examines a program designed to assist eight million poor farm families in Mexico. Reveals that the poorest farmers work with the Mexican government to increase farm output, extend access to electricity, and build roads, schools and health centers. Shows that the government encourages the farmers to make their own decisions about how resources will be used in their communities. Includes teaching notes.
Agriculture; Business and Economics; Geography - World; Social Science; Sociology
Dist - WB **Prod** - WB

Seeds of Revolution 28 MIN
U-matic / VHS / 16mm
Color
Examines the various sectors of Honduran society through interviews with corporate representatives, military officials, labor leaders, missionaries and peasants. Demonstrates the conflicting demands of agribusiness concerns and the new peasant self - help cooperatives.
Agriculture; History - World
Dist - ICARUS **Prod** - ABCNEW 1979

Seeds of success in Bangladesh 17 MIN
U-matic / VHS / BETA
Color; NTSC; PAL; SECAM (J H C G)
PdS58
Shows the agricultural methods used in Bangladesh on the Indian subcontinent. Includes plowing, sowing, transplanting, irrigating, harvesting and threshing rice. Illustrates agriculture without the use of machines and how humans or oxen provide labor at every stage. Reveals that the fight against flood and famine is led by a British agriculturist. He introduces high - yield rice to a people who had never before used fertilizers, insecticides or line sowing. If the first harvest is a failure, high - yield rice will be discredited and the project a write - off, but it turns out to be a great success and the area becomes self - supporting in food for the first time since the founding of Bangladesh.
Agriculture
Dist - VIEWTH

Seeds of Survival 27 MIN
16mm / U-matic / VHS
Color (H C A)
Follows a Nebraska farm family and their farming neighbors through one year in their lives, from planting through harvest.
Agriculture
Dist - ALTSUL **Prod** - ROBPAM 1983

Seeds of the Sixties 60 MIN
VHS / 16mm
Making Sense of the Sixties Series
Color (G)
$59.95 purchase _ #MSIX - N903
Recreates American society in the Fifties, with its rapidly expanding middle class, suburbs, atmosphere of conservatism and conformity, traditional gender roles, anti - communism and rules. Focuses on the institutionalized prejudice against American blacks which kept them in subservience and poverty. Part of a six - part series on the Sixties.
Civics and Political Systems; History - United States; Sociology
Dist - PBS **Prod** - WETATV 1990

Seeds of Tomorrow 58 MIN
U-matic / VHS
Nova Series
Color (H C A)
Shows how the 'green revolution,' a plan based on advanced agricultural technologies to ensure food for the world, now threatens the supply of food for the future. Originally a NOVA television program.
Agriculture
Dist - CORF **Prod** - WGBHTV 1985

Seeds of Trust 29 MIN
16mm
Color
LC 79-700277
Offers a view of childbirth as a family experience. Follows four families of diverse backgrounds through the experience of childbirth and records their responses to the event. Shows how support is given to the families by trained nurse - midwives who interact with the families with sensitivity and care.
Health and Safety; Sociology
Dist - VICTFL **Prod** - VICTFL 1979

Seeds on the move 14 MIN
VHS
Color; PAL (P I)
PdS29.50 purchase
Uses time - lapse and high speed photography to depict methods of seed dispersal. Includes seeds that travel on the wind, in water, by adhesion and even one that walks along the ground.
Science; Science - Natural
Dist - EMFVL **Prod** - STANF

Seeds Scatter 15 MIN
U-matic / VHS / 16mm
Color (K P)
$49.95 purchase _ #Q10909
Utilizes time - lapse photography to illustrate the variety of ways in which seeds are dispersed. Features the drying of seed pods, catapulted seeds, and seeds which bore into the ground.
Science - Natural
Dist - CF **Prod** - IFFB 1984

Seeds to Grow 22 MIN
16mm
Color (I)
LC 74-701236
Shows several new approaches to agricultural education and research now underway in East Africa under the sponsorship of the University of West Virginia.
Agriculture; Geography - World; Guidance and Counseling
Dist - WVAU **Prod** - WVAU 1973

Seeing 20 MIN
16mm
All that I Am Series
B&W (C A)
Fine Arts; Guidance and Counseling
Dist - NWUFLM **Prod** - MPATI

Seeing 20 MIN
VHS / 16mm
Trail Series
Color (I)
$150.00 purchase, $30.00 rental
Teaches wildlife awareness and appreciation, with an introduction to the difference between wild and domestic animals and casual looking and scientific observation.
Science - Natural
Dist - AITECH **Prod** - KAIDTV 1986

Seeing 50 MIN
VHS
Human brain series
Color (H C A)
PdS99 purchase
Highlights recent advances in knowledge about the brain and its functions relative to sight. Uses case histories to illustrate individuals' triumphs over brain injury. Part of a seven-video set focusing on the self, memory, language, movement, sight, fear, and madness.
Psychology
Dist - BBCENE

Seeing 4 MIN
16mm / U-matic / VHS
Most Important Person - Senses Series
Color (K P I)
Introduces Danny, who doesn't mind his new glasses, when he learns how important eyes are.
Science - Natural
Dist - EBEC **Prod** - EBEC 1972

Seeing & doing - children in Europe 75 MIN
VHS
Color; PAL (K P)
PdS35 purchase
Presents five programs of 15 minutes each portraying children from different social and ethnic backgrounds, from rural and urban communities. Includes a blind child. Shows that the differences of the individuals are many, but the factors they have in common are enormous. Encourages viewers to relate to others and places beyond their own immediate experience. Contact distributor about availability outside the United Kingdom.
Education; Social Science; Sociology
Dist - ACADEM

Seeing & doing - design and technology 75 MIN
VHS
Color; PAL (K P)
PdS35 purchase
Presents five programs of 15 minutes each looking at recent developments in science and technology projects for primary school children. Takes a familiar object as an example of everyday technology in each program, and eavesdrops on a primary school classroom where children are busy designing and making their various projects. Contact distributor about availability outside the United Kingdom.
Business and Economics; Education; Science
Dist - ACADEM

Seeing & doing - history 75 MIN
VHS
Color; PAL (K P)
PdS35 purchase
Presents five programs of 15 minutes each introducing history to youngsters as an activity, involving problem solving and investigation. Begins with concepts within the experience of most children and enables schools to develop projects using first - hand historical evidence available in and around the school. Contact distributor about availability outside the United Kingdom.
Education
Dist - ACADEM

Seeing & doing - music 75 MIN
VHS
Color; PAL (K P)
PdS35 purchase
Helps inspire and motivate children towards awareness and a real feeling for music. Features five programs of 15 minutes each. Contact distributor about availability outside the United Kingdom.
Education; Fine Arts
Dist - ACADEM

Seeing & doing - technology 75 MIN
VHS
Color; PAL (K P)
PdS35 purchase
Presents five programs of 15 minutes each covering technology, history, media studies, geography and science. Offers ideas for projects to be pursued in and out of the classroom, around the theme of making things move. Introduces children to people and places outside the children's direct experience using links and similarities to a child's everyday activities. Contact distributor about availability outside the United Kingdom.
Business and Economics; Education; Geography - World; Science
Dist - ACADEM

Seeing and not seeing 30 MIN
VHS
Gospel of Mark series
Color (J H C G A R)
$39.95 purchase, $10.00 rental _ #35 - 819 - 2076
Features New Testament scholar Dr Donald Juel in a historical and cultural consideration of the Gospel of Mark. Produced by Seraphim.
Literature and Drama; Religion and Philosophy
Dist - APH

Seeing beyond the obvious - understanding 40 MIN
perception in everyday and novel environments
VHS
Color (H C)
$14.95 purchase _ #NA201
Looks at the physiological and psychological basis for human perception. Investigates primary depth cues; secondary depth cues and motion depth cues. Covers virtual reality, vestivular systems, the physiology of the eye, depth, convergence, stereopsis and linear perspective. Uses animation to illustrate principles.
Psychology; Science - Natural
Dist - INSTRU **Prod** - NASA

The Seeing Eye 25 MIN
U-matic / VHS
Color
Explains how to safeguard sight in children and adults. Warns about the adult diseases of glaucoma and cataracts and the threats to children's sight of strabismus or amblyopia.
Health and Safety; Science - Natural
Dist - MEDCOM **Prod** - MEDCOM

Seeing God at Christmas 18 MIN
16mm
Seeing God Series
Color
LC 74-702513
Shows a variety of Christmas customs as practiced in the Moravian community in Bethlehem, Pennsylvania.
Religion and Philosophy; Sociology
Dist - FAMF **Prod** - FAMF 1974

Seeing God in Mountain Forests 11 MIN
16mm
Color (P)
Portrays a family spending a day together in the mountain forests. Provides a setting in which children can gain some new appreciation for the wonder of God's creation. Presents popular children's songs including All Things Bright and Beautiful and Thank You.
Fine Arts; Guidance and Counseling; Religion and Philosophy; Sociology
Dist - FAMF **Prod** - FAMF

Seeing God in Signs of Love 10 MIN
16mm
Color (P)
Celebrates the joy of family relationships.
Guidance and Counseling; Religion and Philosophy; Sociology
Dist - FAMF **Prod** - FAMF

Seeing God in the City 14 MIN
16mm
Seeing God Series
Color
LC 74-700111
Shows a group of children journeying throughout the city and experiencing elements of God's world in an urban setting.
Religion and Philosophy; Sociology
Dist - FAMF **Prod** - FAMF 1974

Seeing God Series
Seeing God at Christmas 18 MIN
Seeing God in the City 14 MIN
Dist - FAMF

Seeing God through your parents' eyes and being a peacemaker in your home - Tape 1 60 MIN
VHS
How to get along with your parents series
Color (J H R)
$10.00 rental _ #36 - 876001 - 533
Features Christian youth speaker Dawson McAllister discussing teenagers and their relationship with their parents. Consists of two 30 - minute segments which outline the importance of having a good relationship with parents and consider how teenagers can play the role of peacemaker in the family.
Religion and Philosophy; Sociology
Dist - APH **Prod** - WORD

Seeing is Beautiful 10 MIN
U-matic / VHS
Color
Describes the plastic lens implant procedure for treatment of a cataract.
Health and Safety
Dist - WFP **Prod** - WFP

Seeing is Believing 14 MIN
16mm / U-matic / VHS
Color (J)
LC 79-701803
Illustrates how the human eye can be deceived. Provides examples of confusing activity, optical illusion and misdirection of movement to show how visual perception can be distorted.
Science - Natural
Dist - MCFI **Prod** - NILLU 1977

Seeing is Believing 10 MIN
16mm
Color
LC 81-700421
Spoofs media reports on such topics as incredible inventions and unbelievable world records. Suggests that what is seen is not necessarily to be believed.
Fine Arts; Sociology
Dist - SIPOM **Prod** - SIPOM 1980

Seeing is believing - eye safety 16 MIN
U-matic / BETA / VHS
Color (IND G)
$395.00 purchase _ #600 - 08
Explains the physiology of the eye. Reviews four common categories hazardous to the eye along with the correct protective devices and procedures for guarding against injury.
Health and Safety; Industrial and Technical Education; Psychology; Science - Natural
Dist - ITSC **Prod** - ITSC

Seeing is Deceiving 29 MIN
Videoreel / VT2
Observing Eye Series
Color
Science - Physical; Sociology
Dist - PBS **Prod** - WGBHTV

Seeing Like an Artist - Vegetables 10 MIN
16mm
Color
LC 73-702418
Uses macrocinematography of a variety of vegetables in order to emphasize their different kinds of color, form, shape, texture and design.
Fine Arts; Industrial and Technical Education
Dist - SF **Prod** - MNDLIN 1973

Seeing sense 30 MIN
VHS / U-matic
Supersense series
Color (H C)
$250.00 purchase _ #HP - 5802C
Explains how and what animals really see. Compares the visual abilities of various species with human abilities. Part of a series which deals with different facets of animal awareness.
Psychology; Science - Natural
Dist - CORF **Prod** - BBCTV 1989

Seeing Sound - the Process of Captioning 8 MIN
VHS / U-matic
Captioned; Color (S)
Depicts the videotape captioning process from transcription to final production. Notes educational benefits for deaf students.
Guidance and Counseling; Psychology
Dist - GALCO **Prod** - GALCO 1980

Seeing the soul 30 MIN
BETA / VHS
Developing intuition series
Color (G)
$29.95 purchase _ #S400
States that psychic abilities are a natural function of the soul and spirit, while intellect is a natural function of the ego. Features Carol Dyer, psychic consultant. Part of a four - part series on developing intuition.
Psychology; Religion and Philosophy
Dist - THINKA **Prod** - THINKA

Seeing the World 24 MIN
16mm
B&W
Depicts the Little Rascals gang travelling though Europe.
Fine Arts
Dist - RMIBHF **Prod** - ROACH 1927

Seeing through arithmetic series
Basic math principles 24 MIN
Computation 27 MIN
Division 27 MIN
Dist - CDIAND

Seeing through commercials 15 MIN
VHS / U-matic / 16mm
Color; Captioned (K P I)
$340.00, $270.00, $240.00 purchase _ #A337
Alerts children to the techniques and motivations behind TV commercials. Shows how close - up shots, camera angles, lighting and special effects can make products seem bigger and more exciting than they really are. Reveals that important product information and disclaimers are often hidden. Includes a special commercial for children to analyze.
Business and Economics; Fine Arts; Sociology
Dist - BARR **Prod** - VISF 1982

Seeing windows 28 MIN
VHS
Color (G)
$190.00 purchase, $50.00 rental
Travels to Honduras to demonstrate how self - help programs have helped to alleviate problems of poverty and housing in rural areas.
Fine Arts; Geography - World; Sociology
Dist - FIRS **Prod** - HARROB 1987

Seeing with Sound 8 MIN
16mm / U-matic / VHS
Color
LC 79-701524
Focuses on a technique for improving tunneling methods, which uses acoustical holography to 'see' through rock.
Science - Physical; Social Science
Dist - AMEDFL **Prod** - NSF 1975

Seeing with sound - acoustical holography - 10
U-matic / VHS / BETA
Search encounters in science series
Color; PAL (G H C)
PdS25, PdS33 purchase
Brings modern research efforts of the world's leading scientists into the classroom. Features one of a series of 24 mini - documentaries. Each film is 5 - 7 minutes in length.
Industrial and Technical Education; Science; Science - Physical
Dist - EDPAT **Prod** - NSF

Seeing with the camera 30 MIN
VHS
Photographic vision series
Color (G)
$49.95 purchase _ #RM104V-F
Compares human vision with that of the camera. Presents the technical aspects of photography clearly and simply, including principles of the camera and techniques for controlling exposure, the use of various kinds of lighting, selection of appropriate lenses and film and basic darkroom techniques. Focuses on the world of photographers and photography - its history and evolution, its uses for personal development and expression, and the impact of photography on the world. Part of a 20-part series examining all aspects of the field of photography.
Industrial and Technical Education
Dist - CAMV **Prod** - COAST
CDTEL

Seek and Speak 30 MIN
U-matic
Read all about it - One Series
Color (I)
Teaches reading and writing skills as it continues a story in which Chris's friend Lynn writes a speech to help preserve King's Park and Sam and Chris are trapped in an old factory by Duneedon.
Education; English Language; Literature and Drama
Dist - TVOTAR **Prod** - TVOTAR 1982

Seeking Community I - the North 1877 - 1900 29 MIN
Videoreel / VT2
Black Experience Series
Color
History - United States
Dist - PBS **Prod** - WTTWTV

Seeking Community II - the South 1877 - 1900 29 MIN
Videoreel / VT2
Black Experience Series
Color
History - United States
Dist - PBS **Prod** - WTTWTV

Seeking Community III - the Exodus 29 MIN
Videoreel / VT2
Black Experience Series
Color
History - United States; Sociology
Dist - PBS **Prod** - WTTWTV

Seeking Community IV - African Exodus 29 MIN
Videoreel / VT2
Black Experience Series
Color
History - United States
Dist - PBS **Prod** - WTTWTV

Seeking Community V - the Migration 29 MIN
Videoreel / VT2
Black Experience Series
Color
Sociology
Dist - PBS **Prod** - WTTWTV

Seeking help - but where? 30 MIN
U-matic / VHS
Contemporary health issues series; Lesson 3
Color (C A)
Looks at four different approaches to therapy. Includes biological, behaviorist, intrapsychic and humanist. Provides guidelines for seeking mental health services.
Health and Safety; Psychology
Dist - CDTEL **Prod** - SCCON

Seeking New Laws 58 MIN
16mm
Character of Physical Law Series
B&W (H C A)
LC 70-707489
Features Professor Richard Feynman, California Institute of Technology, who summarizes the state of our knowledge of the physical world and points up some existing mysteries. He discusses the methods used to seek new laws, the art of guessing. The development and trials of some present laws are used as examples.
Science; Science - Physical
Dist - EDC **Prod** - BBCTV 1965

Seeking Permission - Li Desu Ka 28 MIN
U-matic / VHS
Japanese for Beginners Series
Color (C) (JAPANESE)
$249.00, $149.00 purchase _ #AD - 2103
Deals with the unspoken rules of behavior acceptable to Japanese. Shows what is permitted and not permitted in a given situation. Illustrates the appropriate verbalizations. Part of the Japanese for Beginners Series.
Foreign Language; Geography - World; History - World; Psychology; Social Science; Sociology
Dist - FOTH **Prod** - FOTH

Seeking the first Americans 60 MIN
16mm / VHS
Odyssey series
Color (G)
LC 81-700372
Examines the theories of archaeologists who are searching for clues to the identity of the first people to reach North America between 11,000 and 50,000 years ago.
Science - Physical; Sociology
Dist - DOCEDR **Prod** - PBA 1980
PBS

Seen but not Heard 13 MIN
16mm
Color
LC 80-700840
Focuses on the rights of children as set down by the United Nations. Explores the child's point of view and what each child would like to change.
Civics and Political Systems; Sociology
Dist - TASCOR **Prod** - NSWF 1978

See'n tell series

Australian animals	8 MIN
Birds on a seashore	10 MIN
Blackbird Family	12 MIN
Butterfly	8 MIN
Carp in a marsh	7 MIN
Shepherd dog and his flock	8 MIN

Dist - FI

A Segment of Arel 3 MIN
16mm
B&W (G)
$5.00 rental
Tells the story of a deep friendship in which a man carries his confused, emotional state to the bedside of a sick friend. Affirms the somber fidelity between them. Produced by Paul Heilemann.
Fine Arts
Dist - CANCIN

Segmental pulmonary resection 21 MIN
16mm
Color (PRO)
Illustrates the technique of the removal of different individual and groups of pulmonary segments of both upper and lower lobes. Shows the important steps of segmental hilar dissection, treatment of the vascular and bronchial elements and the dissection of the intersegmental plane.
Health and Safety
Dist - ACY **Prod** - ACYDGD 1950

Segmental ureteral achalasia 14 MIN
16mm
Color
Illustrates Dr Victor A Politano's method of handling a large, dilated ureter secondary to ureteral achalasia. Shows that the achalasic segment is resected, the ureter is reduced by removing a longitudinal strip from its entire length and the distal end is reimplanted into the bladder by submucosal tunnel technique.
Health and Safety; Science
Dist - EATONL **Prod** - EATONL 1971

Segmentation - the Annelid Worms 16 MIN
U-matic / VHS / 16mm
Biology (Spanish Series Unit 7 - Animal Classification and 'Physiology; Unit 7 - Animal classification and physiology
Color (H) (SPANISH)
Describes the structure and functions of the segmented worm body systems and shows that the segmented annelid worm represents an important evolutionary development. Illustrates the major classes of the phylum Annelida.
Foreign Language; Science - Natural
Dist - EBEC **Prod** - EBEC

Segmentation - the Annelid Worms 16 MIN
U-matic / VHS / 16mm
Biology Series Unit 7 - Animal Classification and Physiology; Unit 7 - Animal classification and physiology
Color (H) (SPANISH)
Shows the structure and functions of the nervous, digestive and reproductive systems of the earthworm using animated drawings. Illustrates the annelid worm's part in evolution, and the major classes of phylum annelida.
Science - Natural
Dist - EBEC **Prod** - EBEC 1962

The Segmented invertebrates - Pt 5 30 MIN
16mm
Life on Earth series - Vol II; Vol II
Color (J)
$495.00 purchase _ #865 - 9026
Blends scientific data with breathtaking wildlife photography to tell the story of the development of life. Features wildlife expert David Attenborough as host. Part 5 of 27 parts, 'The Segmented Invertebrates,' considers life forms that evolved before insects.
Science; Science - Natural; Science - Physical
Dist - FI **Prod** - BBCTV 1981

The Segovia Legacy 60 MIN
VHS
Color (G)
$29.95 purchase _ #1290
Presents a tribute to classical guitar master Andres Segovia, including rare film footage of the maestro in performance. Hugh Downs narrates.
Fine Arts
Dist - KULTUR

Segovia - the Mirror of Spanish History 35 MIN
U-matic / VHS
Color (C)
$279.00, $179.00 purchase _ #AD - 2148
Chronicles the history of Segovia from the Romans, who built the original walled fortress, through growth in Visigothic times, to its existence as a rich and powerful city in the Spain of the Middle Ages.
Geography - World; History - World
Dist - FOTH **Prod** - FOTH

Segurid Y Salud 17 MIN
VHS
Baby Care Workshop Series
Color (I J H A) (SPANISH)
$175.00 purchase
Presents a version of Safe and Sound. Helps parents understand how to create a safe environment for an infant. Considers home environment, transportation and accident prevention in daily activities.
Guidance and Counseling; Health and Safety; Home Economics; Social Science; Sociology
Dist - PROPAR **Prod** - PROPAR 1988

Seguridad - Control De Perdidas Totales 10 MIN
U-matic / VHS / 16mm
Color (IND) (SPANISH)
Presents a version of the motion picture Safety - Total Loss Control. Points out that industry must direct its accident prevention efforts toward all incidents which might lead to injury of employees. Notes that fire prevention, theft prevention, reduction in pollution and improvement in industrial health and hygiene are of particular importance to loss control.
Business and Economics; Health and Safety
Dist - IFB **Prod** - IAPA 1972

Seikan Undersea Tunnel, Pt 1 32 MIN
16mm
Color
Presents a documentary of the work involved in constructing the longest undersea tunnel in the world, designed as a fundamental solution to link Honshu and Hokkaido by rail.
Geography - World; Industrial and Technical Education; Social Science
Dist - UNIJAP **Prod** - UNIJAP 1967

Seiko at School 7 MIN
16mm
Exploring Childhood Series
Color (J)
LC 76-703946
Shows Seiko fingerpainting and playing with friends on the school playground.
Education; Psychology; Social Science; Sociology
Dist - EDC **Prod** - EDC 1975

Seismic Reflection Processing 35 MIN
VHS / 16mm
Sedimentary Processes and Basin Analysis Series
Color (C)
$150.00, $185.00 purchase _ #269509
Illustrates the key concepts, economic relevance and influence of measurement technology advances in palaeoenvironmental and basin analysis. Observes how large parts of the earth's crust subside and accumulate thick deposits of sediments, possible reservoirs for oil, gas and coal. Divides into four themes - Sedimentary Petrology, Sedimentary Environments, Basin Analysis and North Sea - Western Canada Case Studies. 'Seismic Reflection Processing' uses animation to explain the steps involved in processing seismic data recorder on or sea to ensure that the information can be reliably interpreted. Shot on location at Shell's Exploration and Production Department in London, where discussions center on the North Sea operations.
Business and Economics; Geography - World; Industrial and Technical Education; Science - Physical; Social Science
Dist - ACCESS **Prod** - BBCTV 1987

Seismic Stratigraphy 49 MIN
VHS / 16mm
Sedimentary Processes and Basin Analysis Series
Color (C)
$150.00, $185.00 purchase _ #269510
Illustrates the key concepts, economic relevance and influence of measurement technology advances in palaeoenvironmental and basin analysis. Observes how large parts of the earth's crust subside and accumulate thick deposits of sediments, possible reservoirs for oil, gas and coal. Divides into four themes - Sedimentary Petrology, Sedimentary Environments, Basin Analysis and North Sea - Western Canada Case Studies. 'Seismic Stratigraphy' considers the branch of geology that studies the arrangement of layered rock formations, enhanced by the seismic technique of determining the correct sequence of stratification, even in areas where folding, faulting or erosion has taken place. This will establish a consistent geochronology for the entire earth.
Geography - World; Science - Physical
Dist - ACCESS **Prod** - BBCTV 1987

Seismology - Moving Earth 18 MIN
U-matic / VHS
Color (H C A)
Explores the science of seismology, which is helping predict earthquake and volcanic activity.
Science - Physical
Dist - JOU **Prod** - UPI

Seismos '83 15 MIN
U-matic / VHS
Color (PRO)
Shows a simulated demonstration of the city emergency plan in the simulated aftermath of an earthquake recorded during the International Earthquake Conference in Los Angeles, shows a a simulated demonstration of the city emergency plan in the in the simulated aftermath of an earthquake.
Health and Safety; Social Science
Dist - FILCOM **Prod** - LACFD

Seizure 15 MIN
VHS / U-matic
Color
Deals with a chronic disease, characterized by convulsions and unconsciousness. Shows a strobe light on the faceplate.
Health and Safety
Dist - KITCHN **Prod** - KITCHN

Seizure precautions 11 MIN
VHS
Color (PRO C)
$200.00 purchase, $60.00 rental _ #4393
Explains what a seizure is and educates hospital and long - term care workers on how to best protect the patient having a seizure. Explains the different types of seizures and appropriate patient care response to each type. Stresses seizure safety and the importance of a complete patient assessment. Includes patient education and support.
Health and Safety
Dist - AJN

Seizure - the Story of Kathy Morris 104 MIN
U-matic / VHS
Color (H C A)
Tells of a young music student suddenly afflicted with a brain tumor, the brilliant neurosurgeon in whose hands her life is placed, and the anguish and struggle both patient and doctor must endure when the patient comes out of the operation unable to read or count. Stars Leonard Nimoy and Penelope Milford.
Fine Arts; Health and Safety
Dist - TIMLIF **Prod** - TIMLIF 1983

Seizures 19 MIN
U-matic / VHS
Color (C)
$249.00, $149.00 purchase _ #AD - 1465
Explores how epilepsy is diagnosed and treated. Shows how an EEG measures the electrical activity of the brain and how CAT and RMI scans take pictures of the brain. Shows what to do for someone experiencing a seizure.
Health and Safety; Psychology; Science - Natural
Dist - FOTH **Prod** - FOTH

Seizures 10 MIN
U-matic / VHS
Children's Medical Series
Color (P I)
Explains some of the signs that may precede a seizure, what it may feel like to have a seizure and what should be done for the person having a seizure.
Health and Safety
Dist - CORF **Prod** - HFDT 1982

Sejour En France Series
Arrivee En France 11 MIN
Le Marais 13 MIN
Le Musee Grevin 12 MIN
L'Ile De La Cite 12 MIN
Un Hotel a Paris 11 MIN
Un Repas Chez Francis 11 MIN
Dist - IFB

Selamat Datang 'Welcome to Indonesia' 27 MIN
16mm
Color (C A)
LC FIA68-817
Describes the contrasts of Indonesia, a nation of old kingdoms blending with the republic's modernization. Shows views of temples, scenery, dances and gold and silver handicrafts.
Geography - World; Sociology
Dist - MCDO **Prod** - GARUDA 1967

Selbe - One among many 30 MIN
16mm / VHS
As Women See it - Global Feminism Series
Color (G)
$500.00, $250.00 purchase, $60.00 rental
Offers a view of daily life in Senegal, West Africa. Focuses on the social role and economic responsibility of women in African society. Part of a series of films by and about women in Third World countries which include English voice over.
Fine Arts; Geography - World; History - United States; Sociology
Dist - WMEN **Prod** - FAUST

Selbstverstummelung - self - mutilation 6 MIN
16mm
B&W (A)
$10.00 rental
Emphasizes the surrealistic drama of symbolic self - destruction. Reveals a man covered in white plaster lying surrounded by razor blades and surgical instruments, which are gradually inserted into him in a ritualistic self - operation.
Fine Arts
Dist - CANCIN **Prod** - KRENKU 1965

Select - O - Matic Nozzles - the Original Thinking Nozzles 23 MIN
VHS
Color (G PRO)
$25.00 purchase _ #35377
Illustrates types of automatic nozzles, design construction and materials, flow ranges for different types of automatic nozzles and hose sizes, and the operation and maintenance of automatic nozzles. Trains firefighters.
Agriculture; Health and Safety; Industrial and Technical Education; Psychology; Science - Physical; Social Science
Dist - OKSU

Selected Communication Tasks during the Trial 50 MIN
U-matic / VHS
Effective Communication in the Courtroom Series
Color (PRO)
Explores special problems trial advocates face during voir dire, opening statements, direct and cross - examination and the closing argument. Gives suggestions for making a favorable impression during jury selection, establishing credibility with the jury and persuading through effective communication.
Civics and Political Systems; Psychology; Social Science
Dist - ABACPE **Prod** - ABACPE

Selected communication tasks during the trial 50 MIN
VHS
Effective communication in the courtroom series
Color (C PRO)
$100.00 purchase _ #ZCX03
Features University of Nevada professor Gordon Zimmerman in a discussion of courtroom communication tasks.
Civics and Political Systems
Dist - NITA **Prod** - NITA 1982

Selected films - 1979 - 1988 - Gary Adlestein 39 MIN
VHS
Color & B&W (G)
$60.00 purchase
Presents a set of nine productions made between 1979 - 1988. Includes selections from Optical Lyrics - Swan Boat, an impressionistic image from the Boston Public Gardens; and Pie Plates, an experimental film using images of metal pie plates. Continues with selections from M - 95 Miniatures - Shadow Hunting, an impressionistic cine - painting of the filmmaker out with his dog looking for rabbits; Amish, portrays a quiet shopping center parking lot; Woodswalk, in Oley Valley. Concord, looks at a pool in the Catskills; and Fontana, a self - portrait of the filmmaker as a grotesque Roman fountain. See S - 8 Diaries, also available in 16mm format, for description.
Fine Arts
Dist - CANCIN **Prod** - ADLEST
FLMKCO

Selected films - Dana Plays 35 MIN
VHS
Color (G)
$35.00 purchase
Features five productions by Dana Plays, 1978 - 1988. Includes Arrow Creek, a neo - Western filmed at Crow Agency, Montana, in which the Indians are cowboys; Don't Means Do, a simple encounter between the moods of child and adult; Shards, questions ideas of wholeness and reconstruction in the film form. See individual titles for descriptions of Via Rio and Across the Border.
Fine Arts; Literature and Drama; Psychology; Social Science
Dist - CANCIN

Selected issues in using expert witnesses 240 MIN
VHS / U-matic
Color (PRO)
Focuses on securing the right person as an expert witness, preparing the expert to testify, appproaching attorney work product issues and discovering the opponent's expert witness and information.
Civics and Political Systems
Dist - ABACPE **Prod** - CCEB
ALIABA ALIABA
CCEB

Selected Sonnets by Shakespeare 40 MIN
VHS / U-matic
Color
Analyzes four examples of Shakespeare's sonnets including Sonnet 65, Sonnet 66, Sonnet 94 and Sonnet 127.
Literature and Drama
Dist - FOTH **Prod** - FOTH 1984

Selected Speeches of Franklin Delano Roosevelt - Navy and Total Defense Day Address 26 MIN
16mm / U-matic / VHS
B&W (H A)
Presents a critical speech given by Roosevelt on October 27, 1941, in which he revealed information about Nazi activities. Discusses the historical significance of the speech in light of the Nazi attacks on American ships in September and October 1941.
Biography; English Language; History - United States; History - World
Dist - USNAC **Prod** - USNAC 1941

Selected Speeches of Franklin Delano Roosevelt - State of the Union Message 42 MIN
16mm / U-matic / VHS
B&W (H A)
Presents a speech given by Roosevelt on January 6, 1942, one month after Pearl Harbor. Discusses the history of the Axis powers and their conquests in the 1930's, the monetary cost of the war for the United States and the possibility of an ultimate victory against the Axis powers.
Biography; English Language; History - United States; History - World
Dist - USNAC **Prod** - USNAC 1942

Selected Surgical Approaches to Testis, Bladder, and Prostatic Cancers 38 MIN
16mm
Visits in Urology Series
Color
LC 79-700278
Shows surgery on the bladder and prostate, demonstrating the I - 25 implant. Reviews past techniques and comments on developments in the future.
Health and Safety
Dist - EATONL **Prod** - EATONL 1978

Selected Surgical Approaches to Testis, Bladder, and Prostatic Cancers, Pt 1 19 MIN
16mm
Visits in Urology Series
Color
LC 79-700278
Shows surgery on the bladder and prostate, demonstrating the I - 25 implant. Reviews past techniques and comments on developments in the future.
Health and Safety
Dist - EATONL **Prod** - EATONL 1978

Selected survey of decision - Making procedures for groups
U-matic / VHS
Decision analysis series
Color
Industrial and Technical Education; Mathematics
Dist - MIOT **Prod** - MIOT

Selected topics in chemistry 120 MIN
U-matic / VHS
Engineer - in - training review series
Color
Covers selected topics such as ideal gases, balance sets, electrochemistry, Dalton's Law, vapor pressure and chemical reaction. Presented in two one - hour segments.
Industrial and Technical Education; Science - Physical
Dist - UIDEEO **Prod** - UIDEEO

Selected topics in dynamics
Engineer - in - training review series
Color
Covers fundamental principles, theorems and several kinematic and kinetic problems. Includes velocity, acceleration, work energy and variable mass. Divided into two one - hour segments.
Industrial and Technical Education; Science - Physical
Dist - UIDEEO **Prod** - UIDEEO

Selected topics in electric circuits 120 MIN
U-matic / VHS
Engineer - in - training review series
Color
Focuses on several aspects of both AC and DC circuits. Divided into two one - hour segments.
Industrial and Technical Education
Dist - UIDEEO **Prod** - UIDEEO

Selected topics in engineering economy 120 MIN
VHS / U-matic
Engineer - in - training review series
Color
Stresses that the purpose of engineering economic analysis is to assure optimum use of invested capital and realize the greatest possible return. Includes several economic aspects. Divided into two one - hour segments.
Business and Economics; Industrial and Technical Education
Dist - UIDEEO **Prod** - UIDEEO

Selected topics in fluid 120 MIN
VHS / U-matic
Engineer - in - training review series
Color
Focuses on fluid statics, fluid dynamics and dimensional analysis. Presented in two one - hour segments.
Industrial and Technical Education; Science - Physical
Dist - UIDEEO **Prod** - UIDEEO

Selected topics in mechanics of materials 120 MIN
U-matic / VHS
Engineer - in - training review series
Color
Gives a review of several topics including uniaxial deformation, stress - strain relationships, torsion, bending and buckling. Divided into two one - hour parts.
Industrial and Technical Education; Science - Physical
Dist - UIDEEO **Prod** - UIDEEO

Selected topics in statics 120 MIN
U-matic / VHS
Engineer - in - training review series
Color
Includes fundamental principles, theorems and basic equations, and several problems such as equivalent systems and resultant friction and moment of inertia. Divided into two one - hour parts.
Industrial and Technical Education; Science - Physical
Dist - UIDEEO **Prod** - UIDEEO

Selected topics in systems theory 120 MIN
VHS / U-matic
Engineer - in - training review series
Color
Includes definitions of systems, Laplace transforms review, signal flow graph theory review state variable concepts, classical control systems performance, linear systems compensation techniques and a review. Divided into two one - hour parts.
Industrial and Technical Education
Dist - UIDEEO **Prod** - UIDEEO

Selected topics in thermodynamics 120 MIN
VHS / U-matic
Engineer - in - training review series
Color
Covers thermodynamics as the science of energy and its transformations. Includes energy forms, transfer qualities, the thermodynamic system, equilibrium and properties. Divided in two one - hour parts.
Industrial and Technical Education; Science - Physical
Dist - UIDEEO **Prod** - UIDEEO

Selected Tutti Passages from the Symphonic Literature 30 MIN
VHS / U-matic
Cello Sounds of Today Series
Color (J H A)
Fine Arts
Dist - IU **Prod** - IU 1984

Selected works 1980 - the Cough, Secrets I'll Never Tell, the Shot Heard Round the World 9 MIN
U-matic / VHS
Color
Complete title reads Selected Works 1980 - The Cough, Secrets I'll Never Tell, The Shot Heard Round The World, Rabbit Rabid Rawbit, This Video No Good. Pokes fun at everything from medical etiquette to prevalent truisms. Presented by Teddy Dibble and Peter Keenan.
Fine Arts; Literature and Drama
Dist - ARTINC **Prod** - ARTINC

Selecting a Good Child Care Program 26 MIN
VHS / U-matic
Focus on Children Series
Color (C A)
LC 81-707445
Presents a specialist in early childhood education defining the characteristics of quality child care outside the home and compare the features of three types of child care including the nursery school, the day - care center and the day - care home.
Home Economics; Psychology
Dist - IU **Prod** - IU 1981

Selecting a jury 57 MIN
VHS
Winning at trial series
Color (C PRO)
$115.00 purchase, $95.00 rental _ #WAT01
Uses a wrongful death case to teach the skills of trial advocacy. Covers the strategies involved in selecting a jury. Includes excerpts from the trial, comments from the lawyers involved, and critiques.
Civics and Political Systems; Education
Dist - NITA **Prod** - NITA 1986

Selecting a Jury - a Critique 60 MIN
U-matic
Picking and Persuading a Jury Series Program 2
Color (PRO)
LC 81-706167
Features a panel critiquing the performances of attorneys who have just completed a voir dire. Offers suggestions on analyzing and communicating with a panel of jurors.
Civics and Political Systems
Dist - ABACPE **Prod** - ABACPE 1980

Selecting a Jury - a Demonstration 150 MIN
U-matic
Picking and Persuading a Jury Series Program 1
Color (PRO)
LC 81-706166
Demonstrates the methods attorneys for both sides in a case use to select a jury in a civil suit.
Civics and Political Systems
Dist - ABACPE **Prod** - ABACPE 1980

Selecting a Jury - a Demonstration, Pt 1 50 MIN
U-matic
Picking and Persuading a Jury Series Program 1
Color (PRO)
LC 81-706166
Demonstrates attorneys' methods for selecting a jury in a civil suit.
Civics and Political Systems
Dist - ABACPE **Prod** - ABACPE 1980

Selecting a Jury - a Demonstration, Pt 2 50 MIN
U-matic
Picking and Persuading a Jury Series Program 1
Color (PRO)
LC 81-706166
Demonstrates attorneys' methods for selecting a jury in a civil suit.
Civics and Political Systems
Dist - ABACPE **Prod** - ABACPE 1980

Selecting a Jury - a Demonstration, Pt 3 50 MIN
U-matic
Picking and Persuading a Jury Series Program 1
Color (PRO)
LC 81-706166
Demonstrates attorneys' methods for selecting a jury in a civil suit.
Civics and Political Systems
Dist - ABACPE **Prod** - ABACPE 1980

Selecting a Pattern for a Coat 29 MIN
Videoreel / VT2
Sewing Skills - Tailoring Series
Color
Features Mrs Ruth Hickman showing how to select a pattern for a coat.
Fine Arts; Home Economics
Dist - PBS **Prod** - KRMATV

Selecting an adequate diet 47 MIN
VHS
Introductory principles of nutrition series
Color (C PRO G)
$70.00 purchase, $16.00 rental _ #50696
Presents food composition tables, recommended dietary allowances and enrichment and fortification programs. Part of a 20 - part series on basic principles of nutrition, evaluation of dietary intake, nutritional status, nutrition through the life cycle and world food supplies.
Health and Safety; Social Science
Dist - PSU **Prod** - WPSXTV 1979

Selecting an Investigation 15 MIN
VHS / U-matic
Sci - Fair Series
Color (J)
Provides ideas for research projects for science fairs.
Science
Dist - GPN **Prod** - MAETEL

Selecting and Applying Fire Streams 30 MIN
VHS
Firefighter II - III Video Series
Color (G PRO)
$145.00 purchase _ #35251
Uses dramatization to demonstrate the effects of proper fire stream application. Shows how to predict necessary fire flow and how to assemble nozzles and appliances to produce different types of fire steams. Includes special nozzles and foam - making appliances.
Health and Safety; Industrial and Technical Education; Science - Physical; Social Science
Dist - OKSU **Prod** - OKSU

Selecting and Buying Clothes 13 MIN
Videoreel / VT2
Living Better I Series
Color
Home Economics; Social Science
Dist - PBS **Prod** - MAETEL

Selecting and defining a topic
VHS
Using your library to write a research paper series
Color (J H C G)
$49.95 purchase _ #VA74XV
Shows how to select and define a topic for a research paper, using the library. Walks viewers through the process, offering tips, tricks and insights that make the reseaarch and writing process fast and more productive. Part of a four - part series.
Education
Dist - CAMV

Selecting and Dressing the Grinding Stone of the Sioux Valve Seat Grinder 10 MIN
VHS / 16mm
Auto Mechanics Series
(G PRO)
$61.00 purchase _ #AM21
Shows how to select and dress the grinding stone of the Sioux valve seat grinder.
Industrial and Technical Education
Dist - RMIBHF **Prod** - RMIBHF

Selecting and Handling Glassware
U-matic / VHS
Tableside Series
Color
Home Economics; Industrial and Technical Education
Dist - CULINA **Prod** - CULINA

Selecting and Managing Projects 30 MIN
U-matic / VHS
Management for Engineers Series
Color
Business and Economics; Industrial and Technical Education; Psychology
Dist - SME **Prod** - UKY

Selecting and Researching a Production Topic 5.43 MIN
VHS
On Location
(J)
$180 series purchase, $50 rental, $110 self dub
Demonstrates video production skills for small format student productions. Focuses on brainstorming, evaluating and selecting topics in a group setting. Highlights research options. Third in an eight part series.
Fine Arts
Dist - GPN **Prod** - NCGE

Selecting Books 7 MIN
U-matic
Take Time Series
(A)
Demonstrates the influence of parents and others caring for pre - schoolers on the physical and emotional development of the child.
Health and Safety; Psychology; Sociology
Dist - ACCESS **Prod** - ACCESS 1976

Selecting day care for your child 70 MIN
VHS
Color (H A T G)
$39.95 purchase _ #V500
Incorporates the most commonly asked questions regarding day care issues. Discusses selecting the correct day care, in - home care, nannies, family home facilities, corporate facilities, certified child - care facilities, child - care costs, child safety and health issues.
Health and Safety; Home Economics
Dist - AAVIM **Prod** - AAVIM

Selecting Flowering Trees 29 MIN
Videoreel / VT2
Dig it Series
Color
Features Tom Lied describing the different types of flowering trees and suggesting what to look for and which might be best suited for particular types of yards.
Agriculture; Science - Natural
Dist - PBS **Prod** - WMVSTV

Selecting Forecasting Techinques 60 MIN
VHS / BETA
Manufacturing Series
(IND)
Provides aid for choosing the best forecasting and data acquisitions techniques.
Business and Economics
Dist - COMSRV **Prod** - COMSRV 1986

Selecting Fruit Trees 29 MIN
Videoreel / VT2
Dig it Series
Color
Features Tom Lied offering a close look at different types of fruit trees and giving special hints on how to care for them.
Agriculture; Science - Natural
Dist - PBS **Prod** - WMVSTV

Selecting Goals - Deciding what to Train - no 1 60 MIN
U-matic
Training the Trainer Series
Color (PRO)
Presents training sessions for professional training personnel. Includes goal selection, design and presentation of training material and evaluation and reports.
Industrial and Technical Education
Dist - VTRI **Prod** - VTRI 1986

Selecting Houseplants 30 MIN
U-matic / VHS
Even You Can Grow Houseplants Series
Color
Discusses selecting houseplants to fit individual needs.
Agriculture
Dist - MDCPB **Prod** - WGTV

Selecting long - term care - Tape III 30 MIN
VHS
All about aging series
Color (A G)
$195.00 series purchase, $25.00 series rental
Features Dr Dee Alford, RN, who discusses appropriate and cost effective long - term care, as well as alternative choices and community based care options for the aged. Part three of a four - part series not available separately. Includes workbook and provider's guide.
Health and Safety; Sociology
Dist - AGEVI **Prod** - AGEVI 1990

Selecting Media 19 MIN
16mm
Color
LC 81-700636
Highlights various equipment available to support classroom audiovisual presentations and training situations.
Education
Dist - USNAC **Prod** - USAF 1981

Selecting Patients for Treatment 15 MIN
U-matic / VHS
Treatment of the Borderline Patient Series
Color
Gives reasons therapists resist making a diagnosis on a borderline patient. Discusses evaluating severity of pathology and deciding those likely to become psychotic during treatment.
Health and Safety; Psychology
Dist - HEMUL **Prod** - HEMUL

Selecting Shade Trees 29 MIN
Videoreel / VT2
Dig it Series
Color
Features Tom Lied describing what shade trees can do for a yard and offering a careful and complete explanation of the different varieties of shade trees and how they are sold.

Agriculture; Science - Natural
Dist - PBS Prod - WMVSTV

Selecting the Assembly Method 150 MIN
U-matic
Electronics Manufacturing - Components, Assembly and Soldering 'Series
Color (IND)
Tells how to select an assembly method for electronic components and boards. Outlines general factors to consider, and selection methodology and guidelines.
Business and Economics; Industrial and Technical Education
Dist - INTECS Prod - INTECS

Selecting the Best Alternative 30 MIN
U-matic / VHS
Decision Analysis by Kepner - Tregoe Series
Color
Business and Economics; Education; Psychology
Dist - DELTAK Prod - KEPTRG

Selecting the jury 59 MIN
Cassette
Winning the business jury trial series
Color (PRO)
$125.00, $30.00 purchase, $50.00 rental _ #BUS1-002, #ABUS-002
Provides sophisticated trial skills training for the business litigator. Demonstrates business cases including lender liability, securities fraud and antitrust. Explains how to select the jury, giving the viewer an analytical framework in which to view subsequent demonstrations and discussions. Gives an insider's look at nationally recognized business litigators as they plan their strategies. Includes a psychologist who specializes in persuasive communication strategies and decision - making processes providing analysis based on empirical research and juror interviews. Includes study guide.
Business and Economics; Civics and Political Systems
Dist - AMBAR Prod - AMBAR 1992

Selecting the jury in a civil case 59 MIN
VHS
Art of advocacy - selecting and persuading the jury series
Color (C PRO)
$95.00 purchase, $71.25 rental _ #Z0302
Presents lectures and demonstrations of techniques used in jury selection in civil cases. Draws on social science insights.
Civics and Political Systems
Dist - NITA Prod - NITA 1988

Selecting the jury in a criminal case 56 MIN
VHS
Art of advocacy - selecting and persuading the jury series
Color (C PRO)
$95.00 purchase, $71.25 rental _ #Z0305
Presents lectures and demonstrations of techniques used in jury selection for criminal cases. Draws on social science insights.
Civics and Political Systems
Dist - NITA Prod - NITA 1988

Selecting Toys for Disabled Children 22 MIN
Videoreel / VHS
Color (AMERICAN SIGN)
Presents suggestions for parents and caregivers of developmentally impaired children of 0 - 24 months. Explains the need for stimulation and proper positioning for activities. Stresses the importance of play and use of appropriate selection of educational tools to enhance development. Available in American Sign Language format.
Health and Safety; Home Economics; Psychology
Dist - UNDMC Prod - UNDMC

Selection - 1
U-matic / VHS / BETA
Synergy - EEO, diversity and management series
Color; CC; PAL (IND PRO G)
$895.00 purchase
Reveals that selection practices are critical to EEO compliance and to building a productive workforce. Shows what the law requires and the steps that organizations must take to ensure that people who are hired and promoted are truly the most qualified for the job. Illustrates the ways in which stereotypical thinking interferes with various steps in the selection process. A panel of experts analyze cases from three perspectives - EEO liability, healthy approaches to workforce diversity and management philsophy. Vignettes illustrate gender stereotypes, age discrimination, race discrimination, disparate treatment. Includes 20 participant manuals. Part of a series showing managers how to appy EEO guidelines in managing a diverse workforce.
Business and Economics; Guidance and Counseling
Dist - BNA Prod - BNA

Selection and Adaptation 20 MIN
U-matic / VHS
Evolution Series
Color
Studies plants in the desert and snails in the hedgerow and woodlands to show adaptation and natural selection at work.
Science - Natural; Science - Physical
Dist - FOTH Prod - FOTH 1984

Selection and Location of Trees 29 MIN
Videoreel / VT2
Dig it Series
Color
Features Tom Lied offering ideas for turning driveways and parking areas into inviting and necessary parts of the landscape and looking at the kinds of trees which could be added. Provides tips on effective lighting.
Agriculture; Science - Natural; Science - Physical
Dist - PBS Prod - WMVSTV

Selection and Use of Materials 30 MIN
U-matic / VHS
Basic Education - Teaching the Adult Series
Color (T)
Discusses the selection and use of materials when teaching adult basic education students.
Education
Dist - MDCPB Prod - MDDE

Selection and Use of Wrapping Materials for Sterilization 40 MIN
U-matic
Color
LC 79-707309
Demonstrates techniques for wrapping medical supplies and instruments, discussing the selection of wrapping materials, the proper size and thickness of wrappers for various trays and instruments, and the folding and taping of the finished product.
Health and Safety
Dist - USNAC Prod - USVA 1976

The Selection Interview - Choice or Chance 31 MIN
VHS / U-matic
Color
Shows how the selection interview should be run and how different the prospective employee looks when interviewed properly. Points out several common mistakes, such as failing to prepare for the interview, failing to draw the candidate out and get him/her talking freely and failing to come out with direct, probing questions.
Guidance and Counseling
Dist - VISUCP Prod - VIDART

Selection - interview - race issues - 9 ; 2nd ed.
U-matic / VHS / BETA
Choices - a management training program in equal opportunity series
Color; CC; PAL (IND PRO G)
Contact distributor about price
Shows managers how to deal with employee selection, interviewing and racial issues. Trains both new managers and those with previous EEO training. Part of a 12 - part program providing managers with essential knowledge of EEO and enhancing their skills in in such areas as hiring, interviewing, selecting, performance appraisals and more.
Business and Economics; Guidance and Counseling
Dist - BNA Prod - BNA

The Selection Interview - Screening Candidates with Leo F McManus 38 MIN
VHS / U-matic
Color
Deals with hiring decisions, an important aspect of any manager's job. Works as a tool for the manager who makes or contributes to employment decisions, and presents proven methods for conducting screening interviews within the selection process. Includes a student manual.
Business and Economics; Guidance and Counseling; Psychology
Dist - DELTAK Prod - HBCORP

Selection of Breeding Stock 20 MIN
U-matic / VHS
Color
Presents the characteristics and qualities to consider when selecting boars and gilts for a swine breeding program.
Agriculture
Dist - HOBAR Prod - HOBAR

Selection of Electrode, Gas, Cups and Filler Rod for Gas Tungsten Arc (Tig) Welding 15 MIN
U-matic / VHS
Welding III - TIG and MIG (Industry Welding Series
Color
Health and Safety; Industrial and Technical Education
Dist - CAMB Prod - CAMB

Selection of Electrode, Gas, Cups and Filler Rod for Inert Gas Tungsten - TIG
VHS / U-matic
MIG and TIG Welding - Spanish Series
Color (IND H G) (SPANISH)
Industrial and Technical Education
Dist - VTRI Prod - VTRI

Selection of electrodes for shielded metal arc - welding
VHS / U-matic
Shielded metal arc welding - Spanish series
Color (SPANISH)
Industrial and Technical Education
Dist - VTRI Prod - VTRI

A Selection of Fables 15 MIN
VHS / U-matic
Magic Pages Series
Color (P)
Literature and Drama
Dist - AITECH Prod - KLVXTV 1976

Selection of Mounted Bearings MIN
VHS
Power Transmission Series II - Selection, Application and 'Maintenance Series
Color (A)
$265.00 purchase, $50.00 rental _ #57983
Describes various types of mounted bearings, listing and explaining factors which determine the proper choice of mounting type and whether or not a lubricated installation is required. Defines rated life, average life, static load rating, dynamic load rating, and DN value. Discusses fixed and floating bearings, the importance of bearing - to - shaft relationship, seals, alignment, housing types and materials.
Industrial and Technical Education
Dist - UILL Prod - MAJEC 1986

Selection of Your Horse
BETA / VHS
Captain Mark Phillips Horsemanship Training Series
Color
Physical Education and Recreation
Dist - EQVDL Prod - EQVDL

Selections from the European journals 120 MIN
VHS
B&W (G)
$100.00 purchase
Documents filmmaker Bill Creston's trips to France, Spain and Portugal in 1973 and 1974. Features many noted European artists, several of whom are now regulars on the current American video scene. Excerpts from footage shot with a black and white one - half inch Sony Portapak.
Fine Arts; Geography - World
Dist - CANCIN

Selective Distal Splenorenal Shunt 20 MIN
VHS / U-matic
Color
LC 80-706815
Describes the selective distal splenorenal shunt procedure developed by Dr W Dean Warren and presents the surgical procedure as a more successful alternative to the commonly practiced mesocaval shunt. Shows the actual surgical procedure.
Health and Safety
Dist - USNAC Prod - VAHSL 1980

Selective Esophageal Variceal Decompression by in Situ Distal Splenorenal Shunt 32 MIN
16mm
Color (PRO)
Demonstrates a new approach to the problem of controlling bleeding esophageal varices in the cirrhotic minimizing the risk of progressive hepatic failure, prevalent following standard portacaval shunt.
Health and Safety; Science
Dist - ACY Prod - ACYDGD 1969

Selective Gene Expression 30 MIN
VHS / U-matic
Developmental Biology Series
Color
Discusses the process by which certain genes become active during embryonic development and explores the process of regulation of these genes.
Science - Natural
Dist - NETCHE Prod - NETCHE 1971

Selective memory 9 MIN
16mm
Color (G)

$25.00 rental
Presents concepts of memory. Uses material shot and collected over the years in the second part of a series that examines the nature of remembering.
Fine Arts; Psychology
Dist - CANCIN **Prod** - ZIPPER 1991

Selective Renal Angiography 10 MIN
16mm
Color
LC FIA66-61
Demonstrates the technique of selective renal angiography in obtaining diagnostic information regarding lesions of the kidney. Uses animation and slow motion cineradiology to illustrate the author's technique for percutaneous femoral puncture, catheterization of the renal artery and injection of the contrast media.
Health and Safety
Dist - EATONL **Prod** - EATONL 1965

Selective service system 13 MIN
16mm
Color (G)
$25.00 rental
Documents the proceedings of an alternative to dodging the draft during the Vietnam War other than serving prison sentences or seeking refuge in another country. Records how the selective service system was stepped up during this time and made virtually no exemptions. Produced by Warren Haack.
Fine Arts; History - United States
Dist - CANCIN

Selective Vagotomy and Pyloroplasty 34 MIN
U-matic / VHS
Gastrointestinal Series
Color
Health and Safety; Science - Natural
Dist - SVL **Prod** - SVL

Selective Vagotomy, Antrectomy and Gastroduodenostomy 25 MIN
16mm
Color (PRO)
Shows selective gastric vagotomy in detail upon two patients. Portrays the standard technique for antrectomy and gastroduodenal anastomosis. Depicts the Strauss maneuver for the difficult posterior penetrating duodenal ulcer.
Health and Safety; Science
Dist - ACY **Prod** - ACYDGD 1968

Selectware system
CD-ROM
(G A)
$129.00 purchase _ #2921
Includes demos, specs, pictures and detailed information on a wide variety of PC - based software. Helps dealers who want to minimize inventory expenses and maximize demonstration capabilities. Updated regularly. For IBM PCs and compatibles. Requires at least 640K RAM, DOS Version 3.1 or greater, one floppy disk drive - a hard drive is recommended, one empty expansion slot, and an IBM compatible CD - ROM drive.
Computer Science; Home Economics
Dist - BEP

Self 2 MIN
16mm
Meditation Series
Color (I)
LC 80-700747
Explores the belief that each individual is an important statement made by God.
Religion and Philosophy
Dist - IKONOG **Prod** - IKONOG 1974

Self 50 MIN
VHS
Human brain series
Color (H C A)
PdS99 purchase
Highlights recent advances in knowledge about the brain and its functions relative to the person's self-perception. Uses case histories to illustrate individuals' triumphs over brain injury. Part of a seven-video set focusing on the self, memory, language, movement, sight, fear, and madness.
Psychology
Dist - BBCENE

Self - Acceptance - Role of the Significant Other 30 MIN
16mm
Mental Health Concepts for Nursing Series
B&W (PRO)
LC 73-702641
Helps nursing student understand the role of the significant other in developing self - acceptance and improving their abilities in treating patients.
Health and Safety; Psychology
Dist - GPN **Prod** - SREB 1971

Self - Acceptance - the Key to Self - Esteem 55 MIN
VHS
Self - Esteem Video Series
Color (G)
$69.95 purchase _ #6 - 080 - 101P
Reveals that people, regardless of past performance, have the right to feel good about themselves. Examines how people sabotage themselves and what they can do to exercise their right to feel good, no matter what their past or present circumstances. Features Marilyn Grosboll.
Health and Safety; Psychology
Dist - VEP

Self - Acceptance Training with Dick Olney - Pt I 60 MIN
VHS / U-matic
B&W
Shows a low - key approach to self - acceptance through individual analysis of thought process. Stresses ideas which will turn nervousness into excitement, help meet fears head on and bring about mental and verbal acceptance of one's self.
Psychology; Sociology
Dist - UWISC **Prod** - UWISC 1982

Self - Acceptance Training with Dick Olney - Pt II 60 MIN
U-matic / VHS
B&W
Continues discussion on self - acceptance approach. Stresses use of experience to teach about the fear of the unconscious and the fear of being afraid, the idea of emotional containment versus catharsis or repression and actively accepting one's feelings.
Psychology; Sociology
Dist - UWISC **Prod** - UWISC 1982

Self - Actualization as a Life - Long Phenomenon 30 MIN
U-matic
Growing Old in Modern America Series
Color
Health and Safety; Sociology
Dist - UWASHP **Prod** - UWASHP

Self - advocacy for persons with developmental disabilities
VHS
Color (S T PRO)
$149.00 purchase _ #1014
Shows how to establish informal support systems for mentally handicapped adolescents and adults within the community. Improves self - identity of individuals through self - advocacy, teaches the rights and responsibilities of community citizenship, helps to recognize that prejudice is the result of ignorance. Includes footage of successful self - advocacy activities. Includes teacher's guide.
Civics and Political Systems; Education; Social Science
Dist - STANFI **Prod** - STANFI

Self - advocacy - the road toward independence 25 MIN
VHS
Color (PRO G)
$15.00 purchase
Records a conference of self - advocates from adult with developmental disabilties groups in Kansas and Missouri. Depicts the concept of self - advocacy through members' participation in group meetings and from individual descriptions of what the term means to participants in the conference.
Guidance and Counseling; Health and Safety
Dist - BEACH **Prod** - BEACH 1986

The Self and many Others
U-matic
Growth and Development - a Chronicle of Four Children Series Series '10
Color
Describes growth and development of a child from 46 to 47 months.
Psychology
Dist - LIP **Prod** - JUETHO

Self and society 30 MIN
VHS / BETA
Living philosophically series
Color (G)
$29.95 purchase _ #S183
Asks how an individual can live a meaningful life in a social milieu which lacks clear values. Suggests that one could define the self through a role model such as Christ or the Buddha. Features Dr Jane Rubin, teacher of religious studies, who contrasts this approach with that of modern existentialists who view an idealistic approach to life as an escape from authenticity. Part of a four - part series on living philosophically.
Religion and Philosophy
Dist - THINKA **Prod** - THINKA

Self and universe 30 MIN
BETA / VHS
Living philosophically series
Color (G)
$29.95 purchase _ #S004
Considers, how can there be separate things in a universe which is interconnected and, how can there be separate beings in a universe created by God. Features Arthur M Young who suggests that the ancient deities act in the human psyche as forces which unite the individual with the universe. Part of a four - part series on living philosophically.
Psychology; Religion and Philosophy
Dist - THINKA **Prod** - THINKA

Self - Assessment - a Tool for Career Decision
VHS / 35mm strip
$165.00 film or VHS purchase _ #SB415 film, #SB2208V VHS
Teaches how to use the self - assessment process in evaluating job strengths and talents, examining career options and achieving job satisfaction.
Guidance and Counseling
Dist - CAREER **Prod** - CAREER

Self - Assessment - who are You 29 MIN
VHS / 16mm
Career Planning for Special Needs Series
Color (J)
$200.00 purchase _ #277803
Addresses the concerns of individuals with special needs - the physically disabled, deaf, educable and trainable mentally handicapped, gifted and talented, Native Americans, and gender stereotyped. Suggests positively how they can achieve career satisfaction and success. 'Self - Assessment' explains the purpose and value of self - assessment in considering the importance of one's own needs, values, skills, aptitudes, temperament, personality, family and peer influences.
Business and Economics; Guidance and Counseling; Psychology
Dist - ACCESS **Prod** - ACCESS 1989

Self - awareness 15 MIN
VHS
Skills - work - related themes series
Color (H C)
$49.00 purchase, $15.00 rental _ #316629; LC 91-712551
Shows how important it is for young people to identify their interests and strengths and match them with an occupation requiring these qualities. Part of a series created to complement the Skills - Occupational Programs series, focusing on ways to develop these skills and demonstrate their effectiveness in the workplace. Includes teacher's guide with reproducible worksheets.
Guidance and Counseling; Psychology
Dist - TVOTAR **Prod** - TVOTAR 1990

Self - Awareness 30 MIN
VHS / U-matic
Simple Gifts Series no 5
Color (T)
Education; Psychology
Dist - GPN **Prod** - UWISC 1977

Self - Awareness and the Prospective Parent 29 MIN
U-matic / VHS
Tomorrow's Families Series
Color (H C A)
LC 81-706051
Explains that many factors of heredity and environment affect how a person reacts to parental responsibilities.
Sociology
Dist - AITECH **Prod** - MDDE 1980

Self Awareness and Your Career Options
U-matic / VHS
$98.00 purchase _ #XP800V
Shows students how to identify and organize information about themselves. Talks on the importance of understanding goals, values, personalities, interests, work activity preferences, temperaments, skills, and abilities.
Guidance and Counseling
Dist - CAREER **Prod** - CAREER

Self Awareness and Your Career Options 30 MIN
U-matic / VHS
Career Choices Series
Color (H C)
$125 _ #CC7V
Offers a view of career planning in relation to personal values, interests and abilities.
Business and Economics
Dist - JISTW **Prod** - JISTW

Self awareness and your career options 30 MIN
VHS
Choices today - for career satisfaction tomorrow series

Color (I J H)
$98.00 purchase _ #CTV100
Emphasizes student self awareness. Shows how to identify, articulate and organize goals, values, personalities, interests, work activity preferences, temperaments, skills and abilities. Part of a three - part series on making career choices.
Business and Economics; Guidance and Counseling; Psychology
Dist - CADESF **Prod** - CADESF
JISTW
CAMV

Self - Awareness Increases Independence - Group with Mentally Handicapped Adults 21 MIN
U-matic / VHS
Color
Teaches the importance of making decisions. Uses a consensus vote in a group to facilitate the decision - making process.
Psychology; Sociology
Dist - UWISC **Prod** - LASSWC 1979

Self Blood Glucose Monitoring 17 MIN
16mm
Color
Presents Dr I L Spratt, a group of people with diabetes and a diabetes teaching nurse discussing the benefits of self glucose monitoring, which include greater flexibility of lifestyle, greater accuracy and better blood glucose control.
Health and Safety
Dist - ORACLE **Prod** - ADAS

Self - Breast Examination 8 MIN
VHS / U-matic
Color
Explains reasons for self - breast exam. Presents a step - by - step demonstration.
Science - Natural; Sociology
Dist - MEDFAC **Prod** - MEDFAC

Self - care - 5 33 MIN
U-matic / VHS
Healing families - life's journey home series
Color (G)
$249.00 purchase _ #7479
Teaches that success is the quality of the journey - a journey which may take a long time. Outlines self - care techniques in easy - to - follow steps. Presents tools such as affirmations, reading, keeping a journal, setting boundaries, 12 - step or other support groups, therapy and finding a balance. Part of a five - part series hosted by Art Linkletter.
Health and Safety; Psychology; Sociology
Dist - VISIVI **Prod** - VISIVI 1991

Self - Care Female
VHS / 35mm strip
$185.00 purchase _ #IE8115 filmstrip, $185.00 purchase _ #IE8115V VHS
Talks about good personal grooming habits including makeup, hair care, looks, nail care and finishing touches. Assists in improving one's appearance and self - image.
Health and Safety
Dist - CAREER **Prod** - CAREER

Self - Care for Females
VHS / U-matic
Color (J H)
Presents a practical guide to developing good eating habits, selecting make - up and maintaining a practical wardrobe.
Education; Home Economics; Social Science; Sociology
Dist - GA **Prod** - GA

Self - Care for Males
U-matic / VHS
Color (J H)
Presents information on everyday grooming aids and shows how to shave and how to care for nails, hair and scalp.
Home Economics; Social Science; Sociology
Dist - GA **Prod** - GA

Self - Care Male
VHS / 35mm strip
$185.00 purchase _ #IE8114 filmstrip, $185.00 purchase _ #IE1184V VHS
Emphasizes the importance of a clean neat appearance. Teaches how to obtain good grooming in the least amount of time. Assists in improving one's appearance and self - image.
Health and Safety
Dist - CAREER **Prod** - CAREER

Self - Concept 30 MIN
U-matic / VHS
Interaction - Human Concerns in the Schools Series
Color (T)
Discusses the importance of self - concept in an educational setting.
Education
Dist - MDCPB **Prod** - MDDE

Self Concept - an Image of Me 30 MIN
U-matic
Dimensions of Child Development Series
Color (PRO)
Identifies self knowledge and self esteem as two factors which contribute to the development of self image in childhood.
Education
Dist - ACCESS **Prod** - ACCESS 1983

Self - Concept - How I Know who I Am
VHS
(G)
$139 purchase - #SB2022V
Points out that a realistic self - concept and positive self - esteem arecrucial to emotional growth and success in life. Teaches positive steps that viewers can take to change a poor self - concept and that change is possible as long as we learn to see ourselves in new ways.
Guidance and Counseling
Dist - CAREER **Prod** - CAREER

Self - Concept - I'm OK 15 MIN
VHS / U-matic
It's a Rainbow World
(P)
Designed to teach social studies to primary grade students. Explains concepts in terms of everyday situations. Focuses on self concept.
Psychology; Sociology
Dist - GPN

Self - Concept - I'm Special 15 MIN
U-matic / VHS
It's a Rainbow World
(P)
Designed to teach social studies to primary grade students . Explains concepts in terms of everyday situations. Focuses on children's activities.
Psychology; Sociology
Dist - GPN

Self - confidence 39 MIN
VHS
Color (K P I)
$59.95 purchase _ #B075 - V8
Helps elementary students build the life skills essential for success. Conveys the importance of self confidence through modeling story telling, and songs. Shows puppets Youcan Toucan and Professor Vatzinseid guiding Zach and Sandy through the challenge of taking over household chores while their mom is ill. Includes discussion guide.
Guidance and Counseling; Psychology
Dist - ETRASS **Prod** - ETRASS

Self - confidence
VHS
Synergy subliminal series
Color (G)
$19.98 purchase
Focuses on enhancing self - confidence. Combines the nature cinematography of David Fortney with radiant, kaleidoscopic dances of color by Ken Jenkins, wilderness scenes by Blair Robbins, abstract animation by Jordan Belson and ethereal patterns of light created by Jason Loam. Features filmmaker Richard Ajathan Gero who integrates all of the foregoing imagery with subliminal visual affirmations and the music of Steven Halpern.
Fine Arts; Industrial and Technical Education; Psychology; Religion and Philosophy
Dist - HALPER **Prod** - HALPER

Self Control - Learning to CARE for Yourself 29 MIN
16mm
Color (C A)
LC 76-702687
Preeents Dr Carl E Thoresen demonstrating a model for leading group discussions in helping persons apply self - control strategies in their own lives. Depicts a group of college - age students in a discussion led by Dr Thoresen.
Guidance and Counseling; Psychology
Dist - COUNF **Prod** - COUNF 1976

Self - Creation 2 HRS
VHS
Master of Life Training Series
Color (G)
$29.95 purchase _ #VHS142
Contains two Video Hypnosis Sessions which enhance clarity of focus, release of negative blocks and the experience of balance and harmony.
Health and Safety; Psychology; Religion and Philosophy
Dist - VSPU **Prod** - VSPU

Self - defeating behavior - how to stop it 40 MIN
VHS
Color (J H C)
$199.00 purchase _ #CG - 898 - VS
Describes how many adolescents become involved in self - defeating behavior and negative thought loops. Defines and indentifies this behavior and shows teens how to turn it into self - benefiting thoughs and behavior. Examines four major self - defeating behavior - social anxiety, procrastination, worry and lack of assertiveness. Models appropriate behavior which fosters self - assertiveness, self - esteem and relaxation.
Guidance and Counseling; Health and Safety; Psychology; Sociology
Dist - HRMC **Prod** - HRMC

Self Defense 50 MIN
VHS / BETA
Color
Begins with self - defense techniques that can be used by the elderly, frail or untrained. Progresses to more advanced techniques.
Physical Education and Recreation
Dist - VIPRO **Prod** - VIPRO

Self Defense
U-matic / VHS
$29.95 purchase
Physical Education and Recreation
Dist - BEEKMN **Prod** - BEEKMN 1988

Self - defense 60 MIN
VHS
Martial arts series
Color (H C A)
$39.95 purchase _ #MXS3300V
Teaches concepts of self - defense based on the martial arts. Discusses how to discover an opponent's weak points and one's own strong points.
Physical Education and Recreation
Dist - CAMV

Self - Defense Aerobics
VHS
(C A)
$19.95 _ #WW280V
Combines self - defense and aerobic exercise to form a workout.
Physical Education and Recreation
Dist - CAMV **Prod** - CAMV

Self - Defense for Girls 16 MIN
16mm / U-matic / VHS
Color (J H C)
LC 78-705660
Uses dramatized episodes of threatened attack to introduce fundamental self - defense techniques and to prepare girls and women to meet attacks without panic.
Health and Safety; Physical Education and Recreation; Sociology
Dist - PHENIX **Prod** - PHENIX 1969

Self - defense for women 60 MIN
VHS
Martial arts series
Color (H C A)
$39.95 purchase _ #MXS3400V
Presents self - defense strategies for women. Stresses developing women's confidence to walk alone without fear.
Physical Education and Recreation
Dist - CAMV

Self - Defense for Women - a Positive Approach 13 MIN
U-matic / VHS / 16mm
Color (J)
LC 79-701714
Looks at karate experts Kim Fritz and George A Dillman teaching a class of female students how to defend themselves successfully. Stresses the importance of a positive self - image and positive body language to destroy the helpless woman image and discourage potential attackers.
Physical Education and Recreation; Sociology
Dist - PHENIX **Prod** - FILMPA 1979

Self - defense system
VHS
Bill 'Superfoot' Wallace series
Color (G)
$59.95 purchase _ #PNT021
Presents practical means of self - defense for men, women and children.
Physical Education and Recreation; Psychology
Dist - SIV

Self Defense with Steve Powell, Pt 1 - Self Defense for Men 60 MIN
VHS / BETA
Color
Provides instruction in self defense skills for men. Includes exercises for home practice.

Physical Education and Recreation
Dist - MOHOMV **Prod** - MOHOMV

Self Defense with Steve Powell, Pt 2 - Self Defense for Women 60 MIN
BETA / VHS
Color
Provides instruction in self defense skills for women. Includes exercises for home practice.
Physical Education and Recreation
Dist - MOHOMV **Prod** - MOHOMV

Self - Development - the Key to Success 11 MIN
U-matic / 35mm strip
New Supervisor Series Module 5
Color
Shows that supervisors, not their organizations, are primarily responsible for their own self - development.
Business and Economics; Psychology
Dist - RESEM **Prod** - RESEM

Self - directed evaluation 22 MIN
VHS
Quality - productivity series
Color (PRO G A)
$595.00 purchase, $150.00 rental
Demonstrates ways an employee can evaluate and correct his own work to meet quality standards. Part of a four - part series based on work by Cr. Richard Chang. Workshop materials are available separately.
Business and Economics; Psychology
Dist - EXTR **Prod** - DOUVIS

Self Directed Job Search 120 MIN
VHS / U-matic
(H C)
$295.00 _ #JW1V
Gives a live presentation of a JIST workshop covering techniques that are effective in finding a job on one's own.
Business and Economics
Dist - JISTW **Prod** - JISTW

Self directed work teams 29 MIN
VHS
Color (G A)
$450.00 purchase _ #VTEAM - 721
Explains the concept of self - directed work teams. Shows that such teams are different for their greater latitude to make decisions, different supervisory roles, and greater access to information, among other factors.
Business and Economics; Computer Science; Guidance and Counseling; Psychology
Dist - PRODUC **Prod** - PRODUC

Self - Directed Work Teams
VHS
Color (G)
$450.00 purchase
Explains and demonstrates the benefits, the fundamentals and the follow through for the self - directed process.
Business and Economics; Guidance and Counseling; Psychology
Dist - VLEARN

Self Discipline 30 MIN
U-matic
Parent Puzzle Series
(A)
Shows that the way in which children were raised has a profound effect on their behavior as parents.
Psychology; Sociology
Dist - ACCESS **Prod** - ACCESS 1982

Self - Disclosure 11 MIN
Videoreel / VT2
Interpersonal Competence, Unit 02 - Communication Series; Unit 2 - Communication
Color (C A)
Features a humanistic psychologist who, by analysis and examples, discusses the importance of self - disclosure in communication.
Psychology
Dist - TELSTR **Prod** - MVNE 1973

Self Discovery 16 MIN
U-matic / VHS
Becoming Orgasmic - a Sexual Growth Program Series
Color
Shows a woman looking at her body, exploring her genitals and discovering areas of her body that give her pleasure.
Health and Safety; Psychology; Sociology
Dist - MMRC **Prod** - MMRC

Self Esteem 20 MIN
VHS / 16mm
(H)
$98.00 _ #CC16V
Portrays a high school student with feelings of self - doubt after failing a test. Helps identify the thought patterns that trap kids into unproductive and illogical behavior responses.
Guidance and Counseling; Psychology
Dist - JISTW

Self - Esteem 30 MIN
VHS / 16mm
Power of Choice Series
Color (G)
$84.95, $64.95 purchase _ #8813, 8812
Uses comedy to show young people that they have the power of choice, are responsible for their choices and owe it to themselves to make the best choices in regard to the use of chemicals. Features teen counselor Michael Pritchard. Produced by Elkind Sweet Plus Communications, Inc.
Guidance and Counseling; Health and Safety; Psychology; Sociology
Dist - HAZELB

Self - esteem 30 MIN
VHS
Power of choice series
Color (H)
$89.00 purchase _ #60287 - 025
Features comedian - teen counselor Michael Prichard who helps young people realize that they are responsible for the choices they make, that they owe it to themselves to choose the best. Focuses on the role of self - esteem in making decisions. Part of a twelve - part series on making choices.
Psychology
Dist - GA **Prod** - GA 1992

Self Esteem
VHS
Personal Development Series
Color (H)
$98.00 purchase _ #ABV 101
Points out how to overcome feelings of inadequacy and replace them with feelings of self - worth, self - respect and self - confidence. Also available in Beta or 3/4".
Psychology
Dist - CADESF **Prod** - CADESF 1988

Self esteem 30 MIN
VHS / U-matic
Power of choice series
Color (J H)
$64.95 purchase _ #HH - 6338M
Examines self esteem, what it does for an individual and how to get it. Part of a series featuring Michael Pritchard who uses humor to promote positive, life - affirming values and empowers young people to take charge of their lives.
Psychology; Sociology
Dist - CORF **Prod** - ELSW 1990

Self Esteem 30 MIN
VHS / 16mm
Power of Choice Series
(H)
$75.95 #LW103V
Explains what self esteem is, what it does for you and how to get it.
Guidance and Counseling; Psychology
Dist - JISTW

Self - Esteem 30 MIN
VHS
Personal Development Video Series
(J H C)
$425.00 series of 5 purchase _ #CV200V
Presents tips and techniques for dealing with problems of self esteem. Communicates strategies for understanding self, peers, parents and teachers.
Psychology
Dist - CAMV **Prod** - CAMV

Self esteem 30 MIN
VHS
Raising rainbow kids series
Color (G A R)
$39.95 purchase, $10.00 rental _ #35 - 866 - 2076
Trains parents and teachers in methods of encouraging children's self esteem. Hosted by Lois Brokering. Produced by Seraphim.
Education; Health and Safety; Religion and Philosophy
Dist - APH

Self - esteem 30 MIN
VHS
Teen health video series
Color (J H A T)
$39.95 purchase _ #LVPE6640V-P
Offers teenagers and health educators information about self-esteem. Includes advice from experts and personal testimonies from teens themselves. Does not make judgements on moral issues, but does present options available. One of a series of twelve videos about teen health issues. Available individually or as a set.
Guidance and Counseling; Psychology; Sociology
Dist - CAMV

Self - esteem 7 MIN
U-matic
Take Time Series
(A)
Demonstrates the influence of parents and others caring for pre - schoolers on the physical and emotional development of the child.
Health and Safety; Psychology; Sociology
Dist - ACCESS **Prod** - ACCESS 1976

Self - esteem 28 MIN
VHS
Kidspeak series
Color (I J R)
$48.00 rental _ #36 - 851 - 2028
Explores the concept of self - esteem from a Christian perspective. Produced by Kuntz Brothers.
Religion and Philosophy
Dist - APH

Self - Esteem 30 MIN
VHS
Power Of Choice Series
Color (G)
$64.95 purchase _ #CHOI - 103
Conveys the message that a good sense of self - esteem and good decision making are interrelated. Shows that self - esteem affects every part of life. Hosted by comedian and teen counselor Michael Pritchard.
Guidance and Counseling; Psychology; Sociology
Dist - PBS **Prod** - LWIRE 1988

Self - Esteem and Classroom Management 29 MIN
VHS / 16mm
Breaking the Unseen Barrier Series
Color (C)
$180.00, $240.00 purchase _ #269706
Demonstrates through vignettes teaching strategies to help students with learning disabilities reach their full potential. Offers insight into integrating learning disabled students into the classroom. 'Self - Esteem And Classroom Management' shows that when learning disabled students fail despite their best efforts to succeed, they are devastated. Each failure erodes an individual's faltering self - esteem and some become isolated, unhappy and depressed. Asks what teachers can do to reduce the emotional consequences of learning disabilities and avoid classroom management problems.
Education; Mathematics; Psychology
Dist - AITECH **Prod** - ACCESS 1988

Self - esteem and empowerment 28 MIN
VHS / U-matic / BETA
Men in crisis series
Color (G)
$280.00 purchase _ #803.3
Records the struggles of a number of men in recovery, all at various stages of reclaiming their lives and empowering themselves. Discusses and demonstrates the steps necessary to improve self - esteem. Part of a five - part series on men in crisis.
Health and Safety; Psychology; Sociology
Dist - CONMED

Self - esteem and how we learn - Program 2 30 MIN
VHS
Inside stories - journey into self esteem series
Color (H C G)
$295.00 purchase, $55.00 rental
Focuses on the critical school years of childhood. Points out that it takes only one close relationship with a faculty member to turn around a potentially alienated student. Features Dr H Stephen Glenn. Part of a series on self esteem produced by Knowledge Network and Forefront Productions.
Education; Psychology
Dist - FLMLIB

Self - Esteem And Peak Performance Series
Self - Esteem and Peak Performance, Vol I 90 MIN
Self - Esteem and Peak Performance, Vol II 95 MIN
Dist - CARTRP

Self - Esteem and Peak Performance, Vol I 90 MIN
VHS
Self - Esteem And Peak Performance Series
Color (G)
$99.95 purchase _ #20103
Features Jack Canfield. Presents the three keys to high self - esteem. Reveals the common belief system which engenders feelings of being bad. Considers the steps to peak performance and techniques which help to remove the influence of the past and which clarify one's vision. Part one of two parts.
Guidance and Counseling; Health and Safety; Psychology
Dist - CARTRP **Prod** - CARTRP

Self - Esteem and Peak Performance, Vol I and II 185 MIN
VHS

Color (G)
$149.95 purchase _ #20103, #20107
Features Jack Canfield. Considers self - esteem as seeing why things will work, not why they won't. Self - esteem means solving problems instead of placing blame, and failing, learning and trying again. Shows how improved self - esteem increases confidence, energy and optimism and productivity.
Business and Economics; Guidance and Counseling; Psychology
Dist - CARTRP **Prod** - CARTRP

Self - Esteem and Peak Performance, Vol II 95 MIN
VHS
Self - Esteem And Peak Performance Series
Color (G)
$99.95 purchase _ #20107
Features Jack Canfield. Shows how to visualize positive results through powerful affirmations and how to use a support system to keep focused on goals. Demonstrates how to respond to feedback. Part two of two parts.
Guidance and Counseling; Health and Safety; Psychology
Dist - CARTRP **Prod** - CARTRP

Self - esteem begins in the family - Program 1 30 MIN
VHS
Inside stories - journey into self esteem series
Color (H C G)
$295.00 purchase, $55.00 rental
Discusses parenting. Looks at the situation of a divorced mother, a married couple and a single father. Features Dr H Stephen Glenn. Part of a series on self esteem produced by Knowledge Network and Forefront Productions.
Guidance and Counseling; Psychology; Sociology
Dist - FLMLIB

Self - Esteem - Believe You are Special
VHS / 35mm strip
$35.00 purchase _ #015 - 375 filmstrip, $45.50 purchase _ #015 - 394
Provides guidelines for raising one's self - esteem and feeling better about themselves.
Guidance and Counseling; Psychology
Dist - CAREER **Prod** - CAREER

Self Esteem - Feeling Good about Yourself 22 MIN
16mm / U-matic / VHS
Color (J H)
$50 rental _ #9773
Shows how having confidence and feeling good about oneself helps one deal with problems and enjoy life to the fullest.
Psychology; Sociology
Dist - AIMS **Prod** - SAIF 1984

Self - esteem - I would be perfect if only I didn't have this zit 15 MIN
VHS
Understanding who you are - the personality video series
Color (J H)
$79.00 purchase _ #PVS516; $79.00 purchase _ #SC10117VG
Looks at self - esteem and how it can be increased. Asks if certain personality themes have more self - esteem and how each type can maximize its strengths to achieve a high level of self - esteem. Examines the number one preoccupation of teens - popularity and how one is viewed by one's peers. Part of a ten - part series on personality.
Guidance and Counseling; Psychology; Sociology
Dist - CADESF **Prod** - CADESF 1990
UNL

Self - esteem II 20 MIN
VHS
CC; Color (J H)
$99 purchase _ #NP713VL
Features the story of John Foppe, a young man born without arms, as he faces the dilemmas of building self - esteem throughout high school and into college. Encourages students to examine their own self - worth. Comes with a discussion guide.
Guidance and Counseling
Dist - UNL

Self - Esteem in the Classroom 90 MIN
Cassette / VHS
Color (G)
$150.00 purchase
Presents an interactive media package which includes a videotape, curriculum guide and three audiocassettes. Shows how to build positive self - esteem in any age student, overcome negative learning blocks and create a positive learning environment. Features Jack Canfield.
Education; Psychology; Sociology
Dist - MEDIAI **Prod** - MEDIAI

Self esteem of teens 22 MIN
VHS / U-matic
Teen - family life series
Color (J H G)
$179.00, $229.00 purchase, $60.00 rental
Looks at factors contributing to good self - esteem, vital to the development of healthy autonomous adults, and how parents can nurture good self - esteem within their teenagers. Focuses on defining self - esteem, four crucial factors in determining it and concrete ideas on how to aid in fostering the search for self - identity of teenagers.
Psychology; Sociology
Dist - NDIM **Prod** - FAMLIF 1993

Self - esteem video series 220 MIN
VHS
Self - esteem video series
Color (G)
$249.95 purchase _ #6 - 080 - 100P
Presents a series of four videocassettes on self - esteem. Looks at self - acceptance, taking charge of life, making choices about anger and emotional responses, present thinking and future events. Features Marilyn Grosboll.
Health and Safety; Psychology
Dist - VEP

Self - Esteem Video Series

The choice is yours - accept or resist	55 MIN
Self - Acceptance - the Key to Self - Esteem	55 MIN
Self - esteem video series	220 MIN
Your Present Thinking Creates Future Events	55 MIN
You're in Charge of Your Life, Believe it or not	55 MIN

Dist - VEP

Self - Examination for Oral Disease 15 MIN
16mm
Color
LC 80-700772
Demonstrates a self - examination procedure to detect early signs of oral cancer.
Health and Safety
Dist - USNAC **Prod** - VADTC 1979

Self - Examination of the Testes for Testicular Tumor 10 MIN
16mm
Color
LC 75-702662
Presents a dramatization of an actual case history of a patient with a testicular tumor, emphasizing the importance of early diagnosis and demonstrating the correct procedure for self - examination.
Health and Safety; Science
Dist - EATONL **Prod** - EATONL 1975

Self - Fulfillment - Become the Person You Want to be 50 MIN
VHS / U-matic
Color
LC 81-706683
Emphasizes the importance of recognizing and fulfilling one's potential. Shows young people in various careers, leisure activities and volunteer programs finding self - fulfillment.
Guidance and Counseling; Psychology
Dist - GA **Prod** - CHUMAN 1981

Self - Hardening Clay 51 MIN
VHS / 16mm
Children's Crafts Series
(K P)
$39.00 purchase _ #VT1117
Shows children how to work with self - hardening clay through various techniques. Shows what tools are used for various methods. Demonstrates the coil method, pinch method, and slab technique of clay working. Suggests items to make, such as beads, necklaces, blocks, flat piece designs, tile and pots. Taught by Julie Abowitt, Multi - Arts Coordinator for the Seattle Public Schools.
Fine Arts
Dist - RMIBHF **Prod** - RMIBHF

Self - Healing 30 MIN
Cassette / VHS
Power Pack Series
Color (G)
$59.95 purchase _ #PK106
Offers a package for enhancing the healing process. Includes a 30 - minute video, four 60 - minute audiocassettes which feature instruction and motivation, suggestions, subliminals, sleep and Alpha level programming, and a booklet.
Health and Safety; Psychology
Dist - VSPU **Prod** - VSPU

Self - healing
VHS

Synergy subliminal series
Color (G)
$19.98 purchase
Focuses on self - healing. Combines the nature cinematography of David Fortney with radiant, kaleidoscopic dances of color by Ken Jenkins, wilderness scenes by Blair Robbins, abstract animation by Jordan Belson and ethereal patterns of light created by Jason Loam. Features filmmaker Richard Ajathan Gero who integrates all of the foregoing imagery with subliminal visual affirmations and the music of Steven Halpern.
Fine Arts; Industrial and Technical Education; Religion and Philosophy
Dist - HALPER **Prod** - HALPER

Self - Healing 28 MIN
U-matic / VHS
Color (C)
$249.00, $149.00 purchase _ #AD - 2165
Features Dr Bernie Siegel with host Phil Donahue. Talks about Siegel's experiences in teaching people how to heal themselves and lead longer, healthier lives.
Health and Safety; Science - Natural
Dist - FOTH **Prod** - FOTH

Self healing chi gong 240 MIN
VHS
Color (G)
$39.95 purchase _ #V - SHCG
Shows how to experience the benefits of chi flowing through the body in the practice of mind - body exercises. Illustrates how to strengthen and balance each of the five major organs, discover the energies of the mind and develop individual self - healing powers. Uses concepts from the Tao.
Health and Safety; Religion and Philosophy
Dist - PACSPI

Self - Health 23 MIN
VHS / U-matic
Color (C A)
Shows women sharing their experiences and learning how to do self - examinations of the breasts and vagina and the biomanual examination. Emphasizes what is normal for your own body.
Health and Safety; Psychology; Sociology
Dist - MMRC **Prod** - MMRC

Self - Help Housing 45 MIN
U-matic / VHS
B&W
Describes a relatively new government assisted housing program and current issues facing the housing market, realtors and building and lending institutions. Deals with differences between rural and urban housing and with the organization of self - help housing.
Civics and Political Systems; Psychology; Sociology
Dist - UWISC **Prod** - UWISC 1980

Self Help Subliminal Series

Positively Change Your Life - for Men	60 MIN
Positively Change Your Life - for Women	60 MIN
Wealth, make it Come to You - for Men and for Women by Audio Activation, Inc	60 MIN

Dist - BANTAP

Self - Identity / Sex Roles - I Only Want You to be Happy 16 MIN
16mm / U-matic / VHS
Conflict and Awareness Series
Color (J H)
Depicts the interaction of two sisters and their mother, all sharing conflicting points of view on the role of women.
Sociology
Dist - CRMP **Prod** - CRMP 1975

Self - Identity, Sex Roles - I Only Want You to be Happy 16 MIN
U-matic / VHS / 16mm
Conflict and Awareness Series
Color (H C)
Shows the interactions between three women and their conflicting points of view about 'the female role.'.
Psychology; Religion and Philosophy; Sociology
Dist - MGHT **Prod** - MGHT 1975

Self - Image 19 MIN
U-matic / VHS
Jobs - Seeking, Finding, Keeping Series
Color (H)
Tells how Denise learns that in order to be a successful job - hunter she must know who she is and what she wants.
Guidance and Counseling
Dist - AITECH **Prod** - MDDE 1980

Self - Image 30 MIN
U-matic / VHS
High Performance Leadership Series
Color

Psychology
Dist - DELTAK **Prod** - VIDAI

Self - image and discipline - Tape 1 60 MIN
VHS
Joy in parenting series
Color (G A R)
$10.00 rental _ #36 - 871451 - 460
Covers strategies for building self - image in children. Offers guidelines for discipline. Hosted by Jo Schlehofer.
Psychology; Sociology
Dist - APH **Prod** - FRACOC

Self - image and your career 38 MIN
35mm strip / VHS
Color (J H C A)
$199.00, $175.00 purchase _ #2215 - SK, #2214 - SK
Covers personality type and how it affects career choices. Uses the insights of Carl Jung to show students how to determine their personality type. Distinguishes between aptitudes and attitudes. Stresses the importance of personal values. Includes teacher's guide.
Business and Economics; Guidance and Counseling; Psychology
Dist - SUNCOM **Prod** - SUNCOM

The Self - Image Concepts in Selling
VHS / U-matic
Strategies for Successful Selling Series Module 3
Color
Shows how to identify and organize self - image concepts in selling and shows how they can be enhanced and/or dealt with.
Business and Economics; Psychology
Dist - AMA **Prod** - AMA

Self - Image, Self - Confidence 30 MIN
VHS
Video Reflections Series
Color (G)
$29.95 purchase _ #VSLF
Combines images of nature with music and soothing environmental sounds. Uses visual and auditory subliminal messages for enhancing self - image and confidence.
Health and Safety; Physical Education and Recreation; Psychology
Dist - GAINST **Prod** - GAINST

Self Improvement Video Programs - Stop Smoking 22 MIN
VHS / BETA
Color (I)
Focuses on previous attempts to stop smoking which have failed. Describes 'hypnovision' as a self help program that works. Recommends relaxing and watching the program daily for a month, then thereafter as needed. Provides a unique blend of hypnotic relaxation therapy and subliminal suggestion. Includes instructions.
Health and Safety; Psychology
Dist - CBSC **Prod** - CBSC

Self Improvement Video Programs - Weight Loss 22 MIN
BETA / VHS
Color (I)
Focuses on previous attempts to lose weight which have failed. Describes 'hypnovision' as a self help program that works. Recommends relaxing and watching the program daily for a month, then thereafter as needed. Provides a unique blend of hypnotic relaxation therapy and subliminal suggestion. Includes instructions.
Health and Safety; Psychology; Social Science
Dist - CBSC **Prod** - CBSC

Self - Induction 6 MIN
VHS / 16mm
Electrical Theory Series
Color (S)
$50.00 purchase _ #241307
Illustrates 22 concepts fundamental to the training of second year electrical apprentices using graphic animation. Discusses how self - induction occurs when a change in a magnetic field induces a voltage into its own circuit. The induced voltage is known as a counter EMF, and Lenz's Law is introduced in 'Self - Induction.'.
Education; Industrial and Technical Education; Psychology
Dist - ACCESS **Prod** - ACCESS 1983

Self interest can never know the life of the spirit
VHS
Color (G R)
$29.95 purchase _ #C061
Features spiritual teacher Tara Singh.
Health and Safety; Psychology; Religion and Philosophy
Dist - LIFEAP **Prod** - LIFEAP

Self - Learning 18 MIN
Videoreel / VT2
Interpersonal Competence, Unit 05 - Learning Series; Unit 5 - Learning
Color (C A)
Features a humanistic psychologist who, by analysis and examples, discusses self - learning.
Psychology
Dist - TELSTR **Prod** - MVNE 1973

Self loving 60 MIN
VHS
Color (C A)
$39.95 purchase
Features artist, author and sex - educator Betty Dodson, who has been a spokesperson for women's sexual liberation for two decades. Works with women to confront false modesty, help them love their bodies, enhance sexual desire and find sexual liberation. Shows ten women, aged 28 to 60 completing Dodson's workshop, which includes nude exercises, masturbation, breathing techniques, orgasm and non - sexual intimacy. Produced by Betty Dodson.
Health and Safety; Psychology
Dist - FCSINT

Self - Loving 34 MIN
U-matic / VHS
Color (C A)
Offers a positive cross - cultural statement about female sexuality. Eleven women of heterosexual, bisexual and lesbian lifestyles share their early and later experiences, current patterns, use of vibrators, fantasies and orgasmic patterns.
Health and Safety; Psychology; Sociology
Dist - MMRC **Prod** - NATSF

Self made 40 MIN
VHS
John Bull business series
Color (A)
PdS65 purchase
Features a cross section of British entrepreneurs. Part of a six-part series on British business culture.
Business and Economics
Dist - BBCENE

Self - Management of Behavior 33 MIN
16mm / U-matic / VHS
Color (C A)
Deals with the self - management of behavior. Follows the evaluation of two behavior - problem children and the ensuing development self - intervention behavior modification programs. Includes commentary by B F Skinner.
Psychology
Dist - MEDIAG **Prod** - MEDIAG 1976

The Self - Management Training Program 27 MIN
U-matic / VHS
Color
Teaches specific coping skills needed to function successfully in a vocational setting. Deals with negative self - concepts, motivational difficulties, overreactions to external influences and negative emotionality.
Psychology
Dist - RESPRC **Prod** - RESPRC

Self - managing quality teams 15 MIN
VHS / BETA / U-matic
Total quality leadership series
Color (G PRO)
$395.00, $250.00 rental _ #QU0238 - 14
Features Dr Richard Ruhe in a consultant role in a staged quality team meeting. Includes numerous on - site interviews with public and private sector quality role models. Part of ten parts.
Business and Economics; Guidance and Counseling
Dist - BLNCTD **Prod** - BLNCTD

Self Monitoring of the Blood Glucose 17 MIN
U-matic / VHS
Color (PRO)
Reviews the blood sugar curve of diabetics. Discusses the shortcomings of urine testing. Focuses on self monitoring.
Health and Safety; Science - Natural
Dist - MEDFAC **Prod** - MEDFAC 1982

Self - observation 30 MIN
VHS / BETA
Transforming awareness series
Color (G)
$29.95 purchase _ #S117
Suggests that countless factors mitigate against self - observation in Western society. Features Dr Charles Tart, psychologist and author of 'Waking Up,' who recommends learning to focus on seemingly trivial details such as bodily sensations. Part of a four - part series on transforming awareness.
Psychology
Dist - THINKA **Prod** - THINKA

Self - Pleasuring 5 MIN
U-matic / VHS
Mutuality Series
Color
Highlights the importance of being comfortable within oneself and feeling good about giving pleasure to oneself.
Health and Safety; Psychology
Dist - MMRC **Prod** - MMRC

Self Portrait 29 MIN
U-matic
Artist at Work Series
Color
Demonstrates drawing a self portrait.
Fine Arts
Dist - UMITV **Prod** - UMITV 1973

Self portrait 7 MIN
16mm
Color; B&W (G)
$15.00 rental
Animates old drawings, paintings and photographs of filmmaker Hudina onto film.
Fine Arts
Dist - CANCIN **Prod** - HUDINA 1972

Self portraits 30 MIN
VHS
Palette series
Color (G C)
$70.00 purchase, $12.50, rental _ #36406
Reveals that during his 40 - year 17th - century career, Rembrandt, 1606 - 1669, painted nearly 100 self - portraits; even in his early works he positioned himself in the scenes he painted. Asks if such single - mindedness, unique in the history of art, has a secret meaning. Part of a 13 - part series which examines great paintings in a dynamic and dramatic way by moving into their creative spaces and spending time with the characters and their surroundings. Uses special video effects to investigate artistic enigmas and studies material, technique, style and significance. Narrated by Marcel Cuvelier, directed by Alain Jaubert.
Fine Arts
Dist - PSU **Prod** - LOUVRE 1992

Self - Preservation in an Atomic Bomb Attack 10 MIN
16mm
B&W
Explains individual methods of self - preservation in the event of an A - bomb attack, describing methods of protection for air or underwater explosions. Shows the effects of the blast, heat and radiation.
Health and Safety
Dist - USNAC **Prod** - USDD 1951

Self Propelled Cotton Stripper 8 MIN
16mm
Color
Tells why the 707 and 707XTB Cotton Strippers are machines that are designed to handle the new varieties of high - yielding, storm - proof cotton.
Agriculture
Dist - IDEALF **Prod** - ALLISC

Self - Protection 20 MIN
U-matic / VHS
Safety Sense Series Pt 8
Color (J)
LC 82-706076
Uses a variety of situations to demonstrate sensible techniques for protecting oneself from assault and injury. Encourages the avoidance of panic and thinking of alternatives when a threatening situation arises on the street, at home or at school.
Health and Safety; Physical Education and Recreation
Dist - GPN **Prod** - WCVETV 1981

Self - protection and recovery 18 MIN
VHS / U-matic / BETA
Managing assaultive patients series
Color (C PRO)
$280.00 purchase _ #615.1
Discusses ways in which health care staff can protect themselves, both physically and psychologically, from patient assaults. Describes specific physical techniques that can be used in an assaultive situation to minimize injury to both staff and patient. Includes candid testimonials of staff who discuss the effects of being assaulted and their road to recovery. Part of a series on managing assaultive patients.
Health and Safety; Psychology; Sociology
Dist - CONMED **Prod** - CALDMH

The Self - Protective Level (Section a) 28 MIN
U-matic / VHS
Management by Responsibility Series
Color
Psychology
Dist - DELTAK **Prod** - TRAINS

The Self - Protective Level (Section B) 40 MIN
U-matic / VHS

Management by Responsibility Series
Color
Psychology
Dist - DELTAK **Prod** - TRAINS

Self range of motion for lower extremity stretching
VHS / U-matic
Physical therapy series
Color (PRO C G)
$195.00 purchase _ #C890 - VI - 015
Informs patient educators and patients about the benefits of self range of motion for lower extremity stretching. Teaches effective techniques for minimizing pain and fatigue while enhancing the ability to perform daily activities. Part of a series by the physical therapy staff, St Luke's Hospital, Fargo, North Dakota.
Health and Safety; Physical Education and Recreation; Science - Natural
Dist - HSCIC

Self - reliant lifestyles — 30 MIN
VHS
A House for all seasons series
Color (G)
$49.95 purchase _ #AHFS - 313
Describes how Europe's Woonerf Movement has created urban coexistence between cars and people. Presents innovative programs by the electric utility Southern California Edison. Scrutinizes Scandinavian efforts at renewable resource development.
Home Economics; Science - Natural; Social Science; Sociology
Dist - PBS **Prod** - KRMATV 1986

Self - Scoring Examination - Brazelton Behavioral Assessment Scale — 23 MIN
Videoreel / VHS
Brazelton Neonatal Behavioral Assessment Scale Films Series
B&W
Shows an infant being subjected to the full set of stimuli called for by the Neonatal Scale. Contains no narration, but is intended to allow the viewer to assess the performance of the infant. Must be used with the accompanying score sheet.
Psychology
Dist - EDC **Prod** - EDC

Self Service — 11 MIN
VHS / 16mm
Color (I)
LC 75-703556
Presents an animated, allegorical film portraying the activities of a group of mosquitos who build their city around a man's vital fluids.
Guidance and Counseling; Science - Natural; Social Science
Dist - TEXFLM **Prod** - BOZETO 1975

Self - teaching video learning package series
Advanced troubleshooting and upgrading techniques for the IBM PC and compatibles — 150 MIN
The Help desk analyst's workshop — 120 MIN
Managing and using PC memory — 150 MIN
Troubleshooting and maintaining the IBM PC and compatibles — 150 MIN
Your PC - inside out — 120 MIN
Dist - TECHIN

The Self - testing and intelligence - Parts 15 and 16 — 60 MIN
VHS / U-matic
Discovering psychology series
Color (C)
$45.00, $29.95 purchase
Presents parts 15 and 16 of the 26 - part Discovering Psychology series. Looks at how society shapes an individual's concept of the self. Examines the emotional and motivational consequences of beliefs about oneself. Reveals how intelligence testing assigns values to different abilities, behaviors and personalities - for better and for worse. Two thirty - minute programs hosted by Professor Philip Zimbardo of Stanford University.
Education; Psychology
Dist - ANNCPB **Prod** - WGBHTV 1989

Self - Understanding — 28 MIN
16mm
Tangled World Series
Color (H A)
Discusses self - analysis, the indoor sport of the twentieth century. Presents and interprets different views of man from Socrates to Freud.
Psychology
Dist - YALEDV **Prod** - YALEDV

Self - worth - 4 — 66 MIN
VHS
Virginia Satir - families and relationships series
Color; PAL; SECAM (G)
$85.00 purchase
Features Virginia Satir in Part 4 of a 10 - part series on families and relationships. Shows Satir interacting with families and individuals, creating tableaus and role - plays that illustrate ineffective and effective communication styles, how to change viewpoints and perceptions and get beyond old roles and personal history to honest and direct feeling communication. All levels of NLP, neuro - linguistic programming.
Psychology; Social Science; Sociology
Dist - NLPCOM **Prod** - NLPCOM

Self worth in children and parents — 28 MIN
VHS
Prime time for parents video series
Color (G)
$89.95 purchase _ #RMI202
Stresses the value of self - worth in the healthy development of children and parents. Shows how the concept of self is formed and its effects on the way an individual faces life. Identifies behavior which has a negative impact on self - worth and shows how to create an environment for positive behavior. Part of a series on parenting. Study guide available separately.
Health and Safety; Home Economics; Psychology; Sociology
Dist - CADESF **Prod** - CADESF

The Selfish Giant — 10 MIN
U-matic / VHS
Fairy Tale Series
Color (K P I)
Narrates the Oscar Wilde story of the selfish giant who sees the error of his ways. Comes with teacher's guide.
Literature and Drama
Dist - BNCHMK **Prod** - BNCHMK 1985

Selfish Giant — 14 MIN
16mm / U-matic / VHS
Color; B&W (P I)
LC 71-710678
Based on the short story by Oscar Wilde in which a giant who shuts his garden to prevent children from playing in it realizes that in his selfishness he has shut out happiness and sunshine.
Literature and Drama
Dist - WWS **Prod** - UGA 1963

The Selfish Giant — 27 MIN
U-matic / VHS / 16mm
Color (J H) (FRENCH SPANISH SWEDISH FINNISH)
LC 72-703167
Uses animatiom to tell the story of a selfish giant who builds a wall around his castle garden to keep children from playing there. Explains that for being so nasty, the giant is tormented by snow, frost, wind and hail, which finally force the giant into accepting the children when they sneak back to the garden and make it bloom.
Literature and Drama
Dist - PFP **Prod** - READER 1972

Selfish Sally — 25 MIN
VHS
Color (K P I R)
$14.95 purchase _ #35 - 8556 - 19
Tells the story of a little girl named Sally, who refuses to share her tickets to the carnival. Shows how her friends forgive her and teach her that God wants people to share. Uses an animated format.
Psychology; Religion and Philosophy
Dist - APH **Prod** - CPH

Selig Tribune no. 21 — 10 MIN
16mm
Original issue newsreel series
B&W (G)
$15.00 rental
Features launching of a torpedo boat; Harvard varsity crew; Doiran, Greece takes care of injured French; US fleet at Guantanamo Bay; and more. Presents part of a series of original issue silent newsreels in their entirety.
Civics and Political Systems; Fine Arts; History - World; Literature and Drama
Dist - KITPAR

The Selki Girl — 14 MIN
16mm / VHS
Color (K P I)
$120.00, $245.00 purchase, $25.00 rental _ #VC319V, #MP319
Presents the story from the book, The Selki Girl, by Susan Cooper. A lonely man named Donallan spies three sea maidens on a rock and falls in love with one of them.
Health and Safety; Literature and Drama; Psychology
Dist - WWS **Prod** - WWS 1989

Sell Benefits - Communicating for Results — 13 MIN
VHS / 16mm
Color (H C A PRO)
$495.00 purchase, $150.00 rental _ #122
Illustrates how to create the illusion of strong benefits which seduce the customer and overcome his objections. Use as sales training and in the development of communication skills. Includes Leader's Guide.
Business and Economics; Psychology
Dist - SALENG **Prod** - SALENG 1989

Sell Benefits - the Key to Creative Selling — 9 MIN
U-matic / VHS / 16mm
Color (H C A)
LC 78-700651
Focuses on creative selling. Illustrates the difference between the features of a product or service and the benefits which prospective purchasers may derive from them.
Business and Economics
Dist - SALENG **Prod** - SALENG 1977

Sell it to me series
Features a two - part series that presents a variety of probing, closing and other sales skills. Consists of Preparing the Way, with key training points such as asking open questions and selling benefits, not features, and Doing the Deal, which delves into closing the sale, looking for buying signals and more. Includes a leader's guide and briefcase booklet.
Doing the deal
Preparing the way
Sell it to me series
Dist - EXTR **Prod** - VIDART 1977

Sell it to me - Video, workshop and CD-i program — 46 MIN
VHS
Sell it to me - Video, workshop and CD-i program
Color (IND PRO COR A)
$1,740.00 purchase, $500.00 rental, $50.00 preview
Communicates sales techniques to sales personnel on how to listen to customers, how to ask questions, and on closing the sale. This two-part series includes key messages on asking open questions, keeping control of meetings, listening to customers, explaining the benefits, making objections specific, putting the questions in perspective, setting realistic objectives, preparing alternative closes, and looking for buying signals - then closing.
Business and Economics
Dist - VIDART

Sell it to me - Video, workshop and CD-i program series
Doing the deal - Pt 2 — 23 MIN
Preparing the way - Pt 1 — 23 MIN
Dist - VIDART

Sell it to me - Video, workshop and CD-i program
Sell it to me - Video, workshop and CD-i program — 46 MIN
Dist - VIDART

Sell it to me - Video, workshop and CD-i program series
Doing the deal - Pt 2 — 23 MIN
Preparing the way - Pt 1 — 23 MIN
Dist - VIDART

Sell it to me - Video, workshop and CD-i program
Sell it to me - Video, workshop and CD-i program — 46 MIN
Dist - VIDART

Sell Like an Ace - Live Like a King — 28 MIN
16mm / U-matic / VHS
Color
LC 79-701609
Features a sales consultant explaining how to improve selling performance and close more sales. Based on the book Sell Like An Ace - Live Like A King by John Wolfe.
Business and Economics
Dist - DARTNL **Prod** - DARTNL 1974

Sell proud
16mm
B&W (G)
$317.00 purchase
Features Earl Nightingale who motivates sales personnel to have pride in their product and in their profession.
Business and Economics; Psychology
Dist - DARTNL **Prod** - NIGCON

Sell Safety — 10 MIN
16mm
Safety Management Series
Color
LC 74-705598
Business and Economics; Health and Safety
Dist - NSC **Prod** - NSC

Sell yourself - successful job interviewing 23 MIN
VHS
Color (H)
$89.00 purchase _ #60411 - 025
Teaches students how to sell themselves during a job interview. Uses dramatic and sometimes humorous reenactments to show how an interview can become a disaster, as well as how to survive tough questions. Includes teacher's guide, library kit.
Business and Economics; Guidance and Counseling; Psychology
Dist - GA **Prod** - GA 1992

Sellafield - the contaminated coast 52 MIN
VHS
Color; PAL (H C G)
PdS30 purchase
Focuses on the very controversial nuclear plant in Sellafield. Reveals that it was built in 1950, is best known by its original name, Windscale, and has a long record of accidents, leaks and emergencies. Seven years ago a Yorkshire TV documentary about Sellafield revealed abnormally high rates of childhood leukemia in a nearby village and a disturbing level of radioactive contamination along the Cambrian coast. The investigative team returns to Sellafield to see if anything has changed. Contact distributor about availability outside the United Kingdom.
Fine Arts; History - World; Social Science; Sociology
Dist - ACADEM **Prod** - YORKTV

The Sellin' of Jamie Thomas, Pt 1 24 MIN
U-matic / VHS
Young people's specials series
Color
Tells the story of a slave family's breaking apart due to a slave auction and the hardships they endure in order to reunite.
Fine Arts; History - United States; Sociology
Dist - MULTPP **Prod** - MULTPP

The Sellin' of Jamie Thomas, Pt 2 24 MIN
VHS / U-matic
Young people's specials series
Color
Tells of a slave family's escape through the underground railway and their settlement in a Quaker town.
Fine Arts; History - United States; Sociology
Dist - MULTPP **Prod** - MULTPP

Selling 50 MIN
VHS
Color (A PRO)
$59.95 purchase _ #566VU
Features Zig Ziglar in a motivational video for salespersons. Looks at selling from the perspectives of the new salesperson, the seasoned pro, the sales manager, the recruiter, and the salesperson's family.
Business and Economics; Psychology
Dist - NIGCON **Prod** - NIGCON

Selling 22 MIN
VHS
Video guide to occupational exploration - the video GOE series
Color (J H C G)
$69.95 purchase _ #CCP1009V
Discusses sales careers. Interviews a real estate agent, travel agent, clothing buyer and a home sales representative. Part of a 14 - part series exploring occupational clusters.
Business and Economics; Guidance and Counseling
Dist - CAMV **Prod** - CAMV 1991

Selling 15 MIN
U-matic / VHS / 16mm
Communications and selling program series
Color (A)
Presents the five basic steps that experts generally agree are essential to success in selling. Emphasizes the importance of relating the product or service to the customer's need.
Business and Economics
Dist - NEM **Prod** - NEM

Selling 15 MIN
U-matic / VHS / 16mm
Communications and selling program - Spanish series
Color (SPANISH)
Illustrates the five primary steps a salesperson must know to lead a customer to a purchase. Uses three typical sales situations as examples.
Business and Economics
Dist - NEM **Prod** - NEM

Selling a business 48 MIN
VHS
Color (PRO)
$59.95 purchase _ #TKP2023V-B
Helps business owners sell their businesses. Includes advice on the six steps of the selling process; preparing the business to sell; maintaining confidentiality; dealing with employees; managing the transition; finding buyers that buy; how to set a price; exit planning; reasons to sell; accounting tips; legal advice; and more.
Business and Economics
Dist - CAMV **Prod** - TOMKAT 1994
TOMKAT

Selling - a Great Way to Reach the Top
VHS
$39.95 purchase _ #BZ200V
Talks on how to sell yourself on selling. Discusses how to present a product, relate to a client, and close a deal.
Business and Economics
Dist - CAREER **Prod** - CAREER

Selling - a great way to reach the top 50 MIN
VHS
Color (H C A)
$54.95 purchase
Features motivational speaker Zig Ziglar in an examination of how to get the most out of sales calls. Shares Ziglar's own strategies for success.
Business and Economics
Dist - PBS **Prod** - WNETTV

Selling a Song 29 MIN
U-matic
Music Shop Series
Color
Focuses on the modern business of music.
Fine Arts
Dist - UMITV **Prod** - UMITV 1974

Selling as a Profession 2 MIN
U-matic / VHS / 16mm
Sales Meeting Films Series
Color (C A)
Offers a tribute to the sales team which is the heartbeat of the corporation.
Business and Economics
Dist - CORF **Prod** - MBACC 1983

Selling benefits 28 MIN
VHS
Color (A PRO)
$650.00 purchase, $155.00 rental
Teaches salespeople to seek and emphasize the 'benefits' a product has - that is, the product features that the customer finds most useful. Covers how to determine a customer's needs.
Business and Economics; Psychology
Dist - VLEARN **Prod** - RTBL

Selling by telephone 13 MIN
U-matic / VHS / 16mm
Customer service, courtesy and selling programs - Spanish series
Color (SPANISH)
Demonstrates how to use the telephone effectively as a sales tool.
Business and Economics; Social Science
Dist - NEM **Prod** - NEM

Selling by telephone 13 MIN
16mm / U-matic / VHS
Communications and selling program series
Color
LC 81-700435
Presents a series of vignettes demonstrating the techniques of telephone selling.
Business and Economics
Dist - NEM **Prod** - NEM 1980

Selling Houses for a Living 30 MIN
VHS / 16mm
(PRO G)
$89.95 purchase _ #DGP7
Tells the hows and whys of success in three realtors' careers. Hosted by Dick Goldberg.
Business and Economics
Dist - RMIBHF **Prod** - RMIBHF

Selling in Department Stores 64 MIN
U-matic / VHS
Color
Covers several aspects of department store selling. Includes how to approach a customer and determine customer needs. Discusses how to present merchandise and how to make the sale.
Business and Economics; Psychology
Dist - TRASS **Prod** - DOUVIS

Selling in the 80's 20 MIN
16mm / U-matic / VHS
Color (H C A)
Explains different attitudes towards selling. Shows that by overcoming bad attitudes by learning to be proud of selling as a profession, and by taking the time to help customers solve their problems and safisfy their concerns, a salesperson can find out how very rewarding a sales career can be, both financially and psychologically.
Business and Economics; Psychology
Dist - CRMP **Prod** - CRMP 1981

Selling in the '90s 61 MIN
VHS
Color (H C A)
$99.95 purchase _ #NGC586V
Features sales expert Larry Wilson and corporate executives with tips to succeeding in sales in the 1990s. Covers subjects including what buyers want, partnership selling, escaping the trap of 'never enough,' and more. Includes two audiocassettes and two workbooks.
Business and Economics
Dist - CAMV
GAINST

Selling is a profession - there are no more peddlers 55 MIN
VHS
Color (A PRO)
$169.00 purchase _ #S01131
Stresses the concept of selling as a service activity. Attempts to dispel old images of sales and encourages the development of professional attitudes. Hosted by Jim Cathcart and Michael Harbert.
Business and Economics; Psychology; Social Science
Dist - UILL

Selling Jewelry 101 MIN
U-matic / VHS
Color
Focuses on several aspects of selling jewelry in a store. Discusses how to approach a customer and how to determine customer needs. Covers how to present merchandise and how to make a sale.
Business and Economics; Psychology
Dist - TRASS **Prod** - DOUVIS

Selling Menswear 92 MIN
U-matic / VHS
Color
Discusses several aspects of selling menswear. Shows how to approach a customer and how to determine customer needs. Shows how to present merchandise and how to make a sale.
Business and Economics; Psychology
Dist - TRASS **Prod** - DOUVIS

Selling Movies on Television 55 MIN
BETA / VHS
Color
Presents 69 television commercials advertising various films.
Business and Economics; Fine Arts
Dist - VIDIM **Prod** - UNKNWN

Selling of Local TV News 29 MIN
VHS / U-matic
Inside Story Series
Color
Looks at the hotly contested ratings war in Boston's local news market. Both excesses and improvements were noted but the question remained 'Does it have to be this way?'.
Fine Arts; Sociology
Dist - PBS **Prod** - PBS 1981

The Selling of Terri Gibbs 30 MIN
VHS / U-matic
Enterprise II Series
Color (C A)
LC 83-706196
Describes the marketing campaign which made it possible for Terri Gibbs, a country and western singer, to cross over into the pop field.
Business and Economics; Fine Arts
Dist - LCOA **Prod** - WGBHTV 1983

Selling of the Pentagon 52 MIN
U-matic / VHS / 16mm
Color
LC 71-712037
Presents a documentary from CBS news which examines three areas of Pentagon propaganda - - direct contacts with citizens, filmmaking and use of the communications media. Exposes the breadth and depth of the Pentagon's efforts to influence public opinion.
Civics and Political Systems
Dist - CAROUF **Prod** - CBSTV 1971

Selling of the Pentagon, Pt 1 25 MIN
U-matic / VHS / 16mm
Color
Presents a documentary from CBS news which examines three areas of Pentagon propaganda including direct contacts with citizens, filmmaking and use of the communications media. Exposes the breadth and depth of the Pentagon's efforts to influence public opinion. Based entirely on unclassified material.
Sociology
Dist - CAROUF **Prod** - CBSTV

Selling of the Pentagon, Pt 2 25 MIN
U-matic / VHS / 16mm
Color
Presents a documentary from CBS news which examines three areas of Pentagon propaganda including direct contacts with citizens, filmmaking and use of the communications media. Exposes the breadth and depth of the Pentagon's efforts to influence public opinion. Based entirely on unclassified material.
Sociology
Dist - CAROUF **Prod** - CBSTV

Selling on the phone 20 MIN
VHS
Color (A PRO)
$475.00 purchase, $110.00 rental
Covers all aspects of telephone selling. Explains how to get the customer's attention, gain their trust, discover the customer's wants and needs, and make a winning presentation.
Business and Economics; Psychology; Social Science
Dist - VLEARN **Prod** - AIMS

Selling on the Phone 20 MIN
VHS / U-matic
(PRO)
$475.00 purchase, $110.00 rental
Highlights the latest techniques in telephone sales, from planning to closing the sale.
Business and Economics
Dist - CREMED **Prod** - CREMED 1987

Selling on the Telephone 20 MIN
VHS / U-matic
Reach Out to Help Someone Series
Color (A)
Demonstrates ways of selling by telephone. Includes planning, sales methods, and closing a call.
Business and Economics; Social Science
Dist - AMEDIA **Prod** - AMEDIA

Selling Our Products 20 MIN
U-matic
Exploring Our Nation Series
Color (I)
Investigates a large retail department store in order to illustrate buyer and market, wholesaling and retailing, advertising and display, and selling and the consumer.
Business and Economics
Dist - GPN **Prod** - KRMATV 1975

Selling Out 30 MIN
16mm
Color
Shows Prince Edward Island, Canada's smallest and most picturesque province. Features Vernon Macgoughan, an elderly retired farmer, and Robert Hogg, a local auctioneer. Shows the sale by public auction of the farm and personal possessions of Vernon Macgoughan. Focuses on the gradual loss of the human, cultural and material resources of the Island.
Business and Economics; Geography - World; History - World; Social Science; Sociology
Dist - COPFC **Prod** - JWSKIT
COPFC

Selling Power Every Hour 15 MIN
U-matic / VHS
Color (IND)
Shows how point - of - purchase materials, lighting and case schematics can increase selling power. Discusses importance of service, even in a self - service store.
Business and Economics
Dist - NLSAMB **Prod** - NLSAMB

Selling Quality to Management 32 MIN
U-matic / VHS
Quality Planning Series
Color
Describes several justifications for an increased management commitment to quality, including the threat of product liability.
Business and Economics; Industrial and Technical Education
Dist - MIOT **Prod** - MIOT

The Selling Secrets of Ben Franklin 30 MIN
16mm / U-matic / VHS
Color (PRO)
LC 76-709368
A dramatization in which Ben Franklin demonstrates in modern surroundings that his two - hundred - year - old principles of selling still apply today.
Business and Economics
Dist - DARTNL **Prod** - DARTNL 1967

Selling services 28 MIN
VHS
Color (A PRO)
$550.00 purchase, $125.00 rental
Focuses on four areas of service selling - building credibility and trust, presentation techniques, overcoming objections and closing sales, and servicing the sale. Provides examples from the finance, insurance, and service industries. Includes leader's guide, workbooks, and reminder cards.
Business and Economics; Psychology
Dist - VLEARN

Selling skills 35 MIN
VHS
Color (J H C G)
$79.95 purchase _ #CCP0089V
Uses interviews with professional sales personnel in fashion merchandising to present strategies for enhancing business transactions. Shows how to prepare for a sale, approach customers, determine customer needs, present merchandise, ask for a sale, handle resistance and steps to take after the sale. Applicable to any sales position.
Business and Economics; Guidance and Counseling; Psychology
Dist - CAMV **Prod** - CAMV 1992

Selling skills - have I got a deal for you 15 MIN
VHS
Job skills for career success series
Color (H C G)
$79.00 purchase _ #CDSBED102V
Looks at major sales styles and what happens when the style doesn't match the product being sold. Illustrates effective selling styles and career opportunities from retail sales to industrial sales to telemarketing. Part of a ten - part series which explores basic job skills necessary for a successful career. Includes student guide.
Business and Economics; Guidance and Counseling; Psychology
Dist - CAMV

Selling skills in fashion merchandising 35 MIN
VHS
Color (H C G)
$79.95 purchase _ #CCP0089V
Discusses the sales steps to follow from the time a customer first enters a store to ensure that they leave with a full shopping bag and a smile on their face. Uses interviews with professional sales personnel in fashion merchandising to present strategies for enhancing business transactions. Shows how to prepare for a sale, approach customers, determine customer needs, present merchandise, ask for a sale, handle resistance and steps to take after the sale. Includes student manual.
Business and Economics
Dist - CAMV **Prod** - CAMV 1992

Selling Strategies - Steps to Sale
VHS / U-matic
Making of a Salesman Series Session 7
Color
Discusses idea that success is based on determining the right time, place and person in the right sequence and applying the appropriate strategy. Deals with the organizational aspects of selling. Illustrates twelve sales strategies.
Business and Economics; Psychology
Dist - PRODEV **Prod** - PRODEV

Selling the Dream
VHS / 16mm
Smithsonian World Series
Color; Captioned (G)
$49.95 purchase _ #SMIW - 602
Researches, documents and preserves a collection of American advertisements and advertising techniques from the past. Demonstrates the dramatic effect of television on American life. Part of a series on gender, advertising and artificial intelligence.
Business and Economics; Psychology; Sociology
Dist - PBS **Prod** - WETATV 1990

Selling the feeling 29 MIN
VHS
Consuming hunger series
Color (G)
$14.95 purchase
Focuses on the meaning of the Hands Across America campaign and its emphasis on the needs of American people for food and shelter. Looks at media use of the images. Part 3 of a three - part series.
Business and Economics; Guidance and Counseling
Dist - MARYFA

Selling - the Power of Confidence 20 MIN
16mm / U-matic / VHS
Color (H C A)
LC 81-700330
Shows how a salesperson can often be his or her own worst enemy. Follows one sales representative as he works through his fears toward becoming a more confident, effective and successful salesperson.
Business and Economics
Dist - MGHT **Prod** - CRMP 1981

Selling to Hollywood 86 MIN
VHS
Color (G PRO)
$79.95 purchase
Provides an insider's look at writing and selling scripts for motion pictures and television. Gives tips on protecting material, working with agents and selling to studios and independents.
Business and Economics; English Language; Fine Arts
Dist - WRITEC

Selling to the Customer 24 MIN
U-matic
Occupations Series
B&W (J H)
Shows the qualities of a good sales clerk.
Guidance and Counseling
Dist - TVOTAR **Prod** - TVOTAR 1985

Selling to Tough Customers 23 MIN
16mm / U-matic / VHS
Color (H C A) (SPANISH)
LC 81-706216
Distinguishes four hard - to - sell customer types and explains how to deal with them. Introduces The Complainer, The Know - It - All, The Indecisive Type, and The Unresponsive.
Business and Economics
Dist - CRMP **Prod** - CRMP 1981
MGHT

Selling with service 57 MIN
VHS
Color (A PRO)
$69.95 purchase _ #S01550
Contrasts operational and marketing perspectives in sales, stressing the concept that marketing is a philosophy rather than a department. Hosted by Phillip Wexler.
Business and Economics; Psychology
Dist - UILL

Selling Womenswear 88 MIN
VHS / U-matic
Color
Examines several aspects of selling womenswear. Includes how to approach a customer and determine customer needs. Discusses how to present merchandise and how to make the sale.
Business and Economics; Psychology
Dist - TRASS **Prod** - DOUVIS

Selling Your Home 30 MIN
U-matic / VHS
Personal Finance Series Lesson 12
Color (C A)
Offers guidelines for selling a home, from setting the price to making the house more saleable. Explores alternatives for handling potential tax liabilities.
Business and Economics; Sociology
Dist - CDTEL **Prod** - SCCON

Selling Your Home 28 MIN
U-matic / VHS
Personal Finance and Money Management Series
Color (C A)
Business and Economics; Civics and Political Systems
Dist - SCCON **Prod** - SCCON 1987

Selling Yourself
VHS
(G)
$39.95 purchase _ #IL301V
Teaches students how to sell themselves on paper through resumes, cover letters, and application forms. Explains how to make a good first impression in person, on paper, and on the telephone.
Business and Economics; Guidance and Counseling; Sociology
Dist - CAREER **Prod** - CAREER

Selling yourself in the interview - Tape 4
VHS
Find the job you want and get it series
Color (H A T)
$99.00 purchase _ #ES137
Look at preparation for interviews when job searching. Part of a four - part series on employment.
Business and Economics; Guidance and Counseling; Psychology
Dist - AAVIM

Selma Jam 60 MIN
BETA / VHS / U-matic
Color; Mono (G)
Documents a regular get together of a group of musicians as they share their music on fiddles, banjos, guitars and harmonicas. Folksongs handed down through the generations fill the air as some play and some listen.
Fine Arts
Dist - UIOWA **Prod** - UIOWA 1982

Selman's Justice 12 MIN
16mm
Color
LC 76-703804
Tells how Marshal T J Selman and his deputy ride after his daughter's killer.
Fine Arts
Dist - CONCRU **Prod** - CONCRU 1976

Semantic Mapping 30 MIN
U-matic / VHS
Teaching Reading Comprehension Series
Color (T PRO)
$180.00 purchase,$35.00 rental
Establishes two ways in which a students own base knowledge can be utilized in reading comprehension.
Education; English Language
Dist - AITECH **Prod** - WETN 1986

Semantics and Syntax 168 MIN
VHS / U-matic
Meeting the Communication Needs of the Severely/Profoundly 'Handicapped 1981 Series
Color
Defines the area of 'semantics and syntax' and clarifies the relationship between this and other aspects of child language development.
Psychology; Social Science
Dist - PUAVC **Prod** - PUAVC

Semi - conductor materials and diodes 25 MIN
VHS
Electrical series
Color (H A T)
$45.00 purchase _ #DA405
Introduces semi - conductor material and N - P junctions. Uses those principles to develop diode theory. Discusses the use of diodes through rectifiers and logic circuits. Part of a three - part series on electrical work.
Industrial and Technical Education; Science - Physical
Dist - AAVIM **Prod** - AAVIM 1992

Semi - Direct Products
16mm
B&W
Presents the group theoretic ideas that lead to the general semi - direct product construction.
Mathematics
Dist - OPENU **Prod** - OPENU

Semi - Finished Steel 8 MIN
16mm
Making, Shaping and Treating Steel Series
Color (H C A)
Business and Economics; Science - Physical
Dist - USSC **Prod** - USSC

Semi - Immediate Anterior Fixed Partial Denture with Reverse Pin Facing - Assembly of Bridge 13 MIN
U-matic / VHS
Color
Shows that the proper relationship of the retainers and pontics to the investing tissues is a most important esthetic and physiological consideration in any fixed prosthesis and demonstrates a direct and indirect assembly and finishing procedure to gain optimal appearance and function.
Health and Safety; Science
Dist - AMDA **Prod** - VADTC 1969

Semi - Immediate Anterior Fixed Partial Denture with Reverse Pin Facing - Impression 14 MIN
U-matic / VHS
Color
Depicts the methodology of securing impressions for a fixed prosthesis using mercaptan rubber following gingival retention, the procedures incident to producing accurate stone dies and development of the wax patterns for three - quarter type retainers.
Health and Safety; Science
Dist - AMDA **Prod** - VADTC 1969

Semi - Immediate Anterior Fixed Partial Denture with Reverse Pin Facing - Pontic Preparation 11 MIN
VHS / U-matic
Color
Shows the labial and gingival adaptation, essential for a harmonious relationship with the adjacent teeth and physiologic esthetic contact with ridge tissues.
Health and Safety; Science
Dist - AMDA **Prod** - VADTC 1969

Semi - Immediate Anterior Fixed Partial Denture with Reverse Pin Facing - Preparation of 10 MIN
U-matic / VHS
Color
Shows and describes the procedures necessary to convert a denture tooth into a reverse pin pontic.
Health and Safety; Science
Dist - AMDA **Prod** - VADTC 1969

Semi - Immediate Anterior Fixed Partial Denture with Reverse Pin Facing Series
Assembly of bridge and delivery to patient 13 MIN
Impression Procedure Preparation of the Dies and Waxing Retainers 14 MIN
Dist - USNAC

The Semi - Vowel Rule 15 MIN
16mm / U-matic / VHS
Reading Skill, Set 3 Series
Color (P I)
LC 74-701761
Uses animation, live action and a variety of commonly used words in order to show how the consonants L and R, sometimes called semi - vowels, have a special effect on the sound of single vowels in words.
English Language
Dist - JOU **Prod** - GLDWER 1974

Semiautomatic and Hand Molding of Intricate Parts 16 MIN
16mm
B&W
LC FIE52-298
Shows how to mold a part with undercuts, mold a part with complicated shape and assemble and disassemble a hand mold.
Industrial and Technical Education
Dist - USNAC **Prod** - USOE 1945

Semiconductor Electronics Education Com - Mittee Films Series
Transistor Structure and Technology 38 MIN
Dist - EDC

Semiconductor Electronics Education Committee Films Series
A Computer Generated Random - Walk Model of Diffusion Along a Bar 5 MIN
Dist - EDC

Semiconductor Lasers 40 MIN
VHS / U-matic
Integrated Optics Series
Color (C)
Discusses P - N junction laser structures, threshold conditions for lasing, effects of field confinement, optical mode characteristics, and power and efficiency relationships.
Science - Physical
Dist - UDEL **Prod** - UDEL

Semiconductor Memories Course Series no 1
Memory Functions and Economics 60 MIN
Dist - TXINLC

Semiconductor Memories Course Series no 4
High Speed Random Access Storage Design 60 MIN
Dist - TXINLC

Semiconductor Memories Course Series no 5
MOS Random Access Semiconductor Storage Design 60 MIN
Dist - TXINLC

Semiconductor memories course - No 6 series
Fixed program semiconductor storage design 60 MIN
Dist - TXINLC

Semiconductor memories course - No 8 series
Fixed program and sequentially accessed memory applications 60 MIN
Dist - TXINLC

Semiconductor memories course series
Random access memory applications - Pt 1 60 MIN
Random access memory applications - Pt 2 60 MIN
Random access memory applications - Pt 3 60 MIN
Reliability of semiconductor memories 60 MIN
Semiconductor technology arsenal for storage elements 60 MIN
Sequentially accessed semiconductor storage design 60 MIN
Dist - TXINLC

Semiconductor Memories - Dynamic, Prom Memories
U-matic / VHS
Digital Techniques Series
Color
Industrial and Technical Education
Dist - HTHZEN **Prod** - HTHZEN

Semiconductor Memories 'Dynamic /PROM Memories'
U-matic / VHS
Digital Techniques Video Training Course Series
Color
Industrial and Technical Education
Dist - VTRI **Prod** - VTRI

Semiconductor memories - memory basics
U-matic / VHS
Digital techniques video training series
Color
Industrial and Technical Education
Dist - HTHZEN **Prod** - HTHZEN
VTRI VTRI

Semiconductor memories - read, write memories
U-matic / VHS
Digital techniques video training series
Color
Industrial and Technical Education
Dist - HTHZEN **Prod** - HTHZEN
VTRI VTRI

Semiconductor Memory Devices 30 MIN
U-matic / VHS
Microcomputer Memory Design Series
Color (IND)
Includes array of a memory chip, decoding scheme, address field and memory locations, static RAM, organization and operation, microprocessor memory interface signals, and block diagram of complete memory system.
Industrial and Technical Education; Mathematics; Sociology
Dist - COLOSU **Prod** - COLOSU

Semiconductor Memory Driver Applications 30 MIN
U-matic / VHS
Linear and Interface Circuits, Part II - Interface Integrated 'Circuits Series
Color (PRO)
Describes interface drivers for TTL and MOS memories as well as CMOS logic from TTL and ECL logic levels and discusses specific applications. Stresses difference between an interface with p - channel and n - channel MOS.
Industrial and Technical Education
Dist - TXINLC **Prod** - TXINLC

Semiconductor Principles
VHS / 35mm strip
Electricity and Electronics Series
Color
$35.00 purchase _ #MX8204 filmstrip, $75.00 purchase _ #MX8204V VHS
Explains transistors, the molecular structure of some of the most widely used semiconductors and how natural semiconductors can operate more efficiently.
Education; Industrial and Technical Education
Dist - CAREER **Prod** - CAREER

Semiconductor technology arsenal for storage elements 60 MIN
Videoreel / VT1
Semiconductor memories course series; No 2
Color (IND)
Reviews storage - element design objectives, bipolar and MOS storage cells.
Industrial and Technical Education
Dist - TXINLC **Prod** - TXINLC

Semiconductors, Superconductors, and Catalysts 58 MIN
VHS / 16mm
Royal Institution Crystals & Lasers Lectures for Young People Series
Color (J)
$149.00 purchase, $75.00 rental _ #OD - 2221
Discusses resistance in semiconductors and superconductors and how superconductors might change everything from transportation to medical diagnostics. The third of six installments of The Royal Institution Crystals & Lasers Lectures For Young People Series.
Industrial and Technical Education; Science - Physical
Dist - FOTH

The Seminar and Role - Playing Strategy 30 MIN
16mm
Nursing - Where are You Going, How will You Get There Series
B&W (C A)
LC 74-700180
Illustrates the principles and techniques for conducting seminar and role playing episodes.
Education; Health and Safety
Dist - NTCN **Prod** - NTCN 1971

Seminar for Progress 14 MIN
16mm
B&W
Shows the first Seminar of Afro - Asian Rural Development where delegates from African and Asian countries exchanged views, discussed national development and visited different levels of operation rooms, land development schemes and cottage industries in Kuala Trengganu, Malaysia.
Civics and Political Systems; Geography - World
Dist - PMFMUN **Prod** - FILEM 1967

The Seminole 30 MIN
VHS
Indians of North America video series
Color; B&W; CC (P I J)
$39.95 purchase _ #D6659
Overviews the history of the Seminole. Combines interviews with leading authorities on Native American history with live footage and historic stills. Part of a ten - part series.
Social Science
Dist - KNOWUN

Seminole Indians 11 MIN
16mm / U-matic / VHS
Color (I J H)
LC FIA54-1286
Documents the lives of Seminole Indians living in the Florida Everglades. Shows their open - sided houses with raised floors which offer protection against floods and snakes. Includes scenes of women creating souvenirs for tourists, doing washing and sewing, while the men hunt, fish and skin the frogs they will sell.
Geography - United States; Social Science; Sociology
Dist - IFB **Prod** - UMINN 1951

The Seminole - Muskogee 30 MIN
VHS
Indians of North America series
Color (J H C G)
$49.95 purchase _ #LVCD6659V - S
Interviews Seminole leaders who discuss their nation's history. Includes location footage at reservations where children and elders discuss what it means to be Native American today. Part of a 10 - part series on Indian culture.
History - United States; Social Science
Dist - CAMV

Semiotics of the kitchen 8 MIN
VHS / U-matic
B&W
Features a woman explaining the use of a variety of kitchen tools.
Fine Arts
Dist - KITCHN **Prod** - KITCHN

Semiprecision and Precision Layout 15 MIN
U-matic / VHS
Introduction to Machine Technology, Module 1 Series; Module 1
Color (IND)
Tells how to identify tools for semiprecision and precision layout and how to set up and perform a semiprecision layout and a precision layout.
Industrial and Technical Education
Dist - LEIKID **Prod** - LEIKID

Semiramide 220 MIN
VHS
Color (G)
$39.95 purchase _ #1439
Unites a contemporary cast - Marilyn Horne, June Anderson and Samuel Ramey - in a performance of Semiramide, Rossini's last opera. Includes two cassettes. Filmed at the Metropolitan Opera.
Fine Arts
Dist - KULTUR

Semper Fi 13 MIN
16mm
New Directions Series
Color (G)
Presents an independent production by Geoffrey Luck. Part of a comic series of first film shorts.
Fine Arts; Literature and Drama
Dist - FIRS

The Senate 18 MIN
35mm strip / VHS
US government in action series
Color (J H C T A)
$57.00, $45.00 purchase _ #MB - 510770 - 8, #MB - 509984 - 5
Examines the Senate, part of the legislative branch of the United States government. Emphasizes the Constitutional concept of checks and balances. Uses archival and modern graphics.
Civics and Political Systems
Dist - SRA **Prod** - SRA 1988

Senator Sam 58 MIN
U-matic / VHS
Color (G)
$249.00, $149.00 purchase _ #AD - 2010
Profiles Senator Sam Ervin of North Carolina - a portrait of the Constitution in action. Reviews his legislative record on behalf of first amendment rights as well as his chairmanship of the Senate Select Committee on Presidential Campaign Activities - which showed America and the world how the Constitution works and why a society must be ruled by law.
Biography; Civics and Political Systems; History - United States
Dist - FOTH **Prod** - FOTH

Senator Sam Ervin, Jr - the Constitution Series
The Bill of Rights 12 MIN
The Congress 12 MIN
The Constitution in the 21st Century 12 MIN
Delegates and events of the Constitutional Convention 12 MIN
The First Amendment 12 MIN
The Framing of the Constitution 12 MIN
Historical Origins of the Constitution 12 MIN
The Judiciary 12 MIN
The Presidency 12 MIN
The Separation of Powers 12 MIN
Dist - COUNFI

Send a gorilla 94 MIN
35mm
Color; PAL (G)
Entertains with a look at St Valentine's Day in Wellington, New Zealand, traditionally the busiest day of the year for the ladies of the Send A Gorilla Singing Telegram Company. Lists the troubles they encounter on this day - the boss skips town; Vicki wishes her boyfriend would also skip out; Claire wants custody of her son but fears the judge won't consider a gorilla as a suitable parent and she is being dogged by a truant Doberman who has a price on his head and a lust for her gorilla suit. Directed by Melanie Read for Pinflicks, New Zealand. Contact distributor for price and availability outside the United Kingdom.
Fine Arts; Literature and Drama
Dist - BALFOR

Send in the Marines 29 MIN
VHS
America's drug forum series
Color (G)
$19.95 purchase _ #105
Examines the use of US military personnel in Central and South America in an effort to cut off the supply of drugs at their source. Asks if the United States should export the Drug War to Latin and South America. Guests include Col Charles Beckwith - retired, commander of the elite US Delta Force, Jorge Crespo - Velasco, Bolivian Ambassador to the US, Admiral Gene La Rockque - retired, Director of the Center for Defense Information, Coletta Youngers, Associate at the Washington Office on Latin Affairs.
Civics and Political Systems; Health and Safety; History - United States
Dist - DRUGPF **Prod** - DRUGPF 1991

Send - Receive I / Send Receive II 50 MIN
VHS / U-matic
Color
Presented by Liza Bear and Keith Sonnier. Deals with communications technology.
Fine Arts; Social Science
Dist - ARTINC **Prod** - ARTINC

Send these to Me 15 MIN
U-matic / VHS
Los Peregrinos Modernos - the Modern Pioneers Series
Color (I)
Continues the story of the Martinez family's difficulties in adapting to the new and different culture of America. Stresses the need to conform to customary practices and habits of a new home land.
Geography - World; Sociology
Dist - GPN **Prod** - NETV

Sendak 27 MIN
U-matic / VHS
Color; Mono (I J H C)
Describes the significant events of author Maurice Sendak's life and their impact on his work. Asks who the monsters are in Where The Wild Things Are; why everything good happens while children are asleep; how the Lindberg kidnapping affected the fantasy outside over there; and how did the tragedy of the Holocaust affected his works. Explores these themes candidly, and allows the audience to truly get to know the author.
Biography; Literature and Drama
Dist - WWS **Prod** - WWS 1986

Sending Clear Messages 29 MIN
Videoreel / VT2
Interpersonal Competence, Unit 02 - Communication Series; Unit 2 - Communication
Color (C A)
Features a humanistic psychologist who, by analysis and examples, discusses how to communicate in a manner that can be easily comprehended.
Psychology
Dist - TELSTR **Prod** - MVNE 1973

Sending Your Thoughts with Special Care 26 MIN
16mm
Color
Explores the role of the neighborhood FTD florist. Introduces several generations of florists, involved in family owned businesses, living where they work, helping their neighbors enhance special occasions.
Business and Economics; Sociology
Dist - MTP

Seneca Glass 24 MIN
16mm
Color (A)
LC 77-703132
Recaptures the production of early hand - blown Seneca glassware in Morgantown, West Virginia.
Fine Arts; Geography - United States
Dist - USNAC **Prod** - USNPS 1975

Senile dementia 26 MIN
VHS
Color; PAL (J H G)
PdS25 purchase
Encourages a kinder attitude toward the elderly. Focuses on Edith Brooks, 67, who lives with her daughter Jackie in Manchester. Reveals that Jackie has had to give up employment to look after her mother, whom she says is less independent than her two - year - old daughter. Contact distributor about availability outside the United Kingdom.
Health and Safety
Dist - ACADEM

Senior adults - traffic safety and alcohol 11 MIN
16mm / VHS
Color (G A)
$70.00, $35.00 purchase _ #245, #463
Discusses how the use of alchohol affects the mobility of senior citizens. Looks at the effects of alcohol on pedestrians and drivers as well as the effects of combining alcohol and prescription drugs. Includes a teacher's discussion guide and 50 copies of student pamphlets. Guide and pamphlets also available separately.
Guidance and Counseling; Health and Safety; Psychology
Dist - AAAFTS **Prod** - AAAFTS 1978

Senior Center Programming 30 MIN
U-matic
Growing Old in Modern America Series
Color
Health and Safety; Sociology
Dist - UWASHP **Prod** - UWASHP

Senior Executive Interview 60 MIN
VHS
Color (A PRO)
$595.00 purchase, $95.00 rental _ #245000
Reviews job search skills for the professional or executive seeking employment. Focuses on effective use of contacts for networking, how and when to take control of the interview, dealing with executive search firms, and how to answer and negotiate salary questions.
Business and Economics; Guidance and Counseling
Dist - DBMI **Prod** - DBMI 1988

The Senior Executive Service 30 MIN
U-matic
Launching Civil Service Reform Series WASHINGTON, DC 20409
Color
LC 79-706273
Explains the legal provisions governing the federal senior executive service under the system created by the Civil Service Reform Act.
Civics and Political Systems
Dist - USNAC **Prod** - USOPMA 1978

Senior fitnessize 30 MIN
VHS
Color (A PRO)
$49.95 purchase _ #AH45238
Provides a fitness program for senior citizens, one which allows participants to remain seated while participating. Consists of a videocassette, an audio tape, and an exercise manual.
Health and Safety; Physical Education and Recreation
Dist - HTHED **Prod** - HTHED

Senior flex
VHS
Color (H C A)
$39.95 purchase _ #IV1300V
Presents a special workout program for senior citizens. Includes stretching, calisthenics, and low - impact aerobic exercises.
Health and Safety; Physical Education and Recreation
Dist - CAMV

Senior flex 46 MIN
VHS
Color (A PRO)
$29.95 purchase _ #AH45256
Presents a self - paced approach to exercise for senior citizens.
Health and Safety; Physical Education and Recreation
Dist - HTHED **Prod** - HTHED

Senior flex with Ed Taafe - the exciting new workout program for seniors
VHS
Color (G)
$29.95 purchase _ #IV - 056
Provides a practical, safe and enjoyable way to stay in shape for older people which allows them to progress at their own pace.
Health and Safety; Physical Education and Recreation
Dist - INCRSE **Prod** - INCRSE

Senior Olympics 1980 10 MIN
U-matic / VHS
Color
Highlights events from the first Maryland Senior Olympics. Emphasizes the positive effects that physical activity has for older adults.
Health and Safety; Physical Education and Recreation; Sociology
Dist - LVN **Prod** - BCPL

Senior Power and How to Use it 19 MIN
16mm
Urban Crisis Series
Color
LC 76-700422
Points out practical ways in which older people can deter robbers both at home and on the streets. Illustrates how to foil purse snatchers, muggers, prowlers and obscene phone callers by using common sense rather than muscles or weapons.
Health and Safety; Sociology
Dist - BROSEB **Prod** - BROSEB 1975

Senior Profile, Pt 1 48 MIN
U-matic
B&W (J C)
Profiles of three older San Diegans who have remained active and productive. Interviewed are - William Wichnick, painter - Walter Ballard, pilot - and Ethel Hoffman, sculptor.
Health and Safety; Sociology
Dist - SDSC **Prod** - SDSC 1978

Senior Profiles, Pt 2 10 MIN
U-matic
B&W (J C)
Profile of San Diegans, George Coath, a motorcyclist in his 90's who leads an active and productive life.
Health and Safety; Sociology
Dist - SDSC **Prod** - SDSC 1978

Seniority and discrimination 26 MIN
16mm
Color (G A)
$5.00 rental
Portrays an actual arbitration case on seniority. Reveals that although a union contract provides plant - wide seniority, the company proposes to bring in a new employee on the grounds that a black employee bidding on the job lacks experience. The employee's grievance is not only that he is 'reasonably qualified' for the position as provided for in the contract, but that he is a senior employee who was locked into his job by departmental seniority under previous contracts.
Business and Economics; Psychology
Dist - AFLCIO **Prod** - AARA 1973

Seniority vs ability 30 MIN
16mm
Color (G IND)
$5.00 rental
Shows an actual arbitration hearing for an employee who filed a grievance because he was denied a promotion on the ground that he lacked an advanced education. Examines his claim that the job did not require more than a high school education and his contention that his rights were violated when management selected an employee with less seniority. Provides a background for discussing mistakes in presenting a case. For union use only.
Business and Economics; Psychology; Social Science
Dist - AFLCIO **Prod** - AARA 1977

Seniors - a safe neighborhood is up to you 15 MIN
VHS
Color (G C)
$89.00 purchase, $35.00 rental
Teaches how senior citizens can actively contribute to a safer neighborhood through neighborhood watch programs and similar self - help involvement.
Health and Safety
Dist - TNF

Seniors and alcohol abuse 23 MIN
VHS
Color (G)
$199.00 purchase
Looks at alcohol abuse among older people, which is often subtle and complex. Shows how seniors can be hidden abusers and alcoholics, no longer in the work place and sometimes isolated from society. Seniors take more medications, prescribed or not, than any other age group, and the effects of mixing these medications with alcohol can be devastating.
Guidance and Counseling; Health and Safety
Dist - FMSP

Seniors' esteem issues - Program 4 30 MIN
VHS
Inside stories - journey into self esteem series
Color (H C G)
$295.00 purchase, $55.00 rental
Looks at several elderly persons from a variety of circumstances. Features Dr H Stephen Glenn. Part of a series on self esteem produced by Knowledge Network and Forefront Productions.
Health and Safety; Sociology
Dist - FLMLIB

Sensate Focus, Pt 1 11 MIN
U-matic / VHS
EDCOA Sexual Counseling Series
Color
Shows a couple modeling the initial phase of the sensate focus exercises. Shows each partner taking turns giving and getting nongenital sensual touching.
Health and Safety; Psychology
Dist - MMRC **Prod** - MMRC

Sensate Focus, Pt 2 11 MIN
U-matic / VHS
EDCOA Sexual Counseling Series
Color
Continues the process in part one. Each partner teaches the other by means of direct physical guidance. Emphasizes nongenital touching.
Health and Safety; Psychology
Dist - MMRC **Prod** - MMRC

Sensate Focus, Pt 3 11 MIN
VHS / U-matic
EDCOA Sexual Counseling Series
Color
Shows each partner tactilely exploring the other's genitals under the direct physical supervision of the partner being stimulated.
Health and Safety; Psychology
Dist - MMRC **Prod** - MMRC

Sensate Focus, Pt 4 6 MIN
VHS / U-matic
EDCOA Sexual Counseling Series
Color
Explains the 'silent vagina' form of sensate focus exercise which consists of intravaginal penile containment without any active thrusting.
Health and Safety; Psychology
Dist - MMRC **Prod** - MMRC

Sensation and Perception 30 MIN
VHS / 16mm
Psychology - the Study of Human Behavior Series
Color (C A)
$99.95, $89.95 purchase _ 24 - 06
Demonstrates construction of reality from senses, interpretation and organization into meaningful patterns by the brain.
Psychology
Dist - CDTEL **Prod** - COAST 1990

Sensation and perception - learning - Parts 7 and 8 60 MIN
VHS / U-matic
Discovering psychology series
Color (C)
$45.00, $29.95 purchase
Presents parts 7 and 8 of the 26 - part Discovering Psychology series. Considers how personal experience can influence individual perception. Features learning researchers such as Pavlov, Thorndike, Watson and Skinner. Uses the principles of classical and operant conditioning to show how learning occurs. Two thirty - minute programs hosted by Professor Philip Zimbardo of Stanford University.
Psychology; Science - Natural
Dist - ANNCPB **Prod** - WGBHTV 1989

Sensational 60's
VHS
NFL series
Color (G)
$24.95 purchase _ #NFL2017V
Presents highlights from the National Football League during the 1960s. Produced by NFL Films.
Literature and Drama; Physical Education and Recreation
Dist - CAMV

The Sensational Baby - Newborn Sensory Development, Pt 1 - the Fetus and the Newborn 20 MIN
VHS / U-matic
Color (PRO)
Explores fetal reactions to a variety of sensory stimuli. Presented in terms of what parents actually experience during pregnancy.
Health and Safety
Dist - AMCOG **Prod** - POLYMR

The Sensational Baby - Newborn Sensory Development, Pt 2 - the First Week to Four 20 MIN
U-matic / VHS
Color
Deals with the newborn's sensory skills and ways parents and care givers can tailor their behavior to an infant's level of readiness.
Health and Safety; Home Economics; Psychology
Dist - POLYMR **Prod** - POLYMR

Sensational baby series

Fetal sensory development - Part one	20 MIN
Newborn sensory development - Part Two	20 MIN

Dist - POLYMR

The Sensational Five - the Inside Story of Your Senses 15 MIN
U-matic / VHS
Inside Story with Slim Goodbody Series
Color (P I)
Presents Slim Goodbody who uses models to show how the eye, ear, nose, mouth and skin work with the brain to keep a person in touch with the world. Looks at the deep senses like hunger and the muscle sense.
Science - Natural
Dist - AITECH **Prod** - GBCTP 1981

Sensational Seventies series
Covers the years 1970 - 1979. Features a ten - part series examining the major political, cultural and social issues of the Seventies. Narrated by Peter Jennings. Each cassette is time - coded for easy access to any one of dozens of specific topics.

1970	48 MIN
1971	48 MIN
1972	48 MIN
1973	48 MIN
1974	48 MIN
1975	48 MIN
1976	48 MIN
1977	48 MIN
1978	48 MIN
1979	48 MIN
The Sensational Seventies series	480 MIN

Dist - CNEMAG **Prod** - HOBELP 1981

Sensational soups
VHS
Video cooking library series
Color (J H G)
$19.95 purchase _ #KVC921V
Illustrates the preparation of soups through step - by - step demonstrations. Covers everything needed from ingredients to equipment, with clear explanations of cooking techniques. Includes recipes. Part of a 22 - part series.
Home Economics
Dist - CAMV

Sensationalism Caused by the 19th Century Waltz and Serge Diaghilev's Productions 30 MIN
U-matic / VHS
Shaping Today with Yesterday Series
Color
Fine Arts; Industrial and Technical Education
Dist - ARCVID **Prod** - ARCVID

Sensationsal 70s series

1970 - Year of protest	48 MIN
1971 - Year of disillusionment	48 MIN
1972 - Year of summits	48 MIN
1973 - Year of Watergate	48 MIN
1974 - Year of resignation	48 MIN
1975 - Year after the fall	48 MIN

1976 - Year of the Bicentennial 48 MIN
1977 - Year of the Southern President 48 MIN
1978 - Year of moral dilemma 48 MIN
1979 - Year of overthrow 48 MIN
Dist - KNOWUN

Sense Amplifiers 30 MIN
U-matic / VHS
Linear and Interface Circuits, Part II - Interface Integrated 'Circuits Series
Color (PRO)
Establishes basic requirements and defines characteristics. Discusses system applications and performance variations for a core memory and MOS memory system. Gives direction to similar applications.
Industrial and Technical Education
Dist - TXINLC **Prod** - TXINLC

Sense and Nonsense with Linear Equations
16mm
B&W
Emphasizes that the formulation of a problem by a system of linear equations can suffer from ill - conditioning and therefore needs care. Reviews various methods for solving a system of linear equations and indicates that on the grounds of accuracy and efficiency the Guass elimination method looks like the best candidate.
Mathematics
Dist - OPENU **Prod** - OPENU

The Sense and the Shape 30 MIN
U-matic / VHS
Actor and Shakespeare Series
Color
Examines the imagery and shape of Shakespeare, and explains balance and interance, Shakespeare's own word for the deliberate and insistent repetition of a word or phrase. Features Ronald Watkins, Shakespearean actor and director.
Literature and Drama
Dist - NETCHE **Prod** - NETCHE 1971

Sense in the sun 1 MIN
U-matic / VHS
Color
Features Farrah Fawcett, Cancer Society Chairperson for Women Against Cancer, filmed on the beach and warning against sunburn and, over the long term, possible skin cancer. Uses TV spot format.
Health and Safety
Dist - AMCS **Prod** - AMCS 1982

Sense in the sun 14 MIN
16mm
Color (H C A)
LC FIA65-1887
Presents the story of a fisherman who develops skin cancer. Describes basic facts concerning skin cancer, particularly that it is usually caused by excessive exposure to the sun's rays.
Health and Safety
Dist - AMCS **Prod** - AMCS 1965

A Sense of achievement 12 MIN
VHS / U-matic / BETA
Color (C A G)
$475.00 purchase, $180.00 rental
Teaches managers and leaders how to successfully conduct performance reviews with staff members who could improve. Shows how to match the organization's goals with employee goals and review and reestablish goals.
Business and Economics; Psychology
Dist - VIDART **Prod** - VIDART

A Sense of Balance 27 MIN
16mm
Color (I)
LC 82-700322
Focuses on the experience of two disabled boys, one who suffered a cerebral hemorrhage and another with cerebral palsy, as they participate in a camping program in Minnesota.
Education; Psychology
Dist - IMAGER **Prod** - HALLM 1982

Sense of Balance 29 MIN
Videoreel / VT2
Observing Eye Series
Color
Science - Physical; Sociology
Dist - PBS **Prod** - WGBHTV

A Sense of balance - breast reconstruction 30 MIN
VHS
Color (G)
$99.00 purchase _ #CD - 071
Presents a clear and comprehensive overview to help women who must undergo a mastectomy to make informed decisions about reconstruction. Includes alternatives to breast implants. Study guide.
Health and Safety; Sociology
Dist - FANPRO

A Sense of Color 29 MIN
U-matic / VHS
Flower Show Series
Color
Features Mrs Ascher teaching the importance of color in relation to size, shape and placement in arrangement.
Fine Arts; Home Economics; Science - Natural
Dist - MDCPB **Prod** - MDCPB

A Sense of Community 34 MIN
16mm
Color
LC 75-700313
Presents an overview of activities of affiliated members of the National Community Education Association, telling what consitutes effective community education programs and describing their impact on the entire community.
Education; Social Science; Sociology
Dist - NCEA **Prod** - MOTTCF 1974

A Sense of freedom 58 MIN
VHS
Color (G)
$350.00 purchase, $95.00 rental
Visits Gambia, Africa's smallest country and one of only a few successful multi - party democracies on the continent. Surveys the social and economic reasons underlying this success. African journalist Hilton Fyle interviews President Jawara and other government leaders. Directed by Hilton Fyle.
Civics and Political Systems; Fine Arts; History - World; Sociology
Dist - CNEMAG

A Sense of Hope 13 MIN
16mm
Color (I J H)
LC 83-700605
Portrays a young leukemia patient coping with the disease.
Health and Safety
Dist - LEUSA **Prod** - LEUSA 1983

Sense of Humor - Past and Present 25 MIN
U-matic / VHS
Color (J H C A)
Deals with the question of whether comics have to have a special understanding of people in order to be funny.
Literature and Drama; Psychology; Sociology
Dist - GERBER **Prod** - SIRS

A Sense of Humus 28 MIN
U-matic / VHS / 16mm
Color (J)
LC 77-703280
Focuses on the organic farming movement in Canada today by interviewing farmers whose methods vary somewhat, but who all believe in keeping the soil healthy by natural methods to produce healthy crops.
Agriculture; Science - Natural
Dist - BULFRG **Prod** - NFBC 1977

A Sense of joy 15 MIN
U-matic / VHS / 16mm
Inside-out series
Color (I)
LC 73-702447
Shows the joy which may be found in familiar things and in the surprises of everyday life. Presents Chuck and his sister Jean who take two different routes to the beach - she, eager to enjoy the water, goes directly while he wanders leisurely looking at the girls.
Guidance and Counseling
Dist - AITECH

A Sense of Loss
BETA / VHS
Color
Presents an insightful documentary look at the raging conflict in Northern Ireland.
History - World; Sociology
Dist - GA **Prod** - GA

A Sense of Loss
U-matic / VHS
(J H C A)
$89.00 purchase _ #05918 94
Depicts the effects of the raging conflict in Northern Ireland.
Fine Arts; History - World
Dist - ASPRSS

A Sense of Music 29 MIN
U-matic
Challenge Series
Color (PRO)
Spotlights teachers who challenge the education systems' traditional performance oriented music curriculum.
Fine Arts; Psychology
Dist - TVOTAR **Prod** - TVOTAR 1985

A Sense of Place 55 MIN
Videoreel / VT2
Color
Explains that environmental and esthetic concerns in the township of East Hampton in Long Island, New York, are being threatened by rampant commercial interests.
Geography - United States; Science - Natural; Social Science
Dist - PBS **Prod** - WLIWTV

A Sense of Place 57 MIN
16mm
Color
_ #106C 0176 564N
Geography - World
Dist - CFLMDC **Prod** - NFBC 1976

A Sense of Pride - Hamilton Heights 15 MIN
16mm
Color
Documents the restoration of a neighborhood in Harlem. Focuses on the efforts of one man to bring about the change.
Sociology
Dist - BLKFMF **Prod** - BLKFMF

Sense of proportion 50 MIN
VHS
Spirit of the age series
Color (A)
PdS99 purchase
Examines the evolution of architecture in Britain since the Middle Ages. Part four of an eight-part series.
Fine Arts; Industrial and Technical Education
Dist - BBCENE

A Sense of Purpose 14 MIN
U-matic / VHS / 16mm
Searching for Values - a Film Anthology Series
Color (J)
LC 72-703095
Tells how basketball superstar Hector Bloom, indifferent to the forms and rhetoric of success, contemplates his future with little expectation of finding happiness and meaning.
Guidance and Counseling; Physical Education and Recreation; Psychology; Sociology
Dist - LCOA **Prod** - LCOA 1972

Sense of Responsibility - How it Grows 27 MIN
U-matic / VHS
Vital Link Series
Color (A)
Shows teachers and parents how to encourage responsible attitudes in elementary school children.
Guidance and Counseling; Social Science; Sociology
Dist - EDCC **Prod** - EDCC 1980
CORNRS

A Sense of Responsibility 3 MIN
16mm / U-matic / VHS
Color (I J H C)
LC 73-701288
Uses animation to raise questions about individual responsibility. Shows how a careless mine worker starts a chain reaction of accidents which ultimately brings about the destruction of the entire country.
Civics and Political Systems; Guidance and Counseling; Health and Safety
Dist - PHENIX **Prod** - PHENIX 1972

Sense of Responsibility 4 MIN
VHS / 16mm / U-matic
Color (A)
Offers a humorous story which demonstrates that safety on the job is everyone's personal responsibility.
Health and Safety; Psychology
Dist - SALENG **Prod** - SALENG

Sense of the City 27 MIN
16mm
Eye on New York Series
Color; B&W
LC FIA66-842
Explores the impressions of American poets in a visual tour of New York City, including such writers as Hart Crane, John Dos Passos, Edna St Vincent Millay, John Updike, E E Cummings, Thomas Wolfe and Walt Whitman.
Geography - United States; Literature and Drama; Psychology; Social Science; Sociology
Dist - CBSTV **Prod** - WCBSTV 1966

Sense of timing 30 MIN
VHS / U-matic
Supersense series
Color (H C)
$250.00 purchase _ #HP - 5805C
Shows that animal timing is very much controlled by precision - made internal clocks, timepieces set by the rhythms of the natural world whose organic mechanisms are not yet well understood. Part of a series which deals with different facets of animal awareness.
Psychology; Science - Natural
Dist - CORF **Prod** - BBCTV 1989

A Sense of Touch 7 MIN
U-matic / VHS / 16mm
Color (K P S)
Shows how to use powers of observation to identify and compare a variety of textures, and in doing so learn to touch, smell and taste using the eyes and ears. Explains that if we stretch the use of our senses, we can gain more information.
Education
Dist - MOKIN **Prod** - NFBC 1984

The Sense of touch 28 MIN
VHS
Human body - the senses - series
Color (J H G)
$89.95 purchase _ #UW4176
Looks at the different ways in which humans receive information from the environment. Examines whether some people are more receptive to information than others, how touch functions, why and how we feel hot and cold and what happens to information processing if a major sense is lost. Demonstrates experimentally how different parts of the body respond to stimuli. Part of a 39 - part series featuring computer animation, medical photography, electron micrography, full - color drawings and diagrams and three - dimensional working models to cover the workings of the human body from head to toe and inside out.
Science - Natural
Dist - FOTH

A Sense of touch 6 MIN
VHS
With kids in mind series
Color (T)
Uses dozens of constantly changing images to show how young children respond to touch. Shows fingers, feet and mouths tap, grope, squeeze, lick, brush and stroke all manner of manmade and natural objects.
Psychology; Science - Natural
Dist - VIEWTH **Prod** - NFBC

A Sense of touch and A sense of sound 36 MIN
VHS
Visual literacy series
Color; PAL (P I)
PdS29.50 purchase
Extends the power of visual imagery by showing how it connects with information from other senses to enrich the meaning we gain from our experiences. Part two of a five - part series.
Psychology; Religion and Philosophy; Sociology
Dist - EMFVL

A Sense of tragedy 15 MIN
16mm
Artistry of Shakespeare - the drama and language of Macbeth series
Color (H)
Shows how the play affects the student as a tragedy and how Macbeth is led inevitably by a chain of cause and effect to suffering and death.
Literature and Drama
Dist - SVE **Prod** - SINGER 1968

Sense Organs 18 MIN
16mm / U-matic / VHS
Human Body Series
Color (J H C)
$415, $250 purchase _ #1655
Discusses the five senses that human beings have.
Science - Natural
Dist - CORF

Sense Organs and their Sensitivity, Pt 1 40 MIN
VHS / U-matic
Color (PRO)
Discusses the measurements of sensory thresholds, variations and contrasts of the various senses, and comparisons of visual touch and hearing perception. Uses art and history to illustrate the talk. Examines and discusses all the senses.
Science - Natural
Dist - HOUSEI **Prod** - HOUSEI

Sense Organs and their Sensitivity - Pt 2 46 MIN
U-matic / VHS
Color (PRO)
Illustrates and describes the traveling wave in the cochlea. Discusses various functions of the ear, comparing other animals to man.
Science - Natural
Dist - HOUSEI **Prod** - HOUSEI

Sense Perception 28 MIN
VHS / 16mm
Color (J)
Examines the senses of sight, hearing, touch, taste and smell in terms of structure and function. Presents demonstrations of inverted vision and odors made 'VISIBLE.' Shows that perception actually takes place in the brain, not in the sense organs. Points out how limited our senses are through demonstrations with 'SILENT' ultrasonic sound.
Science - Natural; Science - Physical
Dist - MIS **Prod** - MIS 1968

Sensei 12 MIN
16mm
Color
LC 75-703229
Examines the Karate Kata using a simple story to emphasize the development of the spirit through rigorous physical training.
Physical Education and Recreation; Religion and Philosophy
Dist - USC **Prod** - USC 1966

Sensei - Learning music with Dr Suzuki 54 MIN
VHS
Color (T G)
$149.00 purchase _ #EX3255
Presents Dr Suzuki demonstrating his method of music instruction.
Fine Arts
Dist - FOTH

Sensei - Master Teacher 22 MIN
16mm
Color (J)
LC 72-713857
Presents Manju Inque, a master Japanese potter, who demonstrates the Korean tradition, four hundred years old in Japan. Shows the throwing of porcelain, and the shaping and carving of a large jar.
Fine Arts
Dist - PSUPCR **Prod** - PSU 1971

The Senses 29 MIN
U-matic
Introducing biology series; Program 21
Color (C A)
Provides students with understanding of importance of senses to an animal's survival. Introduces how senses function in humans.
Science - Natural
Dist - CDTEL **Prod** - COAST

The Senses 15 MIN
U-matic / VHS
Well, Well, Well with Slim Goodbody Series
Color (P)
Urges children to pay attention to their senses. Explains eye care and eye safety rules and shows a blind person substituting other senses for sight. Explains the danger of loud noise. Talks about smell and taste and shows touch testing.
Science - Natural
Dist - AITECH **Prod** - AITECH

The Senses 10 MIN
16mm
Color (K P I)
LC FIA68-638
Points out that hearing, seeing, tasting, smelling and touching are senses that help animals to know their world.
Science - Natural
Dist - FILCOM **Prod** - SIGMA 1967

The Senses and Perception, Links to the Outside World 18 MIN
16mm / U-matic / VHS
Color (I)
LC 76-701129
Shows differences in the process of sensory perception in higher animals and in man. Emphasizes that the senses are an animal's link to its environment and are necessary to its survival.
Psychology; Science - Natural
Dist - EBEC **Prod** - EBEC 1975

Senses and the world around you 21.5 MIN
VHS / 16mm / U-matic
Human body systems series
Color (I J)
$505.00, $355.00, $385.00 purchase _ #A516
Explains and illustrates how our five senses of seeing, hearing, smelling, tasting, and touching enable us to know our environment. Uses a combination of live action and animation with narration. Offers details on how our sensory nerves function and how the brain interprets signals of sight, sound, smell, taste and touch.
Science - Natural
Dist - BARR **Prod** - BARR 1987

Senses - do You Remember 20 MIN
VHS / U-matic
Creative Dramatics Series
Color (I)
Introduces a game to aid in exploring the senses of taste, hearing, smell, sight and touch.
Fine Arts; Physical Education and Recreation
Dist - AITECH **Prod** - NEWITV 1977

The Senses - Eyes and Ears 26 MIN
16mm / U-matic / VHS
Living Body - an Introduction to Human Biology Series
Color
Discusses the eyes and the ears. Shows a young reckless driver careening down a road, viewing the events from inside his eye where the image of the potential crash sight is pictured. Looks inside the ear, showing how the linked bones vibrate to a sound, and presents a computer graphic sequence showing how the eye focuses on an image.
Science - Natural
Dist - FOTH **Prod** - FOTH 1985

Senses - how we know 15 MIN
BETA / VHS / U-matic / 16mm
Young viewers series
Color (K P)
$245.00, $68.00 purchase _ #C50780, #C51506
Joins Lizzy and her babysitter who find out how the senses enable finding out about the world. Shows how the babysitter is amusingly inept at teaching and entertaining Lizzy. By playing hide - and - seek, preparing a gourmet meal, avoiding a too - hot bath, Lizzy teaches about sight, hearing, taste, smell and touch. Part of a five - part series which introduces concepts essential to academic and social life.
Psychology; Science - Natural
Dist - NGS **Prod** - NGS 1992

The Senses of Man 18 MIN
16mm
Color (J H C G)
Shows the importance of the external and internal sense receptors. Illustrates the general sense receptors of temperature, pressure, touch and pain. Shows the uses of the special senses of vision, hearing, taste, smell and equilibrium.
Science - Natural
Dist - VIEWTH **Prod** - GATEEF

The Senses of man 18 MIN
U-matic / VHS / 16mm
Human physiology series
Color (H C A)
LC FIA65-1661
Reveals how external stimuli - light, sound, odor, touch and taste - are converted into nerve impulses by sense receptors. Discusses sense receptors which are stimulated by inner organs. An animated film.
Psychology; Science - Natural
Dist - IU **Prod** - IU 1965

The Senses of smell and taste 28 MIN
VHS
Human body - the senses - series
Color (J H G)
$89.95 purchase _ #UW4186
Describes the functions and functioning of the senses of smell and taste - how these senses are stimulated, how they can be used and the combined purpose of smell, taste and sight. Part of a 39 - part series featuring computer animation, medical photography, electron micrography, full - color drawings and diagrams and three - dimensional working models to cover the workings of the human body from head to toe and inside out.
Science - Natural
Dist - FOTH

The Senses - Skin Deep 26 MIN
U-matic / VHS / 16mm
Living Body - an Introduction to Human Biology Series
Color
Looks at the sense receptors that depend on contact with the immediate world, including taste buds, touch sensors and olfactory cells. Points out that these receptors lie in the skin, which also senses heat, pain and pressure.
Science - Natural
Dist - FOTH **Prod** - FOTH 1985

Sensing the future 30 MIN
VHS
Perspectives - science in action - series
Color; PAL; NTSC (G)
PdS90, PdS105 purchase
Looks at developments in medical and agricultural sensors.
Agriculture; Health and Safety; Sociology
Dist - CFLVIS **Prod** - LONTVS

The Sensitive 29 MIN
Videoreel / VT2
Who is Man Series
Color
Features Dr Puryear who looks at persons who are especially attuned to the psychic and whose powers of ESP far surpass those of the average individual.
Psychology
Dist - PBS **Prod** - WHROTV

Sensitive subjects
VHS
Knowing sexual facts series
Color (I J)
$69.00 purchase _ #MC319
Provides a chart of categories embedded in the concept of sexuality. Defines terms such as transvestite, lesbian, voyeur and incest.
Health and Safety; Psychology; Sociology
Dist - AAVIM **Prod** - AAVIM 1992

Sensitivity Analysis, Review 54 MIN
VHS / U-matic
Decision Analysis Series
Color
Industrial and Technical Education; Mathematics
Dist - MIOT **Prod** - MIOT

Sensitivity to the Disabled 29 MIN
U-matic / VHS
Color
Gives suggestions on how library staff can better serve the those with learning, visual or physical limitations.
Education; Psychology
Dist - LVN **Prod** - HCPL

Sensitized learning, parts 1 and 2 - Volume 6 60 MIN
VHS
Creative discipline series
Color (G A R)
$10.00 rental _ #36 - 86 - 1
Explores the subject of sensitized learning as it relates to child discipline. Hosted by Dr Robert A Rausch.
Psychology; Sociology
Dist - APH **Prod** - ABINGP

Sensitometry 29 MIN
U-matic / VHS
Automatic Film Processor Quality Control Series
Color (C A)
Health and Safety; Industrial and Technical Education; Science
Dist - TEF **Prod** - BCAMRT

Senso daughters 54 MIN
VHS / 16mm
Color (G)
$390.00 purchase, $75.00 rental
Investigates an unacknowledged tragedy of the Papua New Guinea occupation by Japanese troops during WWII. Exposes the army's mistreatment of New Guinea women and 'comfort girls' - military prostitutes, generally Koreans or lower class Japanese, conscripted believing they would clean and cook for the troops. 90,000 comfort girls were shipped to battlesites as 'military commodities,' without names, identities or records to be traced by. With testimony from New Guinean women and startling denials by Japanese who were there, the film has provoked considerable controversy in Japan because the filmmaker not only exposes a shameful episode in her nation's past, but indicts the culture which fostered it. Produced by Noriko Sekiguchi.
Fine Arts; History - World; Sociology
Dist - FIRS

The Sensor and its characteristics 30 MIN
U-matic / VHS
Optoelectronics series; Pt I - Optoelectronic emitters, sensors and couplers
Color (PRO)
Discusses the sensor, its structure, design objectives and tradeoffs for the diode or transistor configurations, and its characteristics to aid in sensor application.
Industrial and Technical Education
Dist - TXINLC **Prod** - TXINLC

Sensor and transducer interfaces 180 MIN
U-matic
Microprocessor real - time interfacing and control systems series
Color (IND)
Introduces the fundamental principles of sensors, covering resistive, capacitive and inductive sensor technologies, and performance measurement in terms of sensitivity, linearity, accuracy and repeatability. Discusses sensor and transducer applications in terms of position, temperature and pressure. Explains matching sensor performance to diverse application requirements.
Computer Science
Dist - INTECS **Prod** - INTECS

Sensor applications 30 MIN
VHS / U-matic
Optoelectronics series; Pt I - Optoelectronic emitters, sensors and couplers
Color (PRO)
Highlights sensor use for specific applications by categorizing effects of mounting tolerances, apertures, overlap, and size of openings in the transmission media.
Industrial and Technical Education
Dist - TXINLC **Prod** - TXINLC

Sensorineural Hearing Impairment - Patient Management 56 MIN
U-matic / VHS
Color (PRO)
Presents a discussion of the management of otologic patients with sensorineural hearing impairment, including the use of a hearing aid and other communication devices.
Health and Safety; Science - Natural
Dist - HOUSEI **Prod** - HOUSEI

Sensorineural hearing loss in adults 16 MIN
VHS
Color (PRO A)
$250.00 purchase _ #OT - 14
Explains the problem of sensorineural hearing loss for patients and their families. Explains symptoms, causes, evaluation, medical and surgical treatment options and risks. Uses state - of - the - art animation to depict the anatomy. For use in the practicing otolaryngologist's office and helpful to hospital patient educators or clinical staff.
Science - Natural
Dist - MIFE **Prod** - MIFE 1992

Sensors 30 MIN
VHS / 16mm
Manufacturing insights series
Color (A IND)
$200.00, $190.00 purchase _ #VT257, #VT257U
Demonstrates improved data collection for quality control analysis and up to a seven - fold increase in productivity. Includes case studies.
Business and Economics; Industrial and Technical Education
Dist - SME **Prod** - SME 1988

Sensory changes in the elderly 19 MIN
VHS / 16mm
Color (PRO)
$295.00 purchase, $60.00 rental
Reviews the five senses - touch, sight, hearing, smell and taste. Offers suggestions for corrections and or compensatory interventions.
Health and Safety; Psychology
Dist - FAIRGH **Prod** - FAIRGH 1985

Sensory changes in the elderly 120 MIN
VHS
Virginia Geriatric Education Center Video Conference series
Color (G C PRO)
$149.00 purchase, $55.00 rental
Looks at mental, vision, and hearing changes that occur as one ages and problems that frequently result for older adults. Discusses actions that can help the patient deal effectively with such changes.
Health and Safety; Psychology; Sociology
Dist - TNF **Prod** - VGEREC

Sensory Conduction Studies Median Nerve 10 MIN
16mm
Color
LC 74-705603
Demonstrates the antidromic and orthodromic techniques for recording the evoked potentials for digital sensory nerves.
Science - Natural
Dist - USNAC **Prod** - USPHS

Sensory Deprivation 15 MIN
16mm
Patient in Isolation Series
Color
LC 79-712970
Describes problems and anxiety - provoking situations of patients in isolation and explores the feelings of the nurses who deal with these patients.
Health and Safety; Psychology
Dist - TRNAID **Prod** - TRNAID 1969

Sensory Deprivation and Controlled Sensory Stimulation 29 MIN
U-matic
Understanding Human Behavior - an Introduction to Psychology Series 'Lesson 9
Color (C A)
Discusses effects of prolonged isolation from sensory input. Uses excerpts from Antarctica diary of Richard Byrd to show these effects.
Psychology
Dist - CDTEL **Prod** - COAST

Sensory Experiences 7 MIN
U-matic
Take Time Series
(A)
Demonstrates the influence of parents and others caring for pre - schoolers on the physical and emotional development of the child.
Health and Safety; Psychology; Sociology
Dist - ACCESS **Prod** - ACCESS 1976

Sensory Integration - Clinical Observations of Normal Children to Accompany the SCSIT, Pt 1 42 MIN
VHS / U-matic
Color
Presents visual tracking and convergence, ramp movement of the arms, Diadokokinesis, thumb finger touch, jumping, hopping and skipping.
Health and Safety; Science - Natural
Dist - BUSARG **Prod** - BUSARG

Sensory Integration - Clinical Observations of Normal Children to Accompany the SCSIT, Pt 2 41 MIN
VHS / U-matic
Color
Shows Schilder's Arm Extension Test, Prone extension, Inhibition of the tonic neck reflex, Supine flexion and Equilibrium responses - sitting on a ball, walking on a balance beam.
Health and Safety; Science - Natural
Dist - BUSARG **Prod** - BUSARG

Sensory integration in the Medford school system 12 MIN
VHS / U-matic
B&W
Demonstrates sensory - integrative therapy with a ten - year - old boy with learning disabilities including a review of relevant embryology.
Health and Safety; Science - Natural
Dist - BUSARG **Prod** - BUSARG

Sensory Integration Problems in the Adult Wendy 35 MIN
55 MIN
U-matic / VHS
B&W
Presents an interview with a 24 - year - old learning disabled woman who has severe sensory integration problems. Discusses how her problems have affected her social, emotional, physical and academic development from childhood. Show how she is dysproxic, tactually defensive, posturally insecure and hypersensitive to vestibular input.
Health and Safety; Science - Natural
Dist - BUSARG **Prod** - BUSARG

Sensory Integrative Therapy - Principles of Treatment, Pt I 25 MIN
U-matic
Color (PRO)
Begins a discussion of the relationship between clinical expertise and sensory integrative theoretical constructs while paying attention to the political struggle of the occupational therapist in the school system. Narrated by Virginia Scardina.
Education; Health and Safety; Psychology
Dist - AOTA **Prod** - AOTA 1979

Sensory Integrative Therapy - Principles of Treatment, Pt II 20 MIN
U-matic
Color (PRO)
Concludes a discussion of the relationship between clinical expertise and sensory integrative theoretical constructs while paying attention to the political struggle of the occupational therapist in the school system. Narrated by Virginia Scardina.
Education; Health and Safety; Psychology
Dist - AOTA **Prod** - AOTA

Sensory Psychology 29 MIN
U-matic
Understanding Human Behavior - an Introduction to Psychology Series 'Lesson 6
Color (C A)
Discusses basic skin receptors that detect pressure, temperature and pain. Includes functions of deep receptors and the role of the inner ear in balance and motion.
Psychology
Dist - CDTEL **Prod** - COAST

Sensory Testing
U-matic / 35mm strip
Physical Assessment - Neurologic System Series
Color
Health and Safety; Psychology
Dist - CONMED **Prod** - CONMED

The Sensory World 33 MIN
U-matic / VHS / 16mm
Psychology Today Films Series
Color (H C A)
LC 73-713072
An animated film which shows a voyage through the human body to demonstrate the operation of the senses. Includes experiments showing sensory phenomena and confusion.
Psychology; Science; Science - Natural
Dist - CRMP **Prod** - CRMP 1971

Sent by God - Volume 3 30 MIN
VHS
Jesus of Nazareth series
Color (I J H C G A R)
$29.95 purchase, $10.00 rental _ #35 - 8316 - 1502
Presents excerpts from the Franco Zeffirelli film on the life and ministry of Jesus. Surveys the events of Jesus' bar mitzvah, Jesus' baptism, the ministry of John the Baptist, and the calling of Andrew and Philip.
Literature and Drama; Religion and Philosophy
Dist - APH **Prod** - BOSCO

The Sentence 28 MIN
U-matic / BETA / VHS
Communication skills 1 - basic series
Color (H C G)
$101.95, $89.95 purchase _ #CA - 29
Examines the sentence as a basic unit of communication. Shows that, without this complete communication unit, sentences, paragraphs, compositions, letters and memos would be incomprehensible. Teaches the different parts of a sentence and how to combine sentence parts appropriately and accurately. Part of a series on communication.
Social Science
Dist - INSTRU

The Sentence 1 30 MIN
U-matic / VHS
Writing for a Reason Series
Color (C)
English Language
Dist - DALCCD **Prod** - DALCCD

The Sentence 2 30 MIN
U-matic / VHS
Writing for a Reason Series
Color (C)
English Language
Dist - DALCCD **Prod** - DALCCD

Sentence, characters, sinister, disappeared, vanished 10 MIN
U-matic
Readalong three series
Color (P)
Provides reading instruction for third grade students. Uses animation, humor, music, repetition and audience participation. Comes with teacher's guide and kit.
Education; English Language; Literature and Drama
Dist - TVOTAR **Prod** - TVOTAR 1977

Sentence deferred 28 MIN
BETA / VHS
B&W (G)
Covers the life of John Augustus, whose firm belief in a second chance for everyone led to the founding of the probation system for criminal offenders.
Biography; Sociology
Dist - DSP **Prod** - DSP

The Sentence - ethics and legal compliance in the 1990s 20 MIN
VHS
Color (A)
$525.00 purchase
Dramatizes an ordinarily honest business person's progression from careless to unethical, even criminal conduct and brings out the effect such actions have on the company worked for. Alerts viewers to such problem areas as conflicts of interest, influence dealing and cover - ups.
Business and Economics; Civics and Political Systems; Education
Dist - COMFLM **Prod** - COMFLM

Sentence patterns 30 MIN
U-matic / VHS
Write course - an introduction to college composition series
Color (C A)
Explores the sentence and its rhetorical aspects in order to gain an understanding about the importance of sentence style and its relation to grammar.
English Language
Dist - FI **Prod** - FI 1984
DALCCD DALCCD

Sentence patterns - sentence strategy - Parts 17 and 18 60 MIN
VHS / U-matic
Write course - an introduction to college composition
Color (C)
$45.00, $29.95 purchase
Discusses the importance of sentence style and its relation to grammar in Part 17. Explores the use of specific subjects with active verbs and avoiding sentence fragments and dangling modifiers in Part 18. Parts of a 30 - part series on college composition.
Education; English Language
Dist - ANNCPB **Prod** - DALCCD 1984

Sentence sense 13 MIN
U-matic / VHS / 16mm
Effective writing series
Color (J H)
$315.00, $220.00 purchase _ #3068
Shows the importance of using logical and descriptive sentences.
English Language
Dist - CORF

Sentence strategy 30 MIN
U-matic / VHS
Write course - an introduction to college composition series
Color (C A)
LC 85-700986
Emphasizes sentence revision to fit rhetorical context.
English Language
Dist - FI **Prod** - FI 1984
DALCCD DALCCD

Sentence variety 28 MIN
U-matic / BETA / VHS
Communication skills 1 - basic series
Color (H C G)
$101.95, $89.95 purchase _ #CA - 30
Helps students to identify the four types of sentences - simple, compound, complex and compound - complex. Teaches the use of signal words to achieve transitions between ideas, how to recognize and correct sentence run - ons, fragments and comma splices. Covers using good parallel structure, donation, connotation and concrete and abstract concepts. Part of a series on communication.
Social Science
Dist - INSTRU

Sentenced for life - straight talk about drunk driving 40 MIN
VHS
Color (H)
$209.00 purchase _ #60203 - 025
Interviews survivors of alcohol - related accidents. Shares their feelings of loss, guilt, anger, remorse and frustration. Includes teacher's guide and library kit.
Health and Safety; Sociology
Dist - GA **Prod** - VWA 1992

Sentenced to learn 54 MIN
VHS
Color (G)
$295.00 purchase, $90.00 rental
Examines the problem of illiteracy among America's prison population by portraying a peer - tutoring program in which long - term, educated inmates fill teaching positions left vacant due to budget cuts. Interviews teachers and students in the experimental program who discuss their motivations and educational goals, along with prison life. Filmed inside several different Illinois prisons, both men's and women's facilities. Directed by Zadok Dror.
Education; Fine Arts; Health and Safety; Sociology
Dist - CNEMAG

Sentenced to Survival 90 MIN
U-matic
Color
Explores foundations of Judaism. Surveys religious, ethical and social factors of survival of Judaism.
Religion and Philosophy
Dist - ADL **Prod** - ADL

Sentences 45 MIN
VHS / U-matic
Effective Writing Series
Color
English Language; Psychology
Dist - DELTAK **Prod** - TWAIN

Sentences and paragraphs series

Paragraphs - Like Scenes in a Film	15 MIN
Sentences - many ways to begin	12 MIN
Themes - the day when nothing made sense	10 MIN

Dist - CORF

Sentences and solution sets 33 MIN
16mm
Teaching high school mathematics - first course series; No 36
B&W (T)
Mathematics
Dist - MLA **Prod** - UICSM 1967

Sentences - many ways to begin 12 MIN
U-matic / VHS / 16mm
Sentences and paragraphs series
Color (I J H)
$295.00, $210.00 purchase _ #79527
Talks about the importance of variety in constructing sentences.
English Language
Dist - CORF **Prod** - CENTRO 1981

Sentences, Number Line 30 MIN
16mm
Mathematics for Elementary School Teachers Series no 12
Color (T)
Analyzes word problems and associated number sentences. The number line is used to represent sets of admissible solutions under various operations. To be used following 'DIVISION TECHNIQUES.'.
Mathematics
Dist - MLA **Prod** - SMSG 1963

Sentences - paragraphs 27 MIN
VHS / BETA
Color
Provides instruction in basic sentence - building skills and in constructing paragraphs. Uses stories to present the lessons.
English Language
Dist - PHENIX **Prod** - PHENIX

Sentences - telling and asking 15 MIN
VHS
Planet Pylon series
Color (I)
LC 90712897
Uses character Commander Wordstalker from Space Station Readstar to develop language arts skills. Provides worksheet exercise to be worked on by student with the assistance of series characters. Third installment in a series of 23.
Education; English Language
Dist - GPN

Sentences that ask and tell 11 MIN
16mm / U-matic / VHS
Color (P)
$285, $200 purchase _ #1386
Shows how to use words and phrases to build sentences, and discusses the importance of punctuation and capitalization.
English Language
Dist - CORF **Prod** - CORF 1961

Sentences with Ralph and Stanley 15 MIN
U-matic / VHS / 16mm
Writing Skills Series
Color (P I)
LC 78-701680
Tells how two young boys learn the basic skills involved in writing a complete sentence when they set out to track down the Loch Ness Monster.
English Language
Dist - PHENIX **Prod** - BEANMN 1978

The Sentencing of Bill Thomas 16 MIN
VHS
Color (J H C A)
$89.95 purchase _ #10207VG
Shows the arrest, booking, and court hearing of juvenile Bill Thomas during a drug bust. Presents the guilty plea of Bill, the testimony, and the prosecutor's statements. The viewers are then asked to assume the role of the judge and make the decision whether to place Bill in jail or to continue his probation. Includes a teacher's guide, discussion questions, activities, and blackline masters.
Psychology; Sociology
Dist - UNL

Sentimental punk 5 MIN
16mm
Color (G)
$10.00 rental
Fine Arts
Dist - CANCIN **Prod** - KRENKU 1979

Sentinel of the Sea 25 MIN
VHS / U-matic / 16mm
Color; Mono (G) (FRENCH)
MV $185.00 _ MP $530.00 purchase, $50.00 rental
Documents Norine Rouse's trip beneath the waves to veiw the very special animals that live there. Features sharks, rays, the manatee, moray eels and the giant sea turtle.
Science - Natural
Dist - CTV **Prod** - MAKOF 1981

Sentinel, West Face 27 MIN
U-matic / VHS / 16mm
Color
LC FIA68-162
Pictures two mountain climbers scaling the west face of the Sentinel, an 8100 ft peak in Glacier National Park, Montana.
Geography - United States; Physical Education and Recreation; Science - Natural
Dist - PFP **Prod** - SUMMIT 1967

Sentinels in space 30 MIN
VHS
Color (J H C)

$14.95 purchase _ #NA207
Explains the importance of satellites in everyday life. Shows how they track weather and atmospheric conditions. Illustrates the importance of such information on agriculture, transportation, meteorology and even searching for downed aircraft.
History - World; Science - Physical
Dist - INSTRU **Prod** - NASA

Sentinels in Space 16 MIN
16mm
Color
LC 80-701867
Uses animation and satellite imagery to show what environmental satellites measure and to explain how they transmit information. Provides examples of the type of information gathered by environmental satellites.
Industrial and Technical Education; Science - Physical
Dist - USNAC **Prod** - USNOAA 1980

Sentinels of Survival 12 MIN
16mm
Fire Survival Series
Color (I J)
Describes residential sprinkler systems and their impact upon the fire service and public.
Health and Safety
Dist - FILCOM **Prod** - AREASX 1980

Sentinels of the sea 26 MIN
VHS
Challenge of the seas series
Color (I J H)
$225.00 purchase
Considers the pinnepeds, a class of animals that include sea lions, fur seals and elephant seals. Reveals that these animals feed high on the food chain and are an early warning system about the conditions of the ocean. They are telling humans that the oceans are in trouble. Part of a 26 - part series on the oceans.
Science - Natural; Science - Physical
Dist - LANDMK **Prod** - LANDMK 1991

Seoul of Don Bosco - Seoul, Korea 28 MIN
16mm
Color
Shows the work of the Salesian Missions in Korea where they run a trade school, taking the boys off the streets and out of unskilled jobs and preparing them for well - paid jobs in industry. Offers the story of three boys who have passed through the Don Bosco Center.
History - World; Religion and Philosophy; Sociology
Dist - MTP **Prod** - SCC

Separate but equal 193 MIN
VHS
Color (I J H)
$19.98 purchase _ #344744
Presents the dramatic events leading up to the historic Supreme Court decision outlawing segregation. Stars Sidney Poitier, Burt Lancaster and Richard Kiley.
Civics and Political Systems; Education; History - United States; Sociology
Dist - KNOWUN

A Separate peace
VHS / U-matic
Classic Films - on - Video Series
Color (G C J)
$59.00 purchase _ #05639-85
Re - tells John Knowles' story about the complex relationships between boys in the sheltered world of a preparatory school.
Fine Arts
Dist - CHUMAN

A Separate peace 104 MIN
VHS
Color (G)
$44.95 purchase _ #S00544
Tells the story of two roommates at a 1940s prep school. Shows that jealousy and anger by one of the young men leads to tragedy for the other. Based on the novel by John Knowles. Stars Parker Stevenson and John Heyl. Directed by Larry Peerce.
Literature and Drama
Dist - UILL

A Separate Peace
U-matic / VHS
Color (J C I)
Presents John Knowles' story about relationships within the sheltered world of an eastern preparatory school.
Fine Arts; Literature and Drama
Dist - GA **Prod** - GA

A Separate peace 45 MIN
U-matic / VHS / 16mm
Color (J)
$69.95 purchase _ #4014
An edited version of the feature film A Separate Peace, from the John Knowles book. Describes the friendship of two young men and tells how one eventually betrays the other in the sheltered world of a preparatory school.
Fine Arts; Literature and Drama
Dist - AIMS **Prod** - PAR AIMS 1979

The Separate Self - Terra, 22 Momths 7 MIN
16mm
Growth and Development - a Chronicle of Four Children Series Series '6
Color
LC 78-700687
Psychology
Dist - LIP **Prod** - JUETHO 1976

Separate Skin 26 MIN
16mm / VHS
Color (G)
$500.00, $225.00 purchase, $75.00 rental
Tells about Emily, troubled child of Holocaust survivors. Depicts her struggle with childhood fears and fantasies of love. Intercuts present day reality, flashbacks and fantasy sequences which show Emily trying to cope through relationships with both a man and a woman. Finally, she is forced to confront the pain in her past and make peace with her life. Produced by Deirdre Fishel.
Fine Arts; History - World; Psychology; Sociology
Dist - WMEN **Prod** - DEFI 1987

Separate visions 40 MIN
VHS
Color (H C G)
$295.00 purchase, $40.00 rental _ #37899
Profiles four pioneering American Indian artists - Baje Whitethorne, a Navajo painter; Brenda Spencer, a Navajo weaver; John Fredericks, a Hopi kachina carver; and Nora Naranjo - Morse, a Santa Clara sculptor. Reveals that all four work in the most contemporary modes of the media and all are on the leading edge of change - a fact that invites controversy among critics and collectors as well as their own people. Produced by Peter Blystone and Nancy Tongue for the Museum of Northern Arizona.
Fine Arts; Social Science; Sociology
Dist - UCEMC

Separating Sets 15 MIN
U-matic
Math Factory, Module I - Sets Series
Color (P)
Relates the separation of sets to the operation of subtraction.
Mathematics
Dist - GPN **Prod** - MAETEL 1973

Separation 30 MIN
U-matic / VHS / 16mm
Look at Me Series
Color (C A)
LC 82-700413
Focuses on situations where children are separated from their parents, including entering school, divorce, moving to a new home, and death. Shows how parents can cope with children's anxieties over these separations. Narrated by Phil Donahue.
Guidance and Counseling; Home Economics; Psychology; Sociology
Dist - FI **Prod** - WTTWTV 1980

Separation and Divorce - it has Nothing to do with You 14 MIN
16mm / U-matic / VHS
Color (I J H)
LC 74-701919
Dramatizes the reactions of a young boy who returns home to find his mother crying and his father packing. Describes his perspective toward separation and divorce as he finds himself caught in the middle and depicts the hardships a broken marriage can create.
Sociology
Dist - CRMP **Prod** - CRMP 1974

Separation Anxiety and Wishes to be Rid of Patients 15 MIN
VHS / U-matic
Treatment of the Borderline Patient Series
Color
Discusses the significance of separation - anxiety as being as much a part of the therapists's contribution to the patient - therapist relationship as the patient's contribution. Relates this to the reality and frequency of threats by the borderline patient to leave treatment.
Health and Safety; Psychology
Dist - HEMUL **Prod** - HEMUL

Separation by Crystallization, Dissolution and Sublimation 60 MIN
VHS / U-matic
Chemistry Training Series
Color (IND)
Covers evaporation and crystallization, sublimation and desublimation, freeze - drying, extraction and thin - layer chromatography.
Science; Science - Physical
Dist - ITCORP **Prod** - ITCORP

Separation - divorce - it has nothing to do with you 14 MIN
16mm / U-matic / VHS
Conflict and awareness series
Color (J H)
Tells how 16 - year - old Larry's parents separate and describes his feelings of conflicting loyalties.
Sociology
Dist - CRMP **Prod** - CRMP 1975

Separation of Dry Crushed Coals by High - Gradient Magnetic Separation 20 MIN
16mm
Color (IND)
LC 81-700854
Describes the high - gradient magnetic separation of coal and explains the fundamentals of the process. Shows the development of this technology from the laboratory stage to its introduction in a pilot plant.
Social Science
Dist - USNAC **Prod** - USDOE 1980

The Separation of Powers 12 MIN
16mm
Senator Sam Ervin, Jr - the Constitution Series
Color (J H)
Traces the reasons for dividing the government into interdependent, but unique branches. Explains the distinct responsibilities and rights of the federal government, the state governments and the people.
Civics and Political Systems
Dist - COUNFI **Prod** - CHILBE

Separation of Powers 20 MIN
VHS / 16mm
Citizens all Series
Color (H)
$150.00 purchase, $30.00 rental
Analyzes separation of powers in the U.S. Government as reflected in the conflict between the President and the Congress over U.S. aid to Central America.
Business and Economics; Civics and Political Systems
Dist - AITECH **Prod** - WHATV 1987

A Separation of powers - Congress and the bureaucracy - Congress and the courts - Pt 1 30 MIN
U-matic / VHS
Congress - we the people series
Color
Focuses on the interdependence of Congress in the goals each House pursues and in their conduct with each other.
Civics and Political Systems
Dist - FI **Prod** - WETATV 1984

Separation of Thoracopagus Twins 24 MIN
16mm
Color (PRO)
Explains that successful separation of thoracopagus twins depends upon a careful preoperative evaluation of the extent of twinning and the physiological effects of the anatomical variations on each twin.
Health and Safety; Science
Dist - ACY **Prod** - ACYDGD 1960

Separations and Reunions 36 MIN
16mm
B&W (PRO)
Documents reactions of four children age 14 to 20 months, hospitalized for from five to 24 days. Points out that at reunion with parents, hostility and resentment are combined with joy and relief.
Psychology
Dist - PSUPCR **Prod** - PSUPCR 1968

Separatory funnel - I 10 MIN
VHS
Chemistry master apprentice series
Color (H C)
$49.95 purchase _ #49 - 7211 - V
Demonstrates a simple extraction of iodine from water using an organic solvent in a separatory funnel. Part of the Chemistry Master Apprentice series.
Science; Science - Physical
Dist - INSTRU **Prod** - CORNRS

Separatory funnel - II 13 MIN
VHS
Chemistry master apprentice series
Color (H C)
$49.95 purchase _ #49 - 7212 - V
Presents a more detailed version of Part I. Demonstrates a simple extraction of iodine from water using an organic solvent in a separatory funnel. Covers also extractions that result in gas formation and emulsions. Part of the Chemistry Master Apprentice series.
Science; Science - Physical
Dist - INSTRU **Prod** - CORNRS

Sepharad - Judeo - Spanish music 27 MIN
VHS
Jewish music heritage library series
Color (G)
$39.95 purchase _ #792
Discloses that although over 500 years have passed since the expulsion of the Jews from Spain, Sephardic Jewry has managed to preserive its rich musical heritage. Enables the viewer to hear and learn about the tradition and beautiful singers of Spanish singers of the Middle Ages, as well as lullabies, wedding tunes, synagogue melodies and songs of mourning. Deals with the eternal quest for love, peace, religion, even paradise. Part of a series on Jewish music from around the world, featuring Martin Bookspan as narrator.
Fine Arts; Sociology
Dist - ERGOM **Prod** - IMHP

Sephardic Jewry series
Present a series which illuminates the histories of the Sephardic Diaspora communities and addresses the social and political issues confronting the Sephardim in the 20th century. Covers the era between the Expulsion and modern day. Examines the cultural heritage of the Sephardim and their accomplishments. Consists of four programs on a total of nine films. Some available for separate purchase. In English, Portuguese, French, Arabic or Hebrew with English subtitles.

Braids	90 MIN
Communities in exile - Fez	14 MIN
Communities in exile - Salonika	11 MIN
Embroidered canticles	26 MIN
Ilove you Rosa	84 MIN
The Jews of the Spanish Homeland	13 MIN
The Last Marranos	65 MIN
Pillar of salt	58 MIN
Sallah Shabbati	105 MIN

Dist - NCJEWF

September 10 MIN
VHS / U-matic
Emma and Grandpa series
Color (K P)
$180.00 purchase, $30.00 rental
Uses simple rhyming couplets about an apple orchard to help kindergarteners and first graders understand nature and seasonal changes. Highlights the importance of conservation. Focuses on an apple harvest. Ninth in a 12 part series.
Literature and Drama; Science - Natural
Dist - GPN **Prod** - GRIFN 1983

September 15 5 MIN
16mm
Color
LC 77-702641
Presents an autobiographical portrayal of the filmmaker's wedding day.
Fine Arts; Literature and Drama
Dist - CANFDC **Prod** - HANCXR 1972

September 19, 1356 14 MIN
VHS / 16mm
Newscast from the Past Series
Color (I J H)
$58.00 purchase _ #ZF223V
Uses TV news format to portray September 19, 1356 - features the Hundred Year War, Black Death plague, death of Marco Polo, Inca medicine, Chinese rebel attack on Mongolian capitol of Beijing, and other events. Six different historical dates in series.
History - World
Dist - SSSSV **Prod** - ZENGER 1984

September 30, 1955 101 MIN
16mm
Color
Tells how the death of James Dean affects a group of young people in Arkansas.
Fine Arts; Sociology
Dist - SWANK **Prod** - UPCI

September 20th - Gunter Brus 7 MIN
16mm
B&W (G)
$15.00 rental
Fine Arts
Dist - CANCIN **Prod** - KRENKU 1967

September wheat 96 MIN
U-matic / VHS / 16mm
Color (H C)
Deals with the world trade in wheat and hunger in the poor countries of the Third World. Examines the causes of hunger in a time of abundance.
Agriculture; Civics and Political Systems; Sociology
Dist - NEWTIM **Prod** - KRIEGP 1980
FIRS

Septic shock 23 MIN
U-matic / VHS
Emergency management; The First 30 minutes; Vol II
Color
Discusses diagnosis and treatment of septic shock.
Health and Safety; Science - Natural
Dist - VTRI **Prod** - VTRI

Septic shock 21 MIN
VHS / U-matic
Color (PRO)
Discusses the general pathophysiology of shock, the nine basic parts of evaluation, chronic treatment and differentiation of septic shock from hypovolemia.
Health and Safety
Dist - UMICHM **Prod** - UMICHM 1973

Sequels in transfigured time 12 MIN
16mm
Visual essays series
Color (G)
$25.00 rental
Presents viewers with silent still images that appear as abstractions like frost on a winter window. Pulls back to reveal that they are textures of the emulsion in a frame of a Melies film. Pays verbal tribute to Melies' work through subtitles and narration. Part of the series Visual Essays on the origins of film.
Fine Arts
Dist - CANCIN **Prod** - RAZUTI 1976

Sequence and story 5 MIN
U-matic / VHS / 16mm
Visual literacy series
Color (P I)
Shows how visual and verbal elements are assembled into a story and how the order of these elements affects the message. Features three youngsters who take a collection of photographs that show the sequence of a typical school day. When they rearrange the sequence of the photos, a different story can be told.
Fine Arts; Psychology
Dist - MOKIN **Prod** - NFBC 1984
ILEA EMFVL

Sequence and story 6 MIN
VHS
With kids in mind series
Color (T)
Shows three youngsters who take out a collection of photographs arranged in sequence and rearrange their order, making up different stories. Considers the logical importance of visual images, highlighting the demonstration and development of perception.
Psychology; Religion and Philosophy
Dist - VIEWTH **Prod** - NFBC

Sequences
16mm
B&W
Considers four theorems on sequences.
Mathematics
Dist - OPENU **Prod** - OPENU

Sequences and convergence 30 MIN
VHS
Calculus series
Color (C)
$125.00 purchase _ #6044
Explains sequences and convergence. Part of a 56 - part series on calculus.
Mathematics
Dist - LANDMK **Prod** - LANDMK

Sequences and ratios
VHS
Math vantage videos series
Color (I J H)
$39.00 purchase _ #653903 - HH
Looks at mathematical sequences and ratio. Part of a five - part series using interactive learning, interdisciplinary approaches, mathematical connections, student involvement and exploration to enable students to use patterns to explain, create and predict situations.
Mathematics
Dist - SUNCOM **Prod** - NEBMSI 1994

Sequences and Series 33 MIN
VHS / U-matic
Calculus of Complex Variables Series
B&W
Mathematics
Dist - MIOT **Prod** - MIOT

Sequences - Numbers Growing 20 MIN
U-matic / VHS / 16mm
Mathscore Two Series
Color (I)
Discusses aspects of sequences.
Mathematics
Dist - FI **Prod** - BBCTV

Sequences - what next 20 MIN
16mm / U-matic / VHS
Mathscore one series
Color (I J)
Discusses aspects of sequences.
Mathematics
Dist - FI **Prod** - BBCTV

Sequencing 50 MIN
VHS / U-matic
Computer languages series; Pt 1; Pt 1
Color
Discusses the primitive PROG2, PROGN, and the PROG construct in computer languages.
Computer Science; Industrial and Technical Education; Mathematics
Dist - MIOT **Prod** - MIOT

Sequencing Instruction 30 MIN
U-matic / VHS
Mainstreaming Secondary Special Vocational Needs Student Series
Color
Covers course development, analysis of tasks, sequencing guidelines and examples of programs using task analysis sequencing.
Education; Psychology
Dist - PUAVC **Prod** - PUAVC

Sequential circuits 49 MIN
U-matic / VHS
Digital electronics series; Pt 1
Color (PRO)
Industrial and Technical Education; Mathematics
Dist - MIOT **Prod** - MIOT

Sequential circuits 49 MIN
U-matic / VHS
Digital electronics series; Pt 2
Color (PRO)
Industrial and Technical Education; Mathematics
Dist - MIOT **Prod** - MIOT

Sequential logic circuits - BCD and special counters
U-matic / VHS
Digital techniques video training course series
Color
Industrial and Technical Education
Dist - VTRI **Prod** - VTRI

Sequential Logic Circuits - BCD Special Counters
VHS / U-matic
Digital Techniques Series
Color
Industrial and Technical Education
Dist - HTHZEN **Prod** - HTHZEN

Sequential Logic Circuits - Binary Counters
VHS / U-matic
Digital Techniques Series
Color
Industrial and Technical Education
Dist - HTHZEN **Prod** - HTHZEN

Sequential logic circuits - binary counters
VHS / U-matic
Digital techniques video training course series
Color
Industrial and Technical Education
Dist - VTRI **Prod** - VTRI

Sequential logic circuits - clocks
VHS / U-matic
Digital techniques video training course series
Color
Industrial and Technical Education
Dist - VTRI **Prod** - VTRI

Sequential Logic Circuits - Clocks
U-matic / VHS
Digital Techniques Series
Color
Industrial and Technical Education
Dist - HTHZEN **Prod** - HTHZEN

Sequential logic circuits - register
U-matic / VHS
Digital techniques video training course series
Color
Industrial and Technical Education
Dist - VTRI **Prod** - VTRI

Sequential Logic Circuits - Registers
U-matic / VHS
Digital Techniques Series
Color
Industrial and Technical Education
Dist - HTHZEN **Prod** - HTHZEN

Sequentially accessed semiconductor storage design 60 MIN
Videoreel / VT1
Semiconductor memories course series; No 3
Color (IND)
Discusses the design for sequentially accessed semiconductor storage, including MOS and bipolar shift registers plus advanced concepts, such as chargecouple devices.
Industrial and Technical Education
Dist - TXINLC **Prod** - TXINLC

The Sequoia giant of sequoia national park 28 MIN
BETA / VHS
Color
Examines the Sequoia giant trees and discusses the relationship between this largest of all living things and the other redwood forest inhabitants.
Agriculture; Geography - United States; Science - Natural
Dist - CBSC **Prod** - CBSC

Sera posible el sur - Mercedes Sosa sings 76 MIN
VHS / 35mm strip / U-matic
Color (H C A) (SPANISH (ENGLISH SUBTITLES))
$250 rental
Portrays Argentinian singer Mercedes Sosa. Contains footage of scenes of the Argentine countryside. Directed by Stefan Paul.
Fine Arts; Geography - World
Dist - CNEMAG

Serajkella Chhau - the masked dance of India 38 MIN
VHS
Color (G C H)
$295.00 purchase _ #DL478
Shows Kedar Nath Sahoo performing excerpts from choreographed pieces. Demonstrates basic movement patterns.
Fine Arts; History - World
Dist - INSIM

Serama's mask - Bali 25 MIN
U-matic / VHS / 16mm
World cultures and youth series
Color (I J H A)
$520, $250 purchase _ #4106; LC 80-700083
Portrays the Balinese culture and the ceremonial masks which are made for Balinese dances.
Fine Arts; Geography - World
Dist - CORF **Prod** - SUNRIS 1980

Seraphita's diary 90 MIN
16mm / U-matic / VHS
Color
Presents the story of a famous fashion model who, unable to cope with the fantasies and pressures her beauty induces in others, disappears. Profiles her emotional life and contrasts the fantasies she creates in other people's minds with the strains of her emotional life as revealed in her diaries.
Fine Arts; Psychology
Dist - ZIPRAH **Prod** - WISEF 1982

Sercrets of the cosmos 30 MIN
VHS / 16mm
Conquest of space series
Color (G)
Explores the relationship between humankind and the universe. Examines the human belief that we are the center of existence despite the relative minuteness of earth in relation to the universe.
History - World; Religion and Philosophy; Science - Physical; Sociology
Dist - FLMWST

Serenal 5 MIN
U-matic / VHS / 16mm
Color (H C)
Shows the spirit of fiesta on film as Norman McLaren salutes the West Indies. Examines his work as a flow of abstract images and pyrotechnics of light and color that change in response to the rhythms of a Trinidad orchestra.
Fine Arts; Geography - World
Dist - IFB **Prod** - NFBC 1961

Serendipity 29 MIN
16mm
Apothecary series
B&W
LC 75-703230
Analyzes the role and value of the drug researcher and discusses accidental discoveries of some important drugs. Filmed in Kinescope.
Health and Safety; Science
Dist - USC **Prod** - KNXT 1964

Serendipity series
Follow the reader 14 MIN
Speak up 12 MIN
Wordly Wise 14 MIN
Write on 14 MIN
Dist - MGHT

Serendipity spy glass 30 MIN
U-matic / VHS
Color (I J)
Describes how a pixie - like old man shows a boy the magic in the world around him.
Fine Arts
Dist - JOU **Prod** - CANBC

Serene reflection meditation 31 MIN
VHS / BETA
Color; PAL (G)
PdS15, $30.00 purchase
Features Lama Thubten Zopa demonstrating a number of suitable sitting postures and explains what happens when one 'sits' in the Buddhist tradition. Describes how to carry meditation into everyday life. Produced by Wessex Education Television Consortium.
Fine Arts; Religion and Philosophy
Dist - MERIDT

Serene Velocity 23 MIN
16mm
Color; Silent (C)
Experimental film by Ernie Gehr.
Fine Arts
Dist - AFA **Prod** - AFA 1970

Serengeti 25 MIN
16mm / U-matic / VHS
Untamed world series
Color; Mono (J H C A)
$400.00 film, $250.00 video, $50.00 rental
Examines the national park of Serengeti in Africa looking at its important plant and animal life.
Geography - World; Science - Natural
Dist - CTV **Prod** - CTV 1973

Serengeti diary 59 MIN
VHS / U-matic / 16mm / BETA
Color (G)
$400.00, $90.00 purchase _ #C50533, #C51388
Portrays the diversity of the Serengeti through the eyes of photographer Baron Hugo van Lawick and Masai tribesman Tpilit Ole Saitoti, who have lived in the Serengeti for many years.
Geography - World; Science - Natural
Dist - NGS **Prod** - NGS 1989

The Serengeti Lion 20 MIN
VHS / 16mm
Let Them Live Series
Color (I)
$405.00, $205.00 purchase
Shows George Schaller as he tags and watches some of the lions in the Serengeti Wildlife Preserve.
Geography - World; Science - Natural
Dist - LUF **Prod** - LUF

Serengeti Shall not Die 87 MIN
16mm
Color
Documents a relatively unknown wildlife reservation in East Africa, and makes the point that the wilderness must be kept as it is.
Geography - World; Science - Natural
Dist - WSTGLC **Prod** - WSTGLC 1959

Serenity
VHS
Color (G)
$29.95 purchase _ #U891109047
Presents relaxation exercises, imagery, music and affirmations based on the Twelve - Step programs to aid in relaxation without the use of drugs or other chemicals. Features Emmett E Miller, MD.
Health and Safety; Psychology; Religion and Philosophy
Dist - BKPEOP **Prod** - SOURCE 1989

Serenity Video
VHS
Color (A)
$29.95 purchase _ #6999
Applies twelve step program to discussion of serenity.
Education; Psychology; Religion and Philosophy
Dist - HAZELB

Serge, sew and decorate with fabric 60 MIN
VHS
Serger video series
Color (H C G)
$24.95 purchase _ #NN310V
Discusses serging and sewing table coverings, napkins, placemats, table runners and cloths. Shows how to make a serged double ruffle, flanged and flatlocked pillows and how to use the sewing machine to enhance pillow designs. One of three parts on serging.
Home Economics
Dist - CAMV

The Sergeant 108 MIN
16mm
Color
Stars Rod Steiger as a bullying army sergeant who enslaves a young private.
Fine Arts
Dist - TWYMAN **Prod** - WB 1968

Sergeant Matlovich vs the U S Air Force 98 MIN
16mm / U-matic / VHS
Color (H C A)
LC 80-700028
Presents the story of Sergeant Leonard Matlovich, who was drummed out of the U S Air Force in 1975 because of his revealed homosexuality.
Civics and Political Systems; Fine Arts; History - World; Sociology
Dist - LCOA **Prod** - TOMENT 1979

Sergeant Swell 16 MIN
U-matic / VHS / 16mm
Color (J)
Presents a spoof on the Royal Canadian Mounties in which the hero Sergeant Swell finds himself at odds with a local Indian tribe and a key warrior who always seems to be just a few steps behind.
Literature and Drama
Dist - PFP **Prod** - PFP 1972

Sergei Bongart 30 MIN
U-matic / VHS / 16mm
Profiles in American Art Series
Color
Fine Arts
Dist - KAWVAL **Prod** - KAWVAL

Sergei Obraztsov - USSR 56 MIN
VHS
Jim henson presents the world of puppetry series; Pt 5
Color (I)
$49.00 purchase _ #064 - 9015
Travels the globe to meet puppeteers. Features Muppet creator Jim Henson as host. Features Sergei Obraztsov of the USSR, who is hailed as one of the world's greatest puppeteers and has headed the Moscow State Central Puppet Theatre for the past fifty years.
Fine Arts; Geography - World; Sociology
Dist - FI **Prod** - HENASS 1988

Serger sewing series
Advanced serger sewing - Pt 1 20 MIN
Advanced serger sewing - Pt 2 34 MIN
Basic serger sewing - Pt 1 24 MIN
Basic serger sewing - Pt 2 20 MIN
Dist - CAMV

Serger video series
Presents a three - part series on sewing. Includes stitching, corners, collars, ribbons and rolled edges on tailored clothing, decorative sewing and sportswear.
Serge, sew and decorate with fabric 60 MIN
Serging inspirations 60 MIN
Sportswear - serge it - sew it 60 MIN
Dist - CAMV

Serging inspirations 60 MIN
VHS
Serger video series
Color (H C G)
$24.95 purchase _ #NN415V
Demonstrates the creation of professional looking tailored garments with minimal time and energy. Shows how to use a serger to simplify basic garment construction, add finishing details and embellish garments with decorative served trims. One of three parts on serging.
Home Economics
Dist - CAMV

Serial data transfer devices 60 TO 90 MIN
VHS
Microprocessors module series
Color (PRO)
$600.00 - $1500.00 purchase _ #MISDI
Looks at serial transfer through serial interfacing devices which connect the microprocessor's parallel data bus to devices requiring serial input, such as telephones and many types of printers. Part of an eleven - part series on microprocessors. Includes five student guides, five workbooks and an instructor guide.
Computer Science; Education; Industrial and Technical Education; Psychology
Dist - NUSTC **Prod** - NUSTC

Serial Interface 30 MIN
VHS / U-matic
6809 Interface Programming Series
Color (IND)
Analyzes serial interfaces by software - centered and hardware - centered techniques. Explains teletype interface with programs and schematics, and covers opto - isolator circuits with the MC1488.
Industrial and Technical Education; Mathematics; Sociology
Dist - COLOSU **Prod** - COLOSU

Serial Interfacing, Pt 1 48 MIN
U-matic / VHS
Microprocessor Interfacing Series
Color
Industrial and Technical Education; Mathematics
Dist - MIOT **Prod** - MIOT

Serial Interfacing, Pt 2 41 MIN
U-matic / VHS
Microprocessor Interfacing Series
Color
Industrial and Technical Education; Mathematics
Dist - MIOT **Prod** - MIOT

Serial metaphysics 20 MIN
16mm
Color (G)
$25.00 rental
Examines the American commercial lifestyle. Features existing television advertisements edited to play on the collective unconscious. Sountrack by The Mix Group.
Fine Arts; Sociology
Dist - CANCIN **Prod** - WWDIXO 1986

The Serials - Pt 1 64 MIN
Videoreel / VT2
Toys that grew up series
Color
Fine Arts
Dist - PBS **Prod** - WTTWTV

The Serials - Pt 2 64 MIN
Videoreel / VT2
Toys that grew up series
Color
Fine Arts
Dist - PBS **Prod** - WTTWTV

Series 4 7 MIN
16mm / U-matic / VHS
Color
LC 74-703014
Uses animation to examine the relationship between humans and their environment.
Science - Natural; Sociology
Dist - FI **Prod** - NFBC 1974

Series and parallel circuits ; 2nd ed. 15 MIN
U-matic
Search for science series; Unit V - Electricity
Color (I)
Explains the differences between series and parallel circuits and the values of each.
Science - Physical
Dist - GPN **Prod** - WVIZTV

Series and parallel circuits 8 MIN
16mm
Radio technician training series; Elementary electricity
B&W
Illustrates series and parallel circuits, explaining current flow and voltage drop across each lamp.
Industrial and Technical Education
Dist - USNAC **Prod** - USN 1947

Series and Parallel Resistors 9 MIN
U-matic / VHS / 16mm
Basic Electricity Series
Color (H C A)
Deals with resistors in series, the calculation of current in a circuit of known resistance, resistors in parallel, calculation of current effect on cross - sectional area, resistance of cables and voltage drop.
Science - Physical
Dist - IFB **Prod** - STFD 1979

Series a
First aid - newest techniques
Dist - CAREER

Series circuits 30 MIN
U-matic / VHS
Basic electricity and D C circuits series
Color
Surveys series circuits and rules of their behavior. Teaches identifying of series circuits and calculating of their equivalent resistance, current flow, voltage at various circuit points and power dissipated by each resistor.
Industrial and Technical Education; Science - Physical; Social Science
Dist - TXINLC **Prod** - TXINLC

Series conclusion and talking about deafness
U-matic / VHS
Signing with Cindy series
Color (A)
Shows Cindy Cochran signing for deaf children to the song 'Hit Me With Your Best Shot.' Includes the song 'Fire' and answers questions about deafness and deaf people.
Education; English Language
Dist - GPCV **Prod** - GPCV

Series of positive terms 20 MIN
VHS
Calculus series; No 54
Color (H)
LC 90712920
Discusses series of positive terms. The 54th of 57 installments of the Calculus Series.
Mathematics
Dist - GPN

Series overview 30 MIN
VHS / U-matic
Coping with kids series
Color
Introduces Dr Thomas J Sweeney, Professor of Guidance and Counseling at the Ohio University College of Education. Outlines each program in the Coping With Kids presentation, briefly using excerpts from each of them.
Guidance and Counseling; Sociology
Dist - OHUTC **Prod** - OHUTC

Series, Parallel, and Standby Systems 30 MIN
U-matic / VHS
Reliability Engineering Series
Color (IND)
Describes the reliability calculations for series, parallel and standby systems.
Industrial and Technical Education
Dist - COLOSU **Prod** - COLOSU

Series - parallel circuits 30 MIN
U-matic / VHS
Basic electricity and D C circuits series
Color
Discusses application of circuit reduction techniques and Ohm's Law to more complex, single - supply series - parallel circuits. Introduces practical 'circuit sense' methods to help analyze circuit schematics.
Industrial and Technical Education; Science - Physical; Social Science
Dist - TXINLC **Prod** - TXINLC

Series - parallel circuits 15 MIN
VHS / U-matic
Basic electricity and D C circuits - laboratory series
Color
Industrial and Technical Education; Science - Physical; Social Science
Dist - TXINLC **Prod** - TXINLC

Series parallel circuits - analysis 16 MIN
U-matic / VHS
B&W
LC 84-706411
Describes the circuit analysis of series parallel circuits and discusses resistance, current and voltage distribution, and power. Demonstrates the results of changing both the number of branches and the resistance within a branch.
Industrial and Technical Education; Science - Physical
Dist - USNAC **Prod** - USAF 1983

Series parallel circuits - troubleshooting 19 MIN
U-matic / VHS / 16mm
B&W
Shows the symptoms for opens and shorts in series parallel circuits. Uses an ohmmeter and voltmeter to isolate the faulty component.
Industrial and Technical Education; Mathematics; Science - Physical
Dist - USNAC **Prod** - USAF 1983

Series - parallel resistive circuits 40 MIN
16mm / U-matic / VHS
B&W
Shows combinations of series, parallel and series - parallel circuits. Shows how to identify the type of circuit and solve for current, voltage and resistance.
Industrial and Technical Education; Science - Physical
Dist - USNAC **Prod** - USAF

Series - parallel resistive circuits - circuit analysis 40 MIN
16mm
B&W
LC 74-705610
Shows various combinations of series, parallel and series - parallel circuits. Explains how to identify the type of circuit and how to solve for resistance of individual components and total resistance. Explains how to calculate current and describes and explains the procedure for constructing an equivalent circuit. (Kinescope).
Industrial and Technical Education; Science - Physical
Dist - USNAC **Prod** - USAF 1965

Series RC circuits 15 MIN
16mm / U-matic / VHS
B&W
Reviews the use of vector analysis, the Pythagorean theorem and trigonometric functions as applied to series RC circuits. Constructs the impedance and voltage vectors. Uses an oscilloscope to demonstrate phase relationships and relative amplitudes.
Industrial and Technical Education; Mathematics; Science - Physical
Dist - USNAC **Prod** - USAF 1983

Series RC, RL and RCL circuits 37 MIN
U-matic / VHS / 16mm
B&W
LC 74-705604
Defines a vector quantity. Demonstrates the manner in which reactive circuits differ from resistive circuits. Explains why this difference exists and tells how it affects impedance and phases angle.
Industrial and Technical Education; Science - Physical
Dist - USNAC **Prod** - USAF 1979

Series RC, RL and RCL circuits - trigonometric functions 40 MIN
16mm
B&W
LC 74-705605
Explains the method of solving for the phase angle and impedance by the use of trigonometric functions.
Industrial and Technical Education; Mathematics; Science - Physical
Dist - USNAC **Prod** - USAF

Series RC, RL and RCL circuits - trigonometric solutions 40 MIN
BETA
B&W
LC 79-707525
Explains solutions for phase angle and impedance by using trigonometric functions.
Industrial and Technical Education
Dist - USNAC **Prod** - USAF 1979

Series RCL circuits 16 MIN
16mm / U-matic / VHS
B&W
Constructs a parallel RCL circuit and shows how each branch current is independent of the others. Compares the time - phase relationship of branch currents with reactive components. Determines current and phase angle trigonometrically and vectorially.
Industrial and Technical Education; Mathematics; Science - Physical
Dist - USNAC **Prod** - USAF 1983

Series RCL quality and selectivity 28 MIN
16mm
B&W
LC 74-705606
Determines the relationship between reactance and resistance in series RCL circuits. Explains selectivity, band pass and bandwidth.
Industrial and Technical Education; Science - Physical
Dist - USNAC **Prod** - USAF

Series resistive circuits 15 MIN
U-matic / VHS / 16mm
B&W
Shows how to analyze current, voltage and resistance in a series resistive circuit. Discusses how a change in the total resistance affects each parameter.
Industrial and Technical Education; Science - Physical
Dist - USNAC **Prod** - USAF 1983

Series resistive circuits - DC power 29 MIN
16mm
B&W
LC 74-705607
Defines electrical power in terms of work and rate. Discusses the three formulas for computing power. Gives problems to solve, using the power formulae. (Kinescope).
Industrial and Technical Education; Science - Physical
Dist - USNAC **Prod** - USAF

Series resistive circuits - troubleshooting 35 MIN
16mm
B&W
LC 74-705608
Discusses the process of locating trouble in a circuit. Shows how opens are located by use of a voltmeter and ohmmeter and emphasizes the symptoms. Discusses shorts, points out the symptoms and demonstrates the procedure for locating shorts with a volunteer. (Kinescope).
Industrial and Technical Education; Mathematics; Science - Physical
Dist - USNAC **Prod** - USAF

Series resonant circuits 31 MIN
16mm
B&W
LC 74-705609
Calculates the resonant frequency of a series RCL circuit and compares the magnitude of current and impedance. Vectorially analyzes the series RCL circuit as capacitive, inductive or resistive. Filmed in Kinescope.
Industrial and Technical Education; Science - Physical
Dist - USNAC **Prod** - USAF

Series RL Circuits 18 MIN
16mm / U-matic / VHS
B&W
Reviews the vector and trigonometric methods of computing total impedance and current, phase angle and power factor in series RL circuits. Uses an oscilloscope to show the values and phase relationships of ER, EL and EA.
Industrial and Technical Education; Mathematics; Science - Physical
Dist - USNAC **Prod** - USAF 1983

Series sur les manseuvres de ceremonie 7 MIN
16mm
Ceremonial drill - French series
Color (FRENCH)
LC 77-702843
A French language version of the motion picture Ceremonial Drill. Discusses the historical value of ceremonial drills in the armed forces.
Civics and Political Systems
Dist - CDND **Prod** - CDND 1976

Series Wrap 30 MIN
U-matic / VHS
New Voice Series
Color (H C A)
Reviews the programs of the New Voice series.
Literature and Drama
Dist - GPN **Prod** - WGBHTV

Serigraphs 30 MIN
U-matic
Media and Methods of the Artist Series
Color (H C A)
Demonstrates techniques for creating a silkscreen print.
Fine Arts
Dist - TVOTAR **Prod** - TVOTAR 1971

Serious minded stuff 16 MIN
16mm
Color (I)
Presents the story of a 16 - year - old girl who discovers her natural talent for slapstick and becomes an overnight silent film star. Relates the disappointment of her parents when she stops her ballet training in order to pursue her new career.
Fine Arts
Dist - DIRECT **Prod** - USC 1983

Seriously fresh - for teenagers 21 MIN
VHS
AIDSFILMS series
Color (J H)
$65.00 purchase
Portrays four teenagers during basketball practice who discuss with candor everything from cars to girls, pipes to needles and condoms to AIDS. Shows each youth confronting his own vulnerability to HIV transmission and his own responsibility for using condoms when the group learns that their close friend, Kenny, has AIDS. The four friends compare experiences initiating condom use and challenge each other's risk - taking behaviors. Models effective peer resistance, assertiveness and self - empowerment, and addresses decision - making, limit - setting and sexual negotiating skills. Includes discussion guide.
Health and Safety; Psychology; Sociology
Dist - SELMED

Seriousness of struggle
VHS
Evangelism dimensions for discipleship series
Color (G A R)
$39.95 purchase, $10.00 rental _ #35 - 827 - 2076
Features pastor Jack Aamot in presentations on effective evangelism. Produced by Seraphim.
Religion and Philosophy
Dist - APH

Sermon on the Mount - Now 19 MIN
16mm
Color (H C A)
LC 73-701809
Presents an off - screen reading of the exact text of the Gospel of Matthew, chapters five through seven, commonly known as the Sermon on the Mount. Includes without additional comment a collage of contemporary images relating what is being heard to what is modern and relevant today.
Literature and Drama; Religion and Philosophy
Dist - MMA **Prod** - MMA 1973

Sermons and sacred pictures 29 MIN
VHS / 16mm
Color; B&W (H C G A)
$195.00, $595.00 purchase, $45.00 rental _ #38109, #11412
Profiles the life and work of Reverend L O Taylor, a Black Baptist minister from Memphis, Tennessee. Reveals that Rev Taylor was also a filmmaker who preserved a visual and aural record of the social, cultural, and religious fabric of Black American life in the 1930s and 1940s. Combines Taylor's black and white films and audio recordings with color images of contemporary Memphis neighborhoods and religious gatherings. Produced by Lynne Sachs in association with the Center for Southern Folklore.
Biography; History - United States; Religion and Philosophy; Sociology
Dist - UCEMC

Sermons in wood 27 MIN
16mm
Color
Offers a portrait of Elijah Pierce, a craftsman who has spent many years preserving episodes from the Bible and his life in brightly painted wooden sculptures.
Fine Arts; Industrial and Technical Education
Dist - SOFOLK **Prod** - SOFOLK

Serological Technique - Venipuncture 7 MIN
16mm
Medical Laboratory Techniques Series
Color
LC FIE54-453
Demonstrates how to take a blood sample from the arm.
Health and Safety; Science
Dist - USNAC **Prod** - USN 1954

Serous otitis media 17 MIN
VHS / U-matic
Color (PRO)
Presents methods of diagnosing serous otitis media that have been used through history, an otoscopic and physical examination and hearing tests. Discusses evaluation of diagnostic findings, therapeutic considerations and procedures and follow - up care.
Health and Safety; Science - Natural
Dist - UMICHM **Prod** - UMICHM 1974

The Serpent 80 MIN
VHS
Color (G C H)
$139.00 purchase _ #DL354
Presents the play The Serpent by Jean Claude van Itallie, in which the creation and fall of Man are depicted using poetic language and experimental techniques. An Open Theatre production.
Fine Arts; Literature and Drama
Dist - INSIM

Serpent 15 MIN
16mm
Color
LC 72-700070
An experimental film which uses abstract and concrete images and a composite sound track to suggest the conflict between good and evil. Without narration.
Fine Arts; Religion and Philosophy
Dist - SERIUS **Prod** - BARTLS 1971

The Serpent and the cross 55 MIN
VHS
Color; PAL (G)
PdS100 purchase
Features aboriginal artists who are seeking ways to bridge their native spirituality and Christianity. Covers the religious controversy surrounding this work. A Chris Hilton for Aspire Films production.
Fine Arts; Geography - World; Religion and Philosophy
Dist - BALFOR

Serpent fruits 59 MIN
U-matic / VHS / BETA
Color (G PRO)
$46.00, $155.00 purchase _ #LSTF2
Presents actual case histories of people and communities affected by chemicals and chemical pollution. Considers pharmaceutical, industrial and agricultural chemicals.
Health and Safety; Science - Natural
Dist - FEDU **Prod** - USEPA 1980
AFLCIO EPA

Serpent Mother 27 MIN
U-matic / VHS
Color (C H)
Relates the myth of the Hindu goddess Manasha. Portrays rituals performed during the annual Festival of the Snakes.
Religion and Philosophy
Dist - CEPRO **Prod** - HUFSC 1986

Serrated Slopes for Erosion Control 14 MIN
16mm
Color
LC 74-706400
Discusses slopes that can be prepared during highway construction that will reduce erosion and promote the growth of plant life.
Industrial and Technical Education; Science - Natural
Dist - USNAC **Prod** - USDTFH 1970

Serum cholesterol 9 MIN
16mm
Color
LC FIE67-63
Demonstrates a method of extracting both cholesterol and cholesterol esters from whole serum by treatment with alcohol potassium hydroxide and purification with petroleum ether.
Health and Safety; Science
Dist - NMAC **Prod** - USPHS 1965

Serum cholesterol - Abell - Kendall method - manual 9 MIN
U-matic
Color (PRO)
LC 77-706131
Demonstrates a method of extracting both cholesterol and cholesterol esters from whole serum by treatment with alcohol potassium hydroxide and purification with petroleum ether.
Science; Science - Physical
Dist - USNAC **Prod** - NMAC 1977

Servants of God 30 MIN
VHS / 16mm
Greatest tales from the Old Testament series
Color (P I J)
$29.95 purchase
Tells the stories of young Samuel, of King Solomon and of Daniel in the lion's den, adapted from the Old Testament and presented in animated form. From a Christian perspective.
Literature and Drama; Religion and Philosophy
Dist - CAFM **Prod** - CAFM 1988
APH

Serve 30 MIN
VHS
Tennis with Van der Meer series
Color (C A)
$95.00 purchase, $55.00 rental
Features tennis player and instructor Dennis Van der Meer in a presentation on serves. Uses freeze - frame photography and repetition to stress skill development. Serves as part one of a 10 - part telecourse.
Physical Education and Recreation; Psychology
Dist - SCETV **Prod** - SCETV 1989

The Serve 29 MIN
U-matic / VHS
Vic Braden's Tennis for the Future Series
Color
Physical Education and Recreation
Dist - PBS **Prod** - WGBHTV 1981

The Serve 30 MIN
VHS / U-matic
Tennis Anyone Series
Color (H C A)
LC 79-706889
Physical Education and Recreation
Dist - TIMLIF **Prod** - BATA 1979

The Serve 20 MIN
U-matic / 8mm cartridge
Tennis Series
Color (J)
LC 76-701217
Features a group clinic approach to teaching tennis. Shows how to teach the serve.
Physical Education and Recreation
Dist - ATHI **Prod** - ATHI 1976

Serve and return of serve
VHS
NCAA instructional video series
Color (H C A)
$39.95 purchase _ #KAR2301V
Presents the first of a four - part series on tennis. Focuses on the serve and the return of serves.
Physical Education and Recreation
Dist - CAMV **Prod** - NCAAF

Serve in tennis 30 MIN
VHS
Tennis talk series
Color (J H A)
$24.95 purchase _ #PRO007V
Features tennis instructor Dennis Van der Meer teaching about serving in tennis.
Physical Education and Recreation
Dist - CAMV

Serve or Preserve 29 MIN
U-matic
Edible Wild Plants Series
Color
Shows procedures for preparing wild plants for immediate use or preservation. Explores a variety of wild berries and their habitats.
Health and Safety; Science - Natural
Dist - UMITV **Prod** - UMITV 1978

Service 30 MIN
VHS / 16mm
Growing a Business Series
(H C)
$99.95 each, $1,295.00 series
Emphasizes the role of service in a successful business.
Business and Economics
Dist - AMBROS **Prod** - AMBROS 1988

Service
VHS / 35mm strip
Wiring a house series
$85.00 purchase _ #DXWAH030 filmstrips, $85.00 purchase _ #DXWAH030V
Teaches about overhead service, installing the panel and pulling wire.
Industrial and Technical Education
Dist - CAREER **Prod** - CAREER

Service connected priorities - an overview 17 MIN
U-matic
Color
LC 79-706029
Shows how priority care programs have been implemented in two Veterans Administration medical centers.
Guidance and Counseling; Health and Safety
Dist - USNAC **Prod** - VAHSL 1978

Service connected priorities - back to basics 13 MIN
U-matic
Color
LC 79-706030
Provides examples of priority treatment procedures for service - connected veterans being used by two Veterans Administration health care facilities.
Guidance and Counseling; Health and Safety
Dist - USNAC **Prod** - VAHSL 1978

The Service economy 30 MIN
U-matic
It's everybody's business series; Operating a business; Unit 5
Color
Business and Economics
Dist - DALCCD **Prod** - DALCCD

Service excellence 90 MIN
VHS / 16mm
Color (IND)
$730.00 purchase, $235.00 rental
Shows how to improve customer service. Features authors Ron Zemke, Ken Blanchard, William Ouchi and Karl Albrect. Visits successful enterprises.
Business and Economics
Dist - VIDART **Prod** - NATTYL 1990
VLEARN VIDART

Service first - excellence in health care 16 MIN
VHS / U-matic
Color (PRO C)
$395.00 purchase, $80.00 rental _ #C920 - VI - 003
Discusses how to establish a hospital healthcare program which puts the customer - patient - first. Presented by Rush - Presbyterian St Luke's Medical Center, Chicago.
Health and Safety
Dist - HSCIC

Service - how to keep your customers and build your business 39 MIN
VHS
Color (G)
$495.00 purchase, $150.00 rental _ #91F3186
Features Roger Dow who explains how exceptional customer service can build long - term customer loyalty.
Business and Economics; Psychology
Dist - DARTNL **Prod** - DARTNL

Service interruptions
U-matic / VHS
Distribution system operation series; Topic 12
Color (IND)
Assists participant in dealing with interruptions of customer service, analyzing faults and taking action to normalize the situation. Includes planned and forced outages, customer complaints, clearance procedures and documentation.
Industrial and Technical Education
Dist - LEIKID **Prod** - LEIKID

Service Marketing 30 MIN
U-matic / VHS
Marketing Perspectives Series
Color
Covers the characteristics of the service product, marketing of non - profit service organizations and other aspects of service marketing.
Business and Economics; Education
Dist - WFVTAE **Prod** - MATC

The Service module 5 MIN
16mm
Apollo digest series
Color
LC 74-705611
Reports on the unmanned portion of the Apollo spacecraft, the section providing essential services for the command and lunar modules. Explains the functions of propulsion, fuel storage and advanced instrumentation.
Industrial and Technical Education; Science - Physical; Social Science
Dist - USNAC **Prod** - NASA 1969

Service occupations - Pt 1
VHS
Profiles - people and jobs series
Color (H G)
$50.00 purchase _ #SOCC - 1V
Presents part of a series of 6 videos that introduce high school students to high demand, rewarding occupations of the future. Looks at the careers of Chefs and Cooks; Janitors and Cleaners; Food and Beverage Service Workers; Waiters and Waitresses. Series is based on the Occupational Outlook Handbook.
Guidance and Counseling; Psychology
Dist - CENTER **Prod** - CENTER

Service occupations - Pt 2
VHS
Profiles - people and jobs series
Color (H G)
$50.00 purchase _ #SOCC - 2V
Presents part of a series of 6 videos that introduce high school students to high demand, rewarding occupations of the future. Looks at the careers of Medical Assistants; Homemaker - Home Health Aides; Nursing Aides; Correction Officers - Guards. Series is based on the Occupational Outlook Handbook.
Guidance and Counseling; Psychology
Dist - CENTER **Prod** - CENTER

Service organizations 20 MIN
U-matic / VHS
Clues to career opportunities for liberal arts graduates series
Color (C A)
LC 79-706057
Explains how to find out about existing jobs in the community and about the structure of community agencies.
Guidance and Counseling; Psychology
Dist - IU **Prod** - IU 1978

Service perspective - focus the frontline 13 MIN
VHS
Color (IND)
$95.00 purchase _ #PAC03
Captures Rick Tate answering customer service questions from a group of Frontline employees. Provokes dialogue about service quality issues. Produced by Innovative Thinking, Inc.
Business and Economics
Dist - EXTR

The Service phase 24 MIN
U-matic / VHS
Social work interviewing series
Color
Presents an interview with nurses who are having difficulty communicating with a hospital administrator regarding the severe understaffing at the hospital. Shows ways they can bargain with the hospital administrator without jeopardizing their jobs.
Guidance and Counseling; Psychology; Sociology
Dist - UWISC **Prod** - UCALG 1978

Service Procedure for Ball Bearing 20 MIN
16mm
B&W (H C A) (FRENCH)
Shows how to remove, service and install ball bearings.
Industrial and Technical Education
Dist - GM **Prod** - GM 1950

Service station attendant 15 MIN
16mm / U-matic / VHS
Career awareness
(I)
$130 VC purchase, $240 film purchase, $25VC rental, $30 film rental
Presents an empathetic approach to career planning, showing the personal as well as the professional attributes of service station attendants. Highlights the importance of career education.
Guidance and Counseling; Industrial and Technical Education
Dist - GPN

Service video 3 MIN
VHS
Meeting opener motivation videos series
Color (G)
$89.00 purchase _ #MV2
Presents an 'inspiration' video which incorporates cinematography, music and lyrics to create a mood that enhances the impact of the desired message.
Psychology
Dist - GPERFO

Service with a smile 40 MIN
VHS
Circle square series; Vol 7
Color (J H R)
$11.99 purchase _ #35 - 867608 - 979
Examines helping others from a Biblical perspective.
Religion and Philosophy
Dist - APH **Prod** - TYHP

Service with soul 70 MIN
VHS
Color (G C PRO)
$895.00 purchase, $250.00 rental
Features Tom Peters, who investigates how customer expectations have changed in the past decade and what businesses must do now to meet and exceed those expectations. Presents five diverse, on - location case studies to illustrate exemplary customer service. Identifies the shared philosophies and strategies that propelled the sample organizations. Includes discussion guide.
Business and Economics
Dist - FI **Prod** - VPHI 1995

Services; 2nd ed. 21 MIN
U-matic / VHS
Community series
Color (K P)
$415.00, $385.00 _ #V240
Explores the changing communities where families live and work. Focuses on the public places and services of communities. Looks at parks, libraries, schools, the services of the police and fire departments, roads, and the role of government and taxation in providing services. Part of a three - part series on the community.
Guidance and Counseling; Social Science; Sociology
Dist - BARR **Prod** - CEPRO 1991

Services for the blind and physically handicapped 20 MIN
U-matic
Access series
Color (T)
LC 76-706259
Explains the range of services available to those people who are temporarily or permanently unable to read.
Education; Guidance and Counseling
Dist - USNAC **Prod** - UDEN 1976

Services to elementary - age children 20 MIN
U-matic
Access series
Color (T)
LC 76-706261
Presents ideas for noncompetitive, participation - oriented programs for elementary - age children.
Business and Economics; Education; Guidance and Counseling
Dist - USNAC **Prod** - UDEN 1976

Services to Young Children 48 MIN
16mm
B&W
Features a pediatric neurologist, nurse, therapist, speech pathologist, special educator and social worker who discuss the need for and demonstrate the techniques of serving young children (under three years of age) with cerebral dysfunction.
Education; Psychology
Dist - UCPA **Prod** - UCPA

Servicing a propeller 18 MIN
16mm
B&W
LC FIE52-235
Demonstrates how to inspect and remove a propeller, repair damage to the metal edges, check and correct for out - of - track and for out - of - balance problems and reinstall the propeller.
Industrial and Technical Education
Dist - USNAC **Prod** - USOE 1945

Servicing an airplane 17 MIN
16mm
B&W
LC FIE52-266
Shows how to perform the various routine servicing operations on a plane on the ground - cleaning the airplane, refueling, changing the oil, inflating tires and starting the engine. Shows hand signals for guiding the pilot.
Industrial and Technical Education; Social Science
Dist - USNAC **Prod** - USOE 1945

Servicing and Timing Magnetos 16 MIN
16mm
B&W
LC FIE52-258
Demonstrates how to remove magnetos from the engine, install and adjust points and reinstall and time the magnetos.
Industrial and Technical Education
Dist - USNAC **Prod** - USOE 1945

Servicing Chrysler electronic ignition 25 MIN
VHS / U-matic
Automechanics series
Color (IND)
Identifies the components of the Chrysler ignition system. Explains their operating principles and outlines an on - the - car trouble shooting procedure. Covers distributor service.
Industrial and Technical Education
Dist - LEIKID **Prod** - LEIKID

Servicing Ford electronic ignition 24 MIN
VHS / U-matic
Automechanics series
Color (IND)
Identifies the components of the Ford ignition system. Shows a comprehensive on - the - car checkout and distributor test and service procedure.
Industrial and Technical Education
Dist - LEIKID **Prod** - LEIKID

Servicing GM electronic ignition 36 MIN
VHS / U-matic
Automechanics series
Color (IND)
Demonstrates the GM Hi - energy system, self - contained in the distributor, through a precise on - the - car inspection and test. Shows how to dismantle the distributor and reassemble it on the bench.
Industrial and Technical Education
Dist - LEIKID **Prod** - LEIKID

Servicing parking brakes 10 MIN
VHS / 16mm
Automotive tech series
(G PRO)
$61.00 purchase
Shows how to service parking brakes.
Industrial and Technical Education
Dist - RMIBHF **Prod** - RMIBHF

Servicing spacecraft at space stations 17 MIN
VHS
Color (J H C)
$14.95 purchase _ #NA711
Industrial and Technical Education
Dist - INSTRU **Prod** - NASA

Servicing Spark Plug Wires 8 MIN
VHS / 16mm
Kirkwood Community College Auto Mechanics Series
(G PRO)
$56.00 purchase _ #KTI86
Shows how to service spark plug wires.
Industrial and Technical Education
Dist - RMIBHF **Prod** - RMIBHF

Servicing Spark Plugs 9 MIN
VHS / 16mm
Kirkwood Community College Auto Mechanics Series
(G PRO)
$58.50 purchase _ #KTI87
Shows how to service spark plugs.
Industrial and Technical Education
Dist - RMIBHF **Prod** - RMIBHF

Servicing spark plugs and ignition wiring 22 MIN
16mm
Aircraft work series; Power plant maintenance
B&W
LC FIE52-252
Shows how to remove spark plugs and ignition wires, how to clean, inspect, adjust and reinstall the spark plugs, and how to prepare and install ignition wires.
Industrial and Technical Education
Dist - USNAC **Prod** - USOE 1945

Servicing the Automatic Choke 4 MIN
16mm
Color
LC FI68-242
Points out the main operation features of the choke control, the control spring and the method of adjusting for the variance of volatility of the gasoline.
Industrial and Technical Education
Dist - RAYBAR **Prod** - RAYBAR 1966

Servicing the Distributor Cap, Rotor, and Coil 5 MIN
VHS / 16mm
Kirkwood Community College Auto Mechanics Series
(G PRO)
$48.50 purchase _ #KTI88
Shows how to service the distributor cap, rotor, and coil.
Industrial and Technical Education
Dist - RMIBHF **Prod** - RMIBHF

Servicing the Radiator Pressure Cap 4 MIN
16mm
Color
LC FI68-243
Shows cleaning and test for pressure of an old radiator cap. Includes inspection of filler neck and cams and cleaning of the overflow tube.
Industrial and Technical Education
Dist - RAYBAR **Prod** - RAYBAR 1966

Servicing the small engine 44 MIN
VHS
Small engine - a video manual series
Color (H A)
$319.00 purchase _ #VMA31371V
Presents a comprehensive look at how to service a small automobile engine. Consists of three videocassettes and a program guide.
Industrial and Technical Education
Dist - CAMV

Servicing water - cooled condensers 12 MIN
16mm
Refrigeration service series commercial systems; No 4
B&W
LC FIE52-262
Explains the theory of a counter - flow condenser, the essential elements of a water - cooled system and the operation and regulation of the electric water valve.
Industrial and Technical Education
Dist - USNAC **Prod** - USOE 1945

Serving alcohol with care 30 MIN
VHS
Color (IND)
Sensitizes servers and managers of restaurants and bars to the potential liability associated with alcohol service. Shows methods to judge intoxication and tactfully curtail service when necessary.
Business and Economics; Health and Safety; Industrial and Technical Education; Sociology
Dist - EIAHM **Prod** - EIAHM 1986

Serving and feeding the patient 9 MIN
U-matic / VHS
Color (PRO) (SPANISH)
LC 77-731353
Stresses basic nutritional needs and describes the four basic foods groups. Explains the importance of adequate fluid intake. Emphasizes the importance of stimulating the patient's appetite with attractively prepared meals served in a pleasant atmosphere.
Health and Safety; Industrial and Technical Education
Dist - MEDCOM **Prod** - MEDCOM

Serving and forearm passing
VHS
Essential skills - coaching boys' volleyball series; Pt I
Color (J H C G)
$49.95 purchase _ #TRS575V
Features Bill Neville, USA National Team coach. Teaches the essential skills of serving and forearm passing. Part of a three - part series on essential skills in volleyball and an eight - part series on boys' volleyball.
Physical Education and Recreation
Dist - CAMV

Serving, blocking and individual defense
VHS
N C A A volleyball instructional video series
Color (H C A)
$39.95 purchase _ #KAR1601V
Features Dr Marv Dunphy covering basic volleyball skills. Covers the skills of serving, blocking, and individual defense.
Physical Education and Recreation
Dist - CAMV **Prod** - NCAAF

Serving cakes 11 MIN
U-matic / VHS
Color (IND)
Teaches how to cut various cakes, from sheet cake to wedding cake, with an eye toward reflecting in each slice the beauty of the whole cake.
Home Economics; Industrial and Technical Education
Dist - CULINA **Prod** - CULINA

Serving cheese 9 MIN
U-matic / VHS
Color (IND)
Introduces various types of cheese and suggests suitable accompaniments of wine, bread and fruit for each.
Home Economics; Industrial and Technical Education
Dist - CULINA **Prod** - CULINA

Serving food 11 MIN
16mm
Color (SPANISH)
LC 74-705612
Portrays the hiring of a waitress and shows the orientation and induction training given her by a restaurant hostess, including instruction in the proper storage of cups, dishes and glasses. Shows cleanliness, the correct ways of clearing tables, protecting the waitresses' health and safeguards against disease.
Health and Safety; Home Economics; Industrial and Technical Education
Dist - USNAC **Prod** - NMAC 1954

Serving food and beverage
16mm / U-matic / VHS
Professional food preparation and service program series
Color
Demonstrates basic rules of serving food and beverage. Shows how professional waiters and waitresses place a wide range of menu items in front of the guest. Teaches how to add garnishments, condiments and accompaniments, stressing imaginative use of color.
Home Economics; Industrial and Technical Education
Dist - NEM **Prod** - NEM 1983

Serving others 14 MIN
U-matic / VHS
Life's little lessons series; Self - esteem 4 - 6; Pt 49
Color (I)
$129.00, $99.00 purchase _ #V678
Portrays new owners of a hotel whose reputation had been built on excellent service. Depicts their poor service attitude and how it almost ruined the business. Part of a 65 - part series on self - esteem.
Business and Economics; Guidance and Counseling; Psychology
Dist - BARR **Prod** - CEPRO 1992

Serving the customer 24 MIN
U-matic
Occupations series
B&W (J H)
Gives commentaries from a customer and a student waitress on the proper way to serve in a restaurant.
Guidance and Counseling; Industrial and Technical Education
Dist - TVOTAR **Prod** - TVOTAR 1985

Serving the Four Corners of Our Earth 20 MIN
16mm
Color (H C A)
LC 76-702105
Presents an overview of the National Cash Register Corporation's services and facilities throughout the world.
Business and Economics
Dist - NCR **Prod** - NCR 1974

Serving the Gifted and Talented Series
Bright Hopes for the Future 29 MIN
Evaluation - keys to improvement 24 MIN
Identification - Stairway to Discovery 27 MIN
Important Teaching Areas, Pt I 24 MIN
Important Teaching Areas, Pt II 28 MIN
Putting it all Together 28 MIN
Dist - ACCESS

Serving the victim of elder abuse - a multidisciplinary approach 21 MIN
VHS
Color (G C PRO)
$165.00 purchase, $45.00 rental
Presents a team approach to solving problems that cause abuse of the elderly. Draws together mental health, financial, legal, medical, law enforcement and advocacy professionals to suggest interventions in abuse cases.
Guidance and Counseling; Health and Safety
Dist - TNF

Serving those who have served 27 MIN
U-matic
Color
LC 79-707305
Reviews the history of the Veterans Administration hospital system and explains the structure and organization of both the central office and local hospitals.
Guidance and Counseling; Health and Safety
Dist - USNAC **Prod** - USVA 1978

Serving Time 47 MIN
VHS
Color (S)
$129.00 purchase _ #386 - 9052
Examines the steps zoos are taking to combat the worldwide crisis of extinction. Reveals how everyone can contribute to conservation efforts close to home and around the world.
Science - Natural
Dist - FI **Prod** - CANBC 1988

Servo analysis 40 MIN
16mm
B&W
LC 74-705613
Shows how the need for a servo system is established and analyzes a block diagram of a system. Discusses error voltage. Filmed in Kinescope.
Industrial and Technical Education
Dist - USNAC **Prod** - USAF

Sesame Street 30 MIN
VHS
Pt 1
Color (K P) (ARABIC)
$29.95 purchase _ #AAT001
Presents all the Sesame Street characters in an Arabic language video. Teaches the Arabic language and culture. Part one of a 10 - part series.
Foreign Language; Geography - World; Literature and Drama
Dist - IBC

Sesame Street 30 MIN
VHS
Pt 3
Color (K P) (ARABIC)
$29.95 purchase _ #SUF003
Presents all the Sesame Street characters in an Arabic language video. Teaches the Arabic language and culture. Part three of a 10 - part series.
Foreign Language; Geography - World; Literature and Drama
Dist - IBC

Sesame Street 30 MIN
VHS
Pt 4
Color (K P) (ARABIC)
$29.95 purchase _ #SUF004
Presents all the Sesame Street characters in an Arabic language video. Teaches the Arabic language and culture. Part four of a 10 - part series.
Foreign Language; Geography - World; Literature and Drama
Dist - IBC

Sesame Street 30 MIN
VHS
Pt 5
Color (K P) (ARABIC)
$29.95 purchase _ #SUF005
Presents all the Sesame Street characters in an Arabic language video. Teaches the Arabic language and culture. Part five of a 10 - part series.
Foreign Language; Geography - World; Literature and Drama
Dist - IBC

Sesame Street 30 MIN
VHS
Pt 6
Color (K P) (ARABIC)
$29.95 purchase _ #SUF006
Presents all the Sesame Street characters in an Arabic language video. Teaches the Arabic language and culture. Part six of a 10 - part series.
Foreign Language; Geography - World; Literature and Drama
Dist - IBC

Sesame Street 30 MIN
VHS
Pt 7
Color (K P) (ARABIC)
$29.95 purchase _ #SUF007
Presents all the Sesame Street characters in an Arabic language video. Teaches the Arabic language and culture. Part seven of a 10 - part series.
Foreign Language; Geography - World; Literature and Drama
Dist - IBC

Sesame Street 30 MIN
VHS
Pt 8
Color (K P) (ARABIC)
$29.95 purchase _ #SUF008
Presents all the Sesame Street characters in an Arabic language video. Teaches the Arabic language and culture. Part eight of a 10 - part series.
Foreign Language; Geography - World; Literature and Drama
Dist - IBC

Sesame Street 30 MIN
VHS
Pt 9
Color (K P) (ARABIC)
$29.95 purchase _ #SUF009
Presents all the Sesame Street characters in an Arabic language video. Teaches the Arabic language and culture. Part nine of a 10 - part series.
Foreign Language; Geography - World; Literature and Drama
Dist - IBC

Sesame Street 30 MIN
VHS
Pt 10
Color (K P) (ARABIC)
$29.95 purchase _ #SUF010
Presents all the Sesame Street characters in an Arabic language video. Teaches the Arabic language and culture. Part ten of a 10 - part series.
Foreign Language; Geography - World; Literature and Drama
Dist - IBC

Sesame Street Home Video Series
Dance Along 30 MIN
Monster Hits 30 MIN
Rock and Roll 30 MIN
Sing Yourself Silly 30 MIN
Dist - EDUCRT

Sesame Street home video series
Bedtime stories and songs 30 MIN
Big bird in China 75 MIN
Big bird's story time 30 MIN
Christmas eve on Sesame Street 60 MIN
Don't eat the pictures - Sesame Street at the Metropolitan Museum of Art 60 MIN
Getting ready for school 30 MIN
Learning about numbers 30 MIN
Learning to add and subtract 30 MIN
Dist - PBS

Sesame street home video series
Getting ready to read 30 MIN
I'm glad I'm me 30 MIN
Learning about letters 30 MIN
Play - along games and songs 30 MIN
Dist - PBS
UILL

Sesame Street I
VHS / 16mm
Color (K)
$11.88 purchase _ #GLD13860
Presents Sesame Street characters singing songs for children.
Fine Arts; Literature and Drama
Dist - EDUCRT

Sesame Street II
VHS / 16mm
Color (K)
$11.88 purchase _ #GLD13863
Presents Sesame Street characters singing songs for children.
Fine Arts; Literature and Drama
Dist - EDUCRT

Sesame street videos series
Sesame Street visits the firehouse 30 MIN
Sesame Street visits the hospital 30 MIN
Dist - EDUCRT
KNOWUN

Sesame street videos series
The Alphabet game 30 MIN
The Best of Ernie and Bert 30 MIN
Big Bird in Japan 60 MIN
Count it higher 30 MIN
Dist - KNOWUN

Sesame Street visits the firehouse 30 MIN
VHS
Sesame street videos series
Color; CC (K P)
$12.95 purchase _ #119181; $14.44 purchase _ #RH9-808205
Visits a firehouse with the Sesame Street crew and watches firefighters in action.
Psychology; Social Science
Dist - KNOWUN **Prod** - RH 1990
EDUCRT

Sesame Street visits the hospital 30 MIN
VHS
Sesame street videos series
Color; CC (K P)
$12.95 purchase _ #127884; $14.44 purchase _ #RH9-808221
Joins Big Bird and his friends as they learn about what happens in a hospital.
Health and Safety; Psychology
Dist - KNOWUN **Prod** - RH 1990
EDUCRT

Sesame street - word families - Pt 1 18 MIN
U-matic / 16mm
Color (P I)
LC 84-707325; 84-701240
Encourages reading readiness through recognition of common word families.
English Language
Dist - GA **Prod** - GA 1985

Sesame street - word families - Pt 2 18 MIN
U-matic / 16mm
Color (P J)
LC 84-707825; 84-701240
Encourages reading readiness through recognition of common word families.
English Language
Dist - GA **Prod** - GA 1985

Sesame street - word families - Pt 3 12 MIN
16mm
Color
LC 84-701240
Encourages reading readiness through recognition of common word families.
English Language
Dist - GA **Prod** - GA 1985

Sesshu - great landscape painter of Japan 23 MIN
16mm
Color (H)
$6.50 rental _ #33787; $6.00 rental _ #33787
Documents the life of 15th century artist Sesshu, thought to be Japan's greatest ink painter and named one of the greatest figures of world culture at the 1956 World Peace Conference in Vienna. Examines the artist's expression of Zen Buddhist beliefs in his works.
Fine Arts; Geography - World; Religion and Philosophy
Dist - PSU
USNAC

Session I 20 MIN
U-matic / 16mm / VHS
Color
Shows trainees how to replace schoolroom learning ideas with adult learning techniques and drives home the concept that learning extends far beyond the formal program and that each trainee is accountable for his or her results.
Psychology
Dist - EFM **Prod** - EFM

A Session of Gestalt family therapy 57 MIN
VHS
B&W (C G PRO)
$210.00 purchase, $19.50 rental _ #60901
Offers a brief statement of the basic principles of Gestalt family therapy by Cynthia Harris, segments of two therapy sessions conducted by Sonia Nevis and a concluding discussion by Harris and Nevis that serves as teaching commentary on the therapeutic work. Produced by the Center for the Study of the Intimate Systems of the Gestalt Institute of Cleveland.
Psychology
Dist - PSU

A Session with College Students 60 MIN
16mm
B&W
Shows Dr Frederick Perls, founder of Gestalt therapy, demonstrating his method for discovering and expressing the meaning of dreams of college students.
Psychology
Dist - PSYCHF **Prod** - PSYCHF

Sessions and sand trays 75 MIN
VHS
Color (A PRO)
$275.00 purchase, $75.00 rental _ #D - 224A
Demonstrates therapeutic techniques for treating multiple personality disorders resulting from ritual abuse. Shows how sand tray work by clients can aid in diagnosis, facilitate abreaction and the consolidation of memories and provide a direction for subsequent treatment. Features Dr Roberta Sachs, who also discusses special treatments issues for satanic ritual abuse victims. Two parts.
Guidance and Counseling; Health and Safety; Psychology
Dist - CAVLCD **Prod** - CAVLCD

Set construction - where do I start 72 MIN
VHS
Color (G C H)
$129.00 purchase _ #DL207
Covers building supplies and tools, flats and platforms, stiffeners and jacks, moldings, window frames and door jambs, and set assembly.
Fine Arts
Dist - INSIM

A Set covering approach for optimal ingot size selection
VHS
Color (C PRO G)
$150.00 purchase _ #88.04
Examines a new ingot mold stripping facility at Bethlehem Steel Corp capable of handling taller ingots. Shows how a two - phase computer based model selects optimal and internal ingot mold dimensions consistent with the new

stripper's capability and with mill, foundry and steel making contraints. Uses a set covering approach to select optimal ingot and internal ingot mold sizes from among feasible sizes generated. Reviews results, including annual savings in excess of $8 million.
Business and Economics; Industrial and Technical Education
Dist - INMASC

Set Europe ablaze 26 MIN
16mm
Winston Churchill - the valiant years series; No 19
B&W (GERMAN)
LC FI67-2113
Uses documentary footage to describe Churchill's arrangements with governments - in - exile in London. Examines various underground movements in German - occupied Europe, including the ill - fated Warsaw uprising in 1944.
History - World
Dist - SG **Prod** - ABCTV 1961

Set numeration 15 MIN
U-matic
Math factory series; Module 1 - sets
Color (P)
Provides a basic experience in relating number and numeral.
Mathematics
Dist - GPN **Prod** - MAETEL 1973

Set of five 30 - second health related PSA TV spots 3 MIN
VHS / U-matic
Color (G)
$200.00 purchase
Offers a set of five 30 - second PSA TV spots. Covers drinking during pregnancy, alcohol and driving, the immunization of young Native American children and two spots on traditional health with regular checkups.
Business and Economics; Health and Safety
Dist - SHENFP **Prod** - SHENFP

A Set of slides 30 MIN
U-matic / VHS / 16mm
B&W (J)
LC 75-701997
Uses black - and - white still photographs to present a cross - sectional view of London at the end of the 19th century. Re - creates the life of Londoners of all social classes and occupations.
Geography - World; Sociology
Dist - WOMBAT **Prod** - BAYLSP 1975

Set sail 60 MIN
VHS
Set sail series; Vol 1; No 4
Color (G)
$19.95 purchase _ #0652
Presents Volume 1, Number 4 of Set Sail, a quarterly video magazine on boating which features everything from racing and cruising to the latest news about boats and equipment. Cruises aboard the Bill of Rights. Visits St Maarten, St Barts, San Francisco's Maxi Regatta. Looks at strategy in a J - 24 World Championship. Profiles Anne Gardner Nelson, hearty shrimp creole from Patty's Galley. Talks about custom boat building, how to treat burns, nautical news, boardsailing with Tinho and Susie Dornellas.
Physical Education and Recreation
Dist - SEVVID

Set Sail 60 MIN
VHS
Set Sail series; Vol 1; No 3
Color (G)
$19.95 purchase _ #0651
Presents Volume 1, Number 3 of Set Sail, a quarterly video magazine on boating that features everything from racing and cruising to the latest news about boats and equipment. Covers the America's Cup and San Diego Yacht Club, a cruise on the Sea of Cortez near Mexico, sailing tips with Ken Reed who demonstrates upwind sailing and sail trim, Formula 40 Fever, the basics of bareboating, medical check list, builder's boast, world one - ton update, windsurfing. and equipment.
Physical Education and Recreation
Dist - SEVVID

Set sail 30 MIN
VHS / BETA
Under sail series
Color
Tells what's required to safely take off and return a sailboat. Reviews the balance of forces involved in sailing.
Fine Arts; Physical Education and Recreation
Dist - CORF **Prod** - WGBHTV

Set sail 60 MIN
VHS
Set sail series; Vol 2; No 1
Color (G)
$19.95 purchase _ #0653
Presents Volume 2, Number 1 of Set Sail, a quarterly video magazine on boating which features everything from racing and cruising to the latest news about boats and equipment. Cruises Jamaica aboard trimaran Freestyle, the Pride of Baltimore II on a vooyage to Tampa Bay. Visits the largest US inland regatta. Presents sailing tips from Tom Blackaller. Meets the Whitbread competitors. Offers tips from J World sailing school, a medical checklist, nautical news.
Physical Education and Recreation
Dist - SEVVID

Set sail 60 MIN
VHS
Set sail series; Vol 1; No 2
Color (G)
$19.90 purchase _ #0709
Presents Volume 1, Number 2 of Set Sail, a quarterly video magazine on boating which features everything from racing and cruising to the latest news about boats and equipment. Covers the World 12 meter championships, sailing school, Cabbage Key, sailing tips, maritime photography, tall ships, Salley in the galley, on charter, designer's corner, nautical news, amphibious convertible.
Physical Education and Recreation
Dist - SEVVID

Set sail - premiere issue 60 MIN
VHS
Set sail series; Vol 1; No 1
Color (G)
$19.90 purchase _ #0650
Presents the premiere issue of Set Sail, a quarterly video magazine on boating which features everything from racing and cruising to the latest news about boats and equipment. Covers the Antigua Race Week, America's Cup History, Maui water wonderland, International Sailing School, Pro Sail, Olympic Finns, Chinese junk, new products, windward island cruising, tall ships, fashion, nautical news. quarterly video magazine on boating which features everything from racing and cruising to the latest news about boats and equipment.
Physical Education and Recreation
Dist - SEVVID

Set sail series
Set sail 60 MIN
Set sail - premiere issue 60 MIN
Dist - SEVVID

Set speeches and soliloquies 52 MIN
U-matic / VHS
Royal Shakespeare company series
Color
Presents the rules governing a soliloquy, including that it must arise out of a situation, must have a story and must be spontaneous. Uses examples of Shakespearean soliloquies from The Merchant Of Venice, As You Like It, Richard III and Titus Andronicus.
Literature and Drama
Dist - FOTH **Prod** - FOTH 1984

Set straight on bullies 18 MIN
16mm / U-matic
Color (H)
$200.00, $40.00 purchase
Tells of a bullying victim and how the problem of bullying adversely affects the victim, the bully, other students, parents and educators. Indicates that one in seven students is either a bully or a victim of bullying. Reveals that students rate disruptive and inappropriate behavior by classmates as their chief school - related concern.
Psychology; Sociology
Dist - UNKNWN

Set the Pace 10 MIN
16mm
Foremanship Training Series
Color
LC 74-705614
Shows how the supervisor sets the pace for the workmen to follow safety practices in the coal mining industry by his sincerity and enthusiasm.
Business and Economics; Health and Safety
Dist - USNAC **Prod** - USBM 1968

The Set - up - address position
VHS
N C A A instructional video series
Color (H C A)
$39.95 purchase _ #KAR2351V
Presents the first of a four - part series on golf. Focuses on the set - up and address positions.
Physical Education and Recreation
Dist - CAMV **Prod** - NCAAF

Set up and operation of small format video equipment 9 MIN
VHS
On location
(J)
$180 series purchase, $50 rental, $110 self dub
Demonstrates video production skills for small format student productions. Focuses on setup and operation of video equipment. First of an eight part series.
Fine Arts
Dist - GPN **Prod** - NCGE

Set - up and shut down of oxyacetylene welding equipment
U-matic / VHS
Oxyacetylene welding - Spanish series
Color (SPANISH)
Foreign Language; Industrial and Technical Education
Dist - VTRI **Prod** - VTRI

Set - up for holding work to be milled 15 MIN
U-matic / VHS
Machining and the operation of machine tools series; Module 4 - Milling and tool
Color (IND)
Industrial and Technical Education
Dist - LEIKID **Prod** - LEIKID

Set - up variations and fire attack 27 MIN
VHS
Positive pressure ventilation series; Pt 2
Color (PRO IND)
$125.00 purchase _ #35369
Demonstrates positive pressure during fire attack, salvage and overhaul. Trains firefighters. Part of a two - part series which includes instructor and study guides.
Industrial and Technical Education; Psychology; Social Science
Dist - OKSU **Prod** - OKSU

Set - up variations and fire attack 27 MIN
VHS
Positive pressure ventilation series
Color (G PRO)
$125.00 purchase _ #35369
Demonstrates positive pressure ventilation during fire attack, salvage and overhaul. Trains firefighting personnel.
Health and Safety; Psychology; Social Science
Dist - OKSU **Prod** - OKSU

Set your sails, basic sailing skills 75 MIN
VHS
Color (G A)
$49.90 purchase _ #0479
Introduces sport sailing in three parts. Includes Sailing a Dinghy, Keelboat Sailing and Sailing to Win. Features Rob MacLeod and Liz Grogan as hosts.
Physical Education and Recreation
Dist - SEVVID

Set your sails, cruising skills
VHS
Color (G A)
$49.90 purchase _ #0480
Introduces sailing for the family in three parts. Includes Introduction to Cruising, Advanced Cruising and Chartering. Features Rob MacLeod and Liz Grogan as hosts.
Physical Education and Recreation
Dist - SEVVID

Seth Hill 28 MIN
U-matic
San Francisco Bay Area Filmmakers Series
Color (H C A)
LC 80-706449
Interviews animator and documentary filmmaker Seth Hill. Focuses on the creative process of film production.
Fine Arts
Dist - DANKAR **Prod** - DANKAR 1979

Sets 15 MIN
16mm
Color (I)
Presents the elementary notions of sets and operations with appropriate vocabulary in four lessons - - sets, elements and subsets, operation of intersection, operation of union, cardinal number, sum and product.
Mathematics
Dist - MMP **Prod** - MMP 1963

Sets and borders 60 MIN
VHS
Quilting with Joe Cunningham and Gwen Marston series; Vol 2
(H A)
$39.95 purchase _ #BIQ002V
Illustrates the procedure for setting blocks together, making pieced borders, and making applique borders for quilts.
Fine Arts; Home Economics
Dist - CAMV **Prod** - CAMV

Sets and Locations for Videotape 30 MIN
VHS / U-matic
Video - a Practical Guide and more Series
Color
Demonstrates techniques to create minimum cost sets. Shows how to shoot on location and the use of props.
Fine Arts; Industrial and Technical Education
Dist - VIPUB **Prod** - VIPUB

Sets and Numbers 12 MIN
16mm / U-matic / VHS
Modern Elementary Mathematics Series
Color (P)
LC FIA68-315
Explores the mathematical concept of sets and numbers.
Mathematics
Dist - MGHT **Prod** - MGHT 1968

Sets - empty sets 14 MIN
VHS / U-matic
Hands on - grade 2 - lollipops, loops, etc series; Unit 3 - Classifying
Color (P)
Gives experience in classifying sets versus empty sets.
Mathematics
Dist - AITECH **Prod** - WHROTV 1975

Sets of coins 15 MIN
U-matic / VHS
Math factory series; Module 6 - money
Color (P)
Explains the value of the penny, nickel, dime and quarter and shows different sets of coins that have the same value.
Mathematics
Dist - GPN **Prod** - MAETEL

Sets - union and intersection 6 MIN
16mm
MAA elementary arithmetic series
Color (P I)
Mathematics
Dist - MLA **Prod** - MAA 1967
MLA

Setting and achieving goals
VHS
Big changes, big choices series
Color (I J)
$69.95 purchase _ #LVB - 4A
Discusses the importance of learning to set and achieve goals. Introduces strategies for setting both short - term and long - term goals. Part of a 12 - part video series designed to help young adolescents work their way though the many anxieties and issues they face. Encourages them to make positive and healthful life choices. Features humorist and youth counselor Michael Pritchard.
Guidance and Counseling; Psychology
Dist - CFKRCM **Prod** - CFKRCM

Setting and achieving your goals
VHS
FYI video series
Color (J H C G)
$79.95 purchase _ #AMA84025V
Reveals the dynamic process that brings goals into focus. Shows how to reach goals by setting objectives, creating action plans and evaluating process. Part of a 12 - part series on professional and personal skills for the work place.
Guidance and Counseling; Psychology
Dist - CAMV **Prod** - AMA
MEMIND

Setting business strategy 60 MIN
VHS
Effective manager seminar series
Color (A COR)
$95.00 purchase _ #NGC744V; $95.00 purchase _ #6428
Presents a multimedia seminar on setting business strategy. Consists of a videocassette, a 60 - minute audiocassette, and a study guide.
Business and Economics; Psychology
Dist - CAMV
SYBVIS

Setting career goals the video way 21 MIN
VHS / 16mm
Color (J H)
$98.00 purchase _ #CD6V
Utilizes a stone age setting to offer advice on career planning. Focuses on pitfalls in career planning and offers solutions.
Guidance and Counseling; Psychology
Dist - JISTW **Prod** - JISTW

Setting career goals the video way
VHS / BETA / U-matic
Color (J H)
#SGV 100; $98.00 purchase _ #CD500; $98.00 purchase _ CD001V
Helps students set meaningful career goals. Explores self awareness, career exploration, career participation and career preparation. Looks at eight of the most common goal setting mistakes and the six elements found in a successful career plan. Comes with manual and exercises.
Guidance and Counseling
Dist - CADESF **Prod** - CADESF 1987
CAMV CAMV
CAREER CAREER

Setting educational and vocational goals 25 MIN
VHS
Color (H)
$98.00 purchase _ #CD700V; #EVV102
Explores the pros and cons of three post - secondary educational options - university, community or junior college, and vocational school. Shows the differences among these three school types. Covers educational environment, classroom size, choosing a major, and differences in teaching styles. Includes a manual and worksheets.
Education; Guidance and Counseling
Dist - CAMV **Prod** - CAMV 1987
CADESF CADESF

Setting Educational - Vocational Goals
VHS
$98.00 purchase _ #VP100
Gives major considerations in setting post high school educational goals. Stresses choosing a major, classroom size, and styles of learning emphasized in three different settings.
Guidance and Counseling
Dist - CAREER **Prod** - CAREER

Setting goals 11 MIN
U-matic / VHS
Life's little lessons series; Self - esteem 4 - 6; Pt 50
Color (I)
$129.00, $99.00 purchase _ #V679
Illustrates the importance of being organized by portraying the owner of a boot repair shop in a little Western town who is always confused and behind in his work. Part of a 65 - part series on self - esteem.
Business and Economics; Guidance and Counseling; Psychology
Dist - BARR **Prod** - CEPRO 1992

Setting goals - the road to achievement 30 MIN
VHS
Color (J H)
$189.00 purchase _ #2353 - SK
Teaches techniques for setting and achieving goals. Stresses goal - setting in personal, career, and educational matters. Discusses both short and long - term goals. Includes teacher's guide.
Psychology; Sociology
Dist - SUNCOM **Prod** - SUNCOM

Setting in a Regular Sleeve 3 MIN
16mm
Clothing Construction Techniques Series
Color (J)
LC 77-701205
Shows the conventional method of sewing the underarm seam of the sleeve and garment before inserting the sleeve, then shaping the sleeve cap with ease stitch, pinning, stitching and trimming.
Home Economics
Dist - IOWASP **Prod** - IOWA 1976

Setting in a Shirt Sleeve 5 MIN
16mm
Clothing Construction Techniques Series
Color (J)
LC 77-701211
Demonstrates the open or flat construction method for setting in a shirt - type sleeve. Shows how a row of ease stitches is used over the sleeve cap and how the sleeve is attached before the underarm is stitched.
Home Economics
Dist - IOWASP **Prod** - IOWA 1976

Setting in Stories 15 MIN
U-matic / VHS
Word Shop Series
Color (P)
English Language
Dist - WETATV **Prod** - WETATV

Setting limits 24 MIN
VHS / U-matic
Setting limits series
Color (AMERICAN SIGN)
Highlights important themes from first two parts of the Setting Limits Series. Serves as a guide for discussing sexuality with teenagers. In sign language.
Sociology
Dist - ODNP **Prod** - ODNP

Setting limits series
A Night Out 10 MIN
Setting limits 24 MIN
Dist - ODNP

Setting out and building a half - brick, right - angled return with stop end - the students' attempts - Part two of Unit C - Brickwork - Cassette 6 39 MIN
VHS
Building crafts - the teaching and learning process series
Color; PAL (J H IND)
PdS29.50 purchase
Features part of an 18 - part series which observes teaching and learning in a variety of workshop situations. Includes such skills as plumbing, brickwork, carpentry, painting and decorating.
Industrial and Technical Education
Dist - EMFVL

Setting Overall Objectives 7 MIN
U-matic / VHS
Practical M B O Series
Color
Business and Economics; Education; Psychology
Dist - DELTAK **Prod** - DELTAK

Setting Standards of Performance 20 MIN
VHS / U-matic
Color
Shows what performance standards can do for an organization, discusses kinds of practical performance standards and shows managers how to arrive at meaningful standards of their own.
Business and Economics; Psychology
Dist - AMA **Prod** - AMA

Setting the bandsaws up for sawing and use of accessories
U-matic / VHS
Basic machine technology series
Color (SPANISH)
Industrial and Technical Education
Dist - VTRI **Prod** - VTRI

Setting the Context, Pt 1 42 MIN
U-matic / VHS
Relationship Growth Group Series
B&W
Features lecture by Dr Donald R Bardill on relational family therapy. Focuses on the effect a member's absence has on group cohesiveness, the feeling of respect a person gains knowing that she/he is needed and each member's responsibility to the group.
Guidance and Counseling; Psychology; Sociology
Dist - UWISC **Prod** - WRAMC 1979

Setting the course 28 MIN
VHS / U-matic / BETA
Breaking the mold, breaking the myth - defining the masculine 'identity series
Color (G)
$280.00 purchase _ #804.3
Features psychologist Robert Subby. Illustrates and highlights aspects of change that enable men to overcome their personal problems and establish a healthy program for living. Builds on the theme 'redefining the masculine identity' to pull together all the critical developmental components of change. Part of a three - part series on redefining masculine identity produced by Family Systems, Inc.
Health and Safety; Psychology; Sociology
Dist - CONMED

Setting the scene 21 MIN
VHS / 16mm
Drama reference series
Color (C)
$150.00 purchase _ #268401
Implements elementary drama curriculum. Presents drama content, teaching strategies and resources, and demonstrated drama activities for the classroom. Combines interviews, narrations and scenes from the full series to give an overview. Focuses on the philosophy, goals, continuum, starting points, integration of drama and drama as a separate subject in the classroom.
Education; Literature and Drama
Dist - ACCESS **Prod** - ACCESS 1987

Setting the stage 26 MIN
U-matic / VHS
Color (C)
$89.95 purchase _ #EX1906
Examines the technology behind the onstage scenery in theater. Explores the latest in computerized lighting, stereo sound and video projection. Spotlights Robert Wilson who has created a new theater by blending high - technology with non - traditional performance.
Fine Arts
Dist - FOTH **Prod** - FOTH

Setting the stage 48 MIN
VHS
Color (PRO C G)
$119.00 purchase, $39.00 rental _ #625
Complements Fundamentals of Scenic Painting. Shows alternative approaches to common scene painting problems and emphasizes specific paint mixing formulas. Includes three segments on individual cassettes - Preparing the Surface, Painting Exteriors and Painting Interiors. Produced by the Theater Arts Video Library.
Fine Arts
Dist - FIRLIT

Setting the vision - Pt 2 11 MIN
VHS
Breakthrough improvement in quality series; Pt 2
Color (PRO IND A)
$495.00 purchase, $175.00 rental _ #GP133B
Presents part two of a five - part series developed by Florida Power and Light's - Qualtec Quality Service. Discusses the principles that make up policy management and gives organizations a resource to help achieve and keep a competitive advantage.
Business and Economics
Dist - EXTR **Prod** - GPERFO

Setting up a room - creating an environment for learning 27 MIN
16mm
Color; B&W (C T)
LC FIA67-5330
Uses live dialogue and narration to convey the process of planning a kindergarten classroom, establishing the basic work and play areas and arranging the supplementary materials in order to create a functional, flexible room environment for children.
Education; Psychology
Dist - CFDC **Prod** - CFDC 1967

Setting Up a Worksheet
VHS / U-matic
Using MultiPlan Series
Color
Describes the layout of a MultiPlan worksheet, identifying rows, columns and cells. Describes the areas of a MultiPlan worksheet and defines the term window.
Industrial and Technical Education; Mathematics; Sociology
Dist - COMTEG **Prod** - COMTEG

Setting up aluminum wire feed and running butt, t, and lap joints
U-matic / VHS
MIG and TIG welding - Spanish series
Color (SPANISH)
Industrial and Technical Education
Dist - VTRI **Prod** - VTRI

Setting Up an Aquarium 9 MIN
U-matic
Color (P)
Shows school children preparing a classroom aquarium and learning about the needs of living things in a water environment.
Science - Natural
Dist - GA **Prod** - BOBWIN

Setting Up an Electrocardiograph Machine 15 MIN
BETA / VHS
Color
Explains how to set up an electrocardiograph machine.
Health and Safety
Dist - RMIBHF **Prod** - RMIBHF

Setting up and padding of the inert - gas shielded metal - arc welding
U-matic / VHS
MIG and TIG welding - Spanish series
Color (IND VOC) (SPANISH)
Industrial and Technical Education
Dist - VTRI **Prod** - VTRI

Setting up flux cored wire and running continuous beads
VHS / U-matic
MIG and TIG welding - Spanish series
Color (IND VOC)
Industrial and Technical Education
Dist - VTRI **Prod** - VTRI

Setting up for welding 12 MIN
U-matic / VHS / 16mm
Welding series
Color (IND VOC)
LC 74-701448
Illustrates MIG welding techniques. Shows how the spray arc and short arc work, how to set up the equipment and adjust the shielding gas, welding wire, welding current and torch in preparation for welding.
Industrial and Technical Education
Dist - FI **Prod** - UCC 1972

The Setting up of a club 28 MIN
16mm
Learning for a lifetime - the academic club method series; Pt 2
Color
Explains that in the Academic Club Method used at the Kingsbury Center Lab School, a club is built around a set of academic objectives woven into a theme designed to capture children's interest and involvement. Demonstrates by showing the functioning of the Greek Gods Club.'
Education; Psychology
Dist - KINGS **Prod** - KINGS

Setting up the Korek frame repair 18 MIN
BETA / VHS / 16mm
Color (IND VOC)
$80.00 purchase _ #AB134
Discusses setting up the Korek frame repair.
Industrial and Technical Education
Dist - RMIBHF **Prod** - RMIBHF

Setting your child up for success - anticipating and preventing problems 15 MIN
VHS
Boy's town parenting series
Color (G)
$29.95 purchase _ #FFB206V
Shows parents how to help their children be more successful in daily situations. Illustrates teaching children to plan ahead. Part of an 11 - part series.
Guidance and Counseling; Psychology; Sociology
Dist - CAMV **Prod** - FFBH

Setting your own limits - decision making and sex
VHS / 35mm strip
(J H)
$119.00 purchase _ #HR793 filmstrip, $139.00 purchase _ #HR793V VHS
Discusses the conflicts students face when setting limits on sex such as risking disapproval and anger. Shows methods of establishing a sexual identity based on personal values and rights.
Health and Safety; Psychology
Dist - CAREER HRMC **Prod** - CAREER HRMC 1985

Setting your strategic goals 70 MIN
U-matic
Planning the future and the opportunities for your enterprise series; Module 3
Color (A)
Consists of two lessons - Goal Setting For Your Enterprise and Determining Actions To Achieve Your Goals.
Business and Economics
Dist - VENCMP **Prod** - VENCMP 1986

The Settlers 22 MIN
U-matic / VHS / 16mm
Growth of America's West Series
Color (I J H)
LC 78-700922
Explores the reasons for and the impact of America's westward expansion.
History - United States
Dist - PHENIX **Prod** - AFAI 1978

The Settlers and the land 30 MIN
16mm
Great Plains trilogy series; Explorer and settler - the white man arrives
B&W (H C A)
Discusses the rapid settlement of the Great Plains after the Civil War. Describes the Union veterans and government land policies, how the railroads helped the settlers, Nebraska's advertising campaign to break the Great American Desert myth and the state's melting - pot population.
History - United States
Dist - UNEBR **Prod** - UNEBR 1954

Settling Down 55 MIN
16mm / VHS / U-matic
Making of Mankind Series
Color (G)
Explores the reasons why humans began to plant and harvest cereals in the Fertile Crescent over 12,000 years ago. Traces the shift in humankind from nomadic hunter - gatherer to settled villager and farmer. Narrated by Richard Leakey.
History - World; Science - Physical; Sociology
Dist - TIMLIF **Prod** - BBCTV BBCENE AMBROS 1982

The Settling of the Plains 30 MIN
16mm / VHS / U-matic
Great Plains experience series
Color (H C)
History - United States; Social Science
Dist - GPN **Prod** - UMA 1976

Settling the score - women in sports 30 MIN
U-matic
Currents - 1985 - 86 season series; No 216
Color (G)
Talks to women athletes and explores their mixed feelings of pride and achievement and sorrow and anger over levels of funding, coaching, publicity and acceptance.
Physical Education and Recreation; Sociology
Dist - PBS **Prod** - WNETTV 1985

Setup for holding work to be milled
VHS / U-matic
Milling and tool sharpening series
Color (IND VOC)
Industrial and Technical Education
Dist - VTRI **Prod** - VTRI

Setup for holding work to be milled
U-matic / VHS
Milling and tool sharpening - Spanish series
Color (IND VOC) (SPANISH)
Industrial and Technical Education
Dist - VTRI **Prod** - VTRI

Setup for Rough Line - Boring
16mm
Machine Shop - Operations on the Horizontal Boring Mill Series
B&W
LC FIE51-589
Demonstrates how to position the workpiece on the table and position the spindle for horizontal and vertical centers.
Industrial and Technical Education
Dist - USNAC **Prod** - USOE 1945

Setup for rough line - boring 15 MIN
U-matic
Machine shop work series; Operations on the horizontal boring mill; No 4
B&W
LC 80-706610
Demonstrates how to position the workpiece on the table and position the spindle for horizontal centers and for vertical centers. Issued in 1945 as a motion picture.
Industrial and Technical Education
Dist - USNAC **Prod** - USOE 1980

Setup of the Combination Torch and Cutting of Sheet Metal, Sheet Plate 15 MIN
U-matic / VHS
Welding I - Basic Oxy - Acetylene Welding Series
Color
Health and Safety; Industrial and Technical Education
Dist - CAMB **Prod** - CAMB

Setup of the commercial dishwasher 20 MIN
BETA / VHS
Color (G PRO)
$59.00 purchase _ #QF02
Provides useful steps in the operation of a commercial dishwasher, including the pre - wash setup and drying station. Discusses key parts and maintenance tips.
Home Economics; Industrial and Technical Education
Dist - RMIBHF **Prod** - RMIBHF

Setup reduction for just-in-time 30 MIN
VHS / 16mm
Manufacturing insights series
Color (A IND)
$200.00, $190.00 purchase _ #VT392, #VT392U
Shows how companies can implement setup changes to improve efficiency and reduce cost. Includes case studies.
Industrial and Technical Education; Psychology
Dist - SME **Prod** - SME 1990

Seurat 74 MIN
VHS
Color (I)
$39.95 purchase _ #HV - 664
Explores the life and work of Post - Impressionist painter George Seurat. Looks at his creation of Pointillism.
Fine Arts; History - World
Dist - CRYSP **Prod** - CRYSP

Seurat 29 MIN
U-matic
Meet the masters series
B&W
Features Guy Palazzola as he imitates the painting technique of Georges Seurat to illustrate this nineteenth - century painter's use of pointillism and proportion.
Fine Arts
Dist - UMITV **Prod** - UMITV 1966

7 - 64 - Leda und der Schwan - Materialaktion - Otto Muehl - Leda and the swan - An Otto Muehl happening 3 MIN
16mm
Color (G)

$10.00 rental
Uses juxtaposition to cause a captured gesture to assume a more erotic quality.
Fine Arts; Industrial and Technical Education
Dist - CANCIN **Prod** - KRENKU 1964

Seven ages of fashion
VHS
Color; PAL (J H)
PdS35 purchase
Presents seven 26 - minute programs about the English fashion scene from the time of Elizabeth I to the end of the 20th century. Illustrates the genuine clothing of the periods. Contact distributor about availability outside the United Kingdom.
History - World; Home Economics
Dist - ACADEM

The Seven ages of man 30 MIN
VHS
Hurray for today series
Color; PAL (G)
PdS25
Examines changes in British architecture in recent years. Features Lucinda Lambton, an architectural photographer. Part of a six - part series studying architectural changes in Britain from the years of modernization, comprehensive redevelopment and concrete blocks to a new age of modern buildings.
Fine Arts; Geography - World; History - World
Dist - ACADEM

Seven artists series
Focuses on some of the main features of 20th-century art by exploring the work of seven artists who reflect the multiplicity and profusion of styles of this century. The artists are placed in their own social and geographical environments. Follows the creation of an art object begun and completed under the camera's eye.

Antoni Tapies	30 MIN
Duane Hanson	30 MIN
Edward Ruscha	30 MIN
Johannes Grutzke	30 MIN
Julio Le Parc	30 MIN
Roy Lichtenstein	30 MIN
Victor Pasmore	30 MIN

Dist - BBCENE

Seven artists - seven spaces - in a hospital 20 MIN
VHS / 16mm / U-matic
Color
Observes seven leading artists as they engage in massive installations of commissioned artworks in the Detroit Receiving Hospital and the University Health Center. A unique musical score accompanies each artist's interpretation as the work was completed in 1983.
Fine Arts
Dist - MARXS

The Seven Bridges of Konigsberg 4 MIN
U-matic / VHS / 16mm
Color (H C)
Uses animation to re - create Leonard Euler's analysis of the problem of crossing the bridges of Konigsberg in a single, continuous walk.
Geography - World
Dist - IFB **Prod** - IFB 1965

Seven chances 57 MIN
16mm
B&W (J)
Stars Buster Keaton. Tells the story of a young man who will inherit a fortune providing he is married before seven PM on a designated date.
Fine Arts
Dist - TWYMAN **Prod** - MGM 1925

Seven Chinese Festivals 28 MIN
16mm
Color
Depicts the Chinese way of life as manifested in seven major festivals, including Lunar New Year, the Lantern Festival, the Ching Ming Festival, the Birthday Anniversary of Matsu, the Dragon Boat Festival, the Birthday of Confucius and the Moon Festival.
History - World; Sociology
Dist - MTP **Prod** - RCHINA

Seven day itch 7 MIN
16mm
Vignette series
B&W (T)
LC 71-707970
Views children exploring social relations at Hilltop Head Start Center.
Education; Psychology
Dist - EDC **Prod** - EDS 1969

The 7 - day professional image update 20 MIN
VHS
Color (H C A)
$99.00 purchase _ #MEC3601V-J
Presents students with information about leadership skills and functioning as part of a management team. Shows how to attain credibility as a leader; how to transmit messages via dress style; how to accessorize; and how to send consistent verbal and nonverbal messages. Comes with teacher's guide.
Business and Economics; Psychology
Dist - CAMV

Seven days 20 MIN
16mm
Color (G)
$30.00 rental
Spends seven consecutive days by a small stream on the northern slopes of Mount Carningly in southwest Wales, where one frame was taken every ten seconds throughout the day. Shows a Romantic side of nature. Produced by Chris Welsby.
Fine Arts; Geography - World
Dist - CANCIN

Seven days a week 30 MIN
VHS
Color (G C PRO)
$195.00 purchase, $45.00 rental; $195.00 purchase, $100.00 rental _ #CE-080
Focuses on one nursing home owner's insistence on quality care, demonstrating that a well - run agency is a reachable goal. Calls attention to characteristics of a quality institution.
Health and Safety
Dist - TNF **Prod** - TNF
FANPRO

Seven days a week 30 MIN
16mm
Color; B&W (J H T R)
LC FIA68-586
Attempts to motivate Christian laymen to 'witness' to their Christian faith on the job and off seven days a week.
Religion and Philosophy
Dist - FAMF **Prod** - FAMF 1964

Seven days in Bensonhurst 60 MIN
VHS
Frontline series
Color; Captioned (G)
$300.00 purchase, $95.00 rental _ #FRON - 813K
Examines the racially motivated murder of Yusef Hawkins, a Black teenager, in a primarily White Brooklyn neighborhood. Shows how both Blacks and Whites used the incident for political purposes. Reveals the depth of racial division in New York City.
History - United States; Sociology
Dist - PBS **Prod** - DOCCON 1990

Seven days in May
VHS / U-matic
B&W (J H C A)
$69.00 purchase _ #04164 94
Dramatizes a military plan to overthrow the United States government. Stars Burt Lancaster and Kirk Douglas.
Civics and Political Systems; Fine Arts
Dist - ASPRSS

Seven days in the life of the president 60 MIN
16mm
March of time series
B&W
LC FIA66-536
A behind - the - scenes look at Lyndon B Johnson, President of the United States, during a crucial week of decision making.
Biography; Civics and Political Systems; History - United States
Dist - WOLPER **Prod** - WOLPER 1965

Seven dietary guidelines and Eating a variety of foods 28 MIN
VHS / U-matic
Eat well, be well series
Color (H C A)
Introduces the Seven Dietary Guidelines and features dishes emphasizing guideline No 1 - eat a variety of foods.
Health and Safety; Social Science
Dist - JOU **Prod** - JOU 1983

Seven, eight, lay them straight 8 MIN
16mm
Color (A)
LC 81-700787
Presents teenagers discussing their thoughts and feelings about the use of drugs.
Health and Safety; Psychology; Sociology
Dist - USNAC **Prod** - NIDA 1981
MTP

The 7 elements and 8 principles of design 48 MIN
VHS
Color (G)
$39.95 purchase _ #C - 7
Discusses dominance, contrast, gradation, harmony, variation, alternation, balance and unity. Demonstrates the principles basic to all works of art. Features Tony Couch.
Fine Arts
Dist - COUCHT **Prod** - COUCHT

Seven films by Bruce Conner 42 MIN
16mm
B&W (G)
$90.00 rental
Presents seven films produced by Bruce Conner - Ten Second Film, a commercial designed for the New York Film Festival in 1965; America Is Waiting examines ideals of loyalty, power and patriotism; A Movie uses found footage to metaphorically present the apocalypse; Report looks at society's relationship with violence and destruction; Take The 5 - 10 To Dreamland is a series of images inducing a poetic state; and Valse Triste is an autobiographical portrait of the filmmaker's Kansas boyhood in the 1940s.
Fine Arts
Dist - CANCIN **Prod** - CONNER

Seven films - Mark Street 77 MIN
VHS
Color & B&W (G)
$70.00 purchase
Features productions made by Mark Street between 1983 and 1990. Includes Scratch; January Journal; Spray; The Mission Stop; Winterwheat; Lilting Towards Chaos; and Fractious Array - silent. See individual titles for description and availability for rental in 16mm format.
Fine Arts
Dist - CANCIN **Prod** - STREEM

Seven flames - Ass and stick - Katalina
U-matic / VHS / BETA
European folktale series
Color; PAL (P I)
PdS180, PdS188 purchase
Features folktales from Yugoslavia, the United Kingdom and Rumania. Folktale series presents a series of 6 programs of 18 titles from 12 countries around the world.
Fine Arts; Literature and Drama
Dist - EDPAT **Prod** - HALAS

The Seven Forty - Seven 28 MIN
16mm
Color
LC 77-702291
Tells the story of the Boeing 747 airplane as seen through the eyes of the people whose lives it affects as it circumnavigates the globe.
Industrial and Technical Education; Social Science
Dist - WELBIT **Prod** - BOEING 1977

Seven from San Francisco - new filmmakers, new films 56 MIN
16mm
Color & B&W (G)
$160.00 rental
Introduces a sampling of emerging film artists. Presents a diverse spectrum of styles and themes. Titles and production dates are - Mother - 1983 - silent - by Todd Herman; A Different Kind of Green - 1989 - by Thad Povey; Short of Breath - 1990 - by Jay Rosenblatt; Brain in the Desert - 1990 - by Jennifer Seaman and Jay Rosenblatt; Futility - 1989 - by Greta Snider; Winterwheat - 1989 - by Mark Street; The Passion of Goose Egg Tuffy - 1989 by Ted White. Films also available separately.
Fine Arts
Dist - CANCIN

Seven hundred and thirty days 50 MIN
16mm
Color
Presents a Philippines village diary of four young overseas volunteers from Japan's Peace Corps. Explains some of their projects.
Geography - World; Sociology
Dist - UNIJAP **Prod** - UNIJAP 1970

Seven hundred eighty - four days that changed America series

The Break - in	25 MIN
The Coverup	25 MIN
The Crime	28 MIN
The Impeachment	42 MIN

Dist - FI

Seven little ducks 11 MIN
U-matic / VHS / 16mm
Color; B&W (P)
Portrays the life habits of domesticated Muscovy ducks and shows that a child can care for pets by feeding, watering and sheltering them.
Science - Natural
Dist - PHENIX **Prod** - BAILEY 1967

The Seven Little Foys 95 MIN
U-matic / VHS / 16mm
Color
Based on the true story of Eddie Foy, the famous vaudeville song and dance man, on the road with his seven children. Stars Bob Hope and James Cagney.
Fine Arts
Dist - FI **Prod** - PAR 1955

Seven lucky charms 16 MIN
VHS / 16mm
Color (G)
$55.00 rental, $275.00 purchase
Weaves animated imagery with statistical information to help understand the reality of battered women, especially those who kill their batterers in self - defense. Examines violence and retaliation; inadequate police response; gender inequities in the legal system; and prison sentencing. Produced by Lisa Mann.
Fine Arts; Sociology
Dist - WMEN

Seven magnificent motivational speakers
VHS
Color (G)
$29.95 purchase _ #CF007
Showcases the motivational speaking skills of Daniel Burrus, Don Jolly, Mark Victor Hansen, Les Brown, Rita Davenport, Terry Cole - Whittaker and Jack Canfield.
English Language; Psychology; Social Science
Dist - SIV

The Seven minute lesson 7 MIN
U-matic / VHS / 16mm
Color (J)
Demonstrates the proper techniques most commonly involved in acting as a sighted guide for a blind person.
Guidance and Counseling
Dist - AFB **Prod** - AFB
PHENIX

The Seven minute life of James Houseworthy 28 MIN
16mm / U-matic / VHS
Insight series
B&W (H C A)
Presents the life of a man who has lived only for money and power. Shows how he realizes the emptiness of his life.
Guidance and Counseling; Psychology
Dist - PAULST **Prod** - PAULST 1970

The Seven most common nutrition myths 16 MIN
VHS
Color (G)
$49.95 purchase _ #NHV300V
Uncovers the top nutritional myths and exposes the reality learned through research. Includes discussion of organic and natural food; 'evil' foods vs 'good' foods; vitamins; Recommended Daily Allowance - RDA; milk - and who should drink it; fat content of meat; and nutritional counselors.
Health and Safety; Home Economics; Social Science
Dist - CAMV

Seven nights and seven days 58 MIN
VHS
Color (H C G)
$445.00 purchase, $75.00 rental
Documents a healing ceremony in Senegal. Shows how a community gathers together to heal one of its members who is suffering from postpartum depression. Views the ceremony organized by the Lebou people to honor their ancestral spirits and ask them for a cure. Notes precise set of rules performed over seven days and nights. Produced by Maurice Dores.
Geography - World; Health and Safety; Religion and Philosophy; Sociology
Dist - FLMLIB **Prod** - REALIS 1992

Seven North 56 MIN
VHS / 16mm
Color (PRO G)
$240.00 purchase, $150.00 - $75.00 rental
Looks at the duties and responsibilities of primary nurses at Boston's Beth Israel Hospital.
Health and Safety
Dist - FANPRO **Prod** - FANPRO 1989

The Seven - per - cent solution 113 MIN
16mm
Color (J H G)
Tells how Sherlock Holmes reappears in 1894 (after his presumed death in 1891) with a terrible narcotics addiction. Shows how Sigmund Freud tries to help him. Stars Nicol Williamson, Alan Arkin, Robert Duvall, Vanessa Redgrave and Laurence Olivier.
Fine Arts
Dist - TWYMAN **Prod** - UPCI 1976

The Seven phases of a job interview 38 MIN
VHS / 16mm
Color (G)
Presents job search and interviewing techniques through use of television and film formats. Stresses the importance of being on time to interviews and provides guidance for interview. Outlines follow - up techniques, issues for negotiations and provides decision making strategies.
Guidance and Counseling; Psychology
Dist - JISTW **Prod** - MERIDN 1988
MERIDN JISTW
CAREER CAREER
CAMV CAMV

Seven portraits 22 MIN
16mm
Color (G)
$40.00 rental
Explores the relationship between image and sound in a series of poetic impressions. Presents portraits of Willem de Kooning, Leonard Bernstein, Robert Rauschenberg, Tennessee Williams, Andy Warhol, John Cage and Liv Ullman. An Edvard Lieber production.
Fine Arts
Dist - CANCIN

The Seven ravens 21 MIN
U-matic / VHS / 16mm
Color (K P)
LC 75-710025
Recounts the story of a peasant family with seven sons and one daughter. Relates how a wicked old woman casts a spell on the seven brothers, turning them into ravens, and how the sister frees her brothers.
Literature and Drama
Dist - LCOA **Prod** - ANIMAT 1971

The Seven samurai 140 MIN
U-matic / VHS
B&W (JAPANESE)
Presents Akira Kurosawa's adventure of the samurai. Features Toshiro Mifune and Takashi Shimura.
Fine Arts; Geography - World
Dist - IHF **Prod** - IHF
UILL
CHTSUI

The Seven seas 35 MIN
VHS
Visions of adventure series
Color (P)
$24.95 purchase _ #GE07
Studies the oceans of the world. Part of an eight - part series on geography.
Geography - World; Science - Natural
Dist - SVIP

Seven simple chicken dishes
BETA / VHS
Video cooking library series
Color
Instructs in the preparation of such recipes as stir fry chicken and shrimp, Sherry Chicken and Coq Au Vin.
Home Economics
Dist - KARTES **Prod** - KARTES

The Seven sins 15 MIN
16mm
Color (H C)
Combines the works of Flemish painter Peter Bruegel the Elder and author H Arthur Klein to examine the question of whether humans can alter their self - destructive instincts. Shows that we are primitive beings haunted by the demons of our own behavior.
Fine Arts; Religion and Philosophy; Sociology
Dist - MALIBU **Prod** - MALIBU

Seven stars 13 MIN
16mm
Color (JAPANESE)
Presents Tolstoy's fairy story about the great bear made with shadow - pictures. Tells the story of a kind - hearted girl who prayed sincerely to save her village from a long drought. Explains that since then, the villagers believe the beautiful twinkle of the great bear in the north sky is that of this tender little girl's heart.
Literature and Drama
Dist - UNIJAP **Prod** - UNIJAP 1967

Seven steps to good study habits - Part 1 12 MIN
VHS
Seven steps to good study habits series
CC; Color (I)
$79.95 purchase _ #10069VL
Covers the first four steps of a seven - part program designed to help young students improve study skills. Presents information on forming positive relationships with teachers; good attittude; keeping a 'study place'; and setting up a study schedule. Comes with a teacher's guide and a set of blackline masters. Part one of a two - part series.
Education; Psychology
Dist - UNL

Seven steps to good study habits - Part 2 20 MIN
VHS
Seven steps to good study habits series
CC; Color (I)
$89.95 purchase _ #10070VG
Covers the last three steps of a seven - part program designed to help young students improve their study skills. Contains information on taking notes; reading effectively; and listening actively. Uses blackline masters and quizzes in the video to reinforce the material. Comes with a teacher's guido and a set of blackline masters. Part two of a two - part series.
Education; English Language
Dist - UNL

Seven steps to good study habits series
Employs a step - by - step format to help students form good study habits. Presents information on attitude, listening actively, reading effectively, and taking notes. The narration is interspersed with chances for student participation and computer animation. Comes with a teacher's guide and two sets of blackline masters.
Seven steps to good study habits - Part 1 12 MIN
Seven steps to good study habits - Part 2 20 MIN
Dist - UNL

Seven Steps to TQC Promotion Series
Control is the way to endless progress 28 MIN
How to Use the Seven TQC Tools 27 MIN
Introduction and Implementation of TQC 27 MIN
Promotion of QC Circle Activities 30 MIN
Quality Assurance is the Essence of TQC 28 MIN
Reasons for Implementing TQC 27 MIN
What is Total Quality Control 27 MIN
Dist - TOYOVS

7362 9.5 MIN
16mm
Color (C)
$194.00
Experimental film by Pat O'Neill.
Fine Arts
Dist - AFA **Prod** - AFA 1967

Seven Thousand Three Hundred Sixty - Two 11 MIN
16mm
Color (H C A)
Presents an abstract film exercise.
Fine Arts; Industrial and Technical Education
Dist - CFS **Prod** - CFS 1968

Seven - up 'undo it' advertising program 9 MIN
16mm
Color
LC 78-700398
Follows the creation of a 7 - Up soft drink advertising campaign, from statement of objectives and development of concept to execution in various advertising media, including radio, television and outdoor advertising.
Business and Economics; Psychology
Dist - SEVUP **Prod** - SEVUP 1977

The Seven wishes of a rich kid 30 MIN
U-matic / 16mm / VHS
Color (P I J) (SPANISH FRENCH)
LC 79-700612
Tells the story of Calvin Brundage, a kid who has everything money can buy but who wishes for friends, a special girl and closeness with his father. Shows what happens when a video fairy godmother decides to grant his wishes.
Fine Arts; Guidance and Counseling; Sociology
Dist - LCOA **Prod** - LCOA 1979

The Seven wishes of Joanna Peabody 29 MIN
16mm / VHS / U-matic
Color (I P J) (SPANISH FRENCH)
LC 78-701003
Presents a modern - day Cinderella story. Tells of a young girl who is given seven wishes by a fairy godmother who lives in a television set.
Guidance and Counseling; Literature and Drama
Dist - LCOA **Prod** - LCOA 1978

Seven with one blow 10 MIN
16mm / U-matic / VHS
Grimm's fairy tales series
Color (K P I) (SPANISH)
LC 79-700382
Uses animation to tell the classic fairy tale recorded by the Brothers Grimm about a brave little tailor who kills seven flies with one blow.
Literature and Drama
Dist - CF **Prod** - BOSUST 1978

The Seven wives of Bahram Gur 19 MIN
16mm / U-matic / VHS

Arts of the Orient series
Color (H C A)
Traces the life of the legendary Persian hero, Bahram Gur, including his rise to become King, marriage to seven wives, and final marriage to Fitna. Adapted from the epic poem by Nizami and filmed from 15th and 16th century Persian miniatures.
Literature and Drama
Dist - IU **Prod** - IU 1961

Seven women - seven sins 101 MIN
VHS / 16mm
Color (G) (MULTILINGUAL WITH ENGLISH SUBTITLES)
$125.00, $250.00 rental, $295.00 purchase
Features seven of the world's best - known women directors producing their own version of celluloid sin. Addresses the question of what constitutes a deadly sin in this day and age, and how one may approach such a subject. Presents Gluttony, directed by Germany's Helke Sander; Greed, by New Yorker Bette Gordon; Anger, directed by New Yorker Maxi Cohen; Sloth, by Belgian Chantal Akerman; Lust by Austrian Valie Export; Envy by Laurence Gavron from France; and Pride by German director Ulrike Ottinger. Invites a global survey of women's cinema and the unique styles of each filmmaker. Films are in the native language of the filmmaker with English subtitles.
Fine Arts; Guidance and Counseling
Dist - WMEN

The Seven wonders of the ancient world 60 MIN
VHS
Color (G)
$29.95 purchase _ #QV2226V-S
Reveals the story behind each of the seven wonders of the ancient world, its location, the people responsible for its construction, and the original function of each. Explains that the seven wonders were originally identified by Philo of Byzantium approximately 2000 years ago and covers the significance of the number seven and what happened to the six which no longer remain.
Geography - World; History - World
Dist - CAMV
NORTNJ
SIV

Seventeen 90 MIN
U-matic / VHS
Middletown series
Color (J)
Looks at a group of teenagers who are finishing high school in Muncie, Indiana, and are finding themselves unshielded from the lessons of life and death. Contains strong language.
Geography - United States; Sociology
Dist - FI **Prod** - WQED 1982

The 1780s 27 MIN
U-matic / VHS / 16mm
Color (I J H)
$540.00, $250.00 purchase _ #4880C
Discusses the decade following the revolutionary war in America.
History - United States
Dist - CORF

Seventeen forever 29 MIN
16mm / U-matic / VHS
Color (H C A)
Looks at three people and how they have handled the inevitability of growing older. Shows how each member of this sad but not atypical family has bartered self - knowledge and emotional stability for the outward signs of glamour and sexuality. Stars Rue McClanahan and John Randolph.
Health and Safety; Psychology; Sociology
Dist - MEDIAG **Prod** - PAULST 1976

Seventeen going on nowhere 28 MIN
16mm / U-matic / VHS
Insight series
Color (J)
Describes a father's efforts to reach his son who is immersed in a life of rock music, girls and marijuana. Stars Ramon Bieri and Emilio Estevez.
Guidance and Counseling; Psychology; Sociology
Dist - PAULST **Prod** - PAULST

1700 - The roots of democracy 30 MIN
VHS
American history series
Color (I J H)
$64.95 purchase _ #V - 180530
Looks at the forces that helped shape the United States and its system of justice, including the Constitution and the Bill of Rights. Part of a nine - part series which reviews American history from Colonial times to World War II.
Civics and Political Systems; History - United States
Dist - KNOWUN

Seventeen minutes greenland 17 MIN
16mm
Color
Illustrates life and nature in Greenland.
Geography - World
Dist - AUDPLN **Prod** - RDCG

Seventeen reasons why 20 MIN
16mm
Nathaniel Dorsky series
Color; Silent (G A)
$40.00 rental
Presents the work of filmmaker Nathaniel Dorsky. Examines images of Dorsky's friends and acquaintances, street scenes, close - ups of grass and leaves and other subjects with a variety of 8mm cameras which are projected as unslit 16mm, creating a four - image split screen. Builds to an increasingly kaleidoscopic density of change with an explosion of color, light, pattern and composition.
Fine Arts; History - United States; Industrial and Technical Education
Dist - PARART **Prod** - CANCIN 1987

Seventeen seventy - six 148 MIN
16mm
Color
Features a musical version of the events surrounding the American Revolution.
Fine Arts; History - United States
Dist - TWYMAN **Prod** - CPC 1972

Seventeen seventy - six 54 MIN
16mm / U-matic / VHS
Saga of western man series
Color (I)
LC FIA67-1404
Relates what happened during the 1776 American Revolution and why it happened. Filmed in Lexington, Concord, Boston, Philadelphia, Williamsburg, France and England. Narrated by Frederic March.
History - United States
Dist - MGHT **Prod** - ABCTV 1964

Seventeen seventy - six - American revolution on the frontier 22 MIN
16mm / U-matic / VHS
American challenge series
Color (J H)
Recounts how the lives of two young settlers are disrupted by the Revolutionary War in 1776. Features scenes from the motion picture Drums Along The Mohawk starring Henry Fonda and Claudette Colbert.
History - United States
Dist - FI **Prod** - TWCF 1976

Seventeen seventy - six - Pt 1 27 MIN
U-matic / VHS / 16mm
Saga of western man series
Color (I)
LC FIA67-1404
Relates what happened during the 1776 American Revolution and why it happened. Filmed in Lexington, Concord, Boston, Philadelphia, Williamsburg, France and England. Narrated by Frederic March.
History - United States
Dist - MGHT **Prod** - ABCTV 1965

Seventeen seventy - six - Pt 2 27 MIN
U-matic / VHS / 16mm
Saga of western man series
Color (I)
LC FIA67-1404
Relates what happened during the 1776 American Revolution and why it happened. Filmed in Lexington, Concord, Boston, Philadelphia, Williamsburg, France and England. Narrated by Frederic March.
History - United States
Dist - MGHT **Prod** - ABCTV 1965

Seventeen Sixty - the New York Frontier 24 MIN
U-matic / VHS / 16mm
American Challenge Series
Color (J H)
Analyzes the causes and outcome of the French and Indian War, using excerpts from the motion picture Northwest Passage starring Robert Young and Spencer Tracy. Reveals why the British and Americans formed an uneasy alliance and how the colonists were becoming a threat to the British Empire.
History - United States
Dist - FI **Prod** - MGM 1975

Seventeen - year - old boys and girls talk about their sexuality 52 MIN
VHS / U-matic
Color
Presents differences in sources and knowledge of human sexuality obtained by 17 - year - old males and females from different geographical and cultural backgrounds at home, in school or on the streets. Includes impact of peer and parental pressures, conflicts and difficulties caused by different views and values from parents.
Health and Safety; Psychology; Sociology
Dist - HEMUL **Prod** - HEMUL

Seventeenth century 20 MIN
VHS
ARTV series
Color (J H)
$44.95 purchase _ #E323; LC 90-708447
Offers two music videos which feature the art works of Diego Velasquez in 'Ordinary World' and of Rembrandt van Rijn in 'Heartsight.' Includes Rubens and Caravaggio. Part of a ten - part ARTV series which uses TV format, including 'commercials' which sell one aspect of an artist's style and a gossip columnist who gives little known facts about the artists.
Fine Arts
Dist - GPN **Prod** - HETV 1989

Seventeenth century Dutch masters 15 MIN
VHS
Art history II - survey of the Western world series; Pt 7
Color (I J H)
$125.00 purchase
Discusses Dutch painters of the 17th Century, Rembrandt, Hals, Vermeer, de Hooch and Ruisdael. Presents characteristic works of the artists and connects their works to the literature, religion and history of their times.
Fine Arts; Geography - World; History - World
Dist - AITECH **Prod** - WDCNTV 1989

17th Century Dutch masters 15 MIN
VHS / 16mm
Art history II - survey of the Western World series
Color (I H A C)
$125.00 purchase, $25.00 rental
Presents selected works of Rembrandt, Hals, Vermeer, de Hooch and Ruisdael. Part of a series on art history.
Fine Arts; Foreign Language; Industrial and Technical Education
Dist - AITECH **Prod** - WDCNTV 1989

The Seventh cross
U-matic / VHS
Driving safety series
Color (IND) (SPANISH ARABIC)
Looks at probable cause for an accident that seriously injured the driver while making a trip down Torrey Mountain in California. Focuses on safety, particularly while driving in mountainous terrain.
Health and Safety; Industrial and Technical Education
Dist - GPCV **Prod** - DCC

The Seventh day 30 MIN
16mm
B&W
Explains the significance and manner of observance of the Jewish Friday evening service, using narrations, liturgical music and the enactment of various Sabbath rituals. Notes a sequel - The Fourth Commandment.
Religion and Philosophy
Dist - NAAJS **Prod** - JTS 1951

The Seventh fleet 12 MIN
16mm
B&W
LC FIE63-354
Documents the operations and actions of the Seventh Fleet from August 1949 to 1957.
Civics and Political Systems; History - United States
Dist - USNAC **Prod** - USN 1957

Seventh Heaven 119 MIN
16mm
B&W
Tells the story of Diane, a Parisian street waif who is rescued from a savage beating by Chico, a sewer worker, who takes her home to his seventh floor garret dwelling. Shows that Chico's initial pity slowly turns to love and then heartbreak. Stars Janet Gaynor and Charles Farrell. Directed by Frank Borzage.
Fine Arts
Dist - KILLIS

Seventh infantry division 22 MIN
U-matic / VHS / 16mm
B&W (H A)
Presents the training of the 7th Infantry Division at Ford Ord, California; its participation in four Pacific campaigns - Attu, Leyte, Kwajalein and Okinawa; and occupational duties in Korea.
Civics and Political Systems; History - United States
Dist - USNAC **Prod** - USA 1949

The Seventh Mandarin 13 MIN
U-matic
Color (P)
Explains how a Chinese ruler accidentally learns that his people are living in terrible poverty. Describes how he decides to meet his people and rule them well.
Literature and Drama
Dist - GA **Prod** - BOSUST

The Seventh master of the house 12 MIN
16mm
Color (P I)
LC 76-701335
The story of a traveller seeking food and lodging. Shows the necessity of assuming responsibility.
Guidance and Counseling; Literature and Drama
Dist - MLA **Prod** - MLA 1968

The Seventh seal 96 MIN
VHS
B&W (G)
$29.95 purchase _ #SEV090
Combines symbolic imagery, realistic details, and wry humor in a moving medieval tale of a knight searching for God in a world ravaged by plague. Uses a cast of Ingmar Bergman regulars as an honorable knight, his cynical squire, a troupe of carefree actors, and black - robed Death to portray the cruelty and charity that coexisted during medieval times.
Fine Arts; History - World; Religion and Philosophy
Dist - HOMVIS **Prod** - JANUS 1957

The Seventh voyage of Sinbad 89 MIN
U-matic / VHS / 16mm
Color (I J H C)
Stars Kerwin Mathews as Sinbad, the famous wanderer, sailing for the Isle of Colossa to obtain a fragment of the roc's eggshell which is needed by the magician for a brew to restore Princess Parisa who has been reduced to thumb - size by black magic.
Fine Arts; Literature and Drama
Dist - FI **Prod** - CPC 1958
TIMLIF

The 70s - have a nice decade 60 MIN
VHS
History of rock 'n' roll series
Color (A)
$19.99 purchase _ #0 - 7907 - 2432 - 4NK
Looks at rock 'n' roll of the 1970s - from the Allman Brothers' southern rock to the shock rock of Alice Cooper. Highlights Bob Marley, Fleetwood Mac, Pink Floyd, Elton John, Steely Dan. Part of a ten - part series unfolding the history of rock music. May contain mature subject matter and explicit song lyrics.
Fine Arts
Dist - TILIED

Seventies series
The Great powers 27 MIN
The International Economy 27 MIN
The Middle East 27 MIN
Politics of Violence 27 MIN
Southern Africa 27 MIN
Trends 27 MIN
Dist - JOU

Seventy - Five Years - the Chelsea Flower Show 41 MIN
VHS
Color (S)
$24.95 purchase _ #781 - 9045
Looks back over the last 75 years of the Chelsea Flower Show, which marks Britain's first society event of the season. Uses rare period photographs, film footage and music to reflect the changes in fashon, music and world events.
Agriculture; Science - Natural
Dist - FI **Prod** - BBCTV 1989

Seventy Per Cent 6 MIN
16mm
B&W
LC 76-702887
Shows an unusual occurrence that takes place during a card game late at night.
Literature and Drama
Dist - CMBLGS **Prod** - CMBLGS 1975

77 7 MIN
16mm
Color (C)
$325.00
Experimental film by Robert Breer.
Fine Arts
Dist - AFA **Prod** - AFA 1977

Seventy - Seven Jamboree 28 MIN
16mm
Color
LC 78-701446
Features host Burl Ives as he shows the many ways in which scouting provides opportunities for young people to develop character and expand their horizons.
Social Science; Sociology
Dist - BSA **Prod** - BSA 1978

Seventy - six at home 7 MIN
16mm
Color (G)
$20.00 rental
Compiles still and live action images, video fragments, post cards and photographs into a collage. Juxtaposes several 'histories,' including film, television and American history. Produced by Paul Glabicki.
Fine Arts; History - United States
Dist - CANCIN

72 hours to victory - behind the scenes with Bill Clinton 50 MIN
VHS
Color (J H C G)
$29.95 purchase _ #MH62900V
Captures the last 72 hours of the presidential election campaign by Bill Clinton in 1992. Features Ted Koppel who joins Governor Clinton in the last hours. Views Clinton campaign supporters talking openly about the Governor's plans for the future even before the vote is in. Discusses the 13 months of traveling on buses, going to town meetings and trying everything in their power to be accessible to the people.
Biography; Civics and Political Systems
Dist - CAMV

70 5 MIN
16mm
Color (C)
$224.00
Experimental film by Robert Breer.
Fine Arts
Dist - AFA **Prod** - AFA 1970

Severe emotional disturbance in children 26 MIN
U-matic
Color
Presents an overview of current theories about etiology, symptomatology and treatment related to severely disturbed children. Emphasizes recognition of pathology, individualized treatment and importance of family participation in plan of care.
Psychology
Dist - UWISN **Prod** - UWISN

Severe weather 15 MIN
VHS
Exploring weather series
CC; Color (I J)
$69.95 purchase _ #10034VG
Discusses severe weather conditions and storms that can threaten people and property. Covers thunderstorms, tornadoes and hurricanes. Comes with a teacher's guide and blackline masters. Part three of a three - part series.
Geography - World; Science - Physical
Dist - UNL

Severe Weather Test 30 MIN
U-matic / VHS
Color
Illustrates the hazards of severe weather and the precautions that can be taken to avoid injury. Examines tornadoes, thunderstorms, lightning and high winds.
Health and Safety; Science - Physical
Dist - WCCOTV **Prod** - WCCOTV 1982

The Severely traumatized patient 50 MIN
16mm
B&W (PRO)
Describes how to care for a patient in the emergency room after a severe accident. Discusses the importance of examining for the most major injuries, clearing air passages, and treating shock and chest injuries.
Health and Safety
Dist - LOMAM **Prod** - LOMAM

Sevilla 16 MIN
16mm / U-matic / VHS
Spanish language series
Color (J H C) (SPANISH)
LC 75-707301
Tours the city of Sevilla in Spain. Shows the harbor, La Torre de la Giralda, the Gardens of Alcazar and flamenco dancers.
Foreign Language; Geography - World
Dist - IFB **Prod** - IFB 1969

Sew easy, sew beautiful 90 MIN
VHS
Color (H C G)
$39.95 purchase _ #AH100V
Provides students with a step - by - step, start - to - finish overview of how to make a T - top, an elastic waist shirt and a simple skirt. Features close - up photography detailing each step in construction and decorative variations. Offers a series of tips and techniques to help the beginning sewer.
Home Economics
Dist - CAMV

Sew it reversible
VHS
Color (G A)
$24.95 purchase _ #NN850V
Teaches techniques for sewing reversibles.
Home Economics
Dist - CAMV

The Sew - it - Yourself Workshop 26 MIN
VHS / 16mm / U-matic
Color (J)
LC 77-701113
Demonstrates tools and techniques of sewing through the situation of a sewing shop employee who helps an inexperienced young woman complete a dress. Covers construction of the garment from start to finish.
Home Economics
Dist - PFP **Prod** - READER 1977

Sewage treatment plant
U-matic / VHS
Field trips in environmental geology series; Technical and mechanical concerns
Color
Examines sewage treatment, focusing on the use of water, the collection system, and processing technologies, as used at the Akron Ohio City Water Pollution Control Station. Discusses primary and secondary treatment, sample collection, chemical testing and environmental concerns.
Science - Natural; Science - Physical
Dist - KENTSU **Prod** - KENTSU

Sewers 20 MIN
16mm
Color
LC 78-700390
Describes the huge sewer systems that serve Washington, DC, and shows how they handle sanitary sewage, storm runoff and combined sewage.
Health and Safety; Industrial and Technical Education; Sociology
Dist - FINLYS **Prod** - DCENVS 1978

Sewing ABCs 80 MIN
VHS
Color (A H C J)
$49.00 purchase _ #CCP0124V-D
Stresses basic sewing principles as viewers learn how to select a pattern, how to use the information on the pattern envelope and inside guidesheet and how to use the pattern they select. Demonstrates basic sewing techniques, including sewing elastic waistbands, side pockets, hems, facings, interfacing, darts, seam finishes, zipper application, pleats and fasteners.
Home Economics
Dist - CAMV

Sewing active wear 60 MIN
VHS / BETA
Color
Shows the 'tricks of the trade' in sewing jogging suits, swimwear, leotards, shorts and golf and tennis shorts.
Home Economics
Dist - HOMEAF **Prod** - HOMEAF

Sewing basics
VHS
$36.50 purchase _ #RD88832
Shows students how to adjust the machine, thread bobbins, attach zippers, finish hems, and more.
Home Economics
Dist - CAREER **Prod** - CAREER

Sewing basics I 60 MIN
BETA / VHS
Color
Takes a fresh look at the basics of sewing, giving hints for both the beginner and the experienced sewer.
Home Economics
Dist - HOMEAF **Prod** - HOMEAF

Sewing basics II 60 MIN
BETA / VHS
Color
Specializes in pockets, fast fasteners, zippers, buttons and button holes, along with customary sewing techniques.
Home Economics
Dist - HOMEAF **Prod** - HOMEAF

Sewing basics - reader's digest 120 MIN
VHS
(H A)
$39.95 purchase _ #CK100V
Presents the basics of sewing. Shows dozens of fundamental sewing techniques, how to purchase equipment, equipment usage, how to understand patterns, and more.
Home Economics
Dist - CAMV **Prod** - READER

Sewing Crotch Seams 5 MIN
16mm
Clothing Construction Techniques Series
Color (J)

LC 77-701186
Illustrates three methods of stitching a crotch seam as one continuous seam through the front and back garment pieces. Includes both open and closed construction and construction when there is a center opening.
Home Economics
Dist - IOWASP Prod - IOWA 1976

Sewing - Discovering Patterns, Fabric and Basting 52 MIN
BETA / VHS
Color
Details the necessary information to begin creative sewing for a personal wardrobe. Discusses selection of patterns and fabric, as well as basting.
Home Economics
Dist - RMIBHF Prod - RMIBHF

Sewing Knits 87 MIN
VHS / BETA
Color
Uses five popular shirt projects to show many techniques used on knit projects.
Home Economics
Dist - HOMEAF Prod - HOMEAF

Sewing lingerie 115 MIN
BETA / VHS
Color
Starts with the sewing of delicate fabrics and goes through projects such as slips, teddies, nightgowns and more.
Home Economics
Dist - HOMEAF Prod - HOMEAF

The Sewing machine 10 MIN
16mm
Home economics - clothing series
Color (H C A)
LC 73-709989
Depicts the care and operation of a sewing machine and the threading of a bobbin, upper and lower threads.
Home Economics
Dist - SF Prod - MORLAT 1967

Sewing machine art
VHS
Color (G A)
$24.95 purchase _ #NN560V
Teaches the techniques of using a sewing machine to create art.
Fine Arts; Home Economics
Dist - CAMV

Sewing - Making a Simple Skirt 52 MIN
BETA / VHS
Color
Outlines the tailoring techniques for producing a skirt. Features Stella Warnick.
Home Economics
Dist - RMIBHF Prod - RMIBHF

Sewing materials - preparation 10 MIN
16mm
Home economics - clothing series
Color (H C A)
LC 78-709990
Discusses preparing material for sewing, basic weaves of fabric, grains of materials, straightening material making material grain perfect and pinning material.
Home Economics
Dist - SF Prod - MORLAT 1967

Sewing notions 60 MIN
VHS / BETA
Color
Shows multiple uses for classic notions plus tips on newer notions.
Home Economics
Dist - HOMEAF Prod - HOMEAF

Sewing on Buttons 3 MIN
16mm
Clothing Construction Techniques Series
Color (J)
LC 77-701202
Demonstrates how to locate buttons. Shows the attachment of both flat and shank buttons and a method for determining the amount of thread shank needed for a smooth closure.
Home Economics
Dist - IOWASP Prod - IOWA 1976

Sewing Series
Seams and Hems - Basting 10 MIN
Dist - SF

Sewing skills series
Basic sewing skills 12 MIN
Dist - PHENIX

Sewing Skills - Tailoring Series
Attaching collar and shaping 29 MIN
Attaching interfacing - Pt 1 29 MIN
Attaching interfacing - Pt 2 29 MIN
Attaching lining and completing garment 29 MIN
Attaching the collar 29 MIN
Attaching underlinings and stay stitching 29 MIN
Attaching Waistbands 29 MIN
Buttonhole preparation 29 MIN
Buttonholes 29 MIN
Continuing Buttonholes and Interfacing 29 MIN
Cutting and marking, lining and interfacing 29 MIN
Cutting and marking the suit 29 MIN
Darts and curved seams 29 MIN
Edge stitching the front of the coat 29 MIN
Fabric selection 29 MIN
Facing 29 MIN
Facing and Buttonhole Windows 29 MIN
Hem finishes 29 MIN
Interfacing 29 MIN
Interfacing the Undercollar 29 MIN
Layout Cutting 29 MIN
Lining and Finishing the Details 29 MIN
Lining the Coat 29 MIN
Making and Cutting the Lining 29 MIN
Making Bound Buttonholes 29 MIN
Matching Plaids in Darts and Seams by Slip Stitching 29 MIN
Matching Seams and Pleats in Plaid 29 MIN
Patch Pockets and Fitting 29 MIN
Pattern Alteration 29 MIN
Pattern Layouts for Plaids 29 MIN
Patterns and Fabrics 29 MIN
Preparing pattern for layout 29 MIN
Putting Sleeves on the Coat 29 MIN
Selecting a Pattern for a Coat 29 MIN
Underlining and Stay Stitching 29 MIN
Zipper Installation 29 MIN
Dist - PBS

Sewing - skirts and blouses 62 MIN
BETA / VHS
Color
Discusses techniques for sewing a fashionable wardrobe. Demonstrated by Robert Krause.
Home Economics
Dist - RMIBHF Prod - RMIBHF

Sewing specialty fabrics 60 MIN
VHS / BETA
Color
Presents a segment on specialty fabrics, including cutting, fusible interfacing and finishing steps.
Home Economics
Dist - HOMEAF Prod - HOMEAF

Sewing techniques 113 MIN
VHS / BETA
Color
Presents an encyclopedia of tips and techniques used in almost every sewing project. Includes hints on sewing machine feet and use, zippers, hems, pockets and more.
Home Economics
Dist - HOMEAF Prod - HOMEAF

Sewing Unlike Curved Seams 3 MIN
16mm
Clothing Construction Techniques Series
Color (J)
LC 77-701185
Illustrates the joining of unlike curves, including staystitching and clipping the inside curve, pinning and stitching the two layers together. Shows how to notch the seam allowance of the outer curve in order to reduce bulk.
Home Economics
Dist - IOWASP Prod - IOWA 1976

Sewing video series
Shows how much one can accomplish with basic sewing skills and a minimum of time.
Sewing video series
Dist - CAREER Prod - CAREER 1976

Sewing with leather (#1885) 44 MIN
VHS
Color; Mono (J C)
Expert leather seamstress Jennifer Hurn demonstrates selecting and cutting garment leather. Instruct in pattern preparation and special techniques unique to sewing on leather.
Fine Arts; Home Economics; Physical Education and Recreation
Dist - TANDY Prod - TANDY 1986

Sewing woman 14 MIN
VHS / U-matic / 16mm
B&W (G)
$250.00, $195.00 purchase, $40.00 rental _ #EPF - 771, #EVC - 771, #EHC - 771, #ERP - 771
Draws from oral histories to portray a Chicago - born woman and her journey from a traditional Chinese arranged marriage at the age of 13 to working in a sewing factory in San Francisco's Chinatown. Includes old photographs and film clips from China.
Sociology
Dist - ADL Prod - ADL 1982
CROCUR

Sex 30 MIN
VHS / U-matic
Power of choice series
Color (J H)
$64.95 purchase _ #HH-6343M; $89.00 purchase _ #60292-025; $75.95 purchase _ #LW108V; $64.95 purchase _ #CHOI-108
Shows young people how to make decisions about sex that they can live with. Part of a series featuring Michael Pritchard who uses humor to promote positive, life - affirming values and empowers young people to take charge of their lives.
Guidance and Counseling; Health and Safety; Psychology
Dist - CORF Prod - ELSW 1990
GA GA
JISTW LWIRE
PBS

Sex - a guide for the young 18 MIN
VHS
Color; PAL (I J H)
PdS29.50 purchase
Introduces the subject of one's first sexual experience. Uses colorful animation and humor along with a frank approach.
Health and Safety; Sociology
Dist - EMFVL

Sex - A Lifelong pleasure
Erection 53 MIN
The Female orgasm 55 MIN
Harmony 65 MIN
The Male orgasm 53 MIN
Dist - FCSINT

Sex - a topic for conversation for parents of teenagers 25 MIN
VHS
Sex - a topic for conversation series
Color (A T)
$99.00 purchase _ #MON102V
Discusses the facts about sex, relationships, and responsibility for parents of teenagers. Focuses on reasons for not having sex, how to initiate conversations about sexual responsibility, information on birth control and AIDS, and more. Includes a program guide.
Health and Safety; Psychology; Sociology
Dist - CAMV

Sex - a topic for conversation for teenagers 25 MIN
VHS
Sex - a topic for conversation series
Color (H C A)
$99.00 purchase _ #MON101V
Presents a comprehensive introduction to sex education, targeted to teenagers. Covers subjects including reasons not to have sex, sexual responsibility, birth control, AIDS, and more. Includes a program guide.
Health and Safety; Psychology
Dist - CAMV

Sex - a topic for conversation series 50 MIN
VHS
Sex - a topic for conversation series
Color (H A C)
$198.00 purchase _ #MON100SV
Presents a two - part series which discusses the facts about sex, relationships, and responsibility for teenagers and their parents. Focuses on reasons for not having sex, how to initiate conversations about sexual responsibility, information on birth control and AIDS, and more. Includes a program guide for each part.
Health and Safety; Psychology
Dist - CAMV

Sex - a Topic of conversation for parents of teenagers aged 12 to 16 25 MIN
VHS
Sex - A Topic of conversation series
Color (J H T A PRO)
$99.00 purchase _ #AH45266
Features sex and family educator Dr Sol Gordon in a discussion of sex education for teenagers. Stresses the importance of teaching sex education in a language that young people will understand.
Guidance and Counseling; Health and Safety; Science - Natural
Dist - HTHED Prod - HTHED

Sex - a topic of conversation for parents of young children aged 5 to 11 25 MIN
VHS
Sex - a topic of conversation series
Color (T A PRO)

$99.00 purchase _ #AH45267
Features sex and family educator Dr Sol Gordon in a discussion of sex education for young children aged 5 to 11. Stresses the importance of teaching sex education in a language that young people will understand.
Guidance and Counseling; Health and Safety; Science - Natural
Dist - HTHED **Prod** - HTHED

Sex - a topic of conversation for teenagers 25 MIN
VHS
Sex - a topic of conversation series
Color (J H C G T A PRO)
$99.00 purchase _ #AH45265
Features sex and family educator Dr. Sol Gordon in a discussion of sex education for teenagers. Stresses the importance of teaching sex education in a language that young people will understand.
Guidance and Counseling; Health and Safety; Science - Natural
Dist - HTHED **Prod** - HTHED

Sex - a topic of conversation series 75 MIN
VHS
Sex - A Topic of conversation series
Color (G)
$250.00 purchase _ #AH45600
Features sex and family educator Dr Sol Gordon in a three - part series on sex education for children and teenagers. Targets a different group in each episode. Stresses the importance of teaching sex education in a language that young people will understand.
Guidance and Counseling; Health and Safety; Science - Natural
Dist - HTHED **Prod** - HTHED

Sex - a topic of conversation series
Sex - a Topic of conversation for parents of teenagers aged 12 to 16 25 MIN
Sex - a topic of conversation for parents of young children aged 5 to 11 25 MIN
Sex - a topic of conversation for teenagers 25 MIN
Sex - a topic of conversation series 75 MIN
Dist - HTHED

Sex after 50 90 MIN
VHS
Color (G)
$29.95 purchase
Confronts myths and stereotypes about older people while encouraging honest discussion of sexual feelings. Addresses lack of desire, effects of illness and medications on sexuality, menopause, erection difficulties, hormone replacement therapy, loss of a partner, and the inability to communicate about sexuality. Uses animation and easy - to - understand diagrams to explain techniques, with no scenes of nudity or explicit sex acts. Features Dr Lonnie Barbach as narrator and host, with guest appearances by Betty Dodson, Drs Helen Kaplan, Robert Kessler, Virginia Johnson Masters, William Masters, Mary Polan and Bernie Zilbergeld.
Health and Safety
Dist - FCSINT

Sex, Anatomy and Physiology
VHS / U-matic
Independent Study in Human Sexuality Series
Color (PRO)
Health and Safety; Psychology
Dist - MMRC **Prod** - MMRC

Sex and aging
VHS / U-matic
Continuing medical education - basic sexology series
Color (PRO)
Health and Safety; Psychology
Dist - MMRC **Prod** - TIASHS

Sex and decisions - remember tomorrow 29 MIN
VHS
Color (J H)
$495.00, $370.00 purchase, $60.00 rental
Portrays two teens who manage to have a day alone at a beach house and they must decide whether to - or not - have sex. Follows them through the day as they face temptation, resist and feel good about their decision and about each other. Asks viewers to consider how they might decide in a similar situation. Encourages group discussion.
Guidance and Counseling; Health and Safety; Psychology; Sociology
Dist - CF PEREN **Prod** - WFP BROWN 1985

Sex and Disability
U-matic / VHS
Continuing Medical Education - Basic Sexology Series
Color (PRO)
Health and Safety; Psychology
Dist - MMRC **Prod** - TIASHS

Sex and Disability Series Pt 1
Those People Don't Want it 13 MIN
Dist - AJN

Sex and Disability Series Pt 2
Those People Can't do it 21 MIN
Dist - AJN

Sex and Disability Series Pt 3
Those People Don't Enjoy it 23 MIN
Dist - AJN

Sex and Disability Series Pt 4
Those People Can't have Kids 22 MIN
Dist - AJN

Sex and drugs 27 MIN
VHS
Color (C A)
$99.00 purchase, $50.00 rental
Discusses the effect of chemical use on sexual functioning and other behaviors.
Guidance and Counseling; Health and Safety; Psychology
Dist - FCSINT **Prod** - FCSINT 1990

Sex and drugs - the intimate connection 30 MIN
VHS
Color (H C G)
$385.00 purchase
Reveals that compulsive sex as a substitute for drugs is an issue for over half the men and women in drug and alcohol recovery. Features Dr Arnold Washton and Nannette Stone - Washton, along with three recovering sex and drug addicts, who discuss sex and drugs and related topics.
Guidance and Counseling; Health and Safety; Psychology
Dist - FMSP

Sex and gender 20 MIN
VHS / U-matic
B&W (C A)
Explores the concept of sexuality through candid interviews with transvestites and sequences of professional female impersonators at work.
Health and Safety; Psychology; Sociology
Dist - MMRC **Prod** - MMRC

Sex and gender 30 MIN
VHS
Color (H C)
$89.95 purchase _ #TSI - 116
Examines the lives of three women in terms of gender over several generations. Shows how members of society treat each other differently - unequally - based on gender and sexual differentiation and how that treatment has numerous personal and social results.
Sociology
Dist - INSTRU

Sex and gender - maturing and aging 60 MIN
U-matic / VHS
Discovering psychology series; Pts 17 and 18
Color (C)
$45.00, $29.95 purchase
Examines the differences between women and men and how sex roles reflect social values. Focuses on physical and psychological aging. Shows how society reacts to the last stages of life. Two thirty - minute programs hosted by Professor Philip Zimbardo of Stanford University.
Sociology
Dist - ANNCPB **Prod** - WGBHTV 1989

Sex and justice 76 MIN
VHS
Color (J H C G)
$29.95 purchase _ #FRF01V - S
Presents the dramatic confrontation between Anita Hill and Clarence Thomas at his Supreme Court confirmation hearings. Reveals that at one time charges of sexual harassment could not be made because it was not against the law. Shows how these hearings were a defining moment in history and made monumental changes in the lives of women. Features Gloria Steinem.
Civics and Political Systems; History - United States; Sociology
Dist - CAMV

Sex and money - Dr John Money on sexual identity 50 MIN
VHS
Color (H C G)
$445.00 purchase, $75.00 rental
Focuses on transsexual clients in the United States and in the Netherlands. Features Dr John Money who shares his ideas on gender identity. Examines anatomical and biological factors which steer individuals toward the masculine or feminine as opposed to historical, cultural and sociological influences on stages of human gender - identity development. Introduces Money's student, Prof Louis Gooren, researcher and lecturer at the Free University of Amsterdam and some of his clients who speak candidly about their earliest feelings of gender discomfort. Contains explicit material. Produced by the Humanist League, Amsterdam.
Psychology; Sociology
Dist - FLMLIB

Sex and pregnancy - the power of choice and consequences 25 MIN
VHS
At - risk students video series
Color (I J H)
$98.00 purchase _ #AHV408
Looks at sex within the context of a relationship. Shows how sex changes a relationship and how having a baby changes one's life. Features students and teachers from The Tree of Learning School in Portland, Oregon. Includes a reproducible discussion guide with worksheets. Part of a five - part series on students at risk.
Guidance and Counseling; Health and Safety; Psychology; Sociology
Dist - CADESF **Prod** - CADESF 1990

Sex and religion
U-matic / VHS
Independent study in human sexuality series
Color (PRO)
Health and Safety; Psychology; Religion and Philosophy
Dist - MMRC **Prod** - MMRC

Sex and society 30 MIN
VHS
Sex education series; Pgm 2
Color (I J H)
$189.00 purchase _ #CG - 830 - VS
Presents two parts which illustrate how media, peer pressure, parental and other influences can affect sexual values and behavior. Follows three girls and three boys as they get ready for a party and focuses on Elliott and Karen who are being set up for a blind date and feel tremendous pressures to conform. Part two finds Elliott and Karen tricked into playing a game they don't like, but they find a way to form a relationship based on their own interests and values. Explores issues that arise in dating and friendship and outline criteria for a good relationship. Part two of a five - part series on sex education.
Guidance and Counseling; Health and Safety; Psychology
Dist - HRMC **Prod** - HRMC

Sex and Society
U-matic / VHS
Independent Study in Human Sexuality Series
Color (PRO)
Health and Safety; Psychology; Sociology
Dist - MMRC **Prod** - MMRC

Sex and society - the pressures 29 MIN
VHS
Color (I J)
$189.00 purchase _ #660 - SK
Shows how teenagers' behavior is often manipulated by others. Presents dramatic vignettes illustrating the point that self - respect depends on developing standards and values and being true to self. Examines issues related to dating, friendships, and other relationships. Includes teacher's guide.
Guidance and Counseling; Psychology
Dist - SUNCOM **Prod** - HRMC

Sex and the American teenager 33 MIN
VHS
Color (J H A)
$195.00 purchase
Encourages discussion between teenagers and their parents of issues of sexuality, including values about sexual conduct, the consequences of sexual activity and making choices. Includes a guide for discussions.
Guidance and Counseling; Health and Safety; Sociology
Dist - PFP **Prod** - BELLDA

Sex and the brain 30 MIN
U-matic
Realities series
Color (A)
Delves into the political, social, economic and cultural trends regarding sexuality in the 1980s. Probes a wide range of contemporary concerns. Includes guest speakers who are experts in each field under discussion.
Social Science; Sociology
Dist - TVOTAR **Prod** - TVOTAR 1985

Sex and the family 28 MIN
16mm
Tangled world series
Color (H A)
Portrays the Bible's view of sex. Discusses sex as a gift and a responsibility of human living.
Health and Safety; Religion and Philosophy; Sociology
Dist - YALEDV **Prod** - YALEDV

Sex and the Handicapped 18 MIN
VHS / U-matic
Color (C A)
Develops a forceful argument for new attitudes toward the handicapped. Focuses primarily on helping the handicapped establish sexual contacts.
Health and Safety; Psychology
Dist - MMRC **Prod** - TSISR

Sex and the new you 15 MIN
VHS
Learning about sex series
Color (J R)
$12.95 purchase _ #87EE1025
Covers the subjects of sexual maturation, sexual intercourse, conception and birth. Outlines sexual behavior considered inappropriate for Christians, including pornography, experimentation, premarital sex and homosexuality. Discusses AIDS and venereal diseases.
Guidance and Counseling; Health and Safety; Sociology
Dist - CPH **Prod** - CPH

Sex and the Sandinistas 25 MIN
VHS
Color (A) (SPANISH WITH ENGLISH SUBTITLES)
$225.00 purchase, $60.00 rental
Interviews Nicaraguan lesbians and gays. Explores drag balls, cruising cathedral ruins, lesbian poetry, butch - femme roles and love in uniform. Discusses homosexuality in idigenous mythology and an innovative AIDS education campaign. Features ex - president Daniel Ortega who analyzes the debate on sexuality within the FSLN and the fight for gay and lesbian rights within socialism. Produced by Lucinda Broadbent.
Geography - World; Health and Safety; History - World; Sociology
Dist - WMEN

Sex and the scientist 86 MIN
VHS / 16mm
Color (C A)
$160.00 purchase, $40.00 rental _ #EC2420
Features Virginia Johnson Masters narrating the life of Alfred Kinsey from his childhood and early college years through his work as director of the Institute for Sex Research. Includes candid interviews with Clyde Martin, Wardell Pomeroy and Paul Gebhard and commentary by Indiana University Chancellor Herman B. Wells on academic freedom.
Biography; Psychology
Dist - IU **Prod** - IU 1989

Sex and the single parent 98 MIN
U-matic / VHS
Color (H C A)
Offers a comedy - drama showing how parents re - establish themselves as unattached, available adults and still fulfill their responsibilities as parents. Stars Susan Saint James and Mike Farrell.
Fine Arts
Dist - TIMLIF **Prod** - TIMLIF 1982

Sex and the young child 108 MIN
VHS
Color (G A R)
$98.50 purchase, $10.00 rental _ #35 - 87180 - 460
Stresses the role of parents in shaping their children's sexuality. Includes three different segments, 'Responsible Sex,' 'Becoming Sexed,' and 'Creating Sexuality.' Hosted by Jo Schlehofer.
Psychology; Sociology
Dist - APH **Prod** - FRACOC

Sex at seventy 29 MIN
VHS
Center for marital and sexual studies film series
Color (PRO)
$125.00 purchase, $75.00 rental
Shows a couple, approaching the age of 70, making love despite a diabetes - induced inability to attain erection. Documents sexuality in older people. Graphic. Produced by Hartman and Marilyn Fithian for professional use in treating sexual dysfunction and - or training professional personnel.
Health and Safety
Dist - FCSINT

Sex, Booze and Blues and those Pills You Use 12 MIN
16mm
Color (C A)
LC 82-700512
Explains in a humorous manner how abuse of alcohol and other drugs can lead to sexual dysfunction.
Health and Safety; Psychology
Dist - FMSP **Prod** - SCHUM 1982

Sex, choices, and you 18 MIN
16mm / VHS
Color (J S)
$395.00, $355.00 purchase, $60.00 rental
Provides information designed to help young people make important choices regarding abstinence or sexual activity because of the problems of sexually transmitted diseases and unplanned pregnancies. Discusses emotional aspects of sexual relationships, the importance of being responsible to oneself and one's partner, and the use of condoms.
Guidance and Counseling; Health and Safety
Dist - HIGGIN **Prod** - HIGGIN 1988

Sex differences in children's play 27 MIN
16mm
B&W (C A)
LC 74-702969
Examines the sex differences shown in the playground play of preschool and primary school children. Shows size of play groups, rank, style of play and precourtship behavior during group sessions on the playground.
Psychology; Sociology
Dist - PSUPCR **Prod** - UCHI 1974

Sex differentiation 17 MIN
U-matic / VHS
Color (PRO)
Reviews normal sex differentiation. Synthesizes information from physiology, anatomy, genetics, and biochemistry.
Science - Natural
Dist - HSCIC **Prod** - HSCIC 1977

Sex, drugs and HIV 17 MIN
VHS
Color (J H C)
$295.00 purchase
Updates the video Sex, Drugs and AIDS. Features Rae Dawn Chong who explains HIV and AIDS, how the virus can and cannot be transmitted. Provides peer support for negotiating strategies for safer sex and abstinence and provides understanding for people who are HIV positive or who have AIDS.
Health and Safety; Psychology; Social Science; Sociology
Dist - SELMED **Prod** - ODNP

Sex ed series
The ABCs of STDs 20 MIN
Condoms - more than birth control 11 MIN
No baby now - family planning choices 24 MIN
The Pill - a young woman's guide 11 MIN
Dist - POLYMR

Sex education 18 MIN
16mm / U-matic / VHS
Woman talk series
Color (H C A)
Presents an examination of the parents' role in educating their children about sex, stating that it should begin with the pre - school child. Shows how questions can arise from typical situations, and how the parents must deal with these questions in an honest, straightforward manner.
Health and Safety; Sociology
Dist - CORF **Prod** - CORF 1983

Sex education and AIDS 30 MIN
VHS
Color (G)
$100.00 purchase _ #SEXE - 000
Deals with the question of how school - based sex education courses should address AIDS. Features a debate between sex educator Deborah Haffner and conservative activist Phyllis Schlafly. Presents excerpts from several sex education films that have been made for teenage audiences.
Health and Safety; Psychology; Sociology
Dist - PBS HTHED **Prod** - KQEDTV HTHED 1987

Sex Education for Mentally Handicapped Persons 16 MIN
U-matic / VHS
Color
Discusses and demonstrates sex education for mentally retarded persons. Uses charts and dolls.
Health and Safety; Psychology
Dist - UWISC **Prod** - LASSWC 1979

Sex education for the mentally retarded 28 MIN
U-matic / VHS
Color (G)
$249.00, $149.00 purchase _ #AD - 1733
Looks at educating mentally handicapped people about their bodies and about sex and relationships. Features specialists in the area of sex education and mental retardation, as well as actor Larry Drake, who plays Benny in the television series 'LA Law,' and Heidi Hennessey, who plays his love interest in the show and is herself mentally handicapped.
Education; Health and Safety; Psychology
Dist - FOTH **Prod** - FOTH

Sex Education Programs
VHS / U-matic
Independent Study in Human Sexuality Series
Color (PRO)
Health and Safety; Psychology
Dist - MMRC **Prod** - MMRC

Sex education series
Presents a comprehensive five - part series on sex education. Discusses puberty, sex and society, appropriate sexual behavior in partners, responsible parenthood and sexually transmitted diseases.
Parenthood - Program 4 29 MIN
Partners - Program 3 25 MIN
The Puberty years - Program 1 33 MIN
Sex and society 30 MIN
Sex education series 153 MIN
STDs - Program 5 36 MIN
Dist - HRMC **Prod** - HRMC

Sex education - too little, too late 26 MIN
U-matic / VHS
Color (T)
$249.00, $149.00 purchase _ #AD - 1925
Reveals that sex education continues to be an emotional and controversial topic even though half of all American boys and one - third of all American girls have had sex before the age of 17. Features teachers, policy makers and teenagers in an assessment of sex education in schools.
Guidance and Counseling; Health and Safety; Psychology; Sociology
Dist - FOTH **Prod** - FOTH

Sex Fears 15 MIN
16mm / VHS
Sex, Feelings and Values Series
Color (H C A)
LC 78-701826
Focuses on young people as they share their fears about sex.
Psychology
Dist - LRF **Prod** - DF 1977

Sex, Feelings and Values Series
Early homosexual fears 11 MIN
Parents' Voices 12 MIN
Sex Fears 15 MIN
Sex Games 8 MIN
Sex Mis - Education 11 MIN
Sex Morals 13 MIN
Dist - LRF

Sex for Sale - the Urban Battleground 45 MIN
16mm / U-matic / VHS
Color (C A)
LC 77-701415
Visits a number of major American cities where pornography has become big business for some and a major headache for others. Explores the myth of the victimless crime and shows the decay of various neighborhoods in which sex businesses exist.
Sociology
Dist - MGHT **Prod** - ABCTV 1977

The Sex game 20 MIN
U-matic / VHS / 16mm
Reflections series
Color (J)
LC 79-700812
Presents a dramatization about junior high students which argues that emotional intimacy is ultimately more satisfying than physical intimacy.
Guidance and Counseling; Health and Safety; Psychology; Sociology
Dist - PAULST **Prod** - PAULST 1977

Sex Games 8 MIN
VHS / 16mm
Sex, Feelings and Values Series
Color (H C A)
LC 78-701827
Focuses on a young couple playing a sex game, in which each partner tries to reject the other first.
Psychology; Sociology
Dist - LRF **Prod** - DF 1977

Sex games and toys 90 MIN
VHS / U-matic
Better sex series
Color (PRO C A)
$195.00 purchase _ #C910 - VI - 015
Reveals that adding sex toys and games to an established and loving relationship can be stimulating and fun. Presents and demonstrates the use of sex toys and shows how the use of a creative imagination can add a refreshing newness to lovemaking. Part of a three - part series presented by Drs Judith H Seifer and Roger Libby, the Better Sex Institute.
Guidance and Counseling; Health and Safety; Psychology
Dist - HSCIC

Sex, Geriatrics, Illness and Disability
U-matic / VHS
Independent Study in Human Sexuality Series
Color (PRO)
Health and Safety; Psychology
Dist - MMRC **Prod** - MMRC

Sex histories - interviewing and coding
VHS / U-matic
Independent study in human sexuality series
Color (PRO)
Health and Safety; Psychology
Dist - MMRC **Prod** - MMRC

The Sex history 60 MIN
VHS / U-matic
Color
Offers a discussion and demonstration by Wardell Pomeroy, PhD, co - author of the Kinsey Report, on the art and science of taking a sex history which he has developed in taking 35,000 sex histories. Tells how he gathers the data he is after.
Psychology; Sociology
Dist - HEMUL **Prod** - HEMUL

Sex Hormones and Sexual Destiny 26 MIN
VHS / 16mm
Color (G)
$149.00, $249.00, purchase _ #AD - 1718
Visits a Rutgers University laboratory where research has demonstrated that hormone levels have a distinct and measurable effect on 'masculine' and 'feminine' behavior. Shows how the structure of male and female brains differ. Discusses the effect of right - brain and left - brain communication and the influence of environment on behavior. Features Dr June Reinisch, Director of the Kinsey Institute for Research in Sex, Gender and Reproduction.
Psychology; Sociology
Dist - FOTH **Prod** - FOTH 1990

Sex hormones - oxytocics 30 MIN
16mm
Pharmacology series
B&W (C)
LC 73-703351
Describes and classifies male and female sex hormones, emphasizing their pharmacological effects and clinical uses. Discusses oral contraceptives.
Health and Safety
Dist - TELSTR **Prod** - MVNE 1971

Sex in marriage 50 MIN
VHS
God's blueprint for the Christian family series
Color (R G)
$29.95 purchase _ #6142 - 5
Features Dr Tony Evans. Discusses sex in marriage from a conservative Christian viewpoint. Part of six parts on marriage, parenting and families.
Guidance and Counseling; Health and Safety; Religion and Philosophy; Sociology
Dist - MOODY **Prod** - MOODY

Sex in the '90s 30 MIN
VHS
Facing up to AIDS series
Color; PAL (G)
PdS65 purchase
Addresses the changing attitudes to sex in the AIDS era. Postulates that sex in the '90s will be about communication. Explores the history of sex and attitude in the past 20 years. Part two of a two - part series.
Health and Safety; Psychology; Sociology
Dist - BBCENE

The Sex IQ 25 MIN
16mm / VHS / BETA
Color
LC 73-702523
Features correspondent Michael Maclear reporting on sex education classes in Canada. Also discusses the program in London, Ontario.
Health and Safety
Dist - CTV **Prod** - CTV 1976

Sex is a beautiful thing 27 MIN
16mm
Color
LC 73-701035
A documentary filmed in the Berkeley - San Francisco area. Presents two engaged couples on the Berkeley campus giving an intimate, behind - the - scenes look at their lives as they confront the problems of sexual morality. Discusses morality, sexual freedom and permissiveness.
Guidance and Counseling; Sociology
Dist - FAMF **Prod** - FAMF 1970

Sex is no game 15 MIN
VHS
Price tag of sex series
Color (J H T)
$89.95 purchase _ #UL904V; $89.95 purchase _ #10380VG
Addresses teen sexuality and the consequences of sexual indulgence. Features a speaker who stresses the advantages of abstinence and promotes positive interaction and discussion. Focuses on alcohol and sex; abortion and adoption; date rape; and male and female double standards regarding the student's reputation. Part of a four-part series.
Health and Safety; Psychology; Sociology
Dist - CAMV
UNL

Sex, love and babies - how babies change your marriage 30 MIN
VHS
Color (G)
$69.95 purchase _ #INP200V
Features six couples who openly and honestly explore the common problems and changes that arise in a marriage after the birth of a child. Offers insights on how to lessen their impact. Helps couples to keep communications open and express their feelings, how to deal with the hormonal and physical changes new mothers experience, how to balance sexual desires, how and where to find support, how to nurture each other and the marriage as well as the child, and more.
Health and Safety; Sociology
Dist - CAMV

Sex, love or infatuation 45 MIN
VHS
Color (J H R)
$29.95 purchase, $10.00 rental _ #4 - 85054
Considers the question of how to tell the difference between sex, love and infatuation. Suggests ways to evaluate dating relationships. Hosted by Dr Ray Short.
Health and Safety; Religion and Philosophy; Sociology
Dist - APH **Prod** - APH

Sex Mis - Education 11 MIN
VHS / 16mm
Sex, Feelings and Values Series
Color (H C A)
LC 78-701828
Focuses on young people as they criticize sex education offered at school and at home.
Health and Safety; Psychology
Dist - LRF **Prod** - DF 1977

Sex Morals 13 MIN
VHS / 16mm
Sex, Feelings and Values Series
Color (H C A)
LC 78-701829
Focuses on young people as they express their attitudes about sex.
Psychology; Sociology
Dist - LRF **Prod** - DF 1977

Sex myths and facts 17 MIN
16mm / VHS
Color (J S) (SPANISH)
$380.00, $340.00 purchase, $60.00 rental
Identifies some of the most commonly held sexual myths and provides factual information regarding sex. Typical myths addressed are, 'You can't get pregnant the first time,' and 'A guy has to go all the way or it will hurt him.' Provides a straightforward approach aimed specifically at teenagers.
Health and Safety
Dist - HIGGIN **Prod** - HIGGIN 1988

Sex Offenders
U-matic / VHS
Independent Study in Human Sexuality Series
Color (PRO)
Civics and Political Systems; Health and Safety; Psychology
Dist - MMRC **Prod** - MMRC

Sex, power and the workplace 30 MIN
VHS
Color (G)
$495.00 purchase
Explores the critical issues of sexual harassment and offers insights into improving the work environment. Includes a resource guidebook for both preventing and handling harassment situations. Features Joanna Cassidy as narrator.
Sociology
Dist - LUMINA **Prod** - KCET 1993

Sex - resetting the thermostat 28 MIN
16mm
Color
Presents the concept of sex as tenderness and thoughtfulness as opposed to technique and action.
Psychology
Dist - ECUFLM **Prod** - UMCOM 1982

Sex role development 23 MIN
U-matic / VHS / 16mm
Developmental psychology today film series
Color (H C A)
LC 74-703310
Examines male and female sex roles, focusing on how stereotypes are formed. Discusses ways to avoid transmitting these traditional stereotypes to children.
Psychology; Sociology
Dist - CRMP **Prod** - CRMP 1974

Sex Role Stereotyping in Schools Series
Hey, what about Us 15 MIN
Dist - FAMF

Sex Role Stereotyping in Schools Series
Changing Images - Confronting Career Stereotypes 16 MIN
Hey what about Us 15 MIN
I is for Important 12 MIN
Dist - UCEMC

Sex roles 30 MIN
U-matic / VHS
Focus on society series
Color (C)
Explores those agencies which contribute to sex role expectations in society.
Sociology
Dist - DALCCD **Prod** - DALCCD

Sex Roles and Human Relations 56 MIN
U-matic
Color
Looks at changing sex roles and relationships between men and women.
Sociology
Dist - HRC **Prod** - OHC

Sex rules - becoming savvy in the AIDS era 22 MIN
VHS
Color (I J H G)
$195.00 purchase, $50.00 rental
Tells about the friendship of two girls, Jo and Nik, who don't see eye to eye about the AIDS reality. Reveals that Nik has a new romance which she doesn't want to spoil by insisting on condoms and Jo is committed to spreading the word about safe sex. Even though one of their classmates has been hospitalized with AIDS, Nik seems unconcerned about any risk to herself. As the story develops, Nik wises up and so does her boyfriend. Produced by Pip Karmel of Australia.
Guidance and Counseling; Health and Safety; Sociology
Dist - FLMLIB

Sex Therapy and the Medical Practice
U-matic / VHS
Continuing Medical Education - Basic Sexology Series
Color (PRO)
Health and Safety
Dist - MMRC **Prod** - TIASHS

Sex therapy for a quadriplegic couple 16 MIN
VHS
Center for marital and sexual studies film series
Color (PRO)
$99.00 purchase, $50.00 rental
Documents the exploration of sexuality by a couple in their fifties who are confined to wheelchairs. Shows how they achieved coitus even though the male is paralized from the neck down by mutliple sclerosis and the female has limited mobility because of syringmyelia. Graphic. Produced by Hartman and Marilyn Fithian for professional use in treating sexual dysfunction and - or training professional personnel.
Health and Safety
Dist - FCSINT

The Sexes
VHS / U-matic
Body human series
Color
Explores human sexuality, the intricate mechanisms of the human reproductive systems, from gene - programmed sexual instincts through the advanced years. Covers surgical removal of a fallopian tubal blockage, making motherhood possible for a 29 - year - old woman, corrective surgery and hormone treatments allowing normal female development for a young girl born with the genetic imprint of a male and the anatomy of a female.
Health and Safety; Science - Natural; Sociology
Dist - MEDCOM **Prod** - MEDCOM

The Sexes - breaking the barriers 18 MIN
16mm / U-matic / VHS
Color (H C A)
$350.00 purchase - 16 mm, $280.00 purchase - video, $50.00 rental
Features an interview with Dr William Masters and Dr Virginia Johnson, who discuss their research and the need for sex education, and the treatment of sexual dysfunctions.
Health and Safety; Psychology
Dist - CNEMAG **Prod** - DOCUA 1988

The Sexes II
VHS / U-matic
Body human series
Color
Covers the whole spectrum of human sexuality. follows a young couple from first attraction through courtship to marriage, while taking a psychological look at the emotional side of sexual dysfunction. Demonstrates how

sexuality begins in early embyronic life with brain wiring signaling every cell, imprinting basic sexual instincts that will utimately determine the sex for which the fetus was programmed by genes at the instant of conception. Focuses on physical and emotional maturing process in both sexes.
Health and Safety; Science - Natural; Sociology
Dist - MEDCOM **Prod** - MEDCOM

The Sexes - roles 28 MIN
16mm
Color
Surveys the evolution of male - female roles from pre - history to the industrial age of the 1980s. Presents psychologist Judith Bardwick pointing out the stresses caused by the clash between traditional expectations and new realities, Matina Horner discussing her studies on women's fear of success and sociologist Jean Lipman - Blumen relating how girls are socialized to destroy their own dreams at an early age.
Sociology
Dist - FLMLIB **Prod** - CANBC

The Sexes - What's the Difference 28 MIN
16mm
Color
Addresses the question of whether male and female traits are inborn or learned in childhood. Shows child development experts isolating biological from cultural factors such as the ability to perceive changes in the environment.
Psychology; Sociology
Dist - FLMLIB **Prod** - CANBC

Sexism in religion, another view 29 MIN
U-matic
Woman series 20024
Color
Discusses charges of sex bias in religious organizations.
Sociology
Dist - PBS **Prod** - WNEDTV

Sexism in the school 30 MIN
U-matic
Color
Presents Linda Shuto of the British Columbia Teacher's Federation Status of Women Task Force showing evidence of sexism in the school system.
Sociology
Dist - WMENIF **Prod** - WMENIF

Sexism, stereotyping and hidden values 29 MIN
U-matic / VHS / 16mm
Survival skills for the classroom teacher series
Color (T)
Explores the sources of hidden sexist values in the school setting and offers ways whereby teachers can promote a climate of equal opportunity in their classrooms.
Education; Sociology
Dist - FI **Prod** - MFFD 1978

The Sexological Examination 28 MIN
U-matic / VHS
Color (C A)
Provides physiological information and aids in finding and exploring physical sensations which feel good to each partner. Shows couples how to begin exploration and experimentation.
Health and Safety; Psychology; Sociology
Dist - MMRC **Prod** - MMRC

Sexplanation for parents and children 28 MIN
VHS
Color (G)
$26.95 purchase
Tells the story of a family who must explain sexual matters to their nine - year - old son Nick. Teaches parents how to answer similar questions from their children. Covers subjects including physical changes, menstruation, wet dreams, intercourse, peer pressure, and more.
Health and Safety; Sociology
Dist - PBS **Prod** - WNETTV

Sexploitation of children - pornography and other child abuse 24 MIN
U-matic / VHS
Color
$335.00 purchase
Sociology
Dist - ABCLR **Prod** - KGOTV 1981

Sexual abstinence - making the right choice 23 MIN
VHS
Color (I J H)
$169.00 purchase _ #B012 - V8
Presents a strong rationale for abstinence while confronting the tough issues of teens' emerging sexuality. Features peer educators led by sexuality educator Mary Lee Tatum who look at the expectations and responsibilities of a relationship, abstinence as the only 100 percent effective protection against pregnancy and STD prevention.
Guidance and Counseling; Health and Safety; Psychology; Social Science
Dist - ETRASS **Prod** - ETRASS

Sexual abstinence - making the right choice 30 MIN
VHS
Color (J)
LC 89700228
Features candid interviews and persuasive information from individuals and groups of teens around the country on sexuality and abstinence. Presents the Presents the facts and issues of teens'emerging sexuality.
Health and Safety; Psychology; Sociology
Dist - AIMS **Prod** - HRMC 1989

Sexual abstinence - the right choice 30 MIN
VHS
Color (J H)
$185.00 purchase _ #60138 - 126
Underscores that sexual abstinence is the only 100 percent effective protection against unwanted pregnancy and sexually transmitted diseases such as AIDS. Shows how to resist sexual advances and how to reject negative peer pressure.
Health and Safety; Psychology; Sociology
Dist - GA **Prod** - HRMC

Sexual abuse 17 MIN
VHS / U-matic
Child abuse series
Color (PRO)
Recognizes difficulties in diagnosing sexual abuse in children because of the stigma attached to it. Covers steps to assure a safe home environment and to rehabilitate the parents.
Health and Safety; Sociology
Dist - HSCIC **Prod** - HSCIC 1978

Sexual abuse and harassment - causes, prevention - coping 60 MIN
VHS
Color (J H)
$129.00, 209.00 purchase _ #06817 - 026, #06817 - 126
Alerts students to the wide range of inappropriate, unwanted sexual acts, advances and pressures. Features young people talking about how they have coped with these behaviors and counselors explain where to go for help. Offers special advice to those who are victims of sexual abuse at home. Includes teacher's guide and library kit.
Psychology; Sociology
Dist - GA **Prod** - GA

Sexual abuse and harassment - causes, prevention, coping
VHS
$209.00 purchase _ #IE6817
Discusses inappropriate, unwanted sexual acts, advances and pressure students may face in college or on the job. Provides information on preventing dangerous situations and offers special advice to students who may be the victims of sexual abuse at home.
Health and Safety; Psychology
Dist - CAREER **Prod** - CAREER

Sexual abuse of children 54 MIN
U-matic / VHS
Color
Inspects the phenomenon of adults who use children for sex, revealing it is a crime being committed in Minnesota more frequently than imagined.
Psychology; Sociology
Dist - WCCOTV **Prod** - WCCOTV 1982

Sexual abuse of children 30 MIN
U-matic / VHS
Child abuse and neglect series
Color (H C A)
Home Economics; Sociology
Dist - GPN **Prod** - UMINN 1983

Sexual abuse of children - America's secret shame 28 MIN
U-matic / VHS / 16mm
Color (A)
LC 81-700720
Reveals the extent of sexual abuse of children, offering interviews with past victims and convicted child molesters. Describes the ploys used by the molesters and tells why victims don't report the incidents. Narrated by Peter Graves.
Sociology
Dist - AIMS **Prod** - TGL 1980

Sexual Abuse of Children Series

The Sexually Abused Child - a Protocol for Criminal Justice 26 MIN
A Time for Caring - the School's Response to the Sexually Abused Child 28 MIN
Dist - LAWREN

Sexual abuse prevention
VHS
$149.00 purchase _ #HRSAP
Provides preparation to recognize and deal with the problem of sexual abuse. Teaches how to identify potential danger and to develop solid abuse prevention tactics.
Sociology
Dist - CAREER **Prod** - CAREER

Sexual abuse prevention 28 MIN
VHS
Color (P I J H)
$189.00 purchase _ #CG - 814 - VS
Offers two parts which prepare students to recognize and cope with a problem that one out of four will have to confront - sexual abuse. Dispels old myths about sexual abuse and alerts students to situations they may actually encounter. Part one develops an understanding of what sexual abuse and dispels the myth that it is likely to be committed by strangers. Part two discusses sexual abuse within the family.
Guidance and Counseling; Health and Safety; Sociology
Dist - HRMC **Prod** - HRMC

Sexual abuse prevention - five safety rules for persons who are mentally handicapped 30 MIN
VHS / 16mm
Color (I H A)
$180.00 purchase, $35.00 rental
Utilizes five vignettes designed to focus on the five safety rules that are needed for mentally handicapped persons to protect themselves from sexual assault and exploitation.
Health and Safety; Sociology
Dist - AITECH **Prod** - PPCIN 1987

Sexual abuse - the family 30 MIN
U-matic / VHS / 16mm
We can help series
Color (PRO)
LC 77-703248
Presents a discussion by a physician, a social worker and a psychologist on sexual abuse of children. Includes a role play in which professionals interview a sexually abused child and her family in an emergency room setting.
Home Economics, Sociology
Dist - USNAC **Prod** - NCCAN 1977

Sexual addiction
VHS / U-matic
Color (A PRO)
$89.95, $34.95 purchase _ #6924, #6923
Provides information about sexual addiction for mental health professionals.
Psychology; Sociology
Dist - HAZELB

Sexual addiction 28 MIN
VHS / 16mm
Color (G)
$149.00, $249.00, purchase _ #AD - 1258
Explains that there are men and women, heterosexuals and homosexuals, who are so compulsively driven by sexual appetite that their dependency is comparable to that of gamblers or alcoholics. Compares this addiction with normal sexual drive and discusses the problems of overcoming this fixation.
Health and Safety; Psychology
Dist - FOTH **Prod** - FOTH 1990

Sexual addiction 28 MIN
U-matic / VHS
Color (G)
$249.00, $149.00 purchase _ #AD - 1258
Describes how sexual addiction differs from normal sexual drive. Shows the problems of overcoming this fixation. From a Phil Donahue program.
Health and Safety; Psychology; Sociology
Dist - FOTH **Prod** - FOTH

Sexual anatomy and physiology - male and female
35mm strip / VHS / Slide
Color (C A)
$195.00, $165.00 purchase, $75.00 rental
Presents three parts on sexual anatomy and physiology. Examines the capacity for sexual response of the clitoris, clitoral hood, labia minora, labia majora, mons veneris, peritoneum, perineum, anus, urethra, cervix, breasts, the entire skin surface of women in Part 1. Part 2 reviews the sexual physiology and structure of the penis, scrotum, testes, vas deferens, prostate, and discusses primary erogenous zones in men. Part 3 demonstrates the Masters and Johnson four - stage model of sexual response and describes the refractory period. Produced by Drs Leon Zussman and Shirley Zussman.
Health and Safety; Science - Natural; Sociology
Dist - FCSINT **Prod** - FCSINT 1977

Sexual and Bladder Dysfunction in Spinal Cord Injury 118 MIN
VHS / U-matic
B&W
Describes bladder and sexual dysfunction in spinal cord injured patients and various treatment methods.
Health and Safety; Science - Natural
Dist - BUSARG **Prod** - BUSARG

Sexual and Bladder Dysfunction in Spinal Cord Injury, Pt 1 52 MIN
U-matic / VHS
B&W
Discusses the process of rehabilitation of disabled individuals. Includes diagrams on how the central nervous system affects the bladder.
Health and Safety; Science - Natural
Dist - BUSARG **Prod** - BUSARG

Sexual and Bladder Dysfunction in Spinal Cord Injury, Pt 2 48 MIN
U-matic / VHS
B&W
Describes bladder and sexual dysfunction in spinal cord injured patients and various treatment methods.
Health and Safety; Science - Natural
Dist - BUSARG **Prod** - BUSARG

Sexual assault 20 MIN
VHS / 16mm
Color (G)
$225.00 purchase, $50.00 rental
Explores a rarely addressed question - can rapists be cured while in prison. Interviews prison personnel, psychiatrists, rape crisis counselors and rapists. Considers rehabilitation techniques - biofeedback, aversion therapy and training in social skills. Concludes that some have value but the intensely male, sexually assaultive environment of prisons cancels out rehabilitation. Produced by Ali Kazimi and Premika Ratnam.
Health and Safety; Psychology; Sociology
Dist - WMEN **Prod** - KAZRA 1986

Sexual assault 19 MIN
VHS / 16mm
Color (G)
$149.00, $249.00, purchase _ #AD - 2034
Looks at rape follow up procedures of police, hospital, and counseling personnel. Focuses, also, on DNA printing and discusses not only its use in identifying assailants, but also the possibility of its misuse as a source of personal information.
Health and Safety; Psychology; Science - Natural; Sociology
Dist - FOTH **Prod** - FOTH 1990

Sexual assault crimes 30 MIN
U-matic / VHS
Color
Examines the high incidence of sexual assault crimes in the United States, and challenges long held assumptions about the nature of sexual attacks. Prepares students by offering them practical methods for preventing sexual assault.
Psychology; Sociology
Dist - HRMC **Prod** - HRMC 1985

Sexual assault - emergency room procedures 18 MIN
U-matic / VHS
Color
Presents a step - by - step guide to the correct evidence collection, examination and treatment of a sexual assault victim. Stresses importance of staff sensitivity.
Health and Safety; Sociology
Dist - GRANVW **Prod** - GRANVW

Sexual assault - listening to survivors 9 MIN
VHS
In crime's wake victim assistance training series
Color (C PRO G)
$50.00 purchase
Looks at victims' expectations of victim advocates and the positive impact intervention can have on recovery. Part of a five - part series of in - training videos for victim advocates - social workers, domestic intervention specialists, police officers and other victim services personnel. Includes a guide developed by the Police Executive Research Forum.
Guidance and Counseling; Sociology
Dist - SELMED

Sexual Behavior in Laboratory Monkeys (Macaca Mulatta) 30 MIN
16mm
Color (C T)
Illustrates an investigation intended to identify and quantify the characteristics of sexual behavior in laboratory monkeys. Illustrates how sexual behavior in monkeys is influenced by individual differences in personality. Shows monkeys in pre - estrous, estrous and post estrous phases and depicts their variability of sexual behavior. Pictures vatiations in grooming, masturbation and coitus. Showings restricted.
Psychology; Science - Natural
Dist - PSUPCR **Prod** - YALEU 1955

Sexual Behavior in the American Bison 9 MIN
16mm
Color (C A)
LC 76-703303
Illustrates basic patterns of sexual behavior in adult male and female American bison, largely interpreted in terms of the selective advantages they confer.
Science - Natural
Dist - PSUPCR **Prod** - LOTTD 1976

Sexual Behavior of Normal, Socially Isolated and LSD - 25 Injected Guinea Pigs 17 MIN
16mm
B&W (C T)
Shows the estrous behavior of female guinea pigs, and the various phases of sexual behavior of normal males and the reduced amount of sexual behavior of males, raised in social isolation, when in the presence of an estrous female. Illustrates how an injection of LSD25 disrupts the sexual behavior of the male.
Psychology; Science - Natural
Dist - PSUPCR **Prod** - UKANS 1959

The Sexual Brain 28 MIN
U-matic / VHS
Color (G)
$249.00, $149.00 purchase _ #AD - 1416
Considers that mammalian brains - including human brains - show distinct differences between female and male in the thickness of the cortex and the size of the corpus callosum. Shows some startling effects of hormone injections on brain structure and raises provocative questions about the sexual and reproductive roots of structural differences between male and female.
Psychology; Science - Natural
Dist - FOTH **Prod** - FOTH

Sexual Changes - Boys 19 MIN
16mm / VHS
Facts, Feelings and Wonder of Life - the Early Stages Series
Color (I J PRO)
$295.00, $450.00 purchase, $50.00 rental _ #9978, #9978LD
Describes the changes that occur in boys' reproductive organs during puberty, as well as the function of the organs.
Guidance and Counseling; Health and Safety; Science - Natural
Dist - AIMS **Prod** - PVGP 1988

Sexual Changes - Girls 19 MIN
16mm / VHS
Facts, Feelings and Wonder of Life - the Early Stages Series
Color (I J PRO)
$295.00, $450.00 purchase, $50.00 rental _ #9979, #9979LD
Describes the changes that occur in girls' reproductive organs during puberty, as well as the function of the organs.
Guidance and Counseling; Health and Safety; Science - Natural
Dist - AIMS **Prod** - PVGP 1988

Sexual choices 16 MIN
VHS
Color (J H)
$79.95 purchase _ #10222VG
Provides information on sexual choices a teenager may face. Discusses adolescent sexual behavior, values and options through interviews with teens. Covers peer pressure, homosexuality, insecurity, loneliness, pornography, and acceptance. Includes a leader's guide and blackline masters.
Health and Safety; Psychology
Dist - UNL

Sexual compatibility 30 MIN
U-matic / VHS
Family portrait - a study of contemporary lifestyles series; Lesson 17
Color (C A)
Compares differences in the male and female sex drive. Deals with sexual satisfaction and adjustment.
Psychology; Science - Natural; Sociology
Dist - CDTEL **Prod** - SCCON

Sexual Counseling of Physically Disabled 40 MIN
U-matic
Sexuality and Physical Disability Series
Color
Discusses why it is important for rehabilitation professionals to include sexual counseling with patients. Explores personalities, attitudes and professional roles that influence their work. Features four rehabilitation professionals.
Health and Safety; Psychology
Dist - UMITV **Prod** - UMITV 1976

Sexual Counseling of Physically Disabled Adults 40 MIN
VHS / U-matic
Sexuality and Physical Disability Video Tape Series
Color (C A)
Compares methods of dealing with physically disabled clients with varying lifestyles. Explores ways in which rehabilitation professionals use their own personalities and attitudes to deal with their clients.
Health and Safety; Psychology
Dist - MMRC **Prod** - MMRC

Sexual Development 29 MIN
VHS / 16mm
Facts, Feelings and Wonder of Life - the Teenage Years Series
Color (I J H PRO)
$295.00 purchase, $50.00 rental _ #9974
Shows the reproductive organs in animation and an egg's actual journey through the Fallopian tubes via fiber optic surgery.
Guidance and Counseling; Health and Safety; Science - Natural
Dist - AIMS **Prod** - PVGP 1988

Sexual Development in Children 45 MIN
U-matic / VHS
Color (C A)
Explores the developmental processes of the sexual life of boys and girls from infancy through puberty.
Health and Safety; Psychology; Sociology
Dist - MMRC **Prod** - MMRC

Sexual Dysfunction 19 MIN
VHS / 16mm
Color (G)
$149.00, $249.00, purchase _ #AD - 1415
Examines the psychological causes of sexual disinterest, the use of sex surrogates, and the treatment of male impotence through penile implants.
Health and Safety; Psychology
Dist - FOTH **Prod** - FOTH 1990

Sexual Encounters of a Floral Kind 50 MIN
U-matic / VHS
Color (H A)
Studies the pollination of plants from five continents. Demonstrates how different species have evolved in order to lure insects and other animals to their pollen and 'recruit' them as unwitting carriers for fertilization.
Science - Natural
Dist - FI **Prod** - WNETTV

Sexual encounters of the floral kind 54 MIN
VHS
Color (J H)
$180.00 purchase _ #A5VH 1037
Examines the reproductive methods in the plant world. Looks at relationships between flowering plants and pollinators - orchids that impersonate female wasps to draw male wasps, and nectar producing plants that lure rodents and flowers with the scent of rotting flesh.
Science - Natural
Dist - CLRVUE **Prod** - CLRVUE

Sexual Encounters of the Floral Kind
U-matic / VHS
Science and Nature Series
Color (G C J)
$197 purchase _ #06864 - 851
Explores the events too small to see in the process of flower fertilization.
Science - Natural
Dist - CHUMAN **Prod** - OSF 1988

Sexual Enhancement - the Sexual Realities Project 28 MIN
U-matic / VHS
Color
Demonstrates methods for overcoming performance anxiety, erectile difficulties and ejaculatory and orgasmic problems.
Health and Safety; Psychology
Dist - IRL **Prod** - IRL

Sexual harassment 30 MIN
VHS
Teen health video series
Color (J H A T)
$39.95 purchase _ #LVPE6641V-P
Offers teenagers and health educators information about sexual harassment. Includes advice from experts and personal testimonies from teens themselves. Does not make judgements on moral issues, but does present options available. One of a series of twelve videos about teen health issues. Available individually or as a set.
Sociology
Dist - CAMV

Sexual Harassment 28 MIN
VHS / U-matic
Color
Explores the types of behavior and comments that constitute sexual harassment.
Sociology
Dist - WCCOTV **Prod** - WCCOTV 1981

Sexual Harassment - a Manager - Employee Awareness Program Series Part 1
Sexual Harassment - a Threat to Your Profits 20 MIN
Dist - AMEDIA

Sexual Harassment - a Manager - Employee Awareness Program Series Part 2
Sexual Harassment - That's not in My Job Description 20 MIN
Dist - AMEDIA

Sexual Harassment - a Threat to Your Profits 20 MIN
U-matic / VHS
Sexual Harassment - a Manager - Employee Awareness Program Series 'Part 1
Color (A)
Examines effects of sexual harassment on company productivity and profit. Explains EEOC guidelines.
Business and Economics; Sociology
Dist - AMEDIA **Prod** - AMEDIA

Sexual Harassment - an Introduction 8 MIN
U-matic / VHS
Color
Includes a description and example of possible sexual harassment within a mock job interview. Raises questions to initiate group discussion of sexual harassment.
Guidance and Counseling; Sociology
Dist - UWISC **Prod** - UWISC 1982

Sexual harassment and gender discrimination - Disabilities - hiring and promotion - Tape 1 20 MIN
VHS
Diversity - creating success for business series
Color (PRO IND A)
$495.00 purchase _ #ENT21A
Uses real - life vignettes to deal with all aspects of diversity. Teaches recognition of how biases influence objective decision - making, judgment calls and assessment of others; and distinguishing between diversity and organizational, managerial and personal issues. Parts one and two of an eight - part series. Extensive workshop materials available.
Business and Economics; Sociology
Dist - EXTR **Prod** - ENMED

Sexual harassment awareness package
VHS
Color (C A T PRO IND)
$119.00 purchase _ #CCP0201SV-G
Educates viewers about what constitutes sexual harassment, how it affects people, and specific steps that can be taken to stop a harasser. Contains two videos that deal with sexual harassment in the workplace and school and views actual scenarios. Workbook included.
Sociology
Dist - CAMV

Sexual harassment awareness series
Explains different kinds of sexual harassment, defines the factors motivating harassers and provides specific techniques for dealing with the problem.
Sexual harassment awareness series
Dist - CAMV

Sexual harassment - crossing the line 30 MIN
VHS
Color (H C G)
$89.95 purchase _ #CCP0147V
Explains different kinds of sexual harassment. Defines the factors motivating harassers. Provides specific techniques for dealing with the problem. Teaches the steps to be taken if harassed or in witnessing the harassment of others, such as keeping journals, the broken record technique, talking to supervisors, sending memos, using grievance procedures and filing formal complaints.
Business and Economics; Guidance and Counseling; Sociology
Dist - CAMV **Prod** - CAMV 1993

Sexual Harassment from 9 to 5 26 MIN
U-matic / VHS
Color (G)
$249.00, $149.00 purchase _ #AD - 1711
Looks at the legal and the human side of sexual harassment in the workplace. Portrays women whose lives were deeply affected by this aggressive and largely hidden form of discrimination. Shows the rights of women, the responsibilities of male workers and the companies which employ them. Illustrates some corporate efforts to help employees distinguish among romance, harassment and sexual extortion.
Psychology; Sociology
Dist - FOTH **Prod** - FOTH

Sexual harassment - handling the complaint 30 MIN
VHS
Color (A)
$525.00 purchase
Explains effective strategies managers can use in dealing with sexual harassment complaints and situations in the workplace. Emphasizes the importance of immediate response to subtle problems as well as to more overt harassment. Includes one comprehensive training manual. Additional copies are available separately.
Business and Economics; Education; Sociology
Dist - COMFLM

Sexual harassment - how to protect yourself and your organization 126 MIN
VHS
Color (J H C G)
$249.95 purchase _ #CTK20476V
Presents three clear, comprehensive sections on sexual harassment. Clears up the confusion about what is - and is not - sexual harassment. Shows how to handle sexual harassment if it happens, both as a victim and as a manager. Illustrates how to set policy and handle sexual harassment issues skillfully and legally. Includes three videocassettes and a workbook.
Business and Economics; Social Science; Sociology
Dist - CAMV **Prod** - CARTRP 1993

Sexual harassment in healthcare - relearning the rules 15 MIN
VHS
Color (PRO A VOC)
$295.00 purchase, $100.00 rental
Uses dramatized sexual harassment scenarios to guide healthcare professionals on avoiding sexual harassment of clients and staff. Emphasizes that healthcare professionals are responsible for their actions and how these actions are perceived by patients and coworkers. Covers four steps to use when confronted with sexual harassment - confronting the problem; reporting the incident; documenting the incident; and seeking support.
Sociology
Dist - BAXMED AJN **Prod** - ENVINC 1993

Sexual harassment in our schools 26 MIN
VHS
Sexual harassment series
Color (G)
$150.00 purchase
Addresses the full array of issues surrounding sexual harassment and sexual abuse including identification, investigation, discipline and the problem of mobile molesters in school systems. Defines and illustrates sexual harassment and emphasizes that sexually harassing conduct is no longer acceptable in the school environment. Includes written materials - instructional guidebook and family information sheet. Produced by Mary Jo McGrath.
Education; Guidance and Counseling
Dist - MCGRAT

Sexual harassment in the workplace 23 MIN
VHS
Color (PRO A G)
$550.00 purchase, $130.00 rental
Explores what sexual harassment is and how it can be dealt with. Teaches that employees and companies benefit from good working environments. Includes a training leader's guide and desk reminder cards.
Business and Economics; Psychology; Sociology
Dist - EXTR **Prod** - AMEDIA

Sexual harassment is bad business 22 MIN
VHS
Color (A PRO IND)
$495.00 purchase, $175.00 rental
Uses examples from actual sexual harassment cases to illustrate the laws which deal with sexual harassment in the workplace.
Business and Economics; Guidance and Counseling; Psychology; Sociology
Dist - VLEARN

Sexual harassment - is it or isn't it? 17 MIN
VHS
Color (COR)
$575.00 purchase, $285.00 thirty - day rental, $140.00 five - day rental, $40.00 five - day preview _ #ASE/AMI
Reinforces the message that sexual harassment in the workplace will not be tolerated. Specifically geared to the manufacturing setting. Presents case studies that allow employees to decide whether each situation is considered sexual harassment. Each case study is followed by a brief explanation by the narrator - attorney. Includes Leader's Guide.
Business and Economics; Guidance and Counseling; Sociology
Dist - ADVANM

Sexual Harassment - It's no Laughing Matter 15 MIN
16mm / U-matic / VHS
(PRO A)
$395, $425, $150 Rental 5 days, $35 3 days
Approaches the issue of sexual harassment in its many forms, and the effect it has in office situations.
Business and Economics; Sociology
Dist - ADVANM **Prod** - ADVANM

Sexual harassment - Minimize the risk 48 MIN
VHS
Sexual harassment series
Color (T PRO C)
$750.00 purchase
Presents three parts for educational institutions that address the full array of issues surrounding sexual harassment and sexual abuse, including identification, investigation, discipline and the problem of mobile molesters. Includes Legal Information on School District and Personal Liability in Part 1. Part 2 Shows and Tells How to Investigate - Early Detection, Process and Steps to Handle Complaints, Interview Guidelines. Part 3 looks at Remedial - Disciplinary Actions. Written material includes instructional guide, investigator's handbook, sample policies, McGrath template for processing. Produced by Mary Jo McGrath.
Education; Sociology
Dist - MCGRAT

Sexual Harassment - no Place in the Workplace 30 MIN
U-matic
Color
Features Gloria Steinem and Lynn Farley as they discuss issues facing working women. Offers insights and solutions to the problem of sexual harassment in the work place.
Business and Economics; Sociology
Dist - UMITV **Prod** - UMITV 1980

Sexual Harassment on Campus 11 MIN
U-matic / BETA / VHS
Color; Mono (C)
Demonstrates what constitutes sexual harassment and how to deal with it, both personally and institutionally. Designed specifically for use in institutes of higher education at universities and colleges.
Psychology; Religion and Philosophy; Sociology
Dist - UCALG **Prod** - UCALG 1986

Sexual Harassment on the Job 28 MIN
U-matic / VHS
Color (G)
$249.00, $149.00 purchase _ #AD - 1168
Reveals that over seventy percent of working women experience pressure to exchange favors for advancement or continued employment some time during their working lives. Joins Phil Donahue and Susan Meyer who explain how to handle harassment.
Psychology; Sociology
Dist - FOTH **Prod** - FOTH

Sexual harassment - Pay attention 38 MIN
VHS
Sexual harassment series
Color (I J H C)
$600.00 purchase
Presents two parts addressing the full array of issues surrounding sexual harassment and sexual abuse including identification, investigation, discipline and the problem of mobile molesters. Includes Part 1 which defines and illustrates sexual harassment and Part 2 which shows students how to avoid being a victim and what to do if it happens. Written material includes curriculum, follow - up activities, glossary, support material, instructor's background information. Produced by Mary Jo McGrath.
Education; Guidance and Counseling; Health and Safety
Dist - MCGRAT

Sexual harassment plain and simple 50 MIN
VHS
Color (G PRO)
Presents a two - module compliance and training program. Explains the different kinds of behavior that may be interpreted as sexual harassment and the steps that employees can take to prevent and report unwelcome sexual behavior. Includes two videos, a leader's guide and 20 participant booklets. Video I - Dottie Doesn't Work Here Anymore - demonstrates a wide range of sexual harassment incidents recognized under the law, such as hostile work environment, quid pro quo, verbal harassment and non - verbal harassment. Video II - Wait 'Til Trish Sees This - presents options available for resolving sexual harassment situations, and shows how victims can confront the perpetrator or report the incident to a supervisor or human resource person.

Business and Economics; Sociology
Dist - BNA

The Sexual harassment prevention kit 38 MIN
VHS
Color (A)
$395.00 purchase
Presents sexual harassment training material in two parts. Defines sexual harassment and shows how it damages an organization. Shows how to recognize and deal with harassment in the workplace. Explains company liability and legal repurcussions if the problem is not taken care of. Provides training for employees, managers and supervisors. Produced by Promedion. Includes training manual with suggested policy statements and handout material.
Guidance and Counseling; Psychology
Dist - PFP

Sexual harassment pure and simple series
Dottie doesn't work here anymore - Video I 30 MIN
Wait 'til Trish sees this - Video II 30 MIN
Dist - BNA

Sexual harassment series
Presents a three - part series of six videos addressing the full array of issues surrounding sexual harassment and sexual abuse including identification, investigation, discipline and the problem of mobile molesters. Includes Sexual Harassment - Minimize the Risk for educators and school staff; Sexual Harassment - Pay Attention for students; and Sexual Harassment in Our Schools for community audiences. Extensive written materials support the series. Produced by Mary Jo McGrath.
Sexual harassment - Minimize the risk 48 MIN
Sexual harassment - Pay attention 38 MIN
Sexual harassment in our schools 26 MIN
Dist - MCGRAT

Sexual harassment - shades of gray
VHS
Color (A PRO IND)
$1,495.00 purchase, $300.00 rental
Takes an in - depth look at sexual harassment in the workplace. Stresses resolution and prevention over litigation. Consists of five videocassettes, training manuals, leader's guides, and 25 workbooks.
Business and Economics; Sociology
Dist - VLEARN

Sexual Harassment - Shades of Gray Series
What Am I Supposed to do 12 MIN
What are We Doing Here 12 MIN
What Does the Law Say 12 MIN
What is Sexual Harassment 12 MIN
Why Should I Worry about it 12 MIN
Dist - UTM

Sexual Harassment - That's not in My Job Description 20 MIN
VHS / U-matic
Sexual Harassment - a Manager - Employee Awareness Program Series 'Part 2
Color (A)
Addresses harassing behavior by both sexes, non - employees and employees. Offers suggestions on how to handle harassing situations.
Business and Economics; Sociology
Dist - AMEDIA **Prod** - AMEDIA

Sexual harassment - the new rules 37 MIN
VHS
Color (A)
$895.00 purchase
Uses dramatizations and interviews to clarify what sexual harassment is and how it should be dealt with, emphasizing the importance of compliance to the individual and the company. Includes two video programs, one for management and one for employees at all levels. Also includes one reinforcement guide. Additional copies are available separately.
Business and Economics; Education; Sociology
Dist - COMFLM **Prod** - COMFLM

Sexual harassment - the new rules - a management briefing 19 MIN
VHS
Color (A)
$525.00 purchase
Uses dramatizations and interviews to clarify what sexual harassment is and how it should be dealt with, emphasizing the importance of compliance to the individual and the company. Part I for management of Sexual Harassment - the new rules. A reinforcement guide is available separately.
Business and Economics; Education; Sociology
Dist - COMFLM

Sexual harassment - the new rules - employee awareness 18 MIN
VHS
Color (A)
$525.00 purchase
Uses dramatizations and interviews to clarify what sexual harassment is and how it should be dealt with, emphasizing the importance of compliance to the individual and the company. Part II for employees of Sexual Harassment - the new rules. A reinforcement guide is available separately.
Business and Economics; Education; Sociology
Dist - COMFLM

Sexual Harassment - the Other Point of View 33 MIN
16mm / U-matic / VHS
(PRO A)
$495, $545, $150 Rental 5 days, $35 Preview 3 days
Addresses the issue of sexual harassment and gives examples of the problem in its many forms.
Business and Economics; Sociology
Dist - ADVANM **Prod** - ADVANM

Sexual harassment video - it's not just courtesy, it's the law 26 MIN
VHS
Color (A PRO)
$495.00 purchase _ #VD001
Reveals that sexual harassment in the workplace is one of the more troublesome issues faced by employers today. Shows that employers can minimize exposure by recognizing what constitutes sexual harassment and by taking immediate corrective action with training and sound management policy. Helps all employees understand the negative impact sexual harassment has on individuals and organizations. Teaches employees in both office and industrial settings how to handle unwelcome behavior or demands for sexual favors in return for employment advancement. Includes leader's guide with discussion questions for training.
Business and Economics; Home Economics; Sociology
Dist - COEDMA **Prod** - COEDMA

Sexual harassment video - Serious business 25 MIN
VHS
Color (A)
$495.00 purchase _ #VD012
Teaches all employees that preventing or eliminating sexual harassment in the workplace will benefit them as well as the entire organization. Covers the impact of a hostile environment, the consequences of third - party harassment, proper reporting of complaints, confronting the harasser, handling false accusations and more. Includes leader's guide with discussion questions for training.
Business and Economics; Sociology
Dist - COEDMA **Prod** - COEDMA 1994

Sexual Harassment - Walking the Corporate Fine Line 22 MIN
VHS / 16mm
Color (C A)
$495.00 purchase, $150.00 rental _ #192
Develops effective approaches for preventing sexual harassment in the workplace. Includes Leader's Guide.
Guidance and Counseling; Psychology; Sociology
Dist - SALENG **Prod** - NOWLDF 1988

Sexual Harassment - what is it and what Can We do to Stop it 20 MIN
VHS / 16mm
Color (PRO)
$525.00 purchase, $185.00 rental, $35.00 preview
Teaches employees to recognize sexual harassment and encourages them to report harassment as soon as it starts. Shows both men and women how to deal with harassment.
Business and Economics; Psychology; Sociology
Dist - UTM **Prod** - UTM

Sexual Harrassment - what it is and what We Can do to Stop it 21MIN
U-matic / VHS
(PRO G)
$550.00 purchase, $110.00 rental
Defines and illustrates sexual harrassment. Presents ideas on how stop it before it gets out of control, and shows what happens when it goes unrecognized or unreported.
Business and Economics; Sociology
Dist - CREMED **Prod** - CREMED 1987

Sexual health care in the nursing process 25 MIN
16mm
Directions for education in nursing via technology series
Color (PRO)
LC 76-703345
Defines sexual health care and applies concepts of sexual health care to each phase of the nursing process.
Dramatizes four nurse - patient - family interactions within different health care settings.
Health and Safety
Dist - WSUM **Prod** - DENT 1976

Sexual Identity 25 MIN
VHS / 16mm
Color (A)
$200.00 purchase, $16.50 rental _ #35081
Argues that sexual identity is different from being male or female. Includes discussion of the Identity Scale devised by Havelock Ellis, and the author Radcliffe Hall. Produced by Frances Berrigan.
Psychology; Sociology
Dist - PSUPCR **Prod** - PSUPCR 1988

Sexual Impotence in the Male - the Tragedy of the Bedroom 15 MIN
16mm
Color
LC 80-701416
Uses a simulated patient situation in discussing the problems of impotence. Emphasizes obtaining proper help, evaluation and counseling.
Health and Safety; Sociology
Dist - EATONL **Prod** - EATONL 1980

Sexual Intercourse 16 MIN
VHS / U-matic
Color (C A)
Explains and demonstrates the physiology, psychology and basic technique of sexual intercourse. Contains two explicit sexual episodes, each focusing on a different set of concerns.
Health and Safety; Psychology
Dist - MMRC **Prod** - TSISR

Sexual meditation - Faun's room - Yale 3 MIN
16mm
Color (G)
$10.00 rental, $121.00 purchase
Presents the third film in the Sexual Meditation series.
Fine Arts
Dist - CANCIN **Prod** - BRAKS 1972

Sexual meditation - hotel 8 MIN
16mm
Color (G)
$13.00 rental, $236.00 purchase
Says film director Brakhage, '...takes its cue from that ultimate situation of Sex - Med - masturbation, the loft and lonely hotel room.'
Fine Arts
Dist - CANCIN **Prod** - BRAKS 1972

Sexual meditation no 1 - motel 6 MIN
16mm
Color (G)
$224.00 purchase, $10.00 rental
Presents a film by Stan Brakhage.
Fine Arts
Dist - CANCIN **Prod** - BRAKS 1970

Sexual meditation - office suite 4 MIN
16mm
Color (G)
$10.00 rental, $127.00 purchase
Says Brakhage, '...evolves from several years' observation of the sexual energy which charges the world of business and the qualities of palatial environ which this energy often creates.'
Fine Arts
Dist - CANCIN **Prod** - BRAKS 1972

Sexual Meditation - Open Field 6 MIN
16mm
Color; Silent (C)
$207.20
Experimental film by Stan Brakhage.
Fine Arts
Dist - AFA **Prod** - AFA 1972

Sexual meditation - room with a view 4 MIN
16mm
Color; Silent (C)
$112.00
Experimental film by Stan Brakhage.
Fine Arts
Dist - AFA **Prod** - AFA 1972

Sexual Motivation 29 MIN
U-matic
Understanding Human Behavior - an Introduction to Psychology Series 'Lesson 13
Color (C A)
Explores social and biological factors involved in sexual functioning. Describes Kinsey and Masters and Johnson research.
Psychology
Dist - CDTEL **Prod** - COAST

Sexual orientation - Career mobility - language - Tape 4 20 MIN
VHS
Diversity - creating success for business series
Color (PRO IND A)
$495.00 purchase _ #ENT21D
Uses real - life vignettes to deal with all aspects of diversity. Teaches recognition of how biases influence objective decision - making, judgment calls and assessment of others; and aids in distinguishing between diversity and organizational, managerial and personal issues. Parts seven and eight of an eight - part series. Extensive workshop materials available.
Business and Economics; Sociology
Dist - EXTR **Prod** - ENMED

Sexual orientation in the USA - Part one 60 MIN
VHS
Dealing with diversity series
Color (H C G)
$99.00 purchase _ #GSU - 120
Discusses stereotypes about homosexuality and the difficulties of establishing open relationships for gays and lesbians. Examines homophobia and violence against gays and lesbians. Includes Jovita Barber and Vernon Huls of the Illinois Gay and Lesbian Task Force as studio guests. Part one of two parts on sexual orientation and part of a 23 - part series hosted by Dr J Q Adams, Western Illinois University, which helps students to develop the awareness that society is strengthened by a free and unfettered expression of individuality in all its diverse manifestations.
Civics and Political Systems; Sociology
Dist - INSTRU

Sexual orientation issues in the USA - Part two 60 MIN
VHS
Dealing with diversity series
Color (H C G)
$99.00 purchase _ #GSU - 121
Focuses on the experiences of individuals denied equality because of their sexual preference. Discusses 'The Forgotten Boy Scouts,' an organization of individuals expelled from scouting because of their sexual orientation. Includes Allen Shore, Oakland Men's Project, and Robert Schwitz, Gay and Lesbian Community Alliance, Washington University, St Louis. Part two of two parts on sexual orientation and part of a 23 - part series hosted by Dr J Q Adams, Western Illinois University, which helps students to develop the awareness that society is strengthened by a free and unfettered expression of individuality in all its diverse manifestations.
Civics and Political Systems; Sociology
Dist - INSTRU

Sexual orientation - reading between the labels 26 MIN
VHS
Color (I J H)
$195.00 purchase _ #B043 - V8
Helps build respect between individuals of divergent sexual orientation and tells homosexual teens 'you're not alone.' Uses interviews with gay, lesbian, and bisexual teens, their parents, and professional outreach workers. Discusses the difficult issues facing the over 3 million gay and lesbian teens in the US, including social isolation, discrimination, violence, and the stress of 'coming out.'
Health and Safety; Sociology
Dist - ETRASS **Prod** - ETRASS

Sexual Pelvic Muscle Exercises 10 MIN
U-matic / VHS
EDCOA Sexual Counseling Series
Color
Demonstrates the vaginal muscle tone exam and exercises for strengthening the pubococcygeus muscle.
Health and Safety; Psychology
Dist - MMRC **Prod** - MMRC

Sexual Pleasure Education
U-matic / VHS
Independent Study in Human Sexuality Series
Color (PRO)
Health and Safety; Psychology
Dist - MMRC **Prod** - MMRC

Sexual positions for lovers - Beyond the missionary position 53 MIN
VHS
Color (C A)
$29.95 purchase
Features sex educators Dr Derek C Polonksy of Harvard Medical School and Dr Marian E Dunn. Offers a guide to sexual anatomy as a basis for understanding how various sexual positions stimulate different parts of the body. Four typical couples demonstrate numerous positions in graphic detail. Shows specific positions for deeper penetration, clitoral stimulation and prolonged intercourse, as well as positions for couples with problems such as arthritis, back problems, pregnancy or obesity. Produced by Dr Mark Schoen.
Guidance and Counseling; Health and Safety; Science - Natural
Dist - FCSINT

Sexual problems - Tape 5 40 MIN
VHS
Loving better series
Color (C A)
$34.95 purchase
Helps couples to feel better about themselves and their lovemaking. Uses scenes from the four earlier tapes with new narration to assist couples in solving sexual problems such as lack of desire, conflicting levels of desire, erection difficulties, failure to relax and allow penetration - vaginismus, and failure to achieve orgasm. Includes a reference counter in the lower corner of the screen through the tape to allow easy location. Contains explicit sexual material. Created by Dr Sheldon Kule, Clinical Assoc Prof and Chair, Dept of Psychiatry, New York College of Osteopathic Medicine.
Guidance and Counseling; Health and Safety; Science - Natural
Dist - FCSINT

The Sexual Puzzle 30 MIN
16mm / U-matic / VHS
Color
Explores the options young people face. Shows how sexual intimacy gets its best start in caring values, responsible actions and healthy self - acceptance.
Guidance and Counseling; Health and Safety; Psychology
Dist - KAWVAL **Prod** - KAWVAL

The Sexual realities project - a self - help approach 28 MIN
VHS
Color (C A)
$29.95 purchase
Emphasizes the value of communication skills, rational reevaluation, sensate focus, stop - start techniques, masturbation and positions of intercourse for improving sexual skills. Explicit. Produced by Dr William Golden.
Health and Safety; Psychology; Science - Natural; Social Science
Dist - FCSINT **Prod** - FCSINT 1981

The Sexual Realities Project - a Self - Help Approach 28 MIN
U-matic / VHS
Color (C A)
Provides guidelines to anyone who is interested in enhancing sexual relations and in clarifying sexual myths and misconceptions.
Health and Safety; Psychology
Dist - MMRC **Prod** - MMRC

Sexual reproduction in animals 30 MIN
VHS
Color (J H)
$120.00 purchase _ #A5VH 1196
Offers an instructive primer on animal reproduction. Includes sections on internal and external fertilization, eggs and young and internal development. Discusses the adaptive significance of various modes of reproduction and includes examples from throughout the animal kingdom. Offers an animated portayal of human conception and development.
Psychology; Science - Natural
Dist - CLRVUE **Prod** - BBCTV

Sexual responsibility 20 MIN
VHS
Color (J H)
$89.95 purchase _ #ULNP743V; $89.95 purchase _ #NP743VG
Focuses on teenage pregnancy. Features teens explaining their own experiences and how their choices have affected their lives. Mentions two innovative high school programs that are helping teens to accept responsibility for their sexual actions. Includes discussion guide.
Health and Safety; Sociology
Dist - CAMV
UNL

Sexual responsibility - a two way street 29 MIN
VHS
Color (I J H)
$189.00 purchase _ #B013 - V8
Examines the need for both partners in a relationships to participate in making decisions about sexual issues. Dramatizes the need for making responsible choices about abstinence, intercourse, contraception, HIV - AIDS, pregnancy, and STDs that are comfortable for both partners. Includes Teacher's Guide.
Guidance and Counseling; Health and Safety; Psychology; Social Science
Dist - ETRASS **Prod** - ETRASS

Sexual responsibility - a two - way street 30 MIN
VHS
Color (J H)
$189.00 purchase _ #2294 - SK
Examines issues of sexual responsibility among teenagers. Explores common myths about sex and sexuality. Stresses the need for communication and to consider all the consequences of being sexually active. Includes teacher's guide.
Health and Safety; Psychology; Sociology
Dist - SUNCOM **Prod** - HRMC

Sexual responsibility series
Presents a three - part series on sexual responsibility. Discusses unwanted pregnancy and contraception in Contraption - Ready or Not. Explores myths about AIDS and other sexually transmitted diseases in Close Encounters of the Sexual Kind. Discloses the dangers to young women of infertility resulting from pelvic inflammatory disease - PID - in It Doesn't Hurt to Know.
Contraception - ready or not 12 MIN
It doesn't hurt to know 12 MIN
Sexual responsibility series 36 MIN
Dist - FLMLIB **Prod** - SEVDIM

Sexual responsibility series
Close encounters of the sexual kind 12 MIN
Dist - FLMLIB
SEVDIM

Sexual roulette 17 MIN
VHS
Color (C A)
$250.00 purchase
Tells of two successful couples whose infidelity brings trouble to their marriages, including AIDS. Warns of the need for honesty between partners. Emphasizes that AIDS can be fought only through knowledge and responsibility. By Joseph Productions.
Health and Safety
Dist - PFP

Sexual roulette - AIDS and the heterosexual 26 MIN
VHS / 16mm
Color (PRO G)
$149.00, $249.00, purchase _ #AD - 1952
Points out that, although the groups most at risk of contracting AIDS are homosexuals and intravenous drug users, this does not mean that other groups are not at risk. Explains that every sexually active person faces some risk of getting AIDS, the level of risk depending upon geographic area and type of sexual behavior. Enables viewers to gauge their own probable risk levels against profiles of various segments of the heterosexual community. Emphasizes safety precautions.
Health and Safety
Dist - FOTH **Prod** - FOTH 1990

Sexual selection - why do peacocks have elaborate trains 25 MIN
VHS
Evolution series
Color (G C)
$150.00 purchase, $19.50 rental _ #36261
Reveals that researchers at the Whipsnade Zoo in Great Britain have determined through scientific reasoning that the purpose of the male peacock's train is to attract females. Explores what the male peacock might gain or lose from carrying such a long train. Shows the scientific research method in action. Part of a ten - part series exploring evolutionary selection and adaptation.
Science - Natural
Dist - PSU **Prod** - BBC 1992

Sexual sensitivity in the workplace 25 MIN
U-matic / VHS
Color (G)
$249.00 purchase _ #7498
Examines the gender bias women encounter in the workplace and its origins in the belief systems of Western culture and institutions. Reveals that such belief systems may need to be changed to ensure equality in opportunity for women economically, socially and politically. Features cultural anthropologist Jennifer James.
Sociology
Dist - VISIVI **Prod** - VISIVI 1991

Sexual Suicide 29 MIN
U-matic
Woman Series
Color
Features author George Gildre discussing single men and women, freedom, independence, and sexual diversity.
Sociology
Dist - PBS **Prod** - WNEDTV

Sexual Variations 39 MIN
U-matic
Sexuality and Physical Disability Series

Color
Deals with the variety of human sexual behavior in our society in order to dispel myths and to increase understanding and acceptance.
Sociology
Dist - UMITV **Prod** - UMITV 1976

Sexual Variations
VHS / U-matic
Independent Study in Human Sexuality Series
Color (PRO)
Health and Safety; Psychology
Dist - MMRC **Prod** - MMRC

Sexual Variations 40 MIN
U-matic / VHS
Sexuality and Physical Disability Video Tape Series
Color (C A)
Presents several aspects of the range of sexual behavior, including transvestism, exhibitionism, transsexuality, and homosexuality in order to dispel myths and to increase understanding.
Health and Safety; Psychology
Dist - MMRC **Prod** - MMRC

Sexual war films 50 MIN
16mm
B&W (G)
$90.00 rental
Includes films 18 - 19, 14 - 16, Blockage and Virgin Mary. Portrays concern with violence and memory, often presented in voiceover, with imagery that is based on rephotography at times. Intense footage filled with ideological concerns. Part of a series, Films 1 - 37, of psychoanalytical content, dealing with the 'imaginary' and other phenomena and described as 'gritty and obsessive.'
Fine Arts; Psychology; Sociology
Dist - CANCIN **Prod** - SONDHE 1981

Sexuality 30 MIN
U-matic / VHS / 16mm
Coping with serious illness series; No 3
Color (H C A)
LC 80-701662
Deals with the issue of sexuality and the need for loving during times of serious illness.
Health and Safety; Psychology
Dist - TIMLIF **Prod** - TIMLIF 1980

Sexuality 7 MIN
U-matic
Take Time Series
(A)
Demonstrates the influence of parents and others caring for pre - schoolers on the physical and emotional development of the child.
Health and Safety; Psychology; Sociology
Dist - ACCESS **Prod** - ACCESS 1976

Sexuality - a Woman's Point of View 30 MIN
U-matic / VHS
Color (H C A)
Focuses on how women view themselves sexually. Explores the world of women's attitudes about human sexuality. Narrated by Stephanie Powers.
Health and Safety; Psychology; Sociology
Dist - MMRC **Prod** - MMRC

Sexuality after childbirth - 2 14 MIN
VHS
Postpartum period series
Color (J H C G PRO)
$250.00 purchase, $60.00 rental
Discusses sexual activity for women after giving birth. Informs women recovering from childbirth, their partners, childbirth educators and obstetrical staff. Features new parents in real situations. Hosted by Dr Linda Reid. Part of a five - part series.
Health and Safety
Dist - CF **Prod** - HOSSN 1989

Sexuality - AIDS - Social Skills for Teens Series
In control 27 MIN
Playing it Safe 10 MIN
Taking a Stand 16 MIN
Dist - CHEF

Sexuality, Alcohol and Drugs 26 MIN
U-matic / VHS
Color (J A)
Presents a film that explains how some people deal with tension, fear and guilt.
Health and Safety; Psychology; Sociology
Dist - SUTHRB **Prod** - SUTHRB

Sexuality - an Introduction for Medical Students 21 MIN
16mm
Color
LC 79-713391
Portrays the difficulty of a medical student in maintaining his sensitivity throughout the experience of training to become a physician, as well as the difficulty in reacting sensitively to a patient with a sexual problem.
Health and Safety; Psychology; Sociology
Dist - UMIAMI **Prod** - UMIAMI 1971

Sexuality and Aging 50 MIN
U-matic
Color (J C)
Diversity of options regarding sexuality - - panel of elderly.
Health and Safety; Psychology; Sociology
Dist - SDSC **Prod** - SDSC 1977

Sexuality and aging 60 MIN
VHS
Color (G)
$99.00 purchase _ #AJ - 129
Explores the attitudes of society about sexuality in later life. Presents realistic information about the physiological and emotional changes affecting intimacy. Older women and men speak candidly about their attitudes and relationships, while gerontologists, sex researchers and educators give their perspectives. Produced by Gary Hochman.
Health and Safety; Psychology
Dist - FANPRO **Prod** - KCTSTV 1994

Sexuality and Aging 60 MIN
U-matic / VHS
(G A)
$50 purchase
Provides the general viewer with insights into physical and psychological aspects of the effects of aging on sexuality. Focuses on myths, research, and individual experiences. Narrated by actor Ford Rainey.
Sociology
Dist - GPN

Sexuality and aging series
Menopause and beyond 60 MIN
Dist - FCSINT

Sexuality and Disability Adjustment 40 MIN
VHS / U-matic
Sexuality and Physical Disability Video Tape Series
Color (C A)
Presents a discussion between a psychologist and a disabled man anwoman on the relationships between sexuality and other aspects of adjustment.
Health and Safety; Psychology
Dist - MMRC **Prod** - MMRC

Sexuality and Disability Adjustment 30 MIN
U-matic
Sexuality and Physical Disability Series
Color
Discusses the relationship between sexuality and adjustment to disability. Stresses importance of understanding one's dependency, strength or assertivenes central to both sexual health and overall adjustment to a physical disability.
Health and Safety; Psychology
Dist - UMITV **Prod** - UMITV 1976

Sexuality and Mentally Handicapped Persons 16 MIN
VHS / U-matic
Color
Discusses myths connected with the mentally handicapped and sexuality, such as that the mentally handicapped are not sexual. Points out the need for workshops and classes for mentally handicapped regarding sexuality.
Health and Safety; Psychology; Sociology
Dist - UWISC **Prod** - LASSWC 1979

Sexuality and Physical Diability Video Tape Series
Orientation to the Sexuality of Physical Disability 40 MIN
Dist - MMRC

Sexuality and Physical Disability Series
Anatomy and physiology of sexual response cycles 44 MIN
Body image 38 MIN
Medical and Institutional Aspects 40 MIN
Orientation to Sexuality of the Physically Disabled 39 MIN
Sexual Counseling of Physically Disabled 40 MIN
Sexual Variations 39 MIN
Sexuality and Disability Adjustment 30 MIN
Dist - UMITV

Sexuality and Physical Disability Video Tape Series
Anatomy and physiology of the sexual response cycle 40 MIN
Sexual Counseling of Physically Disabled Adults 40 MIN
Sexual Variations 40 MIN
Sexuality and Disability Adjustment 40 MIN
Dist - MMRC

Sexuality and Sexual Issues for the Severely and Profoundly Retarded, Pt I 60 MIN
U-matic / VHS
B&W
Presents an in - service workshop for social workers at a center for the developmentally disabled. Explores the areas of masturbation, public and private, inadvertent sexual arousal by caretakers and visitors, sex education and inappropriate dress and language. Presents innovative training materials.
Health and Safety; Psychology; Sociology
Dist - UWISC **Prod** - CWCDD 1980

Sexuality and Sexual Issues for the Severely and Profoundly Retarded, Pt II 12 MIN
U-matic / VHS
B&W
Presents the conclusion to sexual issues for the severely and profoundly retarded as it brushes on the complexity of how to deal with situations such as encountering male clients in sexual activity or masturbation. Proposes an enlightened attitude of acceptance of male - male sexual contact among the retarded in contrast to the tradition of attempts at 'normalization.'.
Health and Safety; Psychology; Sociology
Dist - UWISC **Prod** - CWCDD 1980

Sexuality in later life 120 MIN
VHS
Virginia Geriatric Education Center video conference series
Color (G C PRO)
$149.00 purchase, $55.00 rental
Explores aspects of functional and dysfunctional sexual ability in older adults that relate to physical health, social relationships and treatments available for problems.
Health and Safety
Dist - TNF **Prod** - VGEREC

Sexuality - Pt I 29 MIN
VHS / 16mm
Feelings Series
Color (G)
$55.00 rental _ #FEES - 109
Features three young teenagers describing their opinions on subjects ranging from teen pregnancies to suggestive scenes on television.
Health and Safety; Sociology
Dist - PBS **Prod** - SCETV
SCETV

Sexuality - Pt II 29 MIN
VHS / 16mm
Feelings series
Color (G)
$55.00 rental _ #FEES - 110
Discusses sexual attitudes and behavior of young teenagers. Covers topics such as homosexuality and the double standard.
Health and Safety; Sociology
Dist - PBS **Prod** - SCETV
SCETV

Sexuality, self - esteem and friendship 24 MIN
VHS / U-matic
Teen - family life series
Color (J H G)
$179.00, $229.00 purchase, $60.00 rental
Presents teens and counselors discussing values and morals and the difficulty of making choices regarding sexuality and friendship. Looks at issues around 'family of origin,' power and dependency within relationships.
Guidance and Counseling; Health and Safety; Psychology
Dist - NDIM **Prod** - FAMLIF 1993

Sexuality - the Human Heritage 59 MIN
16mm
Thin Edge Series
Color (H C A)
LC 76-702373
Traces the development of human sexual identity from prenatal sex hormones to external influences of family and society. Presents Jerome Kagan, professor of developmental psychology at Harvard, discussing how children acquire gender and role identity. Includes interviews with teenagers and homosexuals explaining how they view themselves in regard to the sexual standards of society.
Guidance and Counseling; Health and Safety; Psychology; Sociology
Dist - IU **Prod** - EDUCBC 1976
MEDCOM MEDCOM

The Sexually Abused Child 30 MIN
U-matic / VHS
Home is Where the Care is Series Module 8; Module 8
Color
Presents a program specialist, foster parent and clinical psychologist exchanging views on the foster parent's role in relation to helping the sexually abused child.

Guidance and Counseling; Sociology
Dist - CORF **Prod** - CORF 1984

The Sexually Abused Child - a Protocol for Criminal Justice 26 MIN
16mm
Sexual Abuse of Children Series
Color (C A)
LC 79-700114
Features district attorneys, a judge, a police sergeant, a pediatrician and a receiving home director discussing how they protect the rights of child sex abuse victims and prosecute their offenders.
Civics and Political Systems; Sociology
Dist - LAWREN **Prod** - BAKRSR 1979

The Sexually Abused Child - Identification/Interview 10 MIN
16mm / U-matic / VHS
Color
Demonstrates various interviewing techniques to be used when sexual abuse is suspected. Examines methods of establishing rapport, interpreting nonverbal cues and dealing with the child's protective feelings toward the abuser.
Civics and Political Systems; Social Science; Sociology
Dist - CORF **Prod** - CAVLCD

Sexually abused children in foster care training videotapes series
Presents an eight - part series training foster parents on the care of sexually abused children. Includes Interview With a Foster Parent; Preplacement Interview; Effective Praise and Teaching Interaction; Seductive Behavior - Communication Between Foster Parents; Interview on Suicide; Interview on Chemical Dependency; Psychological Problems of the Sexually Abused Child; and Special Children, Special Risks. Includes an instructor's manual and a source book.

Effective praise and teaching interaction	5 MIN
Interview on chemical dependency	17 MIN
Interview on suicide	45 MIN
Interview with a foster parent	42 MIN
Preplacement interview	37 MIN
Psychological symptoms of the sexually abused child	39 MIN
Seductive behavior - communication between foster parents	4 MIN
Special children, special risks	15 MIN

Dist - FFBH **Prod** - FFBH

The Sexually Mature Adult 16 MIN
16mm / U-matic / VHS
Human Sexuality Series
Color
LC 73-702365
Covers the physiology and emotions involved in mature sexual behavior during the four stages of sexual response in intercourse. Uses live photography to show responses of couples in each stage of lovemaking and animated diagrams to illustrate internal responses. Features men and women who give accounts of their sexual experiences and concludes with a look at sexual relationships in older men and women.
Health and Safety; Science - Natural; Sociology
Dist - MEDIAG **Prod** - WILEYJ 1973

Sexually single 55 MIN
VHS
Color (G R)
$39.95 purchase
Draws from years of experience of Dr Harold Ivan Smith. Addresses subject of singleness with a positive approach. Includes book - Singles Ask - Answers to Questions about Relationships and Sexual Issues.
Guidance and Counseling; Sociology
Dist - GF

Sexually transmitted disease
U-matic / VHS
Color
Reviews the diverse clinical and laboratory manifestations of four common sexually transmitted diseases, syphilis, gonorrhea, chlamydial and herpes infections. Discusses the need for a careful sexual history with sensitive awareness of differing life styles.
Health and Safety
Dist - AMEDA **Prod** - AMEDA

Sexually transmitted diseases
VHS
Knowing sexual facts series
Color (I J)
$89.00 purchase _ #MC317
Discusses sexually transmitted diseases - STDs. Describes some common symptoms. Gives specific information on six major STDs, with special information on AIDS. Answers student questions. Emphasizes that students of this age are not having sex so they can't get STDs.
Health and Safety
Dist - AAVIM **Prod** - AAVIM 1992

Sexually transmitted diseases
VHS
Color (I J H C G A PRO T)
$49.95 purchase _ #AH55028 ; $79.50 purchase _ #AH46336
Portrays numerous examples of the most common sexually transmitted diseases, including syphilis, gonorrhea, genital herpes and AIDS.
Health and Safety
Dist - HTHED **Prod** - HTHED

Sexually transmitted diseases 30 MIN
VHS
Teen health video series
Color (J H A T)
$39.95 purchase _ #LVPE6643V-P
Offers teenagers and health educators information about sexually transmitted diseases. Includes advice from experts and personal testimonies from teens themselves. Does not make judgements on moral issues, but does present options available. One of a series of twelve videos about teen health issues. Available individually or as a set.
Health and Safety; Sociology
Dist - CAMV

Sexually - transmitted diseases 19 MIN
VHS / 16mm
Color (PRO G)
$149.00, $249.00, purchase _ #AD - 1375
Focuses on chlamydia, herpes, and venereal warts as well as AIDS, strongly emphasizing prevention and early detection through new diagnostic tests. Explains the complications from infection, including infertility, tubal pregnancy, and infections in babies.
Health and Safety
Dist - FOTH **Prod** - FOTH 1990

Sexually transmitted diseases 13 MIN
VHS
Color (J H C G)
$250.00 purchase _ #OB - 103A
Provides an overview of the most frequently contracted sexually transmitted diseases - chlamydia, gonorrhea, syphillis, HPV, herpes and AIDS. Discusses who is most at risk, emphasizing that one out of ten teens is diagnosed with an STD. After explaining that STDs are often discovered on routine examinations when there are no actual symptoms, the tape reviews the symptoms that may be present in men and women. Treatments for curable STDs are reviewed. Abstinence is recommended as the best preventive technique but use of a condom with spermicide is recommended for people who decide they want to be sexually active. Shows female patients throughout but is appropriate for viewing by both sexes.
Health and Safety
Dist - MIFE **Prod** - MIFE

Sexually transmitted diseases 15 MIN
16mm / VHS / BETA / U-matic
Color; PAL (J H C G)
PdS125, PdS133 purchase
Examines STD's, formerly known as venereal diseases, the symptoms and how easily each can be cured if treated in the early stages of the disease.
Health and Safety
Dist - EDPAT **Prod** - TASCOR

Sexually transmitted diseases 30 MIN
U-matic / VHS
Here's to your health series
Color
Health and Safety
Dist - DELTAK **Prod** - PBS
KERA

Sexually transmitted diseases 15 MIN
VHS / 16mm
Color (J H C A PRO)
$250.00 purchase, $75.00 rental _ #8193
Overviews the most common sexually transmitted diseases, explains how they are contracted, describes common symptoms and emphasizes the importance of prompt medical attention. Strongly encourages sexual responsibility and sexual ethics.
Health and Safety
Dist - AIMS **Prod** - MIFE 1989

Sexually transmitted diseases
U-matic / VHS
Color (SPANISH)
Represents a broad overview of the numerous, different diseases that can be sexually transmitted. Describes both diseases and symptoms.
Health and Safety
Dist - MIFE **Prod** - MIFE

Sexually transmitted diseases - causes, prevention and cure 65 MIN
VHS / U-matic
Color (H C)
LC 81-707056
Discusses how and why sexually transmitted diseases have created such a complex set of social and medical problems. Describes the causes, transmissions, detection, prevention and cures of the most prevalent of these diseases - gonorrhea, herpes, genitalis and syphilis.
Health and Safety
Dist - GA **Prod** - GA 1982

Sexually transmitted diseases from a sexological viewpoint
U-matic / VHS
Continuing medical education - basic sexology series
Color (PRO)
Health and Safety; Psychology
Dist - MMRC **Prod** - TIASHS

Sexually transmitted diseases - overview
VHS / U-matic
Sexually transmitted diseases series
Color
Discusses incidence and pattern of sexually transmitted disease. Describes pelvic inflammatory disease, including infertility, tubal pregnancies and surgery.
Health and Safety
Dist - CONMED **Prod** - CONMED

Sexually Transmitted Diseases Series
Bacterial infections
Intervention - Interviewing and Patient Teaching
Sexually transmitted diseases - overview
Syndromes
Viral Infections
Dist - CONMED

Sexually transmitted diseases - STDs - the keys to prevention 35 MIN
VHS
Women's health series
Color (G)
$49.00 purchase _ #WHV3
Offers the most - up - to - date medical information on STDs, reviewed and approved by a national panel of health care professionals. Features medical correspondent Dr Holly Atkinson of NBC News Today. Part of an eight - part series.
Health and Safety
Dist - GPERFO **Prod** - AMEDCO

Sexually transmitted diseases - the hidden epidemic 30 MIN
U-matic / VHS
Contemporary health issues series; Lesson 23
Color (C A)
Discusses trends affecting major sexually transmitted diseases. Refutes numerous myths and misconceptions. Compares methods of prevention and treatment as to effectiveness and potential side effects.
Health and Safety
Dist - CDTEL **Prod** - SCCON

Sexually transmitted diseases - what you should know 26 MIN
35mm strip / VHS
Color (J H)
$169.00, $129.00 purchase _ #2245 - SK, #2244 - SK
Covers all sexually transmitted diseases, focusing on chlamydia. Discusses their symptoms, testing, and consequences if left untreated. Stresses abstinence as the only 100 percent effective protection against STDs.
Health and Safety
Dist - SUNCOM **Prod** - SUNCOM

The Seychelles 25 MIN
U-matic / VHS / 16mm
Untamed Frontier Series
Color; Mono (J H C A)
$400.00 film, $250.00 video, $50.00 rental
Reveals the abundance of marine life found in the waters near this granitic island group in the Indian Ocean.
Geography - World; Science - Natural
Dist - CTV **Prod** - CTV 1975

Seychelles and Maldives - the forgotten islands 25 MIN
VHS
Color (G)
$19.95 purchase _ #S01468
Visits the Seychelles and Maldives, two archipelagos located in the Indian Ocean. Reveals that both have a highly multicultural population.
Geography - World; History - World
Dist - UILL

Seyewailo - the flower world 51 MIN
U-matic / VHS
Words and place series
Color (YAQUI (ENGLISH SUBTITLES))
Yaqui with English subtitles. Shows a skit about coyotes who chase and capture a deer. Shows Yaqui deer songs as they are sung and danced at a fiesta.
Literature and Drama; Social Science
Dist - NORROS **Prod** - NORROS

Seymour's view 32 MIN
U-matic / VHS / BETA
Color; PAL (T PRO)
PdS50, PdS58 purchase
Looks at Seymour, a disembodied being in space whose job it is to monitor the development of the human species, to heighten the awareness of teachers and parents of the ways in which development occurs.
Psychology
Dist - EDPAT

SF to LA 3 MIN
16mm
Color (G)
$20.00 rental
Presents 2.5 minutes of film time - lapsed over a 12 hour period while driving down California's Route 1. May be projected backwards. By Richard Beveridge.
Fine Arts
Dist - CANCIN

SFX and the movies - 112 29 MIN
VHS
FROG series 1; Series 1; 112
Color (P I J)
$100.00 purchase
Offers the twelfth program by Friends of Research and Odd Gadgets. Lifts science off the textbook page into the real world to show how enjoyable and challenging science can be. In this episode, the Froggers make their own scary movie with special effects. Special focus on special effects studios, lighting techniques and makeup. Produced by Greg Rist.
Fine Arts; Science - Physical
Dist - BULFRG **Prod** - OWLTV 1993

SGHWR for Nuclear Power 20 MIN
16mm
Color
Describes, in animation, the design of a commercial Sghwr and the method of refuelling, which contributes to its very high availability for power generation.
Industrial and Technical Education; Science - Physical
Dist - UKAEA **Prod** - UKAEA 1968

The SGHWR System 25 MIN
16mm
Color (IND)
Shows the design, construction and operation of the Winfrith Prototype Reactor and the work of British scientists to develop the process.
Science - Physical
Dist - UKAEA **Prod** - UKAEA 1975

Sh - h - h - cancer 12 MIN
U-matic
Color
Explains the nature of cancer and the methods of treatment.
Health and Safety
Dist - UTEXSC **Prod** - UTEXSC

The Shaco - a Japanese president and his company 45 MIN
VHS
Anatomy of Japan - wellsprings of economic power series
Color (H C G)
$250.00 purchase
Asks why Japanese company presidents work so hard when their average earnings are comparatively low by world standards. Analyzes the power, the salary and the duties of Japanese company presidents to clarify the organization, labor relations, management systems and integrity of Japanese companies. Part of a 10 - part series on the current relations between Japan and the world.
Business and Economics; Civics and Political Systems; Geography - World
Dist - LANDMK **Prod** - LANDMK 1989

Shade 16 MIN
16mm
Color (G)
$30.00 rental
Looks at all the possibilities between camera - aperture and focus - and nature - sun and wind - and presents a poetic study on the undying presence of the natural world.
Fine Arts; Industrial and Technical Education
Dist - CANCIN **Prod** - GRENIV 1975

Shade Gardens 30 MIN
U-matic / VHS
Home Gardener with John Lenanton Series Lesson 23; Lesson 23
Color (C A)
Uses the Sherman Foundation Gardens of Corona Del Mar, California, to illustrate shade gardening. Describes planting and maintenance of shade - tolerant plants.
Agriculture
Dist - CDTEL **Prod** - COAST

A Shade of Difference 31 MIN
16mm / U-matic / VHS
Color (H C A)
LC FIA68-2883
Discusses important principles of traffic safety, stressing the extreme caution necessary at intersections. Illustrates that incorrect assumptions about traffic laws cause accidents.
Health and Safety
Dist - IFB **Prod** - BURROW 1967

Shades of Black 28 MIN
16mm / U-matic / VHS
Understanding Space and Time Series
Color
Explains how Einstein's general theory of relativity applies to the objects known as black holes.
Science - Physical
Dist - UCEMC **Prod** - BBCTV 1980

Shades of Black and White 5 MIN
U-matic / VHS / 16mm
This Matter of Motivation Series
Color (IND)
LC 73-702805
Deals with the problem of racial tension in business. Describes the dilemma of a white boss who chooses between two Black employees for a promotion. Discusses the problems of prejudice that arise when the personnel manager, also black, questions the promotion thinking it was done on grounds of prejudice.
Business and Economics; Psychology; Sociology
Dist - DARTNL **Prod** - CTRACT 1970

Shades of freedom 50 MIN
VHS
Redemption song series
Color; PAL (H C A)
PdS99 purchase
Examines prospects for the future in the Caribbean. Features interviews with native inhabitants who discuss the history of the islands. Seventh in a series of seven programs documenting the history of the Caribbean.
History - World; Sociology
Dist - BBCENE

Shades of gray
VHS
Color (A PRO IND)
$700.00 purchase, $150.00 rental
Takes an in - depth look at sexual harassment in the workplace.
Business and Economics; Guidance and Counseling; Psychology; Sociology
Dist - VLEARN

Shades of Gray 66 MIN
16mm
B&W
LC FIE52-65
Portrays through dramatized situations and case histories various mental disorders of soldiers during training and combat. Relates the early life of the soldier to circumstances precipitating his mental breakdown and demonstrates methods of psychotherapy.
Civics and Political Systems; Psychology
Dist - USNAC **Prod** - USA 1948

Shades of meaning 10 MIN
16mm
Color (G)
$25.00 rental
Meditates on music and meaning in cinema in an Andy Moore film.
Fine Arts; Religion and Philosophy
Dist - CANCIN

Shades of Puffing Billy 11 MIN
16mm
Color (P I)
Presents a lighthearted look at the Victorian Narrow Guage Railway which runs between Emerald and Belgrave in the Dandenong Mountains.
Social Science
Dist - AUIS **Prod** - ANAIB 1967

Shading, Strokes and Striping 29 MIN
Videoreel / VT2
Tin Lady Series
Color
Fine Arts
Dist - PBS **Prod** - NJPBA

Shadow 15 MIN
U-matic / VHS
Draw Man Series
Color (I J)
Deals with form shadows and cast shadows. Shows how shadows dramatize drawings and help give the illusion of depth.
Fine Arts
Dist - AITECH **Prod** - OCPS 1975

The Shadow 25 MIN
16mm
Screen Test Series
Color; Silent (J H C G T A)
Religion and Philosophy
Dist - WHLION **Prod** - WHLION

The Shadow 26 MIN
VHS
Color (J H C A)
$59.95 purchase _ #L11084
Tells the allegorical tale of the Philosopher searching for truth and reason and his lost Shadow, which returns to him in malevolent human form. Depicts a struggle between shadow and master and between the light and dark sides of human nature - where only one will triumph. Adapted from the Hans Christian Anderson story, The Shadow.
Literature and Drama
Dist - CF **Prod** - BERMAN 1990

The Shadow Catcher - Edward S Curtis and the North American Indian 88 MIN
U-matic / VHS / 16mm
Color (H C A)
LC 75-701528
Presents a critical account of the life of Edward S Curtis, a photographer and writer who worked among the Indians of the American Southwest for over 32 years.
Biography; Fine Arts; Social Science
Dist - PHENIX **Prod** - PHENIX 1975

Shadow children 30 MIN
16mm / VHS
Color (H G)
Exposes the plight of homeless children and teenagers through interviews with more than a dozen youngsters living on the streets of California's Bay Area. Records their stories of family rejection, struggle for food and shelter, police harassment and the dangers of drugs, prostitution and pregnancy. Observes that while some of them are runaways, 75 percent of the parents don't want their children back. Commentary by social workers and youth agency officials. Directed by Harry Mathias. Includes study guide. Also available in 30 - minute version in video.
Fine Arts; Sociology
Dist - CNEMAG

Shadow Dance 16 MIN
16mm
Color
LC 79-700531
Records the total eclipses of the Sun across southern Australia in 1976 and the ordinary and extraordinary events taking place during the eclipses.
Science - Physical
Dist - AUIS **Prod** - FLMAUS 1976

Shadow government - the secret war in Central America 29 MIN
U-matic / VHS
Color (C)
$375.00, $345.00 purchase _ #V517
Looks at the conflict in Nicaragua between the Sandinistas and the United States' backed Contras. Discusses a Central Intelligence Agency - CIA - plan to overthrow the Nicaraguan government which was not revealed to the American public, yet millions of US dollars went into the covert operations. Invites debate of the issue, using the Constitution of the United States as a guide.
Civics and Political Systems; Geography - World; Sociology
Dist - BARR **Prod** - CEPRO 1990

Shadow in the sun 90 MIN
16mm / U-matic / VHS
Elizabeth R series; No 3
Color
LC 79-707276
Dramatizes Queen Elizabeth I's flirtation with the Duke of Alencon, heir to the French throne, whom she refused to marry and placated with 60,000 pounds.
Biography; Civics and Political Systems; History - World
Dist - FI **Prod** - BBCTV 1976

The Shadow line 14 MIN
16mm
B&W (G)
$30.00 rental
Adapts a chapter from a novel by Polish science fiction writer, Stanislaw Lem, entitled Solaris.
Fine Arts; Literature and Drama
Dist - CANCIN **Prod** - MERRIT 1985

Shadow of addiction 25 MIN
VHS / U-matic
Color (J H G)
$250.00 purchase, $100.00 rental
Features Richard Farrell, a recovering heroin addict, who portrays the dark side of addiction. Visits a crack house, a medium security prison, death row where a man is facing the death penalty for a murder committed while in a state of alcoholic blackout.
Guidance and Counseling; Psychology; Sociology
Dist - BAXMED

Shadow of breast cancer 50 MIN
VHS
Horizon series
Color; PAL (C H A)
PdS99 purchase
Considers medical research into breast cancer. Notes that Britain has the world's highest mortality rate for breast cancer and asks what British medical science can do to improve survival rates.
Health and Safety; Sociology
Dist - BBCENE

Shadow of Doubt 53 MIN
16mm
Color
Discusses Kamp Westerbork, a round - up point for Holocaust victims. Directed by Rolf Orthel.
History - World
Dist - NYFLMS **Prod** - UNKNWN 1975

The Shadow of God on Earth 58 MIN
U-matic / VHS / 16mm
Crossroads of Civilization Series
Color (A)
Discusses the spread and influence of Islam, beginning with the prophet Muhammad.
History - World; Religion and Philosophy
Dist - CNEMAG **Prod** - CNEMAG 1978

A shadow of herself 30 MIN
VHS
Soapbox with Tom Cottle series
Color (G)
$59.95 purchase _ #SBOX - 509
Shows how the death of pop star Karen Carpenter made people aware of eating disorders. Features several young women who discuss their struggles with eating disorders and the inherent dangers involved. Hosted by psychologist Tom Cottle.
Health and Safety; Psychology; Sociology
Dist - PBS **Prod** - WGBYTV 1985

A Shadow of herself 30 MIN
VHS
Color (J H C G T A PRO)
$59.95 purchase _ #AH45290
Interviews teenage young women who have had problems with anorexia or bulimia. Emphasizes the problems and dangers that these conditions can create.
Guidance and Counseling; Health and Safety
Dist - HTHED **Prod** - PBS

Shadow of suicide 35 MIN
VHS
Open space series
Color; PAL (H C A)
PdS50 purchase
Explores the effects of suicide on those left behind by documenting the conversations of families as they attempt to cope with the loss of a loved one. Part of the Open Space series.
Sociology
Dist - BBCENE

The Shadow of the Eagle 226 MIN
BETA / VHS
Color
Offers 12 episodes of a serial starring John Wayne. Tells how stunt flyer Craig McCoy rescues a kidnapped carnival owner and reveals the identity of the evil Eagle.
Fine Arts
Dist - VIDIM **Prod** - UNKNWN 1932

Shadow of the Rising Sun - Pt 8 50 MIN
VHS
New Pacific Series, the
Color (S)
$79.00 purchase _ #833 - 9115
Explores the cultural, historical, economic and political facets of the Pacific Basin which supports a third of the world's population. No other region contains so great a diversity of race, language and culture. Part 8 of eight parts considers how the prosperity of Pacific Rim Nations is challenging American economic dominence.
Business and Economics; Geography - World; History - World
Dist - FI **Prod** - BBCTV 1987

The shadow of the west 50 MIN
VHS / U-matic
Arabs - a living history series
Color (G)
$495.00 purchase
Focuses on the plight of the Palestinians, and Western involvement in the area from the Crusades to the present.
Geography - World; History - World; Religion and Philosophy
Dist - LANDMK **Prod** - LANDMK 1986

The Shadow of Vesuvius 59 MIN
U-matic / VHS
Color (G)
Looks at the 'flaming mountain' as Mount Vesuvius is called. Shows scientists unraveling secrets of ruined Herculaneum, buried when Vesuvius erupted in A D 79.
Geography - World
Dist - NGS **Prod** - NGS

Shadow on the cross 52 MIN
VHS
Color (H C G)
$195.00 purchase
Examines a history of Christian anti - semitism and looks at the ambivalent role of the church during World War II and the Nazi era. Challenges the church to re - examine Christian - Jewish relationships and acknowledge responsibility for 2,000 years of anti - semitic teaching and preaching.
History - World; Religion and Philosophy; Sociology
Dist - LANDMK **Prod** - LANDMK 1990

The Shadow Project 14 MIN
U-matic / VHS
Color
Records the effort to paint shadows on New York City buildings similiar to those etched by the atomic blast at Hiroshima and the reactions of passers - by to the event and to the possibility of atomic conflict.
Sociology
Dist - GMPF **Prod** - GMPF

Shadow Sister 52 MIN
16mm
Color (J H C)
Reveals the life of Kath Walker, Australia's foremost Aboriginal poet, writer and civil rights campaigner.
Biography; History - World; Literature and Drama; Sociology
Dist - CINETF **Prod** - CINETF 1977

Shadow Space 6 MIN
16mm
Color; Silent (C)
$150.00
Experimental film by Barry Gerson.
Fine Arts
Dist - AFA **Prod** - AFA 1973

Shadowgraph 7 MIN
16mm
Color (G)
$15.00 rental
Explores the filmmaker's shadow which becomes an interplay between abstraction and the intrusion of physical reality. Presents a meditative composition. Original soundtrack. Produced by Jane Dobson.
Fine Arts
Dist - CANCIN

Shadowplay 52 MIN
16mm
Color
LC 78-701569
Tells how a young law school professor attempts to escape from professional pressure and loneliness through an organization that promotes suicide.
Fine Arts; Sociology
Dist - CMBLGS **Prod** - CMBLGS 1977

Shadowplay, Pt 1 26 MIN
16mm
Color
LC 78-701569
Tells how a young law school professor attempts to escape from professional pressure and loneliness through an organization that promotes suicide.
Sociology
Dist - CMBLGS **Prod** - CMBLGS 1977

Shadowplay, Pt 2 26 MIN
16mm
Color
LC 78-701569
Tells how a young law school professor attempts to escape from professional pressure and loneliness through an organization that promotes suicide.
Sociology
Dist - CMBLGS **Prod** - CMBLGS 1977

Shadows and light - Joaquin Rodrigo at 90 70 MIN
VHS
Color (G T)
$250.00 purchase, $85.00 rental
Portrays Joaquin Rodrigo, of Spain, the world - renowned composer of classical music. Looks at his life which, at the age of ninety, has been full of tragedy as well as joy, with a belief in demons that rivals his faith in God. Points out that his art has an outlook which is as sunny as the land from which it comes.
Fine Arts
Dist - BULFRG **Prod** - RHOMBS 1994

Shadows between friends 30 MIN
VHS / U-matic / BETA / 16mm
Color (I J H G)
$60.00, $50.00 purchase
Portrays a friendship between high school students of different backgrounds. Examines the relationship between Charlie and Luis which grows despite pervasive stereotypes about foreigners and Charlie's insensitivity. When Charlie is passed over for a coveted summer job and scholarship in favor of a minority student, he explodes in anger against foreigners and his friend Luis. Coproduced with Chapman College. Includes discussion guide.
Guidance and Counseling; Psychology; Sociology
Dist - ADL **Prod** - ADL

Shadows in the Sunbelt 20 MIN
VHS
Color (G)
$75.00 purchase
Considers the economic problems of the South. Shows how residents of communities in Arkansas, Mississippi, Kentucky and North and South Carolina with high illiteracy rates and low incomes rebuilt their economies and improved their quality of life.
Agriculture; Business and Economics; Geography - United States; Sociology
Dist - SCETV **Prod** - SCETV 1988

Shadows of forgotten ancestors
35mm
Films of Sergei Paradjanov series
Color (G) (RUSSIAN WITH ENGLISH SUBTITLES)
$250.00 rental
Adapts folklore from Ukraine. Directed by Sergei Paradjanov.
Fine Arts; Literature and Drama
Dist - KINOIC

Shadows of forgotten ancestors - Wild horses of fire 96 MIN
VHS
Color (G)
$29.95 _ #SHA060
Tells the tragic tale of two lovers separated by a family feud in the Soviet Union. Depicts a Carpathian legend in a production by Sergei Parajanov.
Fine Arts; Psychology; Religion and Philosophy; Sociology
Dist - HOMVIS **Prod** - JANUS 1964

Shadows of Sound 5 MIN
16mm
Color
Presents a veteran with a service - connected hearing defect who is tested and fitted with a hearing aid at a VA audiology clinic. Features the training given at the clinic so that the veteran can receive maximum benefits from his hearing aid.
Health and Safety; Science - Natural
Dist - USVA **Prod** - USVA 1962

Shadows of the Road 20 MIN
16mm
Color
LC 78-701570
Shows the importance of good land transportation and the role of Oklahoma's Department of Transportation in fulfilling this need.
Civics and Political Systems; Geography - United States; Social Science
Dist - TULSAS **Prod** - OKDT 1977

Shadows on Our Turning Earth 11 MIN
U-matic / VHS / 16mm
Color (P I J)
Two primary youngsters use simple demonstrations to study shadows. They mark the position of a shadow and photograph its change of position. Models of the earth are used to show how the movement of the earth produces day and night.
Science - Physical; Social Science
Dist - PHENIX **Prod** - FA 1962

Shadows on the Grass 30 MIN
VHS / U-matic
(G)
Instrumental performances by the Sheldon trio featuring piano, violin and cello. Filmed in scenic Nebraska locations. Includes excerpts from works by Aaron Copland Charles W. Cadman, and William Schuman.
Fine Arts
Dist - GPN **Prod** - NETV 1987

Shadows on the Grass 29 MIN
VHS / 16mm
Color (G)
$55.00 rental _ #SOTG - 000
Films a concert by the Sheldon Trio at several Nebraska locations, integrating music and the environment.
Fine Arts
Dist - PBS **Prod** - NETCHE

Shadows over the future 93 MIN
VHS / 16mm
Color (G)
$490.00 purchase, $100.00, $150.00 rental
Brings together three sides of a triangle - Israeli, Palestinian and German - in the story of Anath, as Israeli studying in Germany, and Fuad, a West Bank Palestinian who has settled in Munich. Features the producer, Wolfgang Bergmann, as the third character, who asks if he, as a German, can criticize Israel without being an anti - Semite.
Fine Arts; History - World; Psychology; Sociology
Dist - FIRS

Shaffle Bit Horsemanship 30 MIN
BETA / VHS
Western Training Series
Color
Demonstrates training involved in snaffle bit horsemanship.
Physical Education and Recreation
Dist - EQVDL **Prod** - EQVDL

Shaft Alignment - 1 60 MIN
VHS
Equipment Alignment and Testing Series
Color (PRO)
$600.00, $1500.00 purchase _ #GMSA1
Introduces principles and procedures of shaft alignment. Covers basic alignment theory, types of misalignment, how measured and corrected. Explains how to prepare for an alignment, the use of the rim and face method to measure, graph and correct vertical and horizontal misalignment. Part of a four - part series on equipment alignment and testing, part of a larger set on general and mechanical maintenance. Includes 10 textbooks and an instructor guide which provide four hours of instruction.
Education; Industrial and Technical Education; Psychology
Dist - NUSTC **Prod** - NUSTC

Shaft Alignment - 2 60 MIN
VHS
Equipment Alignment and Testing Series
Color (PRO)
$600.00, $1500.00 purchase _ #GMSA2
Explains what parallel and angular misalignments are and how misalignments in the vertical and horizontal planes are corrected. Demonstrates shaft alignment using the reverse dial, laser - optic and computer - assisted methods and aligning vertically mounted equipment by the rim and face method. Part of a four - part series on equipment alignment and testing, part of a larger set on general and mechanical maintenance. Includes 10 textbooks and an instructor guide which provide four hours of instruction.
Education; Industrial and Technical Education; Psychology
Dist - NUSTC **Prod** - NUSTC

Shaft Coupling Alignment 18 MIN
VHS
Power Transmission Series II - Selection, Application and 'Maintenance Series
Color (A)
$265.00 purchase, $50.00 rental _ #57985
Emphasizes the financial savings that can come from proper knowledge of and attention to shaft alignment. Warns that tables of tolerance are misleading, in that they give maximum figures. Explains angular and parallel misalignment. Lists methods for alignment in order of increasing reliability (straight edge and caliper, dial indicator, and computer, laser).
Industrial and Technical Education
Dist - UILL **Prod** - MAJEC 1986

Shaft Coupling Selection 16 MIN
VHS
Power Transmission Series II - Selection, Application and 'Maintenance Series
Color (A)
$265.00 purchase, $50.00 rental _ #57977
Defines situations requiring shaft coupling, lists types of coupling options which exist. Lists criteria for selection as being design characteristics, customer preference, availability, and economics. Elaborates on design characteristics, explaining the formula for the determination of design horsepower, and the use of manufacturers capacity chart tables. Specifies critical factors as being bore size, nature of shaft, key seating arrangement, type of fit, and maximum speed.
Industrial and Technical Education
Dist - UILL **Prod** - MAJEC 1986

Shaft Couplings 16 MIN
VHS
Power Transmission Series I - PT Products Series
Color (A)
$225.00 purchase, $50.00 rental _ #57971
Describes the function and rationale of shaft couplings. Distinguishes rigid from flexible, describing all metal (chain gear, grid, disc) and elastomeric (jaw, molded teeth, tire, bonded element).
Industrial and Technical Education
Dist - UILL **Prod** - MAJEC 1986

Shafting, Couplings and Joining Devices 18 MIN
U-matic / VHS / 16mm
Mechanical Power Transmission Series
Color (IND)
Portrays the development of couplings from the early designs. Demonstrates various joining devices in their different forms of rigid and flexible construction. Shows applications of these devices to illustrate how they handle shaft misalignment using various directional flexing characteristics.
Industrial and Technical Education
Dist - LUF **Prod** - LUF 1977

Shag 28 MIN
VHS
Color (G)
Documents the ever - popular dance, the Shag. Reveals that it originated in North and South Carolina, and was based on the Jitterbug, the Lindy, and the Big Apple dances. Shows that the Shag is done to 'beach music,' upbeat rhythm - and - blues music. Includes numerous examples of vintage film footage and interviews. Available only to public television stations.
Fine Arts
Dist - SCETV **Prod** - SCETV 1987

The Shaggy Dog 104 MIN
U-matic / VHS / 16mm
Color (I J H C)
Stars Fred Mac Murray, Jean Hagen and Tommy Kirk. Follows the comic and unusual adventures of a young man who, prompted by curiosity and the suggestion of a mysterious museum professor utters magical words, is transformed into a shaggy Bratislavian sheep dog.
Literature and Drama
Dist - FI **Prod** - DISNEY

Shah Jahan 30 MIN
VHS
Great Moghuls series
Color (H C G)
$195.00 purchase
Examines the enigma of Shah Jahan. Reveals that he murdered several relatives to secure the throne for himself, but that he was also the builder of the Taj Majal in memory of his beloved wife Mumutz who died giving birth to his 14th child. His reign marked the peak of Moghul architectural achievement. Part of a six - part series on the Moghul Empire.
Fine Arts; History - World
Dist - LANDMK **Prod** - LANDMK 1990

The Shah of Iran 12 MIN
VHS / U-matic
Color (H C A)
Offers a 1974 interview with the Shah of Iran, giving insight into the upheaval that later befell Iran.
Biography; History - World
Dist - JOU **Prod** - UPI

Shahira - nomads of the Sahara 52 MIN
VHS
Color (H C G)
$395.00 purchase, $65.00 rental
Documents the life of a young Muslim woman, trained as an anthropologist, who suffered hardship, professional censure and went against the wishes of her traditional family to live among the Bishari tribe which had lived in the Sahara Desert for 5,000 years but was unknown to Egyptian authorities. Shahira Fawzy discovered the Bishara after their grazing ground was submerged by the construction of the Aswan Dam, studied their customs, fought government bureaucracy on their behalf and helped them to develop skills such as irrigation, well digging and gardening. Produced by Filmcentre in association with Bishari Films.
History - World; Sociology
Dist - FLMLIB

Shake a Leg, Eat Eggs 1 MIN
VHS / U-matic
Color
Shows a nest of country - fresh eggs singing a television spot about their protein value.
Health and Safety; Home Economics
Dist - KIDSCO **Prod** - KIDSCO

Shake it Up - Gospel 15 MIN
U-matic / VHS
Strawberry Square II - Take Time Series
Color (P)
Fine Arts
Dist - AITECH **Prod** - NEITV 1984

Shake, rattle and roll - wheelchair dancing 15 MIN
VHS / U-matic
Color (G)
$195.00 purchase _ #C890 - VI - 042
Shows a group of five paraplegic and quadriplegic people who discuss their feelings about and experiences with wheelchair dancing.
Fine Arts; Health and Safety; Physical Education and Recreation
Dist - HSCIC

Shake the Habit - Learning to Live Without Salt 43 FRS
12 MIN
U-matic / VHS
Color (J H A)
Teaches people of all ages how to live without salt and high sodium foods and why they should. Identifies high sodium foods and suggests alternatives. Offers tips on how to prepare food without the use of salt.
Health and Safety; Psychology; Social Science
Dist - POAPLE **Prod** - POAPLE

Shakedown in Santa Fe 58 MIN
VHS
Frontline Series
Color; Captioned (G)
$300.00 purchase, $95.00 rental _ #FRON - 605K
Documents the 1980 riot at the New Mexico State Penitentiary, which was one of the bloodiest prison riots in American history. Suggests that reform efforts have largely failed to control crime within the prison.
History - United States; Sociology
Dist - PBS **Prod** - DOCCON 1988

Shakers
VHS
Frugal gourmet - taste of America series
Color (G)
$19.95 purchase _ #CCP825
Shows how to prepare American food in the style of the Shakers. Features Jeff Smith, the Frugal Gourmet. Part of a ten - part series on American cooking.
History - United States; Home Economics; Physical Education and Recreation; Religion and Philosophy
Dist - CADESF **Prod** - CADESF

The Shakers 30 MIN
16mm / U-matic
American Traditional Culture Series
Color (A)
Presents an overview of America's oldest and most successful experiment in communal living. Contains interviews and performances of Shaker songs and tales.
Religion and Philosophy; Social Science; Sociology
Dist - DAVT **Prod** - DAVT

The Shakers - Hands to Work, Hearts to God 58 MIN
U-matic / VHS / 16mm
Color (J A G)
Portrays the history and traditions of Shaker life. Features elderly Shakers who carry on the traditions of a religious devotion that at one time embraced many thousands of americans in numerous self supporting communities. Discusses Shaker craftsmanship and the Shaker belief in celibacy.
Fine Arts; Social Science; Sociology
Dist - DIRECT **Prod** - FLRNTN 1985

The Shakers in America 28 MIN
VHS
Color (J H C)
$50.00 purchase
Explores the heritage of the Shakers in America as founders of one of the many Utopian societies of the 18th century. Examines their contributions to American art, architecture, design, music, agricultural and industrial technology. Interviews surviving Shakers and incorporates Shaker songs and dance tunes in the soundtrack.
History - United States; Religion and Philosophy
Dist - APPLAS **Prod** - APPLAS

Shakespeare
CD-ROM
(G)
$49.00 purchase _ #1954p - m
Contains the complete unabridged text of the complete works of William Shakespeare. Provides quick access by word and phrase to his plays, poems and sonnets. For IBM PCs and compatibles, requires at least 640K RAM, DOS 3.1 or later, one floppy disk - hard disk recommended, one empty expansion slot, and an IBM compatible CD - ROM drive. For Macintosh Classic, Plus, SE and II computers, requires 1MB of RAM, one floppy disk, and an Apple compatible CD - ROM drive.
Literature and Drama
Dist - BEP

Shakespeare 12 MIN
U-matic / VHS / 16mm
Poetry for People who Hate Poetry with Roger Steffens Series
Color (J H C A)
$215 purchase - 16 mm, $79 purchase - video
Shows the universality and timelessness of Shakespeare's plots. Includes selected speeches from Julius Caesar.
Literature and Drama
Dist - CF

Shakespeare 21 MIN
VHS
Time quest historical interview series
Color (H G)
$195.00 purchase, $50.00 rental
Entertains with the adventures of a high school teacher and one of his students when they don Elizabethan garb and travel back in time to London 1609 to have lunch with William Shakespeare at the Mermaid Tavern. Features the premeire episode of the Time Quest Historical Interview series.
Literature and Drama
Dist - CNEMAG

Shakespeare 12 MIN
U-matic / VHS / 16mm
Poetry for people who hate poetry series
Color (J H C A)
$49.95 purchase _ #L10768; LC 80-700531
Features actor - poet Roger Steffens acting out certain characters from the play Julius Caesar in a contemporary style, offering an understanding of Shakespeare's plays as universal and timeless.
Literature and Drama
Dist - CF **Prod** - STESHE 1980

Shakespeare - a day at the Globe 38 MIN
VHS
Color (J H)
$99.00 purchase _ #06272 - 026
Traces the development of England's commercial and military power, and social and cultural life. Discusses early theaters and the operations of the Globe, including its architecture, stage design and galleries. Dramatic readings, authentic costumes and sound effects present Shakespearean drama as it may have looked to its original audiences. Includes teacher's guide and library kit.
Education; Fine Arts; Literature and Drama
Dist - GA

Shakespeare - a Mirror to Man 26 MIN
U-matic / 16mm / VHS
Color (J) (SPANISH)
LC 72-710043
Covers some of the highlights from Shakespeare's plays The Taming of the Shrew, Macbeth and Othello.
Fine Arts; History - World; Literature and Drama
Dist - LCOA **Prod** - SCNDRI 1971

Shakespeare and His Stage - Approaches to Hamlet 46 MIN
16mm / U-matic / VHS
Color (H C A)
LC 75-702527
Recreates the theatre of Shakespeare's day through the staging of scenes from Hamlet in an Elizabethan courtyard near Stratford, England. Contrasts styles of Shakespearean role playing with excerpts from performances by Laurence Olivier, John Gielgud, Nicol Williamson and John Barrymore. Includes views of landmarks in London, Stratford and Warwick which shaped Shakespeare's approach to theatrical practice.
Fine Arts; Literature and Drama
Dist - FOTH **Prod** - FOTH 1975

Shakespeare and His Theatre, Pt 1 26 MIN
U-matic / VHS / 16mm
Color (H C A)
Presents a tour of the geography and history of Shakespeare's world which creates a vivid picture of the life and times as well as the plays and theatres of the world's greatest dramatist.
Literature and Drama
Dist - MEDIAG **Prod** - THAMES 1977

Shakespeare and His Theatre, Pt 2 26 MIN
U-matic / VHS / 16mm
Color (H C A)
Presents a tour of the geography and history of Shakespeare's world which creates a vivid picture of the life and times as well as the plays and theatres of the world's greatest dramatist.
Literature and Drama
Dist - MEDIAG **Prod** - THAMES 1977

Shakespeare and Kronborg 10 MIN
16mm
B&W
Presents a series of pictures from Elsinore's famous Kronborg Castle. Shows the way Shakespeare probably would have seen the castle 300 years ago and includes scenes from Hamlet.
History - World; Literature and Drama
Dist - AUDPLN **Prod** - RDCG

Shakespeare and the Globe 31 MIN
U-matic / VHS
Color (C)
$249.00, $149.00 purchase _ #AD - 931
Retraces Shakespeare's life and work. Includes landmarks of Elizabethan London associated with his plays, depictions of the structure and operations of the Globe Theatre, historical sources of the plays in art and architecture and theatrical traditions that influenced the playwright.
Literature and Drama
Dist - FOTH **Prod** - FOTH

Shakespeare and the varieties of human experience
VHS / Cassette
Color (C A)
$149.95, $89.95 purchase _ #LI - B264
Presents eight lectures which portray and analyze the complex drama of William Shakespeare. Features Willard Professor of Drama and Oratory, Dr Peter Saccio of Dartmouth College, and Prof Dennis Huston of Rice University as lecturers.
Literature and Drama
Dist - TTCO **Prod** - TTCO

Shakespeare' country 29 MIN
U-matic / VHS / 16mm
Color (H C A)
Provides a foundation for the study of historical and environmental factors that may have influenced the early development of William Shakespeare. Explores the rural character and regal atmosphere of Elizabethan England.
Geography - World; Literature and Drama
Dist - EBEC **Prod** - VIDTRK 1983

Shakespeare explorations with Patrick Stewart series

As You like it - Rosalind and Celia	20 MIN
Hamlet - Claudius	25 MIN
Hamlet - Polonius	
The Merchant of Venice - Shylock	27 MIN

Dist - BARR

Shakespeare - from Page to Stage Series

As You Like It	30 MIN
Romeo and Juliet	30 MIN
The Taming of the Shrew	30 MIN
The Tempest	30 MIN
Twelfth Night	30 MIN

Dist - BCNFL

Shakespeare in conversation 24 MIN
U-matic / 16mm / VHS
Color (H C)
$495.00, $250.00 purchase _ #HP - 5795C
Portrays a conversation between playwright William Shakespeare and his friend, actor Richard Burbage. Discusses Shakespeare's life, contemporaries, achievements and literary influences. Focuses on Shakespeare's plays and their elements, with extensive quotations of significant passages.
Fine Arts; Literature and Drama
Dist - CORF **Prod** - BBCTV 1989

Shakespeare in Performance - the Globe - the World 58.18 MIN
VHS
Understanding Shakespeare Series
Color (J H C)
LC 88-700287
Provides students with an understanding of William Shakespeare and his works in relation to the world today.
Literature and Drama
Dist - SRA **Prod** - SRA 1986

Shakespeare in perspective 200 MIN
VHS
Color (H C G)
$395.00 purchase _ #PPR548775
Takes a unique and very subjective journey into eight plays by William Shakespeare. Features noted critics, journalists and broacasters who comment on Hamlet, Romeo and Juliet, Julius Caesar, Macbeth, King Lear, The Tempest, A Midsummer Night's Dream, and As You Like It. On two videocassettes.
Literature and Drama
Dist - INSTRU **Prod** - BBC 1984

Shakespeare in perspective series

Anna Raeburn on Anthony and Cleopatra	25 MIN
Anthony Clare on Titus Andronicus	25 MIN
David Hunt on Troilus and Cressida	25 MIN
David Jones on twelfth night	25 MIN
Dennis Potter on Cymbeline	25 MIN
Eleanor Bron on Much Ado about Nothing	25 MIN
Emma Tennant on Love's Labour Lost	25 MIN
George Melly on Henry IV - Pt 1	25 MIN
Jilly Cooper on The Merry Wives of Windsor	25 MIN
John Cleese on The Taming of the Shrew	25 MIN
Michael Wood on Henry VI - Pt 1	25 MIN
Michael Wood on Henry VI - Pt 2	25 MIN
Michael Wood on Henry VI - Pt 3	25 MIN
Peter Parker on Life and Death of King John	25 MIN
Rosemary Ann Sisson on Richard III	25 MIN
Susan Hill on Othello	25 MIN
Wolf Mankowitz on Merchant of Venice	25 MIN

Dist - BBCENE

Shakespeare in Perspective Series

As You Like It	30 MIN
Hamlet	30 MIN
Julius Caesar	30 MIN
King Lear	30 MIN
Macbeth	30 MIN
A Midsummer Night's Dream	30 MIN
Romeo and Juliet	30 MIN
Shakespeare in Perspective - Vol I	50 MIN
Shakespeare in Perspective - Vol II	50 MIN
Shakespeare in Perspective - Vol III	50 MIN
Shakespeare in Perspective - Vol IV	50 MIN
The Tempest	30 MIN

Dist - FI

Shakespeare in Perspective - Vol I 50 MIN
VHS
Shakespeare in Perspective Series
Color (S)
$99.00 purchase _ #548 - 9776
Takes a brisk, enthusiastic guided tour of eight of William Shakespeare's greatest works. Features noted critics, journalists and broadcasters who subjectively explore the time and mind of Shakespeare. Divides the series into four volumes, each containing two plays. Volume I offers 'Hamlet' and writer - broadcaster Clive James who argues that Shakespeare identified with the hero of his most celebrated tragedy. 'Romeo And Juliet' is discussed by author, lecturer and social commentator Dr Germaine Greer within the context of frustrated young love.
Fine Arts; Geography - World; Literature and Drama
Dist - FI **Prod** - BBCTV 1984

Shakespeare in Perspective - Vol II 50 MIN
VHS
Shakespeare in Perspective Series
Color (S)
$99.00 purchase _ #548 - 9778
Takes a brisk, enthusiastic guided tour of eight of William Shakespeare's greatest works. Features noted critics, journalists and broadcasters who subjectively explore the time and mind of Shakespeare. Divides the series into four volumes, each containing two plays. Volume II offers 'King Lear' and Cambridge professor Frank Kermode who treats the play as a fairy - tale plot of a king dividing his land between his wicked daughters becoming a horror story of cruelty and protracted suffering. 'The Tempest' is discussed by writer and traveler Laurens van der Post as an allegory of the achievement of the creative spirit.
Fine Arts; Geography - World; Literature and Drama
Dist - FI **Prod** - BBCTV 1984

Shakespeare in Perspective - Vol III 50 MIN
VHS
Shakespeare in Perspective Series
Color (S)
$99.00 purchase _ #548 - 9779
Takes a brisk, enthusiastic guided tour of eight of William Shakespeare's greatest works. Features noted critics, journalists and broadcasters who subjectively explore the time and mind of Shakespeare. Divides the series into four volumes, each containing two plays. Volume III offers 'A Midsummer's Night Dream' and noted historian Sir Roy Strong who views the play as an entertainment for all tastes - a combination of romance, comedy, broad farce and magic. 'As You Like It' is seen by writer Brigid Brophy as a social comedy about adultery, foolishness and lust. It also indicts humans as usurpers and destroyers of the natural order.
Fine Arts; Geography - World; Literature and Drama; Sociology
Dist - FI **Prod** - BBCTV 1984

Shakespeare in Perspective - Vol IV 50 MIN
VHS
Shakespeare in Perspective Series
Color (S)
$99.00 purchase _ #548 - 9777
Takes a brisk, enthusiastic guided tour of eight of William Shakespeare's greatest works. Features noted critics, journalists and broadcasters who subjectively explore the time and mind of Shakespeare. Divides the series into four volumes, each containing two plays. Volume IV

Presents 'Julius Caesar' and author - TV journalist Jonathan Dimbleby who explains his view of Shakespeare's class examination of the meaning of power. 'Macbeth' is teamed with crime - story writer Julian Symons who gives a new twist to traditional views of the tragedy of an upright man goaded by his ambition, and the mental torment resulting from his crime.
Fine Arts; Geography - World; Literature and Drama
Dist - FI **Prod** - BBCTV 1984

Shakespeare in rehearsal series
Julius Caesar 23 MIN
Romeo and Juliet 25 MIN
The Tempest 25 MIN
The Tragedy of Hamlet - Prince of Denmark 22 MIN
The Tragedy of Macbeth 20 MIN
Dist - CORF

Shakespeare is alive and well in the modern world 47 MIN
VHS
Color (G C H)
$219.00 purchase _ #DL370
Shows that many of the themes in Shakespeare's works - alienation, revenge, ambition, rebellion, and love - parallel the themes of modern literature. Features Here Conrad Geller who uses modern works to help students penetrate the difficult Elizabethan vocabulary. Uses excerpts from some of Shakespeare's works as well as from modern works such as The Outsiders, Lord of the Flies and Animal Farm.
Fine Arts; Literature and Drama
Dist - INSIM

Shakespeare is Alive and Well in the Modern World 38 MIN
U-matic / VHS
Color (J H C)
$219.00 purchase _ #00271 - 161
Presents contemporary versions of Shakespearean dramas that enable students to penetrate complex Elizabethan vocabulary and experience insights into characters' feelings, motives and actions.
Literature and Drama
Dist - GA **Prod** - GA

The Shakespeare mystery 60 MIN
VHS
Frontline series
Color (G)
$59.95 purchase _ #FRON - 710K
Considers the question of whether William Shakespeare was the true author of the poems and plays attributed to him. Reveals that many scholars believe that Edward de Vere, the 17th Earl of Oxford, may have been the real author.
History - World; Literature and Drama
Dist - PBS **Prod** - DOCCON 1989

The Shakespeare mystery 52 MIN
VHS
First Tuesday series
Color; PAL (H C G)
PdS30 purchase
Focuses on the myteries of playwright William Shakespeare. Reveals that he lived in an obscure town in the center of England, had little or no education, died more than 400 years ago and is, today, the most famous writer in the world. Asks if the Bard of Stratford really did write some of the greatest works in literary history. Contact distributor about availability outside the United Kingdom.
History - World; Literature and Drama
Dist - ACADEM **Prod** - YORKTV

Shakespeare of Stratford and London 32 MIN
U-matic / VHS / 16mm
World of William Shakespeare Series
Color (H C A)
LC 78-700746
Traces the life of William Shakespeare, visiting Stratford, the Warwickshire countryside and 16th century London.
Biography; History - World; Literature and Drama
Dist - NGS **Prod** - NGS 1978

Shakespeare Plays Series
Coriolanus 145 MIN
Cymbeline 174 MIN
Dist - INSIM
TIMLIF

Shakespeare Plays Series
All's well that ends well 141 MIN
As You Like It 150 MIN
The Comedy of errors 109 MIN
Hamlet 222 MIN
Henry IV, Part I 147 MIN
Henry IV, Part II 151 MIN
Henry V 163 MIN
Henry VI - Pt I 185 MIN
Henry VI - Pt II 212 MIN
Henry VI - Pt III 210 MIN
Henry VIII 165 MIN
Julius Caesar 161 MIN
King John 120 MIN
King Lear 186 MIN
Love's Labour's Lost 120 MIN
Macbeth 148 MIN
Measure for Measure 145 MIN
The Merchant of Venice 157 MIN
The Merry Wives of Windsor 167 MIN
A Midsummer Night's Dream 110 MIN
Much Ado about Nothing 120 MIN
Othello 202 MIN
Pericles 177 MIN
Richard II 157 MIN
Richard III 120 MIN
Romeo and Juliet 165 MIN
The Taming of the Shrew 127 MIN
The Tempest 150 MIN
Timon of Athens 128 MIN
Titus Andronicus 120 MIN
Twelfth Night 124 MIN
The Winter's Tale 173 MIN
Dist - TIMLIF

Shakespeare - Selection for Children 6 MIN
16mm
Color (P I J)
LC FIA65-1119
Maurice Evans reads the 'ALL THE WORLD'S A STAGE' pasage from the Shakespearean comedy 'AS YOU LIKE IT' and two songs from 'LOVE'S LABOUR LOST.' Uses animation to illustrate the selections.
Literature and Drama
Dist - SF **Prod** - FINA 1965

Shakespeare series
Life and Death of King John 155 MIN
Much ado about nothing 150 MIN
Pericles 275 MIN
Titus Andronicus 167 MIN
Dist - BBCENE

Shakespeare Series
Macbeth
Richard III
Dist - CHUMAN

Shakespeare Series
Julius Caesar
Dist - CHUMAN
GA
UILL

Shakespeare Series
Understanding Shakespeare - His Sources 19 MIN
Understanding Shakespeare - His Stagecraft 25 MIN
William Shakespeare - Background for His Works 14 MIN
Dist - CORF

Shakespeare Series
William Shakespeare - Background for His Works 18 MIN
Dist - CORF
VIEWTH

Shakespeare Series
Orientation to Course - Misconceptions about Shakespeare - Elizabethan Life, no 1 45 MIN
Troilus and Cressida - Shakespeare's most 'Modern' Play - Tragi - Comedy of Disillusionment 45 MIN
Dist - GPN

Shakespeare Series
Antony and Cleopatra 11 MIN
Hamlet 10 MIN
Henry IV - Pt 2 6 MIN
Julius Caesar 14 MIN
Macbeth 11 MIN
Much Ado about Nothing 12 MIN
Othello 10 MIN
Richard II 12 MIN
Richard III 12 MIN
Romeo and Juliet 8 MIN
The Taming of the Shrew 13 MIN
The Tempest 14 MIN
Dist - IFB

Shakespeare series
As You Like It - an introduction 24 MIN
Julius Caesar - an Introduction 28 MIN
King Lear - an Introduction 28 MIN
Macbeth - an Introduction 26 MIN
A Midsummer Night's Dream - an Introduction 26 MIN
Twelfth Night - an Introduction 23 MIN
Dist - PHENIX

Shakespeare - Soul of an Age 54 MIN
U-matic / VHS / 16mm
Color (J)
Uses authentic maps and scenes of English towns and cities to point out landmarks in Shakespeare's life. Features Sir Michael Redgrave, who recites illustrative passages from key speeches in shakespeare's chronicles, comedies and tragedies.
Biography; Literature and Drama
Dist - MGHT **Prod** - NBCTV 1963

Shakespeare - Soul of an Age, Pt 1 27 MIN
U-matic / VHS / 16mm
Color (J H C)
Uses authentic maps and scenes of English towns and cities to point out landmarks in Shakespeare's life. Sir Michael Redgrave recites illustrative passages from key speeches in Shakespeare's chronicles, comedies and tragedies.
Literature and Drama
Dist - MGHT **Prod** - NBCTV 1963

Shakespeare - Soul of an Age, Pt 2 27 MIN
16mm / U-matic / VHS
Color (J H C)
Uses authentic maps and scenes of English towns and cities to point out landmarks in Shakespeare's life. Sir Michael Redgrave recites illustrative passages from key speeches in Shakespeare's chronicles, comedies and tragedies.
Literature and Drama
Dist - MGHT **Prod** - NBCTV 1963

Shakespeare - the man and his times 47 MIN
VHS
B&W (G C H)
$139.00 purchase _ #DL380
Uses footage of significant places in Shakespeare's life as well as archival illustrations, quotations from his plays, and comments from historians to examine the cultural, literary, and political context of Elizabethan England and other influences on Shakespeare.
Fine Arts; History - World; Literature and Drama
Dist - INSIM

Shakespeare - the soul of an age 51 MIN
VHS
Color (G)
$29.95 purchase _ #S00545
Visits the historical sites of Shakespeare's greatest plays. Features Sir Michael Redgrave and Sir Ralph Richardson in a tour of sites in England, Scotland, Wales and France.
History - World; Literature and Drama
Dist - UILL

Shakespeare workshop series
The Comic spirit - Shakespeare workshop 2 60 MIN
The Roman tragedies - Shakespeare workshop 3 60 MIN
The Tortured mind - Shakespeare workshop 1 60 MIN
Dist - EMFVL

Shakespearean drama series
King Lear 182 MIN
The Merry wives of Windsor 140 MIN
Romeo and Juliet 165 MIN
The Taming of the shrew 115 MIN
Dist - SVIP

Shakespearean stage production 28 MIN
VHS
Color (G C H)
$119.00 purchase _ #DL436
Reviews the steps necessary to bring a play to the stage in Shakespeare's day, demonstrating how productions were rehearsed and costumed. Examines the architecture and layout of the theater, the acting company, and how sound effects were created.
Fine Arts; Literature and Drama
Dist - INSIM

Shakespearean Tragedy 40 MIN
U-matic / VHS
Color
Explores the nature of tragedy and the Shakespearean tragic hero. Discusses Shakespearean concepts of action, character and catharsis.
Literature and Drama
Dist - FOTH **Prod** - FOTH 1984

Shakespeare's Heritage 29 MIN
U-matic / VHS / 16mm
Color (H C A)
Describes the history of Strafford - Upon - Avon, the resources and facilities available to students and visitors at the Shakespeare Centre, and the role of the Shakespeare Birthplace Trust in preserving and maintaining Shakespeare properties and other Shakespeariana.
Geography - World; History - World; Literature and Drama
Dist - EBEC **Prod** - VIDTRK 1983

Shakespeare's Macbeth 60 MIN
VHS / U-matic
Drama - play, performance, perception series; Module 3
Color (C)
Fine Arts; Literature and Drama
Dist - MDCC **Prod** - MDCC

Shakespeare's plays series
Troilus and Cressida 190 MIN
Dist - AMBROS
INSIM
TIMLIF

Shakespeare's Sonnets 150 MIN
U-matic / VHS
Color
Analyzes 15 of William Shakespeare's sonnets, some of which are dedicated to famous people and events.
Literature and Drama
Dist - FOTH **Prod** - FOTH 1984

Shakespeare's Theater 13 MIN
16mm
Color (H C)
An excerpt from the 1946 feature film 'HENRY V.' Dramatizes, against a background of Elizabethan music, activities in Shakespeare's theater centered about a presentation of 'HENRY V.'.
Literature and Drama
Dist - IU **Prod** - RANK 1960

Shakespeare's Theatres 145 MIN
U-matic
University of the Air Series
Color (J H C A)
$750.00 purchase, $250.00 rental
Considers the development and control of the theatre in Elizabethan London and the locations, reputations and innovations of the famous theatres of Shakespeare's time. Program contains a series of five cassettes 29 minutes each.
Fine Arts
Dist - CTV **Prod** - CTV 1978

Shakespeare's tragedies - a video commentary 25 MIN
VHS
Color (H C)
$89.00 purchase _ #05530 - 126
Explores the characters, stories and central themes of Shakespearean tragedy.
Literature and Drama
Dist - GA **Prod** - GA

The Shakiest Gun in the West 101 MIN
16mm
Color
Stars Don Knotts as a frontier dentist who gets involved with Indians, gun runners and a beautiful redhead.
Fine Arts
Dist - SWANK **Prod** - UPCI

Shall these Bones Live 30 MIN
16mm
B&W (HEBREW)
Theodore Bikel presents dramatic readings with music to illustrate the living quality of the Hebrew language. (Kinescope).
Religion and Philosophy
Dist - NAAJS **Prod** - JTS 1958

Shallow Water Waves
16mm
B&W
Explains how to analyze shallow water waves mathematically.
Mathematics
Dist - OPENU **Prod** - OPENU

Shalom Aleichem 15 MIN
U-matic / VHS
Other families, other friends series; Red module; Israel
Color (P)
Picture a Roman fortress, a Bedouin family, the Dead Sea and a modern kibbutz in Israel.
Geography - World; Social Science
Dist - AITECH **Prod** - WVIZTV 1971

Shalom of Safed 30 MIN
VHS
Color (G)
$29.95 purchase _ #709
Tells of Shalom of Safed who was a humble watchmaker living in Safed, in the Galilee. Reveals that at the age of 58, he began to paint and was almost immediately acclaimed as a great and unique folk - artist. Presents the artist at work. Explores the scope and detail of his paintings as well as the spiritual and physical sources of his inspiration.
Fine Arts; Sociology
Dist - ERGOM

Shalom Sesame - Chanukah 30 MIN
VHS
Color (K P)
$16.95 purchase _ #20362
Journeys with Jeremy Miller to ancient Modin, home of the Maccabees. Plays 'Draydel of Fortune' with Lavana White.
History - World; Religion and Philosophy
Dist - HAMAKO

Shalom Sesame series
Chanukah 30 MIN
Jerusalem 30 MIN
Journey to secret places 30 MIN
Kibbutz 30 MIN
The Land of Israel 30 MIN
The People of Israel 30 MIN
Sing around the seasons 30 MIN
Tel - Aviv 30 MIN
Dist - ERGOM

Shalom Sesame - Sesame Street visits Israel series 330 MIN
VHS
Shalom Sesame - Sesame Street visits Israel series
Color (K P)
$99.95 purchase _ #21576
Presents 11 Sesame Street shows which present the culture, history, values and traditions of the Jewish people and Israel. Features famous Israeli entertainers and Sesame Street characters.
Geography - World; History - World; Religion and Philosophy; Sociology
Dist - HAMAKO

Shalom Sesame - Sesame Street visits Israel series
Shalom Sesame - Sesame Street visits Israel series 330 MIN
Dist - HAMAKO

Shaman 12 MIN
16mm
Color
LC 76-703082
Depicts a glacial lake and the sound of a man's scream. Tells how a silver shaman appears as the scream reaches a crescendo to return the land to its magic silence.
Social Science
Dist - CANFDC **Prod** - CANFDC 1975

Shaman chanted evening 27 MIN
VHS
Color (G)
$30.00 purchase
Features a wacky and tragic psychodramatic teleplay in which the producer, Karen Redgreene, vies with interpersonal and career issues upon the ground of a fractured psyche. Portrays six characters, all played by the producer, each following a contorted path towards a personal nirvana that results in a clash between the hyper - real and hyper - artificial. These extreme and desperate figures ultimately prove that standing up to one's anima - animus can be fun.
Fine Arts; Literature and Drama; Psychology
Dist - CANCIN

Shaman psalm 7 MIN
16mm
B&W (A)
$15.00 rental
Presents a James Brough and Joel Singer production focusing on the love shaman poetry of Brough.
Fine Arts; Literature and Drama
Dist - CANCIN

Shame and addiction 28 MIN
VHS
Color (J H G)
$395.00 purchase
Features counselor and author John Bradshaw who verifies the role of 'shame' in the addictive person. Provides the shame - based individual with guidelines for recovery. Reveals that once shame is identified and addressed, the transfer from either alcohol or drug dependency to other addictions such as sex, food and gambling can be avoided.
Guidance and Counseling; Health and Safety; Psychology
Dist - FMSP **Prod** - FMSP

Shame and Guilt 28 MIN
VHS / 16mm
Color (G)
$165.00 purchase, $40.00 rental _ #5814H, 5829H, 0477J, 0472J
Builds on the theme that a life of sobriety is contingent upon change and growth from self - defeating behavior to mature behavior. Suggests consideration of the disease concept of alcoholism, and the concepts of powerlessness, reponsibility and accountability. Features Dr. Damian McElrath.
Guidance and Counseling; Health and Safety; Psychology; Sociology
Dist - HAZELB **Prod** - HAZELB

The Shame of American Education 24 MIN
16mm
Color (A)
Presents the essence of B F Skinner's faith in technology and outlines what needs to change in education.
Education
Dist - AACD **Prod** - AACD 1984

Shame, Shame on the Bixby Boys 90 MIN
VHS / U-matic
Color (H C A)
Tells of the hilarious adventures of deputy Mordecai Murphy in the Old West as he tries to cope with the rustling Bixby Boys, the clients of a dentist who keeps taking out the wrong teeth and an aggressive young woman who has selected Mordecai as her one and only. Stars Monte Markham and Sammy Jackson.
Fine Arts
Dist - TIMLIF **Prod** - TIMLIF 1982

Shampoo 5 MIN
U-matic / VHS / 16mm
How It's made Series
Color (K)
Business and Economics
Dist - LUF **Prod** - HOLIA

Shampoo 112 MIN
16mm
Color
Portrays a Beverly Hills hairdresser who tries to juggle four love affairs at the same time. Stars Warren Beatty, Julie Christie, Goldie Hawn, Lee Grant and Carrie Fisher.
Fine Arts
Dist - TWYMAN **Prod** - CPC 1975

The Shamrock and the Rose 68 MIN
Videoreel / VT2
Toys that Grew Up II Series
Color
Fine Arts
Dist - PBS **Prod** - WTTWTV

Shamus 98 MIN
16mm
Color
Stars Burt Reynolds as a private eye.
Fine Arts
Dist - TWYMAN **Prod** - CPC 1972

Shane 60 MIN
VHS
Color
$69.95 purchase
Represents the archetypal American hero who fights for the homesteaders' right to fence the range and bring law to the prairie.
Literature and Drama
Dist - AIMS **Prod** - AIMS

Shane 60 MIN
VHS
Color (G)
$19.95 purchase _ #S00280
Presents a film version of the Jack Schaefer novel Shane, an archetypal tale of the Old West hero. Stars Alan Ladd, Jean Arthur, Van Heflin and others. Directed and produced by George Stevens.
Literature and Drama
Dist - UILL

Shane 117 MIN
16mm / U-matic / VHS
Color (I)
Tells of a reticent drifter and retired gunfighter who takes up the cause of a homesteader family terrorized by an aging cattleman and his hired gun. Directed by George Stevens.
Fine Arts
Dist - FI **Prod** - UNKNWN 1953

Shane 60 MIN
U-matic / VHS / 16mm
Color (J)
An edited version of the feature film Shane. Relates the mythic story of a legendary gunfighter's final battle. Stars Alan Ladd, Jean Arthur and Van Heflin.
Fine Arts
Dist - AIMS **Prod** - PAR 1980

Shanghai Duck 29 MIN
Videoreel / VT2
Joyce Chen Cooks Series
Color
Features Joyce Chen showing how to adapt Chinese recipes so they can be prepared in the American kitchen and still retain the authentic flavor. Demonstrates how to prepare Shanghai duck.
Geography - World; Home Economics
Dist - PBS **Prod** - WGBHTV

Shanghai - the New China 33 MIN
U-matic / VHS / 16mm
Color (J H C)
LC 74-703780
Pictures Shanghai, the largest city in Red China. Captures traditional ways of life coexisting with efforts to modernize the city.
Geography - World; Social Science; Sociology
Dist - PHENIX **Prod** - CBSTV 1974

Shanghaied 25 MIN
U-matic / VHS / 16mm
Charlie Chaplin Comedy Theater Series
B&W (I)
Features Charlie Chaplin, who is hired to shanghai a crew, but becomes shanghaied himself. Shows how he becomes a sorry cook aboard a perpetually rocking boat.
Fine Arts
Dist - FI **Prod** - MUFLM 1915

Shangshung - the artistic treasures of Tsaparang and Tholing 60 MIN
VHS / BETA
Color; PAL (G)
PdS25 purchase
Explores the ruins of two ancient cities in the upper Sutlej Valley in Tibet. Looks at early Mahayana Buddhist art and frecoes, dating between the 10th and 17th centuries, remarkable for their brilliance of color, line and form. Includes images of the Buddhas; male and female Bodhisattvas; the sublime tantric heroes and consorts. These two cities are in the province of Shangshung - as Tibet was known before the advent of Buddhism - and were abandoned in the 1960s. Only a few Westerners have visited these sites, full of temples that miraculously survived the Cultural Revolution, and only one team has thoroughly documented their art treasures on film and video offered here. Directed and photographed by Brian Beresford. Produced by Sean Jones.
Fine Arts; History - World; Religion and Philosophy
Dist - MERIDT

Shannon - Portrait of a River 27 MIN
16mm
Color
Traces the course of the Shannon River in Ireland from source to estuary, including life along the river, monuments and ruins along its banks and the large industrial complex at Shannon.
Business and Economics; Fine Arts; Geography - World
Dist - CONSUI **Prod** - CONSUI

Shantiniketan 12 MIN
16mm
B&W (I)
Presents Shantiniketan, the abode of peace founded as a school of international culture by the Nobel laureate, Rabindranath Tagore. Shows it today as VishWabharati University, where students live in communion with nature.
History - World
Dist - NEDINF **Prod** - INDIA

The Shanwar Telis - or, Bene Israel 40 MIN
16mm
About the Jews of India Series
Color
LC 79-701241
Deals with the customs, ceremonies, rituals and education of the Shanwar Telis, descendants of Jews shipwrecked on the Konkan Coast of India 2,000 years ago.
Geography - World; History - World; Religion and Philosophy
Dist - NJWB **Prod** - SPECJO 1979

Shao Ping the Acrobat 25 MIN
U-matic / VHS / 16mm
World Cultures and Youth Series
Color (J)
$520.00, 250.00 purchase _ #4264
Introduces a Chinese boy named Shao Ping who is working hard to become an acrobat.
Geography - World; Sociology
Dist - CORF **Prod** - SUNRIS 1981

Shaolin Chin Na 70 MIN
VHS
Color (G)
$50.00 purchase _ #1157
Contains over 80 grabbing chin na techniques, many applicable to T'ai chi. Uses closeups, slow motion, and fast motion. Demonstrates chin na for fingers, wrist, elbow, shoulder, waist, and neck. Includes practical examples for self - defense. Intended for beginners but also for experts in other martial arts. Features Dr Yang Jwing - Ming.
Physical Education and Recreation
Dist - WAYF

Shape 10 MIN
U-matic / VHS / 16mm
Art of Seeing Series
Color (I)
LC 75-702565
Explores shapes in nature and in art. Discusses how they function and how people perceive and interpret them.
Fine Arts
Dist - FI **Prod** - AFA 1968

The Shape and Color Game 8 MIN
16mm
Color (K P)
LC FIA68-1644
Shows how concepts of color, form, texture and structure of the physical world are learned by children playing with abstract toys.
Education; Fine Arts; Physical Education and Recreation; Psychology
Dist - SF **Prod** - KORTY 1967

Shape and Competence of Ureteral Orifices 17 MIN
16mm
Color
LC 75-701734
Shows that the causes of ureteral reflux have a direct relation to the shape and position of ureteral orifices rather than ureter length. Categorizes and correlates the shapes and positions to degrees of orifice competence for use in urological examination.
Science - Natural
Dist - EATONL **Prod** - EATONL 1968

Shape and Form 15 MIN
VHS / U-matic
Arts Express Series
Color (K P I J)
Fine Arts
Dist - KYTV **Prod** - KYTV 1983

Shape, color, size
VHS
Lola May's fundamental math series
Color (K)
$45.00 purchase _ #10252VG
Provides exercises to teach the identification of circles, squares and triangles. Uses those figures to teach the interchange and differentiation of properties of size and color. Comes with a teacher's guide and blackline masters. Part two of 30 - part series.
Mathematics; Science - Physical
Dist - UNL

Shape descriptions
VHS
Drafting I series
(H C)
$59.00 _ CA136
Gives means of describing the shape of any object.
Education; Industrial and Technical Education
Dist - AAVIM **Prod** - AAVIM 1989

Shape from shading 45 MIN
U-matic / VHS
Artificial intelligence series; Computer vision, Pt 3
Color (PRO)
Features determining surface orientation from a single image, solving the image irradiance equation by integration along characteristic curves, and exploiting smoothness using pseudolocal, iterative computation.
Psychology
Dist - MIOT **Prod** - MIOT

Shape hunting - circles, semicircles, ellipses 7 MIN
VHS
Shape hunting series
Color; PAL (P)
Introduces primary children to basic math concepts and hands - on art activities. Identifies plane figures derived from curves rather than lines - circles, semicircles, ellipses. Part of a series on shapes.
Fine Arts; Mathematics
Dist - VIEWTH **Prod** - VIEWTH

Shape Hunting - Circles, Semicircles, Ellipses 7 MIN
16mm / U-matic / VHS
Shape Hunting Series
Color (I)
Discusses plane figures created from curves rather than line segments, such as circles, semicircles and ellipses. Introduces the concept of diameter, radius, circumference, concentric, arc and segment.
Mathematics
Dist - CORF **Prod** - CORF 1980

Shape hunting - circles, triangles, rectangles, squares 7 MIN
VHS
Shape hunting series
Color; PAL (P)
Introduces primary children to basic math concepts and hands - on art activities. Identifies circles, triangles, rectangles and squares. Part of a series on shapes.
Fine Arts; Mathematics
Dist - VIEWTH **Prod** - VIEWTH

Shape hunting - cylinders, prisms, pyramids 8 MIN
VHS
Shape hunting series
Color; PAL (P)
Introduces primary children to basic math concepts and hands - on art activities. Identifies space figures formed from planes to encourage comparisons of three dimensional figures and objects in the physical world. Looks at cylinders, prisms and pyramids. Part of a series on shapes.
Fine Arts; Mathematics
Dist - VIEWTH **Prod** - VIEWTH

Shape hunting - lines, angles, triangles, quadrilaterals 13 MIN
VHS
Shape hunting series
Color; PAL (P)
Introduces primary children to basic math concepts and hands - on art activities. Identifies lines, angles, triangles and quadrilaterals. Part of a series on shapes.
Fine Arts; Mathematics
Dist - VIEWTH **Prod** - VIEWTH

Shape hunting series

Circles, semicircles, ellipses	7 MIN
Cylinders, prisms, pyramids	8 MIN
Lines, Angles, Triangles, Quadrilaterals	13 MIN
Shape Hunting - Circles, Semicircles , Ellipses	7 MIN

Dist - CORF

Shape hunting series

Shape hunting - circles, semicircles, ellipses	7 MIN
Shape hunting - circles, triangles, rectangles, squares	7 MIN
Shape hunting - cylinders, prisms, pyramids	8 MIN
Shape hunting - lines, angles, triangles, quadrilaterals	13 MIN

Dist - VIEWTH

The Shape of a Leaf 27 MIN
16mm
Color (P)
LC FIA67-604
Reveals the sensitive responses of retarded children to various types of art training. Demonstrates the artistic creativity and the individuality of style that these children possess in common with all children.
Education; Fine Arts; Psychology
Dist - CMPBL **Prod** - PERKNS 1967

The Shape of a winner 45 MIN
VHS
Color (A PRO IND)
$495.00 purchase, $200.00 rental
Features Tom Peters in a lecture on the ingredients of success for growing companies.
Business and Economics
Dist - VLEARN **Prod** - VPHI

The Shape of Darkness - the Art of Black Africa (1000 - 1900 a D) 54 MIN
16mm
B&W
Shows that the distinction of black African art dating from 1000 to 1900 A D was a terror of nature fused with a deep tenderness for it.
Fine Arts; History - World
Dist - ROLAND **Prod** - ROLAND

The Shape of Language 30 MIN
U-matic / VHS
Language - Thinking, Writing, Communicating Series
Color
English Language
Dist - MDCPB **Prod** - MDCPB

The Shape of Polyester 15 MIN
16mm
Color
LC 79-701386
Shows the rapidly expanding industrial uses of polyester fibers.
Business and Economics; Industrial and Technical Education
Dist - WRKSHP **Prod** - CCOA 1979

The Shape of Speed 53 MIN
16mm / U-matic / VHS
Color
Presents boathandling techniques using a boat that is actually under sail. Covers racing tack, outside set, inside set, jiffy reefing, spinnaker handling, string takedown, staysail and blooper handling.

Physical Education and Recreation
Dist - OFFSHR **Prod** - OFFSHR 1981

Shape of speed
VHS
Color (G A)
$44.90 purchase _ #0230
Looks at sail shape and handling in sailboating. Features Lowell North, John Marshall and Dick Deaver. Covers a wide range of boats.
Physical Education and Recreation
Dist - SEVVID **Prod** - OFFSHR

Shape of the 70's 28 MIN
16mm
Eleventh round series; No 5
Color (C A)
Discusses the role of small towns in rural areas in the 70's and the citizen's responsibility in public policy formation.
Agriculture; Business and Economics; Civics and Political Systems
Dist - UNEBR **Prod** - UNL 1969

The Shape of the '80's 20 MIN
16mm
Color
LC 80-700502
Uses interviews with executives and financial analysts to explore the American economy in the 1980's.
Business and Economics
Dist - BNBFW **Prod** - BNBFW 1980

The Shape of the Land 60 MIN
VHS
America by Design Series
Color (H)
$11.50 rental _ #60951, VH
Examines how the American landscape has been altered by farming, strip mining, bridges, irrigation projects and settlement patterns. Discusses regulation of natural resources. Includes the Eads Bridge in St Louis, Hoover Dam, The Brooklyn Bridge, the Tennessee Valley Authority and the Yosemite National Park. Third in the America By Design Series.
Geography - United States; Industrial and Technical Education; Science - Natural; Social Science; Sociology
Dist - PSU **Prod** - PBS

Shape of the Nation 27 MIN
16mm
Color
LC 76-701364
Documents the state of physical fitness in Canada.
Geography - World; Physical Education and Recreation
Dist - SBRAND **Prod** - SBRAND 1974

The Shape of the winner 68 MIN
U-matic / VHS
Color (G PRO A)
$495.00 purchase, $200.00 rental
Presents an address by Tom Peters to the Conference on Growing Businesses.
Business and Economics; Psychology; Sociology
Dist - MAGVID **Prod** - MAGVID 1989

The Shape of the Winner 68 MIN
VHS / 16mm
Color (PRO)
$495.00 purchase, $200.00 rental, $50.00 preview
Discusses traits of emerging high - growth companies, how they differ from successful companies of the past 50 years. Explains how new companies have a simpler corporate structure, their international character, and their emphasis on technological pioneering.
Business and Economics; Education; Psychology
Dist - UTM **Prod** - UTM

The Shape of Thing 15 MIN
U-matic
Landscape of Geometry Series
Color (J)
Introduces some basic concepts of geometry such as points, lines, planes and congruency.
Education; Mathematics
Dist - TVOTAR **Prod** - TVOTAR 1982

The Shape of things 60 MIN
VHS
Color (G)
$29.95 purchase _ #S02088
Uses microphotography, computer animation, and time - lapse photography to show how things develop and change. From the PBS series 'NOVA.'
Fine Arts; Industrial and Technical Education; Science
Dist - UILL **Prod** - PBS

The Shape of Things 10 MIN
U-matic / VHS / 16mm
Color (H C)
LC 76-712676
Describes the activities and the results of the first symposium of sculpture to take place in North America. Highlights the work of eleven sculptors from nine countries who participated in the event.
Fine Arts
Dist - IFB **Prod** - NFBC 1971

Shape of things 60 MIN
VHS
Nova video library
Color (G)
$29.95 purchase
Uses microscopic footage to show the many - varied shapes of nature, including snowflakes, water droplets, crystals, and more. From the PBS series 'NOVA.'
Science - Physical
Dist - PBS **Prod** - WNETTV

The Shape of Things 15 MIN
U-matic / VHS
Math Mission 2 Series
Color (P)
LC 82-706328
Presents a space robot as he shows his puppet assistant the shapes of various items he has purchased at the grocery store. Tells how they compare the shapes to geometric models of a sphere, cone, cube, rectangular prism, and cylinder, and then discuss curved and flat surfaces, edges, and corners.
Mathematics
Dist - GPN **Prod** - WCVETV 1980

The shape of things to come 30 MIN
VHS
Nature by design series
Color (A PRO C)
PdS65 purchase _ Unavailable in USA and Canada
Takes a look at the future in the world of design. Part of a series which utilizes a visual style blending natural history footage, graphics and video effects - moving back and forth between science and nature. Emphasizes that good design is essential for the success of any product, in the natural world and today's high-tech world.
Psychology
Dist - BBCENE

The Shape of Things to Come 21 MIN
16mm
Color (J H C)
LC 74-706401
Discusses the space research at three centers. Includes chemical and electrical propulsion at Lewis Research Center, miniaturization of circuitry and microelectronics at Langley Research Center and radiation reentry heat and frictional heating at Ames Research Center.
Science; Science - Physical
Dist - USNAC **Prod** - NASA 1965

The Shape of Things to Come - Pt 2 25 MIN
VHS / 16mm
All Change - Management of Change Series
Color (A PRO)
$790.00 purchase, $220.00 rental
Returns to the three managers dramatized in Part 1 of this series. Shows 'H G Wells' intervening to help them grasp the lessons of Part 1 and to consider change as a continual strategy in management. Part 2 of a two - part series on managing change in organizations.
Business and Economics; Guidance and Counseling; Sociology
Dist - VIDART **Prod** - VIDART 1990

Shape - Program 2 15 MIN
U-matic
Artscape Series
Color (I)
Shows children learning about printmaking, geometric, curved and organic shapes and negative space in design.
Fine Arts
Dist - TVOTAR **Prod** - TVOTAR 1983

Shape representation 45 MIN
U-matic / VHS
Artificial intelligence series; Computer vision, Pt 3
Color (PRO)
Describes shapes using Gaussian images, extended Gaussian images to identify 3 - dimensional objects, and finding collision - free paths for objects using the configuration - space transform.
Psychology
Dist - MIOT **Prod** - MIOT

Shape Up 8 MIN
16mm
Mathematics for Elementary School Students - Whole Numbers Series
Color (P)
LC 73-701838
Mathematics
Dist - DAVFMS **Prod** - DAVFMS 1974

Shape up 17 MIN
VHS / U-matic
Safety Management Course Series
Color
Teaches proper lifting methods and techniques for reducing back strain while standing and sitting on the job and at home.
Health and Safety
Dist - EDRF **Prod** - EDRF

Shape Up 15 MIN
U-matic
Color (IND)
Shows workers how to avoid back injuries by demonstrating proper lifting methods and an overall fitness program, including nutrition, rest, and exercise.
Health and Safety
Dist - BNA **Prod** - ERESI 1983

Shape up 18 MIN
U-matic / VHS
Industrial safety series
(H A)
$125.00 purchase
Illustrates proper lifting techniques and industrial safety precautions for heavy lifters.
Health and Safety
Dist - AITECH **Prod** - ERESI 1986

Shape up 7 MIN
VHS
Children's encyclopedia of mathematics - meeting numbers series
Color (K P I)
$49.95 purchase _ #8350
Introduces the concepts of geometry. Part of a six - part series on numbers.
Mathematics
Dist - AIMS **Prod** - DAVFMS 1991

Shape Up 58 MIN
VHS
Color (G)
$19.95 purchase _ #1136
Presents 'Shape Up' by ballet master David Howard, with warm - up, beginner, intermediate, advanced and aerobic routines designed for dancers and non - dancers. Features top Broadway dancers and music by Douglas Corbin.
Agriculture; Fine Arts; Physical Education and Recreation; Science - Natural
Dist - KULTUR

Shape Up, Plants? 29 MIN
U-matic
House Botanist Series
Color
Demonstrates indoor and outdoor pruning. Offers tips on how to prune for shape and health.
Agriculture; Science - Natural
Dist - UMITV **Prod** - UMITV 1978

The Shape Your Stomach's in 25 MIN
VHS / U-matic
Color
Examines gas pains, indigestion, the butterflies, upset stomach and ulcers.
Health and Safety
Dist - MEDCOM **Prod** - MEDCOM

Shaped by Danish Hands 17 MIN
16mm
B&W
Gives examples of applied art in Denmark. Includes contemporary ceramists and furniture designers and their works, and examples of works in precious metals.
Fine Arts; Geography - World
Dist - NATDIS **Prod** - DAINFO 1954

Shaped Up Shore Stations 15 MIN
16mm
Color
LC 75-700580
Discusses problems of environmental pollution. Describes how the problems are being corrected through pollution abatement programs within the Naval Establishment centering on air, water and solid waste removal systems.
Health and Safety; Science - Natural
Dist - USNAC **Prod** - USN 1972

The Shaper 15 MIN
16mm
Machine Shop Work Series Basic Machines
B&W (SPANISH)
LC FIE62-57
Describes the functions, characteristics and basic operations of the shaper.
Industrial and Technical Education
Dist - USNAC **Prod** - USOE

Shaper no 3 - Machining Angles 11 MIN
BETA / VHS
Machine Shop - Shaper Series
Color (IND)
Demonstrates four methods of machining angles, swiveling vise, tilting the table, tilting work in vise, and tilting the head.

Industrial and Technical Education; Psychology
Dist - RMIBHF **Prod** - RMIBHF

Shaper no 2 - Squaring a Block 20 MIN
VHS / BETA
Machine Shop - Shaper Series
Color (IND)
Continues Shaper No. 1. Shows the procedure for machining all six sides of a workpiece parallel and square. Covers tool geometry and setup of tool and work for maximum rigidity.
Industrial and Technical Education; Psychology
Dist - RMIBHF **Prod** - RMIBHF

Shaper - Scroll Saw Safety
VHS / 35mm strip
Wood Safety Series
$28.00 purchase _ #TX1B9 filmstrip, $58.00 purchase _ #TX1B9V VHS
Teaches safety and use of the shaper and scroll saw.
Industrial and Technical Education
Dist - CAREER **Prod** - CAREER

Shapers of Our Time - Eamon De Valera 29 MIN
VHS / 16mm
Color (G)
$55.00 rental _ #SOOT - 000
Portrays Eamon de Valera, the great Irish patriot and statesman who led the fight for Irish independence. Uses old photographs and newreels.
Biography; Geography - World; History - World
Dist - PBS **Prod** - WGBHTV

Shapes 15 MIN
U-matic
Math Patrol Two Series
Color (P)
Presents the mathematical concepts of two dimensional geometry.
Education; Mathematics
Dist - TVOTAR **Prod** - TVOTAR 1977

Shapes 5 MIN
16mm
Color (J)
LC 75-701621
Presents an experimental film which shows a variety of shapes and colors which move in time to a rhythmic background of electronic music.
Fine Arts; Industrial and Technical Education
Dist - CFS **Prod** - DEMOS 1974

Shapes 15 MIN
VHS / U-matic / 16mm / BETA
Young viewers series
Color (K P)
$245.00, $68.00 purchase _ #C50777, #C51505
Shows how to identify shapes in the abstract and in real life. Features Mr William Shakespeare, bard of shapes, who brings circles, triangles, squares, even parallelograms, to life through original songs and music. Part of a five - part series which introduces concepts essential to academic and social life.
Mathematics; Psychology
Dist - NGS **Prod** - NGS 1992

Shapes a La Cart 8 MIN
U-matic / VHS / 16mm
Visual Awareness Series
B&W (I)
LC FIA65-418
A magic grocery cart explores a supermarket and encounters boxes, bottles, jugs and sacks of diverse shapes and styles. Animation is used.
Fine Arts
Dist - IFB **Prod** - RAI 1963

Shapes and colors 30 MIN
VHS
Bill Cosby picture pages series
Color (K P)
$9.95 purchase _ #FRV16004V - K
Helps prepare children for the skills required to recognize shapes and colors. Features Bill Cosby and builds on the fact that children enjoy learning. Includes two activity books. Part of a six - part series of building skills in reading and counting and in color, animal, word and letter recognition.
English Language; Psychology
Dist - CAMV

Shapes and more Shapes 15 MIN
U-matic / VHS
Math Mission 2 Series
Color (P)
LC 82-706327
Tells how a space robot and his puppet assistant help their friend, Mr Beetle, make his way through a maze, as they develop the concepts of flat shapes, space shapes, and a straight line. Shows how to draw and construct different patterns and shapes.
Mathematics
Dist - GPN **Prod** - WCVETV 1980

Shapes and polarities of molecules 18 MIN
VHS / 16mm
Chem study video - film series
Color (H C)
$288.00, $99.00 purchase, $27.00 rental _ #192 W 0870, #193 W 2040, #140 W 4154
Develops the concept of molecular polarity through electrical effects, including a stream of falling liquid by an electrically charged rod. Shows a model based on polar and nonpolar molecules. Extends a molecular dipole model to explain differences in solubility, conductivity and chemical reactivity. Part of a series for teaching chemistry to high school and college students.
Science - Physical
Dist - WARDS **Prod** - WARDS 1990

Shapes and Polarities of Molecules 18 MIN
16mm
CHEM Study Films Series
Color (H)
Uses electrical effects, including deflections of a stream of falling liquid by an electrically charged rod. Introduces the concept of molecular polarity. A molecular dipole model is used to explain differences in solubility, conductivity and chemical reactivity.
Science - Physical
Dist - MLA **Prod** - CHEMS 1962

Shapes of Geometry Series Pt 3
Miniature Geometry 20 MIN
Dist - GPN

Shapes of Geometry Series Pt 4
Tesselations 20 MIN
Dist - GPN

Shapes of Geometry Series Pt 6
Non - Euclidean Geometries 20 MIN
Dist - GPN

Shapes of geometry series
Kaleidoscope geometry 20 MIN
Topology I 20 MIN
Topology II 20 MIN
Dist - GPN

Shapes of Things 57 MIN
16mm / VHS
Nova Series
(J H C)
$99.95 each
Explains the inventive, repetitive patterns of nature, such as seen in honeycombs or seashells.
Science; Science - Physical; Sociology
Dist - AMBROS **Prod** - AMBROS 1982

Shapes, Pt 1 15 MIN
VHS / U-matic
Let's Draw Series
Color (P)
Fine Arts
Dist - AITECH **Prod** - OCPS 1976

Shapes, Pt 2 15 MIN
U-matic / VHS
Let's Draw Series
Color (P)
Fine Arts
Dist - AITECH **Prod** - OCPS 1976

The Shapes We Live with 14 MIN
16mm / U-matic / VHS
Color (P I)
LC 78-708051
Introduces the four basic shapes and demonstrates the sphere, the cylinder, the cone and the cube.
Mathematics
Dist - PHENIX **Prod** - BOUNDY 1970

Shaping 5 MIN
U-matic / VHS
Protocol Materials in Teacher Education - the Process of Teaching, 'Pt 2 Series
Color (T)
Education; Psychology
Dist - MSU **Prod** - MSU

Shaping After Template and Shaping Curved Edges 17 MIN
16mm
Precision Wood Machining Series Operations on the Spindle Shaper, no'2
B&W
LC FIE52-40
Shows how to make a template, install knives, use the template for smoothing squared edges and set up equipment for shaping a curved edge.
Industrial and Technical Education
Dist - USNAC **Prod** - USOE 1945

Shaping and Scheduling 42 MIN
U-matic / VHS
Learning and Liking it Series
Color (T)
Gives ways to encourage children to improve when their performance is poor and reward is not possible.
Education; Psychology
Dist - MSU **Prod** - MSU

Shaping Curriculum 30 MIN
VHS / U-matic
On and about Instruction Series
Color (T)
Examines the first of three dimensions of the R H Anderson model of effective teaching.
Education
Dist - GPN **Prod** - VADE 1983

Shaping Instruction 30 MIN
U-matic / VHS
On and about Instruction Series
Color (T)
Looks at the second of three dimensions of the R H Anderson model of effective teaching.
Education
Dist - GPN **Prod** - VADE 1983

Shaping news for the consumer 17 MIN
U-matic / VHS / 16mm
Color (H C A)
LC 75-704007
Shows the process of preparing a television news story and discusses the capabilities and limitations of television news, newspapers and news magazines.
Literature and Drama; Psychology; Social Science
Dist - PHENIX **Prod** - MEDFO 1975

The Shaping of Traditions - 1st to 9th Centuries CE - Pt 3 60 MIN
16mm / VHS
Heritage - Civilization and the Jews Series
Color (J)
$800.00, $49.00 purchase _ #405 - 9123
Explores more than 3000 years of the Jewish experience and its intimate connections with the civilizations of the world. Uses all available resources to weave an extraordinary tapestry of the Jewish history and people. Hosted by Abba Eban, Israel's former ambassador to the UN and the US. Part 3 chronicles the destruction of the Second Temple, the rise of Chistianity and Islam, and the emergence of Jewish culture in Europe.
History - World; Psychology; Religion and Philosophy; Sociology
Dist - FI **Prod** - WNETTV 1984

Shaping, Prompting, and Fading
U-matic / VHS
Effective Behavioral Programming Series
Color (S)
Offers demonstrations in eating, toileting and eye contact, for retarded persons and how to use and fade verbal, gestural and physical prompts.
Education; Health and Safety; Psychology; Sociology
Dist - RESPRC **Prod** - RESPRC

Shaping the Classroom 30 MIN
VHS / U-matic
On and about Instruction Series
Color (T)
Examines the third dimension of the R H Anderson model of effective teaching.
Education
Dist - GPN **Prod** - VADE 1983

Shaping the future 60 MIN
VHS / U-matic
Body in question series
Color (H C A)
LC 81-706951
Discusses what happens at the moment of conception and shows how the fertilized egg is transformed into a full - grown adult. Looks at traditional theories in this area, arguing that a conceptual leap was necessary for real progress to be made. Based on the book The Body In Question by Jonathan Miller. Narrated by Jonathan Miller. Program seven in the series.
Health and Safety; Science; Science - Natural
Dist - FI **Prod** - BBCTV 1979

Shaping the image 29 MIN
VHS
Consuming hunger series
Color (G)
$14.95 purchase
Questions the impact of dramatic photos of starving peoples on Americans as time passed. Part 2 of a three - part series.
Business and Economics; Guidance and Counseling; Literature and Drama
Dist - MARYFA

Shaping the Personality 20 MIN
16mm
Film Studies of the Psychoanalytic Research Project on Problems in 'Infancy Series
B&W (C T)
Illustrates forms of mother - child relations and their influence on the child.

Psychology; Sociology
Dist - NYU **Prod** - SPITZ 1953

Shaping the Residual Limb - Stump Wrapping and the Temporary Prosthesis 23 MIN
U-matic / VHS
Color
Health and Safety
Dist - UMDSM **Prod** - UMDSM

Shaping Today with Yesterday Series
Ballerinas compare notes on creating roles 30 MIN
Morris Dances - Ancient Ritual English Dances 30 MIN
Sensationalism Caused by the 19th Century Waltz and Serge Diaghilev's Productions 30 MIN
Tracing the Roots of Dance with Hanya Holm 30 MIN
Dist - ARCVID

Shaping up 25 MIN
VHS / U-matic
Developmental biology series
Color (H C)
$250.00 purchase _ #HP - 5981C
Examines the developmental processes of morphogenesis - body pattern formation and maintenance of shape. Studies cell migration, regeneration and cell division, polarity of generation, and the body - patterning roles of epithelial cells, neurons and morphogens. Part of a four - part series on biology which addresses regeneration, internal and external structures, cellular communication, gender influences, growth and stability of form.
Science; Science - Natural
Dist - CORF **Prod** - BBCTV 1990

Shaping up series
Diet 10 MIN
Exercise 10 MIN
Dist - POAPLE

Shaping Up Your Geometry 30 MIN
VHS / U-matic
Adult Math Series
Color (A)
Education; Mathematics
Dist - KYTV **Prod** - KYTV 1984

Shaping your sound series
Presents five videocassettes on recording and mixing sound. Explores mixers and mixing, multitrack recording, equalizers, compressors and gates, reverb and delay, and microphones. Features engineer - producer and master teacher Tom Lubin.
Shaping your sound series
Shaping your sound with equalizers, compressors and gates
Shaping your sound with microphones
Shaping your sound with mixers and mixing
Shaping your sound with multitrack recording
Shaping your sound with reverb and delay
Dist - SONYIN **Prod** - SONYIN 1984

Shaping your sound with equalizers, compressors and gates
VHS
Shaping your sound series
Color (G)
$119.00 purchase
Shows how to use EQ to open up a mix and create room for each instrumental texture, and how to use compressors and gates to add clarity, drama and presence to a recording. Features engineer - producer and master teacher Tom Lubin. Part of a five part video series.
Fine Arts; Industrial and Technical Education; Science - Physical
Dist - SONYIN **Prod** - SONYIN

Shaping your sound with microphones
VHS
Shaping your sound series
Color (G)
$119.00 purchase
Uses audio demonstrations and computer graphics to show how variables of size, mass, type and pattern affect a microphone's performance. Shows how to choose the right mic for each job. Teaches the best making techniques for a wide variety of instruments and situations through extensive live music demos. Features engineer - producer and master teacher Tom Lubin. Part of a five part video series.
Fine Arts; Industrial and Technical Education; Science - Physical
Dist - SONYIN **Prod** - SONYIN

Shaping your sound with mixers and mixing
VHS
Shaping your sound series
Color (G)
$119.00 purchase
Explores the workings of the recording console. Goes through every step of a 16 track mixing session. Uses EQ, reverb and dynamics to blend separate tracks into a polished song. Features engineer - producer and master teacher Tom Lubin. Part of a five part video series.
Fine Arts; Industrial and Technical Education; Science - Physical
Dist - SONYIN **Prod** - SONYIN

Shaping your sound with multitrack recording
VHS
Shaping your sound series
Color (G)
$119.00 purchase
Presents a complete guide to the recording and overdubbing process. Goes through all the steps of a multitrack recording session. Demonstrates techniques for top quality recording, creative editing, tape effects. Features engineer - producer and master teacher Tom Lubin. Part of a five part video series.
Fine Arts; Industrial and Technical Education; Science - Physical
Dist - SONYIN **Prod** - SONYIN

Shaping your sound with reverb and delay
VHS
Shaping your sound series
Color (G)
$119.00 purchase
Shows how to get the most from today's reverb and delays. Demonstrates the behavior of sound in a variety of real environments and shows how to use reverb for duplicatoion. Features engineer - producer and master teacher Tom Lubin. Part of a five part video series.
Fine Arts; Industrial and Technical Education; Science - Physical
Dist - SONYIN **Prod** - SONYIN

Shards 5 MIN
16mm
Color (G)
$15.00 rental
Parallels fragmentation and fragility through explorations that question ideas of wholeness and reconstruction in the film form in a Dana Plays production.
Fine Arts
Dist - CANCIN

Share - a - home 9 MIN
U-matic / VHS / 16mm
American family - an endangered species series
Color (H C A)
Explores the concept of group homes for the elderly.
Sociology
Dist - FI **Prod** - NBCNEW 1979

Share it with Someone 4 MIN
16mm / U-matic / VHS
Most Important Person - Getting Along with Others Series
Color (K P I)
Stresses that, whether it's a toy car, sugar cookies or a super idea, it's more fun to share than to be alone.
Guidance and Counseling; Psychology
Dist - EBEC **Prod** - EBEC 1972

Shared Decision Making 57 MIN
U-matic
Child Welfare Learning Laboratory Materials Series
Color
Provides a generic introduction to a nondirective technique to aid clients in identifying goals and the actions necessary for achieving them.
Guidance and Counseling; Sociology
Dist - UMITV **Prod** - UMITV

Shared decision making 60 MIN
VHS
Color (A T C PRO)
$466.00 purchase, $190.00 rental _ #614 - 253X01
Explores how schools better meet the needs of their students when all members of the school community have input on decisions. Includes two videocassettes, Changing Schools through Shared Decision Making and Shared Decision Making, and a facilitator's guide. Shows how schools successfully seek input from teachers, school support staff, parents and students. Interviews Al Shanker and John Goodlad who explain the importance of this new approach.
Education; Psychology
Dist - AFSCD **Prod** - AFSCD 1993

The Shared Experience 29 MIN
16mm
Color
LC 78-700306
Examines the library as a repository for the transmission of human experience. Features Dr Lewis Thomas talking about the biological basis for culture, Noam Chomsky speculating on the origin of language, Alexander Marshack exploring the mind of ice age man, and John Kenneth Galbraith talking about contemporary information.
Education; Social Science
Dist - PRATTE **Prod** - PRATTE 1978

Shared Illusion 29 MIN
U-matic
Color
Looks at the identification of the normal and abnormal in society today. Hosted by Dr William Rhodes, professor of psychology at the University of Michigan.
Psychology; Sociology
Dist - UMITV **Prod** - UMITV 1978

Shared Labor 47 MIN
16mm
Color
LC 80-701264
Documents a young couple's experience with natural childbirth.
Health and Safety; Sociology
Dist - RAINFI **Prod** - FGCH 1980

Shared labor - Pt 1 24 MIN
16mm
Color
LC 80-701264
Documents a young couple's experience with natural childbirth.
Health and Safety; Sociology
Dist - RAINFI **Prod** - FGCH 1980

Shared labor - Pt 2 23 MIN
16mm
Color
LC 80-701264
Documents a young couple's experience with natural childbirth.
Health and Safety; Sociology
Dist - RAINFI **Prod** - FGCH 1980

Shared Meaning 30 MIN
U-matic / VHS
Couples Communication Skills Series
Color
Discusses skills used to reach a common understanding. Involves a process of feedback in which the listener paraphrases what he or she had heard the other say.
Guidance and Counseling; Psychology; Sociology
Dist - NETCHE **Prod** - NETCHE 1975

Shared realities series
The Artist and Television 1 56 MIN
The Artist and Television 2 58 MIN
The Artist and the Computer 57 MIN
Artists and the Media 55 MIN
At home - Part 1 55 MIN
At home - Part 2 55 MIN
Exploring Dance 1 51 MIN
Exploring Dance 2 57 MIN
Long Beach Community Arts 53 MIN
Long Beach Museum of Art - Video 56 MIN
Music and Performance 58 MIN
Personal Perspectives 53 MIN
Dist - LBMART

A Shared understanding - bridging racial and socioeconomic differences in doctor - patient communication 41 MIN
VHS / U-matic
Color (PRO C)
$395.00 purchase, $80.00 rental _ #C901 - VI - 029
Examines cultural influences on three elements of doctor - patient communication - a shared understanding, a functional relationship and mutually satisfactory outcomes. Depicts a 28 - year - old white, male resident performing the fourth routine follow - up of a 48 - year - old obese, black patient and shows how problems in understanding each other show up in the interview. Includes commentaries from health professionals and specialists in cross - cultural communication. Presented by Drs Barbara F Sharf, John Kahler, Richard P Foley, Dianna Grant, Mona Bomgaars and Stanley Harper.
Health and Safety; Social Science
Dist - HSCIC

Shared visions 20 MIN
VHS
Color (G C)
$79.00 purchase, $45.00 rental
Shares discussions among teen - age and older artists about their inspirations, desires and philosophy. Shows the teens' visit to the elders' studios and the older artists' visit to the teens' school art room.

Fine Arts; Health and Safety; Psychology
Dist - TNF **Prod** - TNF

Shareen Brysac 30 MIN
U-matic / VHS
Eye on dance - dance on television series
Color
Looks at producing dance specials for the mass market.
Fine Arts
Dist - ARCVID **Prod** - ARCVID

Shareware carousel volume 2
CD-ROM
(G)
$219.00 purchase _ #1516
Contains over 16,000 - 550 MB - shareware and freeware programs for IBM, Macintosh, Amiga, Atari, and Commodore computers from Alde Publishing. Compresses all programs. IBM files can be retrieved with Alde PICK program. The rest are in ASCII and need only a text lister or word processor. The entire database can be searched by subject or keyword. IBM and compatibles require at least 640K of RAM, DOS 3.1 or greater, one floppy disk drive - hard disk recommended, one empty expansion slot, and IBM compatible CD - ROM drive. Macintosh requires at least 1 MB of RAM, one floppy disk drive, and an Apple compatible CD - ROM drive.
Computer Science
Dist - BEP

Shareware express
CD-ROM
(G)
$49.00 purchase _ #1742
Contains dozens of shareware programs. Includes roladex and quick - dial programs, Mindreader, PC Outline, word processors, Lotus templates and macros, databases, utilities, typing tutors, investment software, graphics, educational programs, Doctor DOS, and others. For IBM PCs and compatibles, requires 640K RAM, DOS 3.1 or later, one floppy disk - hard disk recommended, one empty expansion slot, and an IBM compatible CD - ROM drive.
Computer Science
Dist - BEP

Shareware gold
CD-ROM
(G A)
$125.00 purchase _ #1931
Includes the normal contingent of shareware and freeware plus a very interesting collection of software - the complete Medlin Accounting package, the ButtonWare set of software with PC - File database manger, PC - Calc, PC - TypePlus, PC - Dial, PC - Ticle, PC - Stylist and more. For IBM PCs and compatibles. Requires at least 640K RAM, DOS Version 3.1 or greater, one floppy disk drive - a hard drive is recommended, one empty expansion slot, and an IBM compatible CD - ROM drive.
Civics and Political Systems; Computer Science
Dist - BEP

Shareware gold
CD-ROM
(G)
$79.95 purchase
Contains DOS programs with reviews of each program. Includes programs written by Jim Button, Marshall Magee, Vern Buerg. Virus free and pressed on gold media for long shelf life.
Computer Science
Dist - QUANTA **Prod** - QUANTA

Shareware grab - bag
CD-ROM
(G)
$88.00 purchase _ #1501
Contains 7000 different shareware programs. Includes text editors, word processors, databases, utilities, graphics, educational programs, communication software, business software, spreadsheet templates, source code, games, and device drivers. For IBM PCs and compatibles, requires 640K RAM, DOS 3.1 or later, one floppy disk - hard disk recommended, one empty expansion slot, and an IBM compatible CD - ROM drive.
Computer Science
Dist - BEP

Sharing 20 MIN
VHS / 16mm
Trail Series
Color (I)
$150.00 purchase, $30.00 rental
Analyzes the web of life and the interdependence of all life forms. Suggests that connections in the natural world affect the web of life.
Science - Natural
Dist - AITECH **Prod** - KAIDTV 1986

Sharing 18 MIN
U-matic / VHS
Becoming Orgasmic - a Sexual Growth Program Series
Color
Shows intercourse with concurrent manual stimulation and demonstrates positions which facilitate this technique.
Health and Safety; Psychology; Sociology
Dist - MMRC **Prod** - MMRC

Sharing 30 MIN
U-matic
Today's special series
Color (K P)
Develops language arts skills in children. Programs are thematically designed around subjects of interest to youngsters. Action takes place in a department store where people, mannequins, puppets, comic characters and special guests present a light hearted approach to language arts.
Guidance and Counseling; Literature and Drama; Psychology
Dist - TVOTAR **Prod** - TVOTAR 1985

Sharing 27 MIN
VHS
Sunshine factory series
Color (P I R)
$14.99 purchase _ #35 - 83552 - 533
Features P J the repairman and kids in his neighborhood as they travel to the Sunshine Factory, a land populated by puppets, a computer and caring adults. Teaches a Biblically - based lesson on sharing.
Religion and Philosophy
Dist - APH **Prod** - WORD

Sharing 9 MIN
U-matic / VHS / 16mm
Moral Decision Making Series
Color (I J)
LC 72-702679
Presents Sally, who has been saving money to buy a transistor radio on sale. Considers the moral values involved in the concepts of sharing, and the factors which affect decision making about generosity.
Guidance and Counseling; Sociology
Dist - AIMS **Prod** - MORLAT 1971

Sharing - 24 6 MIN
U-matic / VHS
Life's little lessons - self - esteem K - 3 - series
Color (K P)
$129.00, $99.00 _ #V623
Tells about Gimme First, an ornery Western town where nobody liked to live because everyone just looked out for themselves. Reveals that one day they learned the secret of sharing and changed the town's name to Give First. Part of a 30 - part series on self - esteem.
Guidance and Counseling; Psychology
Dist - BARR **Prod** - CEPRO 1992

Sharing and cooperation 8 MIN
VHS / U-matic
Songs for us series
Color (P)
$250.00 purchase _ #JC - 67700
Presents a live - action music video which teaches children the importance of sharing and cooperation with others. Part of the Songs for Us series.
Fine Arts; Psychology
Dist - CORF **Prod** - DISNEY 1989

The Sharing and not sharing game 11 MIN
16mm / VHS
Learning responsibility series
Color (P)
$225.00, $205.00 purchase, $50.00 rental
Employs the character of wise Mr Mac to teach little Beverly about things to share and not to share. Shows that it can be fun to share games, toys, and information, but that she should not share a valuable gift from her parents, or, for health reasons, such items as combs, hats, or an ice cream cone.
Health and Safety; Psychology
Dist - HIGGIN **Prod** - HIGGIN 1980

Sharing is Caring 15 MIN
16mm
Color
LC 74-702887
Describes the educational and recreational opportunities made available primarily to inner - city youths through the Kids Corporation, a group of volunteers who are sponsored by business organizations in the Newark, New Jersey, area.
Business and Economics; Social Science; Sociology
Dist - PICA **Prod** - PICA 1974

Sharing is fun 15 MIN
16mm
Our children series
Color; B&W (P I R)
Tells the story of a boy who befriends a new neighbor who is recovering from polio. Shows how the boy learns Christian attitudes of sharing.
Guidance and Counseling; Religion and Philosophy
Dist - FAMF **Prod** - FAMF

Sharing is Unity (Ushirika Ni Umoja) (Kiswahili) 23 MIN
16mm / U-matic / VHS
Color (A)
Explores rural life and feelings of the Iteso peoples of Kenya. Experiences African sense of community through farming and storytelling.
Geography - World; History - World; Religion and Philosophy
Dist - AFFILM **Prod** - AFFILM 1985

Sharing literature with young children series
Jump over the moon - sharing literature with young children - a series
Dist - HRAW

Sharing my feelings 13 MIN
VHS / 16mm
Color (P I) (SPANISH)
$325.00, $260.00 purchase, $50.00 rental _ #8277
Uses animation to help young children express their feelings about adult use of alcohol or other drugs. Helps youngsters to understand that some of the adult behavior which makes them uncomfortable may be caused by alcohol or drug use. Teaches children that their feelings are important. Produced by Mothers Against Drunk Driving - MADD.
Guidance and Counseling; Health and Safety; Sociology
Dist - AIMS

Sharing Orgasm - Communicating Your Sexual Responses 10 MIN
16mm
Color (PRO)
Shows the entire process of genital pleasuring, the crucial step in a series of exercises designed for women learning to have orgasms with a partner. Provides a model for honest communication between partners.
Guidance and Counseling; Health and Safety
Dist - DAVFMS **Prod** - DAVFMS 1978

Sharing the Experience Series
Sharing the Experience with Gavin 28 MIN
Sharing the Experience with June 28 MIN
Sharing the Experience with Peter 28 MIN
Sharing the Experience with Walter 28 MIN
Dist - STNFLD

Sharing the Experience with Gavin 28 MIN
U-matic / VHS / 16mm
Sharing the Experience Series
Color
Describes the situation when the birth of a child with Down's Syndrome resulted in the hospital and community working closely with the parents and grandparents to give the child the best start in life. Presents the parents describing the birth experience, their decision on amniocentesis and future children and their concern about being free to enjoy their child as a delightful addition to their family.
Guidance and Counseling; Psychology
Dist - STNFLD **Prod** - STNFLD

Sharing the Experience with June 28 MIN
U-matic / VHS / 16mm
Sharing the Experience Series
Color
Documents experiences in the life of June, a mentally retarded teenager.
Guidance and Counseling; Psychology
Dist - STNFLD **Prod** - STNFLD

Sharing the Experience with Peter 28 MIN
16mm / U-matic / VHS
Sharing the Experience Series
Color
Documents the experiences of a young boy who is severely handicapped and shows how he is very much a part of his family. Discusses a program called Extend - A - Family which helps form friendships between handicapped and nonhandicapped children.
Guidance and Counseling; Psychology
Dist - STNFLD **Prod** - STNFLD

Sharing the Experience with Walter 28 MIN
16mm / U-matic / VHS
Sharing the Experience Series
Color
Documents the experiences of Walter, who lived most of his life in an institution for the mentally retarded and now has moved into the community and learned to live on his own. Discusses a group of parents of institutional residents who created a 'Community Living Board' to provide services that enable residents to move out into the community.
Guidance and Counseling; Psychology
Dist - STNFLD **Prod** - STNFLD

Sharing the glory 30 MIN
16mm
Color (R)

LC 73-701033
Presents a Bible study in the home of Ron Simmons and his friends. Poses the question - 'Doesn't each one of use have countless opportunities to witness everyday?'
Guidance and Counseling; Religion and Philosophy
Dist - FAMF **Prod** - FAMF 1971

Sharing the God story series
Experiencing the truth - writing our own story 30 MIN
Learning the truth - the Bible as a story 30 MIN
Learning to tell the story 30 MIN
Dist - APH

Sharing the kingdom 6 MIN
VHS / U-matic
Color (R G)
$50.00 purchase, $25.00 rental _ #810, #811, #812
Examines the challenge of blending Christian values with the business of being healthcare providers. Presents text by Sister Juliana Casey, IHM.
Guidance and Counseling; Health and Safety; Psychology; Religion and Philosophy
Dist - CATHHA

Sharing the Leadership 30 MIN
16mm
Dynamics of Leadership Series
B&W (H C A)
Explores three categories of individual action - - selfserving, task and group - serving functions - - and their relationship to group leadership.
Guidance and Counseling; Psychology
Dist - IU **Prod** - NET 1963

Sharing the light 18 MIN
VHS
Color (G)
$18.00 purchase
Records the International Conference of Jewish Women held in Kiev, Ukraine in 1994, organized by Project Kesher. Looks at the participants from around the world sharing common dreams of connecting with one another as Jewish women and rebuilding Jewish life in the former Soviet Union. Directed by Julie Gal.
Fine Arts; Religion and Philosophy; Sociology
Dist - NCJEWF

Sharing the light - Christmas with His Eminence 28 MIN
VHS
Illuminations series
Color (G R)
#V - 1014
Features Archbishop Iakovos in a Christmas visit to St Basil Academy and St Michael's Home for the Aged. Includes the Archbishop's Christmas message.
Fine Arts; Religion and Philosophy
Dist - GOTEL **Prod** - GOTEL 1988

Sharing the Road 15 MIN
16mm
Color
Stresses that the nation's highways can be shared by both motorists and truckers. Demonstrates the kinds of problems truckers encounter on the road.
Health and Safety; Social Science
Dist - MTP **Prod** - ATA

Sharing the road with big trucks 18 MIN
16mm / VHS
Color (H G)
$87.00, $30.00 purchase _ #250, #465
Offers specific suggestions to help motorists safely share the road with big trucks. Illustrates the view of a big truck with its sight limitations and advantages and how others are affected by them.
Health and Safety
Dist - AAAFTS **Prod** - AAAFTS 1985

Sharing the Secret 84 MIN
16mm
Color (A)
LC 82-700350
Documents the pride, pain, anguish and affection of homosexuality by looking at several gay men. Shows them in their homes, with their families and in their various gay relationships.
Sociology
Dist - IFEX **Prod** - CANBC 1981

Sharing the wind 27 MIN
16mm
Color
LC 81-700428
Shows catamaran sailing, including scenes of racing and high - speed lake sailing, dramatic twenty - foot wave surfing and the antics of some of the world's best catamaran sailors.
Physical Education and Recreation
Dist - ALLNRP **Prod** - ALLNRP 1979

Sharing truth and love - Tape 8 30 MIN
VHS
Acts of the Apostles series
Color (I J H C G A R)
$29.95 purchase, $10.00 rental _ #35 - 8369 - 1502
Presents stories of the early Christian church as described in the New Testament book of Acts. Covers the events of Paul and Barnabas' ministry in Jerusalem, the first Council of the Church, and the debate over the role of Gentiles in relation to Jewish Law.
Religion and Philosophy
Dist - APH **Prod** - BOSCO

Sharing with others 30 MIN
VHS
Quigley's village series
Color (K P I R)
$19.95 purchase, $10.00 rental _ #35 - 89 - 2504
Features Mr Quigley and his puppet friends. Tells how Danny, Spike and Bubba entered a contest and agreed to share the prize, only to see Spike try to keep the prize for herself when she wins. Produced by Jeremiah Films.
Literature and Drama; Religion and Philosophy
Dist - APH

Shark 50 MIN
U-matic / 16mm / VHS
Color; Mono (G)
MV $250.00 _ MP $975.00 purchase, $50.00 rental
Relates information regarding many varieties of sharks. Anatomy, sensory systems, reproduction, distribution and behavior are covered in this unique veiw of a marine animal that plays a very important role in the balance and structure of the marine ecosystem.
Science - Natural
Dist - CTV **Prod** - MAKOF 1981

Shark 29 MIN
16mm / U-matic / VHS
Color (I J H C)
LC 76-700285
Shows author Peter Benchley and underwater photographer, Stan Waterman as they dive off the Great Barrier Reef. Follows their encounters with several different types of sharks, including the great white shark.
Geography - World; Science - Natural
Dist - LCOA **Prod** - ABCSRT 1976

Shark - ancient mystery of the sea 15 MIN
16mm
Science in action series
Color (C)
Explains the research being done on sharks. Deals with how sharks can by affected by underwater sound, their pattern of pre - attack behavior, if they can distinguish color and how the shark has survived unchained for millions of years. Examines ways of guarding against the shark while sharing his environment.
Science; Science - Natural
Dist - COUNFI **Prod** - ALLFP

Shark attack 53 MIN
VHS
Color (G)
$29.95 purchase _ #S01425
Features underwater explorers Ron and Valerie Taylor as they study the sharks of Australia's Great Barrier Reef. Shows how the Taylors use fish pieces abd a steel mesh suit to attract a potentially dangerous shark attack.
Geography - World; Physical Education and Recreation; Science - Natural
Dist - UILL

Shark - Danger in the Sea 27 MIN
16mm
Color
LC 74-706576
Discusses how the Navy's shark research programs help in the development of equipment and procedures useful in preventing shark attacks.
Health and Safety; Science; Science - Natural
Dist - USNAC **Prod** - USN 1973

Shark, Danger in the Sea 27 MIN
U-matic
Color
LC 79-706712
Discusses how the U S Navy's shark research programs help in the development of equipment and procedures useful in preventing shark attacks.
Civics and Political Systems; Health and Safety; Science - Natural
Dist - USNAC **Prod** - USN 1979

Shark dissection 26 MIN
VHS
Dissection video II series
Color (J H)
$160.00 purchase _ #A5VH 1225
Shows the dissection of a shark, start - to - finish. Provides clear and detailed presentations of the external anatomy, the correct procedures used for dissection and a review of the internal anatomy and physiological systems. Includes a dissection manual and a written examination. Part of a series on dissection.
Science; Science - Natural
Dist - CLRVUE **Prod** - CLRVUE

The Shark - Maneater of Myth? 24 MIN
U-matic / VHS
Color (I J C)
$89.00 purchase _ #3388
Probes the latest scientific research on the behavior of sharks and looks at new warning and protective devices designed to ward sharks' infrequent but devastating attacks on humans.
Science - Natural
Dist - EBEC **Prod** - AVATLI

Shark reef 60 MIN
VHS / U-matic / 16mm
Last frontier series
Color; Mono (G)
MV $225.00 _ MP $550.00
Probes the depths of the Caribbean Sea in a seach for the resident groups of reef sharks.
History - World; Science - Natural
Dist - CTV **Prod** - MAKOF 1985

The Sharks 59 MIN
VHS / Videodisc / BETA
Color; CLV; Captioned (G)
$35.20, $24.20 purchase _ #C53501, #C50501
Science - Natural
Dist - NGS **Prod** - NGS

Sharks 24 MIN
U-matic / VHS / 16mm
Undersea World of Jacques Cousteau Series
Color (G)
$295 purchase - 16 mm, $99 purchase - video
Explains how sharks make visual discriminations, how their behavior at night differs from their behavior during the day, and how people can protect themselves from sharks.
Health and Safety; Science - Natural
Dist - CF

Sharks
VHS
World around us series
Color (G)
$29.95 purchase _ #IV - 004
Studies sharks. Covers feeding habits, the acute sensory apparatus of sharks, when and why they attack humans, safety against sharks while in the water, shark physiology, repellents, and fresh water sharks.
Health and Safety; Science - Natural
Dist - INCRSE **Prod** - INCRSE

Sharks 60 MIN
VHS
National Geographic video series
Color (G)
$29.95 purchase
Gives the facts about sharks, including that only 20 of the 350 different species of shark are dangerous to humans. Features extensive underwater footage.
Science - Natural
Dist - PBS **Prod** - WNETTV

Sharks 60 MIN
VHS
National Audubon Society specials series
Color; Captioned (G)
$49.95 purchase _ #NTAS - 404
Focuses on the much - feared shark and its prospects for continued survival. Reveals that shark cartilage is being used in cancer research. Includes footage of the birth of lemon sharks and of testing of shark repellents in the open water. Also produced by Turner Broadcasting and WETA - TV. Narrated by Peter Benchley, author of the book 'Jaws.'
Science - Natural
Dist - PBS **Prod** - NAS 1988

Sharks 60 MIN
VHS
Color; Captioned (G)
$29.95 purchase _ #S00869; $29.95 purchase _ #SOO869
Examines sharks and their traits. Discusses the shark's feeding habits, sensory systems, and psychology, among other subjects.
Science - Natural; Science - Physical
Dist - UILL **Prod** - NGS
SEVVID

Sharks 24 MIN
U-matic / VHS / 16mm
Undersea world of Jacques Cousteau series
Color (G) (ENGLISH, SPANISH)
$49.95 purchase _ #Q10611
A shortened version of Sharks. Presents a discussion by Jacques Cousteau's oceanographers about myths associated with sharks. Illustrates how sharks are

attracted to an alien presence, how sharks learn and make visual discriminations, how night affects shark behavior and how people can protect themselves from sharks. Part of a series of 24 programs.
Science - Natural
Dist - CF **Prod** - METROM 1970

Sharks 60 MIN
VHS
Color (G)
$24.95 purchase _ #S02000
Focuses on gaining a true picture of sharks by dispelling myths. Portrays various attempts by humans to gain a sort of coexistence with sharks.
Science - Natural
Dist - UILL **Prod** - SIERRA

Sharks - pirates of the deep 87 MIN
VHS
Color (G)
$29.90 purchase _ #0400
Films a shark attack and other close encounters. Features Glenn Ford as narrator. Directed by Jean Lebel.
Science - Natural; Science - Physical
Dist - SEVVID

Sharks, some facts 17 MIN
16mm / U-matic / VHS
Color (J)
LC 78-702019
Presents factual information about sharks and their behavior patterns in an attempt to dispel common misconceptions about their potential danger to humans.
Science - Natural
Dist - PHENIX **Prod** - COUSJM 1978

Sharks - terror, truth, death 28 MIN
16mm / U-matic / VHS
Planet of man series
Color (J H)
Demonstrates the shark pattern of attack and sensory mechanism. Points out that attacks on people are exceedingly rare. Presents Peter Benchley defending his book Jaws and citing documented attacks on people by sharks.
Science - Natural
Dist - FI **Prod** - ABCNEW 1976

Sharks, the true story 60 MIN
VHS
Color (G)
$29.90 purchase _ #0701
Features Peter Benchley, author of 'Jaws,' and Al Giddings, who travel to where the great white sharks feed. Interviews people who have survived attacks.
Science - Natural; Science - Physical
Dist - SEVVID

Sharon and the birds on the way to the wedding 35 MIN
16mm
Color (G)
$60.00 rental, $40.00 purchase
Blurs the line between fact and fiction, personal and cultural perceptions, and the language of love and romance.
Fine Arts; Religion and Philosophy
Dist - CANCIN **Prod** - KIRBYL 1987

Sharon Doubiago - 10 - 16 - 81 60 MIN
VHS / Cassette
Poetry Center reading series
Color (G)
$15.00 purchase, rental _ #450 - 383
Features the writer reading her works at the Poetry Center, San Francisco State University, with an introduction by Tom Mandel.
Literature and Drama
Dist - POETRY

Sharon Lois and Bram at the Young People's Theatre 30 MIN
16mm / U-matic / VHS
Color (P I J)
Captures the three singers doing what they do best, singing in concert in a manner that establishes instant audience rapport. Shows them performing to children of all ages, moms, dads, grandparents, and in informal workshops. Helps young people to develop appreciation for music.
Fine Arts
Dist - BCNFL **Prod** - CAMBFP 1983

Sharon, Lois and Bram's elephant show - Series 1 - Programs 1 - 13 364 MIN
VHS
Elephant show series
Color (P I)
$975.00 purchase
Presents a music education series that teaches reading readiness and social skills while engaging children in making music. Explores a new theme with each program through adventure, fantasy, mystery and song with recording artists Sharon, Lois and Bram. Uses traditional materials which stress participation - action songs, sing - along songs, story songs, clapping songs, singing games, playground chants and folk songs from many different traditions. Includes teacher's guide co - authored by a music education specialist. Includes Schoolyard, Farm Show, Picnic, Friendship, Food Show, Elephant's Doctor, Amusement Park, Rainy Day, Zoo, Lifestyles, Neighborhood, Party and Camp.
Fine Arts; Sociology
Dist - BULFRG **Prod** - CAMBFP 1988

Sharon, Lois and Bram's elephant show - Series 3 - Programs 27 - 39 364 MIN
VHS
Elephant show series
Color (P I)
$975.00 purchase
Presents a music education series that teaches reading readiness and social skills while engaging children in making music. Explores a new theme with each program through adventure, fantasy, mystery and song with recording artists Sharon, Lois and Bram. Uses traditional materials which stress participation - action songs, sing - along songs, story songs, clapping songs, singing games, playground chants and folk songs from many different traditions. Includes teacher's guide. Includes Duet Show, Treasure Island, Overnight, Caribana, Fairy Tale, Grandma Bessie's Birthday, Who Stole the Cookies, Soap Box, Library, Topsy - Turvy Elephant, There's an elephant in that Tree, Growing Up and Hospital.
Fine Arts; Sociology
Dist - BULFRG **Prod** - CAMBFP 1991

Sharon, Lois and Bram's elephant show - Series 2 - Programs 14 - 26 364 MIN
VHS
Elephant show series
Color (P I)
$975.00 purchase
Presents a music education series that teaches reading readiness and social skills while engaging children in making music. Explores a new theme with each program through adventure, fantasy, mystery and song with recording artists Sharon, Lois and Bram. Uses traditional materials which stress participation - action songs, sing - along songs, story songs, clapping songs, singing games, playground chants and folk songs from many different traditions. Includes teacher's guide co - authored by a music education specialist. Includes Funny Field Day, Masquerade, Reversal, Marathon, Clean - up, Kensington Market, Babysitting, Hobby, Pioneer Village, Dance School, Beach Show, Sleepover and Treasure Hunt.
Fine Arts; Sociology
Dist - BULFRG **Prod** - CAMBFP 1989

Sharp and terrible eyes 87 MIN
VHS / 16mm
A Different understanding series
Color (G)
$240.00 purchase _ #BPN178002
Presents the case studies of 2 young offenders. Features interviews with a broad range of experts in the juvenile justice system, including judges, psychiatrists, caseworkers, probation officers, employers and parents. Gives an inside look at the justice system's institutions. Shows the effects of these institutions on the teenager's ego, identity, and moral values.
Sociology
Dist - RMIBHF **Prod** - RMIBHF
TVOTAR

Sharp as a Razor 15 MIN
16mm
Color (PRO)
Illustrates the use of cutting tools in fighting watershed fires.
Health and Safety; Social Science
Dist - FILCOM **Prod** - PUBSF

Sharp AV500 (Audio Cassette Recorder) 7 MIN
U-matic / VHS
Audio - Visual Skills Modules Series
Color
Education; Industrial and Technical Education
Dist - MDCC **Prod** - MDCC

Sharp Eyes, Sharp Talons 16 MIN
U-matic / VHS / 16mm
North American Species Series
Color (P I J)
Describes the different forms of hawks, their adaptation for aerial hunting and their various habitats.
Science - Natural
Dist - BCNFL **Prod** - KARVF 1984

Sharp - Tail Grouse - a Real Prairie Dandy 8 MIN
16mm
Color (I)
Provides a look at the habits of the sharp - tail grouse of North America. Shows the mating dance of the birds at close range.
Science - Natural
Dist - COLIM **Prod** - COLIM

Sharpen your sales presentation - make it a winner 30 MIN
VHS
Color (G)
$565.00 purchase, $150.00 rental _ #91F6018
Features sales trainer Joe Batten who shows how sales personnel can increase sales volume through planning and organization.
Business and Economics; Psychology
Dist - DARTNL **Prod** - DARTNL 1991

Sharpening a Drill on the Drill Grinder 16 MIN
BETA / VHS
Machine Shop - Drill Press, Radial Drill, Drill Grinder Series
Color (IND)
Industrial and Technical Education; Psychology
Dist - RMIBHF **Prod** - RMIBHF

Sharpening a form relieved cutter 18 MIN
16mm
Machine shop work - operations on the cutter grinder, no 5 -'series
B&W
LC FIE51-603
Tells what constitutes the rake and clearance angles of the form relieved cutter. Shows how to mount the correct attachment, set up for spotting the back of teeth and grind the face of the teeth.
Industrial and Technical Education
Dist - USNAC **Prod** - USOE 1944

Sharpening a Plain Helical Milling Cutter 16 MIN
16mm
Precision Wood Machining Series Operations on the Cutter Grinder, no'2
B&W
LC FIE51-601
Shows how to mount the helical cutter on an arbor and sharpen the secondary clearance angle. Describes how to check and adjust for taper when grinding the primary clearance angle.
Industrial and Technical Education
Dist - USNAC **Prod** - USOE 1944

Sharpening a Reamer between Centers 15 MIN
VHS / U-matic
Machining and the Operation of Machine Tools, Module 4 - Milling and'Tool Series
Color (IND)
Industrial and Technical Education
Dist - LEIKID **Prod** - LEIKID

Sharpening a shell end mill 17 MIN
16mm
Machine shop work - operations on the cutter grinder, no 3 -'series
B&W
LC FIE51-602
Shows how to select the correct arbor, mount the work head and adjust it for clearance settings, and set up for sharpening the outside diameter, corner and face.
Industrial and Technical Education
Dist - USNAC **Prod** - USOE 1944

Sharpening a side milling cutter 23 MIN
16mm
Machine shop work - operations on the cutter grinder, no 1 - series
B&W
LC FIE51-600
Shows how to identify the parts of a cutter, select and mount the correct grinding wheel, mount the cutter, set up the grinder for sharpening, set the correct clearance angle and check for width of land.
Industrial and Technical Education
Dist - USNAC **Prod** - USOE 1944

Sharpening an Angular Cutter 18 MIN
16mm
B&W
LC FIE51-604
Explains how to choose the correct grinding wheel, how to adjust the swivel table for grinding the angular teeth of the cutter, adjust for clearance angle and check the teeth for accuracy of the angle.
Industrial and Technical Education
Dist - USNAC **Prod** - USOE 1944

Sharpening and Tempering Farm Tools 17 MIN
16mm 12 MIN
B&W
LC FIE52-304
Demonstrates how to heat carbon steel tools for forge sharpening. Explains how to identify tempering colors.
Agriculture
Dist - USNAC **Prod** - USOE 1945

Sharpening Brazed Carbide Lathe Tools using a Universal Vise 15 MIN
U-matic / VHS

Machining and the Operation of Machine Tools, Module 4 - Milling and Tool Series
Color (IND)
Industrial and Technical Education
Dist - LEIKID **Prod** - LEIKID

Sharpening Chisels, Plane Irons and Gouges 12 MIN
16mm
Hand Tools for Wood Working Series
Color (H C A)
LC FIA67-961
Demonstrates the sharpening of tools for woodwork, including chisels, plane irons and gouges using the grinder and the oilstone.
Industrial and Technical Education
Dist - SF **Prod** - MORLAT 1967

Sharpening drill bits by hand and machine
VHS / U-matic
Basic machine technology series
Color (ENGLISH, SPANISH)
Industrial and Technical Education
Dist - VTRI **Prod** - VTRI

Sharpening Drill Bits by Hand and Machine
U-matic / VHS
Basic Machine Technology - Spanish Series
Color (SPANISH)
Foreign Language; Industrial and Technical Education
Dist - VTRI **Prod** - VTRI

Sharpening ends of end mills
U-matic / VHS
Milling and tool sharpening series
Color (ENGLISH, SPANISH)
Industrial and Technical Education
Dist - VTRI **Prod** - VTRI

Sharpening - Inlaying and Detailing 86 MIN
Videoreel / VHS
Woodworking Series
Color
Discusses how to properly sharpen woodworkng tools. Goes on into beginning inlaying and detailing.
Industrial and Technical Education
Dist - ANVICO **Prod** - ANVICO

Sharpening Lathe Tools Including N/C Lathe Tools
U-matic / VHS
Milling and Tool Sharpening Series
Color (ENGLISH, SPANISH)
Industrial and Technical Education
Dist - VTRI **Prod** - VTRI

Sharpening periodontal instruments 15 MIN
U-matic
Color (PRO)
LC 79-706756
Demonstrates techniques for sharpening periodontal instruments and presents two methods of testing instruments for sharpness.
Health and Safety; Science
Dist - USNAC **Prod** - MUSC 1978

Sharpening Side Milling Cutters, Slitting Saws and Staggered Tooth Cutters
U-matic / VHS
Milling and Tool Sharpening Series
Color
Industrial and Technical Education
Dist - VTRI **Prod** - VTRI

Sharpening techniques for scalers and curettes 14 MIN
VHS / U-matic
Color (C PRO)
$395.00 purchase, $80.00 rental _ #D830 - VI - 014
Shows how to correctly sharpen scalers and curettes. Covers the three objectives of sharpening, the principles of reestablishing the cutting edge, the criteria for evaluating whether the tool is sharp, precise methods of sharpening and several types of stones used for sharpening. Presented by Dorothy J Slattery.
Health and Safety
Dist - HSCIC

Sharpening the focus
VHS / U-matic
Write course - an introduction to college composition series
Color (C)
Discusses the third of three lessons on the pre - writing stage showing how to develop a specific topic from a wide range of ideas. Reinforces the relationship of the composition to the audience.
Education; English Language
Dist - DALCCD **Prod** - DALCCD
FI

Sharpening the Periphery of an End Mill 15 MIN
U-matic / VHS
Machining and the Operation of Machine Tools, Module 4 - Milling and Tool Series
Color (IND)
Industrial and Technical Education
Dist - LEIKID **Prod** - LEIKID

Sharpening the periphery of end mills
VHS / U-matic
Milling and tool sharpening series
Color (ENGLISH, SPANISH)
Industrial and Technical Education
Dist - VTRI **Prod** - VTRI

Sharpening the Periphery of Plain Milling Cutters and Side Mills 15 MIN
U-matic / VHS
Machining and the Operation of Machine Tools, Module 4 - Milling and Tool Series
Color (IND)
Industrial and Technical Education
Dist - LEIKID **Prod** - LEIKID

Sharpening your legal negotiating skills - how to improve settlement results 285 MIN
VHS
Color (PRO)
$125.00, $250.00 purchase, $79.00 rental _ #CP-52247, #CP-62247
Presents discussion of negotiation to settle a legal case, with emphasis on preparation, disclosure, blocking techniques, inducement of an offer, bargaining, weakening the opposing position, recognizing nonverbal communication, interpreting various cultural and sex - based roles, and ethics. Features Charles B Craver. Includes a handbook with the audio or the video program.
Civics and Political Systems
Dist - CCEB

Sharpening your writing of legal documents 135 MIN
VHS
Color (PRO)
$65.00, $125.00 purchase, $49.00 rental _ #MI-53118, #MI-63118
Instructs in ways to improve writing of letters, contracts, memoranda, pleadings, and briefs. Promotes more effective writing. Includes a handbook.
Civics and Political Systems
Dist - CCEB

Sharps, Flats, Keys and Scales 29 MIN
Videoreel / VT2
Playing the Guitar I Series
Color
Fine Arts
Dist - PBS **Prod** - KCET

Shatter the Silence 29 MIN
16mm
Color (J)
LC 80-701150
Dramatizes the confused world of a child who is the victim of incest. Discusses the need for public awareness of this offense, recognition of the emotional needs of the victim and counseling for real and potential victims.
Health and Safety; Psychology; Sociology
Dist - SLFP **Prod** - SLFP 1980

Shattered 21 MIN
U-matic / VHS / 16mm
Color
Explores the social, emotional and legal aftermath of a rape attack. Dispels current myths about the rapist and the victim. Shows rape crisis personnel working with police, family members and prosecuters to help lessen the women's ordeal. Illustrates the role of peer counseling sessions in helping victims cope with the trauma.
Sociology
Dist - CORF **Prod** - CORF

The Shattered Badge 26 MIN
U-matic / VHS / 16mm
Color (J)
LC 82-700612
Deals with the problem of stress in police work and how various officers cope with it.
Civics and Political Systems; Psychology; Social Science; Sociology
Dist - LCOA **Prod** - ABCNEW 1980

Shattered dishes 28 MIN
VHS
Color (G)
$99.00 purchase _ #CE - 074
Focuses on three young women and men who confront the intense emotions surrounding the breakup of their families. Reveals the ways this experience has affected their own development and relationships. Helps children of divorce to recognize and articulate their feelings of abandonment, anger, loss and depression and adds to an understanding of the subtle impact of family conflict. Produced by Deborah Ellman.

Health and Safety; Sociology
Dist - FANPRO

Shattered Dreams - Schizophrenia and the Family 28 MIN
16mm / VHS
Color (H)
$160.00, $550.00 purchase, $30.00 rental
Tells the story of two victims of schizophrenia as told by their brother, focusing on the emotional toll that this disease takes. Indicates that an enlightened and supportive family environment can be crucial to a patient's well - being.
Health and Safety; Psychology
Dist - IU **Prod** - NFBC 1990

Shattered - if your kid's on drugs 60 MIN
VHS
(A)
$29.95 purchase _ #MCA80430V; $24.95 purchase; $24.95 purchase _ #81901
Dramatizes two families' confrontations with drugs. Explores the epidemic of teenage drug abuse. Discusses, family contracts, peer pressure, parental toughness, and personal respsonsibilties. Lists a series of alcohol and drug help centers.
Guidance and Counseling; Psychology; Sociology
Dist - CAMV **Prod** - CAMV
BRODAT MCATV
CMPCAR

Shattered - if Your Kid's on Drugs 60 MIN
VHS
Color (J H C A)
$24.95 _ #81901
Illustrates how living with a drug abusing teenager shatters a family emotionally, physically, and spiritually. Discusses the dynamics of denial, enabling, and manipulating behaviors. Features Judd Nelson and Burt Reynolds.
Guidance and Counseling; Psychology; Sociology
Dist - CMPCAR **Prod** - MCATV

Shavings 30 MIN
U-matic
Explorations in Shaw Series
Color (H)
Interviews friends and neighbors from the village of Ayot St Lawrence who give a private view of Shaw which differs from his public persona as a cranky, socialistic atheist.
Literature and Drama
Dist - TVOTAR **Prod** - TVOTAR 1974

Shavuoth 15 MIN
16mm
Color
Shows how the Festival of Shavuoth is celebrated in Israel.
Geography - World; Religion and Philosophy; Social Science
Dist - ALDEN **Prod** - ALDEN

Shaw vs Shakespeare - Caesar and Cleopatra 33 MIN
VHS
Color (H C G)
$129.00 purchase _ #DL507
Examines the problem of the progress of the human species as presented in George Bernard Shaw's play which centers around four political murders and Caesar's reactions to them. Presents scenes from the play to examine Shaw's idealization of Julius Caesar.
Fine Arts; Literature and Drama
Dist - INSIM

Shaw vs Shakespeare, Pt 1 - the character of Caesar 33 MIN
VHS
Color (H C G)
Features George Bernard Shaw, portrayed by Donald Moffatt, who analyzes Shakespeare's characterization of Julius Caesar and compares it with his own treatment in Caesar and Cleopatra. Uses scenes from both plays to illustrate the different views of Caesar.
Fine Arts; Literature and Drama
Dist - INSIM
EBEC

Shaw vs Shakespeare, Pt 3 - Caesar and Cleopatra 33 MIN
U-matic / VHS / 16mm
Humanities - the drama series
Color (H C)
Features the character of George Bernard Shaw who develops one of his favorite themes, the problem of the progress of the human species, by analyzing the four political murders in Shakespeare's Caesar And Cleopatra.
Literature and Drama
Dist - EBEC **Prod** - EBEC 1970

Shaw vs Shakespeare, Pt 2 - the Tragedy of Julius Caesar 35 MIN
16mm / U-matic / VHS

Humanities - the drama series
Color (H C)
Discusses Shakespeare's Julius Caesar as a tragedy of 'political idealism.' Features the character of George Bernard Shaw who claims that Shakespeare's portrayal of Brutus as 'the complete idealist' helps make this play 'the most splendidly written political melodrama that we possess.'
Literature and Drama
Dist - EBEC **Prod** - EBEC 1970
INSIM

Shaw vs Shakespeare series
Caesar and Cleopatra 33 MIN
The Character of Caesar 33 MIN
The Tragedy of Julius Caesar 35 MIN
Dist - EBEC

Shaw vs Shakespeare - The Tragedy of Julius Caesar 35 MIN
VHS
Color (H C G)
$129.00 purchase _ #DL506
Focuses on Caesar's death and its aftermath, analyzing Shakespeare's drama as a tragedy of political idealism. Examines the character of Brutus, considering whether he is an idealist, as portrayed by Shakespeare, or the villain of the play.
Fine Arts; Literature and Drama
Dist - INSIM

Shaw's Pygmalion 20 MIN
16mm
B&W (H C)
An excerpt from the 1938 feature film 'Pygmalion' based on George Bernard Shaw's play about the transformation in speech, dress and manners of Eliza Doolittle, the Cockney flower girl.
Literature and Drama
Dist - IU **Prod** - PASCAL 1962

Shaw's St Joan 60 MIN
VHS / U-matic
Drama - play, performance, perception series; Module 3
Color (C)
Fine Arts; Literature and Drama
Dist - MDCC **Prod** - MDCC

Shaw's Women 30 MIN
U-matic
Explorations in Shaw Series
Color (H)
Probes George Bernard Shaw's relationships with actresses, women socialists, admirers, his wife and his mother.
Literature and Drama
Dist - TVOTAR **Prod** - TVOTAR 1974

She chase 10 MIN
16mm
Color (G)
$25.00 rental
Peels away the realities of three office workers until their hidden desires are revealed. Experiments with narrative, seductive imagery and music. Produced by Varda Hardy.
Fine Arts
Dist - CANCIN

She Drinks a Little 30 MIN
16mm / U-matic / VHS
Color (J)
LC 81-701053
Shows how a teenager is burdened and traumatized by an alcoholic mother. Depicts how her exposure to organizations such as Alateen helps her to cope emotionally with the situation.
Guidance and Counseling; Health and Safety; Psychology; Sociology
Dist - LCOA **Prod** - TAHSEM 1981

She had her gun all ready 30 MIN
U-matic / VHS
Color
Explores the relationship between two antithetical types, passive Pat Place and active Lydia Lunch. Characterized by increasingly violent animosity.
Fine Arts
Dist - KITCHN **Prod** - KITCHN

She has a Choice 17 MIN
16mm
Color (H C A)
LC 81-701052
Presents women of different ages and backgrounds who share their real - life experiences of dealing with alcoholism. Explores the myths and realities of alcohol and women.
Health and Safety; Psychology
Dist - MTVTM **Prod** - MTVTM 1978

She, he shall overcome 60 MIN
U-matic
Liberation series
Color
Examines male - female stereotyping. Discusses women's as well as men's liberation.
Sociology
Dist - HRC **Prod** - OHC

She is Away 14 MIN
16mm
Color
LC 77-702642
Presents a tone poem of waiting and anticipation which is based on time in its metaphysical aspects.
Literature and Drama; Religion and Philosophy
Dist - CANFDC **Prod** - LITWKS 1975

She must be seeing things 95 MIN
16mm
Color (A)
Presents an independent production by Sheila McLaughlin. Treats the dynamics of sex and sexuality, career and commitment, fidelity and companionship within the context of a love affair between two women.
Fine Arts; Guidance and Counseling; Psychology; Sociology
Dist - FIRS

She must be Seeing Things 95 MIN
VHS / 16mm
Color (G)
$490.00 purchase
Explores gender and power relations in films and real life.
Fine Arts; Sociology
Dist - ICARUS

She sold candies 13 MIN
16mm
Cuba - a view from inside series
Color (G)
$150.00 purchase, $25.00 rental
Tells a satirical story of a metallurgical engineer who, consistently refused work because she's a woman, decides she's better off making and selling candies. Features part of a 17 - part series of shorts by and about Cuban women. Directed by Gerardo Chijona. Illustrated catalog available. Contact distributor for programming advice and discount package rental fees.
Fine Arts; Literature and Drama; Sociology
Dist - CNEMAG

She Stoops to Conquer 119 MIN
VHS / U-matic
Classic Theatre Series
Color
LC 79-706929
Features Ralph Richardson and Tom Courtenay in Oliver Goldsmith's comedy She Stoops To Conquer.
Literature and Drama
Dist - FI **Prod** - BBCTV 1976

She - va 3 MIN
16mm
Color (G)
$20.00 rental
Presents a young dancer rechoreographed through film editing.
Fine Arts
Dist - CANCIN **Prod** - KELLEM 1971

She was like a wild chrysanthemum 92 MIN
VHS / 35mm
B&W (G) (JAPANESE WITH ENGLISH SUBTITLES)
$350.00 rental
Portrays an old man who returns to the village where he grew up and recalls his unrequited love. Directed by Keisuke Kinoshita.
Fine Arts; Literature and Drama
Dist - KINOIC

She wore a yellow ribbon 103 MIN
U-matic / VHS / 16mm
Color (G)
Stars John Wayne as the captain of a U S Cavalry troop in 1876 just after the Custer massacre combating the Indians' final united attempt to drive out the White man. Depicts the Captain's need to escort his commanding officer's family out of the danger zone, complicated by his own impending retirement.
Fine Arts
Dist - FI **Prod** - RKOP 1949
RMIBHF

Shear, Torsion, Creep and Creep Rupture Testing 60 MIN
BETA / VHS / U-matic
Color
$400 purchase
Shows single and double shear tests.
Industrial and Technical Education; Science; Science - Physical
Dist - ASM **Prod** - ASM

Shearing Day 15 MIN
U-matic / VHS
Encounter in the Desert Series
Color (I)
Deals with the lives of Bedouin nomads. Shows sheep - shearing.
Geography - World; Social Science; Sociology
Dist - CTI **Prod** - CTI

Shearing Yaks - Tajik 9 MIN
16mm
Mountain Peoples of Central Asia Series
B&W (P)
LC 73-702415
Explains that the yak herds who stay high in the mountains where it is cool are brought down to the village for shearing. Shows them being sheared with scissors. Describes what happens to the yak's hair after shearing.
Agriculture; Geography - World; Social Science
Dist - IFF **Prod** - IFF 1972

Shedding light on the European single market - updated edition 45 MIN
VHS
Color (A)
$495.00 purchase
Focuses on the Maastricht Treaty and resulting business developments in Europe, emphasizing the issues related to a common market among the nations. Includes two videocassettes.
Business and Economics
Dist - COMFLM

Shedding some light 95 MIN
VHS
Technical theatre series
Color (J H C G)
$95.00 purchase _ #DSV005V
Teaches stage light without hauling tons of lighting instruments and accessories into the classroom. Tours a typical theater including - using the tools of the trade, light instruments and accessories and more. Includes teacher's guide. Part of a five - part series on theater techniques.
Fine Arts
Dist - CAMV

Shedding some light on pesticide protection 14 MIN
VHS
Color (G H)
Covers how much exposure to toxic pesticide chemicals is too much. Discusses long - term effects of exposure. Trains individuals who mix, load or apply chemical pesticides.
Health and Safety; Psychology
Dist - CORNRS **Prod** - USEPA

Shee butter tree - source of butter for the Sahel women 15 MIN
VHS
Fruits of the earth series
Color (G)
$175.00 purchase
Looks at efforts to improve extraction of plant fats from the Shee butter tree for use in cooking by the women of Mali. Considers more efficient harvest methods that can be developed. Part of a series of 15 videos that describe everyday conditions in regions throughout the earth and look at plants available for environmentally sound, economically productive development.
Geography - World; Science - Natural
Dist - LANDMK

The Sheep - 28 11 MIN
VHS / U-matic
Animal families series
Color (K P I)
$225.00, $195.00 purchase _ #V164
Looks at the farm life of sheep. Looks at the different wool types of sheep - long wool, short wool, fine wool and coarse wool. Covers the processing of wool from the back of a sheep to yarn. Part of a series on animal families.
Agriculture; Home Economics; Science - Natural
Dist - BARR **Prod** - GREATT 1989

Sheep Abnormalities 23 MIN
16mm
Color
Many abnormalities in sheep affect their marketability or use as breeding stock. Identifying the visual signs that characterize these problems can help to decide about treating or culling problem animals in the flock.
Agriculture; Science - Natural; Social Science
Dist - UWISCA **Prod** - UWISCA 1982

Sheep and Goats 12 MIN
U-matic / VHS / 16mm
Looking at Animals Series
Color (I J H)
Depicts the characteristics of various breeds of sheep and goats. Points out the close relations between members of the same family group. Shows shearing and wool

processing operations.
Agriculture; Psychology; Science - Natural; Social Science
Dist - IFB **Prod** - BHA 1966

Sheep brain dissection 22 MIN
VHS
Dissection video II series
Color (H C)
$150.00 purchase _ #A5VH 1225
Shows the dissection of a sheep brain, start - to - finish. Provides clear and detailed presentations of the external anatomy, the correct procedures used for dissection and a review of the internal anatomy and physiological systems. Includes a dissection manual and a written examination. Part of a series on dissection.
Science; Science - Natural
Dist - CLRVUE **Prod** - CLRVUE

Sheep castration 15 MIN
VHS
Sheep processes series
Color (A)
$49.95 purchase _ #6 - 053 - 103P
Explains and demonstrates the emasculation of sheep. Part of a three - part series on sheep modification and care.
Agriculture; Health and Safety; Science - Natural
Dist - VEP **Prod** - VEP

Sheep dipping 22 MIN
VHS
Color; PAL; NTSC (G)
PdS66, PdS77 purchase
Shows how COSHH applies to the process of dipping sheep which involves chemicals that are potentially harmful to the humans using them. Demonstrates strategies and practical engineering controls which inspectors should expect to see at dipping facilities. An HSE medical expert outlines symptoms of exposure to dip chemicals and the main causes of contamination. Reminds viewers of the environmental risks associated with the disposal of used sheep dip solution.
Agriculture; Health and Safety
Dist - CFLVIS

Sheep Docking 14 MIN
VHS
Sheep Processes Series
Color (G)
$49.95 purchase _ #6 - 053 - 104P
Explains and demonstrates the docking - tail removal - procedure for sheep. Part of a three - part series on sheep modification and care.
Agriculture; Health and Safety; Science - Natural
Dist - VEP **Prod** - VEP

Sheep farmer 15 MIN
U-matic
Harriet's magic hats II series
(P I J)
Shows how sheep are cared for by people and sheepdogs. Features wool production, shearing and formation of yarn.
Agriculture; Guidance and Counseling
Dist - ACCESS **Prod** - ACCESS 1983

Sheep handling, using equipment and sheep psychology 18 MIN
VHS / U-matic
Managing a flock series
Color
Demonstrates the need for chutes, gates, foot baths, cradles and pens for sheep. Looks at how to use each item.
Agriculture; Science - Natural
Dist - HOBAR **Prod** - HOBAR

The Sheep in the clover field 14 MIN
VHS
Postman Pat series
Color (P I)
$175.00 purchase
Reveals that sheep have strayed into the clover field and Postman Pat and Ted Glenn have a tough time rounding them up. Part of a 13 - part animated puppet series which teaches values.
Guidance and Counseling; Literature and Drama
Dist - LANDMK **Prod** - LANDMK 1991

Sheep in Wood 10 MIN
16mm
Color (J)
LC 75-710644
Presents Jacques Hnizdovsky working in his studio on a woodcut of two rams locked in combat. Uses close - up photography to show each step in the process of making a woodcut, from preliminary sketches to the artist's proof.
Fine Arts; Industrial and Technical Education
Dist - FLMART **Prod** - ARTSCO 1971

Sheep judging practice
VHS
Livestock judging videos series
Color (G)
$49.95 purchase _ #6 - 089 - 100P
Illustrates front, rear, side and head views of Hampshire ram lambs, Suffolk ewes and Hampshire ewes. Shows student judges giving oral reasons and a professional judge critiquing the students. Part of a series of videos on livestock judging.
Agriculture
Dist - VEP **Prod** - VEP

Sheep Judging (Set H) Series
Judging Breeding Sheep 38 MIN
Judging Market Lambs 35 MIN
Practice Sheep Judging
Dist - AAVIM

Sheep management pracrtices - I 54 MIN
VHS
Sheep production series
(C)
$79.95 _ CV154
Gives fundamentals of sheep management practices including the characteristics of sheep, housing and facilities, handling and restraint, lambing, docking, and castration. Set N of the series.
Agriculture
Dist - AAVIM **Prod** - AAVIM 1989

Sheep management practices - II 43 MIN
VHS
Sheep production series
(C)
$79.95 _ CV155
Teaches sheep management practices including identification, internal and external parasite control, footcare, and shearing. Includes a summary with quizzes and answers. Set N of the series.
Agriculture
Dist - AAVIM **Prod** - AAVIM 1989

Sheep Obstetrics 29 MIN
U-matic / VHS
Raising Baby Lambs Series
Color
Discusses the various positions in which lambs may be born. Looks at procedures for assisting in their delivery.
Agriculture; Health and Safety
Dist - HOBAR **Prod** - HOBAR

Sheep processes series
Sheep castration 15 MIN
Sheep Docking 14 MIN
Sheep shearing 22 MIN
Dist - VEP

Sheep production series
Sheep management pracrtices - I 54 MIN
Sheep management practices - II 43 MIN
Dist - AAVIM

Sheep shearing 22 MIN
VHS
Sheep processes series
Color (G)
$49.95 purchase _ #6 - 053 - 105P
Explains and demonstrates correct procedures for safely and efficiently shearing sheep. Part of a three - part series on sheep modification and care.
Agriculture; Science - Natural
Dist - VEP **Prod** - VEP

Sheep shearing 21 MIN
16mm
Farm work series
B&W (ENGLISH, SPANISH)
LC FIE52-358
Explains how to handle sheep for shearing, the steps for shearing and how to roll and tie the fleece. Focuses on livestock in number one of the series.
Agriculture
Dist - USNAC **Prod** - USOE 1944

Sheep, Shearing and Spinning - a Story of Wool 11 MIN
16mm / U-matic / VHS
Color (K P I)
LC 81-700623
Describes the traditional processes used to fashion a wool garment, including sheep shearing, wool spinning, dyeing, and knitting.
Agriculture
Dist - IFB **Prod** - BERLET 1980

Sheep, Sheep, Sheep 11 MIN
16mm / U-matic / VHS
Animals Series
Color (P I)
$210 purchase - 16 mm, $79 purchase - video
Shows the moods, rhythms, and images of sheep. A Dimension Film, directed by Michael Murphy.
Agriculture; Science - Natural
Dist - CF

Sheep Sheep Sheep 11 MIN
U-matic / VHS / 16mm
Animals Series
Color (P I)
$49.95 purchase _ #Q10521; LC 74-708278
Illustrates the moods, rhythms and images of sheep through natural sounds without commentary. Shows sheep as they graze - - eating, sleeping, waking and moving to the highlands.
Agriculture; Science - Natural
Dist - CF **Prod** - CF 1970

Sheep Showmanship
VHS
Color (G)
$29.95 purchase _ #6 - 011 - 100P
Shows how to select and fit good animals for showing. Demonstrates the fitting and showing techniques necessary to win, emphasizes the basics to be mastered. Stages a test contest and concludes with critiques of each shower.
Agriculture; Science - Natural; Social Science; Sociology
Dist - VEP **Prod** - VEP

Sheepmen - Build the Land 27 MIN
16mm
Color (J H)
LC 77-704983
Presents the sheepman's age - old struggle against loneliness, drought, coyotes and cougars in the American West.
Geography - United States; Guidance and Counseling; Psychology; Sociology
Dist - AUDPLN **Prod** - ASPC 1964

Sheepshead Blues 10 MIN
16mm
B&W
Features Charles Mingus in a performance of his own jazz music.
Fine Arts
Dist - NYU **Prod** - NYU

Sheer craziness 8 MIN
16mm
Color
Presents a brief glimpse into the motorcycle counterculture of motocross racing. Follows a race from tune - up to the checkered flag.
Industrial and Technical Education; Physical Education and Recreation
Dist - UPITTS **Prod** - UPITTS 1974

Sheet Metal Machinery 117 MIN
VHS / 35mm strip
(H A IND)
#518XV7
Shows the foot operated shear, turret punch press, tab notcher, hand operated shear, single station punch, hand operated press brake, finger brake, hand operated bender, and hand operated slip roller (9 tapes). Includes a Study Guide.
Education; Industrial and Technical Education
Dist - BERGL

Sheet Metal - Making a Five - Piece Elbow 13 MIN
16mm
Color (H C A)
Shows the use of patterns and steps in laying out the elbow gores, types of snips and the squaring shear, as they are used in cutting the gores. Explains folding edges of the bar folder, the use of the slip - roll former, making the seams, turning and burring gore edges and the final assembly of the elbow.
Industrial and Technical Education
Dist - SF **Prod** - SF 1969

Sheet Metal - Pattern Development 13 MIN
16mm
Color (J A)
Shows the importance of three - dimensional visualization through demonstrations with various objects. Explains the principles of parallel line development, triangulation and radial line development.
Industrial and Technical Education
Dist - SF **Prod** - SF 1969

Sheet Metal Processing 19 MIN
U-matic / VHS
Manufacturing Materials and Processes Series
Color
Covers types of sheet metal processing, shearing, cutting, bending, drawing, spinning and expanding.
Industrial and Technical Education
Dist - WFVTAE **Prod** - GE

Sheet metal trades 9 MIN
U-matic / VHS / 16mm
Career job opportunity series
Color

LC 73-700513
Shows sheet metal workers assembling helicopter fuselage sections, making kitchens, air - conditioning and air - moving equipment, forming and finishing large electric duct, custom building metal cabinets and commercial alphabets in sheet - metal and joining plastic helicopter cabs to metal framework. Number 14 in the series.
Guidance and Counseling; Industrial and Technical Education
Dist - USNAC **Prod** - USDL 1968

Sheet metal upset 11 MIN
VHS / BETA / 16mm
Color (A PRO)
$63.50 purchase _ #KTI67
Shows metal upset in low crowned panels. Recommends procedure for repair.
Industrial and Technical Education
Dist - RMIBHF **Prod** - RMIBHF

Sheet Metal Work
VHS
Metalworking Industrial Arts Series
(H C G)
$59.00 _ CA217
Shows layout, cutting, bending, joining and use of hand tools, bench anvils, squaring shear, box and pan brake.
Industrial and Technical Education
Dist - AAVIM **Prod** - AAVIM 1989

Sheet metal worker 5 MIN
VHS / 16mm
Good works 3 series
Color (H)
Presents the occupation of a sheet metal worker. Gives a profile of a young person who is either undergoing an apprenticeship or has recently completed training in this field. Takes the viewer on a tour of this person's workplace and explains the practical skills and training offered by employers and schools. Gives a better understanding of the demand for skilled workers today and the potential for personal growth.
Guidance and Counseling
Dist - RMIBHF **Prod** - RMIBHF
TVOTAR

Sheet metal working - advanced equipment 9 MIN
VHS / 16mm / U-matic
Color (J H A G) (ENGLISH, ARABIC)
Teaches the use of the floor shear, electric shears, the Rotex turrent punch and several common sheet metal stakes by making a funnel from sixteen - gauge sheet metal. Covers the anvil horn, the rotary machine, rollers, the Beverly battery shear and the sliproll.
Health and Safety; Industrial and Technical Education
Dist - AAVIM **Prod** - AAVIM 1992
AIMS

Sheet Metal Working - Basic Equipment 8 MIN
16mm / U-matic / VHS
Color (J) (ARABIC)
LC 79-700883
Demonstrates the basic tools and techniques of working with sheet metal. Shows the purposes and operation of each piece of equipment and emphasizes efficient work practices and cleanup.
Industrial and Technical Education
Dist - AIMS **Prod** - AIMS 1978

Sheet metal working - basic equipment 8 MIN
VHS
Color (J H A G)
$49.95 purchase _ #AM9562
Demonstrates basic tools and techniques of sheet metal working through creation of a twelve - inch square dustbin. Shows step - by - step the purposes and operation of equipment and provides useful tips at each stage, emphasizing efficient work practices, cleanup and safety.
Health and Safety; Industrial and Technical Education
Dist - AAVIM **Prod** - AAVIM 1992

Sheet Metalwork 102 MIN
VHS / 35mm strip
(H A IND)
#507XV7
Shows an introduction and overview, straight line pattern development, parallel and radial line pattern development, cutting methods, drilling and forming and bending (pt 1), forming and bending (pt 2), and assembly and fastening (7 tapes). Includes a Study Guide.
Education; Industrial and Technical Education
Dist - BERGL

Sheet rock 30 MIN
U-matic / VHS
You can fixit series
Color
Discusses the installation of sheet rock.
Industrial and Technical Education
Dist - MDCPB **Prod** - WRJATV

Sheffey 135 MIN
16mm
Color (R)
Depicts events from the life of Robert S Sheffey, a nineteenth century circuit rider. Based on the book The Saint Of The Wilderness by Jess Carr.
Religion and Philosophy
Dist - UF **Prod** - UF

Sheila Isham - An Artist's odyssey 28 MIN
U-matic / VHS
Color (H C A)
$39.95, $59.95 purchase
Follows artist Sheila Isham in her travels to Germany, Russia, China, Haiti, India and New York. Documents her search for personal truth as she delves into the foreign cultures, religions and philosophies she encounters. Presents her work as a combination of eastern and western approaches to art.
Fine Arts
Dist - ARTSAM

Sheila Tobias, Political Science, Education 29 MIN
U-matic / VHS
Quest for Peace Series
Color (A)
Civics and Political Systems; Education
Dist - AACD **Prod** - AACD 1984

Sheila Walsh - shadowlands 66 MIN
VHS
Color (G R)
$19.95 purchase _ #35 - 85024 - 533
Presents Christian vocalist Sheila Walsh in a performance of her songs, including 'Turn, Turn, Turn,' 'We're All One,' 'Christian,' and many others.
Fine Arts; Religion and Philosophy
Dist - APH **Prod** - WORD

Sheldon Glashow - unifying forces 16 MIN
VHS
Nobel prize series
Color (J H C)
$49.00 purchase _ #2317 - SK
Features Sheldon Glashow, Nobel Prize winner, whose work in theoretical physics has shown that electromagnetic and weak nuclear forces are actually manifestations of the same force. Includes student notebook and teacher resource book, with additional student workbooks available at an extra charge. Presents the portion of the series focusing on chemistry and physics.
History - World; Science; Science - Physical
Dist - SUNCOM

The Sheldon Trio 29 MIN
Videoreel / VT2
B&W
Features chamber music of the Sheldon Trio at Nebraska's Arbor Lodge State Historical Park.
Fine Arts
Dist - PBS **Prod** - NETCHE

Sheldon Wolin 30 MIN
VHS
World Of Ideas With Bill Moyers - Season I - series
Color (G)
$39.95 purchase _ #BMWI - 121
Interviews Princeton University professor Sheldon Wolin. Unveils Wolin's emphasis on democracy, power and the role of the state. Reviews his years as a professor at the University of California at Berkeley in the tumultuous 1960s. Hosted by Bill Moyers.
Civics and Political Systems; History - United States; Sociology
Dist - PBS

Shelf Sediments - Storms and Tides 17 MIN
VHS / 16mm
Sedimentary Processes and Basin Analysis Series
Color (C)
$150.00, $185.00 purchase _ #269505
Illustrates the key concepts, economic relevance and influence of measurement technology advances in palaeoenvironmental and basin analysis. Observes how large parts of the earth's crust subside and accumulate thick deposits of sediments, possible reservoirs for oil, gas and coal. Divides into four themes - Sedimentary Petrology, Sedimentary Environments, Basin Analysis and North Sea - Western Canada Case Studies. 'Shelf Sediments - Storms And Tides' explores how shelf sediments are influenced by both wave and tidal processes. The Canadian Rockies sedimentary sequence illustrates storm activity, while an English cretaceous site, Leighton Buzzard, reveals tidal action.
Geography - World; Science - Physical
Dist - ACCESS **Prod** - BBCTV 1987

Shelf Sediments - Upper Jurassic of Dorset 17 MIN
VHS / 16mm
Sedimentary Processes and Basin Analysis Series
Color (C)
$150.00, $185.00 purchase _ #269506
Illustrates the key concepts, economic relevance and influence of measurement technology advances in palaeoenvironmental and basin analysis. Observes how large parts of the earth's crust subside and accumulate thick deposits of sediments, possible reservoirs for oil, gas and coal. Divides into four themes - Sedimentary Petrology, Sedimentary Environments, Basin Analysis and North Sea - Western Canada Case Studies. 'Shelf Sediments - Upper Jurassic Of Dorset' examines the Upper Jurassic shelf sediments found in the cliffs of the Dorset coast in the form of a geology field trip. The main sediment sequences analyzed are the Corallian Beds, Nothe Clay and the Bencliff Grit Beds.
Geography - World; Science - Physical
Dist - ACCESS **Prod** - BBCTV 1987

The Shell
U-matic / VHS
UNIX overview series
Color
Describes the UNIX shell as a programming language and as a command interpreter. Illustrates the file name generation, pipes and filters. Unit four of the series.
Business and Economics; Industrial and Technical Education; Mathematics; Sociology
Dist - COMTEG **Prod** - COMTEG

Shell as a command language
U-matic / VHS
UNIX and 'C' language training - a full curriculum series
Color
Industrial and Technical Education; Mathematics; Sociology
Dist - COMTEG **Prod** - COMTEG

Shell files - Pt I 30 MIN
U-matic / VHS
UNIX series
Color (IND)
Lecture tells about shell variables, grave accents, substitution parameters, while ... do, for ... do, Command Search Strategy, and Commands - eval, sh, test, shift, and echo (- n).
Industrial and Technical Education; Mathematics; Sociology
Dist - COLOSU **Prod** - COLOSU

Shell files - Pt II 30 MIN
U-matic / VHS
UNIX series
Color (IND)
Goes into if ... then, case, Arithmetic and Relational Operations, and following commands - read, expr, continue, and test (- f, - r, - w, - d).
Industrial and Technical Education; Mathematics; Sociology
Dist - COLOSU **Prod** - COLOSU

Shell Mounds in the Tennessee Valley 15 MIN
16mm
B&W (H C A)
LC 80-701174
Describes archeological work in the Tennessee Valley Authority's reservoir area prior to impoundment. Shows excavation of shell mounds which mark prehistoric villages.
Geography - United States; Science - Physical
Dist - USNAC **Prod** - TVA 1965

Shell programming
U-matic / VHS
UNIX and 'C' language training - a full curriculum series
Color
Industrial and Technical Education; Mathematics; Sociology
Dist - COMTEG **Prod** - COMTEG

Shelley and Pete - and Carol 23 MIN
16mm / U-matic / VHS
Color (H)
Describes the responsibilities which teenage parents must face, including their changing relationships with their parents, peers, and one another.
Sociology
Dist - USNAC **Prod** - USDHHS 1980

Shelley finds her way 30 MIN
U-matic
Khan Du series
Color (S P I)
LC 78-706323
Tells about a young blind girl who wants to be a creative writer but is afraid to go to class. Explains how she meets a magical creature named Khan Du, who shows her other people with disabilities who can do many things because they have tried.
Education; Guidance and Counseling; Psychology
Dist - USNAC **Prod** - USOE 1978

Shelley Whitebird's first powwow 8 MIN
U-matic / VHS / 16mm
Color (P I)
$49.00 purchase _ #3501; LC 77-703275
Presents a story about a young girl who is preparing for her first powwow. Shows the cultural and artistic heritage of a Native American Indian tribe.
Social Science
Dist - EBEC **Prod** - LIFSTY 1977

Shelley Without Hearing 38 MIN
U-matic
Color (A)
LC 80-706691
Observes a typical day for a four - year - old deaf girl at a day - care center as she interacts with other children and plays by herself.
Guidance and Counseling; Psychology; Science - Natural
Dist - CTVS **Prod** - CTVS 1979

Shellfish 20 MIN
VHS / U-matic
Color (I A)
Shows breeding, harvesting and processing shellfish.
Science - Natural; Social Science
Dist - SUTHRB **Prod** - SUTHRB

Shellfishing in the Chesapeake 25 MIN
16mm
Color (I)
Deals with the methods and equipment used in catching oysters, crabs and clams.
Geography - United States; Physical Education and Recreation; Psychology; Social Science
Dist - VADE **Prod** - VADE 1956

Shells and rushes 14 MIN
16mm
Color (G)
$30.00 rental
Creates a world reminiscent of the surrealists, full of allusions to classical mythology and uses of negative - positive space. Travels to Alaska in the summertime then focuses on the artist's table where a marble chessboard sits.
Fine Arts
Dist - CANCIN **Prod** - COUZS 1987

Shells and the animals inside 20 MIN
16mm
Color
LC 80-700635
Demonstrates how to present the topic of mollusks to children through the use of specimens, discussion, art, creative writing, and fantasy.
Education; Science; Science - Natural
Dist - USNAC **Prod** - SMITHS 1979

Shelly Manne Quartet 28 MIN
VHS
Color (G)
$19.95 purchase
Offers some jazz renditions from the Shelly Manne Quartet.
Fine Arts
Dist - KINOIC **Prod** - RHPSDY

Shelter 11 MIN
U-matic / VHS / 16mm
Color (P I)
LC 80-700711
Looks at the history of housing and community development. Outlines the many uses of shelter.
Social Science; Sociology
Dist - EBEC **Prod** - EBEC 1980

Shelter 11 MIN
VHS / U-matic / 16mm
Basic needs series
Color (P)
$320.00, $250.00 purchase _ #HP - 5928C
Uses animation and live action to explain the form and function of shelter. Stars two aliens who examine how homes are constructed, from tree to finished product. Illustrates the importance of shelter for safety, solitude, family and happiness. Part of a series produced by Bill Walker Productions.
Geography - World; Social Science; Sociology
Dist - CORF

Shelter 55 MIN
VHS
Color (H C G)
$445.00 purchase, $75.00 rental
Reveals that not since the Great Depression have so many Americans been homeless. Examines the causes of homelessness through interviews and portraits of the homeless. Meets a man who has been on the road for five years in search of a job, a mentally ill person who was turned out of a hospital without adequate preparation for independent living, a family with two children who migrated from Maine to Seattle in search of work, representing the new poor, the victims of recession.
Business and Economics; Sociology
Dist - FLMLIB **Prod** - KCTSTV 1987

Shelter Around the World 14 MIN
U-matic / VHS / 16mm
Basic Needs Series
Color (P I)
LC 79-700541
Shows how people throughout the world use the resources of their environment for shelter and how they adapt their housing to their culture and lifestyles.
Social Science; Sociology
Dist - PHENIX **Prod** - MITC 1979

Shelter Construction in Winter 13 MIN
16mm
Color (I J H)
LC FIA68-1288
Explains that comfortable shelters can be constructed easily, even during winter's cold conditions. Shows some of the methods used to build comfortable shelters.
Physical Education and Recreation; Social Science
Dist - SF **Prod** - SF 1967

Shelter for the homeless 27 MIN
VHS / U-matic
Color (H C G)
$420.00, $390.00 purchase _ #V468
Reveals that approximately one - quarter of the world's population does not have adequate housing and lives in appalling conditions. Describes a Sri Lanka program which enables families living under the poverty level to build their own homes with government help. Focuses also on Rio de Janiero's new policy of land tenure which helps shantytowns become functioning neighborhoods.
Geography - World; Sociology
Dist - BARR **Prod** - CEPRO 1988

Shelter stories 14 MIN
VHS
Color (G)
$145.00 purchase, $100.00 rental _ #079
Features five homeless teens who collaborate with a professional videographer to tell their stories about living with their families in homeless shelters. Uses interviews and dramatizations to tell about shelter conditions, the effects on their school and family lives, the harassment they suffer from other children, and their new awareness of how the media and society deal with homelessness. Produced by Meryl Perlson.
Sociology
Dist - FANPRO

Sheltered workshop 5 MIN
16mm / U-matic / VHS
Color
Shows that actual work experience, adjusted to the levels of students' abilities, is offered through the sheltered workshop program. Portrays students working on a sub - contract basis, processing products that are used in the consumer market. Points out that financial proceeds are divided among the trainees who enjoy being useful and productive wage earners.
Education; Guidance and Counseling; Psychology
Dist - IFB **Prod** - THORNE

Sheltered Workshops 26 MIN
16mm
Color (H)
LC 70-711463
Discusses the role of volunteer organizations in setting up special workshops for the training and employment of mentally and physically handicapped people.
Sociology
Dist - AUIS **Prod** - AUSCOF

The Shema - an affirmation of belief, love and trust 15 MIN
VHS / U-matic
Tradition and contemporary Judaism - prayer and the Jewish people series
Color
Explores the three themes of the Shema. Discusses the centrality of learning within Judaism. Program three of the series.
Religion and Philosophy
Dist - ADL **Prod** - ADL

Shenandoah 105 MIN
16mm
Color
Stars James Stewart as an irascible widowed Virginia landowner who fights the forces that attempt to draw him and his sons into the Civil War.
Fine Arts
Dist - TWYMAN **Prod** - UPCI 1965

Shenandoah - Dickey Ridge 14 MIN
U-matic / VHS / 16mm
Color
Shows things to see and do in Shenandoah National Park and on Skyline Drive.
Geography - United States
Dist - USNAC **Prod** - USNPS 1982

Shenandoah - the Gift 19 MIN
16mm / U-matic / VHS
Color
Traces the 40 - year development of Shenandoah National Park from depleted and ravaged land into a wilderness park.
Geography - United States; Science - Natural; Social Science
Dist - USNAC **Prod** - USNPS 1982

The Shepherd 11 MIN
16mm / U-matic / VHS
B&W (H C A)
Tells how the tranquil serenity of a shepherd is broken when he finds signs of a marauder.
Fine Arts
Dist - IFB **Prod** - NFBC 1955

The Shepherd 12 MIN
16mm / U-matic / VHS
B&W (I J)
Portrays a day in the life of a shepherd and his two sheep dogs in British Columbia.
Agriculture; Geography - World
Dist - IFB **Prod** - NFBC 1959

The Shepherd 15 MIN
U-matic / VHS
Encounter in the Desert Series
Color (I)
Deals with agriculture and livestock in the lives of Bedouin people.
Geography - World; Social Science; Sociology
Dist - CTI **Prod** - CTI

Shepherd dog and his flock 8 MIN
U-matic / VHS / 16mm
See'n tell series
Color (P I J)
LC 75-706312
Shows two German shepherd dogs as they help their masters to herd sheep.
Agriculture; Science - Natural
Dist - FI **Prod** - PMI 1970

Shepherd life 14 MIN
16mm
Color; B&W (I)
Illustrates the typical shepherd life of people of Bible times by showing the life of the nomadic shepherds of Palestine, much of which remains unchanged since Biblical days.
Agriculture; Geography - World; Religion and Philosophy; Sociology
Dist - FAMF **Prod** - FAMF 1960

The Shepherd's family 22 MIN
16mm / VHS
Films from Andalusia, Spain series
B&W (G)
$400.00, $200.00 purchase, $45.00, $30.00 rental
Portrays a shepherd's family which remains tied to its traditional occupation and its semi - feudal role in rural society. Reveals that the children help by guarding the flock and by earning additional wages through gathering snails, picking cotton and hoeing. Part of a series.
Geography - World; History - World; Sociology
Dist - DOCEDR **Prod** - MINTZJ 1987

The Shepherd's Hat 16 MIN
16mm
Animatoons Series
Color
LC FIA68-1537
A story about the origin of the perpetual hatred of dogs for cats which resulted after kitten hatmakers sold a shepherd dog's hat to a maharajah.
Literature and Drama
Dist - RADTV **Prod** - ANTONS 1968

The Shepherd's hat - Pt 1 11 MIN
16mm
Animatoons series
Color
LC FIA67-5509
Tells the story of a shepherd dog who orders a hat from kitten hatmakers who prefer catering to nobility.
Fine Arts
Dist - RADTV **Prod** - ANTONS 1968

The Shepherd's hat - Pt 2 11 MIN
16mm
Animatoons series
Color
LC FIA67-5510
Shows how the kitten hatmakers make a hat for the shepherd dog but sell it to a Maharajah, thus initiating the perpetual hatred of dogs for cats.
Fine Arts
Dist - RADTV **Prod** - ANTONS 1968

Sheraton Reservations 14 MIN
16mm
Color
LC 76-702890
Presents a series of musical vignettes and comedy sequences to describe features of a world - wide hotel reservations system.
Business and Economics; Geography - World
Dist - ITTSHE **Prod** - ITTSHE 1976

Sherbets and ice cream
VHS
Frugal gourmet - entertaining series
Color (G)
$19.95 purchase _ #CCP847
Shows how to prepare sherbets and ice cream. Features Jeff Smith, the Frugal Gourmet. Part of a ten - part series on preparing food for entertaining.
Home Economics
Dist - CADESF **Prod** - CADESF

Sheridan's world of society 17 MIN
16mm / U-matic / VHS
Color (H C)
LC 72-702120
Traces the life of dramatist - statesman Richard Brinsley Sheridan and the society in which he lived. Uses paintings, cartoons and portraits by artists of the period to depict events in Sheridan's life, as he went from a popular playwright and theater owner to a gambling, drinking politician who died a pauper.
Biography; Fine Arts; History - World; Literature and Drama
Dist - IFB **Prod** - SEABEN 1972

Sherlock Holmes
CD-ROM
(G)
$49.00 purchase _ #1951
Contains the complete text of all the Sherlock Holmes novels and stories by Arthur Conan Doyle, as well as The Medical Casebook of Dr Arthur Conan Doyle, block prints by George Wells, and Medical Poetry by George Bascom. Enables users to search by phrases, words, and browsing. For IBM PCs and compatibles, requires 640K RAM, DOS 3.1 or later, one floppy disk drive - hard disk recommended, one empty expansion slot, an IBM compatible CD - ROM drive, and a VGA monitor to view the images. For Macintosh Classic, Plus, SE and II computers, requires 1MB of RAM, one floppy disk drive, and an Apple compatible CD - ROM drive.
Literature and Drama
Dist - BEP

Sherlock Holmes and a study in scarlet 67 MIN
U-matic / VHS
Sherlock Holmes series
Color (K P I)
Presents an animated children's version of some of the Sherlock Holmes stories. Peter O'Toole is the voice of Sherlock as he, Dr Watson and the Baker Street Irregulars unravel puzzles and solve mysteries.
Fine Arts; Literature and Drama
Dist - PAV **Prod** - RPTAV 1983

Sherlock Holmes and the Baskerville Curse 67 MIN
U-matic / VHS
Sherlock Holmes series
Color (K P I)
Presents an animated children's version of some of the Sherlock Holmes stories. Features Peter O'Toole as the voice of Sherlock as he, Dr Watson and the Baker Street Irregulars unravel puzzles and solve mysteries.
Fine Arts; Literature and Drama
Dist - PAV **Prod** - RPTAV 1983

Sherlock Holmes and the sign of four 67 MIN
U-matic / VHS
Sherlock Holmes series
Color (K P I)
Presents an animated children's version of some of the Sherlock Holmes stories. Peter O'Toole is the voice of Sherlock as he, Dr Watson and the Baker Street Irregulars unravel puzzles and solve mysteries.
Fine Arts; Literature and Drama
Dist - PAV **Prod** - RPTAV 1983

Sherlock Holmes and the valley of fear 67 MIN
U-matic / VHS
Sherlock Holmes series
Color (K P I)
Presents an animated children's version of some of the Sherlock Holmes stories. Peter O'Toole is the voice of Sherlock as he, Dr Watson and the Baker Street Irregulars unravel puzzles and solve mysteries.
Fine Arts; Literature and Drama
Dist - PAV **Prod** - RPTAV 1983

Sherlock Holmes series
Sherlock Holmes and a study in scarlet 67 MIN
Sherlock Holmes and the Baskerville Curse 67 MIN
Sherlock Holmes and the sign of four 67 MIN
Sherlock Holmes and the valley of fear 67 MIN
Dist - PAV

Sherlock Holmes with Mr Magoo 26 MIN
16mm / U-matic / VHS
Mr Magoo in great world classics series
Color (I J)
Presents Magoo as Dr Watson, the bumbling friend of Sir Arthur Conan Doyle's famed detective who solves baffling crimes by sheer deduction from seemingly unimportant clues.
Fine Arts; Literature and Drama
Dist - FI **Prod** - FLEET

Sherlock Jr 46 MIN
16mm
B&W (J)
Stars Buster Keaton. Tells of a projectionist in a motion picture theatre who falls asleep, enters the plot of the movie he is showing and fulfills his secret desire to become a great detective.
Fine Arts
Dist - TWYMAN **Prod** - MGM 1924

Sherman's March 155 MIN
16mm
Color (G)
Presents an independent production by Ross McElwee which focuses on McElwee's pursuit of women along the original route of General Sherman's Civil War March in search of true romance.
Fine Arts; Guidance and Counseling; Literature and Drama; Psychology
Dist - FIRS

Sherpa 28 MIN
U-matic / VHS / 16mm
Color
Examines the culture of the Sherpa who live at the base of Mount Everest. Focuses on one family.
Geography - World; Sociology
Dist - CEPRO **Prod** - CEPRO

Sherpa high country 20 MIN
16mm / U-matic / VHS
Color
Looks at the Sherpas of the Solu Khumbu highlands in Nepal, near Mt Everest. Focuses on the Mani - Rimdu ceremony, a three - day dance drama performed by monks celebrating Buddhist teachings.
Geography - World; Religion and Philosophy
Dist - UCEMC **Prod** - LISANX 1977

Sherpas 53 MIN
VHS
Disappearing world series
Color (G C)
$99.00 purchase, $19.00 rental _ #51218
Reveals that since 1953, when a Nepalese accompanied Sir Edmund Hillary on the first Expedition to the summit of Mount Everest, Sherpas have become famous as mountain guides. Looks at the contrasting lives of three Himalayan brothers - a Buddhist monk, a farmer and an expedition guide. Features anthropologist Sherry Ortner. Part of a series working closely with anthropologists who lived for a year or more in societies whose social structures, beliefs and practices are threatened by the expansion of technocratic civilization.
Physical Education and Recreation; Sociology
Dist - PSU **Prod** - GRANDA 1977

The Sherpas 25 MIN
16mm / U-matic / VHS
Untamed world series series
Color; Mono (J H C A)
$400.00 film, $250.00 video, $50.00 rental
Looks at life among the Sherpas and the dominance of religious practices in their society.
Geography - World; Religion and Philosophy; Sociology
Dist - CTV **Prod** - CTV 1971

The Sherpas of Everest 30 MIN
U-matic / VHS
Journey into the Himalayas series
Color (J S C A)
MV=$195.00
Shows a pilgrimage to the slopes of Everest by a Sherpa who climbed to the summit in 1975.
Geography - World; Physical Education and Recreation
Dist - LANDMK **Prod** - LANDMK 1986

Sherrill Milnes at Julliard - an Opera Master Class 75 MIN
VHS
Color (S)
$39.95 purchase _ #153 - 9002
Features six advanced voice students performing for renouned baritone Sherrill Milnes. Demonstrates Mr. Milnes critiquing and instructing each student, illustrating vocal techniques and phrasing.
Fine Arts
Dist - FI **Prod** - ROPE 1987

Sherrill Milnes - homage to Verdi 56 MIN
VHS
Color (G)
$19.95 purchase _ #1117
Tours the home region of Giuseppe Verdi, Italy's Po Valley. Features host Sherrill Milnes singing excerpts from Verdi's 'La Traviata,' 'Rigoletto,' and 'Nabucco.'
Fine Arts; Foreign Language; Geography - World
Dist - KULTUR

Sherry Millner Series
Out of the Mouth of Babes 24 MIN
Scenes from the Microwar 24 MIN
Womb with a View 40 MIN
Dist - WMEN

Sherwood Anderson - storyteller's town 29 MIN
VHS / U-matic
Color (H C A)
Tours Clyde, Ohio, the town where Sherwood Anderson grew up and the model for the setting of his novel, Winesburg, Ohio. Examines the people and events that helped shape Anderson's literary career.
Literature and Drama
Dist - GA CEPRO **Prod** - GA CEPRO

Sherwood Anderson's blue ridge country 29 MIN
U-matic
Color (H C A)
Dramatizes Sherwood Anderson's newspaper days in Virginia after he had become famous for his novel Winesburg, Ohio.
Biography; Literature and Drama
Dist - CEPRO **Prod** - CEPRO

She's a Railroader 10 MIN
16mm / U-matic / VHS
Color (J)
LC 81-700794
Presents a portrait of Karen Zaitchik, who works on the railroad, a traditionally male field. Emphasizes that there are alternatives to office jobs for women.
Social Science; Sociology
Dist - PHENIX **Prod** - NFBC 1980

She's in the Army Now 26 MIN
16mm
Color
LC 79-701013
Shows the rigorous training of women for combat duty in the American armed forces. Visits three military bases and includes interviews with recruits, drill sergeants and officers.
Civics and Political Systems; Sociology
Dist - WJLATV **Prod** - WJLATV 1978

She's just growing up, dear 16 MIN
VHS / 16mm
B&W (G)
$55.00 rental, $275.00 purchase
Presents powerful recollections of a woman's emerging realization that she was sexually abused as a child by her father, combined with kitsch 1950s media imagery. Examines the profound emotional complexity of incest and contrasts the constructed images of American family values with the voice of reality. Poses questions about the female psyche, memory and denial, nostagia for childhood and modern ideas about sexuality. A film by Julia Tell.
Psychology; Sociology
Dist - WMEN

She's Nobody's Baby - a History of American Women in the 20th Century 36 MIN
55 MIN
16mm / VHS / U-matic
Color (H C A J) (SPANISH)
Surveys the trends in women's roles and lives through the twentieth century. Hosted by Marlo Thomas and Alan Alda.
History - United States; History - World; Sociology
Dist - CORF **Prod** - ABCNEW 1982

She's pregnant and she's a junkie - mothers, crack and babies 43 MIN
VHS
Color (H C A PRO)
$165.00 purchase
Documents the sometimes hopeless, sometimes hopeful lives of three pregnant drug addicts and the support network of care providers, family members and doctors who treat them and their newborns. Raises the complex issues and challenges of meeting the health, social and educational needs of drug - affected families.
Education; Guidance and Counseling; Psychology; Sociology
Dist - SELMED

She's Waiting for Us 25 MIN
16mm / U-matic / VHS
Insight Series
Color
LC 79-700647
Tells the story of a boy who is taught to accept responsibility for his actions.
Guidance and Counseling
Dist - PAULST **Prod** - PAULST 1977

The Shetland Experience 27 MIN
16mm
Color
Depicts the care and concern for the environment which is being taken by the oil industry in building Europe's biggest transshipment point for oil at the Shetland Islands.
Geography - World; History - World; Social Science
Dist - MTP **Prod** - BPNA

Shew - be - do - Wop - Wah - Wah 29 MIN
VHS / 16mm
Watch your mouth series
Color (H)
$46.00 rental _ #WAYM - 114
Emphasizes language and communication skills for high school students. Notes the difference between formal and informal word usage.
Education; English Language; Psychology; Social Science
Dist - PBS

Shhh - I'm finding a job - the library and your self - directed job search 40 MIN
VHS
Color (H C G)
$79.95 purchase _ #CCP0128V
Details how the library gives job seekers needed information to launch themselves in the job market. Shows how to capitalize on strengths, minimize weaknesses, aggressively build a job network, develop valuable leads through informational interviews, create dynamic resumes and cover letters and become more confident and better - armed for job interviews. Includes manual.
Business and Economics; Guidance and Counseling; Social Science
Dist - CAMV **Prod** - CAMV 1993

Shi no Zadanki 27 MIN
U-matic
Color (JAPANESE)
A Japanese language videotape. Discusses contemporary Japanese poetry with Yoshimasu Gozo and Yoshihara Sachiko, two Japanese poets visiting the International Writing Program at the University of Iowa.
Literature and Drama
Dist - UIOWA **Prod** - UIOWA 1980

Shiatsu massage 90 MIN
VHS
Color (G)
$39.95 purchase _ #HE - 07
Demonstrates shiatsu massage. Features Jerry Lugio.
Health and Safety; Physical Education and Recreation
Dist - ARVID **Prod** - ARVID

The Shield 13 MIN
U-matic
Color
Presents the testimony of men who escaped blindness because they wore eye protection on - the - job. Encourages the use of appropriate 100 per cent eye and face protection on - the - job and for school shop safety.
Health and Safety; Industrial and Technical Education; Science - Natural
Dist - HF **Prod** - HF 1972

The Shield 51 MIN
VHS / U-matic / 16mm
Canada - five portraits series
Color; Mono (G) (FRENCH)
MV $350.00 _ MP 600.00 purchase, $50.00 rental
Tells of the overwhelming influence of the pre - Cambrian Shield on the Canadian way of life. Describes how the meager provisions of the rocky terrain have squeezed the North American population south. Only nomadic people and nomadic - like traders and trappers have been able to eke out a living in this cold and harsh land.
Geography - World; Science - Natural; Science - Physical
Dist - CTV **Prod** - CTV 1973

Shield against invasion 14 MIN
16mm
Color
LC FIE63-122
Emphasizes the need for constant evaluation of America's weapons and aircraft. Shows how these evaluations are accomplished.
Civics and Political Systems
Dist - USNAC **Prod** - USDD 1959

Shield of freedom 28 MIN
16mm
Color
LC 74-706241
Raymond Massey explains the Air Defense Command's dominant role in organizing, training and providing aerospace defense forces to NORAD. Portrays the magnitude of the Command's mission, including the detection, identification, interception and destruction of manned bomber or missile attacks on the North American continent.
Civics and Political Systems
Dist - USNAC **Prod** - USDD 1963

Shield of plenty 29 MIN
U-matic / VHS / 16mm
Planet of man series
Color (H C)
LC 76-703567
Discusses the formation of ancient rock shields during the Precambrian period, the type of mineral resources found in these shields and methods of dating this rock through radioactivity.
Science - Physical
Dist - FI **Prod** - OECA 1976

Shielded Metal - Arc Structural and Pipe Welding 60 MIN
U-matic / VHS
Welding Training Series
Color (IND)
Focuses on practice beads, structural welding, carbon steel pipe, stainless steel pipe and aluminum pipe.
Education; Industrial and Technical Education
Dist - ITCORP **Prod** - ITCORP

Shielded Metal - Arc Welding Principles 60 MIN
U-matic / VHS
Welding Training Series
Color (IND)
Covers introduction and safety, equipment, polarity, voltage/current relationships, electrodes, setting up the machine, adjusting and starting the machine, striking an arc, electrode motion and shutdown.
Education; Industrial and Technical Education
Dist - ITCORP **Prod** - ITCORP

Shielded metal arc welding - Pt 01 14 MIN
16mm
Miller module method series
Color (IND)
LC 74-703671
Industrial and Technical Education
Dist - MILEL **Prod** - MILEL 1975

Shielded metal arc welding - Pt 02 14 MIN
16mm
Miller module method series
Color (IND)
LC 74-703671
Industrial and Technical Education
Dist - MILEL **Prod** - MILEL 1975

Shielded metal arc welding - Pt 03 14 MIN
16mm
Miller module method series
Color (IND)
LC 74-703671
Industrial and Technical Education
Dist - MILEL **Prod** - MILEL 1975

Shielded metal arc welding - Pt 04 14 MIN
16mm
Miller module method series
Color (IND)
LC 74-703671
Industrial and Technical Education
Dist - MILEL **Prod** - MILEL 1975

Shielded metal arc welding - Pt 05 14 MIN
16mm
Miller module method series
Color (IND)
LC 74-703671
Industrial and Technical Education
Dist - MILEL **Prod** - MILEL 1975

Shielded metal arc welding - Pt 06 14 MIN
16mm
Miller module method series
Color (IND)
LC 74-703671
Industrial and Technical Education
Dist - MILEL **Prod** - MILEL 1975

Shielded metal arc welding - Pt 07 14 MIN
16mm
Miller module method series
Color (IND)
LC 74-703671
Industrial and Technical Education
Dist - MILEL **Prod** - MILEL 1975

Shielded metal arc welding - Pt 08 14 MIN
16mm
Miller module method series
Color (IND)
LC 74-703671
Industrial and Technical Education
Dist - MILEL **Prod** - MILEL 1975

Shielded metal arc welding - Pt 09 14 MIN
16mm
Miller module method series
Color (IND)
LC 74-703671
Industrial and Technical Education
Dist - MILEL **Prod** - MILEL 1975

Shielded metal arc welding - Pt 10 14 MIN
16mm
Miller module method series
Color (IND)
LC 74-703671
Industrial and Technical Education
Dist - MILEL **Prod** - MILEL 1975

Shielded metal arc welding - Pt 11 14 MIN
16mm
Miller module method series
Color (IND)
LC 74-703671
Industrial and Technical Education
Dist - MILEL **Prod** - MILEL 1975

Shielded metal arc welding - Pt 12 9 MIN
16mm
Miller module method series
Color (IND)
LC 74-703671
Industrial and Technical Education
Dist - MILEL **Prod** - MILEL 1975

Shielded metal arc welding - Pt 13 14 MIN
16mm
Miller module method series
Color (IND)
LC 74-703671
Industrial and Technical Education
Dist - MILEL **Prod** - MILEL 1975

Shielded metal arc welding - Pt 14 14 MIN
16mm
Miller module method series
Color (IND)
LC 74-703671
Industrial and Technical Education
Dist - MILEL **Prod** - MILEL 1975

Shielded metal arc welding - Pt 15 17 MIN
16mm
Miller module method series
Color (IND)
LC 74-703671
Industrial and Technical Education
Dist - MILEL **Prod** - MILEL 1975

Shielded metal arc welding - Pt 16 14 MIN
16mm
Miller module method series
Color (IND)
LC 74-703671
Industrial and Technical Education
Dist - MILEL **Prod** - MILEL 1975

Shielded metal arc welding series
Carbon arc cutting
Dist - VTRI

Shielded metal arc welding - Spanish series
Electric - arc power sources and minor maintenance
Electric arc welding in flat, horizontal, vertical and overhead butt welds
Multi - pass electric arc welding
Running continuous bead in horizontal and vertical down position
Running continuous beads in vertical up and overhead position
Safety in electric - arc welding and terms
Selection of electrodes for shielded metal arc - welding
Striking an arc, restarting the arc and running a continuous bead in the flat
T - joint, lap joint, outside corner joint in a horizontal position with SMAW
T - joint, lap joint, outside corner joint in a vertical up position with SMAW
T - joint, lap joint, outside corner joint in an overhead position
T - joint, lap joint, outside corner joint in flat position
Welding cast iron in flat position with electric arc, hard facing surfaces
Dist - VTRI

Shielded metal arc welding training systems series
Plate welding - Pt I
Plate welding - Pt II
Dist - CAREER

Shielded metal arc welding training systems
Pipe welding
Dist - CAREER

Shielded stick metal arc welding I 35 MIN
VHS
Color (H A T)
$89.95 purchase _ #CV983
Examines in depth safety, pre - operational inspection of equipment and proper clothing for welding. Provides step - by - step procedure for the set up and adjustment of an AC - DC, a rectifier AC and a standard AC welder. Uses close - up footage of nine welds - stringers, butt welds, lap weld, T - weld, multi - pass weld, five others, performed in a flat position. Demonstrates welds using straight, crescent and up and back motions. Discusses types of electrodes and their uses. Features Prof Billy Harrell of Sam Houston State University.
Health and Safety; Industrial and Technical Education; Psychology
Dist - AAVIM **Prod** - AAVIM 1992

Shielded stick metal arc welding II 35 MIN
VHS
Color (H A T)
$89.95 purchase _ #CV984
Illustrates nine welds including stringer, butt, lap, T - weld and others, performed in horizontal, vertical and overhead positions. Features Prof Billy Harrell of Sam Houston State University.
Health and Safety; Industrial and Technical Education; Psychology
Dist - AAVIM **Prod** - AAVIM 1992

Shielded stick metal arc welding III 35 MIN
VHS
Color (H A T)
$89.95 purchase _ #CV985
Presents two methods of testing welds - guided bend and nick break. Includes preparation of metal for test samples, performing welds and preparation of speciments for testing. Includes a summary of essentials for successful welding, including metal identification. Features Prof Billy Harrell of Sam Houston State University.
Health and Safety; Industrial and Technical Education; Psychology
Dist - AAVIM **Prod** - AAVIM 1992

Shielded stick metal arc welding - Pt 1 35 MIN
VHS
Shielded stick metal arc welding series
Color (G H VOC IND)
$89.95 purchase _ #CEV20810V-T
Describes the basics of safety inspections when performing arc welding. Provides step-by-step procedure for the set-up and adjustment of an AC - DC, a rectifier AC and a standard AC welder. Explains the proper method for doing different types of welds.
Education; Industrial and Technical Education
Dist - CAMV

Shielded stick metal arc welding - Pt 2 35 MIN
VHS
Shielded stick metal arc welding series
Color (G H VOC IND)
$89.95 purchase _ #CEV20811V-T
Demonstrates the proper procedures for shielded stick metal arc welding. Includes information on the correct method to perform nine different welds that include: stringer, lap, butt and T-weld performed in horizontal, vertical and overhead positions. Explains and discusses each type of weld.
Education; Industrial and Technical Education
Dist - CAMV

Shielded stick metal arc welding - Pt 3 35 MIN
VHS
Shielded stick metal arc welding series
Color (G H VOC IND)
$89.95 purchase _ #CEV20818V-T
Describes proper procedures for shielded stick metal arc welding. Includes information on the correct technique to test welds through either the guided bend or the nick break method. Explains the best way to test metal preparation, specimen preparation. Provides a test of metal identification and a summary of welding essentials.
Education; Industrial and Technical Education
Dist - CAMV

Shielded stick metal arc welding series
Shielded stick metal arc welding - Pt - 1 35 MIN
Shielded stick metal arc welding - Pt - 2 35 MIN
Shielded stick metal arc welding - Pt - 3 35 MIN
Dist - CAMV

Shift 9 MIN
16mm
Color (G)
$18.00 rental
Employs extensive montage effects with a series of cars and trucks filmed from a height of several stories. Uses inverted shots to depict a car hanging from the asphalt like a bat from a rafter and angles so severe that the traffic seems to be sliding off the earth. Produced by Ernie Gehr.
Fine Arts
Dist - CANCIN

Shift of stimulus control - a clinical procedure for articulation therapy 37 MIN
16mm
Color (C T)
LC 72-702018
Presents films of work with two mentally retarded children which demonstrate the general strategy of stimulus - shift techniques in which new phoneme responses are developed under precise stimulus control.
English Language; Psychology
Dist - UKANS **Prod** - UKANS 1970

Shift Registers 28 MIN
VHS / 16mm
Digital Electronics Series
Color (H A)
$465.00 purchase, $110.00 rental
Explains the concepts behind shift registers.
Industrial and Technical Education
Dist - TAT **Prod** - TAT 1989

Shifting and reflecting graphs 30 MIN
VHS
College algebra series
Color (C)
$125.00 purchase _ #4017
Explains shifting and reflecting graphs. Part of a 31 - part series on college algebra.
Industrial and Technical Education; Mathematics
Dist - LANDMK **Prod** - LANDMK

Shifting and Reflecting Graphs 30 MIN
VHS
Mathematics Series
Color (J)
LC 90713155
Explains shifting and reflecting graphs. The 79th of 157 installments in the Mathematics Series.
Mathematics
Dist - GPN

Shifting gears 12 MIN
16mm
Time out series
Color
LC 81-701202
Tells how Buddy risks his close friendship with PK in a personal conflict over the violence in both their lives. Proposes another dimension to male friendship and suggests an alternative to male - supported violence.
Sociology
Dist - ODNP **Prod** - ODNP 1982

A Shifting of Risk 29 MIN
U-matic
Life, Death and Taxes Series
Color
Focuses on the function and operation of personal life insurance in estate planning.
Business and Economics
Dist - UMITV **Prod** - UMITV 1977

Shifting sands 31 MIN
U-matic / VHS
Battle for the planet series
Color (H C G)
$160.00 purchase, $30.00 rental _ #CC4253VU, #CC4253VH
Demonstrates how chronic overgrazing and land mishandling have caused one - third of the earth's land to be threatened by desertification. Shows how economic reform and incentives can encourage individual participation in proper management and refoliation of the land. Part of a series.
Agriculture; Geography - World; Science - Natural
Dist - IU **Prod** - NFBC 1987

The Shifting sands - a history of the Middle East 29 MIN
VHS
Color; PAL (J H G)
PdS29.50 purchase
Travels through the history of this region from the beginning of recorded time to the end of the Gulf War. Reveals ancient artifacts that tell of the early Sumerian civilization and of life 5,000 years ago in Mesopotamia. Discusses influences of different cultures including Babylonian and Roman. Contrasts the religious and cultural differences between the Arabs and Israelis.
History - World; Sociology
Dist - EMFVL **Prod** - AIMS

Shigeko Kubota - an Interview 28 MIN
U-matic / VHS
Color
Presented by D L Bean and Jeanine Mellinger.
Fine Arts
Dist - ARTINC **Prod** - ARTINC

Shigeko Kubota - Duchampiana, Video Installations 42 MIN
U-matic / VHS
Color
Draws from the work of Marcel Duchamp.
Fine Arts
Dist - ARTINC **Prod** - ARTINC

Shigeko Kubota - My Father 15 MIN
VHS / U-matic
B&W
Records events from Shigeko Kubota's life.
Fine Arts
Dist - ARTINC **Prod** - ARTINC

Shigeko Kubota - Video Girls and Video Songs for Navajo Skies 26 MIN
U-matic / VHS
Color
Involves Paik - Abe and Rutt - Etra synthesizers.
Fine Arts
Dist - ARTINC **Prod** - ARTINC

Shiites, followers of Ali 27 MIN
U-matic / VHS / 16mm
In the footsteps of Abraham series
Color (J H C A)
MP=$375.00
Documents the rise of the Shiites who were the first dissidents within Islam. They opposed the authority of the Sunni rulers and took their authority from Ali the nephew of Mohammed.
Religion and Philosophy
Dist - LANDMK **Prod** - LANDMK

Shiites, followers of Ali - 3 30 MIN
U-matic / VHS / BETA
Abraham's posterity series
Color; PAL (G H C)
PdS50, PdS58 purchase
Follows the journeys which Abraham made some 4000 years ago. Offers a dramatic interpretation at the events which are today tearing the region apart. Part of a thirteen - part series. A Cine & Tele Production, Brussels, Belgium.
Fine Arts; Religion and Philosophy
Dist - EDPAT

The Shilluk 53 MIN
VHS
Disappearing world series
Color (G C)
$99.00 purchase, $19.00 rental _ #51252
Reveals that in the 16th century a man named Nyikang united the various groups living along the Nile River into one people, the Shilluk. Discloses that Shilluk life revolves around the 'Reth,' believed to be the divine incarnation of the Shilluk people. Shilluk territory is now part of the Sudan and the Reth has been demoted to local magistrate by the central government. Features anthropologists Paul Howell and Walter Kinijwok. Part of a series working closely with anthropologists who lived for a year or more in societies whose social structures, beliefs and practices are threatened by the expansion of technocratic civilization.
Sociology
Dist - PSU **Prod** - GRANDA 1976

Shiloh 16 MIN
16mm / U-matic / VHS
Color
Deals with Shiloh, a two - day battle of the Civil War.
History - United States
Dist - KAWVAL **Prod** - KAWVAL

Shine when you dine
VHS
Kitchen video series
$79.00 purchase _ #FY102V
Teaches the importance of kitchen safety and following directions. Uses kitchen video transfers and graphic photography.
Health and Safety; Home Economics; Industrial and Technical Education
Dist - CAREER **Prod** - CAREER

Shining conquests 60 MIN
VHS
Out of the fiery furnace series
Color; Captioned (G)

$69.95 purchase _ #OOFF - 103
Examines how precious metals such as gold have often served as the impetus for exploration and migration. Traces this phenomena to the legends of the Golden Horn and the Golden Fleece. Hosted by Michael Charlton.
History - World; Religion and Philosophy; Science - Physical
Dist - PBS **Prod** - OPUS 1986

Shinnecock - the Story of a People 20 MIN
U-matic / VHS / 16mm
Color (H C A)
LC 76-702514
Centers on the lost culture and heritage of the East Coast Indians of North America, focusing on the Shinnecock tribe.
Social Science; Sociology
Dist - PHENIX **Prod** - PHENIX 1976

Shinto - Nature, Gods and Man in Japan 49 MIN
16mm
Color (H C A)
LC 78-700218
Traces the development of the Shinto religion and portrays the reconstruction of one of the Shinto shrines according to the specifications of the ancient documents.
Religion and Philosophy
Dist - JAPANS **Prod** - GILWES 1977

Shintoism 15 MIN
16mm
Off to Adventure Series
Color (P I J)
Geography - World; Religion and Philosophy
Dist - YALEDV **Prod** - YALEDV

Shiny is Beautiful 15 MIN
16mm
Fingermouse, Yoffy and Friends Series
Color (K P I)
LC 73-700438
Follows Yoffy and his friends as they collect pretty and shiny objects such as bottle - tops, shells and tiny paper stars.
Guidance and Counseling; Literature and Drama
Dist - VEDO **Prod** - BBCTV 1972

Ship county and city compendium
CD-ROM
(G)
$745.00 purchase _ #1586
Includes three databases - County Statistics, County Income and Employment, and County - City Plus, which includes population, housing and income data for for the US. Updated annually. For IBM PCs and compatibles. Requires 640K RAM, DOS 3.1 or later, floppy disk - hard disk recommended, one empty expansion slot, and an IBM compatible CD - ROM drive.
Social Science; Sociology
Dist - BEP

Ship of Fools 149 MIN
16mm
Color
Portrays an allegorical voyage aboard a passenger freighter bound from Vera Cruz to Bremerhaven in 1933 of a confused world.
Fine Arts
Dist - TIMLIF **Prod** - CPC 1965

Ship of fools 149 MIN
VHS
B&W (G)
$59.90 purchase _ #0323
Adapts the novel Ship Of Fools by Katherine Anne Porter. Portrays the follies and foibles of humanity in the passengers aboard a ship sailing from Mexico to pre - Hitler Germany. Stars Vivien Leigh, Simone Signoret, Jose Ferrer, Lee Marvin, Oskar Werner, Elizabeth Ashley.
Fine Arts; Literature and Drama
Dist - SEVVID **Prod** - CPC

Ship of trade 50 MIN
VHS
Discoveries underwater series
Color; PAL (G)
PdS99 purchase
Explores some of the many sunken trade ships that still carry their cargoes intact. Follows archaeologists as they uncover and explain the finds from those merchant ships. Looks at the growing science of underwater archaeology. Part six of an eight - part series.
Business and Economics; History - World; Physical Education and Recreation
Dist - BBCENE

A Ship reborn 32 MIN
VHS
Color (H)
Follows the construction of a Viking Age merchant ship, which was built using Viking - age technology. Available for free loan from the distributor.
Business and Economics; History - World; Industrial and Technical Education; Social Science
Dist - AUDPLN

The Ship that wouldn't die 53 MIN
VHS
Color (G)
$39.80 purchase _ #0465
Tells of the USS Franklin, the most decorated ship and crew in United States Naval history. Features Gene Kelly as host.
Civics and Political Systems; History - United States
Dist - SEVVID **Prod** - NBCTV

Shipboard Helicopter Operations - Functions 8 MIN
16mm
Color
LC FIE59-238
Discusses the principal missions of the helicopter aboard ship as plane guard, in rescues and during mail transfers.
Civics and Political Systems; Industrial and Technical Education; Social Science
Dist - USNAC **Prod** - USN 1954

Shipboard Helicopter Operations - Landing and Take - Offs 7 MIN
16mm
Color
LC FIE59-239
Shows procedures to be followed in helicopter landings and take - offs during shipboard operations.
Civics and Political Systems; Industrial and Technical Education; Social Science
Dist - USNAC **Prod** - USN 1954

Shipboard Inspection by Medical Department Personnel - Food Preparation 25 MIN
16mm
B&W
LC FIE59-144
Shows how to make an inspection of the various areas of possible contamination in the preparation of food aboard ship. Discusses sanitary equipment and spaces, sanitary personnel and sanitary work habits.
Health and Safety; Social Science
Dist - USNAC **Prod** - USN 1958

Shipboard Inspection by Medical Department Personnel - Food Serving 13 MIN
16mm
B&W
LC FIE59-145
Shows how to make an inspection of such food - serving areas as the mess areas, serving line and the scullery.
Health and Safety; Industrial and Technical Education; Social Science
Dist - USNAC **Prod** - USN 1958

Shipboard inspection by medical department personnel - food storage 12 MIN
16mm
B&W
LC FIE59-146
Shows how to make a sanitary inspection of the storage of food aboard ship. Covers such subjects as cleanliness, air circulation, temperature and stowage.
Health and Safety; Industrial and Technical Education; Social Science
Dist - USNAC **Prod** - USN 1958

Shipboard Inspection by Medical Department Personnel - Living and Working Spaces 20 MIN
16mm
B&W
LC FIE59-147
Shows what and how to inspect in order to insure good conditions of sanitation, ventilation, lighting and safety in the living and working spaces of a ship.
Health and Safety; Social Science
Dist - USNAC **Prod** - USN 1958

Shipboard inspection by medical department personnel - water supply 21 MIN
16mm
B&W
LC FIE59-148
Shows how and where to inspect a ship's fresh - water supply at the points of possible contamination.
Industrial and Technical Education; Science - Natural; Social Science
Dist - USNAC **Prod** - USN 1958

Shipboard Vibrations, Pt 4 - Service Problems and Field Investigation 13 MIN
16mm
B&W
LC FIE53-519
Explains how to report shipboard vibration problems, how they are diagnosed and remedied by vibration engineers and how vibration study as preventive engineering contributes to overall ship design and performance.
Industrial and Technical Education; Social Science
Dist - USNAC **Prod** - USN 1953

Shipboard Vibrations, Pt 1 - Fundamental Principles of Vibrating Systems 22 MIN
16mm
B&W
LC FIE53-516
Explains basic concepts and principles, including longitudinal and torsional vibrations, free and forced vibrations, the time relationship between the force cycle and the amplitude cycle and the phase angle diagram.
Industrial and Technical Education; Social Science
Dist - USNAC **Prod** - USN 1953

Shipboard Vibrations, Pt 3 - Vibration, Excitation and Response 15 MIN
16mm
B&W
LC FIA53-518
Shows vibration excitation in the propulsion machinery due to imbalance and to propeller thrust variation and the response of the ship's structure to this excitation.
Industrial and Technical Education; Science - Physical; Social Science
Dist - USNAC **Prod** - USN 1953

Shipboard Vibrations, Pt 2 - Multi - Mass Systems 23 MIN
16mm
B&W
LC FIE53-517
Explains basic concepts, including those of a uniform system, a lumped system, modes of vibration, relative amplitudes, harmonic analysis, orders of vibration and critical speeds.
Industrial and Technical Education; Social Science
Dist - USNAC **Prod** - USN 1953

Shipbuilding skills series

Covering hot and cold pipes	22 MIN
Cutting and threading pipe on a power machine	17 MIN
Laying out and installing hangers	19 MIN
Making a cold bend on a hand powered machine	13 MIN
Measuring pipe, tubing, and fittings	15 MIN
Pipe fabrication with jigs	22 MIN
Side frames - subassembly of a web frame	17 MIN
Simple foundation Pt 1 - layout	28 MIN
Simple Foundation, Pt 3 - Assembly and Installation	23 MIN
Simple Foundation, Pt 2 - Duplication and Fabrication	17 MIN
Tinning and solder wiping	26 MIN

Dist - USNAC

Shipley Street 28 MIN
U-matic / 16mm
Color
Deals with a black working - class family trying to make it in the city. Focuses on the father and his young daughter. Shows the difficulties of the college educated father in trying to get a promotion and the daughter's problems in the Catholic school she attends.
Sociology
Dist - BLKFMF **Prod** - BLKFMF

Shipmaster 5 MIN
U-matic
Good work series
Color (H)
Provides useful, up to date information on various occupations to aid high school students in career selection. Available in five series of ten jobs each.
Education; Guidance and Counseling; Social Science
Dist - TVOTAR **Prod** - TVOTAR 1981

A Shipment to Saratoga 20 MIN
16mm
B&W
Describes how foreign aid helped the Continental Army defeat the British in the Battle of Saratoga, the turning point in the Revolutionary War.
History - United States
Dist - USNAC **Prod** - USDD 1958

Shippensburg College - Guest Brook Zern , Program B 29 MIN
Videoreel / VT2
Sonia Malkine on Campus Series

Color
Features French folk singer Sonia Malkine and her special guest Brook Zern visiting Shippensburg College in Pennsylvania.
Education; Fine Arts; Foreign Language; Geography - United States
Dist - PBS **Prod** - WITFTV

Shippensburg State College - Guest Brook Zern, Program A 29 MIN
Videoreel / VT2
Sonia Malkine on Campus Series
Color
Features French folk singer Sonia Malkine and her special guest Brook Zern visiting Shippenburg State College in Pennsylvania.
Education; Fine Arts; Foreign Language; Geography - United States
Dist - PBS **Prod** - WITFTV

Shipping and Receiving Clerk 15 MIN
U-matic / 16mm / VHS
Career Awareness
(I)
$130 VC purchase, $240 film purchase, $25 VC rental, $30 film rental
Presents an empathetic approach to career training, showing the personal as well as professional attributes of shipping and receiving clerks. Highlights the importance of career education.
Business and Economics; Guidance and Counseling
Dist - GPN

The Shipping Hooker 8 MIN
U-matic / VHS
Steel Making Series
Color (IND)
Explains the job performed by the shipping hooker with emphasis on safety. Includes the loading of trucks and rail cars.
Business and Economics; Health and Safety; Industrial and Technical Education
Dist - LEIKID **Prod** - LEIKID

Shipping - the Tankard Hazard 12 MIN
U-matic / VHS
Color (H C A)
Explains that as more and more countries import and export crude oil, the seas have become jammed with super tanker traffic. Discusses the increased risk of oil spills and wrecks and looks at methods used to alleviate the problems.
Social Science
Dist - JOU **Prod** - UPI

Ships 15 MIN
VHS / U-matic / 16mm
Goofy's field trips series
Color (P)
$425.00, $280.00 purchase _ #JC - 67242
Stars Goofy who escorts two youngsters on a tour of a passenger ship where they meet the cruise director, engineer, captain, radio officer and visit the galley. Visits a harbor where they watch freighters enter and leave port and meet the harbor master and the berthing officer. Part of a series on transportation.
Social Science
Dist - CORF **Prod** - DISNEY 1989

Ships - a First Film 11 MIN
16mm / U-matic / VHS
B&W (P I)
Shows the differences and similarities in large commercial vessels.
Social Science
Dist - PHENIX **Prod** - BEANMN 1970

Ships, aircraft and weapons of the USN
VHS
Color (G)
$39.80 purchase _ #0466
Profiles 81 classes of fighting ships and aircraft of the United States Navy. Includes carriers such as Nimitz and Eisenhower and the submarines Trident and Polaris. Includes craft and weaponry through 1979.
Civics and Political Systems; History - United States
Dist - SEVVID

Ships and Seafaring 24 MIN
16mm / VHS / U-matic
Ancient Greece Series
Color (J)
LC 82-706461; 82-700374
Focuses on the powerful ships that made Greece master of the sea around 470 - 333 BC, exploring Greek maritime activity in peace and war, boat and harbor construction, and naval and sailing tactics. Includes views of the ruins of a merchant ship which was excavated near Kyrenia, Cypress.
History - World; Social Science
Dist - MEDIAG **Prod** - OPENU 1981

Ships and Seamen - Pt 1 20 MIN
VHS
Tudors Series
Color (I)
$79.00 purchase _ #825 - 9421
Paints a detailed and historically accurate picture of the Tudor period, 1485 - 1603, in British history. Examines historical trends over a broad time period or concentrates on one aspect of the era. The dramatizations are based on source material and the locations are authentic. Part 1 of seven parts details the English contribution during the period of European voyages of discovery.
History - World; Social Science
Dist - FI **Prod** - BBCTV 1987

Ships A'Sail 14 MIN
VHS / U-matic
Under the Yellow Balloon Series
Color (P)
Classifies vessels from kayaks to aircraft carriers according to their source of power and their purpose.
Social Science
Dist - AITECH **Prod** - SCETV 1980

Ship's Blueprints - Basic 22 MIN
16mm
B&W
LC FIE52-1232
Explains how to identify fundamental structural elements in ship construction by orthographic drawings and symbols, to visualize these drawings in three dimensions, to understand the use and function of dotted and hidden lines and to read a ship's blueprints.
Industrial and Technical Education; Social Science
Dist - USNAC **Prod** - USN 1944

Ship's entertainment officers 45 MIN
VHS
Situation vacant series
Color (A)
PdS65 purchase
Watches four entertainers on a 12-day assessment cruise on the liner Canberra. Reveals that at the end of the cruise one of the four will win a lucrative position with P&O, the other three will return to unemployment on shore. Part of a six-part series looking at selection procedures for a wide range of jobs.
Education; Psychology
Dist - BBCENE

Ships master 4.5 MIN
VHS / 16mm
Good works 5 series
Color (A PRO)
$40.00 purchase _ #BPN238009
Presents the occupation of a ships master. Gives a profile of a young person who is either undergoing an apprenticeship or has recently completed training in this field. Takes the viewer on a tour of this person's workplace and explains the practical skills and training offered by employers and schools. Gives a better understanding of the demand for skilled workers today and the potential for personal growth.
Guidance and Counseling; Social Science
Dist - RMIBHF **Prod** - RMIBHF

Ships of war 50 MIN
VHS
Discoveries underwater series
Color; PAL (G)
PdS99 purchase
Observes archaeologists as they apply space - age technology to locate sunken warships. Looks at the growing science of underwater archaeology, its methods and future. Part five of an eight - part series.
Business and Economics; History - World; Physical Education and Recreation
Dist - BBCENE

Ship's Pumps 16 MIN
16mm
B&W
LC 74-706577
Explains uses, functions and construction of ship pumps.
Industrial and Technical Education
Dist - USNAC **Prod** - USN 1951

The Ships that Flew 49 MIN
16mm
Color (J)
LC 76-700572
Takes a look at the history of flying boat services in Australian aviation. Considers in particular the last of these services from Sydney to Lord Howe Island which ended in 1974.
Geography - World; History - World; Industrial and Technical Education; Social Science
Dist - AUIS **Prod** - FLMAUS 1974

Shipwreck 60 MIN
VHS / U-matic / 16mm
Last Frontier Series
Color; Mono (G)
MV $225.00 _ MP $550.00
Depicts the coastline of British Columbia as a savage and unforgiving place where ships and men are lost to the violent seas. Shows divers exploring what is known as the graveyard of the Pacific. The exotic marine life of these waters is showcased.
Geography - World; History - World; Science - Natural
Dist - CTV **Prod** - MAKOF 1985

Shipwreck Island 93 MIN
16mm
Color (P I)
Fine Arts
Dist - FI **Prod** - FI

Shipyard fire and explosion hazards 43 MIN
16mm
Color
LC 77-701240
Presents table top demonstrations to illustrate the principles of fires, with applications to shipyard repairing and building activities. Points out control measures for the prevention of fire and explosion accidents.
Health and Safety; Industrial and Technical Education
Dist - USNAC **Prod** - USDL 1965

Shipyard fire and explosion hazards 41 MIN
U-matic
Color (IND)
LC 77-706132
Presents the basic principles of fire through the use of laboratory experiments and simulation of four ship fires and explosions. Explains the flash point flammable limits and demonstrates sources of ignition. Describes the testing instruments for flammable vapors and the hazards of oxygen excess and deficiency.
Health and Safety; Industrial and Technical Education; Science - Physical; Social Science
Dist - USNAC **Prod** - USDL 1977

Shirim k'tanim - Hebrew songs for children 40 MIN
VHS
Color (K)
$24.95 purchase _ #230
Features Israel TV star Uzi Chitman and his young friends who sing and dance their way through 40 Hebrew nursery rhymes and songs with colorful animation, illustration and special effects. Accompanies musical numbers with either translation, transliteration or the Hebrew lyrics.
Fine Arts; Foreign Language; Geography - World; Sociology
Dist - ERGOM **Prod** - ERGOM

Shirley A Hill
U-matic / VHS
Third R - teaching basic mathematics skills series
Color
Provides an overview of the Third R - Teaching Basic Mathematics Series. Includes a brief segment from each of the other five programs in the series.
Education; Mathematics
Dist - EDCPUB **Prod** - EDCPUB

Shirley Hall Studio 6 MIN
16mm
B&W (G)
$10.00 rental
Delves into the history of the Shirley Hall dormitory, named after Jack Shirley, the famous Grand Canyon trail guide, and constructed by Fred Harvey in 1905 for mule wranglers. Captures a group of artists and filmmakers who convert the building into a makeshift film studio, just before it was torn down. A Mike Quinn production.
Fine Arts; Geography - United States; Geography - World
Dist - CANCIN

Shirley Holmes pursues patient safety - Part 1 18 MIN
BETA / VHS / U-matic
Fundamental concepts in nursing series
Color (C PRO)
$280.00 purchase _ #623.2
Reveals that the Accident Monster and his nemesis, Shirley Holmes, lock horns. Describes patients who tend to be accident - prone and discusses situations in which the healthcare worker may inadvertently contribute to accidents. Emphasizes the importance of a safe environment and illustrates patient safety in the patient unit and in the bathroom. Part one of two parts and part of a three - part series on fundamental concepts in nursing produced by Video Ideas Productions Inc.
Health and Safety
Dist - CONMED

Shirley Holmes pursues patient safety - Part 2 16 MIN
VHS / U-matic / BETA
Fundamental concepts in nursing series
Color (C PRO)
$280.00 purchase _ #623.3
Continues the saga in which the Accident Monster and his nemesis, Shirley Holmes, lock horns. Concentrates on protecting the elderly, the confused and the sedated patient from the harmful intent of the Accident Monster. Shares the strategy of Holmes for protecting such patients. Discusses in detail how to move patients safely, emphasizing transfer technique with wheelchair and stretcher. Part two of two parts and part of a three - part series on fundamental concepts in nursing produced by Video Ideas Productions Inc.
Health and Safety
Dist - CONMED

Shirley Holmes tracks down germs 16 MIN
BETA / VHS / U-matic
Fundamental concepts in nursing series
Color (C PRO)
$280.00 purchase _ #623.1
Introduces inveterate germ fighter Shirley Holmes and her arch enemy Mr Germ. Reveals that she investigates hiding places for organisms and helps caregivers avoid aiding and abetting their growth and transfer. Presents a refreshing look at practical and reliable methods for fighting the battle against harmful organisms in healthcare facilities and homes. Part of a three - part series on fundamental concepts in nursing produced by Video Ideas Productions Inc.
Health and Safety; Science - Natural
Dist - CONMED

Shirley Jones' and Sheila Cluff's complete fitness and beauty program
VHS
Secrets of the stars series
Color (G)
$29.95 purchase _ #IV - 051
Presents a program for health, fitness and beauty by TV star Shirley Jones and beauty and health specialist Sheila Cluff.
Health and Safety; Physical Education and Recreation
Dist - INCRSE **Prod** - INCRSE

Shirley Taylor - 10 - 4 - 87 120 MIN
VHS / Cassette
Poetry Center reading series
Color (G)
#929 - 629
Features the writer reading from her works at the Ruth Witt - Diamant Memorial Reading at the Poetry Center, San Francisco State University. Also includes readings by James Broughton, Robert Duncan, Rosalie Moore, Mark Linenthal, Christy Taylor, Justine Fixel, Lawrence Fixel, Michael McClure, Gail Layton, and Stephen Witt - Diamant. Introduction by Frances Phillips. Slides of Ruth Witt - Diamant courtesy of Caryl Mezey. Available for listening purposes only at the Center; not for sale or rent.
Literature and Drama
Dist - POETRY **Prod** - POETRY 1987

Shirley Temple - biggest little star of the '30s
16mm
Fox Movietone news series
B&W (G)
$15.00 rental
Compiles sequences including Shirley's Oscar acceptance, mingling with stars and dancing with 'Bojangles' Robinson. Presents part of a series of special Movietone issues, 6 - 11 minutes.
Fine Arts; Literature and Drama
Dist - KITPAR **Prod** - FOXNEW 1976

Shirley Verrett 60 MIN
VHS
Color (G)
$19.95 purchase _ #1147
Follows the professional and private life of singer Shirley Verrett for a year. Shows her in many of the dramatic opera roles she has made her own, including Iphigenie at the Paris Opera, Tosca at the Arena di Verona, Dalila at the Royal Opera House Covent Garden and Carmen at La Scala.
Fine Arts
Dist - KULTUR

Shirtless soul 88 MIN
VHS
Color (G)
$35.00 purchase
Carries on the tradition of film as poetry. Explores the world of a sensitive woman whose father claims an immortality strangely connected to a wornout shirt. Journeys into the depths of his soul as the two become estranged. Directed by Kyle Bergersen.
Fine Arts; Religion and Philosophy; Sociology
Dist - ALTFMW

Shirtmaking techniques 45 MIN
VHS
Color (A H)
$69.95 purchase _ #TPR083V-H
Features David Page Coffin teaching sewing techniques for creating high quality shirts and blouses. Demonstrates special skills such as making rolled hems, flat-felled seams and precisely sewn plackets, cuffs and collars, in order to produce the hallmarks of fine shirts - collars that roll beautifully, symmetrical cuffs and carefully topstitched details. Includes the book Shirtmaking - Developing Skills for Fine Sewing.
Home Economics
Dist - CAMV

Shish Kebab and Shish Taouk 30 MIN
U-matic / VHS
Color (PRO)
Presents techniques for making skewered lamb and skewered chicken.
Home Economics; Industrial and Technical Education
Dist - CULINA **Prod** - CULINA

Shiva's Disciples 50 MIN
U-matic
Color (H C A)
Portrays the lifestyle of the people of Kerala, in southern India, whose daily lives revolve around the worship of Shiva, Hindu God of Dance.
Geography - World; History - World; Religion and Philosophy
Dist - CEPRO **Prod** - CEPRO 1986

Shiver My Timbers 21 MIN
16mm
B&W
Features the Little Rascals in a spoof of pirate movies.
Fine Arts
Dist - RMIBHF **Prod** - ROACH 1931

Shiver, Shudder, Stairs, Secrets, Scream, Shriek, Yelling 10 MIN
U-matic
Readalong Three Series
Color (P)
Provides reading instruction for third grade students. Uses animation, humor, music, repetition and audience participation. Comes with teacher's guide and kit.
Education; English Language; Literature and Drama
Dist - TVOTAR **Prod** - TVOTAR 1977

The Shivering King 16 MIN
16mm
Animatoons Series
Color
LC FIA68-1530
Tells the story of a King who suffers from an unbearable cold and constant shivering until he realizes that his cold is the result of having a cold heart.
Literature and Drama
Dist - RADTV **Prod** - ANTONS 1968

Shivering Shakespeare 18 MIN
16mm
B&W
Tells how a classic recitation turns into a pie - throwing brawl. A Little Rascals film.
Fine Arts
Dist - RMIBHF **Prod** - ROACH 1929

Shock 7 MIN
16mm / U-matic / VHS
First Aid - Rev Ed - Series
Color
Describes the characteristics of shock and the shock cycle, the causes, symptoms, and physical and emotional changes associated with physical shock. Illustrates the human nervous system, how it controls the body's vital organs, and how it is directly involved in cases of physical shock. Stresses that shock follows most serious injuries and should not be neglected.
Health and Safety; Science - Natural
Dist - USNAC **Prod** - USMESA 1981

Shock 14 MIN
16mm
Medical self - help series
Color (ENGLISH, SPANISH)
LC 75-702551
Teaches the individual how to take care of his or her medical and health needs in time of disaster when medical assistance might not be readily available.
Presents instructions for treating shock.
Health and Safety
Dist - USNAC **Prod** - USPHS 1960

Shock 29 MIN
16mm
Color (PRO)
Outlines the diagnosis and treatment of shock based on hemodynamic diagnosis and emphasizes the value of measurement of central venous pressure and cardiac output.
Health and Safety; Science; Science - Natural
Dist - ACY **Prod** - ACYDGD 1965

Shock 4 MIN
U-matic / VHS / 16mm
Emergency First Aid Training Series
Color (A)
LC 81-700828
Describes the symptoms of shock and discusses measures to prevent or control shock.
Health and Safety
Dist - IFB **Prod** - CRAF 1980

Shock 13 MIN
U-matic / VHS
Emergency medical training series; Lesson 4
Color (IND)
Presents comprehensive steps in detecting the 'quiet killer' - trauma shock. Shows emergency medical treatment steps for the proper action.
Health and Safety; Industrial and Technical Education
Dist - LEIKID **Prod** - LEIKID

Shock 15 MIN
U-matic
Trauma Series
Color (PRO)
Depicts the signs and symptoms of shock, counter measures to be taken and complications to be avoided or treated in the case of shock.
Health and Safety
Dist - PRIMED **Prod** - PRIMED

Shock corridor 101 MIN
VHS / 16mm
B&W (A)
Features a newsman obsessed with the Pulitzer Prize, schizophrenics and nymphomaniacs. Conveys profound insights about American society. Directed by Samuel Fuller. Digitally remastered with original color sequences.
Fine Arts; Literature and Drama; Psychology
Dist - HOMVIS KITPAR **Prod** - JANUS 1963

Shock Excited Oscillator 36 MIN
16mm
B&W
LC 74-705632
Gives the purpose of each component in the shock excited oscillator circuit and explains the circuit operation and shows the input and output waveshapes graphically. Explains how L and C of the duration of the input gate determine the frequency and duration of the output. (Kinescope).
Industrial and Technical Education; Science - Physical
Dist - USNAC **Prod** - USAF

Shock horror 10 MIN
VHS
Color; PAL; NTSC (G IND)
PdS57, PdS6 purchase
Educates young farm workers about the dangers of overhead powerlines. Reminds workers not to use high machinery such as combines, tipping trailers or long irrigation pipes too close to power lines. Features a burn specialist who explains the consequences of accidents and victims who recall their experience. Recommended that children under the age of 12 watch this program with an adult because of the disturbing content.
Health and Safety; Psychology
Dist - CFLVIS

The Shock of futurism 23 MIN
VHS
Color (G)
$29.95 purchase _ #ACE10V - F
Displays innovative works by Boccioni, Balla, Carra and Severini that are examples of Italian futurism. Expresses the debate between the function and the role of art in culture.
Fine Arts
Dist - CAMV

Shock of the New Series

Culture as Nature	52 MIN
The Future that was	52 MIN
The Landscape of Pleasure	52 MIN
The Mechanical Paradise	52 MIN
The Powers that be	52 MIN
The Threshold of Liberty	52 MIN
Trouble in Utopia	52 MIN
The View from the Edge	52 MIN

Dist - TIMLIF

Shock - recognition and management 17 MIN
16mm
Color (PRO)
LC 70-702865
Uses animation and live - action to illustrate the physiology of shock, and to present procedures for recognizing and managing the shock patient. Explains the need for evaluation and treatment of shock, and emphasizes the importance of aggressive, but orderly, procedures. Follows step - by - step initial counter measures, fluid replacement, venous catheterization, physiological monitoring, and other necessary measures in the management of the patient in shock.
Health and Safety
Dist - AMEDA **Prod** - SKF 1968

Shock septico 23 MIN
U-matic / VHS
Color (PRO) (SPANISH)
A Spanish version of Septic Shock. Discusses the general pathophysiology of shock, the nine basic parts of evaluation (which include vital signs), cultures, CBC differential and a coagulation screen), chronologic treat - ment (which includes fluid therapy, pharmacologic agents and antibiotics) and differentiation of septic shock from hypovolemia.
Health and Safety; Science - Natural
Dist - UMICHM **Prod** - UMICHM 1975

Shock Series Module 2
Perfusion Failure 94 FRS
Dist - BRA

Shock Series Module 3
Cerebral Perfusion Failure 88 FRS
Dist - BRA

Shock Series Module 6
Drug Therapy in Shock 91 FRS
Dist - BRA

Shock Trauma 60 MIN
U-matic
Color
Follows the progress of events from the time a patient is involved in a accident until he is released from the Shock Trauma Unit at the University of Maryland. Features doctors, nurses and patients describing their highly emotional involvement with this medical treatment program.
Health and Safety
Dist - MDCPB **Prod** - MDCPB

Shock Waves 32 MIN
16mm / U-matic / VHS
Color (H C A)
Explores the effects of television in our society. Asks whether nightly exposure to television changes the children watching it.
Sociology
Dist - CORF **Prod** - GANNET

A Shocking Accident 25 MIN
16mm
Color (I)
Tells the story of an English school boy who learns that his father has been killed in a bizarre accident. Relates that his friends tease him and only when he meets a girl who understands, can he shake off the terrible memory of his father's death. Based on the short story A Shocking Accident by Graham Greene.
Literature and Drama
Dist - DIRECT **Prod** - DIRECT 1983

The Shoemaker 34 MIN
U-matic / VHS / 16mm
B&W (H C A)
LC 79-700102
Concerns the effect of the rural exodus in Spain on the life of a poor Andalusian shoemaker. Tells how he attempts to stay in his native village when his children leave to work in a tourist town, but finds that he must close his shop and adjust to a new setting with his children.
History - World; Sociology
Dist - IU **Prod** - MINTZJ 1978

The Shoemaker 45 MIN
VHS / 16mm
Films from Andalusia, Spain series
B&W (G)
$400.00, $200.00 purchase, $45.00, $30.00 rental
Portrays a shoemaker who, deeply attached to his network of family and friends, assumed that he would spend his last years in his native village. Reveals that when his children leave to work in a tourist town, the shoemaker follows and struggles to adapt to the isolation of his new environment.
Geography - World; Sociology
Dist - DOCEDR **Prod** - MINTZJ 1978

The Shoemaker and the elves 14 MIN
16mm / U-matic / VHS
Color (P)
Puppets re - create the story of the elves who slip into the shoemaker's shop and make shoes for him.
English Language; Literature and Drama
Dist - CORF **Prod** - GAKKEN 1962
VIEWTH

Shoemaker and the Elves 15 MIN
U-matic / VHS / 16mm
Color (P I)
Tells how the midnight magic of a pair of cobbler elves reverses the misfortunes of a poor shoemaker.
Literature and Drama
Dist - FI **Prod** - IFFB 1972

The Shoemaker and who's George 30 MIN
VHS
Davey and Goliath series
Color (P I R)
$19.95 purchase, $10.00 rental _ #4 - 8830
Presents two 15 - minute Davey And Goliath episodes. The Shoemaker describes the effects of Davey's spreading false rumors about the new shoemaker in town. Who's George? shows how Davey finds milk bottles piling up at an apartment door, which leads him to the gravely ill tenant inside. Produced by the Evangelical Lutheran Church in America.
Literature and Drama; Religion and Philosophy
Dist - APH

Shoes 30 MIN
U-matic
Today's special series
Color (K P)
Develops language arts skills in children. Programs are thematically designed around subjects of interest to youngsters. Action takes place in a department store where people, mannequins, puppets, comic characters and special guests present a light hearted approach to language arts.
English Language; Literature and Drama; Psychology
Dist - TVOTAR **Prod** - TVOTAR 1985

Shoes for Children 13 MIN
Videoreel / VT2
Living Better I Series
Color
Home Economics; Social Science
Dist - PBS **Prod** - MAETEL

Shoeshine girl 25 MIN
U-matic / VHS / 16mm
Color (I J P) (SPANISH)
LC 79-701411
Tells of a young, feisty daughter who goes to live with her aunt and takes a job as a shoeshine girl. Teaches responsibility.
Guidance and Counseling; Sociology
Dist - LCOA **Prod** - MACPRO 1980

Shoo - Moosh 5 MIN
16mm
Color
LC 76-703805
Tells the story of a mysterious stolen bag.
Literature and Drama
Dist - CONCRU **Prod** - CONCRU 1975

Shoot and cry 51 MIN
16mm / VHS
Color (G)
$995.00, $390.00 purchase, $125.00, $75.00 rental
Focuses on 18 - year - old Tal, about to begin military service on a West Bank kibbutz, and Mohammed, a West Bank Palestinian who cooks in a cafe Tal frequents. Portrays the two trying to speak openly, but their realities are far apart. For Tal the question of Palestine is abstract, and for Mohammed the Israeli occupation is enslavement. Film by Helene Klodawsky.
Fine Arts; History - World; Psychology; Sociology
Dist - FIRS **Prod** - NFBC 1988

Shoot - don't shoot 26 MIN
16mm / U-matic / VHS
Color
Analyzes what its like to be a police officer facing the deadly force dilemma. Addresses the psychological pressures created by shooting incidents, the effects on fellow officers, legal implications and alternatives to shooting.
Civics and Political Systems; Social Science
Dist - CORF **Prod** - BELLDA

Shoot - don't shoot 24 MIN
VHS / U-matic / 16mm
Outdoor survival series
Color (J H G)
$275.00, $325.00, $545.00 purchase, $50.00 rental
Presents a wide variety of dramatic situations that can confront hunters in different locations and circumstances. Exposes the viewer to critical thinking skills that sharpen gun use awareness and increased safety.
Health and Safety; Physical Education and Recreation
Dist - NDIM **Prod** - MADISA 1990

Shoot - don't shoot I 24 MIN
16mm / U-matic / VHS
Color
Presents scenes of incidents during which a police officer would have to decide to shoot or not shoot.
Civics and Political Systems; Social Science
Dist - CORF **Prod** - WORON

Shoot - don't shoot II 25 MIN
16mm / U-matic / VHS
Color
Discusses how policemen should be concerned with the finality of death and the extreme consequences of being wrong in a shooting situation. Covers essential rules for the use of legal force and a definition of local laws and requirements concerning the officer's response to a fleeing felon.
Civics and Political Systems
Dist - CORF **Prod** - WORON

Shoot for the contents 101 MIN
16mm / VHS
Color (G)
$1600.00, $495.00 purchase, $225.00 rental
Explores power and change, politics and culture in China and the effects of the events in Tienanmen Square through the maze of allegorical naming and storytelling of China. Juxtaposes Chinese popular songs and classical music, the sayings of Mao and Confucius, women's voices and the words of artists, philosophers and other cultural workers.
Fine Arts; Geography - World; Literature and Drama
Dist - WMEN **Prod** - TRIMIN 1991

Shoot the piano player - Tirez sur le pianiste 81 MIN
VHS
B&W (G)
$39.95 _ #SHO100
Features a pastiche of Hollywood B - film combining suicide and murder with slapstick humor. Centers on a once - famous concert pianist who is now the piano player in a seedy Paris bar, where he is surrounded by gangsters. A classic of the French New Wave. Produced by Les Films du Carrosse.
Fine Arts; Psychology
Dist - HOMVIS

Shooting
VHS
N C A A instructional video series
Color (H C A)
$39.95 purchase _ #KAR1503V
Presents the third of a three - part series on offensive ice hockey. Focuses on shooting skills.
Physical Education and Recreation
Dist - CAMV **Prod** - NCAAF

Shooting
VHS
NCAA soccer instructional video series
Color (J H A)
$39.95 purchase _ #KAR1402V
Features college soccer coach Bill Muse teaching the skills of shooting a soccer ball.
Physical Education and Recreation
Dist - CAMV **Prod** - NCAAF

Shooting
VHS
NCAA basketball instructional video series
Color (G)
$39.95 purchase _ #KAR1206V
Features former North Carolina State basketball coach Jim Valvano in an instructional video on shooting the basketball.
Physical Education and Recreation
Dist - CAMV **Prod** - NCAAF

Shooting 8 MIN
U-matic / VHS / 16mm
How to play hockey series
B&W (H C)
Shows the techniques of executing various types of shots, such as the forehand, backhand, and slap. Number five in the series.
Physical Education and Recreation
Dist - IFB **Prod** - CRAF 1956

Shooting back - photography by homeless children 30 MIN
VHS
Color (G)
Features photographs taken by homeless children who have participated in the workshops of photographer Jim Hubbard. Expresses the harshness of the children's daily lives as well as their unbroken spirit, creativity and tenderness. Produced by Robin Smith.

Fine Arts; Industrial and Technical Education; Sociology
Dist - FANPRO

Shooting Decisions 25 MIN
16mm / U-matic / VHS
Color
Presents 21 shooting decisions in which the decision had to be made by police officers to shoot or not shoot.
Civics and Political Systems; Social Science
Dist - CORF **Prod** - CORF

Shooting for black and white with Allen Daviau and Denny Lenoir 55 MIN
VHS
Color (C G PRO)
$89.95 purchase
Shows cinematographers Allen Daviau, whose film credits include ET; The Color Purple; Avalon; The Falcon and the Snowman; and Denny Lenoir - Monsieur Hire; L'Enfant D'Hiver; Daddy Nostalgie - in workshop settings. Guides the viewer through lighting problems and their solutions, while comparing the different approaches of the two cinematographers to the problems.
Fine Arts; Industrial and Technical Education
Dist - FIRLIT **Prod** - AFTRS 1994

Shooting for drama with Robby Muller and Peter James 55 MIN
VHS
Color (C G PRO)
$89.95 purchase
Shows cinematographers Robby Muller, whose film credits include Repo Man; Paris, Texas; To Live and Die in LA; and Peter James - Driving Miss Daisy; Alive; Rich in Love - in workshop settings. Guides the viewer through lighting problems and their solutions, while comparing the different approaches of the two cinematographers to the problems.
Fine Arts; Industrial and Technical Education
Dist - FIRLIT **Prod** - AFTRS 1994

Shooting for fantasy with Sacha Vierny and Denny Lenoir 55 MIN
VHS
Color (C G PRO)
$89.95 purchase
Shows cinematographers Sacha Vierny - Belle du Jour; Hiroshima Mon Amour; The Cook, The Thief, His Wife and Her Lover - and Denny Lenoir - Monsieur Hire; L'Enfant D'Hiver; Daddy Nostalgie - in workshop settings. Guides the viewer through lighting problems and their solutions, while comparing the different approaches of the two cinematographers to the problems.
Fine Arts; Industrial and Technical Education
Dist - FIRLIT **Prod** - AFTRS 1994

Shooting for mars 3 MIN
16mm
Screen news digest series
B&W (J H)
LC FIA68-2099
Examines America's Mariner - Mars project. Explores attempts to reach remote regions of the galaxy. Volume seven, issue five of the series.
Science - Physical
Dist - HEARST **Prod** - HEARST 1964

Shooting for realism with Allen Daviau and Sacha Vierny 55 MIN
VHS
Color (C G PRO)
$89.95 purchase
Shows cinematographers Allen Daviau, whose film credits include ET; The Color Purple; Avalon; The Falcon and the Snowman; and Sacha Vierny - Belle du Jour; Hiroshima Mon Amour; The Cook, The Thief, His Wife and Her Lover - in workshop settings. Guides the viewer through lighting problems and their solutions, while comparing the different approaches of the two cinematographers to the problems.
Fine Arts; Industrial and Technical Education
Dist - FIRLIT **Prod** - AFTRS 1994

The Shooting Gallery 5 MIN
16mm
Color (J H)
LC 79-709260
Presents a mannequin - like soldier who enters a shooting gallery in full - dress uniform, and with no apparent feeling, fires at old targets found at a shooting gallery, setting each group of target characters into mechanical motion. Shows the captive figures repeating the same gestures, never quite completing their actions or reaching their goals. Illustrates what happens when a loving couple attempts to break away from the mechanism.
Psychology; Religion and Philosophy; Sociology
Dist - SIM **Prod** - KRATKY 1970

Shooting great underwater videos 39 MIN
VHS
Color (H C)
$29.95 purchase _ #D503
Shows everything from O rings to lens covers, from concepts for a production to delivering the finished product. Produced by Perry Tong, Scuba World TV Show.
Industrial and Technical Education
Dist - INSTRU

Shooting guns 8 MIN
16mm
B&W (G)
$20.00 rental
Documents an excerpt from an unfinished movie. Shows Jonas Mekas directing a sequence from his feature, Guns Of The Trees.
Fine Arts; Industrial and Technical Education
Dist - CANCIN **Prod** - LEVCHI 1966

The Shooting party 105 MIN
35mm / 16mm
Color (G) (RUSSIAN WITH ENGLISH SUBTITLES)
$250.00, $300.00 rental
Adapts the novel by Anton Chekhov. Directed by Emil Lotyanu.
Fine Arts; Literature and Drama
Dist - KINOIC **Prod** - CORINT 1977

Shooting Skills and Air Gun Competition 10 MIN
U-matic / 8mm cartridge
Air Gun Shooting Series no 3
Color (I)
LC 79-700774
Describes the fundamentals of recreational and competitive air gun shooting, with emphasis on safety.
Physical Education and Recreation
Dist - ATHI **Prod** - ATHI 1979

Shooting star 5 MIN
16mm
B&W; Color (G)
$10.00 rental
Entertains with a homespun comedy about transformation. Presents a film by Freude.
Fine Arts
Dist - CANCIN

Shooting straight - guilt - free assertiveness 40 MIN
VHS
Women and leadership series
Color (A PRO)
$79.95 purchase _ #PB08V-B
Focuses on issues of interest to working women. Presents ways for women to stand their ground in a conflict - without guilt. Offers steps to take when asking problem-solving questions that lead to resolution and a six-step confrontation method that works. Part of a four-part series.
Business and Economics; Psychology; Sociology
Dist - CAMV

Shooting techniques
VHS
N C A A instructional video series
Color (H C A)
$39.95 purchase _ #KAR1251V
Presents the first of a three - part series on women's basketball. Focuses on shooting techniques.
Physical Education and Recreation
Dist - CAMV **Prod** - NCAAF

Shooting up AIDS 29 MIN
VHS
America's drug forum series
Color (G)
$19.95 purchase _ #101
Focuses on the controversial work of activist Jon C Parker, a former heroin addict, now in graduate school at the Yale School of Public Health. Reveals that Parker distributes clean needles to injecting drug addicts and was the first person to be acquitted of a drug paraphernalia law when a Boston judged ruled that he acted to save lives. Other guests include Maxie Collier, Health Commissioner of Baltimore, Dr James Curtis, Director of Psychiatry at Harlem Hospital, David Kerr, residential treatment expert.
Guidance and Counseling; Health and Safety; Psychology
Dist - DRUGPF **Prod** - DRUGPF 1991

Shootout in Paradise 26 MIN
16mm
Color
Shows highlights of the 1982 Women's Kemper Open Golf Tournament held in Maui, Hawaii. Includes scenes of golfers JoAnne Carner, Nancy Lopez and Pat Bradley.
Physical Education and Recreation
Dist - MTP **Prod** - MTP

The Shop accident 25 MIN
16mm
Color (G A)
$5.00 rental
Reveals that a serious accident in the shop causes the union safety committee to file a complaint with OSHA. Follows the OSHA inspector who is accompanied by management and union representatives on a walk - around inspection of the plant. Covers the right to file anonymous complaints, the right to walk around with the inspector, how safety hazards are identified. Shows the compliance officer discussing findings with management and the union committee.
Business and Economics; Health and Safety; Social Science
Dist - AFLCIO **Prod** - UWISCA 1976

Shop Assignments 29 MIN
16mm
Color
Covers the method of removing the cylinder head, showing how to remove valves, clean valve seats and replace the head gasket and cylinder head. Examines the removal and replacement of a piston and connecting rod, showing the tools required for the job.
Dist - SF **Prod** - SF 1969

Shop assignments - Pt 1 14 MIN
16mm
Color (J)
Shows the different kinds of shop assignments - - pistons and connecting rods Pt 1 and 2, cylinder head, Pt 1 and 2 and the generator.
Industrial and Technical Education
Dist - SF **Prod** - SF 1968

Shop assignments - Pt 2 15 MIN
16mm
Color (J A)
Shows the removal and replacement of a piston and connecting rod assembly and explains the required tools. Describes how to take apart and reassemble gear and rotor type oil pumps and fuel pumps.
Industrial and Technical Education
Dist - SF **Prod** - SF 1969

Shop Math 45 MIN
VHS / 35mm strip
(J H A IND)
#950XV7
Provides remedial instruction on basic arithmetic operations and covers the highest level of math needed in production shops. Includes basic arithmetic operations, dimensioning calculations for machinists, and basic layout & math techniques for tool & die makers (3 tapes). Includes a Study Guide.
Education; Industrial and Technical Education
Dist - BERGL

Shop Math
VHS / U-matic
Color (J H)
Presents formulas and procedures followed by practice problems and correct answers for immediate reinforcement.
Mathematics
Dist - CAREER **Prod** - CAREER 1981

The Shop on Main Street 128 MIN
VHS
Color (G) (CZECHOSLOVAKIAN (ENGLISH SUBTITLES))
Tells the story of a tragic relationship between a Jew and an 'Aryan' in pre - World War II Czechoslovakia. Stars Ida Kaminska.
Civics and Political Systems; Fine Arts; History - World
Dist - UILL

The Shop on Main Street 125 MIN
VHS
B&W (G)
$24.95 _ #SHO110
Translates the horrors of the Nazi occupation into the simplest of human terms with the heartbreaking story of a friendship between an elderly Jewish woman who owns a button shop and an amiable but weak carpenter appointed by the Nazis as her Aryan controller. Addresses the complex issue of moral responsibility while illuminating the tragedy of racism. Directed by Jan Kadar and Elmar Klos. Produced by IFEX.
Fine Arts; History - World; Psychology; Religion and Philosophy; Sociology
Dist - HOMVIS

Shop safety 22 MIN
U-matic / VHS / 16mm
Color (VOC J H)
Describes common hazards in a vehicle maintenance shop, and shows what precautions should be taken to prevent accidents.
Health and Safety; Industrial and Technical Education
Dist - USNAC **Prod** - USA

Shop safety - a video manual
VHS
(J H VOC)
$379.00 purchase _ #016 - 860
Directs student attention to developing safe work habits. Stresses the importance of personal, group, and equipment safety, including being alert to dangerous situations.
Health and Safety
Dist - CAREER **Prod** - CAREER

Shop safety - a video manual 60 MIN
VHS
Color (H G IND)
$129.00 purchase _ #31373 - 027
Emphasizes the importance of personal safety and shows how students can protect themselves, their fellow workers, the shop equipment and environment. Demonstrates using tools correctly, proper clothing and eye protection and more. Covers the auto shop, the machine shop, woodworking and welding shops. Includes teacher's guide and library kit.
Education; Health and Safety; Industrial and Technical Education
Dist - GA

Shop Safety Series
Safety in the auto shop
Safety in the electronics shop
Safety in the Metal Shop
Safety in the Shop - General
Safety in the Wood Shop
Dist - AAVIM

Shop safety series
Shows how to prevent accidents and injuries by following safety procedures and stresses the different rules to be followed in each type of shop.
Shop safety series
Dist - CAREER **Prod** - CAREER

Shop safety series
Auto shop safety 20 MIN
Electricity - electronics safety 20 MIN
General shop safety 20 MIN
Metal shop safety 20 MIN
Dist - GA

Shop sharply, eat smartly 6 MIN
VHS / U-matic
Color (J H A)
Features a junk - food mother wheeling her baby around the grocery when the baby suddenly 'grows up' and begins giving Mom pointers on wise food shopping and eating.
Health and Safety; Home Economics; Social Science
Dist - NOVID **Prod** - NOVID

Shop sketch theory - one - view working drawings 19 MIN
BETA / VHS
Color (IND T H VOC)
Illustrates the shortcut approach to illustrating an object, such as a fitting or transition, with a one - view working drawing, instead of the typical three - view working drawing as found on most blueprints.
Industrial and Technical Education
Dist - RMIBHF **Prod** - RMIBHF

The Shop steward 22 MIN
16mm
Color (G IND) (SPANISH)
$5.00 rental
Tells the story of a newly elected shop steward learning the responsibilities of the job and solving a difficult grievance at the first step. Originally produced in English and dubbed over.
Business and Economics; Psychology; Social Science; Sociology
Dist - AFLCIO **Prod** - NFBC 1955

Shop stewards 28 MIN
16mm
Are you listening series
Color (IND C H VOC T)
LC 80-701126
Considers the men and women who have experienced the tedium inherent in industrial assembly lines. Talks with workers in the auto, garment, steel, hospital, rubber and electrical unions about the tug - of - war between union and management.
Business and Economics; Social Science; Sociology
Dist - STURTM **Prod** - STURTM 1972

Shop talk 83 MIN
U-matic / VHS / 16mm
Color (A)
Examines contemporary American working class consciousness.
Sociology
Dist - CNEMAG **Prod** - MACHR 1980

Shop talk for trade and industry series
Agriculture and horticulture 30 MIN
Auto mechanics 30 MIN
Business 30 MIN
Construction 30 MIN
Drafting 30 MIN
Electronics 30 MIN
Food service 30 MIN
Health occupations 30 MIN
Home economics 30 MIN
Dist - CAMV

Shoplifters - the Criminal Horde 15 MIN
U-matic / VHS / 16mm
Color (H C A)
$420, $250 purchase _ #83055
Shows shoplifting techniques and explains how store owners and employees can detect thieves.
Sociology
Dist - CORF

Shoplifting 21 MIN
U-matic / VHS / 16mm
Color (J)
Explores the scope of shoplifting today, why people do it and what the results are to the thief and to society. Suggests that everyone should cooperate to reduce shoplifting for the protection of each one's pocketbook.
Psychology; Sociology
Dist - AIMS **Prod** - ACI 1974

Shoplifting 19 MIN
U-matic / VHS
Cop Talk Series
Color (I J)
Depicts what happens when two teenage girls are caught and prosecuted for shoplifting, Phyllis as a first offender and Nancy as a repeated offender.
Sociology
Dist - AITECH **Prod** - UTSBE 1981

Shoplifting 20 MIN
16mm
Community Protection and Crime Prevention Series
Color (G)
LC 73-703199
Features numerous experts who discuss shoplifting while actors dramatize aspects of this type of crime.
Sociology
Dist - SUMHIL **Prod** - SUMHIL 1973

Shoplifting - how it affects your bottom line 9 MIN
VHS
Color (PRO COR A)
$295.00 purchase, $100.00 five - day rental, $30.00 three - day preview _ #CSM
Demonstrates to retailers how to reduce losses from shoplifters and internal theft. Explains how to identify suspicious customer behavior, display merchandise one item at a time, secure display cases, avoid distractions, and be aware of ways employees can steal money and merchandise. Includes a Leader's Guide. Also available in a six - minute version for sales associates.
Sociology
Dist - ADVANM

Shoplifting is stealing 16 MIN
16mm / U-matic / VHS
Color (J H)
LC 76-702135
Shows that the cost of shoplifting is passed on to all consumers. Illustrates increasingly effective surveillance and other techniques to apprehend shoplifters. Emphasizes that shoplifting is a serious crime punishable by law.
Guidance and Counseling; Home Economics; Sociology
Dist - AIMS **Prod** - CAHILL 1975

Shoplifting - It's a Crime 12 MIN
16mm / U-matic / VHS
Color (I)
LC 75-701085
Uses dramatized incidents involving young people of elementary school and high school age in order to show the consequences for shoplifters.
Civics and Political Systems; Guidance and Counseling; Sociology
Dist - ALTSUL **Prod** - ALTSUL 1975

Shoplifting - learn to combat the crime
U-matic / VHS / 16mm
Color (A)
Teaches small business owners how to protect their inventory.
Business and Economics; Psychology; Sociology
Dist - AIMS **Prod** - AIMS 1986

Shoplifting prevented 25 MIN
U-matic / VHS
Color (A)
Shows how to save money by preventing shoplifting. Instructs in the detection of shoplifters. Narrated by Martin Milner.
Sociology
Dist - AMEDIA **Prod** - AMEDIA

Shoplifting - preventing the crime 23 MIN
16mm / VHS
Color (C A)
$360.00, $480.00 purchase, $75.00 rental _ #9839
Teaches small business owners how to protect their inventory. Features a professional shoplifter who narrates the film and shows the tricks of the trade. Offers tips on shoplifting prevention that are precise, but easy to follow. Teaches viewers to be aware of local shoplifing laws, citizen's arrest procedures and how to work with local law enforcement agencies.
Civics and Political Systems; Sociology
Dist - AIMS **Prod** - AIMS 1986

Shoplifting - Sharon's Story 26 MIN
U-matic / VHS / 16mm
Color (J)
LC 77-702444
Tells the story of a young woman who steals from a department store and is subsequently arrested. Shows her reactions as well as those of her parents to the humiliation of search, interrogation, detention, family confrontation and court procedure.
Civics and Political Systems; Guidance and Counseling; Sociology
Dist - LCOA **Prod** - AURO 1977

Shoplifting - you pay for it 16 MIN
U-matic / VHS / 16mm
Color
Deals with the shoplifting problem from a non - accusatory perspective. Points out the cost to consumers in terms of fewer jobs, lower earnings and higher store prices when shoplifting runs rampant. Emphasizes the high risk and low reward of shoplifting.
Sociology
Dist - CORF **Prod** - CORF

Shopping 25 MIN
VHS
Dragon's tongue series
Color (C G) (CHINESE)
$195.00 purchase
Visits the marketplace in the People's Republic of China, using Putonghua, the official language of China based on the dialect of Beijing. Part of a 10 - part series hosted by Prof Colin Mackerras, Co - Director of the Key Center for Asian Languages and Studies at Griffith University.
Foreign Language; Geography - World
Dist - LANDMK **Prod** - LANDMK 1990

Shopping Bag Ladies 45 MIN
U-matic
B&W
Documents the lives of the Shopping Bag Ladies through the city. Presents five intimate portraits of these homeless women who live in doorways, in railway stations and bus stations, on park benches and who carry their belongings in bulging paper and plastic satchels.
Sociology
Dist - WMENIF **Prod** - WMENIF

The Shopping bag lady 21 MIN
U-matic / VHS / 16mm
Color (P I) (SPANISH FRENCH)
LC 75-701067
Tells how a series of experiences of a group of typical 14 - year - old girls make them more sensitive to the needs of elderly people.
Fine Arts; Health and Safety; Psychology
Dist - LCOA **Prod** - LCOA 1975

A Shopping expedition - Paddington and the Old Master - A disappearing trick 17 MIN
U-matic / VHS / 16mm
Paddington Bear 1 series
Color (K P I)
LC 77-700665
Presents an animated adaptation of chapters 4, 5 and 8 from the children's book A Bear Called Paddington by Michael Bond. Tells about a small, dark bear whose attempts at shopping, painting and magic result in a series of misadventures.
Fine Arts; Literature and Drama
Dist - ALTSUL **Prod** - BONDM 1977

Shopping for doomsday 16 MIN
VHS / U-matic
Color (H C A)
Presents the views of a growing number of people who call themselves Survivalists. Explores their beliefs, which include the fact that the West will experience a total breakdown of law and order and a nuclear disaster in the next decade.
History - United States; Sociology
Dist - JOU **Prod** - JOU

Shopping for Insurance 14 MIN
Videoreel / VT2
Living Better II Series
Color
Examines the different types of insurance including, life, property, liablity, automobile and health. Lists specific tips and insurance terms that help plan for a family's security.
Business and Economics; Home Economics
Dist - PBS **Prod** - MAETEL

Shopping for your wedding 60 MIN
VHS
Color (H C G)
$29.95 purchase _ #GHA100V
Focuses on wedding experts who offer valuable tips on everything from catering and photography to dressmaking, tuxedos, music, florists, limousine, jewelry and even travel.
Home Economics; Sociology
Dist - CAMV

Shopping Sense - Self - Defense 15 MIN
U-matic / VHS
Soup to Nuts Series
Color (J H)
Focuses on supermarket psychology and discusses ingredient labels, unit pricing, and open dating.
Health and Safety; Home Economics; Social Science
Dist - AITECH **Prod** - GSDE 1980

Shopping smart - a consumer's guide to healthy food selection 15 MIN
VHS
Color (G)
$149.00 purchase, $45.00 rental
Takes a video tour through a supermarket, from produce counter to deli. Shows how to 'shop the perimeter,' the dairy section, meat and produce, the inner and frozen - food sections and the delicatessen area. Features leading nutritionists who explain how to read labels, understand packaging claims and make smart nutritional choices. Booklet available separately.
Home Economics; Social Science
Dist - GPERFO

Shopping strategies 29 MIN
U-matic / VHS / 16mm
Be a better shopper series; Program 3
Color (H C A)
LC 81-701460
Discusses general shopping strategies, including ideas for preplanning the weekly shopping trip, ways to control impulse spending and supermarket specials.
Home Economics
Dist - CORNRS **Prod** - CUETV 1978

The Shopping Trip 15 MIN
VHS / U-matic
It's all Up to You Series
Color (I J)
Illustrates how institutions, governmental and nongovernmental, vary in form and function.
Guidance and Counseling; Social Science
Dist - AITECH **Prod** - COOPED 1978

Shopping Wisely 14 MIN
U-matic / 35mm strip
Color (H C A)
Details the things to look for and be aware of when shopping for food, clothing or credit. Be Aware Of Easy Credit; Become A Wise Shopper; Breakfast Food Number One; Breakfast Food Number Two; Bright Idea; Buying Clothing - Care Labels; Buying Clothing - Care Labels; Buying Clothing - Generic Names; Buying Clothing - Label; Buying Clothing - Label; Buying Clothing - Label; Buying Credit; Buying Eggs; Buying Is A Matter Of Making Choices; Buying Meat; Buying Steak; Carrying Charges; Compare Credit Cost; Consumerism; Convenience Foods; Convenience Foods - Cost; Deferred Payment Price; Easy Credit Can Be Expensive; Eggs - Size And Grade; Federal Standards - 1; Federal Standards - 2; Finance Charge; Food Is Expensive; Frankfurters; Fresh Meat Stamp; Ground Beef; Help To Buy Wisely; Interstate And Intrastate Sales; Is Organic Food Better For You; It's Your Money - Spend It Wisely; Keys To Quality Buying Number One; Keys To Quality Buying Number Two; Kinds Of Meat And Seafood; Mandatory Labeling; Nutrition Label; Organic Food Cost; Package Weights; Processed Meat Stamp; Shop For Credit; Steaks Have Many Names; USDA Choice; USDA Good; USDA Prime; USDA Stamp; Ways To Save In Buying Food; What Is Important When Buying Beef.
Home Economics
Dist - UTRANS **Prod** - UTRANS

Shore Survival 22 MIN
U-matic / VHS
Fisheries Safety and Survival Series
Color (PRO)
Discusses survival once on shore, including identifying alternative sources of food, boiling water, keeping dry, creating shelter and making signals. Includes interviews with survivors who followed these guidelines.
Health and Safety
Dist - USNAC **Prod** - USCG 1983

The Shoreline doesn't stop here anymore 46 MIN
VHS
Color; CC (G H C A)
$250.00 purchase, $75.00 rental
Looks at erosion, nature's way of transporting sand from one place to another in the ongoing dance between waves, wind and land, as explained by host David Suzuki. Examines how humans interfere with this process as they try various engineering solutions to combat the sea. Shows how an eight million dollar project of the US Army Corps of Engineers at Folly Beach, South Carolina, was destroyed by 1993's storm of the century hurricane - force winds. Produced by the Canadian Broadcasting Corporation's The Nature Of Things. In two parts for schools, 20 and 26 minutes.
Geography - World; Industrial and Technical Education; Science - Physical
Dist - BULFRG **Prod** - CANBC 1994

Shores of Gulf St Vincent 24 MIN
16mm
Color (P I J H)
LC 76-708711
Shows three submerged reefs off the coast of South Australia and their formation. Includes divers exploring the biological aspects of the reefs. Reveals a wide variety of unknown and interesting marine animals.
Geography - World; Science - Natural; Science - Physical
Dist - AMEDFL **Prod** - STEEND 1970

The Shores of Phos - a fable 10 MIN
16mm
Color (G)
$22.00 rental, $420.00 purchase
Says filmmaker Brakhage, 'Phos equals light, but then I did also want that word within the title which would designate place....a specific country of the imagination with tangible shores, etc.'
Fine Arts
Dist - CANCIN

The Shores of the cosmic ocean 60 MIN
16mm / U-matic / VHS
Cosmos series; Program 1
Color (J H C G)
LC 81-701150
Offers a guided tour of the universe, from clusters of galaxies to Earth. Introduces the discoveries of Eratosthenes and discusses the dawn of systematic scientific research and the Alexandrian library. Concludes with a 'cosmic calendar,' a journey through time from the Big Bang to the present. Based on the book Cosmos by Carl Sagan. Narrated by Carl Sagan.
Science; Science - Physical
Dist - FI **Prod** - KCET 1980

Shoring 21 MIN
U-matic
Carpentry Apprenticeship Series
(H)
Demonstrates the main types of shoring and re - shoring.
Industrial and Technical Education
Dist - ACCESS **Prod** - ACCESS 1983

Shoring and trenching 31 MIN
VHS
Color (G A)
$295.00 purchase _ #EO405GA
Shows correct procedure for trenching and shoring operations, with emphasis on soil analysis and safety considerations for particular situations.
Health and Safety; Industrial and Technical Education
Dist - WAENFE

Short and Suite 5 MIN
16mm / U-matic / VHS
Color (H C)
Norman McLaren translates into moving patterns of color and light the moods and rhythms of music written for jazz ensemble by Eldon Rathburn.
Fine Arts
Dist - IFB **Prod** - NFBC 1960

The Short approach shots 9 MIN
Videoreel / VT2
Modern golf instruction in motion pictures series; Unit 3
Color (H C A)
LC 76-703597
Identifies short approach golf swings. Demonstrates adjustments in setup and stroke and explores the results of lengthening a short approach swing.
Physical Education and Recreation
Dist - NGF **Prod** - NGF 1974

Short Block Engine Repair
VHS / 35mm strip
Automotive Technology Series
Color
$40.00 purchase _ #MX8002 filmstrip, $80.00 purchase _ #MX8002V VHS
Education; Industrial and Technical Education
Dist - CAREER **Prod** - CAREER

Short block service 40 MIN
VHS
Color (H C A VOC)
$89.00 purchase _ #MC113
Illustrates how to reassemble the crankshaft, main bearings, rods, pistons, piston rings and other parts in the cylinder block.
Industrial and Technical Education
Dist - AAVIM **Prod** - AAVIM 1990
CAMV

Short Chinese TV plays 180 MIN
VHS
Color (C A G) (CHINESE)
$99.95 purchase
Contains ten short TV plays from China. Text available separately with transcriptions of the plays in both simplified and traditional characters. Teaches intermediate through advanced students of Chinese.
Foreign Language; Literature and Drama
Dist - CHTSUI **Prod** - CHTSUI

Short circuit 45 MIN
16mm
Color (C A)
Asks how an upper - middle - class liberal can make a documentary film about the black population and culture of his Manhattan neighborhood.
Fine Arts; Sociology
Dist - KIRPRO **Prod** - KIRPRO

Short circuiting metal transfer
VHS
Arc welding processes series
(VOC)
$59.95 purchase _ #MJ093117V
Uses high speed photography to show arc welding processes and conditions. Shows how to set up and apply the processes. Portrays industry applications of thin and thick gauge metals.
Industrial and Technical Education
Dist - CAREER **Prod** - CAREER

Short circuiting - mild steel modules
VHS
Gas metal arc welding - plate - series
(VOC H IND)
$350.00 purchase _ #MJ105750V
Provides training in safe, effective techniques in short circuiting.
Education; Industrial and Technical Education
Dist - CAREER **Prod** - CAREER

Short Cuts 29 MIN
Videoreel / VT2
Making Things Grow III Series
Color
Agriculture
Dist - PBS **Prod** - WGBHTV

Short cuts 25 MIN
VHS / 16mm
(C COR A)
$176.00 rental
Presents shortened versions of A Passion for Excellence, Team Excellence, Megatrends, The One Minute Manager, Putting the One Minute Manager to Work, Building the One Minute Manager Skills, and Leadership and the One Minute Manager.
Business and Economics; Education
Dist - VLEARN **Prod** - VPHI 1986
VPHI

Short Day Problems 30 MIN
Videoreel / VT2
Making Things Grow II Series
Color
Agriculture
Dist - PBS **Prod** - WGBHTV

Short Distance Runner 21 MIN
16mm
Color (J H C)
LC 79-700941
Dramatizes the story of a high school student whose increased dependency on alcohol affects his schoolwork and athletic pursuits.
Health and Safety; Psychology; Sociology
Dist - MARTC **Prod** - SIGPRS 1978

Short Eared Owl 17 MIN
U-matic / VHS / 16mm
RSPB Collection Series
Color
Shows the owl, opening at its wintering grounds and follows its southern movements in spring. Examines the link between breeding success and population of meadow mice, its main prey. Reveals that, unlike most owls, the short eared owl often hunts in daylight over open fields and salt marshes.

Science - Natural
Dist - BCNFL **Prod** - RSFPB 1983

Short Field Procedure L - 19 - Bird Dog - Pt 1 - Power Approach and Maximum Performance Takeoff 16 MIN
16mm
B&W
LC 74-706244
Presents a flight training film which shows the start and control of power approach, the effects of wind and temperature and landing techniques. Demonstrates preparation, start and climb for a maximum performance takeoff.
Industrial and Technical Education
Dist - USNAC **Prod** - USA 1960

Short field procedure L - 19 - bird dog - Pt 2 - barrier landing and barrier takeoff 10 MIN
16mm
B&W
LC 74-705634
Shows directional control, power approach and line descent in barrier landing, maximum performance takeoff and climb and normal climb in barrier takeoff.
Industrial and Technical Education
Dist - USNAC **Prod** - USA 1960

Short film compilation number 1 60 MIN
VHS
Color; B&W (G)
$49.00 purchase
Presents ten short films including The Refigerator, 1991, 7 minutes, directed by David Stovall and David Bird; Information Evolution, 1992, 2 minutes, directed by Miles Fawcett; Gay Parade, 1972, 11 minutes, by Sol Rubin; For Which it Stands, 1991, 5 minutes, by Sam Bozzo; The Kite Flies Out of Sight Or Be Positive Ketchup, 1992, 13 minutes, by Peter Steinberg; Doctor Thunder, 1992, 4 minutes, by Christa Myers; Two Sad Cowboys, 1992, 3 minutes, by Russell Hexter and Jim Carden; Airline Saftey Film number 4a, 1991, 4 minutes, by James Keitel; Sweet n Sour, 1993, 9 minutes, by Tag Purvis; and Tossin and Turnin in the Global Economy, 1991, 2 minutes, by Sim Sadler.
Fine Arts
Dist - ALTFMW

Short film compilation number 2 32 MIN
VHS
Color; B&W (G)
$39.00 purchase
Presents four short productions. Includes A Voice from the Streets, 1991, 9 minutes, offering a subjective look at an individual's life on the streets, directed by William Tyler Smith; Allure of the Threshold, 1992, 12 minutes, portraying a woman forced into facing the dark reality of her soul, her descent into madness and return to sanity, directed by Bret Lama; Doug's History, 1987, 4 minutes, a new account of JFK's term of office revealing the secret origin of the US space program, directed by Douglas Underdahl; Sacred Circle, 1992, 7 minutes, a film poem inspired by Native American Coyote trickster stories, in which a wandering woman encounters the conjoined spirits of Hawk and Coyote, directed by Gretchen Widmer.
Fine Arts
Dist - ALTFMW

Short films 1975 - 1 to 10 40 MIN
16mm
Color (G)
$1231.00 purchase, $78.00 rental
Presents a series of ten deliberately untitled films by Stan Brakhage.
Fine Arts
Dist - CANCIN **Prod** - BRAKS 1975

Short films 1976 25 MIN
16mm
Color (G)
$679.00 purchase, $42.00 rental
Stars Jane Brakhage as The Dreamer, Bob Benson as The Magnificent Stranger, Omar Beagle as The Snow Plow Man and Jimmy Ryan Morris as The Poet and as Doc Holliday.
Fine Arts
Dist - CANCIN **Prod** - BRAKS 1976

Short films of D W Griffith - Vol 1 45 MIN
BETA / VHS
B&W (G)
Presents The Battle (1911), The Female Of The Species (1912) and The New York Hat (1912), silent films directed by D W Griffith.
Fine Arts
Dist - VIDIM

The Short films of Pascal Aubier 40 MIN
16mm / U-matic / VHS
Color & B&W (G)
$500.00, $400.00, $250.00 purchase
Presents six short films by Pascal Aubier, born in Paris in 1943. Includes a fatally wounded soldier in Flashback; a young factory worker who locks himself into a bathroom and encounters a vision in Le Petits Coins - The John; the consequences of intolerance - with an anti - smoking slant in La Cendre - The Ash; a dark and humorous exploration of faith and ignorance in L'Apparition - The Apparition; a half - comic meditation on the pain and inhumanity of modern technology in La Mort du Rat - The Death of the Rat; and a playful study of eating strawberries and high - diving in Sauteuse de L'Ange - The Angel Jump Girl.
Fine Arts
Dist - FLOWER

Short form by Terry Dunn 120 MIN
VHS
Color (G)
$29.95 purchase _ #1107
Teaches the 37 - posture Yang style short form created by Cheng Man - Ch'ing. Features an introduction to T'ai chi ch'uan, breathing, posture, and warmup. Includes step by step instruction with video windows showing different angles.
Physical Education and Recreation
Dist - WAYF

The Short Game with John Jacobs
VHS
(J H C A)
$69.95 purchase _ #DG006V
Discusses the short game of golf.
Physical Education and Recreation
Dist - CAMV

Short irons - Volume 2 55 MIN
VHS
Name of the game is golf series
(H C A)
$49.95 purchase _ #SWC420V
Demonstrates basics golf skills, including correct swing, hooks and slices, tempo and proper alignment and more. Features slow motion photography.
Physical Education and Recreation
Dist - CAMV

The Short Life of Lolo Knopke 30 MIN
U-matic / VHS / 16mm
Powerhouse Series
Color (I J)
Reveals that the capture of a would - be killer by the smallest Powerhouse Kid shows that everyone can be big when they use their brains.
Psychology
Dist - GA **Prod** - EFCVA 1982

Short - Lived Radioisotopes in Nuclear Medicine 27 MIN
16mm
Color (PRO)
LC 77-714176
Describes the development of a technetium - 99M generator at Brookhaven National Laboratory and shows the medical applications of the generator at the Argonne Cancer Research Hospital.
Health and Safety; Science; Science - Physical
Dist - USERD **Prod** - ANL 1971

Short of breath 10 MIN
16mm / VHS
Color; B&W (A)
$35.00 rental, $20.00 purchase
Features a haunting emotional collage about birth, death, sex and suicide. Looks at a woman bending over backwards trying to be a good wife and mother. Her head is cut off from her heart, a doctor picks her brain and a boy inherits his mother's depression. A Jay Rosenblatt production. Available for purchase as a package with 'Brain in the Desert.'
Fine Arts; Psychology; Sociology
Dist - CANCIN

Short order cookery 10 MIN
U-matic / VHS / 16mm
Professional food preparation and service program series
Color (H VOC)
LC 74-700231
Presents a training course to the short order cook for greater efficiency and productivity while facing particular problems of organizing work with the added challenge of often performing his duties in the public eye. Stresses ways of coping with traffic, staying ahead of the rush, various foods that must be prepared. Emphasizes details of griddle use and maintenance. Shows that appearance and cleanliness are needed for exhibition cooking.
Home Economics; Industrial and Technical Education
Dist - NEM **Prod** - NEM 1973

Short order food service - grill managment 45 MIN
VHS
Color (H VOC)
$129.00 purchase _ #30810 - 027
Illustrates cleaning and maintaining equipment, cooking zones and techniques for cooking typical menu items. Explains importance of 'prepping' food, managing flow of orders and timing for doneness.
Education; Home Economics; Industrial and Technical Education
Dist - GA

The Short order gourmet 60 MIN
U-matic
(H VOC)
$39.95 _ #EQ500V
Shows the viewer how to choose ingredients and dishes for appropriate occasions, and demonstrates how to prepare a wide variety of those dishes.
Home Economics; Industrial and Technical Education
Dist - CAMV **Prod** - CAMV
UILL

Short order restaurants 27 MIN
VHS
Color (H VOC)
$129.00 purchase _ #30811 - 027
Takes a detailed look at how restaurants are laid out for maximum efficiency, the operating routines, kinds of jobs, labor laws, hygiene and safety. Illustrates preparation of sandwiches, beverages and desserts.
Education; Home Economics; Industrial and Technical Education
Dist - GA

Short Rotation Forestry 29 MIN
VHS
Ecology Workshop Series
Color (J H C G)
$195 purchase, $50 rental
Discusses coppicing or short rotation forestry which is an old technique that saves money for reforestation, prevents erosion, and provides high yields. Points out that fast growing trees such as poplar, willow, and birch are cut, left to resprout, and then cut again a few years later.
Science - Natural; Science - Physical
Dist - BULFRG **Prod** - BULFRG 1987

Short, sharp and shocking 40 MIN
VHS
40 minutes series
Color; PAL (H C A)
PdS99 purchase; Not available in South Africa
Features an experiment designed to deter youth criminals from further criminal activity. Follows seven teenagers, all of whom are on probation, as they visit a high security jail and meet with long - term inmates who give them an insider's perspective on what it means to be imprisoned. The youth are hasseled, demeaned, and sworn at by other inmates as they experience the realities of prison life.
Sociology
Dist - BBCENE

Short sizes and framing faults 9 MIN
VHS
Lessons in visual language series
Color (G C)
$99.00 purchase, $39.00 rental _ #748
Defines the basic shot types of film and video vocabulary, from wide shot to big closeup. Discusses the most effective use of each. Shows how to build up an action sequence from a combination of framings and discusses the psychological impact of common framing errors. Features Peter Thompson as creator and narrator of a ten - part series on visual language. Produced by the Australian Film, Television and Radio School.
Industrial and Technical Education; Social Science
Dist - FIRLIT

Short Socks 30 MIN
16mm
Classic Christie Comedies Series
B&W
Literature and Drama
Dist - SFI **Prod** - SFI

Short stories - a video anthology series
VHS
Short stories - video anthology series
Color (H G)
$479.20 purchase
Offers a collection of 16 short dramas by young American filmmakers. Includes suspense, the supernatural, black comedy, wacky romance and family drama. Each film is between 20 - 40 minutes in length. Purchase of complete set features a savings of $30.00 per film from the single purchase price of $59.95. Also available as a selection of six for $39.95 each.
Fine Arts; Literature and Drama
Dist - CNEMAG

Short Stories by John Cheever and Eudora Welty 29 MIN
Videoreel / VT2
One to One Series
Color
Presents readings from the short stories of John Cheever and Eudora Welty.
Literature and Drama
Dist - PBS **Prod** - WETATV

Short stories - video anthology series
And another honkytonk girl says she will 30 MIN
Assurances 28 MIN
The Badge 30 MIN
Ballyhoo baby 30 MIN
The Boardwalk club 27 MIN
Bronx cheers 30 MIN
Freefall 28 MIN
Many wonder 40 MIN
Ralph's arm 30 MIN
Redlands 28 MIN
Short stories - a video anthology series
Stream of social intercourse 26 MIN
Together and apart 26 MIN
Dist - CNEMAG

The Short Story
U-matic / VHS
Color (H C)
Explains the key elements of the short story and discusses the different techniques and objectives of short story writers such as Poe, Thurber, Saroyan, Hemingway and others. Gives readings from Jean Stafford and Flannery O'Connor with the authors' own insights into their work methods and feelings.
Literature and Drama
Dist - GA **Prod** - GA

A Short story history of processors 29 MIN
U-matic
Radiographic processing series; Pt 3
Color (C)
LC 77-706072
Discusses the development of radiographic processing equipment from the time of manual processing to automatic radiographic processors of the 1970's.
Health and Safety; Industrial and Technical Education; Science
Dist - USNAC **Prod** - USVA 1975

Short Story I 15 MIN
U-matic / VHS
Zebra Wings Series
Color (I)
Discusses the characters, setting and plot of a short story.
English Language; Literature and Drama
Dist - AITECH **Prod** - NITC 1975

Short Story II 15 MIN
U-matic / VHS
Zebra Wings Series
Color (I)
Introduces several mystery writing components, including aliteration, mood and setting.
English Language; Literature and Drama
Dist - AITECH **Prod** - NITC 1975

Short story series
Presents 16 fifteen - minute programs on four videocassettes which introduce American and European short story writers and discusses the technical aspects of short story structure.
The Boarded window 15 MIN
Dave's necklace 15 MIN
The Diary of Adam and Eve 15 MIN
The Dilettante 15 MIN
The Lull 15 MIN
Mrs Ripley's trip 15 MIN
The Queen of spades 15 MIN
Tennessee's partner 15 MIN
The Two Thanksgiving Day gentlemen 15 MIN
The Village singer 15 MIN
Dist - GPN **Prod** - CTI 1975

Short Story Series
The Bet 15 MIN
The Real thing by Henry James 15 MIN
The Tell - Tale Heart by Edgar Allan Poe 15 MIN
Tennessee's Partner by Bret Harte 15 MIN
The Two little soldiers 15 MIN
Dist - GPN
IU

Short story series
The Birthmark - by Nathaniel Hawthorne 15 MIN
The Boarded window - by Ambrose Bierce 15 MIN
Dave's necklace by Charles Chestnutt 15 MIN
The Diary of Adam and Eve by Mark Twain 15 MIN
The Dilettante - by Edith Wharton 15 MIN
The Lull - by Saki 15 MIN
Mrs Ripley's Trip by Hamlin Garland 15 MIN
The Queen of spades by Alexander Pushkin 15 MIN
The Tell - Tale Heart - by Edgar Allan Poe 15 MIN
The Two Little Soldiers by Guy De Maupassant 15 MIN
The Two Thanksgiving Day Gentlemen by O Henry 15 MIN
The Village Singer by Mary Wilkins Freeman 15 MIN
The Yellow Wallpaper by Charlotte Perkins Gilman 15 MIN
Dist - IU

Short Tall Story 5 MIN
U-matic / VHS / 16mm
Color (I)
LC 81-700795
Presents an animated fable about a cloud - covered land inhabited by a group of tall people and a group of short people. Tells how a good fairy removes the clouds and the two groups see that, regardless of their physical differences, they are really all the same.
Fine Arts; Literature and Drama
Dist - PHENIX **Prod** - HALAS

Short - term group psychotherapy for loss patients - a demonstration videotape 55 MIN
VHS
Color (PRO)
$195.00 purchase _ #2948
Demonstrates the time - limited, interpretive approach developed by Dr William E Piper for dealing with persons who have experienced loss. Portrays typical examples of patient discussion, therapist intervention and patient - therapist interaction. Produced by Dr Piper, Mary McCallum, Anthony S Joyce, Scott F Duncan, J Fyfe Bahrey and members of the Short - Term Psychotherapy Seminar.
Psychology
Dist - GFORD

A Short term systems intervention model for family assessment and intervention - Pt 1 60 MIN
VHS / U-matic
B&W (PRO)
Presents a short - term systems intervention model for family assessment and intervention. Discusses its development, methodology and testing as well as assessing the role and function of individual family members.
Sociology
Dist - UWISC **Prod** - TELURN 1978

Short Time Intervals 21 MIN
16mm
PSSC Physics Films Series
B&W (H C)
Presents a study of the extension of senses to deal with very short time intervals. Timing devices - - moving cameras, pen recorders and an oscilloscope - - are shown and explained.
Psychology; Science; Science - Natural; Science - Physical
Dist - MLA **Prod** - PSSC 1960

Short vowel sounds 15 MIN
VHS
Planet pylon series
Color (I)
LC 90712897
Uses character Commander Wordstalker from the Space Station Readstar in series to develop language arts skills. Examines short vowel sounds. Features a worksheet exercise that can be used by viewers with the help of series characters.
English Language
Dist - GPN

The Short vowel sounds 12 MIN
U-matic / VHS / 16mm
Reading skills, set 2 series; 2
Color (P I)
LC 73-700986
Reviews the long and short vowel sounds with emphasis on the latter using animated letter sequences.
English Language
Dist - JOU **Prod** - GLDWER 1972

Short vowels 15 MIN
U-matic / Kit / VHS
Space station readstar series
(P)
$130 purchase, $25 rental, $75 self dub
Teaches phonics in a series designed to supplement second grade reading programs. Focuses on short vowels. First in a 25 part series.
English Language
Dist - GPN

The Short Way Home 14 MIN
16mm
Color (PRO)
LC 74-705636
Discusses how patients, who previously might have been confined to a hospital for a long period of recuperation, can be returned to their homes through the facilities provided by the home health services. Explains that the combined efforts of physicians, community nurses, therapists and technicans bring the hospital to the patient and speed his recovery in familiar surroundings.
Health and Safety
Dist - USPHS **Prod** - USPHS 1967

Shortchanging girls, shortchanging America 15 MIN
VHS
Color (G)
$24.95 purchase
Underscores the need for major changes in the ways girls are taught and treated in American schools. Includes AAUW poll results, interviews with education experts, narratives by public policy leaders and the compelling faces and voices of American girls.
Education; Sociology
Dist - AAUW **Prod** - AAUW 1992

The Shortest distance 60 MIN
VHS
People in motion - changing ideas about physical disability series
Color; CC (G)
$89.95 purchase _ #UW5677
Explores new assistive technologies, as well as the basic research currently underway aimed at reducing or eliminating paralysis. Examines underlying attitudes and stereotypes regarding people with physical disabilities by considering people with disabilities in the performing arts - with a special emphasis on dance. Shows how disability hasn't stopped one wheelchair user from running for Congress. Part one of three parts.
Health and Safety
Dist - FOTH

Shortest - longest 15 MIN
VHS / U-matic
Hands on series; Grade 1 - Measuring; Unit 2
Color (P)
Mathematics; Science; Science - Physical
Dist - AITECH **Prod** - VAOG 1975

Shortgrass Prairie, Pt 1 15 MIN
U-matic / VHS / 16mm
Animals and Plants of North America Series
Color (J)
LC 81-700952
Describes the extremes of climate on the prairie and shows the courtship ritual of the male sage grouse during a period of bitter cold.
Science - Natural
Dist - LCOA **Prod** - KARVF 1981

Shortgrass Prairie, Pt 2 15 MIN
U-matic / VHS / 16mm
Animals and Plants of North America Series
Color (J)
LC 81-700952
Shows the display ritual of a lark bunting, hawks rearing their young and the habits of other animals that inhabit the prairie.
Science - Natural
Dist - LCOA **Prod** - KARVF 1981

Shostakovich - Symphony no 5 - Pt 6 88 MIN
VHS
Story of the symphony series
Color (H C G)
$39.95 purchase _ #833 - 9047
Features Andre Previn conducting the Royal Philharmonic Orchestra in some of the most popular and important works of the concert repertoire. Presents Previn in rehearsal discussing the composer and his music, using pictures, anecdotes and orchestral excerpts to underscore his comments. Each program concludes with a complete and uninterrupted performance of the symphony. Part 6 discusses 20th - century musical trends in different countries from Vaughan Williams in Britain to Shostakovich in the Soviet Union. Under Stalin's regime Shostakovich incurred offical displeasure and lived in constant fear of arrest. His Fifth Symphony was his creative response to criticism by Soviet authorities.
Fine Arts
Dist - FI **Prod** - RMART 1986

The Shot 22 MIN
VHS
Color (G)
$25.00 purchase
Embarks on an intriguing adventure when Marvin Levitch, a sly Paparazzi, disguises himself as a telephone repairman to catch a photograph of Gordon Sunshine, a famous singer who went into hiding ten years earlier. Presents a production directed by Aaron Greene.
Fine Arts; Industrial and Technical Education; Literature and Drama
Dist - ALTFMW

The Shot 12 MIN
U-matic / VHS / 16mm
Athletics Series
Color (H C A)
LC 80-700343
Uses slow - motion scenes to analyze the movements leading up to the release of the shot. Shows athletes and their coach demonstrating training routines, covering both the straight line put and the rotational technique. Concludes with scenes of an international competition in the event.
Physical Education and Recreation
Dist - IU **Prod** - GSAVL 1980

The Shot Heard 'Round the World 32 MIN
U-matic / VHS / 16mm
Johnny Tremain Series
Color (I J H)
LC FIA67-1284
Presents an excerpt from the feature film Johnny Tremain. Describes how younger members of the Sons of Liberty supplied the information about British plans which enabled Paul Revere to alert the Minutemen.
Fine Arts; History - United States
Dist - CORF **Prod** - DISNEY 1966

Shot put 60 MIN
U-matic / VHS
Frank Morris instructional videos series
Color; B&W; Silent; Mono; Stereo (H C A)
Instructs athletes how to execute and improve performance of the Shot Put. Produced and Narrated by coach Frank Morris.
Physical Education and Recreation
Dist - TRACKN **Prod** - TRACKN 1986

Shot put
VHS
Coaching men's field and track series
Color (H C G)
$59.95 purchase _ #TRS1251V
Features men's field and track coach Rick Sloan on the shot put. Starts with the standing throw, goes through the mechanics of the power position, the starting position, the glide and full throws. Offers in - depth demonstrations of how to teach rotational shot techniques. Part of a nine - part series.
Physical Education and Recreation
Dist - CAMV

Shot put 30 MIN
VHS
Track and field techniques series
Color (H C G)
$29.95 purchase _ #WK1105V
Features shot putter Parry O'Brien who discusses the skill and improving performance. Part of a series.
Physical Education and Recreation
Dist - CAMV

Shot put
VHS
Coaching women's track and field series
Color (H C G)
$59.95 purchase _ #TRS1101V
Features women's field and track coaches Bob Meyers and Meg Ritchie on the shot put. Discusses overhead throws, standing throws, foot work and body mechanics leading to full throws. Offers preliminary drills for hip extension, drills to develop the throwing action, step back drill to encourage right leg activity during the shift and drills to enhance the correct mechanics of the complete throw. Includes strength training programs using specific exercises to develop the beginning through advanced thrower. Part of a nine - part series.
Physical Education and Recreation
Dist - CAMV

Shot put technique 12 MIN
VHS
Bill Dellinger's championship track and field series
Color (H C A)
$39.95 purchase _ #WES1708V
Features Bill Dellinger and the University of Oregon coaching staff, who teach the basic techniques of the shot put. Presents drills to develop an athlete's potential and correct common errors in technique. Uses slow - motion film and on - screen graphics.
Physical Education and Recreation
Dist - CAMV

Shot Putting with Thge Big 'O' - Philosophy and Training of Brian Old field 30 MIN
U-matic / VHS
John Powell Associates Videos Series
Color (J H C A)
Provides technical instruction on the shot put event. Features expert Brian Oldfield.
Physical Education and Recreation
Dist - TRACKN **Prod** - TRACKN 1985

Shotgun fundamentals 45 MIN
VHS / BETA
Color (A)
Explains how to choose and fit a gun, correct gun mount, sight picture, trigger pull, dealing with recoil, target acquisition, and methods of lead. Includes an exhibition in trick shooting by the instructor, John Satterwhite - U S skeet shooting champion,dual Gold Medalist from the Pan American games and the U S Olympic Committee Athletic Advisor for shooting.
Physical Education and Recreation
Dist - RMIBHF **Prod** - RMIBHF

Shotgun Joe 25 MIN
16mm
Jason films portrait series
Color (J H C)
LC 75-705662
A cinema verite portrait of Joe Scanlon who is serving time for armed robbery in the Connecticut State Reformatory. Includes interviews with guards, teachers, fellow inmates, family members and with Joe, himself, which reveal that he is moving toward self - destruction.
Psychology; Sociology
Dist - JASON **Prod** - CAMPI 1970

Shotgun or Sidearm 16 MIN
U-matic / VHS / 16mm
Color
Explores situations in which an officer must decide which weapon to use, a sidearm or a shotgun. Demonstrates the advantages and disadvantages of a shotgun and explores its capacities. Looks at what an officer should consider when making his decision and what problems arise when an error is made. Covers both tactical and psychological aspects of the weapons.
Civics and Political Systems; Social Science
Dist - CORF **Prod** - DAVP

Shotgun - Second Weapon 25 MIN
16mm / U-matic / VHS
Color
Discusses the proper use of the law enforcement shotgun, styles and makes of weapons, psychology of the shotgun, car mounts, ammunition, and avoidance of lethal situations caused by an improper understanding of what the shotgun can and cannot do. Includes re - creations of incorrect use which can easily be avoided with knowledge, care and proper attitude.
Civics and Political Systems; Social Science
Dist - CORF **Prod** - WORON

Shotgun shooting and how 11 MIN
U-matic / VHS / 16mm
Color (A)
Features Vic Reinders to emphasize safe handling of guns. Demonstrates such fundamentals as fit of gun, and swing, lead and alignment.
Physical Education and Recreation
Dist - IFB **Prod** - KRAFT 1950

Should Congress Deregulate Interstate Trucking 59 MIN
U-matic
Advocates Series
Color
Shows a debate between Bonnie Frank and Lisle Baker centering around Congressional deregulation of interstate trucking.
Civics and Political Systems; Social Science
Dist - PBS **Prod** - WGBHTV

Should Congress Pass Carter's Energy Program 59 MIN
U-matic
Advocates Series
Color
Asks whether President Carter's energy bill should be approved. Features Morris Udall and Robert Kruger debating the issue.
Civics and Political Systems; History - United States; Social Science
Dist - PBS **Prod** - WGBHTV

Should Congress Pass President Carter's Welfare - Jobs Bill 56 MIN
U-matic
Advocates series
Color (H C)
Presents Franklin Raines and John Kramer debating the question of the passage of President Carter's welfare - jobs bill.
Civics and Political Systems; History - United States; Sociology
Dist - PBS **Prod** - WGBHTV

Should he tell 5 MIN
16mm / VHS
Starting early series
Color (I J H)
$40.00, $25.00 purchase _ #255, #470
Tells about Jeff whose dad has come to take him on a weekend fishing and camping trip. Shows Jeff's mother cautioning his father about drinking. Jeff loves his father, but the weekend is ruined by his father's abusive drinking. Part of a series on alcohol education.
Guidance and Counseling; Health and Safety; Psychology
Dist - AAAFTS **Prod** - AAAFTS 1985

Should I Retire Early? 57 MIN
VHS / U-matic
Color
Designed to assist employees in making the decision to retire early, defer early retirement or continue working until normal retirement age.
Business and Economics; Sociology
Dist - DBMI **Prod** - DBMI

Should oceans meet 30 MIN
16mm
Life around us Spanish series
Color (SPANISH)
LC 78-700078
Presents a discussion by scientists on the potential ecological damage that may result from the excessive building of canals and dams.
Geography - World; Science - Natural; Science - Physical
Dist - TIMLIF **Prod** - TIMLIF 1971

Should Oceans Meet 30 MIN
16mm / U-matic / VHS
Life Around Us Series
Color (I)
LC 73-700961
Stresses the fact that man's prior tampering with water on a large scale has brought about many unforeseen disastrous aftereffects. Discusses the ecological possibilities of joining the two major oceans of the world.
Geography - World; Science - Natural; Science - Physical
Dist - TIMLIF **Prod** - TIMLIF 1971

Should Old Acquaintance be Forgot? 30 MIN
U-matic / VHS
Color
Takes a hard look at society's plan for its elderly, the effects of retirement and a visit to KOPE (Keep Older People Employed).
Health and Safety; Sociology
Dist - WCCOTV **Prod** - WCCOTV 1981

Should public institutions be permitted to give preferential treatment to minorities in hiring and admissions 58 MIN
U-matic / VHS
Advocates series
Color
Considers whether public institutions should be allowed to give preferential treatment to minorities in hiring and admissions. Features attorney Larry Tribe as the proponent and attorney Larry Lavinsky as the opponent.
Psychology; Sociology
Dist - PBS **Prod** - WGBHTV

Should Puerto Rico be a Commonwealth, a State or an Independent Nation 59 MIN
U-matic
Advocates Series
Color
Presents Jaime Foster, Joachim Marquez and Fernando Martin debating whether Puerto Rico should be a commonwealth, a state or an independent nation.
Geography - United States
Dist - PBS **Prod** - WGBHTV

Should the Day Ever Come 26 MIN
16mm
Color
LC 74-705637
Follows Coast Guard reservists as they develop and maintain the skills required to fulfill the missions imposed on the Reserve to meet mobilization assignments.
Civics and Political Systems; Health and Safety; Social Science
Dist - USNAC **Prod** - USGEOS 1967

Should the Federal Government Give Tax Credits to Help Pay for School Tuition 59 MIN
U-matic
Advocates Series
Color
Considers whether or not the federal government should give tax credits to help finance school tuition. Presents Antonin Scalia as the pro advocate and William Van Alstyne as the opponent.
Business and Economics; Civics and Political Systems; Education
Dist - PBS **Prod** - WGBHTV

Should the Federal Trade Commission Ban Advertising on Children's Television 59 MIN
U-matic
Advocates Series
Color
Features Nicholas Johnson and Ed Diamond debating the issue of advertising on children's television.
Business and Economics; Fine Arts
Dist - PBS **Prod** - WGBHTV

Should the United States Agree to United Nations Control of Seabed Mining 59 MIN
U-matic
Advocates Series
Color
Asks whether the United States should agree to UN control of seabed mining. Features pro advocate Randall Robinson and con advocate Lewis Crampton.
Civics and Political Systems; Social Science
Dist - PBS **Prod** - WGBHTV

Should the United States Break the Price - Setting Power of OPEC 59 MIN
U-matic
Advocates Series
Color
Features Avi Nelson and Margaret Marshall debating whether or not the United States should break OPEC's price - setting power.
Civics and Political Systems; Social Science
Dist - PBS **Prod** - WGBHTV

Should the United States Expand its Nuclear Power Program 59 MIN
U-matic
Advocates Series
Color
Presents Charles E Walker and Anthony Z Roisman debating the issue of nuclear power in the United States.
Social Science
Dist - PBS **Prod** - WGBHTV

Should the united states support self - determination for Palestinians in a peace settlement 59 MIN
U-matic
Advocates series
Color
Presents Professor Fouad Ajami and attorney Morris Abram debating U S support of Palestinian self - determination in a Middle East peace settlement.
Civics and Political Systems; Geography - World
Dist - PBS **Prod** - WGBHTV

Should We 30 MIN
U-matic / VHS
Management for the '90s - Quality Circles Series
Color
Business and Economics; Psychology
Dist - DELTAK **Prod** - TELSTR

Should we be worried about Mexico 30 MIN
U-matic
Adam Smith's money world 1985 - 1986 season series; 245
Color (A)
Attempts to demystify the world of money and break it down so that small as well as large businesses and it's people understand and adjust to new social and economic trends. Reports on the major economic stories and discoveries of 1985 and 1986.
Business and Economics
Dist - PBS **Prod** - WNETTV 1986

Should We Cut Back Veterans' Preference for State and Federal Jobs to Provide more 59 MIN
U-matic
Advocates Series
Color
Considers whether or not to cut back veterans' preference for state and federal jobs in order to provide more opportunity for women. Presents Margaret Marshall as the pro advocate and Avi Nelson as the con advocate.
Guidance and Counseling; Sociology
Dist - PBS **Prod** - WGBHTV

Should We Impose Mandatory Controls on Wages and Prices to Stop Inflation 59 MIN
U-matic
Advocates Series
Color
Focuses on mandatory controls on wages and prices to stop inflation. Features Margaret Marshall as the pro advocate and Avi Nelson as the con advocate.
Business and Economics
Dist - PBS **Prod** - WGBHTV

Should We Legislate Sexual Behavior 60 MIN
VHS / U-matic
Color
Discusses the topic of legislating sexual behavior. Concludes that no one should be discriminated against because of sexual preference in the areas of employment, housing and public accommodations.
Psychology; Sociology
Dist - UWISC **Prod** - UWISC 1980

Should we support the new government of Zimbabwe - Rhodesia 59 MIN
U-matic
Advocates series
Color
Presents Avi Nelson and Randall Robinson debating U S support of Zimbabwe.
Civics and Political Systems; Geography - World
Dist - PBS **Prod** - WGBHTV

Should Your State Require a Competency Test for High School Graduation 59 MIN
U-matic
Advocates Series
Color
Presents Lewis Crampton and Renault A Robinson debating whether or not states should require competency tests for high school graduation.
Civics and Political Systems; Education
Dist - PBS **Prod** - WGBHTV

The Shoulder 32 MIN
VHS / U-matic
Cyriax on Orthopaedic Medicine Series
Color
Discusses the examination and treatment of the shoulder for arthritis, bursitis, tendonitis, infraspinatus and subscapularis.
Health and Safety; Science - Natural
Dist - VTRI **Prod** - VTRI

Shoulder and knee injuries
VHS
Athletic clinic series
Color (C A PRO)
$29.95 purchase _ #SVS1606V
Discusses common shoulder and knee injuries, and shows how to recognize and treat them.
Health and Safety; Physical Education and Recreation; Science - Natural
Dist - CAMV

Shoulder Arthoplasty 13 MIN
VHS / U-matic
Color (PRO)
Shows shoulder arthoplasty.
Health and Safety
Dist - WFP **Prod** - WFP

Shoulder Dysfunction 10 MIN
U-matic / VHS
Color (PRO)
Discusses the functional anatomy of the shoulder, conditions which affect the shoulder, management of these conditions and differential diagnostic considerations.
Health and Safety; Science - Natural
Dist - UMICHM **Prod** - UMICHM 1977

Shoulder injuries
VHS
Athletic clinic series
Color (C A PRO)
$29.95 purchase _ #SVS757V
Outlines the basic anatomy and mechanics involved in most shoulder injuries. Describes six common shoulder problems and how to recognize and treat them.
Health and Safety; Physical Education and Recreation; Science - Natural
Dist - CAMV

Shoulder Joint 12 MIN
U-matic / VHS
Upper Extremities Functional Range of Motion Series
Color (PRO)
Enables the therapist to determine what range of motion of the shoulder a patient needs to increase. Part one of a three part series.
Health and Safety; Psychology
Dist - HSCIC **Prod** - HSCIC

Shoulder mobilization exercises
U-matic / VHS
Physical therapy series
Color (PRO C G)
$195.00 purchase _ #C890 - VI - 071
Informs patient educators and patients about the benefits of shoulder mobilization exercises. Teaches effective techniques for minimizing pain and fatigue while enhancing the ability to perform daily activities. Part of a series by the physical therapy staff, St Luke's Hospital, Fargo, North Dakota.
Health and Safety; Physical Education and Recreation; Science - Natural
Dist - HSCIC

Shoulder Prosthesis for Four Part Fracture 19 MIN
VHS / U-matic
Prothesis Films Series
Color (PRO)
Health and Safety
Dist - WFP **Prod** - WFP

Shoulder Prosthesis for 4 - Part Fracture 16 MIN
U-matic
Color (PRO)
Shows surgical procedure, postoperative rehabilitation procedure and results of a case of 4 - part fracture of the proximal humerus treated by prosthetic replacement of the humeral head.
Health and Safety
Dist - MMAMC **Prod** - MMAMC

The Shoulder Region 11 MIN
U-matic / VHS / 16mm
Guides to Dissection Series
Color (C A)
Demonstrates the dissection of the shoulder.
Health and Safety; Science - Natural
Dist - TEF **Prod** - UCLA

Shoulder throw - seoinage 3 MIN
16mm
Combative measures - Judo series
B&W (G)
LC 75-700830
Demonstrates the shoulder throw in judo. Shows steps in maneuvering, setting up and executing a right - or left - shoulder throw.
Physical Education and Recreation
Dist - USNAC **Prod** - USAF 1955

Shoulder to shoulder series
Examines the early 20th century struggle for women's suffrage in Great Britain. Focuses on three members of the Parkhurst family, and others, who led the campaign for suffrage. Reveals that their campaign included public demonstrations, lobbying, marches, hunger strikes and civil disobedience - even violence. Six - part series, originally aired as part of 'Masterpiece Theater,' is hosted by actress Jane Alexander.

Annie Kenney	60 MIN
Christabel Pankhurst	60 MIN
Lady Constance Lytton	60 MIN
Outrage	60 MIN
The Pankhurst family	60 MIN
Sylvia Pankhurst	60 MIN

Dist - PBS **Prod** - MKNZM 1955

Shoulder wheel - Kataguruma 4 MIN
16mm
Combative measures - Judo series
B&W (G)
LC 75-700829
Demonstrates the shoulder wheel in judo. Shows how to set up an opponent and follow through.
Physical Education and Recreation
Dist - USNAC **Prod** - USAF 1955

Shout for joy 58 MIN
VHS
Color (J H C G A R)
$29.95 purchase, $10.00 rental _ #35 - 8660 - 1518
Features surfing champion Rick Irons in a statement of his Christian faith. Shows that the Irons family has set up a ministry to young people in Hawaii.
Physical Education and Recreation; Religion and Philosophy
Dist - APH **Prod** - SPAPRO

Shout it alphabet 11 MIN
U-matic / VHS / BETA
Color; PAL (P I)
PdS30, PdS38 purchase
Brings words to life with simple and vivid collage animation involving all the letters of the alphabet. Plays a game for children to see how many 'A' words, 'B' words, etc they can discover on the screen.
Education; English Language
Dist - EDPAT

The Shout it out alphabet film 11 MIN
U-matic / VHS / 16mm
Color (K P)
LC 70-706107
A film game in which an audience of children tries to see how many words they can recognize by identifying the first letter in the collage of animated happenings on the screen.
English Language
Dist - PHENIX **Prod** - CCVISA 1969

Shout it Out Numbers, from One to Ten 6 MIN
U-matic / VHS / 16mm
Color (P I)
LC 83-700013
Uses animated geometric shapes and lively music to illustrate numbers from one through ten.
Mathematics
Dist - PHENIX **Prod** - FILBUL 1982

Shout Youngstown 45 MIN
U-matic / VHS
Color (A)
Discusses the social and human implications of the closing of three major steel plants in Youngstown, Ohio. Covers 1976 to 1980.
Business and Economics; Geography - United States; Sociology
Dist - CNEMAG **Prod** - CNEMAG 1984

Show 1 30 MIN
U-matic
Half a Handy Hour Series
Color (G)
Discusses and offers repair help on levelling things, pocket knives, the car as a system, help books, hammers and nails.
Industrial and Technical Education
Dist - TVOTAR **Prod** - TVOTAR 1985

Show 2 30 MIN
U-matic
Half a Handy Hour Series
Color (G)
Discusses and offers repair help on under the hood, the lumberyard, attaching things, kid's record players and light switches.
Industrial and Technical Education
Dist - TVOTAR **Prod** - TVOTAR 1985

Show 3 30 MIN
U-matic
Half a Handy Hour Series
Color (G)
Discusses and offers repair help on the fuse box, duplex outlets, soldering, sanding things, the rent all shop.
Industrial and Technical Education
Dist - TVOTAR **Prod** - TVOTAR 1985

Show 4 30 MIN
U-matic
Half a Handy Hour Series
Color (G)
Discusses and offers repair help on pliers, cutters, glues, hinges and handsaws.
Industrial and Technical Education
Dist - TVOTAR **Prod** - TVOTAR 1985

Show 5 30 MIN
U-matic
Half a Handy Hour Series
Color (G)
Discusses and offers repair help on measuring things, chisels, files, the chain saw, glue gun, copper plumbing.
Industrial and Technical Education
Dist - TVOTAR **Prod** - TVOTAR 1985

Show 6 30 MIN
U-matic
Half a Handy Hour Series
Color (G)
Discusses and offers repair help on the hair dryer, planes, cars that won't start, rivets, rivet guns and the fuse box.
Industrial and Technical Education
Dist - TVOTAR **Prod** - TVOTAR 1985

Show 7 30 MIN
U-matic
Half a Handy Hour Series
Color (G)
Discusses and offers repair help on the propane torch, circular saws, sharpening things, and the hardware store.
Industrial and Technical Education
Dist - TVOTAR **Prod** - TVOTAR 1985

Show 8 30 MIN
U-matic
Half a Handy Hour Series
Color (G)
Discusses and offers repair help on the car manual, rope, string, small engines, painting tools, thermostats and furnaces.
Industrial and Technical Education
Dist - TVOTAR **Prod** - TVOTAR 1985

Show 9 30 MIN
U-matic
Half a Handy Hour Series
Color (G)
Discusses and offers repair help on ladders, electric motors, radial and table saws, the Home Show and the hi - fi.
Industrial and Technical Education
Dist - TVOTAR **Prod** - TVOTAR 1985

Show 10 30 MIN
U-matic
Half a Handy Hour Series
Color (G)
Discusses and offers repair help on the pit stop, clamps, wrenches, sockets, the router, the continuity tester and the toilet.
Industrial and Technical Education
Dist - TVOTAR **Prod** - TVOTAR 1985

Show 11 30 MIN
U-matic
Half a Handy Hour Series
Color (G)
Discusses and offers repair help on the humidifier, drains, traps, stacks, spark plugs, adhesive tapes, and the paint store.
Industrial and Technical Education
Dist - TVOTAR **Prod** - TVOTAR 1985

Show 12 30 MIN
U-matic
Half a Handy Hour Series
Color (G)
Discusses and offers repair help on the front end, axes, electric drills, the plumbing store, screws and screwdrivers.
Industrial and Technical Education
Dist - TVOTAR **Prod** - TVOTAR 1985

Show 13 30 MIN
U-matic
Half a Handy Hour Series
Color (G)
Discusses and offers repair help on caulking guns, fireplaces, adjusting TV sets, fluorescent lights, the Do It Yourself Woodworks Shop.
Industrial and Technical Education
Dist - TVOTAR **Prod** - TVOTAR 1985

Show 14 30 MIN
U-matic
Half a Handy Hour Series
Color (G)
Discusses and offers repair help on oil changes, furniture refinishing, volts, amps, watts and campfires.
Industrial and Technical Education
Dist - TVOTAR **Prod** - TVOTAR 1985

Show 15 30 MIN
U-matic
Half a Handy Hour Series
Color (G)
Discusses and offers repair help on brakes, humidifiers, universal motor repair and used cars.
Industrial and Technical Education
Dist - TVOTAR **Prod** - TVOTAR 1985

Show 16 30 MIN
U-matic
Half a Handy Hour Series
Color (G)
Discusses and offers repair help on wire in walls, country plumbing, wood differences, heat pumps and electric furnaces.
Industrial and Technical Education
Dist - TVOTAR **Prod** - TVOTAR 1985

Show 17 30 MIN
U-matic
Half a Handy Hour Series
Color (G)
Discusses and offers repair help on outboard motors, furnaces, Canadian Standards Association and typewriters.
Industrial and Technical Education
Dist - TVOTAR **Prod** - TVOTAR 1985

Show 18 30 MIN
U-matic
Half a Handy Hour Series
Color (G)
Discusses and offers repair help on glycerin, wood stoves, generators and fibreglass.
Industrial and Technical Education
Dist - TVOTAR **Prod** - TVOTAR 1985

Show 19 30 MIN
U-matic
Half a Handy Hour Series
Color (G)
Discusses and offers repair help on Betamax, pumps, glass and heat distribution.
Industrial and Technical Education
Dist - TVOTAR **Prod** - TVOTAR 1985

Show 20 30 MIN
U-matic
Half a Handy Hour Series
Color (G)
Discusses and offers repair help on multimeters, paint stripping, faucets and chain.
Industrial and Technical Education
Dist - TVOTAR **Prod** - TVOTAR 1985

Show 21 30 MIN
U-matic
Half a Handy Hour Series
Color (G)
Discusses and offers repair help on ground fault circuit interrupters, piano repair, electrical service and incandescent lights.
Industrial and Technical Education
Dist - TVOTAR **Prod** - TVOTAR 1985

Show 22 30 MIN
U-matic
Half a Handy Hour Series
Color (G)
Discusses and offers repair help on tap and die, refrigerators, fire extinguishers, masonry.
Industrial and Technical Education
Dist - TVOTAR **Prod** - TVOTAR 1985

Show 23 30 MIN
U-matic
Half a Handy Hour Series
Color (G)
Discusses and offers repair help on central vacuum cleaners, house inspection, door locks and septic tanks.
Industrial and Technical Education
Dist - TVOTAR **Prod** - TVOTAR 1985

Show 24 30 MIN
U-matic
Half a Handy Hour Series
Color (G)
Discusses and offers repair help on R value, diesel engines, building permits and caning.
Industrial and Technical Education
Dist - TVOTAR **Prod** - TVOTAR 1985

Show 25 30 MIN
U-matic
Half a Handy Hour Series
Color (G)
Discusses and offers repair help on car kits, weird toilets, heavy vapors and bicycles.
Industrial and Technical Education
Dist - TVOTAR **Prod** - TVOTAR 1985

Show 26 30 MIN
U-matic
Half a Handy Hour Series
Color (G)
Discusses and offers repair help on induction motors, outboard care, carpenter's square and potpourri.
Industrial and Technical Education
Dist - TVOTAR **Prod** - TVOTAR 1985

Show and Tell 30 MIN
U-matic / VHS
Adult Math Series
Color (A)
Shows adult math students reviewing previous lessons and introduces them to the special mixed number pi.
Education; Mathematics
Dist - KYTV **Prod** - KYTV 1984

Show and tell 20 MIN
U-matic / VHS
Tomes and talismans series
(I J)
$145 purchase, $27 rental, $90 self dub
Uses a science fantasy adventure to define, illustrate and review basic library research concepts. Designed for sixth, seventh and eighth graders. Twelfth in a 13 part series.
Education; Social Science
Dist - GPN **Prod** - MISETV

Show and tell 24 MIN
16mm
Color (G)
$25.00 rental
Presents a comedy full of pathos and feeling for humanity.
Fine Arts
Dist - CANCIN **Prod** - LIPTNL 1968

Show Biz - a Job Well Done 12 MIN
U-matic / VHS / 16mm
Color (P)

LC 75-703870
Shows how a young boy turns a small part in the production of a class play into an important one and gains the satisfaction of a job well done.
Fine Arts; Guidance and Counseling
Dist - BARR **Prod** - CALLFM 1975

The Show Business 24 MIN
U-matic / VHS
Color
Points out that the real purpose of a demonstration is to build a commitment to purchase the product.
Business and Economics
Dist - VISUCP **Prod** - VIDART

Show business 5 MIN
U-matic / VHS
Write on series; Set 2
Color (J H)
Deals with varying sentence length in writing.
English Language
Dist - CTI **Prod** - CTI

The Show Business - How to Demonstrate a Product 23 MIN
U-matic / VHS
Color (A)
Using humor, shows how to successfully demonstrate a product. Emphasizes preparation, presentation and closing of the demonstration. Underlines the close connection between good demonstrations and sales.
Business and Economics; Psychology
Dist - XICOM **Prod** - XICOM

Show business is good business - how US manufacturers expand their markets through exports 14 MIN
U-matic / VHS
Color (PRO)
$65.00, $95.00 purchase _ #TCA18189, #TCA18190
Interviews exhibitors at international trade and textile shows. Discusses how exhibiting at such shows can help the export business.
Business and Economics
Dist - USNAC

Show handling 30 MIN
U-matic / VHS
Training dogs the Woodhouse way
Color (H C A)
Shows Barbara Woodhouse's method of handling show dogs.
Science - Natural
Dist - FI **Prod** - BBCTV 1982

Show Jumping World Cup
VHS / U-matic
Color
Physical Education and Recreation
Dist - MSTVIS **Prod** - MSTVIS

Show leader 1 MIN
16mm
B&W (G)
Features a film leader included at no charge for shows devoted to the work of Bue Baillie, totaling 80 minutes running time or more.
Fine Arts
Dist - CANCIN **Prod** - BAILB 1966

Show Me 24 MIN
16mm
Color (H C A)
Demonstrates the Timken Company's steelmaking capabilities, featuring its melting, strandcasting rolling, piercing, finishing, inspecting and shipping facilities.
Business and Economics; Industrial and Technical Education
Dist - TIMKEN **Prod** - TIMKEN

Show me what you mean 15 MIN
VHS / U-matic
Writer's realm series
Color (I)
$125.00 purchase
Demonstrates how to use improved vocabulary to increase the reader's understanding of the story.
English Language; Literature and Drama
Dist - AITECH **Prod** - MDINTV 1987

The Show must go on 26 MIN
U-matic / VHS
Color (C)
$89.95 purchase _ #EX1905
Looks at the health hazards associated with the performing arts. Examines current research into the biomedics of performance, the facilities and capabilities of arts medicine, performance medicine clinics and a neurological analysis of musical performance.
Fine Arts; Health and Safety
Dist - FOTH **Prod** - FOTH

Show on the Road 29 MIN
VHS / 16mm
Color (G)
$55.00 rental _ #SHRD - 000
Features a drama about the alternately playful and painful relationship between a father and his teenage son. Reveals the complex process by which children test their independent personalities against their parents' love.
Sociology
Dist - PBS **Prod** - WHATV

Show time 15 MIN
VHS
Art's place series
Color (K P)
$49.00 purchase, $15.00 rental _ #295808
Describes how everyone pools artistic talents to put on a show about a lonely witch. Emma and Leo create masks, Jessie and Emma paint a backdrop and everyone acts as Mirror narrates. Part of a series that combines songs, stories, animation, puppets and live actors to convey the pleasure of artistic expression. Includes an illustrated teacher's guide.
Fine Arts
Dist - TVOTAR **Prod** - TVOTAR 1989

Show time - the decline of the Canadian Parliament 30 MIN
VHS
Remaking of Canada - Canadian government and politics in the 1990s 'series
Color (H C G)
$89.95 purchase _ #WLU - 505
Discusses the decline of the House of Commons, the rise of the Senate and proposals for parliamentary reform. Part of a 12 - part series incorporating interviews with Canadian politicians and hosted by Dr John Redekop.
Civics and Political Systems; History - World
Dist - INSTRU **Prod** - TELCOL 1992

Showa 200 MIN
U-matic / VHS
B&W (G)
$599.00, $399.00 purchase _ #AD - 1611
Presents key episodes from the beginning of the reign of Emperor Hirohito of Japan. Offers four parts which document 'The Rising Sun At Versailles,' the Paris Peace Conference, agreement with the last emperor of China which established a puppet state in Manchuria, growing isolation in the 1930s, withdrawal from the League of Nations.
Civics and Political Systems; Geography - World; History - United States; History - World
Dist - FOTH **Prod** - FOTH

Showdown 13 MIN
16mm
Color
LC 74-705638
Tells the story of a young new supervisor who attempts to get full cooperation and support from an older problem worker. Presents comments on the stuation by co - workers and the supervisor's boss. Shows how the relationship between the supervisor and his problem employee deteriorates to the point that the former proposes disciplinary action only to learn that his boss may not support him.
Business and Economics
Dist - USNAC **Prod** - USPHS 1966

The Showdown 30 MIN
U-matic
Read all about it - One Series
Color (I)
Concludes a story in which Chris and his friends Sam and Lynne sent the evil Duneedon on a one way trip back to Trialviron.
Education; English Language; Literature and Drama
Dist - TVOTAR **Prod** - TVOTAR 1982

Showdown at the hoedown 60 MIN
U-matic / 16mm
Color
Captures the color and spectacle of the Smithville, Tennessee Fiddler's Jamboree. Includes highlights of the fiddle, dance and harmonica events and shows the competition between fiddle champion Frazier Moss and the junior champion challenger.
Fine Arts; Geography - United States
Dist - SOFOLK **Prod** - SOFOLK

Showdown at the Hoedown 60 MIN
VHS / 16mm
Color (H A)
$85.00 rental
Documents the fourth annual Tennessee Fiddlers' Jamboree.
Fine Arts
Dist - AFA

Showdown on Tobacco Road 57 MIN
VHS / 16mm
Color (J H A)
$75.00 rental
Questions whether cigarette manufacturers have the right to advertise under the First Amendment. Explores why smoking has become a national dilemma and seeks to motivate people to search for solutions. Overviews smoking in our culture from the 1880s to the present.
Business and Economics; Civics and Political Systems; Health and Safety; Sociology
Dist - VARDIR **Prod** - VARDIR 1987

Shower and locker room 14 MIN
BETA / VHS / U-matic
Medical housekeeping series
(IND)
$225 _ #1014
Appraoches the topic of effective cleaning in showers and locker rooms in various industries such as hospitals and schools. Uses demonstrations and shows tools that can be used.
Education; Guidance and Counseling; Health and Safety
Dist - CTT **Prod** - CTT

Shower and locker room 15 MIN
VHS
Housekeeping series
Color (H A G T)
$225.00 purchase _ #BM114
Explains several different methods for cleaning shower and locker rooms in schools, hospitals, athletic facilities and other institutions. Part of a series on housekeeping.
Home Economics; Industrial and Technical Education; Psychology
Dist - AAVIM **Prod** - AAVIM

Shower and locker room 16 MIN
BETA / VHS / U-matic
Basic housekeeping series
(IND)
$225 _ #1014
Discusses various procedures that are useful in cleaning the showers and locker rooms of institutions such as hospitals, schools and athletic facilities.
Education; Guidance and Counseling; Health and Safety
Dist - CTT **Prod** - CTT

Shower and locker room 14 MIN
VHS / U-matic / BETA
School housekeeping series
(IND)
$225 _ #1014
Exhibits several procedures for keeping the showers and locker rooms in many institutions such as schools, hospitals, and athletic facilities clean.
Education; Guidance and Counseling; Health and Safety
Dist - CTT **Prod** - CTT

Showering and grooming 16 MIN
VHS / 16mm
Quadriplegic functions skills series
Color (H)
$50.00 purchase, $16.00 rental _ #58028
Demonstrates the use of tub and shower stalls by quadriplegic males. Emphasizes testing water temperature, exercising care in transfer from the chair to the bench. Shows several options with regard to soap, brushes, shower attachments. Discusses the use of electric and safety razors, electric toothbrushes. Quadriplegic students demonstrating the devices recommend goal - setting as way to advance in rehabilitation.
Health and Safety
Dist - UILL **Prod** - UILL

Showing dairy cattle 16 MIN
VHS
Dairy fitting and showing series; Set R
(C)
$49.95 _ CV169
Gives the fundamentals of showing including the showing scorecard, leading, posing, showing animal to best advantage, sportsmanship, exhibit appearance, and tips for successful showing courtesy of Dr. David Dickson.
Agriculture; Home Economics
Dist - AAVIM **Prod** - AAVIM 1989

Showing initiative 10 MIN
VHS / U-matic
Young job seekers series
Color (H C VOC)
Shows how to ask relevant questions of job interviewer. Stresses importance of background information about company and job.
Guidance and Counseling
Dist - SEVDIM **Prod** - SEVDIM

Showing livestock video series
Presents three parts on showing livestock. Includes the titles Fitting and Showing Steers, Clipping Dairy Cattle, and Sheep Showmanship.
Fitting and showing market steers
Showing livestock video series
Dist - VEP **Prod** - VEP

Showing off 6 MIN
VHS / U-matic
Life's little lessons - self - esteem K - 3 - series; 25
Color (K P)
$129.00, $99.00 _ #V624
Tells about three cowpokes who got into a lot of trouble when they tried to do some bull riding to show off. Part of a 30 - part series on self - esteem.
Guidance and Counseling; Psychology
Dist - BARR **Prod** - CEPRO 1992

Showmanship 30 MIN
U-matic / VHS / 16mm
Color
Covers grooming and preparation of the horse and exhibitor as well as many do's and don'ts regarding showmanship rules and class routine.
Physical Education and Recreation
Dist - AQHORS **Prod** - AQHORS 1979

Showmanship at Halter 16 MIN
VHS / BETA
Color
Instructs how to show at halter. Includes basic rules, conditioning and grooming techniques, control and style.
Physical Education and Recreation
Dist - EQVDL **Prod** - AMSDHA

Showmanship, the Basics 23 MIN
16mm / U-matic / VHS
Color
Covers grooming and preparation of the horse and exhibitor as well as many do's and don'ts regarding showmanship rules and class routine.
Physical Education and Recreation
Dist - AQHORS **Prod** - AQHORS 1986

Showroom to the World 6 MIN
16mm
Export Development Series
Color
LC 78-701102
Explains what a U S Trade Center is and what it does. Gives brief looks at trade center in New York, Paris and Stockholm and shows how one company had success in utilizing this marketing service.
Business and Economics
Dist - USNAC **Prod** - USIATA 1978

Shows and Tell 30 MIN
U-matic
Polka Dot Door Series
Color (K)
Presents a variety show for pre - school children. Includes songs, mime, stories, film sequences, talk, dance and fantasy figures. Each show emphasizes a particular theme such as numbers, feelings, exploring, music or time. Comes with parent teacher guide.
Fine Arts; Literature and Drama
Dist - TVOTAR **Prod** - TVOTAR 1985

Shred of evidence 52 MIN
VHS
Color; PAL (J H)
PdS30 purchase
Provides a documentary on the secretive world of forensic science in the finest laboratories in the world at Scotland Yard. Shows how modern technology can turn a particle of sand or a thread of material into a revealing clue which can solve all types of crime. Contact distributor about availability outside the United Kingdom.
Guidance and Counseling; Sociology
Dist - ACADEM

Shred of sex 23 MIN
16mm
B&W (A)
$75.00 rental
Attempts to define the sexuality of punk culture and debunk the stereotypical images of the snarling, leather S&M pervert or the other extreme of celibate vegetarians. Ranges from explicit, spontaneous romps to more deliberately choreographed images. A seven - part film of three - minute vignettes, each person starring in his or her own film. Produced by Greta Snider.
Fine Arts; Sociology
Dist - CANCIN

Shrike 25 MIN
VHS
Nature watch series
Color (P I J H C)
$49.00 purchase _ #320207; LC 89-715851
Shows that the sharp cries of the carnivorous shrike in the fall are really a fierce declaration of its territory, where it will do all its hunting, courting, and raising of offspring. Part of a series that explores the curious and uncommon characteristics of a variety of mammals, insects, birds and sea creatures.
Science - Natural
Dist - TVOTAR **Prod** - TVOTAR 1988

Shrimps for a day 19 MIN
16mm
B&W
Features the Little Rascals in a story about a young couple whose encounter with a magic lamp allows them to become children again.
Fine Arts
Dist - RMIBHF

The Shrine 46 MIN
VHS
Color (C G)
$295.00 purchase, $50.00 rental _ #37976
Explores the traditions and mysteries surrounding El Santuario, a small adobe church in northern New Mexico. Reveals that this sacred shrine, with its famed healing dirt and its figure of the Christ child that is said to walk in the night, attracts thousands of people each year in the largest religious pilgrimage in the United States. Traces the history of El Santuario and relates it to New Mexico's Hispanic cultural heritage. Produced by Bob Paris and Christiane Badgley.
Geography - United States; History - United States; Religion and Philosophy; Sociology
Dist - UCEMC

Shrine under siege 42 MIN
VHS
Color (G)
$350.00 purchase, $60.00 rental
Describes the coalition formed by fundamentalist United States Christians and militant Israeli Jews to destroy the Dome of the Rock, Islam's third holiest shrine, and to build a new Jewish temple in its place. Explores the theological background to this unusual coalition and places it within the context of the increased political power of fundamentalism in the United States and the rise of extremist religious parties in Israel.
Religion and Philosophy
Dist - FIRS **Prod** - ZIVILN 1985

Shringar 29 MIN
16mm
Color (G)
Explains that Indian women through the centuries have been famous for their coiffeurs, as can be seen in the frescoes of Ajanta and the sculptures of Konarak and Khajuraho. Surveys the varied hair - styles from ancient times to the present.
Geography - World; Home Economics
Dist - NEDINF **Prod** - INDIA

Shrink or swim - in - store theft 8 MIN
U-matic / VHS
Retail sales power series
Color
Focuses on shoplifting and how to prevent it. Presents cartoon sequences that leave indelible images of shoplifter's characteristic clothing, behavior and techniques. Stresses involvement in the prevention program by security people.
Business and Economics; Sociology
Dist - PRODEV **Prod** - PRODEV

The Shrinking dollar 30 MIN
U-matic / VHS
Money puzzle - the world of macroeconomics series; Module 10
Color
Investigates the causes of inflation. Stresses the difference between anticipated and unanticipated inflation. Discusses the relationship between inflation and increased income taxes.
Business and Economics; Sociology
Dist - MDCC **Prod** - MDCC

Shrove Tuesday 18 MIN
16mm
Color (P I)
Relates that the Chiffy kids enter a pancake race in which the prize is a year's supply of groceries which they intend to give to a needy elderly lady. Explains that they need all their wits about them to win as one of their competitors is very tricky and determined to get the prize.
Literature and Drama
Dist - LUF **Prod** - LUF 1979

Shrubs and vines 30 MIN
VHS / U-matic
Home gardener with John Lenanton series; Lesson 16
Color (G)
Focuses on how to buy and plant shrubs that are appropriate for the home garden. Demonstrates planting process.
Agriculture
Dist - CDTEL **Prod** - COAST

Shua - the human Jesus 60 MIN
VHS
Color (G R)
$49.95 purchase _ #350
Creates a boyhood friend of Jesus, Shua, who narrates fictional stories of Jesus' life from childhood through the crucifixion. Dramatized by Father William Burke.
Literature and Drama; Religion and Philosophy
Dist - ACTAF **Prod** - ACTAF

Shucking Clams
VHS / U-matic
Color
Home Economics; Industrial and Technical Education
Dist - CULINA **Prod** - CULINA

Shucking Oysters
U-matic / VHS
Color
Home Economics; Industrial and Technical Education
Dist - CULINA **Prod** - CULINA

Shui Hu 1610 MIN
VHS
Color (G) (CHINESE)
$600.00 purchase _ #5182
Presents a film from the People's Republic of China. Includes 20 videocassettes.
Geography - World; Literature and Drama
Dist - CHTSUI

Shuk Day 15 MIN
U-matic / VHS
Encounter in the Desert Series
Color (I)
Shows market day among Bedouin nomads.
Geography - World; Social Science; Sociology
Dist - CTI **Prod** - CTI

Shultz 60 MIN
VHS
Color (G)
$49.95 purchase _ #SHTZ - 000
Interviews former Secretary of State George Shultz. Reviews his career and the foreign policy initiatives of the Reagan Administration. Hosted by Meg Greenfield.
Civics and Political Systems; History - United States
Dist - PBS **Prod** - WETATV 1989

Shunka's Story 20 MIN
16mm / U-matic / VHS
Color
Offers a portrait of a Tzotzil Maya woman of Zinacantan in Chiapas, Mexico, conveying her thoughts and feelings about her life, her culture and her children.
Social Science
Dist - UCEMC **Prod** - KREBS 1977

Shunt hartley oscillator - VT 28 MIN
16mm / U-matic / VHS
B&W
Shows the Shunt Hartley oscillator circuit, pointing out identifying features and explaining the purpose of each component. Shows its use in high power circuits and how to troubleshoot it.
Industrial and Technical Education; Science - Physical
Dist - USNAC **Prod** - USAF

Shurtleff on acting 60 MIN
VHS
Color (G C H)
$169.00 purchase _ #DL494
Presents casting director Michael Shurtleff who helps students to find the core of a scene and encourages them to take emotional risks along the way. Interviews actors Gene Hackman and Elliot Gould.
Fine Arts
Dist - INSIM

Shutdown Rules for Variability and the Mean 20 MIN
U-matic / VHS
Statistics for Technicians Series
Color (IND)
Develops shutdown rules for the variance using the chi - square distribution, and for the mean when sigma is not known using the t distribution. Discusses effect of changing sample size.
Business and Economics; Mathematics; Psychology
Dist - COLOSU **Prod** - COLOSU

Shutter speeds and aperture 30 MIN
VHS / U-matic
Taking better pictures series
Color (G)
Explains basic functions of the 35mm camera's most important controls and their creative use. Illustrates depth of field by photographs and a studio demonstration.
Industrial and Technical Education
Dist - GPN **Prod** - GCCED

The Shuttle in close - up 28 MIN
U-matic / VHS
Video encyclopedia of space series
Color (G)

$249.00, $149.00 purchase _ #AD - 2114
Begins with the launch of Columbia on April 12, 1981. Explains step by step what is happening and why as the main engines ignite, solid rocket booster ignition begins, lift - off is achieved and the solid rocket boosters separate and parachute into the ocean. Shows what happens in orbit and how problems are solved, as well as the return to Earth. Part of an eleven - part series on space.
History - World; Industrial and Technical Education; Science - Physical
Dist - FOTH **Prod** - FOTH

Shuttle to tomorrow 11 MIN
16mm
Color (G)
LC 76-704010
Explains the role of the space shuttle, with emphasis on the responsibility of the Marshall Space Flight Center in providing space shuttle engines and the solid rocket booster. Includes a profile of a shuttle mission.
History - World; Industrial and Technical Education; Science - Physical
Dist - USNAC **Prod** - USMSFC 1976

The Shvitz 47 MIN
16mm / VHS
Color; B&W (G)
$300.00 rental, $295.00 purchase
Looks at the unlikely community forged in the 260 degree heat of the last traditional Jewish steambaths in the United States. Uses this vanishing institution to offer a perspective on the evolution of Jewish life, while bringing up issues of ethnicity, nostalgia, spirituality and ritual. Reveals the diversity of the patrons, from businessmen and 'new age' masseuses to poets and rabbis. Produced by Jonathan Berman.
Psychology; Religion and Philosophy; Social Science; Sociology
Dist - NCJEWF

Shy, Withdrawn and Bashful 10 MIN
16mm
Psychology - the Emotions Series
Color (P I)
LC 74-700307
Features George Jammal and several children demonstrating in various ways shyness, withdrawal and bashfulness.
Guidance and Counseling; Psychology
Dist - SUMHIL **Prod** - SUMHIL 1974

Shyness 45 MIN
VHS
Client sessions series
Color; PAL; SECAM (G)
$60.00 purchase
Features Richard Bandler in the first part of a four - part series of client sessions, using NLP, neuro - linguistic programming. Demonstrates clinical applications of NLP methods. Bandler sometimes uses profanity for emphasis, which may offend some people. All levels.
Health and Safety; Psychology
Dist - NLPCOM **Prod** - NLPCOM

Shyness and assertiveness 30 MIN
VHS
Personal development video series
(J H C)
$425.00 series of 5 purchase _ #CV200V
Presents tips and techniques for defeating problems of shyness and for learning how to be assertive. Communicates strategies for understanding self, peers, parents, and teachers.
Psychology
Dist - CAMV **Prod** - CAMV

Shyness and Assertiveness
VHS
Personal Development Series
Color (H)
$98.00 purchase _ #ABV 104
Offers insights into the reasons for shyness and ways to overcome it. Points the viewer toward healthy assertiveness and shows methods for building self - esteem and developing social skills. Also available in Beta or 3/4".
Psychology
Dist - CADESF **Prod** - CADESF 1988

Shyness - Reasons and Remedies
VHS / 35mm strip
$98.00 purchase _ #HR617 filmstrip, $111.00 purchase _ #HR617V VHS
Discusses the causes, effects, and management of shyness.
Guidance and Counseling; Psychology
Dist - CAREER **Prod** - CAREER

Si no Es Demasiado Tarde 9 MIN
16mm / U-matic / VHS
Color (IND) (SPANISH)
A Spanish - language version of the motion picture If It's Not Too Late. Shows how safety control has evolved from injury prevention to loss control management. Identifies some of the causes of incidents which may result in accidents and injury as well as loss of efficiency.
Business and Economics; Foreign Language; Health and Safety
Dist - IFB **Prod** - IAPA 1974

Si Pitagoras no Miente 14 MIN
U-matic / VHS / 16mm
Color (J H) (SPANISH)
A Spanish - language version of the motion picture Possibly So, Pythagoras. Investigates the Pythagorean theorem through inductive experimentation and formal deductive proof.
Foreign Language; Mathematics
Dist - IFB **Prod** - IFB 1963

Si Podemos (Yes, We Can) 22 MIN
16mm
Color
LC 77-702867
Demonstrates to slum and semi - slum residents of Latin American cities what can be done to improve their lives through self - help projects.
Geography - World; Psychology; Science - Natural; Social Science; Sociology
Dist - HF **Prod** - USAID 1967

Si Quiero but not Now 20 MIN
16mm
Color
LC 79-700739
Focuses on a young Spanish - American couple and the conflict of the traditional views on family planning versus their own needs. Shows how they finally receive help from a family planning clinic.
Health and Safety; Sociology
Dist - USNAC **Prod** - PPFRES 1978

Si see sunni 7 MIN
16mm
Color (G)
$22.00 rental
Portrays Sunni, a modern mystic with degrees from Vassar and Harvard. Displays Tarot cards to reveal her past.
Fine Arts; Sociology
Dist - CANCIN **Prod** - LEVCHI 1967

Si Shi Tong Tang 22 HRS
VHS
Color (G) (MANDARIN CHINESE)
$500.00 purchase _ #6036X
Presents a Mandarin Chinese language television program produced in the People's Republic of China.
Geography - World; Industrial and Technical Education; Literature and Drama
Dist - CHTSUI **Prod** - CHTSUI

Si shui wei lan 589 MIN
VHS
Color (G) (CHINESE)
$180.00 purchase _ #5176
Presents a film from the People's Republic of China. Includes six videocassettes.
Geography - World; Literature and Drama
Dist - CHTSUI

Si, Spain 60 MIN
VHS
Traveloguer collection series
Color (G)
$29.95 purchase _ #QU007
Visits Spain. Offers historical and geographic highlights.
Geography - World; History - World
Dist - SIV

Siamese Fighting Fish 17 MIN
U-matic
Color
Examines features of agressive behavior in animals. Uses a series of balsa wood models then real fish in an aquarium with Betta fighting fish to demonstrate the consistency of aggressive behavior patterns in these fish..
Psychology
Dist - UMITV **Prod** - UMITV 1976

Siamese twin pinheads 6 MIN
16mm
B&W (G)
$15.00 rental
Assembles a little talent show starring Mark Ellinger, Curt McDowell and Janey Sneed Ellinger as 'the nun.'
Fine Arts
Dist - CANCIN **Prod** - MCDOWE 1972

Siamese twins 50 MIN
VHS
Horizon series
Color (A)
PdS99 purchase
Focuses on Dao and Duan who are joined at the pelvis with only three legs between them. Reveals that Duan is the stronger and seems destined to thrive at the expense of her sister. Follows their journey from Thailand to the United States where a surgical attempt will be made to turn them into separate individuals.
Health and Safety
Dist - BBCENE

Siberia 25 MIN
16mm / U-matic / VHS
Color (H C A)
Features a journey to Siberia and shows the geography, history and people of this immense land.
Geography - World; History - World
Dist - NGS **Prod** - NGS 1977

Siberia - Ice on Fire 60 MIN
VHS / 16mm
Portrait of the Soviet Union Series
(H C)
$99.95 each, $595.00 series
Looks at the contrasting beauty and harshness of Siberia, the northern region of the USSR.
Geography - World; History - World
Dist - AMBROS **Prod** - AMBROS 1988

Siberia - the endless horizon 51 MIN
U-matic / VHS / 16mm
Color (H J)
LC 79-705663
Shows the struggle for survival in 90 degrees below temperature, the battle with perma frost and the culture and entertainment of the 'Reindeer People.' Visits the Yakee tribesmen and the towns of Irkutsk, Akademgorodak and Bratsk. Stresses the importance of the Trans - Siberian Railroad for communications and supplies to remote villages.
Geography - World
Dist - NGS **Prod** - NGS 1969

Siberiade 210 MIN
16mm
Color (H C A) (RUSSIAN)
LC 82-700446
Offers an epic romantic drama about three generations of two feuding families, the rich Solomins and the poor Ustyuzhanins, from the time of the Russian Revolution to the present - day exploration of hidden resources in Siberian soil.
Fine Arts; Foreign Language; History - World
Dist - IFEX **Prod** - MOSFLM 1982

Siberiade, Pt 1 35 MIN
16mm
Color (H C A) (RUSSIAN)
LC 82-700446
Offers an epic romantic drama about three generations of two feuding families, the rich Solomins and the poor Ustyuzhanins, from the time of the Russian Revolution to the present - day exploration of hidden resources in Siberian soil.
History - World; Literature and Drama
Dist - IFEX **Prod** - MOSFLM 1982

Siberiade, Pt 2 35 MIN
16mm
Color (H C A) (RUSSIAN)
LC 82-700446
Offers an epic romantic drama about three generations of two feuding families, the rich Solomins and the poor Ustyuzhanins, from the time of the Russian Revolution to the present - day exploration of hidden resources in Siberian soil.
History - World; Literature and Drama
Dist - IFEX **Prod** - MOSFLM 1982

Siberiade, Pt 3 35 MIN
16mm
Color (H C A) (RUSSIAN)
LC 82-700446
Offers an epic romantic drama about three generations of two feuding families, the rich Solomins and the poor Ustyuzhanins, from the time of the Russian Revolution to the present - day exploration of hidden resources in Siberian soil.
History - World
Dist - IFEX **Prod** - MOSFLM 1982

Siberiade, Pt 4 35 MIN
16mm
Color (H C A) (RUSSIAN)
LC 82-700446
Offers an epic romantic drama about three generations of two feuding families, the rich Solomins and the poor Ustyuzhanins, from the time of the Russian Revolution to the present - day exploration of hidden resources in Siberian soil.
History - World; Literature and Drama
Dist - IFEX **Prod** - MOSFLM 1982

Siberiade, Pt 5 35 MIN
16mm
Color (H C A) (RUSSIAN)
LC 82-700446
Offers an epic romantic drama about three generations of two feuding families, the rich Solomins and the poor Ustyuzhanins, from the time of the Russian Revolution to the present - day exploration of hidden resources in Siberian soil.
History - World; Literature and Drama
Dist - IFEX **Prod** - MOSFLM 1982

Siberiade, Pt 6 35 MIN
16mm
Color (H C A) (RUSSIAN)
LC 82-700446
Offers an epic romantic drama about three generations of two feuding families, the rich Solomins and the poor Ustyuzhanins, from the time of the Russian Revolution to the present - day exploration of hidden resources in Siberian soil.
History - World; Literature and Drama
Dist - IFEX **Prod** - MOSFLM 1982

Siberian riches 20 MIN
VHS / U-matic / BETA
Soviet Union series
Color (H C A)
$250.00 purchase _ #JY - 5863C
Examines the climactic harshness of Siberia and its 5 million square miles of enormous wealth in timber, oil, gas, coal and minerals. Reveals that temperatures fall to 50 degrees below zero, shortages in food and housing occur, there is little in leisure - time activity, and there are enormous pollution problems. Part of a five - part series on the diverse lifestyles and regions of the USSR.
Civics and Political Systems; Geography - World; History - World; Social Science
Dist - CORF **Prod** - BBCTV 1989

The Sibling perspective 20 MIN
VHS / U-matic
Coping with cancer series
Color (PRO)
$275.00 purchase, $70.00 rental _ #5264S, #5264V
Looks at four children, ages 6 to 16, whose siblings have cancer. Shares their intimate feelings as they grapple with changes in their family, their school life, and their close friendships. Discloses that despite their anxieties, they have gained a greater closeness to their families and a deeper appreciation for life. Part of four- part series that discusses and helps explain what children with cancer and their siblings are feeling.
Health and Safety; Sociology
Dist - AJN **Prod** - MSKCC 1983

Sibling Relationships 7 MIN
U-matic
Take Time Series
(A)
Demonstrates the influence of parents and others caring for pre - schoolers on the physical and emotional development of the child.
Health and Safety; Psychology; Sociology
Dist - ACCESS **Prod** - ACCESS 1976

Sibling Rivalry 28 MIN
VHS / U-matic
Color (G)
Shows a warm, sensitive, entertaining and educational approach to the frequently painful and universal conflict of jealous feelings toward a new baby in the family. Contains a great deal of information for mothers having a baby for the second or third time, on the feelings of children when a new baby is born.
Guidance and Counseling; Sociology
Dist - PRI **Prod** - PRI 1985

Siblingitis 30 MIN
VHS
Beverly Cleary's Ramona series
Color; CC (K P I)
$16.95 purchase _ #132698
Presents a Ramona story by Beverly Cleary.
Literature and Drama
Dist - KNOWUN

Siblingitis 27 MIN
U-matic / VHS / 16mm
Ramona Series
Color (P I)
$3795 purchase - 16 mm (entire set), $435 purchase - 16 mm (per
Tells how Ramona worries that she will be forgotten because a new baby is on its way. From Ramona Forever. A production of Atlantis Films, Ltd. in association with Lancit Media Productions, Ltd. and Revcom Television.
Literature and Drama
Dist - CF

Siblings 30 MIN
VHS / U-matic
Issues of cystic fibrosis series
Color (PRO C)
$395.00 purchase, $80.00 rental _ #C891 - VI - 051
Interviews siblings of cystic fibrosis patients. Tells of the impact of the illness on their lives and the life of their family. Addresses disruption of family plans, fear during acute attacks, guilt, coping with a siblings death and fear of being a carrier. Part of a 13 - part series on cystic fibrosis presented by Drs Ivan Harwood and Cyril Worby.
Health and Safety; Science - Natural; Sociology
Dist - HSCIC

Siblings 10 MIN
U-matic / VHS
You - parents are special series
Color
Explores the subject of siblings, with Fred Rogers.
Psychology; Sociology
Dist - FAMCOM **Prod** - FAMCOM

Siblings as Behavior Modifiers 25 MIN
16mm / U-matic / VHS
Color (C A)
Tells the story of a mentally retarded child whose family chose to keep him at home rather than in an institution. Shows how each sibling was confronted with a different problem and how each was rewarded by their brother's positive responses to their efforts with him.
Guidance and Counseling; Psychology; Sociology
Dist - MEDIAG **Prod** - MEDIAG 1976

Siblings of children with cancer 30 MIN
VHS / U-matic
Color (G)
Presents siblings of young cancer patients discussing their experience and the effect the illness has had on the relationship between siblings.
Health and Safety; Sociology
Dist - UARIZ **Prod** - UARIZ

Sicily - the Yanks are coming 30 MIN
VHS / 16mm
World War II - G I diary series
(J H C)
$99.95 each, $995.00 series _ #20
Depicts the action and emotion that soldiers experienced during World War II, through their eyes and in their words. Narrated by Lloyd Bridges.
History - United States; History - World
Dist - AMBROS **Prod** - AMBROS 1980
TIMLIF

Sick Call - Introduction to Sick Call Techniques 26 MIN
16mm
Color
LC 74-705641
Trains the inexperienced hospital corpsman to conduct sick call by acquainting him with the proper attitudes and procedures.
Civics and Political Systems; Health and Safety
Dist - USNAC **Prod** - USN 1970

Sick Call - Skin Diseases 34 MIN
16mm
Color
LC 74-706579
Shows various skin conditions which most frequently confront the hospital corpsman. Tells how to distinguish between cases to treat and ones to refer to the medical officer.
Civics and Political Systems; Health and Safety
Dist - USNAC **Prod** - USN 1970

Sick of stress 23 MIN
VHS
Color (A PRO IND)
$195.00 purchase, $75.00 rental
Discusses stress and its effects. Teaches viewers how to recognize stress and avoid it.
Business and Economics; Psychology
Dist - VLEARN

Sickle cell anaemia 28 MIN
16mm
Color (J H)
LC 82-700695
Deals with sickle cell anaemia both on a scientific and a human level. Uses microphotography to show the transformation of a normal - looking cell into a sickle cell and the damage that clusters of sickle cells cause in the circulatory system. Presents conversations with the Williams family, who have six children, three of whom are severely affected.
Health and Safety; History - United States
Dist - FLMLIB **Prod** - CANBC 1981

Sickle - cell anemia 18 MIN
16mm
Color (J H)
LC 72-702930
Explains that Puerto Ricans, Latin Americans, Greeks, Italians, Indians from Mediterranean areas and people of African descent are all affected by sickle - cell anemia. Describes the disease and its effects.
Health and Safety; Science - Natural; Sociology
Dist - LEECC **Prod** - LEECC 1972

Sickle cell story
VHS / U-matic
Color (SPANISH ARABIC)
Discusses hemoglobin screening, prenatal diagnosis and current research and development of medication to prevent the occurrence of sickle cell anemia.
Health and Safety; History - United States; Science - Natural; Sociology
Dist - MIFE **Prod** - MIFE

Sid a ids 10 MIN
16mm
Color (A)
$25.00 rental
Articulates a renunciation of the media's coverage of AIDS, which has unleashed a hysteria that indiscriminately calls for a return to traditional values and has caused victimization and discrimination of the sick. Uses verbal text to critique the discourse, images and the production of words surrounding AIDS. Primarily explores the response to the disease in France. Produced by Yann Beauvais.
Fine Arts; Health and Safety; Sociology
Dist - CANCIN

The Sid story 20 MIN
16mm / VHS
Color (H)
LC 89715689
Uses Steve Mulraney's 'The Sid Story' to teach ways of rewarding productivity and focusing on positive behavior. Used in business management training.
Business and Economics; Guidance and Counseling; Psychology
Dist - BARR
VLEARN

SIDA - cambiando las reglas 28 MIN
VHS
AIDSFILMS series
Color (H C G) (SPANISH)
$65.00 purchase
Stresses that changing sexual behavior is the only means of protection against HIV infection. Features Esai Morales and Maria Conchita Alonso. Gives direct and explicit facts about HIV - AIDS transmission, prevention and testing. Also available in an English language version, AIDS - Changing the Rules.
Health and Safety; Psychology; Sociology
Dist - SELMED

Siddhartha 86 MIN
16mm
Color
Offers an adaptation of Herman Hesse's novel Siddhartha.
Fine Arts; Literature and Drama
Dist - TWYMAN **Prod** - CPC 1973

Side Abdominals 29 MIN
Videoreel / VT2
Maggie and the Beautiful Machine - Bellies Series
Color
Physical Education and Recreation
Dist - PBS **Prod** - WGBHTV

Side effects of medication 11 MIN
U-matic / VHS
Supervision of self administration of medication series; Module V
Color (PRO C)
$395.00 purchase, $80.00 rental _ #C920 - VI - 021
Notes that individuals with developmental disabilities cannot report what is going on in their bodies. Stresses that staff must observe closely for clues they can report of possible illness or side effects of medications. Reviews what staff should look for and procedures for them to follow. Part of a five - part series presented by the Richmond State School Staff Development, Texas Dept of Mental Health and Mental Retardation.
Health and Safety; Psychology
Dist - HSCIC

Side frames - subassembly of a web frame 17 MIN
16mm
Shipbuilding skills series; Work of shipfitter and shipwright; 4
B&W
LC FIE52-192
Shows how to lay out the main web plate from a template, fit stiffeners to the web plate and dog the stiffeners to the plate for welding.
Industrial and Technical Education
Dist - USNAC **Prod** - USOE 1942

Side splitter 8 MIN
16mm / VHS
Muppet meeting films series
Color (PRO)
$550.00 purchase, $300.00 rental, $30.00 preview
Presents Jim Henson's muppets who introduce and humorously comment on business meetings and breaks. Consists of three to four segments each approximately two and a half minutes.
Business and Economics; Psychology; Sociology
Dist - UTM

Side - to - side portacaval anastomosis for portal hypertension 24 MIN
16mm
Color (PRO)
Demonstrates the exposure, the approximation, and suture of the portal vein and inferior vena cava by the side - to - side technique.
Health and Safety; Science
Dist - ACY **Prod** - ACYDGD 1958

Side - to - side portacaval shunts 26 MIN
16mm
Color (PRO)
Presents a general discussion of both commonly used shunts and less frequently used shunts between the portal and systemic venous systems. Makes particular reference to the hemodynamics of these shunts.
Health and Safety; Science
Dist - ACY **Prod** - ACYDGD 1959

Side tracks 28 MIN
VHS
Color (G)
$190.00 purchase, $50.00 rental
Features homeless men who leave their refuge, the railroad tunnel under New York City's Riverside Park, to tell their stories. Provides a provocative and unusual insight into the lives of this community of intelligent but invisible men. Produced by Kyle Boyd.
Fine Arts; Sociology
Dist - FIRS

Side - walk - shuttle 41 MIN
16mm
Color (H C A)
$110.00 rental
Explores the relationship between architecture, city streets and the movement on them, the medium of cinema, and patterns of thought. Incorporates straight-forward pans and tilt shots of the city street facades and rooftops while raising and lowering the cameras perspective to give a roller coaster effect. Produced by Ernie Gehr.
Geography - World; Science - Natural
Dist - CANCIN

Sidehorse and vaulting 17 MIN
U-matic / VHS / 16mm
Color (I J H C) (SPANISH ARABIC)
LC 75-714075
Demonstrates basic sidehorse vaulting and support work, with attention to teaching techniques, progressions and spotting performers.
Physical Education and Recreation
Dist - AIMS **Prod** - ASSOCF 1974

Sidereal passage 6 MIN
16mm / VHS
Color (G)
$10.00 rental
Offers a journey into the beyond through a black hole in space, into a fiery world, through a cosmic void, into stellar seas and finally to a crystal city. Features special effects and music from Flight to the Future, a live show performed with George Muncy on his 21 - string electric guitar.
Fine Arts
Dist - CANCIN **Prod** - COHENK 1977

The Sideshow 9 MIN
U-matic / VHS / 16mm
Art of silence, pantomimes with Marcel Marceau series
Color (J H C)
LC 75-703453
Features Marcel Marceau performing a pantomime showing circus performers demonstrating their skills. Includes a juggler, an acrobat, clowns pulling ropes without ropes and a tightrope walker as the major performer.
Fine Arts
Dist - EBEC **Prod** - EBEC 1975

Sidet - forced exile 60 MIN
VHS
Color (G)
$295.00 purchase, $75.00 rental
Documents the life of three women refugees in the Sudan in northern Africa, who fled from the famine, poverty and political strife of Ethiopia. Reveals that one woman sells injera bread and brew to other Ethiopian refugees in order to support her family, a development worker from Addis Ababa endures a painful separation from her sons, and a young single mother receives news of her emigration visa to Australia. Produced by Salem Mekuria.
History - World; Sociology
Dist - WMEN

SideTRACKED 22 MIN
16mm
Color (A)
$50.00 rental
Features a rendition of a feminist quest film. Sets the story of a woman's personal journey through Western Europe against the larger experience of travel. Juxtaposes the mythology of travel with the mythology of romance, and the woman's journey becomes a catalyst for reflection on the relationship between personal expectations and cultural myths. Produced by Lesli Alperin.
Fine Arts; Geography - World; Literature and Drama; Psychology; Sociology
Dist - CANCIN

Sidewalk Santas 10 MIN
VHS
Magnum eye series
Color (G)
$125.00 purchase, $30.00 rental
Looks at the Volunteers of America's Santa Claus training program. Takes the camera beneath the beards and stuffed red coats to reveal the individuals who annually transform into the Western symbol of good will. Every year 40 men from various backgrounds - mostly homeless, often rehabilitating alcoholics or drug addicts - don the suit for the Christmas season. The director travels with them as they take their opportunity to offer their services and be appreciated as they spread good cheer in the streets of New York. Part of a series by photographers from the Magnum Photo Agency.
Fine Arts; Geography - United States; Health and Safety; Religion and Philosophy; Social Science
Dist - FIRS **Prod** - MIYAKE 1993

Sidewalks and Similes 14 MIN
U-matic / VHS / 16mm
Color (P I)
LC 73-701626
Shows how inspiration for children's poetry can be found in common objects in the city, such as traffic signals, street lights and fire escapes.
English Language; Literature and Drama
Dist - AIMS **Prod** - CWRU 1973

Sidewalks of shade 25 MIN
16mm / VHS / U-matic
Color (J H G)
LC 81-701039
Takes a trip to the northeastern part of the United States in order to see successful neighborhood and community tree - planting programs. Deals with community organization, funding, maintenance and information about working with utility companies.
Social Science; Sociology
Dist - CORNRS **Prod** - NYSCAG 1981

Sidney's Family Tree 6 MIN
16mm
Color (P)
Presents the story of an elephant who is adopted by monkeys. Relates what happens when he takes a bride and the two elephants decide to live in a tree.
Literature and Drama
Dist - SF **Prod** - SF 1975

Sie Haben Die Prufung Bestanden 15 MIN
16mm / U-matic / VHS
Guten Tag series; 26
B&W (H) (GERMAN)
LC 76-707339
A German language film. Presents an episode in which the characters employ frequently used expressions and idioms in order to teach conversational German to beginners. Stresses the correct use of the verbs tun and machen, the expression was fur ein, and the preposition tiber (with accusative).
Foreign Language
Dist - IFB **Prod** - FRGMFA 1970

Sieg Im Westen 120 MIN
U-matic / VHS
B&W
Presents a propaganda pageant shown to the German people after one of history's greatest victories by German force of arms, the Nazis' six - week invasion of Holland, Belgium and France in spring of 1940.
Foreign Language; History - World; Sociology
Dist - IHF **Prod** - IHF

Siege 95 MIN
VHS
B&W (G) (HEBREW WITH ENGLISH SUBTITLES)
$79.95 purchase _ #544
Portrays Tamar, an Israeli woman who lost her husband during the Six Day War. Reveals that her husband's friends do not want his memory to be forgotten and this forces her into the role of the ever - mourning widow. Stars Gila Almagor, Dahn Ben Amotz and Yehoram Gaon. Directed by Gilberto Tofano.
Fine Arts; History - World; Literature and Drama; Sociology
Dist - ERGOM **Prod** - ERGOM 1970

Siege 10 MIN
16mm
B&W (J H)
Presents a film made by the last neutral reporter left in Poland in 1931, Julien Bryan, which depicts the horror and confusion of Warsaw during the Blitzkrieg. Describes the chain of events that finally resulted in the capitulation of Warsaw and Poland.
Civics and Political Systems; History - World
Dist - IFF **Prod** - BRYAN 1974

Siege 48 MIN
VHS
Vietnam - the ten thousand day war series; Vol 7
Color (G)
$34.95 purchase _ #S00681
Documents the battle of 3500 Marines to hold Khe Sanh. Shows that the Johnson administration considered Khe Sanh to be critical to its Vietnam policy. Reveals that Americans were beginning to question both the cost and results of the war. Suggests that the Viet Cong used this battle to divert US attention from their Tet offensive plans. Narrated by Richard Basehart.
History - United States
Dist - UILL

The Siege and capture of Charleston, South Carolina 30 MIN
VHS
And then there were thirteen series; Pt 4
Color (H)
$69.95 purchase
Looks at the siege and capture of Charleston, South Carolina. Uses footage shot on battle ground location. Describes command personalities, weapons and uniforms. Part 4 of a twenty - part series on Southern theaters of war during the American Revolution.
Civics and Political Systems; Geography - United States; History - United States
Dist - SCETV **Prod** - SCETV 1982

Siege at Powderham Castle 25 MIN
U-matic / VHS
Color
Records the annual re - enactment of a 16th century British battle, capturing the customs, dress and flavor of the day. Explains the role of women in battle.
Geography - World; History - World; Sociology
Dist - JOU **Prod** - UPI

Siege of Fort Stanwix 20 MIN
16mm
Color (G)
LC 77-703156
Dramatizes the 22 - day siege at Fort Stanwix, New York, by the British and the final surrender of General Burgoyne at Saratoga in 1777. Highlights the critical period when a British victory might have been a deathblow to the fight for American independence.
History - United States
Dist - USNAC **Prod** - USNPS 1976

The Siege of the Alamo 21 MIN
16mm / U-matic / VHS
You are There Series
Color (I J)
LC 75-714895
Recounts the events leading to the Battle of the Alamo, portrays the defeat of the Texans at the Alamo, and covers the subsequent defeat of the Mexicans by Sam Houston.
Biography; History - United States
Dist - PHENIX **Prod** - CBSTV 1971

The Siege of Yorktown 15 MIN
VHS
Color (P I J)
$17.95 purchase _ #HFV - 4
Relives the dramatic events leading to the capture of Cornwallis and the British defeat at Yorktown in the fall of 1781. Explores the historical significance, strategy and tactics of the siege.
Civics and Political Systems; History - United States; Sociology
Dist - KNOWUN

The Siege of Yorktown, Virginia 30 MIN
VHS
And then there were thirteen series; Pt 18
Color (H)

$69.95 purchase
Focuses on the siege of Yorktown, Virgina. Uses footage shot on battleground locations. Describes command personalities, weapons and uniforms. Part 18 of a twenty - part series on Southern theaters of war during the American Revolution.
Civics and Political Systems; Geography - United States; History - United States
Dist - SCETV **Prod** - SCETV 1982

The Siege of Yorktown, Virginia - second phase 30 MIN
VHS
And then there were thirteen series; Pt 19
Color (H)
$69.95 purchase
Focuses on the second phase of the siege of Yorktown, Virgina. Uses footage shot on battleground locations. Describes command personalities, weapons and uniforms. Part 19 of a twenty - part series on Southern theaters of war during the American Revolution.
Civics and Political Systems; Geography - United States; History - United States
Dist - SCETV **Prod** - SCETV 1982

The Sieges of Augusta, Georgia and Ninety - Six, South Carolina 30 MIN
VHS
And then there were thirteen series; Pt 15
Color (H)
$69.95 purchase
Focuses on the sieges of Augusta, Georgia and Ninety - Six, South Carolina. Uses footage shot on battleground locations. Describes command personalities, weapons and uniforms. Part 15 of a twenty - part series on Southern theaters of war during the American Revolution.
Civics and Political Systems; Geography - United States; History - United States
Dist - SCETV **Prod** - SCETV 1982

Siegfried 253 MIN
U-matic / VHS
Wagner Ring Cycle Series
Color
Fine Arts
Dist - FOTH **Prod** - FOTH

Siena 22 MIN
16mm
Treasures of Tuscany Series
Color
LC FIA66-1359
Shows views of the palaces, piazzas and public buildings of Siena in the light of artistic style and social history, including the font in the baptistry and its sculptured panels by Donatello and Jacopo Della Quercia, filmed in Italy.
Fine Arts; Geography - World
Dist - RADIM **Prod** - WESTCB 1965

Siena - chronicles of a medieval commune 29 MIN
VHS
Color (G)
$29.95 purchase _ #412 - 9076
Focuses on the civic and religious institutions of the city of Siena in Tuscany during medieval and Renaissance times. Captures Sienese life and society during its golden age, using contemporary sources and location shooting in Tuscany.
Civics and Political Systems; Geography - World; History - World; Sociology
Dist - FI **Prod** - MMOA 1988

SIER 30 MIN
VHS / U-matic
Effective listening series; Tape 4
Color
Focuses on sending, interpreting, evaluating and responding in personal communication.
English Language
Dist - TELSTR **Prod** - TELSTR

The SIER formula 30 MIN
VHS / U-matic
Effective listening series
Color
English Language; Psychology
Dist - DELTAK **Prod** - TELSTR
TELSTR

Sierpinski's Curve Fills Space 5 MIN
U-matic / VHS / 16mm
Topology Short Films Series
Color (C A)
LC 81-700617
Proves that Sierpinski's curve actually passes through every point in the square.
Mathematics
Dist - IFB **Prod** - IFB 1979

Sifted Evidence 42 MIN
16mm
Color (C)
$600.00 purchase, $60.00, $80.00 rental
Recreates through stills, narration, and enactment a woman's quest for an obscure archeological site in Mexico, which leads her into a psychological misadventure with a man. Experiments with projection screen techniques to create an overlapping of dream and reality. Raises questions about personal motives. Produced by Patricia Gruben.
Fine Arts; Geography - World; Sociology
Dist - WMENIF

Sifted Gold 30 MIN
16mm
Color (H C A)
LC 75-704231
Tells the story of a woman who contracts a fatal disease and is unable to tell anyone about it. Shows how, after her recovery, she relates her feelings and tells of her belief that God was by her side during the ordeal.
Guidance and Counseling; Psychology
Dist - CPH **Prod** - CPH 1975

Siga las instrucciones - follow the directions 20 MIN
U-matic / VHS
Spanish for health professionals series; Program 2
Color (PRO) (SPANISH)
Includes colors, directions and prepositional phrases in Spanish. Gives tips on taking control of the conversation to keep it at your level of understanding.
Health and Safety
Dist - HSCIC **Prod** - HSCIC 1982

Sigaalow - Town of Dust 22 MIN
16mm / U-matic / VHS
Color (H C A)
LC 83-700271
Examines the daily routine of the people of Sigaalow, a refugee camp on the banks of a muddy river in East Africa. Includes their farming methods, educational system and cultural practices. Discusses the problems they face as a result of their crowded, sedentary lifestyle. Produced in Switzerland in 1974.
Geography - World; Sociology
Dist - CRMP **Prod** - CRMP 1983

The Sight of Sound 29 MIN
Videoreel / VT2
Museum Open House Series
Color
Fine Arts
Dist - PBS **Prod** - WGBHTV

Sight Reading and Playing 29 MIN
Videoreel / VT2
Playing the Guitar I Series
Color
Fine Arts
Dist - PBS **Prod** - KCET

Sight Reading in Two Parts 29 MIN
Videoreel / VT2
Playing the Guitar II Series
Color
Fine Arts
Dist - PBS **Prod** - KCET

Sight Restoration - Miracles in the Making 27 MIN
U-matic
Color
Shows how thousands of people have had their sight restored as a result of eye banks and optic surgery. Documents an actual cornea transplant operation. Close - captioned.
Health and Safety; Science - Natural
Dist - MTP **Prod** - IALC

Sight Restoration - Miracles in the Making 15 MIN
16mm
Color
Looks at the operation of Lions Club's eye banks. Views an actual cornea transplant and presents transplant recipients who tell how their lives have been changed by the operation.
Health and Safety; Social Science; Sociology
Dist - MTP **Prod** - MTP

Sight through sound 19 MIN
16mm
B&W
Presents a study of a young engineering student who is shown working on the problem of devising a method, for use by the blind, through which they can hear their world. Explains the device, and allows us to hear the sound patterns which the 'seeing' device produces. Shows the young inventor trying to act blind so as to learn the problems, and see and hear the device he develops.
Guidance and Counseling; Psychology
Dist - UPENN **Prod** - UPENN 1969

Sight unseen 31 MIN
VHS
Color (G)
$35.00 purchase
Traces the existential displacement of an American tourist as he travels through India. Examines the limitations of cultural knowledge and the fragility of personal identity by looking at the tourist's perceptions of India, rather than focusing on merely describing the country. Stories, poetic observations, musical vignettes and humor all serve to explore the ambiguous persistence of the colonial imagination. Directed by Jonathan Robinson.
Fine Arts; Geography - World; History - World; Psychology; Religion and Philosophy
Dist - ALTFMW

Sight - Visual System 18 MIN
U-matic / VHS / 16mm
Anatomical Basis of Brain Function Series
Color (PRO)
Science - Natural
Dist - TEF **Prod** - AVCORP

Sighting Scope 15 MIN
U-matic
Know Your World Series
(I J)
Observes nature and shows students constructing a sighting scope to improve their perception of things in the natural environment.
Science
Dist - ACCESS **Prod** - ACCESS 1981

Sights and sounds of San Francisco 30 MIN
VHS
Color (G)
$29.95 purchase _ #S01978
Presents the various sights and sounds of San Francisco. Reveals the diversity of the city, and tours many of the most popular tourist destinations.
Geography - United States
Dist - UILL

Sightseeing 25 MIN
VHS
Dragon's tongue series
Color (J H G)
$195.00 purchase
Teaches basics of Putonghua, China's official language. Presents one video in a series of nineteen helping students develop comprehension skills by using only Chinese - no subtitles. Shows authentic scenes of Chinese homes, cities and the countryside. Features Colin Mackerras of Griffith University.
Foreign Language
Dist - LANDMK

Sigma Theta Tau International retrospective 6 MIN
VHS
Color (C PRO G)
$15.00 purchase _ #992
Captures the heritage of and the vision for the future of Sigma Theta Tau International. Features statements of Sigma Theta Tau leaders Sister Rosemary Donley, Nell Watts, Virginia Henderson and others. Captures the highlights of the 70 - year - old society.
Health and Safety; Sociology
Dist - SITHTA **Prod** - SITHTA 1991

Sigmund Freud - His Offices and Home, Vienna, 1938 17 MIN
16mm
Color
LC 75-700367
Uses contemporary photographs to show the interior of Freud's home in Vienna in 1938. Explores the political situation in Nazi Vienna and shows why Freud left his home to flee to London.
Biography; Psychology
Dist - FLMLIB **Prod** - FRIEDG 1974

Sign Here 19 MIN
U-matic / VHS
Rights and Responsibilities Series
Color (J H)
Considers various types of contracts, contracts and minors, implications of reaching the age of majority, credit and commercial employment contracts, wage garnishment and the marriage contract.
Civics and Political Systems; Home Economics; Social Science
Dist - AITECH **Prod** - WHROTV 1975

The Sign Language Alphabet 15 MIN
16mm
Quick Flicks Series
Color (I)
LC 75-700659
Shows the American manual alphabet. Includes practice sentences which demonstrate how to form the letters with the hands and how to read the letters from another person's hands.

Guidance and Counseling; Psychology; Social Science
Dist - JOYCE **Prod** - JOYCE 1975

Sign Language and English 8 MIN
16mm
Color (I) (AMERICAN SIGN)
LC 76-701703
Advocates the teaching of sign language in an academic setting to improve a deaf student's ability to read English. Points to comparisons of minority groups being taught in their own language when that language is related to English. Performed in American sign language by Herb Larson.
Education; English Language; Psychology
Dist - JOYCE **Prod** - JOYCE 1975

Sign Language - Exact English 110 MIN
BETA / VHS
Color
Guides parents whose children are learning to sign Exact English at school. Shows vocabulary of 480 signs and practice sentences.
Education
Dist - VIPRO **Prod** - VIPRO

Sign language for the dental team 20 MIN
VHS
Color (PRO)
$395.00 purchase _ #N900VI011
Introduces sign language to aid in the dental care of hearing impaired persons. Demonstrates the basic alphabet in segment one, the numbers 1 through 32 in segment two, and words and phrases used by dentists in segment three.
Education; Guidance and Counseling; Health and Safety; Psychology
Dist - HSCIC

Sign Language - the language of life 16 MIN
U-matic / VHS / 16mm
Color (H C A)
LC 82-700388
Looks at the development of sign language for the deaf, from its earliest forms when it was used to convey basic needs to a complex form capable of expressing emotions and conveying creative thought.
Education
Dist - JOU **Prod** - JOU 1981
GALCO

The Sign of the Beaver
35mm strip / VHS / Cassette
Newbery Award - Winners Series
Color (I)
$66.00, $14.00 purchase
English Language; Literature and Drama
Dist - PELLER

Sign of the First Derivative
U-matic
Calculus Series
Color
Mathematics
Dist - MDCPB **Prod** - MDDE

Sign of Victory 22 MIN
16mm
Color (H C A)
LC 82-700769
Presents a championship high school basketball team where all the girls are deaf. Shows how these girls have overcome the isolation of their handicap by competing in the world of sports. Narrated by Al McGuire and filmed at the Rhode Island School for the Deaf.
Education; Guidance and Counseling; Physical Education and Recreation
Dist - FLMLIB **Prod** - FLMLIB 1982

Sign Off 3 MIN
U-matic / VHS
Color
Presents apocalyptic, anti - military symbols to the Jimi Hendrix' performance of the Star Spangled Banner. Produced as the concluding segment for the Night Flight show on the USA Cable Network.
Fine Arts
Dist - KITCHN **Prod** - KITCHN

Sign on - sign off 24 MIN
16mm
Color (C)
LC FIA68-2700
A non - technical introduction to computer - assisted instruction (CAI). Examines the tutorial method of instruction in the classroom and at the computer terminal. Uses simple animation to show the operation of computer - assisted - instuction systems.
Education; Mathematics; Psychology; Sociology
Dist - PSUPCR **Prod** - PSUPCR 1967

Sign posts 30 MIN
U-matic / VHS
Stage at a time series
Color (P)
Depicts the communications problems arising when a deaf person responds to a Held Wanted notice in a sign shop. Shows the two characters in the play with their own distinctive communications systems.
Education; Guidance and Counseling; Literature and Drama
Dist - GPN **Prod** - WUFT

Sign test
VHS
Probability and statistics series
Color (H C)
$125.00 purchase _ #8056
Provides resource material about sign tests for help in the study of probability and statistics. Presents a 60 - video series, each part 25 to 30 minutes long, that explains and reinforces concepts using definitions, theorems, examples and step - by - step solutions to tutor the student. Videos are also available in a set.
Mathematics
Dist - LANDMK

Sign with me - a family sign language curriculum 140 MIN
VHS
Color (G)
$29.95 purchase _ #V604
Arranges sign language instruction in a development sequence, beginning with words and phrases for toddlers and progressing on to more complicted language. Includes the skills parents need to assist their child in communication, such as directing attention and handling tantrums. Comes with two videocassettes and a workbook. Available in American Sign Language - ASL - and Manually Coded English - based primarily on SEE II.
Education; Social Science
Dist - FFBH **Prod** - FFBH 1993

Signal and Power Conditioning 180 MIN
U-matic
Microprocessor Real - Time Interfacing and Control Systems Series
Color (IND)
Discusses signal conditioning and amplification, featuring noise filtering and common mode rejection. Speaks on isolation and level conversion, dealing with isolation and safety considerations, and the use of opto - isolators, isolation amplifiers and transformers, as well as power control switching vs linear.
Computer Science
Dist - INTECS **Prod** - INTECS

Signal Conditioning for Digital Circuits 59 MIN
U-matic / VHS
Digital Electronics Series
Color (PRO)
Industrial and Technical Education; Mathematics
Dist - MIOT **Prod** - MIOT

Signal Conversion - 1 60 TO 90 MIN
VHS
Distributed Control Systems Module Series
Color (PRO)
$600.00 - $1500.00 purchase _ #DASC1
Focuses on digital - to - analog and analog - to - digital signal conversion. Addresses basic concepts and common methods of conversion. Part of a fourteen - part series on distributed contol systems. Includes five student guides, five workbooks and an instructor guide.
Computer Science; Education; Industrial and Technical Education; Psychology
Dist - NUSTC **Prod** - NUSTC

Signal Conversion - 2 60 TO 90 MIN
VHS
Distributed Control Systems Module Series
Color (PRO)
$600.00 - $1500.00 purchase _ #DASC2
Introduces the concepts of signal multiplexing by discussing the basic concepts of multiplexing and sample and hold circuits. Part of a fourteen - part series on distributed contol systems. Includes five student guides, five workbooks and an instructor guide.
Computer Science; Education; Industrial and Technical Education; Psychology
Dist - NUSTC **Prod** - NUSTC

Signal Generator Operation 9 MIN
U-matic / VHS / 16mm
Radio Technician Training Series
B&W
Shows how to use a signal generator to align a radio receiver. Issued in 1945 as a motion picture.
Industrial and Technical Education
Dist - USNAC **Prod** - USN 1978

Signal - Germany on the air 37 MIN
16mm
Color (G A)
$55.00 rental
Presents the work of filmmaker Ernie Gehr. Offers shifting images of Gehr's return to Berlin, the city from which his parents fled in 1939. Combines chunks of ambient, asynchronous street noise, silence and excerpts of multilingual radio broadcasts. Phrase shards, 'You people are all the same,' 'Don't blame me,' 'What are you accusing me of,' interplay with scenes of the city, including a factory on a barren lot which is identified as the former Gestapo headquarters.
Fine Arts; Geography - World; History - World; Industrial and Technical Education
Dist - PARART **Prod** - FMCOOP 1985

Signal Processing and Control 30 MIN
U-matic / VHS
6809 Interface Programming Series
Color (IND)
Shows how microprocessors do complicated tasks by linearizing a thermocouple. Describes digital control algorithms with low - pass filter example. Tells how proportional - integral - derivative control algorithms are employed in position - independent and modular structured code.
Industrial and Technical Education; Mathematics; Sociology
Dist - COLOSU **Prod** - COLOSU

Signal Syntax 8 MIN
VHS / U-matic
Color (H C A)
Presents comedy by the Brave New World Workshop of the Twin Cities.
Literature and Drama
Dist - UCV **Prod** - JDR

Signal Wiring, Transmission and Conditioning 60 TO 90 MIN
VHS
Distributed Control Systems Module Series
Color (PRO)
$600.00 - $1500.00 purchase _ #DASIT
Examines signal wiring, transmission and conditioning in a control system. Part of a fourteen - part series on distributed contol systems. Includes five student guides, five workbooks and an instructor guide.
Computer Science; Education; Industrial and Technical Education; Psychology
Dist - NUSTC **Prod** - NUSTC

Signaler - forward lunge and bend - Siam squat 15 MIN
U-matic / VHS
Roomnastics series
Color (P)
Presents several exercises which can be performed in a classroom setting.
Physical Education and Recreation
Dist - GPN **Prod** - WVIZTV 1979

Signaling and Modulation 30 MIN
U-matic / VHS
Telecommunications and the Computer Series
Color
Industrial and Technical Education; Mathematics
Dist - MIOT **Prod** - MIOT

Signals 3 MIN
16mm
Color (H C A)
Emphasizes the life - saving potential of cancer's warning signals.
Health and Safety
Dist - AMCS **Prod** - AMCS

Signals 10 MIN
VHS
Stop, look, listen series
Color; PAL (P I J)
Looks at signals used to convey messages, including signals which warn of danger - sirens, bells, flashing lights, signals giving directions such as police signals, indicators on cars, signals giving commands or requests such as the bell on a bus, the guard on a train, a knock at the door, personal signals such as facial expressions. Part of a series of films which start from some everyday observation and show more of what is happening, how and why. Builds vocabulary and encourages children to be more observant.
Social Science; Sociology
Dist - VIEWTH

Signals for Sense 11 MIN
16mm / U-matic / VHS
Color (P)
$280, $195 purchase _ #3730
Discusses sentence structure and punctuation.
English Language
Dist - CORF

Signals for survival 51 MIN
U-matic / VHS / 16mm

Color (H C)
LC 74-709835
Shows the various types of signals and language gulls use in communicating with each other. Includes behavioral aspects such as territoriality, aggression, courtship and mating, alarm signals and flight.
Psychology; Science - Natural
Dist - MGHT **Prod** - TINBGN 1970

Signals for survival - Pt 1 21 MIN
16mm / U-matic / VHS
Color (H C)
Shows the various types of signals and language gulls use in communicating with each other. Includes behavioral aspects such as territoriality, aggression, courtship and mating, alarm signals and flight.
Psychology; Science - Natural
Dist - MGHT **Prod** - TINBGN 1970

Signals for survival - Pt 2 30 MIN
16mm / U-matic / VHS
Color (H C)
Shows the various types of signals and language gulls use in communicating with each other. Includes behavioral aspects such as territoriality, aggression, courtship and mating, alarm signals and flight.
Psychology; Science - Natural
Dist - MGHT **Prod** - TINBGN 1970

Signals of Change - the Junior High Child
VHS / U-matic
Vital Link Series
Color (A)
Helps parents understand and deal with teenage development.
Guidance and Counseling; Sociology
Dist - EDCC **Prod** - EDCC

Signals of Change - the Senior High Child
VHS / U-matic
Vital Link Series
Color (A)
Helps parents understand and deal with teenage development.
Guidance and Counseling; Sociology
Dist - EDCC **Prod** - EDCC

Signals - Read 'Em or Weep 20 MIN
16mm
Color (IND)
LC 82-700260
Depicts a number of unnecessary and fairly common damage - causing situations involving construction equipment. Emphasizes the need for observing maintenance and operating instructions in order to help reduce damage to equipment.
Health and Safety; Industrial and Technical Education
Dist - MTP **Prod** - CTRACT 1982

Signals, sounds, and making sense 29 MIN
VHS / 16mm
Everybody's children series
(G)
$90.00 purchase _ #BPN16109
Explores the development of communication and language skills. Comprises part of a series which examines child raising in modern society.
Education; Psychology; Sociology
Dist - RMIBHF **Prod** - RMIBHF
TVOTAR

Signals without words 15 MIN
VHS
Color; PAL (J H G)
PdS29.50 purchase
Explores non - verbal communication. Shows the many ways humans and animals communicate without using words - facial expressions, body posture, gesture, dress, sounds other than words and sense of smell.
Psychology
Dist - EMFVL **Prod** - EDMI

Signature and Seals 30 MIN
VHS / 16mm
Chinese Brush Painting Series
Color (C A)
$85.00, $75.00 purchase _ 20 - 19
Demonstrates selection, enriching the beauty and personal significance of signature and seals.
Fine Arts
Dist - CDTEL **Prod** - COAST 1987

Signature series
Cabiria 123 MIN
Metropolis 90 MIN
Spiders 137 MIN
Dist - KINOIC

Signatures of the Soul 59 MIN
VHS / U-matic
Color
Shows some of the most spectacular contemporary tattooing in the world. Introduces the artists who practice this most hidden of art forms.
Fine Arts; Sociology
Dist - FLMLIB **Prod** - FLMLIB 1984

Signed by a Woman 60 MIN
U-matic
Color
Attempts to define important issues in women's art and is a significant presentation on the power and skill of women artists today.
Fine Arts; Sociology
Dist - WMENIF **Prod** - WMENIF

Signed, Sealed and Delivered 10 MIN
16mm
Cargo Security Series
Color (A)
LC 78-700820
Points out the fact that cargo loss is a major problem in the United States and has a widespread effect.
Business and Economics; Health and Safety
Dist - USNAC **Prod** - USDT 1978

Signed, sealed and delivered - labor struggle in the post office 40 MIN
VHS / U-matic
Color
Depicts working conditions and a wildcat strike among postal workers, following their struggle to the floor of the American Postal Workers' Union National Convention. Portrays the death of a mailhandler who was crushed to death by postal machinery as the event bringing their struggle to national attention.
Business and Economics; Health and Safety; Social Science; Sociology
Dist - DCTVC **Prod** - DCTVC 1980
TAMERP

The Significance of Malcolm X 30 MIN
16mm
Black History, Section 21 - Protest and Rebellion Series; Section 21 - Protest and rebellion
B&W (H C A)
LC 78-704115
Dr C Eric Lincoln discusses the life and career of the black revolutionary leader Malcolm X and explains the impact of his message.
Civics and Political Systems; History - United States
Dist - HRAW **Prod** - WCBSTV 1969

Significance of the Second Derivative
U-matic
Calculus Series
Color
Mathematics
Dist - MDCPB **Prod** - MDDE

Significance Testing
16mm
B&W
Introduces the idea of significance testing as applied to a simple industrial problem.
Mathematics
Dist - OPENU **Prod** - OPENU

Significant developments in civil and federal practice and procedure - 1990 - 91 legislative and rule - making changes 210 MIN
VHS
Color (PRO C)
$140.00, $200.00 purchase _ #M802, #P276
Updates federal judges, federal civil practitioners and law professors on The Civil Justice Reform Act of 1990, the Federal Courts Study Committee Implementation Act of 1990, proposed Federal Rules of Civil - Appellate Procedure Amendments and more.
Civics and Political Systems
Dist - ALIABA **Prod** - ALIABA 1991

Significant others 24 MIN
VHS
Color (A PRO)
$95.00 purchase, $35.00 rental _ #D - 226
Explains multiple personality disorders. Discusses disorders caused by ritual abuse in satanism. Presents therapy sessions with children and adults.
Psychology; Religion and Philosophy
Dist - CAVLCD **Prod** - KPIXTV

Signing with Cindy series
Family signs
Introduction and beginning sign language instruction
Series conclusion and talking about deafness
Dist - GPCV

Signposts 15 MIN
16mm
B&W (G)
Indicates that a chronic cough and shortness of breath are symptoms of respiratory disease. Shows the results of neglecting the symptoms by describing real case histories.
Health and Safety
Dist - AMLUNG **Prod** - NTBA 1963

Signposts aloft 28 MIN
VHS
Moody science classics series
Color (R I J)
$19.95 purchase _ #6118 - 2
Compares metaphorically the use of instruments in mechanical flight with the guidance of the Christian deity. Features part of a series on creationism.
Literature and Drama; Religion and Philosophy
Dist - MOODY **Prod** - MOODY

Signs 15 MIN
U-matic / VHS
Word Shop Series
Color (P)
English Language; Literature and Drama
Dist - WETATV **Prod** - WETATV

Signs 11 MIN
16mm / U-matic / VHS
Color (P I)
Explains that signs warn, instruct, guide, explain and direct. Presents the many different kinds of signs. Encourages students to discover the various signs and their meanings, in a number of different environments, whether they are on their way to the library, looking for a bus stop, riding a bike in the park, or taking the dog for a walk. Stresses the fact that signs are helpful guides.
Health and Safety
Dist - PHENIX **Prod** - GABOR 1969

Signs 10 MIN
VHS
Stop, look, listen series
Color; PAL (P I J)
Looks at nonverbal communication through signs, badges, road signs, cub pack tracking signs, hotel and pub signs and sign language. Part of a series of films which start from some everyday observation and show more of what is happening, how and why. Builds vocabulary and encourages children to be more observant.
Education; Social Science; Sociology
Dist - VIEWTH

Signs and Lines 11 MIN
16mm
Color
LC 74-700515
Uses animated graphics to emphasize the importance of knowing and heeding traffic signs and markings wherever a person is driving. Encourages people to learn the international traffic signs and marking lines system.
Health and Safety
Dist - MTP **Prod** - GM 1973

Signs and Signals 60 MIN
VHS / U-matic
Discovery of Animal Behavior Series
Color (H C A)
Looks at the phenomena of animal communication through the re - creations of Karl Von Frisch unraveling the language of honeybees, Julian Huxley discovering the possible language in ritual movements of great - crested grebes, Konrad Lorenz recording the visual language of geese and Niko Tinbergen studying the habits of hunting wasps and together with Esther Cullen recording the relationship of temperament in birds to their habitat.
Science; Science - Natural
Dist - FI **Prod** - WNETTV 1982

Signs and signing - 2 20 MIN
VHS
Design and technology starters series
Color; PAL (J H)
PdS29.50 purchase
Begins with a search for worthwhile design possibilities within a particular real - world context. Suggests ways in which pupils might start thinking about certain artifacts, systems and environments, and how well they meet the needs and desires of different people who might use them. Part two of a seven - part series.
Fine Arts; Sociology
Dist - EMFVL

Signs and symptoms of a heart attack 7 MIN
VHS
Color; CC (G C PRO)
$150.00 purchase _ #HA - 35
Identifies signs of a heart attack to help patients and their families know when to seek emergency care. Differentiates symptoms of angina from a possible

infarction. Provides a description of nitroglycerin protocol. Contact distributor for special purchase price on multiple orders.
Health and Safety
Dist - MIFE **Prod** - MIFE 1995

Signs at the Shopping Center 9 MIN
U-matic / VHS / 16mm
Color (P)
Presents a group of children and their mothers in a shopping mall. Shows how they go from store to store, guided by various signs, examining goods and making choices as to what to buy. Key words are flashed on the screen.
English Language
Dist - PHENIX **Prod** - PHENIX 1983

Signs for Time 15 MIN
16mm
PANCOM Beginning Total Communication Program for Hearing Parents of 'Series Level 1
Color (K)
LC 77-700504
Education; Guidance and Counseling; Psychology; Social Science; Sociology
Dist - JOYCE **Prod** - CSDE 1977

Signs of Anxiety 22 MIN
16mm
Color
Illustrates verbal and non - verbal signs of anxiety in three patients seen in a doctor's waiting room and in consultation. Features method actors who effectively demonstrate and relate their experiences with acute anxiety, chronic anxiety associated with somatic complaints and anxiety as it relates to interpersonal behavior in a geriatric patient.
Health and Safety; Psychology; Sociology
Dist - AMEDA **Prod** - HOFLAR

Signs of Change 18 MIN
VHS / 35mm strip
Color (I J H C A)
Shows how a famine was averted in Senegal.
Sociology
Dist - CWS **Prod** - CWS 1985

Signs of His Promise 27 MIN
16mm
Color
Demonstrates how Christian care and training can help mentally retarded persons progress to more normal living opportunities.
Education; Psychology; Religion and Philosophy
Dist - BLH **Prod** - BLH

Signs of Life 27 MIN
16mm
To Get from Here to There Series
Color (H)
Presents a look at the signs, signals and markings that help control traffic.
Health and Safety; Psychology
Dist - PROART **Prod** - PROART

Signs of Life 90 MIN
16mm
B&W (GERMAN (ENGLISH SUBTITLES))
Depicts a wounded German soldier recuperating on a Greek island and staging a lyrical/mad one - man rebellion involving insects, fireworks and windmills. Directed by Werner Herzog. With English subtitles.
Fine Arts; Foreign Language
Dist - NYFLMS **Prod** - UNKNWN 1968

Signs of life 50 MIN
VHS
Horizon series
Color (A PRO C)
PdS99 purchase
Explains that biologists have discovered much about how living things work, while the quality of life remains a mystery. Explores Artificial Life, a line of research which seeks to reveal the secrets of life by using computer simulations of simple living organisms which can evolve autonomously.
Science - Natural
Dist - BBCENE

Signs of the apes, songs of the whales 60 MIN
VHS
Nova video library series
Color (G)
$29.95 purchase
Examines language in the animal world, looking at how animals communicate with one another and whether they could communicate with humans. From the PBS series 'Nova.'
Psychology; Science - Natural
Dist - PBS **Prod** - WNETTV
TIMLIF WGBHTV

Signs of the Times 28 MIN
VHS / 16mm
Color (G)
$200.00 purchase, $15.50 rental _ #35503
Overviews the Old School or Primitive Baptists who once lived in the Northeastern United States. Examines beliefs, architecture and other elements of this group. Produced by Leandra Little.
Religion and Philosophy
Dist - PSUPCR **Prod** - PSUPCR 1989

Signs of the times series
Takes viewers 'through the keyhole' into ordinary late 20th-century homes in Britain to see what people's perceptions of good and bad taste really are. A five-part series.
Big Ben and the Jesus picture 50 MIN
Marie Louise collects bric-a-brac 50 MIN
Red drives me nuts 50 MIN
That little bit different 50 MIN
They're not holding the ceiling up 50 MIN
Dist - BBCENE

Signs, Symbols and Signals 11 MIN
16mm / U-matic / VHS
Color (K)
LC 79-704205
Shows a kaleidoscope of basic visual communication, depicting the signs, symbols and signals that individuals and the community rely on.
Psychology; Social Science
Dist - ALTSUL **Prod** - FILMSW 1969

Signs, tags, labels and placards 17 MIN
8mm cartridge / VHS / BETA / U-matic
Color; PAL (IND G)
$295.00 purchase _ #ELK - 005
Shows that injuries can be prevented and lives saved when signs, tags, labels and placards are used correctly. Explains the meaning of colors, symbols, words and numbers, as well as the three colors identifying the levels of safety and the the safety signal words. Discusses the difference between Haz Comm Standard labels and DOT labels. Covers ANSI label requirements, the NFPA Hazard Warning System requirements and details special packing instructions for hazardous materials. Reveals the necessity for marking hazardous situations or equipment, warning of specific hazardous materials, providing safety procedures and pointing the way out for an emergency evacuation. Includes a leader's guide and test materials for duplication.
Health and Safety
Dist - BNA

Signs Take a Holiday 10 MIN
U-matic / VHS / 16mm
B&W (P I J H)
LC FIA65-1161
Uses a cartoon fantasy to stress the importance of obeying traffic signs. Explains the six sign shapes.
Health and Safety; Social Science
Dist - JOU **Prod** - JOU 1960

Signs you already know 30 MIN
U-matic / VHS
Say it with sign series; Pt 1
Color (H C A) (AMERICAN SIGN)
LC 83-706358
Presents Lawrence Solow and Sharon Neumann Solow introducing American Sign Language used by the hearing - impaired. Emphasizes signs that resemble gestures already used by many people in spoken conversation.
Education
Dist - FI **Prod** - KNBCTV 1982

Sika and sambar 25 MIN
VHS
Nature watch series
Color (P I J H C)
$49.00 purchase _ #320212; LC 89-715856
Profiles the delicate sika deer and the large and powerful sambar deer. Part of a series that explores the curious and uncommon characteristics of a variety of mammals, insects, birds and sea creatures.
Science - Natural
Dist - TVOTAR **Prod** - TVOTAR 1988

Silage Production 15 MIN
VHS / 16mm
Forage for Profit Series
Color (S)
$150.00 purchase _ #284403
Offers proven suggestions for crop establishment, hay and silage production and pasture management. Features successful beef, horse and dairy producers, forage exporters, district agriculturists and other experts who explain techniques. 'Silage Production' explains the use of silage as an alternative management strategy.
Agriculture; Education
Dist - ACCESS **Prod** - ACCESS 1989

Silage Wagons 17 MIN
VHS / U-matic
Agricultural Accidents and Rescue Series
Color
Focuses on a rescue from the beater bars and teeth of an unloading silage wagon.
Agriculture; Health and Safety
Dist - PSU **Prod** - PSU

Silas Marner 92 MIN
VHS
Color (G)
$59.98 purchase _ #S01381
Presents an updated BBC version of the classic tale of a social outcast who finds hope in an abandoned child's face. Stars Ben Kingsley.
Literature and Drama
Dist - UILL

Silas Marner 27 MIN
U-matic / VHS / 16mm
Color (J H)
Dramatizes the story of the lonely weaver whose life changes when a girl called Eppie appears. Based upon SILAS MARNER by George Eliot.
Literature and Drama
Dist - LUF **Prod** - LUF

Silas Marner 65 MIN
16mm
B&W (J H)
LC 73-701851
Presents George Eliot's novel 'SILAS MARNER.'.
Literature and Drama
Dist - FCE **Prod** - THAN 1973

Silbale a Guillermito 6 MIN
U-matic / VHS / 16mm
Color (SPANISH)
A Spanish - language version of the motion picture Whistle For Willie. Tells the story of a boy who badly wants to learn to whistle so that he can call his dog. Based on the book Whistle For Willie by Ezra Jack Keats.
Foreign Language; Literature and Drama
Dist - WWS **Prod** - WWS

Silberaktion Brus - silveraction brus 2 MIN
16mm
B&W (G)
$10.00 rental
Fine Arts
Dist - CANCIN **Prod** - KRENKU 1965

The Silence 95 MIN
VHS
B&W (A)
$24.95 purchase _ #SIL100
Depicts a world in which God is silent, a world of despair. Tells the story of two sisters united since childhood in a love - hate relationship of lesbian incest as they struggle, then part when the younger seeks her freedom in a heterosexual affair. Expresses their conflict in visual terms, with little dialogue, to portray modern man's condition, wherein human relations are grotesquely egocentric and perversely sexual. The third film of Ingmar Bergman's religious trilogy, which also includes Through A Glass Darkly and Winter Light.
Fine Arts; Psychology; Sociology
Dist - HOMVIS **Prod** - JANUS 1963

Silence and cry 79 MIN
VHS / 16mm
Miklos Jansco series
B&W (G) (HUNGARIAN WITH ENGLISH SUBTITLES)
$175.00 rental
Follows a Red soldier, Istvan, who seeks shelter on a lonely farm of a childhood friend following the fall of the first Communist revolution in 1919. Directed by Miklos Jansco.
Civics and Political Systems; Fine Arts; History - World
Dist - KINOIC

The Silence Barrier 30 MIN
U-matic / VHS / 16mm
KnowZone Series
Color (I J H)
$550 purchase - 16 mm, $250 purchase - video _ #5072C
Talks about the problems that deafness causes. Adapted from the Nova series. Hosted by David Morse.
Psychology
Dist - CORF

Silence Equals Death 60 MIN
16mm
Color (G)
Presents an independent production by Rosa von Praunheim in collaboration with Phil Zwickler. Documents the struggle between homosexuals and people with AIDS on one hand, and an indifferent society and government on the other. Focuses on New York's artistic community. Features the work of and interviews with David Wojnarowicz, Keith Haring, Allen Ginsberg, Rafael Gamba and Emilio Cubiero.
Health and Safety; Sociology
Dist - FIRS

The Silencers 105 MIN
U-matic / VHS / 16mm
Color (A)
Stars Dean Martin as Matt Helm, the pleasure - loving playboy super - sleuth who must abandon his indolent life to resume his work for a top - secret U S intelligence agency. Shows how he smashes the 'BIG O,' an organization whose headquarters are in a desert mountain cave.
Literature and Drama
Dist - FI **Prod** - CPC 1966

Silences 12 MIN
U-matic / VHS / 16mm
Color (H C A)
LC 72-702616
Presents a film study of the moral ambiguities created by war as evidenced in the effect of war on the reactions of a Serbian peasant during World War II.
Guidance and Counseling; History - World; Sociology
Dist - MGHT **Prod** - YF 1972

Silent Army 29 MIN
VHS / U-matic
Color
Explores the stories and legends of China's Bronze Age. Uses original music recorded in China with 2400 - year - old bronze chime bells.
Fine Arts; History - World; Sociology
Dist - PBS **Prod** - WTTWTV 1980

Silent Comedy Series
A Bedroom Scandal 25 MIN
Dist - RMIBHF

Silent Countdown 28 MIN
16mm
Color
LC 75-703292
Follows five people on their way home from work, all of whom suffer from high blood pressure, one of whom will not make it home. Reveals their weaknesses and some of the reasons why they discontinued treatment through their discussions with Ben Gazzara.
Health and Safety
Dist - CINSEV **Prod** - CINSEV 1975

Silent Countdown 27 MIN
16mm
Color
Dramatizes the need for detection and continuing treatment of high blood pressure. Features Ben Gazzara.
Health and Safety
Dist - MTP **Prod** - CTHBP

The Silent cry 96 MIN
16mm
Color (G)
$150.00 rental
Exposes a girl in conflict like a kind of diary that reveals her silent cry for help and understanding. Outlines her conflicts, each of which separately may not appear particularly traumatic, but when viewed in conjunction with one another, explain why she can't function in relationships. The film weaves a composite of dreams, distortions, diaries, memories and feelings. Produced by Steve Dwoskin.
Guidance and Counseling; Sociology
Dist - CANCIN

The Silent E Rule 7 MIN
VHS / U-matic
Better Spelling Series
Color
English Language
Dist - DELTAK **Prod** - TELSTR

The Silent Epidemic - Alzheimer's Disease 26 MIN
16mm
Color (A)
LC 82-701112
Examines the disease of senility, Alzheimer's disease. Describes the symptoms of the disease and the difficulty of nursing such patients by family and nursing professionals.
Health and Safety
Dist - FLMLIB **Prod** - GRATV 1982

The Silent explosion 20 MIN
VHS
Color (G)
$15.00 rental
Focuses on the consequences of overpopulation on the world's economies, environments and food supplies. Provides examples of solutions with film footage from developing countries. Stimulates student discussion and awareness of population issues. Produced by the Population Institute.
Business and Economics; Health and Safety; Science - Natural; Sociology
Dist - CMSMS **Prod** - SIERRA 1987

Silent Forest 23 MIN
U-matic / 16mm
Captioned; Color (I J H C)
Explores the kelp forest beneath the ocean's surface along the Pacific coastline of North America. Looks at the community of marine life supported by the kelp and at the pollution that threatens it.
Geography - World; Science - Natural
Dist - BARR **Prod** - TRUSTY

Silent Forest 23 MIN
U-matic / VHS / 16mm
Color (J)
LC 78-700436
Analyzes the kelp forests along the Pacific coastline where thousands of animal species eat, live and die among the towering columns.
Science - Natural
Dist - BARR **Prod** - TRUSTY 1978

The Silent Guard 15 MIN
16mm
Color
Describes the planning, design and sealing of a new Vertical Laminar Flow System for clean rooms. Illustrates proper methods for interior and exterior sealing and caulking.
Industrial and Technical Education
Dist - THIOKL **Prod** - THIOKL 1966

Silent Heritage - the American Indian Series
Myths and Manifest Destiny 20 MIN
The Northern Plains 30 MIN
Dist - UMITV

Silent Heroes 11 MIN
VHS / U-matic / BETA
(G PRO)
Provides the viewer with an informative and visual tour of animal research facilities at University of Texas M. D. Anderson Hospital, and shows how laboratory research animals are contributing to patient care.
Health and Safety; Science
Dist - UTXAH **Prod** - UTXAH 1985

The Silent Killer 12 MIN
16mm / U-matic / VHS
Color (A)
Explores the treatment of hypertension with regimens and medications targeted at bodily renin and sodium levels, as well as more unique causes. Cautions against the overzealous restriction of salt without first testing the patients' sensitivity to sodium.
Health and Safety
Dist - CORF **Prod** - ABCTV 1984

The Silent Killer - a Call to Fitness 20 MIN
16mm
Color
LC 79-700280
Explains how police officers can be aware of physical fitness. Discusses how to gauge and improve fitness.
Civics and Political Systems; Physical Education and Recreation
Dist - TRAVLR **Prod** - TRAVLR 1978

The Silent Killers 19 MIN
U-matic / VHS
Color (C)
$249.00, $149.00 purchase _ #AD - 1393
Focuses on hypertension and silent ischemia. Reveals that from three to five million Americans may have daily episodes of ischemia without being aware of it. High blood pressure is the nation's primary accessory to death, leading to strokes and heart attacks. Profiles a patient struggling to achieve the self - discipline to control high blood pressure.
Health and Safety; Psychology; Science - Natural
Dist - FOTH **Prod** - FOTH

The Silent Killers 60 MIN
U-matic / 16mm / VHS
Last Frontier Series
Color; Mono (G)
MV $225.00 _ MP $550.00
Surveys the different methods used by human beings to protect themselves against shark attacks. Expedition leader John Stoneman tests the devices and concludes tha an understanding of shark behavior is man's best defence against wolves of the sea.
Science - Natural
Dist - CTV **Prod** - MAKOF 1985

Silent Letters - Kn, Wh, Wr, Mb 15 MIN
VHS
Planet Pylon Series
Color (I)
LC 90712897
Uses character Commander Wordstalker from the Space Station Readstar to improve langauge arts skills. Studies silent letters. Includes a worksheet to be completed by students with the aid of series characters.
Education; English Language
Dist - GPN

Silent Lotus - 95
VHS
Reading rainbow series
Color; CC (K P)
$39.95 purchase
Explores the art of communication in a book by Jeanne M Lee and narrated by Lea Salonga. Introduces a little deaf girl who is blessed with the talenet to communicate with her world through dance. LeVar opens the door to nonverbal communication and tries his hand at sign language. Part of a series offering a multicultural approach to generating reading enthusiasm with cross - curricular applications, hosted by LeVar Burton.
Education; English Language; Fine Arts; Guidance and Counseling; Literature and Drama; Social Science
Dist - GPN **Prod** - LNMDP 1993

The Silent Majority 29 MIN
VHS / 16mm
Color (G)
$55.00 rental _ #SMIN - 000
Documents the active and varied lives of the deaf. Explores some myths about deafness. Surveys national legislation, employment and educational needs for the deaf.
Health and Safety
Dist - PBS **Prod** - WHATV

The Silent Minority 26 MIN
U-matic / VHS
Breakthroughs Series
Color
Shows how recent surgical breakthroughs bring fresh hope to victims of Down's Syndrome. Demonstrates that while the condition remains incurable, speech and other defects can now be corrected and appearances radically changed enabling children to integrate with the community.
Health and Safety; Psychology; Sociology
Dist - LANDMK **Prod** - NOMDFI

Silent Minority 60 MIN
VHS / U-matic
Color (K P I J H C G T A S R PRO IND)
Shows a program on the remarkable abilities of the deaf to work and live normal lives. Allows the viewer to experience the world of the deaf and points out some of the difficulties they must overcome.
Education; Guidance and Counseling
Dist - UEUWIS **Prod** - UEUWIS 1978

Silent Movie 20 MIN
16mm
Color
LC 76-702094
Re - creates the style of a 1920's tragicomedy.
Fine Arts
Dist - CANFDC **Prod** - CANFDC 1974

The Silent Neighbor 10 MIN
16mm
Color
Provides a capsule history of the place of abused children in ancient and modern society. Uses a series of vignettes to show typical cases of child abuse and the responsibility of neighbors to make it their business to help.
Sociology
Dist - FILAUD **Prod** - FILAUD 1978

Silent Night 27 MIN
16mm / U-matic / VHS
Color
MP=$400.00Tel. 703 - 241 - 20 30, 800 - 342 - 4336
Pictures in animation the true story of how the popular Christmas carol Silent Night was written in Oberndorf, Germany.
Fine Arts; Religion and Philosophy; Social Science
Dist - LANDMK **Prod** - LANDMK 1981

Silent Night 21 MIN
16mm
Color
LC 78-701627
Tells how a young man, working as a psychiatric technician on Christmas Eve, defies the authority of the head nurse in a subtle way.
Fine Arts
Dist - USC **Prod** - USC 1978

Silent Night - Story of the Christmas Carol 13 MIN
16mm / U-matic / VHS
Color (P I J H C A)
$315, $220 purchase _ #774
Tells how a poem about Christmas was set to music and became one of the most popular carols. Filmed in Austria.
Fine Arts; Social Science
Dist - CORF

Silent Night - Story of the Christmas Carol 13 MIN
16mm / U-matic / VHS
Color (P I J H)
Depicts the events which contributed to the writing of Silent Night, Holy Night in Oberndorf, Austria in 1818.
Religion and Philosophy
Dist - CORF **Prod** - CORF 1953

Silent Night - with Jose Carreras 40 MIN
VHS
Color (G)
$19.95 purchase _ #1189
Journeys to Austria for a traditional 'Salzburg Christmas Eve.' Features Jose Carreras singing Christmas favorites and explaining many holiday customs.
Fine Arts; Religion and Philosophy
Dist - KULTUR

The Silent one
VHS
Color (G)
$24.95 purchase _ #0838
Tells the story of Jonasi, a young Polynesian boy growing up in a remote Pacific village. Reveals that he is isolated from the villagers by his silence and their prejudices, but finds solace in his underwater world, developing a unique bond with a giant white turtle.
History - World; Literature and Drama
Dist - SEVVID

The Silent Partner 105 MIN
VHS / U-matic
Color (C A)
Introduces Miles Cullen, a bank teller who leads a humdrum life until, during a holdup at his bank, the robber unwittingly gives him a chance to pocket most of the money. Reveals that the thwarted thief escapes and then launches a campaign of terror to force Cullen to turn over the loot. Stars Elliott Gould and Christopher Plummer.
Fine Arts
Dist - TIMLIF **Prod** - TIMLIF 1982

Silent pioneers - gay and lesbian elders 42 MIN
VHS / 16mm
Color (H C G)
$650.00, $395.00 purchase, $65.00 rental
Meets eight elderly gays and lesbians who lived through an era when homosexuality was not tolerated, and who battled constantly for self - esteem and survival in a 'straight world.' Includes a male couple still in love after 55 years of living together, a feminist author - political activist living in an intergenerational community in Florida, a former monk turned rancher who has, in his 80s, made peace with being Catholic and gay, a black great - grandmother who revealed her lesbianism to her grandchildren, a feisty ex - waitress from Chicago. Produced by Pat Snyder, Lucy Winer, Harvey Marks and Paula deKoenigsberg in consultation with Senior Action in a Gay Environment - SAGE.
Biography; Health and Safety; Sociology
Dist - FLMLIB

Silent Power 27 MIN
16mm
Color
LC 78-701888
Documents the peaceful uses of nuclear power in the United States space program. Surveys the history of the nuclear power program and discusses developments for the future.
Industrial and Technical Education; Science - Physical; Social Science
Dist - USNAC **Prod** - USDOE 1978

A Silent Rap 6 MIN
16mm
B&W
Presents a romantic encounter whose dramatic action is framed within a racial triangle and sparked by a silent dialogue and a complementary music track.
Sociology
Dist - BLKFMF **Prod** - BLKFMF

Silent reversal 12 MIN
16mm
Color (G)
$25.00 rental
Studies motion with a film that does not end, is never rewound and each frame is seen twice in a single viewing. Resembles a palidrome which illustrates Chicago's 'elevated' shuttling passengers to death. Produced by Louis Hock.
Fine Arts
Dist - CANCIN

The Silent Revolution 23 MIN
16mm
B&W (I)
Shows the transformation of an Indian village through cooperative endeavor and highlights the perseverance and idealism of a 'A GRAM SEVAK' (village worker.).
Social Science
Dist - NEDINF **Prod** - INDIA

Silent Revolution 25 MIN
16mm
B&W
Records the successful outcome of the First Malaysia Five Year Plan due to the formation of a committee system. Tells how this system established a two - way channel of intercommunication between government and the people, providing the rural areas with amenities not existing before.
Civics and Political Systems; Geography - World
Dist - PMFMUN **Prod** - FILEM 1967

Silent Safari Series

Baboon	20 MIN
Elephant	11 MIN
Gazelle	11 MIN
Impala	11 MIN
Wildebeest	20 MIN

Dist - EBEC

Silent Sam 16 MIN
VHS / 16mm
Managing Problem People Series
Color (A PRO)
$415.00 purchase, $195.00 rental
Portrays a noncommunicative staff person who has the answers but clams up in group settings. Part of a series on managing 'problem' employees.
Business and Economics; Guidance and Counseling
Dist - VIDART **Prod** - VIDART 1990

Silent Sentinel 14 MIN
16mm
Color
LC FIE61-120
Explains the basic concept of the fleet ballistic missile program and shows all the necessary steps which the Navy must go through to make the Polaris missile operational.
Civics and Political Systems; Industrial and Technical Education
Dist - USNAC **Prod** - USN 1959

Silent Shame - the Sexual Abuse of Children 50 MIN
VHS / U-matic
Color (H C A)
Reveals facts about the nationwide spread of child sexual abuse and pornography. Includes interviews with young victims and the people who abused them, both pedophiles and professional pornography purveyors. Shows undercover shots of the world's largest producers and distributors of child pornography in Europe. Testifies to the lasting damage and cyclical occurrence from generation to generation.
Sociology
Dist - FI **Prod** - NBCNEW

Silent short films by Wheeler Dixon 20 MIN
16mm
B&W; Color (G)
$20.00 rental
Presents Ceilio Drive, a record of a wedding; Waste Motion which recounts a murder on Christopher Street; Gaze, a photo - document of a mural the filmmaker completed in 1974; A Brief History of Japan 1939 - 1945; and Cutting Room Newsreel which shows pre - editing of his film, Un Petit Examen.
Fine Arts
Dist - CANCIN **Prod** - WWDIXO 1987

Silent skys 26 MIN
VHS
Challenge of the seas series
Color (I J H)
$225.00 purchase
Reveals that Florida Bay lies at the souther edge of the Florida Everglades. Discloses that the Bay is miles of shallow, warm water, bound on its south by the Florida Keys and home to many species of fish, is the breeding ground for lemon sharks and feeding ground for dolphins. Part of a 26 - part series on the oceans.
Geography - United States; Science - Natural; Science - Physical
Dist - LANDMK **Prod** - LANDMK 1991

The Silent sniper 7 MIN
U-matic / BETA / VHS
Color (IND G)
$495.00 purchase _ #801 - 06
Discusses the dangers of hydrogen sulfide, H2S. States emphatically that if a worker goes down, every worker left standing must leave the area immediately, sound an alarm, and don appropriate breathing apparatus before attempting a rescue.
Health and Safety; Industrial and Technical Education; Psychology
Dist - ITSC **Prod** - SOCC

Silent Speech 50 MIN
U-matic / VHS / 16mm
Color (C A)
Reviews the work of French biologist Hubert Montagner in the field of nonverbal communication among young children. Shows that young children exhibit complex social interactions guided entirely by gesture.
Psychology
Dist - FI **Prod** - BBCTV 1981

The Silent Traveler 9 MIN
16mm
Color (PRO)
Demonstrates the techniques of application and interpretation of the Tuberculine Tine Test and includes a statement by Luther Terry, Surgeon General of the U S Public Health Service, on the seriousness of tuberculosis.
Health and Safety
Dist - LEDR **Prod** - ACYLLD 1964

Silent victory 60 MIN
VHS
Color & B&W (G)
$24.99 purchase
Focuses on the role of submarines in the naval battles of World War II.
History - United States
Dist - DANEHA **Prod** - DANEHA 1993

Silent Walls 28 MIN
16mm
No Place Like Home Series
Color
LC 74-706245
Examines deafness and the problems of deaf people who must adjust to a silent world. Shows the training of deaf people to communicate, to find employment and to bridge the gap of isolation and alienation. Demonstrates new office equipment designed especially for the deaf by deaf persons.
Guidance and Counseling; Health and Safety; Psychology
Dist - USNAC **Prod** - USSRS 1973

Silent warnings from the ocean 50 MIN
VHS
Fragile planet series
Color; PAL (G)
PdS30 purchase
Examines marine pollution and its effects on the recycling of ocean water and the environment. Incorporates the latest scientific data and theories, the participation of some of the world's leading scientists and institutions, as well as the cooperation of NASA to examine the 'Fragile Planet.' Asks whether present methods of pollution control, including legal restrictions, are adequate or not. Part of a two - part series. Contact distributor about availability outside the United Kingdom.
Geography - World; Science - Natural; Science - Physical
Dist - ACADEM

The Silent Witness 55 MIN
16mm
Color (H C G T A)
Shows mystery and speculation surrounding the Shroud of Turin since its first public display in the 1350s. Now preserved in the cathedral of Turin, Italy, it bears a remarkable image, a full length, photographic negative imprint of a man's body. Many believe it to be the cloth in which Christ was buried. A fascinating detective story involving art historians, Interpol experts, forensic evidence, JPL NASA image research and Oxford historians. The startling results unfold dramatically, but the conclusions are left up to the viewer.
Fine Arts; Religion and Philosophy
Dist - WHLION **Prod** - WHLION 1979

The Silent witness 55 MIN
VHS
Color (G R)
$69.95 purchase _ #S01417
Presents evidence for the authenticity of the Shroud of Turin, an ancient cloth bearing the image of a man who had been crucified. Reveals that many believe it was the burial cloth of Jesus. Considers evidence ranging from ancient legends to computer image analysis of the cloth. Based on the book 'The Shroud of Turin' by Ian Wilson.
History - World; Religion and Philosophy; Sociology
Dist - UILL

The Silent Witness 55 MIN
U-matic / VHS / 16mm
Color
LC 79-700967
Investigates the possibility that the Shroud of Turin was the burial garment worn by Jesus Christ. Interviews experts from various fields who say that the shroud is either authentic or the most clever fraud in the history of man.
History - World; Religion and Philosophy; Sociology
Dist - PFP **Prod** - SCREEP 1979

Silent World, Muffled World 28 MIN
16mm

Color (PRO)
LC FIA66-634
Relates the difficulties of speech, education and normal living for the deafened, and shows new methods of education and rehabilitation. Uses animation to explain mechanics of hearing and types of impairment. Narrated by Gregory Peck.
Education; Health and Safety; Psychology
Dist - USNAC **Prod** - USPHS 1966

The Silent World of Jim 14 MIN
16mm
Color (S)
LC 74-703672
Describes, without narration, the adventures of a seven - year - old deaf boy in order to help deaf children develop an awareness of safety. Includes an introduction by Nanette Fabray.
Guidance and Counseling; Health and Safety; Psychology; Science - Natural
Dist - INMATI **Prod** - INMATI 1974

Silhouettes 15 MIN
VHS / 16mm
Drawing with Paul Ringler Series
Color (I H)
$125.00 purchase, $25.00 rental
Offers suggestions and reasons for drawing silhouettes that convey information.
Fine Arts; Industrial and Technical Education
Dist - AITECH **Prod** - OETVA 1988

Silhouettes - 19 15 MIN
VHS
Drawing with Paul Ringler Series
Color (I)
$125.00 purchase
Presents suggestions and reasons for drawing silhouettes that convey information. Emphasizes the drawing process, for older students, rather than drawing specific objects. Part of a thirty - part series.
Fine Arts
Dist - AITECH **Prod** - OETVA 1988

The Silhouettes of Gorden Vales 26 MIN
U-matic / VHS
Color
Portrays Gordon Vales, an artist whose life began in a facility for the mentally handicapped but who developed a talent for tearing well - formed silhouettes from paper.
Biography; Fine Arts; Psychology
Dist - MEDIPR **Prod** - MEDIPR 1980

The Silhouettes of Gordon Vales 26 MIN
16mm
Color
LC 81-700468
Introduces Gordon Vales, a 45 - year - old retarded man who discusses his life in an institution and how he subsequently learned to live and care for himself in his own apartment.
Education; Psychology
Dist - ARCS **Prod** - ARCS 1981

The Silicon chip
U-matic / VHS
Audio visual library of computer education series
Color
Provides an explanation of the evolution, appearance, construction and manufacture of integrated circuits. Presents the use of computers as an example for tracing out the history of electronics and the development of miroelectronic techniques.
Business and Economics; Mathematics
Dist - PRISPR **Prod** - PRISPR

Silicon Controlled Rectifiers
VHS
Industrial Electronics Training Program Series
$99.00 purchase _ #RPVCI8
Industrial and Technical Education
Dist - CAREER **Prod** - CAREER

Silicon factor series
And what of the future 40 MIN
Now the Chips are Down 50 MIN
So What's it all about 40 MIN
Dist - FI

Silicone Implant Arthoplasty 17 MIN
VHS / U-matic
Color (PRO)
Shows silicone implant arthoplasty.
Health and Safety
Dist - WFP **Prod** - WFP

Silicone Implant for the Correction of Impotence 10 MIN
16mm
Color
LC 75-702312
Demonstrates a complete repair procedure for impotence using a silicone implant. Illustrates pre - and post - operative measures.
Science
Dist - EATONL **Prod** - EATONL 1965

Silk 22 MIN
16mm / U-matic / VHS
Color (J H)
LC 80-700683
Provides a history of silk and illustrates the production of silk, including the life cycle of the silkworm, reeling the silk thread from the cocoons, and dyeing, weaving, and printing the fabric.
Industrial and Technical Education
Dist - IFB **Prod** - BHA 1977

Silk Flower Making - Part 2 60 MIN
VHS
Morris Flower Series
(A)
$29.95 _ #MX1317V
Complements part one of the silk flower making pair. Continues instruction on techniques used in making silk flowers.
Science - Natural
Dist - CAMV **Prod** - CAMV

Silk Flower Making - Part One 60 MIN
VHS
Morris Flower Series
(A)
$29.95 _ #MX1316V
Teaches the viewer basic techniques involved in making silk flower arrangements.
Science - Natural
Dist - CAMV **Prod** - CAMV

Silk Flower Making, Pt 1 60 MIN
VHS / BETA
Crafts and Decorating Series
Color
Demonstrates making silk flowers. Includes carnations, camellias, peonies, chrysanthemums and rhododendrons.
Fine Arts
Dist - MOHOMV **Prod** - MOHOMV

Silk Flower Making, Pt 1 60 MIN
VHS / 16mm
(G)
$39.95 purchase _ #VT1050
Shows how to make carnations, rhododendrons, camellias, chrysanthemums and peonies out of silk.
Fine Arts
Dist - RMIBHF **Prod** - RMIBHF

Silk Flower Making, Pt 2 60 MIN
BETA / VHS
Crafts and Decorating Series
Color
Demonstrates making silk flowers. Includes roses, gardenias, tulips, daffodils and delphiniums.
Fine Arts
Dist - MOHOMV **Prod** - MOHOMV

Silk Flower Making, Pt 2 60 MIN
VHS / 16mm
(G)
$39.95 purchase _ #VT1051
Shows how to make roses, gardenias, tulips, daffodils and delphiniums out of silk.
Fine Arts
Dist - RMIBHF **Prod** - RMIBHF

Silk Industry in India 28 MIN
16mm
Color (I)
Reports on the silk industry of India today. Describes the scientific methods of breeding silk worms, the cultivation of mulberry leaves, the extraction of silk from cocoons and the weaving of silk.
Agriculture; Business and Economics
Dist - NEDINF **Prod** - INDIA

Silk Moth 7 MIN
U-matic / VHS / 16mm
See 'N Tell Series
Color (K P I)
LC 79-706313
Uses microphotography to reveal the egg - laying process of the silk moth and to show the caterpillars as they emerge from the egg. Follows the process of metamorphosis from the spinning of the cocoon, and the transformation into a chrysalis to the emergence of the silk moth twenty days later.
Science - Natural
Dist - FI **Prod** - PMI 1970

Silk reeling exercises 60 MIN
VHS
Color (G)
$49.95 purchase _ #1176
Presents Zhang Xia Xin, a T'ai chi practitioner, teaching 25 silk reeling cocoon exercises - chan ssu chin. Shows how these non - impact exercises are traditionally done to create relaxation, to loosen the 18 joints of the body, and to increase flexibility and energy. Designed for beginners, the program uses multiple repetitions at a slow pace. Two martial arts applications are shown.
Physical Education and Recreation
Dist - WAYF

Silk road 99 MIN
VHS
Color (G) (JAPANESE WITH ENGLISH SUBTITLES)
$89.95 purchase _ #VMN5508
Stars Toshiyuki Nishada and Anna Nakagawa Kaichi Sato in a story of fierce battles and fighting along the Silk Road. Directed by Junya Sato.
Fine Arts; Literature and Drama
Dist - CHTSUI

The Silk road - China's bridge to the west series
China - glories of ancient Chang - an - Xi - an 45 MIN
Dist - GA
INSTRU

Silk road - China's bridge to the West series
China - 1,000 kilometers beyond the Yellow River 45 MIN
Dist - INSTRU

Silk road II series
Presents a video produced by China Central Television to provide the sights, sounds, and historic dramas of historic and inaccessible locations on the fabled Silk Road. Features the art, culture, and history that live on in artifacts and the daily lives of the residents. Supplements the original The Silk Road series, which also pictured seldom-seen sights on the historic road linking Europe to China that was first traveled by Marco Polo.
A Heat wave called Turfan 55 MIN
Journey into music 55 MIN
Khotan - oasis of silk and jade 55 MIN
Two roads to the Pamirs 55 MIN
Where horses fly like the wind 55 MIN
Dist - CAMV

The Silk Road pack collector's gift box 360 MIN
VHS
Color (G)
$149.95 purchase _ #CPM1008
Presents six documentaries focused on the Silk Road linking China and Europe and traveled by Marco Polo. Explores the art, culture and history of China. Includes a soundtrack by Kitaro. Produced by Central Park Media.
Fine Arts; Geography - World; History - World
Dist - CHTSUI

Silk road series
Through the Tian Shan Mountains by rail 60 MIN
Dist - CAMV
CHTSUI

Silk road series
Across the Taklamakan Desert 60 MIN
Art gallery in the desert 60 MIN
Collector's gift box II 360 MIN
The Dark castle 60 MIN
Glories of ancient Chuang - An 60 MIN
A Heat wave called Turfan - Volume 8 60 MIN
In Search of the kingdom of Lou - lan 60 MIN
Journey into music - south through the Tian Shan Mountains - Volume 10 60 MIN
Khotan - oasis of silk and jade - Volume 7 60 MIN
One thousand kilmeters beyond Yellow River 60 MIN
Two roads to the Pamirs - Volume 12 60 MIN
Where horses fly like the wind - Volume 11 60 MIN
Dist - CHTSUI

Silk Screen Fundamentals 14 MIN
16mm / U-matic / VHS
Color (J H C)
LC 79-711102
Presents an introduction to the art of paper stencil and silk screening. Step by step procedures involved in constructing a 'DO - IT - YOURSELF' stretcher frame, stretching the commerical frame, cutting paper stencils, registering the printing stock, and finally, printing the stencils are demonstrated. Pictures the tools used in silk screen, with emphasis on care and safety.
Fine Arts
Dist - PHENIX **Prod** - PHENIX 1969

Silk Screen Printing 10 MIN
16mm
Color; B&W (H C A)
Demonstrates the technique whereby hand screen printing has been brought up to date. Shows preparation, washing, dyeing, printing and completion.
Fine Arts; Industrial and Technical Education
Dist - AVED **Prod** - ALLMOR 1957

Silk Screen Techniques 14 MIN
16mm / U-matic / VHS
Color (J H C)
LC 72-711103
Presents four professional artists, who demonstrate advanced silk - screen techniques. Includes the clay and glue tusche methods, the lacquer film method and the photo silk - screen process.
Fine Arts
Dist - PHENIX **Prod** - PHENIX 1969

Silkmaking in China 13 MIN
VHS / U-matic
Color (P I J)
Shows the process of silkmaking in a Chinese commune and provides an insight into village life in the People's Republic of China.
Civics and Political Systems; Fine Arts; Psychology; Science - Natural; Sociology
Dist - ATLAP **Prod** - ATLAP

Silkscreen 14 MIN
VHS
Rediscovery Art Media Series
Color
$69.95 purchase _ #4424
Illustrated are the basic principles of silkscreen printing and how to use various materials for making stencils.
Fine Arts
Dist - AIMS **Prod** - AIMS

Silkscreen 14 MIN
U-matic / VHS / 16mm
Rediscovery - Art Media (Spanish Series
Color (I) (SPANISH)
Illustrates the basic principles involved in silkscreen printing and demonstrates the use of various materials for making stencils.
Fine Arts; Foreign Language
Dist - AIMS **Prod** - ACI 1967

Silkscreen 14 MIN
U-matic / VHS / 16mm
(French (from the Rediscovery - Art Media (French Series
Color (I)
Illustrates the basic principles involved in silkscreen printing and demonstrates the use of various materials for making stencils.
Fine Arts; Foreign Language; Physical Education and Recreation
Dist - AIMS **Prod** - ACI 1967

Silkscreen 15 MIN
U-matic / VHS / 16mm
Rediscovery - Art Media Series
Color (I)
LC FIA67-1525
Illustrates the basic principles involved in silk screen printing, shows the building of a screen and demonstrates ways for creating silk screen stencils from simple to more complex film and tusche - and - glue methods. Shows the uses and expressive ideas to which this medium may be adapted.
Fine Arts; Industrial and Technical Education
Dist - AIMS **Prod** - ACI 1967

Silkscreening 30 MIN
VHS / U-matic
Arts and Crafts Series
Color (H A)
LC 81-707006
Demonstrates the materials and equipment needed to develop a silkscreen print. Shows how to cut a master, adhere it to the screen, mask the screen, register the print, print the design, and clean the silkscreen frame.
Fine Arts
Dist - GPN **Prod** - GPN 1981

The Silkworm - 32 11 MIN
VHS / U-matic
Animal families series
Color (K P I)
$225.00, $195.00 purchase _ #V165
Shows silkworms weaving their silk cocoons. Gives a close - up look at a silkworm's life cycle. Looks at the intricate and delicate method for farming silkworms that produces one of the most commercially valuable materials. Part of a series on animal families.
Agriculture; Home Economics; Science - Natural
Dist - BARR **Prod** - GREATT 1989

Silly Sidney 10 MIN
U-matic / VHS
Happy Time Adventure Series
Color (K P)
$29.95 purchase _ #VS007
Presents an adaptation of the book Silly Sidney. Contains a 32 page hardcover book and a video.
English Language; Literature and Drama
Dist - TROLA

Silos 30 MIN
VHS / U-matic
Agricultural Accidents and Rescue Series
Color
Discusses removal of a patient from inside a tower silo. Covers the use of a Z - rig as well as silo gases and Farmer's Lung.
Agriculture; Health and Safety
Dist - PSU **Prod** - PSU

Silver 30 MIN
U-matic
Antiques series
Color
Fine Arts
Dist - PBS **Prod** - NHMNET

Silver Bears 113 MIN
16mm
Color
Centers on a financial speculator who manipulates amorous adventures and the world silver market with equal ease. Stars Michael Caine and Cybill Shepherd.
Fine Arts
Dist - SWANK **Prod** - CPC

Silver Blaze 31 MIN
U-matic / VHS / 16mm
Classics, Dark and Dangerous Series
Color (H C A)
LC 76-703937
Presents an adaptation of the story 'Silver 'Blaze by Sir Arthur Conan Doyle, about the disappearance of a famous racing horse and the murder of his trainer which leads to an investigation by Sherlock Holmes.
Fine Arts; Literature and Drama; Physical Education and Recreation
Dist - LCOA **Prod** - LCOA 1977

Silver Blaze 31 MIN
16mm / U-matic / VHS
Classics Dark and Dangerous (Spanish Series
Color (P) (SPANISH)
Tells the story of the theft of a racehorse, Silver Blaze. Based on a story by Sir Arthur Conan Doyle.
Foreign Language; Literature and Drama
Dist - LCOA **Prod** - LCOA 1977

Silver Brazing and Soft Soldering
U-matic / VHS
Oxyacetylene Welding - Spanish Series
Color (SPANISH)
Foreign Language; Industrial and Technical Education
Dist - VTRI **Prod** - VTRI

The Silver chair 174 MIN
VHS
Chronicles of Narnia - Wonderworks collection series
Color (I J H)
$29.95 purchase _ #SIL02
Presents a segment from the C S Lewis fantasy in which animals speak, mythical creatures roam and children fight an epic battle against evil.
Guidance and Counseling; Literature and Drama
Dist - KNOWUN **Prod** - PBS

Silver City 60 MIN
VHS / U-matic
Rainbow Movie of the Week Series
Color (J A)
Reveals how the four, teenage members of a multi - ethnic rock and soul band pursue a recording career amid the tarnish and gleam of Hollywood.
Fine Arts; Sociology
Dist - GPN **Prod** - RAINTV 1981

The Silver cornet 29 MIN
U-matic / VHS
Long ago and far away series
Color (P)
$250.00 purchase _ #HP - 6078C
Dramatizes the story of Adam, a young English boy who has found a cornet and is determined to learn how to play it. Shows that he tries to get the cornet player from the local orchestra to teach him, to no avail. One day the cornet player is involved in a serious rock - climbing accident. Adam saves him but loses his cornet, and earns a special gift from the musician. Features James Earl Jones as host. Part of the Long Ago and Far Away Series.
Fine Arts; Literature and Drama
Dist - CORF **Prod** - WGBHTV 1989

The Silver Cow 12 MIN
VHS / U-matic
Color; Mono (K P I)
Presents a young cowherd, his harp, and the shining white cow it summons from the depths of a mountain lake. To convey the delicate balance between the tale's concrete storyline and its musical undertones, a haunting musical score, and a narration in melodious Welsh tones have been added to Hutton's luminous watercolor images. This tale of the cowherd's purity, his struggle with a proud and greedy father, and their inevitable confrontation springs from the author's childhood travels to Aberdovey, Wales.
English Language; Literature and Drama
Dist - WWS **Prod** - WWS 1985

The Silver Eagle - Master of the Skies 16 MIN
16mm
B&W
LC 79-700823
Offers a satirical reminder of the importance of physical and mental fitness among aviation pilots. Depicts the Silver Eagle, a pilot who believes he has extraordinary judgment and flying prowess, to illustrate the adverse effects of alcohol, medicines, stress and fatigue.
Industrial and Technical Education
Dist - USNAC **Prod** - USFAA 1979

The Silver fox and Sam Davenport 47 MIN
U-matic / VHS / 16mm
Animal featurettes series; Set 3
Color (I J H)
LC 79-701720
Tells how a fox escapes a foxhunt by jumping on a farmer's haywagon in turn - of - the - century New England. Shows the pursuit that follows as the farmer recognizes the value of the stowaway and begins his own foxhunt.
Literature and Drama
Dist - CORF **Prod** - DISNEY 1962

Silver Fox Rodeo 8 MIN
16mm
Color
LC 75-703702
Shows U S Navy pilots and airmen at work and at play. Shows enlisted personnel and officers flying over the Sierras, riding broncos and wild burros and milking wild cows.
Civics and Political Systems; Physical Education and Recreation
Dist - USNAC **Prod** - USN 1974

Silver Gull 25 MIN
U-matic
Animal Wonder Down Under Series
Color (I J H)
Shows the behavior and ecology of the Silver Gull.
Geography - World; Science - Natural
Dist - CEPRO **Prod** - CEPRO

Silver Harvest 25 MIN
16mm
Color
LC 79-701015
Documents the Italian fishing families that came to Monterey, California, to fish schooling sardines in the 1930's. Shows special equipment that was designed and emphasizes the unique heritage which developed.
Business and Economics; Geography - United States; History - United States; Industrial and Technical Education; Sociology
Dist - MONSAV **Prod** - MONSAV 1979

Silver into Gold 24 MIN
U-matic / VHS / 16mm
Color (J H C G)
$515, $360, $390 _ #C443
Demonstrates that rewards await those who put aside artificial barriers and pursue any worthwhile goals with intelligence and vigor. Shows all viewers the power of venturing forward with determination to make the most of natural talents at any age.
Guidance and Counseling; Literature and Drama; Physical Education and Recreation; Psychology
Dist - BARR **Prod** - BARR 1987

Silver Lining 24 MIN
U-matic / VHS / 16mm
Color (H C A)
LC 77-700871
Surveys art works in Illinois produced under the Work Progress Administration program between 1933 and 1943. Includes scenes of the murals of the old post office building in Murphysboro and stained glass windows at the University of Illinois Medical Center. Conducts interviews with artists who participated in the program and presents archival footage of some of the WPA artists at work.
Fine Arts; History - United States
Dist - MCFI **Prod** - MCFI 1977

Silver Lining 28 MIN
16mm
Color
LC 76-702672
Features two senior citizens who solve their difficult problems through the assistance of the Salvation Army.
Religion and Philosophy; Sociology
Dist - MTP **Prod** - SALVA 1976

Silver Linings 28 MIN
U-matic

Color
Features the Salvation Army's activities which help senior citizens cope with their problems. Focuses on a few members of the group whose lives were altered by the activities. Not available to school audiences.
Guidance and Counseling; Health and Safety; Sociology
Dist - MTP **Prod** - SALVA

The Silver Maiden 12 MIN
U-matic / VHS / 16mm
Color (H C A)
Describes the rediscovered love of an elderly man and woman meeting in a park. Based on the play A Sunny Morning by Joaquin and Serafin Quintero. Stars Eli Wallach and Jacqueline Brookes.
Fine Arts; Literature and Drama
Dist - CAROUF **Prod** - SPIELD

The Silver mine and not for sale 30 MIN
VHS
Davey and Goliath series
Color (P I R)
$19.95 purchase, $10.00 rental _ #4 - 8831
Presents two 15 - minute 'Davey and Goliath' episodes. 'The Silver Mine' deals with the issue of free will, as Davey learns that he, and not God, is responsible for getting into an accident at a mine. 'Not for Sale' finds Davey trying to buy his dad's forgiveness for losing one of his dad's skis. Produced by the Evangelical Lutheran Church in America.
Literature and Drama; Religion and Philosophy
Dist - APH

Silver Nitrate Wet Treatment of Burns 26 MIN
16mm
Color (PRO)
Describes treatment of burns with continuously wet dressings with bacteriostatic control with five - tenths percent silver nitrate.
Health and Safety; Science
Dist - ACY **Prod** - ACYDGD 1996

The Silver Pony 7 MIN
U-matic / VHS / 16mm
Color (K P I)
LC 81-701568
Tells an animated story about a boy who escapes in his imagination on a winged pony, bringing joy to others. Illustrates the power of imagination. Based on the book The Silver Pony by Lynd Ward.
Fine Arts; Guidance and Counseling; Literature and Drama
Dist - CF **Prod** - BOSUST 1981

The Silver Safari 28 MIN
16mm
Color
LC 77-701833
Shows car racing at the 25th Safari Rally in Kenya, a five - day road race which started with 68 cars and ended with only 11 cars still running.
Geography - World; Physical Education and Recreation
Dist - KLEINW **Prod** - KLEINW 1977

Silver shine - jazz musician Andy Hamilton 26 MIN
VHS
Color (H C G)
$295.00 purchase, $55.00 rental
Incorporates archival footage, interviews and performance to capture the social climate of the black urban jazz scene in England. Portrays musican Andy Hamilton and shows the similarity between black experience in the United Kingdom and the United States - prejudice, poverty, creativity. Produced by Sunandan Walia, directed by Yugesh Walia.
Fine Arts; Geography - World; Sociology
Dist - FLMLIB

The Silver trumpeter 26 MIN
VHS / U-matic
Survival in nature series
Color (J H)
$275.00, $325.00 purchase, $50.00 rental
Documents the trumpeter swan's remarkable recovery from near extinction last century.
Science - Natural
Dist - NDIM **Prod** - SURVAN 1990

The Silver Whistle 17 MIN
U-matic / VHS / 16mm
Color (P I)
LC 80-701955
Uses puppet animation to tell the story of a girl who sets out to make her way in the world, aided only by a silver whistle. Based on the children's book The Silver Whistle by Jay Williams.
Literature and Drama
Dist - ALTSUL **Prod** - ALTSUL 1980

Silver Wings and Santiago Blue 59 MIN
U-matic / VHS
Color
Uses old newsreels, Air Force films and footage of the Congressional hearing which gave recognition to the 1,000 women of the Woman's Auxiliary Ferry Squadron and the Women's Air Force Service Pilots for their service during World War II.
Civics and Political Systems; History - United States; Sociology
Dist - PBS **Prod** - ADMKNG 1980

Silver Wires, Golden Wings 28 MIN
16mm
Color
Details the efforts of electric utilities to prevent the electrocution of birds of prey on power lines. Shows how many utilities have installed special nesting platforms on transmission towers.
Industrial and Technical Education; Science - Natural; Social Science
Dist - MTP **Prod** - EEI

Silverberg 28 MIN
16mm
Color (G)
_ #106C 0180 204
Portrays the engraving artist Silverberg as a craftsman and a thinker.
Fine Arts
Dist - CFLMDC **Prod** - NFBC 1980

Silversmith of Williamsburg 44 MIN
16mm / U-matic / VHS
Color (IND)
LC 70-713169;
Documents the handcrafting of a 1765 coffee pot from a crucible of scrap silver to the fashioning of the product by master silversmith William De Matteo. Discusses methods employed, the properties of silver, and the evolution of design.
Fine Arts; Industrial and Technical Education
Dist - CWMS **Prod** - CWMS 1971

The Silversword alliance - the evolution of plants in an island setting 36 MIN
VHS
Evolution series
Color (G C)
$150.00 purchase, $19.50 rental _ #36267
Provides a comparison of morphology, genetic make - up and reproductive characteristics among an alliance of 28 genetically similar Hawaiian plants, consisting of the genera Argyroxiphium, Dubautia and Wilkesia. Shows how proof of common ancestry and probable origin are sought through application of scientific method. Examines environment and survival characteristics of different members. Part of a ten - part series exploring evolutionary selection and adaptation.
History - United States; Science - Natural
Dist - PSU **Prod** - BBC 1992

Similar Shapes 20 MIN
VHS / U-matic
Math Topics - Trigonometry Series
Color (J H C)
Mathematics
Dist - FI **Prod** - BBCTV

Similar Triangles 8 MIN
U-matic / VHS / 16mm
Triangle Series
Color (J H A)
LC 81-700611
Investigates the families of similar triangles. Conveys the concept that triangles are similar if their corresponding angles are equal and their corresponding sides are proportional.
Mathematics
Dist - IFB **Prod** - CORNW 1976

Similar Triangles in Use 11 MIN
U-matic / VHS / 16mm
Color (J H C)
LC 70-713563
Presents the practical value of knowing that corresponding sides of similar triangles are proportional. Shows the use of the surveyor's quadrant and sextant.
Mathematics
Dist - IFB **Prod** - IFB 1962

Similarities in Wave Behavior 27 MIN
Videoreel / VHS
B&W
Considers the similarities in the behavior of waves of various mechanical, electrical, acoustical and optical wave systems. Demonstrates many aspects of wave behavior through the use of several specially built torsion wave machines.
Science - Physical
Dist - EDC **Prod** - NCEEF

Similarity 30 MIN
VHS
Geometry series
Color (H)
$125.00 purchase _ #7008
Explains similarity. Part of a 16 - part series on geometry.
Mathematics
Dist - LANDMK **Prod** - LANDMK

Similarity 30 MIN
VHS
Mathematics Series
Color (J)
LC 90713155
Discusses similarity. The 149th of 157 installments in the Mathematics Series.
Mathematics
Dist - GPN

Simla 29 MIN
VHS / U-matic
Journey into India Series
Color (G)
MV=$195.00
Reveals that Simla was the summer capital of the British Raj. Today it is still the summer retreat of middle class Indians who leave the heat of the plains for the cool hills.
Geography - World; History - World
Dist - LANDMK **Prod** - LANDMK 1986

Simmering and poaching 10 MIN
VHS / 16mm / U-matic
Professional food preparation and service program series
Color (J)
LC 74-700232
Demonstrates methods of cooking in liquids including totally submerged meats and poultry as well as poached items. Defines and differentiates various moist meat preparation techniques. Shows use of steam kettles and top - of - range cooking. Discusses boiling versus simmering and includes techniques in braising and stewing.
Home Economics
Dist - NEM **Prod** - NEM 1973

Simon 5 MIN
VHS
Color (P)
$49.95 purchase _ #8376
Presents an animated film about Simon, a boy who is perfectly normal except that he was born without a nose. Teaches children to understand and value difference and to realize that everyone is special.
Guidance and Counseling; Literature and Drama
Dist - AIMS **Prod** - LENCER 1991

Simon Boccanegra 150 MIN
VHS
Color (S) (ITALIAN)
$39.95 purchase _ #384 - 9609
Presents a stunning Metropolitan Opera production of 'Simon Boccanegra' by Verdi. Features baritone Sherrill Milnes in the role of Boccanegra, an Italian Renaissance rule willing to die to unite his warring people. James Levine conducts, Anna Tomowa - Sintow, Vasile Moldoveanu and Paul Plishka also star in this opera which was disliked by Verdi's 19th - century contemporaries.
Fine Arts; Foreign Language
Dist - FI **Prod** - PAR 1988

Simon Bolivar - the Great Liberator 58 MIN
U-matic / VHS
Color (C)
$299.00, $199.00 purchase _ #AD - 816
Portrays Simon Bolivar, aristocratic revolutionary, victor in battle and loser to those who considered the revolution their personal mandate. Details how and why Spain lost her colonies, the historic trends and the national heroes responsible for the outcome.
Biography; Foreign Language; History - United States; History - World
Dist - FOTH **Prod** - FOTH

Simon Peter, Fisherman 30 MIN
16mm
B&W (J)
Shows the effect of Jesus on the life of strong, impetuous Simon Peter. Shows aspects of home and social life of the time and the place.
Religion and Philosophy
Dist - CAFM **Prod** - CAFM

Simon Wiesenthal - freedom is not a gift from heaven 60 MIN
VHS
Willy Lindwer collection series
Color (G) (DUTCH W/ENGLISH SUBTITLES)
$39.95 purchase _ #658
Focuses on Nazi hunter Simon Wiesenthal who reveals for the first time on camera his life story. Tells of his youth in the Ukraine, his experiences during the war in various concentration camps and of his liberation by American soldiers in 1945. Part of eight documentaries on the Holocaust.
History - World
Dist - ERGOM **Prod** - LINDWE

Simone De Beauvoir - La Femme Rompue 90 MIN
U-matic / VHS
Color (C) (FRENCH)
$299.00, $199.00 purchase _ #AD - 941
Presents 'La Femme Rompue' by Simone de Beauvoir in French.
Foreign Language; History - World; Literature and Drama; Psychology; Sociology
Dist - FOTH **Prod** - FOTH

Simone Forti - Solo no 1 8 MIN
VHS / U-matic
B&W
Features the movements of grizzly and polar bears.
Fine Arts; Science - Natural
Dist - ARTINC **Prod** - ARTINC

Simone Forti - Three Grizzlies 15 MIN
U-matic / VHS
B&W
Features the movements of grizzly and polar bears.
Fine Arts; Science - Natural
Dist - ARTINC **Prod** - ARTINC

Simone Veil 40 MIN
VHS
Women in politics series
Color (G)
$60.00 rental, $99.00 purchase
Focuses on Simone Veil, one of France's most popular politicians. Reveals her girlhood experiences of Auschwitz and Belsen, her lifelong distaste for sectarianism and party politics and her pioneering legislation for abortion. Part of a six part series of documentaries profiling women politicians. Produced by Lowri Gwilym.
Civics and Political Systems; Fine Arts; History - World; Sociology
Dist - WMEN

Simon's Book
VHS / 35mm strip
ALA Notable Children's Filmstrips Series
Color (K)
$33.00 purchase
Presents a children's story. Part of the American Library Association series.
English Language; Literature and Drama
Dist - PELLER

Simon's book - 17
VHS
Reading rainbow series
Color; CC (K P)
$39.95 purchase
Shows how doodles come to 'monstrous' life in the book, narrated by Ruby Dee. Features author - illustrator Henrik Drescher who demonstrates how his ideas formed. Visits a printing plant with Levar Burton to show how the final product - the book - was produced. Part of a series offering a multicultural approach to generating reading enthusiasm with cross - curricular applications, hosted by LeVar Burton.
English Language; Literature and Drama
Dist - GPN **Prod** - LNMDP

Simpatico Means Venezuela 28 MIN
16mm
Color (C A)
LC FIA67-609
Presents an air - travel film about Venezuela, its history and natural resources. Includes scenes of Caracas, the capital city, the nearby jungles and Lake Maracaibo.
Geography - World
Dist - MCDO **Prod** - DAC 1966

Simpatico Means Venezuela 28 MIN
16mm
Color (I) (SPANISH)
LC FIA67-609
Presents an air - travel film about Venezuela, its history and natural resources. Includes scenes of Caracas, the capital city, the nearby jungles and Lake Maracaibo.
Foreign Language; Geography - World
Dist - MCDO **Prod** - DAC 1966

The Simple Accident 10 MIN
16mm / U-matic / VHS
Color (P I)
LC 76-702157
A revised version of the 1952 motion picture Why Take Chances. Presents a direct, positive attack on the accident problem. Points out to boys and girls the dangers they face in living and playing. Shows how easily the accidents can be avoided merely by being smart and careful. Portrays a series of carefully selected situations where children may, through carelessness, get hurt.
Health and Safety
Dist - AIMS **Prod** - DAVP 1969

The Simple acts of life 60 MIN
VHS
Moyers - The Power of the word series
Color; Captioned (G)
$59.95 purchase _ #MOPW - 101
Features the 1988 Geraldine R Dodge Poetry Festival in Waterloo Village, New Jersey. Interviews many of the poets present at the festival, including Robert Bly, Galway Kinnell, Sharon Olds, Octavio Paz and William Stafford. Hosted by Bill Moyers.
English Language; Literature and Drama
Dist - PBS

Simple Addressing Modes 30 MIN
U-matic / VHS
MC68000 Microprocessor Series
Color (IND)
Introduces register direct, address register indirect, absolute, immediate and program counter relative addressing modes using 68000 instruction.
Industrial and Technical Education; Mathematics; Sociology
Dist - COLOSU **Prod** - COLOSU

Simple and Compound Machines - How they Work 22 MIN
U-matic / VHS / 16mm
Color (I)
$50 rental _ #9776
Examines the six simple machines and illustrates how they can be combined to create the more complex machines used every day.
Science; Science - Physical
Dist - AIMS **Prod** - SAIF 1984

A Simple Case for Torture, or How to Sleep at Night 60 MIN
U-matic
Color (C)
Experimental film by Martha Rosler.
Fine Arts
Dist - AFA **Prod** - AFA 1983

Simple Ceramics 10 MIN
16mm
Color; B&W (I)
A fruit bowl is made of clay by the hammock - mold method.
Fine Arts
Dist - AVED **Prod** - ALLMOR 1958

A Simple Choice 18 MIN
16mm
Color (IND)
Asks why many accidents occur in industry. Points out how workers often ignore safety rules because of attitudes developed when they were children.
Health and Safety
Dist - JONEST **Prod** - DRUKRR

Simple Chords 29 MIN
Videoreel / VT2
Playing the Guitar I Series
Color
Fine Arts
Dist - PBS **Prod** - KCET

Simple Distillation 12 MIN
VHS / U-matic
Organic Chemistry Laboratory Techniques Series
Color
Clarifies the theoretical principles behind simple distillation. Examines glassware. Shows various heat sources.
Science; Science - Physical
Dist - UCEMC **Prod** - UCLA

Simple distillation 13 MIN
VHS
Chemistry master apprentice series
Color (H C)
$49.95 purchase _ #49 - 7220 - V
Shows the step - by - step assembly of the ground joint apparatus required to separate a mixture by simple distillation. Part of the Chemistry Master Apprentice series.
Science; Science - Physical
Dist - INSTRU **Prod** - CORNRS

Simple Effects for Cinema 26 MIN
U-matic / VHS / 16mm
Color (I J H)
LC 77-701261
Shows the creative and fun aspects of filmmaking and points out the way to create simple visual effects.
Education; Fine Arts
Dist - CAROUF **Prod** - TWTHON 1977

Simple Equations 40 MIN
16mm
B&W
LC 74-705644
Explains axioms and algebraic rules needed to solve simple linear equations. (Kinescope).
Mathematics
Dist - USNAC **Prod** - USAF

Simple Equations - Fractions 20 MIN
16mm
B&W
LC 74-705645
Applies axioms and algebraic rules to rearrangement of several electronic formulas. (Kinescope).
Mathematics
Dist - USNAC **Prod** - USAF

Simple foundation Pt 1 - layout 28 MIN
16mm
Shipbuilding skills series; The Shipfitter; 1
B&W
LC FIE52-1238
Explains, through animation, the layout of a simple foundation, and shows a workman performing the actual operations. Explains how to mark the template with necessary directions.
Industrial and Technical Education
Dist - USNAC **Prod** - USN 1944

Simple Foundation, Pt 3 - Assembly and Installation 23 MIN
16mm
Shipbuilding Skills Series
B&W
LC FIE52-1209
Demonstrates marking location aboard ship, swinging the assembly aboard and welding the deck and the bulkhead after making corrections.
Industrial and Technical Education
Dist - USNAC **Prod** - USN 1944

Simple Foundation, Pt 2 - Duplication and Fabrication 17 MIN
16mm
Shipbuilding Skills Series
B&W
LC FIE52-1240
Shows how the layout man develops the job from the templates. Depicts fastening the template to the steel plate, marking the plate with the center punch or painting the billing on steel. Shows the use of shears, burning torch, cold press and punch.
Industrial and Technical Education
Dist - USNAC **Prod** - USN 1944

Simple Fractions 12 MIN
16mm
Color (T)
Shows how the basic characteristics of fractions can be taught by cutting familiar objects into parts and then reassembling them.
Mathematics
Dist - SF **Prod** - SF 1970

Simple Gifts 54 MIN
16mm
Color
LC FIA66-843
Describes what people seek and the things they can find on a vacation within a 200 mile radius of New York City. Pictures the feudal setting of architect George Nakashima in Bucks County, a yacht racing champion and his sons in Barnegat Bay, a Shaker festival and fox hunt in Old Chatham, New York, the Harkness Ballet in Rhode Island and a climb to the top of the Adirondack's highest mountain.
Geography - United States; Physical Education and Recreation; Social Science; Sociology
Dist - CBSTV **Prod** - WCBSTV 1965

Simple Gifts Series no 12
Issues 30 MIN
Dist - GPN

Simple Gifts Series no 2
History of the Educational Treatment of the Gifted 30 MIN
Dist - GPN

Simple Gifts Series no 3
Identification - Convergent 30 MIN
Dist - GPN

Simple Gifts Series no 4
Identification - Divergent 30 MIN
Dist - GPN

Simple Gifts Series no 5
Self - Awareness 30 MIN
Dist - GPN

Simple Gifts Series no 6
Qualitatively Different Program 30 MIN
Dist - GPN

Simple gifts series
Creativity 30 MIN
Definition of giftedness 30 MIN
Going deeper - No 9 30 MIN
Going faster - No 8 30 MIN
Going wider - No 10 30 MIN

The Helping adult 30 MIN
Dist - GPN

Simple gifts series
December 25, 1914 13 MIN
The Great frost 15 MIN
Memory of Christmas 12 MIN
No Room at the Inn 13 MIN
Dist - TIMLIF

Simple Gifts
Explores the problems and rewards of working with gifted and talented students. Focuses on identifying and meeting their special needs. Presented in a series of 12 half hour programs.
Simple Gifts 30 MIN
Dist - GPN

A Simple Good Time 30 MIN
VHS / U-matic
Journey into Japan Series
Color (J S C G)
MV=$195.00
Shows a group of Japanese factory workers on a weekend holiday tour.
Geography - World; History - World
Dist - LANDMK **Prod** - LANDMK 1986

The Simple interrupted suture 15 MIN
VHS / U-matic
Color (PRO C)
$395.00 purchase, $80.00 rental _ #C870 - VI - 068
Presents a detailed demonstration of surgical knot - tying with the simple interrupted suture. Shows and describes the instruments used in the procedure and presents the procedure twice, once for a basic understanding and the second time as a guide while practicing. Presented by Bruce Dobbs.
Health and Safety
Dist - HSCIC

Simple Investing 60 MIN
U-matic / VHS
How to be a Financially Secure Woman Series
Color
Presents Dr Mary Elizabeth Schlayer talking with moderator Susan Wright about simple investing for women.
Business and Economics; Sociology
Dist - KUHTTV **Prod** - KUHTTV

The Simple Lens - an Introduction 12 MIN
U-matic / VHS / 16mm
Color (J H)
LC 77-700103
Demonstrates the properties of the simple lens of the camera. Clarifies the principle of light refraction and illustrates the functions of the lens.
Industrial and Technical Education; Science - Physical
Dist - PHENIX **Prod** - VEILX 1976

Simple Linear Regression with Evaluation and Predictive Techniques 30 MIN
U-matic / VHS
Engineering Statistics Series
Color (IND)
Describes how the best straight line may be fit to the data, when it should be fit, how well it fits and how to use the equation to make predictions.
Industrial and Technical Education; Mathematics; Psychology
Dist - COLOSU **Prod** - COLOSU

Simple Looms 13 MIN
U-matic / VHS / 16mm
Weaving Series
Color (J)
LC 77-700827
Presents Erika Semler of the Hand Weavers and Spinners Guild of Australia demonstrating weaving on two simple looms, the weighted warp loom and the backstrap. Shows how to set up the loom, plain weaving, joining threads, adding fringes and wrapping.
Fine Arts; Geography - World
Dist - CORF **Prod** - EDMEDA 1977

Simple Machine - the Lever 10 MIN
U-matic / VHS
Color (I J)
Describes the three parts of a lever and provides the formula for determining the movements in any lever system.
Science - Physical
Dist - PICOLO **Prod** - PICOLO 1971

Simple Machines 15 MIN
VHS / 16mm
Challenge Series
Color (I)
$125.00 purchase, $25.00 rental
Illustrates six simple machines and some of the more complicated machines that incorporate these simple machines.
Science; Science - Physical
Dist - AITECH **Prod** - WDCNTV 1987

Simple machines
VHS
Basic science series
Color (J H) (ENGLISH AND SPANISH)
$39.95 purchase _ #MCV5061
Focuses on simple machines, presenting only basic concepts. Includes teacher's guide and review questions. Combines computer animation and the use of 'sheltered language' to help students acquire content vocabulary, become comfortable with scientific language and achieve success in science curriculum. Part of a series on basic science concepts.
Science; Science - Physical
Dist - MADERA **Prod** - MADERA

Simple Machines 15 MIN
VHS / U-matic
Matter and Motion Series Module Green; Module green
Color (I)
Uses toys, games, recreational facilities and tools to illustrate how simple machines work.
Science - Physical
Dist - AITECH **Prod** - WHROTV 1973

Simple Machines - Inclined Planes 12 MIN
U-matic / VHS / 16mm
Simple Machines Series
Color (I J)
Highlights the important distinction between stationary and moving inclined planes. Demonstrates how the slope of an inclined plane affects the amount of force and its direction.
Science - Physical
Dist - CORF **Prod** - CORF 1984

Simple machines - inclined planes 12 MIN
VHS
Simple machines series
Color; PAL (P I J H)
Presents an animated prehistoric human who teaches youngsters about inclined planes. Distinguishes between stationary and moving inclined planes. Part of a five - part series about simple machines demonstrated by an inspired but accident prone caveman.
Agriculture; Science - Physical
Dist - VIEWTH **Prod** - VIEWTH

Simple Machines - Inclined Planes and Levers 17 MIN
U-matic / VHS / 16mm
Color (J) (SPANISH)
Uses the ramp of a parking garage to illustrate the principles that apply to machines belonging to the lever and plane families. Discusses the concept of work in terms of force and distance.
Foreign Language; Science - Physical
Dist - EBEC **Prod** - EBEC 1983

Simple machines - levers 12 MIN
VHS
Simple machines series
Color; PAL (P I J H)
Presents an animated prehistoric human who teaches youngsters about levers. Part of a five - part series about simple machines demonstrated by an inspired but accident prone caveman.
Agriculture; Science - Physical
Dist - VIEWTH **Prod** - VIEWTH

Simple Machines - Levers 12 MIN
U-matic / VHS / 16mm
Simple Machines Series
Color (I J)
Uses animation and a prehistoric human to introduce the workings of the lever. Explains that a lever can be any bar that tips back and forth on a point or fulcrum and that a lever exchanges distance for force or force for distance and speed.
Science - Physical
Dist - CORF **Prod** - CORF 1984

Simple Machines - Pulleys 12 MIN
U-matic / VHS / 16mm
Simple Machines Series
Color (I J)
Presents an analogy which makes clear now individual rope segments support part of an object's weight. Uses animation to make it clear how combinations of pulleys are brought together in a block and tackle.
Science - Physical
Dist - CORF **Prod** - CORF 1984

Simple machines - pulleys 12 MIN
VHS
Simple machines series
Color; PAL (P I J H)
Presents an animated prehistoric human who teaches youngsters about pulleys. Part of a five - part series about simple machines demonstrated by an inspired but accident prone caveman.
Agriculture; Science - Physical
Dist - VIEWTH **Prod** - VIEWTH

Simple machines series - the lever 10 MIN
U-matic / VHS / 16mm
Simple machines series - the lever
Color (I J)
LC 73-711114
Describes the three parts of a lever and provides the formula for determining the movements in any level system.
Science - Physical
Dist - PHENIX **Prod** - PICOLO 1971

Simple machines series - the lever
Simple machines series - the lever 10 MIN
Dist - PHENIX

Simple Machines Series
Inclined planes 12 MIN
Levers 12 MIN
Pulleys 12 MIN
Simple Machines - Inclined Planes 12 MIN
Simple Machines - Levers 12 MIN
Simple Machines - Pulleys 12 MIN
Simple Machines - Wheels and Axles 12 MIN
Simple Machines - Working Together 12 MIN
Wheels and Axles 12 MIN
Working Together 12 MIN
Dist - CORF

Simple machines series
Simple machines - inclined planes 12 MIN
Simple machines - levers 12 MIN
Simple machines - pulleys 12 MIN
Simple machines - wheels and axles 12 MIN
Simple machines - working together 12 MIN
Dist - VIEWTH

Simple Machines - using Mechanical Advantage 17.5 MIN
VHS / 16mm / U-matic
Elementary Physical Science Series
Color (I J)
$395, $275, $305 purchase _ #A251
Teaches the importance of simple machines. Discusses how we use the mechanical advantage of simple machines. Shows how we can combine simple machines to make more complex machines. Explains that our modern world depends upon machines.
Science - Physical
Dist - BARR **Prod** - BARR 1979

Simple Machines - using Mechanical Advantage 18 MIN
16mm / U-matic / VHS
Elementary Physical Science Series
Color (I J)
LC 79-700571
Relates the importance of simple machines, such as levers, incline planes, wedges, screws, pulleys, wheels and axles.
Science - Physical
Dist - BARR **Prod** - HALDAR 1979

Simple Machines - Wheels and Axles 12 MIN
U-matic / VHS / 16mm
Simple Machines Series
Color (I J)
Introduces animated, prehistoric characters who demonstrate simple machines. Shows how wheels and axles help reduce friction and are used in all sorts of devices to make work easier. Gives examples to depict the exchange between force and distance.
Science - Physical
Dist - CORF **Prod** - CORF 1984

Simple machines - wheels and axles 12 MIN
VHS
Simple machines series
Color; PAL (P I J H)
Presents an animated prehistoric human who teaches youngsters about wheels and axles. Part of a five - part series about simple machines demonstrated by an inspired but accident prone caveman.
Agriculture; Science - Physical
Dist - VIEWTH **Prod** - VIEWTH

Simple machines - working together 12 MIN
VHS
Simple machines series
Color; PAL (P I J H)
Presents an animated prehistoric human who teaches youngsters about levers, pulleys, inclined planes, wheels and axles, all simple machines. Shows how simple machines can be combined to work together. Part of a five - part series about simple machines demonstrated by an inspired but accident prone caveman.
Agriculture; Science - Physical
Dist - VIEWTH **Prod** - VIEWTH

Simple Machines - Working Together 12 MIN
U-matic / VHS / 16mm
Simple Machines Series
Color (I J)
Uses animated characters to show that the lever, pulley, inclined plane, wheel and axle are simple machines and are the basic building blocks of mechanical devices. Explains that the more these simple machines are used, the easier it is to understand the mechanics of input and output work.
Science - Physical
Dist - CORF **Prod** - CORF 1984

A Simple Matter of Justice 26 MIN
U-matic / VHS / 16mm
Color (H C)
LC 78-701273
Examines the debate over the Equal Rights Amendment, focusing on the work of actress Jean Stapleton at the International Woman's Year Conference in Houston, Texas. Features three First Ladies, two congresswomen and several feminist leaders.
Civics and Political Systems; Sociology
Dist - FI **Prod** - HASSA 1978

Simple Method for Tracheal Suction and Bronchoscopy 11 MIN
16mm
Color
LC FIE61-34
Describes the clinical requirement and prescribed method for performing safe and effective tracheal suction and bronchoscopy on patients who have undergone pulmonary surgery.
Health and Safety; Science
Dist - USNAC **Prod** - USA 1961

Simple Method of Ureterocele Repair 12 MIN
16mm
Color (PRO)
Presents ureterocele repair by a simple surgical technique not requiring extensive dissection or ureteral re - implantation. Points out that the method effectively prevents reflux, and there have been no complications. Includes pre - and post - operative pyelograms of illustrative cases.
Health and Safety; Science
Dist - ACY **Prod** - ACYDGD 1970

Simple minds 40 MIN
VHS
Education special
Color (A)
PdS20 purchase
Asks if the graduate scientists and teachers of Great Britain are competent, or have they failed to understand basic scientific concepts. Wonders if the curriculum is too broad; is there a mismatch between the abstract - and the abstruse - material in school textbooks and the common sense world. Features Dr Matt Schnepts, Prof Lewis Wolpert and others who explore the problems of science teaching and suggest ways of recognizing and using children's misconceptions about science in a positive way.
Science
Dist - BBCENE

Simple Molds 10 MIN
U-matic / VHS / 16mm
Craftsmanship in Clay Series
Color (H C A)
Shows a skilled ceramist demonstrating the step - bystep process of making slipcasting, drape and press molds.
Fine Arts
Dist - IU **Prod** - NET 1969

Simple Multicellular Animals - Sponges, Coelenterates, and Flatworms 20 MIN
VHS / U-matic
Modern Biology Series
Color (H C)
Analyzes the comparative anatomical development from protistans through animals with layered body walls. Uses micrography and animation to show specialized cell types.
Science - Natural
Dist - BNCHMK **Prod** - BHA 1985

Simple Organisms - Algae and Fungi 14 MIN
16mm / U-matic / VHS
Major Phyla Series
Color (J H C)
$350, $245 purchase _ #3982
Shows the differences between algae and fungi, their habitats, and their major characteristics.
Science - Natural
Dist - CORF

Simple Organisms - Bacteria 15 MIN
16mm / U-matic / VHS
Major Phyla Series
Color (J H)
$365, $250 purchase _ #3856
Shows the structure, growth, reproduction, and spore formation of bacteria.
Science - Natural
Dist - CORF

The Simple Overcall 30 MIN
VHS / U-matic
Play Bridge Series
Color (A)
Physical Education and Recreation
Dist - KYTV **Prod** - KYTV 1983

Simple Plants - the Algae 18 MIN
U-matic / VHS / 16mm
Biology (Spanish Series Unit 6 - Plant Classification and Physiology; Unit 6 - Plant classification and physiology
Color (H) (SPANISH)
Illustrates typical forms of algae, explaining their structure and describing their evolutionary development. Uses photomicrography to show the reproductive processes of algae. Emphasizes the importance of algae to aquatic animals and man.
Foreign Language; Science - Natural
Dist - EBEC **Prod** - EBEC

Simple Plumbing Repairs 21 MIN
16mm / U-matic / VHS
Home Repairs Series
Color (J)
LC 81-700044
Illustrates several basic tools needed for simple plumbing repairs. Shows common problems and tells how to solve them.
Industrial and Technical Education
Dist - CORF **Prod** - CENTRO 1981

Simple Plumbing Repairs 21 MIN
U-matic / VHS / 16mm
Home Repairs Series
Color (J H C A)
$505, $250 purchase _ #80533
Shows how to make simple plumbing repairs.
Home Economics; Industrial and Technical Education
Dist - CORF

Simple sauces 29 MIN
VHS
Cookbook videos series
Color (G)
$19.95 purchase _ #ALW110
Shows how to prepare simple sauces in short, easy - to - learn segments. Lists each ingredient as it is added in subtitles and visually reinforces spoken instructions. Gives recipe background and nutritional facts. Part of the Cookbook Videos series.
Home Economics; Social Science
Dist - CADESF **Prod** - CADESF

Simple sauces 29 MIN
VHS
Cookbook videos series; Vol 6
Color (G)
$19.95 purchase
Demonstrates easy - to - make gourmet sauces. Includes printed abstract of recipes. Part of a series.
Home Economics; Social Science
Dist - ALWHIT **Prod** - ALWHIT

Simple sentence - basic construction 18 MIN
VHS
Language construction company series
Color (H C G)
$50.00 purchase _ #LCC - 2
Assists students in improving their written and spoken English grammar skills. Bases all programs on a 'construction theme.' Includes review tests as an integral part of each lesson. Students may stop, start and repeat any part of the lesson. Visual cues are given for review purposes. Part of a 15 - part series.
English Language
Dist - INSTRU

Simple Silver Working 10 MIN
16mm
Color; B&W (J)
Demonstrates the method of silver decoration known as repousse, or chasing. Antonio Castillo, famous silver worker of Old Mexico, is shown translating an original design for a bar pin into a finished piece of jewelry.
Fine Arts; Industrial and Technical Education
Dist - AVED **Prod** - ALLMOR 1957

Simple Slab Methods 10 MIN
16mm / U-matic / VHS
Craftmanship in Clay Series
Color (J H)
Demonstrates three slab methods. Shows wedging, rolling out the piece and the correct use of basic tools.
Fine Arts
Dist - IU **Prod** - IU

A Simple Song of Freedom 30 MIN
16mm
Color (J)
Presents an anti - war poetic documentary film.
Psychology; Sociology
Dist - CFS **Prod** - CFS

Simple steps 15 MIN
VHS
Color (G)
$125.00 purchase _ #AH45285
Gives potential patients a full understanding of the processes of total hip or knee - joint replacement.
Health and Safety
Dist - HTHED **Prod** - HTHED

Simple Techniques in Shaping Glass 9 MIN
U-matic / VHS / 16mm
Fundamentals of Chemistry Series
Color (H C)
$245, $170 purchase _ #69095
Shows how glass is handled in a chemistry laboratory.
Science - Physical
Dist - CORF

Simple Time - Interval Measurement System, a, Pt 1 30 MIN
VHS / U-matic
Microprocessors for Monitoring and Control Series
Color (IND)
Shows how a time interval measurement system is designed and implemented. Gives a microprocessor implementation program available in ROM for permanent storage. First of two lectures.
Industrial and Technical Education; Mathematics; Sociology
Dist - COLOSU **Prod** - COLOSU

Simple Time - Interval Measurement System, a, Pt 2 30 MIN
U-matic / VHS
Microprocessors for Monitoring and Control Series
Color (IND)
Shows how a time interval measurement system is designed and implemented. Gives a microprocessor implementation program, available in ROM for permanent storage. Second of two lectures.
Industrial and Technical Education; Mathematics; Sociology
Dist - COLOSU **Prod** - COLOSU

Simple Treasures 30 MIN
U-matic
Visions - Artists and the Creative Process Series
Color (H C A)
Focuses on the artist's impulse to exalt common objects into art.
Fine Arts; History - World
Dist - TVOTAR **Prod** - TVOTAR 1983

Simple Voltage Regulators 22 MIN
16mm
B&W
LC 74-705646
Identifies the purpose of each component in a simple voltage regulator circuit and shows the current paths. Explains the circuit operation when the input voltage and the load are changed. Discusses the effect of placing VR tubes in the series. (Kinescope).
Industrial and Technical Education; Science - Physical
Dist - USNAC **Prod** - USAF

Simple Waves 27 MIN
16mm
PSSC Physics Films Series
B&W (H C)
Shows elementary characteristics of waves by means of pulse propagation on ropes and slinkies. Effects are shown at regular speeds and in slow motion. A torsion bar wave - machine is used to demonstrate reflection.
Science - Physical
Dist - MLA **Prod** - PSSC 1959

Simplemente Jenny 33 MIN
16mm / U-matic / VHS
Color (H C A) (LATIN)
Explores the varied cultural influences, from religion to advertising and popular culture, which shape the lives of women in Latin America.
Geography - World; History - World; Sociology
Dist - CNEMAG **Prod** - IWFP 1977

A Simpler quadratic formula 6 MIN
VHS
Improvements in the teaching of algebra series
Color (J H)
$20.00 purchase
Features a method which is less than half the size of the normal quadratic formula. Presents part of a five - part series on teaching algebra developed by Professor H Paul McGuire.
Mathematics
Dist - MMMATH **Prod** - MMMATH

The Simplest Place in Time 30 MIN
16mm
Color
Features golfer Arnold Palmer as he pursues a new passion of photography in New Zealand, a country of dramatic scenic contrasts with an old world charm that surprises and delights the traveler.
Industrial and Technical Education; Physical Education and Recreation
Dist - MTP **Prod** - ANZ

Simpleton Peter 27 MIN
U-matic / VHS / 16mm
Storybook International Series
Color
Presents the English story of Peter who is stumped by a wise woman's complicated riddles. Reveals that after he marries, he is able to answer the riddles with his wife's help, thus proving the value of a clever wife.
Guidance and Counseling; Literature and Drama
Dist - JOU **Prod** - JOU 1982

Simplicity, Compassion and Freedom
VHS / Cassette
(G)
$49.00, $18.00 purchase _ #U890001190, 1191
Presents a talk by two Theravada Buddhist monks on how to bring spirit and heart into life. Produced by Access Group.
Health and Safety; Psychology; Religion and Philosophy
Dist - BKPEOP

Simplified 24 - movement Taiji and applications 60 MIN
VHS
Color (G)
$49.95 purchase _ #1136
Introduces the history of T'ai chi through archival footage. Shows basics of the standardized 24 position form with different angles, repetitions, and closeups. Shows some self defense applications. With Liang Shouyu and Sam Masich.
Physical Education and Recreation
Dist - WAYF

Simplified Insect Management Program - a Guide to Apple Sampling 28 MIN
VHS
Color (C A)
$40.00 purchase, $20.00 rental
Provides training in the most up - to - date methods for managing insect and mite pests of apples.
Agriculture
Dist - CORNRS **Prod** - CORNRS 1989

Simplify, Simplify 22 MIN
16mm
Color
LC 77-702492
Takes a behind - the - scenes look at the development of Metropolitan Life Insurance Company's corporate advertising campaign from conception to production of television commercials.
Business and Economics; Psychology
Dist - COMCRP **Prod** - MLIC 1977

Simplifying Complex Fractions 30 MIN
16mm
Advanced Algebra Series
B&W (T)
Shows how to manipulate algebraic complex fractions using various techniques such as inverting the divisor and multiplying, combining numerator terms or denominator terms and factoring, and cancelling. Analyzes the simple continued fraction.
Mathematics
Dist - MLA **Prod** - CALVIN 1960

Simplifying outdoor painting 60 MIN
VHS
Color (A G)
$24.95 purchase _ #SIM - 01
Shows the simplicity of the method John Stobart has developed during his 35 - year painting career. Overviews the basic requirements the aspiring artist needs in order to be prepared for painting from nature. Includes a lesson on drawing and perspective, instruction on preparation of a canvas, and a look at the materials needed for a field trip. Part of a series on painting outdoors.
Fine Arts
Dist - ARTSAM **Prod** - WORLDS

Simplifying Radicals 30 MIN
VHS
Mathematics Series
Color (J)
LC 90713155
Discusses simplifying radicals. The 51st of 157 installments of the Mathematics Series.
Mathematics
Dist - GPN

Simplifying radicals
VHS
Intermediate algebra series
Color (J H)
$125.00 purchase _ #3020
Teaches the concepts involved in simplifying radical expressions. Part of a set of 31 videos, each between 25 and 30 minutes long, that explain and reinforce concepts in intermediate algebra. Videos are also available in a set.
Mathematics
Dist - LANDMK

Simply beautiful garnishes 90 MIN
VHS
Color (G IND)
$99.00 purchase _ #ANB01V-H
Designed to teach large volume garnishing techniques. The three 30-minute programs cover classic slices and designs - equipment requirements, produce quality, preservation and storage and planning fruit, vegetable, meat and cheese garnishes, basic carving, cuts, grates and shreds - equipment requirements and care, safety and fruit and vegetable garnishes and herbs, spices, pauses, purees, gelatins and convenience garnishes - complementing with the right flavor, equipment requirements, herb and spice garnishes, sauces and gravies, congealed designs and ready-to-use garnishes.
Home Economics
Dist - CAMV

Simply Making Jewelry 18 MIN
VHS / U-matic
Color
Reveals how unusual pieces can be made with easily available objects and materials, and how jewelry need not require expensive metals and gems. Shows how necklaces, pendants and earrings can be made from wood, metal grids, wire, dowels, screw eyes, suede lace, string and button blanks, all easily obtained from hardware stores, art and garment supply houses.
Fine Arts
Dist - IFF **Prod** - IFF

Simply Metric 19 MIN
U-matic / VHS / 16mm
Color (I J)
LC 76-703291
Presents an animated film giving a whimsical history of measurement standards. Focuses on present use of the metric system introduced by the French. Explains basic metric concepts and terminology through use of familiar situations.
Mathematics
Dist - ALTSUL **Prod** - CRAIGF 1976

Simply Metric 20 MIN
U-matic / VHS / 16mm
Color (I J)
Uses animation to give a history of the circumstances that led up to the introduction of the French metric system. Analyzes the system itself.
Mathematics
Dist - ALTSUL **Prod** - ALTSUL

Simply scientific series
Beyond the stars - a space story 12 MIN
Byron B Blackbear and the scientific method 15 MIN
How to dig a hole to the other side of the world 11 MIN
The Lightning and Thunder Case 14 MIN
Microcomputers - an Introduction or the Computer and the Crook 15 MIN
Dist - LCOA

Simpson Street 22 MIN
16mm / U-matic / VHS
Color (H C A)
LC 80-701151
Examines the sociological and political reasons for the deterioration of the South Bronx.
Geography - United States; Sociology
Dist - ICARUS **Prod** - ICARUS 1980

Simpson's Rule 20 MIN
VHS
Calculus Series
Color (H)
LC 90712920
Discusses Simpson's rule. The 46th of 57 installments of the Calculus Series.
Mathematics
Dist - GPN

Simtameciu Godos 22 MIN
VHS / U-matic
B&W (LITHUANIAN)
Documents the subject of Lithuania's centenarian citizens.
Foreign Language; Health and Safety
Dist - IHF **Prod** - IHF

Simulated experience 9 MIN
16mm
Caroline Avery series
Color (G A)
$10.00 rental
Presents the work of filmmaker Caroline Avery. Creates a collaged expression of television viewing of stock TV images of a man being led away by two policemen and a man surrounded by reporters.
Fine Arts; History - United States; Industrial and Technical Education
Dist - PARART **Prod** - CANCIN 1989

Simulated Home Visits Series
Abuse 36 MIN
The Cirrhotic patient 35 MIN
The Diabetic Patient 20 MIN
The Dialyzed Patient 30 MIN
The Myocardial Infarction Patient 24 MIN
The Stroke Patient 30 MIN
Dist - AJN

Simulated patient training - acute paralysis of both legs in a young woman 36 MIN
VHS / U-matic
Simulated patient training series
Color (PRO C)
$395.00 purchase, $80.00 rental _ #C880 - VI - 031
Demonstrates the use of a simulated patient by presenting an actual training session in which a simulated patient is being prepared to simulate acute paralysis of both legs in a young female patient. Presented by Dr Howard S Barrows. Part of a two - part series on training simulated patients to present symptoms to medical students.
Health and Safety; Psychology
Dist - HSCIC

Simulated patient training series
Presents a two - part series on training simulated patients to present symptoms to medical students presented by Dr Howard S Barrows. Includes simulation of pneumothoras and acute paralysis of both legs.
Simulated patient training - acute paralysis of both legs in a young woman 36 MIN
Simulated patient training - the pneumothorax 31 MIN
Dist - HSCIC

Simulated patient training - the pneumothorax 31 MIN
VHS / U-matic
Simulated patient training series
Color (PRO C)
$395.00 purchase, $80.00 rental _ #C870 - VI - 056
Presents Dr Howard S Barrows working with a young man through the three components of simulation training - history, physical findings and dress rehearsal to present pneumothorax symptomology. Part of a two - part series on training simulated patients to present symptoms to medical students.
Health and Safety; Psychology
Dist - HSCIC

Simulated psychiatric profiles series
Presents a five - part series on psychiatric cases to illustrate theories about those illnesses. Demonstrates therapeutic techniques such as clarification, confrontation and interpretation. Includes adjustment disorders, affective disorders, anxiety disorders, personality disorders and schizophrenia and unspecified psychoses. Presented by Dr Donald C Fidler.
Adjustment disorders - adults and adolescents - Pt I 41 MIN
Affective disorders - mania and depression - Part II 51 MIN
Anxiety disorders - generalized anxiety , agoraphobia, obsesseive - compulsive anxiety - Part III 60 MIN
Personality disorders - antisocial, histrionic, schizotypal behaviors - Part IV 31 MIN
Psychoses - schizophrenia and unspecified psychoses - Part V 21 MIN
Dist - HSCIC

Simulation 30 MIN
U-matic / VHS
Project STRETCH - Strategies to Train Regular Educators to Teach Children with Handicaps Series; Module 9
Color (T S)
LC 80-706645
Presents a dream sequence in which a teacher visits a simulation factory which designs a simulation exercise for her to use in a social studies project.
Education; Psychology
Dist - HUBDSC **Prod** - METCO 1980

Simulation 60 MIN
VHS / U-matic
Introduction to BASIC Series Lecture 8; Lecture 8
Color
Industrial and Technical Education; Mathematics
Dist - UIDEEO **Prod** - UIDEEO

Simulation 28 MIN
VHS / 16mm
Manufacturing insights series
Color (A IND)
$200.00, $190.00 purchase _ #VT253, #VT253U
Shows how several companies used simulation to watch their plans in operation before committing to construction.
Business and Economics; Computer Science; Industrial and Technical Education
Dist - SME **Prod** - SME 1987

Simulation for the Design and Analysis of Manufacturing Systems 4 1/2HR
VHS / 16mm
Color (A IND)
$1595.00
Teaches how to model and analyze system performance, how to choose simulations and animation software, how to interpret data. Instructor is simulation expert Dr. Averill Law. Includes reference guides.
Computer Science; Education; Industrial and Technical Education; Psychology
Dist - SME **Prod** - SME 1990

Simulation - High Green to Training 16 MIN
16mm
Color (C A)
LC 71-706110
Shows how Conduction - Missouri is applying its space technology and manufacturing skills to the development and manufacturing of one of the world's first railroad train simulators. Depicts and explains the operation of the various sub - systems of the simulator. Includes a live dialog sequence that portrays the use of the railroad simulator in a typical training situation.
Social Science
Dist - MCDO **Prod** - CONMIS 1969

Simulation in Pilot Training 20 MIN
16mm
Color
LC 78-702062
Discuses the advantages of using simulators in pilot training, describing the improvements from the days of the Blue Box Simulator of World War II. Features the moon simulator, the combat simulator, C - 5 and DC - 10 simulators, and the research simulator.
Industrial and Technical Education
Dist - USNAC **Prod** - USAF 1978

A Simulation of a Gemini Spacecraft Land Landing System 17 MIN
U-matic
Color
Simulates gliding parachute descent at Ft Hood and continues with analog simulation requirements, map plotting, altitude readouts and its commanding roll, pitch and yaw. Includes a simulated Gemini parasail reentry run.
Industrial and Technical Education
Dist - NASA **Prod** - NASA 1972

Simulation - the next best thing to being there 30 MIN
16mm
Project STRETCH Series; Module 9
Color (T)
LC 80-700616
Shows a dream in which a classroom teacher visits a simulation factory which designs a simulation exercise for her to use in a social studies project.
Education; Psychology
Dist - HUBDSC **Prod** - METCO 1980

Simulation through Role - Playing 69 FRS
U-matic / VHS
Dynamic Classroom Series
Color
Shows how to use role playing as a 'fun' exercise vs a learning process, using complex roles, simple roles, instructor controlled roles.
Education; Psychology
Dist - RESEM **Prod** - RESEM

Simulations and Games 30 MIN
VHS / U-matic
Bits and Bytes Series Pt 8; Pt 8
Color (A)
Investigates computer simulations and games, and the features that make them valuable as educational tools. Explains the concepts of digital and analog communication and 'booting DOS'.
Mathematics
Dist - TIMLIF **Prod** - TVOTAR 1984

Simultaneous Drilling and Production 20 MIN
VHS / 16mm
Color (IND)
$595.00 purchase
Illustrates oil drilling and production procedures for those working on systems where both operations might be in progress. Emphasizes standard safety control concepts.
Health and Safety; Industrial and Technical Education; Social Science
Dist - FLMWST

Simultaneous Drilling and Production 20 MIN
VHS / U-matic
Color
Emphasizes the concepts involved in standard safety controls when both drilling and production are in progress. Illustrates the procedures which must be undertaken by those operating the systems.
Health and Safety
Dist - FLMWST **Prod** - FLMWST

Simultaneous engineering 45 MIN
VHS / 16mm
Manufacturing insights series
Color (A IND)
$200.00, $190.00 purchase _ #VT286, #VT286U
Shows how other companies have improved quality, lowered costs, and reduced their design - to - market cycle.
Business and Economics; Computer Science; Industrial and Technical Education
Dist - SME **Prod** - SME 1989

Simultaneous equations
VHS
Intermediate algebra series
Color (J H)
$125.00 purchase _ #3031
Teaches basic concepts involved in solving simultaneous equations. Part of a 31 - video series, each part 25 to 30 minutes long, that explains and reinforces concepts in intermediate algebra. Uses definitions, theorems, examples and step - by - step solutions to tutor the student. Videos also available in a set.
Mathematics
Dist - LANDMK

Simultaneous Equations 30 MIN
VHS
Mathematics Series
Color (J)
LC 90713155
Explains simultaneous equations. The 62nd of 157 installments of the Mathematics Series.
Mathematics
Dist - GPN

Simultaneous equations, systems of inequalities, repeating decimals and radicals 60 MIN
VHS
Algebra I series; Volume 5
Color (I J H C A)
$29.95 purchase _ #S02150
Covers algebraic concepts of simultaneous equations, systems of inequalities, repeating decimals and radicals. Encourages students to use sight, sound and writing skills in learning the material. Uses modern electronic and computer graphics to illustrate many of the concepts. Includes a workbook, with additional workbooks available at an extra charge.
Mathematics
Dist - UILL

Simultaneous Two - Team Abdominal Perineal Resection of the Rectum 24 MIN
16mm
Color (PRO)
Shows a combined abdominal perineal resection of the lower sigmoid and rectum which has been carried out employing two surgical teams simultaneously. Demonstrates both the drawbacks and advantages of this procedure.
Health and Safety; Science
Dist - ACY **Prod** - ACYDGD 1961

Sin city diary 29 MIN
VHS
Color (G) (FILIPINO WITH ENGLISH SUBTITLES)
$60.00 rental, $250.00 purchase
Explores the lives of women who work as prostitutes around the US Navy base at Subic Bay in the Philippines. Takes the form of a diary to incorporate filmmaker Rachel Rivera's own experience as a Filipina American. Looks at the effects of the decision by the Filipino government to shut down the base, after nearly a century of American presence there. Raises questions about America's responsibility to its former colony. Includes English narration.
Fine Arts; Geography - World; History - World; Sociology
Dist - WMEN

The Sin of Virtue 30 MIN
16mm
B&W
LC FIA64-1180
Presents the story about Rabbi Israel Salanter who convinced the surviving members of the Jewish community of Vilna, during a plague 125 years ago, to break the fast on Yom Kippur so that their lives might be saved.
History - World; Religion and Philosophy
Dist - NAAJS **Prod** - JTS 1963

Sinaga's Family - a Batak Village 18 MIN
16mm
Asian Neighbors - Indonesia Series
Color (H C A)
LC 75-703586
Explores the day - to - day life of a family living in a small village on Lake Taba in Indonesia.
Geography - World; Social Science
Dist - AVIS **Prod** - FLMAUS 1975

Sinai Field Mission 127 MIN
U-matic / VHS / 16mm
Color (H C A)
LC 79-700270
Documents the daily life of American personnel stationed at the U S Sinai Field Mission, located in the buffer zone between Israeli and Egyptian territories.
Civics and Political Systems; Fine Arts; Geography - World
Dist - ZIPRAH **Prod** - WISEF 1978

Sinatra Live in Concert 52 MIN
BETA / VHS
Color (ENGLISH (JAPANESE SUBTITLES))
Presents a live, one - man concert by Frank Sinatra, first presented on Japanese television. Contains Japanese subtitles, commentary and commercials, but Sinatra sings in English.
Fine Arts
Dist - VIDIM **Prod** - UNKNWN 1974

Sinbad 98 MIN
16mm / VHS
Color (G) (HUNGARIAN WITH ENGLISH SUBTITLES)
$175.00 rental
Recreates the world of the capital of Hungary at the turn of the century as seen through the eyes of an aging Don Juan. Directed by Zoltan Huszaruk.
Fine Arts
Dist - KINOIC

Sinbad and the Eye of the Tiger 114 MIN
16mm
Color (P A)
Presents the continuing adventures of Sinbad in the sequel to Golden Voyage Of Sinbad. Directed by Sam Wanamaker. Stars Taryn Power, Patrick Wayne and Jane Seymour. Special effects by Ray Harryhousen.
Fine Arts
Dist - TIMLIF **Prod** - CPC 1977

Sinbad the Sailor 117 MIN
U-matic / VHS / 16mm
Color (I J H C)
Stars Douglas Fairbanks Jr as Sinbad the Sailor, whose oft - told tales are a bit tall for his associates' credulity. Presents the imagined eighth voyage of the fabled prince of voyages.
Literature and Drama
Dist - FI **Prod** - RKOP 1947

Sinbad the Sailor 20 MIN
16mm
Color
Describes the life of the Beggar Boy of Baghdad as brought to the screen through the Mount Puppets, the creations of two San Francisco artists.
Fine Arts; Literature and Drama
Dist - RADIM **Prod** - RLUCE

Since '45 30 MIN
U-matic / VHS / 16mm
Color (J)
LC 81-701608
Uses old film clips and recollections of many notable people to take a nostalgic look at the significant national and world events of the three decades following 1945. Emphasizes those events that reflect a changing culture and the media's pervasive influence on it.
History - United States; Social Science; Sociology
Dist - FI **Prod** - KORM 1980

Since the American Way of Death 59 MIN
VHS / 16mm
Color (G)
$70.00 rental _ #SAWD - 000
Investigates the funeral industry eleven years after Jessica Mitford's 'The American Way Of Death' described the majority of U S funeral directors as unethical.
Sociology
Dist - PBS **Prod** - WTTWTV

Sincerely 14 MIN
16mm
Color; B&W (G)
$35.00 rental
Enters into the issue of abortion and choice. Highlights the filmmaker's belief that every woman should have a choice regardless of economics. The government has ceased funding of abortion except when the woman's life is endangered and the film explores consequences of state funding of abortion.
Civics and Political Systems; Fine Arts; Sociology
Dist - CANCIN **Prod** - KIRBYL 1980

Sincerity I 27 MIN
16mm
Color (G)
$55.00 rental, $897.00 purchase
Says Brakhage, '...a graph of light equivalent to autobiographical thought process.'
Fine Arts
Dist - CANCIN **Prod** - BRAKS 1973

Sincerity II 40 MIN
16mm
Color (G)
$1144.00 purchase, $42.00 rental
Presents a film autobiography by Stan Brakhage composed of film photographed by Bruce Baillie, Jane Brakhage, Larry Jordan and Stan Phillips, among others. Draws footage from some 20,000 feet of home movies and outtakes salvaged from Brakhage's photography over the years.
Fine Arts; Literature and Drama; Sociology
Dist - CANCIN **Prod** - BRAKS 1975

Sincerity III 35 MIN
16mm
Color; Silent (C)
$1221.00
Experimental film by Stan Brakhage.
Fine Arts
Dist - AFA **Prod** - AFA 1978

Sincerity IV 40 MIN
16mm
Color (G)
$1144.00 purchase, $78.00 rental
Presents the sixth film of the Sincerity - Duplicity series. Lurks in the earliest tradition of Brakhage's mind work, Psycho - Drama, as well as in the most recent, Imagnostic, directions.
Fine Arts; Psychology
Dist - CANCIN **Prod** - BRAKS 1980

Sincerity V 45 MIN
16mm
Color (G)
$1264.00 purchase, $78.00 rental
Finishes 11 years of editing and 30 years of photography and the work of the Sincerity - Duplicity series.
Fine Arts; Psychology
Dist - CANCIN **Prod** - BRAKS 1980

Sinclair Lewis - the Man from Main Street 57 MIN
U-matic
Color (H C A)
Chronicles the life and works of Sinclair Lewis, who won both the Pulitzer and Nobel Prizes for literature.
Biography; Literature and Drama
Dist - CEPRO **Prod** - CEPRO

Sinclair Lewis - the man from Main Street 57 MIN
VHS / U-matic
Color (H C A)
$420.00, $395.00 purchase _ #V341
Chronicles the life and works of Sinclair Lewis, the 'great debunker' of the American Myth. Looks at Lewis' unhappy childhood in Sauk Center, Minnesota, and discusses the effects of the adulation he received in later years. Dramatizes scenes from his three most famous novels.
Biography; History - United States; Literature and Drama
Dist - BARR **Prod** - CEPRO 1986

The Sinclair Story 18 MIN
16mm
Color
LC 73-700388
Documents the importance of data and records in comparative medicine. Presents research done with mini - swine at the Sinclair Research Farm of the University of Missouri.
Health and Safety; Science
Dist - UMO **Prod** - UMO 1972

Sind Sie Herr Berger 15 MIN
16mm / U-matic / VHS
Guten Tag Series no 4; No 4
B&W (H) (GERMAN)
LC 74-707317
A German language film. Presents an episode in which the characters employ frequently used expressions and idioms in order to teach conversational German to beginners. Stresses the correct use of questions with was, negations with kein, verb forms with haben and sein, demonstrative pronouns, the article kein/E, the pronoun ending - E, the interrogative pronoun was and the preposition von.
Foreign Language
Dist - IFB **Prod** - FRGMFA 1970

Sindrome De Trastorno Respiratorio Del Adulto 19 MIN
U-matic / VHS
Color (PRO) (SPANISH)
A Spanish version of Adult Respiratory Distress Syndrome. Describes the adult R.D.S entity and its many etiologies including the most common causes, confirming diagnosis and management.
Foreign Language; Health and Safety; Science - Natural
Dist - UMICHM **Prod** - UMICHM 1980

Sine Graph 20 MIN
U-matic / VHS
Math Topics - Trigonometry Series
Color (J H C)
Mathematics
Dist - FI **Prod** - BBCTV

Sine of Obtuse Angles 20 MIN
VHS / U-matic
Math Topics - Trigonometry Series
Color (J H C)
Mathematics
Dist - FI **Prod** - BBCTV

Sinews of war - Program 9 50 MIN
VHS
Soldiers - a history of men in battle series
Color (H C G)
$300.00 purchase, $75.00 rental
Shows how the complexities of modern warfare are matched by the complexities of modern logistiscs. Discusses how the invasion of Normandy was the product of years of staff work. Part of a 13 - part series on soldiers and warfare hosted by Frederick Forsyth and written by John Keenan.
Civics and Political Systems; Guidance and Counseling; History - World; Sociology
Dist - CF **Prod** - BBCTV 1986

Sing a Song and Work Along 10 MIN
U-matic / VHS
Book, Look and Listen Series
Color (K P)
Focuses on the knowledge and skill to recognize and interpret the story lines in songs.
English Language; Literature and Drama
Dist - AITECH **Prod** - MDDE 1977

Sing a song of Seabrook - opposition to a nuclear plant 25 MIN
VHS
Color (H C G)
$295.00 purchase, $55.00 rental
Looks at a citizen action group - Clamshell Alliance - created because of the construction of Seabrook Nuclear Plant on fragile seacoast in New Hampshire. Examines nuclear plant safety, waste disposal and energy sources for the future. Produced by Raymond Stevens.
Science - Natural; Social Science
Dist - FLMLIB

Sing Along 15 MIN
VHS / U-matic
Song Sampler Series
Color (P)
LC 81-707071
Presents songs from the entire Song Sampler Series.
Fine Arts
Dist - GPN **Prod** - JCITV 1981

Sing Along with Israel
VHS
Color (G) (ENGLISH AND HEBREW)
$44.50 purchase _ #V72161
Presents songs in Hebrew and transliterated English against both historical footage and panoramic views of the Israeli countryside.
Fine Arts; Foreign Language
Dist - NORTNJ

Sing along with Israel 56 MIN
VHS
Color (G) (HEBREW WITH ENGLISH SUBTITLES)
$34.95 purchase _ #775
Presents 22 Israeli folksongs. Includes a songbook in Hebrew with an English translation.
Fine Arts; Sociology
Dist - ERGOM **Prod** - ERGOM

Sing and Play Songs that Tickle Your Funny Bone
VHS / 16mm
Color (K)
$9.88 purchase _ #PPI25272
Presents Ruth Roberts singing children's songs.
Fine Arts
Dist - EDUCRT **Prod** - PIONR

Sing and rejoice - Guiding young singers 60 MIN
VHS
Helen Kemp series
Color (G A R)
$69.95 purchase, $10.00 rental _ #35 - 8231 - 19
Outlines Helen Kemp's philosophies and strategies for training children in choirs. Emphasizes her philosophy that the whole person - body, mind, spirit and voice - is involved in singing.
Fine Arts; Literature and Drama
Dist - APH **Prod** - CPH

Sing around the seasons 30 MIN
VHS
Shalom Sesame series
Color (K P)
$19.95 purchase _ #247
Marks the changing seasons of Israel with song and the Muppets from Sesame Street. Part of an eight - part series on Israel with the Sesame Street Muppets.
Fine Arts; Geography - World; Sociology
Dist - ERGOM **Prod** - ERGOM

Sing, beast, sing 9 MIN
16mm / U-matic / VHS
Color (G)
$300.00, $150.00, $100.00 purchase
Presents a Mary Newland cartoon sans endless violence. Offers a grotesquely Dionesyian character entertaining himself and a few friends with a song.
Fine Arts
Dist - FLOWER

Sing Down the Moon
35mm strip / VHS / Cassette
Newbery Award - Winners Series
Color (I)
$66.00, $14.00 purchase
English Language; Literature and Drama
Dist - PELLER

Sing Joyfully 28 MIN
U-matic / VHS / 16mm
Color (J)
LC 76-702264
Shows the work of the Choir School of St Thomas Church in New York City.
Fine Arts; Religion and Philosophy
Dist - PHENIX **Prod** - ROPE 1976

Sing me a story - Rabbi Joe Black in concert 45 MIN
VHS
Color (K P I)
$24.95 purchase _ #838
Bops to the beat of the Aleph Bet Boogie and offers an Afikoman Mambo along with Rabbi Joe Black in concert with acoustic guitar. Collects original songs as well as old favorites from Hanukah, Passover and Sukkot. Includes enthusiastic parents and grandparents who join their children in singing.
Fine Arts; Sociology
Dist - ERGOM **Prod** - ERGOM

Sing of the Border 20 MIN
U-matic / VHS / 16mm
Color (J H C)
LC FIA68-2882
Pictures the Scottish border country, using old Scottish folk songs. Describes the countryside and its history, viewing historic ruins, small villages, the scene of the Battle of Flodden, the home of Sir Walter Scott, barley farmers and fishermen.
Geography - World
Dist - IFB **Prod** - BTF 1967

Sing Out America 25 MIN
U-matic / VHS
Kidsongs Series
(K P I)
Sociology
Dist - BERNGH **Prod** - TAVPI

Sing out for Wales 30 MIN
VHS
World of festivals series
Color (J H C G)
$195.00 purchase
Visits the Eisteddfod held alternately in North and South Wales. Looks at the main events - the Crowning of the Bard and a welcome home to Welsh exiles. Part of a 12 - part series on Europan festivals.

Geography - World; Social Science
Dist - LANDMK **Prod** - LANDMK 1988

The Sing - Song of Old Man Kangaroo 11 MIN
U-matic / VHS / 16mm
Just So Stories Series
Color (K P)
Tells how long ago in Australia, Old Man Kangaroo was gray and woolly like all the other animals, but he wanted to be different. The Big God agreed to his request and sent the dingo to chase him. By five o'clock the kangaroo had been chased right out of his old shape and into one that was very different. Adapted from the short story The Sing - Song Of Old Man Kangaroo by Rudyard Kipling.
Fine Arts; Literature and Drama
Dist - CORF **Prod** - CORF 1983

The Sing - Song of Old Man Kangaroo 11 MIN
16mm / U-matic / VHS
Just So Stories Series
Color (P I)
$275, $170 purchase _ #4589
Tells how the kangaroo got his long legs by wanting to be different and by being chased by a dingo.
Literature and Drama
Dist - CORF

Sing We and Chant it 145 MIN
U-matic
University of the Air Series
Color (J H C A)
$750.00 purchase, $250.00 rental
Examines rehearsal techniques for the choral director and demonstrates methods of conducting.
Fine Arts
Dist - CTV **Prod** - CTV 1978

Sing what You Say 15 MIN
U-matic / VHS
Hidden Treasures Series no 1; No 1
Color (T)
LC 82-706525
Uses the adventures of a pirate and his three friends to explore the many levels of language arts. Focuses on the concept of learning to express oneself through music.
English Language
Dist - GPN **Prod** - WCVETV 1980

Sing Yourself Silly 30 MIN
VHS / 16mm
Sesame Street Home Video Series
Color; Captioned (K)
$14.44 purchase _ #RH 9 - 805192
Features Sesame Street characters singing hit songs.
Fine Arts
Dist - EDUCRT **Prod** - RH

Singapore 30 MIN
VHS
Color (G)
$29.95 purchase _ #ST - IV0356
Strolls across Padang. Visits the Temple of Heavenly Happiness and Sentosa Island and experiences a tour by rickshaw.
Geography - World
Dist - INSTRU

Singapore 20 MIN
U-matic / VHS / 16mm
Color (J)
Visits Singapore which was first settled in 1819 as a port on the route from East Asia to Europe. Shows that it is now one of the best equipped ports of the world as well as a modern, beautiful city.
Geography - World; Sociology
Dist - LUF **Prod** - LUF 1979

Singapore - a success story 27 MIN
VHS
Color (J H)
$195.00 purchase
Looks at several aspects of the multicultural and multiethnic society of Singapore, focusing on its cultural, educational, political and economic characteristics.
Geography - World
Dist - LANDMK

Singapore - Crossroad to the Orient 22 MIN
U-matic / VHS / 16mm
Color; Captioned
Explores the History, Geography, Economic and Multi - Ethnic aspects of the country.
Geography - World; History - World; Social Science; Sociology
Dist - HANDEL **Prod** - HANDEL 1987

Singapore - crossroads of Asia 30 MIN
VHS
Color (G)
$29.95 purchase _ #S01979
Tours the city of Singapore. Visits street festivals and markets, famous hotels, the Temple of Heavenly Happiness, and other sites. Features a rickshaw tour of the city.
Geography - World; History - World; Sociology
Dist - UILL

Singapore - doing it my way 30 MIN
VHS
Business matters series
Color (A)
PdS65 purchase
States that it is over 30 years since the British withdrew from Singapore, leaving high unemployment and a superfluous dockyard. Reveals that now, largely due to the efforts of one man, Lee Kwan Yew, the country is a major financial center with the largest port in the world. However, Singapore's success has been at the price of individual liberty. The population goes along with the strict regime, but there are signs of growing dissent.
Civics and Political Systems; Geography - World
Dist - BBCENE

Singapore - toward tomorrow - Pt 13 30 MIN
U-matic / VHS
Profiles in progress series
Color (H C)
$325.00, $295.00 purchase _ #V558
Highlights the women and men who insure the success of Singapore. Focuses on a variety of endeavors, from education and culture to tourism and finance. Shows how Singapore, a country with few natural resources, has developed into a global giant because of its people and a consistent commitment to free enterprise, good government, education and ethnic harmony. Part of a 13 - part series on people who are moving their tradition - bound countries into modern times.
Business and Economics; Geography - World
Dist - BARR **Prod** - CEPRO 1991

Singendes Deutschland 16 MIN
16mm / U-matic / VHS
B&W (H C) (GERMAN)
A German language film. Fifteen popular German songs are sung and illustrated by appropriate German scenes and dances.
Foreign Language
Dist - IFB **Prod** - IFB 1952

Singer Instaload (Sound/Filmstrip Projector/ Viewer) 11 MIN
U-matic / VHS
Audio - Visual Skills Modules Series
Color
Education; Industrial and Technical Education
Dist - MDCC **Prod** - MDCC

The Singer not the Song 129 MIN
16mm
Color (H C A)
LC FI67-1311
Presents a drama about the conflict between a Catholic priest and a murderous bandit who want to control the people of a fear - gripped Mexican village.
Literature and Drama
Dist - WB **Prod** - RANKOR 1961

Singer of Tales, the, Pt 3 50 MIN
VHS
In Search of the Trojan War Series
Color (H)
$16.50 rental _ #50990
Depicts efforts of historian Michael Wood to demonstrate oral storytelling as it was done by Homer in the courts and festivals of the Aegean. Visits a Gaelic storyteller and travels to Kars in Tukrkish Armenia to hear a professional bard tell a 500 - year - old Turkish epic. Part of the In Search Of the Trojan War Series.
History - World; Literature and Drama
Dist - PSU **Prod** - FI

Singers of Two Songs 30 MIN
U-matic / VHS
Color (I J H C)
Looks into the perceptions of the Indian artists as they 'Weave Traditional Values into Contemporary Life' while living in two worlds. Portrays artists of song, dance, basketry, regalia making, painting, jewelry making, pottery, and wood carving.
Social Science; Sociology
Dist - SHENFP **Prod** - SHENFP 1987

Singhalese Fisherman of Ceylon 14 MIN
16mm
Human Family, Pt 1 - South and Southeast Asia Series
Color (I)
Depicts life in Unakaruva, a fishing village on the southern shore of Ceylon. Tells the story of Upasena, his wife and their four children.
Geography - World; Social Science; Sociology
Dist - AVED **Prod** - AVED 1972

Singing - a Joy in Any Language 56 MIN
16mm
Color (G)
_ #106C 0183 543
Records a tour that three Canadian singers did in China in 1982. Shows the Canadians giving public concerts and master classes at Chinese music conservatories. Introduces 800 year old traditional Chinese opera.
Fine Arts
Dist - CFLMDC **Prod** - NFBC 1983

Singing, acting, art 15 MIN
VHS
Arts and youth series
Color (J H C)
$89.95 purchase _ #EX4458; Program not available in Canada.
Presents young artists discussing the importance of art in their education and life. Focusses on singing, acting and art. Part of a three - part series.
Fine Arts; Sociology
Dist - FOTH

Singing America's songs series

America	10 MIN
America the beautiful	10 MIN
The Battle Hymn of the Republic	11 MIN
God bless America	9 MIN
The Star Spangled Banner	11 MIN

Dist - AIMS

The Singing blacksmith - Yankl der schmid 95 MIN
VHS
Moyshe Oysher film classics series
B&W (G) (YIDDISH WITH ENGLISH SUBTITLES)
$79.95 purchase _ #747
Stars Moyshe Oysher as a blacksmith who sees too many women and drinks too much liquor. Reveals that when he meets Tamare his life appears to change. Adapts the story by Daivd Pinski. With Miriam Riselle and Forence Weiss. Directed by Edgar G Ulmer.
Fine Arts; Literature and Drama; Sociology
Dist - ERGOM **Prod** - ERGOM 1938

The Singing Bone 13 MIN
16mm
Peppermint Stick Selection Series
Color (P I)
LC 76-701279
An excerpt from the motion picture The Wonderful World Of The Brothers Grimm. Presents an adaptation of the fairy tale about a magic flute that sings a song about a servant's unrewarded bravery and his master's treachery. Based on the story Der Singende Knochen by Jakob and Wilhelm Grimm.
English Language; Fine Arts; Literature and Drama
Dist - FI **Prod** - FI 1976

Singing for the Union 30 MIN
U-matic
Color (A)
Records folk singers and composers performing labor songs.
Business and Economics; Fine Arts
Dist - AFLCIO **Prod** - LIPA

Singing Frogs and Toads 11 MIN
U-matic / VHS / 16mm
Color (I)
Shows how various toads and frogs live and develop. Reproduces the sounds of the toads and frogs. Includes pictures of the American toad, leopard frog, gray tree frog, bullfrog and green frog.
Science - Natural
Dist - IFB **Prod** - CRAF 1961

Singing in the dark 86 MIN
16mm
B&W (G)
Presents one of the earliest American feature films to focus on the story of a Holocaust survivor. Centers on the relationship between a hard - luck comedian and a singer who suffers from amnesia. Contains post - war footage of scenes shots on location amidst the ruins of the Berlin Synagogue and a finale staged in the Rivington Street Synagogue on the Lower East Side of New York City. Stars cantor Moishe Oysher. ANO Productions.
History - World; Literature and Drama; Sociology
Dist - NCJEWF

Singing insects - 30 11 MIN
VHS / U-matic / 16mm
Animal families series
Color (K P I)
$275.00, $225.00, $195.00 purchase _ #B569
Examines singing insects such as grasshoppers and crickets. Uses close - ups to reveal how these insects make their sounds - by rubbing their wings together. Reveals that their purpose in singing is to attract a mate. Part of a series on animal families.
Science - Natural
Dist - BARR **Prod** - GREATT 1989

The Singing Marine 106 MIN
16mm
B&W (J)
Stars Dick Powell, Doris Weston and Lee Dixon. Presents the musical numbers created and staged by Busby Berkeley, including 'CAUSE MY BABY SAYS IT'S SO,' 'I KNOW NOW,' 'SONG OF THE MARINES' and 'NIGHT OVER SHANGHAI.'.
Fine Arts
Dist - UAE **Prod** - WB 1937

Singing on the Mountain 12 MIN
16mm
B&W
Presents a photographic record of the annual Singing on the Mountain, an annual gathering of thousands of mountain folk to one of the largest community song festivals in America.
Fine Arts; Physical Education and Recreation
Dist - MORTON **Prod** - MORTON 1958

The Singing Princess
VHS / U-matic
$29.95 purchase
Presents a delightful animated story from the Arabian Nights. Features the voice of Julie Andrews.
Literature and Drama
Dist - BESTF **Prod** - BESTF

The Singing sculpture 20 MIN
VHS
Color (G)
$39.95 purchase _ #SIN - 01
Presents British artists Gilbert & George, famous for their deadpan gallery performances, whose stiff demeanor contrasts sharply with their outrageous behavior. Shows that in 1971, New York's Sonnabend Gallery opened its doors with G&G's 'The Singing Sculpture,' for which they stand atop a table and sing along with a music hall ditty as they slowly dance and turn. Amusing at first, the viewer soon realizes that the song is about homelessness, and the performance takes on a darker side.
Fine Arts; Literature and Drama
Dist - ARTSAM **Prod** - HAASPH

A Singing Stream - a Black Family Chronicle 57 MIN
16mm
American Traditional Culture Series
Color (H)
Traces 20th century black history through the musical and cultural traditions of one Southern black family.
Fine Arts; History - United States; Sociology
Dist - DAVT **Prod** - DAVT 1987

Singing to Millions, Rounding to Thousands - Estimating to Thousands 15 MIN
U-matic / VHS
Figure Out Series
Color (I)
Shows how Alice estimates the revenues Mac will earn on a new recording contract.
Mathematics
Dist - AITECH **Prod** - MAETEL 1982

The Singing Tree 15 MIN
16mm
Color (P I)
LC 82-700468
Presents 100 school children and singer Billy Brennan who use songs to teach scientific concepts about the growth and and function of trees, such as photosynthesis, absorption of soil nutrients and water by roots, and the protective role of bark.
Science - Natural
Dist - UWISCA **Prod** - UWISCA 1980

The Singing Trilogy 15 MIN
VHS / U-matic
Magic Pages Series
Color (P)
Literature and Drama
Dist - AITECH **Prod** - KLVXTV 1976

The singing whales 24 MIN
16mm / U-matic / VHS
Undersea world of Jacques Cousteau series
Color (G)
$49.95 purchase _ #Q10612; LC 75-702734
A shortened version of The Singing Whales. Describes the migration of the humpback whales and discusses the reasons for the annual migration. Part of a series of 24 programs.
Science - Natural; Science - Physical
Dist - CF **Prod** - METROM 1975

Single 60 MIN
U-matic / VHS
Color
Looks at the issues faced by single people and the implications of this large and growing group.
Sociology
Dist - WCCOTV **Prod** - WCCOTV

Single Arm Coordinators / Front and Back Knee Touch / Jumping Leg Crossovers 15 MIN
U-matic / VHS
Roomnastics Series
Color (P)
Presents several exercises which can be performed in a classroom setting.
Physical Education and Recreation
Dist - GPN **Prod** - WVIZTV 1979

Single Armlifts Forward / Sideward Bend with Front and Back Bend / Leg Bend and Crossover 15 MIN
VHS / U-matic
Roomnastics Series
Color (P)
Presents several exercises which can be performed in a classroom setting.
Physical Education and Recreation
Dist - GPN **Prod** - WVIZTV 1979

Single Armlifts Sideward / Trunk Twist with Front and Back Bend / Leg Coordinator 15 MIN
VHS / U-matic
Roomnastics Series
Color (P)
Presents several exercises which can be performed in a classroom setting.
Physical Education and Recreation
Dist - GPN **Prod** - WVIZTV 1979

Single Armstretchers / Trunk Twist and Rotation / Leg Circles 15 MIN
U-matic / VHS
Roomnastics Series
Color (P)
Presents several exercises which can be performed in a classroom setting.
Physical Education and Recreation
Dist - GPN **Prod** - WVIZTV 1979

Single Beam Spectrophotometer, Wavelength Calibration 9 MIN
U-matic
Color (PRO)
LC 79-708036
Demonstrates calibration of a single - beam spectrophotometer using a didymium filter at 585 nanometers.
Science
Dist - USNAC **Prod** - CFDISC 1979

The Single - Celled Animals - Protozoa 17 MIN
U-matic / VHS / 16mm
Biology (Spanish Series Unit 7 - Animal Classification and 'Physiology; Unit 7 - Animal classification and physiology
Color (H) (SPANISH)
Illustrates the characteristics and behavior of each class of protozoans. Demonstrates the processes of digestion and reproduction in protozoans and discusses theories of protozoan evolution.
Foreign Language; Science - Natural
Dist - EBEC **Prod** - EBEC

Single concept drug film series
Alcohol 29 MIN
Dist - USNAC

Single - Concept Films in Physics Series

Absorption spectra A - 4	4 MIN
Coupled Oscillators - Equal Masses M - 1	3 MIN
Coupled Oscillators - Unequal Masses M - 2	3 MIN
Critical temperature H - 1	3 MIN
Double slit L - 2	3 MIN
Ferromagnetic domain wall motion E - 1	3 MIN
Inertial Forces - Centripetal Acceleration M - 5	3 MIN
Inertial Forces - Translational Acceleration M - 4	3 MIN
Michelson Interferometer L - 4	3 MIN
Nonrecurrent Wavefronts W - 3	3 MIN
Paramagnetism of Liquid Oxygen E - 2	3 MIN
Radioactive Decay A - 1	3 MIN
Resolving Power L - 3	3 MIN
Scintillation Spectrometry a - 2	3 MIN
Single Slit L - 1	3 MIN
Tacoma Narrows Bridge Collapse W - 4	35 MIN
Temperature Waves W - 1	3 MIN
The Wilberforce Pendulum M - 6	3 MIN

Dist - OSUMPD

Single Handed Sailing 15 MIN
16mm
Sports Film Olympic Promotion Series
Color (I)
LC 72-705664
Teaches the points of sailing in a bay and racing skills in setting sails and trimming the boat while reaching, running and beating.
Physical Education and Recreation; Social Science
Dist - SPORTF **Prod** - SPORTF 1970

Single Insulator Changeout
VHS / U-matic
Live Line Maintenance Series
Color (IND)
Shows that the objective of a single insulator changeout is to lift and secure one conductor clear of its insulator. Demonstrates use of a temporary conductor holder, rubber gloves and an aerial device.
Industrial and Technical Education
Dist - LEIKID **Prod** - LEIKID

A Single Light 30 MIN
U-matic / 16mm / VHS
Color (J H A)
Presents a story which shows the importance of forgiveness. Based on the novel A SINGLE LIGHT by Maria Wojciechowska.
Guidance and Counseling; Literature and Drama; Psychology
Dist - LCOA **Prod** - LCOA 1984

Single living 30 MIN
U-matic / VHS
Family portrait - a study of contemporary lifestyles series; Lesson 11
Color (C A)
Looks at social and personality characteristics, security, happiness and problems of the unmarried. Examines advantages, disadvantages, myths and stereotypes that surround the single person.
Sociology
Dist - CDTEL **Prod** - SCCON

Single mothers - living on the edge 29 MIN
VHS
Color (J H G)
$250.00 purchase, $60.00 rental
Reveals that in the United States, one in four families is headed by women and half of these families live in poverty because of economic discrimination against women. Visits three women of different ages and backgrounds who tell of their struggle to provide for their families, dead - end jobs, female - male wage inequity, lack of child care, insufficient child support and demeaning social service. Produced and directed by Megan Siler.
Sociology
Dist - CF

Single Parent 42 MIN
U-matic / VHS / 16mm
Color (J)
Presents a portrait of the life of a divorced woman and the burdens she must cope with.
Guidance and Counseling; Sociology
Dist - MEDIAG **Prod** - MEDIAG 1978

The Single Parent 28 MIN
16mm
Look at Me Series no 5
Color (A)
LC 77-700462
Describes how single parents can have fun with their children.
Guidance and Counseling; Physical Education and Recreation; Psychology; Sociology
Dist - USNAC **Prod** - PARLTF 1975

The Single parent 15 MIN
VHS
Family life - transitions in a marriage - a case history - series
Color (A)
Portrays the divorce of Helene and Alan which is now final. Reveals that Helene has custody of the children, Kathy, Bobby and Christine, and is trying to manage the family on a very limited income. Alan takes the children on a jaunt in a rented sailboat with his new girlfriend, obviously financially well off. Helene attends a Parents Without Partners meeting and meets Ray, who is interested in her. Part of a series following a family through divorce, single parenthood and remarriage.
Health and Safety; Sociology
Dist - VIEWTH **Prod** - VIEWTH

The Single Parent Experience 29 MIN
U-matic
Woman Series
Color
Talks about the joys and pitfalls of being a single parent.

Sociology
Dist - PBS **Prod** - WNEDTV

Single - parent families 30 MIN
VHS / U-matic
Family portrait - a study of contemporary lifestyles series; Lesson 27
Color (C A)
Profiles the relationship of adults and children in a single - parent family. Explores the legal, financial, emotional and social problems of single - parent faimlies.
Sociology
Dist - CDTEL **Prod** - SCCON

The Single Parent Family 15 MIN
U-matic / VHS / 16mm
Family Life - Transitions in a Marriage Series
Color (I J H C A)
$355, $250 purchase _ #80543
Shows the different aspects and issues of single parenthood and post - divorce problems.
Sociology
Dist - CORF

Single Parent Family
U-matic / VHS
Vital Link Series
Color (A)
Explores the way in which schools and communities are responding to nearly half the nation's children.
Guidance and Counseling; Social Science; Sociology
Dist - EDCC **Prod** - EDCC

The Single Parent Family 15 MIN
U-matic / VHS / 16mm
Family Life - Transitions in Marriage Series
Color (I)
LC 81-701448
Examines the adjustmentgs that children and parents must make after a divorce. Follows the case of a fictional couple whose divorce results in the woman having to face the problems and issues of single parenthood.
Sociology
Dist - CORF **Prod** - GORKER 1981

The Single parent family 26 MIN
VHS
Color (J H)
$175.00 purchase _ #06863 - 126
Speculates that nearly half of families in the United States may be single parent homes. States that lower achievement in school, discipline and health problems may result. Interviews students and teachers who give personal accounts of the emotional and practical adjustments necessary for this type of family.
Sociology
Dist - GA **Prod** - EDCC

The Single Parent Family 26 MIN
VHS
Color (C A)
$75.00 purchase, $35.00 rental
Addresses the challenge of raising children as a single parent. The dimensions of single parenting are explored and emphasis is placed on its impact on children.
Psychology; Sociology
Dist - CORNRS **Prod** - EDCC 1980

Single Parent, the, Pt 1 22 MIN
16mm
Color (A)
Covers the issues of conflicts faced by single parents in responding both to needs of children and the demands of a job. Covers also the issue of establishing new relationships and loneliness.
Psychology; Sociology
Dist - AACD **Prod** - AACD 1981

Single Parent, the, Pt 2 22 MIN
16mm
Color (A)
Explores remarriage of an ex - spouse, social situations around a two - parent - family, and needs of a single parent for help from family and friends.
Psychology; Sociology
Dist - AACD **Prod** - AACD 1981

Single parenting 30 MIN
VHS
Color (A H)
$39.95 purchase _ #VB300V-H
Explores all the difficulties and joys of being a single parent. Features both single mothers and fathers who give advice from their own experiences on what works and what to watch out for. The children of single parents reveal their true feelings by discussing pictures they have drawn.
Sociology
Dist - CAMV

Single parenting 20 MIN
VHS
Color (J H G)
$97.00 purchase _ #05823 - 126
Covers the issues of discipline, financial problems, family crises within single parent families. Suggests where a single parent can find support, training and guidance.
Health and Safety; Sociology
Dist - GA **Prod** - UNL

Single Parenting
VHS
Practical Parenting Series
$89.95 purchase _ #014 - 120
Provides instruction on how to manage a single parent household.
Sociology
Dist - CAREER **Prod** - CAREER

Single Parenting - a New Page in America's Family Album 25 MIN
U-matic
Color (J H C A)
Examines the new trend of single parenting in America.
Sociology
Dist - CEPRO **Prod** - CEPRO

Single Parenting - a New Page in America's Family Album 25 MIN
VHS
Color (J A)
Presents a positive overview of changes in parenting. Looks at the traditional divorced single mother, the single father, women who have chosen to have children without marriage and co - parenting.
Sociology
Dist - CEPRO **Prod** - CEPRO 1989

Single parenting - one - parent families; 2nd Edition 27 MIN
VHS
Practical parenting series
CC; Color (F A)
$99 purchase _ #283VL
Focuses on single parents and families. Looks at ways to deal with the challenges of having only one parent in the family. Examines ways of minimizing the adverse effects of a death or divorce. Comes with a leader's guide.
Sociology
Dist - UNL

Single parents 28 MIN
U-matic
Are you listening series
Color (I J H C)
LC 80-707405
Highlights the joys and jolts of the single parent experience.
Sociology
Dist - STURTM **Prod** - STURTM 1980

Single Parents - and Other Adults 25 MIN
U-matic / VHS / 16mm
Color (A)
Presents 18 vignettes showing situations single parents are likely to encounter with other adults such as struggling with an ex - spouse over money and visiting arrangements, trying to find a new mate or a date at the same time that children require so much attention, making holidays festive and dealing with grandparents' concern over how a new single parent will manage.
Psychology; Sociology
Dist - CORF **Prod** - CORF

Single Parents and their Children 18 MIN
16mm / U-matic / VHS
Color (A)
Presents 13 vignettes showing stressful situations faced by single parents including the need to be both mother and father, bringing other adult's into children's lives, coping with the simultaneous demands of children, work and household maintenance, and arranging children's visits.
Psychology; Sociology
Dist - CORF **Prod** - CORF

Single Pass Fillet 3 MIN
BETA / VHS
Welding Training (Comprehensive - Metal Inert Gas (M I G Welding 'Series
Color (IND)
Industrial and Technical Education; Psychology
Dist - RMIBHF **Prod** - RMIBHF

Single Pass Fillet (Vertical Down) 2 MIN
BETA / VHS
Welding Training (Comprehensive - Metal Inert Gas (M I G Welding 'Series
Color (IND)
Industrial and Technical Education; Psychology
Dist - RMIBHF **Prod** - RMIBHF

Single pass fillet weld 15 MIN
U-matic / VHS
Arc welding training series
Color (IND)
Industrial and Technical Education
Dist - AVIMA **Prod** - AVIMA

Single - Phase AC Induction Motor Maintenance 60 MIN
VHS
Motors and Motor Controllers Series
Color (PRO)
$600.00, $1500.00 purchase _ #EMSPA
Explains single - phase motor operation. Emphasizes recognizing and distinguishing between different types of single - phase motors and the procedures associated with common single - phase motor maintenance tasks. Part of a ten - part series on motors and motor controllers, which is part of a 29 unit set on electrical maintenance. Includes 10 textbooks and an instructor guide which provide four hours of instruction.
Education; Industrial and Technical Education; Psychology
Dist - NUSTC **Prod** - NUSTC

Single - phase and polyphase circuits 17 MIN
16mm
Electrical work - electrical machinery series; No 1
B&W
LC FIE52-242
Explains a single - phase synchronous generator, the use of sine curves to illustrate flow changes, two - and three - phase systems, and ways of simplifying wiring.
Industrial and Technical Education
Dist - USNAC **Prod** - USOE 1945

Single Phase Boundary Potentials, Electrochemical Potentials, Half - Cells, 53 MIN
VHS / U-matic
Electrochemistry Series
Color
Discusses single phase boundary potentials, electrochemical potentials, half - cells, standard electrode potentials and thermodynamic and other single ion properties.
Science; Science - Physical
Dist - KALMIA **Prod** - KALMIA

Single phase boundary potentials - electrochemical potentials - half - cells - E 53 MIN
U-matic / VHS
Electrochemistry - Pt III - thermodynamics of galvanic cells series
Color
Discusses single phase boundary potentials, electrochemical potentials, half - cells, E not accessible, standard electrode potentials and thermodynamic and other single ion properties.
Science; Science - Physical
Dist - MIOT **Prod** - MIOT

Single Photon Emission Computed Tomography for the Evaluation of Renal Function. 11 MIN
VHS / 16mm
(C)
$385.00 purchase _ #860VI001
Introduces the technology of single photon emission computed tomography - SPECT - and shows some specific examples of how it has been used in patients with renal abnormalities.
Health and Safety
Dist - HSCIC **Prod** - HSCIC 1986

Single piece wheel rim 9 MIN
BETA / VHS / U-matic
Driving safety series
Color (G)
$589.00 purchase, $125.00 rental _ #SIN001
Demonstrates the proper way of changing a tire on a single - piece wheel rim. Corrects some common misconceptions about safe tire changing practices.
Health and Safety; Industrial and Technical Education
Dist - ITF **Prod** - GPCV

Single Process Blonding (Tinting) (#1)
U-matic / VHS
Color
Demonstrates a variety of techniques and coloring effects. Shows how to lighten brown hair that has been permanent - waved, and how to lighten or darken several shades of graying hair while achieving natural results. Explains formulation, experimentation and swatch testing.
Education; Home Economics
Dist - MPCEDP **Prod** - MPCEDP 1984

Single Process Tint Application
U-matic / VHS
Color
Explains the concepts of 'lift' and 'deposit,' oxidation and various volumes of peroxide. Covers the entire procedure of the tinting service from client consultation to after - care advice. Details the strand test procedure, sectioning, and virgin application of tint. Outlines the correct procedure for removal of tint from the hair and finishing procedures.

Education; Home Economics
Dist - MPCEDP Prod - MPCEDP 1984

Single Ram Vertical Surface Broaching 28 MIN
16mm
Machine Shop Work Series Operations on a Broaching Machine, no 2
B&W
LC FIE51-582
Shows how to install broaching inserts for straddle broaching, mount the tool - holder with its assembled broaching tool, mount and adjust the work fixture, and surface - broach at production rate.
Industrial and Technical Education
Dist - USNAC Prod - USOE 1945

Single screw boathandling
VHS
Color (G)
$39.80 purchase _ #0957
Teaches single screw boathandling. Includes the basics of safe trailering, launching, maneuvering, docking and retrieving. Covers all legally required safety equipment.
Physical Education and Recreation
Dist - SEVVID

Single sideband
VHS
Color (G A)
$29.95 purchase _ #0855
Presents step - by - step instructions on the installation and operation of the single sideband transceiver.
Industrial and Technical Education; Physical Education and Recreation; Social Science
Dist - SEVVID

Single Slit L - 1 3 MIN
16mm
Single - Concept Films in Physics Series
Color (H C)
Shows variable width and variable wave length.
Science - Physical
Dist - OSUMPD Prod - OSUMPD 1963

Single Stage Proctocolectomy for Ulcerative Colitis 22 MIN
16mm
Color (PRO)
Shows a two team combined abdomino - perineal approach to proctocolectomy and ileostomy in a young man with severe ulcerative colitis.
Health and Safety; Science
Dist - ACY Prod - ACYDGD 1970

Single Station Digital Controllers 60 MIN
VHS / 16mm
Control Technology and Application Series
Color (PRO)
$595.00 purchase, $125.00 rental
Includes Overview, Features, Automatic Tuning, Benefits, Applications - PID Control, 3 - Element Drum Level Control, Applications - Ratio Control and Batch Control. Part of a seven - part series on control technology and application.
Industrial and Technical Education
Dist - ISA Prod - ISA

Single - Station Hand - Operated Bench Punch 24 MIN
BETA / VHS
Color (IND)
Demonstrates the operation and set - up for changing punches and dies in a hand - operated single - station bench punch.
Industrial and Technical Education; Psychology
Dist - RMIBHF Prod - RMIBHF

Single subscripted variables 29 MIN
U-matic / VHS
Programming for microcomputers series; Unit 18
Color (J)
LC 83-707136
Introduces arrays and subscripted variables and shows how to dimension arrays. Explains the elements of a list and presents programs with one - dimensional arrays. Shows how to use more than one array, how to sort a list of numbers and how a list of names can be printed in alphabetical order.
Mathematics
Dist - IU Prod - IU 1983

Single tactics 30 MIN
VHS
Tennis talk series
Color (J H A)
$24.95 purchase _ #PRO006V
Features tennis instructor Dennis Van der Meer teaching about singles tactics.
Physical Education and Recreation
Dist - CAMV

The Single Thyroid Nodule 19 MIN
16mm
Color (PRO)
Presents the single thyroid nodule. Discusses the selection of cases for surgery and the methods of management including those situations where malignancy is encountered.
Health and Safety; Science
Dist - ACY Prod - ACYDGD 1961

Single Tuned RF Amplifier 26 MIN
16mm
B&W
LC 75-700581
Discusses the single tuned RF amplifiers using capacitive and transformer coupling. Explains circuit operation with respect to a parallel resonant tank in the plate circuit of the capacitance coupled amplifier. Explains circuit operation with respect to a series resonant tank in the grid circuit of the transformer coupled amplifier's second stage.
Civics and Political Systems; Industrial and Technical Education; Science - Physical
Dist - USNAC Prod - USAF

Single Visit Root Canal Treatment on an Upper Premolar 34 MIN
U-matic
Color (C)
Covers a clinical endodontic treatment of a maxillary premolar from anesthesia to polycarboxylate placement.
Health and Safety; Science - Natural
Dist - UOKLAH Prod - UOKLAH 1986

Singleness and marriage - Tape 1 80 MIN
VHS
One is a whole number series
Color (H C G A R)
$10.00 rental _ #36 - 86421 - 1518
Features the comedy team of Hicks and Cohagan in dramatizations of situations Christian single adults often face. Covers topics related to singleness and marriage. Narrated by Dr Harold Ivan Smith. Consists of two 40 - minute episodes.
Guidance and Counseling; Psychology; Religion and Philosophy
Dist - APH Prod - SPAPRO

Singles Strategy 29 MIN
U-matic / VHS
Love Tennis Series
Color
Features Lew Gerrard and Don Candy giving tennis instructions, emphasizing singles strategy.
Physical Education and Recreation
Dist - MDCPB Prod - MDCPB

Singles Strategy, Pt 1 29 MIN
VHS / U-matic
Vic Braden's Tennis for the Future Series
Color
Physical Education and Recreation
Dist - PBS Prod - WGBHTV 1981

Singles Strategy, Pt 2 29 MIN
U-matic / VHS
Vic Braden's Tennis for the Future Series
Color
Physical Education and Recreation
Dist - PBS Prod - WGBHTV 1981

Singles tactics 30 MIN
VHS
Tennis with Van der Meer series
Color (C A)
$95.00 purchase, $55.00 rental
Features tennis player and instructor Dennis Van der Meer in a presentation on singles tactics. Uses freeze - frame photography and repetition to stress skill development. Serves as part five of a 10 - part telecourse.
Physical Education and Recreation; Psychology
Dist - SCETV Prod - SCETV 1989

The Singular Duo 8 MIN
U-matic / VHS
Color (IND)
Shows the use of the Ansul brand model AFFF wheeled fire fighting equipment in extinguishing and securing flammable liquid fires. Teaches how to prevent ignition of a fuel spill during the securing stage. Illustrates recharging extinguishers.
Health and Safety
Dist - ANSUL Prod - ANSUL 1980

Singular illumination of the body 31 MIN
16mm
Color (A)
$90.00 rental
Explore the naked heterosexual male body in relation to issues of language and hysteria. Uses a stuttered text against images analyzing the semiotics of male prowess and abjection. The middle section murders a body in a vacant apartment. The last section is exhibitionist - the filmmaker, naked, in extreme slow motion, manipulates part of his body, created waves of flesh. Set against a text which draws the body into the realm of speech.
Fine Arts; Psychology
Dist - CANCIN Prod - SONDHE 1990

Singular Perturbation Theory and Geophysics 50 MIN
16mm
MAA Mathematics Series
B&W (C A)
LC 74-702789
Discusses how geophysical phenomena, the wind - driven Gulf Stream in the Atlantic and the Kuroshio in the Pacific, from the point of view of singular perturbation theory with extensive comments about the boundary between applied and pure mathematics.
Mathematics; Science - Physical
Dist - MLA Prod - MAA 1974

S'Initier a La Peinture 6 MIN
U-matic / VHS / 16mm
Color (I J H)
LC 79-707258
Shows many examples of art work produced with tempera paint by children three and five, when creativity is great at age six when recognizable figures are introduced and at age seven when skills begin to catch up with ideas.
Fine Arts; Foreign Language
Dist - IFB Prod - CRAF 1957

Sink - Float 14 MIN
U-matic / VHS
Hands on, Grade 2 - Lollipops, Loops, Etc Series Unit 3 - 'Classifying; Unit 3 - Classifying
Color (P)
Gives experience in classifying things that float versus things that sink.
Science
Dist - AITECH Prod - WHROTV 1975

Sink or swim 28 MIN
VHS
Young adult issues series
Color (G R)
$29.95 purchase
Deals with issue of integrity in a scholastic achievement - sports participation situation. Dramatizes a young man's struggle in deciding whether to compromise his values to remain on the swim team, and the consequences involved.
Physical Education and Recreation; Religion and Philosophy
Dist - GF

Sink or swim 48 MIN
U-matic / 16mm / VHS
B&W (G)
$725.00, $295.00 purchase, $145.00 rental
Gives a compelling account of the conflicts and connections between parent and child - particularly father and daughter. Opens up questions of generational, gender and sexual difference within a personal narrative.
Sociology
Dist - WMEN Prod - SUFR 1990

Sink the Bismarck 97 MIN
VHS
B&W (G)
$100.00 rental _ #0965
Dramatizes the true story of World War II of the sinking of the Bismarck. Uses actual combat footage.
Civics and Political Systems; Fine Arts; History - United States; Sociology
Dist - SEVVID

The Sinking Ark - Pt 2 58 MIN
VHS
Only One Earth Series
Color (S)
$129.00 purchase _ #227 - 9002
Explores and demystifies the links between environment and development and illustrates the detrimental clashes between economics and ecology in the first three hour - long programs. Part 2 of eleven reveals that by destroying the environment, we are endangering the future of the planet - and ourselves. Many animals and plants provide us with life - saving medicines. In order to save ourselves, we must protect species and prevent their extinction.
Agriculture; Science - Natural
Dist - FI Prod - BBCTV 1987

The Sinking of the Lusitania 17 MIN
U-matic / VHS / 16mm
World War I Series
B&W (H C)
Tells how the sinking of the Lusitania in 1915 turned the tide of public opinion against Germany and paved the way for America's declaration of war.
History - United States; History - World
Dist - FI Prod - CBSTV 1967

The Sinking of the Lusitania - Unrestricted Submarine Warfare 17 MIN
16mm / U-matic / VHS
World War I Series
B&W
LC FIA67-1772
Shows how the United States was brought to the brink of war in 1915 when Germany violated international law and sank the merchant ship Lusitania without warning, killing 1,200 people, including 128 Americans.
History - United States; History - World
Dist - FI **Prod** - CBSTV 1967

Sino - American Relations - a New Beginning 16 MIN
U-matic / VHS
Color (H C A)
Documents the opening of American - Chinese relations in the early 1970's. Tells how this alliance integrated China into the world community.
Civics and Political Systems; History - World
Dist - JOU **Prod** - UPI

Sinopah trails - Glacier National Park along Canadian Border with Montana, USA 15 MIN
U-matic / VHS / BETA
National park series
Color (P I J H)
$29.95 purchase, $130.00 purchase _ #LSTF108
Travels through the life zones - biomes - on a mountain in Waterton Lakes International Peace Park. Explains how biomes change with elevation and some of the environmental differences that cause changes in plant and animal life. Includes teachers' guide. Produced by Nature Episodes assisted by Glacier National Park.
Geography - United States; Geography - World; Science - Natural
Dist - FEDU

Sins of our mothers 60 MIN
VHS
Color (G)
$59.95 purchase
Recalls the antipathies against women in America's past, the taboos against them and the punishment of their lives. Tells of Emeline who went to work in the Lyon textile mills in Maine at the age of 13 and suffered a shocking fate - her story told only in whispers in the tiny town of Fayette.
History - United States; Sociology
Dist - NEFILM

The Sins of our mothers 60 MIN
VHS
Color; Captioned (G)
$59.95 purchase _ #AMEX - 116
Tells how women in 19th century New England were able to work in the mills of Lowell, Massachusetts. Shows that the women worked in a highly structured environment. Focuses on the story of one woman, Emeline Gurney, who began working in the Lowell mills at age 13. Narrated by actress Amanda Plummer.
History - United States; Sociology
Dist - PBS

The Sins of the Father 29 MIN
16mm
This is the Life Series
Color
Describes how a young woman's marriage is almost destroyed by the memories of her father's incestuous relationship with her.
Psychology; Sociology
Dist - LUTTEL **Prod** - LUTTEL 1983

Sinus Arrhythmias 49 MIN
U-matic
EKG Interpretation and Assessment Series
Color (PRO)
Teaches the criteria for the identification of common arrhythmias originating in the sino atrial node.
Science; Science - Natural
Dist - CSUS **Prod** - CSUS 1984

Sinus beta 6 MIN
16mm
B&W (G)
$15.00 rental
Features a montage of several shots from previous films.
Fine Arts
Dist - CANCIN **Prod** - KRENKU 1967

Sinus or Sinusitis 13 MIN
U-matic / VHS
Color (PRO)
Reviews the physiology of the sinuses. Provides the physician with an appropriate method of evaluation and differential diagnosis of patients who complain of 'sinus trouble.' Discusses treatment plans based on the cause of the disease for both acute and chronic infections.
Health and Safety
Dist - UMICHM **Prod** - UMICHM 1976

Sinusitis and sinus surgery 12 MIN
VHS
Color (PRO G)
$250.00 purchase _ #OT - 10
Explains symptoms, causes, evaluation and treatment of sinusitis. Explains the role of medical therapy and irrigation. Reveals that tests such as rhinoscopy, endoscopy or CT scans may be reeded. Presents internal and external sinus surgery as options when other treatments prove ineffective. Risks are discussed. Developed in cooperation with and endorsed by the American Academy of Otolaryngology - Head and Neck Surgery.
Health and Safety
Dist - MIFE **Prod** - MIFE 1991

Siobhan Mc Kenna 29 MIN
Videoreel / VT2
Elliot Norton Reviews II Series
Color
Presents exchanges and arguments between the dean of American theatre critics, Elliot Norton, and Siobhan Mc Kenna.
Fine Arts
Dist - PBS **Prod** - WGBHTV

Sioux County, Iowa, USA 22 MIN
16mm
Color
LC FIA67-5815
Reports on the activities of farm cooperatives in Sioux County, Iowa, a county which has numerous farm cooperatives and is noted for its many residents of Dutch descent.
Agriculture; Geography - United States
Dist - FARMI **Prod** - FARMI 1966

Sioux legends 20 MIN
VHS
Color (G)
$69.95 purchase _ #S01418
Presents legends of the Sioux Indian culture which reveal much about the religion and philosophy of the Sioux people. Features dramatic footage of the Black Hills and Badlands regions of South Dakota.
Geography - United States; Social Science
Dist - UILL

Sioux Legends 20 MIN
U-matic / VHS / 16mm
Color (I)
LC 74-702141
Presents members of the Sioux tribes in South Dakota acting out some of their legends and folklores. Gives an impression of Indian culture and daily life before the arrival of the white man and shows the universality of folklore.
Social Science
Dist - AIMS **Prod** - NAUMAN 1974

The Sioux Painter 29 MIN
VHS / U-matic
Color (G)
Preserves the Sioux culture by giving visual form to Sioux ideas. Discusses his cultural heritage and its influence on every facet of his painting. Howe's creations derive their uniqueness from his geometric use of lines and aesthetic points. His bright colors and abstract shapes let him paint today's man in a traditional context.
Social Science
Dist - NAMPBC **Prod** - NAMPBC 1973

Sippie Wallace 23 MIN
VHS
Color (G)
$24.95 purchase
Focuses on jazz singer Sippie Wallace.
Fine Arts
Dist - KINOIC **Prod** - RHPSDY

Sips and Songs 28 MIN
U-matic / VHS
Color (J A)
Features entertainer Phil Gordon as he sings familiar songs.
Fine Arts; Health and Safety
Dist - SUTHRB **Prod** - SUTHRB

Siqueiros 56 MIN
U-matic / VHS
Color (C) (SPANISH)
$279.00, $179.00 purchase _ #AD - 2186
Looks at Mexican muralist, Jose David Alfaro Sequeiros. Looks at his pre - Hispanic artistic roots and his role in the political revolution of the 1930s. In Spanish.
Biography; Civics and Political Systems; Fine Arts; Foreign Language; Geography - World; History - World; Social Science
Dist - FOTH **Prod** - FOTH

Siqueiros, El Maestro - March of Humanity in Latin America 14 MIN
16mm / U-matic / VHS
Rasgos Culturales Series
Color; B&W (J H C) (LATIN)
LC 74-704165
Presents a documentary account of the largest mural ever created, 'THE MARCH OF HUMANITY IN LATIN AMERICA,' painted by David Siqueiros in Mexico City. Explains some of the artistic innovations of Siqueiros, emphasizing esculpto - pintura. Includes scenes of the artist as he supervises, paints, plans and discusses his techniques and his philosophy reflected in the theme of the mural.
Fine Arts
Dist - EBEC **Prod** - EBEC 1969

Siqueiros, El Maestro - the March of Humanity in Latin America 14 MIN
U-matic / VHS / 16mm
Color (J H C) (LATIN)
Focuses on The March Of Humanity In Latin America, a mural by David Siqueiros. Shows how Siqueiros employs a combination of sculpture and painting techniques in order to create his murals. Discusses the artist's philosophy and explains how it is reflected in the theme of the mural.
Fine Arts; Foreign Language
Dist - EBEC **Prod** - EBEC

Sir Arthur 'Bomber' Harris - Marshal of the Royal Air Force 52 MIN
16mm / U-matic / VHS
Commanders Series Number 5; No 5
Color (H C A)
LC 79-701085
Looks at the career of Sir Arthur Harris, the Marshal of the Royal Air Force during World War II.
Biography; History - World
Dist - TIMLIF **Prod** - BBCTV 1976

Sir Arthur Harris, marshal of the RAF 60 MIN
VHS
Commanders series
Color; PAL (H C A)
PdS99 purchase; Not available in the United States.
Documents the way in which a few select men strove to make their countries victorious in World War II. Focuses on the man who carried out the controversial policy of bombing German cities like Dresden. Includes archival footage and interviews with family, friends and colleagues. Part two of a seven part series.
History - United States; History - World
Dist - BBCENE

Sir Author Conan Doyle - the man who was Sherlock Holmes 26 MIN
VHS / U-matic
Stamp of greatness series
Color (H G)
$280.00, $330.00 purchase, $50.00 rental
Tells the story of Doyle's life and some of the causes he championed. Reveals that, apart from his career as an author, he ran a front line hospital during the Boer War, introduced cross country skiing into Switzerland, the steel helmet into the Army and the life jacket into the Navy during the First World War. Looks at various reforms he supported along with his active support of Spiritualism.
Fine Arts; Literature and Drama
Dist - NDIM **Prod** - TYNT 1990

Sir Edmund Hillary - Kaipo Wall 53 MIN
VHS
Color; Stereo (G)
$19.98 purchase _ #TT8037
Features legendary adventurer Sir Edmund Hillary as he leads a team of climbers on an expedition to conquer New Zealand's Kaipo Wall.
Literature and Drama; Physical Education and Recreation
Dist - TWINTO **Prod** - TWINTO 1990

Sir Ewart Jones 30 MIN
VHS
Eminent chemists videotapes series
Color (H C G)
$60.00 purchase _ #VT - 038
Meets chemist Sir Ewart Jones. Part of a series glimpsing into the history of chemistry and offering insights into the successes, trials and tribulations of some of the most distinguished names in the world of chemistry.
Science
Dist - AMCHEM

Sir Francis Drake - the Rise of English Sea Power 30 MIN
16mm / U-matic / VHS
B&W (I J H)
Shows how Sir Francis Drake won England the right - of - way into a new continent, captured vast treasures, terrorized the Spanish Navy and persuaded the people of England to 'look to the sea for their strength.'.

History - World
Dist - EBEC **Prod** - EBEC 1957

Sir George Porter 30 MIN
VHS
Eminent chemists videotapes series
Color (H C G)
$60.00 purchase _ #VT - 037
Meets chemist Sir George Porter. Part of a series glimpsing into the history of chemistry and offering insights into the successes, trials and tribulations of some of the most distinguished names in the world of chemistry.
Science
Dist - AMCHEM

Sir Hugh Casson 30 MIN
VHS
Making their mark series
Color (A)
PdS65 purchase _ Unavailable in South Africa
Profiles Sir Hugh Casson, who has a unique drawing style and way of working. Introduces the viewer to practical and aesthetic aspects of the skill of drawing. Part of a six-part series.
Fine Arts
Dist - BBCENE

Sir James Goldsmith 40 MIN
VHS / 16mm
Take it from the Top Series
Color (A PRO)
$295.00 purchase
Interviews Sir James Goldsmith, the only living Englishman to have become a billionaire by his own efforts. Discusses his business philosophy. Part of a series featuring David Frost who interviews successful English businessmen.
Business and Economics; Geography - World; Guidance and Counseling; Psychology; Religion and Philosophy; Sociology
Dist - VIDART **Prod** - VIDART 1991

Sir John Harvey - Jones 32 MIN
VHS / 16mm
Take it from the Top Series
Color (A PRO)
$295.00 purchase
Interviews Sir John Harvey - Jones who ran ICI, England's largest company. Discusses leadership and management. Part of a series featuring David Frost who interviews successful English businessmen.
Business and Economics; Geography - World; Guidance and Counseling; Psychology; Sociology
Dist - VIDART **Prod** - VIDART 1991

Sir John Peck 29 MIN
U-matic
Dana Wynter in Ireland Series
Color
Interviews Sir John Peck, former British ambassador to Ireland. Gives his thoughts on the Irish problem and offers a tour of his home in Ireland.
Biography; Geography - World
Dist - PBS **Prod** - GRIAN

Sir Laurence Olivier dies - Tuesday, July 11, 1989 30 MIN
VHS
Nightline series
Color (H C G)
$14.98 purchase _ #MP6175
Marks the death of Shakespearean actor, Sir Laurence Olivier, age 82.
Fine Arts
Dist - INSTRU **Prod** - ABCNEW 1989

Sir Terence Conran 52 MIN
VHS
Color (S)
$39.95 purchase _ #833 - 9356
Demonstrates the design revolution of Sir Terence Conran by showing a typical 1950s living room, then transforming it, a la Conran, to reflect the cheerful, clean and simple style of the 1960s. Reveals that since he opened the first Habitat store in London, his empire has grown to more than 900 retail outlets. Includes a tour of Conran's mansion in Berkshire.
Fine Arts; Geography - World; Home Economics; Sociology
Dist - FI **Prod** - RMART 1988

Sir Thomas Beecham 83 MIN
VHS
Color (G)
$89.95 purchase _ #EX2838
Presents a portrait of the English conductor, Sir Thomas Beecham. Features Timothy West as Sir Thomas. Includes the Halle Orchestra.
Fine Arts; History - World
Dist - FOTH

Sir Walter Scott 29 MIN
VHS / 16mm
Famous Authors Series
Color (C)
$11.50 rental _ #35509
Chronicles the life of Sir Walter Scott (1771 - 1832) and his immensely popular career as a poet. Although financially successful for most of his life, Scott's investment in a publishing firm ended in financial disaster and he died in debt.
English Language; Fine Arts; Literature and Drama
Dist - EBEC

Sir Walter Scott 29 MIN
VHS
Famous Authors Series
Color (H)
$11.50 rental _ #35509
Follows Sir Walter Scott's life from a time of financial success and popularity to a final period of financial disaster and debt. An installment of the Famous Authors Series, which examines important English writers in the context of their times.
English Language; History - World; Literature and Drama
Dist - PSU **Prod** - EBEC

Sir Walter's Journey 50 MIN
VHS
Horizon series
Color (A PRO C)
PdS99 purchase
Seeks to prove, through the work of geneticist Walter Bodmer, that one's genes can detect Viking invaders in the Lake District of Britain and Flemish settlers in Wales. Ends quest in Orkney, where Bodmer uses latest DNA techniques to search for evidence of Britain's first inhabitants.
Science - Natural
Dist - BBCENE

Sir William Slim - Field Marshal, British Army 62 MIN
16mm / U-matic / VHS
Commanders Series Number 4; No 4
Color (H C A)
LC 79-701084
Examines the career of Sir William Slim, British commander in the China - Burma - India theater during World War II.
Biography; History - World
Dist - TIMLIF **Prod** - BBCTV 1976

Sirene 10 MIN
U-matic / VHS / 16mm
Color (H C)
LC 70-707285
Presents the story of a mermaid in the harbor of a modern city who is charmed by a young man playing a flute and attempts to flee with him but the machines that surround the harbor destroy her. Provides a satirical story of present day commercial life.
English Language; Literature and Drama; Psychology; Social Science; Sociology
Dist - IFB **Prod** - SERVA 1970

Sirens, Symbols and Gamour Girls, Pt 1 26 MIN
16mm
Hollywood and the Stars Series
B&W
LC FI68-249
Discusses the glamour girls of motion pictures and how the movie image of the ideal woman has changed. Includes scenes of Mary Pickford, Gloria Swanson, Greta Garbo, Jean Harlow, Mae West, Bette Davis, Lana Turner, Rita Hayworth and others.
Fine Arts; Home Economics
Dist - WOLPER **Prod** - WOLPER 1963

Sirens, Symbols and Gamour Girls, Pt 2 26 MIN
16mm
Hollywood and the Stars Series
B&W
LC 79-701987
Shows a view of the glamour girls of the screen - Rita Hayworth, Ava Gardner, Marilyn Monroe, Elizabeth Taylor. Analyzes their fame and power and discusses the price they pay. Includes scenes of young ingenues who hope to achieve fame.
Fine Arts; Home Economics
Dist - WOLPER **Prod** - WOLPER 1963

Sirius 51 MIN
U-matic / VHS / 16mm
Featurettes for Children Series
Color (J)
LC 78-701861
Tells a story about a young Czechoslovakian boy, his parents and his beloved dog Sirius during the early years of World War II. Shows how the boy is forced to examine his values when the Nazis demand that all dogs be surrendered for training as attack dogs.
Guidance and Counseling; History - World; Literature and Drama; Science - Natural
Dist - FI **Prod** - CFET 1978

Sirius and the White Dwarf 8 MIN
16mm
Explorations in Space and Time Series
Color (H C A)
LC 75-703982
Uses computer animation to demonstrate the motions of the star system composed of Sirius and its companion Sirius B, a white dwarf star. Discusses the laws and calculations that resulted in the discovery of the first white dwarf.
Science - Physical
Dist - HMC **Prod** - HMC 1974

Sirius, Pt 1 25 MIN
U-matic / VHS / 16mm
Featurettes for Children Series
Color (J)
LC 78-701861
Tells a story about a young Czechoslovakian boy, his parents and his beloved dog Sirius during the early years of World War II. Shows how the boy is forced to examine his values when the Nazis demand that all dogs be surrendered for training as attack dogs.
History - World
Dist - FI **Prod** - CFET 1978

Sirius, Pt 2 26 MIN
16mm / U-matic / VHS
Featurettes for Children Series
Color (J)
LC 78-701861
Tells a story about a young Czechoslovakian boy, his parents and his beloved dog Sirius during the early years of World War II. Shows how the boy is forced to examine his values when the Nazis demand that all dogs be surrendered for training as attack dogs.
Geography - World; History - World
Dist - FI **Prod** - CFET 1978

Sirius Remembered 11 MIN
16mm
Color; Silent (C)
$420.00
Experimental film by Stan Brakhage.
Fine Arts
Dist - AFA **Prod** - AFA 1959

Sisal 22 MIN
16mm
B&W (J H)
Discusses the sisal industry as well as the economy that has grown up around it in Africa.
Agriculture; Geography - World
Dist - VIEWTH **Prod** - GATEEF

Sissela Bok 30 MIN
VHS
World Of Ideas With Bill Moyers - Season I - series
Color (G)
$39.95 purchase _ #BMWI - 116
Interviews philosopher Sissela Bok, whose work explores issues of lying, deception and keeping of secrets. Examines the importance of public leaders mainatining the public trust.
Business and Economics; Civics and Political Systems; Guidance and Counseling; Psychology; Religion and Philosophy
Dist - PBS

Sister 22 MIN
16mm
Color
LC 75-703003
Depicts the thoughts and feelings of ten nuns on their work, the Church and modern life, and their service and commitment to God.
Civics and Political Systems; Religion and Philosophy; Sociology
Dist - CORPRO **Prod** - ARCHCC 1975

Sister Adrian - the Mother Theresa of Scranton 30 MIN
VHS
Color (G)
$59.95 purchase _ #SAMT - 000
Features Scranton, Pennsylvania nun Sister Adrian Barrett. Shows how Sister Adrian devotes her life to helping the poor and disadvantaged. Follows her through the course of a typical day. Narrated by actor Martin Sheen.
Sociology
Dist - PBS **Prod** - WVIATV 1987

Sister Goodwin - 3 - 2 - 85 40 MIN
VHS / Cassette
Poetry Center reading series
Color (G)
#620 - 524
Features the writer reading her works, including selections from A Lagoon Is In My Backyard, at the Poetry Center, San Francisco State University. Available only for listening purposes at the Center; not for sale or rent.
Literature and Drama
Dist - POETRY **Prod** - POETRY 1985

Sister Kenny 52805 116 MIN
BETA
B&W
Stars Rosalind Russell as Sister Elizabeth Kenny, the nurse who crusaded for the treatment of infantile paralysis.
Fine Arts
Dist - RMIBHF **Prod** - UNKNWN 1946

Sister of the Bride 30 MIN
U-matic / VHS / 16mm
Planning Ahead Series
Color (J)
LC 83-700504
Presents the story of two white, middle - class sisters whose mother, although divorced, tries to pressure them into early marriages. Follows the last few days before the elder's sister marriage, probing her doubts and uncertainties while the younger sister realizes that a career as a veterinarian is the most important thing in her life.
Guidance and Counseling; Sociology
Dist - UCEMC **Prod** - BERKS 1982

Sister, Sister - Enhancing Alternatives - 7 15 MIN
VHS
Your Choice - Our Chance Series
Color (I)
$180.00 purchase
Focuses on knowledge, attitudes and behaviors that influence drug free and drug use life styles. Emphasizes that effective drug abuse prevention education must begin before children are established users of tobacco, alcohol or other addictive drugs. Targets children in the vulnerable preteen years. Program 7 reveals that Alicia and Sophia's family is having a rough time, but Alicia makes a friend and buys a bike while Sophia gets involved with drugs.
Guidance and Counseling; Health and Safety; Psychology; Sociology
Dist - AITECH **Prod** - AITECH 1990

Sister, Sister - Health - Enhancing Alternatives 15 MIN
VHS / 16mm
Your Choice - Our Chance Series
Color (I A)
$180.00 purchase, $25.00 rental
Shows how constructive leisure - time activities can enhance physical and mental health and build self - esteem leading to greater wellness and resistence to drug abuse.
Health and Safety; Psychology
Dist - AITECH **Prod** - AITECH 1990

Sister Wendy's odyssey 60 MIN
VHS
Color (A)
PdS99 purchase
Features Sister Bendy Beckett who has lived in solitary religious contemplation for 22 years. Journeys to six of Britain's finest art galleries, where she talks about some of the greatest works of art held in these collections. Throughout the program she conveys her enthusiasm for art while providing some fascinating insights.
Fine Arts
Dist - BBCENE

Sisters 8 MIN
16mm
Color (G)
$15.00 rental
Celebrates Women's International Day march in San Francisco with joyous dancing from a collage of lesbians. Examines images of women doing all types of traditional 'men's work' and features Family of Woman.
Fine Arts; Sociology
Dist - CANCIN **Prod** - BARHAM 1973

Sisters cake decorating made fun and easy 55 MIN
VHS
Sisters cake decorating series
Color (J H G)
$39.95 purchase _ #CCP0044V
Covers, step - by - step, the basics of cake decorating. Features decorators with over 40 years experience. Offers good close - ups of the procedures described. Covers the basic equipment, ingredients and techniques for producing a variety of cakes, including a birthday cake, doll cake, bridal shower, Halloween, santa face and petite fours. Includes shortcuts, do's and don'ts and detailed techniques for making borders, flowers and more. Part of a two - part series.
Home Economics
Dist - CAMV **Prod** - CAMV 1990

Sisters cake decorating series
Presents a two - part series on cake decorating. Includes Sisters Cake Decorating Made Fun and Easy; Sisters Wedding Cake Decorating.
Sisters cake decorating made fun and easy 55 MIN
Sisters wedding cake decorating 47 MIN
Dist - CAMV **Prod** - CAMV 1990

Sisters in Crime 29 MIN
U-matic
Woman Series
Color
Explains why the crime rate among women is increasing several times faster than the male crime rate. Looks at the growing numbers of all - women gangs, the need for women in law enforcement, and the lack of rehabilitation in women's prisons.
Sociology
Dist - PBS **Prod** - WNEDTV

Sisters of the Space Age 29 MIN
16mm
Color (G)
_ #106C 0174 617
Demonstrates the capabilities of a new tribal class of destroyers built for Canada's Maritime Command - versatile peacetime ships for surveillance of territorial waters but also with military capacity. Tours some of the ships' installations and space age technology.
Civics and Political Systems
Dist - CFLMDC **Prod** - NFBC 1974

Sisters Under Siege 60 MIN
VHS
Oil Series
Color (G)
$59.95 purchase _ #OILO - 103
Discusses how seven corporations - Exxon, Mobil, Chevron, Texaco, Gulf, British Petroleum and Royal Dutch/Shell - dominated the world oil market after World War II. Shows that the Iranian crisis of the 1970s challenged this domination. Examines the situation in Iran, including a look at the Iran - Iraq war.
Business and Economics; History - World; Social Science
Dist - PBS

Sisters wedding cake decorating 47 MIN
VHS
Sisters cake decorating series
Color (J H G)
$39.95 purchase _ #CCP0045V
States that making a wedding cake is as simple as making three birthday cakes, that the tricky part is learning how to decorate the cake to make it an impressive, professional looking display. Demonstrates, step - by - step, the techniques for making beautiful wedding and anniversary cakes. Teaches about the tools used, the amount of cake mix and icing needed for different sized cakes and many tricks for creating edible masterpieces. Part of a two - part series.
Home Economics
Dist - CAMV **Prod** - CAMV 1991

Sisyphus 10 MIN
16mm
Color (C A)
LC 72-700404
Shows the destructiveness of materialism by telling the story of a man who was driven out of his mind when his possessions took on an animate force.
Psychology; Religion and Philosophy; Sociology
Dist - MMA **Prod** - ZAGREB 1970

Sisyphus 3 MIN
16mm / U-matic / VHS
B&W (J)
LC 76-701503
Shows a man pushing an ever - larger boulder up an ever - growing mountain with the use of animation.
Fine Arts; Religion and Philosophy
Dist - PFP **Prod** - JANK 1975

Sisyphus and Corinth 12 MIN
VHS / 16mm
Greek and Roman Mythology in Ancient Art Series
Color (I)
LC 90708208
Focuses on three different myths - the curse of Ixion, the tragedy of Tantalus and the rock of Sisyphus.
Fine Arts; History - World; Religion and Philosophy
Dist - BARR

Sit and Stay 30 MIN
VHS / U-matic
Training Dogs the Woodhouse Way
Color (H C A)
Shows Barbara Woodhouse's method of teaching a dog to sit and stay.
Home Economics; Science - Natural
Dist - FI **Prod** - BBCTV 1982

The Sit - down buffet
VHS
Frugal gourmet - entertaining series
Color (G)
$19.95 purchase _ #CCP843
Shows how to prepare a sit - down buffet. Features Jeff Smith, the Frugal Gourmet. Part of a ten - part series on preparing food for entertaining.
History - United States; Home Economics
Dist - CADESF **Prod** - CADESF

Sit Down, Doctor - and Live 11 MIN
U-matic / VHS / 16mm
Color
Points out that sit - down dentistry can prolong a dentist's useful operating life about ten years. Shows the direct approach to the four oral quadrants.
Health and Safety
Dist - USNAC **Prod** - VADTC

Sit Down, Shut Up, or Get Out 60 MIN
16mm
Color
$645 rental
Discusses the problems of 13 - year - old Christopher Bright in school. Discusses his antagonism of teachers and peers, and the failure of teachers to treat him as an individual. Written by Allan Sloane for NBC.
Education; Sociology
Dist - CCNCC **Prod** - CCNCC 1985

Sit Down, Shut Up, or Get Out 58 MIN
16mm / U-matic / VHS
Color (J)
LC 75-703347
Uses an allegorical play about an exceptionally bright junior - high school student in order to show how society and institutions make it difficult to be one's self. Examines the problems of parents, school teachers and others in dealing with exceptional children.
Education; Psychology; Sociology
Dist - FI **Prod** - NBCTV 1975

Sit Down, Shut Up, or Get Out, Pt 1 29 MIN
U-matic / VHS / 16mm
Color (H C)
Explains that society and institutions often make it difficult to be an individual. Features a boy who dares to be different and deals with the threat to individual freedom involved in the expression of dissent. Presents Christopher Bright who is intellectually gifted but has behavior problems because he cannot fit into the pattern of things in junior high school.
Guidance and Counseling; Psychology; Sociology
Dist - FI **Prod** - NBCTV

Sit Down, Shut Up, or Get Out, Pt 2 29 MIN
U-matic / VHS / 16mm
Color (H C)
Explains that society and institutions often make it difficult to be an individual. Features a boy who dares to be different and deals with the threat to individual freedom involved in the expression of dissent. Presents Christopher Bright who is intellectually gifted but has behavior problems because he cannot fit into the pattern of things in junior high school.
Guidance and Counseling; Psychology; Sociology
Dist - FI **Prod** - NBCTV

Sit Down - Sit Danish 14 MIN
16mm
Color
Presents the story of Danish furniture and shows its role in the lives of everyday people.
Fine Arts; Industrial and Technical Education
Dist - AUDPLN **Prod** - RDCG

Sit Housing Report 9 MIN
VHS / U-matic
Color
Features practical advice on coping with housing problems and the local agencies where viewers can go for help.
Sociology
Dist - NOVID **Prod** - NOVID

Sit - up shaped cakes
U-matic / VHS
Cake decorating series
(H A PRO)
$29.95_#CIN130V
Sketches the methods used in baking specialty cakes for many different occasions. Hosted by Frances Kuyper, known in the world of cake baking as the 'Cake Lady.'.
Home Economics; Industrial and Technical Education; Physical Education and Recreation
Dist - CAMV **Prod** - CAMV

Site 10 MIN
16mm
B&W
Deals with a film - document of a dance by Bob Morris and Carolee Schneeman set in a black infinite space.
Fine Arts
Dist - VANBKS **Prod** - VANBKS

Site selection and injection techniques 27 MIN
VHS / U-matic / BETA
Parenteral medication administration series
Color (C PRO)
$280.00 purchase _ #622.4
Begins with a discussion of common intramuscular injection sites and essential assessment consideration. Describes concisely the techniques for administration of intramuscular medications with emphasis on the displacement or Z - track method. Discusses subcutaneous site selection. Illustrates in detail procedures, including specific techniques for insulin and heparin administration. Highlights the use of Universal Precautions. Part of a four - part series on parenteral medication administration produced by Healthcare Media.
Health and Safety
Dist - CONMED

Sites unseen - off the beaten track in Jerusalem 45 MIN
VHS
Color (G)
$29.95 purchase _ #224
Offers a guide to the sights in Jerusalem, looking at lesser - known places, their history, including archival footage.
Geography - World; History - World
Dist - ERGOM

The Sitter 30 MIN
VHS
Join in series
Color (K P)
#362312
Shows that Jacob and Nikki help Zack prepare for his first job babysitting, and together they think up activities, songs, games, nursery rhymes and stories that children will enjoy. Part of a series about three artist - performers who share studio space in a converted warehouse.
Fine Arts; Literature and Drama
Dist - TVOTAR **Prod** - TVOTAR 1989

Sittin' on Top of the World - at the Fiddlers' Convention 24 MIN
U-matic / VHS / 16mm
Color (J)
LC 74-703305
Presents a documentary on the oldest and largest bluegrass music festival of the United States, held in the Smokey Mountains of North Carolina. Presents both contemporary and traditional performances of authentic American mountain music and dance, including many selections on the banjo and dulcimer.
Fine Arts; Geography - United States
Dist - PHENIX **Prod** - PHENIX 1974

Sitting 2 MIN
16mm
Color (G)
$6.00 rental
Features a sitting meditation study.
Dist - CANCIN **Prod** - BALLGO 1977

Sitting Bull - a Profile in Power 26 MIN
U-matic / VHS / 16mm
Profiles in Power (Spanish Series
Color (H C A) (SPANISH)
Produces an appreciation for the controversial and enigmatic native American, Sitting Bull.
Biography; Foreign Language; Social Science
Dist - LCOA **Prod** - LCOA 1977

Sitting Bull - a Profile in Power 26 MIN
U-matic / VHS / 16mm
Color (H C A)
LC 76-702973
Explores, through the use of an imaginary historical interview, the life and role of Chief Sitting Bull.
Biography; Guidance and Counseling; History - United States; Psychology; Social Science
Dist - LCOA **Prod** - LCOA 1976

Sitting on Top of the World 5 MIN
16mm
Screen news digest series; Vol 2; Issue 8
B&W
Sails with the nuclear submarine Sargo under the Arctic ice cap.
Geography - World; Social Science
Dist - HEARST **Prod** - HEARST 1960

Sitting Too Long 10 MIN
Videoreel / VT2
Janaki Series
Color
Physical Education and Recreation
Dist - PBS **Prod** - WGBHTV

Situation Analysis 35 MIN
VHS / U-matic
Situation Management Series
Color
Business and Economics; Psychology
Dist - DELTAK **Prod** - EXECDV

Situation Ethics 30 MIN
U-matic / VHS
Moral Values in Contemporary Society Series
Color (J)
Features Joseph Fletcher of the University of Virginia Medical School talking about situation ethics.
Religion and Philosophy; Sociology
Dist - AMHUMA **Prod** - AMHUMA

Situation Management Series
Decision making 27 MIN
Problem Diagnosis 35 MIN
Problem Prevention 26 MIN
Situation Analysis 35 MIN
Dist - DELTAK

Situation vacant series
Presents a six-part series looking at selection procedures for a wide range of jobs. Examines selection processes for candidates for the Royal Marines, advertising, ship entertainment officers, restoration staff, mangement of a toy store and the police.
Advertising executive 45 MIN
Assistant chief constable 45 MIN
Restoration man 45 MIN
The Royal Marine's office 45 MIN
Ship's entertainment officers 45 MIN
Superstore manager 45 MIN
Dist - BBCENE

The Situational Leader Videocassette Package 90 MIN
U-matic / VHS
(PRO)
$1495 three quarter inch _ #CE55 - AJ, $1495 one half inch VHS _
Outlines the methods and philosophy behind situational leadership. Enables managers to provide accurate and consistent leadership information and to increase managerial participation, committment and motivation. Features Dr Paul Hersey.
Business and Economics; Guidance and Counseling
Dist - UNIVAS

Situational Leadership
16mm / U-matic / VHS
Color (A)
Uses the film 'Twelve O'Clock High' to learn about leadership, motivation, performance and the process of change. Includes a comprehensive leader's guide, three instructional tapes featuring Dr Paul Hershey, key graphics and tapes of 'Twelve O'Clock High.'.
Psychology
Dist - FI **Prod** - FI

Situational Leadership 16 MIN
VHS / U-matic
Color
Introduces concepts of Situational Leadership a technique designed to help leaders assess the performance of others, achieve results, develop people and contribute to organizational success.
Business and Economics; Sociology
Dist - UNIVAS **Prod** - UNIVAS

Situational Leadership - Developing Leadership Skills 20 MIN
U-matic / VHS
Color
Features Dr Paul Hersey in a presentation of his 'Situational Leadership Model.' Provides a visual presentation of the situational leadership model and a follow - up to readings on the theory. Includes a Situational Leadership handout and a Situational Leadership Summary handout.
Business and Economics; Psychology
Dist - DELTAK **Prod** - DELTAK

Situational leadership II - Unit I 31 MIN
VHS / BETA / U-matic
Situational leadership series
Color (G PRO)
$1000.00, $900.00 purchase, $225.00 rental _ #ST0024
Features Ken Blanchard who explains situational leadership. Uses family and work settings to show what happens when employees are given the leadership style they need.
Business and Economics; Guidance and Counseling; Psychology
Dist - BLNCTD **Prod** - BLNCTD

Situational leadership series
Communication skills - Unit II
Situational leadership II - Unit I 31 MIN
Situational leadership skills II - Unit III 27 MIN
Dist - BLNCTD

Situational leadership skills II - Unit III 27 MIN
BETA / U-matic / VHS
Situational leadership series
Color (G PRO)
$1000.00, $900.00 purchase, $225.00 rental _ #ST0010
Portrays supervisors practicing the skills of providing work direction, praising, building self - reliance, delegating and handling performance problems.
Business and Economics; Guidance and Counseling; Psychology
Dist - BLNCTD **Prod** - BLNCTD

Situations of displacement 15 MIN
16mm
Color (G)
$20.00 rental
Presents a fictitious autobiogaphical science - fiction film. Consists of eight episodes, each of which reflects a form of displacement: physical, emotional, intellectual, psychic, spiritual. A Kon Petrochuk production.
Fine Arts; Literature and Drama; Psychology
Dist - CANCIN

Siu Mei Wong - who Shall I be 17 MIN
16mm / U-matic / VHS
Captioned; Color (I J A)
Presents the story of a young girl in Chinatown, Los Angeles, who wants to be a ballerina, against her father's wishes.
Fine Arts; Geography - United States; Psychology; Sociology
Dist - LCOA **Prod** - LCOA 1970

Siu Mei Wong - who Shall I be 18 MIN
U-matic / VHS / 16mm
Many Americans Series
Color (I J)
Tells the story of a young Chinese girl, living in Los Angeles' Chinatown, who yearns to become a ballerina. Describes the family's conflict when her ballet lessons infringe upon her education at the Chinese school where she has been sent by her father to make sure she retains her Chinese culture. Tells how her father decides that he must not let his own deep ties to tradition prevent his daughter from having a chance to pursue her own goals.
Guidance and Counseling; Psychology; Social Science; Sociology
Dist - LCOA **Prod** - LCOA 1971

Siva 2 MIN
16mm
Color (G)
$8.00 rental
Shines a light on the Hindu God, Siva by presenting a 'cinematic tone poem.'
Fine Arts; Religion and Philosophy
Dist - CANCIN **Prod** - LEVCHI 1967

6 - 64 - Mama und Papa - Materialaktion - Otto Muehl - Mama and Papa - An Otto Muehl happening 4 MIN
16mm
Color (G)
$10.00 rental
Introduces subject matter that was considered at that time to be highly revolutionary. Illustrates 'actions' and 'happenings' staged by Otto Muehl and Gunter Brus.
Fine Arts
Dist - CANCIN **Prod** - KRENKU 1964

Six American families series
The Burks of Georgia 56 MIN
The Georges of New York City 53 MIN
The Greenbergs of California 58 MIN
The Kennedys of Albuquerque 59 MIN
The Stephenses of Iowa 58 MIN
The Stephenses of Iowa - Pt 1 29 MIN
The Stephenses of Iowa - Pt 2 29 MIN
Dist - CAROUF

Six American families series
The Burk family 52 MIN
The George family 52 MIN
The Greenberg family 52 MIN
The Kennedy family 52 MIN
The Pasciak family 52 MIN
The Stephens family 52 MIN
Dist - ECUFLM

Six Bells Series
Birth of the Haunted 27 MIN
Dist - NIMBUS

The Six Billion Dollar Sell 15 MIN
U-matic / VHS / 16mm
Consumer Reports Series
Color (I)
LC 77-700413
Examines clips from actual television commercials and makes use of animation, comedy sketches and children talking about their actual experiences to show people how not to be taken in by television commercials.

Fine Arts; Home Economics
Dist - FI **Prod** - CU 1977

Six cardinal rules of customer service
VHS
Telephone doctor series
Color; CC (A PRO)
Presents a training video with Nancy Friedman, customer service consultant. Outlines six hard and fast rules for dealing with the public. Part six of a 16-part series of humorous programs for training in telephone skills.
Business and Economics; Social Science; Sociology
Dist - EXTR **Prod** - TELDOC

Six centuries of verse 416 MIN
VHS
Color; PAL (J H)
PdS15 purchase
Presents 16 half - hour programs on poetry. Appeals to ordinary viewers, as well as to stage 3 and 4 students and university students. Each program is also available separately. Contact distributor about availability outside the United Kingdom.
Literature and Drama
Dist - ACADEM

Six characters in search of an author 60 MIN
VHS
Color (H C G)
$119.00 purchase _ #DL312
Includes the whole central section of the play by Luigi Pirandello and a condensed version of the opening, using a television studio set up as the rehearsal space. Features Ossie Davis who discusses the role of the creator in the theater.
Fine Arts; Literature and Drama
Dist - INSIM **Prod** - BBC 1977

Six Characters in Search of an Author 60 MIN
U-matic / VHS
Drama - play, performance, perception series; Conventions of the theatre
Color (H C A)
Discusses stylization, avantgardism, black theatre and realism in drama. Uses the play Six Characters In Search Of An Author as an example.
Fine Arts; Literature and Drama
Dist - FI **Prod** - BBCTV 1978

Six Colorful Inside Jobs 35 MIN
16mm
Color; Silent (C)
$700.00
Experimental film by John Baldessari.
Fine Arts
Dist - AFA **Prod** - AFA 1977

Six Days in June 14 MIN
16mm
B&W
Presents a compilation of newsreel films from Israel and documentary material from Egypt, showing the events which lead to the Six Day War in June, 1967. Depicts the fighting during the war and Jerusalem liberated and unified.
Geography - World; History - World
Dist - ALDEN **Prod** - ALDEN

The Six Deadly Skids 27 MIN
Videoreel / VT1
Color
Presents competition driver Denise Mc Cluggage demonstrating causes of skids and how to control them. Award winner.
Health and Safety
Dist - MTP **Prod** - LIBMIC

Six English Towns Series
Chichester, Richmond, Tewkesbury - Vol I 86 MIN
Stamford, Totnes, Ludlow - Vol II 86 MIN
Dist - FI

Six Feet of the Country 30 MIN
16mm / U-matic / VHS
Color (H C A)
$575, $250 purchase _ #4089
Tells the story of some South Africans who find the body of an illegal alien on their farm and strive to have it reburied from a potter's grave to their farm. A Perspective film. Based on the story by Nadine Gordimer.
Literature and Drama
Dist - CORF

Six Feet of the Country 29 MIN
16mm / U-matic / VHS
Color (H C A)
LC 81-700545
Tells how a husband and wife abandon the racial tensions of Johannesburg, South Africa, and escape to the country to coexist with black laborers. Based on the short story Six Feet Of The Country by Nadine Gordimer.

Literature and Drama
Dist - CORF **Prod** - PERSPF 1980

Six Filmmakers in Search of a Wedding 13 MIN
16mm / U-matic / VHS
Color
LC 72-702335
Presents six filmmakers. Depicts the different technical and style of each. Provides their views of a simple family wedding.
Fine Arts; Industrial and Technical Education; Sociology
Dist - PFP **Prod** - ENVIC 1971

Six films 18 MIN
16mm
Color (G)
$25.00 rental
Features a reel of six films, including Claude, Evil Is Live Spelled Backwards, Red - Green, Star Spangled Banner, Nine O'Clock News and God Is Dog Spelled Backwards.
Fine Arts; Sociology
Dist - CANCIN **Prod** - MCLAOG

Six films by Bill Creston 59 MIN
VHS
B&W (G)
$100.00 purchase
Includes Bert Lahr, 15 minutes of Carl Methfessel's humorously painful warm - ups to his imitations of Bert Lahr; Cracks, in which a man tries to divine the meaning of the sidewalk; Cripple, 12 minutes of uncomfortable travel on uneven crutches in an unlikely environment; Newsdealer, short portrait of Mickey, the corner philosopher - newsdealer; The Execution, a prophetic tape about the sudden death of a character played by the late Carl Methfessel; and S E G, a humorous experiment with a vintage video special effects generator, and the news story of an altercation between elderly German roomates. Productions made between 1971 - 1974.
Fine Arts; Literature and Drama
Dist - CANCIN

Six films by Bruce Conner 35 MIN
16mm
B&W; Sepia (G)
$75.00 rental
Features a dancing girl as the leitmotiv in Cosmic Ray, 1961, 4 minutes, B&W, which refers to musician Ray Charles whose art is visually transcribed onto film. Introduces a biblical tyrant confronted with a truth he cannot handle in Permian Strata, 1969, 4 minutes, B&W. Mongoloid, 1978, 4 minutes, B&W, depicts a young man who overcomes his mental disability. A Movie, 1958, 12 minutes, B&W, is a montage of facts from newsreels and fiction from old movies. Take the 5 - 10 to Dreamland, 1977, 6 minutes, presents images tinted in sepia tones. Valse Triste, 1979, 5 minutes, B&W, tells the story of Conner's Kansas boyhood.
Fine Arts; Psychology
Dist - CANCIN **Prod** - CONNER 1979

Six films - Claire Bain 26 MIN
VHS
B&W/Color (G)
$25.00 purchase
Features Found Out; Natural Light Essay Number One; ITSME; ITSME part 2; Vel and the Earthquake; and Vel Richards Presents VDT Health. See individual titles for description. Titles available separately for rental in 16mm format.
Fine Arts; Physical Education and Recreation; Psychology; Sociology
Dist - CANCIN **Prod** - BAINCL

6 Films (Fountain/Car; Baseball/TV; Flying; Hand/Water; Rock/String/ Roller Coaster/Reading) 9 MIN
16mm
B&W; Color; Silent (C)
$90.00 for per film, $504.00 for all 6 films
Experimental film by Stuart Sherman.
Fine Arts
Dist - AFA **Prod** - AFA 1980

Six great ideas series
Beauty 60 MIN
Goodness 60 MIN
Liberty 60 MIN
Truth 60 MIN
Dist - FI

Six - gun heroes series 173 MIN
VHS
Six - gun heroes series
Color (G)
Presents excerpts from the Saturday matinee westerns of the 1940s. Features such stars as Tex Ritter, Gene Autry, Roy Rogers and Ken Maynard. Hosted by Republic Pictures cowboy star Sunset Carson. Consists of three videocassettes.
Fine Arts
Dist - SCETV **Prod** - SCETV

Six - gun heroes series
Six - gun heroes series 173 MIN
Dist - SCETV

Six - Gun Territory 16 MIN
16mm
Color; B&W
Shows one of Florida's newest tourist attractions, located near Silver springs. Six - gun territory offers a pioneer western town complete with gun fighters, trading post and a saloon, soft drinks and can - can dancers.
Geography - United States; Physical Education and Recreation; Social Science
Dist - FDC **Prod** - FDC

6 harmonies and 8 methods - Liou Ho Ba Fa 40 MIN
VHS
Color (G)
$49.95 purchase _ #1109
Demonstrates this internal martial art, which resembles T'ai chi in its 'soft' style. Features York Why Loo and his student Terry Dunn.
Physical Education and Recreation
Dist - WAYF

6 harmony - 10 animal Hsing I Chuan - Part 1 75 MIN
VHS
Color (G)
$49.95 purchase _ #1172
Presents an unusual Hsing I form based on movements patterned after 10 animals. Demonstrates the form and the animals' characteristics. Uses basic training exercises and three repetitions of the segments in each sequence. With George Xu.
Physical Education and Recreation
Dist - WAYF

6 harmony - 10 animal Hsing I Chuan - Part 2 58 MIN
VHS
Color (G)
$49.95 purchase _ #1173
Looks at a set entitled 'The Eagle and Bear Fight for Survival.' Demonstrates the form and the animals' characteristics. Repeats the segments in each sequence with different camera angles. With George Xu.
Physical Education and Recreation
Dist - WAYF

Six healing sounds - theory and practice
VHS / Cassette
Guided practice series
Color (G)
$55.00, $9.95 purchase _ #V62 - TP, #C10
Presents a series of arm movements and vocalizations which produce a balanced and healing effect on the internal organs. Features Master Mantak Chia as instructor.
Health and Safety; Physical Education and Recreation; Religion and Philosophy
Dist - HTAOC **Prod** - HTAOC

Six Heavy Fish and a Ton of Sinkers 16 MIN
16mm
Color (J)
LC 72-702255
Portrays the discovery, recovery and restoration of six cannons jettisoned from Captain James Cook's ship 'ENDEAVOUR' on Australia's Great Barrier Reef 200 years ago.
Geography - United States; Geography - World; History - United States; History - World
Dist - AUIS **Prod** - AUSCOF 1972

Six hundred days to Cocos Island 93 MIN
VHS
Color (G A)
$44.90 purchase _ #0281
Follows a young couple with a small sailboat on a 600 - day adventure. Visits Mexico, Central America, Galapagos, Cocos Island.
Geography - World; Physical Education and Recreation
Dist - SEVVID

Six Hundred Millenia - China's History Unearthed 89 MIN
VHS / 16mm
Color (G)
$95.00 rental _ #SMCU - 000
Documents a traveling exhibit of archaeological finds from the People's Republic of China.
Fine Arts; Geography - World; History - World
Dist - PBS **Prod** - KQEDTV

Six Hundred, Sixty - Six 78 MIN
16mm
Color (R)
Describes the moral decisions faced by five men who must feed the best of what man has learned through the centuries into the memory banks of the latest computers.

Guidance and Counseling; Religion and Philosophy
Dist - GF **Prod** - GF

Six in Paris 93 MIN
16mm
Color (FRENCH)
Features six episodes involving Parisians in different parts of the city. Includes tales set in St Germain des Pres, Gare du Nord, Rue St Denis, Place de l'Etoile and Montparnasse et Levallois.
Fine Arts; Foreign Language; Geography - World
Dist - NYFLMS **Prod** - NYFLMS 1966

Six interviews 38 MIN
VHS / 16mm
Six interviews series
Color & B&W (G)
$50.00 rental, $30.00 purchase
Features a six - part series of 'interviews' from 1973 - 1981. Includes Walk That Dog; Observeillance; Cut; A Quiet Afternoon with Strangers; Lincoln Logs for Jesus; and Excess, Black Noise, and Fast Moving Pictures. Produced by Tyler Turkle.
Fine Arts; Guidance and Counseling; Literature and Drama
Dist - CANCIN
FLMKCO

Six interviews series
Excess, black noise and fast moving pictures 1 MIN
Observeillance 3 MIN
A Quiet afternoon with strangers 9 MIN
Six interviews 38 MIN
Dist - CANCIN
FLMKCO

Six keys to service 16 MIN
U-matic / VHS / 16mm
Customer service, courtesy and selling programs series
Color
Dramatizes factors that affect the quality of service offered by a business. Shows how to use them to achieve greater customer satisfaction.
Business and Economics
Dist - NEM **Prod** - NEM

Six keys to service 16 MIN
U-matic / VHS / 16mm
Customer service, courtesy and selling programs - Spanish series
Color (SPANISH)
Dramatizes factors that affect the quality of service offered by a business. Shows how to use them to achieve greater customer satisfaction.
Business and Economics; Foreign Language
Dist - NEM **Prod** - NEM

Six Loop - Paintings 11 MIN
16mm
Color
Shows how sound and image are handmade with the use of acetate adhesive patterned screens and tapes.
Education; Industrial and Technical Education
Dist - FMCOOP **Prod** - SPINLB 1970

6 Loop Paintings 11 MIN
16mm
Color; B&W (C)
$280.00
Experimental film by Barry Spinello.
Fine Arts
Dist - AFA **Prod** - AFA 1971

The Six Months Blues 30 MIN
U-matic
Parent Puzzle Series
(A)
Highlights the various schedule changes that are required to meet a baby's needs.
Psychology; Sociology
Dist - ACCESS **Prod** - ACCESS 1982

Six Murderous Beliefs 12 MIN
16mm
B&W (J H)
Tears down six false ideas of safety, such as 'I DON'T HAVE AN ACCIDENT BECAUSE I'M LUCKY' and 'SAFETY IS FOR SISSIES.' Teenagers dramatize the tragic results of such activities as jay walking and reckless driving.
Health and Safety
Dist - NSC **Prod** - NSC 1955

The Six Nations 26 MIN
U-matic / VHS / 16mm
Native Americans Series
Color
Discusses the Iroquois League, a federation consisting of the Mohawk, Oneida, Onondaga, Seneca, Cayuga and Tuscarora tribes. Shows how these tribes consider themselves to be a sovereign, independent nation and reject the American way of life in favor of a self - sufficient existence on their own land. Focuses on the Seneca Nation which owns valuable property. Presents the President of the Seneca Nation and the mayor of a white community which leases its land from the Seneca nation, discussing the various aspects of Indian and white coexistence.
Social Science; Sociology
Dist - CNEMAG **Prod** - BBCTV

Six O'Clock and All's Well 60 MIN
16mm / U-matic / VHS
Color (H C A)
LC 80-700852
Follows the activities of New York WABC - TV's Eyewitness News team for several weeks during 1977. Shows producers, directors, editors, reporters, technicians and anchormen working on a variety of stories.
Fine Arts
Dist - CNEMAG **Prod** - SPNCRR 1979

Six O'Clock and All's Well, Pt 1 30 MIN
16mm / U-matic / VHS
Color (H C A)
LC 80-700852
Follows the activities of New York WABC - TV's Eyewitness News team for several weeks during 1977. Shows producers, directors, editors, reporters, technicians and anchormen working on a variety of stories.
Literature and Drama
Dist - CNEMAG **Prod** - SPNCRR 1979

Six O'Clock and All's Well, Pt 2 30 MIN
16mm / U-matic / VHS
Color (H C A)
LC 80-700852
Follows the activities of New York WABC - TV's Eyewitness News team for several weeks during 1977. Shows producers, directors, editors, reporters, technicians and anchormen working on a variety of stories.
Literature and Drama
Dist - CNEMAG **Prod** - SPNCRR 1979

Six ordinary people - a drug - free awareness program - II 30 MIN
8mm cartridge / VHS / BETA / U-matic
Drug - free workplace series
Color; CC; PAL (IND G PRO)
$495.00 purchase, $175.00 rental _ #DFE - 200
Portrays the dangers of drug abuse, detailing the bumpy ride from social drug use to addiction. Features six former abusers who recount their personal stories - from their first involvement with drugs, the highs and the lows, how they hit bottom and their steady climb back to being drug free. Part two of two parts.
Business and Economics; Guidance and Counseling; Psychology
Dist - BNA **Prod** - BNA

The Six Penguins 5 MIN
U-matic / VHS / 16mm
Color (P)
LC 70-711909
An animated story in which six penguins and a whale mutually aid each other.
Science - Natural
Dist - MGHT **Prod** - BULGRA 1971

Six self-esteem styles
VHS
Personality games for Macintosh series
Color (H C)
$79 purchase - #CDPVS102M-D
Looks at how each of the six major personality orientations define and deal with self-esteem. Uses interaction to promote the idea that there are many different ways to view the self and to evaluate others. Shows that getting along is a matter of recognizing and acting on certain personality factors.
Business and Economics; Guidance and Counseling; Psychology
Dist - CAMV

Six Short Films 7 MIN
U-matic / VHS / 16mm
Color (H C A)
LC 73-701434
Uses animation to present a sort of contemporary American cinemagraphic primitive, full of visual incongruities in which things are what they seem and then become something else.
Fine Arts; Industrial and Technical Education; Psychology
Dist - PHENIX **Prod** - PHENIX 1973

Six short films by Les Blank 83 MIN
VHS
Color (G)
$99.95 purchase
Collects Blank's best short films from 1960 to 1985. Includes Chicken Real, The Sun's Gonna Shine, God Respects Us When We Work, but Loves Us When We Dance, Dizzy Gillespie, and Running Around Like a Chicken with its Head Cut Off, Blank's first student film.
Fine Arts
Dist - CANCIN **Prod** - BLNKL 1985

Six Short Steps to Sales Disaster 11 MIN
VHS / 16mm
Color (A PRO)
$200.00 purchase
Presents John Cleese in several vignettes to be used at meetings or as a diagnostic exercise in sales. Management training.
Business and Economics; Guidance and Counseling; Literature and Drama
Dist - VIDART **Prod** - VIDART 1991

Six short steps to sales disasters 7 MIN
VHS
Color (PRO IND COR A)
$249.00 purchase, $170.00 rental, $50.00 preview
Presents vignettes from John CLeese's, 'So You Want To Be A Success At Selling?' as part of a diagnostic selling skills exercise.
Business and Economics
Dist - VIDART

Six Spectacular Hours, Reel 1 2 MIN
Videoreel / VT2
Six Spectacular Hours Series
Color
Fine Arts
Dist - PBS **Prod** - WITFTV

Six Spectacular Hours, Reel 2 2 MIN
Videoreel / VT2
Six Spectacular Hours Series
Color
Fine Arts
Dist - PBS **Prod** - WITFTV

Six Spectacular Hours, Reel 3 2 MIN
Videoreel / VT2
Six Spectacular Hours Series
Color
Fine Arts
Dist - PBS **Prod** - WITFTV

Six Spectacular Hours, Reel 4 2 MIN
Videoreel / VT2
Six Spectacular Hours Series
Color
Fine Arts
Dist - PBS **Prod** - WITFTV

Six Spectacular Hours, Reel 5 2 MIN
Videoreel / VT2
Six Spectacular Hours Series
Color
Fine Arts
Dist - PBS **Prod** - WITFTV

Six Spectacular Hours, Reel 6 2 MIN
Videoreel / VT2
Six Spectacular Hours Series
Color
Fine Arts
Dist - PBS **Prod** - WITFTV

Six Spectacular Hours, Reel 7 2 MIN
Videoreel / VT2
Six Spectacular Hours Series
Color
Fine Arts
Dist - PBS **Prod** - WITFTV

Six Spectacular Hours Series
Six Spectacular Hours, Reel 1 2 MIN
Six Spectacular Hours, Reel 2 2 MIN
Six Spectacular Hours, Reel 3 2 MIN
Six Spectacular Hours, Reel 4 2 MIN
Six Spectacular Hours, Reel 5 2 MIN
Six Spectacular Hours, Reel 6 2 MIN
Six Spectacular Hours, Reel 7 2 MIN
Dist - PBS

Six - step reframing 75 MIN
VHS
Color; PAL; SECAM (G)
$75.00 purchase
Features Connirae Andreas who shows how to access and organize unconscious resources for change. Utilizes NLP, neuro - linguistic programming, in a pattern to change undesired habits, feelings and behaviors. Demonstrates with a woman who wants to stop smoking. Includes a follow - up interview. Introductory level.
Health and Safety; Psychology
Dist - NLPCOM **Prod** - NLPCOM

Six steps to developing responsibility 90 MIN
VHS
Color (H C G)
$49.95 purchase _ #SBT106V - K
Presents a practical model for teaching responsibility by setting up an environment of firmness with dignity and respect for both adults and children. Shows how children learn to anticipate limits and consequences and develop problem - solving skills necessary for success in adult life.

Guidance and Counseling; Health and Safety; Psychology; Sociology
Dist - CAMV

Six Thousand Partners 20 MIN
16mm
Color (H C A)
LC FIA52-241
Shows the contribution of the products and services of the 6,000 supplying firms which produce the materials and parts necessary for the production of the Ford automobile.
Business and Economics
Dist - FORDFL Prod - FMCMP 1950

6 to 8 AM 28 MIN
16mm
B&W (G)
$65.00 rental
Tells the story of a young and upwardly mobile black man who, despite his success, is very unhappy as he realizes that he is living his life as others feel he should.
Fine Arts; History - United States
Dist - CANCIN Prod - MERRIT 1975

Six to Eight Months 10 MIN
VHS / U-matic
Teaching Infants and Toddlers Series Pt 3
Color (H C A)
Shows how infants between the ages of six to eight months learn by seeing, hearing, feeling, general imitation and through spatial relationships.
Home Economics; Psychology
Dist - GPN Prod - BGSU 1978

Six to Remember Series
My Partner, Officer Smokey 17 MIN
Dist - AMEDFL

Six windows 7 MIN
16mm / VHS
Color (G)
$20.00 rental
Creates a window of a wall on film by pan and dissolve. Portrays the filmmaker in a luminous space with positive and negative overlays.
Fine Arts
Dist - CANCIN Prod - KELLEM 1979

Six works by Larry Kless 27 MIN
VHS
Color & B&W (G)
$40.00 purchase
Features Cowboys Were Not Nice People; The Negative Kid; and Post - Modern Daydream; see individual titles for description. Includes A Kinder Gentler Nation, an exploration of the banality of this statement by George Bush; Warning Signs juxtaposes images from educational films, broadcast television and video feedback to subvert the original intention meant as information; and Political Gestures studies the urban textures that reflect personal ideologies injected into the public sphere. Made during 1988 - 1991.
Civics and Political Systems; Fine Arts
Dist - CANCIN

16 - 19 - Mathematics and science 114 MIN
VHS
Color; PAL (T)
PdS29.50 purchase
Attempts to integrate mathematics and science teaching in a basic science course for 16 - 19 - year - olds in a multicultural inner city FE college in London. Features two units - BTEC physical science extracts from a three - hour class divided into small groups, covering different experiments in electricity; BTEC mathematics is structured as a formal lecture to the whole class and then works on problem sheets in small groups. 58 and 56 minutes in length respectively.
Mathematics; Science
Dist - EMFVL

Sixteen days of glory - Part 2 147 MIN
VHS
Color (G)
$24.95 purchase _ #S02089
Presents the second of a two - part series profiling the US athletes of the 1984 summer Olympics in Los Angeles. Portrays the athletes in competition and in their personal lives.
History - United States; Physical Education and Recreation
Dist - UILL

Sixteen in Webster Groves 47 MIN
U-matic / VHS / 16mm
B&W (J H C)
LC FIA66-1814
Depicts the shocking results of a survey made by the University of Chicago, at Webster Groves, Missouri, on teenage opinions and goals. Shows that these attitudes stem directly from the parent's expectations and the rigid and constraining level of conformity.
Psychology; Sociology
Dist - CAROUF Prod - CBSTV 1966

Sixteen leaders - Szesnastu 55 MIN
VHS
B&W (G A) (POLISH)
$29.95 purchase _ #V131
Presents the so - called 'trial' of sixteen leaders of the Polish Home Army by a Stalinist court and their fate in Soviet prisons after World War II.
Civics and Political Systems; Fine Arts; History - World
Dist - POLART

The 16mm camera 195 MIN
VHS
Color (PRO G)
$299.00 purchase, $75.00 rental _ #719
Features a two - part session with cinematographer Bill Constable on the 16mm camera. Uses a comprehensive selection of 16mm cameras to demonstrate all major systems and operations. Includes detailed examinations of: viewing systems; motor types and running speeds; magazine types and camera loading technique; turret types and lens mounts; how to avoid camera noise; claw mechanisms; variable shutters; in - camera special effects; the video tape; single system cameras; metering systems; camera support systems; and hand holding technique. Examines 12 major camera systems and offers an evaluation of each system. Produced by the Australian Film, Television and Radio School.
Industrial and Technical Education
Dist - FIRLIT

Sixteen Mm Film - Classroom Filmart 2 MIN
16mm
B&W
LC 73-702933
Shows simple ways of making movies without cameras.
Education; Fine Arts
Dist - FLMMKR Prod - FLMMKR 1973

Sixteen Nineteen - 1860 - Out of Slavery 20 MIN
16mm / U-matic / VHS
History of the Negro in America Series
B&W (J H)
LC FIA67-1374
Traces the history of the Negro from 1619 to 1860, the promise of freedom and equality.
History - United States
Dist - MGHT Prod - MGHT 1965

The Sixteen - Point Program for Spanish - Speaking Americans 24 MIN
16mm
B&W
LC 75-701378
Shows the 16 - point program for providing Spanishspeaking people equal opportunities in Federal employment. Provides guidance for Federal agencies to implement the program and discusses several of the 16 points, including the need for agencies to include Spanish - speaking Americans in their affirmative action programs.
Guidance and Counseling; Sociology
Dist - USNAC Prod - USCSC 1973

Sixteen Tales Series
Ananse and the golden box 15 MIN
The Blind man's daughter 15 MIN
Ma Liang and the Magic Brush 15 MIN
The Tiger and the Rabbit 15 MIN
Dist - AITECH

Sixteenth - Century English 12 MIN
16mm
Color
LC 74-702765
Features excerpts from a 16th - century book on healthy living, read in the original language of the time and illustrated by original drawings on 16th - century examples.
Literature and Drama
Dist - QFB Prod - QFB 1973

Sixteenth Olympiad (Australia) 30 MIN
16mm
B&W
Presents the highlights from all the events in six different films.
Physical Education and Recreation
Dist - SFI Prod - SFI

The Sixth Continent 28 MIN
U-matic / VHS
Color (H C A)
Discusses the many secrets of man's history held by the ocean. Includes the work of international teams cooperating in marine research to discover major sources of energy in the ocean.
Science; Science - Physical
Dist - JOU Prod - JOU

Sixth Day 27 MIN
VHS / U-matic
Color (J A)
Features Keenan Wynn and Marty Feldman in the story of Creation.
Fine Arts; Religion and Philosophy
Dist - SUTHRB Prod - SUTHRB

The Sixth Day 27 MIN
U-matic / VHS / 16mm
Insight Series
Color (H C A)
Depicts God's first man as a creature with angel's wings, a tail and some horns. Demonstrates God's constant evolutionary process. Stars Keenan Wynn and Marty Feldman.
Psychology; Religion and Philosophy
Dist - PAULST Prod - PAULST

The Sixth Face of the Pentagon 28 MIN
16mm
Color
Follows the anti - war demonstrators during the two days in October, 1967 when they met at the Pentagon, were openly blocked by the militia and were forced to find a new strategy to make their protest real.
Sociology
Dist - CANWRL Prod - MARKC

Sixth Infantry Division 20 MIN
16mm / U-matic / VHS
B&W (H A)
Presents scenes from the 6th Infantry Division combat operations in New Guinea, including the securing of the Maffin Bay area, the amphibious landing at Sausapor and the assault at Lingayen Gulf, Luzon.
Civics and Political Systems; History - United States
Dist - USNAC Prod - USA 1948

Sixth sense 30 MIN
VHS / U-matic
Supersense series
Color (H C)
$250.00 purchase _ #HP - 5801C
Speculates about the possibility of a sixth sense in animals. Shows that animals compensate for smaller brains by having at least one heightened sense - birds can see far better than humans, dogs can smell up to a million times better than humans, and insects are extraordinarily sensitive to sound. Part of a series which deals with different facets of animal awareness.
Psychology; Science - Natural
Dist - CORF Prod - BBCTV 1989

The Sixth Sense 27 MIN
U-matic / VHS / 16mm
Color
Shows how people develop their senses from infancy, and how they change with age. Dispels myths surrounding old age. Reveals active older people and medical authorities discussing problems of sensory change among the elderly. Narrated by Arlene Francis.
Health and Safety; Psychology; Sociology
Dist - EXARC Prod - EXARC

The Sixth Sense 15 MIN
16mm
Color (P)
Shows children how to protect themselves from child molestation.
Health and Safety; Home Economics; Sociology
Dist - KLEINW Prod - KLEINW

Sixth Street Meat Club 10 MIN
16mm
Color
Shows the termination of the pacification program of the 'WAR ON POVERTY' as the federal government intervenes in the attempts of a Negro anti - poverty group, to set up their own independent meat cooperative.
Civics and Political Systems; History - United States
Dist - CANWRL Prod - CANWRL

The Sixth Van Cliburn International Piano Competition 180 MIN
U-matic / VHS
Color
Fine Arts
Dist - ABCLR Prod - ABCLR

The Sixth Wheel 27 MIN
U-matic / VHS / 16mm
Color (J H A)
Follows a salesman, a young mother and a teen - age boy through a day of driving. Observes their driving strengths and weaknesses.
Health and Safety
Dist - IFB Prod - IFB 1962

The Sixties 30 MIN
VHS / U-matic
Art America series
Color (H C A)

$43.00 purchase
Examines the emergence of the commercial image in American art. Looks at the techniques and mediums available to the contemporary artist. Provides social and cultural context background information. Part of a 20-part series.
Fine Arts
Dist - CTI **Prod** - CTI
GPN

The Sixties 15 MIN
U-matic / VHS / 16mm
Color (J H)
LC 70-707671
Presents a brief socio - political review of the decade of the sixties.
History - World
Dist - PFP **Prod** - BRAVC 1969

Sixty Cycle Cyclops Show 22 MIN
16mm
Color
LC 80-700881
Presents a statement against television's impact on children during 21 years of broadcasting in Australia.
Fine Arts; Geography - World; Industrial and Technical Education; Psychology; Sociology
Dist - TASCOR **Prod** - WILBRI 1977

Sixty Days Beneath the Sea - Tektite I 15 MIN
16mm
Color
LC 74-705650
Shows how four aquanauts lived and conducted extensive oceanographic studies, during the longest undersea project. Describes how their behavior in isolation was monitored by surface scientists.
Psychology; Science; Science - Physical; Sociology
Dist - USNAC **Prod** - USN 1970

6809 Interface programming series
Advanced interface 30 MIN
Basic interface 30 MIN
Serial interface 30 MIN
Signal processing and control 30 MIN
Dist - COLOSU

6809 Interface Programming Series
Advanced interface 30 MIN
Basic interface 30 MIN
Serial interface 30 MIN
Signal processing and control 30 MIN
Dist - COLOSU

Sixty - Eight Hundred I, O Operations, Interrupts
U-matic / VHS
Microprocessor Series
Color
Industrial and Technical Education; Mathematics
Dist - HTHZEN **Prod** - HTHZEN

Sixty - Eight Hundred Instruction Set, Pt 1 60 MIN
U-matic / VHS
Understanding Microprocessors Series Pt 7
B&W
Industrial and Technical Education; Mathematics
Dist - UAZMIC **Prod** - UAZMIC 1979

Sixty - Eight Hundred Instruction Set, Pt 2 60 MIN
VHS / U-matic
Understanding Microprocessors Series Pt 8
B&W
Industrial and Technical Education; Mathematics
Dist - UAZMIC **Prod** - UAZMIC 1979

Sixty - Eight Hundred Microprocessor
VHS / U-matic
Microprocessor Series
Color
Industrial and Technical Education; Mathematics
Dist - HTHZEN **Prod** - HTHZEN

Sixty - Eight Hundred MPU I/O Operations/Interrupts
U-matic / VHS
Microprocessor Video Training Course Series
Color
Industrial and Technical Education
Dist - VTRI **Prod** - VTRI

Sixty - Eight Hundred MPU Stack Operation/Subroutines
U-matic / VHS
Microprocessor Video Training Course Series
Color
Industrial and Technical Education
Dist - VTRI **Prod** - VTRI

Sixty - Eight Hundred Stack Operations, Subroutines
U-matic / VHS
Microprocessor Series
Color
Industrial and Technical Education; Mathematics
Dist - HTHZEN **Prod** - HTHZEN

Sixty - Four Million Years Ago 12 MIN
16mm / U-matic / VHS
Color (K P)
LC 82-701152
Shows a day in the life of planet Earth when the dinosaur was king. Uses animation and models to show the great reptiles in peaceful life as well as fierce battles.
Science - Natural
Dist - BARR **Prod** - NFBC 1982

Sixty Four Million Years Ago 11.5 MIN
U-matic / VHS / 16mm
Color (K P I)
$260, $180, $210 purchase _ #B341
Shows a day in the life of our planet when the dinosaur was king. Features animated miniatures and models of the great reptiles.
Science - Natural
Dist - BARR **Prod** - BARR

The Sixty Million Germans and their Country 28 MIN
16mm
Color (H C A)
Deals with the people of the Federal Republic of Germany, and discusses who these people are and what their special joys and worries are.
History - World; Sociology
Dist - WSTGLC **Prod** - WSTGLC

The Sixty minute sailor
VHS
Color (G A)
$39.90 purchase _ #0269
Covers all the fundamentals of sailing. Includes launching and beaching. Good for dinghy sailors.
Physical Education and Recreation
Dist - SEVVID

Sixty Minutes on Business 60 MIN
U-matic / VHS
Color (G)
Business and Economics
Dist - VPHI **Prod** - VPHI 1984

Sixty Minutes on Business Series
Closed Market (Price Supports)
Fake (counterfeit products)
I Magnin File
A Modern American Tragedy - Hughes Aircraft Co
The Money Shuttle - Rockwell International Corp
Nobody Saw it Coming (Douglas Fraser, UAW)
Queen Lear (Lear Fan)
The Re - Selling of Tylenol
Trouble Brewing - Adolph Coors Co
Dist - CBSFOX

Sixty Minutes on Business Series
He Bought the Company - Remington Products, Inc
Dist - CBSFOX
VPHI

Sixty Minutes on Business Series
Closed Market - Farmer's Market 60 MIN
Fake 60 MIN
I Magnin 60 MIN
Modern American Tragedy - Hughes Aircraft 60 MIN
The Money Shuttle 60 MIN
Nobody Saw it Coming 60 MIN
Queen Lear 60 MIN
Trouble Brewing 60 MIN
Dist - VPHI

60 minutes to a smoke free life 60 MIN
VHS
Color (J H C G)
$19.95 purchase _ #LA100V; $19.95 purchase _ #SD04
Features behavioral expert and psychotherapist Jonathan Robinson. Combines 'one on one' counseling with scenes from smoking cessation seminars. Shows that cigarette smoking is as much a psychological addiction as a physical one.
Guidance and Counseling; Health and Safety; Psychology
Dist - CAMV
SVIP

60 minutes to meltdown 84 MIN
16mm / VHS
Nova series
(J H C)
$99.95 each
Traces the events and mistakes leading to the Three Mile Island disaster. In 2 parts.
Science; Science - Physical; Social Science; Sociology
Dist - AMBROS **Prod** - AMBROS 1984

Sixty Minutes to Meltdown 84 MIN
16mm / U-matic / VHS
Nova Series
Color (H C A)
Presents a docudrama chronicling the minute - by - minute sequence of malfunctions and mistakes at the Three Mile Island nuclear power plant and follows with a documentary examining the lessons raised by the accident and the critical economic and safety questions confronting nuclear power use.
History - United States; Social Science
Dist - TIMLIF **Prod** - WGBHTV 1984

69 5 MIN
16mm
Color (C)
$224.00
Experimental film by Robert Breer.
Fine Arts
Dist - AFA **Prod** - AFA 1968

Sixty - nine CR 180 - an artist's report 60 MIN
16mm
Artist as a reporter series
Color
Presents a surreal reenactment of the 1968 Democratic Convention turmoil, depicting anti - war activists and cultural revolutionaries, such as Abbie Hoffman, Jerry Rubin, David Dellinger and others. Portrays William Kuntzler and Leonard Weinglass versus Thomas Foran and Richard Schultz, all under the watchful eye of Judge julius Hoffman.
Biography; Civics and Political Systems
Dist - ROCSS **Prod** - ROCSS 1970

Sixty Second Spot 25 MIN
U-matic / VHS / 16mm
Color
Gives an account of the unknown struggles behind the production of a major television commercial. Records a real production, as the producers decide to create a take - off on old desert movies and travel to the desert sands where Beau Geste was filmed.
Business and Economics; Fine Arts
Dist - PFP **Prod** - MNDLIN

Sixty Second Spot - the Making of a Television Commercial 25 MIN
U-matic / VHS / 16mm
Color (J)
LC 74-702417
Traces the steps taken in creating and shooting a television commercial. Shows the cooperation between the advertising agency, the independent producer and the individuals making the film, including the producer, director and actors.
Business and Economics; Social Science
Dist - PFP **Prod** - MNDLIN 1974

Sixty - Seven Thousand Dreams 30 MIN
U-matic / VHS / 16mm
Story of Carl Gustav Jung Series
Color (C A)
LC 72-702066
Explains the development of the major theories and concepts of Carl Gustav Jung, including discussion of the collective unconscious, the psychology of types, the psyche in space and time and the importance of myth and intuition to the complete man.
Biography; Psychology; Religion and Philosophy
Dist - FI **Prod** - BBCTV 1972

66 5 MIN
16mm
Color (C)
$224.00
Experimental film by Robert Breer.
Fine Arts
Dist - AFA **Prod** - AFA 1966

66 was a good year for tourism 66 MIN
VHS
Color (G) (ENGLISH & HEBREW ENGLISH SUBTITLES)
$36.00 purchase
Features filmmaker Amit Goren's story of his family's immigration to the United States from Israel in 1966, when he was nine years old. Explores the question of whether his family members, after 25 years in the US, would consider returning to Israel. Highlights his own immigrant experience which is relevant to millions of immigrants around the world who have uprooted themselves from their own culture to seek a better life elsewhere. Written and directed by Amit Goren.

Fine Arts; History - United States; Religion and Philosophy; Sociology
Dist - NCJEWF

Siyabonga and the baboon 10 MIN
VHS
Siyabonga series
Color (P I J)
$150.00 purchase
Goes along with Zulu boy Siyabonga as he dream - travels to visit with baboons, where he meets one who tells about his species' life in Africa. Ends with Siyabonga, whose name means 'thank you', understanding and identifying with the animals. Part of a six - part series that is available as a set.
Geography - World; Literature and Drama
Dist - LANDMK

Siyabonga and the elephant 10 MIN
VHS
Siyabonga series
Color (P I J)
$150.00 purchase
Goes along with Zulu boy Siyabonga as he dream - travels to visit with elephants, where he meets one with a broken tusk who tells about his species' life in Africa. Ends with Siyabonga, whose name means 'thank you', understanding and identifying with the animals. Part of a six - part series that is available as a set.
Geography - World; Literature and Drama
Dist - LANDMK

Siyabonga and the lion 10 MIN
VHS
Siyabonga series
Color (P I J)
$150.00 purchase
Goes along with Zulu boy Siyabonga as he dream - travels to visit with lions, where he meets one who tells about his species' life in Africa. Ends with Siyabonga, whose name means 'thank you', understanding and identifying with the animals. Part of a six - part series that is available as a set.
Geography - World; Literature and Drama
Dist - LANDMK

Siyabonga and the ostrich 10 MIN
VHS
Siyabonga series
Color (P I J)
$150.00 purchase
Goes along with Zulu boy Siyabonga as he dream - travels to visit with ostriches, where he meets one who tells about his species' life in Africa. Ends with Siyabonga, whose name means 'thank you', understanding and identifying with the animals. Part of a six - part series that is available as a set.
Geography - World; Literature and Drama
Dist - LANDMK

Siyabonga and the rhinoceros 10 MIN
VHS
Siyabonga series
Color (P I J)
$150.00 purchase
Goes along with Zulu boy Siyabonga as he dream - travels to visit with rhinos, where he meets one who tells about his species' life in Africa. Ends with Siyabonga, whose name means 'thank you', understanding and identifying with the animals. Part of a six - part series that is available as a set.
Geography - World; Literature and Drama
Dist - LANDMK

Siyabonga and the warthog 10 MIN
VHS
Siyabonga series
Color (P I J)
$150.00 purchase
Goes along with Zulu boy Siyabonga as he dream - travels to visit with warthogs, where he meets one who tells about his species' life in Africa. Ends with Siyabonga, whose name means 'thank you', understanding and identifying with the animals. Part of a six - part series that is available as a set.
Geography - World; Literature and Drama
Dist - LANDMK

Siyabonga series
Presents a set of six videos in a series that dream - travels with Zulu boy Siyabonga to visit various African animals and see how they live. Ends with Siyabonga, whose name means 'thank you', understanding and identifying with the animals. Videos are also available separately.
Siyabonga and the baboon 10 MIN
Siyabonga and the elephant 10 MIN
Siyabonga and the lion 10 MIN
Siyabonga and the ostrich 10 MIN
Siyabonga and the rhinoceros 10 MIN
Siyabonga and the warthog 10 MIN
Dist - LANDMK

Size 10 18 MIN
16mm
Color (C)
$500.00 purchase, $40.00, $50.00 rental
Celebrates the female body in all sizes and shapes. Rejects the cultural norm of poor self image because of not conforming to the female body image created by advertising and sexism. Discusses body image, sexuality, society's conditioning of what women should look like, pressures of conforming and how fashion industries profit from preying on female insecurity.
Psychology; Sociology
Dist - WMENIF

Size 10 20 MIN
16mm
Color (G)
$450.00 purchase, $50.00 rental
Introduces four women who are striving for a more positive self - image. Shows how a woman's body image has been formed by advertising and sexism. Produced by Susan Lambert and Sarah Gibson of Australia.
Psychology; Sociology
Dist - WMEN

Size and Distance 6 MIN
16mm
Basic Facts about the Earth, Sun, Moon and Stars Series
Color (K P)
Describes the relationship of distance to size.
Science - Physical
Dist - SF **Prod** - MORLAT 1967

Size description
VHS
Drafting I series
(H C)
$59.00 _ CA137
Gives basics of dimensioning a mechanical drawing.
Education; Industrial and Technical Education
Dist - AAVIM **Prod** - AAVIM 1989

The Size of the Molecules in Olive Oil
VHS
Chemistry - from Theory to Application Series
Color (H)
$190.00 purchase
Determines the approximate size of the olive oil molecule through spreading a film of oil over the surface of water. Explains the experiment through the aid of graphs and arithmetic evaluation.
Science; Science - Physical
Dist - LUF **Prod** - LUF 1989

The Size of the Moon 8 MIN
16mm
Science Series
Color (K P)
Explains the calendar, phases of the moon and why the size of the moon appears to change.
Science - Physical
Dist - SF **Prod** - MORLAT 1967

Size, Shape, Color, Texture 15 MIN
VHS / U-matic
Hands on, Grade 1 Series Unit 1 - Observing; Unit 1 - Observing
Color (P)
Science; Science - Physical
Dist - AITECH **Prod** - VAOG 1975

Sizing and Selection 30 MIN
U-matic / VHS
Programmable Controllers Series
Color
Deals with needs assessment and equipment considerations.
Industrial and Technical Education; Sociology
Dist - ITCORP **Prod** - ITCORP

Sizing Solar Collectors, Pt 1 25 MIN
U-matic / VHS
Solar Collectors, Solar Radiation, Insolation Tables Series
Color (H C A)
Explains the use of the Clear Sky Daily Solar Radiation Table and Average Daily Solar Radiation Table to determine the expected average daily insolation for a tilted surface, the first step in sizing solar collectors.
Social Science
Dist - MOKIN **Prod** - NCDCC

Sizing Solar Collectors, Pt 2 25 MIN
U-matic / VHS
Solar Collectors, Solar Radiation, Insolation Tables Series
Color (H C A)
Shows how to calculate the potential harvest of solar collectors. Describes how components affect efficiency and the use of efficiency charts.
Social Science
Dist - MOKIN **Prod** - NCDCC

Sizing Solar Collectors, Pt 3 25 MIN
VHS / U-matic
Solar Collectors, Solar Radiation, Insolation Tables Series
Color (H C A)
Explains how to size collectors to meet various levels of estimated water and space - heating demand.
Social Science
Dist - MOKIN **Prod** - NCDCC

Sizing up animals 15 MIN
VHS / U-matic / 16mm / BETA
Animals around you series
Color (K P)
$245.50, $68.00 purchase _ #C50759, #C51499
Compares the world's largest animals - blue whales, giraffes and African elephants - with tiny beetles and other insects. Shows a six - year - old child using herself and familiar objects as bases for comparison in judging size. Teaches about height, weight and length, the concepts of bigger and smaller, heavier and lighter, taller and shorter. Part of a five - part series on animals.
Mathematics; Science - Natural
Dist - NGS **Prod** - NGS 1992

Sizing up sharks
Videodisc
Laser learning set 3 series; Set 3
Color; CAV (P I)
$375.00 purchase _ #8L5418
Overviews the physical characteristics and behaviors of sharks. Shows sharks as creatures deserving respect, rather than fear or hatred. Part of a series of six theme - based interactive videodisc lessons. Requires a Pioneer LD - V2000 or 2200, with barcode reader and adapter, or a Pioneer LD - V4200 or higher. Includes user's guide, two readers.
Science - Natural
Dist - BARR **Prod** - BARR 1992

Sizwe Bansi is dead 60 MIN
VHS
Color (G C H)
$119.00 purchase _ #DL312
Presents Athol Fugard's play about repressive laws in South Africa. Begins after the first monologue.
Fine Arts
Dist - INSIM **Prod** - BBC

Sizwe Banzi is Dead 60 MIN
VHS / U-matic
Drama - play, performance, perception series; Conventions of the theatre
Color (H C A)
Discusses stylization, avantgardism, black theatre and realism in drama. Uses the play Sizwe Banzi Is Dead as an example.
Fine Arts; Literature and Drama
Dist - FI **Prod** - BBCTV 1978

Sizzlin' skateboards 40 MIN
VHS
Color (I R)
$19.95 purchase, $10.00 rental _ #35 - 821 - 2020
Includes two stories centered around skateboarding. Tells how a man who lost his son in a skateboarding accident set up a program for safe skateboarding. Features a national skateboarding champion who shares her athletic skills and faith.
Literature and Drama; Religion and Philosophy
Dist - APH **Prod** - ANDERK

Skarv - Phalacrocorax Carbo (Cormorant) 12 MIN
16mm
Color
Describes the cormorant in its natural surroundings, accompanied by sound effects.
Science - Natural
Dist - STATNS **Prod** - STATNS 1965

Skate expectations - Episode 4
VHS
McGee and me series
Color (P I R)
$19.95 purchase, $10.00 rental _ #35 - 84155 - 979
Features Nick and his animated friend McGee. Shows how Nick challenges the class bully to a skateboard contest. Emphasizes the importance of doing the right thing, no matter how difficult it may be.
Literature and Drama; Religion and Philosophy
Dist - APH **Prod** - TYHP

The Skateboard Craze 11 MIN
VHS / U-matic
Color
Focuses on skateboarding, a California - initiated fad that became a worldwide sport. Shows skateboarding competitions featuring jumping, downhill racing, and gymnastics.

Physical Education and Recreation
Dist - JOU **Prod** - UPI

Skateboard Fever 12 MIN
16mm
Color
LC 78-700668
Presents an impressionistic musical essay on skateboarding. Shows both amateurs and professionals skateboarding to a variety of accompanying musical themes and rhythms.
Physical Education and Recreation
Dist - NFL **Prod** - NFL 1978

Skateboard Riding Tactics 15 MIN
16mm / U-matic / VHS
Color (J)
LC 78-700626
Outlines elements of safe skateboarding, including proper equipment check, the advantages of a low center of gravity, why laws forbid riding in certain areas, the importance of protective gear, keeping control on steep slopes, dangerous surfaces and how to fall to avoid injury.
Health and Safety; Physical Education and Recreation
Dist - AIMS **Prod** - CAHILL 1978

Skateboard Safety 13 MIN
U-matic / VHS / 16mm
Color (P)
LC 76-701846
Points out that skateboarding is a sport and like other sports requires training skill and experience. Stresses the importance of protective clothing, how to check for safe equipment, where and how to ride and proper techniques for falling without injury.
Health and Safety; Physical Education and Recreation
Dist - PFP **Prod** - MCDONJ 1976

Skateboard Sense 10 MIN
U-matic / VHS / 16mm
Color (P I J H)
Shows how good equipment and proper riding techniques enhance the thrill and safety of skateboarding techniques. Demonstrates the use of elbow and knee pads, helmets and gloves and shows the ways to take a fall.
Health and Safety; Physical Education and Recreation
Dist - AIMS **Prod** - AIMS 1976

Skateboarding to Safety 9 MIN
16mm / U-matic / VHS
Color (P I J) (SWEDISH)
LC 76-703533
Presents safety advice for practicing the sport of skateboarding.
Foreign Language; Health and Safety; Physical Education and Recreation
Dist - PHENIX **Prod** - LORIPR 1976

The Skater 24 MIN
U-matic / VHS
Young people's specials series
Color
Presents the story of a young girl who is told she can no longer skate because of something someone else did. Focuses on parent and child relationships.
Fine Arts; Sociology
Dist - MULTPP **Prod** - MULTPP

Skater Dater 18 MIN
U-matic / VHS / 16mm
Color
LC 71-712412
Portrays a boy's emergence into adolescence as he slowly realizes that his skateboard gang is part of a childhood that he has outgrown.
Psychology
Dist - PFP **Prod** - BACKLR 1971

The skates of Uncle Richard / song of trees 15 MIN
VHS / U-matic
Book bird series
Color (I)
Tells of a young girl's dreams of becoming a famous ice skater and of a black family's attempts to save the singing trees. From the books by Carol Fenner and Mildred Taylor.
English Language; Literature and Drama
Dist - CTI **Prod** - CTI

Skates, Wagons, Cycles and Subways to Far - Away Places 8 MIN
16mm
Crystal Tipps and Alistair Series
Color (K P)
LC 73-700457
Shows Crystal introducing Alistair to wheeled vehicles such as skates, wagons and cycles.
Guidance and Counseling; Literature and Drama
Dist - VEDO **Prod** - BBCTV 1972

Skating 9 MIN
16mm / U-matic / VHS
How to Play Hockey Series no 1; No 1
B&W (J H C)
Shows the fundamentals of balance, stopping, starting, turning and speed skating.
Physical Education and Recreation
Dist - IFB **Prod** - CRAF 1956

The Skating Rink 27 MIN
16mm / U-matic / VHS
Color (I P) (SPANISH)
LC 75-702922;
Centers around a teenager whose early childhood experiences left him with an awkward stutter.
Guidance and Counseling; Psychology; Sociology
Dist - LCOA **Prod** - LCOA 1975

Skating Rink, the 27 MIN
U-matic / VHS / 16mm
Captioned; Color (P)
Centers around a teenager whose early childhood experiences left him with an awkward stutter.
Fine Arts; Physical Education and Recreation; Psychology; Sociology
Dist - LCOA **Prod** - LCOA 1975

A Skating Spectacular 59 MIN
VHS / 16mm
Color (G)
$70.00 rental _ #SKSP - 000
Covers the annual benefit skating exhibition given by the Genesee Figure Skating Club of Rochester, New York.
Physical Education and Recreation
Dist - PBS

Skating techniques
VHS
N C A A instructional video series
Color (H C A)
$39.95 purchase _ #KAR1504V
Presents the first of a three - part series on defensive ice hockey. Focuses on skating techniques.
Physical Education and Recreation
Dist - CAMV **Prod** - NCAAF

Skein 5 MIN
16mm
Color (G)
$11.00 rental, $196.00 purchase
Says Brakhage, 'A loosely coiled length of yarn - story...wound on a reel - my parenthesis. This is a painted film - inspired by Nolde's 'unpainted pictures'.'
Fine Arts
Dist - CANCIN **Prod** - BRAKS 1974

Skeletal Adaptations - Variations on a Theme 24 MIN
U-matic / VHS / 16mm
Color (H C)
LC 82-700407
Outlines skeletal adaptation as a phenomenon of evolution, an instance of natural selection in animals. Deals with the concepts of convergence and divergence in animal skeleton adaptation, pointing out that convergence indicates that a single end has been achieved although organisms have used different methods.
Science - Natural
Dist - MEDIAG **Prod** - BBCTV 1981

Skeletal and muscle action 6 MIN
VHS
Systems of the human body series
Color (I J)
$24.95 purchase _ #L9627
Uses X - ray photography to view bones and muscles during movement. Part of a seven - part series on the human body, using the single - concept format.
Science - Natural
Dist - HUBDSC **Prod** - HUBDSC

Skeletal and muscle action 9 MIN
VHS / 16mm
Systems of the human body series
Color (J H C)
$80.00 purchase _ #194 W 0099, #193 W 2099
Examines the relationship between body movements and skeletal - muscle action through the use of X - ray photographs. Part of a series on the systems of the human body.
Science - Natural
Dist - WARDS **Prod** - WARDS

Skeletal and topographic anatomy series

Introduction to Topographic Anatomy	19 MIN
Postnatal development of the skeleton - Pt 1 - the skull	21 MIN
Postnatal development of the skeleton - Pt 3 - deciduous and permanent dentition	21 MIN
Postnatal development of the skeleton - Pt 2 - vertebral column and extremities	22 MIN
Skeletal Features of the Lower Extremity	18 MIN
Skeletal Features of the Pelvis	16 MIN
Skeletal Features of the Skull, Pt 4 - Neural Structures	20 MIN
Skeletal Features of the Skull, Pt 1 - the Cranium	13 MIN
Skeletal Features of the Skull, Pt 3 - Vascular Structures	19 MIN
Skeletal Features of the Skull, Pt 2 - the Face	18 MIN
Skeletal Features of the Thorax	19 MIN
Skeletal Features of the Upper Extremity	16 MIN
Skeletal Features of the Vertebral Column	20 MIN
Topographic anatomy of articular sites - Pt 1 - general and axial	20 MIN
Topographic anatomy of articular sites - Pt 3 - appendicular (lower extremity)	20 MIN
Topographic anatomy of articular sites - Pt 2 - appendicular (upper extremity)	19 MIN
Topographic Anatomy of the Abdomen	18 MIN
Topographic Anatomy of the Back	20 MIN
Topographic anatomy of the head and neck - Pt 4 - the oral cavity	19 MIN
Topographic anatomy of the head and neck - Pt 1 - the neck	17 MIN
Topographic anatomy of the head and neck - Pt 3 - the cranium	20 MIN
Topographic anatomy of the head and neck - Pt 2 - the face	12 MIN
Topographic anatomy of the lower extremity - Pt 1 - femoral, gluteal and popliteal regions	17 MIN
Topographic anatomy of the lower extremity - Pt 2 - knee, leg, ankle and foot	18 MIN
Topographic Anatomy of the Pelvis, Perineum and Inguinal Regions	18 MIN
Topographic anatomy of the thorax - Pt 1 - external features	19 MIN
Topographic anatomy of the thorax - Pt 2 - internal features	19 MIN
Topographic Anatomy of the Upper and Lower Extremities - Nerve Injury	22 MIN
Topographic anatomy of the upper extremity - Pt 2 - forearm, wrist and hand	15 MIN
Topographic Anatomy of the Upper Extremity, Shoulder, Axilla, Arm and Elbow	15 MIN

Dist - TEF

Skeletal Features of the Lower Extremity 18 MIN
16mm / U-matic / VHS
Skeletal and Topographic Anatomy Series
Color (C A)
Health and Safety; Science - Natural
Dist - TEF **Prod** - UTEXMH

Skeletal Features of the Pelvis 16 MIN
16mm / U-matic / VHS
Skeletal and Topographic Anatomy Series
Color (C A)
Health and Safety; Science - Natural
Dist - TEF **Prod** - UTEXMH

Skeletal Features of the Skull, Pt 4 - Neural Structures 20 MIN
16mm / U-matic / VHS
Skeletal and Topographic Anatomy Series
Color (C A)
Health and Safety; Science - Natural
Dist - TEF **Prod** - UTEXMH

Skeletal Features of the Skull, Pt 1 - the Cranium 13 MIN
U-matic / VHS / 16mm
Skeletal and Topographic Anatomy Series
Color (C A)
Health and Safety; Science - Natural
Dist - TEF **Prod** - UTEXMH

Skeletal Features of the Skull, Pt 3 - Vascular Structures 19 MIN
U-matic / VHS / 16mm
Skeletal and Topographic Anatomy Series
Color (C A)
Health and Safety; Science - Natural
Dist - TEF **Prod** - UTEXMH

Skeletal Features of the Skull, Pt 2 - the Face 18 MIN
U-matic / VHS / 16mm
Skeletal and Topographic Anatomy Series

Color (C A)
Health and Safety; Science - Natural
Dist - TEF **Prod** - UTEXMH

Skeletal Features of the Thorax 19 MIN
U-matic / VHS / 16mm
Skeletal and Topographic Anatomy Series
Color (C A)
Health and Safety; Science - Natural
Dist - TEF **Prod** - UTEXMH

Skeletal Features of the Upper Extremity 16 MIN
U-matic / VHS / 16mm
Skeletal and Topographic Anatomy Series
Color (C A)
Health and Safety; Science - Natural
Dist - TEF **Prod** - UTEXMH

Skeletal Features of the Vertebral Column 20 MIN
U-matic / VHS / 16mm
Skeletal and Topographic Anatomy Series
Color (C A)
Health and Safety; Science - Natural
Dist - TEF **Prod** - UTEXMH

Skeletal Muscle Relaxants, their Antagonists 30 MIN
16mm
Pharmacology Series
B&W (C)
LC 73-703343
Describes the anatomy and physiology of skeletal muscle relaxants, focusing on central acting drugs and the peripheral acting drugs. Explains how antagonists of muscle relaxants work.
Health and Safety; Psychology
Dist - TELSTR **Prod** - MVNE 1971

Skeletal System 12 MIN
U-matic / VHS / 16mm
Color (J H C)
$300, $210 purchase _ #3957
Talks about the skeleton gives the body form and flexibility, protects vital organs, and enables humans to move.
Science - Natural
Dist - CORF

Skeletal traction - 19 12 MIN
VHS
Clinical nursing skills - nursing fundamentals - series
Color (C PRO G)
$395.00 purchase _ #R890 - VI - 074
Presents the equipment and procedures used to maintain skeletal traction. Describes and demonstrates procedures for the patient in balanced - suspension traction, cervical traction with tongs and halo - thoracic vest traction. Part of a 23 - part series on clinical nursing skills.
Health and Safety
Dist - HSCIC **Prod** - CUYAHO 1989

The Skeleton - an Introduction 46 MIN
VHS / U-matic
Color (C A)
Presents an introduction to human skeletal anatomy.
Health and Safety; Science - Natural
Dist - TEF **Prod** - UWO

Skeleton, the 17 MIN
U-matic / VHS / 16mm
Color (J H)
LC 80-700144
Uses x - ray photography, diagrams and detailed close - ups of several types of bones to aid in identifying the structure, function, composition and overall coordination of the skeleton in humans and other vertebrates. Stresses the importance of proper diet and exercise to maintain healthy bones.
Health and Safety; Science - Natural
Dist - EBEC **Prod** - EBEC 1979

Skeletons and Frameworks 29 MIN
VHS / 16mm
Villa Alegre Series
Color (P T)
$46.00 rental _ #VILA - 158
Presents educational material in both Spanish and English.
Education
Dist - PBS

Skeletons of Spitalfields 50 MIN
VHS
Chronicle series
Color; PAL (G)
PdS99 purchase; Not available in the United States or Canada
Observes archaeologists as they remove bodies from the crypt of Christ Church Spitalfields in London. Examines the collaborative work of doctors, dentists and anthropologists as they use the skeletons to make a record of life in early 19th century London. Looks at the benefits of the study to current medical and forensic science.
History - World
Dist - BBCENE

Skenduolis 11 MIN
VHS / U-matic
B&W (LITHUANIAN)
Recreates life in Lithuania before Soviet rule.
Fine Arts; Foreign Language
Dist - IHF **Prod** - IHF

Sketch and Storage Bench 30 MIN
VHS / 16mm
Build Your Own Series
Color (H C A PRO)
$15.00 purchase _ #TA218
Features construction of an indoor storage space with built - in chalkboard and corkboard for kid art.
Industrial and Technical Education
Dist - AAVIM **Prod** - AAVIM 1990

Sketches 1 3 MIN
16mm
Color
LC FIA65-1018
Presents without narration three audio - visual sketches about the sewing machine.
Home Economics
Dist - SVE **Prod** - SINGER 1964

Sketches from the Tempest 7 MIN
16mm
Color
Presents fragments of George Dunning's uncompleted animated version of Shakespeare's classic play The Tempest.
Fine Arts
Dist - FILMWE **Prod** - FILMWE 1979

Sketches in Jazz 30 MIN
VHS / U-matic
Color
Presents paintings of the pastoral American countryside with jazz background music provided by Rosemary Clooney, Johnny Hartman and the Loonis McGlohon Trio.
Fine Arts
Dist - MDCPB **Prod** - WNSCTV

Sketching eyes with expression 29 MIN
U-matic
Sketching techniques series; Lesson 18
Color (C A)
Contains several pieces of information that are useful in drawing eyes. Illustrates key eye expressions.
Fine Arts
Dist - CDTEL **Prod** - COAST

Sketching flowers 29 MIN
U-matic
Sketching techniques series; Lesson 17
Color (C A)
Shows that almost all elements of art can be found in flowers. Discusses points to consider in flower arrangement, such as basic geometrical shapes.
Fine Arts
Dist - CDTEL **Prod** - COAST

Sketching for communication 29 MIN
U-matic
Sketching techniques series; Lesson 6
Color (C A)
Emphasizes communication as one of the most valuable uses of drawing. Explains need for drawing in education.
Fine Arts
Dist - CDTEL **Prod** - COAST

Sketching in architecture 29 MIN
U-matic
Sketching techniques series; Lesson 7
Color (C A)
Explains how to apply alignment in architectural drawings. Illustrates how art elements are added to make architectural drawings more attractive.
Fine Arts
Dist - CDTEL **Prod** - COAST

Sketching interiors 29 MIN
U-matic
Sketching techniques series; Lesson 16
Color (C A)
Demonstrates how interiors can be suggested by objects usually found in a room. Shows how to create interiors with a few simple lines.
Fine Arts
Dist - CDTEL **Prod** - COAST

Sketching technique series
Presents ten programs on sketching techniques. Includes Drawing in Three Dimension; The Two - Pencil Technique; The Thumbnail Sketch; Value, Color and Texture; Proportion; Dominance in Composition; Action; Creating Mood; Special Effects in Sketches; and Tools for Sketching.
Sketching technique series 300 MIN
Dist - CAMV

Sketching techniques series
Action 29 MIN
Animals 29 MIN
Caricature 29 MIN
Creating mood 29 MIN
Design and decoration 29 MIN
Dominance in composition 29 MIN
Drawing in three dimensions 29 MIN
Drawings by the classic artists 29 MIN
The Elements of value, color, and texture 29 MIN
Hands in action 29 MIN
Heads and faces 29 MIN
Proportion 29 MIN
Repetition in sketching 29 MIN
Sketching eyes with expression 29 MIN
Sketching flowers 29 MIN
Sketching for communication 29 MIN
Sketching in architecture 29 MIN
Sketching interiors 29 MIN
Sources of ideas for drawing 29 MIN
Special effects in sketches 29 MIN
Still - life sketches 29 MIN
Styles of sketching 29 MIN
Summary and review of sketching techniques 29 MIN
The Thumbnail sketch 29 MIN
Tools for sketching 29 MIN
The Two - pencil technique 29 MIN
The Use of landscapes in a sketch 29 MIN
Vehicles 29 MIN
Wood and wooden objects 29 MIN
Wrinkles 29 MIN
Dist - CDTEL

Skeye 5 MIN
16mm
B&W
LC 76-701365
Explores some of the aesthetic aspects of astronomical observation.
Science - Physical
Dist - YORKU **Prod** - YORKU 1974

Skezag 73 MIN
16mm
Color (J)
Presents a period of ten hours during which Wayne, a 21 - year - old black living in New York City, talks at length about a variety of topics, including his use of heroin and why he won't become addicted. Shows Wayne four months later as he is preparing to leave New York. Points out that his physical deterioration and depressed attitude show a marked change in contrast to his former confidence in his ability to use heroin without becoming addicted.
Health and Safety; History - United States; Psychology; Sociology
Dist - CNEMAG **Prod** - CINNAP 1970

Ski Classic
16mm
Learn to Ski Series
B&W
Physical Education and Recreation
Dist - SFI **Prod** - SFI

Ski Colorado 30 MIN
VHS / 16mm
Color (H C G)
$29.95 purchase _ #TVC204
Presents recreational possibilities for the vacationer in the Colorado ski country USA.
Geography - United States
Dist - RMIBHF **Prod** - RMIBHF

Ski Country, USA 28 MIN
Videoreel / VT1
Color
Shows sunshine, powder snow, a variety of slopes, action, expert skiing, skiers and lodges. Features some of the nations top eight major ski areas near Denver.
Geography - United States; Physical Education and Recreation
Dist - MTP **Prod** - UAL

Ski Cross Country 22 MIN
16mm / U-matic / VHS
Color (I)
Explores the thrill and enjoyment of cross country skiing amid beautiful Rocky Mountain scenery.
Physical Education and Recreation
Dist - LUF **Prod** - LUF 1981

Ski Esta
16mm

Learn to Ski Series
B&W
Physical Education and Recreation
Dist - SFI **Prod** - SFI

Ski Fever 98 MIN
16mm
Color (C A)
Stars Martin Milner, Claudia Martin and Toni Sailer. Presents a musical comedy about fun on the ski slopes with a new twist.
Fine Arts
Dist - CINEWO **Prod** - CINEWO 1968

Ski Fever 9 MIN
U-matic / VHS / 16mm
Color (I)
LC 73-713135
Portrays the beauty, sport and folly of skiing by presenting scenes of various ski activities.
Physical Education and Recreation
Dist - PHENIX **Prod** - LEMSST 1971

Ski Finesse 28 MIN
16mm
Color
LC 75-701530
Features Stein Ericksen, one of the all - time skiing greats, who shares the secrets of his famous style. Illustrates techniques for the beginner, intermediate and advanced jet turn skiier.
Physical Education and Recreation
Dist - FFORIN **Prod** - BARP 1974

Ski Injuries 35 MIN
16mm
Color
Features Arthur Ellison, M D describing the nature of ski injuries and their mechanism of production. Deals mainly with sprains and fractures of the ankle, leg and knee.
Health and Safety; Physical Education and Recreation; Science - Natural
Dist - JAJ **Prod** - JAJ 1973

The Ski Instructor 15 MIN
VHS / 16mm
Harriet's Magic Hats IV Series
Color (P)
$175.00 purchase _ #207147
Presents thirteen new programs to familiarize children with more workers and their role in community life. Features Aunt Harriet's bottomless trunks of magic hats where Carrie has only to put on a particular hat to be whisked off to investigate the person and the role represented by the hat. 'The Ski Instructor' shows Carrie visiting Murray, a ski instructor, to learn about skiing. In the mountains, Murray teaches Carrie some simple techniques. Murray explains the importance of posture and demonstrates many movements used in skiing. Next, they watch some expert skiers and different forms of skiing.
Business and Economics; Guidance and Counseling; Physical Education and Recreation; Psychology
Dist - ACCESS **Prod** - ACCESS 1986

Ski Instructor 15 MIN
16mm / U-matic / VHS
Career Awareness
(I)
$130 VC purchase, $240 film purchase, $25 VC rental, $30 film rental
Presents an empathetic approach to career planning, showing the personal as well as the professional attributes of ski instructors. Highlights the importance of career education.
Guidance and Counseling; Physical Education and Recreation
Dist - GPN

Ski Moderne
16mm
Learn to Ski Series
B&W
Physical Education and Recreation
Dist - SFI **Prod** - SFI

Ski moderne 10 MIN
16mm
Color (J)
Features the world renowned skier Ernie Mc Culloch and his demonstration team teaching the very latest techniques in parallel skiing. Shows the basic snowplow turn, traversing, side slipping, stem christies and elementary parallel exercises.
Physical Education and Recreation
Dist - AVEXP **Prod** - AVEXP

Ski Mountains of the West 27 MIN
16mm
Color
LC 78-701389
Presents a guide to the ski mountains and accommodations of America's West.
Geography - United States; Physical Education and Recreation
Dist - MTP **Prod** - UAL 1977

Ski New England 90 MIN
VHS
Color (G)
$29.95 purchase _ #S01482
Tours the most popular New England ski resorts, including Sugarloaf, Saddleback, Stowe and Smuggler's Notch. Hosted by U S Olympic ski coach Bob Beattie.
Geography - United States; Physical Education and Recreation
Dist - UILL **Prod** - RMNC

Ski Party 90 MIN
16mm
Color (J)
Stars Frankie Avalon and Dwayne Hickman. Concentrates on two star athletes who seek to extend their sports conquests to a pair of luscious co - eds who have been monopolized by a decidedly non - athletic Romeo.
Literature and Drama; Sociology
Dist - TWYMAN **Prod** - AIP 1965

Ski peak - t'ai chi chi kung ski conditioning program 60 MIN
VHS
Color (G)
$29.95 purchase
Presents a conditioning program for skiers that applies principles of t'ai chi.
Physical Education and Recreation
Dist - DANEHA **Prod** - DANEHA 1994

Ski Right - Beginning to Advanced Skills 90 MIN
VHS
(H C A)
$39.95 purchase _ #BF99645V
Discusses basic and advanced cross country skiing skills, including basic christies, short swing, ski bumps, slalom skiing and more.
Physical Education and Recreation
Dist - CAMV

Ski sense 27 MIN
16mm
Color (H C A)
Describes the nature and causes of most skiing injuries and builds a strong case for year round physical conditioning.
Physical Education and Recreation; Sociology
Dist - AETNA **Prod** - AETNA

Ski sense and safety 17 MIN
U-matic / VHS / 16mm
Color (J H C G)
$395, $275, $305 purchase _ #A533
Introduces Mogul Mike, America's Ski Buddy, using animated comedy. Demonstrates the skiers' responsibility code. Discusses six rules of the road fundamental to snow skiing. Demonstrates race course safety for the racer as well as the spectator courtesy of Christin Cooper, Olympic silver medalist. Informs skiers on safe skiing techniques and etiquette using ski footage.
Health and Safety; Physical Education and Recreation
Dist - BARR **Prod** - BARR 1988

Ski sense and safety 17 MIN
U-matic / VHS / 16mm
Color (A H C I)
LC 88-713505
Informs skiers about ski safety and etiquette. Portrays Christin Cooper, Olympic silver medalist, in skiing situations.
Physical Education and Recreation
Dist - BARR **Prod** - SIERPS 1984

Ski the Outer Limits 25 MIN
U-matic / VHS / 16mm
Color
LC 74-702869
Demonstrates the essential mechanics of skiing. Depicts the inner limits of the sport, the discipline which must be learned before the skier has the capability for freedom of expression.
Physical Education and Recreation
Dist - PFP **Prod** - HRTSKI 1968

Ski touring 29 MIN
VHS / 16mm
Color (G)
55.00 rental _ #SKIT - 000
Follows two former members of the U S Ski Team as they demonstrate the art of cross country skiing through Yosemite National Park back country.
Physical Education and Recreation
Dist - PBS **Prod** - KQEDTV

Ski Vermont 30 MIN
VHS / 16mm
Color (H C G)
$29.95 purchase _ #TVC205
Presents ski areas in Vermont. Discusses lodging, dining, and accessibility.
Geography - United States
Dist - RMIBHF **Prod** - RMIBHF

The Ski Wheelers 14 MIN
16mm
Magnificent 6 and 1/2 Series
Color (P I)
Shows how Genie has the bright idea of fixing a pair of skis to roller skates since there isn't any snow and how Our Gang ends up leaving a trail of destruction behind them as they rush through the shopping center, along the road and through various gardens.
Literature and Drama
Dist - LUF **Prod** - CHILDF 1972

Ski whiz 9 MIN
16mm / U-matic / VHS
Color
LC 73-700760
Presents a fast-paced potpourri of snow sports and daredevil skiers.
Physical Education and Recreation
Dist - PFP **Prod** - PFP 1973

Ski with Andy Mill 73 MIN
VHS
Color (G)
$14.95 purchase _ #SF01
Presents beginning instruction from a former Olympic skier, starting with the first day on skis up to the highly technical aspects of parallel skiing.
Physical Education and Recreation
Dist - SVIP

Skid Control
U-matic / VHS
Driving Safety Series
Color (IND)
Looks at the danger of driving on wet or slippery surfaces and what to do if your vehicle starts to skid.
Health and Safety; Industrial and Technical Education
Dist - GPCV **Prod** - DCC

Skid Correlation Study 14 MIN
16mm
Color
LC 72-701966
Compares various techniques used in testing the coefficients of friction of five specially constructed pavements at Tappahannock, Virginia.
Industrial and Technical Education; Social Science
Dist - USNAC **Prod** - USDTFH 1963

Skid road 55 MIN
VHS
Color (H C G)
$445.00 purchase, $75.00 rental
Examines the moral and political issues cities face in combatting the growing problem of public drunkenness. Visits a Seattle shelter and profiles several indigent alcoholics, illustrating their lives and struggles. Travels to Boston, Portland, Oregon, and St Paul to show how these cities cope with the same problem.
Geography - United States; Health and Safety; Sociology
Dist - FLMLIB **Prod** - KCTSTV 1989

Skids and Skidding 28 MIN
16mm
Sportsmanlike Driving Series no 24
Color (H A)
LC FIA68-915
Demonstrates different kinds of skids and the defensive actions which can aid in regaining control of the car.
Health and Safety
Dist - GPN **Prod** - AAA 1967

Skier's Choice 29 MIN
16mm
Color (J)
LC 77-701319
Stresses the importance of control in making skiing a safe, enjoyable and rewarding recreational sport.
Physical Education and Recreation
Dist - LAWJ **Prod** - SAFECO 1976

The Skiff of Renald and Thomas 58 MIN
16mm
Color
_ #106C 0180 029N
Geography - World
Dist - CFLMDC **Prod** - NFBC 1980

Skiing 3 MIN
16mm
Of all Things Series
Color (P I)
Discusses the sport of skiing.
Physical Education and Recreation
Dist - AVED **Prod** - BAILYL

Skiing
16mm
Learn to Ski Series
B&W
Physical Education and Recreation
Dist - SFI **Prod** - SFI

Skiing Above the Clouds 13 MIN
16mm
Color
Follows a party of experienced outdoorsmen as they traverse glacier - clad Mt Rainier at the 10,000 foot level in mid - winter.
Geography - United States; Physical Education and Recreation
Dist - RARIG **Prod** - RARIG

Skiing - Control is the Goal 25 MIN
U-matic / VHS / 16mm
Color (J H C G)
$525, $370, $400 purchase _ #C532
Discusses skiing safety and the need to be courteous and considerate. Uses animation to enlighten skiers on the dangers of careless skiing.
Health and Safety; Physical Education and Recreation
Dist - BARR **Prod** - BARR 1988

Skiing - Control is the Goal 25 MIN
U-matic / VHS / 16mm
Color (J H C A)
LC 88-713508
Emphasizes need for skiing with control and skiing within one's own ability range.
Health and Safety; Physical Education and Recreation
Dist - BARR **Prod** - SIERPS 1987

Skiing Exercises 7 MIN
16mm
Color (J)
LC FIA67-612
Provides amateurs with exercises to prepare for the skiing season. Shows a high school girl demonstrating her skill on Mt Werner, Steamboat Springs, Colorado.
Physical Education and Recreation
Dist - SCHMUN **Prod** - MANSPR 1967

Skiing in Quebec 11 MIN
16mm
Color (C A)
Shows skiers pluming through powder snow steep trails and toddlers huffing and puffing behind their parents on the nursery slopes.
Physical Education and Recreation
Dist - MORLAT **Prod** - CTFL

Skiing Series

Children have the most Fun	29 MIN
Different techniques are not that different	29 MIN
Don't let the bumps get you down	29 MIN
Eliminating the crutch	29 MIN
Enjoy beginning turns	29 MIN
Getting the skis together	29 MIN
Move to Intermediate Level	29 MIN
Moving toward Parallel Skiing	29 MIN
Open the Door to Advanced Skiing	29 MIN
Parallel for Variety	29 MIN
The Stem is Gone	29 MIN

Dist - PBS

Skiing - with a Difference 17 MIN
BETA / VHS / U-matic
Color; Mono (A)
Presents a training program for ski instructors on methods and techniques used in teaching the physically disabled to ski. Looks at the equipment and methodology employed in step by step training of the various levels of physically handicapped people. Demonstrates three track, four track, blind skiers and sledging, loading and unloading procedures.
Health and Safety; Physical Education and Recreation
Dist - UCALG **Prod** - UCALG 1986

Skill Demonstrations for Counseling Alcoholic Clients - Basic Communication Skills 59 MIN
U-matic / VHS
B&W
Shows how alcoholism counselors can improve their communication skills in one - on - one interactions with clients.
Health and Safety; Psychology; Sociology
Dist - USNAC **Prod** - USNAC

Skill Drills - Paragraph Centering, Block Centering, Spread Centering 30 MIN
Videoreel / VT2
Typewriting, Unit 2 - Skill Development Series
B&W
Business and Economics
Dist - GPN **Prod** - GPN

Skill Drills - Vertical and Horizontal Centering, Typing all Capitals 30 MIN
Videoreel / VT2
Typewriting, Unit 2 - Skill Development Series
B&W
Business and Economics; Guidance and Counseling
Dist - GPN **Prod** - GPN

Skilled Acts 37 MIN
16mm
Color
Discusses the characteristic impairment and disturbance of skilled acts produced by paresis or paralysis of the participating muscles, disorders of coordination and Parkinsonism with akinetic and ideakinetic apraxia.
Health and Safety; Science - Natural
Dist - PSUPCR **Prod** - CMC 1946

Skilled Craftsmen 15 MIN
16mm
Color
LC 80-700876
Shows the lifestyle of five craftsmen, each illustrating a different facet of their craft.
Fine Arts
Dist - TASCOR **Prod** - VICCOR 1978

Skilled Hands and Sure Feet 15 MIN
U-matic / VHS / 16mm
Color (IND)
Emphasizes the importance of hand and foot protection for construction workers. Illustrates the great amount of protection steel - toed boots provide, and shows people using artificial limbs, pointing out the grave danger in inadequate protection.
Health and Safety; Industrial and Technical Education; Psychology
Dist - IFB **Prod** - CSAO

The Skillful Thinker 21 MIN
U-matic
Teaching Skillful Thinking Series
Color (T)
Discusses qualities to develop in students and how to develop them.
Education; Psychology
Dist - AFSCD **Prod** - AFSCD 1986

Skills 30 MIN
U-matic / VHS
Making a Living Work Series
(C A)
$225 _ #JWOT4V
Reveals the necessity of recognizing one's abilities in establishing a successful career. Uses interviews with selected people to emphasize points.
Business and Economics; Education
Dist - JISTW **Prod** - OHUTC

Skills 30 MIN
VHS / U-matic
Making a Living Work Series Program 104
Color (C A)
Shows adults talking about the skills they use in work, education and leisure activities. Focuses on the necessity for skill identification in life/work planning.
Guidance and Counseling
Dist - OHUTC **Prod** - OHUTC

Skills 30 MIN
VHS / 16mm
Making a Living Work Series
Color (C)
$150.00 purchase _ #PAOT4V
Suggests tips for evaluating skills which are transferable to other careers. Features people discussing how they discovered their skills.
Guidance and Counseling; Psychology
Dist - JISTW

Skills 16 MIN
U-matic
Teens and Alcohol Series
(J H)
Demonstrates effective alcohol education using a number of techniques.
Sociology
Dist - ACCESS **Prod** - ACCESS 1984

Skills 30 MIN
VHS
Making a living work series
Color (G A)
$150.00 purchase _ #JW840V
Stresses the importance of being aware of one's skills in career planning. Interviews people who have changed careers, focusing on how they became aware of 'transferrable' skills. Gives tips on how to evaluate skills.
Business and Economics; Psychology
Dist - CAMV

Skills 30 MIN
VHS
Making a Living Work Series
$225.00 purchase _ #013 - 531
Provides tips on how to evaluate one's skills. Emphasizes that a person should know what they are good at for successful career planning.
Business and Economics; Guidance and Counseling
Dist - CAREER **Prod** - CAREER

Skills 29 MIN
VHS / 16mm
Villa alegre series
Color (P T) (SPANISH)
$46.00 rental _ #VILA - 106
Presents educational material in both Spanish and English.
Education
Dist - PBS

The Skills Developed from Career Education 30 MIN
16mm
Color (G)
Presents ten skills developed from career education, which are basic math and communications, good work habits, good work values, basic understanding of private enterprise, understanding of self, decision making skills, job finding skills, making productive use of leisure time, overcoming bias, and humanizing the workplace.
Education; Guidance and Counseling; Psychology
Dist - AACD **Prod** - AACD 1981

Skills enhancement for the legal services team 210 MIN
VHS / Cassette
Color (PRO)
$295.00, $150.00 purchase, $150.00 rental _ #SKI1-000, #ASKI-000
Focuses on how the 'team approach' can achieve increased client satisfaction and cost - effectiveness. Includes all members of the legal services team. Analyzes common law office practices and provides insights on creating more effective procedures. Explores how to manage ethical dilemmas, enhance public relations skills, and utilize ever - changing office technology. Includes study guide.
Business and Economics; Civics and Political Systems; Education
Dist - AMBAR **Prod** - AMBAR 1993

Skills for employment in the information society 30 MIN
VHS / U-matic
On and on about instruction - microcomputers series
Color (C)
$180.00 purchase, $30.00 rental
Discusses the impact of computers on our society and the skills students will need to compete in the Information Age.
Industrial and Technical Education; Mathematics; Psychology
Dist - GPN **Prod** - VADE

Skills for first - time job seekers series
VHS
Skills for first - time job seekers series
Color (T H C)
$395.00 purchase _ #JWRK6SV-J
Presents problems, solutions, experiences, and helpful tips about young adults being out on their own for the first time. Comprises six videos about renting apartments, budgeting, choosing roommates, behaviors on the job, interviewing skills, handling rejection, and more. Videos also available individually.
Guidance and Counseling; Sociology
Dist - CAMV

Skills for first - time job seekers series
Skills for first - time job seekers series
Dist - CAMV

Skills for First Time Job Seekers Series
Presents a series of videos that explores the problems and skills needed when out on your own. Emphasizes the importance of employment and how to get and keep a job.

Downtown deli	29 MIN
First time out	16 MIN
Job Line Reports 1 - How and Where to Look for Work	22 MIN
Job Line Reports 2 - How to Interview for a Job	31 MIN
Skills for first time job seekers series	
The Work Place	14 MIN

Dist - JISTW **Prod** - LGFAMS

Skills for food shopping 15 MIN
VHS
Becoming independent series
Color (H G)

$79.00 purchase _ #CDHEC512V
Emphasizes that healthy eating habits are learned, not inherited, and depend on the ability to read and understand food labels and advertisements. Teaches the art of food shopping, balancing the marketing glitz with sound nutrition. Part of a 13 - part series featuring practical life and consumer skills for teens venturing out into independence.
Guidance and Counseling; Home Economics; Social Science
Dist - CAMV

Skills for living alone
VHS
Family - life skills video series
Color (H G A)
$89.00 purchase _ #ES886
Looks at the many responsibilities of independent living and living alone. Discusses housing, getting involved in community life, and day to day living skills such as cleaning, cooking and budgeting.
Home Economics; Sociology
Dist - AAVIM **Prod** - AAVIM

Skills for living - CPVE 260 MIN
VHS
Color; PAL (J H)
PdS45 purchase
Presents ten 26 - minute programs training young people studying for a Certificate in Pre - Vocational Education or CPVE. Covers the whole range of activities in which students can expect to be involved. Builds on their awareness of industry and economics. Includes a booklet. Contact distributor about availability outside the United Kingdom.
Education
Dist - ACADEM

Skills for Progress 27 MIN
U-matic / VHS / 16mm
Career Job Opportunity Series
Color
Discusses apprenticeship systems, emphasizing the importance of acquiring a skill and explaining the steps involved in learning one.
Guidance and Counseling
Dist - USNAC **Prod** - USDL 1979

Skills for Success 36 MIN
VHS / 16mm
Color (PRO)
$395.00 purchase, $175.00 rental, $75.00 preview ; $595.00 purchase, $200.00 rental, $75.00 preview
Presents career consultant Dr Adele Scheele. Identifies six skills possessed by successful professionals. Teaches how to develop these skills.
Psychology
Dist - UTM **Prod** - UTM

Skills for success 36 MIN
VHS / 16mm
Color (G)
$395.00 purchase, $175.00 rental ; $595.00 purchase, $200.00 rental
Features Dr Adele Scheele. Identifies sustainers and achievers. Explains success techniques that work for the employee and the organization.
Business and Economics; Guidance and Counseling; Psychology
Dist - PROSOR

Skills for successful living series
Building equity in your sales career
Dist - MARS

Skills for successful selling 20 MIN
VHS / 16mm
Color (C A)
$575.00 purchase, $150.00 rental _ #181
Includes Leader's Guide. Shows people skills and product skills used by successful salespeople.
Business and Economics; Psychology
Dist - SALENG **Prod** - SALENG 1985

Skills for the new technology - what a kid needs to know today - a series
Skills for the new technology - what a kid needs to know today - a˚series
Color (I)
Points to skills needed for today's technological world. Basic Communication Skills; Living With Change; Living With Computers.
Industrial and Technical Education; Mathematics; Psychology; Social Science; Sociology
Dist - CORF **Prod** - DISNEY

Skills for the new technology - what a kid needs to know today - a series
Skills for the new technology - what a kid needs to know today - a series
Dist - CORF

Skills for the New Technology - what a Kid Needs to Know Today Series
Basic communication skills 10 MIN
Living with Computers 72 FRS
Dist - CORF

Skills - occupational programs series 270 MIN
VHS
Skills - occupational programs series
Color (H C)
$1299.00 purchase _ #89 - 3199
Presents a series of 27 videos that feature occupations in the skilled trades, in service industries and in business leading to careers in areas of demand and future growth. Includes teacher's guide with reproducible worksheets.
Guidance and Counseling; Psychology
Dist - TVOTAR **Prod** - TVOTAR 1990

The Skills of Football - Soccer 20 MIN
16mm
Color
Presents tips and techniques of particular interest to players who are working to improve their skills on the playing field.
Physical Education and Recreation
Dist - COCA **Prod** - COCA 1969

Skills of Helping Series Program 2
Leading a First Group Session 88 MIN
Leading a First Group Session, Pt 1 44 MIN
Leading a First Group Session, Pt 2 44 MIN
Dist - SYRCU

Skills of Helping Series Program 3
Working with the System 93 MIN
Working with the System, Pt 1 46 MIN
Working with the System, Pt 2 47 MIN
Dist - SYRCU

Skills of Helping Series
Preliminary, beginning, and work phases 96 MIN
Preliminary, beginning, and work phases - Pt 1 48 MIN
Preliminary, Beginning, and Work Phases - Pt 2 48 MIN
Dist - SYRCU

Skills Related Safety Series
Cooking safety
Electricity and Electronics Shop Safety
Fire Safety
Food services safety
Graphic arts safety
Grinder, Buffer, Drill Press and Hand Tool Safety
Introduction to Auto Safety
Lathe Safety
Machine - Metal Shop Safety
Milling Machine Safety
Welding Safety with Oxyacetylene and Arc Welding
Dist - CAREER

The Skills search - knowing your skills is essential for a successful job
VHS
Color (H C G)
$89.95 purchase _ #JWSKV
Introduces the importance of knowing and communicating one's skills during a job search. Provides specific techniques and examples for job search related communications skills. Three Types of Skills defines skills types and gives examples of each. Skills Lists shows representative skills from the three skills types to help viewers identify their own skills. Presenting Skills in an Interview offers an effective and easily - remembered five step format for presenting key skills during an interview. Responding to Problem Questions demonstrates basic interview techniques. Includes the book Getting the Job You Really Want.
Business and Economics; Guidance and Counseling
Dist - CAMV **Prod** - JISTW

Skills to build America 20 MIN
16mm
Color
Portrays the Annual Apprenticeship Contest during which carpenters, cabinet makers and millwrights gather to match their skills and craftsmanship.
Guidance and Counseling
Dist - MTP **Prod** - UBCJ

Skills to Live by
16mm
Color
Provides an overview of individualized instruction in business education.
Business and Economics
Dist - HBJ **Prod** - HBJ

Skills Training for the Special Child 30 MIN
16mm / U-matic / VHS
Color (T)
LC 78-701676
Explains the behavioral procedures used to teach number concepts and arithmetic to retarded and developmentally disabled children.
Education; Psychology
Dist - CORF **Prod** - HUBFLM 1971

Skills - work - related themes series 105 MIN
VHS
Skills - work - related themes series
Color (H C)
$349.00 purchase _ #89 - 316629
Presents a series of seven videos created to complement the Skills - Occupational Programs series, focusing on ways to develop these skills and demonstrate their effectiveness in the workplace. Includes teacher's guide with reproducible worksheets.
Guidance and Counseling; Psychology
Dist - TVOTAR **Prod** - TVOTAR 1990

Skillstreaming Video - How to Teach Students Prosocial Skills 26 MIN
VHS / 16mm
Color (T)
$365.00 purchase, $55.00 rental _ #2910VHS
Demonstrates modeling, role playing, performance feedback and transfer training for use in teaching prosocial skills.
Education; Psychology
Dist - RESPRC **Prod** - RESPRC 1988

Skimming - scanning road 20 MIN
U-matic / VHS
Efficient reading - instructional tapes series; Tape 7
Color
Covers reading flexibility and skimming and scanning in depth.
English Language
Dist - TELSTR **Prod** - TELSTR

Skin 29 MIN
VHS
Color (J H R)
$10.00 rental _ #36 - 81 - 216
Presents a dramatic account of minority teenagers and racial issues. Based on actual incidents, interviews and interracial workshops.
Religion and Philosophy; Sociology
Dist - APH **Prod** - LANDMK

Skin 29 MIN
VHS
Color (I J H)
$195.00 purchase
Dramatizes the situation of visibly minority teenagers and the problems they encounter. Focuses on the experiences of three characters, their friends and others like them. Shows how race relations affect the youth of America.
History - United States; Sociology
Dist - LANDMK **Prod** - LANDMK 1990

Skin 15 MIN
16mm
Color (ITALIAN GERMAN FRENCH)
LC 72-700172
Shows how vinyl skins are made by the casting - on - paper process, and tells how they are used for fashion products.
Home Economics
Dist - ENVIC **Prod** - ENVIC 1971

The Skin 28 MIN
VHS
Human body - the senses - series
Color (J H G)
$89.95 purchase _ #UW4194
Examines the varied tasks performed routinely by the body's largest organ. Examines skin as an important organ of sense, an unmistakable stamp of the individual, the body's first line of defense against invaders from outside, and a regulator of body temperature. Part of a 39 - part series featuring computer animation, medical photography, electron micrography, full - color drawings and diagrams and three - dimensional working models to cover the workings of the human body from head to toe and inside out.
Science - Natural
Dist - FOTH

Skin and foot care for the diabetic
VHS / U-matic
Color (SPANISH)
Addresses the importance of skin and foot care for the diabetic. Provides step by step instructions on proper care. Shows appropriate action to take when injury occurs.
Health and Safety; Science - Natural
Dist - MIFE **Prod** - MIFE

Skin and ink - women and tattooing 28 MIN
VHS / U-matic / 16mm
Color (G)
$650.00, $250.00 purchase, $75.00 rental
Looks at women who have tattoos and the women who create them. Encourages viewers to reassess their perceptions of tattoos and those who wear them. Artists, secretaries, academics and mothers reveal their motivations for becoming heavily tattooed, and the social repercussions - one woman lost custody of her child. Produced by Barbara Attie, Nora Monroe and Maureen Wellner.
Sociology
Dist - WMEN

The Skin as a Sense Organ 12 MIN
U-matic / VHS / 16mm
Color (H C A)
LC 76-701942
Provides an introduction to the variety, function and distribution of sensory receptors in the skin. Traces the path of a stimulus from the sensory receptors in the skin to the reflex arc in the spine.
Science - Natural
Dist - IFB **Prod** - BFL 1975

Skin Bank Storage of Postmortem Homografts, Methods of Preparation, Preservation and Use 23 MIN
16mm
Color (PRO)
Explains that viable homografts are obtained from postmortem sources and used as biological dressings to save lives in severe burns. Shows details of the establishment of a skin bank and of the storage and use of the grafts.
Health and Safety; Science
Dist - ACY **Prod** - ACYDGD 1955

Skin Biopsy Techniques 21 MIN
U-matic
Color (PRO)
LC 79-706521
Demonstrates four techniques for biopsy of the skin. Discusses how and when to perform each of the biopsy procedures and includes a post - test.
Health and Safety
Dist - UMMCML **Prod** - UMICH 1978

Skin Cancer 55 MIN
U-matic
Color
Discusses common nonmelanoma skin cancers and squamous cell cancer.
Health and Safety
Dist - UTEXSC **Prod** - UTEXSC

Skin cancer 26 MIN
VHS
Color (G)
$89.95 purchase _ #UW2365
Discusses basal cell and squamous cell malignancies and melanoma - their symptoms, causes, prevention, treatments and cure rates. Shows types of lesions and explains when and how they should be treated. Indicates when to seek medical attention.
Health and Safety
Dist - FOTH

Skin cancer 30 MIN
VHS
At time of diagnosis series
Color (G)
$19.95 purchase _ #1 - 5757 - 7015 - 6NK
Provides patients who have just been diagnosed with skin cancer and their families with thorough, comprehensive and understandable information. Examines what is going on in the body and what might have caused the condition. Explains the type of medical professionals a patient may encounter and how the condition is monitored. Explores treatment options, including medication, surgery and lifestyle changes. Looks at practical issues surrounding the illness and answers the most common questions. Part of an ongoing series to provide the in - depth medical information patients and their families need.
Health and Safety; Science - Natural
Dist - TILIED **Prod** - TILIED 1996

Skin cancer - Part I 9 MIN
BETA / VHS / U-matic
Color (IND G)
$295.00 purchase _ #840 - 03
Trains employees whose work requires extended exposure to sunlight of the risk of developing skin cancer. Reviews the various forms of skin cancer, methods of identification, specific causes and protective measures that can be taken to prevent the occurrence.
Health and Safety; Industrial and Technical Education; Psychology; Science - Natural
Dist - ITSC **Prod** - SOCC

Skin cancer - Parts I and II 16 MIN
BETA / VHS / U-matic
Color (IND G)
$395.00 purchase _ #840 - 04
Expands the material in Skin Cancer - Part I. Trains employees whose work requires extended exposure to sunlight of the risk of developing skin cancer. Reviews the various forms of skin cancer, methods of identification, specific causes and protective measures that can be taken to prevent the occurrence. Includes specific information on the hazard of skin cancer resulting from working with petroleum and petroleum - based products. Emphasizes safe work practices and personal hygiene.
Health and Safety; Industrial and Technical Education; Psychology; Science - Natural
Dist - ITSC **Prod** - SOCC

Skin cancer - the sun and you 28 MIN
35mm strip / VHS
Color (J H C A)
$93.00, $93.00 purchase _ #MB - 540617 - 9, #MB - 540618 - 7
Documents the growing problem of skin cancer. Traces the growth in skin cancer incidence to two factors - depletion of the ozone layer and the popularity of suntanning. Reveals that although skin cancer is usually treatable and curable, it can be fatal if melanoma develops. Encourages viewers to take precautions to protect their skin.
Health and Safety; Science - Natural
Dist - SRA **Prod** - SRA 1989

Skin cancer - we can beat it 10 MIN
VHS
Color (G)
$195.00 purchase, $100.00 rental _ #8325
Discusses the prevention, recognition and treatment of skin cancer in its various forms.
Health and Safety; Science - Natural
Dist - AIMS **Prod** - CENVID 1992

Skin Care 45 MIN
VHS
Beauty Series
(J H A)
$39.95 _ #KV120V
Introduces viewer to the latest procedures of skin care for more beautiful, youthful looking skin.
Home Economics
Dist - CAMV **Prod** - CAMV

Skin care 30 MIN
U-matic / VHS
Consumer survival series; Health
Color
Presents tips on skin care.
Health and Safety; Home Economics
Dist - MDCPB **Prod** - MDCPB

Skin Care and Diapering Your Baby 11 MIN
VHS / U-matic
Color (SPANISH)
LC 81-730128
Covers preventative measures and treatment for skin disorders which affect the infant. Discusses proper diapering and laundry techniques.
Guidance and Counseling; Health and Safety; Home Economics; Science - Natural
Dist - MEDCOM **Prod** - MEDCOM

Skin Care and Skin Cancer 19 MIN
U-matic / VHS
Color (C)
$249.00, $149.00 purchase _ #AD - 1401
Shows that medical experts agree that there is no such thing as a 'healthy' tan. Reveals that prolonged exposure to the sun is the leading cause of non - melanoma skin cancer. Explains what precautions can be taken to protect the skin from cancer, as well as from other skin problems such as acne.
Health and Safety; Psychology; Science - Natural
Dist - FOTH **Prod** - FOTH

The Skin Game 25 MIN
U-matic / VHS
Color
Shows Mario Machado, with guest celebrities Pat McCormick and Jo Anne Worley exploring the world of skin through a game show format. Has guest authority Dr Marjorie Bauer, a dermatologist, explaining the questions designed to increase an understanding of proper skin care.
Health and Safety; Science - Natural
Dist - MEDCOM **Prod** - MEDCOM

Skin grafting 33 MIN
16mm
Color (PRO)
Demonstrates preparation of the patient and local area, selection of the proper type of graft, the actual cutting of the graft, fixation of the graft and dressing. Includes patient follow - up.
Health and Safety; Science
Dist - ACY **Prod** - ACYDGD 1961

Skin Grafting Techniques 28 MIN
16mm
Color (PRO)
Demonstrates the technique of application of thick split graft to face for infected wound, technique of thick split graft to face for cosmetic improvement, and technique of application of whole thickness graft to flexor surface of finger for post - traumatic scar contracture.
Health and Safety; Science
Dist - ACY **Prod** - ACYDGD 1966

Skin, Hair, and Nails Examination 16 MIN
U-matic
Color (PRO)
LC 79-707723
Demonstrates the inspection and palpation of the skin for color, texture, temperature, hydration, turgor and lesions. Shows examination of the hair for distribution, thickness, texture and lubrication and examination of the nails and nail beds for clubbing, appearance annd color.
Health and Safety
Dist - UMMCML **Prod** - UMICHM 1976

Skin - It's all Around You 15 MIN
U-matic / VHS / 16mm
Color (I J)
LC 79-701421
Explains the anatomy and function of skin. Tells how skin protects, how it heals itself and how it is constructed. Shows how to care for it.
Science - Natural
Dist - HIGGIN **Prod** - HIGGIN 1979

The Skin - its Function and Care 16 MIN
16mm
Nurse's Aide, Orderly and Attendant Series
Color (IND)
LC 73-714719
Gives the structure and function of the skin to increase the awareness and activity for maintaining proper cleansing, lubrication and protection of the patient's skin.
Health and Safety
Dist - COPI **Prod** - COPI 1971

The Skin - its structure and function 21 MIN
U-matic / VHS / 16mm
Color (J H) (SPANISH)
Examines the functions and structures of skin with the aid of reproductions from scanning electron micrographs and animation.
Science - Natural
Dist - EBEC **Prod** - EBEC 1982

Skin Matrix 17 MIN
VHS
Color
Presents Ed Emshwiller's video entry selected from the 1985 Whitney Biennial Film and Video Exhibition.
Fine Arts
Dist - AFA **Prod** - AFA 1986

The Skin of our teeth - Programs 1 and 2 52 MIN
VHS / 16mm
Civilization series
Color (G)
LC 70-708459
Travels from Byzantine Ravenna to the Celtic Hebrides, from the Norway of the Vikings to Charlemagne's chapel at Aachen. Defines civilization and gives a synoptic view of the thousand years between the fall of Rome and the rise of the great Gothic. Illuminates the Dark Ages. Features historian Kenneth Clark as host.
Fine Arts; Sociology
Dist - ARTSAM **Prod** - BBCTV 1970

Skin talk 30 MIN
VHS
Bodymatters series
Color (H C A)
PdS65 purchase
Discusses how skin protects the body. Part of a series of 26 30-minute videos on various systems of the human body.
Science - Natural
Dist - BBCENE

Skin traction - 20 15 MIN
VHS
Clinical nursing skills - nursing fundamentals - series
Color (C PRO G)
$395.00 purchase _ #R890 - VI - 073
Introduces the equipment and procedures used in skin traction. Describes the standard traction setup, including the traction frame bed and various mounting and reinforcement equipment. Demonstrates special traction modifications, including Buck's extension, Russell, pelvic and cervical head halter traction. Part of a 23 - part series on clinical nursing skills.
Health and Safety
Dist - HSCIC **Prod** - CUYAHO 1989

Skin - your amazing birthday suit 13 MIN
16mm / U-matic / VHS
PAL; Color (I J)
$340.00, $240.00 purchase _ #80529; LC 81-701474
Presents information about the skin, including its functions, how pigment determines skin coloration and how fingernails are formed. Examines pores, blood vessels, sweat glands and hair follicles, and illustrates skin care.
Science - Natural
Dist - CORF **Prod** - CENTRO 1981
VIEWTH

Skinfold video 20 MIN
VHS
Color (A T)
$29.95 purchase _ #242 - 28332
Shows physical educators or fitness instructors how to accurately measure body fat using skin folds. Explains techniques to measure and evaluate results.
Education; Physical Education and Recreation; Science - Natural
Dist - AAHPER **Prod** - AAHPER

The Skinner Revolution 23 MIN
U-matic / VHS / 16mm
Color
LC 80-700074
Examines the life of B F Skinner and his scientific and philosophical contributions in the field of psychology.
Biography; Psychology
Dist - MEDIAG **Prod** - RESPRC 1978

Skinny and Fatty 45 MIN
16mm / U-matic / VHS
CBS Children's Film Festival Series
B&W (P I J)
LC 73-702070
Portrays the special friendship between two Japanese children, one shy and unsure of himself and the other outgoing.
Guidance and Counseling; Psychology
Dist - MGHT **Prod** - WRLDP 1969

Skip for health 10 MIN
U-matic
Body works series
Color (J H)
Demonstrates new exercises and presents a recipe for Crunch Lunch, a grated carrot and yogurt sandwich spread.
Physical Education and Recreation; Social Science
Dist - TVOTAR **Prod** - TVOTAR 1979

The Skipjack 25 MIN
16mm
Color
LC 76-705665
Focuses attention on the disappearing skipjack sailing fleet and its effect on the lives of the oyster fishermen in the Chesapeake Bay area of Maryland.
Business and Economics; Geography - United States; Geography - World
Dist - WMALTV **Prod** - WMALTV 1969

Skipper Gets a Piano 15 MIN
U-matic / VHS
Strawberry Square Series
Color (P)
Fine Arts
Dist - AITECH **Prod** - NEITV 1982

Skipping 9 MIN
U-matic / VHS / 16mm
Color (P)
LC 82 - 706601; 79-701678
Shows two young children watching other kids skipping. Teaches skipping through the learning experiences of the two watchers.
Physical Education and Recreation
Dist - CF **Prod** - CF 1979

Skipping 9 MIN
U-matic / VHS / 16mm
Color (P)
$190 purchase - 16 mm, $79 purchase - video
Shows children skipping. Directed by Susan Shippey.
Physical Education and Recreation
Dist - CF

Skippy Peanut Butter 2 MIN
VHS / U-matic
Color
Shows a classic animated television commercial tracing the history of peanut butter.
Business and Economics; Psychology; Sociology
Dist - BROOKC **Prod** - BROOKC

Skirt through history series
Utilizes journals, diaries, and other personal writings to present the stories of ten women in history. Features two women journalists, a slave, a slave owner, a doctor, an artist, a social worker, a composer, and an eighteenth - century lesbian. Covers four centuries of women's history in a series of six programs.

Reputation	30 MIN
Skirt through history series	180 MIN

Dist - BBCENE

Skirt through history

Experiment	30 MIN
Lady's portion	30 MIN
Marriage	30 MIN
Two Marys	30 MIN
Wreckers	30 MIN

Dist - BBCENE

Skokie 28 MIN
16mm
Color (I)
Explores the furor unleashed by the attempted march in Skokie, Illinois during June, 1978 by members of the American Nazi Party. Documents the key events preceding the march and interviews the Jewish attorney who defended the Nazis in court, Nazi leader Frank Collins, Tom Kerr of the American Civil Liberties Union and a family of Holocaust survivors from the community.
Civics and Political Systems; History - United States; Religion and Philosophy
Dist - NJWB **Prod** - NJWB 1979

Skoven (the Forest) 26 MIN
16mm
Color
Presents the things to be seen in a forest during the various seasons if you have good eyes and keep very quiet. Includes music and sound effects.
Science - Natural
Dist - STATNS **Prod** - STATNS 1962

The Skull 27 MIN
U-matic / VHS
Anatomy of the head and neck series
Color (PRO C)
$395.00 purchase, $80.00 rental _ #C901 - VI - 063
Overviews the human skull and the bones forming it. Describes the skull from various angles and demonstrates the external features as well as salient features of individual bones. Part of a series on head and neck anatomy produced by Shakti Chandra, Faculty of Medicine, University of Newfoundland.
Health and Safety; Science - Natural
Dist - HSCIC

The Skull - an Introduction 17 MIN
U-matic / VHS
Skull Anatomy Series
Color (C A)
Presents an overview of the skull. Defines terminology and provides a review of the skull.
Health and Safety; Science - Natural
Dist - TEF **Prod** - UTXHSA

Skull Anatomy Series

The Base of the skull	10 MIN
The Cranial Cavity	17 MIN
The Facial Region	14 MIN
Nasal Cavities	12 MIN
The Oral Cavity	11 MIN
The Orbit	10 MIN
Pterygopalatine Fossa	9 MIN
The Skull - an Introduction	17 MIN
The Temporal and Infratemporal Regions	15 MIN

Dist - TEF

The Skull - foramina, fissures and canals 10 MIN
U-matic / VHS
Anatomy of the head and neck series
Color (PRO C)
$395.00 purchase, $80.00 rental _ #C901 - VI - 069
Points out important apertures in the skull and enumerates the structures traversing the openings. Focuses on foramina, fissures and canals of the skull. Presumes familiarity with skull osteology. Part of a series on head and neck anatomy produced by Shakti Chandra, Faculty of Medicine, University of Newfoundland.
Health and Safety; Science - Natural
Dist - HSCIC

Skullduggery 5 MIN
16mm
Color
Uses double exposure and other methods to include animated collage of live newsreel footage, mixing living scenes and non - living scenes.
Fine Arts; Industrial and Technical Education
Dist - VANBKS **Prod** - VANBKS 1960

The Sky 10 MIN
U-matic / VHS / 16mm
Color (P I)
Presents basic scientific facts about the sky and the objects in it -- sun, moon, stars and clouds.
Science - Physical
Dist - IFB **Prod** - EDMNDS 1961

Sky 10 MIN
16mm
Color (P)
LC FIA67-5543
Looks at the sky over a 24 - hour period, showing thunderheads, a rainstorm and the sunrise.
Science - Physical
Dist - NFBC **Prod** - NFBC 1962

Sky blue water light sign 9 MIN
16mm
Color (G)
$15.00 rental
Features an uplifting film. Contructs a mystery around what exactly the audience is viewing. Produced by J J Murphy.
Fine Arts
Dist - CANCIN

Sky Capers 15 MIN
U-matic / VHS / 16mm
Color (J A)
LC FIA68-2320
Examines the sport of sky diving.
Physical Education and Recreation
Dist - PFP **Prod** - PFP 1968

Sky Chief 26 MIN
U-matic / VHS / 16mm
Color (C)
LC 73-700286
Shows the dramatic cultural and economic clash of different forces and resulting ecological damage. Portrays both collusion and conflict among an international petroleum consortium, a Latin American government, Mestize settlers and traders and the indigenous people.
Business and Economics; Civics and Political Systems; Science - Natural; Social Science; Sociology
Dist - UCEMC **Prod** - SCOTTM 1972

Sky dance 11 MIN
16mm / U-matic / VHS
Color
LC 80-700173
Offers an animated depiction of man's age - old attempt to understand his role in the universe.
Fine Arts; Sociology
Dist - PFP **Prod** - HUBLEY 1980

Sky dive 15 MIN
U-matic / VHS / 16mm
Color
LC 79-700968
Shows skydivers taking part in group jumps and plunging off the 3,000 - foot cliff of Yosemite National Park's El Capitan.
Physical Education and Recreation
Dist - PFP **Prod** - BOENIC

Sky Fox 30 MIN
VHS / 16mm
Marketing Series
Color (C A)
$130.00, $120.00 purchase _15 - 06
Focuses on industrial markets, paperwork and bureaucracy.
Business and Economics
Dist - CDTEL **Prod** - COAST 1989

Sky High
U-matic / VHS
Color
Compares various aspects of flying. Includes aerobatics, sky diving, hang gliding, and the history of flying.
Industrial and Technical Education; Physical Education and Recreation
Dist - ALTI **Prod** - ALTI

The Sky is gray 47 MIN
VHS
American short story collection series
Color (J H)
$49.00 purchase _ #05959 - 126
Portrays a boy who struggles between his mother's insistence on dignity and self - reliance, and the realities of prejudice and poverty. Written by Ernest Gaines.
Guidance and Counseling; History - United States; Literature and Drama
Dist - GA **Prod** - GA

The Sky is gray 47 MIN
16mm / U-matic / VHS
American short story series
Color (J H C)
$835.00, $250.00 purchase _ #4098; LC 80-700095
Offers an adaptation of Ernest Gaines' short story The Sky Is Gray about a young black farm boy's dawning of awareness about himself and society.
Fine Arts; Literature and Drama
Dist - CORF **Prod** - LEARIF 1980
CDTEL

Sky Over Holland 22 MIN
16mm

Color
Pictures a potpourri of visual impressions of Holland. Contrasts the works of Dutch artists from Rembrandt to Van Gogh and Mondrian with scenes of contemporary life.
Fine Arts; Geography - World
Dist - WB **Prod** - SCULMR 1968

The Sky pirate 85 MIN
16mm
Color (G)
$100.00 rental
Dramatizes an escapist Latin fantasy. Features Cuba, the New Left's revolutionary society, the wife's little - theatre Carmen and a hooker from Spanish Harlem. Produced by Andrew Meyer.
Fine Arts
Dist - CANCIN

Skydivers 29 MIN
Videoreel / VT2
Bayou City and Thereabouts People Show Series
Color
Explains that the people who participate in skydiving are as varied as their descriptions of the sport.
Physical Education and Recreation
Dist - PBS **Prod** - KUHTTV

Skyfish 30 MIN
U-matic / VHS
Doris Chase concepts series
Color
Reveals the human change experienced by a woman artist as she paints, and her subconscious mind is made visual.
Literature and Drama; Sociology
Dist - WMEN **Prod** - CHASED

Skylab 30 MIN
U-matic / VHS
Color
Presents Dr Story Musgrave, backup pilot for Skylab I and II, explaining the experiments and findings from these Skylab missions. Research covered the sun, earth's resources, the crew's reactions to conditions in space and more.
History - World; Science; Science - Natural; Science - Physical
Dist - NETCHE **Prod** - NETCHE 1975

Skylab 27 MIN
16mm / U-matic / VHS
Color (I J H)
LC 76-715418
Shows the major objectives of the Skylab mission and explains its principal components and features.
Industrial and Technical Education; Science - Physical
Dist - USNAC **Prod** - NASA 1971

Skylab and the Sun 13 MIN
16mm / U-matic / VHS
Color
Presents information gathered by the Skylab missions on the behavior of the sun, solar energy, plasma flow and mass/thermal transfer. Shows how we can use information about the sun to our advantage.
History - World; Industrial and Technical Education; Science - Physical
Dist - USNAC **Prod** - NASA

Skylab Medical Experiments 31 MIN
16mm
Color
Describes the equipment and experiments of the Skylab Medical Experiments Program. Discusses major experiment items such as the lower body negative pressure device, the ergometer, the rotating litter chair and the experiment support system.
Industrial and Technical Education; Science - Physical
Dist - NASA **Prod** - NASA

Skylab - on the Eve of Launch 11 MIN
16mm
Color
Describes Skylab and its flight plans. Highlights the final preparation of flight articles and crew training up to the eve of launch of the first mission.
Industrial and Technical Education; Science - Physical
Dist - NASA **Prod** - NASA

Skylab Science Demonstrations Series
Fluids in weightlessness 15 MIN
Gyroscopes in Space 15 MIN
Magnetic Effects in Space 14 MIN
Magnetism in Space 19 MIN
Zero - g 15 MIN
Dist - USNAC

Skylights 20 MIN
VHS
Color (J H C A)
Teaches how to install a skylight in a standard, flat ceiling room.
Home Economics; Industrial and Technical Education
Dist - COFTAB **Prod** - AMHOM 1985

Skylights
VHS
Home Improvement Series
(H C G A IND)
$39.95 _ SH318
Shows how to plan, locate, lay out, and cut the opening for a skylight as well as consideration of frame openings and other structural changes having to do with installing skylights.
Education; Home Economics; Industrial and Technical Education
Dist - AAVIM **Prod** - AAVIM 1989

Skylights 28 MIN
VHS
Home improvement video series
Color (G)
$39.95 purchase _ #224
Discusses skylights. Shows how to plan, locate, lay out, cut the opening, make structual changes, frame openings, install skylights and roof windows, and covers flashing, shingle, insulation, drywall installation and finishing the opening.
Home Economics
Dist - DIYVC **Prod** - DIYVC

Skylights 38 MIN
VHS
$39.95 purchase _ #DI - 318
Tells how to plan, locate, lay out, cut the opening, make structural changes, and frame openings, and how to install skylights and roof windows. Provides instruction in installing flashing, shingles, drywall, and finishing the opening.
Industrial and Technical Education
Dist - CAREER **Prod** - CAREER

Skylights 38 MIN
VHS / 16mm
Do it yourself series
(G)
$39.95 purchase _ #DIY318
Details how to install skylights and roof windows. Shows how to plan, locate, lay out, cut the opening, make structural changes and frame opening. Includes installing flashing, shingles, insulation, drywall, and finishing the opening.
Home Economics
Dist - RMIBHF **Prod** - RMIBHF

Skyline 83 MIN
VHS / 35mm / 16mm
Color (G) (SPANISH WITH ENGLISH SUBTITLES)
$200.00, $300.00 rental
Portrays a professional photographer from Madrid who tries to establish himself in New York. Directed by Fernando Colomo and co - scripted by and co - starring Whit Stillman. With English subtitles.
Fine Arts
Dist - KINOIC

Skyline series
Basic training - School of American Ballet 30 MIN
Dist - PBS

Skylines for tomorrow 22 MIN
16mm
Color
LC FIA68-1860
Describes and illustrates lightweight aggregate, its deposits, mining, processing and properties. Pictures samples from different parts of the United States and Canada.
Business and Economics; Science - Natural
Dist - CINEA **Prod** - ESCSI 1967

Skylines of the Northwest 19 MIN
16mm / U-matic
Color
Discusses important dimensions of skyline logging in the Pacific Northwest, showing current research, innovations and a variety of skyline systems.
Science - Natural; Social Science
Dist - OSUSF **Prod** - OSUSF

Skylines of the South 20 MIN
16mm
Color (C A)
Shows that in a variety of ways the gospel message penerates the concrete jungles of the cities in southern Brazil.
Geography - World; Literature and Drama; Religion and Philosophy; Social Science
Dist - CBFMS **Prod** - CBFMS

Skyrider 7 MIN
U-matic / VHS / 16mm
Color
LC 81-700903
Presents an animated fantasy about space travel complete with astronauts, space capsules, witches on broomsticks and flying toasters.
Fine Arts; Science - Physical
Dist - PHENIX **Prod** - HALAS 1978

Sky's the limit 22 MIN
VHS
Color (P I J)
$295.00 purchase
Shows two boys resisting peer pressure to drink alcohol and take other drugs with the help of a positive role model and some useful methods for saying 'No' to others. Provides source material for drug - resistance programs.
Guidance and Counseling; Health and Safety; Psychology
Dist - PFP **Prod** - ARMPIC

The Sky's the Limit 56 MIN
U-matic / VHS / 16mm
Color (H C A)
Introduces Dr Wayne Dyer's theory of no - limit thinking covering such topics as handling stress, dealing with anxiety, improving self - worth, making choices and thinking positively. Emphasizes that mastery is a fundamental approach to life.
Guidance and Counseling; Psychology; Religion and Philosophy
Dist - LCOA **Prod** - LCOA

The Sky's the Limit 23 MIN
16mm / U-matic / VHS
Color
Investigates the causes and consequences of urban air pollution, using the San Francisco Bay Area as a case study. Shows the various case factors and analyzes how much each adds to the daily release of pollutants.
Sociology
Dist - UCEMC **Prod** - WHTKEN 1980

The Sky's the Limit 30 MIN
VHS
Soapbox With Tom Cottle Series
Color (G)
$59.95 purchase _ #SBOX - 501
Focuses on the daily difficulties that physically disabled teenagers face. Shows that the biggest difficulty can be learning to cope with the reactions of their peers. Hosted by psychologist Tom Cottle.
Health and Safety; Psychology; Sociology
Dist - PBS **Prod** - WGBYTV 1985

The Sky's the Limit 15 MIN
16mm
Color (A)
Presents women talking about why they are joining the ranks of apprentices in crafts such as electrician, machinist and operating engineer. Shows why women are entering non - traditional jobs and the problems and advantages resulting from this training.
Business and Economics; Sociology
Dist - AFLCIO **Prod** - USDL 1978

The Sky's the limit 10 MIN
VHS
Color; Captioned (G)
$25.00 purchase
Shows children and adults with disabilities participating in all kinds of recreational activities, including hang gliding, skiing, tennis, bicycling and hiking. Features recreation directors who discuss how recreation affects a person's entire life. People with disabilities and parents of children with disabilities emphasize the importance of focusing on the things that one can do.
Health and Safety
Dist - UATP **Prod** - UATP 1991

Sky's the Limit Series
Part One - Taking Charge 30 MIN
Winning all the Time 30 MIN
Dist - DELTAK

Sky's the Limit, the, Pt 2 - Winning all the Time 26 MIN
16mm
Color (H C A)
Presents Dr Wayne Dyer's philosophy that mastery is a fundamental approach to life.
Business and Economics; Science
Dist - LCA **Prod** - LCA

The Sky's the Limit - with Dr Wayne Dyer 56 MIN
U-matic / VHS / 16mm
Captioned; Color (H C A) (SWEDISH)
Shares Dr Dyer's "no - limit" philosophy as an approach to handling stress, making choices and improving goal setting. Can be used as a structured half - day workshop with facilitator's guide. Captioned in Swedish.
Fine Arts; Foreign Language; Psychology
Dist - LCOA **Prod** - LCOA 1981

The Sky's the limit - women overcoming the odds 13 MIN
VHS

Color (P I)
$99 purchase _ #10211VL
Highlights the lives of some famous women pilots such as Harriett Quimby, Bessie Coleman and Amelia Earhart. Uses the lives of the aviatrices to teach motivation, personal potential, and the important roles of women in history. Comes with a teacher's guide and thematic lesson plans, student activities, discussion questions, and 21 blackline masters.
Industrial and Technical Education; Sociology
Dist - UNL

The Sky's unlimited 26 MIN
U-matic / VHS
Color
Focuses on using the sky as a recreation vehicle, including flying ultra light airplanes, parachuting, hang gliding, antique and small plane flying, soaring and ballooning. Shows model planes as a hobby.
Physical Education and Recreation; Social Science
Dist - BCNFL **Prod** - HARDAP 1983

Skyscraper 15 MIN
VHS / U-matic
Explorers unlimited series
Color (P I)
Explores the inside operation of a skyscraper in Cleveland, Ohio.
Social Science
Dist - AITECH **Prod** - WVIZTV 1971

Skyscraper 80 MIN
VHS
Color; CC (G)
$89.95 purchase _ #EX3057
Focusses on the design and construction of Worldwide Plaza in New York City. Presents a shortened version of the series 'Skyscraper.'
Geography - United States; Industrial and Technical Education
Dist - FOTH **Prod** - WGBH

Skyscraper 290 MIN
VHS
Skyscraper series
Color; CC (G)
$425.00 purchase _ #EX2612; Progam not available in Canada.
Chronicles the construction of Worldwide Plaza, a 47 - story, 770 - foot tower built on the former site of Madison Square Garden in New York City. Consists of five 58 - minute segments. Includes 'Rock and Paper,' 'Time and Money,' 'Steel and Stone,' 'Copper and Diamond,' and 'Higher and Higher.'
Geography - United States; Industrial and Technical Education
Dist - FOTH **Prod** - WGBH

Skyscraper Age 33 MIN
16mm
Color
Focuses on the new development project of highrise apartment houses as an effective means of urban redevelopment. Explains that the Kajima Corporation took the initiative in opening Japan's skyscraper age.
Industrial and Technical Education; Sociology
Dist - UNIJAP **Prod** - KAJIMA 1970

Skyscraper series
Copper and diamond 58 MIN
Higher and higher 58 MIN
Rock and paper 58 MIN
Skyscraper 290 MIN
Steel and stone 58 MIN
Time and money 58 MIN
Dist - FOTH

Skyscrapers and slums 20 MIN
16mm / U-matic / VHS
Brazil series
Color (J H)
Presents the story of Mauro, a 12 - year - old schoolboy who works as a part - time shoe shiner in downtown Sao Paulo, Brazil. Contrasts the spectacular business district where Mauro works, the result of the campaign for industrial growth, with the poverty of his home in the favela or squatter settlement.
Business and Economics; Geography - World; History - World
Dist - FI **Prod** - BBCTV 1982

Skyward the Great Ships 27 MIN
16mm
Color (J H A)
LC FIE67-128
Reports on the various kinds of propulsion being developed for space missions and the applications and advantages of each. Illustrates research in chemical, nuclear and electrical propulsion systems.
Industrial and Technical Education; Science - Physical
Dist - USNAC **Prod** - NASA

Skyworks, the red mile 10 MIN
16mm
Color (G)
$15.00 rental
Documents the conceptual art of Le Ann Bartok Wilchusky, 'Skyworks, the red mile,' dropped from 7500 feet by skydivers, unfurling into a line one mile long. Produced by Le Ann Bartok.
Fine Arts
Dist - CANCIN

Skyworks, wind and fire 8 MIN
16mm
Color (G)
$15.00 rental
Documents the conceptual art of Le Ann Bartok Wilchusky, 'Dropped Objects,' dropped from 8000 feet by skydivers. Complements film 'Skyworks, the Red Mile.' Produced by Le Ann Bartok.
Fine Arts
Dist - CANCIN

SL - 1 60 MIN
U-matic / VHS / 16mm
Color; B&W (H A G)
Recreates the true story of America's first nuclear accident. Features previously repressed government evidence which indicates that perhaps the disaster was caused by the suicidal impulse of an individual technician.
Civics and Political Systems; Industrial and Technical Education; Science - Physical; Sociology
Dist - DIRECT **Prod** - ROBLAR 1984

The SL - 1 accident - Phase 3 57 MIN
U-matic / VHS / 16mm
Color
Shows what was done with the SL - 1 reactor and building following the accidental nuclear accident of January 1961. Re-enacts the accident using animation and postulates about the cause.
Health and Safety; History - World; Industrial and Technical Education; Science - Physical; Social Science; Sociology
Dist - USNAC **Prod** - USNRC 1962
USERD

The SL - 1 Accident - Phases 1 and 2 43 MIN
U-matic / VHS / 16mm
Color
Uses actual and reenacted scenes to show what happened in phases one and two following the nuclear accident of January 3, 1961.
Health and Safety; History - World; Industrial and Technical Education; Science - Physical; Social Science; Sociology
Dist - USNAC **Prod** - USNRC
USERD

Sla - Hal, the Bone Game 27 MIN
16mm
Native Music of the North - West Series
Color
LC 82-700230
Shows the native American Indian bone game called sla - hal, photographed at a Makah Indian celebration in the Pacific Northwest. Presents bone game songs in the context of the games being played, together with comments from game participants explaining facts of the game and its place in their contemporary American culture.
Social Science
Dist - WASU **Prod** - WASU 1982

Slab and coil pots 29 MIN
Videoreel / VT2
Exploring the crafts - pottery series
Color
Features Mrs Vivika Heino demonstrating procedures with various slab and coil pots.
Fine Arts
Dist - PBS **Prod** - WENHTV

Slab City - a Very Special Town 29 MIN
U-matic / VHS / 16mm
Color (J)
LC 82-701218
Shows the lifestyles of retired people who each winter migrate to an abandoned Marine base in California where they live rent - free in their trailers throughout the winter. Documents how the people organize brigades to handle such essentials as water retrieval, sewage and waste disposal, and mail distribution.
Sociology
Dist - WOMBAT **Prod** - VONWET 1982

Slabs and Sawdust 20 MIN
16mm
Color
LC 76-701480
Rresents information about safety procedures in sawmills.
Health and Safety; Industrial and Technical Education
Dist - CENTWO **Prod** - CENTWO 1975

Slalom 80 MIN
U-matic / VHS
Superstar Sports Tapes Series
Color
Focuses on equipment, training and technique for use in slalom skiing on water. Includes the slalom course, boats and driving. Stars Bob LaPoint.
Health and Safety; Physical Education and Recreation
Dist - TRASS **Prod** - TRASS

Slams - Bidding and Play 30 MIN
U-matic / VHS
Play Bridge Series
Color (A)
Physical Education and Recreation
Dist - KYTV **Prod** - KYTV 1983

A Slap in the face 87 MIN
16mm
Color (C A) (RUSSIAN (ENGLISH SUBTITLES))
LC 82-700445
Presents a film about life, love and work in Armenia in the 1930s. Relates that following his father's death, an Armenian boy takes over his father's profession as a saddlemaker for donkeys, which leads to great difficulties in his pursuit of a bride.
Fine Arts; Foreign Language; Literature and Drama
Dist - IFEX **Prod** - SOVEXP 1982

A Slap in the face - Pt 1 29 MIN
16mm
Color (C A) (RUSSIAN (ENGLISH SUBTITLES))
LC 82-700445
A film about life, love and work in Armenia in the 1930s. Relates that following his father's death, an Armenian boy takes over his father's profession as a saddlemaker for donkeys, which leads to great difficulties in his pursuit of a bride.
History - World
Dist - IFEX **Prod** - SOVEXP 1982

A Slap in the face - Pt 2 29 MIN
16mm
Color (C A) (RUSSIAN (ENGLISH SUBTITLES))
LC 82-700445
A film about life, love and work in Armenia in the 1930s. Relates that following his father's death, an Armenian boy takes over his father's profession as a saddlemaker for donkeys, which leads to great difficulties in his pursuit of a bride.
History - World
Dist - IFEX **Prod** - SOVEXP 1982

A Slap in the face - Pt 3 29 MIN
16mm
Color (C A) (RUSSIAN (ENGLISH SUBTITLES))
LC 82-700445
A film about life, love and work in Armenia in the 1930s. Relates that following his father's death, an Armenian boy takes over his father's profession as a saddlemaker for donkeys, which leads to great difficulties in his pursuit of a bride.
History - World
Dist - IFEX **Prod** - SOVEXP 1982

Slap Shot 123 MIN
16mm
Color
Shows how a burned - out hockey coach (Paul Newman) suddenly gains fame and fortune when he recruits some new players who will stop at nothing to win.
Fine Arts
Dist - TWYMAN **Prod** - UPCI 1977

Slapstick 27 MIN
16mm
History of the motion picture series
B&W
Covers the slapstick era of visual comedy. Includes some of the top comics of the 1920s performing deathdefying stunts without benefit of doubles or trick effects. Charlie Chase, Monty Banks, Fatty Arbuckle, Larry Semon and Andy Clyde appear.
Fine Arts
Dist - KILLIS **Prod** - SF 1960

Slate and Vinyl Floors - Slate Floors, Tile Floors 30 MIN
BETA / VHS
Wally's Workshop Series
Color
Home Economics; Industrial and Technical Education
Dist - KARTES **Prod** - KARTES

Slaughter procedures - beef 50 MIN
U-matic / VHS
Animal slaughtering - meat cutting
(PRO)
Shows accepted animal slaughtering techniques for beef.
Agriculture
Dist - GPN **Prod** - NETV

Slaughter procedures - sheep 36 MIN
VHS / U-matic
Animal slaughtering - meat cutting
(PRO)
Shows accepted slaughtering techniques for sheep.
Agriculture
Dist - GPN **Prod** - NETV

Slaughter procedures - swine 28 MIN
U-matic / VHS
Animal slaughtering - meat cutting
(PRO)
Shows accepted slaughtering techniques for swine.
Agriculture
Dist - GPN **Prod** - NETV

Slaughter procedures - turkey 13 MIN
VHS / U-matic
Animal slaughtering - meat cutting
(PRO)
Shows accepted slaughtering techniques for turkey.
Agriculture
Dist - GPN **Prod** - NETV

The Slave Coast 50 MIN
16mm
Black African heritage series
Color (J H)
Features narration by Maya Angelou in an exploration of the slave coast, an area where an estimated 15 million humans were enslaved and shipped to other lands between the 17th and 19th centuries. Depicts the Ashanti of Ghana, the Yoruba of Nigeria, the women warriors of Dahomey and the acrobatic Dan dancers of the Ivory Coast.
Geography - World; History - United States; History - World; Social Science
Dist - WBCPRO **Prod** - WBCPRO 1972

The Slave - Pt 1 53 MIN
16mm
Roots series; The Slave; 03
Color (J)
Explains that the slave rebellion aboard the Lord Ligonier is quickly put down. Tells how the ship anchors in Annapolis and Kunta Kinte is bought by plantation owner John Reynolds.
Fine Arts; History - United States
Dist - FI **Prod** - WOLPER

The Slave - Pt 2 48 MIN
16mm
Roots series; The Slave; 04
Color (J)
Shows how Fiddler, an older slave, is put in charge of training Kunta Kinte. Focuses on Kunta's rebellious attitude, which leads him to an unsuccessful escape attempt.
Fine Arts; History - United States
Dist - FI **Prod** - WOLPER

The Slave trade in the New World 30 MIN
16mm
Black history - Section 04 - slave trade and slavery series; Section 4 - Slave trade and slavery
B&W (H C A)
LC 75-704038
Surveys the contribution of the early African explorers - including Pedro Alonzo, who piloted one of Columbus' ships - and those who settled in the area which later became known as Jamestown. John Henrik Clarke discusses the arrival of slaves in 1619, the extent of slavery, and the revolts of slaves in the West Indies and in North and South America.
History - United States; History - World
Dist - HRAW **Prod** - WCBSTV 1969

Slave trade in the world today
VHS
Color (G)
$34.95 purchase _ #VF003
Reveals the existence of an international industry dealing in human slaves.
Sociology
Dist - SIV

The Slave who Wouldn't Give Up 20 MIN
U-matic
Truly American Series
Color (I)
Discusses the life of Frederick Douglass.
Biography; History - United States
Dist - GPN **Prod** - WVIZTV 1979

Slavery and Personality 29 MIN
Videoreel / VT2
Black Experience Series
Color
History - United States; Psychology; Sociology
Dist - PBS **Prod** - WTTWTV

Slavery and Racism in Historical Debate 29 MIN
Videoreel / VT2
Black Experience Series
Color
History - United States; History - World; Sociology
Dist - PBS **Prod** - WTTWTV

Slavery and sentiment in American abolitionism - Uncle Tom's cabin 60 MIN
VHS
Europe and America in the modern age - 1776 to the present series
Color (H C PRO)
$95.00 purchase
Presents a lecture by David M Kennedy. Focuses on a critical period in European and American history and on leaders of the time. Part of a 20 - part series that looks at the last two centuries in Europe and America. Series presents lectures by David M Kennedy and James Sheehan of Stanford University on such figures as Adam Smith, Marx, Lincoln, Washington, Jefferson, Freud, Margaret Sanger, Susan B Anthony and Jane Adams and their impact on the events of their day. For history resource material and continuing education courses.
Civics and Political Systems; History - United States; History - World; Literature and Drama
Dist - LANDMK

Slavery and slave resistance 26 MIN
16mm
Color (G)
$40.00 rental _ #ERF - 732
Traces the growth and development of the institution of slavery in the United States. Documents the efforts of black men and women who resisted through recalling instances of escape and rebellion.
History - United States; Sociology
Dist - ADL **Prod** - ADL

Slavery and Slave Resistance 26 MIN
U-matic / VHS / 16mm
Color (I)
LC 70-705666
Traces the origins of slavery, examines the basis of racial stereotyping as it developed in the dehumanizing conditions of slave life and work, and describes the varieties of active and passive black resistance.
History - United States
Dist - CORF **Prod** - NYT 1969

Slavery as a Social System 29 MIN
Videoreel / VT2
Black Experience Series
Color
History - United States; Sociology
Dist - PBS **Prod** - WTTWTV

Slavery as an Economic System 29 MIN
Videoreel / VT2
Black Experience Series
Color
History - United States; Sociology
Dist - PBS **Prod** - WTTWTV

Slavery in the Cities 29 MIN
Videoreel / VT2
Black Experience Series
Color
History - United States; Sociology
Dist - PBS **Prod** - WTTWTV

Slaves in ancient Rome 19 MIN
VHS
Color (J H C)
LC 89-700173
Looks at the institution of slavery in ancient Rome.
History - World; Sociology
Dist - EAV **Prod** - EAV 1989

A Slave's Story - Running a Thousand Miles to Freedom 29 MIN
U-matic / VHS / 16mm
Captioned; Color (J)
Dramatizes the Craft family's escape from slavery in 1848.
History - United States
Dist - LCOA **Prod** - OBERCI 1972

A Slave's tale 20 MIN
U-matic / VHS
Matter of fiction series no 2
B&W (J H)
Presents Erik Christian Haugaard's story set in Scandinavia during the Viking Age. Concerns the misadventure of a slave girl's youthful master as he sails to Frankland to return a slave to his family. (Broadcast quality).
Literature and Drama
Dist - AITECH **Prod** - WETATV

The Slaying of the Suitors 15 MIN
U-matic / VHS
Homer's Odyssey Series
Color (C)
$239.00, $139.00 purchase _ #AD - 2047
Reunites Odysseus and Telemachus. Shows Odysseus slaying the suitors of Penelope, his faithful wife. Part of a six - part series.
History - World; Literature and Drama
Dist - FOTH **Prod** - FOTH

Slaying the dragon 60 MIN
VHS / U-matic
Color (G)
$225.00 purchase, $50.00 rental
Chronicles Hollywood's recycling of one - dimensional images of Asian American women through film clips and interviews with media critics and Asian American actresses. Reveals that today's images represent updated versions of the 'evil' Dragon Lady, the 'seductive' Suzy Wong and the 'subservient' Geisha girl. Shows the impact of those stereotypes on Asian American women socially and psychologically. Produced and directed by Deborah Gee for Asian Women United.
Sociology
Dist - CROCUR

Sleazy and The Year 2000 50 MIN
16mm
Color (G)
$100.00 rental
Projects from the present into the future to reveal the interiority of the present in two productions. Analyzes a car crash taken from a 1960s film with interspersed dialogue and sound directly related to the body in Sleazy, made in 1987. The Year 2000 is based on a hypothetical projection of the filmmaker from the present into the future. Psychoanalytical theory informed most of this complex work.
Fine Arts; Psychology
Dist - CANCIN **Prod** - SONDHE 1988

Sleep 28 MIN
VHS
Human body - the brain - series
Color (J H G)
$89.95 purchase _ #UW4177
Explains what sleep is and why it is indispensable. Shows what happens in the brain during sleep and explains the different kinds of sleep and dreaming. Covers tiredness, sleep, sleep disturbances and sleeping pills. Part of a 39 - part series featuring computer animation, medical photography, electron micrography, full - color drawings and diagrams and three - dimensional working models to cover the workings of the human body from head to toe and inside out.
Psychology; Science - Natural
Dist - FOTH

Sleep 29 MIN
VHS / 16mm
Discovery digest series
Color (S)
$300.00 purchase _ #707621
Explores a vast array of science - related discoveries, challenges and technological breakthroughs. Profiles and 'demystifies' research and development currently underway in many fields. Considers sleep apnea and examines a true story of living with narcolepsy, highlights the relaxation techniques of Dr Geoffrey Dawrant, and profiles gerontologist Dr David Schonfield.
Health and Safety; Psychology; Science; Sociology
Dist - ACCESS **Prod** - ACCESS 1989

Sleep 15 MIN
VHS
Zardips search for healthy wellness series
Color (P I)
LC 90-707987
Presents an episode in a series which helps young children to understand basic health issues and the value of taking good care of their bodies. Explains the importance of sleep. Includes teacher's guide.
Education; Health and Safety
Dist - TVOTAR **Prod** - TVOTAR 1989

Sleep 11 MIN
16mm / U-matic / VHS
Color (P I)
LC FIA68-1774
Acquaints children with the importance of sleep. Shows different brain waves made during wakefulness, light sleep, deep sleep and dreaming. Presents a horse asleep on his feet, a bat hanging in a cave, a koala bear in a tree, a tree losing its leaves for months of dormancy and a squirrel in hibernation.
Health and Safety
Dist - ALTSUL **Prod** - FILMSW 1968

Sleep 30 MIN
U-matic
Today's Special Series
Color (K P)
Develops language arts skills in children. Programs are thematically designed around subjects of interest to youngsters. Action takes place in a department store

where people, mannequins, puppets, comic characters and special guests present a light hearted approach to language arts.
Fine Arts; Literature and Drama; Psychology
Dist - TVOTAR **Prod** - TVOTAR 1985

Sleep - a prerequisite for health 18 MIN
VHS
Color (G)
$149.00 purchase, $75.00 rental _ #UW4589
Shows the fallacy of thinking that one can function without sleep. Reveals that fatigue was involved in the Exxon Valdez disaster, the Challenger disaster, the Three Mile Island incident and the Bhopal chemical leak. Looks at lack of sleep as a factor in a large percentage of plane and car accidents. Discloses that medical personnel are also subject to the effects of fatigue. Illustrates how fatigue develops and how it affects reactions and reaction time.
Health and Safety
Dist - FOTH

Sleep Alert 30 MIN
VHS
Color (G)
$150.00 purchase _ #SLAL - 000
Examines the widespread phenomenon of sleep deprivation, which is thought to affect 100 million Americans. Cites statistics showing that chronic sleep loss will negatively affect work, learning and behavior.
Health and Safety
Dist - PBS **Prod** - CORNRS 1989

Sleep and Dream Research 145 MIN
U-matic
University of the Air Series
Color (J H C A)
$750.00 purchase, $250.00 rental
Gives an account of the history of sleep and dream research, problems of dream recall, factors effecting sleep and dreams and the effects of sleep deprivation. Program contains a series of five cassettes 29 minutes each.
Psychology
Dist - CTV **Prod** - CTV 1977

Sleep and Dreaming 30 MIN
VHS / 16mm
Psychology - the Study of Human Behavior Series
Color (C A)
$99.95, $89.95 purchase _ 24 - 05
Gives examples of biological rhythms and mental states.
Psychology
Dist - CDTEL **Prod** - COAST 1990

Sleep and Dreaming in Humans 14 MIN
16mm
Films at the Frontiers of Psychological Inquiry Series
Color (H C A)
LC 72-702268
Demonstrates standarized research techniques used to specify stages of wakefulness, sleep and dreaming. Shows placement of electrodes, recording techniques and arousal from non - REM and REM stages using a human subject.
Psychology
Dist - HMC **Prod** - HMC 1971

Sleep and dreams 25 MIN
U-matic / VHS
Color
Notes that despite the fact one spends one third of his or her life asleep, for years almost nothing has been known about sleep. Says that sleep investigators are only just now learning about the physiological structure of sleep. Shows Dr Ernest Rossi, a psychotherapist, discussing dreams and analyzing their content.
Health and Safety
Dist - MEDCOM **Prod** - MEDCOM

Sleep and the Elderly 16 MIN
VHS / 16mm
Color (PRO)
$295.00 purchase, $60.00 rental
Presents normal sleep patterns, new findings regarding sleep patterns in the aged, and suggestions for addressing sleep problems experienced by the elderly. Addresses possible side effects of medication.
Health and Safety
Dist - FAIRGH **Prod** - FAIRGH 1986

Sleep Apnea - an Overview 29 MIN
U-matic / VHS
Color (PRO)
Describes the diagnostic procedures, signs and symptoms, causes and consequences of sleep apnea.
Health and Safety
Dist - HSCIC **Prod** - HSCIC 1984

Sleep Apnea Hypersomnolence Syndrome 21 MIN
U-matic
Color (C)
Reviews the presenting symptoms, diagnosis and pathogenesis of upper airway obstruction during sleep.
Health and Safety; Science - Natural
Dist - UOKLAH **Prod** - UOKLAH 1978

Sleep Disorders 28 MIN
U-matic / VHS
Color (C)
$249.00, $149.00 purchase _ #AD - 1390
Explores sleep disorders. Interviews Dr William Dement of the Stanford Sleep Disorders Center, and Dr Michael Thorpy of the Sleep - Wake Disorders Center at Montefiore Medical Center, and patients suffering from a variety of sleep disorders.
Health and Safety; Psychology
Dist - FOTH **Prod** - FOTH

Sleep Disorders
U-matic / VHS
Psychiatry Learning System, Pt 2 - Disorders Series
Color (PRO)
Includes disorders of initiating and maintaining sleep, disorders of excessive somnolence, disorders of the sleep - wake schedule, and dysfunctions associated with sleep.
Health and Safety; Psychology
Dist - HSCIC **Prod** - HSCIC 1982

Sleep - Dream Voyage 26 MIN
U-matic / VHS / 16mm
Living Body - an Introduction to Human Biology Series
Color
Discusses what happens to the body during sleep. Explores the mystery of REM sleep, presents a computer display of the waves that sweep across the brain during sleep, and shows footage of a cat 'acting out' its dreams. Uses the analogy of sleep to a ship on automatic pilot to illustrate how some functions must and do continuue while the conscious brain is asleep.
Psychology; Science - Natural
Dist - FOTH **Prod** - FOTH 1985

Sleep, Hole, Up, Down 10 MIN
U-matic
Readalong One Series
Color (K P)
Introduces reading and spelling for preschoolers and children in grades 1 to 3 with animation, puppets, humor and music. Comes with teacher's guide and kit.
Education; English Language; Literature and Drama
Dist - TVOTAR **Prod** - TVOTAR 1975

Sleep - Nursing Action 89 FRS
VHS / U-matic
Pain - Sleep Series
Color (PRO)
LC 75-739168
Psychology; Sociology
Dist - CONMED **Prod** - CONMED 1971

The Sleep of babies - spontaneous cyclical phenomena during neonate sleep 30 MIN
16mm
B&W (C)
Records observable behavior of three-to-five-day-old infants' sleep by means of normal speed, slowed motion, speeded motion and stop motion cinematography. Illustrates methods of classifying and recording various types of behavior during sleep.
Psychology
Dist - PSUPCR **Prod** - PSUPCR 1970

Sleep on it 10 MIN
U-matic
Body Works Series
Color (P I J H)
Teaches children the importance of a good night's sleep. Includes nutritious recipes, exercises and a few facts about sleep.
Physical Education and Recreation; Social Science
Dist - TVOTAR **Prod** - TVOTAR 1979

Sleep Problems 19 MIN
U-matic / VHS
Color (C)
$249.00, $149.00 purchase _ #AD - 1386
Looks at sleep disorders that can kill - sleep apnea and narcolepsy. Shows how sleep labs are helping to diagnose and treat these problems. Demonstrates how uvulo palato pharyngoplasty is opening the air passages of sufferers from sleep apnea and shows how narcolepsy is diagnosed by means of a polysomnogram. Explains the different stages of sleep.
Health and Safety; Psychology
Dist - FOTH **Prod** - FOTH

Sleep, Stress and Relaxation 15 MIN
U-matic / VHS
Well, Well, Well with Slim Goodbody Series
Color (P)
Explains how sleep rests the body and how to relax when negative feelings cause stress.
Guidance and Counseling; Health and Safety
Dist - AITECH **Prod** - AITECH

Sleep - the Dark Side of Life 21 MIN
U-matic
Color (C)
Illustrates different breathing disturbances which occur exclusively during sleep.
Health and Safety; Science - Natural
Dist - UOKLAH **Prod** - UOKLAH 1978

Sleep - Wake Disorders
U-matic / VHS
Color
Reviews the clinical aspects of the more common sleep/wake disorders in relation to appropriate phases of normal and circadian rhythm cycles. Identifies salient clinical features of the more common disorders of sleep in individual patients and establishes a differential diagnosis in the patient.
Health and Safety; Psychology
Dist - AMEDA **Prod** - AMEDA

Sleep well 9 MIN
U-matic / VHS / 16mm
Color (J)
LC 75710758
Uses cut-out animation to tell the story of a man who settles into an armchair to snooze and whose sleep is filled with dreams. Each dream comments on the plight of the individual in society -- bureaucracy, patriotism, jingoism. The dreams become nightmares.
Psychology; Sociology
Dist - AIMS **Prod** - GKF 1968

The Sleepers 16 MIN
16mm
Color (G A)
$40.00 rental
Presents the work of filmmaker Mark Lapore. Uses the assonance of images, decription and the close observation of details to create an ethnology of both home and abroad.
Fine Arts; History - United States; History - World; Industrial and Technical Education
Dist - PARART **Prod** - CANCIN 1989

Sleeping Bear Dunes 9 MIN
16mm / U-matic / VHS
Color
Shows how Sleeping Bear Dunes National Lakeshore in Frankfurt, Michigan, offers visitors an opportunity to see how the larger features of the lakeshore came to be, calls attention to the less obvious features and their formation, and tells what determines which plants will grow in a given environment.
Geography - United States; Science - Natural
Dist - USNAC **Prod** - USNPS 1982

Sleeping bears 8 MIN
U-matic / VHS / 16mm
OWL animal studies series
Color (P I J)
Features entering a bear's den during hibernation. Shows scientists tracking black bears as part of a program to learn more about their habits. They find a mother and newborn cubs, and help weigh and measure the cubs before returning them to their den. Shows why such research is important to help protect black bears.
Guidance and Counseling; Science; Science - Natural
Dist - BULFRG **Prod** - OWLTV 1987

The Sleeping Beauty 170 MIN
VHS / U-matic
Color (A)
Presents three of the Soviet Union's finest dancers in Tchaikovsky's renowned ballet.
Fine Arts
Dist - SRA **Prod** - SRA

The Sleeping beauty
VHS
Color (G)
$39.95 purchase _ #SLE05
Presents a Kirov Ballet production of The Sleeping Beauty. Features choreography by Oleg Vinogradov. Stars Farukh Ruzimatov and Larissa Lezhina.
Fine Arts
Dist - HOMVIS **Prod** - RMART 1990

Sleeping Beauty 75 MIN
16mm
Color
Recounts the adventures of Briar Rose, a beautiful princess who is put into a trance by an evil witch.
Fine Arts
Dist - SWANK **Prod** - DISNEY

Sleeping Beauty 26 MIN
16mm / VHS
Children's classics series
Color (P)
$195.00 purchase
Recreates the story of Sleeping Beauty. Adapted by Ken Donnelly from the classic tale.

Fine Arts; Literature and Drama
Dist - LUF **Prod** - BROVID

The Sleeping beauty 135 MIN
VHS
Color (G)
$39.95 purchase _ #S00130
Presents the Kirov Ballet in a performance of the Tchaikovsky ballet. Features Irina Kolpakova and Sergei Berezhnoi. Choreographed by Marisu Petipa and conducted by Viktor Fedotov.
Fine Arts; Geography - World
Dist - UILL

Sleeping Beauty 10 MIN
16mm
Lotte reiniger's animated fairy tales series
B&W (K P I J H C)
Tells the story of Sleeping Beauty through Lotte Reiniger's animated silhouette figures. Based on shadow plays she produced for BBC Television.
Fine Arts; Literature and Drama
Dist - MOMA **Prod** - PRIMP 1954

Sleeping Beauty 7 MIN
U-matic / VHS / BETA
Classic fairy tales series
Color; PAL (P I)
PdS30, PdS38 purchase
Tells the story of a prince who kisses a princess who has been under a spell for a hundred years and brings her back to life. One part of a six - part series containing stories by the Brothers Grimm, Charles Perrault and Hans Anderson.
Literature and Drama
Dist - EDPAT **Prod** - HALAS 1992

Sleeping Beauty 84 MIN
VHS
Color (G)
$29.95 purchase _ #1280
Presents the Kirov Ballet production of 'Sleeping Beauty' by Tchaikovsky from the 1964 film. Stars Alla Sizova, Yuri Solvyov and the young Natalia Makarova. Choreography by Marius Petipa.
Fine Arts; Foreign Language; Geography - World; Physical Education and Recreation
Dist - KULTUR

The Sleeping Beauty 135 MIN
VHS
Color (S)
$39.95 purchase _ #623 - 9810
Marks the 200th anniversary of the Kirov Ballet in a production of 'The Sleeping Beauty' by Tchaikovsky. Stars Irina Kolpakova.
Fine Arts; Geography - World; Physical Education and Recreation
Dist - FI **Prod** - NVIDC 1986

Sleeping Beauty 7 MIN
U-matic / VHS / 16mm
Color (P) (SPANISH)
Tells how a wicked fairy lays a curse on a baby princess, and how the good fairy is able to protect her and the royal court.
Literature and Drama
Dist - EBEC **Prod** - HALAS

Sleeping Beauty
U-matic / VHS
Color (P I)
Presents an enactment of the classic fairy tale Sleeping Beauty.
Literature and Drama
Dist - GA **Prod** - GA

Sleeping Beauty 3 MIN
16mm
Color
Presents one of the first commercials filmed in Gasparcolor, made with Jean Aurenche for Nicolas Wines and containing Alexander Alexeieff's only example of puppet animation.
Business and Economics; Fine Arts; Literature and Drama
Dist - STARRC **Prod** - STARRC 1934

The Sleeping beauty on ice 85 MIN
VHS
Color (K)
$29.95 purchase _ #1176
Presents 16 of the world's leading skaters from Britain, the US, Canada and Germany in a completely new version of 'The Sleeping Beauty' by Tchaikovsky. Stars Robin Cousins, Britain's world professional champion and Olympic gold medalist, and Rosalynn Sumners, world and US professional ladies champion and Olympic silver medalist.
Fine Arts; Geography - World; Physical Education and Recreation
Dist - KULTUR

Sleeping beauty on ice 65 MIN
VHS
Color; Stereo (G)
$29.95 purchase _ #S02040
Presents a unique performance of Tchaikovsky's 'Sleeping Beauty,' performed by an international cast of ice skaters. Stars Robin Cousins, Rosalynn Sumners, and 16 other well - known ice skaters.
Fine Arts; Physical Education and Recreation
Dist - UILL

Sleeping Beauty, the, Brier Rose - a German Folktale 15 MIN
16mm / U-matic / VHS
Color (P I)
LC 76-708561
Features animated puppets as they dramatize the beloved tale of Sleeping Beauty.
Literature and Drama
Dist - PHENIX **Prod** - OMEGA 1970

The Sleeping brain - an experimental approach 23 MIN
16mm
Films at the frontiers of psychological inquiry series
Color (H C A)
LC 72-702267
Presents De Michel Jouvet who explores neurophysiology and neuropsychology of sleep and dreaming and demonstrates research methodology through a series of experiments on cats. Shows how electrodes are implanted to record REM, EOG and PGO activity and explains how animal research relates to studies of human behavior.
Psychology
Dist - HMC **Prod** - HMC 1971

Sleeping dogs - never lie 9 MIN
16mm
Color (G)
$15.00 rental
Features a series of pictures with views of a gray day in December, a snowstorm, several fogs, a strange puddle and a female Husky induced to howl by humans.
Fine Arts
Dist - CANCIN **Prod** - ONEIPA

The Sleeping Feel Good Movie 6 MIN
U-matic / VHS / 16mm
Feel Good - Primary Health Series
Color (K P)
LC 74-702236
Portrays children experiencing the effects of rest and not having enough rest.
Health and Safety
Dist - CF **Prod** - CF 1974

The Sleeping Giant - Coal 29 MIN
16mm
Energy Sources - a New Beginning Series
Color
Discusses the location of coal beds and how much time is required for exploiting them. Asks how coal's sulfur emission problems can be solved.
Science - Natural; Social Science
Dist - UCOLO **Prod** - UCOLO

Sleeping it off 30 MIN
VHS
QED series
Color; PAL (G A)
PdS65 purchase
Examines the accelerated detoxification methods of psychologist Dr Juan Legarda as he places two heroin addicts under general anesthetic. Follows the treatment of the patients, both hooked on methadone, as Dr Legarda administers his treatment that he claims has a 75 per cent success rate. The program also speculates whether the treatment will ever be available on the British National Health Service due to the skepticism of many doctors.
Guidance and Counseling; Psychology
Dist - BBCENE

Sleeping Sharks of Yucatan 52 MIN
U-matic / VHS / 16mm
Undersea World of Jacques Cousteau Series
Color (I)
Science - Natural; Science - Physical
Dist - CF **Prod** - METROM 1970

Sleepover 28 MIN
VHS
Elephant show series
Color (P I)
$95.00 purchase, $45.00 rental
Presents program 25 in the Sharon, Lois and Bram's Elephant Show series. Teaches reading readiness and social skills while engaging children in making music. Each program explores a new theme through adventure, fantasy, mystery and song with recording artists Sharon, Lois and Bram. Uses traditional materials which stress participation - action songs, sing - along songs, story songs, clapping songs, singing games, playground chants and folk songs from many different traditions. Includes teacher's guide co - authored by a music education specialist.
Fine Arts; Sociology
Dist - BULFRG **Prod** - CAMBFP 1989

Sleepwalk 75 MIN
16mm
Color (G)
Presents an independent production by S Driver. Records strange goings - on in New York City. Also available in 35mm film format.
Fine Arts; Geography - United States; History - United States
Dist - FIRS

Sleepwalk 12 MIN
16mm
Color (G)
$18.00 rental
Explores the juncture of psychology and spirituality as expressed in the writing of the Russian mystic - philosopher Gurdjieff and his student Ouspensky.
Fine Arts; Literature and Drama; Religion and Philosophy
Dist - CANCIN **Prod** - WALLIN 1973

Sleepy haven 15 MIN
16mm
Color (A)
$35.00 rental
Conjures up an erotic daydream that marries found footage and original shots. Features nude bodies of sailors beneath physically altered film emulsion, along with huge ships under steam docked in harbors, while the fade-ins and fade-outs produce the effect of the screen breathing in and out. Pays homage to Kenneth Anger's film Fireworks. Produced by Matthias Mueller.
Fine Arts
Dist - CANCIN

Sleepy heads 10 MIN
16mm / U-matic / VHS
Color; B&W (P)
Explains that animals need nourishing food and plenty of sleep to stay healthy. Depicts sleeping habits of various animals, including goldfish, polar bears, hippopotami, crocodiles, horses, koala bears, snakes, canaries, caterpillars, toads, prairie dogs, ground squirrels and brown bears.
Health and Safety; Science - Natural
Dist - STANF **Prod** - STANF 1964

Sleeve and Increasing 29 MIN
Videoreel / VT2
Busy Knitter I Series
B&W
Home Economics
Dist - PBS **Prod** - WMVSTV

Sleeve Gastrectomy 15 MIN
U-matic / VHS
Color (PRO)
Describes sleeve gastrectomy.
Health and Safety
Dist - WFP **Prod** - WFP

The Sleeve Special 29 MIN
Videoreel / VT2
Designing Women Series
Color
Home Economics
Dist - PBS **Prod** - WKYCTV

Sleeves, Plackets, and Cuffs 24 MIN
VHS / U-matic
Clothing Construction Techniques Series
Color (C A)
Covers setting a regular sleeve, making a continuous lapped placket, making cuffs, attaching a cuff to a sleeve having a continuous lapped placket, making a faced opening for a pleated sleeve closure and setting a shirt sleeve.
Home Economics
Dist - IOWASP **Prod** - IOWASP

Sleight of Hand 60 MIN
U-matic / VHS
Body in Question Series Program 8; Program 8
Color (H C A)
LC 81-706952
Discusses the characteristics and historical backgrounds of official healers, charismatic healers and expert healers. Describes the alleged miracle cures of scrofula by the Royalty of England and France and the flamboyant healing performances during the late 18th century. Based on the book The Body In Question by Jonathan Miller. Narrated by Jonathan Miller.
Health and Safety; Science
Dist - FI **Prod** - BBCTV 1979

A Slice of Bread 13 MIN
16mm
Color
Presents a story about a boy and his trip to a local bakery to discover how wheat is processed into bread.
Social Science
Dist - SF **Prod** - SF 1971

Sliced light 15 MIN
16mm
B&W (G)
$10.00 rental
Sets the landscape atremble and alight.
Fine Arts; Science - Physical
Dist - CANCIN **Prod** - SINGJO 1976

Slick Stagger 5 MIN
U-matic / VHS
Write on, Set 1 Series
Color (J H)
Consists of a lesson on comma splices.
English Language
Dist - CTI **Prod** - CTI

Slide guitar for rock and blues 90 MIN
VHS
Color (G)
$49.95 purchase _ #VD - ROG - GT01
Features the slide guitar of Roy Rogers, whose style is rooted in the Mississippi Delta blues tradition. Shows how to play rhythm and lead and how to incorporate bass lines with slide riffs in the treble. Teaches turnarounds, how to break up chords, use of fretted and slide notes, 'classic' ending licks, use of fretted IV and V chords for short cuts in lower register, plus a wide variety of other spicy licks and patterns. Includes the songs Look Over Yonders Wall, The Sky is Crying, Walking Blues, Tip Walk and Black Cat Bone, as well as music and tablature, and some backup by special guests, the Delta Rhythm Kings.
Fine Arts
Dist - HOMETA **Prod** - HOMETA

Slide preparation 12 MIN
VHS
Microscopy prelab series
Color (J H C)
$95.00 purchase _ #CG - 912 - VS
Introduces students to the prepared slide, the dry mount slide, the wet mount slide, the hanging drop slide and the smear. Shows how to prepare each slide for maximum benefit from the compound microscope. Part of a five - part series on microscopy prelab produced by Bill Pieper.
Science; Science - Natural
Dist - HRMC

The Slide Rule - C and D Scales 24 MIN
16mm
B&W
LC FIE52-164
Explains the C and D scales and markings of the slide rule. Shows how to use the scales for multiplication, division and combined operations.
Mathematics
Dist - USNAC **Prod** - USOE 1943

The Slide Rule - Proportion, Percentage, Squares and Square Roots 21 MIN
16mm
B&W
LC FIE52-163
Shows how to use the slide rule to calculate squares, square roots, proportions and percentages.
Mathematics
Dist - USNAC **Prod** - USOE 1944

The Slide Rule - the C and D Scales 24 MIN
U-matic
Engineering Series
B&W
LC 79-706441
Deals with the purpose and parts of the slide rule and shows how to use the C and D scales in multiplication and division of numbers. Issued in 1943 as a motion picture.
Industrial and Technical Education; Mathematics
Dist - USNAC **Prod** - USOE 1979

The Slide Rule - the 'C' and 'D' Scales 24 MIN
U-matic
B&W
Shows the various uses of the slide rules, its parts and how to use the 'C' and 'D' scales in the multiplication and division of numbers.
Mathematics
Dist - USNAC **Prod** - USNAC 1972

Slide show 20 MIN
16mm
Color (G)
$25.00 rental
Documents a young California couple and their community in the context of a dramatic event happening at a gathering of friends to view a slide show. Attempts to provoke the audience with honesty, narrative technique and a mixture of real and fictional events.
Fine Arts; Psychology
Dist - CANCIN **Prod** - LEHE 1977

Sliding Electric Contacts 48 MIN
U-matic / VHS
Tribology 2 - Advances in Friction, Wear, and Lubrication Series
Color
Industrial and Technical Education
Dist - MIOT **Prod** - MIOT

Sliding Surface Bearings - 1 60 MIN
VHS
Bearings and Lubrication Series
Color (PRO)
$600.00, $1500.00 purchase _ #GMSB1
Describes various types of sliding surface bearings and their associated elements. Examines methods of operation for journal and thrust bearings and typical maintenance problems. Part of a six - part series on bearings and lubrication, part of a larger set on general and mechanical maintenance. Includes 10 textbooks and an instructor guide which provide four hours of instruction.
Education; Industrial and Technical Education; Psychology
Dist - NUSTC **Prod** - NUSTC

Sliding Surface Bearings - 2 60 MIN
VHS
Bearings and Lubrication Series
Color (PRO)
$600.00, $1500.00 purchase _ #GMSB2
Discusses sliding surface bearing maintenance. Includes job preparation, safety, disassembly, inspection, measurements and replacement techniques. Part of a six - part series on bearings and lubrication, part of a larger set on general and mechanical maintenance. Includes 10 textbooks and an instructor guide which provide four hours of instruction.
Education; Industrial and Technical Education; Psychology
Dist - NUSTC **Prod** - NUSTC

A Slight Change in Plans 27 MIN
16mm / VHS / U-matic
Insight Series
Color (H C A)
Explores a young man's struggle to decide whether or not to become a priest.
Guidance and Counseling; Psychology; Religion and Philosophy
Dist - PAULST **Prod** - PAULST

A Slight Drinking Problem 25 MIN
U-matic / VHS / 16mm
Insight Series
Color (J)
LC 79-700648
Presents a man and a woman who both deny his alcohol problem until she attends an Alcoholics Anonymous meeting and learns to assume responsibility for her own life. Shows how she abandons her victim role and forces him to face the truth about himself.
Health and Safety; Psychology; Sociology
Dist - PAULST **Prod** - PAULST 1977

Slight of hand - the magic of cards
VHS
World around us series
Color (G)
$39.95 purchase _ #IV - 3035
Features Derek Dingle, famed for his close - up sleight of hand magicianship. Demonstrates card tricks and shows how each is done.
Physical Education and Recreation
Dist - INCRSE **Prod** - INCRSE

Slim Green - Master Saddlemaker 25 MIN
16mm / U-matic / VHS
Color
Deals with the art and craft of custom saddle making. Tells how Slim Green learned his skills and shows him producing a saddle.
Fine Arts; Physical Education and Recreation
Dist - ONEWST **Prod** - PMEDA

Slima the Dhowmaker 25 MIN
16mm / U-matic / VHS
World Cultures and Youth Series
Color (I J A)
LC 80-700082
Introduces Slima, a Tanzanian youth who makes wooden sailboats called dhows as his ancestors have for over 2,000 years. Relates how he picks the natural curved trees, seals the hull and secures the huge, hand - sewn sails.
Geography - World; Sociology
Dist - CORF **Prod** - SUNRIS 1980

Slimderella 21 MIN
16mm
Color (P I)
Shows what happens when the Chiffy kids must share the church hall where they want to perform a pantomime with a rock group.
Literature and Drama
Dist - LUF **Prod** - LUF 1979

Slime Molds - Plant, Animal or 13 MIN
U-matic / VHS / 16mm
Color
Employs time - lapse photography to show that slime molds exhibit animal - like movement while possessing plant - like fruiting bodies.
Science - Natural
Dist - STANF **Prod** - STANF

Slime molds - plasmodial and cellular 20 MIN
VHS / 16mm
Modern biology series
Color (H C)
$540.00, $485.00 purchase, $55.00, $50.00 rental
Reveals that how slime molds function biochemically is a current issue of international research because it promises important revelations into the nature of cell division and specialization in all living things. Examines two main groups of slime molds - Myxomycetes or Plasmodial slime molds which begin their life cycle by emerging from spores as individual amoeboid organisms which merge into one giant mobile cell, up to 3 feet in diameter, called a plasmodium and containing millions of nuclei, and Acrasiomycetes or cellular slime molds which also emerge from spores but do not merge into a single cell. Part of a series on biology.
Science - Natural
Dist - BNCHMK **Prod** - BNCHMK 1989

Slimming Your Waste 15 MIN
16mm
Color
Defines the various ways that steel cans are being separated from household refuse by municipalities and the several end - use markets available for recycling these 'mined' cans.
Science - Natural
Dist - AIAS **Prod** - AIAS

Slimmons scampi 30 MIN
VHS
Richard Simmons slim cooking series
Color (H C G)
$19.95 purchase _ #FFO383V
Demonstrates step - by - step procedures for low - fat, high - flavor scampi. Part of six - part series featuring Richard Simmons' health cuisine.
Home Economics
Dist - CAMV

Slingerland Multi - Sensory Approach to Language Arts for Specific Language 38 MIN
16mm
Color
Discusses language training techniques for primary - aged children with specific language disabilities. Focuses on the Slingerland classroom adaptation of the Orton Gillingham method, which is based upon the simultaneous inter - sensory association of the auditory, visual and kinesthetic channels.
Education; Psychology
Dist - EDPS **Prod** - EDPS

Slingerland Screening Tests for identifying children with Specific Language Disability Pt B series
Administration of the Slingerland Screening Tests 30 MIN
Dist - EDPS

Slingerland screening tests for identifying children with specific language disability series
Evaluation of student responses to the Slingerland screening tests 30 MIN
Dist - EDPS

Slingerland screening tests for identifying children with specific language series Part A
Maturational lag and specific language disabilities 30 MIN
Dist - EDPS

Slinging Load 17 MIN
16mm
B&W
LC FIE52-1204
Shows how to rig and use slings to handle various types of loads and explains safety precautions to be observed.
Health and Safety; Social Science
Dist - USNAC **Prod** - USN 1948

Slings 21 MIN
VHS / U-matic
Safety in Rigging
Color (A IND)
Explains sling materials and configurations. Highlights the wide variety of fibre ropes, wire ropes, chains and web. Points out the limitations of various slings. Discusses guidelines for choosing the right sling for the job depending on exposure and temperature conditions.
Health and Safety
Dist - IFB **Prod** - CSAO 1985

Slip casting 37 MIN
VHS
Color (J H C G)
$69.95 purchase _ #CPC706V
Illustrates the step - by - step process of preparing a plaster of paris slip casting mold for producing multiple copies of an original. Gives explicit directions on different techniques to create the mold - throwing on the wheel - equipment, lubrication, creating the shape, removing from the hump; trimming the piece for an accurate mold; firing in the kiln; tools to aid in molding; the crucial process of leveling the mold; securing the mold with brackets and clay to prepare the cast; preparing and pouring slips; drying; bisque firing; glazing and electric and gas kiln firing.
Fine Arts
Dist - CAMV

Slip covering wooden chairs 13 MIN
Videoreel / VT2
Living better II series
Color
Explains how to determine the correct amount of material to buy and then shows the steps in covering the chair's seat, back, legs and the rounds. Includes tips on how to pad the chair, make homemade paste and mix material patterns.
Home Economics
Dist - PBS **Prod** - MAETEL

Slip Decoration 29 MIN
Videoreel / VT2
Exploring the Crafts - Pottery Series
Color
Features Mrs Vivika Heino introducing and demonstrating the basic techniques of slip decoration in pottery.
Fine Arts
Dist - PBS **Prod** - WENHTV

Slip rings - brushes - single phase - centrifugal switch and capacitor 60 MIN
U-matic / VHS
Electrical maintenance training motors series; Module 2 - Motors
Color (IND)
Industrial and Technical Education
Dist - LEIKID **Prod** - LEIKID

Slip Roll Forming Machine Operation 22 MIN
BETA / VHS
Color (IND)
Explains the basic operation and set - up of a slip roll forming machine and discusses some of the problems inherent in its operation.
Industrial and Technical Education; Psychology
Dist - RMIBHF **Prod** - RMIBHF

Slipperella 10 MIN
16mm
Color (C)
$336.00
Presents an experimental film by Rudy Burckhardt.
Fine Arts
Dist - AFA **Prod** - AFA 1979

Slippery when wet 20 MIN
VHS
Works series
Color; PAL (G)
PdS50 purchase; Available only in the United Kingdom and Ireland
Explores the world of liquid engineering and the dynamics of substances such as toothpaste, multigrade engine oil and non - drip paint. Sets out to show engineers in a creative light as they apply their skills and knowledge to the varied problems of fluid mechanics. Part two of a six - part series.
Industrial and Technical Education; Science - Physical
Dist - BBCENE

Slippin' away 30 MIN
U-matic / VHS
Money puzzle - the world of macroeconomics series - Module 13
Color
Considers the long - range view of this country's economic growth. Includes an analysis of the case for zero growth.
Business and Economics; Sociology
Dist - MDCC **Prod** - MDCC

Slipping into the darkness 17 MIN
U-matic / VHS
Relapse prevention series
Color (G)
$249.00 purchase _ #7437
Interviews recovering addicts who share their frightening experiences of relapse during the recovery process. Discusses the subtle symptoms of relapse, the denial, self - pity and blame. Part of a two - part series on relapse prevention.
Guidance and Counseling; Health and Safety; Psychology
Dist - VISIVI **Prod** - VISIVI 1991

Slipping patterns 100 MIN
VHS / BETA
Color
Shows how to make patterns from existing articles of clothing.
Home Economics
Dist - HOMEAF **Prod** - HOMEAF

Slips and falls 23 MIN
U-matic / VHS
Color (IND)
Addresses a broad range of hazards associated with on-the-job injuries. Discusses safe use of ladders.
Health and Safety; Industrial and Technical Education
Dist - TAT **Prod** - TAT

Slips and falls 3 MIN
U-matic / VHS / 16mm
Accident prevention series
Color (IND) (SPANISH)
LC 72-702119
Depicts ways in which workers may injure themselves in slip - and - fall accidents by showing what happens to a plant maintenance girl when she carries a carpet incorrectly, lets a ladder slip on a soapy floor and steps on curtains she is trying to hang from a short ladder.
Business and Economics
Dist - IFB **Prod** - IAPA 1972

Slips and falls - the point of no return
VHS / U-matic
Color
Addresses the hazards of slips and falls, and the techniques designed to prevent this type of accident on the job.
Education; Health and Safety
Dist - TAT **Prod** - TAT

Slips, trips and falls 12 MIN
VHS / U-matic
Color
Presents a safety program narrated by Murphy, creator of Murphy's Law, about slips, trips and falls.
Health and Safety
Dist - FILCOM **Prod** - FILCOM

Slips, trips and falls 17 MIN
VHS
Safety on the job series
Color (G IND)
$79.95 purchase _ #6 - 203 - 012A
Reveals that slips, trips and falls are a leading cause of injury and death on the job and that carelessness is often the culprit. Makes practical suggestions regarding awareness, responsibility and traction. Part of a series on job safety.
Health and Safety
Dist - VEP **Prod** - VEP

Slips, trips and falls - no laughing matter - C'est loin d'etre drole 18 MIN
BETA / VHS / U-matic
Canadian specific programs series
Color (IND G) (FRENCH)
$C495.00 purchase _ #602 - 04
Informs employees about the causes and prevention of falls on stairs, slips on slick surfaces and trips over obstacles. Demonstrates simple, effective procedures for reducing work - related accidents and injuries. Discusses the hazards of faulty equipment and the results of deliberate unsafe acts and horseplay.
Health and Safety; Industrial and Technical Education; Psychology
Dist - ITSC **Prod** - ITSC

Slipstream 5 MIN
16mm
Color (G)
$10.00 rental
Shows traveling through a passage in a forest, propelled by a camera.
Fine Arts
Dist - CANCIN **Prod** - OSBONS 1973

Slo Pitch Softball
VHS
(H C A)
$39.,95 _ #ESP100V
Discusses hitting tips and mental imaging methods to raise a softball player's batting average. Explains the 'reflex hitting system', correct swing, grip, and stance. Features slow motion photography to illustrate body mechanics.
Physical Education and Recreation
Dist - CAMV

Slogans and policies - Pt 2 45 MIN
VHS / 16mm
Salisbury's report on China - the revolution and beyond series
Color (J)
$349.00 purchase, $175.00 rental _ #OD - 2227
Examines the successes and failures of China's many land and economic programs, such as the Great Leap Forward program. Features New York Times reporter Harrison Salisbury. The second of three installments of the series Salisbury's Report On China - the Revolution and Beyond.
Geography - World; History - World
Dist - FOTH

Slope 20 MIN
U-matic / VHS / 16mm
Color (J H C)
Introduces slope form and processes with emphasis given to the slope as a product of both the balance between forces of uplift and downwearing and of the interaction between processes at the slope foot and on the slope itself.
Science - Physical
Dist - LUF **Prod** - LUF 1982

Slope and equations of lines
VHS
Beginning algebra series
Color (J H)
$125.00 purchase _ #2022
Teaches fundamental concepts used to determine the slope and equation of a line. Part of a series of 31 videos, each between 25 and 30 minutes long, that explain and reinforce basic concepts of algebra. Tutors the student through definitions, theorems, step - by - step solutions and examples. Videos are also available in a set.
Mathematics
Dist - LANDMK

Slope and forms of equations of lines
VHS
Algebra 1 series
Color (J H)
$125.00 purchase _ #A12
Teaches the concepts involved in writing and interpreting linear equations and determining the slope of a linear equation. Part of a series of 16 videos, each between 25 and 30 minutes long, that explain and reinforce 89 basic concepts of algebra. Includes a stated objective for each segment. Tutors the student through definitions, theorems, step - by - step solutions and examples. Videos are also available in a set.
Mathematics
Dist - LANDMK
GPN

Slope and graphing inequalities
VHS
Beginning algebra series
Color (J H)
$125.00 purchase _ #2013
Teaches fundamental concepts used to determine the slope of a line and to graph an inequality. Part of a series of 31 videos, each between 25 and 30 minutes long, that explain and reinforce basic concepts of algebra. Tutors the student through definitions, theorems, step - by - step solutions and examples. Videos are also available in a set.
Mathematics
Dist - LANDMK

Slope and Graphing Inequalities 30 MIN
VHS
Mathematics Series
Color (J)
LC 90713155
Discusses slope and graphing inequalities. The 29th of 157 installments of the Mathematics Series.
Mathematics
Dist - GPN

Slope, graphing inequalities 30 MIN
VHS
Intermediate algebra series
Color (H)
$125.00 purchase _ #M55
Explains slope and graphing inequalities. Features Elayn Gay. Part of a 27 - part series on intermediate algebra.
Industrial and Technical Education; Mathematics
Dist - LANDMK **Prod** - MGHT

Slope, graphing inequalities 30 MIN
VHS
Beginning algebra series
Color (J H)
$125.00 purchase _ #M29
Explains slope and how to graph inequalities. Features Elayn Gay. Part of a 19 - part series on beginning algebra.
Industrial and Technical Education; Mathematics
Dist - LANDMK **Prod** - MGHT

Slope of a Curve
U-matic
Calculus Series
Color
Mathematics
Dist - MDCPB **Prod** - MDDE

The Slope of a Straight Line 30 MIN
U-matic
Introduction to Mathematics Series
Color (C)
Mathematics
Dist - MDCPB **Prod** - MDCPB

Slope - the Key to Landscape 20 MIN
16mm
Color (H C G)
Introduces concepts of basic slope systems.
Geography - World; Industrial and Technical Education; Science - Physical
Dist - VIEWTH **Prod** - USAMP

Slovak Byzantine Cathedral - Unionville Mass 58 MIN
BETA / VHS
Pope John Paul II
(R G) (FRENCH ITALIAN SLOVAK)
$29.95 purchase _ #5PV 118 _ #5PV 218 _ #5PV 108
Shows the visit of Pope John Paul II to the Slovak Byzantine Cathedral in Canada in 1984.
History - World; Religion and Philosophy
Dist - CANBC

The Slovaks - insuring the American dream 9 MIN
VHS
Columbus legacy series
Color (J H C G)
$40.00 purchase, $11.00 rental _ #12335
Examines the sokol and its pioneering insurance policy system through the story of Chuck Bednarik. Reveals that the sokol was a powerful force in the Slovak community. Part of a 15 - part series commemorating the 500th anniversary of Columbus' journeys to the Americas - journeys that brought together a constantly evolving collection of different ethnic groups. Examines the contributions of 15 distinct groups who imprinted their heritage on the day-to-day life of Pennsylvania.
Business and Economics; History - United States; Sociology
Dist - PSU **Prod** - WPSXTV 1992

Slow and Easy 29 MIN
Videoreel / VT2
Maggie and the Beautiful Machine - Easy Does it Series
Color
Physical Education and Recreation
Dist - PBS **Prod** - WGBHTV

Slow boat from Surabaya series
Presents a six - part series on Southeast Asia covering the Philippines, Thailand, Singapore, Indonesia, Malaysia, Vietnam and Kampuchea. Looks at the colonial history of the area, except for the special case of Buddhist Thailand; feminist women in the Philippines; the variety of religions in the area; the situation of expatriate Chinese; and the contrasting fates of Vietnam and Kampuchea.

Diplomatic Thais - Part 2	55 MIN
Filipinas - the women of the Philippines - Part 3	55 MIN
Five faces of god - Part 4	55 MIN
Post colonial waltz - Pt 1	55 MIN
Red pride, red sorrow - Part 6	55 MIN
Rich, clever, homeless - Part 5	55 MIN

Dist - LANDMK **Prod** - LANDMK

Slow cooking
VHS
Kitchen equipment series
(C G)
$59.00_CA235
Covers slow cooking techniques.
Home Economics
Dist - AAVIM **Prod** - AAVIM 1989

Slow Death of the Desert Water 30 MIN
16mm / U-matic / VHS
Our Vanishing Wilderness Series no 4
Color
LC 77-710658
Shows what is happening to Pyramid Lake, in Nevada, and its wildlife because dams divert its source of water and sonic booms frighten its wildlife.
Geography - United States; Science - Natural
Dist - IU **Prod** - NET 1970

Slow pitch strategy, team defense and sliding 60 MIN
VHS
VIP softball series
Color (G)
$29.95 purchase _ #ASAT11V
Covers the basics of slow pitch softball strategy. Includes defensive positioning, offensive and defensive strategies, and sliding. Taught by Bobby Simpson, Cindy Bristow and Buzzy Keller.
Physical Education and Recreation
Dist - CAMV **Prod** - CAMV

Slow - Speed Flight Characteristics of Swept - Wing Aircraft 18 MIN
16mm
B&W
LC FIE58-26
Shows how the slow - speed flight affects the flow of air over swept - wing aircraft and how a stall originates at the wing tips instead of at the wing roots as in conventional wing aircraft.
Industrial and Technical Education
Dist - USNAC **Prod** - USN 1957

The Slow walker 18 MIN
16mm
Doctors at work series
B&W (H C A)
LC FIA65-1361
Uses models and drawings to depict a congenital hip malformation. Shows how a congenitally shallow hip socket in one child is helped by a putti frame traction while a similar condition in another child requires surgical correction.
Health and Safety; Science - Natural
Dist - LAWREN **Prod** - CMA 1962

Slowing Down the Clock 30 MIN
VHS / 16mm
Color (H)
LC 88712491
Presents both facts and myths about the aging process. Gives guidance on leading a longer and healthier life.
Health and Safety; Science - Natural; Sociology
Dist - BARR

Slowing the Clock 26 MIN
U-matic / VHS
Color (C)
$249.00, $149.00 purchase _ #AD - 1813
Shows how to slow down the effects of the aging process. Focuses on current research on the role that the thymus gland and 'free radicals' play in aging.
Health and Safety; Sociology
Dist - FOTH **Prod** - FOTH

Slowly the Singing Began 23 MIN
16mm / U-matic / VHS
Color (C A)
LC 78-701254
Highlights the poets - in - the - schools program by documenting the work of Michael Moos as poet - in - residence in the Wichita, Kansas, school system.
Education; Literature and Drama
Dist - MEDIAG **Prod** - NENDOW 1978

Sludge Management - an Integrated Approach 27 MIN
16mm
Color (IND)
LC 81-701098
Details research into methods of managing sludge in an ecologically sound way. Shows the use of energized electrons for disinfection of sludges, their direct injection into soil and the effects on soil ecosystems.
Science - Natural
Dist - USNAC **Prod** - NSF 1978

Sluice 6 MIN
16mm
B&W (G)
$144.00 purchase, $10.00 rental
Offers a visual word play on a silver sluice.
Fine Arts
Dist - CANCIN **Prod** - BRAKS 1978

Slums in the Third World 17 MIN
U-matic / VHS / 16mm
Color (J)
Follows the daily life of the Sulayta family who live in a typical slum of a large Third World city. Shows their living conditions, their attempts to find work, and their attitudes about the life they are living.
Geography - World; Sociology
Dist - PHENIX **Prod** - PHENIX 1983

Slurps, burps, and spills
VHS
Amazing advantages for kids series
Color (T K P)
$19.95 purchase _ #AMZ003V-K
Teaches children proper table manners, including using a napkin, setting the table, having polite manners, and making conversation. Presented entirely by children. One of a three-part series that teaches manners and social skills.
Health and Safety; History - World; Psychology
Dist - CAMV

Small Animals 15 MIN
U-matic / VHS
Let's Draw Series
Color (P)
Fine Arts
Dist - AITECH **Prod** - OCPS 1976

Small Animals - Easter 15 MIN
U-matic / VHS
Draw Along Series
(K P)
$125.00 purchase
Explains how to draw dogs, cats and Easter rabbits.
Fine Arts
Dist - AITECH **Prod** - AITECH 1986

Small animals of the plains 15 MIN
U-matic / VHS / 16mm
Vanishing prairie series
Color (SWEDISH NORWEGIAN PORTUGUESE DUTCH GERMAN)
Provides an excerpt from the feature-length film. Shows such animals as the prairie dog and pocket gopher in their daily struggle against attacks from predators.
Science - Natural
Dist - CORF **Prod** - DISNEY 1963

Small appliances 30 MIN
VHS / U-matic
Consumer survival series; Homes
Color
Presents tips on the purchase and care of small appliances.
Home Economics
Dist - MDCPB **Prod** - MDCPB

Small arms, soft targets 50 MIN
VHS
Horizon series
Color; PAL (G A)
PdS99 purchase
Observes military medics and Red Cross surgeons as they struggle to deal with a flood of new injuries caused by advanced anti - personnel weapons. Shows inverviews with the designers trying to produce more damaging weapons. Asks whether the laws of war which limit weaponry could be tightened without reducing soldier's ability to fight.
Civics and Political Systems
Dist - BBCENE

Small boat engine maintenance 56 MIN
VHS / 16mm
(G)
$39.95 purchase _ #VT1057; $39.95 purchase _ #0478
Instructs on the maintenance of inboard and outboard marine engines. Shows what to do if the motor quits while under way, how to gap a spark plug, and good lube techniques. Features Chief Warrant Officer Jim Storey, a Marine Inspector for the US Coast Guard.
Industrial and Technical Education; Physical Education and Recreation
Dist - RMIBHF **Prod** - RMIBHF
SEVVID

Small Boat Engine Maintenance 56 MIN
BETA / VHS
Color
Demonstrates maintenance of outboard and inboard marine engines.
Industrial and Technical Education; Social Science
Dist - MOHOMV **Prod** - MOHOMV

Small Boat Navy 28 MIN
16mm
Color
Reports on the operations of the U S Navy's small boats in Vietnam. Discusses the challenges of riverine and coastal warfare. Shows these boats, accompanied by helicopters, on coastal or river patrols under enemy fire and spearheading invasions into enemy held river territory. Raymond Burr narrates.
Civics and Political Systems; Geography - World; History - United States
Dist - USNAC **Prod** - USN 1968

A Small Body of Still Water 16 MIN
16mm / U-matic / VHS
Color (I A)
Portrays the life in ponds, including protozoa, algae, mosquitoes, damselflies, tadpoles and frogs. Explores the concepts of pond ecology, photosynthesis and metamorphosis.
Science - Natural
Dist - UNKNWN

Small Bowel Resection for Post - Radiation Obstruction 25 MIN
16mm
Color (PRO)
Depicts a segmental resection of a loop of terminal ileum which became obstructed three years after the patient, a 55 year old woman, received radiation treatment for carcinoma of the cervix.
Health and Safety; Science
Dist - ACY **Prod** - ACYDGD 1955

Small Business 21 MIN
VHS / U-matic
Clues to Career Opportunities for Liberal Arts Graduates Series
Color (C A)
LC 80-706235
Stresses that the person considering opening a small business should have significant skills developed through work experience and education. Presents a bank loan officer commenting on financing a small business.
Business and Economics; Psychology
Dist - IU **Prod** - IU 1979

Small Business - Behind Closed Doors - Decisions that Business People Deal with on a Daily Basis
VHS
Entrepreneurs - the Risk Takers Series
$70.00 purchase _ #RPS2V
Talks about business decisions that are not apparent to customers. Portrays how a merchant makes decisions on inventory, pricing, employees and advertising.
Business and Economics
Dist - CAREER **Prod** - CAREER

Small Business (Film B) 22 MIN
U-matic / VHS / 16mm
Job Interview - Whom would You Hire? Series
Color (J H)
$445 purchase - 16 mm, $335 purchase - video
Discusses applicants from the point of view of the employer at a small business firm. A Dimension Film. Directed by Gary Goldsmith.
Psychology
Dist - CF

Small business keeps America working 28 MIN
16mm
Color
LC 79-701387
Presents small business owners discussing their experiences in business, their feelings about their work, and their problems and rewards. Features observations by an economic historian and by the president of the U S Chamber of Commerce.
Business and Economics
Dist - USCHOC **Prod** - USCHOC 1979

Small Business My Way 28 MIN
U-matic
Color (A)
LC 83-706798
Features owners and managers of small businesses in and around Buckhannon, W. Va., pondering the opportunities and obligations that spurred them on, the financial risks and hardships they endured and the dim prospects they see for the survival of enterprises such as theirs.
Business and Economics; Geography - United States
Dist - CWVMA **Prod** - GRIES 1983

Small business representation - Landing, developing and servicing small business clients 210 MIN
VHS
Color (C PRO A)
$25.00, $50.00 purchase _ #M764, #P257
Identifies the substantive issues in organizing a start - up business and the skills necessary to attract and retain small business clients. Pays special attention to businesses owned by minorities and women.
Business and Economics; Civics and Political Systems
Dist - ALIABA **Prod** - ALIABA 1989

Small Business - Triumph or Tragedy 25 MIN
U-matic / VHS
Color (G)
$279.00, $179.00 purchase _ #AD - 2000
Shows why small and medium - size businesses so often fail, despite the dedication, perseverance and hard work of their owners. Features David Susskind who explains what it takes to build a successful business.
Business and Economics
Dist - FOTH **Prod** - FOTH

Small business video libary series
VHS
Small business video library series
Color (J H C G A)
$149.95 purchase _ #VPR100SV
Presents a four - part series for budding entrepreneurs with special emphasis on free or low - cost sources of critical information and assistance. Combines instruction, case studies, personal insights and informal panel discussions. Includes a comprehensive workbook with each program to stimulate thinking and provide step - by - step instructions for writing, analyzing, planning and implementing constructive change for any business. Discusses marketing, planning, promotion and publicity and planning for home - based businesses.
Business and Economics
Dist - CAMV

Small business video library series
The Business plan - roadmap to success
Home - based business - blueprint for success
Marketing - winning customers with a workable plan
Promotion - solving the puzzle
Small business video libary series
Dist - CAMV

Small business video library series
The Business plan - your road map for success - Volume 2 55 MIN
Home based business - a winning blueprint - Volume 4 55 MIN
Marketing - winning customers with a workable plan - Volume 1 45 MIN
Promotion - solving the puzzle - Volume 3 56 MIN
Dist - SVIP

Small business - when small is big - how and why people go into business
VHS
Entrepreneurs - the risk takers series
$70.00 purchase _ #RPS1V
Discusses how certain traits, such as the ability to handle the unexpected and to adjust to new situations, are necessary for success in business. Points out how various entrepreneurs got into business.
Business and Economics
Dist - CAREER **Prod** - CAREER

Small Cabbage White 28 MIN
16mm
Color (JAPANESE)
Observes cabbage white butterflies, and analyzes their behavior through various experiments. Illustrates the behavior pattern they possess for individual and specific preservation.
Foreign Language; Science - Natural
Dist - UNIJAP **Prod** - UNIJAP 1968

Small - carrion penile implant for the management of impotence 12 MIN
VHS / U-matic
Color (PRO)
Shows a method of surgically implanting a silicone prosthesis designed for use in patients with impotence stemming from a variety of causes.
Health and Safety
Dist - WFP **Prod** - WFP

A Small Case of Blackmail 27 MIN
16mm
Color
Shows the dangers of corporate nuclear power plants and the possible lack of safeguards in the transport of fissionable material.
Industrial and Technical Education; Science - Physical; Social Science
Dist - IMPACT **Prod** - GRATV

Small Cell Carcinoma of Unknown Primary 60 MIN
U-matic
Color
Discusses small cell carcinoma from the dermatologist's point of view.
Health and Safety
Dist - UTEXSC **Prod** - UTEXSC

Small Change 7 MIN
16mm
Color
LC 77-702644
Tells how a young man's conscience becomes hostage to an apparently simple impulse to give change to a panhandler. Raises the question of who does the giving and who does the receiving.
Fine Arts; Guidance and Counseling; Sociology
Dist - CANFDC **Prod** - MCMFB

Small Changes 18 MIN
16mm
Color
LC 80-700485
Tells how a young boy goes to a nightclub with his older brother and how he sneaks backstage to meet a stripper.
Fine Arts
Dist - USC **Prod** - USC 1979

Small claims court 30 MIN
VHS / U-matic
Consumer survival series; General
Color
Presents tips on using small claims court.
Civics and Political Systems; Home Economics
Dist - MDCPB **Prod** - MDCPB

Small claims court 15 MIN
VHS / 16mm
You and the law series
Color (S)
$150.00 purchase _ #275907
Employs a mixture of drama and narrative to introduce particular aspects of Canadian law. Presents some of the basic concepts and addresses some of the more commonly asked questions. Emphasis is on those elements of the law which are frequently misunderstood. 'Small Claims Court' details the limited jurisdiction of small claims in handling civil cases and explains how to begin action against a person or a company, whether for damages or breach of contract. Topics discussed include tort law, summonses, seizures and breach of contract.
Business and Economics; Civics and Political Systems; Geography - World; Home Economics
Dist - ACCESS **Prod** - ACCESS 1987

Small companies - true heroes of Japanese industry 30 MIN
VHS
Anatomy of Japan - wellsprings of economic power series
Color (H C G)
$250.00 purchase
Reveals that world - renowned Japanese exports are manufactured by not only large companies but also by a host of small companies. Shows how small companies are the true heroes of Japanese industry and examines their significant role as major sources of vitality in Japan's economy. Part of a 10 - part series on the current relations between Japan and the world.
Business and Economics; Geography - World; History - World
Dist - LANDMK **Prod** - LANDMK 1989

Small Computer in the Chemical Laboratory 30 MIN
16mm
Color
Introduces the mini computer in a basic manner by discussing computer architecture and operation. Explores several applications for using the mini computer in various laboratory automation schemes.
Industrial and Technical Education; Mathematics; Science; Sociology
Dist - VPI **Prod** - VPI 1980

Small Diameter Thermocouples 12 MIN
16mm
Color (IND)
Shows the special techniques, tools and accessories which have been developed to ensure reliability and accuracy in temperature measurement. Makes reference to the use of small diameter thermocouples.
Science; Science - Physical
Dist - UKAEA **Prod** - UKAEA 1975

Small Eatings 29 MIN
Videoreel / VT2
Joyce Chen Cooks Series
Color
Features Joyce Chen showing how to adapt Chinese recipes so that they can be prepared in the American kitchen and still retain the authentic flavor. Demonstrates how to prepare small eatings.
Geography - World; Home Economics
Dist - PBS **Prod** - WGBHTV

Small Electrical Repairs 15 MIN
Videoreel / VT2
Making Things Work Series
Color
Home Economics
Dist - PBS **Prod** - WGBHTV

Small engine - a video manual series 87 MIN
VHS
Small engine - a video manual series
Color (H A)
$569.00 purchase _ #VMAVO53SV
Presents a comprehensive look at how to service and overhaul a small automobile engine. Portrays the complete sequence from disassembly to reassembly. Consists of six videocassettes and two program guides.
Industrial and Technical Education
Dist - CAMV

Small Engine Know - How Series
Fuel System - Ignition - Troubleshooting
Major Overhaul
Routine Maintenance
Small Engine Systems
Dist - CAREER

Small engine mechanic 4.5 MIN
VHS / 16mm
Good works 2 series
Color (A PRO)
$40.00 purchase _ #BPN205605
Presents the occupation of a small engine mechanic. Profiles a young person who is either undergoing an apprenticeship or has recently completed training in this field. Takes the viewer on a tour of this person's workplace and explains the practical skills and training offered by employers and schools. Promotes a better understanding of the demand for skilled workers today and the potential for personal growth.
Guidance and Counseling
Dist - RMIBHF **Prod** - RMIBHF

Small engine mechanic 5 MIN
U-matic
Good work series
Color (H)
Provides useful, up to date information on various occupations to aid high school students in career selection. Available in five series of ten jobs each.
Education; Guidance and Counseling; Industrial and Technical Education
Dist - TVOTAR **Prod** - TVOTAR 1981

Small Engine Systems
VHS / 35mm strip
Small Engine Know - How Series
$85.00 purchase _ #DXSEK010 filmstrip, $85.00 purchase _ #DXSEK010V
Teaches basic principles of small engines, the mechanical system, and lubrication and cooling.
Education; Industrial and Technical Education
Dist - CAREER **Prod** - CAREER

Small engines 75 MIN
VHS / 16mm
Color (H A)
$399.00 purchase _ A15
Examines the basic parts and uses of a small engine. Details basic maintenance, dismounting and common repair procedures.
Industrial and Technical Education
Dist - BERGL **Prod** - BERGL 1990

Small engines 19 MIN
U-matic
Occupations series
B&W (J H)
Shows a student repairing an outboard motor in his occupational course and working at a marine service center.
Guidance and Counseling
Dist - TVOTAR **Prod** - TVOTAR 1985

Small engines
VHS
Color (H A)
$459.00 purchase _ #BXA15V
Presents a comprehensive guide to small automobile engines. Covers basic operations, basic maintenance, disassembly, and more. Consists of six videocassettes.
Industrial and Technical Education
Dist - CAMV

Small Engines Explained 95 MIN
VHS / 35mm strip
(J H A IND)
#450XV7
Provides a detailed description of the operation, reconditioning and assembly of a Briggs and Stratton 3.5 H P Four Stroke Cycle engine (Model Series #92000). Includes basic parts and operations - four stroke cycle engine, engine disassembly, inspection and valve reconditioning, cylinder reconditioning, engine assembly, ignition system, fuel systems, carburetor service, and routine care and maintenance (9 tapes). Includes a Study Guide.
Education; Industrial and Technical Education
Dist - BERGL

Small Enough 25 MIN
16mm
Color
LC 76-702673
Describes the intellectual challenge, social milieu, recreational opportunities and psychological ambience offered by the University of Wisconsin - Superior because of its small size.
Education; Geography - United States; Guidance and Counseling
Dist - UWISCS **Prod** - UWISCS 1976

The Small entrepreneur 30 MIN
VHS
Inside Britain 1 series
Color; PAL; NTSC (G) (BULGARIAN CZECH HUNGARIAN SPANISH POLISH ROMANIAN RUSSIAN SLOVAK UKRAINIAN ENGLISH WITH ARABIC SUBTITLES)
PdS65 purchase
Considers the small business as the backbone of any economy. Shows how in Britain the importance of small businesses to the economy is officially recognized through the great variety of help available to small enterpreneurs.
Business and Economics
Dist - CFLVIS **Prod** - CARLYL 1991

Small events 4 MIN
16mm
Color (G)
$10.00 rental
Fine Arts
Dist - CANCIN **Prod** - MERRIT 1979

Small Farm 10 MIN
16mm
Color (I J)
LC FIA67-613
Shows modern small farm methods in California using a strawberry farm in Downey as an example.
Agriculture; Geography - United States; Social Science
Dist - SF **Prod** - FINA 1966

Small Farm 5 MIN
16mm
Color
LC 77-702645
Shows the activities of farm animals on a small subsistence farm in the Precambrian Shield, a vast region of rock and forest which stretches across the north of Canada.
Agriculture; Geography - World; Science - Natural
Dist - MEPHTS **Prod** - MEPHTS 1977

Small gas engine carburetor one 30 MIN
VHS
Color (G H)
$49.95 purchase _ #CEV00837V-T
Portrays the correct method for disassembling, cleaning, and reassembling the Vacu jet and Flow jet carburetors. Includes safety information. Provides detailed examples of the `removal and cleaning of the high speed needled valve, throttle check, float adjustment, venturi check, and carburetor adjustment procedures.'
Education; Industrial and Technical Education
Dist - CAMV

Small gas engine carburetor two 30 MIN
VHS
Color (G H)
$49.95 purchase _ #CEV00838V-T
Describes the correct method for disassembling, cleaning, and reassembling the vertical and horizontal Pulsa jet carburetors. Provides detailed examples of the `removal and cleaning of the diaphragm, choke linkage and more. Uses classroom instruction and field model engines to demonstrate the proper procedures.
Education; Industrial and Technical Education
Dist - CAMV

Small gasoline engine assembly 47 MIN
VHS
Small gasoline engine series
Color (G H)
$49.95 purchase _ #CEV00831V-T
Describes the correct method for reassembling a small gasoline engine. Includes detailed instruction on installing pistons and rings, the crankshaft, the flywheel, and other engine parts along with information on safety in the shop. Explains the procedure for replacing many of the major components of the small engine including the sump, tappetts, and crankshaft.
Education; Industrial and Technical Education
Dist - CAMV

Small gasoline engine assembly part three 38 MIN
VHS
Small gasoline engine series
Color (G H)
$49.95 purchase _ #CEV00833V-T
Describes the correct method for reassembling a small gasoline engine. Includes detailed instruction on installing pistons and rings, the crankshaft, the flywheel, and other engine parts along with information on safety in the shop. Explains the procedure for replacing many of the major components of the small engine including the cylinder head, breather, pulugs, muffler, carburetor, fuel tank, blower housing and more.
Education; Industrial and Technical Education
Dist - CAMV

Small gasoline engine assembly part two 43 MIN
VHS
Small gasoline engine series
Color (G H)
$49.95 purchase _ #CEV00832V-T
Describes the correct method for reassembling a small gasoline engine. Includes detailed instruction on installing pistons and rings, the crankshaft, the flywheel, and other engine parts along with information on safety in the shop. Explains the procedure for replacing many of the major components of the small engine including the armature, coil, flywheel, and the clutch assembly. Includes a special section on tools.
Education; Industrial and Technical Education
Dist - CAMV

Small gasoline engine disassembly part one 49 MIN
VHS
Small gasoline engine disassembly series
Color (G H)
$49.95 purchase _ #CEV00828V-T
Describes through detailed video footage how to remove the carburetor, valves, linkages, springs, flywheel, and crankshaft using the proper tools and procedures. Explains how to drain oil, remove the air filter and fuel tank and the proper technique to repair the ignition system. Provides information about removal of the blower housing and other parts of the engine. Includes a special part about compression and air gap settings.
Education; Industrial and Technical Education
Dist - CAMV

Small gasoline engine disassembly part three 42 MIN
VHS
Small gasoline engine disassembly series
Color (G H)
$49.95 purchase _ #CEV00830V-T
Describes through detailed video footage how to remove the carburetor, valves, linkages, springs, flywheel, and crankshaft using the proper tools and procedures. Explains how to take apart the armature, breaker points, sump pumps, oil slinger, the cam gears, tappets, pistons, and crankshafts. Details the exact procedures for point-gap settings, breaker-point-plunger, and more.
Education; Industrial and Technical Education
Dist - CAMV

Small gasoline engine disassembly part two 42 MIN
VHS
Small gasoline engine disassembly series
Color (G H)
$49.95 purchase _ #CEV00829V-T
Describes through detailed video footage how to remove the carburetor, valves, linkages, springs, flywheel, and crankshaft using the proper tools and procedures. Explains how to take apart a Briggs and Stratton engine and details how to remove cylinder heads, valve cover, valve, springs, and also how to check the tappet-clearance, flywheel key. Provides information on starter pulley clutch, and flywheel.
Education; Industrial and Technical Education
Dist - CAMV

Small gasoline engine disassembly series
Small gasoline engine disassembly part one 49 MIN
Small gasoline engine disassembly part three 42 MIN
Small gasoline engine disassembly part two 42 MIN
Dist - CAMV

Small gasoline engine series
Small gasoline engine assembly 47 MIN
Small gasoline engine assembly part three 38 MIN
Small gasoline engine assembly part two 43 MIN
Dist - CAMV

Small Group Communication 24 MIN
U-matic / VHS
Communication Series
Color (H C A)
Incorporates puppetry as an instructional device to define and analyze small group communication. Displays and examines such phenomena as the phases of group development, the levels of group conflict, the emergence of leadership and the importance of cohesiveness in a group situation.
English Language; Psychology
Dist - MSU **Prod** - MSU

Small group instruction 28 MIN
16mm
Innovations in education series
Color
Presents Dr Dwight Allen, professor of education at Stanford University, who identifies decisions necessary for establishing productive small group interaction, including leadership selection and group control.

Education; Psychology
Dist - EDUC **Prod** - STNFRD 1966

Small group tutoring - basic literacy tutor training
VHS
Color (G T PRO)
$399.00 purchase _ #49029
Offers an 18-hour video-assisted workshop for trainers of literacy tutors. Uses the discovery process to present sight words, context clues, phonics, word patterns, and an on-going assessment. Package includes two videos, two handbooks, a trainer's guide, the READ Trainer's Kit, and an Administrator's Kit. Items also available separately.
Education; English Language
Dist - LITERA

Small happiness - women of a Chinese village - Pt 1 30 MIN
16mm
Color (J H A)
Presents the first half - hour segment of Small Happiness - Women Of A Chinese Village.
Geography - World; Sociology
Dist - NEWDAY **Prod** - LNGBOW

Small happiness - women of a Chinese village - Pt 2 30 MIN
16mm
Color (J H A)
Presents the second half - hour segment of Small Happiness - Women Of A Chinese Village.
Geography - World; Sociology
Dist - NEWDAY **Prod** - LNGBOW

The Small intestine and appendix
Videodisc
Color (PRO C)
$1300.00 purchase _ #C901 - IV - 028
Presents a hypertext presentation dealing with the small intestine and appendix and acute appendicitis adapted from Chapter 16 of the Surgical Textbook developed by the Association for Surgical Education. Includes a video index which divides surgery for acute appendicitis into the 12 major steps of the appendectomy. Written by Dr Joel A Weinstein, Department of Surgery, Case Western Reserve University and developed by the Surgical Hypermedia Project, Cleveland Metropolitan General Hospital. Includes videodisc, courseware on floppies in 3.5 or 5.25 inch size, user's manual and study guide. Requires IBM InfoWindow Touch Display Monitor, IBM compatible with 20MB hard disk and a videodisc player. Ask distributor about other requirements.
Health and Safety
Dist - HSCIC

Small is beautiful 30 MIN
VHS
Perspective - the environment - series
Color; PAL; NTSC (G)
PdS90, PdS105 purchase
Looks at the economic theory of Ernst Schumacher in practice.
Business and Economics; Science - Natural
Dist - CFLVIS **Prod** - LONTVS

Small is Beautiful - Impressions of Fritz Schumacher 30 MIN
U-matic / VHS / 16mm
Color (J)
LC 83-700180
Profiles British economist E F Schumacher who challenges the doctrine of unbridled economic growth.
Biography; Business and Economics
Dist - BULFRG **Prod** - NFBC 1981

The Small Loan 29 MIN
Videoreel / VT2
Way it is Series
Color
Business and Economics; Home Economics
Dist - PBS **Prod** - KUHTTV

Small Molecules 4 MIN
16mm
Molecular Biology Films Series
B&W (C)
LC 70-709326
Displays a catalog of small molecules generated by the Chempak programs.
Science - Natural
Dist - EDC **Prod** - ERCMIT 1970

Small muscle development - Pt 1 11 MIN
16mm
Color (I)
Encourages the practice of small muscle exercises as paper toys are cut out in easy-to-follow steps, since control and co- ordination of the hands strongly influence academic and physical progress. Demonstrates the safe and correct handling of scissors, cutting along straight and curved lines and differences between cutting paper and fabric.
Fine Arts; Psychology
Dist - SF **Prod** - SF 1968

Small muscle development - Pt 2 12 MIN
16mm
Color
Shows three toys being produced by different folding techniques which require the use of small muscles. Includes folding a letter and folding grocery bags.
Fine Arts; Psychology
Dist - SF **Prod** - SF

Small Muscle Development, Pt 3 12 MIN
16mm
Color
Presents a series of games and activities for children which are really small muscle exercises.
Fine Arts; Psychology
Dist - SF **Prod** - SF

The Small One 26 MIN
U-matic / VHS / 16mm
Color (P I)
LC 79-700819
Tells how a young boy goes to Bethlehem to sell his old donkey and how the auctioneer makes fun of his pet. Shows how he finally sells the donkey to Joseph, who buys him to carry Mary to the manger.
Literature and Drama; Religion and Philosophy
Dist - CORF **Prod** - DISNEY 1978

Small predatory mammals 13 MIN
VHS
Color (P I J)
$59.00 purchase _ #71042; $315.00, $220. purchase _ #71042
Emphasizes the positive role that predatory mammals play for all animals. Examines small predators such as the weasel, raccoon and gray fox. Shows that predators are animals that live by killing and eating other animals, that predators raise only a few young at a time, but the animals upon which they feed usually have larger numbers of young which mature quickly.
Science - Natural
Dist - INSTRU
CORF

Small real estate deal 10 MIN
16mm
B&W
LC 76-703806
Features a story about a man who answers an advertisement and has the surprise of his life.
Business and Economics
Dist - SFRASU **Prod** - SFRASU 1976

Small Repertory Companies and the Importance of Style 30 MIN
U-matic / VHS
Repertory Styles - How Different is One Ballet from Another Series
Color
Fine Arts
Dist - ARCVID **Prod** - ARCVID

Small shop projects - boxes with Jim Cummins 60 MIN
BETA / VHS
Color (IND G)
$29.95 purchase _ #060057
Shows how to make boxes. Demonstrates mitre cuts, clamping odd shapes, the use of scrap stock for boxes. Features carpenter Jim Cummins. Includes illustrated booklet.
Fine Arts; Industrial and Technical Education
Dist - TANTON **Prod** - TANTON 1990

Small shop tips and techniques
VHS
Video workshops series
$29.95 purchase _ #FW900
Offers tips from master craftsmen and techniques for operating a small shop.
Education; Industrial and Technical Education
Dist - CAREER **Prod** - CAREER

Small Shop Tips and Techniques with Jim Cummins 60 MIN
VHS / BETA
Color (H C A)
Presents an associate editor of Fine Woodworking showing various tips and tricks he's found in many years of woodworking. Comes with booklet.
Industrial and Technical Education
Dist - TANTON **Prod** - TANTON

Small Signs Supports 30 MIN
16mm
Color
LC 79-701580
Points out the dangers posed by using certain types of posts for small highway signs in the event of impact by a subcompact car. Shows different kinds of supports and provides recommendations for their use.
Industrial and Technical Education
Dist - USNAC **Prod** - TTI 1979

Small spillage cleanup 18 MIN
U-matic / BETA / VHS
British video programs series
Color; PAL (IND G)
$520.00 purchase _ #500 - 38
Trains employees in the United Kingdom. Instructs viewers in the methods of controlling, containing and cleaning up small spills. Includes step-by-step procedures for repairing punctured and damaged drums.
Health and Safety; Industrial and Technical Education; Psychology
Dist - ITSC **Prod** - ITSC

A Small Statistic 27 MIN
U-matic / VHS / 16mm
Insight Series
Color; B&W (H C A)
LC 74-705442
Shows how the complacent happiness of a young couple is shattered when their first child dies at birth.
Guidance and Counseling; Psychology
Dist - PAULST **Prod** - PAULST 1967

Small Steps 29 MIN
VHS
Color (J)
$195.00 purchase, $100.00, $50.00 rental
Shows Joseph Keiffer, co - founder of the Vermont Food Bank, helping elementary school students to acknowledge the problem of hunger in their community and to do something about it. Illustrates the students learning about nutrition, holding monthly food drives and, with the help of elderly gardening enthusiasts, putting their life science skills to work in their lush and productive gardens.
Health and Safety; Psychology; Social Science; Sociology
Dist - FANPRO **Prod** - FANPRO 1989

Small Steps - Giant Strides 29 MIN
16mm
Color
LC 75-701279
Highlights the 15th anniversary of NASA, 1958 - 1973. Portrays the historic accomplishments during the period and stresses benefits gained from the new technology developed.
Industrial and Technical Education; Science
Dist - USNAC **Prod** - NASA 1973

Small Suzhou restaurant 97 MIN
VHS
Color (G) (MANDARIN)
$45.00 purchase _ #1102B
Presents a movie produced in the People's Republic of China.
Fine Arts
Dist - CHTSUI

Small town library 10 MIN
16mm
B&W (J)
LC FIE52-2104
Explains the benefits and shows some of the operations of a public library in a small town, particularly the weekly delivery of books not owned by the small library loaned from the library of a big city nearby.
Education
Dist - USNAC **Prod** - USA 1952

Small Town Life 30 MIN
U-matic / VHS
Focus on Society Series
Color (C)
Looks at a small town in America and at the nature of relationships, the quality of life and the effects of urbanization.
Sociology
Dist - DALCCD **Prod** - DALCCD

The Small town - Pt II 30 MIN
VHS / U-matic
Legacies of the Depression on the Great Plains series
Color
Looks in detail at the experience of one small town, Broken Bow, Nebraska, during the thirties. Concentrates on the aesthetic aspects of Depression events.
Agriculture; History - United States
Dist - NETCHE **Prod** - NETCHE 1978

Small Tumor Virus and the New Genetics 60 MIN
U-matic
Color
Discusses tumor viruses as model chromosomes for studying the basis of the origins of carcinogens.
Health and Safety; Science - Natural
Dist - UTEXSC **Prod** - UTEXSC

Small White Cabbage 28 MIN
16mm
Color
Observes cabbage white butterflies and analyzes their behavior.
Science - Natural
Dist - UNIJAP **Prod** - IWANMI 1968

Small Wilderness 30 MIN
16mm / VHS
Life Around Us Series
(J H C)
$99.95 each, $695.00 series
Examines the unusual ecosystem of an unsettled area in Western Europe.
Science - Natural; Science - Physical; Sociology
Dist - AMBROS **Prod** - AMBROS 1971

Small wilderness 30 MIN
16mm / U-matic / VHS
Life around us series
Color (I) (SPANISH)
Shows that one of the last patches of unspoiled nature in highly industrialized Western Europe is the salty plain of the Camargue region of southern France. Presents the idea of environmental preservation, and stimulates students to consider what the world will be if people continue to destroy its wilderness.
Science - Natural; Social Science
Dist - TIMLIF **Prod** - TIMLIF 1971

Small wonders 30 MIN
VHS
Join in series
Color (K P)
#322603
Shows how Jacob and Nikki help their young friend Jessie deal with her unhappiness about being small. Presents songs about height and about friendship. Part of a series about three artist - performers who share studio space in a converted warehouse.
Fine Arts; Literature and Drama
Dist - TVOTAR **Prod** - TVOTAR 1989

Small world 60 MIN
VHS
Australian ark series
Color (G)
$19.95 purchase _ #S02061
Portrays Australia's flora and fauna.
Geography - World; Science - Natural
Dist - UILL

Small World 12 MIN
16mm
Color
LC 75-700084
Presents a variety of opinions from adults and children about how to live the good life in today's world.
Guidance and Counseling; Psychology
Dist - CCNCC **Prod** - CCNCC 1974

Small world 30 MIN
VHS
Return to the sea series
Color (I J H G)
$24.95 purchase _ #RTS205
Uses close - up photography to examine the smallest life of the coral reef and to reveal their vital role in the tropical ecosystem. Part of a 13 - part series on marine life produced by Marine Grafics and University of North Carolina Public TV.
Geography - World; Science - Natural; Science - Physical
Dist - ENVIMC

The Small World of the Nursery School 29 MIN
16mm
Color (C T)
Focuses on objectives for a nursery school. Summarized desirable experiences for the pre - school child as identified by leading nursery school educators. Discusses the child's total human make - up, including his attitude, physical development, cognitive growth, behavior, social relationships and ability to manage the elements of the environment.
Education; Psychology
Dist - EDUC **Prod** - EDUC

Smaller than the Smallest 10 MIN
U-matic
Structure of the Atom Series
Color (H C)
Explores Dalton's chemical atomic theory, Proust's law of definite proportions and work by Faraday, Crookes, Thomson and Millikan.
Science; Science - Physical
Dist - TVOTAR **Prod** - TVOTAR 1984

The Smallest Elephant in the World 5 MIN
16mm / U-matic / VHS
Color (K P)
LC 78-700631
Uses the story of a little elephant who finds acceptance and happiness in the circus to show that each individual is important no matter how different.
Guidance and Counseling; Sociology
Dist - AIMS **Prod** - FINART 1977

The Smallest Elephant in the World 6 MIN
16mm / U-matic / VHS
Color (P)
Tells the animated story of an elephant that was no bigger than a house cat.
Fine Arts; Literature and Drama
Dist - LUF **Prod** - LUF

The Smallest foe 20 MIN
16mm
B&W
Portrays the properties and types of viruses. Shows the manufacture of counter vaccines and antibiotics, their effects and problems involved in handling.
Science - Natural
Dist - LEDR **Prod** - LEDR 1956

Smallmouth Bass 30 MIN
VHS / BETA
From the Sportsman's Video Collection Series
Color
Shows how to increase one's success in fishing by using the methods the experts use in lakes and rivers to consistently take smallmouth.
Physical Education and Recreation
Dist - CBSC **Prod** - CBSC

Smallmouth bass 30 MIN
U-matic / 16mm
Color
Gives details on where and how to find smallmouth bass and outlines several methods for catching them throughout the U S and Canada.
Physical Education and Recreation
Dist - GLNLAU **Prod** - GLNLAU 1982

Smallmouth I 60 MIN
VHS / BETA
Color
Includes tactics for catching the summer smallies, the fall run of the river smallmouth, and smallmouth bass Great Lakes style.
Physical Education and Recreation; Science - Natural
Dist - HOMEAF **Prod** - HOMEAF

Smalltown, U S A 50 MIN
16mm
Color
LC FIA65-614
Uses representative small towns in the United States to explore the revolution which is under way in small towns in America. Pictures the life and death of small-town America in the 1950s showing how the small town is managing to exist today and how, in some cases, it is failing.
Psychology; Social Science; Sociology
Dist - NBCTV **Prod** - SAVLF 1964

Smart cookies don't crumble
VHS
Color (H A)
$39.95 purchase _ #JJ300V-G
Presents advice from Dr Sonya Friedman to American women. Provides insights that are designed to increase self - confidence and improve self - image. Addresses questions such as whether life seems full of limitations imposed by others and whether the viewer has trouble making choices that are right for her. Based on the book of the same name.
Psychology; Sociology
Dist - CAMV

Smart Cookies Don't Crumble 45 MIN
VHS
(I J H)
$29.95 purchase _ #JJ300V
Discusses how an adolescent can feel restricted by others, treated unfairly or confused about how to make the right decisions for themselves. Features Dr Sonya Friedman who gives advice on the issue of self confidence and self image.
Guidance and Counseling; Psychology
Dist - CAMV **Prod** - CAMV

Smart heart - guide to cardio - fitness 55 MIN
VHS
Color (G)
$29.95 purchase _ #EQ03V
Explains clearly the cardiovascular system and the physiological and psychological factors that affect the heart. Looks at the causes of heart disease and the importance of exercise, good nutrition and stress reduction in developing and maintaining cardiovascular fitness.
Health and Safety; Physical Education and Recreation; Science - Natural
Dist - CAMV

Smart investing 45 MIN
VHS
Color (G)
$19.95 purchase _ #S01437
Explains the world of investments and personal financial planning through a 'gameboard' format.
Business and Economics
Dist - UILL **Prod** - CU

Smart Investing - Consumer Reports 60 MIN
VHS / U-matic
(H C A)
Instructs the viewer on investing his finances with confidence. Covers key prinicples of investing, stocks and bonds, inflation and recession, capital gains, and more.
Business and Economics
Dist - CAMV **Prod** - CAMV
CADESF

Smart Money 30 MIN
BETA / VHS
On the Money Series
Color
Discusses hidden credit potential. Examines will writing. Looks at the relationship between money and productivity.
Business and Economics; Home Economics
Dist - CORF **Prod** - WGBHTV

Smart Moves 10 MIN
U-matic / VHS / 16mm
Color (A)
Stresses safety techniques for linemen.
Health and Safety
Dist - BCNFL **Prod** - OHMPS 1984

The Smart Parts - the Inside Story of Your Brain and Nervous System 15 MIN
VHS / U-matic
Inside Story with Slim Goodbody Series
Color (P I)
Presents Slim Goodbody who uses displays to illustrate the major brain regions and how impulses flash through the nervous system.
Science - Natural
Dist - AITECH **Prod** - UWISC 1981

Smart Questions 19 MIN
VHS / 16mm
Color (PRO)
Presents business consultant and author Dorothy Leeds who teaches questioning as a business skill. Discusses how to obtain information efficiently, improve listening skills, clarify thinking, develop creativity in problem solving, negotiate comfortably, and reduce mistakes.
Business and Economics; Computer Science; Education; Psychology
Dist - UTM
VLEARN

Smart risk taking 30 MIN
VHS
Color (G PRO)
$79.95 purchase _ #737 - 67
Shows how to minimize risks and maximize success. Tells when and why to take risks, how to assess ability to deal with certain risks and how to identify the strengths and weaknesses brought to risky situations. Discusses recognizing and overcoming personal barriers - lack of confidence, fear of success, love of recklessness - that may block progress in personal and professional life.
Business and Economics; Psychology
Dist - MEMIND **Prod** - AMA

Smart risk taking
VHS
FYI video series
Color (J H C G)
$79.95 purchase _ #AMA84007V
Shows when and why to take risks and how to assess one's ability to deal with certain risks. Looks at how to identify the strengths and weaknesses an individual brings to each risky situation. Part of a 12 - part series on professional and personal skills for the work place.
Business and Economics; Guidance and Counseling; Psychology
Dist - CAMV **Prod** - AMA

Smart risk taking 30 MIN
VHS
FYI video series
Color (H C G)
$79.95 purchase _ #AMA84007V
Teaches when and why to take risks, how to assess one's ability to deal with certain risks and how to identify the strengths and weaknesses brought to each risky situation. Part of a seven - part series on professional and personal skills for the workplace.

Business and Economics; Guidance and Counseling; Psychology
Dist - CAMV **Prod** - AMA 1991

Smart, safe and sure - preventing child abduction 28 MIN
U-matic / VHS
Color (PRO)
$275.00 purchase, $60.00 rental _ #9081S, #9081V
Offers practical and essential advice to parents on preventing child abduction. Suggests how children can protect themselves. Reviews the responsibilities of health care professionals in training the public to identify and avoid high - risk situations. Stresses communication and education, open lines of communication with children, and teaching them to say no to strangers and walk with friends.
Sociology
Dist - AJN **Prod** - HOSSN 1986

The Smart Shopper 30 MIN
U-matic / VHS
Personal Finance Series; 4
Color (C A)
Explains techniques that can aid the consumer in purchasing food, clothing, home furnishings and appliances. Discusses primary causes of poor shopping habits, unit pricing, brand name products versus generic and using coupons.
Business and Economics
Dist - CDTEL **Prod** - SCCON

Smart supermarket shopping with the new food label 23 MIN
VHS
Color (G A)
$89.95 purchase _ #NHV900V
Takes a viewer step-by-stey through a trip to the grocery store and shows them how to make the most nutritional and economic purchases using all of the information found on food packages. Introduces the new label now found on all prepared food packages so shoppers will have the necessary information available to them in order to make informed choices.
Home Economics
Dist - CAMV

Smart Talk - Sexually - Transmitted Disease Prevention 13 MIN
VHS
Color (I)
Emphasizes knowing about and promptly treating all sexually - transmitted diseases - STDs. Advocates abstinence from sex as the best policy. Shows teens talking about delaying sex and enjoying other pursuits together. Produced for Planned Parenthood of Alameda - San Francisco by Eclipse Productions. Includes a discussion guide and additional information on STDs.
Health and Safety; Psychology; Sociology
Dist - MEDIAI
ETRASS

Smart Transmitters 60 MIN
VHS / 16mm
Control Technology and Application Series
Color (PRO)
$595.00 purchase, $125.00 rental
Includes Introduction, Memory and Computation Features, Communications Features, Benefits and Selection Considerations, Tank Gauging Application and Paper Coating Process. Part of a seven - part series on control technology and application.
Business and Economics; Industrial and Technical Education
Dist - ISA **Prod** - ISA

Smart Weapons 26 MIN
U-matic / VHS
Breakthroughs Series
Color
Shows how the silicon chip and cathode tube are making smart weapons smarter with the awesome capability of transforming war into the ultimate video game.
Civics and Political Systems; Industrial and Technical Education; Sociology
Dist - LANDMK **Prod** - NOMDFI

The Smart workplace - developing high performance work systems 51 MIN
VHS
Color (IND)
$895.00 purchase, $300.00 rental _ #FFH27
Presents a program produced by the National Association of Manufacturers on performance - building techniques. Includes two videos, a leader's guide with case studies, assessment guides and organization tools.
Business and Economics; Psychology
Dist - EXTR **Prod** - FOTH

Smarter Together - Autonomous Working Groups 29 MIN
U-matic / VHS
Re - Making of Work Series
Color (C A) (GERMAN)
Documents different approaches aimed at increasing productivity. Demonstrates how profits increase when employees are given a greater measure of identification with their work. Features the Mayekawa Manufacturing plant in Japan and the Berkel Company in Germany.
Business and Economics; Sociology
Dist - EBEC

Smarter together series
Presents two modules faciliating dialog between women and men and improving their communication skills. Includes the titles Insights Into Male - Female Interactions and Male - Female Communications Skills, as well as a trainer's manual and 20 participant manuals for each module.

Insights into male - female interactions - Module I	28 MIN
Male - female communication skills - Module II	20 MIN
Smarter together series	48 MIN

Dist - BNA **Prod** - BNA 1983

Smash 6 MIN
16mm
Color
LC 80-700922
Shows possible causes and effects of vandalism. Follows the story of one boy and links the boy's rejection by society and family to the wrecking of a classroom at night.
Sociology
Dist - TASCOR
EDPAT

Smash the Plates 26 MIN
VHS
Color (C)
$400.00 purchase, $40.00, $50.00 rental
Comments on the politics of housework, state surveillance, and the desire for emotional release through the story of cleaning ladies who launch a campaign to smash unused plates. Produced by Lorna Boschman.
Sociology
Dist - WMENIF

Smashed, loaded, blasted, bombed - what you should know about alcohol
VHS
Color (I J H)
Presents three parts on avoiding peer pressure to drink and abuse alcohol. Interviews teens who tell why they drink. Examines facts and myths about drinking, describes the harmful effects of alcohol and gives practical advice on finding help for alcohol abuse.
Health and Safety; Psychology; Sociology
Dist - CADESF **Prod** - CADESF
GA

The Smashing of the Reich 84 MIN
U-matic / VHS
B&W
Shows the fall of Nazi Germany. Includes the landing at Normandy Beach, bombing of German industrial centers, the liberation of Paris and the freeing of concentration camp survivors.
History - United States; History - World; Sociology
Dist - IHF **Prod** - IHF

Smear and Squash Techniques 7 MIN
16mm / U-matic / VHS
Biological Techniques Series
Color (H C)
Demonstrates a simple method of making slides to study mitosis. Uses onion root tips and flower buds.
Science; Science - Natural
Dist - IFB **Prod** - THORNE 1961

Smell and taste 4 MIN
VHS
Color; PAL (H)
Demonstrates the major components of the senses of smell and taste.
Psychology; Science - Natural
Dist - VIEWTH

Smell - Brain and Ancient Cortex - Rhinencephalon 18 MIN
16mm / U-matic / VHS
Anatomical Basis of Brain Function Series
Color (PRO)
Science - Natural
Dist - TEF **Prod** - AVCORP

The Smell of War 20 MIN
U-matic / VHS
History in Action Series
Color
Analyzes the causes of World War I.
History - World
Dist - FOTH **Prod** - FOTH 1984

Smelt - Chemical Recovery 60 MIN
VHS
Systems Operations Series
Color (PRO)
$600.00 - $1500.00 purchase _ #PKSCR
Covers devices and tasks that convert smelt to white liquor. Overviews the smelt - to - white - liquor conversion process. Describes dissolving tanks, clarifiers, slakers and lime kilns. Includes ten textbooks and an instructor guide to support four hours of instruction.
Education; Health and Safety; Industrial and Technical Education; Psychology
Dist - NUSTC **Prod** - NUSTC

Smelt Recovery Operation
U-matic / VHS
Pulp and Paper Training, Module 2 - Chemical Recovery Series
Color (IND)
Focuses on startup, normal operation and shutdown of the smelt recovery operation.
Business and Economics; Industrial and Technical Education; Science - Physical; Social Science
Dist - LEIKID **Prod** - LEIKID

Smelt Recovery, Pt 1
U-matic / VHS
Pulp and Paper Training, Module 2 - Chemical Recovery Series
Color (IND)
Covers smelt spouts, the dissolving tank, green liquor clarifier and slaker/reaction tanks.
Business and Economics; Industrial and Technical Education; Science - Physical; Social Science
Dist - LEIKID **Prod** - LEIKID

Smelt Recovery, Pt 2
U-matic / VHS
Pulp and Paper Training, Module 2 - Chemical Recovery Series
Color (IND)
Covers several aspects of smelt recovery including white liquor, lime mud and lime kiln.
Business and Economics; Industrial and Technical Education; Science - Physical; Social Science
Dist - LEIKID **Prod** - LEIKID

Smelting and Refractories 45 MIN
U-matic / BETA / VHS
Color
Shows smelting as reduction process and reactions and products in iron blast furnace.
Industrial and Technical Education; Psychology; Science - Physical
Dist - ASM **Prod** - ASM

Smile 113 MIN
16mm
Color
Presents an affectionate satire on beauty pageants and small - town American life. Directed by Michael Ritchie.
Fine Arts
Dist - UAE **Prod** - UNKNWN 1975

The Smile and the Sword 22 MIN
16mm
B&W
LC 75-700583
Depicts an actual case from United States Government files in order to illustrate Communist espionage methods. Designed for defense contractor employees in contact with classified information.
Business and Economics; Civics and Political Systems
Dist - USNAC **Prod** - USA 1967

Smile - don't move 14 MIN
U-matic / VHS
En Francais series
Color (H C A)
Shows a photographer at a village fair and a cameraman shooting a historical film at the 15th century castle at Pierrefonds.
Foreign Language; Geography - World
Dist - AITECH **Prod** - MOFAFR 1970

Smile for Auntie 35 MIN
VHS / 16mm
Children's Circle Video Series
Color (K)
$18.88 purchase _ #CCV003
Presents five children's stories including Make Way For Ducklings, The Snowly Day, Wynken, Blynken And Nod.
Literature and Drama
Dist - EDUCRT

Smile for Auntie 5 MIN
U-matic / 35mm strip
Color (P I)

LC 79-700626; 79-731213
Tells the story of a woman who tries everything she can think of to make a baby smile. Based on the children's book Smile For Auntie by Diane Peterson.
Fine Arts; Literature and Drama
Dist - WWS **Prod** - WWS 1979

Smile Makers - Self - Applied Fluoride Programs for Schools 26 MIN
U-matic / VHS / 16mm
Color
Assists in in - service training for adults involved in school fluoride programs. Gives the steps to instituting a program and raising funds. Details distribution procedures and explains the benefits.
Health and Safety
Dist - USNAC **Prod** - USHHS

The Smile of Reason 52 MIN
U-matic / VHS / 16mm
Civilisation Series; No 10
Color (J)
LC 72-708457
Surveys the development of Western civilization during the 18th century as shown in the art and sculpture of Van Loo, David, de Troy and Houdon. Points out the growth of humanitarianism and the prevailing belief that mankind would advance by conquering ignorance through reason and moderation.
Fine Arts; History - World
Dist - FI **Prod** - BBCTV 1970

The Smile of Reason - Pt 1 24 MIN
U-matic / VHS / 16mm
Civilisation Series; No 10
Color (J)
LC 72-708457
Surveys the development of Western civilization during the 18th century as shown in the art and sculpture of Van Loo, David, de Troy and Houdon. Points out the growth of humanitarianism and the prevailing belief that mankind would advance by conquering ignorance through reason and moderation.
Fine Arts
Dist - FI **Prod** - BBCTV 1970

The Smile of Reason - Pt 2 28 MIN
U-matic / VHS / 16mm
Civilisation Series; No 10
Color (J)
LC 72-708457
Surveys the development of Western civilization during the 18th century as shown in the art and sculpture of Van Loo, David, de Troy and Houdon. Points out the growth of humanitarianism and the prevailing belief that mankind would advance by conquering ignorance through reason and moderation.
Fine Arts
Dist - FI **Prod** - BBCTV 1970

The Smile of the Baby 30 MIN
16mm
Film Studies of the Psychoanalytic Research Project on Problems in 'Infancy Series
B&W (C T)
An experimental study showing the first stage of the infant's response to humans. Illustrates that parental love makes the child friendly and socially secure.
Psychology; Sociology
Dist - NYU **Prod** - SPITZ 1948

The smile of the walrus 22 MIN
16mm / U-matic / VHS
Undersea world of Jacques Cousteau series
Color (G)
$49.9 purchase _ #Q10628; LC 78-701189
A shortened version of The Smile Of The Walrus. Features Jacques Cousteau as he studies the endangered walrus in its annual migration to the Arctic Sea. Emphasizes the importance of the walrus to isolated Eskimos. Shows the crew as it rears an ophaned pup and teaches it to forage on the ocean floor. Part of a series of 24 programs.
Geography - World; Science - Natural
Dist - CF **Prod** - METROM 1977

Smile Please 26 MIN
16mm
B&W
Introduces a man who is both a sheriff and photographer and shows that the latter profession is the most dangerous of the two. Stars Harry Langdon.
Fine Arts
Dist - RMIBHF **Prod** - KEYFC 1924

The Smile that Wins 30 MIN
VHS / U-matic
Wodehouse Playhouse Series
Color (C A)
Presents an adaptation of the short story The Smile That Wins by P G Wodehouse.
Literature and Drama
Dist - TIMLIF **Prod** - BBCTV 1980

Smile You're on 18 MIN
16mm
Color
LC 78-701325
Presents a variety show based on the daily routines of supermarket employees, with a backstage theatrical twist. Points out that employees should adopt a friendly and helpful attitude with regard to customer service.
Psychology
Dist - ALPHAB **Prod** - ALPHAB 1978

Smilemakers - Self - Applied Fluorides, Programs for Schools 25 MIN
16mm
Color (A)
Shows how to plan and implement the school - based, self - applied fluoride program in a community. Discusses and demonstrates the procedure for conducting and supervising the fluoride tablet and fluoride mouth rinse procedures.
Health and Safety
Dist - MTP **Prod** - NIH

Smiles 5 MIN
16mm
Color
LC 78-701481
Demonstrates, in a classroom and in a dentist's office, how to brush and floss teeth properly and the importance of proper diet in preventive dentistry.
Health and Safety
Dist - ECP **Prod** - ECP 1978

Smiles 30 MIN
U-matic
Today's Special Series
Color (K P)
Develops language arts skills in children. Programs are thematically designed around subjects of interest to youngsters. Action takes place in a department store where people, mannequins, puppets, comic characters and special guests present a light hearted approach to language arts.
Fine Arts; Literature and Drama; Psychology
Dist - TVOTAR **Prod** - TVOTAR 1985

Smiles of a summer night 110 MIN
VHS
B&W (G)
$29.95 purchase _ #SMI040
Sets the stage for romantic intrigue at a country estate in turn - of - the - century Sweden when eight characters become four couples during a long, languorous summer night. Shows the mismatched couples switching partners under the influence of a mysterious elixir in an intricate roundelay that is both lyrical and erotic. This satire of social rites and sexual mores was the inspiration for the Sondheim musical, A Little Night Music, and for Woody Allen's Midsummer Night's Sex Comedy. Digitally remastered with new subtitles.
Fine Arts; Literature and Drama; Psychology
Dist - HOMVIS **Prod** - JANUS 1955

Smiley 20 MIN
16mm
Color (P I)
LC 79-700850
Tells how a boy discovers a lost dog and tries unsuccessfully to find the dog's owner while growing more and more attached to it.
Fine Arts; Science - Natural
Dist - SIMONJ **Prod** - SIMONJ 1979

Smiling 8 MIN
16mm
B&W
LC 75-703293
Presents a story about a down - and - out derelict sitting on a park bench ready to take his life. Shows how a curiously smiling little man teaches the derelict, through a series of adventures, how to best cope with life's endless problems and how to come through it all, happy, content and smiling.
Guidance and Counseling; Sociology
Dist - USC **Prod** - USC 1974

Smiling - 51 8 MIN
VHS / U-matic
Life's little lessons - self - esteem 4 - 6 series
Color (I)
$129.00, $99.00 purchase _ #V680
Looks at Camp No - Come - Backee which was well named. Reveals that Rex and Gladys who ran the place infected it with crabbiness. One day the health inspector shut it down because he recognized that the crabbiness disease had taken over. He reopened it when Rex and Gladys learned to smile. Part of a 65 - part series on self - esteem.
Business and Economics; Guidance and Counseling; Psychology
Dist - BARR **Prod** - CEPRO 1992

The Smiling Response 20 MIN
16mm
Film Studies of the Psychoanalytic Research Project on Problems in 'Infancy Series
B&W (C T)
An excerpt from The Smile of the Baby which presents only the experimental part of the film.
Psychology
Dist - NYU **Prod** - SPITZ 1948

Smith
VHS
Campus clips series
Color (H C A)
$29.95 purchase _ #CC0057V
Takes a video visit to the campus of Smith College in Massachusetts. Shows many of the distinctive features of the campus, and interviews students about their experiences. Provides information on the composition of the student body, professors, academics, social life, housing, and other subjects.
Education
Dist - CAMV

Smith - Martin Ambulance Service 35 MIN
U-matic / VHS
Color
Investigates the possible abuse of public safety as the I - Team monitors ambulance calls for three weeks and discovers that some decisions about dispatching ambulances are made for profit, not patient safety.
Health and Safety; Sociology
Dist - WCCOTV **Prod** - WCCOTV

The Smith Systems of Space Cushion Driving 18 MIN
16mm / U-matic / VHS
Color
Presents professional driving instructor Harold Smith's five safe driving habits, including how to aim high in steering, how to get the big picture, how to keep the eyes moving, how to be seen and having an out.
Health and Safety; Industrial and Technical Education
Dist - FORDFL **Prod** - FORDFL

The Smiths Falls Carvers 24 MIN
U-matic / VHS / 16mm
Color (J)
LC 78-702034
Reveals the cultural and historical influences of a tradition of duck decoy carving in the rural community of Smiths Falls, Ontario, Canada. Shows how this art has been passed down through families.
Fine Arts; Geography - World; Sociology
Dist - WOMBAT **Prod** - GARNIA 1978

Smithsonian collection series
Presents a three - part series on the Smithsonian collections. Includes The National Zoo; Our Biosphere - the Earth in Our Hands; and Supertour.
The National zoo 50 MIN
Our biosphere - the Earth in our hands 45 MIN
Supertour
Dist - CAMV **Prod** - SMITHS 1978

The Smithsonian Institution 17 MIN
U-matic / VHS
Color (J C)
$69.00 purchase _ #3188
Provides an inside look of the many and the varied objects of the Institution giving an idea of the scale of the Institution, a sense of its present - day goals, and a knowledge of its early history.
Fine Arts
Dist - EBEC

The Smithsonian Institution 21 MIN
U-matic / VHS / 16mm
Eames Film Collection Series
Color (J H C)
LC FIE67-142
Describes events leading up to the founding of the Smithsonian Institution and the work of those men who set the character of the Smithsonian as we know it.
Fine Arts; Geography - United States
Dist - EBEC **Prod** - EAMES 1965

The Smithsonian Institution with S Dillon Ripley, Secretary 24 MIN
16mm
Color
LC 78-701712
Provides insight into the operations and facilities of the Smithsonian Institution, from the museums in Washington to the Tropical Research Institute in Panama. Touches on the work of the research scientists, artists and scholars employed by the Institution, as well as the secretaries who have headed the Institution since 1846.
Fine Arts; Geography - United States
Dist - USNAC **Prod** - SMITHS 1977

Smithsonian series
American first ladies 24 MIN
American folk art 25 MIN
Catlin and the Indians 24 MIN
A Million Years of Man 24 MIN
Our Vanishing Lands 24 MIN
Tippecanoe and Lyndon too 24 MIN
The World Around Us 25 MIN
Dist - MGHT

Smithsonian super tour 60 MIN
VHS
Color (J H C G)
$29.95 purchase _ #HVS50V
Tours the museums of the Smithsonian with entertainer Dudley Moore. Views an exclusive showing of African art displayed in the National Museum of African Arts. Visits the Smithsonian Zoo, the National Museum of Natural History, the National Museum of American Art, and the National Air and Space Museum.
Fine Arts; History - United States
Dist - CAMV

Smithsonian world series
Introduces a four-part videotape series that looks at some of the topics and issues on display at the Smithsonian Institution, one of the United States' best-known museum complexes. Notes four parts include a look at Americana titled American Pie, a look at outer space and ocean deep titled Where None Has Gone Before, a look at the measurement of time and how stars reveal the past titled Time and Light, and a looks at art and pop culture titled Filling in the Blanks. Details that tapes may be purchased separately.
American pie 55 MIN
Filling in the blanks 55 MIN
Time and light 55 MIN
Dist - CAMV

Smithsonian World Series
Where None has Gone Before 60 MIN
Dist - CAMV
WETATV

Smithsonian World Series
American dream at Groton 60 MIN
American pie 60 MIN
A Certain Age
Doors of perception
The Elephant on the hill 60 MIN
From information to wisdom
Gender - the Enduring Paradox
Islam 60 MIN
The Living Smithsonian 60 MIN
A Moveable Feast 60 MIN
Nigerian Art - Kindred Spirits 60 MIN
The Promise of the land 60 MIN
The Quantum universe 60 MIN
Selling the Dream
Tales of the human dawn 60 MIN
The Vever affair 60 MIN
Voices of Latin America 60 MIN
The Way we wear 60 MIN
Web of life 60 MIN
The Wyeths - a father and his family 60 MIN
Zoo 60 MIN
Dist - PBS

Smithsonian World Series
Crossing the distance 60 MIN
Designs for living 60 MIN
Desk in the jungle 60 MIN
Filling in the blanks 60 MIN
Heroes and the Test of Time 60 MIN
The Last Flower 60 MIN
On the Shoulders of Giants 60 MIN
Speaking without words 60 MIN
Time and Light 60 MIN
A Usable Past 60 MIN
Dist - WETATV

Smithsonian's great battles of the Civil War series
Presents a seven - part series on the Civil War. Features dramatic reenactments of important campaigns, eyewitness accounts, period photographs, paintings and artifacts, expert challenges to traditional historical thinking, contemporary illustrations, computer enhanced maps and the music of the time.
Smithsonian's great battles of the Civil War - Volume I 60 MIN
Smithsonian's great battles of the Civil War - Volume II 60 MIN
Smithsonian's great battles of the Civil War - Volume III 60 MIN
Smithsonian's great battles of the Civil War - Volume IV 60 MIN
Smithsonian's great battles of the Civil War - Volume V 60 MIN
Smithsonian's great battles of the Civil War - Volume VI 60 MIN
Smithsonian's great battles of the Civil War - Volume VII 60 MIN
Dist - CAMV **Prod** - SMITHS

Smithsonian's great battles of the Civil War - Volume I 60 MIN
VHS
Smithsonian's great battles of the Civil War series
Color (J H C G)
$39.95 purchase _ #MST550V
Covers Ft Sumter, the first Manassas, Ft Donelson, the Ironclads and the Navies, the War in the Far West, Shiloh and intervening campaigns in Volume I of a seven - part series on the Civil War.
History - United States
Dist - CAMV **Prod** - SMITHS 1993

Smithsonian's great battles of the Civil War - Volume II 60 MIN
VHS
Smithsonian's great battles of the Civil War series
Color (J H C G)
$39.95 purchase _ #MST551V
Covers the battles for New Orleans and the Mississippi River, Shenandoah Valley, the Peninsula Campaign, the second Manassas and intervening campaigns in Volume II of a seven - part series on the Civil War.
History - United States
Dist - CAMV **Prod** - SMITHS 1993

Smithsonian's great battles of the Civil War - Volume III 60 MIN
VHS
Smithsonian's great battles of the Civil War series
Color (J H C G)
$39.95 purchase _ #MST552V
Covers Antietam, Corinth, Perryville, Fredericksburg, First Drive on Vicksburg and intervening campaigns in Volume III of a seven - part series on the Civil War.
History - United States
Dist - CAMV **Prod** - SMITHS 1993

Smithsonian's great battles of the Civil War - Volume IV 60 MIN
VHS
Smithsonian's great battles of the Civil War series
Color (J H C G)
$39.95 purchase _ #MST553V
Covers Stones River, Chancellorville, Brandy Station, Gettysburg and intervening campaigns in Volume IV of a seven - part series on the Civil War.
History - United States
Dist - CAMV **Prod** - SMITHS 1993

Smithsonian's great battles of the Civil War - Volume V 60 MIN
VHS
Smithsonian's great battles of the Civil War series
Color (J H C G)
$39.95 purchase _ #MST554V
Covers the sieges of Vicksburg and Charleston, Chickamauga, Chattanooga and Lookout Mountain and intervening campaigns in Volume V of a seven - part series on the Civil War.
History - United States
Dist - CAMV **Prod** - SMITHS 1993

Smithsonian's great battles of the Civil War - Volume VI 60 MIN
VHS
Smithsonian's great battles of the Civil War series
Color (J H C G)
$39.95 purchase _ #MST555V
Covers New Market, the Wilderness and Spotsylvania, Cold Harbor, Kennesaw Mountain, Battle of the Crater, Mobile Bay, Battles for Atlanta in Volume VI of a seven - part series on the Civil War.
History - United States
Dist - CAMV **Prod** - SMITHS 1993

Smithsonian's great battles of the Civil War - Volume VII 60 MIN
VHS
Smithsonian's great battles of the Civil War series
Color (J H C G)
$39.95 purchase _ #MST556V
Covers the destruction of the CSS Alabama, Cedar Creek, Franklin, Ft Fisher, siege of Petersburg, Bentonville, Sailor's Creek and Appomattox in Volume VII of a seven - part series on the Civil War.
History - United States
Dist - CAMV **Prod** - SMITHS 1993

Smocking 60 MIN
BETA / VHS
Color
Teaches traditional smocking methods, as well as ways to achieve gathers and stitches for smocking application.
Home Economics
Dist - HOMEAF **Prod** - HOMEAF

Smogbusters 26 MIN
VHS
How to save the Earth series
Color (J H C G)
$175.00 purchase, $45.00 rental
Looks at the work of Eric Mann, a former auto worker now promoting mass transit systems in Los Angeles, and Nei Serra, the green warrior mayor of Cubatao, Brazil, once labeled 'the most polluted place on Earth.' Deals with air pollution, smog, acid rain, ozone depletion and global warming.
Fine Arts; Science - Natural
Dist - BULFRG **Prod** - CITV 1993

Smoke 8 MIN
U-matic / VHS
Safe Child Series
Color
Tells how smoke rises and spreads. Puppets and children demonstrate how to escape from smoke, whether at home or school.
Health and Safety; Home Economics
Dist - FPF **Prod** - FPF

Smoke and Fire - Two Steps to Survival 20 MIN
16mm
Color
LC 78-700219
Explains the dangers of smoke and stresses the importance of early warning and rapid escape from a fire.
Health and Safety
Dist - AETNA **Prod** - AETNA 1977

Smoke - Filled Rooms and Dark Horses 30 MIN
16mm
Structure and Functions of American Government Part VII, Lesson 3 - 'First Semester
B&W
Describes and analyzes the role of organizations and national party conventions.
Civics and Political Systems
Dist - NBCTV **Prod** - NBCTV 1963

Smoke Gets in Your Hair 14 MIN
U-matic / VHS / 16mm
Learning Values with Fat Albert and the Cosby Kids, Set II Series
Color (P I)
Shows the dangerous effects of tobacco on the body and tells how smoking can lead to serious health problems.
Guidance and Counseling; Health and Safety
Dist - MGHT **Prod** - FLMTON 1977

Smoke Screen 5 MIN
16mm / U-matic / VHS
Color (I)
LC 74-711448
Aims to deter children from acquiring the smoking habit through the use of kinestatic images of smokers.
Fine Arts
Dist - PFP **Prod** - WARSHW 1970

Smoke screen - Cigarettes and advertising 15 MIN
VHS / U-matic
Color (I J)
$280.00, $330.00 purchase, $50.00 rental
Features a dramatic production with students discussing the negative aspects of cigarette smoking and how advertising is used to attract new smokers. Provides an analysis and examples of advertising strategies.
Health and Safety; Psychology
Dist - NDIM **Prod** - ALLMED 1991

Smoke Testing a Wastewater Collection System 6 MIN
VHS / BETA
Color
Discusses maintenance and repair, and water and wastewater technology.
Health and Safety; Industrial and Technical Education; Social Science
Dist - RMIBHF **Prod** - RMIBHF

Smokeable cocaine - the Haight - Ashbury crack film 28 MIN
VHS
Color (J H G)
$325.00 purchase
Details how freebase and crack manipulate brain chemistry. Uses animation, computer graphics and interviews with doctors and ex - users. Traces the role of the lungs, transfer point for the smoke from freebase and crack, allowing the absorption of the vaporized drug which is then pumped back to the heart where doses of cocaine rich blood are sent to every organ and tissue of the body, particularly the brain. It takes less than 10 seconds for cocaine molecules to reach and infiltrate the central nervous system, the brain and spinal cord.
Guidance and Counseling; Psychology; Science - Natural
Dist - FMSP

Smokeless Tobacco 16 MIN
16mm
Color (I J H)
Presents the very real dangers of smokeless tobacco in this dramatic film based on the true story of Seqn Marsee, a high school track star and habitual snuff user who died of oral cancer at age 19. Points out that smokeless tobacco is not a safe alternative to smoking.
Health and Safety; Psychology
Dist - CORF **Prod** - DISNEY 1986

Smokeless Tobacco - it Can Snuff You Out 13 MIN
16mm / VHS
Color (J A)
$295.00, $265.00 purchase, $50.00 rental
Explores growing use of snuff and chewing tobacco, use of sports figures to promote the products, and misconception that such products are not as dangerous or addictive as smoking. Cites the concerns of medical authorities who describe the harm of smokeless tobacco to mouth tissue and its contribution to oral cancer.
Health and Safety; Psychology
Dist - HIGGIN **Prod** - HIGGIN 1986

Smokers are hazardous to your health 50 MIN
VHS
Color (G)
$149.00 purchase, $75.00 rental _ #UW4137
Reveals that the hazards of second - hand smoke are becoming more and more apparent. Documents the facts and the growing international battle among those who make money out of tobacco, those who demand the right to destroy themselves - and, evidently, those around them - by smoking, and the rest of the population.
Guidance and Counseling; Health and Safety
Dist - FOTH **Prod** - BBC

Smokers can harm your health 50 MIN
VHS
Horizon series
Color; PAL (C H A)
PdS99 purchase; Not available in the United States
Examines the passive smoking issue, noting there is increasing evidence that inhaling smoke from other people's cigarettes is damaging.
Health and Safety
Dist - BBCENE

Smokers have Rights Too 24 MIN
16mm
Color (A)
LC 79-700942
Dramatizes the story of a congressional aide who says he has a right to smoke. Tells how he meets a man dying of emphysema who teaches him an important lesson.
Health and Safety; Psychology
Dist - NARCED **Prod** - NARCED 1979

Smoker's Luck 50 MIN
16mm / U-matic / VHS
Color (C A)
Explains the risks involved in tobacco smoking, including the danger of carbon monoxide, a possible major factor in heart disease, the effect of a mother's smoking on the unborn child and the danger to non - smokers from inhalation of other's smoke. Uses animation to show how blocking of the arteries can result causing loss of blood supply to the legs.
Health and Safety
Dist - FI **Prod** - BBCTV

Smokey and His Friends 4 MIN
16mm
Color
LC 74-705657
Depicts Smokey meeting some of his wild animal and bird friends and watching them in their forest home. Reminds the viewer that fires destroy the homes of his friends.
Health and Safety; Science - Natural; Science - Physical
Dist - USNAC **Prod** - USDA 1967

Smokey Bear 18 MIN
16mm
Color (K P I)
LC 77-701264
Tells how two children learn from their grandfather the true story of Smokey Bear and how he was found clinging to a burned tree after a devastating forest fire. Relates how Smokey Bear was made the national living symbol of forest fire prevention and was sent to live in Washington DC. Deals with the importance of preserving our forests and being cautious with fire hazards while outdoors.
Health and Safety; Science - Natural; Social Science
Dist - FILCOM **Prod** - USFS 1977

Smokey Joe's hayride 13 MIN
VHS / 16mm
Color (H G)
$80.00, $35.00 purchase _ #260, #475
Presents a film - discussion program to portray the hazardous effects of marijuana on the ability to drive safely. Combines live action and animation to demonstrate the different negative effects of marijuana driving skills. Includes a teacher's discussion guide and 50 copies of student pamphlets. Guide and pamphlets also available separately.
Guidance and Counseling; Health and Safety; Psychology
Dist - AAAFTS **Prod** - AAAFTS 1984

Smokey Joe's Revenge 57 MIN
16mm / U-matic / VHS
Color (P I)
Tells what happens when a man gives some children an old steam roller which they restore and race against the man's new steam roller.
Fine Arts
Dist - LUF **Prod** - CHILDF 1978

Smokey the Bear 5 MIN
U-matic / VHS / 16mm
B&W
LC FIE52-2165
A group of boys on a camping trip are reminded of their responsibility in helping to prevent forest fires. Smokey Bear stars and Eddy Arnold sings.
Health and Safety; Science - Natural
Dist - USNAC **Prod** - USDA 1952

Smokey's Story 12 MIN
16mm
Color
LC 74-705658
Dennis Weaver sees a boy playing with matches in the woods, and so he retells the story of Little Smokey, the cub who survived a forest fire.
Health and Safety; Literature and Drama; Science - Natural
Dist - USNAC **Prod** - USDI 1971

Smoki Snake Dance 12 MIN
16mm
Color (I J)
Shows activities of civic - minded Arizonians as they prepare to learn and present Indian dances in their annual Smoki Dance Festival.
Social Science; Sociology
Dist - MLA **Prod** - DAGP 1952

Smoking
VHS
Personal action system series
Color (G)
$149.00 purchase _ #V205
Teaches employees about the health risks of smoking. Part of a 13 - part series to educate employees on the importance of health.
Guidance and Counseling; Health and Safety; Psychology
Dist - GPERFO

Smoking - a New Focus 15 MIN
8mm cartridge / VHS / U-matic / 16mm
Color (I J H) (SPANISH FRENCH ARABIC)
LC 72-700710;
Examines the problem of smoking from a medical and sociological standpoint. Avoids scare tactics and didactic preaching.
Health and Safety; Psychology
Dist - AMEDFL **Prod** - AMEDFL 1972

Smoking - a New Focus 16 MIN
U-matic / VHS / 16mm
Color (J H C) (SPANISH)
Examines the smoking problem from a medical and sociological viewpoint in order to understand how the smoking myth evolved. Presents the viewpoints of a smoker as to why he started, why he can't stop and whether or not he really wants to quit.
Health and Safety; Psychology
Dist - AMEDFL **Prod** - AMEDFL

Smoking - a Report on the Nation's Habit 17 MIN
U-matic / VHS / 16mm
Life and Breath Series
Color (J)
Outlines information regarding smoking trends, the tobacco industry and dangers associated with smoking. Gives a poignant example of why not to start, or if you already have, to quit.
Health and Safety; Psychology
Dist - JOU **Prod** - JOU 1978

Smoking - a Report on the Nation's Habit 15 MIN
16mm
Color (J)
LC 82-700389
Outlines recent information regarding smoking trends, the tobacco industry and the newest dangers associated with smoking. Provides examples of why not to start smoking and why to quit.
Health and Safety; Psychology
Dist - PELICN **Prod** - PELICN 1978

Smoking against your will 30 MIN
U-matic
(PRO G)
Examines medical research on the effect of the harmful ingredients absorbed into the bloodstream of those in close proximity to smokers.
Health and Safety; Psychology
Dist - ACCESS **Prod** - ACCESS 1985

Smoking and health
VHS
Color (I J H C T A PRO PRO)
$79.50 purchase _ #AH46328
Uses extensive medical photography to demonstrate the medical consequences of smoking - lung cancer, emphysema, bronchitis, heart attacks, bladder cancer, strokes, and other conditions.
Health and Safety; Psychology; Science - Natural
Dist - HTHED **Prod** - HTHED

Smoking and Health - a Report to Youth 13 MIN
16mm / U-matic / VHS
Color (J)
Uses animation to show how the trachea, bronchi and lungs function and how they are affected by smoking. Points out that although bronchitis and emphysema are thought of as 'old folks' diseases, they are striking the younger population.
Health and Safety; Psychology
Dist - PHENIX **Prod** - DESCEN 1969

Smoking and Health - the Answers We Seek 15 MIN
16mm
Color
Seeks to provide a full, free and informed discussion of the smoking and health controversy and to affirm the conviction that the controversy must be resolved by scientific research.
Health and Safety
Dist - MTP **Prod** - TOBCCO

Smoking and Health - the Need to Know 28 MIN
16mm
Color (J)
Presents a scientific documentary on a current controversy that relates the facts about smoking and health.
Guidance and Counseling; Health and Safety; Psychology
Dist - MTP **Prod** - TOBCCO

Smoking and Heart Disease 28387 10 MIN
VHS / U-matic
Color
Uses animated drawings and diagrams to present the effects of nicotine on a smoker's heart and circulation. Shows how subtle body changes, such as narrowing of the blood vessels, become gross, with high blood pressure and heart disease diminishing a smoker's life expectancy.
Health and Safety; Science - Natural
Dist - PRIMED **Prod** - PRIMED

Smoking and human physiology 19 MIN
VHS
Color (G C PRO)
$150.00 purchase _ #GN - 16
Uses dramatic statistics and 'inner body' photography to show just how serious a problem smoking is. Covers the dangers of second - hand smoke and shows how a fetus is harmed. Contact distributor for special purchase price on multiple orders.
Health and Safety
Dist - MIFE **Prod** - AIMS 1995

Smoking and Lung Cancer 19 MIN
VHS / 16mm
Color (PRO G)
$149.00, $249.00, purchase _ #AD - 1365
Explains that smokers are ten times as likely to develop lung cancer as nonsmokers, and that the more they smoke, the higher the risk. Emphasizes that early detection, before cancerous cells can metastasize to other vital organs, is crucial to successful treatment and survival. Profiles a man whose encounter with lung cancer gave him the motivation to quit smoking.
Guidance and Counseling; Health and Safety; Psychology
Dist - FOTH **Prod** - FOTH 1990

Smoking, Drinking and Drugs 15 MIN
U-matic / VHS / 16mm
Healthwise Series
Color (K P I)
Shows how habits like smoking, drinking and drugs are easy to form and hard to break. Demonstrates the effects of smoking on the heart and circulation of a smoker. Explains how some people drink too much, hurting themselves and their families. Presents a puppet dinosaur who makes a statement about drugs when he eats an unfamiliar plant and gets more than he bargained.
Health and Safety
Dist - CORF **Prod** - CORF 1982

Smoking - Emphysema - a Fight for Breath 12 MIN
U-matic / VHS / 16mm
Color (H C A)
Illustrates the difference between the functioning of healthy lungs and diseased ones. Describes the breakdowns that take place as emphysema develops.
Health and Safety
Dist - CRMP MGHT **Prod** - NFBC 1975

Smoking follow - up and cholesterol intervention - Part 4 20 MIN
VHS / U-matic
Family approach to coronary risk reduction series
Color (C PRO)
$395.00 purchase, $80.00 rental _ #C921 - VI - 018
Demonstrates a family approach to the prevention of coronary artery disease. Observes a family physician interviewing a male patient named Terry and his wife about his smoking habits and family dietary cholesterol intake. Covers important information about coronary heart disease, situations that put an individual at risk of having a heart attack and ways to reduce the chances of having a heart attack. Teaches health professionals ways to motivate changes in their patients - stopping smoking, changing eating habits. Part of a four - part series presented by Dr Russ Sawa.
Guidance and Counseling; Health and Safety; Sociology
Dist - HSCIC

Smoking follow - up - Part 3 14 MIN
U-matic / VHS
Family approach to coronary risk reduction series
Color (C PRO)
$395.00 purchase, $80.00 rental _ #C921 - VI - 017
Demonstrates a family approach to the prevention of coronary artery disease. Observes a family physician interviewing a male patient named Terry and his wife about his smoking habits. Covers important information about coronary heart disease, situations that put an individual at risk of having a heart attack and ways to reduce the chances of having a heart attack. Teaches health professionals ways to motivate changes in their patients - stopping smoking, changing eating habits. Part of a four - part series presented by Dr Russ Sawa.
Guidance and Counseling; Health and Safety; Sociology
Dist - HSCIC

Smoking - Games Smokers Play 26 MIN
16mm / U-matic / VHS
Color (J)
LC 76-701179
Points out the hazards of smoking. Shows a psychologist discussing reasons for the teenage smoking habit and shows a simulated discussion by teenagers on smoking.
Guidance and Counseling; Health and Safety; Psychology; Sociology
Dist - CNEMAG **Prod** - HOBLEI 1976

Smoking - Hazardous to Your Health, Pt 1 29 MIN
U-matic / VHS
Here's to Your Health Series
Color
Discusses the effects of smoking on the body, heart and lungs, and the diseases triggered by smoking.
Health and Safety; Psychology; Sociology
Dist - PBS **Prod** - KERA

Smoking - How to Quit
U-matic / VHS
Color
Relates a husband and wife who attempt to quit smoking. Includes practical tips.
Psychology
Dist - MIFE **Prod** - MIFE

Smoking - how to stop 23 MIN
VHS
Color (J H C A)
$195.00 purchase
Explains methods developed by organizations, including the American Cancer Society, to break the smoking habit. Encourages smokers to quit.
Guidance and Counseling; Health and Safety; Psychology
Dist - PFP **Prod** - REIDMA

Smoking - How to Stop 23 MIN
U-matic / VHS / 16mm
Life and Breath Series
Color (A)
Examines the progress of a typical smoker as she advances through a quitters clinic. Portrays useful tips for quitting while positive, encouraging messages for the millions of smokers who would like to quit are relayed.
Health and Safety; Psychology
Dist - JOU **Prod** - JOU 1978

Smoking - It's Your Choice 17 MIN
16mm / VHS
Color (I J)
$395.00, $355.00 purchase, $60.00 rental
Demonstrates that the effects of smoking begin with the very first puff and that nicotine addiction may be stronger than addiction to such drugs as heroin and cocaine. Discusses second - hand smoke, smoking bans in certain public places, and additional warnings now required on cigarette packages. Presents facts about how smoking contributes to emphysema and cancer and discusses how to deal with peer pressure.
Health and Safety; Psychology
Dist - HIGGIN **Prod** - HIGGIN 1989

Smoking - Kicking the Habit, Pt 2 29 MIN
U-matic / VHS
Here's to Your Health Series
Color
Examines some of the many programs aimed at stopping smoking, from hypnosis seminars to aversion - therapy clinics, with warnings about dubious, high - cost programs. Places emphasis on keeping teens from starting smoking.
Health and Safety; Psychology
Dist - PBS **Prod** - KERA

Smoking - Light Up, Strike Out 11 MIN
16mm / U-matic / VHS
Color (I)
LC 76-702136
Presents a witty treatment of the claims made by advertisements for cigarettes. Points out that smoking is like gambling and that one smoker out of seven is likely to die from cancer.
Health and Safety; Psychology
Dist - AIMS **Prod** - NULSEN 1975

Smoking - light up - strike out 11 MIN
VHS
Color (I J H G)
$49.95 purchase _ #AM9450
Uses humor and facts to help turn off would - be smokers. Satirizes the reasons people smoke - to feel mature, sophisticated and fashionable. Examines the history of cigarettes, the medical evidence of the harm of smoking and the clever, manipulative advertising used to seduce people into the habit.
Health and Safety; Psychology; Sociology
Dist - AAVIM **Prod** - AAVIM 1992

Smoking - Nico - Teen 11 MIN
U-matic / VHS / 16mm
Color (I J H)
LC 81-701061
Interviews many teenagers regarding why they first began smoking. Shows that smokers are not proud of the habit and examines how teenage smokers work to stop. Originally shown on the CBS program 30 Minutes.
Health and Safety; Psychology
Dist - PHENIX **Prod** - CBSTV 1981

Smoking - Personal Pollution 18 MIN
U-matic / VHS / 16mm
Color (J H)
Shows how cigarettes affect the human body and can lead to addiction. Demonstrates how even one cigarette can affect the blood pressure and circulatory system.
Health and Safety; Psychology
Dist - PEREN **Prod** - GOLDCF

The Smoking Spiral 60 MIN
16mm
Net Journal Series
B&W (J)
Illustrates the possible crippling effects of smoking by showing one day in the lives of two men suffering from lung ailments linked to smoking. Points out that health education against smoking has had little effect. Interviews representatives of the tobacco industry, politicians and medical officers for comments concerning the various aspects of the problem.
Health and Safety
Dist - IU **Prod** - NET 1967

Smoking - the Choice is Yours 11 MIN
16mm / U-matic / VHS
Color (I J) (THAI)
Explains the hazards of smoking and deals with the root problems of self - image and peer pressure which influence students to begin smoking.
Foreign Language; Health and Safety; Psychology
Dist - CORF **Prod** - DISNEY 1982

Smoking - the road to a smoke - free life package
VHS
Personal action for better health series
Color (A IND)
$299.00 purchase _ #AH45409
Views the process of quitting smoking as a journey. Divides the program into three parts - getting ready to quit, quitting, and staying smoke - free. Includes 125 booklets and three posters.
Health and Safety; Psychology
Dist - HTHED **Prod** - HTHED

Smoking, what are the Facts? 13 MIN
U-matic / VHS
Color
Presents the basic information about the effects of smoking as published in the 1979 Surgeon General's Report.
Health and Safety; Psychology
Dist - MEDFAC **Prod** - MEDFAC 1980

Smokin's Bad for You - Yogi Bear 1 MIN
U-matic / VHS
Color
Features animated cartoon favorite Yogi Bear in a TV spot produced jointly by American Cancer Society, American Lung Association and American Heart Association. Tells youngsters as new and potential smokers that 'Smokin's Bad For You.'.
Health and Safety
Dist - AMCS **Prod** - AMCS 1980

Smoky Mountain hymns - the video 35 MIN
VHS
Color (G R)
$19.95 purchase _ #35 - 85137 - 444
Features the life and music of the people of the Great Smoky Mountains. Combines footage of the countryside with traditional arrangements of hymns. Includes such hymns as 'I'll Fly Away,' 'Amazing Grace,' 'Blessed Assurance,' 'How Great Thou Art,' and others.
Fine Arts; Geography - United States; Religion and Philosophy
Dist - APH

Smoky Mountain video number 2 30 MIN
VHS
Color (G R)
$19.95 purchase _ #35 - 85142 - 444
Features the life and music of the people of the Great Smoky Mountains. Combines footage of the countryside with traditional arrangements of hymns. Includes such hymns as 'The Old Rugged Cross,' 'Love Lifted Me,' 'Mansion Over the Hilltop,' and others.
Fine Arts; Geography - United States; Religion and Philosophy
Dist - APH

Smoky Mountains, Pt 1 14 MIN
Videoreel / VT2
Muffinland Series
Color
English Language; Literature and Drama
Dist - PBS **Prod** - WGTV

Smoky Mountains, Pt 2 14 MIN
Videoreel / VT2
Muffinland Series
Color
English Language; Literature and Drama
Dist - PBS **Prod** - WGTV

Smothering Dreams 23 MIN
VHS / U-matic
Color
Deals with Dan Reeves' experiences as a marine in Viet Nam, as well as the childhood war play and fantasy of violence. Calls into doubt the myths of chivalry and war presented to children.
Fine Arts; Sociology
Dist - KITCHN **Prod** - KITCHN

Smotherly Love 30 MIN
16mm / U-matic / VHS
Moving Right Along Series
Color (J H A)
Recounts that when Pete Wolenski receives the basketball scholarship he's dreamt about, his mother and his girlfriend put him through the hoop about leaving home.
Sociology
Dist - CORF **Prod** - WQED 1983

Smug Duds Suds - in 13 MIN
16mm
Color
Presents twin sisters, Patty the know - how gal and Susie, the goof - off as they swim, ski, bowl, motorcycle ride, go to school and play tennis. Includes tips on wardrobe selection and care and illustrates the differences between easy care and special care fabrics. Provides tips on using laundry aids and selection of procedures for automatic care.
Guidance and Counseling; Home Economics
Dist - MAY **Prod** - MAY

Smush the Fire Out 11 MIN
16mm
Color (P I)
LC 76-702948
Introduces the students of a second grade class, who demonstrate fire survival basics through games and activities.
Health and Safety
Dist - FILCOM **Prod** - FILCOM 1976

SNA - Critical Issues 35 MIN
U-matic / VHS
SNA Management Consideration Series
Color
Discusses the critical issues faced by managers in using the System Network Architecture (SNA) technology. Points out the pitfalls of the product and evaluates its suitability for its intended purpose.
Industrial and Technical Education
Dist - DELTAK **Prod** - DELTAK

SNA Implementation and Operation Considerations 35 MIN
VHS / U-matic
SNA Management Consideration Series
Color
Puts the entire issue of System Network Architecture (SNA) into management perspective. Explores planning and implementation issues, emphasizing the impact of the SNA decision on the people and the organization..
Business and Economics; Industrial and Technical Education
Dist - DELTAK **Prod** - DELTAK

Sna jolobil
VHS
Color (J H G) (SPANISH)
$44.95 purchase _ #MCV5043, #MCV5044
Presents a program on the culture of Mexico.
Geography - World
Dist - MADERA **Prod** - MADERA

SNA management consideration series
Components of SNA 35 MIN
SNA - Critical Issues 35 MIN
SNA Implementation and Operation Considerations 35 MIN
Dist - DELTAK

SNA Management Considerations Series
Principles of SNA 35 MIN
Dist - DELTAK

Snack Cakes 5 MIN
U-matic / VHS / 16mm
How It's made Series
Color (K)
Business and Economics
Dist - LUF **Prod** - HOLIA

The Snacking Mouse 5 MIN
U-matic / VHS
Color (K P)
Shows children what happens when a mouse becomes too fat to fit through his mouse hole as a result of consistently eating only sweet and salty snacks.
Health and Safety; Social Science
Dist - POAPLE **Prod** - POAPLE

Snacking Mouse Goes to School 6 MIN
VHS / U-matic
Color (K P)
Follows Snacking Mouse as he starts his first day of school. Shows the mouse beginning to snack excessively at the expense of regular meals.
Health and Safety; Social Science
Dist - POAPLE **Prod** - POAPLE

Snacks 3 MIN
Videoreel / VT2
Beatrice Trum Hunter's Natural Foods Series
Color
Shows how to make a snack mixture combining all sorts of dried fruits, nuts and seeds. Demonstrates a simple method for drying fruits at home.
Home Economics; Social Science
Dist - PBS **Prod** - WGBH

Snacks and Appetizers 28 MIN
VHS / 16mm
What's Cooking Series
Color (G)
$55.00 rental _ #WHAC - 103
Home Economics
Dist - PBS **Prod** - WHYY

Snacks Count Too 12 MIN
U-matic / VHS / 16mm
Your Diet Series
Color (I J H)
Examines the factors that lead to excess snacking and discusses the nutritive value of popular snack foods.
Health and Safety; Social Science
Dist - JOU **Prod** - JOU 1983

Snaffle Bit and Trail Horse 52 MIN
BETA / VHS
Color
Demonstrates how to calm, saddle and ride an inexperienced horse.
Physical Education and Recreation
Dist - EQVDL **Prod** - ARABSC

The Snail - 31 11 MIN
VHS / U-matic
Animal families series
Color (K P I)
$225.00, $195.00 purchase _ #V166
Follows the snail as it hunts for food up a bamboo shoot to a tasty leaf. Uses close - up footage to show a snail sliding across a glass tabletop and illustrate the combination of the rippling muscles and stretching movements which allow a snail to slide. Part of a series on animal families.
Science - Natural
Dist - BARR **Prod** - GREATT 1989

Snails and scorpions 15 MIN
VHS
Pond life - a place to live series
Color (I J H)
$119.00 purchase _ #CG - 850 - VS
Photographs a water scorpion as it stabs its prey and sucks out its juices. Part of a three - part series which looks at life in and around a typical pond in intimate detail.
Science - Natural
Dist - HRMC **Prod** - HRMC

Snails - Backyard Science 12 MIN
U-matic / VHS / 16mm
Color (P I)
LC 79-701024
Describes the physical characteristics, eating habits and behavior patterns of snails. Explains how they are helpful to man.
Science - Natural
Dist - PHENIX **Prod** - BEANMN 1979

Snake 22 MIN
16mm / U-matic / VHS
Animals, Animals, Animals Series
Color (P I)
Looks at the various habitats and means of locomotion of snakes as well as some medical research being done on using venom to cure disease. Uses stories and poems to tell about the snake and his lifestyle. Hosted by Hal Linden.
Science - Natural
Dist - MEDIAG **Prod** - ABCNEW 1977

Snake Hill to Spring Bank 0 MIN
U-matic
Teachers Teaching Writing Series
Color (T)
Demonstrates classroom techniques of several teachers who have been judged superior in their methods of teaching writing. Each of the six programs, which were taped in regular classes, features a single teacher conducting an actual writing process.
Education; English Language
Dist - AFSCD **Prod** - AFSCD 1986

Snake Hunt 10 MIN
16mm
Science Close - Up Series
Color (P I J)
LC FIA67-5012
Shows how staff members of the Lincoln Park Zoo on a 'SNAKE HUNT' in Central Florida, where they capture snakes in a variety of environments. Describes the equipment used by the hunters, the method of capture and the identification and transportation of snakes.
Geography - United States; Science; Science - Natural
Dist - SF **Prod** - PRISM 1967

Snake locomotion 12 MIN
VHS
Aspects of animal behavior series
Color (J H C G)
$99.00 purchase, $35.00 rental _ #37980
Shows in detail lateral undulation, sidewinding, concertina and rectilinear snake locmotion. Part of a series on animal behavior produced by Robert Dickson and Prof George Bartholomew for the Office of Instructional Development, UCLA.
Science - Natural
Dist - UCEMC

The Snake Prince 18 MIN
U-matic / VHS / 16mm
Color (P I)
LC 84-706037
Employs puppets to tell the story of a young prince who sets out to comb his kingdom for a young woman he can love.
Literature and Drama
Dist - WOMBAT **Prod** - KRATKY 1983

The Snake - Villain or Victim 24 MIN
16mm / U-matic / VHS
Wide World of Adventure Series
Color (I J)
LC 77-701013
Attempts to dispel, through the use of cartoons and scenes of snakes in various habitats, the myths and villainous reputation associated with serpents. Provides physiological information on snakes and demonstrates medicinal uses of their venom. Includes interviews with owners of snakes, who impart advice on the proper care, housing and handling of these animals.
Health and Safety; Science - Natural
Dist - EBEC **Prod** - AVATLI 1976

Snakebite - First Aid 11 MIN
U-matic / VHS / 16mm
Color
LC 73-712189
Discusses the characteristics, habitats and geographical distribution of various species of venomous snakes. Explains the first aid measures that should be taken when treating the victim of a snakebite.
Health and Safety; Science - Natural
Dist - PHENIX **Prod** - WLBPRO 1971

Snakebites and Other Emergencies 25 MIN
U-matic / VHS
Color
Shows two facets of emergency care investigated with on - the - scene filming at an urban emergency ward. Says one is an anti - venom program where patients bitten by poisonous reptiles or insects receive life - saving special care. Notes that the other is emergency medicine as a speciality that attracts young doctors, as two young physicians, a woman and a man, are followed during their tour of duty as residents in an emergency room.
Health and Safety; Science - Natural
Dist - MEDCOM **Prod** - MEDCOM

Snakes 15 MIN
U-matic / VHS / 16mm
Color (I J H)
Presents a wide - ranging survey of snakes focusing on habitats and structural and behavioral adaptations. Shows a representative sampling of the 2200 species from the highly venomous rattlesnakes, copperheads and water moccasins to the gentle and helpful corn and hognose snakes.
Science - Natural
Dist - CORF **Prod** - CORF 1984

Snakes 15 MIN
VHS
Color; PAL (H)
Surveys through representative sampling the 2200 species of snakes. Focuses on habitats and structural and behavioral adaptations to observe how snakes move and feed. Examines closely features such as scutes, tongue, teeth, fangs, jaws, pupils and heat - sensitive pits. Shows how a snake hears without external ears and smells with the aid of its tongue. Looks at venomous rattlesnakes, copperheads and water mocassins, as well as the gentle and helpful corn and hognose snakes.
Psychology; Science - Natural
Dist - VIEWTH

Snakes 3 MIN
16mm
Of all Things Series
Color (P I)
Discusses snakes.
Science - Natural
Dist - AVED **Prod** - BAILYL

Snakes 15 MIN
U-matic / VHS
Up Close and Natural Series
Color (P I)
$125.00 purchase
Provides insights into the anatomy and habitat of the snake.
Agriculture; Education; Science - Natural; Social Science
Dist - AITECH **Prod** - NHPTV 1986

Snakes 11 MIN
VHS
Animal profile series
Color (P I)
$59.95 purchase _ #RB8130
Studies snakes, the slithering reptiles which have inspired myth and misunderstanding. Shows how and why snakes shed their skins, how scales look and feel, and how snakes help control many animal and insect pests. Includes footage of a large Indian python. Part of a series on animals which looks at examples from the mammal, snake and bird classes filmed, in their natural habitat.
Science - Natural
Dist - REVID **Prod** - REVID 1990

Snakes 25 MIN
U-matic / VHS / 16mm
Untamed World Series
Color; Mono (J H C A)
$400.00 film, $250.00 video, $50.00 rental
Presents a detailed program on the evolutionary history, eating habits, and methods of defense of snakes.
Science - Natural
Dist - CTV **Prod** - CTV 1971

Snakes Alive 15 MIN
VHS / U-matic
Color (K P I J)
Focuses on many aspects of snakes.
Science - Natural
Dist - SUTHRB **Prod** - SUTHRB

Snakes and a donkey and worth fighting for - Volume 16 45 MIN
VHS
Superbook series
Color (K P I R)
$11.99 purchase _ #35 - 86777 - 979
Uses an animated format to tell the story of Chris and Joy and their time travels through Biblical places and events. 'Snakes and a Donkey' tells the story of Joshua, while 'Worth Fighting For' is an account of Caleb.
Literature and Drama; Religion and Philosophy
Dist - APH **Prod** - TYHP

Snakes and how they live 12 MIN
U-matic / BETA / 16mm / VHS
Color (P I J)
$295.00, $245.00 purchase, $50.00 rental _ #9985
Uses close - up photography to examine the physical characteristics of different species of snakes. Shows snakes moving on the ground and in water, shedding their skin, eating prey and hibernating. A variety of harmless and poisonous snakes is shown.
Science - Natural
Dist - AIMS **Prod** - CAHILL 1991

Snakes and How they Live 13 MIN
VHS
A Closer Look Series
Color
$69.95 purchase _ #1605
Depicted are characteristics of different species of snakes.
Science - Natural
Dist - AIMS **Prod** - AIMS

Snakes and How they Live 13 MIN
U-matic / VHS / 16mm
Color (I J) (SPANISH FRENCH)
LC 75-700185
Relates major pertinent concepts about snakes, using a great variety of types to show how they move, eat, shed skin, etc. An open - end approach stimulates class discussion.
Foreign Language; Science - Natural
Dist - AIMS **Prod** - CAHILL 1968

Snakes and Ladders 59 MIN
16mm / VHS
Color (G)
$275.00 purchase, $125.00, $90.00 rental
Creates a fictional detective who tours the history of women's education in Australia, which closely parallels women's experience in the United States. Interviews ten women aged sixteen to ninety - four, including Anne Summers, the editor of MS Magazine. Illustrates that women's education has been one step foreward and two steps back, like the children's game, Chutes and Ladders. Produced by Trish Fitzsimmons and Mitzi Goldman.
Education; Geography - World; History - World; Sociology
Dist - WMEN **Prod** - TRIMIG 1987

Snakes and the like 15 MIN
U-matic / VHS
Animals and such series; Module brown - types of vertebrates
Color (I J)
Investigates a variety of reptiles, including turtles, snakes, lizards and crocodiles.
Science - Natural
Dist - AITECH **Prod** - WHROTV 1972

Snakes are Interesting 11 MIN
16mm / U-matic / VHS
Color (I)
Includes sequences on how a snake travels without legs, how it sees and hears, how the poison mechanisms operate and how snakes reproduce.
Science - Natural
Dist - IFB **Prod** - DEU 1956

Snakes, Scorpions and Spiders 15 MIN
U-matic / VHS / 16mm
Animals and Plants of North America Series
Color (J)
LC 81-700953
Shows the snakes, scorpions and spiders of the shortgrass prairie, with special close - ups of the animals' and insects' unusual physical features.
Science - Natural
Dist - LCOA **Prod** - KARVF 1981

Snaketown 40 MIN
16mm
Color (C)
LC 73-702926
Shows archeological tools, techniques and methods of excavation used at the snaketown site, home of the prehistoric Hohokam Indians.
Science - Physical; Social Science
Dist - UCEMC **Prod** - TEIWES 1969

Snap Art 14 MIN
VHS / U-matic
Young at Art Series
Color (P I)
Discusses snap art.
Fine Arts
Dist - AITECH **Prod** - WSKJTV 1980

Snap Bean Pest Management 23 MIN
VHS
Color (C A)
$50.00 purchase, $20.00 rental
Details scouting techniques to identify molds, insect damage, root rot and weeks. Comprehensive information on commercial production of snap beans.
Agriculture
Dist - CORNRS **Prod** - CORNRS 1988

Snap Out of it 1 MIN
U-matic / VHS
Color
Shows Larry Hagman using as his pitch a rubber band which he suggests the smoker snap every time he desires a cigarette. Uses TV spot format. Also available in 10 - second version.
Health and Safety
Dist - AMCS **Prod** - AMCS 1982

Snapshots of the City 5 MIN
16mm
Color
Presents a black statement about the city in which two people represent the populace.
Fine Arts; Industrial and Technical Education; Sociology
Dist - VANBKS **Prod** - VANBKS 1961

Snare drum for beginners 50 MIN
VHS
Maestro instructional series
Color (J H C G)
$29.95 purchase _ #BSPD29V
Supplements class lessons and reinforces private lessons on the snare drum. Offers clear - cut examples and demonstrations on how to unpack and assemble the instrument, proper hand position and instrumental nomenclature. Discusses notes, breathing, posture, reading music and care and maintenance of the instrument. Includes booklet. Part of a ten - part series on musical instruments.
Fine Arts
Dist - CAMV

Snare drum rudiments 30 MIN
VHS
Color (J H C G)
$29.95 purchase _ #CPP01V
Encourages drum students to perfect their basic technique and apply it in creative and innovative ways. Offers a clear and complete guide to the rudiments, including the NARD rudiments and the more advanced set devised by the Percussive Arts Society. Demonstrates each rudiment category - rolls, diddles, flams and drags - slowly with on - screen graphics, then at medium and fast tempos. Covers 30 rudiments. Includes booklet with transcriptions of each rudiment.
Fine Arts
Dist - CAMV **Prod** - CAMV

The Snared Runner 28 MIN
U-matic / VHS
Color
Shows emergency care given to a young family man who suffers a cerebrovascular accident. Depicts loss of speech and right - side paralysis which leaves the man handicapped and in need of an integrated rehabilitation program. Portrays community resources working together throughout the patient's recovery and rehabilitation.
Health and Safety; Science - Natural
Dist - PRIMED **Prod** - PRIMED

Snatches 10 MIN
16mm
Color (J H)
Presents a study of the creative sterility existing in movie making under major studio conditions.
Fine Arts; Industrial and Technical Education
Dist - CFS **Prod** - CFS 1970

Sneakers 5 MIN
U-matic / VHS / 16mm
Color (J)
LC 81-700943
Uuses pixillation to present an amusing story about a worn - out pair of sneakers that are joined by pairs of moccasins, boots and sandals for a merry round of square dancing on the living room floor. Without narration.
Fine Arts
Dist - PHENIX **Prod** - JABA 1978

Sneakin' and peakin' 15 MIN
16mm
Color (G)
$25.00 rental
Travels to Indiana back roads to see and shoot the Miss Nude Universe Contest, held at a 'notorious' nudist colony. Encounters truckers and hundreds of Sunday photographers straining for a shot at the contestants. Also contains shots of the Mr Nude Trucker Contest.
Fine Arts; Geography - United States
Dist - CANCIN **Prod** - PALAZT 1976

The Sneetches 13 MIN
U-matic / VHS / 16mm
Dr Seuss on the Loose Series
Color
LC 74-700291
Points out that differences are only relative. Presents an animated cartoon about various kinds of sneetches, showing that beneath their different kinds of bellies they are really quite alike. Edited from the 1974 motion picture Dr Seuss On The Loose.
Guidance and Counseling; Literature and Drama
Dist - PHENIX **Prod** - CBSTV 1974

Sneezles, Wheezles and Measles 15 MIN
VHS / U-matic
All about You Series
Color (P)
Describes the nature of germs and the body's natural defenses against them.
Science - Natural
Dist - AITECH **Prod** - WGBHTV 1975

Sniff and Snuff Animated Television Spots, Set 1 3 MIN
16mm
Color
Presents the exploits of Sniff and Snuff who are in constant pursuit of those who cause fires. Includes A - Hunting They Will Go, Careless Teenagers and Thoughtless Farmer Brown.
Health and Safety
Dist - FILCOM **Prod** - FILCOM

Sniff and Snuff Animated Television Spots, Set 2 3 MIN
16mm
Color
Presents the exploits of Sniff and Snuff who are in constant pursuit of those who cause fires. Includes Find A Firebug, Make The Forest Kid - Proof and Meet The Most Dangerous Animal In The Forest.
Fine Arts; Health and Safety
Dist - FILCOM **Prod** - FILCOM

Sniff and Snuff on the Moon 5 MIN
16mm
Color
Features Super Fire - Safe Snoopers, Sniff and Snuff as astronauts on the moon. Tells how they wonder if the moon is like it is because of fire and how they conclude that people must prevent forest fires so the earth does not look like the moon.
Health and Safety
Dist - FILCOM **Prod** - PUBSF

Sniffles, Sneezes and Contagious Diseases 14 MIN
U-matic / VHS / 16mm
Healthwise Series
Color (K P I)
Presents the Healthwise puppets who learn how people defend themselves against germs. Uses animation to discuss the body's immune system and to illustrate how the inflammatory reaction helps fight germs that survive the immune system.
Health and Safety
Dist - CORF **Prod** - CORF 1982

Sniffy Escapes Poisoning 6 MIN
16mm / U-matic / VHS
Color (K P I)
LC 77-713353
Attempts to prevent accidental poisoning which continues to be a major hazard to the pre - school and primary grade - level child. Speaks directly to children of this age in language they can understand and enjoy as Sniffy and his young friend give an effective but non - frightening warning about the dangers behind the medicine - cabinet door.
Guidance and Counseling; Health and Safety
Dist - PEREN **Prod** - MARFLE 1967

The Sniper 9 MIN
16mm
B&W
LC 75-703233
Attempts to come to terms with the intimate irony of three characters caught in a war. An experimental film produced by students in the cinema division, University of Southern California.
Fine Arts; Psychology; Sociology
Dist - USC **Prod** - USC 1964

Snips and Shears 13 MIN
16mm
Metalwork - Hand Tools Series
Color (H C A)
Straight, combination, curved blade and aviation snips and foot squaring shears.
Industrial and Technical Education
Dist - SF **Prod** - MORLAT 1967

Snookie, the Adventures of a Black Bear Cub 11 MIN
U-matic / VHS / 16mm
Color (P I)
Tells of the adventures of a bear cub, without the usual slapstick comedy.
Literature and Drama; Science - Natural
Dist - IFB **Prod** - DEU 1948

Snoring 30 MIN
VHS
Doc Martin's casebook series
Color; PAL (G)
PdS40 purchase
Presents the case of Tom, a lifelong snorer, as he goes to a specialist who may be able to help him. Examines the causes and possible cures for snoring. Dr Martin Hughes narrates. Part one of an eight - part series.
Health and Safety
Dist - BBCENE

Snoring and obstructive sleep apnea 14 MIN
VHS
Color (PRO A)
$250.00 purchase _ #OT - 12
Clarifies the problems of snoring and obstructive sleep apnea for patients and their families. Explains symptoms, causes, evaluation, medical and surgical treatment options and risks. Uses state - of - the - art animation to depict the anatomy. For use in the practicing otolaryngologist's office and helpful to hospital patient educators or clinical staff.
Psychology
Dist - MIFE **Prod** - MIFE 1992

Snorkeling Skills and Rescue Techniques 13 MIN
U-matic
Lifesaving and Water Safety Series
Color
Demonstrates correct use of face mask, swim fins and snorkel. Illustrates how to select proper equipment and how to use it safely.
Health and Safety
Dist - AMRC **Prod** - AMRC

Snorkeling Skills and Rescue Techniques 16 MIN
16mm
Color
Demonstrates the uses and functions of the snorkel tube both in water recreation and safety.
Physical Education and Recreation
Dist - AMRC **Prod** - AMRC 1972

Snorkelling Skills and Rescue Techniques 13 MIN
16mm
Lifesaving and Water Safety Series
Color (I)
LC 76-701572
Tells how to select and use masks, fins and snorkels for underwater search and rescue operations. Emphasizes the importance of the buddy system.
Health and Safety
Dist - AMRC **Prod** - AMRC 1975

A Snort History 7 MIN
U-matic / VHS / 16mm
Color (H C A)
LC 72-701788
Uses live action and animation to show how alcohol can distort the preception of an individual to such a point that he is overly optimistic in driving situations.
Health and Safety; Psychology
Dist - AIMS **Prod** - CODHW 1972

Snow 30 MIN
U-matic
Today's Special Series
Color (K P)
Develops language arts skills in children. Programs are thematically designed around subjects of interest to youngsters. Action takes place in a department store where people, mannequins, puppets, comic characters and special guests present a light hearted approach to language arts.
Fine Arts; Literature and Drama; Psychology
Dist - TVOTAR **Prod** - TVOTAR 1985

Snow 6 MIN
16mm
Color
Looks at the clean - up of a big city after a major snowfall.
Fine Arts; Sociology
Dist - IFEX **Prod** - SOLEIL 1982

Snow 7 MIN
U-matic / VHS / 16mm
Color (P I J)
LC 75-712543
A visual poem showing the beauty of the snow when it begins to fall. As the snow grows heavier it becomes a menace which eventually turns into an avalanche.
Literature and Drama
Dist - AIMS **Prod** - MALONS 1975

Snow 10 MIN
U-matic / 16mm / VHS
Primary science series
Color (P I)
LC 91-705322
Explains how snowflakes are formed. Shows how people live, work and play in the snow. Includes two teacher's guides. Part of a series on primary science produced by Fred Ladd.
Physical Education and Recreation; Science; Science - Physical
Dist - BARR

Snow - 9 10 MIN
U-matic / 16mm / VHS
Primary science series
Color (K P I)
$265.00, $215.00, $185.00 purchase _ #B590
Shows how people live in the snow. Describes the difficulties of shoveling snow and keeping roads open. Illustrates the sports potential of snow. Explains the formation of snowflakes. Part of an 11 - part series on primary science.
Physical Education and Recreation; Science - Physical
Dist - BARR **Prod** - GREATT 1990

Snow - a First Film 9 MIN
16mm / U-matic / VHS
Color (P I)
LC 77-706586
Introduces the young student to a variety of observations about snow - - how a snowflake is formed and how it affects plant and animal life.
Science - Natural; Science - Physical
Dist - PHENIX **Prod** - NELLES 1969

Snow Country 144 MIN
VHS
Japan Film Collection from SVS Series
B&W (G) (JAPANESE (ENGLISH SUBTITLES))
$59.95 purchase _ #K0700
Presents a movie produced in Japan. Features Shiro Toyoda as director. Stars Ryo Ikebe, Keiko Kishi and Kaoru Yachigusa. Also called 'Yukiguni.'.
Fine Arts; Geography - World
Dist - CHTSUI **Prod** - SONY

Snow Damage 30 MIN
16mm
Color (JAPANESE)
A Japanese language film. Points out that snow, which covers 80 percent of all Japan in winter, causes great damage to railways, roads and power - transmission lines. Shows the experiments, the counterplan and the solution actually taken against snow damage, by using many new kinds of optical instruments from microscopes to aerial cameras.
Foreign Language; Geography - World; Industrial and Technical Education; Social Science
Dist - UNIJAP **Prod** - UNIJAP 1968

Snow Dogs 15 MIN
VHS / 16mm / U-matic
Color (I J H)
MP=$285.00
Depicts the life of a fur trapper in the cold northern region of Canada. Shows how the Husky snow dog thrives in the severe weather, and the special relationship between man and dog.
Physical Education and Recreation; Science - Natural
Dist - LANDMK **Prod** - LANDMK 1985

Snow Geese 25 MIN
U-matic / VHS / 16mm
Untamed Frontier Series
Color; Mono (J H C A)
$400.00 film, $250.00 video, $50.00 rental
Examines the mating habits, nesting preparations, and unique fasting abilities of the migrating snow geese in Northern Canada.
Geography - World; Science - Natural
Dist - CTV **Prod** - CTV 1975

Snow How 27 MIN
16mm
Color (J H C)
LC 75-709018
Combines fun and scenic beauty with a wilderness emergency. Tells of three people who undertake a three day snowmobile trek into the rugged 'ALPS OF OREGON.' Continues with an accident resulting in the loss of the equipment sled and serious personal injury. Presents snow country survival techniques.
Geography - United States; Health and Safety; Physical Education and Recreation; Social Science
Dist - LSTI **Prod** - LSTI 1969

Snow in the Winter and Flowers in the Spring 8 MIN
16mm
Crystal Tipps and Alistair Series
Color (K P)
LC 73-700453
Follows Crystal and her friends as they play in the snow during the winter and turn to gardening with the coming of spring.
Guidance and Counseling; Literature and Drama
Dist - VEDO **Prod** - BBCTV 1972

Snow job - the media hysteria of AIDS 8 MIN
VHS
Color & B&W (G)
$35.00 purchase
Deconstructs the representation of AIDS in the popular press where distortion and misrepresentation amount to a 'snow job' promoting homophobia, sexual discrimination, and repression of gays. Provokes an awareness and critical attitude in the viewer toward the one - dimensional spectacularizing of AIDS by the mainstream media.
Fine Arts; Health and Safety; Sociology
Dist - CANCIN **Prod** - BARHAM 1986

Snow leopards 13 MIN
VHS
Animal profile series
Color (P I)
$59.95 purchase _ #RB8124
Studies snow leopards, shy and mysterious cats found in the Himalayas and other high regions of Asia. Shows that they are tremendous leapers and climbers and includes footage of snow leopard cubs born at the Woodland Park Zoo in Seattle. Part of a series on animals which looks at examples from the mammal, snake and bird classes, filmed in their natural habitat.
Geography - World; Science - Natural
Dist - REVID **Prod** - REVID 1990

Snow Metamorphism 9 MIN
16mm / U-matic / VHS
Color
Uses time - lapse micrographs to illustrate snow compaction under load, equitemperature and temperature - gradient metamorphism, sintering, melt metamorphism and melt.
Science - Physical
Dist - UWASHP **Prod** - ILTS 1973

Snow Monkeys of Japan 8 MIN
U-matic / VHS / 16mm
Color (I)
LC 75-704398
Views a band of snow monkeys, an endangered animal species. Concentrates on the only snow monkeys in the world that have adapted to hot spring water.
Science - Natural
Dist - AIMS **Prod** - MCGHRY 1975

Snow motion 40 MIN
VHS
Color (G)
$14.95 purchase _ #S02090
Presents excerpts from the skiing movie 'Fire and Ice,' including numerous ski stunts and snow dancing. Features skiers John Eaves, Suzzy Chaffee, and others. Written and directed by Willy Bogner. Music by Harold Faltermeyer.
Physical Education and Recreation
Dist - UILL

Snow movies and Fourth of July 11 MIN
16mm
Color (G)
$39.00 rental
Features two productions. Shows winter landscape of upstate New York and in snowbound Cambridge, Mass, 1983. Fourth of July, 1988, meditates on the simple entreaties of the adolescent streets. Both films on one reel.
Fine Arts
Dist - CANCIN **Prod** - AVERYC

The Snow Queen 21 MIN
U-matic / VHS / 16mm
Color (P I)
LC 81-700078
Traces the adventures of a boy and a girl who grow up together, are separated by evil spirits, and are finally reunited. Based on the story The Snow Queen by Hans Christian Andersen.
Literature and Drama
Dist - PHENIX **Prod** - PHENIX 1981

Snow Queen, the, Pt 1 20 MIN
VHS
Gentle Giant Series
Color (H)
LC 90712920
Tells story of the snow queen. Teaches children universal truths. Stories taken from cultures throughout the world. Tenth of 16 installments in the series.
Health and Safety; Literature and Drama; Psychology
Dist - GPN

Snow Queen, the, Pt 2 20 MIN
VHS
Gentle Giant Series
Color (H)
LC 90712920
Tells the story of the Snow Queen, second of three parts. Features stories from cultures throughout the world. Teaches universal truths. Eleventh of 16 installments.
Health and Safety; Literature and Drama; Psychology
Dist - GPN

Snow Queen, the, Pt 3 20 MIN
VHS
Gentle Giant Series
Color (H)
LC 90712920
Tells story of the Snow Queen, final of three parts. Teaches children universal truths through stories from throughout the world. Twelfth of 16 installments in the series.
Health and Safety; Literature and Drama; Psychology
Dist - GPN

Snow - Show 7 MIN
16mm
Color
Reveals the heart of the symmetry of snow flakes through the center of the microscope's eye.
Fine Arts
Dist - VANBKS **Prod** - VANBKS

Snow Spryte at Olympics 10 MIN
16mm
Color
Shows 1201 Snow Spryte tracked vehicles working at grooming and repairing the ski trails for the 1968 Olympics at Grenoble, france.
Physical Education and Recreation
Dist - THIOKL **Prod** - THIOKL 1968

Snow Time for Comedy 10 MIN
16mm / U-matic / VHS
Meet Professor Balthazar
Color (K P I J H C)
Uses animation to show how Professor Balthazar helps his friends with solutions that are ostensibly magical but actually use the spiritual resources the friends already have.
Guidance and Counseling; Religion and Philosophy
Dist - IFB **Prod** - ZAGREB 1986

Snow what 9 MIN
16mm
B&W
LC 76-701368
Explores the shapes, textures and movement inherent in the fabrication of artificial snow under artificial light.
Fine Arts; Physical Education and Recreation; Science - Physical
Dist - RYERC **Prod** - RYERC 1975

Snow White 26 MIN
VHS / 16mm
Children's Classics Series
Color (P)
$195.00 purchase
Tells the classic tale of Snow White. Adapted by Stu Hample. Animated.
Fine Arts; Literature and Drama
Dist - LUF **Prod** - BROVID

Snow White - a lesson in cooperation 8 MIN
16mm / U-matic / VHS
Disney's animated classics - lessons in living series
Color (P I)
LC 78-701723
Tells how a young boy misses a birthday party because he procrastinates and doesn't cooperate at home. Shows how his friend Uncle Phil and a scene from the animated film Snow White And The Seven Dwarfs help him realize that cooperating with others can be a rewarding experience.
Fine Arts; Guidance and Counseling
Dist - CORF **Prod** - DISNEY 1978

Snow White and Rose Red 13 MIN
16mm
Lotte Reiniger's Animated Fairy Tales Series
B&W (K P I)
Presents the fairy tale Snow White And Rose Red in animated form based on live shadow plays produced by Lotte Reiniger for BBC Television.
Literature and Drama
Dist - MOMA **Prod** - PRIMP 1954

Snow White and the seven dwarfs 60 MIN
VHS
Faerie tale theatre series
Color; CC (K P I J)
$19.95 purchase _ #CBS6394
Stars Elizabeth McGovern and Vanessa Redgrave.
Literature and Drama
Dist - KNOWUN

Snow White and the Seven Dwarfs 11 MIN
U-matic / VHS / 16mm
Favorite Fairy Tales and Fables Series
Color (P)
$280, $195 purchase _ #4142
Tells the classic fairy tale of Snow White and the seven dwarfs, and the prince she marries.
Literature and Drama
Dist - CORF

Snow White and the Seven Dwarfs - a German Fairy Tale 11 MIN
16mm / U-matic / VHS
Favorite Fairy Tales and Fables Series
Color (K P)
Presents the German fairy tale Snow White And The Seven Dwarfs. Tells the story of Snow White who flees to the forest and finds refuge with the seven dwarfs when the wicked queen tries to have her killed.
Literature and Drama
Dist - CORF **Prod** - CORF 1980

Snow White and the Three Stooges 107 MIN
U-matic / VHS / 16mm
Color (I J H C)
Stars the Three Stooges and Carol Heiss in an unusual version of the classic fairy tale story of beautiful Snow White, the wicked queen and the handsome Prince Charming, plus a zany trio of awkward but well - meaning protectors.
Fine Arts
Dist - FI **Prod** - TWCF 1961

Snow White with Mr Magoo 52 MIN
16mm
Color (P I)
Fine Arts
Dist - FI **Prod** - FI

Snow White's Daughter 8 MIN
U-matic / VHS / 16mm
Color (J)
LC 81-701239
Uses an animated story about Snow White, Prince Charming and their little daughter to examine the needs and problems of all children. Celebrates UNICEF's International Year of the Child with an appeal to help alleviate the suffering of two - thirds of the world's children.
Civics and Political Systems; Literature and Drama; Sociology
Dist - PHENIX **Prod** - KRATKY 1981

Snowbabies - the innocent victims 24 MIN
VHS
Color (I J H T PRO)
$50.00 purchase _ #AH45650
Documents the devastating effects alcohol and drug use can have on newborns. Features recovering alcoholic and cocaine abuser Tammy Herman, who tells her story and offers ways to prevent this problem.
Guidance and Counseling; Health and Safety; Psychology
Dist - HTHED **Prod** - HTHED

Snowballs and sandcastles 8 MIN
VHS / 16mm
Look again series
Color (P I J)
$150.00, $195.00 purchase, $25.00 rental
Presents a film in the Look Again series, without dialogue. Builds upon and develops children's natural interest in their surroundings. Provides opportunities for students to examine their assumptions about winter and summer and discuss the effects that changing seasons have on everyday lives.
Psychology; Science - Natural
Dist - BULFRG **Prod** - NFBC 1990

Snowbirds 14 MIN
16mm
Color (G)
_ #106C 0177 538
Follows the acrobatics of the Canadian Forces Air Demonstration.
Civics and Political Systems; Physical Education and Recreation
Dist - CFLMDC **Prod** - NFBC 1977

Snowbound 50 MIN
U-matic / VHS / 16mm
Learning to be Human Series
Color (I J H C)
LC 77-702002
Features two teenagers who learn to understand themselves and each other when they are caught in a desolate area during a snowstorm.
Guidance and Counseling; Psychology; Sociology
Dist - LCOA **Prod** - LCOA 1978

Snowbound 33 MIN
16mm / U-matic / VHS
Color (I J H C)
LC 77-702002
A shortened version of the 1978 motion picture Snowbound. Features two teenagers who learn to understand themselves and each other when they are caught in a desolate area during a snowstorm.
Guidance and Counseling; Psychology; Sociology
Dist - LCOA **Prod** - LCOA 1978

Snowbound 32 MIN
U-matic / 16mm / VHS
Captioned; Color (J H A) (SPANISH)
Relates the story of a teenager who offers a lift to a plain, insecure girl who eventually helps both out of a blizzard. Full version.
Fine Arts; Psychology; Science - Physical; Sociology
Dist - LCOA **Prod** - LCOA 1978

The Snowboy 22 MIN
VHS / 16mm
Chinese Animations Series
Color (K)
Tells of a young boy and his mother who live alone in the winter forest and build a snowboy who comes to life. That night the house catches the fire and the snowboy rescues his playmate but melts in the heat. Directed by Lin Wenziao of the People's Republic of China.
Fine Arts; Geography - World; History - United States; Literature and Drama
Dist - LUF **Prod** - SAFS

Snowdonia - realm of ravens 50 MIN
VHS
Natural world series
Color; PAL (H C A)
PdS99 purchase
Records raven behavior in the wild. Reveals the natural habitat of ravens in Snowdonia.
Science - Natural
Dist - BBCENE

Snowdream 112 MIN
VHS / U-matic
Color (C PRO)
$395.00 purchase, $80.00 rental _ #C871 - VI - 019A,B
Dramatizes one man's childhood and adulthood to provide medical and psychology students with a comprehensive psychiatric case study. Stresses the power of myth, the importance of role modeling, the conception of death at different stages of emotional development and the influence of everyday life and how it shapes individual personality. Presented by Dr Donald C Fidler.
Health and Safety; Psychology
Dist - HSCIC

Snowdrift Wesson Oil 2 MIN
U-matic / VHS
Color
Shows a classic television commercial that uses only three words - 'John, Marcia and Snowdrift.'.
Business and Economics; Psychology; Sociology
Dist - BROOKC **Prod** - BROOKC

Snowfire 79 MIN
16mm
B&W (P I J)
Tells the story of Molly, a little girl who talks to horses and is convinced they talk to her.
Literature and Drama
Dist - CINEWO **Prod** - CINEWO 1958

Snowflakes 7 MIN
VHS / 16mm
Color (P I)
Shows snow as a source for fun activities, winter beauty and food for plants. Studies the physical structure of snowflakes through photomicroscopy. Explains snow as a treasure which God supplies to meet man's needs.

Psychology; Science - Physical; Social Science
Dist - MIS Prod - MIS 1956

The Snowman 35 MIN
VHS / 16mm
Children's Circle Video Series
Color (K)
$18.88 purchase _ #CCV019
Presents the children's story.
Literature and Drama
Dist - EDUCRT

The Snowman 7 MIN
U-matic / VHS
(K P I)
Shows a young boy dream that his snowman comes to life. Together they share the perils and joys of winter. Muted pastels, coupled with an exquisite orchestral score, make this non verbal Christmas tale an experience for all seasons.
Literature and Drama; Science - Physical
Dist - WWS Prod - WWS 1984

The Snowman 26 MIN
16mm / U-matic / VHS
Color
Tells the story of a young boy's dream of his snowman coming to life. Described in muted pastels, with an orchestral score.
Literature and Drama
Dist - WWS Prod - RH

Snowman and Eskimos 29 MIN
Videoreel / VT2
Children's Fair Series
B&W (K P)
Science; Social Science
Dist - PBS Prod - WMVSTV

Snowman's Dilemma 9 MIN
16mm / U-matic / VHS
Color (H C)
LC 79-704607
An animated film about a snowman whose tender feelings for a little girl are turned into icicles on her windowsill.
Literature and Drama
Dist - MGHT Prod - FILBUL 1969

Snowmobile Safety Savvy 15 MIN
16mm
Color
LC 74-702669
Combines live action and animation in order to dramatize the pleasures of snowmobiling and to point out dangers of not conforming to established safety rules.
Health and Safety; Physical Education and Recreation
Dist - DEERE Prod - DEERE 1974

Snowmobiling - Trail and Safari 14 MIN
16mm
Color
LC 74-703759
Outlines the necessary equipment and safety precautions for trail and safari snowmobiling.
Physical Education and Recreation
Dist - SF Prod - MORLAT 1973

Snows of Kilimanjaro 114 MIN
16mm
Color
LC FIA53-870
Shows a successful but disillusioned writer who though near death from the wounds received in Africa, reminisces about his amorous intrigues and experiences as a hunter.
Fine Arts; Literature and Drama
Dist - TWCF Prod - TWCF

Snowscreen - the Art of Michael Snow 50 MIN
16mm
Color (H A)
$1100.00 purchase, $105.00 rental
Features Canadian artist Michael Snow who works in the mediums of photography, painting, music and filmmaking.
Fine Arts
Dist - AFA

Snowshoeing 12 MIN
16mm
Color (J)
Explains that the ungainly looking snow shoes, invented by the Indians long ago can be loads of fun as well as providing for easy walking in deep snow. Demonstrates how to use them correctly.
Physical Education and Recreation; Social Science
Dist - SF Prod - SF 1968

Snowsound 1 MIN
16mm
B&W (G)
$15.00 rental
Sketches white hills and valleys with an occasional barn, fence and tree. Animates pencil drawings. Sound courtesy of an old - fashioned music box. Produced by R Raffaello Dvorak.
Fine Arts
Dist - CANCIN

Snowy '69 24 MIN
16mm
Color (J)
Presents a progress report on the Snowy Mountains hydro - electric scheme.
Geography - World; Industrial and Technical Education; Social Science
Dist - AUIS Prod - ANAIB 1971

Snowy, Chilly, Motley and Me 50 MIN
16mm / U-matic / VHS
Color (I J)
Presents John Paling's experiences with a German Shepherd dog, a Siamese cat and a stray cat, including scenes of the dog mating and delivering her first litter. Shows the interaction of the three pets and presents information on the unique behavior of dogs and cats.
Science - Natural
Dist - FI Prod - BBCTV

The Snowy Day 6 MIN
16mm / U-matic / VHS
Color (K P)
An animated version of the picture book by Ezra Jack Keats, using the original illustrations. Tale of a small boy's delight in a city snowfall.
English Language; Literature and Drama; Social Science
Dist - WWS Prod - WWS 1964

Snowy day - stories and poems - 80
VHS
Reading rainbow series
Color; CC (K P)
$39.95 purchase
Joins LeVar in a wintery wonderland, inspired by the book by Caroline Feller Bauer and illustrated by Margot Tomes. Travels to Jackson Hole, Wyoming, and experiences a variety of ways to beat winter's chills and enjoy all of its snowy thrills. Part of a series offering a multicultural approach to generating reading enthusiasm with cross - curricular applications, hosted by LeVar Burton.
English Language; Literature and Drama
Dist - GPN Prod - LNMDP

So be it Enacted 13 MIN
16mm
Color
Gives an account of the Danish parliamentary procedure. Shows an imaginary bill going through the various legislative processes.
Civics and Political Systems; History - World
Dist - AUDPLN Prod - RDCG

So Can You 15 MIN
16mm
Color (A)
Pictures workers from many different unions talking about why they organized and what the union means to them. Covers wages, working conditions, fringe benefits and job security.
Business and Economics; Sociology
Dist - AFLCIO

So Ein Zufall 15 MIN
U-matic / VHS / 16mm
Guten Tag Series
B&W (H) (GERMAN)
LC 75-707328
Presents an episode in which the characters employ frequently used expressions and idioms in order to teach conversational German to beginners. Stresses the correct use of the dative case, the pronouns welche and man, and the prepositions an, auf, in, neben and vor with the dative case.
Foreign Language
Dist - IFB Prod - FRGMFA 1970

So Etwas Muss Man Mit Gefuhl Machen 15 MIN
16mm / U-matic / VHS
Guten Tag Wie Geht's Series
Color (H C) (GERMAN)
Features Frau Schafer visiting the optical trade fair and becoming so entranced with the television coverage that fantasy runs away with her.
Foreign Language
Dist - IFB Prod - BAYER 1973

So Fair a Land 15 MIN
16mm
Color (J H)
LC 77-703238
Shows the U S foreign aid program operating in the Dominican Republic and how it affects the lives of the Dominican forest people.
Civics and Political Systems; Geography - World
Dist - USNAC Prod - USAID 1977

So Far Apart 19 MIN
16mm
Color (J)
LC 74-702169
Considers the problems of the runaway child. Helps stimulate thought and discussion about the forces within families which can cause children to run away.
Psychology; Sociology
Dist - SCREEI Prod - KBTV 1974

So Far from India 49 MIN
16mm
Color
Describes the tension which occurs in an East Indian family when the husband moves to New York seeking a better life while his wife stays behind in India, depending on her in - laws for sustenance.
Geography - World; Sociology
Dist - FLMLIB Prod - NAIRM 1982

So I Took it 10 MIN
U-matic / VHS / 16mm
Color
Shows how a girl named Sally gets caught in the snowballing nightmare of shoplifting due to peer pressure and how she eventually involves her own brother in the crime.
Sociology
Dist - CORF Prod - SRSPRD

So is this 45 MIN
16mm
B&W (G)
$60.00 rental
Reads as a text in which each shot is a single word, tightly - framed white letters against a black background. Creates a kind of moving concrete poetry.
Fine Arts; Literature and Drama
Dist - CANCIN Prod - SNOWM 1982

So Ist Das Leben 66 MIN
16mm
B&W ((GERMAN SUBTITLES))
A silent motion picture with German subtitles. Illustrates the life of a working class family in a Prague suburb. A significant film from the transitional period from silent to sound films.
Fine Arts; Foreign Language
Dist - WSTGLC Prod - WSTGLC 1929

So Kann Das Nicht Weitergehen 15 MIN
16mm / U-matic / VHS
Guten Tag Wie Geht's Series
Color (H C) (GERMAN)
Features Herr Hoffmann, a Studienrat in Eichstatt and his son Joachim, Frau Schafer, the owner of a small toy factory in Nuremberg, Gabi, a secretary at a balloon factory in Rheinberg and Gunther, the foreman for a construction firm in Hamburg, together with the staff of the Goethe Institute and the Bayerischer Rundfunk, in search of a final episode and each other in the forest.
Foreign Language
Dist - IFB Prod - BAYER 1973

So Kann Es Nicht Weitergehen 15 MIN
16mm / U-matic / VHS
Guten Tag Wie Geht's Series Part 26; Part 26
Color
Foreign Language
Dist - IFB Prod - BAYER 1973

So like you 22 MIN
VHS
Color (PRO IND A)
Discusses sexual harassment in the workplace.
Business and Economics; Psychology; Sociology
Dist - CORF Prod - CORF 1990

So Little Time 11 MIN
U-matic / VHS / 16mm
Color (J)
LC 75-700964
Presents a poetic treatise on the waterfowl of the Midwestern United States that makes a plea for their preservation.
Geography - United States; Science - Natural
Dist - AIMS Prod - LATHAM 1974

So Little Time 27 MIN
U-matic / VHS / 16mm
Insight Series
Color (H C A) (SPANISH)
Portrays a journalist in a civil war who knows he is about to die wishing that he could see his wife just one more time. Shows how God allows him to enter the dream she is having and apologize for his infidelity and selfishness. Stars William Devane.
Foreign Language; Guidance and Counseling; Psychology; Religion and Philosophy
Dist - PAULST Prod - PAULST

So Long Joey 63 MIN
16mm
Color (R)
Reveals the struggle of singer Dave Boyer whose heavy drinking led him to the brink of suicide. Details how the acceptance of Christ changed his life.
Guidance and Counseling; Religion and Philosophy; Sociology
Dist - GF **Prod** - GF

So Long Pal 22 MIN
U-matic / VHS / 16mm
Color (H C A) (SPANISH)
LC 75-700965
Uses fantasy and humor in order to break down the resistance to treatment of people arrested for drunken driving and to promote alcohol safety.
Health and Safety; Psychology
Dist - AIMS **Prod** - NHTSA 1974
LACFU
SUTHRB
IA

So many Children 39 MIN
U-matic / VHS
Color (G)
$249.00, $149.00 purchase _ #AD - 1793
Looks at parents of mentally handicapped children coming to terms with their children's disabilities. First of three parts which document twenty years in the lives of five handicapped people.
Education; Health and Safety; Psychology
Dist - FOTH **Prod** - FOTH

So many Lives, One Story 26 MIN
VHS / 16mm
Color (G) (SPANISH (ENGLISH SUBTITLES))
$225.00 purchase, $50.00 rental
Views a workshop organized by social workers for a community of poor and working class women living outside Santiago, Chile. Shares their realities of daily life, which include abusive relationships, children and welfare.
Geography - World; Sociology
Dist - WMEN **Prod** - TAGA 1984

So many miracles 58 MIN
VHS
Color (G)
$36.00 purchase
Tells the story of the Banya family who offered to hide Israel and Frania Rubinek in their one - room farm house for 28 months during 1942 in the Polish village of Pinczow, as the Germans deported Jews to the gas chambers. Interweaves docu - drama sequences with archival material as it follows the Rubineks on their emotional return journey to Poland to be reunited with Zofia Banya, the peasant woman who saved their lives over 40 years ago. Directed by Katherine Smalley and Vic Sarin.
Fine Arts; History - World; Religion and Philosophy
Dist - NCJEWF

So many Voices - a Look at Abortion in America 30 MIN
U-matic / VHS / 16mm
Color (H C A)
LC 82-700729
Examines both sides of the abortion issue through interviews with people personally affected by the legal right to an abortion. Notes that antiabortion legislation is being considered by the U S Congress and questions the various implications such legislation would have for American women. Hosted by Ed Asner and Tammy Grimes.
Health and Safety; Sociology
Dist - PHENIX **Prod** - NARAL 1982

So many Ways 10 MIN
16mm
Color (I)
Discusses bodily joints, how they work and what happens when they don't. Shows children with arthritis and demonstrates that they are capable of many things despite their illness.
Health and Safety; Science - Natural
Dist - ARTHF **Prod** - ARTHF

So near yet so far 100 MIN
VHS
Color (G) (CHINESE)
$45.00 purchase _ #1044C
Presents a film from the People's Republic of China.
Geography - World; Literature and Drama
Dist - CHTSUI

So Nearly Distant 30 MIN
16mm
Color (H C A)
Studies the institution of marriage, its meaning, the hazards involved and its benefits.
Guidance and Counseling; Sociology
Dist - FAMF **Prod** - FAMF

So Old the Pain 25 MIN
VHS / U-matic
Color
Presents Jane Wyman and host Mario Machado in the filmed program about arthritis, the nation's number one crippler. Shows arthritis victims telling how the disease has changed their lives, and scientists, surgeons and rheumatologists explaining treatment alternatives.
Health and Safety
Dist - MEDCOM **Prod** - MEDCOM

So Others Can Meet You
VHS / 35mm strip
$43.50 purchase _ #XY860 for film, $84.95 purchase _ #XY810 for VHS
Gives the purposes and proper uses of a resume. Presents an in - depth view of the four major sections of a resume.
Business and Economics; Guidance and Counseling
Dist - CAREER **Prod** - CAREER

So others can meet you
VHS
Career process series
Color (H A)
$84.95 purchase _ #ES1200V
Takes a detailed look at successful resumes. Explains what makes a resume effective and how to write good accompanying letters.
Psychology
Dist - CAMV

So Red Hot 12 MIN
16mm
Color
LC 82-700538
Uses four short musical numbers to highlight Parents' Magazine's marketing outlook, their target audience of mothers and their industry status.
Business and Economics
Dist - PARENT **Prod** - PARENT 1982

So sad, so sorry, so what 27 MIN
U-matic / VHS
B&W (G)
$265.00 purchase, $100.00, $50.00 rental _ #056
Reveals that women are the fastest growing group with AIDS in the nation. Looks at the correctional facilities of Massachussetts where a disproportionately high number of HIV infected individuals are women. Produced by Jane Gillooly.
Health and Safety; Sociology
Dist - FANPRO

So this is Love 60 MIN
16mm
B&W
Explains what happens when a male dress designer and a hard - as - nails boxer court the same girl. Directed by Frank Capra.
Fine Arts
Dist - KITPAR **Prod** - CPC 1928

So this is productivity 5 MIN
VHS / U-matic
Color (G)
$250.00 purchase, $125.00 rental
Presents a comic comparison between today's technology and the influential, productive people of fifty years ago. Features Laurel & Hardy and the Keystone Cops. Produced by NVC.
Business and Economics; Guidance and Counseling; Literature and Drama; Psychology
Dist - VLEARN

The So - to - Speak Telephone Boutique 3 MIN
16mm
Color
LC 75-701926
Presents a look at the future in telecommunications.
Social Science
Dist - NORTEL **Prod** - NORTEL 1974

So was Einstein - a Look at Dyslexic Children 29 MIN
VHS / 16mm
Color (G)
$100.00 purchase _ #EINSVHS
Focuses on four dyslexic eastern Kentucky children. Shows how their families and schools combined to help them overcome their learning disability.
Geography - United States; Health and Safety; Science - Natural; Sociology
Dist - APPAL

So we said goodbye 26 MIN
VHS
Color; B&W (G) (HEBREW & YIDDISH ENGLISH SUBTITLES)
$54.00 purchase
Watches as 65 - year - old Yackov who, while saying goodbye to his son and grandchildren leaving Israel, suddenly recalls a moment in his childhood when he said goodbye to his family in Poland in 1937. Looks at his realization that he did not know, and only much later realized, he would never see his mother, brother and sister again. Directed by Jorge Gurvich.
History - World; Religion and Philosophy; Sociology
Dist - NCJEWF

So what if it Rains 17 MIN
16mm
Color (A)
LC 80-700532
Interviews a retired couple, a couple not yet retired, an 80 - year - old widow and a 55 - year - old divorcee to address the topic of financial planning for retirement.
Business and Economics; Health and Safety; Sociology
Dist - FLMLIB **Prod** - ALTERC 1980

So What's it all about 40 MIN
16mm / U-matic / VHS
Silicon Factor Series
Color (C A)
Tells how the development of microelectronics made it possible to put circuits that once were multitudes of electron tubes and wires onto silicon chips the size of a fingernail. Shows how this technology works, what goes on inside a micro - computer, and what the possibilities are for the imitation or replacement of human functions.
Industrial and Technical Education; Mathematics
Dist - FI **Prod** - BBCTV 1981

So Who's Perfect 14 MIN
VHS / 16mm
(C PRO)
$135.00 rental
Shows how to give and receive criticism productively.
Education
Dist - VLEARN

So Who's Perfect - How to Give and Receive Criticism 14 MIN
U-matic / VHS / 16mm
Color
LC 83-701022
Explores some of the common mistakes people make when giving or receiving criticism. Offers a step - by - step method for giving and receiving it productively. Features Dr Hendrie Weisinger and Carrie Snodgrass. Based on the book Nobody's Perfect by Dr Weisinger.
Guidance and Counseling; Psychology
Dist - SALENG **Prod** - SALENG 1984

So You Live by Yourself 29 MIN
Videoreel / VT2
That's Life Series
Color
Guidance and Counseling; Psychology
Dist - PBS **Prod** - KOAPTV

So you think you're going to live for ever 35 MIN
VHS
Color (J H C G)
$89.95 purchase _ #VVS11690V
Tells a story of life and death on the highway presented by Lt Pete Collins of the Mississippi Highway Patrol.
Health and Safety
Dist - CAMV

So you wanna be a gambler series
Casino survival kit
Charting the tables
Horseracing - how to interpret daily racing form charts
How to handicap college football
How to handicap pro football
How to handicap the harness races
Win at baccarat
Win at blackjack - basic course
Win at blackjack - card counting
Win at craps - advanced I
Win at craps - advanced II
Win at craps - beginners
Win at draw poker
Win at Pai Gow - Chinese poker
Win at roulette - advanced
Win at roulette - basic
Win at 7 - card stud poker
Win at slots
Win at video poker
Dist - SIV

So You wanna do a video - a comprehensive, non - technical overview of the video production process 44 MIN
VHS
Color (G)
$495.00 purchase, $125.00 rental _ #629
Provides corporate communicators with the tools necessary to manage the process of video production. Helps to define the purpose and parameters of a project and to shape the preproduction, production and post production

decisions to meet corporate objectives. Includes a producer's workbook, a four - page preproduction worksheet and a video terminology guide.
Business and Economics; Industrial and Technical Education; Social Science
Dist - FIRLIT

So You Wanna' make a Film 9 MIN
U-matic / VHS / 16mm
Color (I J H C A)
$220, $160 purchase _ #80509
Uses animation to show the process of making a motion picture. Provides an overview of the filmmaking process from script through answer print.
Fine Arts
Dist - CORF **Prod** - WMUDIC 1980

So You Wanna make a Film 9 MIN
U-matic / VHS
Color (J H C A)
LC 80-706465
Presents the animated story of a brash businessman who wants a film on the history of aviation for a convention the following Thursday. Shows a filmmaker telling him why it's not possible to produce it so quickly.
Fine Arts
Dist - CORF **Prod** - WMUDIC 1980

So you want to be a doctor 116 MIN
VHS
Color; CC (J H C G)
$89.95 purchase _ #UW2999
Follows a small group of aspiring doctors through the intense rites of passage that make up medical training. Includes memorable points in student training - an anatomy lab where med students dissect a human corpse; the first physical examination of a patient; assisting a birth. Shows how the students experience frustration, exhaustion, exhilaration and, at times, uncertainty about their chosen profession.
Guidance and Counseling; Health and Safety
Dist - FOTH **Prod** - WGBH

So you want to be a manager 30 MIN
VHS
How do you manage series
Color (A)
PdS65 purchase
Shows how to cope with being a manager - managing a boss; how managers should perceive themselves and how others see them; recognizing management styles and how they can be improved; realizing what one is capable of and motivating oneself and others. Part of a six-part series featuring Dr John Nicholson, a business psychologist who specializes in helping people develop new attitudes and ways of thinking to improve both job performance and satisfaction.
Business and Economics; Psychology
Dist - BBCENE

So you want to be a parent; 2nd Edition 29 MIN
VHS
Practical parenting series
CC; Color (F A)
$99 purchase _ #213VL
Examines the process of child rearing from birth to age five. Looks at child care techniques, the modern family and financial issues. Dick Van Patten hosts the program, which features parenting expert Dr Bill Wagonseller. Comes with a leader's guide.
Home Economics; Sociology
Dist - UNL

So You Want to be a Star 15 MIN
VHS / U-matic
Movies, Movies Series
Color (J H)
Examines jobs in the motion picture industry.
Fine Arts; Guidance and Counseling; Industrial and Technical Education
Dist - CTI **Prod** - CTI

So You Want to be a Success at Selling - Pt 1 - the Preparation 26 MIN
VHS / U-matic
Color (A)
Illustrates, in a humorous vein, the work to be done and the techniques to be acquired before one can start to sell effectively.
Business and Economics; Psychology
Dist - XICOM **Prod** - XICOM

So You Want to be a Success at Selling - Pt 2 - the Presentation 25 MIN
VHS / U-matic
Color (A)
Shows how, using sound preparation as a foundation, to build an actual sale.
Business and Economics; Psychology
Dist - XICOM **Prod** - XICOM

So You Want to be a Success at Selling - Pt 3 - Difficult Customers 25 MIN
U-matic / VHS
Color (A)
Demonstrates how to make sales to three different types of difficult subjects - the domineering client, the super - busy decision - maker and the indecisive manager.
Business and Economics; Psychology
Dist - XICOM **Prod** - XICOM

So You Want to be a Success at Selling Series Pt I
The Preparation 25 MIN
Dist - VISUCP

So You Want to be a Success at Selling Series Pt II
The Presentation 26 MIN
Dist - VISUCP

So you want to be a success at selling - Part III - difficult customers 25 MIN
VHS
So you want to be a success at selling series
Color (A PRO)
$790.00 purchase, $220.00 rental
Stars John Cleese of 'Monty Python' fame in a discussion of dealing with difficult sales customers. Covers subjects including how to get rid of objections and 'smokescreens,' and using the customer's anxiety, laziness or vanity to the salesperson's advantage.
Business and Economics; Psychology
Dist - VLEARN **Prod** - VIDART

So you want to be a success at selling - Part IV - closing the sale 29 MIN
VHS
So you want to be a success at selling series
Color (A PRO)
$790.00 purchase, $220.00 rental
Stars John Cleese of 'Monty Python' fame in a discussion of closing the sale. Covers subjects including the importance of 'thinking big,' closing techniques, how to keep contact with customers who ultimately say no, and more.
Business and Economics; Psychology
Dist - VLEARN **Prod** - VIDART

So You Want to be a Success at Selling Series
Closing the Sale - Pt 4 29 MIN
Dist - VIDART

So you want to be a success at selling series
So you want to be a success at selling - Part III - difficult customers 25 MIN
So you want to be a success at selling - Part IV - closing the sale 29 MIN
Dist - VLEARN

So You Want to be President 120 MIN
VHS / BETA
Frontline Series
Color
Presents an inside view of what anyone who wants to run for President must do. Follows Colorado Senator Gary Hart's campaign for the 1984 Democratic Nomination and Presidency. Provides a unique look at how the election process works, from closed door strategy sessions to debates.
Civics and Political Systems
Dist - PBS **Prod** - DOCCON

So, You Want to Buy a Good used Car 15 MIN
16mm / U-matic / VHS
Color (J)
LC FIA67-1762
Outlines basic steps to follow in determining the condition of a used car. Suggests a memory aid for those elements of particular importance for safety.
Guidance and Counseling; Health and Safety; Home Economics; Industrial and Technical Education
Dist - FORDFL **Prod** - FMCMP 1966

So You Want to make a Buck? 145 MIN
U-matic
University of the Air Series
Color (J H C A)
$750.00 purchase, $250.00 rental
Looks at the concepts involved, the quality, costs and relevancy of information in the financial world that allows an individual to gain wealth. Program contains a series of five cassettes 29 minutes each.
Business and Economics
Dist - CTV **Prod** - CTV 1977

So You're Going to be a Parent
VHS
Practical Parenting Series
$89.95 purchase _ #014 - 144
Provides instruction in the basics of child care and child development from birth to age five.
Health and Safety; Psychology; Sociology
Dist - CAREER **Prod** - CAREER

So You're Going to be a Parent 30 MIN
VHS
(H C A)
$89.95 purchase _ #UL213V
Provides an overview of child rearing. Discusses the need for prenatal care and giving care and affection to the newborn and its development through age 5. Discussses the psychological impact of a newborn on parents.
Health and Safety; Home Economics; Sociology
Dist - CAMV **Prod** - CAMV

So you're going to be a parent 20 MIN
VHS
Color (J H G)
$97.00 purchase _ #05660 - 126
Touches on the need for parental care of and affection for the newborn. Decscribes the year - by - year development of the child through age five.
Health and Safety; Psychology; Sociology
Dist - GA **Prod** - UNL

So You're New Around Here - New Worker 13 MIN
16mm
B&W
Presents sound, understandable reasons for having a plant safety program.
Business and Economics; Health and Safety; Psychology
Dist - NSC **Prod** - NSC

So You've Got Diabetes
VHS / U-matic
Color (ARABIC SPANISH)
Explains the nature of diabetes, the method of control and the importance of exercise and diet as well as regular office visits. Stresses that you can live a full life despite being a diabetic.
Health and Safety; Social Science
Dist - MIFE **Prod** - MIFE

Soap 13 MIN
16mm / U-matic / VHS
Color
Outlines the history of soap. Shows how it is made and how it works.
Business and Economics
Dist - KAWVAL **Prod** - KAWVAL

Soap 30 MIN
U-matic
Today's Special Series
Color (K P)
Develops language arts skills in children. Programs are thematically designed around subjects of interest to youngsters. Action takes place in a department store where people, mannequins, puppets, comic characters and special guests present a light hearted approach to language arts.
Fine Arts; Literature and Drama; Psychology
Dist - TVOTAR **Prod** - TVOTAR 1985

Soap box 28 MIN
VHS
Elephant show series
Color (P I)
$95.00 purchase, $45.00 rental
Presents program 34 in the Sharon, Lois and Bram's Elephant Show series. Teaches reading readiness and social skills while engaging children in making music. Each program explores a new theme through adventure, fantasy, mystery and song with recording artists Sharon, Lois and Bram. Uses traditional materials which stress participation - action songs, sing - along songs, story songs, clapping songs, singing games, playground chants and folk songs from many different traditions. Includes teacher's guide co - authored by a music education specialist.
Fine Arts; Sociology
Dist - BULFRG **Prod** - CAMBFP 1991

The Soap Box Derby Scandal 24 MIN
16mm / U-matic / VHS
Color (P I J)
LC 75-701091
Tells the story of a boy's experience in the Soap Box Derby and his involvement with the scandal when the race was won with an illegally designed car. Raises questions about winning, losing and cheating.
Guidance and Counseling; Sociology
Dist - WWS **Prod** - CIHIB 1974

Soap Bubbles and the Forces that Mould Them 24 MIN
16mm
Color (J H C)
Actor Richard Montgomery dramatizes the 1911 Sir Charles V Boys lecture describing the phenomenon and nature of soap bubbles.
Science
Dist - RARIG **Prod** - RARIG 1967

Soap Operas 30 MIN
16mm / U-matic / VHS
Media Probes Series
Color (H C A)
LC 82-700488
Looks behind - the - scenes to see how the daytime soap opera All My Children is made. Shows how a dramatic scene evolves and examines the unique relationship which exists between 35 million soap - watchers and their favorite serials. Presents soap writer Pete Lemay talking about the rigors of writing for the form and expresses concern about the impact of the soap opera on American culture. Hosted by Ruth Warrick.
Fine Arts; Literature and Drama
Dist - TIMLIF **Prod** - LAYLEM 1982

Soap, Scents and the Hard, Hard Sell 16 MIN
U-matic / VHS / 16mm
Color (I J H A)
LC 75-704186
Demonstrates good personal hygiene habits. Presents a humorous analysis of television commercials to explain why expensive, highly advertised products are unnecessarily proper hygiene.
Business and Economics; Health and Safety; Home Economics
Dist - HIGGIN **Prod** - HIGGIN 1975

Soapbox With Tom Cottle Series
Abortion - yes, no, maybe 30 MIN
Adopted teens 30 MIN
Back from drugs 30 MIN
Boys' Locker Room 30 MIN
College pressures 30 MIN
Coming to America 30 MIN
Coping with death 30 MIN
A Couple of Beers 30 MIN
Daddy is 17 30 MIN
Disabled Teens 30 MIN
Gay Teens 30 MIN
Girls' locker room 30 MIN
Heavy Metal 30 MIN
High School 30 MIN
High School Dropouts 30 MIN
I Can't Cope 30 MIN
The In crowd 30 MIN
Let's Party 30 MIN
Parents and Teenagers 30 MIN
Pay Day 30 MIN
The Rights of Teenagers 30 MIN
S - E - X 30 MIN
A shadow of herself 30 MIN
The Sky's the Limit 30 MIN
Sunday Morning 30 MIN
Teen Genius 30 MIN
Teen Mom 30 MIN
Teenage Depression 30 MIN
Teenage Drinking and Drug Use 30 MIN
Teenage pregnancy 30 MIN
Teenage Relationships 30 MIN
Teenage Sexuality 30 MIN
Teenagers and Abortion 30 MIN
Teenagers and Body Image 30 MIN
Teenagers and Divorce 30 MIN
Teenagers and Music 30 MIN
Teenagers and Racism 30 MIN
Teenagers and Religion 30 MIN
Teenagers and Sex Roles 30 MIN
Teenagers and the Nuclear Arms Race 30 MIN
Teenagers in Jail 30 MIN
When Families Divorce - Part I 30 MIN
When Families Divorce - Part II 30 MIN
When Friends Die 30 MIN
When I Grow Up 30 MIN
Why Suicide 30 MIN
Working Teens 30 MIN
You're not Listening 30 MIN
Dist - PBS

The SOAS talk 78 MIN
VHS / BETA
Color; PAL (G)
PdS22.50 purchase
Records the Dalai Lama speaking at the School of Oriental and African Studies in London about Tibetan cultural heritage and the relevance of Buddhism to democracy.
Civics and Political Systems; Fine Arts; Religion and Philosophy
Dist - MERIDT

Sober graduation ... make it to your future 18 MIN
VHS
Color (J H G)
$99.00 purchase
Discusses the consequences of drinking and driving and the effects on the victims and their families and friends. Looks at positive peer pressure which results in positive alternatives to drinking and driving. Challenges young people to 'make it to their future.' Made in cooperation with the California Highway Patrol.
Guidance and Counseling; Health and Safety; Psychology; Sociology
Dist - FMSP **Prod** - FMSP

Soc Sci 127 21 MIN
VHS
B&W; Color (G)
$45.00 rental, $59.00 purchase
Documents the late Bill Sanders, an eccentric hard - drinking tattoo artist, working and rambling on about topics such as Vietnam and lesbians, in his 'painless' tattoo shop. Consists of the only known reproductions of Sanders' photographs of tatooed women. Recommended for photography students. A Danny Lyon production.
Fine Arts; Industrial and Technical Education
Dist - CANCIN

Soccer 25 MIN
U-matic / VHS
Color
Witnesses this exciting sport in North America featuring Pele.
Physical Education and Recreation
Dist - KAROL **Prod** - KAROL

Soccer 5 MIN
16mm / VHS
Sport Lego Series
Color (K)
$220.00, $165.00 purchase
Uses animation with Lego toys to introduce the sport of soccer. Uses music but no narration.
Fine Arts; Physical Education and Recreation
Dist - FLMWST

Soccer Clinics U S a 60 MIN
BETA / VHS
Color (A)
Deals with ball handling and scoring. Teaches techniques needed to advance to higher levels of play. Features Clive Charles and Brian Gant, internationally recognized soccer players.
Physical Education and Recreation
Dist - RMIBHF **Prod** - RMIBHF

Soccer Exercises and Tactics for Everyone 20 MIN
16mm / U-matic / VHS
Color (I J H C) (ARABIC)
LC 77-702329
Presents game - like situations in a series of soccer exercises and drills designed to improve player readiness and ball control. Includes strength - and endurance - building exercises which also increase ball control.
Foreign Language; Physical Education and Recreation
Dist - AIMS **Prod** - ASSOCF 1976

Soccer for everyone 45 MIN
VHS
Color (J H A)
$19.95 purchase _ #CON510V
Instructs in the basics of soccer. Covers the rules of the game, fundamental skills, strength and endurance exercises, and more.
Physical Education and Recreation
Dist - CAMV

Soccer Fundamentals for Everyone 12 MIN
U-matic / VHS / 16mm
Captioned; Color (J H C)
LC 78-700634
Explains the basics of soccer from the dimensions of the playing field to the techniques of ball control. Demonstrates various types of kicks, trapping, passing and heading. Shows practice techniques and drills for ball control.
Physical Education and Recreation
Dist - AIMS **Prod** - ASSOCF 1976

Soccer fundamentals with Wiel Coerver - Part One 62 MIN
VHS
Soccer fundamentals with Wiel Coerver series
Color (H C G)
$34.95 purchase _ #TVSTAOV
Introduces the game of soccer. Discusses basic techniques, suppleness, fast footwork and feinting. Part one of a three - part series on soccer featuring Wiel Coerver.
Physical Education and Recreation
Dist - CAMV

Soccer fundamentals with Wiel Coerver - Part Three 48 MIN
VHS
Soccer fundamentals with Wiel Coerver series
Color (H C G)
$34.95 purchase _ #TVSTEOV
Discusses using one's head in playing soccer, shooting, group games and goal scoring. Part three of a three - part series on soccer featuring Wiel Coerver.
Physical Education and Recreation
Dist - CAMV

Soccer fundamentals with Wiel Coerver - Part Two 49 MIN
VHS
Soccer fundamentals with Wiel Coerver series
Color (H C G)
$34.95 purchase _ #TVSTCOV
Shows how to beat an opponent in soccer. Discusses sliding tackles, group games and kicking techniques. Part two of a three - part series on soccer featuring Wiel Coerver.
Physical Education and Recreation
Dist - CAMV

Soccer fundamentals with Wiel Coerver series
Presents a three - part series on soccer featuring Wiel Coerver.
Soccer fundamentals with Wiel Coerver - Part One 62 MIN
Soccer fundamentals with Wiel Coerver - Part Three 48 MIN
Soccer fundamentals with Wiel Coerver - Part Two 49 MIN
Dist - CAMV

Soccer - Goalkeeping 20 MIN
U-matic / VHS / 16mm
Soccer Series
Color (J)
LC 76-701214
Shows positioning and catching, diving, punching, tipping, clearing, throwing and conditioning drills.
Physical Education and Recreation
Dist - ATHI **Prod** - ATHI 1976

Soccer - Hands Off 16 MIN
U-matic / VHS / 16mm
Color (I J H)
LC 75-703884
Introduces the game play of soccer and shows the basic moves of the game, including traps, dribbles, the instep drive, passing the ball with legs and head and techniques of goal - keeping.
Physical Education and Recreation
Dist - PHENIX **Prod** - PHENIX 1975

Soccer heroes 111 MIN
VHS
Color (G) (CHINESE WITH ENGLISH SUBTITLES)
$45.00 purchase _ #6066C
Presents a film from the People's Republic of China.
Geography - World; Literature and Drama
Dist - CHTSUI

Soccer - Individual Skills 20 MIN
U-matic / VHS / 16mm
Soccer Series
Color (J)
LC 76-701211
Shows the basic kicks, trapping, heading and juggling.
Physical Education and Recreation
Dist - ATHI **Prod** - ATHI 1976

Soccer injuries - a video guide to prevention and treatment 55 MIN
VHS
Color (J H A)
$49.95 purchase _ #SLS008V
Presents a step - by - step guide to preventing and treating soccer - related injuries. Covers preventive measures such as good nutrition and proper warm - up exercises, as well as treatment issues such as how to approach an injured player or how to differentiate between minor and serious injuries. Hosted by Don Taylor, physiotherapist to the Southampton Football Club.
Health and Safety; Physical Education and Recreation
Dist - CAMV

Soccer is Fun Part I
VHS / U-matic
$29.95 purchase
Physical Education and Recreation
Dist - BEEKMN **Prod** - BEEKMN 1988

Soccer - Let's Play 10 MIN
16mm
Color (I J H)
LC FIA65-1550
Demonstrates basic skills of soccer and suggests some class drills to develop skills. Shows plays and fouls that might be encountered in playing the game.
Physical Education and Recreation
Dist - SLFP **Prod** - SLFP 1964

Soccer refereeing series - Tape 1
VHS
Soccer refereeing series
Color (H C A)
$49.95 purchase _ #SLS009V
Presents basic training in soccer refereeing skills. Focuses on 'fair' and 'unfair' challenges, examining the fairness of common physical contact situations and helps referees recognize them. Reveals how to manage set play situations such as free kicks, penalty kicks, and corner kicks.

Physical Education and Recreation
Dist - CAMV

Soccer refereeing series - Tape 2
VHS
Soccer refereeing series
Color (H C A)
$49.95 purchase _ #SLS010V
Presents basic training in soccer refereeing skills. Focuses on unsportsmanlike behavior, explaining the various offenses that can lead to cautions and ejections and how to handle players in those situations. Looks at referee positioning and referee movement on the field.
Physical Education and Recreation
Dist - CAMV

Soccer refereeing series
Soccer refereeing series - Tape 1
Soccer refereeing series - Tape 2
Dist - CAMV

Soccer Rules 14 MIN
U-matic / VHS / 16mm
Color (I J H)
LC 81-700721
Explains basic soccer rules. Demonstrates how to mark and measure the field and discusses systems of play, fouls and penalties.
Physical Education and Recreation
Dist - AIMS **Prod** - AIMS 1979

Soccer Scene Germany Gelsenkirch 28 MIN
16mm
Color (H C A)
Deals with the soccer clubs of Germany and the cities that sponsor them. Includes inside views of soccer and the cities that form the major conference of German Soccer.
History - World; Physical Education and Recreation
Dist - WSTGLC **Prod** - WSTGLC

Soccer series
VHS
N C A A instructional video series
Color (H C A)
$64.95 purchase _ #KAR1404V
Presents a three - part series on soccer skills. Covers the subjects of juggling, dribbling, passing, shooting, and goal keeping.
Physical Education and Recreation
Dist - CAMV **Prod** - NCAAF

Soccer Series
Soccer - Goalkeeping 20 MIN
Soccer - Individual Skills 20 MIN
Dist - ATHI

Soccer U S A 25 MIN
16mm / U-matic / VHS
Color (I)
LC 81-700003
Documents the history of soccer from its origins on muddy fields with poor equipment to its worldwide popularity which has produced local, national and international rivalries.
Physical Education and Recreation
Dist - LCOA **Prod** - SOCCER 1981

Soccer, USA 45 MIN
16mm
Color
Presents an American view of soccer, the fastest - growing spectator and participant sport in the United States. Shows how deeply and rapidly the sport has become a part of the American mainstream.
Physical Education and Recreation
Dist - SOCCER **Prod** - SOCCER 1980

Soccer with the Superstars 30 MIN
VHS
(J H C)
$29.95 _ #SIM6105V
Presents famous soccer stars who explain professional soccer skills.
Physical Education and Recreation
Dist - CAMV

Social action and the compassionate heart 56 MIN
VHS
How then shall we live series
Color (H C A)
$49.95 purchase
Features Ram Dass in a discussion of the importance of developing a personal sense of compassion and then applying it to political decision - making.
Sociology
Dist - PBS **Prod** - WNETTV

Social adjustment for the aphasic 26 MIN
U-matic / VHS
Aphasia series
Color (PRO)
Discusses methods of reorienting the aphasic socially. Demonstrates restraining techniques through group therapy sessions.
Health and Safety; Psychology
Dist - WFP **Prod** - WFP

Social Adjustment for the Aphasic Patient 26 MIN
16mm
Aphasis Series; 3
Color
LC FIE53-105
Emphasizes the problems of social reorientation for the aphasic patient and explains the use and importance of group therapy and of corrective physical therapy for the retraining of the language function.
English Language; Health and Safety; Psychology
Dist - USNAC **Prod** - USVA 1950

Social and Cultural Foundations 30 MIN
VHS
Infusing Gerontological Counseling into Counselor Preparation Series
Color (A PRO)
$65.00 purchase _ #77658
Shares observations and information from the perspective of gerontological experts as well as from older persons.
Education; Guidance and Counseling; Health and Safety
Dist - AACD **Prod** - AACD 1988

Social Animal Series
Authority and man 29 MIN
Becoming Human 29 MIN
Behavior and its Consequences 29 MIN
Bureaucracy 29 MIN
Cultural Threat 29 MIN
Education and man 29 MIN
Ideology and Ecology 29 MIN
Public Man and Private Man 29 MIN
Social Position 29 MIN
Dist - UMITV

The Social Animal - Social Psychology 29 MIN
16mm / U-matic / VHS
Focus on Behavior Series
B&W (H C A)
Investigates some of the ways in which man is influenced and changed by society. Studies group pressures to conform and shows the consequences of publicly stating ideas contrary to one's private belief.
History - United States; Psychology; Religion and Philosophy; Sociology
Dist - IU **Prod** - NET 1963

Social Attitudes toward People with Disabilities 27 MIN
VHS / U-matic
B&W
Presents a lecture about prejudice and negative attitudes toward physically disabled people.
Health and Safety
Dist - BUSARG **Prod** - BUSARG

Social behavior in chickens
VHS
BSCS Classic Inquiries Series
Color (H C)
$59.95 purchase _ #193 W 2205
Poses questions, raises problems and presents experimental data on social behavior in chickens. Part of a series on the life sciences.
Psychology; Science - Natural
Dist - WARDS **Prod** - WARDS

Social Behavior of Rhesus Monkeys 26 MIN
16mm
B&W (C T)
Shows large numbers of rhesus monkeys living in a semi - natural environment. Emphasizes the social interaction of individuals and organized groups. Shows various kinds of behavior - - reproductive, maternal, dominance, fighting, homosexual, play and general.
Psychology; Science - Natural
Dist - PSUPCR **Prod** - PSUPCR 1947

Social Behavior of the Norwegian Lemming, Lemmus, Lemmus in Captivity 9 MIN
16mm
Color (C)
Illustrates the agonistic and sexual behavior of wild Norwegian lemmings in cages. Includes male - male, male - female and male - young fighting, male - female sexual behavior, male - male homosexual behavior and defense against threat by human beings.
Psychology; Science - Natural
Dist - PSUPCR **Prod** - PSUPCR 1967

Social Belief and Alcohol 30 MIN
VHS / U-matic
Fundamentals of Alcohol Problems Series
Color (H C A)
Psychology; Sociology
Dist - GPN **Prod** - UMINN 1978

The Social Cat 25 MIN
16mm / U-matic / VHS
Behavior and Survival Series
Color (I J A)
LC 73-700429
Deals with behavioral relationships between predator and prey, using the lion as an example. Shows how the social structure in a group of lions operates.
Science - Natural
Dist - MGHT **Prod** - MGHT 1973

Social change 30 MIN
VHS
Color (H C)
$89.95 purchase _ #TSI - 126
Shows the inevitability of social change. Presents social change as a historical process as well as an ongoing process affecting individual lives now and in the future, examining social changes occurring on different levels of social organization.
Sociology
Dist - INSTRU

Social Change 30 MIN
U-matic / VHS
Focus on Society Series
Color (C)
Identifies major social changes in the United States and evaluates their consequences.
Sociology
Dist - DALCCD **Prod** - DALCCD

Social choice - III 150 MIN
VHS / U-matic
For all practical purposes - introduction to contemporary 'mathematics series
Color (G)
$130.00, $85.00 purchase
Presents a five - part module on social choice. Includes an overview and the titles 'The Impossible Dream,' 'More Equal Than Others,' 'Zero Sum Games' and 'Prisoner's Dilemma.' Demonstrates how mathematics analyzes decisions and makes them quantifiable in areas as diverse as game theory and social choices. Part of a series on contemporary mathematics produced by the Consortium for Mathematics and Its Applications - COMAP. On three videocassettes. Hosted by Professor Solomon Garfunkel.
Mathematics; Psychology
Dist - ANNCPB

Social choice module - more equal than others - zero sum games - Parts 13 and 14 60 MIN
VHS / U-matic
For all practical purposes - introduction to contemporary 'mathematics series
Color (G)
$45.00, $29.95 purchase
Shows the roles of mathematics and statistics in the issues of weighted voting and winning coalitions in Part 13. Looks at game theory strategies for resolving disputes, mathematical solutions provided by zero sum games and game matrices for real - world problems in Part 14. Parts of a five - part Social Choice module and a 26 - part series on contemporary mathematics. Produced by the Consortium for Mathematics and Its Applications - COMAP. Hosted by Professor Solomon Garfunkel.
Mathematics; Psychology
Dist - ANNCPB

Social choice module - overview - the impossible dream - Parts 11 and 12 60 MIN
U-matic / VHS
For all practical purposes - introduction to contemporary 'mathematics series
Color (G)
$45.00, $29.95 purchase
Overviews the Social Choice module and shows how mathematics analyzes social decisions and makes them quantifiable in areas as diverse as game theory and social choices in Part 11. Discusses five different voting methods and demonstrates that not all voting methods are fair in Part 12. Parts of a five - part Social Choice module and a 26 - part series on contemporary mathematics. Produced by the Consortium for Mathematics and Its Applications - COMAP. Hosted by Professor Solomon Garfunkel.
Mathematics; Psychology
Dist - ANNCPB

Social choice module - prisoner's dilemma - Part 15 and on size and shape module - overview - Part 16 60 MIN
VHS / U-matic
For all practical purposes - introduction to contemporary 'mathematics series
Color (G)

$45.00, $29.95 purchase
Uses the games of 'chicken' and 'prisoner's dilemma' to illustrate issues in corporate takeovers and labor relations. Concludes the Social Choice module in Part 15. Overviews the On Size and Shape module. Draws upon geometric applications - da Vinci's 'window' - to record proper linear perspective in art to symmetry - based classification systems in archaelogy in Part 16. Parts of a 26 - part series on contemporary mathematics produced by the Consortium for Mathematics and Its Applications - COMAP. Hosted by Professor Solomon Garfunkel.
Mathematics; Psychology
Dist - ANNCPB

Social class 30 MIN
VHS
Color (H C)
$89.95 purchase _ #TSI - 114
Explores the concept of social class in the United States by focusing on two teenage girls from different classes. Shows how social class is reflected in their lifestyles and how they look at the world. Shows their life chances, asking the question if social stratification in the US is inherently discriminatory.
Sociology
Dist - INSTRU

Social class issues in the USA 60 MIN
VHS
Dealing with diversity series
Color (H C G)
$99.00 purchase _ #GSU - 115
Presents demographic data illustrating family income by ethnic group. Discusses the increase of people below the poverty level. Focuses on the plight of the homeless. Features Mike Meehan, Center for Creative Non - Violence, and Janice Grady, National Coalition for the Homeless. Part of a 23 - part series hosted by Dr J Q Adams, Western Illinois University, which helps students to develop the awareness that society is strengthened by a free and unfettered expression of individuality in all its diverse manifestations.
Social Science; Sociology
Dist - INSTRU

The Social Classes, 1900 - a World to Win 52 MIN
VHS / 16mm
Europe, the Mighty Continent Series; No 3
Color
LC 77-701558
Examines the forces of unrest which disrupted European stability at the beginning of the 20th century, including colonial nationalism, industrialization, socialism, trade unionism and reform movements. Analyzes the causes and effects of the 1905 revolution in Russia.
History - World
Dist - TIMLIF **Prod** - BBCTV 1976

The Social Classes, 1900 - a World to Win, Pt 1 26 MIN
U-matic
Europe, the Mighty Continent Series; No 3
Color
Examines the forces of unrest which disrupted European stability at the beginning of the 20th Century, including colonial nationalism, industrialization, socialism, trade unionism and reform movements. Analyzes the causes and effects of the 1905 revolution in Russia.
History - World
Dist - TIMLIF **Prod** - BBCTV 1976

The Social Classes, 1900 - a World to Win, Pt 2 26 MIN
U-matic
Europe, the Mighty Continent Series; No 3
Color
Examines the forces of unrest which disrupted European stability at the beginning of the 20th Century, including colonial nationalism, industrialization, socialism, trade unionism and reform movements. Analyzes the causes and effects of the 1905 revolution in Russia.
History - World
Dist - TIMLIF **Prod** - BBCTV 1976

Social Cognition - How and what the Infant Learns about Others, Pt 1
U-matic / VHS
Human Development - a New Look at the Infant Series
Color
Education; Psychology
Dist - CONMED **Prod** - CONMED

Social Cognition - How and what the Infant Learns about Others, Pt 2
VHS / U-matic
Human Development - a New Look at the Infant Series
Color
Education; Psychology
Dist - CONMED **Prod** - CONMED

Social control 30 MIN
VHS
Color (H C)
$89.95 purchase _ #TSI - 111
Examines social control in a general sense. Explores the limitations and dysfunctions of prisons as institutions of social control and socialization, presenting alternatives to prisons.
Sociology
Dist - INSTRU

Social Control 30 MIN
U-matic
Faces of Culture - Studies in Cultural Anthropology Series Lesson 18; Lesson 18
Color (C A)
Studies many forms of controls found in various societies. Shows forms of conflict resolution such as the 'trial by ordeal' method used by the Kpelle of Liberia.
Sociology
Dist - CDTEL **Prod** - COAST

Social dance aerobics 100 MIN
VHS
Step into fitness - sodanceabit series
Color (G A)
$39.95 purchase
Features dance instructors Phil Martin and Betty Griffith Railey, who teach social dances to encourage dancing for fitness. Includes step - by - step instruction, slow motion and close - up patterns, and dance - along sessions.
Physical Education and Recreation
Dist - PBS **Prod** - WNETTV
CAMV

Social dance aerobics encore workout 54 MIN
VHS
Step into fitness - sodanceabit series
Color (G A)
Features dance instructors Phil Martin and Betty Griffith Railey, who teach social dances to encourage dancing for fitness. Includes step - by - step instruction, slow motion and close - up patterns, and dance - along sessions.
Physical Education and Recreation
Dist - PBS **Prod** - WNETTV
CAMV

Social Dances of the American Indian, Square Dancing and the ' Swing' Era 30 MIN
VHS / U-matic
Social Dancing is not Just for Fun Series
Color
Fine Arts
Dist - ARCVID **Prod** - ARCVID

Social dancing is not just for fun series

Ballroom dance as an art form	30 MIN
Dancing at the Cotton Club and the Savoy	30 MIN
Demonstration and discussion of social dance in the Baroque era	30 MIN
Social Dances of the American Indian , Square Dancing and the ' Swing' Era	30 MIN

Dist - ARCVID

Social Development 30 MIN
VHS / U-matic
Learning through Play Series
Color (H C A)
Discusses social development. Presents seven illustrations, including solitary play, sibling play, parallel play and informal team play.
Psychology
Dist - UTORMC **Prod** - UTORMC 1980

Social development 30 MIN
VHS
Beginnings - handicapped children birth to age 5 series
Color (G)
$75.00 purchase _ #BHCH - 108
Emphasizes the importance of parents, friends and relatives in social and emotional development for handicapped children. Features Dr Doris Welcher. Part of a series on child development focusing on handicapped children.
Health and Safety; Psychology; Sociology
Dist - PBS **Prod** - MDDE 1985

Social Development - I Am Me and this is My World 30 MIN
U-matic
Dimensions of Child Development Series
Color (PRO)
Describes the continuum of the social development process in young children and identifies how they learn social skills.
Education
Dist - ACCESS **Prod** - ACCESS 1983

Social Development of the Infant 29 MIN
VHS / U-matic
Tomorrow's Families Series
Color (H C A)
LC 81-706917
Tells how a growing child learns about other people, relationships, rules, and role behaviors.
Home Economics; Psychology
Dist - AITECH **Prod** - MDDE 1980

Social documentary 25 MIN
VHS
Exploring photography series
Color (A)
PdS65 purchase
Looks at how two leading photojournalists, Ian Berry and Don McCullin, depict the British way of life through contrasing styles. Explores the creative possibilities of still photography. Covers the major topics of interest to any photographer. Part of a six-part series hosted by Bryn Campbell.
Fine Arts; Industrial and Technical Education
Dist - BBCENE

Social Dominance in the Male Black Buck 9 MIN
16mm
B&W (C T)
Shows how one male dominates the herd and interferes with the expression of social and sexual behavior by subordinate adult and young males. Demonstrates the gait and postures of the dominant male. Shows patterns of aggressive interaction between males (headwrestling and chasing) and of sexual interactions between male and female ('NECK - STRETCHING,' herding). photographed at the new York zoological park.
Psychology; Science - Natural
Dist - PSUPCR **Prod** - PSUPCR 1960

The Social Drinker and the Anti - Social Driver 21 MIN
16mm / VHS
Color (H C A PRO)
$375.00, $475.00 purchase, $50.00 rental _ #9789, #9789LD
Offers sensible alternatives to drinking and driving. Available also in laser disc.
Health and Safety; Industrial and Technical Education; Psychology
Dist - AIMS **Prod** - AIMS 1984
CMPCAR

Social Drinking - Fun and Fatal 14 MIN
16mm / U-matic / VHS
Alcohol Abuse Series
Color (H C A)
LC 80-700254
Re - creates a tragic accident in order to illustrate the results of driving under the influence of alcohol and to demonstrate the effects of liquor on the driving ability of social drinkers.
Health and Safety; Psychology; Sociology
Dist - JOU **Prod** - NSC 1979

Social Encounter 8 MIN
16mm
Encounter Series
Color (I)
LC 72-703205
Considers the impact of personal values on various everyday situations.
Sociology
Dist - FRACOC **Prod** - FRACOC 1970

Social Factors in the Parenthood Decision 29 MIN
VHS / U-matic
Tomorrow's Families Series
Color (H C A)
LC 81-706894
Discusses the effect of a new baby on the community, family relationships, and the educational and career plans of the parents.
Sociology
Dist - AITECH **Prod** - MDDE 1980

Social Group Work with Families Related to Problems of Child Abuse and Neglect, Pt 1 60 MIN
U-matic / VHS
Color
Outlines a social work program developed to help eliminate conflicts between parents and their abused children.
Sociology
Dist - UWISC **Prod** - VRL 1976

Social Group Work with Families Related to Problems of Child Abuse and Neglect, Pt 2 20 MIN
U-matic / VHS

Color
Discusses the 'buddy' system of evaluation in terms of behavioral modification with children, various aspects of these modification systems and negotiations between children and adults.
Sociology
Dist - UWISC **Prod** - VRL

Social Groups 29 MIN
U-matic
Understanding Human Behavior - an Introduction to Psychology Series
Color (C A)
Defines concept of social groups. Discusses classic research by Asch and Sherif. Focuses on manner in which social groups exert powerful influence upon individual behavior.
Psychology
Dist - CDTEL **Prod** - COAST

Social impacts of new medical knowledge - Program 7 52 MIN
16mm / VHS
Day the universe changed series
Color (H C G)
$695.00, $300.00 purchase, $75.00 rental
Reveals that by the end of the Napoleonic Wars, clinical science was beginning to replace the ignorance that had always characterized medicine. Looks at the rise of modern medicine and public health and their surprising relationships to statistics, which doctors learned to apply to diseases, cures and epidemics. As medicine became more and more a science, patients increasingly became statistics. Part of a ten - part series on Western thought hosted by James Burke.
Health and Safety; Mathematics; Science; Sociology
Dist - CF **Prod** - BBCTV 1986

Social Inequality 30 MIN
VHS / U-matic
Focus on Society Series
Color (C)
Looks at the nature and basis of social stratification, its impact upon life chances and the moneyed nature of American society. Discusses the basis of social inequality and possible alternatives to the present system.
Sociology
Dist - DALCCD **Prod** - DALCCD

Social Insects 20 MIN
VHS / U-matic
Color
Reveals intimate details of insect life within highly structured societies. Reviews societies of bees, wasps, ants and termites. Discusses anatomical structures as they relate to caste and function. A video version of 35mm filmstrip program, but with 'live' open and close.
Science - Natural
Dist - CBSC **Prod** - REXERC

Social Insects 15 MIN
U-matic / VHS / 16mm
Insect Series
Color (J H)
LC 80-700665
Examines the complex organization of insect communities using demonstration hives and nests and close - up photographic techniques to illustrate the social behavior of bees, wasps, ants and termites.
Science - Natural
Dist - IFB **Prod** - BHA 1977

Social Insects - the Honeybee 24 MIN
16mm / U-matic / VHS
Biology series
Color (H) (SPANISH)
Shows that social insects, including the honeybee, live in colonies and are divided into castes. Illustrates the particular adaptation of various castes to reproduction, population control and food gathering.
Foreign Language; Psychology; Science - Natural
Dist - EBEC **Prod** - EBEC

Social interaction, conflict and change 30 MIN
VHS
Sociological imagination series
Color (H C)
$89.95 purchase _ #TSI - 102
Examines social change and social conflict and how they affect each other as well as influence the lives of humans.
Psychology; Sociology
Dist - INSTRU

Social interaction in diverse situations 60 MIN
VHS
Dealing with diversity series
Color (H C G)
$99.00 purchase _ #GSU - 102
Discusses a social interaction model. Provides students with a common basis for understanding groups and differences between groups. Part of a 23 - part series hosted by Dr J Q Adams, Western Illinois University, which helps students to develop the awareness that society is strengthened by a free and unfettered expression of individuality in all its diverse manifestations.
Psychology; Sociology
Dist - INSTRU

Social issue series
America's inland coast 60 MIN
Columbia point 26 MIN
Coping with infertility 28 MIN
Torture 57 MIN
Unwasted Stories 75 MIN
Dist - IAFC

Social Learning Approach to Family Therapy 31 MIN
16mm
Color
LC 74-702670
Presents a case study involving a family with a predelinquent boy progressing through a complete treatment process using social learning - based family intervention procedures developed by Drs G Patterson and J Reid at the Oregon Research Institute.
Education; Guidance and Counseling; Psychology; Sociology
Dist - RESPRC **Prod** - OREGRI 1974

Social life 15 MIN
VHS / U-matic
America past series
(J H)
$125 purchase
Looks at characteristics of nineteenth century Americans, family life, reform movements and population growth.
History - United States
Dist - AITECH **Prod** - KRMATV 1987

Social life 15 MIN
VHS / U-matic
America past series
Color (H)
Presents characteristics of nineteenth - century American social life - family life, reform movements, medical treatment, and population growth.
Social Science; Sociology
Dist - AITECH **Prod** - KRMATV 1987

The Social Life of Small Urban Spaces 58 MIN
16mm
Color
LC 81-700460
Studies how people use the parks and plazas of cities. Describes the importance of seating, food, sunlight, and something to watch.
Sociology
Dist - MASOC **Prod** - MASOC 1981

Social Life of Small Urban Spaces - Pt 1 29 MIN
16mm
Color
LC 81-700460
Studies how people use the parks and plazas of cities. Describes the importance of seating, food, sunlight, and something to watch.
Sociology
Dist - MASOC **Prod** - MASOC 1981

Social Life of Small Urban Spaces - Pt 2 29 MIN
16mm
Color
LC 81-700460
Studies how people use the parks and plazas of cities. Describes the importance of seating, food, sunlight, and something to watch.
Sociology
Dist - MASOC **Prod** - MASOC 1981

Social Movements 30 MIN
U-matic / VHS
Focus on Society Series
Color (C)
Examines the various stages through which social movements progress using the women's movement as an example. Discusses the status of women and social forces affecting the movement.
Sociology
Dist - DALCCD **Prod** - DALCCD

Social Organization in the Red Jungle Fowl 10 MIN
16mm
Color (H C)
LC 76-701854
Shows the pattern of fighting behavior which leads to dominance relations between two red jungle fowl males. Illustrates the normally aggressive interactions among an intergrated flock of eleven males during feeding and in a mixed flock of males and females. Concludes with sequences on sexual courtship and copulation.
Psychology; Science - Natural
Dist - PSUPCR **Prod** - BANKSE 1960

The Social Partnership 24 MIN
16mm
Color (H C A)
Discusses the development of social security in the Federal Republic of Germany after the Second World War, which was marked by expansion and improvement of benefits from welfare insurance programs, including health, accident, pension and unemployment insurance. Explains how these and a variety of other systems work.
Business and Economics; History - World; Sociology
Dist - WSTGLC **Prod** - WSTGLC

Social Position 29 MIN
U-matic
Social Animal Series
Color
Examines social position, no matter what kind of rank, as a measure of happiness.
Sociology
Dist - UMITV **Prod** - UMITV 1974

Social Problems and Classroom Guidance 29 MIN
VHS / U-matic
Dealing with Social Problems in the Classroom Series
Color (T)
Discusses how social problems can be handled in a classroom guidance situation.
Education; Sociology
Dist - FI **Prod** - MFFD

Social Psychology 30 MIN
VHS / 16mm
Psychology - the Study of Human Behavior Series
Color (C A)
$99.95, $89.95 purchase _ 24 - 24
Demonstrates the influence of social roles, norms and rules.
Psychology
Dist - CDTEL **Prod** - COAST 1990

Social Psychology 33 MIN
U-matic / VHS / 16mm
Psychology Today Films Series
Color (H C A)
LC 78-713076
Introduces the field of social psychology and defines some of the key concepts. Shows community reactions to bussing and integration in Westport, Conn, with commentary from a panel moderated by Kenneth B Clark.
Psychology; Sociology
Dist - CRMP **Prod** - CRMP 1971

Social Psychology Series
Conformity and Independence 23 MIN
Human Aggression 22 MIN
Invitation to Social Psychology 25 MIN
Nonverbal Communication 23 MIN
Dist - CORF

Social psychology series
Presents an eight - part series on social psychology produced by the International University Consortium. Includes the titles - Communication - Social Cognitions and Attributions; Communication - Negotiation and Persuasion; Friendship; Prejudice; Conformity; Group Decision Making and Leadership; Aggression; Helping and Prosocial Behavior.
Aggression 30 MIN
Communication - negotiation and persuasion 30 MIN
Communication - social cognitions and attributions 30 MIN
Conformity 30 MIN
Friendship 30 MIN
Group decision making and leadership 30 MIN
Helping and prosocial behavior 30 MIN
Prejudice 30 MIN
Dist - PSU

Social Reaction in Imprinted Ducklings 21 MIN
16mm
Color (C)
LC 77-708678
Shows the effects of a sequence of experimental procedures in which newly hatched ducklings were first imprinted to a moving stimulus and then taught to peck a pole, using presentation of the moving stimulus as the sole response - contingent.
Psychology
Dist - PSUPCR **Prod** - PSUPCR 1968

Social reform 30 MIN
U-matic / VHS
American story - the beginning to 1877 series
Color (C)
History - United States
Dist - DALCCD **Prod** - DALCCD

Social responses to aging care and the caring for older people - a series
Social responses to aging care and the caring for older people'series
B&W
Explains a number of aspects of the problems of aging in contemporary society, including the increased numbers of old people, changing lifestyles, early retirement, inflation and the proliferation of medical problems. Emphasizes the need for more knowledge about the aging process and its effects. Continuum Of Care, The - An Alternative To - - ; Institutionalization - Warehousing Or - - ; Introduction - Overview Of The Field Of - - ; Music - A Bridge To Reality; Social Rehearsal For Dying; Triple 'A' Agency, The - Anger, Advocacy, - - .
Health and Safety; Sociology
Dist - UAZMIC **Prod** - UAZMIC 1976

Social responses to aging care and the caring for older people series
Social responses to aging care and the caring for older people - a series
Dist - UAZMIC

Social Responsibility 29 MIN
VHS / 16mm
Villa Alegre Series
Color (P T)
$46.00 rental _ #VILA - 141
Presents educational material in both Spanish and English.
Education; Psychology
Dist - PBS

Social Responsibility - It's My Hobby 11 MIN
U-matic / VHS / 16mm
Conflict and Awareness Series
Color (I J H)
LC 74-701921
Presents a young boy's reactions when he finds out his friend is selling pills to classmates and younger students. Describes the responsibility of an individual to report the selling of drugs, depicting a conflict between social responsibility and personal loyalty.
Guidance and Counseling; Psychology; Sociology
Dist - CRMP **Prod** - CRMP 1974

Social Roles 30 MIN
VHS / U-matic
Psychology of Human Relations Series
Color
Examines the influence of genetic factors on social behavior and social development, the influences of social environment and learning, social roles of men and women and modeling and socialization.
Psychology
Dist - WFVTAE **Prod** - MATC

Social Science Film Series
Fifth street - skid row 32 MIN
Prejudice - Causes, Consequences, Cures 24 MIN
Dist - CRMP

Social Science - History - Tape 1 45 MIN
U-matic / VHS
CLEP General Examinations Series
Color (H A)
Prepares students for the College Level Examination Program (CLEP) tests in Social Science and History. Focuses on United States history.
Education; History - United States
Dist - COMEX **Prod** - COMEX

Social Science - History - Tape 3 45 MIN
VHS / U-matic
CLEP General Examinations Series
Color (H A)
Prepares students for the College Level Examination Program (CLEP) tests in Social Science and History. Focuses on economics.
Business and Economics; Education
Dist - COMEX **Prod** - COMEX

Social Science - History - Tape 4 45 MIN
U-matic / VHS
CLEP General Examinations Series
Color (H A)
Prepares students for the College Level Examination Program (CLE) tests in Social Science and History. Examines social psychology.
Education; Sociology
Dist - COMEX **Prod** - COMEX

Social Science - History - Tape 5 45 MIN
U-matic / VHS
CLEP General Examinations Series
Color (H A)
Prepares students for the College Level Examination Program (CLEP) tests in Social Science and History. Explores several aspects of sociology.
Education; Sociology
Dist - COMEX **Prod** - COMEX

Social Science Reading 120 MIN
U-matic / VHS
A C T Exam Preparation Series
Color
Education; Social Science
Dist - KRLSOF **Prod** - KRLSOF 1985

Social Science/History, Tape 2 45 MIN
VHS / U-matic
CLEP General Examinations Series
Color (H A)
Prepares students for the College Level Examination Program (CLEP) tests in Social Science and History. Discusses political science and American constitutional government.
Civics and Political Systems; Education
Dist - COMEX **Prod** - COMEX

Social Sciences
VHS / U-matic
Video Career Library Series
(H C A)
$69.95 _ #CJ113V
Covers duties, conditions, salaries and training connected with jobs in the social sciences field. Provides a view of employees in this occupation on the job and gives information concerning the current market for such skills. Revised every two years.
Education; Guidance and Counseling; Social Science
Dist - CAMV **Prod** - CAMV

Social Sciences 26 MIN
VHS / 16mm
Video Career Library Series
Color (H C A PRO)
$79.95 purchase _ #WW103
Shows occupations in the social sciences such as economists, psychologists, sociologists, urban and regional planners, social and recreation workers, clergy, lawyers and others in the field. Contains current occupational outlook and salary information.
Business and Economics; Guidance and Counseling; Social Science
Dist - AAVIM **Prod** - AAVIM 1990

Social Sciences - Household Economics
VHS
Video Career Series
$29.95 purchase _ #MD242V
Shows students going 'on the job' to learn the variety of skills required for this occupation and the special training or educational requirements. Discusses various hiring procedures and what is involved in joining a professional association or union.
Education; Guidance and Counseling
Dist - CAREER **Prod** - CAREER

Social Sciences - Library and Archival Science
VHS
Video Career Series
$29.95 purchase _ #MD244
Shows students going 'on the job' to learn the variety of skills required for this occupation and the special training or educational requirements. Discusses various hiring procedures and what is involved in joining a professional association or union.
Education; Guidance and Counseling
Dist - CAREER **Prod** - CAREER

Social Sciences - Psychology
VHS
Video Career Series
$29.95 purchase _ #MD246
Shows students going 'on the job' to learn the variety of skills required for this occupation and the special training or educational requirements. Discusses various hiring procedures and what is involved in joining a professional association or union.
Education; Guidance and Counseling
Dist - CAREER **Prod** - CAREER

Social Sciences - Social Work
VHS
Video Career Series
$29.95 purchase _ #MD248V
Shows students going 'on the job' to learn the variety of skills required for this occupation and the special training or educational requirements. Discusses various hiring procedures and what is involved in joining a professional association or union.
Education; Guidance and Counseling
Dist - CAREER **Prod** - CAREER

The Social Sciences - what is Economics
VHS / U-matic
Color (H)
Demonstrates that economics is a coherent science. Outlines the major economic systems and examines our own. Shows how values and priorities shape the decisions which direct our economy.
Business and Economics
Dist - GA **Prod** - GA

The Social sciences - what is sociology 45 MIN
VHS
Color (H)
$99.00 purchase _ #06118 - 026
Shows students how sociologists work, the subjects they pursue and the techniques they use. Uses an extended case history of a high school student to explain how sociologists examine individuals, groups, institutions and the interactions among all of these. Encourages students to assume the role of sociologist and apply what they have learned to make specific analyses and predictions. Includes teacher's guide and library kit.
Social Science; Sociology
Dist - INSTRU
GA

Social Security 29 MIN
VHS / 16mm
You Owe it to Yourself Series
Color (G)
$55.00 rental _ #YOIY - 004
Business and Economics
Dist - PBS **Prod** - WITFTV

Social security - 50 years strong 29 MIN
VHS / 16mm
Color (G IND)
$5.00 rental
Commemorates the 50 year anniversary of the enactment of the Social Security Act. Features a panel discussion with former HEW Secretary Wilbur Cohen, former Representative Martha Keyes, and an interview with Representative Claude Pepper. Produced by the American Federation of State, County and Municipal Employees.
Business and Economics; Civics and Political Systems; Social Science; Sociology
Dist - AFLCIO **Prod** - AFLCIO

Social Security - Myths and Realities 48 MIN
U-matic / VHS
Color
$455.00 purchase
From the ABC TV program, Close Up.
Business and Economics; Sociology
Dist - ABCLR **Prod** - ABCLR 1981

Social Security - Time for an Overhaul 29 MIN
VHS / 16mm
Color (G)
$55.00 rental _ #SOSE - 000
Examines the inequities of Social Security provisions for women. Visits Congressional hearings on the subject. Includes interviews.
Social Science; Sociology
Dist - PBS **Prod** - WETATV

Social seminar series
Brian at seventeen 30 MIN
You Got the same Thing, Aincha 17 MIN
Dist - USNAC

Social Services and Child Abuse 28 MIN
U-matic / VHS
Color (G)
$249.00, $149.00 purchase _ #AD - 2070
Examines social service agencies charged with the care of children, who are supposed to protect children from abuse. Reports that many agencies are too understaffed or undertrained or simply uncaring to prevent vicious and sometimes fatal child abuse. From a Phil Donahue program.
Sociology
Dist - FOTH **Prod** - FOTH

The Social Side of Health 10 MIN
16mm / U-matic / VHS
Triangle of Health Series
Color (I J H) (SPANISH ARABIC FRENCH GERMAN)
Focuses on learning how to live with others while retaining one's own individuality.
Foreign Language; Psychology
Dist - CORF **Prod** - DISNEY 1969

Social Skills for the Spinal Cord Injured Patient 28 MIN
U-matic
Color (S)
LC 77-706068
Features eight vignettes which demonstrate how persons with severe physical disabilities can manage common social situations. Portrays aggressive, passive and assertive responses.
Education; Psychology
Dist - USNAC **Prod** - USVA 1976

Social Stereotyping 30 MIN
U-matic
Growing Years Series
Color
Discusses sex and ethnic stereotyping and the factors influencing prejudice.
Psychology
Dist - CDTEL **Prod** - COAST

Social stratification 30 MIN
VHS
Color (H C)
$89.95 purchase _ #TSI - 113
Explains the stratified nature of social structure and examines different types of stratifiication throughout the world, and how they developed.
Sociology
Dist - INSTRU

The social struggle 50 MINS.
VHS
The private life of plants
Color; PAL (H G)
PdS99 purchase; not available in USA, Canada
Focuses on the way certain plants struggle to survive in tight communities and fight over limited resources. Uses computer technology and time - lapse photography to highlight the processes. Fourth in the six - part plant survival series The Private Life of Plants. Hosted by David Attenborough.
Science - Natural
Dist - BBCENE

Social studies curriculum program series
Animals in Amboseli 20 MIN
Dist - MLA

Social studies program series
Corn and the origins of settled life in Meso - America - Pt 1 41 MIN
Corn and the origins of settled life in Meso - America - Pt 2 41 MIN
The Earliest writing 11 MIN
Land and Water in Iraq 14 MIN
Dist - EDC

Social studies program
Archaeology in Mesopotamia 17 MIN
Dist - EDC

Social Studies Series
Why Fathers Work 14 MIN
Dist - EBEC

Social studies through dramatic play 30 MIN
VHS
Calico pie series
Color (C A T)
$69.95 purchase
Presents part 11 of a 16 - part telecourse for teachers who work with children ages three to five. Discusses how dramatic play can be used to teach social studies in the classroom. Hosted by Dr Carolyn Dorrell, an early childhood specialist.
Education; Psychology
Dist - SCETV **Prod** - SCETV 1983

Social Variations 27 MIN
16mm
Language - the Social Arbiter Series; 5
Color
LC FIA67-5265
Points out that the great majority of New Yorkers unconsciously shift their sound patterns as well as their grammar according to changes in situation. Notes that the shift is uniform and that there is agreement among New Yorkers on the norms of careful speech. Explains that differences among people are often revealed in their speech patterns.
English Language; Psychology; Sociology
Dist - FINLYS **Prod** - FINLYS 1966

Social Work 15 MIN
VHS / U-matic / BETA
Career Success Series
(H C A)
$29.95 _ #MX248
Portrays occupations in social work by reviewing required abilities and interviewing people employed in this field. Tells of the anxieties and rewards involved in pursuing a career as a social worker.
Education; Guidance and Counseling; Social Science; Sociology
Dist - CAMV **Prod** - CAMV

Social Work 46 MIN
VHS / U-matic
Color
Follows a case through the Meyer Children's Rehabilitation Institute's routine, with emphasis on the social work department's function as a family intermediary. Features a short segment on training social work graduate students at MCRI.
Education; Guidance and Counseling; Sociology
Dist - UNEBO **Prod** - UNEBO

Social Work 15 MIN
VHS / 16mm
(H C A)
$24.95 purchase _ #CS248
Describes the skills required for a career in social work. Features interviews with people employed in this field.
Guidance and Counseling
Dist - RMIBHF **Prod** - RMIBHF

Social Work Interviewing Series
Exploration Phase - Assessment 35 MIN
The Exploration Phase - Data Collection 35 MIN
The Service phase 24 MIN
The Termination Phase 22 MIN
Dist - UWISC

Social Work Licensure 60 MIN
U-matic / VHS
Color
Looks at the regulation of social work as a profession and as it relates to the mental health industry.
Health and Safety; Sociology
Dist - UWISC **Prod** - VRL 1983

Social work roles in foster care series
Child welfare worker - Pt I 39 MIN
Child welfare worker - Pt II 62 MIN
Foster parent trainer, foster home consultant, Pt I 39 MIN
Foster parent trainer, foster home consultant, Pt II 38 MIN
Dist - UWISC

Social Work with the Hearing Impaired 18 MIN
U-matic / VHS
Color
Gives examples of interpersonal skills necessary in dealing with the deaf and how to use them. Shows several interviews with a deaf client and social worker.
Guidance and Counseling; Psychology; Sociology
Dist - UWISC **Prod** - UWISC 1980

Social Worker 15 MIN
16mm / U-matic / VHS
Career Awareness
(I)
$130 VC purchase, $240 film purchase, $25 VC rental, $30 film rental
Presents an empathetic approach to career planning, showing the personal as well as the professional attributes of social workers. Highlights the importance of career education.
Guidance and Counseling
Dist - GPN

Social worker 20 MIN
VHS
Get a life - a day in the career guidance series
Color (H C A)
$89.00 purchase _ #886696-02-0
Takes viewers through a day in the life of Irene, a social worker. Views her duties in a typical day and how she reached her goals. Describes educational and other professional requirements for the job. Part of a ten-part series.
Business and Economics; Guidance and Counseling; Sociology
Dist - VOCAVD **Prod** - VOCAVD 1995

Social worker
VHS
Day in a career series
Color (C H A J T G)
$89.00 purchase _ #VOC02V-G ; $89.00 purchase _ #VOC02V-J
Presents information about the occupation of social worker, one of the careers that the United States Department of Labor projects as potentially successful by the year 2000. Profiles in detail the work day of a real person, with candid interviews and work situations and information about the educational requirements, credentials, job outlook, salaries, important associations, and contacts in the field. One of a series of ten videos, lasting 15 to 22 minutes, available individually or as a set.
Business and Economics; Guidance and Counseling; Sociology
Dist - CAMV

Socialism 25 MIN
VHS / U-matic / 16mm / BETA
Capitalism, socialism, communism series
Color (J H G)
$390.00, $110.00 purchase _ #C05596, #C51202
Examines the history and practice of socialism. Part of a three - part series.
Business and Economics; Civics and Political Systems
Dist - NGS **Prod** - NGS 1986

Socialism in the Third World - Success or Failure 30 MIN
U-matic
Realities
Color (A)
Delves into the political, social, economic and cultural trends of the 1980s. Probes a wide range of contemporary concerns. Each segment includes a guest speaker who is an expert in the field under discussion.
Business and Economics; Civics and Political Systems; Social Science; Sociology
Dist - TVOTAR **Prod** - TVOTAR 1985

Socialist city 20 MIN
VHS / U-matic / BETA
Soviet Union series
Color (H C A)
$250.00 purchase _ #JY - 5862C
Visits Moscow where the socialist state controls life from cradle to grave - marriage, housing, education, medical care, employment, clothing and food. Interviews Muscovite citizens to show how the new optimism under Gorbachev has changed the outlook of the average person. Part of a five - part series on the diverse lifestyles and regions of the USSR.
Civics and Political Systems; Geography - World; History - World; Social Science; Sociology
Dist - CORF **Prod** - BBCTV 1989

Socialist View of Reaganomics 30 MIN
U-matic
Realities
Color (A)
Delves into the political, social, economic and cultural trends of the 1980s. Probes a wide range of contemporary concerns. Each segment includes a guest speaker who is an expert in the field under discussion.
Business and Economics; Civics and Political Systems; Social Science; Sociology
Dist - TVOTAR **Prod** - TVOTAR 1985

Socialization 30 MIN
VHS
Sociological imagination series
Color (H C)
$89.95 purchase _ #TSI - 105
Shows how the agents of socialization influence the concept of the individual self throughout the life cycle.
Psychology; Sociology
Dist - INSTRU

Socialization - Moral Development 22 MIN
16mm / U-matic / VHS
Color (C A)
LC 79-701562
Explores theories of morality and moral development through the demonstration of classic experimental work in social and developmental psychology.
Psychology
Dist - CORF **Prod** - HAR 1980

Societal Needs - 4 29 MIN
VHS
Interactions in Science and Society - Teacher Programs - Series
Color (T PRO)
$150.00 purchase
Looks at computers, plastics and antibiotics as examples of technological developments influenced by the needs of society during World War II.
Education; Health and Safety; History - United States; Industrial and Technical Education; Mathematics; Sociology
Dist - AITECH **Prod** - WHATV 1990

Societies 30 MIN
VHS
Color (H C)
$89.95 purchase _ #TSI - 108
Shows how small, medium - sized and large - complex societies satisfy basic human needs over space and time, and how societies become more complex as they get larger. Explores the effects of population pressures and changes.
Sociology
Dist - INSTRU

The Society 22 MIN
16mm / U-matic / VHS
Every Two Seconds Series
Color
Discusses the varied systemic and societal causes, settings and perpetrators of crime.
Sociology
Dist - CORF **Prod** - CORF

The Society and family - Programme One and Two 30 MIN
VHS
Inside Britain 2 series
Color; PAL; NTSC (G) (BULGARIAN CZECH HUNGARIAN SPANISH POLISH ROMANIAN RUSSIAN SLOVAK UKRAINIAN ENGLISH WITH ARABIC SUBTITLES LITHUANIAN)

PdS65 purchase
Presents two programs on the family and society in the United Kingdom. Considers that, for most people, family ties are important. Reveals that the average British family size is 2.48 people - but there is no such thing as the typical family. Lifestyles vary enormously and the programs look at four different families.
Sociology
Dist - CFLVIS **Prod** - HEWITT 1992

Society and the Individual 30 MIN
U-matic / VHS
Japan - the Changing Tradition Series
Color (H C A)
History - World
Dist - GPN **Prod** - UMA 1978

Society and You 14 MIN
16mm
Family Life Education and Human Growth
Color (J H)
LC 73-703066
Questions whether disenchantment with parents and discontentment with the way things are is considered valid without alternative initiative.
Guidance and Counseling; Psychology; Sociology
Dist - SF **Prod** - SF 1970

Society of the just 50 MIN
VHS
Color (H C G)
$250.00 purchase
Features George Marty who lived in Tehran, Iran, for many years and witnessed the events of the past 20 years first - hand. Gives a subtle analysis of the political, historical, social and economic situation in the Islamic republic, a look behind the facade of violence and fanaticism.
Geography - World; Religion and Philosophy; Sociology
Dist - LANDMK **Prod** - LANDMK 1987

Society - Part 3 180 MIN
VHS
Chinese series
Color (C A)
Covers Chinese societal structures, focusing on the family, social conflicts, and the attempt to create a broader community. Filmed on location, and interviews Chinese people. Consists of parts five through seven of a 13 - part telecourse on China. Includes three related videos, "Marrying," focusing on the Chinese family, "Caring," which discusses the communitarian goals of China, and "Mediating," which discusses social conflicts. Additional educational materials available.
Geography - World; Sociology
Dist - SCETV **Prod** - SCETV 1984

Society - the Students' Places 15 MIN
16mm
Florida Elementary Social Studies Series
Color (P I J)
Presents society by describing it as a group of people living together and sharing ideas, customs, rules and laws.
Sociology
Dist - DADECO **Prod** - DADECO 1973

Sociobiology - Doing what Comes Naturally 20 MIN
U-matic / VHS / 16mm
Color
Discusses the evolution of man's behavior in society and tells how sociobiology can help man plan and understand his behavior.
Science - Natural; Sociology
Dist - CNEMAG **Prod** - DOCUA

Sociobiology - the Human Animal 57 MIN
U-matic / VHS / 16mm
Nova Series
Color (C A)
LC 78-700564
Focuses on sociobiology, a controversial science which holds that behavior is biologically determined.
Psychology; Science - Natural; Sociology
Dist - TIMLIF **Prod** - WGBHTV 1977

A Sociocultural approach to cognition
VHS
Cognition and learning series
Color (T)
$49.95 purchase
Focuses on a Vygotskian approach to cognition. Addresses three themes - reliance on a developmental method, the belief that higher mental functioning originates in social activity, and belief that human mental activity is mediated by tools and signs. Includes the work of Russian linguist Bakhtin who emphasizes the dialogic nature of the mediational tool of language. Presented by Dr James Wertsch of Clarke University. Part of a six - part series on recent theoretical and empirical work done on cognition and learning.
Education; English Language; Psychology
Dist - UCALG **Prod** - UCALG 1991

Sociological imagination series
Culture 30 MIN
Formal organizations 30 MIN
From social interaction to social structure 30 MIN
Groups and group dynamics 30 MIN
Social interaction, conflict and change 30 MIN
Socialization 30 MIN
Sociological thinking and research 30 MIN
Dist - INSTRU

Sociological thinking and research 30 MIN
VHS
Sociological imagination series
Color (H C)
$89.95 purchase _ #TSI - 103
Describes how sociologists view the world, going beyond empirical observations to employ sociological imagination. Illustrates how the scientific method is adapted to apply to human social life by following sociologists on a research project.
Sociology
Dist - INSTRU

Sociological vs psychodynamic - Edgar Epps vs Nicholas Long 30 MIN
VHS
Video training workshops on child variance series
Color (T PRO)
$135.00 purchase _ #M199j
Presents behavior discussion between Edgar Epps and Nicholas Long representing sociological and psychodynamic viewpoints respectively. Part of a six - part series produced by William C Morse and Judith M Smith.
Psychology; Sociology
Dist - CEXPCN **Prod** - CEXPCN

Sockeye Odyssey 14 MIN
16mm
Color
LC 80-701868
Depicts the life cycle and conservation of the Alaskan sockeye salmon. Emphasizes the migration, color changes and spawning of this species.
Science - Natural
Dist - USNAC **Prod** - USNOAA

Sockeye Salmon 25 MIN
U-matic / VHS / 16mm
Untamed World Series
Color; Mono (J H C A)
$400.00 film, $250.00 video, $50.00 rental
Presents a detailed look at the history, feeding, and incredible migratory habits of the sockeye salmon.
Geography - World; Science - Natural
Dist - CTV **Prod** - CTV 1972

Socks - Gorilla Gorilla 15 MIN
U-matic / VHS
Best of Cover to Cover 1 Series
Color (P)
Literature and Drama
Dist - WETATV **Prod** - WETATV

Socrates 120 MIN
16mm
Color (ITALIAN (ENGLISH SUBTITLES))
Offers a portrait of the Greek philosopher Socrates, pointing out that he was a man of both weakness and strength. Directed by Roberto Rossellini. With English subtitles.
Biography; Foreign Language
Dist - NYFLMS **Prod** - UNKNWN 1970

Socrates for six year olds 60 MIN
VHS
Transformers series
Color (A T C)
PdS99 purchase
Looks at the theories of American philosopher Matthew Lipman. Examines these theories through the educational program, Philosophy for Children. Part of a three-part series which looks at teaching children with learning difficulties.
Education; Religion and Philosophy
Dist - BBCENE

The Sod House Frontier 30 MIN
16mm
Great Plains Trilogy, 3 Series Explorer and Settler - the White Man 'Arrives; Explorer and settler - the white man arrives
B&W (H C A)
Describes the sod house as a symbol of the frontier. Shows the food, furnishings and clothing of the settlers and mentions the problems of wood and water. Describes the cultural, educational, religious and social life of the frontier, and discusses frontier agriculture.
History - United States; Sociology
Dist - UNEBR **Prod** - KUONTV 1954

Sodanceabit dance and fitness video series
Cha cha and polka
East coast swing and Viennese waltz
Folk dance aerobics
West coast swing
Dist - CAMV

Sodanceabit dance series
Presents a six - part series of aerobic workout programs based on social dances. Uses slow motion, step - by - step instructional techniques to teach variations on folk dances, the West and East Coast swings, the Cha Cha, the Polka, and the Viennese Waltz. Consists of six videocassettes.
Sodanceabit dance series
Dist - CAMV

Sodbusters 29 MIN
16mm
Earthkeeping Series
Color (H C A)
LC 73-703400
Explains how Americans have created an environmental crisis by maintaining values which grew out of the frontier experience when there were abundant resources and a scarcity of people. Stresses the need for development of new values which reflect the realities of the urban age - dwindling resources, overpopulation and a polluted environment.
Science - Natural; Sociology
Dist - IU **Prod** - WTTWTV 1973

Sodium hydroxide and potassium hydroxide 28 MIN
VHS
Color (IND PRO)
$395.00 purchase, $150.00 rental
Covers the hazards of handling caustics with emphasis on accident prevention and safety. Outlines emergency procedures to follow in the event of a leak, spill or fire, along with protective clothing configurations, first aid for victims, neutralization of spills and safe clean - up activities. Also studied are the principal hazard properties, toxicity and reactivity of caustics.
Health and Safety; Science - Physical; Sociology
Dist - JEWELR

Sodom 21 MIN
16mm
Color (G)
$40.00 rental
Disturbs through its hypnotic mirage of human fragments absorbed in mutilation. Refers to the biblical story and recreates the destruction through an editing style which breaks images down and produces a collage of moving images. A Luther Price production.
Fine Arts; Religion and Philosophy
Dist - CANCIN

Sodom and Gomorrah 50 MIN
16mm / U-matic / VHS
Greatest Heroes of the Bible Series
Color (I)
Reveals that when Lot and his people find themselves in the sinful cities of Sodom and Gomorrah, an angel tells them to leave the cities and not look back, lest they be turned into pillars of salt. Stars Ed Ames and Dorothy Malone.
Religion and Philosophy
Dist - LUF **Prod** - LUF 1979

Sofa 23 MIN
VHS / U-matic
Color
Documents the engineering of two collaborative performances, the Whisper Project and Freeze Frame - Room For Living Room. Directed by Suzanne Lacy with Doug Smith and Eric La Brecque.
Fine Arts
Dist - ARTINC **Prod** - ARTINC

Sofa - Fire Death - Song 11 MIN
16mm
Color (C A)
Presents a psychedelic mood study of the female form.
Fine Arts; Industrial and Technical Education
Dist - CFS **Prod** - CFS 1968

Sofie 12 MIN
VHS
Wreck of a Marriage
Color (P)
Examines the hardships faced by Sofie, a recently divorced woman, and her young daughter Rikki. Traces the development of their stronger relationship.
Sociology
Dist - CEPRO **Prod** - CEPRO 1989

Soft and hard symplectic geometry 60 MIN
VHS
ICM Plenary addresses series
Color (PRO G)

$49.00 purchase _ #VIDGROMOV - VB2
Presents Mikhael Gromov who discusses soft and hard symplectic geometry.
Mathematics
Dist - AMSOC **Prod** - AMSOC

Soft collisions - dream of a good soldier 15 MIN
16mm
Color (G)
$50.00 rental
Presents a found - footage film about the Gulf War, and the media manipulation thereof. Explains filmmaker Yann Beauvais, 'An evocation against the stupidity of war in seven parts.'
Fine Arts
Dist - CANCIN

Soft fiction 54 MIN
VHS / 16mm
B&W (A)
$95.00 rental, $50.00 purchase
Combines a documentary approach with a sensuous lyrial expressionism to portray the survival power of female sensuality. Works on several different levels to evoke the soft line between truth and fiction that characterizes Strand's own aproach to documentary, and suggests the idea of soft - core fiction, which is appropriate to the film's erotic content and style.
Fine Arts; Sociology
Dist - CANCIN **Prod** - STRANC 1979

Soft furnishing - pelmet making - Unit D 28 MIN
VHS
Furniture, soft furnishing and musical instruments technology - 'teaching and learning process series; Unit D
Color; PAL (J H IND)
PdS29.50 purchase
Part of a four - part series which observes teaching and learning in a variety of workshop situations.
Industrial and Technical Education
Dist - EMFVL

Soft is the Heart of a Child 27 MIN
U-matic
Color
Focus on the impact on children of parents' alcoholism. Deals with such matters as where children can turn for help and support. Close - captioned.
Guidance and Counseling; Health and Safety; Home Economics; Psychology; Sociology
Dist - MTP **Prod** - OPCORK

Soft is the Heart of a Child - How Children are Affected by Alcoholism in the Family 30 MIN
16mm / VHS
Color (G)
$375.00, $250.00 purchase, $60.00, $50.00 rental _ #8057H, 9505H, 0552J, 0484J
Illustrates a classic alcoholic family situation - a father who drinks too much, a mother plagued by frustration, guilt and denial, and three children who also suffer. Portrays the typical roles enacted in dysfunctional families by children - protectors, surrogate parents, troublemakers, victims of misplaced anger and total withdrawal.
Guidance and Counseling; Health and Safety; Psychology; Sociology
Dist - HAZELB **Prod** - OPCORK

Soft Lenses 15 MIN
VHS / 16mm / U-matic
Color (A)
Explains how soft lenses work and demonstrates techniques of handling, inserting and removing them. Shows the proper methods of lens wear and care, including asepticizing soft lenses.
Health and Safety
Dist - PRORE **Prod** - PRORE

Soft Pad 4 MIN
U-matic / VHS / 16mm
Color
Describes a series of chairs by illustrating and analyzing the design concepts.
Fine Arts
Dist - PFP **Prod** - EAMES 1970

Soft Pitch Peddlers 28 MIN
VHS / U-matic
Color
Gives a back - stage look at how a salesperson uses psychology to move money from another's pocket to his.
Business and Economics; Psychology
Dist - WCCOTV **Prod** - WCCOTV 1977

Soft rocks 11 MIN
VHS
Color; PAL (P I J)
PdS29
Introduces the idea that rocks are not necessarily hard by studying three contrasting soft rock areas - the clay of the London Basin - City of London and Epping Forest; sand and gravel of the Hampshire Basin - the New Forest; and the peat and silt of the Fenlands - sedimentary rocks in the process of formation.
Geography - World; Science - Physical
Dist - BHA

Soft Sculpture Dolls 1 60 MIN
BETA / VHS
Color
Gives instructions on the creation of soft sculpture dolls.
Fine Arts
Dist - HOMEAF **Prod** - HOMEAF

Soft Sculpture Dolls 2 103 MIN
BETA / VHS
Color
Shows how to create soft - sculpture dolls and gives instuctions on the painting of eyes and hair for the finished doll.
Fine Arts
Dist - HOMEAF **Prod** - HOMEAF

Soft Sell 30 MIN
U-matic / VHS / 16mm
Enterprise Series
Color (H C A)
Presents various approaches to selling.
Business and Economics
Dist - CORF **Prod** - CORF

Soft shoe 20 MIN
16mm
Color (G)
$60.00 rental
Travels to Romania, Germany and Paris. Links East with West through optical printing with a mosaic of layered and shifting imagery. Produced by Holly Fisher.
Fine Arts
Dist - CANCIN

The Soft skin - La Peau douce 118 MIN
VHS
B&W (G)
$39.95 _ #SOF020
Features a French New Wave classic with a suspenseful mood. Tells the story of a happily married man who meets a beautiful airline hostess on a business trip and begins a reckless affair. A Hitchcockian vision of the disintegration of a marriage. Digitally remastered with new translation. Produced by Les Films du Carrosse.
Fine Arts; Psychology; Sociology
Dist - HOMVIS

Soft Tissue Examination 17 MIN
U-matic / VHS
Color (PRO)
Demonstrates a procedure for performing a systematic examination of the external lips, vestibule, frenum attachments, buccal mucosa, parotid gland and orifice, muscles of mastication, temporalis muscle, gingiva, hard and soft palate, pharynx, tongue, the floor of the mouth and sublingual and submand ibular texture of soft tissue, brimanual and bidigital palpation of muscles, tongue, salivary glands and palate, noting tenderness and/or swelling as well as saliva flow and consistently upon palpation.
Health and Safety; Science - Natural
Dist - UWASH **Prod** - UWASH

Soft tissue injuries
VHS
Athletic clinic series
Color (C A PRO)
$29.95 purchase _ #SVS1608V
Examines the common contusions and abrasions encountered by athletes. Covers first aid treatment and extended procedures for nagging ailments.
Health and Safety; Physical Education and Recreation; Science - Natural
Dist - CAMV

Soft Tissue Injuries to the Face 21 MIN
VHS / U-matic
Color (PRO)
Demonstrates the procedure for a regional physical exam, the preparation of a facial wound for repair, the way to dress a wound, follow - up care and the the principles of repairing injuries of the tongue, oral mucosa, lips, nose, ears, scalp and eyelids.
Health and Safety
Dist - UMICHM **Prod** - UMICHM 1977

Soft tissue syndrome and gout 12 MIN
VHS / 16mm
Learning about arthritis series
Color (H C A PRO)
$195.00 purchase, $75.00 rental _ #8086
Discusses soft tissue syndrome and gout.
Health and Safety; Science - Natural
Dist - AIMS **Prod** - HOSSN 1988

Soft White Death 23 MIN
U-matic / VHS
Color
Follows a mother polar bear and her young on their traditional migratory route from hibernation out to the ice flows of Hudson Bay.
Science - Natural
Dist - NWLDPR **Prod** - NWLDPR

Softball and baseball field maintenance and safety 25 MIN
VHS
Color (H C G)
$99.95 purchase _ #IE100V
Trains maintenance personnel on the important aspects of softball and baseball field preparation and how it relates to player safety and reducing unnecessary risk.
Health and Safety; Physical Education and Recreation
Dist - CAMV

Softball defensive skills 27 MIN
VHS
Color (G)
$59.95 purchase, $13.00 rental _ #35358
Outlines beginning softball coaching techniques. Features Penn State women's softball coach Sue Rankin who shows how to teach the fundamental defensive skills of the game - catching flyballs, fielding ground balls and throwing techniques for infielders and outfielders.
Physical Education and Recreation
Dist - PSU **Prod** - WPSXTV 1988

Softball Fundamentals for Elementary Schools 11 MIN
16mm / U-matic / VHS
B&W (I)
Basic rules, positions of players and teamwork are shown in a beginning class in softball. Demonstrates how to bat, pitch, catch and throw. Also stresses the importance of safety measures and good sportsmanship.
Physical Education and Recreation
Dist - PHENIX **Prod** - FURMAN 1966

Softball - putting it together 70 MIN
VHS
Color (G)
$59.95 purchase _ #WC100V
Presents a comprehensive instructional video of softball skills. Covers subjects including skill analysis, position play, defense, offense, mental preparation, and more.
Physical Education and Recreation
Dist - CAMV **Prod** - CAMV 1988

Softball series
VHS
N C A A instructional video series
Color (H C A)
$49.95 purchase _ #KAR1153V
Presents a two - part series on softball. Focuses on pitching and hitting techniques.
Physical Education and Recreation
Dist - CAMV **Prod** - NCAAF

Softball series
Basic skills in softball 10 MIN
Better hitting and baserunning 10 MIN
Better pitching and defense 10 MIN
Dist - ATHI

Softball - Skills and Practice 13 MIN
16mm / U-matic / VHS
Color (I J) (SPANISH)
LC FIA68-391
Illustrates the correct performance of each softball skill. Uses normal as well as slow - motion photography to give the viewer an opportunity to study each skill in detail. The plays are shown in individual and group action.
Foreign Language; Physical Education and Recreation
Dist - PHENIX **Prod** - FA 1967

Softfire 19 MIN
VHS / U-matic / 16mm
Color (H C G)
$425.00, $315.00, $290.00 purchase _ #E037
Provides an intimate look at an elderly woman approaching her death at home, where she is cared for by the staff of a home care service. Shares her experiences of life, aging and of her approaching death.
Health and Safety; Sociology
Dist - BARR **Prod** - CEPRO 1984

Software 30 MIN
U-matic / VHS
Programming Microprocessors Series
Color (IND)
Uses nine videotapes to bring one up to speed in programming the 6800 microprocessor through several demonstration exercises, showing good and bad

practices. Utilizes twelve demonstrations to lead one through programming exercises, to build up expertise in programming microprocessors and interfacing them to real applications.
Industrial and Technical Education; Mathematics; Sociology
Dist - COLOSU **Prod** - COLOSU

Software 7 MIN
16mm
Color (G)
$20.00 rental
Meditates on the human hand, which serves along with intelligence as the genesis of sucess as a species and as the ability for humanity to destroy itself.
Fine Arts; Psychology
Dist - CANCIN **Prod** - ZIPPER 1976

Software Design - Pt 1 30 MIN
U-matic / VHS
Software Engineering - a First Course Series
Color (IND)
Distinguishes between architectural and detail design. Discusses fundamental design principles. Covers method and notation of design by levels of abstraction.
Industrial and Technical Education; Mathematics
Dist - COLOSU **Prod** - COLOSU

Software Design - Pt 2 30 MIN
VHS / U-matic
Software Engineering - a First Course Series
Color (IND)
Depicts hierarchical structure versus tree structure, the integrated top - down approach to design, coding and testing, design of transaction - driven systems and design - representation techniques.
Industrial and Technical Education; Mathematics
Dist - COLOSU **Prod** - COLOSU

Software Design, Pt 3 30 MIN
U-matic / VHS
Software Engineering - a First Course Series
Color (IND)
Presents definition of the term module. Describes several modularization criteria, including the composite (or structured) design method. Concludes with discussion of detail design.
Industrial and Technical Education; Mathematics
Dist - COLOSU **Prod** - COLOSU

Software Development - Key Issues and Considerations 30 MIN
U-matic / VHS
New Technology in Education Series
Color (J)
Discusses education strategies for introducing software, development models for software, hardware choices and software policies.
Education; Industrial and Technical Education
Dist - USNAC **Prod** - USDOE 1983

Software Development Languages and Systems 180 MIN
U-matic
Software Engineering for Micro and Minicomputer Systems Series
Color (IND)
Discusses development languages, comparing machine, assembly and high - level languages, listing characteristics of assemblers, compilers and interpreters, and covering language impact on cost and schedule. Also discusses software development systems, including using simulators and emulators for debugging, shared - resource networks vs stand - alone systems, and support tools and software libraries.
Computer Science
Dist - INTECS **Prod** - INTECS

Software du jour
CD-ROM
(G A)
$49.00 purchase _ #1507
Provides a wealth of useful software for business, education, recreation and programming. For IBM PCs and compatibles. Requires 640K RAM, DOS Version 3.1 or greater, one floppy disk drive - a hard drive is recommended, one empty expansion slot, and an IBM compatible CD - ROM drive.
Civics and Political Systems; Computer Science
Dist - BEP

Software engineering - a first course series

Coding Standards and Documentation Techniques	30 MIN
Coding Style and Standards	30 MIN
Design summary and language features - Pt 1	30 MIN
Economic issues in software engineering	30 MIN
Formal verification	30 MIN
Introduction - Software engineering, pt 1	30 MIN
Introduction - Software engineering, Pt 2	30 MIN
Language Features, Pt 2	30 MIN
Language Features, Pt 3	30 MIN
Program testing - Pt 1	30 MIN
Program testing - Pt 2	30 MIN
Requirements Analysis	30 MIN
Software Design - Pt 1	30 MIN
Software Design - Pt 2	30 MIN
Software Design, Pt 3	30 MIN
Software Maintenance	30 MIN
Software Requirements Analysis Techniques - Pt 1	30 MIN
Software Requirements Analysis Techniques - Pt 2	30 MIN
Testing, Symbolic Execution and Formal Verification	30 MIN

Dist - COLOSU

Software Engineering for Micro and Minicomputer Systems Series

Design practices and configuration management	180 MIN
Estimating Project Parameters	180 MIN
Implementation, Integration and Test	180 MIN
Planning, Control and Reliability	180 MIN
Software Development Languages and Systems	180 MIN
The Software Engineering Team	180 MIN
The Software Project Life Cycle	180 MIN
System Requirements and Documentation	180 MIN

Dist - INTECS

The Software Engineering Team 180 MIN
U-matic
Software Engineering for Micro and Minicomputer Systems Series
Color (IND)
Discusses team structures, in terms of organizational components, types of software development organizations and combined hardware/software development teams. Also presents a course review and summary, with guidelines for successful development, and key pitfalls to avoid.
Business and Economics; Computer Science
Dist - INTECS **Prod** - INTECS

Software Evaluation 28 MIN
U-matic / VHS
Next Steps with Computers in the Classroom Series
Color (T)
Industrial and Technical Education; Mathematics; Sociology
Dist - PBS **Prod** - PBS

Software Evaluation - Pt 1 30 MIN
VHS / U-matic
On and on about Instruction - Microcomputers Series
Color (C)
Demonstrates the necessity of evaluating software based on specific objectives and outlines procedures for the evaluation process.
Industrial and Technical Education; Mathematics; Psychology
Dist - GPN **Prod** - VADE

Software Evaluation - Pt 2 30 MIN
U-matic / VHS
On and on about Instruction - Microcomputers Series
Color (C)
Looks at and demonstrates methods that can be used when examining and evaluating educational software.
Industrial and Technical Education; Mathematics; Psychology
Dist - GPN **Prod** - VADE

Software for Microprocessors 30 MIN
U-matic / VHS
Designing with Microprocessors Series
Color (PRO)
Provides background and definitions in order to bring the hardware designs up to speed in software technology. Discusses alternatives in addressing modes, and direction in software usage.
Industrial and Technical Education
Dist - TXINLC **Prod** - TXINLC

Software introduction 30 MIN
VHS
Multimedia series
Color (C T PRO)
$79.95 purchase
Introduces multimedia software programs from a basic presentation level to creating an interactive teaching module. Looks at cost savings vs traditional methods of teaching; off - the - shelf software vs repurposing materials vs creating new and original material. Part of a five - part series on multimedia technology as a new learning tool hosted by news anchor Joan Stafford.
Computer Science; Education
Dist - AECT

Software Languages and Systems 180 MIN
U-matic
Microprocessor Technical Fundamentals Series
Color (IND)
Discusses software languages and systems for microprocessors, including higher order languages, and editors, translators and debuggers, and details the steps in using a microprocessor development system.
Computer Science
Dist - INTECS **Prod** - INTECS

Software Maintenance 30 MIN
U-matic / VHS
Software Engineering - a First Course Series
Color (IND)
Discusses life - cycle aspects of software maintenance tools and techniques for maintenance. Tells about personnel aspects of software maintenance.
Industrial and Technical Education; Mathematics
Dist - COLOSU **Prod** - COLOSU

The Software Project Life Cycle 180 MIN
U-matic
Software Engineering for Micro and Minicomputer Systems Series
Color (IND)
Outlines course objectives, structure and content. Discusses unique aspects of developing software for microprocessors and minicomputers, and boosting productivity with software engineering techniques. Reviews phases of software development, covering specification, design, implementation, integration, system test and support, and deliverables and milestones for each phase, with cost, manpower and schedule allocations.
Computer Science
Dist - INTECS **Prod** - INTECS

Software Reliability 30 MIN
U-matic / VHS
Reliability Engineering Series
Color (IND)
Defines software reliability, and presents several models to model software reliability, mean time to failures when errors are reduced and test time is required to reduce errors.
Industrial and Technical Education
Dist - COLOSU **Prod** - COLOSU

Software Requirements Analysis Techniques - Pt 1 30 MIN
VHS / U-matic
Software Engineering - a First Course Series
Color (IND)
Tells about software specification techniques - emphasis on desired attributes, developing quality metrics, developing quality assurance procedures, and use of formal notations.
Industrial and Technical Education; Mathematics
Dist - COLOSU **Prod** - COLOSU

Software Requirements Analysis Techniques - Pt 2 30 MIN
VHS / U-matic
Software Engineering - a First Course Series
Color (IND)
Concludes discussion on use of formal notations with implicit equations, recurrence relations and property lists. Describes use of automated tools for software specification.
Industrial and Technical Education; Mathematics
Dist - COLOSU **Prod** - COLOSU

Software Selection 360 MIN
VHS / U-matic
Next Steps with Computers in the Classroom Series
Color (C T)
Computer Science; Education; Mathematics
Dist - UEUWIS **Prod** - UEUWIS 1985
PBS

Software Selection 28 MIN
U-matic / VHS
Next Steps with Computers in the Classroom Series
Color (T)
Industrial and Technical Education; Mathematics; Sociology
Dist - PBS **Prod** - PBS

Softwood Cuttings 28 MIN
Videoreel / VT2
Making Things Grow III Series
Color
Agriculture
Dist - PBS **Prod** - WGBHTV

Soil 12 MIN
U-matic / VHS / 16mm
Understanding Our Earth Series
Color (I J)
$295, $210 purchase _ #3845
Discusses the elements, formation, and differences between soils.

Science - Natural; Science - Physical
Dist - CORF

Soil - a medium for plant growth - Set 1 39 FRS
VHS / Slide / Cassette
Western fertilizer handbook series
Color (G)
$54.95, $40.00, $8.50 purchase _ #1 - 580 - 601P, #1 - 580 - 201P, #1 - 580 - 531P
Looks at soil and its role in plant growth. Part of a fourteen - part series based on the Western Fertilizer Handbook.
Agriculture
Dist - VEP **Prod** - VEP

Soil - an Introduction 9 MIN
U-matic / VHS / 16mm
Color (P I)
LC 77-700100
Explores soil as an important resource. Shows that soil is renewable but in need of constant attention.
Agriculture; Science - Physical; Social Science
Dist - PHENIX **Prod** - NELLES 1976

Soil and Tissue Testing - Set 9 26 FRS
VHS / Slide / Cassette
Western Fertilizer Handbook Series
Color (G)
$36.25, $40.00, $8.50 purchase _ #1 - 580 - 609P, #1 - 580 - 209P, #1 - 580 - 539P
Looks at soil and tissue testing. Part of a fourteen - part series based on the Western Fertilizer Handbook.
Agriculture
Dist - VEP **Prod** - VEP

Soil and Water - a Living World 16 MIN
16mm / U-matic / VHS
Color (P I)
Looks at the various creatures who live in both soil and water, some of which can be seen with the naked eye and some of which require a microscope.
Science - Natural
Dist - BARR **Prod** - SAIF 1983
SAIF

Soil - Cement in Energy and Water Resources 20 MIN
16mm
Color
LC 82-700040
Shows examples of soil - cement construction to stabilize earth dams, water storage reservoirs, waste water treatment lagoons, settling ponds, spillways and other water resource facilities, illustrating proper design and construction.
Industrial and Technical Education
Dist - PRTLND **Prod** - PRTLND 1980

Soil Compaction on Forest Lands 32 MIN
16mm
Color
Takes an in - depth look at the causes of forest soil compaction, its effects on productivity and some management alternatives for reducing compaction and restoring compacted lands.
Agriculture
Dist - OSUSF **Prod** - OSUSF

Soil development 12 MIN
VHS
Earth materials series
Color (H C)
$24.95 purchase _ #S9800
Discusses the role of physical and chemical weathering in the formation of soil. Part of a ten - part series on the development of minerals, rocks and soil.
Agriculture; Science - Physical
Dist - HUBDSC **Prod** - HUBDSC

Soil Makers 17 MIN
16mm
Color (I J H)
Explains the complex processes that produce fertile top soil, upon which all life on Earth is dependent.
Agriculture; Science - Natural; Science - Physical
Dist - MMP **Prod** - MMP 1966

Soil Organic Material - Set 8 17 FRS
VHS / Slide / Cassette
Western Fertilizer Handbook Series
Color (G)
$23.95, $40.00, $8.50 purchase _ #1 - 580 - 608P, #1 - 580 - 208P, #1 - 580 - 538P
Looks at the addition of organic materials to soils. Part of a fourteen - part series based on the Western Fertilizer Handbook.
Agriculture
Dist - VEP **Prod** - VEP

Soil PH 30 MIN
U-matic / VHS
Home Gardener with John Lenanton Series Lesson 4; Lesson 4
Color (C A)
Defines pH, explains its relationship to soil nutrients and shows the student how to change the pH of garden soil to make it more acid or more basic. Includes charts and tables to help in selection of appropriate plants for various soils.
Agriculture
Dist - CDTEL **Prod** - COAST

Soil Profiles and Factors of Formation 15 MIN
BETA / VHS
Color
Discusses soil composition.
Agriculture; Science - Natural
Dist - RMIBHF **Prod** - RMIBHF

Soil Profiles and Processes 20 MIN
U-matic / VHS
Earth Science Series
Color
Offers a detailed study of a large coniferous plantation surrounded by agricultural land. Discusses podzolization and the nature of pozol soil, the effect of slope position, land use drainage and soil profiles.
Science - Physical
Dist - FOTH **Prod** - FOTH 1984

The Soil We Plough 20 MIN
16mm
Color
Describes the automation of today's Swedish agriculture, in which cooperatives play a significant part.
Agriculture; Geography - World
Dist - AUDPLN **Prod** - ASI

Soil - what it is and what it Does 11 MIN
U-matic / VHS / 16mm
Color (P)
LC FIA66-1731
Points out how mixtures of sand, clay and humus make various kinds of soil. Explains how the weathering of rocks helps make soil. Uses experiments to indicate types of soils in which plants grow well.
Agriculture; Science - Natural; Science - Physical
Dist - CORF **Prod** - CORF 1966

Soils 30 MIN
Videoreel / VT2
Making Things Grow I Series
Color
Features Thalassa Cruso discussing different aspects of gardening. Describes different types of soil.
Agriculture
Dist - PBS **Prod** - WGBHTV

Soils 1 30 MIN
VHS / U-matic
Home Gardener with John Lenanton Series Lesson 2; Lesson 2
Color (C A)
Stresses the importance of soil for good plant growth. Discusses physical properties of sandy, clay and loam soils. Teaches how to test soil to determine its texture.
Agriculture
Dist - CDTEL **Prod** - COAST

Soils 2 30 MIN
U-matic / VHS
Home Gardener with John Lenanton Series Lesson 3; Lesson 2
Color (C A)
Introduces materials that are used to turn sandy or clay soil into soil that has good structure. Discusses various soils and synthetic materials. Gives solutions for 'hardpan,' a hard layer of earth beneath the surface.
Agriculture
Dist - CDTEL **Prod** - COAST

Soils - Profiles and Processes 20 MIN
VHS
Color (J)
$139.00 purchase _ #5250V
Looks at the ways soils can vary even within a small area of a forest. Examines in detail a well - developed podzol soil profile and reveals the process that produces different soil types in the same area.
Agriculture; Science - Natural; Science - Physical
Dist - SCTRES **Prod** - SCTRES

Sojouner Truth 30 MIN
VHS
Black Americans of achievement video collection series
Color (J H C G)
$39.98 purchase _ #LVC6608V
Portrays abolitionist Sojouner Truth through interviews with leading authorities, rare footage and archival photographs. Part of 12 - part series on noted black Americans.
History - United States
Dist - CAMV

Sojourn Earth 29 MIN
U-matic / 16mm
Presente Series
Color
Presents an adventure that looks at the planet earth from an alien perspective. Features a journey across thousands of miles of the earth's surface, landing at intervals to show a variety of living creatures and structures of beauty, grace and humor. Directed by Robert Marien. No dialogue.
Fine Arts; Geography - World; Literature and Drama; Science - Natural; Science - Physical
Dist - KCET **Prod** - KCET

Sojourn in India 13 MIN
16mm
Color (I)
Presents the visit of a group of American tourists to India in 1964 in the course of their overland tour of the world. Shows the India seen by them.
Geography - World; Physical Education and Recreation
Dist - NEDINF **Prod** - INDIA

Sol 5 MIN
16mm
Color; Silent (C)
$162.40
Experimental film by Stan Brakhage.
Fine Arts
Dist - AFA **Prod** - AFA 1964

Sol and Journalist 15 MIN
U-matic
Parlez - moi 2 Series
Color (H C) (FRENCH)
Features a clown named Sol who has various adventures which teach intermediate level French. Comes with teacher's guide.
Education; Foreign Language
Dist - TVOTAR **Prod** - TVOTAR 1978

Sol and the Artist 10 MIN
U-matic
Parlez - moi 1 Series
Color (J H) (FRENCH)
Presents a series of skits featuring a clown named Sol, which introduce basic, functional French. Each program introduces four new French phrases with review. Vocabulary and grammar are presented cumulatively, gradually increasing in difficulty. With teacher's guide.
Education; Foreign Language
Dist - TVOTAR **Prod** - TVOTAR 1978

Sol and the Assembly Line 15 MIN
U-matic
Parlez - moi 2 Series
Color (H C) (FRENCH)
Features a clown named Sol who has various adventures which teach intermediate level French. Comes with teacher's guide.
Education; Foreign Language
Dist - TVOTAR **Prod** - TVOTAR 1978

Sol and the Balloon Race 15 MIN
U-matic
Parlez - moi 2 Series
Color (H C) (FRENCH)
Features a clown named Sol who has various adventures which teach intermediate level French. Comes with teacher's guide.
Education; Foreign Language
Dist - TVOTAR **Prod** - TVOTAR 1978

Sol and the Burgler 10 MIN
U-matic
Parlez - moi 1 Series
Color (J H) (FRENCH)
Presents a series of skits featuring a clown named Sol, which introduce basic, functional French. Each program introduces four new French phrases with review. Vocabulary and grammar are presented cumulatively, gradually increasing in difficulty. With teacher's guide.
Education; Foreign Language
Dist - TVOTAR **Prod** - TVOTAR 1978

Sol and the Carpenter 15 MIN
U-matic
Parlez - moi 2 Series
Color (H C) (FRENCH)
Features a clown named Sol who has various adventures which teach intermediate level French. Comes with teacher's guide.
Education; Foreign Language
Dist - TVOTAR **Prod** - TVOTAR 1978

Sol and the Cinema Ticket 10 MIN
U-matic
Parlez - moi 1 Series
Color (J H) (FRENCH)
Presents a series of skits featuring a clown named Sol, which introduce basic, functional French. Each program introduces four new French phrases with review. Vocabulary and grammar are presented cumulatively, gradually increasing in difficulty. With teacher's guide.

Education; Foreign Language
Dist - TVOTAR **Prod** - TVOTAR 1978

Sol and the Clockmaker 10 MIN
U-matic
Parlez - moi 1 Series
Color (J H) (FRENCH)
Presents a series of skits featuring a clown named Sol, which introduce basic, functional French. Each program introduces four new French phrases with review. Vocabulary and grammar are presented cumulatively, gradually increasing in difficulty. With teacher's guide.
Education; Foreign Language
Dist - TVOTAR **Prod** - TVOTAR 1978

Sol and the Disk Jockey 15 MIN
U-matic
Parlez - moi 2 Series
Color (H C) (FRENCH)
Features a clown named Sol who has various adventures which teach intermediate level French. Comes with teacher's guide.
Education; Foreign Language
Dist - TVOTAR **Prod** - TVOTAR 1978

Sol and the Fisherman 10 MIN
U-matic
Parlez - moi 1 Series
Color (J H) (FRENCH)
Presents a series of skits featuring a clown named Sol, which introduce basic, functional French. Each program introduces four new French phrases with review. Vocabulary and grammar are presented cumulatively, gradually increasing in difficulty. With teacher's guide.
Education; Foreign Language
Dist - TVOTAR **Prod** - TVOTAR 1978

Sol and the Flea Market 10 MIN
U-matic
Parlez - moi 1 Series
Color (J H) (FRENCH)
Presents a series of skits featuring a clown named Sol, which introduce basic, functional French. Each program introduces four new French phrases with review. Vocabulary and grammar are presented cumulatively, gradually increasing in difficulty. With teacher's guide.
Education; Foreign Language
Dist - TVOTAR **Prod** - TVOTAR 1978

Sol and the Fortune Teller 10 MIN
U-matic
Parlez - moi 1 Series
Color (J H) (FRENCH)
Presents a series of skits featuring a clown named Sol, which introduce basic, functional French. Each program introduces four new French phrases with review. Vocabulary and grammar are presented cumulatively, gradually increasing in difficulty. With teacher's guide.
Education; Foreign Language
Dist - TVOTAR **Prod** - TVOTAR 1978

Sol and the Gambler 10 MIN
U-matic
Parlez - moi 1 Series
Color (J H) (FRENCH)
Presents a series of skits featuring a clown named Sol, which introduce basic, functional French. Each program introduces four new French phrases with review. Vocabulary and grammar are presented cumulatively, gradually increasing in difficulty. With teacher's guide.
Education; Foreign Language
Dist - TVOTAR **Prod** - TVOTAR 1978

Sol and the Game Show 10 MIN
U-matic
Parlez - moi 1 Series
Color (J H) (FRENCH)
Presents a series of skits featuring a clown named Sol, which introduce basic, functional French. Each program introduces four new French phrases with review. Vocabulary and grammar are presented cumulatively, gradually increasing in difficulty. With teacher's guide.
Education; Foreign Language
Dist - TVOTAR **Prod** - TVOTAR 1978

Sol and the Garage Mechanic 10 MIN
U-matic
Parlez - moi 1 Series
Color (J H) (FRENCH)
Presents a series of skits featuring a clown named Sol, which introduce basic, functional French. Each program introduces four new French phrases with review. Vocabulary and grammar are presented cumulatively, gradually increasing in difficulty. With teacher's guide.
Education; Foreign Language
Dist - TVOTAR **Prod** - TVOTAR 1978

Sol and the Great Detective 15 MIN
U-matic
Parlez - moi 2 Series
Color (H C) (FRENCH)
Features a clown named Sol who has various adventures which teach intermediate level French. Comes with teacher's guide.
Education; Foreign Language
Dist - TVOTAR **Prod** - TVOTAR 1978

Sol and the Lovers 15 MIN
U-matic
Parlez - moi 2 Series
Color (H C) (FRENCH)
Features a clown named Sol who has various adventures which teach intermediate level French. Comes with teacher's guide.
Education; Foreign Language
Dist - TVOTAR **Prod** - TVOTAR 1978

Sol and the Lumberjack 10 MIN
U-matic
Parlez - moi 1 Series
Color (J H) (FRENCH)
Presents a series of skits featuring a clown named Sol, which introduce basic, functional French. Each program introduces four new French phrases with review. Vocabulary and grammar are presented cumulatively, gradually increasing in difficulty. With teacher's guide.
Education; Foreign Language
Dist - TVOTAR **Prod** - TVOTAR 1978

Sol and the Mailman 10 MIN
U-matic
Parlez - moi 1 Series
Color (J H) (FRENCH)
Presents a series of skits featuring a clown named Sol, which introduce basic, functional French. Each program introduces four new French phrases with review. Vocabulary and grammar are presented cumulatively, gradually increasing in difficulty. With teacher's guide.
Education; Foreign Language
Dist - TVOTAR **Prod** - TVOTAR 1978

Sol and the Optician 15 MIN
U-matic
Parlez - moi 2 Series
Color (H C) (FRENCH)
Features a clown named Sol who has various adventures which teach intermediate level French. Comes with teacher's guide.
Education; Foreign Language
Dist - TVOTAR **Prod** - TVOTAR 1978

Sol and the Photographer 10 MIN
U-matic
Parlez - moi 1 Series
Color (J H) (FRENCH)
Presents a series of skits featuring a clown named Sol, which introduce basic, functional French. Each program introduces four new French phrases with review. Vocabulary and grammar are presented cumulatively, gradually increasing in difficulty. With teacher's guide.
Education; Foreign Language
Dist - TVOTAR **Prod** - TVOTAR 1978

Sol and the Pirates 15 MIN
U-matic
Parlez - moi 2 Series
Color (H C) (FRENCH)
Features a clown named Sol who has various adventures which teach intermediate level French. Comes with teacher's guide.
Education; Foreign Language
Dist - TVOTAR **Prod** - TVOTAR 1978

Sol and the Pizza 10 MIN
U-matic
Parlez - moi 1 Series
Color (J H) (FRENCH)
Presents a series of skits featuring a clown named Sol, which introduce basic, functional French. Each program introduces four new French phrases with review. Vocabulary and grammar are presented cumulatively, gradually increasing in difficulty. With teacher's guide.
Education; Foreign Language
Dist - TVOTAR **Prod** - TVOTAR 1978

Sol and the Policeman 10 MIN
U-matic
Parlez - moi 1 Series
Color (J H) (FRENCH)
Presents a series of skits featuring a clown named Sol, which introduce basic, functional French. Each program introduces four new French phrases with review. Vocabulary and grammar are presented cumulatively, gradually increasing in difficulty. With teacher's guide.
Education; Foreign Language
Dist - TVOTAR **Prod** - TVOTAR 1978

Sol and the Sailboat 10 MIN
U-matic
Parlez - moi 1 Series
Color (J H) (FRENCH)
Presents a series of skits featuring a clown named Sol, which introduce basic, functional French. Each program introduces four new French phrases with review. Vocabulary and grammar are presented cumulatively, gradually increasing in difficulty. With teacher's guide.
Education; Foreign Language
Dist - TVOTAR **Prod** - TVOTAR 1978

Sol and the Scout Tent 10 MIN
U-matic
Parlez - moi 1 Series
Color (J H) (FRENCH)
Presents a series of skits featuring a clown named Sol, which introduce basic, functional French. Each program introduces four new French phrases with review. Vocabulary and grammar are presented cumulatively, gradually increasing in difficulty. With teacher's guide.
Education; Foreign Language
Dist - TVOTAR **Prod** - TVOTAR 1978

Sol and the Spies 15 MIN
U-matic
Parlez - moi 2 Series
Color (H C) (FRENCH)
Features a clown named Sol who has various adventures which teach intermediate level French. Comes with teacher's guide.
Education; Foreign Language
Dist - TVOTAR **Prod** - TVOTAR 1978

Sol and the Tomatoes 10 MIN
U-matic
Parlez - moi 1 Series
Color (J H) (FRENCH)
Presents a series of skits featuring a clown named Sol, which introduce basic, functional French. Each program introduces four new French phrases with review. Vocabulary and grammar are presented cumulatively, gradually increasing in difficulty. With teacher's guide.
Education; Foreign Language
Dist - TVOTAR **Prod** - TVOTAR 1978

Sol and the TV Commercial 10 MIN
U-matic
Parlez - moi 1 Series
Color (J H) (FRENCH)
Presents a series of skits featuring a clown named Sol, which introduce basic, functional French. Each program introduces four new French phrases with review. Vocabulary and grammar are presented cumulatively, gradually increasing in difficulty. With teacher's guide.
Education; Foreign Language
Dist - TVOTAR **Prod** - TVOTAR 1978

Sol and the used Car 15 MIN
U-matic
Parlez - moi 2 Series
Color (H C) (FRENCH)
Features a clown named Sol who has various adventures which teach intermediate level French. Comes with teacher's guide.
Education; Foreign Language
Dist - TVOTAR **Prod** - TVOTAR 1978

Sol and the Vacuum Cleaner 10 MIN
U-matic
Parlez - moi 1 Series
Color (J H) (FRENCH)
Presents a series of skits featuring a clown named Sol, which introduce basic, functional French. Each program introduces four new French phrases with review. Vocabulary and grammar are presented cumulatively, gradually increasing in difficulty. With teacher's guide.
Education; Foreign Language
Dist - TVOTAR **Prod** - TVOTAR 1978

Sol and the Washing Machine 10 MIN
U-matic
Parlez - moi 1 Series
Color (J H) (FRENCH)
Presents a series of skits featuring a clown named Sol, which introduce basic, functional French. Each program introduces four new French phrases with review. Vocabulary and grammar are presented cumulatively, gradually increasing in difficulty. With teacher's guide.
Education; Foreign Language
Dist - TVOTAR **Prod** - TVOTAR 1978

Sol at the Airport 10 MIN
U-matic
Parlez - moi 1 Series
Color (J H) (FRENCH)
Presents a series of skits featuring a clown named Sol, which introduce basic, functional French. Each program introduces four new French phrases with review. Vocabulary and grammar are presented cumulatively, gradually increasing in difficulty. With teacher's guide.
Education; Foreign Language
Dist - TVOTAR **Prod** - TVOTAR 1978

Sol at the Baker's 15 MIN
U-matic
Parlez - moi 2 Series
Color (H C) (FRENCH)
Features a clown named Sol who has various adventures which teach intermediate level French. Comes with teacher's guide.
Education; Foreign Language
Dist - TVOTAR **Prod** - TVOTAR 1978

Sol at the Butcher's 15 MIN
U-matic
Parlez - moi 2 Series
Color (H C) (FRENCH)
Features a clown named Sol who has various adventures which teach intermediate level French. Comes with teacher's guide.
Education; Foreign Language
Dist - TVOTAR **Prod** - TVOTAR 1978

Sol at the Candy Store 10 MIN
U-matic
Parlez - moi 1 Series
Color (J H) (FRENCH)
Presents a series of skits featuring a clown named Sol, which introduce basic, functional French. Each program introduces four new French phrases with review. Vocabulary and grammar are presented cumulatively, gradually increasing in difficulty. With teacher's guide.
Education; Foreign Language
Dist - TVOTAR **Prod** - TVOTAR 1978

Sol at the Doctor's 10 MIN
U-matic
Parlez - moi 1 Series
Color (J H) (FRENCH)
Presents a series of skits featuring a clown named Sol, which introduce basic, functional French. Each program introduces four new French phrases with review. Vocabulary and grammar are presented cumulatively, gradually increasing in difficulty. With teacher's guide.
Education; Foreign Language
Dist - TVOTAR **Prod** - TVOTAR 1978

Sol at the Drug Store 10 MIN
U-matic
Parlez - moi 1 Series
Color (J H) (FRENCH)
Presents a series of skits featuring a clown named Sol, which introduce basic, functional French. Each program introduces four new French phrases with review. Vocabulary and grammar are presented cumulatively, gradually increasing in difficulty. With teacher's guide.
Education; Foreign Language
Dist - TVOTAR **Prod** - TVOTAR 1978

Sol at the Fashion Botique 15 MIN
U-matic
Parlez - moi 2 Series
Color (H C) (FRENCH)
Features a clown named Sol who has various adventures which teach intermediate level French. Comes with teacher's guide.
Education; Foreign Language
Dist - TVOTAR **Prod** - TVOTAR 1978

Sol at the Grocer's 10 MIN
U-matic
Parlez - moi 1 Series
Color (J H) (FRENCH)
Presents a series of skits featuring a clown named Sol, which introduce basic, functional French. Each program introduces four new French phrases with review. Vocabulary and grammar are presented cumulatively, gradually increasing in difficulty. With teacher's guide.
Education; Foreign Language
Dist - TVOTAR **Prod** - TVOTAR 1978

Sol at the Hairdresser's 10 MIN
U-matic
Parlez - moi 1 Series
Color (J H) (FRENCH)
Presents a series of skits featuring a clown named Sol, which introduce basic, functional French. Each program introduces four new French phrases with review. Vocabulary and grammar are presented cumulatively, gradually increasing in difficulty. With teacher's guide.
Education; Foreign Language
Dist - TVOTAR **Prod** - TVOTAR 1978

Sol at the Hardware Store 10 MIN
U-matic
Parlez - moi 1 Series
Color (J H) (FRENCH)
Presents a series of skits featuring a clown named Sol, which introduce basic, functional French. Each program introduces four new French phrases with review. Vocabulary and grammar are presented cumulatively, gradually increasing in difficulty. With teacher's guide.
Education; Foreign Language
Dist - TVOTAR **Prod** - TVOTAR 1978

Sol at the Hotel 10 MIN
U-matic
Parlez - moi 1 Series
Color (J H) (FRENCH)
Presents a series of skits featuring a clown named Sol, which introduce basic, functional French. Each program introduces four new French phrases with review. Vocabulary and grammar are presented cumulatively, gradually increasing in difficulty. With teacher's guide.
Education; Foreign Language
Dist - TVOTAR **Prod** - TVOTAR 1978

Sol at the Record Store 10 MIN
U-matic
Parlez - moi 1 Series
Color (J H) (FRENCH)
Presents a series of skits featuring a clown named Sol, which introduce basic, functional French. Each program introduces four new French phrases with review. Vocabulary and grammar are presented cumulatively, gradually increasing in difficulty. With teacher's guide.
Education; Foreign Language
Dist - TVOTAR **Prod** - TVOTAR 1978

Sol at the Shoe Store 10 MIN
U-matic
Parlez - moi 1 Series
Color (J H) (FRENCH)
Presents a series of skits featuring a clown named Sol, which introduce basic, functional French. Each program introduces four new French phrases with review. Vocabulary and grammar are presented cumulatively, gradually increasing in difficulty. With teacher's guide.
Education; Foreign Language
Dist - TVOTAR **Prod** - TVOTAR 1978

Sol at the Tailor 10 MIN
U-matic
Parlez - moi 1 Series
Color (J H) (FRENCH)
Presents a series of skits featuring a clown named Sol, which introduce basic, functional French. Each program introduces four new French phrases with review. Vocabulary and grammar are presented cumulatively, gradually increasing in difficulty. With teacher's guide.
Education; Foreign Language
Dist - TVOTAR **Prod** - TVOTAR 1978

Sol at the Train Station 15 MIN
U-matic
Parlez - moi 2 Series
Color (H C) (FRENCH)
Features a clown named Sol who has various adventures which teach intermediate level French. Comes with teacher's guide.
Education; Foreign Language
Dist - TVOTAR **Prod** - TVOTAR 1978

Sol at the Travel Agency 10 MIN
U-matic
Parlez - moi 1 Series
Color (J H) (FRENCH)
Presents a series of skits featuring a clown named Sol, which introduce basic, functional French. Each program introduces four new French phrases with review. Vocabulary and grammar are presented cumulatively, gradually increasing in difficulty. With teacher's guide.
Education; Foreign Language
Dist - TVOTAR **Prod** - TVOTAR 1978

Sol Buys a House 10 MIN
U-matic
Parlez - moi 1 Series
Color (J H) (FRENCH)
Presents a series of skits featuring a clown named Sol, which introduce basic, functional French. Each program introduces four new French phrases with review. Vocabulary and grammar are presented cumulatively, gradually increasing in difficulty. With teacher's guide.
Education; Foreign Language
Dist - TVOTAR **Prod** - TVOTAR 1978

Sol Goes through Customs 10 MIN
U-matic
Parlez - moi 1 Series
Color (J H) (FRENCH)
Presents a series of skits featuring a clown named Sol, which introduce basic, functional French. Each program introduces four new French phrases with review. Vocabulary and grammar are presented cumulatively, gradually increasing in difficulty. With teacher's guide.
Education; Foreign Language
Dist - TVOTAR **Prod** - TVOTAR 1978

Sol Goes to Court 10 MIN
U-matic
Parlez - moi 1 Series
Color (J H) (FRENCH)
Presents a series of skits featuring a clown named Sol, which introduce basic, functional French. Each program introduces four new French phrases with review. Vocabulary and grammar are presented cumulatively, gradually increasing in difficulty. With teacher's guide.
Education; Foreign Language
Dist - TVOTAR **Prod** - TVOTAR 1978

Sol Goes to Jail 10 MIN
U-matic
Parlez - moi 1 Series
Color (J H) (FRENCH)
Presents a series of skits featuring a clown named Sol, which introduce basic, functional French. Each program introduces four new French phrases with review. Vocabulary and grammar are presented cumulatively, gradually increasing in difficulty. With teacher's guide.
Education; Foreign Language
Dist - TVOTAR **Prod** - TVOTAR 1978

Sol Goes to the Bank 10 MIN
U-matic
Parlez - moi 1 Series
Color (J H) (FRENCH)
Presents a series of skits featuring a clown named Sol, which introduce basic, functional French. Each program introduces four new French phrases with review. Vocabulary and grammar are presented cumulatively, gradually increasing in difficulty. With teacher's guide.
Education; Foreign Language
Dist - TVOTAR **Prod** - TVOTAR 1978

Sol Goes to the Beach 10 MIN
U-matic
Parlez - moi 1 Series
Color (J H) (FRENCH)
Presents a series of skits featuring a clown named Sol, which introduce basic, functional French. Each program introduces four new French phrases with review. Vocabulary and grammar are presented cumulatively, gradually increasing in difficulty. With teacher's guide.
Education; Foreign Language
Dist - TVOTAR **Prod** - TVOTAR 1978

Sol Goes to the Dentist 10 MIN
U-matic
Parlez - moi 1 Series
Color (J H) (FRENCH)
Presents a series of skits featuring a clown named Sol, which introduce basic, functional French. Each program introduces four new French phrases with review. Vocabulary and grammar are presented cumulatively, gradually increasing in difficulty. With teacher's guide.
Education; Foreign Language
Dist - TVOTAR **Prod** - TVOTAR 1978

Sol Goes West 15 MIN
U-matic
Parlez - moi 2 Series
Color (H C) (FRENCH)
Features a clown named Sol who has various adventures which teach intermediate level French. Comes with teacher's guide.
Education; Foreign Language
Dist - TVOTAR **Prod** - TVOTAR 1978

Sol in the Elevator 15 MIN
U-matic
Parlez - moi 2 Series
Color (H C) (FRENCH)
Features a clown named Sol who has various adventures which teach intermediate level French. Comes with teacher's guide.
Education; Foreign Language
Dist - TVOTAR **Prod** - TVOTAR 1978

Sol in the Garden 10 MIN
U-matic
Parlez - moi 1 Series
Color (J H) (FRENCH)
Presents a series of skits featuring a clown named Sol, which introduce basic, functional French. Each program introduces four new French phrases with review. Vocabulary and grammar are presented cumulatively, gradually increasing in difficulty. With teacher's guide.
Education; Foreign Language
Dist - TVOTAR **Prod** - TVOTAR 1978

Sol in the Haunted House 10 MIN
U-matic
Parlez - moi 1 Series
Color (J H) (FRENCH)
Presents a series of skits featuring a clown named Sol, which introduce basic, functional French. Each program introduces four new French phrases with review. Vocabulary and grammar are presented cumulatively, gradually increasing in difficulty. With teacher's guide.
Education; Foreign Language
Dist - TVOTAR **Prod** - TVOTAR 1978

Sol in the Hospital 10 MIN
U-matic
Parlez - moi 1 Series
Color (J H) (FRENCH)
Presents a series of skits featuring a clown named Sol, which introduce basic, functional French. Each program introduces four new French phrases with review. Vocabulary and grammar are presented cumulatively, gradually increasing in difficulty. With teacher's guide.

Education; Foreign Language
Dist - TVOTAR **Prod** - TVOTAR 1978

Sol in the Jewelry Store 10 MIN
U-matic
Parlez - moi 1 Series
Color (J H) (FRENCH)
Presents a series of skits featuring a clown named Sol, which introduce basic, functional French. Each program introduces four new French phrases with review. Vocabulary and grammar are presented cumulatively, gradually increasing in difficulty. With teacher's guide.
Education; Foreign Language
Dist - TVOTAR **Prod** - TVOTAR 1978

Sol in the Laundry 15 MIN
U-matic
Parlez - moi 2 Series
Color (H C) (FRENCH)
Features a clown named Sol who has various adventures which teach intermediate level French. Comes with teacher's guide.
Education; Foreign Language
Dist - TVOTAR **Prod** - TVOTAR 1978

Sol in the Library 10 MIN
U-matic
Parlez - moi 1 Series
Color (J H) (FRENCH)
Presents a series of skits featuring a clown named Sol, which introduce basic, functional French. Each program introduces four new French phrases with review. Vocabulary and grammar are presented cumulatively, gradually increasing in difficulty. With teacher's guide.
Education; Foreign Language
Dist - TVOTAR **Prod** - TVOTAR 1978

Sol in the Park 15 MIN
U-matic
Parlez - moi 2 Series
Color (H C) (FRENCH)
Features a clown named Sol who has various adventures which teach intermediate level French. Comes with teacher's guide.
Education; Foreign Language
Dist - TVOTAR **Prod** - TVOTAR 1978

Sol in the Post Office 15 MIN
U-matic
Parlez - moi 2 Series
Color (H C) (FRENCH)
Features a clown named Sol who has various adventures which teach intermediate level French. Comes with teacher's guide.
Education; Foreign Language
Dist - TVOTAR **Prod** - TVOTAR 1978

Sol in the Restaurant 10 MIN
U-matic
Parlez - moi 1 Series
Color (J H) (FRENCH)
Presents a series of skits featuring a clown named Sol, which introduce basic, functional French. Each program introduces four new French phrases with review. Vocabulary and grammar are presented cumulatively, gradually increasing in difficulty. With teacher's guide.
Education; Foreign Language
Dist - TVOTAR **Prod** - TVOTAR 1978

Sol in the Sports Shop 15 MIN
U-matic
Parlez - moi 2 Series
Color (H C) (FRENCH)
Features a clown named Sol who has various adventures which teach intermediate level French. Comes with teacher's guide.
Education; Foreign Language
Dist - TVOTAR **Prod** - TVOTAR 1978

Sol Joins the Army 10 MIN
U-matic
Parlez - moi 1 Series
Color (J H) (FRENCH)
Presents a series of skits featuring a clown named Sol, which introduce basic, functional French. Each program introduces four new French phrases with review. Vocabulary and grammar are presented cumulatively, gradually increasing in difficulty. With teacher's guide.
Education; Foreign Language
Dist - TVOTAR **Prod** - TVOTAR 1978

Sol Learns Good Manners 15 MIN
U-matic
Parlez - moi 2 Series
Color (H C) (FRENCH)
Features a clown named Sol who has various adventures which teach intermediate level French. Comes with teacher's guide.
Education; Foreign Language
Dist - TVOTAR **Prod** - TVOTAR 1978

Sol Minds the Fruit Store 10 MIN
U-matic
Parlez - moi 1 Series
Color (J H) (FRENCH)
Presents a series of skits featuring a clown named Sol, which introduce basic, functional French. Each program introduces four new French phrases with review. Vocabulary and grammar are presented cumulatively, gradually increasing in difficulty. With teacher's guide.
Education; Foreign Language
Dist - TVOTAR **Prod** - TVOTAR 1978

Sol on the Bus 15 MIN
U-matic
Parlez - moi 2 Series
Color (H C) (FRENCH)
Features a clown named Sol who has various adventures which teach intermediate level French. Comes with teacher's guide.
Education; Foreign Language
Dist - TVOTAR **Prod** - TVOTAR 1978

Sol on the Stage 15 MIN
U-matic
Parlez - moi 2 Series
Color (H C) (FRENCH)
Features a clown named Sol who has various adventures which teach intermediate level French. Comes with teacher's guide.
Education; Foreign Language
Dist - TVOTAR **Prod** - TVOTAR 1978

Sol on the Telephone 10 MIN
U-matic
Parlez - moi 1 Series
Color (J H) (FRENCH)
Presents a series of skits featuring a clown named Sol, which introduce basic, functional French. Each program introduces four new French phrases with review. Vocabulary and grammar are presented cumulatively, gradually increasing in difficulty. With teacher's guide.
Education; Foreign Language
Dist - TVOTAR **Prod** - TVOTAR 1978

Sol Plays Golf 10 MIN
U-matic
Parlez - moi 1 Series
Color (J H) (FRENCH)
Presents a series of skits featuring a clown named Sol, which introduce basic, functional French. Each program introduces four new French phrases with review. Vocabulary and grammar are presented cumulatively, gradually increasing in difficulty. With teacher's guide.
Education; Foreign Language
Dist - TVOTAR **Prod** - TVOTAR 1978

Sol Plays Hockey 15 MIN
U-matic
Parlez - moi 2 Series
Color (H C) (FRENCH)
Features a clown named Sol who has various adventures which teach intermediate level French. Comes with teacher's guide.
Education; Foreign Language
Dist - TVOTAR **Prod** - TVOTAR 1978

Sol Preparation, Dialysis and Ultrafiltration 57 MIN
U-matic / VHS
Colloid and Surface Chemistry - Lyophobic Colloids Series
Color
Science; Science - Physical
Dist - KALMIA **Prod** - KALMIA

Sol Rents a Room 15 MIN
U-matic
Parlez - moi 2 Series
Color (H C) (FRENCH)
Features a clown named Sol who has various adventures which teach intermediate level French. Comes with teacher's guide.
Education; Foreign Language
Dist - TVOTAR **Prod** - TVOTAR 1978

Sol Rides a Horse 15 MIN
U-matic
Parlez - moi 2 Series
Color (H C) (FRENCH)
Features a clown named Sol who has various adventures which teach intermediate level French. Comes with teacher's guide.
Education; Foreign Language
Dist - TVOTAR **Prod** - TVOTAR 1978

Sol Sets the Table 15 MIN
U-matic
Parlez - moi 2 Series
Color (H C) (FRENCH)
Features a clown named Sol who has various adventures which teach intermediate level French. Comes with teacher's guide.
Education; Foreign Language
Dist - TVOTAR **Prod** - TVOTAR 1978

Sol the Babysitter 10 MIN
U-matic
Parlez - moi 1 Series
Color (J H) (FRENCH)
Presents a series of skits featuring a clown named Sol, which introduce basic, functional French. Each program introduces four new French phrases with review. Vocabulary and grammar are presented cumulatively, gradually increasing in difficulty. With teacher's guide.
Education; Foreign Language
Dist - TVOTAR **Prod** - TVOTAR 1978

Sol the Dishwasher 10 MIN
U-matic
Parlez - moi 1 Series
Color (J H) (FRENCH)
Presents a series of skits featuring a clown named Sol, which introduce basic, functional French. Each program introduces four new French phrases with review. Vocabulary and grammar are presented cumulatively, gradually increasing in difficulty. With teacher's guide.
Education; Foreign Language
Dist - TVOTAR **Prod** - TVOTAR 1978

Sol the Office Boy 15 MIN
U-matic
Parlez - moi 2 Series
Color (H C) (FRENCH)
Features a clown named Sol who has various adventures which teach intermediate level French. Comes with teacher's guide.
Education; Foreign Language
Dist - TVOTAR **Prod** - TVOTAR 1978

Sol the Painter 10 MIN
U-matic
Parlez - moi 1 Series
Color (J H) (FRENCH)
Presents a series of skits featuring a clown named Sol, which introduce basic, functional French. Each program introduces four new French phrases with review. Vocabulary and grammar are presented cumulatively, gradually increasing in difficulty. With teacher's guide.
Education; Foreign Language
Dist - TVOTAR **Prod** - TVOTAR 1978

Solar activity 20 MIN
Videodisc / VHS
Color (J H G)
$395.00 purchase, $50.00 rental _ #8284
Films experiments which explain the nature of the sun's surface and atmosphere. Examines solar activity such as sun spots, solar flares and prominences and how the study of sunlight tells much about the composition of the sun. Visits two observatories.
Science; Science - Physical
Dist - AIMS **Prod** - EDMI 1990

The Solar Advantage 20 MIN
16mm
Color
Discusses passive, active and photovoltaic solar energy. Shows all three types of systems in operation in several locations across the country. Includes interviews with people who are using and installing solar systems giving the audience a good overview of how solar energy can be applied.
Social Science
Dist - COPRO **Prod** - COPRO

The Solar Atmosphere 29 MIN
16mm
B&W (C A)
LC 75-702360
Discusses various aspects of the solar atmosphere including granulation, development of sunspots, spicules, flares and flare waves, surges and prominences.
Science - Physical
Dist - CIT **Prod** - NSF 1972

Solar cell 12 MIN
VHS
Energy and the environment series
Color; PAL (J H)
PdS29.50 purchase
Explores solar cells including their structure, how they work and how they can be most appropriately used to generate electricity. Uses models and demonstrations with the real thing. Part of a three - apart series looking into renewable energy sources at the Centre for Alternative Technology in Powys, North Wales. Produced by CV, United Kingdom.
Geography - World; Science; Social Science; Sociology
Dist - EMFVL

Solar cells - power from the sun 15 MIN
VHS
Color (H C G)
$295.00 purchase, $75.00 rental _ #8392
Examines the use of renewable, alternative sources of energy in the form of solar energy. Uses animation to show how a solar cell converts sunlight into usable energy. Considers the possibility of solar - powered homes, cars, appliances - even generating plants.

Science - Natural; Social Science
Dist - AIMS Prod - IFFB 1992

Solar Collectors 27 MIN
U-matic / VHS
Solar Collectors, Solar Radiation, Insolation Tables Series
Color (H C A)
Discusses the parts of a flat - plate collector and suitable materials for each part. Shows the three types of solar collectors along with practical applications for each type. Covers methods for aiming the solar collector for maximum efficiency.
Social Science
Dist - MOKIN Prod - NCDCC

Solar Collectors, Solar Radiation, Insolation Tables Series
Amount and direction of solar input 26 MIN
Sizing Solar Collectors, Pt 1 25 MIN
Sizing Solar Collectors, Pt 2 25 MIN
Sizing Solar Collectors, Pt 3 25 MIN
Solar Collectors 27 MIN
Dist - MOKIN

Solar Comfort 23 MIN
16mm
Color
LC 80-701621
Shows how proper home design can provide solar heating and cooling with a minimum of commercially produced energy. Includes interviews with owners of passive - solar homes.
Industrial and Technical Education; Social Science
Dist - CALENC Prod - CALENC 1980

The Solar Decision 30 MIN
VHS / 16mm
Solar Energy Series
Color (G)
$55.00 rental _ #SLRE - 106
Examines the role of the U S Government in the development of solar energy.
Science - Physical; Social Science
Dist - PBS Prod - KNMETV

Solar design show 30 MIN
VHS
A House for all seasons series
Color (G)
$49.95 purchase _ #AHFS - 302
Tours energy - saving solar homes in France, Germany and the U S. Tells what energy - saving features are best.
Home Economics; Industrial and Technical Education; Science - Natural; Social Science; Sociology
Dist - PBS Prod - KRMATV 1986

Solar Domestic Hot Water Heater 24 MIN
VHS / U-matic
Active Solar Heating and Cooling Series
Color (H C A)
Explains the basic components of a solar domestic hot water heater and illustrates the function of each.
Home Economics; Social Science
Dist - MOKIN Prod - NCDCC

Solar eclipse
U-matic / VHS / BETA
Search encounters in science series
Color; PAL (G H C)
PdS25, PdS33 purchase
Brings modern research efforts of the world's leading scientists into the classroom. Features one of a series of 24 mini - documentaries. Each film is 5 - 7 minutes in length.
Science; Science - Physical
Dist - EDPAT Prod - NSF

Solar Eclipses 11 MIN
U-matic / VHS / 16mm
Color (I J)
$50 rental _ #1625
Describes solar eclipses. Explains basic concepts at work, and highlights research done on eclipses.
Science; Science - Physical
Dist - AIMS Prod - AIMS 1968

Solar energy
Videodisc
Color; CAV (P I J)
$189.00 purchase _ #8L201
Takes an animated look at how solar energy can be used to power electricity, heating and cooling. Explains how the sun produces light and heat and shows how plants and animals rely on the sun's energy. Barcoded for instant random access.
Science - Physical; Social Science
Dist - BARR Prod - BARR 1991

Solar energy 30 MIN
VHS
Color (G)
$29.95 purchase
Discusses the principles of solar energy and how it can be used in the home and office.
Science - Physical
Dist - PBS Prod - WNETTV

Solar Energy 23 MIN
VHS / 16mm
Energy Series
Color (I)
LC 90713867
Explores how the sun produces light and heat. Discusses how plants and animals use solar energy. Examines the use of solar power.
Industrial and Technical Education; Science - Physical; Social Science
Dist - BARR

Solar Energy 15 MIN
U-matic / VHS
First Films on Science Series
Color (P I)
Demonstrates man's dependence on the sun, explaining that it is the earth's chief source of radiant energy. Shows how the sun's light and heat provide energy for plants to grow, to make food and to create fossil fuels, such as coal and oil. Depicts how solar energy causes an evaporation - condensation rain cycle that ultimately results in electricity.
Science - Natural; Science - Physical; Social Science
Dist - AITECH Prod - MAETEL 1975

Solar Energy and You 19 MIN
16mm
Color
LC 77-701834
Reviews the field of solar energy. Shows efforts at utilizing solar power and projected application for the future.
Science - Natural; Science - Physical; Social Science; Sociology
Dist - CONPOW Prod - FARTC 1977

A Solar energy doghouse - 102 29 MIN
VHS
FROG series 1; Series 1; 102
Color (P I J)
$100.00 purchase
Offers the second program by Friends of Research and Odd Gadgets. Lifts science off the textbook page into the real world to show how enjoyable and challenging science can be. In this episode, the Froggers try heating their doghouse with solar power. Special focus on solar collection, heat pumps and storage batteries. Produced by Greg Rist.
Science - Physical; Social Science
Dist - BULFRG Prod - OWLTV 1993

Solar Energy Fundamentals 50 MIN
U-matic / VHS
Energy Issues and Alternatives Series
Color
Gives the fundamental principles of solar utilization as they relate to solar thermal conversion, photovoltaics, bioconversion and heating/cooling applications. Stresses active and passive solar heating, using actual examples and applications.
Social Science
Dist - UIDEEO Prod - UIDEEO

Solar energy - hope for the future
VHS
World around us series
Color (G)
$29.95 purchase _ #IV - 024
Examines the history of the development of solar energy, current usage and future possibilities of solar energy.
Social Science; Sociology
Dist - INCRSE Prod - INCRSE

Solar Energy - How it Works 16 MIN
U-matic / VHS / 16mm
Captioned; Color (I J H)
LC 79-701733
Demonstrates ways to use the energy from the Sun through experiments by children and by showing commercial applications.
Science - Physical; Social Science
Dist - CF Prod - SMITG 1979

Solar Energy - It's Working in Michigan 10 MIN
U-matic / VHS / 16mm
Color
Focuses on three generic solar systems and presents homeowners who explain them. Features an active and passive solar home, a domestic hot water system and a solar greenhouse.
Science - Physical; Social Science
Dist - BRAURP Prod - MDCEA

Solar Energy Now 30 MIN
U-matic / VHS
Color
Presents a de - mystifying look at solar energy systems at work in the home. Taped at the Farallones Institute's Integral Urban House in Berkeley, California and illustrates the applications and installation of home solar energy heating units.
Social Science
Dist - PBS Prod - GOLHAR 1982

Solar Energy Primer 24 MIN
VHS / U-matic
Color
$335.00 purchase
Social Science
Dist - ABCLR Prod - ABCLR 1979

Solar Energy - Ray of Hope 16 MIN
VHS / U-matic
Color
Looks at solar housing in Minnesota, the farsighted California approach and the future hope of generating solar power.
Social Science
Dist - WCCOTV Prod - WCCOTV 1979

Solar Energy Series
Examines space heating and domestic hot water - DHW - systems in old and new buildings. Discusses solar energy systems and how they work including installation procedures.
Installing Solar Systems
Introduction to Solar Energy
Dist - CAREER Prod - CAREER 1979

Solar energy series
The Do - it - yourself guide to solar living 30 MIN
Phase Zero 30 MIN
Power 30 MIN
The Solar Decision 30 MIN
The Solar Scenario 30 MIN
The Theory is Tested 30 MIN
Dist - PBS

Solar Energy, the Great Adventure 28 MIN
16mm
Color
LC 79-700472
Introduces individuals who have developed their own solar energy systems. Shows how they found methods of putting the Sun to work for them. Narrated by Eddie Albert.
Social Science
Dist - USNAC Prod - USDOE 1978

Solar Energy - to Capture the Power of Sun and Tide 21 MIN
U-matic / VHS / 16mm
Coping with Tomorrow Series
Color (J)
Looks at the potential of solar and tidal power for meeting the earth's energy needs. Gives examples of solar and tidal power stations in France and shows a man's house which uses the rain water and a solar still to heat it.
Social Science
Dist - AIMS Prod - DOCUA 1975

Solar Energy - to Capture the Power of the Sun and Tide 21 MIN
U-matic / VHS / 16mm
Color (J)
LC 76-701514
Examines the prospects for solar energy as the solution to the world's energy needs in the future. Shows work being done now in harnessing tidal and solar energy for practical and experimental purposes.
Industrial and Technical Education; Science; Science - Physical; Social Science; Sociology
Dist - CNEMAG Prod - DOCUA 1975

Solar Energy - Unlimited Power 14 MIN
16mm
Color
LC 77-700007
Discusses the ways in which power can be obtained from the Sun, including solar water and space heating, high temperature conversion to produce electricity, solar architecture and air conditioning. Compares solar energy to other sources of power, showing its advantages and disadvantages.
Social Science
Dist - MNTAGE Prod - MNTAGE 1977

The Solar Film 9 MIN
16mm / U-matic / VHS
Color
LC 80-700851
Depicts the ancient relationship between the Sun and man. Explores the formation of the Earth, traces man's consumption of Sun - created fossil fuels and presents the Sun as a logical source of future power.

Science - Physical; Social Science
Dist - PFP **Prod** - WILDWD

The Solar Frontier 25 MIN
U-matic / VHS / 16mm
Color (J H C)
LC 78-701236
Features architects Nick Nicholson, Greg Allen, and Doug Lorriman and residents as they discuss the cost, performance and technology of three houses in the Canadian snowbelt which are heated by solar energy.
Geography - World; Industrial and Technical Education; Social Science
Dist - BULFRG **Prod** - MELFIL 1978
NFBC
CFLMDC

Solar furnace 10 MIN
VHS
Color; PAL (P I J H)
Studies a solar furnace, whose energy is concentrated on brick which melts the brick.
Science - Physical; Social Science
Dist - VIEWTH **Prod** - VIEWTH

The Solar Furnace 10 MIN
U-matic / VHS
Introductory Concepts in Physics - Light Series
Color (C)
$229.00, $129.00 purchase _ #AD - 1208
Examines a large solar furnace of the heliostat type, containing plane mirrors arranged in tiers and a ten - meter parabolic mirror.
Science - Physical
Dist - FOTH **Prod** - FOTH

The Solar Generation 21 MIN
16mm
Science of Energy Series
Color (J H)
Explores the possibilities, problems and successes in harnessing the Sun's power for energy.
Social Science
Dist - FINLYS **Prod** - FINLYS 1976

Solar Greenhouses 20 MIN
VHS / U-matic
Active Solar Heating and Cooling Series
Color (H C A)
Serves as an introduction to solar - heated sun spaces. Covers orientation of the greenhouse, design factors, the different glazing types, heat loss, heat storage and summer cooling.
Agriculture; Home Economics; Social Science
Dist - MOKIN **Prod** - NCDCC

The Solar Horizon 10 MIN
16mm / U-matic / VHS
Color (I J)
LC 81-700760
Shows how solar energy is being harnessed for man's needs.
Science - Physical
Dist - AIMS **Prod** - LINDH 1981

The Solar House 11 MIN
U-matic / VHS
Color (I J H C A)
Shows with animation how a passive solar system absorbs heat and how an active system circulates generated heat.
Science - Natural; Science - Physical; Social Science
Dist - BNCHMK **Prod** - BNCHMK 1986

The Solar Image 29 MIN
U-matic
Project Universe - Astronomy Series Lesson 14
Color (C A)
Discusses importance of sun to humanity since prehistoric times. Provides basic data on sun's composition. Uses still photographs, time - lapse photography and animation.
Science - Physical
Dist - CDTEL **Prod** - COAST

The Solar Interior 29 MIN
U-matic
Project Universe - Astronomy Series Lesson 15
Color (C A)
Explains fusion of hydrogen atoms into helium. Reports on observations of a slight increase in sun's rotation rates.
Science - Physical
Dist - CDTEL **Prod** - COAST

The Solar Percentage 25 MIN
U-matic / VHS / 16mm
Color (PRO)
Describes the use of solar energy in health care facilities.
Health and Safety; Social Science
Dist - USNAC **Prod** - USDHHS 1981

Solar Power 20 MIN
U-matic / VHS / 16mm
Color (J)
Shows solar power being used for passive solar heating, active thermal heating and photovoltaic production of electricity.
Social Science
Dist - HANDEL **Prod** - HANDEL 1980

Solar Power - the Giver of Life 27 MIN
16mm
Energy Sources - a New Beginning Series
Color
Suggests that the sun's energy could supplement other fuels. Examines solar stills, cookers and collectors and the impact of commercial solar installations on the environment.
Science - Natural; Social Science
Dist - UCOLO **Prod** - UCOLO

Solar Powered Irrigation 29 MIN
16mm
Color
Traces the evolution of the solar energy applications in agriculture from its origins in the nineteenth century to the planning, construction and operation of the present demonstration project.
Agriculture; Social Science
Dist - UARIZ **Prod** - UARIZ 1979

Solar products smorgasbord 30 MIN
VHS
A House for all seasons series
Color (G)
$49.95 purchase _ #AHFS - 205
Focuses on unique applications of solar energy. Tours TV star Pam Dawber's super - insulated solar home. Describes the benefits of converting south wall exposures to solar energy. Concludes with a look at plant beds, containers and soil preparation.
Home Economics; Industrial and Technical Education; Science - Natural; Social Science; Sociology
Dist - PBS **Prod** - KRMATV 1985

The Solar Promise 29 MIN
16mm / U-matic / VHS
Color
LC 83-700189
Demonstrates the basic principles of available solar energy devices. Shows the difference between passive and active systems and stresses the value of passive systems and their cost effectiveness.
Social Science
Dist - BULFRG **Prod** - MAYERH 1979

Solar Radiation - Pt 1 - Sun and Earth 18 MIN
16mm
Color (H)
Discusses the concept that the energy radiated away to space by the earth must balance the energy received from the sun.
Science - Physical
Dist - MLA **Prod** - AMS 1967

Solar Radiation - Pt 2 - the Earth's Atmosphere 21 MIN
16mm
Educational Films in the Atmospheric Sciences Series
Color (H)
LC 76-702576
Examines the effects of solar radiation on the earth. Uses instruments to study the light spectrum and light absorption.
Science - Physical
Dist - MLA **Prod** - AMS 1967

Solar Radiation, Sun and Earth's Rays 18 MIN
16mm
Meteorology Series
Color (J H)
LC FIA67-5972
Discusses the concept that the energy radiated into space by the earth must balance the energy received from the sun. Gives explanations of the roles played by the earth's rotation and the tilt of the earth's axis. Presents effects due to the presence of an atmosphere and a cloud cover.
Science - Physical
Dist - MLA **Prod** - AMS 1967

The Solar Scenario 30 MIN
U-matic
Color
Looks ahead to the time when solar power may be the only energy source man will ever need. Tells how some ideas to exploit the sun's energy border on science fiction.
Industrial and Technical Education; Social Science; Sociology
Dist - PBS **Prod** - KNMETV 1974

The Solar Scenario 30 MIN
VHS / 16mm
Solar Energy Series
Color (G)
$55.00 rental _ #SLRE - 105
Looks ahead to the time when sun power may be the only energy source needed.
Science - Physical; Social Science
Dist - PBS **Prod** - KNMETV

The Solar Sea 60 MIN
16mm / U-matic / VHS
Planet Earth Series
Color (C A)
Looks at the sun as a star that powers the earth, giving life, creating weather and warming the oceans, land and even ice. Shows scientists at the North Pole flying through a supercharged aurora shaped by violent solar storms and infra - red and x - ray satellite eyes peering deep into the interior of the sun. Discusses how the solar wind affects the earth.
Science - Physical
Dist - FI **Prod** - ANNCPB

The Solar sea - Part 6 60 MIN
U-matic / VHS
Planet earth series
Color (G)
$45.00, $29.95 purchase
Investigates the 800 - million - year - old rock record of sun activity in an ancient Australian lake bed. Features ground and satellite photography of the aurora borealis. Part of a seven - part series on Planet Earth.
Science - Physical
Dist - ANNCPB **Prod** - WQED 1986

Solar smorgasbord 30 MIN
VHS
A House for all seasons series
Color (G)
$49.95 purchase _ #AHFS - 305
Explores unique solar energy applications in the home. Features the extensive remodeling of a Colorado solar home. Describes solar water systems.
Home Economics; Industrial and Technical Education; Science - Natural; Social Science; Sociology
Dist - PBS **Prod** - KRMATV 1986

The Solar system 23 MIN
VHS
Bright sparks series
Color (P I)
$280.00 purchase
Explores the nine planets of the solar system as well as the moon. Explains how the radio telescope works. Part of a 12 - part animated series on science and technology.
Science - Physical
Dist - LANDMK **Prod** - LANDMK 1989

The Solar system
VHS
Basic science series
Color (J H) (ENGLISH AND SPANISH)
$39.95 purchase _ #MCV5060
Focuses on the solar system, presenting only basic concepts. Includes teacher's guide and review questions. Combines computer animation and the use of 'sheltered language' to help students acquire content vocabulary, become comfortable with scientific language and achieve success in science curriculum. Part of a series on basic science concepts.
Science; Science - Physical
Dist - MADERA **Prod** - MADERA

The Solar System 19 MIN
U-matic / VHS / 16mm
Exploring Space Series
Color (I J)
$440, $250 purchase _ #3553
Shows the different sizes of the planets and the distances between them.
Science - Physical
Dist - CORF

Solar system 28 MIN
U-matic / VHS / BETA
Color; PAL (G H C)
PdS60, PdS68 purchase
Surveys knowledge of the Sun, Moon and the planets, including Mariner 6 and 7 findings on the planet Mars. Features animated drawings, time - lapse photography of solar prominences and color film of the moon's surface taken by Apollo astronauts.
Science - Physical
Dist - EDPAT

The Solar System 30 MIN
U-matic / VHS
Earth, Sea and Sky Series
Color (C)
Examines the evolution and composition of the planets in our solar system. Concentrates on the exploration of Mars using National Aeronautics and Space administration (NASA) footage.
Science - Physical
Dist - DALCCD **Prod** - DALCCD

The Solar System 18 MIN
U-matic / VHS / 16mm
Color (J H) (SPANISH)
Investigates the structure and composition of the solar system. Describes the origin of the sun and its planets

and surveys the major planetary bodies in the solar system. From the revised edition of Our Solar Family.
Science - Physical
Dist - EBEC **Prod** - EBEC 1977

The Solar system; 2nd ed. 15 MIN
U-matic / VHS
Search for science series; Unit II - Space
Color (I)
Studies the solar system and those physical forces which permit it to exist.
Science - Physical
Dist - GPN **Prod** - WVIZTV

Solar System Debris 29 MIN
U-matic
Project Universe - Astronomy Series Lesson 13
Color (C A)
Presents overview of objects in the solar system smaller than planets and their satellites. Discusses asteroids, meteorites and comets.
Science - Physical
Dist - CDTEL **Prod** - COAST

The Solar System - Islands in Space 17 MIN
U-matic / VHS / 16mm
Color (I) (SPANISH)
LC 75-703538
Discusses and illustrates basic concepts about the solar system.
Foreign Language; Science - Physical
Dist - AIMS **Prod** - CAHILL 1969

The Solar System - its Motions 9 MIN
16mm
Astronomy Series
Color (I J)
LC FIA68-3035
Traces the theories of movement of celestial objects from Ptolemy, Copernicus, Brahe and Kepler to Isaac Netwon. Examines the patterns of motion of the planets, sun, moons, asteroids, meteroids and comets to show that they move under the influence of gravitation and inertia.
Science - Physical
Dist - MGHBCD **Prod** - HABER 1968

The Solar System - Measuring its Dimensions 10 MIN
16mm / U-matic / VHS
Astronomy Series
Color (P I)
LC 73-704751
Uses live photography, animation and special effects to investigate methods astronomers use to determine distances between planets in the solar system and planet size. Explains one of the most important methods used, triangulation.
Mathematics; Science - Physical
Dist - MGHT **Prod** - MGHT 1970

Solar Visions 24 MIN
16mm
Color (J)
LC 79-701746
Focuses on the sun as a pragmatic, partial solution to the energy crisis. Explains the basic principles of solar energy and explores the concepts of solar building design, photovoltaics and solar heating.
Industrial and Technical Education; Social Science
Dist - MALIBU
TAPPRO

Solaris 167 MIN
35mm / 16mm
Color (G) (RUSSIAN WITH ENGLISH SUBTITLES)
$300.00, $350.00 rental
Adapts the science fiction novel of Stanislaw Lem. Portrays Cosmonaut Kris Kelvin who is dispatched to a space station orbiting the mysterius planet Solaris. Reveals that the native beings of the ocean - covered planet have the ability to materialize anyone from the past and Kelvin must face his dead wife and the conflict between them which drove her to suicide. Directed by Andrei Tarkovsky.
Fine Arts; Literature and Drama
Dist - KINOIC **Prod** - CORINT 1972

Sold - a guide to consultative selling 28 MIN
VHS
Color (G)
$595.00 purchase, $150.00 rental _ #V1077 - 06
Presents four fundamentals of consultative selling - researching prospects, clarifying needs, demonstrating benefits and closing the sale. Uses dramatization to emphasize the method. Includes video and leader's guide.
Business and Economics
Dist - BARR **Prod** - BBC

Sold down the river 50 MIN
VHS
Timewatch series
Color; PAL (H C A)
PdS99 purchase
Documents social conditions for Southern blacks in 1915, 50 years after the end of the American Civil War and discovers that little progress had been made to improve racial equality - blacks still had few legal rights and little opportunity for economic independence. Asserts that the North shares an equal responsibility for the continuation of racist policies in the South after the Civil War. Part of the Timewatch series.
History - United States; Sociology
Dist - BBCENE

Sold Gold Hours 30 MIN
U-matic / VHS / 16mm
Color (C A)
Explains that out of 1952 working hours in an average salesman's year, he spends only about 700 of them in face - to - face selling. Shows why and how hundreds of those precious hours can be made much more productive through better sales - management.
Business and Economics; Psychology; Social Science; Sociology
Dist - DARTNL **Prod** - DARTNL

Sold on sport 50 MIN
VHS
More than a game series
Color (A)
PdS99 purchase _ Not available in the United States or Canada
Looks at the commercial shadow that falls over sports. Part of an eight-part series that looks at sports as an integral part of every civilization, offering participation, the opportunity to excel and to belong. Asks if this is a romantic view of sport.
Physical Education and Recreation
Dist - BBCENE

Soldering 13 MIN
16mm
Metalwork - Hand Tools Series
Color (H C A)
LC 72-701845
Describes soldering equipment and techniques - tinning an iron, tinning metal, soldering seams and hand soldering.
Industrial and Technical Education
Dist - SF **Prod** - MORLAT 1967

Soldering and Brazing 17 MIN
U-matic / VHS
Manufacturing Materials and Processes Series
Color
Covers steps in soldering and brazing and soldering and brazing defects.
Industrial and Technical Education
Dist - WFVTAE **Prod** - GE

Soldering and brazing copper tubing 13 MIN
U-matic / VHS
Marshall maintenance training programs series; Tape 19
Color (IND)
Shows how to produce good joinings, using soft solder as well as hard solder in joining copper tubing and capillary fittings.
Industrial and Technical Education
Dist - LEIKID **Prod** - LEIKID

Soldering and Brazing Copper Tubing 13 MIN
16mm
Color (IND)
Shows how to produce good joints, using soft solder as well as hard solder in joining copper tubing and capillary fittings.
Industrial and Technical Education
Dist - MOKIN **Prod** - MOKIN

Soldering Axial Lead Devices 8 TO 15 MIN
VHS
High - Reliability Soldering Series
Color (PRO)
$600.00 - $1500.00 purchase _ #TRSAL
Focuses on preparing and terminating axial lead devices. Part of an eighteen - part series on high - reliability soldering. Requires a solid understanding of digital electronics. Includes one textbook and an instructor guide to support 45 minutes of instruction.
Education; Health and Safety; Industrial and Technical Education; Psychology
Dist - NUSTC **Prod** - NUSTC

Soldering Bifurcated Terminals 8 TO 15 MIN
VHS
High - Reliability Soldering Series
Color (PRO)
$600.00 - $1500.00 purchase _ #TRSBT
Examines various types of bifurcated terminals. Shows how a wire or wires can be terminated to a bifurcated terminal from a side, bottom or top entry. Part of an eighteen - part series on high - reliability soldering. Requires a solid understanding of digital electronics. Includes one textbook and an instructor guide to support 45 minutes of instruction.
Education; Health and Safety; Industrial and Technical Education; Psychology
Dist - NUSTC **Prod** - NUSTC

Soldering Connector Pins and Solder Cups 8 TO 15 MIN
VHS
High - Reliability Soldering Series
Color (PRO)
$600.00 - $1500.00 purchase _ #TRSCP
Focuses on the identification of common connector pins and solder cups. Shows the termination of a wire or wires to a solder cup, how to solder a wire to a connector pin or solder cup. Part of an eighteen - part series on high - reliability soldering. Requires a solid understanding of digital electronics. Includes one textbook and an instructor guide to support 45 minutes of instruction.
Education; Health and Safety; Industrial and Technical Education; Psychology
Dist - NUSTC **Prod** - NUSTC

Soldering for Electronic Repair 51 MIN
VHS / 35mm strip
(H A IND)
#865XV7
Introduces equipment and techniques needed in various applications of electronic repair work. Includes basic techniques, soldering terminals and soldering printed circuit boards (3 tapes). Prerequisites needed. Study Guide included.
Industrial and Technical Education
Dist - BERGL

Soldering Hook and Tab Terminals 8 TO 15 MIN
VHS
High - Reliability Soldering Series
Color (PRO)
$600.00 - $1500.00 purchase _ #TRSHT
Identifies common hook and tab terminals. Explains how to properly terminate a wire or wires to hook and tab terminals. Describes solder techniques for hook and tab terminals. Part of an eighteen - part series on high - reliability soldering. Requires a solid understanding of digital electronics. Includes one textbook and an instructor guide to support 45 minutes of instruction.
Education; Health and Safety; Industrial and Technical Education; Psychology
Dist - NUSTC **Prod** - NUSTC

Soldering Inspection Series
Inspecting Boards and Solder
Inspecting Components and Leads
Dist - VTRI

Soldering Irons and Wire Preparation 8 TO 15 MIN
VHS
High - Reliability Soldering Series
Color (PRO)
$600.00 - $1500.00 purchase _ #TRSIW
Describes requirements for an acceptable soldering iron and soldering iron tip. Explains how to prepare a soldering iron and wire for soldering and make three types of wire splices. Part of an eighteen - part series on high - reliability soldering. Requires a solid understanding of digital electronics. Includes one textbook and an instructor guide to support 45 minutes of instruction.
Education; Health and Safety; Industrial and Technical Education; Psychology
Dist - NUSTC **Prod** - NUSTC

Soldering lugs and splicing stranded conductors 18 MIN
16mm
Electrical work - wiring series
B&W
LC FIE52-141
Demonstrates how to splice stranded conductors and how to make a severed cable splice. Shows the use of soldering tongs, blowtorch, and solder pot and ladle to solder a lug.
Industrial and Technical Education
Dist - USNAC **Prod** - USOE 1945

Soldering Multilead Devices 8 TO 15 MIN
VHS
High - Reliability Soldering Series
Color (PRO)
$600.00 - $1500.00 purchase _ #TRSMD
Shows how to prepare, terminate and solder a multilayer component to a printed circuit board. Part of an eighteen - part series on high - reliability soldering. Requires a solid understanding of digital electronics. Includes one textbook and an instructor guide to support 45 minutes of instruction.
Education; Health and Safety; Industrial and Technical Education; Psychology
Dist - NUSTC **Prod** - NUSTC

The Soldering Process 150 MIN
U-matic
Electronics Manufacturing - Components, Assembly and Soldering 'Series

Color (IND)
Discusses basic factors in soldering, including wetting, spread rate, flux, time and temperature control, and hand soldering techniques.
Business and Economics; Industrial and Technical Education
Dist - INTECS **Prod** - INTECS

Soldering Surface - Mounted Devices 8 TO 15 MIN
VHS
High - Reliability Soldering Series
Color (PRO)
$600.00 - $1500.00 purchase _ #TRSSM
Describes how a surface - mounted device is properly prepared, positioned and soldered to a printed circuit board. Part of an eighteen - part series on high - reliability soldering. Requires a solid understanding of digital electronics. Includes one textbook and an instructor guide to support 45 minutes of instruction.
Education; Health and Safety; Industrial and Technical Education; Psychology
Dist - NUSTC **Prod** - NUSTC

Soldering the fixed bridge 11 MIN
VHS / U-matic
Color (C PRO)
$395.00 purchase, $80.00 rental _ #D860 - VI - 051
Demonstrates soldering which is valuable in two aspects of dentistry - joining two parts as in a fixed bridge assembly and building various parts, as in establishing a proximal contact area or filling a casting void. Presented by Dr Matty F Abbate.
Health and Safety
Dist - HSCIC

Soldering Theory 24 MIN
VHS / BETA
Color (IND)
Discusses the various considerations necessary for a student to understand what soldering is and how it takes place.
Industrial and Technical Education; Psychology
Dist - RMIBHF **Prod** - RMIBHF

Soldering Turret Terminals 8 TO 15 MIN
VHS
High - Reliability Soldering Series
Color (PRO)
$600.00 - $1500.00 purchase _ #TRSTT
Identifies common types of turret terminals. Explains how turret terminals are mounted on circuit boards. Shows how turret terminals are cleaned and tinned and how to solder a wire to a turret terminal. Part of an eighteen - part series on high - reliability soldering. Requires a solid understanding of digital electronics. Includes one textbook and an instructor guide to support 45 minutes of instruction.
Education; Health and Safety; Industrial and Technical Education; Psychology
Dist - NUSTC **Prod** - NUSTC

The Soldier 5 MIN
16mm
Song of the Ages Series
B&W (H C A)
LC 70-702127
Presents a modern interpretation of Psalm 41 using a dramatization about a soldier who is shot while sharing his chocolate bar with a seagull along a deserted beach.
Religion and Philosophy
Dist - FAMLYT **Prod** - FAMLYT 1964

Soldier Boy - Pt 2 58 MIN
VHS
Comrades Series
Color (S)
$79.00 purchase _ #351 - 9023
Follows twelve Soviet citizens from different backgrounds to reveal what Soviet life is like for a cross section of the 270 million inhabitants in the vast country of fifteen republics. Features Frontline anchor Judy Woodruff who also interviews prominent experts on Soviet affairs. Part 2 of the twelve - part series considers Volgograd, an important industrial center and home to Nikolai and Ludmilla Krylov and their son Valera. Valera is eighteen and due to begin two years of compulsory national service.
Civics and Political Systems; Education; Geography - World; Sociology
Dist - FI **Prod** - WGBHTV 1988

Soldier Girls 87 MIN
16mm
Color (G)
Presents an independent production by Nick Broomfield and J Churchill. Follows three females recruits through basic training in the US Army.
Civics and Political Systems; Fine Arts; Sociology
Dist - FIRS

Soldier in Love 76 MIN
VHS / U-matic
Color
Offers a story of the fascinating life of John Churchill, the First Duke of Marlborough and his wife Sarah. Stars Jean Simmons, Claire Bloom and Keith Michell.
Fine Arts; Literature and Drama
Dist - FOTH **Prod** - FOTH 1984

Soldier in the Rain 96 MIN
16mm
B&W (C A)
Stars Steve Mc Queen and Jackie Gleason. Tells the story of two non - commissioned officer buddies in the peace - time army.
Literature and Drama
Dist - CINEWO **Prod** - CINEWO 1963

Soldier Man 33 MIN
16mm
B&W (J)
Stars Harry Langdon as a soldier who has been forgotten at the end of World War I.
Literature and Drama
Dist - TWYMAN **Prod** - MGM 1926

Soldier Man 42 MIN
16mm
B&W
LC 71-713610
A comedy in which Harry Langdon plays the dual role of a World War I doughboy and a perpetually inebriated King of a small European country.
History - United States; History - World; Literature and Drama
Dist - RMIBHF **Prod** - SENN 1971

Soldier of the revolution 15 MIN
16mm / U-matic / VHS
Color (I)
$49.95 purchase _ #P10075
Depicts the American Revolution as seen by an ordinary soldier. Focuses on the uprising, hardships at Valley Forge and the turning of the tide in favor of the Revolutionary Army. Animated illustration.
History - United States; Sociology
Dist - CF

Soldier of Twilight 48 MIN
U-matic / VHS
Color
$445.00 purchase
Civics and Political Systems
Dist - ABCLR **Prod** - ABCLR 1981

The Soldier who Didn't Wash 27 MIN
U-matic / VHS / 16mm
Storybook International Series
Color
Tells the Russian story of a soldier who makes a deal with the devil not to wash for fifteen years. Relates that when the soldier grows wealthy, a king asks for his help but the soldier demands one of the king's daughters as payment. Shows that on the wedding day, the fifteen years end and he is revealed to be quite young and handsome.
Guidance and Counseling; Literature and Drama
Dist - JOU **Prod** - JOU 1982

Soldiering for Uncle Sam 5 MIN
16mm
B&W (G)
$15.00 rental
Looks at the life of a doughboy in boot camp in a Ford production.
Fine Arts; History - World; Literature and Drama
Dist - KITPAR

Soldiering on - Volume 9 48 MIN
VHS
Vietnam - the ten thousand day war series
Color (G)
$34.95 purchase _ #S00682
Interviews Vietnam veterans to get an idea of what the war was like for the average soldier. Suggests many were frustrated at being unable to understand or 'win' the war. Features many veterans' recollections of horrifying experiences. Narrated by Richard Basehart.
History - United States
Dist - UILL

Soldiers - a history of men in battle series 650 MIN
VHS
Soldiers - a history of men in battle series
Color (H C G)
$2595.00 purchase, $845.00 rental
Presents a 13 - part series on soldiers and warfare hosted by Frederick Forsyth and written by John Keenan. Includes the titles The Face of Battle, Infantry, Gunner, Cavalry, Tank, Engineer, Airborne, Commander, Sinews of War, Fighting Spirit, Irregular, Casualties and The Experience of War.
Civics and Political Systems; Guidance and Counseling; History - World; Industrial and Technical Education; Sociology
Dist - CF **Prod** - BBCTV 1986

A Soldier's diary 47 MIN
VHS
Color (G)
$375.00 purchase, $75.00 rental
Takes a look from inside the occupation forces with a videotape by a 42 - year - old Israeli Army sergeant, during 23 days of active duty in the West Bank Palestinian town of Hebron. Depicts the moral dilemma that some Israeli soldiers faced in accepting the occupation along with more militant settlers. Produced by Gideon Gitai.
Civics and Political Systems; Fine Arts; History - World
Dist - FIRS

A Soldier's Duty - Pt 9 58 MIN
VHS
Struggle for Democracy Series
Color (S)
$49.00 purchase _ #039 - 9009
Explores the concept of democracy and how it works. Features Patrick Watson, author with Benjamin Barber of 'The Struggle For Democracy,' as host who travels to more than 30 countries around the world, examining issues such as rule of law, freedom of information, the tyranny of the majority and the relationship of economic prosperity to democracy. Part 9 explores three countries in which democracy has at various times been under fire - Argentina, France and Israel, and considers that democracy is at its most fragile state when facing the threat of insurrection or foreign military invasion.
Civics and Political Systems; Geography - World; History - World
Dist - FI **Prod** - DFL 1989

Soldier's heart - memoirs of a World War II veteran 30 MIN
VHS
Color (I J H)
$99.00 purchase _ #60999 - 026
Explores the aftermath of a soldier's World War II experiences during a visit to the same battle sites 40 years after D - Day. Uses a story of the effects of 'battle fatigue' to emphasize the high personal price soldiers often pay after experiencing the atrocities of war. Includes teachers' guide and library kit.
History - World; Sociology
Dist - INSTRU

Soldier's home 42 MIN
VHS
American short story collection series
Color (J H)
$49.00 purchase _ #04540 - 126
Tells of a young soldier who returns to the United States after service in World War I to find himself out of step with his community and his family. Written by Kurt Vonnegut.
History - United States; Literature and Drama
Dist - GA **Prod** - GA

Soldier's Home
U-matic / 35mm strip / VHS / 16mm
American Short Story Series
(G C)
Re - enacts the short story by Ernest Hemingway about a returning soldier and his attempt to integrate himself into the life that he left.
English Language; Literature and Drama
Dist - CDTEL **Prod** - LEARIF 1977

Soldiers in Greasepaint 28 MIN
16mm
Big Picture Series
Color
LC 80-701966
Tells about entertainers who traveled wherever military personnel were stationed in World War II, bringing them a laugh and a reminder of home.
Civics and Political Systems; History - United States
Dist - USNAC **Prod** - USA 1980

Soldiers in hiding 60 MIN
VHS
Color (G)
$29.95 purchase _ #S01505
Portrays Vietnam veterans who continue to live out the war in their backwoods homes. Includes war footage and interviews with the veterans' wives.
History - United States
Dist - UILL

Soldier's stories 28 MIN
VHS
While soldiers fought series
Color (H C G)
$180.00 purchase, $19.00 rental _ #35754
Offers a multifaceted interpretation of soldiers' experiences, featuring the creations of American novelists, cartoonists and journalists. Part of a seven - part series which examines the impact of war on American society from historical, literary, artistic and philosophical perspectives. Produced by the International University Consortium.
Fine Arts; Literature and Drama; Sociology
Dist - PSU

A Soldier's Story
VHS / BETA
Color
Tells the story of a murder on a black army base during World War II. Stars Howard E Rollins, Jr and Adolph Caesar.
Fine Arts; History - United States; Literature and Drama
Dist - GA **Prod** - GA

A Soldier's Tale 52 MIN
16mm
Color
Combines mime, melodrama and ballet, set to the musical score by Igor Stravinsky. Presents a Russian folk tale, A Soldier's Tale. Features ballet star, Robert Helpmann as the Devil.
Fine Arts; Literature and Drama
Dist - CANTOR **Prod** - CANTOR

Sole Bonne Femme 29 MIN
Videoreel / VT2
French Chef French Series
Color (FRENCH)
Features Julia Child of Haute Cuisine au Vin demonstrating how to prepare sole bonne femme. With captions.
Foreign Language; Home Economics
Dist - PBS **Prod** - WGBHTV

Sole Proprietorships and Partnerships 30 MIN
U-matic
It's Everybody's Business Series Unit 2, Organizing a Business
Color
Business and Economics
Dist - DALCCD **Prod** - DALCCD

Soleil - O 106 MIN
16mm
B&W (FRENCH (ENGLISH SUBTITLES))
An English subtitle version of the French language film. Considers the life of immigrant African blacks in Paris. Centers around the sad, frustrating existence of an educated immigrant from Mauritania.
Fine Arts; Foreign Language; History - World; Sociology
Dist - NYFLMS **Prod** - NYFLMS 1972

The Solicitation - Pt 1 24 MIN
U-matic
Basic Procurement Course Series
Color
LC 80-706738
Describes the proper method for putting together a solicitation for bids on federal contracts.
Business and Economics; Civics and Political Systems
Dist - USNAC **Prod** - USGSFC 1978

The Solicitation - Pt 2 24 MIN
U-matic
Basic Procurement Course Series
Color
LC 80-706738
Describes the proper method for putting together a solicitation for bids on federal contracts.
Business and Economics; Civics and Political Systems
Dist - USNAC **Prod** - USGSFC 1978

Solid Figures 30 MIN
16mm
Mathematics for Elementary School Teachers Series no 26
Color (T)
Introduces solid figures, and discusses related geometric concepts. To be used following Congruence And Similarity.
Mathematics
Dist - MLA **Prod** - SMSG 1963

The Solid Gold Cadillac 99 MIN
16mm
Color (J)
Stars Judy Holliday and Paul Douglas in the story of a naive young lady who is plunged into a merry tug - of- war for control of a large corporation.
Business and Economics; Literature and Drama
Dist - TIMLIF **Prod** - CPC

Solid Ground 27 MIN
16mm
Color (IND)
LC FIA67-2338
Traces the development of the minuteman system from its inception to the delivery of the first operational flight to Strategic Air Command. Includes live and static minuteman missile motor firings.
Civics and Political Systems; Science - Physical
Dist - THIOKL **Prod** - THIOKL 1962

Solid, Liquid, Gas 15 MIN
U-matic / VHS
Color (K P)
Explores the three forms of matter, solids, gases, and liquids. Illustrates basic concepts about the properties of matter as children experiment with everyday materials in their environment.
Science - Physical
Dist - NGS **Prod** - NGS

Solid, liquid, gas 12 MIN
VHS / U-matic / 16mm
Matter and energy for beginners series
Color (P)
$400.00, $250.00 purchase _ #HP - 5939C
Uses animation and live action to teach physical science. Stars Investigator Alligator and his friend Mr E, who investigate the properties of physical states of matter - solid, liquid and gas. Part of a six - part series.
Science - Physical
Dist - CORF **Prod** - CORF 1990

Solid, Liquid, Gas 11 MIN
16mm / U-matic / VHS
Matter, Matter, Everywhere Series
Color (P)
$280, $195 purchase _ #3006
Shows how the three types of matter differ from one another.
Science - Physical
Dist - CORF

Solid Performance Leadership 18 MIN
U-matic / VHS
Leadership Link - Fundamentals of Effective Supervision Series
Color
Business and Economics; Psychology
Dist - DELTAK **Prod** - CHSH

Solid plasterwork & fixing a fibrous plaster cornice - Part two of Unit E - Plastering - Cassette 10 58 MIN
VHS
Building crafts - the teaching and learning process series
Color; PAL (J H IND)
PdS29.50 purchase
Features part of an 18 - part series which observes teaching and learning in a variety of workshop situations. Includes such skills as plumbing, brickwork, carpentry, painting and decorating. This cassette also contains instruction on running insitu moulding, setting a wall and a cornice fixing.
Industrial and Technical Education
Dist - EMFVL

Solid Propellant Rocketry 14 MIN
16mm
Color
Deals with the early history of the Thiokol Corporation, the production of various solid propellant rocket motors and basic theory with actual rocket motors being both static and flight tested.
Business and Economics; Industrial and Technical Education; Science
Dist - THIOKL **Prod** - THIOKL 1959

Solid Punch 27 MIN
16mm
Color (IND)
LC FIA67-2339
Shows and traces the development of the Army's new generation of missiles and rockets.
Industrial and Technical Education; Science - Physical; Social Science
Dist - THIOKL **Prod** - THIOKL

Solid Solutions 45 MIN
BETA / VHS / U-matic
Color
$300 purchase
Shows substitutional and interstitial solid solutions.
Industrial and Technical Education; Psychology
Dist - ASM **Prod** - ASM

Solid - State Devices, Tape 4 - Oscilloscope Operation, Soldering and Troubleshooting 60 MIN
U-matic / VHS
Electrical Equipment Maintenance Series
Color (IND) (SPANISH)
Industrial and Technical Education
Dist - ITCORP **Prod** - ITCORP

Solid - State Devices, Tape 1 - Basic Electronics and Diodes 60 MIN
U-matic / VHS
Electrical Equipment Maintenance Series
Color (IND) (SPANISH)
Industrial and Technical Education
Dist - ITCORP **Prod** - ITCORP

Solid - State Devices, Tape 3 - Transistor Theory and Testing, Silicon Controlled 60 MIN
VHS / U-matic
Electrical Equipment Maintenance Series
Color (IND) (SPANISH)
Industrial and Technical Education
Dist - ITCORP **Prod** - ITCORP

Solid - State Devices, Tape 2 - Rectifiers and Power Supplies 60 MIN
U-matic / VHS
Electrical Equipment Maintenance Series
Color (IND) (SPANISH)
Industrial and Technical Education
Dist - ITCORP **Prod** - ITCORP

Solid State Electronics 17 MIN
U-matic / VHS
Introduction to Solid State Electronics (Spanish Series Chapter 1
Color (IND) (SPANISH)
Explains basic semiconductor theory. Shows types of atomic bonds. Discusses majority and minority carriers.
Education; Foreign Language; Industrial and Technical Education
Dist - TAT **Prod** - TAT

Solid State Electronics Series
Special Purpose Semiconductors 17 MIN
Dist - TAT

Solid - State Motor Control 85 MIN
VHS / 35mm strip
(H A IND)
#816XV7
Introduces the basic components, operations and applications of solid - state motor control. Includes static logic, NAND, NOR and memory, time delay and converters, logic design and applications, and applications and installation (5 tapes). Prerequisite required. Includes a Study Guide.
Education; Industrial and Technical Education
Dist - BERGL

Solid State Motor Controls
VHS
Industrial Electronics Training Program Series
$99.00 purchase _ #RPVCI10
Industrial and Technical Education
Dist - CAREER **Prod** - CAREER

Solid State Motor Controls 13 MIN
VHS / 16mm
Electronics Series
(C A IND)
$99.00 purchase _ #VCI10
Focuses on solid state motor controls. Illustrates open and closed loop motor control systems. Examines the characteristics and functions of stepper motors. Utilizes an additional workbook.
Industrial and Technical Education
Dist - RMIBHF **Prod** - RMIBHF

Solid State Principles 26 MIN
16mm
B&W
LC 74-705659
Identifies the relative energy level of electrons and identifies chemically active and chemically stable atoms. Defines electron pair band and lattice structure and differentiates between conductor, semiconductor and insulator. Describes the effect of donor and acceptor atoms on chemically stable lattice structures and defines and identifies P and N type materials. (Kinescope).
Industrial and Technical Education; Science - Physical
Dist - USNAC **Prod** - USAF 1969

Solid Waste 30 MIN
VHS / U-matic
Living Environment Series
Color (C)
Discusses the origins and volume of solid waste material, methods of recycling waste, waste disposal methods and costs and the economic and political obstacles to recycling.
Science - Natural
Dist - DALCCD **Prod** - DALCCD

Solidaridad - Faith, Hope and Haven 57 MIN
VHS / 16mm
Color (G)
$75.00 rental
Explores the history and work of the Vicaria de la Solidaridad, a Catholic organization in Santiago, Chile that provides aid to victims of human rights abuses.
Geography - World; Sociology
Dist - ICARUS

Solidarity 11 MIN
16mm
Color
LC 74-702767
Commemorates a demonstration by workers at Dare Foods Ltd, a cookie factory in Kitchner, Ontario. Presents an organizer's speech on the labor situation.
Business and Economics; Sociology
Dist - CANFDC **Prod** - WIELNJ 1973

Solidification of Metals 45 MIN
BETA / VHS / U-matic
Color
$300 purchase
Shows metal crystals and solidification of pure metals.
Industrial and Technical Education; Psychology; Science - Physical
Dist - ASM **Prod** - ASM

Solids 15 MIN
U-matic
Math Patrol Two Series
Color (P)
Presents the mathematical concepts of the ways in which objects move and develops definitions for geometric formations based on movement.
Education; Mathematics
Dist - TVOTAR **Prod** - TVOTAR 1977

Solids 30 MIN
VHS
Mathematics Series
Color (J)
LC 90713155
Discusses solids. The 156th of 157 installments of the Mathematics Series.
Mathematics; Science - Physical
Dist - GPN

Solids 30 MIN
VHS
Geometry series
Color (H)
$125.00 purchase _ #7015
Explains solids. Part of a 16 - part series on geometry.
Mathematics
Dist - LANDMK **Prod** - LANDMK

Solids - Liquids 14 MIN
U-matic / VHS
Hands on, Grade 2 - Lollipops, Loops, Etc Series Unit 3 - 'Classifying; Unit 3 - Classifying
Color (P)
Gives experience in classifying solids versus liquids.
Science
Dist - AITECH **Prod** - WHROTV 1975

Soliloquy of a river 26 MIN
16mm
Audubon wildlife theatre series
Color (P)
LC 70-709408
Presents the story of a river from its spring resurgence, running through forests and meadows to its struggle for life as it moves past a city. Shows the river under the water and along its shores and how it slowly turns into a polluted waterway.
Psychology; Science - Natural; Sociology
Dist - AVEXP **Prod** - KEGPL 1969

Soliloquy of a River 19 MIN
16mm
Color (I)
LC 70-702873
Tells the story of a river with emphasis on its continuing beauty and on the life in and around a stream during the changing seasons of the year.
Science - Natural
Dist - AVEXP **Prod** - HDP 1969

Soliloquy to a salmon and the Atlantic salmon
VHS
Color (G)
$29.90 purchase _ #0378
Reflects the thoughts of an angler during the hooking, landing and release of an 18 pound Atlantic salmon on the St Jean River in the province of Quebec, Canada, in Soliloquy, the first of two parts. Shows angling techniques for Atlantic salmon on a Newfoundland river in the second part.
Geography - World; Physical Education and Recreation; Science - Natural
Dist - SEVVID

The Solitary Man 5 MIN
16mm
Song of the Ages Series
B&W (H C A)
LC 70-702119
A modern interpretation of Psalm 6 using the dramatization about a dejected, unemployed man and a little boy who gives him a toy doll.
Fine Arts; Religion and Philosophy
Dist - FAMLYT **Prod** - FAMLYT 1964

The Solitary Man 96 MIN
U-matic / VHS
Color (H C A)
Reveals that Dave Keyes' happiness over his promotion and raise is shattered when he discovers that his wife wants a divorce. Explores the children's reactions, Dave's attempts at reconciliation and the manner in which he constructs a new life for himself. Stars Earl Holliman and Carrie Snodgrass.
Fine Arts; Sociology
Dist - TIMLIF **Prod** - TIMLIF 1982

Solitary Nodule of the Thyroid 21 MIN
16mm
Color (PRO)
Demonstrates a technique for excision of a thyroid nodule. Reviews the role of malignancy in such nodules, their diagnosis and management.
Health and Safety; Science
Dist - ACY **Prod** - ACYDGD 1964

The Solitary Thyroid Nodule 21 MIN
16mm
Color (PRO)
Makes a plea for the removal of the solitary nodule by complete lobectomy. Explains that occult lymphatic involvement which occurs with thyroid tumors may be recognized by careful exploration and judicious biopsy. Presents the thyroid lymphatic pathways and the operative procedure in a typical case.
Health and Safety; Science
Dist - ACY **Prod** - ACYDGD 1961

Solitary Wasps 13 MIN
U-matic / VHS / 16mm
Discovering Insects Series
Color (I J)
Shows wasps excavating and building their nests, laying eggs and providing for their young.
Science - Natural
Dist - CORF **Prod** - MORALL 1982

Solo 15 MIN
U-matic / VHS / 16mm
Color
LC 75-712413
Portrays the efforts and exhilarations that are experienced by the solo mountain climber. Filmed in Mexico, the United States and Canada.
Physical Education and Recreation
Dist - PFP **Prod** - PFP 1971

Solo Basic 28 MIN
16mm
Path of the Paddle Series
Color (J)
LC 78-701075
Demonstrates the fundamental paddling positions, strokes and turns of solo canoeing.
Physical Education and Recreation
Dist - NFBC **Prod** - NFBC 1978

Solo - Behind the Scenes 12 MIN
U-matic / VHS / 16mm
Color
Features an account of the making of the motion picture Solo.
Fine Arts
Dist - PFP **Prod** - PFP 1973

Solo - Chorus Songs - Pt 1 15 MIN
VHS / U-matic
Song Sampler Series
Color (P)
LC 81-707033
Describes the form of the solo - chorus song and the relationship between dotted and flagged notes. Presents the songs Hoosen Johnny, I Caught A Rabbit and Michael Row The Boat Ashore.
Fine Arts
Dist - GPN **Prod** - JCITV 1981

Solo - Chorus Songs - Pt 2 15 MIN
U-matic / VHS
Song Sampler Series
Color (P)
LC 81-707033
Describes the form of the solo - chorus song and the relationship between dotted and flagged notes. Presents the songs Hoosen Johnny, I Caught A Rabbit and Michael Row The Boat Ashore.
Fine Arts
Dist - GPN **Prod** - JCITV 1981

Solo Survival 11 MIN
16mm
Outdoor Education Mountaineering Series
Color
LC 74-703609
Shows how a solitary hiker loses his bearings and becomes lost. Emphasizes the importance of proper hiking equipment.
Physical Education and Recreation
Dist - SF **Prod** - MORLAT 1973

Solo Tribute - Keith Jarrett 102 MIN
VHS
Color (S)
$34.95 purchase _ #726 - 9007
Features pianist Keith Jarrett performing 14 jazz classics. Includes 'The Night We Called It A Day,' 'Round About Midnight,' 'Sweet And Lovely' and 'I Got It Bad And That Ain't Good.'.
Fine Arts
Dist - FI **Prod** - VARJ 1989

Soloing and performing - Video Three 90 MIN
VHS
You can play jazz piano series
Color (G)
$49.95 purchase _ #VD - BER - JP03
Features jazz pianist Warren Bernhardt. Teams up with jazz guitarist Mike DeMicco to discuss scales for soloing and improvisation; 'setting up' a solo; preparing a song for performance; playing with other musicians and more. Includes four original etudes for practice sessions and solos, including Sara's Touch, Pali Lookout, Ain't Life Grand and B - Loose Blues. Includes music. Part three of a three - part series.
Fine Arts
Dist - HOMETA **Prod** - HOMETA

Solos and Ensembles 29 MIN
Videoreel / VT2
American Band Goes Symphonic Series
B&W
Fine Arts
Dist - PBS **Prod** - WGTV

Sol's Birthday Cake 10 MIN
U-matic
Parlez - moi 1 Series
Color (J H) (FRENCH)
Presents a series of skits featuring a clown named Sol, which introduce basic, functional French. Each program introduces four new French phrases with review. Vocabulary and grammar are presented cumulatively, gradually increasing in difficulty. With teacher's guide.
Education; Foreign Language
Dist - TVOTAR **Prod** - TVOTAR 1978

Sol's Dancing Lesson 10 MIN
U-matic
Parlez - moi 1 Series
Color (J H) (FRENCH)
Presents a series of skits featuring a clown named Sol, which introduce basic, functional French. Each program introduces four new French phrases with review. Vocabulary and grammar are presented cumulatively, gradually increasing in difficulty. With teacher's guide.
Education; Foreign Language
Dist - TVOTAR **Prod** - TVOTAR 1978

Sol's First Aid Lesson 15 MIN
U-matic
Parlez - moi 2 Series
Color (H C) (FRENCH)
Features a clown named Sol who has various adventures which teach intermediate level French. Comes with teacher's guide.
Education; Foreign Language
Dist - TVOTAR **Prod** - TVOTAR 1978

Sol's Job Interview 10 MIN
U-matic
Parlez - moi 1 Series
Color (J H) (FRENCH)
Presents a series of skits featuring a clown named Sol, which introduce basic, functional French. Each program introduces four new French phrases with review. Vocabulary and grammar are presented cumulatively, gradually increasing in difficulty. With teacher's guide.
Education; Foreign Language
Dist - TVOTAR **Prod** - TVOTAR 1978

Sol's Physical Training 10 MIN
U-matic
Parlez - moi 1 Series
Color (J H) (FRENCH)
Presents a series of skits featuring a clown named Sol, which introduce basic, functional French. Each program introduces four new French phrases with review. Vocabulary and grammar are presented cumulatively, gradually increasing in difficulty. With teacher's guide.
Education; Foreign Language
Dist - TVOTAR **Prod** - TVOTAR 1978

Sol's Singing Lesson 10 MIN
U-matic
Parlez - moi 1 Series
Color (J H) (FRENCH)
Presents a series of skits featuring a clown named Sol, which introduce basic, functional French. Each program introduces four new French phrases with review. Vocabulary and grammar are presented cumulatively, gradually increasing in difficulty. With teacher's guide.
Education; Foreign Language
Dist - TVOTAR **Prod** - TVOTAR 1978

Sol's Weather Report 10 MIN
U-matic
Parlez - moi 1 Series
Color (J H) (FRENCH)
Presents a series of skits featuring a clown named Sol, which introduce basic, functional French. Each program introduces four new French phrases with review. Vocabulary and grammar are presented cumulatively, gradually increasing in difficulty. With teacher's guide.
Education; Foreign Language
Dist - TVOTAR **Prod** - TVOTAR 1978

Solstice - part three 35 MIN
16mm
Oobieland series
Color (G)
$55.00 rental
Portrays someone attempting to find Oobieland in the world now full of a terrible silence and the viewer is caught up in a cycle of meetings with strange inhabitants of that short space of time called winter solstice. Touches on the oldest instincts of humanity, leaving the viewer saddened and scared by the knowledge that the world will never know freedom through the completion of action. Part three of a five - part series.
Fine Arts; Literature and Drama; Religion and Philosophy
Dist - CANCIN **Prod** - UNGRW 1971

Solubility and Optochine Tests for Streptococcus Pneumoniae 8 MIN
16mm
Color
LC 74-705660
Demonstrates the differentiation of streptococcus pneumoniae from other species by the optochin test or by the addition of sodium desoxycholate.
Science; Science - Natural; Science - Physical
Dist - USNAC **Prod** - NMAC 1969

Solucion familias 22 MIN
VHS
Color (G C) (SPANISH WITH ENGLISH SUBTITLES)
$145.00 purchase, $45.00 rental
Points out the needs of elderly Spanish - speaking adults in the United States. Deals with making resources known and meeting those needs without taking the adult from home and family.
Health and Safety
Dist - TNF

Solution and Interpretation 33 MIN
U-matic / VHS
Nonlinear Vibrations Series
B&W
Mathematics
Dist - MIOT **Prod** - MIOT

Solution Methods for Calculation of Frequencies and Mode Shapes 58 MIN
VHS / U-matic
Finite Element Methods in Engineering Mechanics Series
Color
discusses solution methods for finite element eigen - problems.
Industrial and Technical Education; Mathematics
Dist - MIOT **Prod** - MIOT

Solution of Bent Wire Detour Problem by Children, Monkey and Racoon 14 MIN
16mm
B&W (C T)
Shows how to make and present various patterns of bent wire detour problems. Pictures a two - year - old child, a monkey and a raccoon having difficulty in solving simple bent wire detour problems, especially if solution requires that lure be pushed away from subject. Shows that a five - year - old child easily solves complicated problems, an adult monkey can be trained to solve complicated problems and a raccoon succeeds in solving a simple problem after 45 days of practice.
Psychology; Science - Natural
Dist - PSUPCR **Prod** - SDSU 1959

Solution of Equations Beyond the Second Degree 31 MIN
16mm
Advanced Algebra Series
B&W (T)
Applies the method of synthetic division to finding the roots of a 4th degree equation. Explains the rule of signs for finding the number of possible roots. Discusses rules for upper and lower bounds on roots.
Mathematics
Dist - MLA **Prod** - CALVIN 1960

Solution of Finite Element Equilibrium Equations in Dynamic Analysis 56 MIN
U-matic / VHS
Finite Element Methods in Engineering Mechanics Series
Color
Discusses solution of dynamic response by direct integration.
Industrial and Technical Education; Mathematics
Dist - MIOT **Prod** - MIOT

Solution of Finite Element Equilibrium Equations in Static Analysis 60 MIN
U-matic / VHS
Finite Element Methods in Engineering Mechanics Series
Color
Discusses solution of finite element equations in static analysis.
Industrial and Technical Education; Mathematics
Dist - MIOT **Prod** - MIOT

Solution of Salts - the Variation of Solubility with Temperature 12 MIN
16mm
Experimental General Chemistry Series
B&W
Prepares students to develop a detailed experimental procedure to study the effect of temperature on the solubility of salts. Illustrates the factors that influence the solubility of salts and discusses the use of Le Chateliers' principle.
Science; Science - Physical
Dist - MLA **Prod** - MLA

The Solution of the Linear - Quadratic Problem 47 MIN
VHS / U-matic
Modern Control Theory - Deterministic Optimal Linear Feedback Series
Color (PRO)
Industrial and Technical Education; Mathematics
Dist - MIOT **Prod** - MIOT

Solutions 21 MIN
U-matic
Chemistry 101 Series
Color (C)
Defines solution, solvent, solute, using real substances as examples of the solid, liquid and gaseous. Deals with miscibility and concentrations.
Science
Dist - UILL **Prod** - UILL 1975

Solutions 13 MIN
16mm / U-matic / VHS
Color (J H)
LC 79-303102
Presents experiments demonstrating various characteristics of a chemical solution.
Science; Science - Physical
Dist - PHENIX **Prod** - GAKKEN 1969

Solutions - a File on Canadian Technology 27 MIN
16mm
Color (G)
_ #106C 0180 557
Reflects and promotes the Canadian technological capability in the international market place.
Business and Economics; Geography - World
Dist - CFLMDC **Prod** - NFBC 1980

Solutions and People 26 MIN
16mm / VHS
Water Supply and Sanitation in Development Series
Color (H C A)
$550.00, $150.00 purchase, $25.00 rental _ #NC1826
Shows that the informed support and involvement of people affected by sanitation and water projects are necessary for the success of the projects. Follows health workers and technicians as they interview rural populations in several nations to ensure that the final construction project meets with their needs.
Health and Safety; Psychology; Science - Natural
Dist - IU **Prod** - NFBC 1985

Solutions and Projections 30 MIN
U-matic / VHS
Living Environment Series
Color (C)
Suggests some of the brighter possibilities for the coming generations on earth without attempting to project a specific future for mankind.
Science - Natural
Dist - DALCCD **Prod** - DALCCD

Solutions - Canadian Transit Technology 28 MIN
16mm
Color (G)
_ #106C 0181 570
Demonstrates the Canadian urban transportation capability in comparison with major competitors in world markets. Highlights the technological development of the Canadian urban transportation industry and shows the rapidly accelerating capability of Canadian companies in this field.
Business and Economics; Geography - World; Social Science
Dist - CFLMDC **Prod** - NFBC 1981

Solutions for the 21st century 28 MIN
VHS
Color (J H C G T A)
$75.00 purchase, $40.00 rental
Describes the most critical global problems - nuclear war, poverty, and environmental devastation - and suggests ways of resolving them. Offers both short and long - term actions that can be taken. Suggests that apathy is the main obstacle. Features experts including Norman Cousins, the Reverend William Sloane Coffin, Barbara Wien, Patricia Mische, and others. Produced by Jack Yost.
History - World; Sociology
Dist - EFVP

Solutions in Communications Series

The Air bubble	30 MIN
The Difficult 'TH' sound	30 MIN
Introduction of 'SCHWA,' an	30 MIN
A New Look at Jack be Nimble	30 MIN
Other Pieces of the Puzzle	30 MIN
Spanish Smootheners	30 MIN
Thirty Demons	30 MIN
Troubles with 'S' - the initial 'S'	30 MIN

Dist - SCCOE

Solutions - Ionic and Molecular 23 MIN
16mm / U-matic / VHS
Chemistry Series
Color (J H C)
$480, $250 purchase _ #4364
Depicts the chemical nature of a solution and explains why some substances won't dissolve in water.
Science - Physical
Dist - CORF

Solutions of Lyophilic Colloids, Examples of Macromolecules 55 MIN
U-matic / VHS
Colloid and Surface Chemistry - Lyophilic Colloids Series
Color
Science; Science - Physical
Dist - KALMIA **Prod** - KALMIA

Solutions to Images 30 MIN
VHS / U-matic
Developing Image Series
Color (J H)
Contains a technical survey of the major photographic processes, beginning with the daguerrotype.
Industrial and Technical Education
Dist - CTI **Prod** - CTI

Solutions to ten common parenting problems 30 MIN
VHS
Cambridge parenting series
Color (H C G)
$79.95 purchase _ #CCP0068V
Provides simple and realistic solutions for problems commonly experienced by parents of young children. Looks at temper tantrums, bed - wetting, misbehavior at mealtimes and bedtime, and sibling rivalry. Answers commonly asked questions - how to toilet train, when does an illness require a doctor, is thumb - sucking bad, is television harmful, and what's the difference between active and hyperactive. Includes manual. Part of a two - part series on parenting.
Sociology
Dist - CAMV **Prod** - CAMV 1992

Solutions to Vandalism 35 MIN
U-matic / VHS / 16mm
Color (H C A)
LC 79-700501
Describes successful vandalism prevention programs in six U S towns, cities and counties. Includes comments by Birch Bayh.
Civics and Political Systems; Sociology
Dist - PEREN **Prod** - RNBWP 1978

Solvents
U-matic / VHS
Chemsafe Series
Color
Concentrates on the health and safety precautions to take when working with solvents.
Health and Safety; Psychology; Science - Physical
Dist - BNA **Prod** - BNA

Solvents - III ; Rev. 7 MIN
8mm cartridge / VHS / BETA / U-matic
Chemsafe 2000 series
Color; CC; PAL (IND G)
$395.00 purchase, $175.00 rental _ #CS2 - 300
Reveals that every plant uses solvents - even if only for cleaning or degreasing. Discloses that, if used improperly, solvents can be deadly. Explains how to handle and store

solvents safely and use protective gear. Offers guidance on preventive and emergency measures. Part of a nine - part series providing comprehensive training in chemical safety. Includes a trainer's manual and ten participant handouts.
Health and Safety; Psychology; Science - Physical
Dist - BNA **Prod** - BNA 1994

Solvents - Module 3 7 MIN
BETA / VHS / U-matic
Chemsafe series
Color; PAL (IND G) (SPANISH DUTCH ITALIAN)
$175.00 rental _ #CSF - 300
Looks at the common use of solvents in industry. Shows how to protect against the hazards of solvents with effective storage, handling, personal safety and emergency procedures. Part of a comprehensive nine - part series on chemical safety in the workplace. Includes leader's guide and 10 workbooks which are available in English only. .
Business and Economics; Health and Safety; Psychology; Science - Physical
Dist - BNA **Prod** - BNA

Solvents - Module 3 10 MIN
VHS / U-matic / BETA
Chemsafe series
Color (IND G A)
$546.00 purchase, $150.00 rental _ #SOL045
Examines the widespread use of solvents. Reveals that solvents can be deadly, that they run the range of physical and health hazards such as carcinogens, toxins, irritants, sensitizers or attacks on specific organs. Solvents are capable of causing fires or explosions. Focuses on health and safety precautions to take when working with solvents. Part of a nine - part series which provides basic understanding of chemical safety and training in specific hazard categories. Each module dramatizes key points and is designed to support a one - hour training session.
Health and Safety; Psychology
Dist - ITF **Prod** - BNA

Solving Absolute Value Equations 30 MIN
VHS
Mathematics Series
Color (J)
LC 90713155
Examines solving absolute value equations. The 35th of 157 installments of the Mathematics Series.
Mathematics
Dist - GPN

Solving absolute value equations
VHS
Intermediate algebra series
Color (J H)
$125.00 purchase _ #3004
Teaches concepts of solving absolute value equations. Part of a set of 31 videos, each between 25 and 30 minutes long, that explain and reinforce concepts in intermediate algebra. Videos are also available in a set.
Mathematics
Dist - LANDMK

Solving Absolute Value Inequalities 30 MIN
VHS
Mathematics Series
Color (J)
LC 90713155
Explores solving absolute value inequalities. The 37th of 157 installments of the Mathematics Series.
Mathematics
Dist - GPN

Solving absolute value inequalities
VHS
Intermediate algebra series
Color (J H)
$125.00 purchase _ #3006
Teaches concepts of solving absolute value inequalities. Part of a set of 31 videos, each between 25 and 30 minutes long, that explain and reinforce concepts in intermediate algebra. Videos are also available in a set.
Mathematics
Dist - LANDMK

Solving algebraic equations of the 1st degree and inequalities 57 MIN
VHS
Algebra series
Color (G)
$29.95 purchase _ #6889
Uses careful explanations and repeated examples to teach algebra. Second in a series of five videos.
Mathematics
Dist - ESPNTV **Prod** - ESPNTV

Solving algebraic equations of the first degree and inequalities - Part 2 57 MIN
VHS
Math tutor series
Color (G)
$29.95 purchase
Uses live action and computer graphics to help in the review of how to solve algebraic equations of the first degree and inequalities.
Mathematics
Dist - PBS **Prod** - WNETTV

Solving AX Equals B 17 MIN
U-matic
Basic Math Skills Series Proportions; Proportions
Color
Mathematics
Dist - TELSTR **Prod** - TELSTR

Solving Budget Problems 60 MIN
VHS / BETA
Manufacturing Series
(IND)
Discusses how to monitor budget performance and ways to make sure that the budgeting process works.
Business and Economics
Dist - COMSRV **Prod** - COMSRV 1986

Solving calculus problems I 45 MIN
U-matic / VHS
Artificial intelligence series; Fundamental concepts, Pt 1
Color (PRO)
Presents a fundamental paradigm - heuristic search through goal trees. Shows how heuristics can be used to measure difficulty and focus attention.
Mathematics
Dist - MIOT **Prod** - MIOT

Solving calculus problems II 45 MIN
U-matic / VHS
Artificial intelligence series; Fundamental concepts, Pt 1
Color (PRO)
Features importance of experiment, alternative ways to measure performance. Presents searching alternatives - depth first, breadth first, and best first - and what understanding does to the appearance of intelligence.
Mathematics
Dist - MIOT **Prod** - MIOT

Solving choice of business entity problems 210 MIN
VHS
Color (C PRO A)
$67.20, $200.00 purchase _ #M769, #P259
Features panelists, using hypothetical fact situations, who work through both tax and non - tax considerations for selecting a business format for new or existing businesses. Embraces sole proprietorships, parnerships, S and C corporations, joint ventures and more. Analyzes the impact of recent changes in federal tax rates.
Business and Economics; Civics and Political Systems
Dist - ALIABA **Prod** - ALIABA 1990

Solving Communication Problems
VHS / 16mm
Management Skill Development Series
(PRO)
$89.95 purchase _ #MDS3
Covers essential elements of communication, and presents recent concepts in communication theory.
Business and Economics
Dist - RMIBHF **Prod** - RMIBHF

Solving Conflicts
VHS / U-matic
Color (I J)
Discusses ways for students to handle conflicts among themselves. Directed by Dan Jackson.
Education; Psychology
Dist - CF

Solving design problems 24 MIN
35mm strip / VHS
Color (J H C T A)
$93.00 purchase _ #MB - 512984 - 1, #MB512971 - X
Presents a step - by - step process for visual thinking by art students.
Fine Arts
Dist - SRA **Prod** - SRA 1988

Solving equations 30 MIN
VHS
Intermediate algebra series
Color (H)
$125.00 purchase _ #M37
Explains solving equations. Features Elayn Gay. Part of a 27 - part series on intermediate algebra.
Mathematics
Dist - LANDMK **Prod** - MGHT

Solving equations
VHS
Basic mathematical skills series
Color (J H)
$125.00 purchase _ #1014
Teaches the concepts involved in solving equations of various types. Presents part of a series that provides 27 videos, each between 25 and 30 minutes long, that explain and reinforce basic mathematical concepts. Tutors the student through definitions, theorems, step - by - step solutions and examples. Videos are also available in a set.
Mathematics
Dist - LANDMK

Solving equations 30 MIN
VHS
Beginning algebra series
Color (J H)
$125.00 purchase _ #M19
Teaches about solving equations. Features Elayn Gay. Part of a 19 - part series on beginning algebra.
Mathematics
Dist - LANDMK **Prod** - MGHT

Solving Equations 30 MIN
VHS
Mathematics Series
Color (J)
LC 90713155
Describes solving equations. The 14th of 157 installments in the Mathematics Series.
Mathematics
Dist - GPN

Solving equations - informal approach 28 MIN
16mm
Teaching high school mathematics - first course series; No 39
B&W (T)
Mathematics
Dist - MLA **Prod** - UICSM 1967

Solving Equations of Fractional Form 30 MIN
16mm
Intermediate Algebra Series
B&W (H)
Stresses the importance of properly handling equations in which X appears in the denominator in order that a solution does not make the denominator equal to zero. Presents techniques for manipulating fractional equations. Formulates and solves a typical work problem.
Mathematics
Dist - MLA **Prod** - CALVIN 1959

Solving Everyday Problems
VHS / 16mm
Color (G)
$50.00 purchase _ #V007
Demonstrates Rational - Emotive Therapy - RET techniques with a group of youngsters aged 9 to 14.
Guidance and Counseling; Psychology
Dist - IRL **Prod** - IRL

Solving inequalities 30 MIN
VHS
Intermediate algebra series
Color (H)
$125.00 purchase _ #M38
Explains solving inequalities. Features Elayn Gay. Part of a 27 - part series on intermediate algebra.
Mathematics
Dist - LANDMK **Prod** - MGHT

Solving inequalities
VHS
Algebra 1 series
Color (J H)
$125.00 purchase _ #A6
Teaches the concepts involved in solving mathematical inequalities. Part of a series of 16 videos, each between 25 and 30 minutes long, that explain and reinforce 89 basic concepts of algebra. Includes a stated objective for each segment. Tutors the student through definitions, theorems, step - by - step solutions and examples. Videos are also available in a set.
Mathematics
Dist - LANDMK
GPN

Solving inequalities and applications 30 MIN
VHS
Beginning algebra series
Color (J H)
$125.00 purchase _ #M20
Teaches about solving inequalities and applications. Features Elayn Gay. Part of a 19 - part series on beginning algebra.
Mathematics
Dist - LANDMK **Prod** - MGHT

Solving Landscaping Problems 45 MIN
VHS
Color (G)

$19.95 purchase _ #6113
Shows how to handle steep slopes, ugly foundations, overgrown plantings, shady areas and most other common landscaping problems.
Agriculture; Home Economics; Sociology
Dist - SYBVIS **Prod** - HOMES

Solving landscaping problems 45 MIN
VHS
Better homes and gardens video library series
Color (G)
$19.95 purchase
Offers solutions to many of the most common landscaping problems - steep slopes, ugly foundations, overgrown plantings, shady areas, and more. Includes a landscape guide booklet.
Agriculture; Home Economics
Dist - PBS **Prod** - WNETTV

Solving linear equations
VHS
Intermediate algebra series
Color (J H)
$125.00 purchase _ #3001
Teaches concepts of solving linear equations. Part of a set of 31 videos, each between 25 and 30 minutes long, that explain and reinforce concepts in intermediate algebra. Videos are also available in a set.
Mathematics
Dist - LANDMK

Solving linear equations 30 MIN
VHS
Beginning algebra series
Color (J H)
$125.00 purchase _ #M18
Teaches about solving linear equations. Features Elayn Gay. Part of a 19 - part series on beginning algebra.
Mathematics
Dist - LANDMK **Prod** - MGHT

Solving Linear Equations 30 MIN
VHS
Mathematics Series
Color (J)
LC 90713155
Demonstrates how to solve linear equations. The 32nd of 157 installments of the Mathematics Series.
Mathematics
Dist - GPN

Solving linear equations
VHS
Beginning algebra series
Color (J H)
$125.00 purchase _ #2002
Teaches fundamental concepts used in solving linear equations. Part of a series of 31 videos, each between 25 and 30 minutes long, that explain and reinforce basic concepts of algebra. Tutors the student through definitions, theorems, step - by - step solutions and examples. Videos are also available in a set.
Mathematics
Dist - LANDMK

Solving linear equations 30 MIN
VHS
College algebra series
Color (C)
$125.00 purchase _ #4006
Shows how to solve linear equations. Part of a 31 - part series on college algebra.
Mathematics
Dist - LANDMK **Prod** - LANDMK

Solving linear inequalities
VHS
Beginning algebra series
Color (J H)
$125.00 purchase _ #2003
Teaches fundamental concepts used in solving linear inequalities. Part of a series of 31 videos, each between 25 and 30 minutes long, that explain and reinforce basic concepts of algebra. Tutors the student through definitions, theorems, step - by - step solutions and examples. Videos are also available in a set.
Mathematics
Dist - LANDMK

Solving linear inequalities
VHS
Intermediate algebra series
Color (J H)
$125.00 purchase _ #3003
Teaches concepts of solving linear inequalities. Part of a set of 31 videos, each between 25 and 30 minutes long, that explain and reinforce concepts in intermediate algebra. Videos are also available in a set.
Mathematics
Dist - LANDMK

Solving Linear Inequalities 30 MIN
VHS
Mathematics Series
Color (J)
LC 90713155
Demonstrates solving linear inequalities. The 34th of 157 installments of the Mathematics Series.
Mathematics
Dist - GPN

Solving Money Problems 15 MIN
U-matic
Math Factory, Module VI - Money Series
Color (P)
Reviews addition and subtraction of two - digit numerals by using problems involving money and illustrates how to make change.
Business and Economics; Mathematics
Dist - GPN **Prod** - MAETEL 1973

Solving pairs of equations 10 MIN
VHS
Children's encyclopedia of mathematics - pre - algebra series
Color (I)
$49.95 purchase _ #8374
Shows how to solve pairs of equations. Part of a nine - part series about pre - algebra.
Mathematics
Dist - AIMS **Prod** - DAVFMS 1991

Solving Problems 30 MIN
VHS / U-matic
Stress Management - a Positive Strategy Series; 4
Color (A)
LC 82-706501
Shows ways a manager can handle a highly challenging job and the outside world while maintaining a sense of well - being. Covers the manager's role and responsibility in controling the stress - related aspects of relationships among staff members.
Business and Economics; Psychology
Dist - TIMLIF **Prod** - TIMLIF 1982

Solving Problems Creatively 44 MIN
16mm / U-matic / VHS
Color (C A)
LC 81-701445
Offers a training program in problem solving designed to stimulate creativity in resolving management problems and differences. Shows which techniques work best and makes participants aware that there is no one method of solving a problem.
Business and Economics; Psychology
Dist - CRMP **Prod** - MGHT 1981

Solving Problems in the Workplace 5 MIN
VHS / 16mm
Color (PRO)
$185.00 purchase, $60.00 rental, $25.00 preview
Describes humorously how to solve problems in the workplace. Discusses how to ask questions, look for answers, combine ideas, keep ideas simple, search for new and sell ideas.
Psychology
Dist - UTM

Solving problems together - Part 9 14 MIN
VHS
Employment development series
Color (PRO IND A)
$495.00 purchase, $150.00 rental _ #ITC35
Presents part nine of a ten - part series designed to prepare employees to cope with workplace demands in a skillful and confident manner. Enables supervisors and managers to improve their skills and abilities as they work with their peers. Includes a leader's guide, instructions for self - study and participant's booklet.
Business and Economics; Guidance and Counseling; Psychology
Dist - EXTR **Prod** - ITRC

Solving Problems with the Quadratic Formula 29 MIN
16mm
Advanced Algebra Series
B&W (H)
Uses the quadratic formula to solve for the roots of a quadratic equation. Describes three methods for extracting square roots of numbers - - the square root algorithm, the slide rule and tables of square roots. Also shows the use of tables of cube roots.
Mathematics
Dist - MLA **Prod** - CALVIN 1960

Solving Proportions in Fractions and Decimals 10 MIN
U-matic
Basic Math Skills Series Proportions; Proportions
Color
Mathematics
Dist - TELSTR **Prod** - TELSTR

Solving Proportions in Whole Numbers 15 MIN
U-matic
Basic Math Skills Series Proportions; Proportions
Color
Mathematics
Dist - TELSTR **Prod** - TELSTR

Solving Quadratic Equations 30 MIN
VHS
Mathematics Series
Color (J)
LC 90713155
Describes solving quadratic equations. The 70th of 157 installments of the Mathematics Series.
Mathematics
Dist - GPN

Solving quadratic equations 30 MIN
VHS
Intermediate algebra series
Color (H)
$125.00 purchase _ #M50
Explains how to solve quadratic equations. Features Elayn Gay. Part of a 27 - part series on intermediate algebra.
Mathematics
Dist - LANDMK **Prod** - MGHT

Solving quadratic equations 30 MIN
VHS
College algebra series
Color (C)
$125.00 purchase _ #4008
Shows how to solve quadratic equations. Part of a 31 - part series on college algebra.
Mathematics
Dist - LANDMK **Prod** - LANDMK

Solving quadratic equations
VHS
Algebra 1 series
Color (J H)
$125.00 purchase _ #A16
Teaches the concepts involved in solving quadratic equations. Part of a series of 16 videos, each between 25 and 30 minutes long, that explain and reinforce 89 basic concepts of algebra. Includes a stated objective for each segment. Tutors the student through definitions, theorems, step - by - step solutions and examples. Videos are also available in a set.
Mathematics
Dist - LANDMK
GPN

Solving quadratic equations by completing the square
VHS
Intermediate algebra series
Color (J H)
$125.00 purchase _ #3025
Teaches basic concepts involved in solving quadratic equations by completing the square and then factoring. Part of a 31 - video series, each part 25 to 30 minutes long, that explains and reinforces concepts in intermediate algebra. Uses definitions, theorems, examples and step - by - step solutions to tutor the student. Videos also available in a set.
Mathematics
Dist - LANDMK

Solving Quadratic Equations by Completing the Square 30 MIN
VHS
Mathematics Series
Color (J)
LC 90713155
Discusses solving quadratic equations by completing the square. The 56th of 157 installments of the Mathematics Series.
Mathematics
Dist - GPN

Solving quadratic equations by completing the square
VHS
Beginning algebra series
Color (J H)
$125.00 purchase _ #2029
Teaches a particular technique for solving quadratic equations. Part of a 31 - video series, each part between 25 and 30 minutes long, that explains and reinforces fundamental concepts of beginning algebra. Uses definitions, theorems, examples and step - by - step solutions to instruct the student.
Mathematics
Dist - LANDMK

Solving quadratic equations by factoring
VHS
Intermediate algebra series
Color (J H)
$125.00 purchase _ #3012
Teaches the concept of factoring to solve quadratic equations. Part of a set of 31 videos, each between 25 and 30 minutes long, that explain and reinforce concepts in intermediate algebra. Videos are also available in a set.
Mathematics
Dist - LANDMK

Solving quadratic equations by factoring 30 MIN
VHS
Beginning algebra series
Color (J H)
$125.00 purchase _ #M24
Teaches about solving quadratic equations by factoring. Features Elayn Gay. Part of a 19 - part series on beginning algebra.
Mathematics
Dist - LANDMK **Prod** - MGHT

Solving Quadratic Equations by Factoring 30 MIN
VHS
Mathematics Series
Color (J)
LC 90713155
Discusses solving quadratic equations by factoring. The 24th of 157 installments of the Mathematics Series.
Mathematics
Dist - GPN

Solving quadratic equations by factoring
VHS
Beginning algebra series
Color (J H)
$125.00 purchase _ #2008
Teaches fundamental concepts of solving quadratic equations by factoring. Part of a series of 31 videos, each between 25 and 30 minutes long, that explain and reinforce basic concepts of algebra. Tutors the student through definitions, theorems, step - by - step solutions and examples. Videos are also available in a set.
Mathematics
Dist - LANDMK

Solving quadratic equations by the quadratic formula
VHS
Beginning algebra series
Color (J H)
$125.00 purchase _ #2030
Teaches a particular technique for solving quadratic equations. Part of a 31 - video series, each part between 25 and 30 minutes long, that explains and reinforces fundamental concepts of beginning algebra. Uses definitions, theorems, examples and step - by - step solutions to instruct the student.
Mathematics
Dist - LANDMK

Solving Quadratic Equations by the Quadratic Formula 30 MIN
VHS
Mathematics Series
Color (J)
LC 90713155
Discusses solving quadratic equations by the quadratic formula. The 57th of 157 installments of the Mathematics Series.
Mathematics
Dist - GPN

Solving quadratic equations by the quadratic formula
VHS
Intermediate algebra series
Color (J H)
$125.00 purchase _ #3026
Teaches basic concepts involved in solving quadratic equations by using the quadratic formula. Part of a 31 - video series, each part 25 to 30 minutes long, that explains and reinforces concepts in intermediate algebra. Uses definitions, theorems, examples and step - by - step solutions to tutor the student. Videos also available in a set.
Mathematics
Dist - LANDMK

Solving Simultaneous Equations
16mm
B&W
Discusses the problem of solving simultaneous equations, using the engineering of the Concorde as an example.
Mathematics
Dist - OPENU **Prod** - OPENU

Solving simultaneous equations and inequalities algebraically and geometrically 29 MIN
VHS
Algebra series
Color (G)
$29.95 purchase _ #6891
Uses careful explanations and repeated examples to teach algebra. Fourth in a series of five videos.
Mathematics
Dist - ESPNTV **Prod** - ESPNTV

Solving simultaneous equations and inequalities algebraically and geometrically - Part 4 29 MIN
VHS
Math tutor series
Color (G)
$29.95 purchase
Uses live action and computer graphics to help in the review of solving simultaneous equations and inequalities algebraically and geometrically.
Mathematics
Dist - PBS **Prod** - WNETTV

Solving Simultaneous Linear Equations 29 MIN
16mm
Intermediate Algebra Series
B&W (H)
Shows graphical solutions of two unknowns, X and Y. Explains that the unknowns may be subject to pointvalue conditions or to those conditions that can be expressed as linear equations and which appear as straight lines. Discusses the concept of simultaneous solution of two straight lines.
Mathematics
Dist - MLA **Prod** - CALVIN 1959

Solving the Energy Problem 20 MIN
16mm / U-matic / VHS
Exploring Science Series
Color (J H)
Traces the search for alternative sources of energy, now that stocks of coal, oil and natural gas are running short.
Social Science
Dist - FI **Prod** - BBCTV 1982

Solving the Harmony Puzzle - You're Part 15 MIN
VHS / 16mm
Color (I)
$200.00 purchase _ #292701
Follows up the question posed at the end of 'The Harmony Puzzle - Environment And Economy,' what can you do to help. Shows how individuals can take personal responsbility for sustainable development and that industries and government have been required to be socially responsible. Helps viewers understand that they are not isolated from environment problems or powerless to act.
Business and Economics; Science - Natural
Dist - ACCESS **Prod** - ACCESS 1989

Solving the Linear Equations L(Y)=0 - Constant Coefficients 19 MIN
VHS / U-matic
Calculus of Differential Equations Series
B&W
Mathematics
Dist - MIOT **Prod** - MIOT

Solving the problem 28 MIN
U-matic / BETA / VHS
Communication skills 2 - advanced series
Color (H C G)
$101.95, $89.95 purchase _ #CA - 06
Lists the steps of reflective thinking in correct order and identifies the purpose of each step. Shows how to apply the steps of reflective thinking in problem - solving discussions. Part of a 26 - part series.
Psychology; Social Science
Dist - INSTRU

Solving Travel Problems 22 MIN
16mm
Color (I J H)
Describes how handicapped passengers can respond to such typical travel problems as being late, missing the train or bus, being lost and getting hassled. Includes who to ask for help and the importance of being alert and staying calm.
Education
Dist - PARPRO **Prod** - PARPRO

Solving Verbal Problems in Mathematics 21 MIN
16mm
Project on Interpreting Mathematics Education Research Series
Color
LC 74-705661
Shows effective ways to promote verbal problem solving skills. Intersperses examples of teachers and pupils in action, using various problem solving techniques with examples of actual work that results from the use of multiple approaches.
Mathematics
Dist - USNAC **Prod** - USOE 1970

Solving worded problems 27 MIN
16mm
Teaching high school mathematics - first course series; No 50
B&W (T)
Mathematics
Dist - MLA **Prod** - UICSM 1967

Solzhenitsyn's Children are Making a Lot of Noise in Paris 88 MIN
16mm
Color (C A)
Looks at the New Philosophers, former European leftist activists whose thinking has been radically changed by Alexander Solzhenitsyn. Debates whether they will now influence the electorate decisively.
Civics and Political Systems; History - World; Religion and Philosophy
Dist - NFBC **Prod** - NFBC 1978

Soma 17 MIN
16mm
Color (G)
$25.00 rental
Deals with patterns of loss and cyles of memory through past, present and future. Searches for personal meaning via making the film. First in a loose trilogy of films by Sandra Davis.
Fine Arts
Dist - CANCIN

Soma Touch 12 MIN
16mm
Color
Presents a dancer and artist, for whom the experience of masturbation was purely kinetic, without any accompanying fantasies of other persons. Portrays the possibilities of in - depth involvement with one's own body.
Guidance and Counseling; Psychology; Sociology
Dist - MMRC **Prod** - MMRC

Somalia 29 MIN
VHS / U-matic
Color (J H G)
$245.00, $295.00 purchase, $60.00 rental
Listens to Somalians speak about their situations, their thoughts about the past and present and their hopes for the future. Allows for a case study into the breakdown of a nation - state and the consequences.
Fine Arts; History - World
Dist - NDIM **Prod** - BALFOR 1993

Somalia 26 MIN
16mm
Color (J)
LC 72-701204
Describes the geographical features of Ethiopia and tells about the customs, manners, morals, religions and vocations of the people living there.
Geography - World; History - United States
Dist - AVED **Prod** - AVED 1968

Somalia 28 MIN
Videoreel / VHS
International Byline Series
Color (SOMALI)
Interviews a Somalian ambassador the United Nations. Discusses the refugee problem in Somalia. Hosted by Marilyn Perry. Includes a film clip.
Business and Economics; Civics and Political Systems; Geography - World
Dist - PERRYM **Prod** - PERRYM

Somatic Consequences of Emotional Starvation in Infants 30 MIN
16mm
Film Studies of the Psychoanalytic Research Project on Problems in 'Infancy Series
B&W (C T)
Compares children raised in families with those in a foundling home. Illustrates that the emotional deprivation of the institutionalized children results in bodily retardation and other ill effects.
Health and Safety; Psychology; Sociology
Dist - NYU **Prod** - SPITZ 1949

Somatic - emotional therapy 30 MIN
BETA / VHS
Therapeutic alternatives series
Color (G)
$29.95 purchase _ #S305
States that the characteristic attitudes one takes in life are reflected in the postures and attitudes of the body. Features Stanley Keleman, author of 'Somatic Reality,' 'Your Body Speaks Its Mind' and 'Embodying Experience.' Part of a four - part series on therapeutic alternatives.
Physical Education and Recreation; Psychology; Religion and Philosophy; Science - Natural
Dist - THINKA **Prod** - THINKA

Somatization - Possible Sexual Etiology 30 MIN
U-matic / VHS
Color (PRO)
Shows patients presenting vague physical complaints whose underlying cause may be sex - related. Illustrates physicians' approaches to uncovering the interpersonal and sexual problems which may be presented as physical symptoms. Includes a thorough physical examination and appropriate tests by the physician in their treatment plan, and how the final diagnosis is arrived at through a process of elimination. Illustrates several common physical symptoms which may mask a sexual concern.
Health and Safety
Dist - HSCIC **Prod** - HSCIC

Somatoform and Dissociative Disorders 70 MIN
U-matic / VHS
Psychiatry Learning System, Pt 2 - Disorders Series
Color (PRO)
Explains possible causes, symptoms, and treatment of the somatoform disorders.
Health and Safety; Psychology
Dist - HSCIC **Prod** - HSCIC 1982

Somber accomodations 15 MIN
16mm
B&W (G)
$40.00 rental
Dramatizes a metaphorical story in which the passageway of reality opens up between two worlds. Uses the dark waters of a fountain that part to reveal a hidden world while a forlorn figure is trapped by oppressive forces surrounding him within a stone enclosure. Produced by Thad Povey.
Fine Arts; Literature and Drama
Dist - CANCIN

Some African Tropical Diseases 15 MIN
16mm
Color
LC FIA56-1101
Depicts patients from various parts of Africa exhibiting signs and symptoms of schistosomiasis mansoni, yaws, African sleeping sickness, leprosy, kala azar and kawashlorkor. Presents diagrammatic representations of the epidemiology or etiology of each disease.
Geography - World; Health and Safety; Sociology
Dist - UCLA **Prod** - MARJOM 1956

Some Afrikaners 14 MIN
16mm
B&W (H C A)
LC 76-703921
Examines the white South African's ties to the land, his covenant with God and his determined persistence. Emphasizes the rural foundations of the Afrikaner. Based on the book entitled Some Afrikaners. Photographed by David Goldblatt.
Geography - World; Sociology
Dist - BFPS **Prod** - BFPS 1976

Some American Feminists 56 MIN
16mm
Color (H C A)
Explores the women's movements for equal rights by interviewing such feminists as Ti - Grace Atkinson, Rita Mae Brown, Betty Friedan, Margo Jefferson, Lila Karp and Kate Millett.
Sociology
Dist - MOKIN **Prod** - NFBC 1980

Some Analytical Tools 45 MIN
VHS / U-matic
Economic Perspectives Series
Color
Describes some of the analytic tools used in the study of economics.
Business and Economics
Dist - MDCPB **Prod** - MDCPB

Some babies die 55 MIN
VHS / 16mm
Color (H C G)
$950.00, $295.00 purchase, $60.00 rental _ #11294, #37340
Presents an Australian documentary on the grief of stillbirth and neonatal death narrated by Elisabeth Kubler - Ross. Focuses on a family coping with the death of a newborn and undergoing a unique counseling process in which they are urged to create memories of their baby and work through their grief over its death. Contrasts their experience with that of a young woman who had three stillborn sons, non of which she ever saw or held and who, years later, still experiences depression, grief and regret. Produced by Martyn Langdon Down.
Sociology
Dist - UCEMC

Some Basic Differences in Newborn Infants during the Lying - in Period 23 MIN
16mm
Film Studies on Integrated Development Series
B&W (C T)
Presents actual records of children from moment of birth to show the difference in activity and reactions to presentation, removal and restoration of objects of gratification. Emphasizes the importance in the child's total development and its mother's emotional adjustment to it.
Psychology; Sociology
Dist - NYU **Prod** - FRIWOL 1944

Some Basic Signs for Communicating with Deaf Patients 10 MIN
VHS / U-matic
Color (PRO)
Presents short language course for nurses and doctors to learn simple medical sign to communicate with patients. Partially signed.
Guidance and Counseling; Health and Safety; Psychology
Dist - GALCO **Prod** - GALCO 1980

Some beginnings of social psychiatry 14 MIN
VHS / 16mm
Documentaries for learning series
B&W (C G PRO)
$290.00, $60.00 purchase, $29.00 rental _ #24271
Offers excerpts from lectures delivered in a 1965 seminar by the late Dr Erich Lindemann, a pioneer in community psychiatry who surveyed the developing field of social psychiatry. Contains material of historical importance which remains relevant to the mental health field. Part of a series produced for use by health care professionals and educators.
Health and Safety; Psychology
Dist - PSU **Prod** - MASON 1966

Some behavior characteristics of a human and a chimpanzee infant in the same environment 19 MIN
16mm
Ape and child series; Pt 1
B&W (C T)
Compares the general behavior of a normal human infant between the ages of 10 and 14.5 months with the behavior of a chimpanzee companion between the ages of 7.5 months and 12 months, both develop in typical human civilized surroundings. Illustrates six phases of behavioral development - - upright walking, affectionate behavior toward adult, strength, indoor and outriding vehicles.
Psychology; Science - Natural
Dist - PSUPCR **Prod** - PSUPCR 1932

Some Call it Greed 51 MIN
16mm / U-matic / VHS
Color (J)
LC 80-701164
Describes the contributions of men such as J P Morgan, Andrew Carnegie, J Swift, Henry Ford and Alfred Sloan, whose drive for profit helped to make the United States the most productive economy in the world.
Business and Economics
Dist - LCOA **Prod** - FORBES 1980

Some Call it Software 10 MIN
16mm
Color
LC 72-700598
Shows how people assemble the instructions which enable computers to function and to help solve problems. Illustrates traffic control by computer.
Industrial and Technical Education; Mathematics; Social Science
Dist - MTP **Prod** - IBUSMA 1972

Some Don't 8 MIN
16mm
Color (H C A)
Presents a subjective documentary film exemplifying man's desperate craving for female sensuality.
Psychology; Sociology
Dist - CFS **Prod** - CFS 1967

Some ethical considerations in journalism 23 MIN
VHS
Color (H C)
$39.95 purchase _ #IVMC18
Takes a close look at some of the ethical considerations a journalist should follow when writing and reporting a story. Considers whether a journalist should accept perks and how a reporter can avoid bias. Offers recommendations from the Radio and Television News Assn and the Society of Professional Journalists.
Literature and Drama
Dist - INSTRU

Some Examples of Hypnotic Behavior 11 MIN
16mm
B&W (C T)
An experiment to demonstrate the affects of hypnosis on behavior induces illusions and hallucinations. Tests of depth of trance show that painful stimuli are ignored. Examples of regression, with tests, are shown and may be compared with the behavior of a normal child. Sensory selection and agnosia writing are illustrated along with immediate post - hypnotic disorientation and gradual reorientation.
Psychology
Dist - PSUPCR **Prod** - PSUPCR 1946

Some exterior presence 8 MIN
16mm
Color (G)
$15.00 rental
Interprets interaction of dark and light, tone and form into felt exterior - interior presences. Conveys the starkness of red, black and white tempered by suggestions of violence, church and ritual. The two extremes of stark angular exteriors and mysterious rounded interiors are mediated by a figure who endlessly moves between the two domains.
Fine Arts
Dist - CANCIN **Prod** - CHILDA 1977

Some Flowers of the Narcissus - Frank Lloyd Wright 22 MIN
16mm
Color (C)
LC FIA67-1148
Pictures four churches designed by Frank Lloyd Wright from 1906 to 1961, showing his prolific imagination, innovations, changing forms and constant daring.
Fine Arts
Dist - RADIM **Prod** - MARTNG 1967

Some Friendly Insects 5 MIN
U-matic / VHS / 16mm
Wonder Walks Series
Color (P I)
Explores through up - close photography the characteristics of several harmless insects.
Science - Natural
Dist - EBEC **Prod** - EBEC 1971

Some General Principles of Biliary Tract Surgery 28 MIN
16mm
Color (PRO)
Demonstrates some anatomical features of the extrahepatic biliary tract and some technical aspects of surgeries of the gallbladder and bile ducts.
Health and Safety; Science
Dist - ACY **Prod** - ACYDGD 1961

Some general reactions of a human and a chimpanzee infant after 6 months in the same environment 17 MIN
16mm
Ape and child series; Pt 4
B&W (C T)
Compares the non - experimental behavior of a human infant, age 16 to 19 months and a chimpanzee, age 13.5 to 16.5 months, after six months in the same environment. Shows nine comparisons, upright walking, reaction to colored picture book, difference in climbing ability, eating with spoon, drinking from glass, beginning cooperative play, pointing to parts of the body, imitation of scribbling of experimenter and affectionate behavior toward each other.
Psychology; Science - Natural
Dist - PSUPCR **Prod** - PSUPCR 1932

Some Girls 30 MIN
VHS / 16mm
Color (G)
$265.00 purchase, $100.00, $50.00 rental
Focuses on the lives of four teenagers from rural Appalachia and their participation in the local pregnancy prevention and parenting programs.
Sociology
Dist - FANPRO **Prod** - FANPRO 1989

Some Justice 60 MIN
16mm / U-matic / VHS
I, Claudius Series; No 6
Color (C A)
Explains that Germanicus' death has so roused Rome that not even the arranged suicide of Piso can take popular pressure off Tiberius.
History - World
Dist - FI **Prod** - BBCTV 1977

Some leaders are born women 57 MIN
VHS
Color (C PRO G)
$34.95 purchase _ #42 - 2441
Features Sarah Weddington, the youngest woman ever to argue before the Supreme Court winning the landmark Roe v Wade case in 1973. Shares her knowledge on how to teach leadership. Discusses leadership styles, specific obstacles women must overcome to become leaders, why women should seek to be leaders and why this is the time for nurses to lead the nation to health care reform.
Guidance and Counseling; Health and Safety
Dist - NLFN **Prod** - NLFN

Some Like it Cold 11 MIN
16mm / U-matic / VHS
Reading and Word Play Series
Color (P)
Uses boys and girls and amusing animal characters tasting hot and cold foods and examining hot and cold weather as a framework for understanding new word concepts, including eat, drink, hot, cold, good, best and open.
English Language
Dist - AIMS **Prod** - PEDF 1976

Some Like it Hot 121 MIN
16mm
Color
Stars Jack Lemmon and Tony Curtis as a pair of musicians on the run from the mob. Tells how they dress as women and join an all - girl band. Directed by Billy Wilder.
Fine Arts
Dist - UAE **Prod** - UNKNWN 1959

Some liked it hot 50 MIN
VHS
Horizon series
Color (A)
PdS99 purchase
Explores one of the mysteries of human evolution - why they alone walk upright. Explores the latest thinking, known as the Radiator Theory, that the development of the large human brain was linked to walking upright - but not in the way anyone had imagined. In Africa, the fossil record supports this new idea and explains why other paleontologists may have got it wrong.
Science - Natural; Science - Physical
Dist - BBCENE

Some major research departments of mathematics by Saunders Mac Lane 60 MIN
VHS
AMS - MAA joint lecture series
Color (PRO G)
$59.00 purchase _ #VIDMACLANE - VB2
Provides a historical perspective on the development of mathematical research departments in the United States. Begins with Berlin at the turn of the century and Gottingen in the 1930s to chronicle the influence of those departments on the development of mathematics in the US. Describes the strengths of some of the most influential American departments and evalutes the theory of 'mathematical inheritance' as a method of building an excellent research department. Discusses 'objective rankings' of departments, science policy issues and the ills of calculus textbooks. Recorded in Providence.
History - United States; Mathematics
Dist - AMSOC **Prod** - AMSOC 1988

Some Misconceptions about Language - Pt 1 30 MIN
U-matic / VHS
Language and Meaning Series
Color (C)
English Language; Psychology
Dist - GPN **Prod** - WUSFTV 1983

Some Misconceptions about Language - Pt 2 30 MIN
U-matic / VHS
Language and Meaning Series
Color (C)
English Language; Psychology
Dist - GPN **Prod** - WUSFTV 1983

Some Mother Goose rhymes 10 MIN
VHS
Color (K P)
$34.95 purchase
Presents 'Some Mother Goose Rhymes,' a collection of favorite Mother Goose nursery rhymes. Includes 'Humpty Dumpty,' 'One, Two, Buckle Your Shoe,' 'Gold Lock, Gold Key,' 'The ABC Song,' 'Two Blackbirds,' 'Hickory Dickory Dock,' 'Hey Diddle, Diddle,' 'The House That Jack Built,' and 'Old King Cole.' Illustrated and animated by Jack Otis Moore.
Literature and Drama
Dist - LIVOAK **Prod** - LIVOAK

Some Observations Concerning the Phenomenology of Oral Behavior in Small Infants 20 MIN
16mm
Infant Psychology Series
B&W (C T)
A documentation of variations in oral behavior in a group of infants under 24 weeks of age. Shows that mouth movements depend on neuromuscular maturation, different oral patterns and personal modifications.
Psychology
Dist - NYU **Prod** - MENF 1951

Some of My Best Friends are Bottomless Dancers 18 MIN
16mm
Color (C A)
Presents a cinema - verite study of Roman Balladine, the ex - choreographer for the Follies Bergere.
Fine Arts
Dist - UWFKD **Prod** - UWFKD

Some of Our Airmen are no Longer Missing 52 MIN
U-matic / VHS
Color (J S C G)
$99.00 purchase
Documents the reclaiming of land near Amsterdam. As the waters recede, many Allied aircraft which crashed during World War II are being recovered and identified.
Geography - World; History - World
Dist - LANDMK **Prod** - LANDMK 1983

Some of Our Schoolmates are Blind 20 MIN
16mm
Color (T)
LC FIA65-1226
Describes the education of blind sighted children in a public elementary school in Temple City, California, pointing out how the blind child becomes identified with his peers and with the total school program. Shows the blind children in regular classroom work, on the playground and in sessions where special teachers meet special curriculum needs, such as the teaching of Braille.
Education; Psychology
Dist - AFB **Prod** - AFB 1960

Some of the Presidents' Men 59 MIN
VHS / 16mm
Color (G)
$70.00 rental _ #SOPM - 000
Features four former White House Press Secretaries divulging their versions of the major events and decisions made by the Presidents they served.
Civics and Political Systems
Dist - PBS **Prod** - KCTSTV

Some of the Things that Go on Out There 30 MIN
16mm
Color (G)
$465.00 purchase, $70.00 rental _ #4991, 0526J
Explores adolescence, ancient and current rites of passage, parent - youth relationships, sexual activity, drug and alcohol use and gaining independence. Stimulates youth and adult discussion.
Guidance and Counseling; Health and Safety; Psychology; Sociology
Dist - HAZELB MMRC **Prod** - PEREHR

Some of these Days 60 MIN
VHS / U-matic
Color
Profiles four women grappling with the process of aging in America. Uses the device of cross - cuttting between their present lives and their memories.
Psychology; Sociology
Dist - MEDIPR **Prod** - MEDIPR 1980

Some of Your Best Friends 40 MIN
16mm
Color
LC 72-702423
Documents the Gay Liberation Movement. Contains interviews with articulate gay civil rights leaders with various parades and demonstrations in protest of gays. Presents the case for homosexuality as an alternate life style.
Sociology
Dist - USC **Prod** - USC 1972

Some of Your Bits Ain't Nice 11 MIN
16mm / U-matic
Color (J H A)
Presents an animated program about two teenagers that takes a humorous approach to the need to keep hands, hair, teeth, feet, body and clothes clean.
Fine Arts; Health and Safety; Home Economics; Psychology; Sociology
Dist - PEREN **Prod** - PEREN

Some Other Things to Think about 28 MIN
U-matic / VHS
Business of Effective Speaking Series
Color
Discusses the use of media aids in making effective business - related speeches.
Business and Economics; English Language
Dist - KYTV **Prod** - KYTV

Some Other Time 27 MIN
16mm
Color
Depicts the effects of multiple sclerosis on youth, from the initial stages of depression through gradual emotional rehabilitation to that hopeful time when each day is lived for itself. Tells the story of Rob Paterson who has just learned that he has multiple sclerosis and how he learns to cope with MS with the help of Sarah, an MS volunteer.
Health and Safety; Psychology; Sociology
Dist - NMSS **Prod** - MSCAN 1974

Some People 19 MIN
VHS / U-matic
Contemporary Arts Series
Color (G)
$120.00, $80.00 purchase, $45.00, $30.00 rental
Looks at the lives of seven African - American characters. Reveals their stories through movement, monologues and song as their realities overlap and intertwine. Features dance sequences by three colorfully costumed women. Created and produced by choreographer and poet Mary Easter who is also in the dance sequences with her daughter.
Fine Arts; History - United States
Dist - IAFC

Some People Just Call it the Lake 15 MIN
16mm / U-matic / VHS
Color
Looks at the contrast in landscape surrounding Lake Mead and the Hoover Dam. Shows how wildlife, cacti and brilliant flowers thrive throughout the Lake Mead area. Highlights the Mojave desert and the tributaries of the Colorado River.
Geography - United States; Science - Natural
Dist - USNAC **Prod** - USNPS 1981

Some People Need Special Care 14 MIN
16mm
Color (A)
Emphasizes the assistance the handicapped need to do for them what they may not be able to do for themselves, especially in the area of oral health. Shows both daily personal care and periodic professional treatment occurring in a center for developmentally disabled children.
Education; Health and Safety
Dist - MTP **Prod** - AMDA

Some Personal Learnings about Interpersonal Relationships 33 MIN
U-matic / VHS / 16mm
Management Development Series
B&W (H C A S)
LC FIA68-2204
Dr Carl R Rogers, founder of client - centered therapy, discusses the 'MYSTERIOUS BUSINESS OF RELATING WITH OTHER HUMAN BEINGS.' He contrasts real communication with superficial and unmeaningful communication.
Guidance and Counseling; Psychology
Dist - UCEMC **Prod** - UCLA 1966

Some Points of View 10 MIN
U-matic / VHS
(PRO A)
$395, $100 Rental 5 days, $35 Review 3 days
Emphasizes the need for courtesy in telephone skills, and stresses key points with commentary from various individuals.
Business and Economics
Dist - ADVANM **Prod** - ADVANM

Some Principles of Non - Grading and Team Teaching 60 MIN
16mm
B&W (T)
Features Mrs Madeline Hunter, principal of the University Elementary School, responding to the questions and discussing the two most pervasive aspects of the laboratory schoolteam teaching and nongrading.
Education; Guidance and Counseling
Dist - UCLA **Prod** - UCLA 1965

Some Problems 15 MIN
16mm
PANCOM Beginning Total Communication Program for Hearing Parents of 'Series Level 2
Color (K)
LC 77-700504
Education; Guidance and Counseling; Psychology; Sociology
Dist - JOYCE **Prod** - CSDE 1977

Some Questions about Food Storage 17 MIN
16mm
Color
Shows the school lunch program managers and workers, the important 'DOS - AND - DON'TS' involved in efficient transportation, store - room layout and proper conditions for dry, cool and freezer types of storage.
Health and Safety; Social Science
Dist - NYSED **Prod** - NYSED

Some religious ideas and practices considered by a class of 11 - year - olds in the course of a project on the community 55 MIN
VHS
Color; PAL (I)
PdS35.00 purchase
Pictures children in the classroom grappling with ideas about death, sacrifice and symbolism, stimulated by visits to a church and a temple, and influenced by television. Concentrates on the final stages of a project based on work in the community.
Fine Arts; Religion and Philosophy; Social Science; Sociology
Dist - EMFVL

Some scars do not show 9 MIN
VHS / U-matic
Color (K P I)
$210.00, $260.00 purchase, $40.00 rental
Entertains with a Susan Linn puppetry program. Provides a setting where young children can talk about the problem of emotional abuse with responsible and informed adult supervision. Produced by the Family Information Services.
Guidance and Counseling; Sociology
Dist - NDIM

Some Secrets Should be Told 12 MIN
U-matic / VHS / 16mm
Color (P I)
LC 83-700221
Uses puppets to portray what child abuse is and distinguish it from normal love and affection. Shows the various people available to help children deal with the problem of child abuse and encourages children to express their feelings and concerns about the sexual abuse issue.
Sociology
Dist - CORF **Prod** - FAMINF

Some Small Part of each of Us 30 MIN
16mm
B&W
LC FIA65-1102
Presents a reading in observance of the first anniversary of the assassination of John F Kennedy. Includes photographs and speeches of the late President and excerpts from poems and essays written in tribute.
Biography; Civics and Political Systems; History - United States
Dist - NAAJS **Prod** - JTS 1965

Some Thoughts on Winter Flying 21 MIN
16mm
Color
LC 75-703732
Discusses the hazards and safety precautions associated with cold weather flying. Covers proper winter pre - flighting, air - frame icing, ELT operations, ski flying, survival gear, fueling and the whiteout condition.
Industrial and Technical Education
Dist - USNAC **Prod** - USFAA 1975

Some Unsolved Problems in Geometry 20 MIN
16mm
Color (C)
LC 72-710646
Presents several unsolved geometry problems and shows the solutions for some similar problems. Provides a brief history of the unsolved problems.
Mathematics
Dist - MLA **Prod** - MAA 1970

Somebody Cares 14 MIN
16mm
Color (A)
LC 79-700943
Tells how an unloved, unwanted young boy is sent to Yellowstone Boys Ranch in Montana, where he finds a home, a school and a sense of direction.
Psychology; Sociology
Dist - MARTC **Prod** - YBR 1979

Somebody else's place series
Adam Stanislawski and Rudy Esparza 30 MIN
Andy LaCasse and Emque Entienne 30 MIN
Ann Abraham and Hualalei Lee 30 MIN
Carlos Debalsa and Carlos Rodriquez 30 MIN
Denise Oki and Pamela Aragon 30 MIN
Emma Manzo and James Rizzi 30 MIN
Julie Arias and Gheeva Chung 30 MIN
Michele Delgado and Kate Wojciechowski 30 MIN
Tito Sanchez and Joe Solomon 30 MIN
Todd Jepson and Paul John Ironcloud 30 MIN
Dist - GPN

Somebody else's place series
Cindy Miles and Dana Sanchez Rios 30 MIN
Dist - GPN
SWCETV

Somebody Else's Place
Dai Nguyen and Adrian Etie 30 MIN
Dist - GPN

Somebody help me 25 MIN
U-matic / VHS / BETA
Color; NTSC; PAL; SECAM (H C G)
PdS83
Portrays a train accident and follows three individuals from an emergency medical team, a senior anesthetist, his junior colleague and a surgeon, as they deal with the problems created by seriously injured patients. Serves as a guide to medical students, nurses, ambulance personnel and advanced first aid trainees on the situations presented at the scene of a major disaster.
Health and Safety; Psychology
Dist - VIEWTH

Somebody Stole My Bike 20 MIN
U-matic / VHS / 16mm
Color (P I J)
LC 76-702169
Presents preventive measures and techniques for protection against bicycle thieves.
Guidance and Counseling; Social Science
Dist - AIMS **Prod** - DAVP 1972

Somebody to care - the hostess program at Self Memorial Hospital 8 MIN
VHS
Color (PRO C G)
$395.00 purchase _ #N930 - VI - 032
Reveals that hospitalization causes stress for both patients and their families and that caring can make a difference. Shows how hospital hosts help ease stress experienced by a patient by providing a personal, caring environment. Lists procedures for greeting a new patient in the hospital and outlines the main responsibilities of a host - helping patients with their meals, making sure they are comfortable in their room, assisting them with their personal needs, letting nurses and other hospital staff know the needs of their patients. Produced by Susan Ray and James G Butler, Self Memorial Hospital and Upper Savannah AHEC, Greenwood, South Carolina.
Health and Safety; Psychology; Social Science
Dist - HSCIC

Somebody Told Me 24 MIN
U-matic / VHS / 16mm
Color (A)
Presents a case history of the installation of a new computer system in an office, and tells what was done to allay the fears of the office staff over the change, and how care was taken to provide the most comfortable and least stressful environment for equipment and staff.
Business and Economics; Industrial and Technical Education; Mathematics; Psychology
Dist - IFB **Prod** - MILLBK

Someday 9 MIN
16mm
Color (K)
Presents four simple trip ideas. Depicts the supermarket, sailboat ride, zoo and a baseball game in an unusually imaginative way.
Physical Education and Recreation; Social Science
Dist - SF **Prod** - SF 1967

Someday 11 MIN
16mm
Color
Depicts a utopian ski experience in Aspen, in Vail and in the Canadian Rockies. Shows a helicopter depositing ski enthusiasts on high slopes.
Physical Education and Recreation
Dist - COLIM **Prod** - COLIM

Someday, I'll be an Elder 25 MIN
16mm / VHS
Color (J)
$425.00, $350.00 purchase, $48.00 rental
Examines a pilot substance abuse prevention program, 'Project Renewal.' Features Karuk tribal members as they conduct a three - week summer camp program which emphasizes the renewal of traditional ways and values. Narrated by Will Sampson.
Guidance and Counseling; Psychology; Social Science; Sociology
Dist - SHENFP **Prod** - SHENFP 1990

Someday I'll be Big 13 MIN
U-matic / VHS / 16mm
Growing Up with Sandy Offenheim Series
Color (K P)
LC 82-707059
Shows caterpillar eggs about to hatch, with one asking Who Am I? What Am I? Illustrates the two themes with song and dance and ends with new born caterpillars saying ' 'You'll see, someday I'll be big.'.
Education; Fine Arts; Psychology; Sociology
Dist - BCNFL **Prod** - PLAYTM 1982

Someone Cares 24 MIN
16mm
Good Time Growing Show Series; Show 1
Color (K P I)
Presents two stories designed to show that the Bible is God's word to his people. Tells of a boy who moves to the country from the city and is sad when his city friend breaks a promise to write. Relates what happens when he meets a Christian neighbor who explains that God never breaks his promise. Describes how a lion teaches a dragon that the Bible contains messages from God.
Religion and Philosophy
Dist - WHLION **Prod** - WHLION

Someone Else's Crisis 25 MIN
U-matic / VHS / 16mm
Color
LC 75-702663
Presents five vignettes representing situations a policeman might encounter such as a distressed child, a burglary, an armed robbery, a purse snatching and a rape. Shows the victims before and after their encounter with the police in order to train law enforcement officials to treat victims with empathy and sensitivity.
Civics and Political Systems; Psychology; Sociology
Dist - CORF **Prod** - MTROLA 1975

Someone has to make it Happen - a Conversation with C Jackson Grayson, Jr 22 MIN
16mm
Color
LC 76-703438
Presents C Jackson Grayson Jr, a director of the U S Price Commission. Discusses inflation and the role of the Federal government in a question and answer format with a group of housewives and professional women.
Business and Economics; Civics and Political Systems
Dist - USNAC **Prod** - USOPA 1972

Someone I Once Knew 30 MIN
16mm / U-matic / VHS
Color (H C A)
Looks at Alzheimer's Disease, a progressive mental deterioration which will affect one - sixth of the Americans who live to the age of 65. Offers case studies which reveal the painful changes that victims and their families endure.
Health and Safety
Dist - CORF **Prod** - METROM 1983

Someone is Dying, who Cares 30 MIN
U-matic / VHS
Color (PRO)
Studies the feelings and attitudes of health - care team members in their ineteration with a dying patient. Shows interviews with each member conducted by a social worker shortly after the death.
Health and Safety; Sociology
Dist - UARIZ **Prod** - UARIZ

Someone is watching - version A 25 MIN
VHS
Color (A)
$525.00 purchase
Introduces basic principles of correct business practices and outlines antitrust legislation, including the Sherman Act, Clayton Act, and the Federal Trade Commission Act. Discusses federal sentencing guidelines for white - collar crimes. Presents industry - specific dramatizations of business situations that must be handled correctly. This Version A is for manufacturing industries. Version B is available for service industries.
Business and Economics; Civics and Political Systems; Education
Dist - COMFLM **Prod** - COMFLM

Someone is watching - version B 28 MIN
VHS
Color (A)
$525.00 purchase
Introduces basic principles of correct business practices and outlines antitrust legislation, including the Sherman Act, Clayton Act, and the Federal Trade Commission Act. Discusses federal sentencing guidelines for white - collar crimes. Presents industry - specific dramatizations of business situations that must be handled correctly. This Version B is for service industries. Version A is available for manufacturing industries.
Business and Economics; Civics and Political Systems; Education
Dist - COMFLM **Prod** - COMFLM

Someone Like You 13 MIN
16mm
Color; B&W (H C A)
LC FIA66-622
Demonstrates the wide variety of administrative jobs in Girl Scouting, the many different kinds of people needed to fill them and the opportunities in this country and abroad. Shows scenes of Girl Scouting in action.
Guidance and Counseling; Physical Education and Recreation; Sociology
Dist - VISION **Prod** - GSUSA 1966

Someone New 4 MIN
16mm / U-matic / VHS
Wrong Way Kid Series
Color (J H)
LC 83-700945
Uses animation to present the story of a boy who feels that someone seems to be missing from his house. Shows how he finally realizes that the missing someone is his old self because he has grown and changed. Based on the book Someone New by Charlotte Zolotow.
Guidance and Counseling; Literature and Drama
Dist - CF **Prod** - BOSUST 1983

Someone special 15 MIN
VHS / 16mm / U-matic
Inside-out series
Color (I)
LC 73-702449
Introduces David who has a crush on his teacher, Miss Simpson, and dreams that she is in love with him. Depicts his hurt when he realizes that she doesn't place him above the others, but cares for all of her students equally. Explains that crushes are a normal part of growth and psychological development.
Guidance and Counseling; Sociology
Dist - AITECH

Someone Special 28 MIN
16mm
Color
LC 73-702203
Shows how a blind youth gains self - confidence and is aided in adjustment after spending his vacation at the Beacon Lodge Camp for the Blind.
Guidance and Counseling; Psychology
Dist - GE **Prod** - GE 1973

Someone to vote for 28 MIN
U-matic / VHS
Color (H C G)
$425.00, $395.00 purchase _ #V159; LC 90-705966
Examines voter dissatisfaction with the 1988 election campaigns. Reveals that 61 percent of people surveyed in an NBC - Wall Street Journal poll said they wished they had someone else to vote for.
Civics and Political Systems; History - United States
Dist - BARR **Prod** - KTEHTV 1988

Someone to watch over us 30 MIN
VHS
Metropolis series
Color; PAL (H C A)
PdS65 purchase
Traces the historical and technological evolution of the components of a modern city. Focuses on how modern cities protect their inhabitants. Part two of a six part series.
Geography - World; Sociology
Dist - BBCENE

Someone who Cares 11 MIN
16mm
Color
LC 74-706248
Depicts the rehabilitation of stroke victims.
Health and Safety; Psychology; Science - Natural
Dist - USNAC **Prod** - USSRS 1969

Someone who Cares 23 MIN
U-matic / VHS / 16mm
B&W (C A)
Depicts the role and influence of the mental hospital volunteer in the lives of hospitalized mental patients and the process of orienting and training volunteers.
Psychology; Sociology
Dist - IFB **Prod** - IFB 1955

Someone who cares 14 MIN
VHS
Color (G C PRO)
$145.00 purchase, $45.00 rental
Focuses on the needs of older adults who choose home care. Demonstrates assessment techniques and suggests possible solutions for unusual needs. Looks at the possible caregivers, from family members to professional agency staffers. Teaches family members about home care and home care agencies.
Health and Safety
Dist - TNF

Someone you know - acquaintance rape 30 MIN
U-matic / BETA / 16mm / VHS
Color (H C G)
$550.00, $330.00 purchase _ #KC - 4970M
Reveals that one in seven women will be raped during her lifetime, that over half of these victims of crime will be assaulted by someone they know. Explores what can be done to prevent the crime and aid the victims. Hosted by Collin Siedor. Produced by Dystar Television, Inc.
Education; Sociology
Dist - CORF

Someone You Know Drinks Too Much 29 MIN
VHS / U-matic
Here's to Your Health Series
Color
Discusses alcohol and alcoholism in America.
Health and Safety; Psychology; Sociology
Dist - PBS **Prod** - KERA

Someone's in the Kitchen with Jamie 25 MIN
16mm / U-matic / VHS
Color (J)
LC 81-700956
Tells the story of a young high school baseball star who saves his mother's teaching job by getting his teammates to enroll in her home economics class. Recounts the pressure which the coach applies to the young man because of his unmanly pursuits.
Guidance and Counseling; Home Economics; Sociology
Dist - LCOA **Prod** - LCOA 1981

Someplace You Don't Want to Go 22 MIN
VHS / 16mm
Color (J)
$360.00 purchase, $45.00 rental
Shows the stark reality of the effects of drug and alcohol abuse. Features Paul Ortega who narrates and sings.
Psychology; Social Science; Sociology
Dist - SHENFP **Prod** - SHENFP 1990

Something about Movies 25 MIN
16mm
Color (I J H)
Introduces the art of filmmaking.
Fine Arts
Dist - MOKIN **Prod** - MOKIN

Something about Photography 9 MIN
16mm / U-matic / VHS
Color
LC 76-703158
Shows the importance of the creative side of still photography. Records pointers and insights of Charles Eames on individual choices and opportunities that one has in the making of each photograph.
Fine Arts; Industrial and Technical Education
Dist - PFP **Prod** - EAMES 1976

Something about the Time - Myfanwy Spencer Pavelic 20 MIN
U-matic
Color (C)
$300.00 purchase, $35.00, $45.00 rental
Offers a personal, biographical presentation of the work of the Canadian artist Myfanwy Spencer Pavelic. Produced by Artemisia Productions.
Fine Arts
Dist - WMENIF

Something about the weather
VHS
Color (I J H)
$29.95 purchase _ #IV185
Describes three ways in which weather is being studied and shows how the Space Shuttle can be used to provide more information for weather researchers.
Science - Physical
Dist - INSTRU

Something about their listening 16 MIN
VHS
Color (A PRO IND)
$595.00 purchase, $160.00 rental
Covers the verbal and non - verbal aspects of good listening. Portrays bad listening behavior and shows how it can be corrected.
Business and Economics; English Language; Psychology; Social Science
Dist - VLEARN

Something about their Listening - a Guide to the Verbal and Nonverbal Components of Effective Listening 16 MIN
VHS / 16mm
Color (PRO)
$595.00 purchase each, $160.00 rental, $40.00 preview
Encourages better listening skills and shows how to apply them to solving problems, getting information and ideas, supervising, coaching, interviewing, and team - building.
Business and Economics; Education; Psychology
Dist - UTM **Prod** - UTM

Something besides rice 28 MIN
16mm
Color
Shows that images we may associate with the word "missionary" need to begin changing as the nature of Christian mission itself changes around the world. Explains that mission today is being transformed into a world - wide sharing of skills and witness by Christians of many lands. Features three missionaries of this new global village who tell their personal stories of new forms of mission in medicine, educa tion, evangelism and social action.
Religion and Philosophy; Sociology
Dist - ECUFLM **Prod** - UMCOM

something blue 6 MIN
16mm
Color (G)
$15.00 rental
Introduces a psychodrama of anticipation on a hot summer night.
Fine Arts
Dist - CANCIN **Prod** - ZIPPER 1974

Something Borrowed 20 MIN
16mm
B&W
LC 79-701295
Tells how a young woman must decide between maintaining her family ties by living near home, or following her husband to New York.
Fine Arts
Dist - USC **Prod** - USC 1979

Something Called Dignity 10 MIN
16mm
Color (A)
Features both blue and white collar union members who talk about union membership and why they organized.
Business and Economics; Sociology
Dist - AFLCIO **Prod** - IUD 1983

Something Concrete 26 MIN
U-matic / VHS / 16mm
Color (IND)
Illustrates concrete mix, the formwork and the delivery of the concrete after the formwork is ready. Animated sequences explain hydrostatic pressure. Safety precautions are given and both small and large projects are shown.
Health and Safety; Industrial and Technical Education; Psychology
Dist - IFB **Prod** - CSAO

Something Different 15 MIN
16mm
Color
LC 77-702145
Focuses on the new research approaches being used to find methods of ameliorating the effects of cerebral palsy.
Health and Safety
Dist - UCPA **Prod** - UCPA 1976

Something fishy 5 MIN
VHS
Seahouse series
Color (K P)
$29.95 purchase _ #RB8154
Studies fish and compares their anatomy to that of humans. Examines the differences and broad diversity among fish. Part of a series of ten parts on marine animals.
Science - Natural
Dist - REVID **Prod** - REVID 1990

Something for Everyone 28 MIN
U-matic / VHS / 16mm
Human Face of China Series
Color (H C A)
LC 79-701740
Explains that the basic unit of a Chinese People's Commune is the production team. Introduces the leader of one of these teams and illustrates the entire communal process.
Business and Economics; Civics and Political Systems; Geography - World; History - World; Social Science; Sociology
Dist - LCOA **Prod** - FLMAUS 1979

Something for Nothing 30 MIN
16mm / U-matic / VHS
Powerhouse Series
Color (I J)
Discusses decision - making through the story of a shifty film producer that could cost Powerhouse its city license.
Psychology
Dist - GA **Prod** - EFCVA 1982

Something Hidden 58 MIN
16mm
Color
_ #106C 0181 050N
Geography - World
Dist - CFLMDC **Prod** - NFBC 1981

Something in the Air 15 MIN
U-matic / VHS
Matter and Motion Series
Color (I)
Surveys the causes and the development of air pollution.
Science - Natural
Dist - AITECH **Prod** - WHROTV 1973

Something is missing 7 MIN
VHS
Children's encyclopedia of mathematics - meeting numbers series
Color (K P I)
$49.95 purchase _ #8345
Introduces the concepts of addition and subtraction. Part of a six - part series on numbers.
Mathematics
Dist - AIMS **Prod -** DAVFMS 1991

Something like a war 52 MIN
VHS
Color (G)
$90.00 rental, $295.00 purchase
Presents a chilling examination of India's family planning program from the point of view of the women who are its primary targets. Traces the history of the program and exposes the cynicism, corruption and brutality which characterizes its implementation. Women discuss their status, sexuality, fertility control and health. Establishes that, in the absence of development in areas such as education, healthcare, land reform and employment opportunities, population control is just an empty slogan.
Fine Arts; Geography - World; Sociology
Dist - WMEN **Prod -** DEEDH 1991

Something Magical 30 MIN
VHS
Color (G)
$59.95 purchase _ #SOMG - 000
Focuses on the relationship that developed between a class of typical elementary school kids and a school for children with cerebral palsy. Shows how this relationship was borne out of a skit which was insensitive to disabled persons.
Fine Arts; Health and Safety; Psychology; Sociology
Dist - PBS **Prod -** WHYY 1989

Something more for Christmas 18 MIN
16mm
Color
LC 79-701449
Tells the story of a Christmas tree. Shows the tree as it is grown on a farm by a young girl and follows it to the inner city, where it is bought and decorated by a group of children who want to surprise their mother.
Fine Arts; Social Science
Dist - SOP **Prod -** NCTA 1979

Something new out of Africa 30 MIN
VHS
Maryknoll video magazine presents series
Color (G)
$14.95 purchase
Presents the African - American Catholic's view of Christ and the Church as seen in worship styles and art showing African heritage.
History - United States; Religion and Philosophy
Dist - MARYFA

Something Nobody Else has - the Story of Turtle Trapping in Louisiana 29 MIN
U-matic / VHS
Color (J)
Examines the plight of alligator snapping turtles, trapped and made into soup.
Geography - United States; Science - Natural
Dist - BULFRG **Prod -** BULFRG

Something, Nothing, Feelings 10 MIN
U-matic
Readalong One Series
Color (K P)
Introduces reading and spelling for preschoolers and children in grades 1 to 3 with animation, puppets, humor and music. Comes with teacher's guide and kit.
Education; English Language; Literature and Drama
Dist - TVOTAR **Prod -** TVOTAR 1975

Something of the Danger that Exists 59 MIN
U-matic / VHS
Color
Discusses the pharmacological aspects of alcohol and other drugs. Defines alcoholism as a disease and answers questions.
Health and Safety; Psychology; Sociology
Dist - USNPS **Prod -** ICA

Something of Your Own 29 MIN
VHS / 16mm
Encounters Series
Color (I)
$200.00 purchase _ #269210
Presents a ten - part series on art. Introduces art concepts, encourages students to visually explore their world and the world of art, and demonstrates art techniques such as drawing, printmaking, photography, clay and wire sculpture, painting and fabric arts to motivate art expression. 'Something Of Your Own' encourages self - discovery as the first step in artistic expression.
Fine Arts; Psychology
Dist - ACCESS **Prod -** ACCESS 1988

Something Queer at the Library 10 MIN
16mm / U-matic / VHS
Contemporary Children's Literature Series
Color (K P I)
LC 79-700044
Tells about two children whose discovery of mutilated library books strangely links up with a dog show in which they have entered their dog. Based on the book Something Queer At The Library by Elizabeth Levy.
Literature and Drama
Dist - CF **Prod -** BOSUST 1978

Something Short of Paradise 91 MIN
16mm
Color
Describes the on - again, off - again relationship between a theater operator (David Steinberg) and a magazine reporter (Susan Sarandon).
Fine Arts
Dist - SWANK **Prod -** AIP

Something should be done about Grandma Ruthie 54 MIN
VHS
Color (G)
$195.00 purchase, $100.00 rental _ #CE - 122
Offers a moving and unsettling portrait of the family of filmmaker Cary Stauffacher as they struggle to deal with her 85 - year - old grandmother's deteriorating mental condition due to Azheimer's disease. Reveals that, although she is still physically healthy, Ruth Hammer can no longer be relied on to bathe and feed herself or even to remember where and with whom she is. Her children live out of town and a series of compassionate caregivers find themselves unable to deal with her growing disorientation. Yet Ruthie refuses to leave her long - time home and her family must confront the necessity of medicating her against her will and, eventually, of forcibly moving her into a long - term care facility.
Health and Safety
Dist - FANPRO

Something Special 28 MIN
VHS
Color (I)
$59.95 purchase _ #VC - - 806
Develops an awareness of the importance of the arts for a balanced education. Shows children in classes for visual arts, music, dance and theater, illustrating the value of art for children.
Fine Arts
Dist - CRYSP **Prod -** CRYSP

Something Special - a Navy Career 14 MIN
16mm
Color
LC 74-706581
Deals with careers in the U S Navy. Describes the opportunities in vocational and technical fields open only to high school graduates. Urges students to stay in school.
Civics and Political Systems; Guidance and Counseling; Psychology
Dist - USNAC **Prod -** USN 1970

Something special series
A Laughing matter 28 MIN
Dist - OMFLTD

Something to Build on 22 MIN
16mm
Color
LC 79-701057
Presents the plight of farmworkers who are strapped with low income and no available credit and are unable to obtain decent housing. Depicts various housing programs which Rural America, Inc, is sponsoring to try to ease their plight.
Agriculture; Sociology
Dist - VICTFL **Prod -** RURAM 1979

Something to Crow about 22 MIN
VHS
Color (I)
$59.95 purchase _ #VC - - 805
Follows the drawing process with elementary and middle school students to develop high standard skills. Shows art history in drawing and how students learn to develop critical analysis of their work.
Fine Arts
Dist - CRYSP **Prod -** CRYSP

Something to Die for 35 MIN
16mm
Color
Tells the story of two Chinese high school students, and their desperate search for truth. Through a newly converted Indian youth, they come to a personal knowledge of Jesus Christ.
Religion and Philosophy
Dist - GF **Prod -** YOUTH 1959

Something to do with Safety Reps 24 MIN
U-matic / VHS / 16mm
Color
Presents a fictionalized case study of two newly - trained safety representatives at a factory in England where the appointment of safety representatives is now mandatory. Compares the attitudes of the representatives toward their jobs.
Health and Safety
Dist - IFB **Prod -** MILLBK

Something to do with the Wall 88 MIN
16mm
Color (G)
Presents an independent production by Marilyn Levine and Ross McElwee. Offers a cinematic going - away party for the Iron Curtain by two filmmakers whose childhoods were colored by Cold War lore.
Civics and Political Systems; Geography - World; History - World
Dist - FIRS

Something to Hear 28 MIN
VHS / U-matic
Please Stand by - a History of Radio Series
(C A)
Fine Arts; History - United States; Psychology; Sociology
Dist - SCCON **Prod -** SCCON 1986

Something to Live for 49 MIN
16mm
Color (R)
Explores the experiences of a Chinese - American girl in Hong Kong where she meets a young refugee from mainland China who is devoted to Christianity.
Guidance and Counseling; Religion and Philosophy
Dist - GF **Prod -** GF

Something to Prove 60 MIN
VHS / U-matic
Color (G)
Presents highlight of the 1982 NBA playoffs between the Los Angeles Lakers and the Philadelphia 76ers featuring the outstanding play of greats Julius Dr J Erving, Kareem Abdul Jabbar and Magic Johnson.
Physical Education and Recreation
Dist - CTSC **Prod -** NBA 1986

Something to Work for 30 MIN
16mm / 8mm cartridge
Color (PRO) (FRENCH PORTUGUESE DANISH)
LC FIA66-624; fia66-624
Stresses the importance of setting high standards, communicating clearly and giving encouragement and support to subordinates.
Business and Economics; Foreign Language; Guidance and Counseling; Psychology; Sociology
Dist - RTBL **Prod -** RTBL 1966

Something to Work for 30 MIN
U-matic / VHS / 16mm
Color; B&W (PRO) (SWEDISH DUTCH FRENCH GERMAN NORWEGIAN JAPANESE SPANISH)
LC fia66-624; FIA66-624
Focuses on the problem of motivation from the management point of view. Reveals what happens when demands are high, when communication is open, and when people are given support and encouragement in reaching common goals.
Business and Economics; Foreign Language; Psychology
Dist - RTBL **Prod -** RTBL 1966

Something Ventured 30 MIN
16mm / U-matic / VHS
Powerhouse Series
Color (I J)
Describes how Bobby's impulsiveness gets him involved with jewel thieves.
Psychology
Dist - GA **Prod -** EFCVA 1982

Something Wicked this Way Comes 29 MIN
U-matic / VHS / 16mm
Film as Literature, Series; Series 5
Color (I J H)
Reveals that when a stranger known as Mr Dark brings his traveling carnival to a small town, the task of saving family and friends from its destructive clutches falls on the unlikely shoulders of the town librarian. Based on the novel SOMETHING WICKED THIS WAY COMES by Ray Bradbury.
Literature and Drama
Dist - CORF **Prod -** DISNEY 1983

Something wicked this way comes 94 MIN
VHS
Color; CC (I J H)
$21.95 purchase _ #078453
Portrays a mysterious stranger who promises everyone in a small town a better life - for a price. Adapts the story by Ray Bradbury.
Literature and Drama
Dist - KNOWUN

Something Wonderful is a Foot 25 MIN
U-matic
Not Another Science Show Series
Color (H C)
Examines the foot and how it has evolved in humans and investigates foot problems and their cause.
Physical Education and Recreation; Science; Science - Natural
Dist - TVOTAR **Prod** - TVOTAR 1986

Something Worthwhile 15 MIN
16mm
Color
LC 79-701490
Describes methods of burn prevention and emergency first aid for burns, and presents an example of a cooperative community event designed to call public attention to the importance of fire safety.
Health and Safety
Dist - MTP **Prod** - MLIC 1979

Something's Happening to Tom 15 MIN
16mm
Color (PRO)
LC 81-700491
Presents a case history of a depressive, including his symptoms, diagnosis, therapy and eventual recovery.
Psychology
Dist - MTP **Prod** - CIBA 1981

Something's Missing 8 MIN
16mm
Mathematics for Elementary School Students - Whole Numbers Series
Color (P)
LC 73-701839
Mathematics
Dist - DAVFMS **Prod** - DAVFMS 1974

The Sometime Samaritan 50 MIN
BETA / 16mm / VHS
Color
LC 77-702525
Features correspondent Michael Maclear investigating the fate of refugees who fled Vietnam to find a new life in Canada. Looks into Canada's erratic refugee policy.
Geography - World; History - World; Sociology
Dist - CTV **Prod** - CTV 1976

The Sometime Samaritan - Pt 1 25 MIN
16mm / VHS / BETA
Color
LC 77-702525
Features correspondent Michael Maclear investigating the fate of refugees who fled Vietnam to find a new life in Canada. Looks into Canada's erratic refugee policy.
History - World
Dist - CTV **Prod** - CTV 1976

The Sometime Samaritan - Pt 2 25 MIN
16mm / VHS / BETA
Color
LC 77-702525
Features correspondent Michael Maclear investigating the fate of refugees who fled Vietnam to find a new life in Canada. Looks into Canada's erratic refugee policy.
History - World
Dist - CTV **Prod** - CTV 1976

Sometimes a Great Notion
VHS / BETA
Color
Presents Ken Kesey's story about the life of a modern - day lumberjack's family in Oregon. Stars Henry Fonda, Paul Newman and Lee Remick.
Fine Arts; Literature and Drama
Dist - GA **Prod** - GA

Sometimes a Great Notion
VHS / U-matic
Contemporary Literature Series
Color (G C J)
$89 purchase _ #04119 - 85
Documents the lives of a modern - day lumberjack family in Oregon. Star Paul Newman, Henry Fonda, and Lee Remick. Based on the story by Ken Kesey.
Fine Arts; Literature and Drama
Dist - CHUMAN

Sometimes a Great Notion 113 MIN
16mm
Color
Focuses on an Oregon logging family. Stars Paul Newman and Henry Fonda.
Fine Arts
Dist - TWYMAN **Prod** - UPCI 1971

Sometimes I Look at My Life 79 MIN
U-matic / VHS / 16mm
Color (A)
Portrays the film and musical career of Harry Belafonte. Includes his friendship with Paul Robeson, plus scenes of Belafonte performing in Cuba. English language version.
Fine Arts
Dist - CNEMAG **Prod** - CUBAFI 1982

Sometimes I Wonder 30 MIN
U-matic / VHS / 16mm
Color (P I A)
Tells the story of two children faced with the birth of a new brother who run away from home to their grandmother's ranch. Features the birth of a new colt. Looks at life, death, love and family bonds.
Guidance and Counseling; Sociology
Dist - CORF **Prod** - MEDVEN

Sometimes I Wonder if It's Worth it 30 MIN
U-matic / VHS
Color (H A)
$180.00 purchase,$35.00 rental
Talks on the serious subject of suicide. Explains the emotional trauma involved and methods of dealing with the problems.
Guidance and Counseling; Health and Safety; Sociology
Dist - AITECH **Prod** - CCSW 1987

Sometimes I Wonder who I Am 5 MIN
16mm
B&W (H)
LC 76-700262
Tells about a young woman's struggle to decide whether she is a wife, a mother, a lover, or something else.
Guidance and Counseling; Psychology; Sociology
Dist - NEWDAY **Prod** - BRNDNL 1970

Sometimes it Works, Sometimes it Doesn't 63 MIN
Videoreel / VHS
Color (G)
Reveals a conversation between Merce Cunningham and John Cage discussing their work together in the theater and their concept of the relationship between movement and sound. Includes Cunningham's filmdance, Channels - Inserts.
Fine Arts
Dist - CUNDAN **Prod** - BELTV 1983

Sometimes It's OK to Tattle 12 MIN
U-matic / VHS / 16mm
Color (P I)
Employs puppets to emphasize the community resources available to assist children if they are victims of child abuse.
Sociology
Dist - CORF **Prod** - FAMINF

Sometimes It's Turkey, Sometimes It's Feathers 14 MIN
U-matic / VHS
Magic Pages Series
Color (P)
Literature and Drama
Dist - AITECH **Prod** - KLVXTV 1976

Sometimes Sad but Mostly Glad 10 MIN
U-matic / VHS
Book, Look and Listen Series
Color (K P)
Focuses on the ability to recognize feelings in others.
English Language; Literature and Drama
Dist - AITECH **Prod** - MDDE 1977

Sometimes the metro bus doesn't stop for me 28 MIN
VHS
Color (H C PRO G)
$250.00 purchase, $55.00 rental
Utilizes a variety of creative expressions, including painting, dance, songs, poetry and rap music, allowing the artists to dramatically voice their feelings and experiences as disabled persons. Explores issues such as relationships; love and marriage; integration; sexuality; discrimination; the need for independence and freedom of expression; and public perceptions of the disabled. Directed by Terry Amidei for Artists Unlimited.
Fine Arts; Health and Safety; Psychology; Sociology
Dist - CNEMAG

A Sometimes Vowel 15 MIN
Videoreel / VT2
Listen and Say Series
Color (P)
Develops auditory awareness and discrimination of vowel sounds. Introduces a few common vowel generalizations which are an aid in learning to read.
English Language
Dist - GPN **Prod** - MPATI

Somewhere Before 27 MIN
U-matic / VHS / 16mm
Insight Series
Color; B&W (H C A)
Tells the story of a young unmarried girl who is rushed to the hospital in labor and deserted by the father of her child. Explains how her despair slowly begins to kill her unborn child. Stars Cindy Williams, Ron Howard and Mariette Hartley.
Fine Arts
Dist - PAULST **Prod** - PAULST

Somewhere between Jalostotitlan and Encarnacion 6 MIN
16mm
B&W; Color (G)
$25.00 rental
Offers a handheld travelogue of North America, presented in unbroken 28 - second shots of filmmaker Philip Hoffman's spring - wind camera. Dramatizes Catholic life and death on North American streets, a horn band in Guadalajara and a Catholic procession in Toronto among other images.
Fine Arts; Geography - World; Religion and Philosophy
Dist - CANCIN

Somewhere to run 90 MIN
VHS
Color; PAL (J H)
PdS45 purchase
Presents first - hand interviews with runaways from the Central London Teenage Project, a safe house for young people. Includes 16 - year - old Debbie, a refugee from state 'care' and 14 - year - old Sarah, a middle - class refugee from an abusive father. Shows how by sleeping rough, begging, cheating and stealing, the two young women barely manage to survive. Examines what society has to offer to young people who lack the protection of a family. Contact distributor about availability outside the United Kingdom.
Sociology
Dist - ACADEM

The Sommerfeld Effect 32 MIN
U-matic / VHS
Nonlinear Vibrations Series
B&W
Mathematics
Dist - MIOT **Prod** - MIOT

Sommerfuglen Onsker Tillykke - Happy Birthday from a Butterfly 29 MIN
16mm
Color (DANISH)
A Danish language film. Presents a fairy tale of a child's birthday.
Foreign Language
Dist - STATNS **Prod** - STATNS 1968

Somos plus - We are more 15 MIN
VHS
Color (G)
$130.00 purchase, $40.00 rental
Documents a march by women in Santiago, Chile in demand of democracy and peace. Records their peaceful demonstration which is intercepted and then attacked by the police. Produced by Antu Productions.
Civics and Political Systems; Fine Arts; Social Science
Dist - FIRS

Son of 15 MIN
Videoreel / VT2
Umbrella Series
Color
Fine Arts
Dist - PBS **Prod** - KETCTV

Son of Dinosaurs 60 MIN
VHS
Color; Stereo (K)
$14.98 purchase _ #TT8103
Tells the story of two dinosaur hunters who discover a dinosaur egg containing a live embryo.
History - World; Science - Natural
Dist - TWINTO **Prod** - TWINTO 1990

Son of football follies
VHS
NFL series
Color (G)
$19.95 purchase _ #NFL0045V
Presents a collection of humorous 'bloopers' from the National Football League. Produced by NFL Films.
Literature and Drama; Physical Education and Recreation
Dist - CAMV

The Son of God crucified - Volume 13 30 MIN
VHS
Jesus of Nazareth series
Color (I J H C G A R)
$29.95 purchase, $10.00 rental _ #35 - 8326 - 1502
Presents excerpts from the Franco Zeffirelli film on the life and ministry of Jesus. Surveys the events leading up to and including Jesus' crucifixion and burial.
Literature and Drama; Religion and Philosophy
Dist - APH **Prod** - BOSCO

Son of God - Son of Mary 60 MIN
VHS
Who is Jesus series
Color (R G)
$49.95 purchase _ #WJES7
Examines the mysteries and passion of the God - Man, Jesus, according to the teachings of the Roman Catholic Church. Features Donald Goergen, OP, as instructor. Part seven of an eight - part series on the life and death and resurrection of Jesus.
Religion and Philosophy
Dist - CTNA **Prod** - CTNA

Son of Lono 11 MIN
16mm
Color (J H C)
Portrays the adventures of Captain Cook's cabin boy in 1779 Hawaii.
Geography - United States; History - United States
Dist - CINEPC **Prod** - CINEPC

The Son of Monte Cristo 102 MIN
16mm
B&W
Stars Louis Hayward as the son of the Count of Monte Cristo, foiling a scheme to take over the duchy of Lichtenberg.
Fine Arts
Dist - KITPAR **Prod** - UAA 1940

Son of Oil 15 MIN
U-matic / VHS
Color
Presents a political conversation where one thing leads to another.
Fine Arts
Dist - KITCHN **Prod** - KITCHN

Son of Paleface 95 MIN
U-matic / VHS / 16mm
Color
A sequel to the Bob Hope - Jane Russell 'PALEFACE' that satirizes the movie Western.
Fine Arts
Dist - FI **Prod** - PAR 1952

Son of the Ocean 28 MIN
U-matic / VHS / 16mm
Human Face of China Series
Color (H C A)
LC 79-701739
Follows a riverboat journey on the Yangtze River. Shows some of China's most beautiful, fertile and underdeveloped regions as well as some of its poorest and most populous regions.
Geography - World; History - World; Social Science; Sociology
Dist - LCOA **Prod** - FLMAUS 1979

Son of the Sheik 62 MIN
BETA
B&W
Stars Rudolph Valentino as Ahmed, a desert sheik who wants to seek revenge after a dancing girl betrays him. Tells how he learns of her innocence and goes after the band of desert renegades who exploited her.
Fine Arts
Dist - RMIBHF **Prod** - UNKNWN 1926

Son of the Sheik 72 MIN
16mm
B&W
Presents a Rudolph Valentino romance, where he plays a dual role of father and son.
Fine Arts
Dist - KITPAR **Prod** - UAA 1926

Son of the Sheik 27 MIN
16mm
History of the Motion Picture Series
B&W
Presents the 1926 production of 'SON OF THE SHEIK,' a typical adventure of the golden age of movies. Stars Rudolph Valentino.
Fine Arts
Dist - KILLIS **Prod** - SF 1960

The Son of the Sheik 68 MIN
16mm
B&W
Tells the story of Ahmed, a desert sheik who believes himself betrayed by a dancing girl, whereupon he abducts her and exacts his own form of revenge. Stars Rudolph Valentino and Vilma Banky. Directed by George Fitzmaurice.
Fine Arts
Dist - KILLIS **Prod** - UNKNWN 1926

Son Pantalon 10 MIN
U-matic / VHS
Salut - French Language Lessons Series
Color
Focuses on clothing and possessive adjectives.
Foreign Language
Dist - BCNFL **Prod** - BCNFL 1984

Son riders 60 MIN
VHS
Color (J H C G A R)
$19.99 purchase, $10.00 rental _ #35 - 83605 - 533
Profiles several of the world's top surfers. Includes extensive footage of surfing action.
Physical Education and Recreation; Religion and Philosophy
Dist - APH **Prod** - WORD

Son Seals - 2 - 17 - 82 4 MIN
16mm
B&W (G)
$8.00 purchase
Features bluesman Son Seals in concert.
Fine Arts
Dist - CANCIN **Prod** - STREEM 1982

Son Suyas, Cuidelas Y Protejalas 16 MIN
U-matic / VHS / 16mm
Color (A C) (SPANISH)
Examines protective devices for punch and power presses. Highlights the fixed barrier guard. Emphasizes foot treadle guards, die area lighting and control panel positioning. Stresses the importance of safety precautions.
Health and Safety
Dist - IFB **Prod** - IAPA

The Son Worshipers 30 MIN
16mm
Color
Portrays the new American phenomenon of kids 'Turned On' for Jesus.
Guidance and Counseling; Religion and Philosophy; Sociology
Dist - GF **Prod** - GF 1972

Sonata for Pen, Brush and Ruler 11 MIN
16mm
Color
Expresses the use of color and image and the geometric - visceral patterns of the traditional direct - drawn film.
Fine Arts
Dist - FMCOOP **Prod** - SPINLB 1968

Sonata in A Flat, Opus 110 59 MIN
U-matic
Beethoven - the Last Sonatas Series
Color
Fine Arts
Dist - PBS **Prod** - KQEDTV

Sonata in C Minor, Opus 111 59 MIN
U-matic
Beethoven - the Last Sonatas Series
Color
Fine Arts
Dist - PBS **Prod** - KQEDTV

Sonata in E Flat, Opus 109 58 MIN
U-matic
Beethoven - the Last Sonatas Series
Color
Fine Arts
Dist - PBS **Prod** - KQEDTV

Sonatina and fugue 23 MIN
16mm
B&W (G)
$45.00 rental
Combines images of city and landscape with a piano sonatina by Busoni and figures by JS Bach.
Fine Arts
Dist - CANCIN **Prod** - BURCKR 1980

Sonauto 9 MIN
16mm
Color
LC 77-700313
Presents an experimental film without narration in which highway lines and roadside curbs move in time to original music. Includes captions.
Fine Arts
Dist - CANFDC **Prod** - CANFDC 1976

Song 28
16mm
Color (G)
$132.00 purchase
Presents a film by Stan Brakhage. Offers scenes as texture.
Fine Arts
Dist - CANCIN **Prod** - BRAKS 1966

Song 28 and Song 29 8 MIN
16mm
Color (G)
$12.00 rental
Presents two films by Stan Brakhage. Offers scenes as texture in Song 28. Portrays the artist's mother in Song 29.
Fine Arts
Dist - CANCIN **Prod** - BRAKS

Song 29
16mm
Color (G)
$121.00 purchase
Presents a film by Stan Brakhage. Portrays the artist's mother.
Fine Arts
Dist - CANCIN **Prod** - BRAKS 1986

Song Accompaniment - Pt 1 29 MIN
Videoreel / VT2
Playing the Guitar II Series
Color
Fine Arts
Dist - PBS **Prod** - KCET

Song Accompaniment - Pt 2 29 MIN
Videoreel / VT2
Playing the Guitar II Series
Color
Fine Arts
Dist - PBS **Prod** - KCET

Song and Dance Man
VHS / 35mm strip
Caldecotts on Filmstrip Series
Color (K)
$35.00 purchase
Presents a children's story. Part of the Caldecott Series.
English Language; Literature and Drama
Dist - PELLER

Song at Twilight - an Essay on Aging 59 MIN
VHS / 16mm
Color (G)
$70.00 rental _ #DOCS - 110
Explores the social, political, physical and economic problems of aging in our society. Includes interviews.
Sociology
Dist - PBS **Prod** - KOCETV

Song Dog
16mm
Color
Documents the life cycle of the coyote in Yellowstone National Park. Features a coyote pack in an environment where large mammals are abundant and human influence is minimal.
Science - Natural
Dist - TRAILF **Prod** - TRAILF

A Song for Dead Warriors 25 MIN
16mm
Color
Deals with the people and events surrounding the occupation of Wounded Knee by members of the American Indian Movement in 1973.
History - United States; Social Science
Dist - NEWTIM **Prod** - NEWTIM

A Song for grandmother 30 MIN
VHS
Color (J H C G A R)
$49.95 purchase, $10.00 rental _ #35 - 892 - 2504
Documents the fact that more than three million senior citizens live often lonely lives in nursing homes. Tells how two characters, Katherine and Grace, minister to the needs of senior citizens. Encourages others to do likewise.
Health and Safety; Religion and Philosophy; Sociology
Dist - APH

Song for My Sister 45 MIN
16mm
B&W
Features the realistic portrayal of a teenager and her brother in their wanderings through New York City.
Fine Arts; Sociology
Dist - NYU **Prod** - NYU

A Song for Prince Charlie 18 MIN
16mm
Color (I J H)
Presents the story of the Stuart Rising in 1745 in Scotland. Documents the Scot's traditional use of song for expression of their national sentiments and to present stories.
History - World
Dist - SF **Prod** - SF 1973

Song for Tibet 57 MIN
VHS / BETA
Color; PAL (G)
PdS25 purchase
Features a moving and personal account of two young Tibetans in exile in Canada. Highlights the issues of displacement and cultural preservation.
Fine Arts; Religion and Philosophy
Dist - MERIDT

The Song is Love 54 MIN
16mm
Color
LC 74-702867
Various scenes picture Peter Yarrow, Paul Stookey and Mary Travers as individual people and also show how they relate to the singing group of Peter, Paul and Mary.
Fine Arts
Dist - MILPRO **Prod** - MILPRO 1970

A Song of Beauty 12 MIN
U-matic / VHS / 16mm
Bloomin' Human Series
Color (P I)
LC 76-700424
Takes the viewer on a voyage with a group of elementary school students as they encounter beauty in nature, in each other and finally in themselves.
Guidance and Counseling
Dist - MEDIAG **Prod** - PAULST 1975

Song of Bernadette 156 MIN
VHS
B&W (G)
$24.95 purchase _ #P68
Tells the true story of the appearance and miracle of Our Lady of Lourdes witnessed by a 19th century peasant girl, who claimed to speak to the Virgin Mary near her village in France. Stars Jennifer Jones.
History - World; Religion and Philosophy; Sociology
Dist - HP

A Song of Ceylon 51 MIN
16mm
Color (G)
$125.00 rental
Studies colonialism, gender and the body. Uses the metaphor of a ritual exorcism of a woman possessed by demons to pose the body as if it were a puppet, colonized, forced to speak for itself.
Civics and Political Systems; Fine Arts; History - World; Sociology
Dist - WMEN **Prod** - LAJAY 1985

Song of Ceylon 40 MIN
16mm / U-matic / VHS
B&W (J A)
Contrasts the traditional culture and primitive economy of the people in Ceylon with the influence of modern commerce.
Geography - World; Sociology
Dist - MGHT **Prod** - GRIERS 1934

Song of Ireland 55 MIN
VHS
Traveloguer series
Color (G H)
$24.95 purchase _ #TC17
Travels to Ireland, showing maps, geography, museums, sports, landmarks, historical figures, cuisine, etc. Comes with reference booklet.
Geography - World
Dist - SVIP

The Song of Ireland 60 MIN
VHS
Color (G)
$29.95 purchase _ #QU019
Presents a video vacation combining history, geography, scenery and people.
Geography - World
Dist - SIV

Song of Light 45 MIN
16mm
Color
Gives hope of recovery to crippled children by showing the actual life of the workers and children at the Fukushima Crippled Children's Home in Japan. Depicts the necessary education that is needed while children are being rehabilitated.
Guidance and Counseling; Health and Safety; Sociology
Dist - ISWELC **Prod** - ISWELC

Song of Senegal 27 MIN
16mm
Color (FRENCH)
LC 80-701454
Offers an overall view of the country of Senegal.
Foreign Language; Geography - World
Dist - MCDO **Prod** - MCDO 1980

The Song of Songs 10 MIN
16mm
Color
LC 75-700160
Uses the poetry from the Old Testament book Song of Solomon as dialog for a contemporary dramatic presentation.
Literature and Drama
Dist - MARTC **Prod** - MARTC 1974

Song of survival 60 MIN
VHS
Color (G)
$59.95 purchase _ #S01506
Portrays the Dutch, British and Australian women held in a Japanese prison camp during World War II. Reveals that the women formed a choir to sustain their spirits.
Fine Arts; History - World
Dist - UILL

Song of the ages series

Bonsai	5 MIN
By the wayside	5 MIN
Dead end	5 MIN
The Escape	5 MIN
The Find	5 MIN
His Dwelling Place	5 MIN
Hope	5 MIN
I was once a little boy	5 MIN
The Lord is My Shepherd	5 MIN
Many Men Say	5 MIN
The Mask	5 MIN
Night Flight	5 MIN
Point of view	5 MIN
The Soldier	5 MIN
The Solitary Man	5 MIN
With the Dawn	5 MIN
Wonder	5 MIN

Dist - FAMLYT

Song of the birds - a biography of Pablo Casals 66 MIN
VHS
Color (G)
$24.95 purchase_#1342
Tells the life story of cellist Pablo Casals. Utilizes archival film and recordings, including recently discovered videos of the Puerto Rican Casals Festival that were filmed between 1959 and 1971.
Biography; Fine Arts
Dist - KULTUR

Song of the Canary 30 MIN
16mm
Color (A)
Reports effects of the pesticide DBCP on workers at the Occidental Chemical plant. Raises many questions regarding responsibility for protection of workers and consumers against dangerous chemicals.
Health and Safety; Sociology
Dist - AFLCIO **Prod** - AFLCIO 1978

Song of the Canary - Pt 1 29 MIN
16mm
Color (H C A)
LC 79-701016
Documents the health hazards to workers in the cotton textile industry and in the petrochemical industries. Deals with specific hazards and medical diagnoses.
Health and Safety
Dist - NEWDAY **Prod** - MANTEC 1979

Song of the Canary - Pt 2 29 MIN
16mm
Color (H C A)
LC 79-701016
Documents the health hazards to workers in the cotton textile industry and in the petrochemical industries. Deals with specific hazards and medical diagnoses.
Health and Safety
Dist - NEWDAY **Prod** - MANTEC 1979

The Song of the Earth - Jean Lurcat 17 MIN
16mm
Color (C)
LC FIA67-1142
Describes the last tapestry made by the French artist Jean Lurcat, pointing out the themes of man's precarious mastery over nature and the opposition of evil and good. Pictures the artist at work and shows various aspects of his daily life.
Fine Arts
Dist - RADIM **Prod** - MRCNTN 1967

Song of the exile 100 MIN
35mm / 16mm / VHS
Color (G) (CHINESE (ENGLISH SUBTITLES))
Portrays a mother - daughter relationship in Hong Kong. Follows Hueyin Cheung from London to Hong Kong for her sister's wedding, where she finds herself immediately at odds with her sister and her imperious mother. After the wedding, Hueyin reluctantly accompanies her mother to Japan to visit their long - estranged family. With English subtitles. Directed by Ann Hui.
Fine Arts; Geography - World; Sociology
Dist - KINOIC
CHTSUI

Song of the godbody 11 MIN
16mm
Color (A)
$25.00 rental
Films closeups of the body of filmmaker James Broughton in celebration of male sexual ecstasy. Made with filmmaker Joel Singer.
Fine Arts
Dist - CANCIN

The Song of the Lark 30 MIN
16mm
Eternal Light Series
B&W (H C A)
LC 76-700965
Dramatizes the life of the first Baron Edmond de Rothschild, who contributed to the development of a viable economy in Palestine. (Kinescope).
Business and Economics; Religion and Philosophy
Dist - NAAJS **Prod** - JTS 1967

Song of the North
U-matic / VHS
Color
Focuses on Alaska as spring, summer and fall run together in a single three - month season. Shows some of the wildlife that thrive in that environment.
Geography - United States; Science - Natural
Dist - NWLDPR **Prod** - NWLDPR

Song of the Paddle 41 MIN
16mm
Color (J)
LC 79-700604
Follows a family canoeing across the waterways of Canada.
Geography - World; Physical Education and Recreation
Dist - NFBC **Prod** - NFBC 1979

Song of the Plains - the Story of Mari Sandoz 60 MIN
VHS / U-matic
(G)
Features film clips of Nebraska author Mari Sandoz discussing her writing style and technique. Uses interviews with her family, friends and colleagues. Nebraskans Dick Cavett and Dorothy McGuire interview, narrate and read from Sandoz's work.
Literature and Drama
Dist - GPN **Prod** - NETV

Song of the Punjab 19 MIN
16mm
B&W (I)
Presents the story of a Punjabi soldier returning home, getting married and then leaving home to rejoin his regiment. Features folk songs to tell the story, as sung on various occasions.
Fine Arts
Dist - NEDINF **Prod** - INDIA

Song of the Sandy Mooring 24 MIN
16mm
Color
LC 72-714164
Presents nature scenes and encourages visits to national parks.
Geography - United States
Dist - USNAC **Prod** - USNPS 1971

Song of the Snows 12 MIN
16mm
Color (I)
Shows pictures of the Himalayas, which span the entire northern frontiers of India for 1600 miles. Portrays the majestic heights of the Himalayan peaks and depicts how snow is transformed into glaciers, which give birth to such rivers as the Ganga, Yamuna, Brahmaputra and Kosi, the arteries which sustain life in the Indian plains.
Geography - World
Dist - NEDINF **Prod** - INDIA

Song of the spear 57 MIN
16mm
Color (G)
LC 90-708978
Examines the role of culture in the struggle for national liberation in South Africa. Presents performances of the Amandla Cultural Ensemble while touring in the United Kingdom.
Geography - World; History - World; Sociology
Dist - IDAF **Prod** - IDAFSA 1986
CNEMAG

Song of the Wolves - a Profile of Wildlife Sculpture 45 MIN
16mm
Color (A)
LC 82-700159
Shows wildlife artist Wally Shoop as he creates two life - sized bronze sculptures of wolves. Describes the lost wax casting process and the artist's efforts to educate the general public concerning the plight of wild animals.
Fine Arts
Dist - BORMAS **Prod** - BORMAS 1982

Song of youth 170 MIN
VHS
Color (G) (CHINESE)
$45.00 purchase _ #1019C
Presents a film from the People's Republic of China.
Geography - World; Literature and Drama
Dist - CHTSUI

Song Recital 29 MIN
Videoreel / VT2
Playing the Guitar II Series
Color
Fine Arts
Dist - PBS **Prod** - KCET

The Song Remains the same 136 MIN
16mm
Color
Depicts the 1973 Madison Square Garden appearance by the rock group Led Zeppelin.
Fine Arts
Dist - SWANK **Prod** - WB

Song Sampler - Review 15 MIN
U-matic / VHS
Song Sampler Series
Color (P)
LC 81-707070
Reviews the songs presented in the Song Sampler Series.
Fine Arts
Dist - GPN **Prod** - JCITV 1981

Song sampler series

American Indian music - Pt 1	15 MIN
American Indian music - Pt 2	15 MIN
Animal songs, Pt 1	15 MIN
Animal songs, Pt 2	15 MIN
Ballads - Pt 1	15 MIN
Ballads - Pt 2	15 MIN
Cowboy Music, Pt 1	15 MIN
Cowboy Music, Pt 2	15 MIN
Dialog songs - Pt 1	15 MIN
Dialog songs - Pt 2	15 MIN
Favorite folk songs - Pt 1	15 MIN
Favorite folk songs - Pt 2	15 MIN
February songs - Pt 2	15 MIN
February Songs, Pt 1	15 MIN
Fun and nonsense, Pt 1	15 MIN
Fun and nonsense, Pt 2	15 MIN
Game Songs, Pt 1	15 MIN
Game Songs, Pt 2	15 MIN
Holiday Music, Pt 1	15 MIN
Holiday Music, Pt 2	15 MIN
More about Rhythm, Pt 1	15 MIN
More about Rhythm, Pt 2	15 MIN
Mountain Songs, Pt 1	15 MIN
Mountain Songs, Pt 2	15 MIN
Railroad songs - Pt 1	15 MIN
Railroad songs - Pt 2	15 MIN
Rhythms - Pt 1	15 MIN
Rhythms - Pt 2	15 MIN
Rounds - Pt 1	15 MIN
Rounds - Pt 2	15 MIN
Sing Along	15 MIN
Solo - Chorus Songs - Pt 1	15 MIN
Solo - Chorus Songs - Pt 2	15 MIN
Song Sampler - Review	15 MIN
Spirituals - Pt 1	15 MIN
Spirituals - Pt 2	15 MIN

Dist - GPN

Song Writer Series

Making a Melody	29 MIN
Making Arrangements	29 MIN
Post - Natal Care of a Song	29 MIN
Songs from the Soul - the Negro Spiritual	29 MIN
That Good Old Harmony	29 MIN
Words and Music	29 MIN

Dist - UMITV

Songbird story 13 MIN
VHS
Color (K P I J)
$195.00 purchase, $25.00 rental
Presents a dream of two young children who fly along with migratory songbirds on one of their migration paths to the tropical rainforest. Answers questions about development which is threatening the songbirds' nesting habitats. Without the tropical rainforests, these birds have no place to survive through winter. Produced by Laura Heller - Frameline Productions.
Fine Arts; Science - Natural; Sociology
Dist - BULFRG

Songbirds 13 MIN
16mm / U-matic / VHS
Elementary Natural Science Series
Color (P I J)
$325, $235 purchase _ #73076
Discusses the characteristics that distinguish one songbird from another.
Science - Natural
Dist - CORF

The Songbook 30 MIN
U-matic / VHS
Franco File Series
Color (I)
Dramatizes contemporary Franco - American life in New England. Focuses on prejudice.
Sociology
Dist - GPN **Prod** - WENHTV

Songololo - voices of change 54 MIN
VHS / 16mm
Color & B&W (G)
$850.00, $350.00 purchase, $100.00 rental
Celebrates the culture of black resistance in South Africa with a focus on the lives, philosophies and performances of poet - musican - activist Mzwakhe Mbuli and feminst - writer - storyteller Gcina Mhlophe. Includes examples of hostel dancing, church reunion singing, township jazz and freedom songs. Produced by Marianne Kaplan and Cari Green.
Civics and Political Systems; Fine Arts; Geography - World; Literature and Drama; Sociology
Dist - CNEMAG

Songs 30 MIN
U-matic
Today's Special Series
Color (K P)
Develops language arts skills in children. Programs are thematically designed around subjects of interest to youngsters. Action takes place in a department store where people, mannequins, puppets, comic characters and special guests present a light hearted approach to language arts.
Fine Arts; Literature and Drama; Psychology
Dist - TVOTAR **Prod** - TVOTAR 1985

Songs 16 - 22 49 MIN
16mm
Color (G)
$886.00 purchase, $66.00 rental
Prsents Song 16 - a flowering of sex as in the mind's eye, a joy; Songs 17 and 18 - the movie house cathedral and a singular room; Songs 19 and 20 - women dancing and a light; Songs 21 and 22 - two views of closed - eye vision.
Fine Arts
Dist - CANCIN **Prod** - BRAKS 1984

Songs 24, 25, and 26 15 MIN
16mm
Color (G)
$437.00 purchase, $29.00 rental
Presents a naked boy with recorder and a view from the dump, as well a the emotional properties of talk.
Fine Arts
Dist - CANCIN **Prod** - BRAKS

Songs and Stories of Labor 35 MIN
16mm
Color (A)
Presents portions of U.S. labor history in folk songs, narration and flash - back pictures.
Business and Economics; Sociology
Dist - AFLCIO **Prod** - RLEC 1969

Songs and Symphony 29 MIN
U-matic
Music Shop Series
Color
Demonstrates the interesting differences between composing songs and symphonies.
Fine Arts
Dist - UMITV **Prod** - UMITV 1974

Songs and Tales of Yesteryear 25 MIN
16mm
Color
LC 76-701056
Presents old songs and stories, sung and told by the early Canadian prairie pioneers.
Fine Arts
Dist - FIARTS **Prod** - FIARTS 1974

Songs 8 - 14 30 MIN
16mm
Color (G)
$753.00 purchase, $56.00 rental
Enlarges the 8mm Songs 1 - 14 series into 16mm films to save them from extinction. Includes sea creatures; wedding source and substance; sitting around; fires, windows, an insect, a lyre of rain scratches; verticals and shadows caught in glass traps; a travel song of scenes and horizontals; molds, paints and crystals.
Fine Arts
Dist - CANCIN **Prod** - BRAKS 1966

Songs for a Garden 14 MIN
VHS / U-matic
Strawberry Square Series
Color (P)
Fine Arts
Dist - AITECH **Prod** - NEITV 1982

Songs for a Shabbat 26 MIN
VHS
Color (G)
$25.00 purchase
Features Rabbi Haim Louk and his cantors singing the hazanut in the Buffault Synagogue in Paris. Explains that when the Jews left Morrocco they took with them their religious singing, the hazanut, which are living memories of the community and mark every moment of Jewish life, particularly the time of Shabbat. These love songs, rendered in the modes of Andalusian noubas, free the soul from its terrestrial bindings, carrying it in a mystical ascension to its heavenly home. Produced by Izza Genini. French, Arabic and Hebrew with English subtitles.
Fine Arts; Religion and Philosophy
Dist - NCJEWF

Songs for swinging larvae 6 MIN
16mm
Color (G)
$10.00 rental
Tells the story of a child's perverse fantasy about escaping from his motherwhich becomes reality and a nightmare. Features music by the band Renaldo and the Loaft.
Fine Arts
Dist - CANCIN

Songs for us series

Appreciating differences	10 MIN
Making friends	8 MIN
Sharing and cooperation	8 MIN

Dist - CORF

Songs from the Soul - the Negro Spiritual 29 MIN
U-matic
Song Writer Series
Color
Presents a recital of Negro spirituals conducted by Dr Eva Jessye and sung by a small choir of university students.
Fine Arts
Dist - UMITV **Prod** - UMITV 1977

Songs in Minto Life 29 MIN
VHS / U-matic
Color (G)
Features the first documentary of traditional Athabaskan music of Interior Alaska. Music here is not entertainment. Each song contributes to the survival of the community. A song is made by one person but it cannot be sung without community approval. Shows this program produced and directed entirely by rural Alaskans in cooperation with Minto elders. Every effort for accuracy has been made. The Tanana Athabaskan language spoken in Minto is only now being written down. In this program you will see some words spelled for the first time.
Social Science; Sociology
Dist - NAMPBC **Prod** - NAMPBC 1986

Songs of Bengal 11 MIN
16mm
B&W (I)
Captures the rhythm and pulse of life in a riverside village of Bengal, where songs form part of everyday life. Introduces the fisherman's song and the 'BAUL'S' song, along with the shepherd's flute music.
Fine Arts
Dist - NEDINF **Prod** - INDIA

Songs of Childhood 30 MIN
VHS / 16mm
Music Stories Series
Color (P)
$39.95 purchase _ #CL6903
Presents children's songs.
Fine Arts; Literature and Drama
Dist - EDUCRT

The Songs of Christmas 49 MIN
VHS
Color (I J H C G A R)
$24.95 purchase, $10.00 rental _ #35 - 87147 - 460
Presents the stories behind many of the most popular Christmas carols. Alternates views of a children's choir and scenes set in the time of the carols' writing.
Literature and Drama; Religion and Philosophy
Dist - APH **Prod** - FRACOC

Songs of Christmas and Hanukkah I 14 MIN
U-matic / VHS
Music and Me Series
Color (P I)
Presents some Christmas and Hanukkah songs.
Fine Arts; Social Science
Dist - AITECH **Prod** - WDCNTV 1979

Songs of Christmas and Hanukkah II 15 MIN
VHS / U-matic
Music and Me Series
Color (P I)
Presents some Christmas and Hanukkah songs.
Fine Arts; Social Science
Dist - AITECH **Prod** - WDCNTV 1979

Songs of Halloween 15 MIN
U-matic / VHS
Music and Me Series
Color (P I)
Presents some Halloween songs.
Fine Arts; Social Science
Dist - AITECH **Prod** - WDCNTV 1979

Songs of Maharashtra - Pt 1 9 MIN
16mm
B&W (H C A)
Compiles the folk songs of Maharashtra, the occasions at which they are sung and their significance in the social life of the people.
Fine Arts
Dist - NEDINF **Prod** - INDIA

Songs of Maharashtra - Pt 2 13 MIN
16mm
B&W (H C A)
Compiles the folk songs of Maharashtra, the occasions at which they are sung and their significance in the social life of the people.
Fine Arts
Dist - NEDINF **Prod** - INDIA

Songs of my hunter heart - Laguna songs and poems 34 MIN
U-matic / VHS
Words and place series
Color
Continues the oral tradition of the Laguna pueblo life by incorporating contemporary themes into work which retains Pueblo reverence for the spoken word.
Literature and Drama; Social Science
Dist - NORROS **Prod** - NORROS

Songs of Sappho 25 MIN
VHS
Color (G) (GREEK (ENGLISH SUBTITLES))
$99.95 _ #V72052
Presents five ancient Greek poems in a performance combining words, music and dance to express the pain of love and the sadness of loss. Recreates the style of performance used in ancient Greece.
History - World; Literature and Drama
Dist - NORTNJ

Songs of Thanksgiving 15 MIN
U-matic / VHS
Music and Me Series
Color (P I)
Presents some Thanksgiving songs.
Fine Arts; Social Science
Dist - AITECH **Prod** - WDCNTV 1979

Songs of the Adventurers 47 MIN
16mm
Color (H A)
$800.00 purchase, $100.00 rental
Shows Basotho workers performing their proud, funny and defiant songs in their homes, in meeting places and enroute to work. Explores the hundred - year - old heritage of Basothos who have been exported from Lesotho to labor in South African mines.
Fine Arts
Dist - AFA

Songs of the ages series
All His armies 5 MIN
All you lands 5 MIN
Dist - FAMLYT

Songs of the Auvergne 20 MIN
16mm
B&W
Pictures French village life and the countryside. Includes the singing of ancient provincial songs performed by Phyllis Curtin and members of the Boston Symphony Orchestra.
Fine Arts; Geography - World
Dist - REMBRT **Prod** - MORM 1955

Songs of the labor movement 30 MIN
16mm
Color (G A)
$5.00 rental
Features folklore expert Neil Snortum who interviews Joe Glazer. Tells how many of the labor songs heard at union meetings and conventions across the United States were born of the bitter struggle to organize unions and from issues which sparked long - term strikes. Glazer sings.
Business and Economics; Fine Arts; Social Science
Dist - AFLCIO **Prod** - UNMICH 1961

Songs of the talking drum 57 MIN
VHS / 16mm
Color (I J H C G)
$89.95 purchase, $45.00 rental _ #TTP141
Takes a spirited journey through a multicultural musical and theatrical landscape. Features CBS recording artists Tony Vacca and Tim Moran, two jazz musicians who combine the polyrhythmic sounds of the West African balafon and talking drum with saxophone and flute. Drawing on African - American oral storytelling tradition, playwright and performance artist Andrea Hairston blends dramatic monologue, movement and music to create a 'jazz theatre.' Celebrates the creative diversity of the human spirit. Also available in half - hour version and in 16mm; inquire for sale price.
Fine Arts
Dist - TURTID

Songs 1 - 7 28 MIN
16mm
Color (G)
$650.00 purchase, $49.00 rental
Enlarges the 8mm Songs 1 - 14 series into 16mm films to save them from extinction. Includes a portrait of a lady; fire and a mind's movement in remembering; three girls playing with a ball - hand painted; a childbirth song; the painted veil via moth death; San Francisco.
Fine Arts
Dist - CANCIN **Prod** - BRAKS 1966

The Songwriter's video guide 60 MIN
VHS
Video music lesson series
Color (J H C G)
$29.95 purchase _ #TMV16V
Offers step - by - step songwriting instruction. Features studio musicians, composers, arrangers and educators who lend hands - on instruction about instruments, chord progressions, smooth and fluent style, timing and rhythms, common note combinations, instrument set - up, special sound techniques. Includes examples of chord and scale theory, examples for technical improvement and songs to teach the principles of music writing. Includes booklet. Part of a 16 - part series on musical instruction.
Fine Arts
Dist - CAMV

Sonia 53 MIN
VHS / U-matic
Color (PRO)
$350.00 purchase, $60.00 rental _ #5283S, #5283V
Dramatizes a patient with Alzheimer's Disease and points out the fragility of human existence. Portrays a 58 - year - old woman actively involved in her art career, family and friends. Reveals that she experiences increasing memory lapses accompanied by confusion, irritability and agitation. Shows the mental and emotional suffering experienced by those close to a person with Alzheimer's.
Health and Safety
Dist - AJN **Prod** - NFBC 1988

Sonia Malkine 52 MIN
U-matic / VHS
Rainbow quest sries
Color
Presents Sonia Malkine specializing in songs from France. She sings a French rendition of 'Where Have All the Flowers Gone?'.
Fine Arts
Dist - NORROS **Prod** - SEEGER

Sonia Malkine on Campus Series
Dickinson college - guest Michael Cooney, Program a 29 MIN
Dickinson college - guest Michael Cooney, Program B 29 MIN
Franklin and Marshall College - Guest Billy Faier, Program a 29 MIN
Franklin and Marshall College - Guest Billy Faier, Program B 29 MIN
Lebanon Valley College - Guest Dan Smith, Program A 29 MIN
Lebanon Valley College - Guest Dan Smith, Program B 29 MIN
Millersville State College - Guest Frank Fletcher, Program a 29 MIN
Millersville State College - Guest Frank Fletcher, Program B 29 MIN
Shippensburg College - Guest Brook Zern, Program B 29 MIN
Shippensburg State College - Guest Brook Zern, Program A 29 MIN
Dist - PBS

Sonia Speaks - Going further Out of Our Minds
VHS / Cassette
Color (G)
$29.95, $9.95 purchase _ #U890001223, - 1224
Features Sonia Johnson, author of 'From Housewife To Heretic.'.
History - World; Religion and Philosophy; Sociology
Dist - BKPEOP **Prod** - SJOHN 1989

Sonic Boom - sound waves through air 7 MIN
16mm / U-matic / VHS
Color (I J H)
$49.95 purchase _ #Q10918
Examines sound waves created by an airplane traveling at subsonic and supersonic speeds and explains what causes a sonic boom. Features extensive animation to illustrate points.
Science - Physical
Dist - CF **Prod** - IFFB 1984
MF

Sonntag Morgen 11 MIN
16mm
B&W (J)
Presents candid shots of people's faces moving about, expressing the human experience which has shaped them.
Guidance and Counseling; Sociology
Dist - UWFKD **Prod** - UWFKD

Sonntag platz and Big brother 11 MIN
16mm
Color (G)
$33.00 rental
Features two productions. Pays homage to Paul Klee with a painted, textured film made in 1982. Big Brother, 1983, is a comic book - collage with images taken from commercials. Both films on one reel.
Fine Arts
Dist - CANCIN **Prod** - AVERYC

Sonny and Cornblatt 33 MIN
VHS
Color (G C)
$185.00 purchase, $55.00 rental
Illustrates the importance of relationships among the elderly with the experience of a widower who tries to offer support to a newly widowed acquaintance without betraying each man's self - reliance.
Health and Safety; Psychology
Dist - TNF

Sonny Rollins 37 MIN
VHS / 16mm
Color
Features a performance by Sonny Rollins live at Loren.
Fine Arts
Dist - RHPSDY **Prod** - RHPSDY

Sonny Rollins Live 36 MIN
U-matic / VHS / 16mm
Color
LC 79-700934
Presents a live performance by jazz tenor saxophonist Sonny Rollins, supported by Bob Cranshaw on bass, Walter Davis, Jr, on piano, Masuo on guitar and David Lee on drums. Includes the selections There Is No Greater Love, Don't Stop The Carnival, Alfie, and St Thomas.
Fine Arts
Dist - TIMLIF **Prod** - TCBREL 1979

Sonny Terry and Brownie McGhee 52 MIN
VHS / U-matic
Rainbow quest series
Color
Features Sonny Terry, the blind harmonica player and Brownie McGhee on guitar as they trade songs with Pete Seeger.
Fine Arts
Dist - NORROS **Prod** - SEEGER

Sonny Terry - Shoutin' the Blues 6 MIN
U-matic
Color (J)
LC 80-701140; 80-707165
Focuses on blues harmonica player Sonny Terry.
Fine Arts
Dist - LAWREN **Prod** - AGINP 1976

Sonny's Lucky Dream - How to Chase Decay Away 14 MIN
16mm
Color (K P)
LC FIA68-2413
Illustrates the basic dental health rules, using puppets to dramatize the experiences of a little boy who eats too many sweets, is attacked by the villain decay, and is rescued by the dental health fairy.
Health and Safety
Dist - OSUMPD **Prod** - OHIOSU 1967

Sonoma 9 MIN
16mm
Color (A)
Presents an experimental film by Dennis Pies in which there unfolds like an Oriental scroll, twelve cycles of images derived from the I Ching.
Fine Arts
Dist - STARRC **Prod** - STARRC 1977

The Sonoran desert 11 MIN
BETA / U-matic / VHS
Color (G)
$29.95, $130.00 purchase _ #LSTF106
Highlights the saguaro cactus, indicator plant of the Sonoran desert and state flower of Arizona. Includes teachers' guide. Produced in cooperation with the Arizona Sonoran Desert Museum. Produced by Nature Episodes with Arizona Sonoran Desert Museum.
Science - Natural
Dist - FEDU

Sonrisas series

All in its proper time	29 MIN
Artful Dodger	29 MIN
Bad company	29 MIN
Beautiful people	29 MIN
The Champ	29 MIN
A Chance	29 MIN
The Choice	29 MIN
El Curro	29 MIN
Face the music	29 MIN
Finder's Keepers	29 MIN
Getting it Together - Todos Juntos	29 MIN
The Girl is turning 15 - La quinceanera	29 MIN
A Girl like that	29 MIN
Hey, Wake Up - Oye Despiertate	29 MIN
Horse of Pancho Villa	29 MIN
A Job worth doing	29 MIN
Let's Eat - a Comer	28 MIN
Magician	29 MIN
Misplaced Goals	29 MIN
My Friend Freddy	29 MIN
The Need to Touch	28 MIN
Organization - Organizacion	29 MIN
Pachango - Camp Out	29 MIN
A Place to be Yourself	29 MIN
The Problem with exhaustion	28 MIN
The Return	29 MIN
The Rich Dummy	28 MIN
The Right role	29 MIN
The Right to be - derecho de estar	29 MIN
Room for Us	28 MIN
Sour Grapes	29 MIN
The Surprise - La Sorpresa	29 MIN
Tears of the Apache - Lagrimas De Apache	29 MIN
Understanding - Entendimiento	28 MIN
White Dominoes	29 MIN
The Winners	29 MIN
You Bet Your Burger	28 MIN

Dist - PBS

Sonrisas
Provides 39 programs of 30 minutes each dealing with everyday problems faced by Hispanic children and adolescents. Topics include alcoholism, death, love and ecological concerns.
Sonrisas 30 MIN
Dist - GPN **Prod** - KLRNTV 1992

Sons and Daughters - Drugs and Booze
VHS / 16mm
(J H A)
$475.00 video purchase _ #82032, $525.00 film purchase _ #82024,
Offers advice on dealing with youth and drug and alcohol abuse.
Guidance and Counseling; Health and Safety; Psychology
Dist - CMPCAR

Sons and Daughters - Drugs and Booze 28 MIN
16mm / VHS
Color (G)
$525.00, $425.00 purchase, $70.00 rental _ #4956, 4958, 0429J, 0418J
Uses scenes from everyday family life to offer realistic, pragmatic advice to parents whose children have already begun to use drugs. Explains and reinforces the parents' role in prevention.
Guidance and Counseling; Health and Safety; Psychology; Sociology
Dist - HAZELB **Prod** - ROGGTP

Sons and daughters - parents and problems 35 MIN
VHS
Color (H G)
$295.00 purchase
Addresses common conflicts between parent and adolescent and helps parents and teens learn to communicate. Uses dramatic vignettes as a springboard for discussion, followed by a panel discussion by experts in parenting.
Guidance and Counseling; Psychology; Social Science; Sociology
Dist - FMSP

Sons and lovers 30 MIN
VHS
All black series
Color; PAL (H C A)
PdS65 purchase; Available in the United Kingdom or Ireland only
Features single mothers in the Afro - Caribbean community who speak out about the irresponsibility of men who father their children and then offer them little or no support. Notes that over half the families in this community are headed by single mothers. Second in a series of seven programs documenting the social conditions of blacks.
Sociology
Dist - BBCENE

Sons of Haji Omar 58 MIN
U-matic / VHS
Color
Documents the annual migration, led by the son of a wealthy landowner in northeastern Afghanistan, from the spring lambing camp near Col to the bazaar city of Narin into the rich summer grazing pastures of the Hindu Kush. Chronicles the family and social customs, the religious life and the economic realities of a preindustrial market economy.
Business and Economics; Geography - World
Dist - PSU **Prod** - NFBC

Sons of Raji Omar 58 MIN
U-matic / VHS / 16mm
Color (H C G T A)
Follows Pashtun nomads on their annual sheep herding migration from the Narin Valley in northeastern Afghanistan to the pastures of the Hindu Kuksh, showing their economy, family life, social customs, and religion. Study guide included.
Agriculture; Geography - World; Sociology
Dist - PSU **Prod** - PSU 1982

Sons of Shiva 27 MIN
U-matic / VHS
Color (C H)
Shows the festival of Shiva along with ritual practices and the singing of an order of ecstatic monks.
Religion and Philosophy
Dist - CEPRO **Prod** - HUFSC 1985

Sons of the Anzacs 1939 - 1945 79 MIN
16mm
B&W (H C A)
LC 74-709259
Shows the campaigns in which Australians fought in World War II, with special reference to such battles as Tobruk and the Kokoda Trail.
Civics and Political Systems; History - World
Dist - AUIS **Prod** - ANAIB 1968

Sons of the Desert 66 MIN
16mm
B&W
Explains how Laurel and Hardy trick their wives into letting them attend a fraternal convention.
Fine Arts
Dist - RMIBHF **Prod** - ROACH 1933

Sons of the moon 25 MIN
16mm / VHS
Color (H C G)
$500.00, $195.00 purchase, $45.00 rental _ #11185, #37158
Portrays the Ngas of Jos Plateau, Nigeria, who believe that the moon governs the growth of crops and schedule all important human events, including the symbolic rite of passage of boys into manhood, around the phases of the moon. Traces the moon's influence on the Ngas' work and thought through an entire growing season.
Geography - World; Sociology
Dist - UCEMC **Prod** - PISPE 1984

Sony 19 Inch Trinitron - Color Television Recorder 6 MIN
U-matic / VHS
Audio - Visual Skills Modules Series
Color
Education; Industrial and Technical Education
Dist - MDCC **Prod** - MDCC

Sony AVC - 3260 - Black and White Video Camera 7 MIN
VHS / U-matic
Audio - Visual Skills Modules Series
Color
Education; Industrial and Technical Education
Dist - MDCC **Prod** - MDCC

Sony Walkman 30 MIN
VHS
Design classics 2 series
Color (A)
PdS65 purchase _ Available in the United Kingdom, Ireland and Western Europe only
Uses archive film, period commercials, and interviews with key figures to examine the contribution to design made by some of the most successful products marketed in the 20th century. Part of a four-part series.
Business and Economics; Fine Arts
Dist - BBCENE

Soon There will be no more Me 10 MIN
16mm / U-matic / VHS
Color (H C A)
$190 purchase - 16 mm, $135 purchase - video
Discusses the thoughts and worries of a woman with cancer. A Lawrence Schiller film.
Sociology
Dist - CF

Soon There will be no more Me 10 MIN
16mm / U-matic / VHS
Color (H C A)
LC 72-702425
Tells the story of a 19 - year - old mother who is dying.
Guidance and Counseling; Sociology
Dist - CF **Prod** - ALSKOG 1972

The Sooner the Better 27 MIN
16mm
Non - Sexist Early Education Films Series
Color
LC 78-700383
Shows how nonsexist education is applied to preschool teaching.
Education; Psychology; Sociology
Dist - THIRD **Prod** - WAA 1977

The Sooner the Better - Pt 1 14 MIN
U-matic / VHS
Conrad Series
Color (I)
Focuses on physical assessment.
Health and Safety
Dist - AITECH **Prod** - SCETV 1977

The Sooner the Better - Pt 2 14 MIN
VHS / U-matic
Conrad Series
Color (I)
Explores resources for health care.
Health and Safety
Dist - AITECH **Prod** - SCETV 1977

Soongoora and Simba 15 MIN
U-matic / VHS
Teletales Series
Color (P)
$125.00 purchase
Introduces a children's tale from Zanzibar. Story shows positive ideas and values.
Education; Literature and Drama
Dist - AITECH **Prod** - POSIMP 1984

Sooper goop - short version 10 MIN
VHS
Color (P I)
$250.00, $195.00 purchase, $60.00 rental
Presents an animated story featuring two irreverent characters who concoct a television ad for a swee - e - e - e - t cereal called Sooper Goop. Examines advertising sales techniques and reveals the commercialism behind the fun.
Business and Economics; Guidance and Counseling
Dist - CF **Prod** - CHUSWE 1989

Sooper Puppy - a friend in need 21 MIN
VHS / U-matic / 16mm
Sooper Puppy series
Color (P)
$475.00, $375.00 purchase _ #HH - 6027M
Shows that it's better to tell the truth to a friend than to say nothing and see them get hurt. Dramatizes Baxter, also known as Sooper Puppy, who stands his ground to keep one friend from getting involved in drugs and another from playing with a gun. Reveals that friends appreciate being told when they are doing something dangerous and demonstrates that real friends do what it takes to keep people they care about safe and happy.
Guidance and Counseling; Psychology
Dist - CORF **Prod** - MITCHG 1990

Sooper Puppy - drink, drank, drunk 16 MIN
U-matic / BETA / 16mm / VHS
Sooper Puppy drug education series
Color (P)
$435.00, $335.00 purchase _ #JR - 5716M
Teaches the importance of saying 'no' to alcohol and of staying away from people who encourage youngsters to start drinking. Stars Baxter, also known as Sooper Puppy, who falls under the influence of neighborhood 'characters' who pressure him into attending a party where spiked punch is served. The next day Baxter feels awful, and he turns to his wise old Grandpaw for information on the dangers of alcohol use. Part of a series on drug education.
Guidance and Counseling; Health and Safety; Psychology; Sociology
Dist - CORF **Prod** - MITCHG 1988

Sooper Puppy drug education series
Sooper Puppy - drink, drank, drunk 16 MIN
Sooper Puppy - flying high 17 MIN
Sooper Puppy - puff of smoke 17 MIN
Dist - CORF

Sooper Puppy - flying high 17 MIN
U-matic / BETA / 16mm / VHS
Sooper Puppy drug education series
Color (P)
$435.00, $335.00 purchase _ #JR - 5717M
Teaches the difference between real fun, which contributes to growth and strength, and fake fun, which is an illusion manufactured by drugs. Stars Baxter, also known as Sooper Puppy, and the bumbling and mischievous Grizzle and Stoops, who try to convince Baxter that he can really 'fly high' on drugs. Part of a series on drug education.
Guidance and Counseling; Health and Safety; Psychology; Sociology
Dist - CORF **Prod** - MITCHG 1988

Sooper Puppy - once upon a feeling 19 MIN
U-matic / 16mm / VHS
Sooper Puppy series
Color (P)
$475.00, $375.00 purchase _ #HH - 6028M
Shows why it's important to name feelings and to share them. Explores what happens when bad feelings - jealousy, anger and disappointment - aren't shared and shows ways to handle negative feelings. Stars Baxter, also known as Sooper Puppy, and his Grandpaw and friends. Demonstrates that all kids have difficult feelings as well as good emotions and all should be accepted as a part of human nature.
Guidance and Counseling; Psychology
Dist - CORF **Prod** - MITCHG 1990

Sooper Puppy - puff of smoke 17 MIN
U-matic / BETA / 16mm / VHS
Sooper Puppy drug education series
Color (P)
$435.00, $335.00 purchase _ #JR - 5715M
Teaches the physical and mental effects of cigarette smoking and gives youngsters the information they need to say 'no' to smoking. Stars Baxter, also known as Sooper Puppy. Raises the issue of the difficulties of recovery from addiction. Part of a series on drug education.
Guidance and Counseling; Health and Safety; Psychology; Sociology
Dist - CORF **Prod** - MITCHG 1988

Sooper Puppy - self - esteem 19 MIN
VHS / U-matic / BETA / 16mm
Sooper Puppy series
Color (P)
$450.00, $350.00 purchase _ #JR - 4892M
Teaches the secrets of personal success through the power of a strong self - image. Stars Baxter, also known as Sooper Puppy, who is put out of the house for chewing the rug and for letting two scruffy strays scatter his family's garbage. Reveals that he is on the verge of running away from home when Grandpaw stops him and teaches him to say 'no' to bad things, to be his own best friend, and to believe that he is special.
Guidance and Counseling; Health and Safety; Psychology; Sociology
Dist - CORF **Prod** - MITCHG 1988

Sooper Puppy series
Sooper Puppy - a friend in need 21 MIN
Sooper Puppy - once upon a feeling 19 MIN
Sooper Puppy - self - esteem 19 MIN
Sooper Puppy - what's the difference 20 MIN
Sooper Puppy - whose wuzzit 19 MIN
Sooper Puppy - words can hurt 19 MIN
Dist - CORF

Sooper Puppy - what's the difference 20 MIN
U-matic / 16mm / VHS
Sooper Puppy series
Color (P)
$475.00, $375.00 purchase _ #HH - 6026M
Shows the importance of looking at what's inside someone before making judgements. Reveals that name - calling based on appearance can hurt feelings and that a difference in appearance can take time to get used to. Stars Baxter, also known as Sooper Puppy, who learns that in order to love and accept others, one must be able to accept oneself.
Psychology; Sociology
Dist - CORF **Prod** - MITCHG 1990

Sooper Puppy - whose wuzzit 19 MIN
U-matic / 16mm / VHS
Sooper Puppy series
Color (P)
$475.00, $375.00 purchase _ #HH - 6029M
Shows children the importance of not taking what doesn't belong to them. Demonstrates how TV ads make people want to buy things, and that shoplifting is always wrong. Stars Baxter, also known as Sooper Puppy, who wants a ball that he has seen on television, but his owner gives him something else. When bullies Grizzle and Stoops make fun of his toy, he decides to 'borrow' the new ball from his friend Pickles without her permission.
Guidance and Counseling; Psychology
Dist - CORF **Prod** - MITCHG 1990

Sooper Puppy - words can hurt 19 MIN
VHS / U-matic / BETA / 16mm
Sooper Puppy series
Color (P)
$450.00, $350.00 purchase _ #JR - 5886M
Teaches the importance of self - esteem, understanding emotions, controlling 'hurtful' anger, respecting the feelings of other people and learning to apologize. Stars Baxter, also known as Sooper Puppy, who begins his adventure feeling fine and capable, but after a series of incidents in which he is called stupid and other demoralizing names, his confidence is gone, his behavior is inept and he is engaging in name calling himself. Grandpaw gently helps Baxter to understand the causes of his feelings, as well as those of the name callers.
Guidance and Counseling; Psychology; Sociology
Dist - CORF **Prod** - MITCHG 1989

Soopergoop 13 MIN
16mm / U-matic / VHS
Color (P I) (SPANISH)
LC 75-704266
Uses an animated story, about an actor and an advertising man and their deceptive television commercial for a cereal, to present the problem of false advertising and the need for concern about buying habits.
Business and Economics; Fine Arts; Foreign Language
Dist - CF **Prod** - CF 1976

Sootblower Maintenance 60 MIN
VHS
Boiler Maintenance Series
Color (PRO)
$600.00, $1500.00 purchase _ #GMSBM
Discusses the disassembly and reassembly of sootblowers. Describes the function and operation of various types of sootblowers, recurring maintenance problems, in - place service and the overhaul process. Part of a six - part series on boiler maintenance, part of a larger set on general and mechanical maintenance. Includes 10 textbooks and an instructor guide which provide four hours of instruction.
Education; Industrial and Technical Education; Psychology
Dist - NUSTC **Prod** - NUSTC

Soothing the bruise 18 MIN
16mm
Color (G)
$45.00 rental
Discusses 'Sex roles, consumption and destruction in America.' Produced by Betzy Bromberg.
Fine Arts; Sociology
Dist - CANCIN

Sophia, Wisdom 3 - the Cliffs 64 MIN
U-matic / VHS
B&W
Documents the Ontological/Hysteric Theatre.
Fine Arts
Dist - KITCHN **Prod** - KITCHN

Sophie and Lou - 85
VHS
Reading rainbow series
Color; CC (K P)
$39.95 purchase
Tells about a mouse named Sophie who overcomes her shyness by learning to dance, in a story by Petra Mathers, read by Lola Falana. Shows LeVar mastering some fancy footwork, from mambo to hip - hop. Takes a globe - trotting look at dance around the world, including Bali, Ireland and Australia. Part of a series offering a multicultural approach to generating reading enthusiasm with cross - curricular applications, hosted by LeVar Burton.
English Language; Fine Arts; Literature and Drama
Dist - GPN **Prod** - LNMDP

Sophie and the Scales 8 MIN
16mm / U-matic / VHS
Color (H C A)
Tells the story of prim little Sophie who overcomes the ogress who is her piano teacher.
Literature and Drama
Dist - FI **Prod** - UWFKD

Sophie's place 90 MIN
16mm
Color (G)
$60.00 rental
Presents full hand - painted cut - out animation and unrehearsed development of scenes under the camera. Begins in a garden of paradise then enters the Mosque of St Sophia. Episodes center around various forms of Sophia, an early Greek embodiment of spiritual wisdom.
Fine Arts
Dist - CANCIN **Prod** - JORDAL 1986

Sophisticated Investing 60 MIN
VHS / U-matic
How to be a Financially Secure Woman Series
Color
Presents Dr Mary Elizabeth Schlayer talking with moderator Susan Wright about sophisticated investing for women.
Business and Economics; Sociology
Dist - KUHTTV **Prod** - KUHTTV

Sophisticated Vamp 4 MIN
16mm
Color (J H C)
Creates pure color forms which parade across the screen, zooming, then slowly undulating to the accompanying music of a vamp.
Industrial and Technical Education
Dist - CFS **Prod** - FAYMAN

Sophocles' Antigone 54 MIN
VHS
Great Ideas Series
Color (H)
$14.00 rental _ #51042
Features Mortimer J. Adler in the fourth of five seminars of his Great Ideas Series, which exposes a group of high school students to the most important literary works of Western civilization. This installment examines Sophocles' Antigone.
Education; Fine Arts; Literature and Drama
Dist - PSU **Prod** - EBEC
EBEC

Sophocle's Oedipus Tyrannus 60 MIN
U-matic / VHS
Drama - play, performance, perception series; Module 3
Color (C)
Fine Arts; Literature and Drama
Dist - MDCC **Prod** - MDCC

Sorcerer 121 MIN
16mm
Color
Dramatizes a suicidal mission in which a truckload of nitro must be driven through a South American jungle. Directed by William Friedkin.
Fine Arts
Dist - SWANK **Prod** - UPCI

The Sorcerers 87 MIN
16mm
Color (C A)
Stars Boris Karloff, Susan George and Catherine Lacey. Tells the story of a professor who conducts a successful experiment to dominate a young man by mesmeric techniques, only to have the scheme run amuck.
Literature and Drama
Dist - CINEWO **Prod** - CINEWO 1967

The Sorcerer's Apprentice 14 MIN
U-matic / VHS / 16mm
Color (P)
LC 70-709396
Presents the tale of the sorcerer's apprentice who enchants a broom to carry water in this puppet fantasy to Dukas' well - known scherzo.
Fine Arts; Literature and Drama
Dist - CORF **Prod** - CORF 1970

The Sorcerer's Apprentice 27 MIN
16mm / U-matic / VHS
Color (P I J)
Tells the story of Spellbinder the Sorcerer, who mistakenly hires a supposedly ignorant boy who uses the sorcerer's own magic to defeat him.
Literature and Drama
Dist - PFP **Prod** - ROAESO 1980

The Sorcerer's apprentice 33 MIN
VHS / 16mm
Color (P I J G)
$550.00, $295.00 purchase, $55.00 rental
Introduces the various kinds of music that orchestras can make - rock, disco, heavy metal, classical and opera. Follows a young boy on a fantasy adventure where he tries to lead an orchestra and produces a cacophony which brings jeers from the audience. Pursued by authorities for his audacity, he flees in a nightmarish romp with the town's musicians, realizing that making music takes discipline and experience. Produced by Marion Bloem.
Fine Arts
Dist - FLMLIB

The Sorcerer's Apprentice 10 MIN
16mm / U-matic / VHS
Color
Presents Mickey Mouse as a sorcerer's apprentice who gives life to inanimate objects to the music of Paul Dukas. Taken from the full - length motion picture Fantasia.

Fine Arts
Dist - CORF **Prod** - DISNEY 1980

The Sorcerer's Apprentice 26 MIN
16mm / U-matic / VHS
Color (P I) (SPANISH FRENCH)
Relates the tale of young Hans, apprentice to Spellbinder the Sorcerer, whose ability to read the Book of Magic becomes his secret weapon against the Sorcerer's evil powers, and who defeats his wicked master in a duel of magic.
Fine Arts; Foreign Language; Literature and Drama
Dist - PFP **Prod** - ROAESO

The Sorcerer's Apprentice - a Music Fantasy 14 MIN
U-matic / VHS / 16mm
Color (P I)
$340, $240 purchase _ #3088
Tells the story of a magician's apprentice who cannot stop a spell that he put on some brooms.
Literature and Drama
Dist - CORF

The Sorcerer's Boy 15 MIN
U-matic / VHS
Teletales Series
Color (P)
$125.00 purchase
Presents a popular Russian fable for children.
Education; Literature and Drama
Dist - AITECH **Prod** - POSIMP 1984

The Sorceress - Kiri Te Kanawa 50 MIN
VHS
Color (G T)
$225.00 purchase, $80.00 rental
Weaves contemporary and baroque styles in this performance fantasy expressing the warring forces of good and evil and the power of romantic love through music, song, dance and gesture. Blends stage drama and rock video. Features the music of Handel. Stars Kiri Te Kanawa, conducted by Christopher Hogwood, choreographed by Toronto's baroque Opera Atelier. Opera in Italian with English subtitles.
Fine Arts; Religion and Philosophy
Dist - BULFRG **Prod** - RHOMBS 1994

Sore Throat 10 MIN
VHS / U-matic
Take Care of Yourself Series
Color
Instructs the patient or family about sore throat, including causes, symptoms, control and treatment.
Health and Safety; Science - Natural
Dist - UARIZ **Prod** - UARIZ

Soren Kierkegaard 57 MIN
16mm / U-matic / VHS
Third Testament Series
Color
LC 75-703399
Deals with the life and thought of Soren Kierkegaard.
Biography; Literature and Drama; Religion and Philosophy
Dist - TIMLIF **Prod** - NIELSE 1974

The Sorianos 9 MIN
U-matic / VHS / 16mm
American Family - an Endangered Species Series
Color (H C A)
Studies an extended family.
Sociology
Dist - FI **Prod** - NBCNEW 1979

Sorrow 27 MIN
16mm / U-matic / VHS
Storybook International Series
Color
Tells the Hungarian story of two brothers who are left identical sums of money, but one loses his fortune because of the efforts of Sorrow. Reveals that when the poor brother finally gets rid of Sorrow, he becomes wealthy. Shows the other brother releasing Sorrow in the hopes that he will once more make his brother poor, but that Sorrow instead attacks him, punishing him for his envy.
Guidance and Counseling; Literature and Drama
Dist - JOU **Prod** - JOU 1982

The Sorrow and the Pity 260 MIN
16mm
B&W (H C A)
LC 76-702631
Examines the occupation of France by the Germans during World War II using reminiscences of individuals and officials involved in the events at the time. Concentrates on the themes of collaboration and resistance.
Fine Arts; History - World; Sociology
Dist - CINEMV **Prod** - NPSSRT 1972

Sorrow - the Nazi legacy 33 MIN
VHS
Color (G)
$39.95 purchase _ #646
Documents the pilgrimage of a group of six Swedish teenagers, two of whom are Jewish, to Auschwitz to try to comprehend the incomprehensible. Follows them on a preliminary visit to Wannsee, where the implementation of the 'Final Solution' was determined, to set the stage for the teens' pilgrimage. No amount of intellectual explanation of the facts can adequately prepare the group for their own emotional reactions after spending time at Auschwitz. A meeting with one of the camp's survivors proves to be full of pain and sorrow, yet full of hope for the future. The pilgrimage comes full circle as the group returns to Stockholm for a meeting with the son of Hans Frank, the Nazi official who was governor - general of Poland.
History - World
Dist - ERGOM

The Sorrows of Gin 60 MIN
16mm / U-matic / VHS
Cheever Short Stories Series
Color (H C A)
LC 82-700001
Presents a dramatization of the John Cheever story The Sorrows Of Gin. Centers on an eight - year - old girl's search for a sense of family amid the sophisticated and detached whirl of her parents' lives.
Literature and Drama
Dist - FI **Prod** - WNETTV 1981

Sorry, no Vacancy 27 MIN
16mm
Color (H C A)
LC 76-703639
A shortened version of the 52 minute film Sorry, No Vacancy. Illustrates the urgent conflict confronting the world between uncontrolled population growth and man's merciless consumption of the planet's dwindling resources.
Science - Natural; Sociology
Dist - MALIBU **Prod** - WILHIT 1974

Sorry, no Vacancy 52 MIN
16mm
Color (H C A)
LC 73-701721
Studies the population growth with respect to food production, resource consumption, economic impact and ecological consequence.
Business and Economics; Science - Natural; Social Science
Dist - WILHIT **Prod** - WILHIT 1973

Sorted details 13 MIN
16mm
Color (G)
$25.00 rental
Links shape, color or movement with fragments of urban landscape. Yanks the viewer moment to moment and from spot to spot, each with its own naturalistic sound.
Fine Arts
Dist - CANCIN **Prod** - WRGHTC 1980

The Sorter 14 MIN
16mm
Color (H C A)
Introduces the functioning of the parts of the sorter. Conducts a sorting operation to demonstrate the machine's capacity to read punched cards and to sort alphabetically. Shows how vast amounts of random data can be grouped and organized.
Mathematics; Psychology; Sociology
Dist - SF **Prod** - SF 1968

Sorting casualties for treatment and evacuation 5 MIN
VHS / U-matic
EMT video - group one series
Color (PRO)
LC 84-706986
Illustrates procedures for proper sorting (triage) of casualties. Includes steps for determining the type of wound and condition of the patient in order to classify patients for evacuation.
Health and Safety
Dist - USNAC **Prod** - USA 1983

Sorting Out Sorting 30 MIN
16mm
Color
Employs computer animation to demonstrate nine computer sorting techniques grouped into insertion sorts, exchange sorts and selection sorts. Compares the efficiency of each sort.
Business and Economics; Mathematics
Dist - UTORMC **Prod** - UTORMC

SOS 10 MIN
U-matic / VHS / 16mm
Color
LC 81-700809
Uses animation to follow the journey of a tenacious SOS signal as it searches the world for someone willing to save an endangered vessel.
Fine Arts
Dist - PHENIX **Prod** - KRATKY 1979

An SOS 5 MIN
U-matic / VHS
Write on, Set 2 Series
Color (J H)
Shows the correct use of the words 'Past' and 'Passed' and 'Loose' and 'Lose'.
English Language
Dist - CTI **Prod** - CTI

SOS - skim or scan 20 MIN
VHS / U-matic
Tomes and talismans series
(I J)
$145.00 purchase, $27.00 rental, $90.00 self dub
Uses a science fantasy adventure to define, illustrate and review basic library research concepts. Designed for sixth, seventh and eighth graders. Discusses skimming, scanning, paraphrasing and notetaking. Tenth in a 13 part series.
Education
Dist - GPN **Prod** - MISETV

SOS Soap Suds 3 MIN
U-matic / VHS
Color
Shows a classic live television commercial with Durwood Kirby and Garry Moore.
Business and Economics; Psychology; Sociology
Dist - BROOKC **Prod** - BROOKC

Sosua 30 MIN
VHS
Jewish life around the world series
Color (G)
$34.95 purchase _ #127
Reveals that in 1938, 32 nations met at the Evian Conference to find new homes for endangered European Jews. States that only one, the Dominican Republic ruled by Rafael Trujillo, offered sanctuary. In 1940, a group of Jews escaping the terrors of Nazism found haven on the island.
History - World; Sociology
Dist - ERGOM **Prod** - ERGOM

Soto 15 MIN
16mm
Color (J H C) (SPANISH)
LC 73-702059
Gives a retrospective view of Venezuelan kinetic artist J R Soto. Filmed in Paris and Venezuela.
Fine Arts; Foreign Language; Geography - World
Dist - MOMALA **Prod** - OOAS 1972

Soto Zen Buddhism 42 MINS
VHS / BETA
Color; PAL (G)
PdS17, $34.00 purchase
Features the Venerable Lama Thubten Zopa presenting an overview of the Serene Reflection Meditation Tradition. Explains that the fundamental teachings of this school are the practice of meditation; the keeping of Buddhist precepts; that all beings have Buddha Nature; and that training and enlightenment are one and undivided. Produced by Wessex Education Television Consortium.
Fine Arts; Religion and Philosophy
Dist - MERIDT

Soudain le paradis 13 MIN
16mm
Les Francais chez vous series
B&W (I J H)
LC 77-704478
Foreign Language
Dist - CHLTN **Prod** - PEREN 1967

Soul 150 MIN
VHS
Color (G)
$59.95 purchase _ #V - SOUL
Discusses challenges to the mechanistic view of the universe. Features Stephen Hawking, physicist Paul Davis, philosopher Dana Zohar and author Matthew Fox who discuss the role of soul.
Religion and Philosophy
Dist - PACSPI

Soul 30 MIN
VHS
From Jumpstreet Series
Color (G)
$39.95 purchase _ #FJSG - 110
Reflects the development of soul music as performed by black musicians. Features performances and interviews with several black musicians. Hosted by singer and songwriter Oscar Brown, Jr.

Fine Arts; History - United States
Dist - PBS GPN **Prod** - WETATV 1980

The Soul Bewitched 30 MIN
U-matic
Africa File Series
Color (J H)
Looks at various forms of pre - European education and the changing nature and purpose of European public and missionary schools in Africa.
Business and Economics; Education; Geography - World; History - World
Dist - TVOTAR **Prod** - TVOTAR 1985

Soul City 2 MIN
16mm
Color
LC 79-701058
Uses a hand - tinted animation technique in a sequence of the punk rock group Fleshtones performing the song Soul City.
Fine Arts
Dist - AFA **Prod** - JONESM 1979

The Soul of Christmas 58 MIN
VHS / U-matic
Color (J A)
Looks at Christmas Eve service at the Second Christian Church of the Christian Church (Disciples of Christ) in Indianapolis. Shows the diversity of the music and worship experiences of a fast - growing congregation. Shows the excitement and spontaneity of a black worship experience in the United States within the context of a mainstream Protestant denomination.
Religion and Philosophy
Dist - ECUFLM **Prod** - ABCNEW 1981

The Soul of science 78 MIN
VHS
Color (J H)
$150.00 purchase _ #A5VH 1002
Presents four parts on the world's most influential scientists. Introduces pioneer scientists in Wonders Are Many - Science in Antiquity. Shows how the Middle Ages, the Arab World and the European Renaissance contributed to the Scientific Revolution in O Brave New World - Science in the Middle Ages and Renaissance. Details the expansion of the scientific revolution over Europe and North America and visits Charles Darwin in To a Blind Man Eyes - Science in the 18th and 19th Centuries. Explores the work of 20th - century scientists, including Einstein, Bohr, Curie, Crick and Watson in Dare to Be Naive - Science in the 20th Century. Includes supplementary book.
Science
Dist - CLRVUE **Prod** - CLRVUE

Soul of science series
Presents a four - part series on the history of science from ancient times through the 20th century. Includes the titles Wonders Are Many; O Brave New World; Giving a Blind Man Eyes; Dare to Be Naive. Includes a 64 - page book from the Learning Power series.

Dare to be naive - science in the 20th century	18 MIN
Giving a blind man eyes - science in the 18th and 19th centuries	21 MIN
O Brave new world - science in the Renaissance	19 MIN
The Soul of science series	78 MIN
Wonders are many - science in antiquity	20 MIN

Dist - HAWHIL **Prod** - HAWHIL

The Soul of Spain 59 MIN
U-matic / BETA / VHS
Color (G)
$90.00 purchase _ #C51476
Reveals that after centuries of isolation, Spain is emerging into today's world with new vigor. Looks at the remarkable transformation of the economic, political and social structure taking place in Spain.
Geography - World; History - World
Dist - NGS **Prod** - NGS 1991

The Soul of the Acients - Vol I - Pt I 109 MIN
VHS
World of Joseph Campbell Series
Color (S)
$29.95 purchase
Spotlights famous mythologist Joseph Campbell speaking directly to the camera who explores the myths and symbols which shaped our world and delineated what Campbell calls 'the experience of being alive.' Volume I, Part I of the series has two segments. 'In The Beginning - Origins Of Myth And Man' considers birth, growing up, the rites of passage. 'Where People Live Legends - American Indian Myths' retells an archetypal Navajo myth, bringing to life the landscape in which all aspects of the land and the life force are infused with sacred meaning.
History - World; Religion and Philosophy; Social Science
Dist - FI **Prod** - MYTHL 1988

The Soul of the Acients - Vol I - Pt II 109 MIN
VHS
World of Joseph Campbell Series
Color (S)
$29.95 purchase
Spotlights famous mythologist Joseph Campbell speaking directly to the camera who explores the myths and symbols which shaped our world and delineated what Campbell calls 'the experience of being alive.' Volume I, Part II of the series has two segments. 'And We Washed Our Weapons In The Sea - Gods And Goddesses Of The Neolithic Period' traces the establishment of god - centered religions from the Neolithic goddess centered culture to the emergence of wars of conquest and god - centered religions. 'Pharoah's Rule - Egypt, The Exodus, And The Myth Of Osiris' presents the myths of Isis and Osiris and explores the mythological and historical roots of the Exodus.
History - World; Religion and Philosophy
Dist - FI **Prod** - MYTHL 1988

The Soul of the Acients - Vol I - Pt III 58 MIN
VHS
World of Joseph Campbell Series
Color (S)
$19.95 purchase
Spotlights famous mythologist Joseph Campbell speaking directly to the camera who explores the myths and symbols which shaped our world and delineated what Campbell calls 'the experience of being alive.' Volume I, Part III of the series has one segment, 'From Darkness To Light - The Mystery Religions of Ancient Greece,' which explores the recurring theme of mystery, from the Eleusinian mysteries of ancient Greek religion, the mystical elements of Christianity which contrasted with the historical flow of the Bible - eventually reemergin as the spirit behind the Renaissance.
History - World; Religion and Philosophy
Dist - FI **Prod** - MYTHL 1988

Soul of the Islands 30 MIN
VHS / 16mm
Color (G)
$250.00 purchase, $50.00 rental; LC 89715585
Features renowned Haitian singer Toto Bissainthe who recounts in song a fable that recreates Haiti's past and reveals the continuing tragedy of life in Haiti.
Fine Arts; Geography - World; History - World; Literature and Drama; Sociology
Dist - CNEMAG **Prod** - CNEMAG 1988

Soul to Soul 29 MIN
U-matic
Music Shop Series
Color
Examines the origins of soul music and its important relationship to blues and jazz.
Fine Arts
Dist - UMITV **Prod** - UMITV 1974

Sound 10 MIN
VHS
Take a look 2 series
Color (P)
$49.00 purchase, $15.00 rental _ #353805; LC 91-707968
Explains what sound is and how it travels to our ears. Demonstrates how an oscilloscope measures sound waves. Part of a series that takes a hands - on approach to the principles of science.
Psychology; Science; Science - Physical
Dist - TVOTAR **Prod** - TVOTAR 1990

Sound
VHS / U-matic / 16mm
Matter and energy for beginners series
Color (P)
$400.00, $250.00 purchase _ #HP - 5942C
Uses animation and live action to teach physical science. Stars Investigator Alligator and his friend Mr E, who investigate the basics of sound. Part of a six - part series.
Science - Physical
Dist - CORF **Prod** - CORF 1990

Sound 27 MIN
VHS
B&W (G)
$24.95 purchase
Jazzes around with Rahsaan Roland Kirk and John Cage.
Fine Arts
Dist - KINOIC **Prod** - RHPSDY

Sound 15 MIN
U-matic
Science Alliance Series
Color (I)
Demonstrates that sound travels in waves through gases, liquids and solids and tells what an echo is.
Science; Science - Physical
Dist - TVOTAR **Prod** - TVOTAR 1981

Sound 12.5 MIN
U-matic / VHS / 16mm
Color (K P I)
$295, $205, $235 purchase _ #A398
Introduces children to basic concepts of sound. Explains that sound is actually invisible waves traveling through air, water, or materials such as rock. Demonstrates how sound waves travel outward from their source, much like ripples on a lake. Explains the phenomenon of echoes, and the difference between loud and soft sounds. Explains how different pitches are produced. Demonstrates how sounds are produced through vibrations.
Science - Physical
Dist - BARR **Prod** - BARR 1986

Sound - a first film 10 MIN
U-matic / VHS / BETA
Color; NTSC; PAL; SECAM (I J)
PdS58
Demonstrates how sound is created by vibrations through live action footage and graphics. Illustrates conductors of sound and the function of the ear - and other sensors - for an understanding of the prevalence of sound in human life.
Science - Physical
Dist - VIEWTH

Sound - a First Film 10 MIN
U-matic / VHS / 16mm
Color (P I)
LC 84-707082
Science - Physical
Dist - PHENIX **Prod** - BARJA 1983

Sound about 11 MIN
U-matic / VHS / 16mm
Color (P I) (SPANISH)
LC FIA68-1095
Provides discovery experiences in science study of the concepts in sound. Follows two boys and their dog as they walk along a beach and learn about vibrations, pitch and echos.
Science; Science - Physical
Dist - AIMS **Prod** - CAHILL 1967

Sound, Acoustics, and Recording 14 MIN
U-matic / VHS / 16mm
Physical Science Series
Color (I J H)
$340, $230 purchase _ #4831C
Describes how interior surfaces affect sound waves.
Science - Physical
Dist - CORF

Sound advice - 111 29 MIN
VHS
FROG series 1; Series 1; 111
Color (P I J)
$100.00 purchase
Offers the eleventh program by Friends of Research and Odd Gadgets. Lifts science off the textbook page into the real world to show how enjoyable and challenging science can be. In this episode, the Froggers make a box that sees sound, an oscilloscope. Special focus on pipe organs, synthesizers, electronic signals and sound vibrations. Produced by Greg Rist.
Fine Arts; Science - Physical
Dist - BULFRG **Prod** - OWLTV 1993

Sound advice - hearing conservation - Consejo a toda prueba - conservacion del oido - dite oui a votre ouie 17 MIN
BETA / VHS / U-matic
Color (IND G) (SPANISH FRENCH)
$395.00, $495.00 purchase _ #601 - 04, #602 - 03; $C495.00 purchase _ #602-01
Emphasizes the importance of wearing hearing protection in noisy environments on and off the job. Explains the anatomy of the ear and how noise affects the ability to hear. Satisfies annual training requirements.
Health and Safety; Industrial and Technical Education; Psychology; Science - Natural; Sociology
Dist - ITSC **Prod** - ITSC

Sound and Advanced Graphics Capabilities
U-matic / VHS
Authoring in PASS Series
Color
Explains how to use Professional Authoring Software System (PASS) sound, advanced graphics and video interface facilities to enhance lessons. Introduces the concept of character sets and shows how to use the character set editor.
Industrial and Technical Education; Psychology
Dist - DELTAK **Prod** - DELTAK

Sound and healing 30 MIN
BETA / VHS
Perspectives on healing series
Color (G)
$29.95 purchase _ #S344
Features Jill Purce, author of 'The Mystic Spiral,' who states that the use of sound in healing is based on the principle that the entire universe is composed of vibrations and can be influenced through vibrations. Discusses the role of sound in traditional cultures as a means of harmonizing and healing the human body and promoting harmony between people. Part of a series giving alternative perspectives on healing.
Fine Arts; Health and Safety; Psychology; Religion and Philosophy; Science - Physical
Dist - THINKA **Prod** - THINKA

Sound and Hearing 15 MIN
U-matic / VHS
Why Series
Color (P I)
Discusses sound and hearing.
Science - Physical
Dist - AITECH **Prod** - WDCNTV 1976

Sound and Hearing 14 MIN
VHS / U-matic
Color
Explains in detail how noise can damage the ears. Discusses decibels and sound intensity. Presents principles of hearing protection.
Health and Safety; Science - Natural
Dist - MEDFAC **Prod** - MEDFAC 1977

Sound and its Effects 22 MIN
VHS / U-matic
Mathematics and Physics Series
Color (IND)
Begins by defining sound and telling how it is produced, how it travels and how it is received by a detector. Uses animation to explain wave propagation through various media. Shows air - to - air photography to discuss match numbers and speed of sound. Photography illustrates formation of shock waves in transonic and supersonic flight.
Science - Physical
Dist - AVIMA **Prod** - AVIMA 1980

Sound and Movement 17 MIN
16mm
Color (J)
Illustrates movement improvisations accompanied by sounds of voice, hands and feet and a variety of conventional and unconventional instruments.
Fine Arts
Dist - METT **Prod** - METT 1957

Sound and moving pictures 25 MIN
U-matic / VHS / 16mm
Computer programme series; Episode 6
Color (J)
Discusses computer animation and art and the use of voice synthesizers.
Fine Arts; Mathematics
Dist - FI **Prod** - BBCTV 1982

Sound and Rhythm 30 MIN
U-matic
Polka Dot Door Series
Color (K)
Presents a variety show for pre - school children. Includes songs, mime, stories, film sequences, talk, dance and fantasy figures. Each show emphasizes a particular theme such as numbers, feelings, exploring, music or time. Comes with parent teacher guide.
English Language; Fine Arts; Literature and Drama
Dist - TVOTAR **Prod** - TVOTAR 1985

Sound and the Painter 6 MIN
16mm
B&W (C T)
an experimental presentation of paintings with jazz accompaniment. Attempts to catch the visual mood in sound.
Fine Arts
Dist - NYU **Prod** - NYU 1962

Sound and the Story 26 MIN
16mm
Color
Demonstrates the production of a high - fidelity record of Tchaikovsky's 'Romeo and Juliet' performed by the Boston Symphony Orchestra, directed by Charles Munch.
Fine Arts
Dist - RCA **Prod** - RCA 1956

Sound and vision, station to station 10 MIN
16mm
Color (G)
$10.00 rental
Presents a two - part film by Andy Moore about consuming and producing music.
Fine Arts
Dist - CANCIN

Sound Application for Video 30 MIN
U-matic / VHS
Video - a Practical Guide and more Series
Color
Demonstrates audio recording equipment and use of sound effects and music tracks. Explains how sound alters mood.
Fine Arts
Dist - VIPUB **Prod** - VIPUB

A Sound Approach 13 MIN
16mm
Color
Outlines the technological, operational and regulatory procedures which are leading to significant aircraft noise reduction.
Sociology
Dist - MTP **Prod** - FAAFL

A Sound Approach 13 MIN
16mm
Color
LC 79-700028
Deals with the impact of aviation noise on individuals and communities located near airports. Examines actions being taken by the aviation industry to reduce noise levels.
Sociology
Dist - USNAC **Prod** - USFAA 1978

Sound Around 29 MIN
Videoreel / VT2
Observing Eye Series
Color
Science - Physical; Sociology
Dist - PBS **Prod** - WGBHTV

The Sound Collector 12 MIN
16mm
Color
Presents the story of six - year old Leonard who collects sounds and transforms them into imaginative adventure stories.
Fine Arts
Dist - NFBC **Prod** - NFBC 1982

Sound creations 25 MIN
VHS
Color (H C G A)
$190.00 purchase, $40.00 rental _ #38106
Introduces some of America's most original musicians - men and women who invent their own instruments in order to create the new music of our time. Takes the viewer into the studios and performance spaces of these musicians, where they perform their music and comment on its origins and its future. Relates the importance of noted American composer Harry Partch to the 'new instrument' movement and illustrates the influence of African rhythms and Eastern melodic scales on the new music. Produced by Ken d'Oronzio.
Fine Arts
Dist - UCEMC

Sound Discrimination Capacity of the Hearing Impaired 25 MIN
U-matic / VHS
Color
LC 80-707414
Describes research conducted at Gallaudet College to explore the discrimination capacity of persons with moderate to severe sensoryneural deafness.
Guidance and Counseling; Health and Safety; Psychology
Dist - USNAC **Prod** - USBEH 1980

Sound effects 30 MIN
VHS
Join in series
Color (K P)
#362313
Shows that Nikki's excitement about working with Peter Longo, a top - notch sound technician, turns into frustration when Peter's arrogance gets in the way of a good job. Reveals that to show Peter where he has made an error, Zack suggests that they check the sound effects in a run - through of the show. Part of a series about three artist - performers who share studio space in a converted warehouse.
Fine Arts; Literature and Drama
Dist - TVOTAR **Prod** - TVOTAR 1989

Sound, Energy and Wave Motion 14 MIN
16mm / U-matic / VHS
Physical Science Series
Color (I J H)
$340, $230 purchase _ #4830C
Discusses the relationship among energy, sound, and sound waves.
Science - Physical
Dist - CORF

A Sound Film 15 MIN
16mm
Color
LC 77-702648
Presents an experiment in layered sound, time and movement within and without the frame.
Fine Arts; Industrial and Technical Education
Dist - CANFDC **Prod** - CANFDC 1976

Sound Filmstrip, Set 1 Series
Now Age Reading Programs
Dist - MAFEX

Sound Filmstrip, Set 2 Series
Now Age Reading Programs
Dist - MAFEX

Sound Filmstrips - Young Adult Series
How to eat fried worms
The Secret Life of the Underwear Champ
Dist - PELLER

Sound, form and fluency - refined oral skills - Tape 10 17 MIN
VHS
Teacher to teacher series
Color (T)
$100.00 purchase _ #889 - 7
Shows exerienced teachers in actual classroom settings presenting various instructional approaches to both new and veteran ABE and ESL teachers. Teaches how to balance practice for correct sound and form with practice for fluency. Part ten of a 12 - part series.
Education; English Language
Dist - LAULIT **Prod** - LAULIT

A Sound Idea 30 MIN
U-matic
Magic Ring I Series
(K P)
Helps children discover differences in musical taste, the mechanics of pitch and rhythm and the way in which sound travels.
Education; Literature and Drama
Dist - ACCESS **Prod** - ACCESS 1984

Sound in the Sea 30 MIN
U-matic / VHS
Oceanus - the Marine Environment Series; Lesson 22
Color
Focuses on sound waves in the sea. Explains active and passive sonar and the uses of each. Discusses the shadow zone and the deep sound channel. Compares and contrasts the sound produced by sperm whales and humpback whales.
Science - Natural; Science - Physical
Dist - CDTEL **Prod** - SCCON
SCCON

Sound Level Meter Verification and Data Recording 9 MIN
BETA / VHS
Color
Discusses noise measurement.
Health and Safety; Industrial and Technical Education; Sociology
Dist - RMIBHF **Prod** - RMIBHF

Sound Level Meter Verification and Handling 14 MIN
BETA / VHS
Color
Discusses noise measurement.
Health and Safety; Industrial and Technical Education; Sociology
Dist - RMIBHF **Prod** - RMIBHF

A Sound Motion Picture about Decibels 18 MIN
16mm
Color
Uses simple experiments to illustrate why some sounds please and others annoy.
Science - Natural; Science - Physical
Dist - GM **Prod** - GM

Sound - Noise - Towards a Quieter Environment 20 MIN
U-matic / VHS / 16mm
Color
Describes the effects that the noise of the modern world of technology is having on all of us. Shows that noise affects hearing as well as having serious psychological effects.
Psychology; Science - Natural; Sociology
Dist - CNEMAG **Prod** - DOCUA

The Sound of chartreuse 19 MIN
16mm
Color; B&W (G)
$40.00 rental
Incorporates a surrealistic dream with a sequence from a 1929 Paramount musical.
Fine Arts; Psychology
Dist - CANCIN **Prod** - LEVCHI 1967

A Sound of Dolphins 52 MIN
U-matic / VHS / 16mm
Undersea World of Jacques Cousteau Series
Color (I)
Observes the communication system of dolphins. Shows experiments conducted in an ocean enclosure where the whistle/click conversations between a male and a female dolphin are recorded.
Psychology; Science - Natural
Dist - CF **Prod** - METROM 1977

A sound of dolphins 22 MIN
U-matic / VHS / 16mm
Undersea world of Jacques Cousteau series
Color (G)
$49.95 purchase _ #Q10624; $295.00 purchase - 16 mm, $99.00 purchase - video; LC 77-703457
A shortened version of A Sound Of Dolphins. Documents Jacques Cousteau's investigation of the social behavior and vocal communication of two dolphins caught in the waters off the coast of Spain. Part of a series of 24 programs.
Psychology; Science - Natural
Dist - CF **Prod** - METROM 1977

The Sound of Flesh 11 MIN
16mm
B&W (C A)
Presents a satire on modern mores in society.
Guidance and Counseling; Literature and Drama; Psychology; Sociology
Dist - CFS **Prod** - CFS 1968

Sound of Language Series
Teacher as a Storyteller 20 MIN
Dist - OSUMPD

The Sound of Miles Davis 28 MIN
16mm
B&W
LC FI68-654
Tells the story of Miles Davis. Features music written by Miles Davis and includes performances by Dave Brubeck, Gil Evans, Ahmad Jamal and the Miles Davis Sextet.
Fine Arts
Dist - CBSTV **Prod** - CBSTV 1959

Sound of Music 29 MIN
Videoreel / VT2
Observing Eye Series
Color
Fine Arts; Science - Physical; Sociology
Dist - PBS **Prod** - WGBHTV

The Sound of My Own Name 29 MIN
16mm
Color (T)
LC 75-702488
Shows how the opportunities of adult education can meet the challenge of providing adults with new educational experiences. Examines the problems faced by educationally deprived adult learners and discusses the solutions available through adult education.
Education
Dist - USNAC **Prod** - USOE 1974

Sound of one 12 MIN
16mm
Color (G)
$20.00 rental
Captures the meditative movements of T'ai Chi Ch'uan as the setting behind the solo figure changes from ocean cliff to mountain to studio.
Fine Arts
Dist - CANCIN **Prod** - BARTLS 1976

The Sound of Rushing Water 42 MIN
U-matic / VHS / 16mm
Color
Documents the efforts of the Shuar people of South America to resist the armed might of the Inca and Spanish empires. Tells of their efforts to maintain their cultural identity and traditions in the face of colonizing influences and pressures for social integration from Latin American republics.
History - World; Social Science
Dist - CNEMAG **Prod** - CNEMAG

Sound of Silence 29 MIN
16mm
Color
LC 80-700414
Advocates the preservation of nature while providing a historical account of the Mississippi lands. Reveals what can happen to the land when people begin careless development.
Geography - United States; Science - Natural
Dist - MAETEL **Prod** - MAETEL 1979

The Sound of Silence 26 MIN
16mm / VHS
Color (G)
$450.00 purchase, $70.00 rental _ #8128, 8130, 0424J, 0394J; $450.00 purchase, $55.00 rental _ #81752 film, #81760 video, #81778
Reveals that physical abuse and incest have a high rate of incidence in families where alcohol and drug use is a problem. Addresses the subtle aspects of abuse and enables the recognition of taboo subjects. Produced by Claudia Black.
Guidance and Counseling; Health and Safety; Psychology; Sociology
Dist - HAZELB
CMPCAR

The Sound of Sound 16 MIN
16mm
Color
LC 74-711499
Focuses on industrial noise and its insidious attack on hearing. Industrial workers speak candidly of their occupational deafness in an attempt to motivate industrial employees to wear proper hearing protection.
Health and Safety; Industrial and Technical Education; Science - Natural; Sociology
Dist - AMOPT **Prod** - AMOPT 1970

The Sound of Sounds 15 MIN
16mm
Fingermouse, Yoffy and Friends Series
Color (K P I)
LC 73-700436
Follows Fingermouse and Flash as they collect noises on a tape - recorder to use in a story.
Guidance and Counseling; Literature and Drama
Dist - VEDO **Prod** - BBCTV 1972

Sound of Sunshine, Sound of Rain
16mm / U-matic / VHS
Color (P I)
Looks into the life of a blind, seven - year - old black boy and his intimate world of sounds and touch. Shows how his view of the world is affected by his handicap, his poverty and his race. Shows him on his treasured trips to the park, to the grocery store and into his child's world of sound images.
Education; Psychology
Dist - ALTSUL **Prod** - HALEDA 1983

A Sound of Thanksgiving 30 MIN
16mm
B&W
Features the New York Pro Musica, a group of eleven vocal and instrumental virtuosi. Depicts the use of a variety of rare instruments which provide a musical background for thanksgiving prayers. (Kinescope).
Religion and Philosophy
Dist - NAAJS **Prod** - JTS 1960

Sound of the Lake Country 11 MIN
U-matic
Color (J H C A)
Tells the ecological story of the loon, a northern water bird.
Science - Natural
Dist - CEPRO **Prod** - CEPRO

The Sound of Water 20 MIN
U-matic / VHS
Color
LC 83-706981
Presents three prehistoric cultures of the American Southwest, namely the Anasazi, Hohokam and Sinagua. Spans a period of time between 300 BC to AD 1300.
Geography - United States; Social Science; Sociology
Dist - UARIZ **Prod** - FLNPLN 1983

The Sound of wisdom 60 MIN
VHS
Color (G)
$49.00 purchase _ #HFSW
Presents a documentary about the One World Music Festival of Sacred Chant held at the Cathedral of St John the Divine in New York. Looks at Tibetan Buddhist monks from Gyuto Tantric College and Western composers David Hykes, Pauline Oliveros and Terry Riley. Produced by Robyn Brentano.
Fine Arts; Religion and Philosophy
Dist - SNOWLI **Prod** - SNOWLI

The Sound of Wisdom 57 MIN
VHS / 16mm
Color (H)
$11.00 rental _ #60830
Presents a meeting of the musical traditions of East and West, ancient and modern. Eleven Tibetan Buddhist monks perform their ritual chanting accompanied by Tibetan bells, cymbals, trumpets, and long horns. American composers, such as Philip Glass, whose work is inspired by the sacred music of Tibet, India, and Mongolia, join in the concerts and symposia.
Fine Arts; Religion and Philosophy
Dist - HARTLY **Prod** - CBC 1987
PSU HARTLY

Sound or Unsound 57 MIN
16mm / U-matic / VHS
Music of Man Series
Color (H C A)
Looks at the births of folk, rock and electronic music, which were aided by the long - playing record, the transistor radio and television. Includes the sounds of a Duke Ellington medley, Bing Crosby's crooning, steel drums, Elvis Presley's rock and roll, Bob Dylan's Blowin' In The Wind and punk rock. Gives an account of the additional musical contributions of Faure, Britten, Gagnon, Bartok and Scriabin.
Fine Arts
Dist - TIMLIF **Prod** - CANBC 1981

The Sound Perception Method 39 MIN
16mm
International Education of the Hearing Impaired Child Series
Color
LC 74-705667
Surveys the methods of instruction used at the Institute Voor Doven, Sint Michielsgestel, the Netherlands from home visit through integrated secondary school.
Education; Guidance and Counseling; Psychology
Dist - USNAC **Prod** - USBEH 1970

Sound placement within a word 15 MIN
U-matic / Kit / VHS
Space station readstar series
(P)
$130 purchase, $25 rental, $75 self dub
Teaches phonics in a series designed to supplement second grade reading programs. Focuses on sound placement within words. Fourth in a 25 part series.
English Language
Dist - GPN

Sound sense 30 MIN
U-matic / VHS
Supersense series
Color (H C)
$250.00 purchase _ #HP - 5803C
Explores the world of animal sound production and perception which far exceeds what the human ear can hear. Shows that animals navigate, hunt, find mates, track each other and protect themselves by using sound - and humans are just becoming aware of this complex communication aspect of animals. Part of a series which deals with different facets of animal awareness.
Psychology; Science - Natural; Science - Physical
Dist - CORF **Prod** - BBCTV 1989

A Sound Solution 13 MIN
VHS / U-matic
Color (A)
Stresses that people must share problem of abating noise from aircraft. Covers part of Federal Aviation regulations to show Federal Aviation Administration (FAA) responsibility in this area.
Industrial and Technical Education; Sociology
Dist - AVIMA **Prod** - FAAFL

Sound stills 7 MIN
16mm
Color (G)
$15.00 rental
Presents a series of rephotographed sound sources.
Fine Arts
Dist - CANCIN **Prod** - HUDINA 1975

Sound Waves and Stars - the Doppler Effect 12 MIN
16mm / U-matic / VHS
Color (I J H C) (SPANISH DUTCH)
Explains the Doppler effect, that sound travels in waves, that the waves ahead of a moving source increase in frequency and that the frequency of waves behind such a source decreases. Shows how scientists use the Doppler effect to learn about the universe.
Foreign Language; Science - Physical
Dist - PHENIX **Prod** - FA 1964

Sound Waves in Air 35 MIN
16mm
PSSC Physics Films Series
B&W (H C)
Investigates wave characteristics of sound transmission with large scale equipment, using frequencies up to 5000 cycles. Experiments in reflection, diffraction, interference and refraction are supplemented by ripple - tank analogies.
Science - Physical
Dist - MLA **Prod** - PSSC 1961

Soundaround 30 MIN
16mm / U-matic / VHS
Media Probes Series
Color (H C A)
LC 80-701526
Explores various aspects of the human sound environment. Visits U V Muscio, president of Muzak, whose stimulus programming is contrasted with the experimental music of Obie - winning composer Elizabeth Swados. Looks at the impact of the telephone and discusses the demographic marketing theories of radio programming.
Science - Physical
Dist - TIMLIF **Prod** - LAYLEM 1980

Sounder
U-matic / VHS
Classic Films - on - Video Series
Color (G C J)
$39 purchase _ #05727 - 85
Re - tells William H. Armstrong's story about the lives of the members of a black share - cropper's family. Stars Cicely Tyson and Paul Winfield.
Fine Arts
Dist - CHUMAN

Sounder
Videodisc
Laserdisc learning series
Color; CAV (J H)
$40.00 purchase _ #8L212
Adapts the novel 'Sounder' by William Armstrong. Tells the story of a black family of sharecroppers in rural Louisiana during the Great Depression. A teacher's guide is available separately.
History - United States; Literature and Drama
Dist - BARR **Prod** - BARR 1992

Sounder 105 MIN
VHS
Color; Captioned (G)
$24.95 purchase _ #S00283
Uses a Depression - era Louisiana setting to tell the story of a black sharecropper family and their dog, Sounder. Stars Cicely Tyson, Paul Winfield, and Kevin Hooks. Music by Taj Mahal.
Fine Arts; History - United States
Dist - UILL

Sounder 105 MIN
VHS
Color (J H C)
$39.00 purchase _ #05727 - 126
Stars Cicely Tyson and Paul Winfield in a film adaptation of the William H Armstrong story about a black sharecropper's family.
Fine Arts; History - United States; Literature and Drama; Sociology
Dist - GA **Prod** - GA

Sounder 15 MIN
VHS / U-matic
Storybound Series
Color (I)
Presents passages from William Armstrong's story about a Southern black family and their hunting dog.
Literature and Drama
Dist - CTI **Prod** - CTI
GPN

Sounding Brass 15 MIN
VHS / U-matic
Explorers Unlimited Series
Color (P I)
Observes the assembly of a trombone at the King Instrument Company.
Business and Economics; Fine Arts; Social Science
Dist - AITECH **Prod** - WVIZTV 1971

Sounding for Urethral Strictures 25 MIN
VHS / U-matic
Urology Series
Color (PRO)
Health and Safety; Science - Natural
Dist - MSU **Prod** - MSU

Sounding the alarm - awareness level training 14 MIN
8mm cartridge / VHS / BETA / U-matic
Color; PAL (IND G)
$395.00 purchase, $175.00 rental _ #SOU - 106
Offers HAZWOPER training for any worker who may discover a chemical emergency. Shows workers what to do if they are first on the scene of a HAZMAT incident. Explains the risks associated with hazardous materials, where releases are likely to occur, how to recognize a hazardous material, what can happen in an emergency. Discusses why other specialists are necessary, the types of hazardous materials, the importance of labels and placards to effective spill reporting, the role of awareness - level responder and more. Includes a trainer's manual and ten participant workbooks.
Health and Safety; Psychology
Dist - BNA

Sounds 20 MIN
16mm
All that I Am Series
B&W (C A)
Fine Arts; Guidance and Counseling
Dist - NWUFLM **Prod** - MPATI

Sounds 10 MIN
Videoreel / VT2
Janaki Series
Color
Physical Education and Recreation
Dist - PBS **Prod** - WGBHTV

Sounds 11 MIN
16mm
Color (P I)
LC 75-713638
Presents a multiplicity of common sounds to develop and sharpen language and listening skills through awareness of environmental sounds.
English Language; Fine Arts; Industrial and Technical Education
Dist - FILMSM **Prod** - FILMSM 1971

Sounds 10 MIN
VHS
Stop, look, listen series
Color; PAL (P I J)
Encourages children's awareness of sounds in the environment. Watches a sister and brother getting ready for school as they hear a variety of sounds in and around the home. Presents a short quiz on sounds. Part of a series of films which start from some everyday observation and show more of what is happening, how and why. Builds vocabulary and encourages children to be more observant.
Fine Arts; Psychology; Science - Natural; Sociology
Dist - VIEWTH

Sounds Abound 15 MIN
VHS / U-matic
Strawberry Square II - Take Time Series
Color (P)
Fine Arts
Dist - AITECH **Prod** - NEITV 1984

The Sounds and the Skills 30 MIN
U-matic / VHS
Actor and Shakespeare Series
Color
Outlines and describes the actor's task in interpreting Shakespeare's words. Features Ronald Watkins, Shakespearean actor and director.
Literature and Drama
Dist - NETCHE **Prod** - NETCHE 1971

Sounds Around Us 15 MIN
U-matic / VHS
Matter and Motion Series Module Blue; Module blue
Color (I)
Investigates the origin of sound and how it is received by the human ear.
Science - Natural; Science - Physical
Dist - AITECH **Prod** - WHROTV 1973

Sounds Explored 30 MIN
VHS / U-matic
In Our Own Image Series
Color (C)
Fine Arts
Dist - DALCCD **Prod** - DALCCD

Sounds in the Silent Deep 27 MIN
16mm / VHS
Color (J H C)
LC 73-701165
Studies animal behavior in order to demonstrate the importance of sound to underwater life. Discusses the importance of sound in everyday life.
Psychology; Science - Natural; Science - Physical
Dist - MIS **Prod** - MIS 1972

Sounds interesting 25 MIN
U-matic / VHS / 16mm
Making the most of the micro series; Episode 7
Color (H C A)
Studies how it is possible to generate music with a microcomputer. Introduces Dave Ellis, whose band uses a micro to create music and is provided total freedom to form every aspect of sound. Discusses computer languages and shows a program that works solely on human voice instructions.
Mathematics
Dist - FI **Prod** - BBCTV 1983

Sounds Like Australia 55 MIN
VHS
Color (S)
$129.00 purchase _ #188 - 9026
Brings the vast range of Australia's bird calls, frog croaks and bush sounds together, using an incredible computer to shape, contort and rework them into music. Features composers Kevin Peek and Mars Lasar as the creators. Matches the unique music against superbly photographed wildlife that served as its inspiration.
Fine Arts; Geography - World; Industrial and Technical Education; Science - Natural
Dist - FI **Prod** - FLMAUS 1987

Sounds Like Magic Series
Surprise - Sparkling Stars 15 MIN
There's Magic in Good Speech 15 MIN
Dist - GPN

Sounds like mine series
Mainly for pupils - a very good place to start - melody making - Cassette 5 58 MIN
Mainly for pupils - one plus one - gemini - Cassette 6 57 MIN
Mainly for pupils - pulse, pulse, pulse - Cassette 4 66 MIN
Mainly for teachers - a normal activity - Cassette 1 39 MIN
Mainly for teachers - many voices - talking stick - Cassette 3 58 MIN
Mainly for teachers - sinfonietta education - Cassette 2 58 MIN
Dist - EMFVL

Sounds of Anger, Echoes of Fear 54 MIN
16mm
Color (PRO)
LC 77-702471
Looks at how to deal with the breach in patient and nursing staff relationships. Shows a traumatic situation involving a difficult, abrasive patient and how a clinical nurse, using analysis and techniques of intervention, helps the patient and staff develop insights and solutions.
Health and Safety; Psychology
Dist - AJN **Prod** - AJN 1977

The Sounds of Christmas 29 MIN
VHS / 16mm
Color (G)
$55.00 rental _ #SDSC - 000
Combines Christmas songs with a ballet and puppet version of the Nutcracker.
Fine Arts; Social Science
Dist - PBS

Sounds of Christmas - Songs Performed by the M D Anderson Choir 42 MIN
60 MIN
U-matic
Color
Presents Christmas music performed for the patients at the University of Texas M D Anderson Hospital.
Fine Arts; Social Science
Dist - UTEXSC **Prod** - UTEXSC

Sounds of Cicada 29 MIN
U-matic
B&W
Explores the important role the cicada plays in nature's cycle. Filmed on location in the singing creature's natural habitat.
Science - Natural
Dist - UMITV **Prod** - UMITV 1971

Sounds of Freedom 29 MIN
16mm
Color (H C)
Combines travelogue, consumer education and the economics of the food business in one entertaining and informative documentary. Shows Bob Richards, twice Olympic pole vault champion, on a sight - seeing trip in Europe. Includes the European 'Freedom bell' which rings every day. Leads to facts and conclusions of significance to all Americans.
Geography - World; Home Economics
Dist - NINEFC **Prod** - GEMILL

Sounds of Hope - the Cochlear Implant 50 MIN
U-matic / VHS
Color (PRO)
Presents the concepts of evaluation, placement and rehabilitative measures in the use of the single electrode cochlear implant.
Guidance and Counseling; Health and Safety; Science - Natural
Dist - HOUSEI **Prod** - HOUSEI

The Sounds of Language 32 MIN
16mm
Principles and Methods of Teaching a Second Language Series
B&W (H T) (ENGLISH, SPANISH)
Explains various language sound systems - intonation patterns, rhythms, stresses and sounds. Points out that a problem in learning a second language is the tendency to

carry over sound patterns of one's native speech. Shows a Spanish class for English speakers.
Education; English Language; Foreign Language
Dist - IU **Prod** - MLAA 1962

The Sounds of Love 30 MIN
16mm
Color (R)
Probes the experiences of three well - known Christian women. Examines the lives of Maria Von Trapp, Corrie Ten Boom and Dale Evans.
Guidance and Counseling; Religion and Philosophy; Sociology
Dist - GF **Prod** - GF

Sounds of Love 58 MIN
U-matic / VHS
Color
Presents Dr Leo Buscaglia sharing his inspiring philosophy of interpersonal communication and intimacy. Taped before a live audience at Harvard University's Sanders Theater.
Psychology
Dist - PBS **Prod** - PBS

The Sounds of Mexico 45 MIN
VHS
Color (G)
$39.95 purchase _ #W1469
Focuses on the music characteristic of various regions of Mexico. Features each area's unique rhythms and instruments, including mariachis and marimbas.
Fine Arts
Dist - GPC

The Sounds of Music 15 MIN
U-matic
It's Mainly Music Series
Color (I)
Teaches children the concepts of tone, color, and quality of sound that is special to each voice or instrument.
Fine Arts
Dist - TVOTAR **Prod** - TVOTAR 1983

Sounds of Music 30 MIN
U-matic
Magic Ring II Series
(K P)
Continues the aim of the first series to bring added freshness to the commonplace and assist children to discover more about the many things in their world. Each program starts with the familiar, goes to the less familiar, then the new, and ends by blending new and old information.
Education; Literature and Drama
Dist - ACCESS **Prod** - ACCESS 1986

Sounds of Nature 16 MIN
16mm
Color
Features the use of natural sounds in conjunction with photography. Introduces Dan Gibson, a pioneer in this area who illustrates how such recordings are made and his technique of using blinds to capture wildlife on film.
Fine Arts; Industrial and Technical Education; Science - Physical
Dist - AVEXP **Prod** - AVEXP 1971

Sounds of Nature 26 MIN
16mm
Color
LC 76-702057
Illustrates the ease with which even young children can record bird calls and other sounds of nature with the aid of a cassette recorder and a sound parabola.
Science; Science - Natural; Science - Physical
Dist - KEGPL **Prod** - GIB 1975

The Sounds of New York 60 MIN
VHS / 16mm
Color (G)
$350.00 purchase, $90.00 rental; LC 90706907
Portrays street musicians in New York City. Features performances by a variety of musicians, from students and aspiring amateurs to accomplished musicians who play everything from classical to pop music.
Fine Arts; Geography - United States
Dist - CNEMAG **Prod** - CNEMAG 1990

The Sounds of soul 60 MIN
VHS
History of rock 'n' roll series
Color (G)
$19.99 purchase _ #0 - 7907 - 2429 - 4NK
Examines the soundtrack of the 1960s struggle for civil rights. Features James Brown - Pappa's Got a Brand New Bag; Aretha Franklin - Respect; the Supremes - Stop in the Name of Love; as well as Ray Charles, Otis Redding, the Four Tops, Gladys Knight, Smokey Robinson and more. Part of a ten - part series unfolding the history of rock music. May contain mature subject matter and explicit song lyrics.
Fine Arts; History - United States
Dist - TILIED

The Sounds of Success 30 MIN
U-matic / VHS
Your Speaking Image - When Women Talk Business Series
(C A PRO)
$180.00 purchase
Talks on the techniques that may be used to change a woman's speech patterns to help give a more authoritative and presentable appearance in the office.
English Language
Dist - AITECH **Prod** - WHATV 1986
DELTAK

Sounds of Success 180 MIN
VHS / U-matic
Your Speaking Image - When Women Talk Business Series
Color (H C A)
Business and Economics; Education; Psychology; Sociology
Dist - UEUWIS **Prod** - UEUWIS 1984

Sounds of Success 30 MIN
U-matic / VHS
Your Speaking Image - When Women Talk Business Series
Color
English Language; Psychology
Dist - DELTAK **Prod** - WHATV

Sounds of the Cello 29 MIN
U-matic
Color
Introduces the cello by examining its construction, place in the string family, range and musical qualities. Features Jerome Jelinek, University of Michigan music professor and cellist, as he performs Gabriel Faure's 'Elegy.'.
Fine Arts
Dist - UMITV **Prod** - UMITV 1974

Sounds of the City 30 MIN
U-matic / VHS
In Our Own Image Series
Color (C)
Fine Arts
Dist - DALCCD **Prod** - DALCCD

The Sounds of the Normal Heart 17 MIN
16mm
Color (FRENCH ITALIAN GERMAN SPANISH)
LC FIA65-427;
Demonstrates in a variety of ways the actual phenomena which create the four heart sounds. For first - year medical students.
Health and Safety; Science - Natural
Dist - WSUM **Prod** - WSUM 1964

Sounds of Tibet 120 MIN
VHS / BETA
Color; PAL (G)
PdS18, $36.00 purchase
Features the Tibetan Institute of Performing Arts of India in Brighton, England, August 1988.
Fine Arts; Religion and Philosophy
Dist - MERIDT

The Sounds of Time 28 MIN
U-matic / VHS
Please Stand by - a History of Radio Series
(C A)
Fine Arts; History - United States; Psychology; Sociology
Dist - SCCON **Prod** - SCCON 1986

Sounds of Y 15 MIN
VHS / 16mm
Reading Way Series
Color (P)
$125.00 purchase, $25.00 rental
Demonstrates that "y" at athe beginning of a word is usually a consonant, and a final "y" is usually a vowel.
English Language
Dist - AITECH **Prod** - WXXITV 1988

Sounds on the Sea 28 MIN
16mm
Color
LC 74-705668
Explains that many of the sounds of the sea originate in marine life. Demonstrates how the sounds are analyzed, why the sounds are studied and how they can confuse the sonar operator.
Industrial and Technical Education; Science - Natural; Science - Physical
Dist - USNAC **Prod** - USN 1970

Sounds they make Series
Electronic music 30 MIN
Music in Therapy 30 MIN
Trumpet Music of the Baroque 30 MIN
Writing for the Modern Harp 30 MIN
Dist - OHUTC

Soundtrack 10 MIN
16mm
B&W
Shows how sound and image are conceived together as a unit in the artist's mind and built together frame by frame using the same manual recording process for each.
Fine Arts
Dist - FMCOOP **Prod** - SPINLB 1969

Soup 30 MIN
U-matic
Today's Special Series
Color (K P)
Develops language arts skills in children. Programs are thematically designed around subjects of interest to youngsters. Action takes place in a department store where people, mannequins, puppets, comic characters and special guests present a light hearted approach to language arts.
Fine Arts; Literature and Drama; Psychology
Dist - TVOTAR **Prod** - TVOTAR 1985

Soup and Me 24 MIN
U-matic / VHS / 16mm
Color (I J)
LC 78-701666
Tells about the adventures and misadventures of two boys growing up in a small town in Vermont. An ABC Weekend Special. Based on the books Soup and Soup And Me by Robert Peck.
Guidance and Counseling; Literature and Drama
Dist - CORF **Prod** - ABCTV 1978

Soup for President 24 MIN
16mm / U-matic / VHS
Color (I J)
LC 79-700087
Tells a story about two best friends and their loyalty to each other during election time at school. An ABC Weekend Special. Based on the book Soup For President by Robert Peck.
Guidance and Counseling; Literature and Drama; Social Science
Dist - CORF **Prod** - ABCTV 1979

The Soup of the Day Show 30 MIN
VHS / U-matic
Cookin' Cheap Series
Color
Presents basically crazy cooks Larry Bly and Laban Johnson who offer recipes, cooking and shopping tips.
Home Economics
Dist - MDCPB **Prod** - WBRATV

Soup preparation 15 MIN
U-matic / VHS / 16mm
Professional food preparation and service program series
Color
LC 81-701281
Demonstrates how to prepare various types of soups.
Home Economics
Dist - NEM **Prod** - NEM 1981

The Soup Stone 15 MIN
U-matic / VHS / 16mm
Color (P I)
Relates an old French folk tale about an encounter between two itinerant peddlers and a village of gullible peasants who have hidden all their food. Tells how the peddlers get the villagers to share their food.
Literature and Drama
Dist - LUF **Prod** - LUF 1983

Soup to Nuts Series
The Balancing act 15 MIN
Breaking the fast 15 MIN
Chews for Yourself 15 MIN
Don't weight around 15 MIN
Foodstuff 15 MIN
A Little Bit of Everything 15 MIN
Shopping Sense - Self - Defense 15 MIN
There's no Magic 15 MIN
Tip the Scales in Your Favor 15 MIN
Today, Tomorrow, Forever 15 MIN
Dist - AITECH

Soupa Avgolemono and Pilaf 25 MIN
U-matic / VHS
Color (PRO)
Demonstrates the preparation of avgolemono soup and pilaf, two Middle Eastern dishes. The soup contains lemon juice, eggs and a chicken and rice broth.
Home Economics; Industrial and Technical Education
Dist - CULINA **Prod** - CULINA

Soupe Du Jour 29 MIN
Videoreel / VT2
French Chef - Series
Color (FRENCH)
Features Julia Child of Haute Cuisine au Vin demonstrating how to prepare soupe du jour. With captions.

Foreign Language; Home Economics
Dist - PBS **Prod** - WGBHTV

Soupman 25 MIN
U-matic / VHS / 16mm
Reflections Series
Color (I J H)
LC 81-700676
Tells how a tough 14 - year - old boy breaks into an old woman's house in order to steal her TV, but ends up making friends with her. Explains how he realizes the error of his previous ways and takes to the street to peddle hot soup and sandwiches to old people.
Psychology; Sociology
Dist - PAULST **Prod** - PAULST 1980

Soups
VHS
Frugal gourmet - ancient cuisines from China, Greece and Rome series
Color (G)
$19.95 purchase _ #CCP850
Shows how to prepare soups from the cultures of ancient China, Greece and Rome. Features Jeff Smith, the Frugal Gourmet. Part of a five - part series on ancient cuisines.
History - World; Home Economics; Physical Education and Recreation
Dist - CADESF **Prod** - CADESF

Soups 30 MIN
VHS
Home cooking series
Color (H C G)
$19.95 purchase _ #IVN048V
Features expert chef instructors from the California Culinary Academy in San Francisco who share their secrets on soups. Part of a three - part series on home cooking.
Home Economics
Dist - CAMV

Soups
U-matic
Matter of taste series; Lesson 17
Color (H A)
Describes soup as a creative dish to make, even for the novice cook. Demonstrates basic methods for making meat and chicken stocks.
Home Economics
Dist - CDTEL **Prod** - COAST

Soups 45 MIN
VHS
Le Cordon Bleu cooking series
Color (H C G)
$24.95 purchase _ #LCB003V
Details, with close - up footage, techniques and practical methods needed to prepare a fabulous assortment of soups. Features the world - renowned chefs of Le Cordon Bleu's teaching staff. Part of an eight - part series.
Home Economics
Dist - CAMV

Soups - 132 Clear Soups to 64 Cream Soups - Lesson 3 30 MIN
VHS
International Cooking School with Chef Rene Series
Color (G)
$69.00 purchase
Presents classic methods of cooking that stress essential flavor. Introduces newer, lighter foods. Lesson 3 deals with soups.
Fine Arts; Home Economics; Psychology; Social Science; Sociology
Dist - LUF **Prod** - LUF

Soups and Salads 29 MIN
Videoreel / VT2
Cookin' Cajun Series
Color
Features gourmet - humorist Justin Wilson showing ways to prepare soups and salads with various ingredients.
Geography - United States; Home Economics
Dist - PBS **Prod** - MAETEL

Soups - from Chicken Rice to Shrimp Bisque - Lesson 16 30 MIN
VHS
International Cooking School with Chef Rene Series
Color (G)
$69.00 purchase
Presents classic methods of cooking that stress essential flavor. Introduces newer, lighter foods. Lesson 16 focuses on soups.
Fine Arts; Home Economics; Psychology; Social Science; Sociology
Dist - LUF **Prod** - LUF

Soup's on - mmmmmm...good 24 MIN
35mm strip / VHS
Color (J H C A)
$93.00, $93.00 purchase _ #MB - 481113 - 4, #MB - 512692 - 3
Presents step - by - step instruction in soup making. Teaches how to make brown, white, vegetable and fish soup stocks.
Home Economics; Industrial and Technical Education; Social Science
Dist - SRA **Prod** - SRA

Soups, Salads and Bread 60 MIN
VHS / U-matic
Way to Cook with Julia Child
(C A)
$34.95 _ #KN400V
Features popular American cooking teacher Julia Child as she demonstrates various recipes for soups, salads and bread.
Home Economics; Industrial and Technical Education
Dist - CAMV **Prod** - CAMV

Soups, Salads, and Breads
VHS
Way to Cook - Julia Child Series
$179 purchase _ #5 INCH 45 RPM RECORD700V; $29.95 purchase _ #5 INCH 45 RPM RECORD737V
Features Julia Child showing how to prepare a variety of dishes. Uses a combination of hands - on techniques and practical tips.
Education; Home Economics; Industrial and Technical Education
Dist - CAREER **Prod** - CAREER

Soups, Sauces and Gravies 24 MIN
16mm
Color
LC 74-706582
Shows basic skills and techniques used in the preparation of soups, sauces and gravies.
Home Economics
Dist - USNAC **Prod** - USN 1970

Sour Dough 4 MIN
16mm
Beatrice Trum Hunter's Natural Foods Series
Color
Home Economics
Dist - PBS **Prod** - PBS 1974

Sour Dough 3 MIN
Videoreel / VT2
Beatrice Trum Hunter's Natural Foods Series
Color
Demonstrates two methods of making sour dough. Explains that the easiest way is to take a bit of ordinary yeast bread dough and put it to rest in a crock for a few days. Shows how to make sour dough from scratch by combining water, yeast and flour which, when stored in a crock for a few days, will also become sour dough. Clarifies that either of these added to ordinary bread dough will yield sour dough bread.
Home Economics; Social Science
Dist - PBS **Prod** - WGBH

Sour Grapes 29 MIN
VHS / 16mm
Sonrisas Series
Color (T P) (SPANISH)
$46.00 rental _ #SRSS - 120
Features the children forming their own music group. In Spanish and English.
Fine Arts; Sociology
Dist - PBS

Sour grapes and dog gone - Volume 6 45 MIN
VHS
Flying house series
Color (K P I R)
$11.99 purchase _ #35 - 8955 - 979
Uses an animated format to present events from the New Testament era, as three children, a professor and a robot travel in the 'Flying House' back to that time. 'Sour Grapes' tells the story of Jesus' turning water into wine, while 'Dog Gone' tells how a little girl was healed.
Literature and Drama; Religion and Philosophy
Dist - APH **Prod** - TYHP

The Source 13 MIN
VHS / U-matic
Color (IND)
Deals with the generation and transportation of electricity from the generating station to the home distribution outlet.
Industrial and Technical Education; Social Science
Dist - WHIRL **Prod** - WHIRL

Source of Faith 27 MIN
U-matic / VHS / 16mm
Color (J)
LC 81-700241
Looks at the sights of Israel, focusing on its importance as the source of the Christian faith and depicting sites significant to the Judaic and Islamic religions.
Geography - World
Dist - FI **Prod** - MACMFL 1980

Source of life - water in our environment 22 MIN
VHS
Color (P I J)
$89.00 purchase _ #RB861
Addresses the fact that living things need water to survive. Explains where water is found, how it's used in homes, industry and agriculture. Reveals that the amount of available water cannot be increased and explores the effects of water pollution on humans and other forms of life. Looks at the major causes of water pollution, how society can decrease pollution, and the need for water conservation.
Science - Natural; Science - Physical; Social Science; Sociology
Dist - REVID **Prod** - REVID 1990

Source of Power to Contract 31 MIN
U-matic
Basic Procurement Course Series
Color
LC 80-706739
Explains the legal basis of the authority of federal government contracting officers.
Business and Economics; Civics and Political Systems
Dist - USNAC **Prod** - USGSFC 1978

The Source of Soul 30 MIN
VHS / U-matic
From Jumpstreet Series
Color (J H)
Analyzes the source of soul music by presenting the music of Chuck Brown and the Soul Searchers and Michael Babtunde Olatunji. Hosted by a singer and songwriter Oscar Brown, Jr.
Fine Arts; History - United States; Sociology
Dist - GPN **Prod** - WETATV 1979
PBS

Source of strength 29 MIN
VHS
Color (G C)
$135.00 purchase, $45.00 rental
Shows four elderly people as they consider their Jewish heritage's significance for them in age. Points out that one's ethnicity can be a source of strength and consolation.
Health and Safety; Religion and Philosophy; Sociology
Dist - TNF

Source of the Amazon 11 MIN
16mm / U-matic / VHS
Color (I J H C)
Traces the Amazon from its source in the highest peaks of the Andes through the jungle to the ocean.
Geography - World
Dist - IFB **Prod** - IFB 1947

Source Rocks 24 MIN
VHS / U-matic
Basic and Petroleum Geology for Non - Geologists - Hydrocarbons and '- Series; Hydrocarbons
Color (IND)
Industrial and Technical Education; Science - Physical
Dist - GPCV **Prod** - PHILLP

Source Rocks, Generation, Migration, and Accumulation 33 MIN
U-matic / VHS
Petroleum Geology Series
Color (IND)
Industrial and Technical Education; Science - Physical
Dist - GPCV **Prod** - GPCV

Sourced in God alone 60 MIN
VHS
Guidelines for growing spiritually mature series
Color (R G)
$49.95 purchase _ #GGSM1
Challenges Christians in today's world to hear anew and respond joyfully to the universal call to holiness. Focuses on one phase of the journey to maturity in the spiritual sense. Offers guidelines according to the teachings of the Roman Catholic Church. Features Dr Susan Muto and the Rev Adrian Van Kaam. Part one of six parts.
Religion and Philosophy
Dist - CTNA **Prod** - CTNA

Sources - a Matter of Trust 29 MIN
VHS / U-matic
Inside Story Series
Color
Looks at the use of confidential sources in the wake of the Janet Cooke Pulitzer Prize fiasco in the Washington Post and the explosion of press self - examination that followed.
Literature and Drama; Social Science; Sociology
Dist - PBS **Prod** - PBS 1981

Sources and Uses of Light and Sound 29 MIN
VHS / 16mm
Villa Alegre Series

Color (P T) (SPANISH)
$46.00 rental _ #VILA - 115
Presents educational material about sound and light.
Education; Science - Physical
Dist - PBS

Sources of Capital 11 MIN
16mm
Running Your Own Business Series
Color
Explains methods by which a firm can most economically generate additional sources of capital for either ongoing business or expansion.
Business and Economics
Dist - EFD **Prod** - EFD

Sources of Capital 30 MIN
U-matic
It's Everybody's Business Series Unit 3, Financing a Business
Color
Business and Economics
Dist - DALCCD **Prod** - DALCCD

Sources of Conflict 12 MIN
Videoreel / VT2
Interpersonal Competence, Unit 01 - the Self Series; Unit 1 - The self
Color (C A)
Features a humanistic psychologist who, by analysis and examples, discusses sources of internal conflict.
Psychology; Sociology
Dist - TELSTR **Prod** - MVNE 1973

Sources of conflict - Tape 3 25 MIN
VHS
Church leaders under fire series
Color (A R PRO)
$10.00 rental _ #36 - 83 - 222
Shows that conflict is not unheard of within a church. Suggests that conflict, however, is not part of the image most have of the church. Produced by Priority Publishing.
Religion and Philosophy
Dist - APH

Sources of Dance 15 MIN
U-matic / VHS / 16mm
Dance Experience - Training and Composing Series
Color (J H C)
Deals with origins of ideas for composition and the exploration of those ideas by extending them into studies for choreography.
Fine Arts
Dist - ATHI **Prod** - ATHI 1984

Sources of Electrical Energy 30 MIN
VHS / U-matic
Basic Electricity, DC Series
Color (IND)
Covers sources of electrical energy including chemical reaction, electromagnetic induction, heat, light and pressure. Explains difference between primary and secondary cell and outlines transformer and generator action.
Industrial and Technical Education; Science - Physical
Dist - AVIMA **Prod** - AVIMA

Sources of Foreign Material 20 MIN
U-matic / VHS
Food Safety and Plant Maintenance Series
Color
Discusses actual observations of frequently overlooked sources of foreign materials that can get into food, relating to maintenance activities, with emphasis on participation and cooperation, recognizing and reacting.
Agriculture; Health and Safety; Industrial and Technical Education; Social Science
Dist - PLAID **Prod** - PLAID

Sources of Funds 30 MIN
U-matic / VHS
Engineering Economy Series
Color (IND)
Describes common sources of funds to finance investment projects. Shows examination of financial statement of a corporation as example problem.
Business and Economics
Dist - COLOSU **Prod** - COLOSU

Sources of ideas for drawing 29 MIN
U-matic
Sketching techniques series; Lesson 25
Color (C A)
Suggests where to look for new sketching ideas. Explains the value of researching ideas for drawing.
Fine Arts
Dist - CDTEL **Prod** - COAST

Sources of Income 30 MIN
VHS / U-matic
How People Age 50 and Up Can Plan for a more Successful Retirement 'Series
Color
Discusses sources, adequacy, and methods of increasing retirement income. Presented by Edwin Carey and Wilton Heyliger, Howard University School of Business and Public Administration.
Sociology
Dist - SYLWAT **Prod** - RCOMTV

The Sources of international politics 60 MIN
VHS
Europe and America in the modern age - 1776 to the present series
Color (H C PRO)
$95.00 purchase
Presents a lecture by James Sheehan. Focuses on a critical period in European and American history and on leaders of the time. Part of a 20 - part series that looks at the last two centuries in Europe and America. Series presents lectures by David M Kennedy and James Sheehan of Stanford University on such figures as Adam Smith, Marx, Lincoln, Washington, Jefferson, Freud, Margaret Sanger, Susan B Anthony and Jane Adams and their impact on the events of their day. For history resource material and continuing education courses.
Civics and Political Systems; History - United States; History - World
Dist - LANDMK

Sources of Law 19 MIN
U-matic / VHS
Ways of the Law Series
Color (H)
Takes a historical look at our legal system, tracing the roots of law from the Code of Hammurabi to the American Bill of Rights.
Civics and Political Systems
Dist - GPN **Prod** - SCITV 1980

Sources of stress 21 MIN
VHS / U-matic / BETA
Stress series
Color (C PRO)
$150.00 purchase _ #131.2
Presents a video transfer from slide program which examines the sources of stress ranging from specific physical stresses to complex psychological and social phenomena. Presents Holmes and Rahe's study of major life events as stressors, dramatizing this with a documentary interview. Discusses variables which determine individual stress reactions, including interviews focusing on determining factors such as personal resources and past experiences. Part of a series on stress.
Guidance and Counseling; Health and Safety; Psychology
Dist - CONMED **Prod** - CONMED

Sourdough
VHS
Frugal gourmet - American classics series
Color (G)
$19.95 purchase _ #CCP830
Shows how to prepare American style sourdough bread. Features Jeff Smith, the Frugal Gourmet. Part of the nine - part series, American Classics.
History - United States; Home Economics
Dist - CADESF **Prod** - CADESF

Sourwood Mountain Dulcimers 28 MIN
U-matic / 16mm
Color
LC 77 - 700576
Examines the arts of dulcimer building and playing as part of the Appalachian heritage.
Fine Arts; Geography - United States; Sociology
Dist - APPAL **Prod** - APPAL 1977

Sous Les Mots - La Linquistique 35 MIN
U-matic / VHS
Color (C) (FRENCH)
$279.00, $179.00 purchase _ #AD - 1049
Introduces the basic elements of the French language, structure, sounds and the combination of grammar, vocabulary, syntax, pronunciation and usage. Produced by the French Ministry of Education.
Foreign Language
Dist - FOTH **Prod** - FOTH

Sous Un Jour Nouveau 13 MIN
16mm
Family Relations - Series
Color (K P) (FRENCH)
LC 76-700140
Presents a version of the motion picture New Look. Provides an explanation of family relations.
Sociology
Dist - MORLAT **Prod** - MORLAT 1974

The South 24 MIN
16mm / VHS / U-matic 24 MIN
12 MIN
24 MIN
Color (I J H) (ITALIAN JAPANESE GERMAN PORTUGUESE SPANISH FRENCH)
LC 73-702371
Presents a study of the people who make the South a distinct cultural and geographic entity within the whole of America. Describes the history and geography of the South.
Geography - United States; History - United States; Social Science
Dist - AIMS **Prod** - PAR 1973

South Africa 22 MIN
U-matic / VHS / 16mm
Color (J H)
LC 79-701766
Surveys the industrial activities, agriculture and mining in South Africa. Shows the Zulus and their customs, and views of Kruger National Park.
Geography - World; History - United States
Dist - MCFI **Prod** - HOE 1962

South Africa - a journey of discovery 54 MIN
VHS
Color (G)
$29.95 purchase _ #ST - IV1301
Visits Johannesburg. Discovers the Zulu people in Durban and takes a photo safari at the Londolozi Game Reserve.
Geography - World
Dist - INSTRU

South Africa - after apartheid 25 MIN
VHS / U-matic / 16mm / BETA
Color (J H G)
$390.00, $110.00 purchase _ #C50817, #C51519
Examines the political policy of apartheid, its origins, enforcement and effect upon the people and economy of South Africa. Reveals that apartheid has been abolished by de Klerk, but asks if it is truly dead.
Geography - World; Sociology
Dist - NGS **Prod** - NGS 1992

South Africa and Apartheid 29 MIN
Videoreel / VT2
Course of Our Times II Series
Color
Geography - World; History - World
Dist - PBS **Prod** - WGBHTV

South Africa Belongs to Us 55 MIN
U-matic / 16mm / VHS
Color
Portrays the lives of five typical South African women who convey the economic and emotional burdens borne by black women under apartheid.
History - United States; History - World
Dist - CANWRL **Prod** - CANWRL 1981

South Africa Belongs to Us 57 MIN
U-matic / VHS / 16mm
Color
Views the devastating impact of apartheid on black women and the black family in South Africa. Looks at the life of a domestic servant in a white household, at the experiences in an illegal black shantytown and at a nurse at one of the few family planning clinics in Soweto.
History - World
Dist - ICARUS **Prod** - AUCHWE 1980

South Africa - Best - Kept Secret 27 MIN
VHS
Color (G)
Tours countryside and cities of South Africa. Includes sunset cruise from Hout Bay to Cape Town. Available for free loan from the distributor.
Geography - World
Dist - AUDPLN

South Africa debate - September 4, 1985
VHS
Nightline news library series
Color (J H C)
$19.98 purchase _ #MH6150V - S
Focuses on the political debate in South Africa in a news story by the ABC News Team. Part of a series from the news program, Nightline.
Geography - World; Sociology
Dist - CAMV **Prod** - ABCNEW 1985

South Africa (International Byline) 28 MIN
Videoreel / VHS
International Byline Series
Color
Interviews Mr David Steward, Counselor of the Permanent Mission of South Africa to the United Nations and Mr Carl Frank Noffke, Information Counselor of the Embassy of South Africa to the United States. Includes films on 'Zulu' and on Namibia.
Business and Economics; Civics and Political Systems; Geography - World
Dist - PERRYM **Prod** - PERRYM

South Africa - the Riot that Won't Stop 59 MIN
VHS / 16mm
Color (G)
$70.00 rental _ #SARS - 000
Examines the everyday lives of blacks and whites in South Africa. Shows how individuals are dealing with sharpening lines of conflict and increasing political pressure.
Geography - World; Sociology
Dist - PBS **Prod** - WGBHTV

South Africa - the wasted land 52 MIN
VHS
Color (H C G)
$445.00 purchase, $75.00 rental
Illustrates the link between the Apartheid policy of South Africa and its rapidly eroding environment. Reveals that severe overcrowding of the black population to barely life - sustaining 'homeland' areas has caused land to be over - grazed and severely eroded. Because the homelands lack electricity, trees are cut for fuel, leaving the soil more erosion vulnerable. South Africa also releases substantial amounts of toxic waste into the environment. Many homelands were established close to industrialized areas, increasing incidence of respiratory disease, and asbestos mines closed in the 1970s were not properly sealed off, leaving black families living in the midst of poisonous waste.
Agriculture; Geography - World; Sociology
Dist - FLMLIB **Prod** - CFTV 1991

South Africa - the White Laager 59 MIN
16mm / U-matic / VHS
Color (I)
LC 78-700113
Explores the history of the Afrikaners from the arrival of the Dutch in 1652 to South Africa's adoption of the apartheid system.
Geography - World; History - World; Sociology
Dist - LCOA **Prod** - WGBHTV 1978

South Africa Wildlife 15 MIN
VHS / U-matic
Color
Tells how wildlife in South Africa is endangered by man and discusses an approach to solving this problem.
Geography - World; Science - Natural
Dist - JOU **Prod** - UPI

South African Chronicles 105 MIN
VHS
Color (C)
$490.00 purchase, $90.00 rental
Comprises nine short documentaries produced by twelve young filmmakers at the racially integrated Varan Workshop of Johnannesburg. Presents through their lenses a view of South Africa rarely seen by outsiders. Includes a local election campaign in a small mining town, senior citizens gathering to collect pension checks in Soweto, a meeting of the Afrikaner Resistance Movement led by Eugene Terreblanche, and the work of Process, a shelter for street children in Hibrow, Johannesburg.
Fine Arts; Geography - World; History - United States; Sociology
Dist - ICARUS

South African Essay, Pt 1, Fruit of Fear 59 MIN
U-matic / VHS / 16mm
Changing World Series
B&W (H C A)
LC FIA68-2321
Reports on the South African dual standards of living from the lavish white sections to the black ghettos. Interviews such people as Nobel Peace Prize winner Chief Albert Luthuli, Frank Waring and author Alan Paton as to their attitudes toward this condition.
Geography - World; History - United States; Psychology; Sociology
Dist - IU **Prod** - NET 1965

South African Essay - Pt 2 - One Nation , Two Nationalisms 59 MIN
U-matic / VHS / 16mm
Changing World Series
B&W (H C A)
LC FIA68-2322
Examines the political machinery with which apartheid is enforced. Interviews white and black South Africans. Focuses on the power of the White Nationalist Party.
Civics and Political Systems; Geography - World; History - United States; Psychology; Sociology
Dist - IU **Prod** - NET 1965

A South African farm 51 MIN
16mm / VHS
Color (G)
$700.00, $400.00 purchase, $70.00, $40.00 rental
Observes the everyday workings of apartheid on a farm owned by the filmmaker's godfather. Reveals that the black workers enjoy fairly decent living conditions, although black pupils must walk for miles to school while white pupils take a bus to their school in town. Considers that whites are driven by a fear of losing privilege and blacks are torn between the material benefits of white 'protection' and the desire to be free from oppression. Produced by Paul Laufer.
Geography - World; Sociology
Dist - DOCEDR **Prod** - DOCEDR

South America 25 MIN
16mm / U-matic / VHS
Untamed World Series
Color; Mono (J H C A)
$400.00 film, $250.00 video, $50.00 rental
Features a journey across the plains, mountains, and through the jungles of South America to analyze the diverse animal life.
Geography - World; Science - Natural
Dist - CTV **Prod** - CTV 1973

South America 25 MIN
VHS / U-matic / 16mm / BETA
Physical geography of the continents series
Color (P I J H)
$390.00, $110.00 purchase _ #C50636, #C51441
Journeys to the fourth largest continent, South America. Looks at the world's longest mountain range, the Andes, the driest desert - the Atacama, and the Amazon River with its vast surrounding rain forest. Travels from Lake Titicaca in the Andes' high plateau to the Pampas, fertile plains of Argentina. Part of a six - part series on the physical geography of the continents.
Geography - World
Dist - NGS **Prod** - NGS 1991

South America - a Trilogy Series
Bolivia - the tin mountain 27 MIN
Brazil - Children of the Miracle 27 MIN
Peru - the Revolution that Never was 27 MIN
Dist - MEDIAG

South America and Antarctica - Vol 3
Kit / Videodisc
STV - World geography series
Color (I J H) (ENGLISH, SPANISH)
$225.00 purchase _ #T81577; $325.00 purchase _ #T81601
Unfolds the physical features, climate and plant and animal life of the continents of South America and Antarctica. Includes glossary, photos and more. Basic kit is available at lower price. Expanded kit includes software compatible to Mactinosh only. Volume 3 of 3 volume series.
Geography - World
Dist - NGS

South America - Cartagena, a Colonial City 17 MIN
U-matic / VHS / 16mm
Color (I J H)
Presents a typical day in the life of a young boy in Cartagena, Colombia, to show aspects of life unique to South America. Describes the boy's daily routine of meals, school and errands for his mother.
Geography - World
Dist - PHENIX **Prod** - EVANSA 1970

South America - Estancia in Argentina 21 MIN
16mm / U-matic / VHS
Color (I J H)
Explores agricultural life in contemporary Argentina, showing the estancias (large ranches) on the fertile pampas. Tells how these huge ranches, although modern in some respects, resemble the feudal estates of the Middle Ages in which the wealthy owner feeds, clothes and shelters his workers and their families, most of whom spend their entire lives on the estancia.
Geography - World
Dist - PHENIX **Prod** - EVANSA 1969

South America Films Series
South America - Land of many Faces 15 MIN
South America - the Widening Gap 15 MIN
Dist - MGHT

South America, History and Heritage 17 MIN
16mm / U-matic / VHS
Color (I J H)
LC 78-700934
Presents the history of South America from the 15th century to the 1970s. Deals with Inca civilization, the impact of colonial rule and the struggle for political and economic independence.
History - World
Dist - PHENIX **Prod** - NEMESA 1978

South America - Indians of the Andes 21 MIN
U-matic / VHS / 16mm
Color (J H)
Portrays the primitive way of life of an Inca boy and his family in an isolated Peruvian village in the Andes mountains.
Geography - World; Social Science
Dist - PHENIX **Prod** - EVANSA 1969

South America, Land and People 21 MIN
U-matic / VHS / 16mm
Color (I J H)
LC 78-701001
Presents a geographical and cultural tour of South America, including the resources and economics of its major geographical regions. Presents important cities and historical sites.
Geography - World; Social Science
Dist - PHENIX **Prod** - NEMESA 1978

South America - Land of many Faces 15 MIN
U-matic / VHS / 16mm
South America Films Series
Color (I J)
LC 75-702559
Examines the contrasting characteristics of the nations and cultures of South America. Shows how the geography of South America includes high mountains, jungles and temperate regions.
Geography - World
Dist - MGHT **Prod** - MGHT 1975

South America - Life in the City 10 MIN
U-matic / VHS / 16mm
Color (I J H)
LC 77-713570
Portrays the contrasts of progress and poverty, and old and new that exist in the South American cities of Rio De Janeiro and Sao Paulo in Brazil, Buenos Aires, Argentina, Caracas, Venezuela, Santiago, Chile, and Lima, Peru.
Geography - World; Sociology
Dist - PHENIX **Prod** - EVANSA 1971

South America - Market Day 10 MIN
16mm / U-matic / VHS
Color (I J)
Depicts market day in South America as an exciting, important and colorful event. Allows students to draw many conclusions about economic and social life in South American villages.
Geography - World; Sociology
Dist - PHENIX **Prod** - EVANSA 1971

South America - Overview 17 MIN
16mm
Latin American Series - a Focus on People Series
Color (I J H)
LC 73-703063
Explains that South America's move toward a modern society has been slow. Describes the change in the air.
Geography - World; Social Science; Sociology
Dist - SF **Prod** - CLAIB 1972

South America - the Widening Gap 15 MIN
U-matic / VHS / 16mm
South America Films Series
Color (I J)
LC 75-702560
Examines the widening gap between the rich and the poor in South America and shows how population growth could outstrip South America's resources and its ability to develop these resources.
Geography - World; Science - Natural; Social Science
Dist - MGHT **Prod** - MGHT 1975

South America today 28 MIN
U-matic / VHS / BETA
Color; PAL (G H C)
PdS50, PdS58 purchase
Documents the impressive trans - Amazon highway, the great varieties of people and topography of South America.
Fine Arts; Geography - World
Dist - EDPAT

South American Coast 25 MIN
U-matic / VHS / 16mm
Untamed World Series
Color; Mono (J H C A)
$400.00 film, $250.00 video, $50.00 rental
Focuses on some of the varied animal and plant life found along the shores of the South American continent.
Geography - World; Science - Natural
Dist - CTV **Prod** - CTV 1973

South American Instruments - Pt 1 17 MIN
VHS / U-matic
Musical Instruments Series
Color
Fine Arts; Geography - World
Dist - GPN **Prod** - WWVUTV

South American Instruments - Pt 2 19 MIN
U-matic / VHS
Musical Instruments Series
Color
Fine Arts; Geography - World
Dist - GPN **Prod** - WWVUTV

South American series
Takes a look at South America under the following headings - Agriculture and industry; Blend of cultures; Physical geography; Rural life; and Urban life.
South American series 90 MIN
Dist - EMFVL **Prod** - STANF

South American Tribes 25 MIN
U-matic / VHS / 16mm
Untamed World Series Series
Color; Mono (J H C A)
$400.00 film, $250.00 video, $50.00 rental
Explores the history and culture of some of the South American tribal societies.
Geography - World; Sociology
Dist - CTV **Prod** - CTV 1969

South Americans in Cordoba 13 MIN
16mm
Color (J H C) (SPANISH)
Introduces artists represented at the 1967 Cordoba Biennial in Argentina.
Fine Arts; Geography - World
Dist - MOMALA **Prod** - OOAS MOMALA 1966

South - Ao dai - the tunic dress 3 MIN
VHS
Color (G)
$160.00 purchase, $35.00 rental
Considers the visibility of ao dai, the traditional Vietnamese tunic dress, as a gauge of Vietnam's prosperity. Explains how the custom of wearing the graceful dresses has returned with traditional ceremonies and religious rituals being celebrated again as post - war Vietnam experiences a cultural rebirth. Produced by Le Trac.
Fine Arts
Dist - FIRS

South Asia - using Forest Resources 15 MIN
U-matic / VHS
Global Geography Series
Color (I J)
$125.00 purchase
Researches the use of forest resources in South Asia and its implications for the future.
Agriculture; Geography - World
Dist - AITECH **Prod** - AITECH 1987

The South Atlantic - a coast of contrasts 55 MIN
VHS
On the waterways series
Color (G H)
$29.95 purchase _ #OW05
Travels with the crew of the Driftwood from slavery's origins to the birthplace of flight and through some of the United States most isolated communities. Narrated by Jason Robards. Part of a 13 - part series on the history, geography, culture and ecology of North American waterways.
Social Science
Dist - SVIP

The South Atlantic Region 15 MIN
U-matic / VHS / 16mm
U S Geography Series
Color (J)
LC 76-701775
Examines the people, industry, economy and landscape of the South Atlantic region of the United States.
Business and Economics; Geography - United States; Geography - World; Social Science
Dist - MGHT **Prod** - MGHT 1976

South - Birth of a democracy 25 MIN
VHS
Color (G)
$190.00 purchase, $45.00 rental
Surveys Cameroon's political climate after declaring itself, in 1990, a multi - party democracy after 30 years of totalitarian rule. Provides insights into the complications arising - mobilizing the populace when 70 percent speak neither French nor English, the nation's official languages - and dealing with 40 political parties that emerged one month into its newborn democracy. Produced by Bassek Ba Khobio.
Business and Economics; Civics and Political Systems; Fine Arts; History - World
Dist - FIRS

South Brazil 19 MIN
16mm
Latin American Series - Focus on People Series
Color (I J H)
Depicts the area between Rio De Janeiro, Santos and Sao Paulo, the center of developed wealth and population of Brazil, the largest country on the continent of South America. Shows how Brazil is now well into a period of unprecedented economic growth which has not affected most of the people and has been achieved only at the expense of some personal and institutional liberties.
Geography - World; Social Science
Dist - SF **Prod** - CLAIB 1972

South by northwest series
Aunt Tish 30 MIN
Cayton family 30 MIN
Holmes Vs Ford 30 MIN
Homesteaders 30 MIN
Montana, Pt 1 30 MIN
Montana, Pt 2 30 MIN
The Roslyn Migration 30 MIN
York 30 MIN
Dist - GPN

South Carolina 60 MIN
VHS
Portrait of America series
Color (J H C G)
$99.95 purchase _ #AMB40V
Visits South Carolina. Offers extensive research into the US state's history. Films key locations and presents segments on its history, government, education, folklore, science, journalism, sociology, industry, agriculture and business. Shows what is unique about South Carolina and what is distinctive about its regional culture and how it got to be that way. Includes teacher study guides. Part of a 50 - part series.
Geography - United States; History - United States
Dist - CAMV

South Carolina and the United States 28 MIN
VHS
This Constitution - a history series
Color (H C G)
$180.00 purchase, $19.00 rental _ #35738
Surveys and analyzes the way national and state governments divide sovereignty and share responsibility for public safety and well being. Focuses on South Carolina to examine the complex and shifting political forces and social and economic interests that shaped the American state government system from its origins to the 1980s. Part of a five - part series on the philosophical origins, drafting and interpretation of the US Constitution and its effect on American society, produced by the International University Consortium and Project '87.
Civics and Political Systems; History - United States
Dist - PSU

The South Central Region 15 MIN
16mm / U-matic / VHS
U S Geography Series
Color (J)
LC 76-701776
Examines the people, industry, economy and landscape of the South Central region of the United States.
Business and Economics; Geography - United States; Geography - World; Social Science
Dist - MGHT **Prod** - MGHT 1976

South China Seas 91 MIN
VHS
Rick Ray series
Color (G H)
$29.95 purchase _ #WW08
Explores the South China Seas.
Geography - World
Dist - SVIP

South Dakota 60 MIN
VHS
Portrait of America series
Color (J H C G)
$99.95 purchase _ #AMB41V
Visits South Dakota. Offers extensive research into the state's history. Films key locations and presents segments on its history, government, education, folklore, science, journalism, sociology, industry, agriculture and business. Shows what is unique about South Dakota and what is distinctive about its regional culture and how it got to be that way. Includes teacher study guides. Part of a 50 - part series.
Geography - United States; History - United States
Dist - CAMV

South Dakota Gold Miners 20 MIN
U-matic / VHS
Color
Depicts problems of South Dakota gold miners, focusing on the famous Hearst empire mine, the Homestake Gold Mine. Considers working conditions, lung diseases, loss of pensions and a strike.
Business and Economics; Social Science; Sociology
Dist - DCTVC **Prod** - DCTVC

South Dakota's Black Hills, Badlands and lakes 60 MIN
U-matic / VHS / BETA
National park series
Color (G)
$46.00, $155.00 purchase _ #LSTF104
Explores the variety of vacation spots in South Dakota. Produced by Panacom, Inc.
Geography - United States
Dist - FEDU

South - Democracy in crisis 50 MIN
VHS
Color (G)
$390.00 purchase, $75.00 rental
Covers the 20 months in India following Rajiv Gandhi's ouster in 1989, through his assassination, and the violent and chaotic election which followed it. Moves from countrysides to cities, universities to dusty villages, and from interviews with India's uneducated castes to campaign trips with Prime Ministerial candidates. Examines the strains in India's social fabric caused by the political emergence of the lower castes, who are 52 percent of the population; the revival of Hindu fundamentalism, nurtured by the right wing; and perceived interference by outside organizations. Produced by Manjira Datta.
Civics and Political Systems; Fine Arts; Geography - World; History - World; Religion and Philosophy; Sociology
Dist - FIRS

South - east England 20 MIN
VHS
Regional geography of England series
Color; PAL (P I J)
PdS29
Focuses on the regional geography of southeastern England. Offers teacher's notes upon request. Part of a series.
Geography - World
Dist - BHA

The South - East Nuba 60 MIN
U-matic / VHS / 16mm
Worlds Apart Series
Color (J)
Analyzes the Nuba who live in a very remote part of Africa near the center of the Sudan. Shows that they have their own flamboyant culture which includes body painting and the sport of bracelet fighting.
History - World; Sociology
Dist - FI **Prod** - BBCTV 1982

South - El Rojo para los labios - Red for the lips 12 MIN
VHS
Color (G)
$160.00 purchase, $35.00 rental
Employs a mixture of video graphics, computer animation and documentary footage. Uses the metaphor of a disenchanted and lethargic woman to lament the loss of Cuba's revolutionary ideals and fervor. Produced by Pablo Basulto.
Fine Arts; Geography - World; Literature and Drama
Dist - FIRS

South - Farewell, GDR 25 MIN
VHS
Color (G)
$190.00 purchase, $45.00 rental
Follows the many young people who left Mozambique in the 1980s in search of work and better lives in Germany. Reveals the discrimination and open hostility they encountered, which caused many to repatriate, only to find themselves outsiders in their own land. Produced by Licinio Azvedo.
Fine Arts; History - World; Sociology
Dist - FIRS

South - Female college students in China 26 MIN
VHS
Color (G) (CHINESE WITH ENGLISH SUBTITLES)
$190.00 purchase, $45.00 rental
Surveys current attitudes on Chinese campuses. Interviews a law student, a fashion design student and an activist who took part in the hunger strikes after the Tiananmen Square uprising. The common thread that runs through the discussions is the continued government repression of individuality or any sense of self - worth. All three are looking abroad for opportunities. Produced by Tian Zhuang Zhuang.
Civics and Political Systems; Fine Arts; Geography - World; Psychology
Dist - FIRS

South from Valdez 21 MIN
16mm
Color
LC 80-700387
Documents a a single voyage of a large crude - oil carrier from the port of Valdez to the refinery in San Francisco.
Social Science
Dist - MTP **Prod** - EXXON 1980

South - Guatemalan report 9 MIN
VHS
Color (G)

$160.00 purchase, $30.00 rental
Covers the October 1991 Congress of Indigenous American Peoples held in Guatemala. Looks at how the congress provided a forum for native Americans from both continents to express grievances and to protest the upcoming Columbus quincentennial. Produced by Felix Zurita.
Civics and Political Systems; Fine Arts; Sociology
Dist - FIRS

South - Hado 13 MIN
VHS
Color (G)
$160.00 purchase, $35.00 rental
Portrays Hado Gorgo Leontine, a 60 - year - old grandmother and farmer in Burkina Faso, and the leader of a 22 piece touring orchestra. Follows her troupe of musicians, singers and ten dancers who travel the country performing traditional songs as well as her own compositions. Produced by Gaston Kabore.
Fine Arts; History - World; Sociology
Dist - FIRS

South - Haiti 6 MIN
VHS
Color (G)
$75.00 purchase, $25.00 rental
Reveals Jean Bertrand Aristide's Lavalas - 'avalanche' in English - government, which meant to bring democracy, land reform and human rights to impoverished Haiti. Interviews Aristide in exile since the coup d'etat led by General Raoul Cedras. Produced by Jorge Denti.
Fine Arts; History - World
Dist - FIRS

The South - Health and Hunger 23 MIN
16mm
B&W (H C A)
LC 78-707229
Discusses inadequate nutrition, lack of water, and too few medical facilites - problems which affect both the physical and mental development of southern blacks. Interviews the only black obstetrician in Mississippi and a midwife.
History - United States; Science - Natural; Social Science; Sociology
Dist - IU **Prod** - NET 1969

South - Islam and feminism 25 MIN
VHS
Color (G)
$190.00 purchase, $45.00 rental
Examines the inequities in Pakistan's Islamic law, which does not distinguish among rape, adultery and 'fornication.' Looks at the contradictory laws and lists examples: a man and woman arrested for fornicating were sentenced to 100 lashes and death by stoning; the testimony of two women in Pakistani courts is valued as equal to that of one man; although some of the country's most prominent leaders are women, a rape victim can be charged under Islamic law with having had extramarital sex. Introduces the efforts of organizations like the urban Women's Action Forum to battle this severe discrimination. Produced by Nighat Said Khan.
Civics and Political Systems; Fine Arts; History - World; Religion and Philosophy; Sociology
Dist - FIRS

South - Jagriti - The Awakening 25 MIN
VHS
Color (G)
$190.00 purchase, $45.00 rental
Presents a case study of the political red tape and corruption often encountered by samaritans in poor areas all around the world. Focuses on Motia Khan, a slum in the poorest district of Delhi, home to 5000 shacks, and Jagriti, a school for Motia Khan's children. Weaves interviews with local politicians and administrators of aid organizations, including OXFAM and UNICEF, with satirical sketches of these people performed by the students. Produced by Jugnu Ramaswamy.
Civics and Political Systems; Education; Fine Arts; Geography - World; Sociology
Dist - FIRS

South - Kaiso for July 27th 23 MIN
VHS
Color (G)
$180.00 purchase, $40.00 rental
Examines the tensions in Trinidad and Tobago society which may have led to the July, 27, 1990 coup attempt by the Black Muslim group Jammaat al Muslimeen. Interviews Trinidadians who explain the economic hardships suffered as oil prices fell through the 1980s. Reveals the impact of the coup one year later.
Business and Economics; Fine Arts; History - World
Dist - FIRS **Prod** - MARKAR 1991

South Korea - the Future of Democracy 30 MIN
VHS
World Beat - Great Decisions In Foreign Policy Series
Color (G)
$39.95 purchase _ #WDBT - 104
Uses the example of South Korea to consider the question of how the American government can promote democracy in another nation while ensuring its stability. Features various experts on Korea.
Civics and Political Systems; History - World
Dist - PBS **Prod** - WETATV 1988

South - La Esperanza incierta - Uncertain hope 52 MIN
VHS
Color (G)
$390.00 purchase, $75.00 rental
Looks at the current socio - political climates in four South American countries - Brazil, Uruguay, Argentina and Chile. Interviews heads of state, intellectuals, politicians, journalists, former members of the military regimes, and common people on the streets, giving a wide range of opinions on the future of these nations. Produced by Esteban Schroeder, Augusto Gongora, Regina Festa and Fernando Sanatoro.
Fine Arts; Social Science; Sociology
Dist - FIRS

South - Memories of milk city 10 MIN
VHS
Color (G)
$125.00 purchase, $30.00 rental
Juxtaposes contemporary images with verse read by Madhu Rye to create a mosaic of Ahmedabad, a troubled city in the Gujarat region of India. Looks at the communal violence in a city once home to the ideas of Rajiv Gandhi. Produced by Ruchir Joshi.
Civics and Political Systems; Fine Arts; Geography - World; History - World; Sociology
Dist - FIRS

South - Microchip al chip 18 MIN
VHS
Color (G)
$170.00 purchase, $40.00 rental
Examines the destruction of Chilean forests in which 10,000 hectares disappear every year in order to sustain its paper exports to other countries, notably Japan. Intercuts images of barren land, acres of logs waiting to be shipped to a timber depot, consumer culture and statements from a forest manager and Japanese economist. Uses fictional, documentary and videographic techniques. Produced by Pablo Lavin.
Fine Arts; Science - Natural
Dist - FIRS

South - Mr Foot 20 MIN
VHS
Color (G)
$175.00 purchase, $40.00 rental
Takes a lighthearted look at Cameroon's national obsession - soccer. Reveals that in a country where the populace has not been allowed to participate in politics, soccer serves as the people's primary diversion from the stresses and strains of life. Produced by Jean - Marie Teno.
Fine Arts; History - World; Physical Education and Recreation
Dist - FIRS

South of Deadwood - by Louis L'Amour 60 MIN
U-matic / VHS
L'Amour Series
Stereo (K P I J H C G T A S R PRO IND)
Shows a western fiction short story in multi voice presentation.
Literature and Drama
Dist - BANTAP **Prod** - BANTAP

South of nearly everywhere - Antarctic
U-matic / VHS / BETA
Search encounters in science series
Color; PAL (G H C)
PdS25, PdS33 purchase
Brings modern research efforts of the world's leading scientists into the classroom. Features one of a series of 24 mini - documentaries. Each film is 5 - 7 minutes in length.
Science
Dist - EDPAT **Prod** - NSF

South of the Border 63 MIN
U-matic / VHS / 16mm
Color (H C A) (SPANISH (ENGLISH SUBTITLES))
$895 purchase - 16 mm, $595 purchase - video, $100 rental
Surveys protest music in Central America. Includes scenes of local poverty and militarization, Guatemalan refugee camps in Mexico, death squad killings in El Salvador, U S military exercises in Honduras, and contra atrocities in Nicaragua. Directed by David Bradbury.
Fine Arts; History - World; Sociology
Dist - CNEMAG

South of the Clouds 35 MIN
16mm
Color (J A)
Reveals the gradual and complete transformation of Najila, a high caste Moslem, through her participation in the democratic life of a Christian college in Beirut, Lebanon.
Education; Guidance and Counseling; Religion and Philosophy; Sociology
Dist - YALEDV **Prod** - YALEDV

The South of V O Key 30 MIN
VHS
American South Comes of Age Series
Color (J)
$95.00 purchase, $55.00 rental
Presents a view of the South. Part of a fourteen - part series on the economic, social and political transformation of the South since World War II.
Geography - United States; History - United States; Psychology; Sociology
Dist - SCETV **Prod** - SCETV 1985

South of Waldeyers 20 MIN
16mm
Color (PRO)
LC FIA68-823
Dr J A Hutch presents a study of the physiology of micturition. Includes an examination of the embryological origin of anatomical structures involved in pathological conditions and the rationale for their medical or surgical correction. For physicians and medical students.
Health and Safety
Dist - EATONL **Prod** - EATONL 1968

South Pacific 170 MIN
VHS
Color (H C G)
$39.00 purchase _ #DL228
Presents the 1958 film production of South Pacific starring Mitzi Gaynor and Rossano Brazzi.
Fine Arts
Dist - INSIM

South Pacific collection series
Presents a two-part series on the South Pacific. Teaches about the people, culture and history of New Zealand and Australia. Visits historic buildings, monuments and landmarks. Examines the physical topography of both countries. Also part of a larger series entitled Video Visits that travels to six continents.
Australia - secrets of the land down under 60 MIN
New Zealand - island of adventure 60 MIN
Dist - CAMV **Prod** - WNETTV 1958

The South Pacific - End of Eden 59 MIN
16mm / VHS / U-matic
James Michener's World Series
Color (J)
LC 78-701700; 78-701496
A shortened version of the motion picture The South Pacific - End Of Eden. Follows James Michener as he examines the impact of 20th century life on the cultures of the Pacific Islands, including Easter Island, Tahiti, Pitcairn Island and the Stone Age tribes of the Solomon Islands and New Guinea.
Geography - World; Sociology
Dist - PFP **Prod** - READER 1978

South Pacific - End of Eden 58 MIN
U-matic / VHS / 16mm
Color (SPANISH)
Deals with the life of New Guinea tribesmen, who are still living in the Stone Age, descendants of the H M S Bounty's mutineers, Gaugin's Tahiti and radioactive atolls. Includes a commentary by James Michener.
Foreign Language; Geography - World; History - United States; History - World; Sociology
Dist - PFP **Prod** - READER

South Pacific - Islands of the South Pacific 75 MIN
VHS
Color (G)
$29.95 purchase _ #ST - IV1406
Observes fire - walking rituals in Fiji. Strolls through Suva's market in the Kingdom of Tonga. Watches the creation of tapa fabric and visits Samoan valleys and the island of Tahiti.
Geography - World
Dist - INSTRU

South Pacific Series
On the Island of Taveuni 17 MIN
Dist - MMP

South - Parque central 11 MIN
VHS
Color (G) (SPANISH WITH ENGLISH SUBTITLES)
$160.00 purchase, $35.00 rental
Pays visual homage to Venezuela's capitol city, Caracas. Intercuts pictures of statues, buildings, street performers, parks, mountains, roads, roller coasters and a pick - up basketball game. Produced by Andres Agusti.

Fine Arts; Geography - World
Dist - FIRS

South - Recording the truth 25 MIN
VHS
Color (G)
$190.00 purchase, $45.00 rental
Opens with a journalist's statement that the Islamic revolution is the first since the Renaissance, 400 years ago, to take place outside the sphere of Western thought. Allows Iran's intellectuals, religious leaders and photojournalists to express their views on the fundamentalist movement. Provides insights into a belief and value system which remains largely incomprehensible to most westerners. Produced by Karveh Golestan.
Fine Arts; Guidance and Counseling; History - World; Industrial and Technical Education; Religion and Philosophy
Dist - FIRS

South - Sabemos mirar - We can see 25 MIN
VHS
Color (G)
$190.00 purchase, $45.00 rental
Exposes how rock music has become an outlet for young Argentines' frustrations at repressive regimes. Focuses on a band called Bersuit Bergaravat whose members speak of their powerlessness and how 'being young in Argentina means being a suspect.' Closes with performances by the group along with Mercedes Sosa at a 'No to Impunity' rally in Buenos Aires protesting the death of Walter Bulacio, the beating of filmmaker Pino Solanas and threats against the Mothers of Plaza de Mayo. Produced by Dolly Pussi.
Fine Arts; Social Science; Sociology
Dist - FIRS

South - Sankara 20 MIN
VHS
Color (G)
$175.00 purchase, $40.00 rental
Portrays Thomas Sankara, late President of Burkina Faso. Looks at his idealism and how he engineered drastic improvements, from the symbolic change of the country's name from colonial Upper Volta to Burkina Faso - The Country of Free and Dignified People, to providing real health care for the country's children. Sankara was assassinated in 1987. Produced by Balufa Bakupa - Kanyinda.
Fine Arts; History - World; Social Science
Dist - FIRS

The South Seas 57 MIN
VHS
Color (G)
$24.90 purchase _ #0712
Takes a video tour of Tahiti, Moorea Island, Raiatea and Fiji in the South Seas. Tells about the climate, clothing, food.
Geography - World; History - World
Dist - SEVVID

South - Song of the bicycle 17 MIN
VHS
Color (G) (CHINESE WITH ENGLISH SUBTITLES)
$170.00 purchase, $40.00 rental
Digs into the meaning as well as uses of the bicycle in China, which sees 370 million in use every year. Features scenes of bikes being used to transport huge earthenware urns and bamboo cabinets to market, to haul timber to construction sites and to simply get from place to place. Intersperses these practical uses with observations of a Chinese artist who spent four and a half years cycling around China's perimeter. He notes that while foreigners use bicycles for fun, they are essential to the livelihood of China. Produced by Yang Shu.
Fine Arts; Geography - World; Physical Education and Recreation; Social Science
Dist - FIRS

South - The New bosses 13 MIN
VHS
Color (G)
$160.00 purchase, $35.00 rental
Looks at three successful entrepreneurs who employ several thousand workers under the Vietnamese government's 'Doi Moi' plan encompassing a radical shift toward a market economy that included nurturing private enterprises. Presents their hopes and fears of the government supported plan which may be the foundation of Vietnam's future as it rebuilds under the slogan 'Renewal to move forward.' Produced by Le Trac.
Business and Economics; Fine Arts
Dist - FIRS

South - The Shattered pearl 25 MIN
VHS
Color (G)
$190.00 purchase, $45.00 rental
Documents the ongoing violent struggle which began when Sri Lanka adopted Sinhalese as its official language in 1956. Investigates the civil war waged by Tamil, Sinhala and Muslim groups; the murder of a liberal journalist; human rights abuses; and the women who continue to struggle for justice and peace. Produced by Nimal and Ranjani Mendis.
Fine Arts; Religion and Philosophy; Sociology
Dist - FIRS

South - The Singing sheikh 11 MIN
VHS
Color (G)
$125.00 purchase, $30.00 rental
Portrays Sheikh Imam Mohammad Ahmad Eissa, born 1918, famous in the Arab world for his folk songs indicting the ruling classes. Sets scenes of street life to caustic musical criticisms of his native Egypt's upper classes. Produced by Heiny Srour.
Civics and Political Systems; Fine Arts; Sociology
Dist - FIRS

South - This is not your life 15 MIN
VHS
Color (G)
$175.00 purchase, $40.00 rental
Features an ordinary Brazilian woman, Noeli, telling the world her story to illuminate director Jorge Furtado's decree 'Ordinary people, they have no name.' Uses Noeli's life - raiding tangerine orchards as a kid, having boyfriends, marrying a black man to the displeasure of those around her - to make his point that, although Noeli could be just another demographic statistic, 'Numbers have no name, people have a name. Every one has.'
Literature and Drama; Sociology
Dist - FIRS

South to Fire and Ice - Cousteau in the Antarctic 53 MIN
16mm / U-matic / VHS
Undersea World of Jacques Cousteau Series
Color (SPANISH)
LC 74-700481
Follows Jacques Cousteau as he journeys to the Antarctic where he and his crew study life existing on the ice, rock and water surface, as well as in the 30 - degree summer waters below the polar ice floes. Contrasts the icy expanses of the frozen continent with the boiling pools in the crater of a volcano on Deception Island.
Foreign Language; Geography - World
Dist - CF **Prod** - DUPONT 1973

The South Union Shakers 30 MIN
VHS / 35mm strip
Color (G)
$85.00, $25.00 purchase
Examines the contributions of the Shakers, a communal religious sect, to Kentucky where they prospered for over a century. Provides a glimpse into the history, buildings, arts and culture of the Shaker Colony at South Union, Kentucky.
Fine Arts; History - United States; Religion and Philosophy
Dist - UWKY **Prod** - UWKY 1970

South Viet Nam - Tinderbox in Asia 5 MIN
16mm
Screen news digest series; Vol 4; Issue 9
B&W
Traces the birth and growth of the current crisis in Viet Nam.
Geography - World; History - World
Dist - HEARST **Prod** - HEARST 1962

South Vietnam - the People of Saigon 17 MIN
16mm
Color (J)
LC 76-701205
Explains the effects that has had on South Vietnam. Shows the city of Saigon and describes the life of the people.
Civics and Political Systems; Social Science
Dist - AVED **Prod** - BAILYL 1969

South - Wholes 10 MIN
VHS
Color (G)
$125.00 purchase, $30.00 rental
Satirizes the social ills plaguing Sao Paulo, Brazil, one of the largest cities in the world. Uses the metaphor of potholes, which may or may not be a problem and may or may not even exist, depending on who you ask. Produced by Antonio S Cecilio Neto.
Literature and Drama; Sociology
Dist - FIRS

Southeast 60 MIN
VHS
AAA travel series
Color (G)
$24.95 purchase _ #NA10
Explores the Southeast United States.
Geography - United States; Geography - World
Dist - SVIP

Southeast Asia - a Culture History 16 MIN
U-matic / VHS / 16mm
Color (H C A)
LC 72-703296
Explains the cultures of Viet Nam, Laos, Cambodia and Thailand which are a blend of the indigenous tribal traditions with the high culture of Hindu - Buddhist India. Discusses how former centers of empire stand today as a testimony to the endurance of Buddhist and Brahman idea systems in Southeast Asia.
Geography - World; History - World
Dist - FILCOM **Prod** - SIGMA 1969

Southeast Asia Geography 21 MIN
U-matic / VHS / 16mm
Color (I J H)
LC FIA67-2345
Examines the geographic and climatic characteristics of Burma, Laos, Thailand, Cambodia and Malaya. Pictures the raw materials and the surplus foods that make these nations politically important. Comments on Singapore's strategic position and explores the changing role of the Western powers in Southeast Asia.
Civics and Political Systems; Geography - World
Dist - PHENIX **Prod** - EVANSA 1967

Southeast Asia Report - Cambodia, Vietnam, China, Pt 1 30 MIN
VHS / U-matic
Southeast Asia Report - Cambodia, Vietnam, China Series
Color
Examines the first border conflicts between Vietnam and Cambodia, including footage from the border and an analysis of the situation by journalists, scholars, and United States State Department officials.
Geography - World; History - World; Sociology
Dist - DCTVC **Prod** - DCTVC

Southeast Asia Report - Cambodia, Vietnam, China, Pt 2 30 MIN
U-matic / VHS
Southeast Asia Report - Cambodia, Vietnam, China Series
Color
Covers the China - Vietnam War and the Vietnamese occupation of Cambodia and the carnage left by the Pol Pot regime.
Geography - World; History - World; Sociology
Dist - DCTVC **Prod** - DCTVC

Southeast Asia Report - Cambodia, Vietnam, China Series
Southeast Asia Report - Cambodia, Vietnam, China, Pt 1 30 MIN
Southeast Asia Report - Cambodia, Vietnam, China, Pt 2 30 MIN
Dist - DCTVC

Southeast Asia - Spreading New Ideas about Food Production 15 MIN
VHS / U-matic
Global Geography Series
Color (I J)
$125.00 purchase
Surveys the trends in Southeast Asian food production through scenarios with local farmers and citizens.
Geography - World
Dist - AITECH **Prod** - AITECH 1987

Southeastern Massachusetts University
VHS
Campus clips series
Color (H C A)
$29.95 purchase _ #CC0109V
Takes a video visit to the campus of Southeastern Massachusetts University. Shows many of the distinctive features of the campus, and interviews students about their experiences. Provides information on the composition of the student body, professors, academics, social life, housing, and other subjects.
Education
Dist - CAMV

The Southern 500 28 MIN
16mm
Color (I J H C)
Tells the history of the Southern 500 auto race and some of the racers who have won it, including Bobby Allison, Buddy Baker, Richard Petty, Cale Yarborough and David Pearson.
Physical Education and Recreation
Dist - SF **Prod** - SF 1978

Southern Africa 27 MIN
U-matic / VHS / 16mm
Seventies Series
Color (J)
LC 81-700253
Studies the emergence of black nationalism in South Africa during the 1970s. Describes internal problems, labor disputes, riots, and civil wars.
History - World; Sociology
Dist - JOU **Prod** - UPI 1980

Southern Africa - the right to development - 5 28 MIN
VHS / U-matic
People matter series
Color (H C G)
$385.00, $355.00 purchase _ #V475
Documents how the apartheid system of South Africa violates every concept of human rights, including the right to development. Contrasts scenes of rich, prosperous cities with shantytowns and 'homeland' areas. Interviews both white and black South Africans. Part five of a six - part series on human rights around the globe.
Business and Economics; Geography - World; Sociology
Dist - BARR **Prod** - CEPRO 1989

Southern Appalachians
VHS
Dances of the world series
Color (G)
$39.95 purchase _ #FD100V
Presents performances of dances from the Southern Appalachian region of the United States. Interviews the dancers.
Fine Arts; Geography - United States; Physical Education and Recreation
Dist - CAMV **Prod** - CAMV

Southern Baptist hour series

Baptists of the world, Baptist World Alliance 30 MIN
Conversation with Chief of Chaplains Robert P Taylor 30 MIN
Conversation with Dr Herschel H Hobbs 30 MIN
A Conversation with Dr Porter Routh 30 MIN
A Conversation with Dr Theodore F Adams 30 MIN
Ecce homo 54 MIN
From the most high cometh healing 30 MIN
Dist - NBCTV

Southern Black Children 27 MIN
16mm
Play and Cultural Continuity Series Part 2
Color (H C T)
Presents children's vivid, dramatic play and traditional folk games photographed in Houston and the surrounding countryside. Shows cultural entities such as music, dancing, intricate hand clapping improvisations, call and response and circle games. Brings out the warm, easy interaction between old and young, boys and girls and children of different ages.
Fine Arts; Geography - United States; Physical Education and Recreation; Sociology
Dist - CFDC **Prod** - CFDC 1977

Southern colonies 15 MIN
VHS / U-matic
America past series
Color (H J)
$125.00 purchase
Describes the settlement and ways of life in Britain's southern colonies.
History - United States
Dist - AITECH **Prod** - KRMATV 1987

Southern cookin'
VHS
Frugal gourmet - taste of America series
Color (G)
$19.95 purchase _ #CCP822
Shows how to prepare American food from the South. Features Jeff Smith, the Frugal Gourmet. Part of a ten - part series on American cooking.
Geography - United States; History - United States; Home Economics; Physical Education and Recreation
Dist - CADESF **Prod** - CADESF

Southern Cross Crusade 50 MIN
16mm
B&W
Shows the Billy Graham Team's Crusade in Australia and New Zealand.
Religion and Philosophy
Dist - WWPI **Prod** - GRAHAM 1959

Southern desserts - delights
VHS
Video cooking library series
Color (J H G)
$19.95 purchase _ #KVC935V
Illustrates the preparation of Southern desserts through step - by - step demonstrations. Covers everything needed from ingredients to equipment, with clear explanations of cooking techniques. Includes recipes. Part of a 22 - part series.
Home Economics
Dist - CAMV

Southern Germany - Pt 2 40 MIN
16mm
Color (H C A)
Focuses on a variety of scenes as viewed and described by an American traveler.
Geography - World; History - World
Dist - WSTGLC **Prod** - WSTGLC

Southern Highlands - America's Pictureland 28 MIN
16mm
Color
Covers both natural and man - made attractions in the southern Appalachian mountains. Includes views of the world's largest underground lake, Lookout Mountain, hang - gliding on Grandfather Mountain and Biltmore House in Asheville.
Geography - United States
Dist - EKC **Prod** - EKC 1980

Southern Italy 23 MIN
U-matic / VHS / 16mm
Update Europe Series
Color (J H)
$495 purchase - 16 mm, $250 purchase - video _ #5177C
Discusses recent economic developments in poor regions of southern Italy. Produced by the BBC.
History - World
Dist - CORF

The Southern Literary Renaissance 30 MIN
VHS
Modern American Literature Eminent Scholar - Teachers Video Series
Color (C)
$95.00 purchase
Demonstrates that the defining characteristic of 20th Century Southern American writers is their sense of history and their habit of seeing the present as a product of the past. The 29th of 34 installments of the Modern American Literature Eminent Scholar - Teachers Video Series.
History - United States; Literature and Drama
Dist - OMNIGR

The Southern mountain ranges - Pt 3 25 MIN
16mm
Color (H C A)
Discusses each German region's lifestyles, economy, problems and opportunities for the future. Provides some unusual helicopter views of Germany's geography.
Geography - World; History - World; Sociology
Dist - WSTGLC **Prod** - WSTGLC

Southern Rhodesia - Climate and Cultivation 14 MIN
16mm / U-matic / VHS
Color (I J H)
LC FIA65-1541
Depicts Southern Rhodesia's climate and altitude, native life, subsistence and commercial farming, leading crops, export routes and shipment of produce.
Geography - World; History - United States
Dist - IFB **Prod** - IFB 1962

Southern Star 105 MIN
16mm
Color
Offers a spoof on jungle adventures. Stars George Segal, Ursula Andress and Orson Welles.
Fine Arts
Dist - TWYMAN **Prod** - CPC 1969

The Southern United States - 2 30 MIN
VHS
50 States, 50 capitals - geography of the USA series
Color (H)
$89.00 purchase _ #60314 - 025
Discusses in detail the states included in the southern region of the United States. Includes locations, industries, agriculture, capitals, populations, sizes and areas, climates and points of interest. Part one of four parts on US geography.
Geography - United States
Dist - GA **Prod** - GA 1992

The Southern US - Volume 2b 35 MIN
VHS
Visions of adventure series
Color (P)
$24.95 purchase _ #GE03
Focuses on the United States South. Part of an eight - part series on geography.
Geography - United States
Dist - SVIP

The Southerner 91 MIN
16mm
B&W
Tells the story of a young man who decides to strike out on his own, leaving a safe job to grow cotton on a derelict farm. Stars Zachary Scott, Betty Field and Beulah Bondi. Directed by Jean Renoir.
Fine Arts
Dist - REELIM **Prod** - UNKNWN 1945

Southie 59 MIN
VHS / 16mm
Color (G)
$70.00 rental _ #SOUT - 000
Portrays South Boston, an area of strong ethnic ties. Visits the neighborhood and interviews its residents.
Social Science
Dist - PBS **Prod** - WGBHTV

The South's slave system 30 MIN
VHS
American adventure series
Color (G)
$150.00 purchase _ #TAMA - 116
Examines the institution of black slavery in the South. Explores the relationships between slaves and masters, as well as black culture under slavery. Also considers slave resistance and free blacks.
History - United States
Dist - PBS

Southward 19 MIN
16mm
Color
LC 80-700925
Features The Australian Sydney Hobart Yacht Race as it was filmed aboard several of the competing yachts. Records the journey to Tasmania.
Geography - World; Physical Education and Recreation
Dist - TASCOR **Prod** - TASCOR 1976

The Southwest 17 MIN
16mm / U-matic / VHS
U S Geography Series
Color (J)
LC 76-701777
Examines the people, industry, economy and landscape of the Southwest region of the United States.
Business and Economics; Geography - United States; Geography - World; Social Science
Dist - MGHT **Prod** - MGHT 1976

The Southwest 25 MIN
U-matic / VHS / 16mm
United States Geography Series
Color (I J)
Visits the Southwestern states of Texas, Oklahoma, Arizona and New Mexico which comprise an area with an international border, a rich ethnic mix and a bright future.
Geography - United States
Dist - NGS **Prod** - NGS 1983

Southwest 60 MIN
VHS
AAA travel series
Color (G)
$24.95 purchase _ #NA04
Explores the Southwestern United States.
Geography - United States; Geography - World
Dist - SVIP

Southwest
VHS
Frugal gourmet - taste of America series
Color (G)
$19.95 purchase _ #CCP819
Shows how to prepare American food from the Southwest. Features Jeff Smith, the Frugal Gourmet. Part of a ten - part series on American cooking.
Geography - United States; History - United States; Home Economics; Physical Education and Recreation
Dist - CADESF **Prod** - CADESF

Southwest Africa - the Forgotten Desert 15 MIN
U-matic / VHS / 16mm
Great Deserts of the World Series
Color; PAL (J H C)
$400 purchase - 16 mm, $250 purchase - video _ #5294C
Talks about the Namib and the Kalahari - the two deserts of Southwest Africa. Discusses the Bantu and Bushmen tribes.
Geography - World
Dist - CORF
VIEWTH

Southwest Asia - Nations of Complexity 25 MIN
U-matic / VHS / 16mm
Faces of Man Series
Color (I)
From The Faces Of Man Series. Analyzes the changes in Turkey, Afghanistan, Iran and Pakistan and views the effects of poverty and religion.
Geography - World
Dist - CORF **Prod** - SCRESC 1981

Southwest Conference Football Highlights 1972 29 MIN
16mm
Color (J)
Shows highlights from the 1972 Southwest Conference football season, including portions of 12 regular season games. Includes the Texas victory over Alabama in the

Cotton Bowl and the fifth annual presentation of the Kern Tipps Award to Robert Papelka of Southern Methodist University.
Physical Education and Recreation
Dist - EXXON **Prod** - EXXON 1973

Southwest England 21 MIN
U-matic / VHS / 16mm
Regional Geography - British Isles Series
Color (I J H)
LC FIA68-2881
Shows the location, physical character and climate of southwest England, emphasizing the economic importance of the coastal resort areas and of the tin and china industries.
Geography - World
Dist - IFB **Prod** - BHA 1967

Southwest Indians of Early America 14 MIN
16mm / U-matic / VHS
Color (I J)
$350.00, $245.00 _ #3383; LC 72-702760
Tells how the early Indians of the southwest met their needs through division of labor and use of natural resources. Shows dwellings and remains of the ancestors of the Hopi, Pima and Papago Indians that prospered a thousand years ago.
Social Science; Sociology
Dist - CORF **Prod** - CORF 1973

Souvenir 10 MIN
16mm
B&W (H C A)
Tells the story of a young photographer who becomes emotionally involved with his attractive model.
Industrial and Technical Education; Literature and Drama
Dist - UWFKD **Prod** - UWFKD

Souvenirs 30 MIN
VHS
How do you do - learning English series
Color (H A)
#317724
Reviews all of the programs in the series, as Frankie and Chips look at photographs that remind them of all the fun Chips has had while learning English. Part of a series that helps newcomers learn English or improve their ability. Includes viewer's guide with grammar explanations and vocabulary drills, worksheets and two audio cassettes.
English Language
Dist - TVOTAR **Prod** - TVOTAR 1990

Souvenirs 28 MIN
16mm
Color (G)
$25.00 rental
Celebrates the pathetic, poignant pathos of the filmmaker's home movies and intermixes with the camp value sentiments of Country & Western singers. Addresses the sentiments underlying the concept of the souvenir and chronicles a cyclical process of the realization of the loss of love with quotes from Romantic writers such as Goethe and Thomas Mann. Produced by Jerome Carolfi.
Fine Arts; Literature and Drama
Dist - CANCIN

Souvenirs 15 MIN
16mm
Color
Highlights the workmanship of the Russian artisan. Includes a shopping trip, where even the ordinary shops sell extraordinary wares.
Fine Arts; History - World
Dist - MTP **Prod** - MTP

Souvenirs from Kerala 10 MIN
16mm
B&W (H C A)
Reveals the skill and ingenuity of the artisans of Kerala in their many handicrafts, which answer both aesthetic and functional needs. Explains how things of beauty are created out of waste materials.
Fine Arts
Dist - NEDINF **Prod** - INDIA

Souvenirs from Sweden 27 MIN
16mm
Color
LC FIA66-1393
Shows inanimate souvenirs from Lapland and Sweden springing to life to tell about Swedish culture, economy and people and to show the scenic splendors of Sweden. Presents views of sailing in the Archipelago, of the Orrefors Glass Works in the province of Smaland of the Vasa Ski Race in Mora, of Darlina and of the Nobel Festival in Stockholm.
Geography - World
Dist - SWNTO **Prod** - SWEDIN 1960

The Sovereign Self - Right to Live, Right to Die 60 MIN
U-matic / VHS
Constitution - that Delicate Balance Series
Color
Discusses how personal freedoms and privacy are balanced against state intervention and societal rights in a presentation which touches on abortion, Baby Doe cases and the right to die.
Civics and Political Systems; Sociology
Dist - FI **Prod** - WTTWTV 1984

Soviet and American Journalism 28 MIN
U-matic / VHS
Color (G)
$249.00, $149.00 purchase _ #AD - 1271
Features Phil Donahue who hosts a discussion between American journalists covering the Soviet Union and Soviet journalists covering the US. Focuses on how they view their respective beats, what they consider to be the function of the press and their opinions about the future.
Geography - World; History - United States; History - World; Literature and Drama
Dist - FOTH **Prod** - FOTH

The Soviet Army 60 MIN
U-matic / VHS
Color
Looks behind the iron curtain at the modern armed forces of the Soviet Union. Exemplifies Soviet military training and deceptive Communist propaganda techniques.
History - World
Dist - IHF **Prod** - IHF

Soviet army chorus, band, and dance ensemble 70 MIN
VHS
Color (H C A)
$59.95 purchase
Features the Soviet Army Ensemble in performances of song, dance, and play. Shot on location throughout the Soviet Union.
Fine Arts
Dist - PBS **Prod** - WNETTV

Soviet Army Chorus, Band and Dance Ensemble 78 MIN
VHS
Color (G)
$39.95 purchase _ #1106
Presents the Soviet Army Chorus, Band and Dance Ensemble filmed in various locations in Russia.
Fine Arts; Foreign Language; Geography - World; Physical Education and Recreation
Dist - KULTUR

Soviet Boy 16 MIN
16mm
Color (J H)
Provides an intimate look into the life of a communist family through the experiences of a Soviet boy in Armenia, USSR. Shows the differences as well as the similarities between life in the USSR and in the United States.
Civics and Political Systems; Geography - World; Sociology
Dist - ATLAP **Prod** - ATLAP

Soviet Central Asia 25 MIN
U-matic / VHS
Color (H C A)
Looks at Soviet Central Asia, a part of the USSR which is home for 40 to 50 million Moslems.
Geography - World
Dist - JOU **Prod** - UPI

Soviet Dissidents in Exile 28 MIN
U-matic
Color
Interviews five men who challenged the Soviet regime and were exiled. Discusses the problems of adjusting to a new country.
Geography - World; History - United States; Sociology
Dist - ADL **Prod** - ADL

Soviet Estonia 20 MIN
U-matic / VHS
Color
Reviews the social and economic development of Soviet Estonia, one of the 15 constituent republics of the Soviet Union, and its achievements in industry, science and culture.
Business and Economics; Civics and Political Systems; Geography - World; History - World; Science
Dist - IHF **Prod** - IHF

Soviet - Finnish War of 1939 - 40 66 MIN
16mm
British Universities Historical Studies in Film Series
Color (C)
LC 75-703311
Examines the origins and course of the war between Finland and the Soviet Union in 1939 and 1940. Emphasizes the role of the Red Army and pays special attention to the European reaction to the war.
Civics and Political Systems; History - World; Sociology
Dist - KRAUS **Prod** - BUFVC 1975

Soviet Jews - a Culture in Peril 27 MIN
16mm
B&W
Presents Stuart Novins, former Moscow Bureau Chief and traces the 2000 - year history of the Jewish people in what is now the USSR. Examines the lingering antiSemitism within the Soviet Union and proves the causes of the conflict between socialiam and Judaism. Explores the extent of Jewish identity permitted by Soviet authorities and the reason why so many Jews continue their battle for emigration to Israel.
Geography - World; History - World; Religion and Philosophy; Sociology
Dist - ADL **Prod** - ADL

Soviet Latvia 20 MIN
U-matic / VHS
Color
Portrays Soviet Latvia, one of the 15 equal republics of the USSR. Focuses on the nation's capital, Riga, and its national traditions.
Civics and Political Systems; Geography - World; History - World
Dist - IHF **Prod** - IHF

Soviet leader Mikhail Gorbachev 15 MIN
35mm strip / VHS
In our time series
Color (J H C T A)
$78.00, $48.00 purchase _ #MB - 540369 - 2, #MB - 509120 - 8
Profiles Soviet leader Mikhail Gorbachev, from his origins as a peasant's son to his eventual rise to head of the Soviet Communist Party. Examines the changes Gorbachev made after coming to power. Includes live footage of dramatic arms proposals and other announcements made by Gorbachev.
Civics and Political Systems; Geography - World; History - World
Dist - SRA **Prod** - SRA 1989

Soviet Medicine 30 MIN
U-matic / VHS / 16mm
B&W (H C)
LC 72-706846
Shows the emphasis on the health of Soviet citizens and the differences and similarities between Soviet and US medical practices.
Civics and Political Systems; Geography - United States; Geography - World; Health and Safety
Dist - IU **Prod** - NET 1970

The Soviet mind 30 MIN
16mm / VHS
Color (H)
$185.00, $475.00 purchase, $50.00 rental _ #8143; LC 90705076
Uses interviews with Soviet exchange students to investigate the philosophy and changing political climate in the Soviet Union of the 1990s. Includes discussion of social problems, the Soviet work ethic, and differences and similarities between socialist and capitalist systems of government and economy.
Civics and Political Systems; Geography - World
Dist - AIMS **Prod** - HRMC 1990

The Soviet Paradise 14 MIN
VHS / U-matic
B&W (GERMAN)
Witnesses World War II's greatest land battles. Observes first - hand, life in Russia after 20 years of Soviet rule. Represents its citizenry as starving children, youthful gangs, cowed laborers and wretched peasants barely existing in dilapidated collective farms or in overcrowded city slums.
Foreign Language; History - World; Sociology
Dist - IHF **Prod** - IHF

Soviet People are with Vietnam - Soviet People Support Vietnam 60 MIN
VHS / U-matic
B&W
Deals with Soviet material support given to the Vietnamese during the Vietnam war.
History - World
Dist - IHF **Prod** - IHF

Soviet Russia After Sputnik 29 MIN
Videoreel / VT2
Course of Our Times II Series
Color
History - World
Dist - PBS **Prod** - WGBHTV

Soviet School Children 11 MIN
16mm / U-matic / VHS
Color (I J T)
LC 71-708052
Follows the school day of two Russian schoolgirls, one in the first grade and one in the fifth grade. Focuses on the subjects they study and the political youth groups they may join. Demonstrates how the Communist Party uses education to promote the party program.

Education; Geography - World
Dist - PHENIX **Prod** - BAILEY 1968

Soviet Space Power 30 MIN
VHS / 16mm
Conquest of Space Series
Color (G)
Profiles the Soviet space program and considers its future.
Business and Economics; Geography - World; History - World; Industrial and Technical Education
Dist - FLMWST

Soviet students speak to America 20 MIN
VHS
Color (J H C G T A)
$75.00 purchase, $35.00 rental
Takes a look at Soviet schools. Suggests that Soviet children learn more about the U S than their American peers do about the U S S R. Produced by Shirley Ward and the U S - U S S R Youth Exchange Program.
Civics and Political Systems; Education; Sociology
Dist - EFVP

Soviet Style Series
Farming - Soviet style 27 MIN
A People's Music - Soviet Style 23 MIN
Politics - Soviet Style 27 MIN
School's in - Soviet Style 27 MIN
Working - Soviet Style 27 MIN
Dist - JOU

Soviet Teens 28 MIN
U-matic / VHS
Color (G)
$249.00, $149.00 purchase _ #AD - 1269
Features Phil Donahue. Interviews Soviet teens who talk about their interests which range from music to fashion fads, their political views, and their thoughts for the future.
Geography - World; History - World; Psychology; Sociology
Dist - FOTH **Prod** - FOTH

Soviet Television - Fact and Fiction 110 MIN
VHS
Color (S)
$79.00 purchase _ #825 - 9287
Reveals that Soviets watch as much TV as viewers in western nations. Discloses what Soviets see. The USSR broadcasts through 11 time zones, in 45 languages, to millions of people each day. Includes clips from popular programs as well as lively discussions with Soviet citizens.
Fine Arts; Geography - World; History - World
Dist - FI **Prod** - BBCTV 1986

The Soviet Threat 30 MIN
U-matic
Realities
Color (A)
Delves into the political, social, economic and cultural trends of the 1980s. Probes a wide range of contemporary concerns. Each segment includes a guest speaker who is an expert in the field under discussion.
Business and Economics; Civics and Political Systems; Social Science; Sociology
Dist - TVOTAR **Prod** - TVOTAR 1985

Soviet Turkmenistan 20 MIN
VHS / U-matic
Color
Reviews the social and economic development of Soviet Turkmenistan and its achievements in industry, construction, oil and gas extraction, cotton growing, livestock raising, science and culture.
Agriculture; Business and Economics; Civics and Political Systems; Geography - World; History - World; Science; Social Science
Dist - IHF **Prod** - IHF

Soviet Union 15 MIN
U-matic / VHS
Families of the World Series
Color (I)
Travels to Uzbekistan, where eleven year old Bakhtinisa Marov lives in the capital city of Tashkent. Shows Bakhtinisa's school and family life.
Geography - World
Dist - NGS **Prod** - NGS

Soviet Union 25 MIN
U-matic / VHS
Nations of the World Series
Color (I J H A)
Travels to some of the great cities of the historic Islamic region of the Central Asian portion of the Soviet Union. Shows how irrigation enables the people to farm this arid land.
Geography - World
Dist - NGS **Prod** - NGS

Soviet Union, 1918 - 1920 - Civil War and Allied Intervention 17 MIN
16mm / U-matic / VHS
World War I Series
B&W (H C)
LC FIA67-5249
Describes how Lenin attempted to organize the communist state after the overthrow of the czar, and how he was opposed by Kolchak under the white banner. Shows how the phrase 'Crush the White Opposition' was used and how it determined the outcome of Russia's Civil War. Also explains the Red Army's triumph after World War I and how it was strengthened.
Civics and Political Systems; History - World
Dist - FI **Prod** - CBSTV 1967

The Soviet Union - a new look 26 MIN
U-matic / VHS / BETA
Color; PAL (G H C)
PdS60, PdS68 purchase
Features an opening animated sequence to set the stage for rare newsreel footage of life under the Czars, followed by historical material shot by the late Julien Bryan. Reflects the diversity of this country in its wide range of climate, customs, dress and background.
Fine Arts; Geography - World; History - World
Dist - EDPAT

The Soviet Union - a New Look 26 MIN
VHS / U-matic
Color (J)
LC 78-701921
Demonstrates the vastness and diversity of the Soviet Union's geography, variety of its citizens, and wide range of climate, customs, dress and background. Shows kindergartens, schools and universities, artists at work, a ballet school, tractor factory, new housing construction, a family spending an evening at home in Moscow, and a glimpse of women's roles in the Soviet Union.
Geography - World; History - World
Dist - IFF **Prod** - IFF 1978

The Soviet Union After Khrushchev 29 MIN
Videoreel / VT2
Course of Our Times III Series
Color
Civics and Political Systems; History - World
Dist - PBS **Prod** - WGBHTV

Soviet Union - changing times 22 MIN
16mm / VHS
Color (I J H)
$485.00, $360.00 purchase, $60.00 rental
Visits with Alec, a Moscow teenager, who shares a personal view of his country and daily life. Examines geography, history and the rapidly changing economic system. Discusses the ethnic diversity of the Soviet Union, the 15 different republics and the challenge of creating a market system and democracy. Discovers Alec's love of rock music, the importance of literature and warm friendships in his culture and how uncertain times affect a teenager's life.
Business and Economics; Civics and Political Systems; Geography - World; History - World; Sociology
Dist - CF **Prod** - CF 1990

The Soviet Union chronicles - 1905 - 1924 22 MIN
VHS
Soviet Union chronicles series
Color; PAL (J H G)
PdS29.50 purchase
Shows how the unbalanced economy during the rule Nicholas II led to the Bolshevik Revolution, Russia's involvement in World War I, the murder of the Czar and his family and the civil war. Ends with Lenin's death. Part of a three - part series tracing Russia's political and social history. Features documentary footage.
Civics and Political Systems; History - World
Dist - EMFVL **Prod** - AIMS

The Soviet Union chronicles - 1924 - 1945 22 MIN
VHS
Soviet Union chronicles series
Color; PAL (J H G)
PdS29.50 purchase
Follows Stalin as he collaborates with Hitler, invades Poland and divides Germany. Ends with the beginning of the Cold War. Part of a three - part series tracing Russia's political and social history. Features documentary footage.
Civics and Political Systems; History - World; Sociology
Dist - EMFVL **Prod** - AIMS

The Soviet Union chronicles - 1945 - 1993 29 MIN
VHS
Soviet Union chronicles series
Color; PAL (J H G)
PdS29.50 purchase
Follows Stalin's death; Russia's involvement in foreign conflicts; the leadership of Khruschev, Brezhnev, Andropov, Chernenko and Gorbachev. Part of a three - part series tracing Russia's political and social history. Features documentary footage.
Civics and Political Systems; History - World
Dist - EMFVL **Prod** - AIMS

Soviet Union chronicles series
The Soviet Union chronicles - 1905 - 1924 22 MIN
The Soviet Union chronicles - 1924 - 1945 22 MIN
The Soviet Union chronicles - 1945 - 1993 29 MIN
Dist - EMFVL

Soviet Union - Civil War and Allied Intervention 17 MIN
16mm / U-matic / VHS
World War I Series
B&W (H C)
Discusses Russia's Civil War and looks at the Allies' intervention, which ended by the mid - 1920s.
History - World
Dist - FI **Prod** - CBSTV 1967

Soviet Union - Epic Land 29 MIN
U-matic / VHS / 16mm
Color (J H)
LC 72-700171
Emphasizes the size, political structure and potential of the Soviet Union and explores the cities and industry of European Russia.
Business and Economics; Civics and Political Systems; Geography - World
Dist - EBEC **Prod** - EBEC 1971

The Soviet Union - Faces of Today 26 MIN
U-matic / VHS / 16mm
Color (I J H)
LC 72-703305
Presents individuals from diverse segments of Soviet society to call attention to the size and regional variety of the Soviet Union and their ways of life. Features a member of a farm co - operative in European Russia, a professional in Tiblisi on the Turkish border, an engineer in Leningrad and a student in Siberia.
Geography - World; Social Science; Sociology
Dist - EBEC **Prod** - EBEC 1972

The Soviet Union - Faces of Today 26 MIN
U-matic / VHS
Color (J C)
$59.00 purchase, _ #3160
Reveals the wide diversity but common humanity of the Soviet people as workers, doctors, students, and engineers from across the country reveal their homes, work, and lifestyles.
Geography - World; Social Science
Dist - EBEC

Soviet Union - Foreign Politics and Brezhnev 28 MIN
U-matic / VHS
Color (H C A)
On the occasion of Leonid Brezhnev's death, after ruling the Soviet Union for 18 years, takes a look at his foreign policies which influenced every country in the world. Looks at the future foreign policy of his successor, Yuri Andropov.
Civics and Political Systems; Geography - World; History - World
Dist - JOU **Prod** - JOU

The Soviet Union - Gorbachev's Reforms and the Eastern Bloc 30 MIN
VHS
World Beat - Great Decisions In Foreign Policy
Color (G)
$39.95 purchase _ #WDBT - 107
Examines the Soviet Union's policy shifts under Mikhail Gorbachev. Emphasizes the impact of these policy shifts on Eastern Europe.
Civics and Political Systems; History - World
Dist - PBS **Prod** - WETATV 1988

Soviet Union is Our Home, The Rude Awakening 30 MIN
U-matic / VHS
B&W
Documents the life of Jewish people in the Soviet Union and tells of Soviet Jews who had settled in Israel but returned to a better life in the USSR.
History - World
Dist - IHF **Prod** - IHF

Soviet Union - Nina's world 19 MIN
U-matic / 16mm / VHS
Color (P I J)
$475.00, $365.00, $335.00 purchase _ #A618
Examines the changes taking place in the Soviet Union before its dissolution.
Civics and Political Systems; History - World
Dist - BARR **Prod** - CEPRO 1991

The Soviet Union - Past and Present 21 MIN
U-matic / VHS / 16mm
Color (I J H)
LC 77-706807
Traces Russia's history from Ivan the Terrible to the present, and focuses on current efforts to increase industrial output and improve living conditions.
Business and Economics; Geography - World; History - World
Dist - CORF **Prod** - CORF 1970

Soviet Union - Planning for Economic Development 15 MIN
U-matic / VHS
Global Geography Series
Color (I J)
$125.00 purchase
Outlines the economic direction of the Soviet Union and its global implications.
Geography - World
Dist - AITECH **Prod** - AITECH 1987

The Soviet Union series
Presents a five - part series on the diverse lifestyles and regions of the USSR. Visits various locations in Uzbekistan, Siberia, Moscow, Novokuznetsk, and Georgia.
Collective farm 19 MIN
Siberian riches 20 MIN
Socialist city 20 MIN
Steel town 20 MIN
Villages in the clouds 20 MIN
Dist - CORF **Prod** - BBCTV 1987

Soviet Union - the pioneers series
Storm over Asia 73 MIN
Dist - IHF
KINOIC

Soviet Union - the pioneers series
Aelita, Queen of Mars 90 MIN
Arsenal 65 MIN
Bed and sofa 72 MIN
The Cigarette girl of Mosselprom 85 MIN
Earth 54 MIN
The End of St Petersburg 74 MIN
Girl with the hat box 67 MIN
Mother 87 MIN
Three songs of Lenin 88 MIN
Dist - KINOIC

Soviet women filmmakers 51 MIN
VHS
Color (G)
$90.00 rental, $350.00 purchase
Includes interviews with actresses, critics, technicians and leading directors, Kira Muratova and Lana Gogoberidze, along with clips from films such as Larissa Shepitko's Wings. Contrasts more traditional representations of women in Soviet drama. Since Lenin's fervent embrace of cinema in the 1920s, more women have worked in the film industry in the Soviet Union than in the West. Features a production made during glasnost and prior to the dissolution of the USSR.
Fine Arts; History - World
Dist - WMEN **Prod** - SALPOT 1990

Sow seeds - trust the promise series
Community and self understanding 30 MIN
Planning and resourcing 30 MIN
Dist - ECUFLM

Sow seeds/trust the promise series
Outdoor skills 30 MIN
Theology and faith development 30 MIN
Dist - ECUFLM

Soweto 16 MIN
16mm
B&W (H C A)
LC 76-703922
Looks at the people of Soweto, or South Western Townships, a Bantu suburb of Johannesburg in South Africa. Shows their homes, their environment and examines the restrictive laws which govern their lives.
Civics and Political Systems; Geography - World; Sociology
Dist - BFPS **Prod** - BFPS 1976

Soweto - Class of '76 20 MIN
U-matic / VHS
B&W (G)
$249.00, $149.00 purchase _ #AD - 1623
Documents events in Soweto which crystallized issues in South Africa. Looks at blacks demanding basic human and economic rights in their own land and whites trying to maintain their power and monetary base.
Business and Economics; Civics and Political Systems; Geography - World; History - United States; History - World; Sociology
Dist - FOTH **Prod** - FOTH

Soweto to Berkeley 50 MIN
U-matic / VHS
Color (H C A)
$295 purchase, $60 rental
Tells about the Anti Apartheid Movement at the University of California at Berkeley during 1985 and 1986, which led to other student protests nationwide, and led to confrontations with the police. Includes speeches by South African bishop Desmond Tutu and Berkeley Free Speech activist Mario Savio. Directed by Richard C Bock.
Education; History - World; Sociology
Dist - CNEMAG

Sowing for need or sowing for greed 56 MIN
16mm / VHS
Color (H C G)
$850.00, $350.00 purchase, $85.00 rental
Searches for the results of the miracle seeds, which were planted twenty years ago in the Third World in hopes of yielding improved wheat, corn and rice varieties in quantities sufficient to feed the starving masses. Discovers that the yields did increase, but only for those who could afford the irrigation and agrichemicals necessary. Multinational companies benefit from exporting modern agricultural methods, but economic dependence and environmental poisoning are among the prices the farmer has to pay. Produced by Judith Bourque and Peter Gunnarson.
Agriculture; Fine Arts; Social Science
Dist - BULFRG

Sowing hope 27 MIN
16mm
Color (G)
$485.00 purchase, $55.00 rental
Portrays the role of the church in the FMLN and the struggle for social justice in El Salvador. Includes interviews and speeches by church leaders. Filmed in both city and countryside. Produced by the Film and Television Collective, Radio Venceremos System.
Civics and Political Systems; Fine Arts; Sociology
Dist - FIRS

Soya bean - milk and cheese from Africa's soil 15 MIN
VHS
Fruits of the earth series
Color (G)
$175.00 purchase
Looks at efforts to cultivate soya beans and to produce milk and cheese from the oil produced by the plant. Considers its worldwide importance as a food source. Part of a series of 15 videos that describe everyday conditions in regions throughout the earth and look at plants available for environmentally sound, economically productive development.
Home Economics; Science - Natural
Dist - LANDMK

Soybeans 4 MIN
Videoreel / VT2
Beatrice Trum Hunter's Natural Foods Series
Color
Shows some of the many uses of the soybean, including being baked in a casserole and toasted as nibbles. Explains that soy grits and soy flour are used in baked goods and soy oil is good for a salad dressing. Points out that fermented soybean products include tamari, which is like Worchestershire sauce and miso, a soy paste for soup stock and casseroles. Demonstrates how to make tofu, a cheese made from soy flour.
Home Economics; Social Science
Dist - PBS **Prod** - WGBH 1974
PBS

Soybeans - Food, Feed and Future 20 MIN
16mm
Color
Introduces one of the world's oldest food plants, soybeans. Highlights efforts of soybean breeders to improve the varieties available to U S farmers.
Agriculture
Dist - MTP **Prod** - PHBI

Soyez Un Professionel 14 MIN
U-matic / VHS / 16mm
Color (J H A) (FRENCH)
A French - language version of the motion picture Be A Pro. Explains that professional players use the best equipment to protect themselves from injury when playing. Discusses such techniques as applied to automobile driving and machine work.
Foreign Language; Health and Safety; Physical Education and Recreation
Dist - IFB **Prod** - CHET 1966

Soyuz/Apollo Link - up 20 MIN
U-matic / VHS
Color
Tells the story of the first 'international flight of manned spaceships' which took place during the month of June, 1975. Shows Soviet and American astronauts in various stages of preparation.
Science - Physical
Dist - IHF **Prod** - IHF

SPA - 50 Dry Chemical Systems 10 MIN
VHS
Color (IND)
Teaches proper use of the Ansul brand dry chemical fire fighting system. Includes sequence of operation and a fire test.
Health and Safety
Dist - ANSUL **Prod** - ANSUL

Spa workout series
Offers viewers a set of three videos that contain movements that burn fat, increase cardiovascular fitness, firm and shape muscles, relieve muscle tension and fatigue, and increase flexibility. Presents Canyon Ranch Fitness Director Rebecca Gorrell and Wellness Coordinator Jodina Scazzola-Pozo, who demonstrate modifications for all movements, including spinal, arm, and shoulder rotations. Videos range from 47 to 57 minutes and are available individually or as a set.
Fat burning aerobic workout
Muscle conditioning - metabolic booster
Stretching - the stress reducer
Dist - CAMV

Space 16 MIN
U-matic / VHS / 16mm
Advance of Science Series
Color (J H C A)
$385, $250 purchase _ #3805
Talks about the different events, people, discoveries, and theories that have helped humans to gain knowledge of the universes.
Science - Physical
Dist - CORF

Space 10 MIN
16mm / U-matic / VHS
Art of Seeing Series
Color (I)
LC 73-707909
Uses familiar objects and situations to show how we perceive space and how the artist utilizes it. Shows how space is defined and shaped by the objects which exist within it or enclose it.
Fine Arts
Dist - FI **Prod** - AFA 1970

Space 15 MIN
U-matic / VHS
Watch Your Language Series
Color (J H)
$125.00 purchase
Explores the numerous terms associated with space and space exploration.
English Language; Social Science
Dist - AITECH **Prod** - KYTV 1984

Space 29 MIN
VHS / 16mm
Discovery Digest Series
Color (S)
$300.00 purchase _ #707609
Explores a vast array of science - related discoveries, challenges and technological breakthroughs. Profiles and 'demystifies' research and development currently underway in many fields. 'Space' examines an inflatable planetarium, mining the asteroids, the secret of the Northern Lights and the winners of the national 'Invent - An - Alien' contest.
Industrial and Technical Education; Literature and Drama; Psychology; Science; Science - Natural; Science - Physical; Sociology
Dist - ACCESS **Prod** - ACCESS 1989

Space 16 MIN
VHS
Color (J H C)
$59.00 purchase _ #3805
Chronicles the events, people, theories and discoveries that contributed to knowledge of the universe - from Aristotle's original conception of the universe and Ptolemy's geocentric theory to the current search for extraterrestrial life. Includes illustrations and telescopic and space probe photos.
History - World; Science - Physical
Dist - INSTRU

Space 15 MIN
VHS / U-matic
Arts Express Series
Color (K P I J)
Fine Arts
Dist - KYTV **Prod** - KYTV 1983

Space 30 MIN
U-matic
Polka Dot Door Series
Color (K)
Presents a variety show for pre - school children. Includes songs, mime, stories, film sequences, talk, dance and fantasy figures. Each show emphasizes a particular

theme such as numbers, feelings, exploring, music or time. Comes with parent teacher guide.
Fine Arts; Literature and Drama
Dist - TVOTAR **Prod** - TVOTAR 1985

Space - a closer look
Videodisc
A closer look series
Color (I J)
$189.00 purchase _ #Q11131
Examines scientific concepts in space studies. Focuses on the limits of humans and technology in space and explains how themes of systems and interactions are incorporated into space studies. Includes barcoded teacher's guide. Part of a series of five programs.
Science; Sociology
Dist - CF

The Space age 15 MIN
VHS / U-matic
Discovering series; Unit 5 - Space
Color (I)
Science - Physical
Dist - AITECH **Prod** - WDCNTV 1978

Space Age - Dr Goddard to Project Gemini 18 MIN
16mm
Screen news digest series; Vol 7; Issue 9
B&W
Records the sights and sounds of the Space Age from the pioneering work of Robert Goddard to the cosmic conquests of Project Gemini.
Science; Science - Physical
Dist - HEARST **Prod** - HEARST 1965

Space Age Railroad 18 MIN
16mm
Color
LC 74-705669
Tells the story of high speed test track, a research and development facility at Holloman AFB, New Mexico. Highlights advancements since the first track run in 1950. Illustrates monorail runs and explains principal braking systems. Explains the physical layout of areas and different experiments.
Science; Social Science
Dist - USNAC **Prod** - USAF 1969

Space age series
Presents a six - part series on the space age featuring Patrick Stewart as host. Includes Quest for Planet Mars; Celestial Sentinels; The Unexpected Universe; To the Moon and Beyond; Mission to Planet Earth; What's a Heaven For.
Celestial sentinels - 2
Quest for planet Mars - 1
To the moon and beyond
The Unexpected universe - 3
What's a heaven for - 6
Dist - INSTRU **Prod** - NAOS 1969

Space age series
Mission to planet Earth - 5 60 MIN
Dist - INSTRU
KNOWUN

Space age series
Celestial sentinels 60 MIN
Quest for Mars 60 MIN
Dist - KNOWUN

Space and composition - 4 27 MIN
U-matic / VHS
Think new series
Color (C G)
$129.00, $99.00 purchase _ #V579
Gives theoretical motivation and practical ideas about the concepts of space and composition in the arts. Draws content from mathematics, science, history, human feelings, every human endeavor. Part of an 11 - part series that treats art as an essential mode of learning.
Fine Arts
Dist - BARR **Prod** - CEPRO 1991

Space and the Atom 27 MIN
16mm
Color (PRO)
LC 70-714177
Reports on many of the successes of nuclear energy in space, such as the SNAP generators. Delineates the joint efforts of the U S Atomic Energy Commission and the National Aeronautics and Space Administration to develop a nuclear rocket engine and depicts the future role of nuclear energy in space exploration.
Science - Physical
Dist - USERD **Prod** - ANL 1971

Space between Us - the Family in Transition 24 MIN
U-matic / VHS
Color
$335.00 purchase
From the ABC TV program, Directions.
Sociology
Dist - ABCLR **Prod** - ABCLR 1980

Space Camp 15 MIN
VHS / 16mm
Challenge Series
Color (I)
$125.00 purchase, $25.00 rental
Teaches about the environment of space and the training necessary for space travel through the experience of students in a week - long space camp.
Science; Science - Physical
Dist - AITECH **Prod** - WDCNTV 1987

Space case - 31
VHS
Reading rainbow series
Color; CC (K P)
$39.95 purchase
Asks what it would be like to meet beings from another planet. Tells about a young boy who does - on a spooky Halloween night. LeVar sends a special invitation to all the aliens watching Reading Rainbow to visit Earth, and shows them some of Earth's wonders. Part of a series offering a multicultural approach to generating reading enthusiasm with cross - curricular applications, hosted by LeVar Burton.
English Language; Literature and Drama; Science
Dist - GPN **Prod** - LNMDP

Space Child 28 MIN
16mm
Color
LC 77-702649
Focuses on Paul Van Hoydonck and his conceptual sculpture.
Fine Arts
Dist - CANFDC **Prod** - CANFDC 1972

Space Communications 19 MIN
16mm
Color
LC FIE61-122
Uses animation to highlight the basic communications principles and techniques relating to space. Explains the behavior of electromagnetic waves and discusses factors, such as distance, payloads and telemetry.
Psychology; Science - Physical; Social Science
Dist - USNAC **Prod** - USAF 1960

The Space Connection 10 MIN
16mm
Color
LC 80-701455
Describes a digital communication system which employs satellites to provide extremely wide bandwidth connections anywhere in the United States.
Industrial and Technical Education; Social Science
Dist - FLECKG **Prod** - SATBS 1980

Space Down to Earth 28 MIN
U-matic
Space in the 70's Series
Color
LC 79-706680
Shows how Earth - orbiting satellites are serving mankind in the 1970s and discusses prospects for the next decade. Covers Earth resources surveys, measurement of pollution levels, long - range weather forecasts and improvement of navigation and communication. Issued in 1970 as a motion picture.
Industrial and Technical Education; Science - Physical; Social Science; Sociology
Dist - USNAC **Prod** - NASA 1979

Space Driving Tactics 14 MIN
16mm / U-matic / VHS
Color (J)
LC 81-700742
Demonstrates the importance of keeping a safe distance from other vehicles on the highway, and shows how to determine what distance is safe for various driving conditions.
Health and Safety
Dist - AIMS **Prod** - CAHILL 1980

The Space Duet of Gumdrop and Spider - Apollo 9 28 MIN
16mm
Color
Presents a view of the Apollo 9 astronauts before, during and after their earth orbital mission. Concentrates on the launching, rendezvous and docking of the command module (Gumdrop), lunar module (Spider) and the return and recovery of the crew.
Industrial and Technical Education; Science - Physical; Social Science
Dist - NASA **Prod** - NASA

Space, earth and atmosphere - Volume 1
VHS
Tell me why series
Color (P I J)
$19.80 purchase _ #0148; $19.95 purchase
Shows how big the universe is. Describes the solar system, the origin of the sun, why the moon shines, how fast the Earth moves, and the atmosphere of the Earth. Part one of a two - part series on the Earth.
Science - Physical
Dist - SEVVID **Prod** - WNETTV
PBS

Space education series
Presents a three - part series that provides teachers and students with information regarding the latest experimentation with weightlessness. Includes teacher's guide.
Making sense of our senses 13 MIN
Microgravity 13 MIN
What if 13 MIN
Dist - TVOTAR **Prod** - TVOTAR

Space Expectations 27 MIN
16mm
B&W; Color
Looks at the varied viewpoints of America's space program from a cross section of the general public.
History - World; Industrial and Technical Education; Science - Physical
Dist - NASA **Prod** - NASA 1973
USNAC

Space experience series
Consists of a six - part series which takes the viewer on a guided tour of space exploration hosted by astronaut Marc Garneau, a veteran of the Challenger Space Shuttle. Contains Flying on Fire, rocket power created and controlled; Staying Alive, space as a new environment for humankind; Astroworkers, space environment affects accomplishment of various tasks; Space, Inc, how money is made and lost in space; Exploring the Edge, space exploration leads to a new view of planet Earth; and Outward Bound, the impact of humans in space on our consciousness. Each episode is 26 minutes in length.
Astroworkers 26 MIN
Exploring the Edge 26 MIN
Flying on fire 26 MIN
Outward Bound 26 MIN
Space, Inc 26 MIN
Staying Alive 26 MIN
Dist - CNEMAG **Prod** - BUTNIG 1973

Space experiments - Skylab 15 MIN
VHS / U-matic
Discovering series; Unit 5 - Space
Color (I)
Science - Physical
Dist - AITECH **Prod** - WDCNTV 1978

Space exploration; 2nd ed. 15 MIN
U-matic
Search for science series; Unit II - Space
Color (I)
Explains and illustrates the fundamental laws of inertia.
Science - Physical
Dist - GPN **Prod** - WVIZTV

Space Exploration - a Team Effort 24 MIN
U-matic / VHS / 16mm
Color (I J H)
$59.00 purchase _ #3114; LC 72-702520
Introduces the contributions of scientists, engineers and technicians involved in the space program and who make it possible. Follows an astronaut through various training procedures and learning sessions. Reveals present methods of training and future plans.
Industrial and Technical Education; Science; Science - Physical
Dist - EBEC **Prod** - EBEC 1972

Space exploration - our solar system 30 MIN
VHS
Color (I J)
$125 purchase_#10328VL
Traces the development of the solar system and its planets using footage from NASA, computer graphics and animations. Describes and contrasts the planets. Illustrates the vast distances in space through models and comparisons. Split into two parts, the inner planets and the outer planets. Comes with a teacher's guide; student activities; discussion questions; and six blackline masters.
Science - Physical
Dist - UNL

Space exploration - the rockets 23 MIN
VHS
Color (I J)
$95 purchase _ #10218VG
Describes the development of the rocket and space programs. Contrasts solid and liquid fuel rockets. Covers major accomplishments in space exploration and rocket propulsion development. Comes with a teacher's guide and blackline masters.

History - World; Industrial and Technical Education; Science - Physical
Dist - UNL

Space Filling Curves 26 MIN
U-matic / VHS / 16mm
Topology Series
Color (PRO)
LC 73-700763
Illustrates the concept of a limit curve, as specified by a sequence of approximation curves and applies it to the construction of space filling curves in the production of a 16 - millimeter film.
Fine Arts; Mathematics
Dist - IFB **Prod** - IFB

A Space Flight Around the Earth 12 MIN
U-matic / VHS / 16mm
Color; PAL (P) (GERMAN)
Features the flights of John Glenn and Ed White. Pictures the earth as viewed from space.
Foreign Language; Science; Science - Physical
Dist - CF VIEWTH **Prod** - DF VIEWTH 1965

Space for Man 120 MIN
VHS / 16mm
Color (G)
$120.00 rental _ #SPMN - 000
Looks at the ways space technology has benefited humankind in the past and how it may change the future. Includes interviews with leading space figures.
History - World; Science - Physical
Dist - PBS **Prod** - NPACT

Space for the Mentally Retarded 22 MIN
16mm
Color
Shows existing programs and facilities for the mentally retarded and points out remaining needs and how they might be met. Discusses the importance of a team approach in the provision of services to the mentally retarded.
Health and Safety; Psychology; Sociology
Dist - USD **Prod** - USD 1968

Space for Women 28 MIN
16mm
Color (H C A)
LC 81-701185
Interviews women employed in NASA's space transportation programs and shows the variety of positions that they hold, ranging from electrical engineer, aerial photography analyst and safety specialist to astronaut mission specialist. Notes how the women obtained their training and qualified for their positions.
Business and Economics; Science - Physical; Sociology
Dist - USNAC **Prod** - NASA 1981

Space hunting series
Circles, triangles, rectangles, squares 7 MIN
Dist - CORF

Space in the 70's - Aeronautics 28 MIN
16mm
Color
LC 70-710249
Shows the problems of aeronautical flight and flight operations. Includes pictures of short haul aircrafts.
Industrial and Technical Education; Social Science
Dist - USNAC **Prod** - NASA 1971

Space in the 70's - Challenge and Promise 27 MIN
16mm
Space in the 70's Series
Color
LC 74-705672
Presents an updated overview of the content of space in the 70's series.
Science; Science - Physical
Dist - USNAC **Prod** - NASA 1973

Space in the 70's - Exploration of the Planets 25 MIN
16mm
Space in the 70's Series
Color
LC 77-713562
Summarizes the principal features of the planets and presents the various missions planned for their exploration during the decade of the 1970s.
Science; Science - Physical
Dist - USNAC **Prod** - NASA 1971

Space in the 70's - Man in Space - the Second Decade 28 MIN
16mm
Color
Includes a brief history of where we stand now and views proposed future manned space flight programs. Presents mission activities and reasons behind extended Apollo lunar missions in 1971 and 1972, the first experimental space station called Skylab and the space shuttle later in the decade.
Geography - World; Industrial and Technical Education; Science - Physical
Dist - USNAC **Prod** - NASA 1971

Space in the 70's Series
Space in the 70's - Space Down to Earth 28 MIN
Dist - NASA

Space in the 70's Series

Aeronautics	28 MIN
Challenge and Promise	27 MIN
Exploration of the Planets	25 MIN
The Knowledge Bank	25 MIN
Man in Space, the Second Decade	28 MIN
Space Down to Earth	28 MIN
Space in the 70's - Challenge and Promise	27 MIN
Space in the 70's - Exploration of the Planets	25 MIN
Space in the 70's - the Knowledge Bank	25 MIN

Dist - USNAC

Space in the 70's - Space Down to Earth 28 MIN
16mm
Space in the 70's Series
Color (I)
LC 79-710645
Shows how earth - orbiting satellites are serving mankind and what can be expected during the next decade. Includes earth resources surveys, measurements of pollution levels, long - range weather forecasts, precise earth measurements and improved navigation and communications.
Science - Natural; Science - Physical
Dist - NASA **Prod** - NASA 1970

Space in the 70's - the Knowledge Bank 25 MIN
16mm
Space in the 70's Series
Color
LC 76-713168
Presents the idea that research results are deposits to be accumulated and later drawn upon - with the payoff frequently beyond even the range of science fiction. Takes a broad look at physics and astronomy research performed in the laboratory of space.
Science; Science - Physical
Dist - USNAC **Prod** - NASA 1971

Space, Inc 30 MIN
VHS / U-matic
Innovation Series
Color
Looks at a new breed of entrepreneurs who see outer space as the next frontier for private enterprise. Points out that space exploration so far has been a strictly government - financed operation.
Business and Economics; History - World; Science - Physical
Dist - PBS **Prod** - WNETTV 1983

Space, Inc 26 MIN
16mm / VHS
Space Experience Series
Color (G)
$425.00, $295.00 purchase, $55.00 rental; LC 89715681
Looks at how money is made and lost in space - from immediate and substantial profits in telecommunications to long range gambles on the manufacture of drugs and crystals. Part of a six - part series on space hosted by astronaut Marc Garneau, veteran of the Challenger Space Shuttle.
Business and Economics; History - World; Industrial and Technical Education; Science; Science - Physical
Dist - CNEMAG **Prod** - REIDW 1988

Space - Life Out There 22 MIN
16mm / U-matic / VHS
Color
Discusses the possibilities of there being intelligent life on other planets. Examines the controversy about what these beings look like and the efforts being made to contact outer space with radio waves.
Industrial and Technical Education; Science - Natural; Science - Physical
Dist - CNEMAG **Prod** - DOCUA

Space - Man's Great Adventure Series
The Dream that Wouldn't Down 27 MIN
Dist - NASA

Space Medicine - Serving Mankind 14 MIN
U-matic / VHS
Color
Tells how technologies developed to safely facilitate man's exploration of space are now being used to prolong life and eradicate disease here on earth.
Health and Safety; History - World; Science - Physical
Dist - KINGFT **Prod** - KINGFT

Space Medicine - Serving Manking 13 MIN
16mm
Screen news digest series; Vol 24; Issue 8
Color
Focuses on medical research in space that is reaping benefits for people on earth.
Health and Safety
Dist - AFA **Prod** - AFA 1982

Space Navigation 21 MIN
16mm
Color (J H A)
LC FIE67-120
Illustrates with animation and live - action photography the equipment, techniques and mathematics of space navigation between the earth and moon and between the earth and other planets.
Social Science
Dist - NASA **Prod** - NASA 1967

Space Neighbors 15 MIN
U-matic / VHS
Why Series
Color (P I)
Discusses earth's space neighbors.
Science - Physical
Dist - AITECH **Prod** - WDCNTV 1976

The Space of pottery 26 MIN
VHS
Color (H C G)
$195.00 purchase, $50.00 rental _ #38146
Explores the work, creative process and philosophical perspective of internationally acclaimed ceramicist Paul Mathieu. Illustrates the many stages of the ceramic process as Mathieu creats a complicated piece inspired by the book A Brief History of Time by theoretical physicist Stephen Hawking. Produced by Richard L Harrison.
Fine Arts
Dist - UCEMC

Space Orbits 18 MIN
16mm
Color
LC FIE61-123
Uses animation to present basic facts of orbital patterns and the forces which produce them. Tells how these projects follow natural laws formulated by Sir Isaac Newton.
Science - Physical
Dist - USNAC **Prod** - USAF 1960

Space Patrol - 1951,1953 60 MIN
U-matic / VHS
Color
Presents episodes from the 1951 space series with Commander Cory.
Science; Science - Physical
Dist - IHF **Prod** - IHF

Space Patrol - 1953
VHS / U-matic
Color
Presents Commander Cory with high adventure in the vast regions of space from the 1953 space series.
Fine Arts
Dist - IHF **Prod** - IHF

Space Pioneers - a Canadian Story 53 MIN
VHS / 16mm
Color (G)
$295.00 purchase, $90.00 rental; LC 90708188
Documents the story of the first generation of Canadian space pioneers. Shows how, beginning in the late 1950s, these scientists built a series of rockets and eventually launched the successful Alouette satellite. Blends archival footage with contemporary interviews.
Geography - World; History - World; Industrial and Technical Education; Science
Dist - CNEMAG **Prod** - RUDY 1988

Space planning 30 MIN
Videoreel / VT2
Designing home interiors series; Unit 12
Color (C A)
Explains the basic concepts of furniture arrangement. Defines the general goal of space planning.
Home Economics
Dist - CDTEL **Prod** - COAST

Space Project 15 MIN
16mm
Color
LC FIA67-1839
Shows how drug stores become cluttered and disorganized because of the increase in products and promotion items in the same amount of space. Demonstrates ways in which pharmacists can make the best use of their available floor and display space.
Business and Economics
Dist - JAJ **Prod** - JAJ 1965

The Space Race in Asia 24 MIN
U-matic / VHS
Color (C)
$249.00, $149.00 purchase _ #AD - 2202
Reports on the aggressive space programs of China and Japan. Shows where America's leadership is being challenged. Provides the first in - depth look at China'a highly secret space program.
Business and Economics; Geography - World; History - World; Industrial and Technical Education; Science - Physical
Dist - FOTH **Prod** - FOTH

The Space Race in Europe 24 MIN
U-matic / VHS
Color (C)
$249.00, $149.00 purchase _ #AD - 2203
Looks at space programs underway in western Europe. Presents evidence that western European nations wroking through the European Space Agency - ESA - have surpassed Russia and America in the contest to commercialize space.
Business and Economics; Civics and Political Systems; Geography - World; History - World; Industrial and Technical Education; Science - Physical
Dist - FOTH **Prod** - FOTH

Space Rendezvous 25 MIN
16mm
Color
LC 74-706251
Clarifies the principles and limitations of orbital maneuvering in outer space. Focuses primarily on coplanar orbits but also delineates the complexities of noncoplanar orbits for comparison. Points out the problems involved in transferring a vehicle from one orbit to another for rendezvous with another vehicle.
Social Science
Dist - USNAC **Prod** - USAF 1964

Space Research and You Series
Space Research and You - Your Home and Environment 15 MIN
Space Research and You - Your Transportation 15 MIN
Space Research and Your Health 15 MIN
Dist - USNAC

Space Research and You - Your Home and Environment 15 MIN
U-matic / VHS / 16mm
Space Research and You Series
Color
Illustrates spacecraft studies of Earth for inventory of resources and detection of pollution. Shows advanced technologies for acquiring energy from the sun and wind, sewage treatment facilities and energy - saving household devices.
Science; Science - Physical; Social Science; Sociology
Dist - USNAC **Prod** - NASA

Space Research and You - Your Transportation 15 MIN
U-matic / VHS / 16mm
Space Research and You Series
Color
Examines computer simulation teaching tools for training ships' crews, vertical takeoff and landing planes, electric cars, streamlining trucks, aircraft improvement and the space shuttle.
Education; Industrial and Technical Education; Science; Science - Physical
Dist - USNAC **Prod** - NASA

Space Research and Your Health 15 MIN
U-matic / VHS / 16mm
Space Research and You Series
Color
Shows how NASA research has led to improved medical tools and new health practices. Shows miniaturized spacecraft components adapted into implantable devices for treatment of heart disease and diabetes, computer technology for medical diagnosis and communications systems for rural health care.
Health and Safety; Industrial and Technical Education; Science; Science - Natural; Science - Physical
Dist - USNAC **Prod** - NASA

Space robot 30 MIN
VHS
Limit series
Color (A PRO IND)
PdS30 purchase _ Unavailable in USA and Canada
Explains that the Rosetta Mission requires a robot to take samples from the ice surface of a comet and that Stephen Gorevan is constructing one. Part of a six-part series exploring limits of human achievement in engineering, focusing on international engineers facing their toughest career assignments. Asks how far physical limits can be pushed and what restraints exist in extending the scale of engineering projects.
Computer Science; Industrial and Technical Education
Dist - BBCENE

Space Salvage 30 MIN
U-matic / VHS / 16mm
Enterprise Series
Color (H C A)
Chronicles Lloyd's of London's plan to recover two satellites lost in space that it had insured.
Business and Economics
Dist - CORF **Prod** - CORF

Space Science - an Introduction 14 MIN
16mm / U-matic / VHS
Space Science Series
Color (I J)
LC 77-701880
Presents an introduction to the vocabulary and scientific principles of space travel. Uses animation and a specially designed model to show why some vehicles stay in orbit while others can travel through space.
Science - Physical
Dist - CORF **Prod** - CORF 1977

Space science - comets, meteors and asteroids 12 MIN
VHS
Color; PAL (P I J H)
Looks at comets, meteors and asteroids in space. Charts the course of Halley's comet through telescopic photographs and space probes, from its visit early this century to its most recent passage. Shares information from an Antarctic expedition in which ancient meteorites preserved by the polar cold were discovered.
History - World; Science - Physical
Dist - VIEWTH **Prod** - VIEWTH

Space Science - Comets, Meteors and Planetoids 11 MIN
16mm / U-matic / VHS
Space Science Series
Color (I J H)
Shows how the spectroscope, radio and optical telescopes are used to provide information about the origin of comets, meteors and planetoids. Special effects show the meteor shower of 1833, the approach of Halley's comet and the movements of planetoids.
Science - Physical
Dist - CORF **Prod** - CORF 1963

Space Science - Exploring the Moon 16 MIN
16mm / U-matic / VHS
Space Science Series
Color (J H C)
LC 73-704138
Illustrates the 400 - year - long story of lunar exploration, using ancient maps, photographs and motion pictures, including those taken by the first men on the moon.
Science - Physical
Dist - CORF **Prod** - CORF 1969

Space science - exploring the moon 16 MIN
VHS
Color; PAL (H)
Overviews the exploration of the moon, from Galileo's first telescopic view to the first human steps on its surface. Uses ancient maps, photographs and motion pictures taken through telescopes and by the first people on the moon to identify major surface features and illustrate the 400 - year - long story.
History - World; Science - Physical
Dist - VIEWTH **Prod** - VIEWTH

Space Science - Galaxies and the Universe 14 MIN
U-matic / VHS / 16mm
Space Science Series
Color (J H C)
LC 70-704137
Describes the three types of galaxies. Shows the two types of star populations and quasars and illustrates the three most prominent theories of expansion.
Science - Physical
Dist - CORF **Prod** - CORF 1969

Space science - planets 24 MIN
VHS
Color; PAL (P I J H)
Uses telescopic photography, computer simulation and motion pictures from the NASA space probes of Mercury, Venus, Mars, Jupiter, Uranus and Saturn to take a look at the solar system.
History - World; Science - Physical
Dist - VIEWTH **Prod** - VIEWTH

Space Science Series
Comets, meteors, and asteroids 12 MIN
Galaxies and the universe 14 MIN
Planets 24 MIN
Space Science - an Introduction 14 MIN
Space Science - Comets, Meteors and Planetoids 11 MIN
Space Science - Exploring the Moon 16 MIN
Space Science - Galaxies and the Universe 14 MIN
Space Science - Studying the Stars 13 MIN
Space Science - the Planets 16 MIN
Dist - CORF

Space Science Series
Constellations, Guides to the Night Sky 11 MIN
Dist - IU

Space Science Series
Energy in orbit
Flight to the planets 11 MIN
Orbital Shapes and Paths 11 MIN
Over the Hill to the Moon 8 MIN
Principles of Orbit 11 MIN
Rendezvous 11 MIN
Dist - JOU

Space Science - Studying the Stars 13 MIN
16mm / U-matic / VHS
Space Science Series
Color (I J H)
Shows how optical and radio telescopes can measure the energy - radiation of stars and how distance to the stars can be found by the parallax method and by comparing their brightness or magnitude. Presents methods used to keep track of star movements, and how the star's light gives clues to its heat, composition, movement and size.
Science; Science - Physical
Dist - CORF **Prod** - CORF 1967

Space Science - the Planets 16 MIN
U-matic / VHS / 16mm
Space Science Series
Color (I J H)
Uses telescopic pictures, animation and special effects to survey the nine planets and their satellites. Discusses temperature and atmosphere of the planets, their periods of rotation and revolution, and their distance from the sun. Shows how instruments launched into space aid scientists in their study.
Science - Physical
Dist - CORF **Prod** - CORF 1963

Space Sciences Series
An Introduction 14 MIN
Dist - CORF

The Space Shuttle 28 MIN
U-matic / VHS
Video Encyclopedia of Space Series
Color (C)
$249.00, $149.00 purchase _ #AD - 2113
Explains the technology of the space shuttle and shows the functions of its three components - the orbiter, the external tank and the solid rocket boosters. Covers the design of a reusable space vehicle and shows some of the training required for shuttle personnel. Part of an eleven - part series on space.
History - World; Industrial and Technical Education; Science - Physical
Dist - FOTH **Prod** - FOTH

The Space shuttle 27 MIN
VHS / U-matic
Color (P I J)
$325.00, $295.00 purchase _ #V212
Takes an animated look at the US space program and a flight aboard a space shuttle. Reviews the early days of the space race between the United States and the Soviet Union, and the development of a resuable space craft, the shuttle. Shows how the shuttle is propelled into orbit, the tasks it is designed to perform and what it takes to become an astronaut. Includes live footage of astronauts aboard a shuttle flight.
Fine Arts; History - World; Industrial and Technical Education; Science
Dist - BARR **Prod** - GLOBET 1991

The Space Shuttle 30 MIN
VHS / 16mm
Conquest of Space Series
Color (G)
Introduces the space shuttle and its many applications, including scientific experimentation and strategic defense.
History - United States; History - World; Industrial and Technical Education
Dist - FLMWST

Space shuttle 80 MIN
VHS
Color (G)
$39.95 purchase
Takes a comprehensive look at the U S space shuttle program. Features in - space footage of the shuttle and crews in action.
History - United States; History - World
Dist - PBS **Prod** - WNETTV

Space Shuttle 15 MIN
16mm
Color (J H A)
LC 77-700809
Describes the reusable space shuttle and its capabilities for replacing the expendable launch vehicles how being used. Uses animation sequences to illustrate a typical flight mission and the proposed use of the shuttle.
History - World; Science; Science - Physical
Dist - USNAC **Prod** - NASA 1976

The Space Shuttle 14 MIN
U-matic / VHS
Color
Provides information on the U S Space Shuttle, emphasizing the importance of its success from a military and civilian perspective.
Industrial and Technical Education; Science - Physical
Dist - JOU **Prod** - UPI

The Space Shuttle
U-matic / VHS
(J H C A)
$59.00 purchase _ #04542 94
Features action footage of the United States Shuttle program, vehicles, and crews.
Industrial and Technical Education
Dist - ASPRSS

The Space Shuttle 4 MIN
16mm
Color
LC 75-703074
Gives the rationale for a reusable space launching vehicle for scientific experimentation. Describes a typical shuttle mission from launch to landing at Kennedy Space Center, Florida.
History - World; Industrial and Technical Education; Science; Science - Physical
Dist - USNAC **Prod** - NASA 1973

Space Shuttle - a Remarkable Flying Machine 30 MIN
16mm
Color
LC 81-701641
Describes in detail the first space shuttle flight. Shows the lift - off, in - flight activities and landing at Dryden Flight Research Center, California.
Science - Physical
Dist - USNAC **Prod** - NASA 1981

Space Shuttle After Flight Reports Series
Space Shuttle After Flight Reports - Vol 1 64 MIN
Space Shuttle After Flight Reports - Vol 2 64 MIN
Space Shuttle After Flight Reports - Vol 3 64 MIN
Space Shuttle After Flight Reports - Vol 4 64 MIN
Space Shuttle After Flight Reports - Vol 5 64 MIN
Space Shuttle After Flight Reports - Vol 6 64 MIN
Dist - ASVS

Space Shuttle After Flight Reports - Vol 1 64 MIN
U-matic
Space Shuttle After Flight Reports Series
Color (A)
Shows the post flight procedures for the space shuttle.
Industrial and Technical Education
Dist - ASVS **Prod** - NASA 1986 2

Space Shuttle After Flight Reports - Vol 2 64 MIN
U-matic
Space Shuttle After Flight Reports Series
Color (A)
Shows the post flight procedures for the space shuttle.
Industrial and Technical Education
Dist - ASVS **Prod** - NASA 1986

Space Shuttle After Flight Reports - Vol 3 64 MIN
U-matic
Space Shuttle After Flight Reports Series
Color (A)
Shows the post flight procedures for the space shuttle.
History - World; Science - Physical
Dist - ASVS **Prod** - NASA 1986

Space Shuttle After Flight Reports - Vol 4 64 MIN
U-matic
Space Shuttle After Flight Reports Series
Color (A)
Shows the post flight procedures for the space shuttle.
History - World; Science - Physical
Dist - ASVS **Prod** - NASA 1986

Space Shuttle After Flight Reports - Vol 5 64 MIN
U-matic
Space Shuttle After Flight Reports Series
Color (A)
Shows the post flight procedures for the space shuttle.
History - World; Science - Physical
Dist - ASVS **Prod** - NASA 1986

Space Shuttle After Flight Reports - Vo 6l 64 MIN
U-matic
Space Shuttle After Flight Reports Series
Color (A)
Shows the post flight procedures for the space shuttle.
History - World; Science - Physical
Dist - ASVS **Prod** - NASA 1986

Space Shuttle Columbia Flights 1, 2, 3 and 4 28 MIN
VHS / BETA
Color
Shows the official NASA film on all orbital test flights of the Shuttle Columbia. Includes tests, failures, successes, onboard experiments and landings, plus its scientific space discoveries.
Science - Physical
Dist - CBSC **Prod** - CBSC

Space Shuttle Communications 8 MIN
16mm
Space Shuttle Profile Series
Color
LC 81-701652
Explains the vast communications and tracking support shuttle operations, including the tracking and data relay satellite systems to be used for payloads, the NASA communication network, domestic satellites and the deep space network for interplanetary missions.
Science - Physical
Dist - USNAC **Prod** - NASA 1981

Space Shuttle Economics 6 MIN
U-matic / VHS / 16mm
Space Shuttle Profile Series
Color
Explains the economic advantages of the space shuttle system by pointing out the reusability of elements such as the solid rocket boosters and the orbiter. Discusses the financial gain from transporting satellites into space and the 'Gateway Special' program.
Business and Economics; Science - Physical; Social Science
Dist - USNAC **Prod** - NASA

Space Shuttle Extra Vehicular Activity 12 MIN
16mm
Space Shuttle Profile Series
Color
LC 81-701654
Explains the tools, tethers, space suits, life support systems and maneuvering units of extravehicular activity tasks that are planned for shuttle operations.
Science - Physical
Dist - USNAC **Prod** - NASA 1981

Space Shuttle - Flights STS - 1 through STS - 8 60 MIN
VHS
Color (J)
$29.95 purchase _ #1232V
Features two NASA films, 'Opening New Frontiers' and 'We Deliver.' Summarizes the accomplishments of flights 1 through 8.
History - World; Industrial and Technical Education; Religion and Philosophy; Science - Physical
Dist - SCTRES **Prod** - SCTRES

Space Shuttle Ground Support 8 MIN
16mm
Space Shuttle Profile Series
Color
LC 81-701655
Outlines the role of the key facilities for shuttle operations. Discusses particular installations and their individual responsibilities with regard to the space shuttle program.
Science - Physical
Dist - USNAC **Prod** - NASA 1981

Space shuttle journey 25 MIN
VHS
Sparky's animation series
Color (P I R)
$19.95 purchase, $10.00 rental _ #35 - 815 - 2020
Describes Sparky's disappointment at not being selected for the space shuttle mission. Suggests that God will lead Sparky, and other people, to the best place they can serve God.
Literature and Drama; Religion and Philosophy
Dist - APH **Prod** - ANDERK

Space Shuttle - Mission to the Future 27 MIN
16mm
Color
LC 81-701186
Documents the importance of the space shuttle to America and the world. Shows shuttle tests, the training of astronauts and space specialists at work. Includes brief comments on space exploration by novelists James Michener and Isaac Asimov.
Science - Physical
Dist - USNAC **Prod** - NASA 1981

Space Shuttle Missions and Payloads 14 MIN
16mm
Space Shuttle Profile Series
Color
LC 81-701656
Explains different kinds of missions and payloads that are planned for the space shuttle including placing, servicing and retrieving satellites in space, with a brief explanation of the purpose of these satellites. Looks at the multi - mission modular spacecraft, Long Duration Exposure Facility, space probes and Spacelab.
Science - Physical
Dist - USNAC **Prod** - NASA 1981

Space Shuttle Overview 1980 30 MIN
VHS / U-matic
History of Space Travel Series
Color
Discusses the space shuttle.
Science - Physical
Dist - MDCPB **Prod** - NASAC

Space Shuttle - Overview, may 1980 28 MIN
16mm
Space Shuttle Profile Series
Color
LC 81-700658
Looks at the status of the space shuttle as it is being prepared for its mid - 1980 launch. Features an overall view of the shuttle and its components.
Industrial and Technical Education; Science - Physical
Dist - USNAC **Prod** - NASA 1980

Space Shuttle - Platform to the Stars 14 MIN
U-matic / VHS
Color
Focuses on the Space Shuttle and its role in America's continuing efforts to enlarge, or push back the horizons of space.
History - World; Science - Physical
Dist - KINGFT **Prod** - KINGFT

Space Shuttle Profile Series
Orbiter Thermal Protection System 6 MIN
Space Shuttle - Overview, may 1980 28 MIN
Space Shuttle - the Orbiter 14 MIN
Space Shuttle Communications 8 MIN
Space Shuttle Economics 6 MIN
Space Shuttle Extra Vehicular Activity 12 MIN
Space Shuttle Ground Support 8 MIN
Space Shuttle Missions and Payloads 14 MIN
Space Shuttle Propulsion 12 MIN
Space Shuttle Spacelab 12 MIN
STS - 1 Launch Aborts 5 MIN
Dist - USNAC

Space Shuttle Propulsion 12 MIN
16mm
Space Shuttle Profile Series
Color
LC 81-701657
Explains the key propulsion systems, their use for shuttle operations and how they differ from past expendable systems. Looks at the reusable solid rocket boosters, the external tank, the main propulsion system, the reaction control system and the orbital maneuvering subsystem.
Science - Physical
Dist - USNAC **Prod** - NASA 1981

Space Shuttle Spacelab 12 MIN
16mm
Space Shuttle Profile Series
Color
LC 81-701658
Describes the Spacelab Program, including information about the European Space Agency, the scientific expectations of Spacelab and the eight different Spacelab configurations.
Science - Physical
Dist - USNAC **Prod** - NASA 1981

Space Shuttle - the Orbiter 14 MIN
16mm
Space Shuttle Profile Series
Color
LC 81-701659
Explains the space transportation system in general, including the main components, the Orbiter, external tank and solid rocket boosters. Describes the size configuration and internal design of the Orbiter and the multitude of systems such as propulsion, thermal protection and computer.
Science - Physical
Dist - USNAC **Prod** - NASA 1981

Space Spraying of Insecticides 11 MIN
16mm
Color (SPANISH)
LC FIE61-21
Demonstrates techniques of space spraying for insect control over large areas and shows various types of modern power - spraying equipment.
Agriculture; Health and Safety
Dist - USNAC **Prod** - USPHS 1961

Space station 25 MIN
U-matic / VHS
Color (J H C G)
$305.00, $280.00 purchase _ #V363
Features actor George Takei who portrays Lt Sulu of Star Trek as narrator. Looks at what has happened to the United States space program since the shuttle disaster.
History - United States; History - World; Science - Physical
Dist - BARR **Prod** - CEPRO 1987

Space Station 25 MIN
U-matic
Color (J H C A)
Examines the future of a space laboratory.
History - World; Industrial and Technical Education; Science - Physical
Dist - CEPRO **Prod** - CEPRO

Space station readstar series Space station readstar series
Syllabication skills - Pt 2 15 MIN
Dist - GPN

Space station readstar series
The AW sound 15 MIN
Changing Y to I 15 MIN
Compound words 15 MIN
Contractions - Pt 1 15 MIN
Contractions - Pt 2 15 MIN
Dipthongs and irregular vowel sounds 15 MIN
Doubling final consonant 15 MIN
Dropping final E 15 MIN
Final consonant clusters 15 MIN
Initial and final digraphs 15 MIN
Initial consonant cluster 15 MIN
Long A sound 15 MIN
Long E sound 15 MIN
Long I sound 15 MIN
Long O sound 15 MIN
Long U sound 15 MIN
Magic E 15 MIN
More initial consonant clusters 15 MIN
Prefixes and suffixes 15 MIN
R - influenced vowels 15 MIN
Short vowels 15 MIN
Sound placement within a word 15 MIN
Syllabication skills - Pt 1 15 MIN
Vowel pairs 15 MIN
Dist - GPN

Space Station - Venture Read - Alongs 77 MIN
U-matic / VHS
Venture Read - Alongs Series
(P I)
Contains a read along cassette and 8 paperbacks.
Science; Science - Physical
Dist - TROLA **Prod** - TROLA 1986

Space stations series
Features a three - part series dealing with space exploration. Includes Yesterday's Dream, Today's Reality which traces the origins of space exploration; Zero Gravity - The Space Station's Environment looks at how weightlessness affects all aspects of life - support systems; and Scientific Uses, International Cooperation covers all potential uses of the space station such as furthering planetary exploration and international cooperation. Titles available individually. Produced by Media Craft Communications.
Scientific uses, international cooperation 20 MIN
Yesterday's dream, today's reality 20 MIN
Zero gravity - The Space station's environment 20 MIN
Dist - NDIM

Space - the New Ocean 10 MIN
16mm
Color
LC 75-703758
Explains U S military space research and development activities in relation to overall space exploration, featuring current and future space and missile programs of the U S Air Force.
Civics and Political Systems; Industrial and Technical Education; Science; Science - Physical
Dist - USNAC **Prod** - USAF 1971

Space - the New Perspective - Orbital Photography 21 MIN
16mm
Color
Presents Mr Richard Underwood of the NASA Johnson Space Center, Phototechnology Division, discussing what space photography of Earth reveals to the scientist.
Industrial and Technical Education; Science; Science - Physical
Dist - NASA **Prod** - NASA

Space, time and Albert Einstein 29 MIN
U-matic / VHS / 16mm
Dimensions in science - Pt 2 series
Color (H C)
Presents archival footage featuring Albert Einstein explaining aspects of his Special Theory of Relativity which has been proven correct in predicting the way space and time are modified by relative velocities near the speed of light. Demonstrates the Fitzgerald - Lorentz contraction and time dilation, and concludes by showing how matter affects the structure of time and space.
Science; Science - Physical
Dist - FI **Prod** - OECA 1979

Space, Time and Albert Einstein 30 MIN
U-matic
Dimensions in Science - Physics Series
Color (H C)
Outlines Einstein's ideas on space, time, matter, energy, and gravity.
Science; Science - Physical
Dist - TVOTAR **Prod** - TVOTAR 1979

A Space to Grow 32 MIN
U-matic
B&W
Concentrates on the aims and techniques used by the upward bound program to motivate and rectify the academic disabilities of talented poor youngsters.
Education; Psychology; Sociology
Dist - USNAC **Prod** - USNAC 1972

Space Trace 11 MIN
16mm
Color
LC 80-701379
Uses experimental techniques to show an earthbound dancer spinning into outer space by means of a NASA rocket and ice dancing.
Fine Arts
Dist - ALLPI **Prod** - ALLPI 1980

Space trek 26 MIN
VHS
Wonderstruck presents series
Color (I J)
$99.95 purchase _ #Q11175
Investigates moonballs, positive pressure, the space shuttle, and the possibility of life on other planets in eight segments. Features a student contest to design an alien which could survive on other planets in our solar system. Part of a series of 11 programs produced by the British Broadcasting Corporation and hosted by Bob McDonald.
Science; Science - Physical
Dist - CF

Space Trek - Pt 7 30 MIN
VHS
Wonderstruck Presents Series
Color (I)
$99.00 purchase _ #386 - 9061
Organizes science programs thematically for classroom use. Features Bob McDonald as host who makes learning fun with amazing science information and engaging activities. Part 7 of the eight part series moves from the history of the first spaceships to the future of space exploration to cover space planes, moon balls, creating an alien, UFOs, sailcraft, shuttle compartments, a trip to Mars, and Martian fossils.
History - World; Science - Physical
Dist - FI **Prod** - CANBC 1989

Space worker 57 MIN
VHS
Color (H C A)
$49.95 purchase
Looks at how life - long civilian space workers feel abouth their lives, their commitment and their future in space exploration. Addresses the role of the American public in determining space policy and considers why young people are not as interested as formerly in the space program.
History - United States; History - World; Industrial and Technical Education; Science; Science - Physical
Dist - VARDIR

Spaceborne 14 MIN
U-matic / VHS / 16mm
Color
LC 77-702493
Presents a selection of film footage taken during the manned moon flights.
Science - Physical
Dist - PFP **Prod** - LAWHS 1977

Spacecoast 90 MIN
16mm
Color (G)
Presents an independent production by Ross McElwee. Offers a darkly hilarious story of the demise of Cape Canaveral and its eccentric population.
Fine Arts; Geography - United States; History - United States; History - World
Dist - FIRS

Spacecoast USA 15 MIN
16mm
Color
Presents Florida's Cocoa Beach, a noted vacation spot and headquarters for the nation's space program.
Geography - United States; Industrial and Technical Education; Sociology
Dist - FLADC **Prod** - FLADC

Spacecraft for Apollo 6 MIN
16mm
Apollo digest series
Color
LC 75-701379
Overviews the command, service and lunar landing modules.
Industrial and Technical Education; Science - Physical; Social Science
Dist - USNAC **Prod** - NASA 1969

Spacecut 42 MIN
16mm
Color (G)
$60.00 rental
Features an independent film from Hamburg by Werner Nekes, who founded the Hamburg Cooperative in 1967 and has run the Hamburger Filmschau since then. Makes the frame a very strong feature in which every frame is different, yet the assembly of images results in a picture of one place being filmed. The use of single frames has the effect on the audience of total relaxation.
Fine Arts
Dist - CANCIN

Spaced Out Sports 15 MIN
VHS / U-matic
Color (A)
Offers a look at the world of twentieth - century competitive sports from the supposed point of view of a future civilization. Provides light humor.
Physical Education and Recreation; Psychology
Dist - SFTI **Prod** - SFTI

Spaceflight series
Traces the history of America's efforts to conquer space. Uses previously unavailable U S and Soviet film footage. Four - part series is produced by Blaine Baggett Productions.
One Giant Leap 60 MIN
The Territory Ahead 60 MIN
Thunder in the Skies 60 MIN
The Wings of Mercury 60 MIN
Dist - PBS

Spacelab - the Manned Space Laboratory 9 MIN
16mm
Color
LC 75-702874
Presents an animated conception of the European Space Agency's Spacelab and its projected functions. Shows how the Spacelab will have an integration center in the United States which will be open to worldwide input. Explains that the lab will carry equipment and researchers who will perform experiments sent in by scientists all over the world.
Industrial and Technical Education; Science - Physical
Dist - USNAC **Prod** - EURSPA

Spacemen have landed in Leeds 32 MIN
U-matic / VHS / BETA
Color; PAL (T PRO)
PdS60, PdS68 purchase
Features a project for teachers and others involved in work with educationally subnormal children produced by Eric Beer of Leeds City and Carnegie College in England, and the Leeds Theater in Education.
Education; Psychology
Dist - EDPAT

Spaces 30 MIN
VHS / U-matic
Spaces Series
Color (I J)
Features a Black psychophysiologist and an Hispanic astronaut at work. Also shows high schoolers designing an experiment to be carried on a space shuttle flight and Anasazi Indians developing a solar calendar.
Guidance and Counseling; Psychology; Science
Dist - GPN **Prod** - WETATV 1983

Spaces 15 MIN
U-matic
Adventures of Milo and Maisie Series
Color (K P)
Shows mimes and children in various spaces, including their personal spaces, urban and natural spaces, and imaginative spaces.
Fine Arts
Dist - GPN **Prod** - KRLNTV 1977

Spaces between People 18 MIN
U-matic / VHS / 16mm
Searching for Values - a Film Anthology Series
Color (J)
LC 73-700237
Tells the story of a rookie teacher in England who abandons the traditional curriculum approach in order to attempt contact at the human level because he is faced with a class of rejects from other schools. Points out that small successes are achieved, but much distance remains between teacher and student.
Education; Guidance and Counseling; Sociology
Dist - LCOA **Prod** - LCOA 1972

Spaces Series
The Body 30 MIN
Computers 30 MIN
Ecology 30 MIN
Energy 30 MIN
Spaces 30 MIN
Dist - GPN

Spaceship Earth 88 MIN
VHS
Color (J H)
$150.00 purchase _ #A5VH 1362
Presents six parts designed to bridge the gap between science and the humanities. Includes The Universe, The Biosphere, Living Things, The Cells, Atoms and Molecules, A Little While Aware.
Science; Science - Natural; Science - Physical
Dist - CLRVUE **Prod** - CLRVUE

Spaceship Earth 88 MIN
VHS
Color (I J H)
$150.00 purchase _ #A5VH 1362
Updates a program designed to bridge the gap between science and the humanities. Offers six parts - The Universe; The Biosphere; Living Things; The Cell; Atoms and Molecules; A Little While Aware.
Science - Natural; Science - Physical
Dist - CLRVUE **Prod** - CLRVUE 1991

Spaceship earth - our global environment 25 MIN
VHS
Color (I J H C G A)
$39.95 purchase; $49.95 purchase _ #VPR200V-S
Examines three of the world's most important environmental issues - deforestation, global warming, and the depletion of the ozone layer. Suggests that the earth is a highly interdependent place. Hosted by young people around the world, and features rock star Sting. Includes teacher's guide. Produced by Worldlink.
Agriculture; Geography - World; Science - Natural; Social Science
Dist - EFVP
CAMV

Spaceship Earth series
Presents a ten - part series using SPOT and LANDSAT, the latest satellite technology, to offer a comprehensive view of the earth. Shows how natural and human forces are changing the planet. Reveals rapid shifts in the weather; the drying up of land in Kenya; the smoking of volcanoes in Indonesia; the growth of cities such as London or Washington; and the destruction of rainforests. Contact distributor about availability outside the United Kingdom.
Spaceship Earth series 260 MIN
Dist - ACADEM

Spaceship Skylab - Wings of Discovery 9 MIN
16mm
Color
LC 75-700584
Examines the successes and failures of the Skylab program. Shows how man's ingenuity on the ground and in space helped save the Skylab mission and examines the many experiments made aboard the orbiting laboratory.
Industrial and Technical Education; Science; Science - Physical
Dist - USNAC **Prod** - NASA 1974

Spaceship Warlock
CD-ROM
(G A)
$95.00 purchase _ #2812
Embarks the user on a wonder - filled journey across the galaxy to lead a pirate crew, visit distant worlds, lead a planetary raid, charm a stellar beauty and much more. For Macintosh Plus, SE and II Computers. Requires at least one M of RAM, one floppy disk drive, and an Apple compatible CD - ROM drive.
Computer Science; Literature and Drama
Dist - BEP

Spacing in a Perspective - 7 15 MIN
VHS
Drawing with Paul Ringler Series
Color (I)
$125.00 purchase
Shows how to space objects and details in a one - or two - point perspective drawing. Focuses on the drawing process, for older students, rather than drawing specific objects. Part of a thirty - part series.
Fine Arts
Dist - AITECH **Prod** - OETVA 1988

Spacing in Perspective 15 MIN
VHS / 16mm
Drawing with Paul Ringler Series
Color (I H)
$125.00 purchase, $25.00 rental
Tells how to space objects and details in a one - or two - point perspective drawing.
Fine Arts; Industrial and Technical Education
Dist - AITECH **Prod** - OETVA 1988

Spadework for History Series
The Plains 28 MIN
Salvaging American Prehistory, Pt 1 28 MIN
Salvaging Texas prehistory 28 MIN
The Woodlands 28 MIN
Dist - UTEX

Spain 15 MIN
VHS / 16mm
Art history II - survey of the Western World series
Color (I H A)
$125.00 purchase, $25.00 rental
Presents selected works of El Greco, Velasquez, Goya and Gaudi.
Fine Arts; Geography - World; Industrial and Technical Education
Dist - AITECH **Prod** - WDCNTV 1989

Spain 60 MIN
VHS
Traveloguer Southern Europe series
Color (J H C G)
$29.95 purchase _ #QC108V
Visits Spain and its cities. Illustrates notable landmarks, special events in history and the legends that are part of Spanish culture. Part of a four part series on Southern Europe.
Geography - World; History - World
Dist - CAMV

Spain 29 MIN
Videoreel / VT2
International Cookbook Series
Color
Features home economist Joan Hood presenting a culinary tour of specialty dishes from around the world. Shows the preparation of Spanish dishes ranging from peasant cookery to continental cuisine.
Geography - World; Home Economics
Dist - PBS **Prod** - WMVSTV

Spain 30 MIN
VHS
Essential history of Europe
Color; PAL (H C A)
Pds65 purchase; Not available in Denmark
Provides an insider's perspective on the history and culture of Spain. Third in a series of 12 programs focusing on the history of European Community member countries.
Geography - World; History - World
Dist - BBCENE

Spain ; 1988 16 MIN
16mm
Modern Europe series
Color (I J H)
LC 88-712604; 88-712605
Illustrates the geography, climate, industry, agriculture and government of Spain.
History - World
Dist - JOU **Prod** - INTERF 1987

Spain 60 MIN
VHS
Travelogue collection series
Color (I J H A)
$29.95 purchase _ #QC108V-S
Presents information about the historic past and the current status of Spain, including information about the cities and the countryside. Shows famous landmarks, out-of-the way sites, struggles and hardships, victories and championships, and the legends of the region. Uses live-action footage and historical clips to show the geography, history, and culture. Includes 16 60-minute programs on northern, western, eastern, and southern Europe.
Geography - World
Dist - CAMV

Spain 52 MIN
VHS
Color (G) (SPANISH)
$39.95 purchase _ #W1422, #W1423
Focuses on Spanish culture as seen in its architecture, monuments and sports. Visits Barcelona, Segovia and the Basque country. Features narration by Ricardo Montalbon.
Foreign Language; Geography - World; Sociology
Dist - GPC

Spain 1936 80 MIN
U-matic / VHS
B&W (C)
$279.00, $179.00 purchase _ #AD - 1600
Focuses on Spain, 1936, when a leftist coalition won the February election. Reveals that Rightists rallied immediately crying communism. On July 18, 1936, Franco launched the military campaign that would consolidate Fascism. Documents the war from its beginning to its end with the fall of Madrid, leaving 400,000 dead, 400,000 imprisoned and a half million anti - fascists self - exiled from Spain. Reveals that Nazi Germany and Fascist Italy provided Franco the help needed to win, as well as the battle training and armaments testing useful to the Axis when it went to war officially in 1939.
Civics and Political Systems; Foreign Language; History - United States; History - World
Dist - FOTH **Prod** - FOTH

Spain - 5 15 MIN
VHS
Art history II - survey of the Western World series
Color (I)
$125.00 purchase
Discusses Spanish painters El Greco, Velasquez, Goya and Gaudi. Presents characteristic works of the artists, connects their works to the literature, religion and history of their times.
Fine Arts; Geography - World; History - World
Dist - AITECH **Prod** - WDCNTV 1989

Spain - a Catalonian Menu 28 MIN
U-matic / VHS / 16mm
World of Cooking Series
Color (J)
Introduces the Spanish countryside and describes various Spanish delicacies.
Geography - World; Home Economics
Dist - CORF **Prod** - SCRESC 1979

Spain - a Journey with Washington Irving 25 MIN
U-matic / VHS / 16mm
Color (H C A)
Presents a journey through Spain guided by Washington Irving's diary of the 1820s. Depicts the Festival of San Fermin in Pamplona, Holy Week festivities in Madrid and the richness of Spanish painting in the Prado Museum. Visits San Lucar and Barcelona.
Geography - World; Social Science
Dist - NGS **Prod** - NGS 1973

Spain - everything under the sun 60 MIN
VHS
European collection series
Color (J H C G)
$29.95 purchase _ #IVN102V-S
Tours the cities and countryside of Spain. Includes visits to Madrid, Segovia, Avila, Seville, Costa del Sol, and more. Part of a 16-part series on European countries. Also part of a larger series entitled Video Visits that travels to six continents.
Geography - World
Dist - CAMV **Prod** - WNETTV
UILL

Spain - everything under the sun 50 MIN
VHS
Color (G)
PdS17.50 purchase _ #ML-IVN102
Introduces viewers to some of the sights of Spain. Includes video tours of Madrid's Royal Palace; the Plaza Mayor; Avila, the walled eleventh century home of Saint Teresa; the Alcazar at Segovia; Toledo and its cathedral; Cordoba; Granada, the center of Moorish Spain; Barcelona; and more.
Geography - World
Dist - AVP **Prod** - IVNET

Spain - History and Culture 21 MIN
VHS / 16mm / U-matic
Color (J H C)
$495, $345, $375 _ #A526
Traces major events and dates over 3,000 years of Spanish history. Discusses the cultural, economic, and social imprints left by the Romans' five centuries of rule and the Moors' eight centuries of dominance.
Geography - World; History - World
Dist - BARR **Prod** - BARR 1988
HERZOG

Spain in the Golden Age - painting and piety 26 MIN
VHS
Color (G)
PdS15.50 purchase _ #A4-300494
Explores the relationship between religion and art in Spain during the Golden Age of the 17th century. Elaborates on the commissioned decorative cycles that gave visual form to the mysteries of the faith and illustrated the glorious deeds of their founders and patron saints. Includes works by Velazquez, Zurbaran, Murillo, Ribalta, and Valdes Leal, and footage of the monasteries in Seville and Guadalupe.
Fine Arts
Dist - AVP **Prod** - NATLGL

Spain in the new world series
The Civilization of Mexico 13 MIN
The Conquest of Mexico and Peru 13 MIN
The Discovery of America 13 MIN
End of a Culture 13 MIN
The Incas 13 MIN
A New World is Born 13 MIN
Dist - FOTH

Spain - Land and People 24 MIN
VHS / 16mm / U-matic
Color (J H C)
$515, $360, $390 _ #525
Shows that Spain's many mountain ranges have brought about, over the centuries, the development of six distinct regions. Examines the cultures, major cities, landmarks, landscapes, and economies of these six regions.
Geography - World; History - World
Dist - BARR **Prod** - BARR 1988

Spain - Land of the Conquistadores 29 MIN
VHS / 16mm
Countries and Peoples Series
Color (H C G)
$90.00 purchase _ #BPN128120
Presents a view of Spain and its unique history. Features the architectural wonders of the Romans, Moors, and French. Discusses the Spanish Civil War and its aftermath, the economy, and the traditional bullfight.
Geography - World; History - World
Dist - RMIBHF **Prod** - RMIBHF 1982
TVOTAR TVOTAR

Spain Series
Describes the color and variety of Spain in a series of three films. Discusses Spain's history, culture, geography, ethnic groups, and lifestyles.
Jose and His Family 16 MIN
Dist - BARR **Prod** - BARR 1982

Spain - the Land and the Legend 58 MIN
16mm / U-matic / VHS
James Michener's World Series
Color
LC 78-701497
Features author James Michener in an exploration of the history, culture, folklore and art of Spain.
Geography - World; History - World
Dist - PFP **Prod** - READER 1978

Spain - the Land and the Legend 58 MIN
16mm / U-matic / VHS
Color (SPANISH)
Presents a portrait of the Spanish countryside and character. Explores Spanish history and conveys a sense of the forces that have shaped Spain over the centuries. Includes a commentary by James Michener.
Foreign Language; Geography - World; History - World; Social Science
Dist - PFP **Prod** - READER

Spain - the Land and the Legend 26 MIN
16mm / U-matic / VHS
James Michener's World Series
Color
A shortened version of the motion picture Spain - The Land And The Legend. Features author James Michener in an exploration of the history, culture, folklore and art of Spain.
Geography - World; History - World
Dist - PFP **Prod** - READER

Spain - Years of Revolution 60 MIN
16mm
Color
Provides a history of the Spanish Civil War.
History - World
Dist - HRC **Prod** - OHC

Spalding Gray's Map of L A 28 MIN
VHS / U-matic
Color
Intercuts reminiscing about seminal automobile influences with a narrative about arriving in Los Angeles. Presented by Bruce and Norman Yonemoto.
Fine Arts
Dist - ARTINC **Prod** - ARTINC

Span Gas Calibration of Direct Reading Instruments 5 MIN
VHS / BETA
Color
Discusses calibration and analysis of gases.
Health and Safety; Science
Dist - RMIBHF **Prod** - RMIBHF

The Span of Attention 17 MIN
16mm
B&W (P I J H C)
LC 79-713856
Presents a laboratory test of attention, which projects varying numbers of dots at brief intervals, allowing time after each trial for the student to write down his estimate of the number of dots shown.
Psychology
Dist - PSUPCR **Prod** - NSF 1967

Spaniernes Spanien - the Spain of the Spaniards 15 MIN
16mm
B&W (DANISH)
Points out the responsibility of the free democracies for the development in the Spain of Franco today, comparing the Spain of the tourists with that of the Spaniards.
Foreign Language; Geography - World
Dist - STATNS **Prod** - STATNS 1966

The Spanish Armada 32 MIN
U-matic / VHS / 16mm
Color (J)
LC FIA67-275
Considers the 16th century conflict between England, weak from civil war, and Spain, powerful by the wealth of Mexico and Peru. Shows how the conflict culminated in the dispatch of the Armada to invade England.
History - World
Dist - MGHT **Prod** - NBCTV 1967

The Spanish Armada 1588 56 MIN
VHS
Color (H C G)
$195.00 purchase
Uses models and film clips to recreate key points of the battle between the Spanish Armada and the English navy in 1588. Includes original charts, contemporary illustrations and portraits of the personalities involved - Elizabeth I of England, Philip of Spain, Drake and Hawkins, Howard and Leicester.
History - World
Dist - LANDMK **Prod** - LANDMK 1988

Spanish cartoon classics 90 MIN
VHS
Color (G) (SPANISH)
$26.85 purchase _ #W1462
Features the adventures of cartoon characters Woody Woodpecker, Bugs Bunny and Porky Pig. Set of three videos.
Fine Arts; Foreign Language; Literature and Drama
Dist - GPC

The Spanish Civil War 26 MIN
16mm / U-matic / VHS
Between the Wars Series
Color (H C)
LC 79-700370
Examines the Spanish Civil War and points out that the inadequate response of the great democratic powers heightened the contempt of the Axis powers for the democratic world.
History - World
Dist - FI **Prod** - LNDBRG 1978

The Spanish civil war 360 MIN
VHS
Color (J H C G)
$98.00 purchase _ #MH1366V; $97.00 purchase _ #04087 - 941
Offers a complete history of the Spanish Civil War. Reveals that over 3 million lives were lost and that the war served for many as a dress rehearsal for World War II. Includes archival footage and eyewitness accounts that were virtually inaccessible until the death of Franco in 1975. Includes Prelude to Tragedy, 1931 - 36; Rèvolution, Counter - Revolution and Terror; Battlefield for Idealists; Franco and the Nationalists; The Revolution; Victory and Defeat in two volumes.
Civics and Political Systems; History - World; Sociology
Dist - CAMV
ASPRSS

The Spanish Civil War 29 MIN
Videoreel / VT2
Course of Our Times I Series
Color
History - World
Dist - PBS **Prod** - WGBHTV

The Spanish Civil War 55 MIN
16mm
British Universities Historical Studies in Film Series
B&W; Color; PAL (C)
LC 75-703309
Examines the origins and causes of the Spanish Civil War and the impact of the war on the people of Spain and on the people of Europe and the United States.
History - World
Dist - KRAUS **Prod** - BUFVC 1975
BUFVC

Spanish Community Life 15 MIN
U-matic / VHS / 16mm
Color; B&W (I J H)
Portrays life and customs of a typical Spanish pueblo. Illustrates ways in which Spain's modernization program is breaking down the old type of self - sufficient village.
Geography - World; Social Science
Dist - PHENIX **Prod** - GUM 1961

Spanish Conquest of the New World 18 MIN
16mm / U-matic / VHS
Color; PAL (I J H)
$425 purchase - 16 mm, $250 purchase - video _ #4987C; $425, $250 purchase _ #4987C
Shows how Spain explored and colonized the New World and established their own culture.
History - United States; History - World
Dist - CORF
VIEWTH

Spanish emergency lesson plans - the video 30 MIN
VHS
Color (G) (SPANISH)
$49.95 purchase _ #W1456
Provides short cultural commentary segments filmed in various Central American countries, each followed by vocabulary and grammar exercises and three levels of multiple - choice questions, to be used whenever extra material is needed in the classroom. Includes transcript.
Foreign Language; Geography - World
Dist - GPC

The Spanish Enigma 145 MIN
U-matic
University of the Air Series
Color (J H C A)
$750.00 purchase, $250.00 rental
Features a look at Spain and South America from a historical perspective and a talk on some of the possible futures for these nations. Program contains a series of five cassettes 29 minutes each.
Geography - World; History - World
Dist - CTV **Prod** - CTV 1977

Spanish folk dancing volume I 35 MIN
VHS
Color (G) (SPANISH)
$49.95 purchase _ #W1399
Highlights Spanish folk dances including the Huayno from Peru, Jesucita en Chihuahua from Mexico and Fado Blanquita from Spain as performed by high school students. Includes the video, an audiocassette with music and instructions as well as music alone, and instruction manual with culture notes.
Fine Arts; Foreign Language
Dist - GPC

Spanish folk dancing volume II 35 MIN
VHS
Color (G) (SPANISH)
$49.95 purchase _ #W1570
Highlights Spanish folk dances including the Espunyolet from Catalonia, Caballito Blanco and Danza de los Viejitos from Mexico as performed by high school students. Includes the video, an audiocassette with both music and instructions and music alone, and instruction manual with culture notes.
Fine Arts; Foreign Language
Dist - GPC

Spanish folk dancing volumes I and II 70 MIN
VHS
Color (G) (SPANISH)
$89.90 purchase _ #W6581
Combines volumes I and II of Spanish Folk Dancing. Highlights Spanish folk dances from Mexico, Peru and Spain as performed by high school students. Includes two videos, two audiocassettes with both music and instructions and music alone, and instruction manuals with culture notes.
Fine Arts; Foreign Language
Dist - GPC

Spanish for health professionals series
Donde esta la sala de emergencia - where is the emergency room - introductory program 22 MIN
Siga las instrucciones - follow the directions 20 MIN
Vengo a Ayudarla (I Come to Help You) Program Number 3 20 MIN
Dist - HSCIC

Spanish for Latin America - Headstart - Module 1 - Getting to Know You 150 MIN
VHS / U-matic
Spanish for Latin America - Headstart - Spanish Series
Color (G) (SPANISH)
Presents a two - cassette set of Latin American Spanish instruction.
Foreign Language; Geography - World
Dist - USNAC **Prod** - USFSI

Spanish for Latin America - Headstart - Module 2 - Getting Around 200 MIN
VHS / U-matic
Spanish for Latin America - Headstart - Spanish Series
Color (G) (SPANISH)
Presents a two - cassette set of Latin American Spanish instruction.
Foreign Language; Geography - World
Dist - USNAC **Prod** - USFSI

Spanish for Latin America - Headstart - Module 3 - Shopping 181 MIN
VHS / U-matic
Spanish for Latin America - Headstart - Spanish Series
Color (G) (SPANISH)
Presents a two - cassette set of Latin American Spanish instruction.
Foreign Language; Geography - World
Dist - USNAC **Prod** - USFSI

Spanish for Latin America - Headstart - Module 4 - at the Restaurant 95 MIN
VHS / U-matic
Spanish for Latin America - Headstart - Spanish Series
Color (G) (SPANISH)
Presents a two - cassette set of Latin American Spanish instruction.
Foreign Language
Dist - USNAC **Prod** - USFSI

Spanish for Latin America - Headstart - Spanish Series
Cultural Orientation Tape for Panama 23 MIN
Spanish for Latin America - Headstart - Module 4 - at the Restaurant 95 MIN
Spanish for Latin America - Headstart - Module 1 - Getting to Know You 150 MIN
Spanish for Latin America - Headstart - Module 3 - Shopping 181 MIN
Spanish for Latin America - Headstart - Module 2 - Getting Around 200 MIN
Dist - USNAC

Spanish for medical professionals
Videodisc
(PRO C) (SPANISH)
$1800.00 purchase _ #C911 - IV - 008
Provides a basic background in conversational Spanish to allow health professionals to communicate better with their Spanish - speaking patients. Includes a guide to Spanish pronunciation, anatomical and general vocabulary and sample dialogs. Emphasizes Mexican - American - Spanish. Presented by the Office of Curricular Support, School of Medicine, University of California, Davis. Contact distributor for technical requirements.
Foreign Language; Health and Safety
Dist - HSCIC

Spanish for You Series Unit 1
El Parque De Diversiones - the Amusement Park Film a 15 MIN
El Parque De Diversiones - the Amusement Park Film B 15 MIN
Dist - MLA

Spanish for You Series Unit 3
El Cohete - the Rocket, Film a 15 MIN
El Cohete - the Rocket, Film B 15 MIN
Dist - MLA

Spanish for you - unit 4 series
De compras - shopping - film A 15 MIN
De compras - shopping, film A 15 MIN
Dist - MLA

Spanish for You Series Unit 5
Las Actividades - the Activities, Film A 15 MIN
Las Actividades - the Activities, Film B 15 MIN
Dist - MLA

Spanish for You Series Unit 6
La Entrevista - the Interview, Film a 15 MIN
La Entrevista - the Interview, Film B 15 MIN
Dist - MLA

Spanish for You Series Unit 7
El Zoologico - the Zoo, Film a 15 MIN
El Zoologico - the Zoo, Film B 15 MIN
Dist - MLA

Spanish for You Series Unit 8
La Llamada Telefonica - the Telephone Call, Film a 15 MIN
La Llamada Telefonica - the Telephone Call, Film B 15 MIN
Dist - MLA

Spanish for You Series Unit 9
El Cumpleanos - the Birthday Party, Film a 15 MIN
El Cumpleanos - the Birthday Party, Film B 15 MIN
Dist - MLA

Spanish for You Series Unit 10
El Partido De Beisbol - the Baseball Game, Film a 15 MIN
El Partido De Beisbol - the Baseball Game, Film B 15 MIN
Dist - MLA

Spanish for You Series Unit 11
El Rancho - the Ranch, Film a 15 MIN
El Rancho - the Ranch, Film B 15 MIN
Dist - MLA

Spanish for You Series Unit 12
Atracciones de la Ciudad De Mexico - the sights of Mexico City, film a 15 MIN
Dist - MLA

Spanish for You Series Unit 13
El Restaurante - the Restaurant, Film a 15 MIN
El Restaurante - the Restaurant, Film B 15 MIN
Dist - MLA

Spanish for You Series Unit 14
El Ultimo Dia De Clases - the Last Day of Class, Film a 15 MIN
El Ultimo Dia De Clases - the Last Day of Class, Film B 15 MIN
Dist - MLA

Spanish for you series
En La Playa - at the Beach, Unit 2, Film A 15 MIN
En La Playa - at the Beach, Unit 2, Film B 15 MIN
Spanish for You - Test - Units 8 through 14 15 MIN
Spanish for You - Test - Units 1 through 7 15 MIN
Dist - MLA

Spanish for You - Test - Units 1 through 7 15 MIN
16mm
Spanish for You Series
Color (I)
Foreign Language
Dist - MLA **Prod** - LINGUA 1965

Spanish for You - Test - Units 8 through 14 15 MIN
16mm
Spanish for You Series
Color (I)
Foreign Language
Dist - MLA **Prod** - LINGUA 1965

A Spanish Gallery 29 MIN
Videoreel / VT2
Museum Open House Series
Color
Fine Arts; Geography - World
Dist - PBS **Prod** - WGBHTV

Spanish Gypsies 11 MIN
16mm
B&W (H C)
Shows Spanish gypsies holding a family festival in a grotto in Granada. Juan Salido and a group of artists perform a series of exciting flamenco folk dances and songs.
Fine Arts; Geography - World
Dist - RADIM **Prod** - BRAU 1948

The Spanish in the Southwest 14 MIN
16mm / U-matic / VHS
Growth of America's West Series
Color (I J H)
LC 79-700240
Describes Spain's exploration and conquest in the southwestern United States during the 16th century. Shows the role of the Catholic missions in the exchange of skills and traditions between Indians and Spaniards. Discusses how 300 years of Indian - Spanish culture has influenced American life.
History - United States
Dist - PHENIX **Prod** - CAPFLM 1979

Spanish influences in the United States 13 MIN
VHS
Color (I J)
$59.00 purchase _ #MF - 3310
Examines Spanish influences which still remain in Florida, the Southwest and California, long after the abolition of Spanish rule in these regions. Looks at the legacy of Spain in the language, architecture, home furnishings, place names and lifestyles.
History - United States; History - World
Dist - INSTRU **Prod** - CORF

Spanish Influences in the United States 14 MIN
16mm / U-matic / VHS
Color (I J)
$315.00, $220.00 purchase _ #3310; LC 72-701517
Shows different ways in which the United States has been influenced by its Spanish heritage, such as language, home furnishings, architecture, place names, community development and life styles.
History - United States; Social Science; Sociology
Dist - CORF **Prod** - CORF 1972

The Spanish kitchen
VHS
Frugal gourmet international cooking II series
Color (G)
$19.95 purchase _ #CCP815
Shows how to prepare Spanish food. Features Jeff Smith, the Frugal Gourmet. Part of a five - part series on international cooking.
Geography - World; Home Economics; Physical Education and Recreation
Dist - CADESF **Prod** - CADESF

Spanish language series
Aragon y Navarra 16 MIN
Barcelona 18 MIN
Castilla La Nueva 16 MIN
Castilla La Vieja 16 MIN
El Pais Vasco 16 MIN
Madrid - Capital De Espana 18 MIN
Sevilla 16 MIN
Dist - IFB

Spanish Lesson - No 1 30 MIN
16mm
B&W (T)
Shows how a master teacher of Spanish works with a group of nine - year - olds.
Education; Guidance and Counseling
Dist - UCLA **Prod** - UCLA 1965

Spanish Missions in Colonial Texas 10 MIN
U-matic / VHS / Slide
Hispanic Studies, Ranching and Farming Series
Color; Mono (I J H)
History - United States; Sociology
Dist - UTXITC **Prod** - UTXITC 1973

Spanish Newsreel Series Vol 45, no 52
Cuba Walks Out 7 MIN
Dist - TWCF

Spanish Newsreel Series Vol 45, no 54
Plane Crash 8 MIN
Dist - TWCF

Spanish newsreel series
Glenn welcome 6 MIN
Pope - new cardinals 8 MIN
Dist - TWCF

Spanish plus series
Family facts 4.10 MIN
Finding Your Way 6.37 MIN
Getting down to business 6 MIN
Getting the Information 8 MIN
In the restaurant 5.47 MIN
Making a Call - Getting through 8 MIN
Making a Call - Leaving a Message 7 MIN
Making the Sale 5.35 MIN
Money Talk 6.33 MIN
Travel Plans 7.40 MIN
Dist - AITECH

Spanish Ranching in Texas 10 MIN
U-matic / VHS / Slide
Hispanic, Ranching and Farming Series
Color; Mono (I J H)
Discusses the influences of Spanish rancheros and Mexican vaqueros on American cowboy.
History - United States; Sociology
Dist - UTXITC **Prod** - UTXITC 1973

Spanish Ranching in Texas 7 MIN
U-matic / VHS / Slide
Ranching and Farming Series
Color; Mono (I J H)
Agriculture; History - United States; Sociology
Dist - UTXITC **Prod** - UTXITC 1972

Spanish Series
Speak to Me - Level 1 159 MIN
Speak to Me - Level 2 159 MIN
Speak to Me - Level 3 159 MIN
Dist - NORTNJ

Spanish Smootheners 30 MIN
Videoreel / VT2
Solutions in Communications Series
Color (T)
Education; English Language
Dist - SCCOE **Prod** - SCCOE

Spanky 20 MIN
16mm
B&W
Tells how Spanky causes trouble for big brother Breezy, who's trying to land a part in the Gang's barn play. Shows how the play turns into an egg - throwing free - for - all and Breezy proves remarkably resourceful at finding shields while still performing. A Little Rascals film.
Fine Arts
Dist - RMIBHF **Prod** - ROACH 1932

Spanning Vectors 27 MIN
VHS / U-matic
Calculus of Linear Algebra Series
B&W
Mathematics
Dist - MIOT **Prod** - MIOT

Spare the Rod 30 MIN
16mm
Footsteps Series
Color
LC 79-701554
Explains that discipline is often needed to teach children how to take care of themselves and live in a world with other people. Enumerates some of the different disciplinary techniques available to parents, providing guidelines for choosing the most effective one.
Guidance and Counseling; Home Economics; Sociology
Dist - USNAC **Prod** - USOE 1978

Spare the Rod - Discipline 23 MIN
16mm / U-matic
Footsteps Series
Color
Shows why discipline is necessary for young children. Presents a variety of disciplinary techniques for parents and guidelines for using them.
Psychology; Sociology
Dist - PEREN **Prod** - PEREN

Sparing the rod won't spoil the child 28 MIN
VHS
Prime time for parents video series
Color (G)
$89.95 purchase _ #RMI210
Looks at effective alternatives to discipline. Shows that promoting dignity and esteem in the child and parent results in greater family harmony. Covers ten tools for living which prevent misbehavior and the proper response to negative behavior. Part of a series on parenting. Study guide available separately.
Home Economics; Psychology; Social Science; Sociology
Dist - CADESF **Prod** - CADESF

The Spark 30 MIN
VHS
Over the edge series
Color; PAL (G)
PdS50 purchase; United Kingdom and Eire only
Portrays the experience of Charles, a man with HIV infection, as he travels back to his childhood home in Glasgow. Explores the effects of HIV on character and way of life. Deals with the belief that HIV is the spark that draws people into a better, less selfish way of living.
Health and Safety
Dist - BBCENE

The Spark 29 MIN
16mm
Color (I A)
LC 75-702901
Presents an ethnographic study of the Hasidic communities in New York. Depicts religious service, community activities, traditional services, a farbrengen or meeting called by the head rabbi and a Hasidic wedding ceremony and celebration. Uses paintings to portray the history of the movement.
Religion and Philosophy; Sociology
Dist - VANGU **Prod** - VANGU 1975

Spark among the ashes - a bar mitzvah in Poland 56 MIN
16mm / VHS
Color (H C G)
$850.00, $495.00 purchase, $150.00, $95.00 rental
Focuses on Eric Strom, a 13 - year - old Connecticut boy who journeyed to Cracow, Poland for his bar mitzvah. Reveals that only 200 Jews still remain in Cracow, from a population of 60,000 before World War II, and that the community had not seen a bar mitzvah for over 40 years.
History - World; Sociology
Dist - FLMLIB **Prod** - RDVSKY 1986

A Spark in the dark - static electricity 14 MIN
VHS
Electricity and magnetism series
Color (I)
$55.00 purchase _ #1193VG
Discusses the three primary particles of the atom. Establishes how objects gain or lose charge, and its effect on static electricity. Comes with a teacher's guide and blackline masters. Part one of a five - part series.
Science - Physical
Dist - UNL

A Spark of being 6 MIN
VHS / 8mm cartridge
Color (G)
$10.00 rental, $30.00 purchase
Introduces a pale student of unhallowed arts who infuses life into a hideous pantasm. Uses puppet animation, computer animation, and live electrical effects. Produced by Tom Triman.
Fine Arts; Industrial and Technical Education
Dist - CANCIN

Spark Plug Service 4 MIN
16mm
Color
LC FI68-254
Shows the steps to be followed when removing, cleaning, gapping and replacing spark plugs.
Industrial and Technical Education
Dist - RAYBAR **Prod** - RAYBAR 1966

Spark Plug Story 15 MIN
16mm
Color
Presents the procedures involved in the manufacturing of spark plugs and their testing.
Business and Economics; Industrial and Technical Education
Dist - GM **Prod** - GM

Sparkhill Ave 8 MIN
16mm
Color (G)
$20.00 rental
Presents a Robert Breer production.
Fine Arts
Dist - CANCIN

Sparkling Clearwater 15 MIN
16mm
Color
Explores the variety of entertainment and recreation available in Clearwater, Florida.
Geography - United States; Geography - World; Physical Education and Recreation
Dist - FLADC **Prod** - FLADC

Sparks in Neu - Groenland 112 MIN
16mm
Color (GERMAN (ENGLISH SUBTITLES))
Follows an elderly couple's move to a modern housing project and then back to the city when the husband is unable to adjust to an artificial lifestyle.
Foreign Language; Sociology
Dist - WSTGLC **Prod** - WSTGLC

Sparky Vs the Snat 8 MIN
16mm
Color (I)
LC 80-700388
Presents an animated program in which Sparky, the fire dog, and his niece and nephew produce a musical about fire protection, while the Snat, promoter of carelessness with fire, tries to ruin the show.
Health and Safety
Dist - NFPA **Prod** - NFPA 1979

Sparky's animation series
Lasers from space 25 MIN
Legend of Sunshine Mountain 25 MIN
Lost gold mine 25 MIN
Phantom lake 25 MIN
Space shuttle journey 25 MIN
Dist - APH

The Sparrow Family 3 MIN
16mm
Of all Things Series
Color (P I)
Discusses the family of birds known as sparrows.
Science - Natural
Dist - AVED **Prod** - BAILYL

Sparrows 84 MIN
VHS
B&W (G)
$29.95 purchase
Stars Mary Pickford as a spunky young girl who leads an escape from a cruel orphanage. Directed by William Beaudine.
Fine Arts
Dist - KINOIC
KILLIS

Sparta 13 MIN
VHS / 16mm
Greek and Roman Mythology in Ancient Art Series
Color (I)
LC 90708209
Emphasizes the importance of Sparta to ancient Greece. Focuses on Sparta's military prowess.
Fine Arts; History - World; Religion and Philosophy
Dist - BARR

Spartacus 130 MIN
VHS
Color (S)
$39.95 purchase _ #623 - 9400
Showcases the legendary strengths of Moscow's Bolshoi Ballet in a production of 'Spartacus' composed by Aram Khachaturian. Stars Erek Moukhamedov, Natalia Bessmertnova, Mikhail Gabovich and Maria Bylova. Yuri Grigorovich is the choreographer.
Fine Arts; Geography - World; Physical Education and Recreation
Dist - FI **Prod** - NVIDC 1986

Spartacus 95 MIN
VHS
Color (G)
$29.95 purchase _ #1198
Presents the critically acclaimed dance film of 'Spartacus' produced by the Bolshoi Ballet. Stars Vladimir Vasiliev and Natalia Bessmertnova. Choreographed by Yuri Grigorovich to a musical score by Aram Khachaturian.
Fine Arts; Foreign Language; Geography - World; Physical Education and Recreation
Dist - KULTUR

Spartree 15 MIN
U-matic / VHS / 16mm
Color (J H C A)
$365, $250 purchase _ #80508; LC 80-700781
Illustrates the topping and use of the spartree, emphasizing the extreme physical effort of heavy timber logging. Focuses on the work of the highrigger, a daredevil master lumberjack.
Industrial and Technical Education
Dist - CORF **Prod** - MERPI 1980

Spasticity - a Review of Treatment with Dantrolene Sodium 20 MIN
16mm
Color (PRO)
LC 75-702336
Presents objective and subjective improvements in spastic patients treated with Dantrolene Sodium. Shows a Vietnam veteran with spinal cord injury and two multiple sclerosis patients discussing and illustrating their individual responses to Dantrolene Sodium.
Health and Safety; Science; Science - Natural
Dist - EATONL **Prod** - EATONL 1974

Spatial interaction and location - 12 60 MIN
VHS
Land, location and culture - a geographical synthesis series
Color (J H C)
$89.95 purchase _ #WLU112
Considers movement of all kinds as one of the defining features of modern life. Shows the key role that distance and space plays in determining the volume of goods, services and people that moves from one location to another. Answers the fundamental question of why goods and services move about and considers Ullman's three conditions of interregional trade. Explores in detail a more general and quantifiable approach to interaction through a variety of applications of the gravity model as it has been used to assess consumer spatial behavior. Part of a 12 - part series.
Business and Economics; Geography - World; Social Science
Dist - INSTRU

Spatial Learning in the Preschool Years 22 MIN
VHS / U-matic
B&W (PRO)
Views a 'preoperational' child's understanding of three - dimensional space, such as the look, feel and positioning of objects. Shows gain of understanding through exploration and manipulation of objects and suggests appropriate classroom materials and experiences. Deals with spatial understanding in infancy.
Education; Psychology
Dist - HSERF **Prod** - HSERF

Spatial relationships 40 MIN
16mm
Aecom scales of motorsensory development series
Color (PRO)
Depicts stages in early cognitive development in accordance with Piaget's definitions. Reflects the developmental changes concerning the capacity to adapt to and comprehend properties of physical space from subjective space within the child's visually perceived range of movement to the stage of 'Mental representation.'
Psychology
Dist - NYU **Prod** - VASSAR

Spatula, palette knife painting 30 MIN
VHS / 16mm
Art of decorating cakes series
(G)
$49.00 purchase _ #BCD14
Instructs in the art of cake decorating. Shows how to apply food coloring directly to the top of the cake and use a small spatula to construct a flower design on the cake. Taught by Leon Simmons, master cake decorator.
Home Economics; Industrial and Technical Education
Dist - RMIBHF **Prod** - RMIBHF

Spaulding - Richardson Composite Operation for Uterine Prolapse and Allied Conditions 25 MIN
16mm
Color (PRO)
Portrays an operation for marked degrees of uterine prolapse. Shows that the operation overcomes some of the disadvantages of the Manchester Operation and yet retains some of its virtues.
Health and Safety; Science
Dist - ACY **Prod** - ACYDGD 1954

Spawning in an African Mouthbreeding Fish 16 MIN
16mm
Color (H C A)
LC 70-708679
Shows identification characteristics of male and female tilapia macrocephala, including courtship behavior and construction of nest. Describes how the male takes the eggs of the female into his mouth and stores them in an oral pouch where they are hatched. Uses closeups to show eggs and later embryos in the male's mouth. Shows the young released and at several stages of development.
Science - Natural
Dist - PSUPCR **Prod** - AMNH 1967

Speak Arabic - Arabic Script Version 90 MIN
VHS
Color (G) (ARABIC)
$160.00 purchase _ #SAR202
Teaches beginning students of Arabic using authentic situations and information on local customs. Developed and produced by Tim Francis. Includes videocassette, two audiocassettes, two texts and phrase book.
Foreign Language
Dist - NORTNJ

Speak Arabic - Transliterated Version 90 MIN
Cassette / VHS
Color (G) (ARABIC)
$160.00 purchase _ #SAR201
Teaches beginning students of Arabic using authentic situations and information on local customs. Developed and produced by Tim Francis. Includes videocassette, two audiocassettes, two texts and phrase book.
Foreign Language
Dist - NORTNJ

Speak Easy
16mm / U-matic / VHS
Color
Aims to teach everyday conversational language through a combination of mime, video and a variety of classroom activities.
English Language
Dist - NORTNJ **Prod** - NORTNJ

Speak for me 4 MIN
VHS
Color (G R)
$12.50 purchase _ #S16067
Uses a music video format to present an anti - abortion message. Music by Don Wharton.
Guidance and Counseling; Literature and Drama; Religion and Philosophy
Dist - CPH **Prod** - LUMIS

Speak for yourself - a dynamic vocal workout 26 MIN
VHS
Color (G)
$99.00 purchase, $39.00 rental _ #603
Offers a series of voice and body warmups. Helps to build a strong voice, establish focus and concentration while speaking and expands vocal capacity and skills. Includes relaxation and stretching, face preparation, pitch and resonance exercises and tongue twisters to develop clarity and control. Features voice expert Susan Leigh. Produced by Theater Arts Video Library. Package includes a written guideline, bone prop and vocal health tips.
English Language
Dist - FIRLIT

Speak for yourself - a guide to making effective presentations 25 MIN
VHS
Color (G)
$495.00 purchase, $150.00 rental _ #V0178 - 06
Calls attention to speaking skills needed for effective presentations. Shows how to develop those skills by following a three - point outline. Includes leader's guide and video.
Business and Economics; English Language; Psychology
Dist - BARR **Prod** - BBC

Speak Out, Kids! 23 MIN
U-matic / VHS / 16mm
Elementary Language Skills Series
Color (K P I J)
$515, $360, $390 _ #A510
Explains that oral expression skills are valuable not only for speeches, but also for day to day encounters with one's family and friends, at home and in school.
English Language; Guidance and Counseling; Literature and Drama
Dist - BARR **Prod** - BARR 1987

Speak the language of success - a handbook for communication skills 30 MIN
U-matic / VHS
Color
Provides techniques in gaining communication skills. Includes remembering names, listening, keeping messages brief, and controlling silence. Presented by Ellen Phillips, Director, Speech and Dramatic Arts, Fairfax County Public Schools, Virginia.
English Language; Sociology
Dist - SYLWAT **Prod** - RCOMTV

Speak to me - Chinese
VHS
Color (G)
$950.00 purchase _ #27317
Offers an extensive video ESL course. Consists of 3 volumes suitable for beginners to learners at an advanced intermediate level. Includes 9 videotapes and 3 books.
English Language
Dist - PANASI

Speak to Me - Level 1 159 MIN
VHS
Korean Series
Color (G) (ENGLISH AND KOREAN)
$199.00 set purchase, $547.00 series purchase _ #ISPEAK
Presents the first of a three - part English instruction program for Korean - speaking students. Links video lessons to a bilingual workbook to develop ability to think in English. Program adapts to beginning, intermediate and advanced students. Each level includes a set of three videos and a book.
English Language
Dist - NORTNJ

Speak to Me - Level 1 159 MIN
VHS
German Series
Color (G) (ENGLISH AND GERMAN)
$199.00 set purchase, $547.00 series purchase _ #ISPEAK
Gives part one of a three - part English instruction program for German - speaking students. Links video lessons to a bilingual workbook to develop ability to think in English. Program adapts to beginning, intermediate and advanced students. Each level includes a set of three videos and a book.
English Language
Dist - NORTNJ

Speak to Me - Level 1 159 MIN
VHS
Chinese Series
Color (G) (ENGLISH AND CHINESE)
$199.00 set purchase, $547.00 series purchase _ #ISPEAK
Presents the first in a three - part English instruction program for Chinese - speaking students. Links video lessons to a bilingual workbook to develop ability to think in English. Program adapts to beginning, intermediate and advanced students. Each level includes a set of three videos and a book.
English Language
Dist - NORTNJ

Speak to Me - Level 1 159 MIN
VHS
Vietnamese Series
Color (G) (ENGLISH AND VIETNAMESE)
$199.00 set purchase, $547.00 series purchase _ #ISPEAK
Presents the first of a three - part English instruction program for Vietnamese - speaking students. Links video lessons to a bilingual workbook to develop ability to think in English. Program adapts to beginning, intermediate and advanced students. Each level includes a set of three videos and a book.
English Language
Dist - NORTNJ

Speak to Me - Level 1 159 MIN
VHS
Spanish Series
Color (G) (ENGLISH AND SPANISH)
$199.00 set purchase, $547.00 series purchase _ #ISPEAK
Presents part one of a three - part English instruction program for Spanish - speaking students. Links video lessons to a bilingual workbook to develop ability to think in English. Program adapts to beginning, intermediate and advanced students. Each level includes a set of three videos and a book.
English Language
Dist - NORTNJ

Speak to Me - Level 2 159 MIN
VHS
German Series
Color (G) (ENGLISH AND GERMAN)
$199.00 set purchase, $547.00 series purchase _ #ISPEAK
Gives part two of a three - part English instruction program for German - speaking students. Links video lessons to a bilingual workbook to develop ability to think in English. Program adapts to beginning, intermediate and advanced students. Each level includes a set of three videos and a book.
English Language
Dist - NORTNJ

Speak to me - level 2 159 MIN
VHS
Korean Series
Color (G) (ENGLISH AND KOREAN)
$199.00 set purchase, $547.00 series purchase _ #ISPEAK
Presents the second of a three - part English instruction program for Korean - speaking students. Links video lessons to a bilingual workbook to develop ability to think in English. Program adapts to beginning, intermediate and advanced students. Each level includes a set of three videos and a book.
English Language
Dist - NORTNJ

Speak to me - level 2 159 MIN
VHS
Chinese Series
Color (G) (ENGLISH AND CHINESE)
$199.00 set purchase, $547.00 series purchase _ #ISPEAK
Presents the second in a three - part English instruction program for Chinese - speaking students. Links video lessons to a bilingual workbook to develop ability to think in English. Program adapts to beginning, intermediate and advanced students. Each level includes a set of three videos and a book.
English Language
Dist - NORTNJ

Speak to Me - Level 2 159 MIN
VHS
Spanish Series
Color (G) (ENGLISH AND SPANISH)
$199.00 set purchase, $547.00 series purchase _ #ISPEAK
Presents part two of a three - part English instruction program for Spanish - speaking students. Links video lessons to a bilingual workbook to develop ability to think in English. Program adapts to beginning, intermediate and advanced students. Each level includes a set of three videos and a book.
English Language
Dist - NORTNJ

Speak to Me - Level 2 159 MIN
VHS
Vietnamese Series
Color (G) (ENGLISH AND VIETNAMESE)
$199.00 set purchase, $547.00 series purchase _ #ISPEAK
Presents the second in a three - part English instruction program for Vietnamese - speaking students. Links video lessons to a bilingual workbook to develop ability to think in English. Program adapts to beginning, intermediate and advanced students. Each level includes a set of three videos and a book.
English Language
Dist - NORTNJ

Speak to Me - Level 3 159 MIN
VHS
Chinese Series
Color (G) (ENGLISH AND CHINESE)

$199.00 set purchase, $547.00 series purchase _ #ISPEAK
Presents the third in a three - part English instruction program for Chinese - speaking students. Links video lessons to a bilingual workbook to develop ability to think in English. Program adapts to beginning, intermediate and advanced students. Each level includes a set of three videos and a book.
English Language
Dist - NORTNJ

Speak to Me - Level 3 159 MIN
VHS
Spanish Series
Color (G) (ENGLISH AND SPANISH)
$199.00 set purchase, $547.00 series purchase _ #ISPEAK
Presents part three of a three - part English instruction program for Spanish - speaking students. Links video lessons to a bilingual workbook to develop ability to think in English. Program adapts to beginning, intermediate and advanced students. Each level includes a set of three videos and a book.
English Language
Dist - NORTNJ

Speak to Me - Level 3 159 MIN
VHS
Vietnamese Series
Color (G) (ENGLISH AND VIETNAMESE)
$199.00 set purchase, $547.00 series purchase _ #ISPEAK
Presents the third in a three - part English instruction program for Vietnamese - speaking students. Links video lessons to a bilingual workbook to develop ability to think in English. Program adapts to beginning, intermediate and advanced students. Each level includes a set of three videos and a book.
English Language
Dist - NORTNJ

Speak to Me - Level 3 159 MIN
VHS
Korean Series
Color (G) (ENGLISH AND KOREAN)
$199.00 set purchase, $547.00 series purchase _ #ISPEAK
Presents the third of a three - part English instruction program for Korean - speaking students. Links video lessons to a bilingual workbook to develop ability to think in English. Program adapts to beginning, intermediate and advanced students. Each level includes a set of three videos and a book.
English Language
Dist - NORTNJ

Speak to Me - Level 3 159 MIN
VHS
German Series
Color (G) (ENGLISH AND GERMAN)
$199.00 set purchase, $547.00 series purchase _ #ISPEAK
Gives part three of a three - part English instruction program for German - speaking students. Links video lessons to a bilingual workbook to develop ability to think in English. Program adapts to beginning, intermediate and advanced students. Each level includes a set of three videos and a book.
English Language
Dist - NORTNJ

Speak up 60 MIN
VHS / U-matic
Color (J H C A)
Presents a practical approach to becoming a successful public speaker. Areas covered include developing confidence, analyzing audiences, determining objectives, preparing the message, and delivering the speech.
English Language; Psychology
Dist - UTEX **Prod** - CEC 1983

Speak up 12 MIN
16mm / VHS / U-matic
Serendipity series
Color (P)
LC 76-701767
Shows how speaking shares ideas directly with another person and demonstrates how different ways of speaking can affect the message.
English Language
Dist - MGHT **Prod** - MGHT 1976

Speak Up, Andrew 18 MIN
U-matic / VHS / 16mm
Color (I J)
LC 81-701563
Discusses the importance of developing good speaking skills through the story of a young boy who must make a speech on the subject.
English Language
Dist - CF **Prod** - CF 1981

Speak Up for Yourself 45 MIN
VHS
Safe Child Program - K - 3 - Series
Color (K)
$895.00 purchase
Teaches age appropriate for first grade concepts for the prevention of sexual, emotional and physical abuse, and safety for children in self care. Raises self - esteem and improves self - reliance and is developmentally consistent with the needs of first graders. Multiracial and multicultural. Adapted from 'The Safe Child Book' by Sherryll Kraiser. Part of the Safe Child - K - 3 - Program of seven videotapes.
Education; Health and Safety; Psychology; Sociology
Dist - LUF **Prod** - LUF 1989

Speak up - It's so dark 83 MIN
VHS
Color (G)
$490.00 purchase, $125.00 rental
Presents a fictional story about Jacob, a Jewish psychiatrist, and Soren, a neo - Nazi skinhead. Uses issues of neo - Nazism, Holocaust denial and violence to provide the backdrop for a series of encounters between the two men. Produced by Suzanne Osten.
Civics and Political Systems; History - World; Literature and Drama; Sociology
Dist - FIRS

Speak Up on Television 30 MIN
U-matic / VHS / 16mm
Speak Up with Confidence Series
Color
Provides training in television communication. Includes handling news interviews, press conferences, talk shows and other television presentations.
English Language; Social Science; Sociology
Dist - NEM **Prod** - NEM

Speak Up - Skills of Oral Communication
U-matic / VHS
Color (H)
Teaches the basic rules of speaking and dramatizes the four purposes of oral communication - narration, description, persuasion and argumentation.
English Language; Psychology
Dist - GA **Prod** - CHUMAN

Speak up, speak out - learning to say NO to drugs 15 MIN
VHS
Color (I J H)
$59.00 purchase _ #06882 - 126
Follows teens on a class trip to Washington, DC, where they learn specific techniques to resist peer pressure and say 'no' to drug abuse.
Guidance and Counseling; Psychology; Sociology
Dist - GA **Prod** - GA

Speak up - speak out - strategies for developing oral fluency - Tape 11 24 MIN
VHS
Teacher to teacher series
Color (T)
$100.00 purchase _ #890 - 0
Shows experienced teachers in actual classroom settings presenting various instructional approaches to both new and veteran ABE and ESL teachers. Demonstrates how students' drawings and role playing can spark animated dialogue and vocabulary acquisition. Part eleven of a 12 - part series.
Education; English Language
Dist - LAULIT **Prod** - LAULIT

Speak up, Uncle Sam is hard of hearing 5 MIN
16mm / VHS
Color (G)
$10.00 rental
Encourages audience to become more active in the anti - nuke movement by presenting three short messages telling people what they can do to help end the arms race. Includes images from a variety of sources, such as demonstrations and bumper stickers.
Fine Arts
Dist - CANCIN **Prod** - COHENK 1984

Speak Up with Confidence 30 MIN
U-matic / VHS / 16mm
Speak Up with Confidence Series
Color
Provides instruction in public speaking for beginning and experienced speakers. Offers techniques for overcoming obstacles to effective presentations.
English Language
Dist - NEM **Prod** - NEM

Speak Up with Confidence Series

Speak Up on Television	30 MIN
Speak Up with Confidence	30 MIN
Speak Up with Style	30 MIN

Dist - NEM

Speak Up with Style 30 MIN
16mm / U-matic / VHS
Speak Up with Confidence Series
Color
Shows how to prepare and deliver a successful speech. Covers elements of style which produce clarity of content and audience rapport.
English Language
Dist - NEM **Prod** - NEM

Speakeasy 30 MIN
VHS
Bodymatters series
Color (H C A)
PdS65 purchase
Discusses the voice box and speech. Part of a series of 26 30-minute videos on various systems of the human body.
Science - Natural
Dist - BBCENE

Speakeasy series

Did I say that	30 MIN
First find the facts	30 MIN
Pros and Cons	30 MIN
That's Debatable	30 MIN
Trippingly on the Tongue	30 MIN

Dist - ACCESS

The Speaker - a Film about Freedom 42 MIN
16mm
Color (H C A)
LC 77-700848
Presents a story concerning the First Amendment rights of a controversial university professor to speak at a high school.
Civics and Political Systems; Education
Dist - ALA **Prod** - ALA 1977

The Speaker from Texas 58 MIN
VHS
Color (S)
$79.00 purchase _ #154 - 9001
Traces the life and career of former Speaker of the House of Representatives Jim Wright, from his beginnings in a Texas town to his position as one of Capitol Hill's chief power brokers. Features Wright speaking candidly about the practice and personal costs of leadership, his approach to politics, and the realities of modern democratic government.
Civics and Political Systems; Geography - United States
Dist - FI **Prod** - KERA 1987

Speaker of the House - the Legislative Process 21 MIN
U-matic / VHS / 16mm
Color; B&W (I J H)
Examines responsibilities and activities of the speaker of a typical state assembly during the course of a legislative day. Speaker is shown fulfilling his double role as politician and lawmaker.
Civics and Political Systems
Dist - JOU **Prod** - JOU 1964

The Speaker's purpose and occasion 28 MIN
U-matic / BETA / VHS
Communication skills 1 - basic series
Color (H C G)
$101.95, $89.95 purchase _ #CA - 42
Examines the purpose of the public speaker and the setting in which the speech is delivered. Identifies the three general purposes of speaking and examines several examples of each purpose. Explores the occasion and setting as important considerations for the public speaker. Part of a series on communication.
English Language; Social Science
Dist - INSTRU

Speakers with cerebral palsy 25 MIN
16mm
Physiological aspects of speech series
Color
LC FIA67-103; FIA67 - 103
Illustrates variations in respiratory, laryngeal and articulatory functioning exhibited by individuals with cerebral palsy. Emphasizes the difficulty of describing fully the speech physiology problems of these individuals and of relating specific deviations in the functioning of the speech mechanism to specific speech deficits. Highlights the results of recent research.
English Language; Health and Safety
Dist - UIOWA **Prod** - UIOWA 1966

Speakers with cleft palates 30 MIN
16mm
Physiological aspects of speech series
Color (C)
Uses X-ray photography to show the physiological characteristics of the speech of those with cleft palates. Depicts the effect on speech of deviations in the functioning of the velopharyngeal mechanism.
English Language
Dist - UIOWA **Prod** - UIOWA 1964

Speaking again - options for the laryngectomee 50 MIN
VHS
Color (PRO)
$140.00 purchase, $75.00 rental
Presents two parts which explore five alternatives for communication by laryngectomees -- writing, mouthing, gesturing, the use of mechanical devices and esophageal speech -- and emphasizes the techniques for training laryngectomees in the use of esophageal speech. Produced by Jan Briggs and Pat Sproule.
English Language; Health and Safety
Dist - BUSARG

Speaking Again - Options for the Laryngectomee, Pt 1 25 MIN
VHS / U-matic
Color
Presents communication alternatives for people who have lost their vocal cords or larynx.
Health and Safety; Science - Natural
Dist - BUSARG **Prod** - BUSARG

Speaking Again - Options for the Laryngectomee, Pt 2 25 MIN
U-matic / VHS
Color
Presents techniques for training laryngectomized individuals to use esophageal speech.
Health and Safety; Science - Natural
Dist - BUSARG **Prod** - BUSARG

Speaking American English at work series
Climbing the ladder 30 MIN
You're Hired 30 MIN
Dist - NORTNJ

Speaking and writing standard English - personal pronouns 22 MIN
VHS
Color (I J H)
$169.00 purchase _ #FG - 990 - VS
Uses a storyline and computer graphics to underscore the importance of understanding and using standard American English in school and work. Centers around Mike who is fond of using slang and peer - group dialog with his friends but finds out that his language skills are a disadvantage academically and in the workplace. Mike's dilemma is resolved when he is 'discovered' as a star of a TV game show about grammar and he learns to identify and correct the most common usage errors in personal pronouns. Includes student resource books.
English Language
Dist - HRMC **Prod** - HRMC 1994

Speaking Effectively 30 MIN
U-matic / VHS
Communication Skills for Managers Series
Color (A)
Shows how to keep control of a conversation when one is the initiator in the action. Presents hosts Richard Benjamin and Paula Prentiss advising on ways to get verbal and non - verbal feedback and emphasizing the importance of closing a communication.
Business and Economics; English Language; Psychology
Dist - TIMLIF **Prod** - TIMLIF 1981

Speaking effectively - to one or one thousand 21 MIN
16mm / U-matic / VHS
Color (H C A) (SPANISH)
#107776 - 6 3/4
Offers keys for organizing and delivering conversational remarks and rehearsed speeches. Emphasizes body language, vocal quality, intonation, and the words themselves.
English Language
Dist - CRMP **Prod** - SUNSET 1980
MGHT

Speaking for Ourselves - the Challenge of Being Deaf 26 MIN
16mm
Color
LC 77-701454
Shows the challenge, complexity and intensity of the learning experience at the Lexington School for the Deaf, New York.
Geography - United States; Guidance and Counseling; Psychology
Dist - CFDC **Prod** - LSFTD 1977

Speaking for Results 50 MIN
VHS / 16mm
Color (PRO)
$685.00 purchase, $165.00 rental, $45.00 preview
Features speech trainer Carl Clayton who shows how to prepare and deliver a speech. Explains how to get an audience's attention, organize material, close the speech, use statistics and humor and overcome stage fright. Offers examples of business speaking situations. Includes support material.
Education; English Language; Guidance and Counseling; Psychology
Dist - UTM **Prod** - UTM 1989

Speaking for the Listener 62 FRS
U-matic / VHS
Effective Speaking Series
Color
Emphasizes the advantages of being able to communicate face - to - face and the four major factors involved in planning a speech.
English Language; Psychology
Dist - RESEM **Prod** - RESEM

Speaking for the union 20 MIN
16mm / VHS
Color (G IND)
$5.00 rental
Provides strategies and tips to help union members prepare for appearing on local TV. Shows how to present union perspectives effectively.
Business and Economics; English Language; Social Science
Dist - AFLCIO **Prod** - LIPA 1988

Speaking from Experience 18 MIN
VHS / U-matic
Color (IND)
Explores human error in job - related accidents. Narrated by Pat Summerall.
Business and Economics; Health and Safety; Psychology
Dist - CHARTH **Prod** - CHARTH

Speaking Image - When Women Talk Business Series
Vocal Quality Counts 180 MIN
Dist - UEUWIS

Speaking objectly 36 MIN
VHS
Visual literacy series
Color; PAL (P I)
PdS29.50 purchase
Provides a transition from the literal interpretation of visual imagery to the more abstract concept in which what we see carries implicit subjective messages. Part three of a five - part series.
Psychology; Sociology
Dist - EMFVL

Speaking of Explosions 15 MIN
16mm
Color
LC 74-706253
Cites the hazards of unauthorized entry into armament test areas. Explains the dangers of duds and tells what action to take should certain pieces be found. Shows how ordnance drops are planned for practice and testing.
Civics and Political Systems; Health and Safety
Dist - USNAC **Prod** - USAF 1969

Speaking of Harvey 9 MIN
16mm / U-matic / VHS
Color (J)
Addresses the issue of animal experimentation in the world of science. Recommends special regard for the comfort of laboratory animals and stresses the need for all researchers to remain sensitized to the taking of laboratory life.
Science
Dist - PFP **Prod** - FRIEDL

Speaking of Israel 28 MIN
16mm
Color (I)
LC 72-702955
Portrays Israel as seen through the eyes of its inhabitants. Explores Tel Aviv, Haifa and the Negev Desert. Deals with archaeology, science and the cultural life of Israel.
Geography - World; Social Science; Sociology
Dist - ALDEN **Prod** - ALDEN 1969

Speaking of Love 54 MIN
U-matic / VHS
Leo Buscaglia Series
Color
Psychology
Dist - DELTAK **Prod** - PBS

Speaking of Love 60 MIN
U-matic
Color (A)
LC 81-707486
Presents Dr Leo Buscaglia sharing his thoughts on the 'limitless concept' of love and the human potential for giving.
Psychology
Dist - PBS **Prod** - KVIETV 1981

Speaking of Men 20 MIN
16mm
Color (H C A)
LC 78-701530
Presents three women who discuss their attitudes about men, their relationships with men and the importance of men in their lives.
Psychology; Sociology
Dist - POLYMR **Prod** - GROHER 1977

Speaking of Nairobi 60 MIN
VHS / U-matic / 16mm
Color (C G)
$700.00, $180.00 purchase, $35.00 rental _ #CC338016, #CC3380VU, #CC3380VH
Presents a close - up of Forum '85, the gathering in Nairobi, Kenya, of women from all over the world for ten days of discussion, strategic planning and resolution. Reveals that they discussed world peace, hunger, health care, and unemployment. Color, cultural diversity and energy characterized the conference.
Business and Economics; Civics and Political Systems; History - World; Religion and Philosophy; Sociology
Dist - IU **Prod** - NFBC 1985

Speaking of sex
VHS
Big changes, big choices series
Color (I J)
$69.95 purchase _ #LVB-9A
Tells adolescents that sexual abstinence is normal and desirable at their age. Examines the emotional dangers of sexual activity and why young people often turn to sex to compensate for other emotional needs. Part of a 12-part video series designed to help young adolescents work their way though the many anxieties and issues they face. Encourages them to make positive and healthful life choices. Features humorist and youth counselor Michael Pritchard.
Guidance and Counseling; Health and Safety
Dist - CFKRCM **Prod** - CFKRCM

Speaking of sex - a conversation with Winifred Kempton
VHS
Color (G T PRO A)
$49.00 purchase _ #1024
Presents Winifred Kempton who talks about her work in teaching sexuality to persons with special needs. Answers the most common questions asked her by audiences around the world. Includes a copy of Kempton's book 'Sex Education for Persons with Disabilities that Hinder Learning.'
Education; Health and Safety; Psychology
Dist - STANFI **Prod** - STANFI 1989

Speaking of sex ... and persons with special needs 12 MIN
VHS
Color (I J H T PRO)
$79.00 purchase _ #460 - V8
Presents Winifred Kempton, author of a widely - used sex education program for persons with special needs, answering questions for parents, teachers, and health care professionals on the unique sexual issues of the physically or mentally challenged. Includes 198 - page Teacher's Guide.
Guidance and Counseling; Health and Safety
Dist - ETRASS **Prod** - ETRASS

Speaking of sex - It's more than just talk 60 MIN
VHS
Color (C A)
$29.95 purchase
Shows how to deepen intimacy, create a closer relationship and heighten mutual satisfaction. Combines current, reliable information with explicit sexual instruction. Features five educators in the field of human sexuality with honest answers and guidance - Dr Ron Moglia, Director of Graduate Studies in Human Sexuality, NYU; Dr Shirley Zussman, sex therapist; Isadora Alman, sex therapist; Dr Richard Green; Monica Rodriguez, educator, Planned Parenthood.
Guidance and Counseling; Health and Safety; Physical Education and Recreation; Science - Natural; Social Science
Dist - FCSINT

Speaking of success series
Achieving excellence 55 MIN
The E - myth - why most businesses don't work and what to do about it 40 MIN
The generation gap - how to deal with it 55 MIN
How to achieve success with self management 50 MIN
How to become a top performer 55 MIN
How to become an effective listener 56 MIN
How to build a top performers attitude 56 MIN
How to manage time 55 MIN
How to positively influence anybody 50 MIN
Intervention - the key to recovery 50 MIN

Leadership - people potential now	55 MIN
The new selling with service	56 MIN
Perfecting the art of criticism	48 MIN
Reading people right	56 MIN
Successful stress control	55 MIN
Time for strategic planning	55 MIN
Winning more often	48 MIN

Dist - SVIP

Speaking of Weather 8 MIN
U-matic / VHS / 16mm
Color (K P)
Introduces the phenomena of rain, snow, lightning, thunder and other meteorological mysteries. Explains how the sun, water and air converge to create daily and seasonal weather patterns.
Science - Physical
Dist - CORF **Prod** - DISNEY 1982

Speaking on Camera 6.57 MIN
VHS
On Location
(J)
$180 series purchase, $50 rental, $110 self dub
Demonstrates video production skills for small format student productions. Focuses on speaking on camera, highlighting use of the microphone, gestures, eye contact and controlling volume. Second in an eight part series.
Fine Arts
Dist - GPN **Prod** - NCGE

Speaking our peace 55 MIN
16mm / U-matic / VHS
Color (J H A)
Explores the concept of peace as more than the absence of war. Presents the perspectives of women committed both in their personal and professional lives to attaining social justice and permanent world peace. Based on the conviction that women's skills and experience as peacemakers within families and communities must be applied to the global social and political forum if we are to achieve lasting peace. Filmed in Canada, Britain, and the USSR.
Civics and Political Systems; Social Science; Sociology
Dist - BULFRG **Prod** - NFBC 1985

Speaking persuasively 28 MIN
U-matic / BETA / VHS
Communication skills 2 - advanced series
Color (H C G)
$101.95, $89.95 purchase _ #CA - 13
Identifies the external factors that a speaker should consider in persuasive speaking - audience, speaker, purpose, organization, style and delivery. Shows how to analyze the audience, its general makeup, its relative position on the topic, as well as how to identify the purposes that a persuasive speaker may have. Demonstrates how to effectively prepare a persuasive speech. Part of a 26 - part series.
English Language; Social Science
Dist - INSTRU

Speaking Shakespearean Verse 50 MIN
U-matic / VHS
Color
Presents members of the Royal Shakespeare Company who give a workshop on styles of speaking Shakespearean Verse, discuss approaches to the problem of speaking verse in drama and show how the RSC works on a text in rehearsal.
Literature and Drama
Dist - FOTH **Prod** - FOTH 1984

Speaking the Language 15 MIN
16mm / U-matic / VHS
Adventure of the Mind Series
Color
LC 80-701721; 80 - 701721
Demonstrates how the user communicates with a computer using a program language called BASIC.
Business and Economics; Mathematics
Dist - IU **Prod** - IITC 1980

Speaking through walls - who's disabled 28 MIN
VHS
Color (J H C G)
$250.00 purchase
Follows the cast of the Access Theatre as they perform a play written by and starring Neil Marcus, who is severely disabled. Encourages greater understanding and communication between the disabled and the non - disabled. Produced by Anthony Edwards and Shawn Hardin.
Fine Arts; Health and Safety
Dist - CF

Speaking truth - the voice of the heart 55 MIN
VHS
Color (G)
$39.95 _ #VST - C001
Presents Rachel Naomi Remen reading from a collection of poems written by people with cancer and those who love them. Speaks about the concerns of people living on the edge between illness and death.
Health and Safety; Literature and Drama; Sociology
Dist - NOETIC **Prod** - COMMON
COMMON

Speaking with confidence - oral presentations 24 MIN
VHS
Color (H)
$95 purchase _ #10373VG
Shows students how to be effective speakers by teaching organization, rehearsal and presentation. Explains techniques such as planning, outlining, developing introductions, and relaxation. Comes with a teacher's guide, student activities and projects, discussion questions, and blackline masters.
English Language
Dist - UNL

Speaking without words 60 MIN
U-matic / VHS
Smithsonian world series
Color (J)
Examines the non - verbal ways human beings and other creatures communicate. Discusses the evolutionary history of animal communication. Looks at art, mathematics, roadside architecture and the stories that bones can tell.
Fine Arts; Mathematics; Psychology; Science - Physical
Dist - WETATV **Prod** - WETATV

Spear and sword - a payment of bridewealth on the Island of Roti, eastern Indonesia 25 MIN
16mm / VHS
Color (G)
$550.00, $275.00 purchase, $55.00, $35.00 rental
Focuses on the negotiations between the representatives of two families from the Island of Roti during a payment of bridewealth. Begins with an excerpt from a traditional chant about the origin of bridewealth. Continues with the bride's representatives collecting the required money and animals while discussing the problems which might arise during negotiations. Produced by James Fox, Timothy and Patsy Asch.
Geography - World; History - World; Sociology
Dist - DOCEDR

Spear making - boy's spear fight 9 MIN
U-matic / VHS / 16mm
People of the australian western desert series
B&W (H C G T A)
Shows Minma make a spear from an acacia tree while two of his sons play with toy spears.
Geography - World; Social Science; Sociology
Dist - PSU **Prod** - PSU 1965

Spear Thrower Making, Including Stone Flaking and Gum Preparation 33 MIN
U-matic / VHS / 16mm
People of the Australian Western Desert Series
B&W (H C G T A)
Shows Minma cut and shape a piece of acacia wood, flake a stone for a knife, collect spinifex grass gum, melt it, and fasten knife to handle of spear thrower. He also mounts a peg on spear thrower to receive end of spear shaft.
Geography - World; Social Science; Sociology
Dist - PSU **Prod** - PSU 1965

Spearhead at Juniper Gardens 38 MIN
16mm
B&W (C A)
LC 72-701017
Explains that the Juniper Gardens children's project is a program of research conducted in a deprived area of northeast Kansas City, Kansas. Shows how reinforcement principles are used to develop the language of preschoolers and to motivate slow - learning grade school children. Stresses community cooperation.
Education; Geography - United States; Psychology
Dist - UKANS **Prod** - UKANS 1968

Spearman rank correlation
VHS
Probability and statistics series
Color (H C)
$125.00 purchase _ #8060
Provides resource material about the Spearman rank correlation for help in the study of probability and statistics. Presents a 60 - video series, each part 25 to 30 minutes long, that explains and reinforces concepts using definitions, theorems, examples and step - by - step solutions to tutor the student. Videos are also available in a set.
Mathematics
Dist - LANDMK

Special Analytical Tools 10 MIN
VHS / U-matic
Finance for Nonfinancial Managers Series
Color
Business and Economics
Dist - DELTAK **Prod** - DELTAK

Special applications 54 MIN
BETA / VHS / U-matic
Color
$400 purchase
Presents magnetic particle welding, food and drug packaging.
Industrial and Technical Education; Science; Science - Physical
Dist - ASM **Prod** - ASM

Special applications of tension and compression testing 52 MIN
BETA / VHS / U-matic
Color
$400 purchase
Offers an in depth look at the stress-strain curve.
Industrial and Technical Education; Science; Science - Physical
Dist - ASM **Prod** - ASM

Special baby 40 MIN
VHS
Dovetails series
Color (K P I R)
$12.95 purchase _ #35 - 83 - 2064
Presents the New Testament stories of the annunciation, the birth of Jesus, the three wise men, Jesus in the temple, the Sermon on the Mount, the feeding of the 5,000, Jesus' walking on water, Jesus' healing the blind man, and others.
Literature and Drama; Religion and Philosophy
Dist - APH

Special Care 29 MIN
U-matic
Color (H C A)
Focuses on activities during a few months in a hospital nursery for premature infants.
Health and Safety
Dist - CEPRO **Prod** - CEPRO 1986

Special care - inside a children's hospital 18 MIN
VHS
Color (P I)
$89.00 purchase _ #RB807
Visits a prominent American children's hospital. Shows an attractive, fun - filled, loving, home - like and reassuring atmosphere. Examines all facets of hospital care.
Health and Safety
Dist - REVID **Prod** - REVID

Special Cases 13 MIN
16mm / U-matic / VHS
Pregnancy and Childbirth Series
Captioned; Color (H C A)
Depicts modern techniques that can assure safe childbirth even when complications arise. Discusses special cases, such as pregnancies of very young or very old mothers, late or painful deliveries, breech births, premature deliveries and delivery by midwives.
Health and Safety; Science - Natural
Dist - IFB **Prod** - DALHSU 1977

Special cases - 4 12 MIN
16mm / VHS / BETA / U-matic
Canadian hospitals Pregnancy - birth series
Color; PAL (PRO G)
PdS90, PdS98 purchase
Depicts modern techniques that can assure safe childbirth. Shows techniques such as amniotic taps, induced labor, epidural anesthesia and cesarean section. Part of a four - part series.
Health and Safety
Dist - EDPAT

The Special Challenge Shots 14 MIN
16mm
Color
LC 76-703595
Explains how the design of a golf course and natural forces of weather test a golf player's skill. Demonstrates sand recovery techniques and setup and swing adjustments for uphill, downhill and sidehill situations, along with techniques for coping with headwinds and crosswinds.
Physical Education and Recreation
Dist - NGF **Prod** - NGF

The Special child - maximizing limited potential 26 MIN
U-matic / VHS
Color (G)
$249.00, $149.00 purchase _ #AD - 1812
Reveals that when there is doubt about a child's mental and physical coordination, screening for developmental problems should begin at three to four months to determine whether the underlying cause is behavioral,

neurological or emotional. Covers Down's Syndrome, autism, problems of neurological control, speech problems and avoidance behavior.
Education; Health and Safety; Psychology
Dist - FOTH **Prod** - FOTH

Special Children - Blind, Deaf, Physically Handicapped 11 MIN
16mm
Color (P I)
Shows a class discussion about handicapped children which was precipitated by a boy who saw a girl conversing with her parents in sign language.
Education; Guidance and Counseling; Psychology
Dist - ECI **Prod** - ECC 1977

Special children - responding to their needs series
Case conferencing 15 MIN
Identifying Differences 15 MIN
Implementing the Program Plan 15 MIN
Individualizing the Program Plan 15 MIN
Opportunities for Growth 15 MIN
Parents are Special, Too 15 MIN
Dist - ACCESS

Special children, special needs 22 MIN
16mm
Color (C A)
Documents three adapted learning environments for multi - handicapped children that offer learning experiences based on individual strengths and weaknesses.
Education; Psychology
Dist - NYU CFDC **Prod** - NYU NYUMC 1973

Special children, special risks 15 MIN
VHS
Sexually abused children in foster care training videotapes series
Color (PRO A C G)
$9.95 purchase _ #V521
Features Dr Patricia Sullivan, Director of the Boys Town Natl Research Hospital's Center for Abused Handicapped Children, who explores the reasons for the greater vulnerability of handicapped children to sexual abuse and the importance of therapy afterwards. Offers advice to foster parents when caring for such a child. Part of an eight - part series training foster parents on the care of sexually abused children.
Health and Safety; Sociology
Dist - FFBH **Prod** - FFBH 1993

Special Conditions 25 MIN
16mm
To Get from Here to There Series
Color (H)
Presents prepared decisions for responding successfully to conditions of fog, ice, rain, snow and darkness.
Health and Safety; Psychology
Dist - PROART **Prod** - PROART

Special Consonant Combinations 15 MIN
VHS / 16mm
Reading Way Series
Color (P)
$125.00 purchase, $25.00 rental
Considers three consonant combinations such as sprout, string and scrap. Mrs. Read and Tim change sprout to spout and string to sting.
English Language
Dist - AITECH **Prod** - WXXITV 1988

The Special Court at Christian Island 9 MIN
16mm
Color
LC 76-703085
Concerns legal justice for Indian juveniles.
Civics and Political Systems; Social Science; Sociology
Dist - CANFDC **Prod** - CANFDC 1975

Special cycles 17 MIN
U-matic / VHS
Numerical control - computerized numerical control - advanced programming series module 2
Color (IND)
Includes how to program a face mill operation, a rectangular pocket and a mill boring cycle.
Business and Economics; Industrial and Technical Education
Dist - LEIKID **Prod** - LEIKID

Special - Cyprus 28 MIN
Videoreel / VHS
Marilyn's Manhattan series
Color
Presents an interview with the president of Cyprus, Mr S Kyprianou. Focuses on political questions. Hosted by Marilyn Perry.
Business and Economics; Civics and Political Systems; Geography - World
Dist - PERRYM **Prod** - PERRYM

Special days with special kids 18 MIN
VHS
Color
$30.00 rental, $40.00 purchase
Shares memorable moments with Association for Children with Down Syndrome preschool and alumni children. Views days that include a fashion show, field day, dance recital, fathers' breakfast, walkathon, after - school recreation program, graduation ceremonies and more. Days that are shared with parents, brothers and sisters, grandparents, special friends - special days with special kids - opportunities for growth for everyone.
Guidance and Counseling
Dist - ADWNSS **Prod** - ADWNSS

Special Delivery 20 MIN
VHS / U-matic
Color
Takes a look at some of the new technology and some of the problems and hard decisions faced by parents and doctors in the pre - and post - natal care of infants.
Health and Safety; Sociology
Dist - WCCOTV **Prod** - WCCOTV 1982

Special Delivery 7 MIN
16mm
Color (J)
LC 79-701092
Presents an animated comedy about a couple whose quiet existence is disrupted when the mailman falls on their icy steps.
Fine Arts
Dist - NFBC **Prod** - NFBC 1979

Special delivery - creating the birth you want for you and your baby 45 MIN
VHS
Color (G)
$49.95 purchase _ #INP100V
Helps to plan childbirth. Discusses doctors and midwives, hospitals, birthing centers and home deliveries. Answers questions about breathing and relaxation techniques and how to develop a loving bond with a new baby.
Health and Safety
Dist - CAMV

Special Delivery - Handle with Care 20 MIN
VHS / U-matic
Color
$335.00
Sociology
Dist - ABCLR **Prod** - ABCLR 1983

Special Delivery Series
The Able disabled 19 MIN
The Blind Participate 20 MIN
Colin and Ricky 9 MIN
The Common show 28 MIN
The Deaf Communicate 15 MIN
The Positive Show 28 MIN
The Reinforcement Show 28 MIN
The Special Show 28 MIN
The Why Show 28 MIN
Dist - LAWREN

The special demands of service workers and women employees 10 MIN
VHS / U-matic
Meeting the challenge with Dr Warren Bennis series
Color (C A G)
$250.00 purchase _ #V217
Presents Drs Warren Bennis and Peter Drucker who conduct a seminar on the special demands of service workers and women employees. Gives examples of what has worked in real companies. Focuses on the responsibility of management for providing solutions in a rapidly changing global economy. Part of a five-part series.
Business and Economics; Computer Science; Industrial and Technical Education; Psychology; Sociology
Dist - BARR **Prod** - HILSU 1992

Special Edition 30 MIN
U-matic
Read all about it - One Series
Color (I)
Teaches reading and writing skills as it continues a story in which Chris's friends Sam and Lynne publish a special edition of the Chronicle and the police round up Duneedon's agents.
Education; English Language; Literature and Drama
Dist - TVOTAR **Prod** - TVOTAR 1982

Special education curriculum design - a multisensory approach - a series
16mm / U-matic / VHS
Special education curriculum design series
Color
Illustrates the preparation students and teachers should make in anticipation of mainstreamed handicapped children being placed in their classrooms. Fulfillment Of Human Potential; Mainstreaming Techniques - Life Science And Art; Special Education Techniques - Lab Science.
Education
Dist - MGHT **Prod** - MGHT 1979

Special Education Curriculum Design - a Multisensory Approach Series
Fulfillment of Human Potential 18 MIN
Mainstreaming Techniques - Life Science and Art 12 MIN
Special Education Techniques - Lab Science and Art 24 MIN
Dist - MGHT

Special education curriculum design series
Special education curriculum design - a multisensory approach - a series
Dist - MGHT

Special Education Series
Specific Learning Disabilities - Evaluation 28 MIN
Dist - DAVFMS

Special Education Techniques - Lab Science and Art 24 MIN
U-matic / VHS / 16mm
Special Education Curriculum Design - a Multisensory Approach Series
Color (T)
LC 79-700742
Shows the design, adaptations, teaching strategies and implementation of laboratory science and art activities for elementary - level blind children and science activities for intermediate - level and gifted blind children.
Education
Dist - MGHT **Prod** - MGHT 1979

A Special Effect 14 MIN
16mm
Color
LC 80-700389
Tells the story of the wife of a film director who thinks her husband's special effects are inadequate. Shows how her husband and the film crew try to change her mind by trying the special effects on her.
Fine Arts
Dist - RICRUB **Prod** - RICRUB 1978

Special Effects 13 MIN
16mm / U-matic / VHS
Color
LC 73-702372
Documents the use of mechanical effects used in motion pictures and demonstrates the most common present - day special effects. Covers snow, frosted window panes, rain, lightning, fire, bullet holes and flaming arrows.
Fine Arts; Industrial and Technical Education
Dist - PFP **Prod** - PFP 1973

Special effects in sketches 29 MIN
U-matic
Sketching techniques series; Lesson 22
Color (C A)
Focuses on how to depict the more intangible objects that are not solid, such as fire and smoke. Points out some of the drawing and art elements used in sketching special effects.
Fine Arts
Dist - CDTEL **Prod** - COAST

Special Effects - John Dykstra, Bill Mesa 20 MIN
VHS / 16mm
Action - a Day with the Directors Series
Color (H)
$39.95 purchase, $15.00 rental _ #86460
Tells how John Dykstra, whose entry into production was 'Battlestar Galactica,' began and what he does. Discusses the diminishing role of the optical composite industry and talks about how effects are achieved. Features also miniaturist Bill Mesa from Introvision who explains the use of miniatures as substitute sets and shows clips from half a dozen well known features as examples.
Fine Arts; Industrial and Technical Education; Psychology
Dist - UILL **Prod** - SSN 1987

Special Equipment 25 MIN
VHS / 16mm
Licensed Practical Nursing Assistant Refresher Series
Color (C)
$75.00 purchase _ #270512
Helps nursing assistants make the transition back to their chosen career after an extended absence. Updates nursing techniques and procedures which have changed substantially in the last decade. Provides a practical demonstration of step - by - step nursing procedures. 'Special Equipment' provides an overview of the assembly and - or operation of five basic pieces of equipment - the century tub, mechanical patient lifter, oxygen therapy, croupette and basic orthopedic frame.
Health and Safety; Science
Dist - ACCESS **Prod** - ACCESS 1989

Special Equipment Rescues 9 MIN
16mm
Lifesaving and Water Safety Series
Color (I)
LC 76-701573
Uses stop - action to demonstrate rescues from the water using scuba gear, paddleboard, surfboard, rescue tube, torpedo buoy and rescue line.
Health and Safety
Dist - AMRC **Prod** - AMRC 1975

Special Examining Techniques for Children 10 MIN
VHS / U-matic
Color (PRO)
Emphasizes techniques for reassuring, assessing, and examining uncooperative children. Demonstrates exam techniques for preschoolers.
Health and Safety; Home Economics
Dist - HSCIC **Prod** - HSCIC 1980

Special Eye Care for Burns 11 MIN
16mm
Color
LC 74-705676
Demonstrates the special eye care of patients suffering second and third degree burns of the face to prevent eye infection and corneal laceration.
Health and Safety; Science
Dist - USNAC **Prod** - USA 1969

Special feelings 28 MIN
VHS / U-matic
Color (H C G)
$150.00 purchase, $30.00 rental _ #EC2490VU, #EC2490VH
Affirms the universality of the human need for love, companionship and emotional support. Portrays relationships between persons with severe physical disabilities. Stuart and Diane find unique understanding and acceptance in each other, despite severe speech difficulties and motor limitations. Barbara and Lanny, both wheelchair - bound and dependent on considerable nursing care, contemplate marriage. Produced by Dirk Eitzen.
Guidance and Counseling; Health and Safety; Psychology; Religion and Philosophy
Dist - IU

A Special Friendship 13 MIN
U-matic / VHS / 16mm
Color
LC 83-700546
Illustrates the unique relationship and bond between people and their pets. Emphasizes the need for training and proper care of pets.
Science - Natural
Dist - ALTSUL **Prod** - KLUCLA 1983

A Special Gift 47 MIN
16mm / U-matic / VHS
Teenage Years Series
Color (J)
LC 79-701721
Describes Peter's dilemma as he decides whether or not to give up his ballet training, as his father wishes.
Fine Arts; Sociology
Dist - TIMLIF **Prod** - TAHSEM 1979

Special, give, honest, love - Volume 2 60 MIN
VHS
Our friends on Wooster Square series
Color (K P I R)
$34.95 purchase, $10.00 rental _ #35 - 87161 - 460
Presents religious concepts through storylines, songs and Scripture. Features puppet characters including Smedly, Troll and Sizzle. Explores concepts of specialness, giving, honesty and love.
Fine Arts; Literature and Drama; Religion and Philosophy
Dist - APH **Prod** - FRACOC

The Special Homecoming 29 MIN
U-matic / VHS
Tomorrow's Families Series
Color (H C A)
LC 81-706908
Points out that not all babies are healthy and normal at birth and that a family must adjust to the idea and the reality of a distressed infant.
Home Economics; Sociology
Dist - AITECH **Prod** - MDDE 1980

Special interview challenges - minorities, women and people with disabilities 19 MIN
VHS
Color (H C PRO G)
$98.00 purchase _ #3096
Discusses laws governing discrimination in the hiring of minorities, women and disabled people and the way that people who belong to those groups can counteract the culturally - imposed disadvantages of these groups by being well - prepared and personable. Presents specific questions that cannot be legally asked in an interview and shows how to respond tactfully.
Health and Safety; Sociology
Dist - NEWCAR

Special issues 30 MIN
VHS
Beginnings - handicapped children birth to age 5 series
Color (G)
$75.00 purchase _ #BHCH - 112
Features special education teachers. Outlines the challenges and rewards of working with children with special needs. Part of a series on child development focusing on handicapped children.
Education; Health and Safety; Psychology
Dist - PBS **Prod** - MDDE 1985

Special issues in pain control series
Presents a three - part series on pain management presented by Bethany Geldmaker, RN, Mark Lehman, PharmD, Brenda Jackson, PT, and Janet Kues, PT, Medical College of Virginia, Virginia Commonwealth University. Includes the titles Pediatric Pain, Patient - Controlled Analgesia and Transcutaneous Electrical Nerve Stimulation.

Patient - controlled analgesia	11 MIN
Pediatric pain	19 MIN
Special issues in pain control series	42 MIN
Transcutaneous electrical nerve stimulation	12 MIN

Dist - HSCIC

Special issues in using analgesics 28 MIN
VHS / U-matic
Pain management - Margo McCaffery discusses new concepts series
Color (PRO)
$275.00 purchase, $60.00 rental _ #7338S, #7338V
Explores specific approaches for administering analgesics to patients with acute pain, chronic benign pain, a combination of acute and chronic pain and cancer - related pain. Part of a four - part series on pain management featuring Margo McCaffery.
Health and Safety
Dist - AJN **Prod** - HOSSN 1984

The Special journey 22 MIN
16mm
Color
Presents a humanistic approach to infant feeding and nutrition, centering around mother-child relationships.
Health and Safety; Psychology
Dist - MTP **Prod** - INFFRM

A Special kind of care 14 MIN
16mm
Color
LC 77-702875
Explains how Cancer Care, Inc, stands by with counseling, guidance and funds when a family member is struck down by cancer. Shows how all members of a family benefit from the assistance of a case worker.
Psychology; Sociology
Dist - HF **Prod** - CANC 1968

A Special kind of matter 28 MIN
16mm
Color (SPANISH GERMAN FRENCH)
LC 74-703248
Shows scientists involved in the medical finding who discuss the discovery of prostaglandin, a family of natural substances crucial to many physiologic functions.
Foreign Language; Health and Safety; Psychology; Science; Science - Natural
Dist - UPJOHN **Prod** - UPJOHN 1974

A Special Kind of Morning 28 MIN
16mm
What's New Series
Color (K)
LC 76-706114
Follows two little girls on a trip to the zoo at daybreak, and shows the wonder of being alone with only the animals and their keepers and of sharing these experiences with each other.
Science - Natural; Social Science
Dist - IU **Prod** - KETCTV 1970

A Special kind of mother 15 MIN
U-matic / VHS
B&W (PRO)
Shows interactions between mother and baby which emphasize the mother's ability to understand, interpret and act upon the child's needs. Comments on how the mother thought the baby felt in response to her actions.
Education; Psychology; Sociology
Dist - HSERF **Prod** - HSERF

A Special Letter 5 MIN
16mm / U-matic / VHS
Color (J A G)
Tells a true story of a special love between a mother and her grown daughter in drawn pencil animation. Surrounds the memories of the difficulties faced by a Christian Polish family in a WWII concentration camp which make the daughter aware of how the gift of life is spiritual as well as physical.
Fine Arts; Sociology
Dist - DIRECT **Prod** - NFBC 1985

Special locking devices - guard plates, locks, bolts, and bars 30 MIN
VHS
Forcible entry video series
Color (IND)
$159.95 purchase _ #35612
Demonstrates special locking devices. Discusses higher - than - normal security measures. Explains Fichet - type locks, Mul - T - Lock, and police locks. One part of a five - part series that is a teaching companion for IFSTA's Forcible Entry manual.
Health and Safety; Science - Physical; Social Science
Dist - OKSU **Prod** - FIREEN

A Special love 20 MIN
VHS / U-matic
Color
$335.00 purchase
Presents a program on open adoption from the ABC TV program, 20/20.
Sociology
Dist - ABCLR **Prod** - ABCLR 1984

A Special Love 4 MIN
VHS
B&W
$30.00 rental, $40.00 purchase
Presents a 10 - year - old brother playing with his 6 - year - old sister with Down's Syndrome. The brother describes his perceptions of mental retardation and his feeling toward his sister.
Health and Safety
Dist - ADWNSS **Prod** - ADWNSS

The Special magic of herself the elf 24 MIN
16mm / U-matic
Color (K P I)
Presents an animated film about the adventures of Herself the elf and a madcap band of tiny elves whose magical powers help them protect the workings of nature.
Fine Arts; Literature and Drama
Dist - PERSPF **Prod** - PERSPF 1984
CORF

Special needs 40 MIN
VHS
Town hall
Color; PAL (C H)
PdS65 purchase
Follows the Lewisham borough council as it deals with cuts in education. Highlights the difficulty of budgetary restraint. Seventh in the eight - part series Town Hall, which documents the operation of local government in Great Britain.
Civics and Political Systems
Dist - BBCENE

Special Needs Learner Characteristics 30 MIN
VHS / U-matic
Mainstreaming Secondary Special Vocational Needs Student Series
Color
Identifies special needs learner characteristics of handicapped and disadvantaged learners.
Education; Psychology
Dist - PUAVC **Prod** - PUAVC

Special Needs Students in the Classroom 30 MIN
U-matic / VHS
Teaching Students with Special Needs Series
Color
LC 82-706691
Illustrates the range of problem students, from those with learning and behavioral problems to the medically and emotionally needy. Subject specialists discuss goals and strategies which the teacher can apply in actual classroom situations.
Education; Psychology
Dist - PBS **Prod** - MSITV 1981

Special Olympics 13 MIN
16mm
Color
LC 78-701326
Follows the activities of participants and volunteer workers at the California Special Olympics for the mentally handicapped.
Education; Physical Education and Recreation; Psychology
Dist - VIACOM **Prod** - GOLDNH 1977

The Special Olympics 15 MIN
16mm / U-matic / VHS
Color (H C A)
Captures the spirit of courage, determination and enthusiasm involved in the Special Olympics for the mentally retarded. Follows a group of athletes from the time their plane touches down at Los Angeles International Airport to the final jubilation of the victory celebration.
Education; Psychology
Dist - MEDIAG **Prod** - MEDIAG 1976

Special package 295 MIN
VHS
Color (G C PRO)
$199.95 purchase
Combines in a set four tapes of speeches from the 1989 annual meeting of the American Society on Aging. Includes three tapes featuring logotherapy founder Dr Viktor Frankl and one featuring Dr Melvin Kimble in an overview of logotherapy and its application to aging.
Health and Safety
Dist - TNF

Special package 75 MIN
8mm cartridge
Color; B&W (G A)
$150.00 rental
Offers a special package rental of producer Matthias Mueller's films including Continental Breakfast, Final Cut, Epilogue, The Memo Book and Home Stories.
Fine Arts
Dist - CANCIN

Special package 14 MIN
16mm
B&W; Color (G)
$40.00 rental
Reveals virtually unknown underground films by the pioneer kinetic artist, sculptor and filmmaker, Len Lye. Consists of Color Cry, Particles in Space, Tal Farlow, Rhythm and Free radicals.
Fine Arts
Dist - CANCIN **Prod** - LYEL 1980

Special package by Flip Johnson 12 MIN
16mm
Color; B&W (G)
$42.00 rental
Features a special rental package of Frankenstein Cries Out, Wild Animals in the Zoo and The Roar From Within.
Fine Arts
Dist - CANCIN **Prod** - JOHNF 1982

Special package by Joseph Cornell 49 MIN
16mm
B&W; Color tint (G)
$125.00 rental
Includes all six films by Joseph Cornell consisting of Cotillion, The Midnight Party and Children's Party, which are silent pictures, and Carrousel, Jack's Dream and Thimble Theatre, with sound. Features animation and fully collaged film from the 1940s.
Fine Arts
Dist - CANCIN

Special package by Larry Jordan 50 MIN
16mm
Color (G)
$65.00 rental
Consists of Visions of a City, Duo Concertantes, Cornell 1965, Our Lady of the Sphere, Orb, Moonlight Sonata and Masquerade.
Fine Arts
Dist - CANCIN **Prod** - JORDAL 1985

Special package by Larry Jordan - Magenta Geryon series 32 MIN
16mm
Special package by Larry Jordan - Magenta Geryon series
Color (G)
$65.00 rental
Features the Magenta Geryon series which includes Adagio - part I, In a Summer Garden - part 2 and Winter Light - part 3.
Fine Arts; Religion and Philosophy
Dist - CANCIN **Prod** - JORDAL 1983

Special package by Larry Jordan - Magenta Geryon series
Special package by Larry Jordan - Magenta Geryon series 32 MIN
Dist - CANCIN

Special package - Danny Lyon 397 MIN
VHS
Color (G)
$509.00 purchase
Features a special package purchase price of nine productions by Danny Lyon. Includes Soc Sci 127, Llanito, El Mojado, Los Ninos Abandonados - The Abandoned Children, Little Boy, El Otro Lado - The Other Side, Dear Mark, Born to Film, and Willie. See individual titles for description and availability in 16mm format.
Fine Arts
Dist - CANCIN

Special pain problems - pediatric and elderly patients 28 MIN
U-matic / VHS
Pain management - Margo McCaffery discusses new concepts series
Color (PRO)
$275.00 purchase, $60.00 rental _ #7339S, #7339V
Demonstrates methods of communication to assist nursing staff in assessing and managing pain in pediatric and elderly patients. Discusses the problems of differing rates of metabolism, drug interactions and the difficulties of administering analgesics to pediatric and elderly patients. Part of a four - part series on pain management featuring Margo McCaffery.
Health and Safety
Dist - AJN **Prod** - HOSSN 1984

Special Paragraphs - Conclusions and Transitions 30 MIN
U-matic / VHS
Writing for a Reason Series
Color (C)
English Language
Dist - DALCCD **Prod** - DALCCD

Special Paragraphs - Introductions 30 MIN
U-matic / VHS
Writing for a Reason Series
Color (C)
English Language
Dist - DALCCD **Prod** - DALCCD

Special People - Library Service to Nursing Home Residents 15 MIN
U-matic / VHS
Color
Discusses some of the emotional reactions that nursing home employees and library staff may experience while serving nursing home residents. Describes the kinds of services, programs and materials used at a particular convalescent center.
Education; Health and Safety; Social Science; Sociology
Dist - LVN **Prod** - ANARCL

Special periodical index 6 MIN
U-matic / VHS
Library skills tapes series
Color
Shows how to locate articles in professional journals by such periodical indexes as the Social Science Index.
Education; English Language
Dist - MDCC **Prod** - MDCC

A Special Place 11 MIN
VHS / U-matic
Color (C A)
Shows two women who relate primarily to men sexually while they share an intense sexual and emotional relationship with each other.
Health and Safety; Psychology; Sociology
Dist - MMRC **Prod** - NATSF

A Special place - the garden tomb 30 MIN
VHS
Color (J H C G A R)
$19.95 purchase, $10.00 rental _ #35 - 872 - 8516
Tours Jerusalem and the site of the 'Garden Tomb,' where some believe that Jesus' burial and resurrection took place.
Literature and Drama; Religion and Philosophy
Dist - APH **Prod** - VISVID

Special Problems 30 MIN
16mm
Success in Supervision Series
B&W
LC 74-706254
Discusses techniques useful in problem cases that commonly confront the supervisor. Relates techniques for supervising people stationed at long distances and outlines the job of the part - time supervisor.
Business and Economics; Psychology
Dist - USNAC **Prod** - WETATV 1965

Special Procedures in IV Therapy - Part 3 19 MIN
VHS / U-matic
Parenteral Therapy Series
Color (PRO)
Illustrates two special procedures in IV therapy, the heparin lock and the teflon stylet.
Health and Safety
Dist - HSCIC **Prod** - HSCIC 1982

Special Products and Factoring 31 MIN
16mm
Intermediate Algebra Series
B&W (H)
Defines factoring. Shows how the form of a binomial is obtained by multiplying two generalized linear factors and then used to find the binomial factors. Describes the factor theorem for polynomials.
Mathematics
Dist - MLA **Prod** - CALVIN 1959

Special purpose semiconductors 17 MIN
U-matic / VHS
Introduction to solid state electronics series chapter 7
Color (IND) (SPANISH)
LC 80-707265
Covers four of the more important special purpose semiconductors. Explains construction and characteristics of the SCR.
Education; Industrial and Technical Education
Dist - TAT **Prod** - TAT

Special Purpose Semiconductors 17 MIN
VHS / 16mm
Solid State Electronics Series
Color (H A)
$410.00 purchase, $110.00 rental
Covers SCR, DIAC and TRIAC and shows advantages of silicon controlled rectifiers.
Industrial and Technical Education
Dist - TAT **Prod** - TAT 1980

Special Purpose Tubes - Remote Cutoff and Beam Power Tubes 18 MIN
16mm
B&W
LC 74-705677
Discusses the distinguishing characteristics, operation, and advantages of remote cutoff tubes. Compares remote and sharp cutoff tubes and discusses the operation of a sharp cutoff tube. Discusses beam power tube construction and how the beam forming plates overcome the disadvantage of secondary emission. (Kinescope).
Industrial and Technical Education
Dist - USNAC **Prod** - USAF

Special Reference Materials 7 MIN
VHS / U-matic
Library Skills Tapes Series
Color
Examines special reference books such as the Reader's Advisor, Bartlett's Familiar Quotations and the Nation and Florida Status.
Education; English Language
Dist - MDCC **Prod** - MDCC

Special relativity I - 15 49 MIN
VHS
Conceptual physics alive series
Color (H C)
$45.00 purchase
Explores the concepts of space and time, as well as the view of Albert Einstein concerning these concepts. Follows with a discussion which leads to Hewitt's 12 - minute animated film, Relatavistic Time Dilation. Part 15 of a 35 - part series adapted from the college and high school textbook Conceptual Physics by Professor Paul Hewitt.
Science - Physical
Dist - MMENTE **Prod** - HEWITP 1992

Special relativity II - 16 38 MIN
VHS
Conceptual physics alive series
Color (H C)
$45.00 purchase
Discusses length, momentum, mass and Einstein's famous equation E equals MC squared. Supports these concepts with fanciful examples. Entertains speculations about going faster than the speed of light. Part 16 of a 35 - part series adapted from the college and high school textbook Conceptual Physics by Professor Paul Hewitt.
Science - Physical
Dist - MMENTE **Prod** - HEWITP 1992

Special Report 17 MIN
16mm
Color
LC 71-711502
A scathing satire of the news coverage of the murder of a topless go - go dancer, Candy Parabola.
Fine Arts
Dist - USC **Prod** - USC 1970

The Special Show 28 MIN
16mm
Special Delivery Series
Color (P I)
LC 79-701079
Illustrates difficulties faced daily by people with handicaps, viewed from their perspective.

Education; Psychology
Dist - LAWREN **Prod** - WNVT 1979

Special steering and sailing rules 14 MIN
16mm
B&W
LC FIE52-956
Gives the steering and sailing rules governing a steam vessel under way and a sailing fishing vessel. Defines 'privilege' and 'burden.'
Civics and Political Systems; Health and Safety; Social Science
Dist - USNAC **Prod** - USN 1943

A Special Time for Parents and Children 15 MIN
U-matic / VHS / 16mm
Color (A)
Shows how parents can have fun with their children while improving the quality of their life together through a very special bonding.
Home Economics; Sociology
Dist - PEREN **Prod** - JOWA

Special topics in chemistry 63 MIN
35mm strip / VHS
Color (J H C A)
$186.00, $186.00 purchase _ #MB - 512818 - 7, #MB - 512766 - 0
Presents a four - part program on basic chemistry principles. Covers solutions, acids and bases, organic chemistry, and biochemistry. Consists of two videocassettes or four sound filmstrips.
Science - Natural; Science - Physical
Dist - SRA **Prod** - SRA

Special Tour 15 MIN
16mm / U-matic / VHS
Color (J H A)
LC 77-701114
Presents a science fiction film which contains underlying philosophical and satirical meanings.
Fine Arts; Literature and Drama
Dist - PFP **Prod** - BURPT 1973

A Special trade 17 MIN
VHS / U-matic / 16mm
Color (K P I)
$385.00, $300.00, $270.00 purchase _ #A283
Tells of the friendship of Bartholomew, an old man, and Nelly. Reveals that Bartholomew took Nelly for walks in her stroller every day when she was a baby, that he helped her to learn to walk and skate. As Bartholomew and Nelly grew older, it became Nelly's turn to care for Bartholomew.
Literature and Drama; Psychology
Dist - BARR **Prod** - UNDERR 1979

A Special Trade 17 MIN
16mm / U-matic / VHS
Color (K P I)
LC 79-701685
Presents a story about a friendship between a young girl and an older man. Tells how, as a baby, the young girl is taken for outings and taught to walk by her friend. Explains how one day the man returns home from the hospital in a wheelchair and it is the young girl's turn to take her friend for walks. Based on the book A Special Trade by Sally Whitman.
Fine Arts; Guidance and Counseling
Dist - BARR **Prod** - BARR 1979

Special transportation rates and services 30 MIN
VHS
Business logistics series
Color (G C)
$200.00 purchase, $20.50 rental _ #34975
Examines special transportation rates and services. Part of a 30 - part series on business logistics which deals with movement and storage of raw and finished products, and with managerial activities important for effective control of these operations. Interviews logistics managers of major US corporations and transportation companies. Uses on - site segments to demonstrate logistical carrier operations. Features program author Dr John Coyle.
Business and Economics; Social Science
Dist - PSU **Prod** - WPSXTV 1987

Special Treatment 30 MIN
U-matic / VHS
Loosening the Grip Series
Color (C A)
Health and Safety
Dist - GPN **Prod** - UMA 1980

Special trigonometric limits 30 MIN
VHS
Calculus series
Color (C)
$125.00 purchase _ #6033
Explains special trigonometric limits. Part of a 56 - part series on calculus.
Mathematics
Dist - LANDMK **Prod** - LANDMK

The Special Universe of Walter Krolik 25 MIN
16mm
Color
Describes a family man who has TB. Examines the complex relationships between patient and medical and paramedical staff, with special emphasis on nurses.
Health and Safety
Dist - AMLUNG **Prod** - NTBA 1966

Special Use of Valuation - How and When to Use it 51 MIN
VHS / U-matic
Postmortem Tax Planning After ERTA Series
Color (PRO)
Covers the topic of special use valuation with particular emphasis on farmlands. Explains the cash value formula and alternative methods of valuation.
Civics and Political Systems; Social Science
Dist - ABACPE **Prod** - ABACPE

The Specialists 15 MIN
VHS / U-matic
Real world economic series
Color (J H)
$240.00, $290.00 purchase, $60.00 rental
Includes material on people at work, how living standards increase, specialization in all factors of production, the benefits and disadvantages of specialization.
Business and Economics
Dist - NDIM **Prod** - REALWO 1993

Specialization 15 MIN
U-matic / VHS
Pennywise Series no 6
Color (P)
LC 82-706008
Uses the format of a television program to explain that specialization is an important aspect of production and that it often leads to more efficient production of goods and services. Demonstrates that there are both advantages and disadvantages to specialized tasks and jobs.
Business and Economics
Dist - GPN **Prod** - MAETEL 1980

Specialized Centrifugal Pumps 60 MIN
VHS / U-matic
Mechanical Equipment Maintenance Series
Color (IND) (SPANISH)
Features standardized and suction and vertical pumps.
Industrial and Technical Education
Dist - ITCORP **Prod** - ITCORP

Specialized electronic devices 60 MIN
VHS
Electronic systems and equipment series
Color (PRO)
$600.00 - $1500.00 purchase _ #ICSED
Provides basic information on the construction and operation of zener, tunnel, light - emitting and light - sensing diodes, unijunction transistors, silicon - controlled rectifiers, junction field - effect transistors and insulated - gate field - effect transistors. Part of a nineteen - part series on electronic systems and equipment, which is part of a 49 - unit set on instrumentation and control. Includes five workbooks and an instructor guide to support four hours of instruction.
Education; Industrial and Technical Education; Psychology
Dist - NUSTC **Prod** - NUSTC

Specialized laboratory cleaning for biohazardous and radioactive labs 19 MIN
VHS
Color (IND)
$275.00 purchase _ #6896
Trains laboratory technicians, housekeeping and janitorial staff working in laboratories using radioactive isotopes and biohazardous materials.
Health and Safety; Psychology
Dist - UCALG **Prod** - UCALG 1990

Specialized nondestructive testing methods 55 MIN
BETA / VHS / U-matic
Color
$400 purchase
Overviews principles, equipment, procedures, variables, interpretation of test results, advantages and limitations for the methods.
Science; Science - Physical
Dist - ASM **Prod** - ASM

Specialties 29 MIN
U-matic / VHS
Basically Baseball Series
Color
Presents coach Billy Hunter, players Mark Belanger and Don Baylor and Oriole manager Earl Weaver explaining base running, stealing, sliding and individual aspects of baseball and offering comments on winning attitudes and desire.
Physical Education and Recreation
Dist - MDCPB **Prod** - MDCPB

Specialty appliances
VHS
Kitchen equipment series
(G)
$59.00_CA238
Covers specialty appliances used in the kitchen.
Home Economics
Dist - AAVIM **Prod** - AAVIM 1989

Specialty egg dishes 57 MIN
VHS
Cookbook videos series
Color (G)
$19.95 purchase
Offers easy egg dishes for breakfast, brunch, lunch and supper. Provides brief, practical and easy-to-understand instructions for several recipes. Uses close-up photography and detailed on-screen ingredients, so even a novice can duplicate the dishes demonstrated. Includes an abstract of recipes. Part of a series on cooking.
Home Economics; Social Science
Dist - ALWHIT **Prod** - ALWHIT
CAMV

Specialty shots 30 MIN
VHS
Tennis with Van der Meer series
Color (C A)
$95.00 purchase, $55.00 rental
Features tennis player and instructor Dennis Van der Meer in a presentation on specialty shots. Uses freeze - frame photography and repetition to stress skill development. Serves as part six of a 10 - part telecourse.
Physical Education and Recreation; Psychology
Dist - SCETV **Prod** - SCETV 1989

Specialty strokes 30 MIN
VHS
Tennis talk series
Color (J H A)
$24.95 purchase _ #PRO003V
Features tennis instructor Dennis Van der Meer teaching about specialty strokes.
Physical Education and Recreation
Dist - CAMV

Specialty Strokes 30 MIN
16mm / U-matic / VHS
Tennis Anyone Series
Color (H C A)
LC 79-706889
Physical Education and Recreation
Dist - TIMLIF **Prod** - BATA 1979

Speciation - sexual selection in fruit flies 25 MIN
VHS
Evolution series
Color (G C)
$150.00 purchase, $19.50 rental _ #36269
Studies the phylogeny of Drosophilids, the Hawaiian fruit flies, looking particularly at the way in which a change in courtship behavior can initiate speciation. Shows how this information is being used to develop a population of sterile flies to be introduced into the wild for the purpose of pest control in California. Part of a ten - part series exploring evolutionary selection and adaptation.
History - United States; Science - Natural
Dist - PSU **Prod** - BBC 1992

Species and evolution 24 MIN
U-matic / VHS / 16mm
Color
Defines operationally what evolutionists mean when they use the term species. Proposes that the variability of climate and terrain of places like Hawaii is one reason for the diversity of species in a locale.
Science - Natural
Dist - MEDIAG **Prod** - OPENU 1982

Species - specific aggregation of dissociated sponge cells 3 MIN
16mm
EDC Developmental biology series
Color (J H C)
$21.00 rental _ #140 8240
Examines two species of sponge cells, Microciona prolifera and Haliclona occulata, which are dissociated. Illustrates the reaggregation of the cells when the two species are mixed. Part of a series featuring time - lapse photomicrography which depict events never seen clearly before to illustrate an important problem, process or principle.
Science - Natural
Dist - WARDS **Prod** - WARDS

Specific emergency condition series
Emergency childbirth 23 MIN
Dist - PRIMED

Specific gravity separator 3 MIN
16mm

Principles of seed processing series
Color (H C A)
LC 77-701162
Uses both animation and live footage to illustrate the stratifying action of a vibrating slanted deck combined with air, the uphill movement of heavy seeds and the migration of lighter seeds toward the lower end of the deck.
Agriculture; Science - Natural
Dist - IOWA **Prod** - EVERSL 1975

The Specific is terrific 9 MIN
U-matic / VHS / 16mm
Effective writing series
Color (I)
$245.00, $170.00 purchase _ #81527
Points out that writing general statements does not make a very good impression. Stresses using nouns, verbs, adjectives and adverbs in a specific way to attract the interest of the reader.
English Language
Dist - CENTEF **Prod** - CENTRO 1983
CORF

Specific Learning Disabilities 30 MIN
VHS / U-matic
Promises to Keep Series Module 3
Color (T)
Presents an overview of the basic psychological processes including reception, association and expression and describes how disabilities in any one process may affect learning. Considers ways of accommodating an individual's unique learning style. Concludes with an interview with two young adults who share their experiences as disabled students.
Education
Dist - LUF **Prod** - VPI 1979

Specific Learning Disabilities - Evaluation 28 MIN
16mm
Color (T)
LC 75-704162
Follows two learning - disabled children through a series of evaluative tasks to determine their learning strengths and weaknesses in order to give teachers a practical understanding of evaluative techniques.
Education; Psychology
Dist - DAVFMS **Prod** - MHCF 1975

Specific Learning Disabilities - Evaluation 28 MIN
16mm / U-matic / VHS
Special Education Series
Color (T)
LC 75-704162
Deals with the diagnosis and treatment of children with normal IQs who cannot learn in traditional ways. Follows two learning - disabled children through a series of evaluative tasks to determine their learning strengths and weaknesses in oder to give teachers a practical understanding of evaluative techniques.
Education; Psychology
Dist - DAVFMS **Prod** - DAVFMS

Specific Learning Disabilities in the Classroom 23 MIN
16mm
Color (A)
LC 75-703615
Defines and documents the most common types of specific learning disabilities. Presents a language learning hierarchy, illustrated by film footage, to show how and why learning disabilities impair academic development. Discusses resources outside of the school which can offer evaluative and remedial help.
Education; Psychology
Dist - DAVFMS **Prod** - DAVFMS 1975

Specific learning disabilities - remedial programming 31 MIN
16mm
Color (T)
LC 75-704163
Presents and discusses remedial techniques and procedures which teachers can use in the classroom. Describes how information gained through evaluation and observation can be translated into appropriate individualized remedial plans.
Education; Psychology
Dist - DAVFMS **Prod** - MHCF 1975

Specific material handling series
Metalworking fluids 14 MIN
Dist - ITSC

Specifications and Equipment Details
U-matic / VHS
Drafting - Process Piping Drafting Series
Color (IND)
Industrial and Technical Education
Dist - GPCV **Prod** - GPCV

Specifications and tolerances 32 MIN
VHS / U-matic
Quality control series
Color
Describes procedures to establish specifications and tolerances utilizing the statistical data available from quality control records.
Business and Economics; Industrial and Technical Education
Dist - MIOT **Prod** - MIOT

Specified Perils 29 MIN
U-matic
Life, Death and Taxes Series
Color
Discusses methods of maximizing the after - tax dollars for personal life insurance beneficiaries.
Business and Economics
Dist - UMITV **Prod** - UMITV 1977

Spectacular Canyons 17 MIN
U-matic / VHS / 16mm
Natural Phenomena Series
Color (J H)
Visits several spectacular canyons to investigate how they were formed. Deals with how different rocks contribute to canyon formation and the effects of erosion, uplift and plate tectonics. Discusses the Earth's geological history and speculates on what the Earth's future might be.
Science - Physical
Dist - JOU **Prod** - JOU 1982

Spectacular Roses 56 MIN
BETA / VHS / U-matic
Color (A G)
$14.95 _ #MR607
Shows the secrets to creating a bed of beautiful buds, from fertilization tips to insect control.
Agriculture
Dist - BAKERT

Spectacular roses 56 MIN
VHS
(H C A)
$24.95 purchase _ #MX607V
Presents gardening expert Ed Hume who explains the differences among hybrid tea roses, grandifloras, pillars and miniatures, and climbing roses. Discusses care and maintenance of roses.
Agriculture
Dist - CAMV

Spectra 10 MIN
U-matic
Structure of the Atom Series
Color (H C)
Examines Bohr's proposals which brought atomic structure into the realm of quantum physics.
Science; Science - Physical
Dist - TVOTAR **Prod** - TVOTAR 1984

Spectral Analysis of the Amniotic Fluid in Hemolytic Disease of the Newborn 22 MIN
16mm
Clinical Pathology Series
B&W (PRO)
Discusses amniocentesis, its indications and hazards.
Health and Safety
Dist - USNAC **Prod** - NMAC 1972

Spectral Properties of Soils 30 MIN
U-matic / VHS
Introduction to Quantitative Analysis of Remote Sensing Data Series
Color
Describes an experiment in which chemical and physical studies of 500 soils revealed that spectral properties of soils are related to the organic matter and other variables.
Industrial and Technical Education
Dist - PUAVC **Prod** - PUAVC

Spectrometric Oil Analysis Program 19 MIN
U-matic / VHS
Color
LC 84-706487
Depicts the program for testing engine oil for metal traces from worn parts to predict potential engine trouble.
Industrial and Technical Education
Dist - USNAC **Prod** - USA 1983

Spectrophotometric Study of Complex Ions 15 MIN
16mm
Experimental General Chemistry Series
B&W
Develops a procedure for using the spectrophotometer and illustrates a method for finding the formula of a complex ion, iron thiocyanate.
Science; Science - Physical
Dist - MLA **Prod** - MLA 1970

Spectroscopy 13 MIN
16mm
Experimental General Chemistry Series
Color
Introduces the student to the phenomena by which light is produced when an electrical discharge is passed through gases in an evacuated tube and other experiments.
Mathematics; Science; Science - Physical
Dist - MLA **Prod** - MLA

Spectroscopy 9 MIN
U-matic
Chemistry Videotape Series
Color
Demonstrates the concepts of color, absorption and emission. Introduces the properties of light, wavelength and frequency. Discusses the Balmer series.
Science - Physical
Dist - UMITV **Prod** - UMITV

Spectrum clip art
CD-ROM
(G)
$289.00 purchase _ #1510
Includes over 6500 clip art images, such as decorative letters and alphabets from Dover. Features images scanned at 300 DPI and formatted in PCX and PostScript formats for use with both IBM and Macintosh. For IBM PCs and compatibles, requires 640K of RAM, DOS 3.1 or later, one floppy disk drive - hard disk recommended, one empty expansion slot, an IBM compatible CD - ROM drive, and a VGA monitor to view the images. For Macintosh Classic, Plus, SE and II computers, requires 1MB of RAM, one floppy disk drive, and an Apple compatible CD - ROM drive.
Computer Science; Fine Arts
Dist - BEP

The Spectrum of Literature 30 MIN
U-matic
Communicating with a Purpose Series
(H C A)
Examines the differences between prose and poetry. Illustrates the differences between prose fiction and non - fiction.
Education; Literature and Drama
Dist - ACCESS **Prod** - ACCESS 1982

Spectrum series
Anatomy of violence 30 MIN
Aphasia - the road back 20 MIN
Autism's lonely children 20 MIN
Changing the Weather 29 MIN
The Living Sun 30 MIN
Noise - the New Pollutant 30 MIN
R Buckminster Fuller - Prospects for Humanity 30 MIN
Science and Society - a Race Against Time 30 MIN
Stop or Go - an Experiment in Genetics 29 MIN
To Sleep - Perchance to Dream 30 MIN
The Trembling Earth 30 MIN
The Universe from Palomar 30 MIN
Dist - IU

Spectrum Series
Names We Never Knew 27 MIN
Through the Looking Glass Darkly 51 MIN
Dist - WKYTV

Specula - Nasal and Vaginal 14 MIN
U-matic
Instruments of Physical Assessment Series
Color (PRO)
LC 80-707628
Demonstrates various types of nasal and vaginal specula and discusses their special features. Describes measures for providing safety and comfort for the patient and includes suggestions for care, maintenance, and part replacement.
Health and Safety
Dist - LIP **Prod** - SUNYSB 1980

Speculating and Spreading in Financial Futures 30 MIN
U-matic / VHS
Commodities - - the Professional Trader Series
Color (C A)
Discusses trading on the financial futures market. Features Nancy Johnson and Carla Jane Eyre.
Business and Economics
Dist - VIPUB **Prod** - VIPUB

The Speech 7 MIN
U-matic
Color (C)
$150.00
Presents an experimental film by Doug Hall.
Fine Arts
Dist - AFA **Prod** - AFA 1982

Speech and Language Disorders 30 MIN
U-matic / VHS
Promises to Keep Series Module 8
Color (T)
Demonstrates normal communication development and selected disorders which may be exhibited in the classroom. Discusses how each disorder might be treated and how the regular classroom teacher can support corrective efforts.
Education
Dist - LUF **Prod** - VPI 1979

Speech assessment - speech instruction - Session 7
VHS
English as a second language - tutor training series
Color (G T PRO)
$70.00 purchase _ #93003
Presents a follow - up session after six weeks of tutoring, as an in - service for reading tutors. Seventh of seven videos that support the English as a Second Language - Tutor Training Kit.
Education; English Language
Dist - LITERA

Speech Indicator 5 MIN
16mm
Color (H C A S) (AMERICAN SIGN)
LC 76-701704
Describes the speech indicator in American sign language, telling what it is and how to use it. Signed for the deaf by Herb Larson, who relates a personal experience of what happened when he first used the device at home.
Education; Guidance and Counseling; Psychology
Dist - JOYCE **Prod** - JOYCE 1975

Speech Instruction with a Deaf - Blind Pupil, no 1 6 MIN
16mm
B&W (T)
Depicts tactile lip reading and demonstrates the effort required by the pupil to grasp this technique.
Education; English Language; Health and Safety
Dist - CMPBL **Prod** - CMPBL 1968

Speech, Music and Graphics 18 MIN
U-matic / VHS
Little Computers - See How they Run Series
Color (J)
LC 81-706871
Examines various types of functions which computers can perform such as data plotting, graphic displays and programmed speech.
Mathematics
Dist - GPN **Prod** - ELDATA 1980

Speech Preparation 13 MIN
16mm
B&W (H C A)
Presents the basic steps in preparing a speech.
English Language
Dist - AVED **Prod** - CBF 1958

Speech reading 28 MIN
16mm
B&W
LC FIE53-495
Explains how persons with a hearing loss can learn, by careful interpretation of lip movements, to 'see' what people are saying. Shows how vowel and consonant sounds are formed by the mouth.
English Language
Dist - USNAC **Prod** - USA 1953

Speech reading materials series
Blade - Alveloars 10 MIN
Blade - Prepalatals 10 MIN
Conversational skill tape, Pt I 10 MIN
Conversational skill tape, Pt II 10 MIN
Horizontal Vowels and Semi - Vowels 10 MIN
Introduction to Bilabials 10 MIN
Lingua - Alveloars 10 MIN
Rounded Vowels and Labio - Dentals 10 MIN
Velars and Glottals 10 MIN
Vertical Vowels and Lingua - Dentals 10 MIN
Dist - RMIBHF

Speech techniques 11 MIN
16mm
Military instruction series
B&W (J H)
LC FIE56-247
Discusses the importance of good speech techniques in military instruction and illustrates techniques to be used, including looking at and talking directly to the audience, attention to one's diction, exercising care in the use of mannerisms and speaking slowly enough to be understood.
English Language; Guidance and Counseling
Dist - USNAC **Prod** - USA 1956

Speech understanding using Hearsay 45 MIN
U-matic / VHS
Artificial intelligence series; Expert systems, Pt 2
Color (PRO)
Covers interexpert communication, the role of knowledge on many levels, analysis, islands of reliability, and an illustration.
Industrial and Technical Education; Mathematics
Dist - MIOT **Prod** - MIOT

Speeches collection series
Presents a ten - part series on the addresses of the 20th - century's most powerful speakers. Witnesses the signing of peace treaties, the inciting of world wars, the making of history with words. Includes John F Kennedy, Robert Kennedy, Martin Luther King, Jr, Richard Nixon, Winston Churchill, Dwight D Eisenhower, Franklin D Roosevelt, Adolf Hitler, Harry S Truman, and Douglas MacArthur.
Adolf Hitler
Douglas MacArthur
Dwight D Eisenhower
Franklin D Roosevelt
Harry S Truman
John F Kennedy
Martin Luther King, Jr
Richard Nixon
Robert Kennedy
Winston Churchill
Dist - CAMV

The Speeches of Adolf Hitler 50 MIN
VHS
B&W (H C G)
$21.95 purchase _ #MP1685
Examines the hypnotic grip Hitler held over the German masses. Includes over a decade of oratory, from his first speech to the Reichstag as chancellor of Germany, to a speech before the German Youth - the infamous speech about the 'Thousand Year Reich' - delivered during the heat of World War II.
Civics and Political Systems; History - World
Dist - INSTRU

The Speeches of Douglas MacArthur 60 MIN
VHS
B&W (H C G)
$21.95 purchase _ #MP1687
Offers the collected speeches of General Douglas MacArthur, who graduated with highest honors in his class at West Point, developed, shaped and publicized a military career, and became known as the 'American Caesar' because of his commanding reign in the Pacific theater during World War II and the Korean conflict. Includes speeches from throughout his career, including remarks after he was relieved of command in Korea by President Truman.
Biography; History - United States
Dist - INSTRU

The Speeches of Dwight D Eisenhower 60 MIN
VHS
B&W (G)
$19.95 purchase _ #S02013
Presents selected speeches by Dwight D Eisenhower.
Biography; Civics and Political Systems; History - United States
Dist - UILL

The Speeches of FDR - Address at Chautauqua, New York, August 14, 1936 29 MIN
16mm / U-matic / VHS
Speeches of FDR Series
B&W
Presents U S President Franklin Delano Roosevelt's first address on foreign policy. He notes the tendency to hostile aggression growing in the world, details the areas in which the U S promoted good will and peace and repeats his inaugural statement about the Good - Neighbor Policy.
Biography; Civics and Political Systems; English Language; History - United States
Dist - USNAC **Prod** - USNAC

The Speeches of FDR - Navy and Total Defense Day Address, October 27, 1941 26 MIN
16mm / U-matic / VHS
Speeches of FDR Series
B&W
Presents a speech made by FDR after an American ship was fired upon by Nazi submarines, and the USS Kearny was attacked by a German U - boat and eleven lives were lost.
Biography; Civics and Political Systems; English Language; History - United States
Dist - USNAC **Prod** - USNAC

Speeches of FDR Series
The Speeches of FDR - Address at Chautauqua, New York, August 14, 1936 29 MIN
The Speeches of FDR - Navy and Total Defense Day Address, October 27, 1941 26 MIN
The Speeches of FDR - State of the Union Message, January 6, 1942 42 MIN
Dist - USNAC

The Speeches of FDR - State of the Union Message, January 6, 1942 42 MIN
U-matic / VHS / 16mm
Speeches of FDR Series
B&W
Presents the State of the Union address by U S President Franklin Delano Roosevelt one month after Pearl Harbor. He outlines the steps and sacrifices to be made in order to achieve victory in World War II and gives a history of the Axis powers and their conquests in the 1930's.
Biography; English Language; History - United States
Dist - USNAC **Prod** - USNAC

The Speeches of Franklin D Roosevelt 60 MIN
VHS
B&W (G)
$19.95 purchase _ #S02011
Presents selected speeches by Franklin D Roosevelt.
Biography; Civics and Political Systems; History - United States
Dist - UILL

The Speeches of Harry S Truman 55 MIN
VHS
B&W (H C G)
$21.95 purchase _ #MP1686
Reveals that the presidency of Harry S Truman was not appreciated until after his turbulent stay in office. Presents a collection of speeches featuring a man struggling conscientiously with troubled times - fighting for social and economic reforms, raising the standards of living for workers and farmers, pursuing civil rights reforms.
Biography; History - United States
Dist - INSTRU

The Speeches of John F Kennedy 60 MIN
VHS
B&W (G)
$19.95 purchase _ #S02012
Presents selected speeches by John F Kennedy.
Biography; Civics and Political Systems; History - United States
Dist - UILL

The Speeches of Martin Luther King 60 MIN
VHS
B&W (G)
$19.95 purchase _ #S02010
Presents selected speeches by Dr Martin Luther King Jr.
Biography; Civics and Political Systems; History - United States
Dist - UILL

The Speeches of Richard Nixon 60 MIN
VHS
Color & B&W (H C G)
$21.95 purchase _ #MP1688
Reveals that, unlike most great speakers who have developed a reputation for delivering stirring messages to an eager public, the most famous speeches of Richard Nixon were delivered for other reasons - defending his political life, resigning from the Presidency. Shows a defensive man trying to make sense of public outrage. Glimpses a complicated man, whose ethics are troublesome, and who remains a puzzle of contradictions and intelligence.
Biography; Civics and Political Systems
Dist - INSTRU

The Speeches of Robert F Kennedy 60 MIN
VHS
B&W (H C G)
$21.95 purchase _ #MP1689
Recalls the charisma of Robert F Kennedy in a collection of his most memorable speeches. Touches on his role as Attorney General for the presidency of his brother, John F Kennedy, going after Jimmy Hoffa and union corruption, shaping a comprehensive civil rights reform policy. Examines the confirmation of his appeal to the American public in his 1968 race for the Presidency, when he easily won five out of six primaries before he was assassinated in Los Angeles.
Biography; Civics and Political Systems; History - United States
Dist - INSTRU

The Speeches of Winston Churchill 60 MIN
VHS
B&W (G)
$19.95 purchase _ #S02014
Presents selected speeches by Winston Churchill.
English Language; History - World
Dist - UILL

The Speeches of Winston Churchill 30 MIN
VHS
B&W (H C G)
$21.95 purchase _ #MP1412
Examines the role of Winston Churchill in the early years of World War II, when all the world seemed to cower before Hitler and his was the lone voice, eloquent and filled with heart - felt exhortations. Reveals that through his Parliamentary and radio speeches to the British people, Churchill was able to summon up wellsprings of national pride and fervor, and his poetic words earned him a Nobel Prize for literature. Includes World War II footage.
History - World
Dist - INSTRU

Speed 5 MIN
U-matic
Eureka Series
Color (J)
Shows that force varies with mass and rate of change of speed.
Science; Science - Physical
Dist - TVOTAR **Prod** - TVOTAR 1980

Speed - a - Way 11 MIN
16mm
Color; B&W (J)
Demonstrates the game, Speed-a-way -- a combination of soccer, basketball, speedball, field ball and hockey - in which the player is allowed to run with the ball.
Physical Education and Recreation
Dist - LAR **Prod** - LAR 1952

Speed and explosion - speed improvement for athletes 53 MIN
VHS
Color (H C G)
$49.95 purchase _ #NA100V
Offers step - by - step intruction on how to improve speed and performance in any sport. Includes sections on the importance of speed in team sports, factors affecting speed improvement, fast and slow twitch muscle fibers, and how to self evaluate with 15 tests. Features Drs Bob Ward and George Dintiman.
Physical Education and Recreation
Dist - CAMV

Speed and Heat 30 MIN
16mm
Color
LC FIA65-617
Describes the problems which will be encountered by the supersonic transport of tomorrow and explains how research is helping to solve problems in construction, propulsion and the protection of the passengers by developing a whole new technology as well as a new plane.
Industrial and Technical Education; Science - Physical; Social Science
Dist - RCKWL **Prod** - NAA 1964

Speed and Power 15 MIN
VHS / 16mm
All Fit with Slim Goodbody Series
Color (P I)
$125.00 purchase, $25.00 rental
Utilizes a reaction time experiment to illustrate the importance of speed and power.
Health and Safety; Physical Education and Recreation; Science - Natural
Dist - AITECH **Prod** - GDBODY 1987

Speed cookery
VHS
Kitchen equipment series
(G)
$59.00_CA239
Covers techniques used in speed cookery.
Home Economics
Dist - AAVIM **Prod** - AAVIM 1989

Speed dial
CD-ROM
(G)
$399.00 purchase _ #2051
Provides access to business phone numbers across the US. Enables users to search by business name or Yellow Pages listing, limit by state, city or area code, print and download, browse, dial automatically through a modem, and use a note pad. For IBM PCs and compatibles, requires 640K RAM, DOS 3.1 or later, one floppy disk drive - hard disk recommended, one empty expansion slot, and an IBM compatible CD - ROM drive. Hayes compatible modem required for automatic dialing option. Network versions available.
Business and Economics
Dist - BEP

Speed Drop 5 MIN
16mm
B&W
LC FIE52-1084
Demonstrates how load equalizer is added to the governor to control speed and how the power piston and piston and speeder spring function.
Industrial and Technical Education
Dist - USNAC **Prod** - USN 1948

Speed, INC 27 MIN
16mm
Color (J)
LC FIA68-1440
Highlights the 1966 professional football season, featuring team and individual performances of the Dallas Cowboys.
Physical Education and Recreation
Dist - NFL **Prod** - NFL 1967

Speed is life - get fast or go broke 68 MIN
VHS / U-matic
Color (G PRO A)
$995.00, $895.00 purchase, $250.00 rental
Stresses the factor of time management for competing in the global markets of the 1990s. Visits four time-obsessed companies. Features Tom Peters.
Business and Economics
Dist - MAGVID **Prod** - MAGVID 1991

Speed learning series
Active mind 27 MIN
A Competition with Yourself 27 MIN
Getting it all together 28 MIN
The Pay - Off 27 MIN
Surveying for Hidden Treasure 27 MIN
Dist - AITECH

Speed Learning Series
It's all Right to be Wrong 28 MIN
Dist - AITECH
DELTAK

Speed learning series
Rapid reading 29 MIN
Dist - AITECH
DELTAK
LEARNI

Speed Learning Video Series Show 4
Four on the Floor 30 MIN
Dist - AITECH
DELTAK
LEARNI

Speed learning video series show 6
An active mind 30 MIN
Dist - LEARNI

Speed Learning Video Series Show 9
The Pay - Off 30 MIN
Dist - LEARNI

Speed Learning Video Series
The Art of Reading, Pt 1 28 MIN
A Competition with yourself 30 MIN
Surveying for Hidden Treasure 30 MIN
Dist - LEARNI

Speed of Chemical Changes and Molecular Collision 14 MIN
U-matic / VHS / 16mm
Color (I)
LC FIA68-2113
Demonstrates an experiment which shows that chemical reactions can occur at different speeds. Presents a mechanical model of a reaction. Uses the model to formulate hypotheses concerning the factors that influence the speed of chemical change.
Science - Physical
Dist - PHENIX **Prod** - IWANMI 1968

Speed of Light 21 MIN
16mm
PSSC Physics Films Series
B&W (H C)
Shows Dr Siebert of MIT measuring the speed of light in air at night, using a spark - gap, a photocell, parabolic mirrors and an oscilloscope. Later, shows him studying the speed of light in air and water in his laboratory using a high speed rotation mirror.
Science - Physical
Dist - MLA **Prod** - PSSC 1960

Speed of Light 30 MIN
16mm
Color (H C A)
LC 81-700399
Presents a pre - Kennedy - assassination period film in which a California mother and daughter face paranoia - evoking circumstances in the American Midwest.
Fine Arts
Dist - HANVAN **Prod** - HANVAN 1980

The Speed of Light - Measurement and Applications 14 MIN
16mm / U-matic / VHS
B&W (J H C)
Shows how Galileo, Fizeau, Roemer and Michelson contributed to the measurement of the speed of light and indicates some of the most important applications of this constant today. Michelson's famed experiment is shown in animation.
Science; Science - Physical
Dist - EBEC **Prod** - EBEC 1955

The Speed of living 20 MIN
16mm
Doctors at work series
B&W (H C A)
LC FIA65-1362
Examines the symptoms of hyperthyroidism. Describes the tests, medical therapy and surgery performed on a woman patient.
Health and Safety
Dist - LAWREN **Prod** - CMA 1962

Speed Reading 160 MIN
Cassette / VHS
Color (G)
$199.95, $69.95 purchase _ #XVSR, XASR
Offers a speed reading program by Steve Moidel available in either a videocassette kit with two videos, workbook and audiocassette 'drill,' or six audiocassettes.
Education; English Language
Dist - GAINST

The Speed reading hand 60 MIN
VHS
Color (G)
$19.95 purchase _ #S00876
Presents a course in speed reading. Includes instructional booklet.
English Language; Literature and Drama
Dist - UILL

The Speed reading hand 60 MIN
VHS
Color (G)
$49.95 purchase _ #AR000
Shows how to double, triple, even quintuple reading speed. Features Steve Moidel. Increases concentration, comprehension, recall and self - confidence. Includes two audiocassettes and an instruction booklet.
English Language
Dist - SIV

Speed Reading in One Lesson 11 MIN
16mm
Color (I)
LC 75-701531
Shows that rapid reading is a skill that can easily be mastered at home or in the classroom. Provides step - by - step instruction for increasing reading speed.
English Language
Dist - FFORIN **Prod** - FFORIN 1974

Speed Reading - the Computer Course
VHS / U-matic
Color
Teaches the user to read faster and more efficiently while providing a complete understanding of the theory and basics of speed reading. Includes three diskettes and a complete training manual containing instructional material and practice readings.
English Language
Dist - DELTAK **Prod** - BBP

Speed reading - Vol I and II 176 MIN
Cassette / VHS
Color (G)
$199.95 purchase _ #20111, Vol I, #20113, Vol II
Features Steve Moidel. Discusses the 'mechanics' of speed reading and overcoming common reading problems. Presents reading drills and shows how to take notes, enhance recall and deal with difficult material. Includes a 90 - minute drill audiocassette and a 50 - page workbook.
Business and Economics; English Language; Psychology
Dist - CARTRP **Prod** - CARTRP

Speed tailoring blazers
VHS
Color (G A)
$24.95 purchase _ #NN770V
Teaches tailoring techniques for blazers.
Home Economics
Dist - CAMV

Speeding 21 MIN
16mm
Color (H C A)
LC 78-702017
Consists of dramatized interviews with police officers and with motorists who have been ticketed for speeding, in which both sides express their thoughts on speeding violations.
Health and Safety; Industrial and Technical Education
Dist - DIRECT **Prod** - BLOCK 1978

Speedlearning 240 MIN
VHS
Color (G)
$199.95 purchase
Presents a comprehensive, multi - media program to help students retain and apply more of what they learn. Consists of two audiocassettes with eight half - hour lessons, five paperbacks for practice in reading and learning, three workbooks, and an answer key booklet.
Education
Dist - PBS **Prod** - WNETTV

Speedreading hand 60 MIN
VHS
Color (G)
$19.95 purchase
Presents a unique speedreading program in which the hand is the primary tool. Includes an instruction booklet.
Education
Dist - PBS **Prod** - WNETTV

Speedsailing
VHS
Color (G)
$49.90 purchase _ #0492
Overviews the Speedsailing Grand Prix which pits all kinds of fast sailing craft from monohulls to high tech multihulls in a handicap race off Long Beach, California, a 20 mile race.
Physical Education and Recreation
Dist - SEVVID

The Speedscene - the Problem of Amphetamine Abuse 17 MIN
16mm / U-matic / VHS
Color (H C A) (PORTUGUESE FRENCH GERMAN SPANISH)
LC 70-706584
Offers graphic evidence against the use of amphetamines in any form other than for medical reasons.
Foreign Language; Health and Safety; Sociology
Dist - PHENIX **Prod** - MEDIC 1969

Speedway 79 Power Fuel 1 MIN
VHS / U-matic
Color
Shows a classic animated television commercial with a jingle.
Business and Economics; Psychology; Sociology
Dist - BROOKC **Prod** - BROOKC

Speedway through the Years 30 MIN
16mm
B&W
Shows 50 years of progress at Indianapolis.
Physical Education and Recreation
Dist - SFI **Prod** - SFI

Speedy 72 MIN
U-matic / VHS / 16mm
Harold Lloyd Series
B&W
LC 77-701704
Offers a reissue of the 1928 silent Harold Lloyd comedy Speedy. Presents the story of the hero who comes to the rescue when his girlfriend's grandfather's horsecar is stolen by a gang.
Fine Arts; Literature and Drama
Dist - TIMLIF **Prod** - LLOYDH 1976

Speedy Alka - Seltzer 1 MIN
U-matic / VHS
Color
Shows a classic television commercial.
Business and Economics; Psychology; Sociology
Dist - BROOKC **Prod** - BROOKC

The Speedy Samurai 13 MIN
16mm
Color
Describes Kanagawa with its many attractive resorts and its tourist industry.
Geography - World
Dist - UNIJAP **Prod** - UNIJAP 1970

The Spell of linguistic philosophy 45 MIN
VHS
Men of ideas series
Color; PAL (H C A)
PdS99 purchase; Not available in Canada.
Explains in simple terms the main developments in Western philosophy from the 19th century to the present day. Features a contemporary thinker discussing his ideas on linguistic philosophy with Bryan Magee. Part seven of a fifteen part series.
English Language; Religion and Philosophy
Dist - BBCENE

Spell well flash cards
VHS
Color (P I)
$49.95 purchase _ #CZ200
Builds confidence and skills in spelling. Includes four videocassettes.
English Language
Dist - SIV

Spellbound 112 MIN
U-matic / VHS / 16mm
B&W (J)
Stars Gregory Peck as an amnesia victim who assumes the identity of a noted psychiatrist and is accused of the murder of the man he professes to be. Presents Ingrid Bergman as a fellow psychiatrist who attempts to restore his memory and uncover some lead that would prove his innocence.
Fine Arts
Dist - FI **Prod** - UAA 1945

Spellbound (razor sequence) 10 MIN
16mm
Film study extracts series
B&W (J)
Presents an excerpt from the 1945 motion picture Spellbound. Depicts an amnesiac wandering through a house carrying a razor. Directed by Alfred Hitchcock.
Fine Arts
Dist - FI **Prod** - UNKNWN

Spelling 30 MIN
VHS / U-matic
Project STRETCH - Strategies to Train Regular Educators to Teach Children with Handicaps Series; Module 10
Color (T S)
LC 80-706646
Shows strategies for mainstreaming eligible exceptional children. Presents a magician demonstrating some techniques of evaluating a child's spelling skills, of planning individualized remediate weaknesses and of increasing interest in spelling proficiency.
Education; Psychology
Dist - HUBDSC **Prod** - METCO 1980

Spelling - an Introductory Film 14 MIN
16mm / U-matic / VHS
Spelling Skills Series no 1
Color (P)
LC 77-700658
Describes how spelling and writing began, how spelling is a skill common to both reading and writing, how spelling is based on sounds, how letters in the alphabet stand for sounds, how there are more sounds than letters in the alphabet and how to listen for individual sounds in words.
English Language
Dist - JOU **Prod** - GLDWER 1976

Spelling complex sounds 13 MIN
16mm / U-matic / VHS
Spelling skills series no 3
Color (P)
LC 77-700659
Discusses consonant clusters and how to separate the sounds encountered in them, reviews the alphabet and its sounds, explores vowel sounds and the fact that there are different ways of spelling the long vowel sounds in words and, finally, introduces the dictionary as a spelling tool.
English Language
Dist - JOU **Prod** - GLDWER 1976

The Spelling Dragon 16 MIN
U-matic / VHS / 16mm
Color (P I)
Presents the Spelling Dragon who teaches a basic method for spelling any word, while entertaining with a story of knights and maidens in distress. Animated.
English Language
Dist - PHENIX **Prod** - CHRSTD 1982

Spelling Exercises with the Alphabet 19 MIN
U-matic / VHS / 16mm
Spelling Skills Series no 4
Color (P I)
LC 77-701134
Starts with a brief review of the idea that the letters in our alphabet are symbols that stand for the sounds in words. Takes a trip through the alphabet step - by - step, illustrating the sound or sounds of each letter.
English Language
Dist - JOU **Prod** - GLDWER 1977

Spelling Medical Terminology 18 MIN
U-matic / VHS
Medical Terminology Series
Color (PRO)
Emphasizes the spelling of medical terminology. Analyzes the term's component parts, then links these components together using fundamental spelling rules.
Health and Safety
Dist - HSCIC **Prod** - HSCIC

Spelling plural nouns 13 MIN
16mm / U-matic / VHS
Spelling skills series
Color (P)
LC 79-700312
Deals with changing the singular form of a noun to the plural form.
English Language
Dist - JOU **Prod** - GLDWER 1978

Spelling Simple Sounds 13 MIN
U-matic / VHS / 16mm
Spelling Skills Series no 2
Color (P)
LC 76-703931
Reviews the alphabet as the base of our language, explores words as a sequence of sounds, distinguishes among the first, second and final sounds in short words, presents the idea of capital letters and introduces the capitalization of proper names.
English Language
Dist - JOU **Prod** - GLDWER 1976

Spelling Skills Series no 1
Spelling - an Introductory Film 14 MIN
Dist - JOU

Spelling Skills Series no 2
Spelling Simple Sounds 13 MIN
Dist - JOU

Spelling skills series no 3
Spelling complex sounds 13 MIN
Dist - JOU

Spelling Skills Series no 4
Spelling Exercises with the Alphabet 19 MIN
Dist - JOU

Spelling skills series
Spelling plural nouns 13 MIN
Spelling Verbs 14 MIN
Dist - JOU

Spelling Verbs 14 MIN
U-matic / VHS / 16mm
Spelling Skills Series
Color (P I)
LC 80-700241
Details the use and the corresponding spelling of verbs.
English Language
Dist - JOU **Prod** - GLDWER 1978

Spelling - visualization, the key to spelling success 30 MIN
16mm
Project STRETCH Series; Module 10
Color (T)
LC 80-700617
Demonstrates some techniques of evaluating a child's spelling skills, of planning individualized instruction to remediate weakness, and of increasing interest in spelling proficiency.
Education; Psychology
Dist - HUBDSC **Prod** - METCO 1980

Spence Bay 14 MIN
16mm
Journal Series
Color
LC 77-702863
Takes a look at the life of native peoples 250 miles north of the Canadian Arctic Circle as seen by 15 high school students from Toronto.
Geography - World; Social Science; Sociology
Dist - FIARTS **Prod** - FIARTS 1976

The Spencers
U-matic / VHS / 16mm
Portraits of goodbye series
Color (A)
Looks at the Spencer family after the mother is diagnosed as having terminal cancer. Shows that after the inevitable feelings of anger, fear and self pity begin to subside, the family begins to set goals. Discusses how vacations and holidays take on a special meaning as the Spencers learn to cherish each day they spend together.
Sociology
Dist - ECUFLM **Prod** - UMCOM 1980

The Spencers 12 MIN
16mm
Begin with Goodbye Series
Color
LC 79-700284
Profiles a family's feelings, concerns, fears and hopes as it comes to terms with the impending death of 34 - year - old Sandy Spencer.
Sociology
Dist - MMM **Prod** - UMCOM 1979

Spencer's Mountain 119 MIN
U-matic / VHS / 16mm
Color (H C A)
Stars Henry Fonda and Maureen O'Hara in the story of three generations of a dirt - poor family in a small community. Portrays a quarry worker living in the valley with his family who has not sold off his inheritance like his brothers and desires only to build his wife a dream house on his mountain property.

Fine Arts
Dist - FI **Prod** - WB 1963

Spend and prosper 50 MIN
VHS
Horizon series
Color (A)
PdS99 purchase
Traces the life of John Maynard Keynes through the eyes of people who knew him. Spells out some of his policies which contradicted monetarist policies of the Thatcher administration. Keynes was more than a theoretical economist. He believed economics should have a moral basis and that the state had a duty to patronize the arts.
Business and Economics
Dist - BBCENE

Spend it all 40 MIN
16mm / VHS
Color (G)
$99.95 purchase, $50.00 rental
Documents the Cajuns of southwest Louisiana, still immersed in the culture of their French Acadian ancestors.
Fine Arts
Dist - CANCIN **Prod** - BLNKL 1971

Spend, Spend 11 MIN
U-matic / VHS / 16mm
Color (P I)
LC 78-712927
Explains that the retail purchaser is a universal victim, as witnessed in the story of a young boy who buys a scale model sports car which soon falls apart.
Business and Economics; Guidance and Counseling; Home Economics; Social Science
Dist - PHENIX **Prod** - KINGSP 1971

Spending Money 15 MIN
16mm
Our Children Series
Color; B&W (P I R)
Tells the story about two children who learn there are right and wrong ways of obtaining and spending money.
Guidance and Counseling; Psychology
Dist - FAMF **Prod** - FAMF

A Spending Plan 14 MIN
Videoreel / VT2
Living Better II Series
Color
Discusses how to spend money wisely and how to set up a budget.
Business and Economics; Home Economics
Dist - PBS **Prod** - MAETEL

Spent Reactor Fuel Storage in Granite 13 MIN
16mm
Color
LC 80-701561
Documents the Lawrence Livermore Laboratory experimental program for storing spent nuclear fuel in an underground granite rock mass.
Science; Social Science
Dist - LIVER **Prod** - LIVER 1980

Sperm Maturation in the Male Reproductive Tract - Development of Motility 14 MIN
16mm
Color (PRO)
LC 74-703519
Demonstrates and describes the changes in motility characteristics of rabbit spermatozoa as they pass through the male reproductive tract, from the seminiferous tubules and ductuli efferentes through to the cauda epididymidis and ductus deferens.
Science - Natural
Dist - UWASHP **Prod** - GABLHA 1968

Spetsai 15 MIN
16mm
Color (G)
$30.00 rental
Combines images of a Greek island with text that changes the significance of the images. Sound on cassette. By Yann Beauvais.
Fine Arts
Dist - CANCIN

Spetzler Lumbar Peritoneal Shunt System 13 MIN
VHS / U-matic
Color (PRO)
Shows the Spetzler lumbar peritoneal shunt system.
Health and Safety
Dist - WFP **Prod** - WFP

SPFX - the Making of the Empire Strikes Back 52 MIN
16mm / U-matic / VHS
Color (H C A)
LC 81-700583
Discusses the art of creating illusions on film, emphasizing the special effects used in the motion picture The Empire Strikes Back. Offers a historic overview and clips from Close Encounters of the Third Kind, 2001 - A Space Odyssey and King Kong. Deals with the use of stop motion, miniatures, models, mechanicals, graphics, illustrations and blue screen mats. Includes the specifics of sound effects and musical scores.
Fine Arts
Dist - FI **Prod** - GUSC 1981

The Sphere 15 MIN
Videoreel / VT2
Draw Man Series
Color (I J)
Shows that the sphere is a shape frequently found in everyday objects.
Fine Arts
Dist - AITECH **Prod** - OCPS 1975

Sphere eversions 8 MIN
U-matic / VHS / BETA
Color; PAL (G H C)
PdS40, PdS48 purchase
Illustrates Bernard Morin's invention of a sphere eversion, which is a smooth motion that turns the sphere inside out by passing the surface through itself without making any holes or creases. Includes three shorts using various styles of computer animation - Sphere Eversion I - Wire Mesh; Sphere Eversion II - Opaque Surfaces; Sphere Eversion III - Exploded Views.
Industrial and Technical Education; Mathematics
Dist - EDPAT

Spheres 8 MIN
16mm / U-matic / VHS
Color (P)
LC 75-712038
Presents an animated film in which a ball dances to the music of Bach.
Fine Arts
Dist - IFB **Prod** - NFBC 1969

Spheres
VHS
Now I see it geometry video series
Color (J H)
$79.00 _ #60254 - 026
Connects with students' lives and interests by linking lessons to everyday objects ranging from automobiles to ice cream cones, stereos to honeycombs. Includes reproducible worksheet book and answer key. Part of a nine - part series.
Education; Mathematics
Dist - GA

Spheres We See and Use 9 MIN
16mm / U-matic / VHS
Color (P I) (SPANISH)
LC 70-713134
Gives a clear definition of a sphere and explains that we can use spheres to help us move things and to give strength to things we build. Shows how spheres hold the most volume for a given surface area of any shape known.
Mathematics
Dist - PHENIX **Prod** - BOUNDY 1971

Spherical bearing installation and maintenance 13 MIN
VHS
Power transmission series II - selection, application and maintenance series
Color (A)
$265.00 purchase, $50.00 rental _ #57976
Enumerates unique features and advantages of spherical ball bearings, explaining critical elements in their application such as shaft geometry and maximum allowable variance. Explains bore styles, measurement standards (bearing dimensions are metric, tolerances are in ten thousandths of an inch). Explains how the numbering system is designed to convey clearance information. Emphasizes that clearances must be chosen for specific applications.
Industrial and Technical Education
Dist - UILL **Prod** - MAJEC 1986

Spherical Mirrors 11 MIN
16mm
From the Light Series
B&W (J H)
Covers concave and convex mirrors, formation of mirrors, real and virtual images and caustic curve demonstrations.
Science - Physical
Dist - VIEWTH **Prod** - GBI

Spherical space, No 1 5 MIN
16mm
Color
Presents a metaphor of the change of perspective from the 19th century railroad man to the 21st century space - man.
History - World; Industrial and Technical Education; Religion and Philosophy; Sociology
Dist - VANBKS **Prod** - VANBKS

Sphero, the Reluctant Snowball 15 MIN
U-matic / VHS
Magic Pages Series
Color (P)
Literature and Drama
Dist - AITECH **Prod** - KLVXTV 1976

Sphincterotomy for Stenosis of the Sphincter of Oddi 29 MIN
16mm
Color (PRO)
Presents Doctors Warren H Cole, W H Harridge and S S Roberts who believe there is a definite indication for cutting the sphincter of oddi when stenosis is encountered and shows three cases exemplifying this syndrome.
Health and Safety; Science
Dist - ACY **Prod** - ACYDGD 1962

Sphinxes without secrets 58 MIN
VHS
Color (G)
$75.00 rental, $275.00 purchase
Unravels the mysteries of performance art and ponders the world women confront today. Features performers Diamanda Galas, Holly Hughes - one of the NEA Four - Robbie McCauley and Rachel Rosenthal. Shows how performance art has always provided a forum for those artists whose work challenges the dominant aesthetic and cultural status quo. Intercut with appearances by many others such as Laurie Anderson, Annie Sprinkle and Reno. By Maria Beatty.
Fine Arts; Sociology
Dist - WMEN

Spice island saga
VHS
Ring of fire - an Indonesian odyssey series
Color (G)
$29.95 purchase
Presents the first part of the series 'Ring Of Fire - An Indonesian Odyssey.' Portrays part of the ten - year journey Lorne and Lawrence Blair made through Indonesia.
Literature and Drama
Dist - PBS **Prod** - WNETTV

The Spice of Life 5 MIN
U-matic / VHS
Write on, Set 1 Series
Color (J H)
Shows how to achieve variety in word order in writing.
English Language
Dist - CTI **Prod** - CTI

The Spice of Life 15 MIN
16mm / U-matic / VHS
Color (A)
Tells of an elderly man who has lost all interest in eating and preparing meals since his wife died. Tells how his interest is rekindled after a conversation with his sister about the value of good nutrition.
Health and Safety
Dist - NDC **Prod** - NDC 1983

Spice of life series

Allspice - one spice	26 MIN
Chilies - a dash of daring	26 MIN
Cinnamon - the elegant addition	26 MIN
Cloves - Nature's Little Nails	26 MIN
Curry around the world	26 MIN
Garlic's Pungent Presence	26 MIN
Herbs - aromatic influences	26 MIN
Mustard - the Spice of Nations	26 MIN
Nutmeg - Nature's Perfect Package	26 MIN
Pepper - the Master Spice	26 MIN
Peppercorns - Fresh Ground Flavor	26 MIN
Saffron - Autumn Gold	26 MIN
The Spices of India	26 MIN

Dist - BCNFL

The Spice of wickedness 24 MIN
16mm / U-matic / VHS
Color (H A G)
Presents a story of 18th century marital values. Provides the basis for a discussion about moral bargains and male and female relationships as well as literary adaptation. Based on a short story by Guy de Maupassant.
Fine Arts; Literature and Drama
Dist - DIRECT **Prod** - ELKDOR 1984

The Spices of India 26 MIN
U-matic / VHS
Spice of life series

Color (J A)
Unveils India's talent in mixing spices such as turmeric, fenugreek, coriander, cumin, cardamom, pepper and chili. Illustrates an assortment of dishes.
Health and Safety; Home Economics
Dist - BCNFL **Prod** - BLCKRD 1985

The Spider 18 MIN
16mm / U-matic / VHS
Wild, Wild World of Animals Series
Color
LC 77-701753
Follows the lives of various species of spiders, pointing out varied and unusual behavior patterns. Edited from the television program Wild, Wild World Of Animals.
Science - Natural
Dist - TIMLIF **Prod** - TIMLIF 1976

The Spider 11 MIN
U-matic / VHS / 16mm
Animal Families Series
Color (K P I)
$275, $195, $225 purchase _ #B419
Explains how a spider makes its web using silky, sticky liquid produced from its spinnerets. Documents how a spider catches it prey. Explains the differences between insects and spiders. Uses close - up photography.
Science - Natural
Dist - BARR **Prod** - BARR 1986

The Spider and the Frenchman 26 MIN
16mm
Color
Features skiing champions Spider Sabich and Jean - Claude Killy in a 40,000 dollar duel on identical parallel race courses.
Physical Education and Recreation
Dist - FFORIN **Prod** - BARP

Spider engineers 16 MIN
16mm / VHS
Color (P I J)
Shows the spider as an engineer of great skill and versatility. There are an estimated 100,000 species of spiders. In this study four typical species are considered - the orb weaver, the bolas spider, the diving spider, the trapdoor spider.
Science - Natural
Dist - MIS **Prod** - MIS 1956

Spider - its Life and Web 25 MIN
16mm
Color
Explains that the life of any spider is closely related to its web. Illustrates the features of a spider's body and shows how the life of the spider is centered around its web.
Science - Natural
Dist - UNIJAP **Prod** - TOEI 1970

Spider Man - don't hide abuse 11 MIN
VHS / U-matic
Spider Man safety series
Color (I)
$250.00 purchase _ #HH - 6048L
Enables children to recognize and end a physical or sexual abuse situation. Shows that with the help of Spider Man, a young abuse victim is able to find help both for herself and for her abusing father. Reveals the difference between good and bad secrets, that abuse is not the fault of the victim and that there are concerned adults who can help. Defines physical and sexual abuse. Shows that hiding abuse does not end the problem, and describes where to go for help and the difference between abuse and discipline. Part of a series produced in association with Marvel Entertainment and Advanced American Communications.
Sociology
Dist - LCA **Prod** - LCA 1990

Spider Man safety series
Spider Man - don't hide abuse 11 MIN
Spider Man - smart kids play it safe 11 MIN
Spider Man - what to do about drugs 11 MIN
Spider Man - where do you go for help 11 MIN
Dist - LCA

Spider Man - smart kids play it safe 11 MIN
VHS / U-matic
Spider Man safety series
Color (I)
$250.00 purchase _ #HH - 6047L
Teaches seven safety rules that children should follow when not accompanied by an adult. Stars Spider Man who invites viewers to follow his friends E J, Timmy, Maria and Jason home from school and watch how they handle the secret safety tests he has arranged. Stresses the importance of rules for being alone, for always being careful and for following parental rules for answering the phone and door. Part of a series produced in association with Marvel Entertainment and Advanced American Communications.
Health and Safety; Sociology
Dist - LCA **Prod** - LCA 1990

Spider Man - what to do about drugs 11 MIN
VHS / U-matic
Spider Man safety series
Color (I)
$250.00 purchase _ #HH - 6051L
Illustrates a variety of effective ways for children to refuse drugs while providing an argument for healthy alternatives. Stars Spider Man who teaches Timmy about drugs and making good decisions. Part of a series produced in association with Marvel Entertainment and Advanced American Communications.
Guidance and Counseling; Health and Safety; Psychology; Sociology
Dist - LCA **Prod** - LCA 1990

Spider Man - where do you go for help 11 MIN
U-matic / VHS
Spider Man safety series
Color (I)
$250.00 purchase _ #HH - 6049L
Explains the importance of asking questions and how to find responsible adults who can help. Teaches how to call the police on the phone, and that asking for help can be valuable in solving all kinds of problems. Stars Spider Man. Part of a series produced in association with Marvel Entertainment and Advanced American Communications.
Health and Safety; Psychology; Sociology
Dist - LCA **Prod** - LCA 1990

The Spider Takes a Trip 9 MIN
U-matic / VHS / 16mm
Primary Language Development Series
Color (K P I)
LC 75-703685
Uses a story about the adventures of a spider to develop skills in answering questions and predicting sentence endings.
English Language
Dist - AIMS **Prod** - PEDF 1975

Spiders 137 MIN
VHS
Signature series
Color tint (G)
$29.95 purchase
Presents a reconstructed version of Spiders according to original release instructions. Offers a serial adventure series with Inca treasures, human sacrifice, wild chases and hair - breadth escapes. Directed by Fritz Lang.
Fine Arts
Dist - KINOIC

Spiders 11 MIN
U-matic / VHS / 16mm
B&W (I J H)
Illustrates the distinctive characteristics and habits of spiders, including the spinning of webs and the trapping of insects. Some of the types shown are the marbled spider, the black widow and the tarantula.
Science - Natural
Dist - EBEC **Prod** - EBEC 1956

Spiders - Aggression and Mating 17 MIN
16mm / U-matic / VHS
Bio - Science Series
Color (H C A)
Shows that spiders are not insects but arachnids, members of a much older class of animals, that all spiders spin silk, but not all spin webs and that a female spider must suspend her normally aggressive behavior in order to mate. Shows several kinds of webs which spiders use to trap prey and describes various techniques used to kill prey.
Science - Natural
Dist - NGS **Prod** - NGS 1974

Spiders and how they live 15 MIN
Videodisc / 16mm / VHS
Animals and how they live series
Color (I J)
$395.00, $295.00 purchase, $50.00 rental _ #8224
Observes the building of a spider cage to explore the activities of an orb web spider. Examines the body parts and discusses how spiders eat and reproduce and how they make their webs. Surveys the special characteristics and behaviors of other species such as jumping spiders, house, garden, zebra and crab spiders. Part of a series on invertebrates produced by Cicada Productions and VATV.
Science - Natural
Dist - AIMS

Spiders - Backyard Science 13 MIN
U-matic / VHS / 16mm
Color (P I)
LC 78-701678
Shows parts of a spider's body and explains how spiders function. Describes how spiders spin their webs and how they trap the insects and other small animals on which they feed. Illustrates the spider's life cycle and discusses the ways in which spiders contribute to our environment.
Science - Natural
Dist - PHENIX **Prod** - BEANMN 1978

Spiders help farmers grow safer crops 23 MIN
VHS
One second before sunrise - A Search for solutions - Program 2 'series
Color (J H C G)
$95.00 purchase, $45.00 rental
Presents part two of program two. Looks at how 50 percent of the pesticides applied in the US and 25 percent worldwide are used on cotton. Looks at how cotton growers in Hubei Province in China cut their use of chemical pesticides by 70 - 90 percent. Also a California entomologist introduces the green lacewing, one of many insects farmers are using to control pests. Classroom version on two cassettes.
Agriculture; Fine Arts; Geography - World; Science - Natural
Dist - BULFRG **Prod** - HCOM 1993

The Spider's strategem 97 MIN
16mm
Color (ITALIAN)
Presents a tale that takes place in a sleepy Italian village where a young man arrives to investigate the murder of his father, a local anti-Fascist hero assassinated 30 years before in a box at the opera house. Directed by Bernardo Bertolucci.
Fine Arts; Foreign Language
Dist - NYFLMS **Prod** - NYFLMS 1970

Spielwaren Aus Nurnberg 5 MIN
U-matic / VHS / 16mm
European Studies - Germany (German Series
Color (H C A) (GERMAN)
Presents a version of the motion picture Toys From Nuremberg. Shows the toy-producing center of Nuremberg where some operations are still carried out by hand.
Business and Economics; Foreign Language; Geography - World
Dist - IFB **Prod** - MFAFRG 1973

Spies 90 MIN
VHS
B&W (G)
$29.95 purchase
Presents an espionage thriller told in German Expressionist form. Directed by Fritz Lang.
Fine Arts; Literature and Drama
Dist - KINOIC

The Spies among Us 52 MIN
VHS / U-matic
Color (H C A)
Explores the extent and danger of Soviet bloc spy activities in the U S. Covers the entire range of Soviet intelligence gathering operations and explains how U S counterintelligence is dealing with the situation. Highlights the problem of the illegal transfer of technical equipment and microcircuitry information arranged by the KGB.
Civics and Political Systems; Geography - World
Dist - FI **Prod** - NBCNEW 1981

Spies and Detectives 30 MIN
U-matic
Hooked on Reading Series
Color (PRO)
Portrays a father who builds on his children's interest in a single detective series by introducing them to other kinds of mystery writing.
English Language; Literature and Drama
Dist - TVOTAR **Prod** - TVOTAR 1986

Spies in the Wires 48 MIN
U-matic / VHS
Color (H C A)
LC 85-700905
Portrays the increasingly computerized operation of world banks, businesses, government defense systems and citizens' everyday lives. Discusses how large computers can be broken into, and preventive efforts to preserve privacy.
Industrial and Technical Education; Mathematics; Social Science; Sociology
Dist - FI **Prod** - BBCTV 1984

Spies, Nazis, and Reporters 29 MIN
U-matic
City Desk Series
Color
Discusses editorials and other issues of investigative reporting. Analyzes the 'new' women's page.
Literature and Drama; Social Science; Sociology
Dist - UMITV **Prod** - UMITV 1976

Spike - a Montana Horseman 12 MIN
16mm / U-matic / VHS
Color (J H)
LC 77-700490
Presents a portrait of Spike Van Cleve, a Montana horsebreeder whose lifestyle is based on values of hard work, commitment, loyalty, respect for horses and family continuity.

Geography - United States; Guidance and Counseling; Literature and Drama; Physical Education and Recreation; Sociology
Dist - LCOA **Prod** - VARDIR 1977

The Spike - Epilepsy 50 MIN
U-matic / VHS / 16mm
Color (C A)
LC 82-700619
Demonstrates that epileptic seizures are caused by abnormal brain wave activity of unknown origin. Presents epileptics who discuss their problems and plead for understanding by others who often equate epilepsy with mental illness.
Health and Safety; Psychology
Dist - FI **Prod** - BBCTV 1981

The Spike Jones story 60 MIN
VHS
Color; B&W; Hi-fi; Dolby stereo (G)
$19.95 purchase _ #1637
Combines the personal and professional history of comic musician Spike Jones. Features personal friends Milton Berle and Danny Thomas, family members and numerous musical collaborators with Spike Jones. Includes some of Jones' hits - Laura, Cocktails for Two, Der Fueher's Face, You Always Hurt - the One You Love, and some 1950s rock 'n roll parodies. Syndicated comic disc jockey Dr Demento offers some historical perspective.
Fine Arts; History - United States
Dist - KULTUR **Prod** - KULTUR 1992

Spill assessment and you 12 MIN
VHS / U-matic / BETA
Color (IND G A)
$670.00 purchase, $125.00 rental _ #SPI018
Introduces hazardous spill management. Shows how to size up a spill to determine the hazards to life, property and materials.
Health and Safety; Psychology
Dist - ITF **Prod** - ERF 1991

Spill recovery - navy techniques for oil spill containment and removal in harbors 25 MIN
16mm
Color (C A)
LC 77-700086
Describes in - port oil spill control, reporting procedures and clean - up operations.
Civics and Political Systems; Industrial and Technical Education; Science - Natural
Dist - USNAC **Prod** - USN 1975

Spill response - a refresher session - II 14 MIN
8mm cartridge / VHS / BETA / U-matic
Refresher course in chemical safety series
Color; PAL (IND G)
$495.00 purchase, $175.00 rental _ #REF - 102
Shows workers many examples of chemical spill situations and how to handle them. Demonstrates spill containment and clean - up procedures from major releases requiring Level B response down to common solvent discharges on the shop floor. Addresses notification procedures, different levels of spill response. amd decontamination of people and affected surfaces. Details small spills, along with appropriate actions by nonprofessional responders. Reviews material for HAZMAT teams as well as introducing material for awareness - level personnel. Part of a four - part series on chemical safety. Includes a trainer's manual and ten employee manuals.
Health and Safety; Psychology; Science - Physical
Dist - BNA **Prod** - BNA

Spill response and you 12 MIN
VHS / U-matic / BETA
Color (IND G A)
$670.00 purchase, $125.00 rental _ #SPI017
Introduces hazardous spill management. Shows how to size up a spill to determine the hazards to life, property and materials. Teaches procedures for containing and cleaning up a spill.
Health and Safety; Psychology
Dist - ITF **Prod** - ERF 1991

Spill timing an inline diesel fuel pump - Unit D 54 MIN
VHS
Motor vehicle engineering crafts - workshop practice series
Color; PAL (J H IND)
PdS29.50 purchase
Shows workshop practice lessons with a class of second year public service engineering apprentices. Consists of an introduction and demonstration of spill timing an inline diesel fuel pump, followed by the students' own attempts. Part of a five - part series.
Industrial and Technical Education
Dist - EMFVL

Spilled Milk 5 MIN
16mm
Color (P) (AMERICAN SIGN)
LC 76-701705
Presents Louie J Fant Jr, relating in American sign language for the deaf an incident from his childhood involving a jar of milk and a set of instructions that he failed to follow concerning its disposal.
Guidance and Counseling; Psychology
Dist - JOYCE **Prod** - JOYCE 1975

Spills happen 22 MIN
BETA / VHS / U-matic
Color (IND G A)
$777.00 purchase, $150.00 rental _ #SPI006
Demonstrates spill response and clean - up procedures in comprehensive, step - by - step detail. Begins with the moment a spill occurs and goes through the processes of identifying, reporting, containing, cleaning up and decontaminating the spill. Demonstrates three spill scenarios of different severity - a highly toxic acid spill, an environmental contaminant, a medium - level flammable spill.
Health and Safety; Psychology
Dist - ITF **Prod** - BNA 1991

Spills happen - a training program for small spill response 22 MIN
BETA / VHS / U-matic
Color; PAL (IND G) (SPANISH DUTCH NORWEGIAN PORTUGUESE)
$175.00 rental _ #SSR - 100
Demonstrates spill response and clean - up procedures in comprehensive, step - by - step detail. Begins at the moment a spill happens and goes through the process of identifying, reporting, containing, cleaning up and decontaminating the spill. Illustrates three spill scenarios of differing severity - an environmental contamination, a highly - toxic acid spill and a medium - level flammable spill. Includes leader's guide and 10 workbooks which are available in English only.
Business and Economics; Health and Safety; Psychology
Dist - BNA **Prod** - BNA

Spin cycle - Dreams of passion 10 MIN
16mm
Color (A)
$60.00 purchase
Presents two short films by Aarin Burch. Examines Burch's craft and her relationships as a young black lesbian in Spin Cycle. Portrays intimacy and desire between two black women in a dance studio in Dreams of Passion.
Biography; Fine Arts; Sociology
Dist - WMEN

Spin Out - Pt 1 17 MIN
U-matic / VHS
Color
Explores the domination of the imagination.
Fine Arts
Dist - KITCHN **Prod** - KITCHN

Spinal Cord and its Relations 14 MIN
16mm / U-matic / VHS
Cine - Prosector Series
Color (PRO)
Examines the spinal cord and muscles of the back.
Science - Natural
Dist - TEF **Prod** - AVCORP

Spinal Cord Injuries 39 MIN
U-matic
Color (PRO)
Informs insurance personnel of the effects of spinal cord injuries. Discusses basic anatomy and physiology of the spinal cord, and the relationship of the spinal cord to the brain. Includes discussion of practical problems of daily activity.
Business and Economics; Health and Safety; Science - Natural
Dist - RICHGO **Prod** - STFAIN

Spinal Cord Injuries - Functional Expectations as Related to Level of Injury 25 MIN
16mm
Color
Demonstrates the degree of independence that the average patient can attain after injury at various neurological levels. Tells how this independence is accomplished through a program of strengthening the remaining active muscles and going through appropriate training.
Health and Safety
Dist - RLAH **Prod** - RLAH

Spinal cord injury - avoiding skin injuries and infections 16 MIN
U-matic / VHS
Color (PRO C)
$195.00 purchase _ #C861 - VI - 027
Distinguishes pressure sores from those caused by an accident. Presents ways to avoid, monitor and manage both types. Presented by Learning Resources Center, Veterans Administration Medical Center.
Health and Safety; Science - Natural
Dist - HSCIC

Spinal Cord Injury - Patient Education Series
Activities in your new life 7 MIN
Moving in and Out of Your Wheelchair 5 MIN
Dist - PRIMED

Spinal injuries
16mm / VHS / BETA / U-matic
First aid at work training series
Color; PAL (G)
PdS150, PdS158 purchase
Features part of a six - part series on first aid training.
Health and Safety
Dist - EDPAT

Spinal Injury 19 MIN
U-matic / VHS
Color (C)
$249.00, $149.00 purchase _ #AD - 1469
Offers an in - depth look at paraplegia and quadriplegia. Explains the physical, social, sexual and psychological effects of spinal injury. Profiles a member of the first American expedition to climb Mt Everest and a paraplegic since 1968, a quadriplegic family - sexual counselor who discusses the sexual and psychological effects of paralysis on the family. Emphasizes the need for paralysis education and specialized spinal cord treatment and rehabilitation.
Health and Safety; Psychology; Science - Natural
Dist - FOTH **Prod** - FOTH

Spinal Muscular Atrophies 39 MIN
U-matic
Intensive Course in Neuromuscular Diseases Series
Color (PRO)
LC 76-706103
Presents Dr Theodore L Munsat discussing spinal muscular atrophies.
Health and Safety; Science - Natural
Dist - USNAC **Prod** - NINDIS 1974

Spinal - Part II 42 MIN
U-matic / VHS
Obstetrical anesthesia series
Color (PRO C)
$395.00 purchase, $80.00 rental _ #C850 - VI - 020
Demonstrates and describes techniques for administering spinal anesthesia to obstetrical patients. Discusses complications and how to avoid them. Part two of a two - part series on obstetrical anesthesia presented by Dr Ezzat Abouleish.
Health and Safety
Dist - HSCIC

The Spine 28 MIN
VHS
Human body - muscles and bones - series
Color (J H G)
$89.95 purchase _ #UW4181
Demonstrates the structure and functions of the spine. Explains the development of the spine and nervous system from the same cells in the embryonic stage and how the complexities of the system are responsible for many of the more common aches and pains that people experience. Part of a 39 - part series featuring computer animation, medical photography, electron micrography, full - color drawings and diagrams and three - dimensional working models to cover the workings of the human body from head to toe and inside out.
Science - Natural
Dist - FOTH

Spine Flex 10 MIN
Videoreel / VT2
Janaki Series
Color
Physical Education and Recreation
Dist - PBS **Prod** - WGBHTV

Spinet Making in Colonial America 54 MIN
16mm
Color
LC 77-700005
Shows the stages involved in making a spinet, using the tools and methods of 18th century Williamsburg, Virginia.
Fine Arts; Industrial and Technical Education
Dist - CWMS **Prod** - CWMS 1976

Spinet making in Colonial America - Pt 1 27 MIN
16mm
Color
LC 77-700005
Shows the stages involved in making a spinet, using the tools and methods of 18th century Williamsburg, Virginia.

Fine Arts
Dist - CWMS **Prod** - CWMS 1976

Spinet making in Colonial America - Pt 2 27 MIN
16mm
Color
LC 77-700005
Shows the stages involved in making a spinet, using the tools and methods of 18th century Williamsburg, Virginia.
Fine Arts
Dist - CWMS **Prod** - CWMS 1976

Spinnaker sailing 60 MIN
VHS
Color (G A)
$100.00 rental _ #0826
Demonstrates basic spinnaker handling techniques, including packing, launching, jibing and trimming sail. Features Tom Whiddon, president of North Sails.
Physical Education and Recreation
Dist - SEVVID

Spinning 15 MIN
16mm
B&W
LC 77-702650
Presents an experimental film showing a man spinning from various angles.
Fine Arts; Industrial and Technical Education
Dist - CANFDC **Prod** - CANFDC 1976

Spinning a yarn 20 MIN
VHS
Textile studies series
Color (A)
PdS65 purchase
Discusses woven and knitted fabrics, traditional and modern weaving techniques, and the replacement of nylon by new man-made fibers. Explores the origins of man-made and natural fiber; the processes of spinning, weaving, printing, dyeing, and finishing; and the uses of different textiles in everyday life. Part of a five-part series.
Home Economics; Industrial and Technical Education
Dist - BBCENE

Spinning hair string - getting water from well, binding girl's hair 12 MIN
U-matic / VHS / 16mm
People of the Australian western desert series
B&W (H C G T A)
Shows two women spin human hair into string while a girl brings water from one of the wells at Tika Tika. Girl's hair is then bound with the hair string.
Geography - World; Social Science; Sociology
Dist - PSU **Prod** - PSU 1965

Spinning Memories - Oella 25 MIN
U-matic / VHS
Color
Features interviews with residents of Oella, a small town on the banks of Maryland's Patapsco River.
Geography - United States; History - United States
Dist - LVN **Prod** - BCPL

Spinning out 55 MIN
VHS
Color (G PRO)
$350.00 purchase, $95.00 rental
Explains one of the most misunderstood mental illnesses, schizophrenia, and attempts to dispel the widespread misconceptions, fears and myths about it. Interviews doctors, families of schizophrenics and a cross section of schizophrenics who recount their daily struggles with the illness. Produced and directed by Anne Deveson. Study guide available.
Psychology
Dist - CNEMAG

Spinning tops and ticklebops 30 MIN
VHS
Color (K P I T)
$14.95 purchase _ #S01353
Presents three animated stories, 'The Planet Of The Ticklebops,' 'Spinning Tops,' and 'The Animal's Picnic Day.'
Fine Arts; Literature and Drama
Dist - UILL

Spinnolio 10 MIN
16mm
Color (J)
LC 78-701191
Focuses on communication and human relationships through the satirical story of Spinnolio, who grows up, gets a job, retires and is carried off by motorcycle gangs and garbagemen to be used for diverse purposes, despite his wooden lifelessness.
Guidance and Counseling; Literature and Drama; Psychology; Sociology
Dist - NFBC **Prod** - NFBC 1978

Spinoza and Leibniz 45 MIN
VHS
Great philosophers series
Color; PAL (H C A)
PdS99 purchase
Introduces the concepts of Western philosophy and two of its greatest thinkers. Features a contemporary philosopher who, in conversation with Bryan Magee, discusses Spinoza and Leibniz and their ideas. Part five of a fifteen part series.
Education; Religion and Philosophy
Dist - BBCENE

Spinoza - the apostle of reason 52 MIN
VHS
Color (J H G)
$250.00 purchase
Dramatizes the development of Spinoza's philosophy through events in his life that led him to challenge the orthodox thinking of his times. Explains his questioning of irrational acceptance of ideas without thought.
Religion and Philosophy
Dist - LANDMK

Spiral 12 MIN
16mm
Color (G)
$30.00 rental
Layers ambient sound vs image. Produced by Emily Breer.
Fine Arts
Dist - CANCIN

The Spiral cage 25 MIN
VHS
Color (H C G)
$295.00 purchase, $55.00 rental
Portrays Al Davis, a talented comic book artist who took his own story of overcoming disability and turned it into a unique comic book autobiography. Reveals that Davis was born in 1960 with Spina Bifida. His parents were told that he would never walk and being different made him the butt of hostility from his classmates, but David persevered until he learned to walk, developed skills in martial arts and learned to express himself in comic art. Produced by Fred Bear.
Fine Arts; Health and Safety
Dist - FLMLIB **Prod** - ACGB 1991

Spiral Separator 3 MIN
16mm
Principles of Seed Processing Series
Color (H C A)
LC 77-701158
Shows how descending concentric spiral channels are used to separate seeds based on their rolling velocity. Demonstrates separation of a typical mixture of good and split soybean seeds.
Agriculture; Science - Natural
Dist - IOWA **Prod** - EVERSL 1975

The Spiral Staircase 90 MIN
U-matic / VHS / 16mm
B&W (J)
Stars Dorothy McGuire as a mute girl working in a strange house haunted by a psychotic killer.
Fine Arts
Dist - FI **Prod** - RKOP 1946

Spirals 4 MIN
VHS
B&W (G)
$16.50 rental
Illustrates scenes with concentric circular, spiral and radiating patterns that produce optical illusions of great depth. Concentrates on clever alternations of sequences. One effect creates the feeling that the spectator is actually flying into an infinite vortex.
Fine Arts
Dist - CANCIN **Prod** - FISCHF 1926

Spirit and nature 90 MIN
VHS
Color (G)
$29.95 purchase _ #SPNAVI
Features Bill Moyers who examines religious and ethical beliefs as they pertain to the environment. Interviews the Dalai Lama, Audrey Shendandoah and others.
Religion and Philosophy; Science - Natural
Dist - SNOWLI

Spirit and soma 30 MIN
BETA / VHS
Transformation and the body series
Color (G)
$29.95 purchase _ #S325
Discusses the unity of spirit and soma - body - in the life process. Features Stanley Keleman, author of 'Emotional Anatomy,' 'Somatic Reality, ' Your Body Speaks Its Mind, 'Living Your Dying' and 'The Human Ground.' Part of a four - part series on transformation and the body.
Psychology; Religion and Philosophy; Sociology
Dist - THINKA **Prod** - THINKA

Spirit Bay Series
A Time to be Brave 30 MIN
Dist - BCNFL

Spirit catcher - the art of Betye Saar 28 MIN
16mm / U-matic / VHS
Originals - women in art series
Color (H C A)
LC 80-706119
Profiles the life and work of assemblage artist Betye Saar. Shows how her fascination with the mystical and the unknown merges with her social concerns as a black American.
Fine Arts
Dist - FI **Prod** - WNETTV 1978

The Spirit is Willing 15 MIN
VHS / U-matic
Best of Cover to Cover 2 Series
Color (I)
Literature and Drama
Dist - WETATV **Prod** - WETATV

Spirit of '76 28 MIN
16mm
Color (I)
Tells the story of the air force's minuteman missile and its vital place in America's defense arsenal. Relives the saga of the first minuteman through the eyes of a young air force officer who takes a vital part in the firing and flight of today's minuteman, which is capable of delivering a war head on target more than 6000 miles away.
Civics and Political Systems; Industrial and Technical Education
Dist - RCKWL **Prod** - NAA

Spirit of Albion 58 MIN
16mm
Color (G)
$75.00 rental
Documents Britain's new traveling communities which are objects of authoritarian hatred and brutality. Looks at how they struggle to re - establish the ancient right to gather for solstice celebrations at Stonehenge and search for alternatives to human and ecological exploitation. Augmented with poetry by William Blake. A Richard Philpott production.
Fine Arts; Geography - World; Literature and Drama; Sociology
Dist - CANCIN

The Spirit of Allensworth 29 MIN
VHS / U-matic
Color (I)
LC 81-707290
Offers a portrait of the life of Allen Allensworth, a former slave who attained the rank of lieutenant colonel in the US Army. Focuses on the town which he founded for Black Americans in California.
Biography; Geography - United States; History - United States; Sociology
Dist - KTEHTV **Prod** - KTEHTV 1980

Spirit of America - Volunteers 26 MIN
16mm
Color (A)
LC 83-700612
Describes the story of volunteerism in America and includes scenes of some of the most disastrous fires in American history as well as the contributions of some of America's famous individuals.
Social Science
Dist - NFPA **Prod** - NFPA 1983

Spirit of America with Charles Kuralt - Pt 1 - Vermont, New Hampshire, Massachusetts, Maine 18 MIN
U-matic / VHS / 16mm
Color (I)
LC 77-700104
Presents a segment from the CBS television program On The Road in which news correspondent Charles Kuralt journeys to Vermont, New Hampshire, Massachusetts and Maine for a bicentennial look at our nation's history.
Geography - United States; History - United States
Dist - PHENIX **Prod** - CBSTV 1976

Spirit of America with Charles Kuralt - Pt 2 - Rhode Island, Connecticut, New Jersey, 18 MIN
16mm / U-matic / VHS
Color (I)
LC 77-700106
Presents a segment from the CBS television program On The Road in which news correspondent Charles Kuralt journeys to Rhode Island, Connecticut, New Jersey and New York to seek out places, people and events that contributed to the development of America.
Geography - United States; History - United States
Dist - PHENIX **Prod** - CBSTV 1976

Spirit of America with Charles Kuralt - Pt 3 - Pennsylvania, Delaware, Maryland 13 MIN
16mm / U-matic / VHS
Color (I)
LC 77-700107
Presents a segment from the CBS television program On The Road in which news correspondent Charles Kuralt journeys to Pennsylvania, Delaware and Maryland to seek out places, people and events that contributed to the development of America.
Geography - United States; History - United States
Dist - PHENIX **Prod** - CBSTV 1976

Spirit of America with Charles Kuralt - Pt 4 - Tennessee, Arkansas, Kentucky, West Virginia 18 MIN
16mm / U-matic / VHS
Color (I)
LC 77-700108
Presents a segment from the CBS television program On The Road in which news correspondent Charles Kuralt journeys to Tennessee, Arkansas, Kentucky and West Virgina to seek out places, people and events that contributed to the development of America.
Geography - United States; History - United States
Dist - PHENIX **Prod** - CBSTV 1976

Spirit of America with Charles Kuralt - Pt 5 - Virginia, North Carolina, South Carolina, 18 MIN
U-matic / VHS / 16mm
Color (I)
LC 76-703535
Presents a segment from the CBS television program On The Road in which news correspondent Charles Kuralt journeys to Virgina, North Carolina, South Carolina and Georgia to seek out places, people and events that contributed to the development of America.
Geography - United States; History - United States
Dist - PHENIX **Prod** - CBSTV 1976

Spirit of America with Charles Kuralt - Pt 6 - Florida, Alabama, Mississippi, Louisianna 17 MIN
U-matic / VHS / 16mm
Color (I)
LC 76-703536
Presents a segment from the CBS television program On The Road in which news correspondent Charles Kuralt journeys to Florida, Alabama, Louisianna and Mississippi to seek out places, people and events that contributed to the development of America.
Geography - United States; History - United States
Dist - PHENIX **Prod** - CBSTV 1976

Spirit of America with Charles Kuralt - Pt 7 - Texas, Oklahoma, Kansas, Nebraska 19 MIN
U-matic / VHS / 16mm
Color (I)
LC 77-700109
Presents a segment from the CBS television program On The Road in which news correspondent Charles Kuralt journeys to Texas, Oklahoma, Kansas and Nebraska to seek out places, people and events that contributed to the development of America.
Geography - United States; History - United States
Dist - PHENIX **Prod** - CBSTV 1976

Spirit of America with Charles Kuralt - Pt 8 - Minnesota, Iowa, Wisconsin, Missouri 19 MIN
16mm / U-matic / VHS
Color (I)
LC 76-703537
Presents a segment from the CBS television program On The Road in which news correspondent Charles Kuralt journeys to Minnesota, Iowa, Wisconsin and Missouri to seek out places, people and events that contributed to the development of America.
Geography - United States; History - United States
Dist - PHENIX **Prod** - CBSTV 1976

Spirit of America with Charles Kuralt - Pt 9 - Michigan, Ohio, Indiana, Illinois 18 MIN
16mm / U-matic / VHS
Color (I)
LC 76-703538
Presents a segment from the CBS television program On The Road in which news correspondent Charles Kuralt journeys to Michigan, Ohio, Illinois and Indiana to seek out places, people and events that contributed to the development of America.
Geography - United States; History - United States
Dist - PHENIX **Prod** - CBSTV 1976

Spirit of America with Charles Kuralt - Pt 10 - Montana, South Dakota, North Dakota, Wyoming 17 MIN
U-matic / VHS / 16mm
Color (I)
LC 76-703539
Presents a segment from the CBS television program On The Road in which news correspondent Charles Kuralt journeys to Montana, South Dakota, North Dakota and Wyoming to seek out places, people and events that contributed to the development of America.
Geography - United States; History - United States
Dist - PHENIX **Prod** - CBSTV 1976

Spirit of America with Charles Kuralt - Pt 11 - Colorado, New Mexico, Arizona 12 MIN
U-matic / VHS / 16mm
Color (I)
LC 77-700110
Presents a segment from the CBS television program On The Road in which news correspondent Charles Kuralt journeys to Colorado, New Mexico and Arizona to seek out places, people and events that contributed to the development of America.
Geography - United States; History - United States
Dist - PHENIX **Prod** - CBSTV 1976

Spirit of America with Charles Kuralt - Pt 12 - Washington, Oregon, Idaho, Alaska 18 MIN
U-matic / VHS / 16mm
Color (I)
LC 77-700111
Presents a segment from the CBS television program On The Road in which news correspondent Charles Kuralt journeys to Washington, Alaska, Oregon and Idaho to seek out places, people and events that contributed to the development of America.
Geography - United States; History - United States
Dist - PHENIX **Prod** - CBSTV 1976

Spirit of America with Charles Kuralt - Pt 13 - Nevada, Utah, California, Hawaii 17 MIN
U-matic / VHS / 16mm
Color (I)
LC 77-700112
Presents a segment from the CBS television program On The Road in which news correspondent Charles Kuralt journeys to California, Hawaii, Utah and Nevada to seek out places, people and events that contributed to the development of America.
Geography - United States; History - United States
Dist - PHENIX **Prod** - CBSTV 1976

Spirit of America with Charles Kuralt - Pt 14 - the Declaration of Independence 9 MIN
16mm / U-matic / VHS
Color (I)
LC 77-700117
Presents a segment from the CBS television program On The Road in which news correspondent Charles Kuralt journeys to Philadelphia to visit Independence Hall, where the determination of the Founding Fathers to declare independence from Great Britain was debated and decided.
Geography - United States; History - United States
Dist - PHENIX **Prod** - CBSTV 1976

The Spirit of Bonaire 13 MIN
16mm
Color (GERMAN)
LC 80-701559
Shows how people on the small Caribbean island of Bonaire in the Netherlands Antilles have promoted tourism while maintaining their natural resources and wildlife.
Geography - World
Dist - MORTNJ **Prod** - BONTB 1980

A Spirit of celebration 15 MIN
U-matic / 35mm strip / VHS
Color (A)
Shows different types of people participating in a 'hunger walk.'
Sociology
Dist - CWS **Prod** - CWS 1984

The Spirit of Crazy Horse 60 MIN
U-matic
Color (G)
$59.95 purchase
Chronicles the history of the once indomitable nation of the buffalo - hunting warriors, led by Crazy Horse, who called themselves Lakota, meaning 'the Allies.' Features Milo Yellow Hair who recounts the story of these Native Americans, from the lost battles for their land against the invading whites to the present day revival of the Sioux cultural pride and attempts to regain their lost territory.
Social Science
Dist - NAMPBC **Prod** - PBS

The Spirit of Crazy Horse
VHS
American Indian collection series
Color (J H C G)
$29.95 purchase _ #PAV273V
Tells of the Sioux of South Dakota, their way of life which included hunting for buffalo and their struggle to maintain and preserve their heritage. Part of a five - part series on American Indians.
Social Science
Dist - CAMV

Spirit of Ethnography 19 MIN
16mm
B&W (C)
LC 74-703643
Takes a humorous look at the field of cultural anthropology. Chronicles the field research of a fictitious ethnographer embarking on his first field experience.
Sociology
Dist - PSUPCR **Prod** - PUAVC 1974

Spirit of exploration
VHS
Color (G)
$19.95 purchase
Explores rarely visited areas of the 46,000 acre Carlsbad Caverns National Park. Examines plants and animals of the Chihuahuan Desert and the mass flight of over a million Mexican free - tailed bats. Visits the Caverns and other more remote park caves, including the recently discovered Lechuguilla Cave. Films the experience of the 'caver,' squeezing through tight crawlways and dangling hundreds of feet in the air. Features the videography of Tom Zannes.
Geography - United States; Physical Education and Recreation
Dist - CARLSB **Prod** - CARLSB 1994

Spirit of Freedom 29 MIN
16mm
Color
LC 74-706583
Presents a patriotic panorama of America by the U S Navy Band.
Civics and Political Systems; Psychology
Dist - USNAC **Prod** - USN 1968

The Spirit of God - Acts and First Corinthians 30 MIN
VHS
Holy Spirit - biblical and contemporary perspectives series
Color (H C G A R)
$39.95 purchase, $10.00 rental _ #35 - 835 - 2076
Features author and theologian Richard Jensen in a study of the role of the Holy Spirit. Focuses on the concept of the gifts of the Spirit as described in the books of Acts and First Corinthians. Produced by Seraphim.
Literature and Drama; Religion and Philosophy
Dist - APH

The Spirit of God and Jesus of Nazareth 30 MIN
VHS
Holy Spirit - biblical and contemporary perspectives series
Color (H C G A R)
$39.95 purchase, $10.00 rental _ #35 - 834 - 2076
Features author and theologian Richard Jensen in a study of the role of the Holy Spirit. Focuses on the Holy Spirit in relation to Jesus. Produced by Seraphim.
Literature and Drama; Religion and Philosophy
Dist - APH

The Spirit of God and the 'charismatic' renewal 30 MIN
VHS
Holy Spirit - biblical and contemporary perspectives series
Color (H C G A R)
$39.95 purchase, $10.00 rental _ #35 - 836 - 2076
Features author and theologian Richard Jensen in a study of the role of the Holy Spirit. Focuses on the concept of the gifts of the Spirit as expressed in the modern - day church. Considers the 'charismatic' renewal movement within the mainline denominations. Produced by Seraphim.
Literature and Drama; Religion and Philosophy
Dist - APH

The Spirit of God in the Old Testament 30 MIN
VHS
Holy Spirit - Biblical and contemporary perspectives series
Color (H C G A R)
$39.95 purchase, $10.00 rental _ #35 - 833 - 2076
Features author and theologian Richard Jensen in a study of the role of the Holy Spirit. Focuses on the Old Testament. Produced by Seraphim.
Literature and Drama; Religion and Philosophy
Dist - APH

The Spirit of Kuna Yala 59 MIN
VHS
Color (H C G)
$445.00 purchase, $75.00 rental
Features the Kuna Indians of the San Blas Islands of Panama as they unite to protect their rainforest homeland, Kuna Yala, and the tradition it inspires. Recognizes the rapid destruction of tropical rainforests as a critical global problem causing the extinction of countless indigenous peoples. Produced by Andrew Young and Susan Todd for Archipelago Films.
Geography - World; Science - Natural; Social Science
Dist - FLMLIB

Spirit of Lightning Snake 14 MIN
16mm
Color (P)
LC 76-701920
Shows how a young boy's search for Indian petrographs leads him to discover the legend of the Lightning Snake as danced for him by a Nootka Indian chief.
Literature and Drama; Social Science; Sociology
Dist - INLEAS **Prod** - INLEAS 1975

The Spirit of Malcolm Miller
VHS
Color (G)
$29.95 purchase _ #0011
Joins 39 young men from totally different backgrounds on a two - week Sail Training Association course. Shows them learning to work as a team aboard the schooner Malcolm Miller.
Physical Education and Recreation
Dist - SEVVID

The Spirit of nature - the first wildlife musical program kit 50 MIN
VHS / Kit
(P I J G)
$199.95, $29.95 purchase _ #SN101, #SN102
Presents a wildlife musical program available as a kit or as a videocassette. Includes the video, two audiocassettes containing 120 minutes of natural sounds and a guide in the kit. The video features the wildlife cinematography of Robert Bocking and the songs of Scott Wesson. Produced by Bocking and Wesson.
Fine Arts; Science - Natural
Dist - ENVIMC

Spirit of Patton series

The Goal setters - G rated	6 MIN
The Goal setters - R rated	6 MIN
Morale and the Team Effort	4 MIN

Dist - PROSOR

Spirit of Patton series

Sales and morale - G rated	5 MIN
Sales and morale - R rated	5 MIN
Sales and the competition	6 MIN

Dist - PROSOR
UTM

The Spirit of Punxsutawney - Pt 1 29 MIN
16mm
B&W (H C A)
LC 77-700949
Documents the day - to - day routine of the staff of a small town Pennsylvania newspaper called The Spirit. Illustrates the interaction between the editorial staff and the town's residents in order to present the newspaper as a sensitive institution that reacts to the needs of its rural community.
Geography - United States; Literature and Drama; Social Science; Sociology
Dist - PSU **Prod** - WPSXTV 1976

The Spirit of Punxsutawney - Pt 2 30 MIN
16mm
B&W (H C A)
LC 77-700949
Documents the day - to - day routine of the staff of a small town Pennsylvania newspaper called The Spirit. Illustrates the interaction between the editorial staff and the town's residents in order to present the newspaper as a sensitive institution that reacts to the needs of its rural community.
Geography - United States; Literature and Drama; Social Science; Sociology
Dist - PSU **Prod** - WPSXTV 1976

The Spirit of Rhythms and Blues 30 MIN
16mm
Black History, Section 22 - the Cultural Scene Series; Section 22 - Cultural scene
B&W (H C A)
LC 79-704118
Larry Neal acts as moderator as A B Spellman and Julius Lester discuss the ethos of black America in the 1950's and comment on the influence of the wars on black culture as revealed in music, dance and radio programming.
Fine Arts; History - United States
Dist - HRAW **Prod** - WCBSTV 1969

The Spirit of Romanticism 29 MIN
U-matic / VHS / 16mm
Humanities - Philosophy and Political Thought Series
Color (H C)
LC 78-700453
Presents dramatizations that bring to life key events and personalities of the Romantic movement (1789 - 1838) in literature, music and art. Includes Carlyle describing the French Revolution, Delacroix painting Liberty Leading The People and Shelley as a young rebel and as a friend to Byron.
Fine Arts; Literature and Drama
Dist - EBEC **Prod** - EBEC

The Spirit of Rome 29 MIN
16mm / U-matic / VHS
Color (H C) (SPANISH)
Uses scenes from Shakespeare's Julius Caesar and George Bernard Shaw's Caesar and Cleopatra to depict the tremendous spectacle of ancient Rome. Filmed in Rome and London.
Foreign Language; Geography - World; History - World; Literature and Drama
Dist - EBEC **Prod** - EBEC

The Spirit of St Elmo Village 26 MIN
VHS / 16mm
Color (I H C A)
$325.00, $275.00
Visits St. Elmo village, a slum area in the heart of Los Angeles, which has become a kaleidoscope of color and beauty through the efforts of two African - American artists, Rozzell and Roderick Sykes. Shows how the children of St. Elmo are exposed to art and motivated to beautify their community rather than tear it down.
Fine Arts; Guidance and Counseling; History - United States; Psychology; Sociology
Dist - CAROUF **Prod** - THMACK 1989

The Spirit of St Louis 135 MIN
16mm / U-matic / VHS
Color (G)
Dramatizes Charles Lindbergh's historic solo flight from New York to Paris. Stars James Stewart. Directed by Billy Wilder.
Biography; Fine Arts; History - United States
Dist - FI **Prod** - WB 1957
GA

Spirit of Stone 25 MIN
U-matic / VHS / 16mm
Color (H C A)
LC 74-701763
Shows how ancient art carvings are analyzed by anthropologists, art experts and other scientists in order to determine the full history and significance of these carvings and other artifacts.
Fine Arts; History - World; Sociology
Dist - JOU **Prod** - EFD 1974

The Spirit of Sweden 60 MIN
VHS
Traveloguer collection series
Color (G)
$29.95 purchase _ #QU008
Visits Sweden. Offers historical and geographic highlights.
Geography - World
Dist - SIV

Spirit of the age series
Examines the evolution of architecture in Britain since the Middle Ages. An eight-part series.

All that money could buy	50 MIN
Cult of grandeur	50 MIN
Dreams and awakenings	50 MIN
A Full life and an honest place	50 MIN
Landscape with buildings	50 MIN
Medieval world	50 MIN
New heaven, new Earth	50 MIN
Sense of proportion	50 MIN

Dist - BBCENE

The Spirit of the beehive 94 MIN
VHS
Color (G)
$29.95 _ #SPI080
Portrays the isolation of an introverted child within her own family in rural Spain of 1940. Follows her into a mysterious and poetic imaginary world when she ventures into the forest to find Boris Karloff's Frankenstein, whom she believes to actually exist. Directed by Victor Erice.
Fine Arts; Psychology; Sociology
Dist - HOMVIS

The Spirit of the Dance 21 MIN
16mm
B&W
LC FIA65-1038
Depicts the classical dance and the many facets of the professional activity of a ballerina as illustrated in the life of Nina Vyroubva, star of the Paris Opera Ballet, who performs with other members of the ballet. Highlights the exacting disciplines which this art demands. Includes practice at the barre, executing new positions and rehearsals behind the scenes and on stage with ceaseless work towards perfection.
Fine Arts
Dist - RADIM **Prod** - DELOUD 1965

Spirit of the eagle 30 MIN
VHS
Color (G)
$19.95 purchase _ #MR601; $19.95 purchase _ #MVP9003
Presents traditional American values in a metaphor featuring eagle footage.
Guidance and Counseling; Industrial and Technical Education; Sociology
Dist - VSPU **Prod** - MIRMP 1991
MIRMP

Spirit of the hunt 29 MIN
U-matic / VHS
Color (H C G)
$340.00, $315.00 purchase _ #V371
Introduces the culture and religion of the Plains Indians of North America. Focuses on the material and spiritual importance of the buffalo. Looks at the Chippewa, Cree and Dogrib tribes.
Physical Education and Recreation; Social Science
Dist - BARR **Prod** - CEPRO 1982

The Spirit of the mask
VHS
Color (H C G)
$295.00 purchase, $60.00 rental _ #38145
Explores the spiritual and psychological powers of the masks of the Northwest Coast native people of North America. Shows dramatic, rarely - seen ceremonies and commentary by important Indian spiritual leaders. Relates the colonial history of the Northwest Coast Indians, showing how their most significant ceremonies were banned by Christian Europeans. Considers the role of masks in other cultures, including the European pagan mask tradition and examines the meaning of tribal art both to indigenous cultures and to the contemporary West. Produced Peter von Puttkamer for Gryphon Productions, Ltd.
History - World; Religion and Philosophy; Social Science
Dist - UCEMC

Spirit of the Pueblos - Kachina 15 MIN
16mm
Color (I J)
LC 78-700514
Discusses the historical, religious and cultural significance of kachina dolls, which are used as messenger spirits in the tribal rituals of American Southwest Indians.
Social Science
Dist - SRA **Prod** - SRA 1978

The Spirit of the Tree 12 MIN
16mm
Color (P)
LC FIA68-826
Describes the production of a Bible from the planting of a tree through the making of the paper to printing and binding.
Industrial and Technical Education; Literature and Drama
Dist - ABS **Prod** - ABS 1967

Spirit of the White Mountains 13 MIN
16mm
Color (I J)
Presents pioneering activities of the White Mountain Apaches. Describes their present day activities - farming, cattle raising, recreation and business meetings. Shows many areas that attract visitors to this part of Arizona.
Geography - United States; Social Science; Sociology
Dist - MLA **Prod** - DAGP 1959

Spirit of the wind 29 MIN
VHS / U-matic
Real people series
Color (G)
Emphasizes the place of the horse in the life and culture of the Plateau Tribes. Long ago, horses changed old ways of life by making tribes more mobile, widening hunting areas, and increasing fighting power. Bridging the past and present, two retired rodeo riders from the Colville Tribe talk of their life and experiences on the rodeo circuit. Their reminiscing is enhanced by tribal film footage shot in the 1930's.
Social Science
Dist - NAMPBC **Prod** - KSPSTV 1976
GPN

Spirit of the Wind 10 MIN
U-matic / 16mm / VHS
Color (J)
LC 79-701828; 79-701804
Deals with sailboat racing on inland lakes, emphasizing the spirit of wind, water, competition and friendship. Discusses the emotional attachment sailors have for the sport, the mental preparation for the race and the physical rigors necessary to win.

Physical Education and Recreation
Dist - MCFI **Prod** - TFW 1975

Spirit of trees 200 MIN
VHS
Spirit of trees series
Color (G)
$995.00 purchase, $195.00 rental
Features an eight - part series on trees and their relationship with the world around them, hosted by environmentalist Dick Warner, who meets with conservationists, scientists, folklorists, woodsmen, seed collectors, forest rangers, wood turners and more. Contains Old Oaks, ancient oaks in England and spiritual interest in trees; Restoring Scotland's Native Trees, the danger of losing ancient woodlands; From Wild Woods to Town Gardens, natural growth in modern gardens of scarce species; Management of Coppice Woodland, an ancient method of managing trees; Folklore of Trees, history of customs and rituals; Conservation of Rare Trees; History from Trees; and The Future of Trees, visits giant sequoias in California. 25 minutes each.
Agriculture; Geography - United States; Science - Natural; Social Science
Dist - CNEMAG

Spirit of trees series
Conservation of rare trees - episode 6 25 MIN
Folklore of trees - episode 5 25 MIN
From wild woods to town gardens - episode 3 25 MIN
The Future of trees - episode 8 25 MIN
History from trees - episode 7 25 MIN
Management of coppice woodland - episode 4 25 MIN
Old oaks - episode 1 25 MIN
Restoring Scotland's native trees - episode 2 25 MIN
Spirit of trees 200 MIN
Dist - CNEMAG

The Spirit of Victory 10 MIN
16mm
Color
Shows a re - creation of the last great Revolutionary War battle at Yorktown, Virginia, in 1781. Narrated by Charlton Heston.
History - United States
Dist - MTP **Prod** - USA

The Spirit Possession of Alejandro Mamani 27 MIN
16mm
Faces of Change - Bolivia Series
Color (H C A)
Presents an elderly Bolivian man nearing the end of his life who believes himself possessed by evil spirits. Reveals his personal tragedy as well as the universal confrontation with the unknown, old age and death.
Geography - World; Religion and Philosophy; Sociology
Dist - FLMLIB **Prod** - AUFS 1974

The Spirit travels - immigrant music in America 55 MIN
VHS
Color (J H G)
$350.00 purchase, $95.00 rental
Looks at ethnic music in America. Offers a rich sampling of culturally diverse musical styles with lively performances of Irish, Greek, African - American, Jewish, Central Asian, Chinese, and Puerto Rican music among others. Includes archival footage and photos, and interviews with musicians, cultural historians and record producers. Hosted and narrated by Linda Ronstadt. Produced by The Ethnic Folk Arts Center. Directed by Howard Weiss.
Fine Arts
Dist - CNEMAG

The Spirit Visible 30 MIN
U-matic
Visions - Artists and the Creative Process Series
Color (H C A)
Shows three prairie artists expressing their inner harmonies and conflicts through their work.
Fine Arts; History - World
Dist - TVOTAR **Prod** - TVOTAR 1983

The Spirit World of Tidikawa 50 MIN
U-matic
Color ((ENGLISH NARRATION))
Short version of the documentary Tidikawa And Friends, which explores the daily lives of the Bedamini of Papua, New Guinea. Includes English narration throughout. Filmed in 1971.
Geography - World; Sociology
Dist - DOCEDR **Prod** - BBCTV

Spiritism, U F Os and the occult
VHS
Counterfeits series
Color (H C G A R)
$10.00 rental _ #36 - 84 - 2024
Examines spiritism, U F Os and the occult. Contrasts their ideas with orthodox Christianity. Suggests strategies for evangelism. Hosted by Ron Carlson. Produced by Cinema Associates and Film Educators.
Religion and Philosophy
Dist - APH

SpiritMatters 6 MIN
16mm
Color (G)
$15.00 rental
Delivers a silent monologue on the simultaneous perception of space and time. Dares to construct without a camera by writing directly on clear celluloid and then 'translates' by refilming the resulting strips on a light table so they appear as 'subtitles.' A Peter Rose production.
Fine Arts; Psychology; Religion and Philosophy
Dist - CANCIN

Spirits in stone - aspects of Alberta's prehistory 30 MIN
U-matic
Historical resources series
(A)
Presents a variety of prehistorical archaeological resources found at a number of different locations in Alberta. These include vision quest sites, teepee rings, campsites, medicine wheels, buffalo jumps and petroglyphs.
Geography - World; History - World; Social Science
Dist - ACCESS **Prod** - ACCESS 1985

Spirits of America 19 MIN
16mm
Decisions and Drinking Series
Color
LC 80-701624
Uses still graphics to deal with basic issues and standards of American drinking and the historical and cultural aspects associated with them.
Health and Safety; Psychology; Sociology
Dist - USNAC **Prod** - NIAAA 1978

Spirits on the wing 28 MIN
VHS / U-matic / 16mm
Color (J H G)
$275.00, $325.00, $545.00 purchase, $50.00 rental
Covers the history of birds of prey. Includes the habits, the habitat and the physical characteristics of falcons, osprey, eagles, hawk and owls. Produced by Montana Department of Fish, Wildlife and Parks.
Science - Natural
Dist - NDIM

Spiritual aspects of alcoholism 33 MIN
VHS
Color (G)
$250.00, $10.00 purchase
Addresses alcoholism as a 'soul sickness.' States that recovery must be spiritual in nature.
Guidance and Counseling; Health and Safety; Psychology
Dist - KELLYP **Prod** - KELLYP

Spiritual aspects of patient care - Pt 1 30 MIN
16mm
Directions for education in nursing via technology series; Lesson 32
B&W (PRO R)
LC 74-701805
Presents a panel which includes a rabbi, a Catholic priest, a Protestant minister and a nurse who respond to questions relative to traditional ministrations and other spiritual needs of patients.
Guidance and Counseling; Health and Safety; Religion and Philosophy; Sociology
Dist - WSUM **Prod** - DENT 1974

Spiritual aspects of patient care - Pt 2 30 MIN
16mm
Directions for education in nursing via technology series; Lesson 33
B&W (PRO R)
LC 74-701806
Presents a panel which includes a rabbi, a Catholic priest, a Protestant minister and a nurse who respond to questions relative to traditional ministrations and other spiritual needs of patients.
Guidance and Counseling; Health and Safety; Religion and Philosophy; Sociology
Dist - WSUM **Prod** - DENT 1974

Spiritual Awakening 25 MIN
VHS / 16mm
Color (G)
$165.00 purchase, $40.00 rental _ #5812H, 5827H, 0455J, 0470J
Cautions that spiritual awakening is not a bolt from heaven. Stresses that spirituality consists of insights gradually internalized into the way of life outlined in the Twelve Step program. Features Dr Damian McElrath.
Guidance and Counseling; Health and Safety; Psychology
Dist - HAZELB **Prod** - HAZELB

Spiritual Channeling 30 MIN
VHS / BETA
Channels and channeling series
Color (G)
$29.95 purchase _ #S380
Describes the channeling process. Features Alan Vaughan, psychic intuitive and author of 'Patterns of Prophecy' and 'The Edge of Tomorrow,' who goes into trance and a spiritual entity Li Sung appears and describes his role as a spiritual guide. Part of a four - part series on channels and channeling.
Religion and Philosophy
Dist - THINKA **Prod** - THINKA

Spiritual constructions 10 MIN
16mm / VHS
B&W (A)
$22.00 rental
Introduces a meditation on violence in which the filmmaker poured all his 'loathing of the German penchant for drunkenness and aggression' while also infusing the film with a serene sense of consciousness. Employs slow - motion animation, which may be the first use of this technique.
Fine Arts
Dist - CANCIN **Prod** - FISCHF 1927

Spiritual democracy with Steven Rockefeller 30 MIN
VHS
World of ideas with Bill Moyers - Season II - series
Color; Captioned (G)
$39.95 purchase _ #WIWM - 212
Interviews religion and philosophy professor Steven Rockefeller, the great - grandson of John D Rockefeller. Tells of Rockefeller's personal spiritual quest. Presents Rockefeller's observations on religion in American society. Hosted by Bill Moyers.
Religion and Philosophy
Dist - PBS

Spiritual dimensions of life and the will to meaning 40 MIN
VHS
Color (G C PRO)
$39.95 purchase
Features Dr Leo Missinne addressing the 1989 annual meeting of the American Society on Aging.
Health and Safety
Dist - TNF

Spiritual discipline - the door to liberation 50 MIN
VHS
Celebration of discipline series; Tape 1
Color (H C G A R)
$29.95 purchase, $10.00 rental _ #35 - 867 - 8516
Features Richard Foster in an exploration of the role spiritual disciplines can play in spiritual growth. Based on the book of the same title by Foster.
Religion and Philosophy
Dist - APH **Prod** - VISVID

The Spiritual journey 32 MIN
VHS / U-matic
Color (H G)
$280.00, $330.00 purchase, $50.00 rental
Explores death and the dying process. Looks at the opportunity for spiritual growth and awareness for the dying person and the family, friends and social workers who assist in that journey. Produced by Top Shelf Productions.
Sociology
Dist - NDIM

Spiritual life in a material world 60 MIN
VHS / BETA
Color; PAL (G)
PdS25
Features a practical and engaging talk by the Venerable Geshe Namgyal Wangchen, resident teacher at Manjushri Centre, London, about the need for both material progress and a spiritual dimension to life for human development. Contains advice and encouragement for those who live and practice dharma in the midst of Western society.
Fine Arts; Religion and Philosophy; Social Science
Dist - MERIDT

A Spiritual Ordering - the Metal Arts of Africa 20 MIN
U-matic / VHS
Color (C A)
LC 84-706390
Introduces major objects from Western and Central Africa illustrating how African artists have utilized a rich repertory of sacred gestures and frozen them in metal. Traces important themes such as the equestrian figure and zoomorphic representations of the snake.
Fine Arts; History - World
Dist - IU **Prod** - AFRAMI 1983

Spiritual parenting 44 MIN
VHS
Building the family of God series
Color (R G)
$29.95 purchase _ #6110 - 7
Shows how ordinary Christians can change their world and incorporate spirituality into their parenting. Features Dr John MacArthur.
Literature and Drama; Religion and Philosophy; Sociology
Dist - MOODY **Prod** - MOODY

Spiritual Progress and Psychological Growth 45 MIN
BETA / VHS
Psychological Growth and Spiritual Development Series
Color (G)
Psychology; Religion and Philosophy
Dist - DSP **Prod** - DSP

Spiritual psychology quartet series
Presents a four - part series on spiritual psychology. Includes 'Spirituality and Psychology' with Dr Frances Vaughan, 'Psychotherapy and Spiritual Paths' with Dr Seymour Boorstein, 'Past Life Regression and Spirit Depossession' with Dr Edith Fiore and 'Visonary Experience or Psychosis' with Dr John Weir Perry.
Past life regression and spirit depossession 30 MIN
Psychotherapy and spiritual paths 30 MIN
Spirituality and psychology 30 MIN
Visionary experience or psychosis 30 MIN
Dist - THINKA **Prod** - THINKA

Spiritual training 30 MIN
BETA / VHS
Personal and spiritual development series
Color (G)
$29.95 purchase _ #S058
Describes the bliss, peace and love - as well as the despair, hatred and loneliness - of years of training in the Sufi tradition. Features Irina Tweedie, author of 'Daughter of Fire,' a diary of her intensive spiritual training in India with a Hindu Sufi master. Part of a four - part series on personal and spiritual development.
Psychology; Religion and Philosophy
Dist - THINKA **Prod** - THINKA

Spiritual warfare - the G H O S T campaign 28 MIN
VHS
Color (G)
$30.00 purchase
Documents the 1990 Halloween confrontation between Larry Lea's Commandos for Christ and several thousand San Franciscans as Lea's 'prayer warriors' invade the city to exorcise the demons from the Bay Area. Includes mainstream media coverage, interviews, speeches and street theater by the Pink Jesus - Gilbert Baker; Sadie, Sadie, the Rabbi Lady - Gil Block; and film producer Scarlot Harlot - Carol Leigh dancing nude with a live snake. Note - GHOST is an acronym for Grand Homosexual Outrage at Sickening Televangelists.
Fine Arts; Religion and Philosophy; Sociology
Dist - CANCIN **Prod** - LEIGHC 1990

Spirituality and psychology 30 MIN
VHS / BETA
Spiritual psychology quartet series
Color (G)
$29.95 purchase _ #S010
Stresses that all spiritual traditions ultimately offer a means toward transcendence of the limited self. Features Dr Frances Vaughan, transpersonal psychotherapist and author of 'Awakening Intuition' and 'The Inward Arc.' Part of a series on spiritual psychology.
Psychology; Religion and Philosophy
Dist - THINKA **Prod** - THINKA

Spirituality and the intellect 30 MIN
BETA / VHS
Living philosophically series
Color (G)
$29.95 purchase _ #S032
Considers that the essential tension between material and spiritual natures is often forgotten as contemporary concerns are pursued. Features Dr Jacob Needleman who points to Socrates as the ideal philosopher who, through his attitude toward living, fostered appreciation of a deeper strata of awareness. Part of a four - part series on living philosophically.
History - World; Religion and Philosophy
Dist - THINKA **Prod** - THINKA

Spirituality - choosing peace 19 MIN
U-matic / VHS
Freedom from addiction - breaking the chains series; 7
Color (G)
$249.00 purchase _ #7452
Reveals that spirituality and religion are vastly different and outlines the differences. Defines the concepts of spirituality, acceptance, serenity and letting go. Explains the importance and the joys of a spiritually oriented recovery program. Part of an eight - part series dealing with recovery from addiction hosted by recovery specialist Barbara Allen.
Guidance and Counseling; Health and Safety; Psychology; Religion and Philosophy
Dist - VISIVI **Prod** - VISIVI 1991

Spirituality explored 30 MIN
VHS
Color (J H C G A R)
$39.95 purchase, $10.00 rental _ #35 - 82 - 2076
Features Dr Joseph Sittler in an exploration of the significance of spirituality. Produced by Seraphim.
Religion and Philosophy
Dist - APH

The Spirituality tape
VHS
Color (A)
$34.95 purchase _ #6925
Explores issues of chemical dependency as they relate to spiritual growth.
Education; Psychology
Dist - HAZELB

Spirituality - the poor shall lead us 16 MIN
VHS / U-matic
Color (R G)
$50.00 purchase, $25.00 rental _ #827, #828, #829
Explores the plight of those who live in poverty and their struggles against illness, alcoholism, age or lack of education and job skills in the first part. Presents healthcare professionals who work with the poor in the second part and discusses their gratification as a result of their work.
Health and Safety; Religion and Philosophy; Sociology
Dist - CATHHA **Prod** - CATHHA 1989

Spirituals in concert
CD / Cassette / VHS
(G H A)
$12.95, $17.95, $24.95 purchase _ #19391, #19392, #19222
Features Kathleen Battle and Jessye Norman in a performance of 18 traditional spirituals, including 'Oh, What a Beautiful City,' 'Swing Low, Sweet Chariot,' 'Gospel Train,' and 'He's Got the Whole World in His Hands.'
Fine Arts
Dist - WCAT **Prod** - WCAT

Spirituals - Pt 1 15 MIN
U-matic / VHS
Song sampler series
Color (P)
LC 81-707036
Describes the characteristics of spirituals and shows how to recognize the ABA form. Explains the terms pentatonic and shows how to create an introduction and accompaniment for a song. Presents the songs All Night All Day, Get On Board and Michael Row The Boat Ashore.
Fine Arts
Dist - GPN **Prod** - JCITV 1981

Spirituals - Pt 2 15 MIN
VHS / U-matic
Song sampler series
Color (P)
LC 81-707036
Describes the characteristics of spirituals and shows how to recognize the ABA form. Explains the terms pentatonic and shows how to create an introduction and accompaniment for a song. Presents the songs All Night All Day, Get On Board and Michael Row The Boat Ashore.
Fine Arts
Dist - GPN **Prod** - JCITV 1981

Spiro Malas 29 MIN
Videoreel / VT2
Elliot Norton Reviews II Series
Color
Presents exchanges and arguments between the dean of American theatre critics, Elliot Norton, and Spiro Malas.
Fine Arts; Literature and Drama
Dist - PBS **Prod** - WGBHTV

Spirometry - the early detection of chronic obstructive pulmonary disease 25 MIN
16mm
Color (PRO)
LC 79-702582
Illustrates the functioning of the normal respiratory system and shows what happens when ventilation is impaired.
Health and Safety; Science; Science - Natural
Dist - AMLUNG **Prod** - NTBA 1968
WFP

Spirometry - the Three Elements of Effective Testing 15 MIN
U-matic / VHS
Color (A)
Illustrates proper spirometer testing procedures. Discusses machine preparation, subject preparation, testing execution and test result validation.
Health and Safety; Mathematics
Dist - USNAC **Prod** - USPHS 1980

Spirometry - the three elements of effective testing 16 MIN
VHS / U-matic
Color (PRO C)
$395.00 purchase, $80.00 rental _ #C881 - VI - 025
Demonstrates the correct techniques for using the dry rolling seal spirometer which measures and records lung volume, capacity and flow, essential in the early detection of respiratory health problems.
Health and Safety; Science - Natural
Dist - HSCIC **Prod** - NIOSH 1989

Spite - an African prophet - healer 54 MIN
VHS
Color (H C G)
$445.00 purchase, $75.00 rental
Reveals that people from all over the Ivory Coast seek out prophet - healers for treatment of their medical and emotional problems, some caused by the stress of cultural change and uncurable by Western medicine. Focuses on Sebim Odjo who incorporates Moslem, Christian and traditional African beliefs in his healing ceremonies. He moderates disputes, tracks down the source of illness and uses his powers to heal. Observes a water cure used on a patient ill with spite. Produced by J P Collyn and Catherine De Clippel.
Geography - World; Health and Safety; Religion and Philosophy
Dist - FLMLIB

Spitting image 3 MIN
16mm
Color (G)
$15.00 rental
Involves a personal narrative about the struggle to free oneself of the haunting memories of one's past in a Paula Froehle production.
Fine Arts; Psychology
Dist - CANCIN

SPLASH 12 MIN
16mm / U-matic / VHS
Color (P)
LC 81-701575
Uses animation in a story about water droplets to demonstrate the water cycle, the importance of water in urban living and the impact of pollution on this precious natural resource.
Science - Natural; Social Science; Sociology
Dist - CRMP **Prod** - NFBC 1982

Splash erosion 8 MIN
VHS
Hydrology concept series
Color (H C)
$24.95 purchase _ #S9016
Demonstrates soil movement caused by splash erosion in a single - concept format. Part of an 8 - part series covering water and soil topics.
Science - Physical
Dist - HUBDSC **Prod** - HUBDSC

Splendid stones 59 MIN
BETA / VHS / U-matic
Color (G)
$90.00 purchase _ #C51475
Reveals that of the thousands of minerals in the world, only a few dozen qualify as gems. Explores the mystery as well as the high - stakes business of gems - diamonds, pearls, emeralds and rubies.
Science - Physical
Dist - NGS **Prod** - NGS 1991

Splendor in the grass 124 MIN
16mm / U-matic / VHS
Color (C A)
Stars Natalie Wood and Warren Beatty as the idealistic young lovers in the Puritan atmosphere of a small town in Kansas during the late 1920's, which is faced with the decision of containing their passion or sacrificing their illusions of purity of conscience.
Fine Arts
Dist - FI **Prod** - WB 1961

Splendor Undiminished
16mm
Color
_ #106C 0176 044
Geography - World
Dist - CFLMDC **Prod** - NFBC 1976

Splenectomy 21 MIN
U-matic / VHS
Color (PRO)
Describes the splenectomy.
Health and Safety
Dist - WFP **Prod** - WFP

Splenectomy for Massive Splenomegaly 19 MIN
U-matic / VHS
Color (PRO)
Demonstrates a splenectomy technique that minimizes complications, including pancreatitis, bleeding, infections, and splenic laceration. Traces the surgery of a patient with massive splenomegaly due to hairy - cell leukemia.
Health and Safety
Dist - UARIZ **Prod** - UARIZ

Splenectomy in the treatment of hypersplenism 21 MIN
16mm
Color (PRO)
Demonstrates the technique of splenectomy.
Health and Safety
Dist - ACY **Prod** - ACYDGD 1955

Splenectomy with thoraco - abdominal incision 20 MIN
16mm
Color (PRO)
Explains that a complete exposure of the operative field with a precise control of the vascular supply and minimal subsequent tissue necrosis are fundamental technical requirements for splenectomy with thoraco - abdominal incision.
Health and Safety
Dist - ACY **Prod** - ACYDGD 1958

Splenorenal anastomosis for portal hypertension 19 MIN
16mm
Color (PRO)
Describes operation for relief of cirrhosis of the liver by anastomosing the renal vein to the splenic vein (relief of elevated pressure in the portal system.).
Health and Safety
Dist - ACY **Prod** - ACYDGD 1950

Splenorenal shunt for portal hypertension 27 MIN
16mm
Color (PRO)
Presents the technique of three types of shunts, an end - to - side portacaval shunt for bleeding esophageal varices, a side - to - side portacaval shunt for intractable ascites and an end - to - side splenorenal shunt for bleeding esophageal varices.
Health and Safety
Dist - ACY **Prod** - ACYDGD 1960

Splices and terminations 5 KV - 20 KV 60 MIN
U-matic / VHS
Electrical maintenance training series; Module E - Electrical connection
Color (IND)
Industrial and Technical Education
Dist - LEIKID **Prod** - LEIKID

Splicing a Wooden Spar 21 MIN
16mm
B&W
LC FIE52-274
Demonstrates how to cut a scarf joint on a spar, finish a scarf face by hand, glue and assemble a scarf joint, make, glue and assemble reinforcement plates and trim a spar to shape and size.
Industrial and Technical Education
Dist - USNAC **Prod** - USOE 1945

Splinting - open fracture 11 MIN
U-matic / VHS
EMT video - group two series
Color (PRO)
LC 84-706490
Shows the steps to be followed in treating an open fracture on the battlefield, using Army - issue splints, cravats, and pressure dressings.
Health and Safety
Dist - USNAC **Prod** - USA 1983

Splinting - the basswood splint to the forearm 6 MIN
U-matic / VHS
EMT video - group two series
Color (PRO)
LC 84-706488
Demonstrates the application of a basswood splint to immobolize a fractured forearm, including the sequence of steps for treating fractures.
Health and Safety
Dist - USNAC **Prod** - USA 1983

Splinting - the dislocated or fractured elbow 6 MIN
U-matic / VHS
EMT video - group two series
Color (PRO)
LC 84-706489
Shows the application of a wireladder splint for elbow fractures and explains splinting principles.
Health and Safety
Dist - USNAC **Prod** - USA 1983

Split Brain 13 MIN
16mm
B&W (H C A)
Explains the revolutionary split - brain operation, performed at the California Institute of Technology, in which the two hemispheres of the brain are separated surgically along the corpus callosum. Demonstrates devices developed to test split - brain subjects to provide insight into the functioning of the brain.
Health and Safety; Science - Natural
Dist - IU **Prod** - NET 1964

The Split Brain and Conscious Experience 17 MIN
16mm / U-matic / VHS
Color (C)
LC 77-701272
Presents a study of patients whose brains have been surgically separated in an attempt to control severe epilepsy. Shows surgery as well as experiments conducted on these patients.
Health and Safety; Psychology; Science; Science - Natural
Dist - CORF **Prod** - CONCPT 1977

Split Cherry Tree 25 MIN
U-matic / VHS / 16mm
LCA Short Story Library Series
Color (I)
LC 82-700410
Reveals that a father gains insight into the importance of education when he goes to his son's school to protest the boy's punishment for damaging a cherry tree during a class biology trip. Based on the short story Split Cherry Tree by Jesse Stuart.
Education; Guidance and Counseling; Literature and Drama; Sociology
Dist - LCOA **Prod** - LCOA 1982

Split description 8 MIN
16mm
Color; B&W (G)
$20.00 rental
Portrays gestures rather than statements. Utilizes a concentric split - screen technique to present a kaleidoscopic moving montage of three diverse locales - California, Massachusetts and New York. Plays with different zones within the frames while the hairline borders between them become worlds of color and form. Nonverbal, except for some Morse code. Soundtrack ranges from simple to intricate. Produced by Andy Moore.
Fine Arts; Psychology
Dist - CANCIN

Split - phase motor principles 17 MIN
16mm
Electrical work - electrical machinery series; No 4
B&W (SPANISH)
LC FIE52-241
Describes the construction of stator and rotor, the effects of winding resistances and inductive reactances, and the use of capacitor to produce phase displacement. Compares the winding in two - phase stator with split - phase stator.
Industrial and Technical Education
Dist - USNAC **Prod** - USOE 1945

Split - phase motor - rewinding 28 MIN
16mm
Electrical work - motor maintenance and repair series; No 3
B&W
LC FIE52-183
Shows how to test a split - phase motor for electrical and mechanical faults, dismantle and strip the stator, rewind the stator, form and install skein windings and insulate. Explains how to lace, dip and bake the stator, and how to assemble, lubricate and test motors.
Industrial and Technical Education
Dist - USNAC **Prod** - USOE 1945

Split Rock Light - tribute to the age of steel 22 MIN
VHS
Color (G)
$24.95 purchase _ #V - 001
Tells the story of the building of a landmark lighthouse, Split Rock Light.
History - United States
Dist - MINHS

The Split second 10 MIN
16mm / VHS
Color (IND)
$295.00 purchase, $45.00 rental, $35.00 preview
Motivates employees to be aware and responsible when working in the industrial plant. Illustrates how just one second can make the difference between safety and tragedy.
Business and Economics; Guidance and Counseling; Health and Safety; Psychology
Dist - UTM

Split Second Fastening
16mm
Color (IND)
Illustrates and explains the Nelson stud welding process, and gives a brief history of its inception during World War II.
Business and Economics; Industrial and Technical Education
Dist - NSW **Prod** - NSW

Split Second Safety - a Guide for Electrical Hazard Safety 11 MIN
16mm
Color
LC 74-712855
Uses live action and animation to demonstrate the hazards and results of electrical line - to - ground fault problems. C F Dalziel explains electric circuiting and body resistance to electric current and presents safety precautions.
Health and Safety; Industrial and Technical Education
Dist - FILCOM **Prod** - PASSEY 1968

Split - second self - defense
VHS
Color (H C G)
$29.95 purchase _ #F632
Condenses self - defense into a few essential but easy lessons designed especially for women. Teaches basic escape moves from the most common attacks, the 'natural striking weapons' women always have with them, and the 'key striking areas' to cripple assailants and allow escape time. Includes a lesson guide with photographs of each lesson and a wallet card to keep practitioners in practice and alert.
Physical Education and Recreation; Sociology
Dist - CWOMEN

Splitting the Transference - Group Treatment and Psychopharmacology 15 MIN
U-matic / VHS
Treatment of the Borderline Patient Series
Color
Presents Dr Harold F Searles belief about the use of psychopharmacological medications with borderline patients in analytic treatment. Shares his opinions about the impact of drugs, group and family therapy upon the transference.
Health and Safety; Psychology
Dist - HEMUL **Prod** - HEMUL

Spoiled children 113 MIN
35mm / 16mm
Color (G) (FRENCH WITH ENGLISH SUBTITLES)
$250.00, $300.00 rental
Portrays an aging screenwriter moves into an apartment building engaged in a rent strike. Directed by Bertrand Tavernier.
Fine Arts
Dist - KINOIC **Prod** - CORINT 1977

The Spoiled Priest 60 MIN
U-matic / VHS
World of F Scott Fitzgerald Series
Color (C)
Traces the conflict between rigid moral restraints and the lure of the sensual world in this dramatization of a Fitzgerald story.
Literature and Drama
Dist - DALCCD **Prod** - DALCCD

Spoiled rotten 25 MIN
U-matic
Not another science show series
Color (H C)
Focuses on the microorganisms responsible for contaminating food, mould, yeast and bacteria, and how their growth can be prevented.
Science; Social Science
Dist - TVOTAR **Prod** - TVOTAR 1986

The Spokane River 24 MIN
16mm
Color (I)
LC 73-701096
Traces the Spokane River from its source at Lake Coeur D'alene, Idaho, to its confluence with the mighty Columbia River. Points out historic and geographic highlights.
Geography - United States
Dist - NWFLMP **Prod** - PRYOR 1970

Spoken Language Disabilities 30 MIN
U-matic / VHS
Characteristics of Learning Disabilities Series
Color (C A)
Describes disorders of auditory receptive, auditory expressive, and inner language.
Education; Psychology
Dist - FI **Prod** - WCVETV 1976

The Spoken word 22 MIN
16mm
Color (G)
$40.00 rental
Exposes the current rage for self - improvement the success of which is measured by pre - determined ideas of normalcy. Examines and satirizes an average family's fascination with the self - help and how - to media. The actors speak dialogue taken from instructional records.
Fine Arts; Literature and Drama; Psychology
Dist - CANCIN **Prod** - MICHAL 1988

Spokesman for the future - Thomas E. Dewey
16mm
Fox Movietone news series
B&W (G)
$15.00 rental
Features an amusing political propaganda reel produced for the Republican National Committee. Presents part of a series of special Movietone issues, 6 - 11 minutes.
Civics and Political Systems; Literature and Drama
Dist - KITPAR **Prod** - FOXNEW 1944

Spokey the Clown and His Magic Bike 15 MIN
16mm
Color (P I)
LC 73-701351
Illustrates common bicycle safety problems by showing the correct way to ride safely. Tells a story about a clown who loans his talking bicycle to a boy who then learns that the best driver is a safe driver.
Health and Safety
Dist - SCREEI **Prod** - SCREEI 1973

Spoleto - the Festival of Two Worlds 29 MIN
VHS / 16mm
Color (G)
$55.00 rental _ #SPOL - 000
Examines the Spoleto, Italy Festival of Two Worlds, which serves as a showcase for opera, ballet, symphonic music, dance, chamber music, visual arts and theatre. Presents performance excerpts from the 1976 festival.
Fine Arts
Dist - PBS **Prod** - SCETV

Spondylolisthesis 8 MIN
16mm
Color (H C)
Pictures Dr Ben Wiltberger's operation for spinal fusion in spondylolisthesis of the spine.
Health and Safety
Dist - OSUMPD **Prod** - OSUMPD 1961

The Sponge 20 MIN
VHS / U-matic
Color
$335.00 purchase
Health and Safety; Sociology
Dist - ABCLR **Prod** - ABCLR 1983

Sponge Divers 10 MIN
16mm
Land of Opportunity Series
B&W
Tells of the sponge industry of Florida. Emphasizes that the industry symbolizes opportunity for those who engage in it and also presents some hazards.
Business and Economics; Geography - United States
Dist - REP **Prod** - REP 1950

Sponges and Coelenterates - Porous and Sac - Like Animals 11 MIN
U-matic / VHS / 16mm
Major Phyla Series
Color (J H C)
Studies the life cycles of sponges and coelenterates, the simplest multicellular animals. Describes the cell specialization, sexual and asexual reproduction and other characteristics of sponges, jellyfish, sea anemones, corals and hydras.
Science - Natural
Dist - CORF **Prod** - CORF 1962

Spongeware 30 MIN
U-matic
Antiques series
Color
Fine Arts
Dist - PBS **Prod** - NHMNET

The Sponsor Tape
VHS
Color (A)
$34.95 purchase _ #6927
Explores issues of chemical dependency for members of recovery groups.
Health and Safety; Psychology; Sociology
Dist - HAZELB

Spontaneity 17 MIN
U-matic
Chemistry 102 - Chemistry for Engineers - Series
Color (C)
Defines spontaneity explaining that the process may be slow or fast, endothermic or exothermic. Shows that any process which will increase the entropy of the universe will occur spontaneously.
Industrial and Technical Education; Science - Physical
Dist - UILL **Prod** - UILL 1981

Spontaneous Combustion 2 MIN
U-matic / VHS
Color (H C A)
Presents comedy by the Brave New Workshop of the Twin Cities.
Literature and Drama
Dist - UCV **Prod** - BRVNP

Spook in the Pumpkin Patch 15 MIN
U-matic / VHS
Mrs Cabobble's Caboose
(P)
Designed to teach primary grade students basic music concepts. Highlights melody, rhythm, harmony and the different families of musical instruments. Features Mrs. Fran Powell.
Fine Arts
Dist - GPN **Prod** - WDCNTV 1986

Spook Spoofing 22 MIN
16mm
B&W
Tells how Farina uses his 'mumbo - jumbo' charm to protect him in a fight with Toughy. A Little Rascals film.
Fine Arts
Dist - RMIBHF **Prod** - ROACH 1928

Spooks 8 MIN
16mm
B&W
Describes Flip the Frog's adventures in a haunted house populated by a skeleton dancer, skeleton musicians, and a skeleton dog.
Fine Arts
Dist - RMIBHF **Prod** - UNKNWN 1930

Spooks, Cowboys, Gooks and Grunts 50 MIN
16mm / VHS / BETA
Color
LC 77-702526
Shows correspondent Michael Maclear examining, in a two - part presentation, the fate of American soldiers who used terror and brutality to attempt to win the war in Vietnam, only to become victims of their own excesses. Notes the rejection, frustration and alienation of thse men who, both as victims and scapegoats of the war, were unable to adjust to civilian life.
Guidance and Counseling; History - World; Psychology; Sociology
Dist - CTV **Prod** - CTV 1976

Spooks, Cowboys, Gooks and Grunts, Pt 1 25 MIN
16mm / VHS / BETA
Color
LC 77-702526
Shows correspondent Michael Maclear examining, in a two - part presentation, the fate of American soldiers who used terror and brutality to attempt to win the war in Vietnam, only to become victims of their own excesses. Notes the rejection, frustration and alienation of these men who, both as victims and scapegoats of the war, were unable to adjust to civilian life.
History - United States
Dist - CTV **Prod** - CTV 1976

Spooks, Cowboys, Gooks and Grunts, Pt 2 25 MIN
16mm / VHS / BETA
Color
LC 77-702526
Shows correspondent Michael Maclear examining, in a two - part presentation, the fate of American soldiers who used terror and brutality to attempt to win the war in Vietnam, only to become victims of their own excesses. Notes the rejection, frustration and alienation of thse men who, both as victims and scapegoats of the war, were unable to adjust to civilian life.
History - United States
Dist - CTV **Prod** - CTV 1976

Spooky Boo's and Room Noodles 7 MIN
VHS / 16mm / U-matic
Color (K P)
$175, $125, $155 _ #B406
Deals with transforming children's nighttime fears into feelings of security.
Literature and Drama; Psychology
Dist - BARR **Prod** - BARR 1986

Spoon River Anthology 21 MIN
U-matic / VHS / 16mm
Color (J)
LC 76-702114
Illustrates selections from Edgar Lee Master's Spoon River Anthology.
History - United States; Literature and Drama
Dist - PHENIX **Prod** - PHENIX 1976

Spoonful of Lovin' Series no 2
Starting from Scratch - Birth to Three Years 29 MIN
Dist - AITECH

Spoonful of Lovin' Series no 3
Natural Ingredients - Development of the Preschool and School - Age Child 22 MIN
Dist - AITECH

Spoonful of lovin' series
A Good measure of safety 27 MIN
A Gourmet guide to family home day care 25 MIN
A Recipe for Happy Children 26 MIN
Dist - AITECH

Spor I Lyngen - Traces in the heather 25 MIN
16mm
B&W (DANISH)
A Danish language film. Attempts to perpetuate the Jutland Moorland peasant's background by telling the history of the Moors.
Foreign Language; Geography - World; Sociology
Dist - STATNS **Prod** - STATNS 1962

Spore dispersal in the basidiomycetes 15 MIN
VHS
Color (G C)
$85.00 purchase, $14.50 rental _ #23949
Uses microphotography, time - lapse photography and field and lab demonstrations to document methods of spore dispersal in several species of Basiodomycetes. Examines in detail varying degrees of adaptation several species use to aid dispersal in Hymnomycetidae and Gasteromycetidae.
Science - Natural
Dist - PSU **Prod** - IWIF 1984

Sport 30 MIN
VHS
Inside Britain 3 series
Color; PAL; NTSC (G) (BULGARIAN CZECH HUNGARIAN SPANISH POLISH ROMANIAN RUSSIAN SLOVAK UKRAINIAN ENGLISH WITH ARABIC SUBTITLES LITHUANIAN FRENCH GERMAN JAPANESE)
PdS65 purchase
Shows that in Great Britain a unique mix of public and private funding gives many ordinary people the chance to practice their chosen sport. Reveals that schools, private industry, local councils, volunteers and the Sports Council all help to encourage people of all ages to take part.
Geography - World; History - World; Physical Education and Recreation
Dist - CFLVIS **Prod** - TVFLTD 1993

Sport 30 MIN
VHS
How do you do - learning English series
Color (H A)
#317721
Shows how CHIPS, the amiable robot, learns about the game of golf and then discovers the joys of a variety of other sports. Describes how people keep themselves in shape at a fitness club. Part of a series that helps newcomers learn English or improve their ability. Includes viewer's guide with grammar explanations and vocabulary drills, worksheets, and two audio cassettes.
English Language; Physical Education and Recreation
Dist - TVOTAR **Prod** - TVOTAR 1990

Sport and Physical Activity in Society 145 MIN
U-matic
University of the Air Series
Color (J H C A)
$750.00 purchase, $250.00 rental
Investigates the role played by sports and physical activity in past societies and particularly focuses on present cultures and societies. Program contains a series of five cassettes 29 minutes each.
Physical Education and Recreation
Dist - CTV **Prod** - CTV 1977

Sport cycling 40 MIN
VHS
Color (H C A)

$39.95 purchase _ #JCI8202V
Features record - holding cyclist Michael Shermer in a look at sport cycling. Explains and demonstrates the tricks, techniques, and secrets that make for winning cycling.
Health and Safety; Physical Education and Recreation
Dist - CAMV

Sport fishing series

At your door	30 MIN
Big water, big fish	30 MIN
Big water walleye	30 MIN
Changing Lakes	30 MIN
Cold and deep	30 MIN
Fishing the flow	30 MIN
High Tech	30 MIN
Impounded Bass	30 MIN
In the Weeds	30 MIN
Other Fish, Other Ways	30 MIN
Secret Lake	30 MIN
Trout systems	30 MIN
Urban Wilderness	30 MIN

Dist - TVOTAR

Sport Lego Series

Down hill skiing	5 MIN
Figure skating	5 MIN
Grand prix auto racing	5 MIN
Gymnastics	5 MIN
Soccer	5 MIN

Dist - FLMWST

Sport of Orienteering 24 MIN
16mm / U-matic / VHS
Color (J H A)
Swedish youngsters follow a map over rough terrain, using a compass to find their way. Tells how to use a compass.
Physical Education and Recreation; Social Science
Dist - IFB **Prod** - IFB 1948

A Sporting chance 25 MIN
U-matic / VHS / BETA
Positive approaches to fitness series
Color; PAL (G PRO)
PdS50, PdS58 purchase
Aims to counter the sterotyped image of girls and sports. Explores the influences of sex role conditioning in determining the traditionally rigid limits set for girls and physical activities. Part of a series on fitness.
Physical Education and Recreation; Sociology
Dist - EDPAT **Prod** - TASCOR

A Sporting Chance 25 MIN
16mm
Color (J H)
LC 80-701574
Explains why girls should actively participate in sports and physical activities.
Physical Education and Recreation
Dist - TASCOR **Prod** - TASCOR 1980

A Sporting Chance 16 MIN
VHS / U-matic
Color
Reports on a successful health and sport center which offers the disabled a new lease on life. Shows handicapped people skiing, swimming, horseriding, shooting, and even dogsledding.
Physical Education and Recreation
Dist - JOU **Prod** - UPI

Sporting life 5 MIN
U-matic / VHS / 16mm
Professor Balthazar series
Color (K P I J H C A)
$95 film purchase, $15 film rental, $75 U - matic purchase, $65 VHS
Uses animation to illustrate the importance of regular exercise and moderation. Follows the story of Aunt Agnes, her cat Leopold, and their immoderate pursuit of physical fitness.
Physical Education and Recreation
Dist - IFB

A Sporting life 25 MIN
VHS
Dragon's tongue series
Color (C G) (CHINESE)
$195.00 purchase
Looks at sports activities in the People's Republic of China, using Putonghua - the, official language of China based on the dialect of Beijing. Part of a 10 - part series hosted by Prof Colin Mackerras, Co - Director of the Key Center for Asian Languages and Studies at Griffith University.
Foreign Language; Geography - World; Physical Education and Recreation
Dist - LANDMK **Prod** - LANDMK 1990

Sporting news baseball CD - Mac
CD-ROM
Color (G A)
$125.00 purchase _ #1946m
Contains statistics, personalities and details on Major League games, as well as thousands of stats and hundreds of black and white and color VGA images. For Macintosh Plus, SE and II computers. Requires 1MB RAM, floppy disk drive, and an Apple compatible CD - ROM drive.
Physical Education and Recreation
Dist - BEP

Sporting news baseball CD - PC
CD-ROM
(G A)
$125.00 purchase _ #1946p
Contains statistics, personalities and details on Major League games. Includes thousands of stats and hundreds of black and white and color VGA images. For IBM PCs and compatibles. Requires at least 640K RAM, DOS Version 3.1 or greater, one floppy disk drive - a hard drive is recommended, one empty expansion slot, and an IBM compatible CD - ROM drive.
Physical Education and Recreation
Dist - BEP

The Sporting news baseball guide and baseball register
CD-ROM
(G)
$249.00 purchase
Presents the statistics, personalities and the games of Major League Baseball on CD - ROM. Uses direct word - phrase, boolean and wildcard search capabilities. Includes hundreds of black - and - white and color VGA images with image forward and backward scrolling.
Mathematics; Physical Education and Recreation
Dist - QUANTA **Prod** - QUANTA

Sporting science 30 MIN
VHS
Perspectives - industrial design - series
Color; PAL; NTSC (G)
PdS90, PdS105 purchase
Examines the art of perfecting the design of sports equipment.
Physical Education and Recreation
Dist - CFLVIS **Prod** - LONTVS

A Sporting start 11 MIN
16mm
B&W (H C A)
Highlights the activities of the National Institute of Sports in Patiala, India, set up by the government to train coaches from different parts of the country in all types of games and sports.
Physical Education and Recreation
Dist - NEDINF **Prod** - INDIA

Sports 20 MIN
VHS / U-matic
Contract Series
Color (J H)
English Language
Dist - AITECH **Prod** - KYTV 1977

Sports 15 MIN
U-matic / VHS
Watch your language series
Color (J H)
$125.00 purchase
Sketches the use of specialized vocabulary in sports description.
English Language; Physical Education and Recreation; Social Science
Dist - AITECH **Prod** - KYTV 1984

Sports 30 MIN
U-matic / VHS
Say it with sign series; Pt 16
Color (H C A) (AMERICAN SIGN)
Presents Lawrence Solow and Sharon Neumann Solow introducing American Sign Language used by the hearing - impaired. Emphasizes signs that have to do with sports.
Education; Physical Education and Recreation
Dist - FI **Prod** - KNBCTV 1982

Sports - 1897 - 1969
VHS
Hearst News library series
Color (G)
$29.95 purchase _ #TK042
Witnesses homeruns, touchdowns, knockouts and other history making events in sports in the period 1897 - 1969. Part of a series excerpted from 350 newsreels from the Hearst News Library.
History - United States; History - World; Physical Education and Recreation
Dist - SIV

Sports action and health 22 MIN
U-matic / VHS / 16mm
Color (J) (ARABIC)
LC 77-701286
Uses footage of sports stars and sports action to discuss participation in sports and the concept of fitness as a total lifestyle, including good nutrition, exercise, sleep and avoidance of cigarettes, alcohol and drugs. Gives advice on warming up and down, doing conditioning exercises and taking care of injuries.
Health and Safety; Physical Education and Recreation; Social Science
Dist - AIMS **Prod** - SIDRIS 1976

Sports and Business 29 MIN
16mm
We're Number One Series
Color
LC 79-701399
States that Americans are preoccupied with being number one. Shows that a sense of self - worth does not come from being number one and suggests that Christianity offers an alternative perception regarding self - worth.
Psychology; Religion and Philosophy
Dist - AMERLC **Prod** - AMERLC 1978

Sports and games 30 MIN
VHS
Tell me why video series
Color (P I)
$19.95 purchase _ #51438
Answers approximately 50 questions about sports and games. Uses colorful graphics and attention - grabbing film footage. Part of a series.
Physical Education and Recreation
Dist - KNOWUN

Sports and War 60 MIN
U-matic
Challenge Series
Color (PRO)
Shows a discussion by seven men on the role of sports in men's lives.
Civics and Political Systems; Physical Education and Recreation; Psychology
Dist - TVOTAR **Prod** - TVOTAR 1985

Sports - Attendants and Support Service 15 MIN
VHS / 16mm
(H C A)
$24.95 purchase _ #CS262
Describes the skills necessary to be a sports attendant or support staff. Features interviews with people employed in this field.
Guidance and Counseling
Dist - RMIBHF **Prod** - RMIBHF

Sports Bloopers II 23 MIN
16mm
Color
Presents a variety of sports - oriented antics and pratfalls.
Literature and Drama; Physical Education and Recreation
Dist - MTP **Prod** - COORS

Sports capers 40 MIN
VHS
Color (J H R)
$39.95 purchase, $10.00 rental _ #35 - 85008 - 8936
Interviews pro athletes from baseball, football, basketball and other sports on their Christian faith. Includes sports action and 'blooper' sports footage. Produced by Bridgestone.
Physical Education and Recreation; Religion and Philosophy
Dist - APH

Sports Car Racing 3 MIN
16mm
Of all Things Series
Color (P I)
Discusses sports car racing.
Physical Education and Recreation
Dist - AVED **Prod** - BAILYL

The Sports Cartoon 15 MIN
Videoreel / VT2
Charlie's Pad Series
Color
Fine Arts
Dist - PBS **Prod** - WSIU

Sports clinic basketball 75 MIN
VHS
Color (G)
$19.95 purchase
Features Bill Walton, Walt Hazzard, and Greg Lee, who teach the basics of basketball.
Physical Education and Recreation
Dist - PBS **Prod** - WNETTV

Sports clinic football 75 MIN
VHS
Color (G)
$19.95 purchase
Features coach George Allen and a group of all - pro NFL players, who teach the basics of football. Focuses on line play, receiving, and quarterbacking.
Physical Education and Recreation
Dist - PBS **Prod** - WNETTV

Sports clinic soccer 75 MIN
VHS
Color (G)

$19.95 purchase
Features Hubert Vogelsinger and his staff of experts as they teach the basics of soccer.
Physical Education and Recreation
Dist - PBS **Prod** - WNETTV

Sports Film Olympic Promotion Series
Single Handed Sailing 15 MIN
Dist - SPORTF

Sports Fishing 3 MIN
16mm
Of all Things Series
Color (P I)
Discusses sports fishing.
Physical Education and Recreation
Dist - AVED **Prod** - BAILYL

Sports for Elementary Series
Playing Basketball 13 MIN
Playing Softball 11 MIN
Playing Touch Football 12 MIN
Dist - AIMS

Sports for elementary - Spanish series
Playing basketball 13 MIN
Playing softball 11 MIN
Playing touch football 12 MIN
Dist - AIMS

Sports for Life 22 MIN
U-matic / VHS / 16mm
Color (J)
LC 76-702580
Shows how different people in different walks of life are active in sports as a way to look and feel better in their daily lives.
Guidance and Counseling; Health and Safety; Physical Education and Recreation
Dist - BARR **Prod** - BARR 1976

Sports galaxy 40 MIN
VHS
Color (G R)
$29.95 purchase, $10.00 rental _ #35 - 85009 - 8936
Presents film footage of skydiving, ballooning, ski flying and space flight. Interviews Christians involved in these activities on their faith. Produced by Bridgestone.
Physical Education and Recreation; Religion and Philosophy
Dist - APH

Sports Illustrated - get the feeling - power 60 MIN
VHS
Color (G)
$19.95 purchase _ #HBO080V
Looks at the concept of physical power in sports - as faced by such athletes as sumo wrestlers, boxers, basketball players, and more. Features live action footage and interviews with athletes.
Physical Education and Recreation; Science - Natural
Dist - CAMV **Prod** - CAMV 1987

Sports Illustrated - get the feeling - speed 60 MIN
VHS
Color (G)
$19.95 purchase _ #HBO027V
Looks at the excitement and danger that speed offers in sports - as faced by such athletes as a hockey goalie, a race car driver, a halfback, and more. Features live action footage and interviews with Shirley Muldowney, Angel Cordero Jr, Pat Riley, and others.
Physical Education and Recreation; Science - Natural
Dist - CAMV **Prod** - CAMV 1987

Sports Illustrated - get the feeling - winning 60 MIN
VHS
Color (G)
$19.95 purchase _ #HBO132V
Looks at the concept of winning in sports. Features live action footage and interviews with athletes - the Columbia University football team seeking to snap a record - setting losing streak, Olympic wrestler Jeff Blatnick as he tries to overcome life - threatening disease, and the NCAA basketball Final Four of 1988.
Physical Education and Recreation; Science - Natural
Dist - CAMV **Prod** - CAMV 1987

Sports in America series
The Black Athlete 58 MIN
Children and sports 26 MIN
Children in sports 56 MIN
Women in Sports 26 MIN
Dist - PFP

Sports influence on dance performance 30 MIN
VHS / U-matic
Athleticism in dance series
Color
Fine Arts; Physical Education and Recreation
Dist - ARCVID **Prod** - ARCVID

Sports injuries 29 MIN
U-matic / VHS
Here's to your health series
Color
Explains how to exercise and get into shape without being injured. Includes an on - location visit to the San Francisco 49ers.
Health and Safety; Physical Education and Recreation
Dist - PBS **Prod** - KERA

Sports Injuries and the Liability of the Coach 21 MIN
U-matic / VHS
Sports Medicine Series
Color (C A)
$69.00 purchase _ #1470
Gives examples of liability situations and discusses how coaches can avoid negligence suits through an injury control program that addresses conditioning, skill development, performance, and supervision.
Civics and Political Systems; Health and Safety; Physical Education and Recreation
Dist - EBEC

Sports injuries - care and prevention 33 MIN
VHS
Color (J)
$39.95 purchase _ #V2209 - 10
Conveys information from Dr Russell Gives' book on sport injuries. Covers common injuries and prevention. Gives detailed instructions on how to examine an injury. Treatment and rehabilitation are also covered.
Health and Safety; Physical Education and Recreation
Dist - SCHSCI

Sports injuries today 8 MIN
U-matic / VHS
Sports medicine for coaches series
Color
Prepares the coach to recognize common sports injuries and understand the mechanism of injury. Emphasizes immediate on - site care that can be given by the coach and reviews a safe first aid technique.
Health and Safety; Physical Education and Recreation
Dist - UWASH **Prod** - UWASH

Sports legends series
Bob Petit 20 MIN
Eddie Arcaro 20 MIN
Elgin Baylor 20 MIN
Frank Gifford 20 MIN
Gale Sayers 20 MIN
Hugh Mac Elhenny 20 MIN
Jesse Owens 20 MIN
Joe Di Maggio - the Yankee Clipper 20 MIN
Lenny Moore 20 MIN
Mickey Mantle 20 MIN
Paul Hornung 20 MIN
Red Auerbach 20 MIN
Roger Ward 20 MIN
Roy Campanella 20 MIN
Sam Snead 20 MIN
Dist - COUNFI

Sports Lego Series
International Hockey 5 MIN
Weightlifting 5 MIN
Dist - FLMWST

Sports medicine 12 MIN
16mm
Coaching development programme series; 6
Color
LC 76-701058
Discusses medicines commonly used in sports.
Health and Safety; Physical Education and Recreation
Dist - SARBOO **Prod** - SARBOO 1974

Sports medicine 30 MIN
VHS
Teen health video series
Color (J H A T)
$39.95 purchase _ #LVPE6642V-P
Offers teenagers and health educators information about sports medicine. Includes advice from experts and personal testimonies from teens themselves. Does not make judgements on moral issues, but does present options available. One of a series of twelve videos about teen health issues. Available individually or as a set.
Health and Safety; Physical Education and Recreation; Sociology
Dist - CAMV

Sports medicine 30 MIN
U-matic / VHS
Lifelines series
Color
Discusses sports medicine.
Health and Safety; Physical Education and Recreation
Dist - MDCPB **Prod** - UGATV

Sports Medicine 28 MIN
16mm
A Man and His Sport Series
Color (H C A)
LC 73-709319
Illustrates the use of scientific training methods to improve performances in sports. Focuses on weight training, interval training, fitness testing and treatment of injuries.
Physical Education and Recreation
Dist - AUIS **Prod** - ANAIB 1970

Sports Medicine for Coaches Series
The First step - handling the life threatening emergency 7 MIN
Fueling the Body for Sport 9 MIN
Introduction to the sports medicine for coaches series 6 MIN
The New Woman Athlete 9 MIN
Overuse Injuries - Too Much, Too Fast, Too Soon 10 MIN
Pathway to a Winning Season 8 MIN
Sports injuries today 8 MIN
Dist - UWASH

Sports Medicine in the 80's Series
Care and Transportation of the Seriously Injured 28 MIN
Conditions of the Foot, Ankle and Lower Leg, Part I and II 58 MIN
Conditions of the Hand and Wrist 29 MIN
Conditions of the Knee, Part I and II 58 MIN
Conditions of the Shoulder 29 MIN
CPR Cardiopulmonary Resuscitation 28 MIN
Custom padding 29 MIN
The Female athlete 29 MIN
Injury Recognition 28 MIN
Injury Treatment 30 MIN
Introduction to Sports Medicine and Training Room 28 MIN
Minor Sport Injuries made Major 28 MIN
Physical Conditioning for Prevention of Athletic Injuries 29 MIN
Preventative and Protective Taping and Wrapping 29 MIN
Rehabilitation Procedures, Part I and II 58 MIN
Scientific Bases for Conditioning and Training 29 MIN
The Unconscious Athlete - Conditions of the Head, Neck and Spine 30 MIN
Dist - CEPRO

Sports Medicine Series
Care and Prevention of Heat Injury 22 MIN
Conditioning the Athlete to Prevent Sports Injuries 26 MIN
Drug Problems in Sports 24 MIN
Emergency treatment of acute knee injuries 28 MIN
Introduction to Sports Medicine 20 MIN
Minimal Expectations for Health Supervision of Sports 19 MIN
Overuse Syndromes of the Lower Extremity 27 MIN
Prevention and Field Management of Head and Neck Injuries 23 MIN
Prevention and Treatment of Foot Injuries 25 MIN
Psychology of Sports 25 MIN
Sports Injuries and the Liability of the Coach 21 MIN
Dist - EBEC

Sports medicine series
Field evaluation and care of the injured athlete
Injuries to Runners
Physical Examination of the Injured Athlete
Pre - participation physical examination of the athlete
Dist - VTRI

Sports nutrition - facts and fallacies
VHS
To your health series
Color (G)
$29.95 purchase _ #IV - 014
Introduces nutrition to the beginning athlete.
Health and Safety; Physical Education and Recreation
Dist - INCRSE **Prod** - INCRSE

Sports nutrition for the high school and college athlete 120 MIN
VHS
Color (H C G)
$69.95 purchase _ #ODU100V
Records a videoconference on a variety of sports nutrition topics held at Old Dominion University. Features four nutrition experts, David Costill, Nancy Clark, Mel Williams and Jackie Berning, who share their findings on carbohydrates and fluids, weight control techniques,

eating disorders, nutritional aids to enhance performance, steroid use. Clark Kellogg moderates.
Health and Safety; Physical Education and Recreation; Social Science
Dist - CAMV

Sports odyssey 40 MIN
VHS
Color (J H R)
$39.95 purchase, $10.00 rental _ #35 - 85010 - 8936
Uses the action contained in sports film footage as an analogy to the challenges Christians face in everyday life. Produced by Bridgestone.
Physical Education and Recreation; Religion and Philosophy
Dist - APH

Sports Odyssey 25 MIN
U-matic / VHS / 16mm
Color
Offers an action - packed sports spectacular featuring ski jumping, surfing, hang gliding, water skiing, skateboarding, and comedy.
Physical Education and Recreation
Dist - MCFI **Prod** - MCFI

Sports of Old Hawaii 11 MIN
16mm
Color (J H C)
Recreates the most popular sports of the early days in Hawaii by the students at Kamehameha Schools.
Geography - United States; History - United States; Physical Education and Recreation; Sociology
Dist - CINEPC **Prod** - TAHARA 1985

Sports Omnibus 30 MIN
16mm
B&W
Shows Globetrotters, rodeo, roller derby, Sam Snead and Rams - Bears.
Physical Education and Recreation
Dist - SFI **Prod** - SFI

Sports 1 2 3 Individual Sports Series
The Wrestling Abeline Paradox 21 MIN
Dist - MECC

Sports pages - 65
VHS
Reading rainbow series
Color; CC (K P)
$39.95 purchase
Watches LeVar sweat it out on the basketball court, in the weight room and on a bicycle built for three during a story by Arnold Adoff, illustrated by Steve Kuzma. Shares LeVar's enthusiasm for sports when he takes viewers from sport to sport - soccer, basketball, ice skating, swimming and gymnastics. Meets a variety of young athletes who express the joy of participating in sports. Part of a series offering a multicultural approach to generating reading enthusiasm with cross - curricular applications, hosted by LeVar Burton.
English Language; Literature and Drama; Physical Education and Recreation
Dist - GPN **Prod** - LNMDP

The Sports Photography of Robert Riger
VHS / U-matic
Color
Explores the work of sports photographer and filmmaker Robert Riger. Presents footage from his films, an interview and insights into how he has fulfilled his goals.
Industrial and Technical Education; Physical Education and Recreation
Dist - GA **Prod** - SILVRP

Sports - Power Basics Series
Power Basics of Baseball
Dist - RMIBHF

Sports - Professional Sports
VHS
Video Career Series
$29.95 purchase _ #MD214V
Shows students going 'on the job' to learn the variety of skills required for this occupation and the special training or educational requirements. Discusses various hiring procedures and what is involved in joining a professional association or union.
Education; Guidance and Counseling
Dist - CAREER **Prod** - CAREER

Sports Profile 29 MIN
U-matic / VHS / 16mm
Were You There Series
Color (I)
LC 83-706601
Focuses on Artie Wilson, a celebrity in the Negro Baseball League, as he tours his old Birmingham neighborhood and reminisces. Reenactments highlight his childhood and career. Looks at the life and career of Alice Coachman, a black Olympic Gold Medal high jumper and sprinter.
History - United States; Physical Education and Recreation
Dist - BCNFL **Prod** - NGUZO 1982

Sports Psychology 60 MIN
VHS
(H C A)
$89.95 purchase _ #WE100V
Presents a guide to sports success based on sports psychology. Discusses ways of improving performance by commitment, communication, and attitude. Explains various concentration techniques and focusing skills for added motivation. Offers tips on avoiding burnout and handling stress. In 2 parts.
Physical Education and Recreation; Psychology
Dist - CAMV **Prod** - CAMV

Sports Round - Up 30 MIN
16mm
B&W
Presents the best of events in four showings.
Physical Education and Recreation
Dist - SFI **Prod** - SFI

Sports safety 29 MIN
VHS
Sports science series
Color; PAL (T J H)
PdS29.50 purchase
Presents causes of sports injuries and avoidance through proper warm - up and cool - down; maintenance of proper fitness level; and more. Features part of a seven - part series on the science behind sports and physical activity, suitable for health and physical education courses, coaching and fitness programs.
Physical Education and Recreation
Dist - EMFVL

Sports Safety 22 MIN
16mm / U-matic / VHS
Color (I J H)
Points out that some sports accidents involving a youngster may cause serious problems throughout his or her life. Features famous sports figures who explain what can be done to prevent injuries in such sports as baseball, basketball, football and soccer.
Physical Education and Recreation
Dist - HANDEL **Prod** - HANDEL 1983

Sports Safety - 6 8 TO 37 MIN
VHS
Sports Science Series
Color (H)
$75.00 purchase
Presents the science behind sports and physical activity, including training, acquiring new motor skills and preventing injuries. Alternates scenes of athletes in practice and competition with views of anatomical models, commentary and graphics that explain the science and physiology behind movements. Program 6 shows how to prevent sports injuries through proper warm up and cool down, maintenance of proper fitness level, correct technique and protective equipment. Discusses head, neck and back injuries, and hypothermia. Shows rehabilitation procedures.
Health and Safety; Physical Education and Recreation; Science - Natural
Dist - AITECH

Sports Scholarships, Pt I - Advantages 25 MIN
VHS / U-matic
Color (J H C A)
Interviews Joe Paterno, athletic director at Penn State University, and Eric Zemper, research coordinator at the National Collegiate Athletic Association, on the advantages of sports scholarships.
Physical Education and Recreation; Psychology; Sociology
Dist - GERBER **Prod** - SIRS

Sports Scholarships, Pt II - Disadvantages 25 MIN
VHS / U-matic
Color (J H C A)
Continues discussions with Joe Paterno and Eric Zemper on sports scholarships, this time touching on the disadvantages.
Physical Education and Recreation; Psychology; Sociology
Dist - GERBER **Prod** - SIRS

Sports Science Series
Biomechanics - 2 8 TO 37 MIN
Exercise Physiology - 3 8 TO 37 MIN
Functional Anatomy - 1 8 TO 37 MIN
Motor Skill Acquisition - 5 8 TO 37 MIN
Preparing for Competition - 7 8 TO 37 MIN
Principles of Training - 4 8 TO 37 MIN
Sports Safety - 6 8 TO 37 MIN
Dist - AITECH

Sports science series
Biomechanics 37 MIN
Exercise physiology 40 MIN
Functional anatomy 31 MIN
Motor skill acquisition 19 MIN
Preparing for competition 14 MIN
Principles of training 27 MIN
Sports safety 29 MIN
Dist - EMFVL

Sports Services 15 MIN
VHS / U-matic / BETA
Career Success Series
(H C A)
$29.95 _ #MX262
Portrays occupations in sports services by reviewing required abilities and interviewing people employed in this field. Tells of the anxieties and rewards involved in pursuing a career as a sports serviceman.
Education; Guidance and Counseling; Physical Education and Recreation
Dist - CAMV **Prod** - CAMV

Sports Show 24 MIN
U-matic / VHS
Color
Features a high school tennis player whose goal is to win Wimbledon. Shows weight control programs for young people, handicapped horseback riding, how roller skates are made and activities of the Argonauts scuba diving club.
Physical Education and Recreation; Sociology
Dist - WCCOTV **Prod** - WCCOTV 1982

Sports, Society, and Self 15 MIN
U-matic / VHS
Across Cultures Series
Color (I)
Reveals that games are played and watched in every culture. Shows that the Tarahumara are excellent endurance runners, that physical training is important to the Japanese and that Africa's Baoule people enjoy a fast - paced game of mental skill called Aweie.
Geography - World; Physical Education and Recreation; Social Science; Sociology
Dist - AITECH **Prod** - POSIMP 1983

Sports - Sports - Attendants and Support Service
VHS
Video Career Series
$29.95 purchase _ #MD262V
Shows students going 'on the job' to learn the variety of skills required for this occupation and the special training or educational requirements. Discusses various hiring procedures and what is involved in joining a professional association or union.
Education; Guidance and Counseling
Dist - CAREER **Prod** - CAREER

A Sports Suite 8 MIN
16mm / U-matic / VHS
Color (I)
LC 77-701115
Shows the excitement of participation in sports activities. Presents four vignettes, accompanied by classical music, in which youthful participants demonstrate the exuberance and joy they find in physical education and team sports, including gymnastics, volleyball, swimming and soccer.
Fine Arts; Physical Education and Recreation
Dist - PFP **Prod** - LIBERP 1977

Sports support services 15 MIN
VHS
Career success series
Color (H C A)
$29.95 purchase _ #MX262
Presents an introduction to sports support service careers. Covers the necessary skills, and interviews people in these careers on the rewards and stresses involved.
Education; Physical Education and Recreation
Dist - CAMV

Sports teaching video - aerobics 30 MIN
VHS
Color (I J H G)
$12.95 purchase _ #K45258
Teaches proper running to avoid injuries. Explains how to develop a practical personal fitness program.
Physical Education and Recreation
Dist - HTHED **Prod** - HTHED

Sports Technology 26 MIN
U-matic / VHS
Color (C)
$249.00, $149.00 purchase _ #AD - 1720
Visits sports technology centers. Interviews researchers working to advance sports science. Talks with athletes who are enjoying the benefits of biomechanics - the science of human motion - and advances in sports gear. Covers technical improvements in tennis rackets, using computers to lure fish, and shoes that record time, mileage and calories burned.
Health and Safety; Physical Education and Recreation; Science - Natural
Dist - FOTH **Prod** - FOTH

The Sports that Set the Styles 28 MIN
16mm

Color
Examines the history of women in sports. Shows how the nature of different sports influenced what the women players wore and how the clothes worn on the golf course, tennis court and beach eventually found their way into the home and into society.
Physical Education and Recreation; Sociology
Dist - MTP **Prod** - SEARS

Sports Thrills
16mm
B&W
Shows highlights from hockey, basketball, boxing and track.
Physical Education and Recreation
Dist - SFI **Prod** - SFI

Sports - What's the Score 29 MIN
U-matic
Woman Series
Color
Discusses the value and harm of sports in American life. Explores women's attitudes toward sports.
Physical Education and Recreation
Dist - PBS **Prod** - WNEDTV

Sports Words - 4 15 MIN
VHS
Wordscape Series
Color; Captioned (I)
$125.00 purchase
Uses the word 'cell' approach to teach vocabulary, opening each program - sixteen 15 - minute programs - with several word cells familiar to fourth graders and using these 'cells' to form compound words, birdhouse, girlfriend. Employs animated graphics to dramatize how compounds are 'built' of cells that form a seemingly endless series of new words and to teach that understanding cell words can help to understand the new words composed of them. Program 4 highlights words used in sports and to describe body parts, conditions and actions.
English Language; Psychology
Dist - AITECH **Prod** - OETVA 1990

Sports Year 1969 25 MIN
16mm
Color
LC 70-712878
Pinpoints key sports happenings in 1969, such as the Triple Crown races, major events in baseball, football, track, boxing and tennis and other highlights in competitive sports. Narrated by Red Barber.
Physical Education and Recreation
Dist - SFI **Prod** - UPITN 1971

Sports Year 1970 25 MIN
16mm
Color
LC 76-712877
Highlights the key sports happenings of 1970, including events in football, baseball, boxing, golf and other sports. Narrated by Lindsay Nelson.
Physical Education and Recreation
Dist - SFI **Prod** - UPITN 1971

Sports Year '61 30 MIN
16mm
B&W
Presents highlights from the Kentucky Derby, World Series, NFL, NHL, track and boxing.
Physical Education and Recreation
Dist - SFI **Prod** - SFI

Sportsmanlike Driving Series no 10
Traffic Law Observance and Enforcement 28 MIN
Dist - GPN

Sportsmanlike Driving Series no 18
Night Driving and Seeing 28 MIN
Dist - GPN

Sportsmanlike Driving Series no 19
Reaction, Braking and Stopping Distances 28 MIN
Dist - GPN

Sportsmanlike Driving Series no 1
A Time to Live 28 MIN
Dist - GPN

Sportsmanlike Driving Series no 24
Skids and Skidding 28 MIN
Dist - GPN

Sportsmanlike Driving Series no 26
Traffic Safety, Vehicle Design and Equipment 28 MIN
Dist - GPN

Sportsmanlike Driving Series no 7
Traffic Laws made by Nature 28 MIN
Dist - GPN

Sportsmanlike Driving Series no 8
Traffic Laws made by Man 28 MIN
Dist - GPN

Sportsmanlike Driving Series no 9
Motor Vehicle Laws 28 MIN
Dist - GPN

Sportsmanlike driving series refresher course
Driving in cities and towns 30 MIN
Driving in the country 30 MIN
Driving on freeways 30 MIN
Driving under adverse conditions 30 MIN
Taking Care of Your Car 30 MIN
Dist - GPN

Sportsmanlike Driving Series
Attitude and behavior of a good driver 28 MIN
Basic maneuvers, Pt 1 - turning and backing 30 MIN
Basic maneuvers, Pt 2 - hill starts and parking 30 MIN
Buying and insuring your car 30 MIN
Driver's permit or operator's license 30 MIN
Driving as Your Job 30 MIN
Fundamental driving techniques, pt 1 - automatic transmission 30 MIN
Fundamental Driving Techniques, Pt 2 - Standard Transmission 30 MIN
Getting ready to drive 30 MIN
How the Automobile Runs 30 MIN
Map Reading and Trip Planning 30 MIN
Dist - GPN

Sportsman's Video Collection Series
Bigmouth 50 MIN
Dist - CBSC

Sportsmans workshop video library series
Archery tactics for deer 30 MIN
Bass tactics that work 30 MIN
Decoys and duck calls - two secrets for success 45 MIN
How to Catch Trout 30 MIN
How to hunt whitetail deer 30 MIN
How to hunt wild turkey 30 MIN
How to Troll for Fish 30 MIN
North American Big Game 30 MIN
Secrets for Catching Walleye 30 MIN
Dist - WRBPRO

Sportswear - serge it - sew it 60 MIN
VHS
Serger video series
Color (H C G)
$24.95 purchase _ #NN330V
Demonstrates sewing swim and exercise wear. Shows how to work with 4 - way stretch fabric and swimwear elastics. Looks at serging and sewing activewear, using the latest knit techiques and making fashionable knit tops, shorts and stirrup pants. One of three parts on serging.
Home Economics
Dist - CAMV

The Sportswear Special 29 MIN
Videoreel / VT2
Designing Women Series
Color
Home Economics
Dist - PBS **Prod** - WKYCTV

Sportsworld Series
Grow High on Love 23 MIN
Dist - NBCTV

Spot - Flecki series
The Adventures of Spot 30 MIN
Spot's first video 30 MIN
Spot's first video and The Adventures of Spot 60 MIN
Dist - GPC

Spot Prevention - Measles 14 MIN
U-matic
Color (K P I)
Presents humorous illustrations of the chase and capture of the measles 'germ' and his 'conversion' to protective vaccine. Uses animation for the purpose of promoting immunization against measles in children.
Health and Safety; Home Economics
Dist - USNAC **Prod** - USNAC 1972

Spot Welder Demonstration 21 MIN
BETA / VHS
Color (IND)
Explains the basic operating procedure for a rocker arm foot operated floor model spot welder.
Industrial and Technical Education; Psychology
Dist - RMIBHF **Prod** - RMIBHF

Spot welding 20 MIN
16mm
Aircraft work series; Assembling and riveting; No 9
B&W
LC FIE52-280
Shows how to spot weld parts of an access cover, set up the machine, remove and install electrodes, set pressure, current and time controls, test the setup and clean the electrode tips.
Industrial and Technical Education
Dist - USNAC **Prod** - USOE 1945

Spotlight on Deaf Artists 33 MIN
U-matic / VHS
Color (A)
Narrates a tour of the exhibit of art works by deaf artists on display at Gallaudet College. Presents such artists as Goya, Washburn, Tilden, et al. Signed.
Fine Arts; Guidance and Counseling; Psychology
Dist - GALCO **Prod** - GALCO 1981

Spotlight on Negri Sembilan 16 MIN
16mm
B&W
Reviews the work done in rural development in Negri Sembilan, Malaysia, showing the opening of new land for settlement and cultivation of rubber, coconut, oil palms and other crops and some of the projects for the future.
Agriculture; Business and Economics; Geography - World; Sociology
Dist - PMFMUN **Prod** - FILEM 1961

Spotlight on Pahang 18 MIN
16mm
B&W
Discusses Pahang, Malaysia and its development. Shows how problems peculiar to this vast, largely unexplored state have been tackled to bring new life and hope to the fishermen and farmers who make up the bulk of its population.
Business and Economics; Geography - World
Dist - PMFMUN **Prod** - FILEM 1961

Spotlight on war 91 MIN
VHS
March of time - trouble abroad series
B&W (G)
$24.95 purchase _ #S02177
Presents newsreel excerpts covering events in the US and abroad from June through September of 1938. Covers events including troubles in Czechoslovakia, Gibraltar and Britain, and profiles Americans in a variety of professions. Part four of a six - part series.
History - United States; History - World
Dist - UILL

Spot's first video 30 MIN
VHS
Spot - Flecki series
Color (P I J) (FRENCH SPANISH GERMAN)
$29.95 purchase _ #WF1443, #WS1443, #WG1443
Presents animated adventures of Spot using basic vocabulary and situations familiar to younger students. Teaches beginning language students of French, Spanish or German. The character is called Flecki in the German - language version.
Foreign Language; Literature and Drama
Dist - GPC

Spot's first video and The Adventures of Spot 60 MIN
VHS
Spot - Flecki series
Color (P I J) (FRENCH SPANISH GERMAN)
$55.00 purchase _ #WF1445, #WS1445, #WG1445
Presents a set of two videos showing the animated adventures of Spot. Uses basic vocabulary and situations familiar to younger students. Teaches beginning language students of French, Spanish or German. The character is called Flecki in the German - language version.
Foreign Language; Literature and Drama
Dist - GPC

Spotting common check fraud 18 MIN
VHS
Color (IND PRO)
$525.00 purchase, $225.00 rental _ #BTC10
Provides guidelines for dealing with check fraud, including the goals of the con artist and signs of counterfeiting, forgery and check alterations. Includes a leader's guide. Produced by Banctraining.
Business and Economics
Dist - EXTR

Spotty - Story of a Fawn 11 MIN
U-matic / VHS / 16mm
Color (P I)
$270, $190 purchase _ #309
Talks about the life of a wild fawn. Filmed in the North Woods.
Science - Natural
Dist - CORF

Spouse Abuse - Domestic Conflict Containment Program 87 MIN
VHS
Color (H)
$250.00 purchase, $125.00 rental
Presents a two - part program to re - educate abusive couples. Discusses accepting responsibility for violent behavior, understanding the sequence of violence, anger control, stress management, negotiating conflicts and jealousy and sex role stereotyping.
Guidance and Counseling; Health and Safety; Psychology; Sociology
Dist - SCETV **Prod** - SCETV 1985

Spouse Abuse - who is the Victim?
U-matic / VHS
Color
Combines interviews with professionals and abusing and abused spouses, who are played by actors to highlight essential treatment issues. Features a man who talks candidly about repeating the pattern of abuse set in his parents' marriage.
Psychology; Sociology
Dist - BRUMAZ **Prod** - MDMH

SPR debriefing videotape 30 MIN
VHS / BETA / U-matic
Color (C G PRO)
$195.00 purchase _ #DI 39156
Presents Dr J Clayton Lafferty and Dr Lorraine Colletti - Lafferty discussing the 19 domains of the SPR - Stress Processing Report, their interrelationships and their health implications.
Business and Economics; Guidance and Counseling; Health and Safety; Psychology
Dist - HUMSYN **Prod** - HUMSYN

Spray 9 MIN
16mm
Color (G)
$15.00 purchase
Features an abstract study of color and sound made by painting film.
Fine Arts
Dist - CANCIN **Prod** - STREEM 1986

Spray it on 29 MIN
U-matic
Artist at Work Series
Color
Demonstrates the use of a spray gun to make pictures.
Fine Arts
Dist - UMITV **Prod** - UMITV 1973

Spray paint 15 MIN
VHS
Color (H G)
$150.00 purchase, $30.00 rental
Profiles San Francisco painter and muralist Scott Williams who uses stencils and Krylon to appropriate images from movies, TV, magazines, advertising and other pop culture sources. Features a film directed by Nick Gorski.
Fine Arts
Dist - CNEMAG

Spray transfer - mild steel module
VHS
Gas metal arc welding - plate - series
$69.95 purchase _ #MJ105753V
Provides instruction on welding with spray transfer on mild steel with safe, effective techniques.
Education; Industrial and Technical Education
Dist - CAREER **Prod** - CAREER

Spraying Equipment and Procedures, Pt 1 - Residual Spraying 9 MIN
16mm
Community Fly Control Series
Color (FRENCH)
LC FIE53-199
Explains the meaning of residual spraying for fly control, the necessity for this type of spraying, and the methods of using hand and power spraying equipment.
Health and Safety
Dist - USNAC **Prod** - USPHS 1951

Spread of tumors 10 MIN
VHS
Color (G)
$89.95 purchase _ #UW3423
Illustrates currently recognized modes of malignant growth and metastasis.
Health and Safety
Dist - FOTH

Spread the word - teens talk to teens about AIDS 28 MIN
VHS
Color (J H C)
$169.00 purchase _ #CG - 930 - VS
Presents information, stories, attitudes and feelings shared by teens whose lives have been impacted by AIDS. Presents dramatic pieces by teens in Iowa, California and Washington, DC, and takes viewers on the journey of six deaf teens who made a quilt panel to commemorate the life of their teacher. Documents the last interview by Ryan White and chronicles the stories of two young people who contracted AIDS as teens.
Health and Safety
Dist - HRMC **Prod** - HRMC

Spreading 30 MIN
VHS / U-matic
Commodities - the Professional Trader Series
Color (C A)
Presents Sherman Levine and trader John Carter explaining and discussing the procedures and characteristics of spread trading.
Business and Economics
Dist - VIPUB **Prod** - VIPUB

Spreading Oceans 24 MIN
U-matic / VHS / 16mm
Color (C A)
Explores continental drift, the opening of oceans and the movement of tectonic plates. Uses animation to show undersea structures such as transformed faults and plate boundaries as well as the dynamics of ocean - ocean and continent - continent collisions.
Science - Physical
Dist - MEDIAG **Prod** - BBCTV 1981

Spreading - Surface Films of Insoluble Monolayers 51 MIN
VHS / U-matic
Colloid and Surface Chemistry - Surface Chemistry Series
B&W (PRO)
Science - Physical
Dist - MIOT **Prod** - MIOT

Spreading, Surface Films of Insoluble Monolayers 51 MIN
VHS / U-matic
Colloid and Surface Chemistry - Surface Chemistry Series
Color
Science; Science - Physical
Dist - KALMIA **Prod** - KALMIA

Spreading the good news - Tape 6 30 MIN
VHS
Acts of the Apostles series
Color (I J H C G A R)
$29.95 purchase, $10.00 rental _ #35 - 8367 - 1502
Presents stories of the early Christian church as described in the New Testament book of Acts. Covers the events of James' martyrdom, the scattering of the apostles, and how Jewish and Gentile Christians began to coexist.
Literature and Drama; Religion and Philosophy
Dist - APH **Prod** - BOSCO

Spreadsheet Models for Technical Managers 360 MIN
U-matic / VHS
(A PRO)
$2,160.00 PURCHASE
Show how to use spreadsheet programs to make business tasks more efficient. Covers budgets, time estimates and cash flow estimates.
Computer Science
Dist - VIDEOT **Prod** - VIDEOT 1988

Spreadsheet series

Excel 1.5 introduction	56 MIN
Lotus 2.2 and 3.0 level II	65 MIN
Lotus 2.2 and 3.0 level III	60 MIN
Lotus Level II	74 MIN
Lotus Level III	51 MIN
Lotus 1 - 2 - 3 2.2 and 3.0 introduction	47 MIN
Lotus 1 - 2 - 3 introduction	43 MIN
PFS - database and spreadsheet level II	50 MIN
PFS - putting it all together level III	40 MIN

Dist - CAMV

Spreadsheets 30 MIN
VHS
Computing for the less terrified series
Color (A)
PdS65 purchase
Illustrates the use of computer spreadsheets in different organizations. Part of a seven-part series which aims to allay everyone's fear of the computer, whether an individual is an experienced user or relative novice. Explores the numerous applications of the computer and illustrates some of the pitfalls.
Computer Science; Guidance and Counseling
Dist - BBCENE

Sprechen Sie Deutsch 15 MIN
U-matic / VHS / 16mm
Guten Tag Series
B&W (H) (GERMAN)
LC 73-707314
Presents an episode in which the characters employ frequently used expressions and idioms in order to teach conversational German to beginners. Stresses the correct use of word order, verb forms with ich and sie, compound nouns and the pronoun mein.
Foreign Language
Dist - IFB **Prod** - FRGMFA 1970

Sprigs and Twigs 15 MIN
16mm
Fingermouse, Yoffy and Friends Series
Color (K P I)
LC 73-700437
Follows Fingermouse and Flash on a mission to collect spigs and twigs.
Guidance and Counseling; Literature and Drama
Dist - VEDO **Prod** - BBCTV 1972

Spring 15 MIN
U-matic
Celebrate Series
Color (P)
Social Science
Dist - GPN **Prod** - KUONTV 1978

Spring 3 MIN
16mm
Color (G)
$15.00 rental
Offers a souvenir. Captures, in vain, time lost, passing one by like the shadow of a fast - moving cloud. A Thomas Korschil production.
Fine Arts
Dist - CANCIN

Spring 16 MIN
U-matic / VHS / 16mm
Four Seasons Series
Color (P I)
Looks at the activities and changes common to the spring season such as birds returning from their wintering grounds and ice and snow beginning to melt. Shows the farmer plowing and sowing his fields while animals awaken from hibernation.
Science - Natural
Dist - NGS **Prod** - NGS 1983

Spring 11 MIN
16mm / U-matic / VHS
Seasons Series
Color (P I)
$280, $195 purchase _ #80522
Discusses the changes in human activities and in nature when spring arrives.
Science - Natural
Dist - CORF
CENTRO

Spring 9 MIN
U-matic / VHS / 16mm
Color (I)
LC 73-702375
Records the beauty of the earth as it changes from winter to spring, while a young girl asks her father questions about the seasons.
Science - Natural
Dist - PFP **Prod** - PFP 1973

Spring 30 MIN
U-matic
Polka Dot Door Series
Color (K)
Presents a variety show for pre - school children. Includes songs, mime, stories, film sequences, talk, dance and fantasy figures. Each show emphasizes a particular theme such as numbers, feelings, exploring, music or time. Comes with parent teacher guide.
Fine Arts; Literature and Drama
Dist - TVOTAR **Prod** - TVOTAR 1985

The Spring and Fall of Nina Polanski 6 MIN
U-matic / VHS / 16mm
Working Mother Series
Color (J)
LC 75-703434
Considers a woman's perception of motherhood through the media of paintings and sounds.
Guidance and Counseling; Home Economics; Sociology
Dist - MEDIAG **Prod** - NFBC 1974

Spring and Summer 14 MIN
Videoreel / VT2
Images and Memories Series
Color
Features nature photographer Jim Bones celebrating the beauty of spring and summer.
Fine Arts; Industrial and Technical Education
Dist - PBS **Prod** - KERA

Spring and Summer Come and Go 18 MIN
U-matic / VHS / 16mm
Color (P I)
Shows the changes the coming of spring and summer bring to people, plants and animals. Highlights the emergence of frogs from hibernation, the courtship behavior of birds, the planting of crops and vacation activities.
Science - Natural
Dist - IFB **Prod** - BERLET 1987

Spring brings changes; 3rd ed. 14 MIN
U-matic / Videodisc / VHS / 16mm
Color (K P I)
$99.95, $79.95 purchase _ #Q10059; LC 75-704267
Utilizes music, pictures and children's words to illustrate the change of weather in spring. Focuses on trees, flowers, rain, and planting. Features slow - motion photography to demonstrate root and stem growth in detail. No adult narration.
Science - Natural
Dist - CF **Prod** - CF 1976

Spring - Cleaning the House and Chimney 8 MIN
16mm
Crystal Tipps and Alistair Series
Color (K P)
LC 73-700458
Follows Crystal and her friends as they decide to undertake spring - cleaning of the house and chimney.
Guidance and Counseling; Literature and Drama
Dist - VEDO **Prod** - BBCTV 1972

Spring Comes to the City 11 MIN
U-matic / VHS / 16mm
Seasons in the City Series
Color (P)
LC FIA68-14
Explores the city in the springtime with a young boy named Danny, who looks for such signs of spring as melting snows and warming weather, streets being repaired, gardens being planted and children playing in the park.
Science - Natural
Dist - CORF **Prod** - CORF 1968

Spring Comes to the Forest 11 MIN
U-matic / VHS / 16mm
Seasons Series
Color (P I)
LC 72-700527
Shows, in a light, charming manner, the sequence of change in the plant and animal life of the forest during the spring months.
Science - Natural
Dist - CORF **Prod** - CORF 1972

Spring Comes to the Pond 10 MIN
U-matic / VHS / 16mm
Seasons Series
Color (P I)
$265, $185 purchase _ #3026
Shows the different activities of the plants and animals of a pond when spring comes.
Science - Natural
Dist - CORF

Spring commissioning
VHS
Color (G A)
$29.95 purchase _ #0946
Shows how to bring a boat out of storage in the spring. Illustrates fitting out procedures on the engine, plumbing, batteries, interior, hull, trailer.
Physical Education and Recreation
Dist - SEVVID

Spring Harvest 13 MIN
16mm
Color (I)
LC 76-701635
Explores the process of creating maple syrup from maple sap in Vermont.
Business and Economics; Social Science
Dist - GMCW **Prod** - GMCW 1976

Spring Impressions 9 MIN
16mm
Color
Follows the progress of a little girl in spring through a field where the grass is almost as tall as she is, to a stream where she captures a frog to keep the rabbits in her basket company and to the birch woods where she finds forest wildflowers.
Fine Arts; Psychology; Science - Natural
Dist - SF **Prod** - MORLAT

Spring in Iceland 21 MIN
16mm
Color (C A)
Provides a vivid contrast between hot springs and volcanoes and the great glaciers which sit on top of volcanoes. Shows the varied bird and animal life of Iceland which can best be seen in the spring.
Geography - World
Dist - WSTGLC **Prod** - WSTGLC

Spring in Japan 20 MIN
16mm
Color (H C A)
LC 77-702438
Depicts spring in Japan while touring Japanese gardens, spring festivals, Mount Fuji and feudal castles.
Geography - World
Dist - JNTA **Prod** - JNTA 1972

Spring in Nature 17 MIN
U-matic / VHS / 16mm
Seasons in Nature Series
Color (P I)
LC 79-701831
Illustrates the changes which occur in plants and animals during spring.
Science - Natural
Dist - ALTSUL **Prod** - CASDEN 1979

Spring in the Woods 15 MIN
16mm / U-matic / VHS
Place to Live Series
Color (I J H)
Shows the early signs of life in the woods during the spring. Describes how the environment of the woods supports each form of life that lives there.
Science - Natural
Dist - JOU **Prod** - GRATV

Spring is a Season 11 MIN
U-matic / VHS / 16mm
Color; B&W (P I J)
A young boy describes the signs of spring that he sees in the fielas around his home. He records his discoveries on a calendar and notes the new plant growth, the change in the weather and the baby animals.
Science - Natural
Dist - JOU **Prod** - ALTSUL 1961

Spring is an Adventure 11 MIN
16mm / U-matic / VHS
Color (P I)
Shows changes which come with spring such as flowers budding and blooming, and eggs hatching. Shows activities of spring such as the planting of a garden.
Science - Natural
Dist - CORF **Prod** - CORF 1955

Spring is Here 11 MIN
U-matic / VHS / 16mm
Seasons (2nd Ed Series
Color (P)
LC 80-700462
Focuses on the activities of people and animals and the alterations in nature during spring.
Science - Natural
Dist - IFB **Prod** - IFB 1979

Spring is Here 15 MIN
VHS / U-matic
Pass it on Series
Color (K P)
Looks at all the signs of spring as well as the textures, sizes and shapes of spring.
Education; Science - Natural
Dist - GPN **Prod** - WKNOTV 1983

Spring is Here 10 MIN
U-matic / VHS / 16mm
Captioned; Color (P)
Examines animal and human life during the spring. Shows a group of school children preparing and planting a vegetable garden. Captioned for the hearing impaired.
Science - Natural
Dist - IFB **Prod** - BERLET 1967

Spring Lawn Care 30 MIN
BETA / VHS
Victory Garden Series
Color
Discusses spring lawn care including raking, fertilizing, weed control and tuning up the lawn mower. Gives tips on planting parsnips and strawberries.
Agriculture; Physical Education and Recreation
Dist - CORF **Prod** - WGBHTV

Spring Man and the Ss 16 MIN
U-matic / VHS / 16mm
B&W (H C A)
LC 73-702704
Shows the absurdity of Nazi madness. Presents an anecdote about a rumor that was being spread that a man of springs, a mysterious personage, had appeared in Prague and that he attacked the German invaders. Describes the spies, informers and persecutors in a regime of fear and silence.
History - World; Social Science; Sociology
Dist - PHENIX **Prod** - CFET 1973

Spring marsh 26 MIN
16mm
Audubon wildlife theatre series
Color (I)
LC 72-701737
Uses wildlife scenes filmed in Michigan to stress the importance of the marsh as a refuge for many kinds of wildlife, and as a vital part of wildlife ecology.
Science - Natural
Dist - AVEXP **Prod** - KEGPL 1971

Spring Migration 16 MIN
16mm
Color (I)
LC 75-703974
Portrays the migratory flights of sand hill cranes and Canadian geese.
Science - Natural
Dist - RADIM **Prod** - NOVACK 1975

Spring Nature Hike 10 MIN
16mm
Color (P I)
Stimulates student interest in the real world of nature. Follows two children as they discover the many new flowers and animals of springtime in the woods near their home. Points out that even city dwellers can enjoy and appreciate nature if they take the time to observe the happenings around them.
Science - Natural
Dist - SF **Prod** - SF 1967

Spring - Nature's Sights and Sounds 14 MIN
16mm / U-matic / VHS
Nature's Sights and Sound Series
Color (K P I)
Celebrates the coming of spring in the forest as seen through the rebirth of wild plants and flowers, but principally through the birth of small animals. Shows frogs, woodchucks, honey bees, rabbits, foxes, raccoons, turtles, snakes, fish, snails, crayfish and a host of birds.
Science - Natural
Dist - BCNFL **Prod** - MASLKS 1983

Spring Show 24 MIN
U-matic / VHS
Color
Shows the skills and knowledge of a 14 - year - old champion polo player, the training of police dogs, the art of becoming a cheerleader and some Scottish dancing.
Fine Arts; Physical Education and Recreation; Sociology
Dist - WCCOTV **Prod** - WCCOTV 1981

Spring Silkworms
VHS
Color (G) (MANDARIN CHINESE)
$45.00 purchase _ #6039A
Presents a Mandarin Chinese language television program produced in the People's Republic of China.
Geography - World; Industrial and Technical Education; Literature and Drama
Dist - CHTSUI **Prod** - CHTSUI

Spring - Six Interpretations 14 MIN
16mm / U-matic / VHS
Color (I J H)
LC 75-703858
Uses interpretations of spring to explore methods through which ideas, feelings and perceptions are communicated.
Guidance and Counseling; Psychology; Science - Natural
Dist - BARR **Prod** - BARR 1975

Spring Tunes 10 MIN
U-matic / VHS / 16mm
Color (J H C)
LC 77-707567
Presents an animated dramatization in which an egoist tries to destroy a small boy and his fiddle in order to stop the symphony of life.
Fine Arts
Dist - IFB **Prod** - ZAGREB 1970

Spring wildflowers of the Midwest 30 MIN
U-matic / VHS / BETA
Color (T)
$39.95 purchase _ #5107
Teaches teachers of junior high students and up how to teach concepts in biology. Describes and shows over 50 wildflowers that bloom in the spring in their natural environment. Discusses their scientific and common names. Studies the ecological relationships, similarities and differences that exist among the great variety of spring blooming plants.
Science - Natural
Dist - INSTRU

Spring Winding on the Lathe 15 MIN
VHS / U-matic
Machining and the Operation of Machine Tools, Module 3 - 'Intermediate Engine Lathe Series
Color (IND)

Industrial and Technical Education
Dist - LEIKID **Prod** - LEIKID

Spring Winding on the Lathe
U-matic / VHS
Intermediate Engine Lathe Operation Series
Color (SPANISH)
Industrial and Technical Education
Dist - VTRI **Prod** - VTRI

Springboard 34 MIN
16mm
F C A Sports Film Series
Color; B&W
Shows the Christian perspective being demonstrated by champion athletes who attend the FCA conference making a profound impression on a young baseball pitcher.
Physical Education and Recreation; Religion and Philosophy
Dist - WWPI **Prod** - FELLCA 1960

Springman and the SS 16 MIN
16mm / U-matic / VHS
Color (J H A)
LC 81-700935
Presents an animated story about a chimney sweep who discovers the power of a spring taken from an old love seat and uses it to annoy the SS troops who are occupying Czechoslovakia. Highlights the potential of the individual in the midst of an oppressive society.
Fine Arts
Dist - PHENIX **Prod** - TRNKAJ 1973

Springs and wells 10 MIN
VHS
Hydrology concept series
Color (H C)
$24.95 purchase _ #S9022
Shows how springs and wells are formed in a single - concept format. Part of an 8 - part series covering water and soil topics.
Science - Physical
Dist - HUBDSC **Prod** - HUBDSC

Sprinkler system valve inspections 9 MIN
BETA / VHS / U-matic
Fire sprinkler safety series
Color (IND G)
$295.00 purchase _ #828 - 02
Trains attendants, inspectors and supervisors in proper maintenance, operation and testing of fire sprinkler systems. Part of a three - part series.
Health and Safety; Industrial and Technical Education; Psychology
Dist - ITSC **Prod** - ITSC

Sprinkler systems 13 MIN
VHS
Firefighter II series
Color (IND)
$130.00 purchase _ #35660
Presents one part of a 14 - part series that is the teaching companion for IFSTA's Essentials of Fire Fighting manual. Describes the types and operation of various sprinkler systems. Presents sources of water supply for sprinkler systems. Identifies the location and appearance of controls and operating valves. Based on Chapter 13.
Health and Safety; Science - Physical; Social Science
Dist - OKSU **Prod** - ACCTRA

Sprinklers 30 MIN
VHS
Color (J H C A)
Teaches how to install a manual, underground sprinkler system for lawn and yard on flat, fairly level ground.
Agriculture
Dist - COFTAB **Prod** - AMHOM 1985

Sprinklers 15 MIN
VHS
Firefighter I Video Series
Color (PRO G)
$115.00 purchase _ #35065
Explains the operation of water sprinkler systems, including motor alarms, tapping into sprinkler systems for water supply and opening and closing sprinkler systems. Includes an instruction guide for review. Part of a video series on Firefighter I training codes to be used with complementing IFSTA manuals.
Health and Safety; Psychology; Social Science
Dist - OKSU **Prod** - OKSU

The Sprint 13 MIN
16mm / U-matic / VHS
Athletics Series
Color (H C A)
LC 80-700344
Uses slow - motion and live action photography of the 200 - meter sprint to demonstrate training and performance in high - speed competitive running. Covers warmup activities, sprint drills, and starting drills, and concludes with views of an actual competition.
Physical Education and Recreation
Dist - IU **Prod** - GSAVL 1980

Sprint Conditioning
U-matic / VHS
From the Bill Dellinger's Championship Track and Field Videotape 'Training Library Series.
Color (H C)
Divides sprint event conditioning into strength, flexibility, speed and endurance. Stresses conditioning for short sprint competitors and details drills to improve performance.
Physical Education and Recreation
Dist - CBSC **Prod** - CBSC
CAMV

Sprint technique 18 MIN
VHS
Bill Dellinger's championship track and field series
Color (H C A)
$39.95 purchase _ #WES1709V
Features Bill Dellinger and the University of Oregon coaching staff, who teach the basic techniques of sprinting events. Presents drills to develop an athlete's potential and correct common errors in technique. Uses slow - motion film and on - screen graphics.
Physical Education and Recreation
Dist - CAMV
CBSC

The Sprinter 11 MIN
16mm
B&W (J H)
Describes effective techniques of starting, attaining maxmum speeds quickly, and running at maximum efficinarrated by Ed Temple of Tennessee A and I University.
Physical Education and Recreation
Dist - COCA **Prod** - BORDEN

Sprinting 30 MIN
VHS
Track and field techniques series
Color (H C G)
$29.95 purchase _ #WK1106V
Features sprinter Tommie Smith who discusses the skill and improving performance. Part of a series.
Physical Education and Recreation
Dist - CAMV

Sprinting techniques
VHS
NCAA instructional video series
Color (H C A)
$39.95 purchase _ #KAR2101V
Presents the first of a two - part series on track events. Focuses on sprinting techniques.
Physical Education and Recreation
Dist - CAMV **Prod** - NCAAF

Sprinting with Carl Lewis and coach Tom Tellez 58 MIN
VHS
Color (H C A)
$39.95 purchase _ #ESS901V
Features Olympic sprinter Carl Lewis and his coach, Tom Tellez, in a comprehensive training program for prospective sprinters. Covers techniques, principles, and training systems, all of wich can be applied well to other sports.
Physical Education and Recreation
Dist - CAMV

Sprints, Hurdles and Relays 48 MIN
BETA / VHS
Women's Track and Field Series
Color
Physical Education and Recreation
Dist - MOHOMV **Prod** - MOHOMV

Sprints, hurdles and relays 48 MIN
VHS
Track and field series
Color (J H C A)
$39.95 purchase _ #MXS480V
Features Dr Ken Foreman, former U S Olympic women's track coach, in a comprehensive program to teach skills of sprints, hurdles and relays. Focuses on developing speed for sprints, agility for hurdles, and basic techniques for relay runners.
Physical Education and Recreation
Dist - CAMV

Sprints, Hurdles, Relays APPROXIMATELY 33 MIN
U-matic / VHS
Women's Track & Field Videos Series
Color; B&W; Silent; Stereo; Mono (H C A)
Demonstrates techniques and drills by famous athletes for the sprint, hurdle, and relay events. Prepared and narrated by coach Ken Foreman.
Physical Education and Recreation
Dist - TRACKN **Prod** - TRACKN 1986

Sprints - Relays 60 MIN
VHS / U-matic
Frank Morris Instructional Videos Series
Color; B&W; Silent; Mono; Stereo (H C A)
Instructs athletes how to execute and improve performance of sprints and relays. Produced and Narrated by coach Frank Morris.
Physical Education and Recreation
Dist - TRACKN **Prod** - TRACKN 1986

Spriometry - the Early Detection of Chronic Obstructive Pulmonary Disease 25 MIN
16mm
Color
LC 79-702582
Uses animation to illustrate the functioning of the normal respiratory system and to show what happens when ventilation is impaired. Demonstrates the procedures whereby a doctor, in his office, may evaluate typical patients with respiratory complaints.
Science; Science - Natural
Dist - AMLUNG **Prod** - NTBA 1968

Sprout Wings and Fly 50 MIN
16mm
Color (H A)
$500.00 purchase, $65.00 rental
Presents the folk culture and traditions of the rural South through the monologues, fiddle playing and performances of North Carolina folk singer Tommy Jarrel.
Fine Arts
Dist - AFA **Prod** - BLNKL 1984

The Spruce Bog 23 MIN
16mm
Color (J H C)
Describes the conditions under which a spruce bog is formed, with details of the plant types found at successive stages of development, from open water to mature forest. Uses time - lapse photography to show the growth and decay of vegetation.
Science - Natural
Dist - NFBC **Prod** - NFBC 1958

Spruce House 29 MIN
16mm
To Save Tomorrow Series
B&W (H C A)
Explains that the theory followed by Spruce House is that a patient's behavior is the result of the responses, by other people, to past behavior. Shows that normal behavior must then be rewarded and neurotic behavior ignored if behavior modification is to take place.
Psychology
Dist - IU **Prod** - NET

Sprucin' Up 17 MIN
16mm
B&W
Shows what happens when Spanky and Alfalfa vie for the same girl. A Little Rascals film.
Fine Arts
Dist - RMIBHF **Prod** - ROACH 1935

Spud Webb - reach for the skies 60 MIN
VHS
Color (G)
$19.95 purchase _ #BR0741V
Features five - foot, seven - inch NBA star Spud Webb with his perspectives on what it takes to succeed in basketball. Teaches viewers the basic techniques of the game - dribbling, passing, and shooting. Presents game footage, clinics, and interviews with Webb, coaches, and friends including Dominique Wilkins and Ron Harper.
Physical Education and Recreation
Dist - CAMV **Prod** - CAMV 1990

Spunky the Snowman 7 MIN
U-matic / VHS / 16mm
Color
A story cartoon depicting Spunky the Snowman's visit to Santa.
Literature and Drama
Dist - FI **Prod** - FLEET 1957

Spur Dikes 14 MIN
16mm
Color
LC 74-705689
Depicts the theory, laboratory research and practical application of spur dikes to control scour at bridge abutments in flood conditions. Explains the work of public roads departments in several states to establish a standard method of reducing damage and cost of maintenance at bridge locations.
Industrial and Technical Education; Social Science
Dist - USNAC **Prod** - USDTFH 1965

Spur Eines Maedchens 79 MIN
16mm

B&W (GERMAN)
Depicts the fate of a girl suffering from schizophrenia. Reveals how neither intellectual interests nor her good - humored friend can help her. Concludes with her complete loss of contact with reality.
Foreign Language; Health and Safety; Psychology
Dist - WSTGLC **Prod** - WSTGLC 1967

Sputter Deposition - an Overview 35 MIN
U-matic / VHS
Plasma Sputtering, Deposition and Growth of Microelectronic Films 'for VLSI Series
Color (IND)
Describes variation of yield of neutral species as a function of kinetic energy of the input ion. Says yield from the target following ion impact is the fundamental basis of sputter deposition techniques, whether in magnetron, plasma or ion - beam schemes.
Industrial and Technical Education; Science - Physical
Dist - COLOSU **Prod** - COLOSU

Sputum Specimens - Collection and Preparation 18 MIN
U-matic / VHS
Cytotechnology Techniques Series
Color (PRO)
Health and Safety
Dist - WFP **Prod** - WFP

The Spy 22 MIN
16mm
Unbroken Arrow Series
Color (P I)
Presents an adventure set in the time of the Saxons which tells how Robin is tricked into rescuing a youth and taking him back to the secret camp, not realizing that the youth has agreed with the Baron to spy on the outlaws.
Literature and Drama
Dist - LUF **Prod** - LUF 1977

Spy 2000 Owner Operation and Maintenance 53 MIN
U-matic
Color (IND)
Provides vacuum technology training for workers in the field.
Business and Economics; Industrial and Technical Education
Dist - VARIAN **Prod** - VARIAN 1986

A Spy in the House that Ruth Built 29 MIN
U-matic / VHS
Vanalyne Green Series
Color (G)
$250.00, $200.00 purchase, $50.00 rental
Creates a metaphor about family, loss and sexuality through appropriation of the all - male arena of professional baseball. Reinterprets the womanless symbolism of baseball, its womblike landscapes, cycles and rituals, to construct an iconography that pays homage to the female.
Fine Arts; Physical Education and Recreation; Psychology; Sociology
Dist - WMEN **Prod** - VANGRE 1989

Spy Machines 58 MIN
VHS / U-matic
Nova Series
Color (H C A)
$250 purchase _ #5262C
Shows the role of spy machines and focuses on America's efforts to gather intelligence about the Soviet military. Produced by WGBH Boston.
Industrial and Technical Education
Dist - CORF

The Spy who Broke the Code 60 MIN
VHS
Frontline Series
Color; Captioned (G)
$300.00 purchase, $95.00 rental _ #FRON - 702K
Interviews John Walker and Jerry Whitworth, two ex - Navy men who sold military secrets to the Soviet Union. Reviews their activities, and shows that it was not an isolated incident.
Business and Economics; Civics and Political Systems; Computer Science
Dist - PBS **Prod** - DOCCON 1988

Spyfluen - the Bluebottle 13 MIN
16mm
B&W ((DANISH SUBTITLES))
Describes the anatomy of the bluebottle, its egg - laying and development. Portrays the useful functions of the bluebottle in nature. Includes Danish subtitles.
Foreign Language; Science - Natural
Dist - STATNS **Prod** - STATNS 1950

Spying the Spy 10 MIN
16mm
B&W
Presents a story based on the American spy fever during World War I.
History - United States; Literature and Drama
Dist - STRFLS **Prod** - SPCTRA 1917

SQL/DS and relational data base systems series
Basic facilities of SQL/DS 30 MIN
Management Implications of SQL/DS 30 MIN
Relational Data Base 30 MIN
Dist - DELTAK

Squanto and the first Thanksgiving 30 MIN
VHS
Rabbit Ears series
Color (K P)
$9.95 purchase _ #SQU - 03
Tells about Squanto, a Native American sold into slavery in Spain, who later returned to North America. Shows how he aided the Pilgrims during the severe first years of the colony at Plymouth. Narrated by Graham Greene, music by Paul McCandless.
Biography; Literature and Drama
Dist - ARTSAM **Prod** - RABBIT 1993

The Square 29 MIN
16mm
Color
Portrays a serious and idealistic youth in a middle class college setting, pressured into conformity by his peers and in employment interviews.
Guidance and Counseling; Sociology
Dist - CCNY **Prod** - CAROUF

Square and Rectangular Duct End Cap Layout Drive and Slip 9 MIN
VHS / BETA
Metal Fabrication - Duct End Cap Layout Series
Color (IND)
Industrial and Technical Education; Psychology
Dist - RMIBHF **Prod** - RMIBHF

Square and Rectangular Duct End Cap Layout Slip Pocket 10 MIN
BETA / VHS
Metal Fabrication - Duct End Cap Layout Series
Color (IND)
Industrial and Technical Education; Psychology
Dist - RMIBHF **Prod** - RMIBHF

Square Butt A1 2 MIN
VHS / BETA
Welding Training Comprehensive - Tungsten Inert Gas T I G Welding'Series
Color (IND)
Industrial and Technical Education; Psychology
Dist - RMIBHF **Prod** - RMIBHF

Square Butt Aluminum 5 MIN
BETA / VHS
Welding Training Comprehensive - Oxy - Acetylene Welding'Series
Color (IND)
Industrial and Technical Education; Psychology
Dist - RMIBHF **Prod** - RMIBHF

Square Butt Backhand 7 MIN
BETA / VHS
Welding Training (Comprehensive - - - Oxy - Acetylene Welding 'Series
Color (IND)
Industrial and Technical Education; Psychology
Dist - RMIBHF **Prod** - RMIBHF

Square Butt Bronze 6 MIN
BETA / VHS
Welding Training Comprehensive - Oxy - Acetylene Welding'Series
Color (IND)
Industrial and Technical Education; Psychology
Dist - RMIBHF **Prod** - RMIBHF

Square Butt Horizontal 6 MIN
VHS / BETA
Welding Training Comprehensive - Oxy - Acetylene Welding'Series
Color (IND)
Industrial and Technical Education; Psychology
Dist - RMIBHF **Prod** - RMIBHF

Square Butt Joint 2 MIN
BETA / VHS
Welding Training (Comprehensive - Metal Inert Gas (M I G Welding 'Series
Color (IND)
Industrial and Technical Education; Psychology
Dist - RMIBHF **Prod** - RMIBHF

Square Butt Joint Aluminum with Fixture 4 MIN
BETA / VHS
Welding Training Comprehensive - Tungsten Inert Gas T I G Welding'Series
Color (IND)
Industrial and Technical Education; Psychology
Dist - RMIBHF **Prod** - RMIBHF

Square Butt Joint Filler Rod 6 MIN
BETA / VHS
Welding Training Comprehensive - Oxy - Acetylene Welding'Series
Color (IND)
Industrial and Technical Education; Psychology
Dist - RMIBHF **Prod** - RMIBHF

Square Butt Joint Flat 2 MIN
VHS / BETA
Welding Training (Comprehensive - Metal Inert Gas (M I G Welding 'Series
Color (IND)
Industrial and Technical Education; Psychology
Dist - RMIBHF **Prod** - RMIBHF

Square Butt Joint Flat Aluminum 2 MIN
BETA / VHS
Welding Training Comprehensive - Metal Inert Gas M I G Welding'Series
Color (IND)
Industrial and Technical Education; Psychology
Dist - RMIBHF **Prod** - RMIBHF

Square butt joint single - pass 6 MIN
BETA / VHS
Welding training - comprehensive - basic shielded metal arc welding series
Color (IND)
Industrial and Technical Education; Psychology
Dist - RMIBHF **Prod** - RMIBHF

Square Butt Joint Stainless 4 MIN
VHS / BETA
Welding Training Comprehensive - Tungsten Inert Gas T I G Welding'Series
Color (IND)
Industrial and Technical Education; Psychology
Dist - RMIBHF **Prod** - RMIBHF

Square Butt Joint Stainless Vertical - Up 2 MIN
VHS / BETA
Welding Training Comprehensive - Tungsten Inert Gas T I G Welding'Series
Color (IND)
Industrial and Technical Education; Psychology
Dist - RMIBHF **Prod** - RMIBHF

Square butt joints 15 MIN
VHS / U-matic
Arc welding training series
Color (IND)
Industrial and Technical Education
Dist - AVIMA **Prod** - AVIMA

Square Butt Silver Braze 4 MIN
BETA / VHS
Welding Training Comprehensive - Oxy - Acetylene Welding'Series
Color (IND)
Industrial and Technical Education; Psychology
Dist - RMIBHF **Prod** - RMIBHF

Square Butt Stainless with Fixture 4 MIN
BETA / VHS
Welding Training Comprehensive - Tungsten Inert Gas T I G Welding'Series
Color (IND)
Industrial and Technical Education; Psychology
Dist - RMIBHF **Prod** - RMIBHF

Square Butt Vertical - Up 6 MIN
BETA / VHS
Welding Training Comprehensive - Oxy - Acetylene Welding'Series
Color (IND)
Industrial and Technical Education; Psychology
Dist - RMIBHF **Prod** - RMIBHF

Square Circle 17 MIN
16mm
B&W
Presents an over 30' hippie, who functions in the square world as a planner and architect and in his personal world as a member of the turned on generation.
Guidance and Counseling; Psychology; Sociology
Dist - UPENN **Prod** - UPENN 1968

Square Dancing Fundamentals - Pt 1 19 MIN
U-matic / VHS / 16mm
Color (J)
LC 75-700966
Teaches the first 22 fundamental square dance movements, emphasizing good styling.
Fine Arts; Physical Education and Recreation
Dist - AIMS **Prod** - ASSOCF 1974

Square Dancing Fundamentals - Pt 2 17 MIN
U-matic / VHS / 16mm
Color (I)

LC 75-700967
Teaches the last 13 of the fundamental square dance movements, emphasizing the shuffle step, styling and smooth execution of figures.
Fine Arts; Physical Education and Recreation; Sociology
Dist - AIMS **Prod** - ASSOCF 1974

Square Foot Gardening - Pt 1 60 MIN
VHS / U-matic / BETA
Color (A G)
$14.95 _ #SG101
Shows a method of growing flowers, vegetables and herbs in 80% less space. Gives basics of layout, soil, fertilizer and seeds.
Agriculture
Dist - BAKERT

Square Foot Gardening - Pt 2 60 MIN
VHS / U-matic / BETA
Color (A G)
$14.95 _ #SG103
Shows when to start seed preparation, weeding, thinning, trimming, plant supports, wind screens and wire covers, and harvesting.
Agriculture
Dist - BAKERT

Square Foot Gardening - Pt 3 60 MIN
BETA / VHS / U-matic
Color (A G)
$14.95 _ #SG105
Examines small space gardening with tips on patio layout, frome construction, deck and rooftop gardening and "take it easy" gardening.
Agriculture
Dist - BAKERT

Square Heel and Throat Elbow Layout 29 MIN
VHS / BETA
Color (IND)
Presents the way the square heel and throat elbow layout should be laid out, including the seam allowances.
Industrial and Technical Education; Psychology
Dist - RMIBHF **Prod** - RMIBHF

Square inch field 12 MIN
16mm
Color (G)
$20.00 rental
Surveys the micro - macro universe as contained in the mind of man. Collects archetypal faces then accelerates to 24 per second. Viewed through a kind of telescoped iris aperture peering outward from the mind's eye.
Fine Arts; Psychology
Dist - CANCIN **Prod** - RIMMER 1968

Square Johns 28 MIN
U-matic / VHS / 16mm
Penitentiary Staff Training Series
B&W (PRO)
LC FIA68-1253
Views the work of parole officers with two paroled prisoners.
Guidance and Counseling; Psychology
Dist - IFB **Prod** - NFBC 1967

Square one - an introduction to computers 30 MIN
VHS
Color (J H C G)
$59.95 purchase
Familiarizes viewers with the world of personal computing. Details computer jargon; types of computers; how they are used; mainframes; mini and microprocessing units; keyboards, drives; plotters; word processing; data base; spreadsheets; CAD - CAM; and more. Seeks to teach viewers how to select and use software and hardware. Aimed at those who are neophytes to computing.
Computer Science
Dist - CAMV

Square or Rectangular Transition - Bottom Up, Double Offset, all Sides Slanting 30 MIN
VHS / BETA
Transition 'Top Up' or 'Bottom Up' or Top Down or Bottom Down Series
Color (IND)
Industrial and Technical Education; Psychology
Dist - RMIBHF **Prod** - RMIBHF

Square or Rectangular Transition - Equal Taper, Different Size Openings 18 MIN
VHS / BETA
Color (IND)
Shows the full scale pattern layout working from a shop sketch or one - view working drawing. Discusses the application of triangulation, and emphasizes the seam dimensions to determine whether or not the patterns are laid out accurately.
Industrial and Technical Education; Mathematics; Psychology
Dist - RMIBHF **Prod** - RMIBHF

Square or Rectangular Transition - Equal Taper, same Size Openings 9 MIN
BETA / VHS
Color (IND)
Shows the full scale pattern layout working from a one - view working drawing or shop sketch. Discusses the process of triangulation. Deals with openings that are the same size, but which change from a horizontal to a vertical position.
Industrial and Technical Education; Mathematics; Psychology
Dist - RMIBHF **Prod** - RMIBHF

Square or Rectangular Transition - Flat on Top or Bottom, Offset, Different Openings 18 MIN
BETA / VHS
Color (IND)
Shows the full scale pattern development, working from a shop sketch or one - view working drawing. Emphasizes the application of flat top or bottom.
Industrial and Technical Education; Psychology
Dist - RMIBHF **Prod** - RMIBHF

Square or Rectangular Transition - Three Straight Sides 7 MIN
BETA / VHS
Color (IND)
Shows the use of a shop sketch to illustrate the most simple of transitional fittings, and develops full size patterns, using the best method. Discusses alternative methods.
Mathematics; Psychology
Dist - RMIBHF **Prod** - RMIBHF

Square or Rectangular Transition - Top Up, Double Offset, all Sides Slanting 43 MIN
VHS / BETA
Transition 'Top Up' or 'Bottom Up' or Top Down or Bottom Down Series
Color (IND)
Industrial and Technical Education; Mathematics; Psychology
Dist - RMIBHF **Prod** - RMIBHF

Square or Rectangular Transition - Two Straight Sides Different Size Openings 14 MIN
VHS / BETA
Color (IND)
Illustrates the full scale pattern layout, working from a shop sketch or one - view working drawing. Shows the best seaming method.
Industrial and Technical Education; Psychology
Dist - RMIBHF **Prod** - RMIBHF

Square or Rectangular Transition - Two Straight Sides same Size Openings 21 MIN
BETA / VHS
Color (IND)
Illustrates the pattern layout full scale, working from a shop sketch or one - view working drawing, and shows the best seaming method. Discusses some alternative methods.
Industrial and Technical Education
Dist - RMIBHF **Prod** - RMIBHF

Square Pegs, Round Holes 8 MIN
U-matic / VHS / 16mm
Color (I J H)
Tells how a young cube finds it impossible to fit into the niches society requires. Describes how he finally digs his own hole and discovers his own unique way of life.
Guidance and Counseling
Dist - ALTSUL **Prod** - ALTSUL

Square Root Functions and Ratio
Software / BETA
Instrumentation and Control Mathematics Series
Color (PRO)
$600.00 - $1500.00 purchase _ #IDSRF
Focuses on differential pressure and flow rate and its relationship to square root functions. Uses the concept of ratios to calculate flow rates using square root functions. Part of a five - part series on instrumentation and control mathematics. Interactive training system includes course administrator guide, videodisc and computer software.
Industrial and Technical Education; Mathematics; Psychology
Dist - NUSTC **Prod** - NUSTC

Square Throat Curved Heel Elbow Layout 8 MIN
VHS / BETA
Color (IND)
Illustrates the correct way to lay out the cheek patterns for the square throat curved heel elbow, without choking the cheek off.
Industrial and Technical Education; Psychology
Dist - RMIBHF **Prod** - RMIBHF

Square to Round - Offset One - Way Openings not Parallel 28 MIN
BETA / VHS
Metal Fabrication - Square to Round Layout Series
Color (IND)
Industrial and Technical Education; Psychology
Dist - RMIBHF **Prod** - RMIBHF

Square to Round Transition - Offset One - Way 32 MIN
BETA / VHS
Metal Fabrication - Square to Round Layout Series
Color (IND)
Industrial and Technical Education; Psychology
Dist - RMIBHF **Prod** - RMIBHF

Square Wave Characteristics 16 MIN
16mm / U-matic / VHS
B&W
Compares audio and video wave forms. Discusses frequency composition and characteristics, and time base relationships of square waves in terms of wide band pass requirements.
Industrial and Technical Education; Science - Physical
Dist - USNAC **Prod** - USAF 1983

Squares 2 MIN
16mm
Color
Presents the development of color cell processes.
Fine Arts; Science - Physical
Dist - CFS **Prod** - PFP 1934

Squares 2 MIN
16mm
Color (G)
$16.50 rental
Consists of color reconstruction from original drawings.
Fine Arts
Dist - CANCIN **Prod** - FISCHF 1934

Squares are not Bad 6 MIN
16mm / U-matic / VHS
Golden Book Storytime Series
Color (P)
Presents a story showing geometric shapes overcoming their prejudices toward one another, and together making more elaborate shapes.
Literature and Drama
Dist - CORF **Prod** - CORF 1977

Squaring a Block 39 MIN
VHS / BETA
Machine Shop - Milling Machine Series
Color (IND)
Industrial and Technical Education; Psychology
Dist - RMIBHF **Prod** - RMIBHF

Squash Instructional Programs - Advanced 60 MIN
BETA / VHS / U-matic
Color; Mono (G)
$75.00
Composed of four parts - the swing, footwork, movement, routines and drills.
Physical Education and Recreation
Dist - CTV **Prod** - CTV 1985

Squash Instructional Programs - Intermediate 60 MIN
BETA / VHS / U-matic
Color; Mono (G)
$75.00
Composed of four parts - the boast, the drop shot, the volley and overhead drop, practice techniques.
Physical Education and Recreation
Dist - CTV **Prod** - CTV 1985

Squash Instuctional Program - Beginners 60 MIN
BETA / VHS / U-matic
Color; Mono (G)
$75.00
Includes four parts - basic rules, holding the raquet, correct strokes, tactics.
Physical Education and Recreation
Dist - CTV **Prod** - CTV 1985

Squash series
Fundamentals of squash - basic shots and tactics 10 MIN
Fundamentals of squash - grip - forehand - backhand 10 MIN
Fundamentals of squash - serves - returns - volleys 10 MIN
Dist - ATHI

Squash - the Game - Part 1 60 MIN
VHS
(J H C)
$39.95 _ #BF99625V
Introduces the tennis game, the forehand, and the backhand. Discusses the court, choosing equipment, proper grip, and stroke techniques.
Physical Education and Recreation
Dist - CAMV

Squash - the Game - Part 2 60 MIN
VHS
(J H C)
$39.95 _ #BF99626V
Covers advanced tennis shots, rules, and tactics. Anlyzes one game for both beginning and intermediate tactics.
Physical Education and Recreation
Dist - CAMV

The Squashed Show 30 MIN
U-matic / VHS
Cookin' Cheap Series
Color
Presents basically crazy cooks Larry Bly and Laban Johnson who offer recipes, cooking and shopping tips.
Home Economics
Dist - MDCPB **Prod** - WBRATV

Squatters - the Other Philadelphia Story 27 MIN
U-matic / VHS / 16mm
Color (J)
Tells of the movement of poor people who live in or squat abandoned buildings in order to get places to live and to change housing policy locally and nationally. Centers on the story of a group in Philadelphia.
Geography - United States; History - United States; Sociology
Dist - CNEMAG **Prod** - KOPPEC 1984

Squeak the squirrel; Rev. 10 MIN
U-matic / VHS / 16mm
Color; B&W; Captioned (P I)
$ 79.95 purchase _ #Q10003
Investigates how animals learn problem - solving skills. Follows Squeak, a golden - mantled ground squirrel, as he completes a number of different exercises of graduated difficulty. Includes music and narration.
Science - Natural
Dist - CF **Prod** - CW 1995

Squeakerfoot 27 MIN
U-matic / VHS / 16mm
Ramona Series
Color (P I)
What happens when Ramona shows off her squeaky new shoes at school, and finds that being the center of attention is not always a good thing. From Ramona Quimby, Age 8. A production of Atlantis Films, Ltd. in association with Lancit Media Productions, Ltd. and Revcom Television.
Literature and Drama
Dist - CF

Squeakerfoot - Goodbye, hello 60 MIN
VHS
Beverly Cleary's Ramona series
Color; CC (K P I)
$29.95 purchase _ #KA433
Presents two Ramona stories by Beverly Cleary.
Literature and Drama
Dist - KNOWUN

Squeaky and his playmates 5 MIN
16mm
Otto the auto - pedestrian safety - C series
Color (K P)
$30.00 purchase _ #175
Features Otto the Auto and a chattering squirrel who helps Otto teach about the need to play away from traffic. Part of a series on pedestrian safety.
Health and Safety
Dist - AAAFTS **Prod** - AAAFTS 1959

Squeaky Clean - Pt 1 14 MIN
U-matic / VHS
Conrad Series
Color (I)
Discusses personal hygiene.
Health and Safety
Dist - AITECH **Prod** - SCETV 1977

Squeaky Clean - Pt 2 14 MIN
VHS / U-matic
Conrad Series
Color (I)
Examines the structure and function of the skin and discusses acne.
Science - Natural
Dist - AITECH **Prod** - SCETV 1977

Squeeze Cementing 30 MIN
U-matic / Slide / VHS / 16mm
Color (IND A PRO)
$150.00 purchase _ #11.1122, $160.00 purchase _ #51.1122
Tells what squeeze cementing is, how it is used, and what equipment is necessary.
Business and Economics; Industrial and Technical Education; Social Science
Dist - UTEXPE **Prod** - UTEXPE 1977

Squeeze riveting - stationary and portable riveters 15 MIN
16mm
Aircraft work series
B&W
LC FIE52-278
Explains how to select correct rivet sets for stationary and portable squeezers, and shows how to set up and use the stationary squeezer and the portable squeezer.
Industrial and Technical Education
Dist - USNAC **Prod** - USOE

Squeeze Technique 10 MIN
16mm
Color
Demonstrates the technique first introduced by James Semans in premature ejaculation. Tells that this technique is also used by Masters and Johnson and other therapists. Defines premature ejaculation as the inability to delay ejaculation long enough for the partner to reach orgasm 50 percent of the time. Explores the subjective reactions of both persons to the process.
Guidance and Counseling; Psychology; Sociology
Dist - MMRC **Prod** - MMRC

Squiggles, dots and lines 25 MIN
VHS
Color (K P)
$24.95 purchase _ #KVI1022V - K
Teaches kids to draw using the basic shapes of circles, triangles, squares and rectangles.
Fine Arts; Psychology
Dist - CAMV

Squires of San Quentin 30 MIN
U-matic / VHS / 16mm
Color (A)
LC 79-700093
Deals with the workshops for adolescent delinquent boys sponsored by the inmates of San Quentin Prison. Uses cinema verite footage to capture group meetings where conversation centers on a comparison of the youths' and convicts' actions in order to encourage the boys to become more introspective.
Sociology
Dist - CORF **Prod** - MITCHG 1978

Squirrel - cage rotor principles 10 MIN
16mm
Electrical work - electrical machinery series; No 3
B&W
LC FIE52-239
Describes the laws of magnetism and induced EMF. Explains electron flow in squirrel - cage rotor setting up magnetic poles which create torque. Shows the construction of squirrel - cage rotors.
Industrial and Technical Education
Dist - USNAC **Prod** - USOE 1945

Squirrel on My Shoulder 25 MIN
U-matic / VHS / 16mm
Color
Focuses on an orphaned squirrel who is adopted by humans.
Science - Natural
Dist - FI **Prod** - BBCTV 1980

Squirrel woodlands 10 MIN
U-matic / 16mm / VHS
Wild places series
Color (P)
$290.00, $250.00 purchase _ #HP - 6072C
Observes a variety of woodland mammals, birds, amphibians and insects to witness feeding habits and learn each creature's place in woodland ecology. Part of a series teaching about different kinds of habitats which show how living things adapt to varying environments and how each creature depends upon others for existence. Produced by Partridge Film and Video, Ltd.
Science - Natural
Dist - CORF

Squirrels are Up, Squirrels are Down - Adverbials of Place 10 MIN
U-matic / VHS / 16mm
Reading Motivation Series
Color (P I)
LC 73-701280
Presents both orally and visually words selected from commonly used vocabulary lists for primary readers. Engages rhyme and music to create patterns that aid in retention of the words.
English Language
Dist - PHENIX **Prod** - PHENIX 1972

Sr Thea - her own story 50 MIN
VHS
Color (R)
$29.95 purchase _ #491 - 0
Offers a memoir of Sister Thea Bowman, an African - American woman, made at her home in Mississippi just months before she died. Includes discussion guide.
Religion and Philosophy; Sociology
Dist - USCC **Prod** - USCC 1992

Sredni Vashtar 16 MIN
16mm / U-matic / VHS
Color (J)
LC 80-700271
Presents an adaptation of the short story Sredni Vashtar by Saki about a young boy who seeks escape from his cruel guardian and turns to his pet ferret, Sredni Vashtar, whom he believes to be endowed with magical powers.
Fine Arts
Dist - CRMP **Prod** - WHITS 1979

Sri Gurudev Answers Questions 45 MIN
VHS / U-matic
Camp Saginaw Retreat Series
Color
Answers questions on truth, satsang and health.
Religion and Philosophy
Dist - IYOGA **Prod** - IYOGA

Sri Gurudev Chanting 60 MIN
U-matic / VHS
Camp Saginaw Retreat Series
Color
Answers questions on pregnancy, sex and meditation.
Religion and Philosophy
Dist - IYOGA **Prod** - IYOGA

Sri Gurudev Discusses the Retreat 60 MIN
U-matic / VHS
Camp Saginaw Retreat Series
Color
Presents Sri Gurudev discussing the importance of discipline, relating stories of God, Adam and nonattachment.
Religion and Philosophy
Dist - IYOGA **Prod** - IYOGA

Sri Gurudev, His Early Life 120 MIN
U-matic / VHS
Color
Presents Sri Gurudev answering questions and telling about his early life.
Religion and Philosophy
Dist - IYOGA **Prod** - IYOGA

Sri Gurudev Speaks on Buddhahood 60 MIN
U-matic / VHS
Camp Saginaw Retreat Series
Color
Presents Sri Gurudev discussing Buddhahood and answering question on the spirituality of women, the nature of the mind and recognizing a true teacher.
Religion and Philosophy
Dist - IYOGA **Prod** - IYOGA

Sri Gurudev Speaks on Divine Mother 20 MIN
U-matic / VHS
Camp Saginaw Retreat Series
Color
Presents Sri Gurudev speaking on the aspect of the Divine Mother in all of us.
Religion and Philosophy
Dist - IYOGA **Prod** - IYOGA

Sri Gurudev Speaks on Ramana Maharshi 60 MIN
VHS / U-matic
Camp Saginaw Retreat Series
Color
Answers questions on pure love, child rearing and the ego.
Religion and Philosophy
Dist - IYOGA **Prod** - IYOGA

Sri Lanka - a nation in anguish 18 MIN
VHS
Color (G A)
$20.00 purchase
Chronicles the violent repression of Tamil minorities in Sri Lanka. Produced and directed by Paul Stern.
Civics and Political Systems; Sociology
Dist - AMNSTY

Sri Swami Chidananda 120 MIN
VHS / U-matic
Color
Presents Sri Swami Satchidananda introducing Sri Swami Chidananda, president of the Divine Life Society.
Religion and Philosophy
Dist - IYOGA **Prod** - IYOGA

Sri Swami Satchidananda and Retired Major General Jack Kidd - an Informal Evening
VHS
Color
Covers a discussion of the underlying causes of the nuclear arms race and in particular President Reagan's 'Starwars Proposal.'.
Education; Religion and Philosophy
Dist - IYOGA **Prod** - IYOGA

Sri Swami Satchidananda at Johns Hopkins Medical School 90 MIN
VHS
Color
Features the Swami at Johns Hopkins discussing Yoga and natural approaches to health.
Education; Religion and Philosophy
Dist - IYOGA **Prod** - IYOGA 1977

Sri Swami Satchidananda at Santa Barbara, 12/29/79 60 MIN
VHS
Color
Features the Swami Discussing adwaita philosophy, all is dranging, abortion, and playing the game while remembering the truth.
Education; Religion and Philosophy
Dist - IYOGA **Prod** - IYOGA 1979

Sri Swami Satchidananda at Santa Barbara, 4 - 1/1/80 60 MIN
VHS
Color
Presents the Swami discussing wisdom for the new year, wearing leather, explaining highest consciousness, and Christians practicing toga.
Education; Religion and Philosophy
Dist - IYOGA **Prod** - IYOGA 1980

Sri Swami Satchidananda at Santa Barbara, 1 - 12/30/81 45 MIN
VHS
Color
Presents the Swami discussing four seekers and Dasyamuithi, understanding through stillness, how to find true peace, and energy crisis and modern lifestyle.
Education; Religion and Philosophy
Dist - IYOGA **Prod** - IYOGA 1981

Sri Swami Satchidananda at Santa Barbara, 3 - 12/31/79
VHS
Color
Presents the Swami discussing Integral Yoga School, Virginia Ashram, Maha Vakyas, must one abandon one's family, and how to understand starvation.
Education; Religion and Philosophy
Dist - IYOGA **Prod** - IYOGA 1979

Sri Swami Satchidananda at Santa Barbara, 2 - 12/30/81 60 MIN
VHS
Color
Features the Swami discussing fear of the Guru, plans for Virginia Ashram and LOTUS, kaivalya moksha, Sri Ramakrishna and Ranana Maharshi, attributelessness at Kevalam, and how to get the answer to the riddle of life.
Education; Religion and Philosophy
Dist - IYOGA **Prod** - IYOGA 1981

Sri Swami Satchidananda at Saye, 3/21/81 60 MIN
VHS
Color
Presents the Swami discoursing on vegetarian cats and dogs, meat and alcohol abstinence, spiritual growth at one's own speed, value of mistake - making, danger of supernatural powers, story of Visvamitra, Mahatma Gandhi and Ahimsa, and the value of ashram life.
Education; Religion and Philosophy
Dist - IYOGA **Prod** - IYOGA 1981

Sri Swami Satchidananda at Saye, 8/16//80 - on - - the Thirukural, Pt 3 50 MIN
VHS
Color
Features the Swami telling his disciples about impartiality, self - restraint, righteous behavior, cherishing guests, uttering pleasant words, and gratitude.
Education; Religion and Philosophy
Dist - IYOGA **Prod** - IYOGA 1980

Sri Swami Satchidananda at Saye, 11/16/81 - on - the Thirukural, Pt 2 50 MIN
VHS
Color
Features the Swami telling his disciples about virtuous domestic life, children, and unlimited love.
Education; Religion and Philosophy
Dist - IYOGA **Prod** - IYOGA 1980

Sri Swami Satchidananda at Sayva, 10/16/82 - Pt 2 52 MIN
VHS
Color
Presents the Swami discussing pleasure and pain, reincarnation, intelligence, truth in religion, yantra, inner guidance, and self - will.
Education; Religion and Philosophy
Dist - IYOGA **Prod** - IYOGA 1982

Sri Swami Satchidananda at Sayva, 11/14/81 60 MIN
VHS
Color
Features the Swami telling disciples about how Sri Swamiji speaks on the purpose of human endeavor, arrogance, and the commandments will keep one clean.
Education; Religion and Philosophy
Dist - IYOGA **Prod** - IYOGA 1981

Sri Swami Satchidananda at Sayva, 11/7/81 45 MIN
VHS
Color
Presents the Swami discussing four types of people, work ethics, Mahatma Gandhi receiving donations for the poor, giving one's utmost, and a new chant from Sr Devi.
Education; Religion and Philosophy
Dist - IYOGA **Prod** - IYOGA 1981

Sri Swami Satchidananda at Sayva, 12/11/82 50 MIN
VHS
Color
Presents the Swami discussing a memorial satsang for Swami Venkatesanandai, and who controls the mind.
Education; Religion and Philosophy
Dist - IYOGA **Prod** - IYOGA 1982

Sri Swami Satchidananda at Sayva, 12/22/82 50 MIN
VHS
Color
Features the Swami discussing the way to lead a simple but spiritual life, God's experience being always with one, and how to keep a guru alive a long time.
Education; Religion and Philosophy
Dist - IYOGA **Prod** - IYOGA 1982

Sri Swami Satchidananda at Sayva, 3/682 50 MIN
VHS
Color
Presents the Swami discussing memory power, gratitude, whether or not one should meditate on the heart or crown chakra, developing faith, and facing stressful situations.
Education; Religion and Philosophy
Dist - IYOGA **Prod** - IYOGA 1982

Sri Swami Satchidananda at Sayva, 4/11/81 - 1
VHS
Color
Presents the Swami discussing work and play, a farm worker going to the Nataraja festival, accepting criticism, and worshipping God in the heart.
Education; Religion and Philosophy
Dist - IYOGA **Prod** - IYOGA 1981

Sri Swami Satchidananda at Sayva, 4/11/81 - 2
VHS
Color
Presents the Swami asking how can one share peace and joy with one's mate, making decisions, spiritual healing, Yogi's ego versus the Christian idea of soul and asks if God is sadistre and questions hatha yoga.
Education; Religion and Philosophy
Dist - IYOGA **Prod** - IYOGA 1981

Sri Swami Satchidananda at Sayva, 4/25/81 - 1
VHS
Color
Presents the Swami answering questions on, is Grace necessary for liberation, what are the goals, not reaching for goals, is this going to disturb one's peace, and detachment and renunciation.
Education; Religion and Philosophy
Dist - IYOGA **Prod** - IYOGA 1981

Sri Swami Satchidananda at Sayva, 4/25/81 - 2 30 MIN
VHS
Color
Presents the Swami discussing love and peace, how long it takes to practice sincerely, sculptor and reluctant stone, strengthening will, not ego, and how to use the gunas to reach goal.
Education; Religion and Philosophy
Dist - IYOGA **Prod** - IYOGA 1981

Sri Swami Satchidananda at Sayva, 4/3/82 50 MIN
VHS
Color
Presents the Swami telling his disciples about sense control, diet for purity of heart and body, geological changes in California, value of obedience, and no job is menial.
Education; Religion and Philosophy
Dist - IYOGA **Prod** - IYOGA 1982

Sri Swami Satchidananda at Sayva, 5/23/81
VHS
Color
Presents the Swami discussing why God allows so much suffering, arma, jiva and the mind, enlightenment, sex, and moderation and the draft.
Education; Religion and Philosophy
Dist - IYOGA **Prod** - IYOGA 1981

Sri Swami Satchidananda at Sayva, 5/2/81 - 1 60 MIN
VHS
Color
Presents the Swami discussing guidance for decision - making, Guru and God in one's lives, Dhrona and Eklaiva, and the power of Montra.
Education; Religion and Philosophy
Dist - IYOGA **Prod** - IYOGA 1981

Sri Swami Satchidananda at Sayva, 5/2/81 - 2
VHS
Color
Features the Swami discussing Saint Pulsar who builds a mental temple, attitudes toward work and fatigue, organizational goals, should disciples be more missionary about LOTUS, and how faith redeems.
Education; Religion and Philosophy
Dist - IYOGA **Prod** - IYOGA 1981

Sri Swami Satchidananda at Sayva, 5/2/81 - 3 30 MIN
VHS
Color
Presents the Swami discussing faith and surrender to God, the old saying that the Spirit is willing but the flesh is weak, the benefit of group or sangha, and changing though patterns.
Education; Religion and Philosophy
Dist - IYOGA **Prod** - IYOGA 1981

Sri Swami Satchidananda at Sayva, 5/30/81
VHS
Color
Presents the Swami discussing the Significance of LOTUS flower, evolution of the soul in animals and humans, and why the soul takes a body.
Education; Religion and Philosophy
Dist - IYOGA **Prod** - IYOGA 1981

Sri Swami Satchidananda at Sayva, 7/25/81
VHS
Color
Features the Swami in a special talk made on the anniversary of his 15th year of service in the USA, with the theme 'God is doing all through me.'
Education; Religion and Philosophy
Dist - IYOGA **Prod** - IYOGA 1981

Sri Swami Satchidananda at Sayva, 7/4/81 - 1 60 MIN
VHS
Color
Features the Swami discussing seeing beyond the body, Columbus and his discovery of America, the Devil, does the self know itself after death, sleepers sleep, and the saint who called God a scavenger.
Education; Religion and Philosophy
Dist - IYOGA **Prod** - IYOGA 1981

Sri Swami Satchidananda at Sayva, 7/4/81 - 2
VHS
Color
Presents the Swami duscussing the necessity of doing Yoga practices, the story of a child who wanted to leave his parents for spiritual life, changing one's karma, and adwaita and experience.
Education; Religion and Philosophy
Dist - IYOGA **Prod** - IYOGA 1981

Sri Swami Satchidananda at Sayva, 8/15/81
VHS
Color
Presents the Swami discussing such as how siddhis arise and how they are used, how to make spiritual progress, the nature of a contented mind, discrimination, significance of 108, fear, and helping one's parents.
Education; Religion and Philosophy
Dist - IYOGA **Prod** - IYOGA 1981

Sri Swami Satchidananda at Sayva, 8/16/80 - Pt 1 40 MIN
VHS
Color
Features the Swami discussing educating the mind while learning from the world, letting others influence one, the soul and the mind, the handicapped, and abortion.
Education; Religion and Philosophy
Dist - IYOGA **Prod** - IYOGA 1980

Sri Swami Satchidananda at Sayva, 8/21/81 60 MIN
VHS
Color
Presents the Swami discussing fasting, closeness and refection by guru, karma versus astrology, wants versus needs, and everything is perfect, but how to feel that.
Education; Religion and Philosophy
Dist - IYOGA **Prod** - IYOGA 1981

Sri Swami Satchidananda at Sayva, 8/21/81 and 9/2/81 30 MIN
VHS
Color
Presents the Swami discussing how God gives one everything one needs, negative energy and how to deal with it, guru gita, the nature of the physical universe, and keeping the mind in Bliss.
Education; Religion and Philosophy
Dist - IYOGA **Prod** - IYOGA 1981

Sri Swami Satchidananda at Sayva, 8/9/80 50 MIN
VHS
Color
Presents the Swami discussing how one knows if it's God's will to one's own, after Samadni how one functions on the earth plane, the meaning of OM, use of marijuana, killing of pests, a story from the Mahabharata, different planes in nature, and practicing on one's own, away from the sangha.
Education; Religion and Philosophy
Dist - IYOGA **Prod** - IYOGA 1980

Sri Swami Satchidananda at Sayva, 9/2/81 60 MIN
VHS
Color
Presents the Swami discussing will power development, serving family versus spiritual community, duties of a householder, how to develop a sense of humor, God gives us what we need, and how the New York IYI was obtained.
Education; Religion and Philosophy
Dist - IYOGA **Prod** - IYOGA 1981

Sri Swami Satchidananda at Sayve, 10/16/82 - Pt 1 52 MIN
VHS
Color
Observes the Swami lecturing on happiness, how to get and keep it, being in but not of the world, and settlessness does guarantee happiness.
Education; Religion and Philosophy
Dist - IYOGA **Prod** - IYOGA 1982

Sri Swami Satchidananda at St John the Divine 60 MIN
VHS
Color
Features the Swami delivering a sermon during the Ecumenical Pentacost Service at the Cathedral of St John The Divine. Includes as other celebrants clergy from the Buddhist, Islamic, Jewish and Catholic faiths, with chanting and processional. Edited version.
Education; Religion and Philosophy
Dist - IYOGA **Prod** - IYOGA 1983

Sri Swami Satcidananda at Saye, August, 1980 - on the Thirakkural, Pt 4 35 MIN
VHS
Color
Presents the Swami counseling not to speak profitless words, describing ascetic virtue, benevolence, renunciation, penance, and Karma.
Education; Religion and Philosophy
Dist - IYOGA **Prod** - IYOGA 1980

SRO - Single Room Occupancy 13 MIN
U-matic / VHS / 16mm
Bitter Vintage Series
Color (H C A)
Examines the problems of the old, the ill and the unwanted. Shows occupants in a welfare hotel as they comment on the hopelessness and poverty of their lives.
Health and Safety; Sociology
Dist - CAROUF **Prod** - WNETTV

SSS 5 MIN
16mm
Color (G)
$20.00 rental
Jumps with a dance film starring Pooh Kaye and Sally Silvers, among many others and improvisational music. Covers the streets of the East Village. Produced by Henry Hills.
Fine Arts
Dist - CANCIN

The SSW Test - a Measure of Central Auditory Dysfunction 20 MIN
16mm
Color (PRO)
LC 73-703118
Shows the use of the ssw test (dichotic speech test) as it relates to diagnosing site of lesion in three brain damaged aphasiac patients.
English Language; Psychology
Dist - MEMEC **Prod** - MEMEC 1970

St Adolf II 16 MIN
16mm
Color (H A)
$540.00 purchase, $50.00 rental
Uses the words, music and art of schizophrenic artist, Adolf Wolfli, 1864 - 1930, to present the frightening and exciting world in which he believed he was God, the Devil, a saint, a star - traveller and a potentate with many wives.
Fine Arts; Health and Safety
Dist - AFA **Prod** - ACGB 1971

St Albans - an Ethnic Programme 20 MIN
16mm
Color
LC 80-700837
Presents the St Albans East Primary School in Melbourne, Australia, which has an enrollment of 800 pupils, 80% from non - English speaking backgrounds. Shows how the school runs an imaginative program in ethnic languages and cultures which involves parents, teachers and the community.
Education; Geography - World; Sociology
Dist - TASCOR **Prod** - CANCAE 1978

St Augustine, City of the Centuries 15 MIN
16mm
Color
Features St Augustine, the oldest city in Florida.
Geography - United States; History - United States
Dist - FLADC **Prod** - FLADC

St Augustine - the Oldest City 14 MIN
16mm / U-matic / VHS
Re - discovering America Series
Color (I J H)
LC 74-702051
Presents a field trip through the United States' oldest city, St Augustine in Florida.
Geography - United States; Social Science
Dist - AIMS **Prod** - COP 1973

St Barthelemy 30 MIN
VHS
John Stobart's WorldScape series
Color (A G)
$19.95 purchase _ #STO - 02
Features the island of St Barthelemy in the French West Indies. Follows artist John Stobart as he travels the globe, painting directly from life, and demonstrates the simplicity of the method that has made him the foremost living maritime artist. Demonstrates Stobart's classical maritime style in numerous evocative settings around the world. Part of a series on painting outdoors.
Fine Arts
Dist - ARTSAM **Prod** - WORLDS

St Bonaventure Indian Mission and School 30 MIN
VHS
Faith completed by works series
Color (R G)
$39.95 purchase _ #FCBW2
Witnesses the work of lay missionaries in several mission fields in the United States and abroad. Starts from the premise that all Christians are challenged to become missionaries, to bring the good news of Jesus to the poor and marginalized of the world. Part of six parts on evangelization in the Roman Catholic Church.
Religion and Philosophy; Social Science
Dist - CTNA **Prod** - CTNA 1994

St Croix - Reflections 13 MIN
16mm / U-matic / VHS
Color (J A)
Discusses the river's history, resources and changing uses while meeting old Northwest traders, trappers, explorers and mountain men.
Geography - United States; Physical Education and Recreation
Dist - USNAC **Prod** - USNPS 1985

St Croix - US Virgin Islands
VHS
Color (G)
$39.90 purchase _ #0413
Sails on a 37 foot Striker and a Hobie Cat at St Croix in the US Virgin Islands. Visits white coral reefs to view parrotfish.
Geography - World; Physical Education and Recreation
Dist - SEVVID

St Croix, US Virgin Islands - pier diving 30 MIN
VHS
Scuba World series
Color (G)
$24.90 purchase _ #0432
Visits St Croix in the US Virgin Islands. Dives Fredericksted Pier.
Geography - World; Physical Education and Recreation
Dist - SEVVID

St Flourney Lobos Logo 12 MIN
16mm
Color (C)
$220.00
Experimental film by Will Hindle.
Fine Arts
Dist - AFA **Prod** - AFA 1970

St George and the dragon and Pocahontas 15 MIN
VHS / 16mm
English folk heroes series
Color (I)
Presents Edmond Spencer's St George And The Dragon and William Makepeace Thackery's Pocahontas. The second of six installments of the English Folk Heroes Series, which presents figures from English literature in 15 - minute programs.
Literature and Drama
Dist - GPN **Prod** - CTI 1990

St George's Cay Belize - underwater wedding and more 30 MIN
VHS
Scuba World series
Color (G)
$24.90 purchase _ #0455
Visits the uncrowded dive sites of St George's Cay near Belize. Experiences an underwater wedding.
Geography - World; Physical Education and Recreation
Dist - SEVVID

St Joan 60 MIN
U-matic / VHS
Drama - play, performance, perception series; Dramatis personae
Color (H C A)
Explores methods of character development. Uses the play St Joan as an example.
Literature and Drama
Dist - FI **Prod** - BBCTV 1978

The St John Passion 112 MIN
U-matic / VHS
Color (C)
$299.00, $149.00 purchase _ #AD - 916
Presents the Passion of St John in concert at St Thomas Church in Leipzig, where Bach was the organist. Features Venceslava Hruba - Freiberger, Alain Zaepffel, Peter Schreier, Herman - Christian Polster, Jurgen Kurth and the Choir of St Thomas Church.
Fine Arts; History - World
Dist - FOTH **Prod** - FOTH

St Lawrence Seaway - Pathway to the Atlantic 15 MIN
16mm / U-matic / VHS
Color (I J A)
LC 72-708710
Contrasts the forest industries, fishing trade and handicrafts business with the heavy commercial industries along the St Lawrence River. Tells how fur and lumber are found in abundance, and how cod, halibut, lobster and many other kinds of fish are caught by the millions. Explains why the source of water power provides the greatest prosperity to the area's most important industry, paper manufacturing.
Business and Economics; Geography - World
Dist - PHENIX **Prod** - EVANSA 1969

St Louis 25 MIN
16mm
Color
LC 79-700400
Tours the city of St Louis, Missouri, emphasizing its historic heritage.
Geography - United States; History - United States
Dist - CHROMH **Prod** - CHROMH 1978

St Louis blues 17 MIN
U-matic / VHS / 16mm
B&W (A)
Presents the only film appearance of jazz singer Bessie Smith.
Fine Arts
Dist - CNEMAG STRFLS **Prod** - CNEMAG SPCTRA 1929

St Louis Cardinals - the movie 94 MIN
VHS
Color (G)

$29.95 purchase _ #S00620
Traces the history of the major league baseball St Louis Cardinals.
Geography - United States; Physical Education and Recreation
Dist - UILL

St Martin, Sint Maarten
VHS
Color (G)
$29.95 purchase _ #0843
Visits Saint Martin in the Virgin Islands, which boasts three dozen of the world's prettiest beaches.
Geography - World; Physical Education and Recreation
Dist - SEVVID

St Mary's bridge test 9 MIN
16mm
Color
LC 74-705692
Describes the vibration frequency and live load tests conducted on the St Mary's Bridge, located at St Mary's, West Virginia, a sister bridge to the Point Pleasant Bridge, which collapsed in December 1967.
Industrial and Technical Education; Science - Physical
Dist - USNAC **Prod -** USDTFH 1970

St Matthew Passion 91 MIN
U-matic / VHS
Color (C)
$299.00, $149.00 purchase _ #AD - 993
Presents the Passion of St Matthew in concert at St Thomas Church in Leipzig, where Bach was the organist. Reveals that the placement of the choirs makes clear Bach's choral intentions. Features Regina Werner, Rosemarie Lang, Peter Schreier, Siegried Lorenz, Theo Adam and the Choir of St Thomas Church.
Fine Arts; History - World
Dist - FOTH **Prod -** FOTH

St Matthews is My Home 14 MIN
VHS / U-matic
Under the Blue Umbrella Series
Color (P)
Shows Joe narrating scenes from his life near a small rural town. Describes his family's involvement with the farm.
Agriculture; Sociology
Dist - AITECH **Prod -** SCETV 1977

St Maximilian Kolbe - patron saint of hard times - Sw Maksymilian Kolbe - patron trudnych czasow 48 MIN
VHS
Color (G A) (POLISH)
$29.95 purchase _ #V288, #V287
Tells the story of St Maximilian Kolbe, a Franciscan priest and a worshipper of the Holy Mother of God. Follows his travels throughout the world, from Poland, to Italy and Japan, to preach the word of God. Also available with Polish narration.
Fine Arts; History - World; Religion and Philosophy
Dist - POLART

St Michael's College
VHS
Campus clips series
Color (H C A)
$29.95 purchase _ #CC0112V
Takes a video visit to the campus of St Michael's College in Vermont. Shows many of the distinctive features of the campus, and interviews students about their experiences. Provides information on the composition of the student body, professors, academics, social life, housing, and other subjects.
Education
Dist - CAMV

St Patrick's Day 13 MIN
VHS
Color (K P I)
$69.95 purchase _ #10346VG
Explains the history and traditions of Saint Patrick's Day. Displays some of the parades, dances and special programs for the holiday. Shows how an Irish - American family celebrates with special foods, music, and remembrances of vacations to Ireland. Presents some of the symbols of Ireland such as the shamrock, leprechaun, the harp and shillelagh. Includes a guide.
Civics and Political Systems; Religion and Philosophy; Social Science
Dist - UNL

St Paul past 42 MIN
VHS
Color (G)
$19.95 purchase _ #V - 005
Brings to life the days of lumber barons, steamboats, railroads and waves of early ethnic immigrants in a production celebrating 150 years of St Paul, Minnesota history.
History - United States
Dist - MINHS **Prod -** KTCATV

St Peters, Rome 3 MIN
16mm
Of all Things Series
Color (P I)
Discusses St Peters Cathedral in Rome, Italy.
Geography - World
Dist - AVED **Prod -** BAILYL

St Rose Philippine Duchesne 45 MIN
VHS
Color (R)
$29.95 purchase _ #492 - 9
Offers a biography of St Rose Philippine Duchesne and her 83 - year ministry, including the fulfillment of her dream to work among Native Americans. Includes a study guide.
Religion and Philosophy; Sociology
Dist - USCC **Prod -** USCC 1992

St Rube 16 MIN
16mm
Color; B&W (G)
$35.00 rental
Details a young saint's decline from mystic to saloon - keeper. Features Babth and Mark Wallner with music by Dick Bright and His Sounds of Delight Orchestra.
Fine Arts
Dist - CANCIN **Prod -** JONESE 1977

St Thomas, St John
VHS
Color (G)
$29.95 purchase _ #0842
Visits the islands of St Thomas and St John in the US Virgin Islands.
Geography - World; Physical Education and Recreation
Dist - SEVVID

St Valentine's Day Massacre 12 MIN
16mm
American Film Genre - the Gangster Film Series
Color (H C A)
LC 77-701140
Presents an excerpt from the motion picture St Valentine's Day Massacre, issued in 1967. Features a dramatization of the feud between the gangs of Al Capone and Bugs Moran which resulted in the St Valentine's Day massacre in Chicago in 1929. Exemplifies the gangster film genre.
Fine Arts
Dist - FI **Prod -** TWCF 1975

St Vincent - the Island, the Dream, the Man 14 MIN
16mm
Color
Explores St Vincent Island off Florida in the Gulf of Mexico.
Geography - United States; History - United States
Dist - FLADC **Prod -** FLADC

Stab in the dark 50 MIN
VHS
Trial series
Color; PAL (H C A)
PdS99 purchase
Follows the attempted murder trial of James Robertson through four days of court proceedings in the High Court. Juxtaposes Robertson's vows of innocence with the 24 prosecution witnesses who attest to Robertson's two years of violent conflict with his neighbor prior to the attempted murder. Second in a series of five programs filmed by the BBC in the Scottish courts.
Civics and Political Systems; Sociology
Dist - BBCENE

Stabilization Policy - are We Still in Control 30 MIN
U-matic / VHS
Economics USA Series
Color (C)
Business and Economics
Dist - ANNCPB **Prod -** WEFA

Stabilizing aerial apparatus 20 MIN
VHS
Aerial apparatus series
Color (IND)
$135.00 purchase _ #35450
Presents one of a five - part series that is a teaching companion for IFSTA's Fire Department Aerial Apparatus. Displays function of the hydraulic system that controls the stabilizers. Demonstrates how to engage the power take - off system and to set the stabilizers. Shows how to achieve maximum stability. Based on chapter 5.
Health and Safety; Science - Physical; Social Science
Dist - OKSU **Prod -** ACCTRA

Stabilizing Coastal Bluffs with Plants 27 MIN
VHS / 16mm
(C A H)
$90.00 - $125.00 purchase, $16.00 rental
Covers various methods of stablizing the erosion of land along waterways using plants. Gives details regarding types of plants, angle of slope, and methods of preparing, planting, and caring for the plants.
Science - Natural
Dist - CORNRS

Stable and Safe 20 MIN
16mm
Color
LC 74-705693
Reveals what frequently happens when pilots inadvertently fly marginal or IFR weather and lost their visual reference, becoming dangerously disoriented. Describes the different types of stability augmentation systems available for use in general aviation aircraft to assist pilots in maintaining control.
Industrial and Technical Education; Psychology; Science - Natural; Social Science
Dist - USFAA **Prod -** FAAFL 1969

The Stableboy's Christmas 25 MIN
VHS
Color (K P I R)
$29.95 purchase, $10.00 rental _ #35 - 89 - 8579
Presents a unique version of the Christmas story. Tells how the miserly innkeeper at the Bethlehem Inn rejects rumors of a Messiah, while his stableboy believes it will happen. Shows that the innkeeper's attitude changes when Jesus is born.
Literature and Drama; Religion and Philosophy
Dist - APH **Prod -** VIDOUT

The Stableboy's Christmas
VHS
Color (G R)
$19.95 purchase
Tells the story of a little girl who learns the true meaning of Christmas on a time - travel trip back to Jerusalem, where she sees a stableboy offer his lamb to the Christ Child.
Guidance and Counseling; Literature and Drama; Religion and Philosophy
Dist - CPH **Prod -** LUMIS

The Stack environment (S - machine) 50 MIN
U-matic / VHS
Computer languages series; Pt 1
Color
Discusses identifier collision as motivation for a stack structured environment, definition of the S - machine and control trees in computer languages.
Industrial and Technical Education; Mathematics; Sociology
Dist - MIOT **Prod -** MIOT

Stacking and Firing 11 MIN
16mm / U-matic / VHS
Color (H C A)
Demonstrates the correct stacking of both green and glazed pottery in a small kiln. Shows each step in firing the pieces.
Fine Arts
Dist - IU **Prod -** IU 1949

Stacking the Deck 30 MIN
16mm
Footsteps Series
Color
LC 79-701555
Discusses why competence is needed for sheer survival and offers guidelines and activities for helping children increase competence in certain areas.
Guidance and Counseling; Home Economics; Sociology
Dist - USNAC **Prod -** USOE 1978

Staff burnout 30 MIN
U-matic / VHS
Issues of cystic fibrosis series
Color (PRO C)
$395.00 purchase, $80.00 rental _ #C891 - VI - 050
Conducts an interview with a team of professionals who deal with terminally ill children. Addresses the issues of how and when to decide to send the child home or to leave the patient in the hospital, trying experimental drugs and how and when to involve the child as well as the parents in the decision making. Part of a 13 - part series on cystic fibrosis presented by Drs Ivan Harwood and Cyril Worby.
Health and Safety; Science - Natural; Sociology
Dist - HSCIC

Staff Communication 15 MIN
16mm
Developing Skills in Communications Series
Color
LC 74-712969
Defines communication, stressing the role of empathy. Illustrates the problems, faults and misunderstandings of speaker and listener in the communication process and shows how to overcome obstacles to effective communication.
English Language; Psychology; Social Science
Dist - TRNAID **Prod -** TRNAID 1969

Staff Development 30 MIN
U-matic / VHS
Recruiting and Developing the D P Professional Series

Color
Business and Economics; Guidance and Counseling; Psychology
Dist - DELTAK **Prod** - DELTAK

Staff Development and Training 8 MIN
U-matic
Child Welfare Learning Laboratory Materials Series
Color
Orients supervisory personnel to examination of organizational environment, learning needs assessment and identification of training resources.
Guidance and Counseling; Sociology
Dist - UMITV **Prod** - UMITV

Staff Development Series
Needle Play
Preparing a Child for a Renal Transplant
Preparing a Child for an Appendectomy
Preparing a Child for Anesthesia, or, Recovery Room and ICU
Preparing a Child for Herniorrhaphy
Teaching a Child about Leukemia
Teaching a Child about Nephrosis
Dist - CFDC

Staff education for total hip replacement surgery 40 MIN
VHS
Color (PRO C)
$250.00 purchase, $70.00 rental _ #4421
Discusses the medical and nursing care required by patients who require total hip replacement surgery. Begins with a history of orthopedic surgery specific to hip replacement. Explains the anatomy and physiology of the hip and hip joints. Discusses factors that may exacerbate hip problems, such as osteoarthritis, obesity and menopause. Conservative treatment measures, including non - steroidal and steroidal medications, moist heat and assistive devices, are briefly covered. Shows the surgical procedure and discusses possible complications. Stresses nursing staff role in patient teaching. Produced by the National Assn of Orthopaedic Nurses.
Health and Safety
Dist - AJN

Staff education for total knee replacement surgery 28 MIN
VHS
Color (PRO C)
$250.00 purchase, $70.00 rental _ #4422
Discusses the medical and nursing care required by patients who require total knee replacement surgery. Examines the anatomy and functioning of a normal knee. Covers the treatment plan, beginning with conservative measures. Explains that if conservative measures don't work, surgery is considered. Includes historical background on knee replacement and contraindications to surgery. Shows the surgery, as well as how the replacement device is selected. Considers surgical and non - surgical complications, such as scarring, infection, phlebitis, pulmonary embolism and slow healing. Looks at the nurse's role in the procedure and as a patient teacher. Produced by the National Assn of Orthopaedic Nurses.
Health and Safety
Dist - AJN

Staff Meetings that Work for You 19 MIN
VHS / U-matic
Personal Time Management Series
Color
Business and Economics
Dist - DELTAK **Prod** - TELSTR

Staff training video for Second Step - preschool - grade 5 90 MIN
VHS
Color (T)
$145.00 purchase, $50.00 rental _ #611
Uses live classroom footage and interviews to train educators in how best to present Second Step lessons and implement the program on a school - wide basis. Provides important background information on youth violence issues necessary to successfully implement the curriculum. Designed to be used in conjunction with live training, it uses a start - stop format and training guide in order to facilitate discussion and practice of program strategies.
Education; Sociology
Dist - SICACC **Prod** - SICACC

Staffing 30 MIN
U-matic / VHS
Business of Management Series Lesson 13; Lesson 13
Color (C A)
Discusses the importance of staffing to the success of the organization. Gives an in - depth case study at Reader's Digest headquarters in New York that reveals the anatomy of the staffing process at a major corporation.
Business and Economics; Psychology
Dist - SCCON **Prod** - SCCON

Staffing - Developing the Employee
VHS / 16mm
(PRO)
$150.00 purchase _ #PS110
Discusses the manager's role in developing the employee from day 1, and the importance of this to the employee's success.
Business and Economics
Dist - RMIBHF **Prod** - RMIBHF

Staffing - Developing the Employee
VHS / U-matic
Principles of Management Series
Color
Discusses the manager's role in the induction of employees and the importance of this process to the employee's success.
Business and Economics; Psychology
Dist - RMIBHF **Prod** - RMIBHF

Staffing - Matching People to Jobs
VHS / 16mm
(PRO)
$150.00 purchase _ #PS109
Illustrates the relationship between organizing and staffing. Discusses job analysis, job descriptions, and job specifications in the context of their importance to the staffing process.
Business and Economics
Dist - RMIBHF **Prod** - RMIBHF

Staffing the Executive Branch 30 MIN
VHS / U-matic
American Government 2 Series
Color (C)
Explains the selection of the President's Cabinet and major advisors and the roles they play in the executive office.
Civics and Political Systems
Dist - DALCCD **Prod** - DALCCD

Staffs
16mm
Color tint (G)
$22.00 rental
Covers a variety of different experiments made with roughly the same technique as during Fischinger's Munich period. Characterizes basic imagery of hard - edged parallel bars moving up and down in rhythmic patterns with superimposed layers.
Fine Arts
Dist - CANCIN **Prod** - FISCHF 1923

Stage at a time series
Portraits 30 MIN
Sign posts 30 MIN
Stages 30 MIN
Dist - GPN

Stage at a Time
Portraits 30 MIN
Vaudeville Jazz 30 MIN
Dist - GPN

Stage by stage - Les Miserables 60 MIN
VHS
Color (G C H)
$69.00 purchase
Chronicles the ascent of a hit musical with backstage footage from productions in Oslo, Budapest, and Vienna, and from opening nights in London and on Broadway. Interviews the show's creators and stage designers.
Fine Arts
Dist - INSIM

Stage Door 92 MIN
BETA
B&W
Depicts the disappointments and successes of the women living in a theatrical boarding house. Stars Katharine Hepburn, Ginger Rogers, Lucille Ball and Eve Arden.
Fine Arts
Dist - RMIBHF **Prod** - UNKNWN 1937

The Stage fight director 30 MIN
VHS
Color (PRO C G)
$119.00 purchase, $39.00 rental _ #610
Follows the work of combat choreographer David Boushey as he prepares a production of Romeo and Juliet at the Utah Shakespeare Festival. Shows Boushey working closely with the actors, the director, scenic designer and costume designer. Produced by the Theater Arts Video Library.
Fine Arts
Dist - FIRLIT

Stage for a Nation 52 MIN
U-matic / VHS
Color (C)
$89.95 purchase _ #EX1891
Celebrates the historical and present National Theatre in Washington, DC. Features scenes from some of its biggest hits.
Fine Arts
Dist - FOTH **Prod** - FOTH

Stage fright 13 MIN
U-matic / VHS / 16mm
Art of communication series
Color (J H C A)
$325, $235 purchase _ #78509
Describes different techniques for dealing with stage fright.
Social Science
Dist - CORF

Stage II Recovery Part Two - Identifying Self - Defeating Learned Behaviors 30 MIN
VHS
(A)
$395.00 _ #83204
Presents a seminar by Earnie Larsen on advanced alcohol addiction recovery. Explains how to destroy self defeating learned behaviors.
Guidance and Counseling; Health and Safety; Psychology
Dist - CMPCAR **Prod** - CMPCAR

Stage II Recovery - Pt I
VHS / 16mm
Stage II Recovery Series
Color (G)
$395.00 purchase, $70.00 rental _ #4970, 4974, 0436J, 0440J
Explains the basic issues of life after addiction. Produced by Earnie Larsen.
Guidance and Counseling; Health and Safety; Psychology
Dist - HAZELB

Stage II Recovery - Pt II
VHS / 16mm
Stage II Recovery Series
Color (G)
$395.00 purchase, $70.00 rental _ #4971, 4975, 0437J, 0441J
Considers caretaking, people - pleasing and workaholism. Shows how to identify and correct these behaviors. Produced by Earnie Larsen.
Guidance and Counseling; Health and Safety; Psychology; Sociology
Dist - HAZELB

Stage II Recovery Series
Stage II Recovery - Pt I
Stage II Recovery - Pt II
Dist - HAZELB

Stage lighting - shedding some light 95 MIN
VHS
Color (G C H)
$99.00 purchase _ #DL136
Identifies the mechanics of stage lighting, including the instruments and accessories, how to hang and focus them, and lighting safety.
Fine Arts
Dist - INSIM

Stagecoach 100 MIN
U-matic / VHS / 16mm
B&W
Presents the classic among westerns portraying the saga of a westward stagecoach and intermingling of eight different lives. Stars John Wayne, Claire Trevor, Thomas Mitchell, John Carradine, Andy Devine, George Bancroft, Burton Churchill, Donald Meek and Tim Holt. Based on a story by Ernest Haycox and directed by John Ford.
Fine Arts
Dist - FI **Prod** - UAA 1939

Staged Reconstruction of a Severely Burned Hand 20 MIN
16mm
Color (PRO)
LC 75-702316
Demonstrates procedures for correcting severe burn deformities in the hands of children. Emphasizes the value of early repeated operations.
Health and Safety; Science
Dist - EATONL **Prod** - EATONL 1970

Stagedoor Canteen 132 MIN
16mm
B&W
Tells how a soldier falls in love with a canteen worker.
Fine Arts
Dist - KITPAR **Prod** - UAA 1932

Stages 30 MIN
U-matic / VHS
Stage at a Time Series
Color (P)
Takes place on a miniature stage and explores the hopes and dreams of two stagehands. Instructed by the unseen stage manager to take down a western set and put up an outer space set, the hands find they have no blueprint.

Literature and Drama
Dist - GPN **Prod** - WUFT

Stages 57 MIN
16mm
Color (G)
_ #106C 0180 518
Celebrates Canada's performing artists. Features a small group of artists who show through their work the significance of being an entertainer in Canada.
Fine Arts; Geography - World; History - World; Sociology
Dist - CFLMDC **Prod** - NFBC 1980

Stages in Play 7 MIN
U-matic
Take Time Series
(A)
Demonstrates the influence of parents and others caring for pre - schoolers on the physical and emotional development of the child.
Health and Safety; Psychology; Sociology
Dist - ACCESS **Prod** - ACCESS 1976

The Stages of Instruction - Application, Examination and Review or Critique 20 MIN
16mm
Military Instruction Series
B&W
LC FIE56-245
Explains the importance of learning by doing, of giving examinations to improve learning and to measure the effectiveness of teaching.
Education; Psychology
Dist - USNAC **Prod** - USA 1956

The Stages of Instruction - Preparation 12 MIN
16mm
Military Instruction Series
B&W
LC FIE56-243
Discusses the importance of estimating the instructional situation and checking all arrangements to insure no slip occurs up in the classroom.
Education; Psychology
Dist - USNAC **Prod** - USA 1956

The Stages of Instruction - Presentation 12 MIN
16mm
Military Instruction Series
B&W
LC FIE56-244
Explains the elements of presentation in military instruction and the lecture, conference and demonstration methods of explanation.
Education; Psychology
Dist - USNAC **Prod** - USA 1956

Stages of intimate teenage relationships 23 MIN
VHS / U-matic
Teen - family life series
Color (J H G)
$179.00, $229.00 purchase, $60.00 rental
Presents and examines the different stages teenagers or adults may go through within intimate and family relationships. Illustrates common problems such as guilt, mind games and triangulation.
Guidance and Counseling; Health and Safety; Psychology; Sociology
Dist - NDIM **Prod** - FAMLIF 1993

Stagflation - Why Couldn't We Beat it 30 MIN
U-matic / VHS
Economics USA Series
Color (C)
Business and Economics
Dist - ANNCPB **Prod** - WEFA

Staggerlee 55 MIN
16mm
B&W
Presents the famous interview with jailed Panther leader Bobby Seale broadcasted nationally on N E T. Describes Bobby's experiences in jail, his life before he was a Panther, his reasons for becoming a revolutionary and the goals of the revolution.
History - United States
Dist - CANWRL **Prod** - CANWRL

Staging Classical Tragedy 30 MIN
U-matic / VHS
Color (C)
$249.00, $149.00 purchase _ #AD - 1612
Identifies the physical parts of the acting space as used by ancient Greek dramatists using the theatre at Epidauros as an example. Refers specifically to the 'Oresteia' and shows how the plays would have been staged in the time of Aeschylus.
History - World; Literature and Drama
Dist - FOTH **Prod** - FOTH

Staging Laparotomy for Hodgkin's Disease 17 MIN
U-matic / VHS
Color (PRO)
Uses close - up videography to demonstrate the steps of a staging laparotomy.
Health and Safety
Dist - UARIZ **Prod** - UARIZ

Staging of Lung Cancer 19 MIN
U-matic
Color
Explains the classification of lung cancer into different stages. Discusses when, how and why cancer patients are grouped according to their stage of cancer.
Health and Safety
Dist - UTEXSC **Prod** - UTEXSC

The Staging of Shakespeare's plays 45 MIN
VHS
Color (G C H)
$159.00 purchase _ #DL381
Presents an illustrated lecture by George Walton Williams, professor of English at Duke Univ. Traces the development of theatrical playing areas in pre - Shakespearean England. Using information from recent excavations of the Rose and the Globe Theatres, Williams discusses how certain scenes from Shakespeare's plays might have been performed on the adaptable Elizabethan stage.
Fine Arts; Literature and Drama
Dist - INSIM

Staging the Advanced Cardiac Life Support Providers' Course 30 MIN
16mm
Color (PRO)
LC 78-700954
Provides visual orientation to the logistics of staging the advanced cardiac life support providers' course developed by the American Heart Association.
Health and Safety
Dist - USNAC **Prod** - NMAC 1978

Staid poot 3 MIN
16mm
Trildogy series
Color (G)
$8.00 rental
Features part of the Trildogy with music by Clyde McCoy to be shown with Up and Atom.
Fine Arts
Dist - CANCIN **Prod** - WENDTD 1975

Stain Gauge Transducer 9 MIN
VHS / U-matic
Color (PRO)
Describes preparation of the pressure monitoring device including basic principles of the 3 - way stopcock, flushing the transducer system assembly and bedside setup prior to the connection to arterial and venous lines.
Health and Safety; Psychology; Science - Natural
Dist - UWASH **Prod** - UWASH

Stained Glass 15 MIN
16mm
Color
LC 79-701194
Traces the historical and religious development of stained glass from medieval times to the 20th century.
Fine Arts
Dist - SKYE **Prod** - CROANC 1979

Stained Glass 24 MIN
U-matic / VHS
Color (J H)
Visits two famous glassmaking studios to examine step - by - step how various forms of stained glass are created. Shows techniques for creating a pattern, cutting the glass, and fitting the lead for a stained glass window.
Fine Arts
Dist - CEPRO **Prod** - CEPRO

Stained Glass - a Photographic Essay 8 MIN
U-matic / VHS / 16mm
Color (I)
Shows a young craftsman expressing his love for beauty as he makes a stained glass work of art. Without narration.
Fine Arts
Dist - PHENIX **Prod** - SMALLY 1970

Stained Glass - Basic Techniques 120 MIN
VHS
Color (I)
$59.95 purchase _ #VC - - 732
Presents materials, pattern copying and cutting, scoring and breaking, foiling and soldering, patina and other finishing touches in working with stained glass. Features Jack Loewen who demonstrates making a simple flat panel and a six - panel lampshade. Indludes five patterns.
Fine Arts
Dist - CRYSP **Prod** - CRYSP

Stained Glass Craft 30 MIN
U-matic / VHS
Arts and Crafts Series
Color (H A)
LC 81-706991
Discusses the materials used in stained glass work and demonstrates techniques and processes from the designing of the pattern to soldering the cames.
Fine Arts
Dist - GPN **Prod** - GPN 1981

Stained Glass - Painting with Light 20 MIN
16mm / U-matic / VHS
Color (J)
LC 74-703296
Examines the work of artists and master craftsmen as they design and build glass windows and lamp shades. Explores both traditional and contemporary examples of stained glass construction.
Fine Arts
Dist - BARR **Prod** - BARR 1974

Stained Glass Screens 9 MIN
16mm
Color (H C A)
LC 79-709228
Shows the stained glass screens executed by Australian painter Leonard French for the New National library in Canberra.
Fine Arts
Dist - AUIS **Prod** - ANAIB 1969

Stained Glass Windows 32 MIN
16mm
Color (H C A)
LC 72-701099
Presents complete instructions for making stained glass windows. Includes leaded and faceted glass.
Fine Arts
Dist - PISCES **Prod** - PISCES 1972

Stained images 25 MIN
VHS
Color (J H C G A R)
$29.95 purchase, $10.00 rental _ #35 - 80 - 2549
Uses animation, music and interviews to take a look at some of the common negative impressions people have about Christianity. Considers questions such as 'Why are so many Christians hypocrites?' and 'Why do they think Christianity is the only way?' Produced by Inter - Varsity Christian Fellowship's 2100 Productions.
Religion and Philosophy
Dist - APH

Stained picture 4 MIN
16mm
B&W; Color (G)
$10.00 rental
Looks at reflections, images and fragmentations of a New York street scene filmed in the window of a glass and mirror store. Resembles hand - tinted photographs. Produced by Jane Dobson.
Fine Arts
Dist - CANCIN

Staining and Finishing 18 MIN
VHS
Interior Wood Refinishing Series
$39.95 purchase _ #DI - 116
Describes the techniques needed for staining and finishing interior wood. Includes finishing trim.
Industrial and Technical Education
Dist - CAREER **Prod** - CAREER

Staining Blood Films for Detection of Malaria Parasites 8 MIN
16mm
Color
LC 74-705695
Explains steps in staining blood films with giemsa stain to demonstrate maximum detail of blood parasites. Shows good and poor preparations and discusses errors.
Health and Safety; Science; Science - Natural
Dist - USNAC **Prod** - USPHS 1967

Staining Techniques 32 MIN
U-matic / VHS
Color
Demonstrates how to stain bacterial cells for microscopic observation, using smears made from both broth and agar slant culture. Introduces the different types of dyes and the chemical reaction involved in the staining process in addition to coverage of the theoretical bases and procedures for performing the Gram stain, Ziehl - Neelsen acid - fast stain and Schaeffer - Fulton endaspore stain.
Science; Science - Natural
Dist - AVMM **Prod** - AMSM

Stainless steel crown restorations - indications and primary molar preparations 7 MIN
U-matic / VHS

Color (C PRO)
$395.00 purchase, $80.00 rental _ #D881 - VI - 029
Introduces dental students to the indications and primary molar preparation for stainless steel crown restorations. Describes facets of each indication and shows an example of each. Presents procedures for primary molar preparation and techniques for occlusal reduction, proximal reduction, buccal and lingual reductions, line angle reductions and margin reductions. Presented by Dr Willis W Smith.
Health and Safety
Dist - HSCIC

Stair Terminology 16 MIN
U-matic
Step by Step Series
(A)
Introduces some of the different types of stairs, from simple to complex. Deals with the language of stair design and construction and the importance of using the correct terms.
Industrial and Technical Education
Dist - ACCESS **Prod** - ACCESS 1984

Stairway to the stars 6 MIN
16mm
B&W (G)
$10.00 rental
Presents a version of the myth of Sisyphus in which a Columbus Avenue tenement's stairway replaces the mountain Sisyphus was fated to climb. Features a Fred Safran production.
Fine Arts; Religion and Philosophy
Dist - CANCIN

Stairways to the Mayan gods 28 MIN
VHS
Color (G)
$39.95 purchase
Journeys to the ceremonial centers of the Maya Indians of Mexico and Central America, who were master astronomers and mathematicians and translated their perceptions into spectacular cities of pyramids and palaces. Features Joseph Campbell, expert in world mythology and author of numerous books, narrating and providing insights into reasons for their ascent and decline.
Fine Arts; Literature and Drama; Religion and Philosophy; Social Science
Dist - HP

Stairwell Opening Length Calculations 14 MIN
U-matic
Step by Step Series
(A)
Demonstrates the mathematical calculations required to determine a stairwell opening length.
Industrial and Technical Education
Dist - ACCESS **Prod** - ACCESS 1984

Staking Out the Oceans, a New Age in Marine Explorations 14 MIN
16mm
Screen news digest series; Vol 17; Issue 5
Color; B&W (I)
Examines a new age of exploration in claiming the resources in and under the sea.
Civics and Political Systems; Geography - World; Science - Physical
Dist - HEARST **Prod** - HEARST 1975

Stalemate 20 MIN
VHS / U-matic
History in Action Series
Color
Looks at the beginning of World War I and the disillusionment it caused for both sides.
History - United States; History - World
Dist - FOTH **Prod** - FOTH 1984

Stalemate 29 MIN
16mm
Mediation - Catalyst to Collective Bargaining Series
B&W (C)
Business and Economics
Dist - IU **Prod** - KOACTV 1964

Stalemate 30 MIN
16mm
Color (J)
LC 82-700268
Tells the story of Jeffrey Harbor who, in obtaining his champion chess status, has lost connection with everyday life and shows how he becomes reconnected.
Fine Arts
Dist - WLCHCT **Prod** - WLCHCT 1982

Stalemate of truce and War on the homefront - Volume 4 120 MIN
VHS
Korean war series
Color; B&W (G)
$19.95 purchase _ #1648
Presents two parts on the Korean War. Includes film footage from both North and South Korea and interviews with Korean, American and Russian military and political leaders who personally participated in the events. Part four of a five - part series on the Korean War. Produced by the Korean Broadcast System.
History - World
Dist - KULTUR

Stalin 165 MIN
VHS
Color; PAL (J H)
PdS55 purchase
Presents three 55 - minute programs about Joseph Stalin, one of the most feared dictators the world has ever seen. Travels 11,000 miles from Stalin's death camps on the Arctic Circle to his birthplace in Georgia. Interviews Stalin's relatives, admirers and victims and draws from access to over a million feet of unique Soviet film. Provides a timely reassessment of a man whose legacy still haunts the Soviet Union today. Contact distributor about availability outside the United Kingdom.
History - World
Dist - ACADEM

Stalin 26 MIN
16mm / U-matic / VHS
Biography Series
B&W (J)
Depicts the life of Stalin, under whose strong - arm rule the USSR became a world power. Explains Stalin's part in making Russia a communist state.
Biography; Civics and Political Systems; History - World
Dist - MGHT **Prod** - WOLPER 1963

Stalin and Russian History - 1879 - 1927 29 MIN
16mm / U-matic / VHS
World Leaders Series
B&W (H C A) (RUSSIAN)
$495, $250 purchase _ #76562
Shows the turbulent years in Russian history from 1879 to 1927, including the fall of the Czar, the Bolshevik rise to power, World War I, and the Civil War following the Bolshevik coup.
Civics and Political Systems; History - World
Dist - CORF

Stalin and Russian History - 1928 - 1953 31 MIN
U-matic / VHS / 16mm
World Leaders Series
B&W (H C A)
$515, $250 purchase _ #76565
Examines Stalin's purge of the 1930s, the assassination of Trotsky, Stalin's foreign policy, and the major battles of World War II.
Biography; Civics and Political Systems; History - World
Dist - CORF

Stalin and the Modernization of Russia - Pt 7 20 MIN
16mm
Twentieth Century History Series - Vol II
Color (S)
$380.00 purchase _ #548 - 9234
Illuminates the events and issues which shaped our modern world. Uses archival footage, maps, drawings, feature film segments, paintings and posters to illustrate historic events. The first thirteen programs are available separately on 16mm. Part 7 of Volume II of thirteen programs, 'Stalin And The Modernization Of Russia,' traces the history of the USSR from Lenin's death in 1924 through Stalin's rise to power, his economic policies, and his ruthless political purges.
Civics and Political Systems; Geography - World; History - World
Dist - FI **Prod** - BBCTV 1981

Stalin - Man and Image 24 MIN
U-matic / VHS / 16mm
Color (H C A) (SPANISH)
Documents Stalin's despotic control over the media, secret police and the army.
Biography; Civics and Political Systems; Foreign Language; History - World
Dist - LCOA **Prod** - NIELSE 1979

Stalin - the Power of Fear 24 MIN
16mm / U-matic / VHS
Color (H C A) (SPANISH)
Focuses on big brother Stalin as he tries to forge for his workers a brave new world.
Biography; Civics and Political Systems; Foreign Language; History - World
Dist - LCOA **Prod** - NIELSE 1979

Stalingrad 60 MIN
16mm
World at War Series
Color (H C A)
LC 76-701778
History - World; Sociology
Dist - USCAN **Prod** - THAMES 1975

Stalingrad - June 9 1942 - 1943 52 MIN
U-matic / VHS / 16mm
World at War Series
Color (H C A)
Describes how the Russian industrial city of Stalingrad became a symbol of Russia's desperate and stubborn resistance against Hitler's armies until Germany was defeated and Stalingrad was virtually destroyed. It was a psychological turning point in the war.
History - World
Dist - MEDIAG **Prod** - THAMES 1973

Stalking Immortality 58 MIN
16mm
Color
LC 79-700285
Explores various aspects of aging with emphasis on research to extend life expectancy and ways to live a longer, healthier life.
Health and Safety; Psychology; Sociology
Dist - JANEP **Prod** - JANEP 1979

Stalking Immortality, Pt 1 - what You Can do to Prolong Life 20 MIN
U-matic / VHS / 16mm
Color (A)
LC 80-701750
Studies the role of nutrition, exercise, and heredity in the length of a person's life.
Health and Safety
Dist - CORF **Prod** - JANEP 1980

Stalking Immortality, Pt 2 - what Medical Science is Doing to Prolong Life 20 MIN
U-matic / VHS / 16mm
Color (A)
LC 80-701750
Explains how science is working to prolong life. Offers visits to the Sloan Kettering Institute, the Jet Propulsion Lab, and the National Institutes of Health.
Health and Safety; Science
Dist - CORF **Prod** - JANEP 1980

Stalking the President - a history of American assassins 50 MIN
VHS
Color; B&W (G)
$19.95 purchase _ #1650
Investigates the method and the motivations behind assassinations and attempted assassinations of American Presidents, beginning with the attempt made upon Andrew Jackson. Examines the incidents of Lincoln, Garfield, McKinley, Roosevelt, FDR, Truman, Kennedy, Nixon, Ford and Reagan. Looks at the assassinations of Dr Martin Luther King, Jr, Robert Kennedy and the attempt on presidential candidate George Wallace.
Biography; History - United States; Sociology
Dist - KULTUR **Prod** - KULTUR

Stalling for Safety 18 MIN
16mm
Color
LC 75-703759
Reviews the principles of aerodynamics and shows how stalls and spins occur. Demonstrates the warning signs of an approaching stall and points out the recovery actions that the pilot can take.
Industrial and Technical Education
Dist - USNAC **Prod** - USFAA 1975

Stallions of Distinction 28 MIN
BETA / VHS
Color
Presents the 1983 All Arabian Show at the Griffith Park Equestrian Center.
Physical Education and Recreation
Dist - EQVDL **Prod** - MHRSMP

Stallions of Industry 23 MIN
16mm
Color
LC 79-700402
Depicts comedically the political intrigues and conflicting ego trips of people working in a commercial photography studio, showing how their difficulties extend to the advertising agency and the clients.
Fine Arts; Industrial and Technical Education
Dist - KANE **Prod** - KANE 1979

Stamen 15 MIN
16mm
Color
Presents a sensitive interpretation of a male homosexual relationship. Describes how two young men meet in the city and work out living together. Indicates the warmth of their relationship and their pleasure in one another.
Guidance and Counseling; Psychology; Sociology
Dist - MMRC **Prod** - MMRC

Stamford, Totnes, Ludlow - Vol II 86 MIN
VHS
Six English Towns Series
Color (S)
$29.95 purchase _ #781 - 9035
Joins architectural historian Alec Clifton - Taylor for a tour of England's unspoiled towns. Explores three colorful towns, chosen for their spectacular visual impact and the inventive way the English have chosen to use building materials.
Fine Arts; Geography - World; Sociology
Dist - FI **Prod** - BBCTV 1989

Stamp Clubs are Fun 10 MIN
VHS
Color (G)
Documents the experiences of two Benjamin Franklin Stamp Club members as they learn about stamps during a visit to their local post office. Available for free loan from the distributor.
Fine Arts; Physical Education and Recreation; Social Science
Dist - AUDPLN

Stamp Collecting and more Blacks on U S Stamps 29 MIN
U-matic / VHS
Color
History - United States; Sociology
Dist - SYLWAT **Prod** - RCOMTV 1984

The Stamp of Approval 21 MIN
16mm / U-matic / VHS
Color (H C A)
LC 76-700304
Shows the fundamentals of the metal stamping process from its discovery through the modern, automated process.
Business and Economics; Industrial and Technical Education
Dist - MCFI **Prod** - UMDME 1975

Stamp of greatness series
Dramatizes the lives of six historical figures represented on postage stamps of the world. Focuses on individuals of action, of the arts and of the intellect. Discovers the human being behind the achievement. Includes Robert Burns - The Ploughman Poet; Sir Arthur Conan Doyle - The Man who was Sherlock Holmes; Antonin Dvorak - Bohemian Composer; John Paul Jones - The Father of the American Navy; Martin Luther - Protestant Reformer; Bedrich Smetana - Founder of Czech Romantic Music. In six parts, each 26 minutes. Titles available separately.
Antonin Dvorak - Bohemian composer 26 MIN
Bedrich Smetana - Founder of Czech romantic music 26 MIN
John Paul Jones - Father of the American Navy 26 MIN
Martin Luther - Protestant reformer 26 MIN
Robert Burns - The Ploughman poet 26 MIN
Sir Author Conan Doyle - the man who was Sherlock Holmes 26 MIN
Dist - NDIM **Prod** - TYNT 1975

Stamp Out Hog Cholera 22 MIN
16mm
Color (SPANISH)
LC 74-705697
Shows the impact of this disease on a hog producer who gambled with hog cholera and lost. Tells farmers what needs to be done to eradicate hog cholera, and how and why it should be done.
Agriculture; Foreign Language
Dist - USNAC **Prod** - USDA 1963

Stamps - a Nation's Calling Cards 20 MIN
VHS
Color (G)
Describes the process of developing and printing stamps. Available for free loan from the distributor.
Industrial and Technical Education; Physical Education and Recreation
Dist - AUDPLN

Stamps, a Nation's Calling Cards 19 MIN
16mm
Color
LC 72-701048
Shows the beauty and meaning found in postage stamps as they reflect our nation's history and heritage. Describes the processes of stamp production from the first hand - engraved impression to the final printing of millions of stamps.
History - United States; Industrial and Technical Education
Dist - USPOST **Prod** - USPOST 1970

Stan Bolovan 15 MIN
VHS / U-matic
Teletales Series
Color (P)
$125.00 purchase
Presents a children's tale from Rumania. Suggests happy endings and positive values.
Education; Literature and Drama
Dist - AITECH **Prod** - POSIMP 1984

Stan Getz - A Musical odyssey 60 MIN
VHS
Color (G)
$36.00 purchase
Displays the many talents of Stan Getz, jazz saxophone virtuoso. Records his visit in 1977 to Israel, jamming for three weeks with local musicians. His creative encounters include a Kurdish drummer, an Arab quartet, a Hassidic wedding band and a Yemenite dance troupe. Directed and produced by Herbert Dorfman.
Fine Arts; Geography - World; Religion and Philosophy
Dist - NCJEWF

The Stand - Alone Micro 25 MIN
U-matic / VHS
Electronic Office Series
Color (H C A)
LC 85-700734
Host Ian McNaught Davis examines stand - alone word processors and microcomputers likely to be used by individuals or offices with no previous computing knowledge. Emphasizes the need for reliable software knowledge.
Business and Economics; Industrial and Technical Education
Dist - FI **Prod** - BBCTV 1984

Stand and be counted - reacting to racism 15 MIN
VHS
Color (I J H)
$119.00 purchase _ #CG - 867 - VS; LC 90-700014
Presents two dramatic stories which illustrate how young people and their families can make a difference when a racist incident takes place in their communities. Visits the Howard Beach section of New York City where two racially diverse families talk about their reactions to a violent incident in which a group of young white males with baseball bats chased a black man onto a highway where he was killed. In Philadelphia, a Middle School boy tells how he felt when he went to court to identify the man he saw spray - paint KKK on the house of the first African - American family in his neighborhood.
Guidance and Counseling; History - United States; Sociology
Dist - HRMC **Prod** - NBCNEW 1990

Stand out 16 MIN
VHS
Color (G)
$395.00 purchase, $150.00 rental _ #91F6031
Offers some new and creative approaches to selling.
Business and Economics; Psychology
Dist - DARTNL **Prod** - DARTNL 1991

Stand tall 30 MIN
U-matic
Pacific bridges series
Color (I J)
Focuses on the struggle of Asian - Americans against racism and oppression.
Civics and Political Systems; Sociology
Dist - GPN **Prod** - EDFCEN 1978

The Stand - up buffet
VHS
Frugal gourmet - entertaining series
Color (G)
$19.95 purchase _ #CCP841
Shows how to prepare a stand - up buffet. Features Jeff Smith, the Frugal Gourmet. Part of a ten - part series on preparing food for entertaining.
History - United States; Home Economics
Dist - CADESF **Prod** - CADESF

Stand up for choice series
Thrusts viewers into the front lines of the struggle over abortion rights between members of Operation Rescue, pro - choice demonstrators, clinic staff and patients. Reveals the tactics used by extremist groups to shut down clinics and deny women access to reproductive health services. Filmed during actual clinic confrontations that at times turn shockingly violent. A three - part series with 15 - minute episodes titled The Blockade; Escorts; and From Vigilance to Violence. Recommended for clinic defense trainers and other pro - choice activists. Training booklet available.
The Blockade 15 MIN
Escorts 15 MIN
From vigilance to violence 15 MIN
Dist - CNEMAG **Prod** - WARLIT

Stand up for justice
VHS
Color (G)
$15.00 purchase _ #110 - 003
Presents a lecture by Imam Siraj Wahhaj at Masjid Taqwa in New York City.
Religion and Philosophy
Dist - SOUVIS **Prod** - SOUVIS

Stand up for yourself - peer pressure and drugs 16 MIN
VHS
Color (I J H)
$345.00, $260.00 purchase, $60.00 rental
Uses real - life situations and a peer workshop group to dramatize proven ways young people can say no to street drugs, cigarettes and alcohol. Shows how certain verbal techniques provide the social skills young people need to say no and still keep their friends. Older teens model positive attitudes and offer motivation and encouragement. Directed by Dan Jackson.
Guidance and Counseling; Health and Safety; Psychology; Social Science
Dist - CF

Stand Ups 20 MIN
U-matic / VHS / 16mm
Color
LC 79-700514
Contrasts the lives of three aspiring comedians as they share their hopes, inspirations and sometimes overwhelming frustrations. Views the performers pursuing recreational interests and working out new routines in their homes.
Literature and Drama
Dist - PHENIX **Prod** - ASDA 1978

Stand with us America 5 MIN
16mm / VHS
Color (G IND)
$5.00 rental
Introduces the goals and accomplishments of the labor movement to new members, students, or to the general public. Presents brief interviews with workers talking about their union and their hopes for the future.
Business and Economics; Social Science
Dist - AFLCIO **Prod** - LIPA 1988

Standard Cartoon Cliches 15 MIN
Videoreel / VT2
Charlie's Pad Series
Color
Fine Arts
Dist - PBS **Prod** - WSIU

Standard Clinical Oral Surgery Instruments 13 MIN
U-matic
Color (PRO)
LC 79-706757
Describes the use of oral surgery instruments and illustrates their placement on a tray.
Health and Safety
Dist - USNAC **Prod** - USCAR 1978

Standard error of mean
VHS
Probability and statistics series
Color (H C)
$125.00 purchase _ #8029
Provides resource material about standard error and the mean for help in the study of probability and statistics. Presents a 60 - video series, each part 25 to 30 minutes long, that explains and reinforces concepts using definitions, theorems, examples and step - by - step solutions to tutor the student. Videos are also available in a set.
Mathematics
Dist - LANDMK

Standard error of regression
VHS
Probability and statistics series
Color (H C)
$125.00 purchase _ #8047
Provides resource material about standard error of regression for help in the study of probability and statistics. Presents a 60 - video series, each part 25 to 30 minutes long, that explains and reinforces concepts using definitions, theorems, examples and step - by - step solutions to tutor the student. Videos are also available in a set.
Mathematics
Dist - LANDMK

Standard Food Portions 13 MIN
16mm / 8mm cartridge
Food Service Employee Series
Color (IND)
LC 76-707355
Acquaints the students with the definition of a standard portion, the reasons this standard is used and how it is controlled.
Industrial and Technical Education
Dist - COPI **Prod** - COPI 1969

Standard Plate Count of Pasteurized and Raw Milk - Preparation and Analysis of Yogurt 1 41 MIN
U-matic / VHS
Color
Includes three presentations titled Standard Plate Count Of Pasteurized And Raw Milk, Preparation And Analysis Of Yogurt and Pipetting in one tape numbered 6208. Covers the standard technique for determining viable bacterial populations in both pasteurized and raw milk samples. Covers identification of general sources of milk contamination and which diseases can be transmitted to man by drinking contaminated milk. serial dilution, plating and growth of yogurt bacteria as well as an examination of some distinctive cellular characteristics.
Agriculture; Science; Science - Natural; Social Science
Dist - AVMM **Prod** - AMSM

Standard Techniques of Factoring 29 MIN
16mm
Advanced Algebra Series
B&W (H)
Shows how to simplify by factoring in forms which are quadratic perfect square, sum of two cubes, quadratic not - perfect - square and difference of two cubes.
Mathematics
Dist - MLA **Prod** - CALVIN 1960

Standard video Bible study series
First and Second Corinthians 120 MIN
First and Second Samuel - Tape 1 90 MIN
First and Second Samuel - Tape 2 90 MIN
First and Second Samuel series 180 MIN
Genesis - Tape 1 90 MIN
Genesis - Tape 2 90 MIN
Genesis series 180 MIN
Gospel of John - Tape 1 90 MIN
Gospel of John - Tape 2 90 MIN
Gospel of John series 180 MIN
Gospel of Mark 120 MIN
Jeremiah 120 MIN
Joshua and Judges 120 MIN
Letters of John 60 MIN
Revelation 120 MIN
Dist - APH

Standardization - Engineering Planning 14 MIN
16mm
Color
LC FIE60-359
Shows an analysis of the type of engineering and technical work which is necessary on a planned basis to achieve standardization objectives in large and complicated technical areas.
Business and Economics; Industrial and Technical Education; Psychology
Dist - USNAC **Prod** - USN 1959

Standardized Practices for Conducting and Interpreting Cement Bond Logs 78 MIN
VHS / U-matic
Color (IND)
Details the theory and practice of modern cement bond logging techniques. Shows an example of interpreting a log by means of a new quantitative technique.
Business and Economics; Industrial and Technical Education; Social Science
Dist - UTEXPE **Prod** - FENECO

Standardized Practices for Conducting and Interpreting Cement Bond Logs 78 MIN
VHS / 16mm
(A PRO)
$250.00 purchase _ #40.0536
Discusses in detail the theory and practice of modern cement bond logging techniques and shows an actual example of interpreting a log by means of a new quantitative technique developed by D D Fitzgerald.
Health and Safety; Industrial and Technical Education; Social Science
Dist - UTEXPE **Prod** - UTEXPE 1985

The Standardized Test - an Educational Tool 22 MIN
U-matic / VHS / 16mm
Color (C T)
Examines the criteria used to select an appropriate test, the importance of maintaining standard procedure in test administration and the value of the standardized test.
Education; Psychology
Dist - IFB **Prod** - CALVIN 1961

Standardized video exam review series
Basic English
Math review for the A C T
Math Review for the G R E
Math review for the GMAT
Math review for the S A T - P S A T
Review for the A S V A B
Review for the Armed Forces Exam
Review for the G E D
Review for the L S A T
Review for the M A T
Review for the N T E
Review for the S A T
Review for the T O E F L
Verbal review for the A C T
Verbal review for the G R E
Verbal review for the GMAT
Verbal review for the S A T - P S A T
Dist - CAMV

Standards and Appraisal - Aids to Control 20 MIN
U-matic / VHS
Supervisory Management Course, Pt 1 Series Unit 5
Color
Introduces supervisors to the types of performance standards, how they are developed and how to apply the latest techniques in appraising performance against established standards.
Business and Economics; Psychology
Dist - AMA **Prod** - AMA

Standards and Appraisals - Aid to Control 24 MIN
U-matic / VHS
Color
Analyzes a relationship where the supervisor is not doing the job of 'subordinate developing'. Shows how the use of performance standards and appraisal techniques can correct the problem.
Business and Economics; Psychology
Dist - AMA **Prod** - AMA

Standards for Excellence 29 MIN
16mm
Color (A)
LC 77-700476
Demonstrates the impact of standards and measurements on American society from the time of Thomas Jefferson through the 20th century. Cites important contributions which the National Bureau of Standards has made to scientific measurement.
Civics and Political Systems; Education; Mathematics; Science
Dist - USNAC **Prod** - USNBS 1976

Standards for Life Insurance Investment Products
VHS / U-matic
$25.00 purchase
Business and Economics
Dist - BEEKMN **Prod** - BEEKMN 1989

Standards for Mutual Fund Investments
VHS / U-matic
$25.00 purchase
Business and Economics
Dist - BEEKMN **Prod** - BEEKMN 1988 - 89

Standards for Oil and Gas Investments
U-matic / VHS
$25.00 purchase
Business and Economics
Dist - BEEKMN **Prod** - BEEKMN 1988

Standards for Real Estate Investments 360 MIN
U-matic / VHS
$125.00 purchase
Enables the individual investor, the financial planner and the investment advisor to make judgments about competing investments in such areas as quality, risk and suitability.
Business and Economics
Dist - BEEKMN **Prod** - BEEKMN 1988

Standards for Survival 18 MIN
16mm
Color
Illustrates how the ten standard firefighting orders and thirteen situations that shout 'watch out' can mean life or death in a wildfire.
Social Science
Dist - FILCOM **Prod** - FILCOM

Standards II 91 MIN
VHS
Color (S)
$34.95 purchase _ #726 - 9007
Presents an incomparable jazz trio - Keith Jarrett, Gary Peacock and Jack DeJohnette. Showcases 11 classics including 'All Of You,' 'Blame It On My Youth' and 'Georgia On My Mind.'.
Fine Arts
Dist - FI **Prod** - VARJ 1989

Standards of Cleanliness 17 MIN
8mm cartridge / 16mm
Food Service Employee Series
Color (IND)
LC 70-707356
Acquaints the student with the importance of cleanliness in food service, diseases caused by uncleanliness and standards of health set by government agencies.
Health and Safety
Dist - COPI **Prod** - COPI 1969

Standards of Performance 120 MIN
VHS / U-matic
AMA's Program for Performance Appraisal Series
Color
Describes the value of performance standards in the public sector. Discusses various types of standards that can be used effectively and how staff members can formulate meaningful standards.
Business and Economics; Psychology
Dist - AMA **Prod** - AMA

Standards of Performance 26 MIN
Videoreel / VT2
How to Improve Managerial Performance - the AMA Performance 'Standards Program Series
Color (A)
LC 75-704234
Features James L Hayes, president of the American Management Associations, describing the value of performance standards and the various kinds of standards that can be used.
Business and Economics; Psychology
Dist - AMA **Prod** - AMA 1974

Standards of Performance and Appraisal
VHS / U-matic
Essentials of Management Series Unit V; Unit V
Color
Spells out standards of performance and appraisal relationships in a practical, working formula. Teaches how to appraise subordinates' performances.
Business and Economics; Psychology
Dist - AMA **Prod** - AMA

Standards, Styles and Keys 30 MIN
U-matic / VHS
Language and Meaning Series
Color (C)
English Language; Psychology
Dist - GPN **Prod** - WUSFTV 1983

Standing and Ground Maneuvering 5 MIN
16mm
Combative Measures - Judo Series
B&W
LC 75-700844
Demonstrates standing and ground maneuvers used in judo for getting into position to control and to hold or lock a combative - trained attacker.
Civics and Political Systems; Physical Education and Recreation
Dist - USNAC **Prod** - USAF 1955

Standing guard 30 MIN
VHS / U-matic
Color (H C A)
$425.00, $395.00 purchase _ #V441
Follows the staging and execution of maneuvers conducted in Europe each year by NATO. Focuses on the efforts of the Army National Guard which sends a huge force each year. Explains the purposes of the maneuvers and controversies generated by annual 'American invasion.'
Civics and Political Systems; Geography - World; Sociology
Dist - BARR **Prod** - CEPRO 1988

Standing, Start, Starter 10 MIN
U-matic
Readalong Three Series
Color (P)
Provides reading instruction for third grade students. Uses animation, humor, music, repetition and audience participation. Comes with teacher's guide and kit.
Education; English Language; Literature and Drama
Dist - TVOTAR **Prod** - TVOTAR 1977

Standing Tall, Looking Good 20 MIN
16mm
Color
Looks at the various aspects of a soldier's life, including basic training, teamwork, obstacle courses, challenges, inspections, confidence, graduation and advance training.
Civics and Political Systems
Dist - MTP **Prod** - USA 1982

Standing up for yourself 11 MIN
VHS
Taking responsibility series
Color (P)
Shows that each time children stand up for their personal rights, they gain self - confidence and self - esteem. Presents an animated prehistoric child who discovers constructive verbal and nonverbal responses to put - downs, physical aggression and inappropriate touching. Reminds that sometimes it is important to get help from adults. Part of a series teaching health, safety and responsibility to youngsters.

Guidance and Counseling; Health and Safety; Psychology; Sociology
Dist - VIEWTH **Prod** - VIEWTH

Standing Waves 15 MIN
U-matic / VHS
Introductory Concepts in Physics - Wave Motion Series
Color (C)
$229.00, $129.00 purchase _ #AD - 1203
Shows standing waves through experiments with sound and electric waves captured in exceptional photography.
Science - Physical
Dist - FOTH **Prod** - FOTH

Standing Waves and the Principle of Superposition 11 MIN
16mm / U-matic / VHS
Color (H C) (SPANISH)
Explains the formation and characteristics of Standing Waves, a physics principle basic to the understanding of the behavior of matter. Shows how Standing Waves are produced by the superposition of two identical wave patterns traveling in opposite directions. Extends the principle to an explanation of atomic structure.
Foreign Language; Science - Physical
Dist - EBEC **Prod** - EBEC

Stanford
VHS
Campus clips series
Color (H C A)
$29.95 purchase _ #CC0008V
Takes a video visit to the campus of Stanford University in California. Shows many of the distinctive features of the campus, and interviews students about their experiences. Provides information on the composition of the student body, professors, academics, social life, housing, and other subjects.
Education
Dist - CAMV

Stanford Chorale - Il Festino 27 MIN
Videoreel / VT2
Synergism - Variatims in Music Series
Color
Features the Stanford Chorale performing the Renaissance madrigal comedy, Il Festino, by Adriano Banchieri. Composed in 1908, the madrigals are intended to be sung before supper on Holy Thursday.
Fine Arts
Dist - PBS **Prod** - KQEDTV

The Stanislavsky Century 180 MIN
VHS
B&W (C H A)
$169.00 purchase _ #EX4048
Presents a study of Stanislavsky on film, retracing his life using hitherto unknown footage.
Biography; Fine Arts
Dist - FOTH

Stanislavsky - Maker of the modern theatre 29 MIN
16mm / U-matic / VHS
B&W (H C A)
$89.95 purchase _ #EX115; LC 72-702966
Portrays the life, the times, and the ideas of a theatrical innovator, Stanislavsky, father of method acting and the founder of the Moscow Art Theater.
Biography; Fine Arts; Geography - World
Dist - FOTH **Prod** - MANTLH 1972

Stanley and Livingstone 12 MIN
U-matic / VHS
Color (G)
$229.00, $129.00 purchase _ #AD - 1744
Scrutinizes Dr David Livinstone, Scottish explorer and missionary who disappeared on expedition into the heart of Africa, and English - born American journalist Henry Morton Stanley, sent to Africa to find Livingstone and bring back the story of the century.
Biography; History - World; Literature and Drama
Dist - FOTH **Prod** - FOTH

Stanley and the dinosaurs 16 MIN
VHS
Color (P I)
$435.00, $325.00 purchase, $60.00 rental
Adapts the children's book, Stanley, by Syd Hoff. Reveals that Stanley is no ordinary caveman. He paints pictures, grows flowers, says 'please' and 'thank you,' and thinks about how to make life better. He doesn't mind being different but the other cavemen become suspicious and banish him from their cave. Stanley, serenaded in four - part harmony by his dinosaur friends, builds the world's first house and the other cavemen soon discover that 'being different' may not be so terrible after all. Features dimensional animation. Produced by John Matthews.
Literature and Drama; Science - Natural
Dist - CF

Stanley Baldwin
16mm / VHS
Archive series
B&W; PAL (G)
PdS350, PdS60 purchase
Presents newsreel and Conservative Party Film Unit productions with Baldwin between 1923 and 1939. Features election speech, 1931 and 1935; Ottawa Conference, 1932; Baldwin on democracy, 1939 and newsreel obituary, 1947. Includes a substantial accompanying booklet. Uses material compiled by John Ramsden.
Civics and Political Systems; History - World
Dist - BUFVC **Prod** - BUFVC

Stanley Spencer - a kind of heaven 30 MIN
VHS
Color (A)
PdS65 purchase
Profiles the eccentric artist Stanley Spencer. Reveals that he spent several months in Port Glasgow during World War II; the program includes dramatic sequences of the artist at work in the shipyards. Offers a look at the sketches and finished works which celebrate this important period of social and industrial history.
Fine Arts
Dist - BBCENE

Stanley Turrentine in concert 60 MIN
VHS
Color; Dolby stereo (G)
$29.95 purchase _ #1294
Records jazz tenor saxophonist Stanley Turrentine in concert at Village Gate nightclub, New York, 1990. Features 'Impressions' by John Coltrane, 'My Romance,' Rodgers and Hart, and Turrentine's 'Sugar.' Includes an interview of Turrentine conducted by James Brown, WBGO - FM Jazz Radio.
Fine Arts
Dist - KULTUR **Prod** - KULTUR 1991

Stanley William Hayter - the Artist as Teacher 12 MIN
16mm
B&W
LC 72-711505
A documentary film which presents a brief history of printmaking and covers a visit by Stanley William Hayter to the Ohio State University school of art. Hayter demonstrates the techniques he uses to etch, ink and print intaglio plates, commenting on his methods as he works and discussing printmaking and art in general.
Fine Arts; Industrial and Technical Education
Dist - OSUMPD **Prod** - OSUMPD 1970

Stan's Secret 30 MIN
VHS / U-matic
High Feather Series Pt 3; Pt 3
Color (I J)
LC 83-706049
Focuses on a summer camper's diabetes and explains the effects of sugar on the body.
Health and Safety; Social Science
Dist - GPN **Prod** - NYSED 1982

Stapedectomy
U-matic / VHS
Color
Shows how a frozen stapes causes hearing loss. Shows how the stapes are surgically replaced. Details the operation and post - op recovery.
Health and Safety; Science - Natural
Dist - MIFE **Prod** - MIFE

Stapedectomy - 1980 59 MIN
VHS / U-matic
Color (PRO)
Demonstrates the use of both fascia and perichondrium in stapedectomy.
Health and Safety; Science - Natural
Dist - HOUSEI **Prod** - HOUSEI

Stapedectomy - Causes of Failure 54 MIN
VHS / U-matic
Color (PRO)
Shows the technical and anatomical problems encountered in stapes surgery and their solutions.
Health and Safety; Science - Natural
Dist - HOUSEI **Prod** - HOUSEI

Stapedectomy in the Fenestrated Ear 23 MIN
U-matic / VHS
Color (PRO)
Shows the anatomy and surgical technique of stapedectomy in the fenestrated ear. From the original film.
Health and Safety; Science - Natural
Dist - HOUSEI **Prod** - HOUSEI

Stapedectomy in the Fenestrated Ear 20 MIN
16mm
Color (PRO)
Illustrates the surgical technique necessary to perform a stapes operation superimposed upon a previous fenestration cavity. Explains that the operation is done for the purpose of correcting a hearing loss due to otosclerosis.
Health and Safety
Dist - EAR **Prod** - EAR

Stapedectomy - IRP and TORP 59 MIN
U-matic / VHS
Color (PRO)
Shows the use of a wire from the malleus handle (IRP) and the use of a total ossicular replacement prothesis (TORP) in primary stapedectomy procedures, necessitated by incus problems (short, necrotic, dislocated), idiopathic malleus head fixation, or oval window exposure problems.
Guidance and Counseling; Health and Safety; Science - Natural
Dist - HOUSEI **Prod** - HOUSEI

Stapedectomy, Prefabricated Wire Loop and Gelfoam Technique 14 MIN
16mm
Color (PRO)
Depicts a new surgical technique for the correction of hearing loss due to otosclerosis. Explains that this method has been used successfully in over 3,000 cases of otosclerosis.
Health and Safety
Dist - EAR **Prod** - EAR

Stapedectomy - Prefabricated Wire Loop and Gelfoam Technique 14 MIN
U-matic / VHS / 16mm
Color (PRO)
Shows stapedectomy with prefabricated wire loop and gelfoam technique.
Health and Safety; Science - Natural
Dist - HOUSEI **Prod** - HOUSEI

Stapes Surgery When the Incus is Absent 28 MIN
U-matic / VHS
Color (PRO)
Discusses stapes surgery when the incus is absent.
Health and Safety; Science - Natural
Dist - HOUSEI **Prod** - HOUSEI

Staple Yarn Processing Machines
U-matic / VHS
ITMA 1983 Review Series
Color
Industrial and Technical Education
Dist - NCSU **Prod** - NCSU

The Star 29 MIN
VHS / 16mm
Watch your mouth series
Color (H)
$46.00 rental _ #WAYM - 108
Emphasizes language and communication skills for high school students. Notes the difference between formal and informal word usage.
Education; English Language; Psychology; Social Science
Dist - PBS

STAR - a new dialogue about diversity 8 MIN
VHS
Color (I J H)
$25.00 purchase
Shows the People for STAR - Students Talk About Race - race relations program in action. Includes footage of classroom dialogs from two STAR statewide projects in California and North Carolina.
Psychology; Social Science; Sociology
Dist - PAMWAY **Prod** - PAMWAY 1993

Star Birth in Our Galaxy 30 MIN
VHS / U-matic
Astronomy Series
Color
Explores those known areas of the universe where stars are being born and dying, and points out that the sun is expected to live for 'only' five billion more years.
Science - Physical
Dist - NETCHE **Prod** - NETCHE 1973

The Star class 28 MIN
VHS
Color (G)
$34.80 purchase _ #0231
Reviews the 70 year sailing race history of the International Star Class through the 1981 Worlds in Marblehead, Maine. Looks at many of the technical innovations in the class.
Physical Education and Recreation
Dist - SEVVID **Prod** - OFFSHR

Star Clusters 8 MIN
16mm
Explorations in Space and Time Series

Color (H C A)
LC 75-703984
Uses computer animation to examine two open star clusters, the Pleiades and the Hyades, and two globular clusters in the constellation Hercules.
Science - Physical
Dist - HMC **Prod** - HMC 1974

Star clusters - 6
U-matic / VHS / BETA
Search encounters in science series
Color; PAL (G H C)
PdS25, PdS33 purchase
Brings modern research efforts of the world's leading scientists into the classroom. Features one of a series of 24 mini - documentaries. Each film is 5 - 7 minutes in length.
Science; Science - Physical
Dist - EDPAT **Prod** - NSF

Star - Crossed Love 20 MIN
U-matic / VHS / 16mm
World of William Shakespeare Series
Color (H C A)
LC 78-700748
Describes William Shakespeare's play Romeo And Juliet and the response it received in London in the 1590's.
Literature and Drama
Dist - NGS **Prod** - NGS 1978

Star dancer
VHS
Native American folk tales series
(G)
$79.00 purchase
Tells how Coyote's bragging tongue and his eagerness to take a dare get him in trouble with the Great Spirit when he tries to dance with a star.
Literature and Drama; Social Science
Dist - DANEHA **Prod** - DANEHA 1994

Star film 15 MIN
16mm
Color (G)
$35.00 rental
Stars a handmade emulsion. Suggests using 16fps or 18fps unless the projector is significantly brighter at 24fps.
Fine Arts
Dist - CANCIN **Prod** - LEVINE 1971

Star garden 22 MIN
16mm
Color (G)
$44.00 rental, $742.00 purchase
Says Brakhage, '...depicts - as Brancusi put it - 'One of those days I would not trade for anything under heaven'.'
Fine Arts
Dist - CANCIN **Prod** - BRAKS 1974

A Star in the breaking - Episode 2
VHS
McGee and me series
Color (P I R)
$19.95 purchase, $10.00 rental _ #35 - 84153 - 979
Features Nick and his animated friend McGee. Portrays Nick as he appears on a television game show and learns to be humble.
Literature and Drama; Religion and Philosophy
Dist - APH **Prod** - TYHP

A Star is Born 154 MIN
16mm
Color
Portrays two rock - music superstars, one rapidly on the rise and the other on the long spiral down. Stars Barbra Streisand and Kris Kristofferson.
Fine Arts
Dist - SWANK **Prod** - WB

A Star is born 26 MIN
VHS
Stars series
Color (I J H)
$195.00 purchase
Uses infra - red telescopes to witness the Orion nebula where starbirth is occurring. Looks at stellar photography and double stars. Poses the question of whether there are other life - supporting 'Earths' within this galaxy. Views the discoveries made by IRAS and the revolution JCMT, the world's highest observatory. Part of a six - part series on astronomy.
Science - Physical
Dist - LANDMK **Prod** - LANDMK 1988

A Star is Grown 30 MIN
BETA / VHS
Victory Garden Series
Color
Discusses planting fall crops. Features Chef Marian preparing a garden staple for a special dish.
Agriculture; Physical Education and Recreation
Dist - CORF **Prod** - WGBHTV

Star of Bethlehem 13 MIN
16mm
Color (P)
Presents the story of Christmas based on the Gospels. Opens with the holy family traveling to Bethlehem and closes with the wise men bearing rich gifts. Includes a fascinating interpretation of the story of the wise men and how they may have reached Bethlehem.
Religion and Philosophy
Dist - CAFM **Prod** - CAFM

Star of Bethlehem (1700 - 1750) 12 MIN
16mm
Color
Presents tiny Baroque figurines depicting Christ's Nativity and reflecting the simple awe and piety of the Southern Italian peasants of the 18th century.
Fine Arts
Dist - ROLAND **Prod** - ROLAND

Star of India - Iron Lady of the Seas 29 MIN
VHS / 16mm
Color (G)
$55.00 rental _ #STAR - 000
Commemorates the 114th birthday of the Star of India, the oldest iron - hulled merchantman afloat.
Social Science
Dist - PBS **Prod** - KBPS

The Star of the King 23 MIN
16mm / U-matic / VHS
Color (K J)
Tells young children the story of the Magi following the star to Bethlehem.
Literature and Drama; Religion and Philosophy
Dist - DSP **Prod** - DSP

The Star Seekers 10 MIN
16mm
Color (I)
LC FIA66-1342
Uses animation to show different theories of the universe from Greek to modern times. Theories include Babylonian, Copernican, Pythagorean, Kantian and current interpretations.
Science; Science - Physical
Dist - SF **Prod** - FINA 1966

Star - Spangled Banner 43 FRS
U-matic / VHS / 16mm
Color (K P)
LC 75-735601; 75-703912
Depicts verses from the U S national anthem with illustrations taken from Peter Spier's book The Star - Spangled Banner which interprets Francis Scott Key's commemoration of the battle of Fort Mc Henry during the War of 1812.
Civics and Political Systems; Fine Arts; History - United States; Social Science
Dist - WWS **Prod** - SCHNDL 1975

The Star Spangled Banner 11 MIN
U-matic / VHS / 16mm
Singing America's Songs Series
Color (K P I)
LC 72-702427
Instructs young students in the words, music and importance of our National anthem. Provides a better understanding of the Star Spangled Banner.
Civics and Political Systems; Fine Arts; Social Science
Dist - AIMS **Prod** - EVANSA 1971

Star Spangled Banner 5 MIN
16mm
Color (H C A)
Explores the nature of war. Features music by 'The Grass Roots.'.
Sociology
Dist - VIEWFI **Prod** - PFP 1972

Star spangled banner and nine o'clock news 4 MIN
16mm
Color (G)
Presents a film about the 1968 Democratic National Convention in Chicago and a film about the murder of Dr King, respectively. Notes that these films are not available separately.
Fine Arts; Sociology
Dist - CANCIN **Prod** - MCLAOG

Star Spangled Banner I 2 MIN
16mm
Color (J)
Looks at America at its best and at it worst.
Civics and Political Systems; History - United States; Social Science
Dist - SLFP **Prod** - MCLAOG

The Star, the castle and the butterfly 25 MIN
VHS
Color (G)
$54.00 purchase
Follows Rabbi Hugo Gryn as he visits some of Prague's most evocative sites. Recalls 'ir va'em b'yusraek' - a city and a mother in the family of Israel - who nurtured generations of scholars and sages for over 1000 years - and is no more. Filmed six months before Prague's 1989 'velvet revolution.' Produced and directed by Naomi Gryn.
Fine Arts; History - World; Religion and Philosophy; Sociology
Dist - NCJEWF

Star Trek Episode - Amok Time 55 MIN
16mm
Color
Presents a Star Trek episode in which the Enterprise goes to the planet Vulcan because Spock must mate or die.
Fine Arts; Literature and Drama
Dist - NAFVC **Prod** - NBCTV 1979

Star Trek Episode - Cat's Paw 55 MIN
16mm
Color
Presents a Star Trek episode in which the crew of the Enterprise, pitted against a witch and a warlock, continue their odyssey after Kirk vanquished these evil creatures.
Fine Arts; Literature and Drama
Dist - NAFVC **Prod** - NBCTV 1979

Star Trek Episode - City on the Edge of Forever 52 MIN
16mm
Color
Presents a Star Trek episode in which Kirk travels through time when he has foreknowledge that Hitler will win World War II unless a girl dies in a 1939 traffic accident.
Literature and Drama
Dist - NAFVC **Prod** - NBCTV 1977

Star Trek Episode - Miri 52 MIN
16mm
Color
Tells how the crew of the Enterprise lands on a planet where the only survivors of a killer virus are children. Describes what happens when one of the children falls in love with Kirk and she and the others begin harassing the Enterprise crew.
Literature and Drama
Dist - REELIM **Prod** - NBCTV

Star Trek Episode - Shore Leave 52 MIN
16mm
Color
Describes the adventures of the Enterprise crew as they take shore leave on a bizarre planet.
Literature and Drama
Dist - NAFVC **Prod** - NBCTV

Star Trek Episode - Space Seed 55 MIN
16mm
Color
Presents a Star Trek episode in which warlike, though genetically perfect, barbarians, placed in suspended animation and exiled to float through the voids of space, again threaten peace and civilization until the Enterprise intervenes. Stars Ricardo Montalban.
Literature and Drama
Dist - NAFVC **Prod** - NBCTV 1977

Star Trek Episode - the Trouble with Tribbles 55 MIN
16mm
Color
Presents a Star Trek episode in which the Enterprise crew meet Tribbles, furry animals who love everybody and whom everybody loves. Tells how the death of the Tribbles uncovers the real problem, a threat to grain stores under Kirk's protection.
Literature and Drama
Dist - NAFVC **Prod** - NBCTV 1977

Star Trek - the Motion Picture 130 MIN
16mm / U-matic / VHS
Color
Tells how the refurbished USS Enterprise soars off to solve the mystery of a powerful alien force.
Fine Arts
Dist - FI **Prod** - PAR 1979

Star Wars 30 MIN
VHS / 16mm
Conquest of Space Series
Color (G)
Portrays space as an arena for superpower confrontation.
Business and Economics; History - United States; History - World
Dist - FLMWST

Star wars - a search for security 30 MIN
VHS
Color; PAL (G H C T A)
$350.00 purchase, $50.00 rental; $29.95 purchase; LC 87-705653; 87-705654

Provides a critical look at President Ronald Reagan's proposed Strategic Defense Initiative, featuring leading supporters and opponents of the "Star Wars" program. In common sense language with visuals, this program answers the most asked questions about SDI and examines alternative security plans. Presents a provocative and educational review of the pros and cons of the Strategic Defense Initiative from the perspective of 1986.
Religion and Philosophy; Sociology
Dist - EFVP

Star Wars - Fact or Fiction 28 MIN
U-matic / VHS
Issues in the News Series
Color (J H C)
Debates such questions as whether the USSR started the arms race in space with the only antisatellite ready for deployment, whether an ABM can make nuclear weapons obsolete and whether space - defenses on both sides guarantee peace. Includes interviews with such officials as Admiral Eugene J Carroll, Jr, former commander of the aircraft carrier Midway and Dr Robert Bowman, Director of the Institute for Space and Security studies.
Civics and Political Systems
Dist - CNEMAG **Prod** - FUNPC 1984

Star Wars - the great pork barrel in the sky 30 MIN
U-matic
Adam Smith's money world 1985 - 1986 season series; 225
Color (A)
Attempts to demystify the world of money and break it down so that small as well as large businesses and its people understand and adjust to new social and economic trends. Reports on the major economic stories and discoveries of 1985 and 1986.
Business and Economics
Dist - PBS **Prod** - WNETTV 1986

Stardoom 26 MIN
VHS
Stars series
Color (I J H)
$195.00 purchase
Features experts who discuss their supernovae discoveries and the future death of the sun. Uses computer animation to illustrate a star going supernova and discusses the use of a neutrino telescope to tell if a star is going to blow. Considers how supernova trigger starbirths and the theory that stars created the universe. Part of a six - part series on astronomy.
Science - Physical
Dist - LANDMK **Prod** - LANDMK 1988

Starfish 8 MIN
U-matic / VHS / 16mm
Color (I)
Describes this familiar creature of the tidepools and reefs and its strange ways.
Science - Natural
Dist - AIMS **Prod** - ACI 1972

Starfish dissection 30 MIN
VHS
Dissection video I series
Color (J H)
$70.00 purchase _ #A5VH 1217
Shows the dissection of a starfish, start - to - finish. Identifies difficult - to - locate anatomical structures through graphics and pointers. Includes printed script with numbered frame references and a complete glossary. Part of a series on dissection.
Science - Natural
Dist - CLRVUE **Prod** - CLRVUE 1992

Starfish dissection 8 MIN
VHS
Dissection videos series
Color (H C)
$129.95 purchase _ #193 Y 0024
Covers dissection and anatomy of the starfish. Includes dissection manual. Part of a series on dissection.
Science; Science - Natural
Dist - WARDS **Prod** - WARDS 1990

The Starfish's Realm 14 MIN
16mm
Color
Highlights the rhythmic natural movements achieved by various sea animals as they react to different species of starfish in their natural environment. Includes the true life drama of the events that may occur when a crab and an octopus meet.
Science - Natural
Dist - RARIG **Prod** - WHTCAP 1971

Starlife 20 MIN
U-matic / VHS / 16mm
Color (H C A)
$49.95 purchase _ #Q10921
Traces the long evolution of a star from its birth in the depths of a black nebula to its final extinction. Explains the process of nucleo - synthesis, red giants, 'bursters,' the warping of spacetime, and the mysterious 'black hole.'.
Science - Physical
Dist - CF **Prod** - NFBC 1985

Starlight 5 MIN
16mm
B&W; Color (G)
$1.00 rental
Lists a hodgepodge of images including a Tibetan Lama, his disciple, an old tugboat crossing the Mississippi, a man in his seventh month of solitude, the man's hermitage, his bloodhound, clouds, a mountain stream a girl and the sun.
Fine Arts
Dist - CANCIN **Prod** - FULTON 1970

Starlore - Ancient American Sky Myths 7 MIN
16mm / U-matic / VHS
Color
Presents five animated legends about stars taken from Eskimo, Pawnee, Aztec, Inca and Brazilian Indian mythology. Includes the art styles and music characteristic of each culture.
Social Science
Dist - PFP **Prod** - MUAMIN 1982

Starman in November 25 MIN
16mm
Color
LC 75-700482
Features Albert Fisher, a young cartoonist from the Midwest, who comes to Los Angeles to live with his relatives and sell his cartoons. Explains that on the way to the bus depot, he is picked up by two girls who take him to the commune in which they live. Shows Albert in the commune, imagining himself as one of his cartoon creations, namely Starman.
Fine Arts; Industrial and Technical Education; Literature and Drama; Psychology
Dist - USC **Prod** - USC 1975

Starphac 28 MIN
16mm
Color (J)
LC 77-700781
Illustrates the operations of the Health Delivery System by following the stages of health care administered to an Indian patient on the Arizona Papago Reservation. Explains the functions of Starphac, an acronym for a combined NASA and U S Indian Health Service program.
Geography - United States; Health and Safety; Social Science; Sociology
Dist - USNAC **Prod** - NASA 1976

The Starry Messenger - Pt 1 26 MIN
16mm / U-matic
Ascent of Man Series
Color (H C A)
LC 74-702259
Tells about the early human study of astronomy. Traces the origins of the scientific revolution through the conflict between fact and religious dogma, culminating in the trial and persecution of Galileo by the Roman Catholic Church. Narrated by Dr Jacob Bronowski of the Salk Institute.
Science - Physical
Dist - TIMLIF **Prod** - BBCTV 1973

The Starry Messenger - Pt 2 26 MIN
16mm / U-matic
Ascent of Man Series
Color (H C A)
LC 74-702259
Tells about the early human study of astronomy. Traces the origins of the scientific revolution through the conflict between fact and religious dogma, culminating in the trial of persecution of Galileo by the Roman Catholic Church. Narrated by Dr Jacob Bronowski of the Salk Insitute.
Science - Physical
Dist - TIMLIF **Prod** - BBCTV 1973

Stars 8 MIN
VHS / U-matic
Now I Know Series
Color (K P)
$29.95 purchase _ #VS033
Presents an adaptation of the book Stars. Contains a 32 page hardcover book and a video.
English Language; Literature and Drama; Science - Physical
Dist - TROLA

The Stars 10 MIN
U-matic / VHS / 16mm
Astronomy Series
Color (I J)
LC 70-709421
Follows the curriculum in elementary school astronomy as developed by the Illinois project of the National Science Foundation. Combines live photography, animation and special effects to investigate some basic concepts about the stars.
Science - Physical
Dist - MGHT **Prod** - HABER 1971

Stars 12 MIN
16mm / U-matic / VHS
Color (I J)
LC 73-705056
Examines the relative fixed positions and apparent circular movements of stars. Identifies constellations and depicts our sun and solar system. Illustrates galaxies and nebulae.
Science - Physical
Dist - IFB **Prod** - EDMNDS 1961

Stars - a First Film 13 MIN
U-matic / VHS / 16mm
Color (P I)
LC 78-700923
Points out that people have tried to understand the stars since ancient times. Explains how studying the Sun, constellations, colors of stars, distances of stars from Earth and composition of stars has increased understanding of the entire galaxy.
Science - Physical
Dist - PHENIX **Prod** - AFAI 1978

Stars and Stripes 3 MIN
U-matic / VHS / 16mm
Color (P)
Artist Norman McLaren draws directly upon film with ordinary pen and ink, creating stars and stripes which perform acrobatics to John Phillip Sousa's music.
Fine Arts
Dist - IFB **Prod** - NFBC 1950

The Stars and the water carriers 90 MIN
16mm / VHS
Color (G) (DANISH WITH ENGLISH SUBTITLES)
$150.00 rental
Documents the three - week Giro D'Italia bicycle race and the extended madness surrounding it. Directed by Jorgen Leth.
Fine Arts; Physical Education and Recreation
Dist - KINOIC

The Stars are beautiful 19 MIN
16mm
Color (G)
$713.00 purchase, $43.00 rental
Presents a film by Stan Brakhage extending the realm of his Blue Moses, dedicated to James Broughton.
Fine Arts
Dist - CANCIN **Prod** - BRAKS 1974

Stars of the Russian Ballet - Starring Ulanova and Plisetskaya 80 MIN
VHS
Color (G)
$29.95 purchase _ #1199
Presents the only filmed record of Ulanova and Plisetskaya dancing together, as well as the only extant tape of Galina Ulanova as Odette. Features Ulanova and Maya Plisetskaya dancing together in 'The Fountains Of Bakhchisarai,' and Vakhtang Chabukiani in a performance of 'The Flames Of Paris' by B V Asafiev.
Fine Arts; Foreign Language; Geography - World; Physical Education and Recreation
Dist - KULTUR

Stars on the Homefront 20 MIN
VHS
$75.00 purchase _ #HF113
Shows how the Americans at home during World War II did war work. Shows that in their own way, they fought the war just as their loved ones overseas did.
History - United States
Dist - BFKLP **Prod** - BFKLP

Stars Over Broadway 89 MIN
16mm
B&W (J)
Stars James Melton, Jane Froman and Pat O'Brien. Presents musical numbers created and staged by Busby Berkeley, including Broadway Cinderella, Don't Let Me Down, At Your Service Madame, September In The Rain and Carry Me Back To The Lone Prairie.
Fine Arts
Dist - UAE **Prod** - WB 1935

Stars, Pt 1 9 MIN
16mm
Basic Facts about the Earth, Sun, Moon and Stars Series
Color (K P I)
Discusses the twinkling of stars, the North Star, and the constellations of the Big and Little Dippers and Cassiopeia.
Science - Physical
Dist - SF **Prod** - MORLAT 1967

Stars, Pt 2 8 MIN
16mm

Basic Facts about the Earth, Sun, Moon and Stars Series
Color (K P)
Discusses the constellation Orion, the Milky Way, star charts and a constellarium.
Science - Physical
Dist - SF **Prod** - MORLAT 1967

Stars series
Presents a six - part series on astronomy. Examines star gazing techniques, starbirth, secrets of the sun, interpreting stars, supernovae and the Big Bang theory.
Beyond the big bang 26 MIN
Messages from the stars 26 MIN
Reach for the stars 26 MIN
Secrets of the sun 26 MIN
A Star is born 26 MIN
Stardoom 26 MIN
Dist - LANDMK **Prod** - LANDMK 1967

Stars - the Nuclear Furnace 29 MIN
U-matic
Project Universe - Astronomy Series Lesson 23
Color (C A)
Describes processes which maintain equilibrium within normal main sequence stars. Outlines theoretical process by which interstellar gas and dust gravitationally condense.
Science - Physical
Dist - CDTEL **Prod** - COAST

Starstruck 46 MIN
16mm / VHS / U-matic
Color (J H)
LC 81-701660; 82-700471
An edited version of the motion picture Starstruck. Describes the decision 16 - year - old Alicia must make, either to follow her wishes and become a singer or follow her mother's practical example and become a bookkeeper.
Guidance and Counseling; Sociology
Dist - LCOA **Prod** - HGATE 1981

Start at Confusion 20 MIN
U-matic / VHS
Color (PRO)
LC 79-720267
Defines confusion and discusses the application of reality orientation as a method of regaining memory, dignity and independence. Creates an illusion of confusion for the learner to develop greater understanding of the importance of time, place and identity in carrying out daily living activities. Emphasizes the interdependence of people necessary in maintaining a sense of reality.
Health and Safety; Psychology
Dist - MEDCOM **Prod** - MEDCOM

Start by Loving 29 MIN
16mm
Giving Birth and Independence Series
Color (H C A)
LC 81-701579
Focuses on a mother who cannot accept the differences between her sighted and her blind child. Concludes with the mother and her two children gaining a greater appreciation for one another through the help and insights of others.
Education; Home Economics; Sociology
Dist - LAWREN **Prod** - JRLLL 1981

Start day song 3 MIN
16mm
Color (G)
$8.00 rental
Feataures the New Wave band from Arizona, Blue Shoes, performing its last single, Startin' the Day with a Song. Presents Jim Allen on drums. A Mike Quinn production.
Fine Arts
Dist - CANCIN

Start Decorating with Color and Pattern 20 MIN
VHS / U-matic
Color (A)
Tells about the basics of good interior design and decorating, and is aimed at young adults.
Fine Arts; Home Economics
Dist - KAROL **Prod** - KAROL

Start engines...plus fifty years - a first person history of the 8th Air Force in World War II 58 MIN
VHS
Color (J H G)
$29.95 purchase
Chronicles the history of the American 8th Air Force stationed in England during World War II. Reveals that the company sustained 26,000 dead - nearly one - tenth of all Americans killed during the war, 18,000 wounded and 28,000 taken prisoner. Combines live photography shot during the war and the experiences of the survivors.
History - United States; Industrial and Technical Education
Dist - KAWVAL **Prod** - KAWVAL 1992

Start here - adventure into science series
Fantastic power of air 25 MIN
Jumping molecules 25 MIN
Dist - LANDMK

Start Here - Adventures and Science Series
Air at work 25 MIN
The Amazing magnet 25 MIN
Build your own machines 25 MIN
The Fantastic power of air 25 MIN
The Invisible Force 25 MIN
Jumping Molecules 25 MIN
Make a Noise 25 MIN
Quick as Light 25 MIN
Stop and Go 25 MIN
Dist - LANDMK

Start here - adventures into science series 300 MIN
16mm / VHS
Start here - adventures into science series
Color (I J H) (SPANISH)
$1595.00 purchase
Presents a series of twelve videos that introduce Konrad, a robot, who demonstrates basic principles of science involving liquids, electricity, mixtures, air, gravity and friction, sound, light, inertia, temperature, simple machines, weather and magnetism. Shows how the principles apply to the world around us, and tells how some discoveries were made. Series is also available in Spanish, in 16mm, and all 12 titles are available separately.
Science
Dist - LANDMK

The Start of a Lifetime 28 MIN
U-matic / VHS / 16mm
Color (J A) (FRENCH)
Records the first fourteen months in the life of a child. Highlights nine developmental stages and illustrates the role of experience in developing physical, mental, social, emotional and creative abilities. Reveals a child's drive to learn about the world. Based on latest research.
Foreign Language; Psychology; Sociology
Dist - BCNFL **Prod** - BCNFL 1985

The Start of a trial 22 MIN
VHS
Color (J H)
$99.00 purchase _ #4721 - 026
Follows two men from their arrest through their arraignment and trial, stressing the importance of due process of law.
Civics and Political Systems
Dist - INSTRU **Prod** - EBEC

The Start of a War 15 MIN
U-matic / VHS
Stories of America Series
Color (P)
Gives a fictionalized account of what life was like on the eve of the Revolutionary War.
History - United States
Dist - AITECH **Prod** - OHSDE 1976

The Start of Something Special 12 MIN
16mm
Color
LC 74-705699
Explains the academic nature and benefits of the Naval Junior Officer Training Program as an elective science in secondary schools.
Civics and Political Systems; Education
Dist - USNAC **Prod** - USN 1972

Start Plants Right Video Series
Presents a four - part series on landscaping plants. Includes soil preparation, selection of trees, shrubs, herbaceous plants and ground covers and their fertilization.
Fertilizing landscape plants 26 MIN
Growing Media - Soil Preparation in the Landscape 17 MIN
Planting Techniques Part 1 - Trees and Shrubs 26 MIN
Planting Techniques Part 2 - Herbaceous Plants and Ground Covers 25 MIN
Dist - VEP **Prod** - VEP 1972

Start Sleeves 29 MIN
Videoreel / VT2
Busy Knitter II Series
Color
Home Economics
Dist - PBS **Prod** - WMVSTV

Start the day 100 MIN
VHS
Color; PAL (K P)
PdS30 purchase
Presents ten programs of 10 minutes each answering questions such as who loves me; why do things die; why should I say sorry. Takes one question per episode and uses a simple story and children's own voices to introduce new ideas which can be shared in the classroom or at assembly. Useful as part of a religious education curriculum or to encourage children to think out loud about things which delight them and trouble them. Contact distributor about availability outside the United Kingdom.
Education; Psychology; Religion and Philosophy
Dist - ACADEM

Start the Party 12 MIN
VHS / 16mm
What Now - Deciding What's Right Series
Color (K)
$39.95 purchase
Encourages children to look at their alternatives and to weigh the possible consequences of their actions before reaching a decision or taking an action, by focusing on realistic situations involving disobedience. The complete series is also available in one video, What Now - Deciding What's Right.
Education; Religion and Philosophy
Dist - JANUP **Prod** - JANUP

Start the Revolution Without Me 98 MIN
16mm
Color
Stars Gene Wilder and Donald Sutherland playing dual roles as two sets of twins mixed at birth. Tells how they become involved in the French Revolution.
Fine Arts
Dist - TWYMAN **Prod** - WB 1970

Start to Finish - Effective Discharge Planning 19 MIN
VHS / U-matic
Color (PRO)
Describes the role of the Home Care Coordinator in discharge planning. Demonstrates how the Home Care Coordinator works with the patient and family, other health professionals and community agencies to help the patient make the transition from hospital to home care.
Health and Safety
Dist - UMICHM **Prod** - UMICHM 1979

Start - Up 30 MIN
U-matic / VHS / 16mm
Enterprise Series
Color (C A)
Tells of the difficulties of starting a business as background to the story of John De Lorean, a former General Motors employee who started a company capable of competing with automobile industry giants.
Business and Economics; Industrial and Technical Education
Dist - LCOA **Prod** - WGBHTV 1981

Start with the World 30 MIN
16mm
Eternal Light Series
B&W (H C A)
LC 70-700966
Presents a Hasidic legend in dramatic form and explores aspects of Martin Buber's philosophy.
Religion and Philosophy
Dist - NAAJS **Prod** - JTS 1967

Starter Inspection and Overhaul 33 MIN
U-matic / VHS
Automechanics Series
Color (IND)
Shows how to disassemble a starter motor with a solenoid switch and overrunning clutch drive. Discusses component testing and adjustment for installation on the vehicle.
Industrial and Technical Education
Dist - LEIKID **Prod** - LEIKID

Starting a business series
Are you an entrepreneur 18 MIN
Do You Need a Business Plan? 21 MIN
How Can You Survive Business Crises 21 MIN
How do you buy a business? 21 MIN
How do you buy a franchise? 21 MIN
How Much Capital will You Need? 17 MIN
How will You Find Capital? 21 MIN
How will You Penetrate Your Market? 16 MIN
What Should Your Business Plan Contain? 22 MIN
What will Your New Venture Demand 20 MIN
What's the Best Business for You? 16 MIN
Who will Help You Start Your Venture 20 MIN
Who will Your Customers be 18 MIN
Dist - BCNFL

Starting a Physician Support Group 13 MIN
VHS / 16mm
(C)
$385.00 purchase _ #850VI061
Shows how to start a physician support group to help members better cope with the distress and problems of the profession.
Health and Safety
Dist - HSCIC **Prod** - HSCIC 1985

Starting an Exercise Program
U-matic / VHS
Color (SPANISH)
Discusses benefits of aerobic exercises to improve cardiovascular fitness. Demonstrates how 3 different individuals begin and successfully continue an aerobic exercise program.
Physical Education and Recreation
Dist - MIFE **Prod** - MIFE

Starting an intravenous infusion 21 MIN
U-matic / VHS
EMT video - group three series
Color (PRO)
Illustrates proper methods for preparing and positioning IV equipment, selecting and cleaning the infusion site, applying a tourniquet, and inserting the needle into the vein. Demonstrates method for assembling the plasma protein kit so that the solution will flow freely after the clamp is released.
Health and Safety
Dist - USNAC **Prod** - USA 1983

Starting an IV 10 MIN
VHS / U-matic
Color (PRO)
Shows technique used in starting intravenous therapy.
Health and Safety; Science
Dist - HSCIC **Prod** - HSCIC 1977

Starting and Running a Business 30 MIN
VHS / 16mm
(PRO G)
$89.95 purchase _ #DGP5
Talks about the do's and don'ts of starting and running a small business. Hosted by Dick Goldberg.
Business and Economics
Dist - RMIBHF **Prod** - RMIBHF

Starting and Running a Business
VHS
Business Video Series
$89.95 purchase _ #RPDGP5V
Talks about the do's and don'ts of going into small business.
Business and Economics
Dist - CAREER **Prod** - CAREER

Starting and Running a Restaurant 30 MIN
VHS / 16mm
(PRO G)
$89.95 purchase _ #DGP21
Describes the rewards and difficulties in starting and running a restaurant - from a gourmet establishment to a family - type coffee shop. Hosted by Dick Goldberg.
Business and Economics
Dist - RMIBHF **Prod** - RMIBHF

Starting and Running Retail Stores
VHS
$97 purchase _ #PX4749
Talks about how to take an idea and convert it into a successful retail operation. Discusses how to lease a storefront, stock goods, hire employees, and run the store for a profit.
Business and Economics
Dist - CAREER **Prod** - CAREER

Starting and Running Retail Stores 30 MIN
VHS / 16mm
(PRO G)
$89.95 purchase _ #DGP33
Shows how to successfully take and idea and turn it into a successful retail operation. Covers leasing the store, stocking, hiring, and running the store for a profit. Hosted by Dick Goldberg.
Business and Economics
Dist - RMIBHF **Prod** - RMIBHF

Starting Circuit Testing 18 MIN
U-matic / VHS
Automechanics Series
Color (IND)
Shows procedure for checking starter current draw. Covers free running tests.
Industrial and Technical Education
Dist - LEIKID **Prod** - LEIKID

Starting early 20 MIN
VHS
Starting early series
Color (T PRO A)
$35.00 purchase _ #480
Presents an overview of the Starting Early series for school administrators and teachers. Shows real - life implementation of the program at kindergarten, second and fifth grade levels.
Guidance and Counseling; Health and Safety; Psychology
Dist - AAAFTS **Prod** - AAAFTS 1981

Starting early - Part I 30 MIN
VHS
Straight talk series
Color (J H)
$99.00 purchase
Discusses first experimentation with drugs. Features the frank testimonials of 20 young people aged 13 to 22 who have confronted significant chemical abuse issues. Uses quick - cut editing style and a contemporary soundtrack aimed at attracting the MTV gneration. No adult voices are heard - teen interviews discuss personal issues - parental drug and alcohol use, physical abuse, sexual acting out, chronic low self - esteem, loneliness, alienation and suicidal behavior. Part one of three parts on teens and drugs.
Guidance and Counseling; Psychology; Sociology
Dist - FMSP

Starting early series

Alcohol - the unlabeled drug	14 MIN
Alcohol trigger films for junior high school	7 MIN
Anything to be a big boy	4 MIN
Do we or don't we	4 MIN
Froggy and Dodo help at a wedding	
Hidden dangers	14 MIN
Him or me	4 MIN
Is it time to stop pretending	5 MIN
MTV - it's your right to say 'no'	4 MIN
Should he tell	5 MIN
Starting early	20 MIN

Dist - AAAFTS

Starting Efficiently 30 MIN
U-matic
Energy Efficient Housing Series
(A)
Deals with air infiltration, outlining initially those areas where air leakage occurs then demonstrates how to fix them.
Industrial and Technical Education; Social Science
Dist - ACCESS **Prod** - SASKM 1983

Starting English Early 30 MIN
16mm
Color (T)
LC FIA68-232
Demonstrates techniques of teaching English as a second language to children of elementary school age.
Education
Dist - UCLA **Prod** - UCLA 1967

Starting fire with gunpowder 59 MIN
VHS / 16mm
As long as the rivers flow series
Color (G)
$390.00 purchase, $75.00 rental
Explores the control of the media as a means of Native American self - determination. Chronicles the origins and achievements of the Inuit Broadcasting Corporation, IBC, a model for indigenous broadcasters the world over. Helps keep Inuit culture and language alive through documentary, drama, animation and children's programs, along with addressing topics like alcoholism and wife abuse. Narrated by Ann Neekijuk Hanson. Film by David Poisey and William Hansen. Part of a five - part series dealing with the struggle of Native People in Canada to regain control over their destinies.
Fine Arts; Social Science
Dist - FIRS **Prod** - CULRAY 1991

Starting from Nina 30 MIN
16mm / VHS
Color (G)
$530.00, $290.00 purchase, $55.00 rental
Shows the view of education from Paulo Freire as a liberation process in various settings. Includes immigrants in an English class, teachers discussing students' views of their working class neighborhood and clerical workers talking about the pressures of their jobs. Produced by the Development Education Centre.
Business and Economics; Education; English Language; Fine Arts; Sociology
Dist - FIRS

Starting from Scratch 29 MIN
Videoreel / VT2
Making Things Grow III Series
Color
Agriculture
Dist - PBS **Prod** - WGBHTV

Starting from Scratch - Birth to Three Years 29 MIN
U-matic / VHS
Spoonful of Lovin' Series no 2
Color (H C A)
LC 82-707398
Presents journalist Reynalda Muse highlighting the mental, physical, social and emotional changes in children from birth to three years. Discusses the changing needs of children as they struggle for more independence and illustrates right and wrong methods of toilet training.
Home Economics; Psychology
Dist - AITECH **Prod** - KRMATV 1981

Starting Intravenous Infusions - Part 2 17 MIN
U-matic / VHS
Parenteral Therapy Series
Color (PRO)
Demonstrates the proper procedure for starting an intravenous (IV) infusion.
Health and Safety
Dist - HSCIC **Prod** - HSCIC 1981

Starting Life Too Soon 26 MIN
VHS / 16mm
Color (G)
$149.00, $249.00, purchase _ #AD - 1896
Focuses on the seven per cent of the almost four million babies born in the United States each year who are born prematurely. Shows how many develop jaundice, brain hemorrhages, cardiac or pulmonary complications. Explains that their undeveloped immune system makes them vulnerable to infection and other problems. Examines technological breakthroughs in the care of premature infants.
Health and Safety
Dist - FOTH **Prod** - FOTH 1990

Starting Line 22 MIN
16mm / U-matic / VHS
B&W (C A)
Reports on premature infants and what the Illinois Health Department is doing to reduce infant and maternal mortality.
Health and Safety; Psychology; Sociology
Dist - IFB **Prod** - IFB 1948

Starting Nursery School - Patterns of Beginning 23 MIN
16mm
Studies of Normal Personality Development Series
B&W (C T)
Presents an approach to reducing the anxiety of children when starting nursery school, based on gradual acquaintance with the nursery school and longer periods away from mother.
Guidance and Counseling; Psychology
Dist - NYU **Prod** - NYU 1959

Starting over - the long road back
VHS
Running away, dropping out - voices from Nightmare Street series
Color (I J H)
$79.95 purchase _ #CCP0170V - K
Focuses on the future to help kids who cannot go home realize and consider their options. Offers advice from runaways who have dropped out of school and are struggling to get off the streets, off drugs and out of prostitution. Interviews residents and counselors at homeless shelters who describe life at the shelter - the rules they enforce, the assistance they provide, and their success in helping teens overcome their problems. Reveals the help available to those with no hope, jail records, trapped by drugs and - or prostitution so that they can see that there are ways to start life over, get off the streets and on with their lives. Part of two parts on the reality of teenagers struggling to survive on the streets.
Guidance and Counseling; History - United States; Sociology
Dist - CAMV **Prod** - CAMV 1993

Starting Right Now - Peer Pressure and Smoking 28 MIN
VHS
Color (I H)
Presents an anti - smoking message in a musical - drama format.
Fine Arts; Health and Safety
Dist - CEPRO **Prod** - CEPRO 1989

Starting Right Now - Peer Pressure and Smoking 28 MIN
U-matic / VHS
Color (I J H)
Concentrates on peer pressure to urge children not to start smoking. Done as a musical drama.
Fine Arts; Health and Safety; Psychology
Dist - CEPRO **Prod** - CEPRO 1986

Starting, Running and Finishing 17 MIN
16mm / U-matic / VHS
Women's Track and Field Series no 1
Color (J)
LC 79-700801
Discusses basic techniques in women's track and field.
Physical Education and Recreation
Dist - ATHI **Prod** - ATHI 1976

Starting, Running and Finishing - Men's Track 17 MIN
16mm / U-matic / VHS
Men's Track and Field Series no 1
Color (I)

LC 79-700796
Focuses on starting, running and finishing a race and analyzes the running motions involved.
Physical Education and Recreation
Dist - ATHI **Prod** - ATHI 1976

Starting school 30 MIN
VHS
Effective teacher telecourse series
Color (T)
$69.95 purchase, $50.00 rental
Presents strategies for the initial days and weeks of the school year. Hosted by Dr Loren Anderson.
Education; Psychology
Dist - SCETV **Prod** - SCETV 1987

Starting School 14 MIN
U-matic / VHS / 16mm
Color (K P)
LC 73-702539
Shows the activities of one day in kindergarten class. Includes such lessons as recognition, cooking and communication.
Education; Guidance and Counseling
Dist - EBEC **Prod** - EBEC 1973

Starting Seeds Indoors 20 MIN
VHS / U-matic
Color (A)
$19.95 _ #PS100
Presents an overview of the necessary methods used in starting seeds inside the home.
Agriculture; Science - Natural
Dist - AAVIM **Prod** - AAVIM

Starting Small 30 MIN
BETA / VHS
On the Money Series
Color
Looks at investment clubs. Discusses getting financial aid to start a small business. Defines some economic concepts.
Business and Economics; Home Economics
Dist - CORF **Prod** - WGBHTV

The Starting System Explained 48 MIN
VHS / 35mm strip
(H A IND)
#435XV7
Identifies starting system components and shows how they are tested and serviced. Includes fielf coils, armature and brushes, the drive arrangement and solenoid, starting system testing, and starting motor service and repair (4 tapes). Prerequisites required. Includes a Study Guide.
Education; Industrial and Technical Education
Dist - BERGL

Starting tactics
VHS
Color (G A)
$48.00 purchase _ #0917
Teaches sailing techniques such as start procedures, prestart maneuvers, start sequences, boat handling, crew responsibilities, different conditions of start and tactics, start approaches, fleet situation. Includes graphics. Produced by J - World.
Physical Education and Recreation
Dist - SEVVID

Starting the Interview 20 MIN
16mm / U-matic / VHS
Color
Illustrates typical opening sales errors that turn off the prospect and ruin the salesman's chances before he's even had a chance to start selling. Demonstrates how effective opening techniques can win a customer's confidence and multiply the chances of getting the order.
Business and Economics; Guidance and Counseling
Dist - DARTNL **Prod** - RANKAV

Starting the System 13 MIN
VHS / U-matic
Practical M B O Series
Color
Business and Economics; Education; Psychology
Dist - DELTAK **Prod** - DELTAK

Starting to Dive 10 MIN
U-matic / VHS / 16mm
B&W (I J H)
Demonstrates basic elements and practices in diving. Shows exercises in preparation of more advanced dives, such as the somersault, back dive, arm stand dive and twist jump. Uses slow motion underwater photography.
Physical Education and Recreation
Dist - IFB **Prod** - BHA 1965

Starting to Print 29 MIN
U-matic / VHS
Photo Show Series
Color
Shows the steps necessary before printing enlargements after the negatives are ready.
Industrial and Technical Education
Dist - PBS **Prod** - WGBHTV 1981

Starting to Read Series
County Fair 7 MIN
Ducks 8 MIN
In, Out, Up, Down, Over, Under, Upside Down 8 MIN
One Turkey, Two Turkey 6 MIN
Picnic 8 MIN
Playground 7 MIN
Rain 6 MIN
Safety as We Play 7 MIN
Sun 8 MIN
A Wheel is Round 8 MIN
Wind 8 MIN
Z is for Zoo 8 MIN
Dist - AIMS

Starting to Swim 18 MIN
16mm / U-matic / VHS
B&W (I J H)
Explains sanitary measures and pool safety. Considers breathing, gliding, floating, elementary diving and other movements in the water.
Health and Safety; Physical Education and Recreation
Dist - IFB **Prod** - BHA 1965

Starting to Work 15 MIN
U-matic
Job Skills Series
(H C A)
Stresses the need to adjust to and learn in a new situation. Discusses employer and employee expectations in the new work situation.
Business and Economics; Guidance and Counseling; Science - Physical
Dist - ACCESS **Prod** - ACCESS 1982

Starting to Work Together 20 MIN
U-matic / VHS
Working Together for Action Series
Color
Describes positive and disfunctional roles often played by members of a group, including standard setter, mediator, dominator and aggressor when starting to work together for action.
Sociology
Dist - UWISC **Prod** - SYRCU 1976

Starting Tomorrow 29 MIN
16mm / U-matic / VHS
Human Relations and School Discipline Series
Color (C)
Presents a thought - provoking mix of practical suggestions, workable classroom approaches, helpful tips and a few startling ideas that every teacher can use to improve human relations and school discipline. Features interviews with such therapists as William Glasser, Thomas Gordon and others.
Education; Sociology
Dist - FI **Prod** - MFFD

Starting Tomorrow Series Unit 1 - New Ways in Composition
Planning the Story 30 MIN
Dist - WALKED

Starting Tomorrow Series Unit 2 - Understanding the School's Neighborhood
The School's Environment 30 MIN
Dist - WALKED

Starting Tomorrow Series Unit 3 - Individualizing Your Reading Program
Steps to Mature Reading 30 MIN
The Widening World of Books 30 MIN
Dist - WALKED

Starting Tomorrow Series Unit 4 - New Ways in Elementary Science
A Lesson Doesn't End 30 MIN
The Matter of Air 30 MIN
Dist - WALKED

Starting Tomorrow Series Unit 5 - Introducing Sex Education
Reproduction and Birth 25 MIN
Dist - WALKED

Starting Tomorrow Series Unit 6 - New Ways in Art Education
Discoveries in Three Dimensions 30 MIN
Experiment in Color
Dist - WALKED

Starting Tomorrow Series Unit 7 - Providing for Children's Differences
Individualizing the Math Textbook
Dist - WALKED

Starting tomorrow series
Cycles of life 25 MIN
Developing the vocabulary 25 MIN
The Language of Maps 30 MIN
Dist - WALKED

Starting Up 30 MIN
U-matic / VHS / 16mm
Case Studies in Small Business Series
Color (C A)
Business and Economics
Dist - GPN **Prod** - UMA 1979

Starting with safety - an introduction for the academic chemistry laboratory 35 MIN
VHS
Color; PAL (H C)
$79.95 purchase _ #V - 5100 - 19001
Features high school and college students who demonstrate safe ways to use common laboratory equipment. Shows why safety techniques are vitally important. Demonstrates the lighting and use of a Bunsen burner; safely heating glassware; the use of safety equipment; how to dress appropriately for the lab; how to respond to common accidents; how to use thermometers and glass tubing safely; proper behavior in the lab; how to use the centrifuge safely; how to use safety equipment. Technical advisor, Lois Wickstrom. Includes a teacher's guide.
Health and Safety; Science; Science - Physical
Dist - AMCHEM

Starting with the student 91 MIN
U-matic / VHS
Core skills for field instructors series; Program 1
Color (C T)
Uses role playing and examples to teach agency field instructors how to prepare for the arrival of practicum students, to deal with initial student anxiety and to help the students setle in quickly.
Education; Sociology
Dist - MCGILU **Prod** - MCGILU 1983

Starting your new job 19 MIN
VHS
Color (PRO A G)
$495.00 purchase, $125.00 rental
Emphasizes six work habits that are critical to job success. Covers dependability, courtesy, following instructions and being open to criticism among others.
Business and Economics; Guidance and Counseling
Dist - EXTR **Prod** - EBEC

Starts, turns and individual medley
VHS
N C A A instructional video series
Color (H C A)
$39.95 purchase _ #KAR2202V
Presents the second of a three - part series on swimming and diving. Focuses on starts, turns and the individual medley.
Physical Education and Recreation
Dist - CAMV **Prod** - NCAAF

Starts, Turns and Progressive Drills 23 MIN
16mm / U-matic / VHS
Swimming Series no 3
Color
LC 79-700795
Demonstrates starts, turns and drills for individual swim strokes and conditioning exercises.
Physical Education and Recreation
Dist - ATHI **Prod** - ATHI 1977

Starving 10 MIN
16mm / VHS / BETA / U-matic
Color; PAL (J H C G)
PdS75, PdS83 purchase
Features a dramatized documentary about anorexia nervosa.
Health and Safety
Dist - EDPAT

Starving and binging - 1 16 MIN
VHS
Learning about eating disorders series
Color (G)
$250.00 purchase, $60.00 rental
Covers indications of anorexia nervosa and bulimia. Part of a five - part series which explores the problem of eating disorders.
Health and Safety; Psychology
Dist - CF **Prod** - HOSSN 1989

Starving for sugar 58 MIN
VHS
Color (G)
$14.95 purchase
Looks at how the use of sugar substitutes has depressed the sugar market and national economies of sugar - producing countries.
Business and Economics
Dist - MARYFA

The Starwatchers of Kitt Peak 18 MIN
VHS / U-matic
Color
Presents the dramatic birth, growth and death of a single star as seen through the world's most powerful solar telescope, highlighted in this film about men and women astronomers at work.

Science - Physical
Dist - KINGFT **Prod** - KINGFT

State Constitutions 29 MIN
U-matic
American Government Series
Color
LC 79-706332
Uses the constitutions of Texas, Illinois and California to illustrate the process of state constitutional change. Includes interviews with governors, judges and members of state legislatures who discuss issues involving lawmaking, court structuring and budgeting.
Civics and Political Systems
Dist - DALCCD **Prod** - DALCCD 1979

State Fair 100 MIN
U-matic / VHS / 16mm
Color (I J H C)
Presents a score by Rodgers and Hammerstein about a family's adventures at the Iowa State fair. Stars Dana Andrews and Jeanne Crain.
Fine Arts
Dist - FI **Prod** - TWCF 1945

A State fair scrapbook 60 MIN
VHS
Color (G)
$19.95 purchase _ #V - 006
Celebrates the rich history and traditions of the Minnesota State Fair from covered wagon days to the bungee - jumping present.
History - United States
Dist - MINHS **Prod** - KTCATV

State Government - Resurgence of Power 21 MIN
16mm / U-matic / VHS
Color (J H)
LC 76-701795
Outlines the changing concepts and roles of State government in the United States. Shows how new leaders with fresh ideas have come forth and are willing to take responsibility for meeting the social and economic needs of the states.
Civics and Political Systems; Sociology
Dist - EBEC **Prod** - EBEC 1976

State Intervention in Cities 45 MIN
U-matic
Urban Change and Conflict Series
Color (H C A)
Explores state intervention among cities in diffferent national contexts.
Sociology
Dist - ACCESS **Prod** - BBCTV 1983

A State Labor Body 24 MIN
16mm
Color (A)
Portrays a quest for information, giving a picture of the activities of a state labor body in the legislature, on a political action front and in the community.
Business and Economics; Psychology
Dist - AFLCIO **Prod** - AFLCIO 1960

The State Lawmakers 28 MIN
16mm
Color (J)
LC 73-700024
Documents an actual legislative session during which a bill is introduced and drafted to allow voters the right to decide whether or not the voting age should be lowered from 21 to 18 years.
Civics and Political Systems
Dist - SCREEI **Prod** - SCREEI 1971

State Legislatures 30 MIN
U-matic / VHS
American Government 2 Series
Color (C)
Compares the Texas and California state legislatures as classic examples of state government. Illustrates the relative power between the executive and legislative branches in each state and the way they differ.
Civics and Political Systems
Dist - DALCCD **Prod** - DALCCD

State Legislatures 29 MIN
16mm
Color
LC 77-700577
Dramatizes the day - to - day work of a state legislator as he experiences the frustrations and achievements of his daily responsibilities. Discusses the workings of the legislative process, the mechanics of developing and passing a bill and the effect of this work on the lawmaker's personal life.
Civics and Political Systems; Guidance and Counseling
Dist - NCSLS **Prod** - NCSLS 1976

State Libraries - Materials, Manpower, Money 20 MIN
U-matic
Access Series
Color (T)
LC 76-706262
Gives an overview of what services a typical state library can offer to other libraries in the state, such as special collections and services.
Civics and Political Systems; Education
Dist - USNAC **Prod** - UDEN 1976

The State Machine - Definition of Input and Output Signals 30 MIN
VHS / U-matic
Microprocessors for Monitoring and Control Series
Color (IND)
Introduces concept of a state machine, which serves as a description for any digital system. Tells about timing, based on a clock for the state machine. Develops notation to design input and output signals.
Industrial and Technical Education; Mathematics; Sociology
Dist - COLOSU **Prod** - COLOSU

The State of Aloha - 25 Years 24 MIN
VHS / U-matic
Color
$335.00 purchase
History - United States
Dist - ABCLR **Prod** - ABCLR 1983

The State of Apartheid - South Africa 13 MIN
VHS / U-matic
Color (H C A)
Discusses apartheid in South Africa.
Geography - World; Sociology
Dist - JOU **Prod** - UPI

A State of Danger 28 MIN
VHS / 16mm
Color (G)
$225.00 purchase, $60.00 rental
Presents a tape produced for the BBC covering the Palestine Intifada - uprising. Reveals that it was filmed in Israel to offer a perspective on the Intifada which US mainstream media has failed to cover. Interviews Palestinian women who testify about Israeli treatment of the Palestinians, more than 550 of whom have been killed, thousands injured. A small minority of Israeli women testify in support. Each week 'Women in Black' demonstrate silently in front of government offices, confronted by hecklers.
Civics and Political Systems; Geography - World; History - World; Industrial and Technical Education; Sociology
Dist - WMEN **Prod** - HBJM 1989

The State of English 30 MIN
VHS / U-matic
Language - Thinking, Writing, Communicating Series
Color
English Language
Dist - MDCPB **Prod** - MDCPB

The State of Hawaii 29 MIN
16mm
Color (I)
Illustrates the operation of the state government of the state of Hawaii.
Civics and Political Systems; Geography - United States
Dist - CINEPC **Prod** - CINEPC

The State of Israel is recognized by Palestine - Monday, November 14, 1988 30 MIN
VHS
Nightline series
Color (H C G)
$14.98 purchase _ #MP6170
Focuses on the attempt of Palestine to bring about better international relations in the Middle East through the recognition of the State of Israel.
Civics and Political Systems; Fine Arts
Dist - INSTRU **Prod** - ABCNEW 1988

State of Seizure 25 MIN
U-matic / VHS
Color
Shows that epileptics can suffer as much from social rejection as they do from epilepsy itself. Has actress - singer Ketty Lester and other epileptics helping to explore their unique problems and their progress.
Health and Safety; Psychology
Dist - MEDCOM **Prod** - MEDCOM

State of shock - a native people loses its heritage 55 MIN
VHS
Color (H C G)
$445.00 purchase, $75.00 rental
Reveals that like native Americans, the Austalian aborigines have lost their land and their sense of pride. Observes that they turn their anger inward and drift into alcoholism and violence. Alwyn Peters, a 22 - year - old Aborigine living on the reservation, stabbed his girlfriend to death in a drunken rage, and this death, by some historical quirk, raised national consciousness. Produced by David Bradbury.
Geography - World; Health and Safety; History - World; Sociology
Dist - FLMLIB

State of the art of computer animation 70 MIN
VHS
Color (G)
$39.95 purchase _ #S02091
Presents a compilation of computer animated images by more than 30 artists. Shows a wide spectrum of animation styles.
Computer Science; Fine Arts
Dist - UILL

The State of the Art of Sex Education, Therapy and Counseling 60 MIN
U-matic / VHS
Color
Presents the view of the eminent pioneering educator, Mary Calderone, MD, on the impact of changing sex values and practices on individuals and family life. Makes a plea for openness and truth to replace ignorance concerning human sexuality.
Health and Safety; Psychology; Sociology
Dist - HEMUL **Prod** - HEMUL

State of the Arts 30 MIN
U-matic
Fast Forward Series
Color (H C)
Looks at the impact of the new technologies on the arts including the creation of new art forms such as electronic music and videosynthesis.
Computer Science; Science
Dist - TVOTAR **Prod** - TVOTAR 1979

State of the City 29 MIN
16mm
Color
Documents the consolidation of the government of Jacksonville, Florida.
Civics and Political Systems; Geography - United States
Dist - FLADC **Prod** - FLADC

State of the Greek Orthodox Church in the Americas 28 MIN
VHS
Illuminations series
Color (G R)
#V - 1030
Profiles the growth of the Greek Orthodox Church in North and South America, which now has more than 500 parishes and more than half of the estimated 5 million Orthodox Christians in the U S. Focuses on the spiritual and social concerns that the denomination faces. Discusses the church's philanthropic activities.
Religion and Philosophy
Dist - GOTEL **Prod** - GOTEL 1989

State of the Ummah
VHS
Color (G)
$12.00 purchase _ #110 - 079
Features Dr Mukhtar Moughrouni, Ghulam Muhammad Sufi and Imam Al - Amin Abdul Lateef who survey the situation of Muslims in Algeria, Kashmir and the United States.
Religion and Philosophy
Dist - SOUVIS **Prod** - SOUVIS

State of the Union 5 MIN
16mm
Screen news digest series; Vol 4; Issue 7
B&W
Replays President Kennedy's State of the Union Address of 1962.
Civics and Political Systems; History - United States
Dist - HEARST **Prod** - HEARST 1962

State of the Union 29 MIN
VHS / 16mm
Washington Connection Series
Color (G)
$55.00 rental _ #WACO - 102
Civics and Political Systems; Social Science
Dist - PBS **Prod** - NPACT

The State of the Union - Viet Nam Report 1966 14 MIN
16mm
Screen news digest series; Vol 8; Issue 7
B&W (J)
LC 73-700506
Presents the report by President Johnson to the nation on the war in Vietnam.
Civics and Political Systems; History - United States; History - World
Dist - HEARST **Prod** - HEARST 1966

State of the Unions - 115 30 MIN
U-matic

Currents - 1984 - 85 Season Series
Color (A)
Looks at the current state of the labor union movement in America in the current economic climate.
Business and Economics; Social Science
Dist - PBS **Prod** - WNETTV 1985

State of the World Report 15 MIN
U-matic / VHS
It's all Up to You Series
Color (I J)
Illustrates the opportunities and responsibilities of individuals to participate in politics and government.
Guidance and Counseling; Sociology
Dist - AITECH **Prod** - COOPED 1978

The State of the world with Lester Brown 30 MIN
U-matic / VHS
World of ideas with Bill Moyers - Season 2 series
Color; Captioned (A G)
$39.95, $59.95 purchase _ #WIWM - 231
Features Lester Brown, founder of the Worldwatch Institute, and publisher of over 90 papers on enviromental problems. Draws attention to the daily deterioration of the world and suggests solutions for a wide variety of environmental problems. Stresses that dramatic changes must be made in a very short period of time. Part of a series of interviews with Bill Moyers featuring scientists, writers, artists, philosophers and historians. Produced by Public Affairs Television, New York.
Science - Natural; Sociology
Dist - PBS

State Political Organization and Legislative Procedures 20 MIN
16mm
Government and Public Affairs Films Series
B&W (H A)
Dr Gary Brazier, assistant professor of government, Boston College, describes the important process of making and passing legislation at the state level.
Civics and Political Systems
Dist - MLA **Prod** - RSC 1960

State Political Organization and Legislative Procedures - Dr Gary Brazier 20 MIN
16mm
Building Political Leadership Series
B&W (H C)
Civics and Political Systems
Dist - MLA **Prod** - RSC 1960

The State Structure and Bodies of People's Government in the USSR 20 MIN
U-matic / VHS
Color
Explains the basic structure of the USSR as a federation of Union and autonomous republics, equal and sovereign, in which State power is concentrated in soviets, or councils. Focuses on the activities of the Supreme Soviets of the Turkmenian Soviet Socialist Republic and the Autonomous Republic of Abkhazia. Shows local government operation in the Vasileostrousky District Soviet in Leningrad. Includes episodes from Moscow, Leningrad, Ashkabad, Sukhumi and Leontyevo in Kalinin.
Civics and Political Systems; History - World
Dist - IHF **Prod** - IHF

A State University in the South 17 MIN
16mm
College Selection Film Series
Color (J H A)
LC 76-713109
Notes that while universities in the South are not so large as some of the Midwestern and western state universities, state institutions still require more independence and initiative than smaller, more cohesive schools. Shows how geography influences life - style and campus atmosphere at Louisiana State University.
Education; Guidance and Counseling
Dist - VISEDC **Prod** - VISEDC 1971

State University of New York at Albany
VHS
Campus clips series
Color (H C A)
$29.95 purchase _ #CC0077V
Takes a video visit to the campus of the State University of New York at Albany. Shows many of the distinctive features of the campus, and interviews students about their experiences. Provides information on the composition of the student body, professors, academics, social life, housing, and other subjects.
Education
Dist - CAMV

State Visit of the President of the Republic of Germany to Malaysia 15 MIN
16mm
B&W
Records the state visit of President Leubke and Frau Luebke of the Republic of Germany to Malaysia. Shows the president and his official entourage of 15 visiting Parliament House, the National Operation Room, the University of Malaya and Museum Negara.
Civics and Political Systems; Geography - World; History - World
Dist - PMFMUN **Prod** - FILEM 1967

State Visit to Australia by their Imperial Majesties, the Shahanshah Aryamehr and the Shahbanou of Iran 30 MIN
16mm
Color (J)
LC 76-700573
Documents the visit to Australia in 1974 of the Shahanshah Aryamehr and Shahbanou of Iran. Shows them during official functions while in Australia and also in less formal moments during their visit.
Geography - World; History - World
Dist - AUIS **Prod** - FLMAUS 1976

Stateless in Gaza 30 MIN
VHS
Daughters of Abraham series
Color (H C G)
$195.00 purchase
Features Mary Khass who organizes nursery schools and groups in the nine refugee camps of the Gaza Strip. Reveals that she is a pacifist and a Quaker and wants to see both peace and freedom from occupation for the Palestinians. Part of a trilogy about the daily lives and the hopes of three very different women living in a society fractured by political, military, religious and economic divisions.
History - World; Religion and Philosophy
Dist - LANDMK **Prod** - LANDMK 1988

The States of Matter 59 MIN
U-matic / BETA / VHS
Color
$400 purchase
Presents attractive forces between atoms, types of bonding, properties of metallic bonding, unit cells, lattices, valence numbers, grains, and grain boundaries.
Science; Science - Physical
Dist - ASM **Prod** - ASM 1987

The States of Matter 15 MIN
U-matic / VHS
Matter and Motion Series Module Red; Module red
Color (I)
Introduces the states of matter, including solids, liquids and gases. Discusses the concept of a plasma state.
Science - Physical
Dist - AITECH **Prod** - WHROTV 1973

The States of Matter 18 MIN
16mm / U-matic / VHS
Physical Science Film Series
Color (H C A)
LC 73-701092
Explains the four divisions of matter - liquids, solids, gases and plasma. Points out that the division between these states may in the future prove to be less important than the unity that exists between them.
Science - Physical
Dist - CRMP **Prod** - CRMP 1973

States of Mind 60 MIN
VHS / U-matic
Brain, Mind and Behavior Series
Color (C A)
Discusses today's science of the brain and looks to its future in medicine, artificial intelligence and understanding the mind.
Psychology
Dist - FI **Prod** - WNETTV

States of mind - Part 8 60 MIN
VHS / U-matic
Brain series
Color (G)
$45.00, $29.95 purchase
Explores what scientists do not understand about the brain. Looks to the future of research in medicine, artificial intelligence and genetic manipulation. Part eight of an eight - part series on the brain.
Health and Safety; Psychology; Science - Natural
Dist - ANNCPB **Prod** - WNETTV 1984

A Statewide Educational Computing Network - the Minnesota Educational Computing 23 MIN
U-matic / VHS
New Technology in Education Series
Color (J)
Complete title is Statewide Educational Computing Network, A - The Minnesota Educational Computing Consortium (MECC). Provides information on MECC, an organization created by four public educational systems in Minnesota to coordinate and provide computer services to students, teachers and educational administrators.
Education; Industrial and Technical Education
Dist - USNAC **Prod** - USDOE 1983

Static 93 MIN
35mm
Color; PAL (G)
Features an offbeat perspective on American small - town life. Presents Ernie, a 'spiritual outsider,' who sees and feels things too deeply. He invents a device that will make people happy but his family and friends can't acknowledge it or accept this view of heaven. Directed by Mark Romanek for Necessity Films, USA. Contact distributor about price and availability outside of the United Kingdom.
Geography - United States; History - United States; Literature and Drama
Dist - BALFOR

Static and Current Electricity 16 MIN
16mm / U-matic / VHS
Physical Science Series
Color (I J H)
$365, $250 purchase _ #4601
Shows how static and current electricity works.
Science - Physical
Dist - CORF

Static charges 10 MIN
VHS
Junior electrician series
CC; Color (P I)
$55.00 purchase _ #1323VG
Introduces electrons and protons as the charged particles of atoms. Explains static electricity and how objects can pickup a charge. Comes with a teacher's guide and blackline masters. Part one of a four - part series.
Science - Physical
Dist - UNL

Static Electricity 15 MIN
U-matic / VHS
Why Series
Color (P I)
Discusses static electricity.
Science - Physical
Dist - AITECH **Prod** - WDCNTV 1976

Station, Gait and Cerebellar Function
VHS / U-matic
Physical Assessment - Neurologic System Series
Color
Health and Safety; Psychology
Dist - CONMED **Prod** - CONMED

Station Master 28 MIN
16mm
B&W (H C A)
Presents a drama set in the Ukraine during the 1919 Revolution. Tells the story of an old railway station master who becomes a victim of circumstances when an ammunition train has been delayed because the control switches have not been set.
History - World; Literature and Drama; Social Science
Dist - UWFKD **Prod** - UWFKD

Station of sorrow 25 MIN
VHS / U-matic / 16mm
Color (G)
$495.00, $100.00, $75.00 purchase, $50.00 rental _ #HPF - 734, #HVC - 734, #HHC - 734, #HRF - 734
Portrays the stationmaster at Bobigny, France, a site where Jews actually were herded onto freight trains which bore them to death camps. Reveals that he encounters at midnight a stranger who comes to mourn and learns that the mysterious sounds which wake him up at night are the sounds of the Nazi roundup.
Civics and Political Systems; History - World; Religion and Philosophy; Sociology
Dist - ADL

Stationary ark series

Breeding	27 MIN
A Day at the zoo	27 MIN
Gorillas	27 MIN
How dead is dead	27 MIN
Lemurs	27 MIN
Marmosets	27 MIN
Orang - utans	27 MIN
Pheasants and peacocks	27 MIN
Predators	27 MIN
Surviving	27 MIN
Water fowl	27 MIN
Zoo medicine	27 MIN

Dist - EDPAT

Stationary engineer 4.5 MIN
VHS / 16mm
Good works 4 series
Color (A PRO)
$40.00 purchase _ #BPN225803
Presents the occupation of a stationary engineer. Gives a profile of a young person who is either undergoing an apprenticeship or has recently completed training in this field. Takes the viewer on a tour of this person's workplace and explains the practical skills and training offered by employers and schools. Gives a better understanding of the demand for skilled workers today and the potential for personal growth.

Guidance and Counseling
Dist - RMIBHF **Prod** - RMIBHF

Stationary engineer 5 MIN
U-matic
Good work series
Color (H)
Provides useful, up to date information on various occupations to aid high school students in career selection. Available in five series of ten jobs each.
Education; Guidance and Counseling; Industrial and Technical Education
Dist - TVOTAR **Prod** - TVOTAR 1981

Stationary Power Saws, Vol I
VHS
Power Tool Principles - Safety And Technique Series
Color (G IND)
$79.95 purchase _ #6 - 202 - 101P
Discusses safety and the proper use of the table, radial arm and band saw. Indexes the tape to easily locate specific sequences. Part one of two parts on power tool principles and safety.
Health and Safety; Industrial and Technical Education
Dist - VEP **Prod** - VEP

The Stationmaster's Wife 111 MIN
16mm
Color (GERMAN (ENGLISH SUBTITLES))
Tells about a petty civil servant enslaved, and ultimately undone,by his lust for his sensuous wife. Shows the underlying political forces at work in pre - war Germany.
Fine Arts; Foreign Language
Dist - TLECUL **Prod** - TLECUL

Stations of the Elevated 45 MIN
16mm
Color (G)
Presents an independent production by Manny Kirchheimer. Offers a poetic study of graffiti - covered subway cars in New York City backed with by music by Charles Mingus.
Fine Arts; Geography - United States; History - United States
Dist - FIRS

Statistical Averages - Expectation of a Random Variable 19 MIN
VHS / U-matic
Probability and Random Processes - Statistical Averages Series
B&W (PRO)
Introduces the fundamental concept of expectation.
Mathematics
Dist - MIOT **Prod** - MIOT

The Statistical Design of Experiments 20 MIN
16mm
Color
LC FIE61-124
Explains the fundamental concepts of modern statistical design of scientific experiment.
Science
Dist - USNAC **Prod** - USN 1960

Statistical Independence 19 MIN
U-matic / VHS
Probability and Random Processes - Elementary Probability Theory 'Series
B&W (PRO)
Defines the fundamental concept of statistical independence.
Industrial and Technical Education; Mathematics
Dist - MIOT **Prod** - MIOT

Statistical Independence and Memory
16mm
B&W
Summarizes the rules of probability and illustrates how one of these rules is used by psychologists to distinguish between short - and long - term memory.
Mathematics
Dist - OPENU **Prod** - OPENU

Statistical Process Control - 1 60 MIN
VHS
Systems Operations Series
Color (PRO)
$600.00 - $1500.00 purchase _ #OTSP1
Discusses quality control in process plants and how statistical process control - SPC - contributes. Introduces basic SPC theory by examining histograms and explaing normal distribution. Part of a seventeen - part series on systems operations. Includes ten textbooks and an instructor guide to support four hours of instruction.
Business and Economics; Education; Industrial and Technical Education; Psychology
Dist - NUSTC **Prod** - NUSTC

Statistical Process Control - 2 60 MIN
VHS
Systems Operations Series
Color (PRO)
$600.00 - $1500.00 purchase _ #OTSP2
Explains how to analyze control charts for continuous and batch precesses and how to identify problems. Describes alternative methods of statistical control for process plants. Part of a seventeen - part series on systems operations. Includes ten textbooks and an instructor guide to support four hours of instruction.
Business and Economics; Education; Industrial and Technical Education; Psychology
Dist - NUSTC **Prod** - NUSTC

Statistical Process Control of Distillation Columns 60 MIN
VHS
Systems Operations Series
Color (PRO)
$600.00 - $1500.00 purchase _ #RCSPC
Focuses on column operation through practical application of statistical process control. Emphasizes eliminating process disturbances and optimizing tower operation. Includes ten textbooks and an instructor guide to support four hours of instruction.
Education; Industrial and Technical Education; Psychology
Dist - NUSTC **Prod** - NUSTC

Statistical Process Control Series

Advanced control charts	30 MIN
Control charts for attributes	30 MIN
Control charts for variables	30 MIN
Introduction to Control Charts	30 MIN
Introduction to Statistical Process Control	30 MIN
Machine and Process Capability Studies	30 MIN
Problem Solving Techniques	30 MIN

Dist - ITCORP

Statistical process control - SPC I - basics series
VHS
Statistical process control - SPC I - basics series
Color (G)
$1985.00 purchase
Presents a comprehensive program on the basics of Statistical Process Control, SPC. Trains production employees, support staff and supervisors how to use and analyze SPC. Ancillary materials included.
Business and Economics; Psychology
Dist - VLEARN

Statistical process control - SPC I - basics series
Statistical process control - SPC I - basics series
Dist - VLEARN

Statistical process control - SPC II - master series
VHS
Statistical process control - SPC II - master series
Color (G)
$2065.00 purchase
Presents a comprehensive program on Statistical Process Control, SPC. Trains production employees, support staff and supervisors how to use and analyze SPC. Ancillary materials included.
Business and Economics; Psychology
Dist - VLEARN

Statistical process control - SPC II - master series
Statistical process control - SPC II - master series
Dist - VLEARN

Statistical process controls for breakthrough 15 MIN
BETA / U-matic / VHS
Total quality leadership series
Color (G PRO)
$395.00, $250.00 rental _ #QU0264 - 14
Features Dr Richard Ruhe in a consultant role in a staged quality team meeting. Includes numerous on - site interviews with public and private sector quality role models. Part of ten parts.
Business and Economics; Mathematics
Dist - BLNCTD **Prod** - BLNCTD

Statistical process controls for maintenance 15 MIN
BETA / U-matic / VHS
Total quality leadership series
Color (G PRO)
$395.00, $250.00 rental _ #QU0268 - 14
Features Dr Richard Ruhe in a consultant role in a staged quality team meeting. Includes numerous on - site interviews with public and private sector quality role models. Part of ten parts.
Business and Economics; Mathematics
Dist - BLNCTD **Prod** - BLNCTD

Statistical Quality Control - Process Control 12 MIN
16mm
B&W
LC FIE52-1254
Illustrates the statistical method involved in process control as a means for obtaining better products for the government at a cheaper price.
Business and Economics; Mathematics
Dist - USNAC **Prod** - USN 1951

Statistical Sampling - a Management Tool 26 MIN
16mm
Color
LC 74-705700
Endeavors to bring about the understanding, acceptance and the use of statistical sampling as a management tool.
Business and Economics; Mathematics
Dist - USNAC **Prod** - USGSA 1968

Statistically - Independent Random Variables 25 MIN
U-matic / VHS
Probability and Random Processes - Random Variables Series
B&W (PRO)
Defines statistical independence in terms of probability distribution functions. Illustrates the concept with the derivation of a marginal density function. Introduces the idea of utility.
Industrial and Technical Education; Mathematics
Dist - MIOT **Prod** - MIOT

Statistics 15 MIN
U-matic / VHS
Mathematical relationships series
B&W (I J)
#000539; LC 91-706959
Presents examples of various types of statistics together with an examination of what they mean. Part of a series that presents basic concepts important to a student's math development. Includes program guide.
Mathematics
Dist - TVOTAR **Prod** - TVOTAR 1980

Statistics 15 MIN
VHS
Futures series
Color (J H)
$29.95 purchase _ #6 - 404 - 300A
Discusses the role of statistics in projecting what could happen in the future based on past results. Features Jaime Escalante, the teacher in Stand and Deliver. Includes actor Arnold Schwarzenegger, who discusses the use of statistics in determining the physical fitness of American youth.
Guidance and Counseling; Mathematics
Dist - VEP **Prod** - VEP 1993

Statistics 15 MIN
U-matic
Graphing Mathematical Concepts Series
(H C A)
Uses computer generated graphics to show the relationships between physical objects and mathematical concepts, equations and their graphs. Relates theoretical concepts to things in the real world.
Computer Science; Mathematics
Dist - ACCESS **Prod** - ACCESS 1986

Statistics
VHS
Color (H C)
$119.95 purchase _ #VAD008
Presents three videocassettes teaching statistics.
Mathematics
Dist - SIV

Statistics - Analyzing Data 15 MIN
VHS / U-matic
Math Works Series
Color (I)
Shows children analyzing their own data. Emphasizes the importance of asking questions to determine the validity of statistical information, concerning the source of the information, the size of the sample and how accurately the data are portrayed.
Mathematics
Dist - AITECH **Prod** - AITECH

Statistics and Graphs, Pt 1 20 MIN
U-matic
Mainly Math Series
Color (H C)
Focuses on the types of statistics and graphs.
Mathematics
Dist - GPN **Prod** - WCVETV 1977

Statistics and Graphs, Pt 2 20 MIN
U-matic

Mainly Math Series
Color (H C)
Shows how to organize and construct understandable graphs.
Mathematics
Dist - GPN **Prod** - WCVETV 1977

Statistics and Probability - Pt 1
16mm
B&W
Introduces the concepts of statistics and probability.
Mathematics
Dist - OPENU **Prod** - OPENU

Statistics and Probability - Pt 2
16mm
B&W
Follows the axiomatic approach to probability, stressing the direct link between the physical independence of two events and the definition of statistical independence.
Mathematics
Dist - OPENU **Prod** - OPENU

Statistics and Probability - Pt 3
16mm
B&W
Examines sampling distributions and introduces the concept of a random variable.
Mathematics
Dist - OPENU **Prod** - OPENU

Statistics at a Glance 26 MIN
16mm / U-matic / VHS
Color
LC 73-702376
Introduces descriptive statistics and illustrates the widespread use of statistics in our daily activities. Covers frequency distribution, normal and skewed distributions, measures of central tendency variability, percentiles and correlation.
Education; Mathematics
Dist - MEDIAG **Prod** - WILEYJ 1972

Statistics - Collecting Data 15 MIN
U-matic / VHS
Math Works Series
Color (I)
Shows how data can help people make decisions and why it is important to think carefully about how to collect them. Considers determining what data are needed and deciding about the sample, the method of collecting data and the delineation and allocation of tasks.
Mathematics
Dist - AITECH **Prod** - AITECH

Statistics for managers series
Gathering Info - Sample Statistics
Goodness of fit
A Graph is worth one thousand words
Normal Distribution
One - Sample Testing - Product Evaluation
Probability distributions
Regression analysis
Testing Multiple Means - AOV
Testing Proportions
Time - Series Analysis
Two - Sample Inference
Who Needs Statistics
Dist - COLOSU

Statistics for Technicians Series
Choosing and evaluating sample information 20 MIN
Concepts of Experimental Design 20 MIN
Decision making from samples 20 MIN
Estimation and Sample Size 20 MIN
Gathering and Interpreting Data 20 MIN
Percent Defectives for Small Samples 20 MIN
Process Control 20 MIN
Shutdown Rules for Variability and the Mean 20 MIN
Using the Normal Distribution 20 MIN
Dist - COLOSU

Statistics - II 150 MIN
U-matic / VHS
For all practical purposes - introduction to contemporary 'mathematics series
Color (G)
$130.00, $85.00 purchase
Presents a five - part module on statistics. Includes an overview and the titles 'Behind the Headlines,' 'Picture This,' 'Place Your Bets' and 'Confident Conclusions.' Demonstrates how data is collected, organized and analyzed so statistical conclusions can be valid and unbiased. Part of a series on contemporary mathematics produced by the Consortium for Mathematics and Its Applications - COMAP. On three videocassettes. Hosted by Professor Solomon Garfunkel.
Mathematics
Dist - ANNCPB

Statistics module - behind the headlines - picture this - Parts 7 and 8 60 MIN
VHS / U-matic
For all practical purposes - introduction to contemporary 'mathematics series
Color (G)
$45.00, $29.95 purchase
Demonstrates random sampling to avoid bias and randomized comparative experiments to find cause - and - effect relationships in Part 7. Shows how using graphs, histograms and box plots reveal changes and subtle patterns to be examined in terms of mean, median, quartile and outlier in Part 8. Parts of a five - part Statistics module and a 26 - part series on contemporary mathematics. Produced by the Consortium for Mathematics and Its Applications - COMAP. Hosted by Professor Solomon Garfunkel.
Mathematics
Dist - ANNCPB

Statistics module - place your bets - confident conclusions - Parts 9 and 10 60 MIN
VHS / U-matic
For all practical purposes - introduction to contemporary 'mathematics series
Color (G)
$45.00, $29.95 purchase
Finds patterns in seemingly random situations through sampling distributions, normal curves, standard deviations, expected value and the central limit theorem in Part 9. Explains statistical inference and its basis in calculations of probability, to ensure that results are accurate and to determine the possible percentage of error in Part 10. Parts of a five - part Statistics module and a 26 - part series on contemporary mathematics. Produced by the Consortium for Mathematics and Its Applications - COMAP. Hosted by Professor Solomon Garfunkel.
Mathematics
Dist - ANNCPB

Statistics of Polymer Coil Conformations , Viscosity of Polymer Solutions 40 MIN
U-matic / VHS
Colloid and Surface Chemistry - Lyophilic Colloids Series
Color
Science; Science - Physical
Dist - KALMIA **Prod** - KALMIA

Statistics of Polymer Coil Conformations - Viscosity of Polymer Solutions 40 MIN
VHS / U-matic
Colloids and Surface Chemistry - Lyophilic Colloids Series
B&W
Science - Physical
Dist - MIOT **Prod** - MIOT

Statistics - Sampling 15 MIN
U-matic / VHS
Mathematics for the '80s - Grade Six Series
(I)
$125.00 purchase
Explains how a small group is related to a large group, random samples, percentage of return and determining whether a sample is biased.
Mathematics
Dist - AITECH **Prod** - AITECH 1987

Statistics - Sampling 15 MIN
U-matic / VHS
Math Works Series
Color (I)
Gives examples of when to query an entire population, when to sample and what to consider when selecting a sample in statistics.
Mathematics
Dist - AITECH **Prod** - AITECH

Statistics - Understanding Mean, Median, and Mode 15 MIN
U-matic / VHS
Mathematics for the '80s - Grade Six Series
(I)
$125.00 purchase
Reveals how to understand different interpretations of the same data through mean, median and mode.
Mathematics
Dist - AITECH **Prod** - AITECH 1987

The Statue 86 MIN
16mm
Color (C A)
Shows a college professor who is embarrassed when his sculptress wife makes a nude statue of him. Stars David Niven, John Cleese and Robert Vaughn.
Fine Arts
Dist - TIMLIF **Prod** - CINERM 1970

The Statue of Liberty 58 MIN
U-matic / VHS / 16mm
Color (I A G)
Explores the history of the Statue of Liberty and the meaning of liberty itself on the occasion of the statue's renovation. Focuses on the significance of the statue to American life. Features a series of interviews with ordinary and extraordinary Americans.
History - United States; Sociology
Dist - DIRECT **Prod** - FLRNTN 1985

The Statue of Liberty 11 MIN
U-matic / VHS / 16mm
Color (J)
LC 79-701795
Shows the planning, construction and assembling of the Statue of Liberty in New York Harbor.
Civics and Political Systems; Fine Arts; History - United States; Industrial and Technical Education
Dist - MCFI **Prod** - SWAIN 1977

The Statue of Liberty 14 MIN
16mm / U-matic / VHS
Americana series; no 2
Color (P I J H)
LC FIA66-1071
A history teacher and his son visit the Statue of Liberty and learn the history and meaning of the monument in New York harbor.
Civics and Political Systems; Geography - United States
Dist - HANDEL **Prod** - HANDEL 1966

The Statue of Liberty
U-matic / VHS
Color (J H C A)
$39.00 purchase _ #04552 94
Portrays the lore and legends surrounding the Statue of Liberty.
Fine Arts; Literature and Drama
Dist - ASPRSS

Statue of Liberty, Body of Iron, Soul of Fire 27 MIN
16mm
Color
LC 74-702890
Traces the history of the Statue of Liberty, from the sculptor's conception to its completion, and describes American's changing attitudes towards the meaning of the statue.
Fine Arts; Geography - United States; Social Science
Dist - WSTGLC **Prod** - AMEXCO 1974

Status Epilepticus 20 MIN
U-matic / VHS
Pediatric Emergency Management Series
Color
Discusses status epilepticus, including identification, establishment of vital functions, examination, diagnosis and evaluation of drug usage.
Health and Safety
Dist - VTRI **Prod** - VTRI

Status - Key to Understanding the Customer's Frame of Reference
VHS / U-matic
Strategies for Successful Selling Series Module 4
Color
Shows sales people how to recognize and interpret status symbols to understand a customer's frame of reference.
Business and Economics
Dist - AMA **Prod** - AMA

Status of heart replacement - Volume 4
VHS / 8mm cartridge
Cardiology video journal series
Color (PRO)
#FSR - 507
Presents a free - loan program, part of a series on cardiology, which trains medical professionals. Contact distributor for details.
Health and Safety
Dist - WYAYLA **Prod** - WYAYLA

The Status of Women - Strategy for Change 30 MIN
16mm
Color
LC 77-702652
Provides an account of a conference sponsored by the National Action Committee on the Status of Women.
Sociology
Dist - CANFDC **Prod** - ARMMOI 1972

Stay - anti - dropout program for the student at risk
VHS
Color (I J H G)
$89.00 purchase _ #CX200V
Emphasizes how necessary a high school diploma is for getting and keeping jobs that pay above minimum wage. Offers concrete advice about self - esteem, setting goals and where to get advice and help. Uses music video format and rap.

Education; Psychology
Dist - CAMV

Stay Awake Whenever You Can 29 MIN
16mm
Color (A)
Presents an experimental film by Diana Barrie in which a young man reads a sci - fi comic book which comes to life in his dreams.
Fine Arts
Dist - STARRC **Prod** - STARRC 1982

Stay away from the junkyard - 57
VHS
Reading rainbow series
Color; CC (K P)
$39.95 purchase
Follows Theodora into the forbidden junkyard where she discovers that, although things may appear old and useless at first glance, there are creative ways to give them purpose in a story by Tricia Tusa. Meets an artist who collects what some people may consider junk, then transforms 'junk' into beautiful artwork. Part of a series offering a multicultural approach to generating reading enthusiasm with cross - curricular applications, hosted by LeVar Burton.
English Language; Fine Arts; Literature and Drama; Science - Natural; Sociology
Dist - GPN **Prod** - LNMDP

Stay in School 11 MIN
16mm
Color
Depicts teenagers who are deciding whether to get jobs or to continue their education.
Education; Guidance and Counseling
Dist - CMPBL **Prod** - CMPBL

Stay Sober - the Danger of Relapse 20 MIN
VHS
(H A)
$39.95 _ #83345
Discusses the fatal dangers of relapse while recovering from alcoholism. Defines problems and offers solutions.
Health and Safety; Psychology
Dist - CMPCAR **Prod** - CMPCAR

Stay tuned 29 MIN
VHS
Color; Captioned (G)
$195.00 purchase, $100.00 rental _ #CA - 099
Reveals that people who become hearing impaired as adults may 'tune out' - refusing help, withdrawing from family and friends and becoming even more isolated, depressed and confused. Follows one woman's struggles to return to an active and rewarding life after suffering a mid - life hearing loss. Produced by Dr Menachem Daum and Martin Dornbaum.
Guidance and Counseling
Dist - FANPRO

Stay with Me 28 MIN
U-matic / VHS
B&W (H C A)
LC 82-707308
Tells the story of nurse, activist and lesbian, Karen Clark, whose campaign for state representative from Minneapolis created unprecedented conditions between tenants, senior citizens, gays and lesbians.
Civics and Political Systems; Sociology
Dist - UCV **Prod** - UCV 1982

Staying Alive 26 MIN
16mm / VHS
Space Experience Series
Color (G)
$425.00, $295.00 purchase, $55.00 rental; LC 89715683
Explores survival in space, its impact on people. Part of a six - part series on space hosted by astronaut Marc Garneau, veteran of the Challenger Space Shuttle.
History - World; Industrial and Technical Education; Science - Natural; Science - Physical
Dist - CNEMAG **Prod** - REIDW 1988

Staying Alive 16 MIN
16mm
Color (J H C G)
Deals with the selection of a suitable motorcycle, appropriate protective clothing, and riding for the first time. Focuses on the beginning rider.
Health and Safety
Dist - VIEWTH **Prod** - NORCC

Staying Alive 23 MIN
16mm / U-matic / VHS
Color
Helps employees develop essential safety habits and attitudes necessary for accident prevention both in the shop and out on construction sites.
Health and Safety
Dist - CORF **Prod** - KENNC

Staying Alive - Decisions about Drinking and Driving 39 MIN
VHS / U-matic
Color (J H)
$209.00 purchase _ #06797 - 161
Tells the story of three teens who die in a wreck after a night of drinking. Shows how drinking attacks the body systems crucial to safe driving. Explores efforts that have prevented drunk driving and saved lives.
Health and Safety; Psychology
Dist - GA **Prod** - GA

Staying alive - psychology of human survival 30 MIN
BETA / VHS
Consciousness and modern culture series
Color (G)
$29.95 purchase _ #S110
Suggests that individuals cannot live authentic lives without feeling touched by the major problems of the planet. Urges that through awareness of the roots of global problems within the individual consciousness the individual can begin to heal the insanity of western culture. Features Dr Roger Walsh, psychiatrist and author of 'Staying Alive - The Psychology of Human Survival.' Part of a four - part series on consciousness and modern culture.
Guidance and Counseling; Psychology; Religion and Philosophy; Science - Natural
Dist - THINKA **Prod** - THINKA

Staying away from strangers 11 MIN
VHS
Taking responsibility series
Color (P)
Teaches children how to make new friends while being careful about strangers. Uses the animated story of two children who teach a new friend from another planet how to be safe around strangers and the proper responses to the tricks used by dangerous people. Reminds that sometimes it is important to get help from adults. Part of a series teaching health, safety and responsibility to youngsters.
Guidance and Counseling; Health and Safety; Psychology; Sociology
Dist - VIEWTH **Prod** - VIEWTH

Staying even - coping with balance disorders 29 MIN
VHS
Color (PRO G)
$250.00 purchase _ #NR - 04
Helps patients with chronic balance disorders accept their limitations and learn new ways of doing things. Shows how to eliminate potential hazards of falling in the household. Gives spouses and other family members a new understanding of the patient's problems.
Health and Safety; Science - Natural
Dist - MIFE **Prod** - GSHDME

Staying Fit 19 MIN
U-matic / VHS
Color (C)
$249.00, $149.00 purchase _ #AD - 1383
Explains how a patient recovering from cardiac bypass surgery turned his life around through daily exercise and a change in lifestyle. Features two experts on fitness who demonstrate how heart rate, body fat and lung capacity are all important components in determining optimum levels of exercise.
Health and Safety; Physical Education and Recreation; Psychology; Social Science
Dist - FOTH **Prod** - FOTH

Staying fit at the computer 30 MIN
VHS
Color (A G)
Helps people avoid common physical problems related to working at the computer. Offers a combination of posture and work - positioning guidelines, stretching and relaxation techniques and vision exercises designed specifically for computer users. Helps computer users develop healthier work habits, prevent repetitive strain injuries - including carpal tunnel syndrome - reduce eye strain, and enhance their performance, productivity and comfort.
Health and Safety; Physical Education and Recreation
Dist - BALLIV **Prod** - BALLIV 1993

Staying here 30 MIN
U-matic
Pacific bridges series
Color (I J)
Discusses the lifestyles and the meaning of particular social institutions.
Sociology
Dist - GPN **Prod** - EDFCEN 1978

Staying in Character 20 MIN
16mm
Color
Presents advertising man Maxwell Arnold looking at the Jack Daniel's advertising credibility in terms of image and brand position. Compares the Jack Daniel's campaign with other campaigns of long duration and illustrates how consistency in character is the most valuable equity in Jack Daniel's advertising.
Business and Economics; Psychology
Dist - MTP **Prod** - DANDIS

Staying in school - going the distance 28 MIN
VHS
At - risk students video series
Color (I J H)
$98.00 purchase _ #AHV400
Interviews students who dropped out and then re - entered school. Discusses the effects upon their families, their friends and their self esteem. Helps students to sort out priorities and consequences. Features students and teachers from the Tree of Learning School, Portland, Oregon. Includes a reproducible discussion guide with worksheets. Part of a five - part series on at - risk students.
Education; Psychology; Sociology
Dist - CADESF **Prod** - CADESF 1990

Staying in Tune 9 MIN
U-matic
A Matter of Time Series
(A)
Portrays three friends reflecting on their lifestyle, particularly the importance of doing enjoyable things that produce a sense of self worth and well being.
Sociology
Dist - ACCESS **Prod** - ACCESS 1980

Staying Off Cocaine - Avoiding Relapse 38 MIN
VHS
Color (A)
$295.00 _ #6965
Provides recovering cocaine addicts with guidance for getting off and staying off cocaine. Includes experiences of recovering addicts and suggests how to handle high - risk situations, drug cravings and self - sabotage.
Education; Guidance and Counseling; Health and Safety; Psychology; Sociology
Dist - HAZELB

Staying on the safeside 19 MIN
U-matic / VHS / 16mm
Anti - victimization series
Color (I J)
Presents The Wizard of No who helps a 13 - year - old girl learn to say no and to guard against dangerous strangers.
Civics and Political Systems; Health and Safety; Sociology
Dist - CORF **Prod** - CORF

Staying on top 25 MIN
VHS
Supervisors series
Color (A)
PdS50 purchase
Shows ways in which good supervisors manage to deal with the kinds of changes at work that will affect their staff. Part of an eight-part series designed to help supervisors - particularly newly-appointed ones - to understand the demands of their individual roles through the experience of established supervisors who offer personal insights and strategies from within a framework of good practice.
Business and Economics; Psychology
Dist - BBCENE

Staying Out of Trouble 7 MIN
VHS / 16mm
Color (K)
$100.00 purchase
Uses animal puppets to teach children self - control skills. Encourages children to consider the consequences of their actions. Includes leader's guide.
Guidance and Counseling; Health and Safety; Psychology; Sociology
Dist - CHEF **Prod** - CHEF

Staying Sober, Keeping Straight 35 MIN
16mm / VHS
Color (G)
$500.00 purchase, $100.00 rental _ #4985, 4990, 4986, 0732J, 0731J, 0730J
Follows three individuals recovering from chemical dependency as they confront the threat of relapse. Identifies common relapse triggers. Illustrates management of specific high risk factors.
Guidance and Counseling; Health and Safety; Psychology; Sociology
Dist - HAZELB **Prod** - ROGGTP

Staying Straight
16mm / U-matic / VHS
Color (I)
Demonstrates the physical, emotional and legal consequences of alcohol and drug abuse. Explores ways to say 'no' to peers when confronted with drugs. Seeks to

build self - esteem, assertiveness, and establishes awareness of positive alternatives to drug use among its viewers.
Health and Safety; Psychology; Sociology
Dist - ALTSUL **Prod** - NORWIN 1984

Staying Well 27 MIN
16mm
Color
Features people who tell how practical rules regarding diet, exercise and stress reduction helped them reach new levels of wellness.
Health and Safety
Dist - NABSP **Prod** - NABSP

Staying Well with Harv and Marv 13 MIN
U-matic / VHS / 16mm
Color (P)
LC 83 - 706242; 83-700128
Discusses the importance of good health habits, including proper exercise, sufficient rest, good nutrition, tooth care, personal hygiene and resolvement of emotional concerns.
Health and Safety
Dist - HIGGIN **Prod** - HIGGIN 1983

Staystitching and Directional Stitching 3 MIN
16mm
Clothing Construction Techniques Series
Color (J)
LC 77-701176
Defines the meaning of the terms grain, with the grain and against the grain. Illustrates the use, placement and direction of staystitching and shows how to determine the desirable direction for machine stitching.
Home Economics
Dist - IOWASP **Prod** - IOWA 1976

STDs and Sexual Responsibility 35 MIN
VHS / 16mm
Facts, Feelings and Wonder of Life - the Teenage Years Series
Color (I J H PRO)
$295.00 purchase, $50.00 rental _ #9976
Examines sexually transmitted disease including AIDS, how they are transmitted, preventive measures, and reviews symptoms.
Guidance and Counseling; Health and Safety; Sociology
Dist - AIMS **Prod** - PVGP 1988

STDs - Program 5 36 MIN
VHS
Sex education series
Color (I J H)
$199.00 purchase _ #CG - 833 - VS
Presents two parts on sexually transmitted diseases. Focuses on Molly in part one, who discovers that she has an STD. Features a physician who discusses the signs and symptoms, the prevention and cures for most of the common STDs, including AIDS. Part two focuses on the social and emotional side of STDs. A young man from part one realizes that he needs to inform his sexual partners of his disease and that each of them may have to inform others. Part five of a five - part series on sex education.
Guidance and Counseling; Health and Safety
Dist - HRMC **Prod** - HRMC

STD/VFT Leak Detector Operation 270 MIN
U-matic
Color (IND)
Provides vacuum technology training for workers in the field. Set of 5 tapes, number 925.
Business and Economics; Industrial and Technical Education
Dist - VARIAN **Prod** - VARIAN 1986

Ste Genevieve - a French Legacy 27 MIN
16mm
B&W
Focuses on the architectural and historical aspects of Ste Genevieve, a small prosperous French town in Missouri.
Fine Arts; Geography - United States; Social Science
Dist - KETCTV **Prod** - KETCTV

The Steadfast Tin Soldier 14 MIN
16mm
Color (K)
$280.00 purchase _ #177 - 0001
Tells the classic Hans Christian Andersen fairy tale of a one - legged toy soldier who falls in love with a ballerina doll. Uses puppet animation to show his desperate attempts to win her heart, suffering through a series of mishaps brought about by the evil spells of a goblin jack - in - the - box.
Fine Arts; Literature and Drama; Sociology
Dist - FI

The Steadfast Tin Soldier 9 MIN
VHS / U-matic
Fairy Tale Series
Color (K P I)
Narrates the Hans Christian Andersen story of the tin soldier in love with a paper doll ballerina. Comes with teacher's guide.
Literature and Drama
Dist - BNCHMK **Prod** - BNCHMK 1985

Steady as She Goes 27 MIN
16mm
Color
LC 82-700785
Focuses on John Fulfit, a 70 - year - old retired Canadian who indulges his childhood yearning to go to the sea by crafting rigged ships in bottles. Shows him working at his craft as he sings chanteys and philosophically converses with the camera. Employs archival stills to compare his work to actual vessel construction.
Fine Arts; Physical Education and Recreation
Dist - NFBC **Prod** - NFBC 1982

A Steady Rain 25 MIN
16mm
Color
LC 80-700220
Tells how an eight - year - old boy witnesses a murder while looking through a window and comes to grips with the stormy events of his family's life.
Fine Arts
Dist - MLP **Prod** - MLP 1979

Steady State Availability Applications, Availability Improvement Considerations, 60 MIN
VHS / U-matic
Maintainability, Operational Availability and Preventive Maintenance of Series Pt 5
B&W
Treats steady state availability applications, availability improvement considerations, maintainability - cost considerations, and cost benefits from the implementation of reliability and maintainability engineering.
Industrial and Technical Education
Dist - UAZMIC **Prod** - UAZMIC 1981

Steady - State Kalman - Bucy Filter - Continuous - Time Case 48 MIN
VHS / U-matic
Modern Control Theory - Stochastic Estimation Series
Color (PRO)
Industrial and Technical Education; Mathematics
Dist - MIOT **Prod** - MIOT

Steady - State Kalman Filter - Discrete - Time Case 43 MIN
VHS / U-matic
Modern Control Theory - Stochastic Estimation Series
Color (PRO)
Industrial and Technical Education; Mathematics
Dist - MIOT **Prod** - MIOT

The Steady - State Linear - Quadratic Problem - Continuous - Time Case 51 MIN
U-matic / VHS
Modern Control Theory - Deterministic Optimal Linear Feedback Series
Color (PRO)
Industrial and Technical Education; Mathematics
Dist - MIOT **Prod** - MIOT

The Steady - State Linear - Quadratic Problem - Discrete Time Case 38 MIN
VHS / U-matic
Modern Control Theory - Deterministic Optimal Linear Feedback Series
Color (PRO)
Industrial and Technical Education; Mathematics
Dist - MIOT **Prod** - MIOT

Steady - State Linear - Quadratic Problem with Deterministic Disturbances 41 MIN
U-matic / VHS
Modern Control Theory - Deterministic Optimal Linear Feedback Series
Color (PRO)
Industrial and Technical Education; Mathematics
Dist - MIOT **Prod** - MIOT

The Steady - State Linear Regulator Problem for Constant Disturbances 70 MIN
U-matic / VHS
Modern Control Theory - Deterministic Optimal Linear Feedback Series
Color (PRO)
Industrial and Technical Education; Mathematics
Dist - MIOT **Prod** - MIOT

The Steady State LQG Problem - Continuous - Time Case 68 MIN
VHS / U-matic
Modern Control Theory - Stochastic Control Series
Color (PRO)
Industrial and Technical Education; Mathematics
Dist - MIOT **Prod** - MIOT

Steady state power flow 1
U-matic / VHS
Electric power system operation series; Tape 6
Color (IND)
Includes power demand and supply, synchronism, phase angle limits, load transfer and per unit examples.
Industrial and Technical Education
Dist - LEIKID **Prod** - LEIKID

Steady state power flow 2
U-matic / VHS
Electric power system operation series; Tape 7
Color (IND)
Covers division of power flow, load flow examples, base case, effect of outages and distribution factors.
Industrial and Technical Education
Dist - LEIKID **Prod** - LEIKID

Steady State Theory Computer Programs - Helicopter Example 57 MIN
U-matic / VHS
Modern Control Theory - Stochastic Control Series
Color (PRO)
Industrial and Technical Education; Mathematics
Dist - MIOT **Prod** - MIOT

Steady state voltage control
U-matic / VHS
Electric power system operation series; Tape 8
Color (IND)
Includes voltage control by generators, control by transformers, distribution system voltage, transmission system voltage and case studies.
Industrial and Technical Education
Dist - LEIKID **Prod** - LEIKID

Stealing 12 MIN
16mm / U-matic / VHS
Moral Decision Making Series
Color (I J)
LC 72-702681
Presents principles of honesty through the story of Johnny, a newspaper boy. Focuses on the moral issues which affect one's decision to steal.
Guidance and Counseling; Religion and Philosophy
Dist - AIMS **Prod** - MORLAT 1971

Stealing - 26 8 MIN
VHS / U-matic
Life's little lessons - self - esteem K - 3 - series
Color (K P)
$129.00, $99.00 _ #V625
Follows Bunnie and Claud who lived a life of crime, stealing from one town to the next. Shows how they turned their lives around. Part of a 30 - part series on self - esteem.
Guidance and Counseling; Psychology
Dist - BARR **Prod** - CEPRO 1992

Steam 5 MIN
16mm
Color
LC 74-702768
Examines the history and action of steam engines.
Industrial and Technical Education
Dist - CANFDC **Prod** - SUNDEW 1973

Steam and Gas Safety Valves 60 MIN
U-matic / VHS
Mechanical Equipment Maintenance, Module 14 - Relief Valves Series
Color (IND)
Industrial and Technical Education
Dist - LEIKID **Prod** - LEIKID

Steam and Water Recovery and Effluent Treatment
U-matic / VHS
Pulp and Paper Training - Thermo - Mechanical Pulping Series
Color (IND)
Demonstrates the typical white water loop throughout the mill. Reviews the changes in consistency that take place in the loop. Discusses heat recovery systems. Looks at the treatment and pollution control of effluent discharges from the process.
Industrial and Technical Education
Dist - LEIKID **Prod** - LEIKID

Steam Cooking Equipment 20 MIN
VHS / BETA
Color (G PRO)
$59.00 purchase _ #QF01
Provides operation and safety tips on using two standard steam cookers, a Vischer jet cooker and a steam jacketed kettle.
Home Economics; Industrial and Technical Education
Dist - RMIBHF **Prod** - RMIBHF

Steam Cutoffs 8 MIN
VHS
Color (C)

$34.95 purchase _ #193 E 2075
Depicts natural and flood cutoffs including oxbow lake development. Teacher's guide provided.
Science - Physical
Dist - WARDS

Steam Days 59 MIN
VHS
Color (S)
$29.95 purchase _ #781 - 9019
Joins railway enthusiast Miles Kington as he relives boyhood memories of riding the stately streamlined trains of the steam age. Takes a nostalgic trip on the Duchess of Hamilton, a passenger train built in the 1930s, as it steams along the ruggedly beautiful Settle to Carlisle line. In 'The Fishing Line,' Kington meets some local heroes when he takes a ride through the mountains from Fort William to Mallaig.
Geography - World; History - World; Social Science
Dist - FI **Prod** - BBCTV 1988

Steam days 1 60 MIN
VHS
Color (H C A)
$29.95 purchase
Joins Miles Kington in a rail tour through the British countryside. Consists of two trips - 'Travels With A Duchess' and 'The Fishing Line.' Celebrates the old days of steam - engine travel.
History - United States
Dist - PBS **Prod** - WNETTV

Steam Days 2 58 MIN
VHS
Color (S)
$29.95 purchase _ #781 - 9020
Joins railway enthusiast Miles Kington as he relives boyhood memories of riding the stately streamlined trains of the steam age. Visits Bristol's Temple Meads Station and views the Iron Duke which hauled the passenger expresses of the early Victorian era and includes a fond reflection on British freight trains.
Geography - World; History - World; Social Science
Dist - FI **Prod** - BBCTV 1988

The Steam Engine Comes to the Farm 15 MIN
U-matic / VHS / 16mm
American Scrapbook Series
Color (I)
Shows the inner workings of a steam engine and shows how it was used to power dozens of machines that planted, cultivated and harvested crops.
Agriculture; Industrial and Technical Education
Dist - GPN **Prod** - WVIZTV 1977

The Steam engine - G Stephenson 24 MIN
VHS / U-matic
Color (I J)
$325.00, $295.00 purchase _ #V187; LC 90-706275
Tells the story of George Stephenson and his invention of the steam locomotive. Illustrates how Stephenson adapted and refined steam technology to produce the first steam driven locomotive.
Fine Arts; History - World; Social Science; Sociology
Dist - BARR **Prod** - GLOBET 1989

Steam, Schemes and National Dreams 29 MIN
16mm
Color (G)
_ #106C 0184 501
Describes the historical events surrounding the discovery of hot springs in the Rocky Mountains of Alberta and the subsequent birth of Canada's first national park, Banff National Park. Intercut with scenes of present day Banff.
Geography - World; History - World; Science - Natural
Dist - CFLMDC **Prod** - NFBC 1984

Steam Shovel 7 MIN
16mm
Color
LC 75-703119
Studies the mysterious, comic and beautiful aspects of mechanical works of man. Features a 1920 2 - B Eire steam shovel, a supporting cast of Model T's and curious onlookers.
Industrial and Technical Education; Sociology
Dist - KOESTR **Prod** - KOESTR 1975

Steam Sterilization 25 MIN
U-matic
Color (PRO)
LC 79-707311
Discusses and demonstrates the procedures involved in the steam sterilization of medical instruments and supplies. Covers steam penetration, air pockets, temperature monitoring, and cleaning of sterilizers.
Health and Safety
Dist - USNAC **Prod** - USVA 1977

A Steam Train Passes 21 MIN
16mm
Color (H C A)
LC 75-704207
Recreates the era of steam locomotion in Australia.
History - World; Industrial and Technical Education; Social Science
Dist - AUIS **Prod** - FLMAUS 1974

Steam Traps 60 MIN
VHS
Piping Auxiliaries and Insulation Series
Color (PRO)
$600.00, $1500.00 purchase _ #GMSTR
Introduces the basic function of steam traps and describes the various types of steam traps and their operation. Part of a three - part series on piping auxiliaries and insulation, which is part of a set on general and mechanical maintenance. Includes 10 textbooks and an instructor guide which provide four hours of instruction.
Education; Industrial and Technical Education; Psychology
Dist - NUSTC **Prod** - NUSTC

Steam Traps - Operation and Maintenance 18 MIN
VHS / U-matic
Color
Trains operating and maintenance personnel to identify and correct malfunctioning steam traps. Gives an inside view of steam traps in actual operation, as well as a descriptive walk - through of testing procedures and corrective actions.
Health and Safety; Industrial and Technical Education
Dist - AHOA **Prod** - AHOA 1980

Steam Turbine Operation 60 MIN
U-matic / VHS
Equipment Operation Training Program Series
Color (IND)
Identifies the major parts of the steam turbine. Describes how an impulse steam turbine operates. Covers periodic operational check and reading temperature and pressure gauges.
Education; Industrial and Technical Education; Psychology
Dist - LEIKID **Prod** - LEIKID

Steam Turbine Operations 60 MIN
U-matic / VHS
Equipment Operation Training Program Series
Color (IND)
Identifies the major parts of a steam turbine and tells how it operates. Highlights performing periodic operational checks.
Industrial and Technical Education
Dist - ITCORP **Prod** - ITCORP

Steam turbines 60 MIN
VHS
Equipment operations series
Color (PRO)
$600.00 - $1500.00 purchase _ #OTSTU
Introduces the principles of operation of a typical steam turbine. Outlines the major components of a turbine and shows how turbines work to convert thermal energy into mechanical energy. Part of a twenty - part series on equipment operation. Includes ten textbooks and an instructor guide to support four hours of instruction.
Industrial and Technical Education; Psychology
Dist - NUSTC **Prod** - NUSTC

Steamboat 11 MIN
VHS / 16mm
Color (K P I)
LC 76-702968
Presents a nonverbal exploration of the Delta Queen steamboat, the oldest overnight paddle wheeler on the Mississippi River, presented from a child's viewpoint. Records the actual sound of the boat's operations, combined with steam piano and river songs.
Geography - United States; Physical Education and Recreation; Social Science
Dist - LRF **Prod** - LSP 1976

Steamboat a - comin' 25 MIN
VHS
Mississippi River series
Color (I J)
$89.00 purchase _ #RB831
Traces the history of the Mississippi River during the steamboat era. Part of a series on the Mississippi River.
Geography - United States; History - United States
Dist - REVID **Prod** - REVID

Steamboat Bill 11 MIN
U-matic / VHS / 16mm
American Folklore Series
Color (I)
LC 77-712731
Describes the exploits of Steamboat Bill, the famous riverboat captain.
Geography - United States; Literature and Drama
Dist - PHENIX **Prod** - HRAW 1971

Steamboat Bill Jr 71 MIN
16mm
B&W
Tells the story of riverboat owner Steamboat Bill who must battle his rival JJ King for control of the river's shipping lanes. Relates Bill's initial excitement when his son comes to visit him, anticipating an ally in the battle. Shows what happens when Junior turns out to be a moustachioed, ukelele - playing shrimp in college clothes. Stars Buster Keaton. Directed by Charles F Reisner.
Fine Arts
Dist - KILLIS **Prod** - FOXFC 1928

Steamboat - I Like it Here 20 MIN
16mm
Color
LC 80-701486
Describes the friendliness, warmth and fun of Steamboat Ski Area, a resort in Steamboat Springs, Colorado.
Geography - United States
Dist - STEAMB **Prod** - STEAMB 1980

Steamboat on the River 18 MIN
U-matic / VHS / 16mm
Color (I J H)
LC FIA67-5545
Shows the excitement and significance of river craft used for passengers and for freight in the Civil War period of American history.
History - United States; Social Science
Dist - IFB **Prod** - IFB 1965

Steamboat Willie 8 MIN
U-matic / VHS / 16mm
Mickey Mouse - the Early Years Series
B&W (K P I J H)
LC 78-701071
Presents Mickey Mouse as a crew member on a riverboat captained by Big Bad Pete. Features Minnie Mouse as another passenger who joins Mickey as he uses various props as musical instruments.
Fine Arts
Dist - CORF **Prod** - DISNEY 1978

Steamers and Freighters - a Century and a Half of Great Lakes Shipping 20 MIN
16mm / U-matic / VHS
Color (J H C A)
Relates the story behind the development of the Great Lakes Steamers.
Geography - United States; History - United States; Social Science
Dist - BRAURP **Prod** - BRAURP

Steamfitting - Cast Iron Boiler Assembly 13 MIN
16mm
Color (H C A)
Shows a two - man operation in boiler assembly. Discusses layout of section, base level and square, preparing push - nipples and locations, graphite and methods to ensure an even pull - up all around.
Industrial and Technical Education
Dist - SF **Prod** - SF 1969

Steamfitting - Making a Welded Y - Joint 13 MIN
16mm
Color (H C A)
Explains how to make a welded Y - joint, including quartering, laying on template or marking pipe and branch, mitre and radial cutting with oxyacetylene torch, pre - heating, alignment and welding.
Industrial and Technical Education
Dist - SF **Prod** - SF 1969

Steamfitting - Pipe Bending Techniques 13 MIN
16mm
Color (J A)
Discusses pipe bending techniques, including measurement allowances, hydraulic bending equipment and bending operations. Covers heat bend, heating methods, heated areas and various applications.
Industrial and Technical Education
Dist - SF **Prod** - SF 1969

Steaming - Lesson 4 6 MIN
8mm cartridge / 16mm
Modern basics of classical cooking series
Color (A)
#MB04
Describes the three basic steaming sytems, advantages of steaming, texture and appearance of the steamed foods. Part of a series developed in cooperation with the Swiss Association of Restauranteurs and Hoteliers to train foodservice employees. Includes five instructor's handbooks, a textbook by Eugene Pauli, 20 sets of student tests and 20 sets of student information sheets.
Home Economics; Industrial and Technical Education
Dist - CONPRO **Prod** - CONPRO

Stedicam EFP video training manual 120 MIN
VHS
Film, video and TV production series
Color (H C G)

$179.00 purchase _ #652
Offers technical advice on using a camera - stabilizer harness to ensure smoother shots.
Industrial and Technical Education
Dist - INSTRU

Steel and America - a New Look 29 MIN
U-matic / VHS / 16mm
Color (I J H) (SWEDISH SPANISH DANISH)
Dramatizes the story of steel from prehistoric times to the present. Hosted by Donald Duck.
Foreign Language; Social Science
Dist - CORF **Prod** - DISNEY

Steel and stone 58 MIN
VHS
Skyscraper series
Color; CC (G)
$89.95 purchase _ #EX2615; Program not available in Canada.
Chronicles the construction of Worldwide Plaza, a 47 - story, 770 - foot tower built on the former site of Madison Square Garden in New York City.
Geography - United States; Industrial and Technical Education
Dist - FOTH **Prod** - WGBH

Steel Drum Band 29 MIN
U-matic
Color
Covers the story of the conversion of the common oil drum into a sophisticated musical instrument. Features the Trinidad Tripoli Steel Drum Band.
Fine Arts
Dist - UMITV **Prod** - UMITV 1976

Steel from Inland 28 MIN
16mm
Color
Shows how iron ore, coal and limestone become steel at Inland Steel Company's Indiana Harbor Works at East Chicago, Indiana. Offers a close look at some of the new production and environmental technology that has changed the complexion of steelmaking.
Business and Economics; Geography - United States; Industrial and Technical Education
Dist - MTP **Prod** - INLSTL 1982

Steel Industry 3 MIN
16mm
Of all Things Series
Color (P I)
Discusses the steel industry.
Business and Economics; Industrial and Technical Education
Dist - AVED **Prod** - BAILYL

Steel Lives Here 15 MIN
16mm
Color (IND)
LC FIA68-120
Illustrates designs and uses of steel for use in the building of homes.
Fine Arts; Industrial and Technical Education
Dist - AIAS **Prod** - AIAS 1968

Steel Making Series

Back care basics	8 MIN
Ball mill forge	5 MIN
Blast Furnace Gas Hazards	7 MIN
Bloom and billet mill - personal safety equipment	7 MIN
Coke oven sideman	6 MIN
Coke ovens door machine	8 MIN
Continuous Wire Drawing Machine	10 MIN
Drop Forge Die Set Up	13 MIN
Fire Extinguishers - the First Minute Counts	10 MIN
The Fire Stand Scrap Man	13 MIN
Follow that slab	8 MIN
Fowl Deed	8 MIN
General Safety - Steel Making	6 MIN
Guidesetting	14 MIN
Hand Traps	10 MIN
Hoist Safety	7 MIN
The Hot shear laborer	6 MIN
It Only Takes a Minute (Rolling Mill)	6 MIN
Lift Truck Safety	12 MIN
Operating the Pendant Crane	7 MIN
Operation of an Oxy - Fuel Gas Heating Torch	14 MIN
Rod Mill Trimmers	5 MIN
Roll Threading Setup Procedures	14 MIN
The Safe Handling of Oxy Fuel Gas Heating Equipment	14 MIN
Safety	6 MIN
Scarfing Safely	7 MIN
The Shipping Hooker	8 MIN
Strapping Machine Operator - Rod Mill	8 MIN
Strapping Machine Troubleshooting - Rod Mill	10 MIN
Torch Safety	13 MIN
Working with Chains	5 MIN
Working with Lead	14 MIN

Dist - LEIKID

Steel Mill Soccer - Pt 9 58 MIN
VHS
Comrades Series
Color (S)
$79.00 purchase _ #351 - 9033
Follows twelve Soviet citizens from different backgrounds to reveal what Soviet life is like for a cross section of the 270 million inhabitants in the vast country of fifteen republics. Features Frontline anchor Judy Woodruff who also interviews prominent experts on Soviet affairs. Part 9 of the twelve - part series considers the Lenin Tube - Rolling Mill which makes pipes for the oil industry and hosts a soccer team. This program looks at the players as they prepare for a big match against the Synthetic Rubber Company.
Business and Economics; Civics and Political Systems; Geography - World; Physical Education and Recreation
Dist - FI **Prod** - WGBHTV 1988

Steel on the Rouge 19 MIN
U-matic / VHS / 16mm
Color (J)
LC FIA68-3073
Shows the processes involved in making steel.
Business and Economics
Dist - FORDFL **Prod** - FMCMP 1968

Steel Plus 40 MIN
16mm
B&W (C)
Shows the conversion of steel from the open hearth furnace into sheets and thence into tinplate by the hot - dipping process.
Business and Economics; Industrial and Technical Education
Dist - HEFL **Prod** - BFI 1952

Steel - Pretty, Design, Nice 8 MIN
16mm
Color
LC 79-705671
Presents a free form look at steel in a myriad of applications - in art, in construction and in the home.
Business and Economics; Fine Arts; Industrial and Technical Education
Dist - AIAS **Prod** - AIAS 1969

The Steel Reefs 27 MIN
16mm
Color
Takes an adventure beneath the offshore platforms in the Gulf of Mexico. Shows how these rigs initiate a whole chain of marine life in an area which has been described as the 'richest, most productive marine area that borders North America.'
Science - Natural
Dist - MTP **Prod** - CALCHM

Steel Rule 14 MIN
16mm
Machine Shop Work - Precision Measurement Series no 1
B&W
LC FIE51-1
Discusses the variations found in steel rules, the types of scales found on them and their proper usage, and the procedure for transferring measurements by means of calipers and dividers.
Industrial and Technical Education; Mathematics
Dist - USNAC **Prod** - USOE 1941

Steel - the Metal Giant 12 MIN
U-matic / VHS / 16mm
Color (I J)
LC 81-701116
Shows how steel is made.
Industrial and Technical Education
Dist - CORF **Prod** - CENTRO 1981

Steel - the Metal Giant 20 MIN
16mm
Color
Follows the steel - making process starting with the mining of taconite, limestone and coal, and proceding to the blast furnace and the casting, shaping and rolling of molten steel.
Industrial and Technical Education; Social Science
Dist - MTP **Prod** - AIAS

Steel town 20 MIN
VHS / U-matic / BETA
Soviet Union series
Color (H C A)
$250.00 purchase _ #JY - 5864C
Examines working and living conditions in the planned town of Novokuznetsk. Emphasizes the social detriment of increasing production without regard for worker safety and health. Part of a five - part series on the diverse lifestyles and regions of the USSR.
Civics and Political Systems; Geography - World; Health and Safety; History - World; Social Science; Sociology
Dist - CORF **Prod** - BBCTV 1989

Steel town 17 MIN
U-matic / VHS / 16mm
American scene series
B&W
LC FIE52-778
Discusses the daily lives of steel workers and shows steel mills and blast furnaces in Youngstown, Ohio.
Business and Economics; Social Science
Dist - USNAC **Prod** - USOWI 1949

Steelcase Unitrol 6 MIN
16mm
Color
LC 80-700221
Shows the internal working components and operation of a swivel - tilt control mechanism for office chairs.
Industrial and Technical Education
Dist - STEEL **Prod** - STEEL 1979

Steelmakers 29 MIN
VHS / 16mm
Color (G)
$55.00 rental _ #STEE - 000
Explores the history, tradition and values of Roebling, New Jersey, a former company steel town.
Social Science
Dist - PBS **Prod** - NJPBA

Steelmakers 28 MIN
16mm
Color
LC 77-701455
Offers a picture of the Bethlehem Steel Corporation, based on comments by its employees.
Business and Economics; Industrial and Technical Education
Dist - MTP **Prod** - BSC 1976

Steelyard Blues 92 MIN
16mm
Color
Tells how a bunch of social misfits escape to a utopian society.
Fine Arts
Dist - TWYMAN **Prod** - WB 1973

A Steep and Thorny Path 30 MIN
U-matic / VHS
Money Puzzle - the World of Macroeconomics Series Module 13
Color
Introduces the viewer to the definition of 'less developed country.' Explores the many problems encountered when such a country seeks growth.
Business and Economics; Sociology
Dist - MDCC **Prod** - MDCC

The Steepest Descent Method 45 MIN
VHS / U-matic
Modern Control Theory - Deterministic Optimal Control Series
Color (PRO)
Describes the simple digital computer algorithm to solve deterministic optimal control problems. Comes as package of two videotapes.
Industrial and Technical Education; Mathematics
Dist - MIOT **Prod** - MIOT

Steer Clear 20 MIN
VHS / U-matic
Color
Addresses the issues of chemically impaired driving. Demonstrates the effects of alcohol and marijuana on driving skills.
Health and Safety; Psychology; Sociology
Dist - WHITEG **Prod** - WHITEG

Steer Wrestling Clinic 30 MIN
VHS / BETA
Western Training Series
Color
Demonstrates moves involved in steer wrestling.
Physical Education and Recreation
Dist - EQVDL **Prod** - EQVDL

Steering Clear of Lemons 16 MIN
16mm
Consumer Reports Series
Color
LC 75-703537
Presents a consumer education film, providing information on product evaluation, buying, product safety and the role of Government, as seen through seven specific reports on diet foods, fair trade laws, stereos, pain relievers, 10 - speed bikes, grade labeling of beef and aerosols.
Business and Economics; Guidance and Counseling; Home Economics
Dist - CU **Prod** - CU 1975

Steering, Wheels, Front and Rear Axles 19 MIN
16mm
B&W
LC FIE52-362
Discusses how to check for play in the steering wheel and the front end assembly, correct wheel runout, make a toe - in test and test springs, axles and overall backlash.
Industrial and Technical Education
Dist - USNAC **Prod** - USOE 1945

Stefan Roloff - faces of an artist at work 20 MIN
VHS
Color (C G)
$195.00 purchase, $40.00 rental
Profiles the work of Berlin artist Roloff, now a resident of New York City, who produced an immense variety of original, colorful and provocative art. Reveals the evolution of his fanciful visions and visits him at work in the studio. Directed by Rebecca Runze.
Fine Arts
Dist - CNEMAG

Stefanie Powers' complete video guide to horseback riding and horse care 54 MIN
VHS
Color (G)
$29.95 purchase
Features actress Stefanie Powers and horse trainer Art Gaytan in a comprehensive guide for beginning horse riders. Teaches both English and Western styles of riding.
Physical Education and Recreation
Dist - PBS **Prod** - WNETTV

Steffan the Violinmaker 25 MIN
16mm / U-matic / VHS
World Cultures and Youth Series
Color (I J A)
LC 80-700081
Introduces Steffan, a West German boy who is carrying on a family tradition and becoming a violinmaker. Shows the gluing, oiling and toning process necessary to making a violin.
Fine Arts; Geography - World; Sociology
Dist - CORF **Prod** - SUNRIS 1980

Steichen - a Century in Photography 60 MIN
VHS / U-matic
Color
Profiles the life and work of the late Edward Steichen one of the foremost photographers in the history of the art.
Biography; Fine Arts
Dist - PBS **Prod** - WXXITV 1980

Steina Vasulka - Bad 2 MIN
VHS / U-matic
Color
Involves the subjective framing of space.
Fine Arts
Dist - ARTINC **Prod** - ARTINC

Steina Vasulka - Cantaloup 28 MIN
U-matic / VHS
Color
Involves the subjective framing of space.
Fine Arts
Dist - ARTINC **Prod** - ARTINC

Steina Vasulka - Let it be 4 MIN
U-matic / VHS
B&W
Involves the subjective framing of space.
Fine Arts
Dist - ARTINC **Prod** - ARTINC

Steina Vasulka - Selected Treecuts 9 MIN
U-matic / VHS
Color
Involves the subjective framing of space.
Fine Arts
Dist - ARTINC **Prod** - ARTINC

Steina Vasulka - Summer Salt 18 MIN
U-matic / VHS
Color
Deals with the subjective framing of space.
Fine Arts
Dist - ARTINC **Prod** - ARTINC

Steina Vasulka - Urban Episodes 9 MIN
U-matic / VHS
Color
Involves the subjective framing of space.
Fine Arts
Dist - ARTINC **Prod** - ARTINC

Steinbeck - Born 1914 14 MIN
16mm
B&W
Presents cartoonist Steinbeck's clever, nervous, mocking line as the camera jumps and circles around his witty drawings that so precisely lay bare all our solemn lunacies.
Fine Arts
Dist - ROLAND **Prod** - ROLAND

Steinbeck, the Grapes of Wrath and the Depression - a Video Commentary
VHS / U-matic
American Literature Series
(G C J)
$89 purchase _ #05528 - 85
Provides background information needed to understand the book, The Grapes of Wrath.
Literature and Drama
Dist - CHUMAN

Steinbeck, the grapes of wrath and the Depression - a video commentary 25 MIN
VHS
Color (H C)
$89.00 purchase _ #05528 - 126
Explores the social concerns and personal sympathy that underlie the novel by John Steinbeck. Looks at the relationship of the movie to the book and the documentary photography and filmmaking of the period.
History - United States; Literature and Drama
Dist - GA **Prod** - GA

The Steinitz Style 30 MIN
Videoreel / VT2
Koltanowski on Chess Series
Color
Physical Education and Recreation
Dist - PBS **Prod** - KQEDTV

Steinlager challenge
VHS
Color (G)
$29.95 purchase _ #0934
Profiles Peter Blake, the only competitor to take part in all five around the world sailing races. Tells about his trimaran, Steinlager 1, which won the first Round Australia Race, and Steinlager 2 and its winning part in the fifth Whitebread Round the World Race, 1989 - 1990.
Physical Education and Recreation
Dist - SEVVID

The Stem is Gone 29 MIN
Videoreel / VT2
Skiing Series
Color
Physical Education and Recreation
Dist - PBS **Prod** - KTCATV

Stenciling 1 45 MIN
VHS / BETA
Color
Presents the art of stenciling and gives the basics for beginners. Demonstrates finishing techniques for stencil art.
Fine Arts; Industrial and Technical Education
Dist - HOMEAF **Prod** - HOMEAF

Stenciling 2 65 MIN
VHS / BETA
Color
Demonstrates single and multiple stenciling techniques as well as paint shading and finishing techniques.
Fine Arts; Industrial and Technical Education
Dist - HOMEAF **Prod** - HOMEAF

Stensen's Duct - Key to Parotidectomy 32 MIN
16mm
Color (PRO)
Depicts embryologic and anatomic information significant for parotidectomy. Presents four cases illustrating techniques of dissection and hemostasis. Stresses Stensen's duct as the easiest surgical approach to the parotid and the facial nerve.
Health and Safety; Science
Dist - ACY **Prod** - ACYDGD 1962

Step a Little Higher 18 MIN
16mm / U-matic / VHS
Color (H C A)
LC FIA67-621
Depicts the problems facing a functional illiterate as portrayed in the experiences and feelings of two men who never learned to read well. Shows how the adult reading center of the library aided these men.
Education; English Language; Psychology; Sociology
Dist - FEIL **Prod** - CLEVPL 1966

Step ahead 76 MIN
VHS
Color (G)
$19.98 purchase _ #SVC6006V
Features personal trainer and step aerobics teacher Carolan Brown. Leads through a warm - up, a step aerobics workout, cool - down and stretching routine.
Physical Education and Recreation
Dist - CAMV

Step and repeat made easy 29 MIN
VHS
Color (H C)
$79.95 purchase _ #SE - 5
Shows, step - by - step, a simple, fast and effective system for step and repeat that can be done without the use of complicated and expensive equipment, and how to successfully step a single color job as well as a four color job. Covers tools needed, how to use pins and tabs, how to mask out and make a proof, plus more.
Industrial and Technical Education
Dist - INSTRU

Step Aside, Step Down 20 MIN
16mm
Color
LC 74-705701
Reports on the problems of aging in America, such as income, housing, nutrition and transportation. Shows successful private and government programs aimed at solving them.
Health and Safety; Sociology
Dist - USNAC **Prod** - USSRS 1971

A Step Away from War 28 MIN
U-matic / VT3
(G)
$95.00 purchase, $45.00 rental
Explains why a comprehensive ban on nuclear testing is an essential step towards ending the nuclear arms race. Features Paul Newman as host.
Civics and Political Systems; Sociology
Dist - EFVP **Prod** - EFVP 1986

Step behind series
Ask just for little things 20 MIN
Genesis 25 MIN
I'll Promise You a Tomorrow 20 MIN
Dist - HALLMK

A step beyond 46 MIN
VHS
Forklift operator training series
Color (IND)
$495.00 purchase, $95.00 rental _ #817 - 29
Presents one of a series of four videos covering all aspects of forktrucks and their operation. Discusses inspection and design factors for the hydraulic system, the forks and the major types of tires. Identifies areas to inspect on trailers and loading - unloading procedures. Covers inspection, care and preventive maintenance for battery electrics. Discusses the properties of propane, inspection of cylinders and specific safety aspects of propane handling. Includes leader's guide.
Health and Safety; Psychology
Dist - ITSC **Prod** - ITSC

Step by Step 15 MIN
16mm
Color (H C A)
LC 78-701448
Presents an alternative approach to educating handicapped children through integrating the child into normal classroom activities and through respect for individual differences.
Education; Psychology
Dist - CFDC **Prod** - NYCBED 1978

Step by Step 11 MIN
16mm / U-matic / VHS
Color
LC 79-700059
Uses animation to interpret the world of childhood. Describes the condition of children throughout the world and makes a plea for the basic rights of children.
Fine Arts; Sociology
Dist - PFP **Prod** - HUBLEY 1979

Step by Step 20 MIN
U-matic / VHS / 16mm
B&W (C A)
Describes juvenile delinquency in a city neighborhood where physical and human deterioration has occurred. Shows case workers studying juvenile problems and coping constructively with gang activities.
Psychology; Sociology
Dist - IFB **Prod** - IFB 1954

Step by Step 30 MIN
U-matic
Color (C)
LC 81-706501
Tells how the Leichardt Council proposes to rebuild a park, allowing the community to be involved from design to completion, and to use previously unemployed people from the area to build it.
Civics and Political Systems; Sociology
Dist - TASCOR **Prod** - SYDUN 1980

Step by Step 15 MIN
16mm
Color (SPANISH)
Presents a Spanish language version of the film Step By Step, which presents an alternative approach to educating handicapped children through integrating the child into normal classroom activities and through respect for individual differences.

Education; Foreign Language; Guidance and Counseling; Psychology
Dist - CFDC **Prod** - NYCBED

Step - by - step guide to passing your GED series
VHS
Step - by - step guide to passing your GED series
Color (A H)
$189.95 purchase _ #GTS100S V-G
Offers subject reviews on all GED test subjects in a series of five programs. Covers math, science, social studies, writing skills and literature and the arts. Contains three levels of practice tests; answer explanations; test-taking tips and strategies; what to expect on GED test day; and more. Includes study guides. Each program approximately 30 minutes in length.
Education; English Language; Fine Arts; Literature and Drama; Mathematics; Science; Social Science
Dist - CAMV

The Step - by - Step Process 6 MIN
U-matic / VHS
Practical M B O Series
Color
Business and Economics; Education; Psychology
Dist - DELTAK **Prod** - DELTAK

Step by Step Series

Ballustrades	14 MIN
Basic mathematics for designing a stair	20 MIN
The Cut - out and mitred stringer and the housed stringer	22 MIN
Designing a stair with total run limitations	14 MIN
Headroom calculations from fixed opening lengths	11 MIN
An Introduction to Stair Building	15 MIN
Layout and Construction of a Straight - Run Stair	20 MIN
Stair Terminology	16 MIN
Stairwell Opening Length Calculations	14 MIN
Stringer Types and Attachment Methods	22 MIN

Dist - ACCESS

Step by Step - the Appellate Process 120 MIN
U-matic / VHS / Cassette
Color; Mono (PRO)
Features a court of appeal justice and two experienced appellate lawyers who give their views of procedure in the California courts of appeal. Shows how to evaluate the costs and benefits of an appeal, how to prosecute an appeal through briefing and oral argument and the postdecision procedures for obtaining publication of the opinion.
Civics and Political Systems
Dist - CCEB **Prod** - CCEB

Step - families and blended families and churches and schools - helping the healing - Volume 5 60 MIN
VHS
Divorce - from pain to hope series
Color (G A R)
$24.95 purchase, $10.00 rental _ #35 - 861114 - 1
Focuses on the dynamics of step - families and blended families. Suggests ways in which churches and schools can contribute to the process of recovery from divorce.
Psychology; Sociology
Dist - APH **Prod** - ABINGP

Step Family 13 MIN
U-matic / VHS / 16mm
Family Life - Transitions in Marriage Series
Color (I)
LC 81-701449
Examines the impact of remarriage on both children and adults. Uses the case study of a fictional family to show the problems faced in accepting new parents and siblings.
Sociology
Dist - CORF **Prod** - GORKER 1981

Step family 13 MIN
VHS
Family life - transitions in a marriage - a case history - series
Color (A)
Portrays Helene who has married Ray, second marriages for both. Reveals that their relationship is warm and caring but is strained by the squabbles betwen Helene's three children and Ray's son. Alan, the ex - husband of Helene, has also remarried and has a new baby, and his new wife resents the extra work when Alan's children visit. Ray and Helene vow to work through their problems together. Part of a series following a family through divorce, single parenthood and remarriage.
Health and Safety; Sociology
Dist - VIEWTH **Prod** - VIEWTH

Step Five 31 MIN
VHS / 16mm
Steps One through Five Series
Color (G)
$165.00 purchase, $40.00 rental _ #5810H, 5823H, 0454J, 0467J
Guides through the process of finding a willingness within the self to talk to another about the nature of one's wrongs. Features Genny Carlin.
Guidance and Counseling; Health and Safety; Psychology; Sociology
Dist - HAZELB **Prod** - HAZELB

Step five of AA
Cassette
(G)
$195.00, $10.00 purchase
Explains the fifth step of the twelve - step program of Alcoholics Anonymous.
Guidance and Counseling; Health and Safety
Dist - KELLYP

A Step Forward 22 MIN
16mm
Color
Explains that roofmate is one of the Dow cost - reducing installation construction materials. Describes the benefits, production and application of this foam product.
Business and Economics; Industrial and Technical Education
Dist - DCC **Prod** - DCC

Step Four 32 MIN
VHS / 16mm
Steps One through Five Series
Color (G)
$165.00 purchase, $40.00 rental _ #5809H, 5822H, 0453J, 0466J
Emphasizes the need for truthfulness, self - knowledge and self - discipline. Discusses illness, responsibility, accountability and guilt. Features Dr Damian McElrath, Director of Residential Services at Hazelden.
Guidance and Counseling; Health and Safety; Psychology; Sociology
Dist - HAZELB **Prod** - HAZELB

Step four of AA 15 MIN
U-matic / Cassette
Color (G)
$195.00, $10.00 purchase
Explains the fourth step of the twelve - step program of Alcholics Anonymous.
Guidance and Counseling; Health and Safety; Psychology
Dist - KELLYP **Prod** - KELLYP

A Step from the Shadows 28 MIN
16mm
Color (H C)
Stimulates interest and understanding of alcohol and other drug abuse problems.
Guidance and Counseling; Health and Safety; Psychology
Dist - NINEFC **Prod** - LYNVIL

A Step in Time 29 MIN
U-matic / VHS
Color (I A)
Provides information for young persons on making responsible decisions about drinking.
Health and Safety; Sociology
Dist - SUTHRB **Prod** - SUTHRB

Step into ballet - with Wayne Sleep 50 MIN
VHS
Color (K P I J)
$19.95 purchase_#1378
Features former Royal Ballet star Wayne Sleep giving an easily followed guide to the art of ballet. Includes choosing the correct shoes and clothing and taking the first important steps. Good introduction and at-home practice for beginners.
Fine Arts; Physical Education and Recreation
Dist - KULTUR

Step into fitness - sodanceabit series

Social dance aerobics	100 MIN
Social dance aerobics encore workout	54 MIN

Dist - CAMV
PBS

Step into fitness - sodanceabit series

Cha cha and polka	50 MIN
East coast swing and Viennese waltz	57 MIN
Folk dance aerobics - mizerlou, hora, alunelui, harmonica and savilla se bela loza	64 MIN
West coast swing	76 MIN

Dist - PBS

Step into Space 11 MIN
U-matic
Color
Describes the training activities which all astronauts must experience, followed by more specialized training for a particular mission.
Industrial and Technical Education
Dist - NASA **Prod** - NASA 1972

Step 'n time 45 MIN
VHS
Cory Everson's step exercise series
Color (G)
$19.95 purchase _ #KVC60005V
Offers a step training format for beginning through intermediate exercisers.
Physical Education and Recreation
Dist - CAMV

Step off a ten foot platform with your clothes on 7 MIN
16mm
Color (G)
$20.00 rental
Describes itself as being 'to metaphysics what canned ham is to daylight savings time.' Features a Scott Miller production.
Fine Arts
Dist - CANCIN

Step One 28 MIN
VHS / 16mm
Steps One through Five Series
Color (G)
$165.00 purchase, $40.00 rental _ #5806H, 5819H, 0450J, 0463J
Discusses the factors involved in the admitting of powerlessness and unmanageability. Features Fred Holmquist, Section Manager in Rehabilitation Services at Hazelden.
Guidance and Counseling; Health and Safety; Psychology
Dist - HAZELB **Prod** - HAZELB

Step one of AA 15 MIN
Cassette
Color (G)
$195.00, $10.00 purchase
Explains the first step of the twelve - step program of Alcholics Anonymous.
Guidance and Counseling; Health and Safety; Psychology
Dist - KELLYP **Prod** - KELLYP

Step Parenting 20 MIN
16mm
Color (A)
Defines problems that occur in remarriage when children are involved. Educates general public about issues pertinent to step - parenting and to adults and children going through the experience.
Psychology; Sociology
Dist - AACD **Prod** - AACD 1974

Step - parenting issues 20 MIN
VHS
Color (G A R)
$10.00 rental _ #36 - 84 - 999
Portrays common experiences and problems in step - parenting. Covers topics including sibling rivalries, testing authority, and others. Identifies predictable behavior patterns and suggests ways of dealing with them.
Guidance and Counseling; Sociology
Dist - APH **Prod** - FAMINF

Step Print 7.5 MIN
16mm
Color; Silent (C)
$175.00
Experimental film by George Griffin.
Fine Arts
Dist - AFA **Prod** - AFA 1976

Step Right Up 19 MIN
16mm
Color (J)
LC 77-702502
Illustrates possible hazards and improper procedures when using ladders.
Guidance and Counseling; Health and Safety
Dist - FILCOM **Prod** - FILCOM 1977

Step right up 50 MIN
VHS
White heat series
Color; PAL (G)
PdS99 purchase; Not available in the United States or Canada
Probes the connections between language and the development of technology. Utilizes unusual visual and music styles to display the interaction of innovation and languages. Part three of an eight - part series.
Business and Economics; Foreign Language
Dist - BBCENE

Step style 30 MIN
VHS / 16mm
Movement style and culture series
Color (H C G)
$600.00, $195.00 purchase, $45.00 rental _ #10461, #37254

Shows how the leg and foot movemnts of dances throughut the world relate to social structures, cultural patterns, work movements and sports. Part of a series on movement style and culture.
Fine Arts; Sociology
Dist - UCEMC **Prod** - CHORP 1980

Step Three 28 MIN
VHS / 16mm
Steps One through Five Series
Color (G)
$165.00 purchase, $40.00 rental _ #5808H, 5821H, 0452J, 0465J
Discusses the decision - making aspect of Step Three and the concept of moving from self - will to God - will. Features Ted Laska.
Guidance and Counseling; Health and Safety; Psychology; Religion and Philosophy
Dist - HAZELB **Prod** - HAZELB

Step three of AA 15 MIN
U-matic / Cassette
Color (G)
$195.00, $10.00 purchase
Explains the third step of the twelve - step program of Alcholics Anonymous.
Guidance and Counseling; Health and Safety; Psychology
Dist - KELLYP **Prod** - KELLYP

A Step to Tomorrow 13 MIN
VHS / U-matic
Developing Your Study Skills Series
Color (H C)
Introduces issues and adjustments new students will be forced to deal with on campus. Examines the fears and misconceptions students bring to college. Suggests ways of adapting to a new environment.
Education
Dist - BCNFL **Prod** - UWO 1985

A Step Too Slow 25 MIN
16mm / U-matic / VHS
Insight Series
Color (J)
Reveals that when he is cut from the team, Bill Cameron wallows in self - pity. Shows him evaluating his life with the help of Judge Reinhold.
Guidance and Counseling; Psychology; Religion and Philosophy
Dist - PAULST **Prod** - PAULST

Step training 45 MIN
VHS
Cory Everson's step exercise series
Color (G)
$19.95 purchase _ #KVC60004V
Uses a step training format with sections devoted to different body parts.
Physical Education and Recreation
Dist - CAMV

Step Two 30 MIN
VHS / 16mm
Steps One through Five Series
Color (G)
$165.00 purchase, $40.00 rental _ #5807H, 5820H, 0451J, 0464J
Describes Step Two as a decision to turn to a Higher Power and experience a llife of trust and sharing. Features Dr. Damian McElrath, Director of Residential Services at Hazelden.
Guidance and Counseling; Health and Safety; Psychology
Dist - HAZELB **Prod** - HAZELB

Step two of AA 15 MIN
Cassette
Color (G)
$195.00, $10.00 purchase
Explains the second step of the twelve - step program of Alcholics Anonymous.
Guidance and Counseling; Health and Safety; Psychology
Dist - KELLYP **Prod** - KELLYP

Stepdancing - portrait of a remarried family 27 MIN
VHS
Color (I J H C A)
$295.00 purchase
Shows the effect on the children as divorced parents remarry. Looks at the new family relationships involving parents, stepparents and children. Narrated by Oliver Johnson, an eleven - year - old member of the family in the video.
Sociology
Dist - PFP **Prod** - KENCOM

Stephan Gaskin - 5 - 13 - 76
VHS / Cassette
Poetry Center reading series
Color (G)
#205 - 162
Features an interview with the writer by Mark Linenthal at the Poetry Center, San Francisco State University, with an introduction by Lewis MacAdams. Available only for listening purposes at the Center; not for sale or rent.
Guidance and Counseling; Literature and Drama
Dist - POETRY **Prod** - POETRY 1976

Stephane Grappelli - live in San Francisco - 1985 60 MIN
VHS
Color; Stereo (G)
$29.95 purchase
Records a 1985 live Stephane Grappelli concert from San Francisco.
Fine Arts
Dist - KINOIC **Prod** - RHPSDY

Stephanie 58 MIN
16mm / VHS
Color (G)
$800.00, $295.00 purchase, $125.00, $75.00 rental
Documents an American girl's dreams and disappointments as she journeys through adolescence. Follows the young woman, Stephanie, through six years of her life and sees her becoming disenchanted with high school and the narrowness of the life offered her. Produced by Peggy Stern.
Education; Psychology; Sociology
Dist - WMEN **Prod** - PSTERN 1986

Stephanie Herman's muscle ballet workout 62 MIN
VHS
Color (I J H A)
$19.95 purchase_#1362
Presents Stephanie Herman's Muscle Ballet workout based on ballet principles which are useful for safe development of lean, strong, flexible muscles. Helps individuals who want to work on muscle development without fear of bulky muscles.
Fine Arts; Physical Education and Recreation
Dist - KULTUR

Stephanie takes her medicine 9 MIN
VHS / 16mm
Emotional factors affecting children and parents in the hospital series
Color (C A)
LC 81-701488
Focuses on a hospital encounter in which a student nurse enters a playroom and tries in vain to give an unfamiliar liquid to a five - year - old girl.
Health and Safety; Sociology
Dist - LRF **Prod** - LRF 1979

Stephen Crane 22 MIN
16mm / U-matic / VHS
Authors Series
Color (J)
Portrays American author Stephen Crane telling the story of his life and discussing his major works, including THE RED BADGE OF COURAGE.
Literature and Drama
Dist - JOU

Stephen Crane's Three Miraculous Soldiers 18 MIN
16mm / U-matic / VHS
Color (J)
LC 76-703534
Views the Civil War through the eyes of a young girl who is forced to see the humanity of both sides of a war when she encounters both Confederate and Union soldiers.
Fine Arts; Guidance and Counseling; Literature and Drama; Sociology
Dist - PHENIX **Prod** - PHENIX 1976

Stephen Edlich 30 MIN
U-matic
Art Show Series
Color
Features sculptor - painter Stephen Edlich who discusses his collage paintings. Describes materials used.
Fine Arts
Dist - UMITV **Prod** - UMITV

Stephen Emerson - 11 - 22 - 83
VHS / Cassette
Poetry Center reading series
Color (G)
$15.00 purchase, rental _ #571 - 482
Features the writer reading his stories entitled Race Records; Anchorage; Bruxism; After Fellini; and Terpsichore, at the Poetry Center, San Francisco State University, with an introduction by Robert Gluck.
Literature and Drama
Dist - POETRY

Stephen Foster and His Songs 17 MIN
16mm / U-matic / VHS
Color (J)
Traces Stephen Foster's life, the highlights and the disappointments. Provides the historical background for the creation of his best known songs.
Biography; Fine Arts
Dist - CORF **Prod** - CORF 1960

Stephen Foster's Footprints in Dream and Song 15 MIN
16mm
Color
Presents the biography of Stephen Foster, composer of Florida's state song, Way Down Upon The Suwannee River.
Biography; Fine Arts; History - United States
Dist - FLADC **Prod** - FLADC

Stephen Hawking - the universe within 28 MIN
VHS
Eminent scientist series
Color (J H)
$60.00 purchase _ #A2VH 1015
Features physicist Stephen Hawking. Part of a series on scientists which discusses their childhood, educational backgrounds, decisions affecting their careers and illustrious achievements.
Science; Science - Physical
Dist - CLRVUE **Prod** - CLRVUE

Stephen Spender 15 MIN
VHS
Writer's workshop series
Color (C A T)
$69.95 purchase, $45.00 rental
Features Stephen Spender in a lecture and discussion of his work, held as part of a writing workshop series at the University of South Carolina. Hosted by author William Price Fox and introduced by George Plimpton. Part nine of a 15 - part telecourse.
English Language; Literature and Drama
Dist - SCETV **Prod** - SCETV 1982

Stephen Spender 30 MIN
VHS
Writer's workshop series
Color (G)
$59.95 purchase _ #WRWO - 109
Features British author Stephen Spender in a lecture and discussion at the University of South Carolina. Shares his views of writing, poetry and the importance of reading as a learning tool for writers. Offers recollections of some of his literary friends, including W H Auden, T S Eliot and Christopher Isherwood.
Literature and Drama
Dist - PBS **Prod** - SCETVM 1987

Stephen Spender 52 MIN
VHS
Color (H C G)
$79.00 purchase
Features the writer talking with Al Alvarez about the mission of the poet in society and about the writers he has known, among them T S Eliot, W H Auden and Virginia Woolf. Discusses his works including Life and the Poet, Ruins and Visions; The Oedipus Trilogy of Sophocles, and many others.
Literature and Drama
Dist - ROLAND **Prod** - INCART

Stephen Witt - Diamant - 10 - 4 - 87 120 MIN
VHS / Cassette
Poetry Center reading series
Color (G)
#935 - 629
Features the writer reading from his works at the Ruth Witt - Diamant Memorial Reading at the Poetry Center, San Francisco State University. Also includes readings by James Broughton, Robert Duncan, Rosalie Moore, Mark Linenthal, Shirley Taylor, Christy Taylor, Justine Fixel, Lawrence Fixel, Michael McClure, and Gail Layton. Introduction by Frances Phillips. Slides of Ruth Witt - Diamant courtesy of Caryl Mezey. Available for listening purposes only at the Center; not for sale or rent.
Literature and Drama
Dist - POETRY **Prod** - POETRY 1987

The Stephens family 52 MIN
VHS / U-matic
Six American families series
Color (A)
Looks at an Iowa farm family as it experiences the staggering costs of land and equipment and a government policy which seems to be interfering in the family business. Shows that, although all six children want to stay on the farm, there is not enough land to divide among them and frustrations are beginning to be felt by those who realize that the land will never be theirs.
Psychology; Sociology
Dist - ECUFLM **Prod** - GROUPW 1976

Stephen's going straight 30 MINS.
VHS
Lifestories
Color; PAL (G A)
PdS50 purchase
Documents the struggles of a real life family whose child is in trouble with the law. Covers the challenges facing both

the youth offender as he tries to give up crime and the family as they work to support him. Sixth in the six - part Lifestories series.
Sociology
Dist - BBCENE

Stephen's secret 25 MIN
VHS / Videodisc / U-matic
Color (P I)
$350.00 purchase _ #HH - 6247M
Adapts the Kids on the Block puppet program on physical child abuse created by Barbara Aiello. Uses puppet characters to tell the story of a physically abused boy who overcame his reluctance to tell and found help for his family. Shows that children often blame themselves for the abuse and that they commonly confuse abuse with normal family discipline. Produced by Lil' Apple Productions.
Sociology
Dist - CORF

The Stephenses of Iowa 58 MIN
U-matic / VHS / 16mm
Six American Families Series
Color
LC 78-701774
Profiles a third generation farm family struggling with the staggering costs of land and equipment which threaten their lifestyle in the late 1970's.
Sociology
Dist - CAROUF **Prod** - WBCPRO 1977

The Stephenses of Iowa - Pt 1 29 MIN
U-matic / VHS / 16mm
Six American Families Series
Color
LC 78-701774
Profiles a third generation farm family struggling with the staggering costs of land and equipment which threaten their lifestyle in the late 1970's.
Social Science
Dist - CAROUF **Prod** - WBCPRO 1977

The Stephenses of Iowa - Pt 2 29 MIN
16mm / U-matic / VHS
Six American Families Series
Color
LC 78-701774
Profiles a third generation farm family struggling with the staggering costs of land and equipment which threaten their lifestyle in the late 1970's.
Social Science
Dist - CAROUF **Prod** - WBCPRO 1977

The Stepparent 29 MIN
U-matic
B&W
Views the contemporary stepfamily with understanding in an effort to reverse society's stereotype of the 'cruel stepparent.'.
Sociology
Dist - UMITV **Prod** - UMITV 1971

The Stepparent Family
VHS
Daddy Doesn't Live Here Anymore - the Single - Parent Family Series
Color
Looks at the complications of the stepparent family. Covers areas such as new siblings and differing blood ties.
Guidance and Counseling; Sociology
Dist - IBIS **Prod** - IBIS

Stepparenting 28 MIN
VHS / U-matic
Color (G)
Emphasizes the need for a solid and caring relationship between the two adults to prevent divisiveness and the sabotaging of each other's relationship with the children.
Guidance and Counseling; Sociology
Dist - PRI **Prod** - PRI 1985

Stepparenting 25 MIN
U-matic / VHS
Color
Discusses feeling insecure, conflicts over child rearing practices and confusion as to who has authority over the child in remarriage situations.
Sociology
Dist - POLYMR **Prod** - POLYMR

Stepparenting Issues 20 MIN
U-matic / VHS / 16mm
Color (A)
Presents 13 vignettes illustrating common situations faced by stepparents including no time alone for the new couple, disagreements over having additional children, conflicts over childrearing, testing of authority, exploitation or nonacceptance of the new relationship by children and sibling rivalry.
Psychology; Sociology
Dist - CORF **Prod** - CORF

Stepparenting - New Families, Old Ties 25 MIN
16mm
Color (H C A)
LC 77-701852
Focuses on problems of being a stepparent and ways in which families deal with them.
Guidance and Counseling; Sociology
Dist - POLYMR **Prod** - FELTHM 1977

Steppe in Winter 13 MIN
16mm
B&W (P I)
LC FIA67-1434
Shows how in the chilling cold of the steppe land of southeastern Europe, men, women, horses, dogs, cattle and sheep endure the long winter. Explains that the way of life of these people is influenced but not dominated by wind, cold and snow. Without narration.
Geography - World; Science - Natural
Dist - SF **Prod** - SF 1966

Steppin 56 MIN
VHS
Color (G)
$350.00 purchase, $95.00 rental
Introduces the step show, a dance style popular among black fraternities and sororities. Examines the cultural roots of steppin' in African dancing, military marching and hip - hop music. Also discusses the contemporary social significance on college campuses.
Fine Arts; Sociology
Dist - CNEMAG

Steppin' out
VHS
Color (A G)
$29.95 purchase _ #NUV010V-P
Presents a synthesis of step aerobics and interval training that results in a full-body workout for exercisers at any fitness level. Combines aerobic conditioning and strength training and varies step heights, weights, and intensity to offer beginning, intermediate, and advanced participants the tools to lose weight or get into shape.
Physical Education and Recreation
Dist - CAMV

Stepping into melody series
Abraham Lincoln 84 MIN
Dist - UILL

Stepping into Rhythm Series
Beatiful home, sweet home 14 MIN
Black and gold 14 MIN
A Circle story 14 MIN
City rhythms 14 MIN
Country Road 15 MIN
Gerald McBoing, boing 15 MIN
Happy New Year 14 MIN
The Harpsichord 14 MIN
Hear the Bells Ringing 14 MIN
Hold on 15 MIN
I Like to Sing 14 MIN
The Magic Vine 15 MIN
Major or Minor 14 MIN
Merry Christmas 14 MIN
The Moon is Coming Out 14 MIN
My Twenty Pennies 14 MIN
The Note Machine 14 MIN
Nothing but Sing 15 MIN
Of Thee I Sing 15 MIN
Oh, I Saw a Fox 14 MIN
Winter is 15 MIN
Dist - AITECH

Stepping Out into the World, the Middle Years of Childhood 29 MIN
U-matic
Color (C)
Presents an overview of the developmental stages of the middle childhood period.
Health and Safety; Science - Natural
Dist - UOKLAH **Prod** - UOKLAH 1981

Stepping out, stepping in
VHS
Color (J H A I)
$75.00 purchase _ #SO283V
Reveals that when a woman goes nontraditional in her work life, she can and should expect a total life shake - up. Addresses both the woman thinking about this step and the facilitator wishing to guide and support her efforts. 'Stepping Out' looks at a teacher turned welder, offering insight into what to expect when making this kind of change. 'Stepping In' explains the need to get ready - physically, emotionally, mentally - before stepping into occupations where men predominate and tells how to go about it. Two tapes, handbook, leaflet.
Business and Economics; Guidance and Counseling; Sociology
Dist - CENTER **Prod** - CENTER

Stepping Out - the DeBolts Grow Up 52 MIN
16mm / U-matic / VHS
Color (I)
LC 81-700306
Presents a view of the DeBolt family, with its twenty children, some of which are severely handicapped, who are now living at colleges and earning their own living. Tells how they have benefitted greatly from a loving family life.
Education; Psychology; Sociology
Dist - PFP **Prod** - DAVIPR 1981

Stepping Stones 10 MIN
16mm
Parent Education - Information Films Series
B&W (S)
Introduces the techniques used for teaching specific lip - reading skills and offers suggestions for the selection of a specific lip - reading word.
Guidance and Counseling; Psychology
Dist - TC **Prod** - TC

Stepping Stones in Space 14 MIN
16mm
Screen news digest series; Vol 15; Issue 5
B&W (I)
LC 73-701271
Presents a chronicle of the conquest of space from the pioneering flights of Dr Robert Hutchings Goodard in 1926 to the lunar landing of Apollo 17 in December, 1972.
Industrial and Technical Education; Science; Science - Physical
Dist - HEARST **Prod** - HEARST 1972

Stepping Stones to the Stars - the Air Force Museum 27 MIN
16mm
Color
LC 78-701848
Describes the origin, purpose and contents of the Air Force Museum. Shows how old aircraft are restored, how the museum furnishes data on many subjects and how the museum's resources are made available to everybody on a nonprofit basis.
Civics and Political Systems; Fine Arts; History - United States; Social Science
Dist - USNAC **Prod** - USAF 1973

Stepping up to supervisor 20 MIN
VHS
Color (A PRO IND)
$650.00 purchase, $125.00 rental
Portrays many of the common mistakes new supervisors make - under or over controlling, one - way communication, half - way delegating, and not making decisions. Suggests how to avoid these and other mistakes. Targeted to a blue collar setting.
Business and Economics; Guidance and Counseling; Psychology
Dist - VLEARN **Prod** - CRMF

Stepping Up to Supervisor 20 MIN
16mm / VHS
#109047 - 9 3/4
Presents advice for the person taking on a new leadership role, discussing three major mistakes commonly made by new supervisors.
Business and Economics
Dist - MGHT

Steps 12 MIN
16mm
Color (G)
$30.00 rental
Pays homage to Fernand Leger on the fiftieth anniversary of his film, Le Ballet Mecanique. Incorporates the loop from his film with a new one to make visual rhythms. Music by Levine.
Fine Arts
Dist - CANCIN **Prod** - LEVCHI 1976

Steps 1, 2 and 3 for Young People
VHS
Color (P)
$225.00 purchase _ #5858H
Introduces young people to the risks of drug use by using popular music and personal accounts by young recovering drug abusers. Stresses the importance of understanding and accepting the first three steps of AA.
Education; Health and Safety; Sociology
Dist - HAZELB

Steps in Drawing - 1 15 MIN
VHS
Drawing with Paul Ringler Series
Color (I)
$125.00 purchase
Presents a nine - step procedure for freehand drawing. Focuses on the drawing process, for older students, rather than drawing specific objects. Part of a thirty - part series.

Fine Arts
Dist - AITECH **Prod** - OETVA 1988

Steps in Teaching - and what Happens When You Miss One 30 MIN
13 MIN
16mm
Individualizing in a Group Series
B&W (T)
A shortened version, without commentary, of the film Steps In Teaching - And What Happens When You Miss One. Presents a highly skilled teacher working with inner - city children who are learning to tell time and to record that time in numerals.
Education; Psychology
Dist - SPF **Prod** - SPF

Steps in time - Scenes from 1840 Baltimore 30 MIN
VHS
Color (G)
$39.95 purchase _ #STPS - 000
Focuses on life in a Baltimore household of the 1840s. Describes societal and family situations of the time.
History - United States
Dist - PBS **Prod** - WETATV 1988

The Steps of Age 25 MIN
U-matic / VHS / 16mm
B&W (C A)
Shows the necessity of preparing for retirement and old age during the younger years. Contrasts the emotional weakness of a man who goes into a depression and dies soon after his retirement, and the strength of his wife.
Guidance and Counseling; Psychology; Sociology
Dist - IFB **Prod** - MHFB 1951

Steps One through Five Series
Step Five 31 MIN
Step Four 32 MIN
Step One 28 MIN
Step Three 28 MIN
Step Two 30 MIN
Dist - HAZELB

Steps to Mature Reading 30 MIN
16mm
Starting Tomorrow Series Unit 3 - Individualizing Your Reading 'Program
B&W (T)
LC 75-714209
Illustrates methods for improving reading ability.
Education; English Language
Dist - WALKED **Prod** - EALING 1967

Steps to Recovery - Rehabilitation of the Patient with Pulmonary Tuberculosis 30 MIN
16mm
B&W
LC FIE61-37
Depicts the medical treatment and rehabilitation of tubercular patients as viewed through the eyes of two military patients hospitalized at Fitzsimons Army Hospital in Denver.
Health and Safety; Science - Natural
Dist - USNAC **Prod** - USA 1961

Steps toward Maturity and Health 10 MIN
16mm / U-matic / VHS
Triangle of Health Series
Color (P I) (SPANISH HUNGARIAN ARABIC GERMAN SWEDISH)
LC FIA68-2682
Uses animation to show that as the body matures, responsibility for caring for it passes from nature, to parents and finally to the individual himself. Examines social, mental and physical health.
Health and Safety; Science - Natural
Dist - CORF **Prod** - DISNEY 1968

Stereo photography - places and times remembered 30 MIN
VHS
Color (G)
$39.95 purchase _ #SPP01V - F
Reveals the history of stereo photography through the recollections of professional photographer Philip Brigandi. Looks at early three - dimensional photos of the railroads, the pyramids of Egypt, San Francisco's earthquake, and similar scenes in the Keystone - Mast collection of the California Museum of Photography.
Industrial and Technical Education
Dist - CAMV

Stereoscopics 30 MIN
U-matic
Antiques series
Color
Fine Arts
Dist - PBS **Prod** - NHMNET

Stereotactic Procedures for Parkinson's Disease 25 MIN
16mm
Color (PRO)
Explains that it is now generally recognized that localized surgery within the basal ganglia can alleviate tremor and rigidity in better than 90 percent of cases of Parkinson's disease. Emphasizes that it is of paramount importance to use a precise technique, so as to avoid surrounding structures. Illustrates the beneficial effect of stereotactic procedures.
Health and Safety; Science
Dist - ACY **Prod** - ACYDGD 1963

Stereotyped Motor Mechanisms - the Extrapyramidal System 18 MIN
16mm / U-matic / VHS
Anatomical Basis of Brain Function Series
Color (PRO)
Science - Natural
Dist - TEF **Prod** - AVCORP

Stereotypes 25 MIN
VHS
Color (J H C G T A)
$95.00 purchase, $45.00 rental
Uses an animated format to parody the traditional U S and Soviet stereotypes of one another. Tells the story of a cartoon rivalry which escalates into a full - blown battle, concluding with the symbolic melting of a wall built between the two sides. Produced by Laurien Towers and the Soviet Peace Commitee in a joint U S - Soviet effort.
Civics and Political Systems; Sociology
Dist - EFVP

Stereotypes - Module IV 6 MIN
8mm cartridge / VHS / BETA / U-matic
Brainwaves - case studies in diversity series
Color; PAL (PRO G)
$495.00 purchase
Presents two vignettes 'The Work - Family Tightrope;' 'The Case of Don and Patrick.' Discusses realistic, complex diversity issues, concepts and conflicts. Combines case studies with an interactive learning design to allow trainers to lead participants in a structured, non - threatening exploration of diversity. Part four of six parts. Includes trainer's manual and 20 participant manuals.
Business and Economics; Psychology
Dist - BNA **Prod** - BNA

Stereotyping - Sex 30 MIN
U-matic / VHS
Take Charge Series
Color (A)
LC 81-706070
Points out how sex role stereotyping can inhibit personal growth and suggests how people overcome the limitations imposed by it, particularly among women.
Sociology
Dist - USC **Prod** - USC 1979

Steric Stabilization, Sensitized Flocculation 41 MIN
VHS / U-matic
Colloid and Surface Chemistry - Lyophobic Colloids Series
Color
Science; Science - Physical
Dist - KALMIA **Prod** - KALMIA

Sterile Supply Quality Assurance Control 60 MIN
U-matic
Color
LC 79-707312
Discusses procedures for quality control, monitoring and bacteriological control of medical supplies and equipment.
Health and Safety; Science
Dist - USNAC **Prod** - USVA 1978

Sterile Technique 16 MIN
U-matic / VHS
Basic Clinical Skills Series
Color (PRO)
Demonstrates proper maneuvering in the sterile field, showing steam and gas sterilization, sterile gloving, skin prepping and the handling of sterile bundles and packages.
Health and Safety; Science
Dist - HSCIC **Prod** - HSCIC 1984

Sterile Technique at the Bedside
Videodisc
Color (C)
$350.00 purchase _ #2687
Shows how to prepare and apply dressings while maintaining sterile techniques. Features multiple choice testing and remedial sequences with each unit. Can be played on SONY LDP 1000, 1000A or 2000 series players with Level II capability. Includes user's manual.
Health and Safety; Psychology; Science
Dist - ACCESS **Prod** - ACCESS 1987

Sterile Technique for Tracheotomy Suctioning 16 MIN
U-matic
Color (PRO)
LC 80-706510
Demonstrates sterile tracheotomy suctioning procedures using a model with a cuffed tube.
Science
Dist - USNAC **Prod** - VAHSL 1978

Sterile Techniques for Oral Surgery and Periodontal Surgery Procedures 19 MIN
VHS / BETA
Color (PRO)
Health and Safety
Dist - RMIBHF **Prod** - RMIBHF

Sterilization and Consent 29 MIN
U-matic
Woman Series
Color
Discusses abuse in sterilization cases and describes a suit brought by ten women who were coercively sterilized.
Health and Safety; Sociology
Dist - PBS **Prod** - WNEDTV

Sterilization by Laparoscopy - General Anesthesia
U-matic / VHS
Color (SPANISH)
Presents a woman's experience before, during and after undergoing sterilization by laparoscopy using a general anesthetic.
Foreign Language; Health and Safety; Sociology
Dist - MIFE **Prod** - MIFE

Sterilization by Laparoscopy - Local Anesthesia
U-matic / VHS
Color (ARABIC SPANISH)
Presents the sterilization procedure by laparoscopy using a local anesthesia.
Health and Safety; Sociology
Dist - MIFE **Prod** - MIFE

Sterilization by minilaparotomy 11 MIN
VHS
Color (G)
$250.00 purchase _ #OB - 96
Presents minilaparotomy as a safe but permanent method of sterilzation. Discusses both postpartum and interval sterilization and illustrates how the fallopian tubes are blocked to prevent conception. Tells patients what to expect before, during and after surgery. Briefly explains risks.
Health and Safety
Dist - MIFE **Prod** - MIFE

Sterilization monitoring series
Describes sterilization monitoring with emphasis on chemical and biological monitoring, and how to keep sterilization records.
Sterilization monitoring series 35 MIN
Dist - MMAMC **Prod** - MMAMC

Ste ilization of the Female 23 MIN
16mm
B&W (H C A)
Presents various aspects of the sterilization of the female explaining on which individuals it could be performed, how the operation should be done and what post - operative care should be taken.
Health and Safety
Dist - NEDINF **Prod** - INDIA

Sterilization Problems and Techniques 29 MIN
16mm
Color
LC 74-706255
Discusses various aspects of sterilization in hospital practice.
Health and Safety
Dist - USNAC **Prod** - USPHS 1963

Sterilization Record Keeping 6 MIN
U-matic
Color (PRO)
Illustrates the hospital's need for sterilization records. Outlines components of a complete record keeping program and discusses their proper use. Depicts ways of coding information on load record labels and gives suggested applications for these labels. Illustrates completion of a load record form.
Health and Safety
Dist - MMAMC **Prod** - MMAMC

Sterilizing Oral Surgery Instruments 9 MIN
U-matic
Oral Surgery Clinic Routine Series
Color

LC 79-706762
Demonstrates a step - by - step procedure for sterilizing oral surgery instruments, explaining the importance of each step.
Health and Safety; Science
Dist - USNAC **Prod** - MUSC 1978

A Sterling Education of Craftsmanship 11 MIN
16mm
Color
LC 81-700436
Show the features of a Singer 16mm projector and emphasizes the quality of Singer Education Systems.
Education
Dist - SVE **Prod** - SVE 1981

Sterlization 10 MIN
U-matic
Medical - Legal Issues - Observations Series
(A)
Deals with pertinent medical and legal issues in today's complex world of medicine. Co - produced by the Alberta Law Foundation.
Health and Safety; Sociology
Dist - ACCESS **Prod** - ACCESS 1984

Sterlization - the Mentally Handicapped 10 MIN
U-matic
Medical - Legal Issues - Observations Series
(A)
Deals with pertinent medical and legal issues in today's complex world of medicine. Co - produced by the Alberta Law Foundation.
Health and Safety; Sociology
Dist - ACCESS **Prod** - ACCESS 1984

The Stern - Gerlach Experiment 26 MIN
16mm
College Physics Film Program Series
B&W
LC FIA68-1443
Illustrates the Stern - gerlach experiment which demonstrates that a well collimated beam of cesium atoms is split into two distinct beams when it passes through a non - uniform magnetic field. Compares this result with what might be expected if different types of atoms and a uniform magnetic field were tested.
Science - Physical
Dist - MLA **Prod** - EDS 1967

Steroid alert 20 MIN
U-matic / 16mm / VHS
Color (J H C G)
$545.00, $415.00, $385.00 purchase _ #A570; LC 90-705965
Explains the chemical composition of steroids, how they affect human physiology and how they have been used and abused.
Health and Safety; Physical Education and Recreation; Psychology
Dist - BARR **Prod** - BARR 1989

The Steroid Trap - Turning Winners into Losers 37 MIN
VHS
Color (J H)
Investigates the question of who uses steroids and why. Explains how steroids work, and describes proven and suggested adverse effects associated with taking these drugs.
Guidance and Counseling; Health and Safety; Physical Education and Recreation; Psychology
Dist - GA **Prod** - GA 1989
CAMV

Steroids and Sports 19 MIN
VHS / 16mm
Color (C PRO)
$149.00, $249.00 purchase _ #AD - 1372
Examines how the increasing use of steroids to improve athletic performance is worrying physicians, trainers, officials, and families of athletes. Discusses the risks of cancer, heart disease, and infertility. Features a female athlete who experienced significant effects when she stopped taking steroids. Also features a child who was given growth hormone, and an endocrinologist who offers guidelines on the medical indications for administering hormones.
Physical Education and Recreation; Psychology
Dist - FOTH **Prod** - FOTH 1990

Steroids - Crossing the Line 54 MIN
VHS / 16mm
Color (C PRO)
$149.00, $249.00 purchase _ #AD - 1986
Presents an Olympic medalist determined to win at all costs who crossed the line from honest competition to using anabolic steroids. Offers a straightforward description of the athletic scene and the prevalence of drug abuse. Also presents the testimony of gold medalists Al Oerter and Carl Lewis who describe the scope of the problem.
Physical Education and Recreation; Psychology
Dist - FOTH **Prod** - FOTH 1990

Steroids - Dream drug or nightmare 18 MIN
VHS / U-matic
Color (J H)
$295.00, $345.00 purchase, $50.00 rental
Offers an overview of steroids and their potential effect on the body. Uses student narrators, former steroid users and detailed explanations to warn students of the dangers of this drug.
Physical Education and Recreation; Psychology
Dist - NDIM **Prod** - ALLMED 1990

Steroids - Short Cut to make Believe Muscles 30 MIN
VHS
(J H C)
$125.00 purchase _ #CT400V
Examines steroids and why they are used. Describes the harmful effects of steroids and how to reject peer pressure. Presents world body building champions who offer a drug free body building program and nutrition program.
Health and Safety; Physical Education and Recreation
Dist - CAMV **Prod** - CAMV

Steroids - shortcut to make - believe muscles 35 MIN
VHS
Color (I J H C A)
$145.00 purchase _ #2277 - SK
Takes an in - depth look at steroids. Shows that although steroids have legitimate medical uses, they are more often abused to build muscle. Covers the medical hazards of steroid abuse, and demonstrates that steroid - built muscles will go away when the drug is stopped. Stresses the idea that natural, drug - free bodybuilding can achieve excellent results. Produced by Creative Media Group, Inc. Includes facilitator's guide.
Guidance and Counseling; Psychology; Sociology
Dist - SUNCOM

Steroids - the hormonal time bomb 24 MIN
VHS / U-matic
Color (G)
$295.00 purchase _ #7480
Features a sports medicine doctor who explains the dangers of steroid use on both the physical and psychological well - being of the user. Shows how steroids affect hormonal levels and cause heart, liver and kidney problems and weaken the immune system. Discusses the dangerous effects of steroids on the brain.
Guidance and Counseling; Health and Safety; Physical Education and Recreation; Psychology; Sociology
Dist - VISIVI **Prod** - VISIVI 1991

Stethoscope 15 MIN
U-matic
Instruments of Physical Assessment Series
Color (PRO)
LC 80-707627
Shows the wide variety of stethoscopes and explains each part of the instrument. Demonstrates correct usage and storage.
Health and Safety
Dist - LIP **Prod** - SUNYSB 1980

Steve Addiss and Bill Crofut with Phan Duy 52 MIN
U-matic / VHS
Rainbow quest series
Color
Explores the Vietnamese musical tradition. Features Steve Addiss and Bill Crofut who have traveled in the Far East and Vietnamese musician Phan Duy.
Fine Arts
Dist - NORROS **Prod** - SEEGER

Steve Alford's 50 - minute all - American workout 36 MIN
VHS
Color (G)
$39.95 purchase _ #AWP100V
Features former Indiana basketball star Steve Alford and his father Sam with a workout program for improving basketball players' skills. Uses simple props - such as a chair and broomstick - and stresses that quality of time spent in the gym is more important than quantity.
Physical Education and Recreation
Dist - CAMV **Prod** - CAMV 1987

Steve and Kathy and Al 15 MIN
U-matic / VHS
Other families, other friends series; Blue module; Maine
Color (P)
Features the Thibodeau family of Five Islands, Maine.
Geography - United States; Social Science
Dist - AITECH **Prod** - WVIZTV 1971

Steve Benson - 3 - 10 - 83
VHS / Cassette
Poetry Center reading series
Color (G)
$15.00, $45.00 purchase _ #528 - 448
Features the poet at the Poetry Center, San Francisco State University, reading from his work entitled Danger.
Literature and Drama
Dist - POETRY **Prod** - POETRY 1983

Steve Charging Eagle
VHS
Color (G)
$350.00 purchase, $30.00 rental
Profiles Steve Charging Eagle from Red Scaffold, South Dakota. Reveals a quiet man, proud that he was raised here and 'born to the saddle,' proud that his sons have learned his skills. Introduces Steve's wife, Lorraine.
Biography; History - United States; Social Science
Dist - ABBEY **Prod** - CALUME

Steve Fagin - Virtual Play, the Double Direct Monkey Wrench in Black's Machinery 80 MIN
VHS / U-matic
Color
Combines psychoanalytic theories, biographical snippets, Syberbergian expositions and calculated Child's play.
Fine Arts
Dist - ARTINC **Prod** - ARTINC

Steve Garvey's hitting system 45 MIN
VHS
Color (G)
$29.95 purchase _ #KA705V
Features former major leaguer Steve Garvey in a comprehensive guide to hitting a baseball or softball. Covers subjects including selecting an appropriate bat, establishing a good grip, hitting positions, bunting, and more.
Physical Education and Recreation
Dist - CAMV **Prod** - CAMV 1987

Steve McQueen - man on the edge 60 MIN
VHS
Color (H C T A)
$39.95 purchase _ #S01333
Profiles actor Steve McQueen. Features clips from many of his films, as well as home movies and interviews with his first wife and their children.
Biography; Fine Arts; History - United States
Dist - UILL

Steven Curtis Chapman 60 MIN
VHS
Front row concert video series
Color (G R)
$14.95 purchase _ #VCV3107
Features the music of contemporary Christian artist Steven Curtis Chapman. Presented in an acoustic format.
Fine Arts; Guidance and Counseling; Literature and Drama; Religion and Philosophy
Dist - GF

Steven Gilmartin - 11 - 10 - 88
VHS / Cassette
Poetry Center reading series
Color (G)
$15.00, $45.00 purchase, $15.00 rental _ #831 - 651
Features the writer reading from his works at the Poetry Center, San Francisco State University, with an introduction by Robert Gluck.
Literature and Drama
Dist - POETRY **Prod** - POETRY 1988

Steven Weinberg 30 MIN
VHS
World of ideas with Bill Moyers - Season I - series
Color (G)
$39.95 purchase _ #BMWI - 110
Interviews physics and astronomy professor Steven Weinberg. Discusses modern developments in physics and technology, with particular emphasis to defense - related matters such as nuclear weapons and the Strategic Defense Initiative. Offers Weinberg's views that these projects, along with the super collider, must be viewed objectively. Hosted by Bill Moyers.
Industrial and Technical Education; Science; Science - Physical
Dist - PBS

Stevengraphs 30 MIN
U-matic
Antiques series
Color
Fine Arts
Dist - PBS **Prod** - NHMNET

Stevenson Palfi - piano players rarely ever play together 76 MIN
U-matic / VHS

Color
Documents three generations of New Orleans pianists who strongly influenced each other's music.
Fine Arts
Dist - ARTINC **Prod** - ARTINC

Stevenson's travels 100 MIN
VHS
Omnibus series
Color (A)
PdS99 purchase
Created during the centenary of the death of Robert Louis Stevenson, the program tells the story of his life and travels. Describes how he was dogged by ill health and how he travelled not only to satisfy his curiosity, but also to find a climate that would ease his tuberculosis. In two parts - the first reviews his life up to his marriage to Fanny Osbourne; the second covers the years during which his most enduring literary works were written.
Literature and Drama
Dist - BBCENE

Stevie and the Dinosaurs 30 MIN
U-matic
Educating the Special Child Series
Color (PRO)
Examines the process of educational assessment of special children and the cooperative efforts of parents and teacher to develop a program for a bright child who has trouble concentrating.
Education; Psychology
Dist - TVOTAR **Prod** - TVOTAR 1985

Stew Leonard's 30 MIN
VHS / 16mm
Growing a Business Series
(H C)
$99.95 each, $1,295.00 series
Displays the original and very effective business practices of Stew Leonard's, an enormous market in Connecticut.
Business and Economics
Dist - AMBROS **Prod** - AMBROS 1988

Stew Leonard's - creating the customer's dream 59 MIN
VHS / U-matic
Color (H C COR)
Features Stew Leonard's in Connecticut, a very successful dairy farm and market. Reveals the store's effective business practices, focusing on managerial teamwork, stocking systems, supplier rapport, leadership and customer service. Interviews Stew Leonard, hosted by Tom Peters.
Business and Economics; Social Science
Dist - VPHI **Prod** - VPHI 1989
FI
UTM

Stewardship 15 MIN
VHS / 16mm
Forever Wild Series
Color (I)
$125.00 purchase, $25.00 rental
Explores the constant challenge of managing wilderness in a way that satisfies the philosophies, needs and goals of a diverse society.
Agriculture; Geography - United States; Science - Natural
Dist - AITECH **Prod** - WCFETV 1985

Stewardship of Abilities 15 MIN
16mm
Discussion Series
B&W (H C A)
LC 72-701676
Presents an important personal challenge for adults and young alike by exploring questions such as - are we making proper use of God - given abilities, are we living at our fullest for him, what can we do personally to spread the Gospel.
Religion and Philosophy
Dist - CPH **Prod** - CPH 1963

Stewing - simmering 5 MIN
8mm cartridge / 16mm
Modern basics of classical cooking series; Lesson 15
Color (G)
#MB15
Demonstrates the basic principles of stewing and simmering with special emphasis on the appearance and texture of the prepared foods after each process. Part of a series developed in cooperation with the Swiss Association of Restauranteurs and Hoteliers to train foodservice employees. Includes five instructor's handbooks, a textbook by Eugene Pauli, 20 sets of student tests and 20 sets of student information sheets.
Home Economics; Industrial and Technical Education
Dist - CONPRO **Prod** - CONPRO

Stick down, head up
VHS
Color (J H C G)
Presents a skating skills video produced by Nancy Burggraf, who has coached high school hockey teams in North Dakota and the Fighting Sioux of the University of North Dakota.
Physical Education and Recreation
Dist - TEAMM

Stick metal arc welding - I 42 MIN
VHS
Metal arc welding series
Color (G IND)
$89.95 purchase _ #6 - 040 - 123P
Examines in - depth safety, pre - operational inspection of equipment and proper clothing. Provides step - by - step procedure for the setup and adjustment for an AC - DC, a rectifier AC, and a straight AC welder. Presents closeup footage of nine different welds - stringer, lap, butt, T - weld - performed in a flat position. Uses various techniques to demonstrate the welds, straight, tight, circular, horseshoe, and up and back method. Discusses several types of electrodes and their uses. Part one of two parts on stick metal arc welding. Part of a series on metal arc welding.
Health and Safety; Industrial and Technical Education; Psychology
Dist - VEP **Prod** - VEP

Stick metal arc welding - II 25 MIN
VHS
Metal arc welding series
Color (G IND)
$89.95 purchase _ #6 - 040 - 124P
Features nine welds, including lap, stringer, butt and T - weld, performed in overhead, vertical and horizontal positions. Accompanies each weld with expert narrative followed by an evaluation of each weld. Features two methods of weld testing - guided bend tester and nick break. Part two of two parts on stick metal arc welding. Part of a series on metal arc welding.
Health and Safety; Industrial and Technical Education; Psychology
Dist - VEP **Prod** - VEP

Stick - Slip 43 MIN
VHS / U-matic
Tribology 1 - Friction, Wear, and Lubrication Series
Color
Discusses the relaxation and harmonic forms of frictional oscillations and how they arise. Teaches conditions for stick - slip and their relation to material properties.
Industrial and Technical Education
Dist - MIOT **Prod** - MIOT

The Stick that Helped 15 MIN
U-matic
Two Plus You - Math Patrol One Series
Color (K P)
Presents the mathematical concepts of comparison and estimation of length and the need for a standard unit of length.
Education; Mathematics
Dist - TVOTAR **Prod** - TVOTAR 1976

Stickhandling 6 MIN
U-matic / VHS / 16mm
How to play hockey series; No 2
B&W (J H C)
Illustrates the correct method of holding and manipulating the stick to control the hockey puck.
Physical Education and Recreation
Dist - IFB **Prod** - CRAF 1956

Stickhandling
VHS
N C A A instructional video series
Color (H C A)
$39.95 purchase _ #KAR1501V
Presents the first of a three - part series on offensive ice hockey. Focuses on stickhandling skills.
Physical Education and Recreation
Dist - CAMV **Prod** - NCAAF

Sticking to your word 8 MIN
VHS / U-matic
Life's little lessons - self - esteem 4 - 6 series; No 52
Color (I)
$129.00, $99.00 purchase _ #V681
Looks at Ricky Craigton who needed a summer job badly and was lucky to get one. Reveals that after he'd given his word and committed to his job, he got a better offer, so he left. After following this practice for quite some time, word got around and Ricky lost all the jobs he could have had. Part of a 65 - part series on self - esteem.
Guidance and Counseling; Psychology
Dist - BARR **Prod** - CEPRO 1992

Sticks 30 MIN
U-matic
Media and Methods of the Artist Series
Color (H C A)
Discusses traditional drawing materials such as charcoal, crayons and chalk.
Fine Arts
Dist - TVOTAR **Prod** - TVOTAR 1971

Sticks and Stones 14 MIN
16mm
Fingermouse, Yoffy and Friends Series
Color (K P I)
LC 73-700433
Shows how Yoffy sends Fingermouse to the beach to collect a variety of stones and then how Enoch helps him by building a cart out of sticks for carrying them.
Guidance and Counseling; Literature and Drama
Dist - VEDO **Prod** - BBCTV 1972

Sticks and Stones will Build a House 30 MIN
Videoreel / VT2
Indian Arts Series
Color
Traces the development of the Indian as a builder.
Social Science
Dist - PBS **Prod** - KUEDTV

Sticks on the Move 6 MIN
16mm
Color
Presents Elizabeth Ross and Pooh Kage's film entry selected from the 1985 Whitney Biennial Film and Video Exhibition.
Fine Arts
Dist - AFA **Prod** - AFA 1986

Sticks, stones, and stereotypes - Palos, piedras, y estereotypos 26 MIN
VHS
Color (J H I) (ENGLISH & SPANISH)
$325.00 purchase _ #B022 - V8
Refutes the myth that name - calling is harmless. Reveals that, from 'fatty' or 'four - eyes' to racial slurs, everyone has felt the sting of a verbal jab. Focuses on the reasons why young people participate in name - calling and what they can do to stop it. Models communication skills, problem solving, and the power of an ally in response to name calling incidents. Includes one bilingual videotape, an 89 - page curriculum guide in English, and a 95 - page guide in Spanish.
Guidance and Counseling; Psychology; Social Science; Sociology
Dist - ETRASS **Prod** - ETRASS

Sticky My Fingers, Fleet My Feet 23 MIN
16mm
Color
LC 74-707384
Shows a group of Madison Avenue touch football buffs who are beaten by a teenage boy and begin to feel their age.
Physical Education and Recreation; Social Science; Sociology
Dist - TIMLIF **Prod** - AMERFI 1970

Stigma 20 MIN
U-matic / VHS / 16mm
B&W (C A)
Portrays a young woman who suffers a mental breakdown, recovers fully in a hospital and returns to her former environment where she is virtually ostracized.
Psychology; Sociology
Dist - IFB **Prod** - NFBC 1958

Stigmata 27 MIN
VHS
Color (G)
$60.00 rental, $250.00 purchase
Looks at women who are engaged in unusual forms of body modification such as tattooing, cutting, piercing and branding. Suggests that these activities are no more radical than cosmetic surgery and these women are transforming their bodies against conventional stereotypes of femininity rather than conforming to them. Includes some extremely explicit footage. Produced by Leslie Asako Gladsjo.
Fine Arts; Sociology
Dist - WMEN

The Still and empty center 30 MIN
U-matic / VHS
Art of being human series; Module 7
Color (C)
History - World; Literature and Drama; Religion and Philosophy
Dist - MDCC **Prod** - MDCC

Still Going Places 40 MIN
16mm
B&W
Shows how patients who have incurred cardiovascular accidents can be physically, socially and economically rehabilitated, with the help of all of the medical disciplines.
Health and Safety
Dist - PFI **Prod** - STONEY 1955

Still Got Life to Go 30 MIN
16mm
Color

LC 74-715455
Shows inmates, prison officials and parole officers in Oklahoma City behind prison walls and in streets and alleys as they point out some of the causes of recidivism in the Oklahoma correctional system and the need for a meaningful rehabilitation program for first offenders.
Psychology; Sociology
Dist - WKYTV **Prod** - WKYTV 1971

Still in our hearts - Dopoki w sercach Naszych
VHS
Color; B&W (G A) (POLISH)
$29.95 purchase _ #V108
Depicts Polish history as based on documents and memorabilia accumulated by the Polish Institute and Museum in London.
Fine Arts; History - World
Dist - POLART

Still Killing Us Softly - Advertising's Image of Women 30 MIN
U-matic
(H C A)
$550.00 purchase, $106.00 rental one week
Investigates the advertising industry's continuing assault on the self images of women, men and children. Discusses how advertising is a 100 billion dollar - a - year industry that feeds on the fears and insecurities of consumers. Explores the relationship of media images to actual societal problems such as the imposition of traditional gender roles, discrimination against women, sexual abuse of children, rape, eating disorders, and much more. Uses examples of ads from many contexts. Based on the research of Jean Kilbourne, EdD.
Sociology
Dist - CMBRD **Prod** - CMBRD 1979

Still life 60 MIN
VHS
Learning to paint with Carolyn Berry series
Color (H G)
$49.95 purchase
Offers an easy to follow, step - by - step method for creating a finished painting or drawing from a blank canvas. Features part of an eight - part series covering everything from arranging or selecting your subjects to an explanation of the material needed and the specific techniques to be applied. Professional art instructor Carolyn Berry designed this series for students, hobbyists, amateur painters and professionals seeking new tips. Produced by Artists Video and directed by Christian Surette; 1991 - 1994. Video jackets available.
Fine Arts
Dist - CNEMAG

Still Life 20 MIN
VHS / U-matic
Color
Explores the future territory of drama through interplay of language, music, visuals and structure.
Fine Arts; Literature and Drama
Dist - KITCHN **Prod** - KITCHN

Still life 2 MIN
16mm
Color (G)
$6.00 rental
Features a production from Morning Star.
Fine Arts
Dist - CANCIN **Prod** - BAILB 1966

Still life 3 MIN
16mm
Color (G)
$25.00 rental
Meditates on the American rustic in which various objects are presented in unnatural colors and unusual spatial arrangements. Emphasizes the illusion of movement while exploring film grain and graphic nature. Produced by Bette Gordon.
Fine Arts; Sociology
Dist - CANCIN

Still Life 29 MIN
U-matic
Magic of Oil Painting Series
Color
Fine Arts
Dist - PBS **Prod** - KOCETV

Still Life and Landscape - Basic Simple Shapes 20 MIN
U-matic
Basic Drawing Series
Color (J H C)
LC 79-706381
Shows how to draw basic simple shapes.
Fine Arts
Dist - SRA **Prod** - SRA 1979

Still Life and Landscape - Complex Basic Shapes, Still Life 20 MIN
U-matic
Basic Drawing Series
Color (J H C)
LC 79-706382
Shows how to draw complex basic shapes and still life.
Fine Arts
Dist - SRA **Prod** - SRA 1979

Still Life and Landscape - Irregular Shapes, Still Life 20 MIN
U-matic
Basic Drawing Series
Color (J H C)
LC 79-706383
Shows how to draw irregular shapes and still life.
Fine Arts
Dist - SRA **Prod** - SRA 1979

Still Life and Landscape - Landscape with Perspective 20 MIN
U-matic
Basic Drawing Series
Color (J H C)
LC 79-706387
Shows how to draw a landscape with perspective.
Fine Arts
Dist - SRA **Prod** - SRA 1979

Still Life and Landscape - Light and Shade, Basic Form, Still Life 20 MIN
U-matic
Basic Drawing Series
Color (J H C)
LC 79-706384
Shows how to draw light and shade, basic form, and still life.
Fine Arts
Dist - SRA **Prod** - SRA 1979

Still Life and Landscape - Light and Shade, Drapery Problems 20 MIN
U-matic
Basic Drawing Series
Color (J H C)
LC 79-706385
Shows how to draw light and shade, and discusses drapery problems.
Fine Arts
Dist - SRA **Prod** - SRA 1979

Still Life and Landscape - Perspective, Still Life, One and Two Point 20 MIN
U-matic
Basic Drawing Series
Color (J H C)
LC 79-706386
Demonstrates how to draw one - and two - point perspective and still life.
Fine Arts
Dist - SRA **Prod** - SRA 1979

Still Life and Landscape - Review Complex Detail Drawings 20 MIN
U-matic
Basic Drawing Series
Color (J H C)
LC 79-706388
Presents a review of complex detail drawings.
Fine Arts
Dist - SRA **Prod** - SRA 1979

Still life for woodpecker 28 MIN
VHS / 16mm
Color (I J H C G)
$250.00, $550.00 purchase, $50.00 rental
Incorporates an ancient native myth into the study of forest ecology. Shows how scientists are using pileated woodpeckers as indicator species to judge the health of a forest. Comes with teacher's guide. Produced by Francis Paynter.
Fine Arts; Science - Natural
Dist - BULFRG

Still life no 1 - Cherries 7 MIN
16mm
Color (G)
$10.00 rental
Meditates on a close - up of Bing cherries being pitted. Notes that on first screening it should be seen at sound speed, thereafter at either sound or silent.
Fine Arts
Dist - CANCIN **Prod** - RAYHER 1978

A Still life of postcards 8 MIN
16mm
Color; B&W (G A)
$15.00 rental
Presents the work of filmmaker Ines Sommer. Takes femininity as a series of frozen images to be eviscerated and developed along other lines, other images.
Fine Arts; Industrial and Technical Education; Sociology
Dist - PARART **Prod** - CANCIN 1988

Still - life sketches 29 MIN
U-matic
Sketching techniques series; Lesson 13
Color (C A)
Explains 'still life' as a reference. Shows steps used in drawing a still life. Emphasizes the importance of being able to draw independently from the still life by sketching several different kinds of a particular object.
Fine Arts
Dist - CDTEL **Prod** - COAST

Still life with Barbie 24 MIN
16mm
Color (G)
$40.00 rental
Looks at the nature of myth through the ritual of doll - playing and the conflicts that inevitably arise when childhood myth meets adult reality. Addresses the plastic - world values of Barbie and friends. A Barbara Klutinis produciton.
Fine Arts; Sociology
Dist - CANCIN

Still life with woman and four objects 4 MIN
16mm
B&W (G)
$10.00 rental
Portrays a study of a woman's daily routines and thoughts via an exploration of her as a character. Interweaves threads of history and fiction while paying tribute to a real woman - Emma Goldman. A Lynne Sachs production.
Fine Arts; Sociology
Dist - CANCIN

Still lives 18 MIN
16mm
Color (G)
$50.00 rental
Gathers images of an Arlington, Texas shopping plaza at the rate of one frame per hour for 24 hours each day from September 23, 1973 to September 22, 1974. Transposes meteorological fluctutations and solar and axil planet revolutions as well as human cycles from slow daily change into rapid visual images. Film was shot through a portal in a church. Produced by Louis Hock.
Fine Arts
Dist - CANCIN

Still looking 28 MIN
16mm / VHS
Color (H C G)
$560.00, $195.00 purchase, $45.00 rental _ #11375, #37796
Documents the recent work of Janet Adler, movement therapist profiled in Looking for Me, 1970. Shows her working with 8 women through a practice called Authentic Movement, which is concerned with the relationship between moving and witnessing, assuming complete trust in the body's capacity to remember and to tell the truth. Produced by Virginia Bartlett and Norris Brock.
Fine Arts; Psychology; Sociology
Dist - UCEMC

Still more signs you already know 30 MIN
VHS / U-matic
Say it with sign series; Pt 3
Color (H C A) (AMERICAN SIGN)
Presents Lawrence Solow and Sharon Neumann Solow introducing American Sign Language used by the hearing - impaired. Emphasizes signs that resemble gestures already used by many people in spoken conversation.
Education
Dist - FI **Prod** - KNBCTV 1982

Still point 8 MIN
VHS
B&W; Color (G)
$35.00 rental, $50.00 purchase
Whirls around a point of centeredness as four screens of home and homelessness, travel and weather, architecture and sports signify the constant movement and haste of late twentieth century life. Refers to T S Eliot's point of quiet when he wrote 'At the still point of the turning world, that's where the dance is.'
Fine Arts
Dist - CANCIN **Prod** - BARHAM 1989

Still Sane 60 MIN
U-matic
Color (C)
$500.00 purchase, $50.00, $80.00 rental
Focuses on a woman forced to enter a mental hospital after she expressed her homosexuality and who survived to express her feelings through art. Examines the ceramic art exhibit 'Still Sane' by Sheila Gilhooly and Persimmon Blackbridge. Produced by Brenda Ingratta and Linda Patriasz.
Health and Safety; Psychology; Sociology
Dist - WMENIF

Still separate, still unequal - 228 30 MIN
U-matic
Currents - 1985 - 86 season series; 228
Color (A)
Focuses on the resegregation that has taken place in this society despite twenty years of civil rights laws.
History - United States; Social Science
Dist - PBS **Prod** - WNETTV 1985

Still Waters 59 MIN
U-matic / VHS / 16mm
Nova Series
Color (H C A)
LC 80-700979
Uses specially developed photographic techniques to capture animal life in and around a fresh water pond over a period of a year. Shows microscopic life, insects, amphibians, reptiles, fish, birds and mammals.
Science - Natural
Dist - TIMLIF **Prod** - WGBHTV 1978

Stillbirth 20 MIN
U-matic
Color (H C A)
Offers a portrait of a woman who was the mother of a stillborn child.
Guidance and Counseling; Health and Safety; Sociology
Dist - GPN **Prod** - CHERIO 1979

Stillbirth, Miscarriage, and Beyond - Healing through Shared Experience 29 MIN
16mm / U-matic / VHS
Color (A)
Examines the experience of miscarriage and stillbirth. Intends to help viewers who have experienced either to express their feelings in a therapeutic manner. Emphasizes the opportunity for the professional audience to gain insight.
Health and Safety; Psychology; Sociology
Dist - FAIRGH **Prod** - FAIRGH

Stillwater Runs Deep 24 MIN
U-matic / VHS
Color
Shows how Stillwater Prison has begun a swing toward increased security measures and a decrease in treatment programs after two decades of liberal prison reform.
Sociology
Dist - WCCOTV **Prod** - WCCOTV 1977

The Stillwell Road 51 MIN
U-matic / VHS / 16mm
Campaign Reports Series
B&W
Presents a documentary record of the construction of a supply road through the mountains and jungles of Burma in World War II. Issued in 1949 as a motion picture.
History - United States; History - World
Dist - USNAC **Prod** - USWD 1979

Stillwell Road 49 MIN
U-matic / VHS
B&W
Documents the Signal Corps activity on the China - Burma front, scene of one of the great victories of World War II.
History - World
Dist - IHF **Prod** - IHF

Stilt Dancers of Long Bow Village 27 MIN
16mm / U-matic / VHS
Color (A)
LC 80-701487
Documents a stilt - dancing festival in rural China.
Geography - World
Dist - FI **Prod** - GORDR 1980

Stilts 10 MIN
U-matic
Get it together series
Color (P I)
Teaches children how to make stilts from wood.
Fine Arts
Dist - TVOTAR **Prod** - TVOTAR 1978

Stimulants
VHS
Substance abuse video library series
Color (T A PRO)
$125.00 purchase _ #AH45142
Presents information on the abuse of stimulants. Details the history of stimulants, how they are abused, short - term physical and psychological effects, dependency and overdose risks, and treatment. Developed by Brock Morris and Kevin Scheel.
Guidance and Counseling; Health and Safety; Psychology; Sociology
Dist - HTHED **Prod** - HTHED

Stimulants 10 MIN
16mm / U-matic / VHS
Drug Information Series
Color
Discusses the characteristics of stimulants. Identifies the signs of use and abuse, the pharmacological and behavioral effects, and the short - and long - term dangers.
Health and Safety
Dist - CORF **Prod** - MITCHG 1982

Stimulation and Modeling Techniques 54 MIN
U-matic / VHS
Systems Engineering and Systems Management Series
Color
Presents a review of simulation and modeling techniques (useful for digital, analog and hybrid computers). Illustrates the applicability of simulation and modeling.
Industrial and Technical Education
Dist - MIOT **Prod** - MIOT

Stimuli Releasing Sexual Behavior of Domestic Turkeys 19 MIN
16mm
Color (C)
Shows that the mating activity of turkeys is a stereotyped pattern of behavior, in which each responds to successive cues from its mate. Points out that in normal mating behavior, the male responds with a strutting display to the presence of females, the female crouches, male mounts, female elevates head, male makes cloacal contact, female extrudes oviduct, male inseminates. Through examples, demonstrates that the head is more important than the body in eliciting sexual behavior.
Psychology
Dist - PSUPCR **Prod** - PSUPCR 1958

Stimuli which Reduce Turnover 29 MIN
16mm
Controlling Turnover and Absenteeism Series
B&W
LC 76-703321
Business and Economics; Psychology
Dist - EDSD **Prod** - EDSD

Stimulus Series
The Hunger Gap 38 MIN
Dist - LCA

The Sting 129 MIN
16mm
Color
Describes a colossal con game staged by two grifters in 1930's Chicago. Stars Paul Newman and Robert Redford.
Fine Arts
Dist - TWYMAN **Prod** - UPCI 1973

Sting - Preserving the Rainforest 28 MIN
U-matic / VHS
Color (C)
$249.00, $149.00 purchase _ #AD - 2204
Adapts a Phil Donahue program starring Sting, English rock superstar. Reveals that Sting's main concern is with preserving the dying Amazon rainforest, vital to preserving the entire world's wellbeing. Includes Raoni and Megaron, two Amazon chieftains, executives of the Rainforest Foundation and the Smithsonian.
Fine Arts; Geography - World; Science - Natural
Dist - FOTH **Prod** - FOTH

The Stingiest Man in Town 60 MIN
U-matic / VHS
Color (K P I)
Presents an animated story.
Fine Arts
Dist - ABCLR **Prod** - ABCLR

Stinging - celled animals - coelenterates 17 MIN
16mm / U-matic / VHS
Biology - Spanish series; Unit 7 - animal classification and physiology
Color (H) (SPANISH)
Describes the phylum Coelenterata, including fresh and salt water examples. Shows the typical coelenterate body plan and provides examples of three classes of coelenterates.
Science - Natural
Dist - EBEC **Prod** - EBEC

Stinkybutt 4 MIN
16mm
B&W (G)
$15.00 rental
Presents a psychological comedy and a bizarre satire on works like Polanski's Repulsion.
Fine Arts; Literature and Drama
Dist - CANCIN **Prod** - MCDOWE 1974

The Stirling Engine Brought Up to Date 18 MIN
U-matic / VHS / 16mm
Color (H C A)
LC 70-704598
Explains that a highly efficient engine has been developed from the original hot - air engine invented by Robert Stirling. Illustrates the function of cylinder, piston and the displacer.
Industrial and Technical Education; Science - Physical
Dist - MGHT **Prod** - PHILIS 1968

A Stitch in Time 59 MIN
VHS / 16mm
Color (G)
$70.00 rental _ #STTI - 000
Examines emergency care in the case of an automobile accident.
Health and Safety
Dist - PBS **Prod** - WITFTV

Stitchery 14 MIN
16mm / U-matic / VHS
Rediscovery - art media - French series
Color (I)
LC 75-704578
Encompasses the techniques of embroidery, needlepoint and applique and demonstrates the basic procedures involved in each of these activities.
Fine Arts; Home Economics
Dist - AIMS **Prod** - ACI 1969

Stitchery 14 MIN
VHS
Rediscovery art media series
Color
$69.95 purchase _ #4430
Encourages the exploration of yarn and fabric as a form of artistic expression.
Fine Arts
Dist - AIMS **Prod** - AIMS
ACI

Stitchery 14 MIN
U-matic / VHS / 16mm
Rediscovery - art media - Spanish series
Color (I) (SPANISH)
LC 75-704578
Encompasses the techniques of embroidery, needlepoint and applique and demonstrates the basic procedures involved in each of these activities.
Fine Arts; Home Economics
Dist - AIMS **Prod** - ACI 1969

Stochastic Matrices 30 MIN
U-matic
Introduction to Mathematics Series
Color (C)
Mathematics
Dist - MDCPB **Prod** - MDCPB

Stock footage and news events
VHS / 16mm
Color; B&W (G)
Presents a collection of stock footage containing original film and video images dating from 1896 to the present. Includes Pathe Newsreels and Paramount News, exclusive representation of ABC News with footage dating from 1963 to the present.
Fine Arts
Dist - GRINBE **Prod** - GRINBE

The Stock market 30 MIN
VHS
Color (G)
$29.95 purchase _ #S00558
Presents basic information on the workings of the stock market. Covers subjects including bids, price earning ratios, and how to understand stock information in newspapers.
Business and Economics
Dist - UILL

The Stock Market 28 MIN
VHS / U-matic
Personal Finance and Money Management Series
Color (C A)
Business and Economics; Civics and Political Systems
Dist - SCCON **Prod** - SCCON 1987

The Stock market 30 MIN
U-matic / VHS
Personal finance series; Lesson 17
Color (C A)
Discusses the advantages and disadvantages of stock owner - ship as a form of investing. Shows the stock market in operation. Defines several stock market terms.
Business and Economics
Dist - CDTEL **Prod** - SCCON

The Stock market
VHS
World around us series
Color (G)
$29.95 purchase _ #IV - 029
Takes a comprehensive look at the stock market, its history and terminology.
Business and Economics
Dist - INCRSE **Prod** - INCRSE

The Stock market crash of 1987 - causes and effects 18 MIN
VHS
Color (J H C A)
$57.00 purchase _ #MB - 509197 - 6
Uses the 1987 stock market crash as a case study to illustrate the workings of the American financial markets and how the marketplace reflects economic principles.
Business and Economics
Dist - SRA **Prod** - NYT 1989

The Stock market - investigate before you invest 23 MIN
VHS / U-matic
Color (H C A)
Tells the story of a young man who invests a large money gift into the stock market, to illustrate dangers and benefits of investing.
Business and Economics
Dist - NGS **Prod** - NGS

The Stock market - investigate before you invest 23 MIN
VHS / U-matic / 16mm / BETA
Color (J H G)
$101.50, $79.00 purchase _ #C50094, #C51212
Looks at the stock market. Examines what stock is and how it is traded.
Business and Economics
Dist - NGS **Prod** - NGS 1984

Stock preparation 20 MIN
BETA / VHS
Color (VOC G)
$59.00 purchase _ #QF23
Discusses how to prepare light and dark stock and how to obtain maximum flavor and nutrition in each.
Home Economics; Industrial and Technical Education
Dist - RMIBHF **Prod** - RMIBHF

Stock preparation equipment
U-matic / VHS
Papermaking series; Pulp and paper training; Module 3
Color (IND)
Includes stock chests and papers, jordans and refiners and cleaners and screens used in paper stock preparation.
Business and Economics; Industrial and Technical Education
Dist - LEIKID **Prod** - LEIKID

Stock Strategies for Individuals 25 MIN
U-matic / VHS
Your Money Matters Series
Color
Reveals ten surprising guidelines for stock buying. Discusses discount brokers, tax advantages of utilities and some little - known investment options.
Business and Economics; Social Science
Dist - FILMID **Prod** - SKOKIE

Stockhausen, the percussion, and Tristan Fry 26 MIN
U-matic / VHS / 16mm
Musical Triangle Series
Color (J)
Tells how twentieth - century composer Stockhausen is well - known for his electronic music in which the traditional percussion instrument variables of pitch, vibration, frequency and volume are controlled electronically. Features professional musician Tristan Fry demonstrating some of Stockhausen's music.
Fine Arts
Dist - MEDIAG **Prod** - THAMES 1975

Stockholm - the most, Well, Almost 22 MIN
16mm
Color (C A)
Describes the city of Stockholm, known for its perfection, neatness, urbanity and style.
Geography - World; Sociology
Dist - WSTGLC **Prod** - WSTGLC

Stocking and Location Control 60 MIN
VHS / BETA
Manufacturing Series
(IND)
Summarizes how to store received goods when they have been validated.
Business and Economics
Dist - COMSRV **Prod** - COMSRV 1986

Stocking up 28 MIN
U-matic / VHS / 16mm
Color (G)
LC 82-700649
Presents a young couple who demonstrate various methods for preserving home produce, emphasizing low energy techniques such as drying and storing food in a root cellar. Includes a demonstration of freezing and canning techniques and explains the pros and cons of each method in terms of nutrition and expense.
Home Economics
Dist - BULFRG **Prod** - RPFD 1982

The Stockmarket - a marketplace for the nation 14 MIN
16mm / VHS
Color (H C)
$305.00, $230.00 purchase, $60.00 rental
Shows how stock market trading provides for business expansion, new jobs and financing of new ideas. Uses historical footage to chronicle the growth of the market from the early 1800s to the present. Illustrates how trades are executed through floor brokers and specialists. Animated graphics show how stock exchanges throughout the nation are electronically linked and how the market place is regulated for the protection of investors.
Business and Economics
Dist - CF **Prod** - NYSE 1988

Stocks 10 MIN
U-matic / VHS
Color (VOC G)
Shows how to make, cool and store the four basic stocks, brown, white or neutral, chicken and fish.
Home Economics; Industrial and Technical Education
Dist - CULINA **Prod** - CULINA

Stocks and sauces 30 MIN
VHS
Gourmet techniques series
Color (H C G)
$19.95 purchase _ #IVN047V
Features expert chef instructors from the California Culinary Academy in San Francisco who share their secrets on stocks and sauces. Part of a three - part series on gourmet techniques.
Home Economics
Dist - CAMV

Stocks in Action 30 MIN
16mm
Color
Presents the spills and thrills of the circuit.
Physical Education and Recreation
Dist - SFI **Prod** - SFI

Stocks, sauces and gravies
VHS / 35mm strip
Food preparation series
$119.00 purchase _ #PX1145 filmstrip, $119.00 purchase _ #PX1145V
Uses demonstrations to teach how to make rich, flavorful stock. Shows the preparation of brown, white, chicken and fish stock and the use of many thickening agents.
Home Economics; Industrial and Technical Education
Dist - CAREER **Prod** - CAREER

Stocky Mariano 5 MIN
VHS / U-matic
Write on, Set 1 Series
Color (J H)
Teaches the use of strong verbs in writing.
English Language
Dist - CTI **Prod** - CTI

Stockyards - the end of an era 59 MIN
16mm
Color (H)
Traces the 100 - year history of the Chicago stockyards and the lives of the people in its neighborhood 'back of the yards.'
Agriculture; Geography - United States; History - United States
Dist - IU **Prod** - WTTWTV 1973
PBS

Stoichiometry 15 MIN
U-matic
Chemistry 101 Series
Color (C)
Gives laws which serve as the basis for the relationships between elements and their compounds.
Science; Science - Physical
Dist - UILL **Prod** - UILL 1973

Stolen Child 8 MIN
U-matic / VHS / 16mm
Color (P I)
LC 75-703305
Uses animation and puppets to tell a children's story about a girl who leaves a baby carriage unattended, joins a group of animal friends and returns to find the baby is missing.
Fine Arts
Dist - PHENIX **Prod** - KRATKY 1974

Stolen childhood series
The Best we have to give 26 MIN
Dist - ASTRSK

Stolen Children 15 MIN
VHS / U-matic
Color (H C A)
Explores the plight of children who are kidnapped by their own parents during custody battles. Documents the nine - year battle of a Canadian woman to regain custody of her two boys taken by her husband to Ireland.
Sociology
Dist - JOU **Prod** - CANBC

Stolen for love 22 MIN
VHS / U-matic
Color
Deals with the subject of children kidnapped by a parent as a result of child custody or visitation disputes. Addresses concerns about child kidnapping laws, victimized parents, psychological and sometimes physical harm to the child. Includes case studies and talks with abductors.
Civics and Political Systems; Sociology
Dist - WCCOTV **Prod** - WCCOTV

The Stolen Message 30 MIN
U-matic
Read all about it - One Series
Color (I)
Teaches reading and writing skills as it continues a story in which Chris and his friend Samantha intercept a message ordering their newspaper stopped.
Education; English Language; Literature and Drama
Dist - TVOTAR **Prod** - TVOTAR 1982

The Stolen Necklace 8 MIN
U-matic / VHS / 16mm
Children's Storybook Theater Series
Color (P I)
LC 79-713454
An adaptation of a tale from India, written and illustrated by Anne Rockwell, about a pearl necklace which is stolen from a princess by a monkey.
Geography - World; Literature and Drama
Dist - AIMS **Prod** - CLAIB 1971

Stolen Painting 11 MIN
U-matic / VHS / 16mm
Color
LC 81-700944
Features Spunky Lucius who discovers that his wife and her portrait have been kidnapped by the ruthless criminal, Dr Guard. Tells how Lucius finally succeeds in rescuing his wife, and together they flee to an amusement park. Without narration.
Fine Arts; Literature and Drama
Dist - PHENIX **Prod** - KRATKY 1979

Stolen revolution - Pt 1 60 MIN
VHS
USSR series
Color (J H G)
$250.00 purchase
Looks at the development of the communist government through archival footage. Covers the Bolshevik revolution and the rise of Stalin. Part of a series of three videos covering the rise and decline of the USSR. Videos are also available in a set.
History - World
Dist - LANDMK

Stolen watermelon 26 MIN
VHS
Color (K P I R)
$19.95 purchase _ #35 - 819 - 2020
Explores how Jerry tries to hide the fact that he opened a watermelon without permission. Emphasizes the importance of honesty and forgiveness.
Literature and Drama; Religion and Philosophy
Dist - APH **Prod** - ANDERK

The Stomach Story 15 MIN
U-matic / VHS / 16mm
Healthwise Series
Color (K P I)
Presents the Magnificent Body Model, a lifesize fanciful body replica, that conducts a tour of the human body. Features puppets representing the heart, lungs, stomach, liver and intestines. Shows how excitement, worry, over - eating, motion and germs can upset the stomach.
Health and Safety; Science - Natural
Dist - CORF **Prod** - CORF 1982

Stone Age Americans 21 MIN
U-matic / VHS / 16mm
Color (J H C)
LC 77-707287
Introduces the vanished Indians of the Mesa Verde in Colorado and presents the history of these farmer Indians by examining the cliff dwelling and artifacts discovered in them.
History - United States; Social Science; Sociology
Dist - IFB **Prod** - ABCTV 1970

The Stone and the Mouse 15 MIN
VHS / U-matic
Tales of Wesakechak Series

Color (G)
Presents Wesakechak challenging other creatures to race with him. Shows him challenging a big, round stone to a race, and how a little mouse helps Wesakechak.
Social Science; Sociology
Dist - NAMPBC **Prod** - NAMPBC 1984

The Stone carvers 28 MIN
U-matic / VHS / 16mm
Color (J A G)
Discusses ornamental stone carving. Captures the spirit of a small group of Italian American artisans who have spent their lives carving for the Washington Cathedral, a gothic monument begun in 1907 and still under construction.
Fine Arts
Dist - DIRECT **Prod** - SIFP 1985

Stone circles 10 MIN
16mm
B&W; Color (G)
$35.00 rental
Creates a film poem on the prehistoric stone cultures of Britain. Exposes dolmens and Druid rock formations including Stonehenge. Films colorful arrangements of small stones, dirt, sticks and grasses and animates them.
Fine Arts
Dist - CANCIN **Prod** - BARHAM 1983

Stone Forest 17 MIN
16mm
Color
Uses time - lapse photography to demonstrate the formation of crystals and the process by which fallen trees turn into stone.
Science - Natural; Science - Physical
Dist - USNAC **Prod** - USNPS 1974

Stone fox 15 MIN
VHS
More books from cover to cover series
Color (I G)
$25.00 purchase _ #MBCC - 105
Features Little Willy, a boy who hopes to win a dog sled race to raise money to pay back taxes on his grandfather's farm. Based on the book 'Stone Fox' by John Reynolds Gardiner.
English Language; Literature and Drama
Dist - PBS **Prod** - WETATV 1987

Stone in the River 60 MIN
16mm
Color
Features the concept of behavior control and its implications and considers the way the penal system catches and twists its participants. Uses a dramatic structure.
Civics and Political Systems; Psychology; Sociology
Dist - CCNCC **Prod** - NBCTV

Stone knapping in modern turkey 12 MIN
16mm
B&W (C)
LC 75-700200
Reveals techniques used by modern Turkish flint thieves to obtain blades from a piece of flint. Shows the method of applying direct percussion to the nucleus to strike a blade and the use of flint blades in threshing sledges by the local farmers.
Agriculture; Geography - World
Dist - PSUPCR **Prod** - PSU 1974

Stone Mountain Carving 29 MIN
16mm
B&W (I J H)
LC FIA68-3074
Presents an in - progress report on the carving of Stone Mountain in Georgia. Discusses the modern methods used by the workers, and the mathematical planning that they employ in carving the huge Confederate memorial honoring Davis, Lee and Jackson.
Fine Arts; Geography - United States
Dist - IU **Prod** - NET 1968

Stone Soup 11 MIN
U-matic / VHS / 16mm
Color; B&W (K P)
An iconographic film using the drawings from the book of the same title and narrated by the author, Marcia Brown. Relates the familiar story of soldiers who trick the reluctant villagers into feeding them.
English Language; Literature and Drama
Dist - WWS **Prod** - WWS 1955

The Stone Soup 12 MIN
U-matic / VHS
Magic Pages Series
Color (P)
Literature and Drama
Dist - AITECH **Prod** - KLVXTV 1976

Stone Symposium 30 MIN
U-matic
Color
Presents three internationally renowned sculptors discussing their art and lives - Joan Gambioli, Anna - Maria Kubach - Wilmsen and Olga Janic.
Fine Arts; Sociology
Dist - WMENIF **Prod** - WMENIF

The Stone Whistle 29 MIN
16mm
Color
Features John Forsythe starring in a story about the human need to be remembered. Deals with the religious significance of monuments and includes a visit to Vermont's famous granite quarries.
Guidance and Counseling; History - United States; Psychology
Dist - MTP **Prod** - BGA

The Stonecutter 6 MIN
U-matic / VHS / 16mm
Color (K P I J)
LC FIA66-766
Uses animation to tell an ancient Japanese tale of envy and greed - - the story of Tasaka, the stonecutter, who is granted his wishes to become a prince, the sun, a cloud and, finally, a gigantic mountain.
Literature and Drama
Dist - WWS **Prod** - MDERMG 1965

Stoned adventure 10 MIN
16mm
B&W (G)
$10.00 rental
Presents a self - portrait of the filmmaker, David McLaughlin, while recording a trip in a car.
Fine Arts; Geography - World; Literature and Drama
Dist - CANCIN

Stoned - an anti - drug film 30 MIN
16mm / VHS / U-matic
Captioned; Color (J H A)
Deals with the adolescent need for a positive self - image and friends who support it. Portrays a shy teenager who uses marijuana in order to feel popular. Edited.
Fine Arts; Guidance and Counseling; Psychology; Sociology
Dist - LCOA **Prod** - HGATE 1981

Stoned - an Anti - Drug Film 30 MIN
16mm / VHS / U-matic
Color (J H A)
LC 80-701731; 80-701730
Introduces Jack Melon, a shy teenager who turns to marijuana to become noticed by his friends and family. Shows that after a near - accident while stoned, he realizes that he must be himself.
Guidance and Counseling; Health and Safety; Psychology; Sociology
Dist - LCOA **Prod** - HGATE 1980

Stonehenge 16 MIN
16mm / U-matic / VHS
Color (I J H)
Looks at the archaeological research which has attempted to discover the significance of Stonehenge, the most celebrated megalithic structure in England. Speculates on how the stones were brought to the site and erected.
History - World; Sociology
Dist - LUF **Prod** - LUF 1980

Stonehenge 15 MIN
U-matic / VHS / 16mm
Color (J H)
Presents the latest chronology of the building of Stonehenge. Deals with the sources of the stones, probable methods of transport and erection, and the reconstruction of the stone arrangement.
History - World; Sociology
Dist - VIEWTH **Prod** - GATEEF

Stonehenge 28 MIN
U-matic / VHS
Color (C)
$249.00, $149.00 purchase _ #AD - 1361
Examines the literary roots of Stonehenge which lie in many Arthurian romances, the tales of Chaucer and the Celtic episodes of Shakespeare. Reveals that each June, some 60,000 people - geologists, witches, sun - worshipers and passersby - gather to celebrate the summer solstice.
Literature and Drama; Religion and Philosophy; Sociology
Dist - FOTH **Prod** - FOTH

Stonehenge 50 MIN
VHS
Secrets of lost empires series
Color; PAL (G)
PdS99 purchase; Not available in the United States or Canada
Chronicles the first attempt in 4000 years to recreate Stonehenge. Follows the work of modern engineers as they use practical demonstrations and debate the various possibilities. The program is interspersed with location sequences and explorations of the ancient culture as it tries to uncover some of the mysteries surrounding Stonehenge. Part one of a four - part series.
History - United States; History - World; Industrial and Technical Education
Dist - BBCENE

Stonehenge - if Only the Stones Could Speak 28 MIN
VHS / 16mm
Color (H)
$14.00 rental _ #35252
Explores the literary interest in the roots of Stonehenge, which it shares with many of the strands in the Arthurian romances, the tales of Chaucer, and the Celtic strains in Shakespeare. Each June thousands gather at Stonehenge to celebrate the summer solstice - geologists, witches, sun - worshipers, and passersby - the same intellectual mix that provided the audience for English literature at its dawning.
History - World; Literature and Drama; Social Science
Dist - PSU

Stonehenge - mystery in the plain 24 MIN
U-matic / VHS / 16mm
Color (I J H)
Captures the myths and legends of Stonehenge. Explores the mystery of its origins.
History - World; Sociology
Dist - EBEC **Prod** - VORFLM 1980

Stones in the urinary tract 8 MIN
VHS / U-matic
Take care of yourself series
Color (PRO)
Uses illustrations and graphics to explain to the patient what causes symptoms and where stones in the urinary tract may occur. Describes what the patient can do to improve the condition.
Health and Safety
Dist - UARIZ **Prod** - UARIZ

The Stones of Amiens 29 MIN
16mm
Legacy Series
B&W (J H A)
LC 73-707200
Shows how the Notre Dame Cathedral in Amiens, France, is a symbol of the unity of thirteenth century Christianity and Gothic art. Includes John Ruskin's poetic description of the cathedral and the words of such scholars as St Thomas Acquinas.
Fine Arts; History - World; Religion and Philosophy
Dist - IU **Prod** - NET 1965

Stones of Eden 25 MIN
U-matic / VHS / 16mm
Color (A)
Portrays a year in the life of a farmer and his family in the mountains of Central Afghanistan. Discusses problems common to most farmers in the developing world.
Agriculture; Sociology
Dist - CNEMAG **Prod** - CNEMAG 1966

Stones off Holland 9 MIN
16mm
Color (G)
$30.00 rental
Employs experimental techniques to color perceptions of time, place and national identity in a Richard Philpott production.
Fine Arts; Psychology; Sociology
Dist - CANCIN

Stones - subtracting mixed numbers 9 MIN
VHS / 16mm
Using fractions to add and subtract series
Color (I J H G)
$195.00, $125.00 purchase, $50.00 rental _ #8221
Looks at a hotly contested game between the red stones and the blue stones to determine which team has more 'rock value' and how much more. Part of a series teaching the use of fractions to add and subtract developed by the National Council of Teachers of Mathematics.
Mathematics
Dist - AIMS **Prod** - DAVFMS 1990

Stonewall Jackson's way 27 MIN
16mm
B&W (I)
Reveals the character of Stonewall Jackson and his influence on the men who fought in his command. Traces his military career from his training of troops in 1861 until his death at Chancellorsville in 1863.
Biography; History - United States
Dist - VADE **Prod** - VADE 1963

Stonewall Joe 29 MIN
VHS / U-matic
B&W
Portrays Joe Robertson, grandnephew of Grandma Moses. Displays the dying New England craft of dry - laid stonewall building and the traditions of folk art and Scots - Irish music.
Fine Arts
Dist - KITCHN **Prod** - KITCHN
PBS

Stonewall Joe 29 MIN
VHS / 16mm
Color (G)
$55.00 rental _ #AMRA - 102
Profiles Joe Robertson, the last full - time builder of the dry laid stone walls that once criss - crossed New England.
Fine Arts
Dist - PBS

Stoneware 28 MIN
Videoreel / VT2
Wheels, Kilns and Clay Series
Color
Features Mrs Peterson describing certain ceramic processes for her classroom at the University of Southern California. Demonstrates how to work with stoneware.
Fine Arts
Dist - PBS **Prod** - USC

Stoney knows how 26 MIN
VHS / 16mm
Color (G)
$89.95 purchase, $50.00 rental
Presents an extended interview with Leonard St Clair, a paraplegic dwarf sword - swallower and tattoo artist with a long list of bizarre stories.
Biography; Fine Arts
Dist - CANCIN **Prod** - BLNKL

Stop 11 MIN
U-matic / VHS / 16mm
Color (H C A)
LC 77-703313
Records and elaborates on the satirical messages of hundreds of caricaturists from all over the world who urge man to find an end to such world problems as pollution, overpopulation, drug abuse, war and murder.
Fine Arts; Literature and Drama; Sociology
Dist - IFB **Prod** - VARDFM 1977

Stop a fire before it starts 10 MIN
16mm / U-matic / VHS
Color (IND VOC)
LC 75-702173
Explains the basic ingredients of fire and shows how everyday materials can become explosive in the presence of sparks, cigarettes and other ignited materials. Demonstrates typical on - the - job locations where hazardous fire situations are encountered.
Health and Safety
Dist - JOU **Prod** - NSC 1975

The Stop - and - frisk doctrine 50 MIN
U-matic / VHS
Criminal procedure and the trial advocate series
Color (PRO COR)
Discusses the stop - and - frisk doctrine, its application and exceptions. Discusses reasonableness of police action in hot pursuit and the plain view doctrine.
Civics and Political Systems
Dist - ABACPE **Prod** - ABACPE

Stop and Go 25 MIN
16mm
Start Here - Adventures and Science Series
Color
Presents experiments to show how objects behave when subjected to inertia, action and reaction both on Earth and in deep Space.
Science - Physical
Dist - LANDMK **Prod** - VIDART 1983

Stop and Go, Pt 1 11 MIN
U-matic / VHS
EDCOA Sexual Counseling Series
Color
Includes procedures in interrupted partner stimulation therapy. The female demonstrates interrupted manual stimulation, interrupted stimulation with lubricants, and interrupted oral stimulation.
Health and Safety; Psychology
Dist - MMRC **Prod** - MMRC

Stop and Go, Pt 2 10 MIN
U-matic / VHS
EDCOA Sexual Counseling Series
Color
Demonstrates the proper procedure for female - above penile insertion, intravaginal sensory appreciation and interrupted thrusting by the female.
Health and Safety; Psychology
Dist - MMRC **Prod** - MMRC

Stop back pain now 60 MIN
VHS
Color (G)
$29.95 purchase _ #P21
Offers methods for relieving, rehabilitating and preventing back, neck and shoulder pain. Offers easy to follow exercises. Features Irene Lamberti, DC.
Health and Safety; Science - Natural
Dist - HP

Stop before you drop 12 MIN
VHS
Color (I J H)
$200.00 purchase _ #466 - V8
Presents over 300 mostly African - American youth dancing and rapping the message that smoking isn't healthy, glamorous, or cool. Offers tips for quitting, and peer support for resisting the temptation. 'Fight it, don't light it.'
Guidance and Counseling; Health and Safety; Psychology
Dist - ETRASS **Prod** - ETRASS

Stop date rape 23 MIN
VHS
Color (H C A)
$225.00 purchase, $50.00 rental
Uses theatre and improvisation to stimulate discussion about the problem of date rape and its prevention. College students.
Psychology; Sociology
Dist - CORNRS **Prod** - CORNRS 1987

Stop drunk driving - a call to action 18 MIN
U-matic / VHS
Color (J H A)
Strives to raise public awareness about drunk driving. Discusses what can be done to curtail drinking and driving.
Health and Safety; Psychology; Sociology
Dist - SUTHRB **Prod** - AMINS
MTP

Stop ice cold - a guide to the detection and prevention of drug labs on rental property 15 MIN
U-matic / VHS
Ice series
Color (G)
$199.00 purchase _ #7431
Presents 12 important clues to help recognize the 'cooking' of ice, or a nearly pure form of methamphetamine. Reveals that the chemicals used in producing this drug are corrosive and explosive. Fumes generated from the 'cooking' process can burn mucus membranes and skin contact with the liquid drug can cause neurological problems or death. Part of a series on ice.
Guidance and Counseling; Health and Safety; Psychology; Sociology
Dist - VISIVI **Prod** - VISIVI 1991

Stop in the Marshland 31 MIN
16mm
B&W (A)
LC 73-702754
Portrays the character of a brakeman of a freight train in the middle of Nordic marshland. Follows the brakeman as he incurs the wrath of his co - workers when he decides to stay behind.
Literature and Drama; Psychology
Dist - NLC **Prod** - NLC 1973

Stop, Look and Laugh 78 MIN
16mm
B&W (I J H C)
Presents the three stooges popping up in the stories Paul Winchell tells Jerry Mahoney and Knucklehead Smith in the course of a day.
Fine Arts
Dist - TWYMAN **Prod** - CPC 1960

Stop, look, and laugh series
Life in the herd 30 MIN
Dist - APH

Stop, look, and laugh series
Moms, dads and other endangered species 30 MIN
There's more to life than the weekend 30 MIN
Dist - APH
CPH

Stop, Look and Think 11 MIN
U-matic / VHS / 16mm
Color (K P)
LC 79-700885
Shows how to cross streets safely. Uses animation and live action to demonstrate driver reaction time, braking distance of automobiles and stopping distance of children when walking versus running.
Health and Safety
Dist - AIMS **Prod** - CAHILL 1978

Stop, look, listen series
Aeroplane 10 MIN
Ambulance 10 MIN
Bread 10 MIN
Bricklayer 10 MIN
Building site 10 MIN
Bulldozers and cranes 10 MIN
Canal 10 MIN
The Castle 10 MIN
Cheese 10 MIN
Coal miner 10 MIN
Combine harvester 10 MIN
Fairground 10 MIN
Farm 10 MIN
Fire engine 10 MIN
Fish 10 MIN
Fruit 10 MIN
Garbage 10 MIN
Glass 10 MIN
Growing food - and flowers 10 MIN
Launderette 10 MIN
Lorry driver 10 MIN
Making sausages 10 MIN
Market stall holder 10 MIN
Newspapers 10 MIN
The Park 10 MIN
Pets 10 MIN
Police station 10 MIN
Postcode 10 MIN
Pottery 28 MIN
Rail 10 MIN
Road repairs 10 MIN
Safari park 10 MIN
School meals 10 MIN
Seaside 10 MIN
Signals 10 MIN
Signs 10 MIN
Sounds 10 MIN
Summer camp 10 MIN
Telephone 10 MIN
Television studio 10 MIN
Time 10 MIN
Vehicles 10 MIN
Village 10 MIN
The Wood 10 MIN
Wool 10 MIN
Dist - VIEWTH

Stop or Go - an Experiment in Genetics 29 MIN
16mm
Spectrum Series
Color (H C A)
LC FIA68-2299
Documents an experiment which analyzes the genetic code of a mutant virus. Shows geneticists at Rockefeller University as they separate mutant viruses from non - mutants, grow new generations of mutants, extract mutant genetic material and test this material for its ability to manufacture a certain protein.
Science - Natural
Dist - IU **Prod** - NET 1968

Stop - Police 14 MIN
U-matic / VHS / 16mm
Color
Looks at when a police officer should use deadly force. Analyzes the high level of skill development and training that help make up an officer's decision to use deadly force and the incredible pressures on each officer to make the right decision every time. Narrated by Harry Reasoner and originally shown on the CBS program 60 Minutes.
Civics and Political Systems; Social Science
Dist - CORF **Prod** - CBSTV

Stop Press 15 MIN
16mm / U-matic / VHS
Color (I J)
Presents a musical about punctuation, featuring a song - and - dance man as the period, an English tart as the comma, a mime clown as the question mark and singing - and - dancing twins as the quotation marks.
English Language
Dist - MEDIAG **Prod** - THAMES 1983

Stop procrastinating - act now 23 MIN
VHS / U-matic / 16mm
Color (J H C A)
$520.00, $395.00, $365.00 purchase _ #A388
Profiles six procrastinators who take an honest look at themselves. Look at the four excuses for procrastination - expecting perfection, thinking the task is insignificant, boring or overwhelming, fearing the imagined consequences, lacking a clear goal, the ability to set priorities or lack of sufficient self confidence.
Business and Economics
Dist - BARR **Prod** - CALLFM 1985

Stop Rubella 14 MIN
16mm
Color
LC 74-705703
Explains the dangers of the disease rubella and shows how mothers and their unborn children can be protected from it. This film can be used as part of an immunization program or with parents of handicapped children.
Health and Safety
Dist - USNAC **Prod** - USPHS 1969

Stop Ruining America's Past 22 MIN
16mm
Public Broadcast Laboratory Series
B&W (H C A)
LC FIA68-1943
Documents the campaign to save archeological sites in Illinois from destruction by urban and industrial expansion. Explains the significance of the sites. Shows archeologists and students during an emergency midwinter dig.
Geography - United States; History - United States; Science - Physical
Dist - IU **Prod** - NET 1968

Stop Smoking 30 MIN
VHS / Cassette
Only Subliminals Series
Subliminal; B&W (G)
$36.00 purchase _ #4; $24.95 purchase _ #C834; $11.98 purchase _ #T205
Presents a subliminal program for overcoming addiction to nicotine. Carries the underlying themes of self - esteem and inner calm. Features nature sounds.
Health and Safety; Psychology; Religion and Philosophy
Dist - VSPU **Prod** - VSPU

Stop Smoking 30 MIN
VHS
Video Reflections Series
Color (G)
$29.95 purchase _ #VSM
Combines images of nature with music and soothing environmental sounds. Uses visual and auditory subliminal messages for eliminating addiction to nicotine.
Guidance and Counseling; Health and Safety; Psychology
Dist - GAINST **Prod** - GAINST

Stop Smoking for Life 60 MIN
VHS
(H C A)
$24.95 purchase _ #KA100V
Provides a basic seven day program for quitting the smoking habit.
Health and Safety; Psychology
Dist - CAMV **Prod** - CAMV

Stop Smoking Forever
VHS
Color (G)
$19.95 purchase _ #VHS104
Uses two types of hypnosis and two types of subliminal suggestions to help eliminate nicotine addiction.
Health and Safety; Psychology
Dist - VSPU **Prod** - VSPU

Stop Smoking Forever - for Women and Men 60 MIN
U-matic / VHS
Subliminal Series
Stereo (H C G T A S R PRO IND)
Presents subliminals reinforcement to quit smoking.
Psychology
Dist - BANTAP **Prod** - BANTAP 1986

Stop smoking with affirmations 18 MIN
U-matic / VHS
Color (G)
$249.00 purchase _ #7441
Explains the power of the mental belief system and how it can be used to stop smoking through the use of positive affirmations. Presents a step - by - step outline for programming the mind into believing that it belongs to a nonsmoker.
Health and Safety; Psychology; Religion and Philosophy
Dist - VISIVI **Prod** - VISIVI 1991

Stop smoking with Alf Fowles 60 MIN
BETA / VHS
Color
Presents a program for smokers who want to quit. Combines deep relaxation with visual messages directed at the subconscious.
Health and Safety; Psychology
Dist - MOHOMV **Prod** - MOHOMV 1988
BEEKMN

Stop that fire 12 MIN
16mm / U-matic / VHS
Color (G)
Gives examples of various types of fires, how they start, and how to extinguish them. Safety devices such as sprinkler systems and fire extinguishers are explained, and the need for prevention measures and proper emergency training is stressed.
Health and Safety; Industrial and Technical Education; Psychology; Science - Physical
Dist - IFB **Prod** - IFB

Stop that period - period that stop 18 MIN
U-matic / VHS / 16mm
Punctuation series
Color (I J)
$425, $250 purchase _ #76533
Shows three different punctuation marks that can be used to end a sentence.
English Language
Dist - CORF

Stop the fighting 30 MIN
VHS
Club connect series
Color (J H G)
$59.95 purchase _ #CCNC-503-WC95
Encourages teenagers to walk away from fighting with their peers. Presents alternatives to fighting and methods to avoid potential violence. Includes interviews with entertainers D.J. Jazzy Jeff and the Fresh Prince as well as singer Chris Isaak.
Sociology
Dist - PBS **Prod** - WTVSTV 1992

Stop the World - Maggie Wants to Get Off 30 MIN
U-matic / VHS / 16mm
Moving Right Along Series
Color (J H A)
Reveals that when she presumes that she is responsible for her parents' divorce, Maggie angrily runs out into traffic and is struck by a car. Shows that during her recovery, her family, friends and teacher help her realize she wasn't responsible for the break - up.
Sociology
Dist - CORF **Prod** - WQED 1983

Stop the world, we want to get on 26 MIN
VHS
Color (J H C G)
$195.00 purchase, $45.00 rental
Documents a new civil rights organization, Disabled Peoples International, formed ten years ago at the beginning of the UN's Decade of Disabled People. Informs that it now has a membership in over one hundred countries. People with disabilities all over the world are demanding the right to determine their own lives. Produced by Judy Jackson - Alma Productions.
Civics and Political Systems; Fine Arts; Health and Safety
Dist - CANCIN

Stop, think and choose 14 MIN
VHS / U-matic
Color (I J)
$275.00, $325.00 purchase, $50.00 rental
Covers situations involving conflict resolution and the three step method - stop, think and choose - to assist students in coping with potential problems. Intersperses dramatic vignettes with possible solutions. Narrated by students.
Psychology
Dist - NDIM **Prod** - ALLMED 1992

The Stopover 14 MIN
16mm / U-matic / VHS
B&W (J)
LC 76-701933
Depicts a traveler at a stopover in a bus terminal who demonstrates the possibility of living gourmet style while traveling by Greyhound bus.
Literature and Drama
Dist - PHENIX **Prod** - STEINP 1975

Stopping 15 MIN
Videoreel / VT2
Energy series; Let's go sciencing; Unit 2
Color (K)
Shows that a force is required to stop the motion of an object or to change the direction of a moving object.
Science - Physical
Dist - GPN **Prod** - DETPS

Stopping Drugs 58 MIN
VHS
Frontline Series
Color; Captioned (G)
$150.00 purchase, $95.00 rental _ #FRON - 503K
Focuses on the efforts of six addicts to permanently end their drug abuse. Shows how their addictions have caused them to lose family, friends and opportunities for personal advancement. Reveals that most addicts who seek treatment will relapse sometime down the road, and that the failure rate is high for all types of treatment programs.
Guidance and Counseling; Health and Safety; Sociology
Dist - PBS **Prod** - DOCCON

Stopping foodservice waste
U-matic / VHS / 16mm
Professional food preparation and service program series
Color
Dramatizes ways to avoid wasteful practices and save money in all food service operations. Shows waste caused by discarding perfectly good food, ignoring portion control and being wasteful in the handling and storing of food, dishware and utensils.
Industrial and Technical Education
Dist - NEM **Prod** - NEM 1983

Stopping History 57 MIN
VHS / U-matic
Color (H C A)
LC 84-707811
Provokes viewers to confront the question of nuclear war and to consider their role in impeding nuclear devastation.
Civics and Political Systems; Sociology
Dist - ADAIR **Prod** - KQEDTV 1984

Stopping the coming Ice Age 45 MIN
VHS
Color (J H C G)
$75.00 purchase, $40.00 rental
Suggests that the greenhouse effect may accelerate the natural cycle of ice ages. Gives suggestions for slowing or halting the process, including reducing human contribution to the greenhouse effect, planting fast - growing trees, and remineralizing existing forests for better growth. Produced by Larry Ephron.
Agriculture; Geography - World; Science - Physical
Dist - EFVP **Prod** - EFVP 1988

Storage Batteries and Chargers 60 MIN
VHS
Transformers, Switchgear and Batteries Series
Color (PRO)
$600.00, $1500.00 purchase _ #EMSBC
Focuses on how lead - acid batters operate, how they are maintained and tested to ensure safe and efficient operation. Part of a four - part series on transformers, switchgear and batteries, which is part of a 29 unit set on electrical maintenance. Includes 10 textbooks and an instructor guide which provide four hours of instruction.
Education; Health and Safety; Industrial and Technical Education; Psychology
Dist - NUSTC **Prod** - NUSTC

Storage Classes
U-matic / VHS
'C' Language Programming Series
Color
Explains the position of storage class specifier to the type specifier in a declaration statement. Illustrates the scope, life, implicit and explicit initialization values which a storage class may assume. Describes the characteristics of the automatic, register, external and static storage classes and identifies the reasons for selecting a particular storage class for an identifier.
Industrial and Technical Education; Mathematics; Sociology
Dist - COMTEG **Prod** - COMTEG

The Store 118 MIN
U-matic / VHS / 16mm
Color
Portrays the main Nieman - Marcus store and corporate headquarters in Dallas. Includes sequences on the selection, presentation, marketing, pricing, advertising and selling of a vast array of consumer products. Shows internal management and organizational aspects of a large corporation.
Business and Economics
Dist - ZIPRAH **Prod** - WISEF 1983

Store - it - all Barn 30 MIN
VHS / 16mm
Build Your Own Series
Color (H C A PRO)
$15.00 purchase _ #TA217
Features construction of 8 x 8 rustic design outdoor storage.
Industrial and Technical Education
Dist - AAVIM **Prod** - AAVIM 1990

Storefront 40 MIN
16mm
B&W
Views the training and roles of non - professional aides in a neighborhood storefront center. Pictures the anger and frustrations of ghetto life in South Bronx, New York.
History - United States; Psychology; Science - Natural; Sociology
Dist - USNAC **Prod** - USOEO

Storehouse of minerals 15 MIN
16mm / U-matic / VHS
American legacy series; Pgm 11
Color (I)
Presents John Rugg visiting several Rocky Mountain mining sites, discussing surface and underground operations. Shows an open - pit molybdenum mine, milling, tailing

ponds and land reclamation. Highlights early gold and silver booms through dramatic vignettes showing the roles played by Horace Greeley and H A W Taylor.
Geography - United States; History - United States; Social Science
Dist - AITECH **Prod** - KRMATV 1983

Stories 14 MIN
16mm / U-matic / VHS
Joy of Writing Series
Color (K P I)
LC 77-703301
Shows children working with a teacher and making up a round - robin collaborative story, formulating characters, illustrating how they get ideas for stories and how settings can add to stories and talking about the importance of beginnings and endings.
English Language
Dist - CF **Prod** - CF 1977

Stories and Poems from Long Ago Series

Alice in wonderland	15 MIN
The Captain's favorites - the ballad of William Sycamore, the walrus and the carpenter, the owl critic	15 MIN
The Cremation of Sam McGee	15 MIN
Darius Green and his flying machine	15 MIN
Grandmother's story of Bunker Hill Battle	15 MIN
Heroes and Heroines of the American Revolution - Molly Pitcher, the Little Black - Eyed Rebel, the Swamp Fox	15 MIN
Heroes of the American Revolution - Paul Revere's Ride, Nathan Hale	15 MIN
The Hut in the Forest	15 MIN
John Henry	15 MIN
Johnny Appleseed	15 MIN
The Little Match Girl	15 MIN
The One who Wasn't Afraid	15 MIN
Paul Bunyan	15 MIN
The Pilgrim - Pocahontas, the Landing of the Pilgrims Fathers, the First Thanksgiving, Southern Ships and Settlers	15 MIN
Stories of the sea - Casabianca, Wreck of the Hesperus, Dunkirk	15 MIN
The Tales of Aesop	15 MIN

Dist - GPN

Stories are for fun series
Rapunzel and The golden bird 15 MIN
Dist - NCAT

Stories from Cuscatlan 52 MIN
VHS / 16mm
Color (G)
$390.00 purchase, $75.00 rental
Tells the intimate stories of three ordinary Salvadoran families who reflect on their former peaceful, agrarian way of life. Provides honest insight into Salvadorans' feelings about their country and themselves. Produced by Peter Chappell and Jane Ryder. Written by Manlio Argueta.
Fine Arts; Sociology
Dist - FIRS

Stories from many lands
U-matic / VHS
Picture book parade series
Mono (K P I)
Includes the following titles - The Silver Cow, The Stonecutter, The Treasure, Rikki Tikki Tembo, The Hole In The Dike and One Fine Day.
Literature and Drama
Dist - WWS **Prod** - WWS 1986

Stories in Clay 6 MIN
16mm / U-matic / VHS
Color (P I)
LC 76-701516
Shows children working with clay and creating clay figures, followed by animated sequences featuring the figures.
Fine Arts
Dist - AIMS **Prod** - ACI 1972

Stories in Paper 9 MIN
U-matic / VHS / 16mm
Color (P I)
LC 76-701517
Uses live - action segments, followed by animation, to demonstrate how paper puppets can be utilized to act out a story. Introduces a young girl who makes a movable figure out of paper and, as she works, explains how she makes the figure so that she can move it in telling a story.
Fine Arts
Dist - AIMS **Prod** - ACI 1972

Stories in String 8 MIN
16mm / U-matic / VHS
Color (P I)
LC 76-701518
Uses live action and animated sequences to introduce a technique of making string figures.
English Language; Fine Arts
Dist - AIMS **Prod** - ACI 1972

Stories, myths, ironies and songs 70 MIN
VHS / U-matic
Color
Presents 21 segments relating the author's experiences and ideas about our culture, ethics and myths.
Fine Arts; Religion and Philosophy; Sociology
Dist - KITCHN **Prod** - KITCHN

Stories of America series

America is named	15 MIN
Annie Oakley	15 MIN
Ben Franklin	15 MIN
The California gold rush	15 MIN
Children of the Mayflower	15 MIN
Clara Barton	15 MIN
Daniel Boone	15 MIN
Davy Crockett	15 MIN
Discover America	15 MIN
Father is president	15 MIN
The First Cars	15 MIN
Gretchen Goes West	15 MIN
The Growers	15 MIN
Indian Summer	15 MIN
John Billington and Squanto	15 MIN
Lewis and Clark	15 MIN
Little Yellow Fur	15 MIN
Martin and Abraham Lincoln	15 MIN
Needles and Bread	15 MIN
New Amsterdam	15 MIN
Oregon Trail	15 MIN
Our Country's Birthday	15 MIN
Pecos Bill	15 MIN
Pocahontas	15 MIN
Robert Fulton	15 MIN
Runaway Slave	15 MIN
The Start of a War	15 MIN
Tom Edison	15 MIN
The Transcontinental Railroad	15 MIN
The Underground Railroad	15 MIN

Dist - AITECH

Stories of change 56 MIN
VHS
Color (H A T R PRO)
$79.95 purchase
Teaches about substance abuse and recovery to help individuals in crisis move toward health and wholeness. Created by Theresa Tollini.
Health and Safety; Psychology
Dist - FUTED **Prod** - FUTED 1992

Stories of Christmas Love 60 MINS
VHS
Color (G)
$59.95 purchase _ #LBCL - 000
Features Dr. Leo Buscaglia, a University of Southern California education professor, and his views on personal growth, sharing, coping, love and understanding. Uses Christmas - themed stories to illustrate his principles.
Psychology
Dist - PBS **Prod** - KVIETV 1987

The Stories of Maxine Hong Kingston - Pts I and II 60 MIN
VHS
World of ideas with Bill Moyers - Season II - series
Color; Captioned (G)
$59.95 purchase _ #WIWM - 205D
Interviews author Maxine Hong Kingston. Presents her visions of America as a 'melting pot' including both Puritan and Asian influences. Hosted by Bill Moyers.
Literature and Drama; Sociology
Dist - PBS

Stories of North America - Pt 1 30 MIN
VHS
Storytelling live series
Color (I J)
$70.00 purchase _ #T51700
Presents stories and interviews with storytellers which help explain how cultural and geographic forces shape the oral tradition and elements of storytelling. Offers also live performances in front of children and original illustrations. Includes A Land Full of Stories, African-American Stories and Stories in Song. Provides teacher's guide. Part one of a two-part series.
Literature and Drama
Dist - NGS

Stories of North America - Pt 2 30 MIN
VHS
Storytelling live series
Color (I J)
$70.00 purchase _ #T51701
Offers five complete stories and interviews with storytellers which help explain how cultural and geographic forces shape the oral tradition and elements of storytelling. Presents also footage of live performances in front of children and original illustrations. Includes teacher's guide. Part two of two-part series.
Literature and Drama
Dist - NGS

Stories of stories 20 MIN
VHS / U-matic
Folk book series
Color (P)
Describes the origins of storytelling, presenting the stories Feather Toes and How Anansi The Spider Stole The Sky God's Stories.
Literature and Drama
Dist - AITECH **Prod** - UWISC 1980

Stories of the beginning
VHS
Greatest tales from the Old Testament series
Color (K P I R)
$29.95 purchase, $10.00 rental _ #35 - 828 - 528
Presents five stories from the Old Testament. Includes the Genesis creation account, Adam and Eve, Noah's ark, and the Tower of Babel.
Literature and Drama; Religion and Philosophy
Dist - APH **Prod** - CAFM

Stories of the Beginning 30 MIN
VHS / 16mm
Greatest Tales from the Old Testament Series
Color (P I J H A)
$29.95 purchase
Features animated Bible stories from the Book of Genesis from a Christian perspective.
Religion and Philosophy
Dist - CAFM **Prod** - CAFM 1988

Stories of the earth 52 MIN
VHS
EarthScope series; Pt 2
Color (J H C G)
$50.00 purchase
Presents three documentaries - The Living Arts, an East Indian film about a troup of actors which tours the Indian countryside to teach about the environment; If All the Children Would, a montage of five short Yugoslavian films chronicling environmental efforts in small - town Yugoslavia; and Choices, a music video by King Sunny Ade and Onyenko of Nigeria teaching about family planning. Includes a roundtable discussion on financial planning for improving the environment. Part two of a 12 - part series hosted by Robert Siegel of NPR.
Science - Natural; Science - Physical; Sociology
Dist - GVIEW **Prod** - GVIEW 1990

Stories of the Fox 30 MIN
U-matic
Ukrainian Folktales Series
(P) (UKRAINIAN)
Includes the Ukrainian folktales The Rabbit and the Fox, The Cat And The Rooster, The Sly Godmother and The Fox And the Crane. In the Ukrainian language.
Foreign Language; History - World; Literature and Drama
Dist - ACCESS **Prod** - ACCESS 1985

Stories of the sea - Casabianca, Wreck of the Hesperus, Dunkirk 15 MIN
VHS / 16mm
Stories and poems from long ago series
Color (I)
Uses character of retired sea captain to tell the stories Casabianca, Wreck Of The Hesperus and Dunkirk. The fourth of 16 installments of the Stories And Poems From Long Ago Series, which is intended to encourage reading and writing by young viewers.
Literature and Drama
Dist - GPN **Prod** - CTI 1990

Stories of Tuktu - a Children's Adventure Series

Tuktu and His Animal Friends	14 MIN
Tuktu and His Eskimo Dogs	14 MIN
Tuktu and His Nice New Clothes	14 MIN
Tuktu and the Big Kayak	14 MIN
Tuktu and the Big Seal	14 MIN
Tuktu and the Caribou Hunt	14 MIN
Tuktu and the Clever Hands	14 MIN
Tuktu and the Indoor Games	14 MIN
Tuktu and the Magic Bow	14 MIN
Tuktu and the Magic Spear	14 MIN
Tuktu and the Snow Palace	14 MIN
Tuktu and the Ten Thousand Fishes	14 MIN
Tuktu and the Trials of Strength	14 MIN

Dist - FI

Stories 1 - Planning 15 MIN
U-matic
You Can Write Anything Series
Color (P I)
Teaches writing techniques through Amanda who is told that telling a story from your own point of view is one way of making it seem more exciting.
Education; English Language
Dist - TVOTAR **Prod** - TVOTAR 1984

Stories should be shared 15 MIN
16mm
Color (P I)
As part of their reading enrichment program, elementary school children act out stories they have read.
English Language; Literature and Drama
Dist - WSUM **Prod** - WSUM 1958

Stories, Stories, Stories 10 MIN
U-matic / VHS
Book, Look and Listen Series
Color (K P)
Helps children to develop a sense of personal accomplishment regarding their ability to read or interpret sounds, pictures and stories.
English Language; Literature and Drama
Dist - AITECH **Prod** - MDDE 1977

The Stories they tell 30 MIN
VHS
Natural history in the classroom series
Color (T A PRO)
Presents ways to improve teaching of natural history. Stresses creative activities such as collecting insects, building terrariums, using attractants, and reassembling skeletons. Hosted by Rudy Mancke.
Education; Science - Natural; Science - Physical
Dist - SCETV **Prod** - FI 1989

The Stories they tell - Pt 2 30 MIN
VHS
Natural history in the classroom series
Color (I)
$149.00 series purchase _ #899 - 9002
Shows how to use locally collected materials to pique students' curiosity and enliven the classroom experience. Presents collecting insects, building terrariums, using attractants and reassembling skeletons and other creative activities for teacher training and classroom use. Features instructor Rudy Mancke. Part 2 of three parts suggests how to integrate shells, cocoons, leaves and other 'signs of life' into curriculum. Available only as part of the series.
Agriculture; Education; Mathematics; Science; Science - Natural; Science - Physical
Dist - SCETV **Prod** - FI 1989

Stories 3 - Endings 15 MIN
U-matic
You Can Write Anything Series
Color (P I)
Teaches writing techniques through Amanda who is told about different types of story endings and the elements that make up a good ending.
Education; English Language
Dist - TVOTAR **Prod** - TVOTAR 1984

Stories to grow on 120 MIN
VHS
Color (K P R)
$39.99 purchase _ #DM156
Presents a series of stories by Ethel Barrett which teach Christian values to children through parables about animals.
Religion and Philosophy
Dist - GOSPEL **Prod** - GOSPEL

Stories to remember series
David - God's champion 30 MIN
Here comes Jesus 30 MIN
Look what God made 30 MIN
Walking with Jesus 30 MIN
Dist - APH

Stories to write about - creative writing 30 MIN
VHS
Color (G A)
$19.95 purchase _ #TCC106AE
Presents a collection of human interest stories originally broadcast on CNN, offered as a source for possible creative writing assignments.
English Language; Literature and Drama
Dist - TMM **Prod** - TMM

Stories 2 - Characters 15 MIN
U-matic
You Can Write Anything Series
Color (P I)
Teaches writing techniques through Amanda who is told to correct the spelling and punctuation and edit her story before sending it in to a writing contest.
Education; English Language
Dist - TVOTAR **Prod** - TVOTAR 1984

Storing information 30 MIN
U-matic / VHS
Bits and bytes series; Pt 4
Color (A)
Examines the computer as a tool for the storage and retrieval of information. Demonstrates how to move information from computer to disk or how to use the computer as a filing system.
Mathematics
Dist - TIMLIF **Prod** - TVOTAR 1984

Storing, Retrieving, Printing and Advanced Features
U-matic / VHS
Using MultiPlan Series
Color
Explains how to store a MultiPlan worksheet, retrieve a worksheet and print a worksheet in part or whole, or copy it onto a diskette. Describes advanced features of MultiPlan, including storing, iteration, window creation and linking worksheets.
Industrial and Technical Education; Mathematics; Sociology
Dist - COMTEG **Prod** - COMTEG

The Stork 15 MIN
VHS
Gentle Giant Series
Color (K)
LC 90712405
Uses 'The Stork' to teach children universal truths. Features stories from cultures throughout the world. Fourth of 16 installments of the Gentle Giant Series.
Health and Safety; Literature and Drama; Psychology
Dist - GPN **Prod** - CTI 1988

Storks 25 MIN
16mm / U-matic / VHS
Untamed World Series
Color; Mono (J H C A)
$400.00 film, $250.00 video, $50.00 rental
Talks on the history of the stork and its homeland in the wilds of Africa.
Geography - World; Science - Natural
Dist - CTV **Prod** - CTV 1973

Storm 29 MIN
16mm
Color
LC 75-700879
Documents the flooding that resulted from Tropical Storm Agnes. Focuses on the Wyoming Valley in Pennsylvania, where Wilkes - Barre and other towns safely evacuated 80,000 people when the Susquehanna River reached a crest of 40 feet.
History - World; Science - Physical
Dist - USNAC **Prod** - USFDAA 1974

Storm 15 MIN
U-matic / 16mm / VHS
Color (G A)
$160.00, $95.00 purchase _ #TC009098, #TCA16970, #TCA16972
Documents the flooding that resulted from tropical storm Agnes, focusing on the Wyoming Valley in Pennsylvania.
Civics and Political Systems; Health and Safety; History - United States
Dist - USNAC **Prod** - USDD 1974

A Storm, a Strife 28 MIN
16mm
Color (H C A)
Deals with the relationship between emotional well - being and physical health. Tells the story of Trish, who aggravates an illness worrying about family problems and is able to be helped only after her doctor and her minister get together.
Education; Guidance and Counseling; Health and Safety; Sociology
Dist - AMEDA **Prod** - AMEDA

Storm Boy 33 MIN
16mm / U-matic / VHS
Color (I J)
LC 80-701293
A shortened version of the motion picture Storm Boy. Shows how a boy learns about life from an adopted pelican, an aborigine, and his own father.
Fine Arts; Geography - World; Guidance and Counseling
Dist - LCOA **Prod** - SAFC 1980

Storm boy 90 MIN
U-matic / VHS / 16mm
Color
Details the idyllic existence of Storm Boy, his father and his pet pelican on an isolated portion of South Australia. Shows that when the pelican is shot, Storm Boy is prompted to choose between his current lifestyle and rejoining society.
Fine Arts; Geography - World
Dist - LCOA

Storm from the east series
Presents the story of the Mongol empire. Follows the rise of the Mongols in the 13th century from nomadic herdsman to governors of the largest land - based empire in history. Includes episodes on Genghis Khan and the rise of the Mongol nation, Genhis' son Ogedei and the construction of the city of Quarakorum, the mission of John of Plano Carpini, and the final shift from terror and conquest to trade.
Storm from the east series 180 MIN
Dist - BBCENE

Storm from the east
Birth of an empire 45 MIN
The last Khan of Khans 45 MIN
Tartar crusaders 45 MIN
World conquerors 45 MIN
Dist - BBCENE

The Storm of acid snow 30 MIN
VHS
Icewalk series
Color (G)
$39.95 purchase _ #ICWK - 002
Documents the presence of pollutants in the Arctic's snow and atmosphere. Features experts who predict that the pollution could create warmer conditions in the Arctic, melting the ice cap and causing flooding. Suggests that pollutants are carried from other areas to the Arctic by air currents, being deposited there through acid rain or acid snow.
Sociology
Dist - PBS

Storm of fire - World War II and the destruction of Dresden - Pt 2 11 MIN
16mm / U-matic / VHS
B&W (J)
LC 78-701970
Uses archival footage in presenting an overview of World War II. Documents the German advance, the bombing of London, the 'turning of the tide' and defeat of the Germans, and the bombing of Dresden.
History - United States
Dist - CF **Prod** - CADRE 1978

Storm of Strangers Series
The Irish 30 MIN
Italian American 26 MIN
Jewish American 26 MIN
Jung Sai - Chinese American 29 MIN
Dist - FI

Storm over Asia 70 MIN
U-matic / VHS
B&W
Offers a film directed by P I Podovkin.
Fine Arts
Dist - IHF **Prod** - IHF

Storm over Asia 73 MIN
16mm
Soviet Union - the pioneers series
B&W (G)
$150.00 rental
Portrays the conflicts between the Mongolian people and British occupation troops. Directed by Vsevolod Pudovkin.
Fine Arts; History - World
Dist - KINOIC
IHF

Storm over the Supreme Court 52 MIN
U-matic / VHS / 16mm
B&W (J H C)
LC FI67-758
Emphasizes the writings of great chief justices of the Supreme Court. Deals with various controversies from the Dred Scott case to the Desegregation case and the prayer case under Chief Justice Warren. Includes readings by Mark Van Doren, Archibald Mac Leish, Frederick March and Carl Sandburg.
Civics and Political Systems
Dist - CAROUF **Prod** - CBSTV 1963

Storm Over the Supreme Court, Pt 1 - 1790 - 1932 21 MIN
U-matic / VHS / 16mm
B&W (J)
Traces the development of the Supreme Court as a strong force in American government.
Civics and Political Systems
Dist - CAROUF **Prod** - CBSTV

Storm over the Supreme Court - Pt 1 - 1790 - 1932 21 MIN
U-matic / VHS / 16mm
B&W (H C)
Traces the history of the Supreme Court. Describes the conflicts over federal and states' rights, the Dred Scott case and the judiciary power. Discusses the influence exerted on the U S by Chief Justices such as John Marshall, Roger Taney and Charles Hughes.
Civics and Political Systems; History - United States
Dist - CAROUF **Prod** - CBSTV 1963

Storm Over the Supreme Court, Pt 2 - 1932 - 1963 32 MIN
16mm / U-matic / VHS
B&W (J)
Looks at events in the Supreme Court from the era of Franklin Roosevelt until 1963.
Civics and Political Systems
Dist - CAROUF **Prod** - CBSTV

Storm over the Supreme Court - Pt 2 - 1933 - present 31 MIN
U-matic / VHS / 16mm
B&W (H C)
Analyzes the history of the court. Shows President Roosevelt's fight with the court concerning his 'Court packing.' Reveals the philosophical and ideological differences within the court, such as the clash between Justices Frankfurter and Black. Shows the segregation battle.
Civics and Political Systems; History - United States
Dist - CAROUF **Prod** - CBSTV 1963

Storm Signal
16mm
Color
Shows how the lives of a young married couple disintegrate as they battle heroin addiction.
Psychology; Sociology
Dist - DIRECT **Prod** - DREWAS 1966

Storm water management series
Microcomputers and hydrologic analysis
Dist - AMCEE

Stormalong 30 MIN
VHS
American heroes and legends series
Color (P I J)
$12.95 purchase _ #REV10553V
Features John Candy as narrator of the hilarious story of Old Captain Stormalong, the saltiest sailor to sail the seven seas.
Literature and Drama
Dist - KNOWUN

Storme - the lady of the Jewel Box 21 MIN
16mm / VHS
Color (A)
$450.00, $195.00 purchase, $60.00 rental
Portrays Storme DeLarverie, former MC and female impersonator with the Jewel Box Revue - America's first racially integrated female impersonation show. Reveals that the multi - racial revue was a favorite act of the Black theater circuit and attracted mainstream Black and White audiences from the 1940s through the 1960s.
Fine Arts; Sociology
Dist - WMEN **Prod** - MIPA 1987

Storms
16mm
Color (P I)
Teaches children about the basic elements of weather including lightning, thunder, tornadoes, hurricanes, wind and rain. Features classic clips from Disney films such as Bambi, Fantasia, The Old Mill, and The Little Whirlwind.
Science - Physical; Sociology
Dist - CORF **Prod** - DISNEY 1986

Storms 30 MIN
U-matic
Today's Special Series
Color (K P)
Develops language arts skills in children. Programs are thematically designed around subjects of interest to youngsters. Action takes place in a department store where people, mannequins, puppets, comic characters and special guests present a light hearted approach to language arts.
Fine Arts; Literature and Drama; Psychology
Dist - TVOTAR **Prod** - TVOTAR 1985

Storms - an Introduction 14 MIN
16mm / U-matic / VHS
Color (I J)
LC 81-700237
Offers examples of thunderstorms, hurricanes, tornadoes and blizzards and describes the weather patterns that generate them.
Science - Physical
Dist - PHENIX **Prod** - BEANMN 1981

Storms - the Restless Atmosphere 22 MIN
16mm / U-matic / VHS
Earth Science Program Series
Color (I J H)
LC 74-701894
Describes the atmospheric condition which creates thunderstorms, tornadoes and hurricanes. Shows how stresses built up in atmospheric heat and circulation are dissipated.
Science - Physical
Dist - EBEC **Prod** - EBEC 1974

Stormwater Pollution Control - a New Technology 29 MIN
16mm
Color
LC 74-706585
Describes techniques being developed to solve the problem of handling the overflow of raw sewage from storm sewage systems that occurs after heavy rains.
Health and Safety; Industrial and Technical Education; Science - Natural; Sociology
Dist - USNAC **Prod** - USEPA 1974

Stormy the thoroughbred 46 MIN
16mm / U-matic / VHS
Animal featurettes series; Set 1
Color
LC 77-701895
Presents the story of Stormy, a little horse who didn't belong.
Literature and Drama
Dist - CORF **Prod** - DISNEY 1967

Stormy the thoroughbred - Pt 1 23 MIN
16mm / U-matic / VHS
Animal featurettes series; Set 1
Color
LC 77-701895
Presents the story of Stormy, an outcast thoroughbred horse born weaker and smaller than other yearlings in his class, who finds his identity as a polo pony.
Literature and Drama
Dist - CORF **Prod** - DISNEY 1967

Stormy the thoroughbred - Pt 2 23 MIN
U-matic / VHS / 16mm
Animal featurettes series; Set 1
Color
LC 77-701895
Presents the story of Stormy, an outcast thoroughbred horse born weaker and smaller than other yearlings in his class, who finds his identity as a polo pony.
Literature and Drama
Dist - CORF **Prod** - DISNEY 1967

Story 20 MIN
16mm
Color; B&W (G)
Demonstrates a performance of the dance in Finland during the Dance Company's world tour in 1964.
Fine Arts
Dist - CUNDAN **Prod** - FINBC 1964

A Story, a story 10 MIN
U-matic / VHS / 16mm
Color (K P)
LC 73-703026
Tells the story of how long ago there were no stories on earth for children to hear and that all stories belonged to Nyame, the sky god. Explains that Anase, the spider man, wanted to buy some of these stories, so he spun a web up to the sky and went to bargain with the sky god. Uses narration and woodcuts capturing the flavor of African language, customs and lifestyles to show how Anase paid the price.
English Language; Geography - World; Literature and Drama
Dist - WWS **Prod** - WWS 1973

A Story about feelings 10 MIN
U-matic / 16mm / VHS
Color (K P)
Explains and illustrates for young children the disease of chemical dependency. Uses animation to portray the role that feelings and emotions play in drug abuse. Features narration by children.
Guidance and Counseling; Health and Safety; Psychology; Sociology
Dist - BARR **Prod** - JOHNIN 1982
CMPCAR
EDMI

A Story about people 5 MIN
VHS / 16mm
Color (COR)
$225.00 purchase, $85.00 rental, $25.00 preview
Discusses perception of people. Suggests that conformity is not the way for an organization to succeed.
Psychology; Sociology
Dist - UTM **Prod** - UTM
VLEARN

The Story about Ping 35 MIN
VHS / 16mm
Children's Circle Video Series
Color (K)
$18.88 purchase _ #CCV002
Also includes other stories - Rosie's Walk, Charlie Needs a Cloak, The Best of M. Racine.
Literature and Drama
Dist - EDUCRT

The Story about Ping 10 MIN
U-matic / VHS / 16mm
B&W (K P)
An iconographic motion picture based on the children's book of the same title by Flack and Wiese.
English Language; Literature and Drama
Dist - WWS **Prod** - WWS 1957

Story break video series
Arnold of the ducks 25 MIN
Chocolate fever 25 MIN
C.L.U.T.Z 25 MIN
How to eat fried worms 25 MIN
Dist - KNOWUN

Story development with six - and seven year - olds - Unit A
VHS
Drama forum series
Color; PAL (T)
PdS35.00 purchase
Presents David Redman with his infants class. Shows the fifth session of work on a story revolving around a village cut off by snow storms and journalists interviewing the survivors after they have escaped. Unit one of a ten - unit series of observational material on the work of drama teachers.
Education; Fine Arts
Dist - EMFVL

Story elements 15 MIN
U-matic / VHS
Tuned - in series; Lesson 7
Color (J H)
Shows a ninth - grade class studying television involved in such diverse projects as a documentary on interesting after school jobs, situation comedies, commercials and political commercials for school office candidates.
Fine Arts; Literature and Drama; Sociology
Dist - FI **Prod** - WNETTV 1982

Story idea, where are you hiding 11 MIN
16mm / VHS
Creative writing series
Color (I)
$315.00, $235.00 purchase, $60.00 rental
Discusses where story ideas come from. Part of a four - part series set in a classroom with a small demonstration group of students and a teacher of creative writing. Projector stops are provided to encourage viewer participation in creative thinking and writing paralleling that done by the group onscreen. Directed by Bud Freeman.
English Language; Fine Arts; Literature and Drama
Dist - CF

Story into Film - Clark's the Portable Phonograph 10 MIN
16mm / U-matic / VHS
Humanities - Short Story Showcase Series
Color (J)
LC 77-703471
Presents a commentary by producer/director John Barnes on Walter Van Tilburg Clark's The Portable Phonograph in which he discusses the process and problems of translating the short story to a filmed dramatization.
Literature and Drama
Dist - EBEC **Prod** - EBEC 1977

Story Maker 15 MIN
U-matic / VHS
Word Shop Series
Color (P)
English Language; Literature and Drama
Dist - WETATV **Prod** - WETATV

Story Mapping 15 MIN
VHS / Software / U-matic
Storylords Series
Color (P)
$125.00 purchase,$240.00 software purchase
Traces the structure of a story through the use of a storybook character that children can interact with.
Education; English Language
Dist - AITECH **Prod** - WETN 1986

Story mapping 30 MIN
VHS / U-matic
Teaching reading comprehension series
Color (T)
$180.00 purchase,$50.00 rental
Highlights the benefits of discussing story from a question and answer format in the classroom.
Education; English Language
Dist - AITECH **Prod** - WETN 1986

The Story of '91 30 MIN
16mm
Color
Portrays the function of the local union and its close relationship to members on and off the job. Reflects the history of their union and its hard - won benefits at a special meeting.
Business and Economics; Sociology
Dist - AFLCIO **Prod** - ILGWU 1963

Story of a Book 16 MIN
U-matic / VHS / 16mm
Color (I J)
Tells how author Marguerite Henry conceives and writes a book. Discusses where ideas come from, research in the library and on location, writing and rewriting, creating the illustrations, planning the dummy, and printing.
English Language; Literature and Drama
Dist - CF **Prod** - PPIPER 1980

The Story of a check 11 MIN
U-matic / VHS / 16mm
Color (I J)
LC 81-700238
Illustrates how the checking system works, from writing individual checks to the process by which banks handle millions of dollars in checks every day.
Business and Economics
Dist - BARR **Prod** - WILETS 1981

The Story of a Communist 70 MIN
U-matic / VHS
Color
Presents a biography of Leonid Ilyich Brezhnev, General Secretary of the CPSU Central Committee and Chairman of the Presidium of the Supreme Soviet of the USSR.
Biography; Civics and Political Systems; History - World
Dist - IHF **Prod** - IHF

The Story of a Congressman 25 MIN
16mm
B&W (I)
LC FIA66-1304
Follows the activities of a congressman during his reelection campaign. Discussions between the incumbent and his opponent emphasize that the strength of a free government lies with an intelligent voting public.
Civics and Political Systems
Dist - SF **Prod** - WOLPER 1965

The Story of a Craftsman 21 MIN
16mm
Color
LC 76-700427
Follows the work of Dominic Callicchio, an expert metal craftsman, as he makes a trumpet from a raw piece of brass. Shows how his skills are thriving in an increasing technological age.
Fine Arts; Industrial and Technical Education
Dist - MALIBU **Prod** - TAPDEM 1975

Story of a Dam 17 MIN
16mm
Color (J H C)
Follows the building of the Hoover Dam Reservoir at Columbus, Ohio, over a period of three years.
Geography - United States; Industrial and Technical Education; Science - Natural
Dist - OSUMPD **Prod** - OSUMPD 1955

The Story of a Dancer 26 MIN
16mm
B&W
LC FI67-4
Presents an original ballet which portrays the dance career of Melanie Alexander from her days as a beginner to her debut as a prima ballerina.
Fine Arts
Dist - SF **Prod** - WOLPER 1963

Story of a Hospital Fire 27 MIN
16mm
Color
Shows a hospital fire, describing what can happen when health care personnel aren't trained in basic emergency fire procedures. Based on an actual hospital fire in Sweden.
Health and Safety; Social Science
Dist - FILCOM **Prod** - MINERV

Story of a love affair 102 MIN
16mm
B&W (ITALIAN)
Features the debut of Michelangelo Antonioni as a director. Relates the story of a grubby private detective, a glamorous femme fatale and a pair of lovers conniving to bump off an unwanted spouse.
Fine Arts
Dist - NYFLMS **Prod** - NYFLMS 1950

The Story of a Newspaperman 25 MIN
16mm
B&W (I)
LC FIA66-1306
Shows some of the problems faced by a small town newspaperman, who must report world and local news to his readers and must also solicit advertising and take an editorial stand on matters raised by public officials.
Guidance and Counseling; Psychology; Social Science
Dist - SF **Prod** - WOLPER 1963

The Story of a Policeman 25 MIN
16mm
B&W (I)
LC FI67-2
Reveals how Police Chief Edward Allan strengthened the police force in Santa Ana, California, a city which prior to 1955 had one of the highest unsolved crime rates in the United States.
Guidance and Counseling; Psychology; Social Science; Sociology
Dist - SF **Prod** - WOLPER 1962

The Story of a Prisoner 26 MIN
16mm
B&W (H)
LC FI66-2
Follows a day in the San Ouentin prison life of inmate Jim Britt. Shows his work and school routine and includes a visit from his wife and interview with his parole board. A group therapy session brings out the story of his wasted youth and the drug addiction that led to the criminal acts which put him behind bars. Demonstrates how the penal system gives a weak man the opportunity to mature into a responsible member of society.
Guidance and Counseling; Psychology; Sociology
Dist - SF **Prod** - WOLPER 1962

The Story of a songwriter 27 MIN
16mm
B&W
LC FI67-21
Portrays the life of songwriter Sammy Cahn as he relaxes with his famous show - business friends and as he works on his newest project, a nightclub routine for singer - dancer Juliet Prowse.
Fine Arts; Guidance and Counseling
Dist - SF **Prod** - WOLPER 1963

Story of a Spark Plug 34 MIN
16mm
B&W
Shows the manufacture, operation and care of the spark plug.
Business and Economics; Industrial and Technical Education
Dist - USDIBM **Prod** - USDIBM 1942

Story of a storm 29 MIN
16mm
Color (J H)
LC 74-706586
Describes how the Navy Weather Service helps Navy and cargo ships to avoid adverse weather conditions.
Civics and Political Systems; Science - Physical; Social Science
Dist - USNAC **Prod** - USN 1972

Story of a Story 20 MIN
16mm
B&W
Examines how a newspaper operates by following a simple story, the daily weather report, from the time it first comes into the newspaper office over the teletype, through writing, editing, typesetting composition and printing, until it bocomes part of a newspaper on the way to the newsstand.
Social Science
Dist - UPENN **Prod** - UPENN 1961

The Story of a trial 22 MIN
VHS
Color (J H)
$99.00 _ #4721 - 026
Follows two men from their arrest through their arraignment and trial. Stresses the importance of due process by law. Includes teacher's guide and library kit.
Civics and Political Systems; Education; Fine Arts
Dist - GA **Prod** - EBEC

The Story of a violin 5 MIN
16mm
Screen news digest series; Vol 3; Issue 4
B&W
Follows violin maker Gaggini as he creates a handmade Stradivarius violin. Shows how each step is done without haste and carried out with tender care.
Fine Arts
Dist - HEARST **Prod** - HEARST 1960

The Story of a writer 25 MIN
16mm
B&W (I J H)
LC FIA66-1181
Science fiction writer Ray Bradbury shows how he conceives, ponders and produces such tales as The Martian Chronicles, Dandelion Wine, and Fahrenheit 451.
English Language; Guidance and Counseling; Literature and Drama
Dist - SF **Prod** - WOLPER 1963

The Story of Adam and Eve 20 MIN
U-matic / VHS
Bible According to Kossoff Series
Color (G)
$159.00, $59.00 purchase _ #AD - 1516
Tells the story of Adam and Eve from the Book of Genesis in the Old Testament. Features David Kossoff, storyteller and Biblical scholar, in a thirteen - part series of favorite stories from the Old Testament.
Literature and Drama; Religion and Philosophy
Dist - FOTH **Prod** - FOTH

The Story of Alaska's Sawmills 30 MIN
16mm
Color
Presents an historical documentary of Alaska's timber industry, focusing on the development and operations of Alaska's sawmills from 1850 to the present. Uses historical photographs to show early Russian sawmills before Alaska was purchased by the United States. Explores changing markets and the drive to attract pulp companies in order to stabilize Southeast Alaska's fluctuating, seasonal economy.
Agriculture; Business and Economics; Geography - United States; Social Science
Dist - AKLOGA **Prod** - AKLOGA

The Story of America's canyon country
VHS
Color (G)
$29.95 purchase _ #TK046
Offers a video vacation down the Colorado River and through the American Southwest.
Geography - United States
Dist - SIV

The Story of America's crown jewels
VHS
Color (G)
$29.95 purchase _ #TK045
Offers a video tour of the Grand Canyon, Yosemite and Yellowstone National Park.
Geography - United States; Geography - World
Dist - SIV

The Story of America's Great Northwest
VHS
Color (G)
$29.95 purchase _ #TK047
Offers a video vacation through the glaciers, forests and volcanoes of the Northwest.
Geography - United States
Dist - SIV

The Story of America's great volcanoes
VHS
Color (G)
$29.95 purchase _ #TK048
Covers the background and history of some of America's most famous 'fire mountains,' so named by the Native Americans.
Geography - World
Dist - SIV

The Story of America's great volcanoes 60 MIN
VHS
Color (J H)
$29.95 purchase _ #QV2263
Visits the sites and explores the history of some of the United States' most famous volcanoes, including Mt St Helens, Mt Rainier, Crater Lake, Mauna Loa and more.
Geography - World
Dist - KNOWUN

The Story of an Air Force Base 10 MIN
16mm
B&W
LC FIE63-273
Portrays air pioneers and aviation history as General Thomas D White narrates events linking Bolling Air Force Base to growth and development of the USAF.
Civics and Political Systems; History - United States; Industrial and Technical Education; Social Science
Dist - USNAC **Prod** - USAF 1962

The Story of an Artist 26 MIN
16mm
B&W
LC FI66-3
Portrays artist Ed Keinholz at work as he searches through junkyards, thrift stores and manikin factories to find the raw materials to create sculptures reflective of modern life.
Fine Arts; Guidance and Counseling; Psychology
Dist - SF **Prod** - WOLPER 1962

The Story of Anglicanism - Pt 1 28 MIN
VHS / 16mm
Color (H A)
$29.95 purchase
Tells the story of Anglicanism. Part 1 of a three - part series.
Religion and Philosophy
Dist - CAFM **Prod** - CAFM 1990

The Story of Anglicanism - Pt 2 29 MIN
VHS / 16mm
Color (H A)
$29.95 purchase
Tells the story of Anglicanism. Part 2 of a three - part series.
Religion and Philosophy
Dist - CAFM **Prod** - CAFM 1990

The Story of Anglicanism - Pt 3 25 MIN
VHS / 16mm
Color (H A)
$29.95 purchase
Tells the story of Anglicanism. Part 3 of a three - part series.
Religion and Philosophy
Dist - CAFM **Prod** - CAFM 1990

A Story of Arc Welding 24 MIN
16mm
Color
Explains the advantages of arc welding and shows how it is done. Depicts its uses in industry, on the farm and for the repair of military equipment.
Industrial and Technical Education
Dist - USDIBM **Prod** - USDIBM 1945

The Story of Babe Ruth 55 MIN
VHS
Color (J H G)
$19.95 purchase _ #AV2251
Portrays sports hero Babe Ruth who was taken by the Baltimore Orioles from St Mary's School and made the youngest player, at age 19.
Biography; Physical Education and Recreation
Dist - INSTRU

Story of Bananas 11 MIN
16mm / U-matic / VHS
B&W (I)
Shows the cultivation, harvesting, transporting, inspection and distribution of bananas.
Psychology; Social Science
Dist - IFB **Prod** - PAU 1947

The Story of Camp Century - City Under the Ice 32 MIN
16mm
Color
LC FIE64-179
A nontechnical account of the planning and constuction of camp century, a nuclear - powered U S Army Arctic Research Laboratory buried below the Greenland ice cap. Describes the planning, installation, testing and operation of the nuclear power plant which provides electricity and space heating.
Science; Science - Physical
Dist - USNAC **Prod** - USA 1961

Story of Carl Gustav Jung Series no 3
The Mystery that Heals 30 MIN
Dist - FI

Story of Carl Gustav Jung Series
In Search of the Soul 30 MIN
Sixty - Seven Thousand Dreams 30 MIN
Dist - FI

The Story of Cerro - Bolivar 14 MIN
16mm
Color (H C A)
Revised edition of Iron Ore From Cerro - Bolivar. Tells the story of the discovery of the iron ore mine called Cerro - Bolivar in 1947, the initial planning, clearing of jungles, dredging rivers, construction of docks, railroads, bridges, ore loading facilities, power and water plants and the completed communities.
Business and Economics; History - World; Industrial and Technical Education
Dist - USSC **Prod** - HANDY 1954

The Story of Chaim Rumkowski and the Jews of Lodz 55 MIN
U-matic / VHS / 16mm
B&W
LC 83-700854
Presents the story of Chaim Rumkowski, who was appointed by the Nazis as the Chairman of the Lodz Jewish Council and who was responsible for establishing a vast bureaucracy to administer all social services within the ghetto. Tells how Rumkowski attempted to turn the Lodz ghetto into an industrial center that would become indispensable to the German war effort, thus enabling the Jews of Lodz to survive the war. Depicts the conditions of daily life, the gradual disintegration of the ghetto and the deportations to death camps.
History - World
Dist - CNEMAG **Prod** - CNEMAG 1983

The Story of Charles A Lindbergh 55 MIN
VHS
Color (J H G)
$19.95 purchase _ #AV2252
Portrays the life of aviator Charles A Lindbergh who, in 1927, made the first non - stop, solo trans - Atlantic flight to Paris in 33.5 hours. Reveals that he became a world - famous celebrity and, unfortunately, would become famous again when his 20 - month - old son was kidnapped.
History - United States; Industrial and Technical Education
Dist - INSTRU

The Story of Christmas 8 MIN
U-matic / VHS / 16mm
Color (I J H)
LC 76-701281
Uses medieval settings, music and animation, in order to present a version of the Christmas story.
Religion and Philosophy; Social Science
Dist - FI **Prod** - NFBC 1976

The Story of Cinderella 7 MIN
16mm
Color; B&W (K P I)
Presents the fairy tale of Cinderella as seen and interpreted in water color and crayon drawings by fifth grade children. Provides narration by the children.
Fine Arts; Literature and Drama
Dist - NFBC **Prod** - NFBC 1958

The Story of climate, weather and people
VHS
Keys to science literacy series
Color; CC (I J)
$79.00 purchase _ #403
Presents the basic science involved in weather and climate research and prediction. Contains computer graphics and on - site footage. Part of a 14 - part series for teaching scientific literacy and ranging from 15 to 20 minutes in length. Includes a book from the Learning Power series.
Science - Physical
Dist - HAWHIL **Prod** - HAWHIL 1994

Story of Coffee 11 MIN
U-matic / VHS / 16mm
B&W (I)
Explains how Brazilian coffee is grown, harvested, processed, graded, bagged and transported.
Science - Natural; Social Science
Dist - IFB **Prod** - PAU 1947

A Story of Copper 33 MIN
16mm
Color
Tells the story of the mining and manufacture of copper from the crude ore to the finished product.
Business and Economics; Science - Natural
Dist - USDIBM **Prod** - USDIBM 1951

The Story of Copper 14 MIN
16mm
Color
LC 80-700926
Shows the production of copper from open cut mining operations, crushing, flotation and smelting to final electrolysis.
Industrial and Technical Education
Dist - TASCOR **Prod** - TASCOR 1965

Story of Croesus 30 MIN
U-matic
Herodotus - Father of History Series
Color
Discusses how Croesus, the wealthiest man in the world, sought immortality through continuation of his bloodline and reputation and lost both.
History - World
Dist - UMITV **Prod** - UMITV 1980

The Story of 'dance in America' 30 MIN
VHS / U-matic
Dance on television and film series
Color
Fine Arts; Industrial and Technical Education
Dist - ARCVID **Prod** - ARCVID

The Story of David 16 MIN
16mm
Color (C)
Presents an interview with David, a small boy born without a larnyx who has taught himself to speak. The interviewer, Dr Lawrence Pratt, gives an explanation of this extraordinary phenomenon.
English Language; Health and Safety; Psychology
Dist - WSUM **Prod** - WSUM 1958

The Story of David and Bathsheba 20 MIN
U-matic / VHS
Bible According to Kossoff Series
Color (G)
$159.00, $59.00 purchase _ #AD - 1575
Tells the story of King David who lusted after Bathsheba and caused her husband to be sent to death on the battlefield. Reveals that David is punished for breaking the commandments he was supposed to uphold, but David and Bathsheba are also blessed with a son, Solomon, one of the greatest kings of the Bible. Features David Kossoff, storyteller and Biblical scholar, in a thirteen - part series of favorite stories from the Old Testament.
Literature and Drama; Religion and Philosophy
Dist - FOTH **Prod** - FOTH

The Story of David and Goliath 20 MIN
U-matic / VHS
Bible According to Kossoff Series
Color (G)
$159.00, $59.00 purchase _ #AD - 1519
Tells the story of the great King David when he was a shepherd boy. Recalls David's courage and intelligence in overcoming the giant Goliath. Features David Kossoff, storyteller and Biblical scholar, in a thirteen - part series of favorite stories from the Old Testament.
Literature and Drama; Religion and Philosophy
Dist - FOTH **Prod** - FOTH

The Story of Debbie 25 MIN
16mm
Family life education and human growth series
B&W (I)
LC FIA66-1182
Debbie, who has lived with relatives and in foster homes and institution for 11 years, is shown at the children's Baptist home in Los Angeles as she attempts to adjust to life while awaiting a reunion with her family and a return to a more normal life.
Psychology; Sociology
Dist - SF **Prod** - WOLPER 1963

The Story of Dentistry 20 MIN
16mm
Color
LC 75-703234
Using historical photographs, the history of dentistry is traced from ancient Egypt to the present. Scenes of USC'S School of Dentistry depict modern dental practices.
Health and Safety
Dist - USC **Prod** - USC 1964

A Story of discovery - why plants bend toward light 13 MIN
U-matic / VHS / 16mm
Color (I) (SPANISH)
Replicates experiments performed by Darwin and later scientists to illustrate an historical approach to experimentation.
Science
Dist - EBEC **Prod** - EBEC

The Story of disease and health
VHS
Keys to science literacy series
Color; CC (I J)
$79.00 purchase _ #405
Tells the dramatic story of human progress in conquering disease. Helps students to see the importance of science and of common sense in avoiding disease and achieving health. Stresses the harmful effects of smoking, alcohol and other drugs. Part of a 14 - part series for teaching scientific literacy and ranging from 15 to 20 minutes in length. Includes a book from the Learning Power series.
Health and Safety; Psychology; Sociology
Dist - HAWHIL **Prod** - HAWHIL 1994

The Story of Douglas MacArthur 55 MIN
VHS
Color (J H G)
$19.95 purchase _ #AV2246
Traces the life of Gen Douglas MacArthur through his command of US forces in the Far East during World War II and his acceptance of the Japanese surrender about the USS Missouri. Reveals that in June, 1950, when North Korea invaded South Korea, Gen MacArthur directed UN Forces against the communists.
Biography; History - United States
Dist - INSTRU

The Story of Dwight D Eisenhower 55 MIN
VHS
Color (J H G)
$19.95 purchase _ #AV2250
Tells the story of the Allies' victory in World War II and the 'Eisenhower years,' 1952 - 1960, a period that shaped the second half of the 20th century. Focuses on 'Ike,' Dwight D Eisenhower, Supreme Allied Commander in World War II, who accepted the unconditional surrender of the German Army on May 7, 1945.
Biography; Civics and Political Systems; History - United States
Dist - INSTRU

The Story of ecosystems
VHS
Keys to science literacy series
Color; CC (I J)
$79.00 purchase _ #406
Explains what the science of ecology is all about and how it helps humans to make sense of the living world of which they are a part. Discusses concepts such as food chains, chemical cycles, energy flow and environmental choices. Uses computer graphics and footage from around the

world. Part of a 14 - part series for teaching scientific literacy and ranging from 15 to 20 minutes in length. Includes a book from the Learning Power series.
Science - Natural
Dist - HAWHIL **Prod** - HAWHIL 1994

The Story of electricity - the greeks to Franklin 14 MIN
U-matic / VHS / 16mm
Advance of science series
Color (I J)
LC FIA68-900
Traces the key advances in human knowledge of electricity from the early Greek's electron, or amber, to Benjamin Franklin's single - fluid theory. Illustrates the ideas, methods and inventions of William Gilbert, Stephen Gray, Francis Hauksbee, Pieter Van Musschenbroek and Benjamin Franklin.
Science; Science - Physical
Dist - CORF **Prod** - CORF 1968

The Story of Elijah 20 MIN
U-matic / VHS
Bible According to Kossoff Series
Color (G)
$159.00, $59.00 purchase _ #AD - 1525
Tells the story of Elijah the prophet, who met a widow at the city's gates and asked her for bread and water during a dreadful drought. Reveals that Elijah told the woman she and her son would never lack for flour and oil until the arrival of rain. Features David Kossoff, storyteller and Biblical scholar, in a thirteen - part series of favorite stories from the Old Testament.
Literature and Drama; Religion and Philosophy
Dist - FOTH **Prod** - FOTH

The Story of Eman 26 MIN
VHS
Turning 16 series
Color; CC (G T)
$175.00 purchase, $50.00 rental
Follows Eman, a Cairo girl who doesn't always agree with her parents and, inspite of cultural traditions, wants to attend university. Asks if men and women share the same rights and freedoms. Features part four of an eight - part series that questions whether there is a global teenager. Examines the lives of six teens from different countries and explores the major issues facing young people everywhere - including education, culture, sex and marriage, sports, religion, work and the future.
Education; Fine Arts; Geography - World; Guidance and Counseling; Sociology
Dist - BULFRG **Prod** - HARCOT 1994

The Story of English
VHS
Color (H C)
$149.00 purchase _ #04558 - 126
Journeys through the history of the English language. Encompasses history, geography, sociology, drama, language and the arts.
English Language; History - World
Dist - GA **Prod** - GA

The Story of English 58 MIN
VHS
Story of English Series; Vol V
Color (G)
$199.00 series purchase _ #834-9015
Journeys through the history of the English language with host Robert MacNeil. Travels the world to illustrate the language's global influence. Includes 'Next Year's Words - A Look Into The Future,' which considers that Latin, now considered 'dead,' was once a universal language. Asks if a similar fate awaits English. Available only as part of the complete series.
English Language
Dist - FI **Prod** - BBCTV 1986

The Story of English 115 MIN
VHS
Story of English Series; Vol I
Color (G)
$199.00 series purchase _ #834-9015
Journeys through the history of the English language with host Robert MacNeil. Travels the world to illustrate the language's global influence. Includes two parts, 'An English Speaking World,' which discusses English as the world's first truly global language, and 'Mother Tongue,' which surveys the growth of English from its Anglo - Saxon origins through the Norman conquest to the poetry of Geoffrey Chaucer. Available only as part of the complete series.
English Language
Dist - FI **Prod** - BBCTV 1986

The Story of English 115 MIN
VHS
Story of English Series; Vol II
Color (G)
$199.00 series purchase _ #834-9015
Journeys through the history of the English language with host Robert MacNeil. Travels the world to illustrate the language's global influence. Includes two parts, 'A Muse Of Fire,' which considers the works of William Shakespeare and the King James Bible; 'The Guid Scots Tongue,' which traces Scottish influence from embattled Northern Ireland to American Appalachia. Available only as part of the complete series.
English Language
Dist - FI **Prod** - BBCTV 1986

The Story of English 116 MIN
VHS
Story of English Series; Vol IV
Color (G)
$199.00 series purchase _ #834-9015
Journeys through the history of the English language with host Robert MacNeil. Travels the world to illustrate the language's global influence. Includes two parts, 'The Muvver Tongue,' which examines the spread of English in the 19th century through British colonialism and how Cockney, London's working class English, found new impetus in imperialism; and 'The Loaded Weapon,' which considers the Irish influence on English. More than 43 million Americans claim Irish descent. Available only as part of the complete series.
English Language; Geography - World
Dist - FI **Prod** - BBCTV 1986

The Story of English 116 MIN
VHS
Story of English Series; Vol III
Color (G)
$199.00 series purchase _ #834-9015
Journeys through the history of the English language with host Robert MacNeil. Travels the world to illustrate the language's global influence. Includes two parts, 'Black On White,' which explores Black English and its origins in the slave trade, its migration from southern to northern United States, the Creole influence, jive talk and today's black 'rap;' and 'Pioneers O Pioneers,' which evokes the spirit behind the evolution of American English from the Revolutionary War through the 1920s. Available only as part of the complete series.
English Language
Dist - FI **Prod** - BBCTV 1986

Story of English furniture series
From the late 18th Century to the present day - Pt 2 105 MIN
From the Middle Ages to the 18th century - Pt 1 106 MIN
Dist - FI

Story of English series
An English speaking world 60 MIN
The Guid Scots Tongue 60 MIN
The Loaded weapon 60 MIN
A Muse of Fire 60 MIN
The Muvver Tongue 60 MIN
Next year's words - The Empire strikes back 60 MIN
Pioneers O Pioneers 60 MIN
Dist - BBCENE
FI
PSU

Story of English Series
The Story of English 116 MIN
Dist - FI

The Story of Eric 34 MIN
16mm
Color
LC 72-702183
Follows a young mother through her first childbearing experience to help educate parents about the Lamaze method of prepared childbirth.
Guidance and Counseling; Science - Natural; Sociology
Dist - CENTRE **Prod** - ASPPO 1972

The Story of Esther 50 MIN
U-matic / VHS / 16mm
Greatest Heroes of the Bible Series
Color (I)
Reveals how Queen Esther of Persia, who is secretly a Hebrew, discovers a plot to seize the King's throne. Shows how she tricks one of the plotters into revealing the plot before the King. Stars Victoria Principal and Michael Ansara.
Religion and Philosophy
Dist - LUF **Prod** - LUF 1979

The Story of evolution
VHS
Keys to science literacy series
Color; CC (I J)
$79.00 purchase _ #408
Explains how life has changed through the ages and how the modern theory of evolution by natural selection explains those changes. Includes footage from Darwin's home and study. Part of a 14 - part series for teaching scientific literacy and ranging from 15 to 20 minutes in length. Includes a book from the Learning Power series.
Science - Natural
Dist - HAWHIL **Prod** - HAWHIL 1994

Story of Fashion Series
The Art and Sport of Fashion - Pt 2 63 MIN
Remembrance of Things Past - Pt 1 60 MIN
Dist - FI

A Story of Floating Weeds 89 MIN
16mm
B&W
Concerns a down - at - the - heels acting troupe that reaches the end of the line in a remote mountain town. Explores the relationships between the members of the troupe as they begin to go their separate ways. A Japanese production.
Fine Arts; Foreign Language; Sociology
Dist - NYFLMS **Prod** - NYFLMS 1934

The Story of Franklin Delano Roosevelt 100 MIN
VHS
Color (J H G)
$19.95 purchase _ #AV2247
Portrays the United States' Great Depression, which occurred during the first half of the 20th century, and the role of Franklin Delano Roosevelt in overcoming its effects. Shows how his tough - minded attitude and relief programs altered American life for the rest of the century.
Biography; Civics and Political Systems; History - United States
Dist - INSTRU

The Story of gasoline 23 MIN
16mm
B&W
Traces the story of gasoline from crude oil to finished product and explains in simple terms the complex structural patterns of petroleum molecules making up the fuel that propels millions of automobiles, farm equipment, airplanes and other internal combustion engines.
Business and Economics; Industrial and Technical Education; Social Science
Dist - USDIBM **Prod** - USDIBM 1958

Story of George 19 MIN
VHS / 16mm
Color (G)
Relates the story of George, a high school student who does his homework and writes poetry but is considered by teachers and fellow students to be either dull or arrogant. Explores the differences between individuals that can cause misunderstandings.
Psychology; Sociology
Dist - FLMWST

The Story of GI Joe 55 MIN
VHS
Color (J H G)
$19.95 purchase _ #AV2253
Follows the fortunes of the young men who joined the military - Army, Navy, Marine Corps, Air Corps and Merchant Marines - who became 'Government Issue' GIs.
History - United States
Dist - INSTRU

The Story of Gideon 20 MIN
U-matic / VHS
Bible According to Kossoff Series
Color (G)
$159.00, $59.00 purchase _ #AD - 1521
Tells the story of Gideon who conquered the Midianites with an army of three hundred men armed with trumpets and torches. Features David Kossoff, storyteller and Biblical scholar, in a thirteen - part series of favorite stories from the Old Testament.
Literature and Drama; Religion and Philosophy
Dist - FOTH **Prod** - FOTH

The story of good king Huemac 21 MIN
16mm / VHS
Color (P I J G)
$420.00, $150.00 purchase, $40.00 rental _ #11289, #37260
Uses puppet animation to tell how underworld creatures conspired to bring Evil into the happy Toltec kingdom but the force of Good eventually triumphed. Adapts a Mexican Indian legend. Produced by Richard Fichter.
Literature and Drama; Social Science
Dist - UCEMC

The Story of Harry S Truman 55 MIN
VHS
Color (J H G)
$19.95 purchase _ #AV2248
Tells of the 'Truman years' following the death of President Franklin Delano Roosevelt. Reveals that President Truman approved the dropping of two atomic bombs on Japan in August, 1945, in order to avert an Allied invasion of Japan and the loss of possibly one million Allied and Axis troops.
Biography; History - United States
Dist - INSTRU

The Story of Helen Keller 55 MIN
VHS
Color (J H G)
$19.95 purchase _ #AV2245
Portrays Helen Keller who overcame blindness and deafness in order to write, speak and labor incessantly for the betterment of others.
Biography; Guidance and Counseling
Dist - INSTRU

The Story of Henry Ford 55 MIN
VHS
Color (J H G)
$19.95 purchase _ #AV2244
Reveals that Henry Ford built his first automobile in 1893 by mounting an engine on a frame fitted with four bicycle wheels. Discloses that he also introduced mass ownership of automobiles and sparked the 20th - century industrial revolution in America.
Business and Economics; History - United States; Industrial and Technical Education
Dist - INSTRU

The Story of Human Enterprise 28 MIN
16mm
Color
LC 73-711508
Shows the operations of a forest products firm which uses natural resources as raw materials, and produces from these resources a series of consumable products, including plywood, pulp, paper and containers. Explains the need for good management and a minimal disturbance of the forests in order to meet the continuing demand for these products.
Agriculture
Dist - GAPAC **Prod** - GAPAC 1972

The Story of Idrissa 26 MIN
VHS
Turning 16 series
Color; CC (G T)
$175.00 purchase, $50.00 rental
Follows Idrissa, a boy from Niger who wants to stay close to his parents to learn his nomadic tribe traditions, even though it means leaving school. Asks if values can be preserved in an ever - increasing consumer society. Features part three of an eight - part series that asks whether there is a global teenager. Examines the lives of six teens from different countries and explores major issues facing young people everywhere - including education, culture, sex and marriage, sports, religion, work and the future.
Education; Fine Arts; Geography - World; Guidance and Counseling; Sociology
Dist - BULFRG **Prod** - HARCOT 1994

The Story of Islam 120 MIN
VHS
Color; B&W (J H)
$24.98 purchase _ #MP6024
Journeys through the history of Islam, from its humble beginnings 1300 years ago to its place in the modern world. Introduces the culture, philosophy and fundamentals of this way of life.
Religion and Philosophy
Dist - KNOWUN **Prod** - ABCNEW

The Story of Jacob and Esau 20 MIN
U-matic / VHS
Bible According to Kossoff Series
Color (G)
$159.00, $59.00 purchase _ #AD - 1517
Tells the story of the brothers. Jacob, the second - born of twins and his mother's favorite, tricks his brother Esau out of his inheritance. Features David Kossoff, storyteller and Biblical scholar, in a thirteen - part series of favorite stories from the Old Testament.
Literature and Drama; Religion and Philosophy
Dist - FOTH **Prod** - FOTH

The Story of Jacob's Dream 20 MIN
U-matic / VHS
Bible According to Kossoff Series
Color (G)
$159.00, $59.00 purchase _ #AD - 1574
Tells the story of Jacob. Reveals that God appears to him in a dream to tell him of his future role in the history of his people. Features David Kossoff, storyteller and Biblical scholar, in a thirteen - part series of favorite stories from the Old Testament.
Literature and Drama; Religion and Philosophy
Dist - FOTH **Prod** - FOTH

The Story of John Henry 15 MIN
U-matic
Magic Carpet Series
Color (P)
Retells the American legend of John Henry.
Literature and Drama
Dist - GPN **Prod** - SDCSS 1977

The Story of Jonah 20 MIN
U-matic / VHS
Bible According to Kossoff Series
Color (G)
$159.00, $59.00 purchase _ #AD - 1518
Tells the story of Jonah who is swallowed by a big fish God sends to make sure that he gets to Nineveh. Reveals that he learns humility and appreciation for his blessings in the belly of the fish, and God causes him to be vomited out upon dry land. Features David Kossoff, storyteller and Biblical scholar, in a thirteen - part series of favorite stories from the Old Testament.
Literature and Drama; Religion and Philosophy
Dist - FOTH **Prod** - FOTH

The Story of Joseph
VHS
Greatest tales from the Old Testament series
Color (K P I R)
$29.95 purchase, $10.00 rental _ #35 - 829 - 528
Presents a three - part account of the Old Testament story of Joseph.
Literature and Drama; Religion and Philosophy
Dist - APH **Prod** - CAFM
CAFM

The Story of Joshua 20 MIN
U-matic / VHS
Bible According to Kossoff Series
Color (G)
$159.00, $59.00 purchase _ #AD - 1523
Tells the story of Joshua and the seven trumpets and how they ensured the outcome of the Battle of Jericho. Features David Kossoff, storyteller and Biblical scholar, in a thirteen - part series of favorite stories from the Old Testament.
Literature and Drama; Religion and Philosophy
Dist - FOTH **Prod** - FOTH

The Story of King Midas 11 MIN
16mm / U-matic / VHS
Color; B&W (P I)
LC FIA67-1568
Presents the classic story book tale of the king with the golden touch, who learns that greed can bring unhappiness.
English Language; Guidance and Counseling; Literature and Drama; Psychology
Dist - PHENIX **Prod** - HARRY 1954

The Story of Knute Rockne 55 MIN
VHS
Color (J H G)
$19.95 purchase _ #AV2249
Portrays Knute Rockne, the best known college coach in American football history. Reveals that he was renowned for his great locker room speeches and his unbeaten teams in the 'golden era of sports.'
Biography; Physical Education and Recreation
Dist - INSTRU

The Story of L Sharkey 22 MIN
16mm
Color (H C A)
LC 81-701144
Describes how a young journalist in a small town latches on to a story of an old hermit who hasn't been seen for more than 40 years. Tells how the story could mean a big break for the journalist, but the townspeople don't want him to disturb the hermit.
Fine Arts
Dist - USC **Prod** - USC 1981

The Story of Lili Marlene 22 MIN
U-matic / VHS
B&W
Documents the famous World War II song 'Lili Marlene', with historical footage.
History - World; Sociology
Dist - IHF **Prod** - IHF

The Story of living in space
VHS
Keys to science literacy series
Color; CC (I J)
$79.00 purchase _ #411
Tells the dramatic story of human ventures into outer space during the last half of the 20th century. Challenges students to think big about the possible colonization of space, as well as further exploration. Includes a tribute to junior high school teacher Christa McAuliffe. Part of a 14 - part series for teaching scientific literacy and ranging from 15 to 20 minutes in length. Includes a book from the Learning Power series.
History - World; Science - Physical
Dist - HAWHIL **Prod** - HAWHIL 1994

Story of Liz 30 MIN
VHS / U-matic
K I D S - a Series
Color (H)
Tells about Liz, who hitchhikes after school and is sexually assaulted. Unable to cope, Liz swallows a huge dose of sleeping pills but is saved when family and friends enlist help from a radio station to find her in time.
Sociology
Dist - GPN **Prod** - CPOD

The Story of Lubricating Oil 22 MIN
16mm
Color
Explains in animation how lubricating oil is produced and processed to meet the needs of modern machinery.
Business and Economics; Industrial and Technical Education
Dist - USDIBM **Prod** - USDIBM 1949

The Story of Luggage - from Caveman to Spaceman 20 MIN
16mm
Color
Shows how the story of luggage is also the story of man and his need to travel. Traces the history of luggage as it has been made and used by the Stone Age cave dwellers, Pharaoh, the Greeks, the Romans, through the Renaissance, the New World colonists, the American Indians, the Western Pioneers to the present Jet Age. Narrated by Astronaut Scott Carrenter.
Geography - World; History - World; Social Science
Dist - CROSSC **Prod** - SAMCOR

Story of Measuring Time - Hours, Minutes, Seconds 12 MIN
U-matic / VHS / 16mm
Color (I)
$305, $215 purchase _ #3686
Shows the different ways that time is measured and different devices used to measure it such as sundials and atomic clocks.
Mathematics
Dist - CORF

The Story of Miriam and Leonard 11 MIN
VHS
Color (G C)
$135.00 purchase, $35.00 rental
Tells how meeting an active older gentleman changes Miriam's outlook from one of calm introspection regarding the past to an active anticipation of the future.
Health and Safety; Psychology
Dist - TNF

The Story of Molly Pitcher 15 MIN
U-matic / VHS / 16mm
Magic Carpet Series
Color (P)
Retells the legend of Molly Pitcher, American heroine of the Revolutionary War.
Literature and Drama
Dist - GPN **Prod** - SDCSS 1979

The Story of mothers and daughters 7 MIN
16mm
Family series
Color (G)
$20.00 rental
Presents the third in a series of four short films that deal with an idiosyncratic, personal and conceptual view of aspects of familial relationships. Features optically printed home movie footage and new material. The soundtrack intersperses personal anecdotes about mothers and daughters with the images. A Sandy Maliga production.
Fine Arts; Sociology
Dist - CANCIN

The Story of My Life
Cassette / 16mm
Now Age Reading Programs, Set 2 Series
Color (I J)
$9.95 purchase _ #8F - PN681956
Brings autobiographical form to young readers. Filmstrip set includes filmstrip, cassette, corresponding book, classroom exercise materials and a poster. The read - along set includes student activity book, cassette and paperback.
English Language; Literature and Drama
Dist - MAFEX

The Story of natural resources
VHS
Keys to science literacy series
Color; CC (I J)
$79.00 purchase _ #412
Introduces students to one of the most important concepts in science and society today. Explains what a natural resource is and presents conflicting views of experts on the future. Asks if resources are limited or not. Part of a 14 - part series for teaching scientific literacy and ranging from 15 to 20 minutes in length. Includes a book from the Learning Power series.
Science - Natural
Dist - HAWHIL **Prod** - HAWHIL 1994

The story of naval aviation 27 MIN
16mm
B&W
LC 74-706259
Traces the development of U S naval aviation from its earliest days to its modern role as the primary striking weapon of the fleet. Depicts the first trans - Atlantic flight and the first U S carrier landing.
Civics and Political Systems; History - United States; Industrial and Technical Education; Social Science
Dist - USNAC **Prod -** USN 1961

Story of Nickel Refining 22 MIN
16mm
B&W
Shows steps in nickel refining, including the pouring and casting of nickel, a method of recovering nickel from the furnace slag and the preparation of a black nickel oxide virtually free of sulfur.
Business and Economics
Dist - USDIBM **Prod -** USDIBM 1950

The Story of nuclear power
VHS
Keys to science literacy series
Color; CC (I J)
$79.00 purchase _ #413
Explains how nuclear power was discovered. Discusses the basic concepts needed to understand nuclear reactions and nuclear power plants. Concludes with an examination of the pros and cons of nuclear power today and tomorrow. Part of a 14 - part series for teaching scientific literacy and ranging from 15 to 20 minutes in length. Includes a book from the Learning Power series.
Social Science
Dist - HAWHIL **Prod -** HAWHIL 1994

The Story of Oak Ridge Operations 28 MIN
16mm
Color (J)
LC 72-700020
Covers the major activities of the Atomic Energy Commission Oak Ridge operations office, which supports programs of national defense and the peaceful applications of atomic energy. Portrays the gaseous diff1sion plant production of enriched uranium for fueling nuclear power plants, research activities and the use of radiation to diagnose and treat disease.
Geography - United States; Health and Safety; Science; Science - Physical
Dist - USERD **Prod -** ORNLAB 1972

The Story of Our Money System 11 MIN
16mm / U-matic / VHS
Color (I J H)
Traces the evolution of the unified money system from the ancient practice of bartering to the convenient forms of exchange used today. Illustrates the early use of animals and other mediums of exchange, showing the development of metal coins.
Business and Economics; Psychology; Social Science
Dist - CORF **Prod -** CORF 1958

Story of outdoor advertising 13 MIN
16mm
Color
Demonstrates the effectiveness of outdoor advertising on today's consumers. Points out that the automobile, the connecting link between household and marketplace, had become the recognized basis for determining the market.
Business and Economics; Psychology
Dist - CCNY **Prod -** GOUTAD

The Story of paper - managing people, managing processes 25 MIN
35mm strip / VHS
Our economy - how it works series
Color (J H C A)
$39.00, $39.00 purchase _ #MB - 510670 - 1, #MB - 508864 - 9
Presents the third segment of a six - part series on basic concepts of economics. Focuses on the production and distribution process involved in making paper. Covers the process in a step - by - step fashion, from the cultivation and harvesting of the trees to the finished product.
Business and Economics
Dist - SRA **Prod -** SRA

Story of Peggy at the Farm 16 MIN
U-matic / VHS / 16mm
Color (P I)
Shows a typical farm day, from the time the rooster crows until evening. Observes many farm animals.
Science - Natural; Social Science
Dist - IFB **Prod -** CALVIN 1957

The Story of Peter 30 MIN
VHS
Great Bible stories series
Color (P I R)
$15.95 purchase, $10.00 rental _ #35 - 8284 - 8936
Tells the story of how a Roman soldier prayed to God for guidance. Emphasizes the role of Peter in showing the soldier that God cares for all people in all nations.
Literature and Drama; Religion and Philosophy
Dist - APH

The Story of petroleum - critical risks, potential profits 17 MIN
35mm strip / VHS
Our economy - how it works series
Color (J H C A)
$39.00, $39.00 purchase _ #MB - 510674 - 4, #MB - 508868 - 1
Presents the fourth segment of a six - part series on basic concepts of economics. Focuses on the production and distribution process involved in petroleum production. Covers the process in a step - by - step fashion. Reveals the dependence of the U S industrial economy on fossil fuels.
Business and Economics
Dist - SRA **Prod -** SRA

The Story of Pintinho 26 MIN
VHS
Turning 16 series
Color; CC (G T)
$175.00 purchase, $50.00 rental
Follows Pintinho, a talented young Brazilian athlete who hopes to kick his way out of the slums by becoming a soccer star and who has been training for years to become a member of the Flamengo team. Asks if sports are a ticket to the future. Features part five of an eight - part series that questions whether there is a global teenager. Examines the lives of six teens from different countries and explores the major issues facing young people everywhere - including education, culture, sex and marriage, sports, religion, work and the future.
Fine Arts; Geography - World; Physical Education and Recreation; Sociology
Dist - BULFRG **Prod -** HARCOT 1994

Story of Power 3 MIN
16mm
Of all Things Series
Color (P I)
Tells the story of power.
Science - Physical; Social Science
Dist - AVED **Prod -** BAILYL

The Story of Puttinan 26 MIN
VHS
Turning 16 series
Color; CC (G)
$175.00 purchase, $50.00 rental
Follows Puttinan who, at age 13, left her small village for Bangkok, where she worked under harsh conditions for three years to aid in the support of her family, and now devotes herself to ending child labor exploitation. Features part six of an eight - part series that questions whether there is a global teenager. Examines the lives of six teens from different countries and explores the major issues facing young people everywhere - including education, culture, sex and marriage, sports, religion, work and the future.
Fine Arts; Sociology
Dist - BULFRG **Prod -** HARCOT 1994

The Story of radiation
VHS
Keys to science literacy series
Color; CC (I J)
$79.00 purchase _ #414
Teaches about the electromagnetic spectrum, about nuclear radiation and about the risks and the benefits of radiation in the world. Uses computer graphics and live - action footage to add interest to the basics of radiation. Part of a 14 - part series for teaching scientific literacy and ranging from 15 to 20 minutes in length. Includes a book from the Learning Power series.
Health and Safety; Science - Physical
Dist - HAWHIL **Prod -** HAWHIL 1994

Story of radiation series
Radiation - Can We Control it? (Safety Precautions) 15 MIN
Radiation - can we use it - risks vs benefits 15 MIN
Radiation - does it affect us - human effects 15 MIN
Radiation - is it safe - interpretation of dose 15 MIN
Radiation - what does it do - inter - reaction with matter 15 MIN
Radiation - what effect does it have - biological effects 15 MIN
Radiation - what is it - energy in motion 15 MIN
Radiation - what is it made of - particles and waves 15 MIN
Radiation - where do we go from here - issues 15 MIN
Radiation - where is it - measurement and detection 15 MIN
Dist - EDMI

The Story of Rebild 19 MIN
16mm
Color
Presents the Danish - American Fourth of July celebration at Rebild.
Geography - World; History - World; Social Science
Dist - AUDPLN **Prod -** RDCG

The Story of Renal Calculi 32 MIN
16mm
Color (PRO)
Describes the various etiologic factors associated with the formation of renal calculi and the phases of preoperative investigation that are essential to establishing the underlying causative factor in each individual patient. Outlines the surgical removal of stones by pelviolithotomy, nephrolithotomy and by resection of lower pole of kidney.
Health and Safety; Science
Dist - ACY **Prod -** ACYDGD 1957

The Story of Robin Hood 84 MIN
U-matic / 16mm / VHS
Color
Presents the story of the adventures of Robin Hood with his band of Merrymen in the Sherwood Forest.
Fine Arts; Literature and Drama
Dist - FI **Prod -** DISNEY 1963

The Story of Rocky Mountain Spotted Fever 29 MIN
16mm
Color
LC 74-705705
Shows the tick life - cycle, rodent poisoning, cattle dipping and tick parasite and liveration. Demonstrates the discovery of the yolk sac vaccine and the advent of the therapeutic antibiotics.
Health and Safety; Science
Dist - USNAC **Prod -** NMAC 1969

The Story of Rosie 26 MIN
VHS
Turning 16 series
Color; CC (G T)
$175.00 purchase, $50.00 rental
Looks at the role of the family in Jamaica, where 25 percent of all 16 - year - old girls are pregnant. Asks if they can reconcile their mother roles with their desire for careers and carefree teenage lives. Features part two of an eight - part series that asks whether there is a global teenager. Examines the lives of six teens from different countries and explores major issues facing young people everywhere - including education, culture, sex and marriage, sports, religion, work and the future.
Fine Arts; Geography - World; Sociology
Dist - BULFRG **Prod -** HARCOT 1994

The Story of Ruth 20 MIN
U-matic / VHS
Bible According to Kossoff Series
Color (G)
$159.00, $59.00 purchase _ #AD - 1520
Tells the story of Ruth, the woman who became a symbol of loyalty and devotion because she refused to abandon her mother - in - law after the death of her husband. Features David Kossoff, storyteller and Biblical scholar, in a thirteen - part series of favorite stories from the Old Testament.
Literature and Drama; Religion and Philosophy
Dist - FOTH **Prod -** FOTH

The Story of Samson 20 MIN
U-matic / VHS
Bible According to Kossoff Series
Color (G)
$159.00, $59.00 purchase _ #AD - 1522
Tells the story of Samson, known throughout the kingdom for his colossal strength and bravery. Reveals that he is betrayed and shorn of his strength - giving hair by Delilah but revenges himself against his captors, the Philistines. Features David Kossoff, storyteller and Biblical scholar, in a thirteen - part series of favorite stories from the Old Testament.
Literature and Drama; Religion and Philosophy
Dist - FOTH **Prod -** FOTH

The Story of Samuel 20 MIN
U-matic / VHS
Bible According to Kossoff Series
Color (G)
$159.00, $59.00 purchase _ #AD - 1524
Tells the story of Hannah, a barren second wife who longed for a child. Reveals that after she prayed and made sacrifices, the High Priest Eli told her that she would have a child. She dedicated her son Samuel's life to the service of God. Features David Kossoff, storyteller and Biblical scholar, in a thirteen - part series of favorite stories from the Old Testament.

Literature and Drama; Religion and Philosophy
Dist - FOTH Prod - FOTH

The Story of Soil 15 MIN
16mm
Color
LC 79-700286
Shows a farmer who explains the origin of soil and its importance in conservation.
Agriculture
Dist - ECI Prod - THUPRO 1978

The Story of Solo 20 MIN
U-matic / VHS / 16mm
Color (I J)
Presents a study of the social structure and behavior of a pack of wild dogs, particularly of the relationship of a pup named Solo to the pack and the pack leader.
Psychology; Science - Natural
Dist - FI Prod - FI 1974

The Story of Sonam 26 MIN
VHS
Turning 16 series
Color; CC (G T)
$175.00 purchase, $50.00 rental
Follows Sonam Puljor, who has been a Tibetan Buddhist monk since the age of eight and who, while leading a monastic life, has developed a taste for sports, magazines and video games. Asks if he'll keep his monks robes and if teens believe in God. Features part seven of an eight - part series that questioins whether there is a global teenager. Examines the lives of six teens from different countries and explores the major issues facing young people everywhere - including education, culture, sex and marriage, sports, religion, work and the future.
Fine Arts; Religion and Philosophy; Sociology
Dist - BULFRG Prod - HARCOT 1994

The Story of South Africa 16 MIN
VHS
Color (H)
Examines history of South Africa from time of the Portuguese navigators at Cape Of Good Hope to the present day. Looks at political and socio - economic conditions. Available for free loan from the distributor.
Geography - World; History - United States
Dist - AUDPLN

The Story of Stamps 10 MIN
16mm
Color
Re - creates Israel's history through stamps.
Geography - World; History - World; Social Science
Dist - ALDEN Prod - ALDEN

The Story of Susan McKellar - Cystic Fibrosis 20 MIN
16mm
Color
LC 83-700385
Shows how Susan McKellar has maintained a marriage and career as a nurse although she has suffered from cystic fibrosis all her life. Discusses the disease and how she adapts to its treatment.
Health and Safety; Psychology
Dist - FLMLIB Prod - CANBC

A Story of teen depression 32 MIN
VHS
Color (J H)
$189.00 purchase _ #2290 - SK
Reveals that depression is a common and often serious part of adolescence, and that it can trigger such problems as drug abuse, alienation, dropping out, and suicide. Shows the different forms depression can take in teenagers. Notes that depression can usually be treated by counseling. Includes teacher's guide.
Guidance and Counseling; Psychology; Sociology
Dist - SUNCOM

Story of the 747 28 MIN
16mm
Color
LC 77-702291
Tells the story of the Boeing 747 airplane from the point of view of the people and civilizations whose lives it touches.
Industrial and Technical Education; Social Science; Sociology
Dist - WELBIT Prod - BOEING 1977

The Story of the atom
VHS
Keys to science literacy series
Color; CC (I J)
$79.00 purchase _ #401
Helps students to better understand just what an atom is and how the concept of the atom works in science today. Visits Fermilab; IBM; Oak Ridge, Tennessee; and Los Alamos, New Mexico. Uses computer graphics to teach atomic concepts. Part of a 14 - part series for teaching scientific literacy and ranging from 15 to 20 minutes in length. Includes a book from the Power Learning series.
Science - Physical
Dist - HAWHIL Prod - HAWHIL 1994

The Story of the Aztecs 19 MIN
U-matic / VHS / 16mm
Mexican Heritage Series
Color
LC 76-703907
Presents the accomplishments of the Aztecs, showing ruins of the Aztec empire. Points out their relationship to the Mexican people.
Geography - World; History - World; Social Science; Sociology
Dist - FI Prod - STEXMF 1976

Story of the bells 10 MIN
16mm
Color; B&W (G)
Examines the unique tone characteristics of a carillon bell in terms of the fundamental tones and the overtones. Emphasizes the need for arrangements and compositions for carillon.
Fine Arts; Science - Physical
Dist - IOWA Prod - IOWA

Story of the Blood Stream 24 MIN
VHS / 16mm
Color (J H C)
Shows how the circulatory system supplies each cell of the human body with fuel, with oxygen to burn the fuel and how it carries off the waste products. Studies in detail the red cell, white cell and capillaries. Reveals the aortic and mitral valves of a human heart. Refers to a computer the determination of the optimum shape for a red cell as it relates to its respiratory function.
Science - Natural
Dist - MIS Prod - MIS 1968

The Story of the carol 52 MIN
VHS
Color (H C G)
$195.00 purchase, $75.00 rental
Reveals that Christmas carols were originally dances which date back to the 7th century. Traces the history of carols from pagan beginnings, through the first printed carols, through their condemnation by the Puritans, to their Victorian revival. Features Benjamin Luxon, opera star, as presenter, assisted by singers, dancers and musicians. Performs carols, some in original versions. Produced by John Bartlett.
Fine Arts
Dist - FLMLIB

The Story of the Cat 15 MIN
U-matic / VHS / 16mm
Color
Offers the story of a cat who leads an exciting life until he begins to grow old. Reveals that he spends his old age remembering what it was like to be young.
Science - Natural; Sociology
Dist - IFB Prod - HELNEG 1983

The Story of the changing Earth
VHS
Keys to science literacy series
Color; CC (I J)
$79.00 purchase _ #402
Begins with live-action footage from the highlands of Scotland where James Hutton founded the modern science of geology. Explains important concepts in modern geology - plate tectonics, glaciation, the age of the earth and more. Part of a 14-part series for teaching scientific literacy and ranging from 15 to 20 minutes in length. Includes a book from the Learning Power series.
Geography - World; Science - Physical
Dist - HAWHIL Prod - HAWHIL 1994

The Story of the Dancing Frog 25 MIN
16mm / VHS
Color (K)
$495.00, $295.00 purchase
Adapts from 'The Story Of The Dancing Frog' by Quentin Blake. Follows the ups and downs of Gertrude and her lively companion George the Frog as they dance their way around the world. Narrated by Amanda Plummer.
Literature and Drama
Dist - LUF Prod - LUF 1989

The Story of the Episcopal Church 20 MIN
VHS / 16mm
Color (H A)
$29.95 purchase
Tells the story of the 400 - year history of Anglicanism in America. Part 1 of a two - part series.
Religion and Philosophy
Dist - CAFM Prod - CAFM 1988

The Story of the Episcopal Church - Pt 2 23 MIN
VHS / 16mm
Color (H A)
$29.95 purchase
Tells the story of the 400 - year history of Anglicanism in America. Part 2 of a two - part series.
Religion and Philosophy
Dist - CAFM Prod - CAFM 1988

The Story of the expanding universe
VHS
Keys to science literacy series
Color; CC (I J)
$79.00 purchase _ #409
Explains basic facts and concepts of modern astronomy in a way that students can comprehend. Defines the differences between stars and planets, solar systems and galaxies, and how humans found out about all of these things. Part of a 14 - part series for teaching scientific literacy and ranging from 15 to 20 minutes in length. Includes a book from the Learning Power series.
Science - Physical
Dist - HAWHIL Prod - HAWHIL 1994

The Story of the gene
VHS
Keys to science literacy series
Color; CC (I J)
$79.00 purchase _ #410
Uses computer graphics and on - site footage to show students how DNA was discovered. Looks at how DNA works in cells. Part of a 14 - part series for teaching scientific literacy and ranging from 15 to 20 minutes in length. Includes a book from the Learning Power series.
Science - Natural
Dist - HAWHIL Prod - HAWHIL 1994

Story of the Great Lakes 28 MIN
16mm
B&W
LC FIE54-95
Portrays the economic importance of the Great Lakes in the transportation of iron ore, coal and grain, and the uses of the U S Coast Guard on this waterway.
Geography - United States; Social Science
Dist - USNAC Prod - USCG 1954

Story of the Great Rivers 28 MIN
16mm
Color
LC FIE63-241
Uses animated maps and live footage to show the early days of the Mississippi, Missouri and Ohio Rivers, the advent of the coast guard on those rivers and their early duties.
Geography - United States; Health and Safety; Science - Natural; Social Science
Dist - USNAC Prod - USGEOS 1961

The Story of the Horn 29 MIN
U-matic
Color
Looks at the history of the French horn. Tours one of the most extensive private collections of horns in the United States.
Fine Arts
Dist - UMITV Prod - UMITV 1975

The Story of the Letter Post 18 MIN
U-matic / VHS / 16mm
Color (I)
LC FIA65-317
Uses dramatic scenes and drawings to tell the history of the postal service in England from the time of the War of Roses. Reports on the Royal Mail Service, use of censoring, how costs were paid and reforms of 1840.
History - World; Psychology; Social Science
Dist - IFB Prod - GNRLPO 1964

The Story of the Military Aircraft Storage and Disposition - Desert Bonanza 16 MIN
16mm
Color
LC 74-706260
Depicts the mission of the Military Aircraft Storage and Disposition Center at Davis - Monthan Air Force Base in Arizona. Shows how aircraft no longer needed in active inventory are processed for storage and reclamation of parts.
Civics and Political Systems; Industrial and Technical Education
Dist - USNAC Prod - USAF 1966

Story of the Prodigal Son 22 MIN
16mm
B&W (P)
Explains God's loving forgiveness of repented wrong. Presents a parable about a younger son who takes his inheritance, squanders it in a far country and is reduced to feeding swine. Tells how he returns home repentant and is received by a forgiving father.
Religion and Philosophy
Dist - CAFM Prod - CAFM

Story of the serials 27 MIN
16mm
History of the motion picture series
B&W (H C)
Shows the development of the cliff - hangers of silent days, from 1914 with Pearl White's The Perils Of Pauline to 1929 with the advent of sound in motion pictures. Draws parallels between the reign of serial queens with woman's struggle for social and political equality.
Fine Arts
Dist - KILLIS **Prod** - SF 1960

The Story of the Soviet Constitution 30 MIN
U-matic / VHS
Color
Reviews the political system of the USSR, focusing on the Soviet Constitution.
Civics and Political Systems; History - World
Dist - IHF **Prod** - IHF

The Story of the space age - a special report 19 MIN
16mm
Screen news digest series; Vol 7; Issue 9
B&W
LC FIA68-2100
Traces Space - Age progress, exploring the pioneering genius of Robert Hutchings Goodard to the present work of Project Gemini.
Science - Physical
Dist - HEARST **Prod** - HEARST 1965

The Story of the Star Spangled Banner 10 MIN
16mm
Color (H C A S) (AMERICAN SIGN)
LC 76-701097
Tells the story of the Star - Spangled Banner in American sign language. Filmed at locations where Francis Scott Key wrote this national anthem. Signed by Louie J Fant, Jr.
Fine Arts; Psychology; Social Science
Dist - JOYCE **Prod** - JOYCE 1976

The Story of the Stars and Stripes 28 MIN
VHS
Who, what, where, why and when series
B&W (G)
$14.95 purchase _ #FV - 815
Tells the story of the United States Army newspaper, Stars and Stripes, from its birth during the Civil War in 1861 to its rebirth during World War I in 1917. Includes archival footage of World War II soldiers waiting to see their daily hometown newspaper away from home, and stories from the Korean War.
Civics and Political Systems; History - United States; Literature and Drama
Dist - INCRSE **Prod** - USA

The Story of the symphony - Beethoven 90 MIN
VHS
Color; Stereo (G)
$39.95 purchase _ #S01674
Features Andre Previn and the London Philharmonic Orchestra in an exploration of classical composer Beethoven. Gives background information on Beethoven, and then gives a complete and uninterrupted performance of one of his symphonies.
Fine Arts
Dist - UILL

The Story of the symphony - Berlioz 90 MIN
VHS
Color; Stereo (G)
$39.95 purchase _ #S01675
Features Andre Previn and the London Philharmonic Orchestra in an exploration of classical composer Berlioz. Gives background information on Berlioz, and then gives a complete and uninterrupted performance of one of his symphonies.
Fine Arts
Dist - UILL

The Story of the symphony - Brahms 90 MIN
VHS
Color; Stereo (G)
$39.95 purchase _ #S01676
Features Andre Previn and the London Philharmonic Orchestra in an exploration of classical composer Brahms. Gives background information on Brahms, and then gives a complete and uninterrupted performance of one of his symphonies.
Fine Arts
Dist - UILL

The Story of the symphony - Haydn and Mozart 90 MIN
VHS
Color; Stereo (G)
$39.95 purchase _ #S01673
Features Andre Previn and the London Philharmonic Orchestra in an exploration of classical composers Haydn and Mozart. Gives background information on each of the composers, and then gives complete and uninterrupted performances of a symphony from each composer.
Fine Arts
Dist - UILL

Story of the Symphony Series
Beethoven - Symphony no 7 - and Excerpts from no 5 - Pt 2 89 MIN
Berlioz - Symphonie Fantastique - Pt 3 90 MIN
Brahms - Symphony no 4 - Pt 4 88 MIN
Hayden and Mozart - Symphony no 87 and Symphony no 39 - Pt 1 89 MIN
Shostakovich - Symphony no 5 - Pt 6 88 MIN
Tchaikovsky - Symphony no 6 - the Pathetique - Pt 5 87 MIN
Dist - FI

The Story of the symphony - Shostakovich 90 MIN
VHS
Color; Stereo (G)
$39.95 purchase _ #S01678
Features Andre Previn and the London Philharmonic Orchestra in an exploration of classical composer Shostakovich. Gives background information on Shostakovich, and then gives a complete and uninterrupted performance of one of his symphonies.
Fine Arts
Dist - UILL

The Story of the symphony - Tchaikovsky 90 MIN
VHS
Color; Stereo (G)
$39.95 purchase _ #S01677
Features Andre Previn and the London Philharmonic Orchestra in an exploration of classical composer Tchaikovsky. Gives background information on Tchaikovsky, and then gives a complete and uninterrupted performance of one of his symphonies.
Fine Arts
Dist - UILL

Story of the Unknown Soldier - How they Signed the Kellogg - Briand Pact and Ended War 12 MIN
U-matic / VHS / 16mm
B&W
LC 80-700662
Satirizes man's efforts in the 20th century to end war forever through treaties, pacts and edicts. Uses newsreel footage from 1917 to 1928 to build a montage which is half documentary and half satire. Created by Belgian filmmaker Henri Storck.
History - United States; History - World
Dist - IFB **Prod** - STORCH 1978

The Story of Thomas A Edison 55 MIN
VHS
Color (J H G)
$19.95 purchase _ #AV2254
Reveals that Thomas Alva Edison patented over one thousand inventions during his lifetime.
History - United States
Dist - INSTRU

The Story of Tobias 20 MIN
U-matic / VHS
Bible According to Kossoff Series
Color (G)
$159.00, $59.00 purchase _ #AD - 1526
Tells the story of Tobit, a wealthy merchant who has always been generous to the poor and unfortunate. Reveals that he and his family are reduced to poverty when Tobit is struck blind, but an angel takes Tobit's son Tobias into a land of riches and restores Tobit's vision and the family fortunes. Features David Kossoff, storyteller and Biblical scholar, in a thirteen - part series of favorite stories from the Old Testament.
Literature and Drama; Religion and Philosophy
Dist - FOTH **Prod** - FOTH

The Story of toxic wastes
VHS
Keys to science literacy series
Color; CC (I J)
$79.00 purchase _ #416
Explains exactly what a toxic waste is and how toxic waste problems are being solved today. Points out that there were often toxic waste problems in the past - even worse than those of today - and that people can learn from those problems and from new scientific research. Part of a 14 - part series for teaching scientific literacy and ranging from 15 to 20 minutes in length. Includes a book from the Learning Power series.
Science - Natural; Sociology
Dist - HAWHIL **Prod** - HAWHIL 1994

The Story of Two Men 27 MIN
VHS / BETA
B&W (G)
Probes the relationship of school teacher Mentor Graham and his student Abraham Lincoln.
Biography; Religion and Philosophy
Dist - DSP **Prod** - DSP

The Story of two synagogues 17 MIN
VHS
In the footsteps of Marrano families series
Color (G)
$39.95 purchase _ #186
Depicts the unique design and style of two synagogues. Reveals that the ceiling of the synagogue in Chodorov, Poland was decorated in the 17th century with paintings on Jewish themes. Reconstructs the painting on the ceiling from the artist's point of view, depicting artistic deliberation by a Jewish painter while unfolding a picture of Jewish life in Poland. The second synagogue, built in 1732 in Curacao, the Caribbean, was built in the style of the Portuguese Synagogue in Amsterdam. Intertwines the description of the building with the history of the community. Part of a series on the Marranos - Jews forced to convert and to live as Christians - from the Museum of the Jewish Diaspora - Beth Hatefutsoth.
Religion and Philosophy; Sociology
Dist - ERGOM

The Story of Vinh 60 MIN
VHS / U-matic
Color (G)
$250.00 purchase, $50.00 rental
Tells of Vinh Dinh, son of a United States serviceman and a Vietnamese mother. Shows how Vinh arrives at JFK airport dazed, speaking no English and with minimal education. Explodes the myth of the American dream and follows Vinh on his journey from Vietnamese to American culture, from youth to manhood and from false dreams to harsh reality. Compells the viewer to examine the complex legacy of the Vietnamese conflict through Vinh's eyes and to question the shortcomings of the American foster care system. Reveals that there are still thousands of children at the Amerasian Transit Center in Ho Chi Minh City, many of them the victims of poverty and prejudice in their native land.
History - United States
Dist - CROCUR

The Story of Walter 9 MIN
16mm
Color (H C A)
LC 83-700683
Looks at how a young man copes with leukemia.
Health and Safety
Dist - LEUSA **Prod** - LEUSA 1981

The Story of Washington, DC
VHS
Color (G)
$29.95 purchase _ #TK049
Tells the story of this 200 - year - old city.
Geography - United States
Dist - SIV

The Story of weights and measures 11 MIN
16mm / U-matic / VHS
Color (J)
LC 73-702900
Explores how units were first used to measure, how they became standardized, and how they were organized into systems of measurement. Offers advantages of the metric system.
Mathematics
Dist - CORF **Prod** - CORF 1973

The Story of Wine - Pt 1 90 MIN
BETA / VHS
Color (A)
Features history of wine, and two types of wine - Clarets and Aperitifs. Narrated by Baron Philippe De Rothschild.
Health and Safety
Dist - LCOA **Prod** - LCOA

The Story of Wine - Pt 2 90 MIN
BETA / VHS
Color (A)
Features story of cognac, wine tasting and popularity of wine. Narrated by Baron Philippe De Rothschild.
Health and Safety
Dist - LCOA **Prod** - LCOA

Story of Zachary Zween 13 MIN
16mm
Color (K P I)
LC 73-700521
Presents the story of a schoolboy who is always last suddenly finding himself 'first' when he gets lost in the big city.
Psychology
Dist - SF **Prod** - SF 1972

Story Playing 15 MIN
U-matic / VHS
Word Shop Series
Color (P)
Literature and Drama
Dist - WETATV **Prod** - WETATV

Story Problems 15 MIN
U-matic
Studio M Series
Color (P)
Explains how to write a solution to story problems using addition and regrouping.
Mathematics
Dist - GPN **Prod** - WCETTV 1979

Story Problems with the Four Operations 15 MIN
U-matic
Studio M Series
Color (P)
Gives a story problem to explain when to add, subtract, multiply or divide.
Mathematics
Dist - GPN **Prod** - WCETTV 1979

The Story tellers of the Canterbury tales 17 MIN
16mm
Color (MIDDLE ENGLISH)
LC FIA55-271
Gives excerpts from the General Prologue and the Canon's Yeoman's prologue of Chaucer's Canterbury tales. Narration is in Middle English.
Literature and Drama
Dist - USC **Prod** - USC 1953

Story Telling 15 MIN
U-matic / VHS
Word Shop Series
Color (P)
English Language
Dist - WETATV **Prod** - WETATV

Story - telling 17 MIN
16mm
Color (T)
LC 74-705708
Demonstrates, through the story Jack and the Beanstalk, how story telling can be used as an effective teaching aid in speech and language development of the hearing impaired.
English Language; Guidance and Counseling; Psychology
Dist - USNAC **Prod** - USA

Story Theatre 12 MIN
VHS / 16mm
Drama Reference Series
Color (C)
$150.00 purchase _ #268411
Implements elementary drama curriculum. Presents drama content, teaching strategies and resources, and demonstrated drama activities for the classroom. 'Story Theatre' brings well - known stories to life through movement, mime and characterization.
Education; English Language; Fine Arts; Literature and Drama; Mathematics
Dist - ACCESS **Prod** - ACCESS 1987

Story Time 5 MIN
16mm
Exploring Childhood Series
Color (J)
LC 76-701897
Shows a student carrying out an activity she has planned ahead of time which is reading a story to the children. Depicts roles helpers play in their setting, and the particular interaction that takes place during story time.
Education; Literature and Drama; Psychology; Sociology
Dist - EDC **Prod** - EDC 1975

Storybook International Series

Cap O'Rushes	27 MIN
Clever Manka	27 MIN
The Emperor and the Abbot	27 MIN
The Five loaves	27 MIN
The Foolish brother	27 MIN
The Forbidden Door	27 MIN
The Grief of Pi - Kari	27 MIN
The Haunted Pastures	27 MIN
Hinemoa	27 MIN
The Island of Drums	27 MIN
Morwen of the Woodlands	27 MIN
Moses and the Lime Kiln	27 MIN
Nikorima	27 MIN
The Pedlar's Dream	27 MIN
The Priest Know - all	27 MIN
Riches or Happiness	27 MIN
The Russian and the Tartar	27 MIN
Simpleton Peter	27 MIN
The Soldier who Didn't Wash	27 MIN
Sorrow	27 MIN
The Straw Hat	27 MIN
The Twelve months	27 MIN
The Well of the World's End	27 MIN
The Widow's Lazy Daughter	27 MIN

Dist - JOU

Storybook library series

Beady bear	8 MIN
Cloudy with a chance of meatballs	12 MIN
Ox - cart man	8 MIN

Dist - LIVOAK
PELLER

Storybook Library Series
Ira Sleeps Over
Mop Top
A Rainbow of My Own
Today was a Terrible Day
Dist - PELLER

Storybook Series
Miss Esta Maude's Secret 10 MIN
Dist - MGHT

Storybooks 30 MIN
U-matic
Today's Special Series
Color (K P)
Develops language arts skills in children. Programs are thematically designed around subjects of interest to youngsters. Action takes place in a department store where people, mannequins, puppets, comic characters and special guests present a light hearted approach to language arts.
Fine Arts; Literature and Drama; Psychology
Dist - TVOTAR **Prod** - TVOTAR 1985

Storybound Series
A Wrinkle in Time 15 MIN
Dist - CTI

Storybound Series

Bridge to Terabithia	15 MIN
Call it courage	15 MIN
Escape from Warsaw	15 MIN
Ghosts I have been	15 MIN
Island of the Blue Dolphin	15 MIN
It's not the end of the world	15 MIN
Konrad	15 MIN
Mojo and the Russians	15 MIN
Pilot down, presumed dead	15 MIN
The Pinballs	15 MIN
Pinch	15 MIN
Sounder	15 MIN
Tuck everlasting	15 MIN
The Witch of Blackbird Pond	15 MIN
A Wrinkle in time	15 MIN

Dist - CTI
GPN

Storybound series
Presents 16 fifteen - minute programs on four video cassettes designed to lead viewers to the library to find and finish the stories they encounter in the series.

Lizard music	15 MIN
Storybound series	240 MIN

Dist - GPN **Prod** - CTI 1985

Storyland theater tapes 30 MIN
VHS
Storyland theater tapes series; Vol 1
Color (K P I)
$14.95 purchase _ #510
Features The Remarkable Horse, Donkey and Goose and The Little Dragon in live performance by storytellers Jay O'Callahan, Rafe Martin and Laura Simms. Part of a four - part series.
Literature and Drama
Dist - YELMON **Prod** - YELMON

Storyland theater tapes 30 MIN
VHS
Storyland theater tapes series; Vol 2
Color (K P I)
$14.95 purchase _ #511
Features New Year's Eve, The King of Togo Togo, and Foolish Rabbit in live performance by storytellers Jay O'Callahan, Rafe Martin and Laura Simms. Part of a four - part series.
Literature and Drama
Dist - YELMON **Prod** - YELMON

Storyland theater tapes 30 MIN
VHS
Storyland theater tapes series; Vol 3
Color (K P I)
$14.95 purchase _ #512
Features The Wooden Box, The Three Little Pigs, and The Woolly Mammoth in live performance by storytellers Jay O'Callahan, Rafe Martin and Laura Simms. Part of a four - part series.
Literature and Drama
Dist - YELMON **Prod** - YELMON

Storyland theater tapes 30 MIN
VHS
Storyland theater tapes series; Vol 4
Color (K P I)
$14.95 purchase _ #513
Features The Bird Man, Superbowl Sundae, Moon and Otter, and The Magic Princess in live performance by storytellers Jay O'Callahan, Rafe Martin and Laura Simms. Part of a four - part series.
Literature and Drama
Dist - YELMON **Prod** - YELMON

Storyland theater tapes series
Storyland theater tapes 30 MIN
Dist - YELMON

Storylords Series

Activating prior knowledge before reading	15 MIN
Connecting what You Know with What's on the Page	15 MIN
Decoding words in context	15 MIN
Directed Reading - Thinking Activity	15 MIN
Identifying Main Idea and Details	15 MIN
Inferring Word Meaning in Context	15 MIN
Integrating Comprehension Strategies	15 MIN
Knowing When You Don't Know - in Your Head	15 MIN
Knowing When You Don't Know - on the Page	15 MIN
Pronoun Anaphora	15 MIN
Question - Answer Relationships	15 MIN
Story Mapping	15 MIN

Dist - AITECH

Storymaker 14 MIN
16mm / U-matic / VHS
Color (I J)
LC 73-715531
Presents a documentary through which viewers experience the fervor, depression and elation involved in the creation of a children's book. Features author - illustator Don Freeman as he makes preliminary sketches and talks about the source of a story idea.
Literature and Drama
Dist - CF **Prod** - CF 1972

Storymakers - Percy Trezise and Dick Roughsey 17 MIN
VHS
Color (I)
$129.00 purchase _ #188 - 9046
Reveals how the books of children's authors Percy Trezise and Dick Roughsey are conceived and created. Explores the special relationship between author and illustrator. Also tells one of their delightful stories, which are inspired by Australian aboriginal folktales.
Geography - World; Literature and Drama
Dist - FI **Prod** - FLMAUS 1988

The Storyteller 30 MIN
16mm
Color
LC 79-700287
Portrays a gentlemen recounting a love story to a group of prostitutes in a bordello. Reveals eventually that the story is really about the gentleman and his relationship with a beautiful young girl.
Fine Arts
Dist - CHESLE **Prod** - CHESLE 1978

The Storytellers 28 MIN
U-matic / VHS
Color (H C)
$325.00, $295.00 purchase _ #V561
Highlights three storytellers who are taped on location at the 17th Annual National Storytelling Festival. Features Judith Black who explores the experiences of a Jewish immigrant, Michael Cotter who focuses on the extraordinary qualities of ordinary people, and Rex Ellis who tells stories of the enslavement of Afro - Americans.
History - United States; Literature and Drama
Dist - BARR **Prod** - CEPRO 1991
CNEMAG

Storytellers collection series

Animal stories	35 MIN
Magic tales	35 MIN
Scary stories	35 MIN
Tall tales, yarns and whoppers	35 MIN

Dist - KNOWUN

A Storyteller's town 29 MIN
VHS / 16mm
Color (G)
$55.00 rental _ #AMRA - 112
Eric Vaughn portrays author Sherwood Anderson in a program about life in Northwestern Ohio at the turn of the century.
Fine Arts; Literature and Drama
Dist - PBS **Prod** - WGBUTV

Storytelling 20 MIN
VHS / U-matic
We are one series
Color (G)
Shows the 'First Thunders' or first rain storm of the spring and the family inside the lodge as the children are entertained by uncle who is an excellent storyteller. When the rain stops the stories stop as there is work for all. Mother and daughter go the the river for water. Mother explains the necessity of an escort for young girls and how precious the family and children are to the Omaha. Ni'bthaska and Teson find that both intend to fast as a beginning of their change from adolescence to adulthood as warriors.
Social Science
Dist - NAMPBC Prod - NAMPBC 1986

Storytelling 15 MIN
VHS / 16mm
Drama Reference Series
Color (C)
$150.00 purchase _ #268406
Implements elementary drama curriculum. Presents drama content, teaching strategies and resources, and demonstrated drama activities for the classroom. 'Story Telling' focuses on developing personal speaking skills. All aspects of the storytelling sequence are depicted.
Education; English Language; Literature and Drama; Mathematics
Dist - ACCESS Prod - ACCESS 1987

Storytelling 7 MIN
U-matic
Take time series
(A)
Demonstrates the influence of parents and others caring for pre - schoolers on the physical and emotional development of the child.
Psychology; Sociology
Dist - ACCESS Prod - ACCESS 1976

Storytelling - a Beginning 15 MIN
VHS / U-matic
Color
Stresses that storytellers are people of all ages and backgrounds. Shows how storytellers begin to learn a new story.
Literature and Drama
Dist - LVN Prod - CCPL

Storytelling - Art and Tradition 90 MIN
U-matic / VHS
Color (A)
LC 82-707986
Introduces the custom, craft and experience of storytelling. Includes origins and development, material selection, learning, training and techniques. Includes public library experiences. Presented by Teresa Toscano.
Education; English Language; Fine Arts; Literature and Drama
Dist - CATHLA Prod - TVR

Storytelling in America 58 MIN
VHS / U-matic
Color (J)
LC 84-707093
Presents an engaging look at the traditional art of storytelling and its modern practitioners. Filmed at the tenth National Storytelling Festival at Jonesborough, Tennessee.
English Language; Literature and Drama
Dist - NAPPS Prod - NAPPS

Storytelling - live performance 20 MIN
VHS
Design and technology starters series; No 6
Color; PAL (J H)
PdS29.50 purchase
Begins with a search for worthwhile design possibilities within a particular real - world context. Suggests ways in which pupils might start thinking about certain artifacts, systems and environments, and how well they meet the needs and desires of different people who might use them. Part six of a seven - part series.
Fine Arts; Sociology
Dist - EMFVL

Storytelling live series
Stories of North America - Pt 1 30 MIN
Stories of North America - Pt 2 30 MIN
Dist - NGS

Storytelling Videos from Cynthia Watts Series
Storytime with Cynthia Watts
Dist - EDUCRT

Storytelling with Music 15 MIN
U-matic
Music Box Series
Color (K P)
Re - enacts Little Red Riding Hood to show how music adds to the mood and atmosphere of a story.
Fine Arts
Dist - TVOTAR Prod - TVOTAR 1971

Storytime Series
Ice 15 MIN
The Most Remarkable Cat 15 MIN
Dist - GPN

Storytime with Cynthia Watts
VHS / 16mm
Storytelling Videos from Cynthia Watts Series; Vol 1
Color (K P I)
$28.88 purchase _ #ART V001
Tells four stories for younger viewers.
Literature and Drama
Dist - EDUCRT

Stout heart and a sharp knife 50 MINS.
VHS
Courage to fail
Color; PAL (C PRO H)
PdS99 purchase; not available in South Africa
Covers the progress made in the early days of surgery beginning around 1830. Includes the topics of blood transfusions, anaesthesia and infection prevention. First in the five - part series Courage to Fail, which presents the stories of advancements and pioneers in the field of modern surgery.
Health and Safety
Dist - BBCENE

Stove stoker's guide 30 MIN
VHS
A House for all seasons series
Color (G)
$49.95 purchase _ #AHFS - 203
Tells how wood - burning stoves are effective in home heating. Examines wood - splitting devices, reviewing the history of the wood saw.
Home Economics; Industrial and Technical Education; Science - Natural; Sociology
Dist - PBS Prod - KRMATV 1985

The Stowaway 23 MIN
16mm / U-matic / VHS
Unicorn Tales Series
Color (P I)
LC 80-700548
Presents a contemporary story, based on the fairy tale Pinocchio, about a young Italian stowaway who encounters the lovable baker Gepetto and a dancing striped Pizza Man who leads him on the path to truth.
Fine Arts; Literature and Drama
Dist - MGHT Prod - MGHT 1980

Stowaway, Pt 1 - Disease and Personal Hygiene 17 MIN
16mm
B&W
LC FIE52-1520
Depicts obvious and obscure ways in which disease is spread by food - handling personnel.
Health and Safety
Dist - USNAC Prod - USA 1948

Stowaway, Pt 2 - Balley Sanitation 17 MIN
16mm
B&W
LC FIE52-1521
Shows sanitary measures for use in all food service organizations to prevent spread of disease.
Health and Safety
Dist - USNAC Prod - USA 1948

Strabismus 8 MIN
VHS / U-matic
Color
Discusses the nature of the eye condition strabismus and related problems. Stresses the importance of early and appropriate treatment.
Science - Natural
Dist - MEDCOM MEDFAC Prod - MEDCOM MEDFAC

Strabismus
U-matic / VHS
Color
Reviews the nature of both congenital and acquired Strabismus and the threat of Amblyopia. Depicts the underlying problem in the brain's eye control center and how this results in turned eyes and two - dimensional sight. Explains how treatment can be a long term process of patching, glasses, and surgery. Presents surgery along with risks and recovery. Emphasizes early treatment.
Science - Natural
Dist - MIFE Prod - MIFE

Strabismus 17 MIN
U-matic / 8mm cartridge
Color (PRO) (SPANISH)
Explains how strabismus affects vision. Discusses treatment and the roles of patient and family in therapy.
Health and Safety; Home Economics; Science - Natural
Dist - PRORE Prod - PRORE

Strabismus and Amblyopia 15 MIN
U-matic / VHS
Color (PRO)
Discusses the physiologic procedures of how the retina perceives an image and how both eyes work to produce a binocular image (fusion), deviations in the optical system which inhibit tests used to diagnose these deviations and appropriate management.
Health and Safety; Science - Natural
Dist - UMICHM Prod - UMICHM 1976

Strabismus Surgery 11 MIN
VHS / U-matic
Color (PRO)
Demonstrates a simple and effective approach to operating on ocular muscles.
Health and Safety; Science - Natural
Dist - HSCIC Prod - HSCIC 1984

Straddle and Surface Milling to Close Tolerances 27 MIN
16mm
Machine Shop Work Series Operations on the Milling Machine, no 2
B&W
LC FIE51-520
Demonstrates how to make surface - and straddle - milling cutter setups, to surface - mill four sides of a workpiece and to machine a workpiece to a T shape by straddle - milling.
Industrial and Technical Education
Dist - USNAC Prod - USOE 1941

Straddle Milling 17 MIN
16mm
Machine Shop Work - Operations on the Milling Machine Series no 3
B&W
LC FIE51-522
Demonstrates how to use an indexing fixture for production milling operations, space cutters on an arbor for straddle milling and mill parallel bosses on connecting rods.
Industrial and Technical Education
Dist - USNAC Prod - USOE 1941

Straight Allowance Application on Transitions 28 MIN
VHS / BETA
Color (IND)
Discusses the reason for using a straight allowance when developing patterns for transitions which permits faster assembly of fittings and duct work when doing installations.
Industrial and Technical Education; Psychology
Dist - RMIBHF Prod - RMIBHF

Straight and Narrow 10 MIN
16mm
B&W (C)
$448.00
Experimental film by Tony Conrad.
Fine Arts
Dist - AFA Prod - AFA 1970

Straight and Round 15 MIN
16mm
Fingermouse, Yoffy and Friends Series
Color (K P I)
LC 73-700441
Follows Yoffy as he searches for round and straight objects in order to tell a story about two countries, one in which everything is curved and one in which everything is straight.
Guidance and Counseling; Literature and Drama
Dist - VEDO Prod - BBCTV 1972

Straight at ya 44 MIN
U-matic / VHS
K - 12 drug prevention video series
Color; Captioned (J)
$27.00, $50.00 purchase _ #TCA17514, #TCA17513
Stars Kirk Cameron of ABC's 'Growing Pains,' who discusses with teenagers the pressure to use drugs. Includes teacher's guide and information card.
Guidance and Counseling; Health and Safety; Psychology
Dist - USNAC Prod - USDED 1988

Straight dope on drug testing 18 MIN
VHS / U-matic / BETA
Color; PAL (IND G)
$175.00 rental _ #SDD - 100
Provides employees with information on how drug testing works and why organizations feel testing is necessary for the safety and health of the employees, the organization and the public. Shows the role of drugs in work performance problems and health. Includes 10 employee handout booklets.
Business and Economics; Guidance and Counseling; Health and Safety; Psychology
Dist - BNA Prod - BNA

Straight forward back care for nurses 32 MIN
U-matic / VHS / BETA
Color; NTSC; PAL; SECAM (C PRO G)
PdS95
Presents three parts on the back for nurses and other medical staff. Discusses the anatomy of the back, general principles of lifting and techniques for moving patients. Illustrates the back and limb positions of lifters in the process of moving patients.
Health and Safety
Dist - VIEWTH

Straight from the heart 28 MIN
VHS
Color (J H G)
$280.00 purchase
Tells the stories of mothers recovering from addiction. Portrays six women from different backgrounds in various stages of recovery from substance abuse and discusses the impact of parental substance abuse on children. Part of two parts on chemically dependent women coproduced by the National Organization of Gynecologic, Obstetric and Neonatal Nurses.
Guidance and Counseling; Psychology; Sociology
Dist - VHC **Prod** - VHC

Straight from the heart - A Challenge to care 66 MIN
VHS
Color (PRO A C G)
$457.00 purchase
Presents two programs on chemically dependent women coproduced by the National Organization of Gynecologic, Obstetric and Neonatal Nurses. Portrays six women in various stages of recovery in Straight From the Heart. Overviews guidelines for professionals who work with pregnant chemically dependent women in a A Challenge to Care.
Guidance and Counseling; Health and Safety; Psychology; Sociology
Dist - VHC **Prod** - VHC

Straight from the heart with Mike Ditka 77 MIN
VHS
Color (G A)
$39.95 purchase _ #MVC1001V-P
Offers advice from six heart experts and Mike Ditka about changing lifestyle to live better and longer. Includes sections on what a heart attack is, symptoms of heart attack, what to do in the first minutes of a possible attack, nutritional advice about reducing cholesterol and fat, and recipes for some light dishes that are easy to prepare. Provides one accompanying booklet, with additional booklets available in packages of ten.
Health and Safety; Physical Education and Recreation
Dist - CAMV
HTHED

Straight from the shoulder series
Presents a three - part series on teenage drug abuse. Tells the story of Jim and alcoholism and smoking pot; Marci and teenage suicide and its relationship to substance abuse; and Frank and the relationship of crime and teenaged homicide to drug abuse.
Frank 15 MIN
Jim 15 MIN
Marci 15 MIN
Dist - CAMV

Straight - Hole Drilling Practices 29 MIN
VHS / U-matic
Color (IND)
Covers the principles of straight - hole drilling. Focuses on the well - drilling industry.
Social Science
Dist - UTEXPE **Prod** - UTEXPE 1964

Straight, Huge, Gigantic, Enormous, Dinosaur, Curve 10 MIN
U-matic
Readalong Three Series
Color (P)
Provides reading instruction for third grade students. Uses animation, humor, music, repetition and audience participation. Comes with teacher's guide and kit.
Education; English Language; Literature and Drama
Dist - TVOTAR **Prod** - TVOTAR 1977

Straight Jacket 8 MIN
U-matic
Student Workshop Videotapes Series
Color
Looks at the 'Feminization' of an adult female who models herself, in terms of make - up and postures, on images of women in fashion and movie magazines. Focuses on an active subject against a background of photographs.
Sociology
Dist - WMENIF **Prod** - WMENIF

Straight Line Kinematics 34 MIN
16mm
PSSC Physics Films Series
B&W (H C)
Explains the concepts of distance, speed, acceleration and time. Uses measuring equipment in a test car to illustrate the concepts.
Science - Physical
Dist - MLA **Prod** - PSSC 1960

The Straight - Line Ripsaw 48 MIN
U-matic / VHS
Furniture Manufacturing Series
Color (IND)
Shows all steps of the power fed ripsaw operation. Emphasizes high wood yield.
Industrial and Technical Education
Dist - LEIKID **Prod** - LEIKID

Straight lines, pegs and satellites 21 MIN
VHS
Color; PAL (H C G)
Presents surveying as a science with a great variety of applications and techniques. Outlines the history of surveying. Shows the wide range of work undertaken by the Australian Survey Office - the survey of the route for the Alice Springs to Darwin railway, coastal surveys, aerial surveys for map - making and surveys to monitor the stability of major civil engineering works.
Geography - World; Industrial and Technical Education; Social Science
Dist - VIEWTH **Prod** - VIEWTH

Straight on Till Morning 21 MIN
16mm
Color
LC 79-700288
Tells how a sensitive eight - year - old girl attempts to come to terms with the death of her divorced father by creating a fantasy involving Peter Pan to explain his disappearance.
Fine Arts; Guidance and Counseling; Sociology
Dist - ROPELT **Prod** - ROPELT 1978

Straight talk 31 MIN
VHS
Color (J H C G)
$89.95 purchase, $45.00 rental _ #TTP144
Features five Vietnam veterans speaking to high school students about their first - hand experiences in war. Interweaves clips of the veterans' own home - movie footage and photographs taken during their military tours as they talk about their decisions to enter the military and share stories. Also offers glimpses of current high school military recruitment practices such as the landing of an army helicopter on a high school football field. The recruiters' pitches to students contrast sharply with the poignant and revealing testimonies of the veterans.
Fine Arts; Guidance and Counseling; History - United States; History - World
Dist - TURTID

Straight Talk 15 MIN
16mm
Color (H A)
Examines General Motors Institute, an accredited degree - granting engineering college.
Education; Industrial and Technical Education
Dist - GM **Prod** - GM

Straight Talk 24 MIN
16mm / VHS
Color (J H C A PRO)
$395.00, $475.00 purchase, $75.00 rental _ #9841
Depicts drug addiction from the viewpoint of Roland Abner who was a heroin addict by the age of eleven and an alcoholic by the age of fifteen.
Guidance and Counseling; Psychology; Sociology
Dist - AIMS **Prod** - FULBRO 1988

Straight talk about divorce 17 MIN
VHS
Children of divorce series
Color (G I J)
$79.00 purchase
Helps eleven to fourteen - year - old children deal with problems and questions related to their parents' decision to divorce.
Health and Safety; Sociology
Dist - DANEHA **Prod** - DANEHA 1994

Straight talk about drinking 30 MIN
U-matic / BETA / 16mm / VHS
Color (H)
$595.00, $495.00 purchase _ #JR - 5758M
Adapts the book 'Straight Talk about Drinking - Teenagers Speak Out about Alchohol,' by Wayne Coffey. Helps teenagers make informed decisions about alcohol before they start. Features actress Tracey Gold as host.
Guidance and Counseling; Health and Safety; Psychology; Sociology
Dist - CORF **Prod** - CORF 1989

Straight Talk about Drugs 16 MIN
U-matic / VHS
Color (J A)
Focuses on the widespread nature of drug abuse and how it affects persons of all ethnic origins, income or education.
Health and Safety; Psychology; Sociology
Dist - SUTHRB **Prod** - SUTHRB

Straight Talk about Drugs - Psychedelics, PCP and Dangerous Combinations 39 MIN
U-matic / VHS
Straight Talk about Drugs Series
Color (J H)
LC 82-706873
Identifies drugs classed as psychedelics including LSD, mescaline, psilocybin and PCP. Discusses the reasons why people use these drugs, including their effects and legal implications. Describes the dangers of combining drugs and driving under the influence of drugs.
Health and Safety; Psychology; Sociology
Dist - GA **Prod** - GA 1982

Straight Talk about Drugs Series
Straight Talk about Drugs - Psychedelics, PCP and Dangerous Combinations 39 MIN
Straight Talk about Drugs - Stimulants and Narcotics 50 MIN
Straight Talk about Drugs - Tranquilizers and Sedatives 40 MIN
Dist - GA

Straight Talk about Drugs - Stimulants and Narcotics 50 MIN
U-matic / VHS
Straight Talk about Drugs Series
Color (J H)
LC 82-706872
Identifies stimulants and drugs and discusses the dangers and effects of their use. Explores some of the common reasons that people use drugs and describes programs that help rehabilitate the narcotic addict.
Health and Safety; Psychology; Sociology
Dist - GA **Prod** - GA 1982

Straight Talk about Drugs - Tranquilizers and Sedatives 40 MIN
VHS / U-matic
Straight Talk about Drugs Series
Color (J H)
LC 82-706871
Explores the use of tranquilizers and sedatives, including their dangers and effects. Gives an overview of drug use and explains the differences between drug use and misuse.
Health and Safety; Psychology; Sociology
Dist - GA **Prod** - GA 1982

Straight talk - alcohol and other drugs series
VHS
Straight talk - alcohol and other drugs series
Color (J H T)
$289.00 purchase _ #ATC10SV-P
Features frank testimonials of teens with significant chemical dependency issues in a series of three videos. Includes individuals of various ages and ethnic backgrounds and both sexes who are presented in a quick-cut, MTV editing style and docudrama format as they discuss pre-addiction, addiction, and recovery issues such as home life, abusive relationships, sexual acting out, overdose, staying straight, and coping with relapses. Discussion guides included.
Guidance and Counseling; Health and Safety; Sociology
Dist - CAMV

Straight Talk on Eye Safety 12 MIN
16mm
Color (IND)
LC 76-703855
Stresses the importance of wearing eye protection every minute on the job and of following safety rules in preventing blindness.
Health and Safety
Dist - HF **Prod** - HF 1969

Straight talk on leak detection - with Joe Thursday, Leak Detective 25 MIN
U-matic / VHS / BETA
Color (G PRO)
$46.00, $155.00 purchase _ #LSTF71
Explains various leak detection methods available to owners of underground storage tanks to comply with current UST regulations. Produced by Environmental Media Center.
Industrial and Technical Education
Dist - FEDU

Straight talk on teams series
Enables team building that accomplishes goals with confidence and a mininum of error. Outlines, through a four - part series, insights on successful team building. Features Allan Cox.
Building a foundation for powerful teams - Part 1 — 23 MIN
Getting the most out of your team - Part 4 — 21 MIN
Managing conflict - Part 3 — 21 MIN
Recognizing values - Part 2 — 21 MIN
Dist - EXTR **Prod** - BBP 1990

Straight talk series
Presents three parts on teens and drugs. Includes the titles Starting Early; Hitting Rock Bottom; and Getting Straight. Features the testimonials of 20 young people aged 13 to 22 who have confronted chemical abuse issues. Uses a quick - cut editing style and a contemporary soundtrack aimed at attracting the MTV gneration. No adult voices are heard - teen interviews discuss personal issues - parental drug and alcohol use, physical abuse, sexual acting out, chronic low self - esteem, loneliness, alienation and suicidal behavior.
Getting straight - Part III — 30 MIN
Hitting rock bottom - Part II — 30 MIN
Starting early - Part I — 30 MIN
Dist - FMSP

Straight talking - the art of assertiveness 30 MIN
VHS / U-matic / BETA
Color; CC (C A G)
$870.00 purchase, $240.00 rental
Stars John Cleese who shows how to overcome unproductive standoffs. Reveals that assertive people walk the line between aggressive and submissive behavior. Shows how to be honest about what's relevant, establish a bottom line of negotiation, use the 'instant replay' technique, be helpful, invite others to help solve problems and negotiate as equals.
Business and Economics; Psychology; Social Science
Dist - VIDART **Prod** - VIDART 1990

Straight Thinking for Stress Management 32 MIN
U-matic / VHS
Practical Stress Management with Dr Barry Alberstein Series
Color
Psychology
Dist - DELTAK **Prod** - DELTAK

Straight Time 107 MIN
16mm
Color
Focuses on a man who is paroled after six years in jail but who eventually returns to a life of crime. Stars Dustin Hoffman.
Fine Arts
Dist - SWANK **Prod** - WB

Straight Turning between Centers
VHS / U-matic
Basic Engine Lathe Series
Color (SPANISH)
Industrial and Technical Education
Dist - VTRI **Prod** - VTRI

Straight turning between centers on the lathe 18 MIN
VHS
Color (J H A G)
$49.95 purchase _ #AM1428
Explains the steps in the most common machine lathe operations - cutting the stock to working length, center drilling, mounting the workpiece, tool selection, proper clamping of the cutting tool, selection of spindle speed, adjusting for proper feed, measuring the length of cut and making a trial cut.
Health and Safety; Industrial and Technical Education
Dist - AAVIM **Prod** - AAVIM 1992

Straight Turning between Centers on the Lathe 18 MIN
U-matic / VHS / 16mm
Metal Shop - Safety and Operations Series
Color (J) (ARABIC SPANISH)
LC 72-704809
Demonstrates the straight turning between centers operation on the lathe.
Industrial and Technical Education
Dist - AIMS **Prod** - EPRI 1970

Straight Turning Work of Two Diameters
U-matic / VHS
Basic Engine Lathe Series
Color (SPANISH)
Industrial and Technical Education
Dist - VTRI **Prod** - VTRI

Straight up 90 MIN
U-matic / VHS
K - 12 drug prevention video series
Color; Captioned (I J)
$40.00, $84.00 purchase _ #TCA17529, #TCA17528
Stars Lou Gossett Jr and Chad Allen in a tale of a journey on a 'fate elevator,' which teaches Allen's character valuable lessons on why drugs are harmful and how to avoid them. Includes teacher's guide and information card.
Guidance and Counseling; Health and Safety; Psychology
Dist - USNAC **Prod** - USDED 1988

Straight Up 90 MIN
VHS
Color (G)
$29.95 purchase _ #STTU - 000
Uses an action - oriented format to convey the dangers of substance abuse to children ages nine through 12. Deals with issues including peer pressure, how to gain a strong sense of one's values, and the misleading messages of advertising. Features Louis Gossett Jr. and teen actor Chad Allen. Program consists of six 15 - minute segments.
Business and Economics; Guidance and Counseling; Health and Safety; Psychology; Sociology
Dist - PBS **Prod** - KCET 1988

Straight Up and Away 15 MIN
16mm
Color
LC 74-706587
Depicts opportunities for helicopter pilots offered by the Marine Corps.
Civics and Political Systems; Guidance and Counseling; Psychology
Dist - USNAC **Prod** - USN 1970

Straight up rappin' 29 MIN
VHS
Color (J H C G)
$295.00 purchase, $55.00 rental
Looks at Rap music as performed in the streets of New York, straight up - without backup music. Shows 10 - year - olds rapping about the Bill of Rights, young men who rap about homelessness and child abuse, a young woman who raps about revolution.
Fine Arts; History - United States; Sociology
Dist - FLMLIB **Prod** - ROSVUI 1993

Straightforward Communication 19 MIN
U-matic / VHS
Leadership Link - Fundamentals of Effective Supervision Series
Color
Business and Economics; Psychology
Dist - DELTAK **Prod** - CHSH

The Strained knot - crises in marriage 30 MIN
VHS / U-matic
Family portrait - a study of contemporary lifestyles series; Lesson 20
Color (C A)
Discusses how emotional instability in one or both partners can seriously affect the marriage. Examines the disillusionment and unrealistic expectations that may be created by financial difficulties, having and rearing children, illness or death and parental meddling.
Sociology
Dist - CDTEL **Prod** - SCCON

Strainers, Filters, and Traps 60 MIN
U-matic / VHS
Mechanical Equipment Maintenance, Module 7 - Piping Series
Color (IND)
Industrial and Technical Education
Dist - LEIKID **Prod** - LEIKID

Straining, Stretching, Dividing - Division, Three - Digit Dividend, Two - Digit Divisor 15 MIN
U-matic / VHS
Figure Out Series
Color (I)
Tells how Alice's desire to lose weight creates situations in which she divides by a two - digit divisor. Explains the sequence necessary to find a quotient when using a calculator.
Mathematics
Dist - AITECH **Prod** - MAETEL 1982

Strains, Sprains, Dislocations and Fractures 30 MIN
VHS / U-matic
First Aid in the Classroom Series
Color
Deals with injuries requiring specific types of bandages and splints until a doctor can set the break.
Health and Safety
Dist - NETCHE **Prod** - NETCHE 1973

Straits Detroit - the Detroit River 33 MIN
16mm
Color
LC 72-702182
Presents a view of the cultural, economic and scientific importance of the Detroit River and the influence the river has had on the history of the region through which it flows.
Geography - United States
Dist - WSUM **Prod** - WSUM 1972

A Strand in the web 20 MIN
VHS
Color (G)
$19.95 purchase
Documents the efforts of the residents of a small Navajo community who defeated the construction of a proposed hazardous waste dump on their land.
Science - Natural; Social Science; Sociology
Dist - GRNPCE **Prod** - GRNPCE 1989

Strand - under the dark cloth 81 MIN
35mm / 16mm / VHS
Color; B&W (G)
$300.00 rental
Investigates the mysterious life of pioneering photographer Paul Strand. Traces Strand's path from New York to Mexico to Europe. Directed by John Walker.
Biography; Fine Arts; Industrial and Technical Education
Dist - KINOIC

Stranded 49 MIN
VHS
Color (J)
$24.95 purchase _ #807 - 9003
Explores the mystery of why whales, whose intelligence may equal our own, repeatedly fling themselves onto beaches, apparently bent on mass suicide. Demonstrates the intelligence of whales and dolphins in captivity and considers the various theories that have been advanced to explain the mystery of mass strandings.
Science - Natural
Dist - FI

Stranded on an island and the good bad luck 30 MIN
VHS
Davey and Goliath series
Color (P I R)
$19.95 purchase, $10.00 rental _ #4 - 8832
Presents two 15 - minute 'Davey and Goliath' episodes. 'Stranded on an Island' describes how Sally, Davey and Goliath are stranded when their boat is beached by a tide. 'The Good Bad Luck' tells how Davey and Jonathan, after an incident at school, vow to follow their teacher's instructions from that point on. Produced by the Evangelical Lutheran Church in America.
Literature and Drama; Religion and Philosophy
Dist - APH

Stranden - the Seashore 22 MIN
16mm
Color
Presents different types of seashores, showing bird life, a bathing beach, fishermen starting directly from a flat beach and flocks of birds above the sea. Includes music and sound effects.
Science - Natural
Dist - STATNS **Prod** - STATNS 1962

Strands of development - Unit F 32 MIN
VHS
Looking at size and shape series
Color; PAL (H C T)
PdS35.00 purchase
Shows children experiencing and developing notions of size and shape and documents how the development of children's perception of space is a continuous process. Presents part of a six - part series of observation material.
Psychology
Dist - EMFVL

Strandskade - Haematopus Ostralegus - Oyster Catcher 5 MIN
16mm
Color
Presents a description of the oyster catcher in its natural surroundings, accompanied by sound effects.
Science - Natural
Dist - STATNS **Prod** - STATNS 1965

Strange and Unusual Animals - Adaptation to Environment 10 MIN
16mm / U-matic / VHS
Color (I)
LC 75-700968
Studies several animals including the elephant, the ostrich, the cassowary, the bat, the sloth, the leaf frog, the aardvark, the giant anteater, the echinda, the kangaroo, the duck - billed platypus and the koala bear and discusses man's place in nature.
Science - Natural
Dist - AIMS **Prod** - LATHAM 1974

Strange Bird 10 MIN
16mm / U-matic / VHS
Color (P I)
LC 80-701509
Features the only bird in the forest who has no egg to hatch until a clever old crow finds an extra egg for the unhappy mother bird. Shows how the egg turns into an alarm clock instead of a bird. Stresses the concepts of adoption, parental love and the 'different' child.
Guidance and Counseling; Literature and Drama
Dist - IFB **Prod** - ZAGREB 1975

Strange but true body shapes
VHS
NFL series
Color (G)
$24.95 purchase _ #NFL2022V
Takes a humorous look at some of the 'strange body shapes' of National Football League players. Produced by NFL Films.
Literature and Drama; Physical Education and Recreation
Dist - CAMV

Strange but true football stories
VHS
NFL series
Color (G)
$19.95 purchase _ #NFL1086V
Presents a collection of humorous 'bloopers' from the National Football League. Produced by NFL Films.
Literature and Drama; Physical Education and Recreation
Dist - CAMV

The Strange Case of Mr Finch 16 MIN
U-matic / VHS / 16mm
Color (P I)
LC 83-700252
Discusses the importance of effective listening skills.
English Language
Dist - ALTSUL **Prod** - EBERHT 1983

Strange case of the cosmic rays 55 MIN
VHS
Color (G)
$19.95 purchase _ #355617
Reissues a Frank Capra galactic thriller which reveals the mysteries of the universe. Explores the atom, particles and radiation research. Includes puppetry by Bil and Cora's Marionettes.
Fine Arts; Health and Safety; Science - Physical
Dist - INSTRU **Prod** - CAPRA

The Strange Case of the Cosmic Rays - Pt 1 30 MIN
16mm
Bell System Science Series
Color (H)
Uses live action, animation and documentary film excerpts to probe the mysteries of cosmic rays, their character and behavior, pointing up the work of scientists in their constant search for more knowledge of matter and energy.
Science - Physical
Dist - WAVE **Prod** - ATAT 1957

The Strange Case of the Cosmic Rays - Pt 2 29 MIN
16mm
Bell System Science Series
Color (H)
Uses live action, animation and documentary film excerpts to probe the mysteries of cosmic rays, their character and behavior, pointing up the work of scientists in their constant search for more knowledge of matter and energy.
Science - Physical
Dist - WAVE **Prod** - ATAT 1957

The Strange case of the end of civilization as we know it 55 MIN
VHS
Color (G)
$19.95 purchase _ #1663
Stars John Cleese as a descendent of Sherlock Homes who succeeds in bungling every job he organizes. Reveals that 'Holmes' is summoned to a conference by the desperate Commissioner of police to lay plans for the capture of Moriarty before he gains control of the world. From there, nothing seems to go right. Arthur Lowe portrays the 'bionic' grandson of Doctor Watson and Connie Booth is Mrs Hudson.
Literature and Drama
Dist - KULTUR **Prod** - KULTUR 1993

The Strange Case of the English Language 48 MIN
U-matic / VHS / 16mm
Color; B&W (H C A)
LC 76-702592
Explains that a great way to learn about the idiosyncrasies of the English language, as it is spoken and written, is to study film clips of noted public figures. Harry Reasoner from CBS comments on John F Kennedy, Everett Dirksen, Billy Graham and many others. Points up the stylistic quirks and overuse of pet phrases. Features interviews with various language experts.
English Language
Dist - PHENIX **Prod** - CBSTV 1968

The Strange Case of the English Language - Pt 1 24 MIN
U-matic / VHS / 16mm
Color (H C)
LC 76-702592
Harry Reasoner comments on the idiosyncrasies of the English language, as it is spoken and written today, through the use of film clips of noted public figures. Sequences used point up stylistic quirks and overuse of pet phrases. Features interviews with various language experts.
English Language
Dist - PHENIX **Prod** - CBSTV 1968

The Strange Case of the English Language - Pt 2 24 MIN
16mm / U-matic / VHS
Color (H C)
LC 76-702592
Harry Reasoner comments on the idiosyncrasies of the English language, as it is spoken and written today, through the use of film clips of noted public figures. Sequences used point up stylistic quirks and overuse of pet phrases. Features interviews with various language experts.
English Language
Dist - PHENIX **Prod** - CBSTV 1968

Strange Circle 108 MIN
VHS
Color (G) (MANDARIN CHINESE (ENGLISH SUBTITLES))
$45.00 purchase _ #6019A
Presents a movie produced in the People's Republic of China.
Fine Arts; Geography - World; Literature and Drama
Dist - CHTSUI **Prod** - CHTSUI

Strange Creature - the Echidna 14 MIN
VHS / U-matic
Color (P)
Reveals that only two animals lay eggs like reptiles but suckle their young like mammals, and both live in Australia. Describes the echidna, or spiny ant - eater as one of these strange creatures (the other is the platypus). Shows on film, recorded for the first time, the young hatching from its egg and being carried in its mother's pouch. Notes how the echidna lives by tearing open ant nests and licking up the ants with its sticky tongue.
Geography - World; Science - Natural
Dist - EDMI **Prod** - EDMI 1971

Strange creatures of the night 60 MIN
VHS
Color; CC (I J H)
$19.98 purchase _ #VES5344
Explores the world of nocturnal animals.
Science - Natural
Dist - KNOWUN **Prod** - NGS 1973

Strange creatures of the night 60 MIN
VHS
Animal kingdom series
Color (J H C G)
$19.98 purchase _ #VV5344V - S
Explores the mysterious world of nocturnal creatures. Part of a series visiting remote regions of the world to study exotic wildlife.
Science - Natural
Dist - CAMV **Prod** - NGS

Strange Discoveries 30 MIN
U-matic
Read all about it - One Series
Color (I)
Teaches reading and writing skills through a story in which Chris' friend Lynn goes to the town hall to interview a councillor. There she finds the mayor is Duneedon, ruler of the galaxy Trialaviron.
Education; English Language; Literature and Drama
Dist - TVOTAR **Prod** - TVOTAR 1982

The Strange economics of baseball 30 MIN
U-matic
Adam Smith's money world series; 145
Color (A)
Attempts to demystify the world of money and break it down so that employees of a small business can understand and adjust to new social and economic trends. Reports on the major economic stories and discoveries of the day.
Business and Economics
Dist - PBS **Prod** - WNETTV 1985

Strange friends - a learning guide for students of Chinese 90 MIN
VHS / Videodisc
Color; CAV (C) (CHINESE)
$275.00, $45.00 purchase _ #ILISF, #1047B
Supports the text compiled by Jing - heng Ma, which is available separately.
Foreign Language
Dist - CHTSUI

Strange Fruit 33 MIN
U-matic / VHS / 16mm
Color (H C A)
LC 79-700954
Tells the story of Henry Brown, a Black painter who faces the ugliness of racism while trying to exercise his freedom to vote. Based on the book Strange Fruit by Lillian Smith.
Civics and Political Systems; History - United States; Literature and Drama; Sociology
Dist - LCOA **Prod** - AMERFI 1979

Strange interlude 190 MIN
VHS
Color (G)
$69.95 purchase _ #S02208
Presents a dramatization of the Eugene O'Neill tale 'Strange Interlude.' Stars Glenda Jackson, Jose Ferrer, Ken Howard, David Dukes, Edward Petherbridge, and Rosemary Harris. Consists of two videocassettes.
Fine Arts; Literature and Drama
Dist - UILL

Strange life and death of Dr. Turing 50 MIN
VHS
Horizon series
PAL; Color (H C A)
PdS99 purchase; Not available in the United States
Presents the life of one of the great minds of the twentieth century. Explains how Dr. Turing used computers, artificial intelligence, and cryptography to help the Allies win World War II. Examines his life as a social pariah and how he ended it.
History - United States; Science
Dist - BBCENE

The Strange new science of chaos 58 MIN
VHS / U-matic
Nova series
Color (H C A)
$250.00 purchase _ #HP - 5919C
Shows scientists making sense out of some very chaotic behavior in nature. Speculates that turbulent processes like weather, waterfalls, irregular heartbeats and even brain waves actually have hidden and highly - ordered structures. Indicates that chaos and uncertainty are more often the rule than the exception, diverging from Newtonian physics. Part of the Nova series.
Computer Science; Science; Science - Physical
Dist - CORF **Prod** - WGBHTV 1989

Strange Occurrence at Elm View Library 18 MIN
U-matic / VHS / 16mm
Color (I J)
LC 83-701021
Shows a girl encountering the ghost of Ben Franklin, who teaches her the proper way to do library research. Demonstrates the use of the card catalog and the Reader's Guide to Periodicals.
Education; Social Science
Dist - ALTSUL **Prod** - EBERHT 1983

Strange Partners - Symbiosis in the Sea 12 MIN
16mm
Color
LC 73-702421
Portrays the relationship of marine animals. Includes scenes of small fish riding on the backs of larger fish, a pearlfish living within a sea cucumber, neon gobies cleaning parasites off of large fish and microscopic scenes of parasites in gills.
Science - Natural
Dist - MIAMIS **Prod** - REELA 1968

Strange Sleep 59 MIN
U-matic / VHS / 16mm
Nova Series
Color (H C A)
LC 78-700615
Traces the history of the development of anesthesia.
Health and Safety; Science
Dist - TIMLIF **Prod** - WGBHTV 1976

Strange Sleep 30 MIN
16mm / U-matic / VHS
KnowZone Series
Color (I J H)
$550 purchase - 16 mm, $250 purchase - video _ #5069C
Shows how anesthesiology was discovered. Adapted from the Nova series. Hosted by David Morse.
Health and Safety
Dist - CORF

The Strange story of Napoleon's wallpaper 30 MIN
VHS
Human element series
Color; PAL (G)
PdS65 purchase; Not available in the United States or Canada
Explores the mystery surrounding Napoleon's death. Provides a human look at the world of science, showing that there is more to chemistry than meets the eye. David Jones narrates. Part two of a five - part series.
History - World; Sociology
Dist - BBCENE

Strange Story of the Frog who Became a Prince 12 MIN
U-matic / VHS / 16mm
Color (P)
Points out that being just what you are is the nicest thing of all through the story of a frog who is changed into a prince by a snap - happy witch.
English Language
Dist - GA **Prod** - XEROX BOSUST 1972

The Stranger 104 MIN
U-matic / VHS / 16mm
Color (FRENCH (ENGLISH SUBTITLES))
Portrays the milieu of 1938 - 1939 Algiers and the despondency of the hero's plight. French dialogue with English subtitles.
Foreign Language; History - World
Dist - FI **Prod** - FI 1967

The Stranger 30 MIN
VHS
Classic short stories
Color (H)
#E362; LC 90-708400
Presents 'The Stranger' by Victor Trivas. Part of a series which combines Hollywood stars with short story masterpieces of the world to encourage appreciation of the short story.
Literature and Drama
Dist - GPN **Prod** - CTI 1988

The Stranger 30 MIN
U-matic
Read all about it - One Series
Color (I)
Teaches reading and writing skills through a story in which Chris and his friends say they are using the house of an uncle who disappeared as a place to publish a newspaper. Suddenly the friends, Samantha and Lynne, find themselves wheeling through space.
Education; English Language; Literature and Drama
Dist - TVOTAR **Prod** - TVOTAR 1982

The Stranger 13 MIN
VHS / U-matic
Strawberry Square Series
Color (P)
Fine Arts
Dist - AITECH **Prod** - NEITV 1982

A Stranger among us
VHS
Color (G)
$94.98 purchase
Features Melanie Griffith who portrays a New York City policewoman assigned to investigate a murder in the Hasidic community, in a suspense - filled and controversial study of Hasidic life. Directed by Sidney Lumet.
Fine Arts
Dist - ERGOM

A Stranger at Green Knowe 15 MIN
VHS / U-matic
Best of Cover to Cover 2 Series
Color (I)
Literature and Drama
Dist - WETATV **Prod** - WETATV

Stranger danger 30 MIN
VHS
Color (J H C G)
$79.95 purchase _ #CCP0160V - P
Shows parents and other children's caregivers how to teach safety rules to children, how to help children recognize who is or isn't a stranger; where to instruct children to find safety zones if they are scared or in danger; how to prepare children to become streetwise to potentially dangerous situations. Stresses preparing children vs scaring them.
Health and Safety; Home Economics; Sociology
Dist - CAMV **Prod** - CAMV 1994

Stranger from Kahiki 11 MIN
16mm
Color
Tells the legend of the origin of the ti leaf plant.
English Language; Literature and Drama
Dist - CINEPC **Prod** - CINEPC 1975

The Stranger in our midst 18 MIN
VHS
Mission videos series
Color (G R)
$12.50 purchase _ #S12352
Encourages Lutheran Church - Missouri Synod congregations to begin outreach programs to international college students.
Guidance and Counseling; Literature and Drama; Religion and Philosophy
Dist - CPH **Prod** - LUMIS

Stranger than Hoboken 14 MIN
16mm
Color; B&W (G)
Presents a short film directed by Nan Jorgensen.
Fine Arts
Dist - KINOIC

Stranger than Science Fiction 17 MIN
16mm / U-matic / VHS
Twenty - First Century Series
Color (J)
LC 75-702568
Edited version of the 1969 motion picture of the same title. Shows some of the scientific achievements of today which were depicted in the science fiction literature of the past.
Literature and Drama; Science - Natural; Science - Physical; Sociology
Dist - MGHT **Prod** - CBSTV 1975

Stranger than Science Fiction 27 MIN
16mm / U-matic / VHS
Twentieth - First Century Series
Color (J H)
LC 79-701246
Shows some scientific achievements of today which were depicted in the science fiction literature of the past.
Literature and Drama; Science - Physical
Dist - MGHT **Prod** - CBSTV 1969

Strangers 30 MIN
VHS
Color (I J H C G A R)
$24.95 purchase, $10.00 rental _ #35 - 8151 - 19
Portrays a family that seems fine on the surface, but is actually devoid of understanding and love. Reveals that friends of the family help them to see God's model for family relationships.
Guidance and Counseling; Psychology; Religion and Philosophy; Sociology
Dist - APH CPH **Prod** - CPH

Strangers 14 MIN
16mm
Good Life Series
Color (S)
LC 81-700272
Uses a TV game show format to show how to act with strangers in public.
Education
Dist - HUBDSC **Prod** - DUDLYN 1981

Strangers and Kin 58 MIN
U-matic
Color
Relates the history of images and stereotypes of mountain people and the conflict between modernization and tradition. Juxtaposes Hollywood film clips, network television shows, dramatic sketches and interviews with contemporary Appalachians.
Geography - United States; History - United States; Sociology
Dist - APPAL **Prod** - APPAL

Strangers and Self - Care 27 MIN
VHS
Safe Child Program - K - 3 - Series
Color (A)
$895.00 purchase
Presents a seminar to show parents and professionals how to teach primary children prevention of sexual, emotional and physical abuse, and safety for children in self care. Combines teacher training to ensure consistent presentation, parental involvement to reinforce program goals, videotapes to guarantee the accurate introduction of the concepts to children, and classroom role - playing to develop individual mastery of safety skills. Part of a seven videotape program adapted from 'The Safe Child Book' by Sherryll Kraizer, K - 3.
Education; Health and Safety; Psychology; Sociology
Dist - LUF **Prod** - LUF 1989

Strangers Aren't Bad, They're Just Strangers 27 MIN
VHS
Safe Child Program - K - 3 - Series
Color (K)
$895.00 purchase
Teaches age appropriate concepts for the prevention of abuse and abduction by strangers and safety for children in self care. Raises self - esteem, improves self - reliance, is developmentally consistent with the needs of kindergartners. Multiracial and multicultural. Adapted from 'The Safe Child Book' by Sherryll Kraiser. Part of the Safe Child - K - 3 - Program of seven videotapes.
Education; Health and Safety; Psychology; Sociology
Dist - LUF **Prod** - LUF 1989

Strangers at the Door 28 MIN
16mm / U-matic / VHS
Adventures in History Series
Color (I J H)
LC 82-700049
Tells how an immigrant family is split apart at the immigration clearance center in 1907 Quebec. Shows how their dreams of a bright future are destroyed.
Fine Arts; Sociology
Dist - FI **Prod** - NFBC 1978

Strangers in Good Company 100 MIN
16mm
Color (G)
Presents an independent production produced in association with Bedford Entertainment. Weaves a tale of friendship and courage in the wilds of Northern Quebec where seven old women are stranded at a deserted farmhouse. Features Cynthia Scott as director. Available also in 35mm film format.
Health and Safety; Literature and Drama; Psychology; Sociology
Dist - FIRS

Strangers in the Garden - Pt 4 56 MIN
VHS
First Eden Series
Color (S)
$129.00 purchase _ #825 - 9505
Presents a spectacular portrait of the Mediterranean Sea and the variety of plants and animals that call the region home. Features David Attenborough as narrator. Part 4 of four parts considers the Suez Canal which opened in 1869, and opened the Mediterranean to pollution. Despite efforts to counteract the pollution, areas around the sea are still maltreated. Asks if we can save the remaining landscapes or if they are the last of the First Eden.
Geography - World; History - World; Science - Natural; Social Science; Sociology
Dist - FI **Prod** - BBCTV 1988

Strangers in the Homeland 60 MIN
16mm
Color
Shows a fictional family examining their decisions in pre - Revolutionary War times, in the South of the 1940s and during the Vietnam War.
History - United States; Religion and Philosophy
Dist - CCNCC **Prod** - NBCTV

Strangers in the night 3 MIN
16mm
Color (G)
Uses Barbie and Ken to create a pun on romance. Features mixed media techniques with a mixed soundtrack. A Jackie Leger production.
Fine Arts; Literature and Drama
Dist - CANCIN

Strangers - the Story of a Mother and Daughter 96 MIN
VHS / U-matic
Color (H C A)
Portrays the reunion of an embittered mother who reunites with her daughter after a 20 - year estrangement. Shows that although the reunion starts off shakily, the mother eventually lowers her defenses and both enjoy a happy summer. Stars Bette Davis and Gena Rowlands.
Fine Arts; Sociology
Dist - TIMLIF **Prod** - TIMLIF 1982

Strangers We Meet 10 MIN
16mm / U-matic / VHS
Color (P I)
LC 77-703100
Deals with child molestation prevention. Teaches safety rules to be followed whenever any unknown person speaks to a child.
Guidance and Counseling; Health and Safety; Sociology
Dist - AIMS **Prod** - DAVP 1977

The Strangest Secret
VHS / BETA
Color
Presents a program for developing positive attitudes and setting and achieving goals. Discusses topics such as time management, human relations and self - achievement.

Psychology; Sociology
Dist - NIGCON Prod - NIGCON

Strangleholds on the Therapist - Failure to Leave the Office, Phone Calls and Panic 16 MIN
U-matic / VHS
Treatment of the Borderline Patient Series
Color
Reveals clinical details of difficult and interpersonally controlling emotions of borderline patients. Discusses how to handle these reactions.
Health and Safety; Psychology
Dist - HEMUL Prod - HEMUL

Strangulated Femoral Hernia 12 MIN
16mm
Color (PRO)
Shows the varied pathology of strangulated femoral hernia, including Richter's type of hernia with minimal vascular changes, strangulation of bowel which shows remarkable improvement after release of constriction, strangulation of bowel which is obviously gangrenous and Richter's type hernia with small bowel obstruction.
Health and Safety; Science
Dist - ACY Prod - ACYDGD 1958

Strangulated Obstruction of the Intestine 22 MIN
16mm
Color (PRO)
Shows differences in the known or suspected lethal factors between short, medium and long - loop strangulations of the intestine by means of operative findings in patients, animated drawings and microscopic studies.
Health and Safety; Science
Dist - ACY Prod - ACYDGD 1960

Strapping Machine Operator - Rod Mill 8 MIN
U-matic / VHS
Steel Making Series
Color (IND)
Illustrates the duties of the operator of an automatic strapping machine dispenser and seal magazine.
Business and Economics; Industrial and Technical Education
Dist - LEIKID Prod - LEIKID

Strapping Machine Troubleshooting - Rod Mill 10 MIN
U-matic / VHS
Steel Making Series
Color (IND)
Shows how to correct strapping machine problems and get the machine back on line quickly and safely.
Business and Economics; Industrial and Technical Education
Dist - LEIKID Prod - LEIKID

Straps and Transportation Bridles 15 MIN
16mm
B&W
LC FIE52-1587
Shows how to attach straps and bridles to various types of draughts, and how to use dunnage properly.
Social Science
Dist - USNAC Prod - USA 1949

Strat 26 MIN
16mm
Jason Films Portrait Series
Color (J)
LC 76-705673
A cinema verte portrait of Stratford Sherman, showing how he goes about trying to institute change at his exclusive eastern preparatory school. Includes scenes of him at home and on his European summer vacation.
Fine Arts; Psychology; Social Science; Sociology
Dist - JASON Prod - JASON 1970

Strata - the Earth's Changing Crust 11 MIN
U-matic / VHS / 16mm
Color (I)
LC FIA67-1707
Presents a study of strata, or rock layers, found in many parts of the earth. Points out faulted strata which indicate changes in the earth's crust.
Science - Physical
Dist - PHENIX Prod - FA 1966

Stratasphere - a Portrait of Teresa Stratas 87 MIN
VHS
Color (G)
$29.95 purchase _ #1254
Profiles the work of singer Teresa Stratas in conjuction with director Zeffirelli. Includes scenes from 'Salome' and 'La Boheme.'
Fine Arts
Dist - KULTUR

Strategic considerations 57 MIN
Cassette
Faster, more effective depositions in business cases series
Color (PRO)
$125.00, $30.00 purchase, $50.00 rental _ #DEP3-001, #ADE3-001
Emphasizes that changes in federal and local discovery rules resulting from the Civil Justice Reform Act of 1990 give courts greater control over the extent of discovery, while at the same time clients are demanding more efficiency, accountability and results, forcing effective business litigators to rethink their deposition strategies and practices. Shows how some of the nation's outstanding litigators develop their discovery and trial strategies and conduct depositions in a fraud case. Includes study guide.
Business and Economics; Civics and Political Systems
Dist - AMBAR Prod - AMBAR 1993

Strategic cost management 50 MIN
VHS
Color (PRO IND A) (DUTCH FRENCH)
$695.00 purchase _ #VIM14
Discusses product costing and cost allocations versus cost drivers. Considers misleading results from the use of customary product costing systems and commonly used allocation methods. Assumes that managers addressed by Prof Tony Hope have a good understanding of the accounting system in the areas of planning and controlling.
Business and Economics
Dist - EXTR

Strategic Impact of Information Technology Series
The Impact on Business Operations 30 MIN
The Impact on Office and Home 30 MIN
Managing Information Technology 30 MIN
Dist - DELTAK

Strategic Impact of Technology 44 MIN
VHS / U-matic
Management of Microprocessor Technology Series
Color
Lectures on product categories, intelligent product marketing considerations and the advantages of microprocessor - based products.
Industrial and Technical Education; Mathematics
Dist - MIOT Prod - MIOT

Strategic Job Search Series
Developing job leads - module a 25 MIN
Interviewing with Confidence - Module B 25 MIN
Dist - UTM

Strategic job search series
Developing job leads and interviewing with confidence
Dist - VLEARN

Strategic marketing 53 MIN
VHS
Color (PRO IND A) (DUTCH FRENCH)
$695.00 purchase _ #VIM01
Presents Prof Philippe Naert outlining a marketing plan focused on the customer. Helps executives and senior managers to develop a marketing culture and planning process and to design product positioning and market segmentation - while addressing marketing problems of this decade.
Business and Economics
Dist - EXTR

Strategic Planning and Leadership 50 MIN
U-matic
Color (T)
Illustrates the major elements of the school strategic planning and implementation process. Presents the rationale for the process and describes external and internal scanning processes and mission development.
Education
Dist - AFSCD Prod - AFSCD 1986

Strategic planning for logistics 30 MIN
VHS
Business logistics series
Color (G C)
$200.00 purchase, $20.50 rental _ #34982
Discusses strategic planning for logistics. Part of a 30 - part series on business logistics which deals with movement and storage of raw and finished products, and with managerial activities important for effective control of these operations. Interviews logistics managers of major US corporations and transportation companies. Uses on - site segments to demonstrate logistical carrier operations. Features program author Dr John Coyle.
Business and Economics
Dist - PSU Prod - WPSXTV 1987

Strategic Planning, William S Birnbaum
U-matic / VHS
Management Skills Series
Color (PRO)
Business and Economics; Psychology
Dist - AMCEE Prod - AMCEE

Strategic Public Presentations
VHS / 16mm
(PRO)
Guides the viewer to an understanding of the public presentation situation. Teaches the viewer to create the presentation scenario and effectively plan. Gives different situations for the viewer to consider.
Business and Economics
Dist - MRCC Prod - MRCC

Strategic Selling - a Thinking Person's Guide Series Pt 2
Understanding Buyer Behavior 60 MIN
Dist - TIMLIF

Strategic Selling - a Thinking Person's Guide Series Pt 3
Overcoming Resistance 60 MIN
Dist - TIMLIF

Strategic selling - a thinking person's guide series
Customized closing 60 MIN
Dist - TIMLIF

Strategic thinking - Creating cultures that work - Part IV
VHS / BETA / U-matic
Perspective on new organizations series
Color (C G PRO)
$425.00 purchase _ #DI 04204
Presents part IV of a five - part series on IBM, Gore - Tex and Motorola and how each organization achieved excellence, the indicators that led to success or downfall and how they valued and utilized human resources. Features Drs J Clayton Lafferty and Delmar 'Dutch' Landen as co - hosts and contributors, as well as other corporate visionaries.
Business and Economics; Civics and Political Systems; Psychology
Dist - HUMSYN Prod - HUMSYN 1994

Strategic Trust - the Making of Nuclear Free Palau 58 MIN
U-matic / VHS / 16mm
Color (H C A)
Tells the story of Palau, a tiny Micronesian republic which, despite economic and political pressure from the U S, adopted the world's first nuclear free constitution. Raises the question of whether local citizens have the right to decide if nuclear weapons will be deployed on their soil.
Civics and Political Systems; History - World; Sociology
Dist - CNEMAG Prod - CNEMAG

Strategically managing the future of compliance
VHS
Dream team series
Color (IND PRO)
$295.00 purchase, $150.00 rental _ #MAX03F
Introduces Lucy Griffin and Phillips Gay in part of an eight - part series on competitive banking. Includes a leader's guide. Produced by Marx Communications.
Business and Economics
Dist - EXTR

Strategies 30 MIN
U-matic / VHS
Corporate Computer Security Strategy Series
Color
Deals with strategies for the selection and design of computer security safeguards with special emphasis on the role of corporate management in initiating and sustaining an effective security effort.
Industrial and Technical Education; Psychology
Dist - DELTAK Prod - DELTAK

Strategies and Plans 45 MIN
U-matic / VHS
Data Analysis for End Users Series
Color
Gives users an understanding of how a data strategy is derived from an analysis of the organization and operations of the business entity and how they can work effectively with the analysts in planning the data base.
Business and Economics; Industrial and Technical Education
Dist - DELTAK Prod - DELTAK

Strategies and tactics
U-matic / 16mm
Art of negotiating series; Module 4
Color (A)
Discusses strategy and tactics and negotiations, including the 'when' strategy, forebearance, surprise, fait accompli, withdrawal, reversal, limits, feinting, participation, association, crossroads, random sample and bracketing.

Business and Economics; Psychology
Dist - BNA **Prod** - BNA 1983

Strategies and tactics and counters - with life illustrations 41 MIN
VHS / U-matic
Art of negotiating series
Color
Business and Economics; Psychology
Dist - DELTAK **Prod** - DELTAK

Strategies for a Comprehension - Centered Reading Program 29 MIN
VHS / U-matic
Reading Comprehension Series
Color (T)
Produced by Dorothy Watson for Heinemann Educational Books, Inc.
Education; English Language
Dist - HNEDBK **Prod** - IU

Strategies for classroom management series
Features Pam Wolfe in a four - part series on research - based techniques for improving student attitude and behavior. Includes demonstrations by actual teachers in their classrooms and leader's guides. Offers the titles - Developing and Teaching Classroom Rules, Delivering Clear Directions, Using Transition Time Wisely, Creating a Positive Classroom Climate.
Creating a positive classroom climate
Delivering clear directions
Developing and teaching classroom rules
Using transition time wisely
Dist - NSDC **Prod** - NSDC

Strategies for effective instruction series
Presents a four - part series based on research - proven techniques for improving student achievement. Includes demonstrations by actual teachers in actual classrooms and leader's guides for each part. Offers A Chance for Each Student to Learn, Creating a Mind - Set for Learning, Checking for Understanding - Is What You Taught What They Learned, Motivation - Sparking Student Interest. Pam Robbins and Pat Wolfe are the instructors.
A Chance for all students to learn
Checking for understanding - is what you taught what they learned
Creating a mind - set for learning
Motivation - sparking students' interest
Dist - NSDC **Prod** - NSDC

Strategies for interfacial engineering - seeing in a new way 20 MIN
VHS
Color (C G)
$140.00 purchase, $16.00 rental _ #24495
Describes advances in the understanding of colloidal and interfacial systems by demonstrating and discussing recent technology for use in the direct viewing of microstructures. Covers surfactant numbers, fluorescent life - time apparatus, video - enhanced microscopy, cryo - transmission electron microscopy, flow cells and surface forces apparatus.
Industrial and Technical Education; Science - Physical
Dist - PSU **Prod** - UMINN 1988

Strategies for Language Learning
VHS / U-matic
Increasing Children's Motivation to Read and Write Series
Color (T)
Shows teachers that students are natural readers due to linguistic capabilities. Illustrates learning methods through literature, poetry, music and personal experience.
Education; English Language
Dist - EDCORP **Prod** - EPCO

Strategies for Leadership - Collaboration 30 MIN
U-matic / VHS
Dimensions of Leadership in Nursing Series
Color
Focuses on the need for collaboration with other health workers, clients and families to obtain the best possible health care for clients. Uses vignettes to demonstrate how every person involved in a collaboration can make a unique contribution.
Health and Safety
Dist - AJN **Prod** - AJN

Strategies for Leadership - Conflict Management 30 MIN
16mm
Dimensions of Leadership in Nursing Series
Color (PRO)
LC 77-702476
Discusses conflict management, using three nursing situations which illustrate stages of conflict management and problems that arise at each stage. Emphasizes that knowledge of how to manage the conflict process allows both conflict and change to be more positive and productive.
Health and Safety; Psychology
Dist - AJN **Prod** - AJN 1977

Strategies for Leadership - Confrontation 30 MIN
16mm
Dimensions of Leadership in Nursing Series
Color (PRO)
LC 77-702475
Explores confrontation as a valuable and positive dimension of leadership. Explores the development of different kinds of confrontation and attitudes toward the process, showing specific strategies that can be used to make confrontation an effective element of leadership.
Health and Safety; Psychology
Dist - AJN **Prod** - AJN 1977

Strategies for Leadership - Problem Solving 30 MIN
16mm
Dimensions of Leadership in Nursing Series
Color (PRO)
LC 77-702474
Analyzes problem solving, using two nursing situations that involve application of steps in the problem solving process. Covers defining a problem, collecting relevant data, canvassing alternatives, implementing action and evaluating results.
Health and Safety; Psychology
Dist - AJN **Prod** - AJN 1977

Strategies for Learning - Teaching in the Preschool Classroom with Handicapped and 20 MIN
U-matic / VHS
Color
Demonstrates that mainstreaming at the beginning level can be an effective way to assure equal education for both handicapped and nonhandicapped children. Presents an innovative classroom emphasizing the use of appropriate teaching strategies.
Education; Psychology
Dist - UNEBO **Prod** - UNEBO

Strategies for preventing and handling disputes 57 MIN
VHS
Business litigation series
Color (C PRO)
$95.00 purchase, $71.25 rental _ #LBC01
Covers prevention and handling of disputes in business litigation cases.
Civics and Political Systems
Dist - NITA **Prod** - NITA 1987

Strategies for Solving Word Problems in Algebra - Basic Operations 34 MIN
VHS / U-matic
Color
LC 81-706690
Uses simple age problems as examples to introduce a five - step strategy for solving algebraic word problems.
Mathematics
Dist - GA **Prod** - CHUMAN 1981

Strategies for Solving Word Problems in Algebra - Basic Operations and Formula Problems
U-matic / VHS
Color (H)
Gives a basic approach for solving word problems such as weight and age, electricity, leverage, temperature and distance - rate - time problems.
Mathematics
Dist - GA **Prod** - GA

Strategies for Solving Word Problems in Algebra - Formula Problems 32 MIN
VHS / U-matic
Color
LC 81-706691
Uses simple age problems as examples to introduce a five - step strategy for solving algebraic word problems. Discusses time - rate - distance problems and includes examples of overtaking and interception.
Mathematics
Dist - GA **Prod** - CHUMAN 1981

Strategies for Successful Selling Series Module 1
The Professional Nature of Selling
Dist - AMA

Strategies for Successful Selling Series Module 3
The Self - Image Concepts in Selling
Dist - AMA

Strategies for Successful Selling Series Module 4
Status - Key to Understanding the Customer's Frame of Reference
Dist - AMA

Strategies for Successful Selling Series Module 5
Temperament and Personality in Selling
Dist - AMA

Strategies for successful selling series
A Belief system for success in selling
The Psychological make - Up of a Customer
The Psychology of Persuasion
Dist - AMA

Strategies for trial 54 MIN
VHS / Cassette
Medical malpractice litigation - new strategies for a new era series
Color (PRO)
$125.00, $30.00 purchase, $50.00 rental _ #MED2-003, #AME2-003
Discusses and demonstrates innovative litigation strategies and techniques developed in response to the rapidly changing climate in which medical malpractice cases are litigated. Outlines pretrial strategies. Includes demonstrations by skilled trial lawyers, interviews of those conducting the demonstrations and panel discussions. Includes study guide.
Civics and Political Systems
Dist - AMBAR **Prod** - AMBAR 1987

Strategies in college teaching series
Effective grouping techniques 24 MIN
Leading Discussions, Whole Class 49 MIN
Media in the Classroom 48 MIN
Observing Teaching 50 MIN
Dist - IU

Strategies of effective teaching series
Application to the classroom 29 MIN
Applied observation and analysis techniques 29 MIN
Attention, curiosity, and motivation 29 MIN
Demonstration lessons 59 MIN
Increasing student participation 23 MIN
Individual Teaching Styles 29 MIN
Integration of Teaching Strategies 26 MIN
Overview - Teaching Operations and Associated Strategies 29 MIN
Questioning Techniques and Probing 29 MIN
Dist - AITECH

Strategies that work - Video II 35 MIN
U-matic / VHS
Challenges of health care management in the 1990s series
Color (C PRO)
%i $295.50 purchase, $85.00 rental _ #42 - 2428, #42 - 2429, #42 - 2428R, #42 - 2429R
Examines the role of nurses in interdisciplinary provider teams, nurse - managed community care and patients cared for by their families and nursing staff in 'hospital hotels.' Shares the insights of top nurse executives, managers and physicians, as well as hospital CEOs. Part two of a three - part series developed with the American Organization of Nurse Executives - AONE. Self - study guide available separately.
Health and Safety
Dist - NLFN **Prod** - NLFN

The Strategy and art of negotiating 210 MIN
Cassette
Color (PRO)
$295.00, $150.00 purchase, $150.00 rental _ #NEG1-00F, #ANEG-000
Presents practical information and new insights on effective negotiating approaches, strategies and methods. Analyzes various dramatized negotiating styles and presents proven techniques. Discusses how to establish a positive climate and philosophy for negotiating, how to distinguish between positions and interest, when to take control, and how to avoid misrepresentation. Includes study guide.
Civics and Political Systems
Dist - AMBAR **Prod** - AMBAR 1985

Strategy and Tactics 30 MIN
U-matic / VHS
Tennis Anyone Series
Color (H C A)
LC 79-706889
Physical Education and Recreation
Dist - TIMLIF **Prod** - BATA 1979

Strategy and Tactics in Negotiations 50 MIN
VHS / U-matic
Negotiation Lectures Series
Color (PRO)
Suggests ways to deal with negotiation practices, including threats, promises, ambiguities and mediation.
Civics and Political Systems
Dist - ABACPE **Prod** - NITA

Strategy for change - CALS 19 MIN
U-matic / VHS
Color (PRO)

$50.00, $95.00 purchase _ #TCA18090, #TCA18089
Focuses on the Department of Defense's Computer - Aided Acquisition and Logistic Support program, or CALS, which is designed to lessen paperwork and increase the efficiency of weapon systems.
Business and Economics; Civics and Political Systems; Computer Science
Dist - USNAC

A Strategy for responding to criticism 40 MIN
VHS
Color; PAL; SECAM (G)
$60.00 purchase
Shows how to take feedback comfortably without blowing a stack or feeling bad. Features Steve Andreas. Introductory level of NLP, neuro - linguistic programming.
Psychology
Dist - NLPCOM **Prod** - NLPCOM

Strategy for Singles, Doubles, Cut - Throat 10 MIN
VHS / 16mm / U-matic
Racquetball Series no 4
Color (I)
LC 79-700792
Focuses on the strategy for singles, doubles and cut - throat in racquetball.
Physical Education and Recreation
Dist - ATHI **Prod** - ATHI 1979

Strategy for Winning 20 MIN
16mm / U-matic / VHS
Professional Management Program Series
Color
LC 77-700417
Focuses on the process of gaining acceptance and support for new ideas in an organization. Shows a young manager overcoming obstacles such as disappointment, adamant opposition and politics, as he plots a winning course for himself and his organization.
Business and Economics; Psychology
Dist - NEM **Prod** - NEM 1977

Strategy for winning 20 MIN
U-matic / VHS / 16mm
Communications and selling program - Spanish series
Color (SPANISH)
Stresses the importance of positive attitude, persistence and sensitivity to the opinions of others in gaining acceptance of new ideas.
Foreign Language; Psychology
Dist - NEM **Prod** - NEM

Strategy of crisis response 23 MIN
VHS / U-matic / 16mm
Color (G A)
$245.00, $110.00 purchase _ #TCA11015, #TCA11560, #TCA11562
Documents the 1982 rail accident in Livingston, Louisiana that caused one of the worst chemical spills in the state's history. Shows how the disaster was well - managed.
Civics and Political Systems; Health and Safety; Social Science
Dist - USNAC **Prod** - USEPA 1983

Strategy of the Achiever 27 MIN
16mm
Color
LC 78-701449
Presents a story about a yacht skipper and his crew who win first place in an ocean race by putting into action a systematic plan for achievement.
Physical Education and Recreation; Psychology
Dist - VANTCO **Prod** - VANTCO 1977

Strategy - planning your job search 12 MIN
VHS
From pink slip to paycheck series
Color (A G)
$69.00 purchase _ #4178
Presents job search strategy for older workers experiencing unemployment. Features Richard Bolles, author of What Color Is Your Parachute; William Morin - Drake Beam Morin; and others who offer practical, upbeat advice on developing a job search strategy, feeling positive about oneself, communicating clearly and learning to present oneself as an asset and a resource to potential employees. Part of a five - part series.
Business and Economics; Guidance and Counseling
Dist - NEWCAR

Strategy Shots 15 MIN
16mm
Tennis the Nasty Way Series
Color
LC 76-703087
Features Ilie Nastase explaining and demonstrating various strategy shots in tennis, including the lob, the overhead and the drop shot.
Physical Education and Recreation
Dist - MARMO **Prod** - SLANJ 1975

Stratford Hall and Robert E Lee 24 MIN
VHS
American lifestyle series; Politics and the military
Color (I J H C A)
$70.00 purchase, $50.00 rental _ #9880; $125.00, $70.00 purchase, $50.00 rental _ #9880
Profiles the life of Confederate General Robert E Lee, and pays a visit to Stratford Hall, Lee's Virginia home. Hosted and narrated by E G Marshall.
History - United States
Dist - AIMS **Prod** - COMCO 1986

The Stratford Shakespeare Knew 17 MIN
16mm
Color (J H C)
LC 70-713539
Presents a photographic study of Shakespeare's Stratford properties - his home, Hathaway Cottage, Arden House, Trinity Church, his new house and the English countryside.
Biography; Geography - World; Literature and Drama
Dist - PERFET **Prod** - PERFET 1971

Stratified Flow 26 MIN
U-matic / VHS / 16mm
Fluid Mechanics Series
Color (H C)
LC 70-702593
Analyzes stratified fluid systems through experiments showing that density variations help make possible forces that can generate internal waves, inhibit turbulent diffusion, or create strong velocity gradients and jets. Depicts applications in nature ranging from open - channel flows of water to atmospheric waves in the lee of mountain ranges.
Science - Physical
Dist - EBEC **Prod** - NCFMF 1969

Stravinsky 58 MIN
16mm
B&W
Presents the composer, Igor Stravinsky, at home in California, conducting a rehearsal, holding a press conference, and discussing creativity with Balanchine and his own work with Rolf Lieberman. By Richard Leacock and Rolf Lieberman.
Fine Arts
Dist - PENNAS **Prod** - PENNAS

Stravinsky 43 MIN
16mm / U-matic / VHS
B&W (J)
LC FIA67-65
Shows 73 - year - old Igor Stravinsky as he works and visits with fellow artists like George Balanchine, Alberto Giacometti and Benny Goodman, as he is honored by Pope Paul and as he revisits scenes of past musical triumphs, recalling milestones in his career.
Biography; Fine Arts
Dist - CAROUF **Prod** - CBSTV 1966

The Straw Hat 27 MIN
U-matic / VHS / 16mm
Storybook International Series
Color
Presents the German story of a peasant who is tricked by merchants when selling his house. Shows him retaliating and tricking the merchants with a clever plan involving a straw hat.
Guidance and Counseling; Literature and Drama
Dist - JOU **Prod** - JOU 1982

Straw Hill - Manchester, New Hampshire - Vol 17, No 18 9 MIN
VHS
Project reference file - PRF - series
Color (G A PRO)
$60.00 purchase _ #S37
Visits a condominium project in New Hampshire comprised of 65 detached luxury houses on a 22-acre hillside site. Features George Matarazzo, one of the developers. Addresses the pastoral landscaping concept, site constraints, drainage features and marketing.
Business and Economics; Geography - United States; Sociology
Dist - ULI **Prod** - ULI

Strawberries 47 MIN
VHS
Cookbook videos series; Vol 9
Color (G)
$19.95 purchase
Shows how to buy and store strawberries. Features shortcake, strawberries Vienna, chocolate dipped strawberries and other recipes. Includes printed abstract of recipes. Part of a series.
Home Economics; Social Science
Dist - ALWHIT **Prod** - ALWHIT

Strawberries 47 MIN
VHS
Cookbook videos series
Color (G)
$19.95 purchase _ #ALW116
Shows how to prepare strawberries in short, easy - to - learn segments. Lists each ingredient as it is added in subtitles and visually reinforces spoken instructions. Gives recipe background and nutritional facts. Part of the Cookbook Videos series.
Home Economics; Social Science
Dist - CADESF **Prod** - CADESF

Strawberry Charlotte 6 MIN
VHS / U-matic
Cooking with Jack and Jill Series
Color (P I)
$95.00
Portrays the skills of twins Jack and Jill as they cook nutritious and delicious snacks that are easy to prepare. Kitchen safety is emphasized. Animated.
Home Economics
Dist - LANDMK **Prod** - LANDMK 1986

Strawberry Girl
35mm strip / VHS / Cassette
Newbery Award - Winners Series
Color (I)
$66.00, $14.00 purchase
English Language; Literature and Drama
Dist - PELLER

Strawberry Shortcake in Big Apple City 24 MIN
16mm
Color (K P I)
Uses animation to present a story about Strawberry Shortcake, who becomes a finalist in a baking contest and flies to Big Apple City for the televised bake - off. Describes the troubles Strawberry encounters when the other finalist, Peculiar Purple Pieman, tries to keep her from taking part in the finals. Shows how truth, justice and Strawberry's delicious shortcake recipe triumph and the Purple Pieman earns a well - deserved fate.
Literature and Drama
Dist - CORF **Prod** - CORF 1982

Strawberry Square II - Take Time Series

Can you remember	15 MIN
Country Critters	15 MIN
Farm sense	15 MIN
Festival	15 MIN
Orion	15 MIN
Put - Togetherer	15 MIN
Rhythm and Blues	15 MIN
Ricky	15 MIN
Sculpting on the Square	15 MIN
Shake it Up - Gospel	15 MIN
Sounds Abound	15 MIN
Take Time	15 MIN
The Web	15 MIN
Word Play	15 MIN

Dist - AITECH

Strawberry Square Series

Balloons	15 MIN
Breakfast rolls by	14 MIN
Circles, squares, triangles, and things	15 MIN
Curing the Grumpies	15 MIN
A Day for Trees	15 MIN
Finale	15 MIN
Finish the Job Key	14 MIN
Fizzles and fuzzies	13 MIN
Fly away	15 MIN
Friends	14 MIN
Getting Acquainted	14 MIN
A Gift for Skipper	13 MIN
Goodbye, Mr Jingle	15 MIN
I Like Me	14 MIN
It's Halloween	15 MIN
Jingle Gets the News	15 MIN
Keeping Fit	12 MIN
Let a Song be a Friend	15 MIN
Let's be Flexible	15 MIN
Little by Little	14 MIN
A New Day	14 MIN
On Stage	15 MIN
The Pet Shop	15 MIN
A Rainy Day	14 MIN
Remembering	15 MIN
Skipper Gets a Piano	15 MIN
Songs for a Garden	14 MIN
The Stranger	13 MIN
Tell Me a Story	14 MIN
This Land is Your Land	14 MIN
A Trip to the Forest	15 MIN
We Can do it Too	15 MIN

Dist - AITECH

Strawberry Banke - a New England neighborhood 25 MIN
VHS
Color (I J)

$29.95 purchase _ #ST - FF0146
Documents the evolution of a waterfront neighborhood in Portsmouth, New Hampshire, known as Strawbery Banke, as it survived four centuries of social and economic change. Depicts a history once common to most New England coastal towns.
History - United States
Dist - INSTRU

The Stray 14 MIN
16mm
Parable Series
Color (P I J H)
LC 71-713243
A dramatization about a young child who got lost while visiting the zoo with a group of twelve children, and the celebration which took place when the boy was found.
Guidance and Counseling; Religion and Philosophy; Sociology
Dist - FRACOC **Prod** - FRACOC 1971

Stray Dog 122 MIN
VHS
Japan Film Collection from SVS Series
B&W (G) (JAPANESE (ENGLISH SUBTITLES))
$59.95 purchase _ #K0657VH
Features Akira Kurosawa as director. Stars Toshiro Mifune and Takashi Shimura. Also known as 'Nora Inu.'
Fine Arts; Geography - World
Dist - CHTSUI **Prod** - SONY

Stray Voltage 13 MIN
VHS
Color (C A)
$36.00 purchase, $16.00 rental
Presents potential problems of stray voltage on dairy farms. Gives viewers a basic understanding of electricity so that they can understand how and why it occurs and identify potential sources of stray voltage.
Agriculture; Health and Safety; Industrial and Technical Education
Dist - CORNRS **Prod** - CORNRS 1989

The Stream 15 MIN
VHS / U-matic / VT1
Walking with Grandfather series
Color (G)
$39.95 purchase, $35.00 rental
Tells of a tribe of fishing folk who lived in the icy north but had to migrate every winter to escape Old Giant Northwind. Reveals that Firehawk decides to challenge the wind so that his people won't have to flee good fishing spots because of the bully. Old Giant Northwind is very angry when he sees Firehawk planning to stay all winter and uses all his power to destroy him. But Firehawk, with courage, patience and cleverness, stays and drives the wind away, showing that humbleness and patience can also be very strong. Part of a series on storytelling by elders produced by Phil Lucas Productions, Inc.
Guidance and Counseling; Literature and Drama; Social Science
Dist - NAMPBC

The Stream 15 MIN
U-matic / VHS / 16mm
Living Science Series
Captioned; Color (I J H)
Examines the two basic types of stream environments and describes the life forms especially adapted to both environments. Captioned for the hearing - impaired.
Science - Natural
Dist - IFB **Prod** - IFB 1962

The Stream 15 MIN
U-matic / VHS / 16mm
Living Science Series
Color
LC FIA65-272
Examines through seasonal changes and along the course of a flowing water system the two basic types of stream environments, erosional and depositional habitats. Shows examples of channel cutting at the headwaters and pond - like stretches, where the stream gradient lessens. Views life forms especially adapted to both environments. Describes positions and interrelationships of the aquatic plants and animals in the numerous food chains.
Science - Natural
Dist - IFB **Prod** - IFB 1963

A Stream Community 15 MIN
U-matic / VHS
Why Series
Color (P I)
Discusses the living things found in a stream.
Science - Natural
Dist - AITECH **Prod** - WDCNTV 1976

Stream cutoffs 9 MIN
VHS
Geology stream table series
Color (H C)
$24.95 purchase _ #S9008
Treats stream cutoffs in a single - concept format, using models and NASA footage. Part of a 12 - part series on stream tables.
Geography - World; Science - Physical
Dist - HUBDSC **Prod** - HUBDSC

Stream Deposits 37 MIN
VHS / U-matic
Basic and Petroleum Geology for Non - Geologists - Landforms Series; Landforms
Color (IND)
Industrial and Technical Education; Science - Physical
Dist - GPCV **Prod** - PHILLP

A Stream Environment 9 MIN
16mm / U-matic / VHS
Color (P I)
$180.00, $125.00, $155.00 purchase _ #B174; LC 72-7028741
Explores a stream that begins high in the mountains and slowly grows from the melting snow. Points out that as the stream grows, the variety of life that lives along the stream grows too. Explains that plants are nourished by the water and in turn provide food and shelter for birds, mammals and insects.
Science - Natural
Dist - BARR **Prod** - BARR 1972

Stream erosion cycle 9 MIN
VHS
Geology stream table series
Color (H C)
$24.95 purchase _ #S9009
Treats the cycle of stream erosion in a single - concept format, using models and NASA footage. Part of a 12 - part series on stream tables.
Agriculture; Geography - World; Science - Physical
Dist - HUBDSC **Prod** - HUBDSC

Stream Erosion Cycle 8 MIN
VHS
Color (C)
$34.95 purchase _ #193 E 2076
Shows the complete development of a stream valley - youth, maturity and old age. Teacher's guide provided.
Science - Physical
Dist - WARDS

Stream Flow Processes 38 MIN
U-matic / VHS
Basic and Petroleum Geology for Non - Geologists - Landforms Series; Landforms
Color (IND)
Industrial and Technical Education; Science - Physical
Dist - GPCV **Prod** - PHILLP

Stream of social intercourse 26 MIN
VHS
Short stories - video anthology series
Color (H G)
$59.95 purchase
Portrays an introverted but determined young college student who, upon the advice of his therapist, engages his new social skills at a class party. Events take a comic turn when the therapist crashes the party with worse problems than his patient's. Presents a film directed by Serj Minassians. Part of a sixteen - part anthology of short dramas by young American filmmakers.
Fine Arts; Guidance and Counseling; Literature and Drama; Psychology
Dist - CNEMAG

Stream Piracy 7 MIN
VHS
Color (C)
$34.95 purchase _ #193 E 2077
Depicts various means of one stream capturing another through headwater erosion, deflection. Teacher's guide provided.
Science - Physical
Dist - WARDS

Stream piracy 8 MIN
VHS
Geology stream table series
Color (H C)
$24.95 purchase _ #S9010
Treats the occurence of one stream capturing another in a single - concept format, using models and NASA footage. Part of a 12 - part series on stream tables.
Geography - World; Science - Physical
Dist - HUBDSC **Prod** - HUBDSC

Stream systems and the work of running water 21 MIN
VHS
Color (J H)
$45.00 purchase _ #A1VH 9427
Shows how the Earth's surface is constantly reshaped by running water. Includes the vocabulary terms of delta, alluvium, estuary, rill, arroyo, bayou, oxbow lake.
Geography - World; Science - Physical
Dist - CLRVUE **Prod** - CLRVUE

The Street 10 MIN
16mm
Color (J)
Based on a selection from the novel The Street. Tells the story of the slow death of a grandmother, making a statement about family interaction with the aged.
Guidance and Counseling; Health and Safety; Psychology; Sociology
Dist - NFBC **Prod** - NFBC 1976

The Street 60 MIN
VHS
America by Design Series
Color (H)
$11.50 rental _ #60952, VH
Documents the history of America's transportation system, from rivers and railways to roads and interstate highways. Studies how the established names of roadways mirror a community's character. Examines technological developments in transportation and the affect on landscape and population growth. Fourth in the America By Design Series.
Social Science; Sociology
Dist - PSU **Prod** - PBS

Street 15
16mm / VHS
Color (H A)
$225.00 purchase, $30.00 rental
Presents Ulrich Franzen's urban design proposal to free the street of traffic, create parks and play areas, and concentrate major servies in a river straddling megastructure. He applies his proposal to Manhattan's Upper East Side, one of the most densely populated areas in the United States.
Fine Arts; Sociology
Dist - AFA **Prod** - AFA 1974

Street and Sanitation Department Workers 11 MIN
U-matic / VHS / 16mm
Community Helpers Series
Color (P I)
$280, $195 purchase _ #79525
Discusses the many jobs of the street and sanitation workers such as repairing guard railings, fixing potholes, collecting trash, and operating a landfill dump.
Social Science
Dist - CORF

Street Angel 102 MIN
16mm
B&W
Tells the story of the love between Angelo and Gino, a poor painter who has her pose for a Madonna portrait. Reveals that when she runs afoul of the law and is sent to prison, Gino grows despondent and loses all interest in his work. Shows that when she is released, they are reunited and she convinces him she is still worthy of having posed for a Madonna. Stars Janet Gaynor and Charles Farrell. Directed by Frank Borzage.
Fine Arts
Dist - KILLIS **Prod** - FOXFC 1928

Street Angel 100 MIN
VHS
Color (G) (MANDARIN CHINESE)
$45.00 purchase _ #1006A
Presents a movie produced in the People's Republic Of China.
Fine Arts; Geography - World; Literature and Drama
Dist - CHTSUI **Prod** - CHTSUI

Street circus or What's a busker 39 MIN
VHS
Color (P I J)
$19.95 purchase
Shows Buskers, or street performers, juggling, dancing, jump roping, singing, yodeling and more. Films the 1994 Buskerfest on the 16th Street Mall in Denver, Colorado. Features two children, Julianne and David, as emcees. Interviews Buskers from all over North America and includes a juggling lesson from two of the performers.
Geography - United States
Dist - DICOM **Prod** - DICOM 1994

Street Corner Stories 80 MIN
16mm
B&W
Documents mornings with a group of men who congregate at a corner store each day to socialize before they go to work. Portrays the black story - telling tradition, the spoken blues milieu and black street culture.
Fine Arts; History - United States; Sociology
Dist - BLKFMF **Prod** - BLKFMF

Street Crime - what to do 20 MIN
U-matic / VHS / 16mm
Color
Emphasizes the importance of common sense when riding on buses and trains or returning to a parked car. Provides some good tips on self - defense in situations threatening personal safety.
Guidance and Counseling; Sociology
Dist - CORF **Prod** - RIPOL

Street drugs 30 MIN
VHS
Color (J H C A)
$295.00 purchase
Defines street drugs and considers their effects on the body, both physically and mentally. Shows particular drugs with discussion of first effects, long - term effects and withdrawal processes for each one. Focuses on addiction and the dangers inherent in abusing substances. Features Jimmy Smits.
Guidance and Counseling; Health and Safety; Psychology
Dist - PFP **Prod** - PFP

Street Drugs and Medicine Chests 29 MIN
VHS / U-matic
Here's to Your Health Series
Color
Looks at substance abuse, what it is, how it works and how it can be beaten.
Health and Safety; Psychology; Sociology
Dist - PBS **Prod** - KERA

Street Drugs - Just the Facts 25 MIN
U-matic / VHS
Color
Investigates the world of street drugs and details the physiological effects of LSD, speed, barbiturates, marijuana, heroin and alcohol.
Health and Safety; Psychology; Sociology
Dist - MEDCOM **Prod** - MEDCOM

Street film part IV 30 MIN
VHS
Color & B&W (G)
$35.00 purchase
Portrays essential human handiwork, like corn pressed from the cob by thumbs or hands spinning twine, where simple acts are either profound with meaning or meaningless. Uses a long scene of a native woman patting and baking tortillas to make the filmmaker's point.
Fine Arts; Religion and Philosophy
Dist - CANCIN **Prod** - FULTON

Street Freaks 4 MIN
16mm / U-matic / VHS
Color (J)
LC 81-700886
Offers an animated view of New York City street life, featuring a young street musician who finds the competition too stiff until he joins in the live - and - let - live attitude of the other street people.
Fine Arts; Sociology
Dist - PHENIX **Prod** - CANEJ 1978

Street Gangs - Challenge for Law Enforcement 20 MIN
U-matic / VHS / 16mm
Color (A)
LC 79-700886
Presents interviews with gang members in order to provide police officers with a look at the structure and workings of a street gang and the attitudes of its members.
Civics and Political Systems; Sociology
Dist - AIMS **Prod** - CAHILL 1978

Street Kids 20 MIN
16mm
Color (J H G)
Shows the lifestyle of runaway children on the streets.
Sociology
Dist - CINEPC **Prod** - TAHARA 1985

Street - Meat - Meet 15 MIN
16mm
Color
Documents circumnavigating and compiling images and scenes of New York City.
Geography - United States; Geography - World; Industrial and Technical Education; Social Science; Sociology
Dist - VANBKS **Prod** - VANBKS

Street Musique 9 MIN
16mm
Color (J H A)
LC 73-700235
Records artist Ryan Larkin's reactions to the performance of a group of street musicians.
Fine Arts
Dist - NFBC **Prod** - NFBC 1973

Street of crocodiles 21 MIN
16mm / VHS
Color (G)
$400.00, $220.00 purchase, $45.00 rental
Watches a decrepit caretaker of a run - down museum activate a kinetoscope, conjuring into motion a puppet figure of a man. Follows the puppet's exploration of the rooms where he encounters a strange workshop, is harassed by a mysterious boy and eventually finds himself dissected, remodelled and reclothed by a dubious tailoring shop.
Fine Arts; Literature and Drama
Dist - FIRS **Prod** - QUAY 1986

Street of dreams 78 MIN
VHS
Color; PAL (G)
PdS100
Chronicles the history of Harrison Avenue, Detroit. Reveals the hopes and aspirations of the people who live on this poverty - ridden street, once a mecca of black culture and economy. A Darnell Stephen Summers for Guntram Fink, Germany production.
Business and Economics; Fine Arts; History - United States; Social Science; Sociology
Dist - BALFOR

The Street of ships
VHS
Color (G)
$34.90 purchase _ #0487
Tells about the history of South Street in New York City. Shows how this important harbor became a maritime museum.
History - United States; Physical Education and Recreation; Social Science
Dist - SEVVID

Street of the sardine 21 MIN
16mm
Color (G)
$30.00 rental
Presents Cannery Row in Monterey, California, once the thriving 'sardine capital' of the world, now a desolate testimony of man's mismanagement. Looks at a civilization risen and gone, decayed into a blend of colors, sounds, textures, motion and stillness. Aired on CBS' '60 Minutes' in 1970.
Fine Arts; History - United States
Dist - CANCIN **Prod** - LOTHAR

Street players 118 MIN
VHS
Color (G) (MANDARIN)
$45.00 purchase _ #0233C
Presents a movie produced in the People's Republic of China and directed by Lao She.
Fine Arts
Dist - CHTSUI

Street safe, street smart 13 MIN
U-matic / 16mm / VHS
Mickey's safety club series
Color (P)
$400.00, $280.00 purchase _ #JC - 67258
Uses live action, computer animation, an original song and clubhouse magic to look at street safety. Stresses looking out for cars when going into the street, being careful when taking shortcuts and being aware if a car is following too closely. Part of the Mickey's Safety Club series.
Health and Safety; Sociology
Dist - CORF **Prod** - DISNEY 1989

Street Safety and Car Theft 30 MIN
VHS / U-matic
Burglar - Proofing Series
Color
Discusses street safety and ways of preventing car theft.
Health and Safety; Sociology
Dist - MDCPB **Prod** - MDCPB

Street Scene 28 MIN
16mm
B&W
LC 75-703235
Explains how the misbeliefs and terror of a white college girl bring death at the hands of the police to a non - political middle class black man.
Fine Arts; Sociology
Dist - USC **Prod** - USC 1972

Street Scene 80 MIN
16mm
B&W
Focuses on a young girl whose life is torn apart when her father discovers her mother with another man. Stars Sylvia Sidney, William Collier, Jr, and Estelle Taylor. Based on the play Street Scene by Elmer Rice.
Fine Arts
Dist - REELIM **Prod** - UNKNWN 1931

Street sense 15 MIN
VHS
Color; PAL; NTSC (J H C)
PdS57, PdS67 purchase
Follows the individual routes of five members of a pop music group to a concert performance. Illustrates incidents along the road that could have resulted in serious automobile accidents.
Health and Safety
Dist - CFLVIS

Street Shadows 28 MIN
U-matic / VHS
Color (G)
$249.00, $149.00 purchase _ #AD - 1154
Reveals that every year 1.5 million American youth under the age of 18 leave home - some run away, some are thrown out. Profiles the lives of those children - where they sleep, what they eat, how they get money, how they spend their days - and how they die. Tells the stories of runaways, castaways, children who sleep on building ledges and sell drugs to support themselves.
Psychology; Sociology
Dist - FOTH **Prod** - FOTH

The Street smart job seeker - making opportunities happen 150 MIN
VHS
Color (H C G)
$79.95 purchase _ #VCP100V
Offers a practical plan for success in job seeking. Pulls together diverse aspects of a self - directed job search in an easy - to - use format that helps the job seeker to get organized and save time. Covers the psycological impact of job seeking, organizing the search, networking, selecting a mentor as a business consultant. Emphasizes that it is the exchange of information that gives a 'street smart' job seeker a competitive advantage. Includes 25 pages of reproducible worksheets of schedules, charts, checklists and scripts.
Business and Economics; Guidance and Counseling
Dist - CAMV

Street smart, street safe - a woman's guide to self - defense 58 MIN
VHS
Color (G)
$295.00 purchase, $50.00 rental _ #V1017 - 06
Features karate blackbelt holder Nina Chenault showing ways to deal with dangerous situations through avoidance or counterattack. Presents five lessons and a workout session for viewers to develop skill in reacting to problems.
Health and Safety; Physical Education and Recreation; Psychology
Dist - BARR

Street smarts 7 MIN
VHS / U-matic
Kidzone series
Color (I J)
$110.00, $160.00 purchase, $50.00 rental
Features a program on bike helmet safety and some of the rules of street safety for youngsters.
Health and Safety
Dist - NDIM **Prod** - KNONET 1992

Street smarts - straight talk for kids, teens and parents 50 MIN
VHS
Color (I J H G)
$29.95 purchase _ #JMG100V - K
Features veteran homicide detective J J Bittenbinder who delivers a riveting presentation that empowers young people to make tough, but essential, choices in dealing with the danger of drugs, gangs and personal safety on the streets.
Guidance and Counseling; Health and Safety; History - United States; Psychology; Sociology
Dist - CAMV

Street Talk 8 MIN
U-matic / VHS / 16mm
Color (P)
LC 77-701287
Uses a puppet to tell how to interpret various pedestrian street signs and markings. Illustrates four major types of pedestrian accidents.
Health and Safety; Social Science
Dist - AIMS **Prod** - GOLDCF 1976

Street Vibrato 13 MIN
16mm
B&W
LC 79-701388
Explores the thoughts and feelings of an aspiring classical violinist who plays on the street corners of New York City. Contrasts the musician's views on the value of playing in the streets with those of his peers who believe that it is detrimental to his career.
Fine Arts
Dist - MSAL **Prod** - MSAL 1979

A Streetcar Named Desire
VHS / U-matic
American Literature Series
B&W (G C J)
$79 purchase _ #05698 - 85
Screens the film version of Tennesee Williams' play. Stars Marlon Brando, Vivien Leigh, Kim Hunter, and Karl Malden.
Fine Arts
Dist - CHUMAN

A Streetcar named Desire 122 MIN
VHS
B&W (H C)
$29.00 purchase _ #05698 - 126
Stars Marlon Brando, Vivien Leigh and Kim Hunter in the drama by Tennessee Williams.
Fine Arts; Literature and Drama
Dist - GA **Prod** - GA

A Streetcar Named Desire 122 MIN
16mm
B&W
Provides a filmed adaptation of the play A Streetcar Named Desire. Stars Marlon Brando and Vivien Leigh.
Fine Arts
Dist - UAE **Prod** - UAA 1951

Streetcorner research 30 MIN
16mm / VHS
Documentaries for learning series
B&W (C G PRO)
$430.00, $70.00 purchase, $38.00 rental _ #35702
Teaches nonprofessionals about urban adolescents. Features Dr Ralph Schwitzgebel who uses operant conditioning to involve offending youth in self - research. Part of a series produced for use by health care professionals and educators.
Health and Safety; Psychology; Sociology
Dist - PSU **Prod** - MASON 1967

Streetlife - the invisible family 58 MIN
U-matic / VHS
Color (G)
$265.00 purchase, $50.00 rental _ #AB064
Tells the story of several homeless families in the Rocky Mountain region. Portrays the attempts to provide services for these people in emergency shelters, soup kitchens, food pantries, volunteer meal services, public works programs, schools and clinics. Includes commentary by health care personnel.
History - United States; Sociology
Dist - FANPRO **Prod** - KUEDTV

Streetproofing 28 MIN
VHS / U-matic
Youth Lifeskills Series
Color
Uses short vignettes to illustrate some of the inherent hazards in the environment. Provides the 'know how' to avoid dangerous situations and to have fun safely.
Health and Safety; Sociology
Dist - HMDI **Prod** - SCCL

Streets 8 MIN
16mm
Color (G)
$10.00 rental
Photographs the street of San Francisco at night using 12 frames per second with the camera mounted on the roof of car. Captures Chinatown, Geary Street, Polk Street, California Street and Broadway tunnel. Music by Simon Park and J Saunders. Produced by Craig Ellis.
Fine Arts; Geography - United States
Dist - CANCIN

The Streets Belong to the People 5 MIN
16mm
B&W
Shows a battle between Haight street people and the San Francisco tactical squad. The soundtrack consists of contemporary rock.
Civics and Political Systems; Psychology; Sociology
Dist - CANWRL **Prod** - CANWRL 1967

Streets of Greenwood 20 MIN
16mm
B&W
Documents the civil rights struggle in Greenwood, Mississippi in 1963, while the Student Non - Violent Co - Ordinating Committee was registering black voters.
Civics and Political Systems; History - United States; Sociology
Dist - NEWTIM **Prod** - NEWTIM

The Streets of Saigon 28 MIN
U-matic / VHS / 16mm
Color (J H)
Indicates that in the last ten years the population of Saigon has grown ten times. Tells that American soldiers once came looking for girls and marijuana, but now they are rarely seen and the only reminder of them is the babies they have left behind. Depicts these children, many orphaned and homeless, who have been forced to make a living in the streets.
History - World; Sociology
Dist - FI **Prod** - NFBC 1973

Streets, prairies and valleys - the life of Carl Sandburg 30 MIN
VHS
Color (J H)
$99.00 purchase _ #06204 - 026
Offers a portrait of Sandburg through excerpts from the poet's autobiography, readings of his poems and photographs of the locations he described. Follows the poet's life in Illinois, his travels through America, his personal life and his fascination with Lincoln. Includes teacher's guide and library kit.
Education; Literature and Drama
Dist - GA

The Streetwalker & the gentleman 6 MIN
16mm
Color (A)
$10.00 rental
Satirizes a graphic encounter between a hooker and her trick with a mime, Ralph DuPont of San Francisco, playing both parts fully clothed. Features original piano music by Jeff Ross.
Fine Arts; Literature and Drama
Dist - CANCIN **Prod** - COHENK 1975

Streetwise 92 MIN
VHS
Color (G)
$59.95 purchase _ #S00878
Portrays the daily lives of Seattle's 'street kids.' Reveals that they must survive by their wits, with their only choices being to sell blood for money, beg for handouts, or go into prostitution or drug dealing. Interviews the teenagers to allow them to tell their own story.
Sociology
Dist - UILL

Streetwise - working safely in traffic 22 MIN
VHS
Color (G A PRO)
$59.99 purchase _ #V3800GA
Looks at safe procedures for traffic control during street work, with emphasis on closing lanes, surveying, using street signs and street control lights, and directing traffic around work sites at manholes or other work locations.
Health and Safety
Dist - WAENFE

Strega Nonna 55 FRS
VHS / 16mm / U-matic
Color (K P)
LC 78-731254; 78-700665
Presents an Italian folktale about a wise old woman with a magic pasta pot, who leaves her helper alone with the pot. Depicts the disaster that ensues when the helper tries to show the townspeople how the pot works. Based on the book Strega Nonna by Tomie de Paola.
Literature and Drama
Dist - WWS **Prod** - WWS 1978

Strega Nonna 35 MIN
VHS
Children's circle collection series
Color (K P I)
$14.95 purchase _ #WK117
Contains the title story along with Tikki Tikki Tembo; The Foolish Frog; and A Story - A Story.
Fine Arts; Literature and Drama
Dist - KNOWUN

Strength 10 MIN
VHS
Color (I J H)
$95.00 purchase _ #CG - 962 - VS
Witnesses an increasing cycle of confrontation and misunderstanding between two groups of African - American and white youths. Motivates students to explore non - violent solutions to inter - racial conflicts.
History - United States; Sociology
Dist - HRMC **Prod** - HRMC 1992

Strength and Deformation of Solids Series

Concepts of dislocations	7 MIN
Deformation of crystalline materials - Part 1	5 MIN
Deformation of crystalline materials - Part 2	7 MIN
Introduction to Strengthening Materials	6 MIN

Dist - PSU

Strength and Endurance 15 MIN
VHS / 16mm
All Fit with Slim Goodbody Series
Color (P I)
$125.00 purchase, $25.00 rental
Shows exercises to build strenth and endurance.
Health and Safety; Physical Education and Recreation; Science - Natural
Dist - AITECH **Prod** - GDBODY 1987

Strength in the West 20 MIN
16mm
Color (C)
Presents a general survey of modern steel production, including open - cast mining, blast furnace, steel furnaces, milling operations and making steel pipes.
Business and Economics; Industrial and Technical Education
Dist - HEFL **Prod** - KAISER 1952

Strength of Life - Knokovtee Scott 27 MIN
VHS / U-matic
Color (J H C)
Describes his shellwork jewelry and shares with us his journey of rediscovery as he sought the authentic art of his Creek and Cherokee ancestors. Brings a part of that past into our world today.
Fine Arts; Science - Natural; Social Science; Sociology
Dist - NAMPBC **Prod** - NAMPBC 1984

Strength of the Land 29 MIN
VHS / U-matic
Journey into Thailand Series
Color (J S C A)
MV=$195.00
Follows King Bhumibol on his personal tours of the country. His ceremonial engagements culminate in the barge procession which marks the country's bicentennial celebrations.
Geography - World; History - World
Dist - LANDMK **Prod** - LANDMK 1986

Strength through struggle 29 MIN
16mm
Color (G IND)
$5.00 rental
Contains newsreel footage of some of the major strikes which took place in Ohio during the 1930s, including scenes of the state militia shooting Republic Steel strikers and the 12 - mile picket line around Goodyear plants in Akron. Uses labor folk songs and taped interviews with union leaders to tell the story of this era.
Business and Economics; History - United States; Social Science; Sociology
Dist - AFLCIO **Prod** - OHIOSU 1976

Strength through Struggle - a Chronicle of Labor Organization in Ohio 25 MIN
16mm
Color
Tells the story of labor organization in Ohio.
Business and Economics; History - United States
Dist - HRC **Prod** - OHC

Strength through Weakness 30 MIN
Videoreel / VT2
Koltanowski on Chess Series
Color
Physical Education and Recreation
Dist - PBS **Prod** - KQEDTV

Strength Training 60 MIN
VHS
One on One Coaching Series
(J H C)
$39.95 _ #CVN1090V
Presents football coach Bob Fix who demonstrates his program for building strength through weight exercises.
Physical Education and Recreation
Dist - CAMV **Prod** - CAMV

Strength training
VHS
Coaching women's track and field series
Color (H C G)
$59.95 purchase _ #TRS1109V
Features women's field and track coaches Bob Meyers and Meg Ritchie on strength training for women athletes. Demonstrates a comprehensive program to safely develop strength, speed and flexibility. Includes stretching and general exercise routines, specificity exercises for major intercollegiate sports, combinations to train fast twitch fibers and developing individual programs for each athlete to establish a good cycling pattern using proper sets and reps. Part of a nine - part series.
Physical Education and Recreation
Dist - CAMV

Strength training for football 90 MIN
VHS
Color (J H C G)
$59.95 purchase _ #TRS428V
Features Coach Dana LeDuc who demonstrates the proper techniques for developing functional output on the playing field. Includes advanced pulling, pressing, squatting and ballistic movements, high speed specificity activities as well as stretching programs to develop maximum flexibility and range of motion.

Physical Education and Recreation
Dist - CAMV

Strength training for women athletes 90 MIN
VHS
Color (H C G)
$59.95 purchase _ #TRS1109V
Presents Meg Ritchie who demonstrates a comprehensive program to safely develop strength, speed and flexibility in women athletes. Includes stretching and general exercise routines, specifically exercizes for major intercollegiate sports, combinations to train fast twitch fibers and developing individual programs for each athlete to establish a good cycling pattern using proper sets and reps.
Physical Education and Recreation
Dist - CAMV

Strengthening exercises for the lower extremity
VHS / U-matic
Physical therapy series
Color (PRO C G)
$195.00 purchase _ #C890 - VI - 016
Informs patient educators and patients about the benefits of strengthening exercises for the lower extremity. Teaches effective techniques for minimizing pain and fatigue while enhancing the ability to perform daily activities. Part of a series by the physical therapy staff, St Luke's Hospital, Fargo, North Dakota.
Health and Safety; Physical Education and Recreation; Science - Natural
Dist - HSCIC

Strengthening exercises for the upper extremity
U-matic / VHS
Physical therapy series
Color (PRO C G)
$195.00 purchase _ #C890 - VI - 017
Informs patient educators and patients about the benefits of strengthening exercises for the upper extremity. Teaches effective techniques for minimizing pain and fatigue while enhancing the ability to perform daily activities. Part of a series by the physical therapy staff, St Luke's Hospital, Fargo, North Dakota.
Health and Safety; Physical Education and Recreation; Science - Natural
Dist - HSCIC

Strengthening Mechanisms - Nonferrous Metals 40 MIN
BETA / VHS / U-matic
Color
$400 purchase
Shows techniques used to harden nonferrous metals, including age hardening and strain hardening.
Science; Science - Physical
Dist - ASM **Prod** - ASM

Strengthening Organizational Relationships 30 MIN
16mm
Teaching Role Series
Color; B&W (C T)
LC 73-703327
Teaches the nursing instructor various principles, tools and methods of teaching. Stresses the importance of developing organizational teamwork involving effective communication and influence, decentralized and coordinated decision - making and high performance goals and high motivation.
Education
Dist - TELSTR **Prod** - MVNE 1968

Strengthening your grip series
Features Chuck Swindoll and his insights into developing a more active Christian commitment. Deals with topics including priorities, aging, leisure, godliness, attitudes and authority. Six - part series includes a set of 10 study guides.
Aging - refusing to shift your life into neutral - Tape 2
Attitudes - choosing the food you serve your mind - Tape 5
Authority - hope for a talk - back, fight - back world - Tape 6
Godliness - the perils of hothouse Christianity - Tape 4
Leisure - attention all workaholics and churchaholics - Tape 3
Priorities - freedom from the tyranny of the urgent - Tape 1
Dist - APH **Prod** - WORD 1968

Strengthening your immune system through mind and movement 50 MIN
VHS
Color (G)
$34.50 purchase _ #1106
Presents thirteen simple exercises combined with visualization. Explains key immune organs and the influence on them of imagery and exercise. Designed for beginners. Features Shirley Dockstader.
Physical Education and Recreation
Dist - WAYF

Strengths and Weaknesses - College Students with Learning Disabilities 26 MIN
16mm
Color (H C A)
LC 82-700725
Explores the situation of the learning disabled student in the college environment. Compares four students' perceptions of their problems with current professional opinions and examines the role of assessment, coping behavior and remediation as factors in a successful college experience.
Education; Psychology
Dist - LAWREN **Prod** - IOWA 1981

Stresemann 106 MIN
16mm
B&W (GERMAN (ENGLISH SUBTITLES))
Examines the efforts of German Foreign Minister Stresemann (1923 - 1929) toward the establishment of peace and European unity after Word War I. Demonstrates that personal strength and ethics can be political factors. Approaches the decisive beginning of French - German friendship.
Foreign Language; History - World
Dist - WSTGLC **Prod** - WSTGLC 1956

Stress 30 MIN
VHS
Personal Development Video Series
(J H C A)
$425.00 for series of 5 _ CV200V
Presents tips and techniques for solving problems of stress. Communicates strategies for dealing with peers, parents, and teachers without sacrificing personal needs.
Psychology
Dist - CAMV **Prod** - CAMV

Stress 28 MIN
VHS
Color (A PRO IND)
$495.00 purchase, $95.00 rental
Discusses stress and its effects. Teaches viewers how to recognize stress and avoid it. Focuses on the supervisor and his or her role in recognizing and dealing with stress.
Business and Economics; Guidance and Counseling; Psychology
Dist - VLEARN **Prod** - BBP

Stress
VHS
Personal Development Series
Color (H)
$98.00 purchase _ #ABV 105
Shows the causes and effects of stress and the techniques for controlling it. Covers the psychological, physiological and emotional effects of too much stress. Also available in Beta or 3/4".
Psychology
Dist - CADESF **Prod** - CADESF 1988

Stress 15 MIN
U-matic / VHS / 16mm
Color (A)
Presents the causes, effects and origins of stress. Provides ways to avoid and identify stress and dramatizes ways of controlling it.
Health and Safety; Psychology
Dist - PRORE **Prod** - PRORE

Stress 15 MIN
U-matic / VHS
Color
Teaches how to manage the tension and pressures of everyday living.
Health and Safety; Psychology
Dist - AHOA **Prod** - AHOA

Stress 30 MIN
U-matic / VHS
Color (PRO)
Focuses on the many factors that cause stress and investigates ways that people are successfully coping with it. Examines the fine balance of pressure and relaxation needed to provide a vigorous, stimulating and healthy pattern of life. Includes the tape entitled Back To Square One.
Psychology
Dist - GPN **Prod** - CTVC 1981

Stress 31 MIN
U-matic / VHS
Mind and body series
Color (PRO C)
$395.00 purchase, $80.00 rental _ #C850 - VI - 041
Defines stress and presents its phases. Discusses causes and long and short - term ways of dealing with it. Presented by Dr Jonathan A Freedman. Part of a series.
Health and Safety; Psychology
Dist - HSCIC

Stress 29 MIN
U-matic
Understanding Human Behavior - an Introduction to Psychology Series 'Lesson 14
Color (C A)
Shows that all motivation is based on stress. Describes roles of autonomic nervous system and adrenal glands in stress. Offers suggestions on ways to withstand stress.
Psychology
Dist - CDTEL **Prod** - COAST

Stress 14 MIN
VHS
Color (J H)
$79.95 purchase _ #10228VL
Discusses the causes and effects of stress. Describes situations such as parental conflict, peer pressure, dating, and emotional problems which cause stress. Comes with a leader's guide, discussion questions, and two blackline masters.
Psychology
Dist - UNL

Stress 11 MIN
16mm
B&W (C A)
Dr Hans Selye of the University of Montreal explains his theory of the nature of stress as a general alarm reaction through the pituitary and adrenal glands, set off by disease, injury or mental pressure.
Health and Safety; Psychology
Dist - NFBC **Prod** - NFBC 1956

Stress - a fact of life 19 MIN
BETA / VHS / U-matic
Stress series
Color (C PRO)
$150.00 purchase _ #131.1
Presents a video transfer from slide program which explores widespread interest and discussion of stress, including documentary interviews with subjects from different backgrounds and experiences. Traces the research of Hans Selye and presents his concepts as a working model for defining and discussing stress. Describes 'eustress,' the beneficial stress, and 'distress,' the harmful, emphasizing individual differences in toleration of stress. Part of a series on stress.
Guidance and Counseling; Health and Safety; Psychology
Dist - CONMED **Prod** - CONMED

Stress - a Guide to Better Living 44 MIN
VHS
(J H C A)
$59.00 _ #CAP700V
Explores the subject of stress and its effects on life and health. Discusses various methods for coping with stress including relaxation techniques, biofeedback and meditation therapy.
Health and Safety; Psychology
Dist - CAMV **Prod** - CAMV

Stress - a Personal Challenge 30 MIN
U-matic / VHS / 16mm
Color (H C A)
LC 80-701783
Presents Dr Hans Selye discussing the nature of stress. Looks at the need to adjust to stress and to deal with it through a variety of techniques.
Psychology
Dist - CORF **Prod** - SLUMC 1980

Stress - a Personal Challenge 30 MIN
VHS / 16mm
(G A PRO)
$480.00 purchase _ #AG - AC97
Demonstrates how individuals can make use of stress to rise to new levels of creativity and performance.
Business and Economics; Psychology
Dist - CORF **Prod** - STLU 1980

Stress and Coping 21 MIN
Videoreel / VT2
Interpersonal Competence, Unit 07 - Stress Series; Unit 7 - Stress
Color (C A)
Features a humanistic psychologist who, by analysis and examples, discusses how to cope with stress.
Psychology; Sociology
Dist - TELSTR **Prod** - MVNE 1973

Stress and Disease 30 MIN
U-matic / VHS
Color
Examines stress as a real biological phenomenon, looking at what it is, what it can do to our health, and how we can transform it into a positive force in our lives.

Health and Safety; Psychology
Dist - HRMC **Prod** - HRMC 1985

Stress and Disease 30 MIN
VHS
Color (G)
Examines stress as a real biological phenomenon and discusses the techniques that are used to control it.
Health and Safety; Psychology
Dist - IBIS **Prod** - IBIS 1985

Stress and disease - Part 1 22 MIN
BETA / VHS / U-matic
Stress series
Color (C PRO)
$150.00 purchase _ #131.5
Presents a video transfer from slide program which describes evidence of the relationship between stress and disease. Emphasizes that the stressors, the individual, the individual's stress responses and the diseases must all be examined when study the relationship of stress to disease. Cites studies and theories relating disease to number and intensity of stressors and to the individual's predisposition, personality, behavior and social factors. Cautions against forming false conclusions from study data. Part of a series on stress.
Health and Safety; Psychology
Dist - CONMED **Prod** - CONMED

Stress and disease - Part 2 26 MIN
VHS / U-matic / BETA
Stress series
Color (C PRO)
$150.00 purchase _ #131.6
Presents a video transfer from slide program which discusses ways in which the individual's physiologic stress response and stress reducing behaviors might both be causative factors in cardiovascular disease, gastrointestinal ulcers and mental disorders. Explores theories, research and clinical evidence that stress is a contributory factor in the onsent of other diseases such as diabetes mellitus, respiratory disease, infections, cancer and rheumatoid arthritis. Part of a series on stress.
Health and Safety; Psychology
Dist - CONMED **Prod** - CONMED

Stress and Emotion 60 MIN
VHS / U-matic
Brain, Mind and Behavior Series
Color (C A)
Discusses pain, anxiety and behavior.
Psychology
Dist - FI **Prod** - WNETTV

Stress and emotion - Part 4 60 MIN
U-matic / VHS
Brain series
Color (G)
$45.00, $29.95 purchase
Uses two case histories - a man who suffered an accidental frontal lobotomy and a stress - ridden air traffic controller - to examine pain, anxiety and behavior. Part four of an eight - part series on the brain.
Psychology; Science - Natural; Sociology
Dist - ANNCPB **Prod** - WNETTV 1984

Stress and How to Live with it 29 MIN
U-matic / VHS
Color
Health and Safety; Psychology
Dist - SYLWAT **Prod** - RCOMTV 1982

Stress and How to Manage it 29 MIN
U-matic / VHS
Color
Health and Safety; Psychology
Dist - SYLWAT **Prod** - RCOMTV 1984

Stress and Illness 12 MIN
VHS / 16mm
Stress - Unwinding the Spring Series
Color (H C A PRO)
$195.00 purchase, $75.00 rental _ #8075
Examines the relationship between stress and illness.
Health and Safety; Psychology
Dist - AIMS **Prod** - HOSSN 1988

Stress and Immune Function 26 MIN
U-matic / VHS
Color (C)
$249.00, $149.00 purchase _ #AD - 1803
Examines the relationship between stress and illness and studies that link immune systems malfunctions or misfortunes to stress in both animals and humans. Reveals that study results indicate a connection to higher cancer mortality, respiratory infections, herpes and autoimmune disorders.
Health and Safety; Psychology; Sociology
Dist - FOTH **Prod** - FOTH

Stress and mental fitness 25 MIN
VHS
Color (PRO IND A)
$495.00 purchase, $150.00 rental _ #CRI11
Aids in understanding the relationship between stress and good mental health. Teaches how to identify a useful level of stress and to recognize and control harmful stress. Incorporates mental fitness exercises and activities helpful to workplace personnel and others. Includes a leader's guide and workbooks.
Business and Economics; Health and Safety; Psychology
Dist - EXTR **Prod** - CRISP

Stress and Modern Life 145 MIN
U-matic
University of the Air Series
Color (J H C A)
$750.00 purchase, $250.00 rental
Defines stress from both the layman's and the proffessional's point of view and talks on the sources and possible solutions to stress. Program contains a series of five cassettes 29 minutes each.
Health and Safety; Psychology; Sociology
Dist - CTV **Prod** - CTV 1977

Stress and Relaxation 15 MIN
VHS / 16mm
All Fit with Slim Goodbody Series
Color (P I)
$125.00 purchase, $25.00 rental
Explores causes of stress and how to deal with them.
Health and Safety; Physical Education and Recreation; Science - Natural
Dist - AITECH **Prod** - GDBODY 1987

Stress and Strain 20 MIN
U-matic / VHS
Engineering Crafts Series
Color (H C A)
Industrial and Technical Education
Dist - FI **Prod** - BBCTV 1981

Stress and the Adaptation Syndrome 35 MIN
16mm
Color
Depicts the effects of various physical and psychiatric stresses and the mechanisms by which animals effect adaptation. Reveals Dr Hans Selye's contribution to the understanding of the inter - relationship between stress and disease.
Health and Safety
Dist - PFI **Prod** - SHNKRN 1956

Stress and the caregiver - are we driving each other mad series
A Clear understanding of stress 60 MIN
Recognition of the sources of stress 60 MIN
A Vivid awareness of the consequences of prolonged and intense stress 60 MIN
Ways of decreasing or eliminating the unnecessary stresses in your life 60 MIN
Dist - CTNA

Stress and the Child 10 MIN
U-matic / VHS / 16mm
Prepared Childbirth and Parenting Series
Color (A)
Explores the real stresses children face as they grow from infancy to puberty. Reveals that the time is difficult for parents as they must oftentime stand by helplessly. Offers suggested methods for parents to use in coping with these problems.
Psychology; Sociology
Dist - JOU **Prod** - JOU 1982

Stress and the Hot Reactor 23 MIN
16mm
Color (PRO)
Demonstrates the relationship of stress to cardiovascular disease. Features Dr Robert Eliot at the University of Nebraska Simulation Laboratory.
Health and Safety; Psychology
Dist - GEIGY **Prod** - GEIGY

Stress and the New Family 29 MIN
VHS / U-matic
Tomorrow's Families Series
Color (H C A)
LC 81-706921
Describes how individuals and families develop ways of coping with the tensions which occur when a new child is added to the family.
Sociology
Dist - AITECH **Prod** - MDDE 1980

Stress and You Series
Stress, Health and You 5 MIN
Dist - AMEDFL

Stress control now 10 MIN
VHS
Color (I J H)
$24.95 purchase _ #UNA100V
Focuses on the relationship between stress and performance. Presents a proven method of stress therapy with soothing images and a calming voice guiding the viewer to a more relaxed state. Features Dr Edward Klein consultant in professional sports.
Health and Safety; Psychology
Dist - CAMV

Stress Corrosion of Mg Base Alloys 18 MIN
16mm
B&W (J H C)
Shows how corrosion is controlled by the metallurgy of the alloy - - intergranular or transgranular.
Industrial and Technical Education
Dist - OSUMPD **Prod** - OSUMPD 1952

Stress Corrosion of Stainless Steel 13 MIN
16mm
B&W (J H C)
LC FIA66-21
Uses time lapse photography and photomicrography to show the rapid accumulation of corrosion products which may play a role in the mechanism of stress corrosion cracking in austenitic stainless steel in chloride solutions.
Industrial and Technical Education
Dist - OSUMPD **Prod** - OSUMPD 1959

Stress - Distress 21 MIN
U-matic / VHS / 16mm
Color (H C A)
Discusses stress, pointing out that when stress turns to distress, it can make people sick. Describes the prevalent stressors, the consequences of stress, and novel methods that help to prevent, cope and release stress. Demonstrates home - grown methods as well as scientific treatments which include meditation and biofeedback.
Psychology
Dist - HANDEL **Prod** - HANDEL 1982

The Stress factor 19 MIN
16mm / VHS
Color (G IND)
$5.00 rental
Takes a comprehensive look at job - related stress and what can be done to reduce stress in the workplace. Covers the signs and symptoms of stress, its effects on the worker's health, management's response, and how to recognize stress.
Health and Safety; Psychology; Social Science; Sociology
Dist - AFLCIO **Prod** - CANLAB 1986

Stress, Health and You 18 MIN
U-matic / VHS
Color (C A)
LC 80-706914
Presents Dr Hand Selye and Richard Rahe explaining how a person's health is modified by stressful events and discussing different individuals' responses to it. Offers suggestions on avoiding stress and introduces methods of meditation, biofeedback and relaxation therapy.
Health and Safety; Psychology
Dist - TIMLIF **Prod** - AMEDFL

Stress, Health and You 5 MIN
U-matic / VHS / 16mm
Stress and You Series
Color (H C A)
LC 78-701246
Focuses on the causes and effects of stress and shows how dramatic changes affect the human body.
Health and Safety; Psychology
Dist - AMEDFL **Prod** - MAWBYN 1978

Stress Illustrated 23 MIN
Cassette / VHS / 16mm
Color (PRO)
$550.00 purchase, $125.00 rental, $35.00 preview
Illustrates the negative impact of stress on employees and how managing stress will lead to the overall financial health of an organization. Teaches how to manage stress, increase energy, and become more motivated and self - confident. Includes leader's guide and other support items.
Business and Economics; Guidance and Counseling; Psychology; Sociology
Dist - UTM **Prod** - UTM

Stress in Critical Care Nursing Practice 26 MIN
U-matic
Stress in Critical Illness Series Module 4
Color (PRO)
LC 80-707624
Presents an analysis of aspects of critical care nursing that lead to undesirable stressors affecting patients, nurses and families. Highlights intervention techniques that will reduce these stress factors.
Health and Safety; Psychology
Dist - BRA **Prod** - BRA 1980

Stress in Critical Illness Series Module 1
Physiologic Manifestations of Stress 24 MIN
Dist - BRA

Stress in Critical Illness Series Module 4
Stress in Critical Care Nursing Practice 26 MIN
Dist - BRA

Stress in critical illness series
Family stress in critical illness 22 MIN
Psychologic Stress in Critical Illness 26 MIN
Dist - BRA

Stress in the Foster Family 30 MIN
U-matic / VHS
Home is Where the Care is Series Module 7; Module 7
Color
Presents a professional stress management consultant and foster parents discussing the particular stresses created by the foster care situation and ways to deal effectively with them.
Guidance and Counseling; Psychology; Sociology
Dist - CORF **Prod** - CORF 1984

Stress in the Later Years 24 MIN
U-matic / VHS / 16mm
Color (C A)
$450 purchase - 16 mm, $315 purchase - video
Talks about stress and its causes among older people. Directed by John McDonald.
Health and Safety; Psychology
Dist - CF

Stress in the Later Years 24 MIN
U-matic / VHS / 16mm
Be Well - the Later Years Series
Color (C A)
LC 83-700400
Gives an understanding of how the special stresses of older people, such as loss, loneliness and retirement, can cause physical disorders. Introduces relaxation and other techniques, and offers suggestions for enjoying social activities.
Health and Safety; Psychology; Sociology
Dist - CF **Prod** - CF 1983

Stress intelligence - an approach to stress management series
Avoiding stress - the future manager 30 MIN
The Effects of stress - the shortfall manager 30 MIN
Understanding Stress - the Marginal Manager 30 MIN
Dist - DELTAK

Stress - is Your Lifestyle Killing You 29 MIN
U-matic / VHS
Here's to Your Health Series
Color
Deals with stress and how to control it.
Guidance and Counseling; Health and Safety; Psychology
Dist - PBS **Prod** - KERA

Stress - it's just what you think - 1 20 MIN
VHS / U-matic / 16mm
Health - body and mind series
Color (J H)
$440.00, $340.00, $310.00 _ #A327
Shows young people how to recognize and understand the stress in their lives. Teaches them positive ways of managing stress. Part one of a three - part series on health.
Health and Safety; Psychology
Dist - BARR **Prod** - CASDEN 1982

Stress - Learning How to Handle it 23 MIN
16mm / U-matic / VHS
Color (J H)
Discusses causes of stress and how our bodies react to it. Provides workable solutions for dealing with it. Focuses on self - help group of teenagers as they learn to recognize and handle stress in their lives.
Guidance and Counseling; Psychology
Dist - AIMS **Prod** - SAIF 1984

Stress - learning to cope 15 MIN
16mm / VHS / BETA / U-matic
Color; PAL (G)
PdS115, PdS123 purchase
Offers positive suggestions on avoiding stress and individual response to it. Provides insights on our unique abilities to handle stress.
Psychology
Dist - EDPAT

Stress - Learning to Handle it 23 MIN
16mm / U-matic / VHS
Color (J H)
$50 rental _ #9774
Examines causes and effects of stress and provides workable solutions for dealing with it.
Guidance and Counseling
Dist - AIMS **Prod** - AIMS 1984

Stress, Learning to Handle it 23 MIN
VHS / 16mm
(A)
$350.00 VHS purchase _ #82156, $475.00 film purchase _ #82149, $50.00
Follows the progress of a girl who works through her readjustment problems in a peer assistance group. Discusses methods for coping with pressures from parents, friends, and school. Teaches skills in controlling and minimizing stress.
Psychology
Dist - CMPCAR

Stress management 11 MIN
16mm / U-matic / VHS
Correctional officer series
Color (PRO)
Describes the effects of stress on correctional officers. Offers techniques to handle stress and identifies ineffective methods of dealing with stress, including abuse of alcohol or other drugs, overeating and withdrawal. Presents a program for stress management that includes exercise, talking about problems, developing outside interests and taking time to be alone.
Civics and Political Systems; Sociology
Dist - AIMS **Prod** - AIMS 1981

Stress management 30 MIN
VHS / BETA
Optimal performance series
Color (G)
$29.95 purchase _ #S208
Focuses on practical, easy to use methods for monitoring and managing stress at home and in the workplace. Features Dr Janelle M Barlow, human development specialist and author of 'The Stress Manager.' Part of a four - part series on optimal performance.
Health and Safety; Psychology
Dist - THINKA **Prod** - THINKA

Stress Management 17 MIN
16mm / U-matic / VHS
Survival of the Fittest Series
Color (PRO)
Describes the symptoms of stress and various methods of dealing with it.
Health and Safety; Physical Education and Recreation; Psychology
Dist - PRORE **Prod** - PRORE

Stress management
VHS
Personal action system series
Color (G)
$149.00 purchase _ #V206
Teaches employees about the benefits of stress management. Part of a 13 - part series to educate employees on the importance of health.
Health and Safety; Psychology
Dist - GPERFO

Stress Management 120 MIN
VHS
Color (A PRO)
$200.00 purchase _ #77590
Helps clients learn what causes stress, how to overcome day - to - day pressures, how to control the stress response and think your way out of stress, plus more.
Health and Safety; Psychology
Dist - AACD **Prod** - AACD 1985

Stress Management - 105 30 MIN
U-matic
Currents - 1984 - 85 Season Series
Color (A)
Reveals the growth of social and on the job stress and looks at methods to manage it.
Psychology; Social Science
Dist - PBS **Prod** - WNETTV 1985

Stress Management - a Positive Strategy Series Pt 1
Becoming Aware 30 MIN
Dist - TIMLIF

Stress Management - a Positive Strategy Series Pt 2
Taking Stocks 30 MIN
Dist - TIMLIF

Stress Management - a Positive Strategy Series Pt 3
Managing Yourself 30 MIN
Dist - TIMLIF

Stress Management - a Positive Strategy Series Pt 5
Looking Ahead 30 MIN
Dist - TIMLIF

Stress Management - a Positive Strategy Series
Solving Problems 30 MIN
Dist - TIMLIF

Stress Management - Coping with Stress 30 MIN
VHS / U-matic
Color
Demonstrates the program for dealing with stress. Demonstrates techniques for rational reevaluation, coping self - statements, and other relaxation techniques.
Health and Safety; Psychology
Dist - IRL **Prod** - IRL

Stress Management for Healthcare Personnel 27 MIN
VHS / 16mm
Color (PRO)
$295.00 purchase, $60.00 rental
Reflects the observations of Dr. Michael McKee, PhD, Cleveland Clinic Foundation, and his recommendations to healthcare personnel on how to cope with stress and burnout.
Health and Safety
Dist - FAIRGH **Prod** - FAIRGH 1988

Stress management for nurses 23 MIN
VHS
Color (PRO C)
$250.00 purchase, $70.00 rental _ #4373
Shows nurses how they can deal with stress. Explains the effects of stress, such as sleep disorders, work errors and depression and suggests ways to handle stress. Reviews the General Adaptation Syndrome of Hans Selye. Includes accompanying handout.
Health and Safety; Psychology
Dist - AJN

Stress Management for Professionals 88 MIN
VHS
Stress Management For Professionals Series; Vol 2
Color (G)
$99.95 purchase _ #20119
Features Roger Mellott. Examines how need for approval affects one's stress level. Shows how to take hostility out of the Type A person and how to let off steam without getting burned. Part two of two - parts.
Business and Economics; Health and Safety; Psychology
Dist - CARTRP **Prod** - CARTRP

Stress Management for Professionals 85 MIN
VHS
Stress Management For Professionals Series; Vol 1
Color (G)
$99.95 purchase _ #20115
Features Roger Mellott. Examines the paradox of happiness and risk. Shows six ways to increase self - esteem and balance in life and how to live with change. Part one of two - parts.
Business and Economics; Health and Safety; Psychology
Dist - CARTRP **Prod** - CARTRP

Stress Management For Professionals Series
Stress Management for Professionals 88 MIN
Dist - CARTRP

Stress Management for Professionals - Vol I and II 173 MIN
VHS
Color (G)
$149.95 purchase _ #20115, #20119
Features Roger Mellott. Considers the paradox of happiness and risk, how to increase self - esteem. Reveals that one's need for approval affects one's stress level and shows how to get free of the classic 'values bind.'
Business and Economics; Health and Safety; Psychology
Dist - CARTRP **Prod** - CARTRP

Stress management - or what, me worry 30 MIN
VHS
First - year teacher series
Color (T)
$69.95 purchase, $45.00 rental
Discusses the unique challenges and rewards that first - year school teachers face. Serves as the eighth episode of a 12 - part telecourse. Features discussions between first - year teachers and Winthrop College professor Glen Walter on stress management.
Education; Psychology
Dist - SCETV **Prod** - SCETV 1988

Stress management package
VHS
Personal action for better health series
Color (A IND)
$299.00 purchase _ #AH45413
Identifies the causes and symptoms of stress. Outlines and applies skills in managing stress. Includes 125 booklets and three posters.
Health and Safety; Psychology
Dist - HTHED **Prod** - HTHED

Stress Management System Series Film 1
Introduction to Stress 12 MIN
Dist - CORF

Stress Management System Series Film 2
Trauma Stress Management 12 MIN
Dist - CORF

Stress Management System Series Film 3
Long - Term Stress Management 15 MIN
Dist - CORF

Stress Management System Series
Lifesavers - Fitness and Nutrition 20 MIN
Dist - CORF

Stress Management - the Rational - Emotive Approach 30 MIN
U-matic / VHS
Color
Outlines the rational - emotive approach to stress management. Shows a group of participants doing exercises to reduce stress.
Health and Safety; Psychology
Dist - IRL Prod - IRL

Stress Management - Wedding Daze 23 MIN
U-matic / VHS / 16mm
Color (H C A)
Provides insights into the sources of stress as well as its effects. Presents techniques and strategies for coping with stress. Uses a case study that involves a wedding.
Health and Safety; Psychology
Dist - AIMS Prod - AIMS

The Stress mess 25 MIN
VHS / U-matic / 16mm
Color (H C G)
$550.00, $415.00, $385.00 _ #C316
Shows how to reduce and manage stress. Identifies many common signs of stress and the sources of stress. Explains important time management techniques. Follows the Wilson family - Fred, Stacy and their daughter Karen - through a typical stress filled day. The Wilsons' stressful predicaments are relieved through the fortuitous appearance of Harry, a self - styled expert on stress.
Health and Safety; Psychology
Dist - BARR Prod - UNDERR 1981

Stress of Separation 16 MIN
16mm
Under Fives Series
Color (C A)
Shows that children have the most difficulty coping with separation between the ages of seven months and three years. Visits a day - care center and shows the behavior of children after their parents have left.
Psychology
Dist - FLMLIB Prod - GRATV 1982

Stress overload 20 MIN
VHS
Manage it series
Color (A PRO COR IND)
$95.00 purchase _ #VMIV2
Helps viewers focus on the management part of stress management whether their problems are at home or on the job. Provides relaxation techniques that viewers can use to relieve stress. Focuses on how to identify stress overload. Explores three different strategies for stress management - emergency skills for surviving an immediate crisis; short-term skills for managing chronic, recurring stress; and long-term skills for making healthy lifestyle adjustments. Includes leader guide and five participant guides. Part two of a six-part series.
Psychology
Dist - WHLPSN

Stress proofing 30 MIN
VHS
Color (G)
$49.00 purchase _ #4034 - HDLQ
Teaches viewers how deep relaxation helps prevent illness and enhance mental and physical vitality. Explains the effects of stress and leads viewers through 11 stretching and deep - breathing exercises. Uses a calming beach image to create a relaxing atmosphere. Also available as part of the complete Stress Management Program.
Health and Safety; Physical Education and Recreation; Psychology
Dist - KRAMES Prod - KRAMES

Stress Reduction 30 MIN
VHS
Video Reflections Series
Color (G)
$29.95 purchase _ #VSTR
Combines images of nature with music and soothing environmental sounds. Uses visual and auditory subliminal messages for reducing stress.
Health and Safety; Psychology
Dist - GAINST Prod - GAINST

Stress reduction exercises 74
VHS
Color (G)
$24.95 purchase _ #HE - 03
Shows how to reduce stress through the use of T'ai - chi. Features Master Bob Klein.
Physical Education and Recreation; Psychology; Religion and Philosophy
Dist - ARVID Prod - ARVID

Stress reduction program 60 MIN
VHS
Color (J H C G)
$29.95 purchase _ #FF11011V
Shows how to reduce the amount of stress in life. Teaches how to cancel the effects of stress that cannot be avoided. Contains advice from doctors, helpful hints from people who have conquered stress and relieve its ill effects. Includes a booklet detailing the sources of stress, with checklists to identify stress problems, and a Stress Diary.
Health and Safety; Psychology
Dist - CAMV

Stress reduction strategies that really work 31 MIN
VHS
Color (I J H C)
$189.00 purchase _ #CG - 871 - VS; LC 90-700039
Presents the latest and most up - to - date information about how people react to stress - positive and negative - and details step - by - step techniques proven effective in reducing or eliminating stress symptoms. Demonstrates that each one has an individual coping style and ways of dealing with various types of stressors. Includes an instant calming sequence which is often taught in martial arts classes and which neutralizes negative stress in less than one second, as well as another technique called body tension scan.
Guidance and Counseling; Health and Safety; Psychology
Dist - HRMC Prod - VIDDIA 1990

Stress - Related Disorders and their Management through Biofeedback and Relaxation Training 60 MIN
VHS / U-matic
Stress Series
Color
Features Dr Kenneth Greenspan discussing and demonstrating to Dr Milton Berger some biofeedback and relaxation techniques to relieve patients with migraine headaches and phobic anxiety, as well as integrating these with psychodynamic and pharmacological treatments.
Health and Safety; Psychology
Dist - HEMUL Prod - HEMUL

Stress - relaxation techniques 13 MIN
16mm / VHS / BETA / U-matic
Color; PAL (G)
PdS115, PdS123 purchase
Shows special methods of meditation, biofeedback and relaxation therapy that are highly effective in reducing stress and keeping negative effects to a minimum.
Psychology; Religion and Philosophy
Dist - EDPAT

Stress Relief Techniques
VHS / BETA
R M I Stress Management Series Series
Color
Health and Safety; Physical Education and Recreation; Psychology
Dist - RMIBHF Prod - RMIBHF

Stress Relief Techniques
VHS / 16mm
RMI Stress Management Series
(PRO)
$80.00 purchase _ #RSM1002
Looks at stress relief techniques used in stress management.
Business and Economics; Psychology
Dist - RMIBHF Prod - RMIBHF

Stress Relief - the Heimlich Method 16 MIN
U-matic / VHS / 16mm
Color (H C A)
LC 83-700343
Presents Dr Henry Heimlich who discusses the causes of stress, the symptoms or early warning signs, strategies for cooling off a stressful situation, and strategies for changing attitudes that allow stress to rule.
Psychology
Dist - AIMS Prod - AIMS 1983

Stress series
Managing stress - Part 1 21 MIN
Managing stress - Part 2 28 MIN
Sources of stress 21 MIN
Stress - a fact of life 19 MIN
Stress - the body's response 21 MIN
Stress and disease - Part 1 22 MIN
Stress and disease - Part 2 26 MIN
Dist - CONMED

Stress Series
Hypertension - the Relaxation Response as Adjunct to Medical Treatments 50 MIN
Stress - Related Disorders and their Management through Biofeedback and Relaxation Training 60 MIN
Dist - HEMUL

Stress, success and the type A report card 60 MIN
VHS
Color (A PRO)
$69.95 purchase _ #S01551
Describes the positive and negative impacts of stress in a person's life. Focuses on the negative effects of letting stress get out of hand. Presents a variety of stress mediators. Warns against equating stress and success. Hosted by Dr John W Lee.
Business and Economics; Psychology
Dist - UILL

Stress, Tension, and the Relaxation Response 20 MIN
U-matic / VHS
Color
LC 77-730596
Identifies causes of and physiological responses to stress and explains how stress can lead to high blood pressure. Describes the relaxation response and discusses its importance in counteracting effects of stress and helping to reduce blood pressure.
Health and Safety; Psychology
Dist - MEDCOM Prod - MEDCOM

The Stress Test - with Frank Field
VHS / U-matic
Color
Teaches your students about different types of stress while testing their knowledge through a series of questions and answers.
Health and Safety; Psychology
Dist - HRMC Prod - HRMC 1986

Stress testing on the job 60 MIN
16mm / VHS
Color (G IND)
$5.00 rental
Looks at job stress as a union issue in four parts. Explores the physical toll stress can take, why workers blame themselves or co - workers for problems caused by working conditions, how to handle a stress - related grievance, as well as discussing the stress experienced by stewards in the zone between management and workers. Produced by the Institute for Mental Health.
Business and Economics; Health and Safety; Psychology; Social Science; Sociology
Dist - AFLCIO

Stress - the body's response 21 MIN
VHS / U-matic / BETA
Stress series
Color (C PRO)
$150.00 purchase _ #131.3
Presents a video transfer from slide program which describes stress responses of the neurologic and endocrine systems and their effects on the immunologic system. Discusses how measurements of these responses and their physiologic effects can be used in stress research. Cites experimental studies that illustrate how the body responses differ with the type of stressor and the subject's ability to control it. Part of a series on stress.
Guidance and Counseling; Health and Safety; Psychology; Science - Natural
Dist - CONMED Prod - CONMED

Stress - the Management Challenge 15 MIN
U-matic / VHS
Color
Gives step - by - step instructions on developing a management style that turns unavoidable workplace stress into a positive force.
Business and Economics; Psychology; Sociology
Dist - WHITEG Prod - WHITEG

Stress, the Time Bomb within
VHS / U-matic
Color (J H)
Shows how to help teens recognize stress and handle it. Identifies common causes of stress and outlines methods for breaking patterns of tension.
Psychology
Dist - GA Prod - AVNA

Stress Training for Police Series no 2
Humiliation and Anger 10 MIN
Dist - FMD

Stress training for police series
Fear and anxiety 10 MIN
Feeling good 9 MIN
Dist - FMD

Stress training for teachers series
Black is the Color 17 MIN
Crossing the line 16 MIN
The Crunch 16 MIN
Dist - FMD

Stress traps 20 MIN
VHS
Manage it series
Color (A PRO IND COR)
$95.00 purchase _ #VMIV1
Helps viewers focus on the management part of stress management whether their problems are at home or on the job. Provides relaxation techniques that relieve stress. Focuses on big picture issues and how to identify the causes of stress in their own lives. Outlines three of the most common stress traps - misperception, misspending, and overcontrol. Discusses the importance of such stress management skills as relabeling, prioritizing, and letting go. Includes leadership guide and five participant guides. Part one of a six-part series.
Psychology
Dist - WHLPSN

Stress - Unwinding the Spring Series
Coping with stress 12 MIN
Learning to Relax 14 MIN
The Psychobiology of Stress 10 MIN
Stress and Illness 12 MIN
Understanding Stress 12 MIN
Dist - AIMS

Stress, with Dr Roy Martin 55 MIN
U-matic
Color
Discusses the origin of stress and what we can do about eliminating or overcoming stressful situations.
Health and Safety; Psychology
Dist - UTEXSC **Prod** - UTEXSC

Stress - You Can Live with it 26 MIN
U-matic / VHS / 16mm
Color
$470.00 purchase _ #AG - 6MB
Uses case histories to show the negative effects that stressful lifestyles, attitudes and behaviors can have on a person's health. Shows that stress can cause heart attacks, increased cholesterol levels and other chronic ailments.
Psychology
Dist - CORF **Prod** - MITCHG 1982

Stress - You're in Control 23 MIN
16mm / VHS
Color (PRO)
$595.00 purchase, $130.00 rental, $35.00 preview
Explains how every type of employee experiences stress and how this stress effects his or her health and productivity. Illustrates the warning signs of stress.
Business and Economics; Guidance and Counseling; Psychology; Sociology
Dist - UTM **Prod** - UTM

Stressbreak
VHS
Color (G)
$29.95 purchase _ #U891109045
Presents nature images and soothing music to help harness stress and improve productivity. Features Emmett E Miller, MD.
Health and Safety; Psychology; Religion and Philosophy
Dist - BKPEOP **Prod** - SOURCE 1989

Stressed out 30 MIN
VHS
Color (A PRO)
$49.95 purchase _ #FH100V-H
Defines stress and how it can be controlled. Uses interviews with psychologists and comments from people who experience stress in their personal and professional lives. Viewers learn about the causes of stress and specific steps they can take to cope with and control it. They learn relaxation tips and the effect of attitude, nutrition, exercise and leisure on stress.
Guidance and Counseling; Psychology
Dist - CAMV

Stretch Concepts for Teaching Handicapped Children Series
Label the Behavior 30 MIN
Dist - HUBDSC

Stretch for Life
VHS
(C A)
$24.95
Demonstrates various stretching exercises.
Physical Education and Recreation
Dist - CAMV **Prod** - CAMV

The Stretch of Imagination - the Synthetic Duplication of Natural Rubber 27 MIN
16mm
Color (I J H C)
LC FIA64-161
Shows how scientists have created various synthetics having certain properties of natural rubber. Describes their supreme achievement of 1962, polyisoprene, composed of man - made molecules which duplicate those found in the latex of the rubber tree.
Science; Science - Physical
Dist - USDIBM **Prod** - GTARC 1964

Stretch Strategies for Teaching Handicapped Children Series
Parent Counseling 30 MIN
Dist - HUBDSC

Stretch with Priscilla series
Builds on the 'To Life!' yoga series with more advanced yoga exercises. Includes three different levels, each more demanding than the previous one. Hosted by Priscilla Patrick.
Stretch with Priscilla series 1789 MIN
Dist - SCETV **Prod** - SCETV 1964

Stretcher Transport 16 MIN
16mm
Nurse's Aide, Orderly and Attendant Series
Color (A)
LC 71-704830
Demonstrates standard procedures for the safe utilization of stretchers.
Guidance and Counseling; Health and Safety
Dist - COPI **Prod** - COPI 1969

Stretching and Mobilization for the Parkinson Patient 7 MIN
16mm
Color
LC 74-705710
Demonstrates stretching and mobilization techniques for use with Parkinson patients.
Health and Safety; Psychology
Dist - USNAC **Prod** - USPHS 1967

Stretching Mobile Home Heating Dollars 50 MIN
U-matic / VHS
Color (C A)
LC 83-707106
Describes typical mobile home construction methods and shows where added insulation and materials could save heating money. Gives cost analysis of input materials and resulting dollar savings.
Home Economics; Sociology
Dist - CORNRS **Prod** - CUETV 1983

Stretching Out 3 MIN
16mm
Color (I J H C)
Presents a cartoon film dealing with mind expansion.
Fine Arts; Psychology
Dist - CFS **Prod** - CFS 1968

Stretching - the stress reducer
VHS
Spa workout series
Color (G H A)
$24.98 purchase _ #VEG03V-P
Offers viewers movements that relieve muscle tension and fatigue and increase flexibility by concentrating on specific muscle groups. Presents Canyon Ranch Fitness Director Rebecca Gorrell and Wellness Coordinator Jodina Scazzola-Pozo, who demonstrate modifications for all movements, including spinal, arm, and shoulder rotations. One of a set of three videos, ranging from 47 to 57 minutes, available individually or as a set.
Physical Education and Recreation
Dist - CAMV

Stretching to prevent muscle - related injuries 40 MIN
VHS
Color (J H A)
$49.95 purchase _ #CJC100V
Presents a program of stretching exercises to prevent muscle - related injuries. Includes stretching exercises from the ankles to the neck, exercises to prevent back problems, and breathing techniques for relaxation and concentration.
Health and Safety; Physical Education and Recreation; Science - Natural
Dist - CAMV

Stretching with Priscilla 60 MIN
VHS
Color (G)
$31.95 purchase
Presents yoga exercise by Priscilla Patrick who appears on PBS. Offers a natural progression for those who have mastered 'Take A Break.' Starts with a shortened limbering series and has three twenty minute levels, becoming more demanding at each level.
Physical Education and Recreation; Religion and Philosophy; Science - Natural
Dist - PRIPAT **Prod** - PRIPAT

Stretching your whole body 60 MIN
VHS
Color (G)
$24.95 purchase _ #HE - 04
Demonstrates stretching exercises to help prevent injury during sports activity. Features Jean Goulet.
Physical Education and Recreation
Dist - ARVID **Prod** - ARVID

Stretchout 12 MIN
BETA / VHS / U-matic
Color (IND G A)
$510.00 purchase, $125.00 rental _ #STR031
Explains the physiology of stretching and illustrates the benefits of maintaining a commitment to a regular stretching program. Presents a seven - minute 'stretchout.'
Physical Education and Recreation
Dist - ITF **Prod** - CREMED 1991

Strictly on Your Own 29 MIN
16mm
Color
LC 74-706589
Describes life as a woman recruit in the U S Marine Corps.
Civics and Political Systems; Sociology
Dist - USNAC **Prod** - USN 1971

Strictly propaganda 94 MIN
VHS / 16mm
Color (G)
$490.00 purchase, $100.00 rental
Tells the history of the German Democratic Republic through East Germany's official newsreels and state films. Presents beaming workers and perfect children who populate a bizarre and surreal world. By eliminating narration, interruptions or other means of breaking the spell, producer Wolfgang Kissel has strung together a riveting series of vignettes. Compresses four decades' worth of manipulation to convey just how maddening and debilitating such information can be over time.
Fine Arts; History - World; Sociology
Dist - FIRS

Strictly Speaking 31 MIN
16mm / U-matic / VHS
Color
LC 80-700075
Argues for specific and concrete expression, pointing out that clarity of speech results in improved effectiveness. Based on the books A Civil Tongue and Strictly Speaking by Edwin Newman.
English Language
Dist - CCCD **Prod** - CCCD 1979

Strictly speaking - Attorney General Edwin Meese and Judge Robert Bork 60 MIN
U-matic / VHS
In search of the Constitution series
Color (A G)
$59.95, $79.95 purchase _ #MOYR - 107
Discusses the 'original intent' of the framers of the Constitution - on abortion, presidential powers, and big government. Part of an 11 - part series in which Bill Moyers examines the vitality of our nation's most important document by listening to people who interpret and teach it and people whose lives have been changed by it.
Civics and Political Systems; Sociology
Dist - PBS

Strider - a Film 29 MIN
16mm
Color
LC 74-705711
Depicts campus life and classroom scenes of NROTC midshipmen. Describes the advantages of the NROTC college scholarship program, which leads to a degree as well as a career as a Naval or Marine Corps officer.
Education
Dist - USNAC **Prod** - USN 1970

Strider's House 23 MIN
16mm
B&W
LC 81-700322
Depicts a fictitious novelist named Strider Park, who realizes as he lies near death that he must resolve certain neglected parts of his life before he goes.
Fine Arts; Sociology
Dist - USC **Prod** - USC 1980

Strike 72 MIN
VHS / 16mm
Films of Sergei Eisenstein series

B&W (G)
$150.00 rental
Portrays a widespread labor strike in a rural factory. Presents the first film of director Sergei Eisenstein.
Fine Arts
Dist - KINOIC

Strike 78 MIN
VHS / U-matic
B&W
Addresses the suppression of a 1912 factory workers' strike in Russia.
Fine Arts; History - World
Dist - IHF **Prod** - IHF

Strike Back at Strokes 25 MIN
U-matic / VHS
Color
Notes that the third largest cause of death in the United States is stroke. Shows what a stroke is and how it may be prevented. Demonstrates newest techniques for rehabilitating stroke patients, including a Neuromuscular Asist Device which enables many paralyzed patients to walk. Depicts several stroke victims telling how this affliction has affected their lives.
Health and Safety; Psychology
Dist - MEDCOM **Prod** - MEDCOM

Strike City 30 MIN
16mm
Color
Shows the plantation workers in Mississippi in 1967, going on strike against the exploitation of the plantation system and their decision to form their own collective. Explains how after much effort they obtain permanent housing.
Business and Economics; Geography - United States; Social Science; Sociology
Dist - CANWRL **Prod** - DOJGRI 1967

Strike Command 29 MIN
16mm
Big Picture Series
Color
LC 74-706263
Shows the fighting potential of the U S Strike Command, a joint command which includes fighting men of the Army, Navy and Air Force.
Civics and Political Systems
Dist - USNAC **Prod** - USA 1965

Strike Hard, Strike Home 26 MIN
16mm
Winston Churchill - the Valiant Years Series; No 13
B&W
LC FI67-2114
Documents with actual footage the allied invasion of Sicily July 10, 1943, the collapse of the Mussolini regime two weeks later, the surrender of Italy in September by Marshal Badoglio and the meeting between Churchill and Roosevelt in Washington. Based on the book 'The Second World War,' by Winston S Churchill.
History - World
Dist - SG **Prod** - ABCTV 1961

Strike out - Ron LeFebvre's 'perfect pitch' video - Baseball 41 MIN
VHS
Strike out - Ron LeFebvre's 'perfect pitch' video series
Color (P I J H G)
$29.95 purchase
Features Ron LeFebvre, kinesiologist and board - certified sports hypnotherapist, who says, 'We need to help young athletes develop their own style. Instead of hollering and scolding kids for failing, we need to encourage good habits without interfering with their natural style.' Shows students practicing LeFebvre's proven mechanics of pitching - including proper body and head alignment, improved velocity and control, stride and balance, along with throwing techniques. Emphasizes safety, age - appropriate technique, and how coaches can help young athletes develop their own personal style. Part of a series.
Physical Education and Recreation
Dist - RAETEC **Prod** - RAETEC 1993

Strike out - Ron LeFebvre's 'perfect pitch' video series
Strike out - Ron LeFebvre's 'perfect pitch' video - Baseball 41 MIN
Strike out - Ron LeFebvre's 'perfect pitch' video - Softball 41 MIN
Dist - RAETEC

Strike out - Ron LeFebvre's 'perfect pitch' video - Softball 41 MIN
VHS
Strike out - Ron LeFebvre's 'perfect pitch' video series
Color (P I J H G)
$29.95 purchase
Features Ron LeFebvre, kinesiologist and board - certified sports hypnotherapist, who says, 'We need to help young athletes develop their own style. Instead of hollering and scolding kids for failing, we need to encourage good habits without interfering with their natural style.' Shows students practicing LeFebvre's proven mechanics of pitching - including proper body and head alignment, improved velocity and control, stride and balance, along with throwing techniques. Emphasizes safety, age - appropriate technique, and how coaches can help young athletes develop their own personal style. Part of a series.
Physical Education and Recreation
Dist - RAETEC **Prod** - RAETEC 1993

Strike the original match 40 MIN
VHS
Color (G A R)
$39.95 purchase, $10.00 rental _ #35 - 88 - 597
Interviews seven couples who were all near divorce at one time, but who found the resources to overcome their differences through Christ.
Guidance and Counseling; Religion and Philosophy; Sociology
Dist - APH **Prod** - NEWLIB

Strike - the story of a South African boy 19 MIN
VHS
Color (P I)
$295.00 purchase, $75.00 rental _ #8406
Visits Bophuthatswana in South Africa with Strike and his sister Kedibone of Soweto. Explores the traditional way of life in rural South Africa.
Geography - World; History - United States; Sociology
Dist - AIMS **Prod** - SABCOR 1991

Strike Up the Band 15 MIN
U-matic / VHS
Mrs Cabobble's Caboose
(P)
Designed to teach primary grade students basic music concepts. Highlights melody, rhythm, harmony and the different families of musical instruments. Features Mrs. Fran Powell.
Fine Arts
Dist - GPN **Prod** - WDCNTV 1986

Striker tactics - skills to help you score - Part 1
VHS
Winning at soccer with Bobby Charlton series
Color (J H A)
$29.95 purchase _ #SLS013V
Features English soccer coach Bobby Charlton in an introduction to the striker position in soccer. Explains and illustrates the purpose of the striker, including scoring quickly, performance decisions, shooting, and hitting the target.
Physical Education and Recreation
Dist - CAMV

Striker tactics - skills to help you score - Part 2
VHS
Winning at soccer with Bobby Charlton series
Color (J H A)
$29.95 purchase _ #SLS014V
Features English soccer coach Bobby Charlton in an introduction to the striker position in soccer. Illustrates further striker skills including team playing, one touch control, and awareness of field position.
Physical Education and Recreation
Dist - CAMV

Strikes - Protesting to Gain Power as Well as Economic Advantage 15 MIN
16mm
Color
Examines labor protest against management by contrasting the relatively uncomplicated issues of the 1902 United Mine Workers effort to raise their pay. Promotes an understanding of basic sociological concepts.
Business and Economics; Sociology
Dist - REAF **Prod** - INTEXT

Striking 15 MIN
U-matic / VHS
Leaps and Bounds Series no 16
Color (T)
Explains how to teach primary students to strike with a racket and about the face of the implement, lever length, striking a stationary and a moving ball.
Physical Education and Recreation
Dist - AITECH

Striking a Balance 30 MIN
U-matic
Paths of Development Series
Color (H C A)
Focuses on the development choices open to Malaysia, Peru and Niger in their efforts to meet the needs of their people.
Sociology
Dist - ACCESS **Prod** - ACCESS 1985

Striking Against Objects 3 MIN
U-matic / VHS / 16mm
Accident Prevention Series
Color (IND) (SPANISH)
LC 72-702118
Depicts ways in which workers may injure themselves in striking - against - objects accidents by showing what happens to an office worker when she trips up steps, drops papers into a fan, falls over boxes and slips on the floor.
Business and Economics; Health and Safety; Sociology
Dist - IFB **Prod** - IAPA 1972

Striking an arc, restarting the arc and running a continuous bead in the flat
U-matic / VHS
Shielded metal arc welding - Spanish series
Color (SPANISH)
Foreign Language; Industrial and Technical Education
Dist - VTRI **Prod** - VTRI

Striking arcs with E - 6010 cellulose electrodes 13 MIN
VHS / U-matic
Electric arc welding series; Chap 3
Color (IND)
Education; Industrial and Technical Education
Dist - TAT **Prod** - TAT

Striking Arcs with E - 6010/Cellulose Electrodes Series
Electric Arc Welding 13 MIN
Dist - TAT

Striking arcs with E - 7018 low hydrogen electrodes 13 MIN
U-matic / VHS
Electric arc welding series; Chap 4
Color (IND)
Education; Industrial and Technical Education
Dist - TAT **Prod** - TAT

Striking it Rich 30 MIN
U-matic / VHS
CNN Special Reports Series
(G C J)
$129 purchase _ #31383 - 851
Presents the contemporary issue of striking it rich in America today.
Business and Economics
Dist - CHUMAN

Striking it Rich
U-matic / VHS
CNN Special Reports
(J H C)
$129.00 purchase purchase _ #31383 941
Examines how entrepreneurism has becomoe a vital force in strengtherning America's business and in reinforcing the 'American Dream.'
Business and Economics
Dist - ASPRSS **Prod** - TURNED

Striking skills
VHS
Children and movement video series
Color (H A T)
$29.95 purchase _ #MK806
Teaches about striking skills in children ages 3 to 6 years old. Part of a five - part series which guides in conducting physical education programs.
Physical Education and Recreation; Psychology
Dist - AAVIM **Prod** - AAVIM 1992

Strindberg's Miss Julie 102 MIN
VHS
Color (H C A)
$74.95 purchase
Features the Royal Shakespeare Company in a performance of 'Miss Julie' by Strindberg.
Literature and Drama
Dist - PBS **Prod** - WNETTV

Strindberg's the Ghost Sonata 60 MIN
VHS / U-matic
Drama - play, performance, perception series; Module 2
Color (C)
Fine Arts; Literature and Drama
Dist - MDCC **Prod** - MDCC

The String 19 MIN
16mm
Color (K)
LC 72-700403
A fantasy about a magic ball of twine which, because it cannot be cut, winds in and out of the lives and property of the townspeople who are lifted out of themselves and made more sensitive to one another.
Guidance and Counseling; Psychology; Sociology
Dist - MMA **Prod** - FILMC 1970

String 30 MIN
U-matic
Today's Special Series
Color (K P)
Develops language arts skills in children. Programs are thematically designed around subjects of interest to youngsters. Action takes place in a department store where people, mannequins, puppets, comic characters and special guests present a light hearted approach to language arts.
Fine Arts; Literature and Drama; Psychology
Dist - TVOTAR **Prod** - TVOTAR 1985

The String family 15 MIN
U-matic / VHS
Music machine series
Color (P)
Teaches recognition of string musical instruments.
Fine Arts
Dist - GPN **Prod** - GPN

The String Family - 13 15 MIN
VHS
Music and Me Series
Color (P)
$125.00 purchase
Looks at musical instruments in the string family. Encourages student participation to develop skills in singing, listening, rhythmic expression and playing simple instruments. Part of the Music And Me Series.
Fine Arts
Dist - AITECH **Prod** - WDCNTV 1979

String - Knotting and Weaving 10 MIN
U-matic / VHS / 16mm
Color; Captioned (I)
LC 72-701733
Presents an introduction to the kaleidoscope of creative weaving, knotting and macrame.
Fine Arts
Dist - ALTSUL **Prod** - NORMBP 1972

A String of pearls 30 MIN
VHS
America in World War II - The home front series
Color (G)
$49.95 purchase _ #AWWH - 104
Features U S military successes in Guadalcanal and in North Africa. Discusses the role of American women at home, as exemplified by the fictional character 'Rosie the Riveter.' Suggests that the changing role of women in industry and society during World War II paved the way for the women's movement in future years. Narrated by Eric Severeid.
History - United States
Dist - PBS

String Processing
16mm
B&W
Presents the construction of algorithms for processing strings.
Mathematics
Dist - OPENU **Prod** - OPENU

The string quartet
CD-ROM
Audio notes series
(G)
$66.00 purchase _ #2622
Contains the digital recording of Beethoven's String Quartet No.14 - Opus 131, enhanced by thousands of pictures, additional music, commentaries, analysis, historical information, music glossary, and index. Includes HyperCard 1.2.5. Requires a Macintosh with at least 1 MB of RAM, a hard disk drive with at least 6.5 MB of free space, an Apple compatible CD - ROM drive, and headphones or external speakers.
Fine Arts
Dist - BEP

String Quartet 47 MIN
16mm
Color (H C A)
LC 73-702266
Presents the Debussy Quartet in G Minor as played by the Carl Pini String Quartet. Studies the four players as they talk about their lives and careers and their dedication to chamber music.
Fine Arts
Dist - AUIS **Prod** - ANAIB 1972

String theory and geometry 60 MIN
VHS
ICM Plenary addresses series
Color (PRO G)
$49.00 purchase _ #VIDWITTEN - VB2
Presents Edward Witten who discusses string theory and geometry.
Mathematics
Dist - AMSOC **Prod** - AMSOC

String Trimmer
VHS
Landscape Equipment Maintenance Series
Color (G) (SPANISH)
$65.00 purchase _ #6 - 077 - 100P, #6 - 077 - 200P - Spanish
Presents proper procedures on maintenance, safety and operation of the string trimmer for landscaping. Part of a five - part series on landscaping.
Agriculture; Health and Safety
Dist - VEP **Prod** - VEP

The String Trio 9 MIN
16mm
Listening to Music Series
Color (P I J)
Shows close ups of the violin, viola and violoncello. Shows simple basic techniques for playing string instruments.
Fine Arts
Dist - VIEWTH **Prod** - GATEEF

Stringer Bead 7 MIN
VHS / BETA
Welding Training (Comprehensive - - - Oxy - Acetylene Welding 'Series
Color (IND)
Industrial and Technical Education; Psychology
Dist - RMIBHF **Prod** - RMIBHF

Stringer beads with E - 6010 13 MIN
U-matic / VHS
Electric arc welding series; Chap 5
Color (IND)
Education; Industrial and Technical Education
Dist - TAT **Prod** - TAT

Stringer beads with E - 7018 13 MIN
U-matic / VHS
Electric arc welding series; Chap 6
Color (IND)
Education; Industrial and Technical Education
Dist - TAT **Prod** - TAT

Stringer - Portrait of a Newsreel Cameraman 28 MIN
16mm / U-matic / VHS
Color (J)
LC 79-701075
Relates various escapades of newsreel cameraman Mike Gittinger who, during the 1930s, filled movie theater screens with a sensational array of disastrous, violent, and absurd events. Includes Gittinger's own reminiscences about his career as a stringer.
Fine Arts; Industrial and Technical Education
Dist - FI **Prod** - FORMM 1979

Stringer Types and Attachment Methods 22 MIN
U-matic
Step by Step Series
(A)
Presents five different types of wood stringers. Examines their similarities and differences and looks at the various methods of fastening stringers to upper floor systems.
Industrial and Technical Education
Dist - ACCESS **Prod** - ACCESS 1984

Stringing Along 15 MIN
16mm
Fingermouse, Yoffy and Friends Series
Color (K P I)
LC 73-700439
Follows Yoffy and his friends as they collect various kinds of string.
Guidance and Counseling; Literature and Drama
Dist - VEDO **Prod** - BBCTV 1972

Strings and things 25 MIN
U-matic / VHS / 16mm
Making the most of the micro series; Episode 3
Color (J)
Looks at the way a computer can handle words and presents some of the principles involved in managing a large program.
Mathematics
Dist - FI **Prod** - BBCTV 1983

Strip Mined Lands Can be Reclaimed 20 MIN
16mm
Color
LC 80-701175
Demonstrates the restoration of land following coal strip mining operations.
Science - Natural; Social Science
Dist - USNAC **Prod** - TVA 1974

Strip Mining in Appalachia 29 MIN
U-matic
B&W
Views the destruction left in the wake of strip mining with reports from coal mining company executives as well as interviews with people whose lands have been victims of this operation.
Geography - United States; Science - Natural; Social Science
Dist - APPAL **Prod** - APPAL 1973

Stripe Removal by High Temperature Burning with Excess Oxygen 10 MIN
16mm
Color
LC 80-701085
Demonstrates the removal of the painted lines on road surfaces by a method of burning.
Social Science
Dist - USNAC **Prod** - USFHAD 1980

Striped ice cream 15 MIN
VHS / U-matic
Book bird series
Color (I)
Tells of a girl who wants striped ice cream for her eighth birthday party. From the story by Joan Lexau.
English Language; Literature and Drama
Dist - CTI **Prod** - CTI

Striper Fishing Basics 30 MIN
VHS
Color
Presents Charlie Mayes, long time professional striper guide, demonstrating his methods of catching large striped bass. Shows how he uses live and artificial bait, and discusses proper equipment selection.
Physical Education and Recreation; Science - Natural
Dist - HOMEAF **Prod** - HOMEAF

Stripmining - Energy, Environment and Economics 50 MIN
16mm
Color (H A)
LC 80-700960
Discusses the origin and growth of strip mining, and the consequences of this type of mining for the Appalachian region.
Social Science
Dist - APPAL **Prod** - APPAL 1979

Stripmining in Appalachia 25 MIN
16mm
B&W (J H A)
LC 79-700976
Shows the beauty of the Appalachian hills, the humanity of the people and the attitudes of strip mine operators. Illustrates the effect of strip mining on the land.
Geography - United States; Science - Natural; Social Science
Dist - APPAL **Prod** - APPAL 1971

Stripping and Sanding 25 MIN
VHS
Interior Wood Refinishing Series
$39.95 purchase _ #DI - 115
Describes the techniques for stripping and sanding interior wood.
Industrial and Technical Education
Dist - CAREER **Prod** - CAREER

Stripsfilm 13 MIN
16mm
Color (G)
$15.00 rental
Experiments in multiple views of reality as seen from one space in time. Uses simple matting techniques of long strips of images that are multi - exposed in the camera. A Kon Petrochuk production.
Fine Arts; Psychology
Dist - CANCIN

Striptease 1 MIN
16mm
Color
Depicts an apparent striptease which turns out to be something entirely different.
Literature and Drama
Dist - VIEWFI **Prod** - ZAGREB 1970

Striving for Excellence 3 MIN
VHS / 16mm
Color (A PRO)
$200.00 purchase
Presents an opener or closer for meetings which features individuals and teams striving for their goals. Management training.
Business and Economics; Guidance and Counseling; Psychology
Dist - VIDART **Prod** - VIDART 1991

Stroke 60 MIN
VHS / U-matic
Medicine for the Layman Series
Color
LC 84-706512
Discusses the three kinds of stroke, the warning symptoms and how a stroke affects the central nervous system. Describes rehabilitation and new diagnostic techniques using brain scans.
Health and Safety; Science; Science - Natural
Dist - USNAC **Prod** - NIH 1983

Stroke 19 MIN
U-matic / VHS
Color (PRO)
Describes the clinical course of a stroke. Relates pathology to signs and symptoms. Explains rehabilitation. Stresses need for physical therapy and emotional support.
Health and Safety; Science - Natural
Dist - MEDFAC **Prod** - MEDFAC 1979

Stroke 17 MIN
Videoreel / VHS
Color
Interviews stroke patients and a family member of a stroke patient. Discusses the major types of strokes and details many of the cognitive and social consequences. Provides information about various therapies the stroke patient is likely to need.
Health and Safety
Dist - UNDMC **Prod** - UNDMC

Stroke 10 MIN
U-matic / VHS / 16mm
Cardiovascular Disease Series
Color (H C A)
$230 purchase - 16 mm, $160 purchase - video
Discusses how a stroke results from diseases of the arteries and talks about the importance of proper diet and exercise. A film by Sy Wexler and Bob Churchill.
Health and Safety
Dist - CF

Stroke 19 MIN
U-matic / VHS
Color (C)
$249.00, $149.00 purchase _ #AD - 1405
Focuses on preventing stroke and restoring stroke victims to maximum functional capacity. Covers warning signs associated with transient ischemic attacks, preventive procedures like endarterectomy and physical and psychological therapies.
Health and Safety; Psychology; Science - Natural
Dist - FOTH **Prod** - FOTH

Stroke 30 MIN
VHS
At time of diagnosis series
Color (G)
$19.95 purchase _ #1 - 5757 - 7022 - 9NK
Provides patients who have just been diagnosed with stroke and their families with thorough, comprehensive and understandable information. Examines what is going on in the body and what might have caused the condition. Explains the type of medical professionals a patient may encounter and how the condition is monitored. Explores treatment options, including medication, surgery and lifestyle changes. Looks at practical issues surrounding the illness and answers the most common questions. Part of an ongoing series to provide the in - depth medical information patients and their families need to know.
Health and Safety
Dist - TILIED **Prod** - TILIED 1996

Stroke 18 MIN
16mm
Doctors at Work Series
B&W (H C A)
LC FIA65-1363
Follows the progress of a stroke patient through diagnostic tests, physical therapy and excercises. Explains the nature of various types of brain damage and the treatment indicated.
Health and Safety; Psychology
Dist - LAWREN **Prod** - CMA 1961

Stroke - a Program for the Family 16 MIN
U-matic / 35mm strip
Color
LC 83-730050;
Discusses and describes stroke, and its possible causes and the highly individual symptoms that may occur all for the victim's family. Describes treatment that he may receive, and the roles of various health care proffesionals who may be involved in patient care. Concludes by outlining the important considerations in helping the patient to adjust on his/her return home.
Health and Safety; Science - Natural
Dist - MEDCOM **Prod** - MEDCOM

Stroke Awareness and Prevention
U-matic / VHS
Color (SPANISH ARABIC)
Explains how people often experience temporary symptoms similar to a stroke. Warns not to ignore them in order to avoid a stroke.
Foreign Language; Science - Natural
Dist - MIFE **Prod** - MIFE

Stroke - family support 23 MIN
VHS
Color (G C)
$95.00 purchase, $45.00 rental
Presents the views of stroke victims and family members about emotional and personal needs and about role changes in the family after stroke. Details ways to deal with the changes.
Health and Safety; Sociology
Dist - TNF

Stroke - focus on family 23 MIN
U-matic / VHS / BETA
Color; NTSC; PAL; SECAM (G)
PdS95
Reveals that stroke changes not only its victim's life, but also the lives of individuals in the victim's family. Presents family members of the participants in Stroke - Focus on Feelings who express their feelings and reactions to stroke. Discusses lifestyle changes, role reversal changes in the person with the stroke, dependency, interdependency and family communication. Shows how family members can overcome obstacles and help each other live successfully with stroke.
Health and Safety; Sociology
Dist - VIEWTH

Stroke - focus on feelings 23 MIN
U-matic / VHS / BETA
Color; NTSC; PAL; SECAM (G)
PdS95
Examines the trauma and unexpected effects of stroke. Reveals that its effects are both physical and emotional. Features people of different ages who express their feelings about stroke in a group setting. Discusses grieving, coping with anger and fear, facing a new self - image and taking the responsibility of working through therapy towards recovery. Demonstrates that stroke victims still have choices in life and can regain a sense of self - worth and quality of life after a stroke.
Health and Safety
Dist - VIEWTH **Prod** - ORACLE

Stroke - Frontiers of Hope 26 MIN
U-matic / VHS
Color (C)
$249.00, $149.00 purchase _ #AD - 1898
Reveals that stroke is the nation's third leading killer. Examines the latest advances in prevention and treatment.
Health and Safety; Psychology; Science - Natural
Dist - FOTH **Prod** - FOTH

Stroke Management Decisions 67 MIN
U-matic
Color (PRO)
LC 76-706104
Shows factors influencing the decision to perform lumbar puncture and anticoagulation therapy in the stroke patient. Examines the recommendation for arteriography for the stroke patient and factors influencing the decision to refer the patient for surgical treatment. Discusses prevention of stroke and supportive care of the stroke patient.
Health and Safety
Dist - USNAC **Prod** - WARMP 1970

Stroke Management Decisions - Pt 1 22 MIN
U-matic / VHS
Color
Identifies factors influencing the decision to perform lumbar puncture and to use anticoagulation therapy on the stroke patient.
Health and Safety; Science
Dist - USNAC **Prod** - WARMP

Stroke Management Decisions - Pt 2 23 MIN
U-matic / VHS
Color
Discusses factors influencing the decision to recommend arteriography or surgery for the stroke patient.
Health and Safety; Science
Dist - USNAC **Prod** - WARMP

Stroke Management Decisions - Pt 3 22 MIN
U-matic / VHS
Color
Discusses prevention and supportive care in dealing with the stroke patient or potential stroke patient. Shows film clips of patient interviews to illustrate points of clinical importance.
Health and Safety
Dist - USNAC **Prod** - WARMP

A Stroke of the Pen 16 MIN
U-matic / VHS / 16mm
B&W (I)
LC 75-703002
Presents a study of presidential decision - making. Concentrates on President Kennedy's decision to sign an executive order desegregating housing. Chronicles the deliberations and delays which turn a simple 'stroke of the pen' into something more complex.
Biography; Civics and Political Systems; History - United States
Dist - PFP **Prod** - KENJML 1975

The Stroke Patient 30 MIN
VHS / U-matic
Simulated Home Visits Series
Color
Presents a nurse's home visit to a 45 - year - old stroke victim. Explores patient's family history. Evaluates patient's range of motion and ability to get in and out of bed. Reviews discharge treatment plan, diet and rehabilitative activity.
Health and Safety; Science - Natural
Dist - AJN **Prod** - UTEXN

Stroke Patient Comes Home Series

He learns self - reliance	29 MIN
His Physical Well - Being	27 MIN
His Return to the Community	29 MIN
Understanding His Illness	29 MIN
Understanding His Problems	29 MIN

Dist - IFB

Stroke - Recent Trends and Treatments 80 MIN
VHS / 16mm
Medical Aspects of Disability - Course Lecture Series
Color (PRO)
$50.00, $65.00 purchase _ #8826
Presents one part of a course lecture series on the medical aspects of disability. Discusses recent trends and treatments in the rehabilitation of stroke victims.
Health and Safety; Science - Natural
Dist - RICHGO **Prod** - RICHGO 1988

A Stroke - Recovering Together 24 MIN
VHS / U-matic
Color
Describes why strokes occur, shows the predominant forms of aphasia and reviews coping and communication skills for use with stroke victims. Includes comments from a spouse group and profiles of stroke victims demonstrating various levels of recovery.
Health and Safety; Psychology
Dist - USNAC **Prod** - VAMCSL

Stroke - reducing the risks
VHS
Color (PRO A)
$250.00 purchase _ #HA - 27
Reviews both the treatable and untreatable risk factors of stroke, and offers practical advice to viewers on how to reduce their risk. Uses animation to illustrate the pathyophysiology of stroke and its various causes. Teaches patients about the warning signs of stroke, including transient ischemic attacks - TIAs - and bruits. Explains medical and surgical steps that may be taken to prevent a full - fledged stroke when such warning signs are present. Intended for a wide variety of audiences from the general public to stroke patients and their families.
Health and Safety
Dist - MIFE **Prod** - MIFE 1991

Stroke Rehabilitation 69 MIN
U-matic
Color (PRO)
LC 76-706105
Deals with means of determining the learning ability of the stroke patient so that retraining can be planned. Demonstrates the initial and intermediate phases of retraining patients for independence in self - care activities. Describes techniques for reestablishing ambulation and below - the - waist dressing skills and explains the reasons for speech therapy.
Health and Safety; Psychology
Dist - USNAC **Prod** - WARMP 1970

Stroke rehabilitation - health care options for elderly patients 120 MIN
VHS
Virginia Geriatric Education Center Video Conference series
Color (G C PRO)
$149.00 purchase, $55.00 rental
Considers whether the aged should be offered rehabilitation following a stroke. Also discusses what services should be provided, under what conditions and in what locations for best physiological response.
Health and Safety
Dist - TNF **Prod** - VGEREC

Stroke Story 30 MIN
16mm
Color
LC 80-700308
Looks at the lives of three stroke victims and their families. Explores the problems faced by these families as they help a family member recover from a stroke.
Health and Safety; Sociology
Dist - RICHGO **Prod** - RICHGO 1979

Stroke - the New Treatments 19 MIN
U-matic / VHS
Color (C)

$249.00, $149.00 purchase _ #AD - 2049
Focuses on treatment to prevent or minimize the effects of stroke. Shows the process of a stroke and discusses the pros and cons of tPA and carotid endarterectomy.
Health and Safety; Psychology; Science - Natural
Dist - FOTH **Prod** - FOTH

Stroke - Two Personal Perspectives 25 MIN
U-matic
Color (J C)
Provides an interview format in which a 62 - year old man and a 71 - year old woman describe their feelings, horror, dependency, anger, impatience and a heightened appreciation for family and friends and the struggle to recover from their strokes.
Health and Safety; Psychology; Sociology
Dist - SDSC **Prod** - SDSC 1978

Stroke - what Exactly is a Stroke? 30 MIN
VHS / U-matic
Here's to Your Health Series
Color (C T)
Answers the question of what can be done to minimize the risk of being stricken by stroke and how to ease the anguish of those who have suffered a stroke. Explores the 'cardio - vascular accidents' we call stroke.
Health and Safety; Science - Natural
Dist - DALCCD **Prod** - DALCCD

Strokes 11 MIN
16mm / VHS / U-matic
Cardiovascular Disease Series
Color (H C A)
LC 83-706645;
Uses animation to show diseases of the arteries and how strokes result. Explains the process of recovery and the need for rehabilitation. Urges prevention by proper diet, exercise and stress reduction.
Health and Safety
Dist - CF **Prod** - CF 1983

Strokes 28 MIN
U-matic / VHS / 16mm
Learning to live series
Color (H C A)
Explains how we can be less afraid to ask for and accept recognition and love.
Psychology
Dist - ECUFLM **Prod** - UMCOM 1974

Strokes
VHS / U-matic
Color
Health and Safety
Dist - ABCLR **Prod** - ABCLR

Strokes of genius series
Introduces the series Strokes of Genius, a collection of films about expressionist artists in the post WWII era, including Willem de Kooning, Arshile Gorky, Franz Kline, Jackson Pollock, Mark Rothoko and David Smith.
David Smith - steel into sculpture 58 MIN
Jackson Pollock - portrait 54 MIN
Dist - DIRECT **Prod** - CORTP

Strong dollar 30 MIN
U-matic
Adam Smith's money world series; 102
Color (A)
Attempts to demystify the world of money and break it down so that employees of small business can understand and adjust to new social and economic trends. Reports on the major economic stories and discoveries of the day.
Business and Economics
Dist - PBS **Prod** - WNETTV 1985

The Strong dollar, and trade - how are they connected 30 MIN
U-matic
Adam Smith's money world series; 114
Color (A)
Attempts to demystify the world of money and break it down so that employees of small business can understand and adjust to new social and economic trends. Reports on the major economic stories and discoveries of the day.
Business and Economics
Dist - PBS **Prod** - WNETTV 1985

Strong Families, Safe Families Series
How Can I Tell if I'm Really in Love 51 MIN
How to Stop the One You Love from Drinking and using Drugs 56 MIN
Strong Kids, Safe Kids 45 MIN
When Mom and Dad Break Up 32 MIN
Dist - PAR

Strong feelings 15 MIN
16mm
Inside-out series
Color (I)
LC 73-702450
Presents a sequence of zany dreams in which Edgar discovers how love, fright, embarassment, confusion and disappointment can affect the body. Explains the physical effects of strong emotions in order to lessen fear of such reactions.
Guidance and Counseling; Sociology
Dist - AITECH

Strong kids, safe kids 45 MIN
VHS
Color (G)
$24.95 purchase; $34.95 purchase _ #V2323-10
Features Henry Winkler, Scooby - Doo, Yogi Bear, and the Flintstones in a guide to helping children avoid sexual abuse and other dangerous situations.
Sociology
Dist - PBS **Prod** - WNETTV
GA

Strong Kids, Safe Kids 42 MIN
VHS
Color (G)
$24.95 purchase _ #6341
Teaches basic skills to parents and children which can help prevent sexual abuse, abduction and other dangerous situations.
Health and Safety; Physical Education and Recreation; Sociology
Dist - SYBVIS **Prod** - SYBVIS

Strong Kids, Safe Kids 45 MIN
VHS
Strong Families, Safe Families Series
Color (K)
$24.95 purchase _ #85037
Teaches basic skills to children and to their parents in a nonthreatening way that can help prevent sexual abuse and other dangerous situations. Features Henry Winkler, John Ritter, Mariette Hartley, family counselors, Yogi Bear, Scooby Doo and the Flintstones. Produced and directed by Rick Hauser.
Health and Safety; Sociology
Dist - PAR

The Strong Man 78 MIN
16mm
B&W (J)
Presents a Harry Langdon feature directed by Frank Capra.
Fine Arts
Dist - TWYMAN **Prod** - MGM 1926

The Stronger 18 MIN
16mm / U-matic / VHS
Color (H C A)
LC 81-700915
Portrays an encounter between two actresses in a cafe and the effect that this meeting has on the two women.
Psychology
Dist - PHENIX **Prod** - BURF 1970

Stronger than Before 37 MIN
VHS
Color (H)
$350.00 purchase, $50.00, $60.00 rental
Discusses the role of women in anti - militaristic, anti - imperialistic politics and reproductive rights, economic issues and eliminating racism. Recounts the attempted citizen's arrest by 100 women of Litton Systems Canada, which produced parts for U S cruise missiles. Produced by Emman Productions.
Civics and Political Systems; Science - Physical; Sociology
Dist - WMENIF

Stronger than before 27 MIN
VHS / U-matic
Color (G)
$175.00 purchase, $50.00 rental
Documents a summer of demonstrations and protest at the Seneca Women's Encampment for a Future of Peace and Justice, a visible symbol of protests by American women against US militarism. Produced by the Boston Women's Video Collective.
History - World; Religion and Philosophy; Sociology
Dist - WMEN

Stronger than the Strongest - the Algerian Sahara 30 MIN
U-matic
Africa File Series
Color (J H)
Examines the Sahara from the viewpoint of geography, history, and demography bringing to light the changes effected by technology.
Business and Economics; Geography - World; History - World
Dist - TVOTAR **Prod** - TVOTAR 1985

The Strongest Man 20 MIN
16mm / U-matic / VHS
Color (P I S)
LC 82-701155
Reveals that when Billy fails to make the all - star baseball team, he becomes angry and blames his father, a paraplegic who is unable to practice with him. Shows his father explaining that his handicap is something he cannot change and that they must both learn to accept it.
Education; Psychology
Dist - BARR **Prod** - JNSNR 1982

The Strongest Man in the World 29 MIN
U-matic / VHS
Color (P)
Recounts the success story of Mike Swistum, featured as the strongest man in the world with the 1923 Ringling Brothers, Barnum, and Bailey Circus. Features Swistum speaking in English and Ukrainian, the language of his Manitoba, Canada, hometown.
Biography; Geography - World; Physical Education and Recreation
Dist - KINFIL **Prod** - KINOF 1981

Stroszek 108 MIN
16mm
Color (GERMAN (ENGLISH SUBTITLES))
Tells how three Berlin misfits travel to Wisconsin and find a bleak Eldorado of TV, football, CB radio and mobile homesteading. Directed by Werner Herzog. In German and English, with English subtitles.
Fine Arts; Foreign Language
Dist - NYFLMS **Prod** - UNKNWN 1977

Struck 29 MIN
Videoreel / VT2
Our Street Series
Color
Sociology
Dist - PBS **Prod** - MDCPB

Structural abnormalities of human autosomes 30 MIN
16mm
Clinical pathology series
B&W (PRO)
Discusses the mammalian chromosome and various rearrangements produced by abnormal disruption and rejoining. Explains that sometimes these abnormalities are inherited and at other times they are produced de novo. Demonstrates the karotypes and syndromes found in 4p - , 5p - and 18q syndromes.
Health and Safety; Science - Natural
Dist - USNAC **Prod** - NMAC 1970

Structural Examination - Gross Motion Testing 14 MIN
U-matic / VHS
Osteopathic Examination and Manipulation Series
Color (PRO)
Describes movements in relation to the orientation planes of the body. Details the techniques of motion testing. Tests symmetry of the range of motion and the degree of resistance to motion. Elaborates the palpatory criteria with graphics.
Health and Safety; Science - Natural
Dist - MSU **Prod** - MSU

Structural Examination - Initial Screen 14 MIN
VHS / U-matic
Osteopathic Examination and Manipulation Series
Color (PRO)
Shows how diagnosis of the musculoskeltal problem begins with a screening examination of the entire body in order to narrow down the attention of the examiner to any major dysfunction centering within a particular region. Demonstrates procedures. Examines symmetries of structure, tissue and motion.
Health and Safety; Science - Natural
Dist - MSU **Prod** - MSU

Structural Examination - Local Scan 18 MIN
VHS / U-matic
Osteopathic Examination and Manipulation Series
Color (PRO)
Examines the scan in detail. Demonstrates procedures for testing function segment - to - segment throughout costal, shoulder and spinal regions.
Health and Safety; Science - Natural
Dist - MSU **Prod** - MSU

Structural Examination - Spinal Segmental Definition
VHS / U-matic
Osteopathic Examination and Manipulation Series
Color (PRO)
Gives a brief review of the initial structural examination tests that detect the presence and location of dysfunction in the spinal system. Demonstrates tests that provide segmental definition in each spinal region. Illustrates how this diagnostic information becomes immediately useful in restoring motion function.
Health and Safety; Science - Natural
Dist - MSU **Prod** - MSU

Structural fire attack 21 MIN
16mm
Color (IND)

LC 78-700578
Relates fire spread history to actual fire extension in structures. Covers preplanning for structural fires and techniques of confining and extinguishing fires.
Health and Safety; Social Science
Dist - COURTR **Prod** - FIREF 1978

Structural Fires 31 MIN
16mm
B&W (PRO)
Shows how a variety of fires are extinguished with a minimum of water damage. Depicts all types of engine companies in action at scenes of actual fires.
Health and Safety; Social Science
Dist - LAFIRE **Prod** - LAFIRE

Structural Geology 30 MIN
VHS / U-matic
Earth, Sea and Sky Series
Color (C)
Points out several structurally interesting features of earth. Explains the training of astronauts to become scientific observers and photographers.
Science - Physical
Dist - DALCCD **Prod** - DALCCD

Structural geology - faults 33 MIN
VHS / U-matic
Basic and petroleum geology for non - geologists series
Color (IND)
Industrial and Technical Education; Science - Physical
Dist - GPCV **Prod** - PHILLP

Structural geology - folds 25 MIN
U-matic / VHS
Basic and petroleum geology for non - geologists - series
Color (IND)
Industrial and Technical Education; Science - Physical
Dist - GPCV **Prod** - PHILLP

Structural Homologies and Co - Evolution 20 MIN
VHS / U-matic
Evolution Series
Color
Examines the similarities of structure between different species and co - evolutionary relationships. Emphasizes the similarities of structure between a lizard's leg, a bat's wing, a human arm, a sheep's leg and a porpoise's paddle.
Science - Natural; Science - Physical
Dist - FOTH **Prod** - FOTH 1984

Structural inspections - a way of managing wood - inhabiting insects 23 MIN
U-matic / VHS
Integrated pest management series
Color (IND)
$50.00, $110.00 purchase _ #TCA17367, #TCA17360
Covers inspection procedures for dealing with wood - inhabiting insects. Identifies the types of insect damage to wood, sources of infestation, and signs of insect damage.
Agriculture
Dist - USNAC **Prod** - USNPS 1987

Structure and Functions of American Government Part VII, Lesson 3 - First Semester
Smoke - Filled Rooms and Dark Horses 30 MIN
Dist - NBCTV

Structure and functions of American government - second semester - Pt VI, Lesson 5
The Power to tax 30 MIN
Dist - NBCTV

Structure and Physiology of the Avian Egg 15 MIN
U-matic / VHS / 16mm
Aspects of Animal Behavior Series
Color
Illustrates the enormous variety of shapes and colors of bird eggs. Examines their structure.
Science - Natural
Dist - UCEMC **Prod** - UCLA

Structure, delivery and control systems of the human body 56 MIN
VHS
Color (I J H)
$130.00 purchase _ #A5VH 1064
Explores the structure and function of the major systems of the human body. Offers a thorough overview of the systems and develops vocabulary skills within the discipline. Covers cells and tissue, the skeletal and muscular systems, the circulatory, nervous and endocrine systems. Includes teacher's guide.
Science - Natural
Dist - CLRVUE **Prod** - CLRVUE

Structure Fires 31 MIN
16mm
B&W (H C A)
LC 76-701750
Demonstrates methods of putting out fires with a minimum of water damage. Shows all types of engine companies fighting dwelling, mercantile, warehouse, factory, theater, basement and attic fires. Explains fire - fighting strategy.
Health and Safety
Dist - FILCOM **Prod** - LACFD 1951

Structure in Stories 15 MIN
VHS / U-matic
Word Shop Series
Color (P)
English Language
Dist - WETATV **Prod** - WETATV

The Structure of a computer
16mm
B&W
Introduces computing and tells how a computer can be used as an aid to problem solving.
Mathematics
Dist - OPENU **Prod** - OPENU

Structure of assemblers 50 MIN
U-matic / VHS
Computer languages series; Pt 1
Color
Discusses the translation process, how A(M) works, 1 vs 2 passes and space - time tradeoffs in computer languages.
Industrial and Technical Education; Mathematics; Sociology
Dist - MIOT **Prod** - MIOT

The Structure of crystals - Struktura krysztalu 76 MIN
VHS
B&W (G A) (POLISH WITH ENGLISH SUBTITLES)
$59.95 purchase
Depicts a metropolitan member of the scientific elite who visits an old friend and colleague who has retreated with his wife to a remote meteorological station. Offers a production directed by Krzysztof Zanussi and based extensively on his personal experiences.
Fine Arts; Literature and Drama; Psychology
Dist - POLART

The Structure of Gardens 15 MIN
16mm
Color (I)
Views demonstration gardens in California public parks which can serve as sources of inspiration to homeowners. Includes comments by landscape architects and garden attendants.
Agriculture; Science - Natural
Dist - CRA **Prod** - CRA

The Structure of Lysozyme 24 MIN
U-matic / VHS / 16mm
Color
Describes methods used to establish the molecular structure of the enzyme lysozyme, unique in molecular biology as the first enzyme for which both a catalytic mechanism and a detailed molecular structure had been developed.
Science - Natural
Dist - MEDIAG **Prod** - OPENU 1978

Structure of Minerals, Pt 1 27 MIN
16mm
B&W (C A)
Demonstrating the law of constancy of interfacial angles, outlines crystal systems using length and angular relationships of axes and symmetry planes. Employs X - ray equipment, picture of a path of X - rays through a mineral and an example of an X - ray diffraction pattern to explain internal structure and symmetry.
Science - Physical
Dist - UTEX **Prod** - UTEX 1960

Structure of Minerals, Pt 2 26 MIN
16mm
B&W (C A)
Describes the silicon - oxygen tetrahedron and follows its assembly into chains and sheets to form minerals of Bowen's reaction series. Describes the latter to show major mineral types.
Science - Physical
Dist - UTEX **Prod** - UTEX 1960

The Structure of Protein 16 MIN
U-matic / VHS / 16mm
Color (J H)
LC 76-708754
Traces the development of proteins including the building of amino acids, polypeptides, protein molecules and the message DNA which is transferred to RNA to act as a template for the construction of proteins.
Science - Natural
Dist - PHENIX **Prod** - LEVER 1970

Structure of Proteins 10 MIN
16mm
Molecular Biology Films Series
B&W (C)
LC 73-709327
Presents a detailed study of the structures of myoglobin and lysozyme.
Science - Natural
Dist - EDC **Prod** - ERCMIT 1970

The Structure of systems
16mm
; Pt 2
B&W
Analyzes physical systems whose state is determined by a finite number of variables. Focuses on an electrical system.
Mathematics
Dist - OPENU **Prod** - OPENU

The Structure of systems
16mm
; Pt 1
B&W
Analyzes a mathematical model whose state is defined by a finite number of time dependent qualities.
Mathematics
Dist - OPENU **Prod** - OPENU

Structure of the atom 60 MIN
VHS
Concepts in science - physics series
Color; PAL (J H)
PdS29.50 purchase
Explores the history and development of the model of the atom, from hypotheses of early Greek philosophers to the wave - mechanical model of modern atomic physicists. Contains six ten - minute concepts - The Earliest Models; Smaller than the Smallest; The Rutherford Model; The Bohr Model; Spectra; and The Wave - Mechanical Model. Part of a five - part series.
Science; Science - Physical
Dist - EMFVL **Prod** - TVOTAR

Structure of the Atom 14 MIN
U-matic
Chemistry 101 Series
Color (C)
Explains how the energy of spectral lines can be figured using the Rydberg equation. Recounts the formulation of Bohr's theory, identifies the Lyman series, defines ionization potential.
Science; Science - Physical
Dist - UILL **Prod** - UILL 1974

Structure of the Atom Series

The Bohr model	10 MIN
The Earliest models	10 MIN
The Rutherford Model	10 MIN
Smaller than the Smallest	10 MIN
Spectra	10 MIN
The Wave - Mechanical Model	10 MIN

Dist - TVOTAR

The Structure of the cell 20 MIN
VHS
Introduction to the cell structure series
Color (J H)
$69.95 purchase _ #UL10004VA
Uses live - action photography to introduce the basic parts and functions of plant and animal cells. Covers the nucleus and cytoplasm, sub - cellular organisms, enzymes and more. Presents mitosis in a live action sequence. Includes a teacher's guide. Part of a three - part series on the cell.
Science - Natural
Dist - KNOWUN

Structure of the earth 27 MIN
16mm
B&W (C A)
Illustrates that the continental platform and ocean floors dominate the surface of the earth. Summarizes Pratt and Airy's hypotheses of isostasy and garners evidence from seismographs on the interior of the earth. Illustrates the difference between 'P' and 'S' structure of a continent.
Science - Physical
Dist - UTEX **Prod** - UTEX 1960

Structure within the image 29 MIN
VHS
Photographic vision series
Color (G)
$49.95 purchase _ #RM109V-F
Examines framing, line, shape, tone and pattern in photography. Presents the technical aspects of photography clearly and simply, including principles of the camera and techniques for controlling exposure, the use of various kinds of lighting, selection of appropriate lenses and film and basic darkroom techniques. Focuses on the world of photographers and photography - its history and evolution, its uses for personal development and expression, and the impact of photography on the world. Part of a 20-part series examining all aspects of the field of photography.

Industrial and Technical Education
Dist - CAMV

Structure within the Image 30 MIN
U-matic / VHS
Photographic Vision - all about Photography Series
Color
Industrial and Technical Education
Dist - CDTEL **Prod** - COAST

Structured Design Examples 55 MIN
U-matic / VHS
Introduction to VLSI Series
Color (PRO)
Covers the full - adder (FA) and its NAND gate realization. Gives alternative FA designs. Deals with alternative state machines.
Industrial and Technical Education; Science - Physical
Dist - MIOT **Prod** - MIOT

Structured Dramatic Play 18 MIN
VHS / 16mm
Drama Reference Series
Color (C)
$150.00 purchase _ #268402
Implements elementary drama curriculum. Presents drama content, teaching strategies and resources, and demonstrated drama activities for the classroom. 'Structured Dramatic Play' presents games, exercises and activities to demonstrate the process of developing structured dramatic play skills. Illustrates the lesson components, key teaching techniques and classroom - management strategies necessary to implement any dramatic form.
Education; Literature and Drama; Mathematics
Dist - ACCESS **Prod** - ACCESS 1987

Structured Interviews with Young Children 49 MIN
VHS / U-matic
Color
Presents interviews with young children which facilitate the needs of all family members. Points out that setting limits, sharing information, communication boundaries and handling change represent four important goals.
Guidance and Counseling; Psychology; Sociology
Dist - UWISC **Prod** - WRAMC 1979

Structured Program Design Series
Managing a Structured Programming Project 15 MIN
Dist - EDTRCS

Structured Programming and Software Maintenance 30 MIN
U-matic / VHS
Micros for Managers - Software Series
Color (IND)
Introduces structured programming and illustrates with diagrams and examples. Emphasizes relationship of techniques to reduced software - development and maintenance costs in the software life cycle.
Industrial and Technical Education; Mathematics; Sociology
Dist - COLOSU **Prod** - COLOSU

Structured Settlements 180 MIN
U-matic / VHS
Color (PRO)
Presents the advantages and disadvantages of structured settlements in tort liability claims from the perspective of the plaintiff, the defendent, their respective counsels and the insurer.
Civics and Political Systems
Dist - ALIABA **Prod** - ALIABA

Structured Techniques - an Overview Series
Introduction to Structured Techniques 30 MIN
A Management View of Structured Techniques 30 MIN
Relationships among Structued Techniques 30 MIN
Dist - DELTAK

Structured vs unstructured approaches 20 MIN
U-matic
Executive development and training issues - government and industry'series; Part 1
Color (PRO)
LC 77-700634
Presents a panel discussion of formal and informal approaches to executive development using examples from the public and private sectors. Features participants from the United States Civil Service Commission, the Social Security Administration and the Martin Marietta Corporation, who point out the need for organizations to consciously plan for executive development.
Business and Economics; Civics and Political Systems; Guidance and Counseling; Psychology
Dist - USNAC **Prod** - USCSC 1976

Structures 12 MIN
VHS
Color; PAL (P I)
PdS25.00 purchase
Evaluates major structures such as towers, tunnels, bridges, and more. Includes the use of suitable materials and recognition of the patterns generated.
Industrial and Technical Education
Dist - EMFVL **Prod** - LOOLEA

Structures 30 MIN
Videoreel / VT2
Trains, Tracks and Trestles Series
Color
Physical Education and Recreation
Dist - PBS **Prod** - WMVSTV

Structures and Unions
VHS / U-matic
'C' Language Programming Series
Color
Defines and describes a structure, detailing the types of members which a structure may contain. Describes the syntax for defining, declaring and initializing a structure.
Industrial and Technical Education; Mathematics; Sociology
Dist - COMTEG **Prod** - COMTEG

Structuring Single Attribute Utility Functions 48 MIN
U-matic / VHS
Decision Analysis Series
Color
Industrial and Technical Education; Mathematics
Dist - MIOT **Prod** - MIOT

Structuring the Environment and Managing Behavior of the Physically Handicapped Child 14 MIN
Videoreel / VHS
Color
Covers basic methods used in behavior modification program for children. Discusses positive reinforcement, limit setting, establishing routines, negative reinforcement, time - out, modeling, charting, parental consistency and punishment as communication.
Health and Safety; Home Economics; Psychology
Dist - UNDMC **Prod** - UNDMC

Structuring the Learning Environment
U-matic / VHS
Effective Behavioral Programming Series
Color (S)
Gives the concepts of normalization, the ten - point plan for increasing desirable behavior, why inappropriate behaviors occur, how to handle disruptive students.
Education; Health and Safety; Psychology
Dist - RESPRC **Prod** - RESPRC

Structuring the Topic
VHS / U-matic
Write Course - an Introduction to College Composition Series
Color (C)
Explains why an audience needs clear structured writing by showing 'How - To' strategies to plan and organize the writing.
Education; English Language
Dist - DALCCD **Prod** - DALCCD

Structuring the Topic 30 MIN
VHS / U-matic
Write Course - an Introduction to College Composition Series
Color (C A)
LC 85-700977
Explains why an audience needs clearly structured writing by showing 'how - to' strategies to plan and organize writing.
English Language
Dist - FI **Prod** - FI 1984

Structuring the topic - beginning and ending 60 MIN
VHS / U-matic
Write course - an introduction to college composition; Pt 9 and 10
Color (C)
$45.00, $29.95 purchase
Illustrates new ways to organize, outline and plan writing for a specific audience in Part 9. Reveals that good writing includes strong introductory and concluding paragraphs which help the reader follow the ideas in an essay in Part 10. Parts of a 30 - part series on college composition.
Education; English Language
Dist - ANNCPB **Prod** - DALCCD 1984

Struggle at sea 26 MIN
16mm
Winston Churchill - the valiant years series; No 7
B&W
LC FI67-2115
Using documentary footage shows the results of the Nazi U - boat campaign against British shipping and Churchill's response to this peril in the battle of the Atlantic. Pictures the sinking of the German battleship Bismarck and the United States announcement of a new aid policy towards Britain. Based on the book 'THE SECOND WORLD WAR,' by Winston S Churchill.
History - World
Dist - SG **Prod** - ABCTV 1961

Struggle for a Border
The Border confirmed - the Treaty of Washington (1867 - 1871) 58 MIN
Dangerous Decades (1818 - 1846) 58 MIN
The Friendly fifties and the sinister sixties (1850 - 1863) 58 MIN
The New Equation - Annexation and Reciprocity (1840 - 1860) 58 MIN
A Second transcontinental nation - 1872 57 MIN
The Triumphant Union and the Canadian Confederation (1863 - 1867) 58 MIN
The War of 1812 (1783 - 1818) 58 MIN
Dist - CFLMDC

Struggle for Democracy Series
Chiefs and Strong Men - Pt 3 58 MIN
The First freedom - Pt 7 58 MIN
Genesis - Pt 1 58 MIN
The Last Citizens - Pt 6 58 MIN
The Price of Democracy - Pt 8 58 MIN
Reborn in America - Pt 2 58 MIN
The Rule of Law - Pt 5 58 MIN
A Soldier's Duty - Pt 9 58 MIN
The Tyranny of the Majority - Pt 4 58 MIN
Whither Democracy - Pt 10 58 MIN
Dist - FI

Struggle for dominance 30 MIN
VHS
American adventure series
Color (G)
$150.00 purchase _ #TAMA - 107
Reveals how the French and Indian War helped to reestablish English dominance over the colonies. Discusses the growing outrage over England's mercantile policies.
History - United States
Dist - PBS

Struggle for Los Trabajos 35 MIN
16mm / U-matic / VHS
Color (H C A)
LC 77-700499
Explains the investigation and conciliation processes that result when a complaint of job discrimination is filed with the Equal Employment Opportunity Commission.
Business and Economics; Civics and Political Systems; Sociology
Dist - GREAVW **Prod** - USEEOC 1975

The Struggle for peace - Israelis and Palestinians 57 MIN
VHS
Color (G)
$390.00 purchase, $75.00 rental
Offers a different perspective on the Israeli - Palestinian conflict. Examines several grassroots organizations' efforts to bring about a peaceful settlement. Reveals the large number of Israeli soldiers who risked imprisonment by refusing to serve in the Occupied Territories. Produced by Elizabeth Fernea and Steven Talley. Companion book available.
Civics and Political Systems; Fine Arts; History - World
Dist - FIRS

The Struggle for self acceptance - session I and II - Pt 2 20 MIN
16mm
Color (C G)
Shows a film of Carl Rogers and a client holding a counseling session, and then presents these two people watching the film and making comments on it. Illustrates Rogers' client centered counseling technique. Presents the client discussing how she has been changing and her sexual relationships.
Guidance and Counseling; Psychology
Dist - AACD **Prod** - AACD 1980

The Struggle for self acceptance - session II - Pt 1 20 MIN
16mm
Color (C G)
Shows a film of Carl Rogers and a client holding a counseling session, and then presents these two people watching the film and making comments on it. Illustrates Rogers' client centered counseling technique. Presents the client discussing how she has been changing and her sexual relationships.

Guidance and Counseling; Psychology
Dist - AACD **Prod** - AACD 1980

A Struggle for Shelter 29 MIN
16mm / VHS
Color (C)
$550.00, $160.00 purchase, $30.00 rental _ #CC4138
Illustrates the problems of rapid urbanization in developing nations. Focuses on Quito, Ecuador, where many rural Ecaudorians have settled in hopes of finding work.
Geography - World; Sociology
Dist - IU **Prod** - NFBC 1990

Struggle for the Seas - the Development of Fighting Ships 24 MIN
VHS / 16mm
Blue Revolution Series
Color (J)
$149.00 purchase, $75.00 rental _ #QD - 2289
Documents the history of naval battles, including the Battle of Lepanto and the the British defeat of the Spanish Armada in 1588. The ninth of 16 installments of the Blue Revolution Series.
Civics and Political Systems; Social Science
Dist - FOTH

The Struggle for Vicksburg 19 MIN
U-matic / VHS / 16mm
Color (J H C A)
$435, $250 purchase _ #73067
Talks about the siege of Vicksburg and the military maneuvers that resulted in its surrender to the Union.
History - United States
Dist - CORF

The Struggle of Coon Branch Mountain 13 MIN
16mm
Color (H A)
LC 79-700620
Focuses on Coon Branch Mountain, a small community in West Virginia where the residents are struggling for better roads and schools.
Geography - United States; Sociology
Dist - APPAL **Prod** - APPAL 1972

The Struggle of the meat 4 MIN
16mm
Color (G)
$5.00 rental
Collects accumulating images in sync with the phrase The Struggle Of The Meat, discovered while experimenting with sound loops. Produced by Alice Anne Parker aka Anne Severson.
Fine Arts
Dist - CANCIN

Struggle within 16 MIN
VHS / 16mm
Color (H A)
$325.00, $395.00 purchase, $75.00 rental _ #8129
Shows that Bobby feels guilty because of an automobile accident that leaves his best friend crippled, ending a promising football career. Left alone to confront his feelings of abandonment and isolation, Bobby resorts to alcholoism. Produced by Clip - Buffalo Cherokee.
Guidance and Counseling; Psychology
Dist - AIMS

Struggles For Poland Series
Uses interviews, still footage and archival films to tell the history of Poland from 1900 to the present day. Reviews Poland's history, in nine - part series, as a nation fought over, conquered and divided up by larger nations.

Bright Days of Tomorrow - 1945 - 1956	60 MIN
Bright days of tomorrow - Volume 6	60 MIN
Different world - 1919 - 1943	60 MIN
A False Dawn - 1921 - 1939	60 MIN
A False dawn - Volume 2	60 MIN
Friends and neighbors - 1939 - 1945	60 MIN
Friends and neighbors - Vol 5	60 MIN
In this Life - 1900 - 1979	60 MIN
In this life - Volume 8	60 MIN
Occupation - 1939 - 1945	60 MIN
Occupation - Volume 4	60 MIN
Once upon a Time - 1900 - 1923	60 MIN
The Sweepers of Squares - 1956 - 1970	60 MIN
Sweepers of stairs - Volume 7	60 MIN
The Workers' State - 1970 - 1987	60 MIN

Dist - PBS **Prod** - WNETTV 1989

Struggles For Poland Series
Presents a nine - part series covering the history of Poland in the 20th century. Considers subjects including Poland's struggles to remain independent, the wiping out of Polish Jews in the Holocaust, the rise of a Communist state, the influence of the Roman Catholic Church, and the continuing opposition to Communism among the Polish people.

Bright Days of Tomorrow - 1945 - 1956	60 MIN
Bright days of tomorrow - Volume 6	60 MIN
Different world - 1919 - 1943	60 MIN
A False Dawn - 1921 - 1939	60 MIN
A False dawn - Volume 2	60 MIN
Friends and neighbors - 1939 - 1945	60 MIN
Friends and neighbors - Vol 5	60 MIN
In this Life - 1900 - 1979	60 MIN
In this life - Volume 8	60 MIN
Occupation - 1939 - 1945	60 MIN
Occupation - Volume 4	60 MIN
Once upon a Time - 1900 - 1923	60 MIN
The Sweepers of Squares - 1956 - 1970	60 MIN
Sweepers of stairs - Volume 7	60 MIN
The Workers' State - 1970 - 1987	60 MIN

Dist - PBS **Prod** - WNETTV 1989

Struggles with modernity 50 MIN
VHS
Living Islam
Color; PAL (H C A)
PdS99 purchase; Not available in the United States or Puerto Rico
Examines significant events in Islamic history and focuses on Islamic struggles with modernity. Provides information on the faith and many cultures of Islam with a particular emphasis on what it means to be a Muslim in today's world. Third in a series of six programs.
History - World; Religion and Philosophy
Dist - BBCENE

Struggling into the 20th Century a Little Bit Late - How to Fix Up a Little Old American Town 58 MIN
VHS / BETA
Color (A)
Offers a documentary study of the metamorphosis of small - town America, spotlighting New Bern, NC.
Sociology
Dist - CCMPR **Prod** - CCMPR 1985

The Struggling people - Pt 4 28 MIN
VHS
Only one earth series
Color (G)
$79.00 purchase _ #227 - 9004
Explores and demystifies the links between environment and development and illustrates the detrimental clashes between economics and ecology in the first three programs. Presents positive examples of how development can be achieved without harming the environment in the last eight half - hour programs. Part 4 of eleven shows Africa making progress in solving the problems of food production, education and population pressures. The Kubatsirana Project provides villagers with the knowledge to build a better life.
Business and Economics; Geography - World; Health and Safety; Science - Natural; Social Science; Sociology
Dist - FI **Prod** - BBCTV 1987

Strychnine in the Soup 30 MIN
VHS / U-matic
Wodehouse Playhouse Series
Color (C A)
Presents an adaptation of the short story Strychnine In The Soup by P G Wodehouse.
Literature and Drama
Dist - TIMLIF **Prod** - BBCTV 1980

Strychnine toxicosis in the dog 11 MIN
16mm
Color (C PRO)
LC 83-700622
Follows two dogs receiving different levels of strychnine through clinical signs and includes treatment with sodium pentobarbital and activated charcoal.
Health and Safety; Science
Dist - IOWA **Prod** - IOWA 1983

STS - 1 Launch Aborts 5 MIN
16mm
Space Shuttle Profile Series
Color
LC 81-701651
Depicts launch abort modes for the STS mission, including once - around - abort and the use of the Northrup strip in New Mexico if Edwards Air Force Base in California is unusable or the orbiter must re - enter on an orbit that makes the Northrup a safer alternative to Edwards.
Science - Physical
Dist - USNAC **Prod** - NASA 1981

Stuart Hodes, Liz Thompson and Brann Wry 30 MIN
VHS / U-matic
Eye on Dance - Second Time Around, Career Options for Dancers Series
Color
Fine Arts
Dist - ARCVID **Prod** - ARCVID

Stuart Little 52 MIN
U-matic / VHS / 16mm
Color (K P)
LC FIA68-1762
Tells the story of a boy, born five inches tall and weighing five ounces, with ears, whiskers and tail like those of a mouse. Follows him in his adventures, including a sailboat race across a lake in New York's Central Park, a rescue from a trash boat and a northbound trip in search of Margalo, a bird who has flown away from New York City because of a threatening note.
Literature and Drama
Dist - MGHT **Prod** - NBCTV 1968

Stuart Little, Pt 1 20 MIN
U-matic / VHS / 16mm
Color (K P)
LC FIA68-1762
Tells the story of a boy, born five inches tall and weighing five ounces, with ears, whiskers and tail like those of a mouse. Because of his size, many adventures befall him - a sailboat race across a lake in New York's Central Park, a rescue from a trash boat and a northbound trip in search of Margalo, a bird who has flown away from New York City because of a threatening note.
Literature and Drama
Dist - MGHT **Prod** - NBCTV 1968

Stuart Little, Pt 2 32 MIN
16mm / U-matic / VHS
Color (K P)
LC FIA68-1762
Tells the story of a boy, born five inches tall and weighing five ounces, with ears, whiskers and tail like those of a mouse. Because of his size, many adventures befall him - a sailboat race across a lake in New York's Central Park, a rescue from a trash boat and a northbound trip in search of Margalo, a bird who has flown away from New York City because of a threatening note.
Literature and Drama
Dist - MGHT **Prod** - NBCTV 1968

The Stuart Sherman Collection 30 MIN
U-matic / VHS
Color
Presents a collection of Sherman's famous table - top pieces.
Fine Arts
Dist - EIF **Prod** - EIF

The Stuarts Restored 60 MIN
16mm / U-matic / VHS
Royal Heritage Series
Color (H C A)
Discusses the contributions of the later Stuarts of England, including Newmarket and Royal Ascot, Chelsea Pensioners and the Crown Jewels. Points out that they gave architect Christopher Wren the opportunity to produce great buildings not only for the court but for the nation.
Civics and Political Systems; History - World
Dist - FI **Prod** - BBCTV 1977

Stubborn Hope 28 MIN
VHS / 16mm
Color (C)
$500.00, $280.00 purchase, $55.00 rental
Presents a film by Peggy Stern. Portrays Dennis Brutus, exiled South African poet, after he gained political asylum in the United States.
Civics and Political Systems; Geography - World; History - World; Literature and Drama; Sociology
Dist - ICARUS

Stuck on Cactus 29 MIN
U-matic
House Botanist Series
Color
Examines the Christmas cactus and lesser known varieties.
Agriculture; Science - Natural
Dist - UMITV **Prod** - UMITV 1978

Stuck on quality - customer focus by employee empowerment 25 MIN
VHS / U-matic / BETA
Color (COR)
$870.00 purchase, $240.00 rental
Shows how to build a dynamic quality program involving every level of staff. Demonstrates to managers how to set up flexible criteria that allow for individual action and happier customers.
Business and Economics
Dist - VIDART **Prod** - VIDART

Stuck on quality - how to achieve total quality 26 MIN
VHS
Color (COR)
Uses humor and drama to discuss the merits of employee empowerment - involvement in management decisions.

Business and Economics; Guidance and Counseling
Dist - VIDART **Prod** - VIDART 1990

Stuckgut 90 MIN
16mm
Color (GERMAN (ENGLISH SUBTITLES))
Tells the story of a 49 - year - old truck driver who loses his license because of drunken driving. Details his unsuccessful search for employment as he discovers his age is a disadvantage. He does not give up, and with the help of friends, finds a steady job.
Fine Arts
Dist - WSTGLC **Prod** - WSTGLC 1981

The Stud farm 100 MIN
16mm
Color (HUNGARIAN (ENGLISH SUBTITLES))
Focuses on the workers at a Hungarian horse - breeding farm during the early 1950's. Directed by Andras Kovacs. With English subtitles.
Fine Arts; Foreign Language
Dist - NYFLMS **Prod** - UNKNWN 1978

The Student 29 MIN
Videoreel / VT2
Discover Flying - Just Like a Bird Series
Color
Industrial and Technical Education; Social Science
Dist - PBS **Prod** - WKYCTV

The Student and the client 67 MIN
U-matic / VHS
Core skills for field instructors series; Program 2
Color (C T)
LC 83-706439
Focuses on how a field instructor can help the practicum student develop the skills for 'tuning in' to the client, responding directly to indirect client clues and contracting with the client.
Education; Sociology
Dist - MCGILU **Prod** - MCGILU 1983

The Student and variable modular scheduling 23 MIN
16mm
Color (H C T A)
LC 78-710819
Shows appropriate student behavior in small group discussions, large group presentations and unscheduled time activities. Examines the possible pitfalls for the student in a variable modular schedule. Relates these experiences to non - school situations and varied learning opportunities.
Education; Guidance and Counseling
Dist - EDUC **Prod** - EDUC 1970

The Student - applications 7 MIN
VHS
Foundations and applications of distance education series
Color (T G)
$50.00 purchase
Examines the skills needed for successful distance learning. Part of a series on distance education.
Education
Dist - AECT **Prod** - IODIED 1995

The Student as Interviewer 53 MIN
VHS / U-matic
Process - Centered Composition Series
Color (T)
LC 79-706301
Shows how interviewing is learned and used by students as they keep journals and write papers.
English Language
Dist - IU **Prod** - IU 1977

The Student as Teacher 28 MIN
16mm
Color (T)
Discusses student roles in the educational process, emphasizing the involvement of students in teaching capacities.
Education
Dist - EDUC **Prod** - EDUC

Student assistance program 20 MIN
U-matic / VHS
Color (G)
$149.00 purchase _ #7435
Reveals that American youth has the highest level of illicit drug use of any industrialized country in the world. Offers alternatives for those abusing drugs and discusses drug abuse prevention. Answers questions about drug abuse problems in the early 1990s, including statistics and figures showing how large the problem has become. Provides suggestions for setting up support groups and discusses open - door policies with counselors and seeking outside drug treatment.
Education; Guidance and Counseling; Health and Safety; Psychology; Sociology
Dist - VISIVI **Prod** - VISIVI 1991

Student - athlete recruitment series
VHS
Student - athlete recruitment series
Color (H T)
$54.95 purchase _ #CSP300SV-P
Provides two videos that guide student athletes through the college recruitment process, as coaches and admissions personnel explain details of NCAA eligibility, financial aid, scholarships, and more. Comes with separate videos for male and female high school athletes. Recommends viewing by coaches, players, parents, and guidance counselors.
Physical Education and Recreation
Dist - CAMV

Student - athlete recruitment series
Student - athlete recruitment series
Dist - CAMV

Student Court - Edited Version 28 MIN
VHS / 16mm
Color (I)
$530.00, $295.00 purchase
Tells the story of Jessica, a high school girl taken before Student Court for shoplifting. Reveals that she refuses to cooperate at first, then breaks down and faces her problems when other students share their own fears and failures.
Business and Economics; Guidance and Counseling; Psychology; Religion and Philosophy; Sociology
Dist - LUF **Prod** - LUF 1987

Student - directed curriculum - an alternative educational approach 21 MIN
16mm
Color (H C A T)
LC 72-701995
Focuses on the perception of inner - city students on how education can satisfy their concerns. Shows the strategies taken by the institute for the advancement of urban education in identifying the problems at an inner city high school and in setting up a pilot program that incorporated all the elements of an alternative educational approach.
Education; Sociology
Dist - EDUC **Prod** - EDUC 1971

Student evaluation 11 MIN
VHS / 16mm
Junior high health and personal life skills in - service series
Color (C T)
$175.00, $225.00 purchase _ #271806
Orients teachers to the revised 1986 Junior High Health and Personal Life Skills Curriculum. Introduces a change of emphasis in both content and teaching strategies. Knowledge of the human body is superseded by knowledge, attitudes, skills and lifelong behavior for healthy lifestyles. 'Evaluation' provides an overview of various student evaluation strategies that have been effective in teaching the Health and Personal Life Skills Curriculum.
Education; Guidance and Counseling; Health and Safety; Psychology
Dist - ACCESS **Prod** - ACCESS 1986

A Student involvement program for developing values 29 MIN
U-matic / VHS
Successful teaching practices series
Color (A C T)
$75.00 purchase _ #1485
Points out how values clarification, student involvement in a variety of projects, and interaction with community groups contribute to student self - esteem and the welfare of the community.
Education; Guidance and Counseling; Psychology
Dist - EBEC

Student Know - How 30 MIN
VHS / U-matic / BETA
Student Know - How Series
Color; Stereo (H)
Presents comedy quiz shows used to teach study, speaking and writing skills. Includes workshop material for each program.
Education; English Language
Dist - SEVDIM **Prod** - SEVDIM 1985

Student Know - How Series

Get it Write	10 MIN
Say it with words	10 MIN
Student Know - How	30 MIN
Study is not a Dirty Word	10 MIN

Dist - SEVDIM

Student Needs - an Instructional Approach 28 MIN
U-matic / VHS
Helping Adults Learn Series
Color (C G T A)
Demonstrates how some tutors and teachers incorporate their students' day to day needs into a curriculum. It is the theory of the program that, when adult learners can see the practical results of learning, it gives them a way to gauge their educational accomplishments and inspires them to learn more.
Education
Dist - PSU **Prod** - PSU 1987

Student Nurse 30 MIN
U-matic / VHS / 16mm
B&W (A)
Shows the experiences of a student nurse, from her first day of training to the end of the first year, and her classes in such fields as physiology, biology, medicine and psychology.
Guidance and Counseling; Health and Safety; Psychology
Dist - IFB **Prod** - NFBC 1958

The Student prince 29 MIN
VHS / 16mm
Watch your mouth series
Color (H)
$46.00 rental _ #WAYM - 103
Emphasizes language and communication skills for high school students. Notes the difference between formal and informal word usage.
Education; English Language; Psychology; Social Science
Dist - PBS

Student protest in China - May 5, 1989
VHS
Nightline news library series
Color (J H C)
$19.98 purchase _ #MH6174V - S
Overviews the student protest in China in 1989 in a news story by the ABC News Team. Part of a series from the news program, Nightline.
History - World
Dist - CAMV **Prod** - ABCNEW 1989

Student reflections on social work field training 59 MIN
U-matic / VHS
Color
Consists of instructors and a group of graduate students from the Walter Reed Army Medical Center discussing their definition of social work and their reasons for entering the social work profession. Discusses the differences between social work and other mental health service delivery professions.
Sociology
Dist - UWISC **Prod** - WRAMC 1979

Student self - concept and standards 27 MIN
VHS / U-matic
Successful teaching practices series
Color (C A T)
$75.00 purchase _ #1484
Shows how Joe Michel, a teacher with Richfield Senior High School, Richfield, Minnesota, contributes to student self - concept through techniques such as establishing high standards, encouraging inquisitive learning, and teaching in a humanistic manner.
Education; Psychology
Dist - EBEC

Student services in higher education 33 MIN
U-matic / VHS
Color (C A T)
Presents a panel discussion on higher education counseling issues. Increasing their client base and use of outreach programs helps counselors to improve services. Effective for in - service training programs and for students near completion of their curricula. A user's guide is included.
Education
Dist - AACD **Prod** - AACD 1984

Student Stress - Coping with Academic Pressures
VHS
$149.00 purchase _ #HR815V
Discusses the increase in stress symptoms among young people for the last 15 years. Talks about the physiological nature of stress. Points out specific causes of stress through interviews with students. Illustrates some stress reduction techniques and provides tips for dealing with a variety of stressful situations.
Psychology
Dist - CAREER **Prod** - CAREER

Student stress - coping with academic pressures - dealing with the causes 21 MIN
16mm / VHS
Color (J H C A PRO T)
$195.00, $475.00 purchase, $75.00 rental _ #8159
Interviews students to discover factors of student stress. Presents practical strategies and outlines specific coping mechanisms that can improve student life.

Guidance and Counseling; Psychology
Dist - AIMS **Prod** - HRMC 1990

Student to staff nurse - bridging the gap 120 MIN
U-matic / VHS
Color (PRO)
Describes a preceptorship program designed to help bridge the gap between the nursing student role and the new staff nurse role. Discusses college - hospital collaboration and joint planning, the structure of the program, the roles of participants, the evaluation process and implications of the model for nursing.
Health and Safety
Dist - AJN **Prod** - OHCO

Student workshop: Conflict resolution skills 35 MIN
VHS
Color (I J)
$199 purchase No. 2435-YZ
Teaches students grades 5-9 in workshop format six basic skills of conflict resolution. Provides practice in these skills through discussion questions, role plays. Includes 35-minute video, 20 handouts, teachers guide in three-ring binder.
Education; Psychology
Dist - SUNCOM **Prod** - SUNCOM

Student Workshop Videotapes Series
Art for Whom 8 MIN
Straight Jacket 8 MIN
Sur - face 13 MIN
Dist - WMENIF

Students as their Own Editors 40 MIN
VHS / U-matic
Process - Centered Composition Series
Color (T)
LC 79-706300
Presents a system of teaching students how to edit their own and other's work.
English Language
Dist - IU **Prod** - IU 1977

Students evaluate their own generalizations 22 MIN
16mm
B&W (P I T)
Shows a teaching strategy for developing children's thinking.
Education; Psychology
Dist - AWPC **Prod** - AWPC 1968

The Students' guide to getting into college 48 MIN
VHS
Color (H C G)
$39.95 purchase _ #KNO100V
Helps students to navigate the college admission process. Features Harvard students discussing their experiences in choosing a college and gaining admission to the college of their choice. Discusses each aspect of the admissions process - interviews, how to write personal essays that work, how to deal with parental pressure.
Education
Dist - CAMV

A Student's Guide to IIS Coursewriter
U-matic / VHS
Authoring in IIS Coursewriter Series
Color
Portrays the steps used by a student signing on to the coursewriter authoring course and illustrates the various keywords that are used to request information or to switch topics.
Industrial and Technical Education; Psychology
Dist - DELTAK **Prod** - DELTAK

The Student's impact on the agency system 44 MIN
U-matic / VHS
Core skills for field instructors series; Program 4
Color (C T)
LC 83-706441
Focuses on how to help students deal with questions and concerns about agency policy and procedures which emerge during the course of the school year. Discusses ways in which field instructors can help students assess their role in the system, develop formal and informal means for influencing policy or procedures and communicate effectively with other staff.
Education; Sociology
Dist - MCGILU **Prod** - MCGILU 1983

Students' rights - focus on the First Amendment 20 MIN
VHS
Color (J H C T A)
$81.00 purchase _ #MB - 540342 - 0
Covers the controversy over First Amendment rights as they affect students. Discusses the Supreme Court's Hazelwoodf v Kuhlmeier decision, which held that students' First Amendment rights could be restricted. Includes activities package.
Civics and Political Systems
Dist - SRA **Prod** - SRA 1989

Students track the space age 6 MIN
16mm
Screen news digest series; Vol 6; Issue 7
B&W (J A)
LC FIA68-2078
Presents a group of students who have collected, repaired and modernized more than a million dollars in surplus and obsolete military tracking equipment and who can evesdrop on actual exchanges between the Cape Kennedy control center and American astronauts in orbit.
History - United States
Dist - HEARST **Prod** - HEARST 1964

Students - your choice
VHS / Cassette
(J H)
$95.00, $10.00 purchase
Encourages students to exercise inner strength in resisting peer pressure.
Education; Guidance and Counseling; Health and Safety; Psychology
Dist - KELLYP **Prod** - KELLYP

Studiel 2.5 MIN
16mm
Color (C)
$112.00
Experimental film by Michael Zodorozny.
Fine Arts
Dist - AFA **Prod** - AFA 1978

Studies in aging 19 MIN
U-matic / VHS
Color (G C PRO)
$249.00, $149.00 purchase _ #AD - 1439
Reports on current research to determine the effects of aging. Profiles a 74 - year - old father and his son, 38. Features the community of Roseto, Pennsylvania, a landmark study in aging begun in 1964.
Health and Safety; Sociology
Dist - FOTH **Prod** - FOTH

Studies in bacteriology - Pt 2, motility 4 MIN
16mm
B&W
LC FIE63-633
Uses cinephotomicrography to show the motility of monotrichous, amphitrichous and peritrichous bacteria.
Health and Safety; Science - Natural
Dist - USNAC **Prod** - USPHS 1953

Studies in bacteriology - Pt 3, cell division 4 MIN
16mm
B&W
LC FIE53-664
Uses cinephotomicrography to show the process of cell division of spherical and rod - shaped bacteria.
Health and Safety; Science - Natural
Dist - USNAC **Prod** - USPHS 1953

Studies in chronovision 22 MIN
16mm
Color (G)
$50.00 rental
Investigates temporal composition via single frame - time lapse techniques. Covers film sketches constructed over a period of five years. Produced by Louis Hock.
Fine Arts
Dist - CANCIN

Studies in Interviewing Series
Aid To Families With Dependent Children intake interview - Teal - Justin 72 MIN
Unmarried Mother Interview - Peters - Browning 68 MIN
Unmarried mother interview - Peters - Browning - Pt 1 17 MIN
Unmarried mother interview - Peters - Browning - Pt 2 17 MIN
Unmarried mother interview - Peters - Browning - Pt 3 17 MIN
Unmarried mother interview - Peters - Browning - Pt 4 17 MIN
Dist - USC

Studies in Meteorology 15 MIN
16mm
Science in Action Series
Color (C)
Presents the efforts to decrease the destructive wind velocity of hurricanes, examine physics of clouds and regulate snow and hail formation.
Science - Physical
Dist - COUNFI **Prod** - ALLFP

Studies in movement design 10 MIN
16mm
Creative dance for children series
B&W
Shows Barbara Mettler teaching a group of boys and girls at the Creative Dance Center in 1966.
Fine Arts
Dist - METT **Prod** - METT 1977

Studies of normal personality development - a series
Studies of normal personality development - a series
B&W (C)
Presents studies on normal childhood personality development. Abby's First Two Years - A Backward Look; And Then Ice Cream; Ballons - Aggression And Destruction Games; Finger Painting; Frustration Play Techniques; Incitement To Reading; Learning Is Searching - A Third Grade Studies; Long Time To Grow, Pt 1 - Two - And - - ; Long Time To Grow, Pt 2 - Four - And Five - Year - - ; Long Time To Grow, Pt 3 - Six - , Seven - And - - ; Meeting Emotional Needs In Childhood; Pay Attention - Problems Of Hard Of - - ; Starting Nursery School - Patterns Of - - ; This Is Robert - A Study Of Personality; Understanding Children's Play; When Should Grownups Help; When.
Psychology
Dist - NYU **Prod** - NYU

Studies of normal personality development - a series
Studies of normal personality development - a series
Dist - NYU

Studies of Normal Personality Development Series
Abby's first two years - a backward look 30 MIN
And Then Ice Cream 11 MIN
Balloons - aggression and destruction games 17 MIN
Finger Painting 22 MIN
Frustration Play Techniques 35 MIN
Incitement to reading 37 MIN
Learning is Searching - a Third Grade Studies Man's Early Tools 30 MIN
Long time to grow, Pt 1 - two - and three - year - olds in nursery school 35 MIN
Long Time to Grow, Pt 3 - Six - , Seven - and Eight - Year - Olds - Society of Children 30 MIN
Long Time to Grow, Pt 2 - Four and Five Year Olds in School 40 MIN
Meeting Emotional Needs in Childhood - Groundwork of Democracy 33 MIN
Pay Attention - Problems of Hard of Hearing Children 29 MIN
Starting Nursery School - Patterns of Beginning 23 MIN
This is Robert 45 MIN
Understanding children's play 12 MIN
When Should Grownups Help 14 MIN
When Should Grownups Stop Fights 15 MIN
Dist - NYU

The Studio 30 MIN
U-matic / VHS
Photographic Vision - all about Photography Series
Color
Industrial and Technical Education
Dist - CDTEL **Prod** - COAST

The Studio 29 MIN
VHS
Photographic vision series
Color (G)
$49.95 purchase _ #RM112V-F
Shows how to achieve special effects with light. Presents the technical aspects of photography clearly and simply, including principles of the camera and techniques for controlling exposure, the use of various kinds of lighting, selection of appropriate lenses and film and basic darkroom techniques. Focuses on the world of photographers and photography - its history and evolution, its uses for personal development and expression, and the impact of photography on the world. Part of a 20-part series examining all aspects of the field of photography.
Industrial and Technical Education
Dist - CAMV

The Studio 90 MIN
VHS
On assignment - the video guide for photography series
Color (J H C G)
$29.95 purchase _ #MED106V VHS
Offers practical ideas on how to layout and equip a photographic studio. Part of an eight - part series hosted by nationally known photographer Brian D Ratty.

Industrial and Technical Education
Dist - CAMV

Studio lighting 30 MIN
VHS
Color (H C)
$39.95 purchase _ #600110
Covers a wide range of lighting situations, such as lighting the female and minority executives with darker skin hues, lighting speakers who are working with a slide projector, as well as the balding CEO with eyeglasses.
Business and Economics; Industrial and Technical Education
Dist - INSTRU

Studio M Series

Addition and subtraction facts of 13 and 14	15 MIN
Addition and subtraction facts of 15 and 16	15 MIN
Addition and subtraction facts of 17 and 18	15 MIN
Addition and subtraction facts through 11 and 12	15 MIN
Addition with 2 - 3 digit numbers	15 MIN
Compare and order numbers	15 MIN
Division, Pt 1	15 MIN
Division, Pt 2	15 MIN
Estimating Time to the Nearest One - Minute Interval	15 MIN
Estimation	15 MIN
Fractions, Pt 1 - Studio M	15 MIN
Fractions, Pt 2 - Studio M	15 MIN
Geometry - Three - Dimensional Shapes	15 MIN
Geometry - Two - Dimensional Shapes	15 MIN
Greater than, less than	15 MIN
Liquid volume	15 MIN
Money, Pt 1	15 MIN
Money, Pt 2	15 MIN
Multiplication, Pt 1	15 MIN
Multiplication, Pt 2	15 MIN
Numeration to 999	15 MIN
Odd and Even	15 MIN
Review of Previews - 31 Lessons	15 MIN
Story Problems	15 MIN
Story Problems with the Four Operations	15 MIN
Subtraction - Two - Digit Regrouping	15 MIN
Subtraction Regrouping - Story Problems	15 MIN
Time - Five Minutes	15 MIN
Value of Digits	15 MIN

Dist - GPN

Studio - on - a - budget's guide to home recording 60 MIN
VHS
Color (G)
$119.00 purchase, $39.00 rental _ #604
Introduces basic recording vocabulary and provides instruction in sound - on - sound recording, 4 - track recording and mixing, bouncing tracks, MIDI sequencing. Includes charts, graphics and examples to show how to hook up equipment and plan for recording sesssions. Features Curt Miller as instructor and producer.
Fine Arts
Dist - FIRLIT

Studio seconds - the assistant sound engineer video 80 MIN
VHS
Color (G C)
$179.00 purchase _ #771P
Uses dramatizations and graphics to portray the duties of an assistant engineer before, during and after a recording session. Emphasizes the importance of 'people skills' in booking sessions, handling prospective clients, dealing efficiently with scheduling and billing, and handling client problems with grace and tact. Includes detailed skill modules on tape editing and storage, time code and tape recorder head alignment and a 150 page Assistant Engineer's Handbook. Features sound engineer Tom Lubin. Produced by the Australian Film, Television and Radio School.
Fine Arts; Industrial and Technical Education
Dist - FIRLIT

Studio see series
Uses a television magazine format to introduce children to a wide variety of adventures. Includes activities in art, hobbies, sports and nature. Consists of four programs.
Studio see series
Dist - SCETV **Prod** - SCETV 1991

Studio shortcuts 1 - graphic and production tricks 53 MIN
VHS
Graphic specialties series
Color (J H C G)
$39.95 purchase _ #GFG2060V
Reveals contemporary production tips and tricks used by experienced and innovative graphic professionals. Demonstrates time and money - saving procedures in a variety of projects showcasing processes, tools and techniques. Part of a four - part series on graphic specialties.
Industrial and Technical Education
Dist - CAMV

The Studmill Story 15 MIN
16mm
Color
Looks at the operations of studmills, which convert logs into the 2x4 'studs' that frame homes and buildings.
Agriculture; Social Science
Dist - GPN **Prod** - REGIS

Studs Lonigan 95 MIN
VHS
B&W (H C)
$39.00 purchase _ #04556 - 126
Stars Christopher Knight and Frank Gorshin in a rambling tale about the life and loves of a young drifter on Chicago's southside in the 1920s. Adapted from a story by James Farrell.
History - United States; Literature and Drama
Dist - GA **Prod** - GA

Studs Terkel's Chicago 25 MIN
16mm / U-matic / VHS
Cities Series
Color (H C A)
LC 80-701160
Presents author and television personality Studs Terkel on a tour of the city of Chicago.
Geography - United States; Sociology
Dist - LCOA **Prod** - NIELSE 1980

Study and Work Habits
U-matic / VHS
Study Skills Video Series
$98.00 purchase _ #VP004V
Gives specific study skills and shows how these skills apply to successful work habits.
Education
Dist - CAREER **Prod** - CAREER

Study and Work Habits
U-matic / VHS
Study Skills and Job Success Video Series
(J H T)
$98.00 _ #CD820V
Discusses specific study skills in pointing out the relation of school and work habits. Includes ideas on time management, listening, notetaking, handling pressure and others.
Education; Guidance and Counseling
Dist - CAMV **Prod** - CAMV

Study from life 32 MIN
16mm
Color
Explains why and illustrates how live animals are used in medical research. Demonstrates the value of animals in VA'S Research Program. Stresses the humane procedures employed by VA researchers in handling animals.
Science
Dist - USVA **Prod** - USVA 1963

Study from life - Pt 1 - laboratory animals in laboratory research 32 MIN
16mm
Animal care series
Color
LC FIE65-96
Depicts the personal responsibility of the researcher in the care and use of laboratory animals in medical research. Tells of the development of the artificial heart pacemaker. For hospital personnel and associated community groups.
Health and Safety; Science
Dist - USNAC **Prod** - USVA 1963

The Study game 90 MIN
VHS
Color (H)
$69.00 purchase _ #60496 - 027
Features role models such as Chris Evert, Joe Montana, Magic Johnson and Wayne Gretzky covering the fundamentals of note - taking, good and bad homework techniques, the importance of asking questions, test - taking strategies, time management and more. Explains how preparation affects attitude and performance. Includes student playbook, daily planner, game plan and teacher's guide.
Education; Psychology
Dist - GA

The Study game - 30 ways to better grades - college version 60 MIN
VHS
Study game series
Color (C)
$114.95 purchase _ #SC104V
Teaches students thirty ways to improve their grades. Presents each lesson in a concise and interesting format, using Chris Evert, Wayne Gretzky, Joe Montana and Magic Johnson. Includes study guide and teacher's guide.
Education; Psychology
Dist - CAMV

The Study game - 30 ways to better grades - high school version 60 MIN
VHS
Study game series
Color (H)
$114.95 purchase _ #SC101V
Teaches students thirty ways to improve their grades. Presents each lesson in a concise and interesting format, using Chris Evert, Wayne Gretzky, Joe Montana and Magic Johnson. Includes study guide and teacher's guide.
Education; Psychology
Dist - CAMV

The Study game - 30 ways to better grades - junior high version 60 MIN
VHS
Study game series
Color (J)
$114.95 purchase _ #SC103V
Teaches students thirty ways to improve their grades. Presents each lesson in a concise and interesting format, using Chris Evert, Wayne Gretzky, Joe Montana and Magic Johnson. Includes study guide and teacher's guide.
Education; Psychology
Dist - CAMV

Study game series

The Study game - 30 ways to better grades - college version	60 MIN
The Study game - 30 ways to better grades - high school version	60 MIN
The Study game - 30 ways to better grades - junior high version	60 MIN

Dist - CAMV

Study Guide II - a Videodisc Utility
Videodisc
(T G)
$59.00 purchase _ #VID5511 - 5
Allows up to 200 multiple - choice, completion, true - false or matching questions to be written and includes feedback. Allows still frames or video segments to be matched to each question. Requires an Apple IIe, IIc, or IIGS computer, a Pioneer videodisc player in the LD - V6000 or LD - 4200 series and an Apple Super Serial Card.
Computer Science; Education
Dist - MECC **Prod** - MECC

Study in A and vibrato technique 29 MIN
Videoreel / VT2
Playing the guitar II series
Color
Fine Arts
Dist - PBS **Prod** - KCET

A Study in choreography for the camera 4 MIN
16mm
B&W (C)
Experimental film by Maya Daren.
Fine Arts
Dist - AFA **Prod** - AFA 1945
GROVE

Study in Color Series

Boy - an Experience in the Search for Identity	12 MIN
The Job	29 MIN

Dist - ADL

A Study in Development 10 MIN
16mm
Color
Covers a seminar on development held in Kuala Lumpur. Shows participants in the seminar, who came from various Asian countries, touring some development projects in Malaysia to observe hand development implementation in the country.
Geography - World; Social Science
Dist - PMFMUN **Prod** - FILEM 1970

Study in diachronic motion 3 MIN
16mm
Color (G)
$15.00 rental
Experiments in the simultaneous presentation of an action from several different perspectives in time in a Peter Rose production.
Fine Arts; Psychology; Science - Physical
Dist - CANCIN

Study in Human Development - Pt 1, Six to Thirty Weeks 19 MIN
16mm
B&W (C T)
Shows the reactions of a boy to objects at ages of six, 12, 17, 21, 25 and 30 weeks. Demonstrates supine, prone and sitting postures at 21 weeks, rolling from back to stomach and early patterns of crawling and feeding. Depicts the development of manipulation, the response to soundmaking objects and improvements in postural and locomotor activities at ages between 25 and 30 weeks.
Psychology
Dist - PSUPCR **Prod** - PSUPCR 1946

Study in Human Development - Pt 2, Forty - Two Weeks to Fifteen Months 17 MIN
16mm
B&W (C T)
Pictures a child's development at 42 weeks, 12 and 15 months of age. Emphasizes gross motor development and perceptual - manipulatory reactions to objects including a cup, spoon, bell, hoop, ball and mirror. Shows that child pulls up, stands, crawls, mounts stairs and exhibits walking readiness. At age one tests are given for fine manipulation, imitation and stair climbing. The development of motor skills is further demonstrated at 15 months and interaction with another child is described.
Psychology
Dist - PSUPCR **Prod** - PSUPCR 1946

Study in Human Development - Pt 3, Nineteen Months to Two Years and Eight Months 19 MIN
16mm
B&W (C T)
Emphasizes the child's continued gross and fine development and the beginnings of cooperative play. Shows, at 19 months, imitating building a block tower, drinking by holding a glass with both hands, throwing a ball, exhibiting handedness and playing non - cooperatively. At two years, the boy walks up stairs but hesitates in descending, marks on paper without making patterns but still plays individualistically. At 32 months, the child plays more cooperatively and uses a wide variety of toys and play equipment.
Psychology
Dist - PSUPCR **Prod** - PSUPCR 1946

Study in Human Development - Pt 4, Three Years to Five Years 18 MIN
16mm
B&W (C T)
Demonstrates the child's development of skill in drawing and typical motor coordination at three years, Depicts the improvement in coordination, ability in drawing and rudimentary musical skill. Performance tests for intelligence are applied at four years.
Psychology
Dist - PSUPCR **Prod** - PSUPCR 1948

A Study in Maternal Attitudes 30 MIN
16mm
B&W
Describes a project whose purpose is to make the study and treatment of the emotional life of children and mothers an integral part of pediatrics and child health supervision.
Health and Safety; Home Economics; Psychology; Sociology
Dist - NYU **Prod** - NYU

A Study in Paper 5 MIN
U-matic / VHS / 16mm
B&W (H C)
LC FIA66-767
Uses puppet - like figures that tear themselves from newspapers and move about to show that a simple design can be used to develop a theme without using words. Depicts the theme of war versus peace.
Fine Arts
Dist - IFB **Prod** - HOLMAN 1966

Study in Wet 7 MIN
U-matic / VHS / 16mm
Color (H A)
LC FIA65-461
Uses water as a disciplined instrument to create a musical event and relates it to spectacular film scenes.
Fine Arts
Dist - AIMS **Prod** - GROENG 1966

Study is not a Dirty Word 10 MIN
VHS / U-matic / BETA
Student Know - How Series
Color; Stereo (H)
Presents a guide to effective and efficient study techniques.
Education; English Language
Dist - SEVDIM **Prod** - SEVDIM 1985

Study no 10 4 MIN
16mm
B&W (G)
$16.50 rental
Portrays a collaboration between filmmaker and his brother, Hans Fischinger. Combines styles of both artists.
Fine Arts
Dist - CANCIN **Prod** - FISCHF 1932

Study no 11 4 MIN
16mm
B&W (G)
$16.50 rental
Consists of Mozart's Eine Kleine Nachtmusik which provides a backdrop for spatial movements.
Fine Arts
Dist - CANCIN **Prod** - FISCHF 1932

Study no 12 4 MIN
16mm
B&W (G)
$16.50 rental
Conjures up eel - like figures moving slowly to the Torch Dance from Rubinstein's Bride of Corinth.
Fine Arts
Dist - CANCIN **Prod** - FISCHF 1932

Study no 15 1 MIN
16mm / VHS
Films for music for film series
B&W (G)
$25.00, $60.00 rental
Presents one of a series of films by Lawrence Brose that reconsider the interactive dynamic of sound and image in film. Offers a study in light based on a musical composition of the same name by Conlon Nancarrow who lived in exile in Mexico City. Finding no musicians able to play his difficult compositions, he acquired a player piano roll punching machine and began composing for the player piano.
Fine Arts
Dist - CANCIN

Study no 5 3 MIN
16mm
B&W (G)
$16.50 rental
Transforms a fox trot into an abstract ballet, in which two levels of dancers flow past and through each other. Features popular song I've Never Seen A Smile Like Yours. The dancers are extremely fluid plastic figures which constantly change their consistency and size.
Fine Arts
Dist - CANCIN **Prod** - FISCHF 1930

Study no 6 2 MIN
16mm / VHS
B&W (G)
$16.50 rental
Presents a black and white study with an upbeat mood. Reveals filmmaker's profound mystical imagery. Fandango music, Los Verderones, by Jacinto Guerrero.
Fine Arts
Dist - CANCIN **Prod** - FISCHF 1930

Study no 7 3 MIN
16mm
B&W (G)
$16.50 rental
Provides first complete exploration of absolute darkness as a spacial concept. Features Brahm's Hungarian Dance no 5 which becomes a vehicle for the optical experiments.
Fine Arts
Dist - CANCIN **Prod** - FISCHF 1931

Study no 8 4 MIN
16mm
B&W (G)
$16.50 rental
Captures the essence of filmmaker's complex and stunning black and white studies. Integrates textures and movements of Dukas' The Sorcerer's Apprentice by using the sounds as a jumping off point for a myriad of forms and movements.
Fine Arts
Dist - CANCIN **Prod** - FISCHF 1931

Study no 9 3 MIN
16mm
B&W (G)
$16.50 rental
Interprets Brahms' Hungarian Dance No 6 by synchronizing images of graceful figures dancing.
Fine Arts
Dist - CANCIN **Prod** - FISCHF 1931

A Study of Crystals 17 MIN
16mm / U-matic / VHS
Color (H A)
Shows the crystallization of many compounds through microphotography. Illustrates fusion methods in chemical research by Dr Walter Mc Crone whose studies in crystallography and microscopy are internationally known.
Science; Science - Physical
Dist - JOU **Prod** - JOU 1961

Study of Equivalent and Nonequivalent Stimuli in the Rat 18 MIN
16mm
B&W (C T)
Shows animals which are trained, using the Lashley jumping technique, to respond to the smaller of two black circular areas in a gray background. Depicts the animals being tested to determine the preferences for patterns which differ partially from the original stimuli, in order to discover the attributes of the original pattern which determined the animal's choices. Illustrates Kluever's concept of equivalent stimuli and its relation to the study of perception and transfer of training animals.
Psychology; Science - Natural
Dist - PSUPCR **Prod** - PSUPCR 1937

A Study of Esterification 20 MIN
U-matic / VHS
Experiment - Chemistry Series
Color (C)
$249.00, $149.00 purchase _ #AD - 1069
Illustrates the relationship between the kinetic extent of reaction and the maximum extent of reaction governed by chemical equilibrium in a reaction between an alcohol and an acid. Part of a series on experiments in chemistry.
Education; Psychology; Science; Science - Physical
Dist - FOTH **Prod** - FOTH

Study of Grain Growth in Berylium Oxide using a New Transmitted Light Hot Stage 16 MIN
16mm
Color
LC FIE56-212
Depicts the design and operation of a new hot stage used with a polarizing microscope and transmitted light. Examines time - dependent reactions and structural changes in transparent crystalline materials at temperatures as high as 2,000 oC in vacuum.
Science - Physical
Dist - USNAC **Prod** - USNRC

Study of rocks 49 MIN
VHS / U-matic
Basic and petroleum geology for non - geologists series
Color (IND)
Industrial and Technical Education; Science - Physical
Dist - GPCV **Prod** - PHILLP

A Study of rules and their effects on our everyday life with third - year pupils in a boys' school - Unit H 38 MIN
VHS
Religious education in secondary schools series
Color; PAL (T)
PdS35.00 purchase
Presents religious education in ways which are relevant to pupils in mixed - ability classes. Demonstrates a variety of approaches used by four teachers in very different situations. Part of an eight - part series.
Education; Religion and Philosophy
Dist - EMFVL

The Study of the higher - dimensional Poincare Conjecture - what actually happened on the beaches of Rio de Janeiro by Stephen Smale 60 MIN
VHS
AMS - MAA joint lecture series
Color (PRO G)
$59.00 purchase _ #VIDSMALE - VB2
Presents a personal account of the events surrounding Smale's famous proof of the Poincare Conjecture for dimensions greater than 4. Begins with a statement of the conjecture to provide topological and geometric insight into some of the basic ideas of the proof. Discusses the involvement of Smale in the Free Speech Movement and his subpoena by the House Un - American Activities Committee and the withholding of grant funds from the National Science Foundation. Describes the controversy resulting from his claim as originator of the proof of the conjecture and how politics can affect science policy. Recorded in Phoenix.
Civics and Political Systems; History - United States; Mathematics; Science
Dist - AMSOC **Prod** - AMSOC 1989

A Study of the USSR 30 MIN
16mm
B&W
Explores the Soviet Union in depth tracing its history, expansion, culture, philosophy and advancement in science and education.
Civics and Political Systems; Geography - World; History - World
Dist - USNAC **Prod** - USDD

Study of Things which Influence Behavior 29 MIN
16mm
Controlling Turnover and Absenteeism Series
B&W
LC 76-703321
Business and Economics; Psychology
Dist - EDSD **Prod** - EDSD

Study of twins - Pt 1 17 MIN
16mm
B&W (C)
Presents the growth and development of identical twin boys. Deals primarily with responses to everyday, informal situations and stresses the differences between the developing twins. Illustrates motor growth at 14, 22, 28 and 40 weeks, especially the differences in rate of development among various parts of the body. Emphasizes the cephalocaudal pattern.
Psychology; Science - Natural
Dist - PSUPCR **Prod** - PSUPCR 1947

Study of twins - Pt 2 17 MIN
16mm
B&W (C)
Shows identical twins at 12, 15, 18 and 21 months. Demonstrates the getting up, standing and walking stages. Shows the amount of independent and cooperative play.
Psychology; Science - Natural
Dist - PSUPCR **Prod** - PSUPCR 1947

Study of twins - Pt 3 18 MIN
16mm
B&W (C)
Records the behavior of identical twins at 24, 28 and 32 months. Shows amicable but independent play and the rapidity of development of motor skills and of larger muscles.
Psychology; Science - Natural
Dist - PSUPCR **Prod** - PSUPCR 1949

Study of twins - Pt 4 19 MIN
16mm
B&W (C)
Records the behavior of identical twins at three, four and five years. Illustrates increasingly cooperative play and improved muscular coordination. Shows ultimate self - sufficiency in such activities as eating, washing teeth and playing.
Psychology; Science - Natural
Dist - PSUPCR **Prod** - PSUPCR 1951

Study of young children's strength - push, pull, twist and squeeze 15 MIN
16mm
Color (H C A)
LC 74-700155
Depicts research methods and equipment used by bureau scientists in determining what forces children are capable of exerting when pushing, pulling, twisting and squeezing.
Psychology; Science - Physical
Dist - USNBOS **Prod** - USNBOS 1973

Study preparation for school success
VHS
Video keys to school success series
Color (H C A)
$98.00 purchase _ #CD8003V
Tells the humorous story of Imma Disaster as her efforts at studying are constantly sidetracked by distractions - including phone calls, trips to the market, television shows, and more. Explains and demonstrates effective study techniques.
Education
Dist - CAMV

Study preparation for school success
VHS
(H)
$98.00 purchase _ #KSV 300
Helps students identify and organize key factors for study. Uses travel as an analogy and shows how the traveler must be prepared. Introduces study preparation techniques. Comes with worksheets.
Education
Dist - CADESF **Prod** - CADESF 1989

Study, Research, Library Skills Series
Presents a series on the skills necessary to successfully use a library and the study and research materials a library offers.

Classification systems	20 MIN
How to Study	20 MIN
How to Take a Test	20 MIN
How to Use the Library	20 MIN
Interpreting Graphic Materials	20 MIN
Reading a Bibliography	20 MIN
Reading a Dictionary Entry	20 MIN
Understanding Footnotes	20 MIN
Using a Card Catalog	20 MIN
Using the Encyclopedia	20 MIN
Using the Parts of a Book	20 MIN
Using the Readers Guide to Periodical Literature	20 MIN
Writing a bibliograpy	20 MIN

Dist - COMEX **Prod** - COMEX 1989

Study skills activity pack 120 MIN
U-matic / VHS
(H)
Improves attitudes, study habits, and specific learning skills with this 3 to 4 week teaching unit for average and better students. Focuses on self discipline, organizational skills and time management.
Education; Guidance and Counseling
Dist - WALCHJ **Prod** - WALCHJ 1986

Study skills and job success 15 MIN
VHS / 16mm
(J H)
$98.00 _ #FM218V
Shows how the school environment is like the work environment, and how skills like learning to cooperate, meeting deadlines, planning, organizing and listening can be transferred to any work environment.
Education; Guidance and Counseling
Dist - JISTW

Study Skills and Job Success Video Series
Study and Work Habits
Why Stay in School
Dist - CAMV

Study skills exposed 22 MIN
VHS / 16mm
Color (J H G)
$275.00, $360.00 purchase
Demonstrates good study skills, learning habits, and classroom behavior appropriate for high school students.
Education
Dist - CF **Prod** - LAWRN 1991

Study skills - getting the best results 20 MIN
16mm / VHS
Study skills series
Color (I J)
$440.00, $395.00 purchase, $60.00 rental
Presents basic skills in getting the most out of studying. Teaches how to organize one's work, increase vocabulary, proofreading and re - writing skills, and incorporation of information from outside sources.
Education; English Language
Dist - HIGGIN **Prod** - HIGGIN 1987

Study skills - giving an oral report 19 MIN
16mm / VHS
Study skills series
Color (I J)
$440.00, $395.00 purchase, $60.00 rental
Follows two students, and a mother and father, as they take the preparatory steps in giving an oral report, including choosing a topic, researching the facts, organizing the information, and practicing the presentation.
Education; English Language
Dist - HIGGIN **Prod** - HIGGIN 1989

Study skills I
VHS
Color (H)
$209.00 purchase _ #S11008 - 126
Presents a three - part series on study skills. Teaches effective listening, time management, how to take essay tests. Includes teacher's guides, library kits, 21 subscriptions to Time magazine for 12 weeks, 12 weekly guides.
Business and Economics; Education
Dist - GA **Prod** - GA 1992

Study skills II
VHS
Color (H)
$209.00 purchase _ #S11030 - 126
Presents a three - part series on study skills. Shows how to take notes, how to read a textbook and how to use the library. Includes teacher's guides, library kits, 21 subscriptions to Time magazine for 12 weeks, 12 weekly guides.
Education; Social Science
Dist - GA **Prod** - GA 1992

Study skills - learning to listen and communicate effectively 38 MIN
VHS
Color (H)
$139.00 purchase _ #60280 - 025
Demonstrates the essentials of effective communication - speaking and listening. Shows three students producing a home video on energy conservation for a class project and learning how to communicate more effectively, while their classmates learn strategies for listening. Includes teacher's guide and library kit.
English Language; Social Science
Dist - GA **Prod** - GA 1992

Study skills - library skills for the information age
VHS
Color (H)
$209.00 purchase _ #60201 - 126
Introduces the resources that are available in the major areas of the library. Shows how to use the card catalog, the reference collection and indexes, and the periodical collection and indexes. Follows a group of students as they learn step - by - step procedures for organizing and planning a typical research project. In three parts. Includes teacher's guide, library kit, 25 subscriptions to Time magazine for 11 weeks, 11 weekly guides.
Education; Social Science
Dist - GA **Prod** - GA 1992

Study Skills - Note Taking and Outlining
U-matic / VHS / 16mm
Color (I)
Shows how to take the main ideas from various sources of information and write them in note form. Describes how to organize these notes in outline form and demonstrates why this can be useful, not only in evaluating the importance of information but also in aiding to turn it into a clear and concise report.
Education
Dist - HIGGIN **Prod** - HIGGIN 1984

Study Skills - Organize it
U-matic / VHS / 16mm
Color (I)
Demonstrates the concepts of organization, from basic everyday examples to those needed in classwork. Shows how organizing one's work, in its preparation as well as in its presentation, will yield a better product and simplify the process.
Education
Dist - HIGGIN **Prod** - HIGGIN 1984

Study skills plus attitude - the winning combination 32 MIN
35mm strip / VHS
Color (I J)
$189.00, $129.00 purchase _ #2213 - SK, #2212 - SK
Examines the wide variety of study skills, stressing that the right way is whatever works best for the individual student. Emphasizes the importance of having a good attitude. Presents a self - test for students to see where they are doing well and where they need to improve. Includes teacher's guide.
Education
Dist - SUNCOM **Prod** - SUNCOM

Study Skills - Reading for Information 17 MIN
16mm / VHS
Study Skills Series
Color (I J)
$375.00, $340.00 purchase, $60.00 rental
Illustrates various approaches to reading a range of materials including textbooks, fiction, magazines, newspapers, and encyclopedias. Presents the techniques of skimming, questioning, and reviewing, emphasizing the importance of an organized approach.
Education; English Language; Literature and Drama
Dist - HIGGIN **Prod** - HIGGIN 1987

Study skills series
Presents a three - part series on developing effective study skills. Covers listening, time management, and how to take essay tests. Consists of three videocassettes.

How to take essay tests	15 MIN
Study skills series	46 MIN

Dist - CAMV

Study skills series
Aids to memory - note - taking skills
How to Succeed on Standardized Examinations
Improving your study skills - how to be a better student
Putting Ideas in Order - Outlining Skills
Dist - CHUMAN

Study Skills Series

Study skills - getting the best results	20 MIN
Study skills - giving an oral report	19 MIN
Study Skills - Reading for Information	17 MIN
Study skills - verbal communication made easy	19 MIN

Dist - HIGGIN

Study Skills - Take that Test
U-matic / VHS / 16mm
Color (I)
Discusses how to develop good study habits, learn to follow and understand directions, intelligently answer multiple choice, true - false and essay questions, plan one's time in relation to the test and appropriately respond if stumped.
Education
Dist - HIGGIN **Prod** - HIGGIN 1984

Study skills - verbal communication made easy 19 MIN
16mm / VHS
Study skills series
Color (I J)
$425.00, $385.00 purchase, $60.00 rental
Presents the elements of effective speaking and listening skills, including tone of voice, being prepared, maintaining direct eye contact, not talking too fast or too slow, speaking up, use of formal and informal language, and listening. Illustrates these elements with humorous skits.
Education; English Language
Dist - HIGGIN **Prod** - HIGGIN 1990

Study skills video series
Discusses how important schools can be for future job success.
Study and Work Habits
Why Stay in School
Dist - CAREER **Prod** - CAREER 1990

Study skills - Volume I 50 MIN
VHS
Color (H C A)
$39.95 purchase _ #TN100V
Combines information on study skills with exercises designed to build skills. Covers procrastination, time management, organization, goal setting, and listening. Includes a workbook.
Education
Dist - CAMV

Study skills - Volume II 50 MIN
VHS
Color (H C A)
$39.95 purchase _ #TN200V
Combines information on study skills with exercises designed to build skills. Covers memorization, note taking, when and where to study, test taking, and how to overcome boredom. Includes a workbook.
Education
Dist - CAMV

Study Strategies Series
Assignments 15 MIN
Notes 13 MIN
Dist - CORF

Study Tips 13 MIN
BETA / VHS / U-matic
Color; Stereo (H)
Points out that Wayne's exams are two weeks away and he is in a panic. With Uncle Jack's help he develops a positive attitude towards study and more effective study techniques. With Lance Curtis and Geoff Kelso.
Education; Psychology
Dist - SEVDIM **Prod** - SEVDIM 1983

Studying 7 MIN
U-matic / VHS
Life's little lessons - self - esteem 4 - 6 series; No 53
Color (I)
$129.00, $99.00 purchase _ #V682
Follows Phillip who seems to be a brain, but he has learned how to study. Encourages students to really try and to experience the satisfaction that comes with getting better grades. Part of a 65 - part series on self - esteem.
Education; Guidance and Counseling; Psychology
Dist - BARR **Prod** - CEPRO 1992

Studying an Occupation 15 MIN
U-matic
Career Planning Series
Color (H)
Shows high school students studying an occupation to see if they should plan a career in that field.
Guidance and Counseling
Dist - TVOTAR **Prod** - TVOTAR 1984

Studying and occupation 15 MIN
VHS
Career planning series
Color (H C)
$39.00 purchase _ #BPN207003; LC 89-715840
Encourages self - discovery before making a career choice. Shows Jamie and Susan studying occupations. Includes teacher's guide. Part of a six - part series.
Guidance and Counseling; Psychology; Sociology
Dist - TVOTAR **Prod** - TVOTAR 1989

Studying Chemical Interactions 17 MIN
16mm / U-matic / VHS
Scientific Investigation Series
Color (I J H)
LC 79-700313
Reviews the difference between a physical and a chemical change. Defines atoms, molecules, elements and compounds. Illustrates three basic chemical interactions, combination, decomposition and replacement. Introduces simple chemical formulas and equations and discusses laboratory safety.
Science; Science - Physical
Dist - JOU **Prod** - GLDWER 1978

Studying Children 30 MIN
U-matic
Growing Years Series
Color
Shows how the developmental psychologies approach their subject and discusses the ethics of conducting research with children.
Psychology
Dist - CDTEL **Prod** - COAST

Studying electricity 16 MIN
U-matic / VHS / 16mm
Scientific investigation series
Color (I J H) (ENGLISH, SPANISH)
LC 78-701739
Shows ways electricity can be produced using materials available at home or school. Investigates the relationship between electricity and magnetism and how that relationship is used to produce alternating current. Demonstrates the difference between direct and alternating current.
Science - Physical
Dist - JOU **Prod** - GLDWER 1978

Studying Fluid Behavior 17 MIN
16mm / U-matic / VHS
Scientific Investigation Series
Color; Captioned (I J H)
LC 80-700242
Demonstrates the behavior of fluids. Illustrates that fluids will flow in solids, liquids and gases if given somewhere to go.
Science - Physical
Dist - JOU **Prod** - GLDWER 1979

Studying Gravitation and Mass 16 MIN
U-matic / VHS / 16mm
Scientific Investigation Series
Color (I J)
LC 77-703487
Explores the concept of gravity, the effect of distance and mass and the differentiation between mass and weight.
Science; Science - Physical
Dist - JOU **Prod** - GLDWER 1977

Studying Heat and its Behavior 17 MIN
U-matic / VHS / 16mm
Scientific Investigation Series
Color (I J H)
LC 79-700314
Investigates what heat is, what cold is, how heat relates to the three states of matter, and sources of heat, such as combustion, electricity, friction, agitation and chemical action. Studies the behavior of heat and its relationship to light.
Science - Physical
Dist - JOU **Prod** - GLDWER 1978

Studying lightning
VHS / U-matic
Exploring weather, climate and seasons series
Color (P I J)
$239.00, $219.00 purchase
Focuses on lightning, its causes and effects. Part of a six - part series on meteorology.
Science - Physical
Dist - GA **Prod** - GA 1988

Studying the Behavior of Light 16 MIN
U-matic / VHS / 16mm
Scientific Investigation Series
Color (I J)
LC 77-703373
Uses everyday materials to study the wavelike action of light and determine the spectra of several different light sources. Presents practical scientific uses for these observed phenomena.
Science; Science - Physical
Dist - JOU **Prod** - GLDWER 1977

Studying the Big Cats of Africa 15 MIN
16mm
Science in Action Series
Color (C)
Presents the new scientific studies on the big cats of Africa including the lion, leopard and cheetah. Encompasses population surveys of leopards, observations of the social lives of lions and predator/prey measurements of cheetahs.
Science; Science - Natural
Dist - COUNFI **Prod** - ALLFP

Studying the landscape - Cassette 1 80 MIN
VHS
Studying the landscape series
Color; PAL (J H)
PdS29.50 purchase
Contains four programs including Field trip from Castleton; Study of the Derwent Valley; Hill Farm study; and Study of the coastline. Provides a useful introduction to school fieldwork techniques in a variety of landscapes. Offers relevancy to the GCSE practical fieldwork syllabus and those syllabi which include physical geography studies. Part one of two parts.
Geography - World
Dist - EMFVL

Studying the landscape - Cassette 2 100 MIN
VHS
Studying the landscape series
Color; PAL (J H)
PdS29.50 purchase
Contains four programs including Fieldwork on the Lower Langdale Valley; Fieldwork on the Upper Langdale Valley; A Highland valley today; Drainage and farming of the Fens; and Bourne - a town study. Provides a useful introduction to school fieldwork techniques in a variety of landscapes. Offers relevancy to the GCSE practical fieldwork syllabus and those syllabi which include physical geography studies. Part two of two parts.
Geography - World
Dist - EMFVL

Studying the landscape series
Studying the landscape - Cassette 1 80 MIN
Studying the landscape - Cassette 2 100 MIN
Dist - EMFVL

The Stuff We Throw Away 22 MIN
16mm
Color (J A)
LC 75-714059
Shows innovative demonstration grants and research activities being developed by the Bureau of Solid Waste Management of the federal government in association with local communities.
Science - Natural
Dist - FINLYS **Prod** - USEPA 1970

Stuffed Tomatoes 6 MIN
VHS / U-matic
Cooking with Jack and Jill Series
Color (P I)
$95.00
Portrays the skills of twins Jack and Jill as they cook nutritious and delicious snacks that are easy to prepare. Kitchen safety is emphasized. Animated.
Home Economics
Dist - LANDMK **Prod** - LANDMK 1986

Stumble Bumps 10 MIN
U-matic / VHS / 16mm
Meet Professor Balthazar Series
Color (K P I J H C)
Uses animation to show how Professor Balthazar helps his friends who have problems with solutions that are ostensibly magical but actually use the spiritual resources the friends already have.
Fine Arts; Psychology
Dist - IFB **Prod** - ZAGREB 1986

Stunde Null 108 MIN
16mm
B&W (GERMAN (ENGLISH SUBTITLES))
Relates the events following July 1, 1945, the end of the war in Europe. The Americans are forced to withdraw from Leipzig and leave the territory to the Russians in accordance with the Yalta agreement. Deals with the hopes and fears of the people of Leipzig.
Fine Arts
Dist - WSTGLC **Prod** - WSTGLC 1976

The Stuntman 11 MIN
16mm / U-matic / VHS
Color
Documents a day in the life of a stunt man as Greg Anderson reveals the work he does. Shows how certain stunts are performed and tells why he decided to work in films as a stunt man.
Fine Arts; Guidance and Counseling
Dist - PFP **Prod** - PFP 1973

Stuntman 30 MIN
BETA / VHS
American Professionals Series
Color
Deals with the life and work of Conrad Palmisano, age 34, a Hollywood stuntman, who is one of the two hundred active, working stuntmen. He appears in the film Heart Like A Wheel.
Fine Arts; Guidance and Counseling
Dist - RMIBHF **Prod** - WTBS

Stunts 7 MIN
16mm / U-matic / VHS
Color (J)
LC 84-706807
Reveals the variety of brave and remarkable stunts performed by stunt people. Emphasizes the daring of these highly paid, professional, thrill - seeking athletes.
Fine Arts; Guidance and Counseling
Dist - PHENIX **Prod** - PHENIX 1983

Stunts - Hal Needham 21 MIN
VHS / 16mm
Action - a Day with the Directors Series

Color (H)
$39.95 purchase, $15.00 rental _ #86464
Reviews the background of stuntman and director Hal Needham. Discloses that Needham is of Blackfoot Indian ancestry, tested parachutes in the army, owned a car racing team and wrote - directed 'Smoky And The Bandit.' Discusses with interviewer Peter Brown that it takes coordination, agility, timing, nerve, self - confidence and a willingness to take 8 years out of one's life to prepare to work as a stuntperson. Touches on the problem of finding locations for shooting.
Fine Arts; Industrial and Technical Education; Psychology; Social Science
Dist - UILL **Prod** - SSN 1987

The Stupa of Wisdom 26 MIN
VHS / BETA
Color; PAL (G)
PdS17 purchase
Shows the rituals and construction of the first Kadampa Stupa in the West in memory of Ven Lama Thubten Yeshe at Vajra Yogini Institute in France. Features the final blessing by the Gyuto Tantric monks.
Fine Arts; Religion and Philosophy
Dist - MERIDT

Sturcturing communication 30 MIN
U-matic / VHS
Family portrait - a study of contemporary lifestyles series; Lesson 16
Color (C A)
Covers the appropriateness of communication. Examines what time and location are best and what pressures, personalities, preconceptions and/or unconscious motivations are present.
Psychology; Sociology
Dist - CDTEL **Prod** - SCCON

Stuttering 29 MIN
16mm
B&W (C T)
Presents a TV program sponsored by the Council of adult Stutterers, showing stutterers discussing the nature of stuttering, its problems, and control.
English Language; Psychology
Dist - CMPBL **Prod** - CMPBL

Stuttering and other speech disorders 19 MIN
U-matic / VHS
Color (C)
$249.00, $149.00 purchase _ #AD - 1468
Focuses on stuttering and speech disorders caused by trauma and therapies used to treat them. Profiles a 41 - year - old stutterer. Emphasizes the importance of early recognition of the problem.
Health and Safety; Psychology
Dist - FOTH **Prod** - FOTH

Stuttgart ballet - the miracle lives 60 MIN
VHS
Color (G)
$29.95 purchase _ #1238
Documents the Stuttgart Ballet Company.
Fine Arts; Geography - World; Physical Education and Recreation
Dist - KULTUR

STV - animals
Kit / Videodisc
Color (P) (ENGLISH, SPANISH)
$195.00 purchase _ #T81544
Explores the diversity of the animal world. Visits various animal habitats and observes how both familiar and exotic animals adapt to their environments. Also examines how mammal mothers care for their young and how animals are grouped according to eating patterns. Based in part on the National Geographic film Exploring Our World of Animals.
Agriculture; Science - Natural
Dist - NGS

STV - atmosphere
Kit / Videodisc
Color (I J H) (ENGLISH, SPANISH)
$225.00 purchase _ #T81468; $325.00 _ #T81471
Answers questions about the shield of air surrounding our planet - its layers; how it makes life possible; interactions of gases; its role in creating weather. Addresses pollution, global warming and the greenhouse effect. Includes 70 photographs and 20 minutes of video. More expensive kit includes software for additional browsing.
Science - Physical; Sociology
Dist - NGS

STV - biodiversity
Videodisc / Kit
Color (I J H) (ENGLISH AND SPANISH)
$225.00 purchase _ #T81460; $325.00 purchase _ #T81463
Describes how the increases in human population and destruction of habitats are affecting the balance of the world's ecosystems and endangering thousands of species. Presents case studies of successes in preservation. Challenges students to think of their role in preserving the earth's natural habitats. Higher-priced kit includes software.
Science - Natural; Science - Physical
Dist - NGS

STV - human body series
Videodisc
STV - human body series
Color; CAV (J H)
$877.50 purchase _ #T81530; $607.50 purchase _ #T81556
Presents a three - part series on the human body. Offers medical photography by Lennart Nilsson. Includes videodiscs, software diskettes with NGS magazine and book excerpts, glossary and presenter tool, user's guide with directions for interactive hook - up, barcode directory and activities and library catalog cards. Designed for Macintosh system. Contact distributor for hardware configuration. Basic kit available at lower price.
Science - Natural
Dist - NGS **Prod** - NGS 1992

STV - human body series
Immune and reproductive systems - Vol 3
Nervous, muscular and skeletal systems - Volume 2
Respiratory, circulatory and digestive systems - Vol 1
STV - human body series
Dist - NGS

STV - North America
Videodisc
Color (I J H) (ENGLISH, SPANISH)
$225.00 purchase _ #T80957; $325.00 _ #T80960
Offers six videos in a two-videodisc set, exploring North America's varied regions. Includes 200 photographs and maps for an intense look at specific areas and geographic features. Level III has software for additional browsing. Basic kit available at lower price.
Geography - United States
Dist - NGS

STV - plants
Videodisc
Color; CAV (I J) (ENGLISH, SPANISH)
$325.00 purchase _ #T81531; $225.00 purchase _ #T81538
Offers film clips, animation, time - lapse, closeup photography. Shows how different parts of a plant work together. Incorporates footage of plants from around the world. Includes videodisc, software diskettes with NGS magazine and book excerpts, glossary and presenter tool, user's guide with directions for interactive hook - up, barcode directory and activities and library catalog cards. Designed for Macintosh system. Contact distributor for hardware configuration. More basic kit available at lower price.
Science - Natural
Dist - NGS **Prod** - NGS 1993

STV - rain forest
Videodisc
Color; CAV (I J H)
$325.00 purchase _ #T81500; $225.00 purchase _ #T81553
Gives a closeup view of rain forest environments and the forces which endanger them. Includes videodisc, HyperCard software diskettes with NGS magazine and book excerpts, glossary and presenter tool, user's guide with directions for interactive hook - up, barcode directory and activities and library catalog cards. Designed for Macintosh system. Contact distributor for hardware configuration. Basic kit is available at lower price.
Science - Natural
Dist - NGS **Prod** - NGS 1991

STV - restless Earth
Videodisc
Color; CAV (I J H)
$325.00 purchase _ #81510; $225.00 purchase _ #T81550
Explores volcanoes, earthquakes, plate tectonics, spreading, subduction. Visits Iceland, Djibouti and Japan to witness geologic forces changing the Earth. Includes interactive videodisc, software diskettes, glossary and presenter tool, user's guide with directions for interactive hook - up, barcode directory and activities and library catalog cards. Designed for Macintosh system. Contact distributor for hardware configuration. Basic kit available at lower price.
Geography - World; Science - Physical
Dist - NGS **Prod** - NGS 1992

STV - solar system
Videodisc
Color; CAV (I J H)
$325.00 purchase _ #T81505; $225.00 purchase _ #T81553
Studies the planets in an interactive format. Offers space footage, computer - enhanced imagery and animation to clarify concepts and view planetary phenomena. Includes videodisc, software diskettes with NGS magazine and book excerpts, glossary and presenter tool, user's guide with directions for interactive hook - up, barcode directory and activities and library catalog cards. Designed for Macintosh system. Contact distributor for hardware configuration. Basic kit is available at lower price.
History - World; Science - Physical
Dist - NGS **Prod** - NGS 1992

STV - the cell
Videodisc / Kit
Color (J H) (ENGLISH, SPANISH)
$235.00 purchase _ #T81541; $325.00 purchase _ #T81608
Takes a look at the inner workings of the cell. Uses animation and computer - generated three-dimensional images to show cell components. Examines two important cell functions - mitosis and meiosis. CAV videodisc includes photographs and National Geographic film Discovering the Cell, which explores the early history of microscopes and discovery of cells and introduces students to microscope technology.
Science - Natural
Dist - NGS

STV - water
Videodisc / Kit
Color (I J) (ENGLISH, SPANISH)
$225.00 purchase _ #T81082; $325.00 purchase _ #T81085
Deals with sources and use of water and the need to conserve and protect water resources. Joins students, teachers and scientists traveling to the Great Lakes, Ogallala aquifer, Colorado River watershed and south Florida to learn about challenges to water supplies. Uses animation to teach about the hydrologic cycle. Basic kit available at lower price.
Health and Safety
Dist - NGS

STV - world geography series
Kit / Videodisc
STV - world geography series
Color (I J H) (ENGLISH, SPANISH)
$607.50 purchase _ #T81568; $877.50 purchase _ #T81580
Unfolds the physical features, climate and plant and animal life of the continents of Asia, Australia, Africa, Europe, South America and Antarctica. Basic kit is available at lower price. Expanded kit includes software compatible to Mactinosh only. In 3 volumes.
Geography - World
Dist - NGS

Style 30 MIN
VHS / U-matic
Write Course - an Introduction to College Composition Series
Color (C A)
Discusses achieving an individual style appropriate to the writing situation using voice, tone and point of view.
English Language
Dist - FI **Prod** - FI 1984

Style 30 MIN
U-matic
Communicating with a Purpose Series
(H C A)
Defines the elements of style and focuses on literary style and unique styles of various authors.
Education; Literature and Drama
Dist - ACCESS **Prod** - ACCESS 1982

Style 15 MIN
U-matic
Music Box Series
Color (K P)
Explores different musical styles from baroque to electronic.
Fine Arts
Dist - TVOTAR **Prod** - TVOTAR 1971

Style and design in Slovak furniture - 1250 - 1900 13 MIN
16mm
Color
Studies Slovak furniture from a simple carved Gothic chest still strong with folk art to richly inlaid four - poster beds that seem like ships of sleep, to spindle - legged tables almost too refined to bear.
Fine Arts; History - World
Dist - ROLAND **Prod** - ROLAND

Style in Band Performance 29 MIN
Videoreel / VT2
American Band Goes Symphonic Series
B&W
Fine Arts
Dist - PBS **Prod** - WGTV

Style - new directions 60 MIN
VHS / U-matic
Write course - an introduction to college composition; Pt 29 and 30
Color (C)

$45.00, $29.95 purchase
Reveals how voice, tone and point of view contribute to a writer's style in Part 29. Encourages students to develop and strengthen their writing to satisfy personal and professional goals in Part 30. Parts of a 30 - part series on college composition.
Education; English Language
Dist - ANNCPB **Prod** - DALCCD 1984

Style of Champions 19 MIN
16mm
Color (H C A)
LC 78-709320
John Konrads, former Australian Olympic swimming champion looks at and talks about swimming in Australia. Examines training methods while slow motion and underwater photography is used to show various swimming styles.
Physical Education and Recreation
Dist - AUIS **Prod** - ANAIB 1970

The Style of the classic Japanese Noh theater 17 MIN
VHS
Color (G C H)
$129.00 purchase _ #DL318
Features Sadayo Kita in traditional rehearsal clothes. Explains the movements and stance of the performer and the system of Labanotation. Illustrates how these movements are modified to create different characters in Noh theater.
Fine Arts; History - World
Dist - INSIM

Style sketching series
Presents seven programs on sketching techniques. Includes Drawings by the Classic Artists; Sketching for Communication; Sketching in Architecture; Design and Decoration; Repetition in Sketching; Style of Sketching; and Sources of Ideas for Drawing.
Style sketching series 210 MIN
Dist - CAMV

Styles 15 MIN
VHS / U-matic
Music machine series
Color (P)
Demonstrates varying characteristics of musical sounds.
Fine Arts
Dist - GPN **Prod** - GPN

Styles 22 MIN
U-matic / VHS / 16mm
Color (J)
LC 72-701604
Tells the story of three young adults who are choosing among possible life - styles. Explains that each person has a different choice because of a different inner self.
Guidance and Counseling; Psychology; Sociology
Dist - WOMBAT **Prod** - WOMBAT 1972

Styles in Polish art over the centuries - Epoki i style w sztuce polskiej 115 MIN
VHS
(J H C G) (POLISH)
$29.95 purchase _ #V294
Presents the first in a series designed for young people to show them retrospective styles in Polish art. Contains eight documents that were recorded from 1966 through 1987 by different directors.
Fine Arts
Dist - POLART

Styles in Song Accompaniment 29 MIN
Videoreel / VT2
Playing the Guitar I Series
Color
Fine Arts
Dist - PBS **Prod** - KCET

Styles of leadership 30 MIN
U-matic / VHS
Business of management series; Lesson 16
Color (C A)
Focuses on a number of questions that must be answered in order to understand leadership. Includes what makes an effective leader in today's complex world and how good leaders deal with people they lead. Explores several different styles of leadership such as autocratic, participative and laissez - faire.
Business and Economics; Psychology
Dist - SCCON **Prod** - SCCON

Styles of leadership 26 MIN
U-matic / VHS / 16mm
Color (DUTCH, ENGLISH FRENCH, GERMAN, SPANISH JAPANESE NORWEGIAN SWEDISH)
LC 80-701266
Uses a common business problem to illustrate four management leadership styles.
Business and Economics; Foreign Language; Psychology
Dist - RTBL **Prod** - RTBL 1980

Styles of leadership 72 FRS
U-matic / VHS
Leadership series; Module 2
Color
Looks at the common traits of leaders and gives a definition of leadership.
Business and Economics; Psychology
Dist - RESEM **Prod** - RESEM

Styles of sketching 29 MIN
U-matic
Sketching techniques series; Lesson 21
Color (C A)
Shows examples of contrasting styles and explains how a style is formed. Focuses on guest artist and cartoonist Tom Shannon as he demonstrates his particular drawing style.
Fine Arts
Dist - CDTEL **Prod** - COAST

The Styles that made a Splash 20 MIN
16mm
Color
LC 77-702417
Shows the many transformations of female bathing costumes in America. Traces the evolution of styles and the battles that women waged in quest of a simple, functional suit.
Home Economics; Sociology
Dist - MTP **Prod** - SEARS 1977

Styling for Magazines and TV
U-matic / VHS
Color
Shows a versatile haircut that provides three hairstyles which range from the everyday to the theatrical.
Education; Home Economics
Dist - MPCEDP **Prod** - MPCEDP 1984

Styling for the Total Look
VHS / U-matic
Color
Shows how a different hairstyle can make a person look thinner, taller and lovelier.
Education; Home Economics
Dist - MPCEDP **Prod** - MPCEDP 1984

Stylization and Fantasy 30 MIN
U-matic / VHS
Actor's Face as a Canvas Series
Color
Describes how stylization and fantasy in make - up suspend reality and create something new, in this case, the hare from The Tortoise And The Hare. Deals with costume, which plays an important role as well.
Fine Arts
Dist - NETCHE **Prod** - NETCHE 1973

Stylized Realism 30 MIN
VHS / U-matic
Actor's Face as a Canvas Series
Color
Describes a more intense form of make - up which should be carefully matched with the style and purposes of the play. Involves leaving areas of light and shadow in definite patterns, rather than fusing them.
Fine Arts
Dist - NETCHE **Prod** - NETCHE 1973

Su casa esta en orden 18 MIN
U-matic / VHS / 16mm
Color (SPANISH)
LC 83-700668
A Spanish - language version of the motion picture Your House In Order. Shows how industrial accidents can be the results of poor housekeeping and sloppiness. Uses the examples of a reckless forklift operator, a careless maintenance man, two workers unloading pipe without looking, a lathe operator who doesn't clean up the scrap and other workers leaving tools and trucks in dangerous places.
Health and Safety
Dist - IFB **Prod** - MILLBK

Sub - Costal Approach to the Kidney 15 MIN
16mm
Anatomy of the Flank Series
Color
Depicts the anatomical structure encountered in the approaches to the kidney through the sub - costal incision. Emphasizes the anatomical difference between this approach and other types of incisions.
Science
Dist - EATONL **Prod** - EATONL 1971

Sub - Igloo
16mm / VHS / U-matic
Color (G)
Reports a Canadian scientific expedition that put a plastic bubble on the floor of the Arctic Ocean to serve as a workshop and rest station for scientists working below the Arctic ice.
History - World; Science; Science - Physical
Dist - CFLMDC **Prod** - NFBC 1973
IFB

Sub - Igloo 20 MIN
16mm / U-matic / VHS
Color (J)
LC 75-700616
Presents an account of the third Arctic expedition of Canadian geologist, Joseph Mac Innis. Shows the construction of the sub - igloo, a roomsized plastic bubble filled with air and submerged to the sea bottom below the ice.
Geography - World; Science; Science - Physical
Dist - IFB **Prod** - NFBC 1974

Sub - routines 18 MIN
VHS / U-matic
Numerical control/computerized numerical control - advanced programming series; Module 2
Color (IND)
Includes several aspects of a subroutine such as definition, executing and writing.
Industrial and Technical Education
Dist - LEIKID **Prod** - LEIKID

Subarachnoid Endolymphatic Shunt for Meniere's Disease 13 MIN
16mm
Color (PRO)
Depicts a new concept in the surgical treatment of Meniere's disease. Explains that the fluid of the endolymphatic is shunted into the subarachnoid space to equalize the pressure of the two systems.
Health and Safety
Dist - EAR **Prod** - EAR

Subarctic Cross - Country Mobility, Pt 2 - Summer Operations 11 MIN
16mm
B&W
LC FIE56-212
Illustrates and compares summer and winter aspects of subarctic terrain and shows how various routes are traversed in this area through scenes of a platoon journey through the forest, over the tundra and finally through muskeg.
Civics and Political Systems; Geography - World; Science - Natural; Science - Physical; Social Science
Dist - USNAC **Prod** - USA 1956

Subarctic video enhancement
VHS / BETA / U-matic
Survival simulations series
Color (C G PRO)
$125.00 purchase _ #SM 15105
Simulates a plane crash in an isolated area in northern Canada in an exercise that hones problem - solving skills and shows how to minimize destructive conflicts and communication breakdowns. Supports other materials available from the distributor.
Business and Economics; Psychology; Social Science
Dist - HUMSYN **Prod** - HUMSYN

Subatomic Babies 8 MIN
VHS / U-matic
Color
Deals with technological destruction.
Fine Arts
Dist - KITCHN **Prod** - KITCHN

Subatomic Particles and Energy Considerations 15 MIN
U-matic
Chemistry 101 Series
Color (C)
Lists known subatomic particles, distinguishing three which influence chemical behavior. Considers these in order - electron, proton, neutron.
Science; Science - Physical
Dist - UILL **Prod** - UILL 1977

The Subchapter S Revision Act of 1982 210 MIN
Cassette / U-matic / VHS
Color (PRO)
$150.00, $30.00 purchase _ #P133, #M545
Examines the impact of the Subchapter S Revision Act of 1982 on small business. Discusses basis adjustments and distribution, selection of taxable year and changes in eligibility. Includes three audiocassettes or one video cassette for complete 3.5 hour program.
Business and Economics
Dist - ALIABA **Prod** - ALIABA 1987

Subclavian Catheterization 11 MIN
U-matic / VHS
Color (PRO)
Reviews essential equipment and illustrates the step - by - step analysis of the technique as well as demonstrating the actual procedure on two trauma victims. Indications, cautions and confirmation of placement are also included.

Health and Safety; Psychology; Science - Natural
Dist - UWASH **Prod** - UWASH

Subcontract manufacturing, scheduling and control 60 MIN
VHS / BETA
Manufacturing series
(COR)
Teaches how the subcontract decision makes the most of a company's productive, managerial and financial capabilities and how to control and monitor the flow of material and inventory when subcontracting.
Business and Economics
Dist - COMSRV **Prod** - COMSRV 1986

Subcutaneous and intramuscular injections 30 MIN
16mm
Directions for education in nursing via technology series; Lesson 17
B&W (PRO)
LC 74-701792
Demonstrates procedures and techniques for preparing and administering subcutaneous injections and intramuscular injections.
Health and Safety; Science
Dist - WSUM **Prod** - DENT 1974

Subcutaneous catheter 10 MIN
VHS
Color (C PRO G)
$395.00 purchase _ #R930 - VI - 028
Reveals that a subcutaneous catheter provides a less painful method for patients to receive analgesics intermittently. Discusses optimal subcutaneous catheter site location. Details the equipment needed and outlines basic steps for administering the procedure. Provides guidelines for preparing charts and informing the the patient of the procedure. Produced by Marilyn Lewthwaite, RN, Instructional Media Services, Douglas College, New Westminster, British Columbia.
Health and Safety
Dist - HSCIC

Subcutaneous Injections 8 MIN
VHS / BETA
Color
Describes how to administer subcutaneous injections.
Health and Safety
Dist - RMIBHF **Prod** - RMIBHF

Subdiaphragmatic Abscess 15 MIN
16mm
Color (PRO)
Depicts the common site for such abscesses and the surgical approach for draining two of them in different subphrenic spaces.
Health and Safety; Science
Dist - ACY **Prod** - ACYDGD 1954

The Subject is Flowers 29 MIN
U-matic
Artist at Work Series
Color
Explores the geometry of flowers using pastels.
Fine Arts
Dist - UMITV **Prod** - UMITV 1973

The Subject is HIV 16 MIN
VHS
Color (J H C)
$295.00 purchase
Updates the video The Subject is AIDS. Features Rae Dawn Chong who tells young people clearly and directly what they need to know to avoid getting HIV. Offers strategies and support for negotiating abstinence as a primary means of AIDS prevention.
Health and Safety; Psychology; Social Science; Sociology
Dist - SELMED **Prod** - ODNP

The Subject is water 28 MIN
VHS
Color (H C G)
$19.95 purchase _ #IV184
Explains how the Geological Survey, the nation's largest water resources investigating agency, appraises the quantity, quality, distribution and occurrence of surface and ground water. Focuses on how the Survey monitors and evaluates water resources through its nationwide hydrologic network and how such data and research is used by local, state and federal agencies to help solve a wide range of complex water problems.
Social Science
Dist - INSTRU **Prod** - USGEOS

Subject - Narcotics 21 MIN
16mm
Color; B&W (PRO)
Presents detailed information on how narcotics are used, how they can be identified, and how they affect the addict. (Restricted from the general public and from all youth groups).
Health and Safety
Dist - NEFA **Prod** - ANLAM 1952

Subject to contract - an introduction to land law 23 MIN
VHS
Color; PAL (PRO)
PdS29.50 purchase
Presents an introduction to land law in the form of a situation comedy. Intended for use by students on BTEC, A - level, and surveying and management courses, and those on professional access and degree courses in law.
Business and Economics; Civics and Political Systems
Dist - EMFVL

The Subject was Taxes 16 MIN
U-matic / VHS / 16mm
Color (H C A)
Traces the history of taxes and shows how taxes are used.
Civics and Political Systems
Dist - USNAC **Prod** - USIRS 1980

Subjects sketching series
Presents seven programs on sketching techniques. Includes The Use of Landscapes in a Sketch; Still - Life Sketches; Sketching Interiors; Sketching Flowers; Wood and Wooden Objects; Animals; and Vehicles.
Subjects sketching series 210 MIN
Dist - CAMV

Subliminal Perception 29 MIN
U-matic
Understanding Human Behavior - an Introduction to Psychology Series 'Lesson 11
Color (C A)
Discusses difficulties of attempts to conduct scientific research in areas of parapsychology. Distinguishes between various kinds of perception.
Psychology
Dist - CDTEL **Prod** - COAST

Subliminal series
Play to win - for men and women 60 MIN
Stop Smoking Forever - for Women and Men 60 MIN
Dist - BANTAP

Subliminal way to an 'A' - getting good grades
VHS
Color (G)
$29.95 purchase _ #MVGRD
Presents context for incorporating subliminal visual and auditory messages into standard television viewing. Claims enhancement of one's abilities as a student. Must be used with a MindVision processor, VCR and TV.
Education; Psychology
Dist - GAINST **Prod** - GAINST

Submandibular Triangle 14 MIN
16mm
Anatomy of the Head and Neck Series
Color
LC 74-705717
Demonstrates by dissection and illustrative drawings the boundaries and the structures of the submandibular triangle.
Science; Science - Natural
Dist - USNAC **Prod** - USVA 1959

Submarine 93 MIN
16mm
B&W
Relates how a deep - sea diver interrupts his honeymoon to try and unearth a sunken wreck. Shows what happens when he returns home to find his wife in the arms of his best friend, and describes his dilemma when his friend is trapped in a submarine. Directed by Frank Capra.
Fine Arts
Dist - KITPAR **Prod** - CPC 1928

The Submarine - Pt 4 - operating submerged 18 MIN
16mm
B&W
LC FIE66-334
Shows the operation of a submarine while submerged, including the use of special ballast tanks, trim tanks and submarine speed of contract depths. Describes the snorkel system and the operation of snorkeling.
Civics and Political Systems; Social Science
Dist - USNAC **Prod** - USN 1955

The Submarine - Pt 3 - diving and surfacing 12 MIN
16mm
B&W
LC FIE56-333
Discusses methods used by a submarine in submerging and explains positive, negative and neutral buoyancy. Presents an evaluation of surfacing.
Civics and Political Systems; Social Science
Dist - USNAC **Prod** - USN 1955

Submarine - steel boats - iron men 59 MIN
VHS
Color (G)
$29.95 purchase _ #1654
Overviews the development and strategic use of the submarine in both the world wars. Features an appearance by spy story author Tom Clancy.
Civics and Political Systems; Literature and Drama; Sociology
Dist - INSTRU **Prod** - KULTUR

The Submarines 28 MIN
16mm
Color
LC 74-706267
Shows the specialized skills, duties and responsibilities which keep U S Navy submarines prepared to battle other submarines.
Civics and Political Systems
Dist - USNAC **Prod** - USN 1967

The Submental triangle 8 MIN
16mm
Anatomy of the head and neck series
Color
LC 74-705718
Demonstrates the boundaries of the submental triangle in this dissection and uses drawings for clarification.
Science; Science - Natural
Dist - USNAC **Prod** - USVA 1967

Submerged arc welding
VHS
Arc welding processes series
$59.95 purchase _ #MJ093121V
Uses high speed photography to show arc welding processes and conditions. Portrays the automatic, machine, and semi - automatic methods of applying the process. Shows weld joint configurations and material preparations.
Industrial and Technical Education
Dist - CAREER **Prod** - CAREER

Submerged arc welding
U-matic / VHS
MIG and TIG welding - Spanish series
Color (SPANISH)
Industrial and Technical Education
Dist - VTRI **Prod** - VTRI

Submodalities and hypnosis series
Presents Richard Bandler in a five - part series on submodalities and hypnosis, from a seminar, March, 1987. Uses advanced NLP, neuro - linguistic programming. Includes the titles Amplifying Kinesthetic States and Body Work; Nonverbal Elicitation and Change; Presuppositions and Hypnosis; Redesigning and Chaining States; Convictions, Beliefs and Reality. Recommended that tapes be viewed in order. Bandler sometimes uses profanity for emphasis, which may offend some people.
Amplifying kinesthetic states and body work - 1 117 MIN
Convictions, beliefs and reality - 5 82 MIN
Nonverbal elicitation and change - 2 78 MIN
Presuppositions and hypnosis - 3 63 MIN
Redesigning and chaining states - 4 96 MIN
Dist - NLPCOM **Prod** - NLPCOM

The Suboccipital Region 8 MIN
U-matic / VHS / 16mm
Guides to Dissection Series
Color (C A)
Demonstrates the dissection of the suboccipital region.
Health and Safety; Science - Natural
Dist - TEF **Prod** - UCLA

Suboptimal Nonlinear Filtering Algorithm - Discrete - Time 87 MIN
U-matic / VHS
Modern Control Theory - Stochastic Estimation Series
Color (PRO)
Industrial and Technical Education; Mathematics
Dist - MIOT **Prod** - MIOT

Subphrenic Abscess 19 MIN
16mm
Color (PRO)
Attempts to simplify the complex and confusing anatomy and pathology of the subphrenic spaces. Shows the treatment of right and left sided abscess based upon the concept of the anatomy presented.
Health and Safety; Science
Dist - ACY **Prod** - ACYDGD 1962

Subpoena for Sabine 3 MIN
16mm
Color (G)
$15.00 rental
Examines a filmed love letter made public.

Fine Arts; Literature and Drama
Dist - CANCIN **Prod** - JONESE 1976

Subroutines and Functions 22 MIN
U-matic / VHS
Basic Power Series
Color (H C A)
Explains how to build modular programs using subroutines. Demonstrates how to use the functions built into the BASIC language.
Industrial and Technical Education; Mathematics; Sociology
Dist - UCEMC **Prod** - VANGU

Subroutines - program construction 30 MIN
U-matic / VHS
Programming for microcomputers series; Units 11 and 12
Color (J)
LC 83-707129
Discusses the use of top - down design to implement block structure. Shows how the 'gosub' statement can be used to access the subroutine. Explains 'gosub, return' statements, internal subroutines within the main program, the 'end' statement and 'rem' statements. Examines program output in terms of sequence, repetition, alternation or conditional flow, and logical groups. Deals with the use of planning grids for formulating subroutines and for determining call line numbers for the subroutines.
Mathematics
Dist - IU **Prod** - IU 1983

Subscripted variables 60 MIN
U-matic / VHS
Introduction to BASIC series; Lecture 9
Color
Industrial and Technical Education; Mathematics
Dist - UIDEEO **Prod** - UIDEEO

Subscripted Variables and Arrays 22 MIN
U-matic / VHS
Basic Power Series
Color (H C A)
Introduces dimensioned variables. Shows how to design a 'babble sort' routine.
Industrial and Technical Education; Mathematics; Sociology
Dist - UCEMC **Prod** - VANGU

Subset of a set - developing the concept 29 MIN
16mm
Teaching high school mathematics - first course series; No 43
B&W (T)
Mathematics
Dist - MLA **Prod** - UICSM 1967

Subsistence Level 10 MIN
16mm / U-matic / VHS
Foundations of Wealth Series
Color
Explains the problems of subsistence economies. Discusses the movement from a subsistence economy to a modern industrial state.
Business and Economics
Dist - FOTH **Prod** - FOTH

Substance abuse 20 MIN
VHS
Color (J H)
$89.95 purchase _ #NP753VG
Illustrates the problems of substance abuse in teens. Informs adolescents on drug use prevention; the reasons behind drug and alcohol abuse; and solutions to abuse problems. Includes a discussion and information guide.
Psychology
Dist - UNL

Substance abuse - a management intervention program 17 MIN
U-matic / VHS / 16mm
Color (COR)
LC 83-700344
Discusses the cost of firing an employee who's addicted to alcohol or other drugs. Outlines a program of managerial intervention that will help the decision maker restore the employee to full productivity.
Business and Economics; Psychology
Dist - AIMS
CMPCAR

Substance abuse - a two - part awareness and intervention program 25 MIN
VHS / 16mm
Color (COR)
$550.00 purchase, $125.00 rental, $35.00 preview
Presents a training program in two parts on the problem of substance abuse in the workplace. Discusses economic health losses due to employee substance abuse. Part I uses dramatizations, interviews and information excerpts to communicate to employees how to recognize substance abuse and what they can do about it. Part II teaches supervisors how to help employees with substance abuse problems. Available with union and non - union content.
Business and Economics; Psychology
Dist - UTM **Prod** - UTM

Substance Abuse - Alcoholism and Drug Dependence, Pts 1 - 3 125 MIN
U-matic / VHS
Color (PRO)
Discusses the progressive nature of alcoholism and drug dependence, including diagnosis and treatment. Includes a lengthy question and answer session.
Health and Safety; Psychology; Sociology
Dist - USNAC **Prod** - USVA

Substance Abuse and Physical Disability 41 MIN
VHS / 16mm
Medical Aspects of Disability - Course Lecture Series
Color (PRO)
$50.00, $65.00 purchase _ #8826
Presents one part of a course lecture series on the medical aspects of disability. Discusses how substance abuse can cause physical disability.
Health and Safety; Psychology
Dist - RICHGO **Prod** - RICHGO 1988

Substance abuse and pregnancy - a health professional's guide 30 MIN
VHS
Color (PRO)
$295.00 purchase, $50.00 rental
Reveals that the healthcare community is being asked to deal with a multitute of potentially tragic effects resulting from substance use during, and even before, pregnancy. Explains the scope of the problem and provides an easy - to - understand overview of the nurse - counselor's role. Presents specific techniques for risk assessment and demonstrates good communication skills and ways of offering effective on - going support. Presents pregnancy as an opportunity to change a patient's long - term life behavior. Shows effect ways of encouraging patients to affect those changes. Includes a study guide summarizing program content which can be photocopied as a handout.
Guidance and Counseling; Health and Safety; Psychology
Dist - POLYMR **Prod** - SPECTP

Substance abuse and pregnancy - the affected neonate 25 MIN
VHS
Color (G)
#IF - 844
Presents a free - loan program which discusses the challenge to healthcare professionals posed by substance abuse during pregnancy. Focuses on perinatal nurses and how they need to know more about damages sustained by the baby and how babies can be treated for alcohol, tobacco and drug abuse. Stresses the necessity for neonatal nurses to teach parents about the special needs of the affected neonate.
Health and Safety
Dist - WYAYLA **Prod** - WYAYLA

Substance abuse assessment and intervention series
Presents a four - part series on assessment and intervention in substance abuse produced by M and M Productions. Includes the titles Interview and Assessment; Coping Mechanisms; Treatment Modalities; Recovery and Prevention of Relapse.

Coping mechanisms	25 MIN
Interview and assessment	22 MIN
Recovery and prevention of relapse	21 MIN
Treatment modalities	38 MIN

Dist - CONMED

Substance abuse - awareness and intervention - Abuso de drogas - consciencia y remedio 30 MIN
BETA / VHS / U-matic
Color (IND G) (SPANISH)
$495.00 purchase _ #840 - 06, #840 - 07
Presents two parts on substance abuse. Discusses employee awareness of substance abuse in the workplace, how co - workers can detect the problem and how to find help in Part I. Provides supervisors and managers with specific information on what to look for and how to document and effectively deal with employee substance abuse problems.
Business and Economics; Guidance and Counseling; Health and Safety; Industrial and Technical Education; Psychology
Dist - ITSC **Prod** - ITSC

Substance abuse - everyone's problem 19 MIN
VHS
Color (C PRO)
$250.00 purchase, $70.00 rental _ #4362S, #4362V
Describes for the nursing manager the signs of drug and alcohol abuse and the steps to take if a staff member is suspected of having these problems. Gives the rationale for documenting job performance and changes in behavior. Discusses how to plan and conduct a management conference, what to do when immediate action is necessary and how to motivate staff members to get help. Places emphasis on teaching the manager to help an employee acknowledge a substance abuse problem and to get help. Produced by Vanderbilt University Medical Center.
Business and Economics; Guidance and Counseling; Health and Safety; Psychology
Dist - AJN

Substance Abuse - Help Yourself, Help Another 11.5
VHS / 16mm
Taking Care FOCUS Series
(PRO G)
$270.00 purchase
Encourages employees to adopt healthier lifestyles. Gives strategies and suggestions towards this goal. Focuses on substance abuse.
Business and Economics; Health and Safety
Dist - CNTRHP **Prod** - CNTRHP

Substance abuse in the workplace 11 MIN
16mm / VHS / BETA / U-matic
Color; PAL (COR)
PdS120, PdS128 purchase
Focuses on common questions and misconceptions about alcohol and drug abuse. Features two experts, a recovering alcoholic and the other a specialist in industrial mental health, answering questions from employees during a small group training session.
Guidance and Counseling; Health and Safety; Sociology
Dist - EDPAT

Substance abuse in the workplace - what's at stake, what can be done 11 MIN
VHS / 16mm
Handling a suspected substance abuse problem series
(COR)
$110.00 rental
Helps managers and supervisors recognize the deteriorating patterns of employee performance that signal a substance abuse problem, then deal with the problem effectively. Leader's guide included.
Business and Economics; Health and Safety; Psychology
Dist - FI **Prod** - AMEDIA 1989

Substance abuse in the workplace - what's at stake - what can be done 11 MIN
VHS / 16mm
Handling a suspected substance abuse problem series; Video 1
Color (PRO)
$395.00 purchase, $110.00 rental, $35.00 preview
Introduces supervisors and managers to the problem of substance abuse in their organizations. Teaches how to recognize the signs of a substance abusing employee. Includes a leader's guide.
Business and Economics; Psychology
Dist - UTM **Prod** - UTM

Substance abuse prevention 1 30 MIN
VHS
Club connect series
Color (J H G)
$59.95 purchase _ #CCNC-403-WC95
Describes to teenagers the dangers of substance abuse problems. Explains how teens can help each other avoid using alcohol and drugs. Includes a debate on drug testing in the school environment. Natalie Cosby and singer Johnny Gill are featured.
Guidance and Counseling; Psychology
Dist - PBS **Prod** - WTVSTV 1991

Substance abuse prevention 2 30 MIN
VHS
Club connect series
Color (J H G)
$59.95 purchase _ #CCNC-414-WC95
Presents a rally featuring the Club Connect staff and three thousand students. Describes a good way to have fun without using drugs or alcohol. Features methods teenagers use to turn down `offers of alcohol without feeling embarrassed.'
Psychology
Dist - PBS **Prod** - WTVSTV 1991

Substance abuse prevention 3 30 MIN
VHS
Club connect series
Color (J H G)
$59.95 purchase _ #CCNC-602-WC95
Presents Jimmy Rhoades in a skit designed to teach teenagers the dangers of substance abuse. Parodies talk show television programs as Rhoades plays an `obnoxious' host Jeraldo Noital. Includes an interview with musical group Jodeci.
Psychology
Dist - PBS **Prod** - WTVSTV 1992

Substance abuse training package 12 MIN
VHS
Color (A PRO COR)
$295.00 purchase
Presents the basics on substance abuse. Includes handbook.
Business and Economics; Guidance and Counseling; Psychology
Dist - VLEARN

Substance abuse video library series
Presents information on various substances that are abused. Details the history of a drug, how it is abused, short - term physical and psychological effects, dependency and overdose risks, and treatment. Nine - part series developed by Brock Morris and Kevin Scheel.
Adolescent substance abuse
Alcohol
Cocaine
Depressants
Designer drugs
Hallucinogens
Marijuana
Narcotics
Stimulants
Substance abuse video library series
Dist - HTHED **Prod** - HTHED

Substance dependency 15 MIN
VHS
Color (J H C G)
$85.00 purchase _ #ESGV2504V
Defines substance dependency and provides an in - depth exploration of dependency and its impact on society. Discusses alcohol, its poisonous effects on the body and the concept of genetic predisposition. Defines and details the different classes of drugs, including crack - cocaine. Explains designer drugs, hallucinogens and THC and their effects.
Guidance and Counseling; Psychology
Dist - CAMV

Substance misuse 30 MIN
VHS
Color (G)
$149.00 purchase, $75.00 rental _ #UW4659
Examines a range of substances which, when used as intended, are beneficial; but when misused are often deleterious to health and may be fatal. Looks at the most commonly misused substances to explain the effects of each and the problems it can cause. Covers stimulants, depressants, hallucinogens and opiates.
Guidance and Counseling; Health and Safety; Psychology
Dist - FOTH

Substance use disorders
VHS / U-matic
Psychiatry learning system series; Pt 2 - Disorders
Color (PRO)
Identifies the diagnostic criteria for substance use disorders. Covers the nine categories of abused substances, the clinical picture produced by intoxication, and withdrawal syndromes associated with them.
Health and Safety; Psychology
Dist - HSCIC **Prod** - HSCIC 1982

Substantive Criminal Law - Happy Here 19 MIN
VHS / U-matic
Ways of the Law Series
Color (H)
Using mime sequences, this lesson examines criminal law concepts such as crimes against the person. Includes a stark black - and - white interview with a prisoner.
Civics and Political Systems
Dist - GPN **Prod** - SCITV 1980

Substantive Law - Consent to Treatment 51 MIN
U-matic / VHS
Preparing and Trying a Medical Malpractice Case Series
Color (PRO)
Examines different types of consent, problems involving consent, timeliness of consent and the common - knowledge doctrine in preparation of a medical malpractice case.
Civics and Political Systems; Health and Safety
Dist - ABACPE **Prod** - ABACPE

Substantive Law of the Physician - Patient Relationship 50 MIN
VHS / U-matic
Preparing and Trying a Medical Malpractice Case Series
Color (PRO)
Examines the legal basis for the relationship between patient and physician.
Civics and Political Systems; Health and Safety
Dist - ABACPE **Prod** - ABACPE

Substantive Law - Vicarious Liability and Hospital Records 99 MIN
U-matic / VHS
Preparing and Trying a Medical Malpractice Case Series
Color (PRO)
Discusses vicarious liability of both the physician and the hospital and defenses in medical malpractice cases. Examines various hospital records and the liability of those creating or maintaining the records.
Civics and Political Systems; Health and Safety
Dist - ABACPE **Prod** - ABACPE

Substitution 30 MIN
VHS
Calculus series
Color (C)
4125.00 purchase _ #6024
Explains substitution. Part of a 56 - part series on calculus.
Mathematics
Dist - LANDMK **Prod** - LANDMK

Substitution 30 MIN
VHS
Mathematics Series
Color (J)
LC 90713155
Discusses substitution. The 133rd of 157 installments of the Mathematics Series.
Mathematics
Dist - GPN

Substitution and the linking rule 32 MIN
16mm
Teaching high school mathematics - first course series; No 27
B&W (T)
Mathematics
Dist - MLA **Prod** - UICSM 1967

Subsurface fluid flow mechanics 59 MIN
U-matic / VHS
Basic and petroleum geology for non - geologists series
Color (IND)
Focuses on relationship of landform types to fluid flow.
Industrial and Technical Education; Science - Physical
Dist - GPCV **Prod** - PHILLP

Subsurface Fluids 43 MIN
VHS / U-matic
Basic Geology Series
Color (IND)
Industrial and Technical Education; Science - Physical
Dist - GPCV **Prod** - GPCV

Subsurface Investigation - the Reason Why 20 MIN
16mm
Color
LC 79-701581
Explains how proper soil and topographic studies are important for highway planning in order to identify potential problems which might increase maintenance costs later.
Social Science
Dist - USNAC **Prod** - CDT 1978

Subsurface mapping 27 MIN
VHS / U-matic
Basic and petroleum geology for non - geologists series
Color (IND)
Focuses on sedimentary rocks.
Science - Physical
Dist - GPCV **Prod** - PHILLP

Subterranean termite biology 12 MIN
U-matic / VHS
Integrated pest management series
Color (IND)
$40.00, $95.00 purchase _ #TCA17361, #TCA17360
Presents an overview of the subterranean termite, which is the most common of North American termites.
Agriculture; Science - Natural
Dist - USNAC **Prod** - USNPS 1987

The Subtle flight of birds 4 MIN
16mm
B&W (G)
$10.00 rental
Explores through the eye of a bird, then through a world of landscapes populated with puppets. Moves through conflict, the 'subtle flight' of the soul from the body of a bird into resolution. Produced by Steven Dye.
Fine Arts; Science - Natural
Dist - CANCIN

Subtle Influences of Product Advertisement 30 MIN
U-matic / VHS
B&W
Discusses the use of fear and sex 'sells' in advertising and uses illustrative posters and media ads as examples. Points out the subtle inclusion of sexual imagery in subliminal advertising.
Business and Economics; Sociology
Dist - UWISC **Prod** - UWISC 1977

Subtle racial stereotypes
U-matic / VHS / BETA
Bridges - skills for managing a diverse workforce series; No 3
Color; CC; PAL (PRO G)
$745.00 purchase
Reveals that blatant expressions of prejudice are unacceptable in today's workplace, but stereotypes about race and affirmative action continue to influence thinking and subtle behaviors. Shows how to raise and deal with subtle racial stereotypes while maintaining good work relationships. Part three of an eight - part series on managing a diverse workforce.
Business and Economics; Psychology; Social Science; Sociology
Dist - BNA **Prod** - BNA

Subtle sexual harassment 56 MIN
VHS
Subtle sexual harassment series
Color (PRO IND COR A)
$695.00 purchase, $250.00 rental
Examines the grey areas of sexual harassment, the legal, psychologcial, cultural and moral issues behind the law. Looks at legal responsibilities and liabilities facing management, and elements of a sound policy and how to handle complaints. Includes a total of nine dramatizations on this two-part series, leader's guide, handouts, and sample policy statement.
Sociology
Dist - VIDART

Subtle sexual harassment series
The Issue is respect - Pt 1 28 MIN
Management's new responsibilities - Pt 2 28 MIN
Subtle sexual harassment 56 MIN
Dist - VIDART

Subtle sexual harassment series
The Issue is respect - Program 1 28 MIN
Mangement's new responsibilities - Program 2 28 MIN
Dist - VTCENS

Subtotal gastrectomy for duodenal ulcer perforating into the pancreas 29 MIN
16mm
Color (PRO)
Illustrates a technique which has proved safe for handling the difficult duodenal ulcer without jeopardizing the integrity of the pancreas or bile duct, and yet fulfilling the physiologic obligations of an adequate gastric resection for peptic ulcer diathesis.
Health and Safety; Science
Dist - ACY **Prod** - ACYDGD 1951

Subtotal pancreatectomy for adenoma of islet of Langerhans 15 MIN
16mm
Color (PRO)
Demonstrates the technique employed in the resection of the distal portion of the pancreas for a large islet cell tumor. Describes the various methods of approaching the pancreas.
Health and Safety
Dist - ACY **Prod** - ACYDGD 1954

Subtotal parotidectomy 27 MIN
U-matic / VHS
Head and neck series
Color
Health and Safety; Science - Natural
Dist - SVL **Prod** - SVL

Subtotal Parotidectomy for Inflammatory Disease 26 MIN
U-matic / VHS
Head and Neck Series
Color
Health and Safety; Science - Natural
Dist - SVL **Prod** - SVL

Subtotal Thyroidectomy 17 MIN
VHS / U-matic
Head and Neck Series
Color
Health and Safety; Science - Natural
Dist - SVL **Prod** - SVL

Subtracting 9 MIN
U-matic / VHS / 16mm
Basic Math Series
Color (P)
LC 79-701671
Features a magician who makes snowflakes appear, stay, or disappear in order to illustrate that subtraction is a way of counting backward. Shows the meaning of subtract, less, minus and equal signs.
Mathematics
Dist - PHENIX **Prod** - PHENIX 1979

Subtracting fractions 9 MIN
U-matic
Basic math skills series; Subtracting fractions
Color
Mathematics
Dist - TELSTR **Prod** - TELSTR

Subtracting like mixed numbers 10 MIN
U-matic
Basic math skills series; Subtracting fractions
Color
Mathematics
Dist - TELSTR **Prod** - TELSTR

Subtracting real numbers 30 MIN
16mm
Teaching high school mathematics - first course series; No 14
B&W (T)
Mathematics
Dist - MLA **Prod** - UICSM 1967

Subtracting unlike mixed numbers 8 MIN
U-matic
Basic math skills series; Subtracting fractions
Color
Mathematics
Dist - TELSTR **Prod** - TELSTR

Subtracting with fractions 11 MIN
VHS
Children's encyclopedia of mathematics - using fractions to add and 'subtract series
Color (I J)
$49.95 purchase _ #8220
Illustrates subtraction with fractions. Part of a five - part series on adding and subtracting with fractions.
Mathematics
Dist - AIMS **Prod** - DAVFMS 1991

Subtracting with mixed numbers 9 MIN
VHS
Children's encyclopedia of mathematics - using fractions to add and 'subtract series
Color (I J)
$49.95 purchase _ #8221
Illustrates subtraction with mixed numbers. Part of a five - part series on adding and subtracting with fractions.
Mathematics
Dist - AIMS **Prod** - DAVFMS 1991

Subtraction 14 MIN
U-matic / VHS / 16mm
Beginning Mathematics Series
Color (P) (SPANISH)
LC 73-703360
Shows how subtraction is related to addition and discusses the subtraction algorithm.
Mathematics
Dist - JOU **Prod** - GLDWER 1973

Subtraction 12 MIN
16mm / U-matic / VHS
Math for Beginners Series
Color (P)
$305, $215 purchase _ #4192
Shows the methods children can use to solve subtraction problems.
Mathematics
Dist - CORF

Subtraction, division and mixed numbers 12 MIN
U-matic / VHS / 16mm
Mathematics - an animated approach to fractions series; Pt 3
Color
Presents an animated story dealing with the subtraction and division of fractions and the manipulation of mixed numbers.
Mathematics
Dist - FI **Prod** - FI

Subtraction Facts 16 MIN
U-matic / VHS
Math Cycle Series
Color (P)
Presents basic subtraction facts.
Mathematics
Dist - GPN **Prod** - WDCNTV 1983

Subtraction facts to sums of 10
VHS
Lola May's fundamental math series
Color (P)
$45.00 purchase _ #10258VG
Illustrates the process of subtraction and its relationship to addition. Uses models to teach subtraction facts up to 10. Comes with a teacher's guide and blackline masters. Part eight of a 30 - part series.
Mathematics
Dist - UNL

Subtraction Four 15 MIN
U-matic
Math Patrol Three Series
Color (P I)
Presents mathematical concepts of mental calculation and the development of standard algorithms.
Education; Mathematics
Dist - TVOTAR **Prod** - TVOTAR 1978

Subtraction of tens and ones 15 MIN
U-matic
Math factory series; Problem solving series; Module IV
Color (P)
Introduces two - place subtraction problems that do not require regrouping.
Mathematics
Dist - GPN **Prod** - MAETEL 1973

Subtraction of two and three - digit numbers
VHS
Lola May's fundamental math series
Color (P I)
$45.00 purchase _ #10273VG
Uses models to teach subtraction of two and three - digit numbers. Shows how to subtract by trading one ten for ten ones and one hundred for ten tens when the ones and tens can't be subtracted. Comes with a teacher's guide and blackline masters. Part 23 of a 30 - part series.
Mathematics
Dist - UNL

Subtraction One 15 MIN
U-matic
Math Patrol Two Series
Color (P)
Presents the mathematical concepts of subtraction and addition.
Education; Mathematics
Dist - TVOTAR **Prod** - TVOTAR 1977

Subtraction - 1 - using the Cuisenaire rods 8 MIN
16mm
Color (P I)
Presents the use of the Cuisenaire rods as an aid to the learning of subtraction in the classroom for students and teachers.
Education; Mathematics
Dist - MMP **Prod** - MMP 1962

Subtraction Regrouping - Story Problems 15 MIN
U-matic
Studio M Series
Color (P)
Shows how to use subtraction to solve word problems.
Mathematics
Dist - GPN **Prod** - WCETTV 1979

Subtraction - Sums to Six 15 MIN
U-matic
Measure Up Series
Color (P)
Demonstrates how to write a subtraction fact with 'minus' and 'equal' symbols.
Mathematics
Dist - GPN **Prod** - WCETTV 1977

Subtraction - Sums to Ten, Pt 1 15 MIN
U-matic
Measure Up Series
Color (P)
Explains how to write subtraction facts to a sum of ten.
Mathematics
Dist - GPN **Prod** - WCETTV 1977

Subtraction - Sums to Ten, Pt 2 15 MIN
U-matic
Measure Up Series
Color (P)
Shows comparison of two numbers and the subsequent writing of the corresponding subtraction fact.
Mathematics
Dist - GPN **Prod** - WCETTV 1977

Subtraction Three 15 MIN
U-matic
Math Patrol Three Series
Color (P I)
Presents mathematical concepts of two digit subtraction and an introduction to the hundred board and the number line.
Education; Mathematics
Dist - TVOTAR **Prod** - TVOTAR 1978

Subtraction Two 15 MIN
U-matic
Math Patrol Two Series
Color (P)
Presents the mathematical concepts of subtraction and addition facts that do not involve regrouping.
Education; Mathematics
Dist - TVOTAR **Prod** - TVOTAR 1977

Subtraction - Two - Digit Regrouping 15 MIN
U-matic
Studio M Series
Color (P)
Tells how to regroup one ten as ten ones.
Mathematics
Dist - GPN **Prod** - WCETTV 1979

Subtraction - 2 - using the Cuisenaire rods 9 MIN
16mm
Color (P I)
Presents the use of the cuisenaire rods as an aid to the learning of subtraction in the classroom for students and teachers.
Education; Mathematics
Dist - MMP **Prod** - MMP 1964

Suburb 8 MIN
16mm
B&W (G)
$16.00 rental
Presents poor old men or bums and edits these images with the romantic music of Schubert. Takes its material from documentary elements. Produced by Andras Szirtes.
Fine Arts; Health and Safety; Sociology
Dist - CANCIN

Suburban living - six solutions 59 MIN
U-matic / VHS / 16mm
B&W (H C A)
LC FIA65-373
Shows six suburban neighborhoods, five abroad and one in North America. Discusses the important factors of this way of living.
Psychology; Social Science; Sociology
Dist - IFB **Prod** - NFBC 1960

Suburban Strategies - Dayton Malling, LA, Century City 17 MIN
VHS / U-matic
Color
Contrasts typical images from a suburban shopping mall. Depicts four interrelated natural and artificial environments in Los Angeles.
Fine Arts
Dist - KITCHN **Prod** - KITCHN

Suburban Wall 50 MIN
16mm
Color (J H)
Explores the factors responsible for the deteriorating housing situation in suburban America. Points out that of the 60 million housing units in this country, 11 million are either substandard, overcrowded, or both. Examines restrictive zoning requirements, the flight of jobs to the suburbs without housing for the jobholders and inequities of the property - tax structure.
Sociology
Dist - WBCPRO **Prod** - WBCPRO 1971

Suburbanization in Italy and the United States 30 MIN
VHS
Common issues in world regions series; Location; Pt 2
Color (J)
$180.00 purchase
Looks at families in Milan, Italy, and Baltimore, Maryland, dealing with life in the suburbs. Develops international understanding and geographic literacy for today's students growing up in a global community.
Geography - United States; Geography - World; Sociology
Dist - AITECH **Prod** - AITECH 1991

Suburbs - Arcadia for everyone 58 MIN
16mm / U-matic / VHS
Pride of place series
Color (C)
$40.00, $25.00 rental; $89.95 purchase _ #EX982
Examines the American dream of owning a single family house. Looks at Gothic cottages, mini - castles, detached dwelling in sylvan surroundings, the company town and suburbs. Part of an eight - part series hosted by Robert Stern.
Fine Arts; Geography - United States; Sociology
Dist - PSU **Prod** - FOTH
FOTH

Subvalvular aortic stenosis 6 MIN
16mm
Physiological and clinical aspects of cardiac
Color (PRO)
LC 76-700954
Uses animated sequences at normal and reduced speeds in order to show the events taking place in a single cardiac cycle. Demonstrates the generation of the mitral component of the first sound, the ejection systolic murmur and the aortic component of the second sound.
Health and Safety; Science - Natural
Dist - LIP **Prod** - MEDIC 1976

Subversion
VHS
Inside the CIA series; Pt 3
Color (G)
$29.95 purchase _ #MH1364V-S
Takes a penetrating look inside one of the world's most powerful secret organizations. Discusses the two goals of the CIA - gathering information and influencing the balance of world power. Details how the CIA has used subversion to topple or destabilize governments. Part three of a three-part series.
Civics and Political Systems; History - United States
Dist - CAMV

Subversive 58 MIN
VHS / U-matic
Color (H C A)
Biography of Terry Petters, a Seattle, Washington pariah turned hero. Follows fifty years of his colorful and complicated life.
Biography; Civics and Political Systems
Dist - UCV **Prod** - UCV

Subway 4 MIN
16mm
B&W
LC 75-700483
Portrays on man's experience on a cold speeding subway where all the characters are mere shadows. Demonstrates the anonymity of man in a large society.
Guidance and Counseling; Psychology; Social Science; Sociology
Dist - USC **Prod** - USC 1975

Subway city 51 MIN
VHS
Color (H C G)
$350.00 purchase, $65.00 rental
Explores the underground world of the New York subway in all its diversity, from the frenetic rush hour traffic to the eerie solitude of early morning runs. Introduces the thriving subculture of the subway which is simultaneously frightening and fascinating. Reveals that besides those who use the subway as a means of transport are those who work there, who live there and those who commit crimes there. Produced by Nick Lord.
Geography - United States; History - United States
Dist - FLMLIB **Prod** - YORKTV 1993

Succeed in a home business
VHS
Inc magazine business success program series
Color (H C A)
$29.95 purchase _ #KA094V
Examines what is necessary to get a home - based business started. Interviews successful entrepreneurs on how they got started. Presents practical tips rather than textbook theory.
Business and Economics
Dist - CAMV

Succeeding at reengineering 65 MIN
VHS
Reengineering the corporation - Dr Michael Hammer series
Color (COR)
$1150.00 purchase
Explores six reengineering guidelines. Discovers how reengineering transforms all aspects of an organization. Focuses on employee resistance and how to keep a program on track. Features Dr Michael Hammer, coauthor of Reengineering the Corporation - a Manifesto for Business Revolution. Includes a videocassette, audiocassette, leader's and viewer's guide and a self - assessment guide. Part two of a two - part series.
Business and Economics; Psychology
Dist - FI **Prod** - HAMMIC 1995

Succeeding in the Interview 30 MIN
BETA / VHS / U-matic
Vocational Interviewing Series
Color (G)
#CVO520B
Helps vocational job seekers understand the job interview process. Explains how to create a positive impression during an interview and what to do when the interview is over.
Guidance and Counseling
Dist - CADESF **Prod** - CADESF 1988

Succeeding in your interview 30 MIN
VHS / 16mm
Vocational interviewing series
Color (H)
$125.00 purchase _ #CC11V; $98.00 purchase _ #CVO520V
Presents the job interview in four parts - the introduction, selling yourself, fitting in and departure.
Guidance and Counseling; Psychology
Dist - JISTW
CAMV

Succeeding on your new job 19 MIN
VHS
Color (H C A)
$95.00 purchase _ #10335VG
Takes a look at the critical qualities and attitudes needed to grow in the world of work. Presents guidelines on preparing for a job and succeeding in the critical first few weeks of a new job. Shows rules to follow and why employers feel these are important. Includes a teacher's guide and blackline masters.
Psychology; Sociology
Dist - UNL

Succeeding within Your Company and Industry 60 MIN
VHS / U-matic
$69.95 _ PC1V
Features commentary from authorities on the subject, while giving advice and tactics for planning a successful career.
Business and Economics; Education
Dist - JISTW **Prod** - JISTW

Success by the numbers - the applied vocational math video series
Manufacturing technology 30 MIN
Dist - CAMV

Success Image Series
The Economics of your success image
The Finishing Touch
Suits, Symbols and Success
Dist - GPCV

Success in school - helping teens do their best 60 MIN
VHS
Color (H C A)
$89.95 purchase _ #FAM100V
Deals with how to develop successful school habits in teenagers. Covers subjects including problem identification, communication and discipline, motivation, and more. Provides perspectives from parents, teachers, and teenagers.
Education; Psychology
Dist - CAMV

Success in Supervision Series
Basic principles of supervision, Pt 1 30 MIN
Basic principles of supervision, Pt 2 30 MIN
Basic principles of supervision, Pt 3 30 MIN
Communications - talking and listening 30 MIN
Communications - writing and reading 30 MIN
Participation 30 MIN
Planning, Scheduling, Organizing Work and Work Improvement 30 MIN
Special Problems 30 MIN
Working with People 30 MIN
Dist - USNAC

Success in the classroom series
Effective study skills 30 MIN
Effective test taking 30 MIN
Dist - CADESF

Success in the classroom series
Effective study skills 30 MIN
Effective test - taking 30 MIN
Dist - CAMV

Success in the Job Market Series
Behind Closed Doors 15 MIN
The Company 15 MIN
Let Me Count the Ways I Know Me 15 MIN
Loving Me is Loving You 15 MIN
The Search 15 MIN
Working at the Car Wash Blues 15 MIN
Dist - GPN

Success, Needs and Interests 30 MIN
U-matic / VHS
Basic Education - Teaching the Adult Series
Color (T)
Tells how to take into account the success, needs and interests of adult basic education students.
Education
Dist - MDCPB **Prod** - MDDE

Success on Every Level 2 HRS
VHS
Master of Life Training Series
Color (G)
$29.95 purchase _ #VHS145
Contains two Video Hypnosis sessions which enhance clarity of focus, release of negative blocks and the experience of balance and harmony.
Health and Safety; Psychology; Religion and Philosophy
Dist - VSPU **Prod** - VSPU

Success or failure - it's up to you 15 MIN
VHS / U-matic
Color (A)
Features baseball Hall of Fame member Harmon Killebrew, along with baseball star Rod Carew, emphasizing the importance of confronting situations where failure is possible, rather than dodging them. Offers advice on pulling out of dry spells.
Psychology
Dist - SFTI **Prod** - SFTI

Success Oriented Schools
U-matic / VHS
School Inservice Videotape Series
Color (T)
Presents a process that the educational planner can follow to problem solve and make decisions. Helps develop a system that develops a successful environment for students.
Education
Dist - SLOSSF **Prod** - TERRAS

Success Secrets of Self - made Millionaires 60 MIN
Cassette / VHS
Color (G)
$95.00 purchase _ #XVSSM
Scrutinizes the twenty - one characteristics that rocketed self - made millionaires to the top. Features Brian Tracy. Includes video, audiocassette and guide.
Psychology; Social Science; Sociology
Dist - GAINST

Success Self - Programming - How to Create Success 91 MIN
VHS
Color (G)
$99.95 purchase _ #20123
Features Lee Milteer. Reveals the simple secrets of self - motivation, perseverence and discipline. Examines self - talk and how changing a few words can literally change one's life. Illustrates a critical step in breaking bad habits and ways to put one's brain to work while cooking, exercising and sleeping.
Health and Safety; Psychology
Dist - CARTRP **Prod** - CARTRP

Success series
Better business grammar
Get more done in less time
Get more down in less time - Better business grammar - Power writing - the key to success
Power writing - the key to success
Dist - SIV

Success stories - success ahead 29 MIN
VHS
Color (T PRO)
$170.00 purchase, $16.00 rental _ #35611
Features three Pennsylvania companies which have formed partnerships with educators to teach on - site basic - skills classes. Offers in - service training for teachers and administrators in the areas of adult basic education - ABE; general equivalency diploma - GED; and literacy.
Education
Dist - PSU **Prod** - WPSXTV 1989

Success stories - winners 29 MIN
VHS
Color (G)
$170.00 purchase, $16.00 rental _ #35610
Profiles three adult 'winners' who overcame obstacles to earn their general equivalency diplomas - GEDs. Reveals that the three, whose early schooling was halted because of pregnancy, drug abuse, racial discrimination or illiteracy, were honored by the Pennsylvania Dept of Education for their outstanding achievements.
Education
Dist - PSU **Prod** - WPSXTV 1989

A Success story 11 MIN
VHS
Color (G)
$15.00 purchase
Introduces the viewer to the concepts of family literacy and the services of NCFL. Summarizes social problems in the United States that can be addressed by family literacy, describes and illustrates the concepts of family literacy, and provides information assisting local program planners in starting a family literacy program. Provides an orientation for policy makers, administrators and community groups interested in family literacy.
English Language
Dist - NCFL **Prod** - NCFL

Success Story - How Insects Survive 28 MIN
U-matic / VHS / 16mm
Color (J)
LC 79-701067
Shows how insects have adapted successfully to a variety of environments and how they are capable of utilizing almost every available food form. Explains how their astonishing defense capabilities have evolved through instinctive behavior and physical adaptations.

Science - Natural
Dist - EBEC **Prod** - EBEC

Success, the AMA Course for Office Employees - Course Overview 5 MIN
Videoreel / VT2
SUCCESS, the AMA Course for Office Employees Series
Color
Presents an instructional program for office employees. Explains the SUCCESS course.
Business and Economics; Psychology
Dist - AMA **Prod** - AMA

SUCCESS, the AMA course for office employees series
Getting Completed Staff Work from Others 8 MIN
Give change a chance 8 MIN
How to follow through on an assignment 8 MIN
Invitation and the Plan 6 MIN
Manager's Job Responsibilities 3 MIN
Manager's Operating Realities 10 MIN
Success, the AMA Course for Office Employees - Course Overview 5 MIN
They're Always Changing Things 6 MIN
Three Managerial Styles 13 MIN
While You were Out 9 MIN
Why Communication Goes Wrong 9 MIN
Dist - AMA

Success - the Marva Collins Approach 28 MIN
U-matic / VHS / 16mm
Dealing with Social Problems in the Classroom Series
Color (T)
LC 82-700055
Presents a documentary on the teaching methods used by Marva Collins in her West Side Preparatory School in Chicago where phonics, classical literature and a sincere love of children are emphasized.
Education
Dist - FI **Prod** - BELLDA 1981

Success through education - a salute to Black achievement 19 MIN
VHS
Success through education series
Color (J H)
$95.00 purchase _ #10325VG
Offers discussions with Black students speaking out about education, feelings and values with an emphasis on self - esteem and achievement. Presents some of the difficult obstacles African - American students must face and the importance of role models in education. Rap stars MC Lyte and Heavy D, and TV actress Kellie Williams host the program. Includes a teacher's guide, discussion questions, activities, and blackline masters.
Education; History - United States
Dist - UNL

Success through education - a salute to Hispanic excellence 24 MIN
VHS
Success through education series
Color (J H)
$95.00 purchase _ #10326VG
Presents discussions with Hispanic American students concerning education, self - esteem, role models, and the language barrier. Profiles successful Latinos as they share their feelings on growing up in poverty; overcoming the obstacle of learning English; adapting to a new culture; and getting a higher education. Latino actor and director Edward James Olmos hosts the program. Includes a teacher's guide and blackline masters.
Education; Sociology
Dist - UNL

Success through education series
Success through education - a salute to Black achievement 19 MIN
Success through education - a salute to Hispanic excellence 24 MIN
Dist - UNL

Success through teamwork with Morgan Wootten 20 MIN
VHS / 16mm
(PRO COR)
$150.00 rental
Presents basketball coach Morgan Wootten outlining the benefits of being a good team member. Shows strategies for team building and motivation.
Business and Economics; Psychology
Dist - FI **Prod** - CCMPR 1989

Success with Bedding Plants 23 MIN
VHS
Color (G)
$89.95 purchase _ #6 - 300 - 304P
Shows how to select, install and maintain bedding plants. Offers tips on color and design of landscaping beds.
Agriculture
Dist - VEP **Prod** - VEP

Success with Indoor Plants 57 MIN
VHS / BETA
Lawn and Garden Series
Color
Shows how to care for indoor plants. Demonstrates starting new plants and potting and repotting. Includes proper ways to water and prune and methods of controlling insects and disease.
Agriculture; Physical Education and Recreation
Dist - MOHOMV **Prod** - MOHOMV

Success World 22 MIN
VHS / U-matic
Color (I A)
Features Art Linkletter as he comments on successful entrepreneurs.
Business and Economics
Dist - SUTHRB **Prod** - SUTHRB

Successful Breastfeeding - Right from the Start 24 MIN
VHS / U-matic
Color (C A)
Aims at helping new mothers overcome the minor difficulties associated with breastfeeding. Presents the advantages of breastfeeding, technique and scheduling routines, as well as the possible difficulties.
Health and Safety; Home Economics
Dist - TEF **Prod** - UCOLO

Successful delegation 15 MIN
VHS / 16mm
Color (COR)
$545.00 purchase, $150.00 rental, $40.00 preview
Teaches how managers can empower employees by delegating responsibilities. Explains delegation techniques, selecting appropriate employees, and how to establish control without stifling creativity. Includes a leader's guide.
Business and Economics; Education; Guidance and Counseling; Psychology
Dist - UTM **Prod** - UTM

Successful Delegation 15 MIN
U-matic / VHS / 16mm
Color
Illustrates that managers can actually enhance their position, and their value to the company, by giving subordinates the authority to act independently. Helps them understand that managers who don't delegate are not earning their salaries because they are too busy with routine work to do the organizing, planning and decision making they're paid to do.
Business and Economics; Psychology
Dist - EFM **Prod** - EFM

Successful deployment of management science throughout the operations of a major independent petroleum corporation
VHS
Color (C IND COR)
$150.00 purchase _ #86.01
Shows how optimization based decision support and process control systems aid managers at CITGO in such crucial areas as crude oil acquisition, spot market buying and selling, logistical operations and price volume strategies. Reveals that forecasting models address corporate price and volume. The work was instrumental in turning corporate results from a significant loss to significant earnings during the course of a two - year period, contributing approximately $70 million profit improvement per year. CITGO Petroleum Corp. Darwin Klingman, Nancy Phillips, David Steiger, Ross Wirth, Warren Young, Jim Keyes, Bell Beckert.
Business and Economics; Computer Science; Sociology
Dist - INMASC

Successful Duck Hunting 44 MIN
BETA / VHS
Color
Demonstrates duck hunting. Covers such areas as duck calls, decoy setting and selecting a blind. Shows what works best in various ponds and marshes.
Physical Education and Recreation
Dist - MOHOMV **Prod** - MOHOMV

Successful interviewing
VHS
Job search series
Color (H C G)
$69.95 purchase _ #CCPTU120V
Discusses preparing for an interview, answering questions, asking questions of the interviewer, what recruiters will look for, how to show control during different interviewing techniques, and how to communicate strengths. Shows viewers how to present themselves before, during and after an interview. Part of a three - part series which guides viewers through three stages of a successful job search.
Business and Economics; Guidance and Counseling
Dist - CAMV **Prod** - CAMV 1991

Successful interviewing - how to interview others 30 MIN
VHS / 16mm
(PRO G)
$89.95 purchase _ #DGP32
Shows how the interviewer gets the information he or she wants. Features Joy Booth, University of Wisconsin, Nancy Chellevold, employment consultant, and May Fraydas, career counselor. Hosted by Dick Goldberg.
Guidance and Counseling
Dist - RMIBHF **Prod** - RMIBHF

The Successful manager 62 FRS
U-matic / VHS
Management of work series; Module 1
Color
Defines who managers are, what they do, what is expected of them and what the attributes of a successful managers are.
Business and Economics; Psychology
Dist - RESEM **Prod** - RESEM

Successful marketing for the small and medium - size firm 220 MIN
Cassette
Color (PRO COR)
$295.00, $150.00 purchase, $150.00 rental _ #SMF1-00F, #ASMF-000
Presents practical ways to market profitably and ethically in today's marketplace. Describes how to analyze a practice, identify growth opportunities, formulate strategies and tactics, motivate a 'marketing team,' and develop communication materials.
Business and Economics; Civics and Political Systems; Education
Dist - AMBAR **Prod** - AMBAR 1988

Successful negotiating
VHS
FYI video series
Color (COR)
$79.95 purchase _ #AMA84027V
Teaches the art of win - win negotiating without stressful haggling, pressure tactics or adversarial confrontations. Part of a 12 - part series on professional and personal skills for the work place.
Business and Economics; Psychology; Social Science
Dist - CAMV **Prod** - AMA

Successful negotiation 24 MIN
VHS
Color (A COR)
$495.00 purchase, $150.00 rental
Illustrates successful negotiation in all levels of business, with steps to follow for effective negotiating.
Social Science
Dist - DHB **Prod** - CRISP

Successful negotiation 30 MIN
VHS
Color (G PRO COR)
$79.95 purchase _ #732 - 67
Presents a win - win approach to negotiations that can produce more amicable outcomes and stronger relationships. Shows how to reach goals and maintain healthy work and personal relationships.
Psychology; Social Science
Dist - MEMIND **Prod** - AMA

Successful parenting 30 MIN
U-matic / VHS
Family portrait - a study of contemporary lifestyles series; Lesson 26
Color (C A)
Explores interaction between the couple and the child, child development and disciplinary approaches in parenting.
Sociology
Dist - CDTEL **Prod** - SCCON

Successful Parenting
VHS / BETA
Successful Parenting Series
Color
Focuses on the techniques taught by Ann and John Murphy, who conduct religious parenting seminars, workshops and TV shows.
Guidance and Counseling; Religion and Philosophy; Sociology
Dist - DSP **Prod** - DSP

Successful Parenting Series
Love and Discipline, Self Esteem and Family Communications 60 MIN
School, money, management, television - social responsibility - career planning 60 MIN
Successful Parenting
Dist - DSP

Successful persuasion - a new approach to selling 14 MIN
U-matic / VHS / 16mm

Communications and selling program series
Color (J)
LC 75-702698
Concentrates on the buy - sell relationship. Looks behind what people say to what they might actually mean. Illustrates both successful and unsuccessful attempts at persuasion.
Business and Economics; Psychology
Dist - NEM **Prod** - NEM 1975

Successful persuasion - a new approach to selling 14 MIN
U-matic / VHS / 16mm
Communications and selling program - Spanish series
Color (SPANISH)
Teaches the dynamics of the persuasion transaction using everyday situations. Stresses the importance of listening and feedback in two - way communications.
Business and Economics; Psychology
Dist - NEM **Prod** - NEM

Successful safety committees - they're no accident 15 MIN
VHS
Color (IND)
$250.00 purchase, $75.00 rental _ #SON02
Helps safety committee members with strategies adapted from true - to - life situations. Includes a leader's guide, masters for transparencies and a post - training follow - up memo. Produced by Sonalist.
Guidance and Counseling; Health and Safety; Psychology
Dist - EXTR

Successful self - management 45 MIN
VHS
Color (G)
$195.00 purchase _ #91F61103
Shows how perspective and views about control affect self - management. Looks at purposes and values for life, personality, assertiveness rating, planning and setting goals for the future. Features Dr Paul Timm.
Business and Economics; Health and Safety; Psychology
Dist - DARTNL **Prod** - DARTNL

Successful sewing basics
VHS
Color (G A)
$24.95 purchase _ #NN100V
Covers the basics of sewing, including needlepoint, crocheting, and fundamental stitchery. Also reviews supplies and tools needed for a variety of sewing projects.
Home Economics
Dist - CAMV

Successful singlehood 50 MIN
VHS
God's blueprint for the Christian family series
Color (R G)
$29.95 purchase _ #6143 - 3
Features Dr Tony Evans. Discusses the positive aspects of being single from a conservative Christian viewpoint. Part of six parts on marriage, parenting and families.
Guidance and Counseling; Literature and Drama; Psychology; Religion and Philosophy
Dist - MOODY **Prod** - MOODY

Successful speaker 10 MIN
16mm
B&W (I)
Explains that success in speech depends on enthusiasm and spontaneity, directness, communicative posture, control of nervous tension, movement and gesture, and vocal variety.
English Language; Social Science
Dist - UNEBR **Prod** - UNEBR

Successful Strategies for Manufacturing Management Series

Developing an effective manufacturing strategy	30 MIN
Profile of a Winning Competitor	30 MIN
Winners and Losers - a Worldwide Survey	30 MIN

Dist - DELTAK

Successful stress control 55 MIN
VHS
Speaking of success series
Color (H C G)
$39.95 purchase _ #PD09
Features Dr Layne Longfellow explaining his stress reduction program, which is used daily in many hospitals and other stressful environments. Part of a series.
Business and Economics
Dist - SVIP **Prod** - AUVICA 1993

Successful supervision
Videoreel / VHS
Color (COR)
Teaches supervisory skills to trainees. Explains how to work successfully and confidently with subordinates, how to handle differences, praise workers, correct worker performance and prioritize, analyze, delegate and follow up on work.
Business and Economics; Psychology
Dist - OSDVTE **Prod** - OSDVTE

Successful Teaching Practices Series

Creating a Positive Classroom Atmosphere	19 MIN
Developing leadership skills	27 MIN
A Gifted Program in Action	27 MIN
The Giftedness in all Children	27 MIN
Individualizing Instruction through Contract - a New Approach to Classroom Management	25 MIN
Innovative teaching for student motivation	19 MIN
Motivation in the Classroom	27 MIN
The Politics of Working Together in a Gifted and Talented Program	28 MIN
Positive Discipline in the Classroom	28 MIN
Reading in the content area	26 MIN
A Student involvement program for developing values	29 MIN
Student self - concept and standards	27 MIN
A Teacher's Prescription for Reducing Vandalism	23 MIN
Teaching is an Attitude	27 MIN

Dist - EBEC

Successful telephone collections 38 MIN
U-matic
Color; Mono
Seven steps to successful telephone collections.
Business and Economics; Education; Psychology
Dist - PROEDS **Prod** - PROEDS 1986

Successful termination 42 MIN
VHS / U-matic
Color (A PRO)
$595.00 purchase, $95.00 rental _ #244293
Instructs human resource and other management professionals in the proper procedure for terminating an employee. Focuses on preparation for the termination meeting, how to terminate humanely, legal concerns, Equal Employment Opportunity Commission (EEOC) regulations, and presentation of severance packages.
Guidance and Counseling; Sociology
Dist - DBMI **Prod** - DBMI 1989

Successful termination - hourly employees 42 MIN
VHS
Color (G)
$595.00 purchase, $95.00 rental _ #543800
Shows supervisors and managers how to terminate professional and hourly employees legally and humanely. Discusses presentation of a severance page and union and non - union terminations.
Business and Economics
Dist - DBMI **Prod** - DBMI 1990

Successful working moms 56 MIN
VHS
Breastfeeding techniques that work series
Color (G)
$44.95 purchase _ #GP105V
Presents a network discussion with mothers describing how they each fit breast feeding into their busy lifestyles. Part of a seven - part series on breastfeeding presented by Kittie Frantz, RN.
Health and Safety; Sociology
Dist - CAMV

Successfully defending against the pass 27 MIN
U-matic / VHS
Joe Paterno - coaching winning football series
Color (C A)
$49.00 purchase _ #3768
Shows the techniqes of covering passes, rushing the passer, intercepting passes, and recovering fumbles. Conducted by Joe Paterno, head coach of the Penn State football team.
Physical Education and Recreation
Dist - EBEC

Successfully marketing your production 80 MIN
VHS
Color (G)
$49.95 purchase _ #THP12V - F
Teaches potters how to market their wares. Shows how to get involved in studio shows, art fairs and craft festivals, trade shows, co-ops, consignments, securing commissions, getting media coverage, developing consumer lists, wholesale vs retail, advertising, photography, copy writing, packing and shipping, and more.
Business and Economics; Fine Arts
Dist - CAMV

Succession - from sand dune to forest 16 MIN
U-matic / VHS / 16mm
Biology - Spanish series; Unit 1 - Ecology
Color (H) (SPANISH)
Outlines the principles of ecological succession, the process by which an area changes until it becomes a stable natural community.
Science - Natural
Dist - EBEC **Prod** - EBEC

Succession - how forest communities change through time 20 MIN
VHS / U-matic / Slide
Color (C G)
$130.00 purchase, $25.00 rental _ #948.2
Explains the process of succession in biology. Discusses the role that the actions of a resource manager play in accelerating or inhibiting natural change. Illustrates how foresters can either alter the route of succession or adapt their practices to natural processes. Builds upon concepts introduced in Forest Communities - Composition, Structure and Classification.
Agriculture; Science - Natural; Social Science
Dist - OSUSF **Prod** - OSUSF 1989

Succession on lava 14 MIN
16mm / U-matic / VHS
Biology series; Unit 1 - Ecology
Color (J H) (SPANISH)
LC 77-708915;
Photographs the many stages of succession that exist at different locations in Hawaii at the site of volcanic eruptions. Includes scenes of destruction due to lava flows and pumice, dramatizing how swiftly the surrounding area becomes hostile to all forms of life. Shows how each new form of life that strives for survival further modifies the environment and eventually re - establishes a complex web of life.
Science - Natural; Science - Physical
Dist - EBEC **Prod** - EBEC 1970

Succession planning for the family owned business 50 MIN
VHS
Color (A PRO COR)
$95.00 purchase _ #Y504
Looks at the legal tools used to create succession plans. Describes ways to communicate with clients and their family members to blunt the process's emotional component.
Business and Economics; Civics and Political Systems
Dist - ALIABA **Prod** - CLETV 1993

Succoth 15 MIN
16mm
Color
Shows how the Festival of Succoth is celebrated in Israel.
Geography - World; Religion and Philosophy; Social Science
Dist - ALDEN **Prod** - ALDEN

Succulents 29 MIN
U-matic
House Botanist Series
Color
Shows how to divide, transplant and display succulents.
Agriculture; Science - Natural
Dist - UMITV **Prod** - UMITV 1978

The Succulents 30 MIN
Videoreel / VT2
Making Things Grow I Series
Color
Features Thalassa Cruso discussing different aspects of gardening. Shows how to care for succulents.
Agriculture; Science - Natural
Dist - PBS **Prod** - WGBHTV

Such a beautiful day 15 MIN
16mm
Color
LC 80-700857
Discusses the relationship between alcohol and highway safety.
Health and Safety
Dist - USNAC **Prod** - USHTSA 1975

Such a Place 28 MIN
Videoreel / VT2
Synergism - in Today's World Series
Color
Presents a documentary in cinema verite style about very old people in a nursing home. Focuses on the people who live there, the daily routines, from the distribution of mail to visits to the home's beauty parlor.
Health and Safety; Psychology; Sociology
Dist - PBS **Prod** - JSRI

Such is the Real Nature of Horses 60 MIN
BETA / VHS
Color
Presents a documentary on the habits and behaviour of wild horses. Filmed in France.

Physical Education and Recreation; Science - Natural
Dist - HOMEAF **Prod** - HOMEAF

Sucker Rod Failures - Causes and Prevention 25 MIN
VHS / U-matic
Color (IND)
Discusses methods and techniques of reducing sucker rod failures.
Social Science
Dist - UTEXPE **Prod** - UTEXPE 1975

Sucking doctor 45 MIN
VHS
B&W (C G)
$295.00 purchase, $55.00 rental _ #37454
Records a complete shamanistic curing ceremony performed among the Kashia group of Southwestern Pomo Indians. Reveals that the Indian 'sucking doctor' is a prophet of the Bole Maru religion and the spiritual head of the community.
Health and Safety; Religion and Philosophy; Social Science
Dist - UCEMC **Prod** - HEICK 1964

Sucking wounds of the chest 12 MIN
16mm
Color
LC FIE54-288
Demonstrates five important steps in prompt and proper treatment for a sucking chest wound by means of a simulated casualty on the battlefront.
Health and Safety
Dist - USNAC **Prod** - USN 1953

Suction Biopsy of the Gastrointestinal Mucosa 16 MIN
16mm
Color
LC 74-705719
Shows how suction biopsy tubes are passed under fluoroscopic control. Illustrates techniques for passing the pylorus as well as the necessity for taking small bowel biopsies near the duodenojejunal junction. Depicts the use of the suction biopsy tube in the esophagus, stomach and rectum. Features the detail of handling the biopsy to minimize trauma and to assure perfect orientation. Explains that if the biopsies are not handled atraumatically and if they are not perfectly oriented, then subsequent processing of interpretable biopsies will be impossible.
Health and Safety; Science - Natural
Dist - USNAC **Prod** - USPHS 1967

Suction tip placement 6 MIN
VHS / U-matic
Color (PRO C)
$395.00 purchase, $80.00 rental _ #C901 - VI - 086
Discusses the need for oral evacuation during four - handed dentistry to remove fluids and debris from the mouth of the supine patient. Describes and contrasts the applications of low and high - velocity suctions tips. Demonstrates the proper placement of standard high - velocity evacuation tips in all sextants of the mouth.
Health and Safety
Dist - HSCIC

Suction Tip Placement 8 MIN
16mm
Four - Handed Dentistry Series
Color (PRO)
LC 75-704340
Demonstrates how to position a suction tip in all areas of the mouth for oral evacuation.
Health and Safety
Dist - SAIT **Prod** - SAIT 1973

Suctioning Techniques for the Pediatric Patient 10 MIN
VHS / 16mm
(C)
$385.00 purchase _ #860VI061
Demonstrates the procedures for tracheal suctioning in pediatric patients, stressing the importance of maintaining a clear airway. Includes considerations related to using cuffed tubes and humidifiers.
Health and Safety
Dist - HSCIC **Prod** - HSCIC 1986

Sudamerica - Continente De Gran Porvenir 29 MIN
16mm / U-matic / VHS
Color (J H C) (SPANISH)
A Spanish language film. Describes the historical and geographical forces which have molded South America. Shows development of natural resources and describes industrialization.
Geography - World; History - World
Dist - IFB **Prod** - BRYAN 1961

Sudamerica - Continente De Gran Porvenir - Pt 1 16 MIN
16mm / U-matic / VHS
Color (H C) (SPANISH)
LC FIA67-5552
A Spanish language film. Describes the historical and geographical forces which have molded South America. Discusses the Andes, the Amazon and other great rivers. Pictures the conquistadores and depicts the treatment of native Indians and examines the influence of the church. Explores the aristocratic traditions and parental concepts of hacienda owners.
Foreign Language; Geography - World
Dist - IFB **Prod** - BRYAN 1961

Sudamerica - Continente De Gran Porvenir - Pt 2 13 MIN
U-matic / VHS / 16mm
Color (H C) (SPANISH)
LC FIA67-5553
A Spanish language film. Examines the hacienda and discusses strides taken to convert a hacienda - dominated society into a democratic one. Notes factors in South America's progress, including a growing middle class and a recognition of the limitations of a onecrop economy. Shows development of natural resources and describes industrialization.
Geography - World; History - World
Dist - IFB **Prod** - BRYAN 1961

Sudden Changes - Post Hysterectomy Syndrome 29 MIN
U-matic / VHS / 16mm
Color (A)
Concentrates on both the physical and emotional sides of this common but sometimes controversial surgical procedure. Explores hysterectomy from the point of view of doctors, medical researcherauthors and women's rights activists. Suggests discussion of alternatives by women facing hysterectomy.
Health and Safety; Sociology
Dist - CNEMAG **Prod** - CNEMAG 1985

Sudden death 45 MIN
VHS
Color (J H C G A R)
$29.95 purchase, $10.00 rental _ #35 - 823 - 2020
Reveals how the sudden death of a young man during a basketball game causes many who knew him to reassess both his life and theirs.
Psychology; Religion and Philosophy
Dist - APH **Prod** - ANDERK

Sudden emergencies 5 MIN
16mm
Driver education series
B&W (H)
LC FIA66-1007
Stresses the importance of knowing how to react to sudden emergencies encountered in driving.
Health and Safety
Dist - AMROIL **Prod** - AMROIL 1964

Sudden Impact - Meteors, Asteroids, Comets 23 MIN
35mm strip / VHS
Color (H)
$84.00 purchase _ #PE - 481123 - 1, #PE - 512769 - 5
Explores the variety of cosmic debris and explains the role of galactic debris in forming and shaping major celestial bodies, including the earth. Discusses past collisions of matter and their effects on the landscape, climate and population of our planet.
Science - Physical
Dist - SRA **Prod** - SRA 1987

Sudden Infant Death Syndrome 4 MIN
16mm
Sudden Infant Death Syndrome Series
Color (C A)
LC 77-700087
Explains that sudden infant death syndrome takes the lives of about 8,000 infants each year in the United States. Discusses the area of prediction and prevention.
Health and Safety; Sociology
Dist - USNAC **Prod** - USNCHS 1976

Sudden Infant Death Syndrome - After Our Baby Died 26 MIN
16mm
Color
Communicates the nature and intensity of parents who have lost children to Sudden Infant Death Syndrome.
Health and Safety; Home Economics; Sociology
Dist - TOGGFI **Prod** - USHHS 1975

Sudden Infant Death Syndrome series

After our baby died	20 MIN
A Call for help	19 MIN
Sudden Infant Death Syndrome	4 MIN
You are not Alone	27 MIN

Dist - USNAC

Sudden memories - 'why do people die so young' 30 MIN
VHS
Color (J H G)
$199.00 purchase
Portrays a teenager's attempt to make sense of his best friend's death. Focuses on Todd Stewart and Dane Matthews, best friends. Dane dies suddenly and Todd is left to pass through the processes of anger, denial, bargaining, acceptance and grief.
Guidance and Counseling; Health and Safety; Sociology
Dist - CHERUB **Prod** - CHERUB

Sudden Natural Death 25 MIN
16mm
Clinical Pathology - Forensic Medicine Outlines Series
B&W (PRO)
LC 74-705720
Discusses aspects of sudden natural death, with emphasis on the most common cause - occlusive coronary artery disease.
Health and Safety; Science - Natural
Dist - NMAC **Prod** - NMAC 1970

A Sudden storm and come, come to the fair 30 MIN
VHS
Davey and Goliath series
Color (P I R)
$19.95 purchase, $10.00 rental _ #4 - 8833
Presents two 15 - minute 'Davey and Goliath' episodes. 'A Sudden Storm' describes how parental love helps Davey and Sally lessen their fears of thunderstorms. 'Come, Come to the Fair' centers around Davey's Sunday school class, which shows how different cultures depict the Christ Child. Produced by the Evangelical Lutheran Church in America.
Literature and Drama; Religion and Philosophy
Dist - APH

Sudden unexpected natural death 39 MIN
U-matic
Forensic medicine teaching programs series; No 6
Color (PRO)
LC 78-706056
Presents several cases of individuals who were presumed healthy, but died within 24 hours of the onset of symptoms. Discusses sudden natural deaths causes by various heart diseases, central nervous disorders and respiratory dysfunction.
Health and Safety
Dist - USNAC **Prod** - NMAC 1978

Sudden wealth of the poor people of Kombach 94 MIN
16mm
B&W (GERMAN)
Suggests that superstition and religion, public school teaching and a paternalizing concept of justice make poor people into simpletons who are taught to laugh at their own misfortunes. Follows a true story about seven peasants who, in 1821, robbed a tax collector's wagon and were subsequently caught, tried and executed for their crime.
Fine Arts; Sociology
Dist - NYFLMS **Prod** - NYFLMS 1971

Suddenly and Without Warning 6 MIN
16mm
Color
LC 75-701267; 75-700588
Stresses safety in boating and shows how boating accidents can happen.
Health and Safety
Dist - USNAC **Prod** - USCG 1971

Suddenly I burst into another - The Life of Henry Tanner 28 MIN
16mm
Color (G)
$60.00 rental
Explores a farmer's reaction to nuclear holocaust. Investigates Henry Tanner's cryptic life and death from his automotive fixation to his revelatory trip through Asia leading to his retreat to farm life. A pseudodocumentary by Eric Saks.
Fine Arts; Sociology
Dist - CANCIN

Suddenly, Last Summer 114 MIN
16mm
B&W (C A)
Stars Elizabeth Taylor as a beautiful patient of a neuro - surgeon, played by Montgomery Clift. Describes her on the brink of insanity after witnessing the violent death of her young male cousin.
Fine Arts
Dist - TIMLIF **Prod** - CPC

Sudesha 30 MIN
16mm / VHS
As Women See it - Global Feminism Series
Color (G)
$500.00, $250.00 purchase, $60.00 rental
Presents the story of Sudesha who lives in the foothills of the Himalayas in India. Tells of her active involvement in the 'Chipko' movement founded by Indian peasant women who recognize the consequences of deforestation of their regions. Part of a series of films by and about women in Third World countries which include English voice over.
Agriculture; Civics and Political Systems; Geography - World; Science - Natural; Social Science; Sociology
Dist - WMEN **Prod** - FAUST

Sue and Sandra 6 MIN
U-matic / VHS / 16mm
Being Friends Series
Color (I)
Guidance and Counseling; Literature and Drama; Psychology
Dist - USNAC **Prod** - USHHS

Sue Miller Hurst - Come to the edge 100 MIN
Cassette
1992 conference collection series
Color; PAL (C G T)
$150.00, $25.00 purchase _ #V9203, #T9203
Shares breakthrough research that challenges fundamental assumptions about learning. Discloses that the gap between what one knows and what one does, how one acts and who one is can be bridged by rediscovering the incredible human capacities to learn. Features S M Hurst, whose background includes positions as a high school teacher, principal, curriculum director and author. Part of a three - part series on the 1992 Systems Thinking in Action Conference.
Business and Economics; Education; Psychology
Dist - PEGASU **Prod** - PEGASU 1992

Suemi's story - my modern Mayan home 25 MIN
VHS
Children of many lands series
Color (I J)
$79.95 purchase _ #UL2047VA
Presents the story of Suemi, a young Mexican girl from the state of Yucatan. Follows Suemi as she attends school, completes chores, goes to the market, attends a Mayan wedding and more. Part of a three - part series on children in Latin America.
Geography - World; History - World; Social Science
Dist - KNOWUN

Sue's leg - remembering the thirties - Twyla Tharp and dancers 60 MIN
16mm / U-matic / VHS
Dance in America series
Color (H C A)
LC 77-702340
Presents choreographer Twyla Tharp and her dance company performing her creation, entitled Sue's Legs, to the music of the late jazz artist Fats Waller.
Fine Arts
Dist - IU **Prod** - WNETTV 1977

Suez Canal 13 MIN
U-matic / VHS
B&W
Examines the history of the Suez Canal since its opening in 1869 and looks at the crucial role it has played in the Middle East.
Geography - World; History - World
Dist - KINGFT **Prod** - KINGFT

Suez Canal - Politics of Control 16 MIN
U-matic / VHS
Color (H C A)
Examines the incident in 1956 when President Nassar of Egypt nationalized the Suez Canal. Investigates its role in the Middle East and international politics since that time.
Geography - World; History - World
Dist - JOU **Prod** - JOU

The Suez Crisis - 1956 20 MIN
U-matic / VHS
B&W (G)
$249.00, $149.00 purchase _ #AD - 1621
Looks at the other side of the 1956 Arab - Israeli conflict - the British - French attempt to safeguard their economic interest in the Suez Canal. Goes back in time to explain Britain's role in the Suez area, Britain's history in Egypt, its view of Egyptian competence and its fear of repeating the appeasement policies of Munich, 1938.
Geography - World; History - World
Dist - FOTH **Prod** - FOTH

Suffer Little Children 10 MIN
16mm
B&W
Depicts young children in an institution for the mentally retarded. Raises the questions of how and why they were institutionalized and what has become of them. Shows equally disabled children who live at home and attend a nursery school in their own community.
Psychology; Social Science; Sociology
Dist - CMHRF **Prod** - CMHRF

Suffer the Children 86 MIN
VHS / 16mm
Color (C A)
$210.00 purchase, $35.00 rental _ #CC3909
Profiles five families living in urban poverty and how their situations affect children.
Guidance and Counseling; Health and Safety; Sociology
Dist - IU **Prod** - WCCOTV 1986

Suffer the Children 16 MIN
U-matic / VHS / 16mm
Color (H C A)
Presents children sharing their anguish at having to deal with alcholic parents. Explains that children of alcoholics often grow up to be introverted and friendless.
Psychology; Sociology
Dist - CAROUF **Prod** - CBSTV

Suffer the children - of alcoholic parents 16 MIN
16mm / U-matic / VHS
Color (H C A)
Presents several children who share their anguish and anxiety at having to cater to an alcoholic parent's emotional needs. Shows that these children are likely to be introverted and have alcohol problems themselves when they get older.
Health and Safety; Sociology
Dist - CAROUF **Prod** - DRAYNE

Sufferin' Until Suffrage 3 MIN
U-matic / VHS
America Rock Series
Color (I)
Examines women's struggle to vote, showing suffragettes like Susan B Anthony march in demonstrations, carry signs and spark passage of the 19th amendment.
Civics and Political Systems; History - World; Social Science
Dist - GA **Prod** - ABCTV 1976

Suffering in Silence - Abuse of the Elderly 29 MIN
U-matic
Color (C H)
Presents an overview of elder abuse through interviews with victims, caregivers, and human service professionals.
Guidance and Counseling; Health and Safety; Sociology
Dist - CSUS **Prod** - CSUS 1985

Suffragists After a Century 16 MIN
16mm
Color
LC 77-702656
Focuses on ten Canadian women in a discussion of the status of the women's movement in Canada.
Civics and Political Systems; Geography - World; Sociology
Dist - MARMO **Prod** - OFWTA 1975

The Sufi path 30 MIN
VHS / BETA
Mystical paths series
Color (G)
$29.95 purchase _ #S057
Features Irina Tweedie, Sufi teacher and author of 'Daughter of Fire,' who discusses the Sufis as inheritors of a tradition which has influenced many world religions. Part of a four - part series on mystical paths.
Religion and Philosophy
Dist - THINKA **Prod** - THINKA

Sugar
U-matic
Matter of taste series; Lesson 18
Color (H A)
Shows how to make chocolate truffles with praline filling. Illustrates basic principles of sugar cookery.
Home Economics
Dist - CDTEL **Prod** - COAST

Sugar and Spice and all is not Nice 19 MIN
U-matic / VHS / 16mm
Color (H C A)
Interviews actual rape victims. Points out the need for self defense and a change in social and cultural attitudes.
Psychology; Sociology
Dist - LCOA **Prod** - LCOA 1985

The Sugar Beet - How Sweet it is 13 MIN
16mm / U-matic / VHS
Color (P I J)
Shows the special machines crawling over fields, planting, spraying, weeding and harvesting sugar beets. Demonstrates how inside the plant, giant washing wheels clean and carry the beets to be sliced, diced and boiled. Concludes with huge centrifuges whirling the juice from the syrup, leaving fine white crystals ready for drying, sifting and packaging.
Agriculture; Social Science
Dist - BCNFL **Prod** - BORTF 1983

Sugar Bowl Classic 14 MIN
16mm
B&W
Shows the highlights of the football game between the Naval Academy and the University of Mississippi in the Sugar Bowl at New Orleans, Louisiana, on January 1, 1955.
Physical Education and Recreation
Dist - USNAC **Prod** - USA

Sugar Campaign 15 MIN
U-matic / VHS
Explorers Unlimited Series
Color (P I)
Inspects the complex operation of producing sugar from sugar beets.
Science - Natural; Social Science
Dist - AITECH **Prod** - WVIZTV 1971

Sugar cane 11 MIN
U-matic / VHS / 16mm
Color (J H A)
Looks at the communal life of the workers on the island of Negros in the Philippines as they harvest the sugar cane fields. Shows that the process from harvest to raw sugar crystals takes only 24 hours.
Agriculture; History - World
Dist - LUF **Prod** - LUF 1979

The Sugar Cereal Imitation Orange Breakfast 8 MIN
16mm
Color (I)
LC 75-702796
Shows how advertising can sell the sugar - frosted breakfast cereals even though they may be bad for the teeth and low in nutrition. Examines various orange juice products, discussing water, sugar, chemicals and other additives.
Home Economics; Social Science
Dist - BNCHMK **Prod** - WNETTV 1972

Sugar Country 27 MIN
16mm
Color (I J H)
Depicts the entire operations of the sugar industry from planting cane to packages on the grocery shelf. Discusses labor and environmental problems facing the industry. Shows how the industry is solving these problems.
Agriculture; Business and Economics; Social Science
Dist - FLADC **Prod** - FLADC 1973

The Sugar film 27 MIN
16mm / VHS / U-matic
Color (I J)
LC 81-700335; 80-701816
Discusses the harm sugar does, such as increasing the chance of heart disease, contributing 15 - 20 percent of a person's total caloric intake and producing a craving for more sugar.
Home Economics
Dist - PFP **Prod** - LISNDO 1980

The Sugar film 28 MIN
U-matic / VHS
Color
Points out that the average American consumes 129 pounds of sugar per year, compared with only four pounds 200 years ago. Examines the effects of this enormous dietary change on the physical and mental health of Americans.
Health and Safety; Social Science
Dist - IA **Prod** - LACFU

The Sugar film 57 MIN
VHS / 16mm
Color (I J)
Discusses the harm sugar does to the human body, such as increasing the chance of heart disease, contributing 15 - 20 percent of a person's total caloric intake and producing a craving for more sugar.
Health and Safety; Home Economics; Social Science
Dist - PFP **Prod** - LISNDO 1980

Sugar from beets 5 MIN
16mm / U-matic / VHS
European Studies - Germany Series
Color (H C A)
LC 76-700754
Describes the processes involved in obtaining sugar from beets.
Agriculture; Geography - World
Dist - IFB **Prod** - MFAFRG 1973

Sugar from Queensland 22 MIN
VHS
Color; PAL (J H)
PdS29
Covers the Australian sugar industry, from growing sugar cane through milling and refining processes. Produced by Fraser Castle Productions, Australia.
Agriculture; Geography - World
Dist - BHA **Prod** - CSTL

Sugar in Egypt 13 MIN
U-matic / VHS / 16mm
Man and His World Series
Color (P I J H C)
LC 77-705467
Shows the steps in the productoon of sugar, explains why progress is slow in using modern harvesting methods and tells why sugar has become a major Egyptian product.
Agriculture; Geography - World
Dist - FI **Prod** - FI 1969

Sugar is not Enough 14 MIN
16mm / U-matic / VHS
Just One Child Series
Color (I J)
Depicts the difficult work day of a fourteen - year old son of sugar cane farmers in Ecuador, as head of the family because his father works far away, coming home only occasionally. Shows a never - ending series of tasks, including cutting, crushing and refining the sugar cane as a cash crop for family support, going to school in a nearby town, and helping his mother with younger siblings as well as hunting and fishing.
Geography - World; Psychology; Sociology
Dist - BCNFL **Prod** - REYEXP 1983

The Sugar mill 10 MIN
16mm / U-matic / VHS
Captioned; Color (A) (PORTUGUESE (ENGLISH SUBTITLES))
Discusses the methods of sugar production in the Brazilian Northeast and the character of the mills and the life around them. Portuguese dialog with English subtitles.
Agriculture; Fine Arts
Dist - CNEMAG **Prod** - CNEMAG

Sugar molding 30 MIN
VHS / 16mm
Art of decorating cakes series
(G)
$49.00 purchase _ #BCD9
Instructs in the art of cake decoration. Shows how to mold sugar, sugar coloring, and sugar layon designs. Taught by Leon Simmons, master cake decorator.
Home Economics; Industrial and Technical Education
Dist - RMIBHF **Prod** - RMIBHF

Sugar Mountain Blues 28 MIN
U-matic
Color
Shows diabetic young people monitoring their own blood glucose levels and taking part in vigorous activity, including a mountain climbing weekend. Features mountain scenery.
Health and Safety
Dist - MTP **Prod** - BIODYN

Sugar Ray Leonard 11 MIN
U-matic
Color
Features Sugar Ray Leonard describing the information services available at the library. Focuses on career changes and possibilities.
Education; Social Science
Dist - LVN **Prod** - MDPL

Sugar Sullivan, Al Minns and Jane Goldberg 30 MIN
VHS / U-matic
Eye on Dance - Third World Dance, Tracing Roots Series
Color
Fine Arts
Dist - ARCVID **Prod** - ARCVID

The Sugar trap 57 MIN
VHS
Color (G)
$39.95 purchase _ #S01365
Reveals the potential health hazards of sugar consumption. Features Linus Pauling and Lendon Smith.
Health and Safety; Psychology; Social Science
Dist - UILL

Sugarbaby 86 MIN
VHS / 35mm / 16mm
Color (G) (GERMAN WITH ENGLISH SUBTITLES)
$250.00, $300.00 rental
Portrays a romance between an obese mortuary attendant - female - and a diminutive subway conductor - male. Directed by Percy Adlon.
Fine Arts
Dist - KINOIC

Sugarbush 15 MIN
U-matic / VHS
Explorers Unlimited Series
Color (P I)
Pictures a sugarbush to observe the old - fashioned method of making maple syrup.
Science - Natural; Social Science
Dist - AITECH **Prod** - WVIZTV 1971

Suggers, fruggers and datamuggers 50 MIN
VHS
Horizon series
Color (A)
PdS99 purchase
Looks into growing world of market research. Reveals that 'suggers' try to sell things under the cloak of market research, 'fruggers' fundraise under the same pretense, but it is the fear of 'datamugging' that concerns consumers most. There should be no danger of material from genuine market research being seriously abused - but how reliable is it. Looks at the use of survey methodology in commerce, politics and the media.
Business and Economics
Dist - BBCENE

Suggestion Box 9 MIN
16mm
B&W
Describes how war plant workers in 1944 were encouraged to submit suggestions and how some of these suggestions, when put into practice, resulted in saving of time, labor and materials.
Business and Economics; History - United States; Psychology; Social Science
Dist - USNAC **Prod** - USOE 1945

Suggestion System in Japan 30 MIN
U-matic / VHS
Business Nippon Series
Color (COR)
LC 85-702164
Business and Economics; History - World; Psychology
Dist - EBEC **Prod** - JAPCTV 1984

Suggestion System in Japanese Corporations 30 MIN
U-matic / VHS
Business Nippon Series
Color (COR)
LC 85-702163
Business and Economics; History - World; Psychology
Dist - EBEC **Prod** - JAPCTV 1984

Suggestions about Correcting and Criticizing People 29 MIN
16mm
Controlling Turnover and Absenteeism Series
B&W
LC 76-703321
Business and Economics; Psychology
Dist - EDSD **Prod** - EDSD

Suggestive selling for waiters and waitresses
U-matic / VHS / 16mm
Professional food preparation and service program series
Color
Demonstrates basic principles of suggestive selling and menu merchandising. Distinguishes the unimaginative order - taker from the profit - producing salesperson with special emphasis on the art of suggestive selling. Discusses the importance of the serving staff's understanding the psychology of the customer and having a thorough knowledge of menu items.
Industrial and Technical Education
Dist - NEM **Prod** - NEM 1983

Suho and the White Horse 10 MIN
16mm / U-matic / VHS
Color (K P I)
LC 82-700262
Retells the Mongolian legend about a poor shepherd whose devotion to his horse resulted in the creation of the traditional horse - headed fiddle of the Mongolian steppes. Based on the book Suho And The White Horse by Yuzo Otsuka.
Literature and Drama
Dist - WWS **Prod** - WWS 1982

The Suicidal Patient
U-matic / VHS
Crisis Intervention Series
Color
Shows how proper evaluation and management of suicidal patients may ultimately prevent self - imposed death. Provides techniques necessary for dealing with this crisis.
Psychology; Sociology
Dist - VTRI **Prod** - VTRI

The Suicidal Patient 20 MIN
U-matic / VHS
Medical Crisis Intervention Series
Color (PRO)
Teaches effective inter - activity with the suicidal patient so that assessment of lethality and appropriate disposition can be achieved. Covers common factors precipitating suicidal behavior, interview guidelines and follow - up care.
Health and Safety; Sociology
Dist - LEIKID **Prod** - LEIKID

The Suicidal patient - Part 1 15 MIN
VHS / U-matic
Caring for the psychiatric patient series
Color (PRO)
$200.00 purchase, $40.00 rental _ #4261S, #4261V
Dramatizes the needs of suicidal patients in the emergency room, including physical safety, determining the validity of the attempt, assessing emotional stability, and planning either admission or discharge with follow - up. Urges awareness of personal judgments so that personal views are not inappropriately imposed. Part of a four - part series on psychiatric nursing care which stresses the integration of physical and psychological care.
Health and Safety; Sociology
Dist - AJN **Prod** - SEH 1985

Suicide 30 MIN
VHS / U-matic
Mind and body series
Color (PRO C)
$395.00 purchase, $80.00 rental _ #C850 - VI - 040
Discusses common misconceptions about suicide and the characteristics of those who commit suicide. Look at what others should do when someone is suicidal and the effect of suicide on survivors. Presented by Drs Joseph Himmelsbach and Jonathan A Freedman. Part of a series.
Health and Safety; Sociology
Dist - HSCIC

Suicide 30 MIN
VHS / U-matic
New Voice Series
Color (H C A)
Dramatizes the investigations of the staff of a high school newspaper. Focuses on suicide.
Sociology
Dist - GPN **Prod** - WGBHTV

Suicide 17 MIN
U-matic / VHS
Color (PRO)
LC 77-730531
Explores attempted suicide, an emotional event and a challenge to nursing care. Reveals circumstances commonly observed among depressed persons who become suicidal and the events that may precede their suicide attempts.
Health and Safety; Psychology; Sociology
Dist - MEDCOM **Prod** - MEDCOM

Suicide - a teenage dilemma 30 MIN
U-matic / VHS
Color (G T C)
$195.00 purchase _ #C870 - VI - 058
Portrays a frustrated young woman trying unsuccessfully to talk with her father. Emphasizes the need of young people to feel that someone cares about them and will listen to their problems. Intersperses the young woman's story with clips of a group of young people who have attempted suicide or had friends who committed suicide, parents whose children have committed suicide and two teens, one who feels suicidal and one whose friend committed suicide and comments by producer Dr Evelyn Virshup, clinical psychologist Michael Peck and Norman Faberow, director of the LA Suicide Prevention Center. Discusses clues and behavior changes indicating suicidal tendencies.
Sociology
Dist - HSCIC
HRMC

Suicide and abuse - the vulnerable elderly 120 MIN
VHS
Virginia Geriatric Education Center Video Conference series
Color (G C PRO)
$149.00 purchase, $55.00 rental
Considers elderly persons' reasons for and means of committing suicide and ways the underlying depression can be treated, as well as reasons for abuse of older people by those around them.
Health and Safety; Sociology
Dist - TNF **Prod** - VGEREC

Suicide at 17 18 MIN
16mm
Color (H C A)
LC 77-703493
Investigates the problem of adolescent suicide through interviews with the teammates, neighbors and parents of a high school suicide victim.
Education; Psychology; Sociology
Dist - LAWREN **Prod** - EISBGI 1977

Suicide - but Jack was a Good Driver 15 MIN
U-matic / VHS / 16mm
Conflict and awareness series
Color (I J H)
LC 74-701918
Presents two boys exploring the subject of suicide because of their fear that their friend may have tried to take his own life.

Guidance and Counseling; Sociology
Dist - CRMP Prod - CRMP 1974

Suicide - Call for Help 23 MIN
U-matic / VHS / 16mm
Color (J H)
$50 rental _ #9844
Provides a basis for discussion on why young people try suicide and what can be done to prevent it. Suggestions for lifting oneself out of depressions or severe mood swings are given in the film.
Guidance and Counseling; Sociology
Dist - AIMS Prod - AIMS 1986

Suicide - Causes and Prevention 32 MIN
VHS
Color (J H)
Probes social and psychological causes of suicide. Dispels misconceptions, and argues that most suicides can be prevented. Encourages students to watch for symptoms, and teaches appropriate intervention.
Guidance and Counseling; Health and Safety; Sociology
Dist - HRMC Prod - HRMC 1976

Suicide - causes and prevention series
Causes
Prevention
Dist - IBIS

Suicide Clinic - a Cry for Help 28 MIN
16mm / U-matic / VHS
B&W
LC 74-712839
Examines what may lie behind a suicide attempt. Points out that suicides cross all socioeconomic levels and that these persons are not necessarily less stable emotionally. Shows how suicide clinics can help people who are contemplating suicide.
Sociology
Dist - IU Prod - NET 1971

Suicide for Glory 27 MIN
16mm / U-matic / VHS
Victory at Sea Series
B&W (J H)
Shows highlights of the Battle for Okinawa.
Civics and Political Systems; History - United States; History - World
Dist - LUF Prod - NBCTV

Suicide - I don't want to die young 30 MIN
VHS
Teen - aiders video series
Color (I J H G)
$149.95 purchase _ #NIMBS1V
Examines true - life scenarios from teenagers. Discusses knowing when and how to approach someone thinking of suicide and ways of detecting when someone needs help. Interviews teens to point out that many young people don't know how to approach this sensitive issue. Includes a workbook. Part of a four - part series on teen issues.
Sociology
Dist - CAMV

Suicide - I don't want you to die 29 MIN
VHS
Color (I J H C G)
$149.00 purchase _ #NC106
Describes a teen suicide prevention program. Uses true - life scenarios and answers critical questions regarding the subject. Includes a workbook.
Psychology; Sociology
Dist - AAVIM Prod - AAVIM

Suicide in the elderly 29 MIN
VHS / 16mm
Health care today
Color (H C G)
$90.00 purchase _ #BPN109807
Presents two dramatized case studies of suicide in elderly people. Features discussion by a panel of physicians.
Health and Safety; Sociology
Dist - RMIBHF Prod - RMIBHF
TVOTAR

Suicide - it Doesn't have to Happen 20 MIN
U-matic / VHS / 16mm
Color (H C)
LC 76-702116
Presents a dramatization, based on case histories, about a high school teacher who helps a suicidal student.
Education; Psychology; Sociology
Dist - PHENIX Prod - PHENIX 1976

Suicide Prevention - a Teacher's Training Program 30 MIN
VHS
Color
Looks at underlying social and psychological causes of teenage suicide, and examines the role of the teacher as well as other personnel in the early identification of suicidal behavior in students.
Health and Safety; Sociology
Dist - HRMC Prod - HRMC 1986

Suicide Prevention Center of Los Angeles 19 MIN
16mm
B&W
LC 75-703236
Presents a documentary report showing the research which led to the establishment of the Suicide Prevention Center of Los Angeles. Includes a description of how the center functions and lists some of its purposes and goals. Emphasizes the increasing seriousness of the problem of suicide, the number ten killer in the U S. Produced with an animated camera technique which uses still photographs and a spontaneous narration by the co - directors of the center.
Psychology; Sociology
Dist - USC Prod - USPHS 1962

Suicide Prevention in Hospitals 30 MIN
U-matic / VHS / 16mm
B&W
Shows how hospital personnel can anticipate and prevent suicide attempts. Based on 12 years of research by the VA's unit for the study of unpredicted death.
Health and Safety; Sociology
Dist - USNAC Prod - USVA

Suicide Prevention - the Physician's Role 20 MIN
16mm
B&W
LC FIA67-624
Presents an analysis of suicidal clues. Explains that in the United States in 1966, suicide ranked among the first ten causes of death - - third highest in the age group 15 - 25. Dramatizes, in five case histories, early clues to suicide and their proper management.
Health and Safety; Psychology; Sociology
Dist - AMEDA Prod - ROCHEL 1967

The Suicide squeeze 27 MIN
16mm
Color (G)
$60.00 rental
Employs various techniques from animation, film noir and documentary to avant - garde. Makes active use of optical manipulation, including color xerox, optical printing, animation and high speed cinematography. A Brady Lewis production.
Fine Arts
Dist - CANCIN

Suicide Survivors 26 MIN
U-matic / VHS
Color (C)
$249.00, $149.00 purchase _ #AD - 1942
Reveals that because suicide is sudden, often violent and burdened with guilt and stigma, it may be the most traumatic of all deaths for survivors. Explores the special needs of suicide survivors, the role of suicide survivor groups in helping survivors cope with the bereavement process and changing societal attitudes that enable suicide survivors to come out of the closet.
Health and Safety; Sociology
Dist - FOTH Prod - FOTH

Suicide - Teenage Crisis 10 MIN
16mm / U-matic / VHS
Color (J)
LC 81-700020
Tells how one California community is attempting to offer suicide counseling to parents, teenagers and teachers.
Sociology
Dist - CRMP Prod - CBSTV 1981

Suicide - the Unheard Cry 45 MIN
16mm
B&W
LC 74-706268
Presents an analysis of suicidal personalities and their behavior patterns as may be encountered in military life. Emphasizes the assistance that can be offered to prevent suicide attempts.
Civics and Political Systems; Psychology; Sociology
Dist - USNAC Prod - USA 1969

Suicide - the warning signs 24 MIN
16mm / U-matic / VHS
Color (J H)
LC 82-700739
Presents a dramatization about three teenagers who exhibit some of the most common warning signs of suicide.
Sociology
Dist - CORF Prod - CENTRO 1982

Suicide - the will to Die 60 MIN
16mm
Color
Examines the psychological and emotional context of suicide. Introduces a woman who attempted to take her life, reveals what drove her to the act and explains how she learned to make a successful adjustment to life.
Sociology
Dist - NABSP Prod - NABSP

Suicide - the will to die - Pt 1 30 MIN
16mm
Color
Examines the psychological and emotional context of suicide. Introduces a woman who attempted to take her life, reveals what drove her to the act and explains how she learned to make a successful adjustment to life.
Sociology
Dist - NABSP Prod - NABSP

Suicide - the will to die - Pt 2 30 MIN
16mm
Color
Examines the psychological and emotional context of suicide. Introduces a woman who attempted to take her life, reveals what drove her to the act and explains how she learned to make a successful adjustment to life.
Sociology
Dist - NABSP Prod - NABSP

Suitable for Framing 26 MIN
16mm
B&W
LC 79-700734
Looks at a mystery love triangle set in a film noir milieu.
Fine Arts
Dist - GDG Prod - GDG 1979

Suite California - Stops and passes - Part 1 46 MIN
16mm
(G)
$95.00 rental
Ranges over geography and time with some early Edison footage. Blends irony and nostalgia for Hollywood.
Geography - United States
Dist - CANCIN Prod - NELSOR 1976

Suite California - Stops and passes - Part 2 48 MIN
16mm
(G)
$95.00 rental
Ranges over geography and time with some early Edison footage. Renders personal autobiographical material as a travelogue.
Geography - United States; Literature and Drama
Dist - CANCIN Prod - NELSOR 1978

Suite California Stops and Passes - Pts I and II 93 MIN
16mm
Color (C)
$2240.00
Experimental film by Robert Nelson.
Fine Arts
Dist - AFA Prod - AFA

Suite fantaisiste 9 MIN
VHS / U-matic
Videodance project series; Vol One
Color
Looks at 18th century life seen through dance, poetry and the 'fan language' of the time. Features musical performers Sandra Miller, James Richmond and Sarah Cunningham.
Fine Arts
Dist - ARCVID Prod - ARCVID

Suite of Berber dances 10 MIN
16mm
B&W
Presents a study of three folk dances of the berbers of Morocco. Includes a dance by a group of men providing their own music, a war dance from the foothills of the Atlas Mountains and a fiery 'geudra' by a nomad girl of the western Sahara.
Fine Arts; Geography - World
Dist - RADIM Prod - CENCM 1963

Suite of Faces 11 MIN
16mm
B&W
Reviews the faces from French art in 13th century stone, 16th century oils and wood - cuts and engravings of all periods, surviving today in the people of France.
Fine Arts
Dist - RADIM Prod - FILIM

The Suitors 106 MIN
35mm

Color (G A)
Portrays an Iranian celebration of marriage in a New York City apartment where celebrants shishkebob a live sheep. Reveals that a SWAT team, which thinks the party is a gathering of terrorists, descends upon the party, killing the groom and leaving a bewildered, beautiful widow and four zealous suitors. Produced by Ghasem Ebrahimian.
History - United States; Literature and Drama; Social Science; Sociology
Dist - FIRS

Suits, Symbols and Success
VHS / U-matic
Success Image Series
Color (A)
Examines the suit as a symbol, explaining the importance of color, the best fabrics and styles for busines wear, the basic business looks, importance of attitude, and the need for consistency in a business wardrobe.
Business and Economics; Guidance and Counseling; Psychology
Dist - GPCV **Prod** - GPCV

Sukarno and the Emergence of Indonesia 29 MIN
Videoreel / VT2
Course of Our Times II Series
Color (H C)
History - World
Dist - PBS **Prod** - WGBHTV

Suky Durham - 5 - 10 - 80 60 MIN
VHS / Cassette
Poetry Center reading series
Color (G)
$15.00, $45.00 purchase, $15.00 rental _ #398 - 327
Features the writer at the Women Writers Union reading on the workplace presenting two talks entitled Homecoming and Convictions, at the Poetry Center, San Francisco State University.
Literature and Drama
Dist - POETRY

Suleyman the magnificent 57 MIN
VHS
Color (H C T A)
$39.95 purchase _ #S01334
Profiles the 16th century sultan Suleyman, who ruled the Ottoman Empire. Reveals that Suleyman reigned 46 years, showing strong leadership as a lawgiver and military man. Filmed on location in Turkey, featuring mosques built in that era.
Civics and Political Systems; Geography - World; History - World
Dist - UILL

Suleyman the Magnificent 58 MIN
VHS
Color (G)
$39.95 purchase _ #412 - 9068
Explores breathtaking Ottoman palaces and mosques, focusing on the dramatic life of Sultan Suleyman, audacious military leader, celebrated poet, and enthusiastic patron of art and architecture. Recollects his renown as the second Solomon in the 16th century when he ruled half the civilized world. Filmed on location in Turkey, this program remembers the 46 - year reign of Suleyman when the Ottoman Empire experienced a Golden Age.
Geography - World; History - World
Dist - FI **Prod** - MMOA 1987

Sulfonamides and penicillins 30 MIN
16mm
Pharmacology series
Color (C)
LC 73-703355
Health and Safety
Dist - TELSTR **Prod** - MVNE 1971

Sulfur and its Compounds 14 MIN
U-matic / VHS / 16mm
Color (H C)
Demonstrates the chemical and physical properties of sulfur, including the formation of its allotropic forms. Describes the Frasch process, and emphasizes the importance of sulfur in modern industry, medicine and agriculture.
Science - Physical
Dist - CORF **Prod** - CORF 1962

Sulfuric acid and hydrochloric acid 26 MIN
VHS
Color (IND PRO)
$395.00 purchase, $150.00 rental
Teaches fundamental lessons about identifying corrosives, the hazards of these acids, occupancies where acids are found, reactivity problems, why water may be dangerous, neutralization operations, emergency medical treatment, decontamination and environmental concerns.
Health and Safety; Science - Physical; Sociology
Dist - JEWELR

Sullivan's Travels 91 MIN
16mm
B&W
Tells how Hollywood director John L Sullivan, dissatisfied with his moneymaking escapist entertainments, dons a tramp's garb and sets forth to see how the other half lives. Directed by Preston Sturges.
Fine Arts
Dist - TWYMAN **Prod** - UPCI

Sulmet Sulfamethazine in the Treatment of Livestock Disease 35 MIN
16mm
Color (H C A)
Explains that special attention is given to the major infectious diseases of horses, swine, sheep, beef cattle and dairy cattle. Describes the use of the wonderworking sulfa drug, sulmet sulfamethazine, and shows the results of treatment by those drugs.
Agriculture; Health and Safety
Dist - LEDR **Prod** - TF 1949

Sulphur 21 MIN
16mm
B&W (C)
Shows the mining of sulfur by the Frasch process and its uses both in the elemental form and after conversion of sulfuric acid.
Business and Economics; Industrial and Technical Education; Science - Physical; Social Science
Dist - HEFL **Prod** - TEXGS 1953

Sum and Substance Series

Aldous Huxley	30 MIN
Alfred Kazin	30 MIN
Paul Tillich	30 MIN
Roy Harris	30 MIN
Upton Sinclair	30 MIN

Dist - MLA

The Sum of its parts - regions, nations, state 30 MIN
VHS
Remaking of Canada - Canadian government and politics in the 1990s 'series
Color (H C G)
$89.95 purchase _ #WLU - 512
Discusses regional perspectives on regionalism in Canada's six regions - the Atlantic provinces, Quebec, Ontario, the Prairie provinces, British Columbia and the North. Considers federal - provincial relations in light of the growing influence of regionalism in Canadian government and politics. Looks at Canada's future as whole greater than the sum of its parts - ten provinces, two territories, six regions and many nations in one state. Part of a 12 - part series incorporating interviews with Canadian politicians and hosted by Dr John Redekop.
Civics and Political Systems; History - World
Dist - INSTRU **Prod** - TELCOL 1992

Sumi - E 7.5 MIN
16mm
B&W (C)
Experimental film by Francis Lee.
Fine Arts
Dist - AFA **Prod** - AFA 1975

Summary 35 MIN
U-matic
Holistic Medicine in Primary Care Series
Color (C)
Summarizes the series on holistic medicine and discusses the implications of the cases presented.
Health and Safety; Science - Natural
Dist - UOKLAH **Prod** - UOKLAH 1986

Summary 29 MIN
16mm
Controlling Turnover and Absenteeism Series
B&W
LC 76-703321
Business and Economics; Psychology
Dist - EDSD **Prod** - EDSD

Summary and review of sketching techniques 29 MIN
U-matic
Sketching techniques series; Lesson 30
Color (C A)
Reviews important aspects of sketching. Reemphasizes drawing as a vehicle for the visual communication of ideas.
Fine Arts
Dist - CDTEL **Prod** - COAST

The Summary Court - Martial 45 MIN
16mm
B&W
LC FIE54-374
Presents four typical cases which may be tried in a summary court - martial. Illustrates conditions which prompt a recommendation for trial, relationship of the summary court officer to the accused and the procedure followed in trial, conviction and sentencing.

Civics and Political Systems
Dist - USNAC **Prod** - USA 1954

Summary of Earth Science 30 MIN
U-matic / VHS
Earth, Sea and Sky Series
Color (C)
Completes the geologic history of the USA from 200 million years ago to the present. Provides a summary of the 30 half - hour lessons in the Earth, Sea and Sky Series.
Science - Physical
Dist - DALCCD **Prod** - DALCCD

Summary of the Course 30 MIN
U-matic
Introduction to Mathematics Series
Color (C)
Mathematics
Dist - MDCPB **Prod** - MDCPB

Summation 42 MIN
VHS
Trial masters forum series
Color (C PRO)
$42.00 purchase _ #1V3-93
Examines ways to predicate the final argument on carefully developed case themes, and teaches the fundamental oratorical principles of creating a convincing summation. Excerpts from actual summations are presented by Howard Nations.
Civics and Political Systems
Dist - ATLA

Summation notation 30 MIN
VHS
Calculus series
Color (C)
$125.00 purchase _ #6045
Explains summation notation. Part of a 56 - part series on calculus.
Mathematics
Dist - LANDMK **Prod** - LANDMK

Summations and Notation
U-matic
Calculus Series
Color
Mathematics
Dist - MDCPB **Prod** - MDDE

Summer 11 MIN
U-matic / VHS / 16mm
Seasons Series
Color (K P)
LC 80-701935
Presents an overview of the natural and recreational events of summer, showing traditional holidays of the season.
Science - Natural; Social Science
Dist - CORF **Prod** - CENTRO 1980

Summer 15 MIN
U-matic / VHS / 16mm
Four Seasons Series
Color (P I)
Looks at the activities and changes common to the summer season such as crops developing in the fields and the forest turning green with new growth. Shows bees collecting pollen and nectar, birds feeding their young and a caterpillar becoming a beautiful butterfly.
Science - Natural
Dist - NGS **Prod** - NGS 1983

Summer 30 MIN
U-matic
Polka Dot Door Series
Color (K)
Presents a variety show for pre - school children. Includes songs, mime, stories, film sequences, talk, dance and fantasy figures. Each show emphasizes a particular theme such as numbers, feelings, exploring, music or time. Comes with parent teacher guide.
Fine Arts; Literature and Drama
Dist - TVOTAR **Prod** - TVOTAR 1985

Summer - 1966 20 MIN
16mm
Screen news digest series; Vol 9; Issue 1
B&W
Documents significant events of the summer of 1966, such as the flights of Gemini 9 and 10 and Surveyor, Charles de Gaulle's visit to Russia, the work of archaeologists in Bolivia, and the rebuilding of South Vietnam.
History - World; Science
Dist - HEARST **Prod** - HEARST 1966

Summer, 1966 - a nation builds under fire 4 MIN
16mm
Screen news digest series; Vol 9; Issue 1
B&W (J)
LC 72-700282
Studies the struggle of South Vietnam to defend her freedom and to build her future.

Geography - World; History - World
Dist - HEARST **Prod** - HEARST 1966

Summer, 1966 - conquest in space 4 MIN
16mm
Screen news digest series; Vol 9; Issue 1
B&W (J)
LC 70-700279
A review of space achievements by the United States in the summer of 1966. Includes scenes of the walk around the world by astronaut Eugene Cernan, the lunar photographs made by Surveyor, and the docking in space of Agena 10 and Gemini 10.
History - United States; Science - Physical
Dist - HEARST **Prod** - HEARST 1966

Summer, 1966 - Mission to Moscow 5 MIN
16mm
Screen news digest series; Vol 9; Issue 1
B&W (J)
LC 79-700281
A view of life in Moscow, and a report on the visit of Charles de Gaulle to the Russian capital.
Geography - World
Dist - HEARST **Prod** - HEARST 1966

Summer, 1966 - pilgrimage into the past 4 MIN
16mm
Screen news digest series; Vol 9; Issue 1
B&W (J H C)
LC 75-700280
Shows scenes of an archeological expedition to the land of the Tiwanakus in Bolivia.
Geography - World; Science - Physical
Dist - HEARST **Prod** - HEARST 1966

Summer 68 60 MIN
16mm
Color
Focuses on draft resistance in Boston in an attempt to define the nature of commitment to the 'Movement' against a backdrop of the summer's activity.
Guidance and Counseling; History - United States; Sociology
Dist - CANWRL **Prod** - FRUDOU 1968

Summer Adventure 19 MIN
16mm
Color
LC 77-702147
Tells the story of the Summer Adventure program at the High Country Inn of Winter Park, Colorado, a vacation program which offers challenges in the Colorado outdoors.
Geography - United States; Physical Education and Recreation
Dist - LANGED **Prod** - HIGHCI 1977

Summer at Grandpa's 102 MIN
35mm
Color; PAL (G)
Visits a city boy's summer vacation at his ancestral home in the Taiwanese countryside. Creates a realistic picture about tradition, modernization and basic human emotions. Marble Film Productions, Taiwan. Contact distributor about price and availability outside the United Kingdom.
Geography - World; Psychology; Sociology
Dist - BALFOR

Summer Brenner - 11 - 16 - 76
VHS / Cassette
Poetry Center reading series
B&W (G)
$15.00, $45.00 purchase, $15.00 rental _ #232 - 187A
Features the writer reading from her works at the Poetry Center, San Francisco State University.
Literature and Drama
Dist - POETRY **Prod** - POETRY 1976

Summer Brenner - 5 - 18 - 77 30 MIN
VHS / Cassette
Poetry Center reading series
Color (G)
$15.00, $45.00 purchase, $15.00 rental _ #261 - 215
Features the writer reading from Genetrix and Essays at the Poetry Center, San Francisco State University.
Literature and Drama
Dist - POETRY **Prod** - POETRY 1977

Summer Brenner - 5 - 1 - 75 25 MIN
VHS / Cassette
Poetry Center reading series
Color (G)
$15.00, $45.00 purchase, $15.00 rental _ #123 - 94
Features the writer at the Poetry Center, San Francisco State University, giving a reading dedicated to the National Liberation Front. Includes selections from Elements of Industry - a series.
Literature and Drama
Dist - POETRY **Prod** - POETRY 1975

Summer Brenner - 3 - 15 - 84 30 MIN
VHS / Cassette
Poetry Center reading series
Color (G)
$15.00, $45.00 purchase, $15.00 rental _ #581 - 491
Features the writer at the Poetry Center, San Francisco State University, reading The History of Metal.
Literature and Drama
Dist - POETRY **Prod** - POETRY 1984

Summer Camp 13 MIN
U-matic / VHS / 16mm
Learning Values with Fat Albert and the Cosby Kids, Set I Series
Color (K P I)
Discloses that the kids have mixed feelings about being away from home for the first time when they go off to summer camp. Explains that besides the newness of the situation and meeting children of other races, there is a camp bully who makes things worse with his practical jokes and general nasty disposition. Relates that Russell decides he has had enough and runs away, only to get himself in a real jam. Concludes with Russell being rescued by the camp bully, everyone becoming friends and promising to meet again next year.
Guidance and Counseling; Sociology
Dist - MGHT **Prod** - FLMTON 1975

Summer Camp 30 MIN
U-matic
Today's Special Series
Color (K P)
Develops language arts skills in children. Programs are thematically designed around subjects of interest to youngsters. Action takes place in a department store where people, mannequins, puppets, comic characters and special guests present a light hearted approach to language arts.
Fine Arts; Literature and Drama; Psychology
Dist - TVOTAR **Prod** - TVOTAR 1985

Summer camp 10 MIN
VHS
Stop, look, listen series
Color; PAL (P I J)
Follows the adventures of a group of children spending part of their summer holidays at a summer camp. Explores the relationships and responsibilities of the children. Part of a series of films which start from some everyday observation and show more of what is happening, how and why. Builds vocabulary and encourages children to be more observant.
English Language; Physical Education and Recreation; Social Science; Sociology
Dist - VIEWTH

The Summer children 44 MIN
16mm
B&W (T)
LC FIA67-625
A study of the education of disadvantaged children. Examines an experimental program at a university laboratory school where four teachers carried out a language arts program with a group of four - to eight - year - olds from a depressed area. Shows classroom incidents as they actually occurred, explaining how children and teachers learned from each other.
Education; Psychology
Dist - UCLA **Prod** - FAE 1965

Summer Decision 30 MIN
16mm
Color; B&W (I)
LC FIA66-1336
Tells the story of a high school graduate who is torn between going to college in the fall or having a surfing vacation in Hawaii. Shows that he attends a summer church camp where he learns the importance of faith.
Guidance and Counseling; Psychology; Religion and Philosophy
Dist - FAMF **Prod** - FAMF 1966

Summer Dreams 3 MIN
VHS / U-matic
Color
Presents a whimsical flow of memories from childhood using the process of rotoscoping live - action images.
Fine Arts; Industrial and Technical Education; Psychology
Dist - MEDIPR **Prod** - MEDIPR 1979

Summer Fun 15 MIN
VHS / U-matic
Mrs Cabobble's Caboose
(P)
Designed to teach primary grade students basic music concepts. Highlights melody, rhythm, harmony and the different families of instruments. Features Mrs. Fran Powell.
Fine Arts
Dist - GPN **Prod** - WDCNTV 1986

Summer Hanging Plants 29 MIN
Videoreel / VT2
Making Things Grow III Series
Color
Features Thalassa Cruso discussing different aspects of gardening. Explains how to grow and care for geraniums.
Agriculture; Science - Natural
Dist - PBS **Prod** - WGBHTV

Summer Ice 23 MIN
U-matic / VHS
Color
Visits the seventh continent, Antarctica where Adelie penguins breed by the millions on the summer ice. Follows the nesting and breeding procedures until it's time to return to deep ocean for the winter.
Geography - World; Science - Natural
Dist - NWLDPR **Prod** - NWLDPR

Summer in Nature 14 MIN
16mm / U-matic / VHS
Seasons in Nature Series
Color (P I)
LC 79-701832
Illustrates the changes which occur in plants and animals during summer.
Science - Natural
Dist - ALTSUL **Prod** - CASDEN 1979

Summer in the Parks 15 MIN
16mm
Color
LC 78-707385
Portrays the summer in the parks project. Shows children from the Washington, DC, metropolitan area as they are involved in the varied activities of the program.
Geography - United States; Sociology
Dist - USNPS **Prod** - USNPS 1969

Summer in the Parks, 1968 19 MIN
U-matic
Color
LC 79-706161
Shows the U S National Park Service's Summer in the Parks program and depicts the reactions of participating children in the metropolitan Washington, DC, area. Issued in 1969 as a motion picture.
Geography - United States; Physical Education and Recreation
Dist - USNAC **Prod** - USNPS 1979

Summer Incident 27 MIN
16mm
Color
Uses the Lebanon crisis to emphasize the importance of being able to react quickly to continuous world crises and small war situations. Shows the important role played by the navy and marine corps in supporting the foreign policy of the United States. Features the sixth fleet.
Civics and Political Systems; History - World
Dist - USNAC **Prod** - USN 1959

Summer interlude - Illicit interlude 95 MIN
VHS
B&W (G)
$29.95 purchase _ #SUM050
Features an aging ballerina recalling the delirious summer she experienced with her first love. Introduces themes basic to Ingmar Bergman's future productions. Set on an idyllic island near Stockholm.
Fine Arts; Health and Safety; Psychology; Religion and Philosophy
Dist - HOMVIS **Prod** - JANUS 1950

Summer is Here
U-matic / VHS / 16mm
Seasons - an Introductory Series
Color; Captioned (K P)
Explains why seasons occur. Details the changes in the activities of people and animals and the alterations in nature following the turning of the seasons. One of a four part series.
Science - Natural
Dist - IFB **Prod** - BERLET 1971

Summer is Here 10 MIN
16mm / U-matic / VHS
Captioned; Color (P)
Captures the hot weather fun of camping, swimmming and the Fourth of July. Describes animal life during the summer. Captioned for the hearing impaired.
Science - Natural
Dist - IFB **Prod** - BERLET 1967

Summer is here; 2nd ed. 11 MIN
U-matic / VHS / 16mm
Seasons series
Color (P)
LC 80-700463
Focuses on the activities of people and animals and the alterations in nature during summer.
Science - Natural
Dist - IFB **Prod** - IFB 1979

Summer Landscape 29 MIN
U-matic
Magic of Oil Painting Series
Color
Fine Arts
Dist - PBS **Prod** - KOCETV

Summer Legend 8 MIN
U-matic / VHS / 16mm
Color (P I)
$185 purchase - 16 mm, $140 purchase - video
Tells about a Micmac Indian legend that explains the cycle of the seasons. Produced by the National Film Board of Canada.
Science - Physical
Dist - CF

Summer Magic 109 MIN
16mm
Color
Presents the story of a widow who gives up her home in Boston and brings her three children to a small sleepy village in Maine. Discusses the almost immediate pandemonium and hilarity which ensues.
Fine Arts
Dist - TWYMAN **Prod** - DISNEY 1967

Summer Movements in the Arctic 15 MIN
16mm
B&W
LC FIE55-199
Describes the terrain of arctic and subarctic regions, the difficulties of moving men and supplies and problems of camping and survival.
Geography - World
Dist - USNAC **Prod** - USA 1950

Summer - Nature's Sights and Sounds 14 MIN
16mm / U-matic / VHS
Nature's Sights and Sounds Series
Color (P I)
Shows the effect of the warm sun on wildlife areas from the far northern tundra to the southern forests.
Science - Natural
Dist - BCNFL **Prod** - MASLKS 1984

Summer of '42 102 MIN
16mm
Color
Describes a young boy's coming of age in a small New England community in 1942.
Fine Arts
Dist - TWYMAN **Prod** - WB 1971

Summer of '63 20 MIN
U-matic / VHS / 16mm
Color (J H)
LC 76-702168
Dramatizes how VD touched three of the four main characters in this film and explores the VD problem of yesterday and the VD epidemic of today.
Health and Safety; Sociology
Dist - AIMS **Prod** - DAVP 1974

Summer of Decision - Central America 52 MIN
VHS / U-matic
Color (H C A)
Guides through the labyrinth of Central America. Reveals a Reagan administration, sure of its investments in Central America while depicting a cautious American public reluctant to participate in yet another guerilla war fought on foreign soil.
History - World
Dist - FI **Prod** - NBCNEW

Summer Of Judgement Series
The Impeachment Hearings 60 MIN
The Watergate Hearings 120 MIN
Dist - PBS

Summer of judgment - the impeachment hearings 60 MIN
VHS / U-matic
Color (H C A)
Tells the story of the Articles of Impeachment drafted concerning Richard Nixon by the House Judiciary Committee. Contains footage of the original committee debates as well as interviews with many of the participants several years later.
Civics and Political Systems; History - United States
Dist - WETATV **Prod** - WETATV

Summer of judgment - the Watergate hearings 114 MIN
U-matic / VHS
Color (H C A)
LC 83-707474
Distills the six months of Watergate hearings. Introduces members of the Senate investigating committee and the Nixon aides whose testimonies are heard. Presents personal recollections of participants' thoughts and feelings as events were unfolding. Includes archival stills which are periodically montaged with the interviews. Provdes a contemporary perspective on the impact of Watergate.
Civics and Political Systems
Dist - WETATV **Prod** - WETATV 1983

Summer of My German Soldier 98 MIN
U-matic / VHS / 16mm
Captioned; Color (P J)
LC 79-700439
Tells the story of Patty Bergen, a Jewish girl who is treated as an outsider by her neighbors in Jenkinsville. Shows how she forms a friendship with a German POW being held there during World War II. Stars Kristy McNichol and Bruce Davidson.
Fine Arts; Literature and Drama
Dist - LCOA **Prod** - HGATE 1978

Summer of the Colts 27 MIN
U-matic / VHS / 16mm
Color (J)
LC 79-701787
Presents the bittersweet story of three horses who attempted to achieve harness racing imortality.
Fine Arts; Physical Education and Recreation
Dist - MCFI **Prod** - LANGED 1976

The Summer of the Swans 15 MIN
U-matic / VHS
Best of Cover to Cover 2 Series
Color (I)
Literature and Drama
Dist - WETATV **Prod** - WETATV

Summer picnic 30 MIN
VHS
Join in series
Color (K P)
#362305
Reveals that when Jacob, Nikki and Zack attempt to leave their workship for a picnic they are repeatedly thwarted, but through song, dance, cooperation and a lot of improvisation they help each other deal with some unexpected emergencies. Part of a series about three artist - performers who share studio space in a converted warehouse.
Fine Arts; Literature and Drama
Dist - TVOTAR **Prod** - TVOTAR 1989

Summer Quest 1 MIN
U-matic
Color
Encourages the use of the public library in the summer.
Education; Social Science
Dist - LVN **Prod** - MDPL

Summer snow 30 MIN
VHS
Crossroads of life series
Color (I J H R G A)
$24.95 purchase _ #87EE0809
Depicts a stressed - out businessman who turns to cocaine in hopes of relieving his problems. Shows that the man discovers that cocaine is not the answer, and turns to Christian faith to overcome his drug habit.
Guidance and Counseling; Literature and Drama; Religion and Philosophy
Dist - CPH **Prod** - CPH
APH

The Summer Snowman
VHS / 35mm strip
Children's Sound Filmstrips Series
Color (K)
$33.00 purchase
Adapts a children's story by G Zion. Part of a series.
English Language; Literature and Drama
Dist - PELLER

Summer Solstice 48 MIN
16mm / U-matic / VHS
Color (H C A)
Looks at a couple whose marriage has lasted 50 years. Joins them on a visit to the beach where they met and fell in love and where they recount the joyous moments and the losses in their marriage.
Sociology
Dist - CORF **Prod** - WCVBTV 1983

Summer sports - summer fun 3 MIN
16mm
Of all things series
Color (P I)
Discusses sports and fun activities for summer.
Physical Education and Recreation
Dist - AVED **Prod** - BAILYL

Summer switch 31 MIN
U-matic / 16mm / VHS
Color (I J H)
Tells story of a father and son who trade places, as the father goes to summer camp and the son goes to Hollywood. Full version.
Fine Arts; Sociology
Dist - LCOA **Prod** - HGATE 1985

Summer Vegetables 30 MIN
VHS / BETA
Victory Garden Series
Color
Presents a bumper crop of summer vegetables. Surveys the thriving perennial garden. Checks the progress of a fruit orchard.
Agriculture; Physical Education and Recreation
Dist - CORF **Prod** - WGBHTV

A Summer visitor 13 MIN
VHS
Color (G)
$95.00 purchase _ #S01989
Portrays the life cycle of the Great Blue heron.
Science - Natural
Dist - UILL **Prod** - NFBC

Summer windows time exposure 14 MIN
16mm
Color (G)
$25.00 rental
Contains a collaboration between Lyman and James Mccandless on guitar. Dramatizes the passage of time outside the window of a summer house in Maine. 16mm film hangs in strips off the front porch subject to the ravages of time as the seasons pass.
Fine Arts; Science - Natural
Dist - CANCIN **Prod** - LYMAN 1978

Summerfield 90 MIN
35mm
Color; PAL (G)
Entertains with a mysterious disappearance. Tells the story of Simon, newly - arrived in the town of Bannings Beach, who replaces the former schoolteacher who vanished four months earlier without any community concern. Directed by Ken Hannam for Pavilion Films, Australia. Contact distributor about price and availability outside the United Kingdom.
Fine Arts
Dist - BALFOR

Summerhill 28 MIN
16mm
Color (J H C)
LC FIA68-1250
Visits England's progressive school, Summerhill, founded by Alexander Neill to prove that students can make decisions about their studies without lessening the quality of their education.
Education
Dist - NFBC **Prod** - NFBC 1967

Summering House Plants 29 MIN
Videoreel / VT2
Making Things Grow III Series
Color
Agriculture
Dist - PBS **Prod** - WGBHTV

Summerplay 16 MIN
16mm
Color (J)
Follows several divergent characters at a public beach as they interact with one another. Presents a moving expression of growth, maturity and group pressures.
Guidance and Counseling; Social Science; Sociology
Dist - COUNTR **Prod** - COUNTR 1972

Summer's End 33 MIN
U-matic / VHS / 16mm
Color (P A G)
Deals with the growing pains of young people who face questions about their own place in the world.
Fine Arts; Literature and Drama
Dist - DIRECT **Prod** - NIERNG 1985

Summer's on 29 MIN
U-matic
Edible Wild Plants Series
Color
Discusses the plentiful supply of edible plants found in the wilds in the summer.
Health and Safety; Science - Natural
Dist - UMITV **Prod** - UMITV 1978

Summerskin 96 MIN
16mm
B&W (G) (SPANISH WITH ENGLISH SUBTITLES)
$200.00 rental
Portrays a young woman who helps a sick boy recover from illness by pretending to love him, then cruelly reveals the truth to him. Directed by Leopoldo Torre Nilsson.
Fine Arts; Guidance and Counseling
Dist - KINOIC **Prod** - IFEX 1961

Summertime 100 MIN
16mm / U-matic / VHS
Color
Tells the story of a middle - aged secretary touring Venice who meets and falls in love with a worldly antique shop owner. Features Katherine Hepburn and Rossano Brazzi. Directed by David Lean. Based on the play The Time Of The Cuckoo by Arthur Laurents.

Fine Arts; Literature and Drama
Dist - LCOA Prod - UAA 1955

Summertime - Wintertime 4 MIN
16mm
Mini Movies - Springboard for Learning - Unit 1, who are We Series
Color (P I)
LC 76-703088
Presents a collage of winter and summer activities with numerous ideas for comparison, discussion and language development.
English Language; Science - Natural; Social Science
Dist - MORLAT Prod - MORLAT 1975

Summerwind 14 MIN
16mm
Color (G)
$25.00 rental
Addresses emergence from adolescence. Evokes summer life in the filmmaker's hometown. Third in a trilogy that deals with adolescence. Produced by Nathaniel Dorsky.
Fine Arts; Psychology
Dist - CANCIN

Summing Up 30 MIN
VHS
World Of Ideas With Bill Moyers - Season I - series
Color (G)
$39.95 purchase _ #BMWI - 149
Reviews some of the various issues covered in the 'World of Ideas' series.
Business and Economics; Civics and Political Systems; Guidance and Counseling; Literature and Drama; Religion and Philosophy; Sociology
Dist - PBS

Summit 12 MIN
16mm
Color
Presents world leaders at the crossroads.
Biography; History - World
Dist - VANBKS Prod - VANBKS 1963

The Summit seeker 9 MIN
VHS
Color (A COR)
$335.00 purchase, $95.00 rental
Portrays a mountain climber who is tackling the 'impossible mountain,' comparing the climber's effort to the efforts that must be made for success in business.
Psychology
Dist - VLEARN

Summons for the Queen - Zatykac Na Kralovnu 110 MIN
VHS / U-matic
B&W (CZECH (ENGLISH SUBTITLES))
Tells the story of a carefree woman living beyond her means who is summoned for questioning by the Czech police, but in the meantime is found raped and murdered, leading to the discovery of a black - market network. Directed by Dusan Klein. With English subtitles.
Fine Arts; Foreign Language
Dist - IHF Prod - IHF

Sums Up to Six 15 MIN
U-matic
Measure Up Series
Color (P)
Shows how, if given a model, a student can write an addition fact with 'plus' and 'minus' symbols.
Mathematics
Dist - GPN Prod - WCETTV 1977

Sun 10 MIN
U-matic / 16mm / VHS
Primary science series
Color (P I)
LC 91-705330
Describes the sun. Shows how it produces energy and how humans use that energy. Includes two teacher's guides. Part of a series on primary science produced by Fred Ladd.
Science; Science - Natural; Science - Physical
Dist - BARR

The Sun 9 MIN
16mm
Science Series
Color (K P I)
What the sun is and what its role is in animal and plant life, light and heat energy.
Science - Natural; Science - Physical
Dist - SF Prod - MORLAT 1967

The Sun 15 MIN
16mm
Color (I)
Explores the sun's cultural, philosophical and scientific significance to mankind throughout the ages, including the present and future.
Religion and Philosophy; Science; Science - Physical
Dist - DANPRO Prod - HAPLV 1974

Sun 8 MIN
U-matic / VHS / 16mm
Starting to Read Series
Color (K P)
LC 75-707904
Teaches a sight vocabulary with beautiful photographic settings and folk - song sound track.
English Language
Dist - AIMS Prod - ACI 1970

Sun 15 MIN
U-matic / VHS
Let me see series; No 4
Color (P)
Shows Pocus comparing the brightness of sunny days in winter and summer, and contrasts seasonal temperatures. Presents Hocus studying the factors that affect temperature with a little help from Myrtle and animation.
Science - Natural; Science - Physical
Dist - AITECH Prod - WETN 1982

The Sun 11 MIN
U-matic / VHS / 16mm
Astronomy Series
Color (I J)
LC 76-709420
Follows the curriculum for elementary school astronomy as developed by the Illinois Project. Combines live photography, animation and special effects to investigate some basic concepts about the Sun.
Science - Physical
Dist - MGHT Prod - MGHBLA 1971

The Sun - 10 10 MIN
U-matic / 16mm / VHS
Primary science series
Color (K P I)
$265.00, $215.00, $185.00 purchase _ #B591
Describes what the sun is and how it produces energy. Explains how the sun seems to set and rise. Shows solar panels, and their use for heating and generating energy. Part of an 11 - part series on primary science.
Science - Physical; Social Science
Dist - BARR Prod - GREATT 1990

The Sun and its Energy 10 MIN
U-matic / VHS / 16mm
Exploring Space Series
Color (I J)
$265, $185 purchase _ #3552
Shows how the sun's energy is used presently and may be used in the future.
Science - Physical
Dist - CORF

Sun and Other Stars 10 MIN
U-matic
Take a Look Series
Color (P I)
Teaches about the sun and its relationship to other stars as well as it's effects on the earth.
Science; Science - Physical
Dist - TVOTAR Prod - TVOTAR 1986

The Sun and the Earth 15 MIN
VHS / U-matic
Why Series
Color (P I)
Discusses the sun and the earth.
Science - Physical
Dist - AITECH Prod - WDCNTV 1976

The Sun and the Night 26 MIN
VHS / 16mm
Color (C A)
$160.00 purchase, $30.00 rental _ #CC4139
Documents United Nations High Commission for Refugees, HCR, giving aid to refugees in camps in Thailand and eastern Sudan.
Civics and Political Systems; Geography - World
Dist - IU Prod - NFBC 1990

Sun and the Substance Series
Ray Bradbury 30 MIN
Dist - MLA

Sun Bear - vision of the medicine wheel 60 MIN
VHS
Color (G)
$29.95 purchase _ #P42
Visits the late visionary Sun Bear during the final months of his Earthwalk at the 56th Gathering Ceremony. Reveals his prophecies about Earth changes. Looks at the power of ritual and healing circles by Wallace Black Elk, Brooke Medicine Eagle, Brant Secunda and many others.
Fine Arts; Social Science
Dist - HP

The Sun boy
VHS
Native American folk tales series
(G)
$79.00 purchase
Tells of a boy who learns to value individual differences when he alone can help his people at a time of crisis.
Literature and Drama; Social Science
Dist - DANEHA Prod - DANEHA 1994

Sun Country 18 MIN
16mm
Color (C A)
Describes the 'sun country' as beginning at Miami and Miami Beach, Florida and ending in the Bahamas and the out - islands. Depicts the land and water sports there and its unspoiled natural beauty. Points out that it is for those escapists who want sights, sounds and things to do that are out of the ordinary.
Geography - United States; Geography - World; Physical Education and Recreation; Sociology
Dist - MCDO Prod - MCDO 1968

The Sun dagger 59 MIN
16mm / VHS / U-matic
Color (J)
LC 82-701000; 83-700181
An edited version on the motion picture The Sun Dagger. Tells the story of the discovery in New Mexico of the Sun, an early Indian artifact which marks the extreme positions of both the sun and the moon. Narrated by Robert Redford.
History - United States; Science - Physical; Social Science
Dist - BULFRG Prod - SLSTCE 1983

The Sun Dagger 29 MIN
VHS / U-matic
Color (G)
Tells the story of perhaps the most exciting early Indian discovery in North America. Explores the Anasazi culture that produced this remarkable calendar and thrived over 1,000 years ago in the harsh Chaco Canyon environment.
Social Science
Dist - NAMPBC Prod - NAMPBC 1983

Sun Dried Foods 29 MIN
U-matic / VHS / 16mm
Color (H C A)
LC 81-701552
Focuses on traditional methods of harvesting, preserving and using fruits, vegetables, herbs and meats. Shows a Mexican - American family as they go about the daily routines of an active farm that epitomizes the 'small is beautiful' approach.
Home Economics
Dist - BULFRG Prod - SELFR 1980

The Sun - Earth's Star 20 MIN
16mm / U-matic / VHS
Color (J)
LC 80-700234
Discusses the sun and the impact of its radiation on Earth, including the vital role it plays in photosynthesis and the production of food for mankind. Considers various scientific theories regarding the effects on Earth of sunspot activity and solar flares.
Science - Physical
Dist - NGS Prod - NGS 1980

Sun - Friend or Foe? 11 MIN
U-matic / VHS / 16mm
Color (P I)
$50 rental _ #1624
Discusses the positive and negative aspects of the sun's influence on the Earth and our daily lives. Teaches basic concepts and facts about the sun.
Science; Science - Physical
Dist - AIMS Prod - AIMS 1968

The Sun Interrogator Explained 48 MIN
VHS / 35mm strip
(H A IND)
#492XV7
Includes basic operations, testing procedure, and test link (3 tapes). Includes a Study Guide.
Education; Industrial and Technical Education
Dist - BERGL

The Sun is Alive and Well in Miami 14 MIN
16mm
Color
Presents the wide range of activities and sports in Miami, the sun and fun capital of the world.
Geography - United States; Physical Education and Recreation
Dist - MIMET Prod - MIMET

The Sun is Red 13 MIN
16mm
Color
Investigates the problem of pollution and the individual's role in combating it. Uses animation and real film.

Geography - World; Science - Natural; Sociology
Dist - AUDPLN **Prod** - RDCG

The Sun - its Power and Promise 24 MIN
16mm / U-matic / VHS
Wide World of Adventure Series
Color (I J)
LC 77-701911
Shows how man has paid tribute to the sun throughout history. Examines the sun's role in the creation of familiar energy sources such as food, wind, petroleum, coal and natural gas. Points out the need for the new and cleaner sources of energy. Evaluates the potential of alternative energy sources such as nuclear energy and geothermal energy. Takes a close look at the source of solar energy, the sun itself. Surveys the present and potential uses of solar energy.
Science - Physical; Social Science
Dist - EBEC **Prod** - AVATLI 1977

The Sun king 29 MIN
16mm / U-matic / VHS
Legacy series
B&W (J)
LC 77-707201
Examines the power and ritual of monarchy by focusing on King Louis XIV. Provides quotes from the French king and shows scenes of the Versailles palace.
History - World
Dist - IU **Prod** - NET 1965

Sun Kosi - River of Gold 45 MIN
U-matic / VHS
Color (J H C A)
$99.00
Presents a drama of skill and tenacity, following the adventure of a 200 - mile journey in one - man canoes down the length of the perilous Sun Kosi River in Nepal.
Physical Education and Recreation
Dist - LANDMK **Prod** - LANDMK 1983

Sun - Maid - the World's Favorite Raisin 21 MIN
16mm
Color
Details the history of the Sun - Maid company and the care given to their raisins. Shows how the Sun - Maid raisin girl became one of the world's most recognized trademarks. Presents the various stages of stemming, grading and washing raisins.
Agriculture; Home Economics
Dist - MTP **Prod** - SUNMAD

Sun, moon and feather 30 MIN
16mm / VHS
Color (G)
$425.00, $250.00 purchase, $55.00 rental; LC 89715651
Presents a musical comedy documentary about three Native American sisters growing up in Brooklyn during the 1930s and 1940s. Features Lisa, Gloria and Muriel Miguel who have been performing their family stories together professionally for more than a decade as Spiderwoman Theatre.
Fine Arts; Social Science
Dist - CNEMAG **Prod** - CNEMAG 1989

Sun Movie 10 MIN
16mm
Color
LC 77-702659
Presents an animated film showing the Sun passing and a lone person.
Fine Arts
Dist - CANFDC **Prod** - CANFDC 1973

Sun pictures 25 MIN
VHS
Pioneers of photography series
Color (A)
PdS65 purchase
Pictures how Hyppolyte Bayard in Paris and Hill and Adamson in Edinburgh raised photography to the level of art. Part of an eight-part series that examines the contributions made by pioneers in photography.
Fine Arts; Industrial and Technical Education
Dist - BBCENE

Sun power 13 MIN
VHS / U-matic / 16mm
Color (P I J)
$285.00, $230.00, $200.00 purchase _ #A333
Uses animation to describe solar energy, what it is and what it can do. Features the sun who explains how hydrogen is converted to helium to create radiant energy, how that energy is transferred to life on earth through photosynthesis and the food chain. Shows how solar energy is used to heat homes, power communication satellites and cook food.
Science - Physical; Social Science
Dist - BARR **Prod** - SHIRE 1982

Sun Power for Farms 12 MIN
16mm
Color (J H A)
LC 77-700958
Presents new developments in the use of solar energy in agriculture.
Agriculture; Industrial and Technical Education; Social Science
Dist - USNAC **Prod** - USDA 1977

The Sun - power for our solar system 38 MIN
U-matic / VHS
Color (J H C)
LC 81-706758
Examines the most important aspects of the sun's nature and functioning by explaining its chemical composition and physical structure. Describes the effect of the sun's energy upon Earth and explains the greenhouse effect. Takes a look at those questions about the sun which still remain unanswered.
Industrial and Technical Education; Science; Science - Physical
Dist - GA **Prod** - SCIMAN 1982

The Sun - Prominences and Flares
U-matic / VHS
Experiments in Space Series
Color
Depicts scenes of solar prominences and flares. Shows the relationship between flares and sunspots.
Science - Physical
Dist - EDMEC **Prod** - EDMEC

Sun Ra - a joyful noise 60 MIN
VHS
Color (G)
$29.95 purchase
Offers up a little joyful jazz with Sun Ra.
Fine Arts
Dist - KINOIC **Prod** - RHPSDY

The Sun seekers - a surf odyssey 27 MIN
16mm
Color
LC 74-700377
Communicates the Gospel of Christ by telling about individuals whose lives were changed. Shows the beauty of God's creation, focusing on big - wave surfing.
Guidance and Counseling; Religion and Philosophy
Dist - OUTRCH **Prod** - OUTRCH 1973
CAFM

Sun Song - the Mosaic Art of John De Groot 26 MIN
16mm
Color
LC 75-700484
Examines the work of artist John de Groot as he prepares a large mosaic for downtown Fort Lauderdale, Florida. Traces his years of study and his development of tile murals.
Fine Arts
Dist - LYON **Prod** - LYON 1975

Sun, Sunlight and Weather Patterns 26 MIN
VHS / 16mm
Climate & Man Series
Color (J)
$149.00 purchase, $75.00 rental _ #OD - 2402
Explains origins of tropical storms, tropical rain forests and polar deserts. Speculates about the origins of the Sahara desert and the link between weather, the sun, the cycles of dust storms and volcanic eruptions. The second of six installments of the Climate & Man Series.
Geography - World; Science - Natural; Science - Physical
Dist - FOTH

The Sun Symbol in Art 15 MIN
U-matic / VHS / 16mm
Color (I J)
LC 73-702594
Shows the response of man to the sun through its significance in a number of works of art ranging from early Egyptian times through modern contemporary artists working in many kinds of media. Shows fourth grade students creating their own sun symbols. Emphasizes the sun as a source of inspiration to the artist.
Fine Arts
Dist - PHENIX **Prod** - BURN 1968

The Sun Watchers 30 MIN
U-matic / VHS / 16mm
World We Live in Series
Color (I J H)
LC 77-700243
Studies the sun's normal and unusual activities as seen from the world's major solar observatories.
Science - Physical
Dist - MGHT **Prod** - TIMELI 1968

The Sun will Rise 35 MIN
16mm / U-matic / VHS
Color
Tells the story of young members of the African National Congress, sentenced to death or to life imprisonment in South Africa for their activities to end apartheid. Tells the story through the eyes of these young Nationalists and reflects the parents' growing awareness of their children's commitment and sacrifices.
Civics and Political Systems; History - World; Sociology
Dist - ICARUS **Prod** - IDAF 1983

Sun, wind and wood 25 MIN
16mm
Color (G)
LC 80-701714
Shows how some people are using more solar and wind energy and relying less on non - renewable energy. Looks at a 'bioshelter' home, a house heated by solar power, and a house powered by a windmill.
Social Science
Dist - BNCHMK **Prod** - NFBC 1980

The Sunbeam Solution 50 MIN
U-matic / VHS / 16mm
Energy Crunch Series
Color
LC 77-702019
Examines the prospects of solar energy becoming the world's major energy source. Discusses other untapped sources of energy, such as wind and tidal power, geothermal power and the use of natural elements like hydrogen.
Social Science
Dist - FI **Prod** - BBCTV 1974

Sunbelt City - Phoenix, Arizona 20 MIN
U-matic / VHS / 16mm
America in Transition Series
Color (H C A)
Shows that the city of Phoenix, Arizona is booming with new industry, a new population and, perhaps most importantly, new money. Speculates on the continued attractiveness of a city with such high costs in public services, water, utilities and energy.
Business and Economics; History - United States; Sociology
Dist - FI **Prod** - BBCTV 1983

Sunbelt - Myth and Reality 30 MIN
VHS
American South Comes of Age Series
Color (J)
$95.00 purchase, $55.00 rental
Considers the realities and mythology of Sunbelt economics in the American South. Part of a fourteen - part series on the economic, social and political transformation of the South since World War II.
Agriculture; Business and Economics; Geography - United States; History - United States; Sociology
Dist - SCETV **Prod** - SCETV 1985

Sunbuilders 20 MIN
16mm
Color
LC 80-700163
Explains the basic concepts of passive solar energy design, showing examples of how these concepts are being transformed into reality by architects, builders and other solar advocates.
Social Science
Dist - USNAC **Prod** - USDOE 1979

Sundae in New York 4 MIN
16mm / U-matic / VHS
Color (I A G)
Features claymation caricatures of Ed Koch, Frank Sinatra, Woody Allen and Rodney Dangerfield.
Fine Arts
Dist - DIRECT **Prod** - PICKEJ 1984

Sunday and Monday in Silence 52 MIN
16mm / U-matic / VHS
Color (C A)
Documents the complications of coping successfully with deafness in the family on both a normal weekday and during the weekend. Describes one family in which normal parents raise two children who were born deaf and another family in which all the family's members are deaf except for one girl with normal hearing.
Guidance and Counseling; Psychology
Dist - MEDIAG **Prod** - THAMES 1973

Sunday between Wars 41 MIN
16mm
Color
LC 79-700290
Presents a fictional dialogue between a contemporary woman and Walt Whitman concerning accomplishments and failures in the United States between 1865 and 1917.
History - United States; Literature and Drama
Dist - MADDOW **Prod** - MADDOW 1979

Sunday between wars - Pt 1 21 MIN
16mm
Color
LC 79-700290
Presents a fictional dialogue between a contemporary woman and Walt Whitman concerning accomplishments and failures in the United States between 1865 and 1917.
History - United States; Literature and Drama
Dist - MADDOW **Prod** - MADDOW 1979

Sunday between wars - Pt 2 20 MIN
16mm
Color
LC 79-700290
Presents a fictional dialogue between a contemporary woman and Walt Whitman concerning accomplishments and failures in the United States between 1865 and 1917.
History - United States; Literature and Drama
Dist - MADDOW **Prod** - MADDOW 1979

Sunday Dinner 12 MIN
16mm / U-matic / VHS
Color (J)
LC 76-703657
Tells the story of how an elderly lady and a local junkman collect food, wine and other necessities to make their Sunday dinner cozy and homelike.
Guidance and Counseling; Home Economics; Sociology
Dist - PHENIX **Prod** - LINSAL 1976

Sunday drive 8 MIN
VHS
Color (G)
$30.00 purchase
Explores the inspiration caused by the phantasmagoric closed - eye imagery created by the sun while riding in a car during late afternoon, and a statement made by writer Tom Robbins to set up everyone's computers under the wild apple trees. Combines two layers of Super 8 imagery and one layer of computer - generated graphics.
Fine Arts
Dist - CANCIN **Prod** - ORRJER 1990

A Sunday in hell 112 MIN
35mm / 16mm / VHS
Color (G) (DANISH WITH ENGLISH SUBTITLES)
$150.00, $200.00 rental
Examines the grueling Paris - Roubaix bicycle race, nicknamed The Hell of the North. Directed by Jorgen Leth.
Fine Arts; Physical Education and Recreation
Dist - KINOIC

Sunday lark 12 MIN
16mm / U-matic / VHS
B&W (I)
LC FIA64-376
Pictures a six - year - old girl who wanders into New York's Wall Street on a Sunday afternoon, showing her interest in the staple guns, electric pencil sharpeners, various IBM computers and other office paraphernalia in a huge empty office in a skyscraper.
Literature and Drama
Dist - MGHT **Prod** - CRSCND 1963

Sunday Lunch 12 MIN
U-matic
Color (G)
$250.00 purchase, $50.00, $40.00 rental
Documents a stressful family ritual in which a married son, his wife and their two children come to his parents' house for Sunday lunch and tolerate each other's presence only for as long as they have to for the sake of tradition and respect. Created by Clair Dobbin.
Sociology
Dist - WMENIF **Prod** - WMENIF 1985

Sunday Morning 30 MIN
VHS
Soapbox With Tom Cottle Series
Color (G)
$59.95 purchase _ #SBOX - 511
Reports on the role of religion and spirituality in the lives of teenagers. Notes that many teenagers are attracted to alternative religious movements. Hosted by psychologist Tom Cottle.
Psychology; Religion and Philosophy
Dist - PBS **Prod** - WGBYTV 1985

Sunday Morning 15 MIN
16mm
B&W
Explores religious feeling and the grandeur and oppressive power of the concept of God. Opens with a sequence showing nature existing as beautiful and pure, and then focuses on the actions of a small girl as she prepares for church.
Religion and Philosophy
Dist - UPENN **Prod** - UPENN 1964

Sunday Morning Dance 5 MIN
16mm
B&W
LC 76-701483
Compares studio dance and performance dance.
Fine Arts
Dist - YORKU **Prod** - YORKU 1975

Sunday Night Show 30 MIN
U-matic / VHS
Cookin' Cheap Series
Color
Presents basically crazy cooks Larry Bly and Laban Johnson who offer recipes, cooking and shopping tips.
Home Economics
Dist - MDCPB **Prod** - WBRATV

A Sunday on La Grande Jatte 30 MIN
VHS
Palette series
Color (G C)
$70.00 purchase, $12.50, rental _ #36407
Reveals that the work of Neo - Impressionist Georges Seurat in his 1884 pointilist work shocked 19th - century society with dots of color that create an image only when viewed from a distance. Re - imagines the creation of this piece. Part of a 13 - part series which examines great paintings in a dynamic and dramatic way by moving into their creative spaces and spending time with the characters and their surroundings. Uses special video effects to investigate artistic enigmas and studies material, technique, style and significance. Narrated by Marcel Cuvelier, directed by Alain Jaubert.
Fine Arts
Dist - PSU **Prod** - LOUVRE 1992

Sunday Picnic 11 MIN
16mm
B&W (H C A)
LC 72-700402
Portrays the essence of the generation gap by showing various people who are upset by a young man who flirts with a young girl in their midst. Focuses on the confrontation of the young and the old, which ends in a mutual sense of alienation.
Guidance and Counseling; Psychology; Sociology
Dist - MMA **Prod** - ZAGREB 1970

Sunday's children 120 MIN
VHS / 16mm
Color (G)
$490.00 purchase, $150.00 rental
Tells the story of ten year old Pu in which a magical season with his family in the Swedish countryside transforms into a strange emotional time that will resonate throughout Pu's lifetime. Features a largely autobiographical study of Ingmar Bergman's childhood.
Literature and Drama; Psychology; Sociology
Dist - FIRS **Prod** - BERGMA 1993

Sundown shindig 52 MIN
VHS / 16mm
Color (G)
$55.00 rental _ #SDSN - 000
Features a western - style hoedown in a Nebraska setting. Combines bluegrass music, square dancing and stories.
Fine Arts
Dist - PBS **Prod** - NETCHE

The Sundowners 133 MIN
U-matic / VHS / 16mm
Color (J)
Stars Robert Mitchum, Deborah Kerr and Peter Ustinov. Presents a sheepherder in the 1920's whose preference for a nomadic life style is at odds with his wife's fervent desire to buy a farm and settle down.
Fine Arts
Dist - FI **Prod** - WB 1960

Sunflower - 1 10 MIN
U-matic / 16mm / VHS
How plants grow series
Color (K P I)
$265.00, $215.00, $185.00 purchase _ #B597
Presents a close - up examination of the life cycle of the sunflower. Shows how sunflowers are grown on a farm, and some of the uses for sunflower seeds. Discusses pollination, photosynthesis and the origin of the sunflower's name. Part of a seven - part series on how plants grow.
Agriculture; Science - Natural
Dist - BARR **Prod** - GREATT 1990

Sunflowers - more than a Pretty Face 13 MIN
U-matic / VHS / 16mm
Color (P I J)
Begins with spring seeding, then blossoms into fields of brilliant yellow as the sunflower plants mature and become ready for harvest. Shows the processing plant where the seeds become golden oil ready for salads and cooking.
Agriculture
Dist - BCNFL **Prod** - BORTF 1983

The Sunken Fleet 11 MIN
16mm
B&W
Explains the feats by skilled deep - sea divers whose work makes possible the refloating of a sunken merchant vessel.
Physical Education and Recreation; Social Science
Dist - RADIM **Prod** - FILIM

Sunken treasure 21 MIN
U-matic / VHS / 16mm
Undersea world of Jacques Cousteau series
Color (G)
$49.95 purchase _ #Q10613; LC 73-710109
A shortened version of Sunken Treasure. Shows Jacques Cousteau and his crew exploring the site of a wreck believed to be the command ship of the 1641 New World armada. Features the crew as they test underwater archeological salvaging techniques. Part of a series of 24 programs.
Science - Physical
Dist - CF **Prod** - METROM 1970

Sunken treasure - 70
VHS
Reading rainbow series
Color; CC (K P)
$39.95 purchase
Presents a story by Gail Gibbons, narrated by Robert Morse. Follows LeVar on a tresure hunt at 'Pirates Cove' in California where he uses every device known to humans to find a treasure, including a trusty bloodhound. Meets Dr Robert Ballard of the Woods Hole Oceanographic Institution of Massachussetts who, by using science and technology, located and explored the most famous shipwreck in history - the Titanic. Part of a series offering a multicultural approach to generating reading enthusiasm with cross - curricular applications, hosted by LeVar Burton.
English Language; Literature and Drama; Science; Science - Physical
Dist - GPN **Prod** - LNMDP

Sunken Wrecks 22 MIN
16mm
Color
Explores the depths of Key West where the ocean's great ecosystem has absorbed wreckage of centuries - old Spanish galleons up to World War II fighter aircraft. Shows that these vessels now shelter snapper, amberjack, cobia and a myriad of other species of fish.
Geography - United States; Physical Education and Recreation
Dist - KAROL **Prod** - BRNSWK

Sunlight - a First Film 9 MIN
U-matic / VHS / 16mm
Color (P I)
LC 74-711117
Tells how every day the sun brings light and life to the earth. Describes how sunlight brings out the color of things around us, brings us warmth and gives us shadows and changing seasons. Points out that all life on earth needs sunlight.
Science - Physical
Dist - PHENIX **Prod** - NELLES 1971

Sunlight and Shadow in Painting 11 MIN
16mm / U-matic / VHS
Color (I)
LC FIA68-2114
Shows the effects created by light and dark areas on an artist's subject, and how he uses light and simulates shadows with color, line and shading in his painting.
Fine Arts
Dist - PHENIX **Prod** - STOKSF 1968

Sunlight - floating - afternoon 27 MIN
16mm
Color; Silent (C)
$650.00
Experimental film by Barry Gerson.
Fine Arts
Dist - AFA **Prod** - AFA

The Sunlit chariot 30 MIN
VHS / U-matic
Art of being human series; Module 13
Color (C)
History - World; Literature and Drama; Religion and Philosophy
Dist - MDCC **Prod** - MDCC

Sunlit Night's Land Cruise 15 MIN
16mm
B&W
Portrays an eight day trip by a modern train from southern Sweden to above the Arctic Circle.
Geography - World; Social Science
Dist - AUDPLN **Prod** - ASI

Sunnis and the Prohibited Mecca 27 MIN
VHS / 16mm / U-matic
Color (J H C A)
MP=$475.00
Pictures the Sunnis, the largest faction of Islam, who are the guardians of orthodoxy. The Sunnis of Arabia are also guardians of the Kaaba in Mecca.
Religion and Philosophy
Dist - LANDMK **Prod** - LANDMK 1984

Sunnis and the prohibited Mecca - 13 30 MIN
U-matic / VHS / BETA
Abraham's posterity series
Color; PAL (G H C)
PdS50, PdS58 purchase
Follows the journeys which Abraham made some 4000 years ago. Offers a dramatic interpretation at the events which are today tearing the region apart. Part of a thirteen - part series. A Cine & Tele Production, Brussels, Belgium.
Fine Arts; Religion and Philosophy
Dist - EDPAT

Sunny Beef Salad 30 MIN
U-matic / VHS
Cooking Now Series
(C A)
$19.95 _ #CH280V
Features Franco Palumbo, former chef of Weight Watchers International, as he demonstrates a simple, methodical recipe for preparing sunny beef salad.
Home Economics; Industrial and Technical Education
Dist - CAMV **Prod** - CAMV

A Sunny day 5 MIN
16mm
Adventures in the high grass series
Color (K P I)
LC 74-702124
Portrays an insect community in puppet animation. Shows how human beings appear and cause the community problems and dangers, which the insects cope with.
Literature and Drama; Science - Natural
Dist - MMA **Prod** - MMA 1972

Sunny Scandinavia 29 MIN
16mm
Color
Experiences a leisurely jaunt along Sweden's efficient railway while savoring the scenic Swedish countryside.
Geography - World
Dist - MTP **Prod** - SRAIL

Sunny Side of Life 56 MIN
VHS / 16mm
Color (G)
Documents the Carter family and their music at the Carter Family Fold in southwestern Virginia. Features interviews, dancing and performances by members of the Carter family and other musicians. Includes a visual essay on traditional life and work in the region and the place music holds in it.
Fine Arts; Geography - United States
Dist - APPAL **Prod** - APPAL

Sunnyside Up 7 MIN
16mm
Color (I)
Uses a variety of visual techniques to present trees, signs, buildings, designs and windows reflected in water. Includes more somber scenes of the effect pollution could have on the environment.
Science - Natural
Dist - NYFLMS **Prod** - NYFLMS

Sunrise 120 MIN
VHS
Color (G) (MANDARIN CHINESE (ENGLISH SUBTITLES))
$45.00 purchase _ #1093A
Presents a Mandarin Chinese language movie produced in the People's Republic of China.
Fine Arts; Geography - World; Literature and Drama
Dist - CHTSUI **Prod** - CHTSUI

Sunrise 110 MIN
16mm
B&W
Shows how a vacationing lady from the city engages the interest of a young farmer and enslaves him. Reveals what happens when she persuades him to murder his wife, sell his farm and join her in the city. Details the many reasons why the plot does not go as planned. Stars George O'Brien and Janet Gaynor. Directed by F W Murnau.
Fine Arts
Dist - KILLIS **Prod** - FOXFC 1927

Sunrise at Campobello 143 MIN
U-matic / VHS / 16mm
Color (G)
Stars Ralph Bellamy and Greer Garson in the story of the crucial years in the life of Franklin Delano Roosevelt. Portrays his fight to recover from infantile paralysis. Covers the period from 1921 to 1924, from the time the 39 - year - old Roosevelt was stricken with polio to the Democratic convention in 1924 and his return to public life as nominator for Al Smith.
Biography; Civics and Political Systems; Fine Arts; History - World
Dist - FI **Prod** - WB 1960
GA

Sunrise House - Community Program 30 MIN
VHS / 16mm
Your Choice - Our Chance Series
Color (I A)
$295.00 purchase, $35.00 rental
Considers drug abuse and features Sunrise House in Salinas, California, which provides a center and focus for the community's education, prevention, support and intervention services that are extended to young people and their families.
Health and Safety; Psychology
Dist - AITECH **Prod** - AITECH 1990

Sunrise House - Salinas, California 30 MIN
VHS
Your choice - our chance series
Color (A)
$395.00 purchase
Focuses on knowledge, attitudes and behaviors that influence drug free and drug use life styles. Emphasizes that effective drug abuse prevention education must begin before children are established users of tobacco, alcohol or other addictive drugs. Targets children in the vulnerable preteen years. Program 2 addresses the question of how a community can respond to the needs of children and families facing drug and related crises. In the late 1960s Salinas schools recognized the drug problem and assigned a junior high teacher, Elgie Bellizio, to study the problem. Sunrise House was formed in the early 1970s as part of a Joint Powers Agreement among city government, schools, law enforcement, health and other agencies.
Guidance and Counseling; Health and Safety; Psychology; Social Science; Sociology
Dist - AITECH **Prod** - AITECH 1990

Sunrise special 29 MIN
VHS / 16mm
Color (G)
$250.00 purchase _ #283401
Investigates the Metis, descendants of Indian women and European explorers or fur traders. Explains the term Metis is used commonly to mean 'mixed blood.' In Canada the Metis are a distinct cultural group with their own traditions, spiritual beliefs, customs and languages. Visits St Albert in Alberta, which was the site of the first Metis colony and reveals that there are now eight settlements in Alberta that belong to the Metis people. Shows that the Metis used renewable resources for trapping, hunting, fishing, logging, ranching and farming but they also use non - renewable resources such as oil and gas.
Geography - World; History - World; Sociology
Dist - ACCESS **Prod** - ACCESS 1989

Sunriver 26 MIN
16mm
Color
LC 72-700169
Shows the planner and the architect of Sunriver, a vacation - home community on the Deschutes River in central Oregon which is designed to function without automobiles. Discusses the probability of the site's becoming a year - round recreation area.
Fine Arts; Geography - United States; Industrial and Technical Education; Physical Education and Recreation; Sociology
Dist - GROENG **Prod** - SUNRVP 1971

The Sun's gonna shine 10 MIN
VHS / 16mm
Color (G)
$89.95 purchase, $25.00 rental
Presents a companion piece to 'The Blues Accordin' to Lightnin' Hopkins.' Recreates his decision at age 8 to stop chopping cotton and sing for his living. Part of the video collection 'Six Short Films by Les Blank.'
Fine Arts; History - United States
Dist - CANCIN **Prod** - BLNKL

Sunset 60 MIN
VHS
Workshop in oils with William Palluth series
Color (J H C G)
$29.95 purchase _ #FHF145V
Shows how mixing large pools of color can simplify painting and promote color harmony. Part of a series on oil painting by landscape artist William Palluth.
Fine Arts
Dist - CAMV

Sunset 29 MIN
U-matic
Magic of Oil Painting Series
Color
Fine Arts
Dist - PBS **Prod** - KOCETV

Sunset Boulevard 110 MIN
U-matic / VHS / 16mm
B&W
Stars Gloria Swanson as an aging silent film queen, William Holden as the young screenwriter she loves, and Erich Von Stroheim as the great film director reduced to butler. Directed by Billy Wilder.
Fine Arts
Dist - FI **Prod** - PAR 1950

Sunset Crater, Arizona 5 MIN
16mm
Color
LC 79-701540
Explains the geological phenomena that created Sunset Crater, located in Arizona's Sunset Crater National Monument.
Geography - United States; Science - Physical
Dist - USNAC **Prod** - USNPS 1979

Sunset Division - 41st Infantry Division 13 MIN
16mm / U-matic / VHS
B&W (H A)
Presents the film record of the 41st (Sunset) Infantry Division's role in the Pacific during World War II.
Civics and Political Systems; History - United States
Dist - USNAC **Prod** - USA 1950

Sunset Street 100 MIN
VHS
Color (G) (MANDARIN CHINESE (ENGLISH SUBTITLES))
$45.00 purchase _ #1043B
Presents a Mandarin Chinese language movie produced in the People's Republic of China.
Fine Arts; Geography - World; Literature and Drama
Dist - CHTSUI **Prod** - CHTSUI

Sunshine 29 MIN
Videoreel / VT2
Children's Fair Series
B&W (K P)
Science; Science - Physical
Dist - PBS **Prod** - WMVSTV

Sunshine and Showers 91 MIN
VHS
Color (G) (MANDARIN CHINESE)
$45.00 purchase _ #6027A
Presents a movie produced in the People's Republic Of China.
Fine Arts; Geography - World; Literature and Drama
Dist - CHTSUI **Prod** - CHTSUI

Sunshine factory series

Anger	27 MIN
Courage	27 MIN
Forgiveness	27 MIN
Honesty	27 MIN
Keeping promises	27 MIN
Leading and following	27 MIN
Love	27 MIN
Patience	27 MIN
Respecting adults and others	27 MIN
Responsibility	27 MIN
Sharing	27 MIN
Temptation	27 MIN

Dist - APH

Sunshine Showplace 14 MIN
16mm
Color (I J H C)
LC FIA67-628
Tours five major attractions of the city of St Petersburg in Florida.
Geography - United States
Dist - FDC **Prod** - FDC 1966

The Sunshine sisters 36 MIN
16mm
Color (G)
$35.00 rental
Entertains with an absurd comic book love story of doomed women and handsome men caught in a web of dramatic cliches. Features musical compilation by Bob Cowan.
Fine Arts; Psychology
Dist - CANCIN **Prod** - KUCHAR 1972

The Sunshine State of Florida 16 MIN
16mm
Color (K)
Examines the sunshine state of Florida, America's year round vacationland.
Geography - United States
Dist - BECKLY **Prod** - BECKLY

Sunshine's on the way 30 MIN
16mm / VHS / U-matic
Color (J H)
LC 80-701766; 80-701765
Tells the story of a teenaged assistant at a retirement home who persuades the newest arrival, a jazz trombonist she idolizes, to help the other musicians there to improve their band enough to get a job on the Tonight Show.
Fine Arts; Guidance and Counseling; Health and Safety; Sociology
Dist - LCOA **Prod** - HGATE 1980

Sunshine's on the way 47 MIN
U-matic / 16mm / VHS
Captioned; Color (J H A)
Tells of a teenage girl working at a retirement home who gets a jazz trombonist to help her organize a senior citizen band. Full version.
Fine Arts; Health and Safety; Psychology; Sociology
Dist - LCOA **Prod** - HGATE 1981

The Sunspot Mystery - Sun - Weather Connection 30 MIN
16mm / U-matic / VHS
Nova Series
Color (H C A)
LC 78-700456
Covers research done on predicting the Sun's effect on weather, including the discovery of a 22 - year drought cycle, solar winds, coronal holes and effects on the ozone layer. Explains research ranging from an analysis of tree rings to solar experiments in Skylab.
Science; Science - Physical
Dist - TIMLIF **Prod** - WGBHTV 1977

The Sunspot Mystery - Sunspots Explained 31 MIN
16mm / U-matic / VHS
Nova Series
Color (H C A)
LC 78-700457
Explores how the Sun's changes affect the Earth. Interweaves 20th century research on aurorae, solar constants, sunspot cycles and tree ring analysis with historical scientific records.
Science; Science - Physical
Dist - TIMLIF **Prod** - WGBHTV 1977

Sunspot vacations for winter 90 MIN
VHS
Color (G)
$29.95 purchase
Presents a comprehensive travel guide to Mexico, Hawaii, the Bahamas, Puerto Rico, the Dominican Republic, Barbados, and other Caribbean destinations. Offers money - saving tips for accommodations, food, language, currency, attractions, recreation, range of rates, and more.
Geography - World
Dist - PBS **Prod** - WNETTV

Sunstone 3 MIN
16mm
Color (G)
$10.00 rental
Utilizes a digital paint program to create a film version of computer animation.
Fine Arts
Dist - CANCIN **Prod** - EMSH 1979

Super - Artist, Andy Warhol 22 MIN
16mm
Color (H C A)
LC FIA67-1277
A visit with super - artist, Andy Warhol, showing him at work, reviews his views on pop art and presents examples of his work.
Fine Arts
Dist - GROVE **Prod** - TORBTB 1967

Super Bear - the Grizzly 23 MIN
VHS / U-matic
Color (K)
Introduces the grizzly against the backdrop of Alaska and Yellowstone. Shows a mother grizzly caring for her young.
Science - Natural
Dist - NWLDPR **Prod** - NWLDPR

Super blue
CD-ROM
(G)
$149.00 purchase _ #1515
Contains 612 volumes - 250 MB. Includes games, communications, utilities, business, music, science, math, and graphics. All files come from New York Amateur Computer Club, all available updates have been included. Can be searched by category or volume using subject or keyword. Any of the 612 volumes can be transferred to a 360K floppy disk. IBM and compatibles require at least 640K of RAM, DOS 3.1 or greater, one floppy disk drive - hard disk recommended, one empty expansion slot, and an IBM compatible CD - ROM drive.
Computer Science
Dist - BEP

Super Bowl - Super stakes 30 MIN
VHS
Inside story series
Color (G)
$50.00 purchase _ #INST - 402
Focuses on the media hoopla behind the National Football League's annual Super Bowl. Shows that the NFL, networks, news media and advertisers all have a significant stake in the success of the event. Hosted by Hodding Carter.
Literature and Drama; Physical Education and Recreation; Social Science
Dist - PBS

Super Bowl XI 20 MIN
16mm
Color
LC 77-701456
Presents the story of the 1977 World Championship of pro football.
Physical Education and Recreation
Dist - NFL **Prod** - NFL 1977

Super Bugs 14 MIN
VHS / U-matic
Young at Art Series
Color (P I)
Fine Arts
Dist - AITECH **Prod** - WSKJTV 1980

Super Celsius 3 MIN
VHS / U-matic
Metric Marvels Series
Color (P I)
Introduces animated superhero Super Celsius, who masquerades as a mild - mannered TV weatherman in order to explain the Celsius temperature scale.
Fine Arts; Mathematics; Science - Physical
Dist - GA **Prod** - NBCTV 1978

Super chaperone 29 MIN
VHS / 16mm
Que pasa, U S A series
Color (G)
$46.00 rental _ #QUEP - 113
Social Science; Sociology
Dist - PBS **Prod** - WPBTTV

The Super chargers
VHS
Color (G)
$29.80 purchase _ #0423
Watches Hot Boats skim the water at well over 200 miles per hour. Shows that drivers who plunge into water which is rock hard at that speed are saved only by the parachutes on their backs.
Physical Education and Recreation
Dist - SEVVID

Super cities - Florence 30 MIN
VHS
Color (G)
PdS15 purchase _ #ML-IVN319
Introduces viewers to one of Italy's best-known cities - Florence. Takes viewers on a video tour of the artistic and architectural splendors of this historic city. Winds through streets that take viewers back to ancient and medieval times. Presents some of Florence's famous art galleries, which contain works by Michaelangelo, Giotto, and Donatello.
Fine Arts; Geography - World
Dist - AVP **Prod** - IVNET

Super cities - Munich 30 MIN
VHS
Color (G)
PdS15 purchase _ #ML-IVN334
Introduces viewers to the famous German city of Munich. Touts the south German city's architecture, including the Ludwig-Maxmilians, Germany's largest university; the Theaterkirche, more Italian than German; and the Frauenkirche, with its onion-domed towers. Takes viewers on a video tour of some of Munich's most famous landmarks.
Fine Arts; Geography - World
Dist - AVP **Prod** - IVNET

Super cities - Paris 30 MIN
VHS
Color (G)
PdS15 purchase _ #ML-IVN321
Introduces viewers to one of Europe's most famous cities - Paris. Focuses on Paris' historic cafe society and cultural ambience, which has been an inspiration to writers, thinkers, and artists throughout the centuries. Takes viewers on video tours of Paris' tree-lined boulevards; the Arc de Triomphe, the Eiffel Tower; Notre Dame Cathedral; the Louvre, with its art treasures from David to the Mona Lisa; and more.
Fine Arts; Geography - World
Dist - AVP **Prod** - IVNET

Super cities - Venice 30 MIN
VHS
Color (G)
PdS15 purchase _ #ML-IVN313
Introduces viewers to the sights of Venice. Includes a video tour of the Italian town best-known for its intricate canal system. Offers viewers a chance to take a video ride in a gondola and glide beneath the Bridge of Sighs. Includes such famous sights as the basilica of San Marco, the Doge's Palace, and the Campanile.
Geography - World
Dist - AVP **Prod** - IVNET

Super cities - Vienna 30 MIN
VHS
Color (G)
PdS15 purchase _ #ML-IVN314
Presents the sights of Vienna, Austria. Takes viewers on a video tour of such famed sights as the Hofburg and Schnbrunn palaces, St Stephen's Cathedral, and the Ringstrasse that surrounds the city.
Fine Arts; Geography - World
Dist - AVP **Prod** - IVNET

Super - Companies 57 MIN
16mm / VHS
(I A)
$75.00 rental
Focuses on the role of multinationals, or super - companies, in the aluminum industry, who treat the world as a single market, seeking the cheapest material, the lowest taxes and the best deals. Discloses the social and economic problems suffered by the host countries. Available on two reels for schools.
Business and Economics; Social Science
Dist - BULFRG **Prod** - NFBC 1989

Super creatures 25 MIN
VHS
Filling station series; Vol 8
Color (K P I R)
$11.99 purchase _ #35 - 811386 - 979
Combines live action and animated sequences to teach the message that following God's commandments is in a person's best interests.
Literature and Drama; Religion and Philosophy
Dist - APH **Prod** - TYHP

The Super house 30 MIN
VHS
A House for all seasons series
Color (G)
$49.95 purchase _ #AHFS - 303
Presents a wide variety of products and building techniques for building an energy - efficient, superinsulated home.
Home Economics; Industrial and Technical Education; Science - Natural; Sociology
Dist - PBS **Prod** - KRMATV 1986

Super kicking techniques
VHS
Bill 'Superfoot' Wallace series
Color (G)
$59.95 purchase _ #PNT019
Explains Wallace's style of using legs like hands to get around an opponent's blocks. Features two of Wallace's PKA Full - Contact title fights.
Physical Education and Recreation; Psychology
Dist - SIV

Super marketing at the supermarket 29 MIN
16mm / U-matic / VHS
Be a better shopper series; Program 11
Color (H C A)
LC 81-701468
Deals with techniques supermarkets use to encourage shoppers to buy. Provides an inside look at store layout and displays, games, gimmicks, ad promotions, package design and pricing technique.
Home Economics
Dist - CORNRS **Prod** - CUETV 1978

Super realists 15 MIN
VHS / U-matic
Young at art series
Color (P I)
Fine Arts
Dist - AITECH **Prod** - WSKJTV 1980

Super safety 9 MIN
VHS / U-matic
Kidzone series
Color (I J)
$110.00, $160.00 purchase, $50.00 rental
Presents a program on safety habits in the home and at work. Looks at house painting, slippery floors, cooking and lifting.
Health and Safety
Dist - NDIM **Prod** - KNONET 1992

Super scents 30 MIN
U-matic / VHS
Supersense series
Color (H C)
$250.00 purchase _ #HP - 5804C
Explores how the sense of smell can govern the habits and strongly influence the ability of individuals and species to maintain their niche in complex ecosystems. Reveals that salmon which travel hundreds or thousands of miles to return to the exact location of their birth to spawn are led by their sense of smell. Certain birds use smell to navigate, mammals use 'alarm' smells to warn of danger, and moths release an aphrodisiac scent as a prelude to mating. Part of a series which deals with different facets of animal awareness.
Psychology; Science - Natural
Dist - CORF **Prod** - BBCTV 1989

Super secret federal agency surveillance techniques
VHS
Color (G)
$21.95 purchase _ #SPE001
Reveals methods of high - tech espionage used by the federal agents.
Civics and Political Systems
Dist - SIV

Super sitters 30 MIN
VHS
Color (G)
$39.95 purchase _ #ACVSS101V
Teaches young adults how to become responsible babysitters. Discusses principles of babysitting, things to know before parents leave, meeting the child, what needs to be known about babies, toddlers and older children, and first aid and emergency care. Includes first aid and emergency care manual, a sitters' resource guide, parent's resource guide, write on - wipe off memo board and three emergency phone stickers.
Health and Safety
Dist - CAMV

Super sitters - a training course 25 MIN
VHS
Color (I J H)
$89.95 purchase _ #513VG
Teaches babysitting skills and techniques; child development; and some possible problems in child care. Emphasizes the physical safety and security of the child but points out the need for friendship, patience and understanding. Shows the characteristics of children of different ages. Includes a leader's guide and blackline masters.
Home Economics; Sociology
Dist - UNL

Super sparring techniques and strategy
VHS
Bill 'Superfoot' Wallace series
Color (G)
$59.95 purchase _ #PNT020
Explains over 400 of Wallace's offensive and defensive techniques for scoring high. Features Wallace's 1980 PKA Full - Contact retirement bout.
Physical Education and Recreation; Psychology
Dist - SIV

Super stomach 30 MIN
VHS
Esquire great body series
Color (H C A)
$19.99 purchase _ #EQGB01V
Presents the first of a nine - part exercise series oriented to women. Combines stretches and exercises designed for the abdominal sections. Developed by Deborah Crocker.
Physical Education and Recreation; Science - Natural
Dist - CAMV

Super stretching and conditioning
VHS
Bill 'Superfoot' Wallace series
Color (G)
$59.95 purchase _ #PNT022
Presents Wallace's personal stretching and conditioning routines to improve flexibility, strength and stamina. Recommends viewing prior to Wallace's sparring and kicking videos.
Physical Education and Recreation; Psychology
Dist - SIV

Super Sunday - Laughter and Legend 27 MIN
16mm
Color
Presents the comedy highlights from the first 13 Super Bowl games.
Literature and Drama; Physical Education and Recreation
Dist - MTP **Prod** - ANHBUS

Super Time Saving Tips 30 MIN
VHS

Quick and Easy Sewing Series
(H C A)
$19.95 purchase _ #CH420V
Demonstrates ten sewing and measuring techniques that will save time and aid in developing better sewing skills.
Home Economics
Dist - CAMV

Super - vision series unit f
Acting the ok way 34 MIN
Dist - VCI

Super - Vision Series
Games are not for Fun 36 MIN
Dist - VCI

Super - Volt Radiation 50 MIN
16mm
B&W (PRO)
Shows the use of high voltage X - rays, cobalt radiation and linear accelerators in the treatment of breast and lung cancers, Hodgkin's disease and other types of cancer.
Health and Safety
Dist - LAWREN **Prod** - CMA

The Super weapon 14 MIN
16mm
Color (G)
$30.00 rental
Examines the moral dilemma between humans and their ability to create an Apocalypse with nuclear bombs. Employs the style of a film poem shot in San Francisco, Chicago and various American cities in which missiles, bricks, huts, humanoid - types and people emerge from civilization's whimsical debris. Produced by Donna Cameron.
Fine Arts
Dist - CANCIN

Super workout 30 MIN
VHS
Esquire great body series
Color (H C A)
$19.99 purchase _ #EQGB05V
Presents the fifth of a nine - part exercise series oriented to women. Combines stretches and exercises. Developed by Deborah Crocker.
Physical Education and Recreation; Science - Natural
Dist - CAMV

Superabrasives and precision grinding 30 MIN
VHS / 16mm
Manufacturing insights series
Color (A IND)
$200.00, $190.00 purchase _ #VT391, #VT391U
Explains benefits of using superabrasives including information on air bearing spindles used in high speed, precision grinding.
Business and Economics; Industrial and Technical Education; Psychology
Dist - SME **Prod** - SME 1990

SuperBase 2.0 171 MIN
U-matic / VHS / BETA
Color; PAL; NTSC; SECAM (J H C G)
PdS99.95
Presents the original database for Windows. Features Mike Hayes of SPC Intl.
Computer Science
Dist - VIEWTH

Superbook series
Best news yet and mighty convert - Volume 13 45 MIN
A Dream come true and superbrain - Volume 6 45 MIN
Faithful and true and David the king - Volume 19 45 MIN
The First Christmas and miracles of love - Volume 12 45 MIN
The First king and big fish, little fish - Volume 9 45 MIN
The Flood and double trouble - Volume 2 45 MIN
The Giant killer and the lion's den - Volume 4 45 MIN
A Gift from heaven and burning bush - Volume 22 45 MIN
Good left arm and stick in the mud - Volume 17 45 MIN
The Hostage and family reunion - Volume 21 45 MIN
How it all began and my brother's keeper - Volume 1 45 MIN
Just reward and A wonderful gift 45 MIN
Mighty little shepherd and in all his glory - Volume 24 45 MIN
The Miracle rod and those amazing trumpets - Volume 3 45 MIN
Moses and plagues and Moses and Israelites - Volume 23 45 MIN
Mother's day and the beauty queen - Volume 8 45 MIN
Nehemiah - Walls of Jericho and patience of Job - Volume 10 45 MIN
Pitchers of fire and muscleman - Volume 7 45 MIN
Snakes and a donkey and worth fighting for - Volume 16 45 MIN
The Test and here comes the bride - Volume 5 45 MIN
A Test of faith and obedience and love at first sight - Volume 15 45 MIN
A True prophet and flaming chariots - Volume 11 45 MIN
Where, oh where and hot dog - Volume 14 45 MIN
Wicked queen and a matter of time - Volume 25 45 MIN
Dist - APH

Supercharged - the Grand Prix Car 51 MIN
VHS
Color (S)
$29.95 purchase _ #781 - 9047
Recreates the golden age of Grand Prix racing. Combines restored vintage cars such as the Bugatti, Alfa Romeo, Maserati and Mercedes - Benz, with archival footage. Features Grand Prix driver John Watson.
History - World; Industrial and Technical Education; Physical Education and Recreation
Dist - FI **Prod** - BBCTV 1989

Supercharging and Fuel Injection 20 MIN
16mm
B&W
LC FIE58-115
Discusses the supercharging and fuel injection systems used on army vehicles to provide increased horsepower for engines without increasing the size of the engine. Covers their purpose, components and functions.
Civics and Political Systems; Industrial and Technical Education
Dist - USNAC **Prod** - USA

A Superconducting Magnet for Fusion Research 22 MIN
16mm
Color (C A)
LC 72-702145
Describes the thirteen - ton superconducting magnet now in experimental use at the Lawrence Radiation Laboratory at the University of California at Livermore. Shows how the magnet is used in a supercool environment to confine hydrogen plasma in an attempt to produce controlled fusion energy on earth.
Science - Physical
Dist - USERD **Prod** - USNRC 1972

Superconducting Magnets 13 MIN
16mm
Color (H C A)
LC FIE67-135
Describes the basic design problems of superconducting magnets. Includes pictures of the Argonne National Laboratory's 67,000 Gauss magnet during fabrication and testing.
Science - Physical
Dist - USERD **Prod** - ANL 1966

Superconductivity 30 MIN
VHS / 16mm
Interactions Series
Color (H T PRO)
$180.00 purchase, $35.00 rental
Illustrates the discovery of superconductivity through using ceramics at temperatures considerably higher than absolute zero and how this discovery will have the greatest effects in the areas of energy and transportation.
Science - Physical; Social Science
Dist - AITECH **Prod** - WHATV 1989

Superconductivity - 3 29 MIN
VHS
Interactions in Science and Society - Student Programs - Series
Color (H T)
$125.00 purchase
Considers the discovery of superconductivity and its possibly profound political and economic repercussions. Reveals that the country which develops practical technical applications for the discovery will have a strong competitive advantage, especially in the areas of energy and transportation. Part 3 of a 12-part series on interacting technological and societal issues. Includes teacher in-service. Computer component available which enhances decision - making skills.
Science - Physical; Sociology
Dist - AITECH **Prod** - WHATV 1990

Superconductors 25 MIN
35mm strip / VHS

Color (J H C A)
$99.00, $93.00 purchase _ #MB - 909743 - X, #MB - 909719 - 7
Discusses superconductors and their potential impact on electronics. Reveals that superconductors utilize selected metals to conduct electricity at temperatures near absolute zero.
Science - Physical
Dist - SRA **Prod** - SRA 1990

Superconductors 24 MIN
U-matic / VHS / 16mm
Color
Introduces the phenomenon of electrical superconductivity. Shows how superconductors can help clean up pollution, facilitate brain surgery, provide power through special generators, and solve the rapid transit problem with the magnaplane.
Industrial and Technical Education; Science
Dist - CNEMAG **Prod** - DOCUA

Superconductors - Tomorrow's Energy Breakthrough is Here 20 MIN
U-matic / VHS / 16mm
Coping with Tomorrow Series
Color (J)
Explains what superconductors are and how they work. Shows how they may clean up pollution in air and water, make possible operations deep in the brain, provide power through special generators and solve rapid transit problems with the magneplane, which runs on tracks and can go 100 miles per hour.
Social Science
Dist - AIMS **Prod** - DOCUA 1975

Superconductors - Tomorrow's Energy Breakthrough is Here 21 MIN
16mm
Color (J)
LC 76-701714
Discusses superconductors and future prospects for their application in brain and cancer surgery, for cleaning up pollution in air and water, for providing power and for use in solving rapid transit problems.
Health and Safety; Industrial and Technical Education; Science; Science - Physical; Sociology
Dist - CNEMAG **Prod** - DOCUA

The Superconscious mind 30 MIN
BETA / VHS
Opening to intuition series
Color (G)
$29.95 purchase _ #S218
Features Kevin Ryerson, intuitive consultant and trance channeler, who states that higher states of consciousness and the superconscious mind have important implications for the human identity. Part of a four - part series on opening to intuition.
Religion and Philosophy
Dist - THINKA **Prod** - THINKA

Supercup World International 50 MIN
VHS
Color (G)
$29.95 purchase _ #0856
Records the gathering of some of the best sail racers from Canada, Britain, Japan and the United States at San Diego, California, in competition.
Physical Education and Recreation
Dist - SEVVID

The Superficial Back 10 MIN
16mm / U-matic / VHS
Guides to Dissection Series
Color (C A)
Focuses on the back region. Demonstrates the dissection of the superficial back.
Health and Safety; Science - Natural
Dist - TEF **Prod** - UCLA

The Superficial face, parotid gland and posterior and suboccipital triangles 47 MIN
VHS / U-matic
Anatomy of the head and neck series
Color (PRO C)
$395.00 purchase, $80.00 rental _ #C901 - VI - 065
Describes relevant features of the skull using prosected specimens and diagrams. Focuses on the main muscles of facial expression, the facial vein, artery and nerve, as well as the sensory innervation of the face and scalp. Examines the anatomy of the parotid gland, boundaries, floor and contents of the posterior triangle, relationships to deep back musculature and the contents of the suboccipital triangle. Part of a series on head and neck anatomy produced by Shakti Chandra, Faculty of Medicine, University of Newfoundland.
Health and Safety; Science - Natural
Dist - HSCIC

The Superfluous Citizen 28 MIN
U-matic / VHS
All about Welfare Series
Color
Sociology
Dist - PBS **Prod** - WITFTV

Supergrandpa 20 MIN
16mm
Color (I) (AMERICAN SIGN)
LC 76-701099
Presents in American sign language the story of Gastaf Hakansson and the bicycle race that he won in Sweden in 1951. Signed by Howard Busby.
Guidance and Counseling; Physical Education and Recreation; Psychology
Dist - JOYCE **Prod** - JOYCE 1975

Superhero 10 MIN
16mm
Color (H C A)
$30.00 rental
Tells the story of a Dionysian-like superhero who sometimes has to punch out Batman for being too goody-goody. Presents a personalized humorous response to our traditional cartoon hero story. Produced by Emily Breer.
Fine Arts; Literature and Drama
Dist - CANCIN

Superimposition 15 MIN
16mm
B&W
Includes similies of a slippery television tube gesticulating, breaking and supplying a long view of multiple images.
Social Science
Dist - VANBKS **Prod** - VANBKS 1968

Superior sales management 60 MIN
VHS
Effective manager seminar series
Color (COR)
$95.00 purchase _ #NGC756V
Presents a multimedia seminar on sales management. Consists of a videocassette, a 60 - minute audiocassette, and a study guide.
Business and Economics; Psychology
Dist - CAMV

Superior sales management 60 MIN
Cassette / VHS
Effective manager series
Color (COR)
$95.00 purchase _ #6426
Features Brian Tracy who shows how to build a winning sales team, from recruiting, through training and monitoring. Includes a 60 - minute video, two audiocassettes and two workbooks. Part of a fourteen - part series.
Business and Economics; Civics and Political Systems; Guidance and Counseling; Psychology
Dist - SYBVIS

Superjock 16 MIN
U-matic / VHS / 16mm
Physical Fitness Series
Color (J)
LC 79-700315
Shows how an overweight, middle - aged man and his overweight son learn that improper diet, heavy smoking and lack of exercise greatly diminish one's sense of well - being and seriously endanger one's life.
Health and Safety; Physical Education and Recreation
Dist - JOU **Prod** - ALTSUL 1978

Superjock Scales Down 15 MIN
U-matic / VHS / 16mm
Physical Fitness Series
Color (J)
LC 81-700627
Tells how Superjock loses 45 pounds and makes major modifications to his life style. Stresses the importance of continued exercise and regular dieting.
Health and Safety
Dist - JOU **Prod** - ALTSUL 1980

The Superlative Horse 36 MIN
16mm / U-matic / VHS
Color (P)
LC 76-701934
Tells a tale from ancient China which proves that people should not judge things, animals or even other people by their outward appearances, but by their inner qualities. Based on the folk tale The Superlative Horse by Jean Merrill.
Literature and Drama
Dist - PHENIX **Prod** - NYSED 1975

Superlearning video - Part I 120 MIN
VHS
Color (G)
$25.00 purchase _ #117A
Features Sheila Ostrander, Lynn Schroeder and leading experts in accelerated learning from Japan in a seminar at Kaidanren Hall in Tokyo. Includes remarks by Dr Hideo Seki who developed a system for large engineering classes, Dr N Ogawa, President of the Foreign Language University of Japan, and a demonstration by Prof Charles Adamson, Trident College, Nagoya. Part one of two parts.
Education; Geography - World
Dist - SUPERL **Prod** - SUPERL

Superlearning video - Part II 120 MIN
VHS
Color (G)
$25.00 purchase _ #117B
Features Sheila Ostrander, Lynn Schroeder and leading experts in accelerated learning from Japan in a seminar at Kaidanren Hall in Tokyo. Includes remarks by Dr Hideo Seki who developed a system for large engineering classes, Dr N Ogawa, President of the Foreign Language University of Japan, and a demonstration by Prof Charles Adamson, Trident College, Nagoya. Part two of two parts.
Education; Geography - World
Dist - SUPERL **Prod** - SUPERL

Superlearning video - Parts I and II 240 MIN
VHS
Color (G)
$44.95 purchase _ #117B
Features Sheila Ostrander, Lynn Schroeder and leading experts in accelerated learning from Japan in a seminar at Kaidanren Hall in Tokyo. Includes remarks by Dr Hideo Seki who developed a system for large engineering classes, Dr N Ogawa, President of the Foreign Language University of Japan, and a demonstration by Prof Charles Adamson, Trident College, Nagoya. Presented in two parts.
Education; Geography - World
Dist - SUPERL **Prod** - SUPERL

The Superliners - twilight of an era 59 MIN
U-matic / VHS / 16mm
Color
LC 80-700267
Takes a nostalgic look at the luxury liners such as the Normandie, Titanic, Queen Mary, Queen Elizabeth and the Queen Elizabeth 2, which plied the North Atlantic in the first half of the twentieth century.
Social Science
Dist - NGS **Prod** - NGS 1980
SEVVID

Superman 142 MIN
16mm
Color
Stars Christopher Reeve as Superman, the Man of Steel who disguises himself as mild - mannered Clark Kent. Features Margot Kidder, Marlon Brando and Gene Hackman.
Fine Arts
Dist - SWANK **Prod** - WB

Superman and the Bride 40 MIN
U-matic / VHS / 16mm
Color (J)
Shows how stereotyped images of men and women are perpetuated by messages in the mass media because the phenomenon benefits them financially. Stereotypes are broken when women are portrayed as active, confident and self - reliant, dispelling the myth that all men are Supermen and all women are brides.
Sociology
Dist - MEDIAG **Prod** - THAMES 1977

SuperMap county level
CD-ROM
Color (G)
$990.00 purchase _ #1701
Provides access to 1980 US Census of Population and Housing data in a graphic format. Includes search, retrieval and mapping software, enabling users to incorporate data into reports, spreadsheets, or databases, and to produce color or monochrome maps. Data covers entire US to the county level, tract level versions available separately. For IBM PCs and compatibles, requires 640K of RAM, DOS 3.1 or later, one floppy disk drive - hard disk recommended, one empty expansion slot, an IBM compatible CD - ROM drive, and an EGA adapter and display.
Geography - United States; Sociology
Dist - BEP

SuperMap tract level
CD-ROM
Color (G)
$2240.00 purchase _ #1702
Provides access to 1980 US Census of Population and Housing Data in a graphic format. Includes search, retrieval and mapping software that enables users to incorporate this data into reports, spreadsheets and databases, and to produce color or monochrome maps. Offers Census data to the tract level of one region - Northeast, South, Midwest, or West - additional regions

are available at additional cost. For IBM PCs and compatibles, requires 604K RAM, DOS 3.1 or later, one floppy drive - hard disk recommended, one empty expansion slot, an IBM compatible CD - ROM drive, and an EGA adapter and display.
Geography - United States; Sociology
Dist - BEP

Supermarket 14 MIN
U-matic / VHS / 16mm
Color (P)
LC 83-700655
Takes a behind - the - scenes look at the running of a supermarket. Features the store manager, who explains what kind of skills and how much work is involved. Shows delivery men, butchers, produce people, stockmen and bookkeepers.
Home Economics
Dist - HIGGIN **Prod** - HIGGIN 1984

The Supermarket - a Great American Invention 28 MIN
16mm
Color
LC 80-701622
Show changes in goods and services provided by the supermarket as a result of advanced technology and the changing social needs of Americans.
Industrial and Technical Education
Dist - MTP **Prod** - FMI 1980

Supermarket botany 15 MIN
VHS
Color (I J)
$39.95 purchase _ #49 - 8470 - V
Discusses the principle parts of plants using common supermarket fruits and vegetables as examples. Describes the structure and role of plants in many familiar food items. Still frame.
Home Economics; Science - Natural
Dist - INSTRU **Prod** - CBSC

Supermarket Dollar 14 MIN
Videoreel / VT2
Living Better I Series
Color
Home Economics
Dist - PBS **Prod** - MAETEL

Supermarket savvy 60 MIN
U-matic / VHS
(C A)
$34.95 _ #HPG500V
Features a tour through a grocery store and an interview with a registered dietitian, while covering important information about each of the major food groups. Explains such food concepts as 'polyunsaturated fat' and 'no cholesterol.' Includes accompanying booklet.
Home Economics; Industrial and Technical Education
Dist - CAMV **Prod** - CAMV

Supermarket savvy 52 MIN
VHS
Color (G)
$24.95 purchase _ #S02210
Presents tips for making one's grocery shopping more effective. Covers subjects including labels, calculating the amount of calories from fat, product comparisons, and more.
Home Economics; Social Science
Dist - UILL

Supermarket - Ten Cent Store 29 MIN
Videoreel / VT2
Making Things Grow III Series
Color
Agriculture
Dist - PBS **Prod** - WGBHTV

Supermarket, the Mammoth Mousetrap
U-matic / VHS
Color
Discusses how changes in food shopping habits can effect weight control. Encourages expression of feeling about the problems involved in shopping for food while one is trying to lose weight.
Health and Safety; Home Economics; Psychology
Dist - KORSCR **Prod** - DIETF

Supermarkets 30 MIN
U-matic / VHS
Consumer survival series; Shopping
Color
Presents tips on using supermarkets.
Home Economics
Dist - MDCPB **Prod** - MDCPB

Supermarkets - orthodontics - condominiums
VHS / U-matic
Consumer survival series
Color
Discusses various aspects of supermarkets, orthodontics and condominiums.
Business and Economics; Health and Safety; Home Economics
Dist - MDCPB **Prod** - MDCPB

The Supermilers - the 4 - Minute Mile and Beyond 64 MIN
U-matic / VHS
Color (C)
$199.00, $99.00 purchase _ #AD - 918
Features Roger Bannister, the first runner to break the four - minute mile barrier over 30 years ago, and ten runners who have lowered and held the World Mile Record since then. Features Bannister, John Landy, Derek Ibbotson, Herb Elliot, Peter Snell, Michel Jazy, Jim Ryan, Filbert Bayti, John Walker, Sebastian Coe and Steve Ovett who all come from vastly different backgrounds but share the distinction of having run the mile faster than any one before.
Health and Safety; Physical Education and Recreation; Sociology
Dist - FOTH **Prod** - FOTH

Supermouse 8 MIN
16mm / U-matic / VHS
Color (P I)
Presents an animated film featuring a day in the life of Supermouse, who lives the perfect existence, until he wakes up and finds out it is only a dream.
Fine Arts
Dist - PHENIX **Prod** - KRATKY

Supernovas and pulsars 29 MIN
U-matic
Project universe - astronomy series; Lesson 25
Color (C A)
Contrasts nova with supernova. Describes and illustrates current theories of conditions leading to the supernova event. Discusses properties of the neutron star.
Science - Physical
Dist - CDTEL **Prod** - COAST

Superposition 9 MIN
VHS
History in the rocks series
Color (H C)
$24.95 purchase _ #S9813
Shows how stratification profiles are modified using single - concept format. Part of a ten - part series on rocks.
Science - Physical
Dist - HUBDSC **Prod** - HUBDSC

Superpower diplomacy - should the U S reject detente as its strategy 59 MIN
U-matic
Advocates series
Color
Presents a debate on whether or not the United States should reject detente as its strategy when dealing with the Soviet Union. Features Elmo Zumwalt and Lincoln P Bloomfield.
Civics and Political Systems; Geography - World
Dist - PBS **Prod** - WGBHTV

Supersense series

Making sense	30 MIN
Seeing sense	30 MIN
Sense of timing	30 MIN
Sixth sense	30 MIN
Sound sense	30 MIN
Super scents	30 MIN

Dist - CORF

Supersets 60 MIN
VHS
Muscle building series
Color (G)
$39.99 purchase _ #MFV008V
Presents a body building workout program which develops both the cardiovascular and muscular systems by not allowing rest periods between sets. Recommends at least six months of previous weight lifting experience due to the strenuousness of the program.
Physical Education and Recreation; Science - Natural
Dist - CAMV **Prod** - CAMV 1988

Supersonic Laboratory 16 MIN
16mm
Color
LC 74-706590
Discusses past and present facilities of the supersonic test tract at the Naval Weapons Center in China Lake, California.
Civics and Political Systems
Dist - USNAC **Prod** - USN 1971

Supersonic thunderbirds 14 MIN
16mm
Color
LC FIE63-116
Visits the Supersonic Thunderbirds jet aerobats in their homes. Shows how they live during their offduty time. Includes scenes of the men in action.
Civics and Political Systems; Social Science
Dist - USNAC **Prod** - USDD 1959

Superstar 30 MIN
U-matic / VHS
La Esquina series
Color (H C A)
Presents a story centering on the member of a musical band. Uses the story to try to reduce the minority isolation of Mexican - American students by showing the teenager as an individual, as a member of a unique cultural group and as a member of a larger complex society.
Sociology
Dist - GPN **Prod** - SWEDL 1976

Superstar Sports Tapes Series

Barefoot skiing	120 MIN
Beginning and Intermediate Skiing	45 MIN
Jumping	85 MIN
Overall Skiing	30 MIN
Slalom	80 MIN
Trick Skiing	105 MIN
Waterskiing for Kids	30 MIN

Dist - TRASS

The Superstars of venture capital 30 MIN
U-matic
Adam Smith's money world 1985 - 1986 season series; 224
Color (A)
Attempts to demystify the world of money and break it down so that small as well as large businesses and it's people understand and adjust to new social and economic trends. Reports on the major economic stories and discoveries of 1985 and 1986.
Business and Economics
Dist - PBS **Prod** - WNETTV 1986

Superstars - super salaries 30 MIN
VHS
Adam Smith's money world series
Color (H C A)
$79.95 purchase
Takes a look at the salary structure within the National Basketball Association, comparing the salaries of star players and 'journeymen.' Considers a public financing proposal made by the Boston Celtics team. Features host Jerry Goodman, also known as 'Adam Smith,' and his guests Larry Bird, David Stern, Roy Hinson and Bob Woolf.
Business and Economics
Dist - PBS **Prod** - WNETTV

Superstitions 29 MIN
Videoreel / VT2
Who is Man Series
Color
Features Shirley Winston, psychic author and lecturer, joining Dr Puryear in an examination of modern day superstitions and their origins.
Psychology; Religion and Philosophy; Sociology
Dist - PBS **Prod** - WHROTV

Superstore manager 45 MIN
VHS
Situation vacant series
Color (A)
PdS65 purchase
Reveals that Toys R Us is not really interested in qualifications, that the company looks for energy and commitment. Watches as a first round interview is followed by a roundtable competition against other candidates. Part of a six-part series looking at selection procedures for a wide range of jobs.
Education; Guidance and Counseling; Psychology
Dist - BBCENE

Supertour
VHS
Smithsonian collection series
Color (J H C G)
$39.95 purchase _ #PMV002V
Joins entertainer Dudley Moore and a young friend, Devon, on a whirlwind 'supertour' of the largest museum network in the world, focusing on science, history and the arts. Visits the National Museum of American History, the Air and Space Museum, the Museum of African Art and the National Zoo, as well as ten other museums in the Smithsonian network. Takes part in an American Indian deer dance, examines costumes and artifacts from exotic cultures and tours the globe, discovering everything from Caribbean festivals to ancient Chinese myths. Part of a three - part series on Smithsonian collections.
Fine Arts; History - United States
Dist - CAMV **Prod** - SMITHS 1990

Supervise vocational education personnel 14 MIN
VHS
Color (PRO T)
$30.00 purchase _ #V - LT - D - 2
Presents a day in the life of Phyllis Butler, principal at Jones Vocational School. Illustrates some of the skills necessary for effective supervision of instructional personnel. Assesses her performance using the Administrator Performance Assessment Form - APAF.
Business and Economics; Education
Dist - AAVIM **Prod** - AAVIM

Supervised Clinical Sexology
VHS / U-matic
Independent Study in Human Sexuality Series
Color (PRO)
Health and Safety; Psychology
Dist - MMRC **Prod** - MMRC

Supervising and people problems 21 MIN
U-matic / VHS / 16mm
Supervising for results series
Color (COR)
LC 82-701188
Focuses on skills needed by managers who must deal with employees' personal problems that affect work performances. Uses both dramatized episodes and lectures.
Business and Economics; Psychology
Dist - PHENIX **Prod** - INCC 1982

Supervising and the Organization 21 MIN
U-matic / VHS / 16mm
Supervising for Results Series
Color (A)
LC 82-701189
Deals with the importance of good supervision to an organization.
Business and Economics; Psychology
Dist - PHENIX **Prod** - INCC 1982

Supervising differences - valuing diversity - Part V 30 MIN
VHS
Valuing diversity series
Color (A PRO IND)
$695.00 purchase, $100.00 rental
Presents the fifth of a seven - part series on diversity in the workplace. Argues that diversity can be a strength if properly handled. Dramatizes situations leading to conflict and poor performance, showing how they can be better handled. Focuses on first line supervisors, managers, and others in leadership positions.
Business and Economics; Guidance and Counseling; Sociology
Dist - VLEARN

Supervising for productivity 18 MIN
U-matic / VHS / 16mm
Supervising for results series
Color (COR)
LC 82-701190
Demonstrates how good supervision can aid productivity.
Business and Economics; Psychology
Dist - PHENIX **Prod** - INCC 1982

Supervising for Results Series
Supervising and people problems 21 MIN
Supervising and the Organization 21 MIN
Supervising for productivity 18 MIN
Supervisory communication skills 21 MIN
Dist - PHENIX

Supervising for safety series
Call 'em on the carpet 10 MIN
It's an order 10 MIN
Dist - NSC

Supervising safety - making it happen 15 MIN
BETA / VHS / U-matic
Color (IND COR)
$495.00 purchase _ #827 - 08
Discusses the importance of the supervisor's role as a model for promoting safety, rewarding safe behavior when witnessed, and five steps for correcting unsafe acts.
Business and Economics; Health and Safety; Industrial and Technical Education; Psychology
Dist - ITSC **Prod** - ITSC

Supervising safety - you make the difference - Supervisando la seguridad - usted hace la diferencia 19 MIN
U-matic / BETA / VHS
Color (IND G) (SPANISH)
$495.00 purchase _ #850 - 01, #850 - 03
Trains supervisors in ways to improve the safety of the operations they supervise through modeling and other techniques. Discusses the factors which lead to accidents and the techniques supervisors can use to change employee behavior to reduce the number of accidents.
Business and Economics; Health and Safety; Industrial and Technical Education; Psychology
Dist - ITSC **Prod** - ITSC

Supervising the Disadvantaged Series Module 1
General Problems in Supervising the Disadvantaged 50 FRS
Dist - RESEM

Supervising the Disadvantaged Series Module 2
Motivating the Disadvantaged 10 MIN
Dist - RESEM

Supervising the Disadvantaged Series Module 3
Resolving Interpersonal Conflicts 11 MIN
Dist - RESEM

Supervising the Disadvantaged Series Module 4
Interviewing the Disadvantaged 11 MIN
Dist - RESEM

Supervising the Disadvantaged Series Module 5
Training the Disadvantaged 11 MIN
Dist - RESEM

Supervising the disadvantaged series
Presents five modules on developing an awareness in managers and supervisors of how to work with disabled employees. Includes the titles General Problems in Supervising the Disadvantaged, Motivating the Disadvantaged, Resolving Interpersonal Conflicts, Interviewing the Disadvantaged, Training the Disadvantaged.
Supervising the disadvantaged series 51 MIN
Dist - RESEM **Prod** - RESEM

Supervising the Marginal Teacher 60 MIN
U-matic
Color (T)
Spells out the options available to a supervisor in dealing with a marginal teacher. Strategies include intensive assistance, progressive discipline and teacher dismissal. Available with captions for the hearing impaired.
Education
Dist - AFSCD **Prod** - AFSCD 1986

Supervising Women Workers 11 MIN
16mm
Problems in Supervision Series
B&W
LC FIE52-159
A plant manager advises a foreman to take into account in his supervision the fact that women workers haven't had the same industrial experience as men and that they often have more home responsibilities.
Business and Economics
Dist - USNAC **Prod** - USOE 1944

Supervising workers on the job 10 MIN
16mm
Problems in supervision series
B&W (H A COR IND) (SPANISH)
LC FIE62-83
Dramatizes incidents illustrating good and poor methods of supervision, including the necessity for obtaining 'snoopervising.'
Business and Economics; Foreign Language
Dist - USNAC **Prod** - USOE 1944

Supervision 8 MIN
16mm
Safety and You Series
Color
Examines the role of the supervisor in risk control and demonstrates that effective supervision reduces accidents.
Business and Economics; Health and Safety
Dist - FILCOM **Prod** - FILCOM

Supervision and Management Series
Philosophy of Supervision 17 MIN
Dist - TRNAID

Supervision De Los Obreros En Su Trabajo 10 MIN
U-matic
B&W (SPANISH)
LC 79-706681
A Spanish language videocassette. Uses dramatized incidents to illustrate good and poor methods of supervision, discussing the importance of obtaining the confidence of workers and describing the dangers of 'snoopervising'. Issued in 1959 as a motion picture.
Business and Economics; Foreign Language; Psychology
Dist - USNAC **Prod** - USOE 1979

Supervision Management Course, Pt 1 Series Unit 1
The Nature of Management 20 MIN
Dist - AMA

Supervision of self administration of medication series
Presents a five - part series training staff for supervision of developmentally disabled client self medication. Includes the titles What Is Medication, Legal Aspects, Supervision vs Administration, Degrees of Supervision and Side Effects of Medication. Presented by the Richmond State School Staff Development, Texas Dept of Mental Health and Mental Retardation.
Degrees of supervision - Module IV 8 MIN
Legal aspects - Module II 14 MIN
Side effects of medication 11 MIN
Supervision vs administration 14 MIN
What is medication - Module I 13 MIN
Dist - HSCIC

Supervision prescription 30 MIN
U-matic / VHS
Color (PRO)
Deals with supervision techniques in the health care industry. Uses story format showing a new head nurse who learns fundamentals of management.
Business and Economics; Health and Safety
Dist - AMEDIA **Prod** - AMEDIA

Supervision series
Developing cooperation 14 MIN
Dist - USNAC

Supervision vs administration 14 MIN
VHS / U-matic
Supervision of self administration of medication series; Module 3
Color (PRO C)
$395.00 purchase, $80.00 rental _ #C920 - VI - 019
Reveals that an important job of staff in working with individuals with special needs is to help clients develop individuality and to live the most productive and independent life possible. Discloses that part of developing independence involves the self administration of medications. In most facilities, medications are administered by nursing staff or through self administration supervised by trained residential staff. Trains residential staff in helping clients self administer their medications whenever possible. Part of a five - part series presented by the Richmond State School Staff Development, Texas Dept of Mental Health and Mental Retardation.
Health and Safety; Psychology
Dist - HSCIC

Supervison and Management Series
Performance Evaluation 10 MIN
Dist - TRNAID

The Supervisor 20 MIN
16mm / VHS
Color (IND COR) (FRENCH)
$495.00, $445.00 purchase
Demonstrates the attributes of an effective supervisor. Suggests that supervisors in hazardous environments must have both intelligence and satisfactory relationships with workers.
Business and Economics; Guidance and Counseling; Health and Safety; Psychology
Dist - FLMWST

The Supervisor 15 MIN
16mm
H2S Training Series
Color
LC 77-700318
Observes a foreman at a gas plant and his methods of supervision in a hazardous environment.
Health and Safety; Industrial and Technical Education
Dist - FLMWST **Prod** - AWHSC 1977

The Supervisor 20 MIN
VHS / U-matic
Hydrogen sulphide safety series
Color
Concentrates on supervision on hazardous environments. Shows a supervisor's effectiveness by his intelligent behavior and his ways of relating to the people about him.
Health and Safety
Dist - FLMWST **Prod** - FLMWST

Supervisor and Interpersonal Relations Series Module 1
General Problems of Interpersonal Conflict 62 FRS
Dist - RESEM

Supervisor and Interpersonal Relations Series Module 2
Improving Relations between Peers 12 MIN
Dist - RESEM

Supervisor and Interpersonal Relations Series Module 3
Improving Attitudes toward Subordinates 14 MIN
Dist - RESEM

Supervisor and Interpersonal Relations Series Module 4
Improving Attitudes toward Supervision 64 FRS
Dist - RESEM

Supervisor and Interpersonal Relations Series Module 5
Reducing Conflict in the Organization 66 FRS
Dist - RESEM

Supervisor and interpersonal relations series
Presents five modules which examine the supervisor's role in managing attitudes and interpersonal relations within in the work group. Includes the titles General Problems of Interpersonal Conflict, Improving Relations Between Peers, Improving Attitudes Toward Subordinates, Improving Attitudes Toward Supervision, Reducing Conflict in the Organization.
Supervisor and interpersonal relations series 63 MIN
Dist - RESEM Prod - RESEM

Supervisor and OJT series module 1
Analyzing for training 12 MIN
Dist - RESEM

Supervisor and OJT Series Module 2
Preparing Training Objectives 12 MIN
Dist - RESEM

Supervisor and OJT Series Module 5
Following Up on Training 9 MIN
Dist - RESEM

Supervisor and OJT series
Presents five modules which examine the supervisor's responsibility for on - the - job training - OJT - and a basic three - step procedure for teaching specific skills or procedures. Includes the titles Analyzing for Training, Preparing Training Objectives, How to Do On - the - Job Training, Training for Upward Mobility, Following up on Training.
How to do on - the - job training 65 FRS(0237179)
Training for upward mobility 70 FRS
Dist - RESEM Prod - RESEM

Supervisor as a Classroom Instructor Series Module 1
The Teaching - Learning Process 11 MIN
Dist - RESEM

Supervisor as a Classroom Instructor Series Module 3
Preplanning and Objectives 11 MIN
Dist - RESEM

Supervisor as a Classroom Instructor Series Module 5
Effective Teaching Techniques 12 MIN
Dist - RESEM

Supervisor as a Classroom Instructor Series Module 6
Evaluation and Follow - Up 12 MIN
Dist - RESEM

Supervisor as a classroom instructor series
Presents six modules which provide elementary teaching theory, practical help for writing objectives, classroom teaching techniques and the evaluation of training sessions. Includes the titles The Teaching - Learning Process, Communications and Learning, Preplanning and Objectives, Helping the Learner Learn, Effective Teaching Techniques, Evaluation and Follow - Up.
Communications and learning process 61 FRS
Helping the learner learn 64 FRS
Supervisor as a classroom instructor series 67 MIN
Dist - RESEM Prod - RESEM

The Supervisor as a Communicator 12 MIN(0118812)
U-matic / 35mm strip
Effective Communicating Skills Series
Color
Shows how the supervisor is in a unique position as a communicator because he/she must communicate both up and down the organizational ladder. Shows how to develop essential techniques for communicating effectively in both directions.
Business and Economics; English Language; Psychology
Dist - RESEM Prod - RESEM

The Supervisor as a Leader 27 MIN
U-matic
Problems in Supervision Series
B&W
LC 79-706453
Illustrates poor supervisory practices. Issued in 1944 as a motion picture.
Business and Economics; Psychology
Dist - USNAC Prod - USOE 1979

The Supervisor as a leader - Pt 1 14 MIN
16mm
Problems in supervision series
B&W
LC FIE52-76
Gives four illustrations of poor supervisory practices. Shows the importance of always keeping one's promises, never taking credit for someone else's work, never passing the buck and never playing favorites.
Business and Economics
Dist - USNAC Prod - USOE 1944

The Supervisor as a leader - Pt 2 13 MIN
16mm
Problems in supervision series
B&W
LC FIE52-75
Gives four examples of poor supervision which teach that a supervisor should be a leader not an authoritarian, show appreciation, curb his anger and protect the rights and feelings of his workers.
Business and Economics
Dist - USNAC Prod - USOE 1944

Supervisor - motivating through insight 13 MIN
16mm / U-matic / VHS
Professional management program series
Color (COR)
Shows that food service and hospitality employees must be seen as whole persons with unique individual emotions, tastes and needs.
Business and Economics; Psychology; Sociology
Dist - NEM Prod - NEM

The Supervisor - motivating through insight 12 MIN
U-matic / VHS / 16mm
Professional management program series
Color (COR)
LC 74-700227
Shows techniques of employee motivation. Explains that in order to motivate people to do their work well, the supervisor must develop insight into human emotions, his own as well as those of the employees.
Business and Economics; Guidance and Counseling; Psychology
Dist - NEM Prod - NEM 1971

Supervisors' development program series
Features William Shatner as host. Presents a 13 - part series on employee safety which stresses the four - step SAFE model - Search for hazards, Assess risks, Find solutions, Enforce solutions. Looks at safety management, communications and human relations, employee safety training, safety inspections, accident investigations, industrial hygiene, personal protective equipment, ergonomics, machine safeguarding, hand tool and portable power tool safety, electrical safety, fire safety.
Accident investigations 10 MIN
Communications - human relations 10 MIN
Electrical safety 10 MIN
Employee safety training 10 MIN
Ergonomics 10 MIN
Fire safety 10 MIN
Hand tools and portable power tools 10 MIN
Industrial hygiene 10 MIN
Machine safeguarding 10 MIN
Materials handling and storage 10 MIN
Personal protective equipment 10 MIN
Safety inspections 10 MIN
Safety management 10 MIN
Dist - NSC Prod - NSC 1971

Supervisor's role in food distribution series
Compliance with food law 21 MIN
Involving Hourly Personnel 16 MIN
Pest Management and Programs 14 MIN
Pesticides and Pest Management 26 MIN
Recognition of Defects 24 MIN
Dist - PLAID

The Supervisor's safety meeting
16mm / U-matic
Color (COR)
Shows how to plan, conduct and participate in meetings to establish safety policies and procedures.
Business and Economics; Health and Safety
Dist - BNA Prod - BNA 1983

Supervisors series
Presents an eight-part series designed to help supervisors - particularly newly-appointed ones - to understand the demands of their individual roles through the experience of established supervisors who offer personal insights and strategies from within a framework of good practice. Looks at newly appointed supervisors; establishing new supervisory roles; leadership; motivation; communication; personnel training; discipline; changes at work.
I know I'm a supervisor, but what do I do 25 MIN
I'm in charge 25 MIN
Love or money 25 MIN
The Need to know 25 MIN
Problems, problems 25 MIN
Staying on top 25 MIN
Who's for training 25 MIN
Dist - BBCENE

Supervisory communication skills 21 MIN
U-matic / VHS / 16mm
Supervising for results series
Color (COR)
LC 82-701191
Focuses on the skills supervisors need in order to communicate beneficially with their employees, their fellow managers and their superiors. Uses both dramatized episodes and lectures.
Business and Economics; Psychology
Dist - PHENIX Prod - INCC 1982

Supervisory Development for Law Enforcement Series Part 1
Leadership 18 MIN
Dist - CORF

Supervisory Development for Law Enforcement Series Part 2
Discipline 20 MIN
Dist - CORF

Supervisory Leadership Series
Attitudes of people 29 MIN
Basic skills of effective leadership 29 MIN
Fundamental Duties of the Supervisor 29 MIN
Group Participation 29 MIN
The I Pattern of Behavior 29 MIN
Improving Skills of Communication 29 MIN
Improving Skills of Listening 29 MIN
Levels of Human Need 29 MIN
Dist - EDSD

Supervisory liability, management responsibility and accountability 24 MIN
U-matic / VHS / 16mm
Police civil liability series; Pt 5
Color
LC 79-701702
Stresses the identification and reduction of risks in minimizing areas of responsibility for which police supervisory personnel may be held civilly liable.
Civics and Political Systems
Dist - CORF Prod - HAR 1979

Supervisory Management Course, Pt 1 8 MIN
VHS / U-matic
Color (FRENCH SPANISH)
Presents an inclusive course in the principles and applications of professional management, featuring techniques for team - building and setting objectives.
Business and Economics; Foreign Language; Psychology
Dist - AMA Prod - AMA

Supervisory Management Course, Pt 1 Series Unit 2
Planning - the Future's First Step 20 MIN
Dist - AMA

Supervisory Management Course, Pt 1 Series Unit 3
Organizing - Structuring the Work of the Plan 20 MIN
Dist - AMA

Supervisory management course, Pt 1 series unit 4
Controlling - keeping plans on target 20 MIN
Dist - AMA

Supervisory Management Course, Pt 1 Series Unit 5
Standards and Appraisal - Aids to Control 20 MIN
Dist - AMA

Supervisory Management Course, Pt 1 Series Unit 7
Motivation - the Test of Leadership 20 MIN
Dist - AMA

Supervisory management course, Pt 1 series
Communications 20 MIN
Dist - AMA

Supervisory management course series
Decision - making 20 MIN
Dist - AMA

Supervisory overview - HAZCOM 11 MIN
BETA / VHS / U-matic
Hazard communication - live - action video series
Color (IND G)
$495.00 purchase _ #820 - 02
Informs supervisors of the requirements of the OSHA Hazard Communication Standard. Identifies and explains the role supervisors must play in preparing their companies for compliance with the Standard. Part of a series on hazard communication.
Business and Economics; Health and Safety; Industrial and Technical Education; Psychology
Dist - ITSC Prod - ITSC

The Supervisory Process - Helping Teachers to Improve Instruction 30 MIN
U-matic
Color (T)
Simulates the five stages of the clinical supervision model - the pre - observation conference, observation, analysis and strategy, post - observation conference, and post - conference analysis. Available with captions for the hearing impaired.
Education
Dist - AFSCD **Prod** - AFSCD 1986

Supervisory Responsibility 22 MIN
U-matic / VHS
Food Plant Supervisor - Understanding and Performing Inplant Food 'Safety Insp Series
Color
Explores the concept of food protection, coupled with the ability to see and recognize problems common to food processing plants from the point of view of the supervisor.
Health and Safety; Industrial and Technical Education; Social Science
Dist - PLAID **Prod** - PLAID

Supervisory Safety Course Series
Search for Safety 42 MIN
Dist - BNA

Supervisory series
Training - one - on - one 17 MIN
Dist - AAVIM
CTT

Supervisory Series
Communications - key to leadership 10 MIN
Leadership - Meeting the Challenge 9.3 MIN
Motivation - Leadership in Action 18.20 MIN
P E M - Group Training Formula 19.5 MIN
Training - One on One 16.25 MIN
Dist - CTT

Supervisory training - industry series
Assessing employee performance - industry
Coaching for Improved Performance (Industry)
Dealing with employee complaints - industry
Dealing with employee conflicts - industry
Dealing with employee response to controls - industry
Delegating effectively - industry
Fundamental skills of communicating with people - industry
Fundamental skills of managing people - industry
Getting employee commitment to the plan - industry
Giving orders and instructions
Implementing Change (Industry)
Improving Employee Work Habits (Industry)
Terminating an employee - industry
Using Positive Discipline (Industry)
Dist - CRMP

Supervisory training - office series
Assessing employee performance - office
Coaching for Improved Performance (Office)
Dealing with employee complaints - office
Dealing with employee conflicts - office
Dealing with employee response to controls - office
Delegating effectively - office
Fundamental skills of communicating with people - office
Fundamental skills of managing people - office
Getting employee commitment to the plan - Office
Giving orders and instructions
Implementing Change (Office)
Improving Employee Work Habits (Office)
Terminating an employee - office)
Training the trainer
Using Positive Discipline (Office)
Dist - CRMP

The Superwelder 16 MIN
U-matic / VHS
Color
Features welding and cutting operations with detailed guide to safety precautions before, during and after welding.
Health and Safety
Dist - EDRF **Prod** - EDRF

Superwelder 16 MIN
U-matic / VHS / 16mm
Color
Shows welding processes and applications in maintenance shop settings. Emphasizes basic measures for protecting the body and equipping the work area. Demonstrates how to handle special circumstances or unsafe conditions.
Health and Safety; Industrial and Technical Education
Dist - CORF **Prod** - ERF

Superwelder 17 MIN
U-matic / VHS
Industrial safety series
(H A)
$125.00 purchase
Talks on the basics of welding and cutting and focuses on the most important safety procedures that need to be observed.
Health and Safety; Industrial and Technical Education
Dist - AITECH **Prod** - ERESI 1986

Superwelder 15 MIN
U-matic
Color (IND)
Introduces employees to safe welding and cutting procedures and retrains occasional welders in the safety aspects of their job. Covers proper clothing, personal protective equipment, housekeeping, special circumstances, flashback, and the preparation process.
Health and Safety; Industrial and Technical Education
Dist - BNA **Prod** - ERESI 1985

Superwoman revisited - the Changing roles of Greek American women 28 MIN
VHS
Illuminations series
Color (G R)
#V - 1048
Explores the changing roles of Greek American women. Shows that they must face not only the same problems as other American women, but must also overcome stereotypical roles of Greek women. Interviews Greek American women from a variety of backgrounds.
History - World; Sociology
Dist - GOTEL **Prod** - GOTEL 1990

Supplemental foods 74 FRS
U-matic / VHS
Nutrition for the newborn series; Pt III
Color (J H A)
Teaches how to recognize when babies are ready for more than just milk, and what kinds of food to include.
Home Economics; Psychology
Dist - POAPLE **Prod** - POAPLE

Supplemental nursing system 23 MIN
VHS
Breastfeeding techniques that work series
Color (G)
$44.95 purchase _ #GP107V
Demonstrates a feeding tube device which has made breast feeding possible in many situations such as adopted or premature infants. Part of a seven - part series on breastfeeding presented by Kittie Frantz, RN.
Health and Safety; Sociology
Dist - CAMV

Supplier Performance Measurement 60 MIN
BETA / VHS
Manufacturing Series
(IND)
Examines supplier performance and how to evaluate the total cost of products, monitor supplier delivery performance, evaluate the quality of products and measure supplier services.
Business and Economics
Dist - COMSRV **Prod** - COMSRV 1986

Supply 19 MIN
U-matic / VHS / 16mm
People on Market Street Series
Color (H A)
LC 77-702441
Shows how the amount of goods produced and supplied responds to market price and how anticipated sales, selling prices, costs and profits guide a potential producer.
Business and Economics
Dist - CORF **Prod** - FNDREE 1977

Supply 30 MIN
VHS / U-matic
Economics exchange series; Pgm 3
Color (T)
LC 82-706415
Presents Dr Willard M Kniep of Arizona State University instructing teachers in the strategies and skills of teaching children economics and consumer education concepts. Focuses on the topic of supply by explaining it and then demonstrating specific approaches that teachers can use in their classrooms.
Business and Economics; Education; Home Economics
Dist - GPN **Prod** - KAETTV 1981

Supply and Demand 14 MIN
U-matic / VHS / 16mm
Color (J H)
LC 80-700587
Defines the economic forces of supply and demand, and shows how they influence prices and the types of goods and amounts that are produced. Points out that producers and consumers communicate with each other through these forces, with the result that an equilibrium price is set, but seldom maintained for a long time.
Business and Economics
Dist - PHENIX **Prod** - GREENF 1980

Supply and Demand - Price and the Consumer 10 MIN
U-matic / VHS / 16mm
Foundations of Wealth Series
Color
Introduces the law of supply and demand. Compares markets in which prices are fixed to markets in which prices change in response to demand and supply.
Business and Economics
Dist - FOTH **Prod** - FOTH

Supply and Demand - Price and the Producer 10 MIN
16mm / U-matic / VHS
Foundations of Wealth Series
Color
Shows how supply and demand affect price. Discusses how producers react to changing prices.
Business and Economics
Dist - FOTH **Prod** - FOTH

Supply and Demand - what Sets the Price 30 MIN
VHS / U-matic
Economics USA Series
Color (C)
Business and Economics
Dist - ANNCPB **Prod** - WEFA

Supply Lines 20 MIN
U-matic
Exploring Our Nation Series
Color (I)
Emphasizes the importance of truck, rail and air freight in keeping a city supplied with the needs of a population. Looks at the significance of water, gas and electric lines.
Social Science
Dist - GPN **Prod** - KRMATV 1975

Supply Management 60 MIN
BETA / VHS
Manufacturing Series
(IND)
Describes the supply environments and supply responsibilities.
Business and Economics
Dist - COMSRV **Prod** - COMSRV 1986

The Supply Manager's Dilemma 19 MIN
16mm
Color
LC FIE61-125
Describes the influence of order costs, holding costs and shortages in determining supply management policy.
Business and Economics
Dist - USNAC **Prod** - USN 1960

A Supply Schedule for Wumpets 10 MIN
16mm / U-matic / VHS
Economics Series
Color (H C)
Distills the principles of economists such as Adam Smith, David Ricardo and Alfred Marshall. Defines the law of supply and shows the effect of a change in the quantity supplied and a change in supply.
Business and Economics
Dist - MEDIAG **Prod** - MEDIAG 1981

Supply Side Economics 30 MIN
U-matic
Realities
Color (A)
Delves into the political, social, economic and cultural trends of the 1980s. Probes a wide range of contemporary concerns. Each segment includes a guest speaker who is an expert in the field under discussion.
Business and Economics; Civics and Political Systems; Social Science; Sociology
Dist - TVOTAR **Prod** - TVOTAR 1985

Supply theory - the behaviour of profit - maximising firms 30 MIN
VHS
Introductory economics series
Color; PAL (J H C G)
PdS29.50 purchase
Outlines the theory of the firm, which is based on the assumption of profit maximization. Explains the optimal hiring rule and optimal output decision. Features Professor John Palmer and Ellen Roseman. Part of a four - part series.

Business and Economics
Dist - EMFVL **Prod** - TVOTAR

Support Your Child in School 1 MIN
16mm
Color (A)
LC 75-701991
Stresses the importance of parental involvement in children's school activities.
Education; Social Science
Dist - LEECC **Prod** - LEECC 1975

Supporting a Candidate 15 MIN
VHS / U-matic
By the People Series
Color (H)
Shows how individual citizens can work on behalf of a political candidate.
Civics and Political Systems; Social Science
Dist - CTI **Prod** - CTI

Supporting Family Relationships 29 MIN
VHS / 16mm
Daycare - Caregiver Training Series
Color (C)
$250.00 purchase _ #293002
Assists in the educating of university and college students learning to care professionally for young children and professional caregivers employed in preschool centers. Documents the role and impact of caregivers on children, parents and families. 'Supporting Family Relationships' considers the effect professional childcare givers have on a child's development and their role in support to families. The profession must learn to work in partnership with parents and families and strategies for developing open communication within the team of parent, family and daycare professionals.
Guidance and Counseling; Home Economics; Psychology; Sociology
Dist - ACCESS **Prod** - ACCESS 1990

Supporting Ongoing Operations 45 MIN
VHS / U-matic
User Responsibilities in Information Management Series
Color
Stresses that the information system user must remain involved after the system is implemented and that data accuracy and system evaluation are two major concerns of the user at this phase of the system life cycle.
Business and Economics; Industrial and Technical Education; Psychology
Dist - DELTAK **Prod** - DELTAK

Supporting the arts 30 MIN
VHS
Inside Britain 4 series
Color; PAL; NTSC (G) (BULGARIAN CZECH HUNGARIAN SPANISH POLISH ROMANIAN RUSSIAN SLOVAK UKRAINIAN LITHUANIAN)
PdS65 purchase
Reveals that sustaining a varied mix of artistic projects is an expensive ideal. Shows that in the southwest of Britain, Bristol, a city with a rich artistic heritage, is striving to make access to and participation in the arts possible for all.
Fine Arts
Dist - CFLVIS **Prod** - BRCOI 1993

Supportive Care Measures - Granulocyte and Platelet Transfusions 20 MIN
U-matic
Color
Discusses blood component replacement factors.
Health and Safety; Science - Natural
Dist - UTEXSC **Prod** - UTEXSC

Supportive coaching 30 MIN
VHS / U-matic
Performance reviews that build commitment series; Session 5
Color
Distinguishes between 'boss' and 'manager.' Covers the steps essential for achievement and relates them to the manager's task of stimulating accomplishment by his people.
Business and Economics; Psychology
Dist - DELTAK **Prod** - PRODEV

Suppose that all animals and all plants are represented by the branches of a tree 52 MIN
16mm / U-matic / VHS
Voyages of Charles Darwin series
Color (H C A)
LC 80-700475
Speculates that animals and plants are represented by the branches of a tree, the tree of life. Reveals how Charles Darwin gets more clues on evolution from the Galapagos Island, returns to England after a five - year voyage and settles down to a life of science.
Biography; Science; Science - Natural
Dist - TIMLIF **Prod** - BBCTV 1980
HRC

Suppose there were only people 15 MIN
U-matic / VHS
Dragons, wagons and wax - Set 1 series
Color (K P)
Shows that human beings depend on other living things.
Science; Science - Natural
Dist - CTI **Prod** - CTI

Suppression of Food Intake by Experimental Obesity 18 MIN
16mm
B&W
Shows the surgical preparation of a rat for an experiment to determine whether action of the hypothalmus controls obesity. Explains the rationale behind the psychological experiment, and shows the surgery on the rat in detail.
Health and Safety; Psychology; Science; Science - Natural
Dist - UPENN **Prod** - UPENN 1961

Supraomohyoid Neck Dissection 13 MIN
16mm
Color (PRO)
Demonstrates a supraomohyoid neck dissection following surgery of the lip. Shows the anatomical structures in detail as the entire supraomohyoid lymphatics are removed, together with the sub - maxillary gland.
Health and Safety; Science; Science - Natural
Dist - ACY **Prod** - ACYDGD 1950

The Supraperiosteal and Incisive Injections 20 MIN
16mm
Color
LC 72-700485
Demonstrates for dentists and dental students the local anesthetic injections frequently used in the dental profession. Shows osteological considerations and dissection material on the cadaver, and presents examples of techniques used on patients.
Health and Safety; Science
Dist - LOMA **Prod** - LOMA 1970

Suprapubic Vesico - Urethral Suspension for Stress Incontinence 18 MIN
16mm
Color (PRO)
Explains that suprapubic vesico - urethral suspension for correction of urinary stress incontinence in women has proven to be a valuable operation. Presents the technique of Dr Victor F Marshall.
Health and Safety; Science
Dist - ACY **Prod** - ACYDGD 1969

Supravalvular Aortic Stenosis - Extented Aortoplasty 10 MIN
16mm
Color
LC 77-700418; 77 - 700418
Describes a surgical procedure for the repair of supravalvular aortic stenosis. Compares the traditional approach to this technique and demonstrates the latter procedure on a patient.
Health and Safety; Science; Science - Natural
Dist - UIOWA

The Supreme Court 15 MIN
VHS
More perfect union - the three branches of the federal goverment 'series
Color (J H C G)
$65.95 purchase _ #KUN4012V
Takes a look at the inner workings of the Supreme Court of the United States. Examines some of the important rulings that have altered United States history. Part of a three - part series on the branches of the federal government.
Civics and Political Systems
Dist - CAMV

The Supreme Court 30 MIN
U-matic / VHS / 16mm
Color (J)
Discusses the history and operation of the U S Supreme Court. Includes observations by Chief Justice Warren Burger and Justice Lewis F Powell Jr.
Civics and Political Systems
Dist - GPN **Prod** - WCVETV 1978

The Supreme Court 30 MIN
U-matic / VHS
(I J H C G A)
$65 purchase, $30 rental
Uses interviews with Supreme Court justices to explain the workings of the Court to students at intermediate levels and above. Emphasizes the human element in the judicial process. Narrated by Paul Baier and Catherine Skefos.
Civics and Political Systems; History - United States
Dist - GPN

The Supreme Court 15 MIN
VHS
More perfect union series
Color (J H)
$55.00 purchase _ #KUN4012V-S
Focuses on the judicial powers of the Supreme Court. Explains the workings of the federal government, by introducing in a dramatic way the basic civics concepts needed to understand how the three branches of government work and interact. Looks at the inner workings of the Supreme Court and at some of the important rulings that have altered American history.
Civics and Political Systems
Dist - CAMV

The Supreme Court 15 MIN
VHS
More perfect union series
Color (I J)
$55.00 purchase _ #4012VD
Looks at the inner workings of the United States Supreme Court. Examines some of the important rulings that have altered United States history. Includes a guide. Part of a three - part series on the three branches of the federal government.
Civics and Political Systems
Dist - KNOWUN **Prod** - KNOWUN 1992

The Supreme Court 23 MIN
16mm
Color
LC 75-701208
Examines the role of the Supreme Court in guaranteeing justice. Highlights cases and decisions dealing with freedom of religion and the rights of the accused. Explains how a President is overruled and an Act of Congress is declared unconstitutional.
Civics and Political Systems
Dist - USNAC **Prod** - USDD 1970

The Supreme court 18 MIN
35mm strip / VHS
US government in action series
Color (J H C T A)
$57.00, $45.00 purchase _ #MB - 510762 - 7, #MB - 509976 - 4
Examines the judicial branch of the US government. Emphasizes the Constitutional concept of checks and balances. Uses archival and modern graphics.
Civics and Political Systems
Dist - SRA **Prod** - SRA 1988

The Supreme Court and Civil Liberties - the Bank Secrecy Act of 1970 58 MIN
VHS / 16mm
Color (G)
$70.00 rental _ #SUPR - 000
Dramatizes the highlights of an actual Supreme Court case involving the Bank Secrecy Act of 1970.
Civics and Political Systems
Dist - PBS **Prod** - KCET

Supreme court and society 29 MIN
16mm
Government story series; No 40
Color (J H)
LC 70-707202
Shows how the Supreme Court as a policy - making body directly affects the legal, social and political realities of the nation. Illustrates with cases from the Dred Scott decision of 1857 to the obscenity cases of the 1960's.
Civics and Political Systems; Psychology; Sociology
Dist - WESTLC **Prod** - WEBC 1968

The Supreme Court cases on Public Law 94 - 142 62 MIN
VHS
Legal challenges in special education series; Tape 2
Color (G)
$90.00 purchase
Reveals that the US Supreme Court has ruled six times on special education law in cases which define the term 'appropriate', examined related services such as sign language interpreters, considered school health services and drew the line between medicine and education, reviewed the role Congress intended parents to play in special education, considered IEP requirements, determined when a school must reimburse parents for their expenses, placed limits on expulsion of dangerous students and decided state education agency financial responsibility. Features Reed Martin, JD. Includes resource materials. Part of a 12 - part series on Public Law 94 - 142.
Civics and Political Systems; Education
Dist - BAXMED

Supreme Court Decisions that Changed the Nation Series
Gideon Versus Wainright and Miranda Versus Arizona
Dist - ASPRSS

Supreme Court decisions that changed the nation series
Marbury Vs Madison
McCulloch Vs Maryland
Plessy vs Ferguson
Dist - ASPRSS
GA

Supreme Court Decisions that Changed the Nation Series
Brown Vs Board of Education
The Dred Scott Decision
Dist - GA

Supreme Court decisions that changed the nation series
Roe vs Wade 20 MIN
US vs Nixon 20 MIN
Dist - GA
INSTRU

Supreme Court decisions that changed the nation series
Presents an eight - part series on Supreme Court decisions that changed the course of history in the United States. Includes the titles - US v Nixon; Roe v Wade; Gideon v Wainwright and Miranda v Arizona; Marbury v Madison; McCulloch v Maryland; The Dred Scott decision; Plessy v Ferguson; Brown v Board of Education.
Supreme Court decisions that changed the nation series 102 MIN
Dist - INSTRU

The Supreme Court in American life 45 MIN
VHS
Color (J H C G)
$78.00 purchase _ #SOC126V
Prents a three - part program tracing the United States Supreme Court from its inception until the present. Places the court in the context of contemporary economic, social and political events. Shows the Supreme Court to have been as controversial as it is powerful, somtimes leading, sometimes lagging behind public opinion. Describes how the court greatly increased its scope and power and discusses such landmark cases and issues as the power of judicial review, the Doctrine of Implied Powers, the Dred Scott decision, Brown vs Board of Education, pro and anti - business rulings and the Miranda case. Includes teacher's manual.
Civics and Political Systems
Dist - CAMV

Supreme Court - Influences of Personalities 30 MIN
VHS / U-matic
American Government 2 Series
Color (C)
Studies the Marshall, Taney and Warren Supreme Courts. Demonstrates the ways the prejudices and persuasions, the ideals and ideology of the judges shape the judicial progress of the nation.
Civics and Political Systems
Dist - DALCCD **Prod** - DALCCD

The Supreme Court's Holy Battles 60 MIN
VHS
Color (G)
$59.95 purchase _ #CHST - 000
Traces the historic background of the concept of separation of church and state. Shows that the Founding Fathers disagreed over the concept, but wrote it into the Bill of Rights. Considers current legal issues such as school prayer and church tax exemptions. Provides a wide variety of perspectives.
Civics and Political Systems; Religion and Philosophy
Dist - PBS **Prod** - WHYY 1989

Supremem Court Decisions that Changed the Nation
Brown Versus Board of Education
Dist - GA

Sur - face 13 MIN
U-matic
Student workshop videotapes series
Color
Explores the nature of masks and of identity constructed upon appearances or variations of one's appearance.
Sociology
Dist - WMENIF **Prod** - WMENIF

Sur La Tour Eiffel - on the Eiffel Tower 15 MIN
16mm
Toute la bande series
Color (H) (FRENCH)
LC 71-715481
A French language film. Presents a tour of Eiffel Tower taken by Caroline, Victor and Elisabeth, who encounters a youth named Jacques, who becomes friends with the girls and a bore to Victor.
Foreign Language
Dist - SBS **Prod** - SBS 1970

Sur Le Pont D'Avignon 6 MIN
U-matic / VHS / 16mm
Color (H C) (FRENCH)
A French language film. Puppets in medieval costume dance to the tune of this old and well - known repetitive folk song.
Foreign Language
Dist - IFB **Prod** - NFBC 1951

Sur Le Toit 13 MIN
16mm
En Francais series
Color (J A)
Foreign Language
Dist - CHLTN **Prod** - PEREN 1969

Suramericanos En Cordoba 13 MIN
16mm
Color (H C A)
LC 75-700288
Focuses on the artists represented at the 1967 Cordoba Biennial in Argentina.
Fine Arts; Geography - World
Dist - PAN **Prod** - OOAS 1970

The Sure defense 25 MIN
16mm
Color
Presents a panorama of scenic Washington, DC, including the White House, the Capitol, the Lincoln Memorial and cherry blossoms along the Tidal Basin. Depicts a special meeting in the Pentagon where Billy Graham delivers a stirring message.
Biography; Geography - United States; Guidance and Counseling; Religion and Philosophy
Dist - NINEFC **Prod** - WWP

Sure, I Can Dance 25 MIN
16mm
Color (I)
LC 76-703994
Proceeds from the assumption that anyone can dance and presents professional performers demonstrating exercises designed to teach the novice the basic movements of modern dance.
Fine Arts; Physical Education and Recreation; Sociology
Dist - RADIM **Prod** - HAIJUS 1976

Surefootin' 17 MIN
16mm
Color
LC 78-701510
Discusses skateboard safety, including how to fall, skateboard maintenance and skateboard techniques.
Health and Safety; Physical Education and Recreation
Dist - MTP **Prod** - IDQ 1978

Surface 10 MIN
16mm
Color
LC 76-703260
Depicts a study of the abstract patterns of color and motion reflected in the surface of water.
Fine Arts; Industrial and Technical Education
Dist - CANFDC **Prod** - QUAF 1975

Surface and Subsurface Mapping 45 MIN
VHS / U-matic
Basic Geology Series
Color (IND)
Industrial and Technical Education; Science - Physical
Dist - GPCV **Prod** - GPCV

Surface Blasting in Metal and Nonmetal Mines 18 MIN
U-matic / VHS / 16mm
Color (IND)
Shows some of the most common hazards encountered in surface blasting operations and emphasizes the need for greater safety precautions in the use of explosives.
Health and Safety; Industrial and Technical Education; Social Science
Dist - USNAC **Prod** - USDL

Surface damage 25 MIN
VHS / U-matic
Better than new series
Color (H C A)
Examines differences between veneered and solid furniture. Shows how to repair damage to solid surfaces with stopper, filler and wax, how veneers are made, relaying veneer, stringing and banding and inlay motifs.
Fine Arts; Home Economics; Physical Education and Recreation
Dist - FI **Prod** - BBCTV

Surface Energy Effects 43 MIN
VHS / U-matic
Tribology 2 - Advances in Friction, Wear, and Lubrication Series
Color
Discusses the Leadmedium interface in magnetic recording applications.
Industrial and Technical Education
Dist - MIOT **Prod** - MIOT

Surface Fatigue Wear 37 MIN
VHS / U-matic
Tribology 1 - Friction, Wear, and Lubrication Series
Color
Teaches the mechanism of surface fatigue wear and the laws governing it.
Industrial and Technical Education
Dist - MIOT **Prod** - MIOT

Surface Finishing - You Can't Live Without it 15 MIN
16mm
Color
Looks at the surface finishing industry and its role in America's progress and in providing jobs. Includes footage of the space shuttle Columbia and looks at the role surface finishing played in its construction.
Business and Economics; Industrial and Technical Education
Dist - MTP **Prod** - MTP

Surface Grinder no 8 - Surface Grinding Problems 12 MIN
VHS / BETA
Machine Shop - Surface Grinder Series
Color (IND)
Identifies common surface grinding problems which show up as poor surface finish on the workpiece. Covers basic points in selecting, mounting and dressing the grinding wheel.
Industrial and Technical Education; Psychology
Dist - RMIBHF **Prod** - RMIBHF

Surface Grinder no 5 - Grinding to Remove Warp 19 MIN
VHS / BETA
Machine Shop - Surface Grinder Series
Color (IND)
Explains how to grind work that is bowed by shimming. Includes use of dial indicator to determine amount of bow.
Industrial and Technical Education; Psychology
Dist - RMIBHF **Prod** - RMIBHF

Surface Grinder no 4 - Squaring Up a Block 18 MIN
BETA / VHS
Machine Shop - Surface Grinder Series
Color (IND)
Covers the proper sequence for grinding all six surfaces of a block, using an angle plate. Emphasizes the importance of precise squareness of adjoining surfaces.
Industrial and Technical Education; Psychology
Dist - RMIBHF **Prod** - RMIBHF

Surface Grinder no 1 - Mounting Work on a Magnetic Chuck 16 MIN
BETA / VHS
Machine Shop - Surface Grinder Series
Color (IND)
Introduces permanent and electro - magnetic chucks, and demonstrates safe methods of mounting work of different shapes and sizes. Stresses safe setup with the workpiece well supported.
Industrial and Technical Education; Psychology
Dist - RMIBHF **Prod** - RMIBHF

Surface Grinder no 7 - Grinding a 90 Degree 'V' 25 MIN
VHS / BETA
Machine Shop - Surface Grinder Series
Color (IND)
Demonstrates the setup of a magnetic sine plate to grind a 90 degree 'V'. Includes use of a table of sine bar constants and method of selecting and 'wringing' gage blocks together. Stresses grinding techniques that result in maximum accuracy.
Industrial and Technical Education; Psychology
Dist - RMIBHF **Prod** - RMIBHF

Surface Grinder no 6 - Grinding a Vertical Surface 16 MIN
VHS / BETA
Machine Shop - Surface Grinder Series
Color (IND)
Discusses applications for 'Side wheel' grinding, and explains how to relieve the side of the wheel and the technique for grinding a vertical surface to maximum accuracy.
Industrial and Technical Education; Psychology
Dist - RMIBHF **Prod** - RMIBHF

Surface Grinder no 3 - Grinding Flat Surfaces 14 MIN
BETA / VHS
Machine Shop - Surface Grinder Series
Color (IND)
Describes the proper way to mount the workpiece and how to touch off and traverse grind a flat surface. Stresses care in 'stoning' and cleaning the magnetic chuck and workpiece.

Industrial and Technical Education; Psychology
Dist - RMIBHF **Prod** - RMIBHF

Surface Grinder no 2 - Mounting and Dressing the Wheel 10 MIN
VHS / BETA
Machine Shop - Surface Grinder Series
Color (IND)
Explains how to test a wheel for cracks and the proper mounting procedure. Emphasizes correct positioning of a diamond dresser for truing the wheel.
Industrial and Technical Education; Psychology
Dist - RMIBHF **Prod** - RMIBHF

Surface Hardening 48 MIN
U-matic / BETA / VHS
Color
$400 purchase
Shows surface heating without changes in surface chemistry.
Science; Science - Physical
Dist - ASM **Prod** - ASM

Surface Interference Patterns 8 MIN
U-matic / VHS
Introductory Concepts in Physics - Light Series
Color (C)
$229.00, $129.00 purchase _ #AD - 1217
Examines the relationship between the thickness of the surface of the films and the appearance of light interference.
Science - Physical
Dist - FOTH **Prod** - FOTH

Surface Lures and Buzz Baits 30 MIN
U-matic / 16mm
Color
Explains how to use surface lures and buzz baits.
Physical Education and Recreation
Dist - GLNLAU **Prod** - GLNLAU 1982

Surface Lures and Buzz Baits 30 MIN
BETA / VHS
From the Sportsman's Video Collection Series
Color
Reveals how to learn topwater techniques for taking bass and improve one's fishing success.
Physical Education and Recreation
Dist - CBSC **Prod** - CBSC

Surface Mount Technology - Design for Manufacturability 3 3/4HR
VHS / 16mm
Color (A IND)
$1995.00
Focuses in six videotapes on design and manufacturing process guidelines. Also analyzes equipment types, assembly, quality control, and process control. Instructor is Phil Marcoux. Includes reference guide.
Industrial and Technical Education; Psychology
Dist - SME **Prod** - SME 1990

Surface of the Earth 11 MIN
16mm
Color (P I A)
Shows the process of rock formation and discusses the effect of water and wind on the earth, and causes and effects of glaciers, hot springs, earthquakes and volcanoes. Describes how mountains rise from the earth and are slowly worn away, and how caves and caverns are formed.
Science - Physical
Dist - AVED **Prod** - AVED 1959

Surface Potentials, Structure of the Electric Double Layer 54 MIN
VHS / U-matic
Colloid and Surface Chemistry - Surface Chemistry Series
Color
Science; Science - Physical
Dist - KALMIA **Prod** - KALMIA

Surface Potentials - Structure of the Electric Double Layer 54 MIN
VHS / U-matic
Colloid and Surface Chemistry - Surface Chemistry Series
B&W (PRO)
Science - Physical
Dist - MIOT **Prod** - MIOT

Surface Sampling for Microorganisms - Rodac Method 8 MIN
16mm
Color
LC FIE67-9
Explains techniques of surface sampling for bacteria in hospitals, using the Rodac plate. Includes reasons for surface sampling, preparation of agar sampling plates, description of random and geometric grid sampling methods, and colony counting and reporting.
Health and Safety; Science
Dist - USNAC **Prod** - USPHS 1965

Surface Sampling for Microorganisms - Swab Method 5 MIN
16mm
Color
LC FIE67-8
Explains techniques of surface sampling in hospitals, using the swab and template. Includes reasons for surface sampling, processing of swabs and rinse liquids, techniques on flat and irregular surfaces, counting of microbial colonies, and interpretation of results.
Health and Safety; Science
Dist - USNAC **Prod** - USPHS 1965

Surface Tension and Surface Energies 40 MIN
VHS / U-matic
Colloid and Surface Chemistry - Surface Chemistry Series
Color
Science; Science - Physical
Dist - KALMIA **Prod** - KALMIA

Surface Tension and Surface Structure of Solids 52 MIN
VHS / U-matic
Colloid and Surface Chemistry - Surface Chemistry Series
B&W (PRO)
Science - Physical
Dist - MIOT **Prod** - MIOT

Surface Tension in Fluid Mechanics 29 MIN
U-matic / VHS / 16mm
Fluid Mechanics Series
Color (H C)
LC FIA64-788
Illustrates effects of surface tension in experiments including soap film intersections, break - up of jets and sheets into droplets, capillary action, wetting and non - wetting droplets, generation and motion of bubbles, and chemical and electric effects.
Science - Physical
Dist - EBEC **Prod** - NCFMF 1966

Surface water 12 MIN
VHS / U-matic
Water environment series
Color (J H)
$195.00, $245.00 purchase, $50.00 rental
Looks at oceans, lakes, rivers, streams and wetlands and the different kinds of pollution to which these bodies of water are subjected. Encourages students to look at their roles in protecting surface water resources since pollution to this body of water can monitored and remedied.
Science - Natural
Dist - NDIM **Prod** - WAENFE 1988

Surface water unit
VHS
Color (I J H)
$59.00 purchase _ #Z1255GA
Examines the water cycle and focuses on water quality topics, including pollution. Features Dino Sorrus, an animated character, with computer graphics showing ways young people can help prevent surface water pollution. Package includes one videocassette, one teacher's guide and 20 student workbooks. Additional materials are also available.
Science - Natural
Dist - WAENFE

Surface Work 5 MIN
16mm
Color (A)
Presents an experimental film by Dennis Pies which is an exploration in animation of screen space with vocal sound track mixed from three live performances.
Fine Arts
Dist - STARRC **Prod** - STARRC 1978
AFA

Surfacing on the Thames 8 MIN
16mm
Color (G)
$20.00 rental
Confronts the illusions of space and time in the cinema. Experiments with rear - projecting a ten - second sequence of old World War II footage showing two ships passing on the Thames.
Fine Arts
Dist - CANCIN **Prod** - RIMMER 1970

Surfboards, Skateboards and Big Big Waves 10 MIN
16mm
Color
LC 70-708684
Pictures the famous surfing spots of Ala Moana, Anaheim and Waimea Bay and features acrobatics of the world's best skate - boarders.
Geography - United States; Physical Education and Recreation
Dist - AMEDFL **Prod** - GROENG 1969

Surfclubbing 3 MIN
VHS / U-matic
Color
Deals with a psychedelic day at the beach for people who usually go out at night. By Emily Armstrong and Pat Ivers.
Fine Arts
Dist - KITCHN **Prod** - KITCHN

Surf's up
VHS
Color (G)
$24.50 purchase _ #0153
Covers the World Cup of Surfing in Hawaii. Includes the Jet Ski Championship from the North Shore of Oahu.
Physical Education and Recreation
Dist - SEVVID

The Surgeon General's report on AIDS 20 MIN
VHS
Color (J H C A)
$93.00 purchase _ #MB - 481125 - 8
Presents the facts about AIDS and HIV as reported by the Surgeon General of the United States. Covers how HIV is transmitted, relative risks of infection, and the different means of prevention. Dispels rumors and misconceptions about the disease. Presented in a two - part format, with segments tailored to different audiences.
Health and Safety; Psychology
Dist - SRA **Prod** - SRA 1987

The Surgeon general's report on AIDS - video 20 MIN
VHS
Color (H C)
$121.00 purchase _ #193 Y 0010
Presents the surgeon general's report on AIDS, acquired immune deficiency syndrome. Discusses its transmission, prevention and relative risks.
Health and Safety; Sociology
Dist - WARDS **Prod** - WARDS 1990

Surgery and Radiation 101 FRS
Slide / U-matic
Cancer Series Module 3; Module 3
Color (PRO)
LC 81-720125; 81-707090
Health and Safety
Dist - BRA **Prod** - BRA 1981

Surgery and radiation - 3 14 MIN
VHS
Learning about cancer series
Color (G)
$250.00 purchase, $60.00 rental
Focuses on the treatment of cancer through surgery and radiation. Takes an in - depth look at the detection and treatment of cancer and the emotional impact of the disease on patients and their families. Part 3 of a five - part series.
Health and Safety
Dist - CF **Prod** - HOSSN 1989

Surgery, Anesthesia and Chronic Obstructive Lung Disease 16 MIN
VHS / U-matic
Color (PRO)
Discusses determination of patients predisposed to respiratory complications through an appropriate history and physical exam. Emphasizes utilizing these findings and information to prepare these patients for surgery and anesthesia.
Health and Safety; Science - Natural
Dist - UMICHM **Prod** - UMICHM 1975

Surgery - Employment - Insurance
U-matic / VHS
Consumer Survival Series
Color
Presents tips on arranging surgery, employment and insurance.
Business and Economics; Guidance and Counseling; Health and Safety; Home Economics
Dist - MDCPB **Prod** - MDCPB

Surgery for Advanced Cancer of Pelvic Viscera 35 MIN
16mm
Color (PRO)
Illustrates certain features of the technique of radical pelvic surgery for cancer. Emphasizes total pelvic exenteration for recurrent cancer of the cervix. Shows modifications of the operation for limited lesions and for advanced cancer of the rectum and rectosigmoid.
Health and Safety; Science
Dist - ACY **Prod** - ACYDGD 1961

Surgery for Massive Hemorrhage from Gastroduodenal Ulcer 32 MIN
16mm
Color (PRO)
Discusses the problems of diagnosis and surgical technique by illustrating gastric resection on two elderly patients,

one with penetrating posterior wall duodenal ulcer and one with gastric ulcer. Covers clinical data of a five - year study of the management of severely bleeding gastroduodenal ulcer.
Health and Safety; Science
Dist - ACY **Prod** - ACYDGD 1952

Surgery for Multiple Stones in the Kidney Pelvis and Calyces 17 MIN
16mm
Color
LC 75-702251
Illustrates surgery for multiple stones in the kidney pelvis and calyces. Includes demonstration of surgical technique on a fresh human autopsy kidney along with artists' illustrations. Shows exposure provided for easy access to fragmented or multiple stones in the renal pelvis and calyces.
Health and Safety
Dist - EATONL **Prod** - EATONL 1972

Surgery for urinary incontinence in women 10 MIN
VHS
Color; CC (G C PRO)
$175.00 purchase _ #OB - 135
Looks at surgical treatment of stress incontinence. Covers various types of perations, risks, and recommendations for recovery. Contact distributor for purchase price on multiple orders.
Health and Safety; Sociology
Dist - MIFE **Prod** - MIFE 1995

Surgery for Vesicular Ureteral Reflux 57 MIN
16mm
Visits in Urology Series
Color
LC 79-701326
Demonstrates various surgical techniques of extra - vesicular surgery for reflux and shows the similarities, differences and indications for each technique. Includes a panel discussion by different surgeons.
Health and Safety
Dist - EATONL **Prod** - EATONL 1979

Surgery for Vesicular Ureteral Reflux - Pt 1 28 MIN
16mm
Visits in Urology Series
Color
LC 79-701326
Demonstrates various surgical techniques of extra - vesicular surgery for reflux and shows the similarities, differences and indications for each technique. Includes a panel discussion by different surgeons.
Health and Safety
Dist - EATONL **Prod** - EATONL 1979

Surgery for Vesicular Ureteral Reflux - Pt 2 29 MIN
16mm
Visits in Urology Series
Color
LC 79-701326
Demonstrates various surgical techniques of extra - vesicular surgery for reflux and shows the similarities, differences and indications for each technique. Includes a panel discussion by different surgeons.
Health and Safety
Dist - EATONL **Prod** - EATONL 1979

Surgery of Cancer of the Colon 24 MIN
16mm
Color (PRO)
Shows that there is some leeway in choosing the proper operation for cancer of the colon. Illustrates cancer of the colon located in different portions and the method by which it is handled under different circumstances.
Health and Safety; Science
Dist - ACY **Prod** - ACYDGD 1960

Surgery of Decubitus Ulcer - Wire Button Technique 20 MIN
16mm
Color
Shows the technique of closures of sacral, troachanteric and ischial decubitus ulcers.
Health and Safety; Science - Natural
Dist - USVA **Prod** - USVA 1962

Surgery of Male Genital Lymphadema 13 MIN
U-matic / VHS
Color (PRO)
Describes in detail a surgical treatment for treating genital lymphadema, a grotesque disease which affects especially those in equatorial latitudes.
Health and Safety
Dist - WFP **Prod** - WFP

The Surgery of Primary Aldosteronism 23 MIN
16mm
Color (PRO)
Presents Richard H Egdahl, MD, who discusses the methods of diagnosis and localization preoperatively of aldosterone - secreting tumors. Demonstrates the techniques of both the anterior and posterior approaches to the adrenals, and gives reasons for the author's preference for the posterior approach, if the side of the tumor has been determined pre - operatively.
Health and Safety; Science
Dist - ACY **Prod** - ACYDGD 1968

Surgery of the Adrenal Glands 19 MIN
16mm
Color (PRO)
Presents Dr Victor Richards who demonstrates the surgical exposures of the adrenal glands, the two main approaches, a retroperitoneal subdiaphragmatic approach and a transabdominal approach.
Health and Safety; Science
Dist - ACY **Prod** - ACYDGD 1956

Surgery of the Carpal Tunnel 29 MIN
U-matic / VHS
Color (PRO)
Outlines important anatomical landmarks, covers symptoms and diagnosis, details surgical procedure and its hazards and describes postoperative care of the carpal tunnel patient.
Health and Safety; Science - Natural
Dist - HSCIC **Prod** - HSCIC 1984

Surgery of the Horseshoe Kidney 24 MIN
16mm
Color
LC 75-702298
Presents three patients exhibiting variations of the horseshoe kidney to illustrate a technique in accomplishing the two major surgical objectives of correction of various pathological processes and conservation of a maximal amount of functioning renal tissue. Features aortograms and post - operative intravenous pyelograms which illustrate pre - operative pathology and post - operative function.
Health and Safety; Science
Dist - EATONL **Prod** - EATONL 1966

Surgery of the Parotid Gland - as Aided by Differential Staining 14 MIN
U-matic / VHS
Color (PRO)
Shows surgery of the parotid gland as aided by differential staining.
Health and Safety
Dist - WFP **Prod** - WFP

Surgery of Upper Urinary Tract Stone Disease 39 MIN
16mm
Visits in Urology Series
Color (PRO)
LC 78-701379
Presents Dr Joseph J Kaufman interviewing Professor Jose Marie Gil - Vernet of the University of Barcelona, Spain, who discusses his approaches to upper tract stone disease. Discusses various techniques of treatment.
Health and Safety
Dist - EATONL **Prod** - EATONL 1978

Surgery Without Ligature 13 MIN
16mm
Color (PRO)
Describes and demonstrates a new type of hemostatic clip.
Health and Safety
Dist - UCLA **Prod** - UCLA 1968

Surgical Anatomy of Inguinal Region 29 MIN
16mm
Color (PRO)
Reveals a dissection of the inguinal area on a fresh cadaver specimen, as encountered in hernia repair. Demonstrates Cooper's ligament.
Health and Safety; Science
Dist - ACY **Prod** - ACYDGD 1950

Surgical Anatomy of the Anterior Abdominal Wall 17 MIN
16mm
Color (PRO)
LC 74-702597
Presents cadaver dissection and abdominal anatomy from a surgeon's point of view. Shows the location of the four major incisions and follows the dissection, layer by layer, giving special attention to muscles and the rectus sheath. For surgeons, residents and first year anatomy students.
Science - Natural
Dist - EATONL **Prod** - EATONL 1969

Surgical Anatomy of the Female Pelvis 10 MIN
16mm
Color (PRO)
Demonstrates the surgical anatomy of the female pelvis.
Health and Safety; Science; Science - Natural
Dist - SQUIBB **Prod** - SQUIBB

Surgical Anatomy of the Female Perineum 25 MIN
16mm
Color (PRO)
Uses fresh cadaver material to illustrate the anatomy of the female perineum.
Health and Safety; Science; Science - Natural
Dist - ACY **Prod** - ACYDGD 1952

Surgical Anatomy of the Female Perineum 27 MIN
16mm
Color (PRO)
Shows a systematic cadaver dissection of the female perineum, including the vaginal vault.
Health and Safety; Science - Natural
Dist - LOMAM **Prod** - LOMAM

Surgical Anatomy of the Human Kidney and its Applications 25 MIN
16mm
Color
LC 79-701327
Uses art, animation and corrosion casts of the kidney to demonstrate its surgical anatomy. Emphasizes the arterial distribution within the kidney.
Health and Safety; Science - Natural
Dist - EATONL **Prod** - EATONL 1979

Surgical Anatomy of the Lateral Neck 25 MIN
16mm
Color (PRO)
Demonstrates the important structures of the lateral neck by cadaver dissection.
Health and Safety; Science; Science - Natural
Dist - ACY **Prod** - ACYDGD 1954

Surgical Anatomy of the Lateral Neck 10 MIN
16mm
Color (PRO)
Demonstrates the anatomy encountered during surgical procedures in the lateral neck through the dissection of a cadaver and medical artwork.
Health and Safety; Science; Science - Natural
Dist - SQUIBB **Prod** - SQUIBB

Surgical Anatomy of the Male Perineum 20 MIN
16mm
Color (PRO)
Shows a systematic dissection of the male perineum with particular emphasis on the perineal approach to the prostate.
Health and Safety; Science - Natural
Dist - LOMAM **Prod** - LOMAM

Surgical Anatomy of the Parotid Area 18 MIN
16mm
Color (PRO)
Presents an anatomical study of the parotid gland and facial nerve, using fresh cadaver material for demonstration. Shows the anatomy of this area with particular reference to nerves, blood and vessels and other structures encountered in removal of the parotid gland.
Health and Safety; Science; Science - Natural
Dist - ACY **Prod** - ACYDGD 1953

Surgical Anatomy of the Pulmonary Hilum - Left Lung 29 MIN
U-matic / VHS
Color (PRO)
Presents the surgical anatomy of the pulmonary himum, specifically the left lung.
Health and Safety
Dist - WFP **Prod** - WFP

Surgical Anatomy of the Pulmonary Hilum - Left Lung 20 MIN
16mm
Color
Companion to the film Surgical Anatomy of the Pulmonary Hilum Right Lung. Uses sequences from six different surgical procedures and animated sequences to illustrate the various points of reference which must be recognized in order that lung tissue excision may be accomplished with maximum salvage of healthy tissue.
Health and Safety
Dist - PFI **Prod** - UWASH 1960

Surgical Anatomy of the Pulmonary Hilum - Right Lung 24 MIN
U-matic / VHS
Color (PRO)
Presents the surgical anatomy of the pulmonary hilum, specifically the right lung.
Health and Safety
Dist - WFP **Prod** - WFP

Surgical Anatomy of the Pulmonary Hilum - Right Lung 20 MIN
16mm
Color
Companion to the film Surgical Anatomy of the Pulmonary Hilum - Left Lung. Illustrates the various points of reference which must be recognized in order that lung tissue excision may be accomplished with maximum salvage of healthy tissue. Presents animated sequences and sequences demonstrating six different surgical procedures.
Health and Safety
Dist - PFI **Prod** - UWASH 1960

Surgical Anatomy of the Thyroid Gland 18 MIN
16mm
Color (PRO)
Shows an anatomical dissection of a fresh cadaver. Emphasizes the arterial supply and the relation of the recurrent laryngeal nerve.
Health and Safety; Science; Science - Natural
Dist - ACY **Prod** - ACYDGD 1954

The Surgical Approach to Parotid Tumors 21 MIN
16mm
Color (PRO)
Illustrates the surgical approach to parotid resection utilizing peripheral identification of the facial nerve. Discusses the anatomy, technique and indications.
Health and Safety; Science; Science - Natural
Dist - ACY **Prod** - ACYDGD 1967

Surgical Approaches Series

Surgical Approaches to the Ankle	32 MIN
Surgical Approaches to the Elbow	38 MIN
Surgical Approaches to the Foot	32 MIN
Surgical Approaches to the Hip	36 MIN
Surgical Approaches to the Knee	36 MIN
Surgical Approaches to the Spine and Sacroilliac	28 MIN
Surgical Approaches to the Sternoclavicular and Acromioclavicular Joint	16 MIN
Surgical Approaches to the Wrist	33 MIN

Dist - WFP

Surgical Approaches to the Ankle 32 MIN
U-matic / VHS
Surgical Approaches Series
Color (PRO)
Health and Safety
Dist - WFP **Prod** - WFP

Surgical Approaches to the Ankle Joint 32 MIN
16mm
Color
LC FIE63-106
Shows the anatomy of the dorsolateral and medical aspects of the ankle joint. Shows operations employing approaches to the dorsal, lateral, medial and posterior aspects of the joint.
Science - Natural
Dist - USVA **Prod** - USVA 1952

Surgical Approaches to the Bones of the Foot 32 MIN
16mm
Color
LC FIE53-107
Shows the anatomy of the dorsolateral and medical aspects of the foot. Discusses operations employing approaches to the dorsal, dorsolateral and plantar aspects and an approach for bunionectomy.
Health and Safety; Science - Natural
Dist - USVA **Prod** - USVA 1952

Surgical Approaches to the Bones of the Wrist 34 MIN
16mm
Color
LC FIE53-108
Shows the anatomy of the volar, dorsal and ulnar aspects of the wrist. Presents operations employing approaches to the volar, radio - volar, ulnar and dorsal aspects.
Health and Safety; Science - Natural
Dist - USVA **Prod** - USVA 1952

Surgical Approaches to the Elbow 38 MIN
U-matic / VHS
Surgical Approaches Series
Color (PRO)
Health and Safety
Dist - WFP **Prod** - WFP

Surgical Approaches to the Elbow Joint 39 MIN
16mm
Color
LC FIE53-109
Shows the anatomy of the anterior and the posterior aspects of the joint. Presents operations employing approaches to the anterolateral, lateral, medial and posterior aspects of the joint.
Health and Safety; Science - Natural
Dist - USVA **Prod** - USVA 1950

Surgical Approaches to the Foot 32 MIN
U-matic / VHS
Surgical Approaches Series
Color (PRO)
Health and Safety
Dist - WFP **Prod** - WFP

Surgical Approaches to the Hip 36 MIN
U-matic / VHS
Surgical Approaches Series
Color (PRO)
Health and Safety
Dist - WFP **Prod** - WFP

Surgical Approaches to the Hip Joint 36 MIN
16mm
Color
LC FIE52-2215
Shows the anatomy of the anterior and posterior aspects of the hip joint. Presents operations employing approaches to the anterolateral, straight lateral and posterolateral aspects of the joint.
Health and Safety; Science - Natural
Dist - USVA **Prod** - USVA 1951

Surgical Approaches to the Knee 36 MIN
U-matic / VHS
Surgical Approaches Series
Color (PRO)
Health and Safety
Dist - WFP **Prod** - WFP

Surgical Approaches to the Knee Joint 37 MIN
16mm
Color
LC FIE53-110
Shows the anatomy of the anterior and posterior aspects of the knee joint. Presents operations employing approaches to the anterior and posterior aspects and to the medial and lateral semilunar cartilages.
Health and Safety; Science - Natural
Dist - USVA **Prod** - USVA 1951

Surgical Approaches to the Scapulohumeral Joint 36 MIN
16mm
Color
LC FIE53-111
Emphasizes the anatomy of each aspect of a joint in approaching that joint surgically. Depicts the bones, ligaments, muscles, tendons and neurovascular structures with which the surgeon must deal in various approaches to the shoulder joint. Shows actual surgical operations utilizing anterior, posterior and muscle splitting incisions with emphasis always on the anatomy of the region.
Health and Safety; Science - Natural
Dist - USVA **Prod** - USVA 1949

Surgical Approaches to the Spine and Sacroiliac 28 MIN
16mm
Color
LC FIE53-112
Shows the anatomy of the posterior aspect of the sacroiliac, the anterior and posterior aspects of the region of the spine with emphasis on the lumbar area. Demonstrates approaches to the sacroiliac and the retroperitoneal space.
Health and Safety; Science - Natural
Dist - USVA **Prod** - USVA 1952

Surgical Approaches to the Spine and Sacroilliac 28 MIN
VHS / U-matic
Surgical Approaches Series
Color (PRO)
Health and Safety
Dist - WFP **Prod** - WFP

Surgical Approaches to the Sternoclavicular and Acromioclavicular Joint 16 MIN
VHS / U-matic
Surgical Approaches Series
Color (PRO)
Health and Safety
Dist - WFP **Prod** - WFP

Surgical Approaches to the Sternoclavicular and Acromioclavicular Joints 17 MIN
16mm
Color
LC FIE53-110
Shows the anatomy of the anterior aspect of the two joints as an operation approaching each joint.
Health and Safety; Science - Natural
Dist - USVA **Prod** - USVA 1952

Surgical Approaches to the Wrist 33 MIN
U-matic / VHS
Surgical Approaches Series
Color (PRO)
Health and Safety
Dist - WFP **Prod** - WFP

Surgical asepsis 23 MIN
16mm
Directions for education in nursing via technology series; Lesson 15
B&W (PRO)
LC 74-701789
Discusses methods of sterilization giving advantages and disadvantages. Demonstrates rules of procedure when opening sterile packages, adding sterile equipment and one method of putting on a pair of sterile gloves.
Health and Safety
Dist - WSUM **Prod** - DENT 1974

Surgical asepsis - 21 21 MIN
VHS
Clinical nursing skills - nursing fundamentals - series
Color (C PRO G)
$395.00 purchase _ #R890 - VI - 063
Reveals that preventing the access of microorganisms in the surgical field requires great care and a systematic technique. Discloses that, while the steps differ according to the surgical procedure, certain universal principles apply. Describes and demonstrates procedures for the septic changing of a surgical dressing, techniques for the placement and removal of a urinary catheter in both men and women, proper application of sterile gloves. Discusses types of catheters and the procedures for catheter care. Part of a 23 - part series on clinical nursing skills.
Health and Safety
Dist - HSCIC **Prod** - CUYAHO 1989

Surgical Care of the Injured Hand 29 MIN
16mm
Color (PRO)
Depicts the reconstruction of the flexor and extensor mechanisms in the hand as pertains to specific injuries which are narrated.
Health and Safety; Science
Dist - ACY **Prod** - ACYDGD 1965

Surgical Complications - Thoracic, Biliary Pancreatic, Alimentary 35 MIN
16mm
Color (PRO)
Shows operative management of thoracic duct fistula, common duct stricture, pancreatic pseudocyst, postgastrectomy malnutrition by conversion of Billroth II anastomosis to Billroth I, enterovaginal fistula and pelvic abscess drained through the rectum.
Health and Safety; Science
Dist - ACY **Prod** - ACYDGD 1967

Surgical Consideration in the Treatment of Cerebral Arterial Insufficiency 38 MIN
VHS / U-matic
Color (PRO)
Shows how patients can be helped by surgical correction of extracranial occlusive lesions which cause cerebral arterial insufficiency. Demonstrates preoperative techniques for determining the site of the occlusion or area of narrowing in the artery.
Health and Safety; Science - Natural
Dist - PRIMED **Prod** - PRIMED

Surgical Consideration of Cerebral Arterial Insufficiency 30 MIN
16mm
Color
LC DIA66-63
Discusses the surgical treatment of extracranial occlusive disease causing cerebral arterial insuffiency. Presents four cases illustrating the various lesions and techniques employed in the treatment of this disease, using both bypass graft and endarterectomy.
Health and Safety
Dist - EATON **Prod** - EATON 1961

Surgical Consideration of Occlusive Disease of the Abdominal Aorta, Iliac, Femoral Arteries 30 MIN
16mm
Color
LC FIA66-64
Discusses surgical consideration of occlusive disease of the abdominal aorta, iliac and femoral arteries. Demonstrates in detail the operative techniques as applied to patients. Includes statistics compiled from a study of patients with occlusions.
Health and Safety
Dist - EATON **Prod** - EATON 1961

Surgical Correction of Ankyloglossia 5 MIN
16mm
Color (PRO)
LC 75-701328
Shows how an unusually short fibrous lingual frenum is severed to permit a normal range of mobility of the tongue. Demonstrates the care taken to avoid the submaxillary duct and to create adequate space in the ventral surface where the extrinsic musculature is attached.
Health and Safety; Science
Dist - USNAC **Prod** - USVA

The Surgical Correction of Aortic Stenosis 28 MIN
16mm
Color (PRO)
Presents the transventricular approach in the surgical treatment of aortic stenosis. Gives indications for aortic commissurotomy.
Health and Safety; Science
Dist - ACY **Prod** - ACYDGD 1953

Surgical Correction of Blepharoptosis 15 MIN
16mm
Color
LC FIA66-896
Demonstrates the technique of making the incisions, isolating the levator, determining the extent of resection and proper placing of sutures through the various layers of the eyelid on the correction of certain cases of blepharoptosis.
Health and Safety
Dist - ACY **Prod** - ACYDGD 1962

Surgical Correction of Congenital Deformities 120 MIN
U-matic / VHS
Color (PRO)
Demonstrates Dr Dieter Buck - Gramcko's special technique for treatment of some of the frequently encountered congenital anomalies of the hand. Presents a demonstration of an original technique of pollicization for congenital absence of the thumb.
Health and Safety
Dist - ASSH **Prod** - ASSH

Surgical Correction of Hydronephrosis, Pt 1 - Non - Dismembering Procedures Series
Classical foley Y - plasty in a horseshoe kidney 15 MIN
Modified Davis Intubated Ureterotomy 15 MIN
Non - Dismembering Procedures 20 MIN
Vertical Flap Ureteropelvioplasty 20 MIN
Dist - EATONL

Surgical correction of hydronephrosis - Pt 3 - procedures common to most pyeloplasties series
Procedures common to most pyeloplasties - Pt 1 15 MIN
Procedures common to most pyeloplasties - Pt 2 15 MIN
Procedures common to most pyeloplasties - Pt 3 15 MIN
Dist - EATONL

Surgical Correction of Hydronephrosis, Pt 2 - Dismembering Procedures Series
Cuff Re - Implantation Procedure 15 MIN
The Dismembered Foley Y - Plasty 15 MIN
Dismembering Procedures 15 MIN
Uretero - Ureteral Anastamosis 20 MIN
Dist - EATONL

Surgical Correction of Hypertelorism 9 MIN
16mm
Color
LC FIA66-897
Describes the correction of extreme cases of hypertelorism by revision of the bony framework and adjustment of the contour of the overlying soft tissues. Shows the surgical technique used on the second side after healing of the first side has been accomplished.
Health and Safety
Dist - ACY **Prod** - ACYDGD 1962

Surgical Creation of a Sensitive Thumb 20 MIN
16mm
Color
LC FIA66-65
Presents a detailed demonstration of Dr Johnson's technique in creating a sensitive thumb for a two - and - half - year - old child with a congenital absence of the distal two - thirds of the left hand. Shows the utility and durability of the reconstructed digit.
Health and Safety
Dist - EATON **Prod** - EATON 1962

Surgical Drains 11 MIN
U-matic / VHS
Basic Clinical Skills Series
Color (PRO)
Illustrates how different drains are used and shows how to change surgical drain dressings.
Health and Safety; Science
Dist - HSCIC **Prod** - HSCIC 1984

Surgical Dressings 7 MIN
U-matic / VHS
Basic Clinical Skills Series
Color (PRO)
Discusses the dry, nonadherent, sealed, moist and medicated types of dressings and tells how to determine which to use.
Health and Safety; Science
Dist - HSCIC **Prod** - HSCIC 1984

Surgical Elimination of Periodontal Pockets 13 MIN
16mm
Color (PRO)
LC 77-701401
Explains the procedures involved in the surgical elimination of periodontal pockets for a patient with overall horizontal bone loss, interproximal bone craters and deep interproximal pockets.
Health and Safety; Science
Dist - USNAC **Prod** - VADTC 1977

Surgical Endodontics 15 MIN
8mm cartridge / 16mm
Color (PRO)
LC 75-702135; 78-701242
Demonstrates curettage and root resection. Explains the process of periotic reaction and the techniques and precautions that should be taken when surgery is necessary.
Health and Safety; Science
Dist - USNAC **Prod** - USN 1964

Surgical Endodontics 15 MIN
16mm
Color
LC 74-705724
Emphasizes the importance of correct diagnoses and careful selection of cases for surgical management for the general practitioner. Explains the process of periapical inflammatory reaction and demonstrates two surgical corrective procedures.
Health and Safety; Science
Dist - NMAC **Prod** - USN 1964

Surgical Excision of Mandibular Tori 10 MIN
U-matic / VHS / 16mm
Color (PRO)
Demonstrates an accepted technique for removing a torus.
Health and Safety
Dist - USNAC **Prod** - VADTC

Surgical Excison of Maxillary Torus 10 MIN
U-matic
Color (PRO)
LC 78-706011
Describes the indications for the surgical removal of a maxillary torus and demonstrates a technique for this procedure. Issued in 1972 as a motion picture.
Health and Safety
Dist - USNAC **Prod** - USVA 1977

Surgical Exploration for Obscure Massive Upper Gastrointestinal Hemorrhage 29 MIN
16mm
Color (PRO)
Depicts certain steps in operative technique which should be taken before restoring Blind Gastrectomy for severe upper gastrointestinal hemorrhage. Explains that this method has significantly reduced the need for Blind Gastrectomy with its intrinsic risk of overlooking a surgically correctable source of bleeding.
Health and Safety; Science
Dist - ACY **Prod** - ACYDGD 1956

Surgical Grand Rounds 90 MIN
U-matic
Color (PRO)
LC 76-706107
Shows grand rounds at the University of Washington Department of Surgery. Shows physicians discussing lung metastases in a 60 - year - old male with a brain tumor. Deals with operative and postoperative aspects of a 37 - year - old male with persistent recurrence of polyps. Focuses on postoperative aspects of lung metastases in a brain tumor patient and discusses carcinoma aspects of a patient with obstructive jaundice.
Health and Safety
Dist - USNAC **Prod** - WARMP 1971

Surgical Grand Rounds - Pt 1 22 MIN
U-matic
Color (PRO)
LC 76-706107
Shows grand rounds at the University of Washington Department of Surgery. Shows physicians discussing lung metastases in a 60 - year - old male with a brain tumor. Deals with operative and postoperative aspects of a 37 - year - old male with persistent recurrence of polyps. Focuses on postoperative aspects of lung metastases in a brain tumor patient and discusses carcinoma aspects of a patient with obstructive jaundice.
Health and Safety
Dist - USNAC **Prod** - WARMP 1971

Surgical Grand Rounds - Pt 2 22 MIN
U-matic
Color (PRO)
LC 76-706107
Shows grand rounds at the University of Washington Department of Surgery. Shows physicians discussing lung metastases in a 60 - year - old male with a brain tumor. Deals with operative and postoperative aspects of a 37 - year - old male with persistent recurrence of polyps. Focuses on postoperative aspects of lung metastases in a brain tumor patient and discusses carcinoma aspects of a patient with obstructive jaundice.
Health and Safety
Dist - USNAC **Prod** - WARMP 1971

Surgical Grand Rounds - Pt 3 23 MIN
U-matic
Color (PRO)
LC 76-706107
Shows grand rounds at the University of Washington Department of Surgery. Shows physicians discussing lung metastases in a 60 - year - old male with a brain tumor. Deals with operative and postoperative aspects of a 37 - year - old male with persistent recurrence of polyps. Focuses on postoperative aspects of lung metastases in a brain tumor patient and discusses carcinoma aspects of a patient with obstructive jaundice.
Health and Safety
Dist - USNAC **Prod** - WARMP 1971

Surgical Grand Rounds - Pt 4 23 MIN
U-matic
Color (PRO)
LC 76-706107
Shows grand rounds at the University of Washington Department of Surgery. Shows physicians discussing lung metastases in a 60 - year - old male with a brain tumor. Deals with operative and postoperative aspects of a 37 - year - old male with persistent recurrence of polyps. Focuses on postoperative aspects of lung metastases in a brain tumor patient and discusses carcinoma aspects of a patient with obstructive jaundice.
Health and Safety
Dist - USNAC **Prod** - WARMP 1971

Surgical Implant Replacement of the Fractured Displaced Condyle 8 MIN
16mm
Color (PRO)
LC 74-706410
Points out that failure to reduce and immobilize the fractured mandibular condyle may cause poor articulation of the teeth, open bite or inability to open the mouth. Demonstrates the use of prosthetic implant for correction of these complications.
Health and Safety; Science
Dist - USNAC **Prod** - USVA 1968

Surgical Implantation of an Inflatable Penile Prosthesis 20 MIN
16mm
Color (PRO)
LC 80-701417
Demonstrates the inflatable penile prosthesis.
Foreign Language; Health and Safety
Dist - EATONL **Prod** - EATONL 1980

The Surgical Interview 13 MIN
U-matic
Patient Interview - Science or Art Series
Color (PRO)
Discusses a patient interview conducted by a surgeon. Explains that this case is difficult because of the physical and psychological problems of the patient.
Health and Safety; Psychology
Dist - PRIMED **Prod** - PRIMED

Surgical knot tying 10 MIN
U-matic / VHS
Color (PRO C)
$395.00 purchase, $80.00 rental _ #C901 - VI - 043
Presents step - by - step instructions for producing three types of surgical knots. Features Dr William Young, Dartmouth, Hitchcock Medical Center.
Health and Safety
Dist - HSCIC

Surgical Management of an Axillary Burn Web 12 MIN
16mm
Color
LC 75-702318
Portrays an axilla webbing resulting from a thermal injury on the trunk and arm of a five - year - old child. Illustrates the correction which is carried out through normal tissue and can be performed earlier than most contractures.
Health and Safety; Science
Dist - EATONL **Prod** - EATONL 1967

Surgical Management of Calcific Pancreatitis 22 MIN
16mm
Color (PRO)
Presents the concept that in calcific pancreatitis the calcareous material is intraductal. Includes the surgical procedure employed in three illustrative cases together with roentgenologic demonstration of the calcific disease, pathologic specimens and the results of preoperative and postoperative blood lipid studies.
Health and Safety; Science
Dist - ACY **Prod** - ACYDGD 1955

Surgical Management of Crohn's Disease 30 MIN
U-matic / VHS
Color
Reviews surgical aspects of Crohn's disease. Discusses the indications for surgery and the types of operations performed.
Health and Safety
Dist - ROWLAB **Prod** - ROWLAB

Surgical Management of Eyelid Burns 10 MIN
16mm
Color
LC 75-702317
Demonstrates the use of large, free, full - thickness skin grafts in the correction of eyelid contractures resulting from thermal injuries. Stresses the principles of contracture release and correction with skin grafts. Discusses the essentials of post - operative management and shows long term results.
Health and Safety; Science
Dist - EATONL **Prod** - EATONL 1967

Surgical Management of Primary Hyperthyroidism 21 MIN
16mm
Color (PRO)
Demonstrates the technique of subtotal thyroidectomy for primary hyperthyroidism devised by Dr Frank H Lahey. Emphasizes placing a low collar incision and elevation of the upper flap.
Health and Safety; Science
Dist - ACY **Prod** - ACYDGD 1950

Surgical Management of Visceral Arterial Occlusion 30 MIN
16mm
Color (PRO)
Shows that the two most important abdominal vascular syndromes, renal vascular hypertension and abdominal angina, may both be produced by the same mechanism, extrinsic compression by the crus of the diaphragm or intrinsic occlusion of the major visceral vessels.
Health and Safety; Science
Dist - ACY **Prod** - ACYDGD 1968

Surgical nursing 30 MIN
VHS
B&W; Silent (C PRO G)
$30.00 purchase, $15.00 rental _ #933 - P, #933 - R
Details procedures that nurses in the 1930s were taught to follow with patients in the perioperative period. Reveals that the film was produced as a service project by Epsilon Chapter for the School of Nursing, Ohio State University.
Health and Safety
Dist - SITHTA **Prod** - SITHTA 1932

Surgical Nursing Care of the Eye Patient 22 MIN
16mm
Color
LC FIA66-899
Describes the role of the eye nurse in a hospital and as assistant to the opthalmic surgeon. Discusses the training and abilities which are required for the eye nurse in the surgical nursing care of the eye patient.
Health and Safety
Dist - ACY **Prod** - ACYDGD 1963

Surgical Nursing Skills 21 MIN
VHS / 16mm
(C)
$385.00 purchase _ #851VI027
Introduces five commonly used surgical drains, explains their function and indications for their use. Outlines the procedures for drain shortening and removal, assessing wound healing, and suture and clip removal.
Health and Safety
Dist - HSCIC **Prod** - HSCIC

Surgical Nutrition 52 MIN
VHS / 16mm
(C)
$385.00 purchase _ #850VI113
Discusses the impact of nutritional deficiency on postoperative morbidity and mortality, with special attention to methods of nutritional assessment. Covers the benefits of hyperalimentation and methods of nutritional support.
Health and Safety
Dist - HSCIC **Prod** - HSCIC 1985

Surgical - Orthodontic Correction of Maxillary Protrusions 22 MIN
16mm
Color
LC 70-715308
Depicts the evaluation and treatment of a patient with severe malocclusion, emphasizing the coordinated efforts of the involved dental specialists.
Health and Safety; Science
Dist - MAYO **Prod** - MAYO 1970

Surgical Preparation of the Dog for the Physiology Laboratory 21 MIN
16mm
Color (C)
Demonstrates the preliminary surgical procedures used to prepare the dog for general laboratory work, including administration of an anesthetic and tracheal and arterial cannulation.
Health and Safety
Dist - WSUM **Prod** - WSUM 1959

Surgical Problems in Ulcerative Colitis 26 MIN
16mm
Color (PRO)
Presents certain phases of ulcerative colitis by means of selected X - ray films and by slides of specimens, with special emphasis on the risk of cancer in longstanding cases.
Health and Safety; Science
Dist - ACY **Prod** - ACYDGD 1956

Surgical Procedure for Dog Experiments 25 MIN
U-matic / VHS
Color (PRO)
Demonstrates techniques used to prepare a dog for various physiological experiments.
Health and Safety; Science
Dist - HSCIC **Prod** - HSCIC 1981

Surgical Procedure in the Penetrating Duodenal Ulcer with Massive Uncontrollable 25 MIN
16mm
Color (PRO)
Explains that 421 cases of massive hemorrhage from peptic ulcer have been observed on the fourth surgical division of Bellevue Hospital since 1928. Points out that the cases of uncontrollable hemorrhage in this series represent only 14 percent of the total, including those being operated upon as emergency or dying under conservative management.
Health and Safety; Science
Dist - ACY **Prod** - ACYDGD 1956

Surgical Procedures - an Integral Part of General Practice 180 MIN
U-matic
Color (PRO)
LC 76-706164
Demonstrates oral surgical procedures that are normally done by general practitioners in their offices. Shows removal of an impacted tooth, a dental cyst and a torus palatinus. Demonstrates a biopsy procedure and multiple extractions with insertion of an immediate denture. Discusses time - tested surgical principles.
Health and Safety
Dist - USNAC **Prod** - USDH 1976

Surgical procedures series
Presents a 17 - part series recording surgical procedures in detail, with specialists who explain the ailment, the anatomical function of the part of the body being operated on, how successful surgery might improve the patient's quality of life, hosted by Dr Donna Willis. Includes the titles - Open Heart Surgery; Coronary Bypass Surgery; Endometriosis; Vasectomy - Tubal Ligation; Vasectomy Reversal; Tubal Ligation Reversal; Cornea Transplant; Arthroscopic Knee Surgery; Leg - Straightening Procedure; Brain Surgery; Back Microsurgery; Laparoscopic Gallbladder Removal; Reconstructive Surgery; Cesarean Section; Laparoscopic Hernia Repair; Vocal Cord Repair; Plastic Surgery - Facelift.

Arthroscopic knee surgery	45 MIN
Back microsurgery	45 MIN
Brain surgery	45 MIN
Cesarean section	45 MIN
Cornea transplant	45 MIN
Coronary bypass surgery	45 MIN
Endometriosis	45 MIN
Laparoscopic gallbladder removal	45 MIN
Laparoscopic hernia repair	45 MIN
Leg - straightening procedure	45 MIN
Open heart surgery	45 MIN
Plastic surgery - facelift	45 MIN
Reconstructive surgery	45 MIN
Tubal ligation reversal	45 MIN
Vasectomy - tubal ligation	45 MIN
Vasectomy reversal	45 MIN
Vocal cord repair	45 MIN

Dist - FOTH

Surgical Recognition and Management of Valvular Heart Disease - Pt 3 28 MIN
U-matic
Color (PRO)
LC 76-706108
Discusses surgical management of mitral and aortic stenosis and regurgitation.
Health and Safety
Dist - USNAC **Prod** - WARMP 1969

Surgical Rehabilitation of the Adult Cardiac Patient 33 MIN
16mm
Color (PRO)
Presents the techniques of several common corrective cardiac operations. Emphasizes the selection of adult patients for surgery from the standpoint of expected rehabilitation.
Health and Safety; Science
Dist - ACY **Prod** - ACYDGD 1965

Surgical Rehabilitation of the Atrophied Mandible in Preparation for Denture Prosthesis 25 MIN
16mm
Color
LC 75-702330
Explains that the atrophic mandible usually presents great difficulty of a satisfactory full denture prosthesis. Presents a technique, developed by Professor Hugo Obwegeser of the University of Zurich, Switzerland, which makes the patient's remaining mandibular bone available as a denture base. Shows an actual case from start to finish.
Health and Safety; Science
Dist - EATONL **Prod** - EATONL 1968

Surgical Removal of Lesions in Pulmonary Tuberculosis 2 MIN
U-matic / VHS / 16mm
Color (PRO)
LC FIA68-269
Reproduces a roentgenogram of the chest of a patient with a persistent chronic lesion of tuberculosis. Shows how portions of the right lung are removed and how the tuberculous nodule is removed and cut open to expose the caseous material.
Health and Safety; Science - Natural
Dist - UCEMC **Prod** - UCEMC 1961

Surgical Removal of Mesio - Angular Impacted Third Molar 4 MIN
16mm
Color (PRO)
LC 75-702436; 75-701329
Shows how a mesio - angular impacted lower third molar is surgically removed without sectioning. Emphasizes the importance of obtaining adequate surgical exposure and following prescribed surgical techniques.
Health and Safety; Science
Dist - USNAC **Prod** - USVA 1974

Surgical Repair of Complete Uterine Prolapse 29 MIN
16mm
Color (PRO)
Shows that vaginal hysterectomy (Heaney technique) precedes the anterior and posterior vaginal repair in a 60 - year - old multiparous woman with third degree prosthedentia. Includes the surgical repair of the prolapsed bladder and rectal walls.
Health and Safety; Science
Dist - ACY **Prod** - ACYDGD 1952

Surgical Repair of Direct Inguinal Hernia with Rectus Sheath Graft 20 MIN
U-matic / VHS
Color (PRO)
Health and Safety
Dist - PRIMED **Prod** - PRIMED

Surgical Repair of Facial Lacerations for Optimum Cosmetic Results 20 MIN
16mm
Color
Provides a detailed demonstration of a technique of repair designed to secure optimum cosmetic results for facial lacerations resulting from automobile accidents. Illustrates the use of instruments, sutures and local anesthesia for debridement and subcutaneous and cutaneous closures.

Science
Dist - EATONL **Prod** - EATONL 1957

Surgical Repair of Hydronephrosis 23 MIN
16mm
Color
LC FIA66-66
Uses preoperative X - rays, medical illustrations and postoperative excretory urograms to illustrate the principles of Dr Hamm's operative technique in two patients with a solitary left kidney with serious hydronephrosis and renal stones. Describes modifications of the V - Y plasty and emphasizes the rationale of eliminating splints and nephrostomy tubes.
Health and Safety
Dist - EATON **Prod** - EATON 1965

The Surgical Repair of Hypospadias 25 MIN
16mm
Color
LC FIA66-67
Shows in detail the surgical techniques of repairing hypospadias as demonstrated in operations performed on two patients.
Health and Safety
Dist - EATON **Prod** - EATON 1961

Surgical Repair of Peyronie's Disease with Dermis Graft 14 MIN
16mm
Color
LC 75-702248
Shows how to repair Peyronie's disease by resecting the plaque and covering the defect in the tunica albuginea with a graft of dermis obtained from the skin of the abdomen. Demonstrates the pathology of Peyronie's disease and depicts a surgical procedure using the above technique.
Science
Dist - EATONL **Prod** - EATONL 1973

Surgical Repair of the Adult Cleft Palate 19 MIN
U-matic / VHS
Color (PRO)
Details an unusual case history in which surgery is performed to correct a cleft palate in an adult.
Health and Safety
Dist - WFP **Prod** - WFP

Surgical scrub and gloving 12 MIN
VHS / U-matic
Preparation for oral surgery series
Color (PRO C)
$395.00 purchase, $80.00 rental_ #C920 - VI - 038
Reveals that outpatient oral surgery requires a five - minute scrub which is shown in detail. Shows proper gloving techniques. Stresses that carefully following the procedures shown will help to ensure the safety of surgeon and patient. Part of a three - part series on oral surgery presented by Mary Ann Adkisson, RN, and Dr James B Sweet, University of Texas, Health Science Center at Houston, Dental Branch.
Health and Safety
Dist - HSCIC

Surgical scrub, gowning and gloving - closed method 19 MIN
VHS / U-matic
Color (PRO C)
$395.00 purchase, $80.00 rental_ #C870 - VI - 044
Shows how to properly scrub, gown and glove in preparation for work in the operating or delivery room. Presented by Dr Ethelrine Shaw - Nickerson, Carol Keith, Janet Morgan and Jeanine Watters.
Health and Safety
Dist - HSCIC

Surgical Separation of Conjoined Twins - Three Case Studies 30 MIN
VHS / U-matic
Color (PRO)
Acquaints surgeons, nurses, anesthesiologists, pediatricians, operating room personnel, and medical students with examples of three complex surgical operations for separation of conjoined twins.
Health and Safety
Dist - HSCIC **Prod** - HSCIC 1984

The Surgical Skin Prep 14 MIN
VHS / U-matic
Color (PRO)
Discusses the surgical skin prep.
Health and Safety
Dist - WFP **Prod** - WFP

Surgical Skin Preparation 13 MIN
U-matic / VHS
Color (C A)
Discusses and demonstrates the three phases of surgical skin preparation which minimize the potential of bacterial contamination in a surgical wound.
Health and Safety; Science
Dist - TEF **Prod** - UTEXN

Surgical Technique for Correction of Complete Urinary Incontinence 15 MIN
16mm
Color (PRO)
LC 75-702246
Presents a detailed demonstration of a surgical technique successfully applied for correction of postprostatectomy total urinary incontinence. Uses animation and art work to clarify various steps in the procedure.
Health and Safety; Science; Science - Natural
Dist - EATONL **Prod** - EATONL 1973

Surgical Technique for Multiplex Total Knee Replacement 32 MIN
VHS / U-matic
Prothesis Films Series
Color (PRO)
Health and Safety
Dist - WFP **Prod** - WFP

Surgical Techniques, Incisions, and Closures 30 MIN
16mm
Color
LC 80-700393
Demonstrates correct techniques for performing a surgical incision, closing the wound with sutures and dressing the wound.
Health and Safety
Dist - COM **Prod** - NOEJM 1979

Surgical Techniques of the several Types of Skin Graft 33 MIN
16mm
Color (PRO)
Presents the technique of application of thick - split grafts and whole - thickness grafts of skin. Demonstrates the use of dermatape and the cutting of skin grafts by the dermatome, the electro - dermatome and by hand.
Health and Safety; Science
Dist - ACY **Prod** - ACYDGD 1952

Surgical Treatment for Varicose Veins 20 MIN
16mm
Doctors at Work Series
B&W (H C A)
LC FIA65-1364
Examines the causes of varicose veins and the recommended surgery for the condition. Shows the stripling procedure which is involved in vascular surgery. Emphasizes the danger in neglecting a severe condition.
Health and Safety
Dist - LAWREN **Prod** - CMA 1961

Surgical Treatment of Atrial Septal Defects 20 MIN
16mm
Color (PRO)
Presents case studies illustrating several types of atrial septal defects and the technical problems each presents in surgical repair.
Health and Safety; Science; Science - Natural
Dist - SQUIBB **Prod** - SQUIBB

Surgical Treatment of Benign Breast Diseases 35 MIN
16mm
Color (PRO)
Shows the techniques for diagnosis and treatment, combined with the least deformity, in patients with fibro - adenoma, cystic disease, ectasia, intraductal papilloma, recurring sub and para areolar abscesses.
Health and Safety; Science
Dist - ACY **Prod** - ACYDGD 1969

Surgical Treatment of Bronchogenic Carcinoma 29 MIN
16mm
Color (PRO)
Points out that for the surgical treatment of bronchogenic carcinoma, radical pneumonectomy probably offers the best prognosis to the patients. Emphasizes that in selected cases, however, lobectomy with mediastinal lymphadenectomy should be the elected procedure.
Health and Safety; Science
Dist - ACY **Prod** - ACYDGD 1957

Surgical Treatment of Direct Hernia 31 MIN
16mm
Color (PRO)
Outlines the surgical treatment of direct hernia, emphasizing a major point. Demonstrates that the operation for direct hernia should be a radical one, including steps that may not be necessary for all simpler and direct hernias.
Health and Safety; Science
Dist - ACY **Prod** - ACYDGD 1956

Surgical Treatment of the Tetralogy of Fallot 32 MIN
16mm
Color (PRO)
Demonstrates the creation of an artificial ductus arteriosis in the surgical treatment of tetralogy of fallot.
Health and Safety; Science
Dist - ACY **Prod** - ACYDGD 1953

Surgical Treatment of Ureteral Trauma 15 MIN
16mm
Surgical Treatment of Genito - Urinary Trauma Series
Color
LC 75-702272
Presents a new technique developed by Drs C Eugene Carlton Jr and Russell Scott Jr for the primary watertight repair of ureteral injury. Points out that this technique of watertight non - intubated repair has markedly reduced the incidence of ureteral stricture formation.
Science
Dist - EATONL **Prod** - EATONL 1970

Surgical Treatment of Urethral Trauma 15 MIN
16mm
Color
Points out that the incidence of urethral stricture following significant urethral trauma is extremely high. Shows how Drs C Eugene Carlton Jr and Russell Scott Jr have employed early surgical debridement and primary watertight repair in the treatment of significant urethral trauma and have found that the incidence of structure formation has been virtually eliminated. Illustrates the technique of the primary surgical repair of the injured urethra.
Science
Dist - EATONL **Prod** - EATONL 1970

The Surgical Treatment of Varicose Veins 24 MIN
16mm
Color (PRO)
Demonstrates the ligation of the long and short saphenous veins at their junction with the deep venous system together with stripping of these segments and supplemented with individual ligation of perforators.
Health and Safety; Science
Dist - ACY **Prod** - ACYDGD 1955

Surgical Treatment of Ventricular Septal Defect - Technique and Results in 292 Cases 20 MIN
16mm
Color (PRO)
Examines the surgical treatment of ventricular septal defects in which cardiopulmonary bypass was used.
Health and Safety; Science; Science - Natural
Dist - SQUIBB **Prod** - SQUIBB

Surgical Wound Infections 16 MIN
U-matic / VHS
Hospital Infection Control - Infection Control for Medical Practitioners Series
Color (PRO)
Covers the classification of surgical infections and the etiologic agents involved in nosocomial surgical wound infections. Identifies factors that might predispose patients to surgical wound infections.
Health and Safety
Dist - HSCIC **Prod** - HSCIC

Surgical wound infections 17 MIN
VHS / U-matic
Breaking the chain of nosocomial infections series
Color (C PRO)
$395.00 purchase, $80.00 rental_ #C930 - VI - 006
Helps medical students, nurses, doctors and other hospital and nursing home staff to reduce the risk factors that cause surgical wound infections. Demonstrates techiques and suggests types of drug therapy to lessen the chances of infection. Part of a five - part series on nosocomial infections presented by Crescent Counties Foundation for Medical Care.
Health and Safety
Dist - HSCIC

Surinam - a Song of Democracy 28 MIN
U-matic / VHS / 16mm
Color (J)
Explores the background, customs and occupations of the many ethnic groups which compose the population of Surinam, a Dutch commonwealth in South America.
Geography - World; Sociology
Dist - IFB **Prod** - GORDAJ 1973

Surname Viet given name Nam 108 MIN
16mm
Color (G)
$1500.00 purchase, $225.00 rental
Explores the historical role of Vietnamese women, as well as their role in contemporary society. Uses dance, printed texts, folk poetry and the words and experiences of women both in North and South Vietnam.

Fine Arts; History - United States; History - World; Industrial and Technical Education; Literature and Drama; Physical Education and Recreation; Sociology
Dist - WMEN **Prod** - TRIMIN 1989

The Surprise 15 MIN
VHS / U-matic
Dragons, wagons and wax series
Color (K P)
Shows how properties of matter are used to describe and compare materials.
Science; Science - Physical
Dist - CTI **Prod** - CTI

A Surprise for Otto 4 MIN
16mm
Otto the Auto Series
Color (K P I)
Considers if the green traffic light always means 'go.'
Health and Safety; Social Science
Dist - AAAFTS **Prod** - AAAFTS 1971

The Surprise - La Sorpresa 29 MIN
VHS / 16mm
Sonrisas Series
Color (T P) (SPANISH)
$46.00 rental _ #SRSS - 108
Notes Dona Rosario's contributions to the Carriage House. In Spanish and English.
Sociology
Dist - PBS

Surprise - Sparkling Stars 15 MIN
Videoreel / VT2
Sounds Like Magic Series
B&W (P)
English Language
Dist - GPN **Prod** - MOEBA

Surprised 5 MIN
16mm
Color (G)
$9.00 rental
Entertains with an abstract hand - drawn cartoon set to original music.
Fine Arts
Dist - CANCIN **Prod** - WRGHTC 1973

Surprised - the paintings of Henri Rousseau 20 MIN
VHS
Color (G)
PdS10.50 purchase _ #A4-300463
Traces the development of Rousseau from an official with the Paris toll service to a hero of the avant-garde. Displays paintings of this famous 'naive' artist, who was at first ridiculed but who was eventually recognized by fellow artists like Picasso. Explores the background of Rousseau's art and his strange subjects and child-like vision.
Fine Arts
Dist - AVP **Prod** - NATLGL

The Surprises of Failure Can Lead to the Secrets of Success 28 MIN
16mm
You Can do it - if Series
Color
LC 81-700092
Presents 27 people who have known disappointment and failure but who went on to become successful.
Psychology
Dist - VANDER **Prod** - VANDER 1980

Surprising Amsterdam 28 MIN
16mm
Color
LC 72-700032
Illustrates the diversity of life, history and entertainment in Amsterdam, as a means of encouraging travelers to that city.
Geography - World; Social Science
Dist - KLMRDA **Prod** - KLMRDA 1971

Surreal Cartoon Situations 15 MIN
Videoreel / VT2
Charlie's Pad Series
Color
Fine Arts
Dist - PBS **Prod** - WSIU

Surreal Estate 10 MIN
16mm
Color
LC 78-700312
Relates the story of a man who encounters a house for sale which has doorways, rooms, stairways, restaurants and museums which appear and disappear. Reveals that after several adventures, he makes his way out and is greeted by a peculiar realtor.
Fine Arts
Dist - SLVRMN **Prod** - SLVRMN 1977

Surrealism 15 MIN
VHS
Art history - century of modern art series
Color (I)
$125.00 purchase
Discusses Surrealists Salvador Dali, Joan Miro, Henri Rousseau, Rene Magritte, Giorgio de Chirico and Marc Chagall. Considers selected works, comments on the artists' personal histories and points out their distinctive styles and subjects.
Fine Arts
Dist - AITECH **Prod** - WDCNTV 1988

Surrealism 24 MIN
U-matic / VHS / BETA
Color; PAL (G H C)
PdS50, PdS58 purchase
Studies the mysterious faces of surrealism in the works of Ernst, Klee, Miro, Tanguy, Magritte and Dali, as well as the foreunners of the movement and related painters. Produced with George Barford, Illinois State University.
Fine Arts
Dist - EDPAT **Prod** - IFB

Surrealism 7 MIN
U-matic / VHS / 16mm
Understanding Modern Art Series
Color (J H C)
Explains the modern art style of surrealism which extracts things from their usual settings and places them in unnatural surroundings. Points out how surrealistic symbols provide a quality of mystery and intrigue.
Fine Arts
Dist - PHENIX **Prod** - THIEB 1961

Surrealism 15 MIN
VHS / 16mm
Art history - century of modern art series
Color (I H A)
$125.00 purchase, $25.00 rental
Surveys the works of Surrealists Dali, Miro, Rousseau, Magritte, Giorgio, de Chirico and Chagall.
Fine Arts; Industrial and Technical Education
Dist - AITECH **Prod** - WDCNTV 1988

Surgical Treatment of Megacolon 21 MIN
16mm
Color (PRO)
Demonstrates the technique of resection of the aganglionic segment. Discusses problems related to a preliminary transverse colostomy.
Health and Safety; Science
Dist - ACY **Prod** - ACYDGD 1965

Surgical Treatment of Priapism 14 MIN
16mm
Color
LC 75-702296
Demonstrates Dr Chester C Winter's technique for the anastomosis of the saphenous vein to the corpus cavernosum in a 21 - year - old patient who was seen five days after he experienced a second episode of idiopathic priapism. Follows the patient for a period of five months following surgery.
Health and Safety; Science
Dist - EATONL **Prod** - EATONL 1965

Surgical Treatment of Prolapse of the Rectum 31 MIN
16mm
Color (PRO)
Shows the surgical treatment of true prolapse of the rectum by a one - stage operation with a perineal approach. Explains that the procedure is based upon the concept that true rectal prolapse is essentially a sliding hernia of the cul - de - sac through a defect in the pelvic diaphragm.
Health and Safety; Science
Dist - ACY **Prod** - ACYDGD 1957

Surgical Treatment of Renal Injury 20 MIN
16mm
Surgical Treatment of Genito - Urinary Trauma Series
Color
LC 75-702271
Presents a plan of surgical management which has evolved in the treatment of renal injury from experience with the management of over 100 patients with penetrating renal injury. Shows that certain parts of this plan have been expanded and incorporated into the surgical management of renal neoplasm and calculous disease.
Science
Dist - EATONL **Prod** - EATONL 1969

Surgical Treatment of Renovascular Hypertension 30 MIN
16mm
Color
LC FIA66-556
Deals with the surgical treatment of renovascular hypertension. Demonstrates diagnostic procedures, including renography, the Howard test and a surgical technique used successfully in 1,400 consecutive aortograms. Demonstrates the details of the surgical procedures in several patients.
Health and Safety
Dist - EATON **Prod** - EATON 1961

Surgical Treatment of Small Bowel Obstruction Resulting from Occlusion 15 MIN
16mm
Color (PRO)
Explains that partial intestinal obstruction has been caused by stenosis of the small bowel, secondary to healed infarction and is treated by segmental resection with end - to - end anastomosis.
Health and Safety; Science
Dist - ACY **Prod** - ACYDGD 1964

Surrealism - Inner Space 29 MIN
Videoreel / VT2
Museum Open House Series
Color
Fine Arts
Dist - PBS **Prod** - WGBHTV

Surrealism - poetic vision 59 MIN
VHS
Color (H G)
$350.00 purchase, $95.00 rental
Examines the art movement that flourished in Europe between the two world wars and which derived its inspiration from dreams and illogical and fantastic expressions of the unconscious mind. Traces the history, includes archival footage and interviews scholars and dramatically reenacts key moments. Attempts not to simply explain surrealism, but to convey the surrealist experience itself in an offbeat multimedia presentation.
Fine Arts
Dist - CNEMAG

Surrealism - Seekers of the Dream 29 MIN
Videoreel / VT2
Museum Open House Series
Color
Fine Arts
Dist - PBS **Prod** - WGBHTV

Surrender 77 MIN
16mm
B&W (G)
$50.00 rental
Tells the story of the chief Rabbi in an Austrian village, who functions as the compassionate resolver of disputes and manager of village affairs. Reveals that his daughter Lea encounters a Russian officer and they both suffer many trials and sorrow, before finally reuniting. A film by Universal Pictures Corporation. Directed by Edward Sloman.
Fine Arts; Social Science; Sociology
Dist - NCJEWF

Surrender 2 MIN
16mm / VHS
Caffeine Capers - Reel 2 - Series
Color (PRO)
$175.00 purchase, $99.00 rental
Presents a vignette which humorously comments on the tedium of a business meeting. Available also as part of a series.
Psychology
Dist - UTM

Surrender at Appomattox 52 MIN
16mm
Color (J H)
Shows how America's Civil War ended when two great generals, Robert E Lee and Ulysses S Grant, met to make peace and reunite a nation.
History - United States
Dist - FI **Prod** - WOLPER 1974

Surrender at Appomattox 15 MIN
U-matic / VHS
Color
LC 84-706417
Uses archival stills, original illustrations and quotes from eyewitnesses to relive the surrender of the Confederacy at Appomattox Courthouse in Virginia.
Geography - United States; History - United States
Dist - USNAC **Prod** - USNPS 1982

Surrender at Appomattox - Pt 1 - the Union Triumphant - 1863 - 1865 26 MIN
16mm
Color (J H)
Shows how America's Civil War ended when two great generals, Robert E Lee and Ulysses S Grant, met to make peace and reunite a nation.
History - United States
Dist - FI **Prod** - WOLPER 1974

Surrender at Appomattox - Pt 2 - Appomattox Court House - 1865 26 MIN
16mm
Color (J H)
Shows how America's Civil War ended when two great generals, Robert E Lee and Ulysses S Grant, met to make peace and reunite a nation.
History - United States
Dist - FI **Prod** - WOLPER 1974

Surrender at Fort Donelson 5 MIN
16mm
Color
LC 79-701824
Presents a re - enactment of the night of February 15, 1862, when Confederate Generals Floyd, Pillow and Buckner struggled to decide whether their cold and weary troops could cut through the reinforced Union lines surrounding Fort Donelson or whether they would have to surrender.
History - United States
Dist - USNAC **Prod** - USNPS 1979

Surrender - Volume 12 48 MIN
VHS
Vietnam - the ten thousand day war series
Color (G)
$34.95 purchase _ #S00683
Documents the fall of Saigon in 1975. Shows how more than 100,000 troops encircled the city from five directions, as well as how the rush of refugees tried in vain to catch the last US helicopters out of Saigon. Narrated by Richard Basehart.
History - United States
Dist - UILL

Surrogate mothers 25 MIN
VHS
Where there's life series
Color; PAL (G)
PdS25 purchase
Discusses the pros and cons of surrogate motherhood. Includes the world's first surrogate mother, Elizabeth Kane of Chicago, who says she has changed her mind about the morality of carrying someone else's baby in pregnancy. She begs other would - be surrogate moms to spare themselves the anguish she says she has suffered. Meanwhile, Kim Cotton, the first surrogate mother in Britain, says she would do it all again. Features Dr Miriam Stoppard as host in a series of shows making sense of science and treating controversial subjects in an informed way. Contact distributor about availability outside the United Kingdom.
Sociology
Dist - ACADEM

Surveillance 21 MIN
U-matic
Color (C)
$225.00
Experimental film by Bruce Charlesworth.
Fine Arts
Dist - AFA **Prod** - AFA 1981

Surveillance - Who's Watching 60 MIN
16mm / U-matic / VHS
B&W
Presents an on - the - scene investigation of political surveillance and harassment of individuals with a major focus upon the activities of the Chicago Police Department's Red Squad. Features interviews with persons who have been affected by surveillance, government officials and former FBI agents. Examines the dissemination of information about private citizens by the FBI, city police departments and other agencies.
Civics and Political Systems; Sociology
Dist - IU **Prod** - IU 1973

The Survey 20 MIN
16mm
Color
Demonstrates techniques used in conducting a problem - oriented archaeological survey. Follows a survey team as it moves through the Skagit River Delta in Washington State. Presents processes of surface collecting, measurement and recording.
History - United States; History - World; Science - Physical; Sociology
Dist - SF **Prod** - SF

The Survey Disc - using the Rod and Level
Videodisc
Color (C)
$795.00 purchase _ #2794
Introduces the basic surveying principles of using the rod and level. Divides into four sections - operating the automatic level, parts and functions, field procedures and simulation. Can be played on SONY or Pioneer III videodisc players. The system requires an IBM compatible computer with overlay capability. Includes user's manual.
Education; Industrial and Technical Education; Psychology
Dist - ACCESS **Prod** - ACCESS 1989

Survey of Assembly Methods 150 MIN
U-matic
Electronics Manufacturing - Components, Assembly and Soldering 'Series
Color (IND)
Discusses manual assembly of printed circuit boards and components, operator - assist equipment, and semi and fully - automatic assembly equipment.
Business and Economics; Computer Science; Industrial and Technical Education
Dist - INTECS **Prod** - INTECS

A Survey of Children's Speech Disorders 29 MIN
16mm
Color (C)
Illustrates how children with problems of hearing, cleft palate, cerebral palsy, articulation and stuttering learn to use and understand speech.
Education; English Language; Psychology
Dist - UIOWA **Prod** - UIOWA 1961

Survey of English Literature I Series

Adam unparadised - book IX of Paradise Lost - the triumph of human love	44 MIN
The Age of gold - the Battle of Maldon and the Dream of the Rood	45 MIN
Ancient poets and modern ladies - The Rape of the Lock - the mock - epic	45 MIN
Chaucer's world - general prologue - Canterbury Tales	45 MIN
Cut is the branch - Christopher Marlowe's Dr Faustus	45 MIN
The Dream of Man - the Renaissance in England	45 MIN
End of an Era - Beowulf	45 MIN
Escape into Reality - Pre - Romantic Poetry / Conclusion	45 MIN
Fortunate fall - paradoxical results of original sin - expulsion from the garden	44 MIN
Growing Up in Eastcheap - Shakespeare's Henry IV - Prince Hal's Youth	45 MIN
Hero and Villain - the Role of Satan in Paradise Lost	45 MIN
Horse Sense about Houyhnhnms - the Fourth Voyage of Gulliver's Travels	45 MIN
The Long Voyage Home - Donne's Religious Poetry	45 MIN
Love Conquers all - Love, Human, Divine Unlawful and Domesticated in the Canterbury	45 MIN
Love Story - Donne's Love Poetry	45 MIN
Madness and Method - the Play within the Play - Hamlet as Playwright	45 MIN
The Man in the Ironic Mask - Jonathan Swift - the Modest Proposal and the Second	45 MIN
Miller's Tale	45 MIN
The Name of the Age - James Boswell and Samuel Johnson	45 MIN
New and Novel - the Development of the Novel in England	45 MIN
Ourselves to Know - Alexander Pope's Essay on Man - what Oft was Thought but Ne'er So Well	45 MIN
Pardoner's Secret	45 MIN
Plump Jack - Shakespeare's Henry IV - Prince Hal's Rejection of Falstaff	45 MIN
Poet and Hero - Milton's Paradise Lost - the Triumph of Human Love	45 MIN
Questions of Hamlet - Why Does Hamlet Delay	45 MIN
Theatre of the Mind - John Donne's Metaphysical Style	45 MIN
Through the looking glass - introduction - Caedmon's hymm	45 MIN
Virtue Rewarded - Henry Fielding's Joseph Andrews	45 MIN
Woe that is in Marriage - the Wife of Bath and the Nun's Priest's Tale	45 MIN
Yorick's Skull - Gallows Humor in Hamlet	45 MIN

Dist - MDCPB

Survey of English Verse Series

American pioneers	28 MIN
Chaucer	28 MIN
The Earlier Twentieth Century	28 MIN
Introduction to english poetry	28 MIN
The Later Twentieth Century	28 MIN
The Maturing Shakespeare	28 MIN
Medieval to Elizabethan Poetry	28 MIN
Metaphysical and Devotional Poetry	28 MIN
Milton	28 MIN
Old English Poetry	28 MIN
Restoration and Augustan Poetry	28 MIN
Romantic Pioneers	28 MIN
Romantics and Realists	28 MIN
Victorian Poetry	28 MIN
William Wordsworth	28 MIN
The Younger Romantics	28 MIN

Dist - FOTH

Survey of Multiattribute Utility Theory 53 MIN
U-matic / VHS
Decision Analysis Series
Color
Industrial and Technical Education; Mathematics
Dist - MIOT **Prod** - MIOT

Survey of Office Automation Applications 45 MIN
VHS / U-matic
Management Strategies for Office Automation Series
Color
Provides descriptions of the objectives, implementation strategies and results of office automation applications in a cross section of organizations.
Business and Economics; Industrial and Technical Education; Psychology
Dist - DELTAK **Prod** - DELTAK

A Survey of Refuse Disposal Methods 10 MIN
16mm
Color
LC FIE60-79
Demonstrates advantages and disadvantages of types of refuse disposal ranging from open dumps and dumping in oceans and rivers to scientifically engineered metropolitan incineration and sanitary landfills.
Health and Safety
Dist - USNAC **Prod** - USPHS 1959

Survey of the primates 38 MIN
VHS
Color (G C)
$180.00 purchase, $19.00 rental _ #40502
Compares traits among primates in evolutionary perspective, from tree shrews to prosimians, cercopithecidae, ceboidea and lesser and great apes. Discusses anatomical, social and maturational differences, as well as geographical distribution, habitats, intelligence, diet, dentition, learned behavior, manual dexterity and territoriality. Duane Rumbaugh, Austin H Riesen and Robert E Lee.
Science - Natural
Dist - PSU **Prod** - RRL 1988

Survey of the Primates 38 MIN
VHS / 16mm
Color (C A)
$195.00 purchase, $16.50 rental _ #40502
Defines the characteristics of the order Primates and shows examples of the wide array of similarities and differences within primate behavior and morphology. Serves as a comprehensive introduction to primatology. Revised edition of 1969 film.
Science - Natural
Dist - PSUPCR **Prod** - PSUPCR 1988

Survey of the Primates 38 MIN
16mm
Color (H C)
LC 76-710734
Presents nine of the eleven families which comprise the order of primates and uses forty - nine different primate forms to represent those families. Attempts to encourage respect for non - human primates as unique and valuable forms of life that must be protected from forces which threaten their extinction.
Science - Natural
Dist - PHM **Prod** - APPLE 1970

Survey of wastewater technology 60 MIN
U-matic / VHS / BETA
Color (G PRO)
$46.00, $155.00 purchase _ #LS50
Presents four parts on wastewater technology. Includes the titles Small Diameter Effluent Sewers which describes the practicality of small diameter effluent sewers in comparison to conventional sewers; Planning Wastewater Facilities for Small Communities which explains how planners must take into account the special characteristics of their area; Upgrading Small Community Wastewater Treatment which explores new technology suited to small communities; and Sand Filters which looks at the history of common treatment methods in comparison with this new technology. Coproduced with Small Flows Clearing House, West Virginia University.
Industrial and Technical Education
Dist - FEDU **Prod** - USEPA 1988

Surveying a casualty 9 MIN
VHS / U-matic
EMT video - group one series
Color (PRO)
LC 84-706492
Portrays the process of determining the severity of a victim's wounds, and prioritizing and providing appropriate treatment.
Health and Safety
Dist - USNAC **Prod** - USA 1983

Surveying and Establishing the Context 29 MIN
VHS / 16mm
Diversity in Communication Series
Color (C)
$200.00 purchase _ #277201
Catalogues motivational 'beginnings' for instructional projects. Focuses on language - communication - arts. 'Surveying' shows how a number of teachers establish the context for learning in their classrooms. Illustrates urban, rural, small, large, 'upscale' and middle class classrooms.
Education; Mathematics; Social Science
Dist - ACCESS **Prod** - ACCESS 1989

Surveying for Hidden Treasure 27 MIN
VHS / U-matic
Speed Learning Series
Color (J H)
Shows how to scrutinize a book for hidden meanings. Reveals that the title, front matter, first page and illustrations can reveals a lot to the person who knows what to look for.
English Language
Dist - AITECH **Prod** - LEARNI 1982

Surveying for Hidden Treasure 26 MIN
U-matic / VHS
Art of Reading/Speed Learning Series
Color
English Language
Dist - DELTAK **Prod** - LEARNI

Surveying for Hidden Treasure 30 MIN
VHS / U-matic
Speed Learning Video Series
Color
Discusses surveying as a major step in sharpening purpose for reading and provides an overview of the material that has to be read to help students decide what reading skills to use in dealing with that reading.
Education; English Language; Literature and Drama; Psychology
Dist - LEARNI **Prod** - LEARNI

Surveying the Stars 29 MIN
U-matic
Project Universe - Astronomy Series
Color (C A)
Focuses on methods of determining distances to stars and movement of stars in relation to solar system. Describes use of blink comparator and Doppler effect.
Science - Physical
Dist - CDTEL **Prod** - COAST

Surviva 32 MIN
16mm
Color (G)
$500.00 purchase, $50.00 rental
Combines documentary footage with animation and a nature montage. Examines the artist's relationship to work and community. Produced by Carol Clement and Ariel Dougherty and Artemisia.
Fine Arts; Sociology
Dist - WMEN **Prod** - WMEN

Survival 16 MIN
16mm / U-matic / VHS
Color (J H A)
Demonstrates the training program developed by the Motorcycle Safety Council to provide both safe riding strategies for bikers and basic information about motorcycle maintenance.
Health and Safety
Dist - MEDIAG **Prod** - NFBC 1985

Survival 28 MIN
VHS / U-matic
Color (H C A)
Tells how pollution, population and the depletion of non - renewable resources concern countries of all sizes.
Science - Natural; Sociology
Dist - JOU **Prod** - UPI

Survival 20 MIN
VHS / U-matic
Safety Sense Series
Color (J)
Discusses various aspects of survival safety.
Health and Safety
Dist - GPN **Prod** - WCVETV 1981

Survival 17 MIN
16mm
Color (FRENCH)
LC 77-702660
Shows the need for motorcycle safety instruction and some of the teaching methods used in existing motorcycle training courses.
Health and Safety; Social Science
Dist - CANHSC **Prod** - CANHSC 1976

Survival 85 MIN
VHS
Color (G A)
$59.95 purchase _ #0812
Illustrates in - water survival, individual flotation devices. Discusses hypothermia, distress signals, life rafts and rescue cover survival in all types of water. Includes extensive information on equipment requirements, selection, performance and limitations.
Health and Safety; Physical Education and Recreation
Dist - SEVVID

Survival 18 MIN
16mm
Color (J)
LC 77-700779
Demonstrates the use of satellite communications systems in predicting and coping with natural disasters.
Industrial and Technical Education; Science; Science - Physical
Dist - USNAC **Prod** - NASA 1976

Survival 25 MIN
U-matic / VHS / 16mm
Untamed World Series
Color; Mono (J H C A)
$400.00 film, $250.00 video, $50.00 rental
Studies the ability and the need in the animal kingdom to survive. Looks specifically at the camel and its adaptive strengths.
Science - Natural
Dist - CTV **Prod** - CTV 1973

Survival 10 MIN
16mm / U-matic / VHS
Color (IND)
Describes a new life craft that is now used on many ships, tankers and off - shore oil and gas rigs. Explains the features of this 28 - person survival capsule, revealing that it is unsinkable, impact resistant, radar reflective and fireproof.
Health and Safety; Industrial and Technical Education; Social Science
Dist - IFB **Prod** - IFB 1975

Survival 28 MIN
VHS / U-matic / 16mm
Outdoor safety series
Color (J H G)
$275.00, $325.00, $545.00 purchase, $50.00 rental
Covers the fundamental outdoor skills and knowledge required for intelligent enjoyment of the outdoors. Uses four case histories to present 'how - to' information and the need for developing a healthy respect for the outdoors and the importance of maintaining the right attitude should trouble arise.
Health and Safety; Physical Education and Recreation
Dist - NDIM **Prod** - MADISA 1991

Survival After High School 17 MIN
U-matic / VHS / 16mm
Color (J H)
LC 81-701388
Demonstrates common problems associated with such things as dealing with landlord, paying bills and balancing a checkbook. Shows students who are living on their own for the first time how to handle these everyday problems.
Guidance and Counseling; Home Economics
Dist - CORF **Prod** - CENTRO 1981

Survival Against the Odds 28 MIN
U-matic / VHS
Life of Plants Series
Color (C)
$249.00, $149.00 purchase _ #AD - 1673
Shows how an island newly created by a volcanic explosion becomes a botanical laboratory to show how plants are propagated and spread. Considers lichens and their importance in the growth and spread of vegetation. Part of a series on plants.
Science - Natural
Dist - FOTH **Prod** - FOTH

Survival and Advancement 30 MIN
U-matic / VHS
Business of Management Series
Color (C A)
Discusses the issue of how to survive and advance within an organization.
Business and Economics
Dist - SCCON **Prod** - SCCON

Survival and Evasion in Southeast Asia - Short - Term Evasion 21 MIN
U-matic / VHS
Color
Trains U S pilots on what to do if shot down over enemy territory.
Civics and Political Systems; History - United States; History - World
Dist - IHF **Prod** - IHF

Survival and the Senses 25 MIN
16mm / U-matic / VHS
Behavior and Survival Series
Color (H C A)
LC 73-700430
Uses observations, experiments and animation to show how sense organs make animals aware of their environments and determine their behavior. Points out that there are animal senses which man cannot equal.
Science - Natural
Dist - MGHT **Prod** - MGHT 1973

Survival by permit - II 16 MIN
8mm cartridge / VHS / BETA / U-matic
Confined space training - a program for everyone series
Color; PAL (IND G PRO)
$495.00 purchase, $175.00 rental _ #CST - 200
Provides step - by - step training in the confined space permit procedures of OSHA. Details dramatically how training and preparation saved a man's life in a confined space incident. Shows how even a thoroughly executed permit can still result in an emergency response and rescue. Part two of two parts. Includes trainer's manual and ten employee manuals.
Health and Safety; Psychology
Dist - BNA **Prod** - BNA 1994

The Survival Factor - Defense Mechanisms in the Sea 12 MIN
16mm
Living World of the Sea Series
Color (J)
LC 72-702644
Covers in broad terms the defense mechanisms of sea creatures in deep water in the Benthic environment.
Science - Natural
Dist - MIAMIS **Prod** - REELA 1969

Survival - from My Yondering Days 60 MIN
U-matic / VHS
L'Amour Live Series
Stereo (K P I J H C G T A S R PRO IND)
Talks about his escapades as a merchant seaman plus a reading of the short story 'survival'.
Biography; Literature and Drama
Dist - BANTAP **Prod** - BANTAP 1986

Survival Guide 30 MIN
U-matic / VHS
(PRO A)
$295 Purchase, $100 Rental 5 days, $30 Preview 3 days
Covers basic tactics for preventing and handling emergency first aid situations such as electric shock and burn injuries.
Health and Safety
Dist - ADVANM **Prod** - ADVANM

Survival guide to food 60 MIN
VHS
Color; PAL (G)
PdS99 purchase; United Kingdom and Eire only
Provides an expose of the increasing incidence of food poisoning in the last ten years. Looks at how to reduce the risks of poisoning from bacteria in the preparation of foodstuffs. The video compilation is made up of six 10 - minute programs.
Home Economics; Social Science
Dist - BBCENE

Survival in nature series
Presents a five - part series that deals with animals and plant life adaptation to the environment. Covers a different concern in the importance of ecological niche and in survival mechanisms with each title. Titles include Life on the Edge, The Silver Trumpeter, Technical Animals, Venom, and When the Tide goes Out. Each part 26 minutes and available separately for purchase or rental.

Life on the edge 26 MIN
The Silver trumpeter 26 MIN
Technical animals 26 MIN
Venom 26 MIN
When the tide goes out 26 MIN

Dist - NDIM **Prod** - SURVAN 1992

Survival in the Animal World 11 MIN
16mm / U-matic / VHS
Color (I J)
LC 78-712872
Observes a variety of animal life to show that the different species have developed physical traits and instincts that help them to survive.
Science - Natural
Dist - JOU **Prod** - WER 1971

Survival in the Sahel 15 MIN
16mm
Color
LC 75-702875
Shows the effects of the drought on humans, animals and environment in Central and West Africa and Ethiopia. Stresses the massive relief effort mounted by the United States Government, other nations and private agencies and individuals. Emphasizes the role of the U S Agency for International Development in helping to increase food production and to improve nutrition, health, transportation, reforestation and water supply.
Agriculture; Civics and Political Systems; Health and Safety; Science - Natural; Social Science
Dist - USNAC **Prod** - USAID 1975

Survival in the Sea 30 MIN
U-matic / VHS / 16mm
World We Live in Series
Color (J H)
LC 73-700242
Studies the struggle for survival among sea creatures and explains some of the reasons why fish have become adapted through natural selection.
Science - Natural
Dist - MGHT **Prod** - TIMELI 1968

Survival in the wilderness series
Artificial Respiration 10 MIN
Bush first aid - Pt 1 10 MIN
Bush first aid - Pt 2 10 MIN
Distress signals 20 MIN
Distress signals, Pt 1 10 MIN
Distress signals, Pt 2 10 MIN
Dressing Fish 10 MIN
Drownproofing 10 MIN
Fire Making and Shelters 10 MIN
Fundamental Canoeing 10 MIN
Proper Summer Bush Clothing 10 MIN
Survival Kit 20 MIN
The Survival Kit - Pt 1 10 MIN
The Survival kit - Pt 2 10 MIN
Use and Care of Axes and Knives 10 MIN
Using a Compass 10 MIN
Dist - SF

Survival in the Winter Storm 27 MIN
16mm
Color
LC 75-701380
Deals with dangers inherent in winter weather, giving advice to the average citizen on how to prepare for severe weather conditions and explaining the meanings of specific forecasts. Points up the necessity for emergency planning by local governments.
Geography - United States; Guidance and Counseling; Health and Safety; Science - Physical
Dist - USNAC **Prod** - USFDAA 1974

Survival in the workplace 2000 17 MIN
VHS
Color (COR)
$595.00 purchase, $175.00 rental _ #DSI/DPI
Presents entrepreneur Patricia Fripp in a discussion of the individual employee's relationship with his or her work. Extending beyond management - driven empowerment techniques, Fripp asks viewers to value the process of reconsidering the work relationship as a personal commitment to each one's individual success. Includes a Leader's Guide.
Business and Economics; Guidance and Counseling; Psychology
Dist - ADVANM

Survival Kit 20 MIN
16mm
Survival in the Wilderness Series
Color (I J H)
Details the items in a survival kit and explains how they are designed to combat the seven enemies of survival - fear, pain, cold, thirst, hunger, fatigue and loneliness. Shows how two girls, who lose everything in a serious accident except their survival kit, make themselves comfortable in a short period of time and take positive action to ensure their rescue.
Physical Education and Recreation
Dist - SF **Prod** - MORLAT 1967

The Survival Kit - Pt 1 10 MIN
16mm
Survival in the Wilderness Series
Color (I J H)
LC FIA67-1435
Shows a survival kit which is contained in a box six inches long by four inches wide and two inches deep. Details the items in the survival kit and explains how they are designed to combat the seven enemies of survival.
Health and Safety
Dist - SF **Prod** - MORLAT 1967

The Survival kit - Pt 2 10 MIN
16mm
Survival in the Wilderness Series
Color (I J H)
LC FIA67-1436
Explains that the seven enemies of survival are fear, pain, cold, thirst, hunger, fatigue and loneliness. Shows how two girls who, despite a serious accident in which they lost everything except their survival kit, are about to make themselves comfortable in a short space of time and take positive action to ensure that their rescue is effected.
Health and Safety
Dist - SF **Prod** - MORLAT 1967

Survival of a small city - a documentary on urban renewal 65 MIN
VHS / 16mm
Color (H C G)
$900.00, $495.00 purchase, $85.00 rental
Portrays the New England town of South Norwalk, Connecticut, over a seven - year period. Reveals that the once - thriving industrial town tried to reverse its deterioration and shows the consequences of urban renewal, gentrification and the dissolution of the old community. Interweaves the conflicting perspectives of residents, store owners, artists, politicians, preservationists and developers. Asks - what is a city, the people who live there or a collection of buildings.
Geography - United States; Social Science; Sociology
Dist - FLMLIB **Prod** - FRASAL 1987

The Survival of Sontheary Sou 53 MIN
Videoreel / VHS
Color
Documents the story of a Cambodian refugee in America, and the atrocities in Cambodia of the Khmer Rouge. Intended for relevant secondary school programs and university courses, mental health professionals and religions and community groups. In two parts of 30 minutes and 23 minutes.
Geography - World; History - World; Sociology
Dist - BARND **Prod** - BARND

Survival of spaceship Earth 63 MIN
VHS
Color (J H C G)
$29.95 purchase _ #CMP06V
Reveals that, in the past 25 years, the human population on Earth has increased more than it has in the last million years. Considers that this explosive increase in population tests the ability of Earth's biosphere to cope with increasing environmental problems. Asks if humans can survive on a dying planet, if life is worth living on a dying planet.
Science - Natural; Sociology
Dist - CAMV

Survival of the Black College 29 MIN
U-matic
Like it is Series
Color
Discusses the problems facing black colleges today.
Education; Sociology
Dist - HRC **Prod** - OHC

Survival of the Family Farm in the Netherlands and the United States Human - Environmental Interation - 6 30 MIN
VHS
Common Issues in World Regions Series
Color (J)
$180.00 purchase
Looks at concerns of families in the Western Netherlands and Richmond, Kentucky, trying to survive on small family farms. Develops international understanding and geographic literacy for today's students growing up in a global community.
Agriculture; Geography - United States; Geography - World; Social Science; Sociology
Dist - AITECH **Prod** - AITECH 1991

Survival of the Fittest 52 MIN
16mm / VHS / U-matic
Color (SPANISH)
Covers quarter horse conformation and the relation of form to function. In two parts.
Foreign Language; Health and Safety
Dist - AQHORS **Prod** - AQHORS 1978

Survival of the fittest 60 MIN
VHS
Ark series; Episode 1
Color (G)
$290.00 purchase, $50.00 rental
Begins with the huge deficit of the Regent's Park Zoo in London which must be reduced at the expense of animal keepers initially chosen for their ease with animals and who must now reapply for jobs they already hold. Part of a series on the Zoo, founded 1822 and acclaimed for its scientific research, which has been told that, due to the market economy, it must now pay its own way. Records events at the Ark for over a year as a cost conscious management team moves in, slashing expenditures, including 90 people and 1200 animals - 40 percent of the zoo's stock.
Business and Economics; Fine Arts; Science - Natural
Dist - FIRS **Prod** - DINEEN 1993

Survival of the Fittest 60 MIN
U-matic / VHS / 16mm
Color (J H A)
Uses slow - motion photography to show how a horse's conformation helps or hinders the ability to perform and how it affects health.
Agriculture
Dist - CORNRS **Prod** - CUETV

Survival of the Fittest - Pt 1 26 MIN
16mm / U-matic / VHS
Color (SPANISH)
Covers quarter horse conformation and the relation of form to function.
Physical Education and Recreation
Dist - AQHORS **Prod** - AQHORS 1978

Survival of the Fittest Series
Employee Fitness - Fact or Fantasy 24 MIN
The Fitness formula 27 MIN
The Health Fitness Professionals 18 MIN
Heart Disease - Prevention and Rehabilitation 17 MIN
Stress Management 17 MIN
Dist - PRORE

Survival of the Kit Fox - a Conservation Case Study 15 MIN
U-matic / VHS / 16mm
Color (I J H)
LC FIA68-3153
Observes the kit fox, a small prairie animal, throughout one full year. Shows her in each of the four seasons building her den, raising her young and hunting for food. Studies methods of wildlife conservation.
Science - Natural
Dist - JOU **Prod** - ALTSUL 1967

The Survival of the Species 55 MIN
16mm / VHS / U-matic
Making of Mankind Series
Color (G)
Examines the crucial behavior patterns, including aggression, which has made humans the type of species they are. Looks at new evidence that suggests the human animal will survive.
Science - Natural; Science - Physical; Sociology
Dist - TIMLIF **Prod** - BBCTV 1982
BBCENE
AMBROS

Survival Run 12 MIN
16mm / VHS / U-matic
Color (G)
LC 80-700394
Documents the efforts of Harry Cordellos, a blind marathon runner, as he competes in the Dipsea Race.
Guidance and Counseling; Physical Education and Recreation; Psychology
Dist - PFP **Prod** - MAGUSF 1979

Survival Russian
VHS
Color (G) (RUSSIAN)
$49.95 purchase _ #PO000
Teaches Russian phrases and words useful to travelers. Covers the Cyrillic alphabet. Photographs famous Moscow landmarks and speaks with Russians from many walks of life.
Foreign Language; Geography - World
Dist - SIV

Survival Shooting Techniques 35 MIN
16mm / VHS / U-matic
Color (G)
LC 79-700189
Presents state-of-the-art techniques for survival shooting with a revolver, automatic and shotgun. Includes patterns of encounter instinct shooting, disarming techniques, shooting behind natural cover, shooting in low light level conditions and reloading under fire.
Physical Education and Recreation; Social Science
Dist - CORF **Prod** - CORF 1979

Survival shopping - how to buy healthier foods - 2 17 MIN
VHS
Cholesterol watch series
Color (G)
$195.00 purchase
Provides the how - tos of supermarket shopping for healthy, yet tasty foods. Features the Food Pyramid to graphically illustrate dietary guidelines to improve cholesterol levels. Part two of a four - part series on cholesterol.
Health and Safety; Home Economics; Social Science
Dist - GPERFO

Survival simulations series
Cascades video enhancement
Desert I video enhancement
Desert II video enhancement
Subarctic video enhancement
Dist - HUMSYN

Survival Skills 30 MIN
VHS / U-matic
Teaching Students with Special Needs Series
Color (T C)
Takes a look at the range of competencies that comprise survival skills and ways. Tells how curriculum can introduce some of these skills, such as understanding want ads, locating community resources and learning about health care and personal finances.
Education; Psychology
Dist - PBS Prod - MSITV 1981

Survival skills 20 MIN
VHS
Manage it series
Color (A PRO COR IND)
$95.00 purchase _ #VMIV6
Helps viewers focus on the management part of stress management whether their problems are at home or on the job. Provides relaxation techniques that viewers can use to relieve stress. Focuses on how viewers can develop stress-management skills they can use throughout their lives and can evaluate their coping strategies and their personal values. Includes leader guide and five participant guides. Part six of a six-part series.
Psychology
Dist - WHLPSN

Survival skills for diabetic children 28 MIN
VHS / U-matic
Color (PRO)
$275.00 purchase, $60.00 rental _ #7813S, #7813V
Focuses on the understanding of Type I diabetes required by nursing staff to provide education, supervision and support to insulin - dependent children. Prepares nurses to help diabetic children develop the necessary survival skills of proper nutrition, blood glucose monitoring, maintaining normal blood sugar levels, mastering insulin injection and understanding diabetic emergencies.
Health and Safety; Psychology; Sociology
Dist - AJN Prod - HOSSN 1988

Survival Skills for the Classroom Teacher Series
Coping with teacher stress 29 MIN
Dare to discipline 29 MIN
Glasser on discipline 28 MIN
Multi - Cultural Education - a Teaching Style 29 MIN
Questions for Thinking 28 MIN
Sexism, stereotyping and hidden values 29 MIN
Ten Steps to Discipline 29 MIN
Working in the Integrated Classroom 29 MIN
Dist - FI

Survival skills for the future 22 MIN
VHS
Color (PRO IND A)
$695.00 purchase, $225.00 rental _ #ENT20
Features Jennifer James, PhD, who shows how to be open to the future and how to create change. Teaches individuals in the workplace how to develop future perspective, be receptive to possibilities, change expectations and draw upon new types of intelligence.
Business and Economics
Dist - EXTR Prod - ENMED

Survival skills for urban youth series
Presents a three - part series addressing urban youth and three issues that most affect whether or not urban high school teens will finish high school - drugs, teen sexuality and early parenthood and self esteem. Presents two segments in each program to facilitate student discussion before and after the video.
Choices about drugs - Part one 13 MIN
Choices about sex - Part two 15 MIN
Developing self - esteem - Pt three 15 MIN
Dist - HRMC Prod - HRMC

Survival Skills - Organizing and Maintaining a Home
VHS / U-matic
Color (J H G)
Teaches home management. Gives information on organizing living quarters, and management, upkeep and simple repair of the home. Includes decor development and cleaning.
Home Economics
Dist - EDUACT Prod - EDUACT

Survival Spanish 62 MIN
VHS
Color (G) (ENGLISH AND SPANISH)
$39.95 purchase
Presents a ten - lesson course in the Spanish language. Covers a variety of situations, including getting information, travel, money, restaurants, and more.
Foreign Language
Dist - PBS Prod - WNETTV
UILL

Survival Spanish for general patient care
VHS
Practical Spanish for health - care providers series
Color (A PRO) (SPANISH AND ENGLISH)
$350.00 purchase
Instructs in the basics of Spanish for health - care workers. Develops speaking ability to communicate with Spanish - speaking patients in general patient care situations. Includes facilitator's guide, study guide and audiocassettes. Additional sets for students are available at a nominal charge.
Foreign Language; Health and Safety; Psychology
Dist - UARIZ Prod - UARIZ

Survival Spanish for hospital admissions staff
VHS
Practical Spanish for health - care providers series
Color (A PRO) (SPANISH AND ENGLISH)
$350.00 purchase
Instructs in the basics of the Spanish language for health - care workers. Develops speaking ability to communicate with Spanish - speaking patients in admissions situations. Includes facilitator's guide, study guide and audiocassettes. Additional sets for students are available at a nominal charge.
Foreign Language; Health and Safety; Psychology
Dist - UARIZ Prod - UARIZ

Survival Spanish for labor and delivery personnel
VHS
Practical Spanish for health - care providers series
Color (A PRO) (SPANISH AND ENGLISH)
$700.00 purchase
Instructs in the basics of Spanish for health - care workers. Develops speaking ability to communicate with Spanish - speaking patients in labor and delivery situations. Includes facilitator's guide, study guide and audiocassettes. Additional sets for students are available at a nominal charge.
Foreign Language; Health and Safety; Psychology
Dist - UARIZ Prod - UARIZ

Survival Stresses 30 MIN
16mm
Color (G)
LC FIE61-204
Discusses major physiological stresses that may be encountered by persons facing a survival situation in the Arctic, in the desert, in the tropics and on water.
Health and Safety; Psychology
Dist - USNAC Prod - USAF 1961

Survival Swimming 14 MIN
16mm / VHS / U-matic
Learning to Swim Series
B&W (J H C)
LC FIA67-5546
Demonstrates skills of survival swimming, including floating, side and breast strokes and treading water. Illustrates cases where underwater swimming may be necessary and describes how to jump. Discusses the correct use of a tow line or rope ladder, correct ways of getting into and out of the water, and the use of clothing for support.
Health and Safety; Physical Education and Recreation
Dist - IFB Prod - BHA 1965

Survival Swimming 7 MIN
16mm
Lifesaving and Water Safety Series
Color (I)
LC 76-701574
Reviews how to survive a water accident when burdened by water - soaked clothing and shows floating and treading water techniques.
Health and Safety; Physical Education and Recreation
Dist - AMRC Prod - AMRC 1975

Survival Swimming - to Save a Life 15 MIN
16mm / VHS / U-matic
To Save a Life Series
Color (J) (ARABIC SPANISH)
LC 78-700838
Depicts typical water emergency situations and common sense precautions which can prevent danger. Illustrates swimming with full clothing, clothing inflation techniques and flotation methods by which an individual can survive until a rescue is completed.
Health and Safety; Physical Education and Recreation
Dist - EBEC Prod - EBEC 1977

Survival Tactics 22 MIN
16mm / VHS / U-matic
Color (G)
Deals with the problem of extremist attacks. Describes self - defense tactics for the police officer whenever he encounters situations of extreme and unexpected danger. Explores fighting techniques necessary for survival in a sudden, desperate physical attack. Features attackers wielding knives, homemade flame throwers, bottled acid and other sinister weapons.
Sociology
Dist - CORF Prod - WORON

Survive! 5 MIN
U-matic / 16mm / VHS
Color; Mono (G)
MV $85.00 _ MP 170.00 purchase, $50.00 rental
Recognizes the importance of all the species on this planet and presents a desperate plea for their survival. sequences filmed on locations that range from Kenya to the Artic and Hawaii to the Caribbean.
Science - Natural
Dist - CTV Prod - MAKOF 1982

The Survivers 130 MIN
U-matic / VHS / 16mm
Captioned; Color (A) (SPANISH (ENGLISH SUBTITLES))
Portrays a family of aristocratic origin in Cuba which decides to stay on after the 1959 revolution, isolating themselves in their mansion with their servants until they end in cannibalism.
Civics and Political Systems; Fine Arts; History - World
Dist - CNEMAG Prod - CNEMAG 1978

Surviving 27 MIN
U-matic / VHS / BETA
Stationary ark series
Color; PAL (G H C)
PdS50, PdS58 purchase
Discusses the recreation of humankind, nature and wildlife in part of a 12 - part series. Features Gerald Durrell. Filmed on location in Jersey, England.
Science - Natural
Dist - EDPAT

Surviving 20 MIN
VHS / 16mm
Trail Series
Color (I)
$150.00 purchase, $30.00 rental
Probes ways in which humans change the environment to meet their own survival needs.
Science - Natural
Dist - AITECH Prod - KAIDTV 1986

Surviving 50 MINS
VHS
The private life of plants
Color; PAL (H G)
PdS99 purchase; not available in USA, Canada
Reveals the abilities certain plants have to endure extreme conditions. Uses computer technology and time - lapse photography to demonstrate processes. Sixth in the six - part plant survival series, The Private Life of Plants. Hosted by David Attenborough.
Science - Natural
Dist - BBCENE

Surviving a Presentation 22 MIN
VHS / U-matic
Color
Breaks down a presentation into easy to understand components so facts don't get lost in the delivery. Says after completing the program, trainers will be able to design an introduction, prepare a statement of purpose and develop main ideas. Explores elements crucial to successful delivery.
English Language
Dist - GPCV Prod - GPCV

Surviving anger - yours and others 32 MIN
VHS
Surviving series
Color (H C G A R)
$24.95 purchase, $10.00 rental _ #35 - 87230 - 460
Features Clayton Barbeau in a discussion of anger. Notes the various forms anger takes. Demonstrates strategies for dealing with anger.
Religion and Philosophy
Dist - APH Prod - FRACOC

Surviving broken relationships 21 MIN
VHS
Surviving series
Color (H C G A R)
$24.95 purchase, $10.00 rental _ #35 - 87187 - 460
Features Clayton Barbeau in a discussion of broken relationships. Covers the anger and pain that can result.
Religion and Philosophy
Dist - APH Prod - FRACOC

Surviving cancer - the road ahead 70 MIN
VHS
Color (G)
$29.95 purchase _ #CRV200V
Discusses the complexity of cancer treatment and its seemingly endless tests and 'thousands' of doctors. Provides necessary information to patients and explains the importance of family support, lifestyle and attitude.
Health and Safety
Dist - CAMV

Surviving Columbus - the story of the Pueblo people 120 MIN
VHS
Color (I J H)
$19.95 purchase _ #PBS1016
Tells the other side of the story about the European conquest of North America. Features the historical view of the Pueblo people of the United States' Southwest. Uses dramatic images, words and music.
History - World; Social Science
Dist - KNOWUN **Prod** - KNMETV

Surviving depression 26 MIN
VHS
Surviving series
Color (H C G A R)
$24.95 purchase, $10.00 rental _ #35 - 87185 - 460
Features Clayton Barbeau in a discussion of depression. Outlines the signs of depression and offers tactics for coping.
Health and Safety; Religion and Philosophy
Dist - APH **Prod** - FRACOC

Surviving difficult people 40 MIN
VHS
Surviving series
Color (H C G A R)
$24.95 purchase, $10.00 rental _ #35 - 87231 - 460
Features Clayton Barbeau in a discussion of dealing with difficult people. Suggests that people can unwittingly encourage the behavior of difficult people by how they respond. Holds that all people have times when they are difficult to deal with.
Religion and Philosophy
Dist - APH **Prod** - FRACOC

Surviving edged weapons
VHS
Color (G)
$49.95 purchase _ #CLP000
Explains self defense against knife - wielding attackers.
Physical Education and Recreation
Dist - SIV

Surviving grief 24 MIN
VHS
Surviving series
Color (H C G A R)
$24.95 purchase, $10.00 rental _ #35 - 87232 - 460
Features Clayton Barbeau in a discussion of grief. Outlines the steps of the grieving process, including tears, loneliness, anger and denial. Suggests that losing a loved one may strengthen a person's commitment to life.
Religion and Philosophy
Dist - APH **Prod** - FRACOC

Surviving Hostage Situations 25 MIN
U-matic / VHS / 16mm
Color (SPANISH)
Develops the concept of the kidnap process and examines the types of events and behaviors that occur in each phase involving the terrorists, the victims and third parties.
Civics and Political Systems
Dist - CORF **Prod** - WORON

Surviving Hostage Situations 45 MIN
U-matic / VHS / 16mm
Color
Provides a case history of the kidnapping of a company executive. Analyzes the kidnapping process and the various phases undergone by kidnappers, victims and third parties such as the family, the company and law enforcement. Shows how the victim can cope with every phase.
Business and Economics; Civics and Political Systems; Sociology
Dist - CORF **Prod** - CORF

Surviving Illness with Spirit 30 MIN
VHS
Who's in Charge Series
Color (G)
$19.95 purchase
Shows how to deal with illness emotionally. Features Dr Scott Sheperd. Part of a four - part series.
Health and Safety; Psychology
Dist - WGTETV **Prod** - WGTETV

Surviving in the real world - basic skills series
Dollars and sense 33 MIN
Housing and transportation 25 MIN
Your lifestyle 26 MIN
Dist - HRMC

Surviving life transitions 26 MIN
VHS
Surviving series
Color (H C G A R)
$24.95 purchase, $10.00 rental _ #35 - 87188 - 460
Features Clayton Barbeau in a discussion of life transitions. Acknowledges the fear of the unknown that makes change feel threatening. Offers stories and strategies with insights for accepting change.
Religion and Philosophy
Dist - APH **Prod** - FRACOC

Surviving Lifestyle Drugs 45 MIN
VHS
Color (J)
Presents a comprehensive overview of the most widely used drugs in America, including caffeine, nicotine, over the counter drugs, Valium, alcohol, and marijuana. Uses a non judgmental approach to help students assess the nature, effects, and risks of these drugs. Show them how to weigh potential benefits against possible negative consequences.
Guidance and Counseling; Health and Safety; Psychology
Dist - HRMC **Prod** - HRMC 1982

Surviving lifestyle drugs series
Alcohol and marijuana
Caffeine and nicotine
Over-the-counter drugs and valium
Dist - IBIS

Surviving loneliness 24 MIN
VHS
Surviving series
Color (H C G A R)
$24.95 purchase, $10.00 rental _ #35 - 87186 - 460
Features Clayton Barbeau in a discussion of loneliness. Suggests strategies for counteracting loneliness.
Religion and Philosophy
Dist - APH **Prod** - FRACOC

Surviving office politics - everyone's crazy except you 25 MIN
VHS
Basics of job success series
Color (J H C G)
$98.00 purchase _ #CDJOB504V
Shows that office politics are an inevitable part of the work world. Identifies specific destructive office political behaviors - gossip, back - stabbing and game playing. Illustrates the consequences - both long term and short term - from office politicking to show the price attached to counterproductive behaviors. Emphasizes good communication skills and honest intentions and the importance of understanding one's own values. Includes reproducible worksheets. Part of a three - part series on job success.
Business and Economics; Guidance and Counseling; Psychology; Social Science
Dist - CAMV

Surviving rejection and failure 34 MIN
VHS
Surviving series
Color (H C G A R)
$24.95 purchase, $10.00 rental _ #35 - 87233 - 460
Features Clayton Barbeau in a discussion of rejection and failure. Suggests that self - rejection is the source of the fear of rejection. Proposes that an awareness of one's strengths will aid in dealing with fears of rejection.
Health and Safety; Religion and Philosophy
Dist - APH **Prod** - FRACOC

Surviving series
Features Clayton Barbeau in an eight - part series which considers how to survive various difficulties in life. Deals with such topics as depression, loneliness, broken relationships, anger and others.
Surviving anger - yours and others 32 MIN
Surviving broken relationships 21 MIN
Surviving depression 26 MIN
Surviving difficult people 40 MIN
Surviving grief 24 MIN
Surviving life transitions 26 MIN
Surviving loneliness 24 MIN
Surviving rejection and failure 34 MIN
Surviving series 227 MIN
Dist - APH **Prod** - FRACOC

Surviving sexual abuse 27 MIN
VHS
Color (J H C G)
$295.00 purchase, $40.00 rental _ #37552
Features two women and two men who tell of being abused as children and adolescents. Relates how they survived their trauma to lead healthy, productive lives. Encourages viewers to confront and discuss their experiences and to seek outside help in working through their bitterness, anger and guilt. Includes facilitator's guide. Produced by Show Place Video Productions.
Health and Safety; Sociology
Dist - UCEMC

Surviving the big one - how to prepare for a major earthquake - Como sobrevivir un gran terremoto 30 MIN
VHS
Color; CC (J H G) (SPANISH)
$29.95 purchase _ #MCV4739, #MCV4740
Presents a detailed program showing how to prepare for a major earthquake. Demonstrates how preparation can protect individuals and their property. Lists correct supplies to store at work and home. Shows how to 'safety proof' homes. Answers questions such as, 'What if I'm in a car, a tall building or in a crowded theater.' Illustrates how to deal with damaged utilities such as water and gas lines.
History - World
Dist - MADERA **Prod** - MADERA

Surviving the changing workplace 15 MIN
VHS
Managing job stress series
Color (COR)
$89.00 purchase _ #WSC/WPA
Discusses the stress that can arise from any type of change, even positive change. Presents three skills to help employees adapt to change with flexibility and success. Part of a six - part series.
Guidance and Counseling; Psychology
Dist - ADVANM

Surviving the changing workplace 20 MIN
VHS
Managing job stress series
Color (A COR IND PRO)
$95.00 purchase _ #VJSV5
Takes aim at a problem faced by almost everyone - work-related stress. Addresses various work-environment issues that affect everyone from blue-collar workers to executives to volunteers. Outlines how change of any kind can create stress in the workplace. Teaches three skills that help employees increase their flexibility. Includes leader guide and five participant guides. Part five of a six-part series.
Psychology
Dist - WHLPSN

Surviving the checkout - wise food buying
VHS
Consumer skills series
Color (J H G)
$79.95 purchase _ #CCV702
Shows how to make wise food buying decisions through planning menus for a week and using newspaper ads and the concept of food groups as guides. Looks at the selection of fresh foods, reading labels, comparing brands and unit prices, the open dating of products, USDA grading of meats, how to buy meats and use meat substitutes and extenders. Teaches awareness of marketing techniques which promote impulse buying. Part of a series on consumer skills.
Health and Safety; Home Economics; Social Science
Dist - CADESF **Prod** - CADESF

Surviving the Cold 12 MIN
16mm / U-matic / VHS
Many Worlds of Nature Series
Color (I)
Explores hibernation, migration and other methods used by various animals to survive cold winter weather.
Science - Natural
Dist - CORF **Prod** - SCRESC

Surviving the cold 20 MIN
VHS
Color (J H C A)
$225.00 purchase
Uses reenactments to demonstrate survival techniques for cold weather conditions, including home preparation, travel planning and blizzard survival. Focuses on how to identify and treat hypothermia. Includes discussion guide.
Health and Safety
Dist - PFP **Prod** - AMRC

Surviving with Cancer 19 MIN
U-matic / VHS
Color (C)
$249.00, $149.00 purchase _ #AD - 2050
Examines the special needs of cancer patients. Considers their relationships to others and the possible connections between emotions and the immune response to cancer and the ways in which the mind can affect the course of cancer treatment.
Health and Safety; Psychology
Dist - FOTH **Prod** - FOTH

Surviving your parents divorce - it's never easy
VHS
Color (I J H)

$79.95 purchase _ #CCP0150V
Provides specific coping skills for adolescents caught up in the middle of the separation - divorce process. Features young adults who share their experiences of shock and anger, feelings of divided loyalties, confusions about the legal issues, hardships of new financial problems and increased responsibilities. Covers the skills of realizing the validity of one's feelings; keeping lines of communication open with both parents without being caught in the middle; understanding the choices and rights of children of divorcing parents; where and how to look for help; how to take care of oneself; how to look at the bright side of a confusing and trying experience.
Guidance and Counseling; Sociology
Dist - CAMV **Prod** - CAMV 1993

Survivor 30 MIN
U-matic / VHS
B&W
Presents the memories, stories and experiences, past and present, of Henry Martinson, a 97 - year - old one - time farmer, labor organizer, Socialist Party official, writer, editor, poet and Labor Commissioner of North Dakota.
Biography; History - United States
Dist - NFPS **Prod** - NFPS

The Survivor symphony 15 MIN
VHS / U-matic
Color (G)
$250.00 purchase, $100.00 rental
Provides inspiration from survivors of cancer who act as role models. Offers practical advice to make each step of the battle with cancer a little bit easier. Debunks commonly held myths about cancer, explores the role of family members and deals with the often overlooked problems of survivors. Produced by CanSurvivors, Inc.
Health and Safety; Psychology
Dist - BAXMED

Survivors 30 MIN
U-matic / VHS
Japanese American experience in World War II series
Color (G)
$199.00 purchase, $50.00 rental
Presents the first English language film in which atomic bomb survivors speak for themselves about what happened on the day of the bombing. Exposes the political struggles of 20 Japanese Americans who have either returned or immigrated to the United States and continue to face physical, psychological and social problems. Produced and directed by Steven Okazaki.
History - World; Sociology
Dist - CROCUR

Survivors 60 MIN
VHS
Australian ark series
Color (G)
$19.95 purchase _ #S02062
Portrays Australia's flora and fauna.
Geography - World; Science - Natural
Dist - UILL

Survivors 28 MIN
VHS
Living with spinal cord injury series
Color (G)
$195.00 purchase, $100 rental _ #CE - 044
Explores the problems of growing old with a disability in part of a three - part series on spinal cord injuries.
Health and Safety
Dist - FANPRO **Prod** - CORBTB

The survivors 48 MIN
VHS
Color (C A H J)
$89.95 purchase _ #P11142
Introduces the many ecosystems of Australia, from rainforests to deserts, and focuses on animal adaptation to these changing environments. Features animals unique to Australia and investigates why certain animals have survived while others have not.
History - World; Science - Natural
Dist - CF

The Survivors 5 MIN
16mm
B&W
LC 75-703237
Presents a dramatic confrontation between the last man and woman left on earth after an atomic war. Shows that the woman has lost faith in humanity and sees no hope for any possible future generation.
Fine Arts; Psychology; Religion and Philosophy; Sociology
Dist - USC **Prod** - USC 1967

Survivors 54 MIN
VHS
Red empire series
Color (J H C G)
$19.98 purchase _ #FFO9612V
Discloses that victory in World War II is replaced by the Cold War. Reveals that the communists reject everything that is Western as decadent. Redefines truth as the radio and airplane are said to be invented by Russians, not Westerners, Soviets achieve the first space flight. Stalin dies and Krushchev takes over. Part of a seven - part series tracing Russian history from the fall of the Tsar and rise of Lenin, through World War I, the internal war for communism, the emergence of the brutal and ruthless Stalin, World War II, Krushchev, Brezhnev and Gorbachev.
Civics and Political Systems; History - World; Sociology
Dist - CAMV

Survivors 58 MIN
16mm
Color
Examines the physical, emotional and financial hardships which characterize the lives of over 1000 Japanese - Americans who were trapped in Japan during the war and suffered the tragedy of the atomic blasts.
History - United States; History - World; Sociology
Dist - FIRS **Prod** - FIRS

A Survivor's guide - the essay 11 MIN
VHS
Color (H C)
$150.00 purchase _ #6875
Presents a typical history essay on the conquest of Peru to illustrate the proper development of a student research paper. Includes development of a topic statement, time decisions, research, rough draft and final draft.
English Language; Literature and Drama
Dist - UCALG **Prod** - UCALG 1990

Survivor's guide to learning series

Concentration	15 MIN
Exam preparation	15 MIN
The Power of Questioning	15 MIN
Reading, note - taking and recall	15 MIN
Time Management	15 MIN

Dist - ACCESS

Survivors of the Holocaust 25 MIN
VHS / U-matic
Color & B&W (G)
$75.00 purchase _ #HVC - 735, #HHC - 735
Records the testimony of survivors of the Holocaust and their children. Intersperses photographs and film footage shot in concentration camps. Written and produced by Rich Newberg, filmed and edited by Dan Summerville.
Biography; History - World; Sociology
Dist - ADL **Prod** - ADL

Survivor's pride - building resiliency in youth at risk series

Independence	30 MIN
Initiative	30 MIN
Insight	30 MIN
An Introduction to resiliency	70 MIN
Relationships	30 MIN

Dist - SHENEL

Survivors series

Eagle's story	29 MIN
The Mahogany connections	29 MIN
The Mystery of the million seals	29 MIN
Roo's eye view	29 MIN
Seagull story	29 MIN
Tale of a plague	29 MIN
The Wolf saga	29 MIN

Dist - CORF

Survol De La Provence 7 MIN
16mm / U-matic / VHS
Chroniques De France Series
Color (H C A) (FRENCH)
LC 81-700760
A French language motion picture. Offers an overview of Provence, describing its literary and historical past.
Foreign Language; Geography - World
Dist - IFB **Prod** - ADPF 1980

Susan 60 MIN
VHS
Color (J G)
$72.00 purchase
Tells the story of Susan and her twin sister who were deported to Auschwitz as young children and, with other sets of twins, became victims of Dr Mengele's pseudo - medical experiments. Features Susan bearing witness to their ordeal; her sister perished ten days before liberation. Geared for junior high school students, this program's message is strong without being graphic. Written, directed and produced by Yael Katzir.
Fine Arts; History - World; Religion and Philosophy
Dist - NCJEWF

Susan 5 MIN
16mm
B&W
LC 76-703891
Demonstrates a classroom behavior counseling problem involving a quiet and withdrawn nine - year - old girl who becomes erratic and destructive when she is brought to school against her will by an insistent mother. Shows how the child is classified as mentally retarded and how she makes no friends among her peers.
Education; Psychology
Dist - USNAC **Prod** - HURRO 1971

Susan After the Sugar Harvest 27 MIN
16mm
Color (J)
LC 72-702844
Explains that Susan was disillusioned with life until she signed up to go to Cuba to help with the sugar harvest. Points out that she experienced a sense of profound closeness to her fellow workers as they labored together in the fields, cutting down sugar cane, sweating under the hot sun, working for a common purpose, with everyone sharing his joys, his food and his few possessions without considering himself to be better than the rest.
Agriculture; Geography - World; Guidance and Counseling; Sociology
Dist - RADIM **Prod** - ROBINP 1971

Susan and David 28 MIN
VHS / U-matic
Mutuality Series
Color
Shows a deeply caring couple in a celebration of unrepressed playful, nourishing sexuality. Reveals their feelings about making this film.
Health and Safety; Psychology
Dist - MMRC **Prod** - MMRC

Susan and Mrs Stanton 20 MIN
U-matic
Truly American Series
Color (I)
Offers information on Susan B Anthony and Elizabeth Cady Stanton.
Biography; Civics and Political Systems; History - World; Sociology
Dist - GPN **Prod** - WVIZTV 1979

Susan Gevirtz - 10 - 12 - 89 35 MIN
VHS / Cassette
Poetry Center reading series
Color (G)
$15.00, $45.00 purchase, $15.00 rental _ #859 - 670
Features the writer reading her works at the Poetry Center, San Francisco State University, with an introduction by Robert Gluck.
Literature and Drama
Dist - POETRY **Prod** - POETRY 1989

Susan Griffin - 5 - 15 - 75 30 MIN
VHS / Cassette
Poetry Center reading series
Color (G)
$15.00, $45.00 purchase, $15.00 rental _ #129 - 100
Features the writer reading her works including selections from Let Them Be Said and Woman And Nature at the Poetry Center, San Francisco State University.
Literature and Drama
Dist - POETRY **Prod** - POETRY 1975

Susan Griffin - 3 - 21 - 79 50 MIN
VHS / Cassette
Poetry Center reading series
Color (G)
$15.00, $45.00 purchase, $15.00 rental _ #335 - 279
Features the writer reading her works at the Poetry Center, San Francisco State University.
Literature and Drama
Dist - POETRY **Prod** - POETRY 1979

Susan Griffin - 2 - 15 - 90 40 MIN
VHS / Cassette
Poetry Center reading series
Color (G)
$15.00, $45.00 purchase, $15.00 rental _ #872 - 678
Features the writer reading her works including selections from Another Kind Of Waking; The Chorus Of Stones; Unremembered Country; and The Our Mother Poems at the Poetry Center, San Francisco State University, with an introduction by Robert Gluck and Mark Linenthal.
Literature and Drama
Dist - POETRY **Prod** - POETRY 1990

Susan Hansell - 11 - 17 - 88
VHS / Cassette
Poetry Center reading series
Color (G)
$15.00, $45.00 purchase, $15.00 rental _ #834 - 652
Features the writer performing Drop It and A Day In at the Poetry Center, San Francisco State University, with an introduction by Robert Gluck.
Literature and Drama
Dist - POETRY **Prod** - POETRY 1988

Susan Hill on Othello 25 MIN
VHS
Shakespeare in perspective series
Color (A)

PdS45 purchase _ Unavailable in USA
Films Susan Hill and her commentary on location and includes extracts of the Shakespeare play Othello. Challenges many of the more traditional interpretations of Shakespeare's works. Part of a series produced between 1978 and 1985.
Literature and Drama
Dist - BBCENE

Susan Mogul - Comedy as a Back Up 10 MIN
U-matic / VHS
B&W
Shows Susan Mogul preparing for failure at her art career.
Fine Arts
Dist - ARTINC **Prod** - ARTINC

Susan Mogul - Dressing Up 7 MIN
VHS / U-matic
B&W
Reveals the prices of garments.
Fine Arts
Dist - ARTINC **Prod** - ARTINC

Susan Mogul - Last Jew in America 9 MIN
VHS / U-matic
Color
Presents a lecture on Jewish schooling. Exposes certain entertainers.
Fine Arts; Sociology
Dist - ARTINC **Prod** - ARTINC

Susan Mogul - Take Off 10 MIN
VHS / U-matic
B&W
Presents a parody of Vito Acconci's Undertone. Discusses the history of a vibrator.
Fine Arts
Dist - ARTINC **Prod** - ARTINC

Susan Mogul - Waiting at the Soda Fountain 24 MIN
VHS / U-matic
Color
Tells about women's working process and men's authority to designate talent and control women's economic destiny.
Fine Arts; Sociology
Dist - ARTINC **Prod** - ARTINC

Susan Peterson, Artist - Potter 28 MIN
Videoreel / VT2
Wheels, Kilns and Clay Series
Color
Features Mrs Peterson describing certain ceramic processes for her classroom at the University of Southern California.
Fine Arts
Dist - PBS **Prod** - USC

Susan Rogers - Good Grief 22 MIN
U-matic / VHS
Color
Features a comedy about a young woman artist who dies, then returns home for a nostalgic look at her 'perfect' past.
Fine Arts
Dist - ARTINC **Prod** - ARTINC

Susan Sontag 30 MIN
VHS
Writer's workshop series
Color (G)
$59.95 purchase _ #WRWO - 111
Features writer Susan Sontag in a lecture and discussion at the University of South Carolina. Shows that Sontag has written in a wide variety of genres, including novels, essays, short stories, criticism and screenplays. Discusses her views on the essence of writing, her profession and the lack of financial security in writing as a profession.
Literature and Drama
Dist - PBS **Prod** - SCETVM 1987

Susan Sontag 15 MIN
VHS
Writer's workshop series
Color (C A T)
$69.95 purchase, $45.00 rental
Features Susan Sontag in a lecture and discussion of her work, held as part of a writing workshop series at the University of South Carolina. Hosted by author William Price Fox and introduced by George Plimpton. Part 11 of a 15 - part telecourse.
English Language; Literature and Drama
Dist - SCETV **Prod** - SCETV 1982

Susan Stanford Friedman - 4 - 13 - 85 90 MIN
VHS / Cassette
Poetry Center reading series
Color (G)
$15.00, $45.00 purchase, $15.00 rental _ #637 - 534
Presents the writer participating in a panel discussion on The Impact of Feminist Criticism on Contemporary Women's Writing at the Women Working in Literature Conference at the Poetry Center, San Francisco State University, with moderater Deborah Rosenfelt and panelists Sandra Gilbert and Frances Jaffer.
Literature and Drama; Sociology
Dist - POETRY **Prod** - POETRY 1985

Susan Starr 54 MIN
16mm
B&W (C A)
LC 70-714528
Follows three days in the life of Susan Starr, competitor in the finals of Dimitri Mitropoulos international piano competition. Shows her during the competition at the Metropolitan Opera House, backstage as her rivals perform and onstage as she performs.
Biography; Fine Arts
Dist - DIRECT **Prod** - DREW 1970

Susan through Corn 2 MIN
16mm
Color (C)
$115.00
Experimental film by Kathleen Laughlin.
Fine Arts
Dist - AFA **Prod** - AFA 1975

Susana 25 MIN
16mm / VHS
Color (G)
$500.00, $225.00 purchase, $75.00 rental
Considers the cultural context in which female, sexual and ethnic identity is forged. Looks at Susana who leaves her native Argentina for the US to live her life outside the strictures of Latin American cultural and family pressures. Examines racism, sexism and homophobia.
Geography - World; Psychology; Sociology
Dist - WMEN **Prod** - SUMU 1980

Susan's Image 15 MIN
VHS / U-matic
Chemical People Educational Modules Series
Color (J)
Explores how one's self image affects the decision - making process. Interviews young television stars and recovering drug and alcohol addicts.
Psychology; Sociology
Dist - CORF **Prod** - CORF

Susceptibility Testing 11 MIN
16mm
Color (PRO)
Describes the most commonly used antibiotic sensitivity tests, including the Kirby - Bauer or agar diffusion test, the tube dilution method and the agar dilution method.
Health and Safety; Science
Dist - LEDR **Prod** - ACYLLD 1974

Susceptible to kindness - Miss Evers' boys and the Tuskegee Syphilis Study 45 MIN
VHS
Color (G C)
$89.95 purchase
Examines ethical issues raised by the Tuskegee Study of Untreated Syphilis in the Negro Male - 1932 - 1972, conducted by the US Public Health Service to document long - term effects of syphilis. Reveals the subjects were originally gathered to receive free medical treatment, which they received for two years until the funding ran out. The Service continued to track the men's health hoping that funding would be restored - but the men were never told that the annual medical exams and tests they received were not treatment. In 1946, although penicillin was found to be a successful cure for syphilis, the men in the Tuskegee study were deliberately excluded. In 1972, a medical researcher brought media attention to the study, resulting in public outrage.
Health and Safety; History - United States; Religion and Philosophy; Sociology
Dist - CORNRS

Sushi
VHS
Cooking series
Color (G)
$29.95 purchase _ #IV - 045
Shows how to prepare sushi.
Home Economics
Dist - INCRSE **Prod** - INCRSE

Sushi at Home 40 MIN
VHS / U-matic
(C A)
$39.95 _ #IV500V
Demonstrates methods for preparing the low calorie, nutritional dish, sushi. An experienced cook guides the viewer through a variety of different dishes, including many kinds of seafood.
Home Economics
Dist - CAMV **Prod** - CAMV

Susie, the Little Blue Coupe 8 MIN
16mm / U-matic / VHS
Color (P I)
LC 72-700155
A story of the odyssey of Susie, a little coupe, from showroom, used - car lot and junkyard to her restoration as a hot rod.
Industrial and Technical Education; Literature and Drama; Social Science
Dist - CORF **Prod** - DISNEY 1971

Suspect, Suspicious, Suspicions, Emergency, Rattled, Rattle, Gurgled, Clanked, Hissed 10 MIN
U-matic
Readalong Three Series
Color (P)
Provides reading instruction for third grade students. Uses animation, humor, music, repetition and audience participation. Comes with teacher's guide and kit.
Education; English Language; Literature and Drama
Dist - TVOTAR **Prod** - TVOTAR 1977

Suspects and Witnesses, Pt 4 - Use of the Polygraph in Investigations 26 MIN
16mm
B&W (PRO)
LC 74-705733
Presents a pre - test interview with suspect, test examination procedure, analysis of polygraph indications and post - test interrogation of suspect.
Sociology
Dist - USNAC **Prod** - USA 1967

Suspended dreams - 6 50 MIN
VHS
Developing stories series
Color (H C G)
$150.00 purchase, $75.00 rental
Documents the effects of 16 years of civil war in Lebanon, once the intellectual, cultural and commercial center of the Arab world. Tells the story of four Beirut citizens from very different backgrounds as they struggle to rebuild their lives amid the chaos, broken buildings and unexploded mines of their once beautiful city. Also assesses the appalling impact of modern warfare on the environment and looks ahead to a new conflict in the making over of the Middle East's most precious commodity - water. A film by Mai Masri and Jean Chamoun for BBC Television. Part of a six - part series highlighting debates of the Earth Summit.
Civics and Political Systems; Fine Arts; History - World; Science - Natural
Dist - CANCIN **Prod** - BBCTV 1994

Suspended Monorail in Japan 24 MIN
16mm
Color
Explains that a suspended monorail system, seven kilometers in length, has been constructed in the fast growing Shonan - Enoshima residential area near Tokyo. Points out that this is the world's first monorail for practical purposes using the suspended type system, built to cope with the ever - increasing demand for commuter transportation in the vicinity. Shows how the project has been pushed forward without interfering with the everyday traffic and life of the people, and emphasizes safety of the monorail system.
Geography - World; Social Science
Dist - UNIJAP **Prod** - UNIJAP

Suspended Panel Installation 23 MIN
VHS
Ceilings Series
$39.95 purchase _ #DI - 127
Discusses installing suspended ceilings, including planning, repair, hanging the grid, tools and materials, and how to avoid common mistakes.
Industrial and Technical Education
Dist - CAREER **Prod** - CAREER

Suspension 9 MIN
16mm
Color
LC 77-702661
Presents an interpretation of a state of suspension through visual effects, dance, movement and sound.
Fine Arts; Industrial and Technical Education
Dist - CANFDC **Prod** - HUNNL 1974

The Suspension Bridge 26 MIN
16mm
Color (J)
Shows the many phases of suspension bridge construction with the skill of the bridgemen working hundreds of feet up with perfect precision and accuracy.
Business and Economics; Industrial and Technical Education; Science - Physical
Dist - USSC **Prod** - USSC 1955

Suspension Test 30 MIN
BETA / VHS
Last Chance Garage Series
Color
Shows how to test a car's suspension for cracks. Discusses choosing the right bolt. Looks at tire gauges. Features a Peugot station wagon.
Industrial and Technical Education
Dist - CORF **Prod** - WGBHTV

Suspicion 99 MIN
VHS
B&W; CC (G)
$19.95 purchase _ #2074
Tells about a woman who thinks her husband is trying to kill her. Stars Joan Fontaine, Cary Grant, Cedric Hardwicke, Nigel Bruce, Dame May Whitty and Heather Angel. Directed by A Hitchcock.
Fine Arts; Literature and Drama
Dist - APRESS

Suspicious circumstances 100 MIN
VHS
Color; PAL (H C G)
PdS45 purchase
Opens the laboratory door on the test - tube detectives who are expanding the frontiers of forensic science as they bring the guilty to justice. Presents four 25 - minute programs which follow real investigations from the scene of the crime to the lab. Watches as scientists reopen old casebooks on some of their most intriguing investigations. Contact distributor about availability outside the United Kingdom.
Civics and Political Systems; Sociology
Dist - ACADEM

The Suspicious Client 30 MIN
16mm
Psychiatric - Mental Health Nursing Series
Color (PRO)
LC 77-700134
Presents course instructors Grayce Sills and Doreen James Wise discussing the development of the suspicious client's pattern of behavior, as well as nursing activities aimed at establishing a trust relationship between the nurse and client. Presents brief sketches of nurse - client interactions illustrating the suspicious person's behavior and the responses of the nurse.
Health and Safety; Psychology
Dist - AJN **Prod** - AJN 1977

Suspicious person calls - an analysis of officers killed 17 MIN
VHS
Analysis of officers killed series
Color (PRO)
$295.00 purchase, $100.00 rental _ #8415
Offers reenactments of actual incidents and statistics to enhance officer survival when responding to suspicious person calls. Advises officers to obser from a safe position, confront individuals from cover and maintain a position of advantage over the suspects. Discusses the use of vests. Part of a series utilizing information provided by the Uniform Crime Reporting Section of the Federal Bureau of Investigation.
Civics and Political Systems; Social Science; Sociology
Dist - AIMS **Prod** - AIMS 1992

Sustainable agriculture 29 MIN
VHS
Color (G)
$89.00 purchase _ #6 - 070 - 105A
Discusses sustainable agriculture and its techniques for improving agricultural production. Shows how sustainable agriculture is efficient in the use of natural resources, is ecologically sound, economical, socially responsible and humane. Teaches concepts in improving soil fertility and nutrient cycling, maintaining biological diversity, cover crops and trap crops, integrating farm animals, compost and mulch, reducing soil erosion, conservation tillage techniques, pest management, crop rotation.
Agriculture
Dist - VEP **Prod** - VEP 1993

The Sustainable landscape - ecological design principles 32 MIN
VHS
Color (G)
$89.95 purchase _ #6 - 070 - 107A
Features a landscape designer who specializes in sustainability, a biologist, a wholesale plant grower, a developer, architects, an energy - resource consultant and an environmental engineer. Covers plant selection and grouping to promote water efficiency and micro - climate control, using natural growth patterns to reduce energy needs, landscape grading to promote groundwater recharge and discourage erosion and runoff, landscaping to enhance surrounding greenspace, harvesting the nutrient, energy and water resources of wastes for re - use in the landscape.
Agriculture; Science - Natural
Dist - VEP **Prod** - VEP 1993

Sustaining America's agriculture - High tech and horse sense 29 MIN
VHS / U-matic
Color (J H G)
$275.00, $295.00 purchase, $60.00 rental
Provides case studies throughout American farmlands that show profit with farming systems that conserve land for future generations. Looks at economically and ecologically sound approaches to farming. Shows how careful management and an understanding of nature can minimize impact and maximize yield.
Agriculture; Social Science
Dist - NDIM **Prod** - EPA 1992

Susumu Tonegawa - the key to the immune system 17 MIN
VHS
Nobel prize series - biology
Color (J H C)
$49.00 purchase _ #2320 - SK
Features Susumu Tonegawa, Nobel Prize winner, whose work has increased understanding of the workings of the immune system. Suggests that Tonegawa's discoveries have paved the way for being able to manipulate immune system processes. Includes student notebook and teacher resource book, with additional student workbooks available at an extra charge.
Education; Health and Safety; History - World; Sociology
Dist - SUNCOM

Sutherland, Horne, Bonynge Gala Concert 142 MIN
VHS
Color (G)
$39.95 purchase _ #1214
Records the Sydney Opera House gala which hosted two of the best of 'bel canto,' Joan Sutherland and Marilyn Horne with Richard Bonynge conducting the Elizabethan Symphony Orchestra on June 12, 1985. Includes areas and duets from 'Norma,' 'Semiramide,' 'Lakme' and 'Les Contes D'Hoffman' for the Australian Opera production.
Fine Arts; Geography - World
Dist - KULTUR

The Sutton Hoo Ship Burial 25 MIN
16mm
Color
Provides a day - to - day account of the 1939 discovery and excavation of a ship buried at the site of Sutton Hoo in Sussex 1,300 years ago.
Science - Physical; Social Science
Dist - UTORMC **Prod** - UTORMC 1972

Suture and Staple Removal 11 MIN
U-matic / VHS
Basic Clinical Skills Series
Color (PRO)
Demostrates the removal of running stitches, interrupted stitches and staples.
Health and Safety; Science
Dist - HSCIC **Prod** - HSCIC 1984

Sutures and Suture Books 4 MIN
BETA / VHS
Color
Explains how to prepare sutures, suture books and how to pass sutures.
Health and Safety
Dist - RMIBHF **Prod** - RMIBHF

Sutures, Needles and Skin Closure Materials 21 MIN
U-matic / VHS / 16mm
Color (PRO)
LC 72-702342
Introduces the types, uses and preparation of sutures, needles and skin closure materials.
Health and Safety; Science
Dist - FEIL **Prod** - CWRU 1971

Suwannee Adventure 14 MIN
16mm
Color
Presents a canoe trip down the historic Suwannee River through north Florida to the Gulf of Mexico.
Geography - United States; Physical Education and Recreation
Dist - FLADC **Prod** - FLADC

Suzhou 28 MIN
U-matic / VHS / 16mm
Cities in China Series
Color (J)
LC 82-700345
Explores the Chinese urban experience, past and present. Focuses on the historical sites, scenery and culture in Suzhou, China, and observes the activities of its modern residents.
Geography - World; History - World; Sociology
Dist - UCEMC **Prod** - YUNGLI 1981

Suzuki Violin Concert with - Carolyn Sakura Keen 50 MIN
U-matic
Color (J C)
Shows Miss Keen, 14 years old, perform a varied program of works by Kreisler, Joplin, Saintsaens, Eccles, Ross, Bartok and Schubert. She is joined in a duo by her Suzuki violin techer, Dr Theodore Brunson, music professor at San Diego State University.
Fine Arts
Dist - SDSC **Prod** - SDSC 1979

Suzuki Violin Concert with - Frank Almond III 46 MIN
U-matic
Color (J C)
Shows Frank Almond, 16 years old, perform 'Rondo' by Mozard, 'Sonata for violin Solo, Opus 115' by Prokofiev, 'Sonate' by Ravel and 'The Round of Goblins' by Bazzini.
Fine Arts
Dist - SDSC **Prod** - SDSC 1980

Suzuki Violin Concert with - Laura Caballero 51 MIN
U-matic
Color (J C)
Shows Ms Caballero, 16 years old, perform a program of works by Back, Schubert, Wientawski, Mendelssohn, Kreisler and Bartok. She is a student of Dr Theodore Brunson, professor of music and director of the Suzuki String Program at San Diego State University.
Fine Arts
Dist - SDSC **Prod** - SDSC 1979

Suzuki Violin Concert with - Paul Manaster 28 MIN
U-matic
Color (J C)
Shows Paul Manaster, an 18 year old San Diego State University music student perform 'Poerne, Opus 25' by Ernest Chausson, accompanied by Janie Prim, and 'Sonata in D' for solo violin by Sergei Prokofiev.
Fine Arts
Dist - SDSC **Prod** - SDSC 1984

Suzuki Violin Concert with - Tim Dresselhaus 39 MIN
U-matic
Color (J C)
Shows Tim Dresselhaus, 18 years old, perform 'Partita #3 in E Major' by Copland - 'Concerto in G Minor' by Max Bruch and is joined by Dr Theodore Brunson, his Suzuki instructor at SDSU, in 'Duo' by Mihaud.
Fine Arts
Dist - SDSC **Prod** - SDSC 1980

Suzu's Story 58 MIN
VHS
Color (S)
$79.00 purchase _ #366 - 9032
Tells the story of Suzi Lovegrove who died of AIDS at the age of 31. Documents her last months as she struggled against the disease and the prejudice it invokes. Soon after the birth of their son Troy, Suzi and her husband Vince learned that she had contracted AIDS and passed it on to their son.
Civics and Political Systems; Health and Safety; Psychology; Sociology
Dist - FI **Prod** - TWCF 1988

Suzy's Test - Max's Story - Mrs Mulch's Story 15 MIN
VHS / U-matic
Clyde Frog Show Series
Color (P)
Presents stories presented by Muppet - like Clyde Frog presenting stories emphasizing positive self - images, feelings of optimism and self - confidence.
Psychology
Dist - GPN **Prod** - MAETEL 1977

Suzy's war 24 MIN
VHS / U-matic
Young people's specials series
Color
Relates the story of a ghetto child who fights back against the fear and violence that rules her street in an attempt to make her neighborhood a better place to live.
Fine Arts; Sociology
Dist - MULTPP **Prod** - MULTPP

Svadba - a Balkan Wedding 28 MIN
16mm
Color
_ #106C 0178 693N
Geography - World
Dist - CFLMDC **Prod** - NFBC 1978

The Svea - Newport Incident 3 MIN
16mm

B&W
LC FIE52-950
Shows the collision of the SVEA and the Newport and describes the causes of the accident.
Civics and Political Systems; Health and Safety; History - United States; Social Science
Dist - USNAC **Prod** - USN 1943

Svengali 45 MIN
16mm
Movies - Our Modern Art Series
B&W
Features John Barrymore as Svengali, a man who tries to shape and remold his female subject, Trilby.
Fine Arts
Dist - STRFLS **Prod** - SPCTRA 1933

Svengali 80 MIN
16mm
B&W
Stars John Barrymore, Marian Marsh and Donald Crisp in Du Maurier's story about Svengali's hypnotic powers over the girl who calls herself Trilby.
Fine Arts
Dist - KITPAR **Prod** - WB 1931

Svigna
CD-ROM
Color (G A)
$99.00 purchase _ #1571
Combines the music, sounds and sights of tropical Zimbabwe - over 70 mammals, over 200 insects, over 150 birds, over 75 national parks and safari areas, and more from the Encyclopaedia of Zimbabwe. For Macintosh Plus, SE and II computers. Requires at least one M of RAM, one floppy disk drive, and an Apple compatible CD - ROM drive.
Geography - World; Science - Natural
Dist - BEP

Swaco Super Choke 20 MIN
U-matic / Slide / VHS / 16mm
Color (IND A PRO)
$150.00 purchase _ #11.1053, $160.00 purchase _ #51.1053
Introduces the remote - controlled, adjustable choke made by Dresser Swaco and looks at the special advantages of its design and its function in general well - killing procedures.
Industrial and Technical Education; Social Science
Dist - UTEXPE **Prod** - UTEXPE 1981

Swaco Vacuum Degasser 19 MIN
U-matic / VHS
Color (A PRO IND)
$160.00 purchase _ #11.1054, $170.00 purchase _ #51.1054
Covers the purpose, operation, installation and maintenance of the Dresser Swaco vacuum tank degasser.
Industrial and Technical Education; Social Science
Dist - UTEXPE **Prod** - UTEXPE 1980

Swag 26 MIN
16mm
B&W
LC 75-700326
A drama about a tough boy from the city streets who is temporarily lured away from his usual haunts by the attractions of an older woman.
Literature and Drama; Sociology
Dist - POSTMN **Prod** - POSTMN 1974

Swaging Cable Terminals 12 MIN
16mm
B&W
LC FIE52-267
Depicts how to measure and mark the cable accurately, set up the swaging machine, check the terminal after swaging and remove, clean and reassemble the parts of the machine.
Industrial and Technical Education
Dist - USNAC **Prod** - USOE 1944

The Swallow 11 MIN
VHS / 16mm / U-matic
Animal Families Series
Color (K P I)
$275, $195, $225 purchase _ #B415
Offers a close up view of a swallow family nesting in the rafters of a barn. Follows the early development of swallow chicks as both mother and father take turns nourishing them and preparing them for the day when they will take their first flight.
Science - Natural
Dist - BARR **Prod** - BARR 1986

Swallows 3 MIN
16mm
Of all Things Series
Color (P I)
Discusses the birds known as swallows.
Science - Natural
Dist - AVED **Prod** - BAILYL

Swallows 15 MIN
16mm / U-matic / VHS
Color (I J H)
Covers the life history of swallows including nest building, incubation, feeding the young, foraging flights, leaving the nest and autumn migration.
Science - Natural
Dist - VIEWTH **Prod** - GATEEF

Swallows, crows, chickadees - Volume 4 60 MIN
VHS
Audubon society videoguides to the birds of North America series
Color (G)
$29.95 purchase
Combines live footage and color photography in an Audubon Society bird watching program. Focuses on swallows, crows, chickadees, and several other bird types. Uses bird sights and sounds, visual graphics, and maps to aid in the identification of bird types. Narrated by Michael Godfrey.
Science - Natural
Dist - PBS **Prod** - WNETTV

The Swallowtail Butterfly 11 MIN
U-matic / VHS / 16mm
Animal Families Series
Color (K P I)
$275, $195, $225 purchase _ #B421
Follows the development of a swallowtail butterfly from egg to caterpillar to butterfly.
Science - Natural
Dist - BARR **Prod** - BARR 1986

Swami Chidananda 60 MIN
VHS / U-matic
Color
Introduces Swami Chidananda giving a talk about divine origins, divine path and ultimate goal.
Religion and Philosophy
Dist - IYOGA **Prod** - IYOGA

Swami Chidananda 28 MIN
U-matic / VHS / BETA
Faces of India series
Color; NTSC; PAL; SECAM (J H C G)
PdS58
Visits a yogi from Rishikesh. Follows the camera into his home where it becomes a part of his environment. Part of a series of portraits on film presenting a cross section of characters from real life.
History - World
Dist - VIEWTH

Swami Karunananda 28 MIN
U-matic / VHS / BETA
India called them series
Color; NTSC; PAL; SECAM (J H C G)
PdS58
Visits a Holy Man who migrated to India from Australia because of his interest in the science and philosophy of yoga. Includes sequences on the asanas - postures - and kriyas - cleansing rituals - of yoga. Part of a series on people who have moved to India to study yoga, including rare sequences on the asanas and kriyas, as well as scientific examination of the claims made about feats such as Bhugarbha Samadhi - live burial.
History - World; Religion and Philosophy
Dist - VIEWTH **Prod** - ABBAS 1967

Swami Satchidananda 2 MIN
VHS / Cassette
Mono; Color
Covers a two - part lecture by Sri Swami Satchidananda on himself, life and philosophy.
Psychology; Religion and Philosophy
Dist - IYOGA **Prod** - IYOGA

Swami Sevananda 28 MIN
U-matic / VHS / BETA
India called them series
Color; NTSC; PAL; SECAM (J H C G)
PdS58
Visits the 'Lady Swami' who migrated to India from England because of her interest in the science and philosophy of yoga. Includes sequences on the asanas - postures - and kriyas - cleansing rituals - of yoga. Part of a series on people who have moved to India to study yoga, including rare sequences on the asanas and kriyas, as well as scientific examination of the claims made about feats such as Bhugarbha Samadhi - live burial.
History - World; Religion and Philosophy
Dist - VIEWTH **Prod** - ABBAS 1967

Swami Sivananda
VHS
Color
Includes teachings of the Swami transferred from 16mm film without sound, and a Buddhist festival in Sri Lanka.
Education; Religion and Philosophy
Dist - IYOGA **Prod** - IYOGA

Swamiji in India - Part 3 60 MIN
VHS
Color
Education; Religion and Philosophy
Dist - IYOGA **Prod** - IYOGA 1983

Swamiji in India - Parts 1 and 2 120 MIN
VHS
Color
Education; Religion and Philosophy
Dist - IYOGA **Prod** - IYOGA 1983

Swami's Children 50 MIN
U-matic / VHS
B&W
Documents the dynamic and positive results people receive through their practice of Yoga.
Religion and Philosophy
Dist - IYOGA **Prod** - CBSTV

Swamp 33 MIN
VHS
Color (G)
$75.00 purchase
Uses the soap opera format to play with structures and expectations of the family melodrama. Features enthusiastic overacting and a predictably convoluted plot to set the scene for a tale of submerged connections, masked relationships and disguised identities, lurid intrigue, threatened morality and endless double - crosses.
Fine Arts; Literature and Drama; Psychology; Sociology
Dist - CANCIN **Prod** - CHILDA 1991

Swamp Critters 26 MIN
16mm
Color
Looks at the habits of such animals as the deer, otter and egret which populate America's southern swamps.
Science - Natural
Dist - STOUFP **Prod** - STOUFP 1982

The Swamp Dwellers 40 MIN
U-matic / VHS / 16mm
B&W (A)
LC 76-709822
Presents a drama which deals with the disillusionment and isolation felt by Africans who can no longer identify with the staid tribalism of the past or with the increased changes brought on by industrial and economic development.
Geography - World; Psychology; Sociology
Dist - PHENIX **Prod** - DUERD 1970

A Swamp Ecosystem 25 MIN
U-matic / VHS / 16mm
Color (J)
Looks at the ecosystem of the largest freshwater swamp in North America, the Okefenokee Swamp. Views its inhabitants, such as alligators and giant carnivorous pitcher plants.
Science - Natural
Dist - NGS **Prod** - NGS 1983

Swamp Things 23 MIN
VHS / U-matic
Color
Explores the mysterious waters of the Everglades. Shows underneath the surface and a host of creatures who have adapted to a world that rises and falls from season to season.
Geography - United States; Science - Natural
Dist - NWLDPR **Prod** - NWLDPR

The Swampdwellers 40 MIN
U-matic / VHS / 16mm
B&W (J H A)
LC 81-700945
Features a young African who returns to his village and discovers that he has grown too sophisticated to accept his parent's beliefs. Tells how, disillusioned also by urban life, he is caught between two conflicting cultures, unable to identify with either.
Fine Arts; Geography - World; Psychology
Dist - PHENIX **Prod** - SOYNKA 1973

The Swan
U-matic / VHS
Ice Carving Series
Color
Fine Arts; Industrial and Technical Education
Dist - CULINA **Prod** - CULINA

The Swan 11 MIN
VHS / 16mm / U-matic
Animal Families Series
Color (K P I)
$275, $195, $25 purchase _ #B408
Teaches students all about the swan. Photographs a flock of swans as they feed and frolic in their winter home which is a fresh water lake. Explains the life cycle of swans and includes film footage of swans in flight.

Science - Natural
Dist - BARR **Prod** - BARR 1986

Swan challenge 30 MIN
VHS
Business matters series
Color (A)
PdS65 purchase
Focuses on Polar explorer Robert Swan who believes that the teamwork, leadership and survival skills he acquired as an explorer can be applied to the business world. Watches as three executives accept his challenge to climb Snowdon.
Business and Economics; Guidance and Counseling; Psychology
Dist - BBCENE

Swan Ganz Cathete - the Internal Jugular Approach 22 MIN
U-matic / VHS
Color (PRO)
Describes the technique for inserting a catheter through the jugular vein and heart into the pulmonary artery to monitor hemo - dynamic parameters.
Health and Safety
Dist - WFP **Prod** - WFP

Swan - Ganz Pacing TD Catheter 12 MIN
VHS / U-matic
Color (PRO)
Shows Swan - Ganz pacing TD catheter.
Health and Safety
Dist - WFP **Prod** - WFP

Swan Lake 82 MIN
VHS
Color; Hi-fi; Dolby stereo (G)
$39.95 purchase _ #1104
Presents a Kirov Ballet production of Swan Lake based on the Petipa - Ivanov productions. Stars John Markovsky and Yelena Yevteyeva.
Fine Arts; Geography - World
Dist - KULTUR **Prod** - KULTUR

Swan Lake 140 MIN
VHS
Color (S)
$39.95 purchase _ #623 - 9257
Presents Natalia Makarova as Odette and Anthony Dowell as Prince Sigfried in the Royal Ballet production of 'Swan Lake' by Tchaikovsky. Features choreography by Marius Petipa, complemented by additions from Rudolf Nureyev and Frederick Ashton.
Fine Arts; Geography - World; Physical Education and Recreation
Dist - FI **Prod** - NVIDC 1986
UILL

Swan Lake - London Festival Ballet 116 MIN
VHS
Color (G)
$39.95 purchase _ #SWA06
Presents the London Festival Ballet version of Swan Lake by Tchaikovsky. Stars Peter Schaufuss and Evelyn Hart, with choreography by Natalia Makarova.
Fine Arts
Dist - HOMVIS **Prod** - RMART 1990

Swan Lake - Maya Plisetskaya 81 MIN
VHS
Color (G)
Features prima ballerina Maya Plisetskaya dancing the roles of Odette and Odile in the classical ballet Swan Lake. Shows the performance at the Bolshoi Theatre with the Bolshoi Ballet.
Fine Arts
Dist - KULTUR **Prod** - VAI 1957
VAI
UILL

Swan Lake, Minnesota 60 MIN
U-matic / VHS
Color
Fine Arts
Dist - ABCLR **Prod** - ABCLR

Swan Lake - starring Nina Ananiashvili 132 MIN
VHS
Color (G)
$24.95 purchase_#1365
Presents ballet star Nina Ananiashvili, making her video debut with the Russian State Perm Ballet, in Swan Lake. Stars also Aleksei Fadeyetchev in performance.
Fine Arts
Dist - KULTUR

Swan song 104 MIN
VHS
Color (G) (MANDARIN WITH ENGLISH SUBTITLES)
$45.00 purchase _ #5019B
Presents a movie produced in the People's Republic of China.
Fine Arts
Dist - CHTSUI

The Swarming hordes 58 MIN
U-matic / VHS
Life on Earth series
Color (J)
LC 82-706676
Describes how successfully insects have developed through eons of evolution. Shows examples of moulting, metamorphosis, camouflage and social cooperation as seen in termite colonies, beehives and among army ants.
Science - Natural
Dist - FI **Prod** - BBCTV 1981

The Swarming Hordes - Pt 9 30 MIN
16mm
Life on Earth series
Color (J)
$495.00 purchase _ #865 - 9030
Blends scientific data with breathtaking wildlife photography to tell the story of the development of life. Features wildlife expert David Attenborough as host. Part 9 of 27 parts, 'The Swarming Hordes' examines the explosive proliferation of life forms immediately after the appearance of flowering plants.
Science; Science - Natural; Science - Physical
Dist - FI **Prod** - BBCTV 1981

Swarming in Honey Bees 8 MIN
16mm
Color
LC FIA66-1430
Shows views of honey bees swarming about the captive queen bee, describing how and why they periodically swarm and discussing what scientists are learning through research about the swarming of bees.
Science; Science - Natural
Dist - CORNRS **Prod** - NYSCAG 1964

The Swashbucklers 28 MIN
16mm
Hollywood and the Stars Series
B&W
LC 76-702001
A history of adventure films with colorful heroes from the early silents to the present. Scenes from the mark of Zorro, Sea Hawk, and the Charge of the Light Brigade are shown as well as clips of such stars as Doublas Fairbanks Sr and Errol Flynn.
Fine Arts
Dist - WOLPER **Prod** - WOLPER 1964

Swayze dancing 60 MIN
VHS
Color (G A)
$19.95 purchase
Features the Swayze family - Patsy Swayze, her son Patrick, his wife Lisa, and sister Bambi - in an instructional dance program. Teaches viewers how to 'dirty dance' like the best.
Fine Arts
Dist - PBS **Prod** - WNETTV

Swb 11 MIN
16mm
Color (C A) (FRENCH (ENGLISH SUBTITLES))
A French language film. Tells the story of a modern photographer who searches for a girl to replace his lost model. Includes English subtitles.
Foreign Language; Literature and Drama
Dist - UWFKD **Prod** - UWFKD

Sweat and Steel 16 MIN
16mm
Color (H C A)
LC 78-701622
Introduces the sport of bodybuilding, showing scenes of different bodybuilders going through their workouts at Gold's Gym. Traces the progress of one amateur as he prepares for and competes in a bodybuilding contest.
Physical Education and Recreation
Dist - USC **Prod** - USC 1978

The Sweat of the Sun 52 MIN
U-matic / 16mm / VHS
Tribal Eye Series
Color (H C A)
LC 79-707114; 77-701590
Visits ancient sites of the Incas and Aztecs and examines gold artifacts that escaped the pillaging of the Spanish conquerors. Discusses the significance of these objects and describes how they were used by Aztec and Inca priests in practical and ritual fashion.
Fine Arts; Geography - World; History - World; Social Science; Sociology
Dist - TIMLIF **Prod** - BBCTV 1976

Sweat of the sun - tears of the moon series 360 MIN
VHS
Sweat of the sun - tears of the moon series
Color (J H C G)
$1395.00 purchase
Presents a 12 - part series hosted by Jack Pizzey and traveling to seven countries in South America. Travels to Bolivia, Chile, Peru, Brazil, Ecuador, Colombia and Argentina, exploring the role of tyranny and the Roman Catholic Church in the history of South America.
Civics and Political Systems; Geography - World; History - World; Religion and Philosophy
Dist - LANDMK **Prod** - LANDMK 1986

Sweat Testing for Cystic Fibrosis of the Pancreas 10 MIN
U-matic / VHS
Color (PRO)
Demonstrates the pilocarpine iontophoretic method of performing a sweat test for cystic fibrosis of the pancreas.
Health and Safety; Science - Natural
Dist - HSCIC **Prod** - HSCIC 1981

The Sweater - a Childhood Recollection by Roch Carrier 10 MIN
16mm
Color (I)
LC 81-701528
Presents Roch Carrier recalling a painful incident of having his favorite hockey sweater, which was like those worn by the Montreal Canadians, mistakenly replaced by a sweater like those of their archrivals.
Biography; Literature and Drama
Dist - NFBC **Prod** - NFBC 1981

Sweatin' to the oldies - 2 60 MIN
VHS
Color (G)
$39.95 purchase _ #GHM002V
Features Richard Simmons and old time musical favorites Locomotion, Big Girls Don't Cry, Jailhouse Rock, My Boyfriend's Back and more.
Fine Arts; Physical Education and Recreation
Dist - CAMV

Sweatin' to the oldies - 3 60 MIN
VHS
Color (G)
$39.95 purchase _ #GHM003V
Features Richard Simmons and old time musical favorites The Name Game, California Dreaming, Gimme Some Lovin', Born to Be Wild and more.
Fine Arts; Physical Education and Recreation
Dist - CAMV

Sweatin' to the oldies - 4 60 MIN
VHS
Color (G)
$39.95 purchase _ #GHM005V
Features Richard Simmons and old time musical favorites Heatwave, Proud Mary, Devil With a Blue Dress, Mony Mony and more.
Fine Arts; Physical Education and Recreation
Dist - CAMV

Sweating Indian style 57 MIN
VHS
Color (G)
$75.00 rental, $275.00 purchase
Scrutinizes the appropriation of Native American traditions by non - Natives. Follows the New Age activities of a group of Californian women learning to construct a sweat lodge and perform their own ceremony. Raises important questions about the use of elements of Native culture out of context, apart from the complex realities of American Indian experience. Interviews with diverse Native women point out the problems inherent in this increasingly popular New Age phenomenon and its relationship to traditional forms of colonialism.
Fine Arts; Social Science; Sociology
Dist - WMEN **Prod** - SMITSU 1994

Sweden 29 MIN
Videoreel / VT2
International Cookbook Series
Color
Features home economist Joan Hood presenting a culinary tour of specialty dishes from around the world. Shows the preparation of Swedish dishes ranging from peasant cookery to continental cuisine.
Geography - World; Home Economics
Dist - PBS **Prod** - WMVSTV

Sweden 22 MIN
U-matic / VHS / 16mm
Modern Europe Series
Color (J H)
Shows how Swedes in different provinces lives and work. Looks at the political system of Sweden.
Geography - World; History - World
Dist - JOU **Prod** - JOU

Sweden 60 MIN
VHS
Traveloguer collection series

Color (I J H A)
$29.95 purchase _ #QC114V-S
Presents information about the historic past and the current status of Sweden, including information about the cities and the countryside. Shows famous landmarks, out-of-the way sites, struggles and hardships, victories and championships, and the legends of the region. Uses live-action footage and historical clips to show the geography, history, and culture. Includes 16 60-minute programs on northern, western, eastern, and southern Europe.
Geography - World
Dist - CAMV

Sweden 15 MIN
VHS
Color; PAL (P I J H)
Explains why Sweden has such a high standard of living and how the Swedes maintain such a status. Examines the country's geography and the Swedish people who have adjusted their way of life to the demands of the climate and physical features of Sweden, using fully the natural resources they have inherited.
Business and Economics; Geography - World; History - World; Home Economics; Social Science; Sociology
Dist - VIEWTH **Prod** - VIEWTH

Sweden 60 MIN
VHS
Traveloguer Northern Europe series
Color (J H C G)
$29.95 purchase _ #QC114V
Visits Sweden and its cities. Illustrates notable landmarks, special events in history and the legends that are part of Swedish culture. Part of a four part series on Northern Europe.
Geography - World
Dist - CAMV

Sweden 15 MIN
U-matic / VHS / 16mm
Color (I J A)
Emphasizes the social and economic geography of Sweden, observing the abundant natural resources and the adaptation of the people to climate and physical features. Shows how forest products, tourism, agriculture and shipbuilding help give this nation an excellent export market.
Geography - World; History - World
Dist - LUF **Prod** - LUF 1979

Sweden and Lovely 10 MIN
16mm
Color
Presents the young as well as the old in Sweden.
Geography - World
Dist - SWNTO **Prod** - SWNTO 1967

Sweden Film Shorts - Pt 4 - Sweden's Island Capital 5 MIN
16mm
Color
Portrays Stockholm, including a visit to the remains of the warship Vasa.
Geography - World
Dist - SWNTO **Prod** - SWNTO

Sweden Film Shorts - Pt 1 - Sweden's Sunny Arctic 5 MIN
16mm
Color
Portrays Sweden's Lappland, a delightful northern playground with plenty of opportunity for sightseeing, fishing and skiing.
Geography - World; Science - Natural; Sociology
Dist - SWNTO **Prod** - SWNTO

Sweden Film Shorts - Pt 3 - Sweden's Chateaux Country 5 MIN
16mm
Color
Portrays Sweden's chateaux country.
Geography - World; Science - Natural; Sociology
Dist - SWNTO **Prod** - SWNTO

Sweden Film Shorts - Pt 2 - Midsummer in Sweden's Dalarna 5 MIN
16mm
Color
Features Rattvik and Leksand with the original music of Dalarna and all the richness of the Dalecarlia fiddles.
Geography - World; Science - Natural; Sociology
Dist - SWNTO **Prod** - SWNTO

Sweden in World Affairs 30 MIN
16mm
Face of Sweden Series
B&W
Discusses Sweden's position as a neutral but not neutralist nation.
Geography - World; History - World
Dist - SIS **Prod** - SIS 1963

Sweden - Modern Land of the Vikings 31 MIN
16mm
Color (I)
LC FIA66-1395
Views historic Visby on the Isle of Gotland and describes its Viking memories. Shows the development of Sweden in terms of its industries, sport and people.
History - World
Dist - SWNTO **Prod** - CALTEX 1956

Sweden - Nordic treasure 53 MIN
VHS
Color (G)
$29.95 purchase _ #ST - IV1808
Strolls through Skansen. Roams from the fjords to the cosmopolitan culture of Stockholm. Lingers over a smorgasbord of smoked salmon, reindeer and herring. Visits the hushed forests and wild river of Lapland.
Geography - World
Dist - INSTRU

Sweden - Vikings Now Style 28 MIN
16mm / U-matic / VHS
Color (P)
LC 71-702233
Relates the history of Sweden to its oceanbound geography. Compares the old and new Stockholm, and its industries. Discusses the sources of income and the benefits of the modern welfare state. Includes views of Lappland, the university town of Uppsala, the Hanseatic town of Visby and the world - famous Milles gardens with its sculptures by Carl Milles.
Geography - World; History - World
Dist - HANDEL **Prod** - HANDEL 1969

Swedenborg, the Man who Had to Know 28 MIN
16mm
Color
LC 80-700077
Dramatizes key events in the life of Emanuel Swedenborg, including his breakthroughs in anatomy and brain research, his discovery of endocrine glands, his invention of an aircraft, and his assistance in founding the sciences of crystallography and metallurgy. Explores his religious and philosophical beliefs.
Biography; Science
Dist - MTP **Prod** - SWEDF 1978

Sweden's Forest Heritage 18 MIN
16mm
Color
Illustrates modern forestry in Sweden, showing timber and the transportation and treatment of the wood.
Agriculture; Geography - World; Science - Natural
Dist - AUDPLN **Prod** - ASI

The Swedes - corporate nomads 8 MIN
VHS
Columbus legacy series
Color (J H C G)
$40.00 purchase, $11.00 rental _ #12340
Investigates whether the continuous relocation required by the jobs of some Swedish people is creating a truly international citizen and how such people maintain their Swedish heritage in foreign lands. Provides an introduction to the Swedish influence in early Pennsylvania - before the arrival of William Penn. Part of a 15 - part series commemorating the 500th anniversary of Columbus' journeys to the Americas - journeys that brought together a constantly evolving collection of different ethnic groups and examining the contributions of 15 distinct groups who imprinted their heritage on the day - to - day life of Pennsylvania.
History - United States; Sociology
Dist - PSU **Prod** - WPSXTV 1992

Swedish Cinema Classica 40 MIN
16mm
B&W
Presents sequences from original films to portray the great period of Swedish silent cinema, the epoch of Victor Sjostrom and Mauritz Stiller.
Fine Arts; Geography - World
Dist - SIS **Prod** - SIS

A Swedish Couple Discuss Swedish Social Structures - Pt 1 6 MIN
U-matic / VHS
B&W
Discusses the family in Sweden with a Swedish couple, who characterize it as 'small, weak and often dissolving.' Reviews the family, noting demographic data, the divorce rate and the roles of both parents in the labor force and the family.
History - World; Sociology
Dist - UWISC **Prod** - UWISC 1975

A Swedish Couple Discuss Swedish Social Structures - Pt II 40 MIN
U-matic / VHS
B&W
Continues a discussion with a Swedish couple on the place of the Swedish woman in the labor force, marital relation - ships and children and daycare.
History - World; Sociology
Dist - UWISC **Prod** - UWISC 1975

Swedish Peasant Paintings 13 MIN
16mm
Color
Presents peasant paintings from the province of Dalarna.
Fine Arts; Geography - World; Sociology
Dist - AUDPLN **Prod** - ASI

Swedish Summer Day 20 MIN
16mm
Color
Portrays nature and animal life in the scenic summer surroundings of the Swedish countryside.
Geography - World; Science - Natural
Dist - SIS **Prod** - MTP 1959

Sweeney Todd 139 MIN
VHS
Color (H C A)
$39.95 purchase
Features Angela Lansbury and George Hern in a performance of 'Sweeney Todd' by Stephen Sondheim.
Fine Arts
Dist - PBS **Prod** - WNETTV

Sweep Charge Sealed System Charging Procedure 35 MIN
VHS / 35mm strip / U-matic
Color (IND)
Explains basic sealed system diagnosis and a revised sealed system charging procedure now recommended by Whirlpool for domestic refrigeration products.
Industrial and Technical Education
Dist - WHIRL **Prod** - WHIRL

The Sweep of time - humanity's past and potential future with visionary Barbara Marx Hubbard 60 MIN
VHS
Color (G)
$29.95 purchase _ #P46
Weaves a visionary view of human potential and discusses science, religion, healing, higher consciousness and the present day environmental crisis. Reveals Hubbard's assertion that the world is becoming more conscious at an accelerated rate.
Fine Arts; Literature and Drama; Religion and Philosophy
Dist - HP

The Sweepers of Squares - 1956 - 1970 60 MIN
VHS
Struggles For Poland Series
Color (G)
$59.95 purchase _ #STFP - 107
Focuses on the rule of Wladyslaw Gomulka as head of the Polish Communist Party from 1956 to 1970. Reveals that Gomulka allowed some degree of liberalization, but made no significant changes to the system. Shows that uprisings became commonplace, eventually leading to Gomulka's downfall.
History - World; Sociology
Dist - PBS **Prod** - WNETTV 1988

Sweepers of stairs - Volume 7 60 MIN
VHS
Struggles for Poland series
Color (H C A)
$59.95 purchase
Covers the history of Poland from 1956 to 1970. Focuses on the signs of Polish discontent with Communism, including street riots, workers' revolts, and the Soviet Union's sending of tanks to Poland, Hungary, and Czechoslovakia. Hosted and narrated by Roger Mudd.
History - World
Dist - PBS **Prod** - WNETTV

Sweet 15 110 MIN
VHS
WonderWorks Series
Color (P)
$29.95 purchase _ #766 - 9011
Tells the story of a Mexican - American teen who discovers that her father is an illegal immigrant. Stars Karla Montana, Tony Plana, Susan Ruttan. Part of the WonderWorks Series which centers on themes involving rites of passage that occur during the growing - up years from seven to sixteen. Features young people as protagonists and portrays strong adult role models.
Fine Arts; Literature and Drama; Psychology; Sociology
Dist - FI **Prod** - PBS 1990

Sweet and sour 12 MIN
16mm
Color (G)

$25.00 rental
Presents police footage of the corpse of an accident victim in which masks block out the gruesome or 'sour' parts while pieces of 'sweet' home movies are enriched by handcoloring and looping. Consists of five individual sections using animation, motorized mattes and other techniques. Produced by Victor Faccinto.
Fine Arts
Dist - CANCIN

Sweet and Sour 29 MIN
Videoreel / VT2
Joyce Chen Cooks Series
Color
Features Joyce Chen showing how to adapt Chinese recipes so that they can be prepared in the American kitchen and still retain the authentic flavor. Demonstrates how to prepare sweet and sour sauce.
Geography - World; Home Economics
Dist - PBS **Prod** - WGBHTV

Sweet country 57 MIN
16mm / VHS
Color (G)
$890.00, $390.00 purchase, $100.00 rental
Interviews General Pinochet, a state security agent, the mother of a disappeared prisoner, and an exiled political leader. Illustrates Chile's National Security Doctrine according to each one's experience. The consequences of the economic model adopted by the government are described by an economist and a hunger victim. Produced by Juan Andres Racz.
Business and Economics; Fine Arts; Social Science
Dist - FIRS

Sweet Disaster 30 MIN
U-matic / VHS
Color (C)
$249.00, $149.00 purchase _ #AD - 1384
Illustrates the irony of nuclear Armageddon in a group of cynical short animated tales. Includes 'Death of a Speechwriter,' 'Dreamless Sleep,' 'Conversations by a California Swimming Pool,' 'Paradise Regained,' and 'Babylon.'.
Civics and Political Systems; History - World; Sociology
Dist - FOTH **Prod** - FOTH

Sweet dreamer 31 MIN
VHS
Color (G C)
$95.00 purchase, $35.00 rental
Dramatizes a family's dealing with grief following the death of the father, with a ghost as a symbol of their lingering sorrow.
Guidance and Counseling; Sociology
Dist - TNF

Sweet Dreams 3 MIN
16mm
Color (C)
$125.00
Experimental film by Freude.
Fine Arts
Dist - AFA **Prod** - AFA 1970

Sweet England's pride 90 MIN
16mm / U-matic / VHS
Elizabeth R series; No 6
Color
LC 77-701553
Portrays the last years of the reign of Queen Elizabeth I, focusing on her romance with the Earl of Essex and his execution when he attempted to raise a rebellion against her.
Biography; Civics and Political Systems; History - World
Dist - FI **Prod** - BBCTV 1976

Sweet Fresh Water 55 MIN
U-matic / VHS / 16mm
Living Planet Series
Color (H C A)
Follows the Amazon River from its source in the Peruvian Andes to its huge coastal delta in Brazil. Shows how great waterfalls such as the Angel Falls in Venezuela and Iguassu in Brazil shape the landscape.
Geography - World; Science - Natural
Dist - TIMLIF **Prod** - BBCTV 1984
AMBROS

Sweet Honey in the Rock 60 MIN
U-matic / VHS
Color
History - United States
Dist - SYLWAT **Prod** - RCOMTV 1980

Sweet Jail 48 MIN
U-matic
Color (C)
$700.00 purchase, $60.00, $80.00 rental
Documents four generations of Sikh women and their daughters, the history of the migration of Sikhs to California at the turn of the century, and the erosion of Sikh culture in America. Discusses racism and sexism in this context. Produced by Beheroze F Shroff.
Social Science; Sociology
Dist - WMENIF

Sweet Lavender 10 MIN
16mm
B&W
Examines withdrawal and desertion, the inability to find a positive, fruitful relationship to one's society. Centers on an old woman who sells lavender sachets on a busy city street.
Guidance and Counseling; Psychology; Sociology
Dist - UPENN **Prod** - UPENN 1965

Sweet love, bitter 92 MIN
VHS / 16mm
B&W (G)
$250.00 rental
Documents the private lives of the New York jazz set of the 1960s. Examines the life of a down - and - out saxophonist played by Dick Gregory who is struggling to overcome drug addiction and to keep his career alive. Borrows from the life of Charlie 'Bird' Parker. Includes a jazz score by Mal Waldron featuring Chick Corea and Al Dreares. Directed by Herbert Danska.
Fine Arts; History - United States
Dist - KINOIC

Sweet love remembered 14 MIN
16mm
Color (G)
$28.00 rental
Exemplifies inspiration of two remarks by Freud and Nietzsche. Refers to Freud's comment that 'Eros nowhere makes its intentions more clear than in the desire to make two things one,' and Nietzsche's inquiry, 'What must these people have suffered to have become this beautiful.' Music created on a homemade synthesizer and computer.
Fine Arts; Religion and Philosophy
Dist - CANCIN **Prod** - ELDERB 1980

Sweet potato - 6 10 MIN
U-matic / 16mm / VHS
How plants grow series
Color (K P I)
$265.00, $215.00, $185.00 purchase _ #B598
Explains that sweet potatoes are roots. Shows how farmers grow them. Illustrates how a full - grown potato is used as a seed potato that will sprout new plants and how farmers cut the new plants - called slips - and replant them. Looks at the purpose of the plant's roots and the reason for removing weeds. Reveals that the sweet potato has almost no insect enemies. Part of a seven - part series on how plants grow.
Agriculture; Science - Natural
Dist - BARR **Prod** - GREATT 1990

Sweet Return 8 MIN
16mm
B&W
LC 71-702599
A study of racial consciousness as portrayed in a traditional gun duel, photographed in a turn - of - the - century setting, in which the antagonists, a noble black man and a beautiful white youth are pitted against each other by their domineering female seconds.
Fine Arts; History - United States; Psychology; Sociology
Dist - USC **Prod** - USC 1968

Sweet reunion 46 MIN
VHS / U-matic
Adoption series
Color (G)
$149.00 purchase _ #7438
Interviews birth parents who share the pain of giving up their child, and the joy of being reunited again. Features adoptees who tell stories of searching for their birth parents and the physical and personal similarities they have inherited from them. Includes a message from radio and TV personality Art Linkletter, who was also adopted. Part of a three - part series on adoption.
Sociology
Dist - VISIVI **Prod** - VISIVI 1991

Sweet Sixteen and Pregnant 29 MIN
16mm / U-matic / VHS
Dealing with Social Problems in the Classroom Series
Color (T)
Tells the story of five young girls, ages 13 through 17, each of whom had to deal with an unexpected pregnancy. Reveals the reality of teenage pregnancy through young women who have experienced first - hand the sadness, abandonment, anger and frustration that so often follow the discovery that one is expecting a child.
Education; Health and Safety
Dist - FI **Prod** - MFFD 1983

Sweet Sixteen and Pregnant 28 MIN
16mm / U-matic / VHS
Color (J H)
Tells the stories of five teenaged girls who wrestled with the problems and pressures of pregnancy.
Health and Safety; Psychology; Sociology
Dist - CORF **Prod** - BELLDA

The Sweet Smell of Freedom 27 MIN
16mm
Color
LC FIA68-551
Describes new methods in prison rehabilitation used at the D C men's reformatory, Lorton, Virginia. Shows staff problems and relates aspects of the life of prison inmates. Includes interviews with inmates and officials.
Civics and Political Systems; Psychology; Sociology
Dist - WMALTV **Prod** - WMALTV 1967

The Sweet smell of success 50 MIN
VHS
Relative values series
Color (A)
PdS99 purchase
Explores fine art as big business. Today it is not unusual for art work to be bought as an investment rather than for aesthetic appreciation. Interviews distinguished critics, collectors, and artists to discover just how art is perceived in the modern world, how it is valued and promoted, and why artists are more important than the art they produce.
Fine Arts
Dist - BBCENE

Sweet sorrow 8 MIN
VHS
Color (I J H A C)
$195.00 purchase
Dramatizes how a high school student was killed through misuse of hand guns. Brings out his friends' mourning for him and concern that no one else repeats his mistakes. Made by students of Dr Phillips High School. Includes discussion guide.
Social Science; Sociology
Dist - PFP

Sweetening the medicine 50 MIN
VHS
First Tuesday series
Color; PAL (H C G)
PdS30 purchase
Examines the revelations that some drug company salesmen offer doctors cash and free gifts to buy and prescribe their products, along with lavishly entertaining medical personnel. Asks if the hard sell is putting patients at risk. Contact distributor about availability outside the United Kingdom.
Health and Safety
Dist - ACADEM **Prod** - YORKTV

Sweetheart of the Rodeo 24 MIN
16mm
Color
LC 76-703809
Features Dee Watt, the British Columbia champion of barrel racing.
Geography - World; Physical Education and Recreation
Dist - BCDA **Prod** - BCDA 1975

Sweetness and health 26 MIN
U-matic / VHS
Color (C)
$249.00, $149.00 purchase _ #AD - 1904
Examines scientific evidence in the controversy over the role of sugar in violent behavior. Considers the ability of sugar to stimulate the 'primitive brain,' the effects of sugar used in moderation. Looks at the nature and safety of various sugar substitutes.
Psychology; Social Science; Sociology
Dist - FOTH **Prod** - FOTH

Sweets of Japan 26 MIN
16mm
Color
Traces the beginning of a distinctive confectionery in Japan that is scarcely known outside the country.
Home Economics
Dist - UNIJAP **Prod** - UNIJAP 1965

Sweets series
Presents a three - part series which features expert chef instructors from the California Culinary Academy in San Francisco who share their secrets on sweets. Includes Desserts, Candy and Chocolates, and Ice Cream and Frozen Desserts.
Candy and chocolates 30 MIN
Desserts 30 MIN
Ice cream and frozen desserts 30 MIN
Dist - CAMV

Sweetwater 30 MIN
U-matic / VHS / 16mm
Color (I)
Reveals how barriers can be surmounted when we drop our defenses and admit to human need.

Fine Arts; Psychology; Science - Natural; Social Science; Sociology
Dist - LCOA **Prod** - LCOA 1985

Sweetwater and June - a program about gang membership 30 MIN
VHS
Color (I J H)
$49.95 purchase _ #ST - PZ1000
Dramatizes the true stories of Afro - American gang members Sweetwater and June. Describes their partipation in gangs and activities, as well as consequences of gang membership. Shows how a night with no planned activities or recreational opportunities becomes a night of planned revenge, a gun - point car - jacking, a major gunshot incident resulting in arrest, detention, assassination and suicide.
Sociology
Dist - INSTRU

Sweetwater Junction 38 MIN
16mm / U-matic / VHS
Color (J H A)
LC 81-700819
Presents a documentary on the annual Rattlesnake Round - Up held in Sweetwater, Texas, which includes milking venom from rattlesnakes and an unusual pageant featuring women from the Sweetwater area.
Geography - United States; Sociology
Dist - PHENIX **Prod** - SLUIZR 1980

Swept away
VHS
Color (A)
$59.90 purchase _ #0324
Presents 'Swept Away' directed by Lina Wertmuller. Tells of a woman and a man of totally opposed political viewpoints, she's an aristocrat, he's working class, marooned on a tropical island. Portrays how the island becomes a torrid war zone of political ideologies, personalities and raw sex.
Fine Arts; Literature and Drama; Sociology
Dist - SEVVID

Swept away - A Guide to water rescue operations 30 MIN
VHS / U-matic / 16mm
Outdoor safety series
Color (H G)
$275.00, $325.00, $495.00 purchase, $50.00 rental
Offers a training film for recreational enthusiasts that explains clearly through demonstrations the safest and most effective water rescue techniques.
Health and Safety
Dist - NDIM **Prod** - MADISA 1991

Swifty 30 MIN
VHS / U-matic
High feather series Pt 2; Pt 2
Color (G)
LC 83-706048
Focuses on sensible weight loss and gives tips on self - image, diet, exercise and teamwork.
Health and Safety; Social Science
Dist - GPN **Prod** - NYSED 1982

Swim and trim with Billie in pool 19 MIN
VHS
Color (G)
$19.95 purchase _ #BCL010V-P
Demonstrates aquatic exercises that can increase cardiovascular fitness, increase flexibility, and lessen the effects of arthritis. Uses eight segments that work all parts of the body or allow the viewer to concentrate on certain body parts. Does not require ability to swim.
Physical Education and Recreation
Dist - CAMV

Swim lessons for kids 40 MIN
VHS
Color (P I T A)
$29.95 purchase
Demonstrates proper method for parents teaching their children to swim. Emphasizes water safety and confidence - building techniques for both beginning and more advanced swimmers. Features underwater photography and special musical background. Produced by Sue Royston's water safe fundamentals. Includes illustrated booklet linked by time line to videotape.
Health and Safety; Physical Education and Recreation
Dist - SCANPS **Prod** - SUEROY 1988

Swim Meet 15 MIN
16mm
Color
LC FIA66-539
Explains the duties of the officials at swimming meets as seen by leading United States' coaches. Shows events at the National AAU women's swimming meet in May, 1965.
Physical Education and Recreation
Dist - GROENG **Prod** - GROENG 1965

Swim, play and learn - a parents guide to children's swim skills 30 MIN
VHS
Color (K P I J A)
$19.95 purchase
Shows parents how they can guide their children through swimming lessons, using the Medley Swim Systems method. Includes all children's levels from Mom - Dad and Tot to advanced swimmers. Uses games and songs to work with children to make them more confident swimmers. Features Melody Medley - Craig.
Physical Education and Recreation; Sociology
Dist - MEDSWS **Prod** - MEDSWS 1992

Swim training - men series
Backstroke - men 15 MIN
Breaststroke strokes, drills, starts and turns 15 MIN
Butterfly - men 15 MIN
Butterfly strokes, drills, starts and turns 15 MIN
Freestyle Strokes, Drills, Starts and Turns 15 MIN
Dist - ATHI

Swim training - women series
Backstroke - women 15 MIN
Butterfly - women 15 MIN
Dist - ATHI

Swim with the sharks without being eaten alive 40 MIN
VHS
Color (A PRO)
$595.00 purchase, $249.00 rental
Presents a video version of Harvey Mackey's book 'Swim With The Sharks Without Being Eaten Alive.' Covers sales techniques and motivation for success. Includes an audiotape, leader's guide, and 20 workbooks.
Business and Economics; Psychology
Dist - VLEARN

Swimmer 26 MIN
16mm
Man and His Sport Series
Color (J)
LC 72-701522
Shows how two Australian swimming champions, Karen Moras and Diana Rickard, live and train.
Physical Education and Recreation
Dist - AUIS **Prod** - ANAIB 1972

Swimmer 23 MIN
16mm
Color
LC 75-700087
Shows the construction of a unique and powerful sculpture by artist Don Seiler.
Fine Arts
Dist - KANE **Prod** - KANE 1974

Swimming 13 MIN
16mm
B&W
Jim Gray demonstrates difference between old and new methods of swim instruction, especially for parents faced with challenge of teaching children to swim.
Physical Education and Recreation
Dist - SFI **Prod** - SFI

Swimming - a Case Study 15 MIN
VHS / 16mm
Managing Spinal Injury in Sport Series
Color (C)
$150.00 purchase _ #292602
Presents a standardized, systematic and comprehensive approach to the management of spinal injuries in various sports settings. Reveals that sport and recreational activities are the second most common cause of spinal fractures resulting in paralysis. Improper management of this serious injury may increase the chance of lifetime paralysis or death. Trains sports and recreational professionals in the management of spinal injuries. 'Swimming' demonstrates how to manage a spinal injury while swimming. Specific techniques for handling an injured, conscious patient are highlighted.
Health and Safety; Physical Education and Recreation
Dist - ACCESS **Prod** - ACCESS 1989

Swimming and diving series
VHS
N C A A instructional video series
Color (H C A)
$64.95 purchase _ #KAR2204V
Presents a three - part series on swimming and diving. Focuses on freestyle techniques, starts, turns, individual medleys, and diving techniques.
Physical Education and Recreation
Dist - CAMV **Prod** - NCAAF

Swimming and Diving Today 17 MIN
16mm
Color (J)
LC 74-703505
Uses slow motion, stop action and instant replay to clarify rule interpretations for interscholastic swimming. Describes the rules and correct officiating procedures for the benefit of competitive swimmers and divers, coaches, officials and spectators.
Physical Education and Recreation
Dist - OSFS **Prod** - NFSHSA 1974

Swimming for Fitness with Donna DeVerona 50 MIN
VHS
(H C A T)
$29.95 purchase _ #CH800V
Uses underwater slow motion photography to demonstrate proper swimming technique for all strokes. Offers tips on training and practice drills. Explains maximum heart rate for training and more.
Physical Education and Recreation
Dist - CAMV

Swimming for Survival 18 MIN
16mm
B&W
LC FIE54-367
Stresses the importance of learning basic swimming for emergency situations. Shows survival skills.
Health and Safety; Physical Education and Recreation
Dist - USNAC **Prod** - USN 1954

Swimming Rescues 8 MIN
16mm
Lifesaving and Water Safety Series
Color (I)
LC 76-701575
Reviews fundamental swimming skills required in water rescues, including entries, stroke adaptations, approaches, carries and tired swimmer assists. Emphasizes that rescues that do not require the rescuer to swim should be used whenever possible.
Health and Safety
Dist - AMRC **Prod** - AMRC 1975

Swimming, Scuba Diving and Fishing at the Seashore 8 MIN
16mm
Crystal Tipps and Alistair Series
Color (K P)
LC 73-700450
Follows Crystal and her friends as they spend a pleasant holiday at the seashore, where they swim, dive, play in the sand, explore underwater and go fishing.
Guidance and Counseling; Literature and Drama
Dist - VEDO **Prod** - BBCTV 1972

Swimming Series no 1
Freestyle Stroke and Backstroke Technique 22 MIN
Dist - ATHI

Swimming Series no 3
Starts, Turns and Progressive Drills 23 MIN
Dist - ATHI

Swimming series
Breast stroke and butterfly technique 20 MIN
Dist - ATHI

Swimming skills and drills - back crawl, breaststroke and turns 39 MIN
BETA / VHS
Color (A)
Breaks down the two strokes into progressive steps for coaching or teaching, and demonstrates proper arm and leg action, breathing and turns. Includes a variety of drills swimmers can use to develop these techniques. Uses underwater photography in regular speed, slow motion and stop frames to demonstrate how each stroke should be performed and how to go about developing the strokes through practice drills. Features swimming coach Dick Hannula and world class swimmers.
Physical Education and Recreation
Dist - RMIBHF **Prod** - RMIBHF

Swimming skills and drills - crawl and butterfly 41 MIN
VHS / BETA
Color (A)
Breaks down the crawl and butterfly strokes into progressive steps to be used in teaching, and demonstrates the proper techniques for the arm actions, leg kicks and breathing. Demonstrates numerous drills to be used in developing these techniques. Includes extensive use of underwater photography in regular speed, slow motion and stop frame, showing how each stroke should be performed through practice drills. Features swimming coach Dick Hannula and elite - class swimmers.
Physical Education and Recreation
Dist - RMIBHF **Prod** - RMIBHF

Swimming stone 14 MIN
16mm
B&W; Color (G)
$5.00 rental
Conjures up a myriad of conceptions including the fluidity of stone, subatomic motion asserting a surface, mind loop wandering, visitation of sound matrix, liquid solid, nature transforming a planetary cycle and relations of a timeless void.
Fine Arts
Dist - CANCIN **Prod** - FULTON

Swimming strokes 90 MIN
VHS
(H C A T)
$39.95 purchase _ #BF99618V
Uses underwater photography and animation to depict techniques for basic swimming strokes.
Physical Education and Recreation
Dist - CAMV

Swimming to Cambodia 87 MIN
35mm / 16mm
Color (G)
Features an exhilarating, hilarious and intricately crafted monologue by Spalding Gray, writer - actor - performance artist. Uses only a table, a glass of water, a map and pointer as props to take the viewer on a dizzy escapade stretching from the Gulf of Siam to poolside Beverly Hills to the sex clubs of Bangkok. Produced by R A Shafransky; directed by Jonathan Demme; with Spalding Gray, Sam Waterston and Ira Wheeler. Contact distributer for price.
Civics and Political Systems; Fine Arts
Dist - OCTOBF

Swimming to survive 13 MIN
VHS
Color; PAL (J H G)
PdS29
Shows how to survive disaster situations at sea or far from land, using 'real - life' locations. Demonstrates methods of remaining afloat while conserving energy and warmth, inflating clothes for use as floats, endurance swimming, underwater swimming to avoid obstacles and safe methods of entering water from a height.
Health and Safety; Physical Education and Recreation
Dist - BHA

Swimming with Dick Hannula Series
Olympic Style Back Crawl, Breast Stroke, and Turns 60 MIN
Olympic Style Crawl and Butterfly 60 MIN
Dist - CAMV

Swimmy 6 MIN
16mm / VHS
Color (K P I)
$300.00, $225.00 purchase
Features Swimmy, a tiny fish, who outwits the jaws of a hungry tuna and leads other fish on an exploration of their richly colored underwater world. Stimulates discussion about cooperation and ecology. Based on the fable by Leo Lionni.
Health and Safety; Literature and Drama
Dist - LUF CONNF **Prod** - LUF CONNF 1969

Swimsuit Edition Video 45 MIN
VHS
Color; Stereo (G)
$9.98 purchase _ #TT8100
Presents today's most provocative swimwear and gives fashion tips for women.
Home Economics; Physical Education and Recreation
Dist - TWINTO **Prod** - TWINTO 1990

Swine Abnormalities 26 MIN
16mm
Color
Abnormalities in swine cause marketability or breeding loss. Identifying the visual signs that characterize swine abnormalities can help to decide about treating or culling problem animals in the pen. Dozens of various abnormalities are illustrated; early detection may remove certain animals and save space and money.
Agriculture; Science - Natural; Social Science
Dist - UWISCA **Prod** - UWISCA 1982

Swine Evaluation
VHS
Color (G)
$89.95 purchase _ #6 - 033 - 100P
Teaches swine evaluation. Examines live animals, frozen carcasses and cuts from carcasses to illustrate the relationship of the characteristics of the live animal to the meat cuts.
Agriculture; Business and Economics; Science - Natural; Social Science
Dist - VEP **Prod** - VEP

The Swine Flu Caper 22 MIN
U-matic / VHS / 16mm
Color
Portrays Dr Anthony Morris, a virologist with the National Institute of Health and the Food and Drug Administration, who was fired after objecting to the swine flu vaccine.
Civics and Political Systems; Health and Safety; Religion and Philosophy
Dist - NEWTIM **Prod** - NEWTIM

Swine Handling and Transportation
VHS
Color (G)
$49.95 purchase _ #6 - 081 - 101P
Shows how to prevent livestock loss - particularly swine - during transport from feedlots to market. Shows how to load, control temperature levels of transport, lower stress during transport and improve handling. Produced by the Livestock Conservation Institute.
Agriculture; Business and Economics; Science - Natural; Social Science
Dist - VEP

The Swine Industry in the U S 24 MIN
U-matic / VHS
Color
Provides an overview of the swine industry and describes the characteristics of swine.
Agriculture
Dist - HOBAR **Prod** - HOBAR

Swine Judging (Set G) Series
Judging Breeding Swine 30 MIN
Judging Market Swine 26 MIN
Practice Swine Judging 42 MIN
Dist - AAVIM

Swine - Life - Cycle Feeding
VHS
Livestock Feedstuffs Video Transfers Series
Color (G)
$30.00 purchase _ #1 - 450 - 003VT
Relates swine feeding to stages of development in the life - cycle. Teaches swine nutritional needs. Part of a three - part series on livestock nutrition.
Agriculture; Business and Economics
Dist - VEP **Prod** - VEP

Swine Management Practices - I 23 MIN
VHS
Swine Production (Set M) Series
(C)
$79.95 _ CV151
Highlights the fundamentals of swine management giving the characteristics swine, site selection, housing and facilities, managment of late gestation sows, farrowing and navel cord care.
Agriculture
Dist - AAVIM **Prod** - AAVIM 1989

Swine Managment Practices - II 22 MIN
VHS
Swine Production (Set M) Series
(C)
$79.95 _ CV152
Shows swine management practices inculding clipping needle teeth, tail docking, iron injections, ear notching, castration, weaning, nursery, feeding, finishing, and paint branding.
Agriculture
Dist - AAVIM **Prod** - AAVIM 1989

Swine Production (Set M) Series
Swine Management Practices - I 23 MIN
Swine Managment Practices - II 22 MIN
Dist - AAVIM

Swine Reproduction, Breeding and Farrowing, Pt I 30 MIN
VHS
Swine Reproduction, Breeding And Farrowing Series
Color (G)
$79.95 purchase _ #6 - 040 - 100P
Illustrates sow, gilt and boar selection, functional anatomy of the sow and boar, estrous cycle, estrus period, natural mating, summary, three quizzes. Part one of a two - part series on swine reproduction.
Agriculture
Dist - VEP **Prod** - VEP

Swine Reproduction, Breeding and Farrowing, Pt II 30 MIN
VHS
Swine Reproduction, Breeding And Farrowing Series
Color (G)
$79.95 purchase _ #6 - 040 - 101P
Illustrates semen collection from a boar and processing, artificial insemination, fertilization diagnosis, the developing embryo and fetus, several different farrowings, summary, quizzes, answers. Part two of a two - part series on swine reproduction.
Agriculture
Dist - VEP **Prod** - VEP

Swine Reproduction, Breeding And Farrowing Series
Swine Reproduction, Breeding and Farrowing, Pt I 30 MIN
Swine Reproduction, Breeding and Farrowing, Pt II 30 MIN
Dist - VEP

Swine Reproduction - I 42 MIN
VHS
Swine Reproduction (Set P) Series
(C)
$79.95 _ CV161
Unveils the fundamentals of swine reproduction including boar selection, sow and gilt selection, functional anatomy of the baor and sow, estrous cylce, estrus period, natural mating and a summary with three quizzes of varying difficulty.
Agriculture; Health and Safety
Dist - AAVIM **Prod** - AAVIM 1989

Swine Reproduction - II 30 MIN
VHS
Swine Reproduction (Set P) Series
(C)
$79.95 _ CV162
Includes actual semen collection from the boar, semen processing, pregnancy diagnosis, the developing embryo and fetus and several different farrowings along with a summary with quizzes and answers.
Agriculture; Health and Safety
Dist - AAVIM **Prod** - AAVIM 1989

Swine Reproduction (Set P) Series
Swine Reproduction - I 42 MIN
Swine Reproduction - II 30 MIN
Dist - AAVIM

The Swineherd 13 MIN
16mm / U-matic / VHS
Color (K P)
LC 75-701093
Presents an animated adaptation of Hans Christian Andersen's tale illustrated by Bjorn Wiinblad about a princess who scorns the love of a prince until he disguises himself as a swineherd.
Literature and Drama
Dist - WWS **Prod** - NORDV 1974

Swing and slide into safety 15 MIN
VHS
Color (H A T K P)
$29.95 purchase _ #MK801
Uses real kids, safety robots, puppets and music to demonstrate the 'whys and hows' of playground safety for young children.
Education; Fine Arts; Health and Safety
Dist - AAVIM **Prod** - AAVIM 1992

Swing bass 29 MIN
U-matic
Beginning piano - an adult approach series; Lesson 25
Color (H A)
Reviews scales and chords in A - flat major and E - flat major. Introduces swing bass, one of the most common of accompaniment patterns, and arpeggios.
Fine Arts
Dist - CDTEL **Prod** - COAST

Swing dancing series
Presents three videos on swing and jitterbug dancing. Moves from basic through intermediate to advanced movements and steps.
Advanced swing
Basic swing
Intermediate swing
Dist - SIV

Swing era - Vol 2 50 MIN
VHS
Cal del Pozo's step this way - learn to dance series
Color (G A)
$19.95 purchase
Presents basic instruction in three dances from the Swing Era - the Waltz, the Lindy, and the Foxtrot. Utilizes Cal del Pozo's method, which involves four simple foot movements, and provides computerized footprints to allow viewers to follow along more easily. Taught by del Pozo, who is a national ballroom dance champion and a Broadway dancer and choreographer.
Fine Arts
Dist - PBS **Prod** - WNETTV

Swing fundamentals plus distance and control 25 MIN
VHS
Lee Trevino's priceless golf tips series
Color (J H A)
$29.95 purchase _ #PM12626V
Features Lee Trevino with tips on improving one's golf swing. Offers advice on how to gain distance and accuracy, as well as dealing with swing faults such as slicing and hooking.

Physical Education and Recreation
Dist - CAMV

Swing low sweet chariot 5 MIN
16mm
Color (G)
$10.00 rental
Makes a tongue - in - cheek tribute to the omnipresent four - wheeled beetle. Produced by Bob Giorgio.
Fine Arts; History - United States
Dist - CANCIN

The Swing of Things 29 MIN
Videoreel / VT2
Observing Eye Series
Color
Sociology
Dist - PBS **Prod** - WGBHTV

The Swing that Swung Back 6 MIN
16mm
Color (A)
LC 76-704012
Discusses playground safety equipment using animation and a plot involving two stereotypic detectives investigating an accident.
Health and Safety
Dist - USNAC **Prod** - USCPSD 1976

Swing time 103 MIN
VHS
B&W (G)
$19.95 purchase _ #S01388
Features Fred Astaire and Ginger Rogers in a musical in which their romance is hampered by Fred's engagement to a girl in his hometown. Notable for Astaire's Bojangles production number. Filmed in 1936.
Fine Arts
Dist - UILL

Swinging rhythm 29 MIN
U-matic
Beginning piano - an adult approach series; Lesson 21
Color (H A)
Discusses swinging rhythm, or the unequal division of the beat used universally in many musical forms, including jazz, musical theater, and commercial music. Begins two new pieces.
Fine Arts
Dist - CDTEL **Prod** - COAST

The Swish pattern 71 MIN
VHS
Color; PAL; SECAM (G)
$75.00 purchase
Demonstrates the Swish Pattern, a rapid, powerful intervention for changing habits and feelings. Observes Steve Andreas as he helps a client eliminate a nailbiting habit. Connirae Andreas works with a woman's pattern of going into a rage when her daughter used a certain tone of voice. Introductory level of NLP, neuro - linguistic programming.
Psychology
Dist - NLPCOM **Prod** - NLPCOM

Swish - Science and Curveballs and Gliders 20 MIN
U-matic / VHS / 16mm
Elementary Physical Science Series
Color (I J)
LC 76-703970
Considers curveballs and gliders in terms of the aerodynamics of moving, spinning and soaring against wind and pressure. Portrays students following a variety of paths to find answers to problems posed by a humorous puppet, Professor Higgenbottom.
Industrial and Technical Education; Science - Physical
Dist - CORF **Prod** - CENTRO 1976

Swiss Army Knife with Rats and Pigeons 6 MIN
16mm
Color (C)
Experimental film by Robert Breer.
Fine Arts
Dist - AFA **Prod** - AFA 1981

Swiss family Robinson 126 MIN
VHS
Color; CC (I J H)
$21.95 purchase _ #484749
Adapts the classic story by Johann Wyss about a family shipwrecked on a tropical island.
Literature and Drama
Dist - KNOWUN **Prod** - DISNEY 1960

Swiss Family Robinson 26 MIN
16mm / VHS
Children's Classics Series
Color (P)
$195.00 purchase
Retells the story by Johann Wyss of the Swiss Family Robinson who are marooned on a deserted island. Emphasizes strong family ties and self - reliance. Adapted by William Overgard.
Fine Arts; Literature and Drama
Dist - LUF **Prod** - BROVID

Swiss Graffiti 6 MIN
U-matic / VHS / 16mm
Color
LC 77-701517
Presents a story based on the premise that the primitive graffiti telling the story of the creation and found on walls throughout the world uses symbols of masculine supremacy. Tells how one day Eve gets tired of her role and the symbols change.
Literature and Drama; Religion and Philosophy; Sociology
Dist - PHENIX **Prod** - VEUREN 1977

Swiss Miss 73 MIN
16mm
Laurel and Hardy Festival Series
B&W (I J H C)
Features Laurel and Hardy as mousetrap salesmen in Switzerland and one of their demonstrations in a luxury hotel which backfires. Shows how the boys end up in the kitchen where, for every dish they break, they must put in one more day of duty.
Fine Arts
Dist - RMIBHF **Prod** - RMIBHF 1938

Switch on the Sun
U-matic / VHS
(J H C)
$109.00 purchase _ #05211 94
Explores ways that solar energy can be harnessed and used as a safe and practical alternative to fossil feuls. Features photography of the sun.
Social Science
Dist - ASPRSS **Prod** - WAHRTI

Switch on the Sun 15 MIN
U-matic / VHS / 16mm
Color (I J H)
LC 77-703421
Presents sources of power that are being exhausted by energy consumption. Explains various methods of solar energy conversion and how this source of power is being used in homes and manufacturing plants.
Social Science
Dist - GA **Prod** - XEROXF 1977

Switchboard 28 MIN
U-matic
Are you listening series
Color
LC 80-707153
Presents a group of former drug users who are now working on a drug hotline program. Discusses drug supply and demand, drug - related experiences, and the value of open communication.
Psychology; Sociology
Dist - STURTM **Prod** - STURTM 1972

The Switched - on Kitchen 30 MIN
U-matic / VHS / 16mm
Color (J H A)
Presents Graham Kerr offering a potpourri of ideas on poaching, baking and breading fish.
Home Economics
Dist - CORNRS **Prod** - CUETV 1975

Switchgear - current carrying devices - racking systems - testing 60 MIN
U-matic / VHS
Electrical equipment maintenance series; Module 4; Tape 2
Color (IND)
LC 80-706014
Industrial and Technical Education
Dist - ITCORP **Prod** - ITCORP 1980

Switchgear - current carrying - devices, racking systems - testing trouble 60 MIN
U-matic / VHS
Electrical equipment maintenance series; Tape 2
Color (IND) (SPANISH)
Complete title reads Switchgear, Tape 2 - Current Carrying Devices, Racking Systems, testing Trouble Analysis (Spanish). Provides training in electrical equipment maintenance.
Industrial and Technical Education
Dist - ITCORP **Prod** - ITCORP

Switchgear - introduction - bus apparatus - interrupting devices - air 60 MIN
VHS / U-matic
Electrical equipment maintenance series; Module 4; Tape 1
Color (IND)
LC 80-706013
Education; Industrial and Technical Education
Dist - ITCORP **Prod** - ITCORP 1980

Switchgear - introduction, bus - apparatus, interrupting devices, air circuit 60 MIN
VHS / U-matic
Electrical equipment maintenance - Spanish series; Tape 1
Color (IND)
Complete title reads Switchgear, Tape 1 - Introduction, Bus Apparatus, Interrupting Devices, Air Circuit Breakers (Spanish). Provides instruction in electrical equipment maintenance.
Foreign Language; Industrial and Technical Education
Dist - ITCORP **Prod** - ITCORP

Switching 51 MIN
VHS / U-matic
Telecommunications and the Computer Series
Color
Discusses switching techniques and comparisons.
Industrial and Technical Education; Mathematics
Dist - MIOT **Prod** - MIOT

Switching and isolating devices
VHS / U-matic
Distribution system operation series; Topic 7
Color (IND)
Looks at the various types of switching devices which are installed to interrupt current flow or isolate circuits. Shows how these devices work. Includes circuit breakers, arc suppressing devices and maintenance considerations.
Industrial and Technical Education
Dist - LEIKID **Prod** - LEIKID

Switching on 57 MIN
U-matic / VHS
Color (C A)
LC 82-706229
Surveys the silicon - chip industry and shows how the computer is revolutionizing the ways in which people live and learn. Includes examples of architects, doctors and composers who are applying computers to do their research and work.
Business and Economics; Mathematics; Sociology
Dist - FLMLIB **Prod** - CANBC 1981

Switzerland 33 MIN
16mm / U-matic / VHS
Color (I)
LC 76-714646
Shows life in Switzerland, including farming, skiing, celebrations and traditions.
Geography - World
Dist - CORF **Prod** - DISNEY 1959

Switzerland 29 MIN
VHS / U-matic
International Cookbook Series
Color
Features home economist Joan Hood presenting a culinary tour of specialty dishes from around the world. Shows the preparation of Swiss dishes ranging from peasant cookery to continental cuisine.
Geography - World; Home Economics
Dist - PBS **Prod** - WMVSTV

Switzerland 60 MIN
VHS
Travelogue collection series
Color (I J H A)
$29.95 purchase _ #QC112V-S
Presents information about the historic past and the current status of Switzerland, including information about the cities and the countryside. Shows famous landmarks, out-of-the way sites, struggles and hardships, victories and championships, and the legends of the region. Uses live-action footage and historical clips to show the geography, history, and culture. Includes 16 60-minute programs on northern, western, eastern, and southern Europe.
Geography - World
Dist - CAMV

Switzerland 60 MIN
VHS
Traveloguer Eastern Europe series
Color (J H C G)
$29.95 purchase _ #QC112V
Visits Switzerland and its cities. Illustrates notable landmarks, special events in history and the legends that are part of Swiss culture. Part of a four part series on Eastern Europe.
Geography - World; History - World
Dist - CAMV

Switzerland 19 MIN
U-matic / VHS / 16mm
Modern Europe Series
Color (I J H)
Looks at the people, geography, industries and history of Switzerland.
Geography - World; History - World
Dist - JOU **Prod** - JOU

Switzerland - glacier express 50 MIN
VHS
Color (G)
$19.95 purchase _ #S01469
Portrays the Swiss railway known as the Glacier Express, which travels across most of southern Switzerland. Reveals that the train must travel across 291 bridges, through 91 tunnels, and runs at altitudes as high as 11,000 feet above sea level. Features the Alpine scenery along the route.
Geography - World; Social Science
Dist - UILL

Switzerland - the Alpine wonderland 60 MIN
VHS
European collection series
Color (J H C G)
$29.95 purchase _ #IVN108V-S
Tours the cities and countryside of Switzerland. Including Neuchatel, Lausanne, Geneva, and Zermatt. Part of a 16-part series on European countries. Also part of a larger series entitled Video Visits that travels to six continents.
Geography - World
Dist - CAMV **Prod** - WNETTV

Switzerland Today 17 MIN
16mm / U-matic / VHS
Color (I)
Looks at modern Switzerland, emphasizing the urbanization of a population traditionally skilled in manipulative abilities and the adaptation of industry to the necessity of importing almost all raw materials. Shows the resultant changes in agriculture and the highly organized tourist industry.
Geography - World
Dist - LUF **Prod** - LUF 1980

Switzerland today 17 MIN
VHS
Color; PAL (P I J H)
Visits Switzerland during the 1970s. Emphasizes the urbanization of a highly skilled population and the adaptation of industry to necessity of importing almost all raw materials. Shows the changes in agriculture and the highly organized tourist industry.
Geography - World; History - World; Sociology
Dist - VIEWTH **Prod** - VIEWTH

Switzerland, Yugoslavia, Iceland, California, Connecticut, Tunisia 27 MIN
16mm
Big blue marble - children around the world series
Color (P I)
LC 76-700639
Describes the lives of children in Switzerland, Iceland, California, Connecticut and Tunisia. Relates a Yugoslavian folk tale about a czar who has the ears of a goat. Program A in a series.
Geography - United States; Geography - World; Literature and Drama; Social Science
Dist - VITT **Prod** - ALVEN 1975

Swivel Bar Transfer for Quadriplegia 11 MIN
U-matic
Wheelchair Transfers Series
Color (PRO)
Shows a physical therapist preparing the swivel bar and hi - lo bed for giving minimal assistance to a quadriplegic patient during transfer from wheelchair to bed. Presents the equipment needed and its proper assembly for use. Includes a demonstration of the safety precautions necessary to prevent equipment failure or possibly injury to the patient.
Health and Safety
Dist - PRIMED **Prod** - PRIMED

Swivel Bar Transfer for Quadriplegia, Pt 1 12 MIN
16mm
Color (PRO)
Presents a physical therapist and a quadriplegic patient demonstrating the swivel bar transfer technique.
Health and Safety
Dist - RLAH **Prod** - CINEMP

Swivels, Blocks, Rotaries 25 MIN
U-matic / VHS / 16mm
You Need to Know Series
Color (IND)
Business and Economics; Industrial and Technical Education; Social Science
Dist - UTEXPE **Prod** - UTEXPE

Swivels, Blocks, Rotaries 25 MIN
16mm / VHS
You Need to Know Series
(A PRO)
$275.00 purchase _ #30.0116, $250.00 purchase _ #50.0116
Shows rig personnel the proper maintenance precedures for LTV Energy Products.
Industrial and Technical Education; Social Science
Dist - UTEXPE **Prod** - UTEXPE 1981

Swoon 92 MIN
35mm
B&W; PAL (G)
Tells the story of two 18 - year - old Jewish youths infamous for the kidnapping and murder in 1924 of a boy from their wealthy Hyde Park New York neighborhood. Looks at how many crimes were planned by the academically precocious pair and discovers how this extreme behavior resulted from from a long and complex relationship revolving around the exchange of sex for criminal activity. Directed by Tom Kalin for Intolerance Productions, USA. Contact distributor about price and availability outside the United Kingdom.
Fine Arts; Psychology; Sociology
Dist - BALFOR

Swoosh Away the Glop 29 MIN
Videoreel / VT2
Tin Lady Series
Color
Fine Arts
Dist - PBS **Prod** - NJPBA

The Sword and the Chrysanthemum 55 MIN
VHS / U-matic
Japan Series
Color (H C A)
$125 purchase _ #5849C
Shows the history of the Samurai and Ninja warriors and how they have affected Japan's social structure. A production of WTTW, Chicago.
Civics and Political Systems; History - World
Dist - CORF

The Sword and the Flute 24 MIN
16mm
Color (J)
LC FIA59-522
Uses Indian music and Moghul and Rajput miniature paintings in presenting four facets in the thinking of India - - the courtly conqueror Emperor Akbar, the saintly life of the Yogin and the respect shown the true ascetic, the spiritual meaning of romantic love between man and woman and the adored divine bridegroom, which is one of the symbols as represented by the Lord Krishna.
Fine Arts; Geography - World; Literature and Drama
Dist - RADIM **Prod** - IVORYJ 1959

The Sword in the stone
VHS
Disney classics on video series
Color; CC (K P I)
$29.95 purchase _ #DIS229
Presents the Disney verion of The Sword in the Stone on video.
Fine Arts; Literature and Drama
Dist - KNOWUN **Prod** - DISNEY

Sword of doom 120 MIN
VHS
B&W (G) (JAPANESE WITH ENGLISH SUBTITLES)
$22.95 purchase _ #NEL6142
Portrays a samurai assassin driven by impulse and lusts for revenge. Directed by Kihachi Okomoto.
Fine Arts
Dist - CHTSUI

The Sword of Gideon 12 MIN
16mm
Tales from the Great Book Series
Color
LC 73-713502
A dramatization of the account in the Bible telling how Gideon became convinced of the strength of the Lord.
Literature and Drama; Religion and Philosophy
Dist - HALCOM **Prod** - GDLP 1971

Sword series
Presents 3 videos demonstrating 3 martial arts involving swords. Features kobujutsu, iaido and kendo taught by 10th Dan masters.
Mastering iaido
Mastering kendo
Mastering kobujutsu
Sword series
Dist - SIV

Swords and plough shares 60 MIN
VHS
Out of the fiery furnace series
Color; Captioned (G)
$69.95 purchase _ #OOFF - 102
Reveals that all of history's greatest civilizations gained mastery over metals. Shows that the development of iron brought an end to the Bronze Age and shifted mankind from agriculture to industry. Hosted by Michael Charlton.
History - World; Science - Physical
Dist - PBS **Prod** - OPUS 1986

Swords and Ploughshares 60 MIN
VHS / 16mm
Portrait of the Soviet Union Series
(H C)
$99.95 each, $595.00 series
Interviews Soviet citizens and discusses war history in their country as a means of measuring Russian reaction to the threat of invasion.
Geography - World; History - World
Dist - AMBROS **Prod** - AMBROS 1988

Swords and plowshares - Part III
VHS
America the bountiful series
Color (G)
$89.95 purchase _ #6 - 402 - 003A
Follows Henry Wallace, son of John Wallace, to Iowa where he reestablishes the family farm after the Civil War. Examines the activities of Wallace and Sean A Knapp to bring education into pioneer lives. Shows how American farmers look to the federal government for advice as the 20th century approaches. Part of a six - part series on the history of American agriculture hosted by Ed Begley, Jr.
Agriculture; Biography; Civics and Political Systems; History - United States
Dist - VEP **Prod** - VEP 1993

Swords, Plowshares, and Politics 48 MIN
U-matic / VHS
Color
$455.00 purchase
Looks at the United Nations. From the ABC TV Close Up program.
Civics and Political Systems
Dist - ABCLR **Prod** - ABCLR 1982

SX-70 11 MIN
U-matic / VHS / 16mm
Color
LC 75-703534
Documents the invention, technology and potential of the SX - 70 photographic system developed by Edwin Land.
Industrial and Technical Education
Dist - PFP **Prod** - POLARD 1973

Sybervision golf videos series
The Dave Stockton golf clinic
Difficult shots made easy by Hale Irwin
Golf - the women's game with Patty Sheehan
Dist - CAMV

Sybil
VHS / BETA
Color
Presents the true story of a woman who developed 16 separate personalities, starring Sally Field.
Psychology; Sociology
Dist - GA **Prod** - GA

Sybil's Plight - a Family's Adjustment to Chronic Illness 21 MIN
VHS / U-matic
B&W
Demonstrates the problems of a family in its adjustment to chronic catastrophic illness. Shows edited segments of actual family interviews. Demonstrates the effect of genetic implications on parent - child relationships.
Psychology; Sociology
Dist - PSU **Prod** - PSU

The Sycamore people - Jaworowi ludzie 60 MIN
VHS
Color (K P) (POLISH)
$17.95 purchase _ #V151
Offers a set of six stories.
Fine Arts; Literature and Drama
Dist - POLART

Sydney Harbour Bridge 13 MIN
16mm
Color
LC 80-700882
Presents a panoramic view of Sydney Harbour Bridge popularized in many tourist postcards.
Fine Arts; Geography - World
Dist - TASCOR **Prod** - WINKLP 1978

Sydney Opera House, 1972 9 MIN
16mm
Color (J)
LC 73-702485
Presents a progress report on the Sydney opera house, showing final stages of construction.
Fine Arts; Geography - World
Dist - AUIS **Prod** - FLMAUS 1973

Syllabication Skills, Pt 1 15 MIN
VHS
Planet Pylon Series
Color (I)
LC 90712897
Uses character Commander Wordstalker from the Space Station Readstar to develop language arts skills. Examines syllabication. Worksheet included to be completed with the help of series characters.

Education; English Language
Dist - GPN

Syllabication skills - Pt 1 15 MIN
U-matic / Kit / VHS
Space station readstar series
(P)
$130.00 purchase, $25.00 rental, $75.00 self dub
Teaches phonics in a series designed to supplement second grade reading programs. Focuses on syllabication skills. Twelfth in a 25 part series.
English Language
Dist - GPN

Syllabication skills, Pt 2 15 MIN
VHS
Planet phylon series
Color (I)
LC 90712897
Uses character Commander Wordstalker of the Space Station Readstar to develop language arts skills. Studies syllabication skills. A worksheet is included. Intended for students at the third - grade level.
Education; English Language
Dist - GPN

Syllabication skills - Pt 2 15 MIN
U-matic / Kit / VHS
Space station readstar series******Space station readstar series**
(P)
$130.00 purchase, $25.00 rental, $75.00 self dub
Teaches phonics in a series designed to supplement second grade reading programs. Reviews syllabication skills and introduces the concepts of stressed syllables and sounded vowels. Twenty third in a 25 part series.
English Language
Dist - GPN

A Sylvan Sewer 25 MIN
16mm
Perspective Series
Color
LC 73-700770
Explains that the 33 miles of Washington, D C's Rock Creek is more than a recreational stream flowing through Rock Creek Park. Reveals the stream as a vital element in the Maryland - District of Columbia watershed. Follows a group of college students as they explore sources of pollution and the environmental dangers involved.
Geography - United States; Science - Natural
Dist - WRCTV **Prod** - WRCTV 1972

Sylvester 6 MIN
U-matic / VHS / 16mm
Golden Book Storytime Series
Color (P)
Shows how Sylvester becomes the world's first guitar - playing mouse.
Literature and Drama
Dist - CORF **Prod** - CORF 1977

Sylvia and the phantom 93 MIN
VHS
B&W (G)
$24.95 _ #SYL040
Looks at fantasy, love and growing up with a 16 - year - old lass pining for the one man she can never have - the ghost of her dead grandmother's lover.
Fine Arts; Sociology
Dist - HOMVIS **Prod** - JANUS 1945

Sylvia Gelber - an Interview 28 MIN
U-matic
Color
Presents Sylvia Gelber, Director of the Women's Bureau of Labour Canada, discussing the position of women in the labour force.
Business and Economics; History - World; Sociology
Dist - WMENIF **Prod** - WMENIF

Sylvia Nolan and Paul Moore 30 MIN
VHS / U-matic
Eye on Dance - Behind the Scenes Series
Color
Looks at creativity behind the scenes of a dance production. Features 'Esoterica' with Diana Byers. Hosted by Celia Ipiotis.
Fine Arts
Dist - ARCVID **Prod** - ARCVID

Sylvia Pankhurst 60 MIN
VHS
Shoulder to shoulder series
Color (G)
$59.95 purchase _ #SHOU - 106
Profiles British suffragist Sylvia Pankhurst, who broke with her mother and sister over the issue of British involvement in World War I. Tells how British women won the right to vote after suffragists declared support for the war. Hosted by actress Jane Alexander.
Civics and Political Systems; History - World; Religion and Philosophy
Dist - PBS **Prod** - MKNZM 1988

Sylvia Plath 60 MIN
VHS / 16mm
Voices and Visions Series
Color (H)
$8.00 rental _ #60735
Compares the life and poetry of Sylvia Plath (1932 - 1963) with the symbol of the divided self which she became after her suicide at age 30 - the modern woman torn by unresolvable conflicts. Plath's mother, Aurelia, and Sandra Gilbert, Helen McNeil, Clarissa Roche, Dido Merwin, A Alvarez, and others recount her intense and turbulent life and discuss her poems, most of which were written at top speed in the last nine months of her life.
Literature and Drama
Dist - PSU

Sylvia Plath - Letters Home 90 MIN
U-matic / VHS
Color (C)
$299.00, $199.00 purchase _ #AD - 934
Performs 'Letters Home' which was written by Sylvia Plath to her mother during the years of her development as a poet and degeneration into psychological hell. Features Anna Nigh and June Brown in performance.
Biography; Fine Arts; Literature and Drama
Dist - FOTH **Prod** - FOTH

Sylvia Plath - Part 9 60 MIN
VHS / U-matic
Voices and visions series
Color (G)
$45.00, $29.95 purchase
Recalls the life and poetry of Sylvia Plath. Separates the myth of the woman from the art and symbolic intent of her poetry. Part of a thirteen - part series on the lives and works of modern American poets.
Biography; History - United States; Literature and Drama
Dist - ANNCPB **Prod** - NYCVH 1988

Sylvia Porter Series
Make Yourself House Rich 60 MIN
Dist - BANTAP

Sylvia Porter's Personal Finance - the Video 45 MIN
VHS / U-matic
(H C A)
$34.95 _ #JJ100V
Features Sylvia Porter, financial advisor, as she explains her seven winning techniques for investment. Uses charts, graphs, and examples to cover home buying, mutual funds, tax investments, and other investment concepts.
Business and Economics
Dist - CAMV **Prod** - CAMV

Sylvia - Summer Before College 29 MIN
U-matic / VHS / 16mm
Color; Mono (J H)
Tells the story of an accomplished adolescent.
Psychology; Sociology
Dist - TOGG **Prod** - TOGG 1983

Sylvie Guillem at work 53 MIN
VHS
Color (G)
$39.95 purchase _ #SYL02
Profiles 24 year old dancer and choreographer, Sylvie Guilem. Films her rehearsal and performance of Raymonda by Glazunov, Four Last Songs by Richard Strauss, and In the Middle, Somewhat Elevated, both by Tom Willems.
Fine Arts
Dist - HOMVIS **Prod** - RMART 1990

Symbiosis 10 MIN
U-matic / VHS / 16mm
Color (J H) (SWEDISH)
LC 73-701435
Points out the many examples in nature of organisms living together in mutual dependence. Gives insights into the relationship called symbiosis.
Science - Natural
Dist - PHENIX **Prod** - PHENIX 1973

Symbiosis 4 MIN
U-matic / VHS / 16mm
Color (H C A)
LC 77-703312
Tells the story of an island that runs away from home to avoid destruction by the 'occasionals' who visit it on weekends. Shows the frightened island, who, searching the world for a more suitable home, finds none and returns home to receive a prodigal's welcome.
Fine Arts; Literature and Drama
Dist - IFB **Prod** - COXDA 1977

Symbiotic Nitrogen Fixation 20 MIN
U-matic
Breakthrough Series
Color (H C)
Shows that legumes infected by rhizobium bacteria fix their own nitrogen and become, in effect, partially self fertilizing. Finding out how this nitrogen process works will enable the use of it with other food crops.
Agriculture; Science; Science - Natural; Science - Physical
Dist - TVOTAR **Prod** - TVOTAR 1985

Symbol Boy 5 MIN
16mm
Color (C A)
LC 76-701787
Uses animated drawings in order to introduce the basic vocabulary of Blissymbols. Shows how the Bliss system can be useful in helping the verbally handicapped communicate.
Education; English Language; Psychology
Dist - BNCHMK **Prod** - NFBC 1976

Symbolic Leader 15 MIN
VHS / U-matic
Modern President Series
Color (H C)
$250 purchase
Shows how the president as a symbolic leader affirms the heritage of the United States and help Americans to develop self - confidence. Produced by Focus Enterprises.
Biography; Civics and Political Systems
Dist - CORF

Symbolic Programming Languages 30 MIN
U-matic
Computing for Every Man Series
Color (H A)
Explores the evolution and detailed construction of a typical Symbolic Assembly Program. Discusses the advantages of this mode of programming.
Mathematics
Dist - NYSED **Prod** - NYSED 1973

Symbolism in literature 15 MIN
16mm
Color (J H C)
LC FIA66-973
Uses the UPA cartoon version of Edgar Allen Poe's The Tell Tale Heart to develop concepts of literary symbolism.
Literature and Drama
Dist - FILCOM **Prod** - SIGMA 1966

Symbols - 2 20 MIN
U-matic / VHS / BETA
Religion and civilisation series
Color; PAL (G H C)
PdS40, PdS48 purchase
Looks at the symbolic nature of religious practices. Includes prayers, festivals, places of worship and more. Part of a two - part series exploring religions within their individual traditions. Produced in Britain by Charles Harris.
Religion and Philosophy
Dist - EDPAT

Symbols and Components 33 MIN
16mm
B&W
LC 74-704177
Illustrates a practical electrical circuit, using symbols to represent the electrical components and measuring instruments. Explains electrical grounds, fuses and switches.
Industrial and Technical Education; Science - Physical
Dist - USNAC **Prod** - USAF 1965

Symbols, Equations and the Computer 23 MIN
16mm / U-matic / VHS
Color
Describes the symbols and equations needed to find the answer to the shape of the famous Golden Section. Shows where the symbols come from and explores iteration methods to find the answers.
Mathematics
Dist - MEDIAG **Prod** - OPENU 1979

Symbols for welding 18 MIN
BETA / VHS / U-matic
Welding training series
Color (IND G)
$495.00 purchase _ #821 - 08
Trains welders. Covers all the symbols used in the industrial welding process. Part of a series on welding.
Health and Safety; Industrial and Technical Education; Psychology
Dist - ITSC **Prod** - ITSC 1990

Symbols of expression 26 MIN
16mm
B&W (C T)
Extends the theme of unity of personality (expressive behavior). attempts to demonstrate that an individual's drawings, 'Doodlings,' art productions, dance forms,

signatures or written productions embody the 'Key Symbol' of personality. Demonstrates with children, college students and shows signatures and musical manuscripts of Bach, Beethoven and Mozart.
Education; Fine Arts; Psychology
Dist - PSUPCR **Prod** - PSUPCR 1952

Symbols of Texas 10 MIN
U-matic / VHS / Slide
Color; Mono (K P I)
Presented and explained are Texas' numerous official and unofficial symbols. Includes a series of activities and games to help teach the symbol of Texas to children.
Education; Geography - United States
Dist - UTXITC **Prod** - UTXITC 1986

Symmetricks 7 MIN
16mm
B&W (G)
$15.00 rental
Explores the rapid tracking of drawn line images compounded by the symmetry of multiple images. Uses computer - animated drawing that works at the speed of light. Blends music with the color that comes from the black and white images.
Fine Arts; Industrial and Technical Education
Dist - CANCIN **Prod** - VANBKS 1972

Symmetries of the Cube 14 MIN
U-matic / VHS / 16mm
College Geometry Series
Color (H C)
LC FIA68-831
Examines symmetry in terms of reflections, first by studying the square and then the cube and its reciprocal octahedron. Shows the axis and planes of symmetry in relationship to the 48 symmetries of the cube.
Mathematics
Dist - IFB **Prod** - NSF 1971

Symmetry 13 MIN
16mm
B&W w/color tint (H C A)
$30.00 rental
Tells the tale of the spiral-like downfall of a young woman following a breakup with a boyfriend. Utilizes heavily filtered light, monotone dialogue, and foreboding aerial footage. Produced by Jon Behrens. Screenplay by Duane Wright and music by Common Language.
Guidance and Counseling; Sociology
Dist - CANCIN

Symmetry 11 MIN
16mm / U-matic / VHS
Color (J A)
LC FIA67-5711
Use animated semi - abstract figures to depict and define symmetry. Examines a controlled progression of simple to complex symmetries and points out that symmetries obey strict mathematical principles.
Mathematics
Dist - IFB **Prod** - STGT 1967

Symmetry 15 MIN
U-matic
Math Makers Two Series
Color (I)
Presents the math concepts of symmetry and balance, combining shapes to make symmetrical figures, and shapes with multiple lines of symmetry.
Education; Mathematics
Dist - TVOTAR **Prod** - TVOTAR 1980

Symmetry - a First Film 14 MIN
U-matic / VHS / 16mm
Color (P I J)
Uses attractive visuals of both ordinary and exotic objects to illustrate mirror symmetry, radial symmetry and rhythm.
Fine Arts; Mathematics
Dist - PHENIX **Prod** - PHENIX 1983

Symmetry and Shapes - Mirror Image 20 MIN
U-matic / VHS / 16mm
Mathscore One Series
Color (I J)
Discusses aspects of symmetry and shapes.
Mathematics
Dist - FI **Prod** - BBCTV

Symmetry and Shapes - S for Shapes 20 MIN
16mm / U-matic / VHS
Mathscore Two Series
Color (I)
Discusses aspects of symmetry and shapes.
Mathematics
Dist - FI **Prod** - BBCTV

Symmetry in Physical Law 57 MIN
16mm
Character of Physical Law Series
B&W (C)
LC 75-707490
Professor Richard Feynman, California Institute of Technology, discusses the symmetries of physical phenomena - - translations in space and time, rotations in space, the right and left handedness of fundamental interactions and of living things, the consequences of relative motion and the interconnections of space and time.
Mathematics; Science - Physical
Dist - EDC **Prod** - BBCTV 1965

The Sympathoadrenal system in cardiovascular health and disease
VHS / 8mm cartridge
Color (PRO)
#TE - 40
Presents a free - loan program which trains medical professionals. Contact distributor for details.
Health and Safety
Dist - WYAYLA **Prod** - WYAYLA

Sympathomimetic Blocking Agents, Ganglionic Blocking Agents and Anti - Hypertensive Agents 30 MIN
16mm
Pharmacology Series
Color (C)
LC 73-703340
Health and Safety; Psychology
Dist - TELSTR **Prod** - MVNE 1971

Sympathomimetics 30 MIN
16mm
Pharmacology Series
B&W (C)
LC 73-703339
Reviews the anatomy and physiology of the autonomic nervous system. Shows effects of various sympathomimetric drugs caused by their action of stimulating sympathetic nerve activity.
Health and Safety; Psychology
Dist - TELSTR **Prod** - MVNE 1971

Sympathy for the Devil (1 Plus 1) 110 MIN
16mm
Color (H C A)
Presents Jean - Luc Godard's, Sympathy For The Devil (1 Plus 1) with the accompaniment of the Rolling Stones. Touches on the issues of black power, rape, murder, fascism, acid, pornography, sex and brutality.
Civics and Political Systems; Health and Safety; Sociology
Dist - NLC **Prod** - NLC

Symphone - Windows, Spreadsheets Word Processing 40 MIN
U-matic / VHS
(A PRO)
$275.00 purchase
Explores Symphony's capabilities and includes window functions and spreadsheet functions.
Computer Science
Dist - VIDEOT **Prod** - VIDEOT 1988

Symphonia de erosus 15 MIN
16mm
Color (G)
$40.00 rental
Meditates on nature and the human relationship with it. Explores the consequences of submersion with nature. Organized like a visual symphony and consists of three movements. Produced by Kevin Deal.
Fine Arts
Dist - CANCIN

Symphonic Cello Soli 30 MIN
U-matic / VHS
Cello Sounds of Today Series
Color (J H A)
Fine Arts
Dist - IU **Prod** - IU 1984

Symphonie Diagonale 7 MIN
16mm
B&W
Features hieroglyphic forms moving along an invisible diagonal in a work by Viking Eggeling, recognized by fellow artists as a 'lucid thinker and creator'. Produced 1921 - 25.
Fine Arts
Dist - STARRC **Prod** - STARRC

Symphonie Einer Weltstadt 79 MIN
16mm
B&W (H C) (GERMAN)
LC 79-712386
A German language film. Views the people, industry and recreation of pre - war Berlin against a background of symphonic music.
History - World
Dist - TRANSW **Prod** - LAFRGL 1970

Symphonie Einer Weltstadt - Berlin Wie Es War 79 MIN
16mm / U-matic / VHS
B&W (H C A) (GERMAN)
A German language film. Presents glimpses of the Berlin of the 1930's.
Foreign Language; Geography - World; History - World
Dist - IFB **Prod** - IFB 1939

Symphonie Pastorale 105 MIN
16mm
B&W
Features the story of a girl, blind and orphaned, who is adopted by the village minister. Shows how as time goes by, the minister's affection grows into love.
Literature and Drama; Psychology; Sociology
Dist - TRANSW **Prod** - CON 1964

Symphonie realiste 13 MIN
16mm
Les Francais chez vous series
B&W (I J H)
LC 70-704479
Presents lesson one of the first set in the Les Francais Chez Vous series.
Foreign Language
Dist - CHLTN **Prod** - PEREN 1967

The Symphonist 28 MIN
U-matic / VHS
Beethoven by Barenboim Series
Color (C)
$249.00, $149.00 purchase _ #AD - 1230
Reveals that almost all of Beethoven's music has a symphonic character. Demonstrates his overriding of the boundaries of the piano through Barenboim's performance of excerpts from the Pastoral Sonata, Opus 28, the Hammerklavier and the first movement of Symphony No 8. Part of a thirteen - part series placing Beethoven, his music and his life within the context of his time and the history of music, Beethoven by Barenboim.
Fine Arts; History - World
Dist - FOTH **Prod** - FOTH

Symphony 360 - 480 MIN
Cassette
(A PRO)
$119.00; $1,995.00; $119.00
Includes 4 audio cassettes, diskette and guide.
Computer Science
Dist - VIDEOT **Prod** - VIDEOT 1988

Symphony
VHS
Micro Video Learning Systems Series
(A IND)
$495.00 purchase _ #MV500
Demonstrates the use of the Symphony computer system.
Computer Science
Dist - CAMV

Symphony 2
Videodisc
(H A)
$2195.00 purchase
Explains the basics of four Symphony Release 2 applications that can combine spreadsheet, word processing, graphics, and data management functions. Six to eight hour course.
Computer Science; Education
Dist - CMSL **Prod** - CMSL

Symphony 2.0
VHS
Color (G)
$179.95 purchase _ #SYM20
Provides video PC software training in Symphony 2.0. Includes training guide.
Computer Science
Dist - HALASI **Prod** - HALASI

Symphony Across the Land 50 MIN
16mm
B&W (H A)
LC FIE63-52
Explains the role of music in the U S and features leading symphony orchestras from various states as they perform music by American composers.
Fine Arts
Dist - USIS **Prod** - USIS 1959

Symphony beneath the sea 60 MIN
U-matic / 16mm / VHS
Last frontier series
Color; Mono (G)
$225.00, $550.00 purchase
Demonstrates that the sea is alive with the sounds of many creatures.
Science - Natural
Dist - CTV **Prod** - MAKOF 1985

Symphony - Complete Anderson Set
VHS / U-matic
(A PRO)
$495.00 purchase
Explores system's capabilities for business professionals.
Computer Science
Dist - VIDEOT **Prod** - VIDEOT 1988

Symphony - Graphics, Data Management and Communications 40 MIN
U-matic / VHS
(A PRO)
$275.00 purhase
Introduces graphics, data management and communications capabilities to the business professional. Teaches development and display of various charts and graphs. Includes maintenance of databases.
Computer Science
Dist - VIDEOT **Prod** - VIDEOT 1988

Symphony in Black 9 MIN
16mm
B&W
Features Louis Armstrong and Billie Holiday in a musical short.
Fine Arts; History - United States
Dist - STRFLS **Prod** - SPCTRA 1935

Symphony in D Workshop 53 MIN
VHS
Color (S)
$39.95 purchase _ #833 - 9184
Features the innovative choreography of Kiri Kylian and the Nederlands Dans Theater's performance of 'Symphony In D' by Haydn. Shows Kylian rehearsing the work with students of the Royal Ballet School in London and talking about his exile from Czechoslovakia and life as a dancer and choreographer.
Fine Arts; Physical Education and Recreation
Dist - FI **Prod** - RMART 1987

Symphony in Steel 14 MIN
16mm
Color
LC FIA68-832
Describes an air trip to the West Indies at carnival time. Views the islands and their inhabitants, documenting the hand - crafting of a steel orchestra from discarded oil barrels. Presents the November, 1966, visit of a steel band to Barbados for Independence Week celebrations.
Fine Arts; Geography - World
Dist - PANWA **Prod** - PANWA 1967

Symphony in the Mountains 75 MIN
VHS / U-matic
B&W (GERMAN (ENGLISH SUBTITLES))
Presents a romance about a public - school teacher who teaches singing and skiing instead of the regular curriculum against the advice of his superiors and falls in love with the sister of one of his students. Features songs by the Vienna Boys Choir. With English subtitles.
Fine Arts; Foreign Language
Dist - IHF **Prod** - IHF

Symphony no 1 60 MIN
U-matic
Beethoven Festival Series
Color
Presents the Detroit Symphony Orchestra, under the direction of Antal Dorati, performing Beethoven's Symphony No. 1. Features the conductor discussing the symphony with E G Marshall.
Fine Arts
Dist - PBS **Prod** - WTVSTV

Symphony no 2 60 MIN
U-matic
Beethoven Festival Series
Color
Presents the Detroit Symphony Orchestra, under the direction of Antal Dorati, performing Beethoven's Symphony No. 2. Features the conductor discussing the symphony with E G Marshall.
Fine Arts
Dist - PBS **Prod** - WTVSTV

Symphony no 3 60 MIN
U-matic
Beethoven Festival Series
Color
Presents the Detroit Symphony Orchestra, under the direction of Antal Dorati, performing Beethoven's Symphony No. 3. Features the conductor discussing the symphony with E G Marshall.
Fine Arts
Dist - PBS **Prod** - WTVSTV

Symphony no 4 60 MIN
U-matic
Beethoven Festival Series
Color
Presents the Detroit Symphony Orchestra, under the direction of Antal Dorati, performing Beethoven's Symphony No. 4. Features the conductor discussing the symphony with E G Marshall.
Fine Arts
Dist - PBS **Prod** - WTVSTV

Symphony no 5 60 MIN
U-matic
Beethoven Festival Series
Color (H C A)
LC 79-708047
Presents narrator E.G. Marshall and conductor Antal Dorati discussing Beethoven's Fifth Symphony. Includes a performance of the work by the Detroit Symphony Orchestra.
Fine Arts
Dist - PBS **Prod** - WTVSTV 1979

Symphony no 6 60 MIN
U-matic
Beethoven Festival Series
Color
Presents the Detroit Symphony Orchestra, under the direction of Antal Dorati, performing Beethoven's Symphony No. 6. Features the conductor discussing the symphony with E G Marshall.
Fine Arts
Dist - PBS **Prod** - WTVSTV

Symphony no 7 60 MIN
U-matic
Beethoven Festival Series
Color
Presents the Detroit Symphony Orchestra, under the direction of Antal Dorati, performing Beethoven's Symphony No. 7. Features the conductor discussing the symphony with E G Marshall.
Fine Arts
Dist - PBS **Prod** - WTVSTV

Symphony no 8 60 MIN
U-matic
Beethoven Festival Series
Color
Presents the Detroit Symphony Orchestra, under the direction of Antal Dorati, performing Beethoven's Symphony No. 8. Features the conductor discussing the symphony with E G Marshall.
Fine Arts
Dist - PBS **Prod** - WTVSTV

Symphony no 9 60 MIN
U-matic
Beethoven Festival Series
Color
Presents the Detroit Symphony Orchestra, under the direction of Antal Dorati, performing Beethoven's Symphony No. 9. Features the conductor discussing the symphony with E G Marshall.
Fine Arts
Dist - PBS **Prod** - WTVSTV

Symphony no 94 in G - Surprise - second movement 10 MIN
VHS
Color (I J H)
LC 89-700200
Teaches appreciation of the Symphony No 94 in G, Sunrise, Second Movement, by Franz Josef Haydn.
Fine Arts
Dist - EAV **Prod** - EAV 1989

Symphony of a World City - Berlin as it was 79 MIN
U-matic / VHS / 16mm
B&W (H C A)
LC 80-700690
Uses footage shot in the 1930's to show life in pre - World War II Berlin. Describes the people, their work days and leisure activities, and the various sections and buildings of the city.
History - World
Dist - IFB **Prod** - LAFRGL 1977

Symphony on Ice 10 MIN
16mm
Color
Features the game of hockey, a sport which requires split - second decisions from each player who must travel down the ice at speeds in excess of 50 miles per hour. Explains the gear used by the players and the techniques of playing well.
Physical Education and Recreation
Dist - FILMSM **Prod** - FILMSM

The Symphony orchestra 14 MIN
U-matic / VHS / 16mm
Color (I J H) (SPANISH)
Traces the development of the orchestra from an ensemble of five string players to a large symphonic organization. Uses examples from the musical masterworks of three centuries to demonstrate the contribution of each major development in the orchestra. Features the Vienna Symphony Orchestra.
Fine Arts; Foreign Language
Dist - EBEC **Prod** - EBEC

Symphony series
Graphics, data management, and communications 60 MIN
Windows, Spread Sheets, and Word Processing 60 MIN
Dist - UTM

The Symphony Sound with Henry Lewis and the Royal Philharmonic 27 MIN
16mm / U-matic / VHS
Color (H C A)
LC 71-709017
Henry Lewis discusses the unique characteristics of the Symphony orchestra and describes the instruments and their particular roles within the symphony.
Fine Arts
Dist - LCOA **Prod** - IQFILM 1970

Symphony Training System 100 MIN
U-matic / VHS
(A PRO)
$495.00, $595.00 purchase
Teaches all environments including spreadsheet and work processing, database graphing and telecommunications.
Computer Science
Dist - VIDEOT **Prod** - VIDEOT 1988

Symposium of Popular Songs 16 MIN
16mm / U-matic / VHS
Color (P I J H)
LC 79-700820
Takes a look at various forms of popular songs and how they have changed with the passage of time.
Fine Arts
Dist - CORF **Prod** - DISNEY 1962

The Symptomatic Postgastrectomy Patient 22 MIN
16mm
Color
LC 74-705734
Presents fiberscopic photographs of postoperative complications of the stomach.
Science; Science - Natural
Dist - USNAC **Prod** - NMAC 1969

Symptoms and Treatment of Marine Injuries 18 MIN
U-matic / VHS
Color (PRO)
Demonstrates how to diagnose and treat eight kinds of injuries from marine life.
Health and Safety; Science - Natural
Dist - HSCIC **Prod** - HSCIC 1977

Symptoms in Schizophrenia 18 MIN
16mm
B&W (C A)
Demonstrates various symptoms in schizophrenia, such as social apathy, delusions, hallucinations, hebephrenic reactions, cerea flexibilitas, rigidity, motor stereotypes, posturing and echopraxia in typical cases. For medical and allied groups.
Psychology
Dist - PSUPCR **Prod** - PSUPCR 1938

Symptoms of aging 28 MIN
VHS
Human body - aging - series
Color (J H G)
$89.95 purchase _ #UW4172
Covers some of the symptoms of aging - loss of muscular strength, reduced visual capability, arteriosclerosis - as well as how these might be prevented, postponed or dealt with. Shows how fitness can be maintained and how seniors may have the edge over younger people. Part of a 39 - part series featuring computer animation, medical photography, electron micrography, full - color drawings and diagrams and three - dimensional working models to cover the workings of the human body from head to toe and inside out.
Health and Safety; Science - Natural
Dist - FOTH

Symptoms of Coronary Heart Disease
VHS / U-matic
Color
Discusses symptoms of coronary heart disease.
Health and Safety; Science - Natural
Dist - MEDFAC **Prod** - MEDFAC

Symptoms of Sobriety 45 MIN
U-matic / Cassette
Color; Mono (G)
$495.00, $10.00 purchase
Defines the characteristics of a sober alcoholic. Drawn from the work of Father Joseph C Martin.
Health and Safety; Psychology
Dist - KELLYP **Prod** - KELLYP

Sync Touch
VHS / 16mm
Films of Barbara Hammer Series
Color (G)
$35.00 rental
Juxtaposes lesbian images with common cliches, providing an ironic and humorous inquiry into the lesbian aesthetic. Produced by Barbara Hammer.
Fine Arts; Health and Safety; Literature and Drama; Psychology; Sociology
Dist - WMEN

Synchro Systems 28 MIN
U-matic
Radio Technician Training Series
B&W
LC 78-706304
Explains how a synchro generator controls the movement of a synchro motor and shows the electrical transfer of angular motion between two remote points. Demonstrates the operation of a control transformer and a differential synchro generator and tells how to use a control transformer as a receiver and a differential synchro generator when putting correction into the signal of the circuit. Issued in 1944 as a motion picture.
Industrial and Technical Education
Dist - USNAC **Prod** - USN 1978

Synchro systems, Pt 1 14 MIN
16mm / U-matic
Radio technician training series
B&W (VOC)
LC 78-706304
Explains how a synchro generator controls the movement of a synchro motor and shows the electrical transfer of angular motion between two remote points. Demonstrates the operation of a control transformer and a differential synchro generator and tells how to use a control transformer as a receiver and a differential synchro generator when putting correction into the signal of the circuit. Issued in 1944 as a motion picture.
Civics and Political Systems; Education; Industrial and Technical Education
Dist - USNAC **Prod** - USN 1978

Synchro Systems, Pt 2 13 MIN
16mm
Radio Technician Training Series
B&W
LC FIE52-926
Shows how to use a control transformer as a receiver and a differential synchro generator when putting corrections into the signal of the circuit.
Industrial and Technical Education
Dist - USNAC **Prod** - USN 1948

Synchromy 8 MIN
16mm
Color (P)
LC 72-700225
Uses moving colors to create a visual conception of music. Presents various patterns and frequencies, which represent musical shapes from a corresponding soundtrack.
English Language; Fine Arts; Industrial and Technical Education
Dist - NFBC **Prod** - NFBC 1972

Synchronized Swimming 17 MIN
U-matic / VHS / 16mm
B&W (J H C)
LC FIA68-2888
Introduces synchronized swimming. Shows basic skills required for strokes, summersaults, rotation and figure work. Underwater photography describes various movements.
Physical Education and Recreation
Dist - IFB **Prod** - BHA 1968

Synchronous Belt Drives 10 MIN
VHS
Power Transmission Series I - PT Products Series
Color (A)
$225.00 purchase, $50.00 rental _ #57961
Describes identification, construction, measuring conventions and numbering systems for timing belts (measured in inches) and round - tooth belts (measured metric). Lists advantages of these as fixed ratio, no slippage, no lubrication, diminished bearing load, and good load capacity range and operating efficiency. Explains how to determine belt specs from conventional numbers and for pulleys. Explains the use of flanges and the way to determine if a double flange is required.
Industrial and Technical Education
Dist - UILL **Prod** - MAJEC 1986

Synchronous Combined Protocolectomy for Mucosal Ulcerative Colitis 46 MIN
VHS / U-matic
Gastrointestinal Series
Color
Health and Safety; Science - Natural
Dist - SVL **Prod** - SVL

Synchronous Combined Resection of the Rectum 32 MIN
16mm
Color (PRO)
Shows details of a two - team abdomino - perineal resection of the rectum for carcinoma, using a simple technique of positioning the legs on mayo high stands.
Health and Safety; Science
Dist - ACY **Prod** - ACYDGD 1969

Synchronous Machines - Electromechanical Dynamics 33 MIN
Videoreel / VHS
B&W
Focuses on electromagnetic fields and forces as they interact with moving and deformable media.
Industrial and Technical Education; Science - Physical
Dist - EDC **Prod** - NCEEF

Synchronous Motors and Controller Maintenance 60 MIN
VHS
Motors and Motor Controllers Series
Color (PRO)
$600.00, $1500.00 purchase _ #EMSMC
Covers basic synchronous motor and controller operation. Considers typical preventive maintenance and electrical testing procedures for common electrical problems. Part of a ten - part series on motors and motor controllers, which is part of a 29 unit set on electrical maintenance. Includes 10 textbooks and an instructor guide which provide four hours of instruction.
Education; Industrial and Technical Education; Psychology
Dist - NUSTC **Prod** - NUSTC

Synchros 25 MIN
16mm / U-matic / VHS
B&W (H A)
Describes the construction, operation, and electrical characteristics of a synchro device, emphasizing the voltage induced into the stator with the rotor at various positions. Defines such terms as electrical balance, correspondence, friction and torque.
Industrial and Technical Education
Dist - USNAC **Prod** - USNAC 1984

Synchroscope 38 MIN
16mm
B&W
LC 74-705735
Shows the block diagram of the vertical and horizontal channels of a typical synchroscope and traces a signal through both channels. Uses the Tektronix 502A oscilloscope to demonstrate how the various controls affect signal presentation. (Kinescope).
Industrial and Technical Education
Dist - USNAC **Prod** - USAF

Synchrotron 15 MIN
16mm
Color (H C A)
LC 75-700729
Uses live action and animation to discuss the components and operation of the Cambridge electron accelerator, a high energy physics research laboratory operated by Harvard and the Massachusetts Institute of Technology. Includes scenes of scientists performing experiments to test old and new theories regarding the basic nature of matter.
Science - Physical
Dist - USERD **Prod** - HPP 1968

Syndactylism - Surgical Management 25 MIN
U-matic / VHS
Color (PRO)
Discusses incidence and classification of syndactylism of the hand. Demonstrates three different operations, along with follow - ups to show end result.
Health and Safety
Dist - ASSH **Prod** - ASSH

Syndromes
VHS / U-matic
Sexually Transmitted Diseases Series
Color
Presents five syndromes attributable to sexually transmitted disease. Presents signs and symptoms and treatment for each disease.
Health and Safety
Dist - CONMED **Prod** - CONMED

Synectics 30 MIN
VHS / U-matic
Teaching for Thinking - Creativity in the Classroom Series
Color (T PRO)
$180.00 purchase,$50.00 rental
Explains Synectics, the practice of making the commonplace different and the different commonplace, then offers applications toward reading comprehension.
Education; English Language
Dist - AITECH **Prod** - WHATV 1986

Synectics and Group Investigation 30 MIN
U-matic / VHS
Classroom Teaching Models Series
Color
Demonstrates one aspect of synectics, a strategy for developing and improving creative problem solving ability. Describes synectics activities which enhance the problem - solving capacity and creative thinking processes of the individual student, with the teacher acting as the facilitator. Presents a second model in which the teacher and her students are involved in a group investigation of the concept of communication through social inquiry, which is a more structured model than the synectics model.
Education; Psychology
Dist - NETCHE **Prod** - NETCHE 1979

Synergetics - a completely new experience in exercise 71 MIN
VHS
Color (G)
$49.95 purchase; LC 90-713682
Introduces and explains the concept of 'synergetics' exercise, a fitness routine designed to improve overall fitness, reduce stress, help with weight reduction and provide overall musculature improvement. Demonstrates four different routines for the viewer to follow. Includes book. Video also available separately.
Physical Education and Recreation; Psychology
Dist - SYNHP **Prod** - SYNHP 1990

Synergism - Cities and Towns Series
Promise City 29 MIN
Dist - PBS

Synergism - Command Performance Series
The American highlands 58 MIN
Budaya - the performing arts of Indonesia 59 MIN
O Say Can You Sing 60 MIN
Rochester Philharmonic Orchestra - Unlikely Sources of Symphonic Music 60 MIN
Dist - PBS

Synergism - Encore Series
Art of Bunraku 29 MIN
Dances of Greece 29 MIN
Fantasy in mime 29 MIN
A Gallery of children 29 MIN
Mr Smith and Other Nonsense 29 MIN
The Music of Japan - Koto Music 29 MIN
Dist - PBS

Synergism - Gallimaufry series
Secrets of a Brook 30 MIN
Dist - IU
PBS

Synergism - gallimaufry series
Fence around the amish award series 1967 29 MIN
Gold was where you found it - award series 1966 29 MIN
Only Yesterday - Award Series 1965 29 MIN
Dist - PBS

Synergism - in today's world series
Bill Cosby on prejudice 29 MIN
Chicano 30 MIN
Low View from a Dark Shadow 29 MIN
The Marshes of 'Two' Street 29 MIN
Questions 29 MIN
Such a Place 28 MIN
Underground film 29 MIN
Until I Die 29 MIN
Watts Tower Theatre Workshop 28 MIN
Dist - PBS

Synergism - Profiles, People Series
The Artist of Savitiria 29 MIN
In Pursuit of Discovery - the Memoirs of Joseph Priestly 28 MIN
Mr Thoreau Takes a Trip - a Week on the Concord and Merrimack 27 MIN
Transitions - Conversations with Wendell Castle 30 MIN
Woman as Painter 29 MIN
Dist - PBS

Synergism - the Challenge of Sports Series
Racing on Thin Air 30 MIN
This is Rodeo 30 MIN
Dist - PBS

Synergism - Variatims in Music Series
Stanford Chorale - Il Festino 27 MIN
Dist - PBS

Synergism - Variations in Music Series
Come blow your horn 29 MIN
The Music of Harry Partch 30 MIN
Dist - PBS

Synergy - EEO, diversity and management
VHS / U-matic / BETA
Color; CC (G IND PRO C)
Features Fred Alvarez, Ron Galbraith and Barbara Walker, three experts on EEO and diversity. Offers three modules and an introductory video which examine selection practices, the workplace environment and managing performance. Uses vignettes to illustrate gender stereotyping, age and race discrinimation and disparate treatment. Includes a trainer's manual, 20 partipant manuals for each module and a copy of The Manager's Practical EEO Handbook.
Business and Economics; Psychology
Dist - BNA **Prod** - BNA 1993

Synergy - EEO, diversity and management series
Managing performance - 3
Selection - 1
The Workplace environment - 2
Dist - BNA

Synergy subliminal series
Ideal weight
Improved memory
Inner peace
Prosperity
Relaxation
Self - confidence
Self - healing
Dist - HALPER

Syngerism - Troubled Humanity Series
No Gun Towers, no Fences 59 MIN
Tiger by the Tail 58 MIN
With all Deliberate Speed 59 MIN
Dist - PBS

Synod 85 30 MIN
BETA / VHS
Color
Features an interview with Cardinal Bernard Law, Archbishop of Boston on several social changes at issue within the Catholic Church.
Religion and Philosophy
Dist - DSP **Prod** - DSP

The Synoptiscope - How to Use it 20 MIN
U-matic / VHS
Color (PRO)
Teaches students how to use the synoptiscope for testing simultaneous perception, fusion, stereopsis, retinal correspondence, and cardinal position of gaze.
Health and Safety; Science - Natural
Dist - HSCIC **Prod** - HSCIC 1981

Syntactic and Semantic Development 136 MIN
U-matic / VHS
Meeting the Communications Needs of the Severely/Profoundly 'Handicapped 1980 Series
Color
Addresses three basic questions regarding the nature of early semantic and syntactic development in communication.
Psychology; Social Science
Dist - PUAVC **Prod** - PUAVC

Syntagma 17 MIN
16mm
Color (G)
$35.00 rental
Juxtaposes notions of body language and unity of body, space and time with the final break or end of the body and fragmentation of the world. Depicts the schizophrenic breakdown of identity. Produced by Valie Export.
Fine Arts
Dist - CANCIN

Syntax 13 MIN
16mm
Color (G)
$30.00 rental
Deals with the way in which sounds and images come together. Presents a narration of the process of retaining a narration. Produced by Martha Haslanger.
Fine Arts
Dist - CANCIN

A Synthesis Approach to Reading 30 MIN
U-matic / VHS
Teaching Children with Special Needs Series
Color (T)
Discusses a synthesis approach to reading in children with special needs.
Education
Dist - MDCPB **Prod** - MDDE

Synthesis - Architecture 15 MIN
U-matic / VHS
Arts - a - Bound
(I)
$130.00 purchase, $25.00 rental, $75.00 self dub
Explores the architect's art. Uses a documentary format featuring interviews with architects on location, following projects from inception to completion.
Fine Arts
Dist - GPN **Prod** - NCGE 1985

Synthesis of an organic compound 20 MIN
VHS / 16mm
Chem study video - film series
Color (H C)
Shows the synthesis of 2 - butanone, a ketone, from 2 - butanol, an alcohol, as an example of a common type of organic synthesis. Discusses three basic steps, synthesis, purification and indentification, illustrating the latter by forming a solid derivative of the 2 - butanone, determining its melting point and confirming identification by infrared spectroscopy. Part of a series for teaching chemistry to high school and college students.
Science - Physical
Dist - WARDS MLA **Prod** - WARDS CHEMS 1990

Synthesis of Neuroanatomy, Pt 1 18 MIN
16mm / U-matic / VHS
Anatomical Basis of Brain Function Series
Color (PRO)
Science - Natural
Dist - TEF **Prod** - AVCORP

Synthesis of Neuroanatomy, Pt 2 18 MIN
16mm / U-matic / VHS
Anatomical Basis of Brain Function Series
Color (PRO)
Science - Natural
Dist - TEF **Prod** - AVCORP

Synthesis - opera 15 MIN
VHS / U-matic
Arts - a - bound
(I)
$130.00 purchase, $25.00 rental, $75.00 self dub
Explores the art of opera. Uses a documentary format featuring interviews with artists and performers on location, following a performance from rehearsals to finished production.
Fine Arts
Dist - GPN **Prod** - NCGE 1985

Synthetic Sapphire 7 MIN
16mm
B&W (C)
Examines the manufacture of synthetic sapphire from alumina and gives some examples of its uses.
Business and Economics; Science - Physical; Social Science
Dist - HEFL **Prod** - BFI 1946

The Syphay Family 29 MIN
VHS / U-matic
Color
Traces the lineage of the Syphay's, one of Virginia's oldest black families, to the owner of the Arlington Plantation.
History - United States; Sociology
Dist - SYLWAT **Prod** - RCOMTV 1985

Syphilis 15 MIN
U-matic / VHS
Color
Presents a detailed explanation of the nature of syphilis. Discusses diagnosis. Stresses early and appropriate treatment.
Health and Safety
Dist - MEDFAC **Prod** - MEDFAC 1973

Syphilis 14 MIN
16mm
B&W (PRO)
Covers the diagnosis of early, latent and late syphilis.
Health and Safety
Dist - NMAC **Prod** - USPHS 1941

Syphilitic Venereal Disease 25 MIN
16mm
Color (PRO)
Organizes and clarifies for the physician the stages and types of syphilis with correct diagnosis and treatment discussed.
Health and Safety; Science; Science - Natural
Dist - SQUIBB **Prod** - SQUIBB 1954

Syphilitic Venereal Disease 19 MIN
16mm
Color (PRO)
Examines the types and stages of syphilis, explaining the course of the disease in terms of the pathologic processes initiated by the infecting Treponema pallidum organism. Illustrates the variety of symptoms by clinical material, to the end that correct diagnosis may by made and proper treatment given.
Health and Safety; Science - Natural
Dist - SQUIBB **Prod** - SQUIBB

Syracuse
VHS
Campus clips series
Color (H C A)
$29.95 purchase _ #CC0079V
Takes a video visit to the campus of Syracuse University in New York. Shows many of the distinctive features of the campus, and interviews students about their experiences. Provides information on the composition of the student body, professors, academics, social life, housing, and other subjects.
Education
Dist - CAMV

Syrian Arab Republic 28 MIN
Videoreel / VHS
International Byline Series
Color
Interviews Ambassador Hammoud El - Choufi, permanent representative to the United Nations, on Syria today and the advancement the country has made in the last few years. Includes a film clip on Syria's industrialization.
Business and Economics; Civics and Political Systems; Geography - World
Dist - PERRYM **Prod** - PERRYM

Syringe driver in symptom control 9 MIN
U-matic / VHS / BETA
Color; NTSC; PAL; SECAM (C PRO G)
PdS95 purchase
Demonstrates in detail the use of the Graesby Syringe Driver for continuous administration of drugs by slow subcutaneous infusion.
Health and Safety
Dist - VIEWTH

Systamodules 13 MIN
16mm
Color
LC 77-700420
Shows a new concept in hospital pharmacy patient care, based on a system of unique modular environments. Traces these modules through their conception, documentation, design and application.
Health and Safety
Dist - FISHSC **Prod** - FISHSC 1976

The System 27 MIN
16mm / U-matic / VHS
Insight Series
B&W (J)
LC 72-702003
Tells a story about a happy - go - lucky housewife, who won prizes on many television game shows, in contrast to her husband, whose philosophy is that no one get something for nothing and that one cannot beat the system, in order to show that to live fully one must trust life.
Guidance and Counseling; Psychology; Sociology
Dist - PAULST **Prod** - PAULST 1972

The System 15 MIN
16mm / VHS / BETA / U-matic
Color; PAL (G)
PdS125, PdS133 purchase
Illustrates a basic series of correct procedures to adopt when riding a motorcycle.
Health and Safety; Industrial and Technical Education
Dist - EDPAT

The System 20 MIN
U-matic / VHS
Tomes and talismans series
(I J)
$145.00 purchase, $27.00 rental, $90.00 self dub
Uses a science fantasy adventure to define, illustrate and review basic library research concepts. Designed for sixth, seventh and eighth graders. Fifth in a 13 part series.
Education
Dist - GPN **Prod** - MISETV

The System 14 MIN
16mm
Color
Looks at the American economic system through the eyes of high school students.
Business and Economics
Dist - MTP **Prod** - EXXON 1982

System 12 20 MIN
16mm
Color
LC 82-700191
Explains the function of System 12 components by visiting the various sites in Europe and America where they were developed or are produced. Introduces the actual people involved who explain this digital switching system.
Industrial and Technical Education
Dist - BLUMAR **Prod** - ITTEM 1981

System Analysis - Design 30 MIN
VHS / U-matic
Making it Count Series
Color (H C A)
LC 80-707573
Presents the process of designing a system and the role of the system analyst.
Business and Economics; Mathematics
Dist - BCSC **Prod** - BCSC 1980

System Analysis - Development and Implementation 30 MIN
VHS / U-matic
Making it Count Series
Color (H C A)
LC 80-707574
Shows the development and implementation phases of a system. Discusses the skills required of programmers and their role in system development.
Business and Economics; Mathematics
Dist - BCSC **Prod** - BCSC 1980

System Analysis - Problem Definition 30 MIN
VHS / U-matic
Making it Count Series
Color (H C A)
LC 80-707572
Shows how information systems are developed, starting with user requirements and proceeding through the phases of system design. Outlines the process and examines the first two steps, problem definition and project analysis. Describes the role of the system analyst. Covers techniques of investigation, analysis of information, and planning and control methods.
Business and Economics; Mathematics
Dist - BCSC **Prod** - BCSC 1980

System Classification 27 MIN
U-matic / VHS
Probability and Random Processes - Linear Systems Series
B&W (PRO)
Provides an investigation of the classification of systems according to their input - output properties.
Mathematics
Dist - MIOT **Prod** - MIOT

System Control and Factory Automation 29 MIN
BETA / VHS / U-matic
Color
$400 purchase
Shows programmable logic controller.
Industrial and Technical Education; Science
Dist - ASM **Prod** - ASM

System Descriptions 22 MIN
VHS / U-matic
Probability and Random Processes - Linear Systems Series
B&W (PRO)
Introduces the basic concept of a single - input single - output system, and presents a number of examples and special cases including the important class of of linear systems.
Mathematics
Dist - MIOT **Prod** - MIOT

The System Error Budget 41 MIN
U-matic / VHS
Systems Engineering and Systems Management Series
Color
Illustrates the application of system error analysis to practical systems. Establishes system error budgets based on an analysis of these systems.
Industrial and Technical Education
Dist - MIOT **Prod** - MIOT

A System for handling sports injuries 33 MIN
U-matic / VHS / BETA
Color; PAL (H C T G)
PdS50, PdS58 purchase
Outlines a system which can be applied whenever injury occurs in any sporting event.
Physical Education and Recreation
Dist - EDPAT

A System for Overdenture Retention 14 MIN
VHS / U-matic / 16mm
Color (PRO)
Describes the use of the zest anchor system which consists of a metallic sleeve and nylon post, one of the stud attachments available commercially which can be utilized to enhance the retention of complete removable overdentures.
Health and Safety; Science
Dist - USNAC **Prod** - VADTC

System Functions 35 MIN
U-matic / VHS
Probability and Random Processes - Linear Systems Series
B&W (PRO)
Describes some techniques for measuring system functions (impulse response and frequency response), and also considers the analysis of linear systems characterized by differential equations, or the cascade of several linear systems.
Mathematics
Dist - MIOT **Prod** - MIOT

The System is Based on 10 20 MIN
U-matic
Metric System Series
Color (J)
Emphasizes decimal prefixes and points out that the decimal system uses 10 and multiples of 10 as bases.
Mathematics
Dist - GPN **Prod** - MAETEL 1975

System of change series
Combines units one, two and three of the series in a package. Includes the videos The Vision for Change, The Change Champions, Thinking it Through, Questions of Commitment, The Psychology of Resistance, and The Psychology of Attraction. Also includes workbooks.

The Change champions	14 MIN
Change excellence - Unit 1	27 MIN
Changing people - Unit 3	25 MIN
Implementing change - Unit 2	28 MIN
The Psychology of attraction	14 MIN
The Psychology of resistance	11 MIN
Questions of commitment	16 MIN
Thinking it through	12 MIN
The Vision for change	13 MIN

Dist - EXTR **Prod** - CCCD 1975

System operating manual
U-matic / VHS
Electric power system operation series; Tape 20
Color (IND)
Covers system interties, operation coordination, generator control, interchange, reliability - generation capacity, transmission, maintenance coordination, system disturbances and communications.
Industrial and Technical Education
Dist - LEIKID **Prod** - LEIKID

System Operation Checks 60 MIN
VHS / U-matic
Air Conditioning and Refrigeration - - Training Series
Color (IND)
Explains general system check, checking refrigerant charge, leak testing, maintaining lubrication level and start - up procedures.
Education; Industrial and Technical Education
Dist - ITCORP **Prod** - ITCORP

System Redundancy and Failure Detection Requirements 36 MIN
U-matic / VHS
Systems Engineering and Systems Management Series
Color
Discusses the need for redundancy to improve system reliability. Analyzes grouping and alternative failure, detection techniques for redundancy.
Industrial and Technical Education
Dist - MIOT **Prod** - MIOT

System Reliability, Maintainability and Availability 41 MIN
VHS / U-matic
Systems Engineering and Systems Management Series
Color
Presents definitions and terminology used in the fields of reliability, maintainability and availability. analyzes the basic foundations of a system reliability program. Presents methods for improving maintainability.
Industrial and Technical Education
Dist - MIOT **Prod** - MIOT

System Requirements and Documentation 180 MIN
U-matic
Software Engineering for Micro and Minicomputer Systems Series
Color (IND)
Discusses formulating and developing system requirements, and allocating them to sub - systems. Also discusses 'necessary and sufficient' requirements and production of concrete software specifications. Teaches planning and controlling of documentation for requirements, design, implementation, test and support.
Computer Science
Dist - INTECS **Prod** - INTECS

System Testing Techniques 46 MIN
U-matic / VHS
Systems Engineering and Systems Management Series
Color
Presents the basic foundations of system test. Illustrates an example for testing a large naval shipyard system.
Industrial and Technical Education
Dist - MIOT **Prod** - MIOT

A Systematic approach to hitting
VHS
You can teach hitting series
Color (J H C G)
$29.95 purchase _ #BIT009V - P
Illustrates a systematic approach to hitting through the collaborative teaching of a player, coach and teacher. Part of a three - part series on baseball and batting.
Physical Education and Recreation
Dist - CAMV

A Systematic Approach to Organizing an Energy Audit 45 MIN
VHS / U-matic
Energy Auditing and Conservation Series
Color (PRO)
LC 81-706444
Shows Mr Susemichel discussing how energy resources management fits into management of the total facility, and describes practical plant alterations that save money and can be used in figuring the plant's payback analysis. Also talks about the impact and necessity of energy audits and the importance of the team approach in resource management.
Business and Economics; Science - Natural; Social Science
Dist - AMCEE **Prod** - AMCEE 1979

Systematic Jury Selection Techniques - a Lecture by Hans Zeisel 32 MIN
U-matic / VHS
Color (PRO)
Attacks the mystique of jury selection as Hans Zeisel describes his research and experimentation in the federal courts. Stresses the importance of assembling facts and tangible information during voir dire and questions methods that emphasize surveying demographic information or observing body language.
Civics and Political Systems
Dist - ABACPE **Prod** - ABACPE

Systematic Periodontal Examination and Charting 16 MIN
VHS / U-matic
Color (PRO)
Presents a method for the examination of the periodontally involved dentition and offers a format for the eliciting and recording of diagnostic data.
Health and Safety; Science
Dist - USNAC **Prod** - VADTC 1982

Systematic Procedures and Numerical Example 38 MIN
VHS / U-matic
Modern Control Theory - Stochastic Control Series
Color (PRO)
Industrial and Technical Education; Mathematics
Dist - MIOT **Prod** - MIOT

A Systematic Program Design Model for Therapeutic Recreation 30 MIN
U-matic / VHS
Color (PRO)
LC 80-707596
Provides guidelines for systematically developing a therapeutic recreation program. Includes information on needs assessment, program development and evaluation.
Health and Safety
Dist - USNAC **Prod** - VAMCMM 1980

Systemic Disease and the Eye, Pt 1 12 MIN
VHS / U-matic
Color (PRO)
Discusses the pathogenesis and related ocular findings for congenital and acquired syphilis, tuberculosis, systemic viral infections (herpes simplex, varicella - zoster, rubella), systemic fungal infections (candidiasis, histoplasmosis), toxoplasmosis, Reiter's syndrome, sarcoidosis and connective tissue disorders (systemic lupus erythematosus).
Health and Safety; Science - Natural
Dist - UMICHM **Prod** - UMICHM 1976

Systemic Disease and the Eye, Pt 2 13 MIN
VHS / U-matic
Color (PRO)
Considers the relationship of ocular findings to seven systemic diseases. Presents detailed descriptions of the physician in diagnosing these disease entities.
Health and Safety; Science - Natural
Dist - UMICHM **Prod** - UMICHM 1976

Systemic Disease and the Eye, Pt 3 15 MIN
U-matic / VHS
Color (PRO)
Describes ocular defects which are transmitted genetically. Discusses examples of genetic disorders which involve the eye.
Health and Safety; Science - Natural
Dist - UMICHM **Prod** - UMICHM 1976

Systemic Disease and the Eye, Pt 4 15 MIN
U-matic / VHS
Color (PRO)
Discusses cardiovascular disorders which result in changes in blood vessels within the eye. Describes ocular findings in arteriosclerosis, atherosclerosis and early advanced hypertension. Presents drugs used to treat systemic diseases which cause ocular change.
Health and Safety; Science - Natural
Dist - UMICHM **Prod** - UMICHM 1976

Systemic lupus erythematosus - a brighter tomorrow 40 MIN
VHS / 16mm
Color (G)
$550.00, $275.00 purchase _ #6852F, #6842V
Educates newly diagnosed patients with systemic lupus erythematosus. Shares the experiences of a young teacher - housewife. Discusses the variations in response of the immune system, trends in research and predictive diagnosis.
Health and Safety
Dist - UCALG **Prod** - UCALG 1983

Systemic Lupus Erythematosus (SLE) - it Means some Changes 26 MIN
VHS / U-matic
Color
Provides an insight into patients with systemic lupus erythematosus (SLE). Discusses their reactions to the diagnosis, symptoms, medications and the emotional impact of illness on themselves and their families.
Guidance and Counseling; Health and Safety; Psychology
Dist - UMICHM **Prod** - UMICHM 1981

Systems Analysis
16mm
B&W
Deals with three key ideas in systems analysis.
Mathematics
Dist - OPENU **Prod** - OPENU

Systems Analysis - Means - Ends Diagnosis 29 MIN
16mm
Quantitative Approaches to Decision Making Series
B&W (IND)
LC 74-703326
Business and Economics; Psychology
Dist - EDSD **Prod** - EDSD 1969

Systems analyst 4.5 MIN
VHS / 16mm
Good works 1 series
Color (A PRO)
$40.00 purchase _ #BPN195806
Presents the occupation of a systems analyst. Gives a profile of a young person who is either undergoing an apprenticeship or has recently completed training in this field. Takes the viewer on a tour of this person's workplace and explains the practical skills and training offered by employers and schools. Gives a better understanding of the demand for skilled workers today and the potential for personal growth.
Guidance and Counseling
Dist - RMIBHF **Prod** - RMIBHF

Systems analyst 5 MIN
U-matic
Good work series
Color (H)
Provides useful, up to date information on various occupations to aid high school students in career selection. Available in five series of ten jobs each.
Computer Science; Education; Guidance and Counseling
Dist - TVOTAR **Prod** - TVOTAR 1981

Systems approach for the Turkish housing problem
VHS
Color (C PRO G)
$150.00 purchase _ #88.07
Reveals that, in 1983, at the request of the Turkish Government, the Istanbul Chamber of Industry commissioned an MS group to study causes of available housing decline with the objective of reversing the trend. Shows that the group made a thorough analysis of the economic, social, demographic, technological, financial, legal and institutional aspects of the complex problem using a combination of mathematical tools and expert opinion. Subsequent legislation and implemention largely followed the recommendations, with the annual construction of housing units increasing by 12.4 percent in 1984, 36.3 percent in 1985 and 51.5 percent in 1986. Istanbul Chamber of Industry. Ibrahim Kavrakoglu, Ali Riza Kaylan, Suleyman Ozmucur, Guniz Tamer.
Business and Economics; Sociology
Dist - INMASC

Systems Approach to Social Worker Practices 30 MIN
U-matic / VHS
B&W
Answers questions about how the systems approach to social work practices, coupled with other programs, helps the social worker deal with many elements in a practice situation.
Sociology
Dist - UWISC **Prod** - VRL

Systems Engineering and Systems Management Series

Introduction to Systems Management Techniques	37 MIN
Management Control of System Schedule and Cost	55 MIN
Performance	41 MIN
Scope of Systems Engineering Problem	53 MIN
Stimulation and Modeling Techniques	54 MIN
The System Error Budget	41 MIN
System Redundancy and Failure Detection Requirements	36 MIN
System Reliability, Maintainability and Availability	41 MIN
System Testing Techniques	46 MIN
Systems Management Strategies	55 MIN

Dist - MIOT

Systems for precise observations for teachers series

Devices for self - help task performance	18 MIN
Problems in academic tasks performance - Pt 1	7 MIN

Dist - USNAC

Systems Management Strategies 55 MIN
U-matic / VHS
Systems Engineering and Systems Management Series
Color
Analyzes alternative systems management strategies. Stresses the importance of effective communication concepts in systems management.
Industrial and Technical Education
Dist - MIOT **Prod** - MIOT

Systems Network Architecture 45 MIN
VHS / U-matic
Network Architectures - a Communications Revolution Series
Color
Presents the IBM terminology that is used to describe the various parts of the System Network Architecture (SNA) network. Presents examples of actual IBM hardware implementations, including the new IBM 8100 series.
Industrial and Technical Education; Social Science
Dist - DELTAK **Prod** - DELTAK

Systems of authority, methods of repression 40 MIN
VHS / 16mm
Color & B&W (G)
$10.00 rental, $50.00 purchase
Critiques the intersections of abuse on micro and macro levels. Explains the micro, or personal level, by the filmmaker relating her own history of abuse as a child and the macro level, institutional and political, represented by repressive laws, systems and language that perpetuate abuse. Offers a positive and challenging call to action and resistance against victimization. Produced by Linda Tadic.
Civics and Political Systems; History - United States; Sociology
Dist - CANCIN

Systems of Differential Equations
16mm
B&W
Proves that the general solution of the system of equations (for zero initial velocities) is an arbitrary combination of the three 'normal mode solutions.'.
Mathematics
Dist - OPENU **Prod** - OPENU

Systems of equations
VHS
Beginning algebra series
Color (J H)
$125.00 purchase _ #2014
Teaches fundamental concepts used to solve systems of equations. Part of a series of 31 videos, each between 25 and 30 minutes long, that explain and reinforce basic concepts of algebra. Tutors the student through definitions, theorems, step - by - step solutions and examples. Videos are also available in a set.
Mathematics
Dist - LANDMK

Systems of equations 30 MIN
VHS
Mathematics series
Color (J)
LC 90713155
Discusses systems of equations. The 30th of 157 installments of the Mathematics Series.
Mathematics
Dist - GPN

Systems of linear equations 30 MIN
VHS
Beginning algebra series
Color (J H)
$125.00 purchase _ #M30
Explains systems of linear equations. Features Elayn Gay. Part of a 19 - part series on beginning algebra.
Mathematics
Dist - LANDMK **Prod** - MGHT

Systems of linear equations 30 MIN
VHS
Intermediate algebra series
Color (H)
$125.00 purchase _ #M57
Explains systems of linear equations. Features Elayn Gay. Part of a 27 - part series on intermediate algebra.
Mathematics
Dist - LANDMK **Prod** - MGHT

Systems of linear equations
VHS
Algebra 1 series
Color (J H)
$125.00 purchase _ #A13
Teaches the concepts involved in solving systems of equations. Part of a series of 16 videos, each between 25 and 30 minutes long, that explain and reinforce 89 basic concepts of algebra. Includes a stated objective for each segment. Tutors the student through definitions, theorems, step - by - step solutions and examples. Videos are also available in a set.
Mathematics
Dist - LANDMK
GPN

Systems of linear equations II, matrices 30 MIN
VHS
Intermediate algebra series
Color (H)
$125.00 purchase _ #M58
Explains systems of linear equations and matrices. Features Elayn Gay. Part of a 27 - part series on intermediate algebra.
Mathematics
Dist - LANDMK **Prod** - MGHT

Systems of Linear Equations, Pt 1 30 MIN
U-matic
Introduction to Mathematics Series
Color (C)
Mathematics
Dist - MDCPB **Prod** - MDCPB

Systems of Linear Equations, Pt 2 30 MIN
U-matic
Introduction to Mathematics Series
Color (C)
Mathematics
Dist - MDCPB **Prod** - MDCPB

Systems of linear inequalities
VHS
Beginning algebra series
Color (J H)
$125.00 purchase _ #2027
Teaches basic concepts of systems of linear inequalities. Part of a 31 - video series, each part between 25 and 30 minutes long, that explains and reinforces fundamental concepts of beginning algebra. Uses definitions, theorems, examples and step - by - step solutions to instruct the student.
Mathematics
Dist - LANDMK

Systems of nonlinear equations 30 MIN
VHS
College algebra series
Color (C)
$125.00 purchase _ #4029
Explains systems of nonlinear equations. Part of a 31 - part series on college algebra.
Mathematics
Dist - LANDMK **Prod** - LANDMK

Systems of Nonlinear Equations 30 MIN
VHS
Mathematics Series
Color (J)
LC 90713155
Examines the systems of nonlinear equations. The 91st of 157 installments in the Mathematics Series.
Mathematics
Dist - GPN

Systems of the human body series
Presents a seven - part series on human biology. Includes the titles Fertilization; The Heart and Circulation; Liquid Waste and the Kidney; Lung Action and Function; Passage of Food Through the Digestive Tract; Respiration and Waste; Skeletal and Muscle Action.
Systems of the human body series 35 MIN
Dist - CLRVUE HUBDSC **Prod** - CLRVUE HUBDSC 1989

Systems of the human body series
Fertilization 5 MIN
The Heart and circulation 5 MIN
Liquid waste and the kidney 5 MIN
Lung action and function 5 MIN
Respiration and waste 6 MIN
Skeletal and muscle action 6 MIN
Dist - HUBDSC

Systems of the human body series
Passage of food through the digestive tract 6 MIN
Dist - HUBDSC WARDS

Systems of the human body series
AIDS - facts and fears 9 MIN
Fertilization 9 MIN
The Heart and circulation 9 MIN
The Kidney and homeostasis 9 MIN
Liquid waste and the kidney 9 MIN
Lung action and function 9 MIN
Respiration and waste 9 MIN
Skeletal and muscle action 9 MIN
Dist - WARDS

Systems Operations Series
Advanced operator responsibilities 60 MIN
Basic boiler systems 60 MIN
Bleaching 60 MIN
Boiler fundamentals 60 MIN
Boiler opeations 60 MIN
Centrifuge Operations 60 MIN
Continuous Stirred Reactors 60 MIN
Crude distillation operations 60 MIN
Distillation tower operations 60 MIN
Dryers 60 MIN
Drying Operations 60 MIN
Dust and Mist Removal 60 MIN
Electrical Systems 60 MIN
Evaporation Unit Operations 60 MIN
Filtration and Screening Unit Operations 60 MIN
Furnace fundamentals 60 MIN
Furnace operations 60 MIN
Hydraulic Systems 60 MIN
Introduction to Distillation 60 MIN
Kraft Chemical Recovery 60 MIN
Kraft Pulping Basics 60 MIN
Kraft Pulping Operations 60 MIN
Liquid - Liquid Solvent Extraction 60 MIN
Mechanical - Semichemical Pulping Basics 60 MIN
Mechanical - Semichemical Pulping Operations 60 MIN
Mixing Operations 60 MIN
On - the - Job Training 60 MIN
Organic Chemical Processes 60 MIN
Packaging Operations 60 MIN
Papermaking - 1 60 MIN
Papermaking - 2 60 MIN
Papermaking - 3 60 MIN
Papermaking - 4 60 MIN
Process chemistry 60 MIN
Process Operations Troubleshooting 60 MIN
Process Reactor Fundamentals 60 MIN
Recovery Boiler Operations 60 MIN
Refrigeration systems - 1 60 MIN
Refrigeration systems - 2 60 MIN
Smelt - Chemical Recovery 60 MIN
Statistical Process Control - 1 60 MIN
Statistical Process Control - 2 60 MIN
Statistical Process Control of Distillation Columns 60 MIN
Using System Diagrams 60 MIN
Water Treatment - 1 60 MIN
Water Treatment - 2 60 MIN
Dist - NUSTC

Systems options - computer files and databases - Parts 19 and 20 60 MIN
U-matic / VHS
New literacy - an introduction to computers
Color (G)
$45.00, $29.95 purchase
Investigates batch and real - time processing, on - line direct - access systems, time - sharing, storage, machine capabilities and portable operation systems in Part 19. Traces the development of input - output systems and the characteristics of a well - designed database in Part 20. Parts of a 26 - part series on computing machines.
Computer Science; Mathematics
Dist - ANNCPB **Prod** - SCCON 1988

Systems, Pt 1 39 MIN
VHS / U-matic
Distributed processor communication architecture series
Color
Discusses loop systems, complete interconnect systems, shared memory multiprocessors and global bus multiprocessors.
Industrial and Technical Education; Mathematics
Dist - MIOT **Prod** - MIOT

Systems, Pt 2 42 MIN
VHS / U-matic
Distributed processor communication architecture series
Color
Discusses remote access networks, central control loop systems, central control bus systems, regular network and structured systems.
Industrial and Technical Education; Mathematics
Dist - MIOT **Prod** - MIOT

Systems thinking in action set of audio and videos series
Presents a series including three videos featuring Peter M Senge, Russell L Ackoff and Sue Miller Hurst and 19 audiocassettes featuring business leaders commenting on systems thinking and learning in organizations.
Systems thinking in action set of audio and videos series
Dist - PEGASU **Prod** - PEGASU

Systems working together 15 MIN
U-matic / VHS / 16mm
Human body series
Color (J H C)
$360.00, $250.00 purchase _ #4019
Shows how cells interact with the body's systems.
Science - Natural
Dist - CORF

Syvilla - they Dance to Her Drum 25 MIN
16mm
B&W (G)
$60.00 rental
Portrays Syvilla Fort, a first generation African - American concert dancer. Reflects her choreography, the virtuosity of her dancing and her significance as teacher and force in the history of dance.
Fine Arts; History - United States; History - World
Dist - WMEN **Prod** - AYCH 1979

Syzygy 27 MIN
16mm
Color
LC 71-702600
An introduction to contemporary problems of society and the role of the church, as stimulated by a group discussion of a three - part film dealing with war, cities and people.
Psychology; Sociology
Dist - CCNCC **Prod** - CCNCC 1969

Szechuan and Northern Dishes 60 MIN
VHS / U-matic
Color (J H G)
Demonstrates how to create basic dishes from Szechwan Province and northern China. Includes slicing techniques, rice cookery and advanced skills. Features Chef Rhonda Yee preparing 12 dishes, including Mongolian beef and sweet and sour Shanghai.
Home Economics
Dist - CINAS **Prod** - CINAS 1982

Szechwan and Northern Dishes 60 MIN
VHS / 16mm
(G)
$39.95 purchase _ #VT1123
Presents some favorite Szechwan dishes and how to prepare and make them. Features Pot Stickers, Hot and Sour Soup, Muu Shu Pork with Peking Doilies, and Mandarin dishes such as Mongolian Beef, Sweet and Sour Pork Shanghai, Onion Pancakes, Sizzling Rice Soup, Pon Pon Chicken, and Spicy Shrimp.
Home Economics
Dist - RMIBHF **Prod** - RMIBHF

T

T A C T - telephone answer and call techniques 225 MIN
VHS
Color (G A)
$3,500.00 purchase
Presents a five - part, interactive training package which stresses the importance of telephone skills. Covers basic phone etiquette, understanding customer expectations, handling incoming calls, meeting the needs of the caller, and guidelines for sales, collection and 'calling out' calls. Consists of five videocassettes and facilitator and student guides.
Business and Economics
Dist - PRODUC **Prod** - PRODUC

T A for Teachers 30 MIN
VHS / U-matic
Dealing in Discipline Series
Color (T)
Education; Psychology
Dist - GPN **Prod** - UKY 1980

T. and the small picture frame 12 MIN
16mm
B&W (G)
$30.00 rental
Presents a loving portrait of the filmmaker's family, similar to a slide 'home movie picture show.'
Fine Arts; Sociology
Dist - CANCIN **Prod** - WEISMA 1986

T as in Transportation 15 MIN
16mm
Color (SPANISH)
LC 78-701473
Shows how the Southern Pacific Transportation Company handles a container shipment from the time it arrives at a West Coast port until it reaches its final destination. Uses animation to explain concepts such as minibridge and land bridge.
Foreign Language; Social Science
Dist - SPTC **Prod** - SPTC 1977

T Berry Brazelton - Parts I and II 60 MIN
VHS
World Of Ideas With Bill Moyers - Season I - series
Color (G)
$59.95 purchase _ #BMWI - 131D
Interviews pediatrician T Berry Brazelton, a Harvard pediatrics professor whose behavioral scale is used around the world for newborn babies. Presents his view that child development is harmed when working mothers are forced to return to their jobs. Discusses society's role in providing for the needs of children. Hosted by Bill Moyers.
Psychology; Sociology
Dist - PBS

T - Bones world of clowning
VHS
Children's discovery series
Color (P I J)
$29.95 purchase _ #IV - 052
Teaches the art of clowning. Features T - Bone, Artie, Brian and Jennifer.
Fine Arts; Physical Education and Recreation
Dist - INCRSE **Prod** - INCRSE

T Boone Pickens - is he Robin Hood or Jesse James 30 MIN
U-matic
Adam Smith's money world series; 120
Color (A)
Attempts to demystify the world of money and break it down so that a small business and its employees understand and adjust to new social and economic trends. Reports on the major economic stories and discoveries of the day.
Business and Economics
Dist - PBS **Prod** - WNETTV 1985

T - Cells and the Major Histocompatibility Complex 24 MIN
U-matic / VHS / 16mm
Color
Provides insights into the role of the major histocompatibility complex molecules in the T - cell recognition and regulation which biochemists expect to provide some of the missing clues to future research about immunology. Examines relationships between T - cells and the MHC antigens.
Science - Natural
Dist - MEDIAG **Prod** - OPENU 1978

The T distribution
16mm
B&W
Discusses the problem of making inferences about a population when only small samples are available.

Mathematics
Dist - OPENU **Prod** - OPENU

T - distribution and confidence intervals
VHS
Probability and statistics series
Color (H C)
$125.00 purchase _ #8031
Provides resource material about confidence intervals and the t - distribution for help in the study of probability and statistics. Presents a 60 - video series, each part 25 to 30 minutes long, that explains and reinforces concepts using definitions, theorems, examples and step - by - step solutions to tutor the student. Videos are also available in a set.
Mathematics
Dist - LANDMK

T E T in High School 29 MIN
16mm / U-matic / VHS
Dealing with Classroom Problems Series
Color
Presents Dr Thomas Gordon explaining how the concepts of teacher effectiveness training apply at the the secondary level. Includes Dr Gordon's associate, Noel Burch, demonstrating the 'no lose' method of resolving conflicts.
Education; Psychology
Dist - FI **Prod** - MFFD 1975

T H White - the once and future king 26 MIN
Videoreel / VT2
One to one series
Color (J H G)
Presents readings from The Once And Future King by T H White.
Literature and Drama
Dist - PBS **Prod** - WETATV

T is for tomato 13 MIN
VHS / 16mm
Food from A to Z series
Color (P I)
$335.00, $300.00 purchase
Traces the history of tomatoes from their orgins in South America to their first acceptance by Europeans as a food in Italy. Reveals that they were regarded as poisonous because of their close relationship to the nightshade plant. Examines the many sizes, shapes and colors tomatoes come in and their role as a source of vitamins A and C. Describes the reproductive process of the tomato plant, modern farming methods and the many commercial products made from tomatoes.
Health and Safety; Home Economics; Science - Natural; Social Science
Dist - HANDEL **Prod** - HANDEL 1991

T is for Tumbleweed 18 MIN
U-matic / VHS / 16mm
Color (K A)
Portrays the racing, creeping, leaping travels of a tumbleweed and the encounters it has with people, animals and things. Stimulates creative writing.
English Language; Fine Arts
Dist - PFP **Prod** - PFP 1956

T joint 12 MIN
VHS / BETA
Welding training - comprehensive - basic shielded metal arc welding series
Color (IND)
Industrial and Technical Education; Psychology
Dist - RMIBHF **Prod** - RMIBHF

T joint aluminum braze 5 MIN
BETA / VHS
Welding training comprehensive - oxy - acetylene welding series
Color (IND)
Industrial and Technical Education; Psychology
Dist - RMIBHF **Prod** - RMIBHF

T - Joint Fillet Weld Ten - Gauge Steel Demonstration 5 MIN
BETA / VHS
Color (IND)
Shows the recommended technique for making a fillet weld on ten - gauge material.
Industrial and Technical Education; Psychology
Dist - RMIBHF **Prod** - RMIBHF

T - joint, lap joint, outside corner joint in a horizontal position with SMAW
VHS / U-matic
Shielded metal arc welding - Spanish series
Color (SPANISH)
Foreign Language; Industrial and Technical Education
Dist - VTRI **Prod** - VTRI

T - joint, lap joint, outside corner joint in a vertical up position with SMAW
U-matic / VHS
Shielded metal arc welding - Spanish series
Color (SPANISH)
Foreign Language; Industrial and Technical Education
Dist - VTRI **Prod** - VTRI

T - joint, lap joint, outside corner joint in an overhead position
VHS / U-matic
Shielded metal arc welding - Spanish series
Color (SPANISH)
Industrial and Technical Education
Dist - VTRI **Prod** - VTRI

T - joint, lap joint, outside corner joint in flat position
U-matic / VHS
Shielded metal arc welding - Spanish series
Color (SPANISH)
Foreign Language; Industrial and Technical Education
Dist - VTRI **Prod** - VTRI

T joint - multi - pass weave 6 MIN
VHS / BETA
Welding training - comprehensive - basic shielded metal arc welding series
Color (IND)
Industrial and Technical Education; Psychology
Dist - RMIBHF **Prod** - RMIBHF

T joint - 3 - pass stringer 7 MIN
VHS / BETA
Welding training - comprehensive - basic shielded metal arc welding series
Color (IND)
Industrial and Technical Education; Psychology
Dist - RMIBHF **Prod** - RMIBHF

T - Joint 20 - Gauge to 10 - Gauge Steel Demonstration 4 MIN
BETA / VHS
Color (IND)
Outlines the technique used to weld a thin piece of metal to a heavier piece of metal.
Industrial and Technical Education; Psychology
Dist - RMIBHF **Prod** - RMIBHF

T Minus Two Hours 17 MIN
16mm
Color (IND)
LC FIA67-2340
Reviews the nationwide research and development facilitates of the Thiokol Chemical Corporation. Illustrates the techniques and tools used by the various divisions to develop rocket engines. Comments upon the role of rockets in defense and civilian safety.
Business and Economics; Industrial and Technical Education; Science - Physical
Dist - THIOKL **Prod** - THIOKL 1960

T R Country 14 MIN
16mm
Color
LC 80-701938
Uses the words of Theodore Roosevelt as narrative in showing the Badlands of North Dakota in both winter and summer as Roosevelt saw them. Includes numerous wildlife scenes.
Geography - United States
Dist - USNAC **Prod** - USNPS 1980

T R O T 7 MIN
U-matic / VHS / 16mm
OWL Special Needs Series
Color (P I J)
Shows a day spent with Therapeutic Riding of Tucson's comprehensive program to help disabled children learn to ride horseback. Shows what working with horses means to the children, and shares their riding triumphs.
Education; Guidance and Counseling; Health and Safety; Sociology
Dist - BULFRG **Prod** - OWLTV 1987

T R S 80 Model IV 24 MIN
VHS / BETA
Computer education - programming - operations series
Color
Business and Economics; Mathematics
Dist - RMIBHF **Prod** - RMIBHF

T S Eliot 60 MIN
VHS / 16mm
Voices and Visions Series
Color (H)
$8.00 rental _ #60736
Examines the work of T S Eliot (1888 - 1965), poet and literary critic. Frank Kermode, Stephen Spender, Peter Ackroyd, Quentin Bell, and others discuss Eliot's legacy and offer insights into the man, his poetry, his political and religious convictions, and the way Eliot's poems articulate the feelings of alienation and fragmentation so prevalent in this century.
Literature and Drama
Dist - PSU

T S Eliot 58 MIN
VHS
Modern World - Ten Great Writers Series
Color (H)
$13.00 rental _ #60962
Examines T S Eliot's 'Prufrock And Other Observations,' 'The Waste Land,' 'Murder In The Cathedral' and 'The Cocktail Party.' Examines Eliot's use of idiom in expression to capture the character of his generation. Studies ten important modernist European writers by placing them against turn - of - the century settings, dramatizing their own experiences and looking at their principal works in a ten part series.
Literature and Drama
Dist - PSU **Prod** - FI
FI

T S Eliot - Part 4 60 MIN
VHS / U-matic
Voices and visions series
Color (G)
$45.00, $29.95 purchase
Explores the life and poetry of T S Eliot with photos, archival footage and discussions with friends, critics and scholars. Part of a thirteen - part series on the lives and works of modern American poets.
Biography; History - United States; Literature and Drama
Dist - ANNCPB **Prod** - NYCVH 1988

T S Eliot - Selected Poetry 29 MIN
Videoreel / VT2
One to One Series
Color
Presents the poetry of T S Eliot.
Literature and Drama
Dist - PBS **Prod** - WETATV

T T Liang - Introduction and postures 1 - 22 - Tape 1 45 MIN
VHS
Imagination becomes reality series
Color (G)
$29.95 purchase _ #1181
Teaches the Yang style T'ai chi ch'uan of 93 - year - old T T Liang, who offers a brief introduction on the purpose of T'ai chi. Features Stuart A Olson, Liang's adopted son, who executes the first 22 postures in slow motion with a voiceover. Part one of a three - part series.
Physical Education and Recreation
Dist - WAYF

%t The French programme - year 3 - action tele 100 MIN
VHS
Color; PAL (J H)
PdS30
Instructs third - year French students. Includes five 20 - minute programs.
Foreign Language
Dist - ACADEM

T U R - a Teaching Film 20 MIN
16mm
Color
LC FIA67-636
Demonstrates the usefulness of the motion picture for teaching the processes involved in a transurethral prostatectomy. Includes an introduction to key points using medical illustrations and endoscopic photography.
Education; Health and Safety
Dist - EATONL **Prod** - EATONL 1966

T V - the anonymous teacher 15 MIN
VHS / U-matic
Color (A)
Probes the effect of television viewing on children. Discusses parental concern with regard to violence, commercial advertising and sexual and racial stereotyping. Narrated by Dr Robert M Liebert.
Fine Arts; Sociology
Dist - ECUFLM **Prod** - UMCOM 1976

T V, the anonymous teacher 15 MIN
16mm
Color (H C A)
Suggests that television has a strong influence on children. Interviews experts concerned about the effects of television upon children.
Education; Fine Arts; Social Science; Sociology
Dist - ECUFLM **Prod** - UMCOM 1976

T W U Tel 19 MIN
U-matic
Color (C)
$200.00 purchase, $30.00, $40.00 rental
Documents the takeover by the Telecommunications Workers Union of major telephone centers in British Columbia without the help of any management. Presents operators and union members who discuss strike issues, public support, and improved morale of the workers. Produced by Amelia Productions.
Business and Economics
Dist - WMENIF

Ta fu chih chia
VHS
Color (G)
$50.00 purchase _ #27989
Features a comedy with Kuo - jung Chang produced by Markham.
Fine Arts
Dist - PANASI

Tablatoons 5 MIN
16mm
Color
LC 76-703090
Presents a visual interpretation of Indian drum pieces using scratching and bleaching of film emulsion and rotoscoped spinning bodies in a succession of light and dark flashes.
Fine Arts; Social Science
Dist - CANFDC **Prod** - SHERCL 1975

Table 16 MIN
16mm
Color (G)
$30.00 rental
Represents the celluloid equivalent of a cubist still life. Portrays an ordinary cluttered kitchen table seen from slightly different points of view. Shots are accentuated with blue and red filters. Produced by Ernie Gehr.
Fine Arts
Dist - CANCIN

Table egg production 10 MIN
VHS
Commercial chicken production series
Color (G)
$39.95 purchase _ #6 - 050 - 105A
Discusses egg production. Part of a six - part series on commercial chicken production.
Agriculture
Dist - VEP **Prod** - UDEL

Table Looms 16 MIN
VHS / U-matic
Color (H C)
Introduces the parts of the table loom and tells how the weaver must become fully acquainted with its operation. Notes special attention given to preparing the warp and loading it in the loom. Shows how a beautiful shoulder bag is produced and the steps in finishing it off.
Fine Arts
Dist - EDMI **Prod** - EDMI 1976

Table Manners 16 MIN
16mm
Good Life Series
Color (S)
LC 81-700271
Uses a TV game show format to demonstrate appropriate table manners.
Education; Home Economics
Dist - HUBDSC **Prod** - DUDLYN 1981

Table Manners - Doing it Right 21 MIN
16mm / VHS
Color (J S)
$465.00, $395.00 purchase, $60.00 rental
Demonstrates that use of good table manners puts one at ease in social surroundings and helps create the impression by which we are often judged. Points out that doing it right, and knowing it, helps develop greater self - confidence and poise.
Home Economics; Psychology
Dist - HIGGIN **Prod** - HIGGIN 1990

Table manners for everyday use 41 MIN
VHS
Color (H)
$89.00 purchase _ #60221 - 025; $99.00 purchase, $55.00 rental; $24.95 purchase _ #6350
Covers the basics of behavior at the table when eating meals in restaurants, fast - food places and at home. Shows common foods - pizza, hamburgers, steaks, salads, soup, vegetables, and how to eat them properly - and improperly. Uses short, humorous segments from old films to look at what to avoid when learning table manners.
Home Economics; Sociology
Dist - GA **Prod** - GA 1992
FLMLIB SYBVIS
SYBVIS

Table Representation of the Next State Function and Outputs - Class - 0 Machines 30 MIN
U-matic / VHS
Microprocessors for Monitoring and Control Series
Color (IND)
Introduces use of a table to represent next state and output that is used directly for microprocessor implementation. Shows how digital design systems are broken up into machine classes to aid in design formulation.
Industrial and Technical Education; Mathematics; Sociology
Dist - COLOSU **Prod** - COLOSU

The Table Round 15 MIN
VHS / 16mm
English Folk Heroes Series
Color (I)
Presents the legend of The Table Round. The fourth of six installments of the English Folk Heroes Series, which presents figures from English literature in 15 - minute programs.
Literature and Drama
Dist - GPN **Prod** - CTI 1990

Table Saw and Accessories
VHS
Woodworking Power Tools Videos Series
$89.00 purchase _ #LX6101
Provides instruction on basic and advanced operational techniques for the table saw and accessories. Uses close up photograpy to show how each machine performs cutting, forming, or shaping operations. Stresses safety procedures and considerations including use of each machine's safety guards.
Industrial and Technical Education
Dist - CAREER **Prod** - CAREER

Table service
VHS / 35mm strip
Food service - skills and equipment series
$109.00 purchase _ #PX1133, #PX1131V
Industrial and Technical Education
Dist - CAREER **Prod** - CAREER

Table settings 8 MIN
U-matic / VHS / 16mm
Professional food preparation and service program series
Color (IND) (SPANISH)
LC 75-703057
Shows tables being set for breakfast, lunch and dinner and explains why correct procedures make for smooth service and add to the guests' enjoyment.
Guidance and Counseling; Home Economics; Industrial and Technical Education; Psychology
Dist - NEM **Prod** - NEM 1969

Table Talk 13 MIN
VHS / U-matic
Color
Explores 'food messages.' Shows how family, friends and culture influence choice of foods. Points out how foods and the way people eat affect them.
Health and Safety; Home Economics; Social Science
Dist - AMRC **Prod** - AMRC

Table Tennis 60 MIN
VHS
(G)
$39.95 purchase _ #BF99620V
Describes various aspects of the game of table tennis. Provides demonstrations of basic skills, strokes, and more. Features slow motion photography.
Physical Education and Recreation
Dist - CAMV

Table tennis techniques 20 MIN
U-matic / VHS / BETA
Color; PAL (H C T G)
PdS50, PdS58 purchase
Features a training film that looks at the techniques used by the world's top table tennis stars. Analyzes and considers these skills from the ordinary player's point of view. Former world champions Stellan Bengtsson and Kjell Johansson along with Nicky Jarvis demonstrate their methods.
Physical Education and Recreation
Dist - EDPAT

The Table, the Donkey and the Stick 11 MIN
U-matic / VHS
Fairy Tale Series
Color (K P I)
Tells the story of three brothers who receive magic gifts which are stolen by a wicked innkeeper. The gifts are recovered and there is a happy reunion with their father. Comes with teacher's guide.
Literature and Drama
Dist - BNCHMK **Prod** - BNCHMK 1985

Table Treatment 41 MIN
U-matic / VHS
Proprioceptive Neuromuscular Facilitation Series
Color
Health and Safety
Dist - UMDSM **Prod** - UMDSM

Tableau Vivant 11 MIN
16mm / U-matic / VHS
Inventive Child Series
Color (P I)
Reveals that when Boy is called upon to entertain a child he is babysitting, he makes a crude motion picture machine in a stream. Illustrates the principle of motion pictures and simplifies the phenomenon of persistence of vision, on which the concept of motion pictures is based.
Fine Arts; History - World
Dist - EBEC **Prod** - POLSKI 1983

Tableau Vivant and Honey Harvest 22 MIN
VHS / U-matic
Inventive Child Series
Color (P I J)
$89.00 purchase _ #1584
Presents the character Boy who uses creative abilities to entertain a child he is babysitting (1st part). Demonstrates how Boy and Grandpa use their skills to do a potentially hazardous job more quickly and efficiently (2nd part).
Psychology
Dist - EBEC

Tableaux D'Une Exposition 10 MIN
16mm
B&W
Illustrates a Moussorgsky tone poem with episodes from the composer's childhood in Russia and Alexander Alexeieff's memories of his own childhood there, using two pinboards, a small one that revolves and a stable one behind it. Introduced in English by Alexeieff.
Fine Arts
Dist - STARRC **Prod** - STARRC 1972

Tableros Para Demostracion Y Exhibicion 15 MIN
U-matic / VHS / 16mm
Color (J A) (SPANISH)
A Spanish - language version of the motion picture Display And Presentation Boards. Provides a compact, practical and up - to - date look at display and presentation boards which can be used in a variety of teaching and learning situations. Explores the nature and potential of six different display and presentation boards - felt, hook and loop, magnetic, peg, electric and combination.
Education; Foreign Language
Dist - IFB **Prod** - IFB 1971

Tables, charts and diagrams
VHS
Using maps, globes, graphs, tables, charts and diagrams series
Color (I J H)
$49.50 purchase _ #UL1063VJ
Shows how to read tables, charts and diagrams. Presents part of a five - part series on basic globe skills and understanding data in charts, maps, tables, charts and other graphic representations.
Industrial and Technical Education; Mathematics
Dist - KNOWUN

Tables of Trigonometric Ratios 29 MIN
16mm
Trigonometry Series
B&W (H)
Describes the format and range of conventional trigonometric tables. Shows the compression of the tables resulting from the recognition of the inverse relations. Illustrates the use of the tables.
Mathematics
Dist - MLA **Prod** - CALVIN 1959

Tableside Cooking - Entrees
U-matic / VHS
Tableside Series
Color
Home Economics; Industrial and Technical Education
Dist - CULINA **Prod** - CULINA

Tableside Cooking - Flaming Coffees
VHS / U-matic
Tableside Series
Color
Home Economics; Industrial and Technical Education
Dist - CULINA **Prod** - CULINA

Tableside Cooking - Flaming Desserts
U-matic / VHS
Tableside Series
Color
Home Economics; Industrial and Technical Education
Dist - CULINA **Prod** - CULINA

Tableside Fruit Carving
U-matic / VHS
Tableside Series
Color
Home Economics; Industrial and Technical Education
Dist - CULINA **Prod** - CULINA

Tableside Series
Route Du Champagne
Selecting and Handling Glassware
Tableside Cooking - Entrees
Tableside Cooking - Flaming Coffees
Tableside Cooking - Flaming Desserts
Tableside Fruit Carving
Dist - CULINA

Tabletop cooking
VHS
Frugal gourmet - entertaining series
Color (G)
$19.95 purchase _ #CCP845
Shows how to prepare foods for tabletop cooking. Features Jeff Smith, the Frugal Gourmet. Part of a ten - part series on preparing food for entertaining.
History - United States; Home Economics
Dist - CADESF **Prod** - CADESF

Taboo 85 MIN
VHS
Color; PAL (I J H)
PdS29.50 purchase
Follows the last eighteen months of the life of Jane, a teacher who died from cancer in a hospice at the age of twenty - five. Raises issues such as truth, integrity, honesty, loss, family relationships. Based on the Young Vic's stage adaptation of the book, A Way to Die by Rosemary and Victor Zorza, parents of Jane.
Health and Safety; Sociology
Dist - EMFVL

Tabu 86 MIN
16mm
Silent; Captioned; B&W (GERMAN)
A silent motion picture with German and English subtitles. Shows a lost paradise, with the actors portraying the natives of Tahiti.
Fine Arts
Dist - WSTGLC **Prod** - WSTGLC 1930

The Tabular Tube 29 MIN
VHS / 16mm
Villa Alegre Series
Color (P T)
$46.00 rental _ #VILA - 148
Presents educational material in both Spanish and English.
Education
Dist - PBS

TAC in Action 15 MIN
16mm
B&W
LC 74-706269
Describes TAC'S capabilities in aerial firepower, reconnaissance, guerrilla warfare and assault airlifts. Reviews TAC'S role in the Cuban crisis and in Vietnam coin operations.
Civics and Political Systems
Dist - USNAC **Prod** - USAF 1964

Tachyarrhythmias 19 MIN
VHS / U-matic
Emergency Management - the First 30 Minutes, Vol II Series
Color
Discusses tachyarrhythmias, diagnosis and treatment.
Health and Safety
Dist - VTRI **Prod** - VTRI

Tachyon 20 MIN
VHS
Color (G)
$10.00 purchase _ #V - TACHYON
Explains Takionic and its many uses. Features a presentation from Japan and scientists, Olympic athletes and others.
Physical Education and Recreation
Dist - PACSPI

Tackling productivity in mechanized logging 19 MIN
VHS / U-matic
Color (H C A)
$50.00 purchase, $25.00 rental _ #930
Shows how to reduce inefficiency in mechanical logging. Stresses the concept of teamwork, communication and cross - training. Discusses machine balance, optimal deck levels, avoidance of bottlenecks, the importance of on - site observation, communications and planning.
Agriculture; Industrial and Technical Education; Psychology
Dist - OSUSF **Prod** - OSUSF 1989

Tackling Textbooks 10 MIN
U-matic / VHS
Developing Your Study Skills Series
Color (H C)
Centers around a student having difficulty keeping up with assigned reading. Shows students how to analyze reading habits in order to develop proper reading techniques. Presents the SQ4R technique.
Education; Guidance and Counseling
Dist - BCNFL **Prod** - UWO 1985

Tackling the demons 18 MIN
VHS / U-matic
Better spelling series
Color
Presents lesson four in the Better spelling series.
English Language
Dist - DELTAK **Prod** - TELSTR

Tacoma Narrows Bridge Collapse W - 4 35 MIN
16mm
Single - Concept Films in Physics Series
Color (J)
Pictures the large amplitude resonance vibration of the bridge, nodal lines of the surface of the roadway and the total collapse.
Industrial and Technical Education
Dist - OSUMPD **Prod** - OSUMPD 1963

The Tacoma Narrows Bridge collapses 4 MIN
U-matic / VHS / BETA
Color; NTSC; PAL; SECAM (J H G)
PdS32
Records the November 7, 1940 collapse of the bridge when, in 'moderate winds,' the bridge developed a resonant torsional oscillation and, after 70 minutes, the central span collapsed. Offers footage made by an amateur cameraman using 8mm film that shows part of the construction, the ceremonial opening on July 1, 1940, and the events of November 7.
History - United States; Industrial and Technical Education; Social Science
Dist - VIEWTH

Tactical Air Power 20 MIN
16mm
Color
LC 74-705736
Demonstrates the latest striking power capabilities of the Tactical Air Command and discusses its importance.
Civics and Political Systems; Education
Dist - USNAC **Prod** - USAF 1967

Tactical Bomber in all - Weather Operations 11 MIN
16mm
B&W
LC FIE58-277
Demonstrates the uses and operations of the tactical bomber and the need for close coordination of air, land and sea forces in modern warfare.
Civics and Political Systems; Industrial and Technical Education
Dist - USNAC **Prod** - USAF 1957

The Tactical game 60 MIN
VHS
Color (J H A)
$29.95 purchase _ #VTU102V
Features teaching professional Dennis Van Der Meer with the second of a three - part series on tennis. Focuses on the tactics of the game.
Physical Education and Recreation
Dist - CAMV

Tactical training series
Officer safety 18 MIN
Dist - AIMS

Tactics for Doubles Play 9 MIN
U-matic / VHS / 16mm
Tennis Tactics Series
Color (H C A)
Emphasizes the importance of the first serve and how to take command at the net in tennis.
Physical Education and Recreation
Dist - ATHI **Prod** - ATHI 1980

Tactics for Ground Strokes 9 MIN
U-matic / VHS / 16mm
Tennis Tactics Series
Color (H C A)
Demonstrates the grip, the proper stance and follow through for forehand and backhand ground strokes in tennis.
Physical Education and Recreation
Dist - ATHI **Prod** - ATHI 1980

Tactics for Return of Service 9 MIN
16mm / U-matic / VHS
Tennis Tactics Series
Color (H C A)
Shows how to return a tennis serve down the line, cross court and hit to the server's feet.
Physical Education and Recreation
Dist - ATHI **Prod** - ATHI 1980

Tactics for Singles Play 9 MIN
U-matic / VHS / 16mm
Tennis Tactics Series
Color (H C A)
Covers the proper use of geometry in determining shot placement in tennis.
Physical Education and Recreation
Dist - ATHI **Prod** - ATHI 1980

Tactics for Specialty Shots 9 MIN
U-matic / VHS / 16mm
Tennis Tactics Series
Color (H C A)
Illustrates the use of volleys, overheads, lobs and drop shots in tennis.
Physical Education and Recreation
Dist - ATHI **Prod** - ATHI 1980

Tactics for the Serve 9 MIN
U-matic / VHS / 16mm
Tennis Tactics Series
Color (H C A)
Demonstrates how to use the slice, spin serve and the cannon ball in tennis.
Physical Education and Recreation
Dist - ATHI **Prod** - ATHI 1980

Tactics for thinking
VHS
Color (C A PRO T)
$795.00 purchase 200.00 rental _ #614 - 89145X01
Presents a complete package for training teachers to include thinking skills in their lesson plans. Explains 22 skills that cover learning how to learn, content mastery methods and reasoning principles and provides suggestions for including them in subject teaching. Package includes videotapes, workshop trainer's manual, teacher's manual and blackline activity masters sets for elementary and secondary classes. Contact distributor for more information on the set and on materials available separately.
Education; Psychology
Dist - AFSCD **Prod** - AFSCD 1988

Tactics of Pressure 25 MIN
16mm / U-matic / VHS
Negotiating Successfully Series Part 4
Color (A)
LC 76-702388
Presents a lecture by Chester L Karrass describing various pressure tactics used in negotiations. Tells how to apply pressure and gives defenses against pressure.
Business and Economics; Guidance and Counseling
Dist - TIMLIF **Prod** - TIMLIF 1975

Tad, the Frog 11 MIN
16mm / U-matic / VHS
Color (P)
LC FIA65-328
Shows the growth stages of a frog, including the egg and tadpole periods. Explains how frogs breathe, eat and live. Also instills ideas of pet care and conservation of wild life.
Science - Natural
Dist - CORF **Prod** - CORF 1965

Tadao Ando 58 MIN
16mm / VHS
Color (H C)
$875.00, $290.00 purchase, $110.00 rental
Features the gifted Japanese architect, Tadao Ando who combines a profound respect for traditional Japanese architecture with high regard for LeCorbusier and F.L. Wright.
Biography; Fine Arts; Foreign Language
Dist - BLACKW **Prod** - BLACKW 1989

Tadelloeser and Wolff 205 MIN
16mm
B&W (GERMAN (ENGLISH SUBTITLES))
With English subtitles. Depicts the life of the Kempowski family in Luebeck and Rostock from 1938 until the end of World War II. Based on Walter Kempowski's novel Tadelloeser and Wolff.
Foreign Language; History - World; Literature and Drama; Sociology
Dist - WSTGLC **Prod** - WSTGLC 1975

Tadpoles and Frogs 12 MIN
U-matic / VHS / 16mm
Color (P I)
Follows the transformation of a tadpole into a frog and shows how it begins to swim, grow and develop hindlimbs and forelimbs.
Science - Natural
Dist - NGS **Prod** - NGS 1979

Tae Kwon Do series
Advanced stretching and conditioning
Basic stretching and conditioning
Dist - SIV

Taffy 30 MIN
VHS / U-matic
Color (I J)
Tells how a young girl gets a job at a sugar shack during maple sugar time. Describes the history and methods of the maple sugar industry.
Agriculture; Home Economics
Dist - JOU **Prod** - CANBC

Taffy and the Jungle Hunter 87 MIN
16mm
Color (I J)
Tells of a hunter who captures wild animals for zoos. Shows how he takes his little son and the boy's widowed governess on one of his expeditions.
Literature and Drama
Dist - CINEWO **Prod** - CINEWO 1965

Taffy's imagination 12 MIN
U-matic / VHS / 16mm
Fear of the dark from the forest town fables series
Color (K P I)
$295.00, $210.00 purchase _ #3578; LC 74-700394
Uses a puppet story to present realistic explanations of imagined fantasies so that darkness can be faced with confidence. Explains that Taffy is afraid of the dark until her puppet friends, Butch and Coslo, teach her their night game. Shows how she discovers that things she saw and heard were created in her imagination.
Guidance and Counseling; Literature and Drama
Dist - CORF **Prod** - CORF 1974

Tag Along 29 MIN
U-matic
A Different Understanding Series
Color (PRO)
Shows the problems of a girl whose brain scrambles auditory messages.
Psychology
Dist - TVOTAR **Prod** - TVOTAR 1985

Tag Along 29 MIN
VHS / 16mm
A Different Understanding Series
Color (G)
$90.00 purchase _ #BPN164105
Shows how Janie and her parents come to terms with her learning disability of scrambling auditory messages, and find her the help she needs.
Education; Psychology
Dist - RMIBHF **Prod** - RMIBHF

Tag Der Freiheit - Unsere Wehrmacht 21 MIN
U-matic / VHS
B&W
Depicts a mock battle staged by German troops during the colorful ceremonies at Nuremburg on German Armed Forces Day 1935. Pays special tribute to the Germany Army.
Foreign Language; History - World
Dist - IHF **Prod** - IHF

Tag Der Idioten 110 MIN
16mm
Color (A) (GERMAN (ENGLISH SUBTITLES))
A German language film with English subtitles. Studies a young woman's slow descent into madness. She feels isolated because she proves to be too mad for the outside world and too normal to be institutionalized. Ends when her destructive powers overtake body and mind.
Fine Arts
Dist - WSTGLC **Prod** - WSTGLC 1981

Tahere Tikitiki - the Making of a Maori Canoe 40 MIN
16mm / U-matic / VHS
Color (J A)
Portrays the making of a Maori canoe, showing all the traditions from the felling of the trees to the final launching. Interweaves the process of building with its significance to Maori culture and the changing of the seasons.
Geography - World; Sociology
Dist - UNKNWN **Prod** - NFUNZ

Tahiti - fire waters 60 MIN
VHS
Jacques Cousteau series
Color; CC (G)
$19.95 purchase _ #3045
Travels to Tahiti in the South Pacific with Jacques Costeau. Examines the effects upon nature and the economies of local cultures by the continued testing of nuclear weapons. Part of a series by Jacques Cousteau featuring narration by American English speaking actors and actresses.
Geography - World; History - World; Science - Physical
Dist - APRESS

Tahiti Seaventure 14 MIN
16mm
Color (C A) (FRENCH)
LC 78-713451
Presents scenes of a voyage through six remote islands in French Polynesia, pointing out that the islands are among the last of a vanishing South Sea paradise.
Geography - World
Dist - MCDO **Prod** - MCDO 1971

Tahoe - moving beyond the conflict 19 MIN
16mm / VHS
Color (J H T G)
$395.00, $270.00 purchase, $40.00 rental
Examines the fragile ecology of the Tahoe basin and threats to its balance from increased population, expanding commercial enterprises, tourist activity. Looks at water quality, impact of erosion and nutrient loading on algal blooms and the decreasing transparency of the lake.
Geography - United States; Science - Natural
Dist - UCEMC **Prod** - UCEMC 1987

Tahtonka - Plains Indians buffalo culture 30 MIN
U-matic / VHS / 16mm
Color (I G)
LC FIA67-637
Relates the history of the Plains Indians and their buffalo culture from the pre - horse period to the time of the mountain men, the hide hunters and the destruction of buffalo herds. Reviews the Ghost Dance craze and the massacre of Wounded Knee.
History - United States; Social Science; Sociology
Dist - AIMS **Prod** - PSLI 1966
UILL

Tai chi 45 MIN
VHS
Color (G)
$89.95 purchase, $45.00 rental
Introduces exercises based on moves of Tai Chi with two senior - aged students and an instructor in the art.
Physical Education and Recreation
Dist - TNF

T'ai Chi - a Demonstration 30 MIN
VHS / 16mm
First International Mime Clinic and Festival Series
Color (G)
$55.00 rental _ #FMFI - 004
Physical Education and Recreation
Dist - PBS **Prod** - KTCATV

Tai chi and kung fu workout set 116 MIN
VHS
Color (G)
$34.95 purchase _ #P55
Offers a complete fitness program with David Carradine. Instructs the viewer in kung fu's heightened mental and bodily awareness. Demonstrates the snake, the leopard, the crane and the dragon. Set of two videos, 58 minutes each.
Physical Education and Recreation
Dist - HP

Tai Chi Chi Kung I - theory and practice
VHS
Guided practice series
Color (G)
$55.00 purchase _ #V50 - TP
Shows how to use one's mass in cooperation with the force of gravity and the mind to direct the flow of Chi - life force - and integrate mind, Chi and Earth forces into one unit moving unimpeded through the bone structure. Includes applications of Tai Chi for self - defense. Instructed by Master Mantak Chia.
Health and Safety; Physical Education and Recreation; Religion and Philosophy
Dist - HTAOC **Prod** - HTAOC

Tai Chi Chi Kung II
VHS
Guided practice series
Color (G)
$55.00 purchase _ #V51
Shows how to move quickly in five directions, moving the entire body structure as one unit and to discharge the energy from the Earth through the body structure. Features Master Mantak Chia as instructor.
Health and Safety; Physical Education and Recreation; Religion and Philosophy
Dist - HTAOC **Prod** - HTAOC

T'Ai Chi Ch'uan 8 MIN
16mm / U-matic / VHS
B&W
LC 75-702601
Analyzes the aesthetic and spiritual values of the traditional form of spiritual and physical exercise in China called T'ai Chi Ch'uan. Filmed in Taiwan.
Geography - World; Health and Safety; Physical Education and Recreation; Religion and Philosophy
Dist - DAVT **Prod** - DAVT 1969

T'ai chi chuan - an appreciation featuring three classic Taoist styles 30 MIN
VHS
Color (G)
$24.95 purchase _ #V - TAI
Features Master Ni who presents three styles of T'ai Chi movements - Gentle Path, Sky Journey and Infinite Expression.
Physical Education and Recreation; Religion and Philosophy
Dist - PACSPI

T'ai - chi - ch'uan - Chinese moving meditation 48 MIN
VHS
Color (G)
$24.95 purchase _ #HE - 01
Demonstrates the slow, flowing movements of T'ai - chi - ch'uan, beginning level. Shows how the movements improve health and concentration. Features Master Bob Klein.
Physical Education and Recreation; Religion and Philosophy
Dist - ARVID **Prod** - ARVID

T'ai - chi - ch'uan Kung - fu - Yang short form 120 MIN
VHS
Color (G)
$39.95 purchase _ #MA - 01
Shows the Chinese movements which serve as the basis for Kung - fu. Looks at weight distribution, breathing and beginning 'push hands'. Demonstrates the use of 'chi'.
Physical Education and Recreation; Religion and Philosophy
Dist - ARVID **Prod** - ARVID

T'ai - chi - ch'uan - movements of power and health 120 MIN
VHS
Color (G)
$29.95 purchase _ #HE - 02
Demonstrates the Yang short form of T'ai - chi - ch'uan. Trains in basic coordination, the flow of internal energy, concentration and stress reduction. Features Master Bob Klein.
Physical Education and Recreation; Psychology; Religion and Philosophy
Dist - ARVID **Prod** - ARVID

Tai chi Chuan - Part 1 50 MIN
VHS
Color (G)
$49.95 purchase _ #1162
Demonstrates partial forms of five major styles - Chen, Yang, Wu, Sun, and Wu Jianquan. Includes some forms with push hands and power training. Not a teaching tape.
Physical Education and Recreation
Dist - WAYF

Tai chi Chuan - Part 2 52 MIN
VHS
Color (G)
$49.95 purchase _ #1163
Demonstrates partial forms of five major styles - Chen, Yang, Wu, Sun, and Wu Jianquan. Includes some forms with push hands or weapons forms. Not a teaching tape.
Physical Education and Recreation
Dist - WAYF

T'ai Chi Ch'uan, Program 01 29 MIN
Videoreel / VT2
T'ai Chi Ch'uan Series
Color
History - World; Physical Education and Recreation
Dist - PBS **Prod** - KCET

T'ai Chi Ch'uan, Program 02 29 MIN
Videoreel / VT2
T'ai Chi Ch'uan Series
Color
History - World; Physical Education and Recreation
Dist - PBS **Prod** - KCET

T'ai Chi Ch'uan, Program 03 29 MIN
Videoreel / VT2
T'ai Chi Ch'uan Series
Color
History - World; Physical Education and Recreation
Dist - PBS **Prod** - KCET

T'ai Chi Ch'uan, Program 04 29 MIN
Videoreel / VT2
T'ai Chi Ch'uan Series
Color
History - World; Physical Education and Recreation
Dist - PBS **Prod** - KCET

T'ai Chi Ch'uan, Program 05 29 MIN
Videoreel / VT2
T'ai Chi Ch'uan Series
Color
History - World; Physical Education and Recreation
Dist - PBS **Prod** - KCET

T'ai Chi Ch'uan, Program 06 29 MIN
Videoreel / VT2
T'ai Chi Ch'uan Series
Color
History - World; Physical Education and Recreation
Dist - PBS **Prod** - KCET

T'ai Chi Ch'uan, Program 07 29 MIN
Videoreel / VT2
T'ai Chi Ch'uan Series
Color
History - World; Physical Education and Recreation
Dist - PBS **Prod** - KCET

T'ai Chi Ch'uan, Program 08 29 MIN
Videoreel / VT2
T'ai Chi Ch'uan Series
Color
History - World; Physical Education and Recreation
Dist - PBS **Prod** - KCET

T'ai Chi Ch'uan, Program 09 29 MIN
Videoreel / VT2
T'ai Chi Ch'uan Series
Color
History - World; Physical Education and Recreation
Dist - PBS **Prod** - KCET

T'ai Chi Ch'uan, Program 10 29 MIN
Videoreel / VT2
T'ai Chi Ch'uan Series
Color
History - World; Physical Education and Recreation
Dist - PBS **Prod** - KCET

T'ai Chi Ch'uan, Program 11 29 MIN
Videoreel / VT2
T'ai Chi Ch'uan Series
Color
History - World; Physical Education and Recreation
Dist - PBS **Prod** - KCET

T'ai Chi Ch'uan, Program 12 29 MIN
Videoreel / VT2
T'ai Chi Ch'uan Series
Color
History - World; Physical Education and Recreation
Dist - PBS **Prod** - KCET

T'ai Chi Ch'uan, Program 13 29 MIN
Videoreel / VT2
T'ai Chi Ch'uan Series
Color
History - World; Physical Education and Recreation
Dist - PBS **Prod** - KCET

T'ai Chi Ch'uan, Program 14 29 MIN
Videoreel / VT2
T'ai Chi Ch'uan Series
Color
History - World; Physical Education and Recreation
Dist - PBS **Prod** - KCET

T'ai Chi Ch'uan, Program 15 29 MIN
Videoreel / VT2
T'ai Chi Ch'uan Series
Color
History - World; Physical Education and Recreation
Dist - PBS **Prod** - KCET

T'ai Chi Ch'uan, Program 16 29 MIN
Videoreel / VT2
T'ai Chi Ch'uan Series
Color
History - World; Physical Education and Recreation
Dist - PBS **Prod** - KCET

T'ai Chi Ch'uan, Program 17 29 MIN
Videoreel / VT2
T'ai Chi Ch'uan Series
Color
History - World; Physical Education and Recreation
Dist - PBS **Prod** - KCET

T'ai Chi Ch'uan, Program 18 29 MIN
Videoreel / VT2
T'ai Chi Ch'uan Series
Color
History - World; Physical Education and Recreation
Dist - PBS **Prod** - KCET

T'ai Chi Ch'uan, Program 19 29 MIN
Videoreel / VT2
T'ai Chi Ch'uan Series
Color
History - World; Physical Education and Recreation
Dist - PBS **Prod** - KCET

T'ai Chi Ch'uan, Program 20 29 MIN
Videoreel / VT2
T'ai Chi Ch'uan Series
Color
History - World; Physical Education and Recreation
Dist - PBS **Prod** - KCET

T'ai Chi Ch'uan, Program 21 29 MIN
Videoreel / VT2
T'ai Chi Ch'uan Series
Color
History - World; Physical Education and Recreation
Dist - PBS **Prod** - KCET

T'ai Chi Ch'uan, Program 22 29 MIN
Videoreel / VT2
T'ai Chi Ch'uan Series
Color
History - World; Physical Education and Recreation
Dist - PBS **Prod** - KCET

T'ai Chi Ch'uan, Program 23 29 MIN
Videoreel / VT2
T'ai Chi Ch'uan Series
Color
History - World; Physical Education and Recreation
Dist - PBS **Prod** - KCET

T'ai Chi Ch'uan, Program 24 29 MIN
Videoreel / VT2
T'ai Chi Ch'uan Series
Color
History - World; Physical Education and Recreation
Dist - PBS **Prod** - KCET

T'ai Chi Ch'uan, Program 25 29 MIN
Videoreel / VT2
T'ai Chi Ch'uan Series
Color
History - World; Physical Education and Recreation
Dist - PBS **Prod** - KCET

T'ai Chi Ch'uan, Program 26 29 MIN
Videoreel / VT2
T'ai Chi Ch'uan Series
Color
History - World; Physical Education and Recreation
Dist - PBS **Prod** - KCET

Tai chi Chuan push hands techniques 46 MIN
VHS
Color (G)
$49.95 purchase _ #1161
Presents push hands application techniques for the first four movements of the Yang style, both single hand and two hand. Features Cheng Hsiang, a student of Cheng Man - ch'ing.
Physical Education and Recreation
Dist - WAYF

T'ai Chi Ch'uan Series
T'ai Chi Ch'uan, Program 01 29 MIN
T'ai Chi Ch'uan, Program 02 29 MIN
T'ai Chi Ch'uan, Program 03 29 MIN
T'ai Chi Ch'uan, Program 04 29 MIN
T'ai Chi Ch'uan, Program 05 29 MIN
T'ai Chi Ch'uan, Program 06 29 MIN
T'ai Chi Ch'uan, Program 07 29 MIN
T'ai Chi Ch'uan, Program 08 29 MIN
T'ai Chi Ch'uan, Program 09 29 MIN
T'ai Chi Ch'uan, Program 10 29 MIN
T'ai Chi Ch'uan, Program 11 29 MIN
T'ai Chi Ch'uan, Program 12 29 MIN
T'ai Chi Ch'uan, Program 13 29 MIN
T'ai Chi Ch'uan, Program 14 29 MIN
T'ai Chi Ch'uan, Program 15 29 MIN
T'ai Chi Ch'uan, Program 16 29 MIN
T'ai Chi Ch'uan, Program 17 29 MIN
T'ai Chi Ch'uan, Program 18 29 MIN
T'ai Chi Ch'uan, Program 19 29 MIN
T'ai Chi Ch'uan, Program 20 29 MIN
T'ai Chi Ch'uan, Program 21 29 MIN
T'ai Chi Ch'uan, Program 22 29 MIN
T'ai Chi Ch'uan, Program 23 29 MIN
T'ai Chi Ch'uan, Program 24 29 MIN
T'ai Chi Ch'uan, Program 25 29 MIN
T'ai Chi Ch'uan, Program 26 29 MIN
Dist - PBS

T'ai chi ch'uan - the ultimate exercise 60 MIN
VHS
Color (G)
$29.95 purchase
Presents a total conditioning program that draws from the ancient practice of t'ai chi ch'uan. Taught by David Ross.
Physical Education and Recreation
Dist - PBS **Prod** - WNETTV

Tai chi for health 50 MIN
VHS
Color (G)
$19.95 purchase _ #1100
Teaches a modified form of the first section of the Yang style. Includes postures, stepping procedures, hand movements, warm up exercises, side and back views and reviews of the movements. By Yvette Wong, geared toward older beginners.
Physical Education and Recreation
Dist - WAYF

T'ai chi for health 120 MIN
VHS
Color (G)
$29.95 purchase _ #X005
Introduces the Yang short form of t'ai chi. Features Terry Dunn.
Physical Education and Recreation
Dist - STRUE **Prod** - HEALIN 1993

T'ai chi for health - long form 120 MIN
VHS
Color (G)
$59.95 purchase
Presents a long form program teaching the advanced forms of t'ai chi. Teaches warmups, step - by - step training exercises, and over 100 postures. Hosted by Terry Pang - Yen Dunn.
Physical Education and Recreation
Dist - PBS **Prod** - WNETTV

T'ai chi for health - yang short form 120 MIN
VHS
Color (H C A)
$29.95 purchase
Features Terence Dunn in an introduction to the ancient Chinese practice of t'ai chi. Includes warm - ups, introduction to basic postures, step - by - step instructions in 37 postures, and more.
Health and Safety; Physical Education and Recreation
Dist - YOGAJ **Prod** - YOGAJ

Tai chi for seniors 67 MIN
VHS
Color (G)
$34.95 purchase _ #1121
Presents a set of exercise and self massage techniques for dealing with stiff joints, arthritis, the immune system, high blood pressure, and osteoporosis. Acupressure techniques are shown for stress, headaches, upset stomach and general vitality. Shows a ten movement T'ai chi form that can be done in 4 minutes.
Health and Safety; Physical Education and Recreation
Dist - WAYF

T'ai - chi massage 60 MIN
VHS
Color (G)
$24.95 purchase _ #HE - 06
Demonstrates T'ai - chi massage. Features Bob Klein.
Health and Safety; Physical Education and Recreation
Dist - ARVID **Prod** - ARVID

Tai Chi Qigong 110 MIN
VHS
Color (G)
$49.95 purchase _ #1144
Uses a qigong sequence of 38 - movements as an introduction to T'ai chi and also as an aid to health, flexibility, ch'i development, or martial arts. Teaches with closeups, different angles, and repetition. By Eo Omwake.
Physical Education and Recreation
Dist - WAYF

Tai chi reference series
Demonstrates the 24 - posture simplified form, the 48 - posture combined set, and the 108 - posture traditional Yang style. Features Sam Masich. Not intended as a teaching tape but as a reference.
Tai chi reference series 90 MIN
Dist - WAYF

T'ai - chi sword forms 120 MIN
VHS
Color (G)
$39.95 purchase _ #MA - 02
Shows the movements for the Yang sword form and intermediate fighting form. Demonstrates fighting applications for each movement, sword exercises and freestyle swordfighting practice.
Physical Education and Recreation; Religion and Philosophy
Dist - ARVID **Prod** - ARVID

Tai chi weapons 27 MIN
VHS
Color (G)
$39.95 purchase _ #1105
Shows the orthodox Yang style weapons system, demonstrating sword and sabre , repeating each form three times. Features a clip of host Peter DeBlasio, Jr, MD, sword fencing with T T Liang. Looks at solo and partner exercises to develop skill with staff, plum blosson spear, and halberd.
Physical Education and Recreation
Dist - WAYF

Tai Chi workout
VHS
Color (G)
$29.95 purchase _ #ESA001
Combines Tai Chi with meditation and low - impact aerobics. Features Master Robert Cook.
Physical Education and Recreation; Psychology
Dist - SIV

Tai ki 52 MIN
16mm / VHS
Color (G)
$350.00, $600.00 purchase, $90.00 rental
Uncovers the artifacts of Asian and Central American cultures which anthropologists show have an uncanny resemblance. Wonders if the ancient Chinese could have made a voyage from Southeast Asia to Mexico or South America. Documents the sea adventure designed to test this theory - a 64 - foot replica of a Chinese junk navigated by an international crew.
Fine Arts; Geography - World; Industrial and Technical Education
Dist - CNEMAG **Prod** - HOBELP 1976

The Taiga Ecosystem 15 MIN
VHS / 16mm

Ecosystems of the Great Land Series
Color (I H)
$125.00 purchase, $25.00 rental
Examines the taiga, a dry and cold area with less temperature variation than the tundra, where trees can grow. Outlines also forest succession, interdependence of living things, carrying capacity and predator - prey relationships.
Geography - United States; Science - Natural
Dist - AITECH Prod - ALASDE 1985

Tail loss in lizards 9 MIN
VHS
Aspects of animal behavior series
Color (J H C G)
$99.00 purchase, $35.00 rental _ #37549
Shows the adaptations that enable certain lizards to lose their tails to escape from predators. Part of a series on animal behavior produced by Robert Dickson and Prof George Bartholomew for the Office of Instructional Development, UCLA.
Science - Natural
Dist - UCEMC

Tailgating - How Close is Too Close 11 MIN
U-matic / VHS / 16mm
Color (J) (SPANISH)
LC 76-703738
Shows, through the use of animation, the hazards of tailgating and a simple method to avoid it. Discusses the development of tailgating situations and procedures for correcting them.
Health and Safety; Psychology
Dist - AIMS Prod - CAHILL 1976

The Tailor and early on Sunday 66 MIN
VHS
Glasnost film festival series
Color (H C G T A) (RUSSIAN (ENGLISH SUBTITLES))
$59.95 purchase, $35.00 rental
Presents two of the Soviet films shown at the Glasnost Film Festival. "The tailor" profiles middle - aged Soviets, who are largely disillusioned with their lives. "Early On Sunday" shows several old village women as they go to the forest to chop wood. Features the women as they sit around a fire, talk at length, and go home.
Business and Economics; Civics and Political Systems; History - World; Sociology
Dist - EFVP

The Tailor of Gloucester 30 MIN
VHS
Rabbit ears collection series
Color (K P I J)
$12.95 purchase _ #243241
Tells a Beatrix Potter tale about sharing. Features Meryl Streep as narrator.
Guidance and Counseling; Literature and Drama
Dist - KNOWUN Prod - RABBIT

Tailoring Blazers 60 MIN
VHS / BETA
Color
Shows details of tailoring lined blazers using fusible interfacing and double fusibles, four - point closure, and pressing and shaping techniques.
Home Economics
Dist - HOMEAF Prod - HOMEAF

Tailoring, Pt 4 - Finishing the Simple Suit 29 MIN
Videoreel / VT2
Designing Women Series
Color
Home Economics
Dist - PBS Prod - WKYCTV

Tailoring, Pt 3 - Making a Simple Suit 29 MIN
Videoreel / VT2
Designing Women Series
Color
Home Economics
Dist - PBS Prod - WKYCTV

Tailoring, Pt 2 - Finishing the Simple Coat 29 MIN
Videoreel / VT2
Designing Women Series
Color
Home Economics
Dist - PBS Prod - WKYCTV

Tailoring Shirts for Men and Women 60 MIN
BETA / VHS
Color
Gives instructions on tailoring a man's or woman's shirt including sewing the front ban, double yoke, two - piece collar, sleeve, pocket, and cuffs.
Home Economics
Dist - HOMEAF Prod - HOMEAF

Tailoring Your Proposal to the Funding Source 55 MIN
VHS / U-matic
Winning Grants
(G)
$1,795 member purchase, $1,995 purchase non member
Presents seminars on successful grant writing. Focuses on adapting the proposal to the funding source. Sixth in a series of ten.
Business and Economics; Education
Dist - GPN

Tailoring Your Proposal to the Funding Source 60 MIN
U-matic / VHS
Winning Grants Series
Color (A)
Business and Economics; Education
Dist - GPN Prod - UNEBR

Tails 3 MIN
16mm
Color (G)
$7.00 rental
Ties together a series of tail ends of varied strips of film, with sometimes recognizable images dissolving into light flares, which appear to run through and off of a projector.
Fine Arts
Dist - CANCIN Prod - SHARIT 1976

Tailspin 30 MIN
U-matic / VHS
Enterprise II Series
Color (C A)
LC 83-706197
Presents the story of the Braniff Airline bankruptcy, showing how the chief executive officer tried desperately to restructure the billion - dollar company's operations in a few short months. Illustrates the high level of competition in the airline industry.
Business and Economics; Industrial and Technical Education
Dist - LCOA Prod - WGBHTV 1983

The Tailypo 12 MIN
VHS
Paul Galdone's illustrated spooky stories series
Color (K P I)
$44.95 purchase _ #SAV9025
Tells about an old man, his tired hound dogs and the hairy 'thing' hiding in the woods. Presents part of a four - part series of spooky stories by Paul Galdone.
Literature and Drama
Dist - KNOWUN

Tailypo 20 MIN
VHS / 16mm
Color (P)
$450.00, $195.00 purchase, $50.00 rental
Presents popular Appalachian folktale. Portrays scruffy 1800s hunter who 'hollers' in his three coon dogs and heads home. Empty in hand he arrives at his cabin to find a strange varmint in his bed. A chase follows and ends when the hunter chops off the critter's tail as it flees through a crack. The hunter cooks the tail, eats and goes to sleep. At night the critter returns to fetch its tail.
Literature and Drama
Dist - WADSWB Prod - WADSWB 1990

Taipei story 110 MIN
35mm
Color; PAL (G)
Studies a disintegrating relationship involving a young couple who seem to have everything going for them. Indicates the uncertainties of life in Taipei itself. Directed by Edward Yang for Hang Liu Productions, Taiwan.
Geography - World; Literature and Drama; Sociology
Dist - BALFOR Prod - NATLFM 1985

Taiwan 20 MIN
U-matic
(Formosa - Blueprint for Development (from the Geography for the ' '70's Series
Color (H C)
Geography - World
Dist - GPN Prod - KLRNTV

Taiwan 30 MIN
VHS
On top of the world series
Color (G)
$19.95 purchase _ #WW19
Visits Taiwan, the economic 'Asian tiger.' Looks at the prosperity of Tapei, Taiwan's largest city. Explores the history of Taiwan from the early days when it was called 'La Formosa,' through Japanese occupation to 1949, when Chiang Kai - Shek moved the central government of the Republic of China to the island. Examines Taiwanese society and the prominence of the Buddhist and Taoist religions. Views the colorful 'Lantern Festival' and visits Hualien and the Taroko Gorge. Tours the National Palace Museum and views treasures from the Ch'ing, Ming and Sung dynasties. Hosted by Canadian TV personality, Anne Martin.
Geography - World
Dist - SVIP

Taiwan - exotic blossom of the orient 60 MIN
VHS
Asian collection series
Color (J H C G)
$29.95 purchase _ #IVN353V-S
Teaches about the people, culture and history of Taiwan. Visits historic buildings, monuments and landmarks. Examines the physical topography of the republic. Part of a seven-part series on Asian countries, cities and islands. Also part of a larger series entitled Video Visits that travels to six continents.
Geography - World
Dist - CAMV Prod - WNETTV

Taiwan, Nevada, France, England, Guatemala 27 MIN
16mm
Big blue marble - children around the world series
Color (P I)
LC 76-700640
Describes aspects of life in Taiwan, Nevada, England and Guatemala. Presents a French folk tale about a bridge inspector who makes an agreement with the devil. Part B in a series.
Geography - United States; Geography - World; Literature and Drama; Social Science
Dist - VITT Prod - ALVEN 1975

Tajimoltik - five days without name 30 MIN
VHS / 16mm
Maya series
Color (G)
$550.00, $275.00 purchase, $55.00, $35.00 rental
Examines the Mayan calendar consisting of 18 months of 20 days each, or 360 days - the five remaining days known as 'days without names', or Chaikin, days of Canival. Reveals that these days of transition coincide with Catholic Holy Week and are filled with elements of Spanish Catholicism, traditional rituals and cargo fiestas. French priest Michel Chantea discusses the meaning of these days. Part of a series by Georges Payrastre and Claudine Viallon.
Geography - World; Religion and Philosophy; Social Science
Dist - DOCEDR Prod - DOCEDR 1978

Take a Break 107 MIN
VHS / 16mm
Color (G)
$41.95 purchase
Presents yoga exercise by Priscilla Patrick who appears on PBS. Offers a beginning exercise video which focuses on limbering up, breathing exercises and relaxation techniques.
Physical Education and Recreation; Religion and Philosophy; Science - Natural
Dist - PRIPAT Prod - PRIPAT

Take a Deep Breath 15 MIN
U-matic / VHS
All about You Series
Color (P)
Uses a burning candle to demonstrate the body's need for air. Discusses how air gets in and out of the body. (Broadcast quality).
Science - Natural
Dist - AITECH Prod - NITC 1975

Take a Giant Step 6 MIN
16mm
Human Side of Supervision Series
Color (IND)
LC 73-701929
Presents Hank, the new supervisor, who finds that paperwork goes with management. Shows how, as he flounders in administrative details or ignores what he considers petty details, he loses the respect of his employees.
Business and Economics; Psychology
Dist - VOAERO Prod - VOAERO 1972

Take a Good Look 1959 ABC
U-matic / VHS
Color
Shows Ernie Kovaks hosting an unusual show with Hans Conried, Cesar Romero and Edie Adams.
Fine Arts; Sociology
Dist - IHF Prod - IHF

Take a Guess - Estimation and Problem Solving 20 MIN
U-matic
Let's Figure it Out Series

B&W (P)
Mathematics
Dist - NYSED **Prod** - WNYE 1968

Take a Little Pride 10 MIN
16mm
Color (I)
Shows elementary students planning and participating in projects to beautify and improve their schools under the Project Pride program.
Education; Sociology
Dist - LAWREN **Prod** - PARKRD

Take a Look at Yourself 16 MIN
16mm
Human Values Series
Color (I J)
LC 74-712725
Deals with the need for laws and the necessity for upholding them. Discusses the growing antagonism toward the man who wears the police uniform and suggests that the man in uniform is an individual whose motives, aside from earning a livelihood, may very well be altruistic. Features Bill, a highly sensitive boy antagonistic toward authority, who finally realizes his own helplessness and his need for the protection society has provided for him after his bike is stolen.
Civics and Political Systems; Psychology; Sociology
Dist - MALIBU **Prod** - MENKNS 1970

Take a Look Series
Birds 10 MIN
Boats 10 MIN
Crystals 10 MIN
Eggs 10 MIN
Energy 10 MIN
Flight 10 MIN
Flowers and seeds 10 MIN
Fossils 10 MIN
Growing Things 10 MIN
Insects 10 MIN
Mixtures 10 MIN
The Moon 10 MIN
Plants 10 MIN
Playground Science 10 MIN
Rain 10 MIN
Rocks 10 MIN
Seasons 10 MIN
Sun and Other Stars 10 MIN
Waste 10 MIN
Wind 10 MIN
Dist - TVOTAR

Take a look 2 series
Presents a ten - part children's series that takes a hands - on approach to the principles of science. Teacher's guide available.
Air pressure 10 MIN
Dairy farm 10 MIN
Friction 10 MIN
Heat 10 MIN
Magnets 10 MIN
Matter 10 MIN
Sound 10 MIN
Trees 10 MIN
Dist - TVOTAR **Prod** - TVOTAR 1970

Take a Poetry Break 30 MIN
VHS / U-matic
Color
Presents librarian/educator Dr Caroline Feller Bauer who demonstrates the traditional methods for developing interest in poems, and utilizes a variety of media, such as posters, costumes, puppets, magic tricks and simple props to enhance her presentation.
Education; Literature and Drama
Dist - PBS **Prod** - ALA

Take a sample
16mm
B&W
Shows how a random sample of only 1,000 people from a total population of 50 million allows one to estimate the proportion one is looking for.
Mathematics
Dist - OPENU **Prod** - OPENU

Take a Stand 25 MIN
16mm
Color (A)
LC 82-700786
Documents how a victim - advocate program can help elderly people fight back through the court system when they are the victims of violent crime.
Civics and Political Systems; Health and Safety; Sociology
Dist - FLMLIB **Prod** - TNF 1982

Take Care 30 MIN
U-matic / VHS
Color (A)
Discusses customer relations. Includes suggestions on first impressions, dealing with irate customers and telephone techniques. Uses a fictionalized story.
Business and Economics
Dist - AMEDIA **Prod** - AMEDIA

Take care 30 MIN
16mm / VHS
Color (G IND)
$5.00 rental
Presents a professional musical revue created from the real experiences of RWDSU - 1199 hospital workers from New York City. Features excerpts from a performance of the show intercut with comments from workers talking about the difficulties of their jobs. Produced by the Bread and Roses Culture Project.
Business and Economics; Fine Arts; Social Science
Dist - AFLCIO

Take Care 30 MIN
VHS / 16mm
Color (G)
$240.00 purchase, $100.00 - $50.00 rental
Presents two nurses singing about treating patients, based on hospital experiences.
Fine Arts; Health and Safety
Dist - FANPRO **Prod** - FANPRO 1989

Take Care of Yourself 10 MIN
U-matic
Diabetes Care at Home Series
(A)
Examines health complications which can arise from diabetes. Demonstrates procedures to measure sugar levels. Gives helpful hints on handling travel and eating out.
Health and Safety
Dist - ACCESS **Prod** - ACCESS 1983

Take care of yourself 20 MIN
VHS
Color (PRO)
$48.00 purchase _ #AH46224
Teaches stress reduction techniques for dental hygienists. Covers such techniques as body alignment, three - dimensional breathing and moving, eye relaxation, stretches, self - massage, and others.
Health and Safety; Science - Natural
Dist - HTHED **Prod** - HTHED

Take Care of Yourself Series
Angina pectoris 9 MIN
Colds and flu 9 MIN
Gout 11 MIN
High Blood Pressure 7 MIN
Hyperthyroidism 10 MIN
Hypothyroidism 10 MIN
Infectious Mononucleosis 8 MIN
Iron Deficiency Anemia 8 MIN
Middle Ear Infection 8 MIN
Monilial Vaginitis 7 MIN
Postmenopausal vaginitis 7 MIN
Sore Throat 10 MIN
Stones in the urinary tract 8 MIN
Trichomonal Vaginitis 9 MIN
Urinary Tract Infections 7 MIN
Dist - UARIZ

Take care - understanding preterm labor - Comprendiendo la labor de parto prematura 8 MIN
VHS
Having a baby series
Color (H G PRO) (SPANISH)
$195.00 purchase _ #E910 - VI - 033, #E910 - VI - 045
Reveals that the most significant problem affecting infants today is preterm birth. Discloses that infants born earlier than 37 weeks of pregnancy can have problems that affect them for a lifetime. Teaches mothers how to identify symptoms of preterm labor. Early recognition of these symptoms can help decrease the risk of having a preterm baby. Part of a six - part series on all aspects of birth, from prenatal to postnatal care of the mother and care of the newborn infant.
Health and Safety; Psychology
Dist - HSCIC **Prod** - UTXHSH 1991

Take charge 22 MIN
VHS
Color (PRO IND A)
$695.00 purchase, $225.00 rental _ #WSB07
Draws upon the leadership experience of General H Norman Schwarzkopf who offers insight regarding the nature of successful organizations and people. Inspires supervisors, managers, team leaders. By Washington Productions.
Business and Economics; Guidance and Counseling; Psychology
Dist - EXTR

Take Charge 11 MIN
VHS / 16mm
Color (H A PRO)
$195.00 purchase, $75.00 rental _ #9963
Presents the true story of Dr Lou Schwartz and his fight with cancer.
Health and Safety; Psychology
Dist - AIMS **Prod** - MEDIMP 1988

Take charge 61 MIN
VHS
Color (H C A)
$34.95 purchase _ #MJ200V
Presents a guide to overcoming obstacles to success and happiness. Covers subjects including how to develop effective and loving communication, healing past hurts and resentments, doing less while accomplishing more, and other subjects. Hosted by Harold Bloomfield and Sirah Vettese.
Psychology
Dist - CAMV

Take Charge 61 MIN
VHS
(A PRO)
$34.95 _ #MJ200V
Uses psychotherapeutic methods to help the viewer overcome past crises, master effective communication, and start on the road to success.
Psychology
Dist - CAMV **Prod** - CAMV

Take charge of your life
16mm
B&W (G)
$960.00 purchase _ #6022
Presents five films hosted by Earl Nightingale. Starts with The Strangest Secret followed by four satellite films which amplify the concepts in the first film. Motivates sales personnel and other staff.
Business and Economics; Psychology
Dist - DARTNL **Prod** - NIGCON

Take charge of your life 45 MIN
VHS
Les Brown series
Color (G)
$69.95 purchase _ #TVL 1015
Shows ways to overcome the obstacles, challenges and negative relationships that stand in the way of making progress toward one's dreams.
Guidance and Counseling; Psychology
Dist - JWAVID **Prod** - JWAVID

Take charge of your pregnancy 90 MIN
VHS
Color (J H)
$29.98 purchase _ #462 - V8
Presents a 'visual encyclopedia' with answers to most questions expectant parents may have about pregnancy and childbirth. Features narrator and mother, Candice Bergen, and 22 specialists and health care professionals, who provide complete information on prenatal nutrition and exercise, childbirth preparation, prenatal tests, fetal development, normal or Caeserean delivery, and more. Useful for childbirth classes and prenatal clinics.
Health and Safety
Dist - ETRASS **Prod** - ETRASS

Take Charge Series
Stereotyping - Sex 30 MIN
Dist - USC

Take Charge) - Your Skill in Reading 36 MIN
VHS / U-matic
Color (A)
LC 83-706122
Encourages those individuals who have the ability, but choose not to read, to hone their reading skills.
English Language; Psychology
Dist - CFLA **Prod** - CFLA 1982

Take Command 30 MIN
U-matic / VHS / 16mm
Color
Features astronaut Walter Schirra, Jr in a story to inspire, encourage and stimulate salesmen to overcome every obstacle and surmount every difficulty to reach goals set for them.
Business and Economics
Dist - DARTNL **Prod** - DARTNL

Take downs with Joe Seay 60 MIN
VHS
Wrestling videos series
Color (H C A)
$39.95 purchase _ #DP002V
Features Joe Seay instructing in the methods of wrestling take downs. Includes live - action demonstration of these skills.
Physical Education and Recreation
Dist - CAMV

Take 'Er Down 13 MIN
16mm

B&W
Presents a history of the development of submarines in the U S Navy from 1900 to 1954. Includes scenes of the USS Nautilus, the first nuclear - powered vessel.
Civics and Political Systems; History - United States; Social Science
Dist - USNAC **Prod** - USN 1954

Take 'Er Down / the Nuclear Navy / the Submarines 69 MIN
U-matic / VHS
Color
Tells the history of the development of submarines in the U S Navy from 1900 to the USS Nautilus in 1954 (in black and white). Presents a documentary on the Navy's development of nuclear power and its application in long - range submarines. Focuses on the specialized skills and responsibilities that keep U S Navy submarines ready for battle.
Civics and Political Systems; History - United States; Industrial and Technical Education
Dist - IHF **Prod** - IHF

Take Fewer Steps - Layout Studies 14 MIN
16mm
Color
LC 74-706271
Describes layout studies, focusing on their purpose, use, preparation and application. Discusses how to prepare a layout chart and how to use it to determine distances traveled by people or materials.
Business and Economics
Dist - USNAC **Prod** - USA 1973

Take five 25 MIN
VHS
Color (G R)
$19.95 purchase _ #35 - 885010 - 533
Consists of five music videos by Christian artists. Includes 'Stranger to Danger' by Mylon LeFevre, 'It's Not a Song' by Amy Grant, 'Still Small Voice' by Randy Stonehill, 'Away' by Michael W Smith, and 'Love Calling' by Leon Patillo.
Fine Arts; Religion and Philosophy
Dist - APH **Prod** - WORD

Take five II 22 MIN
VHS
Color (G R)
$19.95 purchase _ #35 - 85035 - 533
Consists of five music videos by Christian artists. Includes 'I'm Not Alone' by Russ Taff, 'Stay for Awhile' by Amy Grant, 'Is It Any Wonder' by Ideola, 'Big Boy Now' by Sheila Walsh, and 'All Is God's Creation' by David Meese.
Fine Arts; Religion and Philosophy
Dist - APH **Prod** - WORD

Take 5 Series
Face Value 10 MIN
Dist - MARHLL

Take heart - a step - by - step guide to open heart surgery 20 MIN
VHS
Color (G)
$75.00 purchase, $25.00 rental _ #840, #841
Helps patients and their families to understand the steps in preparing for and recovering from open heart surgery. Presents the story of Don Hoover as he faces open heart surgery. Follows Hoover and his family through all of the stages of treatment. Includes six parts - Diagnosis, Admissions, Preparations, Surgery, Cardiovascular Intensive Care, Cardiac Recovery Unit. Produced by Cardiac Services and Corporate Communications of Mercy Hospital, Pittsburgh, Pennsylvania.
Health and Safety
Dist - CATHHA

Take it easy and live 27 MIN
16mm
Color (C A)
Revised edition of 'Take It Easy.' Features a housewife, who is a cardiac patient. Demonstrates easy solutions to housework problems and discusses benefits of the work saving programs conducted by Wayne State University and the Heart Association.
Guidance and Counseling; Health and Safety; Psychology; Sociology
Dist - WSUM **Prod** - WSUM 1954

Take it from Here 25 MIN
16mm
Captioned; Color (PRO)
Explains a step by step approach to setting up a continuing education program for deaf adults.
Education; Guidance and Counseling; Psychology
Dist - GALCO **Prod** - GALCO 1977

Take it from the Beginning 15 MIN
U-matic / VHS
Hidden Treasures Series
Color (T)
LC 82-706527
Uses the adventures of a pirate and his three friends to explore the many facets of language arts. Focuses on initial sounds and demonstrates their use in oral and written expression. Number three in a series.
English Language
Dist - GPN **Prod** - WCVETV 1980

Take it from the Pros 16 MIN
16mm
Color
LC 72-701078
Strives to influence portable grinder operators to practice safety measures when mounting grinding wheels and handling portable grinders. Demonstrates safety practices in handling portable grinders.
Industrial and Technical Education
Dist - WSTGLC **Prod** - IRC 1971

Take it from the Top Series
Lord Hanson 32 MIN
Sir James Goldsmith 40 MIN
Sir John Harvey - Jones 32 MIN
Dist - VIDART

Take it from the Top - WP - 2 15 MIN
U-matic
Word Processing Series
(PRO)
$235.00 purchase
Illustrates the importance of executive level involvement in word processing.
Business and Economics
Dist - MONAD **Prod** - MONAD

Take it off 45 MIN
VHS
Color (G)
$29.95 purchase _ #XJ040V
Demonstrates successful weight loss techniques through a plan combining good eating habits, proper food selection, exercise and motivation. Covers setting realistic goals, satisfying nutritional needs, minimizing hunger and fatigue, dining out and weight maintenance.
Health and Safety; Home Economics; Physical Education and Recreation; Social Science
Dist - CAMV

Take it to Heart - Stress, Hypertension, and Heart Disease 30 MIN
U-matic / VHS
Color
Covers the dangers of stressful American lifestyles. Discusses the burden that everyday stress places upon the heart and considers ways of coping with stressful situations.
Health and Safety; Psychology; Science - Natural
Dist - FAIRGH **Prod** - FAIRGH

Take Joy 11 MIN
16mm
Color (P I)
LC 74-702891
Points out that the body and its systems help a person to enjoy life and that it is necessary to take care of these systems.
Health and Safety; Science - Natural
Dist - AMCS **Prod** - AMCS 1973

Take Me Back to Crested Butte 14 MIN
16mm
Color
LC 79-701532
Shows the ambience of Crested Butte, Colorado, which makes it unique among American ski resorts.
Geography - United States; Physical Education and Recreation
Dist - CREBUT **Prod** - CREBUT 1979

Take me to the Kaba - 4
VHS
Adam's world series
Color (P I J)
$19.95 purchase _ #110 - 050
Features the puppet character Adam who teaches educational concepts about Islam and Muslims to children. Teaches about Allah's love for everyone. Features a trip to the three most sacred Masjids in the world, a segment on Allah's Love and Mercy, a segment on the importance of Hajj, a song about the Kaba, the story of a young girl's trip to Hajj, animation showing how to write Kaba in Arabic, plus a trip underwater to see Allah's creations.
Religion and Philosophy
Dist - SOUVIS **Prod** - SOUVIS

Take Me to Your Leader 25 MIN
U-matic / VHS
Color
Visits with Wisconsin and Minnesota residents who have seen UFO's, and with scientists who say there is more to the sightings than meets the eye.
Science - Physical
Dist - WCCOTV **Prod** - WCCOTV 1976

Take me to your leaders 47 MIN
VHS
Raising good kids in bad times series
Color (H C A)
$95.00 purchase
Illustrates problems among people and possible solutions, focusing on child - rearing methods. Provides material for educators and community leaders as well as young people. Written, produced and directed by Carol Fleisher.
Guidance and Counseling; Health and Safety; Sociology
Dist - PFP **Prod** - ASHAP

Take Me Up to the Ballgame 25 MIN
16mm / U-matic / VHS
Color
Depicts ragtag baseball team of rabbit, cow and cat playing intergalactic champions from outer space. Shows how, in animation, earth team turns tables on cheating spacers.
Fine Arts; Literature and Drama
Dist - BCNFL **Prod** - NELVNA 1983

Take My Arm 15 MIN
16mm
Color (J)
LC 77-701858
Shows the staff and trainees of the Texas Center For The Blind and how they describe the purpose, methods and accomplishments of the Center's adult blind rehabilitation program.
Geography - United States; Guidance and Counseling; Health and Safety
Dist - TEXCFB **Prod** - CASTOP 1977

Take Nothing for Granted 19 MIN
U-matic / VHS / 16mm
Harry Sparks Series
Color (IND)
Shows how Harry Sparks, the guardian angel of electrical workers, almost loses an electrician whose only mistake was assuming the power was off when he started repair work.
Health and Safety; Industrial and Technical Education
Dist - IFB **Prod** - IAPA 1975

Take Off 10 MIN
16mm
Color (I)
Presents a series of vignettes on skiing. Uses the camera and background music to create a visual poem on the pleasures of the sport. Without narration.
Fine Arts; Physical Education and Recreation
Dist - VIEWFI **Prod** - SUMMIT 1970

Take - Off 30 MIN
U-matic / VHS / 16mm
Enterprise Series
Color (H C A)
Describes the race to develop a small, fuel - efficient plane to capture the corporate airplane market.
Business and Economics
Dist - CORF **Prod** - CORF

Take off 10 MIN
16mm
B&W (G)
$30.00 rental
Documents a professional stripper going through her paces, baring her body then literally transcending it. Makes a forceful political statement on the image of woman and the true meaning of stripping.
Fine Arts; Sociology
Dist - CANCIN **Prod** - NELSOG 1972

Take - Off and Landings 29 MIN
Videoreel / VT2
Discover Flying - Just Like a Bird Series
Color
Industrial and Technical Education; Social Science
Dist - PBS **Prod** - WKYCTV

Take Off for Opportunities 11 MIN
16mm
Color
Looks at the careers of an air frame and power mechanic, an avionics technician and an aeronautical engineer.
Guidance and Counseling; Industrial and Technical Education
Dist - MTP **Prod** - GEAVMA

Take One 120 MIN
BETA / VHS
Color
Presents a compilation of films and video programs from Appalshop on mountain life and music. Includes major portions of four films, including Sourwood Mountain Dulcimer and Ramsey Trade Fair, as well as excerpts from the Headwaters television series. Includes performances by Nimrod Workman, I D Stamper and many others.
Fine Arts; Geography - United States; Sociology
Dist - APPAL **Prod** - APPAL

Take One with You 26 MIN
16mm
Winston Churchill - the Valiant Years Series
B&W
LC FI67-2116
Presents documentary footage showing the British preparations for a German invasion after the fall of France and the inception of the lend - lease program after Churchill's appeals for assistance to Roosevelt. Based on the book 'The Second World War,' by Winston S Churchill.
History - World
Dist - SG **Prod** - ABC 1961

Take - Out Doubles 30 MIN
U-matic / VHS
Play Bridge Series
Color (A)
Physical Education and Recreation
Dist - KYTV **Prod** - KYTV 1983

Take pride Gulf - wide 18 MIN
U-matic / VHS / BETA
Color (G)
$29.95, $130.00 purchase _ #LSTF77
Describes the Take Pride Gulf - Wide program which involves the federal government, the five Gulf states, the public and industry in dealing with pollution in the Gulf of Mexico.
Science - Natural; Sociology
Dist - FEDU **Prod** - USEPA 1991

Take quantum leaps in your reading speed 30 MIN
VHS
Go to the head of the class collection
Color (H C A)
$29.95 purchase _ #LF702V
Teaches strategies for increasing one's reading speed. Covers a variety of reading styles, including 'idea reading,' skimming, and rapid reading. Includes a booklet.
Education; Psychology
Dist - CAMV

Take Tea and See 1 MIN
U-matic / VHS
Color
Shows a classic television commercial.
Business and Economics; Psychology; Sociology
Dist - BROOKC **Prod** - BROOKC

Take ten for safety series

Basic personal protective equipment	8 MIN
Decision for safety	6 MIN
Elevated areas	9 MIN
Guarding	7 MIN
Hazardous Area Identification	9 MIN
Hot work	9 MIN
Lock - Out	8 MIN
Moment for Decision	8 MIN
Portable Ladders	6 MIN
Vessel Entry	12 MIN

Dist - CORF

Take that First Step 28 MIN
16mm
Color; B&W (J)
LC 71-713897
Tells how a retarded boy and a college student meet by accident, and how the student is influenced to enter the field of special education. Provides information about the problems and challenges of special education.
Education; Guidance and Counseling; Psychology
Dist - NMAC **Prod** - SREB 1967

Take the first step 30 MIN
Videoreel / VT2
Designing home interiors series; Unit 7
Color (C A)
Highlights the points for a prospective buyer or renter to look for in a new home.
Home Economics
Dist - CDTEL **Prod** - COAST

Take the 5 - 10 to dreamland 6 MIN
16mm
Sepia (G)
$300.00 purchase, $15.00 rental
Features very few images edited to invoke a poetic feeling on the viewer's unconscious. Produced by Bruce Conner.
Fine Arts
Dist - CANCIN **Prod** - CONNER 1977

Take the 5 - 10 to dreamland and Valse triste 11 MIN
16mm
Sepia; B&W (G)
$30.00 rental
Presents two short films. Pictures a series of images, tinted soft brown, like a poetic collage, in Take the 5 - 10, 1977, 6 minutes, with music by Patrick Gleeson. Valse Triste, 1979, 5 minutes, is an autobiography of Conner's Kansas boyhood in the 1940s. Features theme music from I love a Mystery radio programs.
Fine Arts
Dist - CANCIN **Prod** - CONNER 1979

Take the mystery out of algebra 30 MIN
VHS
Go to the head of the class collection
Color (H C A)
$29.95 purchase _ #LF706V
Presents a comprehensive guide to algebra. Focuses on explaining concepts, problem solving, and terminology. Includes a booklet.
Education; Psychology
Dist - CAMV

Take the Plunge 30 MIN
BETA / VHS
Great Outdoors Series
Color
Explores an underwater garden. Gives hiking tips. Presents campsite drinking toasts.
Physical Education and Recreation
Dist - CORF **Prod** - WGBHTV

Take the power 7 MIN
Cassette
Color (G H C)
$75.00, $50.00, $35.00 $10.00 purchase, $45.00 rental
Features the sequel to One Fine Day. Celebrates contemporary women's lives and moves from the 'herstorical' into the present and towards the future. Produced by Kay Weaver and Martha Wheelock.
History - World; Sociology
Dist - ISHTAR

Take the Time 18 MIN
16mm
Color
Shows the various guidelines a woman must follow to stay physically fit. Discusses the importance of getting and staying in shape and the nutritious foods that are needed to fuel the body.
Physical Education and Recreation; Sociology
Dist - MTP **Prod** - CRAISN

Take the time 20 MIN
VHS / 16mm
Color (PRO)
$495.00 purchase, $125.00 rental, $35.00 preview
Teaches managers how to build employee strengths and solve problems of low morale. Shows how to coach employees, create an organizational climate, and succeed in teamwork problem - solving. Includes a leader's guide.
Business and Economics; Guidance and Counseling; Psychology
Dist - UTM **Prod** - UTM

Take the Time 20 MIN
U-matic / VHS
Color
Concentrates on creating a 'coaching' management style for executives, managers and supervisors to build on employee strengths. Helps to solve problems of low morale and non - performance. Leader's Guide available to extend course for three hours of training.
Business and Economics; Psychology
Dist - CREMED **Prod** - CREMED

Take this job and keep it - 1 20 MIN
VHS / U-matic
Working on your career series
Color; Captioned (H) (SPANISH)
$275.00, $245.00 purchase _ #V225
Provides high school youth with information on job - keeping skills. Uses dramatic vignettes and documentary - style interviews with teens to emphasize teamwork, preparation, follow - through, honesty and communication. Part of a three - part series on careers.
Business and Economics; Guidance and Counseling; Psychology
Dist - BARR **Prod** - NYSED 1992

Take this job and love it 8 MIN
VHS
Color (A PRO)
$395.00 purchase, $125.00 rental
Introduces new sales associates to the benefits and responsibilities of retail sales.
Business and Economics; Psychology
Dist - VLEARN

Take this job and love it 40 MIN
VHS
Color (H C G)
$79.95 purchase _ #CCP0121V
Discusses positive attitudes, adaptability, dependability, loyalty and interpersonal skills and their role in the workplace. Stresses the importance of preparing for the expectations of bosses, supervisors, co - workers, clients and customers when starting a new job.
Business and Economics; Guidance and Counseling; Psychology
Dist - CAMV **Prod** - CAMV 1993

Take this Woman 25 MIN
U-matic
Color
Surveys lack of equal educational and occupational opportunities for women. Concludes that women, who make up half the population of the United States, are not being used to their full potential.
Sociology
Dist - ADL **Prod** - ADL

Take Time 15 MIN
VHS / U-matic
Strawberry Square II - Take Time Series
Color (P)
Fine Arts
Dist - AITECH **Prod** - NEITV 1984

Take Time Series

Accidents to infants	7 MIN
Accidents to pre - schoolers	7 MIN
Accidents to toddlers	7 MIN
A Child's view of the world	7 MIN
Cooking	7 MIN
Creating an Environment for Play	7 MIN
Dental program	7 MIN
Developing language skills	7 MIN
Discipline	7 MIN
Drawing	7 MIN
Dressing Up and Role Playing	7 MIN
Fear, anger and dependence	7 MIN
Fingerpainting	7 MIN
Hospital Visit	7 MIN
How Parents Speak to Children	7 MIN
How Safe is the Environment	7 MIN
Language Development	7 MIN
Patterns of Development in Art	7 MIN
Physical Development 0 - 3 Months	7 MIN
Physical Development 9 - 12 Months	7 MIN
Physical Development 6 - 9 Months	7 MIN
Physical Development, the Five Year Old	7 MIN
Physical Development, the Four Year Old	7 MIN
Physical Development, the One Year Old	7 MIN
Physical Development, the Three Year Old	7 MIN
Physical Development, the Two Year Old	7 MIN
Physical Development 3 - 6 Months	7 MIN
The Role of the Father	7 MIN
Sculpture	7 MIN
Selecting Books	7 MIN
Self - esteem	7 MIN
Sensory Experiences	7 MIN
Sexuality	7 MIN
Sibling Relationships	7 MIN
Stages in Play	7 MIN
Storytelling	7 MIN
Toys for Infants	7 MIN
Toys for Preschoolers	7 MIN
Toys for Toddlers	7 MIN
A Trip to the Supermarket	7 MIN
Water Play	7 MIN
Ways of Looking at Children's Art	7 MIN
Where Feeding Problems Begin	7 MIN
Why Children Play	7 MIN

Dist - ACCESS

Take time to be a family - holding successful family meetings 15 MIN
VHS
Boy's town parenting series
Color (G)
$29.95 purchase _ #FFB210V
Demonstrates how a weekly get - together can help planning and communication within a family. Explains how to use such sessions to build children's decision - making skills and enhance their sense of responsibility. Part of an 11 - part series.
Guidance and Counseling; Health and Safety; Psychology; Social Science; Sociology
Dist - CAMV **Prod** - FFBH

Take time to listen 19 MIN
VHS / U-matic / BETA
Color; CC (PRO)
$595.00 purchase, $140.00 rental
Shows how to enhance communication through listening and increase listening efficiency nearly 100 percent. Teaches the three basic steps of stop, think and listen. The ability to listen is critical for effective management, leadership and team building. Includes training leader's guide.
Business and Economics; English Language; Social Science
Dist - AMEDIA EXTR **Prod** - AMEDIA 1993

Take Time to Live 12 MIN
16mm
B&W
Tells how hurrying on the job often causes accidents. Suggests allowing a little extra time each day to ensure safety.
Business and Economics; Health and Safety
Dist - NSC **Prod** - NSC

Take two
VHS
Color (A)
$79.95 purchase
Portrays an arrogant Israeli cinematographer who has more on his mind than cinema when he engages as his assistant a young American woman. Contains nudity. Parental discretion advised. With Sherry Ren Smith and Ori Levy.
Fine Arts
Dist - ERGOM

Take two 48 MIN
VHS
Color (R G)
$39.95 purchase, $10.00 rental _ #35 - 81032 - 8936
Profiles Scott, a television video editor whose life changes after he meets a special Christian friend. Produced by Bridgestone.
Psychology; Religion and Philosophy
Dist - APH

Take Two, They're Small 14 MIN
U-matic / VHS / 16mm
Learning Values with Fat Albert and the Cosby Kids, Set II Series
Color (P I)
Shows how shoplifting hurts the storeowner and others.
Guidance and Counseling
Dist - MGHT **Prod** - FLMTON 1977

The Takeaway Babies 25 MIN
BETA / 16mm / VHS
Color
LC 77-702527
Presents correspondent Michael Maclear reporting on international child adoption practices. Notes that countries of the Third World have lenient regulations permitting the adoption of their children.
Civics and Political Systems; Sociology
Dist - CTV **Prod** - CTV 1976

Takedown techniques 22 MIN
U-matic / VHS / 16mm
Wrestling series
Color
LC 79-700806
Demonstrates takedowns in the sport of wrestling. Includes basic arm drags and fireman's carries. Number two in a series.
Physical Education and Recreation
Dist - ATHI **Prod** - ATHI 1976

Takedowns
VHS
N C A A instructional video series
Color (H C A)
$39.95 purchase _ #KAR2501V
Presents the first of a three - part series on wrestling. Focuses on takedown techniques.
Physical Education and Recreation
Dist - CAMV **Prod** - NCAAF

Takedowns with Bobby Douglas - Part I 50 MIN
VHS
Color (H C A)
$39.95 purchase _ #DP010V
Features Arizona State wrestling coach Bobby Douglas in the first of a two - part series on wrestling takedowns. Covers the stance, penetration, tie - up, double leg tackle, fireman's carry, duck under, high crotch, and other maneuvers, all demonstrated by Douglas himself.
Physical Education and Recreation
Dist - CAMV

Takedowns with Bobby Douglas - Part II 50 MIN
VHS
Color (H C A)
$39.95 purchase _ #DP011V
Features Arizona State wrestling coach Bobby Douglas in the second of a two - part series on wrestling takedowns. Covers the single leg tackle, arm drag, foot kicks, head snap, shuck, ankle pick - ups, headlock, and other maneuvers, all demonstrated by Douglas himself.
Physical Education and Recreation
Dist - CAMV

Taken for Granted 15 MIN
16mm
Color
Deals with elevator safety. Discusses what to do if an elevator stalls, what to do in case of fire, when to push the stop button and safe ways to ride an escalator.
Health and Safety
Dist - KLEINW **Prod** - KLEINW

Takeoffs and Landings 12 MIN
U-matic / VHS
Color (A)
Highlights proper safety techniques and procedures while taking off and landing light aircraft under potentially hazardous conditions. Includes three subtitled four - minute segments on Short Field, Soft Field and Crosswind operations.
Industrial and Technical Education
Dist - AVIMA **Prod** - FAAFL

Takeover - Heroes of the New American Depression 58 MIN
VHS / 16mm
Color (G)
$390.00 purchase, $75.00, $125.00 rental
Looks at the 1990 takeover in 8 cities by homeless people who broke locks and took over vacant houses. Tells of Americans who are refusing society's invitation to die quietly on our streets. Takeovers were executed in Detroit, Philadelphia, New York, Minneapolis, Tucson, Oakland, Chicago and Los Angeles with differing results. A film by Peter Kinoy and Pamela Yates.
Fine Arts; Sociology
Dist - FIRS **Prod** - SKYLIT 1990

Takes 5 MIN
16mm
B&W (C)
$350.00
Presents an experimental film by Peter Gidal.
Fine Arts
Dist - AFA **Prod** - AFA 1970

Taking a chance 30 MIN
U-matic / VHS
Edit point series; Pt 5
Color (J H)
LC 83-706437
Presents a fictional story of a talented teenager and two friends who are running a television station while the owner is recovering from an illness. Reviews adjective phrases in a story dealing with two youthful reporters' interviews with a young convict. Shows that good writing skills are necessary in real - life experiences.
English Language
Dist - GPN **Prod** - MAETEL 1983

Taking a Look at Taking Care 16 MIN
U-matic
Color; Mono (H C)
Introduces 4 - H health curriculum. Explains concept of 'Taking Care.' Notes that health involves more than physical aspects - it relates to emotional and spiritual need, and that people with whom we live have a major impact on our health.
Agriculture; Health and Safety; Psychology; Sociology
Dist - UWISCA **Prod** - UWISCA 1984

Taking a sexual history 18 MIN
VHS
Color (C A)
$150.00 purchase, $50.00 rental
Trains physicians, nurse practitioners, social workers and psychologists in the skill of taking sexual histories and in awareness of sexual health care issues. Presents the Glasgow Short Form Assessment of Sexual Health. Reviews common barriers to talking about sex in clinical practice. Produced by Marian Glasgow.
Health and Safety; Social Science
Dist - FCSINT **Prod** - FCSINT 1986

Taking a Stand 16 MIN
VHS / 16mm
Sexuality - AIDS - Social Skills for Teens Series
Color (J)
$180.00 purchase
Shows teens how to be assertive when it comes to relationships, dating and sexual peer pressure. Portrays three teens who need to take a stand with the person they are dating. Presents six steps in expressing personal views.
Guidance and Counseling; Health and Safety; Psychology; Sociology
Dist - CHEF **Prod** - CHEF

Taking a Trip through Visicalc 38 MIN
VHS / U-matic
Color
Features computer expert Barbara McMullen offering a young friend elementary instruction in microcomputer programming, use of the Keyboard and the Apple II power pack. Demonstrates how to maintain a mailing list.
Industrial and Technical Education
Dist - STURTM **Prod** - STURTM 1982

Taking action 15 MIN
16mm / VHS
Color (G IND)
$5.00 rental
Shows how young trade unionists get involved in the democratic process through registering poor people to vote. Looks at other young people working to defeat subminimum wage by collecting signatures on petitions, debating the issue and lobbying their congresspeople.
Civics and Political Systems
Dist - AFLCIO **Prod** - LIPA 1986

Taking Action 15 MIN
VHS / U-matic
Working Together for Action Series
Color
Shows How members of a group working together learn to identify their objectives, identify people in decision - making roles, develop their case through research and outreach and finally, develop tactics.
Sociology
Dist - UWISC **Prod** - SYRCU 1976

Taking action II - frontline against drugs 35 MIN
VHS
Color (PRO IND A)
Educates employees who find themselves working alongside drug abusers. Demonstrates telltale signs of drug use on the job and suggests courses of action to remedy the problem.
Business and Economics; Guidance and Counseling; Psychology
Dist - CORF **Prod** - CORF 1990

Taking advantage of others - 54 12 MIN
VHS / U-matic
Life's little lessons - self - esteem 4 - 6 series
Color (I)
$129.00, $99.00 purchase _ #V683
Follows the Seip family to their uninvited arrival at Ruth and George's house. Reveals that the Seips spent the entire weekend letting Ruth do all the cooking, cleaning and dirty laundry. Part of a 65 - part series on self - esteem.
Guidance and Counseling; Home Economics; Psychology
Dist - BARR **Prod** - CEPRO 1992

Taking and defending a deposition 60 MIN
VHS / Cassette
Faster, more effective depositions in business cases series
Color (PRO)
$125.00, $30.00 purchase, $50.00 rental _ #DEP3-003, #ADE3-003
Emphasizes that changes in federal and local discovery rules resulting from the Civil Justice Reform Act of 1990 give courts greater control over the extent of discovery, while at the same time clients are demanding more efficiency, accountability and results, forcing effective business litigators to rethink their deposition strategies and practices. Shows how some of the nation's outstanding litigators develop their discovery and trial strategies and conduct depositions in a fraud case. Includes study guide.
Business and Economics; Civics and Political Systems
Dist - AMBAR **Prod** - AMBAR 1993

Taking and Defending Depositions 202 MIN
U-matic / VHS
Color (PRO)
Teaches the fundamental skills and techniques involved in preparing for and taking and defending depositions.
Civics and Political Systems
Dist - ABACPE **Prod** - ABACPE

Taking and defending the deposition of a lay witness 57 MIN
Cassette
Taking depositions - VideoLaw seminar - series
Color (PRO)
$125.00, $30.00 purchase, $50.00 rental _ #DEP2-002, #ADEP-002
Teaches the fundamental skills involved in preparing for, taking and defending depositions. Includes demonstrations of preparing and deposing lay witnesses with Professor James McElhaney. Includes study guide.
Civics and Political Systems
Dist - AMBAR **Prod** - AMBAR 1988

Taking and defending the deposition of the expert witness 55 MIN
Cassette
Taking depositions - VideoLaw seminar - series
Color (PRO)
$125.00, $30.00 purchase, $50.00 rental _ #DEP2-004, #ADEP-004
Teaches the fundamental skills involved in preparing for, taking and defending depositions. Includes demonstrations of preparing and deposing expert witnesses with Professor James McElhaney. Includes study guide.
Civics and Political Systems
Dist - AMBAR **Prod** - AMBAR 1988

Taking Back Detroit 55 MIN
16mm / U-matic / VHS
Color (A)
LC 81-701505
Presents Detroit City Councilman Kenneth V Cockrel and Recorder's Court Judge Justin Ravitz promoting their shared Marxist approaches for conquering Detroit's debilitating poverty.
Civics and Political Systems; History - United States; Sociology
Dist - ICARUS **Prod** - ICARUS 1981

Taking back the night 28 MIN
VHS
Color (G)
$30.00 purchase
Documents the 1990 San Francisco Take Back The Night march in remembrance of the 14 female college students murdered for being feminists in the previous year's Montreal Massacre. Reveals a variety of reactions by women to the violence, with an emphasis on the perspectives of strippers and sexual rights activists. The filmmaker encounters a series of conflicts in regard to the presence of men and clashes between sex workers and anti - porn feminists.
Civics and Political Systems; Fine Arts; Sociology
Dist - CANCIN **Prod** - LEIGHC 1990

Taking Better Pictures Series

Composition	30 MIN
Electronic flash	30 MIN
Exposure measurement	30 MIN
Film, Filters and Special Effects	30 MIN
Introduction	30 MIN
Nature Photography	30 MIN
Portraits	30 MIN
Qualities of Light	30 MIN
Shutter speeds and aperture	30 MIN

Dist - GPN

Taking Better Pictures

Exposure measurement	30 MIN
Film, Filters and Special Effects	30 MIN
Interchangeable Lenses	30 MIN
Introduction	30 MIN
Qualities of light	30 MIN

Dist - GPN

Taking Blood Pressure 10 MIN
VHS / U-matic
Color
Explains blood pressure and how it is measured. Describes technique of using a sphygmomanometer step by step.
Health and Safety; Science - Natural
Dist - MEDFAC **Prod** - MEDFAC 1981

Taking Blood Pressure Readings 20 MIN
U-matic / VHS
Blood Pressure Series
Color (PRO)
LC 79-706007
Explains basic terms of blood pressure reading, such as blood pressure, systolic, and diastolic, and demonstrates the reading of an aneroid manometer. Shows a procedure for taking blood pressure, including blood pressure reading trials.
Health and Safety
Dist - IU **Prod** - IU 1978

Taking Care 15 MIN
VHS / U-matic
It's Your Turn Series
Color (J)
Tells the story of a boy who gets a job at a bike shop and learns about the basics of bicycle maintenance and repair.
Health and Safety
Dist - AITECH **Prod** - WETN 1977

Taking Care FOCUS Series

As smoke goes by	12 MIN
The Case of the missing fat	12 MIN
Finding Fitness Your Own Way	8.5 MIN
Healthy Eating through Healthy Choices	10.15 MIN
Hypertension, it Can Happen to Anyone	9.30 MIN
In Distress	12.25 MIN
It's Up to You	12.5 MIN
Never Say Back Pain Again	13.5 MIN
Substance Abuse - Help Yourself, Help Another	11.5
You're Never Too Young	10.5 MIN

Dist - CNTRHP

Taking care of business 19 MIN
VHS
Color (H C G)
$195.00 purchase, $40.00 rental _ #37562
Presents essential informed - consent information to men and their partners considering vasectomy as a means of birth control. Examines the anxieties experienced by most men when contemplating sterilization and surgical contraception. Designed for a multiethnic English - speaking audience. Includes a facilitator's guide. Produced by Terry Looper, University of California, San Francisco.
Health and Safety; Sociology
Dist - UCEMC

Taking care of terrific 61 MIN
VHS
Wonderworks collection series
Color (I J H)
$29.95 purchase _ #TAK010
Portrays three teenagers who plan a fun evening for the bag ladies living in a local park, but their efforts get them into trouble.
Guidance and Counseling; Literature and Drama
Dist - KNOWUN **Prod** - PBS 1992

Taking Care of the Engine 30 MIN
VHS / U-matic
Keep it Running Series
Color
Identifies the parts of an internal - combustion engine, describes the way a four - stroke power cycle internal - combustion engine works and performs a compression check, including recording and interpreting the results.
Industrial and Technical Education
Dist - NETCHE **Prod** - NETCHE 1982

Taking Care of Things You Share 12 MIN
16mm / U-matic / VHS
Beginning Responsibility Series
Color (P)
$295, $210 purchase _ #3718
Shows the importance of taking care of things that are shared with others.
Psychology
Dist - CORF

Taking Care of Your Body 18 MIN
U-matic / 35mm strip
Color (SPANISH)
LC 83-730079;
Notes that since diabetics are more prone to infection, a daily routine of careful examination of skin, teeth, feet and legs is very important. Stresses early recognition and treatment of cuts, bruises, and injuries as essential to good diabetic care.
Health and Safety; Physical Education and Recreation
Dist - MEDCOM **Prod** - MEDCOM

Taking Care of Your Car 105 FRS
VHS / U-matic
Color (J H)
Deals with preventive maintenance and car inspections which can be done by the driver in little time.
Health and Safety; Industrial and Technical Education
Dist - BUMPA **Prod** - BUMPA

Taking Care of Your Car 30 MIN
Videoreel / VT2
Sportsmanlike Driving Series Refresher Course
B&W (C A)
Health and Safety; Industrial and Technical Education
Dist - GPN **Prod** - AAAFTS

Taking Care of Your Own Things 11 MIN
U-matic / VHS / 16mm
Beginning Responsibility Series
Color (P)
$280, $195 purchase _ #3719
Shows how to take care of personal belongings.
Psychology
Dist - CORF

Taking care of your school building 15 MIN
16mm / U-matic / VHS
School citizenship series
Color (P I)
Explains that students are vital elements in the care of the school building. Shows how students unthinkingly damage floors, walls, fixtures, and furniture, thus increasing the workload of the maintenance staff.
Guidance and Counseling; Social Science
Dist - CORF **Prod** - CENTRO

Taking Care of Yourself 8 MIN
VHS / U-matic / BETA
Living with Leukemia Series
(G)
Demonstrates how a patient may take care of himself while he has leukemia, including special methods for daily self care.
Health and Safety
Dist - UTXAH **Prod** - UTXAH 1985

Taking care - The Complete babysitter 23 MIN
VHS / U-matic / 16mm
Color (J H G)
$260.00, $310.00 purchase, $50.00 rental
Explores all the issues that student babysitters need to consider. Provides a guide as a thorough complement to the video. Produced by Parent's Videoguides Inc.
Home Economics; Sociology
Dist - NDIM

Taking chances 22 MIN
U-matic / VHS / 16mm
Color (J H)
Follows the romantic relationship between Kathy and Leigh, interspersing their story with discussion among other teenagers expressing feelings and concerns about their sexual coming - of - age. Stresses communciation and explores some of the reasons that underlie the non - use of birth control among sexually active teenagers.
Health and Safety; Sociology
Dist - CF **Prod** - MOBIUS 1979

Taking Chances 22 MIN
U-matic / VHS / 16mm
Color (J H)
$425 purchase - 16 mm, $300 purchase - video
Discusses a romance between two young people, and the reasons that birth control is not used among sexually active teens. Produced by Mobius Productions, Ltd.
Health and Safety; Sociology
Dist - CF

Taking chances: Teens and risk 27 MIN
VHS
Color (I J)
$169 purchase No. 2295-YZ
Teaches middle-schoolers to look at risk critically and to understand its sources, demonstrating that risk can be positive as well as negative. Teaches students a technique for deciding in advance whether a risk is worth taking. Includes 27 minute video and teacher's guide.
Education; Psychology
Dist - SUNCOM **Prod** - SUNCOM

Taking Charge of Your Health 18 MIN
VHS / U-matic
Color (H C A)
Stresses the potential that each individual has to enhance his or her quality of life. Contains profiles of five people who changed their lifestyles by avoiding such risk factors as smoking, lack of exercise, obesity, drug and alcohol abuse, and chronic stress.
Health and Safety
Dist - PSU **Prod** - PSU 1984

Taking charge - techniques for developing self - directed learners - Tape 12 31 MIN
VHS
Teacher to teacher series
Color (T)
$100.00 purchase _ #891 - 9
Shows exerienced teachers in actual classroom settings presenting various instructional approaches to both new and veteran ABE and ESL teachers. Demonstrates comprehension and analytical skillbuilding activities which challenge the student to take risks. Part twelve of a 12 - part series.
Education; English Language
Dist - LAULIT **Prod** - LAULIT

Taking charge - teens speak out about sexuality and birth control 22 MIN
16mm / VHS / U-matic
Color (H)
$475.00 purchase, $100.00 - $50.00 rental
Looks at the myths and misconceptions teenagers have about sexuality and birth control. Interweaves conversations of five teens and a physician. Stresses that accurate information about birth control is necessary to make mature decisions.
Health and Safety; Sociology
Dist - FANPRO **Prod** - FANPRO 1986

Taking charge - visual impairment 7 MIN
VHS / U-matic
Assistive technology series
Color (C PRO G)
$195.00 purchase _ #N921 - VI - 046
Introduces the accessibility and adaptation strategies of Jim who is visually impaired. Reveals that he is a US attorney and that federal employee status gives him certain opportunities to adapt his environment so that he can function appropriately in his job. Discusses equipment and services and assistance available through government and social service agencies. Part of nine parts produced by Southern Illinois University School of Medicine.
Guidance and Counseling; Health and Safety
Dist - HSCIC

Taking charge - you and AIDS 16 MIN
VHS
Color (H)
$250.00 purchase
Presents graphic footage of complications of AIDS - Pneumocystis pneumonia, Kaposi's sarcoma. Educates on how to avoid AIDS infection.
Health and Safety
Dist - PFP **Prod** - PFP 1987

Taking Children Seriously 50 MIN
VHS
Color (S)
$79.00 purchase _ #322 - 9273
Scrutinizes the dark side of being a child - a side that adults cannot seem to remember and one that children sometimes will reveal only to strangers. Provides a rare opportunity to see the hurt, fear, worry and confusion children often hide - and their reason for concealing these feelings.
Guidance and Counseling; Health and Safety; Psychology; Sociology
Dist - FI **Prod** - NBCNEW 1986

Taking Children Seriously 57 MIN
U-matic / VHS
Color
$300 rental
Explores the problems of child abuse and divorce. Includes interviews with children about their problems.
Sociology
Dist - CCNCC **Prod** - CCNCC 1986

Taking Commas Aside 18 MIN
16mm / U-matic / VHS
Punctuation Series
Color (I J)
$425, $250 purchase _ #76535
Shows the use of commas within a sentence.
English Language
Dist - CORF

Taking control of depression
VHS
Color (G)
$19.95 purchase _ #XJN011
Presents Dr Alan Xenakis, who explains the facts about this common affliction and reveals treatments that work. Features Ed Asner.
Health and Safety; Psychology
Dist - SIV

Taking control - the workers' compensation - return to work connection 26 MIN
VHS
Color (PRO)
Points out attitudes toward workers' compensation within an organization that adversely affect its productivity and costs. Dramatizes the experiences of one company when an employee is injured, and shows how to effectively deal with the workers' compensation process. Includes video and leader's guide.
Health and Safety
Dist - BARR **Prod** - COEDMA
COEDMA

Taking depositions - VideoLaw seminar - series 207 MIN
VHS / Cassette
Taking depositions - VideoLaw seminar - series
Color (PRO)
$295.00, $75.00 purchase, $195.00 rental _ #DEP2-000, #ADEP-000
Teaches the fundamental skills involved in preparing for, taking and defending depositions. Includes demonstrations of preparing and deposing both lay and expert witnesses with Professor James McElhaney. Individual titles include Preparing the Lay Witness for the Deposition, Taking and Defending the Deposition of a Lay Witness, Preparing the Expert Deponent, and Taking and Defending the Deposition of the Expert Witness. Includes study guides.
Civics and Political Systems
Dist - AMBAR **Prod** - AMBAR 1988

Taking Disciplinary Action 10 MIN
VHS / U-matic
Management in Action Series
Color
Provides steps to take when reprimanding an employee. Describes how to encourage change and avoid termination proceedings.
Business and Economics; Psychology
Dist - CORF **Prod** - CORF

Taking good care - inside a children's hospital 25 MIN
VHS / U-matic
Color (H A G)
$295.00 purchase, $100.00, $50.00 rental _ #054
Follows three very different young patients through Children's Hospital in Boston and profiles the wide range of staff persons who care for them. Looks at the variety of interesting and rewarding roles in the care of children in hospitals. Produced by Susan Shaw, RN, and Christine Mitchell, RN, with Ben Achtenberg.
Health and Safety
Dist - FANPRO **Prod** - ACMISH

Taking Good Soil Samples 10 MIN
VHS / 16mm
Color (H C A)
Provides an easy to follow guide for taking soil samples.
Agriculture
Dist - IOWA **Prod** - IOWA 1987

Taking Inside Measurements 9 MIN
U-matic / VHS / 16mm
Power Mechanics Series
Color (J)
LC 73-703252
Presents basic information about taking inside measurements.
Industrial and Technical Education; Mathematics
Dist - CAROUF **Prod** - THIOKL 1969

Taking it in Stride - Positive Approaches to Stress Management 22 MIN
16mm
Color (A)
LC 82-700135
Tells how individuals can manage stress and take responsibility for the way they feel. Identifies stressful situations and investigates the interrelationship of health and habits. Offers suggestions for coping with stress, such as various methods of relaxation, doing fewer things better and adapting to a workable load of responsibilities.
Psychology
Dist - SPEF **Prod** - SPEF 1981

Taking liberties series
Fatal error 20 MIN
Dist - BBCENE

Taking multiple choice - true - false and essay tests
VHS
School solutions video series
Color (I J H)
$98.00 purchase _ #CDSCH118V
Introduces tests, what they are and what they are supposed to do. Presents the various forms of tests, along with tips on how to prepare and study for each type. Features essay test preparation with detailed ways to organize thoughts before beginning to write. Includes reproducible worksheets. Part of a ten - part series to build student success.
Education
Dist - CAMV

Taking notes and organizing your ideas
VHS
Using your library to write a research paper series
Color (J H C G)
$49.95 purchase _ #VA766V
Shows how to take notes and organize ideas for a research paper, using the library. Walks viewers through the process, offering tips, tricks and insights that make the research and writing process faster and more productive. Part of a four - part series.
Education
Dist - CAMV

Taking notes without falling asleep - critical listening skills
VHS
School solutions video series
Color (I J H)
$98.00 purchase _ #CDSCH112V
Looks at how to listen effectively in class by using critical listening skills. Goes to the next step - how to remember what was heard and taking notes, one of the best ways of remembering. Compares the difference between taking notes in a class lecture and taking notes in private study. Discusses outlining and organizational techniques to increase understanding at a later date. Discusses and analyzes using notes for test taking. Includes reproducible worksheets. Part of a ten - part series to build student success.
Education; English Language; Psychology
Dist - CAMV

Taking Off 30 MIN
16mm / U-matic / VHS
Case Studies in Small Business Series
Color (C A)
Business and Economics
Dist - GPN **Prod** - UMA 1979

Taking on Tomorrow 29 MIN
U-matic / VHS / 16mm
Color
Discusses the mainstreaming of handicapped students in postsecondary vocational education programs.
Education
Dist - USNAC **Prod** - USDED 1981

Taking on your opponent - Volume 3 30 MIN
VHS
Graduated soccer method series
Color (J H A)
$29.95 purchase _ #KOD410V
Presents exercises to help young soccer players develop ball - control skills for when they are being pursued by opposing players.
Physical Education and Recreation
Dist - CAMV

Taking Our Bodies Back - the Women's Health Movement 33 MIN
VHS / U-matic
Color (C A)
LC 74-702135
Explores ten critical areas of the women's health movement from the revolutionary concept of self - help to the issue of informed surgical consent. Documents a growing movement of women to regain control of their bodies. Shows women becoming aware of their rights in dealing with the medical industry.
Guidance and Counseling; Health and Safety; Sociology
Dist - CMBRD **Prod** - CMBRD 1974

Taking Ownership 29 MIN
VHS / U-matic
Authoring Cycle - Read Better, Write Better, Reason Better Series
Color (T)
Discusses helping children develop a functional view of learning and re - value reading and writing. Stresses not reducing literacy to a set of rules.
Education; English Language
Dist - HNEDBK **Prod** - IU

Taking responsibility series
On Your Own at Home 12 MIN
Saying no to danger 11 MIN
Dist - CORF

Taking responsibility series
What's wrong with vandalism 11 MIN
Dist - CORF
VIEWTH

Taking responsibility series
On Your own at home 11 MIN
Saying no to danger 11 MIN
Standing up for yourself 11 MIN
Staying away from strangers 11 MIN
Dist - VIEWTH

Taking shape 15 MIN
VHS
Art's place series
Color (K P)
$49.00 purchase, $15.00 rental _ #295802
Visits with Leo and Emma as they explore shapes by using odds and ends to make sculptures. Jessie visits a potter and Mirror tells a tale about a sculptor. Examines Seated Woman by Pablo Picasso and works by Kevin Lockow and Henry Moore. Part of a series combining songs, stories, animation, puppets and live actors to convey the pleasure of artistic expression. Includes an illustrated teacher's guide.
Fine Arts
Dist - TVOTAR **Prod** - TVOTAR 1989

Taking Stock 30 MIN
BETA / VHS
On the Money Series
Color
Surveys various stock strategies. Discusses inheritance taxes and insurance. Makes predictions about the nation's job market.
Business and Economics; Home Economics
Dist - CORF **Prod** - WGBHTV

Taking Stocks 30 MIN
U-matic / VHS
Stress Management - a Positive Strategy Series Pt 2
Color (A)
LC 82-706501
Explains how individuals can develop an awareness of stress in their lives and how they can learn to recognize the first signs of trouble. Examines the relationship between people's responses to stress and their health, as well as their ability to function efficiently as executives.
Psychology
Dist - TIMLIF **Prod** - TIMLIF 1982

Taking the Challenge 30 MIN
VHS / 16mm
Color (PRO)
$545.00 purchase, $150.00 rental
Provides a positive perspective on change. Illustrates the need to adapt and respond proactively to an ever - changing business environment. Trains managers.
Business and Economics; Psychology
Dist - VICOM **Prod** - VICOM 1990

Taking the challenge 32 MIN
VHS
Color (A PRO IND)

$545.00 purchase, $150.00 rental
Examines how changes affect the workplace. Encourages managers to respond to change by overcoming workers' resistance and giving positive motivation.
Business and Economics
Dist - VLEARN **Prod** - EFM

Taking the challenge - Winning through change - Part 1 33 MIN
VHS
Color (PRO G A)
$545.00 purchase, $170.00 rental
Develops skill in dealing positively with changes in a work situation. Helps company leaders anticipate and plan for personnel problems that may arise during periods of adjustment, in order to maintain momentum. Includes leader's guide.
Business and Economics; Guidance and Counseling; Psychology
Dist - EXTR **Prod** - AMA

Taking the patient's temperature 8 MIN
VHS / U-matic
Color (PRO) (SPANISH)
LC 77-731353
Describes the oral and the rectal thermometer and states the average readings and average times required to gain accurate readings for both types of thermometers. Demonstrates the proper methods of inserting both. Emphasizes the importance of cleaning the thermometer before and after it is used and of washing the hands before and after the thermometer is handled.
Health and Safety
Dist - MEDCOM **Prod** - MEDCOM

Taking the Pledge 1 MIN
U-matic / VHS
Color
Focuses on a group of high school girls who agree to quit smoking. As they shake hands on the deal, the announcer says the girls have made a pact to win happier, healthier lives, and asks 'why don't you make a pact and be a winner, too?' Uses TV spot format.
Health and Safety
Dist - AMCS **Prod** - AMCS 1979

Taking the Static Out of Statistics 57 MIN
U-matic / VHS
B&W
Presents beginning concepts in statistics.
Mathematics
Dist - BUSARG **Prod** - BUSARG

Taking the waters 26 MIN
VHS
How to save the Earth series
Color (J H C G)
$175.00 purchase, $45.00 rental
Looks at the people who are fighting to turn the Danube basin wetlands and an important bird migration and nesting lake in Tunisia into national parks. Portrays a Czechoslovakian housewife turned green warrior and a government botanist who stands up to his employers in Tunis.
Fine Arts; Science - Natural
Dist - BULFRG **Prod** - CITV 1993

Taking Time for Ourselves 30 MIN
U-matic
Parent Puzzle Series
(A)
Explores the myth that good parents deny themselves in the continuing interests of their children.
Psychology; Sociology
Dist - ACCESS **Prod** - ACCESS 1982

Taking Time to Feel, Pt 1 8 MIN
U-matic / VHS
Taking Time to Feel Series
Color (C A)
Depicts a man and a woman ejoying the world around them, and themselves, making it vividly clear that being in touch with one's own sexuality helps to feel fulfillment with a partner.
Health and Safety; Psychology; Sociology
Dist - MMRC **Prod** - MMRC

Taking Time to Feel, Pt 2 8 MIN
VHS / U-matic
Taking Time to Feel Series
Color (C A)
Depicts a man and a woman ejoying the world around them, and themselves, making it vividly clear that being in touch with one's own sexuality helps to feel fulfillment with a partner.
Health and Safety; Psychology; Sociology
Dist - MMRC **Prod** - MMRC

Taking Time to Feel, Pt 3 10 MIN
U-matic / VHS
Taking Time to Feel Series
Color (C A)
Shows a couple, married fourteen years, taking genuine pleasure in being together.
Health and Safety; Psychology; Sociology
Dist - MMRC **Prod** - MMRC

Taking Time to Feel Series
Taking Time to Feel, Pt 1 8 MIN
Taking Time to Feel, Pt 2 8 MIN
Taking Time to Feel, Pt 3 10 MIN
Dist - MMRC

The Taking Trilogy - Recent Supreme Court pronouncements on land use regulations 60 MIN
VHS
Color (C PRO A)
$75.00 purchase _ #P226
Examines the holdings and impact of recent Supreme Court cases. Addresses the questions on restrictive land use and the Fifth Amendment and consequences for the regulating authority and land owner when a land use regulation is found to be a taking.
Business and Economics; Civics and Political Systems
Dist - ALIABA

Takli - Shoot
CD-ROM
(G) (HEBREW)
$1299.00 purchase
Contains Tanach, Midrash, Talmud Bavli with Rashi, Rambam and 253 volumes of Responsa literature from Rambam to R'Moshe. Permits user to survey, search and retrieve sources relating to any subject - legal precedents, different opinions relating to Halacha and Jewish tradition. Saves results for import to Hebrew word processors. Requires PC - compatible with Windows 3.0 or above, 2MB RAM, 7MB free disk space, VGA or better video, mouse, CD - ROM drive, MS - DOS 5.0 or above. Comes with Hebrew keyboard stickers and additional software on floppy diskette. Produced by Bar - Ilan University.
Religion and Philosophy; Sociology
Dist - KABALA

Taklit - Torah
CD-ROM
(G) (HEBREW)
$499.00 purchase
Includes the full text of Tanach, Midrash, Talmud Bavli with Rashi, Talmud Yerushalmi and Rambam. Permits user to survey, search and retrieve sources relating to any subject - legal precedents, different opinions relating to Halacha and Jewish tradition. Saves results for import to Hebrew word processors. Requires PC - compatible with Windows 3.0 or above, 2MB RAM, 7MB free disk space, VGA or better video, mouse, CD - ROM drive, MS - DOS 5.0 or above. Comes with Hebrew keyboard stickers and additional software on floppy diskette. Produced by Bar - Ilan University.
Religion and Philosophy; Sociology
Dist - KABALA

Taksu - music in the life of Bali 24 MIN
VHS
Color (H C G A)
$195.00 purchase, $40.00 rental _ #38095
Shows that Balinese music, like Balinese life, reflects community harmony, cooperation, and balance. Serves as a readily accessible window onto Balinese culture. Focuses on the concept of Taksu, the spiritual power found in music, instruments, costumes, and dance. Captures the vibrant rhythm that permeates all Balinese art and culture. Produced by Jann Pasler, professor of music at UC - San Diego.
Fine Arts; Geography - World; Religion and Philosophy
Dist - UCEMC

Tal Farlow 2 MIN
16mm
B&W (A)
Presents an experimental film by Lyn Lye which was completed after his death by assistant Steven Jones.
Fine Arts
Dist - STARRC **Prod** - STARRC 1968

Tal Farlow 2 MIN
16mm
B&W
Presents Len Lye's last scratch film, completed by his assistant, Steven Jones. Features white lines that 'dance' and 'sway' to a jazz guitar solo by Tal Farlow.
Fine Arts
Dist - STARRC **Prod** - STARRC 1980

Tala 8 MIN
16mm
Color
LC 77-702663
Views a crack in the ice, following it through a complex series of variations and repetitions in color distortions and superimposition.
Fine Arts; Psychology
Dist - CANFDC **Prod** - CANCOU 1976

The Tale of a Hare or We're all Different Somewhere 45 MIN
16mm
Color (I)
Describes what cleft lips and palates are and what it's like to have one or the other.
Education; Psychology
Dist - UPITTS **Prod** - UPITTS 1977

Tale of a plague 29 MIN
U-matic / VHS
Survivors series
Color (H C)
$250.00 purchase _ #HP - 6105C
Covers the story of the biggest plague of locusts to invade Africa in thirty years. Demonstrates where locusts fit in the food chain, how humans have contributed to their infestation and what is being done to combat them. Part of a series on the issue of wildlife conservation discussing the enormity of the task of protecting wildlife and wilderness.
Agriculture; Geography - World; Health and Safety; Science - Natural; Social Science
Dist - CORF **Prod** - BBCTV 1990

A Tale of a TV Mouse 14 MIN
16mm
Color (P)
LC 79-701869
Tells the story of a puppet mouse named Lucille whose entire life revolves around the television. Shows how it affects her life and what finally happens to convince her to break the TV habit.
Fine Arts
Dist - FILCOM **Prod** - PUPPET 1979

The Tale of Benjamin Bunny
CD-ROM
Discis Books on CD - ROM
(K P) (SPANISH)
$69.00 purchase _ #2553
Contains the original text and illustrations of The Tale of Benjamin Bunny by Beatrix Potter. Enhances understanding with real voices, music, and sound effects. Every word in the text has an in - context explanation, pronunciation and syllables, available through a click of the mouse. Spanish - English version available for an extra $5 per disc. For Macintosh Classics, Plus, II and SE computers, requires 1MB of RAM, one floppy disk drive, and an Apple compatible CD - ROM drive.
English Language; Literature and Drama
Dist - BEP

A Tale of Bhutan 27 MIN
16mm / U-matic / VHS
Color (K P I)
LC 80-701950
Shows village children in Bhutan pantomiming a story which illustrates UNICEF's work in this country.
Civics and Political Systems; Geography - World
Dist - CAROUF **Prod** - UNICEF 1980

A Tale of Four Wishes 42 MIN
U-matic / VHS / 16mm
Color (K P I)
LC 81-701565
Relates the story of Jane who finds herself trapped in family conflicts until Skeeter offers advice based on the books Hug Me by Pattie Stren, The Man Who Had No Dream by Adelaide Holl, The Silver Pony by Lynd Ward and Jane, Wishing by Toby Tobias.
Fine Arts; Guidance and Counseling; Literature and Drama
Dist - CF **Prod** - BOSUST 1981

The Tale of Heike 27 MIN
16mm
Color (JAPANESE)
Presents the historical facts and Buddhist concept of understanding by depicting the rise and fall of the Heike and Genji clans. Portrays the powers of the Heike clan, the rise of the Genji and the defeat and fall of the Heike, ending with prayers for an everlasting peace in the Buddhist paradise.
Religion and Philosophy; Sociology
Dist - UNIJAP **Prod** - GAKKEN 1969

The Tale of King Midas 18 MIN
16mm / U-matic / VHS
Color (P I) (SPANISH)
LC 74-702305
Tells a tale about a god who grants a wish to a mortal, King Midas, who asks that everything he touches turn to gold. Explains how he soon discovers the consequences of his wish and asks that the god remove it.
Literature and Drama
Dist - EBEC **Prod** - EBEC 1974

The Tale of Mr Jeremy Fisher - The Tale of Peter Rabbit 30 MIN
VHS
Rabbit ears collection series
Color (K P I J)
$12.95 purchase _ #SO626
Tells two Beatrix Potter stories. Features Meryl Streep as narrator.
Literature and Drama
Dist - KNOWUN **Prod** - RABBIT

A Tale of 'O' 27 MIN
U-matic / VHS / 16mm
Color
Tells the story of what happens to any new or different kind of person in a group, and how to manage that situation. Parallels the real - life experience of women and minorities and depersonalizes the situation to allow others to identify with the victim of tokenism.
Sociology
Dist - GOODMI **Prod** - GOODMI

Tale of 'O' 18 MIN
VHS
Color (A PRO IND)
$720.00 purchase, $180.00 rental
Deals with the consequences of being 'different,' especially as they deal with discrimination in the workplace.
Business and Economics; Guidance and Counseling; Psychology; Sociology
Dist - VLEARN

Tale of One City 15 MIN
16mm
Color (J)
LC 78-701233
Portrays the unhappy plight of ordinary people who live in cities where planning has not taken their needs into account. Points out the pressures on City Hall by vested interests to compromise the best interests of citizens.
Sociology
Dist - AUIS **Prod** - FLMAUS 1976

The Tale of Peter Rabbit
CD-ROM
Discis Books on CD - ROM
(K P) (SPANISH)
$84.00 purchase _ #2552
Contains the original text and illustrations of The Tale of Peter Rabbit by Beatrix Potter. Enhances understanding with real voices, music, and sound effects. Every word in the text has an in - context explanation, pronunciation and syllables, available through a click of the mouse. Spanish - English version available for an extra $5 per disc. For Macintosh Classics, Plus, II and SE computers, requires 1MB RAM, one floppy disk drive, and an Apple compatible CD - ROM drive.
English Language; Literature and Drama
Dist - BEP

Tale of Rumpelstiltskin 21 MIN
U-matic / VHS / 16mm
Captioned; Color (P I)
LC 74-701890
Presents an adaptation of the story of Rumpelstiltskin.
Literature and Drama
Dist - EBEC **Prod** - EBEC 1974

A Tale of springtime 103 MIN
VHS
Color (G J H C A)
PdS19.95 purchase _ #ML-ART012
Presents the comic story of Jeanne, a philosophy teacher, and Natasha, a music student. Outlines how the two meet by chance at a party in modern-day Paris. Follows the two as their friendship develops. Directed by Eric Rohmer and produced by Artificial Eye.
Fine Arts; Foreign Language
Dist - AVP

Tale of the Cold Smoke 24 MIN
16mm
Color
LC 78-701572
Tells a tall tale about how Montana's Bridger Bowl originally got its powder snow and shows the pleasures and challenges of recreational skiing.
Geography - United States; Physical Education and Recreation
Dist - BRIBOW **Prod** - BRIBOW 1978

Tale of the comet 29 MIN
VHS
Color (K P I R)
$19.95 purchase, $10.00 rental _ #35 - 813 - 2020
Tells how the ranchers and Gypsies are unable to get along together. Shows that the 'Christian cowboy' Brent Towers becomes their friend and shares the story of Jesus with them.
Literature and Drama; Religion and Philosophy
Dist - APH **Prod** - ANDERK

A Tale of the Ground Hog's Shadow 11 MIN
U-matic / VHS / 16mm
Color (P I)
$270.00, $190.00 purchase _ #969
Tells the legend of the ground hog through an adventure of a raccoon searching for news of coming spring.
English Language; Literature and Drama; Science - Natural
Dist - CORF **Prod** - CORF 1955

The Tale of the Gypsy Robe 30 MIN
VHS / U-matic
Broadway Series
Color
Fine Arts; Industrial and Technical Education
Dist - ARCVID **Prod** - ARCVID

The Tale of the three lost jewels 50 MIN
VHS
Developing stories II series
Color (G T)
$150.00 purchase, $75.00 rental
Tells of a magical love story between two adolescents in a time of war and danger. Portrays the final, agitated days of the Israeli occupation of the Gaza Strip. Introduces Yusef, a 12 - year - old refugee growing up in the Intifada, who meets Aida, a beautiful girl. He becomes infatuated with her, thus beginning a journey for lost jewels in order to win her hand. Presents third video in the second installment of the BBC series in which the BBC, with the guidance of Television Trust for the Environment, commissioned leading filmmakers from developing countries to create programs that deal with issues of people, population, and migration from the perspective of those directly affected by these crises. A film by Michel Kheifi.
Fine Arts; History - World; Social Science; Sociology
Dist - BULFRG **Prod** - BBCENE 1994

Tale of the Ugly Duckling 8 MIN
U-matic / VHS / 16mm
Halas and Batchelor Fairy Tale Series
Color (P) (SPANISH)
LC 73-706203
Tells the story of the Ugly Duckling who, rejected, not belonging to the group, has to live in an alien environment and go through many unhappy experiences before finding his own kind.
Foreign Language; Literature and Drama
Dist - EBEC **Prod** - HALAS 1969

Tale of the Ugly Duckling 8 MIN
U-matic / VHS / 16mm
Color (P) (SPANISH)
Tells the story of the ugly duckling who must live in an alien environment and go through many unhappy experiences before finding his own kind.
Foreign Language; Literature and Drama
Dist - EBEC **Prod** - HALAS

Tale of Three Churches 25 MIN
16mm
Color (C A)
Shows how inflation prevented three overseas congregations from purchasing land and building churches. Explains how each dilemma was solved.
Business and Economics; Religion and Philosophy; Sociology
Dist - CBFMS **Prod** - CBFMS

A Tale of Three Cities 28 MIN
16mm / U-matic / VHS
Color (J H)
LC 74-701770
Visits three different cities on three different continents in three different stages of development. Views their different approaches to the same problems. Discusses population growth and the added stresses that will place on the world's cities. Visits Djakarta, Indonesia, Caracas, Venezuela and Stockholm, Sweden.
Social Science; Sociology
Dist - JOU **Prod** - JOU 1974

A Tale of Till 11 MIN
U-matic / VHS / 16mm
Color (P I J H)
LC 75-701086
Uses puppets in an adaptation of the 14th - century German legend about Eulenspiegel.
Literature and Drama
Dist - ALTSUL **Prod** - MEYRFM 1975

A Tale of Two Cities 117 MIN
16mm
B&W
Tells the classic story of Sydney Carton, a disillusioned lawyer whose life is brightened by love for Lucie Manette, a member of the French revolutionaries. Reveals his sacrifice for her, as he exchanges places with her husband and goes to the guillotine. Features Dirk Bogarde and Dorothy Tutin. Directed by Ralph Thomas. Based on the novel A TALE OF TWO CITIES by Charles Dickens.
Fine Arts; Literature and Drama
Dist - LCOA **Prod** - RANK 1958

A Tale of two cities 122 MIN
VHS
B&W (G)
$24.95 purchase _ #S00546
Presents the 1935 film version of the Dickens novel A Tale of Two Cities, set in the time of the French Revolution. Stars Ronald Colman, Basil Rathbone and Edna Mae Oliver.
Literature and Drama
Dist - UILL

Tale of Two Cities 12 MIN
U-matic / VHS / 16mm
B&W
A documentary of the effects of the atomic bombing of Hiroshima and Nagasaki during World War II.
History - World; Science - Physical
Dist - USNAC **Prod** - USWD 1949

A Tale of Two Cities 44 MIN
16mm
B&W (I J H)
LC FIA52-4978
Re - enacts Dickens' tale of heroism, devotion and tragedy against the background of the French Revolution. Stars Ronald Colman as Sydney Carton.
Literature and Drama
Dist - FI **Prod** - PMI 1935

A Tale of Two Cities 70 MIN
16mm
B&W
Shows how unrequited love leads to a brave sacrifice by an English man who is the exact double of a loved by the woman he Frenchman adores. Stars William Farnum and Jewel Carmen. Directed by Frank Lloyd.
Fine Arts
Dist - KILLIS **Prod** - FOXFC 1917

A Tale of Two Cities
VHS / U-matic
Color (J C I)
Presents a dramatization of Charles Dickens' tale of the French Revolution. Stars Ronald Colman.
Fine Arts; Literature and Drama
Dist - GA **Prod** - GA 1935

A Tale of Two Cities
Cassette / 16mm
Now Age Reading Programs, Set 2 Series
Color (I J)
$9.95 purchase _ #8F - PN681964
Brings a classic tale to young readers. Filmstrip set includes filmstrip, cassette, corresponding book, classroom exercise materials and a poster. The read - along set includes student activity book, cassette and paperback.
English Language; Literature and Drama
Dist - MAFEX

A Tale of two critters 48 MIN
16mm / U-matic / VHS
Animal featurettes series; Set 3
Color (I J H)
LC 78-701718
Tells how a baby raccoon and a bear cub, separated from their families, find themselves unlikely companions on an adventure - filled trek in the Pacific Northwest.
Literature and Drama; Science - Natural
Dist - CORF **Prod** - DISNEY 1977

A Tale of Two Leopards 23 MIN
U-matic / VHS
Color
Focuses on leopards in southern Kenya where they still live in large numbers. Relates their dilemma with the Masai tribesmen.
Science - Natural
Dist - NWLDPR **Prod** - NWLDPR

Tale of Two Neighbors 15 MIN
U-matic / VHS
Neighborhoods Series
Color (P)
Compares two neighbors.
Sociology
Dist - GPN **Prod** - NEITV 1981

A Tale of Two Rivers 40 MIN
16mm / U-matic / VHS
Color (H C A)
LC 74-702906
Shows the significance to the study of human development of the valleys of the Dordogne and Vezere rivers in France. Includes scenes of modern life in the Dordogne and then explores the area's importance in the study of history. Discusses the significance of various archeological sites and examines the concern of present - day inhabitants for preserving their Languedocian customs and language. The narration is edited from interviews with archeologists, historians and art historians.

Fine Arts; Geography - World; History - World; Sociology
Dist - UCEMC **Prod** - SMITCB 1974

Talent for America 30 MIN
16mm
Color
LC 78-701499
Presents an overview of the Affiliate Artists program and tells how the organization sends talented performers to rural communities.
Fine Arts; Sociology
Dist - DREWAS **Prod** - DREWAS 1978

Talent for America 28 MIN
16mm
Color
LC 79-701487
Features the music, dance and performances of three young members of Affiliate Artists, an organization for young performing artists who aim at refining their own talents and creating new audiences for the arts.
Fine Arts
Dist - MTP **Prod** - SEARS 1978

Talent for Disaster 16 MIN
16mm
Color (J H C)
Presents a fire boss in a fire camp explaining the tremendous effort and costs involved in fighting a wildfire. Stresses the importance of fire safety awareness.
Health and Safety; Social Science
Dist - FILCOM **Prod** - PUBSF

A Talent for life - Jews of the Italian Renaissance 58 MIN
16mm
Color
LC 80-700287
Focuses on the Jewish experience during the Italian Renaissance. Traces the history of Jews in Italy from their origins as Roman slaves to their life in the ghettos of Venice. Originally broadcast on the television program The Eternal Light.
History - World; Sociology
Dist - NBCTV **Prod** - NBCTV 1979

A Talent for Life - Jews of the Italian Renaissance - Pt 1 29 MIN
16mm
Color
LC 80-700287
Focuses on the Jewish experience during the Italian Renaissance. Traces the history of Jews in Italy from their origins as Roman slaves to their life in the ghettos of Venice. Originally broadcast on the television program The Eternal Light.
History - World; Sociology
Dist - NBCTV **Prod** - NBCTV 1979

A Talent for Life - Jews of the Italian Renaissance - Pt 2 29 MIN
16mm
Color
LC 80-700287
Focuses on the Jewish experience during the Italian Renaissance. Traces the history of Jews in Italy from their origins as Roman slaves to their life in the ghettos of Venice. Originally broadcast on the television program The Eternal Light.
History - World; Sociology
Dist - NBCTV **Prod** - NBCTV 1979

A Talent for Tony 13 MIN
16mm
Parables Series
Color (K P)
LC 72-703206
Explains that when five - year - old Tony is asked by his artist - father to make some drawings, his fear of failure gets in the way. Shows how he discovers that the one talent to be treasured is belief in himself.
Guidance and Counseling; Psychology
Dist - FRACOC **Prod** - FRACOC 1971

Talent search 60 MIN
VHS
Track and field series
Color (J H C A)
$39.95 purchase _ #MXS490V
Features Dr Ken Foreman, former U S Olympic women's track coach, in a series of tests to determine the most appropriate event for an athlete.
Physical Education and Recreation
Dist - CAMV

Talent Search 60 MIN
VHS / BETA
Women's Track and Field Series
Color
Presents a variety of tests to help determine an athlete's best track and field event.
Physical Education and Recreation
Dist - MOHOMV **Prod** - MOHOMV

Talent Show Today 10 MIN
U-matic / VHS
Book, Look and Listen Series
Color (K P)
Focuses on an awareness of individual talents and physical skills.
English Language; Literature and Drama
Dist - AITECH **Prod** - MDDE 1977

Tales from Aesop 30 MIN
VHS / 16mm
Children's Stories Series
Color (P)
$39.95 purchase _ #CL8805
Presents the fables of Aesop.
Literature and Drama
Dist - EDUCRT

Tales from Africa (Central) 50 MIN
VHS
Fairy Tales from Exotic Lands
Color (K P I)
Presents The Old Man and the Deer, The Origin of the Animals, The Law of Mapaki, and Musar and His Parents. Stories reveal insights into different cultures and traditions of different lands and times.
Literature and Drama
Dist - BENNUP **Prod** - VIDKNW

Tales from Asia 50 MIN
VHS
Fairy Tales from Exotic Lands
Color (K P I)
Presents Hok Lee and the Dwarf, The Rajah's Son and the Princess, and The Jellyfish and the Monkey. Stories reveal insights into different cultures and traditions of different lands and times.
Literature and Drama
Dist - BENNUP **Prod** - VIDKNW

Tales from Europe 50 MIN
VHS
Fairy Tales from Exotic Lands
Color (K P I)
Presents The Ugly Duckling, The Good Woman, The Glass Ax, and The Hobyahs. Stories reveal insights into different cultures and traditions of different lands and times.
Literature and Drama
Dist - BENNUP **Prod** - VIDKNW

Tales from Other Worlds 60 MIN
U-matic / VHS / 16mm
Planet Earth Series
Color (C A)
Presents, through footage shot in space and special effects, a look at the star of Jupiter, the volcano of Io and the full surface of Venus through acid rain clouds. Discusses the yet undiscovered Death Star which may have killed the dinosaurs and millions of other species.
Science - Physical
Dist - FI **Prod** - ANNCPB

Tales from other worlds - Part 4 60 MIN
VHS / U-matic
Planet earth series
Color (G)
$45.00, $29.95 purchase
Visits the great failed star of the planet Jupiter and the raging volcano of the moon Io. Peers through acid rain clouds to see the surface of Venus for the first time. Part of a seven - part series on Planet Earth.
History - World; Science - Physical
Dist - ANNCPB **Prod** - WQED 1986

Tales from the Gimli Hospital 72 MIN
35mm / 16mm
B&W (G)
$300.00, $400.00 rental
Portrays a smallpox epidemic in Gimli, Manitoba, near the turn of the century. Explores the madness and jealousy instilled in two men who share a hospital room. Directed by Guy Madden.
Fine Arts
Dist - KINOIC

Tales from the Great Book Series
The Sword of Gideon 12 MIN
Dist - HALCOM

Tales from the Latin American Indians 50 MIN
VHS
Color (K P I) (SPANISH)
Presents The Magic of the Quetzal Bird, The Legend of Mexico City, The Legend of Quetzalcohuatl, and The Legend of Loiza. Stories reveal insights into different cultures and traditions of different lands and times.
Literature and Drama
Dist - BENNUP **Prod** - VIDKNW

Tales from the map room series
Features actors who re - create significant events in the history of cartography in a series of six programs. Investigates the early roles of maps and map - making in war, navigation, and transportation. Features maps as historical documents and discusses the controversy and discrepancies involved in mapping frontiers and lands.
Tales from the map room series 180 MIN
Dist - BBCENE

Tales from the map room
Fog of war 30 MIN
Metropolis 30 MIN
On the road 30 MIN
On the rocks 30 MIN
Plum pudding in danger 30 MIN
Tissue of lies 30 MIN
Dist - BBCENE

Tales from the North American Indians 50 MIN
VHS
Fairy Tales from Exotic Lands
Color (K P I)
Presents Hiawatha and the Magic Arrows, The Monster of Niagara, The Greedy Mouse and the Buffalo, and Nanook the Eskimo Boy. Stories reveal insights into different cultures and traditions of different lands and times.
Literature and Drama
Dist - BENNUP **Prod** - VIDKNW

Tales from the Odyssey 99 MIN
VHS / U-matic
Tales from the Odyssey Series
Color (I J)
Consists of 1 videocassette.
English Language
Dist - TROLA **Prod** - TROLA 1987

Tales from the Odyssey
VHS
Color (G)
$165.00 purchase _ #0188
Retells seven stories from the Odyssey. Includes The Wooden Horse, The Voyage of Odysseus, Odysseus and the Cyclops, Odysseus and the Giants, Odysseus and the Magic of Circe, Odysseus and the Great Challenge, The Return of Odysseus.
History - World; Literature and Drama; Religion and Philosophy
Dist - SEVVID

Tales from the Odyssey Series
Tales from the Odyssey 99 MIN
Dist - TROLA

Tales from the Vienna Woods 12 MIN
16mm
Color
LC 76-700158
Presents a collage about courtship, love and marriage based on the letters of Sigmund Freud and journals of the period.
Guidance and Counseling; Psychology; Sociology
Dist - MCGILU **Prod** - MCGILU 1974

The Tales of Aesop 15 MIN
VHS / 16mm
Stories and Poems from Long Ago series
Color (I)
Uses the character of a retired sea captain to tell The Tales Of Aesop. The sixth of 16 installments of the Stories And Poems From Long Ago Series, which is intended to encourage reading and writing by young viewers.
Literature and Drama
Dist - GPN **Prod** - CTI 1990

Tales of Edgar Allan Poe 61 MIN
U-matic / VHS
Tales of Edgar Allan Poe Series
Color (I J)
Contains 1 videocassette.
English Language; Literature and Drama
Dist - TROLA **Prod** - TROLA 1987

Tales of Edgar Allan Poe Series
Tales of Edgar Allan Poe 61 MIN
Dist - TROLA

Tales of Gods and Demons 29 MIN
U-matic / VHS
Journey into Thailand Series
Color (J S C A)
$195.00 purchase
Depicts the history of the masked ballet which uses dancers in exotic costumes. The story of the dance drama Ramakien is explained.
Geography - World; History - World
Dist - LANDMK **Prod** - LANDMK 1986

Tales of Hiawatha 19 MIN
16mm
Color (P I J H)

LC FIA67-5308
Presents a puppet film adapted from Henry Wadsworth Longfellow's epic, 'The Song of Hiawatha.' Combines sections of the poem with narration to relate the Indian legend.
Literature and Drama
Dist - SF **Prod** - SF 1967

The Tales of Hoffmann 125 MIN
VHS
Color (G)
$39.95 _ #TAL060
Adapts the fantasy opera by Jacques Offenbach with the Royal Philharmonic Orchestra. Presents three wondrous stories of romance, magic and mystery arising out of the poet Hoffmann's misadventures in love. Directed by Michael Powell and Emeric Pressburger. Unabridged and fully restored; digitally remastered with restored soundtrack.
Fine Arts; Literature and Drama; Psychology
Dist - HOMVIS **Prod** - JANUS 1951

The Tales of Hoffmann 160 MIN
VHS / U-matic
Color (A) (FRENCH)
Portrays three strange love affairs, one with a doll, another with a glittering courtesan, the third with an ambitious but fragile singer in Offenbach's musical, The Tales Of Hoffman.
Fine Arts
Dist - SRA **Prod** - SRA

The Tales of Hoffmann - Les Contes D'Hoffmann 155 MIN
VHS
Color (S)
$39.95 purchase _ #623 - 9548
Stars Placido Domingo, Ileana Cotrubas, Agnes Baltsa and Luciana Serra in the Royal Opera production of 'The Tales Of Hoffmann' by Offenbach. Features John Schlesinger as director.
Fine Arts; Geography - World
Dist - FI **Prod** - NVIDC 1986

Tales of Hoffnung Series
Birds, bees and storks 6 MIN
The Hoffnung Maestro 8 MIN
The Hoffnung Music Academy 8 MIN
The Hoffnung Symphony Orchestra 8 MIN
The Hoffnung Vacuum Cleaner 8 MIN
Professor Ya - Ya's Memoirs 8 MIN
Dist - PHENIX

Tales of New Jersey 25 MIN
16mm
Color
LC 76-701405
Tells legends and folklore of New Jersey set to a background of original music and lyrics.
Fine Arts; Geography - United States; History - United States; Literature and Drama
Dist - NJBTC **Prod** - NJBTC 1976

The Tales of Olga Da Polga 15 MIN
U-matic / VHS
Best of Cover to Cover 1 Series
Color (P)
Literature and Drama
Dist - WETATV **Prod** - WETATV

Tales of Pluto Series
Pluto's Surprise Package 8 MIN
Wonder Dog 8 MIN
Dist - CORF

Tales of Terror 90 MIN
16mm
Color (J)
Stars Vincent Price and Basil Rathbone in three of Edgar Allan Poe's most chilling tales, utilizing all the gripping psychological terror elements which have made his works memorable. Includes The Black Cat, Morella and The Facts In The Case Of M Valdemar.
Fine Arts
Dist - TIMLIF **Prod** - AIP 1962

Tales of the forgotten future - part one - the morning films 35 MIN
VHS / 8mm cartridge
B&W (G A)
$75.00 rental
Presents the work of filmmaker Lewis Klahr. Uses paper cutout animation to create three narratives - 'Lost Camel Intentions,' 'For the Rest of Your Natural Life,' 'In the Month of Crickets.' Chronicles the psychological and mythical themes of mortality, survival, fear of imprisonment and sexual guilt.
Fine Arts; Industrial and Technical Education; Psychology
Dist - PARART **Prod** - FMCOOP 1988

Tales of the human dawn 60 MIN
VHS
Smithsonian world series
Color; Captioned (G)
$49.95 purchase _ #SMIW - 503
Explores cultural factors in evolutionary thought. Suggests that storytelling has played an important role. Interviews Stephen J Gould and Kurt Vonnegut.
History - World; Science - Natural
Dist - PBS **Prod** - WETATV

Tales of the Muscogee 15 MIN
U-matic / 35mm strip
Color (I J H)
Introduces the rich world of Creek Indian folklore as a form of entertainment and moral teaching for children.
Literature and Drama; Social Science
Dist - CEPRO **Prod** - CEPRO

Tales of the rails 31 MIN
U-matic / VHS
Color (J H C G)
$150.00 purchase, $30.00 rental _ #CC4265VU, #CC4265VH
Relates an anecdote of the history of the American railroad in the Midwest. Interviews old - timers who grew up along the tracks in Iowa. Reveals the significance of the railroad to rural communities in the first half of the 20th century. Produced by Dirk Eitzen.
Geography - United States; History - United States; Social Science
Dist - IU

Tales of the Snow Monkey 23 MIN
U-matic / VHS
Color (K)
Tells the story of the amazingly smart and ever - adaptable Japanese snow monkey which has managed to adapt to conditions that have killed off most of Japan's other wildlife species.
Science - Natural
Dist - NWLDPR **Prod** - NWLDPR

Tales of the unknown South series
Presents three Southern short stories, all of which provide a view the South that challenges stereotypes. Julia Peterkin's 'Ashes' tells the story of an independent backwoods woman threatened with eviction by a nearby landowner, while DuBose Heyward's 'The Half - Pint Flask' tells how a visitor to a South Carolina island finds himself confronted by an evil spirit. 'Neighbors,' by Diane Oliver, focuses on a black student who enters a formerly all - white school. Hosted by author James Dickey. Available only to public television stations.
Ashes 38 MIN
The Half - pint flask 45 MIN
Neighbors 33 MIN
Tales of the unknown South series 116 MIN
Dist - SCETV **Prod** - SCETV

Tales of Tomorrow - Our Elders 22 MIN
16mm
Color
Contrasts the lifestyles of several elderly people with handicapping conditions. Shows one couple in which the husband has heart trouble and the wife has Alzheimer's disease moving into a home for the aged while another woman insists on living independently at 80, though wheelchair bound.
Health and Safety; Sociology
Dist - FLMLIB **Prod** - MARTNB 1982

Tales of Washington Irving 45 MIN
16mm
Color
Uses animation to bring some of Washington Irving's favorite places and people to life. Includes the stories of Ichabod Crane and Rip Van Winkle.
Fine Arts; Literature and Drama
Dist - TWYMAN **Prod** - API

Tales of Wesakechak
VHS / U-matic
Tales of Wesakechak Series
Color (G)
Shows fifteen minute programs based on well known Canadian Cree legends. Provides an oral storyteller and shadow puppets to dramatize these stories of Wesakechak. Wesakechak was the teacher of the first Cree Indian people. While there are many different stories of Wesakechak that can be told in many ways, depending on the use of local elements, what remains true are the values and lessons the stories present.
Social Science; Sociology
Dist - NAMPBC **Prod** - NAMPBC 1984

Tales of Wesakechak Series
Ayekis the frog 15 MIN
The Creation of the moon 15 MIN
The Creation of the world 15 MIN
The First spring flood 15 MIN
How the fox earned his name 15 MIN
The Stone and the Mouse 15 MIN
Tales of Wesakechak
Wapoose the Rabbit 15 MIN
Wesakechak and the First Indian People 15 MIN
Wesakechak and the Medicine 15 MIN
Wesakechak and the Whiskey Jack 15 MIN
Why Bees have Stingers 15 MIN
Why the Crow is Black 15 MIN
Why the Rabbit Turns White 15 MIN
Dist - NAMPBC

Tales of wood and water 60 MIN
VHS
Color (G)
$29.95 purchase
Contrasts modern boatbuilding methods with film of the 1919 launching of a four - masted schooner to document the wooden boat culture of the state of Maine. Takes a look at boat yards, boatbuilding schools and WoodenBoat magazine's headquarters.
Fine Arts; History - United States
Dist - NEFILM

Tales Tall and Otherwise 29 MIN
U-matic
Folklore - U S a Series
B&W
Discusses the persistence of tales such as Paul Bunyan and Brer Rabbit. Features a professional storyteller.
Literature and Drama
Dist - UMITV **Prod** - UMITV 1967

Tales the People Tell in China - Favorite Fairy Tales Told in Japan 15 MIN
U-matic / VHS
Best of Cover to Cover 1 Series
Color (P)
Literature and Drama
Dist - WETATV **Prod** - WETATV

Taliesin East 11 MIN
16mm
Color (C A)
LC FIA52-665
Depicts the home of American architect Frank Lloyd Wright, near Madison, Wisconsin.
Fine Arts
Dist - RADIM **Prod** - DAVISJ 1951

Taliesin - the tradition of Frank Lloyd Wright 30 MIN
VHS
Color (J H C G)
$49.95 purchase _ #HVS31V
Journeys back to 1932 when Frank Lloyd Wright and his wife, Olgivanna Lasovich, co - founded the Taliesin Fellowship in which Wright actively participated by sharing his unique theories on organic architecture with his students. Witnesses the beginnings of Taliesin West, interviews its pupils past and present and examines over 1000 structures issuing from Wright's career which spanned more than half a century. Visits Falling Water, the Johnson Wax Administration Building and the Guggenheim Museum.
Biography; Fine Arts; History - United States
Dist - CAMV

Taliesin West 11 MIN
16mm
Color (C A)
LC FIA52-664
Uses a film record to describe the desert house of Frank Lloyd Wright and a brief narration, written by Wright himself. Explains some of his ideas about the relationship between modern art and nature.
Fine Arts
Dist - RADIM **Prod** - DAVISJ 1951

Talisman - Barra 37 MIN
Videoreel / VT2
Color
Describes the restoration of a Scottish castle, the ancestral home of the clan MacNeil.
Geography - World; History - World
Dist - PBS **Prod** - VTETV

Talk Business 15 MIN
U-matic
Keys to the Office Series
Color (H)
Covers the principles of business speaking with telephone etiquette and advice on using the voice effectively.
Business and Economics
Dist - TVOTAR **Prod** - TVOTAR 1986

A Talk in the dark 11 MIN
VHS / 16mm
B&W (G)
$20.00 rental, $19.95 purchase
Adapts a short story by Irish author Walter Macken. Tells of the unexpected and poignant results when two strangers meet on a dark night. Produced by Claddagh Films and directed by Dermot Tynan.

Fine Arts; Literature and Drama; Psychology
Dist - CANCIN

Talk, Listen and Learn 35 MIN
16mm
Color (H C A)
LC 77-703240
Presents actual situations in which young people discuss issues such as alcohol, drugs and sexual behavior in order to demonstrate techniques for leading small group discussions.
English Language; Guidance and Counseling; Health and Safety; Sociology
Dist - USNAC **Prod** - JOB 1967

Talk, Listen, and Learn 35 MIN
VHS / U-matic
Color
LC 80-706842
Presents actual situations in which young people discuss issues such as alcohol, drugs and sexual behavior in order to demonstrate techniques for leading small group discussions.
Guidance and Counseling; Psychology
Dist - USNAC **Prod** - JOB 1980

The Talk of the Town 118 MIN
16mm
B&W
Tells how Cary Grant finds refuge in the summer cottage of a celebrated jurist when he is falsely accused of arson. Follows Jean Arthur's attempts to get the jurist to defend Grant in a new trial. Directed by George Stevens.
Fine Arts
Dist - TIMLIF **Prod** - CPC 1942

Talk so they listen, listen so they talk 28 MIN
VHS
Prime time for parents video series
Color (G)
$89.95 purchase _ #RMI208
Looks at the use of the 'language of acceptance' in enhancing the child, the parent and their relationship. Shows how to read nonverbal behavior and send effective nonverbal messages. Demonstrates constructive listening skills. Part of a series on parenting. Study guide available separately.
English Language; Home Economics; Social Science; Sociology
Dist - CADESF **Prod** - CADESF

Talk, Talk, Talk 10 MIN
16mm
Parent Education - Information Films Series
B&W (S)
Shows the beginning of lip - reading and how an awareness of lip movements can be developed and utilized for the development of lip - reading skills.
Guidance and Counseling; Psychology
Dist - TC **Prod** - TC

Talk, Talk, Talk 15 MIN
U-matic / VHS
All about You Series
Color (P)
Points out that most animals can't learn to talk with words because they lack the nerve network in the brain that makes human speech possible.
English Language; Science - Natural
Dist - AITECH **Prod** - WGBHTV 1975

Talk to Me - a Visit with Mr Carpenter 8 MIN
16mm
Color (J)
LC 76-701175
Presents a statement on growing old, featuring present and past experiences of Authur H Carpenter, an 85 - year - old man who was a singer, an architect and an artist, including his concern for the future.
Health and Safety; Sociology
Dist - ARTCOP **Prod** - TATANA 1974

Talk to the Animals 14 MIN
U-matic / VHS / 16mm
Color (A)
LC 78-701192
Shows scientists communicating with apes by teaching them sign language and through the use of a talking typewriter or computer. Points out that these communication methods can be used to help teach language to the mentally retarded and to brain - damaged children.
Psychology
Dist - MGHT **Prod** - CBSTV 1978

Talk to the Animals 10 MIN
16mm
Peppermint Stick Selection Series
Color (P I)
LC 76-701278
Presents an excerpt from the motion picture Doctor Dolittle. Shows Doctor Dolittle receiving lessons in animal language from Polynesia the Parrot. Introduces communication methods and nonverbal communication or body language. Based on the story Doctor Dolittle by Hugh Lofting.
English Language; Fine Arts; Literature and Drama
Dist - FI **Prod** - FI 1978

A Talk with Carmen D'Avino 6 MIN
16mm
Color (A)
Presents an experimental film by Alfred Kouzel in which artist - animator Carmen D'Avino talks about his scroll - like color doodles.
Fine Arts
Dist - STARRC **Prod** - STARRC 1972

Talk Words - 5 15 MIN
VHS
Wordscape Series
Color; Captioned (I)
$125.00 purchase
Uses the word 'cell' approach to teach vocabulary, opening each program - sixteen 15 - minute programs - with several word cells familiar to fourth graders and using these 'cells' to form compound words such as birdhouse and girlfriend. Employs animated graphics to dramatize how compounds are 'built' of cells that form a seemingly endless series of new words and to teach that understanding cell words can help to understand the new words composed of them. Program 5 centers on words concerned with talk and introduces the dictionary as both a talk word and a source for learning more about words.
English Language; Psychology
Dist - AITECH **Prod** - OETVA 1990

Talking 4 MIN
16mm
Mini Movies - Springboard for Learning - Unit 1, who are We Series
Color (P I)
LC 76-703091
Deals with an extended concept of talking by presenting nonword responses as a form of communication.
English Language; Psychology; Social Science
Dist - MORLAT **Prod** - MORLAT 1975

Talking about Beliefs 14 MIN
16mm
Classroom as a Learning Community Series
B&W (I)
LC 76-714106
Shows students in a fifth - grade class in Newton, Massachusetts, discussing Eskimo beliefs, and in the process examining their own.
Education; Psychology
Dist - EDC **Prod** - EDC 1971

Talking about Breastfeeding 17 MIN
16mm
Color (H C A)
LC 74-703684
Affirms the value of breastfeeding as the simplest, safest and most nutritious way to feed an infant and helps allay common fears. Features a number of nursing mothers who have overcome medical problems and social pressures to breastfeed speaking of their experiences.
Home Economics
Dist - POLYMR **Prod** - POLYMR 1971

Talking about Old People 19 MIN
16mm
Classroom as a Learning Community Series
B&W (I)
LC 72-714105
Shows a classroom situation in which the students have read 'The Kigtak Story' and are discussing the problem that the Netsilik Eskimos have in taking care of their old people.
Education; Psychology; Sociology
Dist - EDC **Prod** - EDC 1971

Talking about Pots 25 MIN
U-matic / VHS
Craft of the Potter Series
Color (H C A)
Features a discussion among a potter, a member of the Crafts Advisory Council, a gallery owner and a collector which centers on appreciation of individual pieces of work by contemporary potters. Shows potters at work.
Fine Arts
Dist - FI **Prod** - BBCTV

Talking about sea turtles 12 MIN
VHS / U-matic
Color (P I J)
$245.00, $295.00 purchase, $60.00 rental
Introduces some of the problems that have pushed sea turtles toward extinction. Offers concrete suggestions about the ways children can help. Produced by Becky Marshall - GDNR.
Science - Natural
Dist - NDIM

Talking Back
VHS / U-matic
Color
Shows how to take positive steps to impact the low back pain problem.
Health and Safety
Dist - VISUCP **Prod** - VISUCP

Talking blues 30 MIN
VHS
All black series
Color; PAL (H C A)
PdS65 purchase; Available in the United Kingdom or Ireland only
Investigates black perceptions of law enforcement and focuses specifically on the relationship between blacks and the police. Seventh in a series of seven programs.
Social Science; Sociology
Dist - BBCENE

Talking cars 15 MIN
VHS
Color; PAL; NTSC (G IND)
PdS57, PdS67 purchase
Features four talking cars who tell all about their owners and the mechanics responsible for their maintenance. Draws attention to some major hazards of motor vehicle repair shops and safeguards.
Health and Safety; Industrial and Technical Education
Dist - CFLVIS

Talking Crime 30 MIN
VHS / U-matic
Color
Answers some common questions about crime. Takes a look at the homicide rate and examines the role of the news.
Sociology
Dist - NOVID **Prod** - NOVID

The talking cure 60 MIN
VHS
Madness
Color; PAL (C PRO H)
PdS99 purchase; Not available in the United States
Covers the history of psychotherapy as treatment for mental illness. Includes psychological perspectives on mental illness. Fourth in the five - part series Madness, which outlines the history of mental illness.
Psychology
Dist - BBCENE

The Talking cure 50 MIN
VHS
Color (H C A)
PdS99 purchase
Features Shahnaz Pakravan in conversations with specialists and patients about therapy techniques and successes. Examines who should seek therapy and why it is effective for certain conditions such as stress.
Health and Safety
Dist - BBCENE

The Talking Cure - a Portrait of Psychoanalysis 56 MIN
VHS / 16mm
Color (C A PRO)
$395.00 purchase, $75.00 rental _ #9958
Describes traditional psychotherapy and the interaction between therapist and client.
Psychology
Dist - AIMS **Prod** - JONDAV 1988

Talking cure and Into the light 58 MIN
16mm
Color & B&W (G)
$80.00 rental
Deals with painful memories of an affair with a young woman. Attempts the therapeutic 'talking cure' that can never work. Voiceover plays against images of Northern California that run, play themselves out, and repeat, slightly out of focus. A 1982 foray into psychoanalytical concerns. Into The Light is the filmmaker's most intense exploration of sexualization and illumination.
Fine Arts; Psychology
Dist - CANCIN **Prod** - SONDHE 1989

The talking eggs 25 MIN
VHS
Color (K P I)
$89.95 purchase _ #L11149
Features the animated story of Selina, a young girl who befriends a mystical elderly woman. Narrates the events that take place after Selina finds three talking eggs. Emphasizes the pursuit of dreams and the discovery of untapped potential in children. Based on a Creole folk tale and narrated by Danny Glover.
Literature and Drama
Dist - CF **Prod** - SPORAN 1993

The Talking Eggs
VHS / 35mm strip
Caldecotts on Filmstrip Series
Color (K)
$35.00 purchase
Presents a children's story. Part of the Caldecott Series.
English Language; Literature and Drama
Dist - PELLER

Talking feet 15 MIN
VHS
Color (P I J)
Presents two talking feet portrayed by junior high children who describe the structure, function and care of the feet. Stresses the selection of correct shoes, foot care and how to deal with warts, athlete's foot and corns.
Science - Natural
Dist - VIEWTH **Prod** - VIEWTH

Talking feet 90 MIN
U-matic / VHS
Color (G)
$600.00, $350.00 purchase
Presents a documentary on Southern - style solo mountain dancing. Showcases clogging, flatfoot, buck, hoedown and rural tap dancing. Includes instructional booklet.
Fine Arts; History - United States
Dist - FLOWER **Prod** - BLNKL 1992

Talking films series
The Big red auk 3 MIN
By the lake 12 MIN
Dead money 6 MIN
Fear is what you find 3 MIN
I D N O 9 MIN
Let's be pals 8 MIN
My day
Dist - CANCIN

Talking Helps 29 MIN
VHS / 16mm
Color (J)
$180.00 purchase
Teaches a series of steps teens can use to help themselves and their friends work through problems. Uses a sequence of vignettes to show young people using this skill in a variety of situations. Includes leader's guide.
Psychology; Sociology
Dist - CHEF **Prod** - CHEF

Talking helps - teaching strategies for educators 27 MIN
16mm / VHS
Color (C A G PRO)
$375.00, $89.00 purchase
Illustrates a community effort to develop a child sexual abuse prevention program in their school. Demonstrates how the film No More Secrets is used with children.
Education; Health and Safety; Social Science; Sociology
Dist - SELMED

Talking history 30 MIN
U-matic / VHS
Asian American heritage collection series
Color (G)
$150.00 purchase, $50.00 rental
Offers a collection of oral histories and historical footage taken of Japanese, Chinese, Korean, Filipino and Laotion women. Features their journeys to the United States and their unique stories as immigrants. Produced and directed by Spencer Nakasako.
History - United States; Sociology
Dist - CROCUR

Talking it Over 20 MIN
U-matic / VHS / 16mm
Literacy Instructor Training Series
Color (T)
LC 78-700890
Demonstrates management skills necessary to sustain a successful tutor - pupil relationship.
Education; English Language
Dist - IU **Prod** - NEWPAR 1978

Talking jobs 60 MIN
VHS
Color; PAL (J H)
PdS30 purchase
Presents a 'fly on the wall' video in which five candidates are interviewed for the position of Communications Operator. Unfold a key message which says that when 'talking jobs,' preparation is the key to success. Includes the job advertisement and the five application forms of the candidates. Contact distributer about availability outside the United Kingdom.
Guidance and Counseling; Social Science
Dist - ACADEM **Prod** - YORKTV

Talking Nicaragua 39 MIN
VHS / BETA
Color
Recounts the highlights of Nicaragua's history since the days of Sandino, through dramatic presentations by actors Susan Sarandon, Edward Herrmann, and others. Recreates the stories of present day Nicaraguans, victims of attacks launched by counterrevolutionary forces along the border with Honduras.
Geography - World; History - World
Dist - ICARUS **Prod** - ICARUS

Talking of Safety 24 MIN
16mm / U-matic / VHS
Color (A)
LC 81-701620
Deals with the effectiveness of safety committee meetings. Shows how a newly - appointed safety supervisor at a brick and manufacturing plant in England makes his committee work more effectively while promoting clearly - defined objectives.
Health and Safety
Dist - IFB **Prod** - MILLBK 1980

Talking on Paper 40 MIN
VHS / U-matic
Effective Writing Series
Color
English Language; Psychology
Dist - DELTAK **Prod** - TWAIN

Talking Ourselves into Trouble 29 MIN
16mm
Language in Action Series
B&W (C A)
Discusses general semantics and how undifferentiated reactions to words lead to lack of communication. Develops the idea that language determines limits of a person's world.
English Language
Dist - IU **Prod** - NET

Talking Out Conflict 15 MIN
U-matic / VHS
Color
Stresses that managers must deal with conflicts or they will only become worse. Points out that the keys to conflict resolution are a positive attitude and an effort to be honest and open with everyone involved.
Business and Economics; Psychology
Dist - EFM **Prod** - EFM

The Talking Parcel 40 MIN
U-matic / VHS / 16mm
Color (I A)
Presents characters and incidents based on ancient myths which come to life in full animation with voices by British personalities and incidental music by a rock composer.
Literature and Drama; Religion and Philosophy
Dist - MEDIAG **Prod** - THAMES 1978

The Talking Plant 54 MIN
VHS / U-matic
Color (I)
Teaches parts of a plant and their functions to stimulate an interest in growing plants and to explain how to use plants in the environment.
Agriculture; Science - Natural
Dist - CORNRS **Prod** - CUETV 1975

Talking Shop 23 MIN
16mm
Color
Presents Hazardous Harry, a bungling hero who shows how not to use hand tools. Shows how injuries can be avoided.
Health and Safety; Industrial and Technical Education
Dist - MTP **Prod** - MTP

Talking things out - a lesson on expressing feelings 13 MIN
VHS
Lessons from the heart - taking charge of feelings series
Color (I)
$89.95 purchase _ #10168VG
Examines the many different ways to communicate and how children can creatively express feelings. Uses vignettes, interviews, and graphics to teach about relationships and being receptive to others' feelings. Comes with a teacher's guide, discussion topics and two blackline masters. Part four of a four - part series.
Guidance and Counseling; Social Science
Dist - UNL

Talking to a machine 25 MIN
U-matic / VHS / 16mm
Computer programme series; Episode 3
Color (J)
Discusses computer languages, comparing BASIC with English and describing holed cards that once programmed a steam organ.
Business and Economics; Mathematics
Dist - FI **Prod** - BBCTV 1982

Talking to strangers 50 MIN
VHS
Trials of life series
Color (J H C G)
$29.98 purchase _ #TUR3092V - S
Looks at inter - species social behavior in animals. Part of a 12 - part series traveling with naturalist David Attenborough and his crew to exotic and dangerous places to observe the animal kingdom.
Science - Natural
Dist - CAMV **Prod** - TBSESI 1991

Talking to the enemy - voices of sorrow and rage 54 MIN
VHS
Color (H C G)
$445.00 purchase, $75.00 rental
Portrays the meeting between young Palestinian journalist Muna Hamzeh and older Israeli editor Chaim Shur who attempt a resolution of the Palestinian - Israeli conflict - and fail. Reveals that Shur invited Hamzeh to visit his kibbutz but her arrival sparks a passionate dialogue as old wounds are reopened. Produced by Mira Hamermesh.
History - World
Dist - FLMLIB

Talking to the team - how to run a meeting 28 MIN
VHS
Color (A PRO IND)
$790.00 purchase, $220.00 rental
Provides guidelines for running meetings successfully.
Business and Economics; Psychology
Dist - VLEARN **Prod** - VIDART

Talking to the Team - How to Run a Team Meeting 27 MIN
VHS / 16mm
Color (A PRO)
$790.00 purchase, $220.00 rental
Shows how to conduct a meeting. Covers planning and preparing information for a meeting and managing its course. Management training.
Guidance and Counseling; Psychology
Dist - VIDART **Prod** - VIDART 1990

Talking too much - 55 8 MIN
U-matic / VHS
Life's little lessons - self - esteem 4 - 6 series
Color (I)
$129.00, $99.00 purchase _ #V684
Portrays Aida Spencer who was more interested in hearing what she had to say herself than in listening to what others were trying to tell her. Shows how foolish she was. Part of a 65 - part series on self - esteem.
English Language; Guidance and Counseling; Psychology
Dist - BARR **Prod** - CEPRO 1992

Talking Turtle 57 MIN
16mm / U-matic / VHS
Nova Series
Color (H C A)
Looks at computers in the classroom through the eyes of MIT's Seymour Papert, inventor of the computer language LOGO and father of the Turtle, a computerized robot that crawls on the floor and communicates in a versatile language even five - year - olds can learn.
Education; Mathematics
Dist - TIMLIF **Prod** - WGBHTV 1984

Talking Turtle 48 MIN
U-matic / VHS / 16mm
Color (C A)
Discusses the uses and potential of Logo, a new computer language developed to meet the need for computers to enrich the range of experience for children. Adapted from the Nova series.
Mathematics; Psychology
Dist - MEDIAG **Prod** - BBCTV 1984

Talking with Pictures 37 MIN
VHS / U-matic
Color
Focuses on three types of visuals which can greatly enhance presentations of ideas, plans, products and results to audiences large and small. Demonstrates the flipchart, the 35mm slide and the overhead transparency. Shows how to design effective visuals and the most effective way to use each type.
Industrial and Technical Education; Social Science
Dist - VISUCP **Prod** - MELROS

Talking with Thoreau 29 MIN
16mm / U-matic / VHS
Humanities - Philosophy and Political Thought Series
Color (H C)
LC 75-702357
Uses a science fiction device of time - travel to present the thoughts of Henry David Thoreau. Stages a visit between Thoreau and four present - day distinguished personages, set in his cabin at Walden Pond.
Biography; Literature and Drama; Religion and Philosophy
Dist - EBEC **Prod** - EBEC 1975

Talking with Young Children about Death 30 MIN
U-matic / VHS
Mister Rogers Talks about Series
Color
Talk about how adults can help children begin to understand death and cope with sadness. This program can be used as a resource for college level courses, parenting and community groups, professional workshops and religious institutions.
Education; Sociology
Dist - FAMCOM **Prod** - FAMCOM

Tall Buildings 5 MIN
16mm / U-matic / VHS
Color (I J H)
LC 74-702825
Tells how the great shift in urban population has necessitated the increasing development of tall buildings. Stresses the importance of developing tall structures which will be ultilitarian, safe and functional for the occupants.
Health and Safety; Industrial and Technical Education; Sociology
Dist - AMEDFL **Prod** - NSF 1975

Tall buildings - psychological problems
U-matic / VHS / BETA
Search encounters in science series
Color; PAL (G H C)
PdS25, PdS33 purchase
Brings modern research efforts of the world's leading scientists into the classroom. Features one of a series of 24 mini - documentaries. Each film is 5 - 7 minutes in length.
Psychology; Science
Dist - EDPAT **Prod** - NSF

Tall Dilemma 21 MIN
16mm
Color
LC 74-702892
Presents the conditions and reasons why firefighters must expect an unusually severe occupant life loss during a serious high rise building fire and discusses what fire departments, building management and occupants can do to prevent it.
Health and Safety; Home Economics; Industrial and Technical Education; Social Science; Sociology
Dist - FILCOM **Prod** - AREASX 1974

Tall grass 12 MIN
16mm
Color (G)
$15.00 rental
Recaps an idyllic summer spent in Mendocino, California in 1968. Portrays close friends including a romantic vision of a high school infatuation.
Fine Arts; Psychology
Dist - CANCIN **Prod** - WALLIN

Tall in the Studio 28 MIN
VHS / U-matic
Please Stand by - a History of Radio Series
(C A)
Fine Arts; History - United States; Psychology; Sociology
Dist - SCCON **Prod** - SCCON 1986

Tall Ships 16 MIN
16mm
Color
Focuses on the Coast Guard training ship Eagle.
Civics and Political Systems; Geography - World; Physical Education and Recreation
Dist - OFFSHR **Prod** - OFFSHR

Tall ships 1976
VHS
Color (G)
$35.90 purchase _ #0086
Joins the 1976 tall ship race from Bermuda to Newport, Rhode Island. Films some collisions at the start in Bermuda.
Physical Education and Recreation
Dist - SEVVID

The Tall Ships are Coming 28 MIN
16mm
Color
LC 76-700716
Shows crews training and sailing in European waters during the summer of 1975 as preparation for Operation Sail 1976. Views the celebration of the 700th birthday of the city of Amsterdam and a sailing spectacle in London called the London Festival of Sail.
Geography - World; Physical Education and Recreation; Social Science
Dist - DREWAS **Prod** - DREWAS 1975

Tall ships, Quebec 1984, Liberty 1986
VHS
Color (G)
$39.80 purchase _ #0288
Joins a crew in training aboard a tall ship sailing from Halifax through the Canso Canal and down the St Lawrence Seaway for a historic rendezvous of the tall ships in Quebec. Follows the ship to Newport, Rhode Island, and on to New York City for a tall ship rendezvous honoring the 100th birthday of the Statue of Liberty.
Geography - World; History - United States; Physical Education and Recreation
Dist - SEVVID

The Tall Spinster of Gimel 30 MIN
16mm
B&W
LC FIA64-1118
Presents a folk tale about the trials and tribulations of a six foot spinster who wants a husband and seeks the help of village leaders on the matter.
Literature and Drama
Dist - NAAJS **Prod** - JTS 1959

Tall Stacks 16 MIN
16mm
Color (PRO)
LC 74-705737
Reports on a five - year study on the effects of large power plants. Presents data on the gaseous and particulate concentrations at various elevations and distances from selected tall - stack installations.
Industrial and Technical Education; Science - Natural
Dist - USNAC **Prod** - USEPA 1972

Tall stacks - steamboats on the Ohio River 35 MIN
VHS
Always a river video collection series
Color (G)
Contact distributor about rental cost _ #92 - 036
Provides a detailed history of Ohio River steamboats through a video produced by the Indiana Historical Society.
Geography - United States
Dist - INDI

The Tall T 80 MIN
16mm
Color
Stars Randolph Scott as a man who encounters a vicious gang of killers.
Fine Arts
Dist - KITPAR **Prod** - CPC 1956

Tall Tales 15 MIN
U-matic / VHS
Word Shop Series
Color (P)
English Language; Literature and Drama
Dist - WETATV **Prod** - WETATV

Tall Tales and Folklore 20 MIN
U-matic / VHS
American Literature Series
Color (H C A)
LC 83-706257
Presents yarns spun around the stove in a country store, including stories of Paul Bunyan, Pecos Bill and some Black American tales, among others.
History - United States; Literature and Drama
Dist - AITECH **Prod** - AUBU 1983

Tall Tales and True 30 MIN
16mm
Color
LC FIA66-857
A documentary film showing the floats, bands and festivities of the floral festival and parade held in Pasadena, California, on New Year's Day, 1960.
Geography - United States; Physical Education and Recreation; Social Science
Dist - TRA **Prod** - TRA 1960

Tall tales, yarns and whoppers 35 MIN
VHS
Storytellers collection series
Color (K P I)
$14.95 purchase _ #ATL422
Offers four examples of tall tales, yarns and whoppers. Features four of the United States' most accomplished storytellers. Part of a four - part series.
Literature and Drama
Dist - KNOWUN

Tall tower 30 MIN
VHS
Limit series
Color (A PRO IND)
PdS30 purchase _ Unavailable in USA and Canada
Asks how tall a skyscraper can be built and if Keizo Shimizu's Millennium Tower is a skyscraper or a city in the sky. Part of a six-part series exploring limits of human achievement in engineering, focusing on international engineers facing their toughest career assignments. Asks how far physical limits can be pushed and what restraints exist in extending the scale of engineering projects.
Industrial and Technical Education
Dist - BBCENE

Tallahassee 15 MIN
16mm
Color
Presents a musical tour of Tallahassee, the state capital of Florida.
Geography - United States; History - United States
Dist - FLADC **Prod** - FLADC

Talley Beatty, Norma Miller 30 MIN
VHS / U-matic
Eye on Dance - Popular Culture and Dance Series
Color
Discusses how popular dance came to the stage. Features Miki Giffune on dance styles in clubs. Hosted by Celia Ipiotis.
Fine Arts
Dist - ARCVID

Tallyho, Pinkerton! 6 MIN
U-matic / VHS
(K P I)
Shows Pinkerton and his feline sidekick, Rose, join their young owner on a trip to the woods. Whom should they bump into but Alaeashs Kibble and her Hunting Academy out in search of the noble fox. From the moment Kibble shouts, 'Tallyho', the zaniness escalates, through a hair raising balloon ride with Pinkerton on board, and the discovery of a striped fox that looks remarkably like a skunk.
English Language; Literature and Drama; Science - Natural
Dist - WWS **Prod** - WWS 1984

Talmage Farlow 58 MIN
VHS / 16mm
Color
Deals with the music and personality of jazz musician Talmage Farlow. Includes Farlow rehearsing with Tommy Flanagan and Red Mitchell.
Fine Arts
Dist - RHPSDY **Prod** - RHPSDY 1980

Talmage Farlow 58 MIN
VHS
Color (G)
$39.95 purchase _ #S02276
Profiles electric guitarist Tal Farlow. Reveals that although Farlow is a well - regarded musician, he maintains a parallel career as a sign painter.
Fine Arts
Dist - UILL

Talons 22 MIN
U-matic / VHS / 16mm
RSPB Collection Series
Color (I J H)
Surveys a variety of birds of prey all sharing features of hooked, tearing beaks, keen eyesight, and taloned feet. Points out how such birds have suffered badly at man's hands, through ignorance, neglect, shooting and the like. Shows the kestrel, hen harrier, red kite, buzzard, goshawk, sparrow hawk, peregine falcon, golden eagle, osprey and short eared, barn and tawny owls.
Science - Natural
Dist - BCNFL **Prod** - RSFPB 1982

Tam Lin 15 MIN
U-matic / VHS / 16mm
Color (J H C)
LC 83-706621
Combines animation with live action to tell the story of a young princess who must rescue the knight, Tam Lin, from an evil abductress.
Fine Arts
Dist - PHENIX **Prod** - KORM 1983

Tamaiti - Children of Samoa 15 MIN
U-matic / VHS
Color (I)
Familiarizes third through fifth grade pupils with other nations' cultures. Builds understanding by studying differences that might divide or cause confusion between various ethnic groups.
Home Economics; Psychology
Dist - GPN

Tamaiti I Hawaii 15 MIN
U-matic / VHS
Color (I)
Familiarizes third through fifth grade pupils with other nations' cultures. Builds understanding by studying differences that might divide or cause confusion between various ethnic groups.
Home Economics; Psychology
Dist - GPN

Tamales 15 MIN
U-matic / VHS
Color (PRO)
Demonstrates the preparation of tamales - corn dough spread over corn husks, filled, and steamed.

Home Economics; Industrial and Technical Education
Dist - CULINA **Prod** - CULINA

Tamanawis illahee - medicine land 58 MIN
16mm
Color (G)
$95.00 rental
Pays homage to the Indian heritage of the Pacific Northwest. Presents the native people, poetry, history and use of their land as opposed to European settlers who lacked a spiritual connection to the region. Experiments with time - lapse photography, archive footage, photos by Edward S Curtis, museum artifacts and other image sources. Produced by Ron Finne.
Fine Arts; Social Science
Dist - CANCIN

Tambor Diego 5 MIN
U-matic / VHS / 16mm
Color (K P) (SPANISH)
Offers a version of the motion picture Drummer Hoff. Adapts a folk verse about the building of a cannon.
Foreign Language; Literature and Drama
Dist - WWS **Prod** - WWS 1969

Tame or wild 15 MIN
U-matic
Tell me what you see series
Color (P)
Explains the relationships between man and animals. Includes affectionate pets, such as dogs and cats, pets that must be kept confined, such as rabbits and parakeets, and animals who have developed a dependence on man, such as mice.
Science - Natural
Dist - GPN **Prod** - WVIZTV

Tame the Wind 28 MIN
U-matic / VHS / 16mm
Color (J H C)
LC 74-701765
Discusses the growing science of weather modification and shows how its techniques are being used today to make rain, suppress hail and lightning and clear fog.
Science; Science - Physical
Dist - JOU **Prod** - UN 1974

The Taming of the Shrew 127 MIN
VHS / 16mm
BBC's Shakespeare Series
(H A)
$249.95
Retells the comical story of Shakespeare's The Taming Of The Shrew, a witty play about the battle of the sexes.
Literature and Drama
Dist - AMBROS **Prod** - AMBROS 1981

The Taming of the shrew 115 MIN
VHS
Shakespearean drama series
Color (I J H C)
$59.95 purchase _ #US29
Presents one of a series in which the Bard's works are staged almost exactly as seen in the 16th century, but without unfamiliar English accents. Stars Franklyn Seales and Karen Austin.
Literature and Drama
Dist - SVIP

The Taming of the shrew
U-matic / VHS
Color (J C I)
Presents Shakespeare's comedy, starring Elizabeth Taylor and Richard Burton.
Fine Arts; Literature and Drama
Dist - GA **Prod** - GA

The Taming of the shrew 127 MIN
VHS
BBC Shakespeare series
Color (G C H)
$109.00 purchase _ #DL466
Fine Arts
Dist - INSIM **Prod** - BBC

The Taming of the Shrew
VHS / U-matic
Classic Films - on - Video Series
Color (G C J)
$89 purchase _ #05652 - 85
Screens Shakespeare's comedy concerning the tempestuous love affair between a man and a woman. Stars Elizabeth Taylor and Richard Burton.
Fine Arts
Dist - CHUMAN

The Taming of the Shrew 13 MIN
16mm / U-matic / VHS
Shakespeare Series
Color (H C A)
Offers an excerpt from the play of the same title. Presents Act I, Scene 2 as Hortensio tells his friend Petruchio of Katharine and Act II, Scene 1 in which Petruchio meets Katharine.
Fine Arts; Literature and Drama
Dist - IFB **Prod** - IFB 1974

The Taming of the Shrew 127 MIN
U-matic / VHS
Shakespeare Plays Series
Color (H C A)
LC 81-706562
Presents William Shakespeare's play which is about a comic confrontation between the sexes.
Literature and Drama
Dist - TIMLIF **Prod** - BBCTV

The Taming of the Shrew 120 MIN
U-matic / VHS
Color
Presents the American Conservatory Theater's interpretation of William Shakespeare's play. Tells the story of a young man's raucous campaign to gain the hand of the uncooperative woman he has decided to marry for her dowry.
Fine Arts; Literature and Drama
Dist - PBS **Prod** - WNETTV

The Taming of the Shrew 122 MIN
16mm
Color
Stars Richard Burton as Petruchio and Elizabeth Taylor as the shrewish Kate. Based on Shakespeare's comedy.
Fine Arts; Literature and Drama
Dist - TIMLIF **Prod** - CPC 1967

Taming of the shrew 122 MIN
VHS
Color (G)
$59.95 purchase _ #S00547
Presents director Franco Zeffirelli's version of Shakespeare's play. Stars Elizabeth Taylor, Richard Burton, Cyril Cusack, Michael York and Victor Spinetti.
Literature and Drama
Dist - UILL

The Taming of the Shrew 30 MIN
VHS / 16mm / BETA
Shakespeare - from Page to Stage Series
Color (J H A)
Presents key scenes from Shakespeare's play bridged with on - camera commentary by one of the actors to reinforce the literary amd thematic aspects of the play. Includes written editions of the complete plays and study guides.
Literature and Drama
Dist - BCNFL **Prod** - CBCEN 1987

Taming the Wild 15 MIN
16mm
Color
Presents Michigan wildlife, including cock pheasant turned mother, black bass fed by man and wolf pup in civilized setting.
Science - Natural
Dist - SFI **Prod** - SFI

Tammy 40 MIN
16mm
Color; B&W (P)
LC FIA55-979
Explains that Tammy, a lovable, lonely little girl, is involved in a serious accident, but that through the efforts of her pastor and the family doctor her life is spared to witness for Christ in her own home.
Guidance and Counseling; Literature and Drama; Religion and Philosophy
Dist - CPH **Prod** - CPH 1953

Tammy the Toad 11 MIN
U-matic / VHS / 16mm
Color (P I)
LC 70-702605
Presents a story about Tammy, a child toad, who decides to leave home in order to achieve rightful appreciation. An adaptation of the parable of the prodigal son.
Fine Arts; Literature and Drama
Dist - PHENIX **Prod** - LEAR 1970

Tampopo 114 MIN
VHS / Videodisc
Color (G) (JAPANESE WITH ENGLISH SUBTITLES)
$35.95, $22.95 purchase _ #REPL2405LD, #NTA4050
Presents a motion picture directed by Juzo Itami.
Fine Arts
Dist - CHTSUI

Tampopo 114 MIN
35mm / 16mm / Videodisc / VHS
Color; PAL (G) (JAPANESE WITH ENGLISH SUBTITLES)
$35.95, $22.95 purchase _ #REPL2405LD, #NTA4050
Concerns a truck driver and his friend who teach a pretty widow how to operate a successful noodle shop. Directed by Juzo Itami for Juzo Itami Productions, Japan. Contact distributor about price and availability outside the United Kingdom.
Fine Arts; Geography - World; Industrial and Technical Education
Dist - BALFOR **Prod** - CHTSUI 198

Tan Sitong 135 MIN
VHS
Color (G) (CHINESE)
$45.00 purchase _ #1080C
Presents a film from the People's Republic of China.
Geography - World; Literature and Drama
Dist - CHTSUI

Tana Hoban's skill building adventures series
Colors and shapes 13 MIN
Over, under and through 10 MIN
Dist - CORF

Tangent Lines 30 MIN
VHS
Mathematics Series
Color (J)
LC 90713155
Discusses tangent lines. The 116th of 157 installments of the Mathematics Series.
Mathematics
Dist - GPN

Tangent lines 30 MIN
VHS
Calculus series
Color (C)
$125.00 purchase _ #6007
Explains tangent lines. Part of a 56 - part series on calculus.
Mathematics
Dist - LANDMK **Prod** - LANDMK

The Tangent Problem 20 MIN
VHS
Calculus Series
Color (H)
LC 90712920
Discusses the tangent problem. The fifth of 57 installments in the Calculus Series.
Mathematics
Dist - GPN

Tangential and Normal Vectors 28 MIN
U-matic / VHS
Calculus of several Variables - Vector - Calculus Series; Vector calculus
B&W
Mathematics
Dist - MIOT **Prod** - MIOT

Tangerine - 7 10 MIN
U-matic / 16mm / VHS
How plants grow series
Color (K P I)
$265.00, $215.00, $185.00 purchase _ #B599
Looks at the stages in the growing season of the tangerine. Describes the climate necessary for growing tangerines and explains how the flowers and fruit of the tangerine develop. Shows how tangerines are harvested and how they go from tree to market. Part of a seven - part series on how plants grow.
Agriculture; Science - Natural
Dist - BARR **Prod** - GREATT 1990

Tangible rewards - Part II 15 MIN
U-matic / VHS
Praise and rewards subseries
Color (G C A)
$275.00 purchase _ #C840 - VI - 020D
Teaches parents how to use praise and rewards to the greatest advantage. Part two of a two - part subseries on praise and rewards and part of a ten - part series on parents and children presented by Dr Carolyn Webster - Stratton.
Health and Safety; Psychology; Sociology
Dist - HSCIC

Tangled Hearts 30 MIN
U-matic / VHS
Wodehouse Playhouse Series
Color (C A)
Presents an adaptation of the short story by P G Wodehouse.
Literature and Drama
Dist - TIMLIF **Prod** - BBCTV 1980

Tangled web, Pt 1 29 MIN
VHS / 16mm
Watch your mouth series
Color (H)
$46.00 rental _ #WAYM - 123
Emphasizes language and communication skills for high school students. Notes the difference between formal and informal word usage.
Education; English Language; Psychology; Social Science
Dist - PBS

Tangled web, Pt 2 29 MIN
VHS / 16mm
Watch your mouth series
Color (H)
$46.00 rental _ #WAYM - 124
Emphasizes language and communication skills for high school students. Notes the difference between formal and informal word usage.
Education; English Language; Psychology; Social Science
Dist - PBS

Tangled Webs 29 MIN
U-matic / VHS / 16mm
Footsteps Series
Color (A)
Focuses on problem behavior in children and how to handle it through the dramatization of a situation in the fictional Tristero family, in which Ann Marie struggles to understand why her young son Paul is constantly lying. Includes a brief introduction and commentary by real - life families and child development experts.
Psychology; Sociology
Dist - USNAC **Prod** - USDED 1980

Tangled World Series
The Affluent society 28 MIN
International Affairs 28 MIN
Self - Understanding 28 MIN
Sex and the family 28 MIN
Dist - YALEDV

Tango 8 MIN
16mm
Color (C A)
LC 83-700153
Offers a metaphoric picture of human fate illustrated by the experiences of many people appearing on the screen at the same time but oblivious to each other.
Fine Arts; Sociology
Dist - IFEX **Prod** - POLSKI 1983

Tango 60 MIN
VHS
Kathy Blake dance studios - let's learn how to dance series
Color (G A)
$39.95 purchase
Features dance instructors Kathy Blake and Gene Russo, who instruct viewers on the basics of the Tango. First of three parts.
Fine Arts
Dist - PBS **Prod** - WNETTV

Tango
VHS
Arthur Murray dance lessons series
Color (G)
$19.95 purchase _ #MC051
Offers lessons in classic ballroom dancing from instructors in Arthur Murray studios, focusing on the tango. Part of a 12 - part series on various ballroom dancing styles.
Fine Arts; Physical Education and Recreation; Sociology
Dist - SIV

Tango 57 MIN
VHS
Color (H C A G)
$39.95 purchase _ #S01575
Features the 28 European dance members of the Grand Company of Geneva in performances of pieces set to the rhythms of the tango. Choreographed by Oscar Ariaz.
Fine Arts; Physical Education and Recreation
Dist - PBS **Prod** - WNETTV
UILL

Tango II 60 MIN
VHS
Kathy Blake dance studios - let's learn how to dance series
Color (G A)
$39.95 purchase
Features dance instructors Kathy Blake and Gene Russo, who instruct viewers on the basics of the Tango. Second of three parts.
Fine Arts
Dist - PBS **Prod** - WNETTV

Tango III 60 MIN
VHS
Kathy Blake dance studios - let's learn how to dance series
Color (G A)
$39.95 purchase
Features dance instructors Kathy Blake and Gene Russo, who instruct viewers on the basics of the Tango. Third of three parts.
Fine Arts
Dist - PBS **Prod** - WNETTV

The Tango is also a history 56 MIN
VHS / 16mm
Color (G)
$390.00 purchase, $100.00 rental
Examines the Tango's development as a record of Argentine political and cultural history. Uses concert footage of several tango artists. Features performances and interviews with Astor Piazzola and Osvaldo Pugliese. Haunting romantic Tango music plays throughout the film. Produced by Humberto Rios.
Civics and Political Systems; Fine Arts
Dist - FIRS

Tango Tangles 10 MIN
16mm
B&W
Tells the story of two men who are smitten with the same hat check girl at a dance. Stars Charlie Chaplin and Fatty Arbuckle.
Fine Arts
Dist - RMIBHF **Prod** - KEYFC 1914

Tangram 3 MIN
16mm / U-matic / VHS
Color (I)
LC 75-704282
Uses animation of the seven geometric pieces of the tangram, an ancient Chinese puzzle, to show the kinds of patterns which can be created from it.
Fine Arts; Mathematics
Dist - PFP **Prod** - SLASOR 1975

Tanjuska and the 7 devils 80 MIN
VHS
Color; PAL (G)
PdS100 purchase
Unfolds the tragedy of a 12 - year - old Estonian girl who stops eating, talking and growing and hence is subjected to brutal religious ceremonies in an attempt to exorcise the seven devils who are believed to have possessed her. Follows the girl and her family over the course of a year. Produced by Pirjo Honkasalo for Baabeli KY, Finland.
Fine Arts; Religion and Philosophy; Sociology
Dist - BALFOR

Tank Calibration 32 MIN
U-matic / VHS
Color (IND)
Explains current API recommendations for strapping cylindrical upright tanks that contain petroleum or petroleum products.
Business and Economics; Industrial and Technical Education; Social Science
Dist - UTEXPE **Prod** - UTEXPE

Tank Platoon in Fire and Movement 26 MIN
16mm
Color
LC 80-701843
Demonstrates basic techniques of mass movement and of fire and movement operations, with emphasis on the platoon leader's responsibilities. Deals with factors that the platoon leader must consider when making decisions under combat conditions.
Civics and Political Systems
Dist - USNAC **Prod** - USA 1980

Tank - Program 5 50 MIN
VHS
Soldiers - a history of men in battle series
Color (H C G)
$300.00 purchase, $75.00 rental
Presents the entire history of the tank, from experimental models to today's high - speed, radar - controlled machines. Shows how the tank came to play a decisive role in modern warfare. Illustrates the experience of living, fighting and dying as a tank soldier. Part of a 13 - part series on soldiers and warfare hosted by Frederick Forsyth and written by John Keenan.
Civics and Political Systems; History - World; Sociology
Dist - CF **Prod** - BBCTV 1986

Tanka 9 MIN
16mm
Color
LC 76-703160
Portrays a vision of the peaceful and wrathful gods, derived from the Tibetan Book Of The Dead and photographed from Tibetan paintings in major American collections.
Fine Arts; Religion and Philosophy
Dist - CFS **Prod** - LEBRUD 1976

Tanker operations series
Elements of tanker construction 30 MIN
Pre - Fire Planning for Tankers 30 MIN
Rural Tanker Evolutions 30 MIN
Dist - OKSU

Tanker Safety Depends on You 13 MIN
16mm / U-matic / VHS
Color
Shows the explosion and fire of the Sensenina in Los Angeles Harbor. Explores the causes of tanker fires and explosions and stresses safety in elimination of all ignition sources.
Health and Safety; Social Science
Dist - USNAC **Prod** - USCG

Tankers - the Ocean's Pipeline 26 MIN
VHS / U-matic
Color
LC 83-706984
Follows several supertankers and their crews along international routes, documents life at sea for the men of Chevron Shipping Company.
Geography - World; Social Science
Dist - MTP **Prod** - CHEVRN 1983

Tanks, Super - Agreeables, and Complainers - Pt II 19 MIN
VHS / 16mm
Coping with Difficult People Series
Color (PRO)
$475.00 purchase, $110.00 rental
Features Dr Robert M Bramson. Presents descriptions and coping methods to use with people who must always be in control, people who avoid action by agreeing with everything and people who blame others for all problems. Part II of a two - part series.
Business and Economics; Psychology
Dist - VICOM **Prod** - VICOM 1990

Tanner 19 Procedure for Afferent Loop Syndrome 23 MIN
U-matic / VHS
Gastrointestinal Series
Color
Health and Safety; Science - Natural
Dist - SVL **Prod** - SVL

Tannhauser 176 MIN
VHS
Metropolitan opera series
Color (G) (GERMAN WITH ENGLISH SUBTITLES)
$39.95 purchase
Stars Richard Cassilly, Eva Marton, Tatiana Troyanos, and Bernd Weiki in a performance of Wagner's opera. Conducted by James Levine. Includes a brochure with plot, historic notes, photographs, and production credits.
Fine Arts
Dist - PBS **Prod** - WNETTV 1982

Tannhauser 176 MIN
VHS
Color (S) (GERMAN)
$39.95 purchase _ #384 - 9371
Offers the Metropolitan Opera production of Wagner's opera. Features James Levine as conductor, Eva Marton and Richard Cassilly as leads.
Fine Arts; Foreign Language
Dist - FI **Prod** - PAR 1988

Tanto tiempo 26 MIN
16mm / VHS
Color (G)
$60.00, $75.00 rental, $195.00 purchase
Tells the story of Mia, a young Mexican - American woman, and her Mexican mother, Luz, who have adapted themselves to an Anglo lifestyle. Reveals Mia's confrontation with her past which leads her to rediscover the value of her Aztec ancestry and brings it and Luz back into her life.
Social Science; Sociology
Dist - WMEN **Prod** - LEADER 1992

Tantra of Gyuto - sacred rituals of Tibet 52 MIN
VHS
Color (G)
$29.95 purchase _ #X014
Records secret Tibetan Buddhist ceremonies of the Gyuto monks. Features the Dalai Lama who introduces the ceremonies, Francis Huxley who narrates Tibetan history, historical footage from the early 1920s until the Chinese occupation in 1959, including scenes of a 1933 German expedition to Tibet.
Religion and Philosophy
Dist - STRUE **Prod** - MFV 1993

Tantra - the experience of transformation 60 MIN
VHS / BETA
Color; PAL (G)
PdS25 purchase
Presents the Venerable Lama Thubten Yeshe giving a clear and concise talk covering not only the three principles of the path but also the process of psychological transformation at the heart of tantric practice. Explains this feature in terms of its methods for utilizing emotional energy and turning what would usually become a neurotic disturbance into the experience of 'blissful wisdom energy.' This talk was given to introduce a tantric empowerment by His Holiness the Dalai Lama. Recorded at Lama Tzong Khapa Institute in Pomaia, Italy.
Fine Arts; Religion and Philosophy
Dist - MERIDT

Tanya the Puppeteer 25 MIN
U-matic / VHS / 16mm
World Cultures and Youth Series
Color (J)
Introduces a Russian girl and shows her efforts to master the art of puppeteering.
Geography - World; Sociology
Dist - CORF **Prod** - SUNRIS 1981

Tanzania - the Quiet Revolution 60 MIN
16mm / U-matic / VHS
Changing World Series no 11; No 11
B&W (H C A)
LC FIA66-1245
Depicts the geography and peoples of Tanzania. Reveals problems of poverty, illiteracy and racism. President Nyerere explains his policy of nonalignment.
Civics and Political Systems; Geography - World; History - United States; Sociology
Dist - IU **Prod** - NET 1964

Tao chien hsiao
VHS
Color (G)
$100.00 _ #27986
Features a Chinese kung fu movie with actress Lin Ch'ing - hsia. Features a two - volume set produced by Markham.
Physical Education and Recreation
Dist - PANASI

Tao Li Mei 119 MIN
VHS
Color (G) (CHINESE)
$45.00 purchase _ #2010C
Presents a film from the People's Republic of China.
Geography - World; Literature and Drama
Dist - CHTSUI

Taoism 22 MIN
U-matic / VHS
Color
Looks at Taoist philosophy in contemporary China.
Religion and Philosophy
Dist - HP **Prod** - HP

Taoism - a Question of Balance 52 MIN
16mm / U-matic / VHS
Long Search Series no 11
Color (H C A)
LC 78-700481
Examines the different types of religious beliefs that make up the spiritual life of Taiwan, including a Confucian respect for the past, the cosmic pattern of the Tao that manifests itself through oracles and the worship of local gods who dispense justice and favors.
Religion and Philosophy; Sociology
Dist - TIMLIF **Prod** - BBCTV 1978

Taoism - a Question of Balance - China 52 MIN
16mm / VHS
Long Search Series
(H C)
$99.95 each, $595.00 series
Unveils the mysticism and meaning surrounding the Buddhist and Taoist religions of Taiwan.
Religion and Philosophy
Dist - AMBROS **Prod** - AMBROS 1978

Taoist 8 immortals double edged sword form 60 MIN
VHS
Color (G)
$49.95 purchase _ #1175
Demonstrates this difficult internal sword form and gives basic training exercises. Repeats segments 3 times and gives applications for the form movements. Sword techniques and principles are given. With George Xu.
Physical Education and Recreation
Dist - WAYF

Taoist eight treasures 120 MIN
VHS
Color (G)
$39.95 purchase _ #1142
Presents a form of Eight Treasures unique to the family of Ni Hua Ching. Stimulates the eight extra meridians of the body. Eight sets of breathing techniques, stretching, and meditative movement are taught by Dr Maoshing Ni, son of Ni Hua Ching.
Physical Education and Recreation
Dist - WAYF

The Taos Pueblo 9 MIN
16mm / U-matic / VHS
OWL North American Indians Series
Color (P I J)
Views the dramatically beautiful 1000 year old pueblo in Taos, New Mexico to discover more about the traditions that the resident Indians are trying to preserve. Shows young children doing ceremonial dances. Teaches about building homes with adobe clay, breadbaking, and making pottery in age old ways.
Geography - United States; Social Science
Dist - BULFRG **Prod** - OWLTV 1987

Tap and Die Threading on the Lathe
U-matic / VHS
Intermediate Engine Lathe Operation Series
Color (SPANISH)
Industrial and Technical Education
Dist - VTRI **Prod** - VTRI

Tap Collar Closed Corners Fabrication 9 MIN
VHS / BETA
Metal Fabrication - Tap Collar Type of Fittings Series
Color (IND)
Industrial and Technical Education; Psychology
Dist - RMIBHF **Prod** - RMIBHF

Tap Collar Open Corners Fabrication 13 MIN
BETA / VHS
Metal Fabrication - Tap Collar Type of Fittings Series
Color (IND)
Industrial and Technical Education; Psychology
Dist - RMIBHF **Prod** - RMIBHF

Tap dance for adults 60 MIN
VHS
Kathy Blake dance studios - let's learn how to dance series
Color (G A)
$39.95 purchase
Features dance instructors Kathy Blake and Gene Russo, who instruct viewers on the basics of tap dance for adults.
Fine Arts
Dist - PBS **Prod** - WNETTV

Tap dance for kids 60 MIN
VHS
Kathy Blake dance studios - children's dancing lessons series
Color (P I)
$39.95 purchase
Presents an introduction to tap dance for children between the ages of six and 11. Allows the children to proceed at their own pace and repeat any difficult steps.
Fine Arts
Dist - PBS **Prod** - WNETTV

Tap dance for preschoolers 60 MIN
VHS
Kathy Blake dance studios - children's dancing lessons series
Color (K)
$39.95 purchase
Presents an introduction to tap dance for preschool - age children. Allows the children to proceed at their own pace and repeat any difficult steps.
Fine Arts
Dist - PBS **Prod** - WNETTV

The Tap Dance Kid 49 MIN
16mm / VHS / U-matic
Color (P) (SPANISH FRENCH)
Tells about an eight - year - old boy who dreams of being on Broadway as a tap dancer, and the opposition he encounters from his father. Full length.
Fine Arts; Literature and Drama; Sociology
Dist - LCOA **Prod** - LCOA 1979

The Tap dance kid 49 MIN
U-matic / 16mm / VHS
Captioned; Color (P I J H)
LC 78-701989; 78-701988
Tells about an eight - year - old boy who dreams of being on Broadway a tap dancer, and the opposition he encounters from his father. Edited.
Fine Arts; Literature and Drama
Dist - LCOA **Prod** - LCOA 1978

Tap Dancing for Beginners 31 MIN
VHS
Color (G)
$19.95 purchase _ #1135
Presents dance lessons by Henry Le Tang, choreographer, tap choreographer and teacher of tap since 1937. Provides fitness benefits such as coordination, agility, timing and rhythm.
Agriculture; Fine Arts; Physical Education and Recreation; Science - Natural
Dist - KULTUR

Tap dancing for beginners 60 MIN
VHS
Color (G)
$39.95 purchase
Presents step - by - step instruction in tap dancing for beginners. Taught by Henri Le Tang, the choreographer of Sophisticated Ladies. Features a guest appearance by Honi Coles.
Fine Arts
Dist - PBS **Prod** - WNETTV

Tap dancing - intermediate and advanced 40 MIN
VHS
Color (J H A)
$19.95 purchase_#1307
Outlines a proven method for learning tap dancing with Broadway dancer Charles Goddertz. Includes full front, rear and wide-angled views, technique demonstrations and original tap choreography.
Physical Education and Recreation
Dist - KULTUR

Tap tape 73 MIN
VHS
Color (G)
$29.95 purchase
Presents step - by - step instruction in tap dancing for beginners. Includes special tap routines to allow viewers to practice their skills. Taught by Diane Davison and Georgie Tapps.
Fine Arts; Physical Education and Recreation
Dist - PBS **Prod** - WNETTV

The Tap tape
VHS
To your health series
Color (G)
$29.95 purchase _ #IV - 047
Teaches the basics of tap dancing.
Fine Arts; Physical Education and Recreation
Dist - INCRSE **Prod** - INCRSE

Tap the power of teamwork 45 MIN
VHS
Color (J H C G)
$79.00 purchase _ #CBR1048V
Shows employees what they must know - and do - to play on a winning team. Offers ideas on dealing with conflict on the job, how teamwork can improve customer service, using the double bottom line to win, handling hostile team members, boosting productivity, avoiding time wasting interruptions, using non - verbal signals, and more.
Business and Economics; Guidance and Counseling; Psychology; Social Science
Dist - CAMV

Tapas 25 MIN
16mm
Color (G)
$65.00 rental
Focuses on the Spanish Civil War through the voices and stories of various generations of refugees gone to America. Includes the poetry of Rosalia de Castro, a 19th - century Galician writer, to blend different historical events. Uses techniques of experimental cinema within a documentary format. Produced by Pia Cseri - Briones.
Fine Arts; History - World; Literature and Drama; Sociology
Dist - CANCIN

A Tape for Sam 15 MIN
VHS
Wediko series
Color (C G PRO)
$50.00 purchase, $16.00 rental _ #24268
Presents a videotape prepared by a Camp Wediko supervisor after more than six weeks of work with Sam, a 13 - year - old emotionally disturbed boy, which enabled Sam to view the tape during the winter away from camp to reinforce the positive behaviors he acquired during the summer months. Includes print material. Part of a series recording spontaneous behavior at Camp Wediko, a pioneer facility for therapeutic camping in Hillsboro, New Hampshire.
Health and Safety; Physical Education and Recreation; Psychology; Sociology
Dist - PSU **Prod** - MASON 1982

Tape Four - Communicating by phone, internal customers, special customers 29 MIN
VHS
You're hired - customer service for youth series
Color (H C A)
$149.00 purchase _ #10357VG
Teaches telephone communication skills, teamwork in customer service, and how to treat special customers such as seniors or children. Covers the fundamentals of customer service. Includes two videos, leader's guides and blackline masters. Part three of a three part series.
Psychology; Social Science
Dist - UNL

Tape Kit Windshield Installation with Exposed Wipers 28 MIN
BETA / VHS / 16mm
Color (A PRO)
$106.00 purchase _ #KTI31
Demonstrates windshield installation from wire cutout to pinch welt primer to tape installation.
Industrial and Technical Education
Dist - RMIBHF **Prod** - RMIBHF

Tape of 15 behavior sequences 30 MIN
VHS
Video training workshops on child variance series
Color (T PRO)
$135.00 purchase _ #M199m
Presents behavior sequences. Part of a six - part series produced by William C Morse and Judith M Smith.
Psychology; Sociology
Dist - CEXPCN **Prod** - CEXPCN

Tape placement and specialty production machinery 50 MIN
U-matic / BETA / VHS
Composites I the basics series
Color
$400 purchase
Presents a one phase tape placement machine for airframe structures.
Industrial and Technical Education; Science
Dist - ASM **Prod** - ASM

Tape Three - Handling problems 26 MIN
VHS
You're hired - customer service for youth series
Color (H C A)
$149.00 purchase _ #10356VG
Demonstrates techniques for handling customer service problems. Covers areas of objections, complaints and difficult customers. Presents the funadmentals of customer service. Includes two videos, leader's guides and blackline masters. Part two of a three - part series.
Psychology; Social Science
Dist - UNL

Tape Two - Customer expectations 25 MIN
VHS
You're hired - customer service for youth series
Color (H C A)
$149.00 purchase _ #10355VG
Features three typical failures in customer service and how to avoid them. Teaches the necessity of customer service and how to maintain the proper perspective. Includes tapes one and two, leader's guides and blackline masters. Part one of a three - part series.
Business and Economics; Psychology
Dist - UNL

Taper key, installation and removal 14 MIN
VHS / U-matic
Marshall maintenance training programs series; Tape 10
Color (IND)
Shows how to measure the keyway for correct size and taper, how the key is machined and how to fit the key for the best results. Demonstrates three different ways of removing a stubborn key.
Industrial and Technical Education
Dist - LEIKID **Prod** - LEIKID

Taper Key Installation and Removal 14 MIN
16mm
Color (IND)
Shows how to measure the keyway for correct size and taper, how the key is machined and how to fit the key for the best results. Demonstrates three different ways of removing a stubborn key.
Industrial and Technical Education
Dist - MOKIN **Prod** - MOKIN

Taper Turning 14 MIN
U-matic / VHS / 16mm
Vocational Skillfilms - Machine Shop Skills Series
Color (IND) (SPANISH)
Shows operation, application and limitations of the compound slide, taper turning attachment, form tools, free hand turning, profile turning attachment and offset tailstock.
Industrial and Technical Education
Dist - RTBL **Prod** - RTBL 1982

Taper Turning on the Lathe
VHS / U-matic
Basic Engine Lathe Series
Color (SPANISH)
Industrial and Technical Education
Dist - VTRI **Prod** - VTRI

Tapestry 25 MIN
U-matic / VHS
Craft of the Weaver Series
Color (J)
Portrays some of the work of the Edinburgh Tapestry Company. Presents the work of Fiona Mathison and Archie Brennan. Includes Coptic and Peruvian work from the Royal Scottish Museum.
Fine Arts
Dist - FI **Prod** - BBCTV 1983

Tapestry of the tropics - Barro Colorado Island and San Blas Island, Panama 24 MIN
16mm / VHS
Amateur naturalist series
Color (I J H C G)
$495.00, $195.00 purchase
Explores a tropical rain forest and tropical reef. Describes the survival strategies of several species - leaf cutter ants, howler monkeys, fig wasps and the three - toed sloth. Snorkels over a reef to display camouflage techniques of fish - the damsel fish and blue headed wrasse. Part of a 13 - part series featuring a naturalist and a zoologist, Gerald and Lee Durrell, on field trips to different habitats.
Geography - World; Science - Natural
Dist - LANDMK **Prod** - LANDMK 1988

Taping and Topcoating 25 MIN
VHS
Wallboard Series
Color (J H C A)
Reviews the steps to be followed to tape the wallboard and apply top and finish coats.
Home Economics; Industrial and Technical Education
Dist - COFTAB **Prod** - AMHOM 1985

Tapir distribution 15 MIN
VHS / 16mm
Yanomamo series
Color (G)
$270.00, $140.00 purchase, $30.00, $25.00 rental
Reveals that several days after the conflict chronicled in The Ax Fight disrupted the political stability of Mishimishmabowei - teri village, Moawa, the most prominent headman, killed a tapir and presented it to his brothers - in - law to reinforce his shaken alliance with them. Shows how the meat is prepared, cooked and distributed - choice meat to the most important men in the village, scraps and fat to the women and children, whatever is left to the dogs. Part of a series on the Yanomamo Indians of Venezuela by Timothy Asch and Napoleon Chagnon.
Geography - World; Social Science; Sociology
Dist - DOCEDR **Prod** - DOCEDR 1975

Tapping into your creativity 30 MIN
VHS
FYI video series
Color (H C G)
$79.95 purchase _ #AMA84002V
Uncovers simple devices to help open up the imagination with proven methods of unlocking innate intuition and playfulness. Part of a series on professional and personal skills for the workplace.
Business and Economics; Guidance and Counseling; Psychology
Dist - CAMV **Prod** - AMA 1991
MEMIND

Tapping out the source of change 42 MIN
VHS
Color; CC (IND)
$695.00 purchase, $250.00 rental _ #VTC04
Teaches basic steps toward making business changes. Contains two tapes and a facilitator's guide. Produced by Video Training, Inc.
Business and Economics
Dist - EXTR

Tapping the Source 18 MIN
16mm
Color
LC 78-701511
Traces the history of the Sun's role as a primary energy source. Includes interviews which reveal how solar power is used in providing energy for home use.
Science - Physical; Social Science
Dist - LILC **Prod** - LILC 1978

Tapping threads on the engine lathe 22 MIN
BETA / VHS
Machine shop - engine lathe series
Color (IND)
Industrial and Technical Education; Psychology
Dist - RMIBHF **Prod** - RMIBHF

Tar Baby 18 MIN
16mm
B&W
LC 76-701407
Shows the dynamics at work when three inner - city residents encounter each other and find their lives altered by that encounter.
Psychology; Social Science; Sociology
Dist - UMD **Prod** - UMD 1975

Tar beach - 81
VHS
Reading rainbow series
Color; CC (K P)
$39.95 purchase
Takes viewers up on the roof to a 'tar beach,' an urban oasis in the sky, in the story by Faith Ringgold, narrated by Ruby Dee. Celebrates life above the city in a profile of a pigeon keeper and a rooftop gardener and goes to new heights in a tribute to the George Washington Bridge. Part of a series offering a multicultural approach to generating reading enthusiasm with cross - curricular applications, hosted by LeVar Burton.
English Language; Geography - United States; Literature and Drama
Dist - GPN **Prod** - LNMDP

Tar Sands - Future Fuel 27 MIN
16mm
Energy Sources - a New Beginning Series
Color
Considers the practicality of the United States' development of tar sands deposits. Asks if the deposits are needed to supplement and thereby conserve conventional fuels.
Home Economics; Science - Natural
Dist - UCOLO **Prod** - UCOLO

Tara, the Stonecutter 8 MIN
U-matic / VHS / 16mm
Color (K P I) (SPANISH)
Presents a Japanese folktale of a poor stonecutter who desires to be emperor, the sun, the mountain and finally himself once again.
English Language; Literature and Drama
Dist - AIMS **Prod** - CAHILL 1955

The Tarahumara 15 MIN
VHS / U-matic
Across Cultures Series
Color (I)
Introduces the Tarahumara Indians of Mexico, an independent, hardworking people who live and farm in the mountain valleys and canyons. Shows that their isolation helps ensure stability and so they ask little of and extend little to the world beyond their mountains.
Geography - World; Social Science; Sociology
Dist - AITECH **Prod** - POSIMP 1983

The Tarahumara 30 MIN
16mm
Color (J H A)
LC 85-703553
Offers insight into the workings of the Tarahumara Indians of Mexico Shows the famous runners of Tarahumara.
History - World; Physical Education and Recreation; Social Science
Dist - EBEC **Prod** - BYU 1983

Taram - a Minangkabau Village 22 MIN
16mm
Asian Neighbors - Indonesia Series
Color (H C A)
LC 75-703587
Examines the matrilineal social structure of a Minangkabau village in Indonesia.
Geography - World; Social Science
Dist - AVIS **Prod** - FLMAUS 1975

Taras bulba 125 MIN
VHS
Color (G)
$24.95 purchase _ #S01818
Stars Yul Brynner and Tony Curtis in the Nikolai Gogol tale of the 16th century conflicts between Ukrainians and Poles. Centers on Cossack life and fighting.
Fine Arts; Literature and Drama
Dist - UILL

Tara's Mulch Garden 21 MIN
U-matic / VHS / 16mm
Color (J)
LC 76-703833
Explains the principle of mulching and demonstrates planting, transplanting, watering and harvesting. Discusses soil - testing and various ways of preserving vegetables.
Agriculture
Dist - WOMBAT **Prod** - NFBC 1976

Taraweeh at Makkah - Quran in the Haram
VHS
Color (G)
$19.95 purchase _ #110 - 029
Features Qari Al - Hudhaifi who leads taraweeh prayers in the last night of Ramadan in the Masjid al Haram at Makkah. Echoes the Quran gently around the holy precincts of the Kaba, with a moving Dua after prayers. The last 27 surahs are recited.
Religion and Philosophy
Dist - SOUVIS **Prod** - SOUVIS

Tarflowers 52 MIN
U-matic / VHS
Winners from Down Under Series
Color (K)
$349.00, $249.00 purchase _ #AD - 1359
Reveals that the problem with tarflowers is that not everyone can see them. Presents a magical story of Kevin and the community which loves and supports him, in contrast with the people from welfare. Part of an eight - part series on children's winning over their circumstances produced by the Australian Children's Television Foundation.

Fine Arts; Literature and Drama; Psychology
Dist - FOTH **Prod** - FOTH

Target - America
U-matic / VHS
CNN Special Reports
(J H C)
$129.00 purchase _ #31381 941, #31381 841
Discusses what the American government is doing to fight back and protect Americans at home and abroad from terrorism.
Civics and Political Systems; Sociology
Dist - ASPRSS **Prod** - TURNED CHUMAN

Target - America 30 MIN
U-matic / VHS
CNN Special Reports Series
(G J C)
$129 purchase _ #31381 - 851
Presents the contemporary issue of America and its citizens being the targets of terrorist organizations.
Sociology
Dist - CHUMAN

Target city hall 26 MIN
VHS / U-matic
Color (G)
Includes a wide range of commentary on the massive demonstration by ACTUP at New York's City Hall on March 28, 1989. Emphasizes the role of women in ACTUP - the AIDS Coalition To Unleash Power.
Health and Safety; History - United States; Sociology
Dist - ACTUP **Prod** - DIVATV 1990

Target Five 48 MIN
U-matic / VHS
Color
Demonstrates four manipulative response forms shown by a family situation. Describes the three essential qualities of an actualizing relationship.
Guidance and Counseling; Psychology
Dist - PSYCHF **Prod** - PSYCHF

Target Five, Pt 1 26 MIN
16mm
Color (C A)
LC 74-703169
Features psychologist Virginia Satir as she demonstrates the four manipulative response forms in cooperation with Everett L Shostron.
Guidance and Counseling; Psychology; Sociology
Dist - PSYCHF **Prod** - PSYCHF 1969

Target Five, Pt 2 22 MIN
16mm
Color (C A)
LC 74-703169
Provides a description of the three essential qualities of an actualizing relationship, hearing and listening, understanding and mutual meaning.
Guidance and Counseling; Psychology; Sociology
Dist - PSYCHF **Prod** - PSYCHF 1969

Target - for Antares 16 MIN
16mm
Color (J)
LC 78-700313
Uses micro - cinematography and animation to describe the fabrication of microscopic targets, which are used to generate energy through laser - fusion techniques.
Industrial and Technical Education; Religion and Philosophy
Dist - LASL **Prod** - LASL 1978

Target for Today 92 MIN
U-matic / VHS
B&W
Presents a detailed account of the operations of a bombing mission by the U S 8th Air Force from planning to execution. Features actual 8th Air Force personnel on location.
Civics and Political Systems; Education; History - United States
Dist - IHF **Prod** - IHF

Target for Tonight 50 MIN
U-matic / VHS
B&W
Views a single action of war, involving a Wellington bomber whose crew are ordered to Germany to destroy oil - storage tanks at Kiel during World War II.
History - World
Dist - IHF **Prod** - IHF

Target Markets 30 MIN
U-matic / VHS
Marketing Perspectives Series
Color
Explains 'market segmentation,' demographic factors which can be used for segmentation. Addresses psychographics and their relationship to the segmentation process.
Business and Economics; Education
Dist - WFVTAE **Prod** - MATC

Target Moon 24 MIN
16mm / U-matic / VHS
Man into Space - the Story of Rockets and Space Science Series
Color (I)
Presents a study of American and Russian attempts to reach the moon that emphasizes the physics and reasons for the effort. Reviews man's age - old striving to go to the moon, indicating how scientific curiosity and national rivalries have spurred it on. Focuses on the Apollo project.
History - United States; History - World; Science - Physical
Dist - AIMS **Prod** - ACI 1974

Target Moon 30 MIN
VHS / 16mm
Conquest of Space Series
Color (G)
Presents the scientific and technological difficulties of reaching the moon.
History - World; Industrial and Technical Education
Dist - FLMWST

Target Nevada 14 MIN
U-matic / VHS / 16mm
Color
Tells the story of the USAF support of the Atomic Energy Commission in atomic testing. Shows all phases of preparation, detonation and aftereffects of a nuclear test.
Civics and Political Systems; History - World; Science - Physical; Social Science; Sociology
Dist - USNAC **Prod** - USDD

Target Nicaragua - 1983 40 MIN
U-matic / VHS / 16mm
Color
Reports on a covert war carried out by the CIA against the Sandinista government of Nicaragua.
Civics and Political Systems; History - World; Sociology
Dist - NEWTIM **Prod** - STDC

Target - Pearl Harbor 70 MIN
VHS
Color (J H C G)
$39.95 purchase _ #JJ0152V
Offers a thorough and definitive account of the Pearl Harbor bombing which killed 2400 young American military personnel. Shows what actually happened, how it happened and why it happened. Interviews many survivors and includes historic footage and captured Japanese war film.
History - United States; History - World; Sociology
Dist - CAMV

Target - Quackery 12 MIN
VHS / U-matic
B&W
Discusses the first efforts to combat quack medicine in the treatment of arthritis. Includes footage from hearings held by the U S Senate in 1962.
Health and Safety
Dist - WSTGLC **Prod** - WSTGLC

Target Suribachi 27 MIN
16mm / U-matic / VHS
Victory at Sea Series
B&W (J H)
Shows the Battle for Iwo Jima during World War II.
Civics and Political Systems; History - United States; History - World
Dist - LUF **Prod** - NBCTV

Target Tokyo 22 MIN
16mm / U-matic / VHS
B&W
Follows the training of a B - 29 crew from the training center at Grand Island, NE, to a mission over Tokyo in World War II.
Civics and Political Systems; History - World
Dist - USNAC **Prod** - USAF

Target - Tokyo 30 MIN
VHS / U-matic
World War II - GI Diary Series
Color (H C A)
History - United States; History - World
Dist - TIMLIF **Prod** - TIMLIF 1980

Target within Range - the Key Role of the USAF Navigator 19 MIN
16mm
Color
Depicts the diversified mission of the USAF navigator who works around the clock and around the world to keep America's defensive and offensive power effectively poised.
Civics and Political Systems
Dist - USNAC **Prod** - USDD 1960

The Target Zone - Aiming for Whole Body Fitness 30 MIN
U-matic / VHS / 16mm
Color (A)
Explains how to design an optimum, aerobic conditioning program.
Physical Education and Recreation
Dist - PFP **Prod** - LISNDO 1984

Targeting Private Funding Sources - Foundations and Corporations 55 MIN
VHS / U-matic
Winning Grants
(A)
$1,795.00 member purchase, $1,995.00 non member purchase
Presents seminars on successful grant writing. Focuses on approaching private funding sources, corporations and foundations. Ninth in a series of ten.
Business and Economics; Education
Dist - GPN

Targets 19 MIN
16mm / U-matic / VHS
Anti - victimization series
Color (J H C)
Emphasizes that teenagers do not have to be alone when dealing with such personal problems as molestation, domestic violence, alcoholism or peer pressure.
Civics and Political Systems; Health and Safety; Sociology
Dist - CORF **Prod** - CORF

Tarjetas De Seguridad 18 MIN
16mm / U-matic / VHS
B&W (J) (SPANISH)
LC 72-707259
Presents a version of the motion picture It's In The Cards. Illustrates the importance of obeying rules of safety rather than depending on luck.
Health and Safety
Dist - IFB **Prod** - ABPPCO 1963

Tarnished Badge 24 MIN
U-matic / VHS / 16mm
Color
Details the downfall of an experienced sergeant who succumbs to the temptations of corruption. Looks at the consequences of the sergeant's act to his self - esteem, financial security, family, fellow officers and department.
Civics and Political Systems; Social Science
Dist - CORF **Prod** - WORON

Tarot - read your own 60 MIN
VHS
Color (G)
$29.95 purchase _ #V207
Teaches the meaning of the 78 cards in a tarot deck.
Religion and Philosophy
Dist - LIBSOR

Tarp 20 MIN
16mm
Color (H C A)
$40.00 rental
Explores the way Americans cover up and protect things and the strange locations in which they do it. Focuses on the basic visual themes of color, shape and "found object" filmmaking. Produced by Richard Myers.
Fine Arts; Sociology
Dist - CANCIN

Tarpon 22 MIN
16mm
Color
Looks at the behavior of tarpon and highlights the mysterious occurance known as daisy chaining.
Physical Education and Recreation; Science - Natural
Dist - KAROL **Prod** - BRNSWK

Tarsus, Jerusalem, Antioch - Tape 1 30 MIN
VHS
Paul - apostle to the nations series
Color (J H C G A R)
$39.95 purchase, $10.00 rental _ #35 - 860739 - 1
Considers the significance of the Apostle Paul's letters and sermons to the Christian church. Focuses on Paul's ministry in Tarsus, Jerusalem and Antioch. Filmed on location.
Literature and Drama; Religion and Philosophy
Dist - APH **Prod** - ABINGP

Tartar crusaders 45 MIN
VHS
Storm from the east
Color; PAL (C H)
PdS99 purchase; Not available in the United States or Pacific Rim countries
Covers the heyday of Mongol conquest. Includes the mission of John of Plano Carpini. Third in the four - part series Storm from the East, which presents the history of the Mongol empire.
Civics and Political Systems; History - World
Dist - BBCENE

Tartes Aux Fruits 29 MIN
Videoreel / VT2
French Chef Series
Color (FRENCH)
Features Julia Child of Haute Cuisine au Vin demonstrating how to prepare tartes aux fruits. With captions.
Home Economics
Dist - PBS **Prod** - WGBHTV

Tartuffe 110 MIN
VHS
Color (H C A)
$39.95 purchase
Features the Royal Shakespeare Company in a performance of 'Tartuffe' by Moliere. Stars Anthony Sher as Tartuffe.
Literature and Drama
Dist - PBS **Prod** - WNETTV

Tartuffe 140 MIN
VHS
Color (H C G) (FRENCH WITH SUBTITLES)
$109.00 purchase _ #DL391
Stars Gerard Depardieu and Francois Perier in Moliere's drama about religious and sexual hypocrisy, based on a stage production directed by Jacques Lasalle of the Theatre National de Strasbourg.
Fine Arts; History - World; Literature and Drama
Dist - INSIM

Tartuffe 71 MIN
16mm
B&W; Silent (GERMAN (GERMAN SUBTITLES))
Tells the story of Tartuffe, loosely based on Moliere's classical work of the same name.
Fine Arts; Foreign Language
Dist - WSTGLC **Prod** - WSTGLC

Tarzan Doesn't Live Here Anymore 60 MIN
U-matic
Africa File Series
Color (J H)
Examines the impressions of the film crew during their journey through Ghana, Dahomey, Niger and Nigeria.
Business and Economics; Geography - World; History - World
Dist - TVOTAR **Prod** - TVOTAR 1985

Tarzan of the Apes 66 MIN
16mm
B&W
Tells how an English infant is lost in the jungle and emerges as a brawny hero. Stars Elmo Lincoln.
Fine Arts
Dist - KITPAR **Prod** - UNKNWN 1918

The Tasaday - Stone Age People in a Space Age World 30 MIN
U-matic / VHS / 35mm strip
(J H C)
$109.00 purchase, $99.00 _ #07966 94, #07966 026
Uses on location photographs and tape recordings to document the Tasaday people, a small and isolated group of people living in a jungle island in the Philippines who maintain a Stone Age way of life. Traces the effects of modern civilization on their culture. In 2 parts.
History - World; Sociology
Dist - ASPRSS GA **Prod** - PATED

The Tasaday - stone age people in a space age world 30 MIN
VHS
Color (J H)
$99.00 _ #07966 - 026
Documents a group of people discovered on a Philippine island in 1971. Features tape recordings to illustrate their Stone Age way of life and trace the effects of modern civilization on their culture. Includes teacher's guide and library kit.
Education; Fine Arts; History - World; Sociology
Dist - GA

Tasha and the magic bubble 20 MIN
U-matic / 16mm / VHS
Color (P I)
$415.00, $315.00, $290.00 purchase _ #E051
Follows a little girl's fantastic journey floating through the air inside a magic bubble. Encourages children to use their imagination.
Literature and Drama
Dist - BARR **Prod** - CEPRO 1987

Task Analysis 16 MIN
VHS / 16mm
Teaching People with Developmental Disabilities Series
Color (A PRO)
$150.00 purchase, $55.00 rental _ #3125VHS
Demonstrates task analysis for teaching people with developmental disabilities.
Mathematics; Psychology
Dist - RESPRC **Prod** - OREGRI 1988

Task Centered Casework, Pt I 60 MIN
U-matic / VHS
Color
Consists of two role play sessions with a client and therapist. Provides suggestions for improving study habits of college students having problems with school.
Psychology; Sociology
Dist - UWISC **Prod** - UWASH

Task Centered Casework, Pt II 50 MIN
VHS / U-matic
Color
Presents two role play sessions between a therapist and client, who is not sure she wants to complete her pregnancy.
Psychology; Sociology
Dist - UWISC **Prod** - UWASH

Task - Centered Family Contracting Session with Jim Goetz 30 MIN
U-matic / VHS
B&W
Presents a contracting session with a marital couple in which the social worker explores potential target problems, arrives at an agreement on priority problems and beginning task work is developed.
Psychology; Sociology
Dist - UWISC **Prod** - UWISC 1979

Task Centered Interviews with a Phobic Client 30 MIN
VHS / U-matic
B&W
Consists of several short interviews with a phobic client who is afraid to go outside alone. Shows how the client progresses by following exercises prescribed by therapist.
Psychology; Sociology
Dist - UWISC **Prod** - UCHI 1976

Task - Centered Treatment with a Marital Couple 60 MIN
U-matic / VHS
Color
Presents a task - centered session with a marital couple. Develops tasks in an attempt to interrupt and change the identified cycle. Includes narration, charts of main points and a discussion by Prof Rooney.
Sociology
Dist - UWISC **Prod** - UWISC 1980

Task Descriptions - Task Analysis
VHS / U-matic
Learning System Design Series Unit 3
Color (T)
Education; Psychology
Dist - MSU **Prod** - MSU

Task force
VHS
Color (G)
$39.80 purchase _ #0462
Presents three parts on military sea power and attack carriers. Includes the titles 'Hook Down, Wheel Down,' 'Seapower - Plymouth Rock to Polaris,' 'The Rise of the Soviet Navy.'
Civics and Political Systems; History - United States; Physical Education and Recreation
Dist - SEVVID

Task Force South - the Battle for the Falklands 120 MIN
U-matic / VHS
Color (H C A)
$29.95 purchase _ #781 - 9006
Reveals the background which led to Britain's battle for the Falkland Islands, Britain's biggest and bloodiest military operation since World War II.
Civics and Political Systems; History - World
Dist - FI **Prod** - BBCTV 1982

Task of the Teacher 43 MIN
16mm
Color (T)
LC 73-703424
Illustrates and analyzes the qualities, talents, skills and techniques necessary for teachers in informal English schools. Shows children through age 12 in eight schools. Depicts buildings with modern open - plans and older structures in both suburban and urban settings. Describes team teaching, resource centers, individual and group studies and work with children of mixed abilities.
Education
Dist - AGAPR **Prod** - STOCKC 1973

Tasks of Teaching, Pt 1 30 MIN
VHS / U-matic
Protocol Materials in Teacher Education - the Process of Teaching, 'Pt 1 Series
Color (T)
Education; Psychology
Dist - MSU **Prod** - MSU

Tasks of Teaching, Pt 2 20 MIN
U-matic / VHS
Protocol Materials in Teacher Education - the Process of Teaching, 'Pt 1 Series
Color (T)
Education; Psychology
Dist - MSU **Prod** - MSU

Tasmania, Australia 18 MIN
16mm
Color
LC 80-801575
Describes the business potential and personal satisfaction that can be achieved by migrants establishing themselves in Tasmania.
Geography - World
Dist - TASCOR **Prod** - TASCOR 1980

The Tasmanian Devil 20 MIN
16mm
B&W (G)
$25.00 rental
Uses the cinema verite technique to create a documentary about the roadster automobile - the Tasmanian Devil - built for drag racing, and the men who built and raced it to a world record in the AA - A class.
Fine Arts; Industrial and Technical Education
Dist - CANCIN **Prod** - UNGRW 1964

Tasmanian Forests - Where and Why 7 MIN
16mm
Color
LC 80-700927
Features a variety of Tasmanian forests and explains why particular types of forests may be found in particular areas.
Agriculture; Geography - World; Science - Natural
Dist - TASCOR **Prod** - TASCOR 1976

Tasmanian Military Tattoo 28 MIN
16mm
Color
LC 80-700928
Presents a record of Tasmania's first Tattoo which was modeled on the Edinburgh Tattoo.
Fine Arts; Geography - World
Dist - TASCOR **Prod** - TASCOR 1976

Tasmanian silent films 18 MIN
16mm
Color (G)
$30.00 rental
Concerns itself with exoticism, unemployment, Tasmania and tourism. Alternates still images with text created on a dining room table. Includes Tasmania - the last wilderness; The Vision; and Justice Finds its Own Reward.
Fine Arts
Dist - CANCIN **Prod** - SONDHE 1983

Tassili N'ajjer - Prehistoric Rock Paintings of the Sahara (Neolithic - 2000 BC) 16 MIN
16mm
Color
Presents prehistoric rock paintings of the Sahara Desert from the Neolothic period to 2000 BC.
Fine Arts; History - World
Dist - ROLAND **Prod** - ROLAND

Taste of America series
VHS
Frugal gourmet cooking series
Color (G)
$169.00 purchase _ #CCP827
Presents a ten - part series on American cooking. Features Jeff Smith, the Frugal Gourmet. Includes Early American, New England, Southwestern, the American breakfast, Philadelphia, Southern, Colonial, Pennsylvania Dutch, Shaker and New Orleans dishes.
History - United States; Home Economics; Physical Education and Recreation
Dist - CADESF **Prod** - CADESF

Taste of China, Pt 5 - Buffet of Chinese Food 38 MIN
U-matic / VHS
Taste of China Series
Color (J)
Presents Kenneth Lo, foremost authority on Chinese food, assisted by gourmet personality Vincent Price and well - known Chinese chefs preparing and serving a complete Chinese meal.
Home Economics
Dist - MEDIAG **Prod** - THAMES 1983

Taste of China, Pt 4 - Chicken and Duck 38 MIN
U-matic / VHS
Taste of China Series

Color (J)
Presents Kenneth Lo, a foremost authority on Chinese food, assisted by gourmet personality Vincent Price and well - known Chinese chefs preparing and serving a complete Chinese meal.
Home Economics
Dist - MEDIAG **Prod** - THAMES 1983

Taste of China, Pt 1 - Rice 38 MIN
U-matic / VHS
Taste of China Series
Color (J)
Presents Kenneth Lo, a foremost authority on Chinese food, assisted by gourmet personality Vincent Price and well - known Chinese chefs preparing and serving a complete Chinese meal.
Home Economics
Dist - MEDIAG **Prod** - THAMES 1983

Taste of China - Pt 3 - meal and fish 38 MIN
VHS / U-matic
Taste of China series
Color (J)
Presents Kenneth Lo, a foremost authority on Chinese food, assisted by gourmet personality Vincent Price and well - known Chinese chefs preparing and serving a complete Chinese meal.
Home Economics
Dist - MEDIAG **Prod** - THAMES 1983

Taste of china - Pt 2 - noodles 38 MIN
VHS / U-matic
Taste of china series
Color (J)
Presents Kenneth Lo, a foremost authority on Chinese food, assisted by gourmet personality Vincent Price and well - known Chinese chefs preparing and serving a complete Chinese meal.
Home Economics
Dist - MEDIAG **Prod** - THAMES 1983

Taste of China Series
Taste of China - Pt 3 - meal and fish 38 MIN
Taste of china - Pt 2 - noodles 38 MIN
Taste of China, Pt 5 - Buffet of Chinese Food 38 MIN
Taste of China, Pt 4 - Chicken and Duck 38 MIN
Taste of China, Pt 1 - Rice 38 MIN
Dist - MEDIAG

Taste of China series
Presents a four - part series on traditional Chinese cuisine. Includes the titles Masters of the Wok, Food for Body and Spirit, The Family Table, Water Farmers.
The Family table 29 MIN
Food for body and spirit 29 MIN
Masters of the Wok 29 MIN
Water farmers 29 MIN
Dist - UCEMC **Prod** - YUNGLI 1983

The Taste of democracy 58 MIN
VHS / U-matic / BETA
Inside Gorbachev's USSR series
Color (H C A)
$125.00 purchase _ #JY - 6268C
Captures the exhilaration of reform and renewal as Soviet President Mikhail Gorbachev attempts to transform a political system shaped by decades of terror and stagnation. Examines the revolutionary nature of the new democratic parliament of the USSR and the power struggles within this new Congress. Considers the disintegration of the Communist party. Part of a four - part series narrated by Hedrick Smith on the clash of modernization with Soviet tradition.
Civics and Political Systems; Geography - World; History - World; Sociology
Dist - CORF **Prod** - WGBHTV 1990

A Taste of freedom 45 MIN
VHS
Color (G A)
$29.95 purchase _ #TNO105OE
Portrays the growing spirit of freedom in the Soviet Union, begun in the late 1980s, as 'glasnost' and 'perestroika' reforms have lifted some totalitarian practices in that country.
Civics and Political Systems; History - World; Social Science
Dist - TMM **Prod** - TMM

The Taste of new wine - Part 1
VHS
Keith Miller - new wine series
Color (H C G A R)
$10.00 rental _ #36 - 87401 - 533
Proposes the theory that living one's faith can provide good opportunities for evangelism. Based on the Keith Miller book 'A Taste of New Wine.'
Religion and Philosophy
Dist - APH **Prod** - WORD

A Taste of Paradise 26 MIN
16mm
Color
Tells the history of the pineapple and how it is planted, cultivated and harvested in Hawaii. Highlights the discovery of pineapple by Columbus, its introduction to the western world and the development of the Hawaiian pineapple.
Agriculture; History - United States; Home Economics
Dist - MTP **Prod** - PGAOH 1982

Taste, Smell, Hearing 29 MIN
U-matic
Understanding Human Behavior - an Introduction to Psychology Series 'Lesson 7
Color (C A)
Compares senses of taste, smell, and hearing. Describes functions and physiology of these senses with special attention to hearing. Shows footage of sound waves.
Psychology; Science - Natural
Dist - CDTEL **Prod** - COAST

Tasteful Romance 6 MIN
16mm
Color
LC 79-700291
Uses animation to create comedy, romance and adventure around a boy - meets - girl theme in a fantasy candyland inhabited by two walking lip characters.
Fine Arts
Dist - COLCLI **Prod** - COLCLI 1978

Tasteless trilogy 16 MIN
16mm
B&W (G)
$35.00 rental
Gives a good example of McDowell's interest in motion picture plots that are gripping but go nowhere, seemingly random.
Fine Arts
Dist - CANCIN **Prod** - MCDOWE

The Tastemakers 26 MIN
U-matic / VHS
Color (C)
$249.00, $149.00 purchase _ #AD - 1894
Focuses on foods created by scientists. Visits the General Foods Research Lab. Shows scientists creating foods with new flavors, tastes and textures, imitating 'natural' ingredients with artificial, convenient and affordable compounds.
Health and Safety; Psychology; Science - Natural; Social Science
Dist - FOTH **Prod** - FOTH

Tasting and Smelling 20 MIN
16mm
All that I Am Series
B&W (C A)
Fine Arts; Guidance and Counseling; Psychology
Dist - NWUFLM **Prod** - MPATI

Tasting Party 4 MIN
16mm / U-matic / VHS
Most Important Person - Nutrition Series
Color (K P I)
Views Fumble, bird and the children enjoying blueberry blintzes, tacos, ravioli and stuffed peppers.
Guidance and Counseling; Health and Safety; Home Economics; Social Science
Dist - EBEC **Prod** - EBEC 1972

Tatara - an old iron making process of Japan 30 MIN
16mm
Color
Explains that the word 'Tatara' was recorded as early as the 8th Century, referring to the traditional process of making iron and steel from iron sand with charcoal. Advocates that this process still produces excellent iron and steel.
Business and Economics; Geography - World
Dist - UNIJAP **Prod** - IWANMI 1970

Tater Tomator 15 MIN
16mm
New Directions Series
Color (G)
Presents an independent production by Phil Morrison. Part of a comic series of first film shorts.
Fine Arts; Literature and Drama
Dist - FIRS

The Tatooed man 35 MIN
16mm
Color (G)
$50.00 rental
Fuses short dreamy moments together by using the tension of motion - picture time. Composes a death - haunted dream of color and imagery. Produced by Storm De Hirsch.
Fine Arts
Dist - CANCIN

Tatort series - Abendstern 89 MIN
16mm
Tatort series
Color (GERMAN)
Features Inspector Haferkamp trying to solve a murder case complicated by the prime suspect's wife's clumsy attempt to clear him of the accusations. An episode from the television series Tatort.
Foreign Language; Literature and Drama; Sociology
Dist - WSTGLC **Prod** - WSTGLC 1976

Tatort series - Acht Jahre Spaeter 95 MIN
16mm
Tatort series
Color (GERMAN)
Discloses that Inspector Haferkamp may be in danger because an ex - convict, whose brother Haferkamp had killed, has sworn revenge on him and on a former mistress. An episode from the television series Tatort.
Foreign Language; Literature and Drama; Sociology
Dist - WSTGLC **Prod** - WSTGLC 1974

Tatort series - AE 612 Ohne Landeerlaubnis 107 MIN
16mm
Tatort series
Color (GERMAN)
A German language motion picture Pursues an airplane flight leading to the capture of a terrorist who was responsible for the death of the hero's wife. An episode from the television series Tatort.
Sociology
Dist - WSTGLC **Prod** - WSTGLC 1977

Tatort series - blechschaden 113 MIN
16mm
Tatort series - blechschaden
Color (GERMAN)
Features Inspector Finke resolving a complicated case involving adultery, disloyalty, blackmail, intrigue, fears, and finally murder. An episode from the television series Tatort.
Fine Arts
Dist - WSTGLC **Prod** - WSTGLC 1977

Tatort series - blechschaden
Tatort series - blechschaden 113 MIN
Dist - WSTGLC

Tatort series - Die Abrechnung 87 MIN
16mm
Tatort series
Color (GERMAN)
Features Inspector Haferkamp, who suspects a woman of having killed her father - in - law but whose evidence is torn apart by a friend of the murdered man at the first trial. An episode from the television series Tatort.
Foreign Language; Literature and Drama; Sociology
Dist - WSTGLC **Prod** - WSTGLC 1975

Tatort series - Eine Todsichere Sache 92 MIN
16mm
Tatort series
Color (GERMAN)
Shows Inspector Konrad tracking down a kidnapper. An episode from the television series Tatort.
Foreign Language; Literature and Drama; Sociology
Dist - WSTGLC **Prod** - WSTGLC 1973

Tatort series - Kurzschluss 94 MIN
16mm
Tatort series - Kurzschluss
Color (GERMAN)
Presents Police Sergeant Freidall as a victim of blackmail by the bank robber he has under investigation. An episode from the television series Tatort.
Literature and Drama; Sociology
Dist - WSTGLC **Prod** - WSTGLC 1977

Tatort series - Kurzschluss
Tatort series - Kurzschluss 94 MIN
Dist - WSTGLC

Tatort series - Platzverweis Fuer Trimmell 105 MIN
16mm
Tatort series
Color (GERMAN)
Features Inspector Paul Timmell trying to discover the true identity of a corpse found at a soccer stadium and a possible connection with the scandal surrounding the national soccer league. An episode from the television series Tatort.
Literature and Drama; Sociology
Dist - WSTGLC **Prod** - WSTGLC 1977

Tatort series - Reifezeugnis 117 MIN
16mm
Tatort series
Color (GERMAN)
Tells a story of love, jealousy, and death. An episode from the television series Tatort. Stars Nastassja Kinski.

Foreign Language; Literature and Drama; Sociology
Dist - WSTGLC **Prod** - WSTGLC 1976

Tatort series - Tod Eines Einbrechers 85 MIN
16mm
Tatort series
Color
Indicates Inspector Gerber's unusual capability of consolidating facts in his investigation of the blackmail of a married woman whose lover kills a burglar in her villa while her husband is away.
Literature and Drama; Sociology
Dist - WSTGLC **Prod** - WSTGLC 1975

Tatort series - wodka bitter lemon 94 MIN
16mm
Tatort series
Color (GERMAN)
Focuses on Inspector Haferkamp's investigation of a murder case in which all the evidence points to the prime suspect, but no motive is apparent. An episode from the television series Tatort.
Foreign Language; Literature and Drama; Sociology
Dist - WSTGLC **Prod** - WSTGLC 1974

Tatort series - Zwei Leben 97 MIN
16mm
Tatort series
Color (GERMAN)
A German language motion picture. Focuses on a former prosecution witness against the Mafia who is forced to kill a Mafia member in self - defense. An episode from the television series Tatort.
Foreign Language; Literature and Drama; Sociology
Dist - WSTGLC **Prod** - WSTGLC 1975

Tatort Series - Zweikampf 97 MIN
16mm
Tatort Series - Zweikampf
Color (GERMAN)
Traces Inspector Haferkamp's tracking down of, and legal battle with, a kidnap and blackmail suspect. An episode from the television series Tatort.
Foreign Language; Literature and Drama; Sociology
Dist - WSTGLC **Prod** - WSTGLC 1973

Tatort Series - Zweikampf
Tatort Series - Zweikampf 97 MIN
Dist - WSTGLC

Tatort series
Tatort series - Abendstern 89 MIN
Tatort series - Acht Jahre Spaeter 95 MIN
Tatort series - AE 612 Ohne Landeerlaubnis 107 MIN
Tatort series - Die Abrechnung 87 MIN
Tatort series - Eine Todsichere Sache 92 MIN
Tatort series - Platzverweis Fuer Trimmell 105 MIN
Tatort series - Reifezeugnis 117 MIN
Tatort series - Tod Eines Einbrechers 85 MIN
Tatort series - wodka bitter lemon 94 MIN
Tatort series - Zwei Leben 97 MIN
Dist - WSTGLC

Tatting, Hairpin Lace and Broomstick Lace 52 MIN
BETA / VHS
Color (G)
$39.95 purchase _ #VT1055
Explains how to tat with heavy or fine cord and string. Describes the proper way to thread a shuttle and how to make a shawl, blanket and belt.
Fine Arts; Home Economics
Dist - RMIBHF **Prod** - RMIBHF

Tatting, Hairpine Lace and Broomstick Lace 52 MIN
VHS / BETA
Crafts and Decorating Series
Color
Shows how to tat with heavy or fine cord and string. Demonstrates the proper way to thread a shuttle. Shows how to make a shawl, blanket and belt.
Fine Arts; Home Economics
Dist - MOHOMV **Prod** - MOHOMV

Tattle 30 MIN
VHS
Color (I J H)
$345.00 purchase _ #B058 - V8
Asks 'when should friends tell on friends.' Reveals that when two members of a championship swim team become addicted to cocaine, the other members must decide whether or not to tell. Argues that chemical dependency is dangerous, and the best way to protect a friend in trouble is to get help as soon as possible. Stimulates discussion in grades 7 - 12.
Guidance and Counseling; Psychology
Dist - ETRASS **Prod** - ETRASS 1989

Tattoo 26 MIN
16mm
Color
LC 79-700292
Explores reasons for the popularity of tattoos and examines the American subculture associated with tattooing and heavily tattooed people.
Psychology; Sociology
Dist - DECDER **Prod** - DECDER 1979

Tattooed lady 14 MIN
16mm
Color (G)
$30.00 rental
Recalls an encounter with the tattooed lady at an old amusement park in Chicago. Sets the story against the park's atmosphere from morning to night as a beautiful love affair between the tatooed lady and the sword swallower unfolds.
Fine Arts; Literature and Drama; Religion and Philosophy
Dist - CANCIN **Prod** - PALAZT

The Tattooed Man 35 MIN
16mm
Color
Presents an underground art film about the children of the water and the tattooed man.
Fine Arts
Dist - IMPACT **Prod** - IMPACT

Tattooed Tears 85 MIN
16mm / U-matic / VHS
Color (H C A)
Looks inside a California youth detention center and training school. Captures the oppressive daily routine and encounters between inmates and their guardians. Raises questions about the presumed goal of rehabilitation or the system's ability to cause any real change in such alienated young men.
Sociology
Dist - CF **Prod** - CF 1978

Tatyana Mamonova, Russian Feminist 60 MIN
U-matic
Color
Introduces Tatyana Mamonova, Russian Feminist on her visit to Canada. She answers questions about her life and the condition of women in the Soviet Union.
Sociology
Dist - WMENIF **Prod** - AMELIA

Tatyana Zaslavskaya 40 MIN
VHS
Women in politics series
Color (G)
$60.00 rental, $99.00 purchase
Focuses on Tatyana Zaslavskaya, the inventor of perestroika and one of Gorbachov's closest advisors. Looks at how she played an active role in the second major revolution in Russian society in this century. Part of a six part series of documentaries profiling women politicians. Produced by Lowri Gwilym.
Civics and Political Systems; Fine Arts; History - World
Dist - WMEN

The Taurus - Gulf Trade incident 3 MIN
16mm
B&W
LC FIE52-946
Describes the collision of the Gulf Trade and the Taurus and the causes of the accident.
Civics and Political Systems; Health and Safety; History - United States; Social Science
Dist - USNAC **Prod** - USN 1944

tausendjahrekino 3 MIN
16mm
Color (H C A)
$15.00 rental
Features a short film produced by Kurt Kren with sound from the film Der Verlorene by Peter Lorre.
Fine Arts; Industrial and Technical Education
Dist - CANCIN

Tauu - En Atoll I Stillehavet (Tauu - an Atoll in the Pacific) 32 MIN
16mm
Color
A Danish langauge film. Portrays the daily life of the population on Tauu, a Pacific atoll. Shows how different articles are manufactured for local use.
Foreign Language; Geography - World
Dist - STATNS **Prod** - STATNS 1967

Tauw 27 MIN
16mm
Color
LC 77-711517
A study of the new generation in Africa as evidenced in the life of 20 - year - old Tauw. Demonstrates the young man's hopes and frustrations, the gap between his life style and that of his parents and his struggle with the realities of life in a developing nation. Filmed in Dakar.
Geography - World; History - World; Social Science; Sociology
Dist - CCNCC **Prod** - CCNCC 1970

A Tavern Celebration 15 MIN
16mm
Rudolf Nureyev's Film of Don Quixote Series
Color
LC 78-701880
Fine Arts
Dist - SF **Prod** - WRO 1978

Tawny Scrawny Lion 6 MIN
U-matic / VHS / 16mm
Golden Book Storytime Films Series
Color (P)
Relates the story of how a scrawny, irritable lion learns how to be healthy and happy from a rabbit.
Literature and Drama
Dist - CORF **Prod** - CORF 1977

Tawny Scrawny Lion 7 MIN
16mm / U-matic / VHS
Color (K P)
LC 75-700397
Presents a story about how a proud, fat, little rabbit helps his animal friends by outwitting a hungry, tawny, scrawny lion. Shows that through the things he does, the little rabbit not only makes a friend of the lion but also finds a way to satisfy the lion's hunger. Emphasizes that it is not one's size that is important but rather it is the quality of thinking and doing that counts.
Guidance and Counseling; Literature and Drama
Dist - BARR **Prod** - WPES 1974

Tax aspects of divorce with professor Frank E A Aander - Pt 1 52 MIN
U-matic / VHS
NPI video CLE series vol 6
Color (PRO)
LC 80-706567
Examines income, estate and gift tax problems arising from marriage dissolution or separation, including alimony and separate maintenance, child support, transfers of property and use of alimony trusts.
Civics and Political Systems; Sociology
Dist - NPRI **Prod** - NPRI 1978

Tax aspects of divorce with Professor Frank E A Sander - Pt 2 52 MIN
U-matic / VHS
NPI video CLE series Vol 6
Color (PRO)
LC 80-706567
Examines income, estate and gift tax problems arising from marriage dissolution or separation, including alimony and separate maintenance, child support, transfers of property and use of alimony trusts.
Civics and Political Systems; Sociology
Dist - NPRI **Prod** - NPRI 1978

Tax aspects of divorce with Professor Frank E A Sander - Pt 3 53 MIN
VHS / U-matic
NPI video CLE series Vol 6
Color (PRO)
LC 80-706567
Examines income, estate and gift tax problems arising from marriage dissolution or separation, including alimony and separate maintenance, child support, transfers of property and use of alimony trusts.
Civics and Political Systems; Sociology
Dist - NPRI **Prod** - NPRI 1978

Tax aspects of divorce with Professor Frank E A Sander - Pt 4 53 MIN
VHS / U-matic
NPI video CLE series Vol 6
Color (PRO)
LC 80-706567
Examines income, estate and gift tax problems arising from marriage dissolution or separation, including alimony and separate maintenance, child support, transfers of property and use of alimony trusts.
Civics and Political Systems; Sociology
Dist - NPRI **Prod** - NPRI 1978

Tax - exempt organizations 14 MIN
VHS / U-matic
Tax tips on tape series
Color; Captioned (A PRO IND)
$20.00, $40.00 purchase _ #TCA17597, #TCA17596
Discusses tax law for tax - exempt organizations. Covers the differences between taxable and non - taxable activities for such organizations. Explains the new rules which restrict political activities by tax - exempt organizations.
Business and Economics; Civics and Political Systems; Social Science; Sociology
Dist - USNAC **Prod** - USIRS 1988

Tax planning for individuals and businesses under OBRA 1990 50 MIN
VHS
Color (C PRO A)
$95.00 purchase _ #Y138
Discusses the impact on individuals and businesses of the deficit - reduction measure passed by Congress in November 1990.
Civics and Political Systems
Dist - ALIABA **Prod** - CLETV 1990

Tax practitioners' analysis of the Revenue Reconciliation Act of 1993 270 MIN
VHS
Color (A PRO C)
$185.00, $230.00 purchase _ #M107, #P292
Provides a concise overview and analysis of the major provisions of the Revenue Reconciliation Act of 1993 in a program cosponsored by the ABA Section of Taxation.
Civics and Political Systems
Dist - ALIABA **Prod** - ALIABA 1993

Tax Reform Act of 1984 - Overview 30 MIN
U-matic / VHS
Tax Reform Act of 1984 Series
Color (PRO)
Business and Economics; Civics and Political Systems; Social Science
Dist - ALIABA **Prod** - ALIABA

Tax Reform Act of 1984 Series
Accounting, deferred payments, time value of money and related party transactions 30 MIN
Corporate Provisions - Subchapter C 30 MIN
Domestic relations 30 MIN
Foreign tax 30 MIN
Fringe benefits and cafeteria plans 30 MIN
Government and tax - exempt entity leasing 30 MIN
IDB's 30 MIN
Insurance 30 MIN
Partnerships 30 MIN
Provisions Affecting Qualified Plans 30 MIN
Tax Reform Act of 1984 - Overview 30 MIN
Tax Shelters 30 MIN
VEBA's 30 MIN
Dist - ALIABA

The Tax Reform Act of 1986 - Changes Affecting Accounting Procedures, Tax Exempt Bonds 210 MIN
Cassette / U-matic / VHS
Color (PRO)
$150.00, $45.00 purchase _ #P192, #M675
Presents private attorneys and current and former staff of the federal government who helped draft the Tax Reform Act Of 1986 as they discuss various significant changes wrought by this landmark legislation. Covers fiscal year to calendar year change, effect on installment sales, simplified LIPO for small businesses. Also reviews impact on private activity and government bonds and the effect on information reporting and bank interest deductions. Includes three audiocassettes or one videocassette and study material for complete 3.5 - hour program.
Business and Economics; Civics and Political Systems; Social Science
Dist ALIABA **Prod** - ALIABA 1987

The Tax Reform Act of 1986 - Changes Affecting Business Enterprises, Foreign Taxation 210 MIN
Cassette / U-matic / VHS
Color (PRO)
$150.00, $45.00 purchase _ #P194, #M677
Examines alternative minimum tax, corporations, partnerships, small business, ACRS, and repeal of investment tax credit. Also reviews foreign tax credit provisions, US shareholders of foreign corporations, foreign currency exchange and technical corrections to the Tax Reform Act of 1984. Includes three audiocassettes or one videocassette for complete 3.5 hour program.
Business and Economics; Civics and Political Systems; Social Science
Dist - ALIABA **Prod** - ALIABA 1987

The Tax Reform Act of 1986 - changes affecting corporations 210 MIN
Cassette / U-matic / VHS
Color (PRO)
$150.00, $45.00 purchase _ #P191, #M674
Presents private attorneys and current and former staff of the federal government who helped draft the Tax Reform Act of 1986 as they discuss various significant changes wrought by this landmark legislation. Topics include the alternative minimum tax, section 382 'change of ownership,' repeal of the General Utilities doctrine, and impact on Subchapter S and C Corporations. Includes three audiocassettes or one videocassette and study materials for complete 3.5 - hour program.
Business and Economics; Civics and Political Systems; Social Science
Dist - ALIABA **Prod** - ALIABA 1987

The Tax Reform Act of 1986 - changes affecting individual taxpayers, estates and trusts, generation skipping 210 MIN
Cassette / U-matic / VHS
Color (PRO)
$150.00, $45.00 purchase _ #P190, #M673
Presents private attorneys and current and former staff of the federal government who helped draft the Tax Reform Act of 1986 as they discuss various significant changes wrought by this landmark legislation. Topics range from changes in basic rate structure to alternative minimum tax, as well as 'kiddie tax,' section 212 expenses and generation skipping. Includes three audiocassettes or one videocassette for complete 3.5 hour program.
Business and Economics; Civics and Political Systems; Social Science
Dist - ALIABA **Prod** - ALIABA 1987

The Tax Reform Act of 1986 - changes affecting pensions and compensation matters 210 MIN
Cassette / U-matic / VHS
Color (PRO)
$150.00, $45.00 purchase _ #P193, #M676
Presents private attorneys and current and former staff of the federal government who helped draft the Tax Reform Act of 1986 as they discuss various significant changes wrought by this landmark legislation. Topics range from changes affecting IRAs and 401(k)s to technical amendments to the Retirement Equity Act (RCA). Includes three audiocassettes or one videocassette and study materials for complete 3.5 - hour program.
Business and Economics; Civics and Political Systems; Social Science; Sociology
Dist - ALIABA **Prod** - ALIABA 1987

The Tax Reform Act of 1986 - changes affecting real estate and tax shelters 210 MIN
Cassette / U-matic / VHS
Color (PRO)
$150.00, $45.00 purchase _ #P189, #M672
Presents private attorneys and current and former staff of the federal government who helped draft the Tax Reform Act of 1986 as they discuss various significant changes wrought by this landmark legislation. Topics range from accelerated cost recovery systems (ACRS) to real estate investment trusts (REITs). Includes three audiocassettes or one videocassette and study materials for complete 3.5 - hour program.
Business and Economics; Civics and Political Systems; Social Science
Dist - ALIABA **Prod** - ALIABA 1987

Tax - saving strategies 30 MIN
VHS / U-matic
Personal finance series lesson 26
Color (C A)
Presents some of the more common strategies that can be used to minimize the amount of federal income tax that must be paid. Includes tax exempt and tax-deferred income, income splitting and tax shelters. Explores procedures for filing tax returns and surviving an audit.
Business and Economics
Dist - CDTEL **Prod** - SCCON

Tax Saving Strategies 28 MIN
VHS / U-matic
Personal Finance and Money Management Series
Color (C A)
Business and Economics; Civics and Political Systems
Dist - SCCON **Prod** - SCCON 1987

Tax Shelters 30 MIN
U-matic / VHS
Tax Reform Act of 1984 Series
Color (PRO)
Presents questions on tax shelters as affected by the Tax Reform Act of 1984 with answers by the individuals from government who developed the legislation.
Business and Economics; Civics and Political Systems; Social Science
Dist - ALIABA **Prod** - ALIABA

Tax tips on tape series
Presents a 15 - part series on taxation. Targets each program to a particular group - children with income, clergy, fishermen, medical personnel, and many others. Provides information on what records to keep and what forms must be filed. Tells how to get free information and advice from the IRS.
Children with income 14 MIN
Clergy 14 MIN
Daycare providers 14 MIN
Educators 14 MIN
Farmers 14 MIN
Fisherman 14 MIN
Medical personnel 14 MIN
Military 14 MIN
Moonlighters 14 MIN
Municipal and civil servants 14 MIN
Older Americans 14 MIN
Overseas taxpayers 14 MIN
People who move 14 MIN
Tax - exempt organizations 14 MIN
Tip income 14 MIN
Dist - USNAC **Prod** - USIRS

Taxation 11 MIN
16mm
Running Your Own Business Series
Color
Shows that with proper planning and record keeping, a businessman can avoid paying more taxes that the law intends.
Business and Economics
Dist - EFD **Prod** - EFD

Taxation 10 MIN
U-matic
Calling Captain Consumer Series
Color (P I J)
Outlines the purpose of taxation, the responsibilities of taxpayers and problems that confront governments in making decisions.
Business and Economics; Civics and Political Systems; Home Economics
Dist - TVOTAR **Prod** - TVOTAR 1985

Taxation 30 MIN
VHS / U-matic
Making government work
(H)
Uses dramatizations and interviews to familiarize high school students with the functions of government. Focuses on taxation.
Civics and Political Systems
Dist - GPN

Taxation and Public Policy 30 MIN
U-matic / VHS
Accounting Series; Pt 9
Color (C)
Discusses taxation and public policy.
Business and Economics; Guidance and Counseling
Dist - GPN **Prod** - UMA 1980

Taxation - what and When 30 MIN
VHS / U-matic
This is My will Series
Color
Presents a comprehensive look at the wide variety of taxes from estate tax to tax on capital gains. Also looks at tax exclusions and deductibles, required taxes and post - mortem tax planning.
Business and Economics; Social Science; Sociology
Dist - PBS **Prod** - WMHTTV 1983

Taxation without representation 16 MIN
U-matic / VHS / 16mm
American history - birth of a nation series; No 2
Color (I)
$69.95 purchase _ $1802; #501508; LC FIA68-1116
Shows the Colonial American merchants' refusal to trade with Britain after Grenville initiated the Sugar and Stamp Acts. Discusses the Townshend Acts and Boston under military rule.
History - United States
Dist - AIMS **Prod** - CAHILL 1967
UILL

Taxco 56 MIN
U-matic / VHS
Color (C) (SPANISH)
$279.00, $179.00 purchase _ #AD - 2180
Focuses on Taxco, a mining town in Mexico's mountains. Looks at its silver mines and industry and architecture.
Geography - World; History - World; Industrial and Technical Education; Social Science
Dist - FOTH **Prod** - FOTH

Taxco - Village of Art 17 MIN
U-matic / VHS / 16mm
Color
Shows the home life of the people and their market place activities. Emphasis is given their handicrafts of basket making and silver work. Modern application of Aztec designs to costume jewelry is depicted.
Fine Arts; Geography - World
Dist - MCFI **Prod** - HOE 1957

Taxes 30 MIN
U-matic
Adam Smith's money world series; 101
Color (A)
Attempts to demystify the world of money and break it down so that a small business and its employees understand

and adjust to new social and economic trends. Reports on the major economic stories and discoveries of the day.
Business and Economics
Dist - PBS **Prod** - WNETTV 1985

Taxes 27 MIN
U-matic / VHS
How to be more Successful in Your Own Business Series
Color (G)
$279.00, $179.00 purchase _ #AD - 2007
Explains some basics of tax accounting for small business owners. Features Donald C Alexander, former Commissioner and Director of IRS. Part of an eight - part series on successful business management moderated by David Susskind.
Business and Economics
Dist - FOTH **Prod** - FOTH

Taxes and Services - who Pays 28 MIN
U-matic
Color (A)
Gives an account of the efforts of citizens and workers in Hawaii, California and Maryland to equalize tax burdens. Followed by a discussion.
Business and Economics; Civics and Political Systems
Dist - AFLCIO **Prod** - LIPA 1984

Taxes in US History Series
Fairness and the Income Tax - 1892 - 1913 - 3 15 MIN
The First federal taxes - 1787 - 1794 - Part 1 15 MIN
The Protective Tariff Issue - 1816 - 1833 - Pt 2 15 MIN
Teacher Program 15 MIN
Dist - AITECH

Taxes, Taxes 27 MIN
U-matic / VHS / 16mm
Color
Discusses the U S tax system including who pays, how much and the possibilities of reform.
Civics and Political Systems
Dist - MRMKF **Prod** - SCHLP 1978

Taxes - who Needs Them 25 MIN
16mm / U-matic / VHS
Color (I)
LC 74-702234
Enumerates some of the taxes the average citizen has to pay, such as taxes on income, property, sales and excise taxes on certain items. Points out the many services that are financed by taxes, such as the police, courts, fire departments, health services and others.
Business and Economics; Civics and Political Systems
Dist - HANDEL **Prod** - HANDEL 1974

Taxes - Why We have Them 14 MIN
16mm / U-matic / VHS
Color
LC 78-701959
Explains why taxes have increased during the history of the United States. Describes the kinds of taxes collected by the three levels of government. Defines progressive and regressive taxes and the advantages and disadvantages of each and classifies some criteria needed to balance taxes and services.
Business and Economics; Civics and Political Systems
Dist - PHENIX **Prod** - GREENF 1978

Taxi 58 MIN
VHS / U-matic
Color (A)
LC 84-707118
Interviews drivers, fleet owners and dispatchers and pairs their comments with images revealing cab school students unable to pinpoint major streets and locations and cabbies dealing with assorted colorful customers.
Guidance and Counseling
Dist - NFBC **Prod** - HAMMOA 1983

Taxi Driver 112 MIN
16mm
Color
Focuses on a New York cab driver who becomes compulsively involved with the city's 'night people.' Directed by Martin Scorcese.
Fine Arts
Dist - SWANK **Prod** - CPC

A Taxing Task 10 MIN
U-matic
Calling Captain Consumer Series
Color (P I J)
Reveals a man angrily calculating his income tax return.
Business and Economics; Civics and Political Systems; Home Economics
Dist - TVOTAR **Prod** - TVOTAR 1985

A Taxing woman 127 MIN
Videodisc / VHS
Color (G) (JAPANESE WITH ENGLISH SUBTITLES)
$79.95, $45.95 purchase _ #FLV1001, #IMALLVD8903
Stars Nobuko Miyamoto as an eager beaver female tax inspector determined to track down every case of small - scale tax fraud, despite being harassed, humiliated and harmed by the people she pursues. Directed by Juzo Itami.
Fine Arts; Literature and Drama
Dist - CHTSUI

A Taxing woman returns 127 MIN
VHS
Color (G) (JAPANESE WITH ENGLISH SUBTITLES)
$79.95 purchase _ #NYV58590
Stars Nobuko Miyamoto as an eager beaver female tax inspector who investigates a corrupt fundamentalist religious order. Directed by Juzo Itami.
Fine Arts; Literature and Drama
Dist - CHTSUI

Taxonomy - How Living Organisms Differ
U-matic / VHS
Color (H)
Introduces the principles of taxonomy and explains Linnaeus' system of classification of related groups. Examines different types of organisms and explains why scientists research fossils, genes, anatomy and physiology in their efforts to determine how organisms should be classified.
Science - Natural
Dist - GA **Prod** - GA

Taylor Approximations
16mm
B&W
Deals with Taylor approximations, Taylor's theorem, and the three different forms of remainder of the Taylor polynomial.
Mathematics
Dist - OPENU **Prod** - OPENU

Taylor Chain 33 MIN
16mm
Color (A)
Reveals the actions of participants in a seven - week strike at a small chain factory in Indiana. Follows the dispute from the beginning of the contract negotiations to the settlement. Focuses on conflicts within the union between the elected officers, the international representative and the militant rank and file. The film is only available to union staff.
Business and Economics; Psychology
Dist - AFLCIO **Prod** - KART 1980

Taylor Polynomials 24 MIN
16mm / U-matic / VHS
Color
Discusses Taylor polynomials.
Mathematics
Dist - MEDIAG **Prod** - OPENU 1979

Taylor series 30 MIN
VHS
Calculus series
Color (C)
$125.00 purchase _ #6052
Explains the Taylor series. Part of a 56 - part series on calculus.
Mathematics
Dist - LANDMK **Prod** - LANDMK

Taylor series
Discusses the convergence of general complex power series and the definition of the circle of convergence. Asks whether the function defined by a convergent power series is analytic. Describes the result of analytic continuation which guarantees uniqueness when a real power series is extended to include complex variables.
Taylor series
Dist - OPENU **Prod** - OPENU

Taylor Slough 5 MIN
16mm
New Directions Series
Color (G)
Presents an independent production by Kurt Hall. Part of a comic series of first film shorts.
Fine Arts; Literature and Drama
Dist - FIRS

Taylor's formula 30 MIN
VHS
Calculus series
Color (C)
$125.00 purchase _ #6021
Explains Taylor's formula. Part of a 56 - part series on calculus.
Mathematics
Dist - LANDMK **Prod** - LANDMK

Taylor's Formula 30 MIN
VHS
Mathematics Series
Color (J)
LC 90713155
Discusses Taylor's Formula. The 130th of 157 installments of the Mathematics Series.
Mathematics
Dist - GPN

Taylor's Theorem 20 MIN
VHS
Calculus Series
Color (H)
LC 90712920
Explains Taylor's theorem. The 57th of 57 installments of the Calculus Series.
Mathematics
Dist - GPN

TB or not TB - new guidelines for prevention and treatment 19 MIN
VHS
Color (PRO C)
$285.00 purchase, $70.00 rental _ #4392
Includes updated OSHA guidelines for prevention of tuberculosis and explains the epidemiology of the disease, how to screen and assess for TB, and the multidrug treatment regimen. Covers how to prevent transmission and how to use respiratory protection programs and personal protective equipment, including NIOSH - approved respirators equipped with high efficiency particulate air - HEPA - filters and 'fit testing.'
Health and Safety
Dist - AJN **Prod** - AJN 1995

TB or not TB - prevention and treatment 20 MIN
VHS
Color (C PRO)
$285.00 purchase, $70.00 rental _ #4364S, #4364V
Presents up - to - date information on the resurgence of tuberculosis, methods of diagnosis, treatment and precautions that need to be taken by health care providers. Reveals that multiple drug resistant TB - MDR - TB - has dramatically increased the fatality rates and increased the risk to health care workers. Include information on surveillance and vaccination.
Health and Safety
Dist - AJN **Prod** - AJN 1993

TB - the forgotten plague 50 MIN
VHS
Horizon series
Color (H C A)
PdS99 purchase
Discusses the increasing incidence of tuberculosis and how it has become resistant to antibiotics, making it the most virulent disease. Notes that TB and AIDS are more frequently seen together and examines the increasing threat to public health.
Health and Safety
Dist - BBCENE

Tch, Tch, Tch, what a Way to Build a Railroad 10 MIN
16mm
Color
LC 70-712854
Follows the steps in building a railroad from planning to completion, covering engineering, machines and machinists. Includes animation and split - screen optical effects.
Industrial and Technical Education; Social Science
Dist - FILCOM **Prod** - SPRRC 1969

Tchaikovsky and the Russians 26 MIN
U-matic / VHS / 16mm
Ballet for all Series
Color (H C A)
Tells how a new form of classical choreography resulted from the fusion in Russia of French and Italian traditions. Presents the grand pas de deux from Sleeping Beauty and from The Bluebird.
Fine Arts
Dist - MEDIAG **Prod** - THAMES 1978

Tchaikovsky and Vivaldi - Israel Philharmonic Orchestra conducted by Zubin Mehta 48 MIN
VHS
Huberman Festival series
Color (G)
$19.95 purchase_#1407
Features violinist Henryk Szeryng performing Tchaikovsky's Concerto for Violin in D Major, Op. 35. Combines talents of Szeryng with Chaim Taub in performing Vivaldi's Concerto for Two Violins and String Orchestra in A Minor, Op. 3, No. 8.
Fine Arts
Dist - KULTUR

Tchaikovsky Competition - Violin and Piano, Victoria Mullora Et Al 90 MIN
VHS / U-matic
Color
Fine Arts
Dist - MSTVIS **Prod** - MSTVIS

Tchaikovsky - Symphony no 6 - the Pathetique - Pt 5 87 MIN
VHS
Story of the symphony series
Color (S)
$39.95 purchase _ #833 - 9046
Features Andre Previn conducting the Royal Philharmonic Orchestra in some of the most popular and important works of the concert repertoire. Presents Previn in rehearsal discussing the composer and his music, using pictures, anecdotes and orchestral excerpts to underscore his comments. Each program concludes with a complete and uninterrupted performance of the symphony. Part 5 reveals Tchaikovsky as a popular composer who was frowned upon by the music establishment for precisely that reason. 'The Pathetique' is Tchaikovsky's last composition, first performed barely a week before his death.
Fine Arts
Dist - FI **Prod** - RMART 1986

Tchebychev's approximation
VHS
Probability and statistics series
Color (H C)
$125.00 purchase _ #8024
Provides resource material about Tchebychev's approximation for help in the study of probability and statistics. Presents a 60 - video series, each part 25 to 30 minutes long, that explains and reinforces concepts using definitions, theorems, examples and step - by - step solutions to tutor the student. Videos are also available in a set.
Mathematics
Dist - LANDMK

Tea 16 MIN
16mm
B&W (J H)
Traces the story of tea from its legendary beginnings through modern aspects of its industry. Covers rules for tea brewing.
Agriculture; Home Economics
Dist - VIEWTH **Prod** - GATEEF

Tea for Elsa 10 MIN
16mm
B&W (J)
Contrasts the tense excitement of a museum robbery with the monotonous routine of a charwoman to make a powerful statement about apathy and non - involvement.
Social Science
Dist - COUNTR **Prod** - COUNTR 1972

Tea for two 5 MIN
16mm
B&W (G)
$20.00 rental
Shows the filmmaker visiting himself, then revealing the frustration of loneliness.
Fine Arts; Psychology
Dist - CANCIN **Prod** - WONGAL 1970

Tea fortunes 52 MIN
VHS
Commodities series
Color (G)
$400.00 purchase, $75.00 rental
Documents the history of the tea industry in China, India, Sri Lanka and East Africa. Profiles Sir Thomas Lipton. Shows how he and his competitors controlled every stage of tea manufacture, from planting to blending, packaging to retailing. Part of a seven - part series which looks at the way banks, corporations, governments, workers and consumers are affected by such ordinary items as coffee, tea and sugar. Examines the nature of exchange between Third World commodities producers and the people who control their processing, financing and marketing. Shows how producers try to increase profits. Considers the roles of cartels, financiers and multi - nationals. Produced by Sue Clayton and Jonathan Curling.
Business and Economics; Fine Arts; History - World; Social Science
Dist - FIRS **Prod** - CFTV 1986

Tea in the harem 110 MIN
VHS
Color (G)
$238.50 purchase
Presents a semi - autobiographical exploration of the plight of young, second - generation Algerians living in Paris. Focuses on the friendship betwen Madjid and Patrick, out of school and unemployed, who are victims of subtle French racism and victimizers as well - stealing, picking pockets and pimping women. A first film by director Mehdi Charef based on the book Le The Au Harem D'Archi Ahmed. Produced by Costa - Gavras.
Business and Economics; Fine Arts; Sociology
Dist - OCTOBF

A Tea Jar Bake 20 MIN
U-matic / VHS
Japanese Cuisine Series
Color (PRO)
Demonstrates baking shrimp, chicken and mushrooms in a tea jar, and filling colored and salted clamshells with other delicacies. The whole is served among miniature colored flames.
Home Economics; Industrial and Technical Education
Dist - CULINA **Prod** - CULINA

TEACCH program for parents 45 MIN
U-matic / VHS
Treatment and education of autistic children in North Carolina 'series
Color (A G C)
$395.00 purchase, $80.00 rental _ #C901 - VI - 082
Introduces parents of autistic children to the TEACCH program of North Carolina. Explores ways of understanding and helping the child who lives in an autistic world. Part of a two - part series by Dr Eric Schopler, UNC Medical School, University of North Carolina.
Education; Health and Safety; Sociology
Dist - HSCIC

TEACCH program for teachers 67 MIN
VHS / U-matic
Treatment and education of autistic children in North Carolina 'series
Color (T C)
$395.00 purchase, $80.00 rental _ #C901 - VI - 081
Shows the TEACCH program of North Carolina in operation. Demonstrates the emphasis on collaboration between professionals and parents. Shows older autistic children entering the school system and shows how structured teaching learned by the parents is transferred to school and incorporated into the classroom. Part of a two - part series by Dr Eric Schopler, UNC Medical School, University of North Carolina.
Education
Dist - HSCIC

Teach a Child to Talk 15 MIN
16mm
Color (A)
LC 76-700270
Follows the development of normal speech and language from birth to 3 years with suggestions for parents.
English Language; Psychology; Sociology
Dist - PFLAU **Prod** - DEVLSC

Teach for transfer - Pt 1 21 MIN
16mm
Color (T)
Presents Dr Madeline Hunter discussing the main factors which facilitate and those which prevent the transfer of pupils' learning to new situations. Illustrates each of these factors with specific examples of classroom teaching situations.
Education; Psychology
Dist - SPF **Prod** - SPF

Teach for transfer - Pt 2 20 MIN
16mm
Color (T)
Presents Dr Madeline Hunter discussing the main factors which facilitate and those which prevent the transfer of pupils' learning to new situations. Illustrates each of these factors with specific examples of classroom teaching situations.
Education; Psychology
Dist - SPF **Prod** - SPF

Teach Me 10 MIN
16mm
Color (C T)
Presents a report of the practical side of a unique special education center now in its third year. Shows that the Warren Development Center has gained the reputation of an intricate combination course of work where Maryland's school systems can attempt to close the breach between the need and supply of teachers trained to work with special problem children.
Education; Psychology; Sociology
Dist - HALLMK **Prod** - HALLMK

Teach me 20 MIN
16mm
Color (J)
LC FIA68-2500
Excerpted from the 1967 feature length film 'Up the Down Staircase' directed by Mike Nichols. A beginning teacher discovers that the rewards of motivating disadvantaged students outweigh environmental handicaps.
Education; Fine Arts
Dist - IU **Prod** - TFC 1968

Teach Me How I Can do it Myself 29 MIN
16mm / U-matic / VHS
Color (C A)
LC 76-712274
A documentary account of the philosophy and practices of the Montessori method of elementary education. Presents scenes of children at a Montessori kindergarten and at a public elementary Montessori school in The Netherlands. Explains that the Montessori method is a total way of life that involves the child, the parents and the teachers.
Education
Dist - IFB **Prod** - STNEON 1971

Teach Me to Dance 28 MIN
U-matic / VHS / 16mm
Adventures in History Series
Color (I J H)
Shows how a young Ukrainian immigrant is assigned a school recitation which sends her into despair, since she has difficulty with English. Describes her relationship with a friend who helps her overcome her problem.
Fine Arts; Sociology
Dist - FI **Prod** - NFBC 1978

Teach more faster - Pt 1 29 MIN
16mm
B&W (C T)
LC 82-701103
Shows how to apply psychological principles in planning material to be taught. Demonstrates the most effective way to sequence lessons, the importance of making material meaningful, how some material can be taught faster and the effect of previously learned material.
Education; Psychology
Dist - SPF **Prod** - SPF 1970

Teach more faster - Pt 2 29 MIN
16mm
B&W (C T)
LC 82-701103
Deals with psychological principles that eliminate the need for a great deal of practice. Reviews importance of motivation, meaning, vividness and sequence of material. Discusses overt and covert participation of the learner, clarifies the influence of positive and negative transfer and shows how the reinforcement theory is related to cognitive learning as well as behavior.
Education; Psychology
Dist - SPF **Prod** - SPF 1970

Teach more faster - Pt 3 29 MIN
16mm
B&W (C T)
LC 82-701103
Describes the three essential elements of planned practice - - how much to practice, how long to practice and how often to practice. Reviews the principles of learning taught in the entire series.
Education; Psychology
Dist - SPF **Prod** - SPF 1970

Teach Safety 15 MIN
16mm
Foremanship Training Series
Color
LC 74-705741
Stresses the importance of the supervisor's responsibility for teaching minors the correct, safe and efficient methods of performing their jobs.
Business and Economics; Health and Safety
Dist - USNAC **Prod** - USBM 1968

Teach your child to swim 55 MIN
VHS
Color (G T)
$29.95 purchase _ #SWI501V-K
Presents a step-by-step approach to teach parents how to help children develop water safety and swimming skills. Incorporates specific cues to help children progress. Directed at novice as well as professional instructors. Features Aquatic Director at University of Florida's College of Health and Human Performance.
Health and Safety; Physical Education and Recreation
Dist - CAMV

Teach your children 60 MIN
VHS
Learning in America series
Color; Captioned (G)
$49.95 purchase _ #LEIA - 103
Considers issues of classroom curriculum, including textbook reform, technology, values and teaching of humanities. Suggests that schools are behind the rest of the nation in adapting to and adopting technology. Hosted by Roger Mudd.
Education
Dist - PBS **Prod** - WETATV 1989

Teach Your Horse to Bow for Easy Mounting 17 MIN
BETA / VHS
Color
Shows how to teach a horse to bow for easy mounting.
Physical Education and Recreation
Dist - EQVDL **Prod** - MHRSMP

Teach yourself how to swim - adult learn to swim program 30 MIN
VHS
Color (C G A)
$19.95 purchase
Teaches adults who have a fear of water how to swim. Uses underwater photography of strokes to help learners visualize skills. Features Melody Medley - Craig.
Education; Physical Education and Recreation
Dist - MEDSWS **Prod** - MEDSWS 1992

Teacher 15 MIN
U-matic / 16mm / VHS
Career awareness
(I)
$130.00, $240.00 purchase, $25.00, $30.00 rental
Presents an empathetic approach to career planning, showing the personal as well as the professional attributes of teachers. Highlights the importance of career education.
Education; Guidance and Counseling
Dist - GPN

The Teacher - a Community Helper 10 MIN
16mm
Color; B&W (P A)
LC FIA67-1908
Describes a typical day in the life of a primary school teacher. Shows her as she plans the lesson, teaches, confers with a parent, attends the university and performs other duties as a mother, homemaker and responsible member of the community.
Education; Guidance and Counseling; Psychology; Social Science
Dist - FILCOM **Prod** - SIGMA 1967

Teacher and Peer Attitudes 30 MIN
VHS / U-matic
Teaching Students with Special Needs Series
Color
Presents consultants discussing the complexities of teacher attitudes toward students and how to manage student attitudes.
Education
Dist - PBS **Prod** - MSITV 1981

Teacher and School Effectiveness 21 MIN
U-matic
Color (T)
Discusses the importance of academic focus, selection of activities, and grouping of students. Lists five characteristics of effective teachers and schools. Available with captions.
Education
Dist - AFSCD **Prod** - AFSCD 1986

The Teacher and Technology 49 MIN
16mm
Communication Theory and the New Educational Media Series
Color; B&W (T)
LC FIA68-833
Presents a series of pictorially documented programs which illustrate some of the ways in which technology is being used to meet the dual problems of masses of students and the need for individualized instruction.
Education
Dist - USNAC **Prod** - USOE 1967

The Teacher - applications 18 MIN
VHS
Foundations and applications of distance education series
Color (T G)
$50.00 purchase
Examines the skills needed for successful distance teaching. Part of a series on distance education.
Education
Dist - AECT **Prod** - IODIED 1995

Teacher as a Storyteller 20 MIN
16mm
Sound of Language Series
Color
LC FIA-640
Bill Martin reads poetry, tells stories, and engages children in oral reponses to what they have heard. He shows how he believes language is learned through the ear, not the eye. He also discusses three levels of language - home rooted, public and life lifting.
Education; English Language; Literature and Drama
Dist - OSUMPD **Prod** - OHIOSU 1967

The Teacher as Club Leader 25 MIN
16mm
Learning for a Lifetime - the Academic Club Method Series Part 5
Color
Discusses the role of the teacher in the Academic Club Method developed at the Kingsbury Center Lab School.
Education; Psychology
Dist - KINGS **Prod** - KINGS

The Teacher as Conductor 20 MIN
VHS / 16mm
Classroom Roles of the English as a Second Language Teacher Series
Color (H C A)
Shows a beginning level grammar - vocabulary class in a pre - academic intensive English as a second language, ESL, program. Using visual aids as well as humor, the teacher leads the students from repetition of basic phrases to manipulation of the new patterns for a limited but realistic communication about themselves.
Education; English Language
Dist - IOWA **Prod** - IOWA 1984

The Teacher as Consultant 20 MIN
VHS / 16mm
Classroom Roles of the English as a Second Language Teacher Series
Color (H C A)
Shows an intermediate - level class in scientific English within an intensive English as a second language, ESL, program on a college campus. The teacher sets up a problem for the students to work out together, then steps back and lets them proceed until they need help or advice.
Education; English Language
Dist - IOWA **Prod** - IOWA 1984

The Teacher as Guide 20 MIN
VHS / 16mm
Classroom Roles of the English as a Second Language Teacher Series
Color (H C A)
Shows a low - proficiency intensive English as a second language, ESL, reading class. By employing visual aids and encouraging student interaction the teacher helps students develop strategies for discovering meaning and monitoring performance.
Education; English Language
Dist - IOWA **Prod** - IOWA 1984

The Teacher as Integrator 20 MIN
VHS / 16mm
Classroom Roles of the English as a Second Language Teacher Series
Color (H C A)
Shows a groups of graduate students from an advanced English as a second language, ESL, course. Integrating real - world experiences with instruction, the teacher takes the students to an art gallery and gives them tasks to complete that require listening, speaking and note - taking skills.
Education; English Language
Dist - IOWA **Prod** - IOWA 1984

The Teacher as Mentor 20 MIN
VHS / 16mm
Classroom Roles of the English as a Second Language Teacher Series
Color (H C A)
Shows English as a second language teachers, ESL, with multinational third through seventh grade pupils in classrooms and tutorial settings. Includes an interview with one teacher about the program's philosophy and techniques.
Education; English Language
Dist - IOWA **Prod** - IOWA 1986

The Teacher as Parent 20 MIN
VHS / 16mm
Classroom Roles of the English as a Second Language Teacher Series
Color (H C A)
Shows a group of preschool children from Southeast Asia participating in American songs and games and listening to stories. The teacher explains for the viewer some of the crosscultural and pedagogical problems that were overcome as the English as a Second Language, ESL, program was developed.
Education; English Language
Dist - IOWA **Prod** - IOWA 1984

Teacher Attitude I 30 MIN
U-matic / VHS
Teaching Children with Special Needs Series
Color (T)
Discusses the importance of teacher attitude when dealing with children with special needs.
Education
Dist - MDCPB **Prod** - MDDE

Teacher Attitude II 30 MIN
U-matic / VHS
Teaching Children with Special Needs Series
Color (T)
Discusses the importance of teacher attitude when dealing with children with special needs.
Education
Dist - MDCPB **Prod** - MDDE

Teacher decision making 26 MIN
16mm
Translating theory into classroom practice series
B&W (C R)
Discusses daily teaching decisions which are identified and grouped in three categories -- academic content, behavior of the learner and behavior of the teacher. Presents the relationship of these decisions to the most recent research in learning so that teachers can increase their efficiency and effectiveness in the classsroom.
Education
Dist - SPF **Prod** - SPF 1967

Teacher - directed television instruction 28 MIN
U-matic
B&W
Demonstrates a television facility which frees university and school faculties from some of the restrictions inherent in traditional television presentations, permitting push - button control of the medium.
Education; Social Science
Dist - USNAC **Prod** - USNAC 1972

Teacher effectiveness training 29 MIN
16mm / U-matic / VHS
Human relations and school discipline series
Color
Outlines the methods created and developed by Dr Thomas Gordon, originator of Teacher Effectiveness Training, a system of techniques now widely used by teachers in building more effective classroom relationships. Illustrates and explains the concepts of 'active listening,' ''I' messages' and the 'no-lose method' for resolving conflicts.
Education; Psychology; Sociology
Dist - FI **Prod** - MFFD

A Teacher in Reflection 11 MIN
16mm
One to Grow on Series
Color (T)
LC 73-701939
Presents a grade school teacher who uses class meetings to help work through students' personal and classroom problems. Features the teacher talking about her teaching style and her successes and failures in accomplishing the classroom environment she seeks.
Education
Dist - USNAC **Prod** - NIMH 1973

The Teacher - inservice 15 MIN
U-matic / VHS
Sci - fair series
Color (T)
Shows how to organize and implement the investigative experience for science fairs.
Education; Science
Dist - GPN **Prod** - MAETEL

Teacher, Lester Bit Me 9 MIN
U-matic / VHS / 16mm
Color (J)
LC 76-701898
Presents an animated story about a preschool day when everything goes wrong. Exaggerates and makes manageable some of the students' worst fears. Discusses some of the common difficulties and how they might be responded to.
Education
Dist - IFB **Prod** - EDC 1975

Teacher, look at me 30 MIN
VHS
Celebrating with children series
Color (G A R)
$39.95 purchase, $10.00 rental _ #35 - 897 - 2076
Features teacher Kathy Wise in lessons on how to maintain order in a classroom and how to encourage children's development of positive self - images. Produced by Seraphim.
Education; Sociology
Dist - APH

Teacher - made Tests 11 MIN
U-matic / VHS
Tests Series
Color (T)
Explains how to prepare relevant and effective teacher - made tests.
Education
Dist - AITECH **Prod** - WTVITV 1980

Teacher Program 15 MIN
VHS
Taxes in US History Series
Color (T)
Introduces the series to teachers and provides an overview of the content and design of the three student programs. Uses classroom sequences to show teachers and students using the materials effectively. Presents the economics of taxation within the context of key events in the American past.
Business and Economics; Civics and Political Systems; Education; History - United States
Dist - AITECH **Prod** - AITECH 1991

Teacher - Pupil interactions 30 MIN
U-matic / VHS
Interaction - human concerns in the schools series
Color (T)
Looks at teacher/pupil interactions in an educational setting.
Education
Dist - MDCPB **Prod** - MDDE

Teacher, Shaker, Sweet 10 MIN
U-matic
Readalong One Series
Color (K P)
Introduces reading and spelling for preschoolers and children in grades 1 to 3 with animation, puppets, humor and music. Comes with teacher's guide and kit.
Education; English Language; Literature and Drama
Dist - TVOTAR **Prod** - TVOTAR 1975

Teacher stress - Pt 1 20 MIN
VHS / U-matic
On and about instruction series
Color (T)
Explains various ways in which stress affects the productivity of educators.
Education; Psychology
Dist - GPN **Prod** - VADE 1983

Teacher stress - Pt 2 29 MIN
U-matic / VHS
On and about instruction series
Color (T)
Gives various techniques that both groups and individuals can use to relieve stressful situations.
Education; Psychology
Dist - GPN **Prod** - VADE 1983

Teacher - Student Interaction Analysis 18 MIN
U-matic / VHS
Color (PRO)
Helps clinical and classroom instructors in allied health, nursing, and medicine to understand more fully their role in the teaching - learning process and how to improve it. Covers instructor's behavior when working with a student, a process for objectively analyzing that behavior, and the establishment of goals for promoting more desirable teacher behavior.
Health and Safety
Dist - HSCIC **Prod** - HSCIC

Teacher Support 15 MIN
16mm
League School for Seriously Disturbed Children Series
Color
LC 75-702438
Shows how the emotionally handicapped student at the League School for seriously disturbed children is afforded the full range of clinical treatment and therapy through an elaborate teacher support system.
Education; Psychology
Dist - USNAC **Prod** - USBEH 1973

Teacher, Take Us Orienteering 14 MIN
16mm / U-matic / VHS
Color (I J H)
Shows a group of school children becoming acquainted with the sport of orienteering, which requires participants to use a map and compass to check in at various control points and be the first to finish a pre - defined course.
Physical Education and Recreation
Dist - IFB **Prod** - OFA 1982

Teacher to teacher on individualization - Pt 1 - how to get an individual started 26 MIN
16mm
Color (C T)
Emphasizes the steps that need to be taken by the classroom teacher to individualize instruction.
Education; Psychology
Dist - SPF **Prod** - SPF 1969

Teacher to teacher on individualization - Pt 2 - how to get an individual started, further 26 MIN
16mm
Color (C T)
Provides the viewer with specific illustration of individualization and shows how the teacher analyzes each situation.
Education; Psychology
Dist - SPF **Prod** - SPF 1969

Teacher to teacher series

The ABCs of ESL - developing literacy - Tape 3	26 MIN
Actively interactive - teaching reading comprehension strategies - Tape 8	36 MIN
Anatomy of a lesson - pacing and structure in the basic education classroom - Tape 5	23 MIN
Chapter 1, page 1 - beginning reading for adults - Tape 2	26 MIN
Every student has a story - developing a community of learners - Tape 1	24 MIN
From real life - using student experiences in reading and writing - Tape 6	36 MIN
Listen, ask and answer - enhancing aural ability and oral facility - Tape 4	35 MIN
Love to write - creating an environment for writers - Tape 9	25 MIN
Sound, form and fluency - refined oral skills - Tape 10	17 MIN
Speak up - speak out - strategies for developing oral fluency - Tape 11	24 MIN
Taking charge - techniques for developing self - directed learners - Tape 12	31 MIN
Teaching reading two ways - the tired and the true - Tape 7	52 MIN

Dist - LAULIT

Teacher to teacher set 352 MIN
VHS
Color (T)
$750.00 purchase _ #879 - X
Shows exerienced teachers in actual classroom settings presenting various instructional approaches to both new and veteran ABE and ESL teachers in a twelve - part series. Includes user's guide and video table of contents.
Education; English Language
Dist - LAULIT **Prod** - LAULIT

Teacher Training Experiences and Issues 47 MIN
U-matic / VHS
New Technology in Education Series
Color (J)
Presents experiences and issues in training teachers for computer use in the classroom and discusses Computer Using Educators (CUE), a teachers' organization for computer education.
Education; Industrial and Technical Education
Dist - USNAC **Prod** - USDOE 1983

Teacher Training Introduction to Catalysis 13 MIN
16mm
CHEM Study In - Service Training Films Series
B&W (T)
Science; Science - Physical
Dist - MLA **Prod** - CHEMS 1966

Teacher Training Introduction to Chemical Bonding 14 MIN
16mm
CHEM Study In - Service Training Films Series
B&W (T)
Science; Science - Physical
Dist - MLA **Prod** - CHEMS 1966

Teacher Training Introduction to Chemical Families 7 MIN
16mm
CHEM Study In - Service Training Films Series
B&W (T)
Science; Science - Physical
Dist - MLA **Prod** - CHEMS 1966

Teacher Training Introduction to Crystals and their Structures 7 MIN
16mm
CHEM Study In - Service Training Films Series
B&W (T)
Science; Science - Physical
Dist - MLA **Prod** - CHEMS 1966

Teacher Training Introduction to Electrochemical Cells 8 MIN
16mm
CHEM Study In - Service Training Films Series
B&W (T)
Science; Science - Physical
Dist - MLA **Prod** - CHEMS 1966

Teacher Training Introduction to Equilibrium 5 MIN
16mm
CHEM Study In - Service Training Films Series
B&W (T)
Science; Science - Physical
Dist - MLA **Prod** - CHEMS 1966

Teacher Training Introduction to Gases and How they Combine 12 MIN
16mm
CHEM Study In - Service Training Films Series
B&W (T)
Science; Science - Physical
Dist - MLA **Prod** - CHEMS 1966

The Teacher Training Introduction to Hydrogen Atom - as Viewed by Quantum Mechanics 9 MIN
16mm
CHEM Study In - Service Training Films Series
B&W (T)
Science; Science - Physical
Dist - MLA **Prod** - CHEMS 1966

Teacher Training Introduction to Introduction to Reaction Kinetics 16 MIN
16mm
CHEM Study In - Service Training Films Series
B&W (T)
Science; Science - Physical
Dist - MLA **Prod** - CHEMS 1966

Teacher Training Introduction to Ionization Energy 8 MIN
16mm
CHEM Study In - Service Training Films Series
B&W (T)
Science; Science - Physical
Dist - MLA **Prod** - CHEMS 1966

Teacher Training Introduction to Mechanism of an Organic Reaction 9 MIN
16mm
CHEM Study In - Service Training Films Series
B&W (T)
Science; Science - Physical
Dist - MLA **Prod** - CHEMS 1966

Teacher Training Introduction to Vanadium - a Transition Element 7 MIN
16mm
CHEM Study In - Service Training Films Series
B&W (T)
Science; Science - Physical
Dist - MLA **Prod** - CHEMS 1966

The Teacher Variable - an Interview with Vera Milz 29 MIN
VHS / U-matic
Reading Comprehension Series
Color (T)
Education; English Language
Dist - HNEDBK **Prod** - IU

Teachers 13 MIN
16mm
Color (C T)
Satirizes four types of teachers in order to show that the teacher is the most important audio - visual 'aid' in the classroom.
Education
Dist - FRAF **Prod** - DAWSON 1958

The Teachers 19 MIN
VHS
Let's talk about it series
Color; PAL (I J)
PdS29.50 purchase
Summarizes the first three films, Male and Female; Birthday; and Puberty, and includes a discussion by the teachers themselves. Part of a five - part series on sex education.
Health and Safety
Dist - EMFVL

Teacher's Aides - a New Opportunity 21 MIN
16mm
B&W (T S R)
LC 74-705744
Depicts the training of para - professional teacher's aides for pre - schools.
Education
Dist - USNAC **Prod** - USOEO

Teachers ask 30 MIN
VHS / U-matic
Creative dramatics - teacher series
Color (T)
Contains an overview of the Creative Dramatics series and its philosophy. Answers questions most commonly asked by teachers during creative dramatics workshops.

Fine Arts
Dist - AITECH **Prod** - NEWITV 1977

Teacher's Beau 19 MIN
16mm
B&W
Tells how the Gang tries to discourage their teacher from marrying, fearing what the 'new' teacher might be like. A Little Rascals film.
Fine Arts
Dist - RMIBHF **Prod** - ROACH 1935

Teachers, Friends and Roller Skaters 22 MIN
16mm
Color
Follows the progress of one young couple as they learn to roller skate, showing their initial awkwardness and gradual development into proficient skaters. Offers demonstrations and explanations of basic roller skating techniques.
Physical Education and Recreation
Dist - MTP **Prod** - MTP

Teachers of adults 60 MIN
VHS
Creative teaching series
Color (G A R)
$29.95 purchase, $10.00 rental _ #35 - 860399 - 1
Trains teachers in creative teaching methods. Presents insights into how people learn. Includes workbook.
Education; Religion and Philosophy
Dist - APH **Prod** - ABINGP

Teachers of elementary 60 MIN
VHS
Creative teaching series
Color (G A R)
$29.95 purchase, $10.00 rental _ #35 - 860410 - 1
Trains teachers in creative teaching methods. Presents insights into how people learn. Includes workbook.
Education; Religion and Philosophy
Dist - APH **Prod** - ABINGP

Teachers of preschool 60 MIN
VHS
Creative teaching series
Color (G A R)
$29.95 purchase, $10.00 rental _ #35 - 860402 - 1
Trains teachers in creative teaching methods. Presents insights into how people learn. Includes workbook.
Education; Religion and Philosophy
Dist - APH **Prod** - ABINGP

Teachers of youth 60 MIN
VHS
Creative teaching series
Color (G A R)
$29.95 purchase, $10.00 rental _ #35 - 860453 - 1
Trains teachers in creative teaching methods. Presents insights into how people learn. Includes workbook.
Education; Religion and Philosophy
Dist - APH **Prod** - ABINGP

Teachers, Parents and Children - Growth through Cooperation 17 MIN
VHS / U-matic
Early Childhood Development Series
Color
Psychology
Dist - DAVFMS **Prod** - DAVFMS

Teachers, Parents, Children 17 MIN
16mm
Color (J)
Explains how to construct alliances between families and teachers to ease a child's entrance into school.
Education; Psychology; Sociology
Dist - DAVFMS **Prod** - DAVFMS 1974

Teachers' perspectives - Video 2
VHS
Neither damned nor doomed series
Color (T PRO A G)
$95.00 purchase
Focuses on teachers who confront the multiple challenges of children prenatally exposed to drugs and their impact on classroom environments. Part 2 of a three - part series on children prenatally exposed to drugs and alcohol produced by the Elementary School Center - ESC.
Education; Guidance and Counseling; Psychology; Sociology
Dist - SELMED

A Teacher's Prescription for Reducing Vandalism 23 MIN
U-matic / VHS / 16mm
Successful Teaching Practices Series
Color (T)
Reveals how art teacher Gary Obermayer and his students at Seward Junior High School have transformed an old, ugly building into a cheerful place through creative expression. Shows how this has altered the attitude of all students and reduced vandalism.
Education
Dist - EBEC **Prod** - UNIDIM 1982

Teachers Teaching Writing Series
Bones 0 MIN
Flight 0 MIN
Puppet Plays 0 MIN
Snake Hill to Spring Bank 0 MIN
Writers 0 MIN
Writing and Sharing 0 MIN
Dist - AFSCD

Teachers who make a difference 90 MIN
VHS
Color (H C G T)
$49.95 purchase _ #SBT108V - K
Tells about a teacher with an unusual gift for empowering students as learners. Identifies and discusses five essential principles of empowerment in teaching.
Education; Guidance and Counseling
Dist - CAMV

Teaching 20 TO 30 MIN
U-matic
Opportunity Profile Series
(H C A)
$99.95 _ #AI210
Illustrates the daily activities involved in a career in teaching. Working professionals in related occupations present the negative and positive aspects of such jobs.
Education; Guidance and Counseling
Dist - CAMV **Prod** - CAMV

Teaching
VHS / U-matic
Opportunity Profile Series
$99.95 purchase _ #AJ109V
Provides advice on the skills and educational background desired by companies, the day to day activities of various careers, and the positive and negative aspects of various careers from corporate vice presidents, managers, and other working professionals.
Guidance and Counseling
Dist - CAREER **Prod** - CAREER

Teaching 25 MIN
VHS
Face to face series
Color (C H A)
$39.95 purchase _ #KARCA03V-G; #KARCAO3V-J
Offers unrehearsed interviews between actual company representatives and college students seeking employment. Provides strategies for improving interview style by Dr. Larry Simpson, director of career planning and placement at the University of Virginia. Part of a five-part series.
Business and Economics; Education; Guidance and Counseling
Dist - CAMV

Teaching 25 MIN
VHS
Career encounters series
Color (J H C A)
$95.00 purchase _ #MG3409V-J
Presents a documentary-style program that explores a career in teaching. Features professionals at work, explaining what they do and how they got where they are. Emphasizes diversity of occupational opportunities and of men and women in the field. Offers information about new developments and technologies and about educational and certification requirements for entering the profession. One of a series of videos about professions available individually or as a set.
Business and Economics; Education; Guidance and Counseling
Dist - CAMV

Teaching 30 MIN
VHS / U-matic
Black literature series
Color
Discusses the teaching of black literature, which, for a white teacher is often difficult because there is a temptation to alter the language and experience of the black writer. Emphasizes that accuracy is essential for an understanding of the black experience.
History - United States; Literature and Drama; Sociology
Dist - NETCHE **Prod** - NETCHE 1971

Teaching a Child about Leukemia
U-matic
Staff Development Series
Color (PRO)
Shows how to teach children about leukemia. Treats pre - teaching conference with parent, family reaction to illness, understanding of diagnostic tests, symptoms of illness and use of visual aids.
Guidance and Counseling; Health and Safety; Home Economics
Dist - CFDC **Prod** - CFDC

Teaching a Child about Nephrosis
U-matic
Staff Development Series
Color (PRO)
Presents a situation where a child with nephrosis is unprepared for hospitalization and refuses to cooperate. Discusses feelings about hospitalization, understanding of the illness, use of body outline to present anatomy and physiology, and use of equipment for explanation.
Guidance and Counseling; Health and Safety; Home Economics
Dist - CFDC **Prod** - CFDC

Teaching a language structure by the Australian situational method - Pt 1 15 MIN
16mm
B&W (C T)
LC 73-702486
Explains the teaching of English as a foreign language.
Education; English Language; Foreign Language
Dist - AUIS **Prod** - FLMAUS 1973

Teaching - a Question of Method 6 MIN
16mm / U-matic / VHS
Citizenship - Whose Responsibility, 1 Series; Set 1
Color (T)
LC FIA65-403
Questions the degree to which a high school teacher has the right to deliberately attempt to alter his students' beliefs in capitalism, democracy, the home, and Judaic - Christian ethical and religious teachings.
Civics and Political Systems; Education
Dist - IFB **Prod** - HORIZN 1964

Teaching a skill 6 MIN
VHS
B&W (T IND)
Shows a lecturer in building techniques teaching plastering. Reveals that he shows the complete skill then breaks the technique down into its components. The students practice the components guided by the lecturer and gradually assemble the elements into the complete technique.
Education; Home Economics; Industrial and Technical Education
Dist - VIEWTH **Prod** - VIEWTH

Teaching Adults 29 MIN
16mm
Teaching Series
Color
Education; Literature and Drama; Religion and Philosophy
Dist - BROADM **Prod** - BROADM 1977

Teaching and Learning - Grades 5 - 6 21 MIN
U-matic / VHS / 16mm
Color (T)
Shows children building a time ladder to gain a concept of long past events in history and preparing their own dramatization of the events leading to the revolt after Solomon's death. Features teachers holding a critique session afterward to analyze their own successes and failures in the unit.
Education; Guidance and Counseling; Psychology
Dist - AIMS **Prod** - GENEVA 1971

Teaching and Learning - Grades 1 - 2 17 MIN
U-matic / VHS / 16mm
Color (T)
Demonstrates teacher preparation, interaction between pupils, teachers and materials and the selection of appropriate learning experiences in light of the session objectives.
Education; Psychology; Sociology
Dist - AIMS **Prod** - GENEVA 1971

Teaching and Learning - Grades 7 - 8 22 MIN
16mm / U-matic / VHS
Color (T)
Uses the inquiry approach with junior high level students, as they try to understand the social concerns involved in the period of Amos. Covers the unit from introduction to conclusion and shows two teachers working cooperatively, student - teacher interaction and student - to - student interaction.
Education; Psychology; Sociology
Dist - AIMS **Prod** - GENEVA 1971

Teaching and Learning - Grades 3 - 4 21 MIN
U-matic / VHS / 16mm
Color (T)
Provides an opportunity to observe team teaching, the interaction process and the opening, developing and concluding of a unit of study.
Education; Psychology; Sociology
Dist - AIMS **Prod** - GENEVA 1971

Teaching and Testing for Results 30 MIN
VHS / U-matic
On and about Instruction Series
Color (T)
Presents a working example of an approach to adaptive education to increase effectiveness and efficiency in instruction.

Education
Dist - GPN **Prod** - VADE 1983

Teaching and the World Wide Web - global online projects for science, math, language, literature, arts and foreign language teachers
VHS
Color (C PRO G T)
$89.00 purchase _ #505
Shows how to expand classroom resources by making people and information from around the world available to your students.. Surveys Internet potential and benefits for K - 12 education. Gives examples of text, graphics, software, and more available online for a large variety of subjects, and lists resources. Features Rich Enderton as instructor.
Computer Science; Education; Fine Arts; Foreign Language; Literature and Drama; Mathematics; Science
Dist - EDREGR **Prod** - EDREGR 1995

Teaching Babies, Creepers and Toddlers at Church 29 MIN
16mm
Teaching Series
Color
Education; Literature and Drama; Religion and Philosophy
Dist - BROADM **Prod** - BROADM 1977

Teaching Basic Reading 30 MIN
VHS / U-matic
Basic Education - Teaching the Adult Series
Color (T)
Explains how to teach basic reading to adult basic education students.
Education
Dist - MDCPB **Prod** - MDDE

Teaching Basic Skills with Film 90 MIN
VHS / U-matic
Color (T)
LC 80-707451
Presents a workshop session offering suggestions for effective and creative teaching with film.
Education; English Language; Literature and Drama
Dist - LCOA **Prod** - LCOA 1980

Teaching basketball offensive tips with Morgan Wootten 60 MIN
VHS
Color (G)
$39.95 purchase _ #WES1615V
Features the legendary high school basketball coach Morgan Wootten teaching basketball offensive skills. Consists of several short sessions focusing on particular offensive skills, with techniques, drills and explanations. Covers subjects including rapid fire shot drills, playing under control, fast break, point guard tips, and more.
Physical Education and Recreation
Dist - CAMV **Prod** - CAMV 1988

Teaching breast self - examination 28 MIN
U-matic / VHS
Color (PRO)
$275.00 purchase, $60.00 rental _ #7618S, #7618V
Shows an experienced nurse teaching a woman how to examine her breasts. Gives advice on how to motivate someone in overcoming her fears in performing the examination. Includes various screening methods - self - exam, physical exam, mammography - changes to expect during the menstrual cycle, various risk factors and the anatomy of the breast.
Health and Safety; Sociology
Dist - AJN **Prod** - HOSSN 1986

Teaching Breast Self - Examination - Baseline 24 MIN
U-matic / VHS
Focus on Cancer - Prevention and Early Detection Series
Color
Presents incorporation of Breast Health Education Protocol into history/physical exam.
Health and Safety; Science - Natural
Dist - UWASH **Prod** - UWASH

Teaching Breast Self - Examination - Office Visit 22 MIN
U-matic / VHS
Focus on Cancer - Prevention and Early Detection Series
Color
Demonstrates use of Breast Health Education Protocol to teach health education.
Health and Safety; Science - Natural
Dist - UWASH **Prod** - UWASH

Teaching by Guided Discussion 21 MIN
16mm
B&W
LC FIE58-279
Presents an air university academic course instructor conducting a seminar in teaching psychology.
Education; Psychology
Dist - USNAC **Prod** - USAF 1957

Teaching career encounters 28 MIN
VHS
Career encounters video series
Color (J H)
$89.00 purchase _ #4256
Offers a documentary on careers in the field of teaching. Visits workplaces and hears professionals explain what they do, how they got where they are and why they find the work so rewarding. Emphasizes human diversity in the professions. Dispels myths, misconceptions and stereotypes and offers practical information about the requirements for entering the field. Part of a 13 - part series.
Business and Economics; Education; Guidance and Counseling
Dist - NEWCAR

Teaching chemistry with demonstrations
Videodisc
Color (H A)
$325.00 purchase
Presents demonstrations of difficult, dangerous or time - consuming experiments for the chemistry lab such as halogen reactions, electrochemistry and rates of combustion. Helps teachers develop clear presentations of chemical principles. Illustrates lab errors and the consequences, emphasizing the need for care in the laboratory. Includes one videodisc and teacher's manual. Contact distributor for system requirements.
Computer Science; Science; Science - Physical
Dist - FALCSO

Teaching Children Poison Prevention 14 MIN
16mm
Color
LC 76-703161
Informs children and their parents of potential poison hazards contained in the medicine cabinet.
Guidance and Counseling; Health and Safety; Home Economics
Dist - MTP **Prod** - PD 1976

Teaching Children Self - Control 26 MIN
16mm
Color (T)
LC 79-701119
Demonstrates problem - solving techniques for dealing with defiant and assaultive classroom behavior. Illustrates the methods of an experienced teacher as she joins her children in their struggle to acquire impulse control and self - mastery.
Education; Psychology
Dist - NYU **Prod** - PSW 1978

Teaching children self - control 26 MIN
VHS
Color (T A)
$49.95 purchase _ #S00704
Demonstrates techniques and activities for developing self - control in children with behavior problems. Narrated by Peter Thomas.
Health and Safety; Psychology; Sociology
Dist - UILL

Teaching Children to Read Series

Building on what children know	29 MIN
Developing effective reading materials	30 MIN
Helping the reluctant reader	29 MIN
Human Behavior and Reading	29 MIN
Organizing the Reading Environment	29 MIN
Planning for Change	29 MIN
Reading as a Part of Life	29 MIN
The Role of Phonics	29 MIN
Thinking, Writing and Reading	29 MIN
Using Human Resources	29 MIN
Ways of Assessing Reading Progress	29 MIN
What about Reading Systems	29 MIN

Dist - FI

Teaching children to write poetry 26 MIN
VHS / U-matic / 16mm
Color (T)
$250.00, $300.00, $495.00 purchase, $50.00 rental
Focuses on the teaching methods of a master teacher as he works with young children to show how creative expression can be fostered in the classroom environment. Offers a production designed primarily for school teachers and education departments of universities and teachers' colleges.
Literature and Drama; Sociology
Dist - NDIM **Prod** - EDFLM 1990

Teaching Children with Special Needs - Preview 30 MIN
U-matic / VHS
Teaching Children with Special Needs Series
Color (T)
Offers a preview of the Teaching Children With Special Needs Series.
Education
Dist - MDCPB **Prod** - MDDE

Teaching Children with Special Needs - Review 30 MIN
U-matic / VHS
Teaching Children with Special Needs Series
Color (T)
Reviews the main points of the Teaching Children With Special Needs Series.
Education
Dist - MDCPB **Prod** - MDDE

Teaching Children with Special Needs Series

An Analytic approach to reading	30 MIN
Behavior Problems I	30 MIN
Behavior Problems II	30 MIN
Informal Assessment of Reading	30 MIN
Mathematical Problems I	30 MIN
Mathematical Problems II	30 MIN
Observation of Behavior	30 MIN
Oral Expressive Language	30 MIN
Oral Receptive Language	30 MIN
The Referral Process	30 MIN
A Synthesis Approach to Reading	30 MIN
Teacher Attitude I	30 MIN
Teacher Attitude II	30 MIN
Teaching Children with Special Needs - Preview	30 MIN
Teaching Children with Special Needs - Review	30 MIN

Dist - MDCPB

Teaching Cohesion Comprehension 30 MIN
U-matic / VHS
Teaching Reading Comprehension Series
Color (T PRO)
$180.00 purchase,$50.00 rental
Focuses on the necessity of making inferences between subjects to create a total understanding of the reading material.
Education; English Language
Dist - AITECH **Prod** - WETN 1986

Teaching Communications - a New Draft
VHS / 16mm
(T)
$55.00 purchase _ #TV102
Provides a K - 12 model for communications learning. Features peer interaction, individual conferences, and use of multiple technologies.
Education
Dist - MECC **Prod** - MECC 1989

Teaching critical thinking about conflict resolution series
Presents a three - part series which features teacher Roger Halstead in three in - class demonstrations. Includes Clarifying Moral and Personal Responsibility, Handling Controversial Issues, Resolving Personal Conflict. Produced by the Educational Film and Video Project.

Clarifying moral and personal responsibility - Part 1	20 MIN
Handling controversial issues - Part 2	21 MIN
Resolving personal conflict - Part 3	22 MIN

Dist - CF

Teaching Crutch Walking 9 MIN
U-matic / VHS
Color (PRO)
Shows how to fit a patient with crutches and how to instruct a patient in walking, sitting, and climbing stairs with them. Demonstrates guarding against a fall, the four - point gait, the three - point gait, the swing - through gait, and the proper method of negotiating stairs without rails.
Health and Safety
Dist - HSCIC **Prod** - HSCIC

Teaching Crutch Walking 13 MIN
16mm
B&W (A)
LC FIE52-411
Explains how to teach the patient to walk in a walker, and how to learn the various methods of crutch walking - - two - point, four - point and swinging. Shows how to sit, rise and climb stairs and discusses the safety factors involved in crutch walking.
Health and Safety; Psychology
Dist - USNAC **Prod** - USOE 1945

Teaching early reading series

How Can I Help Them - Effective Instruction	30 MIN
How do they understand - comprehension	30 MIN
What do they do - Word Recognition	30 MIN
When are they Ready - Reading Readiness	30 MIN

Where do they Come from - Language Development 30 MIN
Where do they Go from Here - Motivating the Use of Reading 30 MIN
Dist - CTI

Teaching early reading series
Presents six 30 - minute programs on teaching early reading. Includes three videocassettes.
Effective instruction - Part 5 30 MIN
How do they understand - Part 4 30 MIN
Reading readiness - Part 2 30 MIN
What do they do - Part 3 30 MIN
Where are they coming from - Part 1 30 MIN
Where do they go from there - Part 6 30 MIN
Dist - GPN **Prod** - CTI 1945

Teaching English Conversation 23 MIN
U-matic
B&W (T)
LC 78-706150
Presents the hearing and speaking method of teaching English as a foreign language. Issued in 1963 as a motion picture.
English Language
Dist - USNAC **Prod** - USIA 1978

Teaching English in Kindergarten - ESL 14 MIN
16mm
JAB Reading Series
Color (T)
LC 75-703880
Shows a bilingual kindergarten with an ESL (English as a second language) orientation, attended by children who speak predominantly Spanish.
Education; English Language
Dist - JBFL **Prod** - JBFL 1973

Teaching English in Kindergarten - ESL 14 MIN
16mm
Color (T) (SPANISH AND ENGLISH)
Uses an English as a second language approach, ESL, and examines a day in the life of kindergarten students who are bilingual and who speak Spanish in the home. Demonstrates how the class can be conducted in English.
English Language; Foreign Language
Dist - JBFL **Prod** - JBFL

Teaching episodes
VHS
Color (T PRO)
$245.00 purchase _ #V1
Presents 19 classroom vignettes at numerous grade levels, featuring a diverse student population. Uses classroom observation and script taping to teach supervision and coaching skills for teachers. Includes script.
Education
Dist - NSDC **Prod** - NSDC

Teaching Episodes - Resources for the Analysis of Instruction - a Videodisc Minicourse
Videodisc
(T)
$250.00 purchase _ #VID5701
Provides examples of effective teaching behavior. Includes a two - sided videodisc and manual.
Education
Dist - MECC **Prod** - MECC

Teaching evolution series
Presents a series of two videos for teaching evolution. Demonstrates the 'discovery' method of science education. Includes the titles How Scientists Know about Human Evolution and How Scientists Know about Punctuated Equilibria, both produced by the National Center for Science Education.
Teaching evolution series 38 MIN
Dist - UCEMC

Teaching family life education 40 MIN
VHS
Color (T)
$69.95 purchase _ #488 - V8
Provides educators with the concrete skills necessary to teach sex education to elementary through high school students. Combines interviews with five experienced family life teachers with candid footage from their classrooms. Looks at the following strategies - the anonymous question box; brainstorming; role plays; small and large groups; motivating tools; and wrap - up techniques.
Education; Health and Safety
Dist - ETRASS **Prod** - ETRASS

Teaching for Retention 30 MIN
U-matic / VHS
Aide - ing in Education Series
Color
Provides a summary of principles of learning. Identifies and illustrates five critical principles of learning which have the power to increase retention of what has been learned.
Education
Dist - SPF **Prod** - SPF

Teaching for Thinking 30 MIN
U-matic
Teaching Skillful Thinking Series
Color (T)
Explains how teachers can promote student thinking in the process of teaching regular academic content.
Education; Psychology
Dist - AFSCD **Prod** - AFSCD 1986

Teaching for thinking - creativity in the classroom series
Conceptual - thematic approaches 30 MIN
Conceptual Approach - a Demonstration in History 30 MIN
Convergent thinking - analysis - synthesis and evaluation 30 MIN
Divergent thinking - fluency, flexibility , originality, and elaborateness 30 MIN
Enhancing Writing Skills 30 MIN
Group Techniques for Enhancing Thinking 30 MIN
An Inquiry Approach 30 MIN
Metaphoric Thinking and Analogic Thought 30 MIN
Problem Solving - a Demonstration in Social Studies 30 MIN
Problem solving and decision - making 30 MIN
The Psychologically Safe Environment 30 MIN
Synectics 30 MIN
Dist - AITECH

Teaching for tomorrow series
Presents eleven programs using real teachers and schools to evaluate ideas and support professional development for primary and secondary teachers. Stimulates discussion on classroom management, handling curriculum changes and developing new teaching techniques. Includes the topics of curriculum change; assessment; progression and continuity; pupil diversity; equality of opportunity - race, gender; teaching styles and methods; promoting good behavior; personal and social development. Contact distributor about availability outside the United Kingdom.
Assessment - 3
Assessment - 4
Curriculum change - 1
Curriculum change - 2
Equality of opportunity - race, gender - 7
Personal and social development - 10
Personal and social development - 11
Progression and continuity - 5
Promoting good behaviour - 9
Pupil diversity - 6
Teaching styles and methods - 8
Dist - ACADEM

Teaching Fours and Fives at Church 29 MIN
16mm
Teaching Series
Color
Education; Literature and Drama; Religion and Philosophy
Dist - BROADM **Prod** - BROADM 1977

Teaching health choices - strategies for substance - use prevention in grades K - 2 50 MIN
VHS
Color (T PRO)
$95.00 purchase
Presents three parts of a substance - use prevention program to train teachers, counselors and administrators how to implement Project Healthy Choice. Examines the personal concerns of teaching personnel in Self Assessment. Follows four teachers implementing the program in Healthy Choices in Action. Demonstrates how to coordinate staff in Getting Started. Produced by the Bank Street College of Education.
Business and Economics; Education; Guidance and Counseling
Dist - SELMED

Teaching high school mathematics - first course series
Adding real numbers 35 MIN
Advent of awareness 29 MIN
Basic principles for real numbers, 1, principles of arithmetic for numbers of 39 MIN
Basic principles for real numbers, 2, distributive principles for numbers of 40 MIN
Basic principles for real numbers, 3, principles of arithmetic for real numbers 21 MIN
Basic principles for real numbers, 4, discovery and patterns 36 MIN
Bound variables - matching language with awareness 38 MIN
Comparing real numbers - the number line 18 MIN
Dividing real numbers 29 MIN
Equation transformation principles in practice - Part 1 31 MIN
Equation transformation principles in practice - Pt 2 24 MIN
Equivalent equations - developing the concept 43 MIN
Equivalent equations and transformation principles 30 MIN
Functions - foreshadowing the concept 22 MIN
Inverses of operations 26 MIN
Isomorphism - developing the concept 46 MIN
Logical basis for equation transformation principles - Pt 1 32 MIN
Logical basis for equation transformation principles - Pt 2 33 MIN
Logical basis for equation transformation principles - Pt 3 35 MIN
Multiplying real numbers 37 MIN
Naming sets - the set abstractor 33 MIN
Number line graphs of solution sets 22 MIN
Numbers and numerals - Pt 1 26 MIN
Numbers and numerals - Pt 2 25 MIN
Numerical variables - developing the concept, 1 31 MIN
Numerical variables - developing the concept, 2 30 MIN
Operation machines 24 MIN
Operations - binary, singulary 24 MIN
Organizing knowledge by deduction 47 MIN
Prelude to deduction 30 MIN
Prelude to proof - making 40 MIN
Prerequisite to communication 22 MIN
Principles and discovery in algebraic manipulation - Pt 4 - some other common cases 29 MIN
Principles and discovery in algebraic manipulation - Pt 1 - equivalent expressions 21 MIN
Principles and discovery in algebraic manipulation - Pt 3 - manipulating fractions 39 MIN
Principles and discovery in algebraic manipulation - Pt 2 - simplification 31 MIN
Proving generalizations - Pt 1 - test pattern principle 32 MIN
Proving generalizations - Pt 2 - classroom examples 31 MIN
Punctuation and conventions in mathematics - Pt 1 - punctuation 29 MIN
Punctuation and conventions in mathematics - Pt 2 - conventions 33 MIN
Real numbers - developing the concept 32 MIN
Sentences and solution sets 33 MIN
Solving equations - informal approach 28 MIN
Solving worded problems 27 MIN
Subset of a set - developing the concept 29 MIN
Substitution and the linking rule 32 MIN
Subtracting real numbers 30 MIN
Transformation principles for inequations - Pt 1 31 MIN
Transformation principles for inequations - Pt 2 28 MIN
Verbalizing generalizations in the classroom 20 MIN
Dist - MLA

Teaching History, Geography and Civics 27 MIN
16mm
Learning for a Lifetime - the Academic Club Method Series Part 4
Color
Shows the Academic Club Method at the Kingsbury Center Lab School where study of the social development of man is achieved through clubs organized around six periods of history.
Education; Psychology
Dist - KINGS **Prod** - KINGS

Teaching Infants and Toddlers Series Pt 1
One to Three Months 9 MIN
Dist - GPN

Teaching Infants and Toddlers Series Pt 3
Six to Eight Months 10 MIN
Dist - GPN

Teaching Infants and Toddlers Series Pt 4
Nine to Eleven Months 11 MIN
Dist - GPN

Teaching Infants and Toddlers Series Pt 7
Twenty - One to Twenty - Nine Months 13 MIN
Dist - GPN

Teaching infants and toddlers series
Fifteen to twenty months 13 MIN
Four to five months - Pt 2 9 MIN
Twelve to fourteen months 12 MIN
Dist - GPN

Teaching Interpersonal Skills to Health Professionals 100 MIN
U-matic
Color (T)
LC 79-706871
Presents an overview of the interpersonal skills program. Discusses elements in preparing for instruction, shows how to explain the instructional intentions, demonstrates skills to be learned, reviews effective and ineffective feedback and documents and critiques practice experiences.
Health and Safety; Psychology
Dist - USNAC **Prod** - NMAC 1978

Teaching interpersonal skills to health professionals - Program 1 - overview 15 MIN
VHS / U-matic
Color (T)
Presents a brief overview of the Interpersonal Skills Programs to help potential users determine if the series is appropriate to their needs.
Education; Health and Safety; Psychology
Dist - USNAC **Prod** - NMAC

Teaching interpersonal skills to health professionals - Programs 2 - 7 85 MIN
VHS / U-matic
Color (T)
Discusses the importance of advance planning in preparing for instruction, demonstrating skills to be learned, providing practice opportunities, documenting and critiquing practice experiences, making video recordings and other key elements used in teaching interpersonal skills.
Education; Health and Safety; Psychology
Dist - USNAC **Prod** - NMAC

Teaching introductory chemistry 120 MIN
VHS
Color (C PRO T)
$100.00 purchase _ #V - 6200 - 27306
Stars leading educators from all over the United States. Illustrates chemical demonstrations that are safe, inexpensive and easy to perform in the classroom. Offers fresh approaches to teaching chemistry and ways to present chemical concepts in terms relevant to students in their everyday lives. Features Diane M Bunce, Catholic Univ of America; Julie B Ealy and James L Ealy, Jr, Peddie School; Edmund J Escudero, Summit Country Day School; and Robert G Silberman, State Univ of NY. Includes a course study guide.
Science - Physical
Dist - AMCHEM **Prod** - AMCHEM 1993

Teaching is an Attitude 27 MIN
U-matic / VHS / 16mm
Successful Teaching Practices Series
Color (T)
Features teacher John Robinson showing how innate attitudes can be used in areas of student classroom behavior, racial issues, values clarification and the cooperative learning process.
Education
Dist - EBEC **Prod** - UNIDIM 1982

The Teaching - Learning Process 11 MIN
U-matic / 35mm strip
Supervisor as a Classroom Instructor Series Module 1
Color
Looks at the basic elements of the teaching - learning process, including the teacher, the learner, the subject matter and the environment in which the learning takes place.
Business and Economics; Education; Psychology
Dist - RESEM **Prod** - RESEM

The Teaching Learning Process 25 MIN
VHS / U-matic
How to of Patient Education Series
Color
Explains the basics of the teaching/learning process and defines the roles of both the teacher and the learner in patient education. Discusses the components of the teaching/learning process, including assessment, formulation of objectives, motivation and reinforcement, establishment of the learning environment, learning activities and evaluation.
Health and Safety
Dist - FAIRGH **Prod** - FAIRGH

Teaching Machines 30 MIN
U-matic / VHS
Basic Education - Teaching the Adult Series
Color (T)
Discusses the use of teaching machines with adult basic education students.
Education
Dist - MDCPB **Prod** - MDDE

Teaching Machines and Sidney Pressey 12 MIN
16mm
Communication Theory and the New Educational Media Series
B&W (J H C)
LC 74-705748
Introduces Sidney Pressey, emeritus professor at Ohio State University, and the teaching machine he invented in 1925. Comments on forms of programmed instruction and concludes with a prediction by Pressey about the relation of automated instruction to the teacher.
Education; Psychology; Sociology
Dist - USNAC **Prod** - USOE 1966

Teaching Mathematics - Basic Level 30 MIN
VHS / U-matic
Basic Education - Teaching the Adult Series
Color (T)
Shows how to teach basic level mathematics to adult basic education students.
Education
Dist - MDCPB **Prod** - MDDE

Teaching Mathematics Effectively 30 MIN
U-matic
Color (T)
Demonstrates, with actual classroom episodes, the steps in the effective mathematics lesson. Discusses beginning activities, development, seatwork, and homework.
Education; Psychology
Dist - AFSCD **Prod** - AFSCD 1986

Teaching Methods 10 MIN
VHS / 16mm
Secondary Physical Education Series
Color (C)
$95.00 purchase _ #264003
Familiarizes teachers with Secondary School Physical Education, an expanded curriculum that emphasizes the lifestyle implications of regular physical activity. 'Teaching Methods' models teaching methods based upon the premise that instruction is a chain of decision - making.
Education; Mathematics; Physical Education and Recreation
Dist - ACCESS **Prod** - ACCESS 1986

Teaching Middle and Younger Children 29 MIN
16mm
Teaching Series
Color
Education; Literature and Drama; Religion and Philosophy
Dist - BROADM **Prod** - BROADM 1977

Teaching ministry 20 MIN
VHS
Color (G A R)
$24.95 purchase, $10.00 rental _ #4 - 85080
Outlines the various options for the teaching ministry. Designed for both new and experienced teachers.
Religion and Philosophy
Dist - APH **Prod** - APH

Teaching Modern School Mathematics - Struc - Ture and Use Series
Beginning Concepts in Logic, Dr Ernest Duncan 20 MIN
Fractional Number Concepts, Dr Marilyn J Zweng 19 MIN
Introducing Addition and Subtraction, Dr W G Quast 20 MIN
Introducing Division, Dr Marilyn J Zweng 21 MIN
Introducing Multiplication, Dr Marilyn J Zweng 19 MIN
Introducing Sets, Dr Lelon R Capps 18 MIN
Meaning of Addition and Subtraction, Dr W G Quast 20 MIN
The Meaning of Multiplication, Dr Marilyn J Zweng 19 MIN
Number Sentences, Dr Ernest Duncan 20 MIN
Dist - HMC

Teaching Modern School Mathematics - Structure and Use Series
Decimals and Percents, Dr Ernest Duncan 22 MIN
Dist - HMC

Teaching Observed
U-matic / VHS / 16mm
Color
Shows six teachers from different countries in Africa and Asia at work in their own environment teaching English.
English Language
Dist - NORTNJ **Prod** - NORTNJ

Teaching of and about Thinking 22 MIN
U-matic
Teaching Skillful Thinking Series
Color (T)
Deals with instruction in thinking skills and development of metacognition.
Education; Psychology
Dist - AFSCD **Prod** - AFSCD 1986

The Teaching of Buddha in everyday life 90 MIN
VHS / BETA
Color; PAL (G)
PdS31 purchase
Presents His Eminence Sakya Trizin, the 41st spiritual head of the Sakya school of Tibetan Buddhism and recognized as the emanation of Manjushri, the enlightened prinicple of Wisdom. Gives practical advice on how best to integrate Buddhism into daily life. Recorded at Rigpa, London.
Fine Arts; Religion and Philosophy
Dist - CANCIN

Teaching Older Children 29 MIN
16mm
Teaching Series
Color
Education; Literature and Drama; Religion and Philosophy
Dist - BROADM **Prod** - BROADM 1977

Teaching our children about feelings - 9 38 MIN
VHS / U-matic
Glendon programs - a series
Color (J H C G)
$305.00, $275.00 purchase _ #V598
Features a lively discussion between Dr Firestone and several teenagers. Discusses competitive feelings, anger and other 'unacceptable' feelings and the importance of acknowledging and being responsible for one's feelings. Part of a 12 - part series featuring Dr Robert W Firestone, who is noted for his concept of the 'inner voice' and Voice Therapy.
Guidance and Counseling; Psychology; Social Science; Sociology
Dist - BARR **Prod** - CEPRO 1991

Teaching patients about foot care - Part IV 14 MIN
VHS
Foot care for the older adult series
Color (C PRO G)
$395.00 purchase _ #R921 - VI - 013
Provides information to nurses on four areas of foot care patient education - teaching patients a routine for daily foot care which includes inspecting the feet, care of the nails, hygiene and exercise; discussing with patients various foot problems they may experience, including corns and calluses; explaining the importance of appropriate footwear, including socks and stockings, and recommendations for buying shoes; discussing poor health habits that adversely affect the condition of feet - cigarette smoking, overeating and lack of exercise. Part of a four - part series on foot care for the elderly.
Health and Safety; Physical Education and Recreation; Sociology
Dist - HSCIC **Prod** - CESTAG 1993

Teaching Patients - Three Vignettes 19 MIN
U-matic / VHS
Color (PRO)
Consists of three 5 - minute, unrehearsed patient education vignettes characteristic of typical interactions. Discusses the teaching of patients.
Health and Safety
Dist - UMICHM **Prod** - UMICHM 1981

Teaching People with Developmental Disabilities Series
Error correction 30 MIN
Prompting 25 MIN
Reinforcement 17 MIN
Task Analysis 16 MIN
Dist - RESPRC

Teaching programs in child development series
Case studies in child development - David 31 MIN
The End is My Beginning - an Interdisciplinary Approach to the Assessment 40 MIN
Handicapped Child - Issues in Professional - Parent Communication 25 MIN
Dist - UARIZ

Teaching Reading as Thinking 30 MIN
U-matic
Color (T)
Translates current theory and research on teaching reading comprehension into an instructional model for the classroom. Includes workshop materials.
Education; English Language
Dist - AFSCD **Prod** - AFSCD 1986

Teaching Reading Comprehension 30 MIN
U-matic / VHS
Basic Education - Teaching the Adult Series
Color (T)
Explains how to teach reading comprehension to adult basic education students.
Education
Dist - MDCPB **Prod** - MDDE

Teaching reading comprehension series
Basic inference 30 MIN
Becoming Strategic Readers - Becoming Strategic Teachers 30 MIN
The Current view of reading comprehension series 30 MIN
Developing active - constructive readers within the basal - reader structure 30 MIN
Independent seat work 30 MIN
Integrating Word Analysis - There's more to Reading than Decoding, 30 MIN
Main Idea 30 MIN
Questioning 30 MIN
The Reading - Writing Relationship 30 MIN
Semantic Mapping 30 MIN
Story mapping 30 MIN
Teaching Cohesion Comprehension 30 MIN
What is the Nature of Reading Comprehension Series Instruction Today - 30 MIN
Word Meaning 30 MIN
Dist - AITECH

Teaching Reading to Spanish Speakers 14 MIN
16mm
JAB Reading Series
Color (T)
LC 75-703879
Reports on an experiment to begin reading instruction in both English and Spanish for Spanish - speaking children in kindergarten.
Education; English Language; Foreign Language
Dist - JBFL **Prod** - JBFL 1973

Teaching Reading to Spanish Speakers 14 MIN
16mm
Color (T) (SPANISH)
Presents a teaching experiment that introduces reading to Spanish - speaking kindergarteners in their native language. Shows how the experimental program functions and teacher attitudes toward the program.
English Language; Foreign Language
Dist - JBFL **Prod** - JBFL

Teaching reading two ways - the tired and the true - Tape 7 52 MIN
VHS
Teacher to teacher series
Color (T)
$100.00 purchase _ #892 - 7
Shows exerienced teachers in actual classroom settings presenting various instructional approaches to both new and veteran ABE and ESL teachers. Demonstrates a traditional ESL reading lesson. Compares it to one which helps students to take risks and use the strategies practiced by good readers. Part seven of a 12 - part series.
Education; English Language
Dist - LAULIT **Prod** - LAULIT

Teaching responsible behavior 50 MIN
VHS
Common sense parenting series
Color (G)
$39.95 purchase _ #FFB355V
Shows parents how to correct children's misbehavior, help them accept responsibility for homework and household chores, negotiate positive changes in behavior and help children set and achieve realistic goals. Part of a two - part series.
Guidance and Counseling; Health and Safety; Sociology
Dist - CAMV **Prod** - FFBH 1992

Teaching Role of Nursing Supervisors 12 MIN
U-matic / VHS
Color
Focuses on how the nursing supervisor provides ongoing instruction to nurses. Includes 12 half - hour lessons.
Health and Safety
Dist - TELSTR **Prod** - TELSTR

Teaching Role Series
Creative problem solving 30 MIN
Essential Methods of the Teaching - Learning Process, Pt 1 30 MIN
Essential Methods of the Teaching - Learning Process, Pt 2 30 MIN
Evaluation of Student Performance 30 MIN
Faculty Self - Development 30 MIN
The formulation of objectives 30 MIN
How People Learn 30 MIN
How to Motivate the Student 30 MIN
Instructor Skills in Supportive Evaluation 30 MIN
Role of the Instructor 30 MIN
Strengthening Organizational Relationships 30 MIN
Understanding and Dealing with Student Attitudes and Behavior 30 MIN
Dist - TELSTR

Teaching Safety on the Job 10 MIN
16mm
Human Factors in Safety Series
Color; B&W
Shows how to make the instruction understood, checking and follow - up. Shows how to build safety into job training.
Business and Economics; Health and Safety
Dist - NSC **Prod** - NSC

Teaching Self - examination of the Breasts 20 MIN
U-matic / VHS
Color (PRO)
Includes both a demonstration of the techniques which a health professional may use in teaching self - examinations of the breasts and a demonstration of a woman doing a complete self - examination of the breasts. Discusses specific areas where metastases commonly occur and the characteristics of a breast mass which should be reported.
Health and Safety
Dist - UMICHM **Prod** - UMICHM 1975

Teaching Series
Teaching Adults 29 MIN
Teaching Babies, Creepers and Toddlers at Church 29 MIN
Teaching Fours and Fives at Church 29 MIN
Teaching Middle and Younger Children 29 MIN
Teaching Older Children 29 MIN
Teaching Young Adults 29 MIN
Teaching Youth 29 MIN
Dist - BROADM

Teaching sex education in high school 14 MIN
U-matic / VHS
Color (G)
$249.00, $149.00 purchase _ #AD - 1994
Introduces a singularly effective sex education teacher who unflinchingly faces the issues and minces no words in instructing a class on sexual abstinence, the consequences of sexual activity and AIDS, as well as other sexually transmitted diseases. Features Ed Bradley of '60 Minutes' as host.
Guidance and Counseling; Health and Safety; Psychology; Sociology
Dist - FOTH **Prod** - FOTH

Teaching sign language to the chimpanzee - Washoe 48 MIN
16mm
B&W (H C A)
LC 74-702783
Documents Project Washoe, in which two - way communication was established with a chimpanzee by means of the sign language of the American deaf, Ameslan. Illustrates the range of Washoe's vocabulary, including signs for objects, proper names and actions and the development of sentence - like sequences of signs.
Guidance and Counseling; Psychology; Science - Natural
Dist - PSUPCR **Prod** - UNEV 1973

Teaching Skillful Thinking Series
Issues in Teaching Thinking 30 MIN
The Skillful Thinker 21 MIN
Teaching for Thinking 30 MIN
Teaching of and about Thinking 22 MIN
Dist - AFSCD

Teaching Social and Leisure Skills to Youth with Autism 35 MIN
U-matic / VHS
Color (C A)
LC 84-706391
Documents the activities of five autistic students, illustrating their problems relating socially, using leisure time and coping in the community. Outlines skill objectives which deal with feelings, touching, communication, leisure and other social activities.
Education; Psychology
Dist - IU **Prod** - IU 1983

Teaching strategic for the development of auditory verbal communication series
The development of auditory memory span and sequencing 60 MIN
Dist - BELLAG

Teaching strategies for the development of auditory verbal communication series
Auditory attention, localization and vocal play 60 MIN
Auditory discrimination, feedback and feedforward 60 MIN
Dist - BELLAG

Teaching strategies for the development of auditory verbal communication series
Development of auditory memory span and sequencing 60 MIN
Development of symbolic language - auditory processing 60 MIN
Preparation for mainstreaming 60 MIN
Preparing for mainstreaming 60 MIN
Dist - BELLAG

The Teaching strategies library - part one 180 MIN
VHS
Teaching strategies library series
Color (C A PRO)
$895.00 purchase, $200.00 rental _ #614 - 146X01
Provides information on and demonstrations of four effective strategies for teaching. Demonstrates application of the strategies in classes from kindergarten through high schoool by expert teachers. Package includes four videotapes of the strategies, one overview tape and one workshop leader's manual.
Education
Dist - AFSCD

The Teaching strategies library - Part One 270 MIN
VHS
Teaching strategies library series
Color (T C PRO)
$895.00 purchase, $200.00 rental _ #614 - 146X01
Presents a 4 - part video program offering instructional strategies explaining tried - and - true classroom approaches. Features approaches developed by consultants Richard Strong, Harvey Silver and Robert Hanson. Experienced teachers guide through a step - by - step implementation of each strategy. Covers concepts such as the mastery lecture; concept attainment; concept formation; peer practice; compare and contrast; reading for meaning; synectics; circle of knowledge. Helps teachers align lesson plans and classroom teaching with four important learning outcomes - mastery, understanding, synthesis and involvement. Includes an overview tape to explain the research basis for the strategies, four strategy tapes, and a trainer's manual.
Education
Dist - AFSCD **Prod** - AFSCD 1987

The Teaching strategies library - part two 180 MIN
VHS
Teaching strategies library series
Color (C A PRO)
$795.00 purchase, $200.00 rental _ #614 - 164X01
Provides information on and demonstrations of four effective strategies for teaching. Demonstrates application of the strategies in classes from kindergarten through high schoool by expert teachers. Package includes four videotapes of the strategies, one overview tape and one workshop leader's manual.
Education
Dist - AFSCD

The Teaching strategies library - Part Two
VHS
Color (T C PRO)
$795.00 purchase, $200.00 rental _ #614 - 164X01
Presents a 4 - part video program offering instructional strategies explaining tried - and - true classroom approaches. Features approaches developed by consultants Richard Strong, Harvey Silver and Robert Hanson. Experienced teachers guide through a step - by - step implementation of each strategy. Covers concepts such as the mastery lecture; concept attainment; concept formation; peer practice; compare and contrast; reading for meaning; synectics; circle of knowledge. Helps teachers align lesson plans and classroom teaching with four important learning outcomes - mastery, understanding, synthesis and involvement. Includes an overview tape to explain the research basis for the strategies, four strategy tapes, and a trainer's manual.
Education
Dist - AFSCD **Prod** - AFSCD 1989

Teaching strategies library series
Presents two 4 - part video programs offering eight instructional strategies explaining tried - and - true classroom approaches. Features approaches developed by consultants Richard Strong, Harvey Silver and Robert Hanson. Experienced teachers guide through a step - by - step implementation of each strategy. Covers the mastery lecture; concept attainment; concept formation; peer

practice; compare and contrast; reading for meaning; synectics; circle of knowledge. Helps teachers align lesson plans and classroom teaching with four important learning outcomes - mastery, understanding, synthesis and involvement. Includes an overview tape to explain the research basis for the strategies, eight strategy tapes, and two trainer's manuals.

The Teaching strategies library - Part One 270 MIN
The Teaching strategies library - part two 180 MIN
The Teaching strategies library - part one 180 MIN
Dist - AFSCD **Prod** - AFSCD 1989

Teaching Students with Special Needs Series
Presents instructional techniques and strategies for teaching students with learning deficiencies. Fifteen - part series uses role - playing exercises and commentary from educational experts to train teachers in instruction, classroom management, discipline and dealing with parents.

Behavior Problems in the Classroom 30 MIN
Career and Vocational Education 30 MIN
Employability and the World of Work 30 MIN
Instruction in Mathematics 30 MIN
Instruction in Reading 30 MIN
Instruction in Social Studies and Science 30 MIN
Instruction in Written Expression 30 MIN
Management of Classroom Environment 30 MIN
Medical Problems 30 MIN
Parent Conferencing 30 MIN
Special Needs Students in the Classroom 30 MIN
Survival Skills 30 MIN
Teacher and Peer Attitudes 30 MIN
The Team Approach 30 MIN
Dist - PBS **Prod** - MDINTV 1989

Teaching Styles 29 MIN
U-matic / VHS
On and about Instruction Series
Color (T)
Shows the importance of incorporating a variety of materials and methods into one's personal teaching style.
Education
Dist - GPN **Prod** - VADE 1983

Teaching styles and methods - 8
VHS
Teaching for tomorrow series
Color; PAL (C T)
PdS20 purchase
Uses real teachers and schools to evaluate ideas and support professional development for primary and secondary teachers in the areas of teaching styles and methods. Stimulates discussion on classroom management, handling curriculum changes and developing new teaching techniques. Contact distributor about availability outside the United Kingdom.
Education
Dist - ACADEM

Teaching teachers series
Positive discipline - the key to building self - image 60 MIN
Preparation of the participants 60 MIN
Dist - CTNA

Teaching teams to score - Scott
VHS
Basketball small college winners series
Color (H C G)
$29.95 purchase _ #SAM081V - P
Features Coach Scott who discusses teaching basketball teams to score. Part of an 11 - part series featuring innovative basketball coaches at the small college level.
Physical Education and Recreation
Dist - CAMV

Teaching the Child who is Retarded 20 MIN
16mm
Color
Depicts classroom situations for retarded children at the University of South Dakota summer school program. Illustrates various methods of teaching retarded children.
Education; Psychology
Dist - USD **Prod** - USD

Teaching the elephant to dance 40 MIN
VHS
Color (COR)
$795.00 purchase, $250.00 rental _ #MTE/MA
Offers material to help overcome organizational stagnation through discussions of selling the vision; hiring the right people; measuring and evaluating; creating heroes; setting an example; and rewarding employees. Based on the work of change management expert Dr James Belasco. The video traces Belasco's visits to four organizations that have successfully incorporated his concepts of managing organizational change. Includes a Leader's Guide and course manual. Special twenty - minute versions are available for Government, Healthcare, and Manufacturing.
Business and Economics; Guidance and Counseling; Psychology
Dist - ADVANM

Teaching the gynecologic examination of the disabled patient 29 MIN
U-matic / VHS
Color (PRO C)
$395.00 purchase, $80.00 rental _ #C891 - VI - 014
Demonstrates how to teach the gynecologic examination of the disabled patient using a course instructor, a trained gynecologic teaching associate and a medical student. Emphasizes proper patient communication to facilitate a good physician - patient relationship. Presented by Wendy Baugniet - Nebrija, Drs Susan Daniels, Sterling Sightler and Warren C Plauche.
Health and Safety
Dist - HSCIC

Teaching the Severely Handicapped 14 MIN
16mm
Exceptional Learners Series
Color (T S)
LC 79-700714
Visits classrooms where special equipment and systematic instruction are used to help severely handicapped children achieve their potential.
Education; Psychology
Dist - MERILC **Prod** - MERILC 1978

Teaching the Vietnam war - classroom strategies 72 MIN
VHS
Color (T)
$49.95 purchase _ #CSS100V
Features 40 teachers, including 16 Vietnam veterans who demonstrate classroom strategies they have found effective in teach about the conflict in Vietnam. Contains helpful guides and exercises to understand the geography and culture of Vietnam, promote critical thinking and aid curriculum development. Includes teacher's guide.
Civics and Political Systems; History - United States; Sociology
Dist - CAMV

Teaching throwing - the skills and drills 20 MIN
VHS
VIP softball series
Color (G)
$29.95 purchase _ #ASAT01V
Covers the basics of throwing a softball and how to drill players in this skill. Taught by Bobby Simpson, Cindy Bristow and Buzzy Keller.
Physical Education and Recreation
Dist - CAMV **Prod** - CAMV

Teaching to develop independent learners - 29 MIN
Pt 1 - 4 - 8 years
U-matic / VHS
Color
Describes the educational and emotional values achieved by teaching students to become independent learners and stresses the importance of the teacher's skill in attaining that goal.
Education
Dist - SPF **Prod** - SPF

Teaching to develop independent learners - 29 MIN
Pt 2 - 4 - 8 year olds
U-matic / VHS
Color
Follows same group of students from Part 1 two months later. Relationships on the teaching - learning process which make an increasing degree of independence possible are identified.
Education
Dist - SPF **Prod** - SPF

Teaching to develop independent learners - 29 MIN
Pt 3 - 4 - 8 year olds
VHS / U-matic
Color
Observes the same group of students from Part 2 five months later. Summarizes the skills which must be taught in order to foster independent learning and suggests many practical techniques for use in the classroom.
Education
Dist - SPF **Prod** - SPF

Teaching to develop independent learners - 29 MIN
Pt 4 - 9 - 13 year olds
U-matic / VHS
Color
Reviews the values inherent in helping students become independent learners and introduces a list of skills which must be acquired before that objective can be attained.
Education
Dist - SPF **Prod** - SPF

Teaching to learning styles 30 MIN
VHS
Color (T C PRO)
$328.00 purchase, $125.00 rental _ #614 - 242X01
Introduces teachers in every grade level and subject area to practical approaches for teaching which allows for differences in learning styles. Presents three fundamental guidelines for teaching. Uses classroom scenes from elementary, middle and high schools to show teachers applying the guidelines in a variety of subjects. Includes a leader's guide which offers key information, outlines and activities for implementing an effective workshop on teaching to learning styles, and the ASCD book Marching to Different Drummers by Pat Guild and Stephen Garger.
Education
Dist - AFSCD **Prod** - AFSCD 1992

Teaching to learning styles 30 MIN
VHS
Color (A C PRO)
$398.00 purchase, $125.00 rental _ #614 - 242X01
Helps teachers identify learning styles most effective for individual students and adapt their teaching styles to meet students'needs. Shows how teachers can expand their skills in providing educational activities for individualized instruction. Provides a leader's guide and text along with the video that can be used to hold a seminar or workshop for administrators, teachers or parents.
Education; Psychology
Dist - AFSCD

Teaching to objectives - Pt 1 30 MIN
U-matic / VHS
On and about instruction series
Color (T)
Divides the classification of instructional objectives into three categories - informational, conceptual and procedural.
Education
Dist - GPN **Prod** - VADE 1983

Teaching to objectives - Pt 2 30 MIN
U-matic / VHS
On and about instruction series
Color (T)
Divides the classification of instructional objectives into three categories - informational, conceptual and procedural.
Education
Dist - GPN **Prod** - VADE 1983

Teaching Tomorrow 12 MIN
16mm
Color (P I T)
LC 74-712804
Shows a primary school classroom in rural Kenya, where African children learn science in new ways by using local materials and modern methods. A teacher training film.
Education; Geography - World; Science
Dist - EDC **Prod** - EDC 1970

Teaching Transurethral Surgery using a Cow's Udder 15 MIN
16mm
Color (PRO)
LC FIA66-22
Uses a cow's udder, which simulates in many respects the obstructed human bladder to indicate the technique of transurethral surgery.
Health and Safety
Dist - OSUMPD **Prod** - OSUMPD 1964

The Teaching Triad 17 MIN
U-matic / VHS / 16mm
Color (S)
LC 75-700969
Focuses on the direct involvement of the educational therapist with the family of the handicapped child as well as with the child himself. Defines the teacher - parent - child component as the teaching triad and demonstrates ways teachers and parents together can help to bring the child to his optimal level of development.
Education; Guidance and Counseling; Health and Safety; Psychology; Sociology
Dist - AIMS **Prod** - DUBSET 1974

Teaching vocabulary 13 MIN
VHS / 16mm
English as a second language series
Color (A PRO)
$165.00 purchase _ #290308
Demonstrates key teaching methods for English as a Second Language - ESL teachers. Features a teacher - presenter who introduces and provides a brief commentary on the techniques, then demonstrates the application of the technique to the students. Outlines the process of selecting vocabulary items, assisting students in learning new vocabulary items, and shows how a simple review of new items might be conducted.
Education; English Language; Mathematics
Dist - ACCESS **Prod** - ACCESS 1989

Teaching with Pilote - inset package
VHS
French language for primary - pilote series
Color; PAL (I J T)
PdS29.50 purchase
Helps teachers introduce French into the primary curriculum. Addresses coping with French as a non - specialist teacher; how to bring native speakers to the classroom; building links with Europe; French right across the curriculum; and cross - phrase links. Part of a four - part series on French for beginners at key stage 2 and 3. Includes teacher's notes. Produced by KETV in the United Kingdom.
Foreign Language
Dist - EMFVL

Teaching with Video - Reir, Jugar, Hablar 120 MIN
VHS
Color (T) (SPANISH)
$44.50 purchase - #V72191
Shows innovative methods using poems, dialogs, activities, games and songs to teach beginning Spanish to young children. Includes one videocassette and a booklet of puzzles, jingles and other activity suggestions.
Foreign Language
Dist - NORTNJ **Prod** - NORTNJ

Teaching Word Recognition 30 MIN
U-matic / VHS
Basic Education - Teaching the Adult Series
Color (T)
Explains how to teach word recognition to adult basic education students.
Education
Dist - MDCPB **Prod** - MDDE

Teaching Writing 30 MIN
U-matic / VHS
Basic Education - Teaching the Adult Series
Color (T)
Demonstrates how to teach writing to adult basic education students.
Education
Dist - MDCPB **Prod** - MDDE

Teaching writing - a process approach series 261 MIN
VHS
Teaching writing - a process approach series
Color (G)
$650.00, $830.00 purchase _ #TWPA - 000
Presents theories and practices in instruction of writing. Considers topics such as diagnosis, evaluation, organizing to write, rewriting and other topics. Nine - part series stresses the importance of writing for success in later life.
Education; English Language
Dist - PBS **Prod** - MDINTV 1982

Teaching Writing - the Process 28 MIN
16mm / U-matic / VHS
Dealing with Social Problems in the Classroom Series
Color (T)
LC 82-700489
Presents authors and teachers sharing the writing exercises which they initiate to prompt written expression from their students' life experiences and imaginations. Observes the application of these writing procedures in fourth grade through high school classes.
Education; English Language
Dist - FI **Prod** - MFFD 1982

Teaching Young Adults 29 MIN
16mm
Teaching Series
Color
Education; Literature and Drama; Religion and Philosophy
Dist - BROADM **Prod** - BROADM 1977

Teaching Your First Class 30 MIN
U-matic / VHS
Training the Trainer Series
Color (T)
Discusses preparing for a first class and keeping the lesson on track.
Education; Psychology
Dist - ITCORP **Prod** - ITCORP

Teaching Your Wings to Fly 19 MIN
U-matic / VHS / 16mm
Color (K P)
Deals with the importance of movement, using the mind and body as one to help a child reach his or her full potential. Shows children involved in activities such as the clapping orchestra, invisible strings, train engineers, and trees and hammocks.
Physical Education and Recreation
Dist - ALTSUL **Prod** - BARAL 1978

Teaching Your Wings to Fly - Learning through Movement 19 MIN
16mm
Color
LC 78-701762
Presents dance instructor Anne Lief Barlin demonstrating how to teach young children 19 movement activities designed to enhance body control, self - esteem, spatial awareness, coordination, relating to others and relaxation.
Physical Education and Recreation; Psychology
Dist - LAWREN **Prod** - BARAL 1978

Teaching Youth 29 MIN
16mm
Teaching Series
Color
Education; Literature and Drama; Religion and Philosophy
Dist - BROADM **Prod** - BROADM 1977

The Teahouse 129 MIN
VHS
Color (G) (CHINESE WITH ENGLISH SUBTITLES)
$45.00 purchase _ #6072C
Presents a film from the People's Republic of China. Text available.
Geography - World; Literature and Drama
Dist - CHTSUI

Tealia 10 MIN
U-matic / VHS / 16mm
Color
LC 77-701457
Gives a presentation of an original ballet choreographed and performed by dancers of the San Francisco Ballet.
Fine Arts; Physical Education and Recreation
Dist - PHENIX **Prod** - ROARP 1977

The Team 29 MIN
16mm
Color
Documents the work and scope of Magen David Adom, Israel's Red Cross service.
Health and Safety; Sociology
Dist - ALDEN **Prod** - YANIV

The Team Approach 30 MIN
VHS / U-matic
Teaching Students with Special Needs Series
Color
Presents a discussion of student interdisciplinary action and its composition and usefulness in considering problems recommending solutions.
Education
Dist - PBS **Prod** - MSITV 1981

A Team Approach 30 MIN
U-matic
Investigating Sudden Death Series
(PRO)
Provides an understanding of the science of forensic medicine and the interpersonal cooperation needed.
Health and Safety; Sociology
Dist - ACCESS **Prod** - ACCESS 1978

A Team Approach to Patient Management 20 MIN
U-matic / VHS
Life with Diabetes Series
Color (PRO)
LC 81-707065
Discusses the health care team as it applies to the treatment of people with diabetes. Emphasizes the facts that quality care is based on each team member performing his defined role, the agreement of each member in the team philosophy of treatment, and the effectiveness of the team leader.
Health and Safety
Dist - UMICH **Prod** - UMICH 1980

The Team backstage - sets, lighting, costumes, design 15 MIN
VHS / U-matic
Arts - a - bound
(I)
$130.00 purchase, $25.00
Explores the art of stage set and lighting design. Uses a documentary format featuring interviews with artists, technicians and performers on location, from rehearsal to finished production.
Fine Arts
Dist - GPN **Prod** - NCGE 1985

Team - based quality - Volume 1 30 MIN
VHS
Leading the nation series
Color (PRO IND A)
$595.00 purchase, $595.00 rental _ #ENT14A
Presents volume one of a two - volume series. Uses a government agency's experience to help managers understand how quality can be beneficial and how to implement a quality model within their own organization. Facilitator's Guide and Participant's Workbook are available.
Business and Economics; Civics and Political Systems
Dist - EXTR **Prod** - ENMED

Team Building 18 MIN
16mm / VHS
#109010 - X 3/4
Presents specific suggestions on how to build and maintain good work teams that recognize that the task is the real boss. Explores how to avoid counterproductive human tendencies without eliminating the positive interpersonal side of work teams.
Business and Economics
Dist - MGHT

Team Building 15 MIN
16mm
ICARE Training Series
Color
LC 75-704050
Shows a mock classroom session of instruction on team building for hospital employees.
Health and Safety
Dist - USNAC **Prod** - BHME 1975

Team building 25 MIN
VHS
Color (PRO IND A)
$495.00 purchase, $150.00 rental _ #CR129
Outlines a plan for moving groups into becoming teams. Employs examples and exercises to assist managers in planning, organizing, motivating, setting goals, controlling, building trust, dealing with conflict and emphasizing positive results - leading to improved employee productivity and communication. Includes a leader's guide and workbooks. Based on the book by Robert B Maddux.
Business and Economics; Psychology
Dist - EXTR **Prod** - CRISP

Team Building 18 MIN
U-matic / VHS / 16mm
Color (C A) (SPANISH)
LC 82-701199
Outlines necessary steps to follow and describes common pitfalls to avoid in order to change a group of people into an effective team.
Business and Economics; Foreign Language
Dist - CRMP **Prod** - CRMP 1982

Team building 23 MIN
VHS
Color (PRO IND A)
Helps managers and team members deal with a change in management structure. Covers the issues of groups vs teams, planning and organizing and effective people skills.
Business and Economics; Guidance and Counseling; Psychology; Social Science
Dist - ACTIVM **Prod** - ACTIVM 1990

Team building - an exercise in leadership 22 MIN
VHS
Color (A PRO)
$495.00 purchase, $150.00 rental
Trains managers in organizing, motivating, and making use of teams for best performance. Alerts leaders to errors that can destroy a team's effectiveness.
Business and Economics; Guidance and Counseling; Psychology
Dist - DHB **Prod** - CRISP

Team building - choosing the right individuals for a team 35 MIN
VHS / BETA / U-matic
Color (G)
$495.00 purchase, $130.00 rental
Recognizes that a group of diverse personalities and abilities is desirable in a team. Shows how to use the BEST system for choosing individuals to create an effective team - Balance the team, Exploit diversity, Share the goal, Trust the team. Includes two videos.
Business and Economics; Guidance and Counseling; Psychology
Dist - AMEDIA **Prod** - WYVERN

Team Building for Administrative Support Staff Series
Developing on - the - job communication skills
Making the most of on - the - Job Changes
Using Managerial Techniques on the Job
Working Effectively with Different Managerial Styles
Working with Others
Dist - AMA

Team building - how to motivate and manage people - Vol I 99 MIN
VHS
Team building series
Color (G)
$99.95 purchase _ #20126
Features Mark Sanborn. Explores personnel motivation. Discusses competition in relationship to staff self - esteem

and productivity and the role of the company mission statement. Part one of two parts.
Business and Economics; Psychology
Dist - CARTRP **Prod** - CARTRP

Team building - how to motivate and manage people - Vol II 89 MIN
VHS
Team building series
Color (G)
$99.95 purchase _ #20129
Features Mark Sanborn. Shows how to encourage staff teams to take risks and innovate. Discusses team meetings, monetary v nonmentary rewards and methods of communication. Part two of two parts.
Business and Economics; Psychology
Dist - CARTRP **Prod** - CARTRP

Team building - how to motivate and manage people - Volume 1 90 MIN
VHS
Team building series
Color (H C A)
$99.95 purchase _ #CTKTBL1V
Focuses on the importance of teamwork to any successful group. Discusses how not competing can increase personal self - esteem, how to recruit team members, how to deal with problem team members, and more. Hosted by Mark Sanborn.
Psychology
Dist - CAMV

Team building - how to motivate and manage people - Volume 2 90 MIN
VHS
Team building series
Color (H C A)
$99.95 purchase _ #CTKTBL2V
Focuses on the importance of teamwork to any successful group. Discusses how to increase risk - taking and innovation, what constitutes an effective team meeting, different rewards, and more. Hosted by Mark Sanborn.
Psychology
Dist - CAMV

Team building series
Presents a two - part series which focuses on the importance of teamwork to any successful group. Hosted by Mark Sanborn.
Team building - how to motivate and manage people - Volume 1 90 MIN
Team building - how to motivate and manage people - Volume 2 90 MIN
Team building series 180 MIN
Dist - CAMV

Team building series
Team building - how to motivate and manage people - Vol I 99 MIN
Team building - how to motivate and manage people - Vol II 89 MIN
Dist - CARTRP

Team building - Vol I and II 188 MIN
VHS
Color (G)
$149.95 purchase _ #20126, #20129
Features Mark Sanborn. Explores ways to create a staff team which is motivated to achieve manager and company goals. Discusses how to recruit and hire the best talent and keep them on as employees.
Business and Economics; Psychology
Dist - CARTRP **Prod** - CARTRP

Team compatibility - the truth option 25 MIN
VHS
Color (A)
$595.00 purchase, $150.00 rental _ #V280 - 06
Examines the roles of individuals as part of independent teams as determined in discussions among corporate trainers and executives. Features Will Schutz. Presents questions each team member should ask himself or herself about contributing effectively to the group. Includes a group leader's guide with the video.
Business and Economics; Guidance and Counseling; Psychology
Dist - BARR **Prod** - BARR

Team Conferences 30 MIN
16mm
Nursing - R Plus M Equals C, Relationship Plus Meaning Equals 'Communication Series
B&W (C A)
LC 74-700212
Presents and identifies communication elements in a team conference to observe and analyze specific communication skills in problem solving groups.
Health and Safety; Psychology
Dist - NTCN **Prod** - NTCN 1971

Team development and maintenance 20 MIN
VHS
Color (PRO IND A)
$695.00 purchase, $150.00 rental _ #VCO02
Reflects the current view that authoritarian - style supervision hinders productivity. Probes the supervisor's role in effective team development. Includes a leader's guide and overheads.
Business and Economics; Psychology
Dist - EXTR

Team drills
VHS
Team tactics and team drills - coaching boys' volleyball II series
Color (J H C G)
$49.95 purchase _ #TRS581V
Features Bill Neville, USA National Team coach. Focuses on team drills in volleyball. Part of a three - part series on team tactics and team drills in volleyball and an eight - part series on boys' volleyball.
Physical Education and Recreation
Dist - CAMV

Team excellence 60 MIN
U-matic / 16mm / VHS
Color (G PRO A)
$1295.00, $1095.00, $995.00 purchase, $350.00, $250.00 rental
Visits three companies where teamwork is practiced. Emphasizes the concept of bringing together diverse people with better ideas for better products. Features Walter Cronkite.
Business and Economics; Fine Arts; Guidance and Counseling; Psychology
Dist - MAGVID **Prod** - MAGVID 1986

Team Excellence 60 MIN
U-matic / VHS / 16mm
Color (G)
Brings together diverse people with better ideas for production.
Business and Economics
Dist - VPHI **Prod** - VPHI 1986

Team Leader's Module 26 MIN
U-matic
Color
LC 79-707306
Summarizes the rationale for the employee training program within the Veterans Administration Medical Administration Service.
Guidance and Counseling; Psychology
Dist - USNAC **Prod** - USVA 1978

Team meeting skills 19 MIN
VHS
Tools for continual improvement - one series
Color (IND PRO)
$395.00 purchase _ #ELI01
Presents a newscast format and team demonstration for training employees. Includes trainer's notes, wall charts and reference cards. Available in healthcare and general business versions. Produced by Executive Learning, Inc.
Business and Economics
Dist - EXTR

A Team of champions 52 MIN
VHS
Color (PRO A G)
$695.00 purchase, $195.00 rental
Demonstrates team - building concepts through interviews with successful managers who have implemented principles taught by John Parker Stewart.
Business and Economics; Guidance and Counseling; Psychology
Dist - EXTR **Prod** - EXTR

Team of champions - short version 28 MIN
VHS
Color (PRO IND A)
$595.00 purchase, $195.00 rental _ #ETC18
Presents John Parker Stewart describing skills needed to form a work team that is empowered and motivated towards improvement. Gives supervisors workable guidelines for goal - oriented leadership. Includes leader's guide. Related material also available.
Business and Economics; Guidance and Counseling; Psychology
Dist - EXTR

A Team of eagles 17 MIN
VHS
Color; CC (IND)
$595.00 purchase, $175.00 rental _ #DAR50
Illustrates the methodology of team work through the views of former middle linebacker for the Chicago Bears, Mike Singletary.
Business and Economics; Psychology
Dist - EXTR **Prod** - DARTNL

A Team of eagles - with Mike Singletary, role model and motivator 17 MIN
VHS
Color (H)
$125.00 purchase _ #10349VG
Features Mike Singletary, former NFL football player, as he presents his views on teamwork, motivation and role modeling. Shows the importance of having personal and team goals together and the evolution of a team into a committed group.
Psychology
Dist - UNL

Team Planning in the Cognitively Oriented Curriculum 18 MIN
U-matic / VHS
B&W (PRO)
Shows two preschool teachers at important points of the school day, planning activities, sharing observations of children and evaluating the effectiveness of planned activities.
Education; Psychology
Dist - HSERF **Prod** - HSERF

Team player 21 MIN
VHS / BETA / U-matic
Color; CC (G)
$650.00 purchase, $175.00 rental
Trains organization individuals in functioning as a team while understanding the importance of each individual on the team. Shows how to set common ground rules to make teams more successful, how to solve problems in a structured manner, encourages everyone to participate, to avoid derogatory comments by asking questions, to understand and put into practice key skills needed to be an effective team player. Includes a course materials guide and building block exercise package.
Business and Economics; Psychology
Dist - AMEDIA **Prod** - AMEDIA 1993

Team problem - solving and decision - making 23 MIN
VHS
Color (A PRO)
$495.00 purchase, $150.00 rental
Outlines steps of problem - solving and techniques of analysis, along with ways to improve communication and apply learned skills to practical problems. Based on Sandy Pokras' book Systematic Problem - Solving and Decision - Making.
Business and Economics; Psychology
Dist - DHB **Prod** - CRISP 1994

Team Roping 26 MIN
U-matic / VHS / 16mm
Color
Deals with team roping including techniques and pointers on the selection and use of rope, and the training and selection of team roping horses.
Physical Education and Recreation
Dist - AQHORS **Prod** - AQHORS 1978

Team Roping Clinic 30 MIN
VHS / BETA
Western Training Series
Color
Demonstrates how to win team roping.
Physical Education and Recreation
Dist - EQVDL **Prod** - EQVDL

A Team Show 30 MIN
U-matic / VHS
Musical Encounter Series
Color (P I)
Features three musical teams, including a 14 - piece string orchestra, a group of eight violinists, and The Haydn Trio. Points out that while it is important to be able to play solo, it is also very important and great fun to learn to play with others. Presents Heiichiro Ohyama, principal viola of the Los Angeles Philharmonic Orchestra. Hosted by Florence Henderson.
Fine Arts
Dist - GPN **Prod** - KLCSTV 1983

Team skills for meeting together - Part 6 14 MIN
VHS
Employment development series
Color (PRO IND A)
$495.00 purchase, $150.00 rental _ #ITC32
Presents part six of a ten - part series designed to prepare employees to cope with workplace demands in a skillful and confident manner. Enables supervisors and managers to improve their skills and abilities as they work with their peers. Includes a leader's guide, instructions for self - study and participant's booklet.
Business and Economics; Guidance and Counseling; Psychology
Dist - EXTR **Prod** - ITRC

Team Spirit 18 MIN
16mm
Color
LC 78-701900
Depicts joint American and Korean military operations in the Pacific.
Civics and Political Systems
Dist - USNAC **Prod** - USDDI 1978

Team Spirit 10 MIN
VHS
MacNeil - Lehrer Newshour Series
Color (G)
$49.95 purchase _ #MLNH - 100
Explores the unique motivational strategies of Jack Stack, president and CEO of Springfield Re - Manufacturing Corporation. Shows how the SRC strategy emphasizes team identity and pride within work units.
Business and Economics; Guidance and Counseling
Dist - PBS **Prod** - MLPRO 1990

Team strategies and containment 16 MIN
VHS / U-matic / BETA
Managing assaultive patients series
Color (C PRO)
$280.00 purchase _ #615.2
Describes ways in which health care staff can work together as a cohesive team, including instruction on safe and humane restraining maneuvers suitable for staff of any age or level of physical fitness. Discusses the different roles that each staff member plays in the containment process. Illustrates the value of post - incident reviews and staff support. Part of a series on managing assaultive patients.
Health and Safety; Psychology; Sociology
Dist - CONMED **Prod** - CALDMH

Team tactics 90 MIN
VHS
Beginning girls' volleyball series
Color (J H C G)
$49.95 purchase _ #TRS602V
Follows a natural progression of team tactics from simple front court setting to more advanced backcourt setting concepts. Includes discussions and demonstrations of serve - receive formations critical to determining the success of offense. Part of a three - part series on girls' volleyball.
Physical Education and Recreation
Dist - CAMV

Team tactics and team drills - coaching boys' volleyball II series
Defensive tactics
Offensive tactics
Team drills
Dist - CAMV

The Team that Hustles - the Inside Story of Your Bones and Muscles 15 MIN
U-matic / VHS
Inside Story with Slim Goodbody Series
Color (P I)
Presents Slim Goodbody and a friendly skeleton who chat about bones and their structure. Shows different types of bones, joints, and muscles, and how they work together. Stresses good food and exercise.
Science - Natural
Dist - AITECH **Prod** - UWISC 1981

Team - Work 11 MIN
U-matic / VHS / 16mm
Color
LC 83-700222
Offers a nonverbal parable from the People's Republic of China about three monks and their development of a cooperative system of collecting water from a spring at the foot of the mountain.
Fine Arts; Literature and Drama
Dist - ALTSUL **Prod** - ALTSUL 1982

Team Work for a Controlled Environment 24 MIN
16mm
Color
LC FIE59-232
Stresses the importance of healthful living and working conditions at Air Force installations and shows how a successful preventive - medicine program is dependent upon the continuing joint efforts of the various activities concerned.
Civics and Political Systems; Health and Safety; Sociology
Dist - USNAC **Prod** - USAF 1958

Teambuilding - a blueprint for success 19 MIN
VHS
Color (A PRO IND)
$595.00 purchase, $150.00 rental
Uses the setting of an architectural firm to demonstrate effective team - building techniques. Emphasizes overcoming employee resistance, creating cooperative work attitudes, and the development of team management techniques.
Business and Economics; Psychology
Dist - VLEARN **Prod** - EFM

Teambuilding - an exercise in leadership 25 MIN
VHS
Color (A PRO IND)
$395.00 purchase
Uses case studies and exercises to present a step - by - step program for developing a workplace team. Covers subjects including planning, organizing, motivating, controlling, goal - setting, and more. Includes leader's guide and workbooks.
Business and Economics; Psychology
Dist - VLEARN

Teaming up 28 MIN
VHS
Quality - productivity series
Color (PRO G A)
$595.00 purchase, $150.00 rental
Explains the use and implementation of team concepts in a work setting. Dramatizes team concepts applied to professional, service and manufacturing organizations. Part of a four - part series based on material by Dr. Richard Chang. Workshop materials are available separately.
Business and Economics; Psychology
Dist - EXTR **Prod** - DOUVIS

Teams and leaders 23 MIN
VHS
Color (A PRO IND)
$795.00 purchase, $185.00 rental
Trains new managers in team formation. Covers subjects including determining objectives, gaining commitment, utilizing diverse personalities, and more.
Business and Economics; Psychology
Dist - VLEARN **Prod** - MELROS

Teams and Leaders
VHS
Management Development Series
Color (G)
$795.00 purchase, $185.00 rental
Presents insights into an office problem which are gained during a walking expedition in Wales. Part of a five - part series on management development.
Business and Economics; Guidance and Counseling; Psychology
Dist - VLEARN **Prod** - MELROS

Teamwork
U-matic / VHS
Implementing Quality Circles Series
Color
Emphasizes communication and participation by quality circle members. Stresses reacting to ideas rather than to the person presenting them.
Business and Economics; Psychology
Dist - BNA **Prod** - BNA

Teamwork 8 MIN
U-matic / VHS
Color (A)
Shows how commitment to a team can make the difference between success and failure in sports and business. Narrated by Jack Whitaker.
Physical Education and Recreation; Psychology
Dist - SFTI **Prod** - SFTI

Teamwork - a Film from the People's Republic of China 11 MIN
16mm / U-matic / VHS
Color (H C A)
LC 83-700001
Uses a story about three feuding monks, who must replenish their temple's water, in order to demonstrate the importance of teamwork. Shows how the monks develop a new and ingenious method for sharing the task. Designed to illustrate the dynamics of groups and how these dynamics affect group performance.
Geography - World; Guidance and Counseling; Psychology
Dist - SALENG **Prod** - SAFS 1982

Teamwork - an Introduction to Group Dynamics 24 MIN
16mm / U-matic / VHS
Color (C A)
LC 84-706177
Presents the film Teamwork, a short animated film from China, after which Dr Frank Wagner analyzes the film, indicating the six sources of conflict illustrated.
Psychology
Dist - SALENG **Prod** - SALENG 1984

Teamwork and Leadership 29 MIN
Videoreel / VT2
Interpersonal Competence, Unit 08 - Groups Series; Unit 8 - Groups
Color (C A)
Features a humanistic psychologist who, by analysis and examples, discusses teamwork and leadership.
Psychology; Sociology
Dist - TELSTR **Prod** - MVNE 1973

Teamwork - Business and Government - Relationships between Business and Government
VHS
Entrepreneurs - the Risk Takers Series
$70.00 purchase _ #RPS4V
Discusses the relationships of business with government as expressed by various entrepreneurs and politicians.
Business and Economics
Dist - CAREER **Prod** - CAREER

Teamwork for Safety 10 MIN
16mm
Human Factors in Safety Series
Color; B&W
Illustrates making a group of people feel like part of a team and function like one. Shows how team effort helps prevent accidents.
Business and Economics; Health and Safety
Dist - NSC **Prod** - NSC

Teamwork - gaining cooperation and commitment 30 MIN
VHS
Color (A PRO IND)
$645.00 purchase, $150.00 rental
Stresses the need to build and maintain commitment and cooperation within a project team. Covers how best to utilize individual strengths, diversity, and encouraging an environment where creative solutions are welcomed.
Business and Economics; Psychology
Dist - VLEARN

Teamwork in Action 33 MIN
16mm
Color
Tells what happens to an Ontario workman and his family when he is disabled by an industrial accident. Shows the roles of various members of the team with whom the victim comes into contact as a result of his accident.
Guidance and Counseling; Health and Safety
Dist - ISWELC **Prod** - ISWELC

Teamwork on call 25 MIN
VHS
Color (G)
$495.00 purchase, $140.00 rental _ #91F6092
Identifies attitudes and behaviors that characterize good teamwork. Focuses on hospital staff.
Business and Economics; Health and Safety; Social Science
Dist - DARTNL **Prod** - DARTNL

Teamwork on the Nevada Range 18 MIN
16mm
Color
LC FIE63-217
Tells the story of rural development through the combined efforts of government agencies and Nevada ranchers.
Geography - United States; Sociology
Dist - USNAC **Prod** - USDA 1963

Teamwork on the Potomac 29 MIN
16mm
Color
LC FIA66-790
A story about pollution in the Potomac River. Shows the river at its worst and describes the difficult climb toward restoration. Discusses pollution and waste - disposal methods. Explores water - management problems in detail.
Geography - United States; Health and Safety; Science - Natural; Sociology
Dist - FINLYS **Prod** - FINLYS 1965

Teamwork, pride and professionalism 22 MIN
VHS
Color (A PRO)
$525.00 purchase, $110.00 rental
Features Notre Dame football coach Lou Holtz and his perspectives on working together, meeting customers' expectations, developing self - esteem, and more.
Guidance and Counseling; Psychology
Dist - VLEARN

Teamwork, Pride, and Professionalism - an Interview with Lou Holtz 22 MIN
VHS / 16mm
Color (PRO)
$525.00 purchase, $110.00 rental, $35.00 preview
Presents football coach Lou Holtz who encourages members of a company to work together. Teaches how to create and maintain a successful sales team, how to please customers and how personal pride in the company can help it to be a success.
Business and Economics; Education; Guidance and Counseling; Psychology
Dist - UTM **Prod** - UTM

Teamwork - safe handling of a hazardous materials incident 37 MIN
VHS / U-matic
Color (G PRO)
$50.00, $25.00 purchase _ #35331, #35330
Presents an incident an overturned tank truck leaking flammable poisonous material. Covers every aspect of the incident from time it happens through cleanup and critique. Trains firefighting personnel and other handlers of hazardous materials.
Health and Safety; Psychology; Social Science; Sociology
Dist - OKSU **Prod** - CHEMMA

Teamwork video 3 MIN
VHS
Meeting opener motivation videos series
Color (G)
$89.00 purchase _ #MV3
Presents an inspiration video which incorporates cinematography, music and lyrics to create a mood that enhances the impact of the desired message.
Business and Economics; Psychology
Dist - GPERFO

Teamwork with Pat Riley 24 MIN
VHS / 16mm / U-matic
Color (J H C G)
$520.00, $365.00, $395.00 _ #A514
Explains to viewers how to develop a team attitude, motivate a continuous stream of contributions from individuals, combine individual talents to yield a greater whole than the sum of talents, and focus competitive drives outward from the team toward the competition.
Business and Economics; Education; Psychology; Social Science
Dist - BARR **Prod** - BARR 1988

Teamwork with Pat Riley 24.5 MIN
16mm / U-matic / VHS
Color (H C)
LC 88-3387878
Demonstrates specific concepts and techniques that can help viewers build a more focused and motivated team.
Guidance and Counseling; Physical Education and Recreation
Dist - BARR **Prod** - BARR 1988

Teamwork - working well with others - module 4 60 MIN
Software / VHS
Attributes for successful employability series
Color (H)
$395.00 purchase
Presents four 60 - minute Level III interactive video modules - available for Macintosh and IBM InfoWindow - dealing with realistic work situations which call for choices. Makes it clear that while some choices are better than others, often there is no right answer, just different answers with different results. Each module includes five scenes filmed at a variety of work environments. Each scene includes a computerized dictionary of terms which define the attributes demonstrated in the scene. The learner views, reviews and experiments with alternative solutions to problems presented. Module 4 stresses proper grooming, loyalty, communication, teamwork, cooperation and integrity.
Business and Economics; Education; Guidance and Counseling; Psychology
Dist - AITECH **Prod** - BLUNI 1990

Teamworking 13 MIN
U-matic / VHS / 16mm
Color (J)
Observes the creative efforts of three teams, a group of ecologically - minded architects, a crew of Ford automobile design engineers and talented members of a ballet company.
Fine Arts; Industrial and Technical Education
Dist - PHENIX **Prod** - WILANH

Teapots 28 MIN
Videoreel / VT2
Wheels, Kilns and Clay Series
Color
Features Mrs Peterson describing certain ceramic processes for her classroom at the University of Southern California. Includes a demonstration with teapots.
Fine Arts
Dist - PBS **Prod** - USC

Tear Gas and Self - Defense 14 MIN
16mm / U-matic / VHS
Color (H C A)
Presents tear gas as an effective and safe self - defense weapon, but one that is controlled by law. Describes the effect of the gas on the criminal and shows how to use the cannisters. Distinguishes between legal and illegal use, stressing that tear gas should be used only to allow the user to escape.
Physical Education and Recreation
Dist - AIMS **Prod** - AIMS 1981

Tear on the Dotted Line 28 MIN
U-matic
A Different Understanding Series
Color (PRO)
Looks at the emotional and practical problems of two teenagers in a foster home.
Sociology
Dist - TVOTAR **Prod** - TVOTAR 1985

Tear on the dotted line 28 MIN
VHS / 16mm
A Different understanding series
Color (G)
$90.00 purchase _ #BPN178018
Looks at the emotional and practical problems of 2 teenagers living in a foster home. Features discussion between the two teens and their social worker about their daily lives and how they help each other.
Sociology
Dist - RMIBHF **Prod** - RMIBHF

Tear - Or 4 MIN
16mm
Color (G)
$10.00 rental
Refers to a poem by Erik Kiviat.
Fine Arts
Dist - CANCIN **Prod** - LEVINE 1967

Tearing down the walls - the GEO change forces 22 MIN
VHS / U-matic
Color (H C A G)
$695.00 purchase _ #V224
Shows how globalization, empowerment and orchestration are changing the global marketplace, the work - force and technology. Produced by GEO.
Business and Economics; Guidance and Counseling
Dist - BARR

Tears 30 MIN
U-matic
Today's Special Series
Color (K P)
Develops language arts skills in children. Programs are thematically designed around subjects of interest to youngsters. Action takes place in a department store where people, mannequins, puppets, comic characters and special guests present a light hearted approach to language arts.
Fine Arts; Literature and Drama; Psychology
Dist - TVOTAR **Prod** - TVOTAR 1985

Tears of the Apache - Lagrimas De Apache 29 MIN
VHS / 16mm
Sonrisas Series
Color (T P) (SPANISH)
$46.00 rental _ #SRSS - 113
Shows a young Native American child coming to grips with his heritage. In Spanish and English.
Social Science; Sociology
Dist - PBS

Teasing and Being Teased 22 MIN
16mm
I Am, I Can, I will, Level II Series
Color (K P S)
LC 80-700571
Presents Mr Rogers explaining how teasing can make people feel bad. Discusses growing up with a physical handicap and other personal differences.
Guidance and Counseling; Psychology
Dist - HUBDSC **Prod** - FAMCOM 1979

Teasing, Breeding and Semen Collection in the Horse 25 MIN
VHS / BETA
Color
Gives examples of estrus in mares. Tells how to wash a horse's penis. Discusses condoms and artificial vaginas for semen collection.
Health and Safety; Physical Education and Recreation
Dist - EQVDL **Prod** - UMINN

Teatro 60 MIN
VHS
Color (R) (SPANISH)
$29.95 purchase _ #579 - 8, #578 - X
Takes a look at the acting troupe of Teatro la Fragua - The Forge Theater - in Honduras. Includes discussion guide. Funded by the Catholic Communication Campaign.
Fine Arts; Religion and Philosophy
Dist - USCC

Teatro - theater and the spirit of change 58 MIN
16mm / VHS
Color (H C G) (SPANISH)
$850.00, $445.00 purchase, $125.00, $85.00 rental
Explores the realities of life in Honduras, the Latin American nation best known as a haven for the Contras. Reveals that illiteracy and malnutrition are a way of life in Honduras and that political opposition is stifled, but a grassroots theater company - Teatro la Fragua - led by a Jesuit priest, Jack Warner, travels the backroads of Honduras to bring a message of social justice to people who have never seen a play. Produced by Edward Burke and Ruth Shapiro.
Civics and Political Systems; Fine Arts; History - World
Dist - FLMLIB

Tech Island 14 MIN
U-matic
Color
Profiles four Long Island engineers and their work.
Civics and Political Systems; Sociology
Dist - WSTGLC **Prod** - WSTGLC

Tech prep - A Future to look forward to 10 MIN
VHS
Color (J H PRO T)
$99.50 purchase _ #TMTPA - A
Informs parents, teachers, counselors, and business leaders about CFKR's JOB - O Tech Prep programs. Includes testimonials from a business leader, a college Tech Prep coordinator and a college administrator who outline the 'teamwork' approach that will make Tech Prep work.
Business and Economics; Guidance and Counseling
Dist - CFKRCM **Prod** - CFKRCM

Tech prep and business occupations 17 MIN
VHS
Color (J H T)
$129.95 purchase _ #MEC107V-J
Informs viewers about business and office related occupations and how a tech prep program builds the necessary skills for entry into the field. Includes careers as secretaries, legal assistants, auditing personnel, computer programmers, court reporters, administrative assistants, office managers, computer bookkeepers, and accountants. Includes teacher's guide.
Business and Economics; Guidance and Counseling
Dist - CAMV

Tech prep careers of the future video series
Presents a five - part video series which examines careers in a variety of fields in a program developed in conjunction with the Carl Perkins Applied Technology Act. Discloses what the technical preparatory, vocational student or community college graduate can expect from the work place and how the student's interest, values and skills relate to each of the clusters presented. Balances relevant career data with what to expect from the day to day workplace. Features three in - depth interviews in each program. Includes Family, Social and Human Services; Business and Management; Production and Technology; Environmental, Physical and Health Sciences; and Communication.

Business and management	25 MIN
Communications	25 MIN
Environmental, physical and health science	25 MIN
Family, social and human services	25 MIN
Production and technology	25 MIN
Tech prep careers of the future video series	125 MIN

Dist - CAMV

Tech prep - It's where the action is 8 MIN
VHS
Color (J H PRO T)
$99.50 purchase _ #TMTPT - A
Presents an MTV - style video that explains to students about options in their education. Highlights the advantages of CFKR's Tech Prep programs, applied academics, earning power, and lifelong learning. Balanced ethnic and gender representation in non - traditional roles. Includes worksheets and a teacher's guide.
Business and Economics; Guidance and Counseling
Dist - CFKRCM **Prod** - CFKRCM

The Tech prep video series
Explores three career areas in terms of related academic - vocational coursework and innovative business - industry - school relationships such as mentor, apprenticeship programs, coop programs and company tuition programs. Looks at tech prep for schools and teachers, students, business and industry.

The Tech prep video series	30 MIN

Dist - CAMV

Technical animals 26 MIN
VHS / U-matic
Survival in nature series
Color (J H)
$275.00, $325.00 purchase, $50.00 rental
Documents the select number of animals around the world that have discovered tool technology. Looks at how they have developed tool skills as a means of survival.
Science - Natural
Dist - NDIM **Prod** - SURVAN 1990

Technical Considerations in Hemipelvectomy 16 MIN
16mm
Color (PRO)
Demonstrates a tumor of the upper femur for which hemipelvectomy is indicated. Shows the case of a 60 year old woman with a chondrosarcoma of the left pubis with details of the operative procedures.
Health and Safety; Science
Dist - ACY **Prod** - ACYDGD 1955

Technical Data Management and Documentation 42 MIN
16mm
B&W
LC 74-706272
Presents a panel discussion on the status of the Department of Defense management program. Discusses program weaknesses, problems and improvement possibilities.
Business and Economics; Civics and Political Systems
Dist - USNAC **Prod** - USAF 1965

Technical manager 85 MIN
VHS
Color (A PRO IND)
$965.00 purchase, $375.00 rental
Trains technical specialists for management positions. Presents a framework for managing and motivating other technical people. Consists of two videocassettes.
Business and Economics; Psychology
Dist - VLEARN **Prod** - EFM

Technical - Manufacturing cluster 1 20 MIN
U-matic / VHS
Vocational visions series
Color
Discusses the requirements and duties for such jobs as welder, drafter, sheet metal worker and instrumentation technician.
Guidance and Counseling; Psychology
Dist - GA **Prod** - GA

Technical - Manufacturing cluster 2 25 MIN
U-matic / VHS
Vocational visions series
Color
Discusses the requirements and duties for such jobs as computer programmer, engineering technician, fluid power technologist, avionics technician and parts merchandiser.
Guidance and Counseling; Psychology
Dist - GA **Prod** - GA

Technical Occupations 33 MIN
VHS / U-matic
Video Career Library Series
(H C A)
$69.95 _ #CJ118V
Covers duties, conditions, salaries, and training connected with jobs in the technical field. Provides a view of employees in technical related occupations, and gives information on the current market for such skills. Revised every two years.
Education; Guidance and Counseling; Industrial and Technical Education
Dist - CAMV **Prod** - CAMV

Technical Occupations 33 MIN
VHS / 16mm
Video Career Library Series
Color (H C A PRO)
$79.95 purchase _ #WW108
Shows technical occupations such as clinical laboratory technicians, medical records technicians, electrical engineering technologists, drafters, chemical technologists, air traffic controllers, computer programers, technical writers and others. Contains current occupational outlook and salary information.
Business and Economics; Guidance and Counseling
Dist - AAVIM **Prod** - AAVIM 1990

Technical Occupations - Dental Hygienics
VHS
Video Career Series
$29.95 purchase _ #MD151V
Shows students going 'on the job' to learn the variety of skills required for this occupation and the special training or educational requirements. Discusses various hiring procedures and what is involved in joining a professional association or union.
Education; Guidance and Counseling
Dist - CAREER **Prod** - CAREER

Technical Occupations - Drafting
VHS
Video Career Series
$29.95 purchase _ #MD153V
Shows students going 'on the job' to learn the variety of skills required for this occupation and the special training or educational requirements. Discusses various hiring procedures and what is involved in joining a professional association or union.
Education; Guidance and Counseling
Dist - CAREER **Prod** - CAREER

Technical Occupations - Graphic Arts
VHS
Video Career Series
$29.95 purchase _ #MD155
Shows students going 'on the job' to learn the variety of skills required for this occupation and the special training or educational requirements. Discusses various hiring procedures and what is involved in joining a professional association or union.
Education; Guidance and Counseling
Dist - CAREER **Prod** - CAREER

Technical Occupations - Mechanics
VHS
Video Career Series
$29.95 purchase _ #MD158V
Shows students going 'on the job' to learn the variety of skills required for this occupation and the special training or educational requirements. Discusses various hiring procedures and what is involved in joining a professional association or union.
Education; Guidance and Counseling
Dist - CAREER **Prod** - CAREER

Technical Occupations - Medical Laboratory Technology
VHS
Video Career Series
$29.95 purchase _ #MD159V
Shows students going 'on the job' to learn the variety of skills required for this occupation and the special training or educational requirements. Discusses various hiring procedures and what is involved in joining a professional association or union.
Education; Guidance and Counseling
Dist - CAREER **Prod** - CAREER

Technical occupations - part 1
VHS
Profiles - people and jobs series
Color (H G)
$50.00 purchase _ #TOCC - 1V
Presents part of a series of 6 videos that introduce high school students to high demand, rewarding occupations of the future. Looks at the careers of Engineering Technicians; Science Technicians; Computer Programmers. Series is based on the Occupational Outlook Handbook.
Business and Economics; Guidance and Counseling
Dist - CENTER **Prod** - CENTER

Technical occupations - part 2
VHS
Profiles - people and jobs series
Color (H G)
$50.00 purchase _ #TOCC - 2V
Presents part of a series of 6 videos that introduce high school students to high demand, rewarding occupations of the future. Looks at the careers of Clinical Laboratory Technicians; Licensed Practical Nurses; Radiologic Technologists. Series is based on the Occupational Outlook Handbook.
Business and Economics; Guidance and Counseling
Dist - CENTER **Prod** - CENTER

Technical Occupations - Performing Arts Technologies
VHS
Video Career Series
$29.95 purchase _ #MD161V
Shows students going 'on the job' to learn the variety of skills required for this occupation and the special training or educational requirements. Discusses various hiring procedures and what is involved in joining a professional association or union.
Education; Guidance and Counseling
Dist - CAREER **Prod** - CAREER

Technical Occupations - Photographic Processing
VHS
Video Career Series
$29.95 purchase _ #MD162V
Shows students going 'on the job' to learn the variety of skills required for this occupation and the special training or educational requirements. Discusses various hiring procedures and what is involved in joining a professional association or union.
Education; Guidance and Counseling
Dist - CAREER **Prod** - CAREER

Technical Occupations - Printing
VHS
Video Career Series
$29.95 purchase _ #MD163
Shows students going 'on the job' to learn the variety of skills required for this occupation and the special training or educational requirements. Discusses various hiring procedures and what is involved in joining a professional association or union.
Education; Guidance and Counseling
Dist - CAREER **Prod** - CAREER

Technical Occupations - Radio and Television Production
VHS
Video Career Series
$29.95 purchase _ #MD164
Shows students going 'on the job' to learn the variety of skills required for this occupation and the special training or educational requirements. Discusses various hiring procedures and what is involved in joining a professional association or union.
Education; Guidance and Counseling
Dist - CAREER **Prod** - CAREER

Technical Occupations - Utilities Equipment Operation
VHS
Video Career Series
$29.95 purchase _ #MD175V
Shows students going 'on the job' to learn the variety of skills required for this occupation and the special training or educational requirements. Discusses various hiring procedures and what is involved in joining a professional association or union.
Education; Guidance and Counseling
Dist - CAREER **Prod** - CAREER

Technical Procedures for Diagnosis and Therapy in Children 27 MIN
16mm
Color (PRO)
LC 74-705752
Gives step - by - step procedures for femoral venipuncture, internal jugular puncture, lumbar puncture, subdural tap, gastric lavage, scalp venipuncture and cutdown.
Health and Safety; Science - Natural
Dist - USNAC **Prod** - USN 1965

Technical Proposal Evaluation 19 MIN
VHS / U-matic
Color
LC 80-706762
Describes the methodology of evaluating technical proposals.
Civics and Political Systems
Dist - USNAC **Prod** - USDL 1978

The Technical Side of Production 30 MIN
VHS / U-matic
Behind the Scenes Series
Color
Fine Arts
Dist - ARCVID **Prod** - ARCVID

The Technical side of TV 12 MIN
VHS / U-matic
Getting the most out of TV series
Color (P I J)
$195.00, $245.00 purchase, $50.00 rental
Looks at how TV pictures are made and broadcast. Visits a TV studio, set and control room. Part of a seven - part series.
Fine Arts; Industrial and Technical Education
Dist - NDIM **Prod** - YALEU 1981
CORF TAPPRO

Technical studies 375 MIN
VHS
Technical studies series
Color (A PRO IND)
PdS450 purchase
Presents a series designed to take students out of the classroom setting and into the world of engineering. Highlights key topics which show how fundamental concepts in materials and engineering science are applied to manufacturing.
Business and Economics; Industrial and Technical Education
Dist - BBCENE

Technical studies series
Bearing materials 25 MIN
Capstan and turret lathes 25 MIN
Cutting tool materials 25 MIN
Non - ferrous metals and alloys 25 MIN
Technical studies 375 MIN
Welding techniques 25 MIN
Dist - BBCENE

Technical studies series
Die and investment casting 25 MIN
Engineering design 25 MIN
Forging 25 MIN
Heat Treatment 25 MIN
Manufacturing with Plastics 25 MIN
Micro - Electronics 25 MIN
Pressworking 25 MIN
Properties of Plastics 25 MIN

Rolling 25 MIN
Sand casting 25 MIN
Dist - FI

Technical theatre series
Presents a five - part series on theater techniques. Includes the titles Where Do I Start; How Do I Paint It; Shedding Some Light; The Basic Costume; The Make - Up Workshop.
The Basic costumer 73 MIN
How do I paint it 83 MIN
The Make - up workshop 90 MIN
Shedding some light 95 MIN
Technical theatre series 413 MIN
Where do I start 72 MIN
Dist - CAMV

Technical Venture Strategies 49 MIN
U-matic / VHS
Management of Technological Innovation Series
Color
Discusses entrepreneurial alternatives, investments in small companies, joint ventures and new venture spin - offs, internal venture generation and directions for enhancing new venture results.
Business and Economics; Industrial and Technical Education
Dist - MIOT **Prod** - MIOT

Technical Writing 150 MIN
U-matic / VHS
Color
Teaches how to convey technical material with specific audiences in mind. Reveals how to develop an organizational approach to technical writing that communicates effectively.
Education; English Language; Literature and Drama; Science - Physical
Dist - AMCHEM **Prod** - AMCHEM

Technical writing series
Applied technical writing 15 MIN
Efficient technical writing 15 MIN
Technical Writing Techniques 15 MIN
Dist - DELTAK

Technical Writing Techniques 15 MIN
VHS / U-matic
Technical Writing Series
Color
Business and Economics; English Language; Industrial and Technical Education
Dist - DELTAK **Prod** - DELTAK

Technicians in Our Changing World 14 MIN
16mm / U-matic / VHS
Color; B&W (J H)
LC FIA65-1820
Explains the impact of recent advances in science and automation. Points out the work of technicians in industry, business and medicine. Underscores the growing need for competent people and describes the educational and attitudinal requirements.
Guidance and Counseling; Psychology; Sociology
Dist - STANF **Prod** - STANF 1965

Technicians of tomorrow 20 MIN
16mm
Color
Describes the training of specialists -- the engineering technicians in two - year technical colleges -- and points out the increasing need for them in American industry.
Business and Economics; Industrial and Technical Education
Dist - USOE **Prod** - SGF 1966

Technicolor fashion parade 9 MIN
16mm
Color (G)
$15.00 rental
Features a Gatsby - era short in two - strip Technicolor in which some Hollywood starlets show off the latest fashions.
Fine Arts; Home Economics; Literature and Drama
Dist - KITPAR

Technique 29 MIN
U-matic / VHS / 16mm
Photography - the Incisive Art Series
B&W (H C A)
LC FIA66-1124
Illustrates from the collection of Ansel Adams the use of light, filters, exposure, magnification and interpretation. Demonstrates the use of these techniques to achieve given effects.
Fine Arts; Industrial and Technical Education
Dist - IU **Prod** - NET 1962

Technique for Making a Slide Culture 18 MIN
U-matic
Color
LC 80-706766
Demonstrates step - by - step mycological techniques used to identify a fungal culture.
Science
Dist - USNAC **Prod** - CFDISC 1979

Technique for Propelling Standard Wheelchair by Hemiplegic Patient 8 MIN
16mm
Color
LC 74-705753
Demonstrates the manner in which a hemiplegic can be taught to use a wheelchair.
Health and Safety; Psychology
Dist - USNAC **Prod** - USPHS 1966

Technique of Brain Surgery of the Cat with Observations on Vestibular Disfunction 15 MIN
16mm
B&W (C)
Describes surgical operation on a cat to section the eighth cranial nerve and shows the many classical symptoms of vestibular disfunction.
Science
Dist - PSUPCR **Prod** - NESMKA 1939

Technique of Clinical Electromyography 17 MIN
16mm
Color (PRO)
Demonstrates the use of the electromyograph and shows procedures employed in the use of the electrode needle. Illustrates the impulses caused from muscular contractions.
Health and Safety
Dist - LOMAM **Prod** - LOMAM

Technique of Fresh - Frozen Section Histochemistry as Applied to Muscle Biopsies 15 MIN
U-matic
Intensive Course in Neuromuscular Diseases Series
Color (PRO)
LC 76-706109
Presents Dr Guy Cunningham lecturing on the technique of fresh - frozen section histochemistry as applied to muscle biopsies.
Health and Safety; Science; Science - Natural
Dist - USNAC **Prod** - NINDIS 1974

Technique of Intra - Articular and Peri - Articular Injection 20 MIN
16mm
Upjohn Vanguard of Medicine Series
Color (PRO)
LC 79-703007
Uses animation and live action to show Dr Edward Boland's technique of injecting the most commonly - affected sites. Shows where the needle penetrates, and discusses contraindications and necessary precautions.
Health and Safety; Science - Natural
Dist - UPJOHN **Prod** - UPJOHN 1969

The Technique of Intra - Articular and Peri - Articular Injection 20 MIN
U-matic / VHS
Color (PRO)
Describes the technique for correct injection of the principle joints in the body by means of actual demonstration and anatomical drawings.
Health and Safety
Dist - WFP **Prod** - WFP

The Technique of Intracellular Perfusion of Squid Giant Axon 10 MIN
16mm
Color
LC 74-706274
Demonstrates the introduction of perfusion fluid into the inlet and outlet cannulas of the axon by means of the micromanipulator.
Science; Science - Natural
Dist - USNAC **Prod** - NIMH 1969

The Technique of Menisectomy 20 MIN
U-matic / VHS / 16mm
Color (PRO)
Shows the principles involved in different menisectomy techniques, such as exposure through skin incision, preservation of idle structures, retention and evaluation of posterior horn and excision of the posterior portion.
Health and Safety; Science
Dist - USNAC **Prod** - WRAIR

Technique of Microvascular Anastomosis 45 MIN
VHS / 16mm
(C)
385.00 purchase _ #841VJ110
Teaches how to use the operating microscope; what position to take in relation to the operating table; how to control hand tremor; how to suture; how to use tools effectively; how to provide counteraction to prevent wild movements; and, how to tie knots. Demonstrates, through an actual operation, the steps in mocrovascular anastomosis.
Health and Safety
Dist - HSCIC **Prod** - HSCIC 1985

Technique of Platelet Transfusion - Om - 1284 22 MIN
16mm
Color (PRO)
Demonstrates a medical technique that is substantially reducing leukemia deaths due to hemorrhaging. Demonstrates the method of obtaining blood platelets by plasmapheresis.
Health and Safety; Science; Science - Natural
Dist - USNAC **Prod** - NIH 1966

The Technique of Radical Cystectomy 42 MIN
16mm
Color (PRO)
LC 75-702233
Demonstrates a systemic and meticulous approach to radical cystectomy with en bloc pelvic lymph node dissection.
Health and Safety; Science; Science - Natural
Dist - EATONL **Prod** - EATONL 1974

The Technique of television commercials 23 MIN
VHS
Exploring mass communication series
Color (J H C)
$39.95 purchase _ #IVMC04
Explores the 14 different categories of television commercials. Introduces and defines each type and shows how they were used in television commercials.
Business and Economics; Guidance and Counseling
Dist - INSTRU

A Technique of Total Hip Replacement 25 MIN
16mm
B&W (PRO)
Demonstrates the Charnley technique for creating new joints.
Health and Safety
Dist - LAWREN **Prod** - CMA

Technique - Program four 47 MIN
VHS
European art school series
Color (G)
$79.95 purchase
Discusses composition. Looks at natural composition, geometrical and abstract shapes, the picture area, positive and negative shapes, movement and rhythm, color in composition, abstract and realistic composition and experiments in composition. Part four of a four - part series on art techniques.
Fine Arts
Dist - ARTSAM **Prod** - EURART 1984

Technique - Program one 35 MIN
VHS
European art school series
Color (G)
$79.95 purchase
Introduces drawing techniques. Discusses pencil technique, contour drawing, gesture drawing, modeling, three dimensinal form and comments on pencil fabrication. Part one of a four - part series on art techniques.
Fine Arts
Dist - ARTSAM **Prod** - EURART 1984

Technique - Program three 47 MIN
VHS
European art school series
Color (G)
$79.95 purchase
Discusses color. Looks at color theory, the color circle, primary, secondary and tertiary colors, complementary colors, warm and cold colors, mixing values, intensity, light and shadow, and comments on fabrication of artists' colors, textures in oil, watercolor, gouache and acrylics. Part three of a four - part series on art techniques.
Fine Arts
Dist - ARTSAM **Prod** - EURART 1984

Technique - Program two 47 MIN
VHS
European art school series
Color (G)
$79.95 purchase
Discusses drawing techniques. Looks at basic forms, creating volume and space, charcoal techniques, values, keys, moods, light and shadow, ink techniques, perspective and comments on the fabrication of brushes. Part two of a four - part series on art techniques.
Fine Arts
Dist - ARTSAM **Prod** - EURART 1984

Techniques
VHS / U-matic
Metropolitan Museum Seminars in Art Series
Color
Describes the technical aspects of working in various media and presents examples of works by artists who have excelled in the various techniques.
Fine Arts
Dist - GA **Prod** - GA

Techniques 33 MIN
VHS / 16mm
Basketry of the Pomo series
Color (G C)
$660.00, $360.00 purchase, $24.50 rental _ #31554
Uses slow - motion close - ups and animation to show Pomo Indian techniques used to form and decorate baskets - plain twining, diagonal twining, wrapped twining, wicker, single - rod coiling and three - rod coiling. Part of a series.
Social Science
Dist - PSU **Prod** - UCEMC 1962

Techniques 30 MIN
VHS / U-matic
Corporate Computer Security Strategy Series
Color
Provides an overview of the basic security controls that can be applied to computer systems. Discusses security controls in terms of physical controls, logical controls, administrative controls and legal/social controls.
Industrial and Technical Education
Dist - DELTAK **Prod** - DELTAK

Techniques 40 MIN
U-matic / VHS
Active learning for youth series
Color
Highlights creative teaching methods to begin productive discussionS. Focuses on church youth group training.
Religion and Philosophy; Sociology
Dist - ECUFLM **Prod** - UMCOM

Techniques and Applications of Infrared 120 MIN
16mm
B&W (IND)
LC 79-701626
Introduces the theory of infrared radiation absorption and demonstrates techniques of sample handling and the uses of various instruments.
Science
Dist - AMCHEM **Prod** - AMCHEM 1976

Techniques and applications of infrared - Pt 1 60 MIN
16mm
Color (IND)
LC 79-701626
Introduces the theory of infrared radiation absorption and demonstrates techniques of sample handling and the uses of various instruments.
Science; Science - Physical
Dist - AMCHEM **Prod** - AMCHEM 1976

Techniques and applications of infrared - Pt 2 60 MIN
16mm
Color (IND)
LC 79-701626
Introduces the theory of infrared radiation absorption and demonstrates techniques of sample handling and the uses of various instruments.
Science; Science - Physical
Dist - AMCHEM **Prod** - AMCHEM 1976

Techniques and Practices for Equipment Operators 60 MIN
VHS / U-matic
Equipment Operation Training Program Series
Color (IND)
States basic safety practices and relates them to specific plant safety regulations and procedures. Provides guidelines for responding to problems. Identifies guidelines for monitoring operations and for making changes to equipment.
Industrial and Technical Education
Dist - ITCORP **Prod** - ITCORP

Techniques and technologies for dealing with learning disabilities - Tape 4
VHS
Adults with learning disabilities teleconferences series
Color (PRO)
$35.00 purchase
Presents Drs Richard J Cooper, Dale R Jordan and Edna D Copeland. Overviews techniques and technologies for learning disabilties. Part four of a four - part series on adults with learning disabilities.
Education; Psychology
Dist - KET **Prod** - KET 1991

Techniques for classroom observation 90 MIN
VHS
Another set of eyes - techniques for classroom observation and 'conferencing skills series
Color (T C PRO)
$445.00 purchase, $75.00 rental _ #614 - 153X01
Presents two videos which introduce supervisors and peer coaches to six techniques for observing and recording student - teacher interactions in the classroom - selective verbatim; verbal flow; at task; class traffic; interaction analysis; global scan. Features Keith Acheson who explains observation techniques. Observes experienced teachers and teacher supervisors demonstrating how the techniques help teachers reflect on their practices. Shows six observation techniques that give teachers the objective data they need to improve student - teacher interactions. The second video serves as a practice model. Includes trainer's manual. Part of a series on observation and conferencing skills.
Education
Dist - AFSCD **Prod** - AFSCD 1988

Techniques for deep water worm fishing
VHS
Color (G)
$29.95 purchase _ #0887
Shows how to catch bass in up to 40 feet of water using worms as bait. Features Larry Nixon.
Physical Education and Recreation; Science - Natural
Dist - SEVVID

Techniques for deposing and defending lay witnesses 100 MIN
VHS
Color (A PRO C)
$95.00 purchase _ #Y803
Describes and demonstrates techniques for eliciting crucial information from non - expert witnesses during depositions. Explains the way to handle objections and other troublesome tactics of opposing counsel. A combination format of lecture, demonstrations and audience participation is led by David A Sonenshein.
Civics and Political Systems
Dist - ALIABA **Prod** - CLETV 1993

Techniques for Handling Difficult People and Listening to Yourself 16 MIN
VHS / U-matic
Listening - the Forgotten Skill Series
Color
English Language; Psychology
Dist - DELTAK **Prod** - DELTAK

Techniques for making a slide culture 12 MIN
VHS / U-matic
Color (C PRO)
$395.00 purchase, $80.00 rental _ #C860 - VI - 042
Demonstrates and explains the preferred equipment and techniques for a slide culture. Shows each every step of the procedure - from preparing the slide culture chamber to making a permanent mount of the culture. Discusses different types of cultures and their purposes. Describes three potentially hazardous cultures - histoplasma capsulatum, blastomyces dermatitidis and coccidioides immitis. Presented by Amy Stine Collins.
Health and Safety; Science - Natural
Dist - HSCIC

Techniques for soloing and improvisation - flatpick style 90 MIN
VHS
Color (G)
$49.95 purchase _ #VD - FLY - FL01
Features Nashville guitarist Pat Flynn who carefully breaks down his own method for improvising across the entire guitar fingerboard. Shows how to find the 'chord centers' on which to base scales and ultimately create sizzling guitar solos. Demonstrates how to work up the neck, combining various scale positions with open, ringing notes. Includes chords and tablature.
Fine Arts
Dist - HOMETA **Prod** - HOMETA

Techniques for supporting the laboring woman 34 MIN
U-matic / VHS
Color (PRO)
$330.00 purchase _ #830VI065
Outlines guidelines for nurse's role in helping the woman in labor to relax, minimize her discomfort, and stay in control during the first and second stages of labor.
Health and Safety
Dist - HSCIC **Prod** - HSCIC 1982

Techniques for the phone sales representative 12 MIN
U-matic / VHS / 16mm
Telemarketing series
Color (H C A)
$450.00, $250.00 purchase _ #83030
Shows the steps involved in telemarketing.
Business and Economics
Dist - CORF

Techniques in Anaerobic Bacteriology 30 MIN
U-matic
Color (C)
Provides instruction in the majority of methods used for isolation and identification of obligate anaerobic bacteria.
Health and Safety; Science - Natural
Dist - UOKLAH **Prod** - UOKLAH 1977

Techniques in basic infrared spectrophotometry 85 MIN
VHS
Color (C PRO)
$395.00 purchase _ #V - 3200 - 11922
Presents five parts on basic infrared spectrophotometry. Includes basic IR spectroscopy, liquid sampling techniques, solid sampling techniques, computer - aided spectrophotometry and quantitative analysis and maintenance and troubleshooting. Includes a course study guide.
Science; Science - Physical
Dist - AMCHEM

Techniques in flower judging 24 MIN
VHS
Flower industry series
Color (G)
$49.95 purchase _ #6 - 104 - 100A
Demonstrates flower juding, staging and giving reasons as methods for learning industry standards. Part of a series on the flower industry.
Agriculture; Science - Natural
Dist - VEP **Prod** - VEP 1993

Techniques in hanging wallpaper 21 MIN
U-matic / VHS / 16mm
Home repairs series
Color (J)
$505.00, $250.00 purchase _ $80532; LC 81-700045
Illustrates basic equipment needed for hanging wallpaper. Tells how to remove the old paper and how to measure, cut and apply the new wallpaper.
Home Economics
Dist - CORF **Prod** - CENTRO 1981

Techniques in Plant Identification 27 MIN
VHS
Color (G)
$89.95 purchase _ #6 - 042 - 100P
Introduces the skill of plant identification to students of horticulture. Starts with the identifying characteristic of foliage, moves to stems and branches, flowers, scents, fruit, growth habits and other aspects of identity. Explores identification of dormant deciduous plants, techniques for learning the common and botanic names of plants and how botanic names are interpreted.
Agriculture; Science - Natural
Dist - VEP **Prod** - VEP

The Techniques of Army News Photography 27 MIN
16mm
B&W
LC FIE64-24
Shows experts in photojournalism who design and illustrate essentials of superior news photography, covering still and motion picture techniques.
Industrial and Technical Education
Dist - USNAC **Prod** - USA 1963

Techniques of Ball Handling 20 MIN
VHS / 16mm / U-matic
Basketball Series no 1; No 1
Color (I)
LC 79-700779
Explains the fundamentals of basketball by focusing on ball handling, the seven basic passes, dribbling and drills.
Physical Education and Recreation
Dist - ATHI **Prod** - ATHI 1976

Techniques of birding 69 MIN
VHS
Color (G)
$29.95 purchase
Features Arnold Small in a wilderness search for birds of every size and sort. Portrays 109 species of North American birds. Shows how to select binoculars and field glasses, when and where to look for birds, how to attract birds, and more.
Science - Natural
Dist - PBS **Prod** - WNETTV

Techniques of Bone Marrow Aspiration 8 MIN
U-matic
Color
Gives the indications for performing bone marrow aspiration and biopsy. Demonstrates the two - needle technique for performing the aspiration, then the biopsy.
Health and Safety
Dist - UTEXSC **Prod** - UTEXSC

Techniques of Cell Assembly 6 MIN
16mm
B&W (PRO)
Examines the procedures of taking the nucleus, the cytoplasm and the cell membrane from different amoebas and combining them to form new amoeba - like organisms.
Health and Safety; Science; Science - Natural
Dist - SQUIBB **Prod** - SQUIBB

Techniques of Decision Making 28 MIN
16mm
You in Public Service Series
Color (A)
LC 77-700969
Presents practical methods for making decisions and applying them to typical on - the - job situations.
Business and Economics; Guidance and Counseling
Dist - USNAC **Prod** - USOE 1977

Techniques of Defense 20 MIN
VHS / 16mm / U-matic
Basketball Series no 4; No 4
Color (I)
LC 79-700782
Explains the fundamentals of basketball by focusing on techniques of defense.
Physical Education and Recreation
Dist - ATHI **Prod** - ATHI 1976

Techniques of defensive driving film series
The Car Ahead 11 MIN
Driving expressways 11 MIN
The Mystery Crash 8 MIN
Who's to Blame 10 MIN
Dist - NSC

Techniques of defensive driving series
The Head - on crash 10 MIN
Dist - NSC

Techniques of Drownproofing 20 MIN
VHS / U-matic
Color
Teaches the exact techniques for survival in water as they are taught to trainees assigned to the United States Navy Underwater Survivor's School.
Health and Safety; Physical Education and Recreation
Dist - PRIMED **Prod** - PRIMED

Techniques of Endometrial Biopsy 12 MIN
U-matic
Color
Demonstrates the instruments and techniques of the endometrial biopsy. Describes the cytologic examination of the biopsied tissue.
Health and Safety
Dist - UTEXSC **Prod** - UTEXSC

Techniques of Exhaled - Air Artificial Respiration 12 MIN
16mm
B&W
LC FIE60-121
Shows how to administer mouth - to - mouth artificial respiration.
Health and Safety
Dist - USNAC **Prod** - USAF 1959

The Techniques of Extrication 45 MIN
VHS
Extrication Video from Carbusters Series
Color (G PRO)
$149.95 purchase _ #35342
Stresses options and illustrates proper techniques of extrication using hydraulic rescue tools. Demonstrates specific tips, tricks and procedures to enhance safety and efficiency in a variety of situations.
Health and Safety; Psychology; Social Science
Dist - OKSU

Techniques of Flying 29 MIN
Videoreel / VT2
Discover Flying - Just Like a Bird Series
Color
Industrial and Technical Education; Social Science
Dist - PBS **Prod** - WKYCTV

Techniques of Implanting the Port - a - Cath for Hepatic Artery Access 8 MIN
U-matic
Color
Illustrates the technique of inserting an implantible drug - delivery device known as a port - a - cath.
Health and Safety
Dist - UTEXSC **Prod** - UTEXSC

Techniques of inventory management 30 MIN
VHS
Business logistics series
Color (G C)
$200.00 purchase, $20.50 rental _ #34962
Examines techniques of inventory management. Part of a 30 - part series on business logistics which deals with movement and storage of raw and finished products, and with managerial activities important for effective control of these operations. Interviews logistics managers of major US corporations and transportation companies. Uses on - site segments to demonstrate logistical carrier operations. Features program author Dr John Coyle.
Business and Economics
Dist - PSU **Prod** - WPSXTV 1987

Techniques of Microvascular Anastomosis 45 MIN
U-matic / VHS
Color (PRO)
Outlines and illustrates in detail how to perform microvascular anastomosis.
Health and Safety; Science; Science - Natural
Dist - HSCIC **Prod** - HSCIC 1984

Techniques of Non - Verbal Psychological Testing 20 MIN
16mm / U-matic / VHS
Color (C A)
LC FIA65-1885
Depicts psychological evaluation of children who cannot be examined by the usual intelligence tests because of very young age, physical handicaps or foreign culture. Shows use of non - verbal techniques such as Gesell development scales, Leiter international performance scale, parts of the Merrill - Palmer scale and Peabody vocabulary test.
Education; Psychology
Dist - IFB **Prod** - ROSSCJ 1965

Techniques of Offense 20 MIN
U-matic / VHS / 16mm
Basketball Series no 3; No 3
Color (I)
LC 79-700781
Explains the fundamentals of basketball by focusing on the offensive game.
Physical Education and Recreation
Dist - ATHI **Prod** - ATHI 1976

Techniques of paper sculpture 10 MIN
16mm
Color (I)
Techniques of paper sculpturing are demonstrated and varied uses of this medium from party favors to lifesize figures for drapery displays are illustrated. (Also known as 'paper sculpture').
Fine Arts
Dist - AVED **Prod** - ALLMOR 1958

Techniques of Parenteral Injection 22 MIN
16mm
Color (PRO)
Focuses on the techniques involved in giving medications by injection and includes the four most common methods of parenteral injection, the intramuscular injection, the subcutaneous, the intradermal and the intravenous.
Health and Safety; Science
Dist - SCITIF **Prod** - BECDIC 1970

Techniques of physical diagnosis - a visual approach series
The Abdomen 22 MIN
The Head and neck - Pt A 17 MIN
The Head and neck - Pt B 20 MIN
The Heart 17 MIN
Male genitalia 12 MIN
Musculoskeletal examination 20 MIN
Neurological exam, Part A 26 MIN
Neurological exam, Part B 22 MIN
Pelvic examination 17 MIN
The Thorax and Lungs 22 MIN
Dist - MEDMDS

Techniques of play therapy - a clinical demonstration 50 MIN
VHS
Color (C PRO)
$95.00 purchase _ #2983
Features Nancy Boyd Webb who describes and demonstrates effective play therapy techniques. Views unrehearsed segments of sessions, follow - up sessions and scenes from an initial parent interview. Includes comprehensive program manual.
Psychology
Dist - GFORD

Techniques of Shooting 19 MIN
U-matic / VHS / 16mm
Basketball Series no 2; No 2
Color (I)
LC 79-700780
Explains the fundamentals of basketball by focusing on the shooting game and a series of drills designed to improve offensive play.
Physical Education and Recreation
Dist - ATHI **Prod** - ATHI 1976

Techniques of Sigmoidoscopy, Bone Marrow Aspiration, and Endometrial Biopsy 34 MIN
BETA / VHS / U-matic
(PRO)
Demonstrates oncologic biopsy techniques, includes examination of the large bowel using a flexible sigmoidoscope, instruments and techniques of endometrial biopsy, and describes the cytologic examination of the biopsy specimen.
Health and Safety
Dist - UTXAH **Prod** - UTXAH 1984

Techniques of Spiritual Direction and Religious Counseling 180 MIN
VHS / BETA
Color
Expounds the religious and psychological counseling techniques of Father Groeschel, PhD in Psychology, who aims his teachings at counselors and clergy.
Psychology; Religion and Philosophy
Dist - DSP **Prod** - DSP

Techniques of therapeutic communication - 606.1 20 MIN
VHS
Nurse patient interaction series
Color (PRO)
Dramatizes interactions which define and illustrate techniques for talking with patients - ways of encouraging conversation, helping patients explore their thoughts and feelings, and ensuring mutual understanding between nurse and patients. Part 1 of 3 - part series.
Health and Safety; Psychology; Social Science
Dist - CONMED **Prod** - CONMED

Techniques of Thyroid Surgery 29 MIN
16mm
Color (PRO)
Shows techniques of operations for cancers of the thyroid, multinodular goiters, solitary nodules and intrathoracic goiters. Shows the diagnosis and treatment of thyroiditis.
Health and Safety; Science
Dist - ACY **Prod** - ACYDGD 1955

Techniques of Titration 13 MIN
16mm / U-matic / VHS
Basic Laboratory Techniques in Chemistry Series
Color (J H A)
Shows the preparation of a buret for titration and the correct techniques for performing simple acid - base titrations. Follows the steps outlined for cleaning, filling and preparing for titration.
Science; Science - Physical
Dist - LUF **Prod** - LUF 1981

Techniques of TV interviewing 20 MIN
VHS
Color (PRO G)
$149.00 purchase, $49.00 rental _ #740
Highlights the ingredients of a dynamic and successful interview. Uses interview excerpts that include great interview techniques as well as the pitfalls that await the unwary interviewer. Offers the classic interview in which Margaret Thatcher turns the tables on an ill - prepared journalist and subjects him to the third degree. Features television journalist Mike Minehan as host. Produced by the Australian Film, Television and Radio School.
Fine Arts; Guidance and Counseling
Dist - FIRLIT

The Techniques of Venipuncture 10 MIN
U-matic
Color (C)
Provides an introduction to the materials and procedure of venipucture.
Health and Safety; Science - Natural
Dist - UOKLAH **Prod** - UOKLAH 1972

Techniques of Working with Addicts 50 MIN
16mm
Films and Tapes for Drug Abuse Treatment Personnel Series
Color
LC 73-703451
Uses a series of simulated counseling sessions to describe behavior patterns of drug addicts and to depict counseling methods used to deal with them.
Psychology
Dist - NIMH **Prod** - NIMH 1973

Techniques - Session 3
VHS
English as a second language - tutor training series
Color (G T PRO)
$70.00 purchase _ #31048
Presents how - to's of repetition drills, substitution drills, transformation drills, box drills, dialogues, conversation and interview. Third of seven videos that support the English as a Second Language - Tutor Training Kit.

Education; English Language
Dist - LITERA

Techniques that work - Program 2 28 MIN
VHS
Saving a generation I and II series
Color (T PRO C)
$95.00 purchase
Demonstrates concrete HIV education strategies. Offers methods for teaching about HIV - AIDS in a variety of settings and disciplines including health, science and social studies. Covers the issues of transmission, societal attitudes, self - esteem building techniques and skills - based learning, including refusal skills. Part two of a two - part series offering teachers strategies for teaching about HIV and AIDS prevention in grades 4 - 12.
Education; Health and Safety; Social Science
Dist - SELMED **Prod** - SACVP

Technological Man 25 MIN
16mm
Science of Life Series
Color (J)
LC 81-700850
Compares biological adaptation with technological invention and points out the differences in the rates of change. Looks at social factors contributing to the development of western technology. Argues the pros and cons of modern technology.
Sociology
Dist - WARDS **Prod** - CRIPSE 1981

The Technological revolution - toward the future - Parts 51 and 52 60 MIN
VHS / U-matic
Western tradition - part II series
Color (G)
$45.00, $29.95 purchase
Presents two thirty - minute programs tracing the history of ideas, events and institutions which have shaped modern societies hosted by Eugen Weber. Examines how keeping up with the ever increasing pace of change became the standard of the day in part 51. Part 52 considers how modern medicine, atomic energy, computers and new concepts of time, energy and matter all have important effects upon life in the twentieth century. Final two parts of a 52 - part series on the Western tradition.
Geography - World; Health and Safety; Mathematics; Science - Physical; Sociology
Dist - ANNCPB **Prod** - WGBH 1989

Technologies and terminology primer - foundations 14 MIN
VHS
Foundations and applications of distance education series
Color (T G)
$50.00 purchase
Explains telecommunications technologies. Part of a series on distance education.
Education
Dist - AECT **Prod** - IODIED 1995

Technology 45 MIN
VHS / U-matic
Corporate Network Strategy Series
Color
Discusses some of the most powerful of the new information technologies, including video conferencing, communications satellites, computer networks, computer manufacturer influences and common carrier contributions.
Industrial and Technical Education; Social Science
Dist - DELTAK **Prod** - DELTAK

Technology and environment - economic development of America 25 MIN
VHS
American foundations - wilderness to world power series
Color (J H C G)
$59.95 purchase _ #BU903V
Explores the economic development of the United States and its impact on the environment. Part of a seven - part series on American history.
History - United States
Dist - CAMV

Technology and the Disabled 30 MIN
U-matic / VHS
Innovation Series
Color
Discusses technology that may eventually allow the crippled to walk or the blind to see.
Guidance and Counseling; Health and Safety; Sociology
Dist - PBS **Prod** - WNETTV 1983

Technology and values - the energy connection 19 MIN
VHS / 16mm / U-matic
Color (I J H C G)
$430.00, $300.00, $330.00 purchase _ #A270
Discusses the energy problem. Explains that we must develop alternative energy resources and learn to depend less on energy in our daily lives. Suggests that solving the energy problem means caring enough about ourselves and our world to change our way of life.
Science - Natural; Science - Physical
Dist - BARR **Prod** - BARR 1979

Technology at Your Fingertips 20 MIN
16mm
Color
LC 76-702701
Describes how private firms have made practical use of NASA technology, including the technical information retrieval services made available through the agency's technology utilization program.
Business and Economics; Industrial and Technical Education; Science - Physical
Dist - USNAC **Prod** - NASA 1970

Technology - Catastrophe or Commitment 22 MIN
16mm / U-matic / VHS
Color (J)
Predicts that the technological systems of the future will feed and protect us, clothe and comfort us, inform and enrich us, and still retain the potential for killing us. Provides a perspective analysis of the advantages and disadvantages of the shape of technology in the future.
Sociology
Dist - CNEMAG **Prod** - DOCUA 1971

Technology - Catastrophe or Commitment 20 MIN
U-matic / VHS / 16mm
Color
Questions the idea that advanced technology offers the ultimate solution to all of society's problems, pointing out that some solutions kill even as they cure. Examines the dilemma of increasing industrialization and dwindling natural resources.
Sociology
Dist - CNEMAG **Prod** - DOCUA

A Technology for Spacecraft Design 12 MIN
16mm
Living in Space Series Part 3
Color (J H C)
Shows technology being developed to enable scientists and engineers to design and build a flyable regenerative life support system for manned space missions of months or years.
Science - Physical
Dist - NASA **Prod** - NASA 1966

A Technology for spacecraft - living in space - Pt 2 12 MIN
16mm
Color
Shows the features that must be incorporated into a spacecraft intended for long duration manned space flight and the technology that is being developed to solve the numerous problems.
Industrial and Technical Education; Science - Physical; Social Science
Dist - NASA **Prod** - NASA

Technology for the Disabled 29 MIN
VHS / 16mm
Discovery Digest Series
Color (S)
$300.00 purchase _ #707606
Explores a vast array of science - related discoveries, challenges and technological breakthroughs. Profiles and 'demystifies' research and development currently underway in many fields. 'Technology For The Disabled' looks at a telecommunications device for the deaf, hi - tech aids for the blind, a paraplegic pilot and a cerebral palsy victim who's a computer whiz.
Computer Science; Health and Safety; Mathematics; Psychology; Science
Dist - ACCESS **Prod** - ACCESS 1989

Technology for the third age 18 MIN
VHS
(I J H)
PdS25.50 purchase
Explains the needs of the aged including diet and nutrition, planning a kitchen, leisure activities, residential homes and security. Focuses on technology in housing developed to help the aged overcome health problems. Includes pupils' and teachers' notes.
Health and Safety
Dist - BRIGAS **Prod** - BRIGAS

Technology in America - the Age of Invention 18 MIN
U-matic / VHS / 16mm
Color (J H C I A)
$425.00, $250.00 purchase _ #5099C
Shows how technology developed and America became industrialized during the late 1800s.
History - United States; Sociology
Dist - CORF

Technology in America - the Age of Material Progress 18 MIN
U-matic / VHS / 16mm
Color (I J H C A)
$425, $250 purchase _ #5100C
Discusses new inventions and labor - saving devices that transformed America in the early 1900s.
History - United States
Dist - CORF

Technology in dialogue with human values 28 MIN
VHS / U-matic
Color
$325.00 rental
Discusses the impact of computers in the classroom and other educational settings. Includes debates by scientists, psychologists, and clerby about the impact of the computer.
Sociology
Dist - CCNCC **Prod** - CCNCC 1986

Technology in Education 28 MIN
16mm
Innovations in Education Series
Color (T)
Educational technology as a useful ally in the education.
Education
Dist - EDUC **Prod** - EDUC

Technology, Innovation, and Industrial Development Series

A Dynamic View of the Economy	51 MIN
A Dynamic View of the Firm	51 MIN
Dynamics of an Economy	33 MIN
Dynamics of Change in the Automobile Industry	71 MIN
Dynamics of Change in the Electronics Industry	52 MIN
Dynamics of Change in the Industrial Gas Industry	37 MIN
Dynamics of Change in the Textile Industry	53 MIN
Effects of change on productivity and labor in industry	37 MIN
The Importance of Technology and Innovation	43 MIN
Innovative Dynamism and International Trade	56 MIN
Policies and Programs of Other Governments	34 MIN
Possible Programs and Policies of the U S	27 MIN
R and D and innovation	45 MIN
Regulation and Innovation	51 MIN
Venturing - Old and New Firms	54 MIN
Views of the Council on Economic Development	18 MIN

Dist - MIOT

Technology on a large scale 30 MIN
VHS
Computing for the terrified series
Color (A)
PdS65 purchase
Takes a look at the London Underground and other operations using computers. Part of a seven-part series which introduces some of the growing range of computer applications in the home, office and industry, aimed at those returning to work.
Computer Science; Guidance and Counseling
Dist - BBCENE

The Technology spiral 20 MIN
U-matic / VHS
You, me, and technology series
(H C A)
$150.00 purchase
Discusses four major technological revolutions in history, such as the wheel, petroleum, and the industrial and agricultural revolutions.
Social Science; Sociology
Dist - AITECH **Prod** - NJN 1986

Technology Starts Here 30 MIN
U-matic / VHS
Perspective II Series
Color (J H C A)
$150.00
Explores a variety of science and technology subjects dealing with light and its use as a medium of communication. Shows how they work and discusses the implications of this new knowledge.
Science - Physical
Dist - LANDMK **Prod** - LANDMK 1981

Technology transfer 30 MIN
VHS
Inside Britain 4 series
Color; PAL; NTSC (G) (BULGARIAN CZECH HUNGARIAN SPANISH POLISH ROMANIAN RUSSIAN SLOVAK UKRAINIAN LITHUANIAN)
PdS65 purchase
Reveals that the successful duplication of products in new markets as a result of research conducted elsewhere is called Technology Transfer. Shows that the benefits to be gained are many, with joint ventures and international partnerships becoming increasingly important.
Business and Economics
Dist - CFLVIS **Prod** - ASPBUS 1993

Technology, transformation - wonder woman 7 MIN
U-matic / VHS
Color
Presents a stutter - step progression of the moments of transformation within the television show Wonder Woman.
Fine Arts
Dist - KITCHN **Prod** - KITCHN

Technology Utilization 30 MIN
16mm
Color
LC 76-702702
Describes how private firms have made practical use of NASA technology, including the technical information retrieval services made available through the agency's technology utilization program.
Education; Industrial and Technical Education; Science - Physical
Dist - USNAC **Prod** - NASA 1970

Technology's Heartbeat 30 MIN
U-matic / VHS
Time's Harvest - Exploring the Future Series
Color (C)
Sociology
Dist - MDCPB **Prod** - MDCPB

Tecnicas Bacteriologicas 6 MIN
16mm / U-matic / VHS
Biological Techniques (Spanish Series
Color (H C) (ENGLISH, SPANISH)
A Spanish language version of the English language film, Bacteriological Techniques. Illustrates how to make cotton plugs, sterilize wire loops and transfer cultures.
Foreign Language; Science
Dist - IFB **Prod** - THORNE 1960

Tecnicas De Medicion 15 MIN
16mm / U-matic / VHS
Biological Techniques (Spanish Series
Color (H C) (ENGLISH, SPANISH)
A Spanish language version of the English language film, Measuring Techniques. Demonstrates the basic techniques and equipment used to measure length and volume and to determine concentrations.
Foreign Language; Science
Dist - IFB **Prod** - THORNE 1960

Tecnicas Histologicals 10 MIN
16mm / U-matic / VHS
Biological Techniques (Spanish Series
Color (H C) (ENGLISH, SPANISH)
A Spanish language version of the English language film, Histological Techniques. Shows how to make microscope slides. Illustrates several finished slides through photomicrography.
Foreign Language; Science
Dist - IFB **Prod** - THORNE 1960

Tecnicas Para Manejar La Neurospora 8 MIN
16mm / U-matic / VHS
Biological Techniques (Spanish Series
Color (H C) (ENGLISH, SPANISH)
A Spanish language version of the English language film, Nuerospora Techniques. Presents methods used in culturing and handling neurospora or pink bread mold to demonstrate genetic principles. Demonstrates genetic crossing with the result of genetic segregation.
Foreign Language; Science
Dist - IFB **Prod** - THORNE 1961

Tecnicas Para Pesar 9 MIN
U-matic / VHS / 16mm
Biological Techniques (Spanish Series
Color (H C) (ENGLISH, SPANISH)
A Spanish language version of the English language film, Weighing Techniques. Shows techniques and and principles of handling basic laboratory scales, including the hand scale, the triple beam balance, the analytical balance and others.
Foreign Language; Science
Dist - IFB **Prod** - THORNE 1960

Tectonic plates 100 MIN
VHS
Color (G T)
$275.00 purchase, $95.00 rental
Tells the story of an art student in Venice meeting a large number of characters who, twenty years later, provide the inspiration for her paintings. Moves between actual locations in Venice and a stage containing a pool that mirrors the watery streets of the city. Dreamlike in imagery, the geology of continental drift becomes a metaphor for the evolution of human culture in this 'adaptation - integration' of the Theatre Repere stage production of Robert Lepage's Tectonic Plates. Produced by Rhombus Media and Hauer Rawlence Productions; a film by Peter Mettler.
Fine Arts; Literature and Drama; Psychology
Dist - BULFRG **Prod** - RHOMBS 1994

Ted Baryluk's Grocery 10 MIN
U-matic / VHS
B&W (J)
LC 83-707256
Looks at Canadian Ted Baryluk's beliefs and background as he ponders retirement and the futile hope that his daughter will take over his grocery store.
History - World; Sociology
Dist - NFBC **Prod** - SCOTTM 1983

Ted Berrigan - 4 - 25 - 79 30 MIN
VHS / Cassette
Poetry Center reading series
Color (G)
$15.00, $45.00 purchase _ #343 - 286
Features the writer reading his works at the Poetry Center, San Francisco State University.
Literature and Drama
Dist - POETRY **Prod** - POETRY 1979

Ted Berrigan - 3 - 6 - 75 40 MIN
VHS / Cassette
Poetry Center reading series
Color (G)
$15.00, $45.00 purchase _ #104 - 78
Features the writer reading his works at the Poetry Center, San Francisco State University, with an introduction by Kathleen Fraser.
Literature and Drama
Dist - POETRY **Prod** - POETRY 1975

Ted Greenwald - 11 - 10 - 76 43 MIN
VHS / Cassette
Poetry Center reading series
Color (G)
$15.00 purchase, rental _ #227 - 182
Features the writer reading his works at the Poetry Center, San Francisco State University, with an introduction by Lewis MacAdams.
Literature and Drama
Dist - POETRY **Prod** - POETRY 1976

Ted Shawn and His Men Dancers Series
The Dome 20 MIN
Kinetic Molpai 20 MIN
Labor Symphony 20 MIN
Dist - IU

Ted Turner - How He Did it 30 MIN
VHS / 16mm
(PRO G)
$89.95 purchase _ #DGP37
Talks about Ted Turner's career from the age of 24, in his own words. Hosted by Dick Goldberg.
Business and Economics
Dist - RMIBHF **Prod** - RMIBHF

Ted Turner looks ahead 30 MIN
VHS / 16mm
(PRO G)
$89.95 purchase _ #DGP38
Looks at the future of broadcasting, how cable will affect entertainment, and how Ted Turner plans to position himself to be a winner. Hosted by Dick Goldberg.
Business and Economics
Dist - RMIBHF **Prod** - RMIBHF

Ted Williams and the Atlantic Salmon 28 MIN
16mm
Color
LC 75-702664
Shows sportsman Ted Williams as he attempts to catch Atlantic salmon on the Miramichi River in Canada.
Physical Education and Recreation; Science - Natural
Dist - MTP **Prod** - SEARS 1974

Teddy at the throttle 20 MIN
16mm
B&W (I A)
LC 79-711886
Features Gloria Swanson, Wallace Berry and Bobby Vernon in the 1916 Sennet Comedy, 'Teddy at the Throttle.' Presents a typical 'villain - sweetheart - hero' triangle, including automobile chases and close calls with speeding trains.
Fine Arts
Dist - RMIBHF **Prod** - MSENP 1916

The Teddy Bear who Wanted to Go Home 15 MIN
U-matic
Two Plus You - Math Patrol One Series
Color (K P)
Presents the mathematical concepts of set, group or collection of real things and set membership.
Education; Mathematics
Dist - TVOTAR **Prod** - TVOTAR 1976

The Teddy Bear's Balloon Trip 14 MIN
16mm / U-matic / VHS
Color (P)
LC 74-709397
Provides a background for language arts activities such as story - telling, creative dramatics and reading. Features a trip across Europe to Asia as a German girl sends her teddy bear by balloon with a gift for Chinese children.
Literature and Drama
Dist - CORF **Prod** - CORF 1970

Teddy Dibble - selected works 1985, the man who made faces, new findings in medical science, what a difference a day makes, the moustache 4 MIN
U-matic / VHS
Color
Presents comedy hijinks.
Fine Arts; Literature and Drama
Dist - ARTINC **Prod** - ARTINC

Teddy Dibble - the KCPT tapes, if looks could kill, the sound of music, the sound of defiance, practice makes perfect, a scar - y story 10 MIN
VHS / U-matic
Color
Makes fun of everything from medical etiquette to prevalent truisms.
Fine Arts; Literature and Drama
Dist - ARTINC **Prod** - ARTINC

Teddy on Time 8 MIN
U-matic / VHS
Happy Time Adventure Series
Color (K P)
$29.95 purchase _ #VT012
Presents an adaptation of the book Teddy On Time. Contains a 32 page hardcover book and a video.
English Language; Literature and Drama
Dist - TROLA

Teddy Roosevelt - the right man at the right time 28 MIN
U-matic / VHS / 16mm
Color (J) (SPANISH)
LC 73-702725
Explains that America was in severe crisis when Theodore Roosevelt came to the presidency in 1901. Shows how the power of big business was virtually unchecked by the government and that organized labor was still relatively weak. Features Roosevelt, known as the great Trust - Buster, who later changed his views to favor both business and labor.
Biography
Dist - LCOA **Prod** - LCOA 1974

Teen addiction 19 MIN
VHS / 16mm
Color (C PRO)
$149.00, $249.00 purchase _ #AD - 1367
Presents a profile of a high school student recovered from addiction to drugs and alcohol. He discusses the factors that led to his addiction, and how his addiction led him to contemplate suicide. The student's parents talk about the effect on family life and what compelled them to force him into treatment. Also discusses how parents and siblings may act as 'enablers.'
Psychology
Dist - FOTH **Prod** - FOTH 1990

The Teen - Age Mother 26 MIN
U-matic / VHS
Color
Addresses the complex issue of adolescent mothers who discover that the adult world of single parenting at age 16 is not attractive.
Psychology; Sociology
Dist - WCCOTV **Prod** - WCCOTV 1981

Teen - age Weight Control 16 MIN
U-matic / VHS
Color
Focuses on proper nutrition for teenagers. Discusses weight control. Stresses problems of snacking and junk foods.
Health and Safety; Social Science; Sociology
Dist - MEDFAC **Prod** - MEDFAC 1981

Teen - Age Whiz Kids 11 MIN
16mm
Color (I)
LC 81-701506
Focuses on two exceptionally bright young teenagers who are accelerating their studies in a special program at the University of Washington. Shows the teenagers in college courses and with college classmates, while the remarks of their parents and a university administrator voice some of the cautions with which they approach this acceleration of academics. Originally shown on the CBS program 30 Minutes.
Education; Psychology
Dist - MOKIN **Prod** - CBSTV 1981

Teen - aiders video series 120 MIN
VHS
Teen - aiders video series
Color (I J H G)
$549.00 purchase _ #NIMBS14V
Presents a four - part series on teen issues. Includes the titles Suicide - I Don't Want to Die; Peer Pressure - When the Heat's On; Violence - Where Have All the Children Gone; Drug Free Kids - What They're On and How You Can Get It. Accompanying workbooks.
Guidance and Counseling; Psychology; Sociology
Dist - CAMV

Teen AIDS in focus 17 MIN
VHS
Color (J H C)
$115.00 purchase _ #BO69 - V8
Personalizes the risk of HIV and AIDS by bringing teenage audiences face to face with peers who are HIV positive - 'I expect this to be my last summer.' Replaces fears about people with AIDS with compassion, and convinces teens of their own vulnerability to the virus. Argues that 'unsafe sex is NOT cool,' and 'AIDS does not discriminate.'
Guidance and Counseling; Health and Safety; Sociology
Dist - ETRASS **Prod** - ETRASS

Teen awareness - Sexual harassment - What it is, what to do 24 MIN
VHS / U-matic
Color (J H)
$295.00, $345.00 purchase, $60.00 rental
Heightens student awareness of what constitutes sexual harassment in the classroom - school context and positive ways it can be countered. Uses dramatic vignettes and teen focus group discussions to provide a range of information and observations about the issue.
Health and Safety; Sociology
Dist - NDIM **Prod** - VIDDIA 1992

Teen Contraception 13 MIN
16mm / VHS
Color (I) (SPANISH)
$295.00, $250.00 purchase, $75.00 rental _ #8155; LC 90705084
Presents the straight facts about how and when pregnancy occurs. Tells the truth about AIDS and other sexually transmitted diseases - STDs. Explores the pros and cons of each contraceptive method.
Guidance and Counseling; Health and Safety; Sociology
Dist - AIMS **Prod** - MIFE 1989

Teen Crime 25 MIN
U-matic / VHS
Color (J H C A)
Discusses crime prevention, creative rehabilitation and the types of young adults who get into trouble and why.
Psychology; Sociology
Dist - GERBER **Prod** - SIRS

Teen Dads 52 MIN
U-matic / VHS
Color (G)
$249.00, $149.00 purchase _ #AD - 1528
Looks at a group of teenage fathers who are responsibly accepting psychological and financial nurturance of their children, some of whom have married, and some who have not. Considers the importance of the role of a father in a child's life.
Psychology; Sociology
Dist - FOTH **Prod** - FOTH

Teen Dads - 222 30 MIN
U-matic
Currents - 1985 - 86 Season Series
Color (A)
Explores the social and personal problems of teenage fathers and their inability to financially provide for their family.
Social Science; Sociology
Dist - PBS **Prod** - WNETTV 1985

Teen dads' point of view 30 MIN
VHS
Teenage pregnancy - from both sides series
Color (H J T)
$79.95 purchase _ #CCP0174V-G
Presents teen pregnancy from the viewpoint of the teen father. Discusses how young men deal with sex, birth control, and the pregnancy of a girlfriend. Features interviews with professionals who relate relevant facts. Advises teen fathers to establish paternity, develop parenting skills. Advises teenage viewers to abstain from sex as long as possible and to be responsible with their sexuality.
Sociology
Dist - CAMV

Teen dads' point of view
VHS
Teen pregnancy series
Color (H)
$79.95 purchase _ #CCP0174V-D
Addresses issues surrounding teen-age fatherhood. Looks at individual issues of how teen-age boys deal with sex, birth control, and pregnant girlfriends, as well as broader social issues such as how society views teen-age fathers. Breaks into four sections, including attitudes toward sex, attitudes toward pregnancy, attitudes toward fatherhood, and responsible parenting.
Health and Safety; Sociology
Dist - CAMV

Teen decisions for a lifetime 15 MIN
VHS
Teen issues video series
Color (I J H)
$99.00 purchase _ #ES750V
Helps teenagers to understand the reasons for saying no to adolescent sex, the effects of peer pressure and good decision - making and the realities of love vs sex. Part of a three - part series confronting the issues of teen pregnancy prevention, the confusions and misconceptions as teens face the pressures of dating, the realities of being a parent and parenting skills.
Guidance and Counseling; Health and Safety; Psychology; Sociology
Dist - CAMV

Teen depression and suicide 30 MIN
VHS
Video encyclopedia of psychoactive drugs series
Color (J H G)
$44.95 purchase _ #LVP6620V
Presents the most up - to - date research in clinical and laboratory studies on teen depression and suicide. Part of a series.
Psychology; Sociology
Dist - CAMV

Teen - Family life series 258 MIN
VHS / U-matic
Teen - family life series
Color (J H G)
$1675.00 purchase, $495.00 rental
Offers an 11 - part series for and about teenagers. Features 7 programs directed to teens to raise a variety of issues germane to growing up in today's world as a teenager. The other 4 programs are targeted for teens and their parents. Titles include Teen Years - Part 1; Teen Years - Part 2; Youth Leadership - Part 1; Youth Leadership - Part 2; Intimate Relationships; Stages of Intimate Teenage Relationships; Sexuality, Self Esteem and Friendship; Parenting Your Teen; Responsibility for Teens; Self Esteem of Teens; Communicating with Your Teen. Each title 20 - 26 minutes in length and available for separate rental or purchase.
Social Science; Sociology
Dist - NDIM **Prod** - FAMLIF 1993

Teen - family life series

Communicating with your teen	22 MIN
Intimate relationships	26 MIN
Parenting your teen	23 MIN
Responsibility for teens	19 MIN
Self esteem of teens	22 MIN
Sexuality, self - esteem and friendship	24 MIN
Stages of intimate teenage relationships	23 MIN
Teen - Family life series	258 MIN
Teen years - Part I	24 MIN
Teen years - Part II	26 MIN
Youth leadership - Part I	23 MIN
Youth leadership - Part II	25 MIN

Dist - NDIM

Teen Fashion Basics - a Photo Started it all 15 MIN
16mm
Color (I J)
Teaches the basic fundamentals of good grooming and dress which give a sense of individualism and self esteem that comes from feeling good about oneself.
Health and Safety; Home Economics
Dist - MTP **Prod** - SEARS

Teen Genius 30 MIN
VHS
Soapbox With Tom Cottle Series
Color (G)
$59.95 purchase _ #SBOX - 410
Shows that gifted teenagers face both good and bad consequences because of their intellectual status. Reveals that peer pressure is often less important than the gifted teenager's self - imposed high standards. Hosted by psychologist Tom Cottle.
Guidance and Counseling; Psychology; Sociology
Dist - PBS **Prod** - WGBYTV 1985

Teen health video series
Offers teenagers and health educators information in a series of twelve videos about common teen concerns and issues from AIDS to pregnancy to abusive relationships to cancer to eating disorders to sports medicine. Includes advice from experts and personal testimonies from teens themselves. Does not make judgements on moral issues, but does present options available. Videos also available individually.

Abusive relationships	30 MIN
AIDS	30 MIN
Birth control	30 MIN
Cancer	30 MIN
Child abuse	30 MIN
Eating disorders	30 MIN
Self - esteem	30 MIN
Sexual harassment	30 MIN
Sexually transmitted diseases	30 MIN
Sports medicine	30 MIN
Teen pregnancy	30 MIN
Teen sexuality	30 MIN

Dist - CAMV

Teen Issues 27 MIN
16mm / U-matic / VHS
Color (J H)
$695 purchase
Discusses some young actors who tackle issues of importance to teens. A production of KPBS - TV, San Diego.
Psychology; Sociology
Dist - CF

Teen issues - date rape 27 MIN
VHS
Teen issues series
Color (J H)
$395.00, $265.00 purchase, $60.00 rental
Reveals that as much as half of all teen rape is committed by acquaintances. Uses dramatizations to examine the definition of date rape and provide some guidelines to help lessen the chances of its occurance - how to spot and deal with potentially dangerous situations, how to set limits and express them clearly, how to be aware of behavior that makes one uncomfortable or suspicious and how to stand up for one's rights. Part of a three - part series featuring the New Image Teen Theatre which tackles issues of crucial interest to teens, blending seriousness, frankness and humor.
Guidance and Counseling; Health and Safety; Sociology
Dist - CF **Prod** - KPBS 1988

Teen issues - peer pressure 27 MIN
16mm / VHS
Teen issues series
Color (J H)
$395.00, $265.00 purchase, $60.00 rental
Uses song and satire in a series of vignettes to help teens deal realistically with their need to be accepted. Examines drugs, alcohol, sex, the perfect body and more. Helps teens to feel good about themselves and comfortable with the way they are. Focuses on the options teens have and how they can make responsible decisions despite peer pressure. Part of a three - part series featuring the New Image Teen Theatre which tackles issues of crucial interest to teens, blending seriousness, frankness and humor.
Guidance and Counseling; Psychology
Dist - CF **Prod** - KPBS 1988

Teen issues series
Presents a three - part series featuring the New Image Teen Theatre which tackles issues of crucial interest to teens, blending seriousness, frankness and humor. Includes date rape, peer pressure and teen - parent communication.

Teen issues - date rape	27 MIN
Teen issues - peer pressure	27 MIN
Teen issues - teen - parent communication	27 MIN

Dist - CF **Prod** - KPBS 1988

Teen issues - teen - parent communication 27 MIN
16mm / VHS
Teen issues series
Color (J H)

$395.00, $265.00 purchase, $60.00 rental
Explores how teens communicate with their parents and with each other about issues they face. Illustrates helpful as well as harmful approaches. Examines the sensitive issues of lying to get something, dealing with manipulation by divorced parents and the threat of AIDS. Part of a three - part series featuring the New Image Teen Theatre which tackles issues of crucial interest to teens, blending seriousness, frankness and humor.
Psychology; Social Science; Sociology
Dist - CF **Prod** - KPBS 1988

Teen issues video series
Presents a three - part series confronting the issues of teen pregnancy prevention, the confusions and misconceptions as teens face the pressures of dating, the realities of being a parent and parenting skills. Includes the titles Teen Decisions for a Lifetime; Teens, Temptations, Troubles; and Proms and Pacifiers.
Proms and pacifiers 15 MIN
Teen decisions for a lifetime 15 MIN
Teens, temptations, troubles 15 MIN
Dist - CAMV

Teen Jobs and the Minimum Wage 28 MIN
U-matic
Color (A)
Focuses on the efforts of a Bronx teenager to protest the proposed subminimum wage. Shows a panel discussion on the issue.
Business and Economics; Civics and Political Systems; Sociology
Dist - AFLCIO **Prod** - LIPA 1984

Teen Menstruation
U-matic / VHS
Color
Addresses the two major menstrual problems encountered by teenagers, irregularity and late onset. Covers other helpful information on menstruation.
Health and Safety
Dist - MIFE **Prod** - MIFE

Teen Mom 30 MIN
VHS
Soapbox With Tom Cottle Series
Color (G)
$150.00 purchase _ #SBOX - 403
Portrays the lives of teenage mothers through interviews with several young women. Shows that many young mothers faced unpleasant home situations and were largely ignorant about effective birth control. Hosted by psychologist Tom Cottle.
Health and Safety; Psychology; Sociology
Dist - PBS **Prod** - WGBYTV 1985

Teen mom 30 MIN
VHS
Color (J H T A PRO)
$59.95 purchase _ #AH45179
Interviews teenage mothers. Reveals that most lacked basic information about birth control before having sex, and that one of every six U S babies is born to a teenage mother.
Guidance and Counseling; Health and Safety; Sociology
Dist - HTHED **Prod** - PBS

Teen Mother - a Story of Coping 24 MIN
U-matic / VHS / 16mm
Color (J H)
$440.00, $310.00 purchase
Discusses the problems of being a teenage mother. Discusses child care, housing, finances, education, and social life. Produced by Mobius Production, Ltd.
Health and Safety; Sociology
Dist - CF **Prod** - MOBIUS 1988

Teen - parent conflict - making things better 30 MIN
VHS
Color (J H)
$189.00 purchase _ #2274 - SK
Deals with conflict between teenagers and their parents. Examines the nature of such conflict, and presents techniques for dealing with it. Covers subjects including trust, negotiation, and the roles of teens and parents. Stresses the idea that teens should act like adults if they want to be treated as adults. Includes teacher's guide.
Guidance and Counseling; Psychology; Sociology
Dist - SUNCOM **Prod** - SUNCOM

Teen pregnancy 30 MIN
VHS
Teen health video series
Color (J H A T)
$39.95 purchase _ #LVPE6644V-P
Offers teenagers and health educators information about teen pregnancy . Includes advice from experts and personal testimonies from teens themselves. Does not make judgements on moral issues, but does present options available. One of a series of twelve videos about teen health issues. Available individually or as a set.
Guidance and Counseling; Sociology
Dist - CAMV

Teen pregnancy series
Going it alone 35 MIN
Teen dads' point of view
Dist - CAMV

Teen Rights 25 MIN
VHS / U-matic
Color (J H C A)
Discusses the Youth Policy Institute, a unique organization founded by the late Robert F Kennedy Memorial where young adults monitor and publish reports on all litigation that affects the lives of American youth.
Civics and Political Systems; Psychology; Sociology
Dist - GERBER **Prod** - SIRS

Teen runaways - Pt I - causes and effects 25 MIN
U-matic / VHS
Color (J H C A)
Interviews Rev Leonard Scheider, director of emergency shelter in New York City and Father Bruce Ritter, founder and director of 'Under 21/Convenant House' in New York City on the subject of runaway teenagers.
Psychology; Sociology
Dist - GERBER **Prod** - SIRS

Teen runaways - Pt II - effects and solutions 25 MIN
VHS / U-matic
Color (J H C A)
Continues the discussion about runaway teenagers.
Psychology; Sociology
Dist - GERBER **Prod** - SIRS

Teen Scene 38 MIN
16mm
Color
LC 72-702343
Provides birth control information for teenagers and their parents.
Guidance and Counseling; Sociology
Dist - PPFA **Prod** - PPFA 1972

Teen self - esteem - the right rites of passage
VHS
Family formula - video basics of parenting series
Color (G)
$79.00 purchase _ #CDFAM108V
Discusses the difficulties of passing through the teenage years in modern society. Integrates cross - cultural and cross - generational wisdom with the street culture of today. Part of a seven - part series.
Education; Guidance and Counseling; Health and Safety; Psychology; Sociology
Dist - CAMV

Teen sexuality 30 MIN
VHS
Teen health video series
Color (J H A T)
$39.95 purchase _ #LVPE6645V-P
Offers teenagers and health educators information about teen sexuality . Includes advice from experts and personal testimonies from teens themselves. Does not make judgements on moral issues, but does present options available. One of a series of twelve videos about teen health issues. Available individually or as a set.
Guidance and Counseling; Sociology
Dist - CAMV

Teen Sexuality - What's Right for You 29 MIN
U-matic / VHS / 16mm
Color (J H)
Presents teenagers discussing such topics as masturbation, pornography, homosexuality and venereal disease with a pair of doctors.
Health and Safety; Sociology
Dist - PEREN **Prod** - UUAMC

Teen suicide 35 MIN
VHS
Color (T A H J)
$89.95 purchase
Looks at the reasons teens consider, attempt, or commit suicide while stressing specific measures to help prevent unhappy teens from becoming suicide statistics. Viewers learn how to recognize the signals of suicide which they can look for in friends or relatives considering taking this drastic measure, the importance of communication, what to do to help and where to go for assistance. Viewers who may be considering suicide learn they are not alone in their problems, how to conquer these feelings and become aware of specific people and organizations who want to help.
Psychology; Sociology
Dist - CAMV

Teen Suicide 28 MIN
U-matic / VHS
Color (G)
$249.00, $149.00 purchase _ #AD - 1250
Brings together Heather Locklear of TV's 'Dynasty' who has lost members of her own family to suicide, parents of teen suicide victims, teens who have attempted suicide and psychotherapist Karen Blaker. Discusses recognizing the warning signals of potential suicides.
Psychology; Sociology
Dist - FOTH **Prod** - FOTH

Teen Suicide - who, Why and How You Can Prevent it
VHS / U-matic
Color (J H)
Tells which teens are most likely to attempt suicide and why. Shows how to recognize critical signs and where and how to seek help.
Guidance and Counseling; Psychology; Sociology
Dist - GA **Prod** - GA

Teen Times - Neither Fish Nor Fowl 30 MIN
VHS / U-matic
Coping with Kids Series
Color
Discusses techniques for coping with the challenging period of development known as the teen years. Looks at the time between the dependence of the child and the autonomy of the adult as being difficult years for both parent and child.
Guidance and Counseling; Sociology
Dist - OHUTC **Prod** - OHUTC
FI MFFD

Teen Tutor 38 MIN
16mm
B&W
LC 70-705682
Shows the operation of the Teen Tutor Program, in which seventh - grade boys and girls study child development, tutor kindergarten children and work in an integrated curriculum toward self - knowledge and social development. Portrays a Teen Tutor with his teachers and his classmates as he struggles with feelings about himself, his parents and younger children .
Education; Guidance and Counseling; Psychology; Sociology
Dist - OSUMPD **Prod** - SOUCS 1969

Teen violence 29 MIN
U-matic / VHS
Private violence - public crisis series
Color (J H C G)
$395.00 purchase _ #HH - 5891M
Reveals that homicide is the second leading cause of death for youths aged 15 to 24. Examines the effectiveness of violence prevention strategies for youth seeking a way out of the cycle of gangs, guns and crime.
Sociology
Dist - CORF **Prod** - WGBHTV 1989

Teen years - Part I 24 MIN
VHS / U-matic
Teen - family life series
Color (J H G)
$179.00, $229.00 purchase, $60.00 rental
Features fourteen and fifteen - year - olds engaged in a frank discussion about their changing role within their family and peer group system. Deals with self - image, peer groups and changing relationships with parents.
Psychology; Sociology
Dist - NDIM **Prod** - FAMLIF 1993

Teen years - Part II 26 MIN
VHS / U-matic
Teen - family life series
Color (J H G)
$179.00, $229.00 purchase, $60.00 rental
Features teens discussing social stereotypes that influence them in their everyday life. Examines pressure from the media to wear certain clothing or use certain types of products in order to feel needed and a part of a group.
Psychology; Sociology
Dist - NDIM **Prod** - FAMLIF 1993

Teenage Addiction - Alcohol and Drugs 30 MIN
VHS / U-matic
Color
Tells the story of the nation's chemically dependent teenagers, focusing on eight recovering, addicted teenagers from the Twin Cities.
Health and Safety; Psychology; Sociology
Dist - WCCOTV **Prod** - WCCOTV 1981

Teenage alcoholism - the personal struggle - 11 25 MIN
VHS / U-matic
Adolescent alcoholism - recognizing, intervening and treating series

Color (PRO C)
$195.00 purchase _ #C901 - VI - 018
Focuses on the personal struggle of adolescent alcoholics in recovery. Provides a framework for caregiver awareness. Presents facts and information and outlines current thinking regarding teenage alcoholism and substance abuse using the disease model of alcoholism. Part 13 of a 13 - part series presented by Drs Patrick J Fahey, Lawrence L Gabel, Jeptha Hostetler, John S Monk and Robert E Potts, Ohio State University, Depts of Family Medicine, Preventive Medicine and Biomedical Communications.
Guidance and Counseling; Health and Safety; Psychology; Sociology
Dist - HSCIC

Teenage anger 50 MIN
VHS
Color (G A R)
$10.00 rental _ #36 - 89 - 533
Stresses that teenage anger is not wrong, but must be dealt with appropriately by parents. Suggests strategies for ensuring that teenagers turn to family for emotional fulfillment. Hosted by Christian psychiatrist Ross Campbell.
Guidance and Counseling; Psychology; Religion and Philosophy; Sociology
Dist - APH **Prod** - WORD

Teenage birth control - why doesn't it work?
VHS
(G)
$159.00 purchase _ #SB2193V
Emphasizes that sexual activity requires emotional maturity and clearly defined personal goals. Presents information in a counselor led discussion on the safety and effectiveness of various forms of birth control.
Guidance and Counseling; Sociology
Dist - CAREER **Prod** - CAREER

Teenage Blues - Coping with Depression
VHS / U-matic
Color (J H C)
Introduces students to the concept of depression, some common causes and symptoms, where and how to get help. Suggests self - help methods for alleviating mild depression while cautioning that some severe cases require outside assistance. Includes teacher's guide.
Guidance and Counseling; Health and Safety; Psychology
Dist - SUNCOM **Prod** - SUNCOM

Teenage Challenge 30 MIN
16mm
Teenage Film Series
B&W (J H T R)
LC FIA67-1924
Portrays how a school essay contest is the basis for an examination of the problem of how a Christian teenager can seek God's will and still be popular.
Religion and Philosophy
Dist - FAMF **Prod** - FAMF 1958

Teenage Christmas 30 MIN
16mm
Teenage Film Series
Color; B&W (J H T R)
LC FIA67-1923
Points out how a group of teenagers, caught in the pressures of a commercial Christmas season, realize the true meaning of Christmas as they tell the story of the coming of Christ to two small children.
Guidance and Counseling; Psychology; Religion and Philosophy
Dist - FAMF **Prod** - FAMF 1959

Teenage Code 30 MIN
16mm
Teenage Film Series
B&W (J H T R)
LC FIA67-1922
Dramatizes a situation in which a Christian boy must choose between conflicting ideas about cheating.
Guidance and Counseling; Psychology; Religion and Philosophy
Dist - FAMF **Prod** - FAMF 1958

Teenage Conflict 30 MIN
16mm
Teenage Film Series
B&W (J H T R)
LC FIA67-1921
Describes how a boy and his sister, who have rejected the Christian faith for new scientific concepts, are shown by a scientist the relationship between the scientific approach and Christian concepts.
Guidance and Counseling; Psychology; Religion and Philosophy
Dist - FAMF **Prod** - FAMF 1959

Teenage crises - the fateful choices 28 MIN
VHS
Color (I J H)
$189.00 purchase _ #FG - 980 - VS
Addresses many of the significant problems facing today's teens - addiction, violence, pregnancy, AIDS and depression - suicide. Shakes up the notion of teen invincibility by talking to young people who have paid a price for poor choices and have come through hard times with tough, articulate assessments. Includes kids in prison, teen women with children and young adults who have overcome adverse circumstances to shine as achieving members of society. Looks at choosing not to do drugs or drink and avoiding risky behavior, choosing good role models, seeking help when life is too difficult, getting through despair.
Guidance and Counseling; Health and Safety; Sociology
Dist - HRMC **Prod** - HRMC 1994

Teenage Crusade 30 MIN
16mm
Teenage Series
B&W (J H T R)
LC FIA67-1920
Portrays two boys involved in planning a visitation crusade with their youth group. Tells how their plans to bring other youths to church were almost wrecked by a rough crowd. Shows how they meet the problem with sincerity and friendliness and accomplish their goal.
Guidance and Counseling; Psychology; Religion and Philosophy
Dist - FAMF **Prod** - FAMF 1960

Teenage dating I 30 MIN
VHS
Color (I J H)
$89.95 purchase _ #DGP - 49
Asks if the sexual revolution and feminism of the '70s and '80s have filtered down to the high school dating scene.
Guidance and Counseling; Health and Safety; Psychology; Sociology
Dist - INSTRU

Teenage dating II 30 MIN
VHS
Color (I J H)
$89.95 purchase _ #DGP - 50
Features four teenagers who talk about what it means to go steady in the 1980s.
Guidance and Counseling; Health and Safety; Psychology; Sociology
Dist - INSTRU

Teenage Depression 30 MIN
VHS
Soapbox With Tom Cottle Series
Color (G)
$59.95 purchase _ #SBOX - 206
Reveals that depression is a common problem for teenagers. Shows that depression is normal and suggests ways to cope. Hosted by psychologist Tom Cottle.
Psychology; Sociology
Dist - PBS **Prod** - WGBYTV 1985

Teenage drinking 30 MIN
VHS
Video encyclopedia of psychoactive drugs series
Color (J H G)
$44.95 purchase _ #LVP6612V
Presents the most up - to - date research in clinical and laboratory studies on teenage drinking. Discusses the effects of alcohol on the mind and body, addiction and abuse, recovery and rehabilitation, medical uses, importation and distribution facts, user methodology and current trends. Part of a series.
Guidance and Counseling; Health and Safety; Psychology
Dist - CAMV

Teenage Drinking - a National Crisis 32 MIN
16mm / U-matic / VHS
Color (J)
Presents four young people who discuss graphically why teenage drinking is a national problem. Offers advice on how to recognize a drinking problem, how young people can handle friends who urge them to drink and how parents can help youngsters who are struggling with alcohol abuse.
Health and Safety; Sociology
Dist - CORF **Prod** - ABCTV 1982

Teenage Drinking and Drug Use 30 MIN
VHS
Soapbox With Tom Cottle Series
Color (G)
$59.95 purchase _ #SBOX - 201
Gives a teenage perspective on alcohol and drug use. Focuses on issues ranging from peer pressure to parental responsibilities. Hosted by psychologist Tom Cottle.
Health and Safety; Psychology; Sociology
Dist - PBS **Prod** - WGBYTV 1985

Teenage drinking and drug use 30 MIN
VHS
Color (J H C G A)
$59.95 purchase _ #AH45185
Examines the growing problem with alcoholism and drug abuse among teenagers. Reveals that teenagers begin drinking at an average age of 12, and that 10 percent of all teenagers are alcoholics. Considers the roles of peer pressure and parental influence in determining what a teenager will do. Encourages parents to be confidants rather than watchdogs.
Guidance and Counseling; Psychology; Sociology
Dist - HTHED **Prod** - PBS

Teenage Drinking - Hey, How about Another One 15 MIN
U-matic / VHS / 16mm
Conflict and Awareness Series
Color (I J H)
Portrays two high school boys who, during a study break at home, decide to have a drink to relax. Shows how one drink can lead to another, resulting in studying becoming the last thing on their minds. Considers why people start drinking, whether alcohol relieves anxieties and whether it is a crutch.
Health and Safety; Psychology; Sociology
Dist - CRMP **Prod** - CRMP 1974

Teenage Dropouts - Wasted Wealth 60 MIN
U-matic / VHS
Color (I)
Documents the problems of teenage dropouts. Includes discussions with parents, teachers, police and judges. Looks at some alternative educational programs.
Civics and Political Systems; Education; Social Science; Sociology
Dist - WETATV **Prod** - WETATV

Teenage drug and alchohol abuse
VHS
Children's discovery series
Color (P I J H)
$29.95 purchase _ #IV - 005
Shows how to deal with teenagers who are involved in drug and alcohol abuse. Provides information about agencies and organizations whose purpose is to aid families in putting their lives back together.
Guidance and Counseling; Health and Safety; Psychology; Sociology
Dist - INCRSE **Prod** - INCRSE

Teenage Drug and Alcohol Abuse 30 MIN
VHS
Color (A)
$39.95 purchase _ #V2322 - 10
Tells parents how to deal with teenage drug and alcohol abuse. Provides information about preventive measures and lists agencies and organizations which provide assistance.
Health and Safety; Psychology
Dist - SCHSCI

Teenage entrepreneurs - Pt I - teenagers learning about entrepreneurship 25 MIN
U-matic / VHS
Color (J H C A)
Focuses on teenage entrepreneurs who own their own businesses. Profiles four student businesses and discusses regulating competition on campus.
Business and Economics; Psychology; Sociology
Dist - GERBER **Prod** - SIRS

Teenage entrepreneurs - Pt II - teenagers design programs for home computers 25 MIN
VHS / U-matic
Color (J H C A)
Illustrates the increasing popularity among teenagers of designing computer programs and becoming involved in computer - related businesses.
Business and Economics; Psychology; Sociology
Dist - GERBER **Prod** - SIRS

Teenage father 30 MIN
16mm
Color (J H C A)
LC 79 - 701017
Looks at teenage parenthood from the points of view of the unmarried father, the mother, peers, and both sets of parents.
Health and Safety; Sociology
Dist - CHSCA **Prod** - NEWVIS 1978

Teenage father 38 MIN
VHS
Color (J H)
$199.00 purchase _ #2298 - SK
Focuses on the unique problems that teenage fathers face - despite being partly responsible, they are often left out of the eventual decision. Profiles three teenage fathers, who face different situations. Stresses the idea that the young

father should be involved in the decision. Includes teacher's guide.
Guidance and Counseling; Health and Safety; Psychology; Sociology
Dist - SUNCOM **Prod** - SUNCOM

Teenage Film Series

Called to serve	30 MIN
Teenage Challenge	30 MIN
Teenage Christmas	30 MIN
Teenage Code	30 MIN
Teenage Conflict	30 MIN
Teenage Loyalty	30 MIN
Teenage Romance	30 MIN
Teenage Testament	30 MIN
Teenage Witness	30 MIN
Teenager's Choice	30 MIN
Teenagers' Parents	30 MIN

Dist - FAMF

Teenage Girls 58 MIN
U-matic / VHS
Color (A)
LC 81-707244
Focuses on three lower - class urban families in which the relationships among family members are marred by constant strife.
Sociology
Dist - CCABC **Prod** - CCABC 1980

Teenage Health Teaching Modules Program Series
Violence Prevention Curriculum for Adolescents 60 MIN
Dist - EDC

Teenage Homosexuality 11 MIN
16mm / U-matic / VHS
Color (J)
LC 80-701951
Presents five gay teenagers describing their lifestyles. Interviews a psychiatrist who works with gay teenagers and offers the opinions of a mother of a gay teenager. Originally shown on the CBS television series 30 Minutes.
Sociology
Dist - CAROUF **Prod** - CBSTV 1980

Teenage idols - Pt 1 26 MIN
16mm
Hollywood and the stars series
B&W
LC FI68-269
Presents stars popular with teenagers since World War II, including singers Frank Sinatra, Elvis Presley, Pat Boone and Ricky Nelson, disc jockey Dick Clark, and actors James Dean, Marlon Brando and Sandra Dee.
Fine Arts
Dist - WOLPER **Prod** - WOLPER 1964

Teenage idols - Pt 2 26 MIN
16mm
Hollywood and the stars series
B&W
LC FI68-270
Discusses the career of teenage idol Fabian, and discusses the publicity prior to his appearance, his rise to stardom, his loneliness and decision to buy out his contract in order to attempt an acting career.
Fine Arts
Dist - WOLPER **Prod** - WOLPER 1964

Teenage Immigrants 25 MIN
U-matic / VHS
Color (J H C A)
Illustrates how teenage immigrants have the burden of coming to terms with where their home is.
Psychology; Sociology
Dist - GERBER **Prod** - SIRS

Teenage Loyalty 30 MIN
16mm
Teenage Film Series
B&W (J H T R)
LC FIA67-1919
Dramatizes circumstances that make a high school leader realize that her first loyalty should be to Christ.
Religion and Philosophy
Dist - FAMF **Prod** - FAMF 1959

Teenage Marriage 25 MIN
U-matic / VHS
Color (J H C A)
Presents a 'family living' course in which young couples are paired and taught to deal with wedding plans, insurance, apartment seeking, finance and emotional trauma.
Psychology; Sociology
Dist - GERBER **Prod** - SIRS

Teenage mother - a broken dream 15 MIN
16mm / U-matic / VHS
Color (J)
LC 77-703012
Explores the problem of teenage pregnancy. Shows a young girl who attended a state school for unwed mothers and must face the problems of handling her dream of home and family and the reality of the responsibility of caring for a child.
Guidance and Counseling; Psychology; Sociology
Dist - CAROUF **Prod** - CBSTV 1977

Teenage Mothers - a Global Crisis 55 MIN
VHS / 16mm
Color (J)
$295.00 purchase, $90.00 rental; LC 90709144
Examines the world - wide crisis in teenage pregnancies through four case studies of teenage mothers in Ghana, England, Cuba and the US. Addresses the hazards to the health and wellbeing of such young mothers, as well as their unpreparedness, emotionally, medically and financially, for motherhood. Discusses ways to cope with the problem.
Guidance and Counseling; Health and Safety; Psychology; Sociology
Dist - CNEMAG **Prod** - BWORLD 1990

Teenage Parents 11 MIN
16mm / VHS / U-matic
Color (J H)
LC 81-700018; 81-706013
Documents the lifestyles of two teenaged married couples who are discovering what it is like to assume the responsibilities of marriage and parenthood while still teenagers.
Sociology
Dist - CRMP **Prod** - CBSTV 1981

Teenage parents - making it work 17 MIN
VHS
Color (J H A)
$49.00 purchase _ #CSK200V1
Follows a teenage mother through a day, raising issues concerning various needs and offering solutions teen mothers have found successful.
Guidance and Counseling; Sociology
Dist - CENTER **Prod** - CENTER

Teenage parents - making it work
VHS
$59.00 purchase _ #013 - 314
Explores the needs of teenage mothers and the solutions they have found successful.
Psychology; Social Science; Sociology
Dist - CAREER **Prod** - CAREER

Teenage parents - their lives have changed 23 MIN
16mm / VHS
Color (J S)
$495.00, $395.00 purchase, $60.00 rental
Shows, in interviews with young mothers and fathers, how having a baby has drastically changed their lives. Describes, in their own words, the hardships of child - raising, the change in plans for their future, and the inability to enjoy the usual activities of teen life.
Guidance and Counseling; Social Science; Sociology
Dist - HIGGIN **Prod** - HIGGIN 1987

Teenage pregnancy
VHS
Knowing sexual facts series
Color (I J)
$89.00 purchase _ #MC318
Discusses the consequences of an unwanted pregnancy. Emphasizes that the best way to avoid pregnancy is by not having sex.
Health and Safety; Psychology; Sociology
Dist - AAVIM **Prod** - AAVIM 1992

Teenage pregnancy; 2nd Ed. 29 MIN
VHS
Practical parenting series
CC; Color (H C A)
$99.00 purchase _ #253VL
Provides teenagers with a picture of the struggles of pregnancy and the responsibilities of raising a child. Addresses myths and takes one teenager through pregnancy. Comes with a leader's guide and 11 blackline masters.
Health and Safety; Sociology
Dist - UNL

Teenage Pregnancy 29 MIN
U-matic
Woman Series
Color
Examines the implications of teenage pregnancy.
Health and Safety; Sociology
Dist - PBS **Prod** - WNEDTV

Teenage pregnancy 26 MINI
VHS
Color (J H G)
$89.95 purchase _ #UW2378
Follows several teenage women through the births of their children and subsequent changes in their lives. Looks at the realities and responsibilities of teenage pregnancy. Explains that nurses' visits during pregnancy and the first two years of the baby's life can relieve some of the problems caused by depression and poverty.
Health and Safety; Psychology; Sociology
Dist - FOTH

Teenage pregnancy 30 MIN
VHS
Soapbox with Tom Cottle series
Color (G)
$59.95 purchase _ #SBOX - 212
Features teenage mothers who discuss their experiences. Considers many of the social and personal consequences of teenage pregnancy. Hosted by psychologist Tom Cottle.
Guidance and Counseling; Health and Safety; Psychology; Sociology
Dist - PBS **Prod** - WGBYTV 1985

Teenage Pregnancy 14 MIN
16mm
Family Life Education and Human Growth Series
Color (J)
Shows that a teenage daughter's pregnancy brings emotional and psychological upheaval to the entire family.
Guidance and Counseling; Psychology; Sociology
Dist - SF **Prod** - SF 1970

Teenage Pregnancy - an American Crisis 55 MIN
U-matic
Color
Looks at the increasing number of teenage pregnancies, the sexual attitudes of young people, and the roles that parents, peers, church, school and society play in sex education.
Health and Safety; Psychology
Dist - HRC **Prod** - OHC

Teenage pregnancy and prevention 36 MIN
U-matic / VHS
Color (J H)
Explores the emotional, social, and economic difficulties that face teenage parents. Students confront the reasons behind the growing problem of teenage pregnancy, and identify the need for mature sexual attitudes and greater responsibility.
Health and Safety
Dist - HRMC **Prod** - HRMC 1980

The Teenage Pregnancy Experience 26 MIN
U-matic / 16mm
Parenting Experience Series
Color (I J H C A)
LC 81-706053
Follows two school - age mothers through pregnancy, labor and birth. Shows them caring for their young infants.
Health and Safety; Sociology
Dist - COURTR

Teenage pregnancy - from both sides series
VHS
Teenage pregnancy - from both sides series
Color (H J T)
$149.95 purchase _ #CCP0175SV-G
Looks at teen pregnancy from the father's point of view and from the mother's. Includes information about how teen parents deal with sex, birth control, paternity, and day-to-day life. Presents difficulties of taking care of mother's needs while coping with emotional, psychological, and physical needs of infant. Features interviews with experts. Recommended for use in class discussions. Includes two videos.
Sociology
Dist - CAMV

Teenage pregnancy in America 18 MIN
VHS
Color (G)
#TP - 520
Presents a free - loan program which reveals that one in ten female teenagers gets pregnant and two - thirds of these carry their pregnancies to term. Gives insights into the sexual activities of teenagers. Discusses major causes of the pregnancy epidemic and preventions.
Health and Safety; Sociology
Dist - WYAYLA **Prod** - WYAYLA

Teenage Prenancy 25 MIN
VHS / U-matic
Color (J H C A)
Examines the problem of teenage pregnancy from the perspective of education and the difficult process of decision making.
Psychology; Sociology
Dist - GERBER **Prod** - SIRS

Teenage Relationships 30 MIN
VHS
Soapbox With Tom Cottle Series
Color (G)
$59.95 purchase _ #SBOX - 310
Explores the nature of teenage relationships. Questions whether teenage sexual activity is as prevalent as commonly believed. Suggests that most teenagers are more interested in companionship than in sex. Hosted by psychologist Tom Cottle.
Guidance and Counseling; Health and Safety; Psychology; Sociology
Dist - PBS **Prod** - WGBYTV 1985

Teenage Revolution 52 MIN
16mm
B&W
LC FIA66-652
Studies American teenagers and their activities, their economic power, their idols and their social life. Deals with the teenage scientist, the dropout and many other facets of teenage life.
Psychology; Sociology
Dist - WOLPER **Prod** - FI 1965

Teenage Romance 30 MIN
16mm
Teenage Film Series
B&W (J H T R)
LC FIA67-1917
Discusses teenage dating and the problems and adjustments of going steady.
Guidance and Counseling; Psychology
Dist - FAMF **Prod** - FAMF 1959

Teenage runaways - society's victims 18 MIN
35mm strip / VHS
Color (J H C T A)
$57.00, $48.00 purchase _ #MB - 909529 - 1, #MB - 909532 - 1
Examines the world of the teenage runaway. Shows that many, if not most, end up as prostitutes, drug addicts, or dead. Portrays the work of organizations dedicated to helping runaway teenagers.
Sociology
Dist - SRA **Prod** - NYT 1990

Teenage Series
Teenage Crusade 30 MIN
Dist - FAMF

Teenage Sexuality 29 MIN
VHS
Color (C A)
$75.00 purchase, $35.00 rental
Traces the changes in social attitudes towards sexuality over the past fifty years. The pressures confronting today's teenagers are discussed.
Health and Safety
Dist - CORNRS **Prod** - EDCC 1986

Teenage Sexuality
U-matic / VHS
Color (J H)
Helps students identify and clarify their own values regarding their sexual activity after viewing these filmstrips.
Health and Safety; Psychology; Sociology
Dist - CAREER **Prod** - CAREER 1980

Teenage Sexuality 30 MIN
VHS
Soapbox With Tom Cottle Series
Color (G)
$59.95 purchase _ #SBOX - 203
Cites statistics suggesting that while teenagers are beginning to have sex at about age 16, most feel the experience comes too soon for them. Suggests that peer pressure is often the reason. Hosted by psychologist Tom Cottle.
Health and Safety; Psychology; Sociology
Dist - PBS **Prod** - WGBYTV 1985

Teenage Sexuality and Contraception 13 MIN
16mm
Color (J H)
LC 79-701684
Discusses contraceptive methods available with and without a prescription, describing procedures for their proper use and pointing out the advantages, disadvantages and failure rate of each.
Health and Safety; Sociology
Dist - MIFE **Prod** - MIFE 1979

Teenage Shoplifting 10 MIN
U-matic / VHS / 16mm
Color (J)
LC 81-700010
Focuses on the city of Muskegon, Michigan, where store owners, social workers, police and parents work together to reduce the incidence of shoplifting.
Sociology
Dist - CRMP **Prod** - CBSTV 1981

Teenage Stess - Causes and Cures
VHS
(J H)
$89.00 purchase _ #MG2003V
Discusses how stress is a cause of many physiological and psychological problems among teenagers. Explains what stress is and how it can be avoided and treated. Attempts to put problems in perspective.
Guidance and Counseling; Psychology; Sociology
Dist - CAMV **Prod** - CAMV

Teenage Stress
U-matic / VHS
Color (J H)
Helps teenagers understand and accept stress in their lives so that they are better able to cope with the problems encountered during the teen years.
Psychology
Dist - CAREER **Prod** - CAREER 1981

Teenage Stress - Causes and Cures
VHS
$89.00 purchase _ #LX2023V
Assists teens in understanding what stress is, what causes stress, and how to avoid and treat stress. Teaches students to put their problems in perspective and seek help when needed.
Psychology
Dist - CAREER **Prod** - CAREER

Teenage stress - causes and cures
VHS
Color (J H)
$95.00 purchase _ #MC704
Looks at stress as a major factor in many physiological and psychological problems in teens, sometimes leading to suicide. Helps teens to understand what stress is, what some of the causes are and how it can be avoided and treated.
Health and Safety; Psychology; Sociology
Dist - AAVIM **Prod** - AAVIM

Teenage stress management - learning to cope 51 MIN
VHS
Color (H)
$209.00 purchase _ #60116 - 126
Combines vignettes with statements from experts in stress management to show what stress is, what can happen when it is overwhelming, and how to use the mind and body to control it. Teaches students important skills in handling stress.
Health and Safety; Psychology; Sociology
Dist - GA **Prod** - GA

Teenage substance abuse - an open forum with John Callahan 23 MIN
U-matic / 16mm / VHS
Color (J H)
$495.00, $325.00 purchase _ #JC - 67271
Features cartoonist John Callahan whose work is popular with teenagers. Reveals that he is a recovering alcoholic whose alcoholism began in childhood. Shows how difficult it was for him to acknowledge his addiction - even becoming wheelchair bound as the result of a drunk - driving accident was not enough. Includes a cross - section of teenagers who respond to Callahan's candor by sharing their own coping strategies.
Guidance and Counseling; Health and Safety; Psychology; Sociology
Dist - CORF **Prod** - DISNEY 1989

Teenage suicide 20 MIN
VHS
Color (H)
$89.95 purchase _ #NP723VG
Deals with the issue of teenage suicide by talking with teens who have attempted suicide. Tells the teens' experiences with suicide and what brought them to that choice. The importance of talking out problems is stressed as the first step in suicide prevention. Includes a discussion guide.
Sociology
Dist - UNL

Teenage Suicide 19 MIN
U-matic / VHS
Color (G)
$249.00, $149.00 purchase _ #AD - 1382
Explores some of the reasons teenagers commit suicide and the recent increase in reported suicides. Describes some behavior patterns to which family members and friends should be alert.
Psychology; Sociology
Dist - FOTH **Prod** - FOTH

Teenage Suicide 16 MIN
U-matic / VHS / 16mm
Color (A)
LC 79-700625
Examines the reasons for the number of teenage suicides. Interviews parents, professional authorities and emotionally disturbed youths.
Psychology; Sociology
Dist - CORF **Prod** - CBSTV 1979

Teenage Suicide 25 MIN
U-matic / VHS
Color (J H C A)
Explores the growing problem of teenage suicide in America. Shows how organizations such as the National Suicide Hotline in Denver have been formed to help young adults overcome serious depression.
Guidance and Counseling; Psychology; Sociology
Dist - GERBER **Prod** - SIRS

Teenage suicide 12 MIN
16mm / U-matic
Prime time series
Color; Mono (J H C A)
$200.00, $200.00 purchase, $50.00 rental
Explores the problem of teenage suicide and attempts to uncover the cause and some possible solutions.
Sociology
Dist - CTV **Prod** - CTV 1977

Teenage Suicide 60 MIN
U-matic / VHS / 16mm
Color (H C A)
Explores the lives and deaths of four American teenagers. States that every day in America, 18 young people commit suicide. Narrated by Timothy Hutton.
Sociology
Dist - FI **Prod** - LNDBRG 1981

Teenage suicide - is anyone listening 22 MIN
VHS
Color (I J H)
$49.95 purchase _ #ST - BR3030
Informs troubled youth that they are not alone and how to seek help. Educates the friends of suicidal teenagers on how to understand and listen to friends who are depressed and isolated.
Health and Safety
Dist - INSTRU

Teenage Suicide Series
Dangers Signs and Myths of Suicide, Pt 1 50 MIN
Types of Suicide Adolescents, Pt 2 50 MIN
Dist - GPN

Teenage suicide - the ultimate dropout 29 MIN
U-matic / VHS
Color
$55.00 rental _ #TESU - 000
Offers advice by psychiatrists and social workers to families facing a potential suicide crisis.
Sociology
Dist - PBS **Prod** - KAETTV 1980

Teenage Testament 30 MIN
16mm
Teenage Film Series
B&W (J H T R)
LC FIA67-1916
Presents how a teenage boy with active Christian convictions reacts to a situation in which his faith is seriously tested.
Religion and Philosophy
Dist - FAMF **Prod** - FAMF 1959

Teenage Troubles - How to Survive the Teenage Years 31 MIN
16mm / VHS
Color (J H A PRO)
$185.00, $495.00 purchase, $50.00 rental _ #8147
Features four young adults who look back on their high school years and discuss their difficulties and how they dealt with them.
Guidance and Counseling; Health and Safety; Psychology
Dist - AIMS **Prod** - HRMC 1990

Teenage Turn - on - Drinking and Drugs 37 MIN
16mm / U-matic / VHS
Color (J)
LC 77-703258
Investigates the problems of drinking and drug abuse among teenagers. Shows how readily accessible alcohol and drugs are abused and how their abuse cuts across economic and social boundaries.
Guidance and Counseling; Health and Safety; Sociology
Dist - MGHT **Prod** - ABCTV 1977

Teenage Turn - on - Drinking and Drugs 38 MIN
16mm / U-matic / VHS
Color (J H)
Presents addicted teenagers telling their stories. Visits a drug treatment center and a half - way house.
Health and Safety; Sociology
Dist - CRMP **Prod** - ABCNEW 1977

Teenage turn - on - drinking and drugs - Pt 1 18 MIN
U-matic / VHS / 16mm
Color (J)
LC 77-703258
Investigates the problem of drinking and drug abuse among teenagers. Shows how readily accessible alcohol and drugs are abused and how their abuse cuts across economic and social boundaries.
Psychology
Dist - MGHT **Prod** - ABCTV 1977

Teenage turn - on - drinking and drugs - Pt 2 19 MIN
U-matic / VHS / 16mm
Color (J)
LC 77-703258
Investigates the problem of drinking and drug abuse among teenagers. Shows how readily accessible alcohol and drugs are abused and how their abuse cuts across economic and social boundaries.
Psychology
Dist - MGHT **Prod** - ABCTV 1977

Teenage Witness 30 MIN
16mm
Teenage Film Series
B&W (J H T R)
LC FIA67-1915
Tells the experiences of a boy who, despite unhappy school and home situations, continues to share his Christian faith.
Guidance and Counseling; Psychology; Religion and Philosophy
Dist - FAMF **Prod** - FAMF 1958

The Teenage Years 56 MIN
U-matic
Color
Reveals the stories of two disabled adults and their parents as they look back on how they coped with the special problems they faced as teenagers. Covers such topics as sexuality, self - esteem and school relationships.
Psychology
Dist - ESST **Prod** - ESST 1983

Teenage years series

The Amazing cosmic awareness of Duffy Moon	32 MIN
Blind Sunday	31 MIN
The Body human - facts for girls	30 MIN
The Body human - the facts for boys	30 MIN
The Bridge of Adam Rush	47 MIN
The Bridge of Adam Rush - Pt 1	23 MIN
The Bridge of Adam Rush - Pt 2	23 MIN
The Escape of a One - Ton Pet	41 MIN
Follow the north star	47 MIN
Follow the north star, Pt 1	23 MIN
Follow the north star, Pt 2	24 MIN
Gaucho	47 MIN
Heartbreak Winner	47 MIN
Hewitt's Just Different	47 MIN
A Home Run for Love	47 MIN
Home to Stay	47 MIN
The Horrible Honchos	31 MIN
The House at 12 Rose Street	32 MIN
I Don't Know who I Am	30 MIN
It's a Mile from Here to Glory	47 MIN
Lost in Death Valley	47 MIN
Me and Dad's New Wife	33 MIN
Mighty Moose and the Quarterback Kid	31 MIN
Mom and Dad Can't Hear Me	47 MIN
My Mom's Having a Baby	47 MIN
New York City, Too Far from Tampa Blues	47 MIN
No Other Love	58 MIN
P J and the President's Son	47 MIN
Portrait of a Teenage Shoplifter	47 MIN
The Rocking Chair Rebellion	30 MIN
Rookie of the Year	47 MIN
Rookie of the Year - Pt 1	23 MIN
Rookie of the Year - Pt 2	24 MIN
Sara's summer of the swans	33 MIN
The Secret Life of T K Dearing	47 MIN
A Special Gift	47 MIN
Tell Me My Name	52 MIN
The Terrible Secret	47 MIN
What are Friends for	47 MIN
Where do Teenagers Come from	47 MIN
Which Mother is Mine	47 MIN

Dist - TIMLIF

Teenagers and Abortion 30 MIN
VHS
Soapbox With Tom Cottle Series
Color (G)
$59.95 purchase _ #SBOX - 311
Gives teenagers' views of abortion. Explores the implications of the fact that 30 percent of all abortions are performed on teenagers. Hosted by psychologist Tom Cottle.
Health and Safety; Psychology; Sociology
Dist - PBS **Prod** - WGBYTV 1985

Teenagers and Body Image 30 MIN
VHS
Soapbox With Tom Cottle Series
Color (G)
$59.95 purchase _ #SBOX - 301
Demonstrates that teenagers are often influenced by media images of what their bodies should look like. Explores how such perceptions influence eating disorders and similar problems. Emphasizes the importance of a good self - image. Hosted by psychologist Tom Cottle.
Guidance and Counseling; Health and Safety; Psychology; Sociology
Dist - PBS **Prod** - WGBYTV 1985

Teenagers and Divorce 30 MIN
VHS
Soapbox With Tom Cottle Series
Color (G)
$59.95 purchase _ #SBOX - 304
Features teenagers whose parents have divorced. Shows that divorce is a growing phenomenon in American society. Hosted by psychologist Tom Cottle.
Psychology; Sociology
Dist - PBS **Prod** - WGBYTV 1985

Teenagers and Music 30 MIN
VHS
Soapbox With Tom Cottle Series
Color (G)
$59.95 purchase _ #SBOX - 209
Views the punk movement among teenagers. Scrutinizes the social and political agenda of the movement. Hosted by psychologist Tom Cottle.
Fine Arts; Psychology; Sociology
Dist - PBS **Prod** - WGBYTV 1985

Teenagers and Racism 30 MIN
VHS
Soapbox With Tom Cottle Series
Color (G)
$59.95 purchase _ #SBOX - 303
Features teenagers discussing racism from a wide variety of perspectives. Explores issues such as interracial dating and whether future generations will have to deal with racism. Hosted by psychologist Tom Cottle.
Guidance and Counseling; Psychology; Sociology
Dist - PBS **Prod** - WGBYTV 1985

Teenagers and Religion 30 MIN
VHS
Soapbox With Tom Cottle Series
Color (G)
$59.95 purchase _ #SBOX - 306
Shows that many teenagers feel religion is important to their lives. Features teenagers sharing their differing views. Hosted by psychologist Tom Cottle.
Guidance and Counseling; Psychology; Religion and Philosophy; Sociology
Dist - PBS **Prod** - WGBYTV 1985

Teenagers and Sex Roles 30 MIN
VHS
Soapbox With Tom Cottle Series
Color (G)
$59.95 purchase _ #SBOX - 207
Explores the changing roles of masculine and feminine behavior. Shows how teenagers are dealing with the changes. Hosted by psychologist Tom Cottle.
Health and Safety; Psychology; Sociology
Dist - PBS **Prod** - WGBYTV 1985

Teenagers and the Nuclear Arms Race 30 MIN
VHS
Soapbox With Tom Cottle Series
Color (G)
$59.95 purchase _ #SBOX - 204
Explores teenagers' views of the nuclear arms race. Hosted by psychologist Tom Cottle.
Civics and Political Systems; Guidance and Counseling; Psychology; Religion and Philosophy; Sociology
Dist - PBS **Prod** - WGBYTV 1985

Teenagers and tough decisions
VHS
Color (J H PRO)
$44.95 purchase
Reveals that at least half of the teenagers in the '90s are sexually active and of this number, 2.5 million will contract a sexually transmitted disease. Stimulates discussion on the difficult issues facing teens of the '90s - peer pressure, safe sex, pregnancy, substance abuse and more. Designed to be viewed in segments with small groups of teens and one teacher, church leader, guidance counselor, social worker, psychologist or parent in order to stimulate individual participation. Includes teaching guide and student quiz.
Guidance and Counseling; Health and Safety; Sociology
Dist - PINCOM **Prod** - PINCOM 1993

Teenagers and tough decisions 55 MIN
VHS
Color (I J H)
$49.95 purchase _ #PIC100V
Stimulates discussion on the difficult issues facing teens today. Presents brief segments depicting peer pressure, safe sex, pregnancy, substance abuse, money management, the working world, families and divorce, teenage stress, life goals and more. Includes teacher's guide.
Business and Economics; Guidance and Counseling; Health and Safety; Psychology; Sociology
Dist - CAMV

Teenager's Choice 30 MIN
16mm
Teenage Film Series
B&W (J H T R)
LC FIA67-1914
Uses a dramatization about two teenagers who, on a dare from friends, decide to elope, to explain that marriage is not an escape or a situation to be taken lightly, but that it is a God - given relationship.
Guidance and Counseling; Psychology; Religion and Philosophy
Dist - FAMF **Prod** - FAMF 1959

Teenagers - How to Get and Keep a Job
U-matic / VHS / 16mm
Color
Explores the importance of a positive attitude, promptness, honesty and good customer relations.
Guidance and Counseling; Sociology
Dist - HIGGIN **Prod** - HIGGIN

Teenagers in Jail 30 MIN
VHS
Soapbox With Tom Cottle Series
Color (G)
$59.95 purchase _ #SBOX - 313
Focuses on three young men who are serving time in prison. Shows that criminal behavior is not uncommon among teenagers. Hosted by psychologist Tom Cottle.
Psychology; Sociology
Dist - PBS **Prod** - WGBYTV 1985

Teenagers' Parents 30 MIN
16mm
Teenage Film Series
B&W (J H T R)
LC FIA67-1918
Presents a teenage discussion on parents as people and disciplinarians. Shows the reactions of the parents when they hear a tape recording of the discussion.
Guidance and Counseling; Psychology; Religion and Philosophy
Dist - FAMF **Prod** - FAMF 1959

Teenagers Talk - Getting through Adolescence 12 MIN
U-matic / VHS / 16mm
Color (J H)
LC 75-704008
Uses animation to present problems of adolescence. Discusses relationships with parents and friends and decisions about freedom, sex and drugs. Describes this as a time for finding one's identity.
Guidance and Counseling; Psychology
Dist - PHENIX **Prod** - WEISSM 1975

A Teenager's Underground Guide to Understanding Parents 25 MIN
16mm / U-matic / VHS
Color (J)
Provides information which helps teens understand how parents feel about chemical abuse and how to make life easier for everyone.
Psychology; Sociology
Dist - CORF **Prod** - WQED

Teenagers - Vol 3 52 MIN
VHS / 16mm
Art of parenting video series
Color (G)
$69.95 purchase
Offers tips, suggestions and solutions to parenting problems. Focuses on teenagers. Considers curfews, why teens take risks, step families, jobs, parent stress, reducing arguments, new drivers, love vs trust, and more. Part of a three - part series on the art of parenting which features Evelyn Peterson, family life education expert.
Psychology; Social Science; Sociology
Dist - PROSOR

Teens and alcohol series

Adolescents, alcohol and approaches	18 MIN
Attitudes and values	15 MIN
Skills	16 MIN

Dist - ACCESS

Teens and alcohol - the hidden problem 37 MIN
VHS
Color (J H)
$199.00 purchase _ #2296 - SK
Presents three dramatic scenarios in which teenagers face issues of alcohol use and abuse. Shows that alcoholism is not the only consequence of drinking. Includes teacher's guide.
Guidance and Counseling; Psychology; Sociology
Dist - SUNCOM **Prod** - SUNCOM

Teens and Teeth - the Orthodontic Years 14 MIN
U-matic
Color
Discusses questions concerning orthodontics that often arise during the teen years. Presents teachers, teenagers and orthodontists addressing these concerns.
Health and Safety; Sociology
Dist - MTP **Prod** - AAORTH

Teens - clean and sober 20 MIN
VHS
Color (J H)
$29.95 purchase _ #VB800V
Features five teens discussing the quality of their lives before and after becoming sober. Examines the mental and physical self - destruction they experienced before realizing that they must choose between sobriety and death.
Guidance and Counseling; Health and Safety; Psychology
Dist - CAMV

Teens Having Babies 20 MIN
U-matic / VHS
Color (I J H)
LC 83-707044
Offers teenage mothers - to - be an opportunity to become acquainted with childbirth. Shows adolescent girls talking with nurses, physicians and social workers, who clearly explain the procedures for prenatal visits as they use or describe essential medical instruments. Enumerates the indications of labor and cesarean delivery and shows an actual childbirth.
Health and Safety
Dist - POLYMR **Prod** - POLYMR 1983

Teens in changing families - making it work 26 MIN
VHS
Color (J H C)
$169.00 purchase _ #2300 - SK
Interviews two young people who lived in a stepfamily, and who discuss their experiences. Focuses on the problems of facing differing rules between stepfamilies. Includes teacher's guide.
Guidance and Counseling; Psychology; Sociology
Dist - SUNCOM **Prod** - SUNCOM

Teens in Turmoil 26 MIN
U-matic / VHS
Color (G)
$249.00, $149.00 purchase _ #AD - 1929
Looks at what it's like to be a teenager in America. Examines a high school crisis prevention program, peer counseling. Considers two distinct schools for handling teenagers, tough - love and the concept of parents learning how to communicate their love to their children.
Psychology; Sociology
Dist - FOTH **Prod** - FOTH

Teens in Turmoil - 214 30 MIN
U-matic
Currents - 1985 - 86 Season Series
Color (A)
Explores the psychological, emotional, and social problems of being a teenager and the discord this can bring to the youth and those around him.
Social Science; Sociology
Dist - PBS **Prod** - WNETTV 1985

Teens, Sex and AIDS 28 MIN
VHS / 16mm
Color (PRO G J H C)
$149.00, $249.00, purchase _ #AD - 2038
Combines an open and candid discussion between teens about their AIDS concerns with dramatizations of teens dealing with decisions about sex. Portrays a young man being pressured by a friend to have sex with his girlfriend and a sexually active couple using birth control responsibly but uncertain how to proceed in the face of the AIDS crisis. Features screen personalities Jim J. Bullock and Rebecca Street and commentary by sex educationalists Lynda Madaras and Christian Haren.
Health and Safety; Psychology; Sociology
Dist - FOTH **Prod** - FOTH 1990

Teens, singles and love vs sex 50 MIN
VHS
Creating family series
Color (H C G A R)
$10.00 rental _ #36 - 871504 - 460
Features marriage counselor and therapist Clayton Barbeau in an exploration of issues facing teenagers and single adults. Focuses on the difference that can exist between love and sex.
Guidance and Counseling; Psychology; Religion and Philosophy; Sociology
Dist - APH **Prod** - FRACOC

Teens stopping rape 25 MIN
VHS
Color (J H)
$99.00 purchase _ #10398VL
Features conversation about rape, power games, relationships, peer pressure and partying. Shows stories from survivors of acquaintance rape and from experts and educators. Teaches techniques for stopping rape, from communication to volunteering at a local rape crisis center. Comes with a teacher's guide; student activities; discussion questions; script; and blackline masters.
Guidance and Counseling; Sociology
Dist - UNL

Teens, temptations, troubles 15 MIN
VHS
Teen issues video series
Color (I J H)
$99.00 purchase _ #ES751V
Confronts the confusions encountered as adolescents develop and enter the dating age. Discusses the myths and misconceptions about sex and the issue of looking for love in the form of a baby. Part of a three - part series confronting the issues of teen pregnancy prevention, the confusions and misconceptions as teens face the pressures of dating, the realities of being a parent and parenting skills.
Guidance and Counseling; Health and Safety; Psychology; Religion and Philosophy; Sociology
Dist - CAMV

Teens who Choose Life - the Suicidal Crisis
U-matic / VHS
Color (J H C)
Explores the dynamics of teen suicide, using the moving stories of three teenagers who attempted suicide and survived. Emphasizes strategies to cope with stress and depression. Demonstrates that the first step is to choose life. Includes teacher's guide.
Guidance and Counseling; Health and Safety; Psychology; Sociology
Dist - SUNCOM **Prod** - SUNCOM

Teens with tiny strangers
VHS
Color (I J H)
$195.00 purchase, $50.00 rental
Emphasizes the importance of learning parenting skills, especially for adolescent parents. Examines exemplary parenting programs, including the nationally acclaimed Beethoven Project on the south side of Chicago, where young parents learn more about their babies, more about parenting and more about themselves.
Guidance and Counseling; Sociology
Dist - NEWIST **Prod** - NEWIST

Teeny - Tiny and the Witch - Woman 14 MIN
U-matic / VHS / 16mm
Color (K P)
LC 79-701809
Presents a Turkish folktale about three brothers who, despite their mother's warnings, go into the forest to play and encounter a witch - woman who eats little children.
Literature and Drama
Dist - WWS **Prod** - WWS 1979

Teeny - tiny and the witch - woman 35 MIN
VHS / 16mm
Children's circle video series
Color (K)
$18.88 purchase _ #CCV005
Presents the children's story.
Literature and Drama
Dist - EDUCRT

The Teeny - tiny woman
VHS
Paul Galdone's illustrated spooky stories series
Color (K P I)
$44.95 purchase _ #SAV9026
Tells about a teeny - tiny woman who has a problem with a teeny - tiny voice in her teeny - tiny cupboard. Presents part of a four - part series of spooky stories by Paul Galdone.
Literature and Drama
Dist - KNOWUN

Teeth 12 MIN
U-matic / VHS / 16mm
Exploring the Body Series
Color (P I J H)
LC 72-702861
Illustrates the growth and care of teeth and the development of teeth including incisors, canine teeth, molars and premolars, from the formation of milk teeth to their replacement by permanent teeth. Describes the inner structure of teeth and the dental treatment of decay and application of braces to correct the chewing position of the teeth.
Health and Safety; Science - Natural
Dist - FI **Prod** - FI 1972
IFFB

Teeth 15 MIN
VHS
Zardips search for healthy wellness series
Color (P I)
LC 90-707991
Presents an episode in a series which help young children understand basic health issues and the value of taking good care of their bodies. Explains the function of teeth. Includes teacher's guide.
Education; Health and Safety
Dist - TVOTAR **Prod** - TVOTAR 1989

Teeth are for Chewing 11 MIN
U-matic / VHS / 16mm
Color (P I) (FRENCH HUNGARIAN THAI ARABIC)
LC 72-700147
Reviews normal tooth development in human beings and studies the process of replacement of primary teeth. Demonstrates proper tooth care and explores the many varieties of teeth found in the animal kingdom.
Foreign Language; Health and Safety; Science - Natural
Dist - CORF **Prod** - DISNEY 1971

Teeth are Good Things to have 13 MIN
16mm
Color (P)
Portrays the necessity of a personal, in - home program of preventive hygiene.
Health and Safety
Dist - JAJ **Prod** - JAJ 1973

Teeth are to keep 11 MIN
16mm
Color (P I)
Animated drawings show the four essentials of good teeth care -- eat proper food, avoid sweets, brush teeth after each meal and visit the dentist twice a year.
Health and Safety
Dist - NFBC **Prod** - NFBC 1950

Teeth - People are Smarter than Germs 10 MIN
16mm
Health Series
Color
LC 75-704341
Demonstrates how people who are taking care of their teeth are also looking after their health.
Health and Safety
Dist - MORLAT **Prod** - MORLAT 1974

Teeth - some facts to chew on 14 MIN
U-matic / VHS / 16mm
Color (I J)
$360.00, $250.00 purchase _ #80525; LC 81-701475
Illustrates the location and function of incisors, cuspids, bicuspids and molars. Uses animation to show the components of teeth and to demonstrate how plaque can result in tooth decay. Provides information on the proper care of teeth.
Health and Safety; Science - Natural
Dist - CORF **Prod** - CENTRO 1981
VIEWTH VIEWTH

Teeth - the better to eat with 15 MIN
VHS / U-matic / 16mm / BETA
Color (K P)
$245.00, $68.00 purchase _ #C50660, #C51449
Shows how animals use their teeth for defense, communication and eating. Illustrates how the shape of an animal's jaw and teeth reveals what type of food it eats. Looks at stages in the development of human teeth and discusses the importance of good dental hygiene.
Health and Safety; Science - Natural
Dist - NGS **Prod** - NGS 1990

Teeth White - Teeth Bright 10 MIN
16mm
Color (P I)
LC FIA65-1121
Shows a young boy caring for his teeth and emphasizes the importance of brushing correctly, drinking milk, eating the right foods and having regular check - ups.
Health and Safety
Dist - SF **Prod** - MORLAT 1965

Tehching Hsieh - One Year Performance, Time Clock Piece 7 MIN
U-matic / VHS

Color
Represents the time of labor and life in images of spinning clock hands and growing hair.
Fine Arts
Dist - ARTINC **Prod** - ARTINC

Teiman - music of Yemenite Jewry 27 MIN
VHS
Jewish music heritage library series
Color (G)
$39.95 purchase _ #793
Reveals that an unusual sense of togetherness and an abundance of musical talent pervades Yemenite Jewry. Discloses that mourning for the destruction of the Second Temple resulted in the prohibition of using musical instruments and the stringent Yemenite Jews accepted this ban literally, perfecting singing and rhythm, drumming and dancing as an alternative. The songs sung by Yemenite men are inspired by the Diwan, a compilation of poetry dating back 300 years, while the women sing ballads of love and family. Performances by Yemenite vocalists Ofra Haza and Noa - Achinoam Nini. Part of a series on Jewish music from around the world, featuring Martin Bookspan as narrator.
Fine Arts; Sociology
Dist - ERGOM **Prod** - IMHP

Teine Samoa - a Girl of Samoa 26 MIN
16mm / U-matic / VHS
Girl of Series
Color (J H)
Views life in a village in Western Samoa through the eyes of a young educated girl who is faced with the choice of either remaining with her family or seeking a life further afield. Examines her role in the traditional family structure, her daily duties, moments of relaxation and the tensions brought about when the outside world appears to offer opportunities of a new and different life.
Geography - World; Social Science; Sociology
Dist - JOU **Prod** - JOU 1982

Tejst - Cepphus Grylle - Black Guillemot 4 MIN
16mm
Color
Presents a description of the black quillemot in its natural surroundings, accompanied by music and sound effects.
Science - Natural
Dist - STATNS **Prod** - STATNS 1965

Tekenfilm 3 MIN
U-matic / VHS / 16mm
Color
LC 79-701687
Presents a cartoon in which a figure drawn in pencil prances and frolics on the drawing board until he is threatened by an eraser.
Fine Arts
Dist - IFB **Prod** - REUSN 1977

Tel - Aviv 30 MIN
VHS
Shalom Sesame series
Color (K P)
$19.95 purchase _ #241
Features Itzhak Perlman who guides the viewer through Tel - Aviv. Part of an eight - part series on Israel with the Sesame Street Muppets.
Geography - World; Sociology
Dist - ERGOM **Prod** - ERGOM

Telecommunications 28 MIN
VHS / U-matic
Next Steps with Computers in the Classroom Series
Color (T)
Industrial and Technical Education; Mathematics; Social Science; Sociology
Dist - PBS **Prod** - PBS

Telecommunications 360 MIN
VHS / U-matic
Next Steps with Computers in the Classroom Series
Color (C T)
Computer Science; Education; Mathematics
Dist - UEUWIS **Prod** - UEUWIS 1985

Telecommunications 30 MIN
U-matic / VHS
Innovation Series
Color
Demonstrates how communications satellites work, and what new programming is under development.
Industrial and Technical Education; Social Science
Dist - PBS **Prod** - WNETTV 1983

Telecommunications 29 MIN
VHS / 16mm
Discovery digest series
Color (S)
$300.00 purchase
Explores a vast array of science - related discoveries, challenges and technological breakthroughs. Profiles and 'demystifies' research and development currently underway in many fields. 'Telecommunications' reports that a national newspaper crosses the continent in seconds via satellite, telecommunications close the gap between teachers and distance learners, and 'Bell's baby,' the telephone, grows up.
Computer Science; Health and Safety; Psychology; Science; Science - Physical; Social Science
Dist - ACCESS **Prod** - ACCESS 1989

Telecommunications 10 MIN
VHS
Skills - occupational programs series
Color (H C)
$49.00 purchase, $15.00 rental _ #316622; LC 91-712452
Features young people who work in the growing telecommunications industry, including a self - employed video producer, technicians who service cable systems, telephone systems and photocopiers and a computer engineer technologist. Part of a series that features occupations in the skilled trades, in service industries and in business leading to careers in areas of demand and future growth. Includes teacher's guide with reproducible worksheets.
Guidance and Counseling; Psychology; Social Science
Dist - TVOTAR **Prod** - TVOTAR 1990

Telecommunications 30 MIN
VHS
Inside Britain 2 series
Color; PAL; NTSC (G) (BULGARIAN CZECH HUNGARIAN SPANISH POLISH ROMANIAN RUSSIAN SLOVAK UKRAINIAN ENGLISH WITH ARABIC SUBTITLES LITHUANIAN)
PdS65 purchase
Presents a brief history of telecommunications. Illustrates, with four case histories, how the efficient exploitation of telecommunications helps to promote good business and generate profits.
Business and Economics; Social Science
Dist - CFLVIS **Prod** - KANNMI 1992

Telecommunications and the Computer Series
Multiplexing 45 MIN
Dist - AMCEE

Telecommunications and the Computer Series
Computer Networks 60 MIN
Data base distribution 51 MIN
Error control 43 MIN
Introduction to Data Communication 35 MIN
Link Control Procedures 56 MIN
Management of Data Communications 42 MIN
Multiplexing 44 MIN
Network Architecture 48 MIN
Security in Data Communications 46 MIN
Signaling and Modulation 30 MIN
Switching 51 MIN
Terminal Equipment and Interfaces 49 MIN
Dist - MIOT

Telecommunications for Distributed Processing 720 MIN
U-matic / VHS
(PRO A)
$4,320.00
Provides training for managers, engineers and communications specialists on modern communications theory.
Business and Economics; Computer Science
Dist - VIDEOT **Prod** - VIDEOT 1988

Teleconference highlights 60 MIN
Cassette / VHS
Color (G A)
$25.00, $10.00 purchase
Presents the highlight speeches of the Causes and Cures national teleconference on the narcotics epidemic. Includes the keynote address of the Rev Dr Joseph Lowery.
Civics and Political Systems; Guidance and Counseling; Health and Safety; Sociology
Dist - CRINST **Prod** - CRINST

Teleconference - the US Congress and the Constitution 57 MIN
VHS
Color (J H C G)
$49.99 purchase _ #CUP837V - S
Records a teleconference with Sen Orrin Hatch, Republican, Utah, ranking member of the Senate Labor and Human Resource Committee. Examines the evolving relationship between Congress and the US Constitution, using case examples and questions from college students in Texas. Covers balancing the interests of small and large states, distribution of power at the federal level and what the framers intended when they created the bicameral system. Discusses Iran - Contra, line - item vetoing, Roe v Wade, mandatory drug testing and the Fourteenth Amendment. Includes teacher's guide.
Civics and Political Systems
Dist - CAMV

Teleconference videos and audios
VHS / U-matic / Cassette
Color (G A)
$200.00, $100.00, $50.00 purchase
Documents the November 9, 1991, teleconference on the narcotics epidemic at the Marble Collegiate Church in New York. Includes dialogues between nearly 200 local gatherings nationwide and the New York conference, sponsored by Causes and Cures. Includes five videocassettes or audiocassettes.
Civics and Political Systems; Guidance and Counseling; Health and Safety; Sociology
Dist - CRINST **Prod** - CRINST

Teledetection - a New Look at the Earth 30 MIN
U-matic / VHS
Color (C)
$249.00, $149.00 purchase _ #AD - 1140
Shows how satellite scanning and temperature maps - thermal imaging - are aiding the search for oil and mineral deposits, improving land use and crop conditions and counteracting the effects of pollution.
Agriculture; Industrial and Technical Education; Science - Physical; Social Science; Sociology
Dist - FOTH **Prod** - FOTH

Telefrancais Series
Program 1 10 MIN
Program 10 10 MIN
Program 11 10 MIN
Program 12 10 MIN
Program 13 10 MIN
Program 14 10 MIN
Program 15 10 MIN
Program 16 10 MIN
Program 17 10 MIN
Program 18 10 MIN
Program 19 10 MIN
Program 2 10 MIN
Program 20 10 MIN
Program 21 10 MIN
Program 22 10 MIN
Program 23 10 MIN
Program 24 10 MIN
Program 25 10 MIN
Program 26 10 MIN
Program 27 10 MIN
Program 28 10 MIN
Program 29 10 MIN
Program 3 10 MIN
Program 30 10 MIN
Program 4 10 MIN
Program 5 10 MIN
Program 6 10 MIN
Program 7 10 MIN
Program 8 10 MIN
Program 9 10 MIN
Dist - TVOTAR

Telegraph Line 3 MIN
VHS / U-matic
Science Rock Series
Color (I)
Features the human nervous system and shows how it functions as the body's communications system.
Science - Natural
Dist - GA **Prod** - ABCTV

Telemarketing for Better Business Results Series
Handling Customer Objections 9 MIN
Handling Incoming Calls 12 MIN
Identifying and Developing Customer Needs 16 MIN
Making Product Recommendations and Closing the Call 15 MIN
Opening a Telemarketing Call 14 MIN
Product and Competitive Knowledge 9 MIN
Prospecting and Planning 7 MIN
Dist - DELTAK

Telemarketing series
Becoming a Pro on the Phone 13 MIN
Controlling the collection call 17 MIN
Customer service - a backup sales force 14 MIN
Dealing with customer objections 17 MIN
Getting the order 17 MIN
Techniques for the phone sales representative 12 MIN
Dist - CORF

Telemarketing site selection
VHS
Color (C PRO G)
$150.00 purchase _ #89.05
Reveals that over 180,000 telemarketing centers in the US employ more than 2 million people. Shows that site selection in the telemarketing business has become a critical problem. AT&T developed a DSS to help customers determine locations for such centers. A mixed integer programming model swiftly assisted 46 customers in selecting sites, while committing $375 million in annual

network services and $31 million in equipment. AT&T. Thomas Spencer III, Anthony J Brigandi, Dennis R Dargon, Michael J Sheehan.
Business and Economics
Dist - INMASC

Telemetry in Emergency Care 30 MIN
U-matic / VHS
Color
Explores the mobile intensive care program of Northwest Community Hospital in Arlington Heights, Illinois, and gives behind - the - scene details of how to start and operate a life - saving, two - way radio - telemetry communications network.
Health and Safety
Dist - TEACHM **Prod** - TEACHM

Teleological and Cosmological Arguments 25 MIN
U-matic / VHS
Introduction to Philosophy Series
Color (C)
Religion and Philosophy
Dist - UDEL **Prod** - UDEL

Telepathic communications with animals 46 MIN
VHS
Color (G)
$29.95 purchase _ #V - T2A
Features Penelope Smith who gives documented proof of her ability to 'talk' with all creatures. Gives tips on how to learn the skill of communication with animals.
Social Science
Dist - PACSPI

Telepathic healing 30 MIN
BETA / VHS
Frontiers of psychic research series
Color (G)
$29.95 purchase _ #S346
Describes various experiments showing positive healing results - even when there was no healer present. Hypothesizes that positive expectations may play a very important role in psychic and spiritual healing. Features Jerry Solfvin, parapsychologist. Part of a four - part series on the frontiers of psychic research.
Health and Safety; Psychology
Dist - THINKA **Prod** - THINKA

Telephone 10 MIN
VHS
Stop, look, listen series
Color; PAL (P I J)
Observes the school telephone ringing and the headmaster answering it. Shows how the voice of student cannot be heard at a distance, but a teacher goes to a telephone booth outside of the school, dials the school number and one of the students answers the call. Part of a series of films which start from some everyday observation and show more of what is happening, how and why. Builds vocabulary and encourages children to be more observant.
English Language; Industrial and Technical Education; Social Science
Dist - VIEWTH

Telephone 30 MIN
VHS
How do you do - learning English series
Color (H A)
#317707
Shows that CHIPS discovers the telephone, how to answer it, how to take a message and call the operator. Teaches how to use a telephone directory and how to make a long distance call. Part of a series that helps newcomers learn English. Includes viewer's guide with grammar explanations and vocabulary drills, worksheets and two audio cassettes.
English Language; Social Science
Dist - TVOTAR **Prod** - TVOTAR 1990

Telephone behavior - the power and the perils 29 MIN
VHS
Color (A PRO IND)
$790.00 purchase, $220.00 rental
Teaches effective call answering skills. Covers identification, gathering the facts, giving help where needed, and more. Stars John Cleese of 'Monty Python' fame.
Business and Economics; Industrial and Technical Education; Social Science; Sociology
Dist - VLEARN **Prod** - VIDART
VIDART

Telephone call 5 MIN
VHS
English plus series
(J H A)
Explains how to ask for someone on the phone, and the use of regular and irregular verbs in the past tense.
English Language
Dist - AITECH **Prod** - LANGPL 1985

Telephone communications 28 MIN
VHS
Basic clerical skills series
Color (H C A)
$119.00 purchase _ #VMA30728V; #PX1183V; #30728 - 126
Examines the use of the telephone in clerical jobs. Covers subjects including intercoms, area codes, directory and operator assistance, direct dial, station - to - station, person - to - person, WATS lines, and more. Includes reproducible masters and a teacher's guide.
Business and Economics
Dist - CAMV **Prod** - CAREER
CAREER GA
GA

Telephone Concept 6 MIN
VHS / U-matic
Color (I)
Uses archival photographs and drawings that depict Alexander Graham Bell's telephone concept.
Fine Arts; History - United States; Industrial and Technical Education
Dist - NFBC **Prod** - CRAF 1981

Telephone courtesy and customer service 26 MIN
VHS
Color (A PRO)
$495.00 purchase, $150.00 rental
Illustrates effective telephone communication skills from use of the voice to negotiating techniques. Emphasizes the importance of telephone etiquette to customer service.
Business and Economics; Social Science
Dist - DHB **Prod** - CRISP

Telephone Courtesy - Healthcare 22 MIN
VHS
Telephone Courtesy Pays Series
Color
Business and Economics; Home Economics; Social Science; Sociology
Dist - ADVANM **Prod** - ADVANM

Telephone courtesy - industry specific 8 MIN
U-matic / VHS
(PRO A)
$395.00 purchase, $100.00, $35.00 rental
Demonstrates effective telephone skills that apply specifically to industries such as aerospace, car dealerships, and government.
Business and Economics
Dist - ADVANM **Prod** - ADVANM

Telephone Courtesy - Insurance 22 MIN
VHS
Telephone Courtesy Pays Series
Color
Business and Economics; Social Science; Sociology
Dist - ADVANM **Prod** - ADVANM

Telephone Courtesy - Large Retail Business 22 MIN
VHS
Telephone Courtesy Pays Series
Color
Business and Economics; Home Economics; Social Science; Sociology
Dist - ADVANM **Prod** - ADVANM

Telephone Courtesy - Law Enforcement 22 MIN
VHS
Telephone Courtesy Pays Series
Color
Business and Economics; Home Economics; Social Science; Sociology
Dist - ADVANM **Prod** - ADVANM

Telephone courtesy - lodging - hotel motel 22 MIN
VHS
Telephone courtesy pays series
Color
Business and Economics; Home Economics; Social Science; Sociology
Dist - ADVANM **Prod** - ADVANM

Telephone Courtesy - Manufacturing 22 MIN
VHS
Telephone Courtesy Pays Series
Color
Business and Economics; Home Economics; Social Science; Sociology
Dist - ADVANM **Prod** - ADVANM

Telephone courtesy pays 15 MIN
16mm / U-matic / VHS
Courtesy under pressure series
(PRO A)
$495.00 purchase, $150.00, $35.00 rental; $199.00 purchase _ #012 - 805
Points out that courtesy in telephone skills is an asset to both client and business, even under pressure.
Business and Economics
Dist - ADVANM **Prod** - ADVANM
CAREER CAREER

Telephone Courtesy Pays 14 MIN
U-matic / VHS / 16mm
(A PRO)
$495.00, $520.00 purchase, $150.00, $35.00 rental
Provides information and training for people in business involved in communications, especially telephone answering.
Business and Economics
Dist - ADVANM **Prod** - ADVANM

Telephone courtesy pays 23 MIN
VHS
Color (COR)
$495.00 purchase, $150.00 five - day rental, $35.00 three - day preview _ #TCR
Demonstrates and teaches 27 basic telephone techniques that are essential for increasing employee efficiency, for satisfying customers, and increasing profits. Teaches handling of multiple calls, call transferring, handling problems, taking messages, and voice mail etiquetts. Includes support materials. Available for three - day preview and five - day rental, as well as for lease or purchase.
Business and Economics; Guidance and Counseling
Dist - ADVANM

Telephone Courtesy Pays Off 19 MIN
VHS / U-matic
(PRO)
$475.00 purchase, $110.00 rental
A version of 'Handling Incoming Calls,' differs in focus on telephone courtesy rather than selling techniques.
Business and Economics
Dist - CREMED **Prod** - CREMED 1987
VLEARN AIMS

Telephone Courtesy Pays Series
Telephone Courtesy - Healthcare 22 MIN
Telephone Courtesy - Insurance 22 MIN
Telephone Courtesy - Large Retail Business 22 MIN
Telephone Courtesy - Law Enforcement 22 MIN
Telephone courtesy - lodging - hotel motel 22 MIN
Telephone Courtesy - Manufacturing 22 MIN
Telephone Courtesy - Real Estate 22 MIN
Telephone Courtesy - Small Retail Business 22 MIN
Telephone Courtesy - Utility Company 22 MIN
Dist - ADVANM

Telephone Courtesy - Real Estate 22 MIN
VHS
Telephone Courtesy Pays Series
Color
Business and Economics; Home Economics; Social Science; Sociology
Dist - ADVANM **Prod** - ADVANM

Telephone Courtesy - Small Retail Business 22 MIN
VHS
Telephone Courtesy Pays Series
Color
Business and Economics; Home Economics; Social Science; Sociology
Dist - ADVANM **Prod** - ADVANM

Telephone courtesy under pressure series
Assertive problem solving
Dealing with the irate customer
Games Customers and Customer Service People Play
Listening Under Pressure
Winning Customers through Service
Dist - CAREER

Telephone Courtesy - Utility Company 22 MIN
VHS
Telephone Courtesy Pays Series
Color
Business and Economics; Home Economics; Social Science; Sociology
Dist - ADVANM **Prod** - ADVANM

Telephone Creek 26 MIN
16mm
Color; B&W (I J H C G T A)
Analyzes the reflective side of the smokejumpers, otherwise known as forest fire fighters. Story of eight smokejumpers who spot a forest fire in central Idaho in 1950, and how they put the fire out.
Agriculture; Geography - United States; Guidance and Counseling; Social Science
Dist - FO **Prod** - FO 1987

Telephone doctor series
Proactive customer service
Six cardinal rules of customer service
Dist - EXTR

Telephone doctor series
How to deal with the foreign accent 22 MIN
How to handle the irate caller 10 MIN
How to treat every caller as a welcome guest 9 MIN
On outgoing calls 17 MIN
Dist - EXTR
TELDOC

Telephone doctor series
From curt to courteous 27 MIN
How to avoid emotional leakage 6 MIN
Dist - EXTR
TELDOC
VLEARN

Telephone doctor series
Determining caller needs 22 MIN
Five forbidden phrases 18 MIN
Dist - EXTR
VLEARN

Telephone doctor series
Hall of shame 20 MIN
Dist - VLEARN

The Telephone Film 7 MIN
16mm
B&W
LC 74-703020
Presents a humorous compilation of telephone scenes from old movies.
Business and Economics; Industrial and Technical Education
Dist - CANFDC

Telephone for Help 9 MIN
16mm / U-matic / VHS
Color; B&W (P I)
LC FIA68-1275
Shows three situations in which children call the police, the firemen and the telephone operator for help. Explains that giving information clearly and precisely helps rescuers.
Guidance and Counseling; Health and Safety; Social Science
Dist - PHENIX **Prod** - RBNETT 1968

Telephone Installer 15 MIN
U-matic
Harriet's Magic Hats I Series
(P I J)
Shows how telephones work and that the telephone system is a huge wire network that transports sound as electricity.
Guidance and Counseling
Dist - ACCESS **Prod** - ACCESS 1980

Telephone line 17 MIN
VHS / U-matic
Kidzone series
Color (I J)
$195.00, $245.00 purchase, $50.00 rental
Traces the history of the telephone and the contemporary communications possible through the telephone line. Explains the principles of the telephone, its history, fiber optics, use of the 911 number and broad band networking through the telephone.
Industrial and Technical Education
Dist - NDIM **Prod** - KNONET 1992

Telephone Lineman 15 MIN
16mm / U-matic / VHS
Career Awareness
(I)
$130.00, $240.00 purchase, $25.00, $30.00 rental
Presents an empathetic approach to career planning, showing the personal as well as the professional attributes of telephone linemen. Highlights the importance of career education.
Guidance and Counseling; Industrial and Technical Education; Social Science
Dist - GPN

Telephone manners 10 MIN
U-matic / VHS / 16mm
Communications and selling program - Spanish series
Color (SPANISH)
Discusses telephone courtesy as a vital element in both internal and external communications in any organization. Demonstrates important steps in placing and answering a phone call.
Business and Economics; Foreign Language; Industrial and Technical Education; Psychology
Dist - NEM **Prod** - NEM

Telephone manners 10 MIN
16mm / U-matic / VHS
Communications and selling program series
Color (J)
LC 74-700225
Presents a basic training for every person who must use the telephone in business. Includes tips on courtesy when answering the phone, taking messages, and transferring and placing a call. Gives special attention to warmth and friendliness. Stresses the fact that the voice on the phone is the voice of the business or organization it represents.
Business and Economics; Guidance and Counseling; Psychology
Dist - NEM **Prod** - NEM 1973

Telephone manners 2 11 MIN
U-matic / VHS / 16mm
Customer service, courtesy and selling programs series
Color (SPANISH)
Demonstrates courteous and effective use of the telephone in business.
Business and Economics; Social Science
Dist - NEM **Prod** - NEM

Telephone medicine series
Presents a teaching package for training in telephone medicine. Includes a videocassette, three audiocassettes, an instructor's manual and a student workbook. Offers 13 audio vignettes which trigger discussion, role play and evaluation by the learners. Presented by Dr Peter Curtis, Susan Evens, Nathan Berolzheimer and Madeline Beery.
Telephone medicine series
Dist - HSCIC

Telephone Operator 15 MIN
U-matic / 16mm / VHS
Career Awareness
(I)
$130.00, $240.00 purchase, $25.00, $30.00 rental
Presents an empathetic approach to career planning, showing the personal as well as the professional qualities of telephone operators. Highlights the importance of career education.
Guidance and Counseling; Industrial and Technical Education; Social Science
Dist - GPN

Telephone Perfection
VHS
Color (G)
$795.00 purchase, $185.00 rental
Teaches telephone courtesy and skills to office staff.
Business and Economics; Industrial and Technical Education
Dist - VLEARN **Prod** - MELROS

Telephone Selling - a New Approach 30 MIN
VHS / 16mm
Color (A PRO)
$790.00 purchase, $220.00 rental
Trains in telephone sales and setting appointments. Shows how to make contacts, communicate content and bring about a satisfactory conclusion.
Business and Economics; Industrial and Technical Education
Dist - VIDART **Prod** - VIDART 1991

Telephone Selling Series
Meeting Objections
Dist - COLOSU

Telephone Skills - Hospitality on the Line 27 MIN
VHS / 16mm
Color (A)
LC 90711943
Teaches telephone skills for people who work in the hospitality industry. Emphasizes training for hotel employees.
Business and Economics; Industrial and Technical Education
Dist - EIAHM **Prod** - UNKNWN 1990

Telephone skills - techniques for customer types 15 MIN
VHS
Job skills for career success series
Color (H C G)
$79.00 purchase _ #CDSBED112V
Shows how to convert telephone nightmares into public relations and sales opportunities. Presents various kinds of callers along with specific response techniqes. Part of a ten - part series which explores basic job skills necessary for a successful career. Includes student guide.
Business and Economics; Guidance and Counseling; Psychology
Dist - CAMV

Telephone skills - why they're important 15 MIN
VHS
Job skills for career success series
Color (H C G)
$79.00 purchase _ #CDSBED110V
Shows how customer service representatives with poor telephone skills can ruin the reputation of a good company. Explores the importance of good telephone skills in all careers. Part of a ten - part series which explores basic job skills necessary for a successful career. Includes student guide.
Business and Economics; Guidance and Counseling; Psychology
Dist - CAMV

Telephone Talk - How to Deal with People Over the Telephone 20 MIN
U-matic / VHS / 16mm
(A)
Illustrates sharpening people skills and practical skills over the telephone thereby making it more efficient, more successful, and more enjoyable.
Business and Economics
Dist - SALENG **Prod** - SALENG 1984

Telephone Tips for Kids 21 MIN
VHS
Color (K)
$22.50 purchase _ #V3011 - 10
Uses humor and life - sized puppets to teach children the proper use of phones. Tells story of Auntie Bella and her young guests. Children are instructed by Nancy J. Friedman, an expert on phone techniques, in how to take messages and make emergency phone calls.
Health and Safety; Industrial and Technical Education
Dist - SCHSCI

The Telephone - Tool or Tyrant 23 MIN
U-matic / VHS / 16mm
Color (A)
Explains how to use the telephone efficiently in an office setting.
Business and Economics
Dist - CCCD **Prod** - CCCD 1983

Telephones 30 MIN
U-matic / VHS
Consumer survival series; Homes
Color
Presents tips on the care of telephones.
Home Economics
Dist - MDCPB **Prod** - MDCPB

Telephoning by TTY 7 MIN
16mm
Color (J) (AMERICAN SIGN)
LC 76-701706
Records in American sign language a conversation between a deaf husband and wife on using the TTY (teletypewriter) more efficiently, he for his social work and she for her women's club activities. Signed for the deaf by Mr and Mrs Kyle Workman.
Education; Guidance and Counseling; Industrial and Technical Education; Psychology
Dist - JOYCE **Prod** - JOYCE 1975

Telesales - your line of business - simplifying the telephone sales call 30 MIN
VHS / U-matic
Color (C A PRO)
$790.00 purchase, $220.00 rental
Divides the process of telephone sales into three stages - Contact, Content and Conclusion. Emphasizes brevity and directness - say who's calling and why, then listen to see if the prospect is available and find the right person to talk to.
Business and Economics; English Language; Social Science
Dist - VIDART **Prod** - VIDART 1991

The Telescope 8 MIN
VHS / U-matic
Color (K P I J C A)
$49.00 purchase _ #3547
Relates the story of Jonelle, a little girl who builds a telescope. Examines the power of imagination when her telescope is destroyed.
Literature and Drama
Dist - EBEC **Prod** - AESOP 1987

The Telescope - Window to the Universe 16 MIN
16mm / U-matic / VHS
Color; Captioned (I J)
Shows different types of telelscopes and their use and care. Two students construct a basic refractor telescope, and learn the concepts of focal length, inversion, terrestrial and celestial viewing as well as the difference between refractors and reflectors.
Science - Physical
Dist - HANDEL **Prod** - HANDEL 1986

Telescopes 15 MIN
VHS / U-matic
En Francais series
Color (H C A)
Visits a hilltop overlooking the countryside and the Observatory of Saint - Michel - de - Provence.
Foreign Language; Geography - World
Dist - AITECH **Prod** - MOFAFR 1970

Telespanol Uno series
The Adjectives (Los Adjetivos) 30 MIN
Dist - GPN

Teletales series

The Bargain	15 MIN
Bianchinetta	15 MIN
Caliph stork	15 MIN
The Charmed ring	30 MIN
The Chenoo	15 MIN
Fiddy wow wow	15 MIN
Half Chick and the Squire's Bride	15 MIN
Hansel and Gretel	15 MIN
Long Nose	15 MIN
Molly O'Mally	15 MIN
Paka's	15 MIN
Soongoora and Simba	15 MIN
The Sorcerer's Boy	15 MIN
Stan Bolovan	15 MIN
The Willow Tree	15 MIN

Dist - AITECH

Teletherapy and Brachytherapy 18 MIN
16mm
Color
LC FIE63-192
Shows the diagnostic and therapeutic uses of such radioisotopes as CP - 60, CS - 137, EU - 152 - 154, I - 131 and Y - 90 in teletherapy and brachytherapy by using machines that aim a high - energy beam at a tumor or by using implants of radioactive materials in the form of needles, beads, sterile tubing or seeds.
Health and Safety; Science; Science - Physical
Dist - USNAC **Prod** - USNRC 1958

Television 30 MIN
U-matic
Today's Special Series
Color (K P)
Develops language arts skills in children. Programs are thematically designed around subjects of interest to youngsters. Action takes place in a department store where people, mannequins, puppets, comic characters and special guests present a light hearted approach to language arts.
Fine Arts; Literature and Drama; Psychology
Dist - TVOTAR **Prod** - TVOTAR 1985

Television - 113 29 MIN
VHS
FROG series 1; Series 1; 113
Color (P I J)
$100.00 purchase
Offers the thirteenth and final program in series 1 by Friends of Research and Odd Gadgets. Lifts science off the textbook page into the real world to show how enjoyable and challenging science can be. In this episode, the Froggers create their own Public Service Announcement. Special focus on filming commercials, community television and how TV cameras work. Produced by Greg Rist.
Industrial and Technical Education; Science - Physical
Dist - BULFRG **Prod** - OWLTV 1993

Television - a Political Machine 14 MIN
16mm
Public Broadcast Laboratory Series
B&W (H C A)
LC FIA68-3075
Discusses how politics has been affected by the use of television, as evidenced in the 1968 Indiana presidential primary.
Civics and Political Systems; Psychology; Social Science
Dist - IU **Prod** - NET 1968

Television, a teaching assistance, presenting patterns of inter-institutional and inter-regional teaching 28 MIN
U-matic
B&W
Presents examples of patterns of inter - institutional and inter - regional teaching on television in selected areas of the United States, including the educational advantages to both staff and students of cooperative uses of television in college teaching.
Education; Social Science
Dist - USNAC **Prod** - USNAC 1972

Television and Politics 25 MIN
U-matic / VHS / 16mm
Color (J)
Outlines the history of political television commercials, beginning in 1948. Examines many campaign commercials that use Madison Avenue techniques to package and sell politicians. Newsman Mike Wallace questions politicians and political consultants who plan and produce the candidates' commercials.
Biography; Civics and Political Systems; Social Science
Dist - PHENIX **Prod** - CBSTV 1971

Television and the presidency
VHS
Color (G)
Free _ #V94 - 19
Presents a three - part series, hosted by Sander Vanocur examining the impact of television on the presidency.
Biography; Sociology
Dist - FREEDM **Prod** - FREEDM 1994

Television assassination 14 MIN
16mm
B&W (H C A)
$600.00 purchase, $45.00 rental
Transforms the experience of seeing the familiar images of the assassination of John F. Kennedy. Uses humor to relieve the sadness of the material. Produced by Bruce Conner and Patrick Gleeson.
Civics and Political Systems; Sociology
Dist - CANCIN

Television - Behind the Scenes 23 MIN
VHS / U-matic
Color (I J)
$79.00 purchase _ #3610
Looks at the creative process of producing a network television program and the job responsibilities of the production staff and stars. Filmed on the set of the Donny and Marie Osmond Show.
Fine Arts
Dist - EBEC

Television - Behind the Scenes 23 MIN
U-matic / VHS / 16mm
Wide World of Adventure Series
Color (I J H)
LC 79-700834
Provides a behind - the - scenes look at the filming of a network television show. Explores the job responsibilities of the production staff and stars.
Fine Arts
Dist - EBEC **Prod** - AVATLI

Television Delivers People 6 MIN
U-matic / VHS
Color
Focuses on broadcasting as corporate monopoly and imperialism. Uses irony.
Fine Arts
Dist - KITCHN **Prod** - KITCHN

The Television Designer 27 MIN
U-matic / VHS
BBC TV Production Training Course Series
Color (C)
$279.00, $179.00 purchase _ #AD - 2084
Follows the designer through the complete production of a half - hour episode of a sitcom. Touches upon costing, coordinating with construction crews, working on location, buying props and working on the studio floor. Part of a twelve - part series on TV production by the BBC.
Fine Arts; Geography - World; Industrial and Technical Education
Dist - FOTH **Prod** - FOTH

The Television Explosion 57 MIN
VHS / U-matic
Nova Series
Color (H C A)
LC 83-706192
Explains that, of all the technical innovations of the past, none has pervaded people's daily lives so much as television. Looks at the new technologies that are creating a second television revolution which could well transform people's lives again.
Fine Arts; Sociology
Dist - TIMLIF **Prod** - WGBHTV 1982

Television in the Classroom
U-matic
Visual Learning Series Session 3
Color (T)
Describes how to use television in the classroom, showing a variety of teachers, environments and techniques.
Education; Fine Arts; Industrial and Technical Education
Dist - NYSED **Prod** - NYSED

Television - it's done with mirrors 15 MIN
VHS
Field trips series
Color (I J)
$34.95 purchase _ #E337; LC 90-708558
Tours a television studio and station. Follows the process of television program production through its various stages. Looks at both studio and remote production. Part of a series which provides visual opportunities for children to 'visit' a variety of locations and activities as if they were on a field trip.
Education; Fine Arts; Geography - United States; Industrial and Technical Education
Dist - GPN **Prod** - MPBN 1983

Television Land 12 MIN
16mm / U-matic / VHS
Color
LC 74-713371
Uses live and taped film clips from programs from 1948 to the present to give an overview of the range of American television.
History - United States; Industrial and Technical Education; Social Science
Dist - PFP **Prod** - BRAMAN 1971

Television - Line by Line 11 MIN
16mm / U-matic / VHS
Color (H C)
LC 70-707288
Uses animation to explain principles of television. Demonstrates how light energy is converted to electrical energy which is transmitted to a distant place by radio signal, and how the receiving picture - tube changes the radio signal to an image that is formed like the original scenes line by line.
Fine Arts; Psychology; Science - Physical; Social Science
Dist - IFB **Prod** - IFB 1970

The Television Newsman 28 MIN
U-matic / VHS / 16mm
Color (J)
LC 76-700717
Traces the workings of a television news operation and the job of a TV field reporter. Spotlights Bill Redeker of television station KABC in Los Angeles.
Education; Fine Arts; Literature and Drama; Social Science
Dist - PFP **Prod** - BRAVC 1975

The Television Perspective 30 MIN
VHS / U-matic
ITV Utilization Series
Color
Introduces the technical aspects of ITV utilizations.
Education; Fine Arts
Dist - NETCHE **Prod** - NETCHE 1970

The Television Picture and those who make it 24 MIN
16mm / U-matic / VHS
Color (H C A)
LC 80-701957
Surveys the realities and excitement of working in television production, from advertising to news.
Fine Arts; Guidance and Counseling
Dist - PHENIX **Prod** - BARLOW 1980

Television - revolution in a box 49 MIN
VHS / U-matic / BETA
Color (H C A)
$250.00 purchase _ #JY - 6215M
Looks at how television is being used in and by the Soviet Union as an extremely powerful social safety valve to report delicate issues and promote public image. Features Ted Koppel as host.
Fine Arts; Geography - World; Sociology
Dist - CORF **Prod** - ABCNEW 1989

Television Serves its Community 15 MIN
U-matic / VHS / 16mm
Color (I J H)
Shows how television programs are prepared for transmission to the homes of a community. Follows three programs as they are planned, rehearsed and televised. Shows the use of live cameras, film, magnetic tape and remote pick - ups from trucks and helicopters.
Psychology; Social Science
Dist - PHENIX **Prod** - GOLD 1960

Television studio 10 MIN
VHS
Stop, look, listen series
Color; PAL (P I J)
Begins with a television scene of children dancing. Moves the camera to observe the work at a television studio. Looks at television photography in the control room and production procedures. Part of a series of films which start from some everyday observation and show more of what is happening, how and why. Builds vocabulary and encourages children to be more observant.
English Language; Fine Arts; Industrial and Technical Education; Social Science
Dist - VIEWTH

The Television studio 15 MIN
U-matic / VHS
Tuned - in series; Lesson 2
Color (J H)
Accompanies a ninth - grade class as it tours a television studio and gets a demonstration of the equipment. Shows an editor selecting video segments for the news and reveals that television news must be brief and is therefore often incomplete.
Fine Arts; Literature and Drama; Sociology
Dist - FI **Prod** - WNETTV 1982

Television - Testing the Future 11 MIN
VHS / U-matic
Color
LC 81-707114
Explores experiments in television broadcasting in three different locales where television is used to deliver services to the elderly, as a training tool for firefighters and as an aid in teaching English, spelling and arithmetic.
Fine Arts
Dist - USNAC **Prod** - NSF 1979

Television - the electric art 30 MIN
VHS / U-matic
Art of being human series; Module 9
Color (C)
History - World; Literature and Drama; Religion and Philosophy
Dist - MDCC **Prod** - MDCC

Television's Vietnam 115 MIN
VHS
Color (J H C G)
$29.95 purchase _ #BRD0492V
Presents two parts on the Vietnam war asking if the 58,132 Americans killed in the war died for a good cause. Offers the views of military experts, scholars, journalists and Vietnamese exiles. Includes The Real Story stating that early media coverage of the war misrepresented the realities of the politics, the soldiers and the conflict; The Impact of Media stating that misleading reporting from Vietnam contributed significantly to the loss of will to do what was necessary to keep South Vietnam from falling to the communists.
History - United States; Sociology
Dist - CAMV

Television's Vietnam - the impact of media 102 MIN
VHS
Color (G)
$29.95 purchase _ #S01534
Provides a two - part rebuttal to the PBS series 'Vietnam - A Television History.' Suggests that the media were in some part responsible for 'losing' the Vietnam War. Narrated by Charlton Heston.
History - United States; Psychology
Dist - UILL

Tell me a story 15 MIN
Videoreel / VT2
Art corner series
B&W (P)
Encourages students to use crayons to tell a story about their own family and what their mother or father does during the day.
Fine Arts
Dist - GPN **Prod** - CVETVC

Tell Me a Story 14 MIN
U-matic / VHS
Strawberry Square Series
Color (P)
Fine Arts
Dist - AITECH **Prod** - NEITV 1982

Tell Me a Story Series
Beauty and the beast video 30 MIN
Chuck Larkin video 30 MIN
Lynn Rubright Video 30 MIN
Mary Carter Smith Video 30 MIN
Michael 'Badhair' Williams Video - Vol I 30 MIN
Michael 'Badhair' Williams Video - Vol II 30 MIN
Nancy Schimmel Video 30 MIN
Ruthmarie Arguello - Sheehan Video 30 MIN
Dist - UPSTRT

Tell Me a Story, Sing Me a Song 29 MIN
VHS / 16mm
Color (G)
$100.00 purchase _ #STORYVH
Features black, Jewish and Appalachian independent theater companies. Uses interview and performance footage to illustrate the three companies' common concerns.
Fine Arts; Geography - United States; Sociology
Dist - APPAL

Tell me about yourself 27 MIN
U-matic / VHS / 16mm
Color (A) (NORWEGIAN SPANISH DUTCH SWEDISH JAPANESE)
LC 82-701181
Presents the entire interview process, emphasizing the thought processes of the interviewer as she attempts to achieve her interview objectives.
Foreign Language; Guidance and Counseling; Psychology
Dist - RTBL **Prod** - RTBL 1976

Tell Me all about it - what Makes a Friend So Special 9 MIN
16mm / U-matic / VHS
Read on Series
Color (P)
LC 72-701540
Relates incidents involving children and their friends, and what their friendships mean to them. Encourages written and oral expressions among young students.
English Language; Guidance and Counseling; Psychology
Dist - AIMS **Prod** - ACI 1971

Tell Me My Name 52 MIN
U-matic / VHS / 16mm
Teenage Years Series
Color (J)
Tells the story of a young adopted woman who tracks down her natural mother. Explains how she is met with shock and shame.
Fine Arts; Sociology
Dist - TIMLIF **Prod** - SUSSK

Tell me what you saw 52 MIN
VHS
Color; PAL (G)
PdS100 purchase
Journeys into the mysterious world of memory and oblivion through the portrait of a family of six siblings and their mother who suffers from dementia. Presents a Kiti Luostarinen for Kinotuotanto Oy, Finland production.
Fine Arts; Psychology; Sociology
Dist - BALFOR

Tell me what you see series
Are legs really necessary 15 MIN
The Cats 15 MIN
Coral life 15 MIN
Do all birds fly 15 MIN
Other Clawed Animals 15 MIN
Primates 15 MIN
Sea Life that Doesn't Crawl 15 MIN
Tame or wild 15 MIN
What Can Birds do 15 MIN
Dist - GPN

Tell Me Where to Turn 27 MIN
16mm
Color (A)
Provides a background for training union community service counselors. Helps people with problems to contact the community agency or counselor that can help.
Guidance and Counseling; Psychology; Sociology
Dist - AFLCIO **Prod** - PUAC 1970

Tell Me who I Am 30 MIN
U-matic
North of Sixty Degrees - Destiny Uncertain Series
Color (H C)
Investigates the dilemma presented by recent attempts to provide relevant and useful educational opportunities to an ethnically diverse population.
Geography - United States; Geography - World; History - World
Dist - TVOTAR **Prod** - TVOTAR 1985

Tell Me who You are 15 MIN
VHS / U-matic
It's all Up to You Series
Color (I J)
Promotes a recognition and acceptance of other world views.
Social Science
Dist - AITECH **Prod** - COOPED 1978

Tell me why - Americana 30 MIN
VHS
Color (P I J)
$19.95 purchase _ #ST - BM4656
Answers questions about United States history. Visits national landmarks and discusses American government.
Civics and Political Systems; Geography - United States; History - United States
Dist - INSTRU

Tell me why series
Animals and arachnids 30 MIN
Fish, shellfish and other underwater life 30 MIN
Insects 30 MIN
Life forms, animals and animal oddities 30 MIN
Mammals 30 MIN
Dist - CLRVUE

Tell me why series
Birds and rodents - Volume 8 30 MIN
Dist - CLRVUE
PBS

Tell me why series
Americana - Vol 6 30 MIN
Animals and arachnids - Volume 10 30 MIN
Fish, shellfish, and other underwater life - Volume 11 30 MIN
Flowers, plants, and trees 30 MIN
Gems, metals, and minerals - Volume 4 30 MIN
A Healthy body - Volume 13 30 MIN
Insects - Volume 5 30 MIN
Life forms, animals, and animal oddities - Volume 7 30 MIN
Mammals - Volume 9 30 MIN
Prehistoric animals, reptiles, and amphibians - Volume 12 30 MIN
Dist - PBS

Tell me why series
Space, earth and atmosphere - Volume 1
Water and weather - Volume 2
Dist - PBS
SEVVID

Tell me why series
Marine hurricane preparedness
Dist - SEVVID

Tell me why video series
Anthropology, science, sound and energy 30 MIN
Beginnings - civilization and government 30 MIN
Customs and superstitions 30 MIN
Flight 30 MIN
Geography 30 MIN
How things work 30 MIN
Science, sound and energy 30 MIN
Sports and games 30 MIN
Time, money and measurement 30 MIN
Dist - KNOWUN

Tell My Wife I Won't be Home for Dinner 32 MIN
16mm / U-matic / VHS
Color (H C A)
LC 80-700607
Presents three humorous exaggerations of time mismanagement. Contends that effective use of time is measured by results, not by the number of hours spent on a job.
Business and Economics; Psychology
Dist - CORF **Prod** - MTLTD 1980

Tell someone 5 MIN
VHS
Color (P I J H)
$89.00 purchase
Portrays five different kids in situations that revolve around alcohol abuse in the home. Shows the effects of alcholism on the entire family. Urges viewers from dysfunctional families to seek help.
Guidance and Counseling; Health and Safety; Sociology
Dist - LANDMK **Prod** - LANDMK 1990

Tell someone music video 4 MIN
VHS
Color (I J H C)
$89.95 purchase _ #AH45211
Uses a music video format to portray families with alcoholic parents. Encourages teenagers in such families to talk to an adult about it.
Guidance and Counseling; Health and Safety; Psychology; Sociology
Dist - HTHED **Prod** - HTHED

The Tell - tale heart 25 MIN
U-matic / VHS / 16mm
B&W (J)
LC 80-701648
Presents an adaptation of the Edgar Allen Poe story, 'The Tell- Tale Heart,' a study in psychological suspense and terror.
Literature and Drama
Dist - CF **Prod** - AMERFI 1974

The Tell - Tale Heart 8 MIN
16mm / U-matic / VHS
Color (J H)
Presents an animated version of Edgar Allen Poe's short story The Tell - Tale Heart, with James Mason as the narrative voice of the killer. Shows how a man's guilt becomes his undoing.
Fine Arts; Literature and Drama
Dist - LCOA **Prod** - BOSUST 1969

The Tell - Tale Heart 20 MIN
U-matic / VHS
Edgar Allan Poe - the Principle Works Series
Color (C)
$249.00, $149.00 purchase _ #AD - 1700
Retells 'The Tell - Tale Heart' by Edgar Allan Poe. Features Conrad Pomerleau as presenter.
Fine Arts; Literature and Drama
Dist - FOTH **Prod** - FOTH

The Tell - Tale Heart 23 MIN
16mm
B&W (I J H)
LC FI68-656
From his cell, a madman relates how he committed murder, revealing an obsessed and guilt - ridden mind.
Literature and Drama
Dist - CBSTV **Prod** - CBSTV 1959

The Tell - tale heart 26 MIN
16mm / U-matic / VHS
Color (J H C A)
$450.00, $315.00 purchase
Tells the story of an old man whose sightless eye becomes the focus for his servant's obsession. An AFI Film.
Literature and Drama; Psychology
Dist - CF

The Tell - tale heart 30 MIN
VHS
American short story collection series
Color (J H)
$49.00 purchase _ #60390 - 126
Portrays a murderer who is so consumed by guilt that he hears the beating of his victim's heart. Written by Edgar Allan Poe.
Literature and Drama
Dist - GA **Prod** - GA

The Tell - Tale Heart 20 MIN
16mm
B&W (J H C)
LC FIA52-4355
Presents Edgar Allen Poe's story of the apprentice who killed his master and then was driven to confession by what he thought was the sound of the dead man's beating heart.
Literature and Drama
Dist - FI **Prod** - MGM 1953

The Tell - Tale Heart - by Edgar Allan Poe 15 MIN
U-matic / VHS / 16mm
Short Story Series
Color (J H C A)
LC 83 - 706129
Presents a tale of terror about an imagined or actual murder and the very real guilt and its consequences experienced by the murderer. Based on the short story The Tell - Tale Heart by Edgar Allan Poe.
Literature and Drama
Dist - IU **Prod** - IITC 1982

The Tell - Tale Heart by Edgar Allan Poe 15 MIN
16mm / U-matic / VHS
Short story series
Color (J)
LC 83-700046
Presents a tale of terror about an imagined or actual murder and the very real guilt and its consequences experienced by the murderer. Based on the short story The Tell - Tale Heart by Edgar Allan Poe.
Literature and Drama
Dist - IU **Prod** - IITC 1982
GPN CTI

TELL - Techniques in Early Language Learning 17 MIN
U-matic / VHS / 16mm
Color (T)
LC 70-713055
Describes a pre - school language curriculum based on environmental assistance that attempted to stimulate two - year - old children's language functioning.
Education; English Language; Psychology
Dist - AIMS **Prod** - SPRKET 1971

Tell Them about Us 28 MIN
16mm
Color
LC 77-700063
Describes the prevocational program at Aneth Community School in Aneth, Utah, which was begun in 1965 with Title I funds. Shows how the school helps Navajo teenagers obtain training in a variety of vocational skills.
Education; Guidance and Counseling; Psychology; Social Science
Dist - BAILYL **Prod** - USBIA 1976

Tell Them for Us 28 MIN
VHS / 16mm
Color (G)
$195.00 purchase, $50.00 rental
Discusses MADRE, a National Friendship Committee, which brings together diverse peoples in a call for peace. Reveals that its purpose is to stop US intervention through developing a true exchange between the people of the US and the people in Central America and the Caribbean. Follows thirteen American women who traveled to Nicaragua in 1985.
Civics and Political Systems; Geography - World; Religion and Philosophy; Sociology
Dist - WMEN **Prod** - JLBRAD 1985

Tell Them I'm a Mermaid 23 MIN
U-matic / VHS
Color
Presents seven women with disabilities in a musical theatre piece. Reveals their memories and aspirations, their joys and sorrows, expressed candidly and without bitterness.
Psychology
Dist - EMBASY **Prod** - TAPEME

Tell Us How You Feel 4 MIN
16mm / U-matic / VHS
Most Important Person - Health and Your Body Series
Color (K P I)
Stresses the importance of communicating feelings. Explains the need to tell a shoe salesman if a shoe doesn't fit.
Guidance and Counseling; Health and Safety; Science - Natural
Dist - EBEC **Prod** - EBEC 1972

Teller's ticket 25 MIN
VHS / U-matic
Color (C A)
$225.00, $195.00 purchase _ #V539
Dramatizes a short story by Robert Flanagan. Tells of Byron Teller, whose sex drive is greater than that of his wife Nina. Shows that they devise a system of IOUs so that if Byron wants sex and Nina doesn't, she presents a ticket which Byron redeems when she's 'in the mood.' When Byron runs out of money during a poker game, he bets and loses one of Nina's IOUs. Portrays Byron's frantic attempts to redeem the ticket before Nina discovers what he's done.
Literature and Drama
Dist - BARR **Prod** - CEPRO 1991

Telling secrets - 56 8 MIN
VHS / U-matic
Life's little lessons - self - esteem 4 - 6 series
Color (I)
$129.00, $99.00 purchase _ #V685
Tells about Douglas who confided his deepest, darkest secret to his friend Harry who said his lips were sealed. Reveals that soon after, Douglas' secret was all over town because Harry wasn't loyal. Part of a 65 - part series on self - esteem.
Guidance and Counseling; Psychology
Dist - BARR **Prod** - CEPRO 1992

Telling Stories to Children 27 MIN
U-matic
Color
Presents the essentials of story telling techniques through observation of two experienced story tellers and the development of skill in a young librarian. Indicates the integration of art and music with folk and fairy tales.
Education; Literature and Drama
Dist - UMITV **Prod** - UMITV 1959

Telling stories without words 55 MIN
VHS
Color (K P I J H T)
$19.95 purchase _ #S00882
Features mime T Daniel, a former student of Marcel Marceau, in a demonstration of basic miming moves.
Fine Arts
Dist - UILL

Telling teens about AIDS 52 MIN
VHS / 16mm
Color (PRO G J H C)
$149.00, $249.00, purchase _ #AD - 1688
Seeks to break down the 'it can't happen to me' attitude that teenagers erect when warned of any danger by adults. Features teens and those who contracted AIDS in their teens speaking directly to teenagers. Helps parents and teachers confront the issue with respect to their own children.
Health and Safety; Psychology; Sociology
Dist - FOTH **Prod** - FOTH 1990

Telling teens about sex 28 MIN
VHS / 16mm
Color (G)
$149.00, $249.00, purchase _ #AD - 1243
Investigates what teenagers know about sex. Features a panel of sex educators in discussion with an audience of teenagers about what teens know and what they want to know.
Health and Safety
Dist - FOTH **Prod** - FOTH 1990

Telling the story 19 MIN
VHS
Color (G A R)
$19.95 purchase, $10.00 rental _ #4 - 85073
Uses five key phases of storytelling to show how the Bible can be presented successfully to young children.
Literature and Drama; Religion and Philosophy
Dist - APH **Prod** - APH

Telling their Own Story 27 MIN
VHS / 16mm
Color (G)
$190.00 purchase, $50.00 rental
Presents two examples of how developing areas are coping with the news and information demands of their national audiences. Shows Asiavision coordinating the exchange of national TV programs between national broadcasters throughout Asia. In Papua New Guinea, the needs are different for its widely scattered population.
Fine Arts; Geography - World; Industrial and Technical Education; Literature and Drama; Sociology
Dist - FIRS **Prod** - FIRS 1988

Telling Time 11 MIN
U-matic / VHS / 16mm
Basic Math Series
Color (P)
LC 80-700726
Presents a musician who uses magic tricks to explain how to read time in hours, half hours and quarter hours.
Mathematics
Dist - PHENIX **Prod** - SYKES 1980

Telling time - 25 30 MIN
VHS
English 101 - Ingles 101 series
Color (H)
$125.00 purchase
Focuses on a specific topic in order to emphasize a particular grammatical point or set of idioms. English is used from the beginning as the primary language of instruction but Spanish translations are included to ensure understanding. Part 25 considers units of time, parts of the day, telling time by the clock, questions and answers. Part of a series of 30-minute programs in basic English for native speakers of Spanish.
English Language; Foreign Language
Dist - AITECH **Prod** - UPRICO 1988

Telling Time with Count Clock 15 MIN
U-matic / VHS / 16mm
Color (P)
LC 83-700077
Introduces Count Clock who teaches two children how to tell time.
Mathematics
Dist - HIGGIN **Prod** - HIGGIN 1983

The Tellington touch video for cats 60 MIN
VHS
Color (G)
$39.95 purchase _ #V - TTCAT
Illustrates a new way to communicate with pets and get results. Purports to improve the health and behavior of cats.
Health and Safety; Social Science
Dist - PACSPI

The Tellington touch video for dogs 60 MIN
VHS
Color (G)
$39.95 purchase _ #V - TTDOG
Illustrates a new way to communicate with pets and get results. Purports to help dogs suffering from stress, fear of loud noises, arthritis, hip displasia, itching, hyperactivity or other ailments.
Health and Safety; Social Science
Dist - PACSPI

The Tellington touch videos for dogs and cats 120 MIN
VHS
Color (G)
$69.95 purchase _ #V - TTSET
Presents two videos which illustrate a new way to communicate with pets and get results. Purports to improve the health and behavior of dogs and cats.
Health and Safety; Social Science
Dist - PACSPI

Tembo - the Baby Elephant 10 MIN
16mm / U-matic
Captioned; Color (K P I)
Tells the story of a baby African elephant, his dependence on his mother and the herd, and shows some of the other animals who share his natural home.
Science - Natural
Dist - BARR **Prod** - BARR

Temiscaming Quebec 64 MIN
16mm
Color
_ #106C 0175 197N
Geography - World
Dist - CFLMDC **Prod** - NFBC 1975

Temores 8 MIN
16mm
Project Bilingual Series
Color (P)

LC 75-703540
Uses live - action and animation to show how making an acquaintance with a frightening thing or person can help to overcome fear of it.
Guidance and Counseling
Dist - SUTHLA **Prod** - SANISD 1975

Tempera as Watercolor 15 MIN
VHS / U-matic
Young at Art Series
Color (P I)
Discusses the use of tempera as watercolor.
Fine Arts
Dist - AITECH **Prod** - WSKJTV 1980

Temperament and Personality in Selling
VHS / U-matic
Strategies for Successful Selling Series Module 5
Color
Teaches sales people to recognize basic characteristics of temperament and personalities and how to deal with them in selling.
Business and Economics; Psychology
Dist - AMA **Prod** - AMA

The Temperate Deciduous Forest 17 MIN
16mm / U-matic / VHS
Biology (Spanish Series Unit 2 - Ecosystems; Unit 2 - Ecosystems
Color (H) (SPANISH)
Reveals the complex network of plant and animal relationships in the temperate deciduous forest community. Shows typical forest inhabitants in each season of the year.
Foreign Language; Science - Natural
Dist - EBEC **Prod** - EBEC

Temperate deciduous forest 13 MIN
U-matic / 16mm / VHS
Biomes series
Color (J H)
$350.00, $250.00 purchase _ #HP - 5937C
Reveals that deciduous forests are governed by the cycle of seasons and undergo dramatic changes within the year. Shows that the plant and animal population has adapted a variety of coping mechanisms. Documents an entire year to show how the deciduous nature of different species of trees affects the herb layer beneath them and the animals which depend on each for food and shelter. Part of a series on biomes produced by Partridge Films, Ltd.
Science - Natural
Dist - CORF

The Temperate Rain Forest 16 MIN
U-matic / VHS / 16mm
Color (I J H A)
Examines the characteristics and ecology of the coastal rain forest of the Pacific Northwest. The high canopy of tall trees and the fragrant decay of the damp woodland floor display a lush mix of majestic conifers and deciduous growth. Tangled undergrowth teems with frogs and salamanders. Reminds us of the exquisite beauty of the temperate rain forest and of an obligation to preserve its place in nature.
Agriculture; Geography - United States; Science - Natural; Science - Physical
Dist - BULFRG **Prod** - NFBC 1985

Temperature 60 MIN
VHS / 16mm
Industrial Measurement Series
Color (PRO)
$695.00 purchase, $125.00 rental
Includes Introduction to Temperature Measurement, Common Mechanical Devices, Thermocouple, Resistance Temperature Detectors, Thermisters, Radiation Pyrometers and Thermocouple Temperature. Part of a five - part series on industrial measurement.
Industrial and Technical Education; Mathematics
Dist - ISA **Prod** - ISA

Temperature 25 MIN
U-matic / VHS
Metric Education Video Tapes for Pre and Inservice Teachers (K - 8 'Series
Color
Explains the origin and usage of a Celsius thermometer. Presents common Celsius temperatures to use as reference points.
Mathematics
Dist - PUAVC **Prod** - PUAVC

Temperature 30 MIN
U-matic
Today's Special Series
Color (K P)
Develops language arts skills in children. Programs are thematically designed around subjects of interest to youngsters. Action takes place in a department store where people, mannequins, puppets, comic characters and special guests present a light hearted approach to language arts.
Fine Arts; Literature and Drama; Psychology
Dist - TVOTAR **Prod** - TVOTAR 1985

Temperature 15 MIN
U-matic
Math Makers One Series
Color (I)
Presents the math concepts of degrees Celsius, significant temperatures, comparative temperatures and rate.
Education; Mathematics
Dist - TVOTAR **Prod** - TVOTAR 1979

Temperature and Concentration in Chemical Reactions 14 MIN
VHS
Chemistry - from Theory to Application Series
Color (H)
$190.00 purchase
Indicates that magnesium strips and hydrochloric acid react at different temperatures. Demonstrates a model showing particle velocity distribution - Maxwell.
Science; Science - Physical
Dist - LUF **Prod** - LUF 1989

Temperature and gas laws - engine of nature - Parts 45 and 46 60 MIN
VHS / U-matic
Mechanical universe...and beyond - Part II series
Color (G)
$45.00, $29.95 purchase
Reveals that discoveries about the behavior of gases makes the scientific connection between temperature and heat in Part 45. Presents the first part of two parts on the Carnot engine, beginning with simple steam engines in Part 46. Parts of a 52 - part series on the mechanics of the universe.
Science; Science - Physical
Dist - ANNCPB **Prod** - SCCON 1985

Temperature and Kinetic Theory 15 MIN
U-matic / VHS
Experiment - Physics Level 1 Series
Color (C)
$249.00, $149.00 purchase _ #AD - 1964
Introduces concepts such as absolute temperature, ideal gas laws and the molecular theory of gases. Includes gas laws, phase changes and triple point. Part of a series of videos demonstrating physics experiments which are impractical to perform in a classroom laboratory.
Education; Psychology; Science - Physical
Dist - FOTH **Prod** - FOTH

Temperature and Temperature Measurement - 1 60 MIN
VHS
Fundamentals of Instrumentation and Control Series
Color (PRO)
$600.00 - $1500.00 purchase _ #ICTT1
Covers the basic operating principles and use of fluid, filled - system and bimetallic thermometers. Shows how to to convert a temperature reading from any of the four temperature measuring scales to any of the other scales through simple mathematical computations. Part of a nineteen - part series on the fundamentals of instrumentation and control, which is part of a 49 - unit set on instrumentation and control. Includes five workbooks and an instructor guide to support four hours of instruction.
Mathematics; Psychology
Dist - NUSTC **Prod** - NUSTC

Temperature and Temperature Measurement - 2 60 MIN
VHS
Fundamentals of Instrumentation and Control Series
Color (PRO)
$600.00 - $1500.00 purchase _ #ICTT2
Explains how thermocouples, RTDs, thermistors and infrared temperature sensors operate. Shows how certain electrical properties and temperatures are related and applied in electrical temperature - measuring instruments. Part of a nineteen - part series on the fundamentals of instrumentation and control, which is part of a 49 - unit set on instrumentation and control. Includes five workbooks and an instructor guide to support four hours of instruction.
Industrial and Technical Education; Mathematics; Psychology
Dist - NUSTC **Prod** - NUSTC

Temperature and temperature measurement series
Filled systems and bimetallic thermometers
Introduction to Temperature Measurement
RTDs and Thermistors
Thermocouples
Dist - NUSTC

Temperature and the Gas Laws 16 MIN
VHS / U-matic
Mechanical Universe - High School Adaptation Series
Color (H)
Science - Physical
Dist - SCCON **Prod** - SCCON 1986

Temperature and Wind 8 MIN
U-matic / VHS / 16mm
Weather - Air in Action Series
Color (I J)
Defines weather as the condition of the atmosphere which surrounds the Earth. Shows how weather reports are made by observing and measuring air temperature, movement, moisture and pressure.
Science - Physical
Dist - AIMS **Prod** - CAHILL 1965

Temperature Compensation and Maintenance
Software / BETA
Liquid Level Measurement Series
Color (PRO)
$600.00 - $1500.00 purchase _ #IDTEC
Focuses on a typical closed - tank, wet - leg systems and how changes in temperature affect the operation of the system. Part of a six - part series on liquid level measurement. Interactive training system includes course administrator guide, videodisc and computer software.
Industrial and Technical Education; Mathematics; Psychology
Dist - NUSTC **Prod** - NUSTC

Temperature Control 18 MIN
VHS / 16mm
Catering with Care Series
Color (H)
$205.00 purchase
Outlines the risks associated with subjecting foods to improper temperatures during preparation and storage. Uses time lapse photography and computer - generated animation to illustrate the effects of temperature on food. Includes support materials.
Health and Safety; Home Economics; Industrial and Technical Education
Dist - FLMWST

Temperature Control Devices 14 MIN
16mm
Color (H C)
Discusses thermometers and their function in relation to a modern air conditioning complex, transducers and transmitters, thermometer location, central control panels, meters and recorders.
Industrial and Technical Education
Dist - SF **Prod** - SF 1970

Temperature Control of Complex Batch Processes
VHS / 16mm
Batch Control Series
Color (PRO)
$300.00 purchase, $90.00 rental
Describes Control of an Exothermic Process, Using a Heat Exchanger on the Heating - Cooling Source, Using an External Heat Exchanger for Reflex Control and Temperature Ramping. Part of a four - part series on batch control.
Home Economics; Industrial and Technical Education
Dist - ISA **Prod** - ISA

Temperature Control System 29 MIN
U-matic
Radiographic Processing Series Pt 9
Color (C)
LC 77-706078
Discusses temperature control components, including intrinsic and extrinsic factors. Describes their functions and problems and emphasizes the heat exchanger, the thermostatic missing valve, water supply problems and calibration of thermometers.
Health and Safety; Industrial and Technical Education; Science
Dist - USNAC **Prod** - USVA 1975

Temperature controls - Pts 1 and 2
VHS
Refrigeration training seminars by Bob Graham series
Color (G IND)
$75.00 purchase
Presents the operation and function of temperature controls on two videocassettes. Discusses limited vapor controls, cross - ambient controls and liquid - filled controls. Covers proper selection and installation of constant differential and constant cut - in controls. Part of a series of refrigeration training seminars by Bob Graham.
Industrial and Technical Education; Psychology; Science - Physical
Dist - AACREF **Prod** - AACREF 1990

Temperature, energy and thermal equilibrium 3 MIN
16mm
Kinetic theory by computer animation series
Color (H C A)
LC 73-703242
Introduces temperature as a measure of kinetic energy. Uses spikes corresponding to speeds of particles and a meter displaying average kinetic energy to indicate gas 'temperature.'
Science; Science - Physical
Dist - KALMIA **Prod** - KALMIA 1973

Temperature, pressure and fluids - Pt 1 gases 30 MIN
U-matic / VHS
Mathematics and physics series
Color (IND)
Covers laws of physics relating to gases. Sketches Boyle's Law's, Charles' Law's, and Gay Lusac's help in developing absolute temperature scales. Shows laboratory experiments to explain temperature and pressure effects on gases.
Science - Physical
Dist - AVIMA **Prod** - AVIMA 1980

Temperature, pressure and fluids - Pt 2 liquids 16 MIN
U-matic / VHS
Mathematics and physics series
Color (IND)
Introduces fluid dynamics. Uses animation to show relationship between forces, area and pressure of confined liquids.
Science - Physical
Dist - AVIMA **Prod** - AVIMA 1980

Temperature, pressure and wind 16 MIN
VHS
Meteorology series
Color (J H)
$34.95 purchase _ #193 W 0058
Shows the principles of a barometer and applies those principles to the understanding of winds caused by the differential heat gain and loss over the Earth. Part of a six - part single concept series which uses NASA footage to complement experimental devices and laboratory set - ups to demonstrate basic meteorological principles.
Science - Physical
Dist - WARDS **Prod** - WARDS

Temperature, pressure, and wind - Part I 8 MIN
VHS / 16mm
Color (C)
$80.00, $34.95 purchase, _ #194 E 0086, #193 E 2086
Demonstrates the principle of a barometer and the action of high and low pressure systems.
Science - Physical
Dist - WARDS **Prod** - AMS

Temperature, pressure, and wind - Part II 8 MIN
VHS / 16mm
Color (C)
$80.00, $34.95 purchase, _ #194 E 0087, #193 E 2087
Uses global pressure and wind maps to demonstrate simple air circulation resulting from three unequally heated areas.
Science - Physical
Dist - WARDS **Prod** - AMS

Temperature, Pulse and Respiration 14 MIN
VHS / U-matic
Color (J)
An instructional film on cardinal symptoms and TPR equipment, oral and rectal thermometers, reading care of thermometers, taking temperatures and taking a pulse and respirations.
Health and Safety
Dist - SF **Prod** - SF 1969

Temperature, pulse and respiration - theory 27 MIN
16mm
Directions for education in nursing via technology series; Lesson 8
B&W (PRO)
LC 74-701781
Uses animation to show the physiology of temperature, pulse and respiration and their interrelation.
Health and Safety; Science - Natural
Dist - WSUM **Prod** - DENT 1974

Temperature, Pulse, Respiration 15 MIN
16mm
B&W (J H)
Demonstrates how to take the pulse, temperature and respiration. Explains how to accomplish it methodically and points out the locations where the pulse beat may be found.
Health and Safety
Dist - MLA **Prod** - MLA 1943

Temperature Regulation 13 MIN
U-matic / VHS / 16mm
Color (H C)
LC 80-700112
Deals with the human body's temperature mechanisms, using thermography to illustrate the normal range of body temperature as well as reactions to temperature changes. Describes the function of dermal papillae capillaries, sweat glands and sensory receptors in the skin and around the hypothalamus.
Health and Safety; Science - Natural
Dist - IFB **Prod** - IFFB 1979

Temperature Regulation 12.5
U-matic / VHS / 16mm
Color (H C)
Explains the normal range of body temperatures as well as reactions to temperature changes. Illustrates the systems involved in cooling and warming the body and the control systems that regulate temperature. Highlights dermal papillae capillary networks and sweat glands.
Science - Natural
Dist - IFB **Prod** - IFFB 1984

Temperature Vs Heat 5 MIN
U-matic
Eureka Series
Color (J)
Explains that heat refers to quantity of hotness and is determined by the mass and speed of molecules.
Science; Science - Physical
Dist - TVOTAR **Prod** - TVOTAR 1980

Temperature Waves W - 1 3 MIN
16mm
Single - Concept Films in Physics Series
Color (J H C)
Thermometers are inserted in holes in a brass rod to show a wave front as one end of the rod is cycled in temperature.
Science - Physical
Dist - OSUMPD **Prod** - OSUMPD 1963

Tempering of steel 48 MIN
U-matic / BETA / VHS
Color
$400.00 purchase
Gives methods of obtaining a combination of strength, hardness, ductility and toughness in steel to ensure product reliability.
Science; Science - Physical
Dist - ASM **Prod** - ASM

Tempers - 57 8 MIN
VHS / U-matic
Life's little lessons - self - esteem 4 - 6 series
Color (I)
$129.00, $99.00 purchase _ #V686
Shows that hanging around people with nasty tempers can be bad for people. Looks at Arnie Wallis who threw his golf clubs whenever the game wasn't going the way he wanted. Part of a 65 - part series on self - esteem.
Guidance and Counseling; Psychology
Dist - BARR **Prod** - CEPRO 1992

The Tempest 25 MIN
U-matic / 16mm / VHS
Shakespeare in rehearsal series
Color (H C)
$495.00, $250.00 purchase _ #HP - 5924C
Dramatizes Shakespeare and his leading actors putting the final touches on 'The Tempest.' Follows the characters Caliban, Prospero and Ariel as they work through their important lines and block out the staging under Shakespeare's direction. Discusses theme and plot interpretation, character motivation and development, pertinent historical references, line delivery and staging. Part of a series on Shakespeare in rehearsal.
Fine Arts; Literature and Drama
Dist - CORF **Prod** - BBCTV 1989

The Tempest 150 MIN
VHS / 16mm
BBC's Shakespeare Series
(H A)
$249.95
Depicts Shakespeare's play The Tempest, a dramatic romance.
Literature and Drama
Dist - AMBROS **Prod** - AMBROS 1980

Tempest
VHS
Color (G)
$79.90 purchase _ #0326
Stars John Cassavetes, Gena Rowlands, Susan Sarandeon, Molly Ringwald and Raul Julia in 'Tempest,' directed by Paul Mazursky. Tells of Phillip who flees with his daughter from his stormy marriage to a nearly deserted island near Greece. Presents a modern version of the Shakespeare play.
Fine Arts; History - United States; Literature and Drama; Sociology
Dist - SEVVID

The Tempest 126 MIN
16mm / U-matic / VHS
Color (H C A)
Dramatizes Shakespeare's The Tempest. Serves as an introduction to Elizabethan theater, as a companion to reading the play, or, by itself, as a teaching tool.
Literature and Drama
Dist - EBEC **Prod** - BARDPR 1983

The Tempest 150 MIN
VHS
BBC Shakespeare series
Color (G C H)
$109.00 purchase _ #DL467
Fine Arts
Dist - INSIM **Prod** - BBC

Tempest 27 MIN
16mm
History of the motion picture series
B&W (H C)
Presents the 1928 production of 'Tempest,' a colorful romance with Russian Revolution background. Stars John Barrymore. Directed by Sam Taylor.
Fine Arts
Dist - KILLIS **Prod** - SF 1960

The Tempest 30 MIN
VHS / U-matic
Shakespeare in Perspective Series
Color (J)
LC 84-707155
Presents an adaptation of the Shakespearean play The Tempest, a romantic drama of the timeless struggle to create an ordered society and the cost that this entails. Includes the plays A Midsummer Night's Dream, King Lear and As You Like It on the same tape.
Literature and Drama
Dist - FI **Prod** - FI 1984

The Tempest 30 MIN
BETA / VHS / 16mm
Shakespeare - from Page to Stage Series
Color (J H A)
Presents key scenes from Shakespeare's plays bridged with on - camera commentary by one of the actors to reinforce the literary amd thematic aspects of the play. Includes written editions of the complete plays and study guides.
Literature and Drama
Dist - BCNFL **Prod** - CBCEN 1987

The Tempest 127 MIN
U-matic / VHS
Color (A)
Presents Shakespeare's classic story of the fantasy world of spirits, sorcery, monsters, maidens and shipwrecked scheming noblemen.
Literature and Drama
Dist - KULTUR **Prod** - KULTUR 1985

The Tempest 14 MIN
U-matic / VHS / 16mm
Shakespeare Series
Color (H C A)
An excerpt from the play of the same title. Shows Miranda and Ferdinand in Act I, Scene 2 as they meet and fall instantly in love and Act III, Scene 1 as Miranda offers to help Ferdinand carry wood.
Fine Arts; Literature and Drama
Dist - IFB **Prod** - IFB 1974

The Tempest 150 MIN
U-matic / VHS
Shakespeare Plays Series
Color
LC 79-707319
Presents Shakespeare's play The Tempest, which revolves around an enchanted island, an exiled duke, young lovers and a framework of conspiracy as they affect dramatic and emotional romances.
Literature and Drama
Dist - TIMLIF **Prod** - BBCTV 1980

The Tempest 127 MIN
VHS
Color (G)
$89.95 purchase _ #S01593
Presents a film version of Shakespeare's 'The Tempest,' a tale of the fantasy world come to life. Stars Efrem Zimbalist Jr, William H Bassett, Ted Sorel and Ron Palillo.
Fine Arts; Literature and Drama
Dist - UILL

Tempest 102 MIN
16mm
B&W
Tells the story of an enlisted sergeant of the dragoons in the Imperial Army of the Czar Nicholas the second and a stunning princess, daughter of a general. Stars John Barrymore and Camilla Horn. Directed by Sam Taylor.
Fine Arts
Dist - KILLIS **Prod** - UNKNWN 1928

The Tempest 76 MIN
U-matic / VHS
Color
Offers a production of Shakespeare's play The Tempest starring Maurice Evans, Richard Burton, Tom Poston and Lee Remick.
Fine Arts; Literature and Drama
Dist - FOTH **Prod** - FOTH 1984

Template Functions of DNA 23 MIN
U-matic / 35mm strip
Color (H C)
$43.95 purchase _ #51 2514
Explains the molecular basis for the storage of genetic information. Describes the process of DNA replication and RNA synthesis. Includes a teacher's guide.
Science - Natural
Dist - CBSC **Prod** - BMEDIA

The Temple 59 MIN
VHS
Glasnost film festival series
Color (H C G T A) (RUSSIAN (ENGLISH SUBTITLES))
$59.95 purchase, $35.00 rental
Presents a Soviet film shown at the Glasnost Film Festival. Examines the role of religion in Soviet society, with emphasis on the Orthodox Church. Reveals that Christianity has been in Russia for more than 1,000 years. Takes viewers to a monastery and a restoration effort for a church that burned down. Interviews a young monk and Nikolai, an 80 - year - old Orthodox priest.
Business and Economics; Civics and Political Systems; History - World; Sociology
Dist - EFVP

The Temple 30 MIN
16mm
Color (R)
Captures the essence of modern Israel. Focuses on efforts made by Israelis to learn the ancient rites of temple worship by digging among the rocks of their native land.
Guidance and Counseling; History - World; Religion and Philosophy
Dist - GF **Prod** - GF

Temple
VHS
Campus clips series
Color (H C A)
$29.95 purchase _ #CC0093V
Takes a video visit to the campus of Temple University in Pennsylvania. Shows many of the distinctive features of the campus, and interviews students about their experiences. Provides information on the composition of the student body, professors, academics, social life, housing, and other subjects.
Education
Dist - CAMV

Temple of Apollo at Bassae 16 MIN
U-matic / VHS / 16mm
Color
Explores the temple near Bassae, a small Greek village southwest of Athens. Explains that the structure with its Doric columns was created by the designer of the Parthenon, Ictinus.
Fine Arts; History - World
Dist - IFB **Prod** - MCBRID 1974

Temple of the godmakers 26 MIN
VHS
Color (J H C G A R)
$49.95 purchase, $10.00 rental _ #35 - 81 - 2504
Reveals the content of many of the secret ceremonies held in Mormon temples. Suggests that these ceremonies are based on Masonic rituals.
Religion and Philosophy
Dist - APH

The Temple of Twenty Pagodas 21 MIN
16mm
Color (J)
LC 73-702487
Views the daily life of a Buddhist Monastery and the village which it serves in northern Thailand.
Geography - World; Religion and Philosophy; Sociology
Dist - SF **Prod** - FLMAUS 1973

Temple Priests and Civil Servants 25 MIN
16mm / U-matic / VHS
Ancient Lives Series
Color
Examines such subjects as the relationship between pharaoh, gods, priests and common people in ancient Egypt.
Geography - World; History - World; Sociology
Dist - FOTH **Prod** - FOTH

The Temples of Malta 11 MIN
VHS
Color; PAL (J H)
PdS29
Reveals that, during the period 3000 - 2000 BC, the peoples of the small islands of Malta and Gozo in the central Mediterranean built some remarkable megalithic temples of unique design. Discloses that the temples, together with rock - cut tombs, indicate a high level of culture unparalleled in western Europe at that time. Shows the evolution of the trefoil temple plan and discusses the influence of contemporary civilizations upon art, sculpture and pottery in these islands.
History - World
Dist - BHA

Temples of Time 42 MIN
16mm
Color (G)
_ #106C 0171 002
Shows a mountain is a living thing with an ecological balance. Depicts mountain solitudes and wildlife, natural splendor in all its changing moods in the Canadian Rockies and in Garibaldi Park.
Geography - World; Science - Natural
Dist - CFLMDC **Prod** - NFBC 1971

Temples of tomorrow 12 MIN
16mm
B&W (H C A)
Surveys the hydro - electric projects in India, which the late Jawaharlal Nehru described as 'Temples of Tomorrow.' Discusses projects which are transforming the lives of the people.
Industrial and Technical Education
Dist - NEDINF **Prod** - INDIA

Tempo 29 MIN
U-matic
Beginning piano - an adult approach series; Lesson 14
Color (H A)
Reviews A - major scale. Introduces the principal tempo indications found in music notation.
Fine Arts
Dist - CDTEL **Prod** - COAST

Tempo and Dynamics 15 MIN
U-matic / VHS
Music and Me Series
Color (P I)
Discusses tempo and dynamics in music.
Fine Arts
Dist - AITECH **Prod** - WDCNTV 1979

Tempo - Australia in the seventies 24 MIN
16mm
Color (H C A)
LC 72-702254
Emphasizes the growth and development in Australia in the 1970s.
Geography - World
Dist - SF **Prod** - ANAIB 1972

The Temporal and Infratemporal Regions 15 MIN
U-matic / VHS
Skull Anatomy Series
Color (C A)
Describes the boundaries, demonstrates the bones and identifies the bony regions of the temporal and infratemporal areas of the skull.
Health and Safety; Science - Natural
Dist - TEF **Prod** - UTXHSA

The Temporal Bone from Above - the Mid - Cranial Fossa Approach 29 MIN
16mm
Color (PRO)
Demonstrates in detail the surgical anatomy of the temporal bone from above. Serves as a teaching aid for those interested in learning to approach the contents of the temporal bone and posterior fossa through the mid - cranial fossa. Demonstrates the anatomy of this area as a surgeon would encounter it and then correlates the anatomical points demonstrated with practical surgical uses of the approach.
Health and Safety; Science - Natural
Dist - EAR **Prod** - EAR

Temporal Mandibular Joint Eminectomy 19 MIN
16mm
Color
LC 77-705684
Shows pre - operative live action films and radiographs of the patient's distress, following through with surgery and a description of the patient's post - operative relief.
Health and Safety; Science - Natural
Dist - OSUMPD **Prod** - OSUMPD 1969

Temporal Parameters of Auditory Stimulus Response Control 10 MIN
16mm
Color (C A)
LC 78-701611
Demonstrates a test which presents signals in random or alternating order with nonaudible control periods. Illustrates accident safeguards and their effect on test results and subject behavior.
Psychology
Dist - UKANS **Prod** - UKANS 1974

Temporalis Muscle Transfer for Lagophthalmos 18 MIN
VHS / U-matic
Color (PRO)
Presents temporalis muscle transfer for lagophthalmos.
Health and Safety
Dist - WFP **Prod** - WFP

Temporary Admission 27 MIN
16mm / U-matic / VHS
Five Billion People Series
Color
Looks at the contemporary situation of immigrant laborers. Traces the history of the great waves of immigration and explores the social, economic and legal aspects of immigration.
Sociology
Dist - CNEMAG **Prod** - LEFSP

Temporary arrangements 8 MIN
16mm
B&W (G)
$10.00 rental
Contains an absurdist collage - film made from mostly found footage. States it is useful for starting arguments. A Dirk Kortz production.
Fine Arts
Dist - CANCIN

Temporary dwellings 28 MIN
VHS
Color (H C G)
$295.00 purchase, $55.00 rental
Looks at a group of Seattle's homeless community which took matters into their own hands and erected a series of large, tattered, gray tents. Reveals that Tent City was run by the homeless with firm ground rules - no drugs or alcohol, no weapons, no violence. All decisions were put to a vote in this experiment in self government. Tent City lasted until the mayor of Seattle provided a shelter which was to be run and managed by the residents themselves. Produced, written and directed by Michael Regis Hilow.
Geography - United States; Social Science; Sociology
Dist - FLMLIB

Temporary Grounding for De - Energized Maintenance
U-matic / VHS
Live Line Maintenance Series
Color (IND)
Demonstrates procedures for grounding an overhead distribution line on a tangent structure, a vertical running corner and a vertical deadend.
Industrial and Technical Education
Dist - LEIKID **Prod** - LEIKID

Temporary Plastic Bridges 19 MIN
16mm
Color
LC 74-705758
Gives a clinical demonstration of the construction of a temporary plastic bridge of four teeth.
Health and Safety; Science
Dist - USNAC **Prod** - USA 1964

Temporary Restoration of a Class II Mesio - Occlusal Cavity Preparation with Zinc 10 MIN
16mm
Restoration of Cavity Preparation with Amalgam and Tooth - Colored 'Materials Series Module 11a
Color (PRO)
LC 75-702876
Demonstrates placing a mechanical retainer and matrix band, placing and contouring the zinc - oxide and eugenol materials and adjusting occlusion in a manikin. Shows four - handed procedures.
Health and Safety; Science
Dist - USNAC **Prod** - USBHRD 1974

Temporary Support Structures 21 MIN
16mm / U-matic / VHS
Color
Shows the errors and omissions which cause a temporary support structure to collapse. Stresses the need for sound design of framework, good choice of equipment and materials, and ample financial support. Covers operations from a simple propping system support to large and complex support structures for major engineering projects.
Health and Safety; Industrial and Technical Education
Dist - IFB **Prod** - NFBTE

The Temporomandibular Joint 8 MIN
U-matic
Anatomy of the Head and Neck Series
Color (PRO)
LC 78-706254
Demonstrates the anatomy and function of the temporomandibular joint.
Health and Safety; Science - Natural
Dist - USNAC **Prod** - USVA 1978

Temporomandibular Joint Arthroplasty - Intracapsular 13 MIN
16mm
Color (PRO)
LC 77-700855
Describes and demonstrates the surgical procedures of a temporomandibular joint arthroplasty and evaluates postoperative results.
Health and Safety; Science
Dist - USNAC **Prod** - VADTC 1977

Temps de metre 17 MIN
16mm
Color (G)
$30.00 rental
Questions the measure of the Maitre - the meter. By Yann Beauvais.
Fine Arts
Dist - CANCIN

Temptation 27 MIN
VHS
Sunshine factory series
Color (P I R)
$14.99 purchase _ #35 - 83597 - 533
Features P J the repairman and kids in his neighborhood as they travel to the Sunshine Factory, a land populated by puppets, a computer and caring adults. Teaches a Biblically - based lesson on temptation.
Religion and Philosophy
Dist - APH **Prod** - WORD

The Temptation of Power 43 MIN
U-matic / VHS / 16mm
Color (H C A)
LC 79-701637
Probes the reasons for widespread discontent among Iran's population during the rule of the Shah. Focuses on elements such as poverty, the roles of the military and police, the demolition of ancient buildings and villages, the erosion of the traditional way of life, land reform, and rapid westernization.
Civics and Political Systems; History - World
Dist - ICARUS **Prod** - ICARUS 1979

The Temptation of Red Yisroel 30 MIN
16mm
Eternal Light Series
B&W (H C A)
LC 73-700975
Presents a fantasy drawn from Hasidic legend, in which the story moves from the Polish town of Bialystok to the Heavenly Court. Portrays such characters as a bevy of cantankerous angels, a magnanimous pickpocket and an unworldly rabbi and his wife. (Kinescope).
Literature and Drama; Religion and Philosophy
Dist - NAAJS **Prod** - JTS 1968

Tempting providence 50 MIN
VHS
Fire in the blood series
Color (A)
PdS99 purchase
Looks at the Spain that has evolved since Franco's death, especially in light of the 1992 Olympic Games in Barcelona, EXPO in Seville, and the quintentenary of Columbus' landing in the Americas. Examines the unacceptable face of freedom.
Civics and Political Systems; Geography - World; History - World
Dist - BBCENE

The Ten Billion Dollar Rip - Off 22 MIN
U-matic / VHS / 16mm
Color (J)
Dramatizes the story of a young girl who steals from her employer and the tragic consequences of her actions. Shows five key rules developed by security experts to help employees curb theft and avoid trouble themselves.
Sociology
Dist - CORF **Prod** - GIFL 1983

The Ten billion dollar ripoff 22 MIN
35mm strip / 16mm / U-matic / BETA
Color (A)
$450.00, $150.00, $150.00purchase _ #FC42
Presents an approach to fighting employee theft. Wins employees over to honesty. Presents five key rules employees can use to stay out of trouble.
Guidance and Counseling; Sociology
Dist - CONPRO **Prod** - CONPRO

Ten Cents a Dance - Parallax 30 MIN
16mm / VHS
Color (G)
$500.00 purchase, $75.00 rental
Uses the split screen device from classic cinema to consider contemporary sexuality and communication in three segments. Features two women in the first segment who timidly discuss their mutual attraction. The second segment depicts anonymous bathroom sex between two men and the third is a particularly cynical episode of heterosexual phone sex. Produced by Midi Onodera.
Fine Arts; Health and Safety; Psychology; Sociology
Dist - WMEN **Prod** - MION 1986

The Ten commandments 220 MIN
VHS
Color (G R)
$29.95 purchase _ #S02092
Presents the Biblical epic of Moses' life, beginning with his birth and abandonment through the Jewish Exodus out of Egypt. Stars Charlton Heston, Yul Brynner, Edward G Robinson, and many others. Produced by Cecil B DeMille.
Fine Arts; Religion and Philosophy
Dist - UILL **Prod** - PAR 1956

The Ten commandments of communicating with people with disabilities 26 MIN
VHS
Color (G S T)
$195.00 purchase _ #PDA100V-G
Presents a program that uses humor to teach students and others how to communicate with individuals who have disabilities. Offers insights of Tim Harrington, a man with cerebral palsy, and features people with all types of disabilities in vignettes. Suggests speaking directly to people with disabilities, offering to shake hands when introduced, relaxing, listening closely, and treating adults as adults.
Health and Safety; Psychology
Dist - CAMV

The Ten Commandments of Cross - Examination 60 MIN
U-matic / VHS
Color (PRO)
Describes qualities of an effective cross - examiner and a method for recognizing a persuasive argument. Outlines Irving Younger's ten commandments of cross - examination.
Civics and Political Systems
Dist - ABACPE **Prod** - ABACPE

The Ten commandments of cross examination 60 MIN
VHS
Basic concepts in the law of evidence series
B&W (C PRO)
$100.00 purchase, $50.00 rental _ #EYX14
Features the late law professor Irving Younger in a presentation of basic concepts of the law of evidence. Outlines ten 'commandments' of cross examination.
Civics and Political Systems
Dist - NITA **Prod** - NITA 1975

Ten Commandments of Gun Safety 12 MIN
16mm
Color (I)
LC 74-704575
Fundamentals of gun handling and behavior when hunting.
Health and Safety; Physical Education and Recreation
Dist - SF **Prod** - MORLAT 1967

The Ten commandments of networking 25 MIN
VHS
Color (PRO A)
$39.95 purchase
Uses seminar discussion, action vignettes and humor to illustrate each of the ten commandemnts of networking. Takes a look at the right and sometimes wrong way to network. Consultant and author Sandy Vilas discusses the Two Rs of networking; the Lone Ranger Complex; the '3 - foot rule' and the art of powerful introductions.
Business and Economics; Social Science
Dist - TOMKAT **Prod** - TOMKAT 1994
CAMV

Ten common mistakes and how to correct them
VHS
You can teach hitting series
Color (J H C G)
$24.95 purchase _ #BIT010V - P
Addresses ten common mistakes in batting through the collaborative teaching of a player, coach and teacher. Part of a three - part series on baseball and batting.
Physical Education and Recreation
Dist - CAMV

Ten Common Mistakes made by New Parents
VHS
$79.00 purchase _ #FY350V
Provides instruction in solving the problems encountered by new parents. Discusses feeding, toilet training, sleeping habits, rewards and discipline. Tells why certain procedures are preferable.
Health and Safety; Psychology; Science - Natural; Sociology
Dist - CAREER **Prod** - CAREER

Ten Days in Calcutta
16mm
Color
Portrays Mrinal Sen, one of India's most famous directors.
Fine Arts
Dist - TLECUL **Prod** - TLECUL

Ten Days Per Man 26 MIN
16mm
Color
Discusses today's highway problems.
Social Science
Dist - GM **Prod** - GM

Ten Days, Ten Years - the Nicaraguan Elections of 1990 54 MIN
VHS / 16mm
Color (G)
$295.00 purchase, $90.00 rental
Documents the Nicaraguan elections of 1990. Follows the surprise upset victory by Violeta Chamarro with coverage of emotional post - election press conferences by both candidates, Chamarro and Daniel Ortega, and a series of impassioned street corner debates about the significance of the election.
Civics and Political Systems; Geography - World
Dist - CNEMAG **Prod** - FRIMAC 1990

Ten days that shook the world 80 MIN
VHS
Color (J H C)
$39.98 purchase _ #MH1365V-S
Relates the story of the 1917 Russian Revolution. Features participants in the revolution who tell their eyewitness stories of what happened to them in those dramatic ten days. For them, this time held a promise and hope for a new era. For others, the events plunged the world into a state of despair.
Civics and Political Systems; History - World
Dist - CAMV

Ten Days that Shook the World 75 MIN
U-matic / VHS
B&W
Recreates the historic events of the Bolshevik Revolution in many of the actual locations. Based on John Reed's book of the same title.
Fine Arts; History - World
Dist - IHF **Prod** - IHF

Ten days that shook the world 77 MIN
VHS
B&W (G)
$29.95 purchase _ #ST - MP1365
Tells the complete story of the 1917 Russian Revolution, narrated by Orson Welles. Depicts the extravagances of Czar Nicholas, the poverty of the people of Russia, soldiers fighting without hope in World War I in rare archival footage.
Civics and Political Systems; History - World; Sociology
Dist - INSTRU

The Ten deadly sins of communication 15 MIN
VHS
Color (IND)
$495.00 purchase, $150.00 rental _ #VCO13
Identifies ten common communication pitfalls. Includes a leader's guide. Produced by Video Communications.
Business and Economics; Social Science
Dist - EXTR

Ten Dollars or Nothing 12 MIN
VHS / 16mm
Color (G)
$250.00 purchase, $50.00, $40.00 rental
Tells the story through the narrative of a native woman of the unionization of women working in fish canneries in the 1940s. Presented by Sara Diamond.
Business and Economics; Sociology
Dist - WMENIF **Prod** - WMENIF 1989

Ten factors 30 MIN
VHS / U-matic
Effective listening series; Tape 3
Color
Presents ten factors that help make a good listener. Discusses the differences between good and poor listeners.
English Language
Dist - TELSTR **Prod** - TELSTR

Ten Factors of Good Listening 30 MIN
U-matic / VHS
Color
Gives ten differences between good and poor listeners. Includes a drama showing a communication breakdown and the listening failures that caused it.
English Language
Dist - DELTAK **Prod** - TELSTR

The Ten fastest growing careers - jobs for the future
VHS
Color (H)
$209.00 purchase _ #60130 - 025
Interviews working professionals from the fastest growing career areas. Includes the areas of computers, accounting, sales, nursing, paralegal, human resources, teaching and hospitality. Includes teacher's guide, library kit, 25 subscriptions to Time magazine for 12 weeks and 12 weekly guides.
Business and Economics; Guidance and Counseling; Psychology; Sociology
Dist - GA **Prod** - GA 1992

Ten for Gold 28 MIN
VHS / U-matic
Color (A)
Tells the story of Bruce Jenner's triumph in the 1976 Olympic decathlon. Emphasizes how he motivated himself to come back from defeat to reach new heights.
Psychology
Dist - SFTI **Prod** - SFTI

Ten for our time series
Commandments five through ten - Tape 2 30 MIN
Introduction and first four commandments 30 MIN
Dist - APH

Ten from your show of shows 92 MIN
16mm
B&W
Presents an anthology of skits from the early '50s television comedy Your Show Of Shows. Stars Sid Caesar, Imogene Coca and Carl Reiner.
Fine Arts
Dist - TWYMAN **Prod** - WB 1972

Ten Haiku 8 MIN
16mm
Color; B&W (G)
Presents vignettes which reflect the simplicity and beauty of Japanese haiku poetry. Includes study guide.
Fine Arts; Literature and Drama
Dist - CRAR **Prod** - CRAR 1976

Ten has its Place 15 MIN
U-matic
Two Plus You - Math Patrol One Series
Color (K P)
Presents the mathematical concepts of cardinal aspects of numbers from one to 30 and place values of our number system.
Education; Mathematics
Dist - TVOTAR **Prod** - TVOTAR 1976

Ten Little Engines 8 MIN
16mm
Color (H C A)
LC FIA68-246
Pictures automobile drivers violating the rules of the road and causing accidents as a result of driving too fast for conditions, improper passing and drinking.
Health and Safety
Dist - AETNA **Prod** - AETNA 1967

Ten Little Indians 92 MIN
16mm / U-matic / VHS
B&W (H C A)
Stars Hugh O'Brian in Agatha Christie's suspense tale of strangers gathered in an ancient, inaccessible castle where the 'ten little indians' systematically decrease in number.
Fine Arts; Literature and Drama
Dist - FI **Prod** - WB 1965

Ten Long Minutes 13 MIN
16mm
Color; B&W
Illustrates the story of a worker whose wife and children are on vacation and who may have been in an accident. Provides a memorable lesson in off - job safety.
Health and Safety
Dist - NSC **Prod** - NSC

Ten Million Books - an Introduction to Farley Mowat 25 MIN
16mm
Color (G)
_ #106C 0181 014
Shows an abridged version of the film In Search of Farley Mowat. Introduces us to the probably most read Canadian writer.
Biography; Literature and Drama; Science - Natural
Dist - CFLMDC **Prod** - NFBC 1981

Ten Minutes of Protection 8 MIN
16mm
Color (IND)
LC 77-703347
Describes a variety of fire tests conducted on lightweight steel roof supports. Shows how tests evaluated the insulating materials which are applied to steel joints in order to provide them with ten minutes of fire protection.
Health and Safety; Industrial and Technical Education
Dist - USNAC **Prod** - USGSA 1977

The Ten most asked questions about fat 30 MIN
U-matic / VHS
Bodywatch series
Color (H C G)
$80.00 purchase _ #HH - 6013M
Shows the difference between cholesterol and saturated fat and whether eating vegetable oil is healthy. Addresses hundreds of questions about diet. Part of the Bodywatch series.
Health and Safety; Psychology; Social Science
Dist - CORF **Prod** - WGBHTV 1989

Ten, Nine, Eight and on Market Street
VHS
Caldecott Videos Series
Color (P)
$66.00 purchase
Literature and Drama
Dist - PELLER

Ten Occupational Fields - How do I Explore Them
U-matic / VHS
Employability Skills Series
Color
Explores ten occupational fields and describes specific jobs in depth according to a set of specific criteria for analyzing jobs.
Guidance and Counseling
Dist - CAMB **Prod** - ILCS

Ten Per Cent of the Pie 29 MIN
VHS / 16mm
About Women Series
Color (S)
$250.00 purchase _ #678603
Examines issues raised by the women's movement. Focuses on matters crucial to an understanding of the position of women in contemporary society. Four main topics are considered - the personal and domestic sphere, economic and work - related issues, women's health and well - being, and the politics and strategies of working for change. 'Ten Per Cent Of The Pie' documents that some four million Canadian women live below the level of poverty and their numbers are increasing. Globally, almost seventy per cent of the world's work is done by women, yet only ten per cent of the world's wealth is owned by women. Studies the feminization of poverty, the experiences of several poor women and the social causes of their conditions.
Sociology
Dist - ACCESS **Prod** - ACCESS 1986

Ten Seconds that Shook the World 50 MIN
U-matic / VHS / 16mm
B&W (J H C)
LC FIA64-790
Portrays the joint efforts of the United States and Great Britain which produced the atomic bomb that brought the war in the Pacific to an end. Shows how peaceful uses of atomic energy can help to create a new and better world.
Civics and Political Systems; History - World; Science - Physical
Dist - FI **Prod** - PMI 1963

Ten short films by Chuck Hudina 64 MIN
VHS
Color & B&W (G)
$75.00 purchase
Includes Egg; Ikarus; Bicycle; On the Corner; Sound Stills; Baby in a Rage; Plaster; Black Heat; Parents' Visit; and Ruby Red. Produced between 1972 - 1985. See individual titles for description and availability for rental in 16mm format. See also Five Short Films.
Fine Arts
Dist - CANCIN

Ten Shots in a Boarding House 3 MIN
16mm
B&W
LC 77-702667
Deals with the mystery of a boarding house by presenting ten shots of scenes there.
Sociology
Dist - CANFDC **Prod** - CANFDC 1976

Ten speed stays home - a child's eye view of God 45 MIN
VHS
Childcrafting - a predictive guide to creative parenting series
Color (G R)
$24.95 purchase, $10.00 rental _ #35 - 87298 - 460
Discusses the balance parents must maintain between being loving and supportive and instilling discipline and responsibility.
Religion and Philosophy; Sociology
Dist - APH **Prod** - FRACOC

Ten steps of bussing tables 6 MIN
BETA / VHS / U-matic
Color (A)
#FC46
Introduces the busser to his duties in the restaurant. Emphasizes efficiency and speed. Teaches the value of teamwork and cooperation.
Industrial and Technical Education
Dist - CONPRO **Prod** - CONPRO

Ten Steps to Discipline 29 MIN
VHS / U-matic
Survival Skills for the Classroom Teacher Series
Color (T)
Presents ten steps for disciplining in the classroom.
Education
Dist - FI **Prod** - MFFD

Ten steps to effective youth ministry 100 MIN
VHS
Color (G A R)
$59.95 purchase, $10.00 rental _ #35 - 81 - 2104
Presents ten segments on developing a youth ministry within a congregation. Includes segments on organization, leadership, evaluation and different types of youth ministry. Hosted by Roland Martinson. Produced by the Evangelical Lutheran Church in America.
Religion and Philosophy
Dist - APH

Ten Tahun Herdeka 24 MIN
16mm
B&W
Shows the celebrations of ten years of independence in Malaysia.
Civics and Political Systems; Geography - World
Dist - PMFMUN **Prod** - FILEM 1967

Ten Takes Flight 14 MIN
16mm
Color (C A)
Presents the final minutes just prior to and including the first flight of the DC - 10. Features scenes of construction and rollout of the aircraft.
Industrial and Technical Education
Dist - MCDO **Prod** - MCDO 1970

Ten the Magic Number 13 MIN
16mm
Color (I)
LC 75-700222
Presents an animated story about a man who finds out about metric measurement in a time - travel voyage to the future. Shows how the differences between the metric and English systems cause him many problems.
Mathematics
Dist - NFBC **Prod** - CAMETR 1975

Ten times empty - Greece) 21 MIN
U-matic / VHS / 16mm
Village life series
Color (J)
LC 77-703024
Features an eleven - year - old boy from the Greek island of Simi describing how the one - time shipping center is losing its population due to pollution and over - fishing.
Geography - World; Science - Natural
Dist - JOU **Prod** - JPFLM 1977

Ten Ugly Pounds 29 MIN
Videoreel / VT2
Maggie and the Beautiful Machine - Eating Series
Color
Physical Education and Recreation
Dist - PBS **Prod** - WGBHTV

Ten vital rules for giving incredible speeches and why they're irrelevant 32 MIN
VHS / U-matic
Color (G PRO A)
$595.00, $495.00 purchase, $200.00 rental
Features Tom Peters. Takes a humorous look at some 'vital rules' of speech making and why Peters doesn't use them. Shows how to become more at ease with speeches and presentations. Reviews Peters' simple guidelines for presentations.

Business and Economics; English Language; Social Science
Dist - MAGVID VPHI Prod - MAGVID VPHI 1990

Ten ways to a better job - back to the basics 30 MIN
VHS
Color (C A)
$79.95 purchase _ #CCP0183V-G; #CCP0183V-D
Offers basics of job hunting, including gaining as much education and computer knowledge as possible; naming ten people who will be included in your job search network; learning where the jobs are and aren't; knowing what you do well and being able to discuss it; and learning how to move vertically as well as horizontally within a company. Advocates remaining aware of opportunities that may help in future job searches, rather than focusing only on the nick-of-time.
Business and Economics; Guidance and Counseling
Dist - CAMV

Ten ways to be a better parent 25 MIN
VHS
Cambridge parenting series
Color (H C G)
$79.95 purchase _ #CCP0064V
Teaches methods to improve parenting skills. Shows how to develop trust, the importance of spending time together, the benefits of communication and how to provide experiences fostering growth and learning. Illustrates methods for building positive self - esteem and positive attitudes about health and nutrition, encouraging the expression of emotions and feelings, and providing consistent guidelines for behavior and safety. Includes teacher's instruction manual. Part of a two - part series on parenting.
Sociology
Dist - CAMV Prod - CAMV 1991

Ten ways to measure training's effectiveness and return on investment - Scott B Parry 120 MIN
VHS
Color; PAL (C G PRO)
$89.95, $69.95 purchase _ #85AST - V - T26
Examines 10 criteria for evaluating performance attributable to training and ways of measuring each item. Features the President of Training House, Inc, Princeton NJ, Scott B Parry.
Business and Economics; Education; Psychology
Dist - MOBILE Prod - ASTD 1985

Ten Ways to Tell if You're in Love 29 MIN
16mm / U-matic / VHS
Color (H C A)
LC 81-701037
Presents Rev Jack F Paul offering advice and guidance to an audience of college students on the subject of forming lasting relationships. Discusses 10 practical guidelines for helping young people, especially women, decide if they are really in love and emphasizes the importance of moral values for establishing a lasting marriage.
Guidance and Counseling; Psychology
Dist - PHENIX Prod - BANHST 1980

Ten who Dared 92 MIN
16mm
Color
Presents ten rugged adventurers who undertake a perilous journey from which only six will return. Features the story of Major Powell's first daring conquest of the Colorado River in 1869.
Fine Arts; History - United States
Dist - TWYMAN Prod - DISNEY 1963

Ten who dared series

Alexander Von Humboldt	52 MIN
Alexander Von Humbolt - Venezuela, 1799, Pt 1	26 MIN
Alexander Von Humbolt - Venezuela, 1799, Pt 2	26 MIN
Burke and Wills	52 MIN
Burke and Wills - Australia, 1860 - Pt 2	26 MIN
Captain James Cook	52 MIN
Captain James Cook - South Pacific, 1768, Pt 1	26 MIN
Captain James Cook - South Pacific, 1768, Pt 2	26 MIN
Charles Doughty	52 MIN
Charles Doughty - Arabia, 1877 - Pt 1	26 MIN
Charles Doughty - Arabia, 1877 - Pt 2	26 MIN
Christopher Columbus	30 MIN
Christopher Columbus - the Americas, 1492 Pt 1	26 MIN
Christopher Columbus - the Americas, 1492 Pt 2	26 MIN
Francisco Pizarro	52 MIN
Francisco Pizarro - Inca Nation, Peru , 1532, Pt 1	26 MIN
Francisco Pizarro - Inca Nation, Peru , 1532, Pt 2	26 MIN
Henry Morton Stanley	52 MIN
Henry Morton Stanley - Congo River, 1874, Pt 1	26 MIN
Henry Morton Stanley - Congo River, 1874, Pt 2	26 MIN
Jedediah Smith	30 MIN
Jedediah Smith - America, 1826, Pt 1	26 MIN
Jedediah Smith - America, 1826, Pt 2	26 MIN
Mary Kingsley	52 MIN
Mary Kingsley - West Africa, 1893, Pt 1	26 MIN
Mary Kingsley - West Africa, 1893, Pt 2	26 MIN
Roald Amundsen	52 MIN
Roald Amundsen - South Pole, 1911 - Pt 1	26 MIN
Roald Amundsen - South Pole, 1911 - Pt 2	26 MIN

Dist - TIMLIF

Ten Years After 52 MIN
16mm
B&W
LC 77-702153
Uses the tenth - year reunion of the filmmaker's high school class as a backdrop and examines the lives of six individuals from the Class of '65, the changes they have undergone and the realities they now face.
Education; Psychology; Sociology
Dist - TEMPLU Prod - TEMPLU 1977

Ten years after - Pt 1 26 MIN
16mm
B&W
LC 77-702153
Uses the tenth - year reunion of the filmmaker's high school class as a backdrop and examines the lives of six individuals from the Class of '65, the changes they have undergone and the realities they now face.
History - United States
Dist - TEMPLU Prod - TEMPLU 1977

Ten years after - Pt 2 26 MIN
16mm
B&W
LC 77-702153
Uses the tenth - year reunion of the filmmaker's high school class as a backdrop and examines the lives of six individuals from the Class of '65, the changes they have undergone and the realities they now face.
History - United States
Dist - TEMPLU Prod - TEMPLU 1977

Ten Years of the Berlin Wall 19 MIN
VHS / U-matic
Color (H C A)
Documents the building of the Berlin Wall and the East - West relationships during the ten - year period following it.
Civics and Political Systems; History - World
Dist - JOU Prod - UPI

Ten Years to Tomorrow 25 MIN
16mm
Color
LC 73-700785
Points out the value of the communication satellite network. Shows how in Quito, Ecuador, an international team under the guidance of COMSAT connects another seven million people to the worldwide communication satellite network.
Geography - World; Social Science
Dist - GUG Prod - COMSAC 1973

The Tenants' Act 5 MIN
16mm
B&W
LC 74-702769
Deals with the issue of women's liberation in the context of the class struggle.
Sociology
Dist - CANFDC Prod - REDTRK 1973

A Tender balance 17 MIN
U-matic / VHS / 16mm
Color (J)
Discusses the problem of communication between teenagers and their parents. Shows a young man talking to his parents about his girlfriend and his sister's struggle to avoid her father's protectiveness. Intended to trigger discussion among students.
Guidance and Counseling; Psychology; Sociology
Dist - FI Prod - PALLP

Tender duplicity 30 MIN
VHS / 16mm
Color (G)
$35.00 purchase
Interviews dancer and choreographer Margaret Jenkins, who discusses her sources and influences. Describes her experiences in the early days of modern dance in New York, the building of her own company in San Francisco and the joys and difficulties of keeping her modern dance troupe alive and well. Looks at her dancers as they rehearse and develop a new piece in collaboration with Yoko Ono.
Fine Arts
Dist - CANCIN Prod - SHEREL 1992

Tender images 6 MIN
16mm
Color (G)
$10.00 rental
Features fifteen imaginative three - dimensional paintings in black, sepia and white light in a Sara Kathryn Arledge production.
Fine Arts
Dist - CANCIN

Tender loving care - the coach's role in labor and delivery 26 MIN
U-matic / VHS
Color (PRO)
$250.00 purchase, $60.00 rental _ #4272S, #4272V
Follows first - time parents from their arrival at the hospital through the birth of their eight pound, nine ounce daughter. Demonstrates important coaching variations during labor. Provides a live birthing experience and coaching model for nurses, fathers and all significant others who might coach during labor and delivery.
Health and Safety; Sociology
Dist - AJN Prod - HTHSA 1986

The Tender Mansion 17 MIN
16mm
Color (J H)
Discusses the cause and effects of environmental pollution, exploring the consequences of many commonly suggested solutions. Encourages the adoption of a meaningful ecological awareness by all citizens and the application of that awareness in their daily lives.
Science - Natural; Sociology
Dist - DRPEP Prod - DRPEP

Tender negative 2 MIN
16mm
B&W (G)
$15.00 rental
Presents a high - contrast love dance and struggle over space in the frame.
Fine Arts
Dist - CANCIN Prod - HUDINA 1990

The Tender Tale of Cinderella Penguin 10 MIN
16mm
Color (I J A)
LC 82-700484
Presents an animated story, without words and set to a wide variety of musical selections, which spoofs the traditional tale of Cinderella, with penguins playing the story's characters.
Fine Arts; Literature and Drama
Dist - NFBC Prod - NFBC 1981

Tenderloin blues 58 MIN
VHS
Color (G)
$75.00 purchase
Introduces the people in the streets of San Francisco's Tenderloin District. Allows them to express themselves fully. Produced by Chuck Hudina.
Fine Arts; Social Science
Dist - CANCIN

Tending towards the horizontal 32 MIN
16mm
Color (G)
$75.00 purchase
Creates three images that recur alternately throughout the film - a bird tirelessly flapping its wings; a figure sitting on a hay bale, watching the city below; and a woman in a library who reads only what others have left behind. Uses voiceover text, written and performed by France Daigle. Filmed images are mostly houses, dissolving in and out of light and shadow. Produced by Barbara Sternberg.
Fine Arts
Dist - CANCIN

Tendon Injuries 26 MIN
16mm
Color (PRO)
Presents a brief demonstration of the healing process of tendons to illustrate the principles underlying tendon suturing. Depicts the details of the operative technic of the insertion of a tendon graft into a digit.
Health and Safety; Science
Dist - ACY Prod - ACYDGD 1953

Tendon Transfers in the Quadriplegic Hand 60 MIN
VHS / U-matic
Color (PRO)
Presents Professor Eric Moberg, MD's lecture on the study of surgical techniques and treatment of the quadriplegic upper extremity.
Health and Safety
Dist - ASSH **Prod** - ASSH

Tenent 5 MIN
16mm
Color (G)
$15.00 rental
Explains filmmaker Barnett, 'A meditation on a few frames of film in which a woman turns earth with a spade.'
Fine Arts
Dist - CANCIN **Prod** - BARND 1977

Tengboche - a threatened sanctuary
VHS / U-matic / BETA / 16mm
Everest connection series
Color (G)
$480.00, $292.00, $270.00 purchase
Glimpses inside a Himalayan monastery for Tibetan Buddhism, Tengboche in Nepal. Reveals that Sherpa migration from Tibet 400 years ago created a monastery which survived intact while most monasteries in the Tibetan motherland were destroyed by the Chinese. Shows how Tengboche is now threatened by the invasion of Western tourism - 8,000 visitors a year are undermining the local economy and corrupting traditional values with their wealth of cash and consumer goods. Features Sir Edmund Hillary.
Geography - World; Religion and Philosophy
Dist - MEDCIN **Prod** - MEDCIN

Tengboche - a threatened sanctuary - 3 28 MIN
VHS / U-matic
Everest connection series
Color (H C)
$205.00, $175.00 purchase _ #V698
Presents a rare glimpse into a Himalayan monastery, Tengboche. Shows how it is threatened by Western tourism. Shows how the monastery is being assisted by Sir Edmund Hillary and funding from Canada to revitalize itself through building a new school combining religious and secular studies. Part three of a three - part series on the Sherpa people of the Himalayan region.
Geography - World; Religion and Philosophy
Dist - BARR **Prod** - CEPRO 1991

Tenn - Tom - a New Waterway for America 28 MIN
16mm
Color
Tours the Tennessee - Tombigbee Waterway, a 234 - mile waterway which joins two of the busiest navigation systems in the Southeast.
Geography - United States; Social Science
Dist - MTP **Prod** - USAE

Tennant Creek in Passing 7 MIN
16mm
Color (J)
LC 75-702392
Presents impressions of life in Tennant Creek, a small town in the Australian outback.
Geography - World
Dist - AUIS **Prod** - FLMAUS 1974

Tenneco - Night and Day 17 MIN
16mm
Color
Traces the global operations of Tenneco, Inc. Shows how Tenneco balances strong energy production and exploration operations with a variety of consumer and industrial businesses.
Business and Economics; Social Science
Dist - MTP **Prod** - FENECO

Tennessee 60 MIN
VHS
Portrait of America series
Color (J H C G)
$99.95 purchase _ #AMB42V
Visits Tennessee. Offers extensive research into the state's history. Films key locations and presents segments on its history, government, education, folklore, science, journalism, sociology, industry, agriculture and business. Shows what is unique about Tennessee and what is distinctive about its regional culture and how it got to be that way. Includes teacher study guides. Part of a 50 - part series.
Geography - United States; History - United States
Dist - CAMV

Tennessee Birdwalk 6 MIN
U-matic
Color (P)
Features bald birds, birds flying north in the winter, and other aviary improbabilities.
Science - Natural
Dist - GA **Prod** - NBCTV

Tennessee River - Conservation and Power 14 MIN
U-matic / VHS / 16mm
Color (I J H)
LC 76-711626
Discusses the Tennesse Valley Program which has proved that man can alter his environment to his advantage and correct past ecological mistakes. Tells how the development of this area by the Federal government has resulted in benefits to both the people living in the area and to those beyond the valley. Points out that the quality of life in the area has been greatly affected by the wise use of this river resource.
Geography - United States; Science - Natural
Dist - PHENIX **Prod** - EVANSA 1971

Tennessee Sampler 15 MIN
16mm / U-matic / VHS
Color (J A G)
Explores the state of Tennessee, its culture, crafts, and characters.
Fine Arts; Geography - United States; Sociology
Dist - DIRECT **Prod** - MOURIS 1977
PHENIX PHENIX

Tennessee - Tombigbee Waterway - slicing through the South 55 MIN
VHS
On the waterways series
Color (G H)
$29.95 purchase _ #OW13
Travels with the crew of the Driftwood on the nation's newest waterway, the Tenn - Tom, completed in 1985, connecting the Great Lakes and the Ohio River with the Gulf of Mexico. Narrated by Jason Robards. Part of a 13 - part series on the history, geography, culture and ecology of North American waterways.
Social Science
Dist - SVIP

The Tennessee Valley 15 MIN
16mm / U-matic / VHS
American legacy series
Color (I)
Presents John Rugg reviewing the history of the Tennessee Valley through scenes of the British at Fort Loudon, early pioneers at Rocky Mount, a flatboat trip down the river and the slow deterioration of the valley's resources. Gives a first - hand look at how the Tennessee Valley Authority helped reclaim the region.
Geography - United States; History - United States
Dist - AITECH **Prod** - KRMATV 1983

Tennessee Vs Garner - June 1985
VHS
Crime to Court Legal Specials Series
Color (PRO)
$99.00 purchase
Reviews the case of an officer being sued for shooting a fleeing felon - Tennessee vs Garner. Trains law enforcement personnel. Part of an ongoing series to look in depth at cases which impact the field of law enforcement. Produced in cooperation with the South Carolina Criminal Justice Academy and the National Sheriff's Association.
Civics and Political Systems; Psychology; Social Science; Sociology
Dist - SCETV **Prod** - SCETV

Tennessee Williams - theater in progress 29 MIN
VHS
Color (G C H)
$119.00 purchase _ #DL415
Follows the creation of The Red Devil Battery Sign from first rehearsals to opening night. Shows how Williams rewrote parts of the play as production progressed, and how director Edwin Sherwin coached Anthony Quinn, Claire Bloom, and others in the cast.
Fine Arts
Dist - INSIM

Tennessee's partner 15 MIN
VHS
Short story series
Color (J H)
#E373; LC 90-713153
Develops the theme of love and friendship in an account of two friends in a gold mining town in 'Tennessee's Partner' by Bret Harte. Part of a 16 - part series which introduces American and European short story writers and discusses the technical aspects of short story structure.
Literature and Drama
Dist - GPN **Prod** - CTI 1978

Tennessee's Partner by Bret Harte 15 MIN
16mm / U-matic / VHS
Short Story Series
Color (J)
LC 83-700055
Tells a story of genuine love and friendship between two men whose characters and appearances belie their sentimental hearts. Based on the short story Tennessee's Partner by Bret Harte.
Literature and Drama
Dist - IU **Prod** - IITC 1978
GPN CTI

Tennis Anyone - Introduction 30 MIN
U-matic / VHS
Tennis Anyone Series
Color (H C A)
LC 79-706889
Physical Education and Recreation
Dist - TIMLIF **Prod** - BATA 1979

Tennis Anyone Series
The Backhand 30 MIN
The Forehand 30 MIN
The Serve 30 MIN
Specialty Strokes 30 MIN
Strategy and Tactics 30 MIN
Tennis Anyone - Introduction 30 MIN
Dist - TIMLIF

Tennis - Basic Tactics for Doubles 13 MIN
U-matic / VHS / 16mm
Tennis Series
Color (J) (SPANISH)
LC 78-711118
Demonstrates doubles tactics through strategic court positions, service net approach, return of serve, lobbing, poaching, net play and other fundamentals.
Foreign Language; Physical Education and Recreation
Dist - PHENIX **Prod** - PHENIX 1968

Tennis - basic tactics for singles 13 MIN
U-matic / VHS / 16mm
Tennis series
Color (J H A) (SPANISH)
LC 71-711119
Explains that the basic strategy for beginners is to keep the ball in play. Shows that once that is mastered, placing the ball where opponents least expect it is good strategy, since a running shot is considerably harder to make. The basic stroke fundamentals are followed by the correct positions, the changing of shot directions, the ways to take advantage of an opponent's weaknesses and ways to regain position.
Physical Education and Recreation
Dist - PHENIX **Prod** - PHENIX 1968

Tennis by Vic Braden
VHS
Tennis by Vic Braden Series
(J H C)
$29.95 _ #HSV7055V
Presents coach Vic Braden who introduces the game of tennis. Discusses techniques for improving basic strokes and more.
Physical Education and Recreation
Dist - CAMV

Tennis by Vic Braden Series
Court etiquette
Playing Doubles
Practice with the Pros
Tennis by Vic Braden
Dist - CAMV

Tennis equipment 30 MIN
VHS
Tennis talk series
Color (J H A)
$24.95 purchase _ #PRO012V
Features tennis instructor Dennis Van der Meer teaching about tennis equipment.
Physical Education and Recreation
Dist - CAMV

Tennis Everyone 15 MIN
16mm
Color
Examines Florida's tennis facilities and presents hints to improve your game.
Geography - United States; Physical Education and Recreation
Dist - FLADC **Prod** - FLADC

Tennis Everyone 26 MIN
U-matic / VHS
Color
Explores the growth and popularity of this sport with plenty of action.
Physical Education and Recreation
Dist - KAROL **Prod** - KAROL

Tennis Grips and Strokes 11 MIN
U-matic / VHS / 16mm
Color; B&W (J)
LC FIA67-1438
Uses slow - motion, hold frames and identification titles to demonstrate in detail tennis fundamentals, such as forehand and backhand grips and drives, backhand volley, serves and the overhead smash.
Physical Education and Recreation
Dist - PHENIX **Prod** - SLACK 1966

The Tennis Lesson 9 MIN
U-matic / VHS / 16mm
Color (H C A)
LC 78-700462
Deals with the issue of the increasing human dependence on technology by telling a story about a woman who has an affair with a tennis ball machine.
Fine Arts; Guidance and Counseling; Physical Education and Recreation; Sociology
Dist - PHENIX **Prod** - KARGL 1977

The Tennis match 15 MIN
U-matic / VHS / 16mm
Color (A)
LC 78-701801
Portrays the intense competition, petty bickering and ego clashes that erupt during the weekly tennis matches among four friends.
Physical Education and Recreation; Psychology
Dist - PHENIX **Prod** - KARPS 1978

Tennis Mothers 14 MIN
16mm / U-matic / VHS
Color (I)
Presents a typical day in the life of a 12 - year - old girl and her mother, who is determined that her daughter become a champion tennis star.
Physical Education and Recreation; Sociology
Dist - CAROUF **Prod** - CBSTV

Tennis our way 151 MIN
VHS
Color (G)
$39.95 purchase
Features tennis stars Arthur Ashe, Stan Smith, and Vic Braden in a comprehensive guide to tennis.
Physical Education and Recreation
Dist - PBS **Prod** - WNETTV

Tennis Our Way 150 MIN
VHS
(J H C A)
$49.95 _ #WV2004V
Discusses the fundamentals of tennis, including forehand, serving fundamentals, practice methods, court strategies, rules, ball spin, and more. Features various tennis stars.
Physical Education and Recreation
Dist - CAMV

Tennis Philosophy and the Forehand Stroke 29 MIN
VHS / U-matic
Vic Braden's Tennis for the Future Series
Color
Physical Education and Recreation
Dist - PBS **Prod** - WGBHTV 1981

Tennis racquet 7 MIN
U-matic / VHS / 16mm
Goofy over sports series
Color (P I J) (SPANISH)
LC 77-701888
Features Goofy as the scorekeeper in a slapstick version of the traditionally polite game of tennis.
Physical Education and Recreation
Dist - CORF **Prod** - DISNEY 1977

Tennis series
VHS
NCAA instructional video series
Color (H C A)
$74.95 purchase _ #KAR2305V
Presents a four - part series on tennis. Focuses on serving, returning serves, the volley, the forehand, and the backhand.
Physical Education and Recreation
Dist - CAMV **Prod** - NCAAF

Tennis series
Applying forehand and backhand strokes 20 MIN
Forehand and Backhand Strokes 23 MIN
Net Play 21 MIN
The Serve 20 MIN
Dist - ATHI

Tennis series
Tennis - Basic Tactics for Doubles 13 MIN
Tennis - basic tactics for singles 13 MIN
Dist - PHENIX

Tennis, Spin and You 30 MIN
VHS
Color (G)
$49.95 purchase _ #CCP0007
Shows how to add spin to your tennis game. Illustrates the proper stance, grip and follow - through. Covers top spin, under spin, service spin and tips for practice and match situations.
Physical Education and Recreation
Dist - CADESF **Prod** - CADESF 1986

Tennis, spin and you 30 MIN
VHS
Color (J H A)
$29.95 purchase _ #CCP0007V
Features teaching pro John Smallfield teaching about the importance of spin in tennis. Explains the proper stance, grip, and follow - through for each type of spin - top spin, under spin, and service spin.
Physical Education and Recreation
Dist - CAMV

Tennis Tactics Series
The Importance of Practice 9 MIN
Tactics for Doubles Play 9 MIN
Tactics for Ground Strokes 9 MIN
Tactics for Return of Service 9 MIN
Tactics for Singles Play 9 MIN
Tactics for Specialty Shots 9 MIN
Tactics for the Serve 9 MIN
Dist - ATHI

Tennis talk series
Backboard tennis 30 MIN
Backhand drive 30 MIN
Corrective tennis 30 MIN
Doubles tactics tennis 30 MIN
Forehand drive 30 MIN
Instant tennis 30 MIN
Mixed doubles 30 MIN
Serve in tennis 30 MIN
Single tactics 30 MIN
Specialty strokes 30 MIN
Tennis equipment 30 MIN
The Volley 30 MIN
Dist - CAMV

Tennis teaching methods of Dennis Van Der Meer series
Presents a three - volume series that comprehensively covers every aspect of tennis. Features Dennis Van Der Meer. Includes the titles Essential Strokes, The Tactical Game and The Attacking Game.
The Tennis teaching methods of Dennis Van Der Meer series 180 MIN
Dist - CAMV

Tennis the Nasty Way Series
Tennis with Ilie Nastase - Backhand 13 MIN
Tennis with Ilie Nastase - Forehand 12 MIN
Tennis with Ilie Nastase - serve and volley 13 MIN
Tennis with Ilie Nastase - Strategy Shots 10 MIN
Dist - AIMS

Tennis the nasty way series
Backhand 15 MIN
Forehand 15 MIN
Strategy Shots 15 MIN
Dist - MARMO

Tennis - Tut Bartzen 13 MIN
16mm
B&W
Shows Davis cup star and national clay courts champ demonstrating how to serve, play the net and how to stroke forehand and backhand.
Physical Education and Recreation
Dist - SFI **Prod** - SFI

Tennis with Ilie Nastase - Backhand 13 MIN
16mm / U-matic / VHS
Tennis the Nasty Way Series
Color (J)
LC 76-701873
Presents Ilie Nastase explaining the different backhand grips. Reviews the stroke and shows that the swing and follow - through is similar to the forehand.
Physical Education and Recreation
Dist - AIMS **Prod** - SF 1975

Tennis with Ilie Nastase - Forehand 12 MIN
16mm / U-matic / VHS
Tennis the Nasty Way Series
Color (J)
LC 76-701874
Presents Ilie Nastase demonstrating the fundamentals of the forehand and the importance of watching the ball and keeping the knees flexed. Shows the backswing. Explains and reviews basic strokes and variations, how to hit flat, topspin and slice forehands and when to use each most effectively.
Physical Education and Recreation
Dist - AIMS **Prod** - SF 1975

Tennis with Ilie Nastase - serve and volley 13 MIN
U-matic / VHS / 16mm
Tennis the nasty way series
Color (J)
LC 76-701876
Explains that a service is broken down into three component parts. Shows slow motion shots of increasing the power in the serve by snapping the wrist and straightening the body at the moment of impact. Demonstrates putting spin on the ball. Discusses and demonstrates three important elements of the volley.
Physical Education and Recreation
Dist - AIMS **Prod** - SF 1975

Tennis with Ilie Nastase - Strategy Shots 10 MIN
16mm / U-matic / VHS
Tennis the Nasty Way Series
Color (J)
LC 76-701877
Considers three storkes, the overhead, the lob and the drop shot. Shows the similarity between the overhead and service, offensive and defensive lobs and demonstrates the drop shot.
Physical Education and Recreation
Dist - AIMS **Prod** - SF 1975

Tennis with Van der Meer series
Features tennis player and instructor Dennis Van der Meer in a 10 - part telecourse on the basics of the sport. Uses freeze - frame photography and repetition to stress skill development. Covers topics inclusing serving, returns, specialty shots, strategies for doubles and singles matches, and mental aspects of the game.
Doubles tactics 30 MIN
Drill 30 MIN
Ground strokes 30 MIN
Mental aspects 30 MIN
Physical aspects 30 MIN
Practice 30 MIN
Return of the serve 30 MIN
Serve 30 MIN
Singles tactics 30 MIN
Specialty shots 30 MIN
Dist - SCETV **Prod** - SCETV 1975

Teno 12 MIN
U-matic
Color (G)
$300.00 purchase, $50.00, $40.00 rental
Examines through interview and narrative the effects of repetitive labor and overwork on women in traditionally female jobs. Created by Margo Nash.
Health and Safety; Sociology
Dist - WMENIF **Prod** - WMENIF 1984

Tense - imperfect 11 MIN
U-matic / VHS / 16mm
Critical moments in teaching series
Color (C T)
LC FIA67-644
Portrays the experiences of a young teacher, formerly assigned to an outstanding high school, who is unable to adjust to teaching students in a lower income area. Describes how her problem is increased through her inability to understand and communicate with a student in one of her classes.
Education; Psychology; Sociology
Dist - PHENIX **Prod** - CALVIN 1966

Tense - Unit 1 41 MIN
VHS
French language file series
Color; PAL (I J H)
PdS29.50 purchase
Covers verb tense in two cassettes. Supports the process of foreign language learning by developing pupils' awareness of how the language is structured and how it functions. Part one of a three - part series on French language.
Foreign Language
Dist - EMFVL

Tension and Relaxation 13 MIN
16mm
Creative Dance for Children Series
B&W
Shows Barbara Mettler teaching a group of boys and girls at the Creative Dance Center in 1966.
Fine Arts
Dist - METT **Prod** - METT 1977

Tension Application on Rear - End Collision, Ford Hardtop 19 MIN
VHS / BETA / 16mm
Color (A PRO)

$83.50 purchase _ #KTI60
Demonstrates tension application on rear end collision on a Ford hardtop.
Industrial and Technical Education
Dist - RMIBHF **Prod** - RMIBHF

Tension Hook Up and Accessories 8 MIN
BETA / VHS
Color (A PRO)
$56.00 purchase _ #KTI84
Deals with auto body repair. Demonstrates pull hook up and hardware on damages.
Industrial and Technical Education
Dist - RMIBHF **Prod** - RMIBHF

Tension Testing 21 MIN
16mm
B&W
LC FIE52-219
Demonstrates how a hydraulic tension testing machine operates.
Industrial and Technical Education
Dist - USNAC **Prod** - USOE 1944

Tension, Worry and Ulcers 50 MIN
16mm
Color (PRO)
Shows the diagnosis and management of duodenal ulcers and the removal of a major portion of a patient's stomach in a corrective procedure to prevent recurrence of persistent ulcers.
Health and Safety
Dist - LAWREN **Prod** - CMA

Tensions increase 76 MIN
VHS
March of time - trouble abroad series
B&W (G)
$24.95 purchase _ #S02175
Presents newsreel excerpts covering events in the US and abroad in 1937. Covers events including the 20th birthday of Finland, a crisis in Algeria, the largest cotton mill in the world, predictions that airplane flight would replace the luxury liner for transatlantic travel, and more. Part two of a six - part series.
History - United States; History - World
Dist - UILL

Tent 4 MIN
16mm
Color (G)
$8.00 purchase
Features the last of a trilogy chronicling a journey to Alaska.
Fine Arts; Geography - United States; Geography - World
Dist - CANCIN **Prod** - STREEM 1985

Tent Flaps and Flapjacks 26 MIN
16mm
Color
LC FIE63-218
Portrays the recreational opportunities in the national forests in the northcentral states.
Geography - United States; Physical Education and Recreation; Science - Natural; Social Science; Sociology
Dist - USNAC **Prod** - USDA 1962

Tentacles 96 MIN
16mm
Color (H A)
Describes a giant octopus that leaves its victims as skeletons washed up on a California beach. Stars Shelley Winters, John Huston and Henry Fonda.
Fine Arts
Dist - TIMLIF **Prod** - ECE 1982

10 basics of business etiquette 22 MIN
VHS
Color (H COR T G)
$99.00 purchase _ #MEC3602V-J
Instructs viewers in professional etiquette in such situations as making introductions, business dining, using the telephone, and attending meetings. Uses humor to present the 'rules of the game.' Comes with teacher's guide.
Business and Economics; Guidance and Counseling
Dist - CAMV

The Tenth dancer 52 MIN
VHS / 16mm
Color (G) (CAMBODIAN WITH ENGLISH SUBTITLES)
$110.00, $130.00 rental, $295.00 purchase
Provides a rare glimpse into women's lives in Cambodia, a country under cultural and political reconstruction following the brutal Pol Pot regime, in which over 90 percent of Cambodia's artists were killed, including most of the classical dancers of the Royal Court Ballet. Tells the story of the tenth dancer - only one in ten survived - and her relationship with one pupil. An Australian production by Sally Ingleton.
Fine Arts; Sociology
Dist - WMEN

Tenth Decade Series
The End of an Era, Episode 8 58 MIN
Dist - CANBC

10 easy ways to keep your job 30 MIN
VHS
Color (G H C VOC T)
$189.00 purchase _ #GW - 127 - VS
Parodies a late - night talk show to show students the importance of career planning. Helps students to identify common - sense concepts often taken for granted by first - time employees - until they receive their first 'pink slip.' Explores the daily practice that all employees should follow - take initiative, increase skills, leave personal problems at home, get along with co - workers, help make the company profitable, develop problem - solving skills, learn to take direction from superiors, create good relations with the boss, go the extra mile and learn to enjoy the job. Interviews a career education consultant and the regional manager for a chain of sports stores. Includes a teacher's resource book.
Business and Economics; Guidance and Counseling
Dist - HRMC

10 easy ways to lose your job 25 MIN
VHS
Color (H C VOC T G)
$169.00 purchase _ #CG - 882 - VS
Explores the ten most common reasons employers give for dismissing beginning workers: poor work quality; not following directions; poor customer service; dishonesty; undependability; lack of respect for the boss; chronic lateness; sexual harassment; socializing; and stealing. Illustrates each cause for dismissal with a dramatic vignette modeling the undesired behavior. Presents positive steps toward job - retention skills.
Business and Economics; Guidance and Counseling
Dist - HRMC **Prod** - HRMC

The Tenth good thing about Barney 12 MIN
U-matic / VHS / 16mm
Color (K P I)
Presents a story of a boy remembering his pet cat. Based on the book by Judith Viorst.
English Language; Literature and Drama
Dist - AIMS **Prod** - WILETS 1986

Tenth International Games for the Deaf 40 MIN
16mm
Color
LC FIA66-670
Shows the strength and skill of deaf contestants participating in an Olympic sports spectacle.
Education; Health and Safety; Physical Education and Recreation; Psychology
Dist - MONUMT **Prod** - MONUMT 1965

10 keys to a more powerful personality 64 MIN
VHS
Color (H C G)
$69.00 purchase _ #NGC571V
Features Brian Tracy who shares his ten keys to success - clarity, competence, concentration, common sense, creativity, consideration, consistency, commitment, courage and confidence. Explains thoroughly the importance of each quality and motivates students.
Guidance and Counseling; Psychology
Dist - CAMV **Prod** - NIGCON

The Tenth Month 123 MIN
U-matic / VHS
Color (H C A)
Tells the story of a female journalist who finds herself single, middle - aged and pregnant. Shows how she rebuffs family pressure to get rid of the baby, rents a cheap flat in a rough New York neighborhood and begins an ever hopeful vigil for the birth of the child. Stars Carol Burnett.
Fine Arts; Sociology
Dist - TIMLIF **Prod** - TIMLIF 1982

10 new easy biographies book bags 11 MIN
VHS / U-matic
Easy biography book bags series
(I J)
Contains one hard cover library book with a word for word cassette.
Social Science
Dist - TROLA **Prod** - TROLA 1986

10 rules for personal success 32 MIN
VHS
Color (I J H)
$39.95 purchase _ #SD200V
Features Dr Steve Bell who shares some of the ways students can quickly develop a personal plan that works. Stresses that, like developing a golf swing, the important thing is to find 'the groove' and through practice and commitment make certain that it is not changed or lost.
Guidance and Counseling; Psychology
Dist - CAMV

10 steps to improved customer service 23 MIN
BETA / U-matic / VHS
Color (G COR PRO)
$495.00 purchase, $160.00 rental
Shows how to improve customer service by asking questions; finding out what the competition is doing; taking responsibility for problems; understanding the business of customers; being aware of cultural differences; investing in self - improvement; and building organizational pride.
Business and Economics
Dist - AMEDIA **Prod** - AMEDIA 1993

The Tenth symphony of Abel Gance 87 MIN
35mm
Color; PAL; Silent (G)
Resurrects Abel Gance's 1929 film 'Napoleon,' in which a melodramatic plot revolves around the fortunes of a rich young woman who is blackmailed by adventurers, and the emotional havoc this causes in her subsequent marriage to a composer, who uses his music as an outlet for his suffering. Features restoration by Bambi Ballard, of Paris, who is dedicated to bringing director Abel Gance and his works back into prominence. Contact distributor about price and availability outside the United Kingdom.
Fine Arts; Sociology
Dist - BALFOR

10 x 17 20 MIN
16mm
B&W (A)
$100.00 rental
Follows the filmmaker's first days in Chicago, nearly living on the skids, working at Manpower for $9 per day. Documents his relationship with his girlfriend.
Fine Arts; Psychology; Sociology
Dist - CANCIN **Prod** - ANGERA 1971
FLMKCO

Tents, Gear and Horseback Tour 30 MIN
BETA / VHS
Great Outdoors Series
Color
Introduces a tentmaker. Discusses choosing a campsite and gear. Features a Los Angeles urban wilderness and a horseback tour.
Physical Education and Recreation
Dist - CORF **Prod** - WGBHTV

Teotihuacan 56 MIN
U-matic / VHS
Color (C) (SPANISH)
$279.00, $179.00 purchase _ #AD - 2189
Examines the history and archeological sites of Teotihuacan, City of the Gods. Reveals that it was once the largest city in Mesoamerica and birthplace of the creation myth that held sway for 1800 years. Despite its enormous political and economic power, it disappeared without explanation, leaving buildings, paintings and the oral tradition of the Nahuas.
Foreign Language; Geography - World; History - World; Religion and Philosophy; Social Science; Sociology
Dist - FOTH **Prod** - FOTH

Tepatitlan
VHS
Color (J H G)
$44.95 purchase _ #MCV5039
Presents a program on the culture of Mexico.
Geography - World
Dist - MADERA **Prod** - MADERA

Tepoztlan 30 MIN
16mm / U-matic / VHS
Color (C A)
LC 71-709218
Documents traditional lifeways in Tepoztlan including daily activities of the people, the cultivation of maize, planting, harvesting and grinding.
Geography - World; History - World; Social Science; Sociology
Dist - PHENIX **Prod** - GRISWD 1970

Tepoztlan in Transition 20 MIN
U-matic / VHS / 16mm
Color (C)
LC 76-709814
Tells how the village of Tepoztlan emerges from its traditional isolation through mechanization which brings modern methods of irrigation and cultivation and a new type of employer - employee relationship as skilled labor develops in the village.
Agriculture; Business and Economics; Geography - World; Psychology; Social Science; Sociology
Dist - PHENIX **Prod** - HRAW 1970

Tepozton 11 MIN
U-matic / VHS / 16mm
American Folklore Series
Color (I J)

LC 73-713789
Presents a Mexican legend of the mischevous boy who is half Aztec God and half human.
Geography - World; Literature and Drama
Dist - PHENIX **Prod** - HRAW 1971

Teresa Venerdi 90 MIN
16mm / U-matic / VHS
Captioned; B&W (A) (ITALIAN (ENGLISH SUBTITLES))
Portrays the story of a young girl in an orphanage in this romantic comedy with social overtones.
Fine Arts
Dist - CNEMAG **Prod** - CNEMAG 1941

Terex 33 - 15 11 MIN
16mm
Color
LC 75-703437
Demonstrates the largest diesel electric hauler built and designed in Canada.
Social Science
Dist - GMCAN **Prod** - GMCAN 1973

Tereza 91 MIN
U-matic / VHS
B&W (CZECH (ENGLISH SUBTITLES))
Tells of a female police officer who solves a complicated murder. Based on motifs from the novel by Anna Sedlmaye Rovia. Directed by Pavel Blumenfeld and starring Jirina Suorcova. With English subtitles.
Fine Arts
Dist - IHF **Prod** - IHF

Terezin Diary 88 MIN
16mm
Color (G)
Presents an independent production by Dan Weissman who also directs. Focuses on Helga Kinsky and nine other survivors of the Nazi concentration camp for Central European Jews created in Terezin near Prague. Reveals that the Nazis tried to give Terezin the semblance of a normal town and encouraged the staging of operas, plays and concerts by the well - known musicians, artists, writers and performers incarcerated there. Describes the paradox of concerts at night and transport to death the next day. Written by Zuzana Justman and narrated by Eli Wallach.
History - World; Religion and Philosophy; Sociology
Dist - FIRS

Terminal Equipment and Interfaces 49 MIN
U-matic / VHS
Telecommunications and the Computer Series
Color
Industrial and Technical Education; Mathematics
Dist - MIOT **Prod** - MIOT

Terminal Illness 30 MIN
VHS / 16mm
Color (PRO)
$225.00 purchase
Provides support to workers whose video display terminals cause eyestrain and contribute to high stress levels. Encourages VDT operators to acknowledge their physical problems and use their experiences to help others. Resource guide available.
Business and Economics; Health and Safety; Psychology; Sociology
Dist - FLMWST

Terminal Illness Series

The Grieving Process	25 MIN
Grieving Process, the 1	45 MIN
Interviews with the Patient	25 MIN
Pain Management	37 MIN
Religion and the Clergy	35 MIN
The Role of the Physician	41 MIN

Dist - UWASHP

Terminal Illness - the Patient's Story 28 MIN
U-matic / VHS
Color (C)
$249.00, $149.00 purchase _ #AD - 1735
Reveals that Joan Robinson, writer and social worker, was 41 when she learned she had ovarian cancer. Films her account of endurance and death, finally, over five years. Adapted from a Phil Donahue show.
Health and Safety; Psychology; Sociology
Dist - FOTH **Prod** - FOTH

Terminal illness - when it happens to you 50 MIN
VHS
Color (G)
$149.00 purchase, $75.00 rental _ #UW5691
Profiles a terminally ill patient, his courageous battle against cancer and the emotional toll his illness has taken on his family. Reveals that, at the age of 46, Chris Brotherton was diagnosed with a brain tumor and given only a few months to live. Follows the last six months of his life and shows how he, his wife and young son and the medical staff at a hospice deal with his illness.
Health and Safety; Sociology
Dist - FOTH

The Terminal Man 103 MIN
16mm / U-matic / VHS
Color
Stars George Segal as a man who submits to a controversial operation in order to control his violent blackouts.
Fine Arts
Dist - FI **Prod** - WB 1974

A Terminal on My Desk - the Impact of Data Processing in the Office 29 MIN
U-matic / VHS
Re - Making of Work Series
Color (C A)
Presents case studies of two large firms in England and Paris which demonstrate how the new technology is revolutionizing working conditions. Focuses on the need for involving individual workers in the process of implementing change.
Business and Economics; Industrial and Technical Education
Dist - EBEC

Terminal Self 9 MIN
16mm
Color
LC 72-700681
An experimental film in which a photograph of the head of a girl is reproduced in pink vapors which change to multiple images that flutter in circular motion and finally converge into a single expression, that of the death mask.
Guidance and Counseling; Industrial and Technical Education
Dist - UWFKD **Prod** - WHIT 1971

Terminal - VDTs and women's health 23 MIN
VHS / 16mm
Color (G IND)
$5.00 rental
Examines the possible linkage of birth defects to VDTs and the role of unions in protecting workers. Reveals that some unions are sponsoring legislation restricting exposure to VDTs while others have gotten contract language addressing the problem.
Health and Safety; Mathematics; Social Science; Sociology
Dist - AFLCIO **Prod** - GRATV 1985

Terminating an employee - industry
16mm / U-matic / VHS
Supervisory training - industry series
Color (A)
Shows how to terminate an employee in industrial setting.
Business and Economics
Dist - CRMP **Prod** - CRMP 1983

Terminating an employee - office)
16mm / U-matic / VHS
Supervisory training - office series
Color (A)
Shows how to terminate an employee in an office setting.
Business and Economics
Dist - CRMP **Prod** - CRMP 1983

Termination 5 MIN
16mm
B&W (G)
$10.00 rental
Features a small community of Indian people near Laytonville, California. Presents a Canyon Cinema documentary film unit by Tulley and Baillie.
Fine Arts; Social Science
Dist - CANCIN **Prod** - BAILB 1966

The Termination interview 21 MIN
VHS / 16mm / U-matic
Color (C G A PRO)
$495.00, $345.00, $375.00 _ #A449
Discusses the importance of preparation and correct handling of termination interviews. Demonstrates proper planning and preparation steps for a termination interview.
Business and Economics; Psychology; Social Science
Dist - BARR **Prod** - BARR 1986

Termination - making the best of it and The Termination handbook 21 MIN
VHS / U-matic / BETA
Color (PRO)
$195.00 purchase
Offers advice on firing and being fired, avoiding legal complications and reducing negative impact on morale. Includes the book The Termination Handbook by Robert Coulson.
Business and Economics; Psychology; Social Science
Dist - AARA

Termination of Cardiac Arrhythmias 11 MIN
U-matic
Cardiopulmonary Resuscitation Series
Color (PRO)
Discusses the use of electrical energy for external defibrillization of the heart.
Health and Safety; Science; Science - Natural
Dist - PRIMED **Prod** - PRIMED

Termination of Life 48 MIN
VHS / U-matic
Color
$455.00 purchase
Sociology
Dist - ABCLR **Prod** - ABCLR 1983

Termination of Parental Rights 59 MIN
VHS / U-matic
Legal Training for Children Welfare Workers Series Pt IV
Color
Discusses procedural requirements for termination of parental legal rights.
Civics and Political Systems; Sociology
Dist - UWISC **Prod** - UWISC 1975

Termination on trial 25 MIN
VHS
Color (A PRO IND)
$250.00 purchase
Presents the first part of a two - part series on the legal implications of job terminations. Reviews a wrongful termination lawsuit, showing the 'do's' and 'don'ts' of terminations.
Business and Economics; Psychology
Dist - VLEARN **Prod** - COMFLM

Termination on trial 25 MIN
VHS
Wrongful termination series
Color (A)
$450.00 purchase
Details company and individual policies and actions that could lead to wrongful termination litigation under the law. Outlines seven principles for hiring, reviewing and firing. Part I of two parts in the series.
Business and Economics; Civics and Political Systems; Education
Dist - COMFLM **Prod** - COMFLM

Termination on trial and termination - six expert views 60 MIN
VHS
Color (A PRO IND)
$295.00 purchase, $150.00 rental
Presents a two - part series on the legal implications of job terminations. 'Termination On Trial' reviews a wrongful termination lawsuit, showing the 'do's' and 'don'ts' of terminations. 'Termination - Six Expert Views' presents a panel of personnel professionals and attorneys, who discuss wrongful dismissal cases and problem areas.
Business and Economics; Psychology
Dist - VLEARN **Prod** - COMFLM

The Termination Phase 22 MIN
VHS / U-matic
Social Work Interviewing Series
Color
Presents the final segment in the series as a young woman shows marked improvement in her situation during the course of her session. Indicates that her placement in a temporary shelter has had a beneficial effect and she displays an awareness of her past child abuse.
Guidance and Counseling; Psychology; Sociology
Dist - UWISC **Prod** - UCALG 1978

Termination - Pt 8 50 MIN
U-matic / VHS
Relationship growth group series
Color
Discusses the feelings of members of a relational growth group as group termination draws near. Explores feelings of withdrawal.
Guidance and Counseling; Psychology; Sociology
Dist - UWISC **Prod** - WRAMC 1979

Termination - six expert views 30 MIN
VHS
Wrongful termination series
Color (A)
$350.00 purchase
Shows a panel discussion among personnel professionals and attorneys regarding actual cases of termination litigation. Presents debate concerning particular problem areas in company hiring practices. Part II of two videos in the series.
Business and Economics; Civics and Political Systems; Education
Dist - COMFLM **Prod** - COMFLM

Termination - six expert views 35 MIN
VHS
Color (A PRO IND)
$45.00 purchase
Presents the second part of a two - part series on the legal implications of job terminations. Features a panel of attorneys and personnel professionals, who discuss wrongful dismissal cases and problem areas.
Business and Economics; Psychology
Dist - VLEARN **Prod** - COMFLM

Terminaton in the Task - Centered Approach 60 MIN
VHS / U-matic
B&W
Uses the task - centered approach to demonstrate the steps in termination. Interviews a practitioner who works with the elderly about issues in termination with this population sub - group.
Sociology
Dist - UWISC **Prod** - UWISC 1980

Terminus 26 MIN
16mm
B&W (I)
LC FIA65-1122
Candidly studies, without narration, London's Waterloo Station. The fragmented sound score -- jazz, half - heard dialogue and signal box noises -- underscores the fragmentary nature of the peoples' experiences in a railroad station. termite, types of termites and how science copes with the problems created by these insects.
Geography - World; Social Science
Dist - SF **Prod** - BTF 1964

Termites - Architects of the Underground 9 MIN
16mm / U-matic / VHS
Real World of Insects Series
Captioned; Color (P) (SPANISH)
Presents an interesting study of termites, including their sensitivity to light, alien sound and movement.
Science - Natural
Dist - LCOA **Prod** - PEGASO 1973

Terms and Conditions 30 MIN
U-matic
North of Sixty Degrees - Destiny Uncertain Series
Color (H C)
Presents the northerners' views on large scale energy projects.
Geography - United States; Geography - World; History - World
Dist - TVOTAR **Prod** - TVOTAR 1985

Terms and safety
VHS
Pieper - zoology prelab dissections - series
Color (J H C)
$95.00 purchase _ #CG - 896 - VS
Discusses zoology laboratory terminology and reviews lab safety. Includes a brief post test to gauge student retention. Part of a 15 - part series on zoological lab dissection, including a lab safety review, produced by Bill Pieper.
Health and Safety; Science; Science - Natural
Dist - HRMC

Terms of Endearment
BETA / VHS
Color
Chronicles a mother and daughter's difficult relationship. Stars Shirley MacLaine, Debra Winger and Jack Nicholson.
Guidance and Counseling; Sociology
Dist - GA **Prod** - GA

Tern 25 MIN
VHS
Nature watch series
Color (P I J H C)
$49.00 purchase _ #320218; LC 89-715861
Examines the tern. Part of a series that explores the curious and uncommon characteristics of a variety of mammals, insects, birds and sea creatures.
Science - Natural
Dist - TVOTAR **Prod** - TVOTAR 1988

Ternary diagrams derived from binaries 6 MIN
16mm
Phase equilibria series
Color (C)
LC 78-700705
Depicts the relationship of phase diagrams to real cases of materials technology. Uses computer animation to show the construction of a ternary system from three binary systems. Explains the projection of the upper curved surfaces onto the base of the solid model. Demonstrates that the projection contains information about composition, primary phase fields and temperature in a given ternary system.
Industrial and Technical Education
Dist - PSU **Prod** - NSF 1976

Ternary Phase Diagram 7 MIN
16mm
Color
LC 74-705761
Depicts the development of a new and rapid technique for preparation of ternary phase diagrams required in the search for useful alloys. Shows techniques for determining ternary phase alloy diagrams that make it possible to circumvent a previously tedious, time consuming and costly research procedure.
Science; Science - Physical; Social Science
Dist - USNAC **Prod** - USNRC 1965

Terra Maria 23 MIN
16mm
Color (J H)
Presents the complete story of ancient St Mary's City, the first capital of Maryland.
Geography - United States
Dist - SHUGA **Prod** - SHUGA 1973

Terra nullius 21 MIN
VHS / 16mm
Color; B&W (G)
$65.00 rental, $275.00 purchase
Confronts the Australian government's policy of assimilation in which Aboriginal children were removed from their families and placed in white foster homes. Focuses on a young Aboriginal girl absorbing the fear, shame and incestuous abuse of her adoptive white parents. Exposes the connections between racial and sexual violence and the social effects of cultural genocide. Expressionist images disrupt the narrative echoing the denial of racial and sexual abuse. By Anne Pratten.
Fine Arts; Sociology
Dist - WMEN

Terra - Our World Series

Energy	20 MIN
Energy Alternatives	20 MIN
Environments	20 MIN
Food and people	20 MIN
Food in the environment	20 MIN
The Future	20 MIN
Non - Renewable Resources	20 MIN
Places Where People Live	20 MIN
Quality of Life	20 MIN
Renewable Resources	20 MIN

Dist - AITECH

Terra Sancta - a film of Israel 31 MIN
16mm / U-matic / VHS
Color (J H C)
LC 78-701740
Presents a view of Israel, a nation on the brink of war since its creation. Contrasts young Israel's vitality with the ruins and spirit of the Holy Land's past.
Geography - World; Religion and Philosophy
Dist - IFB **Prod** - UARIZ 1969

Terradynamics 21 MIN
16mm
Color (H C A)
LC FIE68-96
Explains that the Earth penetration program at Sandia Laboratories is concerned with determining the nature and composition of sub - surface soil using earth - penetrating, ballistic vehicles. Shows early experimentation, the evolution of the program, the delivery techniques and design of several penetration vehicles, plus a typical recovery operation and post - recovery analysis. Discusses the unique soil - motion studies conducted by the Terradynamics Division of Sandia.
Agriculture; Science - Natural
Dist - USERD **Prod** - USNRC 1968

Terrain investigation techniques 16 MIN
16mm
Color
LC FIA68-838
Describes preliminary engineering problems involved in choosing the best location for a new highway. Presents four techniques used to analyze terrain -- photo investigation, seismic refraction, electrical resistivity and confirmation borings.
Industrial and Technical Education; Social Science
Dist - OSUMPD **Prod** - OHIOSU 1967

Terrains 30 MIN
U-matic / VHS
Color
Presents three nude studies by Jeff Bush. Shows the video screen becoming a window upon image composition which shifts in response to contrasting contours.
Fine Arts
Dist - ARCVID **Prod** - ARCVID 1978

The Terrarium - classroom science 12 MIN
U-matic / VHS / 16mm
Color (P I)
LC FIA68-79
Explains that a terrarium is a small copy of part of the out - of - doors. Shows how to build two types of terraria -- a copy of an area where there is moss and sufficient water to sustain it and a copy of a desert area. Shows the kinds of plants and animals which can live in each terrarium.
Science; Science - Natural
Dist - PHENIX **Prod** - BEANMN 1967

Terre D'Alsace 12 MIN
16mm
Aspects De France Series
Color (H) (FRENCH)
A French language film. Explores Strasbourg and provides a close - up of a hard - working family of farmers.
Foreign Language
Dist - MLA **Prod** - WSUM 1966

Terremoto 28 MIN
16mm
Color
Depicts the aftermath of the earthquake in Guatemala and spotlights the assistance of the international organizations who sent help to the striken country.
Geography - World; History - World; Sociology
Dist - MTP **Prod** - SALVA

Terri - Birth 16
U-matic
Video birth library series
Color (J H G)
$100.00 purchase
Follows the childbirth experiences of Terri, 25, single, black, and having her third baby. Reveals that when she arrives at the hospital she is found to already be 8 cm dilated. Labor progresses very quickly and without complications. She delivers a little girl weighing almost 7 pounds. Shows an uncomplicated delivery with no medical intervention. Part of a 15 - part series on childbirth education.
Health and Safety
Dist - POLYMR **Prod** - POLYMR

The Terrible mother - part four 25 MIN
16mm
Oobieland series
Color (G)
$50.00 rental
Visits the kitchen of a Vermont farmhouse where four people have gathered in silence during the solstice to have a ritualized meal and tell a story. Relates their ominous tales yet, as in part one, they are incomplete. The Terrible Mother has passed her powers to a young woman who arrives to restore the old order. Touches on the oldest instincts of humanity, leaving the viewer saddened and scared by the knowledge that the world will never know freedom through the completion of action. Part four of a five - part series.
Fine Arts; Literature and Drama; Religion and Philosophy
Dist - CANCIN **Prod** - UNGRW 1972

The Terrible News 25 MIN
16mm
Color
LC 73-702382
Points out that the production of concentrated energy at fossil fuel plants generates concentrated wastes which alter the balance of the natural energy system. Focuses on Montana, offering examples of the tangible effects of industrial operations on their immediate surroundings.
Home Economics; Science - Natural
Dist - BITROT **Prod** - BITROT 1972

The Terrible Secret 47 MIN
U-matic / VHS / 16mm
Teenage Years Series
Color (I J H)
LC 79-700855
Tells how two teenagers experience fear and guilt when one becomes involved in a hit - and - run accident and the other cheats in order to win a tennis scholarship. Based on Hope Dahle Jordan's book Haunted Summer.
Guidance and Counseling; Literature and Drama; Sociology
Dist - TIMLIF

The Terrible tiles 15 MIN
U-matic / VHS
Dragons, wagons and wax - Set 1 series
Color (K P)
Shows how objects can be classified by a given property.
Science; Science - Physical
Dist - CTI **Prod** - CTI

Terrible Tuesday 23 MIN
U-matic / VHS / 16mm
Color (J A)
Portrays the devastating tornado which struck Wichita Falls, Texas in 1979. Reports the impressions of survivors, records the city's annual disaster drill, and features tornado footage. Discusses how to survive a tornado.
Geography - United States; History - United States; Science - Physical
Dist - USNAC **Prod** - NOAA 1984

Terrible Two's and Trusting Three's 22 MIN
16mm / U-matic / VHS
Color (H C A)
Views two - and three - year - old children in order to show how their behaviors and abilities develop.
Home Economics; Psychology
Dist - CRMP **Prod** - NFBC 1951

The Terrible Twos and Trusting Threes 21 MIN
U-matic / VHS / 16mm
Ages and Stages Series
Color (H C)
Presents a study of child behavior at two and three years of age, showing what to expect from youngsters of these ages and suggesting how parents can deal constructively with the problems they present.

Home Economics; Psychology; Sociology
Dist - MGHT **Prod** - NFBC 1951

A Terribly Strange Bed 24 MIN
VHS / U-matic
Orson Welles Great Mysteries Series
Color (I J C)
$89.00 purchase _ #3423
Presents a classic crime story in which a reckless young man patronizes a sleazy gambling house looking for excitement. Shows how he learns a sobering lesson after being convinced by a 'kindly' stranger to stay the night since he has had too much to drink. Written by Wilkie Collins.
Literature and Drama
Dist - EBEC

A Terribly Strange Bed 24 MIN
16mm / U-matic / VHS
Orson Welles Great Mysteries Series
Color (I J H C)
LC 75-702358
Tells a story about an organized band of criminals who operate a gambling house in the slums of Paris and their sinister method of reclaiming their losses and disposing of the winners. Televised on CBS in the Orson Wells Great Mystery Series.
Literature and Drama
Dist - EBEC **Prod** - ANGLIA 1975

Terrific brunches for 2 to 20 40 MIN
VHS
Everyday gourmet series
Color (A)
$19.95 purchase _ #KVC0097V-H
Demonstrates fast, easy, and delicious recipes and shows how to entertain with style without spending a lot of time, energy, or money. Offers practical suggestions on everything from shopping and hospitality to decorating and cleaning up.
Home Economics
Dist - CAMV

Terrific Brunches for Two to Twenty - a Delicious Way to Entertain Family and Friends 40 MIN
VHS
Color (C G A)
$14.95_KC203
Gives menu items for gatherings.
Home Economics; Sociology
Dist - AAVIM **Prod** - AAVIM 1989

Terrific, Teriffically 10 MIN
U-matic
Readalong Three Series
Color (P)
Provides reading instruction for third grade students. Uses animation, humor, music, repetition and audience participation. Comes with teacher's guide and kit.
Education; English Language; Literature and Drama
Dist - TVOTAR **Prod** - TVOTAR 1977

Terrific trips series
Presents an eight - part series on the community. Includes trips to the post office, a family farm, firehouse, zoo, a trip on a hot air balloon, a magic show, an aquarium and an amusement park.

A trip in a hot air balloon 14 MIN
A trip to a magic show 14 MIN
A trip to the amusement park 14 MIN
A trip to the aquarium 14 MIN
A trip to the farm 14 MIN
A trip to the firehouse 14 MIN
A trip to the post office 14 MIN
A trip to the zoo 14 MIN
Dist - CF **Prod** - LNMDP 1977

The Terrific Twos 15 MIN
U-matic / VHS
Color
Presents practical suggestions to parents experiencing the trying times of raising two year olds. Discusses the significance of a child's first rebellious and independent feelings.
Guidance and Counseling; Health and Safety; Sociology
Dist - PRI **Prod** - PRI 1986

Terrific twos 20 MIN
VHS
Training for child care providers series
Color (H A)
$89.95 purchase _ #CEVK20362V
Discusses how to provide care for two - year olds. Focuses on developing the child's self - esteem through the use of visual art, manipulatives, eating, cleaning up, putting away toys and creative play centers. Includes a leader's guide and reproducible study materials.
Health and Safety; Psychology
Dist - CAMV

Terrific twos 21 MIN
VHS
Color (H A T G)
$59.95 purchase _ #CV964
Illustrates how interactions between caregivers and energetic two- year-olds can enhance self-esteem through the use of visual art, manipulatives, eating, cleaning up, putting away toys and creative play centers. Emphasizes the importance of showing two year olds that they can accomplish simple tasks and develop an 'I can do it' attitude at an early age. Guide available separately.
Health and Safety; Psychology
Dist - AAVIM **Prod** - AAVIM

Terrines and Pates 29 MIN
Videoreel / VT2
French from the French Chef - French Series
Color
Features Julia Child of Haute Cuisine au Vin demonstrating how to prepare pates. With captions.
Foreign Language; Home Economics
Dist - PBS **Prod** - WGBHTV

The Territory 30 MIN
VHS
Color (A)
$525.00 purchase
Details the progression from friendly discussions between competitors to actual violations of fair business practices possible in companies' marketing plans. Illustrates through actual cases how such violations develop, are discovered and are prosecuted. Warns of the penalties of competition rigging.
Business and Economics; Civics and Political Systems; Education
Dist - COMFLM **Prod** - COMFLM

The Territory Ahead 60 MIN
U-matic / VHS
Spaceflight Series
Color
Studies current and future directions in space, including the unveiling of the first reusable space vehicle, the space shuttle, the first woman in space, Sally Ride, the rapid commercialization of space, the 'Star Wars' scenario and the growing militarization of space. Ends with an eye to the future, including N A S A's unmanned planetary program, and explores the possibilities of space stations, colonies, and traveling on to the stars.
Science - Physical
Dist - PBS **Prod** - PBS

Territory and space 30 MIN
U-matic / VHS
Art of being human series; Module 7
Color (C)
History - World; Literature and Drama; Religion and Philosophy
Dist - MDCC **Prod** - MDCC

Territory in Conflict 28 MIN
U-matic / VHS / 16mm
Color
Portrays the conflict between the people of a small Colorado mountain town and a huge corporation intent on mining one of the largest molybdenum deposits in the world.
Social Science
Dist - CEPRO **Prod** - CEPRO

Terror by Night 60 MIN
BETA
B&W
Tells how Holmes and Watson are hired to protect a huge diamond on a train trip to Scotland. Stars Basil Rathbone and Nigel Bruce.
Fine Arts
Dist - VIDIM **Prod** - UNKNWN 1946

The Terror of Anaphylaxis 14 MIN
VHS / U-matic
Color (PRO)
Describes the early and late signs and symptoms of an anaphylactic reaction. Differentiates airway obstruction due to bronchospasm from that due to upper airway obstruction. Details the proper treatment and lists the precautions which minimize the risk of a serious anaphylactic reaction.
Health and Safety
Dist - UMICHM **Prod** - UMICHM 1974

Terror - to Confront or Concede 52 MIN
16mm / U-matic / VHS
Color (C A)
LC 78-700520
Examines the question of whether nations should submit to terroristic blackmail. Includes interviews with Canadian and South American terrorists who discuss their political ambitions and terrorist tactics.
Sociology
Dist - FI **Prod** - BBCTV 1978

The Terror trade - buying the bomb 55 MIN
VHS
Color (H C G)
$150.00 purchase, $55.00 rental
Reports on the international black market in nuclear material. Interviews a Belgian arms trader who brokered illicit plutonium sales to aspiring nuclear powers throughout the Third World. Features Senator John Glenn, former President Jimmy Carter and the Director of the International Atomic Energy Agency. Coproduced by Claudia Milne.
Civics and Political Systems; Sociology
Dist - FLMLIB **Prod** - BWORLD 1989

Terror trail 20 MIN
16mm
B&W (G)
$25.00 rental
Pays homage to the old Western movies. Splices together footage from old films and pictures Gary Cooper, William Boyd, Tom Mix and more. Edited by Lyle Pearson.
Fine Arts; Literature and Drama
Dist - CANCIN **Prod** - PEARLY

Terrorism 21 MIN
U-matic / 16mm
CTV Reports Series
Color; Mono (J H C A)
$250.00 film, $250.00 video, $50.00 rental
Examines the problem of international terrorism and the steps being taken to prevent it in the future.
Sociology
Dist - CTV **Prod** - CTV 1978

Terrorism - the Russian Connection
VHS / U-matic
Color (J H C A)
$97.00 purchase _ #04563 94
Investigates the recruitment and training techniques of the PLO and other terrorist groups.
Sociology
Dist - ASPRSS

Terrorism - the World at Bay 119 MIN
VHS / U-matic
Color
Presents an investigation of the causes and effects of worldwide terrorism on people, governments, diplomacy and political decision - making.
Civics and Political Systems; Sociology
Dist - PBS **Prod** - WHYY 1978

Terrorist group profiles - Mac
CD-ROM
(G A)
$129.00 purchase _ #2841m
Contains detailed information, statistics and chronologies of some of today's most dangerous organizations. Includes group name, date formed, membership, headquarters, area of operation, leadership, sponsors, objectives, targets, background and chronology of terror incidents. For Macintosh Plus, SE and II Computers. Requires at least one M of RAM, one floppy disk drive, and an Apple compatible CD - ROM drive.
Civics and Political Systems; Computer Science
Dist - BEP

Terrorist group profiles - PC
CD-ROM
(G A)
$129.00 purchase _ #2841p
Contains detailed information, statistics and chronologies of some of today's most dangerous organizations. Includes group name, date formed, membership, headquarters, area of operation, leadership, sponsors, objectives, targets, background and chronology of terror incidents. For IBM and compatibles. Requires 640K RAM, DOS version 3.1 or greater, one floppy disk drive - a hard disk drive is recommended, one empty expansion slot, and and IBM compatible CD - Rom dirve.
Civics and Political Systems; Computer Science
Dist - BEP

Terrytoons Cartoon Series
The Heat's Off 7 MIN
Dist - TWCF

Tesla - the zenith factor 28 MIN
U-matic / VHS
Color (H C A)
$250.00 purchase, $50.00 rental
Examines the career of inventor Nikola Tesla. Tells how he helped bring in the electrical age by inventing fluorescent, neon, and strobe lighting, robotics, poly phase motors, laser beams, and the particle beam. Directed by Sky Fabin.
History - United States
Dist - CNEMAG

Tess 170 MIN
VHS
Color (H C)
$129.00 purchase _ #04564 - 126
Stars Nastassia Kinski and Peter Firth in a film version of the Thomas Hardy novel. Directed by Roman Polanski.
Fine Arts; Literature and Drama
Dist - GA **Prod** - GA

Tess Gallagher - 3 - 11 - 82 30 MIN
VHS / Cassette
Poetry Center reading series
Color (G)
$15.00 purchase, rental _ #479 - 407
Presents the writer reading her works at the Poetry Center, San Francisco State University.
Literature and Drama
Dist - POETRY **Prod** - POETRY 1982

Tesselations 20 MIN
VHS / U-matic
Shapes of Geometry Series Pt 4
Color (H)
LC 82-707390
Presents teachers Beth McKenna and David Edmonds investigating many aspects of tesselations including regular, semiregular and demiregular, as well as Islamic mosaics. Views transformational geometry by presenting Escher's tesselations and showing how to create them.
Mathematics
Dist - GPN **Prod** - WVIZTV 1982

Tesselations and Area - a Cover Up 20 MIN
16mm / U-matic / VHS
Mathscore One Series
Color (I J)
Discusses aspects of tesselations and area.
Mathematics
Dist - FI **Prod** - BBCTV

Tesselations and Area - Space Count 20 MIN
U-matic / VHS / 16mm
Mathscore Two Series
Color (I)
Discusses aspects of tesselations and area.
Mathematics
Dist - FI **Prod** - BBCTV

Tessellations 15 MIN
U-matic
Math Makers Two Series
Color (I)
Presents the math concepts of tessellations involving rectangles, squares and triangles.
Education; Mathematics
Dist - TVOTAR **Prod** - TVOTAR 1980

Tessellations
VHS
Math vantage videos series
Color (I J H)
$39.00 purchase _ #653803 - HH
Looks at geometric shapes. Part of a five - part series using interactive learning, interdisciplinary approaches, mathematical connections, student involvement and exploration to enable students to use patterns to explain, create and predict situations.
Mathematics
Dist - SUNCOM **Prod** - NEBMSI 1994

The Test 11 MIN
U-matic / VHS
Tests Series
Color (T)
Emphasizes the importance of helping students learn how to take standardized achievement tests. Gives tips for reducing trauma experienced by teachers and students on test day.
Education
Dist - AITECH **Prod** - WTVITV 1980

The Test and here comes the bride - Volume 5 45 MIN
VHS
Superbook series
Color (K P I R)
$11.99 purchase _ #35 - 86610 - 979
Uses an animated format to tell the story of Chris and Joy and their time travels through Biblical places and events. 'The Test' tells the story of Abraham, while 'Here Comes The Bride' tells the story of Rebecca.
Literature and Drama; Religion and Philosophy
Dist - APH **Prod** - TYHP

Test and Maintenance Equipment 60 MIN
VHS / U-matic
Air Conditioning and Refrigeration - - Training Series
Color (IND)
Covers gauge manifolds, temperature sensors, leak detection devices, vacuum pumps and suction line filter dryers.
Education; Industrial and Technical Education
Dist - ITCORP **Prod** - ITCORP

A Test Can Teach 10 MIN
U-matic / VHS / 16mm
Color (I J H)
LC FIA68-3155
Demonstrates that a returned teacher - graded test can be a useful educational tool and can be helpful in improving future test performance. Suggests specific techniques that will enable the student to review and to react to the returned test paper.
Education; Psychology
Dist - JOU **Prod** - ALTSUL 1968

Test instruments - megohmmeters - voltage testers - clamp - on ammeters 60 MIN
VHS / U-matic
Electrical maintenance basics series; Pt 3
Color (IND) (SPANISH)
Industrial and Technical Education
Dist - ITCORP **Prod** - ITCORP

Test instruments - miscellaneous - bridges - phase rotation - phase sequence, variable current tester 60 MIN
U-matic / VHS
Electrical maintenance basics - spanish series; Pt 4
Color (IND) (SPANISH)
Complete title reads Test Instruments, Pt 4 - Miscellaneous, Bridges, Phase Rotation, Phase Sequence, Variable Current Tester (Spanish). Provides instruction in electrical maintenance.
Foreign Language; Industrial and Technical Education
Dist - ITCORP **Prod** - ITCORP

Test instruments - multimeter use 60 MIN
U-matic / VHS
Electrical maintenance basics series; Pt 2
Color (IND) (SPANISH)
Industrial and Technical Education
Dist - ITCORP **Prod** - ITCORP

Test instruments - multimeters - basic circuits - movements 60 MIN
VHS / U-matic
Electrical maintenance basics series; Pt 1
Color (IND) (SPANISH)
Industrial and Technical Education
Dist - ITCORP **Prod** - ITCORP

A Test of faith and obedience and love at first sight - Volume 15 45 MIN
VHS
Superbook series
Color (K P I R)
$11.99 purchase _ #35 - 86776 - 979
Uses an animated format to tell the story of Chris and Joy and their time travels through Biblical places and events. 'A Test of Faith and Obedience' tells the story of Abraham and Isaac, while 'Love at First Sight' is an account of Isaac and Rebecca.
Literature and Drama; Religion and Philosophy
Dist - APH **Prod** - TYHP

A Test of Japanese management - Japanese cars made in the USA 45 MIN
VHS
Anatomy of Japan - wellsprings of economic power series
Color (H C G)
$250.00 purchase
Asks if Japanese - style management can be transferred to other countries. Focuses on a joint venture in Fremont, California by Toyota and General Motors. Part of a 10 - part series on the current relations between Japan and the world.
Business and Economics; Geography - World; History - United States
Dist - LANDMK **Prod** - LANDMK 1989

Test of Standard Written English 120 MIN
U-matic / VHS
SAT Exam Preparation Series
Color
Education; English Language
Dist - KRLSOF **Prod** - KRLSOF 1985

A Test of Violence 20 MIN
16mm
Color (H C A)
Presents a view of violence in contemporary society as visualized in the paintings of noted Spanish artist Juan Genoves.
Biography; Fine Arts; Sociology
Dist - UWFKD **Prod** - UWFKD

Test preparation series
Be prepared for the act 30 MIN
Be prepared for the S A T and the P S A T 30 MIN
Don't be afraid, it's only a test 16 MIN
Dist - CF

Test Preparation Video Series
Armed services exams 120 MINUTES
Civil service exams
Firefighter Exams
Math review for the A C T 120 MIN
Math Review for the GED 120 MINUTES
Math Review for the SAT - PSAT 120 MINUTES
Police officer exams
Post office exams
Review for the SAT 120 MINUTES
Verbal review for the A C T 120 MIN
Verbal Review for the GED 120 MINUTES
Verbal Review for the SAT - PSAT 120 MINUTES
Dist - CADESF

Test - Pt 1 29 MIN
Videoreel / VT2
Maggie and the beautiful machine - general shape - up series
Color
Physical Education and Recreation
Dist - PBS **Prod** - WGBHTV

Test - Pt 2 29 MIN
Videoreel / VT2
Maggie and the beautiful machine - general shape - up series
Color
Physical Education and Recreation
Dist - PBS **Prod** - WGBHTV

Test Taking 20 MIN
VHS / U-matic
Art of Learning Series
Color (H A)
Shows how to develop strategies to study for and take exams. Tells how to analyze test results.
Education
Dist - GPN **Prod** - WCVETV 1984

Test taking - GED series
VHS
Test taking - GED series
Color (H A)
$224.95 purchase _ #VA901SV-G
Presents a series of five videos that help students study for the GED high school equivalency test. Uses a test-taking instructor to guide viewer through every GED subject - writing skills, social studies, science, math and literature and the arts. Outlines what to expect on the test, how to prepare, and tips to getting a higher score. Each video 120-160 minutes in length.
Education; English Language; Fine Arts; Literature and Drama; Mathematics; Science; Social Science
Dist - CAMV

Test taking - SAT I series
VHS
Test taking - SAT 1 series
Color (H A)
$269.95 purchase _ #VA91XSV-G
Presents a series of five videos helping students study for the SAT scholastic aptitude test. Uses a test-taking instructor to guide viewer. Outlines what to expect on the test, how to prepare, and tips to getting a higher score. Each program 120-160 minutes in length.
Education
Dist - CAMV

Test taking - SAT I series
Mathematical reasoning - problem solving and grid - ins
Mathematical reasoning - quantitative comparisons
Tips, tricks, and traps
Verbal reasoning - analogies
Verbal reasoning - critical reading
Verbal reasoning - sentence completions
Dist - CAMV

Test taking - SAT 1 series
Test taking - SAT I series
Dist - CAMV

Test - Taking Skills - Effective Study Techniques
U-matic / VHS
Color (H)
Reviews skills that help students prepare for objective and essay test questions.
Education
Dist - GA **Prod** - GA

Test - Taking Skills - How to Succeed on Standardized Examinations 37 MIN
VHS / U-matic
Color
LC 81-706695
Shows how to relieve anxieties when taking standardized tests by preparing and becoming familiar with the types of questions on the test. Reviews mathematics problems, reading, antonyms, sentence completions, analogies and standard written English.

Education
Dist - GA Prod - CHUMAN 1981

Test Taking Strategies Activity Pack 90 MIN
VHS / U-matic
(J H)
Designed to guide students toward greater achievement on both teacher made and standardized tests. Excellent preparation for SATs and ACTs.
Education; Guidance and Counseling
Dist - WALCHJ **Prod** - WALCHJ 1985

Test - Tube Babies - a Daughter for Judy 57 MIN
16mm / U-matic / VHS
Nova Series
Color (H C A)
LC 83-700021
Looks at the intriguing science which has made it possible to conceive human babies outside the womb. Discusses the disturbing social issues it raises.
Health and Safety
Dist - TIMLIF **Prod** - WGBHTV 1982

Test tubes for the sea
U-matic / VHS / BETA
Search encounters in science series
Color; PAL (G H C)
PdS25, PdS33 purchase
Brings modern research efforts of the world's leading scientists into the classroom. Features one of a series of 24 mini - documentaries. Each film is 5 - 7 minutes in length.
Science; Science - Physical
Dist - EDPAT **Prod** - NSF

Test Tubes in the Sea 6 MIN
U-matic / VHS / 16mm
Color (J)
LC 79-701525
Focuses on an international team of scientists as they measure pollutants in the sea in an attempt to find out how much pollution the ocean can absorb.
Science; Science - Natural; Science - Physical; Sociology
Dist - AMEDFL **Prod** - NSF 1975

Test Your Suggestability 8 MIN
16mm
Professional Selling Practices Series 2 Series
Color (H C)
LC 77-702356
Demonstrates when and how to suggest related items and multiple quantities in making a sale. Shows how to determine what to suggest, how to make the suggestion specific, time the suggestion appropriately and explain additional purchase benefits to the customer.
Business and Economics
Dist - SAUM **Prod** - SAUM 1968

Test yourself - the hazard communication review 20 MIN
VHS
Color (IND)
$495.00 purchase, $95.00 rental _ #801 - 01
Reviews and reinforces employees' understanding of OSHA's Hazard Communication Standard, plus MSDSs and labels. Contains workplace vignettes for employees to evaluate, plus a self test.
Health and Safety; Psychology
Dist - ITSC **Prod** - ITSC

Testability and Producibility 180 MIN
U-matic
Electronics Testing, Quality/Reliability and Manufacturing Control 'Series
Color (IND)
Discusses elements of testability and producibility of printed circuit boards and components, including goals and methods, problems and solutions, programs, costs, and design impacts.
Business and Economics; Industrial and Technical Education
Dist - INTECS **Prod** - INTECS

Testament 20 MIN
16mm
Color (G)
$40.00 rental
Features Broughton discussing his role as a major figure in avant - garde film and poetry since the 1940s. Includes clips from earlier films.
Fine Arts; Literature and Drama
Dist - CANCIN **Prod** - BROUGH 1974

Testament
16mm
B&W; Color (G)
$70.00 rental
Introduces a film of a film which chronicles Berkeley between 1965 and 1966 and was later remade as The Death of Alex Litsky.
Fine Arts
Dist - CANCIN **Prod** - DEGRAS 1970

Testament
BETA / VHS
Color
Tells the story of a mother of three who struggles to keep her family together after a nuclear attack. Stars Jane Alexander and William Devane.
Civics and Political Systems; Science - Physical; Sociology
Dist - GA **Prod** - GA
ASPRSS

The Testament of Dr Mabuse 112 MIN
VHS
B&W (G)
$24.95 _ #TES020
Uses a sinister mood throughout this crime drama about an insane asylum inmate who plots to crush society in a wave of violence. Follows the devious Mabuse as he hypnotizes the hospital's director into carrying out his evil mission. Fritz Lang used the production to expose Hitler's monstrous intentions, as a result the film was banned in Germany and the director forced to flee the country.
Fine Arts; Psychology; Sociology
Dist - HOMVIS **Prod** - JANUS 1933

Testament of Orpheus 79 MIN
VHS
Orpheus trilogy series
B&W/Color (G)
$29.95 _ #TES010
Portrays an 18th - century poet who travels through time on a quest for divine wisdom and meets symbolic phantoms who bring about his death and resurrection. Features an eclectic cast including Yul Brynner and Pablo Picasso. The third in Cocteau's Orphic trilogy, which began with Blood of a Poet and continued in Orpheus.
Fine Arts; Literature and Drama; Sociology
Dist - HOMVIS **Prod** - JANUS 1960

Testament - the Bible and history series
As it was in the beginning 52 MIN
Chronicles and kings 52 MIN
Gospel truth 52 MIN
Mightier than the Sword 52 MIN
Paradise Lost 52 MIN
The Power and the Glory 52 MIN
Thine is the Kingdom 52 MIN
Dist - FOTH

Testicular Autotransplantation After Laparoscopic Localization 11 MIN
U-matic / VHS
Color (PRO)
Covers laparoscopy used to localize the nonpalpable testes in a one - year - old male and subsequent testicular autotransplantation performed to correct the high position of the child's testes and the short card.
Health and Safety; Psychology; Science - Natural
Dist - HSCIC **Prod** - HSCIC 1984

Testicular self - examination 11 MIN
VHS / U-matic
Cancer education series
Color (G C PRO)
$195.00 purchase _ #C920 - VI - 045
Provides a complete explanation of testicular cancer. Identifies individuals who are at risk for the disease - young men between 15 and 40 - the disease is rare in African - Americans and Asians. Discusses the importance of early detection of the disease through self - examination. Considers risk factors and signs and symptoms and demonstrates the self - examination procedure. Part of a four - part series presented by the University of Texas, MD Anderson Center.
Health and Safety; Sociology
Dist - HSCIC

Testicular Self Examination 8 MIN
U-matic
Color
Explains the importance of testicular self - examination and demonstrates the procedure.
Health and Safety
Dist - UTEXSC **Prod** - UTEXSC

Testifying in Court 9 MIN
8mm cartridge / 16mm
Color (H C A)
LC 75-701985
Helps police officers become acquainted with procedures for testifying in court. Discusses pretrial preparation, demeanor outside the courtroom and proper behavior on the witness stand.
Civics and Political Systems; Social Science
Dist - MCCRNE **Prod** - MCCRNE 1975

Testimony 17 MIN
16mm
B&W (G)
$20.00 rental
Reveals a cinema - verite portrait of a Pentecostal religious group in Athens, Ohio. Interviews several parishioners, looks at members giving public testimony in downtown Athens and counters with shots of dancing, preaching and singing in the church. Produced by Brian Patrick.
Fine Arts; Religion and Philosophy
Dist - CANCIN

Testimony of expert witnesses under the federal rules of evidence 51 MIN
VHS
The Art of advocacy - expert witnesses series
Color (C PRO)
$90.00 purchase, $67.50 rental _ #Z0110
Features law professor Abraham P Ordover in a discussion of pertinent rules for testimony of expert witnesses under the Federal Rules of Evidence.
Civics and Political Systems
Dist - NITA **Prod** - NITA 1988

Testimony of love and war and Some features of US chemical warfare in South Vietnam 36 MIN
16mm
B&W (G)
$60.00 rental
Looks at the effects of warfare upon the social order in two productions. Recounts a hypothetical rape occurring during the bombing of Hiroshima in the first film. The second is a restoration of a North Vietnam film of the same name from 1971 which was restored, duplicated and new soundtrack added. Documents the effects of Agent Orange, napalm and other defoliants.
Fine Arts; History - United States; Sociology
Dist - CANCIN **Prod** - SONDHE 1982

Testing 60 MIN
U-matic / VHS
Quality Assurance Series
Color (IND)
Explains various types of inspections and tests. Compares destructive and non - destructive tests. Covers tensile, bend torsion, impact and vibration, ultrasonic, dye penetrant and eddy current.
Business and Economics; Industrial and Technical Education
Dist - LEIKID **Prod** - LEIKID

Testing and individual therapy for aphasia 28 MIN
VHS / U-matic
Aphasia series
Color (PRO)
Shows tests for determining the nature and extent of an individual's aphasia. Follows retraining of aphasics from each category (motor, sensory and formulation).
Health and Safety; Psychology
Dist - WFP **Prod** - WFP

Testing - Assembled Boards 180 MIN
U-matic
Electronics Testing, Quality/Reliability and Manufacturing Control 'Series
Color (IND)
Discusses testing assembled printed circuit boards, including opens, shorts and in - circuit testing, static and dynamic functional testing, and special board testing methods.
Business and Economics; Industrial and Technical Education
Dist - INTECS **Prod** - INTECS

Testing Children with Multiple Handicaps 30 MIN
16mm
B&W (S)
Demonstrates the educational evaluation of preschool children with single and multiple handicaps. Illustrates the function of the multi - disciplinary team.
Education; Psychology
Dist - UCPA **Prod** - UCPA

Testing - Components and Bare Boards 180 MIN
U-matic
Electronics Testing, Quality/Reliability and Manufacturing Control 'Series
Color (IND)
Discusses all phases of electronics testing of components and bare boards, including testing equipment, techniques and processes.
Business and Economics; Industrial and Technical Education
Dist - INTECS **Prod** - INTECS

Testing Digital Circuits 28 MIN
VHS / 16mm
Digital Electronics Series
Color (H A)
$465.00 purchase, $110.00 rental
Explains the concepts in testing digital circuits.
Industrial and Technical Education
Dist - TAT **Prod** - TAT 1989

Testing dirty 47 MIN
VHS / U-matic
Color (J H)
$425.00, $395.00 purchase _ #V169
Looks at random drug testing. Shows how a student's good reputation has been ruined after a cold medicine results in

a false positive test when he is tested for drugs at school. Examines the ethics of random drug testing and its implications for the citizens of the United States.
Guidance and Counseling; Health and Safety; Psychology; Religion and Philosophy; Sociology
Dist - BARR **Prod** - ASSELI 1991

Testing Equipment and Approaches 29 MIN
Videoreel / VT2
Who is Man Series
Color
Features Dr Puryear and his guest Elmer Green (director of research on voluntary control, the Menninger Foundation) who discuss and demonstrate contemporary methods and modern sophisticated equipment developed for more precise measurement of ESP and related phenomena.
Psychology
Dist - PBS **Prod** - WHROTV

Testing Generator Output 4 MIN
16mm
Color
LC FI68-275
Points out the use of the tachometer and the proper reading of the ampmeter and voltmeter.
Industrial and Technical Education
Dist - RAYBAR **Prod** - RAYBAR 1966

Testing Headlight Aim 4 MIN
16mm
Color
LC FI68-276
Shows steps taken before adjusting headlight aim. Demonstrates the method of fixing the meter bulb, points out different parts and shows how to align the headlights.
Industrial and Technical Education
Dist - RAYBAR **Prod** - RAYBAR 1966

Testing Irradiated Steel 16 MIN
16mm
Color
Shows the performance of crack arrest tests on steel specimens after they have been irradiated. Includes shots of the actual irradiation and the remote handling techniques made necessary by the radioactivity of the specimens.
Industrial and Technical Education; Science - Physical
Dist - UKAEA **Prod** - UKAEA 1964

Testing Multiple Means - AOV
U-matic / VHS
Statistics for Managers Series
Color (IND)
Defines this testing as a way of making comparisons of two or more products. Discusses Completely Randomized and Randomized Block Design. Illustrates use of the LSD test to determine which means are different.
Business and Economics; Mathematics; Psychology
Dist - COLOSU **Prod** - COLOSU

Testing multiply handicapped children 30 MIN
16mm
B&W
LC FIA67-1280
Illustrates techniques for evaluating children with multiple disabilities. Shows case studies of three children -- one with a severe cerebral palsy condition and a related speech problem, another with severe visual and auditory impairments and a third who is hyperactive - distractible with mental retardation. Emphasizes the importance of the examiner being adaptible and flexible.
Education; Psychology
Dist - UCPA **Prod** - UCPA 1963

Testing New Waters 57 MIN
VHS / 16mm
(I A)
$75.00 rental
Documents a decade of dealing with pollution in the Niagra river. Considers the interests of industry and government in both the United States and Canada, and explains complex concepts emerging in the national hazardous waste agenda. In three parts for schools. With teacher's guide.
Science - Natural; Social Science; Sociology
Dist - BULFRG

Testing - None of the Above 33 MIN
16mm
Color (C A)
LC 78-701450
Presents a school counselor as she looks at several aspects of standardized tests. Examines the effect of test scores on teacher expectations, the scarcity concept of education, and the validity of test items.
Education; Psychology
Dist - UWISC **Prod** - UWISC 1978

Testing Objectives 30 MIN
U-matic / VHS
Eager to Learn Series
Color (T)
Education; Psychology
Dist - KTEHTV **Prod** - KTEHTV

Testing of antimicrobial agents - coagulase and antibody reactions 29 MIN
VHS / U-matic
Color
Includes two presentations on one tape number 6206. Presents basic techniques employing filter paper discs to determine antimicrobial effectiveness of disinfectants/antiseptics and antibiotics/sulfonamides. Identifies land measures zones of inhibition and considers factors influencing the size of such zones.
Science; Science - Natural
Dist - AVMM **Prod** - AMSM

Testing 1 - 2 - 3 25 MIN
U-matic
Not Another Science Show Series
Color (H C)
Explains how sound is reproduced on records, tapes and digital machines.
Industrial and Technical Education; Science
Dist - TVOTAR **Prod** - TVOTAR 1986

Testing Proportions
U-matic / VHS
Statistics for Managers Series
Color (IND)
Defines as a formalized to decision making involving go/no - go data. Uses normal approximation to test one - and two - sample proportions, while the chi - square is used to test one or more proportions.
Business and Economics; Mathematics; Psychology
Dist - COLOSU **Prod** - COLOSU

Testing, Symbolic Execution and Formal Verification 30 MIN
U-matic / VHS
Software Engineering - a First Course Series
Color (IND)
Concludes discussion of current issues in program - testing. Covers symbolic execution and relationship of testing to formal verification.
Industrial and Technical Education; Mathematics
Dist - COLOSU **Prod** - COLOSU

Testing, Tension and Competition 25 MIN
U-matic / VHS
Color (J H C A)
Interviews Dr Slack and Dr Porter of Beth Israel Hospital in Boston about their criticism of the emphasis placed on standardized testing in high school. Discusses their belief that the Scholastic Aptitude Test in particular provokes anxiety and that the results often leava negative mark on a student's self - esteem.
Education; Psychology; Sociology
Dist - GERBER **Prod** - SIRS

Testing the Multiply Handicapped Children, Millicent 30 MIN
16mm
B&W
Depicts the testing of Millicent, age four and one - half who is hyperactive, distractable and mentally retarded.
Education; Psychology
Dist - UCPA **Prod** - UCPA

Testing the Waters 57 MIN
U-matic / VHS / 16mm
Color (H)
$375.00, $350.00 purchase, $75.00 rental
Considers the future of the Niagara River, which is threatened by toxic chemical wastes. Reveals that the area around Niagara Falls has the largest concentration of leaking hazardous waste dumps in North America. Examines the competing interests of industry and the citizens and governments of the United States and Canada.
Business and Economics; Geography - United States; Geography - World; Science - Physical; Social Science; Sociology
Dist - BULFRG **Prod** - LCORC 1988

Testing the Waters 30 MIN
VHS / 16mm
Marketing Series
Color (C A)
$130.00, $120.00 purchase _ 15 - 10
Features the service strategy used aboard the SS Azure Seas.
Business and Economics
Dist - CDTEL **Prod** - COAST 1989

Testing water systems 30 MIN
VHS
Firefighter II - III video series
Color (G PRO)
$145.00 purchase _ #35246
Demonstrates how to test and read water flow pressures and determine discharge capacities for water systems. Shows how to predict hydrant usability and determine the causes of friction loss in water mains. Throroughly views the technical aspects of water supply systems for training firefighters.
Health and Safety; Industrial and Technical Education; Psychology; Science - Physical; Social Science
Dist - OKSU **Prod** - OKSU

Testing - What's it all about?
U-matic / VHS
Vital Link Series
Color (A)
Provides information to parents about testing experiences children undergo during their elementary and secondary schooling.
Guidance and Counseling; Psychology; Social Science; Sociology
Dist - EDCC **Prod** - EDCC

Testis, Epididymis, VasDeferens, Ampulla 330 MIN
VHS / 16mm
Histology review series; Unit XIII
(C)
$330.00 purchase _ #821VI057
Covers anatomy, functions and histological organization of the testis, epididymis, vas deferens, and ampulla. Part 1 of the Male Reproductive System Unit.
Health and Safety
Dist - HSCIC **Prod** - HSCIC 1983

Testmaster - ACT video review 120 MIN
VHS
Color (J H)
$109.00 purchase _ #RN1000V
Conducts an intensive review of all four sections of the ACT test, including Math, Vocabulary, Grammar, Reading Comprehension and Science. Includes a diagnostic pretest based on questions similar to actual test questions, as well as a study guide and a teacher's guide.
Education
Dist - CAMV

Testport 29 MIN
16mm
Color
LC 74-706593
Describes the mission and services of the Naval Air Test Center in Patuxent River, Maryland.
Industrial and Technical Education
Dist - USNAC **Prod** - USN 1971

Tests and Stress 12 MIN
U-matic / VHS
Making it Work Series
Color (H A)
Reveals that Susan, Alan and Lucy are all nervous about the typing test. Explains that Susan doesn't listen or ask for instructions, Alan arrives late and is tired, hungry and hostile while Lucy has practiced at home, listens carefully, asks questions and does well.
Guidance and Counseling; Psychology
Dist - AITECH **Prod** - ERF 1983

Tests for qualitative data - proportions 30 MIN
U-matic / VHS
Engineering statistics series
Color (IND)
Uses normal and Chi - Square tests for determining if goals are met (a specific proportion defective) or for comparison of several production lines or procedures.
Industrial and Technical Education; Mathematics; Psychology
Dist - COLOSU **Prod** - COLOSU

Tests Series
Know the Score 11 MIN
Teacher - made Tests 11 MIN
The Test 11 MIN
Tests, Tests, Tests 11 MIN
Dist - AITECH

Tests, Tests, Tests 11 MIN
VHS / U-matic
Tests Series
Color (T)
Explains the purpose of tests and looks at the differences among the various types of tests.
Education
Dist - AITECH **Prod** - WTVITV 1980

Tet, 1968 60 MIN
U-matic / VHS / 16mm
Vietnam - a television history series; Episode 7
Color (H C A)
Shows that one of the big turning points in the war in Vietnam came when the Americans thought they were winning but were actually in a stalemate. Reveals that on the Tet holiday, attacks came in areas the U S thought to be secure, including Saigon. States that the defeats caused second thoughts in Washington that eventually resulted in President Johnson's decision to call a partial bombing halt.

History - United States; History - World
Dist - FI **Prod** - WGBHTV 1983

Tet, 1968 and Vietnamizing the war, 1969 - 1973 - Volume 4 120 MIN
VHS
Vietnam - a television history series
Color (H C A)
$14.95 purchase
Presents the seventh and eighth episodes of a 13 - part series covering the history of the Vietnam War. Includes the episodes 'Tet, 1968' and 'Vietnamizing The War, 1969 - 1973.'
History - United States
Dist - PBS **Prod** - WNETTV

Tet - Volume 4 120 MIN
VHS
Vietnam - a television history series
Color (G)
$29.95 purchase _ #S01530
Consists of two 60 - minute episodes examining the US involvement in Vietnam - 'Tet' and 'Vietnamizing the War.' Covers the years from 1968 to 1973.
History - United States
Dist - UILL **Prod** - PBS

Tetanus Prophylaxis and Management 25 MIN
16mm
Color (PRO)
Explains that tetanus is a dire, but completely preventable disease. Depicts aspects of tetanus treatment and prevention.
Health and Safety; Science
Dist - ACY **Prod** - ACYDGD 1965

Teton - Decision and Disaster 58 MIN
VHS / 16mm
Color (G)
$70.00 rental _ #DOCS - 114
Examines the Teton Dam collapse of 1976. Includes footage of the disaster and interviews the victims.
Agriculture; Science - Natural
Dist - PBS

Tetralogy of Fallot 30 MIN
16mm
Color (PRO)
Presents a review of the embryonic development of the heart and examines the Blalock - Taussig and Potts - Smith surgical procedures for correcting Tetralogy of Fallot.
Health and Safety; Science - Natural
Dist - SQUIBB **Prod** - SQUIBB

Tevye 96 MIN
16mm / 35mm
B&W (G) (YIDDISH WITH ENGLISH SUBTITLES)
Adapts Sholem Aleichem's play which deals with intermarriage. Centers on Khave, daughter of the dairyman Tevye, who falls in love with Fedye, the son of a Ukrainian peasant. Her courtship and marriage pit Tevye's love for his daughter against his deep - seated faith and loyalty to tradition. Contact distributor for rental fee. Also available in 35mm.
Religion and Philosophy; Sociology
Dist - NCJEWF

Tevye - Tevye der Milkhiker 96 MIN
VHS
Maurice Schwartz films series
B&W (G) (YIDDISH WITH ENGLISH SUBTITLES)
$89.95 purchase _ #742
Adapts the Sholom Aleichem story. Tells how Tevye's daughter falls in love with and marries a gentile, placing Tevye's paternal affection in conflict with his deep commitment to religious tradition. Stars Maurice Schwartz who also directs. Features Miriam Riselle and Leon Liebgold.
Literature and Drama; Sociology
Dist - ERGOM **Prod** - ERGOM 1939

Tex 26 MIN
16mm / U-matic / VHS
Film as Literature, Series 4 Series; Series 4
Color (J H)
LC 82-700736
Offers an abbreviated version of the motion picture Tex about the coming of age of a 15 - year - old boy in rural Oklahoma who must deal with family conflicts, peer pressure, emotional instability, and experimentation with sex and drugs. Based on the novel TEX by S E Hinton.
Fine Arts; Literature and Drama
Dist - CORF **Prod** - DISNEY 1982

Tex
VHS / U-matic
Adolescent Literature Series
Color (G C J)
$89.00 purchase _ #04565 - 85
Follows the life of a teenager coming of age in a small Texas town. Stars Matt Dillon and Meg Tilly. Based on the novel by S.E. Hinton.
Fine Arts; Literature and Drama
Dist - CHUMAN

Tex - Mex accordion 70 MIN
VHS
Color (G)
$39.95 purchase _ #VD - FLO - AC01
Features accordionists Flaco Jimenez and Tim Alexander with special guest Max Baca on bajo - sexto. Shows how to play the main dance forms of Tex - Mex music in note - for - note detail on G - C - F three - row accordions. Allows even beginners to master tunes such as La Napolera, La Piedrera, Atotonilco, Viva Seguin, La Tuna, La Paloma and Flor Marchita. Teaches the importance of grace notes, trills, bellows shaking, hammer - ons, glissandos and more.
Fine Arts
Dist - HOMETA **Prod** - HOMETA

The Texaco - Pennzoil case - is a handshake a deal 30 MIN
U-matic
Adam Smith's money world 1985 - 1986 season series; 223
Color (A)
Attempts to demystify the world of money and break it down so that a small business and its employees understand and adjust to new social and economic trends. Reports on the major economic stories and discoveries of 1985 and 1986.
Business and Economics
Dist - PBS **Prod** - WNETTV 1986

Texane Ceskeho Puvodu - the Czech Texans 7 MIN
Slide / VHS / U-matic
Ethnic Studies Series
Color; Mono (J H)
Biography; History - United States; Sociology
Dist - UTXITC **Prod** - UTXITC 1971

Texas 15 MIN
16mm / U-matic / VHS
United States expansion series
Color (J H)
$420.00, $250.00 purchase - _ #5764C
Discusses the conflicts with the Indians and Mexico, and the important men who shaped the history of Texas. A Donald Klugman Communication production.
History - United States
Dist - CORF

Texas 60 MIN
VHS
Portrait of America series
Color (J H C G)
$99.95 purchase _ #AMB43V
Visits Texas. Offers extensive research into the state's history. Films key locations and presents segments on its history, government, education, folklore, science, journalism, sociology, industry, agriculture and business. Shows what is unique about Texas and what is distinctive about its regional culture and how it got to be that way. Includes teacher study guides. Part of a 50 - part series.
Geography - United States; History - United States
Dist - CAMV

Texas
VHS / U-matic
Portrait of America Series
Color
Presents five segments about the state of Texas, a vast and sprawling land that brings to mind images of cowboys, wide open spaces, oil rigs, millionaires and the magic of myth and legend.
Geography - United States; History - United States
Dist - TBSESI **Prod** - TBSESI

Texas and its Natural Resources 27 MIN
16mm
Color
Describes the magnitude of Texas mineral and energy resources. Also discusses agriculture, cattle and sheep raising, transportation facilities, and climate. Made in co - operation with the Texas Gulf Sulphur Co.
Geography - United States; Science - Natural
Dist - USDIBM **Prod** - USDIBM 1955

Texas and the American Revolution 10 MIN
U-matic / VHS / Slide
Texas military history series
Color; Mono (J H)
Describes Texas's limited participation in American Revolution and the impact of the Revolution on Spanish Texas and Texas history.
History - United States; Social Science; Sociology
Dist - UTXITC **Prod** - UTXITC 1976

Texas Indians series
The Alabama Coushatta Indians 8 MIN
The Indian Texans 8 MIN
The Tigua Indians - Our Oldest Texans 8 MIN
Dist - UTXITC

Texas - instant 40 MIN
VHS
Architecture at the crossroads series
Color (A)
PdS99 purchase _ Unavailable in Europe
Examines the main themes running through the world of architecture. Demonstrates how pop-up cities show the 21st century in the making. The fifth program in a ten-part series.
Fine Arts; Industrial and Technical Education
Dist - BBCENE

Texas Military History Series
The Mexican Texans to 1865 10 MIN
Texas and the American Revolution 10 MIN
Dist - UTXITC

Texas, Virgin Islands, Holland 27 MIN
16mm
Big Blue Marble - Children Around the World Series Program O; Program O
Color (P I)
LC 76-700627
Portrays a minicycle contest in Texas, a salt pond in the Virgin Islands and a circus school in Holland. Relates a folk tale from Bulgaria about a spoiled girl.
Geography - United States; Geography - World; Literature and Drama; Social Science
Dist - VITT **Prod** - ALVEN 1975

The Texas Wiretap Law 15 MIN
U-matic
Color (H C A)
LC 82-707074
Explains Texas' 1981 wiretap law that allows state law enforcement officers to tap phones to determine drug - related offenses. Interviews with an undercover narcotics agent and an attorney provide comparisons of this law with those in other states. Discusses privacy and surveillance techniques.
Civics and Political Systems; History - United States
Dist - SWINS **Prod** - SWINS 1981

Text editor - Part I 30 MIN
U-matic / VHS
UNIX Series
Color (IND)
Explains editor command line, addressing, search capability, and editor commands - ed, p, a, i, c, u, and q.
Industrial and Technical Education; Mathematics; Sociology
Dist - COLOSU **Prod** - COLOSU

Text editor - Part II 30 MIN
VHS / U-matic
UNIX series
Color (IND)
Goes into file backup, file recovery, and editor commands - d, s, m, t, j, w, e, f, and r.
Industrial and Technical Education; Mathematics; Sociology
Dist - COLOSU **Prod** - COLOSU

Text of light 73 MIN
16mm
Color; Silent (C)
$1680.00
Presents an experimental film by Stan Brakhage.
Fine Arts
Dist - AFA **Prod** - AFA 1974

Textile Art 15 MIN
VHS / U-matic
Young at Art Series
Color (P I)
Discusses textile art.
Fine Arts
Dist - AITECH **Prod** - WSKJTV 1980

Textile Design Series
Batik 10 MIN
Tie Dye 16 MIN
Weaving with Looms You Can make 16 MIN
With Fabric and Thread 15 MIN
Dist - AIMS

Textile Industry 3 MIN
16mm
Of all Things Series
Color (P I)
Discusses the textile industry.
Business and Economics; Home Economics
Dist - AVED **Prod** - BAILYL

Textile Printing 29 MIN
Videoreel / VT2
Exploring the Crafts - Silk Screen Printing Series

Color
Fine Arts; Home Economics
Dist - PBS **Prod** - NHN

Textile studies series
Explores the origins of man-made and natural fiber; the processes of spinning, weaving, printing, dyeing, and finishing; and the uses of different textiles in everyday life. Shows designers conceptualizing new clothing, new fibers being introduced, and how color is introduced to fabrics. A five-part series.

Clothes talk	20 MIN
Fashion makers	20 MIN
The Right stuff	20 MIN
Riot of colour	20 MIN
Spinning a yarn	20 MIN
Textile studies series	100 MIN

Dist - BBCENE

Textile Testing using the Instron 22 MIN
U-matic / VHS
Measuring the Performance of Textiles - Textile Testing Series no 2
Color (C A)
LC 81-707150
Offers basic examples of textile testing using the Instron to execute ASTM standard test procedures. Includes four test procedures, tensile properties of fabrics, tear strength of woven fabrics, tensile properties of fibers and compression testing of carpets.
Home Economics; Industrial and Technical Education; Science
Dist - CORNRS **Prod** - CUETV 1981

Textile Testing using the Instron 16 MIN
VHS / 16mm
Measuring the Performance of Textiles - Textile Testing Series
(C A PRO)
$125.00 purchase, $16.00 rental
Gives basic examples of textile testing using the Instron to execute ASTM Standard test procedures. Includes such procedures as - tensile properties of fabrics, tear strength of woven fabrics, tensile properties of fibers. Interprets each of the stress - strain diagrams.
Business and Economics; Industrial and Technical Education; Science
Dist - CORNRS **Prod** - CORNRS 1981

Textiles 20 MIN
VHS
Color (H C G)
$120.00 purchase _ #DE143V
Covers fabrics, yarns and fibers. Examines the Textile Fibers Products Identification Act, fiber content, generic names and brand names. Discusses and shows examples of natural fibers such as cotton, flax, silk and wool. Looks at artificial fibers such as rayon and polyester. Includes script, discussion questions and unit quiz.
Industrial and Technical Education
Dist - CAMV

Textiles 29 MIN
VHS / 16mm
Villa Alegre Series
Color (P T)
$46.00 rental _ #VILA - 103
Presents educational material in both Spanish and English.
Education; Industrial and Technical Education
Dist - PBS

Textiles 21 MIN
VHS / 16mm
Manufacturing Materials Series
Color (I)
LC 90713865
Investigates the creation and use of natural and synthetic fibers. Focuses on their use in clothing.
Business and Economics; History - World; Home Economics
Dist - BARR

Textiles and Ornamental Arts of India 12 MIN
16mm / U-matic / VHS
Color (H C A)
LC 79-706837
Records an exhibition of East Indian arts and crafts shown by the museum of modern art in New York in 1955. Motion is created by using the metric - cutting film technique.
Fine Arts; Geography - World
Dist - EBEC **Prod** - EAMES 1955

Textiles and Ornamental Arts of India 11 MIN
U-matic / 8mm cartridge
Color (J C H)
$59.00 purchase _ #3189
Combines color, sound, texture, poetry and rhythm in an interpretation of an exhibition at the Museum of Modern Art. Shows intricately woven and embellished textiles, jewelry, brightly painted dolls. Reflects Indian tradition and philosophy and explores the spiritual significance that relates art to everyday life.
Fine Arts
Dist - EBEC **Prod** - EBEC

Texture 15 MIN
VHS / U-matic
Arts Express Series
Color (K P I J)
Fine Arts
Dist - KYTV **Prod** - KYTV 1983

Texture in Drawing - 17 15 MIN
VHS
Drawing with Paul Ringler Series
Color (I)
$125.00 purchase
Shows how three kinds of texture describe an object and how distance affects the appearance of texture. Emphasizes the drawing process, for older students, rather than drawing specific objects. Part of a thirty - part series.
Fine Arts
Dist - AITECH **Prod** - OETVA 1988

Texture - Program 5 15 MIN
U-matic
Artscape Series
Color (I)
Shows children entering a magic texture tent where they learn what texture is and how to use it in creating art.
Fine Arts
Dist - TVOTAR **Prod** - TVOTAR 1983

Textures and Shapes 15 MIN
U-matic
Is the Sky Always Blue Series
Color (P)
LC 80-706688
Explores the texture and shapes of objects with the purpose of stimulating young children to use their tactile and visual perceptions in the creation of graphic designs and compositions. Introduces basic geometric shapes and shows their texture through rubbings, which children can make and use to create their own designs.
Fine Arts
Dist - GPN **Prod** - WDCNTV 1979

Textures of the Great Lakes 6 MIN
16mm
Creative Motivational Series
Color (J H C)
LC FIA66-769
Presents an artistic interpretation of the textural qualities of the waters, beaches, dunes and woods of the Great Lakes region. Synchronizes visual images with harp accompaniment.
Fine Arts; Geography - United States
Dist - LOH **Prod** - LOH 1966

Texturing Clay 28 MIN
Videoreel / VT2
Wheels, Kilns and Clay Series
Color
Features Mrs Peterson describing certain ceramic processes for her classroom at the University of Southern California. Demonstrates how to texture clay.
Fine Arts
Dist - PBS **Prod** - USC

TGIS - thank goodness it's Shabbat - a guide to Sabbath traditions 28 MIN
VHS
Jewish home video series
Color (G) (RUSSIAN)
$29.85, $34.95 purchase _ #841, #841R
Portrays a man delayed on the train ride home one Friday afternoon who recalls for his wife his childhood memories of visits with his uncle and aunt on Shabat. Stars Theodore Bikel as the uncle. Includes study guide. Part of a three - part series on Jewish holidays and observance produced by WJUF of Chicago.
Religion and Philosophy; Sociology
Dist - ERGOM

Thai Images of the Buddha 14 MIN
16mm
Arts of the Orient Series
Color; B&W (H C A)
Uses ancient statuary from the arts of Thailand exhibit to show the transformation of the Buddha image from that of revered teacher to that of a supreme diety. Discusses the historical course of Buddhism.
Fine Arts; Religion and Philosophy; Sociology
Dist - IU **Prod** - IU 1963

Thailand 25 MIN
U-matic / VHS / 16mm
Untamed world series series
Color; Mono (J H C A)
$400.00, $250.00 purchase, $50.00 rental
Reveals the ancient arts, social traditions, and the physical geography of Thailand.
Geography - World; Sociology
Dist - CTV **Prod** - CTV 1969

Thailand 13 MIN
16mm
New Horizons Series
Color
Shows the hundreds of canals which crisscross the countryside of Thailand and run through the city of Bangkok carrying 80 percent of the bustling internal traffic.
Geography - World; Social Science
Dist - PANWA **Prod** - TWCF

Thailand 28 MIN
Videoreel / VHS
International Byline Series
Color
Interviews Ambassador Birabhongse Kasemri, permanent representative of Thailand to the United Nations. Discusses the people and attractions of Thailand. Includes two film clips of Thailand.
Business and Economics; Civics and Political Systems; Geography - World
Dist - PERRYM **Prod** - PERRYM

Thailand 10 MIN
VHS
People living in other lands
Color; PAL (P I J H)
Visits Thailand, a flat country in the tropical zone. Reveals that there is a wide network of rivers and much flooding, even in the capital of Bangkok. The country is extremely fertile and a large exporter of rice. Buddhism is the dominant religion. Part of a series of eight films selecting a place with a particular climate and geography and describing the life of the inhabitants.
Geography - World; History - World; Religion and Philosophy; Science - Natural
Dist - VIEWTH **Prod** - VIEWTH

Thailand 51 MIN
VHS
Asian insight series; Part 6
Color (S)
$79.00 purchase _ #118 - 9017
Introduces the people and the cultures of the Asian Pacific. Presents a balanced, objective interpretation of the region's history. Illuminates past and present social structure, mores, beliefs, art and architecture to give a well - rounded look at this newly influential area. Part 6 of six parts examines Thai society through the history of Buddhism and the Thai monarchy. Thailand is different from its neighbors in that the majority of its people are Buddhists and Thailand has never known colonial rule.
Geography - World; History - World; Religion and Philosophy
Dist - FI **Prod** - FLMAUS 1987

Thailand - Ally Under Fire 20 MIN
16mm
Screen news digest series; Vol 9; Issue 7
B&W
Discusses various aspects of Thailand, such as its history, economy, agriculture, aid from the United States and commitment in Vietnam.
Civics and Political Systems; Geography - World; History - World
Dist - HEARST **Prod** - HEARST 1967

Thailand - Bicentennial 27 MIN
U-matic / VHS
Color (H C A)
Presents Thailand celebrating the bicentennial of its Royal Family - the Chakri dynasty. Examines the history of the dynasty as well as the social, political and economic problems facing contemporary Thailand.
Geography - World; History - World
Dist - JOU **Prod** - JOU

Thailand - convicts of the sea 48 MIN
VHS
Jacques Cousteau II series
Color; CC (G)
$19.95 purchase _ #3049
Sails into the Gulf of Siam with Cousteau and his crew to examine the effects of tin mining and overfishing on the sea floor surrounding Thailand. Reveals that they find an uncharted coral reef and explore its wonders. Part of a six - part series by Cousteau.
Geography - World; Industrial and Technical Education; Science - Natural
Dist - APRESS

Thailand - land of freedom 16 MIN
U-matic / VHS / BETA
Color; PAL (G H C)
PdS40, PdS48 purchase
Tours exotic Bangkok, cosmopolitan Pattaya and resort areas near the border with Burma. Highlights fishing and tin mining on the islands of the Isthmus of Kra as well as traditional village life. Includes the lowlands; the annual elephant roundup; Buddhism and religious ceremonies.
Fine Arts; Geography - World
Dist - EDPAT **Prod** - POLNIS

Thailand - Land of Smiles 27 MIN
U-matic / VHS / 16mm
Color (J)
LC 77-700797
Presents traditional aspects of the culture of Thailand. Discusses the geography, emphasizing the importance of water for travel and agriculture. Shows dances, festivals, handicrafts and the influence of religion on Thailand's culture.
Geography - World; Sociology
Dist - CORF **Prod** - CFDLD 1977

Thailand - Life Along the Khlongs 22 MIN
16mm / U-matic / VHS
Color
Looks at the life of a family who lives along the canals or Khlongs of Thailand. Views the family's morning swim, their trip to a floating market, their water school bus and their water festival.
History - World
Dist - HANDEL **Prod** - HANDEL 1983

Thailand - the golden kingdom 60 MIN
VHS
Asian collection series
Color (J H C G)
$29.95 purchase _ #IVN364V-S
Teaches about the people, culture and history of Thailand. Visits historic buildings, monuments and landmarks. Examines the physical topography of the kingdom. Part of a seven-part series on Asian countries, cities and islands. Also part of a larger series entitled Video Visits that travels to six continents.
Geography - World; History - World
Dist - CAMV **Prod** - WNETTV

Thailand Today 16 MIN
U-matic / VHS / 16mm
Color (J H) (SWEDISH)
LC 81-700692;
Describes traditions and life styles in Thailand.
Geography - World
Dist - IFB **Prod** - WOVIEN 1980

Thanatopsis 6 MIN
16mm
B&W
LC 75-703239
Presents a somber study of the ornamented steps, windows, doors and elaborately designed railings and trimmings of an old deserted house about to be demolished.
Industrial and Technical Education; Psychology; Social Science; Sociology
Dist - USC **Prod** - USC 1965

Thanatos 9 MIN
VHS
Color & B&W; Silent (G)
$30.00 purchase
Confronts death in the form of a 600 - year - old female skeleton. Uses image processing and digitilizing to rework the configuration of visuals and text into a postmodern context. Combines a live performance with quotations from poetry and visuals from Druer's woodcuts.
Fine Arts; Literature and Drama; Sociology
Dist - CANCIN **Prod** - BARHAM 1990

Thanh 9 MIN
16mm
Rebop Series
Color (I J H)
LC 79-700477
Introduces Pham Thanh, a 15 - year - old refugee from Vietnam who tells his classmates of the tragedy of seeing American soldiers destroy his village and kill his mother, father and grandmother. Relates his daily struggle to deal with the loneliness, fear and depression that have been part of his life since he was airlifted out of Vietnam.
Guidance and Counseling; History - World; Sociology
Dist - IU **Prod** - WGBHTV 1979

Thanh's war 58 MIN
VHS
Color (H C G A)
$195.00 purchase, $50.00 rental _ #38085
Tells the story of Pham Thanh, a remarkable Vietnamese - American whose family was killed when he was 12 by a US grenade that also blew his throat apart. Reveals that Thanh was rescued by US soldiers and taken to American where he built a new life. Tells Thanh's courageous and poignant story as he grapples with the emotional legacy of the war and attempts to make his way in two vastly different cultures. Produced by Elizabeth Farnsworth for KQED San Francisco.
History - United States; History - World; Sociology
Dist - UCEMC

Thank God and the Revolution 50 MIN
16mm / U-matic / VHS
Color (H C A)
LC 82-700188
Focuses on the role of organized religion in the Nicaraguan guerrilla movement. Shows members of the Roman Catholic clergy serving as government officials and various Nicaraguans as they testify to the inspirational and unifying force of Christianity in the revolutionary struggle and reforms in Nicaragua.
History - World; Religion and Philosophy
Dist - ICARUS **Prod** - TERCIN 1981

Thank God and the Revolution 55 MIN
16mm
Color
$645 rental
Examines the bond between socialist communities and the church in Nicaragua. Describes cooperative efforts for social and economic reform.
History - World; Religion and Philosophy; Sociology
Dist - CCNCC **Prod** - CCNCC 1985

Thank god I'm a lesbian 55 MIN
VHS / 16mm
Color (G)
$90.00, $140.00 rental, $295.00 purchase
Documents the diversity in the lives of several lesbians. Entertains with uplifting and frank discussions on issues ranging from coming out, racism and bisexuality to the evolution of the feminist and lesbian movements. Proposes an alternate vision of self and community that is realistic and positive. Edited by Geraldine Peroni; film by Laurie Colbert and Dominique Cardona.
Fine Arts; History - World; Sociology
Dist - WMEN

Thank Heaven 3 MIN
16mm
Color (H C A)
Uses animation to tell of a new recruit from earth who makes some very surprising discoveries about God's plumbing.
Literature and Drama
Dist - UWFKD **Prod** - UWFKD

Thank you Allah - 6
VHS
Adam's world series
Color (P I J)
$19.95 purchase _ #110 - 052
Features the puppet character Adam who teaches educational concepts about Islam and Muslims to children. Tells about shukr, or being grateful to Allah. Shows how the prospect of becoming very rich brings Adam face to face with the concept of thanking God in word and deed. Visits Morocco. Adam, the Wonder Journalist, looks for people who thank Allah for His blessings, a story from the Quran about shukr, a segment on the importance of zakat, an animated segment on the letter 'tha,' a rendition of the famous 'Allah, there's only One God' song by Yusuf Islam.
Religion and Philosophy
Dist - SOUVIS **Prod** - SOUVIS

Thank you for calling - effective telephone techniques 30 MIN
VHS
Clerical skills series
Color (H C G)
$79.95 purchase _ #CCP0037V
Teaches entry level employees how to conduct themselves on the phone and how to handle all types of business telephone communications in two parts. Shows how to deal with a host of incoming calls including proper procedures for answering the telephone, taking messages, screening calls and handling irate callers in the first part. The second part presents steps for placing calls, including a brief look at the telephone directory, local and long distance calls, efficient use of the telephone and more. Includes workbook. Part of a series on clerical skills.
Guidance and Counseling; Psychology; Social Science
Dist - CAMV **Prod** - CAMV 1991

Thank You, Jesus, for the Eternal Present Part I 5.5 MIN
16mm
Color; B&W (C)
$398.00
Experimental film by George Landow (aka Owen Land).
Fine Arts
Dist - AFA **Prod** - AFA 1973

Thank You, Jesus, for the Eternal Present Part II 11.5 MIN
16mm
Color (C)
$465.00
Experimental film by George Owen (aka Owen Land).
Fine Arts
Dist - AFA **Prod** - AFA 1974

Thank You M'am 12 MIN
16mm / U-matic / VHS
Color (I J H)
LC 76-703956
Presents an adaptation of the short story Thank You M'am by Langston Hughes about an older Black woman who makes a Black youth pay the consequences for trying to steal her pocketbook.
Fine Arts; Literature and Drama; Sociology
Dist - PHENIX **Prod** - SUGERA 1976

Thank you, m'am and a father like that 30 MIN
VHS
Color (K P I J)
$89.00 purchase _ #S01101
Presents two stories about boys. 'Thank You, M'am,' based on a Langston Hughes short story, tells how a young boy who tries to steal an old woman's purse ends up learning a valuable lesson. Charlotte Zolotow's 'A Father Like That' finds a boy named Greg having to write a school essay about his father, who he has never seen. Shows that Greg ends up writing about the father he would like to have.
Literature and Drama; Sociology
Dist - UILL **Prod** - PHENIX
PHENIX

Thank you, masked man 8 MIN
16mm
Color (G)
Presents a animated short film created by Jeffrey Hall and Lenny Bruce.
Fine Arts; Literature and Drama
Dist - KINOIC

Thank you, Mr President 45 MIN
VHS
Color (G)
$19.95 purchase _ #S00050; $34.95 purchase
Presents the wit and wisdom of John F Kennedy as shown in excerpts from his bi - weekly press conferences. Provides JFK's unique perspectives on issues including U S - Soviet relations, nuclear war, and women's rights. Narrated by E G Marshall.
Biography; History - United States
Dist - UILL **Prod** - WNETTV 1984
PBS

Thank you, Poles - Dziekujemy wam Polacy 95 MIN
VHS
Color; B&W (G A) (POLISH)
$29.95 purchase _ #V109
Presents the history of General Maczek Brigade based on archival documents, photos and films from World War II, and his unique relationship with officers of the 1 Pancer Division.
Fine Arts; History - World
Dist - POLART

Thank you, thank you
VHS
Bippity boppity bunch series
Color (K P I R)
$14.95 purchase _ #35 - 819 - 8579
Portrays Maxine, who forgets to thank her friends for throwing her a surprise birthday party. Teaches the importance of gratitude.
Literature and Drama; Religion and Philosophy
Dist - APH **Prod** - FAMF

Thankfulness - 27 8 MIN
VHS / U-matic
Life's little lessons - self - esteem K - 3 - series
Color (K P)
$129.00, $99.00 _ #V626
Tells about Gracy and Greta, identical twin sister singing act, except that Gracy was grateful and Greta was grumpy. Shows how grumpiness almost ruined their careers. Part of a 30 - part series on self - esteem.
Guidance and Counseling; Psychology
Dist - BARR **Prod** - CEPRO 1992

Thanks a' Plenty Boss Series
The Correct Way of Correcting 24 MIN
The Rewards of Rewarding 24 MIN
Dist - RTBL

Thanks - but no Thanks - Peer Pressure 15 MIN
VHS / 16mm
Your Choice - Our Chance Series
Color (I A)
$180.00 purchase, $25.00 rental
Dramatizes the intensity of peer pressure and the difficulty of resisting it. Demonstrates that self - esteem and a sense of responsibility provide a foundation for resisting this pressure.
Health and Safety; Psychology
Dist - AITECH **Prod** - AITECH 1990

Thanks, but no Thanks - Peer Pressure -5 15 MIN
VHS
Your Choice - Our Chance Series
Color (I)
$180.00 purchase
Focuses on knowledge, attitudes and behaviors that influence drug free and drug use life styles. Emphasizes that effective drug abuse prevention education must begin before children are established users of tobacco, alcohol or other addictive drugs. Targets children in the vulnerable preteen years. Program 5 tells of Lenora, who, before entering junior high, joins friends at the mall. Some of her 'friends' want to involve her in shoplifting, smoking and drinking.
Guidance and Counseling; Health and Safety; Psychology; Sociology
Dist - AITECH **Prod** - AITECH 1990

Thanks for the memories 30 MIN
VHS
America in World War II - The home front series
Color (G)
$49.95 purchase _ #AWWH - 108
Shows how Americans, increasingly uneasy at the number of war casualties, turned to popular entertainment for relief. Highlights the efforts of celebrities such as Bob Hope and Dinah Shore in performing USO shows both at home and abroad. Reviews military developments, including MacArthur's return to the Philippines, the German V - 2 bomb, and the Soviets' conquest of Warsaw. Narrated by Eric Sevareid.
History - United States
Dist - PBS

Thanks for the Memory 24 MIN
BETA / VHS / 16mm / U-matic
Color; Stereo
Shows 'Sam Nesia' a salesman who has the world's worst memory. After an office mishap, he dreams he meets Tracey, who is in charge of his memory. Through this dream the workings of Sam's brain are demonstrated. Sam then applies the techniques of memory retention he learned in the dream after he wakes up. A program to improve memory skills.
Business and Economics; Computer Science
Dist - SEVDIM **Prod** - SEVDIM 1984

Thanks for the Memory 14 MIN
U-matic / VHS
Funny Business Series
Color
Business and Economics; Psychology
Dist - DELTAK **Prod** - LCOA

Thanks for the One Time 45 MIN
U-matic / VHS / 16mm
Color (J H A)
LC 81-706000
Presents the story of an alcoholic physician who can't bring himself to admit that he has a drinking problem. Illustrates the techniques of intervention in order to help the alcoholic take the first step toward help.
Health and Safety; Psychology; Sociology
Dist - LCOA **Prod** - SHANDA 1981

Thanks girls and goodbye 51 MIN
VHS / 16mm
Color (G)
$450.00, $900.00 purchase, $100.00, $80.00 rental
Documents the history of the Australian Women's Land Army during World War II which was created to reverse the shortage of 'man' - power during the war. Presented by Sue Maslin and Sue Hardisty.
Geography - World; History - United States; Sociology
Dist - WMENIF **Prod** - WMENIF 1988

Thanks to You 13 MIN
16mm
Color
LC 77-700422
Tells the story of Sharon, a child inflicted with cystic fibrosis and gives brief glimpses of others helped by United Fund contributions.
Health and Safety; Psychology; Sociology
Dist - CPTCO **Prod** - UFCMD 1976

Thanksgiving 15 MIN
U-matic / VHS
Draw Along Series
(K P)
$125.00 purchase
Focuses on drawing faces by locating the features. A Pilgrim man and woman are drawn.
Fine Arts
Dist - AITECH **Prod** - AITECH 1983

Thanksgiving
VHS
Why We Celebrate - Video Series
Color (P)
$39.95 purchase
English Language; Literature and Drama; Religion and Philosophy; Social Science
Dist - PELLER

Thanksgiving 10 MIN
VHS
Color (K P I)
$69.95 purchase _ #10011VG
Presents the story of Thanksgiving Day through a historically accurate reenactment. Gives facts on harvest festivals around the world. Shows some of the games children may have played at the first Thanksgiving. Includes a guide.
Civics and Political Systems; Religion and Philosophy; Social Science
Dist - UNL

Thanksgiving 5 MIN
16mm
Color
LC 75-703438
Presents a story about a plucked and ready - to - cook turkey that suddenly drops off the stove and attempts to escape.
Literature and Drama; Social Science
Dist - CANFDC **Prod** - CANFDC 1974

Thanksgiving - 10 15 MIN
VHS
Draw man series
Color (I)
$125.00 purchase
Demonstrates developing an illustration by arranging people, settings and costumes. Focuses on Thanksgiving. Features Paul Ringler, the 'Draw Man,' as instructor. Part of 'The Draw Man' Series.
Fine Arts; Religion and Philosophy
Dist - AITECH **Prod** - KOKHTV 1975

Thanksgiving Day 15 MIN
VHS
America's special days series
Color (K P) (SPANISH)
$23.95 purchase
Looks at the background of the first Thanksgiving Day to explain reasons behind Americans' celebration. Shows how families gather to remember many things to be thankful for. Looks at different ethnic foods and how various cultures celebrate, along with visits with homeless people and different types of families.
Civics and Political Systems; Social Science
Dist - GPN **Prod** - GPN 1993

Thanksgiving Dinner
BETA / VHS
Video Cooking Library Series
Color
Demonstrates Thanksgiving recipes such as baked turkey, dressings, vegetables and pies.
Home Economics; Social Science
Dist - KARTES **Prod** - KARTES

Thanksgiving in Peshawar 17 MIN
VHS / U-matic
Color
LC 84-706401
Presents a documentary by Kirk Douglas on his visit to Afghan refugee camps near Peshawar, Pakistan. Reviews the history of Afghanistan and discusses the Soviet invasion, emphasizing the plight of the refugees.
Geography - World; History - World; Sociology
Dist - USNAC **Prod** - USIA 1983

Thanksgiving - let's draw 15 MIN
U-matic / VHS
Let's draw series
Color (P)
Fine Arts
Dist - AITECH **Prod** - OCPS 1976

Thanksgiving Recipes 29 MIN
VHS / 16mm
Holiday Chef Series
Color (G)
$55.00 rental _ #HLDC - 001
Features restaurant owner and chef Jim Haller preparing a Thanksgiving meal.
Home Economics
Dist - PBS **Prod** - NHMNET

Thanksgiving - the Pilgrims 14 MIN
Videoreel / VT2
Muffinland - Holiday Specials Series
Color
Literature and Drama; Social Science
Dist - PBS **Prod** - WGTV

Thanksgiving - the Things I Like Best 14 MIN
Videoreel / VT2
Muffinland - Holiday Specials Series
Color
Literature and Drama; Social Science
Dist - PBS **Prod** - WGTV

Thanos and Despina 96 MIN
16mm
B&W (C A) (GREEK (ENGLISH SUBTITLES))
Shows the battle between the sexes, classes and generations in contemporary Greece. With English subtitles.
Foreign Language; Sociology
Dist - GROVE **Prod** - GROVE

That Certain Thing 70 MIN
16mm
B&W
Tells how a rich boy is disinherited when he marries the girl who works in a cigar store. Shows what happens when the young couple launches their own thriving business and causes the boy's father to reconsider. Directed by Frank Capra.
Fine Arts
Dist - KITPAR **Prod** - CPC 1928

That Cold Day in the Park 105 MIN
U-matic / VHS / 16mm
Color (C A)
Stars Sandy Dennis and Michael Burns. Describes what ensues when a 32 - year - old Canadian spinster finds a handsome young hippie in the park on a cold rainy day, brings him in, gives him a bath and offers him a place to stay.
Fine Arts
Dist - FI **Prod** - UNKNWN 1969

That Fabulous Face 4 MIN
16mm
Color; B&W (I)
LC 78-714215
An art film which presents a series of black and white photographs of a Negro woman using dramatic movements to music by Chopin and then converts the photographs with special graphic effects and color painting - in techniques.
Fine Arts
Dist - ZINNJ **Prod** - ZINNJ 1971

That Feeling of Falling 9 MIN
16mm
Color
LC 76-703439
Discusses product improvements that can prevent stairway falls, glass door accidents and bathtub slips and falls. Suggests handrails on stairways, handgrips on bathroom walls and slip - resistant surfaces on stairways.
Guidance and Counseling; Health and Safety
Dist - USNAC **Prod** - USCPSD 1976

That fellow Shakespeare 78 FR
VHS
Color (H G)
$27.50, $29.95 purchase _ #P - F37, P - M205
Tells the life story of William Shakespeare through colorful drawings and humorous narrative. Lists his plays with brief comments on each. Filmstrip includes cassette soundtrack and script.
Biography; English Language; Literature and Drama
Dist - CONDS

That Funny Fat Kid 24 MIN
U-matic / 16mm / VHS
Color (K)
$495.00, $349.00, $249.00 purchase _ #AD - 1536
Portrays an overweight teenager who decides he is tired of being the classroom clown. Shows that Tony borrows his sister's diet pills with serious consequences.
Literature and Drama; Psychology; Sociology
Dist - FOTH **Prod** - FOTH

That Good Old Harmony 29 MIN
U-matic
Song Writer Series
Color
Shows how harmony fits into song writing.
Fine Arts
Dist - UMITV **Prod** - UMITV 1977

That Hamilton Woman 125 MIN
U-matic / VHS / 16mm
B&W
Stars Laurence Olivier as Lord Nelson and Vivien Leigh as his paramour.
Fine Arts
Dist - FI **Prod** - UNKNWN 1941

That it may Never Die - a Record of the Chattooga River 28 MIN
16mm
Color (I J H C)
Presents the story of one of the last free flowing unpolluted rivers in the southeastern United States and explains how it is being preserved in its natural state.
Geography - United States; Science - Natural
Dist - GCCED **Prod** - GCCED 1972

That little bit different 50 MIN
VHS
Signs of the times series
Color (A)
PdS99 purchase
Takes viewers 'through the keyhole' into ordinary late 20th-century homes in Britain to see what people's perceptions of good and bad taste really are. Explores how matters of taste may serve as indicators of social status. Part five of a five-part series.
Fine Arts; Home Economics; Industrial and Technical Education
Dist - BBCENE

That Long Night in '43 110 MIN
U-matic / VHS / 16mm
B&W (A) ((ENGLISH DUBBING))
Presents a wartime tale of a Fascist massacre of partisans. English dubbed version.
Civics and Political Systems; Fine Arts; History - World
Dist - CNEMAG **Prod** - CNEMAG 1960

That Makes Two of Us 44 MIN
VHS / U-matic
Color (A)
Presents story of relationship of two deaf people, one from an oral background and the other from a sign language background. Signed.
Education; Guidance and Counseling; Psychology
Dist - GALCO **Prod** - GALCO 1982

That March Incident 4 MIN
16mm
B&W
LC 80-701267
Illustrates the nuclear power plant accident at Three Mile Island in Pennsylvania and the effect it had on the area's inhabitants.
History - United States
Dist - TEMPLU **Prod** - VINBKS 1980

That obscure object of desire 104 MIN
VHS
Color (G)
$29.95 purchase _ #OBS010
Follows a genteel widower who becomes obsessed with his sexy but elusive maid. Blends satire and surrealism while creating a twist when two actresses alternate as the coquette who humiliates her suitor continually.
Fine Arts; Literature and Drama; Psychology
Dist - HOMVIS **Prod** - JANUS 1977

That Old Time Religion - 210 30 MIN
U-matic
Currents - 1985 - 86 Season Series
Color (A)
Examines the resurgence of fundamentalism in America and the political power such groups are trying to wield.
Religion and Philosophy; Social Science
Dist - PBS **Prod** - WNETTV 1985

That Others may Live - the Mission of the Air Rescue Service 22 MIN
16mm
Color
LC FIE63-325
Points out the ability and dedication of the Air Rescue Service (ARS) in saving imperiled civilians. Explains how ARS, with its top - flight capsule recovery teams, is geared to the space age.
Civics and Political Systems; Health and Safety
Dist - USNAC **Prod** - USDD 1963

That our children will not die 60 MIN
VHS
Color (G)
Examines three different community - based approaches to the delivery of primary health care services in culturally and geographically distinct regions of Nigeria. Reveals that Nigeria, with over 75 million people, is the most populous state in sub - Saharan Africa. Despite the fact that it is among the most richly endowed in natural, mineral and oil resources and has rapidly modernized, Nigeria continues to have one of the highest mortality rates in the world, particularly among children and mothers. Most of the health problems involved are preventable, such as malnutrition and infection, fever, diarrhea and coughs, by simple cures administered by non - professionals.
Geography - World; Health and Safety
Dist - DOCEDR **Prod** - CHOPRA

That our children will not die - Pt 1 30 MIN
16mm
Color
LC 78-701501
Shows primary health care services in various parts of Nigeria which use specially trained community health workers and nurses in an expanded role.
Sociology
Dist - DOCEDR **Prod** - FDF 1978

That Rhythm, those Blues 58 MIN
VHS
American Experience Series
Color (H)
$9.50 rental _ #60945, VH
Documents the establishment of rhythm and blues as a uniquely American art form during the 1940s and 1950s. Depicts racial tensions and the many one - night stands endured by black singers who hoped to star in the Apollo, a Harlem theater which featured the best black singers in the nation. Third installment of the American Experience Series.
Fine Arts; History - United States
Dist - PSU **Prod** - PBS

That Rhythm, those Blues 60 MIN
VHS / 16mm
American Experience Series
Color; Captioned (G)
$59.95 purchase _ #AMEX - 110
Recounts the history of black rhythm - and - blues singers who performed in warehouses, tobacco barns, movie theaters and halls as steps toward the recognition of appearing at the Apollo Theatre on 125th Street in Harlem. Interviews singer Ruth Brown who recalls Jim Crow laws in the South during the '40s and '50s. Part of an ongoing series which highlights personal stories behind the historic events of America. Produced by WGBHTV, WNETTV and KCETTV.
Fine Arts; History - United States; Sociology
Dist - PBS

That the Deaf may Speak 42 MIN
16mm
Color
Studies the problems of the deaf child. Describes the parents' reaction when they learn their child is deaf. Traces the training and development of a deaf child from nursery school to the eighth grade.
Education; Psychology; Sociology
Dist - CFDC **Prod** - LSFTD 1951

That the Last be the Best 28 MIN
16mm
Color
LC 74-705768
Reports on initiatives of the Conference on Aging and shows film clips of President Nixon as he addresses the final session on December 2, 1971.
Health and Safety; Sociology
Dist - USNAC **Prod** - USSRS 1971

That these Things Shall not be Forgotten 30 MIN
U-matic
Herodotus - Father of History Series
Color
Discusses Herodotus' view that while facts are important, what they tell about human behavior is more important.
History - World
Dist - UMITV **Prod** - UMITV 1980

That they may Learn 30 MIN
16mm
Color (T)
LC 75-702929
Uses examples from Navajo Indian schools to show how Title I funds are to be used in assisting students from low income families to reach the educational goals established for them.
Education; Social Science
Dist - AVED **Prod** - USBIA 1975

That Uncertain Paradise 58 MIN
16mm
Color (H C A)
LC 74-703250
Examines conditions in the United States Trust Territory of the Pacific Islands, or Micronesia. Explores the native cultures of the islands, describes the history of the area and discusses its governmental system, its political future and its relationship with the United States.
Geography - World; History - World
Dist - WGTV **Prod** - WGTV 1974

That uncertain paradise - Pt 1 29 MIN
16mm
Color (H C A)
LC 74-703250
Examines conditions in the United States Trust Territory of the Pacific Islands, or Micronesia. Explores the native cultures of the islands, describes the history of the area and discusses its governmental system, its political future and its relationship with the United States.
Civics and Political Systems; Geography - World; Sociology
Dist - WGTV **Prod** - WGTV 1973

That uncertain paradise - Pt 2 29 MIN
16mm
Color (H C A)
LC 74-703250
Examines conditions in the United States Trust Territory of the Pacific Islands, or Micronesia. Explores the native cultures of the islands, describes the history of the area and discusses its governmental system, its political future and its relationship with the United States.
Civics and Political Systems; Geography - World; Sociology
Dist - WGTV **Prod** - WGTV 1973

That War in Korea 79 MIN
U-matic / VHS / 16mm
Color (J H C)
LC FIA66-1838
Uses newsreel footage to present an overview of the Korean conflict, the first unified international action against aggression. Commentary by Richard Boone.
History - United States; History - World
Dist - FI **Prod** - NBCTV 1966

That war in Korea - Pt 1 39 MIN
U-matic / VHS / 16mm
Color (J H C)
LC FIA66-1838
Uses newsreel footage to present an overview of the Korean conflict, the first unified international action against aggression. Commentary by Richard Boone.
History - World
Dist - FI **Prod** - NBCTV 1966

That war in Korea - Pt 2 40 MIN
16mm / U-matic / VHS
Color (J H C)
LC FIA66-1838
Uses newsreel footage to present an overview of the Korean conflict, the first unified international action against aggression. Commentary by Richard Boone.
Dist - FI **Prod** - NBCTV 1966

That We may Serve 28 MIN
16mm
Color
Presents the story of the supply service of the Department of medicine and surgery of the VA. Discusses its program of quality control so that thousands of professional and support personnel may better serve their veterans.
Sociology
Dist - USVA **Prod** - USVA 1960

That which is between 8 MIN
VHS
Color (G)
$200.00 purchase, $50.00 rental
Explores native American spirituality and the process of living with AIDS day - to - day. Includes cuts of Indian healing ceremonies. Produced by Mona Smith, a Lakota videomaker, and Nan Toskey.
Health and Safety; Religion and Philosophy; Social Science; Sociology
Dist - WMEN

The Thatch of night 10 MIN
16mm
Color (G)
$224.00 purchase, $20.00 rental
Offers homage to Marie Menken's Notebooks.
Fine Arts
Dist - CANCIN **Prod** - BRAKS 1990

Thatching 15 MIN
U-matic / VHS / 16mm
Color (I J H)
LC 74-707289
Depicts a seasoned worker at the Plymonth plantation in Massachusetts using authentic tools and techniques to thatch the roof of a newly constructed cottage. Covers all the steps of thatching which usually take one man from eight to ten weeks to complete.
History - United States; Psychology; Social Science
Dist - IFB **Prod** - PLIMOT 1970

That's a Killer 15 MIN
U-matic
Workers at Risk Series
(A)
Depicts the short and long term effects of occupational accidents and the hazard of work related disease.
Health and Safety
Dist - ACCESS **Prod** - ACCESS 1982

That's all We Need 16 MIN
16mm
Magnificent 6 and 1/2 Series
Color (I J)
Presents the 'six and a half' gang who decide to erect an old hut as headquarters for an 'adventure playground' on some local wasteland without anticipating the confusion in store with the demolition gang and the police.
Fine Arts
Dist - LUF **Prod** - CHILDF 1972

That's black entertainment 60 MIN
VHS
Color (H C A)
$29.95 purchase
Presents a sampling of the films created by the underground black film industry during the 1930s and 1940s. Stars include Paul Robeson, Lena Horne, Sammy Davis Jr, Nat King Cole, and others.

History - United States
Dist - PBS **Prod** - WNETTV

That's Bluegrass 56 MIN
16mm
Color (I)
LC 79-700459
Examines Bluegrass Music as a unique form of American music and culture. Interviews musicians who made contributions to the growth of this musical form and shows them performing the songs that made them famous.
Fine Arts
Dist - MNTFLM **Prod** - MNTFLM 1979

That's business series
The Accounting process 27 MIN
Accounts receivable 34 MIN
The Balance sheet 21 MIN
Cash flow forecasting 30 MIN
Financing Growth 34 MIN
Profit Forecasting 30 MIN
Dist - OWNMAN

That's Debatable 30 MIN
U-matic
Speakeasy Series
(J H)
Shows a formal high school debate with teams of two speakers complete with affirmatives and negatives, mutual cross examinations and rebuttals. Explains debate strategies and conduct.
English Language
Dist - ACCESS **Prod** - ACCESS 1981

That's entertainment 132 MIN
VHS
Color (G)
$59.95 purchase _ #S01223
Presents a collection of nearly 100 scenes from MGM musicals. Features numbers by Fred Astaire, Bing Crosby, Gene Kelly, Peter Lawford, Clark Gable, Jimmy Durante and more.
Fine Arts
Dist - UILL

That's entertainment part 2 126 MIN
VHS
Color (G)
$29.95 purchase _ #S01224
Presents a sequel to the 1974 film 'That's Entertainment.' Includes musical, comedy and drama scenes from classic MGM films. Features performances by John Barrymore, Clark Gable, Greta Garbo, the Marx Brothers, W C Fields, Judy Garland and many others. Hosted by Fred Astaire and Gene Kelly, who perform a few song - and - dance numbers of their own.
Fine Arts
Dist - UILL

That's incredible - New Orleans 15 MIN
U-matic / VHS
Color
Uses the familiar format of television's 'That's Incredible' show to take a look at the variety of ways parents can get involved in their kids' education.
Education; Sociology
Dist - NOVID **Prod** - NOVID

That's just how I feel - a lesson on emotions 11 MIN
VHS
Lessons from the heart - taking charge of feelings series
Color (I)
$89.95 purchase _ #10165VG
Presents the idea that all feelings, good and bad, are valid. Shows young children methods of understanding and handling emotions. Uses interviews, graphics, and dramatic vignettes to guide children to an acceptance of complex feelings. Comes with a teacher's guide, discussion topics and two blackline masters. Part one of a four - part series.
Guidance and Counseling
Dist - UNL

That's Life Series
The Great debate 29 MIN
Is Anybody Listening 29 MIN
It's OK to be Angry 29 MIN
Kids are People, Too 29 MIN
Make Up Your Mind 29 MIN
A New Life 29 MIN
So You Live by Yourself 29 MIN
Turn Yourself on 29 MIN
Who Am I 29 MIN
You are not Alone 29 MIN
A Zest for Living 29 MIN
Dist - PBS

That's life special series
Fire safety 45 MIN
Dist - BBCENE

That's me 9 MIN
16mm
Amazing life game theater series
Color (K)
LC 72-701742
Encourages a child to take a look at himself and the world around him. Allows him to identify with the grown - up world and everyday activities.
Guidance and Counseling; Psychology
Dist - HMC **Prod** - HMC 1971

That's Mine 15 MIN
16mm
Color (K P)
LC 76-703640
Uses games, dramatizations and candid camera interviews with children to explain the concepts of individual ownership, responsibilities of group ownership and causes and solutions of conflict over possessions.
Guidance and Counseling
Dist - MALIBU **Prod** - TAPDEM 1976

That's My Bike 12 MIN
16mm / U-matic / VHS
Learning Laws - Respect for Yourself, Others and the Law Series
Color (I)
Tells the story of Lawrence, an industrious teenager who is tempted by a friend to move some stolen merchandise, but refuses. Shows him finding an honest way to make money, even after his bike is stolen.
Civics and Political Systems; Guidance and Counseling; Psychology
Dist - CORF **Prod** - DISNEY 1982

That's My Name - Don't Wear it Out 26 MIN
16mm / U-matic / VHS
Color (P)
LC 76-701755
Tells the story of troublesome but sensitive adolescent who befriends a deaf youngster. Shows how both boys mature from this relationship, the older boy becoming less wary of involvement and the younger boy learning to push beyond the limitations of this handicap.
Education; Guidance and Counseling; Psychology
Dist - LCOA **Prod** - OECA 1976

That's My Name - Don't Wear it Out 26 MIN
U-matic / VHS / 16mm
Color; Captioned (P) (SPANISH)
Tells the story of a troublesome adolescent who befriends a deaf youngster.
Fine Arts; Foreign Language; Psychology
Dist - LCOA **Prod** - OECA 1977

That's Nice 3 MIN
16mm
Color (I)
Presents a sensitive cinepoem of a merry - go - round ride, emphasizing the abstract imagery latent there.
Fine Arts; Literature and Drama
Dist - CFS **Prod** - CFS 1968

That's no tomato, that's a work of art 30 MIN
U-matic / VHS
Creativity with Bill Moyers series
Color (H C A)
States that the tomato is one of America's favorite vegetables, with the average American consuming 50 pounds or more each year. Tells how a great deal of creative effort is still being poured into producing more profitable and valuable tomatoes.
Agriculture; Fine Arts; Psychology
Dist - PBS **Prod** - CORPEL 1982
DELTAK PBS

That's not fair 30 MIN
VHS
Quigley's village series
Color (K P I R)
$19.95 purchase, $10.00 rental _ #35 - 85 - 2504
Features Mr Quigley and his puppet friends. Portrays Danny, Bubba and Spike as they fight over a watermelon they grew together. Shows Mr Quigley and Doc teaching the importance of sharing. Produced by Jeremiah Films.
Literature and Drama; Religion and Philosophy
Dist - APH

That's not me they're talking about 30 MIN
U-matic
Color
Looks at the presentation of women in TV, movies, advertising, music, fashion and the visual arts, decodes the images and examines the connections between them and women's lives. Discusses the problems created by these images along with suggestions for improving the portrayal of women in the media.
Sociology
Dist - WMENIF **Prod** - WMENIF

That's not My Job 26 MIN
8mm cartridge / U-matic / 16mm / VHS
Color; B&W; Captioned (PRO) (NORWEGIAN SWEDISH DUTCH JAPANESE)
LC fia67-645; FIA67-645
Discusses the importance of training each employee of a large organization to understand his role and his relationship to other employees. Demonstrates that cooperative effort contributes to the end product or service of the group.
Business and Economics; Foreign Language; Psychology; Sociology
Dist - RTBL **Prod** - RTBL 1967

That's not my problem 8 MIN
VHS
Color; CC (G PRO)
$295.00 purchase, $145.00 rental
Uses animation to teach employees to acknowledge problems and act on them before they get out of hand. Shows what results from people not taking responsibility for situations. Includes support materials.
Business and Economics; Psychology
Dist - AMEDIA **Prod** - AMEDIA 1993

That's Our Baby 22 MIN
16mm
Color (H C A)
LC 75-703304
Uses the example of the filmmaker, his wife and their first child to demonstrate the techniques of Lamaze training in childbirth.
Health and Safety; Home Economics
Dist - LAWREN **Prod** - LAWREN 1975

That's Rich - and a Little about Long Distance 28 MIN
16mm
Color
LC 70-713389
Features entertainer Rich Little doing a series of impersonations to demonstrate how zero - plus and one - plus long distance telephone calls are made.
Social Science
Dist - SWBELL **Prod** - SWBELL 1971

That's right 15 MIN
VHS
Color (P I)
Takes a look at the rights of children and at the work of UNICEF. Visits two children in rural Ghana and two children in rural Ontario.
Civics and Political Systems; Geography - World; Health and Safety; Sociology
Dist - ASTRSK **Prod** - ASTRSK 1989

That's Right Edie 15 MIN
VHS / U-matic
Picture Book Park Series Blue Module; Blue module
Color (P)
Presents the children's story That's Right, Edie by Johanna Johnston.
Literature and Drama
Dist - AITECH **Prod** - WVIZTV 1974

That's risky business 28 MIN
U-matic
Color (IND)
Shows dramatizations of actual antitrust situations, how to spot anticompetitive practices, acts and practices that must be avoided to stay within the law, defenses against antitrust charges, when to check with legal counsel, and more.
Business and Economics; Civics and Political Systems
Dist - BNA **Prod** - FISSCI 1986

That's Show Business - the Rules of Exhibiting 35 MIN
VHS / 16mm
Color (A PRO)
$790.00 purchase, $220.00 rental
Concentrates on three points to keep in mind when planning for an exhibition. Stresses knowledge of the objectives of self and organization, targeting prospects, and presenting an attractive and accessible exhibit.
Business and Economics; Psychology
Dist - VIDART **Prod** - VIDART 1990

That's Stealing 17 MIN
16mm / U-matic / VHS
Color (P I)
Presents the story of two girls in sixth grade and how one of them develops the bad habit of stealing. Shows how the girls deal with the problem.
Guidance and Counseling; Social Science; Sociology
Dist - ALTSUL **Prod** - EBERHT 1984

That's the Flower Business 20 MIN
U-matic
Occupations Series

B&W (J H)
Interviews an occupational course student about his work as a commercial florist.
Guidance and Counseling
Dist - TVOTAR **Prod** - TVOTAR 1985

That's the Rule 15 MIN
U-matic
Color (IND)
Educates supervisors in effective techniques to enforce rules and motivate employees to work safely. Instructs supervisors in the purpose of safety rules and techniques for the development of safety rules.
Guidance and Counseling; Health and Safety
Dist - BNA **Prod** - ERESI 1983

That's the Rule) 30 MIN
U-matic / VHS
Color
Presents a practical and effective way to help supervisors enforce safety rules without employee resentment and rebellion.
Business and Economics; Health and Safety
Dist - EDRF **Prod** - EDRF

That's what drugs took me to 25 MIN
VHS
Color (J H T PRO)
$59.95 purchase _ #CWL4549V - K
Features Lisa who traces the history of her troubled teenage years, during which she gave birth to three children, became involved with and addicted to drugs, lost custody of a son, suffered the death of another child and began the process of getting her life together.
Guidance and Counseling; Health and Safety
Dist - CAMV

That's what It's all about 29 MIN
16mm
Regional Intervention Program Series
Color
LC 75-702439
Depicts all aspects of the Regional Intervention Program for unmanageable children, from initial intake through the various behavior modification modules to the child's return to a normal public school within the community.
Education; Psychology
Dist - USNAC **Prod** - USBEH 1973

That's what the circus is for 15 MIN
8mm cartridge / VHS / BETA / U-matic
Color; PAL (IND G)
$295.00 purchase, $175.00 rental _ #MOB - 001
Follows a small circus through its routine of setup, rehearsal and performance, drawing powerful parallels to working safely on the job. Covers the topics of teamwork, awareness, safety meetings, thinking through actions, protective equipment, housekeeping, working deliberately and following established procedures. Makes the point that the difference between professional success and personal tragedy depends upon the choices made. Includes a leader's guide.
Health and Safety; Psychology
Dist - BNA

That's what We're Here for 32 MIN
16mm
Color
LC 76-702719
Depicts all phases of Veterans Administration hospital dentistry, including the various residency programs, graduate training and continuing education. Features Veterans Administration dental personnel at six major hospitals throughout the United States.
Health and Safety
Dist - USNAC **Prod** - USVA 1975

That's why we're here 28 MIN
VHS
Mission videos series
Color (G R)
$12.50 purchase _ #S12365
Examines the Lutheran Church - Missouri Synod's Volunteer Youth Ministry program in Japan and Taiwan.
Guidance and Counseling; Literature and Drama; Religion and Philosophy
Dist - CPH **Prod** - LUMIS

That's Worth Noting 15 MIN
VHS / U-matic
Writer's Realm Series
Color (I)
$125.00 purchase
Explains the importance of taking notes that may apply to creative writing in areas of organization and future reference.
English Language; Literature and Drama; Social Science
Dist - AITECH **Prod** - MDINTV 1987

Thea 27 MIN
16mm / U-matic / VHS
Insight Series
Color (H C A)
Demonstrates how a male chauvinist, who has made his wife assume a subservient role, learns how God transcends human categories. Shows how this leads to a joyous reconciliation with his wife. Stars Julie Sommars and Jess Walton.
Guidance and Counseling; Psychology; Religion and Philosophy
Dist - PAULST **Prod** - PAULST

Theater 20 MIN
16mm
B&W (C A) (FINNISH)
An English and Finnish language motion picture. Presents an impressionist documentary of the Finnish National Theatre's production of Beckett's Waiting For Godot. Delves beneath the surface of acting, lighting, set and costume design to study the interrelationships among these basic elements of theater.
Fine Arts; Foreign Language
Dist - MOMA **Prod** - SRKTJ 1957

Theater Fur Kinder 5 MIN
U-matic / VHS / 16mm
European Studies - Germany (German Series
Color (H C A) (GERMAN)
Shows children as both spectators and participants in the theater as they help to produce plays.
Fine Arts; Foreign Language; Geography - World
Dist - IFB **Prod** - MFAFRG 1973

The Theater in Shakespeare's Time 14 MIN
16mm / U-matic / VHS
Color (J)
LC 73-701436
Visualizes the many facets and traditions of the Elizabethan Theater and the unique characteristics of the stage within the context of the society of Shakespeare's time. Explains that Shakespeare wrote his plays for the stage on which they were performed, for the actors and for an audience which represented a cross - section of the citizens of London.
Fine Arts; History - World; Literature and Drama
Dist - PHENIX **Prod** - PHENIX 1973

Theater of the Night - the Science of Sleep and Dreams 45 MIN
VHS
Color (J)
LC 85-703878
Visits sleep labs and describes the most current research on sleep and dreams. Details sleep stages and causes and treatments of sleep disorders.
Health and Safety; Psychology
Dist - HRMC **Prod** - HRMC

Theater of the palms 30 MIN
VHS
Color (G C H)
$295.00 purchase _ #DL478
Observes the 1000 - year - old tradition of puppet theater in China, including a look at puppet master Lee - Tien - lu.
Fine Arts; History - World
Dist - INSIM

Theatre 30 MIN
U-matic
Explorations in Shaw Series
Color (H)
Interviews actors who describe Shaw as a rebellious playwright, a demanding director and a generous friend.
Literature and Drama
Dist - TVOTAR **Prod** - TVOTAR 1974

Theatre and the revolution - 8 51 MIN
VHS
Eastern Europe - breaking with the past series
Color (H C G)
$50.00 purchase
Presents three segments on actors and artists behind the revolution - Theatre at the End of November, which reveals that in support of the November, 1989 revolution actors closed theatres across Czechoslovakia and Poland; The Other Europe, an excerpt showing the communist use of theater in the 'show trials' of the 1950s to purge the State of dissenting opinions; and Gardzienice, an excerpt from a performance by the Polish avant garde theater group, Gardzienice. Part eight of 13 parts.
Civics and Political Systems; Fine Arts; History - World
Dist - GVIEW **Prod** - GVIEW 1990

Theatre arts discoveries series
Introduces and illustrates concepts and activities involved in presenting dramas with youth. Also includes supplementary print and resource materials. Divided into three parts - 1. The first step - demonstrates how 4 - H leaders can use simple theatre games to assess their 4 - Hers cooperation, concentration, and expression skills. 2. Informal drama activities - introduces three kinds of activities - Theatre Games, Story Dramatization and Group Improvisation. three 4 - H leaders conduct drama sessions with their pupils and talk about selecting activities and leading drama. 3. Leader strategies.
Theatre arts discoveries series 44 MIN
Dist - UWISCA **Prod** - UEUWIS 1990

The Theatre at Work 30 MIN
VHS / U-matic
In Our Own Image Series
Color (C)
Fine Arts
Dist - DALCCD **Prod** - DALCCD

Theatre D'Enfants (Les Marionnettes) 7 MIN
U-matic / VHS / 16mm
Chroniques De France Series
Color (H C A) (FRENCH)
LC 81-700769
A French language motion picture. Looks at the marionette theaters of France.
Foreign Language; Geography - World
Dist - IFB **Prod** - ADPF 1980

Theatre for Children - Designing the Setting 27 MIN
16mm
Color
Emphasizes the importance of scenic elements for the child audience. Demonstrates the designer's approach, script requirements, style, form, facility and stock pieces. Shows the designer in production with plans, paint, props and lights.
Fine Arts
Dist - USC **Prod** - HALLJL 1975

Theatre Fundamentals - Backstage, is it Safe 21 MIN
16mm / U-matic / VHS
Color (C A)
LC 83-700662
Examines the issue of stage safety through the comments of technical directors and theater safety experts interspersed with documentary footage of practices backstage. Uses original footage of Buster Keaton with appropriate music by theater organist Dennis James.
Fine Arts; Health and Safety
Dist - IU **Prod** - IU 1983

Theatre Fundamentals - Breath of Performance 14 MIN
16mm / U-matic / VHS
Color (H C A)
LC 80-700653
Demonstrates the proper blend of speech and body training which leads to effective use of the voice in theater. Shows theater students performing exercises designed to develop a sense of proper body alignment, foster efficient breathing, and refine coordination of movement.
English Language; Fine Arts
Dist - IU **Prod** - IU 1980

Theatre Fundamentals - Costumes on Stage 26 MIN
16mm / U-matic / VHS
Color (H C A)
Illustrates the step - by - step creation of costumes for a theatricalproduction. Begins with pre - production conferences, and demonstrates costume research, design, cutting, assembling, and fitting.
Fine Arts
Dist - IU **Prod** - IU 1985

Theatre Fundamentals - Stage Lighting 16 MIN
U-matic / VHS / 16mm
Color (H C A)
LC 81-700112
Demonstrates four properties of light and shows their functions in stage lighting.
Fine Arts
Dist - IU **Prod** - IU 1981

Theatre in the Streets 59 MIN
Videoreel / VT2
Festivals of Pennsylvania Series
Color
Presents the Philadelphia Street Theatre which consists of a truckful of actors coming into the community to entertain.
Fine Arts; Geography - United States; Literature and Drama
Dist - PBS **Prod** - WHYY

Theatre of China 29 MIN
U-matic
Off Stage Series
Color
Examines Chinese Theatre, from the classical to the contemporary. Discusses proletariat drama.
Fine Arts; History - World
Dist - UMITV **Prod** - UMITV 1975

The Theatre of Etienne Decroux 23 MIN
16mm
B&W
Documents the efforts of Etienne Decroux to establish mime as an art in its own right in an autonomous branch of theatre.
Fine Arts
Dist - RADIM **Prod** - FILIM

The Theatre of Social Problems - Ibsen, Hedda Gabler 45 MIN
U-matic / VHS / 16mm
History of the Drama Series
Color (H C A)
LC 76-700971
Presents an abridged version of Ibsen's play, Hedda Gabler, the story of a woman's tormented search for self - fulfillment in a world dominated by men.
Fine Arts; Literature and Drama; Sociology
Dist - FOTH **Prod** - FOTH 1976

The Theatre of Social Problems - Ibsen, Hedda Gabler 60 MIN
U-matic / VHS / 16mm
History of the Drama Series
Color (J)
LC 76-700971
Presents an abridged version of Ibsen's play, Hedda Gabler, the story of a woman's tormented search for self - fulfillment in a world dominated by men.
Fine Arts; Literature and Drama
Dist - FOTH **Prod** - MANTLH 1976

Theatre of the absurd - pirandello, six characters in search of an author 58 MIN
U-matic / VHS / 16mm
History of the drama series
Color (J)
LC 76-703608
Presents an adaptation in English of Pirandello's play, Six Characters In Search Of An Author, in which six characters seek to exchange their fixed, frozen form in art for the uncertainty of life.
Fine Arts; Literature and Drama
Dist - FOTH **Prod** - FOTH 1976
MANTLH

Theatre of the Mind - John Donne's Metaphysical Style 45 MIN
U-matic / VHS
Survey of English Literature I Series
Color
Analyzes John Donne's metaphysical style.
Literature and Drama
Dist - MDCPB **Prod** - MDCPB

Theatre of the palms - puppet master Lee - Tien - lu 30 MIN
VHS
Color (H C G)
$295.00 purchase, $55.00 rental
Focuses on the puppetry of the I Wan Ran troupe of Taiwan and its 80 - year - old puppet master Lee - Tien - lu. Reveals that Master Lee began his vocation in puppetry at age 9 and has passed his knowledge on to his sons and other apprentices. Explores the development of Chinese puppetry using archival material.
Fine Arts; History - World
Dist - FLMLIB **Prod** - RDVSKY 1990

The Theatre - One of the Humanities 30 MIN
U-matic / VHS / 16mm
Humanities - the Drama Series
Color (H C)
Considers the three main elements of any play and considers their interrelationship. Examines the play itself, the actors and the audience.
Fine Arts
Dist - EBEC **Prod** - EBEC 1959

Theatre, Opera, the Concert Stage 30 MIN
VHS / U-matic
Afro - American Perspectives Series
Color (C)
Discusses black trends in the theatre, opera and the concert stage.
History - United States
Dist - MDCPB **Prod** - MDDE

Theatre - Why Criticize? 29 MIN
U-matic
Off Stage Series
Color
Debates the validity of criticism, who should criticize and how they should criticize.
Fine Arts
Dist - UMITV **Prod** - UMITV 1975

Theatrical Cartooning 15 MIN
Videoreel / VT2
Charlie's Pad Series
Color
Fine Arts
Dist - PBS **Prod** - WSIU

Theatrical Devices in Classical Theatre 20 MIN
U-matic / VHS
Color (C)
$249.00, $149.00 purchase _ #AD - 1637
Covers the purpose, design and uses of the 'ekkyklema' for showing the victims and perpetrators of off - stage violence, the 'deus ex machina,' Charonian steps and other means of entrance and exit. Explains the reasons for New Comedy, its audience and its physical requirements.
History - World; Literature and Drama
Dist - FOTH **Prod** - FOTH

Theban Plays Series

Antigone	120 MIN
Oedipus at Colonus	120 MIN
Oedipus the King	120 MIN

Dist - FOTH

Theban Plays Series

Antigone - Pt 3	120 MIN
Oedipus at Colonus	120 MIN
Oedipus at Colonus, Pt 2	120 MIN
Oedipus the King	120 MIN
Oedipus the King, Pt 1	120 MIN

Dist - PSU

The Theft 27 MIN
16mm / U-matic / VHS
Insight Series
Color; B&W (J)
LC 75-700943
Presents a story about a married couple who fight constantly. Tells how they discover a burglar in their home and begin another fight while the burglar becomes the referee.
Guidance and Counseling; Sociology
Dist - PAULST **Prod** - PAULST 1974

The Theft 25 MIN
16mm / VHS
Color (I J)
LC 76-700430
Presents a story about a jobless youngster who agrees to go along with an older boy on a burglary and about the anxiety he faces afterwards.
Guidance and Counseling; Sociology
Dist - LRF **Prod** - KLINGL 1975

The Theft of Fire 15 MIN
U-matic / VHS
Gather Round Series
Color (K P)
Literature and Drama
Dist - CTI **Prod** - CTI

Their Best Teacher - PhDs Learn from Mr Boy 10 MIN
16mm
Color (C A)
Presents two professors in special education who tell how they have learned from their mentally retarded son.
Education; Psychology
Dist - LAWREN **Prod** - CBSTV 1983

Their Finest Hour 27 MIN
U-matic
Color
Relates five incidents in which lives were actually saved by people who remembered what Red Cross had taught them in first aid, cardiopulmonary resuscitation (CPR) or water safety courses.
Health and Safety
Dist - AMRC **Prod** - AMRC 1979

Their Finest Paragraph 5 MIN
U-matic / VHS
Write on, Set 2 Series
Color (J H)
Deals with emphasis in writing. See also the title The Rocking Horse Writer.
English Language
Dist - CTI **Prod** - CTI

Their first mistake 20 MIN
35mm
B&W (G)
Features Laurel and Hardy in over their heads when Ollie adopts a baby and Stan 'helps' take care of it. Contact distributor for rental price.
Fine Arts; Psychology; Sociology
Dist - KITPAR **Prod** - ROACH 1932

Their First Teachers 15 MIN
16mm
B&W (C T)
Deals with the relationships between parents and children. Shows the effects of parental understanding on the personal adjustment and maturation of children.
Psychology; Sociology
Dist - PSUPCR **Prod** - CCNY 1956

Their Game was Golf 28 MIN
16mm
Color
Presents St Lucie, Florida, as a favorite site for the Ladies Professional Golf Association tournaments.
Geography - United States; Physical Education and Recreation
Dist - FLADC **Prod** - FLADC

Their Own Brand 30 MIN
U-matic / VHS / 16mm
Case Studies in Small Business Series
Color (C A)
Business and Economics
Dist - GPN **Prod** - UMA 1979

Their Right to Belong 15 MIN
16mm
B&W
Shows a sheltered workshop program including special special training classes for the trainable mentally retarded.
Education; Psychology
Dist - OARC **Prod** - OARC

Their Royal Highnesses Princess Margrethe and Prince Henrik Visit Canada 12 MIN
16mm
Color
Follows the royal couple on their official visit to Canada in September 1967.
Geography - World; History - World
Dist - AUDPLN **Prod** - RDCG

Theirs is the kingdom 5 MIN
16mm
Beatitude series
Color (J)
LC 72-700775
Features two high school boys, attempting to solve the problems of poverty in a Mexican border town, cause a near riot because of their insensitivity. Depicts that they re-examine their motives and return to try again.
Guidance and Counseling; Sociology
Dist - FRACOC **Prod** - FRACOC 1972

Them 94 MIN
U-matic / VHS / 16mm
B&W (J)
Stars James Whitmore. Presents gigantic creatures emerging from a desert crater and causing mysterious killings in the Mojave Desert. Pictures the jeopardy of the human race when two of the creeping monsters escape.
Fine Arts
Dist - FI **Prod** - WB 1954

Them not - So - Dry Bones 3 MIN
U-matic / VHS
Science Rock Series
Color (P I)
Uses animation to discuss the topic of human anatomy.
Fine Arts; Science - Natural
Dist - GA **Prod** - ABCTV 1979

Them People 43 MIN
16mm
Color (J)
LC 70-705685
Shows the operation of urban welfare systems as exemplified by systems in Cleveland, which are supposed to help the poor, but instead work to their detriment. Describes efforts by various church and civic groups to change these systems.
Psychology; Sociology
Dist - UMCBM **Prod** - UMCBM 1970

Them thar trains 50 MIN
VHS
Color (H C A)
$24.95 purchase
Presents vintage color railroad films from the steam engine days. Includes the films 'Safety In Railroading,' produced in 1947 by the Nickel Plate Road, 'Safety In Railroading,' produced in 1940 by the Missouri Pacific Railroad, and others.
History - United States
Dist - PBS **Prod** - WNETTV

The Theme 100 MIN
VHS / 35mm
Color (G) (RUSSIAN WITH ENGLISH SUBTITLES)
$300.00 rental
Portrays a state - approved, middle - aged playwright who questions the true value of his commercially successful work. Directed by Gleb Panfilov.
Fine Arts; Guidance and Counseling
Dist - KINOIC

Theme and variation - pt 21 30 MIN
16mm
Life on Earth series; Vol VI
Color (J)
$495.00 purchase _ #865 - 9042
Blends scientific data with wildlife photography to tell the story of the development of life. Features wildlife expert David Attenborough as host. Part 21 of 27 parts is entitled 'Theme And Variation.'
Science; Science - Natural; Science - Physical
Dist - FI **Prod** - BBCTV 1981

Theme and variations 58 MIN
U-matic / VHS
Life on Earth series; Program 10
Color (J)
LC 82-706682
Describes some of the diverse specializations which mammals have evolved to obtain food, to move, to navigate and, in some instances, to communicate.
Science - Natural
Dist - FI **Prod** - BBCTV 1981

Theme and Voice in Poetry 30 MIN
U-matic / VHS
Communicating through Literature Series
Color (C)
Literature and Drama
Dist - DALCCD **Prod** - DALCCD

Theme I - Self - Awareness and Acceptance - Theme II - Relating to Others 16 MIN
VHS / 16mm
Junior High Health and Personal Life Skills in - Service Series
Color (C)
$175.00, $225.00 purchase _ #271802
Orients teachers to the revised 1986 Junior High Health and Personal Life Skills Curriculum. Introduces a change of emphasis in both content and teaching strategies. Knowledge of the human body is superseded by knowledge, attitudes, skills and lifelong behavior for healthy lifestyles. 'Themes I and II' explores curriculum orientation toward self - awareness and acceptance, and interpersonal relationships.
Education; Guidance and Counseling; Health and Safety; Psychology
Dist - ACCESS **Prod** - ACCESS 1986

Theme III - Life Careers 13 MIN
VHS / 16mm
Junior High Health and Personal Life Skills in - Service Series
Color (C)
$175.00, $225.00 purchase _ #271803
Orients teachers to the revised 1986 Junior High Health and Personal Life Skills Curriculum. Introduces a change of emphasis in both content and teaching strategies. Knowledge of the human body is superseded by knowledge, attitudes, skills and lifelong behavior for healthy lifestyles. 'Theme III' compares the career decisions faced by students in the early part of this century with those faced by today's adolescents. Explains the need to develop skills and attitudes that deal with a rapidly changing environment.
Education; Guidance and Counseling; Health and Safety; Psychology
Dist - ACCESS **Prod** - ACCESS 1986

Theme IV - Body Knowledge and Care 13 MIN
VHS / 16mm
Junior High Health and Personal Life Skills in - Service Series
Color (C)
$175.00, $225.00 purchase _ #271804 ial Self Help And Self Awareness ^Social Group And Interpersonal Processes^Sexual Education^Sexual Hygiene
Orients teachers to the revised 1986 Junior High Health and Personal Life Skills Curriculum. Introduces a change of emphasis in both content and teaching strategies. Knowledge of the human body is superseded by knowledge, attitudes, skills and lifelong behavior for healthy lifestyles. 'Theme IV' illustrates the rational for providing health and life skills education to adolescents. Emphasizes taking responsibility for making positive, healthy lifestyle choices.
Education; Guidance and Counseling; Health and Safety; Psychology
Dist - ACCESS **Prod** - ACCESS 1986

Theme Maps 10 MIN
U-matic
Geography Skills Series
Color (J H)
Explores several techniques for mapping population density.
Computer Science; Education; Geography - World
Dist - TVOTAR **Prod** - TVOTAR 1985

Theme Song 30 MIN
U-matic / VHS
B&W
Deals with the direct address of the viewer by the performer. Explores the intimacy of the television viewing situation.
Fine Arts
Dist - KITCHN **Prod** - KITCHN

Theme V - Human Sexuality - Optional 17 MIN
VHS / 16mm
Junior High Health and Personal Life Skills in - Service Series
Color (C)
$175.00, $225.00 purchase _ #271805
Orients teachers to the revised 1986 Junior High Health and Personal Life Skills Curriculum. Introduces a change of emphasis in both content and teaching strategies. Knowledge of the human body is superseded by knowledge, attitudes, skills and lifelong behavior for healthy lifestyles. 'Theme V' stresses local decision making on and the optional nature of human sexuality education for adolescents. Emphasizes the importance of parent - teacher meetings in allaying parental concern about school - based sex education.
Education; Guidance and Counseling; Health and Safety; Psychology
Dist - ACCESS **Prod** - ACCESS 1986

Themes and moods 30 MIN
Videoreel / VT2
Designing home interiors series; Unit 5
Color (C A)
Shows the design principle of harmony as the key to establishing the theme or mood of a room. Discusses formal and informal themes.
Home Economics
Dist - CDTEL **Prod** - COAST

Themes and variations at the National Gallery - saints 21 MIN
VHS
Color (G)
PdS10.50 purchase _ #A4-300435
Uses the National Gallery's collection to present images of saints in Western European art of the Middle Ages and the Renaissance. Notes the prolific use of saints in everything from large public altarpieces to small private devotional works. Explores why the saints were so frequently represented, how they were recognized, and how their roles in society were reflected in the images made of them.
Fine Arts
Dist - AVP **Prod** - NATLGL

Themes and variations - pictures in pictures 25 MIN
VHS
Color (G)
PdS10.50 purchase _ #A4-300449
Features National Gallery pictures which contain pictures within them. Notes that the effect gives the artist an opportunity to imitate other artists' styles, to show how pictures were once displayed, or to comment on the main action or subject. Explores the use of pictures within pictures to allude seriously or playfully to notions of reality and resemblance.
Fine Arts
Dist - AVP **Prod** - NATLGL

Themes in Fiction 30 MIN
VHS / U-matic
Communicating through Literature Series
Color (C)
Literature and Drama
Dist - DALCCD **Prod** - DALCCD

The Themes of Macbeth 28 MIN
VHS
Color (G C H)
$119.00 purchase _ #DL499
Focuses on Lady Macbeth, Macduff, and Banquo to analyze what the narrator calls the play's many 'contradictions, seeming truths, concealed meanings, and double meanings.'
Fine Arts; Literature and Drama
Dist - INSIM

Themes - the day when nothing made sense 10 MIN
U-matic / VHS / 16mm
Sentences and paragraphs series
Color (I J H)
$265.00, $185.00 purchase _ #79529; LC 81-700054
Illustrates the need for logical order by showing how a teenage boy struggles through a day in which nothing follows in a logical sequence. Demonstrates the need for organization in writing themes.
English Language
Dist - CORF **Prod** - CENTRO 1981

Then and now 30 MIN
U-matic
Pacific bridges series
Color (I J)
Highlights and summarizes the Pacific Bridges series, which deals with Asian - American culture.
Sociology
Dist - GPN **Prod** - EDFCEN 1978

Then Came Man 15 MIN
U-matic
North America - Growth of a Continent Series
Color (J H)
Explains how the arrival of different races in North America shaped the social, political and economic face of the continent.
Geography - United States; Geography - World
Dist - TVOTAR **Prod** - TVOTAR 1980

Then One Year 20 MIN
U-matic / VHS / 16mm
Color (I J) (SPANISH)
Discusses the primary and secondary changes at adolescence in boys and girls.
Health and Safety; Psychology
Dist - CF **Prod** - CF 1984

Thenow 14 MIN
16mm
Color (A)
Presents a single Black girl moving through a dream of her past lives, when she was Black and when she was White, when her lovers were Black and when her lovers were White. Shows interracial couples together at play and in sexual intercourse. Describes thenow as a liberation of the habit of labels in interracial understanding, a deeper understanding of our common flow of life, our common ties as people working out Our destinations.
Guidance and Counseling; Psychology; Sociology
Dist - MMRC **Prod** - MMRC

The Theodolite 13 MIN
VHS / U-matic
Marshall maintenance training programs series; Tape 42
Color (IND)
Teaches how to set up the theodolite and center it over a point. Emphasizes the method for reading horizontals as well as angles and double checking these readings.
Industrial and Technical Education
Dist - LEIKID **Prod** - LEIKID

The Theodolite on site - Cassette 2 45 MIN
VHS
Using surveying instruments series
Color; PAL (J H IND)
PdS29.50 purchase
Deals with leveling, one of the operations carried out in the field of site surveying, which determines relative heights between different building components or between different positions on the ground. Concentrates on one aspect - setting up a dumpy level prior to taking readings, ie the temporary adjustments. Part two of two parts.
Industrial and Technical Education
Dist - EMFVL

Theodore Bikel and Rashid Hussain 52 MIN
VHS / U-matic
Rainbow quest series
Color
Presents Israeli and Arabic music and poetry in their original language and in translation. Features Pete Seeger on banjo and Theodore Bikel on guitar.
Fine Arts
Dist - NORROS **Prod** - SEEGER

Theodore Enslin - 2 - 12 - 87 40 MIN
VHS / Cassette
Poetry Center reading series
Color (G)
$15.00, $45.00 purchase, $15.00 rental _ #736 - 589
Features the writer reading his works at the Poetry Center, San Francisco State University, with an introduction by Frances Phillips.
Literature and Drama
Dist - POETRY

Theodore Gericault 26 MIN
16mm / U-matic / VHS
Romantic Vs Classic Art (Spanish Series
Color (H C A) (SPANISH)
Fine Arts; Foreign Language
Dist - PFP **Prod** - VPSL

Theodore M Hesburgh, education, religion - Pt 2 29 MIN
VHS / U-matic
Quest for peace series
Color (A)
Education; Religion and Philosophy
Dist - AACD **Prod** - AACD 1984

Theodore Roosevelt 26 MIN
VHS / U-matic
Biography series
B&W/Color (H C)
$79.00 purchase _ #HH - 6227C
Examines the life and political career of Theodore Roosevelt. Reveals that as President of the United States, Roosevelt threw the nation into the arena of international politics, pushed the development of the Panama Canal and battled trusts. Part of a series portraying a diverse group of personalities who shaped some aspect of world and cultural history.
Biography; History - United States; History - World
Dist - CORF **Prod** - WOLPER 1963
MGHT

Theodore Roosevelt - American 27 MIN
16mm
B&W
LC FIE58-38
Presents the highlights of Roosevelt's life, from his boyhood out West through his role in national and international affairs. Particular emphasis is given to the development of his political career.
Biography; Civics and Political Systems; History - United States
Dist - USNAC **Prod** - USDD 1958

Theodore Roosevelt - cowboy in the White House 29 MIN
U-matic / VHS / 16mm
Biographies series
Color (J H C A)
$635.00, $250.00 purchase _ #77531
Portrays Theodore Roosevelt telling his grandchildren about his past life as a cowboy. Includes information about Roosevelt's role in peace negotiations at the end of World War I.
Biography; Civics and Political Systems
Dist - CORF

Theodore Roosevelt - He who has Planted will Preserve 28 MIN
VHS / 16mm
Naturalists Series
Color (G)
$55.00 rental _ #NTRL - 102
Portrays Theodore Roosevelt, an ardent conservationist. Focuses on Roosevelt as a concerned naturalist who did more than any other American president to preserve our woods and wildlife. Filmed at Sagamore Hill, his home.
Biography; Science - Natural
Dist - PBS **Prod** - KRMATV

Theodore Roosevelt's Sagamore Hill 23 MIN
VHS
Color (H C T A)
$69.95 purchase _ #S01335
Tours Sagamore Hill, the Long Island home of Theodore Roosevelt and his family. Hosted by E G Marshall.
Biography; Fine Arts; History - United States
Dist - UILL

Theodore Roosevelt's Sagamore Hill 23 MIN
U-matic / VHS / 16mm
American lifestyle series; U S Presidents
Color (J)
Tours the summer home of Theodore Roosevelt on Long Island. Shows how the home, Sagamore Hill, is testimony to Roosevelt's energy and to the rich and happy life he shared there with his wife and six children.
Biography; Geography - United States; History - United States; Sociology
Dist - AIMS **Prod** - COMCO 1975

Theodore Roosevelt's Sagamore Hill 25 MIN
16mm
American Life Style Series
Color
LC 73-700491
Presents E G Marshall who conducts a tour of Sagamore Hill, the home of Theodore Roosevelt, at Cove Neck, New York. Reveals the personal and public history of President Roosevelt and gives insight into his character.
Biography; Geography - United States
Dist - SHOWCO **Prod** - BASFIN 1972

Theodoric - Ostrogoth 30 MIN
VHS
Saints and legions series
Color (H)
$69.95 purchase
Profiles Theodoric of the Ostrogoths. Part 14 of a twenty - six part series which introduces personalities, movements and events in ancient history responsible for the beginnings of Western Civilization.
Biography; Civics and Political Systems; History - World
Dist - SCETV **Prod** - SCETV 1982

Theology and faith development 30 MIN
U-matic / VHS
Sow seeds/trust the promise series
Color (J A)
Discusses experimental Bible study and planning Bible study. Examines theologizing models and theologizing with music. Features Walter Wink and Charles McCullough.
Religion and Philosophy
Dist - ECUFLM **Prod** - UMCOM

Theology and the kingdom of God
VHS / U-matic
Color (A)
Features a presentation by Marjorie Hewit Suchocki, professor of theology and director of the Doctor of Ministry program at Pittsburg Theological Seminary.
Religion and Philosophy
Dist - ECUFLM **Prod** - WHSPRO 1983

Theology of the marketplace 30 MIN
VHS
Christian values in the business world series
Color (H C G A R)
$39.95 purchase, $10.00 rental _ #35 - 895 - 2076
Explores the creative tension that can exist between one's job and one's faith. Hosted by Bill Bockelman. Produced by Seraphim.
Business and Economics; Religion and Philosophy
Dist - APH

Theology on tap - an introduction to God, Jesus, Church and moral living 120 MIN
VHS
Color (G R)
$49.95 purchase _ #365
Presents a program which introduces contemporary Roman Catholic theology to young adults developed by the Young Adult Ministry of the Archdiocese of Chicago. Features Fathers John Cusick, Patrick Brennan and Charles Schutte and John Horan and Maureen Shields.
Religion and Philosophy; Sociology
Dist - ACTAF **Prod** - ACTAF

Theonie - Arni Me Kolokithakia - Lamb with a little zucchini 15 MIN
Videoreel / VT2
Theonie Series
Color
Shows Theonie preparing kolokithakia and arni which are prepared separately and combined before baking. Tells the difference between spring lamb, yearling lamb and mutton.
Home Economics
Dist - PBS **Prod** - WGBHTV

Theonie - Baklavas 15 MIN
Videoreel / VT2
Onie Series
Color
Shows Theonie making baklavas, the sweet of a thousand layers made with walnuts, spices and many layers of phillo, a paper - thin pastry sheet. Demonstrates the process of clarifying butter, the Greek way of peeling an orange or lemon so the entire rind peels off in a single strip and how to crush walnuts with a wooden mortar and pestle so that there are pieces as well as powdered walnuts for the filling.
Home Economics
Dist - PBS **Prod** - WGBHTV

Theonie - Dolmathes - Stuffed Grape Leaves 15 MIN
Videoreel / VT2
Onie Series
Color
Shows how to make stuffed grape leaves. Explains that the stuffing is a basic meat sauce with pine nuts, dill weed and rice.
Home Economics
Dist - PBS **Prod** - WGBHTV

Theonie - Fasoulakia Fresca 15 MIN
Videoreel / VT2
(Fresh Green Beans (from the Theonie Series
Color
Demonstrates three ways to prepare fresh green beans.
Home Economics
Dist - PBS **Prod** - WGBHTV

Theonie - Garithes Me Fetta - shrimp baked with feta cheese 14 MIN
Videoreel / VT2
Theonie Series
Color
Demonstrates how to peel and devein fresh shrimp. Shows that after preparing the sauce with olive oil, onions, tomatoes, parsley, garlic, wine, salt and pepper, Theonie sears the shrimp and squeezes lemon juice over them. Explains that the ingredients are assembled in layers in the baking dish and cooked for a short time in a very hot oven.
Home Economics
Dist - PBS **Prod** - WGBHTV

Theonie - Ghighes Me Arni (Giant Beans with Lamb) 14 MIN
Videoreel / VT2
Onie Series
Color
Shows how to prepare the shoulder chops, browning them in hot olive oil before adding onion, celery, tomato paste, salt and pepper, cumin, water and pre - soaked beans. Gives instructions for the cooking, draining and chilling of beans combined with onion, celery and tomato paste and dressed as a salad with latholemono, an olive oil, lemon and garlic dressing.
Home Economics
Dist - PBS **Prod** - WGBHTV

Theonie - Hilopittas - noodles 15 MIN
Videoreel / VT2
Onie Series
Color
Shows how to make hilopittas. Suggests serving the noodles with butter, butter and kephalotiri or Parmesan cheese, or with a combination of honey, cinnamon and crushed sesame seeds.
Home Economics
Dist - PBS **Prod** - WGBHTV

Theonie - Lahano Dolmathes - cabbage leaves stuffed with pork 14 MIN
Videoreel / VT2
Theonie Series
Color
Demonstrates how to select a good head of cabbage, how to core it and steam it to make the leaves pliable for stuffing. Shows how to make the stuffing for lahano dolmathes by combining rice, scallions, dill weed, egg, tomato paste, salt and pepper. Explains that a saucepan is lined with some of the outer cabbage leaves to prevent the stuffed leaves from scorching, then the rolled leaves are layered and olive oil and chicken broth is poured over them.
Home Economics
Dist - PBS **Prod** - WGBHTV

Theonie - melopitta nissiotiki - island honey and cheese pie 15 MIN
Videoreel / VT2
Theonie series
Color
Demonstrates the preparation of honey cheese pie. Shows how to make the filling by mixing sugar and ricotta cheese, honey, slightly - beaten eggs and grated lemon rind.
Home Economics
Dist - PBS **Prod** - WGBHTV

Theonie - moussaka - eggplant 15 MIN
Videoreel / VT2
Onie series
Color
Shows how to select an eggplant and prepare Moussaka.
Home Economics
Dist - PBS **Prod** - WGBHTV

Theonie - ornitha kokkinisti - pot - roasted chicken 15 MIN
Videoreel / VT2
Onie series
Color
Shows how to prepare chicken for stuffing. Explains how to make the stuffing using chicken liver, olive oil, scallions, ground beef, rice, tomato paste, pine nuts, thyme, parsley, salt and pepper. Outlines the rest of the cooking procedures necessary in making pot - roasted chicken.
Home Economics
Dist - PBS **Prod** - WGBHTV

Theonie - pastitsion - baked spaghetti and meat sauce 15 MIN
Videoreel / VT2
Theonie series
Color
Shows how to cook pastitsion made with ground lamb, olive oil, onion, tomato sauce, crushed garlic, parsley, salt, pepper and wine. Explains how to layer the meat sauce and spaghetti in a crumbed baking pan and gives instructions for making a white sauce to top the dish.
Home Economics
Dist - PBS **Prod** - WGBHTV

Theonie - phinikia - spiced bars in lemon syrup 14 MIN
Videoreel / VT2
Onie series
Color
Shows how to combine ground walnuts, sugar, cinnamon and egg to make phinikia, a Greek Christmas cookie.
Home Economics
Dist - PBS **Prod** - WGBHTV

Theonie - portokalli glyko - orange sweets 14 MIN
Videoreel / VT2
Onie series
Color
Shows how to select medium - sized naval oranges for candied orange peel. Explains how to cut the skin in six sections and remove the peels. Features the skins being formed into tight rolls which are cooked in syrup.
Home Economics
Dist - PBS **Prod** - WGBHTV

Theonie - psari plaki and horiatiki salata - baked fish and peasant salad 15 MIN
Videoreel / VT2
Onie series
Color
Shows how to make psari plaki. Suggests using scup, bluefish, snapper, striped bass or any delicately flavored fish and tells how to see if the fish is fresh. Prepares a peasant salad with Greek olives and crumbled feta cheese with a vinegar, garlic and olive dressing.
Home Economics
Dist - PBS **Prod** - WGBHTV

Theonie - psaria nissiotika - island fish soup 15 MIN
Videoreel / VT2
Onie series
Color
Suggests using perch for making fish soup, since it is the closest fish to the scorpios. Shows how to bone the fish, saving the fillets to add later to the soup. Shows Theonie combining the fish bones, tomato, potato, onion, parsley, olive oil, white wine and water, cooking the stock, straining it through a fine sieve, mashing the vegetables and adding the fillets.
Home Economics
Dist - PBS **Prod** - WGBHTV

Theonie - ravanie - walnut cake 15 MIN
Videoreel / VT2
Onie series
Color
Shows how to make ravanie. Explains that the secret of a successful cake is the rapid and thorough combining of the dry and wet ingredients. Stresses that since the cake contains no baking powder to make it rise, the egg whites must not be allowed to collapse in mixing.
Home Economics
Dist - PBS **Prod** - WGBHTV

Theonie - salates kalorkerines - summer salads 14 MIN
Videoreel / VT2
Onie series
Color
Shows how to select a cucumber and also how to prepare a yogurt and cucumber salad and eggplant salad sauce.
Home Economics
Dist - PBS **Prod** - WGBHTV

Theonie Series

Theonie - Arni Me Kolokithakia - Lamb with a little zucchini	15 MIN
Theonie - Garithes Me Fetta - shrimp baked with feta cheese	14 MIN
Theonie - Lahano Dolmathes - cabbage leaves stuffed with pork	14 MIN
Theonie - melopitta nissiotiki - island honey and cheese pie	15 MIN
Theonie - pastitsion - baked spaghetti and meat sauce	15 MIN
Theonie - tarama and tahi - appetizers with tarama and tahi	15 MIN
Theonie - zouzoukakia - meatball sausages in wine sauce	14 MIN

Dist - PBS

Theonie - souppa avgolemono - egg lemon soup 14 MIN
Videoreel / VT2
Onie series
Color
Shows how egg and lemon are combined to make avgolemono sauce which crowns many Greek dishes. Presents Theonie making souppa avgolemono.
Home Economics
Dist - PBS **Prod** - WGBHTV

Theonie - souppes hymoniatikes - winter soups 14 MIN
Videoreel / VT2
Onie series
Color
Prepares souppa fakki made with lentils, onion, celery, minced garlic, tomato paste and olive oil. Demonstrates the preparation of another favorite Greek soup, lahaniki souppa, or winter vegetable soup.
Home Economics
Dist - PBS **Prod** - WGBHTV

Theonie - spanikopitta - spinach pie 15 MIN
Videoreel / VT2
Onie series
Color
Demonstrates the kneading and rolling of the pie crust for spanikopitta and the preparation of the filling of spinach, scallions, onion and dill.
Home Economics
Dist - PBS **Prod** - WGBHTV

Theonie - stiffato - beef stew 14 MIN
Videoreel / VT2
Onie series
Color
Shows that staffato is cooked with onions, wine and herbs during the winter months in Greece. Presents several different cuts of chuck beef which could be used in preparing this stew. Shows how to trim and cut walnut - sized chunks of meat which are then browned in hot olive oil.
Home Economics
Dist - PBS **Prod** - WGBHTV

Theonie - tarama and tahi - appetizers with tarama and tahi 15 MIN
Videoreel / VT2
Theonie series
Color
Shows that the secret of making tarama is crushing the eggs with pestle and wooden bowl and using wet, stale bread to cut the saltiness. Explains how to make the basic tahi sauce and a variation of it with crushed chick peas.
Home Economics
Dist - PBS **Prod** - WGBHTV

Theonie - tiropittes - cheese triangles 15 MIN
Videoreel / VT2
Onie series
Color
Shows how to make tiropittes, a combination of feta and mizithra cheese, eggs, parsley and white pepper. Demonstrates another variation of cheese pastry, tirotrigonas or cheese pie.
Home Economics
Dist - PBS **Prod** - WGBHTV

Theonie - youvetsi - lamb with orzo 15 MIN
Videoreel / VT2
Onie series
Color
Demonstrates how to bone a leg of lamb and how to make the little barley, or kritharaki pasta, by pinching off bits of dough and rolling them between the fingers to form little seed - shaped bits.
Home Economics
Dist - PBS **Prod** - WGBHTV

Theonie - zouzoukakia - meatball sausages in wine sauce 14 MIN
Videoreel / VT2
Theonie series
Color
Shows how to make the Greek dish zouzoukakia using ground meat mixed with damp stale bread bits, eggs, garlic, parsley, grated cheese, ground cumin, salt and pepper. Prepares the wine sauce with tomato sauce, garlic, red wine, olive oil and pepper.
Home Economics
Dist - PBS **Prod** - WGBHTV

The Theorem of the Mean 10 MIN
16mm
MAA Calculus Series
Color
States the theorem of the mean and how it is derived from Rolle's theorem. Develops the intermediate function to which Rolle's theorem is applied.
Mathematics
Dist - MLA **Prod** - MAA

The Theorem of the Mean 28 MIN
16mm
Maa Calculus Series
Color (H C)
LC FIA68-2216
Derives the theorem of the mean from Rolle's theorem. Gives particular attention to developing the intermediate function to which Rolle's theorem is applied. An animated film narrated by Felix P Welch.
Mathematics
Dist - MLA **Prod** - MAA 1967

Theorem Painting 55 MIN
BETA / VHS
Color
Introduces the art of theorum painting and gives basic techniques.
Fine Arts
Dist - HOMEAF **Prod** - HOMEAF

Theorem Proving 18 MIN
U-matic / VHS
Probability and Random Processes - Elementary Probability Theory 'Series
B&W (PRO)
Introduces lecture on theorem proving.
Industrial and Technical Education; Mathematics
Dist - MIOT **Prod** - MIOT

The Theories of the press 25 MIN
VHS
Color (J H C)
$39.95 purchase _ #IVMC12
Reveals that mass communication specialists have placed all of the world's press systems into five categories - authoritarian, libertarian, Soviet - totalitarian, social responsibility and developmental. Explains how each of these five theories were developed, their chief purpose for existence, who has the right to use mass media, how the media is controlled, who owns the media and what is forbidden under each type. While the United States more or less follows the Social Responsibility school of press, it is vital to understand other systems in order to understand global media.
Sociology
Dist - INSTRU

Theories on the Origin of Life 14 MIN
U-matic / VHS / 16mm
Biology Series Unit 10 - Evolution; Unit 10 - Evolution
Color; B&W (H C)
LC 71-702923
Discusses four theories which explain the origin of life.
Science; Science - Natural
Dist - EBEC **Prod** - EBEC 1969

Theory 18 MIN
16mm
Search for Solutions Series
Color (J)
LC 79-701464
Points out that in scientific investigation, theories explain and set in motion other processes of problem solving. Narrated by Stacy Keach.
Science
Dist - KAROL **Prod** - PLYBCK 1979

Theory and Layout 15 MIN
VHS / BETA
Color (IND)
Deals with square and rectangular duct layout. Illustrates the various methods of making a straight piece of duct work, and discusses seaming techniques.
Industrial and Technical Education; Psychology
Dist - RMIBHF **Prod** - RMIBHF

Theory and practice - Video I 37 MIN
VHS
Therapeutic touch - healing through human energy fields series
Color (C PRO)
$275.00 purchase, $75.00 rental _ #42 - 2485, #42 - 2485R
Explores the theoretical framework of Therapeutic Touch. Covers its evolution from Eastern healing arts and how human energy fields respond. Defines key concepts and highlights research which document its clinical effectiveness. Includes a CE - certification education - self study guide and reprints of research studies and relevant articles. Part of a three - part series featuring Janet Quinn with Dora Kunz, Janet Macrae and other experts.
Business and Economics; Health and Safety
Dist - NLFN **Prod** - NLFN

Theory and research - foundations 13 MIN
VHS
Foundations and applications of distance education series
Color (T G)
$50.00 purchase
Examines the implications of research for distance education practice. Part of a series.
Education
Dist - AECT **Prod** - IODIED 1995

Theory and testing of lead acid batteries 30 MIN
U-matic / VHS
Basic electricity, dc series
Color (IND)
Illustrates the storage battery as portable electric energy. Shows primary and secondary cells and the theory of operation of the most popular secondary cell, the lead acid battery. Tells how to service and maintain this battery and discusses safety procedures and servicing equipment.
Industrial and Technical Education; Science - Physical
Dist - AVIMA **Prod** - AVIMA

Theory into Practice 29 MIN
U-matic / VHS / 16mm
Human Relations and School Discipline Series
Color
Documents individualized instruction as practiced at University Elementary School on the campus of UCLA, with commentary by Dr Madeline Hunter, principal of the

school and creator of the program. Includes sequences filmed at an inner - city school where the theories and techniques are being field - tested.
Education; Sociology
Dist - FI **Prod** - MFFD

The Theory is Tested 30 MIN
VHS / 16mm
Solar Energy Series
Color (G)
$55.00 rental _ #SLRE - 102
Looks at the prospect of a home fully heated by solar energy.
Science - Physical; Social Science
Dist - PBS **Prod** - KNMETV

The Theory of cooking, in brief - lesson 1 8 MIN
8mm cartridge / 16mm
Modern basics of classical cooking series
Color (A)
#MB01
Introduces basic knowledge required for the 14 following lessons in the series. Discusses the four elements of the cooking process - food, untensils, basic methods and heat source - types of heat and the essentials of modern nutrition. Part of a series developed in cooperation with the Swiss Association of Restauranteurs and Hoteliers to train foodservice employees. Includes five instructor's handbooks, a textbook by Eugene Pauli, 20 sets of student tests and 20 sets of student information sheets.
Home Economics; Industrial and Technical Education
Dist - CONPRO **Prod** - CONPRO

Theory of Debye and Huckel, Effect of the Ionic Atmospheres on Activities, Energy 46 MIN
U-matic / VHS
Electrochemistry Series
Color
Discusses the theory of Debye and Huckel, effect of the ionic atmospheres on activities, energy, applications, solubility of sparingly soluble salts, dissociation constants of weak acids and kinetics of reaction.
Science; Science - Physical
Dist - KALMIA **Prod** - KALMIA

Theory of Debye and Huckel - effect of the ionic atmospheres on activities - energy 46 MIN
U-matic / VHS
Electrochemistry - Pt II - thermodynamics of electrolytic solutions series
Color
Discusses the theory of Debye and Huckel, effect of the ionic atmospheres on activities, energy, free energy of ionic atmospheres, osmotic coefficient, activity coefficient, application of Debye and Huckel theory to osmotic coefficients and to the heat of dilution, application of Debye and Huckel theory to activity coefficients, solubility of sparingly soluble salts, dissociation constants of weak acids and kinetics of reaction.
Science; Science - Physical
Dist - MIOT **Prod** - MIOT

Theory of Electrophoresis 29 MIN
VHS / U-matic
Colloid and Surface Chemistry - Electrokinetics and Membrane Series
Color
Science; Science - Physical
Dist - KALMIA **Prod** - KALMIA

Theory of Equations and Synthetic Division 29 MIN
16mm
Advanced Algebra Series
B&W (H)
Uses the technique of plotting by completing the square to graph a variety of parabolas, displaced from their axes in various ways. Shows use of synthetic division to test for roots of cubic equations.
Mathematics
Dist - MLA **Prod** - CALVIN 1960

Theory of evolution 29 MIN
U-matic
Introducing biology series; Program 34
Color (C A)
Discusses Charles Darwin and the development of the theory of evolution. Shows films of Gallapogos Islands where Darwin formulated his theory. Covers five parts of the theory.
Science - Natural
Dist - CDTEL **Prod** - COAST

The Theory of Helicopter Flight 22 MIN
16mm
Color
LC 74-705770
Describes how the helicopter obtains lift, direction stability and control. Shows the use of the helicopter in war and peace.
Industrial and Technical Education; Science - Physical; Social Science; Sociology
Dist - USNAC **Prod** - USN 1969

Theory of limits - Pt 1 - limits of sequences 34 MIN
16mm
Mathematics today series
B&W (H C)
LC FIA66-1270
Professor E J Mc Shane, with the aid of animation, defines the limit of a sequence using the concept of an advanced set.
Mathematics
Dist - MLA **Prod** - MAA 1963

Theory of limits - Pt 2 - limits of functions and limit processes 38 MIN
16mm
Mathematics today series
B&W (H C)
LC FIA66-1270
Professor E J Mc Shane applies the method of advanced sets to the definition of a limit of a real valued function and to the definition of an integral.
Mathematics
Dist - MLA **Prod** - MAA 1963

Theory of limits - Pt 3 13 MIN
16mm
Mathematics today series
B&W (H C)
LC FIA66-1270
Professor E J Mc Shane applies the method 'advanced sets' to cauchy convergence.
Mathematics
Dist - MLA **Prod** - MAA 1963

Theory of Optical Waveguides 34 MIN
VHS / U-matic
Integrated Optics Series
Color (C)
Presents a comparison of geometric or 'ray optic' approach to wavelength theory with the electromagnetic field or 'physical optic' approach. Discusses theoretical derivation of the mode profiles and cutoff conditions for planar waveguides.
Science - Physical
Dist - UDEL **Prod** - UDEL

Theory of Processing 29 MIN
U-matic
Radiographic Processing Series Pt 2
Color (C)
LC 77-706071
Reviews formation of latent image and development of visable image, developer oxidation, relationship of time and temperature to development, calculation of film development time in a processor, standard processing or cycle time and standard radiographic processing.
Health and Safety; Industrial and Technical Education; Science
Dist - USNAC **Prod** - USVA 1975

The Theory of relativity 20 MIN
U-matic / VHS / BETA
Color; PAL (G H C)
PdS55, PdS63 purchase
Shows how Einstein's special theory of relativity explains how the concept of time is affected in experiments dealing with objects moving at high velocities.
Science; Science - Physical
Dist - EDPAT **Prod** - IFB

Theory of Relativity - an Introduction 20 MIN
U-matic / VHS / 16mm
Color (H C)
LC 81-700689
Depicts everyday examples of the relativity of motion, then postulates the unchanging velocity of light. Deduces the time - dilation formula and applies it to atomic clocks, atmospheric mesons, and daily experience.
Science - Physical
Dist - IFB **Prod** - IFB 1981

Theory of the Lead - Acid Storage Battery 25 MIN
16mm
B&W
LC FIE60-215
Shows in detail, by use of animation, how chemical energy is converted into electrical energy to produce electromotive force.
Science - Physical
Dist - USNAC **Prod** - USN 1959

Theory on Concept Formation 30 MIN
16mm
B&W (P I J H)
Shows Dr Anthony Mc Naughton lecturing on children developing satisfactory understanding through wide experience.
Education; Psychology
Dist - AWPC **Prod** - AWPC 1968

Theory Vs Practice - Bennis on Leadership 30 MIN
U-matic
Decision Makers Series
Color
Features an interview with Dr Warren Bennis, former president of the University of Cincinnati. Deals with qualities necessary for leadership and problems that face leaders.
Biography; Civics and Political Systems
Dist - HRC **Prod** - OHC

Theory X and Theory Y - Two Sets of Assumptions in Management 10 MIN
U-matic / VHS / 16mm
Color
LC 74-700702
Presents Douglas Mc Gregor's Theory X and Theory Y assumptions about people. Shows how assumptions influence managerial style and how managerial style can determine the effectiveness of a manager.
Business and Economics; Psychology
Dist - SALENG **Prod** - SALENG 1974

ThePrizewinners - Pt 2 29 MIN
16mm
Color
LC 79-700110
Focuses on Rosalyn Yallow, Roger Guillemin and Andrew Schally, the Veterans Administration's Nobel laureates of 1977. Presents a portrait of their personalities and describes their scientific backgrounds, research methods and the impact of their research on patient care.
History - World
Dist - USNAC **Prod** - USVA 1978

Therapeutic Activity for Perceptual - Motor Dysfunction through Use of a Scooter 15 MIN
16mm
B&W
LC 74-700851
Shows a variety of tasks, all using a scooter and designed to provide specific types of sensory input to enchance sensitory integration and the ability to motor plan.
Health and Safety
Dist - USC **Prod** - USC 1969

Therapeutic alternatives series

Biofeedback and self - control	30 MIN
Humanistic psychotherapy	30 MIN
Putting psychotherapy on the couch	30 MIN
Somatic - emotional therapy	30 MIN

Dist - THINKA

Therapeutic child rearing - 12 47 MIN
VHS / U-matic
Glendon programs - a series
Color (C A)
$305.00, $275.00 purchase _ #V599
Interviews Dr Firestone to summarize his approach to parent - child relationships. Includes conversations with Dr Richard Seiden - suicidologist and psychologist, Barry Langberg - attorney, and Joyce Catlett - child mental health specialist. Part of a 12 - part series featuring Dr Robert W Firestone, who is noted for his concept of the 'inner voice' and Voice Therapy.
Health and Safety; Psychology; Sociology
Dist - BARR **Prod** - CEPRO 1991

The Therapeutic Community 28 MIN
16mm
Color
LC 74-705686
The model therapeutic community at a Michigan State Hospital is described by staff, administrators and patients. Presents the strains and stresses, pleasures and rewards involved in the attempt of the hospital community to duplicate life outside the hospital.
Psychology; Sociology
Dist - UMICH **Prod** - UMITV 1969

Therapeutic Exercise Equipment with Pulleys 30 MIN
VHS / U-matic
B&W
Demonstrates various therapeutic exercise equipment used with patients that have muscular weakness. Explains the concept of mechanical advantage in relation to fixed and movable pulleys. Includes demonstrations of different wall weights, the elgin table and various springs and slings for therapeutic exercise.
Health and Safety; Science - Natural
Dist - UWASH **Prod** - UWASH

Therapeutic Exercise - Orthopedics 28 MIN
16mm
B&W
LC FIE52-1726
Demonstrates therapeutic exercises suitable in the management of orthopedic cases.

Health and Safety
Dist - USNAC Prod - USA 1950

Therapeutic exercise procedures 150 MIN
U-matic / VHS
Color (H A PRO)
$180.00, $230.00 purchase, $100.00 rental
Demonstrates therapeutic exercise procedures. In 3 parts. Part I discusses Rolling And Prone Progression, Part II, Low Trunk Procedures, and Part III, Sitting and Standing Progressions.
Health and Safety
Dist - BUSARG Prod - PATSUL 1987

Therapeutic Exercise Procedures for the Hemiplegic Patient 40 MIN
VHS / U-matic
Color; Mono (C A)
Demonstrates the integrated approach of treatment techniques for renewal of the skill level for motor control. In 2 parts. Part I explains the theory and techniques of this program through a demonstration on a male patient. Part II explains the same through a demonstration on a female patient.
Health and Safety
Dist - BUSARG Prod - PATSUL 1985

Therapeutic Interaction with a Schizophrenic Patient 10 MIN
U-matic / VHS
B&W
Simulates nurse - patient interaction in the setting of an inpatient treatment environment where the patient displays schizophrenic behaviors.
Psychology
Dist - UWASHP Prod - UWASHP

Therapeutic Intervention in Assaultive Behavior 19 MIN
VHS / 16mm
(C PRO)
$385.00 purchase _ #861VI074
Helps nurses develop and review skills to deal with assaultive behavior.
Health and Safety
Dist - HSCIC Prod - HSCIC 1986

Therapeutic Intervention in Assaultive Behavior 19 MIN
U-matic / VHS
Color (PRO)
Discusses three elements in the intervention of assaultive behavior - verbal intervention, defense skills and physical intervention. Intended for VA nurses and mental health care personnel.
Psychology
Dist - USNAC Prod - VAMCNY 1984

Therapeutic massage for sports and fitness 102 MIN
VHS
Color (G)
$39.95 purchase _ #ESS801V
Features massage therapist Rich Phaigh with instruction in therapeutic massage for sports and fitness. Presents step - by - step instruction for each area of the body. Explains and demonstrates various massage regimens and techniques.
Physical Education and Recreation; Science - Natural
Dist - CAMV Prod - CAMV 1988

Therapeutic Physical Intervention - Vol II 26 MIN
VHS / 16mm
Nonviolent Crisis Intervention Series
Color (PRO)
$375.00 purchase
Demonstrates basic principles of personal safety when dealing with a physically aggressive individual, as well as passive blocking skills, flails and punches. Shows how to utilize physical and psychological advantage during physical assaults, release techniques for grabs, hairpulls, bites and chokes, basic blocks against kicks, therapeutic restraint, moving the aggressive individual and maintaining a therapeutic attitude during the violence.
Education; Psychology; Sociology
Dist - NCPI Prod - NCPI 1989

Therapeutic Silence 30 MIN
U-matic / VHS
Rapeutic Relationships Series
Color
Illustrates how a skillful, understanding nurse helps improve the outlook of a severely depressed adolescent who has been hospitalized following a suicide attempt.
Guidance and Counseling; Health and Safety; Psychology
Dist - AJN Prod - AJN

Therapeutic techniques for Hispanic, Black and American Indian clients - Pt I 60 MIN
U-matic / VHS
Color
Discusses therapeutic techniques in working with Hispanic, Black and American Indian clients. Points out historical, cultural and social factors which are relevant in assessing client problems.
Sociology
Dist - UWISC Prod - UWISC 1981

Therapeutic techniques for Hispanic, Black, and American Indian Clients - Pt II 30 MIN
VHS / U-matic
Color
Continues the discussions on working with minority clients.
Sociology
Dist - UWISC Prod - UWISC 1981

Therapeutic techniques - Pt I - interpretations, silence and how silence is 30 MIN
U-matic / VHS
Treatment of the borderline patient series
Color
Emphasizes the need of the therapist's sensitivity to the patient's skill in coercing the therapist into making too many early interpretations.
Health and Safety; Psychology
Dist - HEMUL Prod - HEMUL

Therapeutic Techniques, Pt II - 'Good Mothering' 15 MIN
U-matic / VHS
Treatment of the Borderline Patient Series
Color
Discusses the non - constructive value of certain kinds of supper and so - called 'good mothering' in the treatment of borderline patients who become guilty at their inability to be equally feeling or caring.
Health and Safety; Psychology
Dist - HEMUL Prod - HEMUL

Therapeutic techniques - Pt III - communications between therapist and patient 24 MIN
U-matic / VHS
Treatment of the Borderline Patient Series
Color
Stresses the value of the therapist communicating free - associations, fears and other feelings and inner subjective data which occur during a session with a therapist.
Health and Safety; Psychology
Dist - HEMUL Prod - HEMUL

Therapeutic Touch - a New Skill from an Ancient Practice 28 MIN
VHS / 16mm
Color (C PRO)
$275.00 purchase, $60.00 rental _ #7538S, #7538V
Features demonstrations with actual patients to explore benefits of Therapeutic Touch, a scientific use of touch to diminish anxiety and alleviate pain. Approved for CE credit. Includes study guide.
Health and Safety
Dist - AJN Prod - HOSSN 1990

The Therapeutic Touch - Healing in the New Age 35 MIN
16mm
Color (H C A)
LC 79-700606
Focuses on the work of Dr Dolores Krieger, specialist in hemoglobin research and professor of nursing at New York University. Shows her teaching a seminar, doing research in the laboratory, and utilizing the special techniques involved in her 'therapeutic touch' method while working with patients.
Health and Safety; Science
Dist - HP Prod - HP 1979

Therapeutic touch - healing through human 127 MIN
energy fields series
VHS
Therapeutic touch - healing through human energy fields series
Color (C PRO)
$675.00 purchase _ #42 - 2488M
Presents a three - part series featuring Janet Quinn with Dora Kunz, Janet Macrae and other experts. Introduces viewers to Therapeutic Touch. Includes the titles Theory and Practice; The Method; Clinical Applications.
Business and Economics; Health and Safety
Dist - NLFN Prod - NLFN

Therapeutic Use of Toys 28 MIN
U-matic / VHS
B&W
Demonstrates the use of toys to elicit a specific motor response such as prone extension, supine flexion, postural support with push pattern, finger and wrist extension and grasp with wrist stabilization.
Health and Safety
Dist - BUSARG Prod - BUSARG

Therapeutic uses of heat and cold - Pt 1 - administering hot applications 21 MIN
16mm
Nursing series
B&W
LC FIE52-336
Discusses body reactions to heat and the use of heat to alleviate pain. Shows how to apply hot water bottles, electric pads, chemical pads and paraffin baths. Shows how to use hot soak, compresses, infra - red lamps and shortwave diathermy.
Health and Safety
Dist - USNAC Prod - USOE 1945

Therapeutic Vocal Cord Injection - a Seventeen Year Overview 25 MIN
VHS / U-matic
Color (PRO)
Gives a history and summary of vocal cord injection for therapeutic purposes. Includes a demonstration of the technique and its results.
Health and Safety; Science
Dist - USNAC Prod - USVA 1981

Therapeutic Vs Nontherapeutic Communication 20 MIN
VHS / 16mm
(C)
$330.00 purchase _ #780VI001
Shows a health professional communicating with a patient in a nontherapeutic way, then a second version of the same situation instructing the viewers in the techniques of therapeutic communication.
Health and Safety
Dist - HSCIC Prod - HSCIC

Therapeutically Radiated Breast 29 MIN
U-matic
Color
Speaks about the advantages of radiation therapy over surgery.
Health and Safety
Dist - UTEXSC Prod - UTEXSC

Therapeutive alternatives quartet 120 MIN
VHS / BETA
Color (G)
$69.95 purchase _ #Q344
Presents a four - part discussion about therapeutic alternatives. Includes 'Biofeedback and Self - Control' with Dr George Fuller - Von Bozzay, 'Humanistic Psychotherapy' with Dr James Bugental, 'Putting Psychotherapy on the Couch' with Dr Bernie Zilbergeld and 'Somatic - Emotional Therapy' with Stanley Keleman.
Health and Safety; Psychology; Religion and Philosophy
Dist - THINKA Prod - THINKA

Therapist(S) - Couple Communication 55 MIN
U-matic / VHS
Family Communication Series
Color
Reveals the 'what and how' of communication between married co - therapists and four couples in a program which focuses on reinforcement rather than on discounting for more functional marriages.
Psychology; Sociology
Dist - HEMUL Prod - HEMUL

Therapist(S) - Family Communication 60 MIN
VHS / U-matic
Family Communication Series
Color
Reveals how therapists communicate openly and directly with a family to establish a working alliance, minimize scapegoating, disqualifications, vindictiveness and guilt provoking, while increasing objectivity and responsibility in the parents for the children as well as themselves.
Psychology; Sociology
Dist - HEMUL Prod - HEMUL

Therapy and pain management 13 MIN
VHS / 16mm
Learning about arthritis series
Color (H C A PRO)
$195.00 purchase, $75.00 rental _ #8088
Examines therapy for arthritis and discusses various methods of pain management.
Health and Safety; Science - Natural
Dist - AIMS Prod - HOSSN 1988

Therapy Can be Fun - a Look at Sensory Integrative Activities
U-matic / VHS
Color
Presents an introduction to the use of sensory integrative treatment activities and demonstrates a variety of activities that may be used. Addresses areas of sensory integration including tactile, vestibular, proprioception, equilibrium vestibular - bilateral integration and motor planning.
Health and Safety; Psychology
Dist - UWASH **Prod** - UWASH

Therapy Choices 30 MIN
VHS / 16mm
Psychology - the Study of Human Behavior Series
Color (C A)
$99.95, $89.95 purchase _ 24 - 23
Discusses alternatives and evaluation of various kinds of therapy.
Psychology
Dist - CDTEL **Prod** - COAST 1990

Therapy in Motion 13 MIN
U-matic / VHS / 16mm
Color
Demonstrates how arthritis sufferers can help themselves to feel better. Emphasizes the importance of establishing a daily routine that balances rest with proper exercise.
Health and Safety
Dist - CORF **Prod** - MINIP 1980

The Therapy of Prayer 30 MIN
16mm
B&W
Depicts emotional difficulty encountered by the parents of a boy who stutters. Shows the mother enrolled in a prayer therapy treatment course at the University of Redlands where she discovers the true cause of the son's affliction.
Psychology; Religion and Philosophy; Sociology
Dist - WWPI **Prod** - GUIDAS 1959

Therapy - what do You Want Me to Say 15 MIN
16mm / U-matic / VHS
Conflict and Awareness Series
Color (I J H)
LC 74-701926
Dramatizes a young girl who is pressured into seeing a psychologist. Describes her initial hostility and fear, the role of psychologist, what therapy is and how it works.
Guidance and Counseling; Psychology
Dist - CRMP **Prod** - CRMP 1974

Therayattam 18 MIN
16mm
B&W
Presents a documentary on one of the oldest forms of organized dance worship of North Malabar in South India, performed in the courtyard of the village shrine in honor of the heroes of legend, faith or family.
Fine Arts; Geography - World; Sociology
Dist - RADIM **Prod** - JOHN

There Ain't no Flies on Us 28 MIN
U-matic
Color
Illustrates camping and recreational activities and facilities for physically handicapped youngsters as seen from their viewpoint with their thoughts, ideas and feelings expressed.
Psychology; Sociology
Dist - ESST **Prod** - ESST 1978

There are Alternatives 29 MIN
U-matic / VT3
(G)
$95.00 purchase, $45.00 rental
Looks at the growing international science of Peace Research. Features Professor Johann Galtung summarizing the results of Peace Research to date.
Civics and Political Systems; Sociology
Dist - EFVP **Prod** - EFVP 1987

There are Choices 18 MIN
16mm
Color
LC 78-701133
Tells the story of how former world champion cowboy Jim Shoulders became a small businessman. Juxtaposes his story with that of Blue Bell, an American corporation which makes Wrangler jeans.
Business and Economics
Dist - WSTGLC **Prod** - BLUBEL 1978

There are no Clowns
VHS / U-matic
Color (IND) (FRENCH)
Features Glenn Ford in a dramatic demonstration of the power of carbon dioxide and nitrogen in well servicing operations. Discusses proper bleed back procedures and safe work practices.
Business and Economics; Industrial and Technical Education; Social Science
Dist - GPCV **Prod** - GPCV

There are yachts at the bottom of my garden 10 MIN
U-matic / VHS / 16mm
Color (J)
LC 74-703291
Shows sailing on Sydney Harbor, Australia, where a number of boat owners have harbor - front homes and there are yachts at the bottom of the garden.
Geography - World; Sociology
Dist - JOU **Prod** - ANAIB 1974

There but for Fortune 60 MIN
16mm
Color
Chronicles the Latin American concert tour taken by Joan Baez, a journey impeded by government intimidation due to her public position as a humanist activist.
Civics and Political Systems; Geography - World
Dist - FIRS **Prod** - FIRS

There Comes a Time 30 MIN
16mm
Footsteps Series
Color
LC 79-701556
Discusses some of the things parents need in order to do a good job raising their children, enumerates resources that are available to help meet these needs and suggests ways in which parents can go about finding the help they need.
Guidance and Counseling; Home Economics; Sociology
Dist - USNAC **Prod** - USOE 1978

There Go I 26 MIN
16mm
Color (H C A)
LC 81-701029
Dramatizes a successful manager's view of the barriers facing the disabled worker. Discusses job modifications, workplace accommodations and the sensitive relations with coworkers.
Education; Guidance and Counseling; Psychology
Dist - MALIBU **Prod** - MALIBU 1981

There Goes the Bride 29 MIN
Videoreel / VT2
Our Street Series
Color
Sociology
Dist - PBS **Prod** - MDCPB

There Goes the Neighbourhood 13 MIN
16mm
Color
LC 76-703331
Poses possible solutions to housing problems as a reaction to the rising demolition of neighborhoods in Montreal. Focuses on the St Louis district in downtown Montreal.
Geography - World; Sociology
Dist - CANFDC **Prod** - CANFDC 1975

There is a Law Against it 8 MIN
U-matic / VHS / 16mm
Consumer Education Series
Color (J)
Introduces four familiar consumer problems - garnishment of wages, unauthorized auto repair work, payment demanded for a debt already paid and a housewife pressured into signing a purchase contract by a door - to - door salesman. Dramatizes how new consumer laws in California protect the consumer in each case.
Civics and Political Systems; Guidance and Counseling; Home Economics; Sociology
Dist - ALTSUL **Prod** - ALTSUL 1972

There is a Law Against it 8 MIN
16mm / U-matic / VHS
Color (J) (SPANISH)
Shows how laws in the state of California protect consumers from unfair garnishment of wages, unauthorized auto repair work, payment demanded for a debt already paid and being pressured into signing a contract by a door - to - door salesman.
Civics and Political Systems; Foreign Language; Home Economics
Dist - ALTSUL **Prod** - ALTSUL 1973

There is a Place Called Sesame Place 12 MIN
U-matic / 16mm
Color
Discusses Sesame Place, an innovative people powered park where families with children ages 3 to 13 play and learn together.
Education; Home Economics; Physical Education and Recreation; Psychology
Dist - MTP **Prod** - ANHBUS

There is a road 1 MIN
U-matic / VHS
Color
Employs TV spot format and voice-over technique to stress need for volunteers to drive cancer patients to and from treatment along 'The Road To Recovery.'
Health and Safety
Dist - AMCS **Prod** - AMCS 1982

There is a way 27 MIN
16mm
Color
LC 74-705772
Portrays the life of F - 105 pilots who fight the air war in Southeast Asia daily. Pictures their hazardous missions against a determined enemy in the North, while pilots and crews tell about the job they are doing and why.
Civics and Political Systems; History - World
Dist - USNAC **Prod** - USAF 1967

There is no Global Population Problem, and Geroethics
VHS / Cassette
Humanist Voices Speak Out Series
Color (G)
$49.95, $9.00 purchase
Offers two programs. Features Garrett Hardin who suggests that there are no global solutions to the problem of population growth in the first program. 'Geroethics' features Gerald A Larue and considers the ethical treatment of the growing population of elderly. Part of a series which examines social issues in light of humanist values.
Business and Economics; Health and Safety; Religion and Philosophy; Science - Natural; Social Science; Sociology
Dist - AMHUMA **Prod** - AMHUMA

There is no One Like Me 20 MIN
16mm
All that I Am Series
B&W (C A)
Fine Arts; Guidance and Counseling
Dist - NWUFLM **Prod** - MPATI

There is no one way to teach
VHS
(T PRO)
$10.00 purchase _ #A30
Feature Madeline Hunter who urges educators to view teaching as a situational, contextual profession.
Education
Dist - NSDC **Prod** - NSDC 1991

There must be a Catch 12 MIN
16mm / U-matic / VHS
Color
LC 74-702609
A study of interviewing and hiring practices. Presents a job interview between a high school drop - out and a personnel manager of a coffee plant to show the effect of an inept and insensitive interviewer, both from the point of view of a youth who deserves a better reception and an employer who desperately needs employees.
Business and Economics; Guidance and Counseling; Psychology
Dist - USNAC **Prod** - USBES 1968

There must be another way 60 MIN
VHS
Color (G R)
$24.95 purchase _ #C062
Features spiritual teacher Tara Singh in a workshop which discusses what precipitated the writing of 'A Course in Miracles' by Dr Helen Shucman.
Health and Safety; Psychology; Religion and Philosophy
Dist - LIFEAP **Prod** - LIFEAP

There Ought'a be a Law 25 MIN
16mm
Color
Looks at the litter problem and workable solutions to it. Studies Bottle Bill legislation and two viable alternatives, Resource Recovery and the Clean Community System.
Health and Safety; Sociology
Dist - MTP **Prod** - AIAS

There they Go 25 MIN
16mm
Color (A)
Goes behind the scenes to show how fine race horses are developed. Visits famous trainers and jockeys at thoroughbred farms and race track stables. Hosted by Jack Kramer.
Physical Education and Recreation
Dist - HLYWDT **Prod** - HLYWDT

There was a Child 28 MIN
VHS / 16mm
Color (G)
Allows parents suffering the loss of a perinatal child to express their feelings and demonstrates the ways they come to terms with their losses and move on.
Health and Safety; Sociology
Dist - FANPRO **Prod** - FANPRO 1989

There was an Unseen Cloud Moving 60 MIN
VHS / U-matic
Color (G)
$295.00, $250.00 purchase, $75.00 rental
Presents a deliberately fragmented biography of Isabelle Eberhardt, a Victorian traveller who dressed as an Arab man, became a Moslem and writer in Algeria at the turn of

the century. Reveals that even her death was romantic she died in a flash flood in the desert and most of her writings were lost in the sands.
Biography; Education; Literature and Drama; Religion and Philosophy; Sociology
Dist - WMEN **Prod** - LETH 1987

There were times, dear - a film about living with alzheimer's disease 60 MIN
16mm / U-matic / VHS
Color (H A G)
Illustrates the symptoms of Alzheimer's disease. Tells tho story of how one family, the Millards, deals with the problem. Presents facts and statistics.
Health and Safety; Physical Education and Recreation; Sociology
Dist - DIRECT **Prod** - LILAC 1986

There's a Message for You 15 MIN
U-matic / VHS
Reading for a Reason Series no 3
Color (J)
LC 83-706574
Uses a dramatic approach to reading and understanding expository texts. Focuses on techniques that get the author's purpose and message across, previewing techniques and clues to textbook messages.
Education; English Language
Dist - AITECH **Prod** - WETN 1983

There's always a question 8 MIN
16mm
Color
LC 75-700353
Tells a story about two unseen beings who observe the function of the Earth, the development of life forms there and man's evolution to the energy crisis. Designed to raise questions about alternative energy sources.
Guidance and Counseling; History - World; Science - Natural; Sociology
Dist - SCE **Prod** - SCE 1974

There's an elephant in that tree 28 MIN
VHS
Elephant show series
Color (P I)
$95.00 purchase, $45.00 rental
Presents program 37 in the Sharon, Lois and Bram's Elephant Show series. Teaches reading readiness and social skills while engaging children in making music. Each program explores a new theme through adventure, fantasy, mystery and song with recording artists Sharon, Lois and Bram. Uses traditional materials which stress participation - action songs, sing - along songs, story songs, clapping songs, singing games, playground chants and folk songs from many different traditions. Includes teacher's guide co - authored by a music education specialist.
Fine Arts; Sociology
Dist - BULFRG **Prod** - CAMBFP 1991

There's Magic in Good Speech 15 MIN
Videoreel / VT2
Sounds Like Magic Series
B&W (P)
English Language
Dist - GPN **Prod** - MOEBA

There's money where your mouth is 46 MIN
VHS
Elaine Clark voice - over series
Color (J H C G)
$39.95 purchase _ #DES01V
Teaches the fundamentals of voice - over acting. Part of a three - part series by Elaine Clark on the field of voice - overs.
English Language; Fine Arts
Dist - CAMV

There's more to Life 25 MIN
16mm
Captioned; Color (S)
Encourages participation in continuing education courses. Shows deaf people involved in a variety of continuing education classes.
Education; Guidance and Counseling; Psychology
Dist - GALCO **Prod** - GALCO 1977

There's more to life than the weekend 30 MIN
VHS
Stop, look, and laugh series
Color (J H R)
$19.95 purchase, $10.00 rental _ #35 - 831 - 19
Compares the excitement of the Christian life to the life of teenagers in a rut, complaining about boredom. Uses humor, comic vignettes and a question - and - answer session to present a Christian perspective. Hosted by Pat Hurley.
Literature and Drama; Religion and Philosophy
Dist - APH **Prod** - CPH
CPH

There's more to Me than what You See 29 MIN
16mm
Color (H C A)
LC 82-700189
Depicts the experiences of three disabled persons, their attitudes about themselves and the attitudes of others toward them. Focuses on the barriers society has erected against the disabled and the daily challenges that they must face.
Education; Psychology
Dist - APH **Prod** - AMERLC 1981

There's no Business Like Show Business 117 MIN
U-matic / VHS / 16mm
Color (C A)
Stars Ethel Merman and Donald O'Connor in the story of a vaudeville family who made their way from the Hinterlands to Broadway. Depicts the trials and tribulations of the Donahues and includes such Irving Berlin greats as Alexander's Ragtime Band, Simple Melody and There's No Business Like Show Business.
Fine Arts
Dist - FI **Prod** - IDEAL 1954

There's no Business Like Show Business 15 MIN
VHS / U-matic
Movies, Movies Series
Color (J H)
Explores the motion picture industry. Interviews people involved in making movies.
Fine Arts; Industrial and Technical Education
Dist - CTI **Prod** - CTI

There's no Excuse - using Safe Operating Procedures
16mm / U-matic
Color (A)
Stresses that good safety procedures are the first line of defense in accident prevention.
Health and Safety
Dist - BNA **Prod** - BNA 1983

There's no limit 29 MIN
U-matic
A Different understanding series
Color (PRO)
Describes the difficulties of two men with cerebral palsy and their quest for acceptance as normal adult human beings.
Psychology
Dist - TVOTAR **Prod** - TVOTAR 1985
RMIBHF RMIBHF

There's no Magic 15 MIN
U-matic / VHS
Soup to Nuts Series
Color (J H)
Explains that wise decisions about food affect physical, mental and emotional development. Shows how Lee learns that she doesn't need a genie to look and feel better.
Health and Safety; Social Science
Dist - AITECH **Prod** - GSDE 1980

There's no Place Like Home 15 MIN
16mm
Color
Recounts how Senior Companions help elderly citizens maintain their independence and continue to live in their own homes. Shows the volunteers helping with shopping, light housework and heavier chores.
Health and Safety; Social Science; Sociology
Dist - MTP **Prod** - ACTON

There's no such Thing as an Aunt in an Ant 9 MIN
VHS
Color
Discusses the structure of the any colony and the development of complex social behavor in these insects. Shows their communal achievements, including nomadic hunting behavior of army ants and the architecture and animal husbandry of weaver ants.
Science - Natural
Dist - CBSC **Prod** - CBSC

There's no such thing as an aunt in an ant colony 13 MIN
VHS
Natural history series
Color (I J H)
$60.00 purchase _ #A5VH 1107
Illustrates the communal achievements of ant colonies. Examines the structure of the colonies and their social behavior. Observes the nomadic hunting pattern of army ants as well as the architecture and animal husbandry of weaver ants. Part of a series on natural history.
Psychology; Science - Natural
Dist - CLRVUE **Prod** - CLRVUE

There's no such thing as women's work 30 MIN
VHS / U-matic
Color (C A PRO IND)
$45.00, $110.00 purchase _ #TCA17865, #TCA17864
Traces the history of women in the workplace in the 20th century. Describes the effect of various legislation on women in the workplace. Shows the role of the Department of Labor Women's Bureau.
Sociology
Dist - USNAC **Prod** - USDL 1987

There's no such thing as women's work 30 MIN
16mm / VHS
Color (G IND)
$5.00 rental
Presents a fast moving decade - by - decade history of 'women's work' in the United States. Offers images ranging from Eleanor Roosevelt to Alice Kramden and music by Aretha Franklin and Doris Day. Sketches the debate over protective legislation, the fight for the right to vote and the role of unions in winning rights for women workers.
History - United States; Social Science; Sociology
Dist - AFLCIO **Prod** - USDL 1988

There's Nobody Else Like You 14 MIN
U-matic / VHS / 16mm
Color (P I) (SPANISH)
LC 74-700030
Reveals that it is both natural and desirable that people have different appearances, interests and skills. Documents a trip to the zoo, a classroom discussion and a recreation of a school recess. Uses the events of the day and the words of children to show that everyone is truly an individual.
Foreign Language; Guidance and Counseling; Sociology
Dist - ALTSUL **Prod** - FILMSW 1973

There's something about a story 27 MIN
16mm
Color (P)
LC 71-704569
Uses the comments of storytellers and sequences from storytelling situations to show the value of storytelling with children 6 through 12 years of age. Discusses where to find stories and the basic techniques for preparing and presenting them.
English Language; Literature and Drama
Dist - CONNF **Prod** - PULIDO 1969

There's the Rub 8 MIN
16mm
Color
LC 77-702668
Focuses on the massage parlors of Toronto, Canada, and the attitudes of the people who operate them, work in them, patronize them or want to have them closed down.
Geography - World; Sociology
Dist - CANFDC **Prod** - CANFDC

There's Trouble Underfoot 15 MIN
16mm
Color (J)
Presents techniques for cleaning carpets, including shampoo, steam and dry cleaning. Shows how to establish a daily vacuuming regimen.
Home Economics
Dist - KLEINW **Prod** - KLEINW

Theresa - a change of face 29 MIN
VHS
Color (H C G)
$195.00 purchase, $45.00 rental _ #37894
Follows a young woman through a major maxillofacial surgery that dramatically alters the shape of her face. Explores the effects this change of face has upon her confidence, self - image and self - esteem. Produced by Mac and Ava Motion Picture Productions.
Health and Safety; Sociology
Dist - UCEMC

Therese 90 MIN
35mm / 16mm
Color (G) (FRENCH WITH ENGLISH SUBTITLES)
$300.00 rental; $59.95 purchase
Adapts the diary of Therese Martin, a nun who died at age 24 in 1897. Offers an intimate revelation of life in a convent by a nun who was canonized after her untimely death. Directed by Alan Cavalier. Based on Martin's Journal, published as a book.
Fine Arts; Religion and Philosophy
Dist - KINOIC
UILL

Therese 90 MIN
VHS
Color (G R) (FRENCH (ENGLISH SUBTITLES))
$59.95 purchase _ #S02280
Dramatizes the life of Therese Martin, who eventually was canonized as St Theresa. Based on Martin's journal, published as a book.

History - World; Literature and Drama; Religion and Philosophy; Sociology
Dist - UILL

Theresienstadt - gateway to Auschwitz 58 MIN
VHS / U-matic
Color (H C A) (ENGLISH, GERMAN, AND HEBREW (ENGLISH SUBTITLES))
$395.00 purchase, $90.00 rental
Features recollections of survivors of the transit camp Theresienstadt, which was established by Nazi officials in 1941. Includes rare archival photos, painting and drawings by ghetto inmates and scenes from a survivor's reunion at Theresienstadt House at Kibbutz Givat Chaim Ichud in Israel. Produced by Paul Tyras and Jan Fantl.
Civics and Political Systems; History - World
Dist - CNEMAG

Thermal Environment of the Neonate 14 MIN
U-matic / VHS
Color (PRO)
Discusses the modalities of heat loss, the infants' metabolic responses to heat loss or gain, the effect of birth weight on thermoregulation, thermal stress in low birth weight infants and the prevention of cold stress.
Health and Safety; Science - Natural
Dist - UMICHM **Prod** - UMICHM 1983

Thermal insulation 60 MIN
VHS
Piping Auxiliaries and Insulation Series
Color (PRO)
$600.00, $1500.00 purchase _ #GMTIN
Introduces the concept and types of thermal insulation. Shows how to select the right insulation for a particular application. Part of a three - part series on piping auxiliaries and insulation, which is part of a set on general and mechanical maintenance. Includes 10 textbooks and an instructor guide which provide four hours of instruction.
Education; Industrial and Technical Education; Psychology
Dist - NUSTC **Prod** - NUSTC

Thermal Interactions 15 MIN
Videoreel / VT2
Just Wondering Series
B&W (P)
Science - Physical
Dist - GPN **Prod** - EOPS

Thermal Metal Refining 45 MIN
U-matic / BETA / VHS
Color
Gives methods of refining.
Industrial and Technical Education; Psychology; Science - Physical
Dist - ASM **Prod** - ASM

Thermal Separation 60 MIN
VHS / U-matic
Chemistry Training Series
Color (IND)
Goes into evaporation and condensation, vapor pressures and boiling points of liquids, distillation, fractional distillation, continuous rectification and fractionation of petroleum.
Science; Science - Physical
Dist - ITCORP **Prod** - ITCORP

The Thermal Wilderness 29 MIN
16mm
Color (I)
LC 76-702108
Follows the fortunes of a backpacking party through two days of a heat wave. Demonstrates pacing, exposure avoidance and water and salt intake. Emphasizes prevention of heat disorders but demonstrates identification and early treatment of salt depletion, dehydration and incipient heat stroke.
Health and Safety; Physical Education and Recreation
Dist - LAWJ **Prod** - SAFECO 1975

Thermochemistry 29 MIN
U-matic
Chemistry 102 - Chemistry for Engineers - Series
Color (C)
Demonstrates how bonding characteristics affect fuel value. Relates bond energy to molecular structure and uses bond energies to calculate heats of reaction.
Industrial and Technical Education; Science - Physical
Dist - UILL **Prod** - UILL 1984

Thermocouples
Software / BETA
Temperature and Temperature Measurement Series
Color (PRO)
$600.00 - $1500.00 purchase _ #IDTHE
Identifies the parts of a thermocouple. Describes how a thermocouple works. Part of a four - part series on temperature and temperature measurement. Interactive training system includes course administrator guide, videodisc and computer software.
Industrial and Technical Education; Mathematics; Psychology
Dist - NUSTC **Prod** - NUSTC

Thermodynamics of Electrochemical Corrosion - Application of Stability Diagrams 52 MIN
U-matic / VHS
Corrosion Engineering Series
Color (PRO)
Industrial and Technical Education; Science - Physical
Dist - GPCV **Prod** - GPCV

Thermodynamics of Electrochemical Corrosion 1 - the Nernst Equation 58 MIN
VHS / U-matic
Corrosion Engineering Series
Color
Develops a measure of the relative tendency of metals to corrode. Illustrates the fundamental thermodynamic expression relating single electrode potentials to the effective concentration of species in solution, the Nernst equation.
Industrial and Technical Education; Science - Physical
Dist - MIOT **Prod** - MIOT

Thermodynamics of electrochemical corrosion - stability - pourbaix diagrams 51 MIN
U-matic / VHS
Corrosion engineering series
Color (PRO)
Industrial and Technical Education; Science - Physical
Dist - GPCV **Prod** - GPCV

Thermodynamics of Electrochemical Corrosion - the Nernst Equation 58 MIN
VHS / U-matic
Corrosion Engineering Series
Color (PRO)
Industrial and Technical Education; Science - Physical
Dist - GPCV **Prod** - GPCV

Thermodynamics of Electrochemical Corrosion 3 - Application of Stability Diagrams 52 MIN
U-matic / VHS
Corrosion Engineering Series
Color
Considers the corrosion of iron in terms of important anodic (metal dissolution, passivation, etc) and cathodic (proton and oxygen reduction) partial processes with the aid of stability diagrams. Illustrates the utility of such diagrams in terms of corrosion control.
Industrial and Technical Education; Science - Physical
Dist - MIOT **Prod** - MIOT

Thermodynamics of electrochemical corrosion 2 - stability - pourbaix - diagrams 51 MIN
VHS / U-matic
Corrosion engineering series
Color
Tells how stability (Pourbaix) diagrams are the electrochemical equivalent of metallurgical phase diagrams and shows, in a compact form, phase stability as a function of electrode potential and solution ph.
Industrial and Technical Education; Science - Physical
Dist - MIOT **Prod** - MIOT

Thermodynamics of fluid interfaces 48 MIN
U-matic / VHS
Colloid and surface chemistry - surface chemistry series
B&W/Color (PRO)
Science - Physical
Dist - MIOT **Prod** - MIOT
KALMIA KALMIA

Thermodynamics of polymer solutions, osmotic pressure 52 MIN
VHS / U-matic
Colloid and surface chemistry - lyophilic colloids series
Color
Science; Science - Physical
Dist - KALMIA **Prod** - KALMIA
MIOT MIOT

Thermodynamics of Solutions 18 MIN
U-matic
Chemistry 102 - Chemistry for Engineers - Series
Color (C)
Describes solubility in terms of the thermodyamic functions G, H and S.
Industrial and Technical Education; Science - Physical
Dist - UILL **Prod** - UILL 1981

Thermodynamics - potential ph diagrams 54 MIN
U-matic / BETA / VHS
Color
$400.00 purchase
Shows changes in a metal's equilibrium with its environment, the Nernst equation, and the electromotive force series.
Science; Science - Physical
Dist - ASM **Prod** - ASM

Thermography 28 MIN
Videoreel / VT2
Interface Series
Color
Business and Economics; Science - Physical
Dist - PBS **Prod** - KCET

Thermometers and how they work 11 MIN
U-matic / VHS / 16mm
Color (P) (SPANISH)
Demonstrates thermometers made with liquids, those made with gases and those made with solids. Explains expansion and contraction of materials. Shows how thermometers are used in various occupations.
Science; Science - Physical
Dist - EBEC **Prod** - EBEC 1963

Thermometers - the Hot and Cold of it
16mm / U-matic / VHS
Color
Shows how a thermometer works. Covers a variety of thermometers and their purposes.
Science
Dist - HIGGIN **Prod** - HIGGIN

Thermometric Titrations 20 MIN
U-matic / VHS
Experiment - Chemistry Series
Color (C)
$249.00, $149.00 purchase _ #AD - 1070
Uses the exothermicity of the reactions of ions in solution during titration to indicate the stoichiometry of the precipitates and complexes formed. Part of a series on experiments in chemistry.
Education; Psychology; Science; Science - Physical
Dist - FOTH **Prod** - FOTH

Thermoplastics 13 MIN
16mm
Plastics and fiber glass series
Color (J)
LC 76-712913
A thermoplastic project -- forming, shaping, finishing and joining.
Industrial and Technical Education
Dist - SF **Prod** - MORLAT 1967

These are Our Children 20 MIN
16mm
Color (PRO)
Shows the education and training of cerebral palsied children at the Eastern New York Orthopedic Hospital School.
Education; Health and Safety; Psychology; Science
Dist - UCPA **Prod** - UCPA 1951

These are Our Forests 14 MIN
16mm
Color
LC 79-700828
Examines the role of timber in the Southwestern United States, where wood is often the primary energy source for cooking and heating. Describes various types of woodburning stoves and the different kinds of timber they burn.
Home Economics; Social Science
Dist - USNAC **Prod** - USFS 1979

These are the Days 20 MIN
16mm
Color
Looks at a group of elderly people who have formed an acting ensemble whose purpose is to dramatize the aspects of aging through the use of satire and vignettes.
Health and Safety; Sociology
Dist - FILMID **Prod** - CLNTCR 1982

These are the directions I give to a stranger 15 MIN
16mm
Color (G)
$30.00 rental
Diagrams an exploration between imagination and reality with an old man circling outside a house, looking for water with a dousing rod, and a young woman circling inside a labyrinth of connecting rooms which are dimly lit. Reveals the conflicts between what is inside and what is outside; the woman is searching for something and the old man thinks he knows what it is.
Fine Arts; Literature and Drama; Psychology; Religion and Philosophy
Dist - CANCIN **Prod** - PIERCE 1984

These Faces I've Seen 29 MIN
VHS / 16mm
Color (G)
$55.00 rental _ #AMRA - 120
Profiles five members of the Puerto Rican community in Springfield, Massachusetts.
Sociology
Dist - PBS

These Items on Sale 20 MIN
16mm
Color
LC 73-713387
A study of the reaction of three women who meet at the funeral of their old, beloved teacher.
Sociology
Dist - GCCED **Prod** - GCCED 1971

These kids are tough 22 MIN
VHS
Color (J H)
$189.00 purchase, $75.00 rental _ #8342
Presents Samina, Ryan and Davida in true stories of real teens resisting drugs, overcoming alcoholic parenting, dysfunctional families and child molestation.
Health and Safety; Psychology; Sociology
Dist - AIMS **Prod** - HRMC 1991

These kids are tough 30 MIN
VHS
Color (J H T PRO)
$189.00 purchase _ #AH45654
Interviews teenagers who have successfully resisted pressure from their peers, neighbors and even family members to take or sell drugs.
Guidance and Counseling; Health and Safety; Psychology; Sociology
Dist - HTHED **Prod** - HTHED

These People are Working 23 MIN
VHS / 16mm
Color (G)
$55.00 rental _ #TPAW - 000
Features four people who have achieved successful careers despite physical and mental challenges.
Health and Safety
Dist - PBS **Prod** - KAETTV

These People - Focus on Community Care for the Mentally Disabled 29 MIN
16mm / U-matic / VHS
Color (A)
LC 79-701734
Uses Wilkes - Barre, Pennsylvania, as a case study to examine the issues involved in providing alternative treatment of mentally disabled individuals in small community care facilities. Includes a segment of a public forum on the subject, in which community leaders, neighbors, legislators and mental patients express their views and reactions to the issues.
Psychology; Sociology
Dist - PEREN **Prod** - HORIHS 1979

These people may pass 21 MIN
16mm / VHS
Color (G)
$395.00, $210.00 purchase, $45.00 rental
Records the impressions of United States citizens who travelled to Nicaragua to help with the coffee harvest, despite the Contras. Provides narration by one of the volunteers, a veteran of the Abraham Lincoln Brigade, who reads from his diary. Presents an INCINE production, Nicaragua's film studio created by the Sandinistas, whose films reveal the country's own perceptions of their revolution. Film by Rossana Lacayo.
Fine Arts; Social Science
Dist - FIRS

These Special People 14 MIN
16mm
Color
Shows how computer guided tools bring new sophistication, accuracy and speed to air traffic control. Looks at the thousands of navigational aids beaming radio signals to pilots and instrument landing systems at all major airports.
Industrial and Technical Education; Social Science
Dist - MTP **Prod** - FAAFL

These Special People 16 MIN
16mm
Color
LC 79-700824
Explores the work of electronics technicians in the Federal Aviation Administration. Tells how they install, operate and maintain the nation's complex airway facilities network.
Industrial and Technical Education
Dist - USNAC **Prod** - USFAA 1979

These Stones Remain 27 MIN
16mm
Color
Depicts Irish stone carving from the earliest times to the 12th century, shown in its natural surroundings along with many locations in the west of Ireland.
Fine Arts; Geography - World
Dist - CONSUI **Prod** - CONSUI

These things are ours 26 MIN
16mm
Audubon wildlife theatre series
Color (I)
Follows a long walk through a wilderness area of the Midwestern United States with naturalist - photographers Mary Jane Dockeray and Walter Berlet. Examines a profusion of plants and animals and the careless destruction of wildlife through the use of insecticides and man - made hazards.
Geography - United States; Industrial and Technical Education; Science - Natural
Dist - AVEXP **Prod** - AVEXP

These Too are Our Children 40 MIN
16mm
Color
Demonstrates methods of working with mentally retarded and physically handicapped persons, as practiced by the Boulder County Board of Developmental Disabilities in Colorado.
Education; Psychology
Dist - UCOLO **Prod** - UCOLO

These were the Maya 19 MIN
16mm / U-matic / VHS
Mexican Heritage Series
Color
LC 76-703910
Focuses on the Yucatan Peninsula, the site of the Mayan ruins of Chichen Itza, Uxmal, Dzibilchaltun and Tulum. Features the Mayas who populate the cities of the Yucatan and shows architecture and industry along with the old customs.
Fine Arts; Geography - World; History - World; Social Science; Sociology
Dist - FI **Prod** - STEXMF 1976

These women mean business - Kamsky Associates of the China trade 30 MIN
U-matic
Adam Smith's money world series; 143
Color (A)
Attempts to demystify the world of money and break it down so that a small business and its employees can understand and adjust to new social and economic trends. Reports on the major economic stories and discoveries of the day.
Business and Economics
Dist - PBS **Prod** - WNETTV 1985

Theseus and the Labyrinth 20 MIN
16mm / U-matic / VHS
Mythology of Greece series
Color (I J H)
$470.00, $330.00, $360.00 purchase _ #A505; LC 88-713596
Show some of Theseus' early heroic achievements before he became king of Athens.
History - World; Literature and Drama
Dist - BARR **Prod** - BRIANJ 1987

Theseus and the Minotaur 21 MIN
U-matic / VHS / 16mm
Color
LC 79-712544
Presents the Greek myth about Theseus and his encounter with the Minotaur.
Literature and Drama; Religion and Philosophy
Dist - PHENIX **Prod** - KINGSP 1970

Theseus and the Minotaur
VHS / 35mm strip
Timeless Tales - Myths of Ancient Greece - Set II
Color (I)
$39.95, $28.00 purchase
Recreates the myth of Theseus and the minotaur. Part of a five - part series on Greek mythology.
English Language; History - World; Literature and Drama; Religion and Philosophy
Dist - PELLER

Theseus and the Minotaur - a Greek Folk Tale 5 MIN
U-matic / VHS / 16mm
Color (P I)
Presents the story of Theseus, a young prince of Athens, who was a great warrior even as a boy. Explains how he outwitted Minos, the cruel King of Crete, and slew Minotaur, the monster.
Geography - World; Literature and Drama; Religion and Philosophy
Dist - LUF **Prod** - PIC 1972

They 16 MIN
U-matic / VHS / 16mm
Color (P I) (SPANISH)
$365.00, $250.00 purchase _ #72051
Shows the importance of including other people in one's life and provides insights into human relationships.
Psychology
Dist - CORF

They all Can Work 28 MIN
16mm
Color (H C A)
Looks at the employees of the Natural Recovery Systems, who are all physically and mentally handicapped. Shows them on and off the job, learning new skills and generally relaxing among themselves in the company cafeteria.
Education; Guidance and Counseling; Psychology
Dist - NFBC **Prod** - NFBC 1977

They all learn 28 MIN
16mm
Color
Explores the remaking of twelve schools in a poor rural Southern district, from a traditional, self contained arrangement to a more informal, continuous, child - centered program. This project was intended to eliminate deficiencies and improve achievement in one of the poorest and most underfunded counties in the United States.
Education; Psychology
Dist - PROMET **Prod** - PROMET

They all Learn to Read 26 MIN
16mm / U-matic / VHS
B&W (C)
Shows a reading class divided into four groups of varying reading ability and the teaching of each group at its own speed.
Education; English Language
Dist - IFB **Prod** - SYRCU 1956

They Also Learn 14 MIN
16mm
B&W
Discusses the program of a residential school for both educable and trainable children at the University of South Dakota. Depicts teacher training, psychological diagnosis and staff evaluation procedures in a summer school.
Education; Psychology
Dist - USD **Prod** - USD

They Appreciate You more 16 MIN
16mm
Working Mother Series
Color (H C A)
LC 75-701057
Looks at a family in which both adults work and share in the household responsibilities.
Sociology
Dist - NFBC **Prod** - NFBC 1974

They are their own gifts 52 MIN
16mm
Color (C A)
$295.00 purchase, $125.00 rental; LC 78-702046
Uses documentary photographs and interviews to present the lives and contributions of poetess Muriel Rukeyser, portrait artist Alice Neel and choreographer Anna Sokolow. Includes commentary by the artists.
Biography; Fine Arts; Literature and Drama
Dist - RHOMUR **Prod** - RHOMUR 1978
WMEN

They Call Him Ah Kung 24 MIN
16mm
Faces of Change - Taiwan Series
Color
Profiles Ah Kung, a Taiwanese schoolboy who will inherit the family farm but may leave it in favor of industry and an urban lifestyle. Explains that this is faced by many of his fellow schoolmates and that it affects Taiwan's ability to feed its population properly.
Education; Geography - World; Sociology
Dist - WHEELK **Prod** - AUFS

They Call it Pro Football 27 MIN
16mm
Color
LC FIA68-372
Describes the violence and excitement in professional football today and its effect on players, coaches and spectators.
Physical Education and Recreation
Dist - NFL **Prod** - AMEXCO 1967

They Call it Wildcat 32 MIN
16mm
Color (J)
LC 75-702966
Shows the efforts of the Vera Institute of Justice, through its creation of the Wildcat Services Corporation. Explains how the institute helps drug addicts and criminal offenders find work in New York City.
Guidance and Counseling; Social Science; Sociology
Dist - KAROL **Prod** - FDF 1975

They Call Me Names 22 MIN
16mm / U-matic / VHS
Color (H C A S)

LC 73-700194
Portrays the lives of mentally different young people and explores how they perceive a world in which they are told often and in many ways that they are retarded.
Education; Guidance and Counseling; Psychology
Dist - PHENIX **Prod** - EFFEX 1972

They Call the Wind Energy 29 MIN
U-matic
Color
LC 79-707935
Traces the history of the use of wind as an energy source and examines the concept and details of wind generation.
Social Science
Dist - UMICH **Prod** - UMICH 1979

They Called Me Stupid 20 MIN
VHS / U-matic
Color (H C A)
Focuses on dyslexia, the perceptual disorder which impairs the individual's ability to receive and communicate information accurately.
Psychology
Dist - JOU **Prod** - CANBC

They Called the Island Long 22 MIN
16mm
Color (I)
LC FIA68-840
Explores Long Island and the activities of its resi dents, in all its seasons, at work and at play. Learning and putting knowledge to use.
Geography - United States
Dist - LILC **Prod** - LILC 1967

They Came to Cordura 123 MIN
U-matic / VHS / 16mm
Color (H C A)
Stars Gary Cooper and Rita Hayworth. Portrays a career officer who once showed cowardice in battle, assigned to lead five medal - of - honor candidates back from the front to receive their decorations, accompanied by the daughter of a disgraced politician.
Psychology; Sociology
Dist - FI **Prod** - CPC 1959

They came to race 30 MIN
16mm
Color
Tells the story of men and machines in record - breaking competition at Indy in 1965 and the outcome as Jim Clark comes in first.
Physical Education and Recreation
Dist - SFI **Prod** - SFI

They Came to Stay 12 MIN
16mm
Color
Examines the effects of terrorism on the lives of Israelis in border development towns, focusing on Kiryat Shemona and Ma 'Alot. Shows what must be done to maintain these towns as viable parts of Israeli society.
Geography - World; History - World; Sociology
Dist - ALDEN **Prod** - UJA

They Came to Stay 30 MIN
U-matic
North of Sixty Degrees - Destiny Uncertain Series
Color (H C)
Investigates the reign of the Hudson's Bay Company, the growth of the fur and whaling industries and the role of the federal government.
Geography - United States; Geography - World; History - World
Dist - TVOTAR **Prod** - TVOTAR 1985

They Can be Helped 22 MIN
16mm / U-matic / VHS
Color (H C A)
LC 76-700916
Shows the methods used to help four severely handicapped children at the National Children's Home in England. Studies the children's progress over a period of six months.
Education; Psychology
Dist - IFB **Prod** - NACHH 1981

They Can be Helped 21 MIN
16mm / U-matic / VHS
Color (H C A)
LC 76-700916
Shows methods used to help four severely handicapped children. Studies the procedures used and the children's progress over a period of six months. Made in England.
Education; Psychology
Dist - IFB **Prod** - BADDH 1975

They can do it 53 MIN
16mm
Early childhood education study of Education Development Center series
B&W (T)
LC 75-707939
Deals with 26 first graders in the Pastorius Public School in Philadelphia who have never been in school before. Starts with the second day of school, following the class on five visits throughout the year.
Education
Dist - EDC **Prod** - EDS 1969

They Can do it 34 MIN
16mm
B&W (T)
LC 75-707939
Visits the classroom of Lovie Glenn with her 26 underprivildged children. Emphasizes the task of teaching the child in such a way as to provide learning and experiences for his education. The child must not only learn specific subjects, but must be taught how to learn in an educational framework.
Education; Psychology
Dist - EDC **Prod** - EDS 1968

They can't break our union 50 MIN
VHS
Color (H C G)
$89.95 purchase, $45.00 rental _ #TTP135
Chronicles the experiences of 68 members of United Auto Workers Local 430 on strike at Sterling Radiator, an industrial plant in Westfield, Massachussetts. Interviews strikers, their families and union officials. Examines the conditions which led to the walkout and the consequences on familly life of this longest strike in the state's history. Studies the breakdown in American labor relations in the past decade in which companies fire strikers and replace them with new workers. More companies are using strikebreakers, 'take - backs' and replacement workers to defeat unions. Culminates in an act of civil disobedience in which 91 union members are arrested for blockading a bus delivering strikebreakers to the plants.
Business and Economics; Fine Arts; History - United States; Social Science
Dist - TURTID

They Change their Tune 20 MIN
Videoreel / VT2
Learning Our Language, Unit 2 - Dictionary Skills Series LINCOLN, NB˚68501; Unit 2 - Dictionary skills
Color (P)
English Language
Dist - GPN **Prod** - MPATI

They Clear the Way 29 MIN
16mm
Big Picture Series
Color
LC 74-706277
Describes U S Army engineers whose job it is to build bridges, airfields and roads in Vietnam in order to bring mobility to combat forces.
Civics and Political Systems; History - World; Industrial and Technical Education; Sociology
Dist - USNAC **Prod** - USA 1967

They do Recover 22 MIN
16mm
Color
LC 78-700221
Shows Dinah Shore interviewing guest celebrities who discuss the effect of alcohol on their lives and careers, as well as how and why they were able to recover.
Health and Safety; Sociology
Dist - SUTHRB **Prod** - SUTHRB 1978

They don't build them like they used to 22 MIN
16mm
Color
LC 77-702669
Juxtaposes the use of building materials and techniques of the 1970s with the work of yesteryear.
Industrial and Technical Education
Dist - INCC **Prod** - HUDAC 1975

They Don't Come with Manuals 29 MIN
VHS / 16mm
Color (G)
$195.00 purchase, $100.00, $50.00 rental
Looks at what it is like to parent children with mental or physical challenges.
Health and Safety; Sociology
Dist - FANPRO **Prod** - FANPRO 1989

They Go Boom 21 MIN
16mm
B&W
Tells what happens when Oliver Hardy comes down with a roaring cold and Stan Laurel plays doctor.
Fine Arts
Dist - RMIBHF **Prod** - ROACH 1929

They Hailed a Steamboat Anyplace 30 MIN
16mm
B&W (P I J H)
Recreates the period from 1840 to 1918 in Oregon's Williamette Valley, when the river was the main route of travel and trade.
Geography - United States; History - United States; Psychology; Social Science
Dist - PCCOL **Prod** - PCCOL 1973

They Hailed a Steamboat Anyplace 28 MIN
U-matic / VHS
B&W
Features four oldtimers recalling the days when steamboats went up and down the Willamette River in Oregon. Uses still photography, old documentary footage and period music.
History - United States; Social Science
Dist - MEDIPR **Prod** - MEDIPR 1974

They Harness Nature 20 MIN
16mm
B&W
Describes the work done by the Drainage and Irrigation Department of Malaysia together with the farmers to create new productive areas.
Agriculture; Geography - World
Dist - PMFMUN **Prod** - FILEM 1958

They Knew they were Pilgrims 12 MIN
16mm
Color
LC 72-701077
A documentary narrative, which traces the Pilgrim adventure from its origins in Babworth, England, to the arrival of the Pilgrims at Plymouth in New England.
History - United States
Dist - PLIMOT **Prod** - PLIMOT 1971

They Know what they Want 8 MIN
16mm
Professional Selling Practices Series 2 Series
Color (H C)
LC 77-702354
Encourages sales people to interpret customer requests in terms of available stock. Demonstrates effective techniques for presenting and selling appropriate substitute merchandise.
Business and Economics
Dist - SAUM **Prod** - SAUM 1968

They laid it on the line 29 MIN
Videoreel / VT2
Turning points series
Color
Presents people who have risked their jobs and reputations to help fight pollution.
Science - Natural; Sociology
Dist - PBS **Prod** - WVIZTV

They lied to us 45 MIN
VHS
Color (J H R)
$60.00 rental _ #36 - 82 - 533
Profiles several young people who based their values and actions on the messages of television, music, movies and friends. Suggests that doing so only led to trouble.
Psychology; Religion and Philosophy; Sociology
Dist - APH **Prod** - WORD

They live by water 26 MIN
16mm
Audubon wildlife theatre series
Color (P)
LC 74-709409
Shows the world of an ordinary pond including the hydra, a multi - armed creature, a tiger that lives under water and a scorpion that looks like a dead twig.
Science - Natural
Dist - AVEXP **Prod** - KEGPL 1969

They made Me a Criminal 92 MIN
U-matic
B&W
Stars John Garfield as a boxing champion who becomes a fugitive on the run.
Fine Arts
Dist - VIDIM **Prod** - UNKNWN 1939

They never asked our fathers 58 MIN
VHS / U-matic / VT1
Color (G)
$59.95 purchase, $35.00 rental
Visits Nunivaaq, 'Island,' home for 2,000 years to the Yup'ik Eskimos, hunters and gatherers, seafarers and fishers. Reveals that other peoples were laying claim to their land - first the Russians and then the United States government. Discloses that the culture of the Yup'ik was irrevocably altered, that although they were never consulted, never conquered in war, never persuaded by treaty or negotiation, the Yup'ik were robbed of their land in a process that barely recognized them as a people. Interweaves historic photographs, documents, interviews with Eskimo elders and scenes of island life on the Bering Sea. Produced by KYUK - TV, John McDonald and Alexie Isaac.
History - United States; History - World; Social Science
Dist - NAMPBC

They never call it rape 21 MIN
BETA / VHS / U-matic
Color (H C G)
$250.00 purchase _ #KC - 6281M
Presents a shocking picture of double standards in institutions of higher education wherein victims of rape become the accused and universities do everything but openly protect the rapist. Demonstrates that gang rape has become so commonplace that many fraternities have given the term code names. Debunks the myth that so - called 'nice guys' and athletes do not commit sexual assault offenses.
Education; Sociology
Dist - CORF **Prod** - ABCNEW 1990

They Promised to Take Our Land 26 MIN
U-matic / VHS / 16mm
Native Americans Series
Color
Looks at the exploitation of Indian resources. Presents members of various tribes who discuss how their people have lost land to government encroachments. Notes the conflict of interest created by charging a single government agency with responsibility for both Indian affairs and the development of natural resources.
Psychology; Social Science; Sociology
Dist - CNEMAG **Prod** - BBCTV

They risked their lives - rescuers of the Holocaust 54 MIN
VHS
Color (G)
$39.95 purchase _ #628
Reveals that more than 8,500 non Jewish rescuers have been honored by Vad Vashem in Jerusalem for saving Jewish lives during the Holocaust. Discloses that thousands more remain unknown. From 1986 - 1988 Gay Block and Malka Drucker interviewed and photographed over 100 Holocaust rescuers from 12 countries. Meets the 'Righteous Gentiles' who risked their lives and the lives of their families to save Jews. Directed by Gay Block.
History - World
Dist - ERGOM **Prod** - ERGOM 1993

They Served, We Remember and Honor 20 MIN
16mm
Color
LC 80-700768
Shows Memorial Day services at Arlington National Cemetery in 1979, including the placing of wreaths at the Tomb of the Unknowns and at a plaque honoring Vietnam veterans. Shows the ceremony entitled No Greater Love, which was presented by children of servicemen killed, disabled or missing in action during the Vietnamese conflict.
Civics and Political Systems; Social Science
Dist - USNAC **Prod** - USVA 1979

They Shall See 5 MIN
16mm
Color (J)
LC 73-701881
Presents the wonder of the everyday world around us as seen through the human eye.
Psychology; Sociology
Dist - FRACOC **Prod** - FRACOC 1972

They shouldn't call Iceland, Iceland 28 MIN
16mm
Color (GERMAN FRENCH SPANISH NORWEGIAN)
LC 77-700423
Presents a travelog on Iceland.
Foreign Language; Geography - World
Dist - ICETB WSTGLC **Prod** - ICETB WSTGLC 1976

They sing of a heaven 16 MIN
16mm
Color
LC 72-702179
Documents sacred harp singing, a 200 - year - old tradition of religious singing which survives today in the rural South.
Fine Arts; Geography - United States; Religion and Philosophy; Sociology
Dist - UMISS **Prod** - UMISS 1972

They Steamed to Glory 22 MIN
U-matic / VHS / 16mm
Color (I J H)
LC FIA67-5547
A documentary of the steam engine and its role in the Westward expansion of the United States, from its earliest beginnings in 1831, when the John Bull was brought from England, to the last run of a mainline steam locomotive in 1960. Shows historically important locomotives in action, such as the Tom Thumb, the William Mason and the Pioneer. Illustrates the development in design and increase in size and power of locomotives over the years.
History - United States; Industrial and Technical Education; Social Science
Dist - IFB **Prod** - IFB 1962

They used to Call 'Em Trailers 16 MIN
16mm
Color
LC 79-701018
Uses on - location interviews to offer varying points of view regarding trailer park living. Attempts to dispel the notion that trailer living is undesirable.
Sociology
Dist - JEFFIL **Prod** - DEANZA 1978

They went that - a - way 26 MIN
16mm
B&W
LC FI68-309
Explores the Western movie from 'The Great Train Robbery' made in the early 1900s to 'How the West Was Won' made in 1963. Includes scenes which feature William S Hart, Tom Mix, John Wayne, Gary Cooper, Roy Rogers and Gene Autry.
Fine Arts
Dist - WOLPER **Prod** - WOLPER 1963

They Went that - a - Way and that - a - Way 106 MIN
16mm
Color
Tells how two bumbling deputies are planted inside a federal prison to track down stolen government bonds. Stars Tim Conway.
Fine Arts
Dist - TWYMAN **Prod** - UNKNWN 1978

They were Cars 11 MIN
U-matic / VHS / 16mm
Reading Vocabulary Series
Color (P I J)
Presents a musical tour of an auto wrecking yard which teaches action verb concepts while supplying material for independent observations about obsolescence and reliability.
English Language
Dist - PHENIX **Prod** - KINGSP 1971

They were ten 105 MIN
VHS
B&W (G) (HEBREW WITH ENGLISH SUBTITLES)
$79.95 purchase _ #521
Recreates the establishment of a 19th - century settlement in Palestine by ten Russian Jews. Shows how they contended with both Arab resentment and the Turkish military. Stars Ninette, Oded Teomi and Leo Filer. Directed by Baruch Dienar.
Fine Arts; History - World; Literature and Drama; Sociology
Dist - ERGOM **Prod** - ERGOM 1961

They Won't Forget 94 MIN
16mm
B&W
Explores the murder of a Southern high school girl. Tells how an innocent Northern teacher is accused, unleashing a crazed and vengeful mob determined to see the murderer hang. Stars Lana Turner and Claude Rains. Directed by Mervyn LeRoy.
Fine Arts
Dist - UAE **Prod** - UAA

They're Always Changing Things 6 MIN
Videoreel / VT2
SUCCESS, the AMA Course for Office Employees Series
Color
LC 75-704211
Presents an instructional course for office employees. Offers a case study which identifies and evaluates the ways in which people react to change. Discusses the merits of each type of reaction.
Business and Economics; Psychology
Dist - AMA **Prod** - AMA 1972

They're Doing My Time 56 MIN
16mm / VHS
Color (G)
$895.00, $495.00 purchase, $95.00 rental; LC 89708695
Examines the plight of the children of women in America's prisons. Reveals that every day thousands of children deal with the loneliness, confusion, anger and helplessness created by a parent's imprisonment. Examines the social dilemma between the need to carry out justice and the need to care for innocent children who are often abandoned while their parents do time.
Sociology
Dist - CNEMAG **Prod** - CNEMAG 1988

They're Murdering Our Children 20 MIN
VHS / U-matic
Color
$335.00
Sociology
Dist - ABCLR **Prod** - ABCLR 1984

They're not holding the ceiling up 50 MIN
VHS
Signs of the times series
Color (A)
PdS99 purchase
Takes viewers 'through the keyhole' into ordinary late 20th-century homes in Britain to see what people's perceptions of good and bad taste really are. Looks at associations and prejudices evoked by 'antique' interiors and furniture. Part four of a five-part series.
Fine Arts; Home Economics; Industrial and Technical Education
Dist - BBCENE

They're Out to Get You 13 MIN
16mm
Color
LC 70-705012
A dramatization about two cellmates, one a professional shoplifter, who form a shoplifting team and plot their future crimes against retail store operators. Designed to motivate small retailers to take preventive measures that will limit shoplifting in their stores.
Business and Economics; Psychology; Sociology
Dist - USSBA **Prod** - USSBA 1969

They're Your People 29 MIN
16mm
To Save Tomorrow Series
B&W (H C A)
Shows how to aid short - term patients and help local communities develop their own mental health facilities.
Psychology
Dist - IU **Prod** - NET 1971

They've killed President Lincoln 52 MIN
16mm
Color (I)
LC 79-712185
Uses authentic still pictures to recreate the events and intrigue leading up to the assassination of President Lincoln and the aftermath. Emphasizes the futility of political assassinations and explains that while a great public leader can be murdered, his ideas often live on to inspire succeeding generations.
Biography; History - United States
Dist - FI **Prod** - QUO 1971

They've killed President Lincoln - Pt 1 26 MIN
16mm
Color (I)
LC 79-712185
Uses authentic still pictures to recreate the events and intrigue leading up to the assassination of President Lincoln and the aftermath. Emphasizes the futility of political assassinations and explains that while a great public leader can be murdered, his ideas often live on to inspire succeeding generations.
History - United States
Dist - FI **Prod** - QUO 1971

They've killed President Lincoln - Pt 2 26 MIN
16mm
Color (I)
LC 79-712185
Uses authentic still pictures to recreate the events and intrigue leading up to the assassination of President Lincoln and the aftermath. Emphasizes the futility of political assassinations and explains that while a great public leader can be murdered, his ideas often live on to inspire succeeding generations.
History - United States
Dist - FI **Prod** - QUO 1971

Thicker than water 40 MIN
VHS
John Bull business series
Color (A)
PdS65 purchase
Takes a look at five different family businesses. Part of a six-part series on British business culture.
Business and Economics
Dist - BBCENE

Thicker than Water 22 MIN
16mm
B&W
Tells the story of a man who has a bill to pay and makes the mistake of asking a friend to take the money to the store for him. Stars Stan Laurel and Oliver Hardy.
Fine Arts
Dist - TWYMAN **Prod** - ROACH 1935

Thicker than water 10 MIN
VHS
Color (G C PRO)
$69.95 purchase, $25.00 rental
Looks at ways nursing home staff can deal with an Alzheimer's patient's emotionally upset family members. Part four of a series.
Health and Safety; Sociology
Dist - TNF

The Thief and the hangman 30 MIN
16mm
B&W
LC FIA64-1138
Explores the question, 'Who May Administer Justice' in the style of a morality fable. Deals with the time of moral man in an immoral society and shows that all men sin.
Civics and Political Systems; Religion and Philosophy
Dist - NAAJS **Prod** - JTS 1953

Thief in the night - SIDS 25 MIN
VHS / U-matic
Color
Profiles four families who have lost their children to Sudden Infant Death Syndrom (SIDS). Shows how to deal with the guilt, fear and ignorance.
Health and Safety; Home Economics; Sociology
Dist - MEDCOM **Prod** - MEDCOM

Thief in the Soil 10 MIN
16mm
Color
Explains the danger of underground soil destruction and suggests fumigation as a solution to the problem.
Agriculture; Science - Natural
Dist - DCC **Prod** - DCC

Thief of Bagdad 27 MIN
16mm
History of the Motion Picture Series
B&W (H C)
Presents 'THIEF OF BAGDAD,' showing Douglas Fairbanks as he battles monsters and mongol hordes led by a renegade who has designs on a princess.
Fine Arts
Dist - KILLIS **Prod** - SF 1960

The Thief of Bagdad 140 MIN
16mm
B&W
Presents an Arabian night fantasy about Ahmed, a notorious thief who reforms when he falls in love with the Princess. Recounts that in order to prove himself worthy, he has to undergo a series of adventures. Stars Douglas Fairbanks, Sr. Directed by Raoul Walsh.
Fine Arts
Dist - KILLIS **Prod** - UNKNWN 1924

The Thief of Baghdad 109 MIN
16mm / U-matic / VHS
B&W (I J H C)
Stars Sabu and Conrad Veidt in the tale of the love between the Prince of Baghdad and the Princess of Basra and the various adventures of the Grand Vizier and the light - fingered Urchin, Abu.
Literature and Drama
Dist - FI **Prod** - UAA 1940

The Thief tax 20 MIN
VHS / 16mm
(A PRO)
$160.00 purchase _ #40.0535
Looks at the theft of tools, equipment, and crude oil and examines the toll it takes on the company, consumer and employee. Gives information on prevention of theft for the field operators and supervisors.
Industrial and Technical Education; Social Science; Sociology
Dist - UTEXPE **Prod** - UTEXPE 1984
TEXACO

Thieves of Time 29 MIN
VHS / 16mm
Color (G)
$55.00 rental _ #THOT - 000
Examines the destruction of Arizona's priceless archaeological resources by pothunters who dig up ancient ruins in search of artifacts to sell or collect.
Sociology
Dist - PBS **Prod** - KAETTV

Thigh and Gluteal Region - Unit 23 27 MIN
U-matic / VHS
Gross Anatomy Prosection Demonstration Series
Color (PRO)
Discusses the anterior aspect of the thigh, including the anterior and medial compartments and their innervation and vascular supply, the gluteal region and the posterior compartment of the thigh.
Health and Safety; Science - Natural
Dist - HSCIC **Prod** - HSCIC

Thigh line lyre triangular 7 MIN
16mm
Color (G)
$16.00 rental, $282.00 purchase
Says filmmaker Brakhage, 'I wanted a childbirth film which expressed all of my seeing at such a time.'
Fine Arts
Dist - CANCIN **Prod** - BRAKS 1961
AFA AFA

A Thin Dime 10 MIN
16mm
Color (C)
Presents a surrealistic study of a beautiful woman with an artificial leg.
Fine Arts
Dist - CFS **Prod** - PIKE

Thin dining - diabetes 20 MIN
VHS
Color (G) (SPANISH)
$79.95 purchase _ #NHV400V
Assists diabetic adults in selecting low - fat, low - calorie but good - tasting restaurant cuisine. Shows how to choose nutritional food in restaurants, fast food establishments, salad bars, airline meals, parties and discusses diet saboteurs.
Health and Safety; Home Economics; Social Science
Dist - CAMV

Thin dining - weight management 20 MIN
VHS
Color (G) (SPANISH)
$79.95 purchase _ #NHV410V
Assists weight - conscious adults in selecting low - fat, low - calorie but good - tasting restaurant cuisine. Shows how to choose nutritional food in restaurants, fast food establishments, salad bars, airline meals, parties and discusses diet saboteurs.
Health and Safety; Home Economics; Social Science
Dist - CAMV

Thin dreams 21 MIN
U-matic / VHS
Color (G)
$295.00 purchase, $100.00 rental
Combines documentary interviews and dramatic improvisations to explore the obsession of many young women with thinness.
Health and Safety; Sociology
Dist - BAXMED **Prod** - NFBC

Thin Edge of the Bay 22 MIN
U-matic / VHS / 16mm
Color
Uses San Francisco Bay as a focus to study the economic and political conflicts over shrinking environmental resources in urban areas. Highlights the complex factors involved in all environmental and land - use decision - making.
Science - Natural
Dist - UCEMC **Prod** - LANDYR 1980

Thin Edge Series
Depression - the shadowed valley 59 MIN
Guilt - the Psychic Censor 59 MIN
Dist - IU

Thin edge series
Aggression - the explosive emotion 59 MIN
Anxiety - the endless crisis 59 MIN
Sexuality - the Human Heritage 59 MIN
Dist - IU
MEDCOM

Thin Edge Series
Depression - the shadowed valley 60 MIN
Guilt - the Psychic Censor 60 MIN
Dist - MEDCOM

The Thin Hyper Shell 27 MIN
16mm
Color
Describes the erection of a hyperbolic paraboloid roof at Purdue University under an advanced concept of construction.
Industrial and Technical Education
Dist - DCC **Prod** - DCC

Thin layer chromatography 10 MIN
VHS
Chemistry master apprentice series
Color (H C)
$49.95 purchase _ #49 - 7221 - V
Separates a mixture of strongly colored dyes using a silica gel TLC plate and a wide - mouthed bottle as a developing chamber. Demonstrates how to make a micropipet and how to use this pipet to spot the plate. Uses ultraviolet light and iodine to make colorless spots visible. Part of the Chemistry Master Apprentice series.
Science; Science - Physical
Dist - INSTRU **Prod** - CORNRS

Thin Layer Chromatography 13 MIN
VHS / U-matic
Organic Chemistry Laboratory Techniques Series
Color
Emphasizes the similarities in the principles of thin layer and column chromatography. Considers choosing a stationary phase and solvent.
Science; Science - Physical
Dist - UCEMC **Prod** - UCLA

A Thin line 35 MIN
VHS
Color (PRO IND A)
Features Peter Bell, executive director of the Institute of Black Chemical Abuse. Discusses how to deal with Afro - Americans in substance abuse counseling.
Guidance and Counseling; History - United States; Psychology; Social Science
Dist - CORF **Prod** - CORF 1990

The Thin Red Line 99 MIN
16mm
B&W (C A)
Tells of a soldier on Guadalcanal who constantly and compulsively risks his life in combat to smother his fear of becoming a coward and of his ironic friendship with a sergeant who masks his every human feeling with a cold, impersonal attitude.
Literature and Drama
Dist - CINEWO **Prod** - CINEWO 1964

Thin Twin Laundry System 27 MIN
VHS / 35mm strip / U-matic
Color (IND)
Highlights key installation points and service procedures for the Thin Twin laundry system.
Industrial and Technical Education
Dist - WHIRL **Prod** - WHIRL

Thine inward - looking eyes 2 MIN
16mm
Color (G)
$10.00 rental
Advises the viewer to relax and take a deep breath while watching this Thad Povey production. Winner of Will Hindle Award, 1994 Onion City Film Festival, Chicago.
Fine Arts
Dist - CANCIN

Thine is the Kingdom 52 MIN
U-matic / VHS
Testament - the Bible and History Series
Color (G)
$279.00, $179.00 purchase _ #AD - 1729
Follows Christianity from the transformation of the Roman Empire into a Christian Empire. Part of a seven - part series on the Bible and history.
History - World; Literature and Drama; Religion and Philosophy
Dist - FOTH **Prod** - FOTH

Thine is the Power 50 MIN
U-matic / 16mm / VHS
Window on the World Series
Color; Mono (J H C A)
MV $350.00 _ MP $600.00 purchase $50.00 rental
Probes the potential dangers of nuclear power generators. Includes interveiws with scientists, public officials, interested citizens about the possibilities of nuclear accidents, problems of waste disposal, and need for greater awareness of nuclear power.
Industrial and Technical Education; Sociology
Dist - CTV **Prod** - CTV 1977

The Thing 30 MIN
VHS
Join in series
Color (K P)
#362306
Shows that Nikki and Zack try to guess what a large, wrapped object left for Jacob might be, but when Jacob uncovers the mysterious thing, they still don't know what it is. Discovers that it is all right not to have the answer for everything. Part of a series about three artist - performers who share studio space in a converted warehouse.
Fine Arts; Literature and Drama
Dist - TVOTAR **Prod** - TVOTAR 1989

The Things a Teacher Sees 19 MIN
U-matic / VHS / 16mm
Color (C T)
LC FIA65-273
Stresses the value of teacher observation for detecting physical and emotional health problems of pupils.
Education; Psychology
Dist - IFB **Prod** - UOKLA 1964

Things are Different Now 15 MIN
16mm / U-matic / VHS
Bloomin' Human Series
Color (I J)
LC 78-701250
Focuses on a 12 - year - old boy and his perception of the recent divorce of his parents.
Fine Arts; Guidance and Counseling; Sociology
Dist - MEDIAG **Prod** - PAULST 1978

Things Aren't what they used to be 12 MIN
16mm
Color
Pictures the problems of the elderly pedestrian and follows some elderly pedestrians as they try to handle today's traffic complexities. Explains rules for safe walking.

Health and Safety; Social Science; Sociology
Dist - AAAFTS **Prod** - AAAFTS 1975

Things Begin to Change on Planet Purple 28 MIN
16mm
Purple Adventures of Lady Elaine Fairchilde Series Program 5
Color (K P S)
LC 80-700581
Presents Mr Rogers talking, singing and using puppets to tell what happens when Paul and Pauline return to Planet Purple and introduce change so that everyone wants to be different. Discusses individual differences, handicaps, uniqueness and change.
Fine Arts; Guidance and Counseling; Literature and Drama
Dist - HUBDSC **Prod** - FAMCOM 1979

Things Change - Solids, Liquids, Gases 10 MIN
U-matic / VHS / 16mm
Color; B&W (P)
LC 75-702924
Explains how to identify solids, liquids and gases, and shows how matter can change from one state to another in different environments and temperatures.
Science - Physical
Dist - EBEC **Prod** - EBEC 1969

Things gone and things still here 58 MIN
VHS
Color (G)
$350.00 purchase, $95.00 rental
Traces Paul Bowles' career from a young musical protege to novelist, short story writer, translator, North African musicologist and composer for films and theater. Interviews numerous colleagues and Bowles himself, who also reads from his writings. Directed by Clement Barclay.
Fine Arts; Literature and Drama
Dist - CNEMAG

Things of Beauty 29 MIN
U-matic
Creation of Art Series
Color
Explores why artists paint still lifes and how viewers react to them.
Fine Arts
Dist - UMITV **Prod** - UMITV 1975

Things of Value 14 MIN
Videoreel / VT2
Living Better II Series
Color
Gives background information about old bottles, depression glass, barbed wire, fruit jars and wire insulators. Explains that by knowing what objects are in demand by collectors, the home viewer can gain satisfaction from owning them, or he can get fair prices by selling them.
Business and Economics; Home Economics
Dist - PBS **Prod** - MAETEL

Things seen in Madras 52 MIN
16mm
Phantom India series; Part 2
Color
Presents a religious festival, movie studios, man - drawn carts, a dancing school where girls learn the sacred dances of India and other aspects of the Madras area's culture.
Geography - World; Social Science; Sociology
Dist - NYFLMS **Prod** - NYFLMS 1967

Things that Go Bump - in Your G I Tract 29 MIN
U-matic / VHS
Here's to Your Health Series
Color
Examines the digestive system and efforts to treat and prevent ulcers.
Science - Natural
Dist - PBS **Prod** - KERA

Things that Go Wrong in the Night
VHS
Ater of the Night - the Science of Sleep and Dreams Series
Color
Examines causes and treatments of sleep disorders. Explores circadian sleep rhythms and dramatizes an experiment of a researcher's months in a dark cave.
Health and Safety; Psychology
Dist - IBIS **Prod** - IBIS

The Things that matter most 30 MIN
VHS
Author's night at the Freedom Forum series
Color (G)
$15.00 purchase _ #V94 - 09
Focuses on conservative commentator Cal Thomas, author of the book of the same title, in part of a series on freedom of the press, free speech and free spirit.
Civics and Political Systems; Guidance and Counseling; Social Science; Sociology
Dist - FREEDM **Prod** - FREEDM 1994

Things to come 26 MIN
U-matic / VHS / 16mm
Computer programme series; Episode 10
Color (J)
LC 82-701106
Looks at computer technology and its effects on society, focusing on agriculture and information processing.
Business and Economics; Mathematics
Dist - FI **Prod** - BBCTV 1982

Things to Come 3 MIN
16mm
Color (I)
Presents an abstract film exercise.
Fine Arts
Dist - CFS **Prod** - CFS 1954

Things to do 30 MIN
U-matic
Polka Dot Door Series
Color (K)
Presents a variety show for pre - school children. Includes songs, mime, stories, film sequences, talk, dance and fantasy figures. Each show emphasizes a particular theme such as numbers, feelings, exploring, music or time. Comes with parent teacher guide.
Fine Arts; Literature and Drama
Dist - TVOTAR **Prod** - TVOTAR 1985

Things to do When You Visit the Zoo 15 MIN
U-matic / VHS / 16mm
Color (K P I)
LC FIA68-1203
Follows a group of children on a visit to the zoo in order to explain concepts about the animal world and to examine some of its individual members, including the elephant, the giraffe, the lion, the monkey and the snake. Stresses rules of conduct and safety and explains reasons for maintaining a zoo.
Guidance and Counseling; Psychology; Science - Natural; Social Science
Dist - JOU **Prod** - JOU 1967

Things Worth Saving 14 MIN
16mm
Color
Explores the potential of large - scale resource recovery from America's growing volume of municipal solid waste, trash and garbage. Shows that future systems will separate valuable resources for recycling and use as fuel for heat and electrical systems.
Science - Natural; Social Science
Dist - FINLYS **Prod** - FINLYS 1972

Things You Should Know about Your Financial Institution 25 MIN
U-matic / VHS
Your Money Matters Series
Color
Discusses money market, super now accounts and what deregulation means to the average customer.
Business and Economics; Social Science
Dist - FILMID **Prod** - FILMID

Things your mother never told you 58 MIN
VHS
Color (H C G)
$295.00 purchase, $75.00 rental
Shares the perceptions of forty women of diverse ages and backgrounds of being a mother. Includes a blind and deaf woman who had no doubts that she could meet the challenges of motherhood. Another woman tells of being one of the first single women to adopt a child. Produced by Rhyena Halpern.
Sociology
Dist - FLMLIB

Think about Your Back
U-matic / 16mm
Color (A)
Alerts workers to the painful reality of back injuries and demonstrates how they can protect themselves against such injuries.
Health and Safety
Dist - BNA **Prod** - BNA 1983

Think Ahead 15 MIN
VHS / U-matic
Out and about Series
Color (P)
Describes Molly's anger when she is told by her brother that she is too young to go with them to the hobby shop. Explains that when she storms into the library, Sam helps her think of the possible consequences of the revenge she's planning and she decides on another approach with good results.
Guidance and Counseling
Dist - AITECH **Prod** - STSU 1984

Think back 9 MIN
VHS
Color (G)
$95.00 purchase _ #4002 - HDLQ
Demonstrates good body mechanics, using a slide show format. Available also as part of Back to Backs Program.
Health and Safety; Science - Natural
Dist - KRAMES **Prod** - KRAMES

Think it through with Winnie the Pooh series
One and only you 14 MIN
Responsible persons 15 MIN
Dist - CORF

Think Like a Mountain 28 MIN
16mm
Color
LC 74-705775
Deals with rare and endangered species of wildlife and the Forest Service's concern with protecting them. Shows mountain men, cowboys, wolf trappers and a hermit on the desert recall the changes they have witnessed in the land and its wildlife, the former abundance of species now considered endangered.
Agriculture; Science - Natural; Social Science
Dist - USNAC **Prod** - USDA 1972

Think Metric 10 MIN
16mm
Color (I)
LC 75-701532
Uses animated characters to demonstrate metric measurement of length, liquid volume and mass.
Mathematics
Dist - FFORIN **Prod** - FFORIN 1974

Think Metric Series
Measure Length - Think Metric 9 MIN
Measure volume - think metric 9 MIN
Measure Weight - Think Metric 9 MIN
Dist - BARR

Think new series
Presents an 11 - part series which gives theoretical motivation and practical ideas about viewing art. Draws content from mathematics, science, history, human feelings, every human endeavor. Look at art as an essential mode of learning. Includes design, drawing, painting, composition, puppetry, sculpture, fiber art, murals, bookbinding, printmaking, and viewing art.
Bookbinding - 9 22 MIN
Design is everywhere - 1 28 MIN
Drawing - 2 22 MIN
Fibers - 7 31 MIN
Looking at art - 11 24 MIN
Murals and celebrations - 8 22 MIN
Painting - 3 28 MIN
Printmaking - 10 31 MIN
Puppets - 5 34 MIN
Space and composition - 4 27 MIN
Working in 3D sculpture - 6 30 MIN
Dist - BARR **Prod** - CEPRO 1974

Think Nutrition - Consuming Interest 26 MIN
16mm
Color
Takes a tour of a typical U S supermarket and suggests how to get the best food buys.
Health and Safety; Home Economics; Social Science
Dist - LOMA **Prod** - LOMA

Think Nutrition - Meals Without Meat 26 MIN
16mm
Color
Tells why a vegetarian diet is preferable to a meat diet. Offers a history of vegetarian diet at the Loma Linda Medical Center. Outlines the four basic food groups and shows how the vegetarian diet can be a balanced diet.
Health and Safety; Social Science
Dist - LOMA **Prod** - LOMA

Think Nutrition - Overweight 25 MIN
16mm
Color
Explores the basic causes of overweight, emphasizing the need for balanced diet and plenty of exercise. Compares the caloric levels of various foods and discusses different types of exercise.
Health and Safety; Social Science
Dist - LOMA **Prod** - LOMA

Think Nutrition - Vitamins 22 MIN
16mm
Color
Discusses the use of vitamins, pointing out that taking excessive vitamin supplements can be harmful. Shows how a balanced vitamin intake can be derived from a balanced diet.
Health and Safety; Social Science
Dist - LOMA **Prod** - LOMA

Think of a Cloud 11 MIN
U-matic / VHS / 16mm
Color (P I)

LC 74-702008
Uses photography and narration in order to stimulate interest in aesthetics from a scientific point of view.
Guidance and Counseling; Industrial and Technical Education; Psychology
Dist - STANF **Prod** - STANF 1973

Think or sink - professional team decision thinking 26 MIN
VHS / U-matic
Color (C A PRO)
$790.00 purchase, $220.00 rental
Takes a new look at team leadership. Looks at the dangers of egocentricity and being overbearing in management. Shows how to encourage contributions from everyone on the team, elicit alternative considerations and create competition between ideas - not people. Includes the book 'The Professional Decision Maker' and a discussion leader's guide.
Business and Economics; Fine Arts; Guidance and Counseling; Psychology
Dist - VIDART **Prod** - VIDART 1991

Think Positive 20 MIN
U-matic / VHS / 16mm
Color (A)
Discusses the importance of attitude to a successful career in selling.
Business and Economics
Dist - RTBL **Prod** - SANDYC

Think Tall - Sell Up to Quality 8 MIN
16mm
Professional Selling Practices Series 2 Series
Color (H C)
LC 77-702357
Encourages a positive, professional point of view in selecting and presenting quality merchandise. Shows how to trade through emphasis on quality instead of price.
Business and Economics
Dist - SAUM **Prod** - SAUM 1968

Think Tanks - Prophets of the Future 20 MIN
16mm / U-matic / VHS
Color
Looks at the work of the Hudson Institute of New York, a think tank which evaluates the prospects of mankind, advises major corporations and government agencies, and seeks out solutions for energy problems and poverty.
Sociology
Dist - CNEMAG **Prod** - DOCUA

Think Twice - the Persuasion Game 19 MIN
16mm / U-matic / VHS
Color (J H C)
$355.00, $89.00 purchase
Discusses ways in which certain groups appeal to the emotions of people to get them to think a certain way or buy a certain thing. Directed by William Haugse.
Psychology
Dist - CF

Think Twice - They're Confusing You 19 MIN
U-matic / VHS / 16mm
Color (J H C)
LC 78-701974
Illustrates kinds of faulty or misleading information, such as oversimplification, distortion of facts and logical fallacies.
Psychology; Religion and Philosophy
Dist - CF **Prod** - CF 1978

Think Win 30 MIN
16mm / U-matic / VHS
Color (PRO)
LC 72-700989
Features star football player and salesman, George Blanda, relates his philosophy and personal experiences in football and sales to inspire the sales training and motivation of others.
Business and Economics; Physical Education and Recreation
Dist - DARTNL **Prod** - TAKTEN 1971

Thinkabout Series Giving and Getting Meaning
Meaning is more than Words 14 MIN
Dist - AITECH

Thinking 60 MIN
VHS
Mind Series
Color; Captioned (G)
$59.95 purchase _ #MIND - 108
Outlines the importance of the frontal lobe and prefrontal cortex parts of the brain. Shows that these two locations are where memory, emotion and intelligence join together to encourage conscious activity. Interviews a stroke victim and a concert violinist who, each in their own way, show the importance of brain activity.
Psychology
Dist - PBS **Prod** - WNETTV 1988

Thinking 30 MIN
VHS
Mind/Brain Classroom Series
Color (H G)
$59.95 purchase _ #MDBR - 110
Explores the processes of human thought. Reveals that two parts of the brain, the frontal lobe and the prefrontal cortex, are essential to thought. Intended for high school students.
Psychology
Dist - PBS **Prod** - WNETTV

Thinking about drinking 18 MIN
U-matic / 16mm / VHS
Color (J)
LC 91-705284
Teaches the basics about alcholic beverages to enable youngsters to make thoughtful decisions about the use of alcohol. Stresses the dangers of drinking and driving. Includes teacher's guide.
Guidance and Counseling; Health and Safety; Sociology
Dist - HIGGIN **Prod** - HIGGIN 1991

Thinking about Hands - Laboratory 12 MIN
16mm / U-matic / VHS
Color
Illustrates how normally safe tasks in the laboratory can become hazardous because of inattention to routine, poor position, improper tools, lack of protective equipment or failure to follow procedure. Analyzes incidents according to primary cause and other contributing factors.
Health and Safety; Science
Dist - CORF **Prod** - OLINC

Thinking about Hands - Manufacturing 12 MIN
16mm / U-matic / VHS
Color
Illustrates how normally safe tasks in manufacturing can become hazardous because of inattention to routine, poor position, improper tools, lack of protective equipment or failure to follow procedure. Analyzes incidents according to primary cause and other contributing factors.
Business and Economics; Health and Safety
Dist - CORF **Prod** - OLINC

Thinking about Rocks 15 MIN
U-matic / VHS
Matter and Motion Series Module Red; Module red
Color (I)
Looks at the way rocks are broken down by the forces of nature.
Science - Physical
Dist - AITECH **Prod** - WHROTV 1973

Thinking about school bus safety 8 MIN
VHS / 16mm
Color (P I)
$40.00, $25.00 purchase _ #285, #483
Discusses proper and safe school bus behavior.
Health and Safety
Dist - AAAFTS **Prod** - AAAFTS 1983

Thinking about thinking 30 MIN
VHS / BETA
Critical self - awareness series
Color (G)
$29.95 purchase _ #S140
Describes 'evaluation phobia' as the fear that individuals and organizations have about carefully examining the logic of their own decisions. Features philosopher Dr Michael Scriven whose specialty is the process of thinking. Part of a four - part series on critical self - awareness.
Psychology; Religion and Philosophy
Dist - THINKA **Prod** - THINKA

Thinking Ahead 30 MIN
U-matic
Inside Japan Series
(H C A)
Looks at some of the activities which make large Japanese companies successful. Illustrates the need for the flexibility to expand.
Geography - World; History - World
Dist - ACCESS **Prod** - ACCESS 1980

Thinking and Drinking - a RET Approach to Staying Stopped 18 MIN
VHS
Color (G) (SPANISH)
$85.00 purchase _ #V009, #V010
Introduces the early warning signs of alcoholism. Outlines a proven method for reducing dependency on alcohol consistent with the effective self - help techniques of AA. Rational - Emotive Therapy - RET techniques. Includes ten workbooks.
Guidance and Counseling; Health and Safety; Psychology
Dist - IRL **Prod** - IRL

Thinking and library skills series
Critical thinking - how to evaluate information and draw conclusions
Decision - making skills
Dist - CHUMAN

Thinking and Reasoning in Preschool Children 23 MIN
VHS / U-matic
B&W (PRO)
Takes an overview of important concepts and reasoning abilities that children develop during the 'preoperational' period. Shows how preschool children's understanding of the world affects their behavior and problem - solving methods.
Education; Psychology
Dist - HSERF **Prod** - HSERF

Thinking Exercises 29.42 MIN
VHS
Critical Thinking Exercises
Color (J H C)
LC 88-700273
Teaches students the thinking skills necessary to set out to find a career.
Business and Economics
Dist - SRA **Prod** - SRA 1986

Thinking for our children
VHS
Islamic videos on family and education series
Color (G)
$14.95 purchase _ #110 - 040
Features Imam M Naseem, Shabbir Monsoori and Yahya Emerick who discuss mistakes parents make, misinformation about Islam in public school textbooks and youth teaching youth.
Religion and Philosophy; Sociology
Dist - SOUVIS **Prod** - SOUVIS

Thinking in Action Series Module 2
Improvement, Review and Productivity 13 MIN
Dist - FI

Thinking in Action Series Module 3
People, Communication and Negotiation 13 MIN
Dist - FI

Thinking in Action Series Module 4
Problems, Crises and Opportunities 13 MIN
Dist - FI

Thinking in action series - Module 5
Decision, choice and evaluation 13 MIN
Dist - FI

Thinking in action series module 6
Action, planning and implementation 13 MIN
Dist - FI

Thinking in action series
Creativity, design and innovation 13 MIN
Dist - FI

Thinking in Sets 11 MIN
16mm
Pathways to Modern Math Series
Color (I J H)
LC FIA64-1445
Shows how to think in sets and explains their relation. Introduces the idea of things being naturally grouped together by their likenesses or their position. Instills a feeling for the relations between groups of numbers, such as 3, 6, 15, 33 and 87 belonging together as a result of their divisibility by 3. Describes the relations between geometric figures, such as line segments.
Mathematics
Dist - GE **Prod** - GE

Thinking in the future tense 28 MIN
VHS / U-matic
Color (A)
Centers around an ecumenical conference with futurist Dr Edward Lindaman who examines the shape of things to come. Includes genetic engineering, communication technology, sharing of natural resources and pollution. Intended to stimulate discussion of how our Christian belief can and should affect our response to the future.
Religion and Philosophy; Sociology
Dist - ECUFLM **Prod** - DCCMS 1981

Thinking it through 23 MIN
16mm / U-matic / VHS
Color (C A) (DUTCH SWEDISH)
Presents a checklist for management problem solving, including identifying the problem, gathering facts, identifying alternatives, evaluating and selecting alternatives, implementing the decision and evaluating the decision.
Business and Economics; Foreign Language; Psychology
Dist - RTBL **Prod** - PILSBY 1978

Thinking it through 12 MIN
VHS
System of change series
Color (PRO G A)
$465.00 purchase, $130.00 rental
Presents a systematic approach to change that encourages thorough preparation for change. Points out that anticipating reactions of others helps in planning for smooth changes. Part of Implementing Change, Unit 2.

Business and Economics; Guidance and Counseling; Psychology
Dist - EXTR **Prod** - CCCD

Thinking it through - the mark of the professional supervisor 22 MIN
U-matic / BETA / VHS
Color (IND G)
$495.00 purchase _ #801 - 05
Features Arthur Miller, professor of law, Harvard University. Informs employees, first line supervisors and managers about the importance of personal compliance with safety and health procedures. Covers accountability, consequences and liabilities of both employer and employee.
Business and Economics; Health and Safety; Industrial and Technical Education; Psychology
Dist - ITSC **Prod** - ITSC 1990

Thinking it through - the mark of the professional supervisor 18 MIN
VHS
Color (IND PRO COR VOC)
$495.00 purchase, $150.00 five - day rental, $35.00 three - day preview, _ #ITT/ITS
Discusses the liabilities of the company and supervisors in relation to safety and health requirements, presented by Harvard Law School Professor Arthur Miller. Includes guidelines for handling OSHA and workers' compensation cases. Provides information on 'thinking it through' to facilitate adherence with company safety procedures and to maintain a safer workplace. Includes a Leader's Guide.
Business and Economics
Dist - ADVANM

The Thinking machine 50 MIN
VHS
Dream machine series
Color; PAL (G)
PdS99 purchase; Not available in the United States
Discusses the limitations of computers and progress toward artificial intelligence. Traces the development of the computer, the machine that changed the world. Part four of a five - part series.
Computer Science
Dist - BBCENE

The Thinking machine 25 MIN
U-matic / VHS / 16mm
Computer programme series; Episode 8
Color (J)
Reveals how computers are almost taught to think so that they can perform tasks ranging from playing games to performing medical diagnosis.
Business and Economics; Mathematics
Dist - FI **Prod** - BBCTV 1982

The Thinking machine and meditation 60 MIN
VHS
Krishnamurti - 1982 talks in the Oak Grove series
Color (G)
$39.95 purchase _ #P75e
Features one of humanity's greatest religious philosophers in the idyllic setting of the Oak Grove in Ojai, California. Captures the intensity and passion of Krishnamurti. Part of a five - part series.
Literature and Drama; Religion and Philosophy
Dist - HP

Thinking made Visible 70 MIN
16mm
What is Good Writing Series
Color
LC 76-702720
Presents two lectures by Dr George D Linton, who explains the importance of proper writing in communicating to others.
English Language; Psychology
Dist - USNAC **Prod** - USFAA 1964

Thinking metric
VHS
Basic mathematical skills series
Color (I J H)
$125.00 purchase _ #1024
Expands the concepts of the metric system of weights and measures. Presents part of a series that provides 27 videos, each between 25 and 30 minutes long, that explain and reinforce basic mathematical concepts. Tutors the student through definitions, theorems, step - by - step solutions and examples. Videos are also available in a set.
Mathematics
Dist - LANDMK

Thinking of her 4 MIN
16mm
B&W (G)
$15.00 rental
Fine Arts
Dist - CANCIN **Prod** - PALAZT 1993

Thinking of Others 4 MIN
U-matic / VHS / 16mm
Most Important Person - Getting Along with Others Series
Color (K P I)
Portrays Nancy's feelings, as she realizes that being selfish is no fun since you end up being alone.
Guidance and Counseling; Psychology
Dist - EBEC **Prod** - EBEC 1972

Thinking patterns - Module I 7 MIN
8mm cartridge / VHS / BETA / U-matic
Brainwaves - case studies in diversity series
Color; PAL (PRO G)
$495.00 purchase
Presents the vignette, 'The Coffee Break.' Discusses realistic, complex diverisity issues, concepts and conflicts. Combines case studies with an interactive learning design to allow trainers to lead participants in a structured, non - threatening exploration of diversity. Part one of six parts. Includes trainer's manual and 20 participant manuals.
Business and Economics; Psychology
Dist - BNA **Prod** - BNA

Thinking positive 24 MIN
VHS
Color (J H C)
$250.00 purchase
Provokes thought and discussion among youths about risks associated with unsafe sex and the AIDS virus. Urges taking responsibility for one's behavior.
Guidance and Counseling; Health and Safety; Psychology
Dist - LANDMK **Prod** - NFBC

Thinking Professionally 29 MIN
VHS / 16mm
Daycare - Caregiver Training Series
Color (C)
$250.00 purchase _ #293001
Assists in the educating of university and college students learning to care professionally for young children and professional caregivers employed in preschool centers. Documents the role and impact of caregivers on children, parents and families. 'Thinking Professionally' provides an understanding of the profession of childcare and its requirements of in - depth knowledge of child development and a desire to constantly improve professional competence.
Guidance and Counseling; Home Economics; Psychology; Sociology
Dist - ACCESS **Prod** - ACCESS 1990

Thinking - Program 8 60 MIN
VHS
Mind series
Color (G)
$69.95 purchase
Presents the eighth program of a nine - part series exploring the human mind. Looks at the higher processes of thought and reasoning.
Psychology
Dist - PBS **Prod** - WNETTV

Thinking Skills - Introduction to Critical Thinking 68 MIN
VHS
Color (J)
LC 85-703
Presents thinking as a skill which can be improved. Illustrates successful learning techniques, distinguishes inductive from deductive reasoning, and tells how to improve insight and imagination.
Psychology
Dist - HRMC **Prod** - HRMC

Thinking through Safety - the Job Safety and Health Analysis
16mm / U-matic
Color (A)
Illustrates how to gather information, write job safety and health analyses and set up procedures to perform jobs safely.
Business and Economics; Health and Safety
Dist - BNA **Prod** - BNA 1983

Thinking Twice 30 MIN
16mm
Color
Shows an American family coming to grips with the arms race and nuclear war. Views the past, present and future consequences of nuclear war.
Sociology
Dist - SKYE **Prod** - SKYE 1981

Thinking, Writing and Reading 29 MIN
U-matic / VHS / 16mm
Teaching Children to Read Series
Color (T)
Examines the total - language approach to learning, emphasizing the thinking - writing - reading continuum.
Education; English Language
Dist - FI **Prod** - MFFD 1975

Thinking your way to better S A T scores 130 MIN
VHS
Color (G)
$125.00 purchase _ #TYBS - 000
Features Dr Gary Gruber and his strategies for improving Scholastic Aptitude Test scores, which have declined over the past 20 - 25 years. Stresses the importance of good thinking skills in test taking. Includes a 50 - page resource guide.
Education
Dist - PBS **Prod** - PBS 1989

Thinner Usage by Temperature Range 10 MIN
BETA / VHS
Color (A PRO)
$61.00 purchase _ #KTI45
Deals with auto body repair. Gives the usual temperature breaks for thinness, using Dupont and Ditzler thinners as examples.
Industrial and Technical Education
Dist - RMIBHF **Prod** - RMIBHF

The Thinnest Line 10 MIN
16mm / VHS
Color (G)
$300.00, $125.00 purchase, $30.00 rental
Portrays the intimate friendship between two young black women, one a filmmaker, the other a mother. Examines the strains in their relationship, the underlying jealousy and competition between women friends.
History - United States; Sociology
Dist - WMEN **Prod** - DKYI 1988

The Thinnest Slice 21 MIN
16mm
B&W
LC FIA52-176
Tissue is sliced to 1/500,000th of an inch on a microtome by Dr Daniel Pease in a technique which he and Dr Richard Baker developed in the U S C laboratories.
Science
Dist - USC **Prod** - USC 1949

The Third angel 58 MIN
VHS / U-matic
Color (J H G)
$280.00, $330.00 purchase, $60.00 rental
Explores the world of Birute Galdikas who has lived for 20 years in the heart of the Borneo rainforest to study the Red Ape, the Orangutan. Reveals that this primate is one of the closet relatives to humans, sharing 95 percent of their genetic makeup. Paleontologist Louis Leakey chose three women to study the great apes as a window on early man - Jane Goodall, who rose to international fame studying chimpanzees in Africa; Dian Fossey, whose legendary heroic fight to protect the African mountain gorilla led to her murder; the third of 'Leakey's Angels,' Galdikas, has devoted her life to saving a major species and the rainforest in which it lives.
Fine Arts; Science - Natural
Dist - NDIM **Prod** - CANBC 1992

The Third Attribute 30 MIN
16mm
B&W
Relates the story of an arrogant young scholar who becomes embittered after a crippling illness. Tells how the target of his bitterness is his servant, who tries to teach him justice, mercy and humility.
Religion and Philosophy
Dist - NAAJS **Prod** - JTS 1953

Third Avenue 60 MIN
U-matic
Color (A)
LC 80-706227
Presents a look at the seamy side of urban life by focusing on six people who live or work along New York's Third Avenue.
Geography - United States; Sociology
Dist - DCTVC **Prod** - DCTVC 1979

Third Avenue El 11 MIN
U-matic / VHS / 16mm
Color (J H C)
LC FIA64-1087
Presents a study of New York's now departed railway, the Third Avenue El, coordinated with the music of Haydn and the artistry of the late Wanda Landowska on the harpsichord. Depicts a poetic and nostalgic train ride through old New York.
Fine Arts; Psychology; Social Science; Sociology
Dist - AIMS **Prod** - DAVC 1957

The Third Coast 55 MIN
VHS
Color (H C G)
Portrays the city of Houston, Texas, during one of its boom years. Looks at the promises and problems of a city emerging as America's third most powerful urban center.
Geography - United States; History - United States
Dist - VIDVER **Prod** - VIDVER 1981

The Third coast - Pt 1 28 MIN
16mm
World exchange series
Color
LC 81-700502
Examines life in Houston, Texas, as rapid growth, booming economy, the oil industry, and the Bible Belt meet the western frontier in the 1980s.
History - United States
Dist - DIRECT **Prod** - VIDVER 1981

The Third coast - Pt 2 27 MIN
16mm
World exchange series
Color
LC 81-700502
Examines life in Houston, Texas, as rapid growth, booming economy, the oil industry, and the Bible Belt meet the western frontier in the 1980s.
History - United States
Dist - DIRECT **Prod** - VIDVER 1981

The Third Cod War 17 MIN
VHS / U-matic
Color (H C A)
Describes a dispute between the United Kingdom and Iceland which centered on the extent of territorial waters and fishing rights.
History - World; Industrial and Technical Education
Dist - JOU **Prod** - UPI

The Third cry 72 MIN
VHS
Color (G A R)
$29.95 purchase, $10.00 rental _ #35 - 874 - 8516
Reveals how a couple learned to deal with their first child's cerebral palsy.
Guidance and Counseling; Health and Safety; Sociology
Dist - APH **Prod** - VISVID

3rd degree 24 MIN
16mm
Color (G)
$55.00 rental
Looks at the fragility of the film medium and human vulnerability in which both the filmic and the human images resist threat, intimidation and mutilation.
Fine Arts
Dist - CANCIN **Prod** - SHARIT 1982

The Third dimension 7 MIN
VHS
Lessons in visual language series
Color (PRO G C)
$99.00 purchase, $39.00 rental _ #749
Shows how human eyes and brains use a variety of visual cues to construct three dimensional space. Looks at how to use these cues to define spacial relationships or to fool the eye. Includes a number of startling optical illusions. Features Peter Thompson as creator and narrator of a ten - part series on visual language. Produced by the Australian Film, Television and Radio School.
Industrial and Technical Education; Social Science
Dist - FIRLIT

Third Eye Series
Namibia - Africa's Last Colony 52 MIN
Dist - CANWRL

The Third Generation 111 MIN
16mm
Color (GERMAN (ENGLISH SUBTITLES))
Follows a band of German urban guerrillas, created by a computer tycoon who knows that terrorism sells surveillance devices. Directed by Rainer Werner Fassbinder. With English subtitles.
Foreign Language
Dist - NYFLMS **Prod** - UNKNWN 1979

The Third Generation 50 MIN
16mm / U-matic / VHS
Color (H C A)
$795 purchase - 16 mm, $295 purchase - video, $60 rental
Deals with the attempts by modern Germans and Jews to relate to one another, and to interact socially. Shows the activities of the German Israeli Youth Exchange Program. Directed by Yeshayahu Nir.
History - World; Sociology
Dist - CNEMAG

Third grade science 11 MIN
16mm
Programmed instruction - the teacher's role series
B&W (C T) (SPANISH)
LC 74-705776
Discusses various uses of programmed instruction in teaching third grade science.
Education; Science - Natural
Dist - USNAC **Prod** - USOE 1966

The Third Lantern for the Third Century 28 MIN
16mm
Color
LC 75-704437
Shows the April 1975 ceremony in the Old North Church in Boston commemorating the 200th anniversary of Paul Revere's ride. Includes an address by President Ford.
Biography; History - United States
Dist - USNAC **Prod** - USARBA 1975

The Third Law 18 MIN
U-matic
Chemistry 102 - Chemistry for Engineers - Series
Color (C)
Explores the relationship between entropy and probability. S is calculated from W, the number of microstates corresponding to a given macrostate. Presents the third law of thermodynamics and compares absolute entropies of various substances.
Industrial and Technical Education; Science - Physical
Dist - UILL **Prod** - UILL 1984

The Third man 104 MIN
VHS
B&W (G)
$24.95 purchase _ #THI110
Features an American writer who goes to Europe to look for a friend, but finds instead intrigue along the back streets of postwar Vienna. Stars Joseph Cotten and Orson Welles. Directed by Carol Reed.
Fine Arts
Dist - HOMVIS **Prod** - JANUS 1949

The Third Millenium 95 MIN
16mm / U-matic / VHS
Color
Examines the people, the ecology and the fate of the Amazon basin. Chronicles Senator Evandro Carreira's political campaign tour by boat through a remote jungle between Brazil, Columbia and Peru where he meets with his constituency, the Indian population of the region.
History - World; Social Science
Dist - CNEMAG **Prod** - STOPFM

The Third person 18 MIN
VHS / U-matic / 16mm
Color (H G)
$275.00, $325.00, $375.00 purchase, $50.00 rental
Presents a primer on the parenting experience with a first child. Documents the range of emotions experienced by one couple's expectations, their adjustments to being parents and their hopes.
Sociology
Dist - NDIM **Prod** - NFBC 1985

The Third planet 60 MIN
VHS
Miracle planet - the life story of Earth series
Color (I J H)
$100.00 purchase _ #A5VH 1320
Explores the origins of the Earth and the events that made the planet conducive to life. Reveals that violent collisions with meteorites left clues in the craters - witnesses to the beginning of Earth and possible clues to the sudden disappearence of the dinosaurs. Part of a six - part series examining the intricate balance of systems known as planet Earth.
Science - Natural; Science - Physical
Dist - CLRVUE

The Third Pollution 23 MIN
16mm
Color (I)
LC FIA67-652
Portrays America's solid waste problem and its relation to air pollution and water contamination. Outlines alternatives for community action, including procedures for obtaining federal or state assistance.
Psychology; Science - Natural; Sociology
Dist - FINLYS **Prod** - FINLYS 1966

Third r - teaching basic mathematics skills series
Calculators and computers in the school math program
Developing computational skills
Geometry and Measurement in a Balanced Math Curriculum
An Overview of School Mathematics in the 80's
Problem - solving 1 - the basic skill
Using Math in Everyday Situations
Dist - EDCORP

Third R - Teaching Basic Mathematics Skills Series
Carol Dodd Thornton
Frank K Lester
Phares O'Daffer
Ross Taylor
Shirley A Hill
Zalman P Usiskin
Dist - EDCPUB

Third Reich and roll 5 MIN
16mm
Color (G)
$10.00 rental
Introduces The Residents, an underground performance group, in their first film. Features renditions of Land of a Thousand Dances and Wipeout. Produced by Cryptic Corporation aka Ralph Records.
Fine Arts
Dist - CANCIN

Third Review Week 1 10 MIN
U-matic
Readalong Two Series
Color (P)
Provides young viewers with a flexible range of reading experiences through active involvement in reading and writing. Comes with teacher's guide and kit.
Education; English Language; Literature and Drama
Dist - TVOTAR **Prod** - TVOTAR 1976

Third Review Week 2 10 MIN
U-matic
Readalong Two Series
Color (P)
Provides young viewers with a flexible range of reading experiences through active involvement in reading and writing. Comes with teacher's guide and kit.
Education; English Language; Literature and Drama
Dist - TVOTAR **Prod** - TVOTAR 1976

Third Review Week 3 10 MIN
U-matic
Readalong Two Series
Color (P)
Provides young viewers with a flexible range of reading experiences through active involvement in reading and writing. Comes with teacher's guide and kit.
Education; English Language; Literature and Drama
Dist - TVOTAR **Prod** - TVOTAR 1976

Third Sister Liu 110 MIN
VHS
Color (G) (MANDARIN CHINESE (ENGLISH SUBTITLES))
$45.00 purchase _ #1034B
Presents a movie produced in the People's Republic of China.
Fine Arts; Geography - World; Literature and Drama
Dist - CHTSUI **Prod** - CHTSUI

The Third Team on the Field - Umpiring Baseball 17 MIN
U-matic / VHS / 16mm
Color (H C A)
Explains the individual responsibilities of the plate and base umpire, with special emphasis on the two - person system. Shows how the two umpires can get into postion to make the right call anywhere.
Physical Education and Recreation
Dist - ATHI **Prod** - NCAA 1982

The Third Temple 17 MIN
16mm
Color
Portrays modern Israel marching forward in the wake of the persecuted wandering Jew.
Geography - World; History - World; Sociology
Dist - ALDEN **Prod** - ALDEN

Third Testament Series
Blaise Pascal 57 MIN
Dietrich Bonhoeffer 57 MIN
Leo Tolstoy 57 MIN
Saint Augustine 57 MIN
Soren Kierkegaard 57 MIN
William Blake 57 MIN
Dist - TIMLIF

Third Times Luck, Dan Spock 20 MIN
16mm
Cellar Door Cine Mites Series
Color (I)
LC 74-701552
Fine Arts
Dist - CELLAR **Prod** - CELLAR 1972

The Third Trimester 29 MIN
U-matic / VHS
Tomorrow's Families Series
Color (H C A)
LC 81-706901
Shows how the fetus grows during the third trimester of pregnancy and how the parents prepare for the birth, often in childbirth classes.
Health and Safety
Dist - AITECH **Prod** - MDDE 1980

The Third Voyage of Captain James Cook 15 MIN
16mm
Color (J H C)
Traces Cook's third voyage with sketches made by the official artist on board and contrasts them with the same areas as they look today.

Geography - United States; History - United States; History - World; Sociology
Dist - CINEPC **Prod** - TAHARA 1980

Third Wave Series
The Changing Business Environment 30 MIN
Management Faces the Waves of Change 30 MIN
Managing the Transition 30 MIN
The New Age of Diversity 30 MIN
Tomorrow's Tools 30 MIN
Dist - DELTAK

The Third World - an Introduction 21 MIN
U-matic / VHS / 16mm
Color (J)
LC 84-707084
Presents an introduction to the concept of the Third World. States that most Third World nations were once colonies of First World nations and still depend on their ex - rulers for much of their trade and military assistance. Discusses the problems, the solutions and the future of a huge part of our world.
Civics and Political Systems; Geography - World; History - World
Dist - PHENIX **Prod** - PHENIX 1983

The Third World and the U S national interest 27 MIN
16mm
B&W
LC FIE65-22
Roger G Mastrude interviews Frank M Coffin, who explores in depth and detail the political and philosophical justifications for United States economic assistance to the 'Third World.'
Business and Economics; Civics and Political Systems
Dist - USNAC **Prod** - USAID 1964

Third World Dance - Beyond the White Stream Series
Defining Black dance 30 MIN
Ethnic Dance and How those of Other Cultures See it 30 MIN
Historical Perspectives on Black Dancers in the U S a 30 MIN
Toward a Broader Understanding of Ethnic Dance 30 MIN
Dist - ARCVID

Third World Dance - Tracing Roots Series
Black Ballet in America 30 MIN
Legendary Women in Dance - Syvilla Fort and Thelma Hill 30 MIN
Origins and Influences of Ethnic Dance 30 MIN
Rhythm's the Name of the Game 30 MIN
Dist - ARCVID

Third world on the Mississippi 30 MIN
VHS
Color (G A)
$19.95 purchase _ #TCO110E
Reveals the depth of poverty that now exists for the people living along the Mississippi River, as high illiteracy rates, growing unemployment, inadequate health care, and rising poverty have become common. Suggests that a joint effort between government, business, and private industry may be necessary to alleviate the situation. Hosted by CNN correspondent Larry Woods.
History - United States; Social Science; Sociology
Dist - TMM **Prod** - TMM

Thirdstring 15 MIN
16mm
Color
LC 72-702434
Shows how a young boy suffers from a domineering sister and a mother who has failed to understand her son. Explains how he seeks escape in fantasies but his sister is determined to rid him of the 'evil spirit' which possesses him.
Fine Arts; Guidance and Counseling; Sociology
Dist - USC **Prod** - USC 1972

Thirsty people in thirsty lands 15 MIN
VHS
Mission videos series
Color (G R)
$12.50 purchase _ #S12367
Profiles the Meinzen family and its efforts over three generations to provide water resources and ministry to the people of India.
Guidance and Counseling; Literature and Drama; Religion and Philosophy
Dist - CPH **Prod** - LUMIS

Thirsty work 26 MIN
VHS
Alcohol - breaking the habit series
Color (G)
$149.00 purchase, $75.00 rental _ #UW3292
Reveals that alcoholism is a primary cause of days lost at work, inefficiency, carelessness and accidents. Shows a model corporate program designed to teach employees the guidelines for safe drinking and offer to those in need of treatment a way to seek it without endangering their employment. Part of a four - part series on alcoholism, how alcohol affects the body, how much alcohol can be safely consumed and how to break the alcohol habit.
Guidance and Counseling; Health and Safety; Psychology; Sociology
Dist - FOTH

Thirteen Minutes to Wait 51 MIN
U-matic
Color
Shows Toronto's Steve Podborski waiting 13 minutes to find out his World Cup downhill ski racing rival beat him by 28/100ths of a second. Explains how he went on to become ranked best in the world.
Physical Education and Recreation
Dist - LAURON **Prod** - LAURON

The Thirteenth Chamber of the Copper Prince 9 MIN
U-matic / VHS / 16mm
Color (I)
LC 84-707085
Tells the story of a corpulent, meat - eating prince who falls in love with a beautiful vegetarian princess. Because the prince wants to marry the princess, he tells her he has become a vegetarian, but in the 13th chamber the prince has hidden stores of meat. Describes what happens when the princess finds out about the prince's secret hoard.
Fine Arts; Sociology
Dist - PHENIX **Prod** - KRATKY 1983

The Thirteenth floor 10 MIN
16mm / VHS / BETA / U-matic
Color; PAL (PRO)
PdS120, PdS128 purchase
Features a humorous slant on all the safety errors committed in a short time in a typical office.
Health and Safety
Dist - EDPAT **Prod** - EUSA

Thirty Days Beneath the Sea 15 MIN
16mm
Color
LC 74-705778
Shows the drifting voyage of the Ben Franklin submersible under the Gulf Stream and how the new knowlege is derived from the cruise to the addition of the understanding of the oceans.
Science; Science - Physical
Dist - USNAC **Prod** - USN 1971

Thirty Demons 30 MIN
Videoreel / VT2
Solutions in Communications Series
Color (T)
Education; English Language
Dist - SCCOE **Prod** - SCCOE

Thirty - eight proven ways to close that sale 87 MIN
VHS
Color (G)
$99.95 purchase _ #20000
Features Mark Victor Hansen on sales techniques. Shows five ways to overcome a customer's objections as well as how to make a friend as well as a sale. Illustrates specific words and phrases which make effective closings and how to use referrals.
Business and Economics
Dist - CARTRP **Prod** - CARTRP

Thirty - Five - C, 45 - C Tractor Shovels 16 MIN
16mm
Color
LC 78-701575
Shows common applications for two tractor shovels produced by Clark Equipment Company and provides specifications which are important to potential purchasers.
Agriculture
Dist - PILOT **Prod** - CLARK 1978

Thirty - Five Mm Photography Basic Part 1 80 MIN
U-matic / VHS
Color (J)
LC 83-706444
Shows the beginner or casual user of 35mm cameras the use of the controls and such materials as films, flash units, tripods, winders and lenses. Tells how to choose additional equipment. Signed for the deaf.
Fine Arts; Industrial and Technical Education
Dist - MEMREP **Prod** - MEMREP 1983

Thirty - Four Years After Hitler 19 MIN
16mm / U-matic / VHS
Color (J) (GERMAN)
LC 79-700680
Reports the ways in which the Hitler legacy lives on in Germany and is supported through an American operation in Lincoln, Nebraska. Tells how neo - Nazi groups in Germany destroy Jewish cemeteries, paint swastikas on the street and distribute anti - Semitic propaganda. Originally shown on the CBS television program 60 Minutes.
Geography - World; History - World; Sociology
Dist - CAROUF **Prod** - CBSTV 1979

The Thirty - fourth hour 27 MIN
U-matic / VHS / 16mm
Insight series
B&W (H C A)
LC 76-705448
Features participants in a marathon basic encounter group, including a priest, a nymphonmaniac and a bitter man, who examine their 'hang - ups' and come to a new appreciation of themselves.
Guidance and Counseling; Psychology; Sociology
Dist - PAULST **Prod** - PAULST 1968

Thirty - Nine, Single and Pregnant 18 MIN
16mm
Color (A)
LC 82-700662
Tells about Jane Davis, who decided to carry through her pregnancy and become a single parent. Shows the difficulties she faced in being separated from her child, forfeiting jobs, seeking a larger place to live, and raising him without a father and on a limited budget.
Home Economics; Sociology
Dist - FLMLIB **Prod** - WYNNC 1982

The 39 steps 87 MIN
VHS
B&W (G)
$24.95 purchase _ #THI100
Features Alfred Hitchcock's first man - on - the - run thriller. Contains breathtaking action and mischievous humor to tell the story of an innocent man pursued by the police and murderous spies.
Fine Arts; Literature and Drama
Dist - HOMVIS **Prod** - HITCH 1935

Thirty Pieces of Silver 15 MIN
16mm
Living Bible Series
Color; B&W (J H A)
Mary anoints Jesus' head and feet in the house of Simon in Bethany. Judas speaks scornfully of this waste and Jesus rebukes him. Judas makes his way to the chief priests to bargain with them to betray Jesus for thirty pieces of silver.
Religion and Philosophy
Dist - FAMF **Prod** - FAMF

The Thirty Second Dream 15 MIN
16mm
Color (J)
LC 78-701078
Presents a montage of television commercials, pointing out the messages conveyed by their portrayal of family life, intimacy, vitality and success.
Business and Economics; Fine Arts; Home Economics; Psychology
Dist - MMM **Prod** - LABRSE 1977

The Thirty - second dream 15 MIN
VHS
Color (J H R)
$10.00 rental _ #36 - 85 - 1521
Uses a fast - paced collage of television commercials and commentary to reveal the idea behind advertising. Shows that advertising attempts to tap into people's deepest needs and desires.
Religion and Philosophy; Sociology
Dist - APH **Prod** - MMM

Thirty - Second Infantry Division 18 MIN
16mm / U-matic / VHS
B&W
LC FIE54-405
Traces the history of U S Army's 32nd Infantry Division through the Civil War, Spanish - American War, Mexican Border Campaign, World War I and World War II.
Civics and Political Systems; History - United States
Dist - USNAC **Prod** - USA 1954

The Thirty - Second President 55 MIN
VHS / U-matic
Walk through the 20th Century with Bill Moyers Series
Color
Examines the role of advertising in politics in the 20th century, featuring an interview with the late Rosser Reeves, an advertising executive who worked on early political television advertising for Dwight D Eisenhower. Includes a discussion with media whiz Tony Schwartz

about how electoral politics have changed with the increased use of television advertising. Hosted by Bill Moyers.
Business and Economics; Sociology
Dist - PBS **Prod** - CORPEL

Thirty - Second Seduction 27 MIN
VHS
Color (S)
$79.00 purchase _ #410 - 9022
Investigates the methods advertisers use to capture the public attention - and its dollars. Interviews top creative directors who share the secret of their craft. A leading sociologist explains how commercials tap our basic fears and desires, and a food stylist demonstrates how he makes food irresistibly appetizing.
Business and Economics; Home Economics; Industrial and Technical Education; Psychology
Dist - FI **Prod** - CU 1985

30 second shot clock offense - Conrad
VHS
Basketball small college winners series
Color (H C G)
$29.95 purchase _ #SAM090V - P
Features Coach Conrad who discusses the 30 - second shot clock offense in basketball. Part of an 11 - part series featuring innovative basketball coaches at the small college level.
Physical Education and Recreation
Dist - CAMV

Thirty Second Spot 11 MIN
U-matic / VHS
Joan Braderman Series
Color (G)
$250.00, $200.00 purchase, $50.00 rental
Focuses on media and power. Tells about buying network time in 1976 for counter - bicentennial activities.
Civics and Political Systems; History - United States; Psychology; Sociology
Dist - WMEN **Prod** - JBRAD 1988

Thirty Second Spots - TV Commercials for Artists 15 MIN
VHS / U-matic
Color
Makes miniature statements with economy of time in mind.
Fine Arts
Dist - KITCHN **Prod** - KITCHN

37 - 73 60 MIN
16mm
B&W (G)
$90.00 rental
Experiments with dreams, memory, nightmares and magic. Evokes the crazy pain of being an artist.
Fine Arts
Dist - CANCIN **Prod** - MYERSR 1974

The Thirty - seven practices of a Bodhisattva 300 MIN
VHS / BETA
Color; PAL (G)
PdS62 purchase
Travels to Rikon, Switzerland, where His Holiness the Dalai Lama gives a three day teaching on the classic 12th - century verse text by Thogme Zangpo, one of His favorite texts on the Mahayana path of the Bodhisattva - the individual who acts out of wisdom and compassionate awareness to become enlightened in order to help all other beings on the path to liberation. Includes the Dalai Lama explaining these practices from his own personal experience along with their traditional meaning. Translated by Prof Jeffrey Hopkins.
Fine Arts; Religion and Philosophy
Dist - MERIDT

Thirty - Six 30 MIN
16mm
B&W
LC FIA64-1136
Re - tells an old European legend that in every generation there are thirty - six secret Tzaddikim, or saints, simple men unmarked by any distinction.
Literature and Drama; Religion and Philosophy
Dist - NAAJS **Prod** - JTS 1957

36 forms Chen style Taijiquan 120 MIN
VHS
Color (G)
$49.95 purchase _ #1180
Teaches the style created by Prof Kan Gui Xiang of the Beijing Institute of Physical Education. Includes repetitions, closeups, and front and back views. Demonstrated by Prof Kan and Dr Paul Lam. Assumes some knowledge of T'ai chi or other martial art. Book version also available separately.
Physical Education and Recreation
Dist - WAYF

Thirty Six Inch Modular Cooktop with Self Ventilating Down Draft Exhaust 45 MIN
U-matic / VHS
Color (IND)
Shows how the cookstop is used, demonstreates correct installation and details mechanical teardown and electrical diagnosis.
Home Economics; Industrial and Technical Education
Dist - WHIRL **Prod** - WHIRL

Thirty - Sixth Infantry Division 21 MIN
16mm / U-matic / VHS
B&W (H A)
Presents the 36th Infantry Division's part in the battles at Salerno, San Pietro, Cassino, Anzio and Germany.
Civics and Political Systems; History - United States
Dist - USNAC **Prod** - USA 1953

30,000 legal malpractice claims - an analysis 22 MIN
VHS
Color (PRO)
$95.00 purchase, $50.00 rental _ #LMC1 - 000
Discusses the causes of legal malpractice claims. Examines the results of a four - year research project by the ABA National Legal Malpractice Data Center. Illustrates the frequency of claims based on categories such as area of the law, type of lawyer activity, kind of error, client status, size of the firm and age of the attorney. Includes study guide.
Civics and Political Systems
Dist - AMBAR **Prod** - AMBAR 1987

Thirty three
16mm
B&W
Illustrates some of the abstract ideas of Galois theory by using the television studio floor to represent a collection of numbers in the complex field C and constructing physical objects to take on the role of mathematical entities.
Mathematics
Dist - OPENU **Prod** - OPENU

Thirty - Three Men 30 MIN
16mm
Color
A picture story of Rodger Ward's second win at Indianapolis in 1962.
Physical Education and Recreation
Dist - SFI **Prod** - SFI

33 Yo Yo Tricks 8 MIN
16mm
Color (C)
$201.00
Experimental film by P White.
Fine Arts
Dist - AFA **Prod** - AFA 1976

Thirty Ways to make more Time
VHS
Management Development Series
Color (G)
$795.00 purchase, $185.00 rental
Presents thirty ways to make more time for managers. Part of a five - part series on management development.
Business and Economics; Guidance and Counseling; Psychology
Dist - VLEARN **Prod** - MELROS

Thirty ways to make more time 25 MIN
Transp / VHS / 16mm
Color (PRO)
$695.00 purchase, $150.00 rental; $795.00 purchase, $185.00 rental
Teaches first - time and middle managers how to plan and control their time. Includes leader's guide and OHP transparencies.
Business and Economics; Education; Psychology; Sociology
Dist - UTM **Prod** - UTM
VLEARN MELROS

30 years ago they didn't talk about kissing 4 MIN
16mm
Family series
Color (G)
$10.00 rental
Presents the second in a series of four short films that deal with an idiosyncratic, personal and conceptual view of aspects of familial relationships. Features faded home movie footage, from a party in 1947, which is slowed down and manipulated through optical printing while a voice - over pushes the images with questions about kissing. A Sandy Maliga production.
Fine Arts; Sociology
Dist - CANCIN

Thirty years in service - a tribute to Archbishop Iakovos 28 MIN
VHS
Illuminations series
Color (G R)
#V - 1018
Documents the life and work of Archbishop Iakovos, leader of the Greek Orthodox Church in the Americas. Highlights film footage of his march with Dr Martin Luther King Jr in Selma, AL. Includes comments and salutations from George Bush, John Sununu, Michael Dukakis, Cardinal John O'Connor, and others.
Fine Arts; Religion and Philosophy
Dist - GOTEL **Prod** - GOTEL 1988

Thirty Years of Fun 85 MIN
U-matic / VHS / 16mm
B&W
Presents a compilation of film comedies from the industry's earliest days to the advent of talking pictures. Includes glimpses of Laurel and Hardy, Buster Keaton, Harry Langdon and Snub Pollard.
Fine Arts
Dist - CAROUF **Prod** - YNGSNR

This a Way, that a Way 30 MIN
U-matic
Polka Dot Door Series
Color (K)
Presents a variety show for pre - school children. Includes songs, mime, stories, film sequences, talk, dance and fantasy figures. Each show emphasizes a particular theme such as numbers, feelings, exploring, music or time. Comes with parent teacher guide.
Fine Arts; Literature and Drama
Dist - TVOTAR **Prod** - TVOTAR 1985

This Bloody, Blundering Business 30 MIN
U-matic / VHS / 16mm
B&W (A)
Discusses the history of American intervention in the Philippines following the Spanish American War.
Civics and Political Systems; History - World
Dist - CNEMAG **Prod** - CNEMAG 1978

This Business of Numbers 20 MIN
16mm
Color
Gives a completely animated study of arithmetic from cavemen to the present day. Includes man's need for numbers for counting and use in the modern data processing system.
Mathematics
Dist - UNIVAC **Prod** - UNIVAC 1969

This Business of Turkeys 17 MIN
16mm
Color (I J H C)
Surveys the history of turkeys and turkey growing. Studies the development of the bird from egg to maturity. Indicates the best methods of turkey raising.
Agriculture; Psychology; Science - Natural; Social Science
Dist - OSUMPD **Prod** - OSUMPD 1957

This businesss of gleaning 20 MIN
16mm
Color
Examines the development of the gleaning tool used for harvesting of wheat. Shows how modern combines are designed, tested and manufactured.
Agriculture
Dist - IDEALF **Prod** - ALLISC

This Cat Can Play Anything 28 MIN
VHS / U-matic
Color
Features Emmanuel 'Manny' Sayles, one of New Orleans' greatest banjo and guitar jazzmen, in this documentary which aired nationally on PBS. Traces the historical and musical milestones in Sayles' life while visiting the places where he evolved into a working musician.
Fine Arts
Dist - NOVID **Prod** - NOVID

This child is mine 29 MIN
VHS
Color (H C G)
$195.00 purchase, $50.00 rental _ #37774
Explores the ethical and social issues surrounding parenting by women with developmental disabilities. Focuses on four such women, showing that many mildly handicapped women are perfectly capable of being good mothers if some specialized support services are available. Produced by Winter Schumacher.
Health and Safety; Psychology; Sociology
Dist - UCEMC

This Child is Rated X 54 MIN
U-matic / VHS / 16mm
Color (I A)
LC 72-700267
Examines the inequities of juvenile justice and abuse of children's rights in America. Focuses on two types of

children - - the child who committed a child's crime and the child who has committed a very serious crime.
Psychology; Sociology
Dist - FI **Prod** - NBCTV 1971

This child is rated x - Pt 1 27 MIN
16mm
Color (I A)
LC 72-700267
Examines the inequities of juvenile justice and abuse of children's rights in America. Focuses on the child who has committed a child's crime and the child who has committed a very serious crime.
Sociology
Dist - NBCTV **Prod** - NBCTV 1971

This child is rated x - Pt 2 27 MIN
16mm
Color (I A)
LC 72-700267
Examines the inequities of juvenile justice and abuse of children's rights in America. Focuses on the child who has committed a child's crime and the child who has committed a very serious crime.
Sociology
Dist - NBCTV **Prod** - NBCTV 1971

This City is Milwaukee 27 MIN
Videoreel / VT2
Color
Points out the many works of art which combine to make the 'look' of the city complete. Portrays its parks, large office buildings, churches and public buildings which possess qualities of distinction and aestheticism.
Fine Arts; Geography - United States; Social Science
Dist - PBS **Prod** - WHATV

This Constitution - a history series 140 MIN
VHS
This Constitution - a history series
Color (H C G)
$720.00 purchase
Presents a five - part series on the philosophical origins, drafting and interpretation of the US Constitution and its effect on American society, produced by the International University Consortium and Project '87. Includes the titles The Federal City; South Carolina and the United States; Prayer in the Classroom; The Pursuit of Equality; The Rise and Fall of Prohibition.
Civics and Political Systems
Dist - PSU

This Country Called Deutschland 27 MIN
16mm
Color
Presents a visual portrait of Germany through the eyes of a young German woman who receives a letter from friends overseas announcing their impending arrival. Includes the Kurfurstendamm in Berlin, Hamburg's 'Reeperbahn,' the Munich 'Oktoberfest,' and museums, cathedrals, romantic castles and medieval towns.
Geography - World; History - World
Dist - WSTGLC **Prod** - WSTGLC

This Dog is Real 15 MIN
16mm
Color
LC 80-701052
Tells the story of a little girl whose family buys a dog. Shows how the animal is selected and focuses on the responsibilities of each family member in caring for it. Highlights the services of the veterinarian and obedience trainer.
Guidance and Counseling; Science - Natural
Dist - KLEINW **Prod** - KLEINW 1978

This England 26 MIN
16mm
Audubon wildlife theatre series
Color (I A)
LC 72-701987
Demonstrates how wildlife wilderness areas have been preserved in modern, industrialized England.
Geography - World; Science - Natural; Social Science
Dist - AVEXP **Prod** - KEGPL 1970

This film has no title 5 MIN
16mm
B&W
LC 75-703240
Presents a visual mood piece of a young girl rediscovering the shape and textures of the world. Shows how the young Caucasian girl is brought face to face with a young Negro girl on the other side of a fence, exchanging glances and going in opposite directions.
Fine Arts; Guidance and Counseling; History - United States; Psychology; Social Science; Sociology
Dist - USC **Prod** - USC 1965

This film has no title 30 MIN
VHS / U-matic / 16mm
(PRO G)
$89.95 purchase _ #DGP23
Relates the obstacles and opportunities in starting a child care operation and the daily details of running it.
Business and Economics
Dist - RMIBHF **Prod** - RMIBHF

This Film is about Rape 30 MIN
U-matic / VHS / 16mm
Color
Offers suggestions for reducing vulnerability to rape and for responding both physically and psychologically should an attack occur. Presents various methods for dealing with the rape problem including assertiveness training, self - defense classes and rape crisis hotlines.
Sociology
Dist - CORF **Prod** - CORF

This guy Denenberg 29 MIN
Videoreel / VT2
Turning points series
Color
Looks at Herbert Denenberg, a relatively unknown professor from the Wharton School of Finance, who was sworn in on January, 1971 as Insurance Commissioner for the Commonwealth of Pennsylvania and whose name three months later was practically a household word throughout the state. Explains Denenberg's conflicts with the State Medical Society.
Biography; Business and Economics; Geography - United States
Dist - PBS **Prod** - WQED

This happy breed 110 MIN
VHS
Color (G)
$39.95 purchase _ #THI030
Adapts the play by Noel Coward which looks at an English family's struggle for stability between the two World Wars. Uses imaginative camera direction to examine human nature. Directed by David Lean and Anthony Havelock - Allan. Remastered.
Fine Arts; Sociology
Dist - HOMVIS **Prod** - JANUS 1947

This Hazardous planet - 7 60 MIN
VHS
Land, location and culture - a geographical synthesis series
Color (J H C)
$89.95 purchase _ #WLU107
Examines the basic hazards of life on Planet Earth - hurricanes, earthquakes and tornadoes - which geographers study as natural hazards. Emphasizes that such hazards are solely products of the physical world but result through the interaction of people and the environment. Closes by considering the adjustments people can make to minimize the risks people can make to minimize the risks they face from damaging events. Part of a 12 - part series.
Geography - World; History - World
Dist - INSTRU

This Honorable Court 120 MIN
VHS
Color; Captioned (G)
$90.00 purchase _ #THHC - 000
Provides a two - part look behind the scenes at the U.S. Supreme Court. Traces the history of the Supreme Court from its beginnings in 1789 to the modern - day controversy over the Supreme Court nomination of Robert Bork in Part One, 'A History of the Court.' Part Two, 'Inside the Supreme Court,' uses the Louisiana creationism case of Edwards v Aguillard to show how a case is considered by the Supreme Court.
Civics and Political Systems
Dist - PBS **Prod** - WETATV 1988

This is a Cooperative 28 MIN
U-matic / VHS / 16mm
Color (J H C)
LC FIA68-842
Host Lorne Greene discusses the role of consumer cooperatives in urban and rural society, showing the activities of a health cooperative, a housing cooperative, a credit union and a farm family.
Business and Economics; Social Science; Sociology
Dist - JOU **Prod** - CLUSA 1967

This is a Football 28 MIN
16mm
NFL Action Series
Color
LC 77-702615
A study of the football, its effect on the game and the men who play it. Includes scenes from games played by the teams in the National Football League.
Physical Education and Recreation
Dist - NFL **Prod** - NFL 1967

This is a Laboratory School 29 MIN
16mm
B&W (T)
LC FIA65-475
Shows the role of the laboratory school in education. Includes views of social studies, art, mathematics and science classes with comments by the children and teachers.
Education
Dist - UCLA **Prod** - UCLA 1964

This is a recorded message 10 MIN
16mm
Color (J H C)
LC 74-702428
Includes cut - out color ads projected in fragmented, rapid succession to represent the barrage of advertising that assails the individual almost from the time of entrance into the world. Suggests the reality hidden behind the false images.
Psychology
Dist - NFBC **Prod** - NFBC 1973

This is a test - this is only a test - test - taking techniques 30 MIN
VHS
Better grades series
Color (J H C)
$69.95 purchase _ #CCP0074V
Teaches the art of stress - free test - taking. Offers tips for reviewing and retaining information with easy - to - implement effective study techniques. Shows how test scores and anxiety levels are affected by preparing, organizing, cramming and anticipating. Includes How to Study book.
Education; Psychology
Dist - CAMV **Prod** - CAMV 1992

This is Advertising 27 MIN
16mm
Color
Explains the vital role of advertising to salesmen, dealers, employees and community groups.
Business and Economics; Psychology
Dist - CCNY **Prod** - ANA

This is an Emergency 25 MIN
VHS / U-matic
Color
Gives a patient's eye view of an emergency, from treatment on the scene by a fire department paramedic squad through an ambulance ride and concluding with the treatment in the emergency room, complete with life - restoring measures.
Health and Safety
Dist - MEDCOM **Prod** - MEDCOM

This is an Emergency 29 MIN
16mm
Color (H C A)
LC 80-701814
Points out that industry consumes half of North America's energy. Shows how factories in Sweden conserve energy and how Canadian factories are trying to do the same.
Business and Economics; Social Science
Dist - NFBC **Prod** - NFBC 1980

This is Ben Shahn 17 MIN
U-matic / VHS / 16mm
Color (J)
LC FIA68-2115
Ben Shahn discusses his personal philosophy and how it is reflected in his paintings. He discusses some of his works and the impulses and events which prompted their creation.
Fine Arts
Dist - PHENIX **Prod** - CBSTV 1968

This is Betty Crocker 23 MIN
16mm
Color (H C)
Pictures the seven kitchens of the world at General Mills, Inc., to show the many employees at work through a day of developing and testing products and recipes for packages and cookbooks, preparing food for photography and answering Betty Crocker's mail. Contains close - ups of beautiful foods and time - saving techniques which homemakers can adapt to their own cooking needs.
Business and Economics; Home Economics; Industrial and Technical Education
Dist - NINEFC **Prod** - GEMILL

This is Boeing 13 MIN
16mm
Color
LC 79-701060
Traces the history of Boeing's involvement in air travel and looks ahead to its activities in space. Describes employment opportunities for graduating engineers and scientists.
Business and Economics; Guidance and Counseling; Social Science
Dist - CORPOR **Prod** - BOEING 1979

This is British Nuclear Fuels Limited 23 MIN
16mm
Color
Features the process of uranium fuel manufacturing at British Nuclear Fuels Limited plant at Springfields. Shows their enrichment plant at Capenhurst and their processing and plutonium fuel manufacturing plants at Windscale. Shows that BNFL provides a comprehensive nuclear fuel service to reactor operators throughout the world.
Industrial and Technical Education; Science - Physical
Dist - UKAEA **Prod** - UKAEA 1971

This is Camping 18 MIN
16mm / U-matic / VHS
Color (I)
LC 73-700536
Presents a look at organized camping and the many facilities and activities offered campers. Shows how the campers learn cooperation, conservation and ecology through their involvement with nature and each other.
Physical Education and Recreation; Science - Natural; Sociology
Dist - IU **Prod** - IU 1972

This is dedicated - grieving when a partner dies 24 MIN
VHS
Color (H C G)
$295.00 purchase, $55.00 rental
Reveals that the feelings of bereavement suffered by lesbians or gay men who have lost lovers are intensified because society does not recognize such losses. Discloses that whether the death occurred because of accident or illness, there are no traditions for expressing sympathy, and that the straight world is often insensitive and even cruel to survivors whose relationships were not considered legitimate. Produced by Alleycat Productions.
Sociology
Dist - FLMLIB

This is Edward R Murrow 44 MIN
16mm / U-matic / VHS
B&W (J)
LC 76-703287
Highlights the career of newsman Edward R Murrow, including excerpts from many of his most famous broadcasts.
Biography; Fine Arts
Dist - CAROUF **Prod** - CBSTV 1976

This is Edward Steichen 27 MIN
U-matic / VHS / 16mm
B&W (J)
LC FIA67-61
Portrays Edward Steichen, who has elevated photographic portraiture to an art. Shows some of his world famous photographs and his renowned 'Family of Man' exibit.
Fine Arts; Industrial and Technical Education
Dist - CAROUF **Prod** - WCBSTV 1966

This is fraud 9 MIN
16mm / U-matic / VHS
Consumer education series
Captioned; Color (J) (ENGLISH, SPANISH)
LC 72-703424
Illustrates the 'bait and switch' technique and other methods of a crafty door - to - door salesman.
Business and Economics; Home Economics
Dist - ALTSUL **Prod** - ALTSUL 1972

This is Frederica 25 MIN
U-matic / 16mm
Color
LC 79-706162; 77-703157
Re - creates scenes of town life in the early 18th century village of Fort Frederica on Saint Simon's Island, Georgia. Relates the importance of the fort as a buffer against Spanish expansion from the south.
History - United States
Dist - USNAC **Prod** - USNPS 1979

This is going to hurt me more than it hurts you 25 MIN
VHS
Color (A PRO IND)
Discusses those situations where a manager must give bad news to an employee. Suggests an approach in which the manager focuses on the employee's point of view. Stars John Cleese of 'Monty Python' fame.
Business and Economics; Guidance and Counseling; Psychology
Dist - VLEARN **Prod** - VIDART
VIDART

This is Guatemala 24 MIN
16mm
Color (I)
LC 77-701859
Features a tour of Guatemala, showing areas where various stages of the culture and history of Central America are still visible.
Geography - World; History - World; Social Science; Sociology
Dist - CASTOP **Prod** - CASTOP 1975

This is Ham Radio 15 MIN
U-matic / VHS / 16mm
Color
LC 72-700973
Presents Matt Futterman describing some of the lure of ham radio, and discussing licensing requirements, low - cost rigs and the relative ease of earning a novice class ticket from the FCC and getting on the air. Includes scenes of young people operating mobile rigs, testing emergency gear, relaying messages across the ocean and talking with friends across town.
Industrial and Technical Education; Physical Education and Recreation; Social Science; Sociology
Dist - ALTSUL **Prod** - BELLDA 1970

This is Harness Racing 15 MIN
U-matic / VHS / 16mm
Color (J)
LC 79-701788
Focuses on the sport of harness racing. Shows those who train, drive and look after the horses. Explains the difference between a pacer and a trotter and uses slow motion techniques to describe each gait.
Physical Education and Recreation
Dist - MCFI **Prod** - LANGED 1975

This is Hawaii 14 MIN
16mm
Color (I J H C)
LC FIA61-805
Presents Hawaii industrially and socially through visits to schools, churches, factories and tourists attractions.
Geography - United States
Dist - CLI **Prod** - CLI 1961

This is Hawaii 28 MIN
16mm
Color
LC 73-711524
Features Don Ho, singing star, as he tours the Hawaiian Islands. Captures the beauty, color and splendor of this little corner of the world through background music of Hawaiian songs.
Geography - United States
Dist - MTP **Prod** - UAL 1971

This is Hope Enterprises 25 MIN
U-matic / VHS / 16mm
Color (H C A)
LC 77-700737
Explores Hope Enterprises, which serves developmentally disabled people whose needs have not been met by the traditional community resources for rehabilitation, education and employment.
Health and Safety; Psychology
Dist - STNFLD **Prod** - STNFLD 1976

This is how we live - Homecoming 47 MIN
VHS
Glasnost film festival series
Color; B&W (H C G T A) (RUSSIAN (ENGLISH SUBTITLES))
$59.95 purchase, $35.00 rental
Presents two of the Soviet films shown at the Glasnost Film Festival. This Is How We Live is a color film which portrays the alienation and depravity of some Soviet young people, focusing in particular on the Fascists. Homecoming shows an interview of Soviet veterans of the Afghan War.
Business and Economics; Civics and Political Systems; History - World; Sociology
Dist - EFVP

This is Israel 53 MIN
VHS
Color (J H C G A R)
$10.00 rental _ #36 - 839 - 8579
Takes viewers on a tour through the Holy Land.
Geography - World; History - World; Religion and Philosophy
Dist - APH **Prod** - VIDOUT

This is it 45 MIN
16mm
Color (C)
$196.00 purchase
Experimental film by James Broughton.
Fine Arts
Dist - AFA **Prod** - AFA 1971

This is Jennifer 21 MIN
16mm
Color (G)
$40.00 rental
Examines the heroine, a real - life 'Savior' type, dedicated to saving the world. Presents her delivering a William Burrough's - like sermon to spellbound youths in a San Francisco ghetto backyard. Produced by Bob Giorgio.
Fine Arts; History - United States
Dist - CANCIN

This is Livestock Pooling 5 MIN
16mm
Color
LC 74-705780
Shows the selling of livestock through auction marketing pooling. Explains the advantages of marketing livestock by this method.
Agriculture; Business and Economics
Dist - USNAC **Prod** - USDA 1964

This is Mack 17 MIN
16mm
Color
LC 75-700486
Surveys the history and accomplishments of the firm Mack Trucks and takes a look at Mack's power, facilities and service capabilities today.
Business and Economics; Industrial and Technical Education; Social Science
Dist - MACKT **Prod** - MACKT 1974

This is Magnesium 15 MIN
16mm
B&W
Depicts the unlimited resources, methods of extraction and countless uses of magnesium, which is obtained from sea water.
Industrial and Technical Education; Science - Physical
Dist - USDIBM **Prod** - USDIBM 1952

This is Marina City 18 MIN
16mm
Color
Describes the planning, building and use of twin circular towers at one edge of Chicago's central business district.
Industrial and Technical Education
Dist - PRTLND **Prod** - PRTLND 1966

This is Marshall McLuhan - the medium is the massage 53 MIN
U-matic / VHS / 16mm
Color (H C A)
Presents Marshall McLuhan's ideas about the manner in which all media of communication shape and alter society. Concentrates on the electronic media and instruments which speed up life, process information, and shape sensibilities.
Education; Psychology; Social Science; Sociology
Dist - CRMP **Prod** - NBCTV 1967
MGHT

This is Marshall McLuhan - the medium is the massage - Pt 1 26 MIN
U-matic / VHS / 16mm
Color (H C A)
LC FAI67-5710
Presents Marshall McLuhan's ideas about the manner in which all media of communication shape and alter society. Concentrates on the electronic media and instruments which speed up life, process information, and shape sensibilities.
Social Science; Sociology
Dist - CRMP **Prod** - NBCTV 1967
MGHT

This is Marshall McLuhan - the medium is the massage - Pt 2 27 MIN
16mm / U-matic / VHS
Color (H C A)
Presents Marshall McLuhan's ideas about the manner in which all media of communication shape and alter society. Concentrates on the electronic media and instruments which speed up life, process information, and shape sensibilities.
Social Science; Sociology
Dist - CRMP **Prod** - NBCTV 1967
MGHT

This is me 4 MIN
U-matic / VHS / 16mm
Most important person - creative expression series
Color (K P I)
Depicts Fumble's dissatisfaction when he decides that his painting is not perfect. Follows, as a friend reminds him that what matters is that he tried and that 'it's an original.'
English Language; Fine Arts; Guidance and Counseling; Psychology
Dist - EBEC **Prod** - EBEC 1972

This is Mexico 27 MIN
16mm
Color (I)
Shows modern Mexico and how successive civilizations, arts and cultures - - Mayan, Toltec and Spanish - - have left their marks in city, town and countryside. Depicts progress in industry, education and recreation.
Geography - World
Dist - AVED **Prod** - BARONA 1963

This is Mission, USA 10 MIN
16mm
B&W (R)
LC 73-702060
Presents a kaleidoscopic view of the variety of ministries and needs of the Baptist missions in the United States. Includes a short narration taken from the book See How Love Works by Walker L Knight and Don Rutledge.
Religion and Philosophy
Dist - BHMB **Prod** - BHMB 1972

This is montage 7 MIN
16mm
Color (G)
$10.00 rental
Affirms and contradicts Sergei Esenstein's theory of film montage. Concentrates on film and language. Produced by Holly Fisher.
Fine Arts
Dist - CANCIN

This is My Friend 10 MIN
16mm / U-matic / VHS
Color (P I)
Presents a visual poem of friendship involving a boy and a girl.
Guidance and Counseling; Sociology
Dist - PHENIX **Prod** - KINGSP

This is my garden 26 MIN
VHS
Color (H C G)
$295.00 purchase, $55.00 rental
Describes the emotional impact of AIDS on the lives of five men who recently lost their partners to the disease. Uses interviews and photographs to describe each relationship, from the first meeting to daily life together, to the onset of illness. Each man reveals what he thought as he cared for his partner during the course of the illness. Produced by Alex Benedict.
Guidance and Counseling; Health and Safety; Sociology
Dist - FLMLIB

This is My Grandmother 15 MIN
16mm
B&W
LC 77-702671
Portrays 80 - year - old Gertrude Day. Shows how the widow of 20 years relives memories with family and friends.
Biography; Sociology
Dist - CANFDC **Prod** - CANFDC 1976

This is My Home Series
A Historic Fort Town - Fort St James 14 MIN
An Island Below the Sea - Westham Island 14 MIN
A Mining Community - Kimberley 14 MIN
A Rocky Mountain Town - Revelstoke 14 MIN
A Seacoast port city - Port of Vancouver 14 MIN
Dist - BCNFL

This is My Own - the Rockwell Kent Collection 44 MIN
16mm
Color
LC 80-700396
Examines the complexity of the work of artist Rockwell Kent as seen in collections of his work at his former home, at SUNY College, and in the Soviet Union.
Fine Arts
Dist - SUNY **Prod** - SUNY 1979

This is my own - the Rockwell Kent collection - Pt 1 22 MIN
16mm
Color
LC 80-700396
Examines the complexity of the work of artist Rockwell Kent as seen in collections of his work at his former home, at SUNY College, and in the Soviet Union.
Fine Arts
Dist - SUNY **Prod** - SUNY 1979

This is my own - the Rockwell Kent collection - Pt 2 22 MIN
16mm
Color
LC 80-700396
Examines the complexity of the work of artist Rockwell Kent as seen in collections of his work at his former home, at SUNY College, and in the Soviet Union.
Fine Arts
Dist - SUNY **Prod** - SUNY 1979

This is my son 60 MIN
16mm
Color
$345.00 rental
Discusses the birth of a child with Down's Syndrome to a professional couple, and their experience in coping with his problem.
Education; Health and Safety; Psychology
Dist - CCNCC **Prod** - CCNCC 1985

This is My will Series
How to go about it 30 MIN
Taxation - what and When 30 MIN
Why 30 MIN
Dist - PBS

This is New Jersey 30 MIN
16mm
Color
Presents the state of New Jersy - - its history, character, people, beauty, industry, agriculture and recreational areas.
Geography - United States
Dist - NJBTC **Prod** - NJBTC 1958

This is New York 12 MIN
U-matic / VHS / 16mm
Picture Book Parade Series
Color (P I)
An iconographic motion picture, using original illustrations from the children's book by Miroslav Sasek, about a young French boy's visit to New York City and his witty and informative reactions.
English Language; Geography - United States; Social Science
Dist - WWS **Prod** - WWS 1962

This is Noel Coward 60 MIN
16mm
Color (J)
Documents the life of British playwright and humorist, Noel Coward. Includes an interview with Coward, filmed shortly before his death and intercut with biographical photographs, scenes from stage and film productions of his work and interviews with close acquaintances. Narrated by Sir John Gielgud.
Biography; Fine Arts; Literature and Drama
Dist - CANTOR **Prod** - CANTOR

This is not a Museum 13 MIN
VHS / U-matic
Color
Comments humorously on the intellectualization of modern art. Makes visual references to the work of such artists as Picasso, Rousseau, Goya, Magritte and Oldenburg. Uses animation.
Fine Arts
Dist - MEDIPR **Prod** - HAUGSE 1974

This is Our Farm 11 MIN
16mm
Color
Shows a unique children's farm in Israel.
Geography - World; Social Science; Sociology
Dist - ALDEN **Prod** - ALDEN

This is philosophy 27 MIN
16mm
Color (H C)
LC 74-702393
Introduces high school students to the field of philosophy. Shows the possibilities for study in philosophy and examines the contribution of philosophy to the solution and clarification of issues and problems.
Education; Religion and Philosophy
Dist - AUIS **Prod** - FLMAUS 1974

This is Robert 45 MIN
16mm
Studies of Normal Personality Development Series
Color
Presents a longitundinal study tracing the growth of Robert, an agressive but appealing child, from nursery school at two to the public school at seven.
Psychology; Sociology
Dist - NYU **Prod** - VASSAR

This is Rockwell 22 MIN
16mm
Color
LC 74-700379
Tours several of Rockwell International's facilities and shows the kinds of products Rockwell makes.
Business and Economics
Dist - RCKWL **Prod** - RCKWL 1974

This is Rodeo 30 MIN
Videoreel / VT2
Synergism - the Challenge of Sports Series
Color
Captures the excitement of the Western rodeo from bulldogging to chuck wagon racing.
Geography - United States; Physical Education and Recreation
Dist - PBS **Prod** - KRMATV

This is sailing
VHS
Color (G A)
$35.90 purchase _ #0074
Presents a three - part course on sailing. Discusses the theory of sailing, the components of the boats, sailing skills such as steering and sail trim, tacking and jibing. Refines techniques for spinnaker work, maximizing speed, heavy weather sailing.
Physical Education and Recreation
Dist - SEVVID

This is Sailing - First Essential Skills 19 MIN
16mm
Color (J)
LC 74-703810
Presents the first essential skills in sailing. Covers sailing terms, points of sail, force vectors, tacking, jibbing, sail trim, hull balance, picking up a mooring and landing at a dock and on the bench.
Physical Education and Recreation
Dist - SAIL **Prod** - SAIL 1974

This is Sailing - Introduction to a Boat 19 MIN
16mm
Color (J)
LC 74-703809
Presents an introduction to a sailboat. Discusses the important parts of a boat, the mainsail draft, stepping the mast, hoisting sail, launching from shore and dock, steering and getting underway.
Physical Education and Recreation
Dist - SAIL **Prod** - SAIL 1974

This is Sailing - more Advanced Techniques 19 MIN
16mm
Color (J)
LC 74-703811
Depicts advanced techniques in sailing, including spinnaker gear, hoisting, trimming, jibbing and lowering the spinnaker, spilling wind, reefing and shortening sail in heavy weather, capsize recover, planing and trapeze.
Physical Education and Recreation
Dist - SAIL **Prod** - SAIL

This is Sea World 9 MIN
16mm
Color
Presents Sea World, Florida's largest marine life park.
Geography - United States; Physical Education and Recreation; Science - Natural
Dist - FLADC **Prod** - FLADC

This is Switzerland 60 MIN
VHS
Traveloguer collection series
Color (G)
$29.95 purchase _ #QU009
Visits Switzerland. Offers historical and geographic highlights.
Geography - World; History - World
Dist - SIV

This is TB 10 MIN
16mm
B&W (I)
Outlines the cause, spread and prevention of tuberculosis.
Health and Safety
Dist - AMLUNG **Prod** - NTBA 1946

This is the Beginning 28 MIN
16mm
Color; Mono; B&W (I J H C G T A)
Constructs a larger than usual church building known as 'Cathedral Of The Rockies' at Boise, Idaho. This film reveals the splendor part of the community. The expression is orthodox Christian. The particular theme presented is 'Onward Christian Soldiers.' Content has worshipful tone.
History - United States; Religion and Philosophy
Dist - FO **Prod** - FO 1963

This is the day 30 MIN
VHS
Color (J H C G A R)
$19.95 purchase, $10.00 rental _ #35 - 88119 - 87
Features continuous scenes of natural wonders, combined with music and Scripture readings. Produced by Zondervan.
Industrial and Technical Education; Literature and Drama; Religion and Philosophy
Dist - APH

This is the film in which you are forgiven and This is the film in which I am lost 12 MIN
16mm
B&W (G) (SUBTITLES IN ENGLISH)
$20.00 rental
Features two works which deal with memory and filmmaking. Interweaves sections from footage shot in Tasmania and New York which play off the text, documenting politics and political torture.

Civics and Political Systems; Fine Arts; Psychology
Dist - CANCIN **Prod** - SONDHE 1984

This is the Home of Mrs Levant Graham 15 MIN
16mm / U-matic / VHS
B&W (H C A)
LC 77-711525
Focuses on a Washington, D C, mother in a Black ghetto and her large, loose - knit family.
History - United States; Psychology; Sociology
Dist - PFP **Prod** - PFP 1970

This is the John Birch Society - an Invitation to Membership 115 MIN
16mm
B&W (A)
LC 73-700815
Presents G Edward Griffin, author and active member of the John Birch Society, who lectures on the purposes, organizational structure and plan of action of the John Birch Society.
Civics and Political Systems
Dist - AMMED **Prod** - AMMED 1970

This is the life 30 MIN
VHS
Color (H C A R)
$19.95 purchase
Presents dramas with Christian themes. Produced by the International Lutheran Laymen's League.
Guidance and Counseling; Literature and Drama; Religion and Philosophy
Dist - CPH **Prod** - LUMIS

This is the life 15 MIN
U-matic / VHS
Dragons, wagons and wax - Set 2 series
Color (K P)
Examines human movement, growth, eating, breathing and reproduction.
Science; Science - Natural
Dist - CTI **Prod** - CTI

This is the Life - a Voice Crying 29 MIN
VHS / U-matic
Color (J H A)
Talks about a seminary graduate who decides to pursue a career in hunger advocacy instead of pastoral work. Produced by the Aid Association for Lutherans.
Psychology; Sociology
Dist - CWS

This is the life series
A Warm place inside 29 MIN
Dist - CPH

This is the life series
Elm Street Divided 29 MIN
The Hunger Next Door 29 MIN
Only Hooked a Little 29 MIN
Project compassion 29 MIN
The Sins of the Father 29 MIN
Dist - LUTTEL

This is the microscope 16 MIN
VHS
Color (J H C)
$39.95 purchase _ #49 - 8135 - V
Describes the compound microscope. Explains the different types of compound light microscopes in use, as well as their history, the different parts of a modern microscope and its use and care. Still frame.
Science - Natural
Dist - INSTRU **Prod** - CBSC

This is Toronto 30 MIN
VHS
Color (G)
$29.95 purchase _ #S01980
Presents the sights and sounds of Toronto. Features such sites as the CN Tower, Ontario Place, museums, shopping centers, and the many green spaces within the city.
Geography - World; Sociology
Dist - UILL

This is TV - America 30 MIN
VHS
Color (G)
$40.00 purchase
Combines interviews, off - air footage and a performance by the Air Farce players to create docu - satire. Presents news programs, commercials, soap operas, sports and game shows as deconstructivist video collage. Pantomime, stand - up comedy and animation are used for the satire.
Fine Arts; Literature and Drama
Dist - CANCIN **Prod** - DEWITT 1979

This is Volleyball 30 MIN
16mm
Color (H C A)
Presents an overview of individual skills and basic team tactics in volleyball from the 1976 Olympics.
Physical Education and Recreation
Dist - CVA **Prod** - CVA 1977

This is what we think - Asi Pensamos 29 MIN
16mm / VHS
Color (G)
$515.00, $290.00 purchase, $55.00 rental
Documents a community of 100 peasants in Ecuador's mountainous countryside who organized against their feudal landlord. Looks at their seven year struggle in which they were able to gain, by peaceful and legal means, a portion of his estate. Interviews these people of Pillachiquir who began an agricultural cooperative on their land as they talk about their lives and working conditions. Produced by Camilo Luzuriaga.
Fine Arts; Social Science; Sociology
Dist - FIRS

This is Where it all Began 24 MIN
16mm
Color
Tells the history of Christianity in the Holy Land.
Geography - World; History - World; Religion and Philosophy
Dist - ALDEN **Prod** - ALDEN

This is William Brose Productions, Incorporated 4 MIN
16mm
Color
LC 76-703165
Uses clips from films of William Brose Productions to demonstrate the firm's image - building potential for prospective clients. Documents the firm's day - to - day activities, emphasizing the creative process.
Business and Economics; Fine Arts
Dist - BROSEB **Prod** - BROSEB 1975

This is You
VHS / U-matic
Color (J H)
Focuses on students' real problems and presents solutions. Includes teenage pregnancy. Discusses love and the elements of successful relationships.
Psychology; Sociology
Dist - EDUACT **Prod** - EDUACT

This is you - health series
You - and your ears 8 MIN
You - and your eyes 8 MIN
You - and your five senses 8 MIN
You - and Your Food 8 MIN
You - and Your Sense of Smell and Taste 8 MIN
You - and your sense of touch 8 MIN
You - the human animal 8 MIN
You - the living machine 8 MIN
Dist - CORF

This is you series
The Human animal 9 MIN
The Living machine 13 MIN
You and your ears 14 MIN
You and your eyes 13 MIN
You and your five senses 13 MIN
You and your food 12 MIN
You and your sense of touch 13 MIN
You and your senses of smell and taste 14 MIN
Dist - CORF

This is Your Lung 17 MIN
U-matic / VHS / 16mm
Color (H C A)
LC 72-700799
Presents essential facts about cigarette smoking and lung cancer. Shows how cilia regularly subjected to irritants and tars of smoke are gradually destroyed.
Guidance and Counseling; Health and Safety
Dist - IFB **Prod** - VERITY 1966

This is Your Museum Speaking 14 MIN
U-matic / VHS / 16mm
Color (I J)
LC 81-701249
Shows the exhibits in a museum coming alive as a night watchman and his guard dog patrol the darkened corridors.
Fine Arts
Dist - FI **Prod** - NFBC 1981

This Isn't Wonderland 57 MIN
U-matic / VHS
Color
Attempts to identify the cultural factors that generate women's role dilemmas, and the madness which can result. Explores a woman's attempts to deal with severe depression. Discusses other women's confrontation with madness.
Sociology
Dist - WMENIF **Prod** - WMENIF

This just in - Columbus has landed 42 MIN
VHS
Color (I J H)
$49.95 purchase _ #QC2000V-S
Celebrates the quincentennial of Christopher Columbus' expeditions and discovery of the New World. Features material delivered as a modern news broadcast - reporters follow the voyage and report the happenings as they occur. Interviews actors portraying Columbus, John II, the King of Portugal, sailors, and others. Viewers learn of the trouble Columbus experienced when he first tried to get royal support for his theories and desire to explore, the success and fame he received later, and his attempt to return to the New World to inhabit it.
History - United States; History - World
Dist - CAMV

This Land 15 MIN
16mm
Color
LC FIE67-141
Describes a land settlement project in Kenya as seen by a Peace Corps volunteer working as a land settlement officer, pointing out the transition between old and new in Kenya.
Civics and Political Systems; Geography - World; History - United States; History - World
Dist - USNAC **Prod** - USPC 1966

This Land 17 MIN
16mm
Color (I)
LC FIE67-80
Highpoints the history of the United States, from its Beginnings through to the Civil War. Shows places in U S National Parks where historical events occurred.
Geography - United States; History - United States
Dist - USNAC **Prod** - NEWSPX 1967

This Land is 58 MIN
16mm
Color
LC 70-705690
Traces the history and character of the southern Illinois region, utilizing folk stories and contemporary witticisms.
Geography - United States; Literature and Drama; Social Science
Dist - SIUFP **Prod** - SILLU 1969

This land is our land 30 MIN
VHS
Color (G)
$14.95 purchase
Shows how land use and market access disagreements bring violence and disruption to Brazil's agricultural economy. Focuses on the family farm in contrast to the large corporation.
Agriculture; Business and Economics; Sociology
Dist - MARYFA

This Land is Our Land 15 MIN
VHS / 16mm
First Americans Series
Color (I)
Examines American Indian culture and how it relates to the culture of the United States. The third of six installments of The First Americans Series, which attempts to present a more accurate portrait of American Indians than has been presented in the media.
Psychology; Social Science
Dist - GPN **Prod** - CTI 1990

This Land is Your Land 14 MIN
VHS / U-matic
Strawberry Square Series
Color (P)
Fine Arts
Dist - AITECH **Prod** - NEITV 1982

This Life of Mine 110 MIN
VHS
Color (G) (MANDARIN CHINESE (ENGLISH SUBTITLES))
$45.00 purchase _ #6003A
Presents a Mandarin Chinese language movie produced in the People's Republic of China.
Fine Arts; Geography - World; Literature and Drama
Dist - CHTSUI **Prod** - CHTSUI

This man must die 115 MIN
16mm
Color (C A) (FRENCH (ENGLISH SUBTITLES))
Tells the story of a grief - stricken father who sets out to find the killer of his son and to gain revenge in a small village on the French coast.
Literature and Drama
Dist - CINEWO **Prod** - CINEWO 1970

This Matter of Motivation 30 MIN
16mm / VHS / U-matic
This Matter of Motivation Series
Color (IND)

LC 75-703994
Introduces a series of case - study films designed to help managers and supervisors handle employee problems effectively. Discusses the effectiveness of behavioral science motivational techniques, focusing on the theories of Dr Federick Herzberg. Describes how to apply these techniques to personnel problems.
Psychology
Dist - DARTNL **Prod** - CTRACT 1971

This Matter of Motivation Series
The Ball of fire 4 MIN
The Gilded Lily 5 MIN
Harry's Hangover 5 MIN
The Indispensable Miss Spencer 5 MIN
The Nice Guy 4 MIN
The Pacesetter 6 MIN
People will Talk 4 MIN
The Perfect Job for Jim 4 MIN
The Puzzle 6 MIN
The Roadblock 6 MIN
Shades of Black and White 5 MIN
This Matter of Motivation 30 MIN
Dist - DARTNL

This matter of motivations series
Among the missing 9 MIN
Dist - DARTNL

This Means that 30 MIN
U-matic
Magic Ring II Series
(K P)
Continues the aim of the first series to bring added freshness to the commonplace and assist children to discover more about the many things in their world. Each program starts with the familiar, goes to the less familiar, then the new, and ends by blending new and old information.
Education; Literature and Drama
Dist - ACCESS **Prod** - ACCESS 1986

This most Gallant Gentleman 10 MIN
16mm
Color
Describes the life of Roger Casement, using the 1965 state funeral as background.
Biography; Geography - World
Dist - CONSUI **Prod** - CONSUI

This My Life 23 MIN
16mm
Color
Explores the opportunities for service in the physical therapy field.
Health and Safety; Science
Dist - LOMA **Prod** - LOMA

This Nuclear Age 29 MIN
16mm
Color (G)
_ #106C 0173 629
Shows the many areas of nuclear research and recent developments in Canada. Shows Canadian atomic reactors and laboratories where experimentation is carried out in pure and applied nuclear science.
Science - Physical; Social Science
Dist - CFLMDC **Prod** - NFBC 1973

This old house 60 MIN
VHS
Color (G)
$19.95 purchase
Presents numerous ideas for home repair and restoration projects. Based on the PBS television series.
Home Economics; Industrial and Technical Education
Dist - PBS **Prod** - WNETTV

This old house 60 MIN
VHS
Color (A)
$24.95 purchase _ #S01375
Features Bob Vila and Norm Abram of the PBS series This Old House, as they demonstrate various home improvement projects.
Business and Economics; Home Economics; Industrial and Technical Education
Dist - UILL **Prod** - PBS

This Old House, Pt 1 - the Dorchester Series
Ceiling and renovation 30 MIN
A Closer Look 30 MIN
Finishing Touches 30 MIN
Flooring and masonry 30 MIN
Heating and Insulation 30 MIN
History Preserved 30 MIN
Landscape Design 30 MIN
Paint Stripping Hints 30 MIN
Parquet and Tile Floors 30 MIN
Unforeseen Problems 30 MIN
Dist - CORF

This Old House, Pt 2 - Suburban '50s Series
Counter Top Installation 30 MIN
Dry Wall 30 MIN
Energy Audit 30 MIN
Framing and Addition 30 MIN
Master Bathroom 30 MIN
Mistake - Proof Wallpapering 30 MIN
No - Wax Floors 30 MIN
Proposal for Expansion 30 MIN
Roof Check 30 MIN
Trimming and Painting 30 MIN
Waterproofing the Basement 30 MIN
Wiring and Insulation 30 MIN
Dist - CORF

This old house series
Plasterers, roofers, carpenters 30 MIN
Dist - CORF

This Old house - the Dorchester series
First impression 30 MIN
The Question of heating Pt 1 30 MIN
Dist - CORF

This old pyramid 86 MIN
VHS
Color; CC (G)
$89.95 purchase _ #EX3836
Reveals the secret of how the ancient pyramids were built by constructing one.
Fine Arts; History - World; Industrial and Technical Education
Dist - FOTH **Prod** - WGBH

This One for Dad 18 MIN
U-matic / VHS / 16mm
Reflections Series
Color (J)
LC 78-701486
Addresses the acceptance of death with a story about a boy who idolized his father and had to face the reality of his father's death.
Sociology
Dist - PAULST **Prod** - PAULST 1978

This one with that one 10 MIN
16mm / U-matic / VHS
Math readiness series
Color (P)
$255.00, $180.00 purchase _ #3642
Shows how sets of things match using a fisherman matching lines, baits, and fish to illustrate the concept.
Mathematics
Dist - CORF

This Other Eden 60 MIN
16mm
Color
LC 80-700288
Traces the history of England, emphasizing the role of religion. Includes scenes of Stonehenge, the sanctuary at Glastonbury, the fortress of Maiden Castle, and Bamburg Castle.
History - World
Dist - NBCTV **Prod** - NBCTV 1979

This other Eden - Pt 1 30 MIN
16mm
Color
LC 80-700288
Traces the history of England, emphasizing the role of religion. Includes scenes of Stonehenge, the sanctuary at Glastonbury, the fortress of Maiden Castle, and Bamburg Castle.
History - World
Dist - NBCTV **Prod** - NBCTV 1979

This other Eden - Pt 2 30 MIN
16mm
Color
LC 80-700288
Traces the history of England, emphasizing the role of religion. Includes scenes of Stonehenge, the sanctuary at Glastonbury, the fortress of Maiden Castle, and Bamburg Castle.
History - World
Dist - NBCTV **Prod** - NBCTV 1979

This other Haiti 58 MIN
VHS
Color (G)
$350.00 purchase, $95.00 rental
Examines the activities of a nationwide peasant movement for social change in Haiti. Interviews key members of the MMP - Peasant Movement of Papay - and shows their success in establishing agricultural co - ops, a credit bank, educational and training programs and health dispensaries, thus revealing 'this other,' little known Haiti. Directed by David Korb. Creole dialog with English voiceover and narration.
Fine Arts; Social Science; Sociology
Dist - CNEMAG

This Our India 9 MIN
16mm
Color (H C A)
Presents the basic geographic and economic facts about India. Uses animated maps and diagrams to show how the people of India are striving to achieve a fuller and better life.
Geography - World; History - World
Dist - NEDINF **Prod** - INDIA

This Question of Violence 59 MIN
16mm
B&W (H C A)
LC FIA68-3077
Reports on the historical, social and psychological factors which underline violence in modern life. Presents a discussion by psychiatrists of the problem of agression. Traces the history of violence in the United States, emphasizing that periods of dramatic social change have most often been associated with outbreaks of violence. Examines the responsibilities of the mass media with respect to violence.
History - United States; Psychology
Dist - IU **Prod** - NET 1968

This Shattered Land - the Devastated Land of Cambodia 48 MIN
U-matic / VHS
Color
$455.00 purchase
From the ABC TV Close Up program.
Civics and Political Systems; Sociology
Dist - ABCLR **Prod** - ABCLR 1980

This Side is Good 18 MIN
16mm
Color
Focuses on 72 - year - old Sidney Keller six years after a severe stroke left him paralyzed on his right side and moderately aphasic. Shows his activities of daily living, his day - to - day struggles and adjustments, his interactions with family and friends and his volunteer work as a messenger at a Veterans Administration Hospital.
Health and Safety
Dist - FLMLIB **Prod** - FLMLIB 1983

This Side of Eden 27 MIN
16mm / U-matic / VHS
Color
LC 78-701488
Dramatizes how Adam and Eve, guilt - stricken over being thrown out of Eden and appalled at Cain's murder of Abel, complain to God about their unhappiness. Tells how God forgives them and how they learn to forgive Cain.
Religion and Philosophy
Dist - MEDIAG **Prod** - PAULST 1977

This Thing Called Change 9 MIN
U-matic / VHS / 16mm
Color (IND)
Suggests that new realities are here and the comfortable past will never return.
Business and Economics; Sociology
Dist - CCCD **Prod** - CCCD 1974

This time, next time 54 MIN
VHS
Color (H C G)
$445.00 purchase, $75.00 rental
Outlines the frightening and irreversible effects that alcohol consumption can have on the brain. Shows that alcohol related brain damage - ARBD - is not limited to a particular population. Interweaves documentary material of doctors, health workers and ARBD patients with a dramatic narrative about Paula who is researching premature babies, discovers a baby with fetal alcohol syndrome born to an ARBD mother and realizes that her own husband may be suffering from ARBD. Produced by Robin de Crespigny.
Guidance and Counseling; Health and Safety; Psychology
Dist - FLMLIB

This time on my own 33 MIN
16mm / U-matic / VHS
Color (J H C)
LC 84-706730
Tells the story of Kim Williams, a promising teenage swimmer whose discovery that she has epilepsy forces her into a dramatic re - evaluation of her future. Reveals that her coach, teachers, family and friends begin to treat her differently. Explains how Steve Connors, a new boy in school, helps her overcome the attitude of those people who assume that epilepsy has to be a disability.
Education; Psychology
Dist - CF **Prod** - CANBC 1984

This Time Sweden 25 MIN
16mm
Color
Features Sweden away from the large cities, the country itself with the people who are hospitable and proud to show the visitor their modern country.

Geography - World; Social Science
Dist - SWNTO **Prod** - SWNTO

This tiny world 15 MIN
U-matic / VHS / 16mm
Color
LC 74-700709
Reveals the life found in a group of old - fashioned toys.
Guidance and Counseling; Physical Education and Recreation
Dist - PHENIX **Prod** - PHENIX 1973

This Trembling Earth 22 MIN
U-matic / VHS
Phenomenal World Series
Color (J C)
$129.00 purchase _ #3971
Examines a violent but fascinating phenomenon, the earthquake, cause by a sudden jump of slabs of rock that grind and slide past one another.
History - United States; History - World; Science - Physical
Dist - EBEC

This was the Beginning, Pt 1 - the Invertebrates 13 MIN
16mm / U-matic / VHS
This was the Beginning Series
Color (J H C)
Presents the first invertebrates which appeared in the oceans, including algae, sponges, coelenterates, worms, mollusks, arthropods and echinoderms.
Science - Natural
Dist - IFB **Prod** - NFBC 1982

This was the Beginning, Pt 2 - the Vertebrates 11 MIN
U-matic / VHS / 16mm
This was the Beginning Series
Color (J H C)
Considers the classification of vertebrates, including cartilaginous fish, bony fish, amphibians, reptiles, birds and mammals. Highlights physical characteristics, environmental adaptations and reproductive behaviors which differentiate the groupings. Shows that man is a remarkable primate set apart by his brain and hand.
Science - Natural
Dist - IFB **Prod** - NFBC 1982

This was the Beginning Series
This was the Beginning, Pt 1 - the Invertebrates 13 MIN
This was the Beginning, Pt 2 - the Vertebrates 11 MIN
Dist - IFB

This way to an A - wise study habits 30 MIN
VHS
Better grades series
Color (J H C)
$69.95 purchase _ #CCP0075V
Teaches the Empty 'V' system which stresses the importance and effectiveness of deciding the purpose of each lesson in order to better understand key information. Offers proven techniques for studying, reviewing and retaining information that fit into any lifestyle or class structure. Includes How to Study book.
Education; Psychology
Dist - CAMV **Prod** - CAMV 1992

This Way to Heaven 30 MIN
16mm
B&W (I)
LC 72-701661
A story about a young boy who asks his sunday school superintendent about the way to heaven.
Guidance and Counseling; Religion and Philosophy
Dist - CPH **Prod** - CPH 1956

This Way to Safety 10 MIN
16mm
Drugs and Medicine Series
Color
LC 76-702571
Depicts a pharmacist and his assistant who present examples of how people knowingly or unknowingly misuse medicines designed to relieve mental and physical distress.
Health and Safety
Dist - MORLAT **Prod** - MORLAT 1975

This way to the White House 13 MIN
16mm
Screen news digest series
B&W (J H)
LC 73-701272
Shows the making of a President. Depicts the color and excitement of the American electoral process of nomination, election and inauguration. Volume 15, issue six of the series.
Biography; Civics and Political Systems
Dist - HEARST **Prod** - HEARST 1973

This week - Silent epidemic 26 MIN
VHS
Color; PAL (G)
PdS30 purchase
Investigates the affliction of osteoporosis, a bone - weakening condition. Reveals that it affects one - fifth of the female population in Britain. Contact distributor about availability outside the United Kingdom.
Health and Safety
Dist - ACADEM

This World is not for Children 54 MIN
16mm
Color (H C A)
LC 76-701399
Concerns children everywhere as victims of superstition, ignorance and the indifference of the privileged. Shows children in scenes from Peru, Africa, Columbia, Thailand, Japan and India, who are overworked, socially rejected, exploited and have short life expectancies. Narrated by Peter Ustinov. Made In England.
Sociology
Dist - MMA **Prod** - PRICER 1975

This year, next year, sometime 19 MIN
16mm
B&W (C T)
Describes the work of Dr Joshua Bierer, who extended the day - hospital concept for treatment of emotionally disturbed children. Depicts the center's facilities and the basic idea behind it.
Psychology; Sociology
Dist - NYU **Prod** - CASH 1962

This Year's Hero 12 MIN
16mm
Color
LC 77-702673
Demonstrates the economic, social and physical hardships that can affect family life when excessive drinking is a problem.
Health and Safety; Psychology; Sociology
Dist - ODH **Prod** - ODH 1975

Thom Gunn - 11 - 22 - 86 34 MIN
VHS / Cassette
Poetry Center reading series
Color (G)
#728 - 585
Features the writer reading his works at the Poetry Center, San Francisco State University, with an introduction by Frances Phillips. Available for listening purposes only; not for sale or rent.
Literature and Drama
Dist - POETRY **Prod** - POETRY 1986

Thom Gunn - 11 - 20 - 74 31 MIN
VHS / Cassette
Poetry Center reading series
Color (G)
$15.00, $45.00 purchase, $15.00 rental _ #90 - 63
Features the writer reading his works at the Poetry Center, San Francisco State University, with an introduction by Kathleen Fraser.
Literature and Drama
Dist - POETRY **Prod** - POETRY 1974

Thom Gunn - 12 - 13 - 90 34 MIN
VHS / Cassette
Poetry Center reading series
Color (G)
$45.00 purchase, $15.00 rental _ #957 - 722
Features the writer reading his works at the Poetry Center, San Francisco State University, with an introduction by Robert Gluck.
Literature and Drama
Dist - POETRY **Prod** - POETRY 1990

Thomas - aged two years, four months, in foster care for 10 days 38 MIN
VHS / 16mm
Young children in brief separation series
B&W (C G PRO)
Presents the story of a boy named Thomas who is briefly in fosster care. Reveals that because he is mature, Thomas is able to keep his mother in mind and talk about her. Discloses that daily visits by his father help him understand his situation. Although in need of mothering care, Thomas cannot easily accept affection because it arouses conflicts with loyalty to his mother. He often shows hostility to the foster mother while simultaneously demanding her attention. Part of a series on children in brief sepration.
Health and Safety; Psychology
Dist - PSU **Prod** - ROBJJ 1969
NYU VASSAR

Thomas Alva Edison - the wizard of Menlo Park 25 MIN
16mm / U-matic / VHS
Americana series
Color (I)
Discusses the life of Thomas Alva Edison. Tells how he created the phonograph, the incandescent light bulb, the electric railroad, the motion picture projector and the storage battery.
Biography; History - United States; Science - Physical
Dist - HANDEL **Prod** - HANDEL 1982

Thomas and the fiscal fighters 30 MIN
VHS / U-matic
Money puzzle - the world of macroeconomics series
Color
Differentiates between the two main types of discretionary fiscal policies - increased government expeditures or decreased taxes. Module nine of the series.
Business and Economics; Sociology
Dist - MDCC **Prod** - MDCC

Thomas Aquinas and early reformers - Tape 3 40 MIN
VHS
Cloud of witnesses series
Color (R)
$39.95 purchase, $10.00 rental _ #35 - 860038 - 1
Profiles St Thomas Aquinas and several of the early church reformers. Filmed on location.
Religion and Philosophy
Dist - APH **Prod** - ABINGP

Thomas Berry - Dreamer of the universe 57 MIN
VHS / 16mm
Color (G)
$295.00 purchase, $75.00 rental
Features an in - depth interview with the man Newsweek magazine called 'the most provocative figure among the new breed of ecotheologians.' Looks at Berry's life, educated as a Catholic priest, a historian of cultures, poet, environmental activist and author of The Universe Story. Produced by Arcadia Productions.
Fine Arts; History - United States; Literature and Drama; Science - Natural
Dist - FIRS

Thomas Cook and son 60 MIN
VHS
Great Britons
Color; PAL (C H)
PdS99 purchase
Presents the story of Thomas Cook. Describes Cook's accomplishments in making travel possible for the common man. Focuses on Cook's visionary business sense. Second in the six - part series Great Britons, which examines the lives of important figures in British culture.
Geography - World; History - World
Dist - BBCENE

Thomas Corwin 51 MIN
16mm / U-matic
Profiles in Courage Series
B&W (I J H C A)
LC 83-706546
Explains how Senator Corwin forfeited his presidential chances because he spoke against his country's involvement in a war he did not believe justifiable. Discusses Manifest Destiny, the Mexican War and foreign intervention.
Biography; Civics and Political Systems; History - United States
Dist - SSSSV **Prod** - SAUDEK 1965

Thomas Corwin - Pt 1 25 MIN
16mm
Profiles in courage series
B&W (H C A)
Explains how Senator Corwin forfeited his presidential chances because he spoke against his country's involvement in a war he did not believe justifiable. Discusses Manifest Destiny, the Mexican War and foreign intervention.
Biography; Civics and Political Systems; History - United States
Dist - SSSSV **Prod** - SAUDEK 1965

Thomas Corwin - Pt 2 25 MIN
16mm
Profiles in courage series
B&W (H C A)
Explains how Senator Corwin forfeited his presidential chances because he spoke against his country's involvement in a war he did not believe justifiable. Discusses Manifest Destiny, the Mexican War and foreign intervention.
Biography; Civics and Political Systems; History - United States
Dist - SSSSV **Prod** - SAUDEK 1965

Thomas E Dewey 26 MIN
16mm
Biography Series
B&W (I)
LC FI67-260
Uses rare actuality footage to portray the personal life and history - making deeds of Thomas E Dewey.
Biography; Civics and Political Systems; History - United States
Dist - SF **Prod** - WOLPER 1963

Thomas Eakins - a motion portrait 60 MIN
VHS / U-matic
Color (G)
$39.95 purchase _ #EAK-01
Portrays Thomas Eakins, an artist who flouted Victorian conventions by painting nudes and whose talent was unappreciated until after his death in 1916. Combines dramatic sequences with archival footage and still portraits. Kevin Conway portrays Eakins, Sam Waterston narrates.
Fine Arts
Dist - ARTSAM **Prod** - MMOA
FI

Thomas Edison 26 MIN
16mm / U-matic / VHS
Biography Series
B&W (I J H)
Traces the life of inventor Thomas Alva Edison from his early boyhood until his death in 1931. Provides historical scenes of early lighting and transportation systems and of the customs and costumes of the times.
Biography; History - United States; Science
Dist - MGHT **Prod** - WOLPER 1963

Thomas Edison 15 MIN
U-matic / VHS
Color (G)
$229.00, $129.00 purchase _ #AD - 1748
Looks at Thomas Edison, authentic American genius, who patented over one thousand inventions. Reveals that he was determined and eccentric, but he brought light, sound and direct long distance communication to the world.
Biography; History - United States; History - World; Industrial and Technical Education; Science
Dist - FOTH **Prod** - FOTH

Thomas Edison - Lightning Slinger 51 MIN
U-matic / VHS / 16mm
Great Americans Series
Color (I J H)
Recreates the turning point in the life of young Thomas Edison, focusing on the hardships he overcame to become one of the world's greatest inventors.
Biography; History - United States
Dist - LUF **Prod** - LUF 1979

Thomas Edison - reflections of a genius 27 MIN
16mm / U-matic / VHS
Color (I J H)
$455.00, $250.00 purchase _ #5059C
Shows the many inventions, life, and achievements of Thomas Edison.
Biography; History - United States; Science
Dist - CORF

Thomas Edison - the electric light 24 MIN
VHS / 16mm
Color (I)
LC 90706265
Relates the story of Thomas Edison's invention of the incandescent electric light bulb.
Biography; History - United States; Science - Physical
Dist - BARR

Thomas Edison's Glenmont 23 MIN
16mm / U-matic / VHS
American lifestyle series; Industrialists and inventors
Color (I)
LC 79-700025
Presents a guided tour of the residence of Thomas Edison, Glenmont. Describes the life and inventions of Edison.
Biography; Business and Economics; Industrial and Technical Education; Sociology
Dist - AIMS **Prod** - COMCO 1978

Thomas Edison's Glenmont 23 MIN
VHS
Color (H C T A)
$69.95 purchase _ #S01336
Tours Glenmont, the Victorian mansion where Thomas Edison perfected the phonograph, the motion picture camera, and incadescent and fluorescent lighting. Hosted by E G Marshall.
Biography; Fine Arts; History - United States; Science
Dist - UILL

Thomas Hardy 30 MIN
VHS
Famous authors series
Color (H C)
$11.50 rental _ #35511
Uses Hardy's favorite folk tunes in an examination of his life and work. An installment of the Famous Authors Series, which examines important English writers in the context of their times.
English Language; Literature and Drama
Dist - PSU **Prod** - EBEC 1984
EBEC

Thomas Hardy and Dorset 15 MIN
U-matic / VHS
Color (C)
$249.00, $149.00 purchase _ #AD - 1704
Examines Dorset, the setting for most of the novels and poems by Thomas Hardy.
Fine Arts; Literature and Drama
Dist - FOTH **Prod** - FOTH

Thomas Hardy - man of Wessex 37 MIN
VHS
Color (G)
$39.95 purchase
Traces the relationships between the life work of Thomas Hardy and the scenes of Wessex. Blends commentary and readings from his work with the scenery of Wessex, historic and modern.
Geography - World; History - World; Literature and Drama
Dist - WSEXAM

Thomas Hart Benton 50 MIN(0123198)
U-matic / VHS
Profiles in Courage Series
B&W (I J H)
LC 83-706547
Dramatizes the role of Missouri Senator Thomas Hart Benton in opposing the extension of slavery into California and preventing Missouri from seceding from the Union. Analyzes interpretations of the Constitution that led the country into a civil war. Based on book Profiles In Courage by John F Kennedy.
Biography; Civics and Political Systems; History - United States
Dist - SSSSV **Prod** - SAUDEK 1964

Thomas Hart Benton - Pt 1 25 MIN
16mm
Profiles in courage series
Color (I)
Describes Thomas Benton's risk to his Senate career through his opposition to slavery in the new states.
History - United States
Dist - SSSSV **Prod** - SAUDEK 1965

Thomas Hart Benton - Pt 2 25 MIN
16mm
Profiles in courage series
Color (I)
Describes Thomas Benton's risk to his Senate career through his opposition to slavery in the new states.
History - United States
Dist - SSSSV **Prod** - SAUDEK 1965

Thomas Jefferson 28 MIN
U-matic / VHS / 16mm
Americana series; No 3
Color (P I J H C)
LC FIA67-722
Shows Jefferson's self - written epitaph stating that he was the father of the University of Virginia, and the author of the Declaration of Independence and the Virginia Statute for Religious Freedom. Discusses the many other accomplishments of Jefferson and the riddle of why he chose to mention only these three. Describes Jefferson's contributions to science and agriculture and his love for the arts.
Biography; Civics and Political Systems; History - United States
Dist - HANDEL **Prod** - HANDEL 1967

Thomas Jefferson 13 MIN
U-matic / VHS / 16mm
Great Americans Series
Color (I J)
LC 80-701799
Outlines the achievements and career of Thomas Jefferson.
Biography
Dist - EBEC **Prod** - EBEC 1980

Thomas Jefferson - architect of liberty 26 MIN
VHS
Color (J H)
$89.00 purchase _ #06089 - 026
Includes teacher's guide and library kit.
Biography; Education; History - United States
Dist - GA

Thomas Jefferson - Man from Monticello 14 MIN
16mm
Color
LC 76-700431
Offers a tour of Monticello and the University of Virginia in an exploration of the architectural ideas of Thomas Jefferson. Shows how these ideas included the use of brick and other materials.
Biography; Fine Arts; Geography - United States; Industrial and Technical Education
Dist - SCPI **Prod** - SCPI 1975

Thomas Jefferson's Monticello 24 MIN
VHS
Color (H C T A)
$69.95 purchase _ #S01337
Tours Monticello, the home of Thomas Jefferson. Features Jefferson's collections of paintings and furniture. Hosted by E G Marshall.
Biography; Fine Arts; History - United States
Dist - UILL

Thomas Jefferson's Monticello 24 MIN
16mm / U-matic / VHS
American lifestyle series; U S Presidents
Color (J)
Tours Jefferson's spacious home in Virginia. Shows how Monticello reflects Jefferson's life style.
Biography; Geography - United States; History - United States; Sociology
Dist - AIMS **Prod** - COMCO 1975

Thomas Mann 58 MIN
VHS
Modern world - ten great writers series
Color (H)
$13.00 rental _ #60961
Examines Thomas Mann's confrontation with spiritual controversies of 20th century life in his works Death In Venice and The Magic Mountain. Studies ten important modernist European writers by placing them against turn - of - the century settings, dramatizing their own experiences and looking at their principal works in a ten part series.
Literature and Drama
Dist - PSU **Prod** - FI 1987
FI

Thomas Mann - 1875 - 1955 - Volume V 58 MIN
VHS
Modern world - ten great writers series
Color (G)
$129.00 purchase _ #S01956
Profiles German author Thomas Mann, whose works included 'Buddenbrooks' and 'The Magic Mountain.' Uses drama, documentary, and literary criticism to portray Mann's experience, background and personal philosophy. Available for educational use only.
Literature and Drama
Dist - UILL

Thomas Mann - Pt 6 58 MIN
VHS
The Modern world - ten great writers series
Color (S)
$129.00 purchase _ #833 - 9380
Profiles ten great Modernist writers whose work helped shape our world. Dramatizes the author's experiences and examines in - depth their various works. Part 6 presents Thomas Mann who confronted the spiritual controversies of the 20th - century human experience. Considers Buddenbrooks which established Mann as a leading author at the age of 25, and Death In Venice and The Magic Mountain.
Fine Arts; Geography - World; Literature and Drama
Dist - FI **Prod** - LONWTV 1988

Thomas Paine 14 MIN
U-matic / VHS / 16mm
Color (J H C)
$59.00 purchase _ #3427; LC 75-702359
Presents the life of Thomas Paine and his major writings on democracy and individual rights. Shows the influence Paine had on the course of events leading up to the American Revolution.
Biography; Civics and Political Systems; History - United States; Literature and Drama
Dist - EBEC **Prod** - EBEC 1975

Thomas' snowsuit
CD-ROM
Discis Books on CD - ROM
(K P) (SPANISH)
$74.00 purchase _ #2554
Contains the original text and illustrations of Thomas' Snowsuit by Robert Munsch. Enhances understanding with real voices, music, and sound effects. Every word in the text has an in - context explanation, pronunciation and syllables, available through a click of the mouse. Spanish - English version available for an extra $5 per disc. For Macintosh Classics, Plus, II and SE computers, requires 1MB of RAM, one floppy disk drive, and an Apple compatible CD - ROM drive.
English Language; Literature and Drama
Dist - BEP

Thomas Stearns Eliot - 1888 - 1965 - Volume VIII 58 MIN
VHS
Modern world - ten great writers series
Color (G)
$129.00 purchase _ #S01959
Profiles the American - born British poet and dramatist T S Eliot, whose works included 'The Waste Land' and 'The Hollow Men.' Uses drama, documentary, and literary criticism to portray Eliot's experience, background and personal philosophy. Available for educational use only.
Literature and Drama
Dist - UILL

Thomas Stearns Eliot - Pt 9 58 MIN
VHS
The Modern world - ten great writers series
Color (S)
$129.00 purchase _ #833 - 9376
Profiles ten great Modernist writers whose work helped shape our world. Dramatizes the author's experiences and examines in - depth their various works. Part 9 presents poet Thomas Stearns Eliot who consciously devised a new idiom of expression to capture the quality of his generation in Prufrock And Other Observations, The Wasteland, Murder In The Cathedral, and The Cocktail Party.
Fine Arts; Literature and Drama
Dist - FI **Prod** - LONWTV 1988

Thomas Szaz - maverick psychiatrist 29 MIN
VHS
America's drug forum second season series
Color (G)
$19.95 purchase _ #224
Interviews psychiatrist Dr Thomas Szaz who defends the premise of his book, Our Right to Drugs - The Case for a Free Market.
Civics and Political Systems; Psychology
Dist - DRUGPF **Prod** - DRUGPF 1992

Thomas the imposter 94 MIN
16mm
B&W (FRENCH (ENGLISH SUBTITLES))
Tells how an ambiguous young man plays with fiction and reality in the great theatre of World War I. Directed by Georges Franju. With English subtitles.
Fine Arts
Dist - NYFLMS **Prod** - UNKNWN 1965

Thomas - the Orienteer 22 MIN
16mm
Color (J H C G)
Shows training for the new sport of orienteering, a complicated version of cross country running. Provides detailed instructions of orienteering events.
Physical Education and Recreation
Dist - VIEWTH **Prod** - SOLFIL

The Thomas the Tank Engine man 50 MIN
VHS
Bookmark series
Color (A)
PdS99 purchase
Profiles the Reverend Wilbert Awdrey, England's most popular children's author, creator of Thomas the Tank Engine. Discloses that between 1945 and 1972 he wrote a new story every year, and sales of Thomas merchandise alone are estimated at $1 billion per year.
Literature and Drama
Dist - BBCENE

Thomas Wolfe - Look Homeward Angel 45 MIN
U-matic / VHS
Color (C)
$249.00, $149.00 purchase _ #AD - 935
Examines Asheville, North Carolina, home of Thomas Wolfe. Features Richard Walser of NC State University as narrator.
Biography; Fine Arts; Literature and Drama
Dist - FOTH **Prod** - FOTH

Thor Heyerdahl's incredible voyage 25 MIN
VHS
Color (G)
$29.95 purchase _ #S01872
Documents the 3000 - mile transatlantic journey of Thor Heyerdahl's papyrus boat.
Geography - World; History - World; Physical Education and Recreation
Dist - UILL

Thor Heyerdahl's Incredible Voyage 25 MIN
U-matic / VHS
Color
Describes Thor Heyerdahl's journey on the RA - 2 from North Africa to the West Indies, which was designed to prove a link between the Egyptian and Mexican cultures.
Geography - World
Dist - JOU **Prod** - UPI

Thoracentesis 9 MIN
U-matic / VHS
Medical Skills Films Series
Color (PRO)
Health and Safety
Dist - WFP **Prod** - WFP

Thoracentesis 23 MIN
VHS / U-matic
Color (PRO)
Describes situations in which thoracentesis is used and presents the information needed to perform the procedure successfully.
Health and Safety
Dist - HSCIC **Prod** - HSCIC 1977

Thoracic cage - Pt 1 - true ribs 14 MIN
U-matic / VHS
Osteopathic examination and manipulation series
Color (PRO)
Demonstrates basic rib movements of the true ribs during respiration. Shows how to test rib function for signs of disturbances in both the inhalation and exhalation phase. Demonstrates articulatory and muscle energy manipulative procedures.
Health and Safety; Science - Natural
Dist - MSU **Prod** - MSU

The Thoracic Mediastinum 18 MIN
16mm / U-matic / VHS
Cine - Prosector Series
Color (PRO)
Outlines the boundaries of the mediastinum within the thoracic cavity.
Science - Natural
Dist - TEF **Prod** - AVCORP

Thoracic outlet syndrome 22 MIN
16mm
Color (PRO)
Reviews the anatomy, symptomatology and physical examination of thoracic outlet syndrome. Demonstrates the surgical treatment using the axillary approach for first rib resection.
Health and Safety
Dist - ACY **Prod** - ACYDGD 1970

Thoracic region - Pt 1 14 MIN
U-matic / VHS
Osteopathic examination and manipulation series
Color (PRO)
Focuses on manipulative procedures and diagnosis in the upper thoracic region. Explains the principle of a direct technique. Shows three types of direct procedures in detail.
Health and Safety; Science - Natural
Dist - MSU **Prod** - MSU

Thoracic region - Pt 2 12 MIN
U-matic / VHS
Osteopathic examination and manipulation series
Color (PRO)
Demonstrates examination and manipulative techniques for the thoracic spine with the patient seated astride the table. Emphasizes localization of operator forces and careful monitoring of the segmental dysfunction. Presents three types of direct technique.
Health and Safety; Science - Natural
Dist - MSU **Prod** - MSU

Thoracic Series

Gastric Cardioplasty	29 MIN
Gastroplasty and Hiatus Hernia Repair	45 MIN
Pectus Excavatum	29 MIN
Right Lower Lobectomy	18 MIN
Right Upper Lobectomy	39 MIN
Thoracotomy for Benign Mesenchymoma of the Mediastinum	19 MIN
Trans - Cervical Thymectomy	17 MIN

Dist - SVL

The Thoracic Spine 19 MIN
U-matic / VHS
Cyriax on Orthopaedic Medicine Series
Color
Gives seven manipulative techniques for the treatment of the thoracic spine.
Health and Safety; Science - Natural
Dist - VTRI **Prod** - VTRI

Thoraco - abdominal approach to the kidney 14 MIN
16mm
Anatomy of the flank series
Color
Shows that the thoraco - abdominal incision provides excellent exposure for renal surgery, particularly in cases of superior pole or large renal tumors. Describes the anatomy encountered in this approach including views of an actual operation.
Health and Safety; Science - Natural
Dist - EATONL **Prod** - EATONL 1970

Thoraco - abdominal nephrectomy 26 MIN
16mm
Color (PRO)
Demonstrates the removal of kidney tumors through the abdominothoracic approach. Explains that the excellent exposure obtained reduces trauma to the growth, permits early occlusion of the vascular pedicle and allows complete removal of the neoplasm with the adjacent tissue and lymph nodes.
Health and Safety
Dist - ACY **Prod** - ACYDGD 1954

The Thoracoabdominal retroperitoneal lymph node dissection 25 MIN
16mm
Color
LC 75-702245
Explains that radical retroperitoneal lymph node dissection is an effective and proven way of curing patients with non - seminomanous testis tumors. Demonstrates the thoracoabdominal approach to retroperitoneal lymph node dissection, including both the right and left side approach, first in a patient without metastatic disease and then in a patient with extensive left retroperitoneal metastases.
Health and Safety; Science
Dist - EATONL **Prod** - EATONL 1973

Thoracotomy for Benign Mesenchymoma of the Mediastinum 19 MIN
U-matic / VHS
Thoracic Series
Color
Health and Safety; Science - Natural
Dist - SVL **Prod** - SVL

The Thorax and Lungs 22 MIN
U-matic / VHS
Techniques of Physical Diagnosis - a Visual Approach Series
Color
Reviews the techniques of thoracic inspection, palpation, percussion and auscultation. Examines the trachea and rib excursion. Concludes with a review of auscultation maneuvers used to accentuate abnormal breath sounds.
Health and Safety; Psychology
Dist - MEDMDS **Prod** - MEDMDS

Thorax and Lungs 30 MIN
VHS / U-matic
Health Assessment Series
Color (PRO)
Views a physical assessment by a nurse practitioner of the thorax and lungs of a live patient.
Health and Safety; Science - Natural
Dist - BRA **Prod** - BRA

Thorax and lungs 18 MIN
16mm
Visual guide to physical examination - 2nd ed - series
Color (PRO)
LC 81-701525
Demonstrates the physical examination of the thorax and lungs, showing necessary procedures, manipulations, pacing, positions and patient - examiner interactions.
Health and Safety
Dist - LIP **Prod** - LIP 1981

Thoreau's Maine Woods 20 MIN
16mm / VHS / U-matic
America's wildlife heritage series
Color (I J H C)
LC 79-700090
Re - traces the routes of Henry David Thoreau's trips through the Maine woods in the mid - 19th century. Narrated by Richard Wilbur. Based on selections from The Maine Woods by Henry David Thoreau.
Biography; Geography - United States; History - United States; Literature and Drama; Science - Natural
Dist - FENWCK **Prod** - FENWCK 1978
FI

Thoreau's Walden 28 MIN
U-matic / VHS
Color (C)
$249.00, $149.00 purchase _ #AD - 1946
Recreates the two - year period, 1845 - 1847, when Henry David Thoreau withdrew to a cabin on Walden Pond. Features visuals of the passing of the seasons and commentary from Thoreau.
Fine Arts; Literature and Drama
Dist - FOTH **Prod** - FOTH

Thoreau's Walden - a video portrait 27 MIN
VHS
Color (J H C A)
$99.95 purchase _ #L11139
Combines footage of the changing seasons at Walden Pond with Thoreau's writings to illustrate the world he saw when he wrote Walden. Features Thoreau's words on why he built his cabin in the woods, his observations of the natural world, and his insights from living there.

Literature and Drama
Dist - CF

Thorne Family Film 85 MIN
U-matic / VHS
Color; B&W
Traces the story of the descendants of Jonathan C and Margaretta Williams Thorne, who came to Umatilla County, Oregon, in the 1880s to become farmers. Focuses on their values and on the challenge from mechanization.
Biography; Guidance and Counseling; History - United States; Sociology
Dist - MEDIPR **Prod** - MEDIPR 1977

Thornton Wilder 24 MIN
U-matic / VHS / 16mm
B&W (J)
LC FIA68-415
Examines the life and work of Thronton Wilder. Presents the humanist, the scholar and the dramatic innovator behind the facade of the popular playwright - novelist.
Literature and Drama
Dist - FOTH **Prod** - MANTLH 1967

Thornton Wilder's our town 120 MIN
VHS
Color (H C A)
$74.95 purchase; $74.95 purchase _ #SO1359
Presents a performance of the Thornton Wilder play Our Town, a tale of life in a small New England town. Stars Hal Holbrook, Robby Benson, and Sada Thompson.
Literature and Drama
Dist - PBS **Prod** - WNETTV
UILL

Thornton Wilder's Our Town
U-matic / VHS
Color
Fine Arts; Literature and Drama
Dist - MSTVIS **Prod** - MSTVIS

Thoroughbred Affair 14 MIN
16mm
B&W
LC 73-700619
Presents a high - society horse show on the Main Line in Philadelphia which provides an opportunity for some oblique commentary on the American social system.
Physical Education and Recreation; Social Science; Sociology
Dist - TEMPLU **Prod** - TEMPLU 1971

Thoroughbred Heroes 55 MIN
BETA / VHS
Color
Highlights 25 years of thoroughbred history. Includes races and training scenes.
Physical Education and Recreation
Dist - EQVDL **Prod** - EQVDL

Thoroughbreds 29 MIN
Videoreel / VT2
Maggie and the Beautiful Machine - Eating Series
Color
Physical Education and Recreation
Dist - PBS **Prod** - WGBHTV

Thoroughbreds 14 MIN
16mm / U-matic / VHS
Color (P I)
LC 80-700763
Shows the various stages of development of thoroughbred racehorses and explains how they are bred, trained and raced.
Physical Education and Recreation; Science - Natural
Dist - LUF **Prod** - MEDLIM 1979

Thoroughly Modern Millicent 14 MIN
16mm
Color (J)
LC 81-701574
Shows the dawn - to - past - dusk day of U S Congresswoman Millicent Fenwick, documenting the energy and dedication with which she serves her New Jersey constituents. Includes some family and archival photographs. Originally shown on the CBS program 60 Minutes.
Civics and Political Systems; Sociology
Dist - MOKIN **Prod** - CBSTV 1981

Thoroughly Modern Molly 14 MIN
16mm
Color
LC 74-706595
Depicts various jobs, duty stations and training of modern women marines.
Civics and Political Systems; Education; Sociology
Dist - USNAC **Prod** - USN 1968

Those Bad Dude Laundry Germs 8 MIN
VHS / U-matic
Color
Designed to train laundry personnel in hospitals and other institutions where preventing disease transmission is of paramount importance. Illustrates growth and transmission of germs, demonstrates correct hand washing, and provides six basic rules to prevent infection.
Health and Safety
Dist - HSCIC **Prod** - HSCIC

Those Calloways 131 MIN
16mm
Color (I J H C)
Stars Brian Keith, Vera Miles and Walter Brennan. Portrays a family of rural Vermont establishing a permanent lake sanctuary for the great geese flocks who migrate south through their New England town each year.
Fine Arts
Dist - UAE **Prod** - DISNEY 1964

Those Crazy Canucks 47 MIN
U-matic
Color
Features Canada's outstanding downhill ski team as it competes in one of the most dynamic and dangerous sports in the world.
Physical Education and Recreation
Dist - LAURON **Prod** - LAURON

Those First Years 17 MIN
U-matic / VHS / 16mm
Behaviorally Speaking Series
Color
Explores the first years of human development, showing that investigation and exploration, development of coordination, compliance and role modeling are typical features of this age level.
Psychology
Dist - USNAC **Prod** - NMAC 1979

Those five hundred kings 50 MIN
VHS
The great palace: the story of parliament
Color; PAL (C H)
PdS99 purchase
Presents the history of the House of Commons. Follows the growth of the House and details the role of the Queen. Second in the eight - part series The Great Palace: The Story of Parliament, which documents the significance of the institution.
Civics and Political Systems; History - World
Dist - BBCENE

Those Flying Canucks 53 MIN
U-matic
Color
Highlights two talented young men who train and work together while competing against each other and the world for ski jumping sumpremacy.
Physical Education and Recreation
Dist - LAURON **Prod** - LAURON

Those Four Cozy Walls 52 MIN
16mm
B&W
LC 79-702610
Discusses the mission of the church in the world of today.
Religion and Philosophy
Dist - UMCOM **Prod** - UMCOM 1968

Those good old golden rule days 15 MIN
U-matic / VHS
We are one series
Color (I)
Features Grandpa singing a song from his schooldays about the presidents of the United States, and telling Caroline about the schools in the pioneer days.
History - United States; Sociology
Dist - GPN **Prod** - NEITV 1983

Those incredible diving machines 22 MIN
U-matic / VHS / 16mm
Undersea world of Jacques Cousteau series
Color (G)
$295.00 purchase - 16 mm, $99.00 purchase - video
Shows the different methods man has used to explore the depths of the ocean.
History - World; Science - Physical
Dist - CF

Those incredible diving machines 23 MIN
16mm / U-matic / VHS
Undersea world of Jacques Cousteau series
Color (G)
$49.95 purchase _ #Q10606; LC 79-710105
A shortened version of Those Incredible Diving Machines. Traces the history of attempts to improve techniques and equipment to explore or exploit the riches of the sea. Describes future possibilities in this area. Part of a series of 24 programs.
Science - Physical
Dist - CF **Prod** - METROM 1970

Those Mail Order Millions 10 MIN
U-matic / VHS / 16mm
Consumer Fraud Series
Color (I)
LC 76-700810
Shows how to avoid misleading and fraudulent mail order practices.
Business and Economics; Home Economics
Dist - PFP **Prod** - PART 1976

Those Miracle Drugs 145 MIN
U-matic
University of the Air Series
Color (J H C A)
$750.00 purchase, $250.00 rental
Considers primitive and folk medicines and the role they play in modern therapeutics as well as the cost, effectiveness and dangers of modern drug therapy. Program contains a series of five cassettes 29 minutes each.
Health and Safety
Dist - CTV **Prod** - CTV 1977

Those Other Guys 15 MIN
U-matic
Workers at Risk Series
(A)
Shows that such factors as noise, the push for productivity and peer pressure can influence a worker's perception of risk. Demonstrates the link between off the job behavior and on the job accidents.
Health and Safety
Dist - ACCESS **Prod** - ACCESS 1982

Those Paris Years 51 MIN
VHS / 16mm
Color (H)
$220.00, $250 purchase, $19.00 rental _ #50898
Presents poet Archibald Macleish, who discusses Paris in the 1920s and reads poems related to the period. Includes reminiscences about Ernest Hemingway, Gertrude Stein, John dos Passos and other writers and artists from the period.
Literature and Drama
Dist - PSU

Those Paris Years 51 MIN
VHS / 16mm
Color (H)
$19.00 rental _ #50898
Presents a series of conversations, completed in 1977, between Archibald MacLeish (1892 - 1982) and Samuel Hazo, president of the International Poetry Forum, about the 'literary 1920's' in Paris. MacLeish reads his poems related to the era and reminisces about his friendships with Ernest Hemingway, Gertrude Stein, John Dos Passos, F Scott Fitzgerald, Pablo Picasso, Gerald Murphy, and other artists and writers.
Literature and Drama
Dist - PSU

Those people - AIDS in the public mind 30 MIN
VHS
Color (G)
$100.00 purchase _ #THOS - 000; $100.00 purchase _ #AH45177
Documents the lives of people living with AIDS or AIDS - related complex. Shows how they, family and friends have had to deal with both the disease and the fears of society as a whole. Tells of the work of several San Francisco AIDS service organizations. Depicts Bobby Reynolds, a long - term survivor of AIDS and outspoken AIDS activist.
Health and Safety; Sociology
Dist - PBS **Prod** - KQEDTV 1987
HTHED

Those People Can't do it 21 MIN
VHS / U-matic
Sex and Disability Series Pt 2
Color
Health and Safety; Psychology
Dist - AJN **Prod** - MLLRE

Those People Can't have Kids 22 MIN
U-matic / VHS
Sex and Disability Series Pt 4
Color
Health and Safety; Psychology
Dist - AJN **Prod** - MLLRE

Those People Don't Enjoy it 23 MIN
U-matic / VHS
Sex and Disability Series Pt 3
Color
Health and Safety; Psychology
Dist - AJN **Prod** - MLLRE

Those People Don't Want it 13 MIN
VHS / U-matic
Sex and Disability Series Pt 1
Color

Health and Safety; Psychology
Dist - AJN **Prod** - MLLRE

Those were the days 22 MIN
16mm
Color; B&W (G)
A look at life at the turn of the century, including a barnstorming pilot, cotton picking, threshing machines, steam engines, an old turkey farm, an early barbershop, a horse and buggy, and a blacksmith shop.
History - United States; Social Science
Dist - FO **Prod** - FO 1971

Those who Go 33 MIN
16mm
B&W
LC 79-700293
Presents a statement about the world based on Georg Trakl's poem Offenbarung Und Untergang.
Literature and Drama
Dist - POORI **Prod** - POORI 1979

Those who Know Choose Gleaner Combines 15 MIN
16mm
Color
Shows the Gleaner Combines as seen by qualified observers.
Agriculture
Dist - IDEALF **Prod** - ALLISC

Those who know don't tell 25 MIN
16mm / VHS
Color (G IND)
$5.00 rental
Presents historical footage of workers in Hawk's Nest, West Virginia, digging a tunnel through pure silica and other workers standing knee - deep in floating asbestos fibers. Considers that many employers have deliberately misled workers about the safety of certain jobs and that change has come only through the education and collective action of workes. Features Studs Terkel as narrator. Produced by Abby Ginzberg.
Health and Safety; Social Science; Sociology
Dist - AFLCIO

Those who know don't tell - the ongoing battle for worker's health 29 MIN
VHS
Color (H C G)
$295.00 purchase, $55.00 rental
Chronicles the struggle to rid the workplace of occupational hazards. Uses archival footage, union songs and interviews to tell the story of both labor activists and those in the medical profession who became their advocates. Reveals that the fight for occupational health began around 100 years ago with the discovery of lead - caused industrial disease by Dr Alice Hamilton. She was followed by others such as Dr Harriet Hardy of MIT who discovered the dangers of beryllium. Recently, Dr Irving Selikoff uncovered the danger of asbestos to workers and publicized his findings despite pressures from the asbestos industry to silence him. Narrated by Studs Terkel and produced by Abby Ginzberg.
Business and Economics; Health and Safety; History - World
Dist - FLMLIB

Those who Mourn 5 MIN
16mm
Beatitude Series
Color (H A)
LC 72-700776
Describes a young wife's struggles to overcome grief at the loss of her husband and her growth through suffering.
Guidance and Counseling; Religion and Philosophy
Dist - FRACOC **Prod** - FRACOC 1972

Those who Sing Together 28 MIN
U-matic / VHS / 16mm
Color (J H)
LC 78-701261
Introduces Indian culture through songs, dances and mythology reflecting the cycle of life from birth to death. Compares the instruments and songs of the Plains Indians with those from the Pacific Northwest.
Social Science; Sociology
Dist - MGHT **Prod** - DEVGCF 1978

Those who Stay Behind 16 MIN
16mm
Color
LC 74-705785
Shows the problems of the isolated and disadvantaged rural family and emphasizes those problems that face a family having an afflicted child.
Sociology
Dist - USNAC **Prod** - USSRS 1969

Those wonderful dogs 59 MIN
BETA / VHS / 16mm
Color; Captioned (G)
$400.00, $24.20 purchase _ #C53527, #C50408
Science - Natural
Dist - NGS **Prod** - NGS

Thot - Fal'N 9 MIN
16mm
Color (G)
$408.00 purchase, $25.00 rental
Describes a psychological state 'kin to moon - struck.'
Fine Arts
Dist - CANCIN **Prod** - BRAKS 1978

Thou Shalt Teach Them Diligently 30 MIN
16mm
B&W
Explains some of the religious observances in a Jewish home - Mezuzah, Tefillin, Siddur and Birkat Hamazon. (Kinescope).
Religion and Philosophy
Dist - NAAJS **Prod** - JTS 1951

Though I walk through the valley 30 MIN
16mm / U-matic / VHS
Color (J) (ENGLISH, GERMAN)
Presents a powerful statement on death and religious faith, which documents the last months of terminal cancer patient, Tony Brouwer, in a straightforward, unsentimental style. Includes the comments and reactions of Brouwer and his family.
Biography; Guidance and Counseling; Psychology; Religion and Philosophy; Sociology
Dist - PFP **Prod** - GF

Though the Earth be Moved - the Alaskan Earthquake 45 MIN
16mm / U-matic / VHS
B&W
Shows the Good Friday earthquake of 1964 which struck Alaska, causing death, damage and leaving cities helpless in the wave of shock, fire and seismic sea waves.
Geography - United States; Science - Physical
Dist - USNAC **Prod** - USOCD 1965

Thought 15 MIN
16mm
Color (G)
$30.00 rental
Analyzes the site of speech in relation to 'jumbled' thought, and both in relation to preconscious material. Presents images almost invisible and text ona a computer readout.
Fine Arts; Psychology
Dist - CANCIN **Prod** - SONDHE 1991

Thought and the source of disorder 60 MIN
VHS
Krishnamurti - 1982 talks in the Oak Grove series
Color (G)
$39.95 purchase _ #P75c
Features one of humanity's greatest religious philosophers in the idyllic setting of the Oak Grove in Ojai, California. Captures the intensity and passion of Krishnamurti. Part of a five - part series.
Literature and Drama; Religion and Philosophy
Dist - HP

Thought Dreams 3 MIN
16mm
Color
Presents an experimental film based on a game of hide and seek by Barbar Linkevitch.
Fine Arts; Industrial and Technical Education
Dist - CANCIN **Prod** - CANCIN 1972

Thought for Food - the World Food Conference of 1976 28 MIN
16mm
Color
LC 77-700581
Documents the 1976 World Food Conference. Describes the gravity of the food situation in the 1970's, presents issues related to production, distribution and consumption of food, identifies available solutions and considers the possible consequences of inaction.
Health and Safety; Social Science; Sociology
Dist - IOWA **Prod** - WFDI 1977

Thought Processes - Conscious and Subconscious 30 MIN
U-matic / VHS
Personal Development and Professional Growth - Mike McCaffrey's 'Focus Seminar Series
Color
Psychology
Dist - DELTAK **Prod** - DELTAK

Thought viruses and the wholeness pattern - Part One 50 MIN
VHS
Healing patterns of Jesus of Nazareth series
B&W; PAL; SECAM (G)
$60.00 purchase
Features Robert Dilts. Presents part one of a two - part series capturing Dilts' modeling of the healing patterns of Jesus Christ through his in - depth study of the New Testament. Intermediate level of NLP, neuro - linguistic programming. Produced by Western States Training Associates.
Health and Safety; Psychology; Religion and Philosophy
Dist - NLPCOM

Thoughtfulness _ 28 8 MIN
U-matic / VHS
Life's little lessons - self - esteem K - 3 - series
Color (K P)
$129.00, $99.00 _ #V627
Looks at the 13th division of the Cavalry - a thoughtless, lazy, good - for - nothing group of men who were a disgrace. Shows what thoughtlessness did to them. Part of a 30 - part series on self - esteem.
Guidance and Counseling; Psychology
Dist - BARR **Prod** - CEPRO 1992

Thoughts and Feelings about Pregnancy
VHS
$79.00 purchase _ #FY750V
Discusses the positive and negative consequences of pregnancy, investigates the self - destructive reasons teens get pregnant, and talks about how pregnant teenagers and their partners feel. Portrays the effects of pregnancy on teenagers' self - images, their free time, and their social, home, and working lives.
Health and Safety; Psychology; Sociology
Dist - CAREER **Prod** - CAREER

Thoughts on capitalism with Louis Kelso 30 MIN
U-matic / VHS
World of ideas with Bill Moyers - session 2 - series
Color; Captioned (A)
$39.95, $59.95 purchase _ #WIWM - 227
Features Louis Kelso, co - author with Mortimer Adler of The Capitalist Manifesto, and developer of the Employee Stock Ownership Plan - ESOP. Discusses Kelso's advocacy of a more democratic calpitalism in which the US would adopt a national economic policy that recognizes that capital is a main source of productive input and a human right. Reveals that Kelso wants to change the American economic policy of full employment to full employment and capital ownership.
Business and Economics
Dist - PBS **Prod** - PBS

Thoughts on the Run 9 MIN
U-matic / VHS / 16mm
Color (A)
Discusses how jogging has impacted the lifestyles of millions of Americans. Presents Dr George Sheehan offering his thoughts on the importance of physical fitness in building the complete person.
Physical Education and Recreation
Dist - CORF **Prod** - SPORP 1979

Thoughts, Words and Promises
VHS / U-matic
Increasing Children's Motivation to Read and Write Series
Color (T)
Presents a variety of methods to stimulate children's desire to read and write. Illustrates strategies to help teachers guide students from single words to paragraphs.
Education; English Language
Dist - EDCORP **Prod** - EPCO

A Thousand and One Naughts 8 MIN
16mm
Mathematics for Elementary School Students - Whole Numbers Series
Color (P)
LC 73-701849
Mathematics
Dist - DAVFMS **Prod** - DAVFMS 1974

A Thousand and One Years Ago - Inca Art of Peru (400 - 1000 a D) 12 MIN
16mm
Color
Presents Inca art of Peru dating from 400 to 1000 A D, showing scenes of war, daily life, demons and vivid animals. Shows that the whole range of Inca life and death is preserved in these artifacts of a lost culture in clay, stone, wood and paper - thin gold.
Fine Arts; History - World
Dist - ROLAND **Prod** - ROLAND

A Thousand cranes 57 MIN
VHS / U-matic
Color (J H C G A)
Reveals how Americans and Soviets have worked together to save the rare Siberian crane from extinction. Features footage of Russian wilderness, village life, and other scenes. Narrated by Joanne Woodward. Produced by Artemis Wildlife Foundation.

Civics and Political Systems; Science - Natural
Dist - EFVP Prod - EFVP 1986
UILL

A Thousand Days - a Tribute to John F Kennedy 22 MIN
16mm
B&W
LC FIA65-476
Uses the words of John Fitzgerald Kennedy, drawn from his speeches, his press conferences and his interviews to describe the goals which he had set for himself as President and the future he had envisioned for himself and his country. Surveys the accomplishment of Kennedy as President of the United States.
Biography; Civics and Political Systems; History - United States; History - World
Dist - WOLPER Prod - WOLPER 1964

The Thousand days - Sicily - key to victory 40 MIN
VHS / U-matic
B&W
Presents Canada's preparations to become the 'machine shop of the empire' during the first thousand days of World War II, including the expansion of its army and air force and the construction of a tank factory and machine - gun factory. Records the achievements of Canada's First Division in the Sicilian campaign of June 1943, where British, American and Canadian forces were combined for the first time in a large military operation.
Civics and Political Systems; History - United States; History - World
Dist - IHF Prod - IHF

A Thousand eyes 11 MIN
VHS / U-matic / 16mm
Color; PAL; B&W (P I J)
Studies the many different types of eyes possessed by animals. Contrasts the eyes of insects, which are composed of many small eyes, with the eyes of fish and various other animals, including man. Includes references to the importance of care for eyes.
Science - Natural
Dist - VIEWTH Prod - VIEWTH
STANF STANF

A Thousand Flowers will Suddenly Blossom 25 MIN
16mm
Color (I)
LC 72-702954
Explains that thousands of spectators fill the slopes of the natural amphitheater at kibbutz Dahlia, to watch the annual folk dance festival. Shows different ethnic groups displaying their national costumes through their traditional folk dances.
Fine Arts; Social Science; Sociology
Dist - ALDEN Prod - YEHU 1970

The Thousand Mile Journey 26 MIN
16mm / U-matic / VHS
Insight Series
B&W (H C A)
LC 78-705451
Tells the story of a socialite who searches for brotherhood in the slums of New York City.
Guidance and Counseling; Psychology
Dist - PAULST Prod - PAULST 1965

A Thousand Million Ants - a Study of Social Organization
U-matic / VHS
Science and Nature Series
Color (G C J)
$197 purchase _ #06878 - 851
Explores the intricate social organization and structure of the ant world.
Science - Natural
Dist - CHUMAN Prod - OSF 1988

Thousand pieces of gold 105 MIN
Videodisc / VHS
Color (G)
$79.95, $45.95 purchase _ #HEM7064, #HEML8006LD
Portrays a 19th century Chinese woman sold by her own father into slavery in the Old West of America. Reveals that years after slavery was abolished in the United States Asians were still held in involuntary servitude - sometimes by their own people. Based on the novel by Ruthanne Lum McCunn, directed by Nancy Kelly, written by Anne Makepeace and produced by Hemdale Home Video, Inc.
History - United States; Literature and Drama; Sociology
Dist - CHTSUI

A Thousand red flowers 28 MIN
U-matic / VHS / 16mm
Insight series
B&W (H A)
LC 74-705450
Shows how after a college sophomore kills himself, his mother, father, girlfriend and counselor come together at an imaginary trail to ask 'why?'
Guidance and Counseling; Psychology; Sociology
Dist - PAULST Prod - PAULST 1969

A Thousand Suns 9 MIN
16mm / U-matic / VHS
Color
LC 74-701337
Shows how people in the United States have used energy capabilities to create luxuries never dreamed possible, but have also created a throw - away society where little of value endures. Emphasizes the importance of creating values that last, such as self - respect and respect for all other living things.
Guidance and Counseling; Science - Natural; Social Science; Sociology
Dist - BARR Prod - BARR 1974

A Thousand Victories 17 MIN
16mm
Color
LC 75-701736
Documents the daily life of young Michael Radcliff, born without hands, as he adapts to the use of his surgically - separated forearm bones.
Health and Safety; Psychology
Dist - USNAC Prod - WRAMC 1973

A Thousand Words 29 MIN
Videoreel / VT2
Museum Open House Series
Color
Fine Arts
Dist - PBS Prod - WGBHTV

Thousand Years of Gujarat 20 MIN
16mm
B&W (H C A)
Presents the rich heritage of Gujarat dating back more than a thousand years and shows historical temples, fortresses, gateways, mosques and minarets scattered all over the state.
Fine Arts; History - World
Dist - NEDINF Prod - INDIA

Thousands Watch 7 MIN
U-matic / VHS
Color
Presented by Dan Reeves and Jon L Hilton.
Fine Arts
Dist - ARTINC Prod - ARTINC

Thracian Gold 29 MIN
VHS / 16mm
Color (G)
$55.00 rental _ #TGLD - 000
Overviews the gold, silver and bronze artifacts from the Thracian Treasures exhibit displayed at Boston's Museum of Fine Arts.
Fine Arts; History - World
Dist - PBS Prod - WGBHTV

The Thread 11 MIN
16mm
Color
LC 76-701377
Presents a dramatization based on a true story of the death of an old seamstress.
Literature and Drama; Sociology
Dist - SFRASU Prod - SFRASU 1973

Thread of history 48 MIN
VHS
China moon series
Color (I J G)
$295.00 purchase
Shows how, since the time of Marco Polo, the silk trade has linked China with the outside world. Dicloses that, despite a stall during the Cultural Revolution, silk trade again is a link between China and the rest of the world. Part of a series on China.
Civics and Political Systems; Geography - World; History - World; Industrial and Technical Education
Dist - LANDMK Prod - LANDMK 1989

A Thread of Hope 19 MIN
16mm
Color
LC 77-701837
Presents a dramatized case study of the application of a cancer treatment teachnique. Shows the process of hyperthermic perfusion in which the patient's extremity is isolated, the blood in the area is heated and artificially circulated and drugs are injected into the bloodstream.
Health and Safety; Literature and Drama; Science
Dist - MFCFP Prod - STEHLN 1977

The Thread of Life 55 MIN
16mm
Bell System Science Series
Color (J H)
Shows the development of the science of genetics, beginning with the cross - pollination experiments by Gregor Mendel in the middle of the nineteenth century through recent findings on genes, chromosomes and the chemical substance DNA.
Science; Science - Natural
Dist - WAVE Prod - ATAT 1960

The Thread of life - Pt 1 28 MIN
16mm
Bell system science series
Color
Shows the development of the science of genetics, beginning with the cross - pollination experiments by Gregor Mendel in the middle of the nineteenth century through recent findings on genes, chromosomes and the chemical substance DNA.
Psychology; Science - Natural
Dist - WAVE Prod - ATAT 1960

The Thread of life - Pt 2 27 MIN
16mm
Bell system science series
Color
Shows the development of the science of genetics, beginning with the cross - pollination experiments by Gregor Mendel in the middle of the nineteenth century through recent findings on genes, chromosomes and the chemical substance DNA.
Psychology; Science - Natural
Dist - WAVE Prod - ATAT 1960

Threading Taps and Dies, Pt 7 15 MIN
16mm
B&W
LC FIE58-8
Shows sequences and close - ups of the operations involved in tapping and threading as the worker views them in performance of the task. Explains the uses of taper, plug and bottoming taps and shows die adjustments for obtaining the desired fit of threads to tapped holes.
Industrial and Technical Education
Dist - USNAC Prod - USN 1954

Threads 110 MIN
U-matic / VHS / 16mm
Color (C A)
Gives an account of what might happen during and after a nuclear attack on Britain, based on scientific, medical, agricultural and psychological research. Covers a time span from a month before to 13 years after the war and relates events through the experiences of two families, one working - class and one middle - class. Portrays the breakdown of the supporting threads of a technologically advanced society.
Sociology
Dist - FI Prod - BBCTV

Threads of Tradition 14 MIN
VHS
Color (I)
$59.95 purchase _ #VC - - 804
Documents the rebirth of the traditional crafts of weaving and embroidery in the Hispanic culture of southern Colorado. Shows carding, spinning, dyeing and weaving and other examples of folk art.
Fine Arts; Geography - United States; Sociology
Dist - CRYSP Prod - CRYSP

Threat - Car Bomb 20 MIN
16mm
Color
LC 77-702294
Demonstrates the effects of various explosive devices on a standard automobile. Explains how to protect a vehicle and how to conduct a cursory vehicle search, stressing reliance on professional ordnance technicians.
Sociology
Dist - MCCRNE Prod - MCCRNE 1977

The Threat from beyond 13 MIN
BETA / VHS / U-matic
Color; PAL (IND G)
$175.00 rental _ #ASF - 148
Reveals that despite repeated warnings, many workers neglect to wear personal protective equipment. Uses humor to show employees that accidents may be just around the corner, waiting to happen, and that only by using personal protective equipment can they avoid injury. Includes leader's guide and 10 workbooks.
Business and Economics; Health and Safety; Psychology
Dist - BNA Prod - BNA

The Threat from Japan 58 MIN
VHS / U-matic / BETA
Nova - the genius that was China series
Color (H C A)
$250.00 purchase _ #JY - 6183C
Chronicles the conflict between East and West in the 19th century over trade and power. Looks at why Japan was successful in its encounters with the West while China failed. Part of a four - part series which details the rise, fall and re - emergence of science in China.
Civics and Political Systems; History - World
Dist - CORF Prod - WGBHTV 1990

Threatened
Videodisc
Laser learning set 2 series; Set 2
Color; CAV (P I)
$375.00 purchase _ #8L5412
Presents six examples of endangered species of animals and their special means of adaptation. Expresses hope for the future in the form of protective legislation and controlled land use. Part of a series of six theme - based interactive videodisc lessons. Requires a Pioneer LD - V2000 or 2200, with a barcode reader and adapter, or a Pioneer LD - V4200 or higher. Includes a user's guide and two readers.
Science - Natural
Dist - BARR **Prod** - BARR 1992

Threatened forests 19 MIN
VHS / U-matic / 16mm
Color (J H G)
$265.00, $315.00 purchase, $50.00 rental
Explores the problems of forest death caused by airborne pollution from toxic gases in the air and release of dangerous metals in the soil from acidification transported by rain, snow or dust. Looks at possible solutions to the growing worldwide problem which has created palpable tensions between the US and Canada as well as in domestic governmental policies.
Science - Natural
Dist - NDIM **Prod** - RIVPIX 1988

Threatened Paradise 30 MIN
Videoreel / VT2
Color
Explains that people are the cause of environmental decay in Florida. Features fishermen who discuss the industrial threat to Florida's fish supply. Narrated by Cliff Robertson.
Geography - United States; Physical Education and Recreation; Science - Natural
Dist - PBS **Prod** - WPBTTV

Threatened waters 19 MIN
VHS / U-matic
Color (J H G)
$265.00, $315.00 purchase, $50.00 rental
Addresses the serious dilemma of polluted rain and snow turning living waters into dying lakes and streams. Looks at water acidification, a mounting problem in the lakes, streams and ground waters of North America and Europe.
Science - Natural
Dist - NDIM **Prod** - RIVPIX 1988

Threatening behaviour 40 MIN
VHS
Town hall
Color; PAL (C H)
PdS65 purchase
Reveals the strife encountered by members of the Lewisham borough council as they negotiate decisions. Focuses on the tension between councillors and officers. Fourth in the eight - part series Town Hall, which documents the operation of local government in Great Britain.
Civics and Political Systems
Dist - BBCENE

The Threatening sky 40 MIN
16mm
B&W
Presents a sober, well documented assessment of the bombing of North Vietnam, including the destruction of civilian areas, crops and factories. Shows the reactions and defense measures taken by the population. Introduction by Bertrand Russell.
Civics and Political Systems; Geography - World; Psychology; Sociology
Dist - CANWRL **Prod** - VDR 1967

Threats 30 MIN
U-matic / VHS
Corporate Computer Security Strategy Series
Color
Deals with threats to which computer systems are potentially vulnerable and describes the various types of threats, relating them to the concepts of computer security, accuracy and privacy.
Industrial and Technical Education
Dist - DELTAK **Prod** - DELTAK

Three 8 MIN
16mm
B&W (I J H C)
Records the imaginery love triangle of a frustrated introvert.
Fine Arts; Sociology
Dist - CFS **Prod** - JORDAL

Three 19th Century watercolorists 30 MIN
U-matic
Antiques series
Color
Fine Arts
Dist - PBS **Prod** - NHMNET

3 - 60 - Baume im Herbst - Trees in autumn 5 MIN
16mm
B&W (G)
$15.00 rental
Embodies the concept of structural activity in cinema where the camera as subjective observer is constrained within a systematic structural prodecure. Furthers the theory that art forms experience.
Fine Arts; Industrial and Technical Education
Dist - CANCIN **Prod** - KRENKU 1960

Three Against the World 25 MIN
U-matic
Color
Focuses on ski racing and the racer, illustrating that success is largely determined by the excellence of the equipment and the best technical strategy.
Physical Education and Recreation
Dist - LAURON **Prod** - LAURON

Three American guns 35 MIN
U-matic / VHS / 16mm
Color (H C A G)
Introduces three people who purchased guns for protection and used them. Re - enacts the events using most of the real participants.
Health and Safety; Physical Education and Recreation; Sociology
Dist - CORF **Prod** - BELLDA 1983

Three Appeals 60 MIN
U-matic / VHS
Color
Examines the state appeals process, focusing on three cases presented to the New York State Court of Appeals. Includes the oral arguments, interviews with the defendants, the plaintiffs, and their attorneys, and commentary by Professor Charles Nesson, Associate Dean at Harvard Law School. Concludes with the decisions in each case, an explanation of how they were reached, and what they mean for the parties involved.
Civics and Political Systems
Dist - PBS **Prod** - WNETTV

Three Appendectomies 30 MIN
VHS / U-matic
Pediatric Series
Color
Health and Safety
Dist - SVL **Prod** - SVL

Three approaches to group therapy - Pt 1 38 MIN
16mm
Color (H C A)
LC 75-701108
Features Dr Everett L Shostrom discussing his theories as presented in his book entitled Actualizing Therapy.
Literature and Drama; Psychology
Dist - PSYCHF **Prod** - PSYCHF 1974

Three approaches to group therapy - Pt 2 40 MIN
16mm
Color (H C A)
LC 75-701112
Features Dr Albert Ellis demonstrating his techniques of rational - emotive therapy as presented in his book entitled Reason And Emotion In Psychotherapy.
Literature and Drama; Psychology
Dist - PSYCHF **Prod** - PSYCHF 1974

Three Approaches to Group Therapy, Pt 3 38 MIN
16mm
Color (H C A)
LC 75-701113
Features Dr Harold Greenwald using his type of therapy as presented in his book entitled Decision Therapy.
Literature and Drama; Psychology
Dist - PSYCHF **Prod** - PSYCHF 1974

Three Approaches to Psychotherapy II Series
Actualizing therapy 48 MIN
Client - centered therapy 48 MIN
Multimodal Behavior Therapy 48 MIN
Dist - PSYCHF

Three Approaches to Psychotherapy, no 1 - Dr Carl Rogers 48 MIN
16mm
Color; B&W (C T)
LC FIA66-1379
Describes client - centered therapy as practiced by Dr Carl Rogers. Shows his interview with patient Gloria and gives a summation of the effectiveness of the interview. Correlated with the textbook Therapeutic Psychology by L Brammer and E Shastrom.
Psychology
Dist - PSYCHF **Prod** - PSYCHF 1965

Three Approaches to Psychotherapy, no 3 - Dr Albert Ellis 42 MIN
16mm
Color; B&W (C T)
LC FIA66-1381
Describes rational - emotive psycho - therapy as practiced by Dr Albert Ellis. Shows his interview with patient Gloria and gives a summation of the effectiveness of the interview. Includes an evaluation by Gloria of her therapy with doctors Carl Rogers, Frederick Perls and Albert Ellis. Correlated with the textbook Therapeutic Psychology by L Brammer and E Shastrom.
Psychology
Dist - PSYCHF **Prod** - PSYCHF 1965

Three Approaches to Psychotherapy, no 2 - Dr Frederick Perls 32 MIN
16mm
Color; B&W (C T)
LC FIA66-1380
Describes the Gestalt therapy as practiced by Dr Frederick Perls. Shows his interview with patient Gloria and gives a summation of the effectiveness of the interview. Correlated with the textbook Therapeutic Psychology by L Brammer and E Shastrom.
Psychology
Dist - PSYCHF **Prod** - PSYCHF 1965

Three Artists in the Northwest 29 MIN
VHS / 16mm
Color (G)
$55.00 rental _ #TAIN - 000
Explores the link between artist and nature through the works of three men whose art was influenced by the Northwest - Guy Anderson, George Tsutakawa and Theodore Roethke.
Fine Arts; Literature and Drama
Dist - PBS **Prod** - KCTSTV

Three A'S, Three B'S and One C 48 MIN
16mm
University of Illinois Arithmetic Project Series
B&W (T)
LC 74-702617
An unrehearsed teacher - training film in which David Page demonstrates methods of presenting material as he teaches one of the University of Illinois arithmetic project topics to a class of fifth - graders. The class uncovers several of the surprising things that happen with number line rules.
Education; Mathematics
Dist - AGAPR **Prod** - EDS 1969

Three Axis CNC Milling 60 MIN
VHS / 16mm
Color (H A)
$199.00 purchase _ G10
Defines absolute zero. Introduces tool definition statement and demostrates tool length offsets at machines.
Industrial and Technical Education
Dist - BERGL **Prod** - BERGL 1987

Three axis CNC milling series
Presents a four - part series which covers three axis CNC milling. Deals with the subjects of positioning theory, part programming, entering the program, and setting up the machine. Consists of four videocassettes and a study guide.
Three axis CNC milling series
Dist - CAMV

Three - Axis Linear Milling 18 MIN
VHS / U-matic
Numerical Control/Computerized Numerical Control, Module 1 - 'Fundamentals Series
Color (IND)
Covers a compound angle, the dimensions of compound angle and 3 - axis milling.
Business and Economics; Industrial and Technical Education
Dist - LEIKID **Prod** - LEIKID

Three Bad Men 92 MIN
16mm
B&W
Presents the story of three outlaws who join a girl on the Western trail and decide to protect her after her father is killed by a rival gang. Stars George O'Brien and Lou Tellegen. Directed by Lou Ford.
Fine Arts
Dist - KILLIS **Prod** - FOXFC 1926

Three Billion Years of Life - the Drama of Evolution 70 MIN
Slide / U-matic / VHS
Color (J H)
Follows the chronology of organic evolution through three billion years, from the origins of life to the appearance of Homo sapiens.
Science - Natural
Dist - GA **Prod** - SCIMAN

The Three billy goats gruff - The Three little pigs 30 MIN
VHS
Rabbit ears collection series
Color (K P I J)
$12.95 purchase _ #095424
Features Holly Hunter as narrator of two beloved folk tales.
Literature and Drama
Dist - KNOWUN **Prod** - RABBIT

Three bits of comic relief without humans 3 MIN
16mm
B&W (G)
$5.00 rental
Features three little films. Includes A Penguin Comes to Call, which looks at two penguins by a Cape Cod house on a hot summer afternoon; Babies, a sequel to the Penguin; and From the Left Side, a study for an animated political satire involving the right and left sides of place settings at the dinner table. A Rob Savage production.
Fine Arts; Literature and Drama
Dist - CANCIN

The Three books of Bizarrov 192 MIN
16mm
Color (A)
$400.00 rental
Offers a special rental package of The Angry God, Doctor Petronious Seducer of Women and Salivation of Professor Bizarrov. Includes the trailer for The Angry God free of charge.
Fine Arts; Religion and Philosophy
Dist - CANCIN **Prod** - DEGRAS

The Three Brothers - an African Folk Tale 7 MIN
16mm
Folk Tales from Around the World Series
Color (P I)
LC 80-700744
Tells of three brothers who go on a journey because the one who brings back the most extraordinary gift will win the hand of the prettiest girl in the village.
Literature and Drama
Dist - SF **Prod** - ADPF 1980

Three Brothers in Haiti 17 MIN
16mm / U-matic / VHS
Man and His World Series
Color (P I J H C)
LC 74-705469
Describes farm life in Haiti and explains government attempts to improve farming methods.
Agriculture; Geography - World
Dist - FI **Prod** - FI 1969

Three Brothers, Playing a Broken Tune - Crescendos and Climaxes 11 MIN
VHS / U-matic
Color
Reflects upon childhood innocence. Confronts a basic contradiction between representation and reality.
Fine Arts
Dist - KITCHN **Prod** - KITCHN

Three Buoys Houseboat Vacations 30 MIN
U-matic
Frontrunners Series
Color (H C A)
Profiles two young entrepreneurs who discovered an untapped vacation market and in three years were millionaires.
Business and Economics
Dist - TVOTAR **Prod** - TVOTAR 1985

3 by Cornell 25 MIN
16mm
B&W; Color tint (G)
$75.00 rental
Consists of the first three of six films Joseph Cornell gave to Larry Jordan to finish before Cornell's death. Features the first known fully collaged films made from found footage completed in the 1940s. Cornell combines Vaudeville jugglers, animal acts, circus performers, children dancing and science demonstrations in Cotillion, The Midnight Party and Children's Party. Jordan made the films printable without changing the editing structure.
Fine Arts
Dist - CANCIN

Three by Martha Graham, Pt 1 - Cortege of Eagles 38 MIN
U-matic / VHS / 16mm
Color
Presents Cortege Of Eagles as performed by the Martha Graham Dancers.
Fine Arts
Dist - PFP **Prod** - PFP 1969

Three by Martha Graham, Pt 3 - Seraphic Dialog 25 MIN
U-matic / VHS / 16mm
Color
Presents Seraphic Dialog as performed by the Martha Graham Dancers.
Fine Arts
Dist - PFP **Prod** - PFP 1969

Three by Martha Graham, Pt 2 - Acrobats of God 22 MIN
16mm / U-matic / VHS
Color
Presents Acrobats Of God as performed by the Martha Graham Dancers.
Fine Arts
Dist - PFP **Prod** - PFP 1969

Three by Scorsese - The Big shave, ItalianAmerican, American boy 109 MIN
VHS / 16mm
Color (G)
$350.00 rental
Presents three films by Martin Scorsese. Portrays a morning shave which turns into a musical bloodletting in The Big Shave. Invites the viewer into the home of Scorsese's parents, Catherine and Charles, in ItalianAmerican. Interviews actor Steven Prince who portrayed gun salesman Easy Andy in Taxi Driver in American Boy.
Fine Arts; History - United States; Literature and Drama
Dist - KINOIC

Three by the Sea 30 MIN
U-matic / VHS
Reading Rainbow Series no 12
Color (P)
Relates that as LeVar Burton strolls on the beach reading Three By The Sea, he learns that stories can be created out of the sea, the sand, the air and imagination.
English Language; Social Science
Dist - GPN **Prod** - WNEDTV 1982

Three by three 82 MIN
16mm
Color (G)
$140.00 rental
Entertains with an off - beat visual portrait of Ricardo, a gay Cuban refugee, and his two American friends, Sharon and Wes. Operates on two levels of consciousness by intertwining reality and illusion as the three character examine their contrasting backgrounds, attitudes, prejudices and uncertain futures. Includes video documents and cinema verite. Filmed in San Francisco.
Fine Arts; Psychology; Sociology
Dist - CANCIN **Prod** - SALVOC 1986

Three Caballeros 72 MIN
16mm / U-matic / VHS
Color
Depicts an animated musical invasion of Mexico and South America.
Fine Arts
Dist - FI **Prod** - DISNEY 1945

Three cases of murder 99 MIN
VHS
B&W (G)
$39.95 purchase _ #THR120
Portrays a doomed museum guard who is magically transported into his favorite painting. Looks at two friends who fall in love with the same woman who is suddenly killed. The third story stars Orson Welles as a statesman driven mad by guilt after he destroys his political rival. Adapts three mysteries by writers Somerset Maugham, Roderick Wilkinson and Brett Halliday. Digitally remastered. Directed by Wendy Toye, David Eady and George More O'Ferrall.
Fine Arts; Literature and Drama; Psychology; Sociology
Dist - HOMVIS **Prod** - JANUS 1954

Three Cheers on a June Day 14 MIN
16mm
Color
LC 74-705439
Shows June Week and graduation at the Naval Academy at Annapolis, Maryland.
Education
Dist - USNAC **Prod** - USN 1968

Three chimes 9 MIN
U-matic / VHS
Color (J A)
Recreates the story of Peter's betrayal of Christ. Uses an unusual photographic technique and a modern setting.
Religion and Philosophy
Dist - ECUFLM **Prod** - UMCOM

Three Cognitive Skills - Middle Childhood 20 MIN
16mm / U-matic / VHS
Developmental Psychology - Infancy to Adolescence Series
Color (H C A)
LC 78-701010
States that reading, memory and creativity provide the foundations of a child's ability to assimilate into society. Shows the factors which have an effect on these three cognitive skills.
Psychology
Dist - MGHT **Prod** - MGHT 1978

Three Commemorative Stamps 5 MIN
16mm
Color
LC 74-703243
Presents three short vignettes about three well - known commemorative stamps.
History - United States; Social Science
Dist - USPOST **Prod** - USPOST 1974

Three Cornered Flag 26 MIN
16mm / U-matic / VHS
Insight Series
Color; B&W (J H A)
LC 72-705447
Uses flashbacks to review the impact of a boy's mother, uncle, fiancee and priest on his decision to violate his own conscience and enter the army.
Civics and Political Systems; Guidance and Counseling; Psychology; Sociology
Dist - PAULST **Prod** - PAULST 1968

Three - D Defense Self Defense for Women 7 MIN
U-matic / VHS
Color
Instructs women of all ages in delaying, discouraging and disabling tactics to be used in a variety of threatening or potentially dangerous situations.
Physical Education and Recreation; Sociology
Dist - AFFVID **Prod** - AFFVID

Three - D Shapes 15 MIN
U-matic
Math Makers Two Series
Color (I)
Presents the math concepts of solids in the environment, definitions of solid parts and constructing solid models from nets or maps.
Education; Mathematics
Dist - TVOTAR **Prod** - TVOTAR 1980

Three Dances from Cholla - do, Korea 23 MIN
16mm
Ethnic Music and Dance Series
Color (J)
LC 72-700238
Presents three types of dance from the Cholla region of South Korea. Features the dance of a Buddhist monk, who expresses his joy at having attained enlightenment. Includes a solo improvisational dance, Salp'uri, and a popular dance, Kang Kang Su Wol Le.
Fine Arts; Geography - World
Dist - UWASHP **Prod** - UWASH 1971

Three Day Gold 70 MIN
BETA / VHS
Color
Features the U S Three - Day Team's preparation and the 1976 Olympic Three - Day Equestrian Event in Quebec.
Physical Education and Recreation
Dist - EQVDL **Prod** - USCTA

Three days 30 MIN
VHS
Color (H C A R)
$19.95 purchase
Portrays Jesus' disciples, who have hidden following his death, as they learn of his resurrection.
Guidance and Counseling; Literature and Drama; Religion and Philosophy
Dist - CPH **Prod** - LUMIS

Three Days in Szczecin
16mm
World Series
Color (H C A)
Re - creates a confrontation between striking Polish dock - workers and the head of the Polish Communist Party. Based on tape recordings kept by Polish workers.
Business and Economics; Civics and Political Systems; Geography - World
Dist - GRATV **Prod** - GRATV 1977

Three Days in the County Jail 19 MIN
16mm / U-matic / VHS
Under the Law, Pt 2 Series
Color (I J H C)
LC 75-703576
Dramatizes the life and daily routine of a large county jail. Illustrates methods and programs of rehabilitation. Presents the story through the eyes of a young man who was arrested for drunk driving and hit - and - run.

Civics and Political Systems; Sociology
Dist - CORF Prod - USNEI 1975

Three Days on a River in a Red Canoe 30 MIN
VHS / U-matic
Reading Rainbow Series
Color (P)
Presents the story Three Days On A River In A Red Canoe. Shows Levar Burton encountering fun and exciting challenges as he goes camping with a group of enthusiastic young friends.
English Language; Social Science
Dist - GPN Prod - WNEDTV 1982

Three Days Respite 15 MIN
16mm / U-matic / VHS
Color (H C A)
LC 74-701567
Explores the joy and release of carnival time in a town in the northeast of Brazil.
Geography - World; Physical Education and Recreation; Social Science; Sociology
Dist - PHENIX Prod - SLUIZR 1974

Three Decades of Donald Duck Series
Donald's nephews 8 MIN
Fire chief 8 MIN
Up a Tree 8 MIN
Dist - CORF

Three - dimensional art 15 MIN
VHS / 16mm
Art - i - facts series
Color (I)
$125.00 purchase, $25.00 rental
Presents artists explaining how they have chosen a particular media to convey their ideas and how a successful three - dimensional piece lets the viewer see different things from different angles.
Fine Arts
Dist - AITECH Prod - HDE 1986

Three - dimensional art 15 MIN
VHS
Art - i - facts series; Pt 7
Color (I)
$125.00 purchase
Visits the studios of two Hawaiian sculptors - a ceramicist and a metalsmith. Explains how these artists choose particular media to convey their ideas, and how a successful three - dimensional piece lets the viewer see different things from different angles. Part of the Art - I - Facts Series to give third and fourth graders a foundation in the visual arts.
Fine Arts; Geography - United States; History - United States; Industrial and Technical Education
Dist - AITECH Prod - HDE 1986

Three Dimensional Discipline
U-matic / VHS / 16mm
Dealing with Social Problems in the Classroom Series
Color (T)
Discusses classroom discipline techniques.
Education
Dist - FI Prod - MFFD 1983

Three - Dimensional Graphics
U-matic / 35mm strip
All about Computer Graphics Series
Color (A J)
Industrial and Technical Education; Mathematics
Dist - SRA Prod - SRA

Three Dimensional Vectors 26 MIN
U-matic / VHS
Calculus of several Variables - Vector - - Arithmetic Series; Vector arithmetic
B&W
Mathematics
Dist - MIOT Prod - MIOT

Three Directions in Australian Pop Music 11 MIN
16mm
Color (J)
LC 73-702488
Presents three contrasting styles of performance illustrating some of the latest developments in the Australian pop music scene.
Fine Arts; Geography - World
Dist - AUIS Prod - FLMAUS 1973

Three domestic interiors 42 MIN
VHS
Color (G)
$60.00 purchase
Features three characters giving soliloquies to the outside world. Uses each person's home telephone to address these moments of public expression. Fragments of conversation, legs of couches, bits of potted plants become the revealing components of each character's domestic environment - one that simultaneously protects and imprisons its inhabitants.
Fine Arts; Psychology; Social Science; Sociology
Dist - CANCIN Prod - KIRBYL 1992

Three early films - The DC five memorial film, Quick constant and solid instant, Wedding 20 MIN
16mm
Color & B&W (G)
$30.00 rental
Includes The DC Five Memorial Film, in five sections picturing a young man writhing in ecstasy, home movies from childhood, a farm in upstate New York, a party at a disco and a group of young women walking arm - in - arm through the Port Authority Bus Terminal in New York City in the dead of night. Continues with Quick Constant and Solid Instant, featuring John Wallington, a British painter, Rod Townley, and Gerard Malanga on the soundtrack, doing a poetry reading at Rutgers University. Wedding captures the ceremony of two dear friends in the spring of 1969.
Fine Arts; Geography - United States; Psychology
Dist - CANCIN Prod - WWDIXO 1969

Three E's 29 MIN
16mm
Color (I)
Reviews the interrelationship between the three E's, energy, economics and environment. Describes the problems that have arisen in each area and presents some possible solutions. Explains some possibilities, as well as actual accomplishments, in the application of technology to our environmental problems.
Business and Economics; Science - Natural; Social Science; Sociology
Dist - EXXON Prod - EXXON 1973

Three Ethiopian Jewry videos 73 MIN
VHS
Color (G)
$80.00 purchase
Presents three videos on Jews in Ethiopia and their migration to Israel. Includes the titles The Falashas, Operation Moses - a Documentary and Again...the Second Time.
Geography - World; History - World; Sociology
Dist - ERGOM Prod - ERGOM

Three Excerpts from a Group Dance Improvisation 31 MIN
U-matic / VHS
Color
Shows three excerpts from a group dance improvisation.
Fine Arts
Dist - METT Prod - METT

Three faces of beauty 30 MIN
VHS
New faces on make - up series
Color (G A)
$24.95 purchase _ #PRO204V
Provides make - up tips for three different situations - casual, work, and night.
Home Economics
Dist - CAMV

Three Faces of Iceland 25 MIN
16mm
Color (C A)
Traces the history of Iceland in words and images through the centuries, and uses the celebration of eleven hundred years of settlement in 1974 as a springboard. Describes Icelandic history from Viking days to modern times.
Geography - World
Dist - WSTGLC Prod - WSTGLC

Three Faces of Stanley 10 MIN
16mm
Color (H C A)
Presents an animated cartoon with a humorous approach to some of the fears that Stanley has of the 'procto' examination. Outlines the value of the exam in detecting early cases of cancer of the colon and rectum.
Health and Safety
Dist - AMCS Prod - AMCS

Three Facets of Adventure 28 MIN
16mm
Color (C A)
LC FIA66-868
Examines the scenic attractions, social background and other items of interest to tourists and students in Holland, Italy and Israel.
Geography - World
Dist - MCDO Prod - DACKLM 1965

Three Families 52 MIN
U-matic 30 MIN
Everybody's Children Series
Color (PRO)
Looks at three families' different approaches to child rearing.
Home Economics; Psychology; Sociology
Dist - TVOTAR Prod - TVOTAR 1985

Three Families 30 MIN
U-matic / VHS
Japan - the Changing Tradition Series
Color (H C A)
History - World; Sociology
Dist - GPN Prod - UMA 1978

Three Families 29 MIN
VHS / 16mm
Everybody's Children Series
(G)
$90.00 purchase _ #BPN16116
Presents an abbreviated version of 'Three Families' #BPN 176111. Looks at the family, and observes three families' different approaches to child rearing. Comprises part of a series which examines child raising in modern society.
Education; Psychology; Sociology
Dist - RMIBHF Prod - RMIBHF

Three films - Bluewhite, Blood's Tone, Vein 10 MIN
16mm
Color (G)
$25.00 rental, $397.00 purchase
Includes three short films - Bluewhite, 'an intonation of childbirth,' Blood's Tone, 'a golden nursing film,' and Vein, 'a film of baby Buddha masturbation,' according to filmmaker Brakhage.
Fine Arts
Dist - CANCIN Prod - BRAKS 1965

Three films by Alexis Krasilovsky 10 MIN
16mm
B&W; Color (G)
$30.00 rental
Includes Charlie's Dream, Charlie Dozes Off & the Dog Bothers Him - silent B&W - and La Belle Dame Sans Merci. Comments on lovers unaware of love in Charlie's Dream. Charlie Dozes Off & the Dog Bothers Him concerns itself with an erotic study in texture. And La Belle Dame Sans Merci, filmed over the course of a year and a half, pays homage to the feminist poet May Gruening as she struggles to recall passages of her own poems while going blind and deaf. None of these films are available to rent separately.
Fine Arts; Industrial and Technical Education; Literature and Drama; Religion and Philosophy; Sociology
Dist - CANCIN Prod - KRASIL 1973

Three films by Fred Padula 31 MIN
VHS
B&W (G)
$29.00 purchase
Includes Ephesus, Little Jesus - Hippy Hill and David and My Porch.
Fine Arts
Dist - CANCIN Prod - PADULA 1969

Three films by Karl Cohen 34 MIN
VHS
Color (G)
$30.00 purchase
Includes Adios America; Speak Up, Uncle Sam is Hard of Hearing; and Sidereal Passage. See individual titles for description and availability for rental in 16mm format.
Fine Arts
Dist - CANCIN Prod - COHENK

Three films by Lyle Pearson 13 MIN
VHS
Color (G)
$50.00 purchase
Includes Ahead in Paris; The Grand Canary; and The Secret of Quetzalcoatl. See individual titles for description and availability for rental in 16mm format.
Fine Arts
Dist - CANCIN Prod - PEARLY

Three films - Chick Strand 29 MIN
VHS
B&W (G)
$50.00 purchase
Includes Cartoon Le Mousse; Fever Dream; and Kristallnacht. See individual titles for description and availability for rental in 16mm format.
Fine Arts
Dist - CANCIN Prod - STRANC 1979

Three films - Craig Baldwin 98 MIN
VHS
Color (G)
$60.00 purchase
Includes Wild Gunman; Rocketkitkongokit; and Tribulation 99 - Alien Anomalies Under America. See titles for descriptions. Available separately for rental in 16mm format.
Business and Economics; Civics and Political Systems; Fine Arts; Psychology; Sociology
Dist - CANCIN

Three films - Marjorie Keller 23 MIN
VHS
Color; Silent (G)
$70.00 purchase
Includes a trilogy of in - camera edited productions, Ancient Parts; Foreign Parts; and Private Parts. Begins with a small portrait watching a young boy play Narcissus and Oedipus in three minutes. Foreign Parts is a single camera roll of a few familiar faces in a strange landscape and the third portrays Blake Sitney on summer days.
Fine Arts; Sociology
Dist - CANCIN

Three films - Michael Wallin 55 MIN
VHS
Color (G)
$90.00 purchase
Presents a hand - painted film whose emotionally referential shapes and colors are interwoven with words, in English, from the first Hymn to the Night by the late 18th - century mystic poet Friedrich Philipp von Hardenburg, whose pen name was Novalis.
Fine Arts
Dist - CANCIN **Prod** - WALLIN

Three films - Silvianna Goldsmith 36 MIN
VHS
Color (G)
$50.00 purchase
Includes Mexico; Lil Picard, Art is a Party; and Memories of Havana in Queens, 1973 - 1975. See individual titles for description and availability for rental in 16mm format.
Fine Arts
Dist - CANCIN

The Three Fools 9 MIN
16mm
Color (P)
Describes the odd and humorous behavior of three heroes shown trying to hatch eggs, shifting a tree to lie under its shade and building a bridge.
Literature and Drama
Dist - SF **Prod** - SF 1972

Three - Foot Squaring Shear Operation 12 MIN
VHS / BETA
Color (IND)
Illustrates the operation of a three - foot squaring shear that has been converted from a manual to a hydraulic operation.
Industrial and Technical Education; Psychology
Dist - RMIBHF **Prod** - RMIBHF

Three for the City 15 MIN
16mm
Color
LC 78-700821
Documents the initial tests and demonstrations of three innovative buses of radical design and engineering, collectively named Transbus.
Industrial and Technical Education; Social Science
Dist - USNAC **Prod** - USUMTA 1978

Three for the Road Series
The Alcohol you 25 MIN
Power Under Control 22 MIN
Dist - IFB

Three Fox Fables 11 MIN
16mm / U-matic / VHS
B&W (P I)
Uses real - life photography to portray three Aesop fables, the Fox and the Grapes, the Fox and the Crow and the Fox and the Stork.
English Language; Literature and Drama
Dist - EBEC **Prod** - EBEC 1948

The Three generation family 30 MIN
VHS / U-matic
Issues of cystic fibrosis series
Color (PRO C)
$395.00 purchase, $80.00 rental _ #C891 - VI - 049
Offers excerpts from a discussion with the parents and grandparents of a seven - month - old girl recently diagnosed with cystic fibrosis. Includes reactions to the diagnosis and the effect of the disease on family relationships. Part of a 13 - part series on cystic fibrosis presented by Drs Ivan Harwood and Cyril Worby.
Health and Safety; Science - Natural; Sociology
Dist - HSCIC

Three generations of Javanese women 29 MIN
U-matic
Are you listening series
Color (J H C)
LC 80-707406
Presents a group of Javanese women talking about sex roles, family life, village society and family planning. Describes the changes that have taken place in their lives as a result of using contraception.
Sociology
Dist - STURTM **Prod** - STURTM 1980

Three Generations of the Blues 60 MIN
U-matic
Color (J C)
Captures the essence of three great blues singers representing sixty years of unique American music, Sippie Wallace, Willie Mae 'Big Mama' Thornton and Jeannie Cheatham.
Fine Arts
Dist - SDSC **Prod** - SDSC

Three Gifts 16 MIN
U-matic / VHS / 16mm
Color (K P)
LC 74-702297
Features a puppet presentation of a fairy tale where two greedy characters try to steal the three magic gifts.
Literature and Drama
Dist - PHENIX **Prod** - CZECFM 1974

Three gifts to give yourself for personal growth and renewal
VHS
(T PRO)
$10.00 purchase _ #A28
Features Judy - Arin Krupp who presents three gifts that educators must first give themselves before they can give them to students.
Education
Dist - NSDC **Prod** - NSDC 1990

Three Golden Hairs 12.5 MIN
16mm / U-matic / VHS
Color (P I J)
$275.00, $79.00 purchase
Shows how an evil queen's attempts to destroy a princess result in defeat because of the queen's greed. A Bosustow Production.
Literature and Drama
Dist - CF

Three Golden Hairs 13 MIN
U-matic / VHS / 16mm
Grimm's Fairy Tales Series
Color (K P I) (SPANISH)
LC 78-700154
Uses animation to tell the story of the girl who needs three golden hairs from the chin of the devil in order to win her prince and kingdom. Based on the fairy tale Der Teufel Mit Den Drei Goldenen Haaren by the Brothers Grimm.
Literature and Drama
Dist - CF **Prod** - BOSUST 1977

Three great leaders
VHS
Greatest tales from the Old Testament series
Color (K P I R)
$29.95 purchase, $10.00 rental _ #35 - 830 - 528
Presents the stories of three of the great leaders of the Old Testament. Includes accounts of Moses, Isaiah, and David.
Literature and Drama; Religion and Philosophy
Dist - APH **Prod** - CAFM
CAFM

Three great monasteries - Ganden, Drepung and Sera 60 MIN
VHS / BETA
Color; PAL (G)
PdS25 purchase
Follows the life inside three monasteries during the New Year festivities, the Great Prayer festival and beyond as the monks return to their normal daily routine. Tells the history of these three Gelugpa monasteries, which were the largest in Tibet prior to 1959 and greatly renowned for their refined system of education in Buddhist philosophy. Destroyed by the Chinese during the Cultural Revolution, they were reconstructed in India after 25 years of hard work. Recorded in Mundgod and Bylakuppe, South India. Directed by Greta Jensen.
Fine Arts; Religion and Philosophy
Dist - MERIDT

Three Great Salespeople 30 MIN
VHS / 16mm
(PRO G)
$89.95 purchase _ #DGP66
Presents three successful sales people who share the secrets of their trade. Looks at what motivates the motivators. Hosted by Dick Goldberg.
Business and Economics
Dist - RMIBHF **Prod** - RMIBHF

Three Guesses 29 MIN
U-matic / VHS / 16mm
Color (H C A)
LC 73-702750
Studies Miss Jackie Burroughs of Toronto, representing the many roles that she, as one individual, assumes in the course of one day. Explains that she is, at the same time, actress, mother, daughter, woman and estranged wife.
Biography; Fine Arts; Guidance and Counseling
Dist - PHENIX **Prod** - NFBC 1973

Three hand - painted films series
Night music, Rage net, Glaze of cathexis 4 MIN
Dist - CANCIN

A Three hat day - 41
VHS
Reading rainbow series
Color; CC (K P)
$39.95 purchase
Shows how, inspired by the story by Laura Geringer and illustrated by Arnold Lobel, LeVar can go anywhere just by changing his hat. Reveals that when he puts on a jockey's cap, he visits a racetrack where he rides in a horse race and experiences the thrill of the winner's circle. LeVar changes a hat and joins the New York Islanders professional hockey team and learns what it's like to be a goalie. Part of a series offering a multicultural approach to generating reading enthusiasm with cross - curricular applications, hosted by LeVar Burton.
English Language; Literature and Drama; Physical Education and Recreation
Dist - GPN **Prod** - LNMDP

The Three - headed dragon - the threefold barrier to recovery 27 MIN
VHS
Color (G)
Exposes the threefold barrier to recovery from alcoholism - drinking, which affects thinking, which affects feeling. Shows how to dramatically increase acceptance of self - change and effectively aids alcoholics in their ongoing program of recovery.
Guidance and Counseling; Health and Safety; Psychology
Dist - FMSP **Prod** - SUTHRB
SUTHRB

Three Herding Societies - Lapp, Quechua , Masai 13 MIN
16mm / U-matic / VHS
Color (P I J)
$315.00, $220.00 purchase _#4071
Examines three herding societies, showing that the three different cultures share many common elements due to their focus on herding. Looks at Lapps herding reindeer in northern Finland, Quechuas herding alpacas and llamas in Peru, and Masais herding cattle in the Great Rift Valley of Equatorial Africa in Kenya.
Geography - World; Social Science
Dist - CORF **Prod** - CORF 1981

Three Heroes 22 MIN
16mm
Color (I)
LC 73-702729
Presents three Carnegie Medal winners and the heroic deeds that entitled them to this award. Features each hero relating how he saved the life of another human being.
Biography
Dist - IU **Prod** - WGBHTV 1973

Three historic trials 8 MIN
16mm
B&W (G)
$15.00 rental
Offers film clips of the Sacco - Vanzetti demonstrations and trial plus the Scopes Monkey Trial and the court martial of Billy Mitchell.
Civics and Political Systems; Fine Arts; Literature and Drama
Dist - KITPAR

Three - Hundred Feet to the Moon 22 MIN
16mm
Color
Shows the history and development of the Lunar Landing Training Vehicle from its conception through the various design stages and tests to the present configuration.
Industrial and Technical Education; Science - Physical
Dist - NASA **Prod** - NASA

The 300 million years war 30 MIN
VHS
QED series
Color; PAL (H C A)
PdS65 purchase; Not available in Australia
Examines the interactions between plants and insects. Describes the advantages held by the insects, and contrasts them with the defenses of plants.
Science - Natural
Dist - BBCENE

Three Husbands 43 MIN
U-matic / VHS
Color (PRO)
Shows three husbands, 34 - 52 years old, discussing their feelings about their wives' breast cancers. Includes effects of the illness on marriage and children, sexual functioning, reactons to mastectomy, perspectives about medical treatment, concerns about the future and ways husbands support thier wives emotionally.

Health and Safety; Psychology
Dist - UMICHM **Prod** - UMICHM 1982

Three Imams discuss family in the West
VHS
Islamic videos on family and education series
Color (G)
$15.00 purchase _ #110 - 038
Features the Imams M Naseem, Siraj Wahhaj and Jamal Zarabozo who spell out problems facing families and Islamic solutions.
Religion and Philosophy; Sociology
Dist - SOUVIS **Prod** - SOUVIS

Three in a Round 7 MIN
16mm
B&W
Presents a dance short in which two or more roles are performed simultaneously by the same person, appearing sometimes as a mirror image, sometimes moving in counterpoint to himself. Provides a series of dance patterns embracing techniques from popular ballet, modern dance and jazz.
Fine Arts
Dist - RADIM **Prod** - WEAVRR

3 Indian Health TV Spots
VHS / U-matic
Color
Presents three public service announcements.
Social Science; Sociology
Dist - SHENFP **Prod** - SHENFP 1987

Three is a Magic Number 41 FRS
VHS / U-matic
Multiplication Rock Series
Color (P I)
LC 75-733959
Uses songs and cartoons to explore the mathematical possibilities of the number three.
Mathematics
Dist - GA **Prod** - ABCTV 1974

Three Island Women 17 MIN
16mm
Faces of Change - China Coast Series
Color
Introduces a young woman, a middle - aged woman and an old woman who all agree that life on a small Chinese island in Hong Kong waters is better for them now than in the past. Shows them participating fully in the island's decision - making and economic life, while sharing with men the rigors of manual labor.
Geography - World; Sociology
Dist - WHEELK **Prod** - AUFS

Three Islands 50 MIN
U-matic / 16mm
Assignment Maclear Series
Color; Mono (J H C A)
$500.00 film, $350.00 video, $50.00 rental
Discusses the islands of Nauru, Papua, and the Cayman. Examines each island's individual problems and then shows common bonds that could provide solutions.
Geography - World; Social Science
Dist - CTV **Prod** - CTV 1977

Three Key Controls 29 MIN
U-matic / VHS
Photo Show Series
Color
Shows camera control, how to use the aperture, the shutter speed and the focus.
Industrial and Technical Education
Dist - PBS **Prod** - WGBHTV 1981

Three Key Questions in Coronary Disease 90 MIN
16mm
B&W (PRO)
Presents a panel of doctors discussing and debating the value and role of surgery, dietary fat and anticoagulant therapy in heart disease. Shows Dr Charles P Bailey of the Hahnemann Medical College performing an inverse endarterectomy.
Health and Safety; Science - Natural
Dist - UPJOHN **Prod** - UPJOHN

A Three Letter Word for Love 27 MIN
U-matic / VHS / 16mm
Color
Features a discussion between young men and women who speak frankly about their thoughts, feelings, misconceptions, and fantasies about sex. Photographed in Harlem.
Sociology
Dist - CNEMAG **Prod** - DOCUA

The Three little pigs 60 MIN
VHS
Faerie tale theatre series
Color; CC (K P I J)
$19.95 purchase _ #CBS6794
Stars Billy Crystal and Jeff Goldblum.
Literature and Drama
Dist - KNOWUN

Three Little Pigs 8 MIN
16mm / U-matic / VHS
Color (K P I) (FRENCH)
LC 72-700156
Tells the story of the Three Little Pigs.
Literature and Drama
Dist - CORF **Prod** - DISNEY 1956

The Three Little Pigs 15 MIN
16mm
Color
Tells the story of the three little pigs and how they leave home and Ma Hog to gain their independence. Discusses how each of the little pigs deal with adversity.
Guidance and Counseling; Religion and Philosophy
Dist - BROADM **Prod** - BROADM 1976

The Three Little Pigs - Background for Reading and Expression 10 MIN
U-matic / VHS / 16mm
Color (P)
$265.00, $185.00 purchase _ #844
Uses real animals to retell the story of the Three Little Pigs.
English Language; Literature and Drama
Dist - CORF **Prod** - CORF 1956

The Three Little Pigs - Pt 5 15 MIN
VHS
Words and Pictures Series
Color (P)
$49.00 purchase _ #548 - 9869
Uses animated stories to improve reading and vocabulary skills. Discusses the story content of each program and suggests several activities that relate to the story and the lessons learned. Part 5 of the seven part series gives a fabulous treatment to the famous fairy tale of the three little pigs.
English Language; Fine Arts; Literature and Drama
Dist - FI **Prod** - BBCTV 1984

Three Little Rabbits 6 MIN
16mm / U-matic / VHS
Color (P I) (SPANISH)
LC 74-700473;
Tells the story of a magpie who overhears three little rabbits planning to change their menu from carrots to fox meat.
Literature and Drama
Dist - LCOA **Prod** - HUNGAR 1974

The Three Little Tramps 25 MIN
16mm / VHS
Color (P)
$470.00, $285.00 purchase
Presents an animated tale about three abandoned dogs who set off in search of a new home. Reveals the three venture out on their own but vow to be reunited on Christmas Eve. Their wish comes true and they discover the meaning of friendship.
Fine Arts; Health and Safety; Literature and Drama; Psychology
Dist - LUF **Prod** - LUF

Three Little Wizards - an Adventure in Color 7 MIN
16mm
Color (P I)
LC FIA66-1183
The story of three wizards, red, yellow and blue, who discover that colors - and people, too - are at their best when in harmony.
Fine Arts; Literature and Drama; Science - Natural
Dist - SF **Prod** - VIKING 1966

Three Lives 70 MIN
16mm
Color
Brings together without pretense or parallel, the lives of three women, Mallory Millett - Jones, Lillian Shreve, a reflective middle - aged woman and Robin Mide, a liberated woman.
Guidance and Counseling; Psychology
Dist - IMPACT **Prod** - WLIBCC 1970

Three lives - counseling the terminally ill 52 MIN
16mm / VHS / U-matic
Color (G)
$75.00 purchase
Shares the counseling process between psychologist Dr Charles Garfield and three women who are dying of cancer.
Health and Safety; Sociology
Dist - CANCIN PELICN **Prod** - SPINLB 1976

The Three Lives of Thomasina 97 MIN
16mm / U-matic / VHS
Color
Tells the story of an unusual cat who has the power to change human lives.
Fine Arts
Dist - FI **Prod** - DISNEY 1967

Three Looms Waiting 50 MIN
16mm / VHS
Omnibus series
Color (C G)
PdS99 purchase; LC 73-700014
Tells about drama teacher Dorothy Heathcote who left school at the age of 14 to work in a mill where she wove parachutes during World War II. Reveals that, when she was 20, she won a place at a theater school and her fees were paid by the mill owner. Four years later, she was a lecturer in educational drama at Newcastle University. Interviews Heathcote and shows her work on Tyneside with a variety of young people.
Literature and Drama
Dist - BBCENE **Prod** - BBCTV 1972

Three - M Brand Oil Sorbent 18 MIN
16mm
Color
LC 76-702305
Explains what oil sorbents are and shows how to store, use and dispose of oil wastes.
Industrial and Technical Education
Dist - MMAMC **Prod** - MMAMC 1976

Three - M Toolbox for Imagineering 18 MIN
16mm
Color
LC 75-700323
Pictures a wide and largely unrelated group of products manufactured by 3M Company Industrial Specialties Division. Uses two mimes who appear with a toolbox and demonstrate an assortment of products used for cushioning, reinforcing, joining and protecting.
Business and Economics; Industrial and Technical Education
Dist - MMAMC **Prod** - MMAMC 1974

Three Managerial Styles 13 MIN
Videoreel / VT2
SUCCESS, the AMA Course for Office Employees Series
Color
LC 75-704210
Presents an instructional course for office employees. Portrays three different managerial styles. Shows the difference of each style as it is applied to the same managerial situation.
Business and Economics; Psychology
Dist - AMA **Prod** - AMA 1972

Three masked pieces 3 MIN
16mm
Color (G)
$5.00 rental
Presents a series of self - portraits where the filmmaker pokes fun at himself.
Fine Arts; Literature and Drama
Dist - CANCIN **Prod** - MERRIT 1979

Three Meals a Day, Plus 29 MIN
16mm
Food for Youth Series
Color
LC 76-701597
Emphasizes that although lunch is only one of a child's three or more meals a day, it may be the only nutritionally balanced meal he has. Points out the importance of proper food served at breakfast and dinner. Makes suggestions for adding nutritious snacks to daily food intake.
Health and Safety; Home Economics; Social Science
Dist - USNAC **Prod** - USFNS 1974

Three Meals a Day, Plus 28 MIN
U-matic / VHS
Food for Youth Series
Color (J H A)
Industrial and Technical Education; Social Science; Sociology
Dist - CORNRS **Prod** - CUETV 1975

Three Men in a Tub 10 MIN
16mm
B&W
Depicts a boat race between Alfalfa and Waldo which becomes a contest for Darla's affections. A Little Rascals film.
Fine Arts
Dist - RMIBHF **Prod** - ROACH 1938

Three Methods of Facing Work to Length
VHS / U-matic
Basic Engine Lathe Series
Color
Industrial and Technical Education
Dist - VTRI **Prod** - VTRI

Three Methods of Facing Work to Length
U-matic / VHS
Basic Engine Lathe - Spanish Series
Color (SPANISH)
Foreign Language; Industrial and Technical Education
Dist - VTRI **Prod** - VTRI

Three Miles High 50 MIN
U-matic / VHS / 16mm
Great Railways Journeys of the World Series
Color (J)
Presents reporter Miles Kingston who begins a trip from Cuzco, Peru on the highest railway in the world, across the Andes mountains to La Paz, Bolivia. Observes all types of South American scenery, including the lost Inca city of Machu Pichu.
Geography - World; Social Science
Dist - FI **Prod** - BBCTV 1981

Three Minute Warning 15 MIN
16mm
Color
LC 80-701053
Presents television commentator Martin Agronsky who discusses smoke detectors. Covers the various kinds of smoke detectors and their installation in the home.
Health and Safety; Home Economics
Dist - KLEINW **Prod** - KLEINW 1978

Three Minutes to Live 33 MIN
VHS / U-matic / 16mm
Hydrogen Sulphide Safety Series
Color
Pits hydrogen sulphide and death against human intelligence. Uses a plot in which 'Death' is personified as a black - cloaked motorcyclist and hydroogen sulphide as an invisible vicious killer, represented by a hidden voice.
Health and Safety
Dist - FLMWST **Prod** - FLMWST 1974

Three Modes of Visualization for the Larynx 7 MIN
U-matic / VHS / 16mm
Color (PRO C)
$385.00 purchase _ #840VI066
Demonstrates three methods the viewer can use to visualize the larynx and surrounding anatomical landmarks.
Science - Natural
Dist - HSCIC **Prod** - HSCIC 1984

The Three Monks 22 MIN
16mm / VHS
Chinese Animations Series
Color (K)
Retells the beloved Chinese tale - if you send one monk for water he returns with two buckets, if you send two monks they return with one - if you send three monks they return empty - handed. Directed by A Da.
Fine Arts; Geography - World; History - United States; Literature and Drama
Dist - LUF **Prod** - SAFS

Three Moods 8 MIN
16mm
B&W
Presents later visions based on Moussorgsky's music, with slow - moving shadows on a sleepless night, an accelerated passage of drawings and sketches moving across the screen and a third mood of conflict between material goods and artistic aims. Produced by Alexander Alexeieff and Claire Parker.
Fine Arts
Dist - STARRC **Prod** - STARRC 1980

3 more by Cornell 24 MIN
16mm
B&W; Color tint (G)
$75.00 rental
Consists of the last three of six films Joseph Cornell gave to Larry Jordan to finish before Cornell's death. Features the first known fully collaged films made from found footage completed in the 1940s. Jack's Dream is a puppet animation piece. Carrousel is a fully edited animal film. Also includes Thimble Theatre. Jordan made the films printable without changing the editing structure and added soundtracks using Cornell's notes.
Fine Arts
Dist - CANCIN

Three Movers 26 MIN
16mm / U-matic / VHS
Color (H C A)
LC 81-700227
Shows what happens to a traffic law violator after receiving three moving violations in Illinois. Dramatizes the more frequent moving traffic violations and explains modern technology used to apprehend drivers, including radar units and air surveillance. Emphasizes that careless driving endangers the driver's life as well as the lives of others.
Health and Safety
Dist - IFB **Prod** - CCBC 1980
EDPAT

The Three musketeers 127 MIN
VHS
Color (G)
$24.95 purchase _ #S00548
Presents the 1948 film version of Dumas' swashbuckling tale. Stars Gene Kelly as D'Artagnan, along with Lana Turner, June Allison, Van Heflin, Angela Lansbury and Vincent Price.
Fine Arts; Literature and Drama
Dist - UILL

The Three Musketeers
Cassette / 16mm
Now Age Reading Programs, Set 2 Series
Color (I J)
$9.95 purchase _ #8F - PN681972
Brings a classic tale to young readers. Filmstrip set includes filmstrip, cassette, corresponding book, classroom exercise materials and a poster. The read - along set includes student activity book, cassette and paperback.
English Language; Literature and Drama
Dist - MAFEX

The Three Musketeers with Mr Magoo 52 MIN
16mm
Color (P I)
Fine Arts
Dist - FI **Prod** - FI

Three New Orleans 18 MIN
16mm
Color
LC 75-703295
Depicts a dramatic story based on the premise that man has the power to control his future, which tells about a house in New Orleans, Louisiana, covering its past, present and future.
Geography - United States; Literature and Drama; Sociology
Dist - UNORL **Prod** - UNORL 1975

Three New York Painters 29 MIN
U-matic
Art Show Series
Color
Focuses on three young painters living in the Soho section of New York City.
Fine Arts
Dist - UMITV **Prod** - UMITV

Three no sweat designs - making children's clothing out of old sweatshirts
VHS
Color (A)
$19.95 purchase _ #JCP001V-K
Offers instructions for making children's clothing out of old sweatshirts. Uses step-by-step method to guide viewer through process of making three different jumpsuits that each zip in a different way and take into account easy diapering access.
Health and Safety; Home Economics
Dist - CAMV

Three of us 15 MIN
VHS
Color (P I J)
Explores the feelings of hostility, jealousy, responsibility, friendship and rejection, and a growing awareness among three boys of their common need for friendship.
Health and Safety; Psychology; Sociology
Dist - VIEWTH **Prod** - VIEWTH

The Three of Us 30 MIN
16mm
B&W
LC 77-702676
Presents a documentary about the filmmaker's parents, focusing on their lives, marriage and relationship to their son, who reveals details of his life previously unknown to them.
Industrial and Technical Education; Sociology
Dist - CANFDC **Prod** - ROWBR 1976

Three on a Couch 109 MIN
U-matic / VHS / 16mm
Color (H C A)
Stars Jerry Lewis as an artist engaged to a psychiatrist who will not marry him until she has cured three beautiful patients of their man - hating neuroses. Shows the complications which result when he tries to court all three girls simultaneously.
Fine Arts
Dist - FI **Prod** - CPC 1966

Three painters series
Explores the work of great painters from different periods, hosted by painter and critic Sir Lawrence Gowing. Based on the concept that each artist's work represents a distinct stage in the development of European painting between the Renaissance and the present day. Discusses the historical and social backgrounds against which the artists worked, but concentrates on examining a small number of canvases. Includes views of the places which particularly inspired the artist. See 'Three painters series - series 1, series 2, and series 3.' Series 2 is available only in the United Kingdom.
Three painters series 360 MIN
Dist - BBCENE

Three painters 1 series
Explores the work of great painters from different periods, hosted by painter and critic Sir Lawrence Gowing. Based on the concept that each artist's work represents a distinct stage in the development of European painting between the Renaissance and the present day. Discusses the historical and social backgrounds against which the artists worked, but concentrates on examining a small number of canvases. Includes views of the places which particularly inspired the artist.
Bruegel 40 MIN
Goya 40 MIN
Matisse 40 MIN
Dist - BBCENE

Three painters 2 series
Explores the work of great painters from different periods, hosted by painter and critic Sir Lawrence Gowing. Based on the concept that each artist's work represents a distinct stage in the development of European painting between the Renaissance and the present day. Discusses the historical and social backgrounds against which the artists worked, but concentrates on examining a small number of canvases. Includes views of the places which particularly inspired the artist.
Cezanne 40 MIN
Masaccio 40 MIN
Vermeer 40 MIN
Dist - BBCENE

Three painters 3 series
Explores the work of great painters from different periods, hosted by painter and critic Sir Lawrence Gowing. Based on the concept that each artist's work represents a distinct stage in the development of European painting between the Renaissance and the present day. Discusses the historical and social backgrounds against which the artists worked, but concentrates on examining a small number of canvases. Includes views of the places which particularly inspired the artist.
Giotto 40 MIN
Rembrandt 40 MIN
Turner 40 MIN
Dist - BBCENE

3 - part cataract series 19 MIN
VHS
3 - part cataract series
Color (G)
$250.00 purchase _ #5321S
Presents a three - part series on cataract and cataract surgery. Includes the titles Cataract and Cataract Surgery, YAG Laser Capsulotomy, and Phacoemulsification.
Health and Safety; Science - Natural
Dist - AJN **Prod** - VMED

3 - part cataract series
Cataract and cataract surgery 7 MIN
Phacoemulsification 7 MIN
3 - part cataract series 19 MIN
YAG laser capsulotomy 5 MIN
Dist - AJN

3 - part pediatric ophthalmology series 20 MIN
VHS
3 - part pediatric ophthalmology series
Color (G)
$250.00 purchase _ #5304S
Presents a three - part series on pediatric ophthalmology. Includes the titles Amblyopia, Esotropia and Exotropia.
Health and Safety; Science - Natural
Dist - AJN **Prod** - VMED

3 - part pediatric ophthalmology series
Amblyopia 7 MIN
Esotropia 7 MIN
Exotropia 6 MIN
3 - part pediatric ophthalmology series 20 MIN
Dist - AJN

Three Paths - Hinduism, Buddhism, and Taoism 18 MIN
16mm
Color (J)
LC 82-700099
Examines Hinduism, Buddhism and Taoism and the worshippers of each religion.
Religion and Philosophy
Dist - HP **Prod** - HP 1981

Three - penny opera 100 MIN
VHS
Color (H C)

$39.00 purchase _ #04575 - 126
Portrays a world of thieves, murderers, beggars, prostitutes and corrupt officials presided over by Mack the Knife. Adapts the Kurt Weill - Bertold Brecht operetta.
Fine Arts; History - World; Literature and Drama; Sociology
Dist - GA **Prod** - GA

Three - Phase AC Induction Motor Maintenance 60 MIN
VHS
Motors and Motor Controllers Series
Color (PRO)
$600.00, $1500.00 purchase _ #EM3PH
Focuses on the basics of three - phase AC induction motor maintenance. Looks at how three - phase motors are constructed, how they operate and how they are tested, maintained, disassembled, inspected and reassembled. Part of a ten - part series on motors and motor controllers, which is part of a 29 unit set on electrical maintenance. Includes 10 textbooks and an instructor guide which provide four hours of instruction.
Education; Industrial and Technical Education; Psychology
Dist - NUSTC **Prod** - NUSTC

Three - phase circuits - motors - transformers 60 MIN
VHS / U-matic
Electrical maintenance training series; Module A - AC and DC theory
Color (IND)
Industrial and Technical Education
Dist - LEIKID **Prod** - LEIKID

Three - phase motor - Pt 1 - preparing to rewind 17 MIN
16mm
Electrical work - motor maintenance and repair series; No 4
B&W
LC FIE52-184
Shows how to interpret and record nameplate data of a three - phase motor, identify the line and finish leads, remove coils and determine coil span, use a coil winding machine, and end - tape machine wound coils.
Industrial and Technical Education
Dist - USNAC **Prod** - USOE 1945

Three - phase motor - Pt 2 - rewinding 17 MIN
16mm
Electrical work - motor maintenance and repair series; No 5
B&W
LC FIE52-185
Shows how to insert mush coils and separators, fold, trim, and wedge slot insulation around windings, insert phase insulation and make a delta connection.
Industrial and Technical Education
Dist - USNAC **Prod** - USOE 1945

Three phase power 23 MIN
VHS / 16mm
Applied electricity series
Color (H A)
$465.00 purchase, $110.00 rental
Describes three phase circuits and how to calculate voltage and current.
Industrial and Technical Education
Dist - TAT **Prod** - TAT 1987

The Three Phases of a Therapeutic Relationship 17 MIN
U-matic
Color (PRO)
LC 79-707736
Uses a simulation of an actual clinical case in which a nurse performed therapy for seven months to demonstrate the initiation, working and termination phases of a therapeutic relationship.
Health and Safety
Dist - UMMCML **Prod** - UMICHM 1975

A Three - Pipe Problem 28 MIN
16mm
Color (C A)
LC 72-701859
Describes an approach to problem solving and decision making based on an actual case study from the files of social psychologist Charles Kepner and sociologist Benjamin Tregoe.
Psychology; Sociology
Dist - VOAERO **Prod** - VOAERO 1972

Three Poems 10 MIN
16mm
B&W
LC 77-702675
Presents three poems, the first a literal look at the bathroom sink, tub and toilet, the second a peaceful winter in Toronto, the third a short pan of Yonge Street.
Literature and Drama
Dist - CANFDC **Prod** - CANFDC 1975

The Three - Point Contact 7 MIN
16mm / U-matic / VHS
Color (IND)
Demonstrates safe ways of mounting and dismounting heavy construction equipment. Discusses other hazards and recommends modifications to improve hand and foot holds. Gives tips for safe operation.
Health and Safety; Industrial and Technical Education; Psychology; Science - Physical
Dist - IFB **Prod** - CSAO

Three point play 40 MIN
VHS
Color (G)
$39.95 purchase _ #WES1616V
Presents NBA coach Mike Fratello in a discussion of the three - point shot. Explains who should take the shot, when it should be taken, and the appropriate places to take it on court. Diagrams and demonstrates several plays to set up the shot. Discusses relevant drills and exercises.
Physical Education and Recreation
Dist - CAMV **Prod** - CAMV 1988

Three Polish Jewry videos 188 MIN
VHS
Color; B&W (G)
$140.00 purchase
Presents three videos which trace the history of Jews in Poland before World War II and visit the Jewish survivors in present - Poland. Includes the titles Image Before My Eyes, The Jews of Poland and Pilgrimage of Remembrance - Jews in Poland Today.
History - World; Sociology
Dist - ERGOM **Prod** - ERGOM

3 portraits series
Includes three 20 - minute portraits - Anna Neel, painter; Muriel Rukeyser, poet; and Anna Sokolow, choreographer. Portrays the three artists as daring individualists whose art mirrors the challenges of their lives and their times.
Alice Neel - painter 20 MIN
Anna Sokolow, choreographer 20 MIN
Muriel Rukeyser, poet 20 MIN
Dist - RHOPRO **Prod** - RHOPRO

The Three principles of the path 105 MIN
VHS / BETA
Color; PAL (G)
PdS32.50 purchase
Shares two lectures by the Venerable Lama Thubten Yeshe which were given as a preparation for a tantric empowerment that occured on the following day by His Holiness the Dalai Lama. Looks at the ritual which must introduce the disciple to the principle features of Mahayana practice so the initiation into tantra has a proper foundation. Lama Yeshe follows Je Tzong Khapa's encapsulation of this in the 'three principle aspects of the spiritual path,' namely the determination to achieve liberation from suffering; the activation of the altruistic attitude of the awakening mind; and the cultivation of perfect awareness of reality in the profound view of emptiness. Two lectures recorded at the Vajra Yogini Institute in Lavaur, France.
Fine Arts; Religion and Philosophy
Dist - MERIDT

Three - Ring Government 3 MIN
U-matic / VHS
America Rock Series
Color (P I)
Uses animation and rock music in examining the government by comparing its three branches to a three - ring circus.
Civics and Political Systems; Fine Arts
Dist - GA **Prod** - ABCTV 1977

The Three Robbers 6 MIN
U-matic / VHS / 16mm
Color (K P)
LC 72-701865
Explains that three fierce robbers terrify the countryside until they meet a little girl named Tiffany. Points out that under Tiffany's golden charm the robbers turn their gold to good use and all ends happily.
Guidance and Counseling; Literature and Drama
Dist - WWS **Prod** - WWS 1972

The Three Robbers 35 MIN
VHS / 16mm
Children's Circle Video Series
Color (K)
$18.88 purchase _ #CCV005
Presents four stories including 14 Rats and a Rat - Catcher, The Island of the Skog, and Leopold the See - Through Crumbpicker.
Literature and Drama
Dist - EDUCRT

Three R's for Healthy Smiles 15 MIN
16mm
Color
LC FIA64-246
A puppet film exhorting the importance of good health habits in the care of teeth.
Health and Safety
Dist - USC **Prod** - USC

The Three Rs of growing up
VHS
Big changes, big choices series
Color (I J)
$69.95 purchase _ #LVB - 1A
Looks at the three Rs - Responsibility, Respecting ourselves and doing the Right thing. Part of a 12 - part video series designed to help young adolescents work their way though the many anxieties and issues they face. Encourages them to make positive and healthful life choices. Features humorist and youth counselor Michael Pritchard.
Guidance and Counseling; Psychology
Dist - CFKRCM **Prod** - CFKRCM

Three Rules (1 - 1 - 1, Doubling, Silent E) 15 MIN
VHS
Planet Pylon Series
Color (I)
LC 93712897
Uses character Commander Wordstalker from the Space Station Readstar to develop language arts skills. Examines three spelling rules are examined. Includes a worksheet to be used by student with the help of series characters. Intended for third - grade students.
Education; English Language
Dist - GPN

The Three sages of Bally Bunion 5 MIN
16mm
Color (G)
$7.50 rental
Tells an Irish fable for adults and children in a production by Fred Wellington with Robert Mitchell.
Fine Arts; Literature and Drama
Dist - CANCIN
FLMKCO

Three schools - drug free 27 MIN
VHS
Color (G T PRO)
$225.00 purchase
Features three high school principals who openly discuss how they made their schools drug free. Shows model programs which offer concrete solutions to the drug problems in American high schools. Presents a complete K - 12 curriculum and policy guides for school administrators, counselors, teachers, parents and community leaders.
Education; Guidance and Counseling
Dist - FMSP

Three score years and then 180 MIN
VHS
Color; PAL (G)
PdS50 purchase
Presents six 30 - minute programs on the realities of life after age 60. Looks at health, housing, relationships, caring, opportunities and bereavement. Contact distributor about availability outside the United Kingdom.
Health and Safety
Dist - ACADEM

The Three servants 8 MIN
VHS / U-matic
Timeless tales series
Color (P I)
$110.00, $160.00 purchase, $60.00 rental
Portrays a wicked queen who declares that anyone who can perform three tasks can marry her beautiful daughter. Reveals that a handsome prince meets three servants who help him with the seemingly impossible tasks so he can marry the daughter.
Guidance and Counseling; Literature and Drama
Dist - NDIM **Prod** - TIMTAL 1993

The Three Sillies 15 MIN
VHS
Gentle Giant Series
Color (K)
LC 90712405
Uses story to teach children universal truths. Third of 16 installments in the Gentle Giant Series featuring stories from cultures throughout the world.
Health and Safety; Literature and Drama; Psychology
Dist - GPN **Prod** - CTI 1988

The Three sillies 8 MIN
VHS / U-matic
Timeless tales series
Color (P I)
$110.00, $160.00 purchase, $60.00 rental
Tells about an honest farmer who agrees to marry a local girl. Shows how he attempts to help her family whom he believes to harbor silly fears and vows to postpone his marriage until he finds in a single day, three people who are sillier than his wife - to - be's family.

Guidance and Counseling; Literature and Drama
Dist - NDIM Prod - TIMTAL 1993

he Three Sisters 60 MIN
VHS / U-matic
Drama - play, performance, perception series; Playrights and plotting
Color (H C A)
Develops an appreciation of the playwright's craft in shaping the elements of plot, theme and character. Uses the play The Three Sisters as an example.
Literature and Drama
Dist - FI Prod - BBCTV 1978

'he Three Sisters 135 MIN
U-matic / VHS / 16mm
Classic Theatre Series
Color
LC 79-706930
Presents Anton Chekhov's play The Three Sisters, featuring Janet Suzman.
Literature and Drama
Dist - FI Prod - BBCTV 1976

The Three sisters 60 MIN
VHS
Color (H C G)
$129.00 purchase _ #DL305
Presents the last part of Act I and an almost complete presentation of Act III of Chekhov's The Three Sisters. Includes a documentary section examining Chekhov's reputation as a master of mood and character.
Fine Arts; Literature and Drama
Dist - INSIM Prod - BBC

Three Songs by Leadbelly 8 MIN
16mm
Color (J)
LC 75-701089
Shows Huddie Ledbetter in 1945 singing three of his best known folk songs.
Fine Arts
Dist - RADIM Prod - SEEGER 1975

Three songs of Lenin 88 MIN
16mm / VHS
Soviet Union - the pioneers series
B&W (G)
$150.00 rental
Presents three short films which pay homage to the life of Russia's revolutionary leader, Lenin. Directed by Dziga Vertov.
Fine Arts; History - World
Dist - KINOIC

The Three sopranos
VHS
Color (G)
$24.95 purchase _ #KU035
Brings together Renata Scotto, Ileana Cotrubas, and Elena Obraztsova at Italy's Siracuse Roman Amphitheatre.
Fine Arts
Dist - SIV

Three sovereigns for Sarah 180 MIN
VHS
Color (G)
$150.00 purchase _ #TSFS - 000
Tells the story of Sarah Cloyce, a woman who, along with her sisters, was accused of witchcraft in Salem, Massachusetts in 1692. Traces the story from 1692, when the Salem witch trials began, to 1703, when Cloyce is called to defend herself in court. Stars Vanessa Redgrave, Patrick McGoohan, Phyllis Thaxter and Kim Hunter. Produced by NightOwl Productions. Presented in three 60 - minute episodes.
History - United States; Literature and Drama
Dist - PBS

Three Soviet Jewry videos 83 MIN
VHS
Color (G)
$90.00 purchase
Presents three videos which examine present - day life for Jews in the Soviet Union and record Jewish life in the Soviet before and up to Babi Yar. Includes the titles Dosvedanya Means Goodbye, Visions of Russia - a Granddaughter Returns and The Last Journey.
Geography - World; History - World; Sociology
Dist - ERGOM Prod - ERGOM

Three stars 12 MIN
16mm
Color; B&W (G)
$25.00 rental
Travels with a couple who leave their home in Califonia once a year to eat their way through France. Features the Michelin guide's recommendations for three - star ratings. The filmmaker follows them around in a second car. Title reads as '***'.
Fine Arts; Geography - World; Home Economics
Dist - CANCIN Prod - OSTROV 1987

Three - State Bus Concepts 55 MIN
U-matic / VHS
Digital Electronics Series
Color (PRO)
Industrial and Technical Education; Mathematics
Dist - MIOT Prod - MIOT

Three States of Matter 19 MIN
U-matic
Chemistry 101 Series
Color (C)
Shows how any particular substance such as water can exist as a gas, liquid or solid depending on the conditions of temperature and pressure.
Science; Science - Physical
Dist - UILL Prod - UILL 1974

Three Stone Blades 16 MIN
16mm / U-matic / VHS
Color (I J H)
Presents a dramatization of an Eskimo legend of the Bering Strait region which reconstructs aboriginal Eskimo customs and values concerning family, reciprocal sharing, shamanism and transmigration of souls. Describes how man must cope with the environment in order to survive and shows methods of hunting, skinning, preserving food and making shelter.
Geography - World; Social Science; Sociology
Dist - IFB Prod - IFB 1976

The Three Stooges Go Around the World in a Daze 94 MIN
16mm / U-matic / VHS
B&W (I J H C)
Stars the Three Stooges as the servants of Phileas Fogg III, great - grandson of the great globe - girdler of the legendary Around the World in 80 Days.
Fine Arts
Dist - FI Prod - CPC 1963

The Three Stooges in Orbit 87 MIN
U-matic / VHS / 16mm
B&W (I J H C)
Stars the Three Stooges as they become involved with an ultra - secret military weapon and the Martian spies determined to steal it.
Fine Arts
Dist - FI Prod - CPC 1962

The Three Stooges Meet Hercules 89 MIN
U-matic / VHS / 16mm
B&W (I J H C)
Stars the Three Stooges as they meet Hercules, the strongest hero in history. Describes how the three manage to make a shambles out of such serious matters as a minor war, gladiatorial combat and the ancient triremes with their slave - oarsmen rowing to the beat of a drum.
Fine Arts
Dist - FI Prod - CPC 1962

Three story suite 30 MIN
U-matic / VHS
Doris Chase concepts series
Color
Presents a trio of folktales performed by storyteller Laura Simms. Uses video effects to make visual the magic of these myths.
Fine Arts; Literature and Drama
Dist - WMEN Prod - CHASED

Three styles of marital conflict 14 MIN
VHS / 16mm
Color (C G PRO)
$255.00 purchase, $17.50, $16.00 rental _ #21929
Presents reenacted case studies based on clinical experience and research on common types of dysfunctional marital conflict - hidden agendas, the role of the aggressive partner, and the overadequate - inadequate partner.
Guidance and Counseling; Sociology
Dist - PSU Prod - RESPRC 1976
RESPRC

Three - Ten to Yuma 92 MIN
16mm
B&W
Shows how Western conventions are reversed with the heroic virtues portrayed in the character of the villain. The film pits Van Heflin's all - too - fallible dirt farmer against Glenn Ford's outlaw, whom Heflin has been hired to guard until the three - ten can take him away.
Fine Arts; History - United States
Dist - TIMLIF Prod - CON 1957

Three the Hard Way 92 MIN
16mm
Color (H C A)
Features Jim Brown as star and Gordon Parks, Jr as director in a study of the problems of three black business executives who are forced into a struggle with a secret racist organization.

Fine Arts; Sociology
Dist - CINEWO Prod - CINEWO 1974

Three Themes in Variation 4 MIN
16mm
B&W (A)
Presents squares and bars moving in careful rhythms to develop formal, contrapuntal themes. The animation was done with paper cut - outs photographed in stop - motion by Dwinell Grant.
Fine Arts
Dist - STARRC Prod - STARRC 1945

Three Thirty - Six 3 MIN
16mm
B&W
LC 76-701437
Shows a campus guard finding a suicide victim hanging in a storeroom.
Education; Sociology
Dist - SFRASU Prod - SFRASU 1975

Three times tables 25 MIN
VHS / U-matic
Better than new series
Color (H C A)
Demonstrates frame drop - leaf and pedestal tables in visits to a variety of old houses. Gives tips on repairing each type.
Fine Arts; Home Economics; Physical Education and Recreation
Dist - FI Prod - BBCTV

Three to Get Ready 25 MIN
VHS / U-matic
Color
Presents a filmed history of a group of children taken at various times during their first three years. Shows their mental and physical development, then a nursery school teacher tells and demonstrates how to prepare the unpredictable and sometimes assertive three - year - old for nursery school.
Home Economics; Psychology
Dist - MEDCOM Prod - MEDCOM

Three to Go 90 MIN
16mm
B&W (H C A)
LC 75-713559
Presents three stories, entitled Michael, Judy and Toula, which portray some of the problems of modern youth.
Psychology; Sociology
Dist - AUIS Prod - ANAIB 1971

Three to Go, Pt 1 - Michael 31 MIN
16mm
B&W (H C A)
Shows how a young man is caught between the opposing pulls of a conventional middle - class family and his pad - dwelling, pot - smoking friends.
Guidance and Counseling; Sociology
Dist - AUIS Prod - ANAIB 1971

Three to Go, Pt 3 - Toula 30 MIN
16mm
B&W (H C A)
Presents Toula, a Greek girl, whose family has been in Australia four years. Explains how she and her brother must reconcile the Greek and Australian way of life.
Sociology
Dist - AUIS Prod - ANAIB 1971

Three to Go, Pt 2 - Judy 30 MIN
16mm
B&W (H C A)
Presents the story of a young middle - class girl, in a country town, wanting to leave for the big city against the wishes of parents and boyfriends.
Guidance and Counseling; Sociology
Dist - AUIS Prod - ANAIB 1971

Three Track 18 MIN
16mm
Color (J)
Looks at a ski school for pupils with learning disabilities. Shows the pupils being taught by volunteer instructors from the Canadian Ski Alliance.
Education; Physical Education and Recreation; Psychology
Dist - NFBC Prod - NFBC 1979

Three trout to dream about and Minipi's discovery
VHS
Color (G)
$29.90 purchase _ #0387
Presents the first fishing film to be aired on a national television network. Features Lee Wulff who hooks and lands three great brook trout on a single cast with three flies on his leader in the Minipi area of Newfoundland.
Geography - World; Physical Education and Recreation; Science - Natural
Dist - SEVVID

3 - 2 - 1 Classroom contact - scientific investigation videodisc
Videodisc
Color (I)
$119.95 purchase _ #E566
Presents four science curriculum supplemental programs adapted from the television series 3 - 2 - 1 Contact that focus on the scientific method of investigation. Provides interactive capabilities to enhance presentations. Includes an index and teacher's guide with discussion ideas.
Science
Dist - GPN **Prod** - CTELWO 1993

3 - 2 - 1 Contact - architecture 150 MIN
VHS
Color (I J)
$110.00 purchase _ #E567
Presents five videos that focus on construction principles as seen in houses, tents, office buildings, birds' nests, and similar objects. Individual videos include Raising the Big Top, Home, Stack It Up, Made to Fit, and Light, But Strong. Set includes a teacher's guide for all five programs. Each program is 30 minutes in length.
Fine Arts; Science - Natural
Dist - GPN **Prod** - CTELWO

3 - 2 - 1 Contact Series
Exploring Weather, Climate and Seasons
Your Body Systems at Work
Dist - CHUMAN

Three - Two - One Contact Space - What's it Like Out There
U-matic / VHS
Color
Presents a visit to NASA's high - tech facilities as astronauts prepare for a space flight. Includes an interview with Sally Ride and views of the planets, with a discussion on the possibility of extraterrestrial life.
Science - Physical
Dist - GA **Prod** - CTELWO

The Three Types of Oxyacetylene Flames - Neutral, Oxidizing, Carburizing
U-matic / VHS
Oxyacetylene Welding - Spanish Series
Color (SPANISH)
Foreign Language; Industrial and Technical Education
Dist - VTRI **Prod** - VTRI

Three voices 5 MIN
16mm
Color (G)
$20.00 rental
Presents the second in a series shot from the filmmaker's apartment windows. Narrates possible scenarios of neighbor's lives as people move in and out of their apartments.
Fine Arts; Sociology
Dist - CANCIN **Prod** - KIRBYL 1983

The Three Ways and the Levels of Maturity 45 MIN
VHS / BETA
Psychological Growth and Spiritual Development Series
Color (G)
Psychology; Religion and Philosophy
Dist - DSP **Prod** - DSP

Three ways to draw a tree 30 MIN
VHS
Called - the ministry of teaching series
Color (G A R)
$39.95 purchase, $10.00 rental _ #35 - 860 - 2076
Offers tips in classroom instruction for teachers. Includes study guide. Hosted by Sharon Lee. Produced by Seraphim.
Education; Religion and Philosophy
Dist - APH

Three Wheeled Fairytale 20 MIN
16mm
Color
LC 70-713386
Presents a modern musical fairytale about a little girl and a meter maid who go out to find the world together.
Fine Arts; Literature and Drama
Dist - USC **Prod** - USC 1972

Three - Wire Handshake 30 MIN
U-matic / VHS
IEEE 488 Bus Series
Color (IND)
Shows how two or more asynchronous devices can communicate over same set of wires. Describes three - wire handshake flowchart by using a logic timing diagram.
Industrial and Technical Education; Mathematics; Sociology
Dist - COLOSU **Prod** - COLOSU

Three - wire service entrance 24 MIN
16mm
Electrical work - wiring series
B&W
LC FIE52-102
Describes how to mount and connect an outdoor meter connection box and a service control box, ground a three - wire service entrance installation and install a concentric service entrance cable.
Industrial and Technical Education
Dist - USNAC **Prod** - USOE 1945

Three Wise Boys 30 MIN
16mm
Color; B&W (P)
Tells a story about three boys who are brought face to face with meaning of Christmas when a destitute young couple and their sick baby take up temporary quarters in an abandoned farm house down the road.
Literature and Drama; Religion and Philosophy
Dist - FAMF **Prod** - FAMF

The Three wishes 8 MIN
VHS / U-matic
Timeless tales series
Color (P I)
$110.00, $160.00 purchase, $60.00 rental
Tells about a woodcutter who meets a fairy in a tree in the forest. Reveals that the fairy begs him to leave the tree alone in return for three wishes. Continues with the woodcutter and his wife who make grandiose plans for their future but end up squandering the wishes in foolish haste.
Guidance and Counseling; Literature and Drama
Dist - NDIM **Prod** - TIMTAL 1993

Three Women 110 MIN
VHS
Color (G) (MANDARIN CHINESE (ENGLISH SUBTITLES))
$45.00 purchase _ #6001A
Presents a Mandarin Chinese language movie produced in the People's Republic of China.
Fine Arts; Geography - World; Literature and Drama
Dist - CHTSUI **Prod** - CHTSUI

Three Women Alone 49 MIN
16mm
Color
LC 74-702518
Presents socio - economic profiles of three women pioneering their newly emerging role of women without men in today's society.
Guidance and Counseling; Sociology
Dist - SSC **Prod** - RKOTV 1974

The Three worlds of Bali 59 MIN
16mm
Color (G)
$600.00 purchase, $60.00 rental
Discloses that art permeates every aspect of daily life on the island of Bali. Examines Gamelan music, wayang - shadow puppet - theater, dance, elaborately constructed offerings of foods and flowers representing attempts to please gods and placate demons. Reveals that demons dwell in the watery underground, gods in the upper world and humans in the middle realm. Balinese religious practice is directed toward maintaining a balance of the worlds and balance between growth and decay. Records the 1979 ritual Eka Dasa Rudra, held once every 100 years, during which 11 demons - Rudra is the most powerful - must be transformed into beneficial spirits. Produced by Ira R Abrams and Michael Ambrosino.
Geography - World; Religion and Philosophy
Dist - DOCEDR **Prod** - DOCEDR

The Three Worlds of Bali 60 MIN
VHS
Odyssey Series
Color; Captioned (G)
$59.95 purchase _ #ODYS - 208
Explores daily life on the Indonesian island Bali. Displays examples of Balinese art, primarily in pageantry, poetry and song. Emphasizes the importance of art to the Balinese culture.
History - World
Dist - PBS **Prod** - PBA 1980

Three Worlds of Childhood 29 MIN
16mm
Color (H C A)
LC 81-701483
Presents Dr Urie Bronfenbrenner examining how children are raised in the Soviet Union, China and the United States. Offers suggestions for improving the American system of child rearing.
History - World; Home Economics; Sociology
Dist - CORNRS **Prod** - CORNRS 1975

The Three Worlds of Gulliver 100 MIN
16mm
Color (I J H C)
Stars Kerwin Mathews as the real - size Gulliver, traveling through the fabulous nation of beings only six to seven inches high, and then to Brobdingnag, the land of 40 - foo giants.
Literature and Drama
Dist - TIMLIF **Prod** - CPC 196

Three Years of Adolf Hitler
VHS / U-matic
Pre - War German Featurettes Series
B&W
Shows scenes of Hitler's speeches and colorful rallies in an effort to mold the image of the Fuehrer in the eyes of the average German citizen.
History - World
Dist - IHF **Prod** - IHF

The Threepenny opera 113 MIN
VHS
B&W (G)
$39.95 _ #THR110
Adapts the Threepenny Opera by Bertolt Brecht and Kurt Weill. Features a dark satire of respectable society, with dashing thieves, saucy prostitutes and lingering melodies. Directed by G W Pabst. Newly remastered with new subtitles.
Fine Arts; Literature and Drama; Sociology
Dist - HOMVIS **Prod** - JANUS 1931

Three's a Crowd 65 MIN
16mm
B&W (J)
Stars Harry Langdon in a story about an unmarried tenement boy who works long hours for a wagon owner, lives alone and dreams of having a wife and family.
Literature and Drama
Dist - TWYMAN **Prod** - MGM 1927

Threes on the threshold 20 MIN
VHS
Training for child care providers series
Color (H A)
$89.95 purchase _ #CEVK20363V
Discusses how to provide care for three - year olds. Focuses on the development stages of these children as they participate in outdoor activities, use a puppet stage, take risks by trying new things, and practice listening skills. Includes a leader's guide and reproducible study materials.
Health and Safety; Psychology
Dist - CAMV

Threes on the threshold 21 MIN
VHS
Color (H A T G)
$59.95 purchase _ #CV967
Examines the varying developmental stages of three year olds as they participate in outdoor activities, utilize a puppet stage, take risks by trying new things and practice their listening skills. Emphasizes the importance of providing activities which are appropriate for the individual as well as for the group. Guide available separately.
Fine Arts; Health and Safety; Home Economics; Psychology; Social Science
Dist - AAVIM **Prod** - AAVIM

Threshing Wheat 9 MIN
16mm
Mountain Peoples of Central Asia Series
B&W (P)
LC 73-702412
Shows the Tajik farmers threshing the wheat, as they drive their oxen to pull a wooden sledge over the grain in order to separate the grain from the husks.
Agriculture; Geography - World; Social Science
Dist - IFF **Prod** - IFF 1972

Threshing Wheat - Tajik 9 MIN
U-matic / VHS
Mountain Peoples of Central Asia (Afghanistan Series
B&W
Agriculture; Geography - World; History - World
Dist - IFF **Prod** - IFF

The Threshold 28 MIN
16mm
Color (C A)
LC 70-713504
A behind - the - scenes look at some unusual Spanish industries, both ancient and modern. Demonstrates how air cargo is contributing to the industrial progress of Spain.
Business and Economics; Geography - World; Social Science
Dist - MCDO **Prod** - MCDO 1971

Threshold 25 MIN
U-matic / VHS / 16mm
Color (H C A)
LC 70-711531
Presents a lyrical fantasy on the meanings of life and death.
Religion and Philosophy
Dist - PFP **Prod** - LEVINS 1970

Threshold 27 MIN
16mm
Color
LC 74-705788
Illustrates the relationship between research and medical care. Shows the broad scope of modern research - based anesthesiology - surgery, respiratory and intensive care units for the critically ill and the diagnosis and treatment of persistent pain.
Health and Safety; Science
Dist - USNAC **Prod** - USHHS 1969

The Threshold of Liberty 52 MIN
U-matic / VHS / 16mm
Shock of the New Series
Color (C A)
LC 80-700988
Discusses the impact of surrealism and shows examples of art and architecture produced by this movement, including the Ideal Temple built in rural France, the Watts Towers, and paintings by Miro, Dali, Magritte and others.
Fine Arts
Dist - TIMLIF **Prod** - BBCTV 1980

Threshold - the Blue Angels experience 89 MIN
VHS
Color (PRO H C A)
$59.95 purchase
Captures the excitement of special peak experiences encountered in the flight, with the Blue Angels Jet Aerobatic Airshow. Puts viewers in the cockpit of a 1600 mile per hour F - 4 Phantom, flying through violent buffeting jet streams in 8 - G formation aerobatics.
Industrial and Technical Education
Dist - PBS **Prod** - WNETTV

Thriller 35 MIN
16mm
Color (C)
Analyzes the cultural pattern of women as romantic victims in fiction using the opera 'La Boheme' as an example. Discusses how the opera, a classic example of this fiction, subtly sustains class and sexual stereotyping. Juxtaposes clips from the opera with references to suspense thrillers and other literary and psychoanalytic texts to communicate how these stereotypes cause real psychological damage. Produced by Sally Potter.
Fine Arts; Guidance and Counseling; Literature and Drama; Sociology
Dist - WMENIF **Prod** - SALPOT 1979

Thriving on chaos 60 MIN
VHS / U-matic
Color (COR)
$995.00, $895.00 purchase, $250.00 rental; $225.00 rental; $895.00, $995.00 purchase, $250.00 rental
Presents a one - hour overview of the three - part series Thriving on Chaos. Discusses the changes which have occurred in the workplace and the choices to be made in such volatile, complex economic circumstances. Shows how to cope with change and thrive on it. Features Tom Peters.
Business and Economics; Psychology; Sociology
Dist - MAGVID **Prod** - MAGVID 1989
DARTNL VPHI
EXTR

Thriving on Chaos - Part I 62 MIN
VHS / U-matic
Thriving on Chaos Series
Color (G PRO)
$895.00, $794.00 purchase, $225.00 rental
Shows the disorienting and invigorating aspects of chaos as well as considering present and futur change. Deals with management technology. Part 1 of a series of three on Thriving On Chaos by Tom Peters.
Business and Economics; Guidance and Counseling; Psychology
Dist - VPHI **Prod** - VPHI 1989

Thriving on chaos - Pt 1 65 MIN
VHS
Thriving on chaos series
Color (COR)
Features Tom Peters in an exploration of how businesses are adjusting to the chaotic situations they face. Suggests that constant change creates this chaos, and that not all companies are flexible enough to respond properly. Profiles three companies that are making it - Answer Products, SoftAd Group, and KG Retail Stores. Contains interviews with Joel Kotkin and Stanley M Davis.
Business and Economics
Dist - VLEARN **Prod** - VPHI
MAGVID MAGVID
VPHI VPHI
VICOM VICOM

Thriving on chaos - Part 2 - if it ain't broke, fix it anyway 60 MIN
VHS
Thriving on chaos series
Color (COR)
Features Tom Peters in an exploration of how businesses are adjusting to increased competition and information technologies. Suggests that successful companies will encourage taking risks and responding quickly to changes. Profiles four organizations that are doing so - MCI, the Social Security Administration, Bergen Brunswig, and KG Retail Stores. Interviews a host of experts, including Rosabeth Moss Kanter of Harvard Business School.
Business and Economics
Dist - VLEARN **Prod** - VPHI
MAGVID MAGVID
VPHI VLEARN
VICOM VICOM

Thriving on chaos - Pt 3 - brains are in 60 MIN
VHS
Thriving on chaos series
Color (COR)
Features Tom Peters in an exploration of how businesses and employees are adapting to an information - based economy. Profiles companies that have made successful adjustments, including QuadGraphics, CRSS, and the 3M facility in Austin, Texas. Interviews a host of experts, including Rosabeth Moss Kanter of Harvard Business School.
Business and Economics
Dist - VLEARN **Prod** - VPHI
MAGVID MAGVID
VPHI VICOM
VICOM

Thriving on chaos series
Thriving on chaos - Part 2 - if it ain't broke, fix it anyway 60 MIN
Thriving on chaos - Pt 1 65 MIN
Thriving on chaos - Pt 3 - brains are in 60 MIN
Dist - MAGVID
VICOM
VLEARN
VPHI

Thriving on chaos series
Presents the complete three - part series Thriving on Chaos. Discusses the dramatic changes which have occurred in the workplace and the choices to be made in such volatile, complex economic circumstances. Shows organizations how to cope with change and thrive on it. Features Tom Peters.
Thriving on chaos series 197 MIN
Dist - MAGVID **Prod** - MAGVID
VLEARN VPHI
VPHI

Thriving on Chaos Series
Thriving on Chaos - Part I 62 MIN
Dist - VPHI

Throat Culture 6 MIN
BETA / VHS / U-matic
Basic Clinical Laboratory Procedure Series
Color; Mono (C A)
Demonstrates proper equipment, procedures, attention to critical details and efficient, accurate methods for proper collection of specimens.
Health and Safety; Science
Dist - UIOWA **Prod** - UIOWA 1985

Thrombectomy for ileofemoral and axillary vein thrombosis 25 MIN
16mm
Color (PRO)
Shows how venous thrombosis in the early stages is properly treated by anticoagulants. Demonstrates two procedures, one for iliofemoral thrombosis and one for axillary vein thrombosis.
Health and Safety
Dist - ACY **Prod** - ACYDGD 1964

Thrombin clotting time - fibrinogen assay 13 MIN
U-matic / VHS
Blood coagulation laboratory techniques series
Color
LC 79-707606
Describes the use of thrombin clotting time as a tool for monitoring heparin therapy and a simple, rapid assay for clottable fibrinogens. Demonstrates selected blood coagulation methods.
Health and Safety; Science
Dist - UMICH **Prod** - UMICH 1977

Thrombolytic therapy in the treatment of MI 30 MIN
VHS
Color (PRO C)
$285.00 purchase, $70.00 rental _ #6534
Emphasizes the key role nurses play in assessing and identifying the myocardial infarction - MI - patient who is a candidate for thrombolytic therapy. Overviews thrombolytic therapy as the current standard for treatment of acute MI. Discusses methods used to identify the patient, including patient history, physical examination and diagnostic tests. Reviews current methods and expanded indications for thrombolytics in relation to infarct location, criteria for patient selection, contraindications, expanded indications and complications. Provides practical information for administration of thrombolytics, monitoring after therapy and evaluation of patient outcomes. Dramatizes a patient arrival in the ER to clarify key concepts.
Health and Safety
Dist - AJN **Prod** - HESCTV

Thrombosis, embolism and infarction 12 MIN
VHS
Color (G)
$89.95 purchase _ #UW3419
Introduces a conceptual framework for understanding the phenomena of thrombosis, embolism and infarction. Uses computer graphics to stress the generalized nature of the processes involved.
Health and Safety
Dist - FOTH

Throne of blood 105 MIN
Videodisc
B&W; CAV (G) (JAPANESE WITH ENGLISH SUBTITLES)
$89.95 purchase _ #CC1252L
Presents an adaptation of Shakespeare's Macbeth set in 16th century Japan during the Sengoky civil wars. Combines the energy and pacing of the modern American Western with the stylization of Japanese Noh theater. Directed by Akira Kurosawa.
Literature and Drama
Dist - IHF **Prod** - IHF 1957
CHTSUI

Throne of blood - first meeting with the spirit 12 MIN
16mm
Film study extracts series
Color
Presents the story of Washizu and Miki who are on their way home from battle when they get lost in a labyrinthine forest where they meet a spirit who prophesies Washizu's ascendancy and the succession by Miki's son. Designed to create images of symbolic meaning which give visual expression to the themes and motifs of Shakespeare's Macbeth without retaining any of the original text.
Fine Arts
Dist - FI

Through a father's eyes - a birth film for both parents 22 MIN
VHS
Color (G)
$295.00 purchase, $45.00 rental
Acknowledges the feelings of men and shows a diverse group of men actively participating in the births of their babies. Presents four deliveries, including a nurse - midwife assisted delivery in a hospital setting without medical intervention and using a variety of labor positions; an overdue, induced delivery showing the use of pitocin and an epidural; a delivery illustrating breathing techniques with a minimum of pain medication and a husband acting as the labor coach; and a couple using massage and other techniques to minimize discomfort. Shows warm, moving examples of how a father can support and reassure his partner, no matter what may happen as the birth experience unfolds, giving a variety of positive role models with which men can identify.
Health and Safety; Sociology
Dist - POLYMR **Prod** - FIE

Through a glass darkly 90 MIN
VHS
B&W (G)
$29.95 purchase _ #THR100
Studies one family's search for God in a time of crisis. Follows Karin, a young woman who finds little respite from her schizophrenia when she vacations with her husband, father, and adolescent brother. The first film of Ingmar Bergman's religious trilogy, which also includes Winter Light and The Silence. Digitally remastered.
Fine Arts; Psychology; Religion and Philosophy; Sociology
Dist - HOMVIS **Prod** - JANUS 1961

Through a Glass Darkly 480 MIN
U-matic / VHS
Color (G)
$15.50 rental _ #2131 - A
Presents upper - class families of 18th century England and France. Tells the story of Barbara Alderley, her grandmother, mother and the man she loves.
Fine Arts; History - World
Dist - BKSOTP **Prod** - BKSOTP 1988

Through Adam's Eyes 13 MIN
16mm
B&W
LC 78-701576
Presents a portrait of a 7 - year - old boy who underwent dramatic facial reconstructive surgery.

Health and Safety
Dist - TEMPLU **Prod** - SAGETB 1978

Through all time 58 MIN
VHS / 16mm
Color (G)
$70.00 rental _ #TALT - 000
Documents the search for community and the quality of life in the American small town. Illustrates the character of the small town and the changes it has undergone. Presented in two parts.
Social Science; Sociology
Dist - PBS **Prod** - KPBS

Through and through 63 MIN
16mm
Color & B&W (G)
$100.00 purchase
Deals with control and anger and the pressure of history on one's identity in relation to a man and woman's relationship. Presents a visual, perceptual production of common human struggles, focusing on life and death. A Barbara Sternberg production.
Psychology; Sociology
Dist - CANCIN

Through animal eyes 50 MIN
VHS / 16mm
Color (J H)
Attempt to visualize the natural world through various animal eyes, using special video techniques and cameras. Presents images as seen by a chameleon's eyes moving in two directions at once, a night hunting animal seeking prey in the dark and the compound eyes of shrimp, crabs and insects.
Science - Natural
Dist - FI **Prod** - WNETTV
BBCENE

Through Artists' Eyes Series
Caravaggio - the crucifixion of St Andrew 12 MIN
David - Brutus 11 MIN
Poussin - Le Deluge 8 MIN
Velasquez - Las Meninas 9 MIN
Vermeer - Woman Holding a Balance 13 MIN
Dist - AFA

Through Conflict to Negotiation 47 MIN
U-matic / VHS / 16mm
Organizing for Power - the Alinsky Approach Series
B&W
LC 77-706606
Shows what occurs when a community action group in Rochester, New York, confronts the largest employer in the community on the issue of corporate responsibility and employment of minority groups.
History - United States; Psychology; Social Science; Sociology
Dist - FI **Prod** - NFBC 1970

Through Different Eyes 15 MIN
16mm
Color (H C A)
LC 79-709689
Features retarded children in a day - training program receiving specialized training for their handicaps. Emphasizes need of retarded children for training and highlights the areas in which training must be applied. Examines social needs of the children as well as the impact a retarded child has on the rest of the family.
Education; Guidance and Counseling; Psychology; Sociology
Dist - PCHENT **Prod** - PECKM 1970

Through gates of splendor 36 MIN
16mm
Color
Tells the story of five young missionaries killed by the Aucas in Ecuador, and presents film taken on the beach by the men themselves shortly before they were killed. Narrated by Betty Elliott, who with her small daughter went to live among the people who killed her husband.
History - World; Religion and Philosophy
Dist - GF **Prod** - YOUTH

Through Grandpa's Eyes 20 MIN
U-matic / VHS / 16mm
Color (K P I G)
$470, $330, $360 _ #A448
Deals with the bond between a blind man and his grandson. Discusses different ways of seeing the world.
Literature and Drama; Psychology
Dist - BARR **Prod** - BARR 1987

Through Heaven's Gate 30 MIN
U-matic
Color
Dramatizes the encounter between a black man and a white man in the subterranean depths of the New York transit system.
Psychology; Sociology
Dist - BLKFMF **Prod** - BLKFMF

Through hell and high water 60 MIN
VHS
Color & B&W (G)
$24.99 purchase
Focuses on the Merchant Marine's role during World War II.
History - United States
Dist - DANEHA **Prod** - DANEHA 1993

Through joy and beyond - the life of C S Lewis 60 MIN
VHS
Color (G R)
$39.95 purchase _ #S02183; $39.95 purchase, $10.00 rental _ #35-82033-8936
Recalls the life and work of Oxford don and Christian author C S Lewis. Combines live footage of important sites, photographs of Lewis and his friends, and narratives from a friend to give additional insight into Lewis. Features Peter Ustinov reading excerpts from Lewis's works.
Guidance and Counseling; Literature and Drama; Religion and Philosophy
Dist - UILL
APH

Through joy and beyond - the life of C S Lewis - Pt 1 - the formative years 52 MIN
16mm
Color (H C A)
LC 79-700593
Documents the life, works and times of author C S Lewis.
Biography; Literature and Drama
Dist - YOUTH **Prod** - LRDKNG 1979

Through joy and beyond - the life of C S Lewis - Pt 2 - the informed years 52 MIN
16mm
Color (H C A)
LC 79-700593
Documents the life, works and times of author C S Lewis.
Biography; Literature and Drama
Dist - YOUTH **Prod** - LRDKNG 1979

Through joy and beyond - the life of C S Lewis - Pt 3 - Jack remembered 54 MIN
16mm
Color (H C A)
LC 79-700593
Documents the life, works and times of author C S Lewis.
Biography; Literature and Drama
Dist - YOUTH **Prod** - LRDKNG 1979

Through madness 30 MIN
VHS
Color (H C G)
$295.00 purchase, $55.00 rental
Investigates the psychotic illnesses of schizophrenia and manic depression. Focuses on three victims of psychosis - Eileen, a once promising actress now living in a half - way house with a severe form of schizophrenia requiring a sheltered atmosphere; Lionel, former NFL star with the Green Bay Packers diagnosed as paranoid schizophrenic anf once forced to live on the streets; and Joe, troubled with dilusions and hallucinations since childhood, diagnosed as manic - depressive, who describes with his wife their struggles with sickness and recovery. Includes original music and narration by Elizabeth Swados. Produced by Dr Kenneth Paul Rosenberg, psychiatrist.
Psychology
Dist - FLMLIB

Through media 36 MIN
U-matic / VHS
Active learning for youth series
Color
Introduces the novice or experienced media person to the numerous uses of readily available media tools. Focuses on church youth group training.
Religion and Philosophy; Sociology
Dist - ECUFLM **Prod** - UMCOM

Through moon and stars and night skies
VHS
Reading rainbow series; No 89
Color; CC (K P)
$39.95 purchase
Tells about a family formed through adoption in the story by Ann Turner, illustrated by James Graham Hale. Features people from everywhere talking about the ups and downs of life as fathers, mothers, sisters, brothers and more - a show everyone can 'relate' to. Part of a series offering a multicultural approach to generating reading enthusiasm with cross - curricular applications, hosted by LeVar Burton.
English Language; Sociology
Dist - GPN **Prod** - LNMDP

Through my eyes - Kilkenny 31 MIN
16mm
Through my eyes series
Color (T)
LC 75-702394
Illustrates the open plan school technique at the primary school level using the example of Kilkenny Primary School in Kilkenny, South Australia.
Education
Dist - AUIS **Prod** - FLMAUS 1974

Through my eyes series
Through my eyes - Kilkenny 31 MIN
Through my eyes - Stradbroke 26 MIN
Dist - AUIS

Through my eyes - Stradbroke 26 MIN
16mm
Through my eyes series
Color (T)
LC 75-702395
Examines the operation of an open plan school system at the infants school level using the example of Stradbroke Infants School in Stradbroke, South Australia.
Education
Dist - AUIS **Prod** - FLMAUS 1974

Through simulation games 47 MIN
VHS / U-matic
Active learning for youth series
Color
Describes the value of simulation games. Illustrates this method of learning which church youth groups can play.
Religion and Philosophy; Sociology
Dist - ECUFLM **Prod** - UMCOM

Through the genetic maze 60 MIN
U-matic / VHS
Color (H C G T A)
Explores the ethical implications of genetic technology and the care of the genetically defective. The issues raised by this technology are discussed by parents, genetic counselors, doctors, government administrators, ethicists, and religious leaders. Study guides available.
Health and Safety; Religion and Philosophy; Science - Natural
Dist - PSU **Prod** - PSU 1982

Through the Genetic Maze Series
Beautiful baby boy, but 60 MIN
A 50 - 50 chance 60 MIN
To Build Our Future 60 MIN
A Two Edged Sword 60 MIN
We Can Decide 60 MIN
Dist - PSU

Through the hoop - corporate teambuilding 20 MIN
VHS / 16mm
Color (COR)
$495.00 purchase, $150.00 rental, $45.00 preview; $495.00 purchase, $150.00 rental
Uses the example of the Chicago Bulls basketball team to demonstrate principles of corporate teambuilding. Motivates members of an organization to work together. Includes a teacher's guide and ten pocket guides.
Business and Economics; Education; Psychology
Dist - UTM **Prod** - UTM
VLEARN EBEC

Through the language barrier series
Alone - with language 15 MIN
At home - with language 15 MIN
Early experience 15 MIN
In the Beginning 15 MIN
Venturing Out 15 MIN
Dist - ACCESS

Through the Lens 30 MIN
VHS / U-matic
In Our Own Image Series
Color (C)
Fine Arts
Dist - DALCCD **Prod** - DALCCD

Through - the - lock - cylinders and key tools 22 MIN
VHS
Forcible entry video series
Color (IND)
$159.95 purchase _ #35609
Demonstrates the simplicity of locks. Shows the tumblers mechanism. Explains the two simple tool shapes. One part of a five - part series that is a teaching companion for IFSTA's Forcible Entry manual.
Health and Safety; Science - Physical; Social Science
Dist - OKSU **Prod** - FIREEN

Through the Looking Glass 10 MIN
16mm
Color
Presents new abstract forms by applying principles of distortion to familiar forms and principles of nature.
Fine Arts
Dist - RADIM **Prod** - DAVISJ

Through the looking glass and Video 13 47 MIN
VHS
Secrets of science series; Physical science
Color (I J H C)
$49.95 purchase
Presents two parts in two segments each, tracing the evolution of telescopes and explaining how they work, showing how photography captures images on film and how telescopes and cameras work together to see far into space. Looks at how television works and influences human life and the many tasks performed by satellites in space. Includes About Telescopes; Focus on Photography and Looking Into Deep Space in Part I, On Television and Surrounded by Satellites in Part II. Hosted by Discover Magazine Editor in Chief Paul Hoffman. Third of four parts on physical science.
Fine Arts; Industrial and Technical Education; Science - Physical
Dist - EFVP **Prod** - DSCOVM 1994

Through the Looking Glass Darkly 51 MIN
16mm
Spectrum Series
Color
LC 74-700380
Presents a historical documentary on the black man in Oklahoma.
Geography - United States; History - United States; Sociology
Dist - WKYTV **Prod** - WKYTV 1973

Through the looking glass - introduction - Caedmon's hymm 45 MIN
U-matic / VHS
Survey of English literature I series
Color (H C)
Introduces English literature by analyzing the content of Caedmon's Hymm.
Literature and Drama
Dist - MDCPB **Prod** - MDCPB

Through the Magic Mirror 12 MIN
16mm
Color
LC 74-700511
Presents a series of vignettes about the dental future of infants in which all adult roles, except that of the dentist, are played by children.
Health and Safety; Psychology
Dist - ASODFC **Prod** - ASODFC 1973

Through the mask - oceanography 25 MIN
U-matic / VHS
Color
Takes viewers to underwater worlds ranging from a Paris pond to a Red Sea reef.
Science - Physical
Dist - DAVFMS **Prod** - DAVFMS

Through the Milky Way 19 MIN
VHS
Color (G)
$60.00 rental, $250.00 purchase
Looks at a Korean woman's experience of emigrating to Hawaii at the turn of the century and her sense of displacement arising from the conflict between native identity and adopted culture. Features two women who may represent a mother and a daughter, different stages of one person's life or Native Land and New Land. By Yun - ah Hong.
Fine Arts; Sociology
Dist - WMEN

Through the Northwest Passage 28 MIN
16mm
Color (J H)
Documents the well - publicized voyage of the S S Manhattan, through the Northwest Passage to Alaska's north slope. Explains that in addition to shipping crude oil to eastern markets, the ship was a floating laboratory of oceanographers and geologists.
Geography - United States; Science - Physical
Dist - MTP **Prod** - HUMBLE

Through the Pages Series no 10
Lafcadio, the Lion who Shot Back 15 MIN
Dist - GPN

Through the pages series no 3
Anansi, the spider man 15 MIN
Dist - GPN

Through the Pages Series no 5
Mummies made in Egypt 15 MIN
Dist - GPN

Through the Pages Series no 7
What's the Big Idea, Ben Franklin 15 MIN
Dist - GPN

Through the pages series
Family secrets - five very important stories 15 MIN
The Great Pete Penny 15 MIN
How I hunted the little fellows 15 MIN
Jabberwocky / the Ice Cream Cone Coot and Other Rare Birds 15 MIN
Jumanji 15 MIN
Poetry 15 MIN
Dist - GPN

Through the Spring 29 MIN
U-matic
Edible Wild Plants Series
Color
Discusses eight unusual edible wild plants. Shows where to find them.
Health and Safety; Science - Natural
Dist - UMITV **Prod** - UMITV 1978

Through the Tian Shan Mountains by rail 60 MIN
VHS
Silk road series; Vol 9
Color (G)
$29.95 purchase _ #CMP1011; $29.95 purchase _ #CPM1056V-S
Travels by rail through the Tian Shan Mountains along the fabled Silk Road linking Europe and China and traveled by Marco Polo. Features the art, culture, and history of the residents and a soundtrack by Kitaro. Part of a series.
Geography - World; History - World
Dist - CHTSUI
CAMV

Through the wire 68 MIN
16mm / VHS
Color (J H G)
$1000.00, $350.00 purchase, $100.00 rental
Documents the history of an alleged secret political prison in the US. Reveals that in 1986 a high security unit was opened in the underground chamber of the federal prison in Lexington, Kentucky. Its only inmates, Silvia Baraldini, Susan Rosenberg and Alejandrina Torres, received sentences of 43, 58 and 35 years respectively, for non - violent, politically - motivated crimes. Discusses the treatment these women received during incarceration. Features Susan Sarandon as narrator.
Civics and Political Systems; Sociology
Dist - CNEMAG **Prod** - ROSWHI 1990

Through this darkest night 12 MIN
U-matic / VHS
Color & B&W (C G)
$50.00, $40.00 purchase _ #EVC - 737, #EHC - 737
Discloses the tragedy of reservation life for generations of Native Americans. Uses archival photographs and documentary film footage as three voices recount experiences that spelled the destruction of a culture.
Social Science
Dist - ADL **Prod** - ADL

Through young people's eyes 29 MIN
16mm / U-matic / VHS
Color (J)
Looks at the daily lives of poor urban Black and Hispanic teenagers, primarily girls. Uses candid interviews to explore the advantages and disadvantages of adolescence in a poor urban neighborhood.
Sociology
Dist - CNEMAG **Prod** - RMMB 1983

Throw away the key 29 MIN
VHS
America's drug forum second season series
Color (G)
$19.95 purchase _ #202
Asks if new mandatory prison terms for drug crimes - ten years in prison without hope for parole for a first time drug offense - are a deterrent to the crime. Looks at who is going to jail and whether or not sentences are meted out impartially. Considers whether overburdened United States prisons can handle the load of the new laws. Guests include William Otis, assistant United States attorney, Kevin Zeese, former criminal defense attorney and currently counsel of the Drug Policy Foundation, Victoria Toensing, former deputy attorney general, Richard Rehbock, criminal defense attorney.
Civics and Political Systems; Health and Safety; Sociology
Dist - DRUGPF **Prod** - DRUGPF 1992

Throw Me a Rainbow 12 MIN
16mm
Color
Relates the story of some elderly women who love to paint and how they are affected by the appearance of noted art collector Joseph Hirshhorn.
Fine Arts
Dist - CELLAR **Prod** - CELLAR

Throwaway Kids - the Oklahoma Department of Health Services 20 MIN
U-matic / VHS
Color
$335.00 purchase
From the ABC TV program, 20 - 20.
Sociology
Dist - ABCLR **Prod** - ABCLR 1982

Throwaway people 60 MIN
VHS
Frontline series
Color; Captioned (G)
$300.00 purchase, $95.00 rental _ #FRON - 805K
Shows how Shaw, a historic African - American neighborhood in Washington, D C has become plagued by drugs, death and poverty. Reviews Shaw's glorious past as the home of Duke Ellington, women's rights advocates, educators and attorneys who fought segregation.
Sociology
Dist - PBS **Prod** - DOCCON 1990

Throwaway world 20 MIN
U-matic
Challenge to science series
Color (J H C)
Examines the components of garbage with the aim of recycling and reusing waste. Viewers are challenged to develop a system that produces little or no garbage.
Science - Natural; Sociology
Dist - TVOTAR **Prod** - TVOTAR 1985

Throwing 25 MIN
VHS / U-matic
Craft of the Potter Series
Color (H C A)
Demonstrates different types of pottery wheels - hand, kick and power - and how to throw different clay bodies on the wheel. Shows stoneware being prepared and thrown and porcelain being thrown in a variety of shapes.
Fine Arts
Dist - FI **Prod** - BBCTV

Throwing 11 MIN
16mm / U-matic / VHS
Craftsmanship in Clay Series
Color
Demonstrates the shaping of various clay pieces on a potter's wheel, showing each step in making a bowl and special steps in completing a low, flat plate and pitcher.
Fine Arts
Dist - IU **Prod** - IU 1950

Throwing and catching
VHS
Children and movement video series
Color (H A T)
$29.95 purchase _ #MK805
Teaches about throwing and catching skills in children ages 3 to 6 years old. Part of a five - part series which guides in conducting physical education programs.
Physical Education and Recreation; Psychology
Dist - AAVIM **Prod** - AAVIM 1992

The Throwing Events - Men 21 MIN
U-matic / VHS / 16mm
LeRoy Walker Track and Field - Men Series
Color (J H C)
Emphasizes correct form and technique for the discus, shot and javelin. Provides drills and coaching points.
Physical Education and Recreation
Dist - ATHI **Prod** - ATHI 1976

The Throwing Events - Women 20 MIN
U-matic / VHS / 16mm
LeRoy Walker Track and Field - Women Series
Color (J H C)
Presents the discus, shot and javelin events showing correct form, technique and recommended drills. Shows key points to help the competitor reach the highest performance levels.
Physical Education and Recreation
Dist - ATHI **Prod** - ATHI 1976

Throwing on the Run 11 MIN
16mm
B&W (J H)
Features coach John Mc Kay of the University of Southern California who discusses the football technique of throwing on the run.
Physical Education and Recreation
Dist - COCA **Prod** - BOR

Throwing Pitchers, Pulling Handles 28 MIN
Videoreel / VT2
Wheels, Kilns and Clay Series
Color
Features Mrs Peterson describing certain ceramic processes for her classroom at the University of Southern California. Demonstrates how to throw pitchers and pull handles.
Fine Arts
Dist - PBS **Prod** - USC

Throwing - Pt 1 29 MIN
Videoreel / VT2

Exploring the crafts - pottery series
Color
Features Mrs Vivika Heino introducing and demonstrating basic techniques in throwing.
Fine Arts
Dist - PBS **Prod** - WENHTV

Throwing - Pt 2 29 MIN
Videoreel / VT2
Exploring the crafts - pottery series
Color
Features Mrs Vivika Heino introducing and demonstrating basic techniques in throwing.
Fine Arts
Dist - PBS **Prod** - WENHTV

Thru the Eyes of a Child 30 MIN
16mm
Color
LC 73-700799
Shows the floats, bands and horses of the Rose Parade held in Pasadena, California, on New Years Day, 1971.
Civics and Political Systems; Social Science; Sociology
Dist - TRA **Prod** - TRA 1971

Thru the Mirror 8 MIN
U-matic / VHS / 16mm
Mickey Mouse - the Early Years Series
Color (K P I J H)
LC 78-701072
Presents Mickey Mouse in an adaptation of the book Through The Looking Glass by Lewis Carroll. Tells how Mickey falls asleep and dreams that he steps through the mirror into a world where furniture comes to life and where he has to do battle with a pack of cards.
Fine Arts
Dist - CORF **Prod** - DISNEY 1978

Thrufeed grinding a straight pin 29 MIN
16mm
Machine shop work series; Operations on the centerless grinding machine; No 1
B&W
LC FIE52-8
Explains the principle of centerless grinding and describes the basic elements of the centerless grinding machine. Shows how to set up the machine and true the grinding and regulating wheels.
Industrial and Technical Education
Dist - USNAC **Prod** - USOE 1944

Thrufeed grinding a straight pin 28 MIN
16mm
Machine shop work series; Operations on the centerless grinding machine; No 2
B&W
LC FIE52-1
Shows how to balance the grinding wheel, position work for grinding, adjust work guides, take a trial grind, eliminate taper in the grinding wheel, use a crown cam to dress the grinding wheel and check the workpieces.
Industrial and Technical Education
Dist - USNAC **Prod** - USOE 1944

Thulani 26 MIN
16mm / U-matic / VHS
Doris Chase concepts series
(H C A)
Explores the variety of critical issues and experiences facing women today.
Sociology
Dist - CHASED **Prod** - CHASED 1984

Thulani Davis - 4 - 13 - 85 80 MIN
VHS / Cassette
Poetry Center reading series
Color (G)
$15.00, $45.00 purchase, $15.00 rental _ #635 - 533
Features African - American writer Thulani Davis participating in a panel discussion on New Issues at the Women Working in Literature conference at the Poetry Center, San Francisco State University.
Literature and Drama
Dist - POETRY **Prod** - POETRY 1985

Thumb Nail Sketches 29 MIN
U-matic
Artist at Work Series
Color
Focuses on arranging and rearranging one's picture.
Fine Arts
Dist - UMITV **Prod** - UMITV 1973

Thumb reconstruction by fifth digit transportation 20 MIN
16mm
Color
LC FIA66-68
Discusses three methods of thumb reconstruction. Illustrates digit migration on neurovascular pedicles in four subjects exhibiting various results of series trauma. Shows surgically, graphically and with follow - up demonstration the provision of a hand with a reconstructed thumb.
Health and Safety
Dist - EATONL **Prod** - EATONL 1964

Thumb reconstruction by toe transfer 15 MIN
16mm
Color
LC FIA66-69
Illustrates the successful transplantation of the second toe to the residual head of the proximal phalanx. Pictures the seven - year follow - up which shows excelent growth of the distal phalanges and shaft.
Health and Safety
Dist - EATONL **Prod** - EATONL 1960

Thumbelina 10 MIN
16mm
Lotte Reiniger's Animated Fairy Tales Series
B&W (K P I)
Presents the fairy tale Thumbelina in animated silhouette form. Based on the live shadow plays Lotte Reiniger produced for BBC Television.
Literature and Drama
Dist - MOMA **Prod** - PRIMP 1955

Thumbelina 9 MIN
U-matic / VHS / 16mm
Classic Tales Retold Series
Color (P I)
LC 77-700692
Presents the Hans Christian Andersen story of Thumbelina, about a tiny girl who encounters many unusual experiences before she finds the home where she really belongs.
Fine Arts; Literature and Drama
Dist - PHENIX **Prod** - PHENIX 1977

Thumbelina 16 MIN
U-matic / VHS / 16mm
Color (K P)
$385.00, $250.00 purchase _ #4186
Explains how a miniature girl escapes marriage to an ugly toad and a mole by flying to a faraway country on the back of a dove. Relates how she meets a king who is just her size.
Fine Arts; Literature and Drama
Dist - CORF **Prod** - CORF 1981

Thumbelina 30 MIN
VHS
Rabbit ears collection series
Color (K P I J)
$12.95 purchase _ #095225
Features actress Kelly McGillis narrating this Hans Christian Anderson fairy tale.
Literature and Drama
Dist - KNOWUN **Prod** - RABBIT

The Thumbnail sketch 29 MIN
U-matic
Sketching techniques series; Lesson 5
Color (C A)
Teaches how to think with a pencil. Shows how to jot down the main idea of a sketch with the greatest economy of time.
Fine Arts
Dist - CDTEL **Prod** - COAST

Thumbnail sketches 7 MIN
16mm
Color (G)
$20.00 rental
Demonstrates the transformation of some images from a flipbook, with each page containing a cyle of eight drawings in a rectangular ring, through cutting the drawings apart with scissors and performing a brief 'autopsy' illustrating the mechanics of movement, to the eventual animated rebirth. Suggests that a moving line is not as simple as it seems. Produced by George Griffin.
Fine Arts
Dist - CANCIN

Thumbs Down - Hitchhiking 17 MIN
U-matic / VHS / 16mm
Color (P)
LC 74-703270
Demonstrates the variety of potential dangers to both the hitchhiker and driver, using dramatizations of hitchhiking and interviews with victims of hitchhiking - related crimes and accidents.
Guidance and Counseling; Health and Safety; Sociology
Dist - ALTSUL **Prod** - ALTSUL 1974

Thumbs up for kids - AIDS education
16mm / VHS
Color (K P)
$250.00, $445.00 purchase, $75.00 rental _ #8160
Teaches preschool and primary children about disease prevention in general and about AIDS in particular. Features Ruby Petersen, former 'Romper Room' teacher and producer.
Health and Safety
Dist - AIMS **Prod** - MEDIEX 1990

Thunder and lightning 14 MIN
U-matic / 16mm / VHS
Color (K P I)
$350.00, $275.00, $245.00 purchase _ #A610
Uses clay animation to portray the Hopi creation story. Tells of a young god Kowitoma, from the dark underworld, who desperately longs to see the world above where there is sun and light. Depicts his journey to this world through three other worlds and the challenges he faces, including the trickster Coyote. When he arrives, Kowitoma performs a rain dance, rain begins to fall and a rainbow appears, a blessing from the rain gods. Produced by Dr Jon Nordlicht.
Fine Arts; Social Science
Dist - BARR

Thunder in Munich 28 MIN
U-matic / VHS / 16mm
Insight Series
B&W (H C A)
LC 70-705449
Tells of a German war hero who faces a crisis of conscience when confronted with the anti - semitic policies of the Third Reich.
Guidance and Counseling; Psychology
Dist - PAULST **Prod** - PAULST 1965

Thunder in my head 30 MIN
VHS
Saying goodbye - on bereavement series
Color (H C G)
$295.00 purchase, $55.00 rental
Portrays a young woman's journey through the grief of widowhood. Reveals that Becky's husband was killed in an automobile accident. Illustrates that her insistence on going to the morgue to identify the body helps her confront death and adjust to reality. Part of a series on bereavement produced in cooperation with Insight Production.
Guidance and Counseling; Sociology
Dist - FLMLIB **Prod** - TVOTAR 1990

Thunder in the dells 28 MIN
VHS
Color (G)
$19.95 purchase
Social Science
Dist - CARECS

Thunder in the skies 52 MIN
16mm / U-matic / VHS
Connections series; No 6
Color (H C A)
LC 79-700861
Details the changes in building construction and energy usage which occurred when the climate of Europe changed dramatically in the 13th century. Shows how the scarcity of firewood contributed to the invention of the steam engine, which was the predecessor of gasoline - powered engines.
History - World; Sociology
Dist - TIMLIF **Prod** - BBCTV 1979
AMBROS

Thunder in the Skies 60 MIN
VHS / U-matic
Spaceflight Series
Color (GERMAN)
Traces the early history of man's adventures in space, including the career of inventor Robert Goddard, the early development of the rocket as a weapon of war in Germany, pilot Chuck Yeager's breaking the sound barrier, the launching of the Soviet satellite, Sputnik 1. Details the challenge to America's technical excellence, the formation of N A S A, and the selection of the Mercury astronauts.
Science - Physical
Dist - PBS **Prod** - PBS

Thunder mountain 15 MIN
16mm
Color; B&W (G)
Presents vacationers on a trail ride into the Idaho Wilderness Area where they experience the mountains and forests at their midsummer best. Features wildflowers, lakes and streams, big game wildlife. Shows the presence of good fishing in this place where only foot travel is permitted. Contains scenes of the pack horses negotiating the crossing of wild alpine streams and the old town of Roosevelt, which lies at the bottom of a clear mountain lake.
Geography - United States; Physical Education and Recreation
Dist - FO **Prod** - FO 1961

Thunder out of Asia 12 MIN
16mm
Screen news digest series; Vol 8; Issue 8
B&W
Presents a biography of Mao Tse Tung and his rise to power in China.

History - World
Dist - AFA Prod - AFA 1966

Thunder out of China 20 MIN
U-matic / VHS
B&W (J H C)
Documents the Japanese - Chinese war that preceded America's entry into the Pacific war.
History - World
Dist - IHF Prod - IHF

Thunderbird 23 MIN
16mm
B&W (J A)
LC FIA68-2355
Retells the Indian legend of the thunderbird on Mount Olympus and pictures the lore of the Indians of Northwest. Shows how Indians hew a sea - going canoe from a cedar log. Includes views of sea lions, of seagull hatching and of a traditional hunt from an open canoe.
Literature and Drama; Social Science
Dist - RARIG Prod - RARIG 1963

The Thunderbirds 6 MIN
16mm
Color (I)
LC 77-700967
Shows historical highlights of the U S Air Force Thunderbirds in action, without narration.
Civics and Political Systems; Industrial and Technical Education
Dist - USNAC Prod - USAF 1975

Thunderbirds - a team portrait
VHS
Color (G)
$19.95 purchase _ #EK104
Presents aerial and in - cockpit footage of the USAF's precision flying team.
Social Science
Dist - SIV

The Thunderbirds - supersonic thunderbirds - crossover 35 MIN
U-matic / VHS
Color
Presents the Thunderbirds flying various aircraft from the 4 - 84G through the 44 - E. Shows the jet aerobats flying Super Sabres in power climbs, cloverleaf turns, loops, 360 - degree turns and the 'bomb burst.' Presents a documentary of the Thunderbirds on a goodwill tour of South America giving aerial demonstrations.
Industrial and Technical Education; Physical Education and Recreation
Dist - IHF Prod - IHF

Thunderbolt 43 MIN
16mm
Color
LC 74-705789
Tells the story of the members of the 57th Fighter Group participating in Operation Strangle in Italy in 1944 while flying the P - 47 Thunderbolt fighter - bomber from bases in Corsica.
Civics and Political Systems; Industrial and Technical Education
Dist - USNAC Prod - USAF 1946

Thunderbolt 45 MIN
VHS
Color (H G)
Relates the activities of the 57th Fighter Group during Operation Strangle, which destroyed vital supply routes behind German lines in World War II. Features introduction by James Stewart and narration by Lloyd Bridges.
History - United States; Industrial and Technical Education
Dist - IHF Prod - IHF

The Thunderbolts - Ramrod to Emden 33 MIN
16mm
B&W
LC 75-700590
Shows the planning for an escort of P - 47 airplanes to accompany a bombing mission over Emden, German, during World War II. Includes combat scenes showing fighters downing German planes and shows the pilots being debriefed after the mission.
History - World
Dist - USNAC Prod - USAF 1943

Thundercake 14 MIN
VHS
Color (K P)
$44.95 purchase _ #SAV9024
Presents the story by Patricia Polacco about how a grandmother helped her young granddaughter to overcome her fear of thunder.
Guidance and Counseling; Literature and Drama
Dist - KNOWUN

The Thunderstorm 29 MIN
Videoreel / VT2
Weather series
Color (I J)
Features meteorologist Frank Sechrish introducing the largest thunderstorm model ever made and illustrating where rain, hail and tornadoes come from.
Science - Physical
Dist - PBS Prod - WHATV

Thunderstorm 119 MIN
VHS
Color (G) (MANDARIN CHINESE)
$45.00 purchase _ #1060A
Presents a movie produced in the People's Republic Of China.
Fine Arts; Geography - World; Literature and Drama
Dist - CHTSUI Prod - CHTSUI

The Thunderstorm 9 MIN
U-matic / VHS / 16mm
Color (P I)
LC 78-700605
Tells a story about a boy who, during a search for his lost dog, discovers the interdependence of all living things in nature.
Guidance and Counseling; Literature and Drama
Dist - LCOA Prod - LCOA 1969

Thunderstorms 24 MIN
VHS
Color (I)
$79.95 purchase _ #ESD 2221
Uses filmed footage and animated diagrams of thunderstorms to explain how they develop and their resultant rain, hail and lightning. Explains downbursts and wind shears.
Science; Science - Physical
Dist - SCTRES Prod - SCTRES

Thunderstorms - nature's fury 20 MIN
Videodisc / VHS
Earth sciences video library series
Color (J H)
$99.95, $69.95 purchase _ #ES8480; $99.95, $69.95 purchase _ #Q18482
Combines live footage with animated computer graphics to explain how thunderstorms develop to produce rain, hail and lightning. Part of a series which takes a contemporary look at Planet Earth, its natural resources and the human impact on the global environment.
Science - Physical
Dist - INSTRU
CF

Thurgood Marshall 30 MIN
VHS
Black Americans of achievement video collection series
Color (J H C G)
$39.98 purchase _ #LVC6605V
Portrays Supreme Court Justice Thurgood Marshall through interviews with leading authorities, rare footage and archival photographs. Part of 12 - part series on noted black Americans.
Civics and Political Systems; History - United States
Dist - CAMV

Thurgood Marshall - Portrait of an American Hero 30 MIN
VHS
Color (G)
$39.95 purchase _ #TMAR - 000
Sets forth the life and career of Supreme Court Justice Thurgood Marshall. Highlights his career achievements in private practice, as a civil rights litigator for the NAACP, and as the first black Supreme Court justice.
Biography; Civics and Political Systems
Dist - PBS

Thursday 5 MIN
16mm
Color (G)
$20.00 rental
Looks at the filmmaker's Thursdays, between 11am and 1pm while his infant son was sleeping. Deals with sensory pleasure of momentary solitude in a domestic setting.
Fine Arts; Sociology
Dist - CANCIN Prod - PIERCE 1991

Thursday's Children 28 MIN
16mm
Color (T S)
LC 72-708248
Visits a special school which helps children with learning disabilities related to emotional problems overcome such problems. Features four pre - school children and ways their emotional problems are recognized and dealt with by the school staff.
Education; Psychology
Dist - KETCTV Prod - KETCTV 1970

THX 1138 88 MIN
16mm / U-matic / VHS
Color
Centers around a man and a woman in the 25th century who rebel against their rigidly controlled society. Directed by George Lucas.
Fine Arts
Dist - FI Prod - WB 1971

Thy sins are forgiven 15 MIN
16mm
Living Bible series
Color; B&W (R)
Tells the Biblical story of Jesus' healing of a sick man, saying to the man, 'Thy sins are forgiven." Also contains Jesus' call to Matthew to 'Follow me,' the Pharisees' question to Jesus about fasting and his reply with three parables.
Religion and Philosophy
Dist - FAMF Prod - FAMF

Thy will be Done 25 MIN
16mm / VHS / BETA
Color
LC 77-702530
Presents correspondent Michael Maclear examining the issue of capital punishment and considering pros and cons of the debate.
Sociology
Dist - CTV Prod - CTV 1976

Thy will be done 90 MIN
VHS / U-matic
Color
Features an investigation of mind control as related to religious cults.
Psychology; Religion and Philosophy
Dist - WCCOTV Prod - WCCOTV 1980

Thymus, spleen 15 MIN
VHS / 16mm
Histology review series; Unit VIII - the immune system; Pt 2
(C PRO VOC)
$330.00 purchase _ #821VI044
Identifies the histological characteristics and the functions of the thymus and spleen. Also covers the blood vessels supplying the two. Part 2 of the Immune System Unit.
Health and Safety
Dist - HSCIC Prod - HSCIC 1983

Thyration Sawtooth Generator 25 MIN
16mm
B&W
LC 74-705506
Shows an electron beam moving across the face of an oscilloscope and points out that the thyration saw - tooth generator produces the waveshapes required to move the electron beam. Gives a detailed analysis of the circuit operation and constructs a time amplitude graph of the sawtooth waves, explaining its physical and electrical length. (Kinescope).
Industrial and Technical Education; Science - Physical
Dist - USNAC Prod - USAF

Thyristors and optoelectronics 60 MIN
Videoreel / VT1
Understanding semiconductors course outline series; No 9
Color (IND)
Describes representative applications, operating principles and key specifications of devices in both thyristors and optoelectronics, SCR, TRIAC, photodiode, phototransistor and light - emitting diode.
Industrial and Technical Education
Dist - TXINLC Prod - TXINLC

Thyroglossal Duct Cyst Resection 12 MIN
U-matic / VHS
Head and Neck Series
Color
Health and Safety; Science - Natural
Dist - SVL Prod - SVL

Thyroid and antithyroid drugs 30 MIN
16mm
Pharmacology series
B&W (C PRO VOC)
LC 73-703353
Reviews the synthesis of the thyroid hormones and explains what an underproduction or an overproduction of these hormones will produce. Illustrates how antithyroid drugs interfere with the action of the thyroid gland.
Health and Safety
Dist - TELSTR Prod - MVNE 1971

The Thyroid Area 6 MIN
16mm
Anatomy of the Head and Neck Series
Color

LC 75-702145; 74-705790
Demonstrates dissection of deeper structures of the thyroid area and reviews the entire pretracheal area diagrammatically.
Health and Safety; Science - Natural
Dist - USNAC **Prod** - USVA 1969

Thyroid Cancer 22 MIN
16mm
Color (PRO)
LC 74-706127
Presents a dramatic narrative between a resident doctor and a specialist who answers questions regarding thyroid cancer. Uses animation, live action photography of actual cases, X - rays, surgery and radioactive isotope therapy to illustrate points in the narrative.
Health and Safety; Science
Dist - AMCS **Prod** - AEGIS 1969

Thyroid Cancer - Diagnosis and Treatment 20 MIN
16mm
Color (PRO)
Demonstrates diagnostic procedures used for thyroid gland tumors including palpation, radioactive isotope scans, radiography and biopsy. Presents patterns of metastasis, and surgical approaches to management ranging from radical to conservative with rationale for each.
Health and Safety; Science
Dist - AMCS **Prod** - AMCS 1969

Thyroid disorder 30 MIN
VHS
At time of diagnosis series
Color (G)
$19.95 purchase _ #1 - 5757 - 7020 - 2NK
Provides patients who have just been diagnosed with thyroid disorder and their families with thorough, comprehensive and understandable information. Examines what is going on in the body and what might have caused the condition. Explains the type of medical professionals a patient may encounter and how the condition is monitored. Explores treatment options, including medication, surgery and lifestyle changes. Looks at practical issues surrounding the illness and answers the most common questions. Part of an ongoing series to provide the in - depth medical information patients and their families need to know.
Health and Safety
Dist - TILIED **Prod** - TILIED 1996

The Thyroid Gland 30 MIN
U-matic / VHS
Color
Discusses the role of the thyroid gland and the malfunctions that can occur. Looks at symptoms of thyroid diseases. Covers medical and surgical corrections.
Health and Safety; Science - Natural
Dist - AL **Prod** - UILCCC

Thyroid Physiology and Disease - Hyperthyroidism and Thyroiditis 55 MIN
16mm
Clinical Pathology Series
B&W (PRO)
Reviews the classification of hyperthyroidism. Includes a discussion of Graves' disease, its pathogenesis, clinical manifestation and treatment.
Health and Safety; Science - Natural
Dist - USNAC **Prod** - NMAC 1970

Thyroid Physiology and Disease - Hypothyroidism 49 MIN
16mm
Clinical Pathology Series
B&W (PRO)
Discusses the classifications of hypothyroidism, reviews the types of cretinism due to inborn errors in metabolism and gives clinical manifestations of hypothyroidism.
Health and Safety; Science - Natural
Dist - USNAC **Prod** - NMAC 1970

Thyroid physiology and disease - normal physiology and diagnostic tests - Pt 1 33 MIN
16mm
Clinical pathology series
B&W (PRO)
Discusses the normal anatomy and physiology of the thyroid as related to clinical problems.
Health and Safety; Science - Natural
Dist - USNAC **Prod** - NMAC 1970

Thyroid Physiology and Disease - Thyroid Nodules and Cancer 34 MIN
16mm
Clinical Pathology Series
B&W (PRO)
Discusses the varieties of thyroid cancer, the management of the thyroid nodule and attempts to formulate a rational approach to the problem.
Health and Safety; Science - Natural
Dist - USNAC **Prod** - NMAC 1970

Thyroid Today 30 MIN
16mm
Color
LC 76-701065
Discusses thyroid disease and therapy.
Health and Safety; Science - Natural
Dist - BAXLAB **Prod** - BAXLAB 1974

Thyroid Uptake and Scan
U-matic / VHS
X - Ray Procedures in Layman's Terms Series
Color
Health and Safety; Science
Dist - FAIRGH **Prod** - FAIRGH

Thyroidectomy - a Half Century of Experience 30 MIN
16mm
Color (PRO)
Demonstrates the Lahey clinic technique of thyroidectomy, originally developed by Dr Frank H Lahey. Explains that an adequate incision, high mobilization of the skin flap, and the routine division of the strip muscle, make possible the actual visualization of every important structure encountered in a thyroidectomy.
Health and Safety; Science
Dist - ACY **Prod** - ACYDGD 1963

Thyroidectomy - a Safe Operation 24 MIN
16mm
Color (PRO)
Emphasizes techniques that have made thyroidectomy a safe procedure. Presents scenes from operations done for four different pathological conditions to show positioning, anesthesia, exposure, hemostasis, avoidance of injury to vital structures and closures.
Health and Safety; Science
Dist - ACY **Prod** - ACYDGD 1960

Thyroidectomy for Papillary Carcinoma of Thyroid with Cervical Metastases 18 MIN
16mm
Color (PRO)
Shows the complete removal of one lobe and isthmus of the thyroid involved by papillary carcinoma. Demonstrates resection of the regional lymph nodes, care being taken to preserve the recurrent laryngeal nerve.
Health and Safety; Science
Dist - ACY **Prod** - ACYDGD 1951

TI - 99/4A Home Computer
U-matic / VHS
Basic Computer Operations Series
Color
Presents basic operation procedures for the TI - 99/4A Home Computer.
Industrial and Technical Education; Mathematics
Dist - LIBFSC **Prod** - LIBFSC

Ti - Grace Atkinson - radical activist - political theorist 28 MIN
U-matic
Color
Features Ti - Grace Atkinson talking about feminism and class, socialist feminism, and the role of men in the women's movement. Suggests a few 'mechanisms for survival,' and describes marriage and motherhood as anti - feminist institutions.
Civics and Political Systems; Sociology
Dist - WMENIF **Prod** - WMENIF

Ti - Jean goes lumbering 16 MIN
VHS / U-matic
Color; Captioned (P I)
Presents a French - Canadian folktale about the fantastic exploits of a mysterious little boy who one day rides into a winter logging camp on a big white horse. Shows that his exploits dwarf those of even the hardiest lumberjack as he fells lumber, cuts, carries and plies heavy logs, and comes out the victor in every contest. Portrays typical life in a Canadian logging camp.
Literature and Drama
Dist - IFB

Ti - Jean goes lumbering 16 MIN
16mm
Captioned; Color (P I) (SPANISH)
Presents a French - Canadian folktale about the fantastic exploits of a mysterious little boy who one day rides into a winter logging camp on a big white horse. Shows that his exploits dwarf those of even the hardiest lumberjack as he fells lumber, cuts, carries and plies heavy logs, and comes out the victor in every contest. Portrays typical life in a Canadian logging camp.
Literature and Drama
Dist - IFB **Prod** - NFBC 1953

Tiberias - Land of the Emperors 14 MIN
16mm
Color
Points out that the ancient town of Tiberias on the Sea of Galilee was built by Herod as a tribute to the Roman emperor Tiberius. Points out its historic and religious significance, the natural beauty of its surroundings and boating, water skiing and cultural activities.
Geography - World; History - World
Dist - ALDEN **Prod** - ALDEN

Tibet - a seed for transformation 34 MIN
VHS
Color (G)
$25.00 purchase _ #JVTST
Looks at the Chinese takeover of Tibet and how it affects the rest of the world. Contains a discussion of Tibet's location, customs and culture, a look at China's nuclear activities, human rights violations, the environmental destruction of Tibet - and what might be done to help Tibetans. Filmed in Tibet and northern India.
Civics and Political Systems; Geography - World; History - World; Religion and Philosophy; Sociology
Dist - SNOWLI **Prod** - SNOWLI

Tibet in exile 30 MIN
VHS / BETA
Color; PAL (G)
PdS15 purchase
Portrays the Tibetan struggle for survival and their attempts to preserve Tibet's unique culture. Focuses on the arrival of refugee children in India and Nepal. Includes historical footage of the Dalai Lama's 1959 flight from India to Tibet.
Fine Arts; Religion and Philosophy
Dist - MERIDT

Tibet in exile 30 MIN
VHS
Color (G)
$29.95 purchase
Follows the story of ten children who were smuggled by relatives out of Chinese - occupied Tibet - and separated from their families - to Dharamsala, India, home of their exiled leader, the Dalai Lama. Looks at their families' hopes for education, medical care and cultural knowledge no longer allowed under China's rule. Documents the exiled community efforts to preserve Tibetan Buddhist values. Produced by Barbara Banks.
Fine Arts; History - World; Religion and Philosophy; Sociology
Dist - CANCIN

Tibet in India 110 MIN
VHS / BETA
Color; PAL (G)
PdS25 purchase
Features the inauguration, attended by thousands, of a new monastery of the Drikung Kagyu Order of Tibetan Buddhism, Jangchub Ling. Looks at the monastery in northern India as marking an important changing point for an old mystical line of Tibetan Buddhism. Includes interviews, historical footage and scenes of the Dalai Lama leading most of the ceremonies. Includes trance dances, musical performances, meditations and rituals. Two parts in one cassette - 'The little Lamas' and 'In the sign of the gods.' Produced by Angelique and Michael Pakleppa and Inka Jochum.
Fine Arts; History - World; Religion and Philosophy
Dist - MERIDT

Tibet - the cultural evolution 60 MIN
VHS / BETA
Color; PAL (G)
PdS25, $50.00 purchase
Presents a picture of how, as a result of the 'relaxation' in China's policy toward Tibet in the mid 1980s, the Tibetans are eager to continue their former spiritual pursuits and reassume their own cultural identity. Produced by Belgische Radio en Televisie.
Fine Arts; History - World; Religion and Philosophy
Dist - MERIDT

Tibet - the end of time 50 MIN
VHS
Lost civilizations video series
Color (G)
$19.99 purchase _ #0 - 7835 - 8278 - 1NK
Looks at the history of a young boy, viewed as the reincarnation of the Tibetan god - king, who witnesses the collapse of his culture. Visits a modern Shangri - la and views its struggle to survive in a hostile contemporary world. Part of a ten - part series incorporating the newest research, evidence and discoveries; orginal cinematography in 25 countries on 5 continents; dramatized recreations of scenes from the past; three - dimensional computer graphics to reconstruct ancient cities and monumental feats of engineering; historic footage; and computer - animated maps.
History - World; Religion and Philosophy
Dist - TILIED **Prod** - TILIED 1995

Tibet - the ice mother 50 MIN
VHS
Horizon series
PAL; Color (H C A)
PdS99 purchase; Not available in the United States, Canada, Germany or Switzerland
Delves into the studies of Maureen Raymo in Tibet that attempt to discover what caused the Ice Ages. Investigates the ideas that link geological forces and our climate. Includes footage of a trip to the plateau of Tibet where her theories are examined. Part of the Horizon series.
Fine Arts; Science - Physical
Dist - BBCENE

Tibet - the survival of the spirit 92 MIN
VHS
Color (G)
$29.95 purchase _ #TISUSP
Portrays conditions in occupied Tibet and the confrontation between two opposing worlds. Witnesses the rebuilding of Tsurphu Monastery. Includes footage of the Jokhang temple being stormed by Chinese police where monks were beaten to death.
History - World; Religion and Philosophy
Dist - SNOWLI

Tibet - where continents collide 45 MIN
VHS
Color (G)
$45.00 purchase _ #EVT
Melds geologic history with glimpses into the culture of Tibet. Visits the Yarlung Tsangpo suture, the Gangdise volcanic arc and looks at the Indian tectonic plate as it descends beneath Eurasia. Features David Howell of the US Geological Survey who uses simple diagrams and animation to describe the history of India's collision with the Asian continent.
Geography - World; Science - Physical
Dist - SNOWLI **Prod** - SNOWLI

Tibetan Buddhist meditation 30 MIN
BETA / VHS
Meditative experience series
Color (G)
$29.95 purchase _ #S316
Goes step by step through teaching Buddhist meditation in the Kagupa tradition - first quieting the mind, focusing on the four motivations for meditation and finally taking refuge in the Buddha, the Dharma and the Sangha. Discusses the significance of the Lama in Tibetan tradition and the use of sound and imagery. Features Dr Ole Nydahl, trained Tibetan meditation master. Part of a four - part series on the meditative experience.
Fine Arts; Religion and Philosophy
Dist - THINKA **Prod** - THINKA

Tibetan medicine - a Buddhist approach to healing 29 MIN
VHS
Color (G)
$49.95 purchase _ #MFTM
Visits the Tibetan Medical Center in Dharamsala, India. Features Ama Lopsang Dolma, Tibet's first woman doctor, who explains the making of medicine and how acupuncture and moxibustion are used.
Health and Safety; Religion and Philosophy
Dist - SNOWLI **Prod** - SNOWLI

Tibetan medicine - a Buddhist approach to healing 30 MIN
16mm
Color (H C PRO)
LC 76-702211
Discusses Tibetan medicine, including the use of medicines gathered in the mountains, acupuncture and moxabustion. Explains how ignorance, passion and aggression are considered the causes of disease.
Health and Safety; Religion and Philosophy
Dist - HP **Prod** - HP 1976

Tibetan medicine - an introductory lecture 120 MIN
VHS / BETA
Color; PAL (G)
PdS35 purchase
Features Dr Lobsang Rabgay, a Buddhist monk and scholar of the new generation of Tibetans in exile, who outlines the physical and mental principles behind Tibetan medicine. Points out parallels he feels exist between these principles and those behind natural approaches to health in the West. Recorded at Rigpa, London.
Fine Arts; Health and Safety; Religion and Philosophy
Dist - MERIDT

The Tibetan question 12 MIN
VHS / BETA
Color; PAL (G)
PdS10, $20.00 purchase
Examines the present political situation in Tibet. Presents the Dalai Lama's views on nonviolence as the only means of resolving the Tibetan situation. Produced for television.
Civics and Political Systems; Religion and Philosophy
Dist - MERIDT **Prod** - MERIDT

Tibetan rites of rejuvenation 30 MIN
VHS
Color (G)
$29.95 purchase _ #V - RITES
Presents the five rites of rejuvenation practiced in Himalayan monasteries for thousands of years. Shows how Tibetan monks practice five exercises to strengthen and align their physical and ethereal bodies to prepare for intense spiritual practice. Includes a copy of the book originally published in 1939.
Health and Safety; Physical Education and Recreation; Religion and Philosophy
Dist - PACSPI

Tibetan Traders 22 MIN
U-matic / 16mm
Color (J H C)
LC 71-702619
A study of the way of life of a semi - nomadic Himalyaya tribe. Shows the semi - nomadic traders journeying across the Himalayas into Tibet where they barter with other traders from the heartland of Asia. Portrays their family life, education, recreation, government, religion and crafts and their dependence of saddlecarrying goats for transportation.
Business and Economics; Geography - World; Social Science
Dist - ATLAP **Prod** - ATLAP 1968

Tibetans celebrate the birthday of His Holiness the Dalai Lama 60 MIN
VHS / BETA
Color; PAL (G)
PdS25 purchase
Joins the Tibetan Community in Britain gathering at the Camden Centre, London, on the Dalai Lama's 49th birthday. Presents a series of traditional songs, dances and formal offerings for the continuing good health and long life of their spiritual and temporal leader.
Fine Arts; Religion and Philosophy
Dist - MERIDT

A Tibeten new year 43 MIN
VHS / BETA
Color; PAL (G)
PdS25 purchase
Documents the Tibetan New Year celebrations carried out by the monks of the only Bonpo community outside Tibet. Records the preparations and enactment of the annual ceremony while the monks and local villagers perform the rituals. The foothills of the Himalayas in northern India provide the backdrop. Produced by Jon Jerstad.
Fine Arts; History - World; Religion and Philosophy
Dist - MERIDT

TIC - Index to Energy 6 MIN
16mm
Color (A)
LC 77-703416
Visits the Technical Information Center at the Department of Energy in Oakridge, Tennessee. Focuses on the Center's computerized capability to gather, abstract and catalog technical reports and scientific papers at the rate of one million per year.
Business and Economics; Civics and Political Systems; Industrial and Technical Education; Mathematics; Sociology
Dist - USNAC **Prod** - USERD 1977

Tic Toc Time Clock 11 MIN
16mm / U-matic / VHS
Color (P I)
LC 76-701297
Uses a group of students forming a living clock under the direction of a coach in order to show how to tell time and read a clock.
Mathematics
Dist - PHENIX **Prod** - PHENIX 1976

Tick tock 25 MIN
U-matic
Not another science show series
Color (H C)
Explores new ways of keeping time and gives a history of man made units of time. Looks at sundials, water clocks and quartz and liquid crystals.
Business and Economics; Mathematics
Dist - TVOTAR **Prod** - TVOTAR 1986

Tick tock - all about the clock 16 MIN
VHS
Color (K P)
$89.00 purchase _ #RB858
Discusses why it is important to know what time it is. Shows various types of clocks and watches and the function of the clock hands, seconds, minutes, half hours and hours. Looks at the sundial, hour glass and stop watch. Shows how the earth spinning on its axis causes night and day.
Mathematics
Dist - REVID **Prod** - REVID 1990

A Ticket home 10 MIN
VHS / 16mm
Color (G)
$30.00 rental
Translates old friends and old places. Ventures home from west to east and the cross - country return while sharing visual fragments; a journal in color language in which parts of home movie footage jump around wildly full of color and motion.
Fine Arts; Geography - United States; Psychology; Sociology
Dist - CANCIN FLMKCO **Prod** - ANGERA 1982

Ticket to ride
VHS
Color (G)
$24.94 purchase _ #0868
Looks at surfing, skiing, jet skiing, sky diving, hot air ballooning.
Physical Education and Recreation
Dist - SEVVID

Ticket to Sydney 10 MIN
16mm
Color (J)
LC 72-702253
Presents a portrait of life in Sydney, Australia's largest city, as commuters hurry to arrive at work on time.
Geography - World; Social Science; Sociology
Dist - AUIS **Prod** - ANAIB 1972

Ticket to Utopia 29 MIN
U-matic
Color
Features actors, folk singers and artists giving a video tour of some of humanity's most beautiful visions of utopia. Focuses on why these visions persist.
Fine Arts; Religion and Philosophy
Dist - UMITV **Prod** - UMITV 1975

Ticking bombs - defusing violence in the workplace 47 MIN
VHS
Color (IND PRO)
$795.00 purchase, $195.00 rental _ #COR01
Adapts the book by Michael Mantell, PhD. Helps prevent the risk of violence at work. Delves into the seven 'must' questions every employment interview should include, along with a list of early warning signs to watch for. Includes key training points, such as the legal aspects of preparedness and how to establish liaison and communication channels. Includes a leader's guide and a hardback copy of the book.
Business and Economics; Guidance and Counseling; Health and Safety; Social Science; Sociology
Dist - EXTR

Ticks and tick - borne diseases 19 MIN
16mm
Color (PRO A) (SPANISH)
LC FIE61-46
Discusses ticks, their importance in transmitting diseases, their biology and their control.
Health and Safety; Home Economics; Science - Natural
Dist - USNAC **Prod** - USPHS NMAC 1960

Ticonderoga - a Classic Under Sail 13 MIN
16mm
Color
LC 77-700583
Documents the history, launching and racing records of the classic sailboat Ticonderoga.
Physical Education and Recreation
Dist - PICNIC **Prod** - PICNIC 1977

A Tidal flat and its ecosystem 20 MIN
U-matic / VHS / 16mm
Color (I J)
LC 80-700230
Discusses the organisms that flourish in tidal flats and explains the food chains that exist in these areas.
Science - Natural
Dist - NGS **Prod** - NGS 1979

Tide Commercial 1 MIN
VHS / U-matic
Color
Shows a classic television commercial.
Business and Economics; Psychology; Sociology
Dist - BROOKC **Prod** - BROOKC

Tidepool - a Miracle Where Sea Meets Land 11 MIN
16mm
Color (I J)
LC 74-703050
Examines the variety of plants and animals which live in a tidepool.
Science - Natural
Dist - AVED **Prod** - CROCHI 1974

Tides 13 MIN
16mm
Color (A)
$25.00 rental
Deals with the theme and image of woman and ocean. Features extreme slow motion so that the surge and flow of the woman's nude body and the waves become a continually moving cinematic experience. Produced and performed by Amy Greenfield. A counterpart film to Element. Element and Tides may be rented together for the special price of $45.00.
Fine Arts
Dist - CANCIN

Tides of the Ocean - what they are and How the Sun and Moon Cause Them 17 MIN
16mm
Color (J H C)
LC FIA64-47
Uses animation to explain the causes of ocean tides, showing the effect of centrifugal force and the gravitational attraction of the sun and the moon on the waters. Discusses the uses of the ocean tides and points out that the activities of man must be planned to fit the rhythm of the tides.
Science - Physical
Dist - ACA **Prod** - ACA 1964

The Tides of time 26 MIN
U-matic / VHS
Color (C H G)
$249.00, $149.00 purchase _ #AD - 1825
Explores the short - term fight to save endangered coastlines and the long - term implications of the 'greenhouse effect.'
Geography - World; Science - Natural
Dist - FOTH **Prod** - FOTH

Tidewater to Piedmont 15 MIN
U-matic / VHS / 16mm
American legacy series; Pgm 4
Color (I)
Shows that tobacco is very important in Virginia's tidewater area while cotton and the textile industry is important on the Piedmont. Discusses George Washington Carver and the development of peanut farming.
Geography - United States; History - United States
Dist - AITECH **Prod** - KRMATV 1983

Tidikawa and friends 82 MIN
U-matic
Color ((ENGLISH NARRATION))
Presents a long version of the documentary The Spirit World Of Tidikawa. Focuses on a spirit medium of the Bedamini of Papua New Guinea. Includes English narration at the beginning only.
Geography - World; Sociology
Dist - DOCEDR **Prod** - BBCTV 1971

Tidikawa - at the edge of heaven 50 MIN
VHS
Color (H C G)
$445.00 purchase, $75.00 rental
Returns with Susan Cornwell to Papua New Guinea and the Bedamini people. Reveals that when Cornwell first encountered the Bedamini in 1971, as portrayed in Tidikawa And Friends, they were aggressive and practiced cannibalism and Tidikawa was a powerful religious leader. Upon her return Cornwell encounters people in Western dress, converted to Christianity and having abandoned traditional ritual. Shows the people perform tribal dances for money and using calculators to determine the charges. Tidikawa, now an old man, lives deep in the jungle where he still practices his sorcery. Produced by Look Film Productions.
Geography - World; Sociology
Dist - FLMLIB

Tie Dye 16 MIN
16mm / U-matic / VHS
Textile Design Series
Color (J)
LC 74-702619
Demonstrates the techniques and design elements of tie dyeing in step - by - step procedures. Suggests possibilities for exploration and experimentation and shows a number of finished tie - dyed fabrics.
Fine Arts; Home Economics
Dist - AIMS **Prod** - TETKOW 1974

The Tie that binds 27 MIN
VHS
Color (PRO)
$450.00, $295.00 purchase, $45.00 rental
Discusses the biological basis for bonding in humans, the bonding of a mother to a premature infant and the importance of paying attention to the needs of a newborn's older siblings. Suggests ways to improve interaction between parent and infant through speech, gesture, touch, scent and paying attention to the baby's cues.
Health and Safety; Psychology; Social Science; Sociology
Dist - POLYMR

Tiempo del bano 17 MIN
VHS
Baby care workshop series
Color (I J H A) (SPANISH)
$175.00 purchase
Teaches how to bathe a baby in a safe comfortable manner. Addresses cord care, sponge bath, basin bath and preventing cradle cap.
Guidance and Counseling; Health and Safety; Home Economics; Sociology
Dist - PROPAR **Prod** - PROPAR 1988

Tiempo del juego 17 MIN
VHS
Baby care workshop series
Color (I J H A) (SPANISH)
$175.00 purchase
Demonstrates simple, enjoyable activities for parents to share with their infants. Encourages flexibility and spontaneity in play activities, using readily available household items without purchasing special equipment.
Guidance and Counseling; Health and Safety; Home Economics; Sociology
Dist - PROPAR **Prod** - PROPAR 1988

Tierra Mexicana 22 MIN
U-matic / VHS / 16mm
B&W (I J H) (SPANISH)
Portrays animated maps of geographic aspects of Mexico. Describes daily activities in both rural and urban areas, natural resources and industries.
Geography - World
Dist - IFB **Prod** - IFB 1949

Tierra Y Cultura 38 MIN
16mm / U-matic / VHS
Color (H C A) (SPANISH (ENGLISH SUBTITLES))
$495 purchase - 16 mm, $295 purchase - video, $70 rental
Examines the recuperacion movement among Indian communities in Colombia, where a group of Indians is engaged in guerrilla warfare with a counterinsurgency force of Colombian army troops. Directed by Magdalena V and Sigi S.
History - World; Social Science; Sociology
Dist - CNEMAG

The Ties that Bind 27 MIN
U-matic / VHS
Color (A)
LC 81-707012
Describes and illustrates the evolving process of parents' attachment to their baby during pregnancy, delivery and the first weeks of the child's life.
Health and Safety; Sociology
Dist - POLYMR **Prod** - POLYMR

The Ties that Bind 55 MIN
16mm
B&W (G)
$700.00 purchase, $125.00 rental
Tells the story of filmmaker Su Friedrich's mother who lived in the time of Nazi Germany.
Fine Arts; History - World; Sociology
Dist - WMEN **Prod** - SUFR 1984

Ties that bind - fibres 55 MIN
VHS
Hand and eye series; Vol III; Pt 6
Color (S)
$99.00 purchase _ #386 - 9020
Melds together the past and the present in a celebration of handcrafted art. Traverses the globe to present the world's finest examples of weaving and fiber products such as baskets and rope. Part of a series about sculpture, jewelry, glass, pottery, gardening, weaving and woodworking. Contemporary artisans demonstrate the ancient and innovative techniques they use to create their modern masterworks.
Fine Arts; Home Economics
Dist - FI **Prod** - CANBC 1988

Ties that Bind - Images of Canada
16mm
Color
_ #106C 0176 012
Geography - World
Dist - CFLMDC **Prod** - NFBC 1976

Ties that bind - super love vs super kids 45 MIN
VHS
Childcrafting - a predictive guide to creative parenting series
Color (G R)
$24.95 purchase, $10.00 rental _ #35 - 87299 - 460
Suggests that parents can stimulate and motivate their children without interfering with the children's individuality. Also considers the difference between quality and quantity time.
Psychology; Sociology
Dist - APH **Prod** - FRACOC

TIG structural and pipe welding 60 MIN
U-matic / VHS
Welding training series
Color (IND)
Addresses topics of structural aspects, carbon steel pipe, stainless steel pipe, combination of TIG and 'stick.'
Education; Industrial and Technical Education
Dist - ITCORP **Prod** - ITCORP

TIG Welding
VHS / 35mm strip
Welding Series
Color
$42.00 purchase _ #LX84C filmstrip, $62.00 purchase _ #LX84V VHS
Illustrates proper operates and types of jobs best accomplished by the TIG (Tungsten Inert Gas) systems.
Education; Industrial and Technical Education
Dist - CAREER **Prod** - CAREER

TIG welding 84 MIN
35mm strip / VHS
Color (H A IND)
#905XV7
Explains the basic operations, procedures and applications of TIG welding equipment. Includes introduction and applications, power supply, torches and accessories, welding mild steel, welding stainless steel, and welding aluminum (6 tapes). Prerequisite required. Includes a Study Guide.
Education; Industrial and Technical Education
Dist - BERGL

Tiger - 5 10 MIN
U-matic / 16mm / VHS
Zoo animals series
Color (K P I)
$265.00, $215.00, $185.00 purchase _ #B606
Describes the tiger's natural habitat and behavior. Shows tigers living in a wild animal park. Discusses the hunting ability of the tiger. Looks at the differences and similarities of the tiger with other cats. Part of a six - part series on zoo animals.
Science - Natural
Dist - BARR **Prod** - GREATT 1990

The Tiger and the Brahmin
CD / VHS / Cassette
Color (K P G)
$9.98, $16.98, $8.98 purchase _ #8512, #D390, #390
Tells of an East Indian holy man and his quest to discover the ways of the world. Features Ben Kingsley as narrator with music by Ravi Shankar.
Fine Arts; Literature and Drama; Religion and Philosophy
Dist - MULIPE **Prod** - MULIPE

The Tiger and the Rabbit 15 MIN
U-matic / VHS
Sixteen Tales Series
Color (P I)
Tells a story from Puerto Rico and Africa of a rabbit outsmarting a tiger three times.
Geography - World; Literature and Drama
Dist - AITECH **Prod** - KLCSTV

Tiger at the Gate 20 MIN
U-matic / VHS
History in Action Series
Color
Analyzes the underpinnings of Hitler's appeal and his rise to power.
History - World
Dist - FOTH **Prod** - FOTH 1984

Tiger by the Tail 35 MIN
16mm
Color (H C A)
LC 77-715307
Describes some aspects of alcoholism - its causes, problems and a method of treatment - using the experiences of an actual alcoholic.
Health and Safety; Psychology
Dist - IU **Prod** - UARIZ 1971

Tiger by the Tail 58 MIN
Videoreel / VT2
Syngerism - Troubled Humanity Series
Color
Presents a documentary study of the causes, problems and treatment of alcoholism. Features two actual alcoholics. Explores the work of Dr Richard L Reilly and his staff of the Tucson General Hospital Detoxification, Rehabilitation and Research Center. Interviews experts in the field of alcoholism and depicts the actual experiences of alcoholics.
Health and Safety; Psychology; Science; Sociology
Dist - PBS **Prod** - KUATTV

Tiger crises 50 MIN
VHS
Color; PAL (H C A)

PdS99 purchase; Not available in the United States
Documents the trading of poached tiger products in Nepal and China. Indicates that poaching has become easier as the tiger's habitat becomes smaller.
Science - Natural
Dist - BBCENE

Tiger in the House 14 MIN
16mm
Fire Survival Series
Color (I J)
Stresses the need for fire warning devices in the home. Details operation, placement, maintenance, costs and limitations of detectors.
Health and Safety
Dist - FILCOM **Prod** - AREASX

A Tiger in the pond 15 MIN
VHS
Pond life - a place to live series
Color (I J H)
$119.00 purchase _ #CG - 851 - VS
Shows how tiny baby frogs and toads grow into adults. Examines pond insects, including the ferocious water tiger, a kind of beetle. Part of a three - part series which looks at life in and around a typical pond in intimate detail.
Science - Natural
Dist - HRMC **Prod** - HRMC

Tiger of the highlands 30 MIN
VHS
Wildlife on one series
Color; PAL (H C A)
PdS65 purchase; Not available in the United States
Investigates the wildcats that live in the scottish highlands. Indicates that while they remain elusive, sightings have been made near agricultural lands where rabbits live.
Science - Natural
Dist - BBCENE

Tiger rag 3 MIN
16mm
Color (G)
Shows a stylized cartoon adaptation of the Les Paul - Mary Ford recording of Tiger Rag.
Fine Arts
Dist - CFS **Prod** - SAXOND

Tiger, tiger 60 MIN
VHS
Color (G)
$24.95 purchase _ #S02001
Portrays tigers, focusing on their predatory natures. Shows how one man has gone to great lengths to save tigers from extinction.
Science - Natural
Dist - UILL **Prod** - SIERRA

Tigers 13 MIN
VHS
Animal profile series
Color (P I)
$59.95 purchase _ #RB8129
Studies tigers. Includes footage of a Siberian tiger - largest of all cats, a Bengali tiger and a Sumatran tiger. Part of a series on animals which looks at examples from the mammal, snake and bird classes, filmed in their natural habitat.
Science - Natural
Dist - REVID **Prod** - REVID 1990

Tigers in a cage 30 MIN
U-matic
Educating the special child series
Color (PRO)
Relates how a teacher can modify classroom teaching methods to suit the needs of the hostile and disruptive student.
Education; Psychology
Dist - TVOTAR **Prod** - TVOTAR 1985

The Tiger's nest 25 MIN
U-matic / VHS
Land of the dragon series
Color (H C)
Demonstrates how Buddhism has shaped the history of Bhutan, focusing on 'The Tiger's Nest,' where it is said the demons standing in the way of the spread of Buddhism were conquered. Includes biographical information about Padma Sambhava, a revered Buddhist figure because he brought Buddhism to Bhutan in the ninth century.
Religion and Philosophy; Science - Natural; Sociology
Dist - LANDMK **Prod** - NOMDFI

Tigertown 29 MIN
VHS / U-matic / 16mm
Color (J H G)
$260.00, $310.00, $495.00 purchase, $65.00 rental
Studies a community that goes to extremes in support of its high school football team. Offers a mirror to the viewer and to communities on the drive for excellence in sports at any price. Produced by Dan Snipes.
Fine Arts; History - United States; Physical Education and Recreation
Dist - NDIM

Tight budgets 50 MIN
VHS
Prisoners of the sun - Natural world series
Color; PAL (H C A)
PdS99 purchase; Not available in the United States, Canada or Japan
Points out the necessity of conserving energy. Indicates that while most animals are careful with energy resources, man is more profligate.
Science - Natural; Social Science
Dist - BBCENE

Tight Lines North 32 MIN
16mm
Color
Presents Red Fisher fishing the waters of northern Manitoba for brook trout.
Geography - World; Physical Education and Recreation
Dist - KAROL **Prod** - BRNSWK

Tight packers and loose packers 57 MIN
U-matic / VHS / 16mm
Fight against slavery series; No 4
Color
LC 78-700503
Examines the conflicts between the abolitionists and those with vested interests in the slave trade during the late 18th century.
History - United States; Sociology
Dist - TIMLIF **Prod** - BBCTV 1977

Tight times 30 MIN
U-matic / VHS
Reading rainbow series; No 1
Color (P)
Presents LeVar Burton introducing the book Tight Times and showing his friends how to have a great time without spending a dime, including checking out the public library.
English Language; Social Science
Dist - GPN **Prod** - WNEDTV 1982

Tighten security by knowing your customer 25 MIN
VHS
Color (COR)
$665.00 purchase, $225.00 rental _ #BTC10
Explains how to recognize and get rid of con artists, including how to spot phony IDs. Includes a leader's guide. Produced by Banctraining.
Business and Economics
Dist - EXTR

Tighten the drums - self - decoration among the Enga 58 MIN
VHS / 16mm
Institute of Papua New Guinea Studies series
Color (G)
$800.00, $400.00 purchase, $80.00, $60.00 rental
Shows the diverse forms of body art in both daily life and ritual in Enga village society in the Western Highlands of Papua New Guinea. Looks at the use of earth paints, tree oils, bird plumes, human hair and a variety of plants to turn the body into a medium for an expressive and dramatic symbolism. Part of a series by Chris Owen.
Fine Arts; History - World; Sociology
Dist - DOCEDR **Prod** - IPANGS 1983

Tighten up workout
VHS
Rotation and motivation exercise series
Color (H C A)
$19.95 purchase _ #BW603V
Presents the third of a three - part series of exercise programs. Focuses on muscle firming and toning exercises designed to add definition to the body and its muscle groups.
Physical Education and Recreation; Science - Natural
Dist - CAMV

Tighten Your Belts, Bite the Bullet 48 MIN
U-matic / VHS / 16mm
Color (A)
LC 81-701571
Uses animation, archival photography and on - site photography to show how New York City and Cleveland grappled with their financial woes. Reveals that while New York City sought solvency through financial arrangements with its banks, Cleveland refused to have its largest bank buy it out of default. Points out that cities, not financial institutions, should have control of their governments.
Business and Economics; Civics and Political Systems; Sociology
Dist - ICARUS **Prod** - CCFG 1981

Tightrope 12 MIN
VHS / U-matic / BETA
Working in the hazard zone series
Color; PAL (IND G A) (SPANISH)
$175.00 rental _ #OSH-500; $775.00 purchase, $175.00 rental _ #TIG003
Looks at common non - chemical, physical hazards often encountered by hazardous waste workers. Shows how to avoid safety hazards such as slips, trips, falls, electrical hazards, natural hazards, oxygen deficiency and heat stress. Part of a five - part series on working with hazardous substances in compliance with OSHA and EPA - RCRA training regulations.
Health and Safety; Psychology
Dist - BNA **Prod** - BNA 1991
ITF

Tightrope 30 MIN
16mm
Footsteps Series
Color
LC 79-701557
Demonstrates how attitudes toward child rearing have changed over the past fifty years and how children are affected by extreme approaches. Emphasizes that moderation is the best policy in parenting.
Guidance and Counseling; Home Economics; Sociology
Dist - USNAC **Prod** - USOE 1978

The Tightrope walkers 30 MIN
U-matic / VHS
Money puzzle - the world of macroeconomics series; Module 15
Color
Focuses on the complexities of the exchange rate. Includes the meaning of the 'balance of trade' and the 'balance of payments.'
Business and Economics; Sociology
Dist - MDCC **Prod** - MDCC

Tigris - Euphrates Valley 36 MIN
VHS
Daily life in the ancient world series
Color (I J)
$50.00 purchase _ #CLV0201
Explores daily life in the ancient civilizations of the Tigris - Euphrates Valley through the eyes of an ordinary citizen. Covers the physical environment of the period, government and society, religious and educational beliefs and more. Part of a three - part series on daily life in the ancient world. Video transfer from filmstrips.
History - World
Dist - KNOWUN

The Tigua Indians - Our Oldest Texans 8 MIN
U-matic / VHS / Slide
Texas Indians Series
Color; Mono (J H)
Discusses the settlement of Tigua Indians in Texas from 1680 to present.
History - United States; Social Science; Sociology
Dist - UTXITC **Prod** - UTXITC 1971

Tikal 5 MIN
16mm
Color
LC 76-703332
Shows the Mayan ruins of Tikal in Guatemala.
Geography - World; Sociology
Dist - SUMHIL **Prod** - SUMHIL 1974

Tikal 23 MIN
16mm
Color (H C A)
LC 78-700711
Presents an introduction to Mayan civilization through the architecture of Tikal in Guatemala.
Fine Arts; Geography - World; History - World; Sociology
Dist - PSUPCR **Prod** - HEIDK 1977

Tikinagan 59 MIN
VHS / 16mm
As long as the rivers flow series
Color (G)
$390.00 purchase, $75.00 rental
Visits Tikinagan, a native - run child care agency operating out of Sioux Lookout in northwestern Ontario. Touches on the peril of reservations where gas sniffing and alcoholism are major problems and the bitterness and distrust left by years of conflict with provincial child welfare agencies. Directed by Gil Cardinal. Part of a five - part series dealing with the struggle of Native People in Canada to regain control over their destinies.
Fine Arts; Social Science
Dist - FIRS **Prod** - CULRAY 1991

Tikits 17 MIN
VHS / U-matic
Color (J H G)
$280.00, $330.00 purchase, $60.00 rental
Adapts a short story about a 10 - year - old dyslexic boy who copes with the selfish and thoughtless behavior of adults by issuing tickets for misdeeds. Presents a morality tale with a poignant epiphany when the boy returns home and the viewer learns the child is himself the victim of an abusive childhood. Produced by Benjamin Hershleder.

Literature and Drama; Religion and Philosophy; Sociology
Dist - NDIM

Tikki Tikki Tembo 9 MIN
U-matic / VHS / 16mm
Color (K P)
LC 74-701454
Uses the pictures and text of the book of the same title, retold by Arlene Mosel and illustrated by Blair Lent. Shows why parents today give their children short names.
Literature and Drama
Dist - WWS **Prod** - SCHNDL 1974

Tiko's adventures in Kash Koosh 28 MIN
VHS
Color (P I)
$150.00 purchase
Follows the adventures of the shepherd boy Tiko who discovers a space ship in the desert.
Fine Arts; Literature and Drama
Dist - LANDMK **Prod** - LANDMK 1992

Til death do us part 16 MIN
VHS
Color (I J H)
$225.00 purchase _ #B040 - V8
Combines rap music and dance to tell a chilling tale about AIDS, peer pressure, drug abuse, and personal responsibility. Targets at - risk youth in grades 7 - 12, triggers class discussion.
Guidance and Counseling; Health and Safety; Sociology
Dist - ETRASS **Prod** - ETRASS

Til death do us part 20 MIN
VHS
Color (A)
$335.00 purchase
Presents a story on widowhood from the ABC TV series 20 - 20.
Sociology
Dist - ABCLR **Prod** - ABCLR 1983

Til death do us part 25 MIN
VHS / 16mm
Color (J H)
$375.00, $350.00 purchase, $57.00 rental
Films a theater play created by the young adults of the Everyday Theater in Washington, DC, discussing the decisions that young people and their peers must make concerning intravenous drug use and unprotected sex in the face of the AIDS epidemic.
Guidance and Counseling; Health and Safety; Psychology
Dist - DURRIN **Prod** - DURRIN 1988

Til death do us part 30 MIN
U-matic
Currents - 1985 - 86 season series; Pt 205
Color (A)
Examines the current trends in marriage and family in this country.
Social Science; Sociology
Dist - PBS **Prod** - WNETTV 1985

Tile Installation 16 MIN
VHS
Ceilings Series
$39.95 purchase _ #DI - 128
Discusses installing ceiling tiles, including planning, tools and materials, safety, and tips, installing tracks and tiles.
Industrial and Technical Education
Dist - CAREER **Prod** - CAREER

Tiling countertops with Michael Byrne 60 MIN
BETA / VHS
Color (G A)
$29.95 _ #060027
Shows how to install tile on countertops. Features carpenter Michael Byrne. Also available in book format.
Home Economics; Industrial and Technical Education
Dist - TANTON **Prod** - TANTON

Tiling floors with Michael Byrne 60 MIN
VHS / BETA
Color (G A)
$29.95 _ #060031
Shows how to install tile on floors. Features carpenter Michael Byrne. Also available in book format.
Home Economics; Industrial and Technical Education
Dist - TANTON **Prod** - TANTON

Tiling walls with Michael Byrne 75 MIN
BETA / VHS
Color (G A)
$29.95 _ #060029
Shows how to install tile on walls. Features carpenter Michael Byrne. Also available in book format.
Home Economics; Industrial and Technical Education
Dist - TANTON **Prod** - TANTON

Till divorce do us part 30 MIN
U-matic / VHS
(A)
$180 purchase, $30 five day rental
Discusses the emotional and psychological consequences of divorce. Focuses on the steps from survival to recovery.
Guidance and Counseling; Sociology
Dist - GPN **Prod** - CTVC 1984

Till my head caves in 5 MIN
16mm
B&W (G)
$40.00 rental
Presents Rock Ross' first anti - intellectual production.
Fine Arts
Dist - CANCIN

Till the Butcher Cuts Him Down 53 MIN
16mm / VHS
Color
Documents the music and life of New Orleans jazz trumpeter Kid Punch Miller.
Fine Arts
Dist - RHPSDY **Prod** - RHPSDY 1971

Till the Clouds Roll by 137 MIN
16mm
Color
Presents a fictionalized version of the life of songwriter Jerome Kern. Stars Robert Walker, Judy Garland, and Van Heflin.
Fine Arts
Dist - REELIM **Prod** - MGM 1946

The Tillerman 15 MIN
16mm
Color (H C A)
LC 76-701751
Presents the story of the tillerman or the back seat driver on a fire apparatus. Describes the tillerman's duties and gives instructions on negotiating all types of corners.
Health and Safety
Dist - FILCOM **Prod** - LACFD 1958

Tillie, the Unhappy Hippopotamus 12 MIN
16mm / U-matic / VHS
Color; Captioned (P I)
LC 79-700957
Tells the story of Tillie the hippo, who requests to be changed into a butterfly, a fish and a bird.
Guidance and Counseling; Literature and Drama
Dist - LCOA **Prod** - TRNKAJ 1979

Tillie's punctured romance 73 MIN
VHS
B&W (G)
$29.95 purchase
Tells the story of a city slicker who marries country bred Tillie for her inheritance, which he intends to share with his former sweetheart. Teams Charlie Chaplin, Mabel Normand and the Keystone Kops in the first full - length comedy produced. Includes Chaplin's short film, Mabel's Married Life. Directed by Mack Sennett.
Fine Arts
Dist - KINOIC
VIDIM

Tilling compacted forest soils 25 MIN
VHS / U-matic / Slide
Color (C PRO IND A)
$140.00 purchase, $25.00 rental _ #876
Introduces soil tillage as a means of alleviating forest soil compaction problems. Compares the relative effectiveness of four tilling implements - brush blades, rock rippers, winged rippers and disk harrows. Includes information to improve tillage management decisions and operations.
Agriculture; Science - Natural
Dist - OSUSF **Prod** - OSUSF 1985

Tilling the Land 15 MIN
U-matic
North America - Growth of a Continent Series
Color (J H)
Gives a history of agricultural progress from pioneer farming to the highly scientific agricultural operations of today.
Geography - United States; Geography - World
Dist - TVOTAR **Prod** - TVOTAR 1980

Tilson's Book Shop Series
Mommies - are You My Mother - the Way Mothers are 15 MIN
Dist - GPN

Tilt 19 MIN
U-matic / VHS / 16mm
Color (J)
LC 73-702267
Explains that in the first decade of development of the Information and Public Affairs Department of the World Bank, 1960 to 1970, much was learned from the successes and failures in seeking to change the quality of life in the poorer parts of the globe.
Business and Economics; Sociology
Dist - MGHT **Prod** - NFBC 1973

Tilt and turn with Gene Mills 60 MIN
VHS
Wrestling videos series
Color (H C A)
$39.95 purchase _ #DP008V
Features Gene Mills covering basic wrestling skills, focusing on tilt and turn techniques. Includes live - action demonstration of these skills.
Physical Education and Recreation
Dist - CAMV

Tilting pad, oil film, trust bearings 60 MIN
U-matic / VHS
Mechanical equipment maintenance series; Bearings and lubrication; Module 4
Color (IND)
Industrial and Technical Education
Dist - LEIKID **Prod** - LEIKID

Tim - His Sensory - Motor Development 31 MIN
U-matic / VHS / 16mm
Color (PRO)
LC 75-703050
Shows Dr Clair Kopp as she records the pattern of growth of an infant in a study based on the work of Jean Piaget. Examines new evidence that the origins of intelligence develop in the sensory - motor period, the time from birth to about two years of age.
Psychology
Dist - CORF **Prod** - UCLA 1974

Tim Miller, Pooh Kaye and Ishmael Houston - Jones 30 MIN
VHS / U-matic
Eye on Dance - the Experimentalists Series
Color
Fine Arts
Dist - ARCVID **Prod** - ARCVID

Timber and Totem Poles 11 MIN
16mm
Color
LC 74-705806
Shows the timber resources of the Tongass National Forest in southeast Alaska and explains the meaning of the totem poles of the Indians.
Geography - United States; Science - Natural
Dist - USNAC **Prod** - USDA 1949

Timber - EAC in Canada 23 MIN
16mm
Color
Shows what humans have done with the one - million acre Tahsis forest area on Vancouver Island.
Agriculture; Geography - World
Dist - AUDPLN **Prod** - RDCG

Timber in Finland 15 MIN
16mm / U-matic / VHS
Man and his world series
Color (I J H)
LC 79-705470
Shows how natural highways of lakes and rivers are used to carry pulp to the paper mills. Discusses reconstruction efforts to reclaim bottom land for the use of forestry and safeguards employed to avoid the exhausting of natural resources.
Geography - World; Science - Natural; Social Science
Dist - FI **Prod** - FI 1969

Timber Today and Tomorrow 20 MIN
16mm
Color
Shows how by scientific forestry, grazing lands are protected, erosion is prevented and wild life is preserved.
Agriculture; Science - Natural
Dist - CALVIN **Prod** - CALVIN 1953

Timber Town 13 MIN
16mm
Color (J)
LC 73-702489
Explains that the logging industry provides the livelihood of a small town nestled in the hardwood forests of the southwestern corner of Australia. Views the life of the townspeople and the operations of the logging industry - timber getting, re - forestation and control of brush fires.
Geography - World; Science - Natural; Social Science
Dist - AUIS **Prod** - FLMAUS 1973

Timberlane, a Sculpture Garden 17 MIN
16mm
Color
LC 78-701634
Presents a history of the sculpture garden at Timberlane, the Wurtzburger family estate in Pikesville, Maryland. Includes a look at the sculptures by 20th century artists.
Fine Arts; Geography - United States
Dist - PSU **Prod** - PSU 1978

Timberline 16 MIN
U-matic / VHS / 16mm
Mountain Habitat Series
Color (I J H)
Illustrates the mixture of flora and fauna that flourishes at the ill - defined zone above which trees will not grow, but tundra life teems.
Geography - United States; Science - Natural
Dist - BCNFL **Prod** - KARVF 1982

Timberline lodge - legacy of the 30s 29 MIN
VHS / 16mm
Color (G)
$55.00 rental _ #TLLT - 000
Tells the story of Timberline Lodge, an all - season recreation center in Oregon. Reveals how the lodge was built by unemployed blacksmiths, woodworkers and artisans under the auspices of the WPA project.
History - United States
Dist - PBS **Prod** - KOAPTV

Timbromania 29 MIN
U-matic / VHS / 16mm
Color (G)
Offers a guided tour of one of the world's most popular hobbies, stamp collecting, tracing it from the stamp craze of the 1880s through its current popularity. Includes scenes of stamps being printed and developed by the Bureau of Engraving and Printing.
Industrial and Technical Education; Physical Education and Recreation
Dist - PSU **Prod** - PSU 1984
AUDPLN

Time 15 MIN
U-matic
Mathematical Relationship Series
Color (I)
Looks at the importance of the measurement of time and considers both its philosophical and historical aspects.
Education; Mathematics
Dist - TVOTAR **Prod** - TVOTAR 1982

Time 14 MIN
16mm / U-matic / VHS
Science Processes Series
Color (P I)
Teaches that time is another form of measurement which is determined by different standards according to different needs.
Mathematics
Dist - MGHT **Prod** - MGHT 1970

Time 30 MIN
U-matic
Polka dot door series
Color (K)
Presents a variety show for pre - school children. Includes songs, mime, stories, film sequences, talk, dance and fantasy figures. Each show in the series emphasizes a particular theme, such as numbers, feelings, exploring, music or time. Comes with parent - teacher guide.
Fine Arts; Literature and Drama
Dist - TVOTAR **Prod** - TVOTAR 1985

Time 10 MIN
VHS
Stop, look, listen series
Color; PAL (P I J)
Observes the activities of people at different times of the day. Looks at the work and activities of different classes of people. Part of a series of films which start from some everyday observation and show more of what is happening, how and why. Builds vocabulary and encourages children to be more observant.
Psychology; Social Science; Sociology
Dist - VIEWTH

Time After Time 122 MIN
16mm
Color
Tells how H G Wells travels forward in time in order to catch Jack the Ripper. Describes Wells' adventures in 1979 San Francisco. Stars Malcolm McDowell and Mary Steenburgen.
Fine Arts
Dist - SWANK **Prod** - WB

A Time and a Place 9 MIN
U-matic / VHS / 16mm
Color (K P)
LC 79-701776
Tells the story of a young bug named Bucky who hates school and wants to spend his time playing. Shows how he runs away only to realize that he belongs at home.
Guidance and Counseling
Dist - BARR **Prod** - BARR 1978

Time and Clocks 28 MIN
16mm
PSSC Physics Films Series
B&W (H C)
Discusses concepts of time measurement and shows various devices used to measure and record time intervals. Points out that the accuracy of a clock can be judged only by comparison with another clock.
Mathematics; Science; Science - Physical
Dist - MLA **Prod** - PSSC 1958

Time and Dateline 9 MIN
VHS / 16mm
Color (C)
$80.00, $34.95 purchase _ #194 E 0084, 193 E 2084
Simplifies the concept of 24 time zones, the dateline and the passage of day.
Science; Science - Physical
Dist - WARDS **Prod** - AAS

Time and dateline 10 MIN
VHS
Astronomy series
Color (J H)
$34.95 purchase _ #193 W 0053; $24.95 purchase _ #S9105
Shows the concepts of 24 time zones and the passage of days. Part of a six - part series presenting a single concept about astronomy.
Mathematics; Science - Physical
Dist - WARDS **Prod** - WARDS
HUBDSC HUBDSC

Time and destiny 30 MIN
VHS / BETA
New pathways in science series
Color (G)
$29.95 purchase _ #S460
Focuses on the qualitative and cyclical nature of time. Draws on quantum physics and geometry to understand the cyclic patterns in time through cultivation of intuition and feeling with resonant timing. Features mathematician, physicist and philosopher Dr Charles Muses, author of 'Destiny and Control in Human Systems' and 'The Lion Path.' Part of a four - part series on new pathways in science.
Mathematics; Psychology; Religion and Philosophy; Science - Physical
Dist - THINKA **Prod** - THINKA

Time and Direction 7 MIN
16mm
Science Series
Color (K P I)
Explores sundials and compasses as indicators of time and direction, and discusses where the sun rises and sets.
Mathematics; Science - Natural; Science - Physical; Social Science
Dist - SF **Prod** - MORLAT 1967

Time and Light 60 MIN
U-matic / VHS
Smithsonian World Series
Color (J)
Explores time measured by the evolution of the sea urchin and the changes in bamboo. Tours a collection of time pieces. Visits the birthplace of our present - day calendar. Examines 19th - century artist Thomas Moran's use of light to portray earth's timetable in the Grand Canyon.
Science - Natural; Science - Physical
Dist - WETATV **Prod** - WETATV

Time and light 55 MIN
VHS
Smithsonian world series
Color (G)
$19.95 purchase _ #FFO9863V-F
Describes the third segment in a four-part videotape series focusing on the Smithsonian Institution and the subjects to which it devotes its museum space. Focuses on time and light, how time can be measured by plants, humans, and animals. Details how looking at the light emitted from stars can give humans a glimpse into the ancient past. This segment may be purchased separately or as part of the four-tape package.
Mathematics; Science - Physical
Dist - CAMV

Time and light - a film about photographs 24 MIN
VHS
Color (H G)
$250.00 purchase, $50.00 rental
Examines the nature of photography and its powers of expression. Combines photos with commentary by photographers such as Marc Camille Chaimowicz and the late Jo Spence and critics such as Halla Beloff and John Berger. Directed by Roger Elsgood.
Fine Arts
Dist - CNEMAG

Time and meta - programs - 5 77 MIN
VHS
Building and maintaining generalizations series
Color; PAL; SECAM (G)
$75.00 purchase
Features Richard Bandler in the fifth part of a six - part series on building and maintaining generalizations, using submodalities from advanced NLP, neuro - linguistic programming. Shows how people are motivated, learn, become convinced and generalize. Contains the first recorded descriptions of Bandler's time model. Recommended that tapes be viewed in order. Bandler sometimes uses profanity for emphasis, which may offend some people.
Health and Safety; Psychology
Dist - NLPCOM **Prod** - NLPCOM

Time and money 58 MIN
VHS
Skyscraper series
Color; CC (G)
$89.95 purchase _ #EX2614; Program not available in Canada.
Chronicles the construction of Worldwide Plaza, a 47 - story, 770 - foot tower built on the former site of Madison Square Garden in New York City.
Geography - United States; Industrial and Technical Education
Dist - FOTH **Prod** - WGBH

Time and money - making the most of scarce resources - Tape 5 60 MIN
VHS
Management skills for church leaders series
Color (G R PRO)
$10.00 rental _ #36 - 85 - 223
Reviews time and money management techniques, including how to hold effective meetings.
Business and Economics; Religion and Philosophy
Dist - APH

Time and Motion 30 MIN
U-matic / VHS
Photographic Vision - all about Photography Series
Color
Industrial and Technical Education
Dist - CDTEL **Prod** - COAST

Time and motion 29 MIN
VHS
Photographic vision series
Color (G)
$49.95 purchase _ #RM113V-F
Examines action photography. Presents the technical aspects of photography clearly and simply, including principles of the camera and techniques for controlling exposure, the use of various kinds of lighting, selection of appropriate lenses and film and basic darkroom techniques. Focuses on the world of photographers and photography - its history and evolution, its uses for personal development and expression, and the impact of photography on the world. Part of a 20-part series examining all aspects of the field of photography.
Industrial and Technical Education
Dist - CAMV

Time and physical existence according to Buddhist philosophy 36 MIN
VHS / BETA
Color; PAL (G)
PdS18 purchase
Features the Dalai Lama's talk to the IBM Conference titled 'Science Revisited,' in London, March of 1991.
Fine Arts; Religion and Philosophy
Dist - MERIDT

Time and Place 17 MIN
16mm
Color (H C A)
Presents an impressionistic study of Australia's living environment, including architecture and urban development.
Fine Arts; Geography - World; Sociology
Dist - AUIS **Prod** - ANAIB 1971

A Time and Place for Everything 15 MIN
U-matic / VHS / 16mm
Color (A)
Shows how planning can expedite getting a job done, by an example from the construction industry. An on-site examination reveals much better results could be obtained through planning deliveries, scheduling operations and using a flow chart.
Industrial and Technical Education; Psychology
Dist - IFB **Prod** - CSAO

Time and places 9 MIN
16mm
Color (G)
$25.00 rental
Embarks on a personal journey where images of the phenomenal world are woven with those gathered during the Vietnam War, as the former triggers the latter. Shares a common human experience in which a singular event or experience causes one to cross the point of no return - and the world is never quite the same.

Fine Arts; History - United States; Psychology
Dist - CANCIN **Prod** - ZIPPER 1982

Time and Suzie Thompson 20 MIN
16mm
Doctors at Work Series
B&W (H C A)
LC FIA65-1365
Presents the case of a young housewife who delays medical attention after detecting a lump in her breast. Surveys various courses of treatment including biopsy, frozen section and mastectomy.
Guidance and Counseling; Health and Safety
Dist - LAWREN **Prod** - CMA 1963

Time and Terri Adams 16 MIN
16mm
B&W (H C A)
LC FIA65-1356
A hysterectomy is performed after a malignant cystic growth is found in an ovary of a mother of four children.
Health and Safety; Science - Natural
Dist - LAWREN **Prod** - CMA 1963

Time and Territory Management
U-matic / VHS
Making of a Salesman Series Session 8
Color
Helps sellers to develop plans and strategies of account territory coverage. Includes such topics as selling versus managing accounts, time wasters and savers, sales forecasting game plan, call frequency and time apportionment.
Business and Economics; Psychology
Dist - PRODEV **Prod** - PRODEV

Time and territory management - turning time into gold 30 MIN
VHS
Color (IND PRO)
$495.00 purchase, $95.00 rental _ #BBP05
Shows how to identify and eliminate time wasting procedures. Includes a companion leader's guide.
Business and Economics
Dist - EXTR **Prod** - BBP

Time and the hour 25 MIN
VHS
Book tower series
Color; PAL (I J)
PdS20 purchase
Adapts a book by Jan Mark. Tells about a class competition - with money on the side - to see how much time can be wasted in a week. Part of a series reviewing new books and adapting them as drama serials. Contact distributor about availability outside the United Kingdom.
Education; Literature and Drama
Dist - ACADEM

Time and Two Women 18 MIN
16mm
Color (H C S) (SPANISH)
Dr Joe V Meigs, consulting visiting gynecologist to the Vincent Memorial Hospital at the Massachusetts General Hospital, Boston, explains how cancer of the uterus can be detected in the earliest stages through cell examination - 'PAP' test - as part of annual health checkups.
Health and Safety; Sociology
Dist - AMCS **Prod** - AMCS 1957

Time being 8 MIN
16mm
B&W (G)
$20.00 rental
Shapes a delicate portrait of the filmmaker's mother through time and refracted light while unfolding the relationship between them as well.
Psychology; Sociology
Dist - CANCIN **Prod** - NELSOG 1991

The Time Bomb 27 MIN
VHS / 16mm
Color (G) (ENGLISH, SPANISH)
$250.00 purchase, $55.00 rental; LC 89715652
Examines the debt crisis in Latin America which has created a volatile political situation threatening fragile democracies throughout the region. Features interviews with economists and government leaders in the Dominican Republic, Mexico, Chile, Peru, Bolivia, Argentina and Venezuela.
Business and Economics; Civics and Political Systems; Geography - World; History - World; Sociology
Dist - CNEMAG **Prod** - UN 1989

Time bomb 35 MIN
VHS / U-matic
Color (COR)
Tells the story of a computer department overtaken by a series of disasters because security systems were not developed or enforced. Highlights such areas as program change controls, back - up, user checks, documentation, management of key staff and physical security.
Business and Economics; Mathematics; Psychology
Dist - VISUCP **Prod** - MELROS
VLEARN

Time Bomb in the River 24 MIN
16mm
Color
LC 74-705794
Documents the search, recovery and salvage of four huge tanks of dangerous liquid chlorine from the Mississippi River near Natchez, Mississippi. Covers the emergency planning of several agencies to protect the health and welfare of 80 thousand residents in a radius of 30 miles of the sunken barge.
Science; Social Science; Sociology
Dist - USNAC **Prod** - USAE 1963

The Time bomb within 14 MIN
U-matic / VHS / 16mm
Managing stress series
Color (H C A)
Tells how uncontrolled stress is a significant factor in absenteeism and loss of efficiency. Outlines major health consequences of unrelieved stress and suggests ways to lessen its effects.
Health and Safety; Psychology
Dist - CENTEF **Prod** - CENTRO 1984
CORF

Time Capsule of Electrical Progress 3 MIN
16mm
Color
LC 78-706128
Discusses major developments in the history of electricity from Thomas Edison to the moon flights.
Industrial and Technical Education; Science; Science - Physical
Dist - STEEGP **Prod** - GE 1969

Time changes the land - geology of Zion - Bryce 23 MIN
U-matic / VHS / 16mm
Color; Captioned (J H G)
Pictures the land formations in Zion and Bryce canyons and explains their development. Studies the geological and ecological aspects of the region.
Geography - United States; Science - Natural
Dist - MCFI **Prod** - HOE 1963

Time Dilation - an Experiment with Mu - Mesons 36 MIN
16mm
PSSC College Physics Films Series
B&W (H A)
LC FIA67-5925
Depicts an experiment at Massachusetts Institute of Technology and on top of Mt Washington, New Hampshire, using radioactive decay of cosmic ray mu - mesons to show the dilation of time. Features David H Frisch, Mit, and James H Smith, University of Illinois.
Science; Science - Physical
Dist - MLA **Prod** - PSSC 1966

Time Exposure - William Henry Jackson, Picture Maker of the Old West 28 MIN
16mm
Color
LC 79-701062
Depicts William Henry Jackson's photographic documentation of the American West during the late 19th century.
Fine Arts; History - United States; Industrial and Technical Education
Dist - CRYSP **Prod** - CRYSP 1979

Time - Five Minutes 15 MIN
U-matic
Studio M Series
Color (P)
Tells how to estimate and tell the time to the nearest five minutes on different types of clocks.
Mathematics
Dist - GPN **Prod** - WCETTV 1979

Time Flies 15 MIN
16mm
Color (P I)
Presents Our Gang on a map - reading exercise and tells how they become completely lost. Shows how they take the advice of a seafarer and end up creating havoc through lanes, hedges, restaurants, shops and even a deep freeze plant.
Literature and Drama
Dist - LUF **Prod** - CHILDF 1972

Time Flies 25 MIN
16mm
Color (H A)
Traces the history of commercial air service in Europe. Includes scenes of the first 'flying boat,' an early catapult launch for planes and the first airmail service between Europe and the Americas. Narrated by Frank Blair.
History - World; Social Science
Dist - WSTGLC **Prod** - WSTGLC

Time for action 30 MIN
U-matic
Read all about it - one series
Color (I)
Teaches reading and writing skills as it continues a story in which Chris and his friends put together a new edition of the newspaper featuring an interview with Captain Hook. Lynne gives her speech to save the park.
Education; English Language; Literature and Drama
Dist - TVOTAR **Prod** - TVOTAR 1982

Time for caring 41 MIN
U-matic / VHS
Color (H C A)
Presents an in - depth look at the role of the volunteer in hospice care. Focuses on quality of life rather than on dying. Shows how the skills and talents of volunteers are incorporated into the program.
Health and Safety; Sociology
Dist - NFBC **Prod** - NFBC
AJN

Time for Caring 42 MIN
16mm
Color
Presents the experiences and resourcefulness of volunteers working on a palliative care team.
Psychology; Social Science
Dist - NFBC **Prod** - NFBC 1982

A Time for Caring - the School's Response to the Sexually Abused Child 28 MIN
16mm
Sexual Abuse of Children Series
Color (C A)
LC 79-700480
Presents professionals, experienced in recognizing sexually abused children, who explain what steps can be taken by schools to protect a child from further abuse.
Education; Guidance and Counseling; Sociology
Dist - LAWREN **Prod** - BAKRSR 1979

Time for clocks 10 MIN
U-matic / VHS / 16mm
Color; B&W (P)
LC FIA63-599
Shows how clocks help people to use their time wisely. A time for work, play, rest and other activities is explained through poetic narration and stylized settings. Introductory techniques for telling time are also given.
Mathematics; Social Science
Dist - EBEC **Prod** - EH 1967

A Time for Decision 16 MIN
16mm
Color (A)
LC FIA67-656
Uses animation to illustrate the history and hazards of cigarette smoking. Designed for presentation to community leaders.
Health and Safety
Dist - AMCS **Prod** - AMCS 1966

A Time for Decision 29 MIN
U-matic / VHS / 16mm
Color (H C) (SPANISH)
LC 73-701069
Focuses on emotional, social and economic problems affecting an alcoholic's family and associates and develops a practical approach of family guidance.
Guidance and Counseling; Health and Safety; Sociology
Dist - AIMS **Prod** - HOLF 1967
LAC

A Time for Decision 7 MIN
U-matic / VHS / 16mm
Citizenship - Whose Responsibility, Set 2 Series; Set 2
Color (J H)
LC FIA68-2877
Describes the dilemma of a high school student who must choose between supporting a personal friend or another student for class president.
Guidance and Counseling; Psychology
Dist - IFB **Prod** - IFB 1967

Time for Decision 28 MIN
VHS / U-matic
Color (J A) (SPANISH)
Tells the story of a housewife whose attorney husband is an alcoholic.
Fine Arts; Psychology; Sociology
Dist - SUTHRB **Prod** - SUTHRB

A Time for Every Season 30 MIN
16mm
Color
Summarizes Dr Everett L Shostrom's Actualizing Therapy, which uses the idea that man's nature consists of four major polarities - anger, love, strength and weakness, analogous to winter, summer, spring and fall.
Psychology
Dist - PSYCHF **Prod** - PSYCHF

A Time for Georgia 15 MIN
16mm
B&W (H C A)
LC 78-711422
Presents a documentary film which describes the pathology of a three - year - old girl with infantile autism. Portrays the value and urgency of placing autistic children in a pre - school nursery school for seriously disturbed children.
Education; Psychology
Dist - NYU **Prod** - PSW 1971
UILL

Time for Horatio - values, mental and emotional
VHS
Key concepts in self - esteem
Color (K P)
$79.95 purchase _ #MF9368RA
Presents one of an 11 - part series teaching key curriculum concepts such as independence, freedom and responsibility, and peer pressure. Includes video, storybook and teaching guide with activities and games. In this video, a kitten can't understand why everyone is so mean until he learns that the world is running on 'mean time.' Through Horatio, young people gain a vision of a peaceful, more compassionate world.
Education; Psychology
Dist - CFKRCM **Prod** - CFKRCM

A Time for Living 12 MIN
16mm
Color
LC 75-703616
Discusses courses and training programs for those over age 50 to learn how to retire.
Physical Education and Recreation; Sociology
Dist - UCONN **Prod** - UCONN 1975

Time for Living 20 MIN
16mm
Color
LC 72-700595
Portrays the summer resort program of young life, a non - sectarian Christian organization, for high school students at seven resorts and ranches in Colorado.
Geography - United States; Physical Education and Recreation; Religion and Philosophy
Dist - YLC **Prod** - YLC 1972

Time for Myself 30 MIN
U-matic / VHS
Y E S Inc Series
Color (J H)
Points out that part of becoming mature is accepting different realities like sickness and aging - how to live with the inevitable and how to deal with personal conflicts and needs without deserting others in the process.
Guidance and Counseling; Psychology
Dist - GPN **Prod** - KCET 1983

A Time for Rain 8 MIN
U-matic / VHS / 16mm
Wonder Walks Series
Color (P I)
LC 74-713442
Follows a young boy on a walk through an urban environment during a rain shower to show the effects brought about by the rain.
Social Science
Dist - EBEC **Prod** - EBEC 1971

Time for strategic planning 55 MIN
VHS
Speaking of success series
Color (H C G)
$39.95 purchase _ #PD16
Features Dr Pete Johnson and his 'Balanced Strategy Concept' - a six - step process to develop and implement a management strategy that makes practical sense. Part of a series.
Business and Economics
Dist - SVIP **Prod** - AUVICA 1993

A Time for Sun 6 MIN
16mm / U-matic / VHS
Wonder Walks Series
Color (P I)
LC 70-713441
Shows effects of the sun on plants, animals and a variety of materials.
Science - Natural; Science - Physical
Dist - EBEC **Prod** - EBEC 1971

Time for Survival 25 MIN
16mm / U-matic / VHS
Color
LC 79-701195
Shows the role of natural diversity in maintaining environmental stability and discusses the importance of all species. Shows how some of man's activities simplify the environment and thereby go against nature's direction.
Science - Natural
Dist - PHENIX **Prod** - NAS 1979

Time for table manners 6 MIN
VHS / U-matic / 16mm
Color (P I)
$190.00, $140.00 purchase _ #JC - 67682
Presents a practical mealtime guide for children. Includes washing before meals, setting the table, the use of eating utensils and standard etiquette such as 'please,' 'thank you,' and cleaning up the eating area. Encourages responsibility and self - respect and socialization. Animated.
Home Economics; Psychology; Social Science; Sociology
Dist - CORF **Prod** - DISNEY 1987

A Time for Winning 23 MIN
16mm
Color
Focuses around the address delivered by Fran Tarkenton at the Scholarship Award Banquet in Chattanooga, Tennesse, for the Fellowship of Christian Athletes.
Physical Education and Recreation; Religion and Philosophy
Dist - FELLCA **Prod** - FELLCA

Time for work and time for play 15 MIN
16mm
Color
Explores Denmark as an industrial nation. Shows its development from an agricultural to an industrial nation.
Agriculture; Business and Economics; Geography - World; History - World; Sociology
Dist - AUDPLN **Prod** - RDCG

Time Form Color 18 MIN
16mm
Color
Records the fossilization of trees, plants, shells, driftwood and debris from distant ships blended with their original colors, textures and dimensions.
Fine Arts; Mathematics
Dist - RADIM **Prod** - FILIM

The Time Game 14 MIN
U-matic / VHS / 16mm
Professional Management Program Series
Color (IND) (SPANISH)
LC 75-702665
Teaches time management using the analogy of a card game in which the stakes are managerial success and the chips are segments of time. Suggests keeping time log, and ways of controlling crises and establishing priorities.
Business and Economics
Dist - NEM **Prod** - NEM 1975

The Time has Come 22 MIN
16mm
Non - Sexist Early Education Films Series
Color (A)
LC 78-700385
Explores the elements of a non - sexist home environment and deals with influences outside the home, such as television and school.
Home Economics; Sociology
Dist - THIRD **Prod** - WAA 1977

The Time has Come - 1964 - 1965 60 MIN
VHS
Eyes On The Prize - Part II - Series
Color; Captioned (G)
$59.95 purchase _ #EYES - 201
Traces the influence of Malcolm X on the early years of the black civil rights movement. Shows how the philosophy of Malcolm X influenced the activities of the Student Nonviolent Coordinating Committee. Part of a series on the black civil rights movement.
Biography; History - United States; Sociology
Dist - PBS **Prod** - BSIDE 1990

The Time has come - 1964 - 1966 - Two societies - 1965 - 1968 120 MIN
VHS
Eyes on the prize II series
Color & B&W (G)
$19.95 purchase _ #PBS 1056
Reveals that the second generation in the civil rights movement includes the charismatic leaders Malcolm X and Stokely Carmichael and gives birth to the cry of 'Black Power' from both the Student Nonviolent Coordinating Committee - SNCC - and the more radical Black Panther Party. Shows how the battle lines are drawn in Watts, Cicero and Detroit as civil unrest shakes the very foundation of the movement, revealing the rifts that exist between blacks and whites in major cities across the United States in Two Societies.
Civics and Political Systems; History - United States; Sociology
Dist - INSTRU **Prod** - PBS

Time - How We Measure it 24 MIN
VHS / 16mm
Color (I)
LC 90706267
Explains the importance of time measurement. Shows how repetitive natural phenomena create seasons, days and nights, months and years.
Business and Economics; Mathematics; Science - Natural
Dist - BARR

Time - how we measure it
Videodisc
Color; CAV (P I J)
$189.00 purchase _ #8L181
Explores the development of the methods used to measure time in an animated format. Looks at primitive forms of measuring time, including the Greek sundial, the Chinese water watch and the first clock developed by Huygens, which led to today's method of telling time through the use of the Greenwich Meridian and the Atomic Clock. Barcoded for instant random access.
Mathematics
Dist - BARR **Prod** - BARR 1991

Time I 30 MIN
VHS / U-matic
Say it with sign series; Pt 11
Color (H C A) (AMERICAN SIGN)
Presents Lawrence Solow and Sharon Neumann Solow introducing American Sign Language used by the hearing - impaired. Emphasizes signs that have to do with time.
Education
Dist - FI **Prod** - KNBCTV 1982

Time II 30 MIN
VHS / U-matic
Say it with sign series; Pt 12
Color (H C A) (AMERICAN SIGN)
Presents Lawrence Solow and Sharon Neumann Solow introducing American Sign Language used by the hearing - impaired. Emphasizes signs that have to do with time.
Education
Dist - FI **Prod** - KNBCTV 1982

Time III 30 MIN
U-matic / VHS
Say it with sign series; Pt 13
Color (H C A) (AMERICAN SIGN)
Presents Lawrence Solow and Sharon Neumann Solow introducing American Sign Language used by the hearing - impaired. Emphasizes signs that have to do with time.
Education
Dist - FI **Prod** - KNBCTV 1982

Time immemorial 59 MIN
VHS / 16mm
As long as the rivers flow series
Color (G)
$390.00 purchase, $75.00 rental
Portrays the Nisga'a tribe of northwestern British Columbia, who have long led the fight for indigenous peoples' rights in Canada. Chronicles their struggle as they take their case for land rights to the Supreme Court of Canada. Uses documentary footage, archival material and interviews to recount the cultural clash of over four generations of Nisga'a. Directed by Hugh Brody. Part of a five - part series dealing with the struggle of Native People in Canada to regain control over their destinies.
Fine Arts; Social Science
Dist - FIRS **Prod** - CULRAY 1991

Time is 30 MIN
U-matic / VHS / 16mm
Color
Presents the major historical developments of the concept of time.
History - World; Sociology
Dist - MGHT **Prod** - MGHT 1964

Time is for Taking 23 MIN
16mm
Color
LC FIA65-478
Gives insight into the world of the retarded child through everyday situations involving children at a residential camp for the retarded. Shows how problems develop and are solved by skillful counselors.
Education; Psychology
Dist - FINLYS **Prod** - FINLYS 1964

Time is Money 30 MIN
U-matic / VHS / 16mm
Color
Presents techniques in time management for salespeople. Points out that salespeople sell more when they make better use of their time, but that most salespeople waste 80 percent of their time. Stars Burgess Meredith and Ron Masak.
Business and Economics; Psychology
Dist - CCCD **Prod** - CCCD 1976

The Time is Out of Joint 20 MIN
U-matic / VHS / 16mm
World of William Shakespeare Series
Color (H C A)
LC 78-700753
Explores the reasons why William Shakespeare chose a medieval setting for Hamlet, with special emphasis on the political and social situation in England at that time.
History - World; Literature and Drama
Dist - NGS **Prod** - NGS 1978

Time Lag
U-matic / VHS
Red Tapes Series
B&W
Pictures a drawing, rehearsal space acting out a new America. Uses street - theatrical language.
Fine Arts
Dist - KITCHN **Prod** - KITCHN

Time - Lapse Studies of Glacier Flow 14 MIN
16mm
B&W
Offers a time - lapse study of glacier motions including material collected over several years from Pacific Northwest glaciers by the University of Washington and the U S Geological Survey. Illustrates the flow of glacier ice over an icefall during periods of three to four months.
Science - Physical
Dist - UWASHP **Prod** - LACHAP 1973

Time Line 10 MIN
16mm / U-matic / VHS
Color (P I)
LC 72-701734
Shows a time line unfolding to show the succeeding ages of the earth and their distinctive plant and animal life, ending with a depiction of man's own history in relationship to the Earth's past.
History - United States; Science - Natural; Science - Physical
Dist - ALTSUL **Prod** - GERDNC 1972

Time, line and events 15 MIN
16mm / VHS
Color (I J)
$325.00, $230.00 purchase, $60.00 rental
Uses terms meaningful to young students to visualize time as a system for measuring events. Gives an understanding of the vastness of geological time. Shows how to make a timeline. Uses animation.
Mathematics; Science - Physical
Dist - CF **Prod** - DF 1979

The Time Line - Managing the Moment for Safety 13 MIN
VHS / U-matic
Color (H C A)
Looks at how accidents can happen when people lose control of the present because their minds are on the past or the future.
Health and Safety
Dist - CORF **Prod** - ATBELL

Time, Lines, and Events 15 MIN
16mm / U-matic / VHS
Color (I J)
LC 80-700535
Uses animation to present a visualization of time as a system for measuring events. Shows how to make a timeline and discusses the vastness of geologic time.
Mathematics
Dist - CF **Prod** - DF 1980

Time lines and history 13 MIN
VHS
Color; PAL (P I J H)
Illustrates the value of time lines in establishing the relativity of time. Introduces the concept of understanding geologic time.
Education; Science - Physical
Dist - VIEWTH

Time Machine 105 MIN
16mm / U-matic / VHS
Color (J)
Presents the story of a scientist who invents a machine which allows him to travel back and forth through time. Based on the story The Time Machine by H G Wells.
Fine Arts; Literature and Drama
Dist - LUF **Prod** - LUF 1979

The Time Machine
16mm / Cassette
Now Age Reading Programs, Set 1 Series
Color (I J)
$9.95 purchase _ #8F - PN681867
Brings a classic tale to young readers. The filmstrip set includes filmstrip, cassette, book, classroom materials and a poster. The read - along set includes an activity book and a cassette.
English Language; Literature and Drama
Dist - MAFEX

The Time machine 103 MIN
VHS
Color (J H)
$29.00 purchase _ #04576 - 126; $24.95 purchase _ #S01578
Stars Rod Taylor and Yvette Mimieux in a screen version of The Time Machine by H G Wells.
Literature and Drama
Dist - GA **Prod** - GA
UILL

The Time machine 29 MIN
U-matic / VHS / 16mm
Dimensions in science - Pt 2 series
Color (H C)
Focuses on the work at Fermilab near Chicago, one of the largest laboratories of physics in the world. Shows how scientists use the tools of high energy physics to peel away layer after layer of the innermost structure of matter. Describes how, as the energy increases, the target area takes on the properties that existed when the exploding universe emerged from the primeval fireball of the Big Bang.
Science; Science - Physical
Dist - FI **Prod** - OECA 1979

Time Machine 45 MIN
U-matic / VHS / 16mm
Classic Stories Series
Color (J)
Describes the adventures of a scientist who invents a machine that can travel back and forth through time. Based on the story The Time Machine by H G Wells.
Literature and Drama
Dist - LUF **Prod** - LUF 1979

The Time Machine 30 MIN
U-matic
Dimensions in Science - Physics Series
Color (H C)
Looks at an experiment at Fermilab which attempts to accelerate electrons to the energy level of the big bang and allow scientists to observe electron behavior at this speed.
Science; Science - Physical
Dist - TVOTAR **Prod** - TVOTAR 1979

The Time Machine - a Novel by H G Wells 15 MIN
16mm / U-matic / VHS
Novel Series
Color (J)
LC 83-700039
Presents a fictional trip from Victorian England to a society of the future. Based on the novel The Time Machine by H G Wells.
Literature and Drama
Dist - IU **Prod** - IITC 1982

Time magazine compact almanac
CD-ROM
Color (G)
$195.00 purchase _ #1901
Contains full text of Time magazine for 1989, full color charts, opinion polls, Man of the Year covers from 1980 through 1989, a quiz on 1989 news events, an almanac of facts and figures drawn from the US Statistical Abstract, full color maps of the world, fax and phone numbers from the Congressional Directory, and documents of American history. Allows users to search by browsing, keywords, and an index to the full text articles. Articles can be marked, saved, and printed. For IBM PCs and compatibles, requires 604K RAM, DOS 3.1 or later, one floppy disk drive - hard disk recommended, one empty expansion slot, an IBM compatible CD - ROM drive, and an EGA or VGA card and monitor.
Geography - United States; Geography - World; History - United States; Literature and Drama; Sociology
Dist - BEP

Time Management 15 MIN
VHS / 16mm
Survivor's Guide to Learning Series
Color (S)
$185.00 purchase _ #288802
Introduces general processes and pointers through interviews with study skills specialists and students who have mastered the techniques. Covers five theme areas and includes five booklets which deal with each theme. 'Time Management' illustrates a process of management which follows these steps - assessment of current use of time, establishment of goals, setting priorities, planning and assessing results.
Agriculture; Business and Economics; Education; Psychology
Dist - ACCESS **Prod** - ACCESS 1989

Time management
VHS
Personal action system series
Color (G)
$149.00 purchase _ #V217
Teaches employees about the benefits of time management as a means of keeping a handle on stress. Part of a 13 - part series to educate employees on the importance of health.
Health and Safety; Psychology
Dist - GPERFO

Time management 30 MIN
VHS
Color (J H C G)
$19.95 purchase _ #NAC11008V
Features Mark McCormack, founder and CEO of International Management Group. Shows how to take control of one's business life and manage time like a champion. Discusses the time bombs that can blow up a business day; how to take control of transition times; how to use the biggest time waster of all, the telephone; how to make the most of leisure time and the art of doing buiness on the road.
Business and Economics; Social Science
Dist - CAMV **Prod** - NIGCON

Time Management 30 MIN
VHS / U-matic
Management for Engineers Series
Color
Business and Economics; Industrial and Technical Education; Psychology
Dist - SME **Prod** - UKY

Time management 50 MIN
VHS
Color (A PRO IND)
$395.00 purchase, $130.00 rental
Gives suggestions on how professionals can make better use of their time. Hosted by Merrill Douglas and Larry Baker of the Time Management Center.
Business and Economics; Psychology
Dist - VLEARN **Prod** - CVIDE

Time management 54 MIN
VHS
Color (A PRO)
$69.95 purchase _ #S01552
Proposes that time is the most important resource of all, and one that must be managed. Suggests time management techniques. Stresses advance planning.
Business and Economics; Psychology
Dist - UILL

Time Management 30 MIN
VHS
Color (G)
$69.95 purchase _ #6232
Shows how to increase productivity, control the flow of paperwork, delegate, eliminate trivia. Includes guidebook.
Business and Economics; Mathematics
Dist - SYBVIS **Prod** - SYBVIS

Time management
VHS
Color (A PRO IND)
$995.00 purchase, $165.00 rental
Presents a day - long workshop on time management. Covers subjects including taking responsibility for one's own time management, how to determine what needs to be changed, and strategies for improvement.
Business and Economics; Psychology
Dist - VLEARN **Prod** - ITRC

Time management 22 MIN
VHS
Color (A PRO)
$495.00 purchase, $150.00 rental
Teaches how to analyze personal use and misuse of time, with ways to better use time through organization. Based on the book Personal Time Management by Marion Haynes. Includes video and book with case studies, logs and charts.
Business and Economics
Dist - DHB **Prod** - CRISP

Time Management - a Basic Exercise 15 MIN
VHS
Color (H C A)
$79.95 purchase, $26.00 rental _ #57704
Illustrates with two case histories the traps most people fall into which prevent their controlling their time. Includes advice on avoiding each trap, how to build on small successes toward control. Stresses keeping track of and re - using the most successful techniques.
Psychology
Dist - UILL **Prod** - UILL 1985

Time Management - a Practical Approach Series
Avoiding time traps
Getting Things Done
Planning Your Time
Dist - DELTAK

Time Management - a Second Chance 22 MIN
16mm / U-matic / VHS
Color (C A)
Summarizes principles and practices of time management proven effective for faculty and staff in colleges and universities.
Business and Economics; Mathematics; Psychology
Dist - IU **Prod** - IU 1984

Time Management, E Byron Chew
U-matic / VHS
Management Skills Series
Color (PRO)
Business and Economics; Psychology
Dist - AMCEE **Prod** - AMCEE

Time Management for Management Series Pt 1
Principles of Time Management 30 MIN
Dist - TIMLIF

Time Management for Management Series Pt 5
Managing Interruptions 30 MIN
Dist - TIMLIF

Time Management for Management Series Pt 6
Managing Time - Professional and Personal 30 MIN
Dist - TIMLIF

Time management for management series
Decision - making 30 MIN
Dist - TIMLIF

Time Management for Managers and Professionals Series
Collecting subordinate - imposed time - the amateur 20 MIN
Controlling boss - imposed time 30 MIN
Controlling system - imposed time - making the solutions work 20 MIN
Freedom and Leverage 24 MIN
Getting Rid of Subordinate - Imposed Time - the Professional 25 MIN
Managing Your Molecule 15 MIN
The Molecule of Management 22 MIN
Time Management Problem - Peers 20 MIN
Time Management Problem - Subordinates 12 MIN
Time Management Problem - the Boss 20 MIN
Using Time Management 19 MIN
Vocational Time Vs Management Time 20 MIN
Dist - DELTAK

Time Management for Managing Stress 27 MIN
VHS / U-matic
Practical Stress Management with Dr Barry Alberstein Series
Color
Psychology
Dist - DELTAK **Prod** - DELTAK

Time Management for Supervisors 14 MIN
U-matic / VHS / 16mm
Color
Provides supervisors with specific practical time management techniques that can be used immediately, shows them the advantages of written daily plans in keeping their schedules on target and how to take control of their employees' time.
Business and Economics; Psychology
Dist - EFM **Prod** - EFM

Time management ideas that work 47 MIN
VHS
Color (J H C G)
$79.00 purchase _ #CBR1031V
Shows how to minimize time wasters such as interruptions; paperwork; meetings; long - winded writing; poor delegation; procrastination and more.
Business and Economics
Dist - CAMV

Time management - keeping the monkey off your back 30 MIN
VHS
Color (PRO IND A)
$595.00 purchase, $95.00 rental _ #BBP15
Presents insights developed by William Oncken, Jr, on how to manage people, time and priorities. Assists supervisors in controlling work loads rather than being controlled by them. Includes extensive workshop materials.
Business and Economics
Dist - EXTR **Prod** - BBP

Time management - one way to prevent stress 10 MIN
VHS
Color (PRO C G)
#12322, call for price
Explores the relationship between time - consuming activities and stress. Shows some simple strategies to use to increase control over time spent on daily activities.
Produced by the Coordinating Council for Continuing Education in Health Care at Penn State.
Business and Economics; Health and Safety; Psychology
Dist - PSU

Time Management Problem - Peers 20 MIN
U-matic / VHS
Time Management for Managers and Professionals Series
Color
Business and Economics; Psychology
Dist - DELTAK **Prod** - DELTAK

Time Management Problem - Subordinates 12 MIN
VHS / U-matic
Time Management for Managers and Professionals Series
Color
Business and Economics; Psychology
Dist - DELTAK **Prod** - DELTAK

Time Management Problem - the Boss 20 MIN
VHS / U-matic
Time Management for Managers and Professionals Series
Color
Business and Economics; Psychology
Dist - DELTAK **Prod** - DELTAK

Time management skills 28 MIN
VHS
Management skills series
Color (C PRO)
$285.00 purchase, $70.00 rental _ #6003S, #6003V
Explains how to budget and manage time wisely. Explains the causes and effects of poor time management. Shows how to take control of time by using the total management planning concept. Discusses methods of setting priorities and learning the causes of poor time management and how to minimize them. Part of a five - part series on management skills produced by Health and Sciences Network.
Business and Economics; Health and Safety
Dist - AJN

Time marches in 85 MIN
VHS
March of time - the great depression series
B&W (G)
$24.95 purchase _ #S02135
Presents newsreel excerpts covering the period from February to May of 1935. Covers events including Japanese political conflicts, bootlegging of illegal liquor in the US, new traffic lights in London, the opening of the Metropolitan Opera, and more. Part one of a six - part series.
History - United States
Dist - UILL

Time - Measurement and Meaning 26 MIN
U-matic / VHS / 16mm
Man and the Universe Series
Color (H C)
LC 74-702070
Reviews the means by which man has recorded time in the past. Introduces modern methods by which scientists measure time, examine the psychology of subjective time and relate the concepts of entropy and relativity to current ideas about the nature of time.
Mathematics; Science; Science - Physical
Dist - EBEC **Prod** - EBEC 1974

Time, money and measurement 30 MIN
VHS
Tell me why video series
Color (P I)
$19.95 purchase _ #K645
Answers approximately 50 questions about time, money and measurement. Uses colorful graphics and attention - grabbing film footage. Part of a series.
Business and Economics; Mathematics
Dist - KNOWUN

Time - Nagara - Video 4
VHS
Video - cued structural drills series
Color (G) (JAPANESE)
$79.95 purchase _ #VJ - 04
Uses short, often humorous sketches portraying contemporary life in real Japanese schools, offices, restaurants and homes to illustrate expressions of time - Nagara - in Japanese. Incorporates oral drills, grammar patterns and reviews and shows gestures and expressions unique to the Japanese. Part four of a seven - part series by Professor Ken'ichi Ujie, produced by Tokyo Shoseki Co.
Foreign Language
Dist - CHTSUI

A Time of AIDS - the medical and political aspects of AIDS series 240 MIN
VHS
Time of AIDS - the medical and political aspects of AIDS series
Color (G C PRO)
$549.00 purchase _ #UW4562
Presents a four - part series on the history of AIDS. Includes the titles The Zero Factor; The Hunt for the Virus; Fighting for Life; The End of the Beginning.
Health and Safety
Dist - FOTH

The Time of Apollo 28 MIN
16mm
Color (J H A)
LC 75-703841
Examines the statement that President Kennedy made in 1961, stating that America should commit itself to achieving the goal, before this decade is out, of landing a man on the Moon and returning him safely to Earth. Proves the success of the Apollo program.
Biography; History - World; Science; Science - Physical
Dist - USNAC **Prod** - NASA 1975

A Time of challenge 27 MIN
16mm
Color (J H G)
Commemorates the 100th anniversary of the AFL - CIO and organized labor, portraying the struggle of working men and women for fair wages, decent working conditions and economic security. Features various union leaders.
Business and Economics; Social Science
Dist - AFLCIO **Prod** - AFLCIO
MTP

A Time of daring 40 MIN
16mm / VHS
Color (G)
$680.00, $400.00 purchase, $85.00 rental
Takes a provocative look at both sides of the civil war in El Salvador. Juxtaposes scenes of United States advisors with government troops and guerrilla fighters with their supporters. Produced by the Film and Television Collective, Radio Venceremos System.
Fine Arts
Dist - FIRS

Time of darkness 50 MIN
VHS
Horizon series
Color; PAL (H C A)
PdS99 purchase; Not available in the United States
Discusses the warnings in 1992 to inhabitants of the northern hemisphere about skin cancer and cataracts due to the depletion of the ozone layer. Uses images from NASA and recent research findings to link the ozone loss to volcanic eruptions.
Geography - World; Science - Physical
Dist - BBCENE

The Time of diagnosis - 2 8 MIN
VHS
Learning about cancer series
Color (G)
$250.00 purchase, $60.00 rental
Focuses on cancer diagnosis. Takes an in - depth look at the detection and treatment of cancer and the emotional impact of the disease on patients and their families. Part 2 of a five - part series.
Health and Safety
Dist - CF **Prod** - HOSSN 1989

A Time of Hope 14 MIN
16mm
Color
LC FIA66-664
Depicts efforts of the U S Agency for International Development in producing measles vaccines and conducting mass immunization programs in new African nations. Shows American, French and African teams at work.
Health and Safety
Dist - MESHDO **Prod** - MESHDO 1965

Time of Life 18 MIN
16mm
Doctors at Work Series
B&W (H C A)
LC FIA65-1367
Discusses the nature and symptoms of the menopause and describes satisfactory ways of meeting the psychological and physiological problems of this period.
Guidance and Counseling; Psychology; Science - Natural; Sociology
Dist - LAWREN **Prod** - CMA 1962

The Time of Our Lives 63 FRS
VHS / U-matic
Management of Time Series Module 1
Color
Stresses the necessity of good planning if work is to fit into time available and introduces the key elements of good

time management.
Business and Economics; Psychology
Dist - RESEM **Prod** - RESEM

The Time of Our Lives 27 MIN
Videoreel / VT1
Color
Stresses the importance of keeping fit and specific ways to do it. Endorsed by the President of the United States in connection with his physical fitness program.
Biography; Physical Education and Recreation
Dist - MTP **Prod** - AMDAS

Time of the Cree 26 MIN
16mm
Color
LC 77-702677
Investigates the way of life and the past of a Cree family whose ancestors have inhabited Manitoba's Boreal Forest for 6,000 years.
Geography - World; History - World; Social Science; Sociology
Dist - CANFDC **Prod** - SINROD 1974

Time of the Grizzly 26 MIN
16mm
Color
LC 83-700333
Examines the entire spectrum of man's attitudes toward the grizzly.
Science - Natural
Dist - STOUFP **Prod** - STOUFP 1982

Time of the Horn 7 MIN
16mm / U-matic / VHS
B&W (P)
LC FIA65-1160
A small negro boy retrieves a discarded trumpet and loses himself in a jazz fantasy of his own imagining. Musical background is a Duke Ellington composition interpreted by Jonah Jones. No narration is used.
English Language; Fine Arts; Literature and Drama
Dist - JOU **Prod** - JOU 1965

Time of the Jackal 50 MIN
U-matic / VHS / 16mm / BETA
Window on the World Series
Color; Mono (J H C A)
MV $350.00 _ MP $600.00 purchase, $50.00 rental; LC 77-702828
Examines the phenomenon of terrorism and its implications for society.
Sociology
Dist - CTV **Prod** - CTV 1976

Time of the Jackal, Pt 1 25 MIN
BETA / 16mm / VHS
Window on the World Series
Color
LC 77-702828
Examines the phenomenon of terrorism and its implications for society.
Sociology
Dist - CTV **Prod** - CTV 1976

Time of the Jackal, Pt 2 25 MIN
16mm / VHS / BETA
Window on the World Series
Color
LC 77-702828
Examines the phenomenon of terrorism and its implications for society.
Sociology
Dist - CTV **Prod** - CTV 1976

Time of the Jackals 51 MIN
U-matic / VHS / 16mm
Color (H C A)
LC 76-703986
Recreates the 1975 terrorist assaualt on OPEC headquarters in Vienna. Illustrates graphically the modus operandi of the terrorist group and profiles their leader. Considers the general question of political conspiracy and international terrorism.
Civics and Political Systems; History - World; Sociology
Dist - FI **Prod** - CTV 1976

Time of the Jackals, Pt 1 25 MIN
U-matic / VHS / 16mm
Color (H C A)
LC 76-703986
Recreates the 1975 terrorist assault on OPEC headquarters in Vienna. Illustrates graphically the modus operandi of the terrorist group and profiles their leader. Considers the general question of political conspiracy and international terrorism.
Sociology
Dist - FI **Prod** - CTV 1976

Time of the Jackals, Pt 2 26 MIN
16mm / U-matic / VHS
Color (H C A)
LC 76-703986
Recreates the 1975 terrorist assault on OPEC headquarters in Vienna. Illustrates graphically the modus operandi of the terrorist group and profiles their leader. Considers the general question of political conspiracy and international terrorism.
Sociology
Dist - FI **Prod** - CTV 1976

Time of the Locust 12 MIN
16mm / U-matic / VHS
B&W
Uses footage shot by American, Japanese, and Vietnamese cameramen, revealing the agonies of the war in South Vietnam.
History - World; Psychology; Sociology
Dist - CNEMAG **Prod** - AMFSC 1966

Time of the Saviour 24 MIN
16mm
Color
LC 74-700251
Deals with Guru Maharj Ji and his movement, focusing on the main figures of the movement. Raises questions about financing, authenticity of teaching and sentimental exploitation of followers.
Religion and Philosophy; Social Science; Sociology
Dist - PACE **Prod** - PACE 1973

Time of women 20 MIN
16mm / VHS
Color (G) (SPANISH (ENGLISH SUBTITLES))
$225.00 purchase, $60.00 rental
Portrays the rhythms of life in a village in Ecuador populated almost entirely by women. Reveals that the village follows the pattern of many Third World countries where men, out of economic necessity, have migrated to work. Focuses on the women and their responsibilities.
Business and Economics; Geography - World; Sociology
Dist - WMEN **Prod** - MOVAS 1988

Time of wonder 13 MIN
U-matic / VHS / 16mm
Color (K P)
Uses watercolor illustrations from the children's picture book of the same name by Robert McCloskey. Shows the wonders of nature on an island in Maine.
English Language; Literature and Drama
Dist - WWS **Prod** - WWS 1961

Time of Your Life 15 MIN
16mm
Color
Features Panama City, on Florida's Miracle Strip.
Geography - United States; Geography - World; Physical Education and Recreation
Dist - FLADC **Prod** - FLADC

The Time of your life 59 MIN
VHS
Color (J H G)
$225.00 purchase
Looks at society's view of aging and the aged in contrast to medical and scientific improvements that will extend the average person's life. Points out ways society's ideas can change as the number of older citizens increases.
Health and Safety
Dist - LANDMK

The Time of Your Life 28 MIN
16mm / U-matic / VHS
Color
LC 75-703296
Offers insights into the need for time management and suggests techniques for managing time so that more work can be accomplished with less effort.
Business and Economics; Guidance and Counseling; Psychology
Dist - CCCD **Prod** - CCCD 1974

Time of Youth Series
On the Road to Find Out 70 MIN
Dist - WCVBTV

Time offed 13 MIN
16mm
B&W (G)
$20.00 rental
Features a strange and haunting vision of the catharsis involved in the work and leisure expenditure of an apparently nondistinct punch clock worker, a human with its face masked in bandages. Contains special effects.
Fine Arts; Social Science
Dist - CANCIN **Prod** - WENDTD 1971

Time on the line 14 MIN
VHS
Color (A PRO IND)
$395.00 purchase, $100.00 rental
Emphasizes telephone practices in a look at the right and wrong ways to use time on the job. Covers subjects including keeping telephone tools handy, preparing for telephone discussions, keeping personal talk to a minimum, and more.
Business and Economics; Industrial and Technical Education; Psychology; Social Science
Dist - VLEARN **Prod** - EBEC

Time on Your Hands 12 MIN
U-matic / VHS
Developing Your Study Skills Series
Color
Revolves around a student's inability to schedule his time and the obvious consequences. Illustrates the importance of time management and provides suggestions for developing a system of monitoring and evaluating specific goals.
Education; Guidance and Counseling
Dist - BCNFL **Prod** - BCNFL 1985

Time out and other penalties - Part II 33 MIN
VHS / U-matic
Handling misbehavior subseries
Color (G C A)
$385.00 purchase _ #C840 - VI - 020I
Teaches parents how to use time outs and other penalties for misbehavior. Part two of a three - part subseries on handling misbehavior and part of a ten - part series on parents and children presented by Dr Carolyn Webster - Stratton.
Health and Safety; Psychology; Sociology
Dist - HSCIC

Time Out for a Review - 28 30 MIN
VHS
English 101 - Ingles 101 Series
Color (H)
$125.00 purchase
Presents a series of thirty 30 - minute programs in basic English for native speakers of Spanish. Focuses on a specific topic in order to emphasize a particular grammatical point or set of idioms. English is used from the beginning as the primary language of instruction but Spanish translations are included to ensure understanding. Part 28 reviews the verb 'to be,' countinuous present tense, future with 'going to,' future with 'will,' questions.
English Language; Foreign Language
Dist - AITECH **Prod** - UPRICO 1988

Time - Out for Basketball
VHS / U-matic
Color
LC 83-706826
Contains teaching aids which give a better comprehension of the rules of high school basketball.
Physical Education and Recreation
Dist - NFSHSA **Prod** - NFSHSA

Time Out for Hilarious Sports Bloopers 30 MIN
VHS
(G)
$19.95 purchase _ #FRV14004V
Presents TV bloopers from many different sports.
Physical Education and Recreation
Dist - CAMV

Time Out for Life 10 MIN
16mm
Color (H C A)
Dramatizes the life of a young mother who was persuaded to have a pap test. Shows that as a result of the test, uterine cancer was detected and subsequently removed.
Health and Safety; Science
Dist - AMCS **Prod** - AMCS

Time Out for Man 28 MIN
16mm
Color
LC 72-702435
Shows the visits of a team of humanists in the national humanities series in a small South Dakota town.
Geography - United States; Literature and Drama
Dist - WWNFF **Prod** - WWNFF 1972

Time out for science - benefits and uses of nuclear technology 24 MIN
VHS
Color (J H)
$95.00 purchase _ #823VG
Explains the discoveries within nuclear power and physics during the last 30 years. Tells the story of kids from the 1990s who travel through time to the 1950s and discuss nuclear energy with a science club in the '50s. Comes with a teacher's guide, student activities, tests, and blackline masters.
Industrial and Technical Education; Science - Physical; Social Science
Dist - UNL

Time Out for Trouble 22 MIN
U-matic / VHS / 16mm
B&W (H C A)
Illustrates the most common accidents causing serious injury in the home and explains that mental attitudes are the real cause of the trouble. Suggests a course of action to eliminate such injuries.

Guidance and Counseling; Health and Safety; Psychology
Dist - IFB **Prod** - IFB 1962

Time Out - Graffiti 10 MIN
16mm / U-matic / VHS
Color (I J H) (SPANISH)
LC 82-701177
Presents various arguments against graffiti - writing which are climaxed by the realistic arrest, trial and conviction of a young graffitist.
Guidance and Counseling; Sociology
Dist - ALTSUL **Prod** - KLUCLA 1982

Time out of war 22 MIN
VHS / U-matic / 16mm
Color (I J H G)
$260.00, $310.00 purchase, $50.00 rental
Features a classic story about the absurdity of war, based on a popular short story.
Literature and Drama; Sociology
Dist - NDIM **Prod** - SANTER 1954

Time out series
Deck the halls 18 MIN
Shifting gears 12 MIN
Up the Creek 15 MIN
Dist - ODNP

Time out series
Presents three films with a perspective on domestic violence. Includes the titles Deck the Halls which portrays the cycle of violence, Up the Creek which reveals legal and personal consequences to abusive partners, Shifting Gears which explores non - abusive and non violent ways of dealing with stress.
Time out series 47 MIN
Dist - SELMED

Time out - the truth about HIV, AIDS, and you 42 MIN
VHS
Color (J H C)
$19.95 purchase _ #BO68 - V8; $29.95 purchase _ #PM85070V
Uses Magic Johnson's credibility with teens to teach them the truth about AIDS. Features Magic and Arsenio Hall as hosts, and includes celebrity appearances and music videos to convince teens of their vulnerability to HIV and AIDS, to encourage abstinence or protected sex, and to question the myths and fears surrounding HIV transmission.
Guidance and Counseling; Health and Safety; Sociology
Dist - ETRASS CAMV **Prod** - ETRASS

Time out - Volume 10 40 MIN
VHS
Circle square series
Color (J H R)
$11.99 purchase _ #35 - 867632 - 979
Uses an incident where a young person oversleeps and misses the school bus to examine time management. Deals with the subject from a Biblical perspective.
Religion and Philosophy
Dist - APH **Prod** - TYHP

Time Piece 8 MIN
U-matic / 8mm cartridge
Color (J A)
LC FIA67-1680
Zany comedy and serious comment are combined to show one man's life in today's urban 'RAT RACE.' as the hero, a typical young executive, is hospitalized, his daily tasks flash before his eyes, alternating between realism and wild dreams. Modern man's helplessness in his complex world is suggested.
Guidance and Counseling; Psychology; Religion and Philosophy; Science - Natural; Sociology
Dist - MGHT **Prod** - MUPPTS 1966

TIME presents - perspectives on the 1991 Russian revolution 40 MIN
VHS
Color (H)
$39.00 purchase _ #TEP976 - 025
Examines the historical precedents for the Russian Revolution of 1991. Speculates on conditions in years to come. Features round - table discussions.
Geography - World; History - World
Dist - GA **Prod** - TIMLIF 1992

Time, Pt 1 15 MIN
U-matic
Measure Up Series
Color (P)
Shows how to use the hour hand on the clock.
Mathematics
Dist - GPN **Prod** - WCETTV 1977

Time, Pt 2 15 MIN
U-matic
Measure Up Series
Color (P)
Shows how to read multiples of five minutes on a clock.
Mathematics
Dist - GPN **Prod** - WCETTV 1977

Time quest historical interview series
Shakespeare 21 MIN
Dist - CNEMAG

A time remembered 42 MIN
VHS
Color (J H C A)
$99.95 purchase _ #P10486
Utilizes interviews, narration, archival film footage and photography to tell the story of the 3000 Japanese - American citizens who were evacuated from their home on Terminal Island, a small fishing community in Los Angeles harbor, and placed in internment camps shortly after the attack on Pearl Harbor in 1941. Features family members who describe the shock of being forced to leave their homes because of their ethnic background.
History - United States; History - World
Dist - CF

Time - Series Analysis
U-matic / VHS
Statistics for Managers Series
Color (IND)
Says this analysis amounts to understanding the effects of seasonal, cyclical, and trend factors to make forecasts. Covers traditional smoothing and decomposition techniques in detail.
Business and Economics; Mathematics; Psychology
Dist - COLOSU **Prod** - COLOSU

Time Space and Spirit
Radiation 36 MIN
Women in Science 35 MIN
Dist - RH

Time structures 30 MIN
VHS / 16mm / U-matic
Learning to live series
Color (A)
Discusses how the use of our time affects the priorities in our lives. Examines how we can gain control of direction in our use of time. Uses transactional analysis to discuss the issues.
Psychology; Sociology
Dist - ECUFLM TRAFCO **Prod** - UMCOM 1974

Time study for union members 30 MIN
16mm
Color (G IND)
$5.00 rental
Outlines the basic steps required in establishing job standards through a stopwatch time study. Deals with the subject on an elementary level but moves rapidly through complex areas and requires a trained person to handle discussion after the film.
Business and Economics; Psychology; Social Science
Dist - AFLCIO **Prod** - PSU 1977

Time study - the why and the how 60 MIN
BETA / VHS / U-matic
Color (A PRO)
$200.00 purchase
Treats the necessity for - and the techniques used - in the establishment of direct labor standards. Emphasizes stopwatch time study. Includes materials which enable participants to actually take a time study, record watch readings, apply the performance rating factor, add the PD&B allowance, and calculate the standard.
Business and Economics; Psychology
Dist - TAMMFG **Prod** - TAMMFG

Time Table 8 MIN
U-matic / VHS / 16mm
Color (J)
LC 81-700225
Offers an animated comment on air travel. Shows a man discovering Icarus - like wings and attempting to fly. Depicts the same man making a frustrating and dangerous jet flight.
Fine Arts; Social Science
Dist - IFB **Prod** - ZAGREB 1980

The Time table of arts and entertainment
CD-ROM
(J H C G)
$99.00 purchase _ #BO97R5CD
Contains over 4200 original stories that cover the most significant events in global culture, from the first cave paintings to today's computerized choreography and animation. Allows access to artists, writers, sculptors and performers from all ages. Offers the multimedia effects of zoom - in maps, bibliographic and museum references, pictures, animations and pertinent quotes.
Fine Arts
Dist - CAMV

Time table of history - business, politics and media
CD-ROM
Time Table of History series
(G)
$129.00 purchase _ #1323
Includes over 6000 stories covering the key events in business, politics, and the media, from the Trojan Horse to Operation Desert Shield. Features multimedia capabilities that link many of the stories to graphics, sounds, maps and charts. Includes a time line with voice - over narration that describes the event's significance. For Macintosh Classic, Plus, SE and II computers, requires 1MB RAM, one floppy disk drive, and an Apple compatible CD - ROM drive.
History - World
Dist - BEP

Time table of history - science and innovation
CD-ROM
Time Table of History series
(G)
$129.00 purchase _ #1321
Includes over 6000 stories covering the key events in understanding science. Features multimedia capabilities that link many of the stories to graphics, sounds, or animated sequences. Includes a time line with voice - over narration that provides a historical context for the advances in science. For Macintosh Classic, Plus, SE and II computers, requires 1MB RAM, one floppy disk drive, and an Apple compatible CD - ROM drive.
History - World; Science
Dist - BEP

Time Table of History series
Time table of history - business, politics and media
Time table of history - science and innovation
Dist - BEP

Time, the most Precious Resource 30 MIN
U-matic / VHS
Organizational Transactions Series
Color
Discusses how we use our time and influence others to use theirs. Explores the opportunities for leadership in dealing with the intra - and inter - personal factors. Shows the relationship between the need for recognition and time structure.
Psychology
Dist - PRODEV **Prod** - PRODEV

Time - The Next dimension of quality 20 MIN
VHS
Color (PRO IND A)
$745.00 purchase, $190.00 rental _ #AMA74
Utilizes a combination of explanation and dramatic vignettes to show how time - based principles can be used in the office with results that can be gauged. Includes Leader's Guide.
Business and Economics
Dist - EXTR **Prod** - AMA

A Time there was - a profile of Benjamin Britten 102 MIN
VHS
Color; Stereo (G)
$59.95 purchase _ #S02041
Profiles the life and work of 20th century British composer Benjamin Britten. Shows that Britten's work covered nearly every music genre, including grand opera, symphony, and children's pieces.
Fine Arts
Dist - UILL

A Time There was - a Profile of Benjamin Britten 102 MIN
VHS
Color (G)
$39.95 purchase _ #1158
Profiles Benjamin Britten, prolific 20th - century composer. Characterizes his work as passionate, traditional but with an acutely modern touch.
Biography; Fine Arts; Geography - World
Dist - KULTUR

A Time to be Brave 30 MIN
U-matic / VHS
Spirit Bay Series
Color (I J)
Tells the story of a young Indian girl who is afraid of trains, the only link between the wilderness and outside world, because her sick mother left on the train and did not return, and her brother entrained for school. Explains how her father teaches her to hunt and track and survive under adversity. Proves she can conquer fear when her father is hurt and she must flag down the train for much needed help.
Education; English Language; Social Science
Dist - BCNFL **Prod** - TFW

A Time to be old, a time to flourish - the special needs of the elderly at risk 18 MIN
U-matic / VHS
Color (R G)
$50.00 purchase
Examimines the problems of the elderly and proposed solutions. Looks at the role of Catholic healthcare services in the care of the elderly.
Health and Safety; Religion and Philosophy
Dist - CATHHA **Prod** - CATHHA 1989

A Time to build 60 MIN
VHS
Color (R)
$29.95 purchase _ #443 - 0
Examines the 40 - year repression of the Catholic Church in Poland, Hungary and Czechoslovakia and the role of the Church more recently. Includes a study guide.
Civics and Political Systems; Religion and Philosophy
Dist - USCC **Prod** - USCC 1991

Time to care - the nursing home clinical 16 MIN
U-matic / VHS
Color (C PRO)
%i $175.00 purchase, $60.00 rental _ #42 - 2415, #42 - 2414, #42 - 2415R, #42 - 2414R
Chronicles the educational growth of students from the Community College of Philadelphia, a participating program in the Community College - Nursing Home Partnership project funded by the W K Kellogg Foundation. Captures senior nursing students' clinical experiences as they care for elderly residents. Interviews educators associated with the Philadelphia project, as well as nursing leaders Patricia Moccia, Lucille Joel and Em Olivia Bevis.
Health and Safety
Dist - NLFN **Prod** - NLFN

A Time to choose 35 MIN
VHS / U-matic / 16mm
Across five Aprils series
Color (J H G)
$595.00, $250.00 purchase _ #HH - 5974L
Adapts Across Five Aprils, a book by Irene Hunt. Deals with the early rumors of civil war in the southern United States and the confusion and controversy over what such a war would mean to the members of one Illinois family. Part one of a two - part series.
History - United States; Literature and Drama; Sociology
Dist - CORF **Prod** - LCA 1990

A Time to dance 29 MIN
U-matic / VHS / 16mm
Time to dance series
B&W (C A)
Discusses and illustrates three major forms of dance - ethnic, ballet and modern. Shows two performances of European ethnic dances and examples of a 17th century court dance, classical ballet and dance satire to introduce forms of the modern dance. Filmed in Kinescope.
Fine Arts
Dist - IU **Prod** - NET 1960

Time to dance series

A Choreographer at work	29 MIN
Classical ballet	29 MIN
Dance - a Reflection of Our Times	29 MIN
Ethnic Dance - Roundtrip to Trinidad	29 MIN
Great performance in dance	29 MIN
Invention in Dance	29 MIN
The Language of Dance	29 MIN
Modern Ballet	29 MIN
A Time to dance	29 MIN

Dist - IU

A Time to Decide 15 MIN
VHS / 16mm
Color (PRO)
$260.00 purchase, $120.00 rental, $35.00 preview
Discusses the ethical dilemmas of health care professionals. Presents dramatizations of life or death situations which require instant decisions. Discusses principles of ethical decision making. Includes support material.
Business and Economics; Health and Safety; Home Economics; Psychology
Dist - UTM **Prod** - UTM

A Time to Die 49 MIN
16mm / U-matic / VHS
Death and Dying Series
Color
LC 83-701007
Follows the lives of three people courageously facing death from terminal illness. Focuses on the support groups of an organization called Omega, which was formed to help people deal with the fears and burdens of impending death and to help ease the bereavement of the surviving spouses.
Sociology
Dist - CORF **Prod** - CBSTV 1983

A Time to Die - who Decides 34 MIN
VHS / U-matic
Color (C A H)
$285.00 purchase
Focuses on the issue of euthanasia and the ethical and legal viewpoints regarding it. Produced by Dave Bell Associates.
Civics and Political Systems; Sociology
Dist - CF

Time to 5 minutes
VHS
Lola May's fundamental math series
Color (P)
$45.00 purchase _ #10264VG
Presents clocks and the placement, meaning and reading of the hands. Teaches students to read time by hours and to each five minutes. Comes with a teacher's guide and blackline masters. Part 14 of a 30 - part series.
Mathematics
Dist - UNL

A Time to gather stones together 29 MIN
VHS
Color (G)
$34.95 purchase _ #105
Reveals that, during the summer of 1992, genealogist Miriam Weiner organized and led a group of Holocaust survivors and genealogists searching for their roots on a tour of pre - war Galicia - now Poland and Ukraine. Shows that, with the help of Polish and Ukrainian archivists, the tour participants were granted access to previously 'off - limits' materials, enabling them to locate hundreds of family records, track down ancestral homes, burial places, and in one case, a long lost relative.
History - World; Sociology
Dist - ERGOM

Time to Grow 28 MIN
16mm
Color (H C A)
Shows an innovative idea in elementary education, the pre - first grade class. Explains that these classes are based on the idea that many children need maturing before they are ready for the demanding work of first grade. Portrays testing and two classes of pre - first grade in action.
Education; Psychology
Dist - CMPBL **Prod** - CMPBL

A Time to Heal
VHS
Color (G)
$29.95 purchase _ #U891109046
Presents imagery experiences and soothing music to enhance healing response in patients and to back up nursing care. Features Emmett E Miller, MD.
Health and Safety; Psychology; Religion and Philosophy
Dist - BKPEOP **Prod** - SOURCE 1989

Time to learn 30 MIN
VHS
Effective teacher telecourse series
Color (T)
$69.95 purchase, $50.00 rental
Discusses management of classroom time. Hosted by Dr Loren Anderson.
Education; Psychology
Dist - SCETV **Prod** - SCETV 1987

A Time to Learn - Reality Orientation in the Nursing Home 28 MIN
U-matic
Color
LC 78-706260
Emphasizes the implementation process of reality orientation in three nursing home settings. Illustrates staff training in the facilities using various teaching techniques and demonstrates methods of implementing reality orientation. Issued in 1973 as a motion picture.
Health and Safety; Psychology
Dist - USNAC **Prod** - VAHT 1978

Time to Leave - a Time to Return 22 MIN
16mm
Color (H C A)
Tells the story of political upheavals punctuated by missionary evacuations and re - entries in the country of Zaire.
Geography - World; Religion and Philosophy; Sociology
Dist - CBFMS **Prod** - CBFMS

A Time to Live 55 MIN
VHS / U-matic
Color
Presents a documentary of the Ninth Annual Communist Youth Festival held in Sofia, Bulgaria in 1968. Attacks the Vietnam War and stresses solidarity, world peace and freedom. Opens with a parade with groups from Europe, China, Japan, Vietnam, Africa and South America. Features songs, ethnic dances, native costumes and a carnival. Portrays deserters from the U S armed forces criticizing America.
Civics and Political Systems; Fine Arts; History - United States; History - World
Dist - IHF **Prod** - IHF

A Time to Live 29 MIN
U-matic
On to Tomorrow Series
Color
Focuses on the introduction of technology in the area of health care.
Business and Economics
Dist - UMITV **Prod** - UMITV 1976

A Time to Live 28 MIN
16mm
Sportsmanlike Driving Series no 1
B&W (H A)
LC FIA68-913
Discusses the responsibility of the individual to protect himself and others from traffic accidents.
Guidance and Counseling; Health and Safety
Dist - GPN **Prod** - AAA 1967

A Time to Live 50 MIN
U-matic / VHS
Leo Buscaglia Series
Color
Psychology
Dist - DELTAK **Prod** - PBS

The Time to live and the time to die 147 MIN
35mm
Color; PAL (G)
Tells the story of the film director's own early years and the trials of his family in Taiwan in the late 1950s and early 1960s. Deals with the conflicts between ancient superstitions and modern education, along with economic struggles. Produced by Central Motion Picture Corporation, Taiwan. Contact distributor about price and availability outside the United Kingdom.
Geography - World; Literature and Drama; Sociology
Dist - BALFOR

A Time to live - healer of my soul 4 MIN
VHS / U-matic
Color (R G)
$35.00 purchase _ #845, #844
Adapts Healer of My Soul to portray the elderly working toward spiritual wholeness and personal growth through prayer, conversation and therapy.
Health and Safety; Psychology; Religion and Philosophy
Dist - CATHHA

A Time to Live - with Leo Buscaglia 50 MIN
U-matic / VHS
Color
LC 82-707324
Before a throng of California picnickers, Leo Buscaglia delivers a secular sermon on the importance and uses of time. He urges listeners to value the present moment and grow through learning, listening, giving, loving and fun.
Psychology
Dist - PBS **Prod** - KVIETV 1982

Time to 1 minute
VHS
Lola May's fundamental math series
Color (P)
$45.00 purchase _ #10265VG
Teaches to read the minutes represented by dots on the clock and how to tell time when there are no markings between the hour marks. Builds upon knowledge of finding time to the hour and to five minutes. Comes with a teacher's guide and blackline masters. Part 15of a 30 - part series.
Mathematics
Dist - UNL

A Time to Plant 30 MIN
16mm
Color (H C A)
LC 73-715495
Uses a dramatization about a doctor who begins practice in a small community and helps others discard their prejudices, in order to show that a person is not prejudiced if he adheres to his Christian convictions.
Guidance and Counseling; Psychology; Religion and Philosophy; Sociology
Dist - CPH **Prod** - CPH 1969

A Time to Rejoice 14 MIN
16mm
Color
Explores the difficult and day - to - day problems of absorbing new immigrants from the Soviet Union into Israeli society.
Geography - World; Sociology
Dist - ALDEN **Prod** - UJA

A Time to Remember 20 MIN
16mm / U-matic / VHS
B&W
Provides scenes of Jewish life in Eastern Europe before World War II and provides a moving oral history of the holocaust from the perspective of four survivors.
History - World
Dist - CNEMAG **Prod** - CNEMAG

A Time to Remember 19 MIN
16mm
Color (J)
Uses graphic scenes to convey the horror of the Holocaust.
History - World
Dist - NJWB **Prod** - NJWB 1980

A Time to remember and Witness to the Holocaust 150 MIN
VHS
B&W (G)
$100.00 purchase
Overviews the Holocaust through the oral history of four survivors in A Time to Remember. Presents a seven - part series in Witness to the Holocaust. Includes Rise of the Nazis, Ghetto Life, Deportations, Resistance, The Final Solution, Freedom and Reflections. Asks 'could the Holocaust happen here?' Coproduced with the National Jewish Center for Learning and Leadership. Includes study guide.
Civics and Political Systems; Guidance and Counseling; History - World; Sociology
Dist - ADL **Prod** - ADL

Time to Run 97 MIN
16mm
Color (R)
LC 75-702383
Presents Christian answers to problems of alienation, loneliness, and frustration that divide families.
Guidance and Counseling; Sociology
Dist - WWPI **Prod** - WWPI 1973

Time to spare 15 MIN
VHS
Color (P I J)
Focuses on leisure time activities for children.
Fine Arts; Physical Education and Recreation; Sociology
Dist - VIEWTH **Prod** - VIEWTH

A Time to Speak 30 MIN
16mm
Color; B&W (J H T R)
LC FIA67-1913
A story of a man who works faithfully at his job and his Christian living. Although some people feel that he overdoes it in matters of religion, he continues to put his Christian testimony into action as well as into words.
Guidance and Counseling; Psychology; Religion and Philosophy
Dist - FAMF **Prod** - FAMF 1966

The Time to Stop is Now 5 MIN
16mm
Color (H C)
Emphasizes that the time to stop cigarette smoking is now. Explains that the body shows determination to repair itself if given the chance.
Health and Safety
Dist - AMCS **Prod** - AMCS

A Time to Tell - Teen Sexual Abuse 20 MIN
16mm
Color (J H)
Encourages students to talk about their feelings and fears regarding their own sexuality and personal values. Shows teenagers who learn to protect themselves as they come to understand the importance of sharing troubling secrets with those who can help them. Promotes classroom discussion on topics of urgent concern to teens such as self esteem and peer pressure.
Health and Safety; Psychology
Dist - CORF **Prod** - DISNEY 1985

Time to tell time 16 MIN
VHS / U-matic / 16mm
Color (K P)
$350.00, $275.00, $245.00 purchase _ #A349
Stars Clarence, the kindly old household cat, who teaches a confused cuckoo bird how to tell time. Teaches about years, months and days, hours, minutes and seconds, the o'clocks, the thirtys and quarter hours. Produced by Timothy Armstrong and Robert Sheehy.
Fine Arts; Mathematics
Dist - BARR

Time to Think 20 MIN
VHS / 16mm / U-matic
Color (A)
Discusses time management and delegation.
Business and Economics
Dist - RTBL **Prod** - RANKAV

Time to think about media studies 200 MIN
VHS
Color; PAL (J H)
PdS55 purchase
Presents ten programs, 20 minutes each, to show how messages, information and opinions are communicated to mass audiences. Examines the way messages are created and the ways in which truth and reality can be colored or distorted. Examines the press, radio, television and advertising. Gives practical examples of how schools can work with local radio, newspapers and in - house broadcast systems. Includes a substantial amount of copyright - free material for easy duplication. Contact distributor about availability outside the United Kingdom.
Fine Arts; Literature and Drama; Social Science; Sociology
Dist - ACADEM

A Time to Understand 20 MIN
U-matic / VHS
Color
LC 80-706133
Presents a series of vignettes documenting a survey of a VA medical center, conducted by representatives of the Joint Commission on Accreditation of Hospitals.
Health and Safety
Dist - USNAC **Prod** - USVA 1978

A Time to Weep 26 MIN
VHS / 16mm
Color (C A)
$160.00 purchase, $30.00 rental _ #CC4139
Relates the plight of displaced Ethiopians who seek shelter in eastern Sudanese refugee camps.
Civics and Political Systems; Geography - World
Dist - IU **Prod** - NFBC 1990

Time Together 14 MIN
16mm
Family Relations Series
Color (K P)
LC 74-703452
Tells a story about a boy who wants his father to love him but whose father is too busy to show that he cares.
Sociology
Dist - MORLAT **Prod** - MORLAT 1974

Time - Tokoro - Video 3
VHS
Video - cued structural drills series
Color (G) (JAPANESE)
$79.95 purchase _ #VJ - 03
Uses short, often humorous sketches portraying contemporary life in real Japanese schools, offices, restaurants and homes to illustrate expressions of time - Tokoro - in Japanese. Incorporates oral drills, grammar patterns and reviews and shows gestures and expressions unique to the Japanese. Part three of a seven - part series by Professor Ken'ichi Ujie, produced by Tokyo Shoseki Co.
Foreign Language
Dist - CHTSUI

The Time Trap 28 MIN
U-matic / VHS
(PRO G)
$550.00 purchase, $110.00 rental
Presents time management problems and techniques to overcome them. Based on the book, 'The Time Trap,' by Dr Alex MacKenzie.
Business and Economics
Dist - CREMED **Prod** - CREMED 1987

The Time Trap 28 MIN
VHS / U-matic
Color (A)
Focuses on proper use of time in business and industry. Identifies and provides solutions for several time wasters. Uses story format. Based on books by Dr R Alec Mackenzie.
Business and Economics; Guidance and Counseling
Dist - AMEDIA **Prod** - AMEDIA

The Time trap II 23 MIN
VHS
Color (PRO IND A)
$595.00 purchase, $130.00 rental _ #AM168
Defines the problem of being trapped by the tendency to waste time. Enables employees to use techniques developed by Dr Alec Mackenzie to escape the trap of time wasting and put time on their side. Includes training leader's guide.
Business and Economics
Dist - EXTR **Prod** - AMEDIA

Time Trap II 23 MIN
VHS / 16mm
Color (PRO)
$595.00 purchase, $130.00 rental
Features Dr Alec Mackenzie. Demonstrates effective time management in the workplace.
Business and Economics; Guidance and Counseling; Psychology
Dist - VICOM **Prod** - VICOM 1990

Time travel - the next frontier 30 MIN
VHS
Antenna series
Color (A PRO C)
PdS65 purchase
Reveals that Dr David Deutsch believes there is nothing in the laws of physics making time travel impossible, and the only barriers are technological. Describes Professor Stephen Hawking's opposing viewpoint - time travel is impossible given our current understanding of physics.
Science
Dist - BBCENE

Time travel through the Bible series
Uses archeological and historical insights to explore the Biblical world from the time of Abraham to the earthly ministry of Jesus. Consists of two episodes. Hosted by Jonathan Frakes of 'Star Trek - The Next Generation.'
The centuries before Christ 48 MIN
Time travel through the Bible series 107 MIN
The world of Jesus and John 59 MIN
Dist - CPH **Prod** - LUMIS 1992

Time traveler
CD-ROM
Color (J H C G)
$159.00 purchase _ #NMS01
Allows students to hurtle through time to lost civilizations and thousands of important events from the past 6000 years. Includes graphics, maps, videos, music and social sketches of empires, past and present. Offers a detailed control panel and on - screen help that allows user to navigate through time and space in virtually every historical period. Explores five geographic areas. Accompanies graphics with an information window containing facts about the period selected. A click of the mouse provides the sound of speech, native music, cultural facts and innovations specific to the time. Requires MAC 6.0.7 or later, 2MB RAM, 8 - bit color and CD - ROM drive.
Geography - World; History - World
Dist - CAMV

The Time traveler's guide to energy 27 MIN
16mm / U-matic / VHS
Color (I J)
Traces the historical persistence of human ingenuity in harnessing various sources of energy, including coal, wind, natural gas, solar and nuclear power.
Social Science
Dist - CORF **Prod** - DISNEY

The Time Value of Money - Original Issue Discount (OID) 120 MIN
Cassette / U-matic / VHS
Color (PRO)
$150.00, $30.00 purchase _ #P187, #M669
Reviews proposal regulations and amendments issued by the US Treasury Department in April, 1986, regarding the Original Issue Discount (OID). Discusses rules affecting imputed interest, installment obligations and treatment of debt instruments outside the scope of OID rules. Includes two audiocassettes or one videocassette for complete 2 - hour program.
Business and Economics
Dist - ALIABA **Prod** - ALIABA 1987

Time values 29 MIN
U-matic
Beginning piano - an adult approach series; Lesson 4
Color (H A)
Reviews scale forms and earlier pieces. Presents new pieces. Introduces concepts of time values and rhythm.
Fine Arts
Dist - CDTEL **Prod** - COAST

Time well spent 28 MIN
VHS
Color (G)
$598.00 purchase, $150.00 rental _ #91F0876
Shows why planning and organization is a vital part of selling.
Business and Economics; Psychology
Dist - DARTNL **Prod** - DARTNL 1991

The Time will be 3 MIN
16mm
Color
Stresses that the crises of pollution and dimishing fuel supplies are only now beginning to make an impression on the public. Presents a view of what the rapidly increasing auto population and the subsequent pollution may someday result in.
Geography - United States; Science - Natural; Social Science; Sociology
Dist - SLFP **Prod** - SLFP

Time will tell - inner city kids rap with elders 16 MIN
VHS / 16mm
Color (H C G)
$375.00, $275.00 purchase, $45.00 rental
Shows the unlikely coming together of inner city kids from the New York school system and old folks in a nursing home. Shows that the old folks love the breath of fresh air that the young people bring in, that the youngsters find love and acceptance from the residents, bolstering their self - esteem. Produced by Holly Jacobs.
Health and Safety; Sociology
Dist - FLMLIB

Time without pity 88 MIN
VHS
B&W (G)
$39.95 purchase _ #TIM030
Features a psychological thriller about an alcoholic who has one day to save his son from the gallows and a demented millionaire who would hide the truth at any cost. Directed by Joseph Losey. Digitally mastered.
Fine Arts; Sociology
Dist - HOMVIS

Time Zero 11 MIN
16mm
Color
LC 80-701456
Depicts parallels between the interactive process of art and the use of instant photography as a responsive medium.
Fine Arts; Industrial and Technical Education
Dist - POLARD **Prod** - POLARD 1980

Timehoppers 29 MIN
VHS
Color (J H)
$250.00 purchase
Portrays two students struggling to find a topic for their science fair project. Reveals that a pair of strangers appear in the physics lab who have come from the year 2050 in their Timehopper to deliver a message. Transports the students to the year 2050 where they encounter 21st century applications and realize the importance of technology.
Literature and Drama; Science; Sociology
Dist - LANDMK **Prod** - LANDMK 1992

The Timekeeper 22 MIN
16mm
Color
LC 75-700312
Presents an account of man's early record in Minnesota, using today's timepieces as a point of reference. Depicts activities of the Minnesota Historical Society in recording today's events for tomorrow.
History - United States; History - World
Dist - MINHS **Prod** - MINHS 1974

Timeless Tahiti 14 MIN
16mm
Color
LC 78-700669
Attempts to capture the romance of French Polynesia by showing the islands of Tahiti, Moorea, Bora Bora, Raiatea and Rangiroa.
Geography - World
Dist - MCDO **Prod** - UTA 1978

Timeless Tales - Myths of Ancient Greece series
Jason and the Golden Fleece
The Judgement of Paris
Dist - PELLER

Timeless Tales - Myths of Ancient Greece, Set 1 51 MIN
VHS / 16mm
Timeless Tales Series
Color (I)
$149.95 purchase
Introduces Greek mythology through a series of watercolor and ink illustrations. Combines five units previously available separately as filmstrips or enhanced videos - Prometheus and the Gift of Fire, The 12 Labours of Heracles, Persephone, Atalanta, and The Judgement of Paris.
Education; History - World; Literature and Drama; Religion and Philosophy
Dist - JANUP **Prod** - JANUP

Timeless Tales - Myths of Ancient Greece, Set 2 77 MIN
VHS / 16mm
Timeless Tales Series
Color (I)
$149.95 purchase
Introduces Greek mythology through a series of watercolor and ink illustrations. Combines five units previously available separately as filmstrips or enhanced videos - Jason and the Golden Fleece, Theseus and the Minotaur, Perseus and Medusa, and Arachne and Athene.
Education; History - World; Literature and Drama; Religion and Philosophy
Dist - JANUP **Prod** - JANUP

Timeless Tales - Myths of Ancient Greece - Set I
VHS / 35mm strip
Color (I)
$149.95, $130.00 purchase
Introduces Greek mythology. Includes five titles - 'Prometheus And The Gift Of Fire,' 'The Twelve Labours Of Heracles,' 'Persephone,' 'Atalanta' and 'The Judgement Of Paris.' Also available as single titles.
History - World; Literature and Drama; Religion and Philosophy
Dist - PELLER

Timeless Tales - Myths of Ancient Greece - Set II
VHS / 35mm strip
Color (I)
$149.95, $130.00 purchase
Introduces Greek mythology. Includes five titles - 'Jason And The Golden Fleece,' 'Theseus And The Minotaur,' 'Perseus And Medusa,' 'Narcissus And Echo' and 'Arachne And Athens.' Also available as single titles.
History - World; Literature and Drama; Religion and Philosophy
Dist - PELLER

Timeless Tales - Myths of Ancient Greece - Set II
Arachne and Athene
Narcissus and Echo
Perseus and Medusa
Theseus and the Minotaur
Dist - PELLER

Timeless Tales - Myths of Ancient Greece - Set I
Atalanta
Persephone
Prometheus and the Gift of Fire
Dist - PELLER

Timeless tales - myths of ancient Greece
The Twelve labours of Heracles
Dist - PELLER

Timeless Tales Series
Timeless Tales - Myths of Ancient Greece, Set 1 51 MIN
Timeless Tales - Myths of Ancient Greece, Set 2 77 MIN
Dist - JANUP

Timeless tales series
The Fir tree 13 MIN
Rumplestiltskin 15 MIN
Dist - LUF

Timeless tales series
Presents 13 tales based on children's stories from feudal times with kings and princesses, giants and fairies as well as the common folk, dramatically presented by actors. Raises moral issues in a gentle fashion. Includes The Golden Bird; The Three Servants; The Magic Flute; The Three Sillies; The Baker's Shop; The Three Wishes; King Grizzly Beard; The Well; The Poor Princess; The Two Brothers; The Pony, The Table and the Stick; The Fairy Ointment; and Tom Tit Tot. Each 8 minutes in length and available for separate rental or purchase.
The Baker's shop 8 MIN
The Fairy ointment 8 MIN
The Golden bird 8 MIN
King Grisly Beard 8 MIN
The Magic fiddle 8 MIN
The Pony, the table and the stick 8 MIN
The Poor princess 8 MIN
The Three servants 8 MIN
The Three sillies 8 MIN
The Three wishes 8 MIN
Tom tit tot 8 MIN
The Two brothers 8 MIN
The Well 8 MIN
Dist - NDIM **Prod** - TIMTAL

Timeless Temiar 55 MIN
16mm
Color
LC FIA64-1385
Portrays the life cycle of the nomads. Describes their communal way of living, extended families, beliefs and rudimentary divisions of labor. Includes chants instrumental music and dances of the nomads.
Geography - World; History - World; Psychology; Sociology
Dist - PMFMUN **Prod** - MALAYF 1956

Timeline video series
The Black Death - March 27, 1361 30 MIN
The Crusades - October 2, 1187 30 MIN
Fall of Byzantium - may 29, 1453 30 MIN
Granada - January 2, 1492 30 MIN
The Mongol Empire - November 18, 1247 30 MIN
The Vikings - September 25, 1066 30 MIN
Dist - ZENGER

Timepiece 10 MIN
16mm
Color
Tells the story of a young executive caught up in the urban rat race. Shows how a typical day flashes before his eyes during a recuperative stay in the hospital. Concludes with a frantic, surrealistic chase sequence that is half - comedy and half - nightmare.
Fine Arts
Dist - FLMLIB **Prod** - HENASS

Timerman - the News from Argentina 30 MIN
VHS
Inside Story Series
Color (G)
$50.00 purchase _ #INST - 410
Interviews Argentine journalist Jocobo Timerman, who was often imprisoned by his government for practicing his trade. Examines the political situation in Argentina, focusing particularly on the mothers of the 'disappeared.' Discusses freedom of the press within Argentina.
History - World; Social Science
Dist - PBS

Times 3 6 MIN
16mm
B&W
LC 76-701382
Points out that life is an ongoing process and each person is a thousand selves blending and fading from one to the other.
Fine Arts; Guidance and Counseling; Religion and Philosophy
Dist - SFRASU **Prod** - SFRASU 1973

Times for 80 MIN
16mm
Color (A)
$150.00 rental
Tells the tale of a man who wandered onto an island of women whose presence induces his fantasies. Enters into dream reality as an unfulfilled man renders himself to the unrealized sensuality of four women. Produced by Steve Dwoskin.
Fine Arts
Dist - CANCIN

Time's harvest - exploring the future series 224 MIN
VHS
Time's harvest - exploring the future series
Color (C G PRO)
$1152.00 purchase
Presents an eight - part series which explores philosophies underlying the analytical techniques used by futurists to forecast key issues of global concern and explains methodologies used in future research. Includes the titles The Coming Transformation; Planning for Tomorrow; Technology's Heartbeat; Running Out of Water; The Computer Comes Home; Becoming an American; Inheriting the Earth; and Question of Growth. Produced by International University Consortium.
Sociology
Dist - PSU

Time's Harvest - Exploring the Future Series
Becoming an American 30 MIN
The Coming transformation 30 MIN
The Computer comes home 30 MIN
Inheriting the Earth 30 MIN
Planning for Tomorrow 30 MIN
A Question of Growth 30 MIN
Running Out of Water 30 MIN
Technology's Heartbeat 30 MIN
Dist - MDCPB

Time's harvest - exploring the future series
Time's harvest - exploring the future series 224 MIN
Dist - PSU

Times, lines and events; Rev. 15 MIN
VHS
Color (K P I J)
$59.95 purchase _ #Q10510
Describes times as a system used to measure events in terms meaningful to young students. Illustrates geological time and demonstrates how to make a timeline. Features animation. A Dimension Film.
Mathematics; Science - Physical
Dist - CF

Time's Lost Children 30 MIN
U-matic
Color (J C)
Examined is the private and mysterious world of the autistic child by parents, teachers, and doctors. Parents of autistic children discuss how their children seemed normal until the age of two or three when their inability to relate to reality became noticeable. The causes and cures for

autism remain elusive, but at San Diego's Los Ninos Remedial Center dedicated individuals are observed working with autistic children, some of whom are successfully returned to the real world.
Psychology
Dist - SDSC **Prod** - SDSC

Time's Lost Children 29 MIN
Videoreel / VT2
Color
Explores the world of the autistic child from the perspective of parents, teachers and doctors. Examines the traits of autism, often obscured until a seemingly normal child reaches the age of two or three and describes the effects of autism on the children's families.
Psychology
Dist - PBS **Prod** - KPBS

The Times of Harvey Milk 87 MIN
16mm
Color (G)
Documents the rise to power of Harvey Milk, the first openly gay person elected to office in the United States, and one of the gay rights movement's most charismatic and powerful activists. Takes place in San Francisco in the 1970s. Both Mayor George Moscone and Supervisor Milk were shot and killed by Dan White, a fellow supervisor and former policeman and fireman. Captures Harvey's ebullient spirit and stands as a testament to the courage and pride he instilled in both gays and straights. Produced by Richard Schmiechen; directed and co - produced by Robert Epstein. Contact distributor for price.
Biography; Civics and Political Systems; Fine Arts; Sociology
Dist - OCTOBF

Times passes 18 MIN
16mm
Color (G)
$30.00 rental
Weaves personal recollections with cinematic symbols that tap into our collective memory. Contains graphic land and seascapes along with scenes that are moody and witty. Produced by Philip Perkins.
Fine Arts; Psychology
Dist - CANCIN

Times Square 15 MIN
16mm
Color (G)
$50.00 rental
Features a modern - day fairy tale about New York City. Begins with a rapid approach to the skyline at night then follows a young man wandering the streets of Times Square. Focuses on the video games he plays in an arcade as the characters - cops and robbers, monsters, aliens, etc - come to life and cause trouble. A Steve Siegel production.
Fine Arts
Dist - CANCIN

Times Square Show 7 MIN
U-matic / VHS
Color
Documents the June 1980 show in which the Downtown Art/Fashion/Street scene and some uptown affiliates met in order to give this decade a right start.
Fine Arts
Dist - KITCHN **Prod** - KITCHN

Time's Up 21 MIN
VHS / 16mm
Color (G)
$375.00 purchase, $75.00, $60.00 rental
Follows the Australian Council of Trade Unions in its test case for equal pay through the centralized wage fixing system. Links the stories of five women and their struggles for financial equality. Presented by Cynthia Connop.
Business and Economics; Geography - World; Sociology
Dist - WMENIF **Prod** - WMENIF 1986

Timewatch series
Children of the Third Reich 50 MIN
Cuban Missile Crisis 100 MIN
Flames of war 50 MIN
Gladio 150 MIN
Memo from Machiavelli 50 MIN
The Pill 50 MIN
Sold down the river 50 MIN
True story of the Roman arena 45 MIN
Typhoid Mary 50 MIN
Dist - BBCENE

Timewatch
The age of Charles II 50 MIN
Napoleon's last battle 65 MIN
Dist - BBCENE

Timid dinosaurs 15 MIN
VHS
Magic library series
Color (P)
LC 90-707935
Presents a story about dinosaurs. Raises the awareness of children of the sense of story in order to enrich and motivate language, reading and writing skills. Includes teacher's guide. Part of a series.
English Language; Literature and Drama
Dist - TVOTAR **Prod** - TVOTAR 1990

Timing an Engine 4 MIN
16mm
Color
LC FI68-280
Shows the timing of an engine with the use of a timing list and includes the hook up and adjustment of the distributor.
Industrial and Technical Education
Dist - RAYBAR **Prod** - RAYBAR 1966

Timing Belts and Flat Belts 28 MIN
VHS / U-matic
Color (IND)
Focuses on timing belts and includes a short discussion of flat belts. Explains belt construction and compares types.
Education; Industrial and Technical Education
Dist - TAT **Prod** - TAT

Timing Examples 30 MIN
U-matic / VHS
Digital Sub - Systems Series
Color
Uses two detailed examples to show how to deal with timing design problems of both asynchronous and synchronous systems.
Industrial and Technical Education; Mathematics; Sociology
Dist - TXINLC **Prod** - TXINLC

Timing of valve replacement - Volume 14
VHS / 8mm cartridge
Cardiology video journal series
Color (PRO)
#FSR - 508
Presents a free - loan program, part of a series on cardiology, that trains medical professionals. Contact distributor for details.
Health and Safety
Dist - WYAYLA **Prod** - WYAYLA

Timon of Athens 128 MIN
VHS
BBC Shakespeare series
Color (G C H)
$109.00 purchase _ #DL468
Retells the Shakespearean drama of money's virtues and vices, Timon Of Athens.
Literature and Drama
Dist - INSIM AMBROS **Prod** - BBC 1982

Timon of Athens 128 MIN
U-matic / VHS
Shakespeare Plays Series
Color (H C A)
LC 82-707354
Presents William Shakespeare's play Timon Of Athens which details the transformation of a noble Athenian from a reckless spendthrift to a mad misanthrope.
Literature and Drama
Dist - TIMLIF **Prod** - BBCTV 1981

Timothy the turtle 5 MIN
16mm / VHS
Otto the auto - pedestrian safety - C series
Color (K P)
$30.00 purchase _ #190
Features Otto the Auto and a slow moving turtle who tells Otto about safety and watching for turning cars. Part of a series on pedestrian safety. Complete series available on 0.5 inch VHS.
Health and Safety
Dist - AAAFTS **Prod** - AAAFTS 1959

Timpani Techniques 20 MIN
16mm / U-matic / VHS
Musical Instruments Series
Color (J H C)
LC 76-707450
Describes kettle drums of four sizes. Discusses plastic heads versus calf, stick selection, French and German grips, instructions on fourth and fifth tuning, the tuning range, the correct position at the drum, strikes, proper beating area, dampening and muting, sticking, sustained roll and roll ending. Includes demonstrations by Donald Kiss.
Fine Arts
Dist - MCFI **Prod** - CROWB 1969

Tin Lady series
Copying, cuttin' and cussin' 28 MIN
The Final Touch 28 MIN
Now You're an Artist 29 MIN
Shading, Strokes and Striping 29 MIN
Swoosh Away the Glop 29 MIN
Dist - PBS

Tin Mining 10 MIN
16mm / U-matic / VHS
Color (J H A)
Explores Malaysia, which is the world's leading producer of tin and has been mining it for 500 years. Shows how gravel pumps and dredging are used to mine the metal. Views the communal lives of the workers who live in company housing.
Geography - World; History - World; Industrial and Technical Education; Social Science
Dist - LUF **Prod** - LUF 1979

Tin pan fire drill 15 MIN
16mm
Color
Shows school fire drill and young boy who is interested in trying the drill idea at home. Firemen come to his home to make plans with the family for a safe exit, including a tin pan alarm.
Health and Safety
Dist - FILCOM **Prod** - PUBSF

Tina Darragh - 11 - 29 - 84 29 MIN
VHS / Cassette
Poetry Center reading series
Color (G)
$15.00, $45.00 purchase, $15.00 rental _ #607 - 514
Features the writer reading her works at the Poetry Center, San Francisco State University.
Literature and Drama
Dist - POETRY **Prod** - POETRY 1984

Tina's Tea Party 29 MIN
Videoreel / VT2
Children's Fair Series
B&W (K P)
Science
Dist - PBS **Prod** - WMVSTV

Tinikling - the Bamboo Dance 17 MIN
16mm
Physical Fitness Series
Color (I J H C)
LC FIA68-2553
Shows adaptation of popular Philippine folk dance into a modern physical education activity.
Fine Arts; Physical Education and Recreation
Dist - MMP **Prod** - MMP 1967

Tinka's planet 12 MIN
VHS
Color (K P I T)
$55.00 purchase, $30.00 rental
Tells the story of Tinka, a girl who begins a recycling program in her house and gradually expands it to the rest of her neighborhood. Shows how she learns that recycling can help preserve the environment.
Science - Natural; Sociology
Dist - EFVP

The Tinkerer 20 MIN
U-matic
Challenge to Science Series
Color (J H C)
Challenges students to tinker, making use of the air cushion principle, heat exchangers, a candle powered radio and hand powered refrigerator.
History - United States; History - World; Science
Dist - TVOTAR **Prod** - TVOTAR 1985

Tinning and solder wiping 26 MIN
16mm
Shipbuilding skills series; Coppersmithing; 4
B&W
LC FIE52-247
Shows how to clean copper tubing for tinning, apply flux to copper, tin copper tubing by hand and by dipping, and how copper reacts to heat when being dipped and solder wiped.
Industrial and Technical Education
Dist - USNAC **Prod** - USOE 1944

Tinnitus Masking 37 MIN
U-matic / VHS
Color (PRO)
Discusses the indications for a tinnitus masker in various types of cases. Presented by Dr J Vernon, authority on tinnitus masking.
Health and Safety; Science - Natural
Dist - HOUSEI **Prod** - HOUSEI

Tinnitus - Patient Management 55 MIN
VHS / U-matic
Color (PRO)
Presents a round table discussion on tinnitus and various methods of management of the patient with this complaint. Discusses the use of hearing aids, tinnitus maskers, and biofeedback treatment.

Health and Safety; Psychology; Science - Natural
Dist - HOUSEI **Prod** - HOUSEI

Tinnitus - Treatment with Biofeedback 56 MIN
U-matic / VHS
Color (PRO)
Discusses tinnitus and the use of biofeedback in its treatment.
Health and Safety; Psychology; Science - Natural
Dist - HOUSEI **Prod** - HOUSEI

Tinplate 27 MIN
16mm
Color
Traces the history of tinplate and contrasts the slow hand methods used in medieval Europe with more modern methods. Shows how raw materials are converted into thin sheet steel, and tinplating by two processes - hot dip and electrolytic.
Business and Economics; History - World; Industrial and Technical Education
Dist - USDIBM **Prod** - USDIBM 1949

Tinsel Town and the Big Apple 24 MIN
VHS / U-matic
American people and places series
Color (K)
$79.00 purchase _ #EX1332
Takes a 'kid's - eye' view of Los Angeles and New York City. Features four young reporters who offer commentary on the qualities of each city. Part of a twelve - part series on American people and places.
Geography - United States; Sociology
Dist - FOTH **Prod** - FOTH

Tinseltown and the Big Apple 24 MIN
16mm
Young people's specials series
Color
LC 80-700284
Presents four young reporters who provide a tour of New York City and Los Angeles to prove why their respective city is the best and most exciting one in which to live.
Geography - United States; Sociology
Dist - MULTPP **Prod** - MULTPP 1979

Tinsmithing 29 MIN
Videoreel / VT2
Commonwealth Series
Color
Guidance and Counseling; History - United States; Industrial and Technical Education
Dist - PBS **Prod** - WITFTV

Tint Retouch - No 3
U-matic / VHS
Color
Examines factors determing the need for a retouch, examining hair for formula change and methods of matching the regrowth to the ends. Analyzes protective measure for the client's safety. Details the bottle method of application with correct subsectioning, application of color and timing factors. Demonstrates 'soap capping,' correct removal and styling techniques.
Education; Home Economics
Dist - MPCEDP **Prod** - MPCEDP 1984

Tintinnabula 8 MIN
16mm
Color (G)
$30.00 rental
Presents a dozen improvised fairy tales, filmed on the shore of Lake Michigan near an overgrown ruin. By Dawn Wiedemann and Dick Blau.
Fine Arts; Literature and Drama
Dist - CANCIN

Tintoretto 29 MIN
U-matic
Meet the Masters Series
B&W
Examines the innovations of Tintoretto's painting techniques. Discusses how he anticipated both the Baroque and the Mannerist styles and influenced later painters.
Fine Arts
Dist - UMITV **Prod** - UMITV 1966

Tintoretto 52 MIN
VHS / U-matic
Color (G)
$39.95 purchase _ #TIN-01
Looks at the life and works of Venetian artist Tintoretto with narration from writings by Jean Paul Sartre. Reveals that Sartre was fascinated by the Venetian master's rebellion against 16th-century convention and by his visionary style. Explores the influence of Venice on Tintoretto's art.
Fine Arts
Dist - ARTSAM **Prod** - RMART 1984
FI

Tintypes 110 MIN
VHS / U-matic
Color
Industrial and Technical Education
Dist - ABCLR **Prod** - ABCLR

Tintypes 11 MIN
16mm
B&W
Presents the pictorial beauty of the tintype pictures of the 1800's accompanied by the fragmentary comments of the youth of today.
Fine Arts; Industrial and Technical Education
Dist - FINLYS **Prod** - FINLYS

Tinwork of Northern New Mexico 14 MIN
U-matic / VHS / 16mm
Color
Portrays Emilio and Senaida Romero, artisans who carry on the centuries old Hispanic tradition of tinwork.
Biography; Fine Arts; Geography - United States; Sociology
Dist - ONEWST **Prod** - BLUSKY

Tiny 19 MIN
16mm
B&W
LC 76-701383
Uses animation to tell a story about a growing dinosaur.
Fine Arts
Dist - CONCRU **Prod** - CONCRU 1975

Tiny and Ruby - Hell Divin' Women 30 MIN
16mm / U-matic / VHS
Color (H C A)
$425 purchase - 16 mm, $295 purchase - video, $55 rental
Profiles jazz trumpeter Ernestine 'Tiny' Davis and drummer Ruby Lucas, lovers and partners for over 40 years. Includes interviews with Tiny and Ruby, archival material, musical performances, computer animation, and narration by poet Cheryl Clarke. A film by Greta Schiller and Andrea Weiss.
Fine Arts; Sociology
Dist - CNEMAG

The Tiny Carnivores 25 MIN
U-matic
Animal Wonder Down Under Series
Color (I J H)
Pictures the Ningaui, believed to be the smallest mammal on earth. Also shows other tiny carnivores in Australia.
Geography - World; Science - Natural
Dist - CEPRO **Prod** - CEPRO

Tiny tales series
Presents four videocassettes, each one containing two animated stories narrated in rhyme by Ivor the spider. Includes the titles Puffins and Ladybirds, Lizards and Hermit crabs, Bumblebees and Butterflies, Woodpeckers and Spiders.
Bumblebees and butterflies 10 MIN
Lizards and Hermit crabs 10 MIN
Puffins and Ladybirds 10 MIN
Woodpeckers and Spiders 10 MIN
Dist - LANDMK **Prod** - LANDMK

Tip income 14 MIN
VHS / U-matic
Tax tips on tape series
Color (A PRO IND) (SPANISH CHINESE)
$20.00, $40.00 purchase _ #TCA17640, #TCA17639
Discusses who must report tip income to the IRS. Explains how to file the required monthly tip report with an employer.
Business and Economics; Civics and Political Systems; Social Science
Dist - USNAC **Prod** - USIRS 1988

Tip the Scales in Your Favor 15 MIN
U-matic / VHS
Soup to Nuts Series
Color (J H)
Tells how Linda and Bones, who are unhappy about their weight for opposite reasons, learn to choose appropriate patterns of eating and exercise.
Health and Safety; Social Science
Dist - AITECH **Prod** - GSDE 1980

Tippecanoe and Lyndon too 24 MIN
U-matic / VHS / 16mm
Smithsonian series
Color (I J H)
LC FIA67-657
Demonstrates the changes in presidential election campaigns since Washington.
Biography; Civics and Political Systems; History - United States
Dist - MGHT **Prod** - NBCTV 1966

Tippecanoe and Tyler too 12 MIN
16mm
B&W (I)
Focuses on the presidential campaign of 1840. Traces the careers of President William Henry Harrison and President John Tyler from their youth to their terms in the White House. Reveals their political growth and achievements.
Biography; Civics and Political Systems; History - United States
Dist - VADE **Prod** - VADE 1960

Tipping the Scales 55 MIN
16mm
Nature of Things Series
Color (H C A)
LC 82-701186
Discusses the problems of overweight and underweight. Shows how the body stores and uses food, with regard to metabolism, fat cell storage and appetite regulation. Describes research being done on the effects of prenatal diet and childhood eating patterns and examines some drastic measures that are needed by the extremely overweight. Provides information on anorexia nervosa, investigating the psychological pattern that leads to this sometimes fatal condition.
Health and Safety
Dist - FLMLIB **Prod** - CANBC 1982

Tippy's new collar 13 MIN
VHS / 16mm
Alcoholism in the home series
Color (K)
$125.00 purchase
Introduces Tippy, a puppy troubled by his father's drinking and unpredictability. Deals with alcoholism and the disruption it causes within the family in a manner appropriate for very young children. Leader's guide included.
Health and Safety; Psychology; Sociology
Dist - CHEF **Prod** - CHEF

Tips
VHS / Slide
Color (S T PRO)
$399.00 purchase _ #1010
Presents over 150 tips on social skills for the mildly to moderately retarded student. Includes seven programs and a teacher's guide.
Education; Psychology; Social Science
Dist - STANFI **Prod** - STANFI

Tips for a successful interview 22 MIN
VHS
Color (G A COR)
$89.00 purchase _ #JWPA26DV; $89.00 purchase _ #JW900; $89.00 purchase _ #PA26V
Outlines techniques for successful job interviewing, presenting perspectives from both job - seekers and employers. Suggests that researching a company beforehand, and asking relevant questions about the company, will impress interviewers greatly. Lists questions that should never be asked on the first interview.
Business and Economics; Psychology
Dist - CAMV **Prod** - AAVIM 1989
AAVIM
JISTW

Tips for effective training 27 MIN
VHS
Color (G)
$595.00 purchase, $150.00 rental _ #V1072 - 06
Uses the experiences of a supervisor to clarify principles of learning and promote communication. Teaches a basic training program that can be used in many situations to improve learning. Includes video and leader's guide.
Business and Economics; Guidance and Counseling; Psychology
Dist - BARR

Tips for Fuel Savers 15 MIN
16mm
Driving to Survive Series
Color
Deals with the continuing need for fuel - efficient driving, and presents ten tested and proven tips.
Health and Safety; Industrial and Technical Education
Dist - BUMPA **Prod** - BUMPA

Tips for the Beginning French Horn Player 37 MIN
VHS / BETA
Color (FRENCH)
Provides instruction in learning to play the French horn.
Fine Arts
Dist - MOHOMV **Prod** - MOHOMV

Tips from the Pros 30 MIN
BETA / VHS
Victory Garden Series
Color
Talks about soil preparation, crop varieties and harvesting.
Agriculture; Physical Education and Recreation
Dist - CORF **Prod** - WGBHTV

Tips from top pros - grip 13 MIN
16mm
Tips from top pros series; 4
B&W
Physical Education and Recreation
Dist - SFI **Prod** - SFI

Tips from top pros - how to handle each club 13 MIN
16mm
Tips from top pros series; 1
B&W
Physical Education and Recreation
Dist - SFI **Prod** - SFI

Tips from top pros - long irons 13 MIN
16mm
Tips from top pros series; 3
B&W
Physical Education and Recreation
Dist - SFI **Prod** - SFI

Tips from top pros series
Tips from top pros - grip 13 MIN
Tips from top pros - how to handle each club 13 MIN
Tips from top pros - long irons 13 MIN
Tips from top pros - trouble lies 13 MIN
Dist - SFI

Tips from top pros - trouble lies 13 MIN
16mm
Tips from top pros series; 2
B&W
Physical Education and Recreation
Dist - SFI **Prod** - SFI

Tips on Basic Beauty - Grooming, Fashion and Dating
U-matic / VHS
Color (J H)
Covers essential beauty basics including how to attain a fresh look and healthy skin, coordinate fashions, and develop pleasant personality traits.
Health and Safety; Home Economics
Dist - CAREER **Prod** - CAREER 1972

Tips on Working with Children in Groups 18 MIN
VHS
Color (C A)
$40.00 purchase, $18.00 rental
Helps adults deal with confusing and disruptive behavior of school age children in group situations.
Education; Mathematics; Sociology
Dist - CORNRS **Prod** - CORNRS 1987

Tips to save time sewing - Pt 1 22 MIN
VHS
Tips to save time sewing series
Color (A)
$39.95 purchase _ #SWE782V-H
Shows students how to organize their sewing areas and sewing processes to save time. Viewers learn quick ways to fit a pattern, put in buttons and button holes and add patch pockets and yolks. Includes tips for using interfacing and what types to use for collars and pockets.
Home Economics
Dist - CAMV

Tips to save time sewing - Pt 2 19 MIN
VHS
Tips to save time sewing series
Color (A)
$39.95 purchase _ #SWE783V-H
Demonstrates how to make pull-on and fitted shirts. Teaches basic skills of fitting, zippers, sealing off seam allowances, finishing seams, invisible hems and interfacing.
Home Economics
Dist - CAMV

Tips to save time sewing series
Shows students how to organize sewing areas and processes to save time. Viewers learn quick ways to fit patterns, using interfacing, and finishing seams, among many other techniques.
Tips to save time sewing - Pt 1 22 MIN
Tips to save time sewing - Pt 2 19 MIN
Tips to save time sewing series
Dist - CAMV

Tips, tricks, and traps
VHS
Test taking - SAT I series
Color (H A)
$49.95 purchase _ #VA898V-G
Helps students study for the SAT scholastic aptitude test. Uses a test-taking instructor to guide viewer. Outlines what to expect on the test, how to prepare, and tips to getting a higher score. Each program 120-160 minutes in length. Part of a five-part series.
Education
Dist - CAMV

Tire Changing and Right of Way 14 MIN
16mm
Color (H)
Shows the proper way to change a tire. Covers parking the car in a safe place, the use of emergency flashers and flares, and the dangers involved in tire changing. Discusses the issue of right of way in different situations.
Health and Safety
Dist - SF **Prod** - SF 1974

Tire Traveller 10 MIN
U-matic
Get it together series
Color (P I)
Teaches children how to make a dual purpose wagon sled.
Fine Arts
Dist - TVOTAR **Prod** - TVOTAR 1978

Tire Wise 15 MIN
16mm / U-matic / VHS
Color (H C A)
LC 77-701288
Presents what to know when buying and using a set of automobile tires. Explains how tires are manufactured and the differences between the three main types of tires. Tells how to get maximum tire mileage and driving safety. Examines details on skids, chains, changing a tire, hydroplaning and other aspects of tire use, care and behavior.
Health and Safety; Home Economics; Industrial and Technical Education; Psychology
Dist - AIMS **Prod** - CAHILL 1976

Tires 11 MIN
16mm
Color (I)
LC 77-702873
Observes tire sculptor William Weisz as he recycles discarded tires into dragons, elephants and other creative shapes and structures.
Fine Arts
Dist - IFF **Prod** - YANIVY 1977

Tires and Wheels 5 MIN
16mm / U-matic / VHS
Basic Motorcycle Maintenance Series
Color (H C A)
LC 81-700698
Describes how to check motorcycle tires for wear and damage, tread depth, valves, spoke tension and wheel bearings. Includes methods for changing tires and verifying speedometer drive and drive chain connections.
Industrial and Technical Education
Dist - IFB **Prod** - PACEST 1980

Tiropetes, spanakopetes and bourach bi lahmeh 32 MIN
U-matic / VHS
Color (PRO)
Demonstrates three ways to use phyllo dough, in the creation of cheese pies, spinach pies and meat pies.
Home Economics
Dist - CULINA **Prod** - CULINA

Tirso De Molina - El Burlador De Sevilla 120 MIN
U-matic / VHS
Color (C) (SPANISH)
$399.00, $249.00 purchase _ #AD - 956
Presents the play that introduced the theme of Don Juan into European literature, 'El Burlador De Sevilla' by Tirso de Molina.
Foreign Language; History - World; Literature and Drama; Sociology
Dist - FOTH **Prod** - FOTH

Tis pity she's a whore 106 MI
VHS
Color (H C G)
$69.00 purchase _ #DL474
Adapts the novel by John Ford. Stars Charolette Rampling, Oliver Tobias and Fabio Testi.
Fine Arts; History - World; Literature and Drama
Dist - INSIM

'Tis the Seasoning 30 MIN
VHS / 16mm
Marketing Series
Color (C A)
$130.00, $120.00 purchase _15 - 21
Focuses on the key issues of selling.
Business and Economics
Dist - CDTEL **Prod** - COAST 1989

Tissant De La Laine 6 MIN
16mm / U-matic / VHS
Color (I J H)
LC 77-707260
Describes techniques in building a simple loom out of an old broom and a few pieces of wood.
Fine Arts; Foreign Language
Dist - IFB **Prod** - CRAF 1957

Tisser De La Laine 6 MIN
U-matic / VHS / 16mm
Color (I J H)
Describes techniques in building a simple loom out of an old broom and a few pieces of wood.
Fine Arts; Foreign Language
Dist - IFB **Prod** - CRAF 1957

Tissue Culture Approach in Studying Normal and Diseased Muscles 39 MIN
U-matic
Color
LC 76-706111
Uses illustrative slides to present an approach to studying normal and diseased muscles.
Health and Safety; Science
Dist - USNAC **Prod** - NINDIS 1974

Tissue Culture of Normal and Abnormal Human Muscles 45 MIN
U-matic
Intensive Course in Neuromuscular Diseases Series
Color (PRO)
LC 76-706112
Presents Dr Robert I Roelofs lecturing on tissue culture of normal and abnormal human muscles.
Health and Safety; Science - Natural
Dist - USNAC **Prod** - NINDIS 1974

Tissue of lies 30 MIN
VHS
Tales from the map room
Color; PAL (H C A)
PdS65 purchase; Not available in the United States
Features actors who re - create significant events in the history of cartography. Focuses on the difficulties of producing accurate maps. Sixth in a series of six programs.
Geography - World
Dist - BBCENE

Tissue Paper Art 60 MIN
VHS / 16mm
Children's Craft Series
(K P)
$39.00 purchase _ #VT1100
Shows how to make tissue paper collages using bits of torn paper, starch, paste, or polymer medium. Teaches what a collage is, what overlapping and symmetry mean, and what hot and cool colors (or hues) are. Taught by Julie Abowitt, Multi - Arts Coordinator for the Seattle Public Schools.
Fine Arts
Dist - RMIBHF **Prod** - RMIBHF

Tissues 29 MIN
U-matic
Introducing biology series; Program 6
Color (C A)
Describes characteristics and functions of the four types of tissues found in multicellular animals. Gives examples of different types of tissues including those in the leaf of a plant and in a blood vessel.
Science - Natural
Dist - CDTEL **Prod** - COAST

Tissues
VHS
Basic Biology And Biotechnology Series
Color (G)
$75.00 purchase _ #6 - 083 - 113P
Looks at the fertilization and early divisions of an egg cell. Identifies and describes the four types of tissues found in multicellular animals and the four major types of cells in plants. Part of a series on basic biology.
Science - Natural
Dist - VEP **Prod** - VEP

Tissues of the human body 16 MIN
16mm / U-matic / VHS
Color (J H)
A detailed explanation of the various types of tissues found in the body. Discusses skin, muscle, tendons, nerves and blood. Utilizes animation techniques as well as live photography.
Science - Natural
Dist - CF **Prod** - CF 1963

Tit for tat 19 MIN
16mm
B&W (G)
Presents the antics of Laurel and Hardy, who decide to run an appliance store. The denouement to Them Thar Hills.
Fine Arts
Dist - RMIBHF KITPAR **Prod** - ROACH 1935

Titan 5 30 MIN
16mm
Color (H C A R)

LC 72-701667
A fictional account of an astronaut who, confused about the purpose of his life and the moon mission, questions his beliefs. Introduces a close friend who is an unbeliver and a missionary who has recently left the seminary cause the man to realize his responsibility and to renew his faith in God's will.
Guidance and Counseling; Religion and Philosophy
Dist - CPH **Prod** - CPH 1966

Titanic 14 MIN
16mm
B&W
LC 74-713146
Uses a composite of motion picture sequences to depict the sinking of the Titanic in 1912.
History - World; Social Science
Dist - RMIBHF **Prod** - RMIBHF 1960

Titanic 9 MIN
16mm
B&W (G)
$15.00 rental
Features footage which experts agree is actually scenes of a sister ship.
Fine Arts; Literature and Drama
Dist - KITPAR

Titanic in a tub - the golden age of toy boats 28 MIN
16mm / VHS / U-matic
Color (G)
LC 82-700316
Looks at the golden age of toy boats, featuring a bathtub re - creation of the sinking of the Titanic. Uses archival stills and footage to show their full - scale counterparts from the 1890's to the 1930's. Narrated by Rex Harrison.
Fine Arts; Physical Education and Recreation; Social Science
Dist - DIRECT **Prod** - SEVSEA NIERNG 1982

The Titanic - July 18, 1986
VHS
Nightline news library series
Color (J H C)
$19.98 purchase _ #MH6156V - S
Overviews recent discoveries and photography of the wreckage of the Titanic in a news story by the ABC News Team. Part of a series from the news program, Nightline.
History - World
Dist - CAMV **Prod** - ABCNEW 1986

Titbits, and, Nightlife 57 MIN
VHS
Color (S)
$24.95 purchase _ #781 - 9022
Chronicles a year in the life of a pair of birds, the blue tits, which are similar to the American chickadee in 'Titbits.' Tells the story of an eventful night in the English countryside through the eyes and ears of the barn owl, the fox, the nightingale and other nocturnal creatures in 'Nightlife.' Narrated by David Attenborough.
Geography - World; Science - Natural
Dist - FI **Prod** - BBCTV 1988

Titian 57 MIN
VHS
Color (G)
$39.95 purchase _ #TIT-01
Reappraises in depth the work of Titian, master painter of the Venetian Renaissance, who had an inestimable influence on the course of European art. Reveals that Titian was a master of self-promotion and could be ruthless in his pursuit of wealth and prestige. Features the evaluative work art film director Didier Baussy.
Fine Arts
Dist - ARTSAM HOMVIS **Prod** - RMART 1990

Titian - the Venetian colorist 27 MIN
VHS
Color (G)
$29.95 purchase _ #ACE14V - F
Focuses on the unique view of color, light and composition that Titian brought to his art, with emphasis on his influence on later artists.
Fine Arts
Dist - CAMV

The Titicut follies 89 MIN
16mm / U-matic / VHS
Color; B&W (H C A)
LC 79-707491
Describes life behind the walls of an institution for the criminally insane showing the daily life of the men and their talent show.
Health and Safety; Psychology; Sociology
Dist - ZIPRAH **Prod** - WISEF 1967

Title Drive 20 MIN
16mm
Color (G)
LC 70-706131
Describes the role of Evinrude Motors in boat racing. Shows Cesare Scotti's drive for the World Outboard Championship at Lake Havasu, Arizona. Discusses the two major European marathons, the six hours of Paris and the six hours of Berlin, as well as the Gold Coast Marathon in Miami and the Lake Elsinore Marathon in California.
Physical Education and Recreation
Dist - SS **Prod** - OMC 1970

Title IX - Fair Play in the Schools 29 MIN
U-matic
Woman Series
Color
Focuses on the ramifications of Title IX of the Education Amendments of 1972, which prohibits sex discrimination in school athletics and other programs receiving federal assistance.
Civics and Political Systems; Education
Dist - PBS **Prod** - WNEDTV

Title Withdrawn 50 MIN
VHS / U-matic
Color
Illustrates the song Night Sport from the performance process Automatic Writing. Deals with the architecture of self - description.
Fine Arts
Dist - KITCHN **Prod** - KITCHN

Titles 17 MIN
16mm
B&W (G)
$30.00 rental
Says critic Linda Gross, 'the filmmaker is obsessed with shifting time, weird memories and the play of light with film frames. A bride keeps reappearing, evoking an atmosphere that might be from the Tibetan Book of the Dead.' Film by Beth Block.
Fine Arts
Dist - CANCIN

Tito and me 104 MIN
35mm / 16mm
Color (G) (CROATIAN WITH ENGLISH SUBTITLES)
Portrays 10 - year - old Zoran who lives with his family in Belgrade, Yugoslavia, 1954. Reveals that Zoran has a mad crush on Jasna, 12 - year - old orphan of the state who idolizes Tito. In order to join Jasna on the 'Children's Walk Through Tito's Native Country,' Zoran writes an original prize - winning essay on 'Why I Love Tito.' Directed by Goran Markovic.
Fine Arts; Sociology
Dist - KINOIC

Tito and the Balkan Tinderbox 29 MIN
Videoreel / VT2
Course of Our Times I Series
Color
History - World
Dist - PBS **Prod** - WGBHTV

Tito and the Strategy of Non - Alignment 29 MIN
Videoreel / VT2
Course of Our Times III Series
Color
Civics and Political Systems; History - World
Dist - PBS **Prod** - WGBHTV

Tito - Power of Resistance 24 MIN
U-matic / VHS / 16mm
Leaders of the 20th century - portraits of power series
Color (H C A)
LC 80-700911
Documents how Yugoslavian President Tito used resistance to achieve power and then used that power to change the course of history. Narrated by Henry Fonda.
Biography; Guidance and Counseling; History - World; Psychology
Dist - LCOA **Prod** - NIELSE 1980

Tito Profile 25 MIN
VHS / U-matic
Color (H C A)
Chronicles the rise to power of Yugoslavian leader Tito.
Biography; History - World
Dist - JOU **Prod** - UPI

Tito Sanchez and Joe Solomon 30 MIN
VHS / U-matic
Somebody else's place series
Captioned (J H)
$65.00 purchase, $25.00 five day rental
Uses dramatization of a visit between two young people of different backgrounds to encourage appreciation of ethnic and geographic diversity. Sixth in a 12 part series.
Sociology
Dist - GPN **Prod** - SWCETV 1982

Tito Visits Moscow 30 MIN
U-matic / VHS
B&W (RUSSIAN (ENGLISH SUBTITLES))
Presents the 1956 Moscow visit of Josip Broz Tito, Communist president of Yugoslavia, in three Soviet newsreels. Includes a synchronous - sound Russian - language speech by Tito. With English subtitles.
Biography; Civics and Political Systems; Foreign Language; History - World
Dist - IHF **Prod** - IHF

Titration 30 MIN
U-matic / VHS / BETA
Color (T)
$39.95 purchase _ #5205
Focuses on titration, often the most frustrating experiment that a first - year chemistry student performs. Demonstrates the proper procedure for running a good titration experiment. Illustrates the proper procedure to clean glassware so that good results may be obtained. Shows how to calculate the results. Part of a series teaching teachers of senior high students and up how to teach chemistry. Covers important concepts, assists substitute teachers. Shows how to deal with student absenteeism, compensate for differences in learning rates, improve preparation time and review lessons.
Health and Safety; Science; Science - Physical
Dist - INSTRU

Titration
Software / Videodisc / Kit
Annenberg - CPB Project Interactive Science Instruction Videodisc
(H)
$495 purchase
Enables high school students to conduct simulated chemistry experiments on titration without coping with the constraints of time, temperature and luck.
Science
Dist - GPN

Titration 10 MIN
VHS
Chemistry master apprentice series
Color (H C)
$49.95 purchase _ #49 - 7205 - V
Shows how a sample of acid is titrated with base using a buret. Follows a rough titration to approximate endpoint by accurate determination. Uses close - up photography to show the proper reading of the meniscus. Part of the Chemistry Master Apprentice series.
Science; Science - Physical
Dist - INSTRU **Prod** - CORNRS

Titration I 10 MIN
VHS / U-matic
Chemistry - master apprentice series; Program 3
Color (C A)
LC 82-706037
Demonstrates how a sample of acid is titrated with base, using a buret, first performing a rough titration to approximately locate the endpoint, then accurately determining the endpoint.
Health and Safety; Science; Science - Physical
Dist - CORNRS **Prod** - CUETV 1981

Titration II 13 MIN
U-matic / VHS
Chemistry - master apprentice series; Program 101
Color (C A)
LC 82-706048
Shows how a sample of acid is titrated with base using a buret. Explains many of the accepted procedures in volumetric titrations, demonstrating the fine points such as splitting drops by rapid rotation of the stopcock.
Health and Safety; Science; Science - Physical
Dist - CORNRS **Prod** - CUETV 1981

Titus Andronicus 120 MIN
U-matic / VHS
Shakespeare Plays Series
Color (H C A)
Presents William Shakespeare's tragedy Titus Andronicus which draws on mythology for the rape and mutilation of Lavinia and for the banquet at which Tamora is served the flesh of her sons.
Literature and Drama
Dist - TIMLIF **Prod** - BBCTV 1984

Titus Andronicus 167 MIN
VHS
Shakespeare series
Color (A)
PdS25 purchase
Stars Trevor Peacock, Eileen Atkins, Brian Protheroe and Anna Calder - Marshall. Part of a series of plays by Shakespeare performed by leading stage and screen actors and interpreted by directors and producers such as Jonathan Miller, Elijah Mohinsky and Jack Gold.
Literature and Drama
Dist - BBCENE

Titus Andronicus 120 MIN
VHS / 16mm
BBC Shakespeare series
Color (H A C)
Presents Titus Andronicus, Shakespeare's mythological tale of brutality and bravery.
Literature and Drama
Dist - AMBROS INSIM **Prod** - BBC 1983

Tivoli 10 MIN
16mm
Color
LC 74-711535
Shows people of all ages enjoying the rides, music, games, playgrounds, food and fun at Tivoli Gardens in Copenhagen, Denmark.
Geography - World; Physical Education and Recreation; Social Science
Dist - COMCO **Prod** - COMCO 1970

Tivoli Rhythms 10 MIN
16mm
Color
Presents the Tivoli Gardens from morning until night.
Geography - World
Dist - AUDPLN **Prod** - RDCG

Tjurunga 19 MIN
16mm
Color (I)
LC 73-702490
Views the trees and wild flowers of Central Australia, tribal elders in a ceremony, fire making, cooking of emus and witchery grubs and aboriginal children at play.
Geography - World; Sociology
Dist - AUIS **Prod** - FLMAUS 1973

Tlaxcala
VHS
Color (J H G) (SPANISH)
$44.95 purchase _ #MCV5009, #MCV5010
Presents a program on the history of Mexico.
History - World
Dist - MADERA **Prod** - MADERA

TMJ Prosthesis Implant - a Surgical Treatment for Temporomandibular Disease 19 MIN
U-matic / VHS
Color (PRO)
Demonstrates how properly diagnosed patients with TMJ disease may have many of their symptoms relieved by surgical restoration of the temporomandibular joint by means of a metal implant.
Health and Safety
Dist - WFP **Prod** - WFP

TMP Equipment
VHS / U-matic
Pulp and Paper Training - Thermo - Mechanical Pulping Series
Color (IND)
Demonstrates thermo - mechanical process. Gives examples of equipment used. Includes types of steaming vessels, feeders, refiners and various equipment layouts.
Industrial and Technical Education
Dist - LEIKID **Prod** - LEIKID

TMX - a Tandem Mirror Nuclear Fusion Experiment 18 MIN
16mm
Color
LC 80-701562
Uses animation to show one of the significant advances in plasma physics, the tandem mirror concept. Shows the assembly of a research facility and a typical experimental run in this nuclear fusion project conducted for the U S Department of Energy.
Science; Science - Physical
Dist - LIVER **Prod** - LIVER 1980

TNRC Presents - Health and Self Series
American heartbeat 15 MIN
Choices 15 MIN
A Friend a day 15 MIN
The Great American smoke out 15 MIN
High and Dry 15 MIN
Name that Label 15 MIN
Out of the Blue 15 MIN
Dist - AITECH

TNT Teens 'n Theatre 28 MIN
U-matic / VHS
Color (J)
Traces the development of a group of San Francisco multi - ethnic teenagers from audition - line hopefuls to a full - fledged peer education, family life theater company. Highlights issues of sexual stereo - types, peer pressure and peer support.
Health and Safety; Psychology; Sociology
Dist - MMRC **Prod** - UCSFLT

To a Babysitter 21 MIN
16mm / VHS
Color (J A)
$465.00, $395.00 purchase, $60.00 rental
Observes young babysitters handling various situations on the job, emphasizing safety and responsibility. Practical advice is offered by a nurse, a fireman, and a policeman. Shows that babysitting is a serious job which helps to prepare the sitter for future parenthood.
Guidance and Counseling; Home Economics
Dist - HIGGIN **Prod** - HIGGIN 1987

To a Good, Long Life 20 MIN
16mm / U-matic / VHS
Color (J)
LC 76-702142
Focuses on three elderly people who are leading vigorous, interesting lives. Reveals some of the difficulties that each has gone beyond in learning to live creatively rather than merely coping.
Guidance and Counseling; Health and Safety; Psychology; Sociology
Dist - PHENIX **Prod** - PHENIX 1976

To a new land 30 MIN
U-matic
Pacific bridges series
Color (I J)
Explains how some of the first Asian - Americans arrived in the United States.
History - United States; Sociology
Dist - GPN **Prod** - EDFCEN 1978

To a Safer Place 58 MIN
16mm / VHS
Color (H A PRO)
$195.00, $795.00 purchase, $75.00 rental _ #8046
Shows Shirley Turcotte now in her thirties, having built a rich and successful life, returning to the people and places of her childhood where she was sexually abused by her father. Focuses on her efforts to raise public awareness on the issue of child abuse and to help others who were abused.
Psychology; Sociology
Dist - AIMS **Prod** - NFBC 1987

To age is human
U-matic / VHS / 16mm
Color; B&W
Shows that aging has assumed ever increasing significance in a society where people are living longer and expecting more out of life. Explores the realities and problems of old age from a number of perspectives. The documentary format enables the viewer to observe life in nursing home, to share intimate moments with a dying patient, and to learn what communities can provide for the elderly.
Health and Safety; Sociology
Dist - PSU **Prod** - PSU 1975

To Age is Human Series
The Faces of 'a' wing 58 MIN
The Final, Proud Days of Elsie Wurster 58 MIN
More than a Place to Die 59 MIN
Dist - PSU

To Alter Human Behavior - Without Mind Control 20 MIN
U-matic / VHS / 16mm
Color
Investigates some of the techniques of modifying human behavior. Deals with some of the issues involved, asking if behavior should be modified without the subject's knowledge or consent and discussing how to make sure that the altering of human behavior, once developed, remains in the right hands.
Psychology
Dist - CNEMAG **Prod** - DOCUA

To be 30 13 MIN
16mm
Color (I J H)
LC 77-700039
Produced in commemoration of the U N's 30th anniversary, the film presents a capsulization of the organization's history as interpreted by a fictional U N employee who is also celebrating his 30th birthday. Discusses some major international problems and assesses the U N's strengths and weaknesses in dealing with these problems. Features music of the British rock group Pink Floyd.
Civics and Political Systems
Dist - SF **Prod** - UN 1976

To be a Bedouin 15 MIN
VHS / U-matic
Encounter in the Desert Series
Color (I)
Shows the Bedouin way of life.
Geography - World; Social Science; Sociology
Dist - CTI **Prod** - CTI

To be a Butterfly - a Study of Protective Strategies
VHS / U-matic
Science and Nature Series
Color (G C J)
$197 purchase _ #06879 - 851
Studies the complex methods of protection, invisible to the naked eye, that the butterfly uses in order to survive in the wild.
Science - Natural
Dist - CHUMAN **Prod** - OSF 1988

To be a Clown 24 MIN
U-matic / VHS / 16mm
Color (J)
Shows the steps one must take in order to be a clown. Presents an eight - week workshop at Ottawa's National Arts Center in Canada, where students dance in baggy pants, juggle, walk tightropes, practice gags and experiment with masks and makeup.
Education; Fine Arts; Physical Education and Recreation; Sociology
Dist - AIMS **Prod** - SALZP 1975

To be a Doctor 52 MIN
16mm / U-matic / VHS
Color (H C A)
Examines the world of medical students and interns from the point of view of the students themselves. Presents the students discussing their fears about their abilities and their worries about conflicts between treating a patient as a human being or simply as an experiment in learning.
Health and Safety; Science
Dist - FI **Prod** - NBCNEW 1980

To be a Doctor 30 MIN
16mm
Doctors at Work Series
B&W (H C)
LC FIA65-1368
An overview of the life of a doctor - his training, his work and his interest in community affairs.
Guidance and Counseling; Health and Safety; Social Science; Sociology
Dist - LAWREN **Prod** - CMA 1961

To be a Friend 14 MIN
16mm
Circle of Life Series
Color (J H)
LC 73-700928
Presents the issue of friendship. Discusses new and old friends, best friends, lost friends, and other forms of attachment.
Guidance and Counseling; Psychology; Sociology
Dist - BBF **Prod** - BBF 1973

To be a Man 58 MIN
16mm
Color
LC 78-700225
Studies the American male's historical and traditional role in society. Profiles men's changing status and values through interviews with several prominent men and women.
Sociology
Dist - BLACKW **Prod** - BLACKW 1977

To be a Man 44 MIN
U-matic / VHS / 16mm
Color (H C A)
$665, $250 purchase _ #4034
Talks about stereotypes concerning men and how some men decided to do their own thing rather than conform to it. A Perspective film.
Sociology
Dist - CORF

To be a Man 14 MIN
16mm
Circle of Life Series
Color (J H)
LC 78-705695
A verite soundtrack of live interviews forms the basis for a study of boyhood, personhood, masculinity, anti - stereotypes, sexuality and idealism. Includes impressionistic visuals.
Guidance and Counseling; Psychology; Sociology
Dist - BBF **Prod** - BBF 1970

To be a man - Pt 1 29 MIN
16mm
Color
LC 78-700225
Studies the American male's historical and traditional role in society. Profiles men's changing status and values through interviews with several prominent men and women.
Sociology
Dist - BLACKW **Prod** - BLACKW 1977

To be a man - Pt 2 29 MIN
16mm
Color
LC 78-700225
Studies the American male's historical and traditional role in society. Profiles men's changing status and values through interviews with several prominent men and women.
Sociology
Dist - BLACKW **Prod** - BLACKW 1977

To be a Parent 15 MIN
16mm
Circle of Life Series
Color
LC 73-701411
Focuses on aspects of being a parent. Covers such topics as using children as weapons, using children as shields and information on human sexuality. Examines young people as they look at their parents, parents as they look at themselves and grandparents as they look back on both.
Guidance and Counseling; Sociology
Dist - BBF **Prod** - BBF 1972

To be a Person 19 MIN
16mm
Circle of Life Series
Color
LC 73-701412
Deals with the identity, self - awareness and personality of an individual.
Psychology; Sociology
Dist - BBF **Prod** - BBF 1972

To be a Teacher 52 MIN
VHS
Color (S)
$129.00 purchase _ #322 - 9282
Looks at what inspires some of our best teachers. Examines how they cope in the classroom. Reveals the positive outlook that helps them meet the professional challenges they face. An NBC special.
Education; Mathematics
Dist - FI **Prod** - NBCNEW 1987

To be a Winner, Back Your Winners 17 MIN
VHS / U-matic
Color
Attempts to convince managers that they must downplay functional tasks and concentrate on people in order to be really effective as managers. Illustrates that the three most important jobs they do are to communicate expectations, inspect results and provide feedback. Helps trainees get maximum return on their efforts by showing them where to put 80 percent of their time.
Business and Economics; Psychology
Dist - EFM **Prod** - EFM

To be a Woman 14 MIN
16mm
Circle of Life Series
Color (J H)
LC 74-705694
A verite soundtrack of live interviews forms the basis for a study of girlhood, personhood, femininity, anti - stereotypes, sexuality and idealism. Includes impressionistic visuals.
Guidance and Counseling; Psychology; Sociology
Dist - BBF **Prod** - BBF 1970

To be a woman soldier 50 MIN
VHS / 16mm
Color (G)
Analyzes the types of tasks performed by women in the Israeli armed forces and how they are striving to perform jobs other than clerical, answering phones and delivering mail. Illustrates the realities of army service for women in Israel. Produced by Shuli Eshel.
Civics and Political Systems; Geography - World; History - World
Dist - NJWB **Prod** - NJWB 1981
ERGOM

To be Afraid 15 MIN
16mm
Inner Circle Series
Color (J H)
LC 79-701070
Focuses on different categories of fear, including fear of physical things, fear of failure, fear of rejection and fear of the future.
Guidance and Counseling; Psychology
Dist - BBF **Prod** - BBF 1975

To be Afraid 14 MIN
16mm
Circle of Life Series
Color
Suggests that repressed and unspoken fears exert a powerful inhibiting force on the development of human potential. Traces several kinds of fear and seeks the root causes.
Guidance and Counseling; Psychology
Dist - BBF **Prod** - BBF

To be Alone 15 MIN
16mm
Inner Circle Series
Color
LC 75-702666
Focuses on the difference between loneliness and aloneness. Shows how young people are taken by surprise when they find themselves alone for the first time in such situations as a new school, neighborhood or job. Shows how loneliness can be a source for refreshment and creativity and also a source of pain if caused by inner conflict or by an alienating society.
Fine Arts; Guidance and Counseling; Psychology
Dist - BBF **Prod** - BBF 1975

To be an American 50 MIN
VHS / U-matic
Color (J H)
$250.00 purchase _ #HH - 6200M
Tells the true story of Cambodian refugees who fled the repression and oppression to make new lives for themselves in America. Focuses on the point of 'entry cities' of Lowell and Chelmsford, Massachussetts and Cranston, Rhode Island. Features teenager Tong Chin and her family as they experience the joys and challenges of immigration.
Sociology
Dist - CORF **Prod** - NBCNEW 1989

To be an Ingenor 29 MIN
U-matic
Future Without Shock Series
Color
Gives a perspective on engineering. Includes the ideas of ingenuity at work and technological substitution as characteristics of today.
Industrial and Technical Education; Sociology
Dist - UMITV **Prod** - UMITV 1976

To be Assertive 16 MIN
16mm
Inner Circle Series
Color
Discusses how to be assertive without being aggressive.
Psychology; Sociology
Dist - BBF **Prod** - BBF

To be Aware of Death 14 MIN
16mm
Inner Circle Series
Color
Focuses on death and dying. Shows how people are becoming aware that there are stages of death and that these stages can be anticipated and dealt with by family, medical personnel and spiritual advisors.
Sociology
Dist - BBF **Prod** - BBF 1974

To be Continued 14 MIN
16mm
Circle of Life Series
Color
Deals with disappointment, loss, setback, hurt, failure and personal catastrophes. Explains that life must somehow go on in spite of these blows. Suggests that the purpose of life is to get on with it, that life is meant to be continued.
Guidance and Counseling; Psychology
Dist - BBF **Prod** - BBF

To be Continued 15 MIN
16mm
Inner Circle Series
Color
Focuses on a rebirth, or a new life and a second chance.
Guidance and Counseling; Psychology; Sociology
Dist - BBF **Prod** - BBF

To be Creative 15 MIN
16mm
Inner Circle Series
Color
Focuses on the subject of creativity. Shows how some people find it everywhere while others maintain it belongs only to the few.
Fine Arts; Sociology
Dist - BBF **Prod** - BBF

To be employed 28 MIN
VHS
Ready, willing and able - a videotape series
Color (H A)
$89.00 purchase _ #RSG200E
Looks at personal growth, education, career and employment problems and successes experienced by 12 women who have faced disabilities and struggled through restructuring their lives to gain a personal identity and job satisfaction. Discusses how to tell an employer about one's disability, searching for a job, preparing a resume, interviewing and protecting one's rights as a woman with a disability.
Business and Economics; Guidance and Counseling
Dist - CENTER **Prod** - CENTER

To be Growing Older 14 MIN
16mm
Circle of Life Series
Color
LC 73-701413
Discusses aging. Points out that miracle drugs have prolonged our life span and added to our life problems. Explains that children must face the challenge of aging parents and seek for a truly human response. Includes such topics as retirement, intimations of mortality, scrap heap mentality and the nuclear versus extended family.
Guidance and Counseling; Health and Safety; Sociology
Dist - BBF **Prod** - BBF 1972

To be Human is to be Different 30 MIN
U-matic
Challenge Series
Color (PRO)
Deals with innovative approaches to life with changes in the areas of creativity, medicine, men in transition and multiculturalism.
Psychology
Dist - TVOTAR **Prod** - TVOTAR 1985

To be in Love 14 MIN
16mm
Circle of Life Series
Color (J H A)
Focuses on the issue of being in love. Covers such topics as first love, friendship, loving people for themselves, sexual relations. Includes the thoughts of Aristotle, Ovid, Jesus, Mohammed, Chaucer, Shakespeare and Disraeli.
Psychology; Religion and Philosophy
Dist - BBF **Prod** - BBF 1971

To be independent 28 MIN
VHS
Ready, willing and able - a videotape series
Color (H A)
$89.00 purchase _ #RSG200D
Looks at personal growth, education, career and employment problems and successes experienced by 12 women who have faced disabilities and struggled through restructuring their lives to gain a personal identity and job satisfaction. Stresses career assessment, work values, personality profiles, job opportunities, nontraditional careers, exploring and training, setting goals and making decisions as experienced by women who have lived through these processes and achieved success.
Business and Economics; Guidance and Counseling
Dist - CENTER **Prod** - CENTER

To be Irish in Boston 29 MIN
VHS / 16mm
Color (G)
$55.00 rental _ #TBIB - 000
Illustrates the strong sense of Irish pride and spirit that go into the St. Patrick's Day festival and parade in Boston.
Social Science
Dist - PBS **Prod** - WGBHTV

To be Married 14 MIN
16mm
Circle of Life Series
Color (H C A)
LC 73-700532
Opens up for discussion such areas of marriage as communication, signs of affection, wedding day, types of wedding ceremonies, divorce, building together, living together and friends in marriage.
Guidance and Counseling
Dist - BBF **Prod** - BBF 1971

To be married to be a person 14 MIN
16mm
Circle of life series
Color
Discusses various aspects of marriage. Includes such topics as communication, the wedding day, living together, building together, and divorce. Introduces the topic of being a person. Discusses topics such as belonging and apartness, individual and group, loneliness and other important issues.
Sociology
Dist - BBF **Prod** - BBF

To be me 28 MIN
VHS
Ready, willing and able - a videotape series
Color (H A)
$89.00 purchase _ #RSG200C
Offers a series which looks at personal growth, education, career and employment problems and successes experienced by 12 women who have faced disabilities and struggled through restructuring their lives to gain a personal identity and job satisfaction. Focuses on learning

skills, building support systems and working at personal growth to achieve a state of wellness. Illustrates self esteem, values clarification, sexuality, marriage, family, assertiveness and rights of people with disabilities, by looking at real life situations.
Business and Economics; Guidance and Counseling
Dist - CENTER **Prod** - CENTER

To be me - Tony Quon 10 MIN
VHS / U-matic / 16mm
Color (G)
$75.00 purchase, $30.00 rental
Follows Tony Quon, an active 10 - year - old Chinese immigrant from Hong Kong who is learning to adjust to an American school. Follows him through Los Angeles from Beverly Hills to Chinatown as Tony describes his first impressions of strange new classrooms.
Sociology
Dist - CROCUR ADL **Prod** - VISCOM ADL 1974

To be old, Black and poor 52 MIN
VHS
Color (G)
$149.00 purchase, $75.00 rental _ #UW4590
Reveals what it means to be Black, poor and elderly in the United States. Documents the life of Leonard and Sarah Bass on and off for six months, recording their struggle to survive. Watches as well - meaning neighbors and opportunists come and go.
Health and Safety; History - United States; Sociology
Dist - FOTH

To be or not to be - Mel Brooks version 108 MIN
16mm
Color (G)
$105.00 rental
Remakes the 1942 version of a Polish acting troupe headed by the hammy Mr Bronski - Mel Brooks - who helps a freedom fighter stop a counter - agent from killing off the Polish underground. Stars Anne Bancroft, Tim Matheson, Charles Durning and Jose Ferrer. Directed by Alan Johnson.
Fine Arts
Dist - NCJEWF

To be Precise 12 MIN
16mm
Color
Touches on the evolution of precision in terms of getting from here to there, describing the role of inertial sensors in such precision. Documents the achievements of corporation that results in achieving measurements as precise as millionths as a routine occurance.
Mathematics
Dist - MTP **Prod** - NIT

To be Somebody 29 MIN
16mm / VHS
Color (H C)
Records the progress of a young Mexican - American woman going out into the unfamiliar world of the Anglo in search of employment. Shows how, after several unsuccessful attempts to find work, she receives help from a counselor in a local training program for youth.
Guidance and Counseling; Psychology; Sociology
Dist - ATLAP **Prod** - ATLAP 1974

To be Somebody 35 MIN
U-matic
Color (H C A)
Depicts the progress of a young Mexican woman as she faces the prospects of searching for a job in the unfamiliar world of the Anglo.
Psychology; Sociology
Dist - ATLAP **Prod** - ATLAP 1971

To be the Best 25 MIN
U-matic
Color (FRENCH GERMAN)
A condensed version of the film The Best Downhill Racer. Dramatizes the story of downhill ski racing star Steve Podborski who became the first non - European male to capture downhill racing's highest honor.
Physical Education and Recreation
Dist - LAURON **Prod** - LAURON

To be the most You Can be 15 MIN
16mm
Inner Circle Series
Color
Emphasizes how each person should do their best. Discusses the idea that winning is not everything.
Psychology; Sociology
Dist - BBF **Prod** - BBF

To be True to Yourself 15 MIN
16mm
Inner Circle Series
Color (J H)
LC 79-701071
Looks at a person's identity as part of the maturing process. Points out that a sense of identity and worth comes, in part, from being true to oneself.
Psychology
Dist - BBF **Prod** - BBF 1976

To be Young, Gifted and Black 90 MIN
U-matic / VHS / 16mm
Color (H C A)
LC 72-702967
Presents a play depicting the life and works of the late black playwright, Lorraine Hasberry. Portrays her struggles, from her first visit to the South, to the streets of Harlem. Stars Ruby Dee, Al Freeman, Claudia Mc Neil, Barbara Barrie and Lauren Jones.
Fine Arts; History - United States; Literature and Drama
Dist - IU **Prod** - NET 1972

To Bear Witness 41 MIN
16mm / U-matic / VHS
Color (H C A)
Documents the liberation of Nazi concentration camps. Includes first person accounts, historical footage and still photographs, and speeches from the first International Liberators Conference.
Civics and Political Systems; History - World
Dist - PHENIX **Prod** - USHMC 1984

To Bear Witness 42 MIN
U-matic / VHS
Color
Uses the framework of the National Liberators Conference to recount the liberation of the Nazi Death Camps. Includes interviews with survivors and with liberators from some of the 14 armies, on rare historic footage.
Geography - World; History - World
Dist - USNAC **Prod** - USNAC 1983

To bear witness 41 MIN
U-matic / 16mm / VHS
Color (G)
$575.00, $340.00 purchase, $50.00 rental _ #HPF - 743, #HVC - 743, #HHC - 743, #HRF - 743
Records the 1981 Liberators Conference in Washington, DC. Interviews survivors and liberators of the Nazi concentration camps.
Civics and Political Systems; History - World; Sociology
Dist - ADL **Prod** - ADL 1981

To boldly go 58 MIN
U-matic / VHS
Nova series
Color (H C A)
$250.00 purchase _ #HP - 6374C
Examines the Voyager program's 12 - year mission to explore the solar system's outer planets. Overviews Voyager I and Voyager II transmissions as they flew by Jupiter, Saturn and Uranus. Provides information on the planets, their moons and the technological capacities of the two spacecraft. Part of the Nova series.
History - World; Industrial and Technical Education; Science; Science - Physical
Dist - CORF **Prod** - WGBHTV 1990

To Bottle the Sun 5 MIN
16mm
Color (I J H)
LC 73-701364
Explores the possibility of fusion power reactors as an alternative way of satisfying our future expanding energy needs with coal, gas and oil in limited supply.
Industrial and Technical Education; Science - Natural; Science - Physical; Social Science
Dist - AMEDFL **Prod** - NSF 1973

To bottle the Sun - 3
U-matic / VHS / BETA
Search encounters in science series
Color; PAL (G H C)
PdS25, PdS33 purchase
Brings modern research efforts of the world's leading scientists into the classroom. Features one of a series of 24 mini - documentaries. Each film is 5 - 7 minutes in length.
Science; Science - Physical
Dist - EDPAT **Prod** - NSF

To brave a dream 27 MIN
VHS
Color (G) (HEBREW)
$36.00 purchase
Depicts the 1866 journey of a group of God - fearing Americans from Maine, who sailed to the Holy Land to prepare for the second coming of Christ. Relates how, under the influence of their charismatic Reverend, the group shipped pre - fabricated wooden houses and modern farming equipment to Jaffa with the hope of establishing an agricultural settlement. Many died and others returned to America when faced with disease, drought and the Sultan's disapproval of their presence. Some of the wooden houses still stand in Tel Aviv, symbolizing the pioneers' courage to act on a dream. Written, directed and produced by Yael Katzir.
Fine Arts; History - World; Religion and Philosophy; Sociology
Dist - NCJEWF

To Breathe or not to Breathe - a Test on Lungs and Smoking 23 MIN
U-matic / VHS
Color (H C A)
Offers a quiz which tests knowledge of the lungs, breathing, and smoking.
Health and Safety; Science - Natural
Dist - CAROUF **Prod** - WNBCTV

To breathe, to breathe, to live 15 MIN
16mm / VHS / U-matic
Color (C PRO)
LC 75-701742
Demonstrates the diagnostic differences between high and low respiratory obstructive syndromes in young children with acute infectious disease.
Health and Safety; Science - Natural
Dist - BANDER **Prod** - CARNA 1968

To Bridge the Gap 31 MIN
16mm
B&W
Portrays a study tour of Scandinavian and English facilities for the mentally retarded.
Geography - World; Psychology; Sociology
Dist - WCCOTV **Prod** - COUKLA 1967

To Brooklyn with love 23 MIN
16mm / VHS / U-matic
Color
LC 78-700226
Presents a tour of the cultural institutions in Brooklyn that serve the people of New York. Narrated by actress Geraldine Fitzgerald.
Geography - United States
Dist - BEMPS BUGAS **Prod** - BAILYB 1977

To Build a fire 56 MIN
VHS
Color (I J H)
$15.95 purchase _ #VC1088
Features Orson Welles who narrates the Jack London story about a lone man traveling through the Alaskan wilderness.
Literature and Drama
Dist - KNOWUN

To build gigantic ships 29 MIN
16mm
Color
Introduces an outline of the research activities, manufacturing facilities and engineering techniques for building the largest ship of the time 'Vergefus' at a Nagasaki shipyard.
Business and Economics; Industrial and Technical Education; Social Science
Dist - UNIJAP **Prod** - UNIJAP 1968

To Build Our Future 60 MIN
VHS / U-matic
Through the Genetic Maze Series
Color (H C G T A)
Traces the development of amniocentesis and explores prebirth options for parents of children with genetic defects, focusing on abortion.
Health and Safety; Religion and Philosophy; Science; Science - Natural
Dist - PSU **Prod** - PSU 1982

To Capture the Power of Sun and Tide 24 MIN
16mm / U-matic / VHS
Color
Focuses on the sun and the moon as our oldest inexhaustible and non - polluting sources of energy. Illustrates applications of solar energy and experiments to harness tidal power, a by - product of the moon's gravitational pull.
Social Science
Dist - CNEMAG **Prod** - DOCUA 1973

To capture the sun 20 MIN
16mm
Color
Focuses on the current state of solar energy. Discusses its future and its partnership with natural gas to meet energy needs.
Science - Physical; Social Science
Dist - BUGAS **Prod** - BUGAS

To Care - America's voluntary spirit 26 MIN
VHS / 16mm
Color (G)
$70.00 purchase, $12.50 rental _ #36011
Discusses the phenomenon of private sector contributors and volunteers who contribute billions of dollars and countless hours of labor without seeking recognition. Encourages support of private sector activities. Produced by Francis Thompson, Inc, for Independent Sector.
Social Science; Sociology
Dist - PSU FI

To Care Enough 18 MIN
16mm
Patients are People Series
Color (H C)
Describes the importance of the nursing aide in the health care team. Stresses the habits, appearance and attitudes of a good nursing aid and dramatizes the challenges and rewards that come from caring about patients' needs.
Health and Safety; Science
Dist - MLA **Prod** - CALVIN 1967

To Care for Them 28 MIN
16mm
Color
LC 78-701151
Deals with the scope and complexity of nursing services performed by members of the Veterans Administration Nursing Service.
Health and Safety
Dist - USNAC **Prod** - USVA 1978

To Catch a Cloud - a Thoughtful Look at Acid Rain 27 MIN
16mm
Color
Attemps to dispel the propoganda surrounding the acid rain issue by offering a rational presentation about the nature of the atmosphere. Leading scientists provide insight into research concerning acid rain and man's impact, both good and bad, on the environment.
Science - Natural; Science - Physical
Dist - MTP **Prod** - EEI

To Catch a Dream 27 MIN
16mm
Color (C A)
Visits the castles and historical monuments of Spain and views the resorts of Mallorca and the countrysides of the Canary Islands.
Geography - World; History - World
Dist - MCDO **Prod** - MCDO 1963

To Catch a Meal - Feeding in the Sea 13 MIN
16mm
Color
LC 71-705696
Discusses the variety of marine feeding techniques in the planktonic, nektonic and benthic regions.
Science - Natural; Science - Physical
Dist - MIAMIS **Prod** - REELA 1969

To catch a porpoise 29 MIN
16mm
Color
LC FIA65-497
Follows a collecting crew from the Miami seaquarium as they go on a trip to catch porpoises. Includes underwater scenes which depict the man - against - the sea aspect of capturing three of these animals. Shows the return of the porpoises at the seaquarium where they are trained to take part in the show at the new York world's fair.
Science; Science - Natural
Dist - MIAMIS **Prod** - MIAMIS 1964

To Catch a Rhino 27 MIN
16mm / VHS
Color (G)
Documents the capture of square - lipped rhinos as part of an effort to save them from extinction.
Geography - World; Science - Natural
Dist - AUDPLN

To catch a thief 106 MIN
U-matic / VHS / 16mm
Color
Features Cary Grant as a reformed jewel thief who's suspected of a new rash of gem thefts. Directed by Alfred Hitchcock.
Fine Arts
Dist - FI **Prod** - PAR 1955

To Catch a Thrill 102 MIN
U-matic
Color (J H A)
Shows a variety of fishing experiences from a number of places in the world.
Physical Education and Recreation
Dist - APOLLO **Prod** - APOLLO 1986

To Change the Picture 12 MIN
16mm
Color
Presents youths from kindergarten through university and discusses the areas of increased support that the United Jewish Appeal must give to the youth of Israel in light of the Yom Kippur War.
History - World; Sociology
Dist - ALDEN **Prod** - UJA

To Choose a Camera 29 MIN
U-matic / VHS
Photo Show Series
Color
Introduces a variety of cameras, how they came to exist and how they are used.
Industrial and Technical Education
Dist - PBS **Prod** - WGBHTV 1981

To choose the sea 14 MIN
16mm
Color
LC 75-700880
Presents high school senior John Rodgers as he faces the decision of which college and career to choose. Tells how he decides on the Coast Guard Academy and is shown in classrooms, labs, off - duty activities and summer cruises aboard the sailing ship Eagle. Shows John in several assignments - shipboard duty, aviation and postgraduate work.
Civics and Political Systems
Dist - USNAC **Prod** - USCG 1965

To Climb a Mountain 15 MIN
U-matic / VHS / 16mm
Color (I)
LC 75-702540
Shows how blindness is a handicap that can be overcome. Presents a story about a young man and woman and a group of their friends who successfully climb a mountain. Explores their feelings about their accomplishment as blind people and examines the attitudes of society about blindness.
Guidance and Counseling; Psychology
Dist - PHENIX **Prod** - PHENIX 1975

To climb a mountain 25 MIN
16mm / U-matic / VHS
Insight series
Color (J) (SPANISH)
Relates the trouble that Steve has when he sells his car to help a black family. Shows the importance of unselfish love. Stars Emilio Estevez.
Psychology; Religion and Philosophy
Dist - PAULST **Prod** - PAULST

To communicate is the beginning 30 MIN
16mm
Color
LC 76-701408
Illustrates the dramatic growth of communications in the United States and shows key people involved in its history and process. Emphasizes the role of the Bell System in this history.
Industrial and Technical Education; Social Science
Dist - SANDIA **Prod** - SANDIA 1976

To Conquer addiction series
Enabling - masking reality 22 MIN
Dist - AIMS

To Conquer addiction series
Back to reality 31 MIN
Dist - AIMS
BARR

To Conquer addiction series
Intervention - facing reality 31 MIN
Dist - AIMS
BARR
HAZELB

To Cook a Duck 10 MIN
16mm
Color (J)
LC 80-701823
Follows the game bird from the time it is harvested until it is ready to eat. Discusses the field dressing and processing of waterfowl.
Home Economics
Dist - WESTWN **Prod** - WESTWN 1977

To Dance for Gold 90 MIN
U-matic / VHS
Color
Fine Arts
Dist - ABCLR **Prod** - ABCLR

To Defeat the Doomsday Doctrine - the World Isn't Running Out of Everything Quite 20 MIN
U-matic / VHS / 16mm
Color
Explains that too much pessimism about the environment can be as damaging as too much optimism, since doomsday attitudes can breed inaction and turn justifiable fear into a self - fulfilling prophecy.
Science - Natural
Dist - CNEMAG **Prod** - DOCUA

To Defend a killer - Part 2 60 MIN
VHS / U-matic
Ethics in America series
Color (G)
$45.00, $29.95 purchase
Features Supreme Court Justice Antonin Scalia, defense attorney Jack Litman and philosopher John Smith of Yale. Discusses ethical dilemmas in the American criminal justice system, such as the rights of the guilty. Part two of a ten - part series on ethics in America, produced by Fred W Friendly.
Civics and Political Systems; Sociology
Dist - ANNCPB **Prod** - COLMU 1989

To define true madness 60 MIN
VHS
Madness
Color; PAL (C PRO H)
PdS99 purchase; Not available in the United States
Discusses early theories about mental illness. Describes early treatments. Explains why a common definition of madness remains elusive. First in the five - part series Madness, which covers the history of mental illness.
Psychology
Dist - BBCENE

To Die for Ireland 50 MIN
VHS
Color (C G)
Documents the conflicts in Northern Ireland. Examines the role of the British Army on the battleground of terrorism and counterterrorism. Interweaves the factions of the conflict - the British Army, the Irish Republican Army, Catholic and Protestant citizenry.
Geography - World; History - World; Religion and Philosophy; Sociology
Dist - VIDVER **Prod** - VIDVER 1982

To die for Ireland - the Irish Republican Army 48 MIN
U-matic / VHS
Color
$455.00 purchase
From the ABC TV Close Up program.
Civics and Political Systems; Sociology
Dist - ABCLR **Prod** - ABCLR 1980

To die like a man 99 MIN
VHS
Color (G) (CHINESE)
$45.00 purchase _ #6049C
Presents a film from the People's Republic of China by Sima Wensen. The sequel 'Between Life and Death' is also available.
Geography - World; Literature and Drama
Dist - CHTSUI

To Die, to Live - the Survivors of Hiroshima 63 MIN
16mm / U-matic / VHS
Color (H C A)
Presents the thoughts and feelings of survivors of the atomic bomb blast at Hiroshima, including their guilt at being alive when others are dead and their worries about the still - remaining dangers of radiation.
Civics and Political Systems; History - World; Sociology
Dist - FI **Prod** - BBCTV 1982

To die today 50 MIN
16mm
B&W (H C A)
LC 72-703198
Focuses on Dr Elizabeth Kubler Ross, whose work has called attention to the 'Crisis of Dying.' Presents her theory of the five emotional stages through which patients pass and interviews a young patient with Hodgkins disease who seems to have reached an acceptance of his condition.
Health and Safety; Psychology; Sociology
Dist - FLMLIB **Prod** - CANBC 1972

To Die with Dignity - to Live with Grief 29 MIN
U-matic
Color
Focuses on coping with death and living with grief after the loss of a loved one. Interviews a terminally ill leukemia patient, a physician who works with the terminally ill and others including relatives, counselors and patients.
Sociology
Dist - UMITV **Prod** - UMITV 1978

To Discover a New Psychic Force 20 MIN
16mm / U-matic / VHS
Color
Explores what is known about psychokinesis, which may be a natural ability for all people and looks at its future potential.
Psychology
Dist - CNEMAG **Prod** - DOCUA

To Discover Our Body's Time Clock - Anticipate the Rhythm of Your Ecstasy and Blues 20 MIN
16mm / U-matic / VHS

Color
Explores biorhythms, looking at the rise and fall of energy and the rhythmic patterns that affect people.
Psychology
Dist - CNEMAG **Prod** - DOCUA

To do Battle in the Land 27 MIN
U-matic / VHS / 16mm
Color (J A)
Portrays conditions in the North and South that led to abolitionist John Brown's raid on the Federal Arsenal at Harper's Ferry, Virginia, in 1859. Uses archival photographs. Portrays Brown's involvement during the 1855 Kansas slavery skirmishes.
History - United States
Dist - USNAC **Prod** - USNPS 1985

To Dream 12 MIN
U-matic
Color (A)
Documents the contributions made by Martin Luther King in the struggle for human rights and economic justice.
Biography; History - United States
Dist - AFLCIO **Prod** - AFLCIO 1985

To drive at night 13 MIN
VHS / 16mm
Color (H G)
$65.00, $30.00 purchase _ #290, #485
Uses the latest technology in night photography to give a vivid, realistic visual presentation of driving conditions at night appropriate for both new and experienced drivers. Emphasizes the need for motorists to modify daytime driving habits and maneuvers to meet the specific problems of reduced visibility at night.
Health and Safety
Dist - AAAFTS **Prod** - AAAFTS 1976

To Ecuador for marlin 30 MIN
VHS
Color (G)
$29.90 purchase _ #0385
Travels to Ecuador in South America to fish for striped marlin and Pacific sailfish in the Humboldt Current.
Geography - World; Physical Education and Recreation; Science - Natural
Dist - SEVVID **Prod** - NDPC

To Eliminate all Unreasonable Risk 15 MIN
16mm
Color
LC 75-700091
Uses a narrative centered around a Bogart type character in order to explain the identity and purpose of the Consumer Product Safety Commission.
Business and Economics; Civics and Political Systems; Home Economics
Dist - USCPSD **Prod** - USCPSD 1974

To engineer is human 50 MIN
VHS
Horizon series
Color; PAL (G A)
PdS99 purchase
Shows how engineering science is subject to human limitations. Observes Professor Henry Petroski as he contends that structures can fail in ways that have been dismissed as virtually impossible. Professor Petroski illustrates some of the world's major civil engineering disasters using graphic film footage such as the explosion of the space shuttle Challenger.
Health and Safety; Industrial and Technical Education
Dist - BBCENE

To Expect to Die - a Film about Living 59 MIN
VHS / 16mm
Color (G)
$$70.00 rental _ #TETD - 000
Documents San Francisco journalist Robert Hardgrove's struggle from the time he learned he had cancer to his ultimate acceptance of death.
Sociology
Dist - PBS **Prod** - KQEDTV

To fall or not to fall 9 MIN
16mm
Color (A)
LC FIA67-660
Shows humans, from the caveman to the modern industrial worker, falling down on things, from things and over things. Points out that injuries and deaths from falls can be avoided by wearing proper footwear, avoiding unsafe actions and conditions, practicing good housekeeping and using common sense.
Guidance and Counseling; Health and Safety; Home Economics
Dist - AETNA **Prod** - AETNA 1966

To Feed the hungry 12 MIN
VHS
Color (J H C G)
$125.00 purchase, $30.00 rental _ #37746
Documents how Mickey Weiss created an innovative and successful program in Los Angeles in which merchants at the central Wholesale Produce Market donate fresh ripened fruit to charities for distribution to the hungry and homeless. Produced by Judy Chaikin.
Home Economics; Sociology
Dist - UCEMC

To Feed the Hungry of the Earth 20 MIN
16mm
Color (H C A)
$365 purchase, $45 rental
Examines the problems of feeding the earth's hungry people by the year 2000 when the population will be doubled. Includes an interview with plant scientist Dr. Norman Borlaug.
Sociology
Dist - CNEMAG **Prod** - DOCUA 1988

To Fill a Need 27 MIN
U-matic / VHS / 16mm
Career Job Opportunity Film Series
Color
LC 74-706524
Dramatizes how computers serving as job banks provide faster, better service for jobless applicants as well as employers.
Guidance and Counseling; Industrial and Technical Education; Sociology
Dist - USNAC **Prod** - USDLMA 1971

To fill the gap 16 MIN
VHS
Color (P I J H)
$18.95 purchase _ #IV175
Documents how US Geological Survey geologists and geophysicists search for possible oil and gas - bearing rocks beneath the seafloor of Lower Cook Inlet, Alaska. Shows how a research program, combining both onshore and offshore investigations, describes the methods and tools used to locate petroleum target areas.
Social Science
Dist - INSTRU **Prod** - USGEOS

To Find a Friend 15 MIN
16mm
Growing Up - Growing Older Series
Color
Shows what can be accomplished when people of different generations draw together in friendship.
Guidance and Counseling; Health and Safety; Sociology
Dist - MTP **Prod** - SEARSF 1982

To Find a Market 19 MIN
16mm
Color
LC 79-700294
Documents the grain marketing exchange in which farmers, operators of terminal elevators, the Minneapolis Grain Exchange, and the American public take part.
Agriculture
Dist - BOYD **Prod** - MGE 1979

To Find a Way 34 MIN
16mm
B&W (C A)
LC 75-701395
Follows a teacher education program given by Lowell State College in Massachusetts, based on the workshop process in order to initiate and involve future teachers in open education.
Education
Dist - EDC **Prod** - EDC 1971

To Find Answers 29 MIN
16mm
To Live Again Series
Color
LC 74-704796
Discusses research for the handicapped and demonstrates several devices to illustrate how science is improving life for the disabled.
Health and Safety; Science
Dist - USNAC **Prod** - USSRS

To find our life - the peyote hunt of the Huichols of Mexico 65 MIN
16mm
Color (C T)
Follows a group of Indians on their ritual journey to obtain peyote in the high desert country. Shows ritual eating of peyote and subsequent trance.
Social Science; Sociology
Dist - UCLA **Prod** - UCLA 1969

To find the Baruya story - an anthropologist at work with a New Guinea tribe 64 MIN
VHS / 16mm
Baruya series
Color (G)
$800.00, $400.00 purchase, $80.00 rental
Illustrates the actual fieldwork techniques of an anthropologist and personal relationships among the Baruya. Provides an in - depth view of the Baruya's traditional salt - based economic system. Follows French anthropologist Dr Marice Godelier in his attempt to understand the complexities of Baruya culture. Filmed in 1969 and 1982. Part of a series by Allison and Marek Jablonko and Stephen Olsson.
History - World; Sociology
Dist - DOCEDR **Prod** - DOCEDR 1982

To Fly 27 MIN
16mm
Color
LC 76-702901
Shows how Americans moved westward across the continental United States and developed transportation as they went. Explains how this trend culminated in the achievement of flight and the venture into space.
Industrial and Technical Education; Social Science
Dist - CONOCO **Prod** - CONOCO 1976

To forget Venice 108 MIN
16mm
Color (ITALIAN (ENGLISH SUBTITLES))
Explores the lives of five people who gather at a country house. Addresses aging, homosexuality, love and death.
Fine Arts; Foreign Language
Dist - TLECUL **Prod** - TLECUL

To form a more perfect union 31 MIN
16mm / U-matic / VHS
Decades of decision - the American Revolution series
Color (H C A)
Presents a re - creation of the events leading up to the ratification of the U S Constitution. Explains that its ratification depended upon a compromise with the forces advocating strong state government. Shows Governor John Hancock and Samuel Adams proposing amendments which assured its acceptance.
History - United States
Dist - NGS **Prod** - NGS 1975

To Free their Minds 34 MIN
16mm / U-matic / VHS
Color (T)
LC 77-700500
Discusses the methods by which a teacher trained to teach a homogeneous racial group of children adjusts to the demands of an integrated classroom.
Education; Sociology
Dist - GREAVW **Prod** - GREAVW 1974

To Get from Here to There Series

City driving	34 MIN
Expressway driving	30 MIN
Handling Emergencies	23 MIN
It Takes more than Cars	23 MIN
It's a Moving World	23 MIN
Jungle on Wheels	22 MIN
A Look at the Equipment	26 MIN
Rural Driving	35 MIN
Signs of Life	27 MIN
Special Conditions	25 MIN
Where do We Go from Here	33 MIN
The World Outside	34 MIN

Dist - PROART

To go on the floor 13 MIN
16mm
B&W
Examines the confusion and frustration of the first months in the life of a student nurse, when she is forced to work with graphics and mock - ups, and never sees a real patient. Ends with the frightening and challenging day when she gets her cap and 'goes on the floor.'
Health and Safety
Dist - UPENN **Prod** - UPENN 1966

To Halt Man's Physical Collapse 20 MIN
16mm
Color (H C A)
$365 purchase, $45 rental
Discusses the adverse effects of too little exercise and includes discussions by physiologists, sports writers, and athletes.
Health and Safety; Physical Education and Recreation
Dist - CNEMAG **Prod** - DOCUA 1988

To have and not to Hold - Helping Parents of Premies Cope 21 MIN
VHS / U-matic
Color
Contains a series of interviews with parents of premature babies. Gives valuable information to parents to help them understand and accept the experience of the Neonatal Intensive Care Unit.
Health and Safety; Sociology
Dist - POLYMR **Prod** - POLYMR

To have and to hold 30 MIN
VHS
Perspectives - health and medicine - series
Color; PAL; NTSC (G)
PdS90, PdS105 purchase
Looks at the latest solutions to male and female infertility and to babies' inheriting defects or congenital diseases.
Health and Safety; Science - Natural
Dist - CFLVIS **Prod -** LONTVS

To Hear Again 19 MIN
U-matic / VHS
Color (C)
$249.00, $149.00 purchase _ #AD - 1967
Describes the major risk factors for hearing impairment. Stresses the importance of early diagnosis in infants and demonstrates two infant hearing tests. Focuses on new technology to aid the hearing impaired.
Guidance and Counseling; Health and Safety; Science - Natural
Dist - FOTH **Prod -** FOTH

To hear or not to hear 10 MIN
16mm / VHS / BETA / U-matic
Color; PAL (H C T)
PdS90, PdS98 purchase
Demonstrates what is is like to be deaf, both in visual and audible terms. Features Jill Mansfield of Bournemouth, England, who wrote and directed this film and who suffers from a perceptive hearing loss.
Guidance and Counseling; Health and Safety
Dist - EDPAT

To Hear Your Banjo Play 16 MIN
16mm / U-matic / VHS
B&W (I J H C)
Presents the origin of the banjo, the development of southern folk music and its influence upon Americans. Pete Seeger plays his banjo and narrates the story.
Fine Arts
Dist - FI **Prod -** LERNER 1947

To Help a Child 22 MIN
16mm
Color
LC 79-701451
Reports on a comprehensive preventive dentistry demonstration program involving over 20,000 school children in ten cities in the United States.
Health and Safety; Sociology
Dist - KAROL **Prod -** RWJF 1979

To Honor Art 10 MIN
U-matic / VHS / 16mm
Color (J H C A T)
$25 rental _ #9803
Supports and substantiates efforts to strengthen the study of art in schools.
Fine Arts
Dist - AIMS **Prod -** RUSD 1983

To Humanize Our Police - no more TV - Image Cops 20 MIN
U-matic / VHS / 16mm
Color
Investigates the reality behind the paramilitary, pursuit - car image of the police portrayed by television and feature films. Suggests how the police role can be revamped in order to humanize the police and turn the cop on the beat into an accomplished public servant.
Civics and Political Systems; Social Science
Dist - CNEMAG **Prod -** DOCUA

To Humanize the Assembly Line - Freeing Us from Dull, Boring Work 20 MIN
16mm / U-matic / VHS
Color
Discusses the boredom of work on an assembly line. Investigates a successful attempt at a Volvo plant in Sweden to take human values into account, to make work more meaningful and satisfying, and still obtain what only the modern factory can produce. Explains that it is possible to change dull, boring work and that alienation, violence and sabotage, so long accepted as part of the assembly line, can be halted.
Business and Economics; Psychology
Dist - CNEMAG **Prod -** DOCUA

To Hurt and to heal - Part I 45 MIN
VHS
To Hurt and to heal series
Color (C G)
$295.00 purchase, $75.00 rental _ #37556
Converses with the parents of a premature infant who survived just six weeks. Describes their child's struggle to live, his doctors' extensive efforts and the many emotional and ethical conflicts faced by everyone involved in making decisions about the child's life. Part one of two parts produced by Laura Sky.
Sociology
Dist - UCEMC

To Hurt and to heal - Part II 60 MIN
VHS
To Hurt and to heal series
Color (C G)
$295.00 purchase, $75.00 rental _ #37557
Offers six portraits - two families, two nurses, two doctors. Reveals that the families have been affected in very different ways by the intervention of medical technology into their children's lives. The medical professionals discuss their frustrations and doubts about bringing pain to children who may not heal and about facing ever present ethical and clinical dilemmas that elude clear right or wrong answers. Part one of two parts produced by Laura Sky.
Health and Safety; Sociology
Dist - UCEMC

To Hurt and to heal - Parts I and II 105 MIN
VHS
To Hurt and to heal series
Color (C G)
$595.00 purchase
Presents a two - part series exploring ethical dilemmas in neonatal and pediatric medicine, produced by Laura Sky. Converses with the parents of a premature infant who survived just six weeks. Part II interviews families, nurses and doctors about the intervention of medical technology into the lives of children.
Health and Safety; Sociology
Dist - UCEMC

To Hurt and to heal series
To Hurt and to heal - Part I 45 MIN
To Hurt and to heal - Part II 60 MIN
To Hurt and to heal - Parts I and II 105 MIN
Dist - UCEMC

To Imitate the Sun 33 MIN
16mm
Color (H C A)
LC 76-714165
Covers controlled thermonuclear research over two decades. Includes the philosophy of two - X - two, Scylla IV, scyllac, astron, stellerators and tokamaks.
Science - Physical
Dist - USERD **Prod -** USNRC 1971

To Kayak 33 MIN
16mm
Color (I)
LC 77-702503
Offers a look at whitewater kayaking and covers aspects such as buying and making equipment, safety practices and organizations to contact in order to learn about kayaking, cruising and racing.
Health and Safety; Physical Education and Recreation
Dist - BODFIL **Prod -** BODFIL 1975

To keep a heritage alive 20 MIN
VHS / U-matic
Forest spirits series
Color (G)
Shows how the Oneida are reversing the erosion of their heritage by teaching their children their native tongue. Oneida children also are learning about artifacts and mementos, the ethic, a respect for elders, and a regard for the land.
Social Science
Dist - NAMPBC GPN **Prod -** NAMPBC NEWIST 1975

To Keep Our Liberty 23 MIN
U-matic / VHS / 16mm
Color
Describes critical issues and events connected with the decision of the Colonies to declare independence from Great Britain. Covers the period from 1763 to 1775. Issued in 1974 as a motion picture.
History - United States
Dist - USNAC **Prod -** USNPS 1978

To keep our liberty - the Minute Men of the American Revolution 35 MIN
VHS
National park series
Color (J H C G)
$34.95 purchase _ #FHF133V
Explores the issues at play in the critical decades preceding the outbreak of the Revolutionary War in 1775. Explains relations between American colonists and the government of Great Britain. Part of a five - part series on United States' national parks.
Geography - United States; History - United States
Dist - CAMV

To Keep Them Well 18 MIN
U-matic / VHS / 16mm
Color; B&W (A)
LC FIA61-579
Tells how a mother discovers deafness in her older daughter when she questions the doctor during the preschool examination of her younger child. Points out that regular physical examinations would have revealed the disability much earlier.
Health and Safety; Sociology
Dist - IFB **Prod -** OFP 1959

To Kill a Mockingbird
U-matic / VHS
Contemporary Literature Series
B&W (G C J)
$59 purchase _ #05640 - 85
Re - creates Harper Lee's novel about a southern lawyer defending a black man accused of rape. Stars Gregory Peck.
Fine Arts; Literature and Drama
Dist - CHUMAN

To kill a mockingbird 110 MIN
16mm / VHS / U-matic
B&W (I J H)
Presents the film version of the Harper Lee novel about a black man falsely accused of rape in the 1930s South. Stars Gregory Peck, Brock Peters, Phillip Alford and Mary Badham.
Civics and Political Systems; Fine Arts; Literature and Drama
Dist - SWANK GA UILL **Prod -** UPCI GA 1962

To kill a mockingbird
Videodisc
Laserdisc learning series
Color; CAV (J H)
$40.00 purchase _ #8L204
Tells of a distinguished southern lawyer who defends a black man accused of rape. Reveals that his actions causes the loss of many friendships but earns him the admiration of his two motherless children. From the novel by Harper Lee. A teacher's guide is available separately.
History - United States; Literature and Drama; Sociology
Dist - BARR **Prod -** BARR 1992

To Kill the Future 16 MIN
16mm / U-matic / VHS
Color (J)
Describes the fight for tougher drunk driving laws and penalties. Encourages closer parent - teenager communication.
Guidance and Counseling; Health and Safety; Psychology; Sociology
Dist - CORF **Prod -** NBCNEW

To Know the Sound of the World 21 MIN
16mm
Color
LC 79-700326
Focuses on patients at the Boys Town Institute for Communication Disorders in Children. Shows examples of communication disorders and tells how the institute's team approach provides services to handicapped children and their parents.
Education; Health and Safety; Psychology
Dist - CPF **Prod -** FFBH 1978

To Last a Lifetime 16 MIN
VHS / U-matic
Color (IND)
Examines methods to prevent industrial accidents. Focuses on back injuries. Investigates the relationship of the worker's mental attitude and protection for the back.
Business and Economics; Psychology
Dist - CHARTH **Prod -** CHARTH

To Lead 5 MIN
U-matic / VHS / 16mm
Color (I J H)
LC 83-700014
Uses animation to present the story of a group of birds that sing harmoniously until interrupted by a crow. Tells how the birds try to eliminate the crow but find a more workable solution in making the crow their conductor.
Fine Arts
Dist - PHENIX **Prod -** FILBUL 1982

To lead a new life 17 MIN
16mm / VHS / BETA / U-matic
Color; PAL (G)
PdS125, PdS133 purchase
Features disabled persons questioning the term 'disabled.'
Health and Safety
Dist - EDPAT

To life series
Teaches basic yoga stretches and exercises. Allows viewers to perform at their own pace. Hosted by Priscilla Patrick.
To life series 1840 MIN
Dist - SCETV **Prod -** SCETV 1990

To Lighten the Shadows 20 MIN
16mm / U-matic / VHS
B&W (S)
LC FIA65-480
Depicts techniques to be used in handling mentally retarded children, particularly during recreation and camping periods. Pictures personnel training sessions and lectures on mental retardation.

Education; Psychology
Dist - IFB Prod - SILLU 1963

To live again 25 MIN
16mm
Color (J)
Explores a new concept in treatment of alcoholism through a conventional hospital program combined with a special Outward Bound program. Explores how a holistic approach strengthens personal development, interpersonal effectiveness, environmental awareness and redefines personal values.
Guidance and Counseling; Health and Safety
Dist - CRYSP Prod - DURNCD 1982

To Live Again Series

After the accident	29 MIN
The Black Curtain	28 MIN
Drugs	29 MIN
The Glass wall	29 MIN
Great expectations	29 MIN
The Last Chance	29 MIN
A New Start	29 MIN
To Find Answers	29 MIN

Dist - USNAC

To Live and Breathe 12 MIN
16mm
Color
LC 72-702436
Identifies the leading causes of air pollution and tells how they affect the environment. Focuses on the thoughts and actions of people concerned about air pollution and explains what can be done by individuals or as members of the community to combat the problem.
Science - Natural
Dist - AETNA Prod - AETNA 1971

To Live and Move According to Your Nature is Called Love 29 MIN
16mm
To Save Tomorrow Series
B&W (H C A)
Shows attempts to organize residents to cope with community problems. Explains that on the belief that social problems contribute to mental illness, these problems must be identified and solutions seen before real in - roads to mental health can begin.
Psychology
Dist - IU Prod - NET

To Live for Ireland 30 MIN
U-matic / VHS / 16mm
Color (H C A)
$250 purchase, $55 rental
Examines sectarian violence and political turmoil in Northern Ireland. Focuses on the Irish Republican Army and the Social Democrat and Labor Party. Directed by Mary Pat Kelly.
Civics and Political Systems; History - World; Religion and Philosophy; Social Science
Dist - CNEMAG

To Live in Christ 60 MIN
BETA / VHS
Color
Shows Cardinal Law, Archbishop of Boston, talking with a group of teenagers and addressing their problems.
Religion and Philosophy
Dist - DSP Prod - DSP

To live in darkness 13 MIN
16mm
B&W
LC FIE54-228
Portrays three men who lost their eyesight because of carelessness.
Guidance and Counseling; Health and Safety
Dist - USNAC Prod - MOGULS 1947

To Live in Freedom 54 MIN
16mm
Color
Presents a critique of the Israeli reality, analyzes the Israeli and Palestinian class structure, and contains material filmed on the West Bank.
Geography - World; History - World; Sociology
Dist - ICARUS Prod - ICARUS 1975

To Live on 26 MIN
16mm
Color (H C A)
Shows how a group of physically handicapped people worked and fought their way back to lead productive, independent lives.
Health and Safety; Psychology
Dist - FLMLIB Prod - HESS

To Live Until You Die 57 MIN
U-matic / VHS / 16mm
Nova Series
Color (H C A)
Presents an intimate portrait of Dr Elizabeth Kubler - Ross and her work with the dying.
Sociology
Dist - TIMLIF Prod - WGBHTV 1982

To Live with Dignity 29 MIN
16mm
Color
LC 73-701120
Examines a three - month action research project at Ypsilanti State Hospital in which 20 very disoriented people received group therapy.
Psychology; Sociology
Dist - UMICH Prod - UMITV 1972

To Live with Herds 70 MIN
16mm / U-matic / VHS
B&W
Demonstrates the effects of nation - building in pre - Amin Uganda on the semi - nomadic, pastoral Jie. Looks at life in a traditional Jie homestead during a harsh dry season.
History - World
Dist - UCEMC Prod - MCDGAL 1974

To Love 25 MIN
16mm / U-matic / VHS
Color (J)
LC 73-702217
Presents an example of love expressed by the creation of a center of tenderness. Encourages an examination of love and caring in our lives.
Psychology; Sociology
Dist - WOMBAT Prod - WOMBAT 1973

To Love and Let Go 47 MIN
BETA / VHS / U-matic
Color (J H)
Deals with the grieving process experienced when teen mothers surrender their children for adoption. Explores the impact the decision to surrender has had on the lives of surrenderers, parents of a pregnant teen, a teenage father, an adoptive couple and an adoptee. Advocates the need for professional support services in school and in the community for pre and postpartum single parents.
Education; Guidance and Counseling; Home Economics; Sociology
Dist - UCALG Prod - UCALG 1986

To make a buche 29 MIN
Videoreel / VT2
French chef series
Color
Features Julia Child of Haute Cuisine au Vin demonstrating how to prepare a buche. With captions.
Home Economics
Dist - PBS Prod - WGBHTV

To make Man Immune from Disease 20 MIN
U-matic / VHS / 16mm
Color
Explores research into the human immune system.
Health and Safety
Dist - CNEMAG Prod - DOCUA

To make Man into Superman 20 MIN
16mm / U-matic / VHS
Color
Interviews Professor Robert Ettinger, an exponent of the cryonic movement which will freeze people into a state of suspended animation in which they could remain until they could be cured of their diseases.
Health and Safety
Dist - CNEMAG Prod - DOCUA

To make the Balance 33 MIN
16mm / U-matic / VHS
B&W (H C A)
LC 75-70571
Observes procedures used in a bi - lingual Spanish - Zapotec town in Mexico for the settlement of disputes in the town court. Features five cases portraying settlement of family, neighborhood and inter - village disputes.
Civics and Political Systems; Social Science; Sociology
Dist - UCEMC Prod - NALA 1970

To make the most of Today 14 MIN
16mm
Color
Explains the physical, economic, social and emotional problems of multiple sclerosis patients and their families. Concentrates on those services which are provided by an MS chapter, including transportation assistance, special equipment in the home, job counseling and placement and coordination of social services such as the Visiting Nurse Service.
Health and Safety; Psychology; Sociology
Dist - NMSS Prod - VISION 1974

To market, to market 30 MIN
VHS / U-matic
Come alive series; No 5
Color (H C A)
LC 82-706072
Shows the importance of the resume and job interview through the portrayal of a 40 - year - old unemployed man who is trying to organize his job search in some logical way. Uses a dream sequence to show how he learns to develop a proper resume and sharpen his interviewing skills.
Guidance and Counseling
Dist - GPN Prod - UAKRON 1981
CAREER CAREER
JISTW UAK

To market to market and Tagged 3 MIN
16mm
Color (G)
$10.00 rental
Depicts in a nutshell the painful subjection of an elderly person to the callousness of a world which has no place for her. Hopes to stimulate discussion about the nature and sources of the indignities of old age. Two slice - of - life films on one reel.
Health and Safety
Dist - NCJEWF

To market, to market - Spread your enthusiasm around 60 MIN
U-matic / VHS
JIST conference presentations
(C A P)
$60 _ #JWCV61V
Features David Swanson, life and work planning and motivation expert, as he speaks on career issues.
Business and Economics
Dist - JISTW Prod - JISTW

To Measure the Earth 30 MIN
U-matic
Maps - Horizons to Knowledge Series
Color
Explains the geometry of Eratosthenes and the difficulty of transferring a globe to flat paper. Discusses the history and methodology of surveying. Demonstrates surveying equipment.
Geography - United States; Geography - World; Social Science
Dist - UMITV Prod - UMITV 1980

To Meet the Challenge 19 MIN
16mm
Color
Points out many new and unique manufacturing techniques applied in the foundry industry.
Business and Economics; Industrial and Technical Education
Dist - GM Prod - GM

To Mend the World 90 MIN
VHS
Color (S)
$149.00 purchase _ #386 - 9051
Expresses the horror of the Holocaust through the eyes of artists. Features hundreds of paintings, never before seen publicly, by brilliant artists who are survivors of concentration camps. Co - produced with Harry Rasky.
Fine Arts; History - United States; History - World
Dist - FI Prod - CANBC 1988

To new horizons 60 MIN
VHS
B&W (G)
$39.95 purchase _ #S02287
Presents archival clips from films produced between 1931 and 1945. Shows the futuristic orientation that dominated American advertising and films in that period.
Fine Arts; History - United States
Dist - UILL

To Open a Closed Door 15 MIN
16mm
Child Abuse and Neglect Series
Color
LC 78-701589
Highlights two aspects of a social worker's involvement in a child abuse case, the initial interview with suspected abusive family members and testifying as an expert witness in court.
Civics and Political Systems; Sociology
Dist - UKANS Prod - UKANS 1977

To Orbit and Back 14 MIN
16mm
Color (I)
Describes a space shuttle mission of the mid - 1970's. Depicts a shuttle booster and orbiter being launched, the orbiter's rendezvous and docking with an earth orbiting space station and the orbiter's return to a runway landing on the earth.
Industrial and Technical Education
Dist - RCKWL Prod - NAA

To Parsifal 16 MIN
16mm
Color (C)
$436.00
Experimental film by Bruce Baillie.
Fine Arts
Dist - AFA **Prod** - AFA 1963

To Planet Earth with Love 30 MIN
16mm
Color (R)
Tells of the many jobs and short - term positions open to men and women willing to serve the Christian community. Explores the spiritual needs and opportunities in a changing world and how they must be met.
Guidance and Counseling; Religion and Philosophy; Sociology
Dist - GF **Prod** - GF

To Predict and Control Earthquakes 20 MIN
U-matic / VHS / 16mm
Color
Investigates scientists' efforts to understand and predict earthquakes. Discusses the concept of continental drift and examines the San Andreas Fault.
Science; Science - Physical
Dist - CNEMAG **Prod** - DOCUA

To Prepare a Child 23 MIN
16mm
Color
LC 76-700434
Uses the experiences of three children and their families to stress the importance of preparing a child emotionally for a hospitalization experience.
Guidance and Counseling; Health and Safety; Home Economics; Psychology; Sociology
Dist - CHNMC **Prod** - CHNMC 1975

To Preserve the Constitution 26 MIN
16mm / U-matic / VHS
American Challenge Series
B&W (J H)
Reveals how a military takeover could occur in the United States given the right set of political circumstances. Adapted from the motion picture Seven Days In May starring Burt Lancaster and Kirk Douglas.
Civics and Political Systems
Dist - FI **Prod** - PAR 1976

To Preserve, to Resist, to Protect 22 MIN
16mm
Color (A)
LC 78-700949
Shows 200 years of coastal defense as seen through the changes evident at Fort Moultrie, South Carolina.
Civics and Political Systems; Geography - United States
Dist - USNAC **Prod** - USNPS 1977

To Reach the Dawn 48 MIN
16mm
Color (J H)
LC 76-702320
Tells the story of R S Reynolds Sr and his founding of the Reynolds Metals Company. Documents the events in his life from the turn of the century through world War II.
Biography; Business and Economics; Industrial and Technical Education; Social Science
Dist - REYMC **Prod** - REYMC 1967

To remember or to forget 100 MIN
16mm
Color (C A) (RUSSIAN (ENGLISH SUBTITLES))
LC 83-700203
Relates how a contemporary Soviet woman decides to have baby against her doctor's orders hoping that it will improve relations with her husband. Reveals that the newborn baby dies and that she adopts an abandoned baby resulting in an unusual twist of fate.
Fine Arts; Sociology
Dist - IFEX **Prod** - RIGAFS 1982

To remember or to forget - Pt 1 33 MIN
16mm
Color (C A) (RUSSIAN (ENGLISH SUBTITLES))
LC 83-700203
Relates that against her doctor's orders, a contemporary Soviet woman decides to have a baby in hopes that it will improve relations with her husband. Shows that when the newborn baby dies, she adopts an abandoned baby and experiences an unusual twist of fate.
History - World; Sociology
Dist - IFEX **Prod** - RIGAFS 1982

To remember or to forget - Pt 2 33 MIN
16mm
Color (C A) (RUSSIAN (ENGLISH SUBTITLES))
LC 83-700203
Tells the story of a Soviet woman, who against her doctor's orders, decides to have a baby in hopes that is will improve relations with her husband. Relates that the newborn baby dies, and that she adopts an abandoned baby which leads to her experiencing an unusual twist of fate.
Fine Arts; History - World; Sociology
Dist - IFEX **Prod** - RIGAFS 1982

To remember or to forget - Pt 3 34 MIN
16mm
Color (C A) (RUSSIAN (ENGLISH SUBTITLES))
LC 83-700203
Relates the story of a contemporary Soviet woman, who against her doctor's orders, decides to have a baby hoping to improve relations with her husband. Shows that when the newborn baby dies, she adopts an abandoned baby and experiences an unusual twist of fate.
Fine Arts; Foreign Language
Dist - IFEX **Prod** - RIGAFS 1982

To Remember the Fallen - Conflict in Japan 27 MIN
U-matic / VHS / 16mm
(H A)
Examines the controversy and ongoing political struggle over the proposed nationalization of Yasunkuni Shrine in Tokyo which is dedicated to the spirits of the Japanese war dead. Shows the pressure on Japan to rearm itself against Western interests in Asia.
Civics and Political Systems; Geography - World
Dist - RTVA **Prod** - RTVA 1979

To roast a turkey 29 MIN
Videoreel / VT2
The French Chef series
Color
Features Julia Child of Haute Cuisine au Vin demonstrating how to roast a turkey. With captions.
Foreign Language; Home Economics
Dist - PBS **Prod** - WGBHTV

To Run 11 MIN
16mm
Color (J)
LC 73-702261
Studies a cross - country ski racer, revealing the training and determination required for this demanding sport. Shows the skier in training and in competition.
Physical Education and Recreation
Dist - AUIS **Prod** - ANAIB 1971

To Save a Life 14 MIN
16mm
Color; B&W (C G T A S R PRO IND)
Focuses on a method of turning an airplane around when inadvertently caught within a cloud, a procedure developed by the University of Illinois, Department of Aeronautics Training.
Industrial and Technical Education; Social Science
Dist - FO **Prod** - FO 1957

To save a life series
Burns - emergency procedures 15 MIN
Choking - to save a life 12 MIN
CPR - to Save a Life 13 MIN
Survival Swimming - to Save a Life 15 MIN
Dist - EBEC

To Save a Life Test
VHS
$69.00 purchase _ #HRV105
Shows viewers that many lives of accident victims could be saved if people were aware of the correct measures to take. Uses experts in first aid safety and fire safety to provide explanations about different situations, many times dismissing what is commonly thought to be the correct procedure.
Health and Safety
Dist - CAREER **Prod** - CAREER

To Save a Life - Trauma Centers 20 MIN
U-matic / VHS / 16mm
Color (H C)
Describes the concept of trauma centers and analyzes some of the difficult social policy issues it poses.
Health and Safety
Dist - CORF **Prod** - ABCNEW 1980

To Save a Species 15 MIN
16mm
Science in Action Series
Color (C)
Details several projects now underway to protect threatened North American species. Examines an intensive ecological study of the endangered prairie pronghorn of the American Northwest.
Science; Science - Natural
Dist - COUNFI **Prod** - ALLFP

To Save a Whale 60 MIN
VHS / U-matic / 16mm
Last Frontier Series
Color; Mono (G)
MV $225.00 _ MP $550.00
Explains how, in Newfoundland, man has learned to coexist with the great whale.
Science - Natural
Dist - CTV **Prod** - MAKOF 1985

To Save Our Environment - Conservation 13 MIN
U-matic / VHS / 16mm
Color (I J H)
LC 70-715427
Presents a high school student who gives his view of the environment, and discusses how to implement those measures which would conserve human resources, clean air, and pure water.
Science - Natural
Dist - JOU **Prod** - ALTSUL 1971

To Save the Amazon's Green Hell 20 MIN
U-matic / VHS / 16mm
Color
Discusses the Amazon River which permeates the greatest tropical rain forest and the most complex eco - system in the world. Presents an interview with Peruvian conservationist Philippe Benavides who claims that unless something is done, the Amazon people and the rain forest around them will be gone by the end of the twentieth century.
Geography - World; Science - Natural
Dist - CNEMAG **Prod** - DOCUA

To Save Tomorrow Series
Fountain house 29 MIN
Horizon House 29 MIN
Operation Reentry 30 MIN
Spruce House 29 MIN
They're Your People 29 MIN
To Live and Move According to Your Nature is Called Love 29 MIN
Wellmet House 30 MIN
Dist - IU

To Say I Am 29 MIN
U-matic
Color (C A)
LC 80-701133; 80-707162
Focuses on children who cannot use their speech mechanism and have limited body movement because of several handicaps. Tells how they are learning to use non - oral communications to 'speak.'
Psychology
Dist - LAWREN **Prod** - KOCETV 1980

To Search for America 17 MIN
16mm / U-matic / VHS
Color (J)
LC 73-702209
Searches into the romantic American past and into the superreal present for an answer to the question, 'WHY ARE WE THE WAY WE ARE TODAY.' Employs various film techniques. Introduces E G Marshall as narrator.
Sociology
Dist - PFP **Prod** - PFP 1973

To Secure these Rights 22 MIN
16mm
Color
LC 76-703470
Examines the sentiments of average Virginians of 1775. Reveals their concerns and explains why they supported their leaders so strongly during the American Revolution.
History - United States
Dist - VADE **Prod** - VADE 1976

To See Again - Corneal Transplant 37 MIN
16mm
B&W (PRO)
Presents patients before and after they have have their sight restored through corneal transplant. Provides a step - by - step view of the surgical procedure used.
Health and Safety
Dist - LAWREN **Prod** - CMA

To See Clearly 9 MIN
VHS / U-matic
Color (PRO)
Describes the surgical procedure, Radial Keratotomy, to correct myopia.
Health and Safety
Dist - WFP **Prod** - WFP

To See Ourselves 13 MIN
16mm
Color; B&W (H C A)
LC 72-702438
Shows how Jim Morrow learns to see himself from the other man's point of view. Through the magic of camera he is allowed to see himself as others see him.
Guidance and Counseling; Psychology
Dist - AETNA **Prod** - AETNA 1972

To see the summer sky
Videodisc
Laser learning set 2 series; Set 2
Color; CAV (P I)
$375.00 purchase _ #8L5409
Looks at the messages of poets such as Emily Dickinson and Langston Hughes. Guides through a variety of poetic images. Considers the use of the metaphor. Part of a series of six theme - based interactive videodisc lessons. Requires a Pioneer LD - V2000 or 2200, with barcode reader and adapter, or a Pioneer LD - V4200 or higher. Includes user's guide, two readers.
Literature and Drama
Dist - BARR **Prod** - BARR 1992

To Seek, to Teach, to Heal 29 MIN
16mm
Color
LC 74-705799
Focuses on the way the nation's network of medical centers, medical research institutions and medical schools can mobilize and bring man's newest knowledge into life - saving use through a dramatization about a young boy's fight for life.
Health and Safety; Science
Dist - USNAC **Prod** - USNIH

To Sense the Wonder 27 MIN
16mm
Color (G)
_ #106C 0178 502
Deals with the evolution of the Canadian landscape and the formation of the present system of national parks. Shows we can preserve our environment or we can destroy it.
Science - Natural; Social Science
Dist - CFLMDC **Prod** - NFBC 1978

To Serve all, Pt 1 30 MIN
16mm
Color (PRO)
Presents interviews with each of the living past presidents of the American College of Surgeons. Describes important events that took place during the administration of each of these past presidents.
Education; Health and Safety; Science
Dist - ACY **Prod** - ACYDGD 1963

To Serve all, Pt 2 35 MIN
16mm
Color (PRO)
Presents interviews with past presidents of the American College of Surgeons.
Education; Health and Safety; Science
Dist - ACY **Prod** - ACYDGD 1970

To serve the gods 33 MIN
16mm / VHS
Caribbean culture series
Color (G)
$650.00, $350.00 purchase, $55.00, $40.00 rental
Observes a week - long ceremony given by a Haitian family in honor of its ancestral spirits which occurs only every 20 to 30 years. Involves drumming, song, dance, possession, animal sacrifice and sharing food with the gods and with friends, family and neighbors. Part of a series on Caribbean culture by Karen Kramer.
Geography - World; History - World; Religion and Philosophy; Sociology
Dist - DOCEDR **Prod** - DOCEDR 1982

To Shoot or not to Shoot 18 MIN
U-matic / VHS
Color (H C A)
Discusses the dilemma police face when deciding whether or not to shoot. Hosted by NBC News' Lloyd Dobyns, who took part in a unique course being offered in Miami to help train and advise cops in dealing with these situations.
Civics and Political Systems; Social Science; Sociology
Dist - FI **Prod** - NBCNEW 1983

To Sing Our Own Song 50 MIN
U-matic / VHS / 16mm
Color (J)
Presents Jose Diokno, a man who is active in the anti - Marcos movement in the Philippines. Argues that he sees a rich and selfish elite benefiting from the wealth of his land while the poor become more and more convinced that change can come only through violence. Criticizes the United States for supporting a repressive regime.
Civics and Political Systems; History - World
Dist - FI **Prod** - BBCTV 1982

To Sir, with Love 105 MIN
16mm
Color
Tells the story of a teacher who gets his first job in a tough London slum school. Stars Sidney Poitier.
Fine Arts
Dist - TIMLIF **Prod** - CPC 1967

To Sleep - Perchance to Dream 30 MIN
16mm / U-matic / VHS
Spectrum Series
B&W (H C A)
LC FIA68-1379
Documents several experiments to determine the relationship of dreams to stomach secretions, the amount of time infants spend dreaming, and the effect of depriving a subject of his dreams. Filmed at the sleep laboratory at UCLA.
Health and Safety; Psychology; Science - Natural
Dist - IU **Prod** - NET 1967

To Solve the ESP Mystery 20 MIN
U-matic / VHS / 16mm
Color
Shows experiments in extra - sensory perception, precognition, and telepathy.
Psychology
Dist - CNEMAG **Prod** - DOCUA

To Speak Again 16 MIN
16mm
Color (H C A)
Provides insight to the laryngectomy patient and his family.
Health and Safety
Dist - AMCS **Prod** - AMCS

To Speak or not to Speak 11 MIN
U-matic / VHS / 16mm
Color (J H C)
LC 72-702117
Uses an animated film to demonstrate that people who lack knowledge of their political affairs are ripe for manipulation or takeover by special interests or by totalitarian governments. Without narration.
Civics and Political Systems; Social Science
Dist - IFB **Prod** - SERVA 1972

To Speak with Friends 28 MIN
16mm
B&W
LC FIE61-206
Illustrates advanced instructional practices in both elementary and secondary schools. Shows how language laboratories, television, motion pictures and other special audio - visual facilities help students to understand and speak foreign languages.
Education; Foreign Language
Dist - USNAC **Prod** - USOE 1960

To Speak with Friends 29 MIN
U-matic
B&W
Illustrates instructional practices in elementary and secondary schools using language laboratories, television, motion pictures, recordings, slides and other special audio - visual facilities to help students in understanding and speaking foreign languages.
Education; Foreign Language
Dist - USNAC **Prod** - USNAC 1972

To Spring 20 MIN
VHS
Gentle Giant Series
Color (H)
LC 90712920
Uses children's story to teach certain universal truths and morals. The 16th of 16 installments of The Gentle Giant Series, which draws on cultures throughout the world for stories.
Health and Safety; Literature and Drama; Psychology
Dist - GPN

To Stem the Black Tide 14 MIN
16mm
B&W
LC 76-703892
Shows the U S Coast Guard's role in the detection, location and prevention of oil spills and pollution. Features technology and manpower being employed in handling oil spills and pollution.
Civics and Political Systems; Industrial and Technical Education; Science - Natural; Social Science
Dist - USNAC **Prod** - USCG 1976

To Stuff a Cabbage 29 MIN
Videoreel / VT2
French from the French Chef - French Series
Color
Features Julia Child of Haute Cuisine au Vin demonstrating how to stuff a cabbage. With captions.
Foreign Language; Home Economics
Dist - PBS **Prod** - WGBHTV

To Stuff a Sausage 29 MIN
Videoreel / VT2
French from the French Chef - French Series
Color
Features Julia Child of Haute Cuisine au Vin demonstrating how to stuff a sausage. With captions.
Foreign Language; Home Economics
Dist - PBS **Prod** - WGBHTV

To Take a Hand 20 MIN
16mm
Color
Portrays a young nurse in a specialized cancer hospital as she experiences a period of adjustment and change in pre - conceived attitudes, ultimately gaining not only an awareness that there is hope for the cancer patient but also that, by becoming sincerely involved with the patient, she as an individual nurse can make a vital contribution.
Health and Safety; Psychology
Dist - AMCS **Prod** - AMCS 1972

To Take a Hand 17 MIN
16mm
Color
LC 75-711538
Follows a young nurse in a specialized cancer hospital through her period of adjustment, her change in attitudes and concepts, her realization that cancer can be cured, that there is hope and that she as an individual nurse can contribute to helping every cancer patient.
Health and Safety; Sociology
Dist - UTEXSC **Prod** - UTEXSC 1970

To Taste Victory 18 MIN
16mm
Color
LC 72-702015
Shows the activities of the Special Olympic training program for retarded children. Includes participation of retarded boys from the Parsons State Hospital and Training Center at Parsons, Kansas.
Education; Physical Education and Recreation; Psychology; Sociology
Dist - PSHTCA **Prod** - UKANS 1970

To Teach Our Own 30 MIN
U-matic
Africa File Series
Color (J H)
Looks at education in west Africa today where it is seen as essential to development.
Business and Economics; Education; Geography - World; History - World
Dist - TVOTAR **Prod** - TVOTAR 1985

To Tell or not to Tell 7 MIN
16mm / U-matic / VHS
Citizenship - Whose Responsibility, Set 2 Series; Set 2
Color (J H)
LC FIA68-2887
Describes the dilemma of a girl who sees a fellow student cheating during a college scholarship test.
Guidance and Counseling; Psychology
Dist - IFB **Prod** - HORIZN 1967

To Tell the Tooth 10 MIN
U-matic
Body Works Series
Color (P I J H)
Teaches children about different kinds of teeth, shows proper flossing techniques and they receive a surprise visit from the dental care expert Dracula.
Physical Education and Recreation; Social Science
Dist - TVOTAR **Prod** - TVOTAR 1979

To tell the truth 14 MIN
VHS
Color (P I)
$330.00, $245.00 purchase, $60.00 rental
Tells about a little girl who tells some lies at school and learns the consequences for her and others. Includes optional discussion stops within the story to allow children to acquire thinking skills as they predict what will happen. Directed by Beth Brickall.
Guidance and Counseling; Psychology; Social Science
Dist - CF

To the bitter end - fight for an Afrikaner Volkstaat 26 MIN
VHS
Color; PAL (G)
PdS50 purchase
Explores the white right - wing efforts to establish volkstaat, a nation - state for Afrikaners. Presents an Anthony Shaw, South Africa, production.
Fine Arts; Geography - World; Sociology
Dist - BALFOR

To the Edge of Outer Space 12 MIN
16mm
Color
Shows man's flight in the X - 15 aircraft.
Industrial and Technical Education; Science
Dist - THIOKL **Prod** - THIOKL 1959

To the edge of the Earth - ecology and environment 60 MIN
VHS
Infinite voyage series
Color (H C A)

$24.95 purchase _ #ST - ZC5448
Travels from the Arctic to a Costa Rican jungle to places seldom seen by human eye. Combines film footage, special effects, computer graphics and soundtracks to bring scientific concepts to life for students. Includes instructor's guide with terms and definitions, learning objectives and follow-up activities. Part of a 20-part series.
Geography - World; Science - Natural
Dist - INSTRU **Prod** - WQED
INTM

To the Edge of the Universe 23 MIN
16mm
Color (H C)
LC 78-709477
Describes the construction and use of a radio telescope to measure a specific quasar. Shows basic concepts as the size of the universe, light years as a means of measuring astronomical distances, the doppler shift to determine direction of movement, the need for careful observation and measurement in scientific research and some of the methods of astronomers.
Science - Physical
Dist - NFBC **Prod** - NFBC 1970

To the Gates of Japan 50 MIN
U-matic / VHS
B&W
Explains Japanese strategy in the Pacific war. Shows good action scenes on the Solomon islands and Marianas. Shows excellent aircraft carrier footage.
History - World
Dist - IHF **Prod** - IHF

To the honey tree 12 MIN
16mm
Color (I)
Shows a children's trip through a wooded area where they discover the tooth of an unknown animal and the habits of honey bees.
Science - Natural
Dist - SF **Prod** - SF 1973

To the last drop 50 MIN
VHS
Water wars series
Color; PAL (H C A)
PdS99 purchase; Not available in the United States and Canada.
Examines water as a powerful element and the focus of many of the world's conflicts. Focuses on water as the cause of much of the hostility in the Middle East. Part two of a three part series.
Geography - World; History - World
Dist - BBCENE

To the lighthouse 115 MIN
VHS
Color (H C)
$97.00 purchase _ #04577 - 126
Reveals that a proper British holiday turns into a summer of disillusionment. Adapts a novel by Virginia Woolf. Stars Rosemary Harris, Michael Clough.
Literature and Drama
Dist - GA **Prod** - GA

To the moon and beyond
VHS
Space age series; Pt 4
Color (G)
$24.95 purchase _ #SPA090
Explores the possibilities for human colonization of the Moon. Features Patrick Stewart as host. Part four of a six - part series.
History - World; Science - Physical
Dist - INSTRU **Prod** - NAOS

To the north and A different war 120 MIN
VHS
Korean war series; Vol 3
Color; B&W (G)
$19.95 purchase _ #1647
Examines in two parts events in North Korea and the aspects of the war which which made it historically different from previous wars. Includes film footage from both North and South Korea and interviews with Korean, American and Russian military and political leaders who personally participated in the events. Part three of a five - part series on the Korean War. Produced by the Korean Broadcast System.
History - World
Dist - KULTUR

To the Nth Dimension 26 MIN
U-matic / VHS
Color (G)
$249.00, $149.00 purchase _ #AD - 1823
Explores modern mathematics and the emerging crisis in American mathematical education. Considers that America may be unable to compete in the marketplace of ideas.
Business and Economics; Education; Mathematics; Psychology
Dist - FOTH **Prod** - FOTH

To the People of the World 21 MIN
16mm / U-matic / VHS
Captioned; Color (A) (SPANISH (ENGLISH SUBTITLES))
Discusses human rights and the conditions of political prisoners in Chile since the military coup in 1973. Spanish dialog with English subtitles.
Fine Arts; History - World
Dist - CNEMAG **Prod** - MARGIB 1975

To the Pond 13 MIN
16mm
Color (I)
Presents scenes of children on their way to a pond where they discover how to make flour from cattail, find fresh herbs, carve apples, make scale prints and paint with natural dyes.
Fine Arts; Literature and Drama
Dist - SF **Prod** - SF 1973

To the rescue 30 MIN
VHS
Davey and Goliath series
Color (P I R)
$19.95 purchase, $10.00 rental _ #4 - 8834
Features Davey and his friends leading a rescue party to help an injured father and daughter. Focuses on interdependence and teamwork. Produced by the Evangelical Lutheran Church in America.
Literature and Drama; Religion and Philosophy
Dist - APH

To the Rescue 30 MIN
U-matic
Read all about it - One Series
Color (I)
Teaches reading and writing skills by recounting a story in which Chris sends a message that he is trapped on Trialviron. The genie from Aladdin's lamp transports Sam and Lynne to the shifting sands.
Education; English Language; Literature and Drama
Dist - TVOTAR **Prod** - TVOTAR 1982

To the Shores of Iwo Jima 19 MIN
U-matic / VHS / 16mm
Color
Presents a documentary account of the American invasion of Iwo Jima. Shows ship bombardment, rocket fire, air bombing, the use of flame throwers and scenes of individual and group combat.
Civics and Political Systems; Geography - World; History - World
Dist - USNAC **Prod** - USN

To the Top 27 MIN
16mm
Color (G)
_ #106C 0177 033
Shows the construction of the CN tower in Toronto, from the soil tests and the enormous excavations to the 'topping off' with the communications mast by helicopter. The tower is the world's largest free standing structure and provides a link in nationwide communications.
Geography - World; Industrial and Technical Education; Social Science
Dist - CFLMDC **Prod** - NFBC 1977

To the Waterfall 13 MIN
16mm
Color (I)
Shows scenes of children on their way to a waterfall where they learn how Indians used mud, berries and feathers to decorate themselves.
Fine Arts; Social Science
Dist - SF **Prod** - SF 1973

To the Wild Country Series

The Great Canadian southwest	55 MIN
The Great gulf - the Saint Lawrence	55 MIN
Land of the Big Ice	55 MIN
Wild Corners of the Great Lakes	55 MIN
Wild Corners of the Great Lakes, Pt 1	27 MIN
Wild Corners of the Great Lakes, Pt 2	28 MIN
A Wild Lens in Algonquin	55 MIN

Dist - KEGPL

To Think of Dying 58 MIN
VHS / 16mm
Color (G)
$70.00 rental _ #TTOD - 000
Features a conversation about death between Orville Kelly, a terminal cancer patient, and Lynn Caine, whose husband died of cancer.
Psychology; Sociology
Dist - PBS **Prod** - KTCATV

To Tommy with Love 22 MIN
16mm
Color
Depicts a family where the father is constantly away on business trips, and shows how the Cub Scout program brings the family closer together.
Sociology
Dist - BSA **Prod** - BSA 1982

To Touch a Dream 3 MIN
U-matic / VHS / 16mm
Color (J H A)
Shows a young girl realizing her fantasy of dancing.
Fine Arts
Dist - MTOLP **Prod** - RITWAX 1984

To touch, to heal 12 MIN
VHS / U-matic
Color (R G)
$59.00 purchase, $25.00 rental _ #850, #851, #852
Celebrates the historical roots and tradition of Catholic healthcare ministry in the United States. Features Helen Hayes as narrator.
Health and Safety; History - United States; Religion and Philosophy
Dist - CATHHA

To Touch Today 24 MIN
VHS / U-matic
Color (PRO)
Sensitizes viewers to the feelings and experiences that bereaved parents must face. Explains purpose and value of the support group, SHARE.
Health and Safety; Sociology
Dist - HSCIC **Prod** - HSCIC 1984

To Train and Protect 15 MIN
16mm
Color
LC 75-700591
Shows five segments of Arctic survival training, including the water survival training, the research vessel thunderbolt training, the helicopter simulator program and pilot screening. Insures the safety and protection of Air Force flying personnel and emphasizes proficiency, safety and savings.
Geography - World; Health and Safety
Dist - USNAC **Prod** - USAF 1974

To Try Again and Succeed 8 MIN
U-matic / VHS / 16mm
Color (I J H C A) (NORWEGIAN)
$225.00 purchase, $160.00 purchase; LC 82-706597; 80-700104
Portrays the little eagle who fears flying, learns self - confidence and finally succeeds. An animated short story narrated by Orson Welles. A Bosustow production.
Fine Arts; Literature and Drama; Psychology
Dist - CF **Prod** - BOSUST 1980

To Walk in Faith 30 MIN
16mm
Color (H A)
LC FIA68-1495
Tells the story of Doug North, an olympic trainee, whose skiing skiing career ended by a crippling accicent. Reveals that he returns to college to earn his diploma, and is led back to a meaningful Christian life through the effort of a campus Pastor and the genuine concern of a coed.
Guidance and Counseling; Psychology; Religion and Philosophy
Dist - CPH **Prod** - CPH 1968

To Walk on the Moon 17 MIN
16mm
Color (I)
Summarizes the Apollo program from its beginning in 1961 through the historic moon walk of astronauts Armstrong and Aldrin in July, 1969. Includes motion picture and still photographs taken during the Apollo Seven, Eight, Nine, Ten and 11 flights.
History - World; Industrial and Technical Education; Science; Science - Physical
Dist - RCKWL **Prod** - NAA

To what are mutual attachments due 3 MIN
16mm
B&W (A)
$12.00 rental
Uses experimental imagery and numerous overlapping soundtracks to tell the story of a couple who had dated and broken up. Produced by Gorman Bechard.
Fine Arts; Guidance and Counseling
Dist - CANCIN

To what end 60 MIN
VHS
Color (G)
$59.95, $99.95 purchase, $45.00 rental _ #TWEN - 000
Explores four policy options for American nuclear weapons policy - continued buildup without arms control, established arms control policy, strategic defense and disarmament. Interviews advocates for each position, including Edward Teller, Jonathan Schell and Robert McNamara. Hosted by Marvin Kalb.

Civics and Political Systems; Geography - World
Dist - PBS Prod - WNETTV 1988
EFVP

To Whom it may Concern 27 MIN
VHS
(J H C A)
$89.95 purchase _ #UL113V
Examines the growing epidemic of teen suicide. Presents interviews with friends and relatives of suicide victims and attempted suicides. Discusses depression, threats, self destructive behavior, and listlessness as signs of a serious problem. Deals with methods of prevention.
Health and Safety; Sociology
Dist - CAMV Prod - CAMV

To Whom it may Concern
VHS
Is Anyone Listening - a Documentary Series
$89.95 purchase _ #ULTWC
Uses interviews with teenagers who have made serious suicide attempts to help students deal with their own suicidal feelings and with friends who might need their help.
Psychology; Sociology
Dist - CAREER Prod - CAREER

To whom it may concern - a program confronting teen suicide 27 MIN
VHS
Color (J H A)
$95.00 purchase _ #113VG
Interviews friends and relatives of teen suicide victims and with young people who have seriously tried to commit suicide. Deals with issues of suicide from a professional perspective as people around the United States try to understand and put an end to the increasing number of suicides among teenagers. Includes a leader's guide and a blackline master.
Sociology
Dist - UNL

To win at all costs - the story of America's Cup 50 MIN
BETA / VHS
Color
Presents an overview of the history of the America's Cup.
Geography - World; Physical Education and Recreation
Dist - OFFSHR Prod - GRANBN 1983
SEVVID MYSTIC
MYSTIC

To Work 27 MIN
16mm / U-matic / VHS
Five Billion People Series
Color
Examines work as seen from a historical perspective and as it is in the modern world. Questions the present mode of work by setting it within a critical and historical context.
Business and Economics
Dist - CNEMAG Prod - LEFSP

To Work with the Forest 14 MIN
16mm
Color
Tells of the work of professional foresters.
Agriculture; Guidance and Counseling; Science - Natural
Dist - SAFO Prod - SAFO

To Your Good Health 30 MIN
16mm
Captioned; Color (S)
Presents typical health care situations that help hearing - impaired people become better consumers of health care services.
Guidance and Counseling; Health and Safety; Psychology
Dist - GALCO Prod - GALCO

To Your Health 49 MIN
VHS / U-matic / 16mm
Inquiry Series
Color; Mono (H C A)
MV $350.00 _ MP $600.00 purchase, $50.00 rental
Reports that there is little response to programs calling for controls on alcohol consumption. Researchers set up a road block to conduct breathalyzer tests on local drivers in Ontario. It was found that one in every 12 drivers registered a blood alcohol content of .06, the level of impairment recognized by most researchers. Establishes the fact that most people recognize that alcohol can become a habit and a problem, but are unwilling to do anything to control their own consumption.
Sociology
Dist - CTV Prod - CTV

To your health series
Aerobic dancing, medicine, health, exercise
Aerobics, medicine, health and exercise
Dieting
Jazz and exercise
Massage for everyone
Sports nutrition - facts and fallacies
The Tap tape
Weightlifting training and conditioning
Your first baby
Dist - INCRSE

To Your Heart's Content - Positive Approaches to Fitness 26 MIN
16mm
Color (A)
LC 83-700502
Promotes cardiovascular fitness by offering advice from a cardiologist, an exercise physiologist and a world champion cyclist who suggests a gradual but steady inauguration of an exercise regime. Introduces such people as 86 - year - old Hulda Crooks, who enjoys mountain climbing.
Health and Safety; Physical Education and Recreation
Dist - SPEF Prod - SPEF 1982

Toad a Trois 3 MIN
VHS / U-matic
Color (C A)
Presents three beanbag toads engaging in animated sexual activity.
Health and Safety; Psychology
Dist - MMRC Prod - MMRC

Toadskin spell 50 MIN
VHS
Natural world series
Color; PAL (H C A)
PdS99 purchase; Not available in the United States or Canada
Discusses the chemicals found in amphibian skins, especially toad's skins. Examines toads in their natural habitats to discover how toads use their skin.
Science - Natural
Dist - BBCENE

Toast 12 MIN
VHS / 16mm
Color (P I J H C G)
$260 film, $65 video, $25 rental
Illustrates our underlying dependence on fossil fuels, and takes as its example the production and distribution of a commonplace item, bread. Uses images set to music while documenting all the fossil fuel inputs, from the oil well head to the toaster.
Science - Natural; Social Science
Dist - BULFRG Prod - BULFRG 1977

A Toast to Missouri - a video guide to Missouri wine country 20 MIN
VHS
Color (G)
$19.95 purchase
Leads viewers on a flavorful trip through some of the best wines the state of Missouri has to offer. Samples vintner's wares in Hermann, Augusta, Arrow Rock, Rocheport and St James. Also features white - water rafting, bicycling on historic trails, professional theater productions and other recreational offerings. Includes road maps and tourist information numbers displayed on screen. Features Kansas City news anchor Dave Eckert as host.
Geography - United States
Dist - VINESY Prod - VINESY 1993

Tobacco 3 MIN
16mm
Of all Things Series
Color (P I)
Discusses the tobacco industry.
Business and Economics
Dist - AVED Prod - BAILYL

The Tobacco action curriculum 15 MIN
VHS
Color (P I J)
$130.00 purchase _ #CG - 979 - VS
Presents a classroom - tested activity - based curriculum which explores health issues and decision making related to tobacco smoking and chewing. Includes a binder and reproducible worksheets.
Guidance and Counseling; Health and Safety; Psychology
Dist - HRMC Prod - HRMC 1992

Tobacco and Human Physiology 21 MIN
16mm / VHS
Color (J H A)
$380.00, $475.00 purchase, $75.00 rental _ #9855, #9855LD
Shows how the human respiratory system works and how it is damaged by the particulate matter in cigarette smoke. Describes diseases caused by smoking - emphysema, cancer, heart attacks, and the effects of smoking on unborn children. Features Dr Mark Robinson. Available on laser disc.
Psychology; Science - Natural
Dist - AIMS Prod - SANDE 1986

Tobacco and you 20 MIN
VHS
Color (I J)
$149.00 purchase _ #2341 - SK
Combines talk - show segments with interviews with young, teenage smokers to discusss the health risks of smoking and why teens smoke. Considers related issues such as 'smokers' rights,' addiction, and the role of education in preventing smoking. Includes teacher's guide.
Health and Safety; Psychology
Dist - SUNCOM Prod - SUNCOM

Tobacco fable - Dolphin meets ol' coyote 12 MIN
VHS
Color (K P I J)
$250.00 purchase, $45.00 rental
Presents a children's story which details the effects of smoking and chewing tobacco. Tells how Whikil - dolphin - meets Coyote - trickster - and illustrates why it's not 'cool' to smoke or chew even though promoted by peer pressure.
Health and Safety; Literature and Drama; Social Science
Dist - SHENFP Prod - SHENFP 1993

Tobacco Fantasy 2 MIN
16mm
Color
Presents tobacco fragments which come to life in sweeping pictorial images of a great toreador's encounter with a celebrated bull.
Fine Arts
Dist - IFEX Prod - ANIMAF 1983

Tobacco road - a dead end 30 MIN
VHS
Color (I J H G)
$79.95 purchase _ #CCP0065V
Reveals that, according to American Medical Association figures, over 1,000 people die each day and over 4 million people have died since 1980 from tobacco - related diseases. Discloses that 60 percent of current tobacco users begin by age 14 and 90 percent by age 18. Exposes graphically the high occurrence of lung cancer, emphysema, heart disease and vascular disease directly attributed to tobacco use.
Guidance and Counseling; Health and Safety; Psychology
Dist - CAMV Prod - CAMV 1991

Tobacco - the Follower's Habit
VHS / 35mm strip
Addiction Series
$37.50 purchase _ #015 - 714 filmstrip, $47.50 purchase _ #015 - 733
Shows the harmful effects of smoking and tells how to avoid manipulation by advertising campaigns.
Health and Safety; Psychology
Dist - CAREER Prod - CAREER

Tobacco - the Idiot's Delight 19 MIN
16mm
Color (J H C)
LC 76-703181
Uses a series of satirical vignettes to show how social pressures influence young people to accept smoking. Shows cases of tobacco addiction and points out possible adverse physical effects of tobacco.
Guidance and Counseling; Health and Safety; Psychology
Dist - MTVTM Prod - MTVTM 1976

Tobacco - the pushers and their victims 38 MIN
VHS
Color (I J H)
$225.00 purchase
Draws attention to the tobacco industry's efforts to lure young people into smoking through advertising that focuses on teenagers' need for approval, acceptance and independence. Shows ways to combat the tobacco industry's appeal to young people.
Guidance and Counseling; Health and Safety; Psychology
Dist - PFP

Tobelo marriage 106 MIN
VHS
Color (C G A)
$395.00 purchase, $75.00 rental _ #38012
Chronicles a remarkable marriage ritual on a Moluccan island of eastern Indonesia. Reveals that the ritual includes a large - scale exchange of valuables that requires highly diplomatic negotiations, numerous ceremonies, and lengthy preparatory activities. Produced by Dirk Nijland.
Geography - World; Sociology
Dist - UCEMC

Tobias on the Evolution of Man 18 MIN
U-matic / VHS / 16mm
Color (H C A)
LC 76-703412
Summarizes Phillip Tobias' contributions to paleoanthropology in the field and in the laboratory. Presents Tobias discussing the evolution of man, considering various hominid species and their relationship to Homo sapiens.

History - World; Science - Natural; Sociology
Dist - NGS Prod - NGS 1975

Tobruk el Ghazala 42 MIN
VHS
(G A) (POLISH)
$29.95 purchase _ #V143
Offers a newly - released film based on original documents, photos and relations from soldiers who took part in battles in Ghazala and Tobruk.
Fine Arts; History - World
Dist - POLART

Tobruk to Tarakan 30 MIN
16mm
B&W (H C A)
Examines the Australian Army in World War II.
Civics and Political Systems; History - World
Dist - AUIS Prod - ANAIB 1965

Toby Tyler or Ten Weeks with a Circus 96 MIN
16mm / U-matic / VHS
Color
Tells how a runaway boy joins the circus.
Fine Arts; Literature and Drama
Dist - FI Prod - DISNEY 1967

Toccata for toy trains 14 MIN
U-matic / VHS / 16mm
Color (K)
LC FIA59-724
Shows toy trains as they journey from roundhouse and yards, into stations and out, through countryside and village, and on to their destination. All characters, architecture and objects with which the sets are built are toys, most of them made a number of years ago.
Fine Arts; Physical Education and Recreation; Social Science
Dist - PFP Prod - EAMES 1957

Tocqueville's Europe 60 MIN
VHS
Europe and America in the modern age - 1776 to the present series
Color (H C PRO)
$95.00 purchase
Presents a lecture by James Sheehan. Focuses on a critical period in European and American history and on leaders of the time. Part of a 20 - part series that looks at the last two centuries in Europe and America. Series presents lectures by David M Kennedy and James Sheehan of Stanford University on such figures as Adam Smith, Marx, Lincoln, Washington, Jefferson, Freud, Margaret Sanger, Susan B Anthony and Jane Adams and their impact on the events of their day. For history resource material and continuing education courses.
Civics and Political Systems; History - United States; History - World
Dist - LANDMK

Today and Tomorrow 28 MIN
16mm
Color
LC 74-705802
Shows VA youth volunteers in both career explorations and indirect patient service assignments.
Health and Safety; Social Science; Sociology
Dist - USNAC Prod - USVA 1973

Today and Tomorrow 60 MIN
VHS / U-matic
James Galway's Music in Time Series
Color (J)
Presents flutist James Galway discussing how modern music is more difficult to understand or assess. Includes example of the music of Lennon and McCartney, Copland and Stravinsky.
Fine Arts
Dist - FOTH Prod - POLTEL 1982

Today for tomorrow 15 MIN
16mm
Color
LC 74-705803
Explains that keeping aviation's mushrooming growth on safety's centerline is FAA's most important job. Summarizes FAA's major research and development projects and the outstanding personnel and unique testing and simulation facilities that enable NAFEC to create or re - create any kind of flight situation, all in the name of safety.
Industrial and Technical Education; Social Science
Dist - USFAA Prod - FAAFL 1969

Today I am a man, I think 22 MIN
16mm
Color
LC 80-700489
Tells how a young boy approaching his bar mitzvah questions its traditions and meaning as his parents try to turn it into a Hollywood party.
Fine Arts; Religion and Philosophy; Sociology
Dist - USC Prod - USC 1980

Today in America, Sex is Politics
VHS / Cassette
Humanist Voices Speak Out Series
(G)
$49.95, $9.00 purchase
Discusses sex and politics in the US, and how they affect each other. Features Sol Gordon. Part of a series which discusses social issues in humanist terms.
Civics and Political Systems; Guidance and Counseling; Psychology; Religion and Philosophy; Sociology
Dist - AMHUMA Prod - AMHUMA

Today, Tomorrow, Forever 15 MIN
VHS / U-matic
Soup to Nuts Series
Color (J H)
Points out that it's up to each individual to decide whether or not to age in a healthy way. Explains that changes in body and lifestyle require new food choices throughout life.
Health and Safety; Social Science
Dist - AITECH Prod - GSDE 1980

Today was a terrible day 8 MIN
VHS
Color (K P)
$34.95 purchase
Presents a video version of the Patricia Reilly Giff book 'Today Was A Terrible Day.' Tells the story of how young Ronald Morgan has a horrible day at school - but is able to finally smile when he realizes that he can read all by himself. Companion book illustrated by Susanna Natti.
Literature and Drama
Dist - LIVOAK Prod - LIVOAK

Today was a Terrible Day
VHS / 35mm strip
Storybook Library Series
Color (K)
$34.95, $32.00 purchase
Reveals that after a totally calamitous school day, Ronald Morgan discovers that he can read all by himself. By Patricia Reilly Giff.
English Language; Literature and Drama
Dist - PELLER

Today's Army is an Education 18 MIN
16mm
Color
Shows the many opportunities available for higher education in the U S Army including apprenticeship programs, tuition assistance, ROTC, scholarships, resident medical programs, appointments to West Point and other programs leading to college degrees.
Civics and Political Systems; Education; Guidance and Counseling
Dist - MTP Prod - USA

Today's Broadway Gypsies 30 MIN
U-matic / VHS
Broadway Dance Series
Color
Fine Arts; Industrial and Technical Education
Dist - ARCVID Prod - ARCVID

Today's challenge series
Rapping it up (student protest in other countries) 30 MIN
Dist - NCAT

Today's Children 28 MIN
16mm
Color (C T)
Describes the model Early Childhood Program, a program funded under Title III, Elementary and Secondary Act of 1965, as amended. Shows effective ways of introducing young children to the wide world of learning. Portrays children engaged in individualized activities in the areas of language skills, reading and mathematical concepts.
Education; English Language; Psychology
Dist - HALLMK Prod - HALLMK

Today's computers, what they are, how they work
U-matic / VHS
Computer literacy and understanding series
Color (J H)
Introduces the different kinds of computers - main frame, mini and micro computers. Shows and describes the functions of computer hardware.
Industrial and Technical Education; Mathematics
Dist - EDUACT Prod - EDUACT

Today's Culture - Options After High School 17 MIN
16mm / U-matic / VHS
Color (H)
LC 76-701922
Presents interviews with various people in order to show the wide range of opportunities now open to high school graduates.
Education; Guidance and Counseling
Dist - CORF Prod - CORF 1976

Today's entrepreneur 120 MIN
VHS / 16mm
(COR G)
$89.95 purchase _ #BB01; $89.95 purchase _ #RPBB01V
Shows how 20 successful entrepreneurs made it. Reveals what a person needs to know to become a successful entrepreneur.
Business and Economics
Dist - RMIBHF CAREER Prod - RMIBHF CAREER

Today's Family - Adjusting to Change
VHS / U-matic
Vital Link Series
Color (A)
Looks at how family members are coping with change.
Guidance and Counseling; Psychology; Sociology
Dist - EDCC Prod - EDCC

Today's family - adjusting to change 28 MIN
VHS / U-matic
$185.00 purchase _ #IE05504; $75.00 purchase, $35.00 rental
Explores the varieties of family styles from the single mother to the double income family. Considers the traditional two parent, father supported family also. Discusses daycare options developed to meet the requirements of working parents and 'latchkey' kids.
Health and Safety; Sociology
Dist - CAREER CORNRS GA Prod - CAREER EDCC GA 1986

Today's History Series
Inflation - who Wins 26 MIN
Invisible History 26 MIN
The Oil Age 26 MIN
Poland 26 MIN
Utopias 26 MIN
Whatever Happened to Marx 26 MIN
Why War 26 MIN
Why Work 26 MIN
Women and Society 26 MIN
Dist - JOU

Today's newspaper 22 MIN
16mm / U-matic / VHS
Color (H C) (SPANISH)
LC 72-702439
Tells exactly what goes on in the production of a daily periodical. Covers editorials, advertising, photography, art, composition, printing and circulation.
Guidance and Counseling; Literature and Drama; Social Science
Dist - AIMS Prod - COP 1972

Today's Special Series
Adventure 30 MIN
Babies 30 MIN
Balloons 30 MIN
Being Alone 30 MIN
Birthdays 30 MIN
Bliss symbols 30 MIN
Books 30 MIN
Boxes and boxes 30 MIN
Brushes 30 MIN
Building 30 MIN
Butterflies 30 MIN
Buttons 30 MIN
Camping 30 MIN
Cars 30 MIN
Changes 30 MIN
Christmas - Part 1 30 MIN
Christmas - Part 2 30 MIN
Circus 30 MIN
Cookies 30 MIN
Costumes 30 MIN
Cousins 30 MIN
Daisies 30 MIN
Dance 30 MIN
Dancing Shoes 30 MIN
Dinosaurs 30 MIN
Ears 30 MIN
Eyes 30 MIN
Family 30 MIN
Flight 30 MIN
Food 30 MIN
Friends 30 MIN
Fruit 30 MIN
Fun 30 MIN
Games 30 MIN
Gardens 30 MIN
Going out 30 MIN
Grandmothers 30 MIN
Hair 30 MIN
Halloween 30 MIN
Hands 30 MIN
Hats 30 MIN
Help 30 MIN
Heroes 30 MIN
Homes 30 MIN

Hospitals	30 MIN
Imagination	30 MIN
Jeans	30 MIN
Letters	30 MIN
Live Show Special	30 MIN
Lost and found	30 MIN
Movies	30 MIN
Moving	30 MIN
Newspapers	30 MIN
Night	30 MIN
Noses	30 MIN
Opera	30 MIN
Our Story - Part 1	30 MIN
Our Story - Part 2	30 MIN
Pets	30 MIN
Pianos	30 MIN
Plays	30 MIN
Police	30 MIN
Records	30 MIN
Sam's speech	30 MIN
School	30 MIN
The Sea	30 MIN
Sharing	30 MIN
Shoes	30 MIN
Sleep	30 MIN
Smiles	30 MIN
Snow	30 MIN
Soap	30 MIN
Songs	30 MIN
Soup	30 MIN
Storms	30 MIN
Storybooks	30 MIN
String	30 MIN
Summer Camp	30 MIN
Tears	30 MIN
Television	30 MIN
Temperature	30 MIN
Trains	30 MIN
Travel	30 MIN
Treasure Hunts	30 MIN
Vacations	30 MIN
Waldo's Hat	30 MIN
Water	30 MIN
Wheels	30 MIN
Wild West	30 MIN
Wood	30 MIN
Work	30 MIN

Dist - TVOTAR

Today's Veterinarian 23 MIN
16mm
Color
Looks at the duties of the modern veterinarian, including small animal care, public health, agriculture and zoo medicine. Accompanies veterinarians as they make their daily rounds seeing to the health of their animal charges.
Guidance and Counseling; Health and Safety; Science
Dist - MTP **Prod** - AMVMA

Todd Bridges - on a mission 30 MIN
VHS
Color (J H C)
$295.00 purchase
Features actor and recovering addict Todd Bridges in interviews with former addicts and jail inmates as well as hospital and prison therapists. Shows that drug abuse can lead to crime, prostitution, jail time, even death. Ends with a visit to a morgue.
Guidance and Counseling; Health and Safety; Psychology
Dist - PFP

Todd - Growing Up in Appalachia 14 MIN
16mm / U-matic / VHS
Many Americans Series
Color; Captioned (P I J)
LC 74-709721
Tells the story of Todd, a boy from an Appalachian family of very limited means, who finds a purse full of food stamps. Reveals Todd's character by the decision he makes when he sees the owner's name and address in the purse.
Geography - United States; Guidance and Counseling; Psychology; Social Science; Sociology
Dist - LCOA **Prod** - ENGLE 1971

Todd Jepson and Paul John Ironcloud 30 MIN
U-matic / VHS
Somebody else's place series
Captioned; Color (J H)
$65.00 purchase, $25.00 five day rental
Uses dramatization of a visit between two young people of different backgrounds to encourage appreciation of ethnic and geographic diversity. Eighth in a 12 part series.
Sociology
Dist - GPN **Prod** - SWCETV 1982

The Toddler 15 MIN
VHS
Feeding with love and good sense series
Color (G)
$59.95 purchase _ #BUL003V
Offers advice on what to do when a toddler plays with food, along with other tips on getting a toddler to eat. Part of a four - part series featuring real parents, child care providers and children who show what works and doesn't work in feeding, as well as helping children to eat well, staying out of eating struggles with children, understanding feeding from the child's perspective and knowing when to hold the line.
Health and Safety; Sociology
Dist - CAMV

Toddler 40 MIN
U-matic / VHS
Infancy through Adolescence Series
Color
Demonstrates significant spheres of development, including physical, cognitive and psychosocial. Stresses accident prevention.
Health and Safety; Psychology; Sociology
Dist - AJN **Prod** - WSUN

Toddler management 19 MIN
16mm
Regional intervention program series
Color
LC 75-702440
Explains how mothers are taught to modify unacceptable behavior in their preschool children through a program run entirely by mothers who are nonprofessional in the clinical sense, but who have been through the program themselves and are now using their experiences to help others.
Education; Psychology; Sociology
Dist - USNAC **Prod** - USBEH 1973

Toddler self - esteem - I'm OK, what's your problem
VHS
Family formula - video basics of parenting series
Color (G)
$79.00 purchase _ #CDFAM104V
Shows how to interact with toddlers without damaging their self - esteem. Integrates cross - cultural and cross - generational wisdom with the street culture of today. Part of a seven - part series.
Education; Guidance and Counseling; Psychology; Social Science; Sociology
Dist - CAMV

The Toddler's Hours of Hazard 14 MIN
16mm
Color (H C A)
LC FIA66-659
Examines the problem of home accidents which involve the very young and suggests ways in which the annual toll of deaths and injuries can be reduced. Depicts a day in the life of an average American family and shows how minor irritations can breed accidents.
Guidance and Counseling; Health and Safety
Dist - AETNA **Prod** - AETNA 1965

Todd's Birthday Present 30 MIN
U-matic
Hooked on Reading Series
Color (PRO)
Portrays a father who meets children's authors at a bookstore and asks them for advice on helping children become active readers.
English Language; Literature and Drama
Dist - TVOTAR **Prod** - TVOTAR 1986

Todd's story 20 MIN
VHS
Color (J H)
$95.00 purchase _ #M2629A
Presents a portrait of a young man whose risk - taking behavior led to substance abuse and a tragic death in a motorcycle accident at age 21. Poses strong questions to teens about risk taking and substance abuse. Narrated by Todd's mother.
Guidance and Counseling
Dist - CFKRCM **Prod** - CFKRCM

Todos Santos Cuchumatan 29 MIN
16mm / U-matic
Color
Profiles the plight of the Mam Indians of the Cuchumatan highlands in Guatemala. Explains how Guatemala is run by and for the Ladinos, people of mixed European and Indian ancestry who make up almost half of the population, while the rest are Indians who have been isolated geographically until roads were cut into the mountains for cheap labor on cotton farms. Reveals the detrimental changes in the Indian traditions and lifestyle. In Indian and Spanish with English voice - over.
Agriculture; Geography - World; History - World; Social Science
Dist - KCET **Prod** - KCET

Todos Santos Cuchumatan - Report from a Guatemalan Village 41 MIN
16mm / U-matic / VHS
Color
Offers an intimate portrait of everyday life in one Mam Indian village called Todos Santos Cuchumatan, nestled in a valley of the Cuchumatanes mountains of Guatemala at an altitude of nearly 9,000 feet above sea level. Documents the annual sequence of harvest, the elaborate fiesta of Todos Santos and the mass seasonal migration out of the mountain village to work in the cotton plantations of Guatemala's hot and humid lowlands.
History - World; Sociology
Dist - ICARUS **Prod** - CARREO

Todos Santos - the Survivors 58 MIN
VHS / 16mm
Color (G)
$450.00 purchase
Shows how political turmoil has affected the village of Todos Santos in Guatemala.
Geography - World; History - World; Social Science
Dist - ICARUS

Toe to Hand Transfer for Thumb Reconstruction 14 MIN
U-matic / VHS
Color (PRO)
Discusses the technique of reconstructing a thumb by free toe transfer. Describes and shows preoperative planning, operative technique and long term results. Assumes microsurgery technical expertise.
Health and Safety
Dist - ASSH **Prod** - ASSH

Toes Tell 6 MIN
U-matic / VHS / 16mm
Magic Moments, Unit 3 - Let's See Series
Color (K P I)
LC 72-705928
A barefoot girl steps on and feels many textures with her toes.
English Language
Dist - EBEC **Prod** - EBEC 1969

Together 52 MIN
VHS / U-matic
Leo Buscaglia Series
Color
Psychology
Dist - DELTAK **Prod** - PBS

Together 35 MIN
VHS
Center for Marital and Sexual Studies film series
Color (C A)
$125.00 purchase, $75.00 rental
Depicts the exchange of warmth and tenderness between a couple in their fifties who have been together for a long time and are actively engaged in coitus. Demonstrates that both take responsibility for their own orgasm and respond openly to each other. Graphic. Produced by Hartman and Marilyn Fithian for professional use in treating sexual dysfunction and - or training professional personnel.
Health and Safety; Sociology
Dist - FCSINT

Together 3 MIN
16mm
B&W (G)
$10.00 rental
Depicts a single - frame portrait of Broughton's disembodied heads coming slowly together. Features images by Joel Singer and poetry by Broughton.
Fine Arts
Dist - CANCIN

Together 37 MIN
16mm
Color
Examines the explosive structural changes going on in the entire Swedish society which is leaving a very definite mark on Swedish consumer cooperation.
Geography - World; Home Economics; Sociology
Dist - AUDPLN **Prod** - ASI 1964

Together Alone 30 MIN
U-matic / VHS / 16mm
Color (A)
Looks at three couples through various stages of their attempt to conquer infertility. Looks at some of the causes of sterility, several tests administered to both partners, the characteristics patients seek in trusted physicians and some treatments undergone to ameliorate the chances of conception.
Health and Safety; Science - Natural
Dist - PEREN **Prod** - PEREN 1981

Together and apart 26 MIN
VHS / 16mm / U-matic

Short stories - video anthology series
Color (H C A)
$59.95 purchase
Features a musical drama about two former gay lovers who meet again years later, after one has apparently gone straight and married. Reflects, through song and memories, the feelings they experience during this painful yet liberating reunion. Presents a film directed by Laurie Lynd. Part of a sixteen - part anthology of short dramas by young American filmmakers.
Fine Arts; Literature and Drama; Sociology
Dist - CNEMAG **Prod** - DOCUA 1986

Together at last 58 MIN
VHS
Color (G)
$39.95 purchase _ #106
Focuses on businessman Aaron Ziegelman who has always thought that he, along with his mother and sisters, were the only Ziegelmans to have survived the Holocaust. Discloses that a few years ago he hired a genealogist to help put together a family tree and, through a series of fortuitous events, he discovered that a large branch of the family had survived the war. In celebration, Ziegelman brought all of his relatives from around the world to New York City for a reunion.
History - World; Sociology
Dist - ERGOM

Together - Families in recovery 30 MIN
VHS
Color (H G)
$295.00 purchase
Presents a relapse prevention video written by Dennis Daley, expert in the chemical dependency field. Depicts necessary relapse prevention techniques for addicted and non - addicted family members. Follows three families as they are confronted with the threat of relapse - Bob finds himself angry and frustrated with his wife's successful recovery; Otis and Laverne, parents of a recovering addict, fall into old behaviors of enabling; finally, a family's recovery is threatened when two teenagers discover their father is using again.
Guidance and Counseling; Psychology
Dist - FMSP

Together for Children 6 MIN
U-matic / VHS / 16mm
Color
LC 82-700013
Provides an animated look at racial prejudice and the development of tolerance and harmony.
Fine Arts; Sociology
Dist - PHENIX **Prod** - UNICEF 1981

Together - Pt 1 - the early years 33 MIN
16mm
Color
LC 74-700002
Features psychologists Fred S Keller and B F Skinner who discuss their undergraduate experiences, their associations with such notable contemporaries as Boring and Dallenbach and their first attempts to teach a new science.
Biography; Psychology
Dist - PHM **Prod** - APPLE 1973

Together - Pt 2 - 1930 to tomorrow 28 MIN
16mm
Color
LC 74-700003
Features psychologists Fred S Keller and B F Skinner who discuss the growth of modern psychology and its future direction.
Biography; Psychology
Dist - PHM **Prod** - APPLE 1973

Together, sweetly 15 MIN
16mm
Color (C A)
LC 76-703918
A short version of the film How To Make A Woman. Reveals the anatomy of a marriage in which a wife gives up her identity to please and serve her husband. Shows what can happen in such a relationship as seen from a feminist point of view.
Sociology
Dist - POLYMR **Prod** - POLYMR 1973

Together - Teams 7 MIN
VHS / 16mm
Color (PRO)
$295.00 purchase, $110.00 rental
Motivates teamwork. Dramatizes several youngsters using teamwork to walk a train rail.
Business and Economics; Guidance and Counseling; Psychology
Dist - VICOM **Prod** - VICOM 1990

Together they Learn 28 MIN
U-matic / VHS

Integration of Children with Special Needs in a Regular Classroom 'Series
Color
Presents a program for elementary school children who are retarded or emotionally handicapped. Includes math, reading and science. Emphasizes social interaction between the retarded children and other classmates.
Education; Psychology
Dist - AITECH **Prod** - LPS 1975

Together they Stand 55 MIN
VHS / U-matic
Color (I H C A)
Follows a dwarf mongoose family and observes its highly organized society.
Psychology; Science - Natural
Dist - BNCHMK **Prod** - BNCHMK 1987

Together we can 22 MIN
BETA / U-matic / VHS
Color (G)
$545.00 purchase, $150.00 rental
Promotes teamwork. Shows employees how to be good team members and what personal actions they can take to work together effectively as a team.
Psychology; Social Science
Dist - AMEDIA **Prod** - AMEDIA 1993

Together with Leo Buscaglia 52 MIN
VHS / U-matic
Color
Presents Dr Leo Buscaglia discussing the concept of how togetherness and sharing leads to fulfillment in loving relationships.
Psychology
Dist - PBS **Prod** - KVIETV 1952

Together, with Love 29 MIN
16mm
Color (A)
LC 82-700136
Tells the stories of two couples and their experiences at the time of their baby's birth with the prepared childbirth process.
Health and Safety
Dist - CENTRE **Prod** - CENTRE 1981

Together with Love 30 MIN
U-matic / VHS
Color
Follows a couple's preparation for childbirth from classes through the birth experience.
Health and Safety
Dist - CENTRE **Prod** - CENTRE

Together - working together toward a common goal 7 MIN
BETA / U-matic / VHS
Color (G)
$325.00 purchase, $110.00 rental
Offers a session starter or icebreaker for team building sessions.
Business and Economics; Guidance and Counseling; Psychology
Dist - AMEDIA **Prod** - AMEDIA

Togetherness 15 MIN
VHS / U-matic
Dragons, wagons and wax series; Set 1
Color (K P)
Shows that living things must depend on other living things for survival.
Science; Science - Natural
Dist - CTI **Prod** - CTI

Toi Derricotte - 10 - 9 - 86 40 MIN
VHS / Cassette
Poetry Center reading series
Color (G)
$15.00, $45.00 purchase, $15.00 rental _ #713 - 575
Features the African - American writer reading selections from her works, Natural Birth and The Black Notebook, at the Poetry Center, San Francisco State University, with an introduction by Frances Phillips.
Literature and Drama
Dist - POETRY **Prod** - POETRY 1986

Toilet training 52 MIN
U-matic / VHS
Color (S T)
Presents the most salient points of Dr. Richard M. Foxx's and Dr. Nathan H. Azrin's toilet training program for retarded persons.
Health and Safety; Psychology
Dist - RESPRC **Prod** - RESPRC

Toine 15 MIN
16mm / U-matic / VHS
Color (H C A)
Presents the hilarious story of a brutish husband who is domesticated by his wife and mother.
Fine Arts; Literature and Drama
Dist - FI **Prod** - JANUS 1979

Token Economy - Behaviorism Applied 23 MIN
16mm / U-matic / VHS
B F Skinner Series
Color (H C A)
LC 72-702557
Psychologist B F Skinner outlines his theories on the treatment of the mentally ill, criminals and retardates, showing the successful application of these theories in a mental health facility.
Biography; Psychology; Sociology
Dist - CRMP **Prod** - CRMP 1972

A Token Gesture 8 MIN
U-matic / VHS / 16mm
Color (H C A)
LC 77-701156
Presents a satiric portrayal of the stereotypes that are applied to the sexes. Examines the historical development of these attitudes, starting at birth and continuing through adulthood.
Psychology; Sociology
Dist - MGHT **Prod** - NFBC 1977

A Token System for Behavior Modification 10 MIN
16mm
Color
LC 72-702014
Demonstrates the use of a token economy in a behavioral reinforcement education program to teach moderately and severly retarded girls self - help and occupational skills.
Education; Psychology
Dist - PSHTCA **Prod** - UKANS 1971

Tokens of Love 15 MIN
16mm
Our Children Series
Color; B&W (P I R)
Tells a story which teaches Christian attitudes of cooperation and sharing in everyday home chores. Shows how three children learn to have more appreciation and affection for their parents.
Guidance and Counseling; Psychology; Religion and Philosophy
Dist - FAMF **Prod** - FAMF

Tokyo 21 MIN
VHS / 16mm
Paradise Steamship Co Series
Color (I H C A)
$300.00, $225.00 purchase
Takes a look at contemporary life in Japan through looks at a subway station, a fish market, an elementary school, and the shops of some rising Japanese designers.
Geography - World
Dist - CAROUF **Prod** - KCBS 1989

Tokyo breaks the quake barrier - the Kasumigaseki high - rise building project - Pt 1 27 MIN
16mm
Color
Explains that Japan is a volcanic land and every year there are numerous earthquakes, most of them minor, but so frequent that until now high buildings have been impractical. Points out that today, however, with improved building methods a 36 story building has been constructed in Tokyo. Shows how such a structure is made not only practical but safe.
Geography - World; Industrial and Technical Education; Science - Physical
Dist - UNIJAP **Prod** - UNIJAP 1966

Tokyo crusade 28 MIN
16mm
Color
Points out that Japan is primarily a Buddhist country and Christians are an extreme minority. Depicts the overwhelming response to the Billy Graham crusade in Tokyo. Features a personal word of witness from English 'pop' star Cliff Richard and former baseball star, Bobby Richardson, as well as an address by Billy Graham.
Biography; Geography - World; Guidance and Counseling; Religion and Philosophy
Dist - NINEFC **Prod** - WWP

Tokyo, in old times and today 25 MIN
16mm
Color
Catches phases of Tokyo in olden times and today, introducing important paintings, cultural inheritances and actual landscapes. Describes history, culture and living of the castle town of Edo (Tokyo).
Geography - World; Sociology
Dist - UNIJAP **Prod** - TOEI 1971

Tokyo in Tennessee 16 MIN
U-matic / VHS / 16mm
Color (J H G)
LC 83-700386
Shows how Nissan Motors of Japan is opening a 69 - acre automotive plant in Smyrna, Tennessee and hoping to teach American workers the Japanese work ethic of

'master your equipment, love your fellow worker.' Offers the remarks of a core of Smyrna plant workers who were trained in Japan who are optimistic about the undertaking and the comments of United Auto Workers President Douglas Fraser who voices skepticism. Originally shown on the CBS program 60 Minutes.
Business and Economics
Dist - CAROUF **Prod** - CBSTV 1983

Tokyo Industrial Worker 17 MIN
U-matic / VHS / 16mm
Man and His World Series
Color (P I J H C)
LC 72-705471
Shows a metropolitan area in Tokyo with old customs and new western customs side by side. Shows the transition of an industrial worker from a modern factory to his Japanese cultural home.
Business and Economics; Geography - World; History - World; Sociology
Dist - FI **Prod** - FI 1969

Tokyo moves skywards - the Kasumigaseki high - rise building project - Pt 2 35 MIN
16mm
Color
Shows the first high - rise building construction in Japan from its beginning to the completion of erecting the steel frame. Points out that the steel framework is an embodiment of the essence of Japanese architecture at the world's highest level.
Fine Arts; Industrial and Technical Education
Dist - UNIJAP **Prod** - UNIJAP 1967

Tokyo story 134 MIN
16mm
B&W (H C) (JAPANESE WITH ENGLISH SUBTITLES)
Explores the potential violence found in a Japanese family and looks at the sad and necessary differences between generations of the same family.
Fine Arts; Foreign Language; Sociology
Dist - NYFLMS
CHTSUI

The Tokyo Summit 30 MIN
U-matic
Adam Smith's money world 1985 - 1986 season series; 236
Color (A)
Attempts to demystify the world of money and break it down so that small as well as large businesses and it's people understand and adjust to new social and economic trends. Reports on the major economic stories and discoveries of 1985 and 1986.
Business and Economics
Dist - PBS **Prod** - WNETTV 1986

The Tokyo Trial 279 MIN
U-matic / VHS
B&W (G)
$699.00, $499.00 purchase _ #AD - 1649
Presents a concise and complete history of the events in the Far East from the Sino - Japanese War of 1894 through 1952. Uses well documented footage to illustrate events and brings to life the people and actions of a turbulent period little understood in America.
History - World
Dist - FOTH **Prod** - FOTH

Tokyo's Giant Landmark - the Kasumigaseki High - Rise Building Project 42 MIN
16mm
Color
Points out that the Kasumigaseki - Mitsui building was until recently the tallest in all Asia. Shows the various techniques by which it was made, the labor and imagination which went into its construction and its successful completion. Emphasizes that in an earthquake prone land, in a city where much of the land is reclaimed, its construction posed many difficult and unusual construction problems.
Geography - World; Industrial and Technical Education
Dist - UNIJAP **Prod** - UNIJAP 1968

Tokyo's New National Museum of Modern Art 18 MIN
16mm
Color
Explains that the National Museum of Modern Art at Tokyo was born in the Kitanomaru Park of the Imperial Palace. Records the construction process, explains some examples of Japanese art works exhibited at this museum and mentions its function as a quiet retreat for the people of Tokyo.
Fine Arts; Geography - World; Social Science; Sociology
Dist - UNIJAP **Prod** - UNIJAP 1969

Tole painting 1 60 MIN
BETA / VHS
Color
Demonstrates several strokes and techniques on a teddy bear, then shows the instructor illustrating the variety obtainable from alternating basic techniques.
Fine Arts
Dist - HOMEAF **Prod** - HOMEAF

Tole painting basics 60 MIN
VHS
Color (G)
$29.95 purchase _ #S00113
Teaches the traditional folk art of tole painting. Trains viewers in brush strokes, floating, loading the brush, and more.
Fine Arts
Dist - UILL **Prod** - UILL
HOMEAF

The Toll gate 59 MIN
16mm
B&W
Introduces Black Deering, an Old West outlaw who risks capture and his life to rescue a drowning child and to warn an outlying post of Indian uprisings. Stars William S Hart and Anna Q Nilsson. Directed by Lambert Hillyer.
Fine Arts
Dist - KILLIS
RMIBHF

Toller 26 MIN
16mm / U-matic / VHS
Color (J)
LC 77-701608
A shortened version of the 1976 motion picture entitled Toller. Shows Canadian world figure skating champion Toller Cranston executing some of his most difficult routines.
Biography; Geography - World; Physical Education and Recreation
Dist - WOMBAT **Prod** - INST 1977

Toller Cranston - Imagery and Ice 9 MIN
16mm
Color
LC 77-702681
Presents an interview with Canadian ice skating champion Toller Cranston in which he discusses both his skating and his painting.
Fine Arts; Physical Education and Recreation
Dist - INCC **Prod** - CANBC 1973

The Toltec Mystery 26 MIN
16mm
Color (I)
LC FIA66-1400
Explores the mysterious fact that, while the Mayan people exist today, the Toltecs are completely extinct. Reveals clear - cut evidences in the ancient city of Chichen Itza of the infiltration of the Mayan culture by that of the Toltecs.
History - World; Sociology
Dist - AVED **Prod** - HENSON 1966

Toluene - xylene 7 MIN
BETA / VHS / U-matic
Hazard communication series
Color (IND G)
$295.00 purchase _ #830 - 05
Informs employees of the health and physical hazards associated with toluene and xylene. Describes the characteristics of toluene and xylene. Discusses the symptoms of exposure to either chemical. Covers the exposure limits, appropriate work practices, emergency first aid procedures and what to do in case of a spill or fire. Part of a series on hazard communication.
Health and Safety; Industrial and Technical Education; Psychology
Dist - ITSC **Prod** - ITSC

Tom - a study of child abuse 45 MIN
VHS
Color; PAL (T PRO)
PdS35.00 purchase
Provides a basis for discussion about the issues involved for members of staff in primary schools when there is a suspicion that a child is being physically abused at home. Contains four sequences dealing with different situations. Produced for teaching and non - teaching staff to increase their understanding of abuse and to help them create clear school policies and procedures.
Education; Psychology; Sociology
Dist - EMFVL

Tom and Virl Osmond 15 MIN
16mm / U-matic / VHS
Truly Exceptional People Series
Color (I)
LC 79-701263
Profiles Tom and Virl Osmond, who are both hard of hearing. Shows how the brothers are an integral part of the Osmond family of performers in spite of their hearing problem.
Biography; Psychology
Dist - CORF **Prod** - DISNEY 1979

Tom Cat's Meow 13 MIN
16mm / U-matic / VHS
Color (P I J)
LC 76-703957
Uses animation and puppets in an adaptation of a classic Czechoslovakian fairytale about a little girl whose mistreatment by her stepmother and stepsister brings rewards from the tomcat she has befriended. Made in Czechoslovakia.
Literature and Drama
Dist - PHENIX **Prod** - SFSP 1976

Tom Clark - 10 - 25 - 73 60 MIN
VHS / Cassette
Poetry Center reading series
B&W (G)
$15.00, $45.00 purchase, $15.00 rental _ #17 - 14
Features the poet reading selections from Suite, from Blue, and from Expeditions by Lewis and Clark, a collaboration with Lewis MacAdams at the Poetry Center, San Francisco State University, with an introduction by Lewis MacAdams.
Literature and Drama
Dist - POETRY **Prod** - POETRY 1973

Tom Clark - 10 - 27 - 76 30 MIN
VHS / Cassette
Poetry Center reading series
Color (G)
$15.00, $45.00 purchase, $15.00 rental _ #223 - 178
Features the poet reading selections from his works at the Poetry Center, San Francisco State University, with an introduction by Lewis MacAdams.
Literature and Drama
Dist - POETRY **Prod** - POETRY 1976

Tom Clark - 3 - 12 - 87 70 MIN
VHS / Cassette
Poetry Center reading series
Color (G)
$15.00, $45.00 purchase, $15.00 rental _ #741 - 593
Features the poet reading selections from his works at the Poetry Center, San Francisco State University, with an introduction by Frances Phillips.
Literature and Drama
Dist - POETRY **Prod** - POETRY 1987

Tom Edison 15 MIN
VHS / U-matic
Stories of America Series
Color (P)
Spans Thomas Edison's life from his first failing experiment at four to his many adult successes.
Biography; History - United States; History - World
Dist - AITECH **Prod** - OHSDE 1976

The Tom Harper Story 13 MIN
16mm
Color
LC 79-700327
Tells how a young man pulled himself through the rigors of cancer.
Health and Safety
Dist - AMCS **Prod** - AMCS 1978

Tom Horn 98 MIN
16mm
Color
Stars Steve McQueen as a gunfighter who lives by his own code of honor.
Fine Arts
Dist - SWANK **Prod** - WB

Tom Jones 14 MIN
U-matic / VHS
Color (PRO)
Shows Tom Jones, American medical illustrator, demonstrating and talking about his techniques to a group of students at the University Of California at Los Angeles (UCLA).
Health and Safety
Dist - WFP **Prod** - WFP

Tom Jones 127 MIN
16mm
Color (H C)
Presents an adaptation of Henry Fielding's novel Tom Jones, following the adventures of a country lad who leaves home to explore the world. Stars Albert Finney and Susannah York. Directed by Tony Richardson.
Fine Arts; Literature and Drama
Dist - UAE

Tom Keating on painters series
Features Tom Keating who recreates the painting style as done by the artists featured and gives biographical information in a six - part series on painters. Includes the titles Rembrandt, Restoration, Manet, Renoir, Van Gogh, Plein Air.

Manet	30 MIN
Plein Air	30 MIN
Rembrandt	30 MIN

Renoir 30 MIN
Restoration 30 MIN
Van Gogh 30 MIN
Dist - LANDMK **Prod** - LANDMK 1963

Tom Landry Football Series
Defensive line 60 MIN
Offensive Line 60 MIN
Playing to win for backs and receivers 60 MIN
Quarterbacking to win 60 MIN
The Winning Linebacker 60 MIN
Dist - CAMV

Tom Lehrer Sings Pollution 3 MIN
16mm
Color
LC FIE68-23
Presents a musical satire on the effects of air and water pollution.
Fine Arts; Science - Natural
Dist - USPHS **Prod** - USPHS 1967

Tom Magee, Man of Iron 30 MIN
U-matic / VHS
Color (I A)
Shows the rigorous training that enabled Canadian Tom Magers to become the youngest super heavyweight world power lifting champion in 1982. Documents Magee's competition performance in Munich, Germany.
Physical Education and Recreation
Dist - MOBIUS **Prod** - MOBIUS 1983

Tom Parente piano video - Part 1 55 MIN
VHS
Tom Parente series
Color (J H C G)
$29.95 purchase _ #VNO100V
Explains the basics of rhythm and reading simple music notations. Features music teacher Tom Parente. Part one of two parts.
Fine Arts
Dist - CAMV

Tom Parente piano video - Part 2 55 MIN
VHS
Tom Parente series
Color (J H C G)
$29.95 purchase _ #VNO101V
Introduces pick up beats, left hand melody, tied notes, sharps, repeat and more. Features music teacher Tom Parente. Part two of two parts.
Fine Arts
Dist - CAMV

Tom Parente series
Presents two programs of piano instruction by Tom Parente. Explains the basics of rhythm and reading simple music in Part 1. Introduces pick up beats, left hand melody, tied notes, sharps, repeat and more in Part 2.
Tom Parente piano video - Part 1 55 MIN
Tom Parente piano video - Part 2 55 MIN
Tom Parente series 110 MIN
Dist - CAMV

Tom Paxton, the Clancy Brothers and Tommy Makem 52 MIN
U-matic / VHS
Rainbow quest series
Color
Presents the Clancy Brothers and Tommy Makem from Ireland singing traditional and contemporary Irish songs.
Fine Arts
Dist - NORROS **Prod** - SEEGER

Tom Peters - Excellence in the Public Sector 48 MIN
U-matic / VHS
Color (G)
$595.00, $645.00 purchase, $225 rental _ #TPEP - 000
Features business author Tom Peters, who shows how government and nonprofit agencies can improve their management practices. Reveals the importance of such practices as worker recognition, participative management and attention to customer needs. Focuses on five public organizations that have adopted these principles.
Business and Economics; Guidance and Counseling; Psychology
Dist - PBS **Prod** - ENMED 1988

Tom Peters' thriving on chaos - shortcut 60 MIN
VHS / BETA / U-matic
Color (COR)
$995.00, $895.00 purchase, $250.00 rental _ #MC0033
Offers the most popular segments from the full - length version of Thriving on Chaos.
Business and Economics; Guidance and Counseling; Psychology
Dist - BLNCTD **Prod** - BLNCTD

Tom Sawyer
Cassette / 16mm

Now age reading programs series; Set 1
Color (I J)
$9.95 purchase _ #8F - PN681794
Brings a classic tale to young readers. The filmstrip set includes filmstrip, cassette, book, classroom materials and a poster. The read - along set includes an activity book and a cassette.
English Language; Literature and Drama
Dist - MAFEX

Tom Sawyer 26 MIN
16mm / VHS
Children's Classics Series
Color (P)
$195.00 purchase
Relates the classic story of American folk hero Tom Sawyer created by Mark Twain. Adapted by Bob Littell. Animated.
Fine Arts; Literature and Drama
Dist - LUF **Prod** - BROVID

Tom Thumb 10 MIN
16mm / U-matic / VHS
Grimm's fairy tale - Spanish series
Color (P I J) (SPANISH)
Depicts the adventures of Tom Thumb. Shows that avarice is punished.
Literature and Drama
Dist - CF **Prod** - BOSUST

Tom Thumb 10 MIN
U-matic / VHS / 16mm
Grimm's Fairy Tales Series
Color (K P I)
LC 79-700383
Presents an animated adaptation of the classic fairy tale about tiny Tom Thumb, who is able to overcome dangerous obstacles despite his size.
Literature and Drama
Dist - CF **Prod** - BOSUST 1978

Tom Thumb in King Arthur's court 20 MIN
U-matic / VHS / 16mm
Color (P I)
$455.00, $250.00 purchase _ #1383
Tells the story of a man, no bigger than a thumb, who becomes a Knight of the Round Table.
Literature and Drama
Dist - CORF **Prod** - CORF 1963

Tom tit tot 8 MIN
VHS / U-matic
Timeless tales series
Color (P I)
$110.00, $160.00 purchase, $60.00 rental
Tells about a king who decides to marry a young woman after hearing her mother's bragging song that her daughter can spin five bales of cloth a day; if it happens that the young woman cannot he will chop off her head. Finds the young woman locked away in a castle room until she lives up to her mother's false boasting when a funny little man appears to help her - if she can guess his name - if not, she must marry him.
Guidance and Counseling; Literature and Drama
Dist - NDIM **Prod** - TIMTAL 1993

Tom, Tom the piper's son 115 MIN
16mm
Color; B&W; Silent (C)
Experimental film by Ken Jacobs.
Fine Arts
Dist - AFA **Prod** - AFA 1969

Tom Tutko's coaching clinic 77 MIN
VHS
Color (G)
$49.95 purchase
Discusses common personality and competition situations faced by athletic coaches. Hosted by sports psychologist Dr Tom Tutko.
Physical Education and Recreation
Dist - PBS **Prod** - WNETTV

Tom Wolfe 15 MIN
VHS
Writer's workshop series
Color (C A T)
$69.95 purchase, $45.00 rental
Features Tom Wolfe in a lecture and discussion of his work, held as part of a writing workshop series at the University of South Carolina. Hosted by author William Price Fox and introduced by George Plimpton. Part three of a 15 - part telecourse.
English Language; Literature and Drama
Dist - SCETV **Prod** - SCETV 1982

Tom Wolfe 60 MIN
VHS
World of ideas with Bill Moyers series; Season I; Pts I and II
Color (G)
$59.95 purchase _ #BMWI - 134D
Interviews author and social critic Tom Wolfe. Features Wolfe's observations about greed, New York City and the nature of freedom.
Business and Economics; Guidance and Counseling; Literature and Drama; Religion and Philosophy; Sociology
Dist - PBS

Tom Wolfe 50 MIN
VHS
Color (H C G)
$79.00 purchase
Features the writer talking with Peter York about the relationship between journalism and fiction, and experimental forms in literature. Discusses his writings including The Last American Hero; The Right Stuff; From Bauhaus to Our House; and the novel The Bonfire of the Vanities.
Literature and Drama
Dist - ROLAND **Prod** - INCART

Tom Wolfe 30 MIN
VHS
Writer's workshop series
Color (G)
$59.95 purchase _ #WRWO - 103
Features author Tom Wolfe in a lecture and discussion at the University of South Carolina. Explains how Wolfe's 'new journalism' style began. Shares his views on how to get published, past writers and developing a writing style.
Literature and Drama
Dist - PBS **Prod** - SCETVM 1987

Tom Zenanko's Fishing Tips and Secrets Series
Crankbait Fishing Tricks no 49 1 MIN
Dist - TVSS

Toma live 60 MIN
VHS
Color (J H C G)
$49.95 purchase _ #CEA200V
Presents David Toma, pioneer of substance abuse awareness, an ex - cop and an ex - drug addict.
Guidance and Counseling; Health and Safety; Psychology
Dist - CAMV

Tomato salad plates 4 MIN
U-matic / VHS
Color (IND)
Shows how to make tomato poinsettias stuffed with a filling and arranged on a bed of lettuce with thin - sliced cucumber and boiled egg quarters. Contains tips on the preparation of lettuce and peeling tomatoes.
Home Economics; Industrial and Technical Education
Dist - CULINA **Prod** - CULINA

Tomatoes 10 MIN
U-matic / VHS / 16mm
Inventive Child Series
Color (P I)
Shows how a bountiful tomato crop which they cannot personally eat prompts Boy and Grandpa to use the principle of the screw and lever to invent a press to squeeze out the juice. Demonstrates the interrelationship between machines and food preparation and preservation.
History - World; Home Economics; Science - Physical
Dist - EBEC **Prod** - POLSKI 1983

Tomatoes - from Seed to Table 11 MIN
16mm / U-matic / VHS
Color (K P I)
LC 70-708896
Presents the story of tomatoes, from planting and harvesting, canning and transporting to the market, thus into our homes. Stresses people and machines involved.
Agriculture; Business and Economics; Home Economics
Dist - ALTSUL **Prod** - FILMSW 1971

Tomatoes - the homecoming of the paradise apple 15 MIN
VHS
Fruits of the earth series
Color (G)
$175.00 purchase
Looks at efforts to return cultivation of the tomato to Panama, where the plant originated. Considers cooperative efforts that make the plant an important income - producing commodity. Part of a series of 15 videos that describe everyday conditions in regions throughout the earth and look at plants available for environmentally sound, economically productive development.
Home Economics; Science - Natural
Dist - LANDMK

Tomes and talismans series
Direction unknown
Fact or fiction 20 MIN
Final report 20 MIN
Guide to light 20 MIN
Hidden meaning 20 MIN

In the cards	20 MIN
Information quick	20 MIN
Preference for reference	20 MIN
Show and tell	20 MIN
SOS - skim or scan	20 MIN
The System	20 MIN
Tomes entombed	20 MIN
Under cover	20 MIN

Dist - GPN

Tomes entombed 20 MIN
VHS / U-matic
Tomes and talismans series
(I J)
$145.00 purchase, $27.00 rental
Uses a science fantasy adventure to define, illustrate and review basic library research concepts. Designed for sixth, seventh and eighth graders. Presents an overview of library research skills and concepts. First in a 13 part series.
Education; Social Science
Dist - GPN **Prod** - MISETV

Tomi Ungerer, Storyteller 21 MIN
U-matic / VHS / 16mm
Color
LC 81-701271
Interviews author and illustrator of children's books Tomi Ungerer. Discussses his thoughts and feelings about his work, his world and his personal life. Includes scenes from the motion pictures The Three Robber, The Beast Of Monsieur Racine and Moon Man.
Literature and Drama
Dist - WWS **Prod** - WWS 1981

Tommie, Suzie and the Cardboard Box 15 MIN
16mm
Creative Writing Skills Series
Color (P I)
LC 74-703611
Uses three stories about a young boy and girl and their cardboard box to illustrate story structure.
English Language; Literature and Drama
Dist - MORLAT **Prod** - MORLAT 1973

Tommorow's Families Series

The Family Adapts	29 MIN

Dist - AITECH

Tommy 18 MIN
16mm
Color (J H G)
Presents a shortened version of the rock opera Tommy about a 'deaf, dumb and blind boy' and his parents' attempt to cure him. Stars Roger Daltry, Ann - Margret and Jack Nicholson.
Fine Arts
Dist - TIMLIF **Prod** - WGBHTV 1982

Tommy Cat 8 MIN
16mm / U-matic / VHS
Tommy, Tubby, Tuffy Series
Color (K P)
LC 75-704347
Presents a story which has two alternate endings. Considers the implications and meanings of each ending.
Literature and Drama
Dist - LUF **Prod** - MORLAT 1974

Tommy Manion - Western Pleasure 50 MIN
VHS
Color (G)
$89.95 purchase _ #6 - 029 - 101P
Shares the Western Pleasure training and showing techniques developed by Tommy Manion, quarter horse champion. Includes movement, headset, attitude and tack.
Agriculture; Physical Education and Recreation
Dist - VEP **Prod** - VEP

Tommy, Suzie and the Cardboard Box 15 MIN
U-matic / VHS / 16mm
Creative Writing Series
Color (I J)
LC 73-701686
Portrays the cardboard box as one of the earliest means of make - believe for a child. Stimulates creative imagination to produce stories and plays of a student's very own.
English Language; Fine Arts
Dist - AIMS **Prod** - MORLAT 1971

Tommy Tricker and the stamp traveller 101 MIN
VHS
Color (K P I J H)
$39.95 purchase _ #S02119
Tells the story of Tommy Tricker, a young stamp collector who discovers that one of his stamps can be used for travel. Shows the adventures Tommy and his friends find through their stamp travels.
Literature and Drama
Dist - UILL

Tommy, Tubby, Tuffy Series

Tommy Cat	8 MIN
Tubby Bunny	12 MIN
Tuffy Puppy	9 MIN

Dist - LUF

The Tommy Ungerer library 35 MIN
VHS
Children's circle collection series
Color (K P I)
$14.95 purchase _ #WK1197
Offers a collection of stories by children's author Tommy Ungerer. Includes The Three Robbers; Moon Man: The Hat; The Beast of Monsieur Racine; and a conversation with Ungerer.
Fine Arts; Literature and Drama
Dist - KNOWUN

Tommy's first car 11 MIN
U-matic / VHS / 16mm
Color (J) (SPANISH)
Describes how to go about buying a used car. Shows where to look for clues regarding the car's condition and possible necessary repairs and how to road test a car. Explains the importance of having a mechanic examine the car before buying it.
Home Economics; Industrial and Technical Education
Dist - ALTSUL **Prod** - LEARN 1972

Tomorrow again 16 MIN
16mm
B&W (G)
LC 72-701541
A fictional story, presented in the form of a documentary, about a sweet, old lady who lives in a shabby hotel for senior citizens. Pictures the psychological problems which develop because of her loneliness and isolation.
Literature and Drama; Sociology
Dist - VIEWFI **Prod** - PFP 1972

Tomorrow and Yesterday - Modern Technology and Ancient Culture 28 MIN
16mm
Color (H C A)
LC 82-700624
Looks at the daily events in the life of the Kimuras, a modern Japanese family headed by a design engineer in a large construction company.
Geography - World; Guidance and Counseling; History - World; Social Science; Sociology
Dist - LCOA **Prod** - FLMAUS 1982

Tomorrow Begins Yesterday 29 MIN
16mm
Color
LC 77-711541
Describes a program in industrial arts for children on the seventh - grade level. Presents the background, rationale and application of the program, and depicts the educational processes as well as some of the projected outcomes.
Education; Industrial and Technical Education
Dist - UMD **Prod** - UMD 1970

The Tomorrow builders 22 MIN
VHS
Cutting edge series; Pt 3
Color (G)
$150.00 purchase _ #8025
Examines research in engineering and computer sciences - the measurement of building deformation, downhole drillstem instrumentation development, VLSI chip design, digital mapping techniques employing 3 - D computer graphics and satellite photography and computer graphic 'soft' animation. Part of a five - part series on the latest research and technology developments in Western Canada.
Computer Science; Geography - World; Industrial and Technical Education; Science
Dist - UCALG **Prod** - UCALG 1989

Tomorrow came much later - a journey of conscience 58 MIN
U-matic / VHS / 16mm
Color (J H C A)
LC 81-701546
Recounts a journey by a high school class, their teacher and a survivor of the Holocaust. Includes visits to Warsaw, Auschwitz and the Majdanek and Mauthausen concentration camps and an interview with famed Nazi - hunter Simon Wiesenthal.
History - World
Dist - CORF **Prod** - WVIZTV 1981

Tomorrow Comes Early 25 MIN
16mm
Color
Provides an opportunity for adults to discuss the psychological and spiritual problems of growing older, from the Christian perspective by presenting the story of Paul Butram, a middle - aged college professor who is forced to come to grips with his own advancing maturity. Depicts the depth of his personal search for meaning and self - affirmation.
Guidance and Counseling; Health and Safety; Psychology; Religion and Philosophy; Sociology
Dist - FAMF **Prod** - FAMF

Tomorrow i'll be there 11 MIN
U-matic / VHS / 16mm
Growing up with Sandy Offenheim series
Color (K P)
LC 82-707059
Shows a youngster offering new reflections on his ideas about life and growing up as he writes in his diary, and songs and dance illustrate his ideas.
Education; Fine Arts; Psychology; Sociology
Dist - BCNFL **Prod** - PLAYTM 1982

Tomorrow is Here 12 MIN
16mm
Color
LC 76-700202
Takes a look at the activities of insulation contractors.
Guidance and Counseling; Psychology
Dist - NICA **Prod** - NICA 1975

Tomorrow is Maybe 59 MIN
Videoreel / VT2
Environment - Today and Tomorrow Series
Color
Science - Natural; Sociology
Dist - PBS **Prod** - KRMATV

Tomorrow is Today 21 MIN
16mm
Color
Tells about the programs and services of the National Holstein Association from production testing, classification and sire summaries to procedures at the National Office in Brattleboro, Vermont and the Genetic Evaluation and Management Service and International Marketing Service of HFS, Inc.
Agriculture
Dist - HFAA **Prod** - HFAA

Tomorrow is too late 16 MIN
16mm
Doctors at work series
B&W (PRO A)
LC FIA65-1369
A medical examination produces X - ray evidence of a lung lesion and biopsy shows a malignancy. Shows the surgical procedure for a lung cancer operation - - from the removal of the ribs and excision of the upper right lobe to closure of the bronchus.
Health and Safety
Dist - LAWREN **Prod** - CMA 1961

Tomorrow is Too Late 28 MIN
16mm
Color (G)
_ #106C 0174 545
Shows what Canadian fisheries are doing to ensure that Canada's fishing industry continues as a flourishing resource. Shows that some species of fish are badly depleted, but that conservation and scientific management of fishing grounds and water can maintain the balance.
Industrial and Technical Education; Science - Natural; Social Science
Dist - CFLMDC **Prod** - NFBC 1974

Tomorrow, Megalopolis 20 MIN
U-matic
Exploring Our Nation Series
Color (I)
Investigates the elements of a megalopolis and the need for young people to understand the problems of the future and the plans to solve them.
Sociology
Dist - GPN **Prod** - KRMATV 1975

Tomorrow mind 22 MIN
16mm
Color (VOC IND) (SPANISH JAPANESE GERMAN)
LC 80-701315
Looks at the research projects carried out by the General Motors Research Laboratories.
Business and Economics
Dist - GM **Prod** - GM 1980

Tomorrow the world 60 MIN
VHS
Color (A)
PdS99 purchase
Presents a series of six 10-minute programs designed to build up viewer confidence in everyday situations. Covers developing self-confidence; saying 'no;' giving feedback; making requests without giving offense or being overlooked; receiving criticism.
Health and Safety; Psychology
Dist - BBCENE

Tomorrow - today 29 MIN
VHS / U-matic
Tomorrow - today series; No 5
Color (G)
Segments cover experimental NASA aircraft Tiltrotor XV - 15 and Quiet Shorthand Research Aircraft, photovoltaic solar energy and spinal rehabilitation methods.
Sociology
Dist - KTEHTV **Prod** - KTEHTV 1981

Tomorrow - today 29 MIN
VHS / U-matic
Tomorrow - today series; N0 6
Color (G)
Segments include Lick Observatory's search for the birth of the universe lasers used in eye surgery, welding and fusion power, recycling toxic chemicals, think tanks and self - fulfilling prophecies.
Sociology
Dist - KTEHTV **Prod** - KTEHTV 1981

Tomorrow - today 29 MIN
VHS / U-matic
Tomorrow - today series; No 4
Color (G)
Segments feature Stanford Linear Accelerator Center and the search for sub - atomic 'quarks,' Northern Elephant Seals' recovery from near extinction, computer crime and comments of Linus Pauling.
Sociology
Dist - KTEHTV **Prod** - KTEHTV 1981

Tomorrow - today 29 MIN
U-matic / VHS
Tomorrow - today series; No 9
Color (G)
Features alternatives to shots and pills such as transdermal disc and time - release devices for drug delivery, computers in the classroom, and the defense factor in Bay Area electronics industries.
Sociology
Dist - KTEHTV **Prod** - KTEHTV 1981

Tomorrow - today 28 MIN
VHS / U-matic
Tomorrow - today series; No 10
Color (J)
Features CAD/CAM computer design and manufacture, biofeedback, and Japanese semiconductor manufacturers competing for US markets.
Sociology
Dist - KTEHTV **Prod** - KTEHTV 1981

Tomorrow - today 29 MIN
U-matic / VHS
Tomorrow - today series; No 7
Color (G)
Segments include USGS efforts to predict earthquakes, independent inventors, and medical costs.
Sociology
Dist - KTEHTV **Prod** - KTEHTV 1981

Tomorrow - today 29 MIN
U-matic / VHS
Tomorrow - today series; No 2
Color (G)
Segments include non - chemical pest control, space shuttle, food additives as a possible cause of hyperactivity, Feingold Diet and Stewart Brand discussing space colonies.
Sociology
Dist - KTEHTV **Prod** - KTEHTV 1981

Tomorrow - today 29 MIN
VHS / U-matic
Tomorrow - today series; No 3
Color (G)
Segments include Itelsat - V, the Metcalf Site archeological dig, safety hazards in electronic industries and Third World countries being exploited by earth resources satellites.
Sociology
Dist - KTEHTV **Prod** - KTEHTV 1981

Tomorrow - today 29 MIN
U-matic / VHS
Tomorrow - today series; No 12
Color (G)
Feature SP Communications competing with the Bell System for toll service, Christen Eagle Kitbuilt aerobatic biplane, and Interferon linked to Downs Syndrome.
Sociology
Dist - KTEHTV **Prod** - KTEHTV 1981

Tomorrow - today 29 MIN
U-matic / VHS
Tomorrow - today series; No 11
Color (G)
Shows artificial intelligence in PUFF computer programs which diagnoses lung diseases, San Francisco's Exploratorium which is a hands - on science/technology museum, earthquake effects and preparedness.
Sociology
Dist - KTEHTV **Prod** - KTEHTV 1981

Tomorrow - today 29 MIN
U-matic / VHS
Tomorrow - today series; No 1
Color (G)
Segments concern ultrasonic imaging used in medicine, history of microelectronics, genetic engineering patents and comments of biologist Paul Ehrlich on the need for better public understanding of science.
Sociology
Dist - KTEHTV **Prod** - KTEHTV 1981

Tomorrow - today 29 MIN
VHS / U-matic
Tomorrow - today series; No 13
Color (G)
Includes safety of oral contraceptives, the MFTF - B fusion experiment at Lawrence Livermore Labs, and a portrait of electronic music pioneer Bernie Krause.
Sociology
Dist - KTEHTV **Prod** - KTEHTV 1981

Tomorrow - today 29 MIN
U-matic / VHS
Tomorrow - today series; No 8
Color (G)
Contains segments concerning computers learning to speak and listen (speech recognition and synthesis circuits), ethanol and methanol, and a summary of Voyager missions to Saturn and Jupiter.
Sociology
Dist - KTEHTV **Prod** - KTEHTV 1981

Tomorrow - today series
Tomorrow - today 29 MIN
Tomorrow - today 29 MIN
Dist - KTEHTV

Tomorrow will not Wait - Air, Water and Land Conservation 13 MIN
16mm
Color
LC 74-705805
Cites people for befouling the air, water and soil and shows attempts by the Air Force to do something to stop pollution where possible.
Science - Natural; Sociology
Dist - USNAC **Prod** - USAF 1970

Tomorrow's Canberra 35 MIN
16mm
Color (H C A)
LC 73-702491
Shows how Canberra, Australia's national capital, is being developed from a design by Chicago architect Walter Burley Griffin.
Fine Arts; Geography - World; Social Science; Sociology
Dist - AUIS **Prod** - FLMAUS 1973

Tomorrow's child 52 MIN
16mm / VHS
Color (C A PRO)
Describes the experiments being done with frozen embryos to produce a test - tube baby at the Queen Victoria Medical Centre in Melbourne, Australia by the Monash University Medical Team. Discusses the ethical aspects of such experiments.
Health and Safety
Dist - LANDMK **Prod** - NOMDFI 1982

Tomorrow's children 55 MIN
16mm
B&W
Tells how a young woman about to get married finds herself under pressure from townspeople, who consider her a derelict and insist that she be sterilized so that she won't have any unacceptable children. Directed by Bryan Foy, Jr.
Fine Arts
Dist - REELIM

Tomorrow's Children 17 MIN
16mm / 8mm cartridge
Color (J) (SPANISH)
Points out the responsibility involved in having a child, stating that each child is a part of the Earth and tomorrow's small child affects the whole planet.
Science - Natural; Social Science; Sociology
Dist - PEREN **Prod** - MAYERH

Tomorrow's Drivers 10 MIN
16mm
B&W
Records what one city is doing to solve the problem of tomorrow's (and today's) drivers, narrated by James Stewart.
Health and Safety; Psychology
Dist - GM **Prod** - GM

Tomorrow's Energy 20 MIN
16mm
Color
Looks at future sources of gas energy. Highlights solar energy through biomass conversion, methane from water hyacinths, cattle manure and giant brown kelp.
Science - Physical; Social Science
Dist - BUGAS **Prod** - BUGAS

Tomorrow's Energy Today 33 MIN
16mm
Color (J)
Describes a number of successful attempts to obtain energy from renewable sources. Shows how alternative energy sources can be combined with conventional fossil fuels and established energy systems and how dependency on fossil fuels can be alleviated by adopting unconventional ways to use them.
Social Science
Dist - NFBC **Prod** - NFBC 1981

Tomorrow's families series
Caring for the infant 29 MIN
The Decision for nonparenthood 29 MIN
The Decision for parenthood 29 MIN
Economic factors in the parenthood decision 29 MIN
Emotional Development of the Infant 29 MIN
The First trimester 29 MIN
The First year in review 29 MIN
Help for families 29 MIN
The Infant's Hospital Experience 29 MIN
Intellectual Development of the Infant 29 MIN
Labor and Delivery 29 MIN
Medical Care during Pregnancy 29 MIN
The New Family Homecoming 29 MIN
The Newborn 29 MIN
The Parents' Hospital Experience 29 MIN
Physical Development of the Infant 29 MIN
Physical Factors in the Parenthood Decision 29 MIN
Pregnancy Occurs 29 MIN
Preparation for Homecoming 29 MIN
The Role of Others 29 MIN
The Role of the Father 29 MIN
The Role of the Mother 29 MIN
The Second Trimester 29 MIN
Self - Awareness and the Prospective Parent 29 MIN
Social Development of the Infant 29 MIN
Social Factors in the Parenthood Decision 29 MIN
The Special Homecoming 29 MIN
Stress and the New Family 29 MIN
The Third Trimester 29 MIN
Dist - AITECH

Tomorrow's Government Today 27 MIN
U-matic / VHS / 16mm
Color (H C A)
LC FIA65-1884
Discusses problems facing municipal governments, the need for trained personnel to deal with problems and the teamwork necessary among the various departments.
Civics and Political Systems; Psychology; Social Science; Sociology
Dist - IFB **Prod** - IFB 1964

Tomorrow's harvest 29 MIN
VHS / U-matic
Color (H C G)
$425.00, $395.00 purchase _ #V511
Profiles two American farming families as they endure hardships and struggle to survive against the growing wave of corporate farming. Relates the history, present status and future prospects of farming in the United States.
Agriculture; History - United States; Sociology
Dist - BARR **Prod** - CEPRO 1989

Tomorrow's Newspaper 11 MIN
16mm
B&W (J)
LC 72-700401
Portrays the oppressive day - by - day life of a small newspaper boy as he is shaped prematurely into an adult by the sordid events in the world which he cannot understand.
Guidance and Counseling; Psychology; Sociology
Dist - MMA **Prod** - ZAGREB 1971

Tomorrow's oil today 16 MIN
U-matic / VHS / 16mm
Color
Describes the role of the Bartlesville Energy Technology Center and the U S Department of Energy in the development of enhanced oil recovery and improved drilling technology. Includes animation.
Civics and Political Systems; Industrial and Technical Education; Social Science
Dist - USNAC **Prod** - USDOE 1983

Tomorrow's people 150 MIN
VHS
Color; PAL (J H)
PdS30 purchase
Presents ten programs, 15 minutes each, designed to increase student awareness of the richness and diversity of the different backgrounds, customs and languages to be found within the United Kingdom. Confronts questions of prejudice and bigotry inside and outside the classroom. Contact distributor about availability outside the United Kingdom.
Civics and Political Systems; Psychology; Sociology
Dist - ACADEM

Tomorrow's People 17 MIN
16mm
Color (H A)
LC 80-700961
Combines mountain music with views of Appalachian people and places.
Geography - United States; Sociology
Dist - APPAL **Prod** - APPAL 1973

Tomorrow's Power - Today 6 MIN
16mm
Color
LC FIE66-150
Introduces the fundamentals of atomic power. Describes the advantages of nuclear power and considers how it is used to generate electricity.
Science - Physical
Dist - USNAC **Prod** - USNRC 1964

Tomorrow's quake - earthquake prediction 20 MIN
U-matic / VHS / BETA
Color; PAL (G H C)
PdS50, PdS58 purchase
Explores continental drift; dilatency; plate tectonics; earthquake waves; seismic velocity changes; tiltmeters; and more. Concludes with motion pictures of an actual earthquake - one that was predicted. Uses animation and live action.
Geography - World; History - World; Science - Physical
Dist - EDPAT **Prod** - HALLL
AMEDFL

Tomorrow's Salmon 25 MIN
16mm
Color (G)
_ #106C 0176 563
Describes the joint program of the Canadian and British Columbian governments to protect and strengthen stocks of Pacific salmon on which depend, directly or indirectly, the jobs of 75,000 people and a $250 million industry.
Industrial and Technical Education; Science - Natural
Dist - CFLMDC **Prod** - NFBC 1976

Tomorrow's Space Powers - China, India , Brazil 30 MIN
VHS / 16mm
Conquest of Space Series
Color (G)
Introduces the programs of three countries that are not considered space powers but, nevertheless, manufacture their own satellites, giving them telecommunications and surveillance capabilities.
Business and Economics; Geography - World
Dist - FLMWST

Tomorrow's Television - Get what You Like or Like what You Get 62 MIN
16mm
B&W (H C)
LC 70-706848
Shows how the competitive struggle between various segments of the communication industry inhibits and influences what is shown on television.
Business and Economics; Civics and Political Systems; Fine Arts; Psychology; Social Science
Dist - IU **Prod** - NET 1970

Tomorrow's Tools 30 MIN
U-matic / VHS
Third Wave Series
Color
Business and Economics; Sociology
Dist - DELTAK **Prod** - TRIWVE

Tomorrow's world 24 MIN
16mm / U-matic
Color (G)
Shows how Mexico, Algeria and Thailand are working to control the rate of population growth.
Social Science; Sociology
Dist - PEREN **Prod** - UN

Tomorrow's Yesterday 29 MIN
16mm
Color (I)
LC 73-700090
Presents a documentary on Amerian Indians, as they were, as they are, and as they hope to be, emphasizing the positive things they are doing to improve their circumstances and prepare themselves to live in a modern world.
Social Science
Dist - BYU **Prod** - BYU 1972

Tompkins Park 8 MIN
16mm
Color (G)
$10.00 rental
Gives an account of the thousands of young people who enjoy outdoor rock concerts. Begins with showing Tompkins Park in New York's East Village in 1967 then takes off into fantasy with music by the Grateful Dead to produce emotional effects.
Fine Arts
Dist - CANCIN **Prod** - COHENK 1971

Tom's midnight garden 15 MIN
VHS
More books from cover to cover series
Color (I G)
$25.00 purchase _ #MBCC - 112
Presents the book 'Tom's Midnight Garden' by Philippa Pierce. Tells how Tom, while visiting his aunt and uncle, makes a strange and wonderful discovery. Hosted by John Robbins.
Education; English Language; Literature and Drama
Dist - PBS **Prod** - WETATV 1987

Tom's new house 15 MIN
VHS / U-matic
Dragons, wagons and wax series; Set 1
Color (K P)
Shows how wedges and screws work.
Science; Science - Physical
Dist - CTI **Prod** - CTI

The Tomten 8 MIN
U-matic / VHS / 16mm
Color (K P)
LC 82-700263
Reveals that at a lonely old farmhouse on a crisp winter night everyone is sleeping except old Tomten, the troll. Shows that Tomten goes about comforting the animals in his silent language. Based on the book The Tomten by Astrid Lindgren.
Literature and Drama
Dist - WWS **Prod** - WWS 1982

Tone Color 15 MIN
U-matic
Music Box Series
Color (K P)
Demonstrates that sounds as well as things can have color using Tchaikovsky's Waltz Of The Flowers.
Fine Arts
Dist - TVOTAR **Prod** - TVOTAR 1971

Tone color 15 MIN
VHS / U-matic
Music machine series
Color (P)
Discusses the basics of sound recognition.
Fine Arts
Dist - GPN **Prod** - INDIPS 1981

Tone Production, Vibrato and Dynamics 29 MIN
Videoreel / VT2
Playing the Guitar I Series
Color
Fine Arts
Dist - PBS **Prod** - KCET

Tone tales 10 MIN
U-matic / VHS
Book, look and listen series
Color (K P)
Focuses on the ability to associate stories and characters with orchestral music and single instruments.
English Language; Fine Arts; Literature and Drama
Dist - AITECH **Prod** - MDDE 1977

Tong Tana - a journey into the heart of Borneo 88 MIN
16mm
Color (G)
Focuses on Bruno Manser, a 34 - year old Swiss who has rejected civilization to live with the nomadic Penan Indians to help them confront the loggers threatening their existence and historic rainforests in Borneo. Reveals that Manser has a $85,000 price on his head, dead or alive. Available also in 35mm film format.
Science - Natural; Sociology
Dist - FIRS

Tonga Royal - Tonga 20 MIN
16mm / U-matic / VHS
Village Life Series
Color (J)
LC 78-700840
Views the Pacific island kingdom of Tonga. Shows the natural beauty, the people and the ceremonies of the island.
Geography - World; Sociology
Dist - JOU **Prod** - JPFLM 1977

Tongpan 63 MIN
16mm
B&W (H C) (THAI (ENGLISH SUBTITLES))
LC 79-701023
Uses the story of a poverty - stricken farmer in Northeast Thailand to depict political conditions there in the mid - 1970s. Tells how the farmer loses his land when a hydroelectric dam cuts off his water supply, forcing him to support his family with menial jobs. Shows how his life drastically changes when he meets a student who involves him in a seminar to discuss the possibility of another hydroelectric project.
Fine Arts; Foreign Language; History - World
Dist - ISANFG **Prod** - ISANFG 1979

Toni Morrison 52 MIN
VHS
Color (S)
$39.95 purchase _ #833 - 9360
Presents Toni Morrison whose novel Beloved won the 1988 Pulitzer Prize. Reveals the true story on which Beloved was based and discusses the problems of slavery and its legacy which served as the basis of the book.
History - United States; Literature and Drama; Sociology
Dist - FI **Prod** - RMART 1988

Toni Morrison 42 MIN
VHS
Color (H C G)
$79.00 purchase
Features the Nobel Prize - winning writer talking with A S Byatt about using visual images and spoken language to focus writing, and the literary place of African American writers. Discusses her work including The Bluest Eye; Song of Solomon; Tar Baby; and Beloved.
History - World; Literature and Drama
Dist - ROLAND **Prod** - INCART

Tonia the tree - growing is changing
VHS
Key concepts in self - esteem
Color (K P)
$79.95 purchase _ #MF9342RA
Presents one of an 11 - part series teaching key curriculum concepts such as independence, freedom and responsibility, and peer pressure. Includes video, storybook and teaching guide with activities and games. In this video, encouraged by the example of her friends, Tonia learns that growth is exhilarating, life is an adventure, and that courage makes anything possible.
Education; Psychology
Dist - CFKRCM **Prod** - CFKRCM

Tonio Kroger 88 MIN
16mm
B&W
Depicts a writer - hero's feelings as he travels to southern Italy to visit the homeland of his mother.
Fine Arts; Geography - World
Dist - TRANSW **Prod** - CON 1965

Tonometry 16 MIN
16mm
Color (PRO)
LC 78-700892
Depicts two methods of conducting glaucoma tests, using the Schiotz tenometer and using an electronic tonographer. Explains the effects of pressure on eye functions, stresses the importance of sterilizing equipment and shows how to calibrate instruments and record test results.
Science; Science - Natural
Dist - USNAC **Prod** - USA 1977

Tonometry 9 MIN
16mm
Medical skills library series
Color
LC 74-702523
Shows step - by - step procedures of using a Schiotz tonometer to measure intraocular pressure. Discusses basic components of the Schiotz tonometer.
Health and Safety; Science - Natural
Dist - SUTHLA **Prod** - AMCP 1974

The Tonsillar Ring 9 MIN
U-matic
Microanatomy Laboratory Orientation Series
Color (C)
Reviews the tonsillar or Waldeyers ring, those lymphoid structures which surround the pharynx, including the palatine, pharyngeal and lingual tonsils.
Health and Safety; Science - Natural
Dist - UOKLAH **Prod** - UOKLAH 1986

Tonsillectomy 16 MIN
16mm
B&W (H C A)

LC FIA65-1370
A doctor explains the necessity for the removal of a child's adenoids and tonsils. Describes the emotional preparation of the child for hospitalization. Follows the doctor as he performs the operation.
Health and Safety; Psychology
Dist - LAWREN **Prod** - CMA 1961

Tonsillectomy and adenoidectomy 10 MIN
VHS
Color (PRO G) (ARABIC)
$250.00 purchase _ #OT - 08
Explains why the removal of tonsils and - or adenoids often becomes necessary. Teaches viewers about preoperative preparations, what will occur at the hospital and what to expect during recovery. Cautions parents to watch for excessive bleeding and gives tips on what foods are best to eat during recovery. Developed in cooperation with and endorsed by the American Academy of Otolaryngology - Head and Neck Surgery.
Health and Safety
Dist - MIFE **Prod** - MIFE 1991

Tonsils and Adenoids 9 MIN
16mm / 8mm cartridge
Color (A) (SPANISH)
Discusses the indications and results of surgery of the tonsils and adenoids. Covers the parental role in assisting the child and gives instructions for home care.
Health and Safety; Home Economics
Dist - PRORE **Prod** - PRORE

Tony and the Election 6 MIN
16mm / U-matic / VHS
Being Friends Series
Color (I)
Guidance and Counseling; Literature and Drama; Psychology
Dist - USNAC **Prod** - USHHS

Tony Couch Watercolor Series
Controlling watercolor 55 MIN
Watercolor Symbols - Rocks, Puddles and Weeds 55 MIN
Watercolor Symbols - Trees and Water 55 MIN
Winter's Soft Mantle 115 MIN
Dist - CRYSP

The Tony Fontane Story 80 MIN
16mm
Color
Tells the story of Tony Fontane, a singer. Discusses the role of Christ in his life.
Religion and Philosophy
Dist - GF **Prod** - YOUTH

Tony Gwynn's baseball 60 MIN
VHS
Color (J H C G)
$49.95 purchase _ #PHV1100SV
Presents two volumes on improving the game of baseball. Covers five keys to hitting, secrets of the swing, power hitting vs contact hitting, the inner game, the stance, the stride, timing and specific drills in Volume 1 - The King of Swing. Volume 2 - Play to Win covers baserunning, taking a lead, how to steal a base, sliding, fielding and the throw.
Physical Education and Recreation
Dist - CAMV

Tony Oursler - Evol 60603 28 MIN
VHS / U-matic
Color (A)
Features primitive psychoanalytic 'bad boy' actings.
Fine Arts
Dist - ARTINC **Prod** - CAT

Tony Oursler - son of oil 18 MIN
VHS / U-matic
Color (A)
Contains primitive psychoanalytic 'bad boy' actings.
Fine Arts
Dist - ARTINC **Prod** - ARTINC

Tony Oursler - the weak bullet 14 MIN
VHS / U-matic
Color (A)
Presents an expressionistic reverie. Incorporates phantasmagoric sets.
Fine Arts
Dist - ARTINC **Prod** - ARTINC

Too big too soon 50 MIN
VHS
Horizon series
Color (H C A)
PdS99 purchase
Calls attention to expanding uses of human growth hormone. Explains that it is still used to promote growth of hormone-deficient children, but is also used to help HIV patients and the elderly. Discusses questions regarding the future of medical research into the uses of such hormones.
Science - Natural
Dist - BBCENE

Too busy to cook series
Presents a four - part series from Bon Appetite magazine showing time - saving techniques for preparing delicious, quick and creative meals. Includes Light and Fresh Cooking, Weeknight Inspirations, Festive Desserts and Easy Entertaining and recipe cards.
Easy entertaining 60 MIN
Festive desserts 60 MIN
Weeknight inspiration 60 MIN
Dist - CAMV

Too close for comfort 27 MIN
VHS
Color (J H C)
$189.00 purchase _ #BO21 - V8
Cuts to the heart of fears and teen misconceptions about HIV, AIDS, and homosexuality. Portrays Nick who is fired from his job after he tests HIV positive. As rumors fly, he faces the fear, blame, and homophobic stereotypes of those around him, including his best friend. Some of his more discriminating friends make a video about HIV and AIDS, homosexuality and discrimination, and interview people who are HIV positive, have AIDS, and are homosexual. Includes an eight - lesson Discussion Guide.
Guidance and Counseling; Health and Safety; Sociology
Dist - ETRASS **Prod** - ETRASS

Too close to home 50 MIN
VHS
Color (G)
$90.00 purchase
Follows five men during their one - month reserve duty along the northern border of the Golan Heights. Records their comments, full of humor and pathos, as the withdrawal from the Golan Heights becomes an imminent possibility making their future uncertain. Directed by Ori Inbar.
Fine Arts; History - World; Sociology
Dist - NCJEWF

Too close to the sun 50 MIN
VHS
Horizon series
Color (C G)
PdS99 purchase _ Unavailable in Canada
Describes the 1989 discovery by Fleischmann and Pons of endless, cheap energy through nuclear fusion. Tells how their discovery was scorned by the scientific establishment. Shows how the Japanese are about to invest in Fleischmann and Pons' latest work in the area of cold fusion.
Social Science
Dist - BBCENE

Too dangerous to work with 24 MIN
VHS
Color (H IND COR)
$350.00 purchase
Shows what can happen when drugs are used at the workplace. Points out that not only is the user at a greater risk of injury, but the chances of injuring a co - worker also increase dramatically. Emphasizes the importance of Employee Assistance Programs - EAP - and lets workers and managment know that help is available. Demonstrates how attitudes toward fellow employees who abuse drugs can make a difference.
Business and Economics; Guidance and Counseling; Health and Safety; Psychology
Dist - FMSP

Too Far, Too Fast 20 MIN
U-matic / VHS / 16mm
Japan - the Crowded Islands Series
Color (J H C)
Visits a new development in the town of Oita, a scheme designed to attract industries to areas away from the overcrowded East Coast of Japan. Discusses the environmental problems created by the development. Examines the future of Japan and asks if the system will be able to adjust to the probably inevitable task of slowing things down.
Geography - World; Sociology
Dist - FI **Prod** - BBCTV 1982

Too Few Too Far to Matter 12 MIN
16mm
Color
LC 78-701617
Depicts the problems of rural health delivery systems in Montana, New Mexico and South Dakota. Explains the contrast between rural and urban health delivery systems, especially as it relates to services for developmental disabilities.
Geography - United States; Health and Safety; Psychology
Dist - USNAC **Prod** - USDDIS 1978

Too Good to be True 20 MIN
U-matic / VHS
$335.00 purchase
Fine Arts
Dist - ABCLR **Prod** - ABCLR 1983

Too good to be true 29 MIN
16mm / VHS
Color (G IND)
$5.00 rental
Alerts the consumer to the dangers of telemarketing fraud. Reveals that every year millions of people are bilked out of their savings by telephone scam artists who fraudulently sell gold, commodities, travel packages or investment opportunities. Produced by the American Federation of State, County and Municipal Employees Labor News Network of the AFL - CIO.
Sociology
Dist - AFLCIO **Prod** - AFLCIO 1988

Too good to waste 20 MIN
VHS
Color (I J H)
$195.00 purchase
Shows young people that it's okay not to drink or use drugs. Features youth who have 'been there.' Does not 'talk at' kids about the problem of drug and alcohol abuse but simply shows young people living in the solution, enjoying life in their sobriety.
Guidance and Counseling; Psychology
Dist - FMSP **Prod** - FREDER

Too hot to handle series
Acceptable risks 16 MIN
Cores and effects 23 MIN
The Nature of Radioactivity 20 MIN
Radiation - Boon and Bane 17 MIN
Dist - FOTH

Too Late for Questions 20 MIN
U-matic / VHS
Color (IND)
Describes survival equipment and its use upon abandonment of a marine tanker vessel. Details lifeboats and rafts and the gear found on them.
Business and Economics; Health and Safety; Industrial and Technical Education; Social Science
Dist - UTEXPE **Prod** - TEXACO

Too Late to Wait 28 MIN
16mm
Color (J)
LC 73-701572
Features an unrehearsed rap session with a group of black students and closes with an explanation of how anyone can know Christ personally.
Guidance and Counseling; Religion and Philosophy
Dist - CCFC **Prod** - CCFC 1972

Too little too late 30 MIN
U-matic
Currents - 1984 - 85 season series; No 122
Color (A T)
Examines the state of sex education in the schools and those who oppose it and those who approve of it.
Health and Safety; Social Science
Dist - PBS **Prod** - WNETTV 1985

Too little, too late 48 MIN
VHS / 16mm
Color (C A)
$295.00 purchase, $100.00, $50.00 rental
Shows what it feels like to have AIDS affect someone close. Features several families sharing their pain and frustration as well as the solace they derived from helping a loved one toward a peaceful death.
Health and Safety
Dist - FANPRO **Prod** - FANPRO 1989

Too many Bozos 6 MIN
U-matic / VHS / 16mm
Golden Book Storytime Series
Color (P)
Tells the story of a boy who tries out several kinds of pets before he finds just the right one.
Literature and Drama
Dist - CORF **Prod** - CORF 1977

Too many Elephants 25 MIN
U-matic / VHS / 16mm
Behavior and Survival Series
Color (H C A)
LC 73-700431
Features scientists who investigate the migrations and feeding habits of elephants in the Serengeti area. Examines questions of behavior and ecology.
Science - Natural
Dist - MGHT **Prod** - MGHT 1973

Too many People 8 MIN
16mm / U-matic / VHS
Caring about Our Community Series
Color (P I J)
Describes the problem of population growth in terms that a child can understand. Depicts the results of overpopulation in traffic, litter and pollution. Illustrates zero population growth as the answer.
Guidance and Counseling; Science - Natural; Social Science; Sociology
Dist - AIMS **Prod** - GORKER 1973

Too many people, too little space 60 MIN
VHS
Land, location and culture - a geographical synthesis series; Pt 2
Color (J H C)
$89.95 purchase _ #WLU102
Reveals that one of the most persistent themes of the modern world is that there are too many people and that the world's population is growing too fast for humans to cope. Considers the legitimacy of the theme in view of observations of population growth from the earliest beginnings of humanity which note that current population growth is without historical precedent. Discusses the meaning and significance of demographic terms and explores aspects of current population issues, including the trend toward enormous urban centers. Closes with some thoughtful commentary on how to deal with the very serious problems facing the world today. Part of a 12 - part series.
Geography - World; Sociology
Dist - INSTRU

Too much 30 MIN
VHS
Young adult issues series
Color (G R)
$29.95 purchase
Illustrates through a day in a teenager's life the destructive effects of alcohol abuse. Exemplifies by means of a sports participation situation the role of peer pressure in teenage drinking.
Health and Safety; Physical Education and Recreation; Sociology
Dist - GF

Too much noise 15 MIN
VHS / U-matic
Words and pictures series
Color (K P)
Introduces an old man who is beleaguered by the normal noises of his daily life. Tells what happens when a wise man advises him to get noisy animals such as a cow, a hen, a dog and finally a cat.
Literature and Drama
Dist - FI **Prod** - FI

Too Much of a Good Thing 13 MIN
16mm / U-matic / VHS
Learning Laws - Respect for Yourself, Others and the Law Series
Color (I)
Shows how different TV viewing habits have enormous consequences for people throughout their lives.
Fine Arts; Psychology
Dist - CORF **Prod** - DISNEY 1982

Too much off the top 6 MIN
U-matic / VHS / 16mm
Paddington Bear series
Color (K P I)
LC 77-700668
Features an animated adaptation of chapter 13 from the children's book Paddington At Work by Michael Bond. Tells about Paddington, a small, dark bear, whose attempts at haircutting bring unexpected rewards.
Fine Arts; Literature and Drama
Dist - ALTSUL **Prod** - BONDM 1977

Too much speed 11 MIN
16mm
Warner - Pathe newsreel series
B&W (G)
$15.00 rental
Collects crackups and spills on wheels that are accented by jolting sound effects. Presents part of a series by Robert Youngson for Warner - Pathe Newsreels.
Fine Arts; Literature and Drama; Physical Education and Recreation
Dist - KITPAR **Prod** - WARPAN 1951

Too much to handle - living with stress 20 MIN
VHS
Behavior - values - middle school survival kit series
Color (I J)
$99.00 purchase _ #RB8191
Observes that stress is a part of everyday life and that it is important to learn how to deal with it. Examines ways in which young people can keep their stress levels down. Focuses on a teenager who is preparing an oral report, doing regular homework assignments, is part of a baseball team, babysits for his sister in the afternoon and has other chores. Shows that some stress is good, too much is bad, that proper diet, exercise and rest are necessary, that big problems can be broken down into little ones and that talking with an adult can help sometimes to solve a problem. Part of a three - part series on behavior and values.
Guidance and Counseling; Psychology; Sociology
Dist - REVID **Prod** - REVID 1993

Too Much Too Soon 15 MIN
U-matic / VHS
Color (H C A)
$195 purchase, $30 rental
Examines women's bodybuilding. Focuses on bodybuilder Sue Ann McKean. Features scene of McKean practicing aikido techniques, working out in the gym, and participating in bodybuilding competitions. Directed by Mark Schwartz.
Health and Safety
Dist - CNEMAG

Too much too soon 30 MIN
U-matic
Currents - 1984 - 85 season series; No 103
Color (A)
Takes a look at infant intelligence and development.
Psychology; Social Science
Dist - PBS **Prod** - WNETTV 1985

Too much trouble 20 MIN
VHS
Color; PAL; NTSC (G IND)
PdS60, PdS70 purchase
Shows why everyone involved in building maintenance should be concerned about safety. Illustrates how tragedy can strike during the simplest of tasks - the job where, too often, it is just too much trouble to take the necessary safety precautions. Looks at some of the wide range of access equipment now available. Demonstrates the high standards of performance in work being carried out at the Old Vic and the tower of Big Ben.
Health and Safety
Dist - CFLVIS

Too Proud to Beg 29 MIN
Videoreel / VT2
Our Street Series
Color
Sociology
Dist - PBS **Prod** - MDCPB

Too smart for strangers 40 MIN
VHS
Color (K P I T)
$29.95 purchase _ #S00062
Teaches children ages three to ten how to deal with strangers and protect themselves from harm. Features Winnie the Pooh and popular stars such as Tyne Daly, Michael Warren, Patty Duke, and Gavin MacLeod.
Health and Safety
Dist - UILL

Too splendid to lose 29 MIN
VHS
California Capitol restoration series
Color (J H C G)
$175.00 purchase, $40.00 renta _ #37187
Illustrates the imaginative architectural and structural achievement of the restoration of the State Capitol of California. Part of a three - part series which documents the seven - year effort to restore the California State Capitol.
Fine Arts; History - United States
Dist - UCEMC **Prod** - TELENS 1985

Too Tough to Care 18 MIN
16mm
Color (I J)
Delivers an anti - smoking message by telling about the Finster Tobacco Company who must find an advertising theme they can use to hook kids on smoking and combat all this talk about lung cancer, heart disease and respiratory illness.
Health and Safety; Psychology
Dist - LAWREN **Prod** - PARKRD

Too young 3 MIN
16mm
Color (G)
$10.00 rental
Takes a hard, humorous look at the pressures and frustrations young people - women - girls - feel as they rush out to explore their sexuality with all the taboos and fears that sexuality entails. An Elizabeth Sher production.
Fine Arts; Sociology
Dist - CANCIN

Too Young to Burn 26 MIN
16mm
Color
Focuses on how to teach children about fire and emphasizes the necessity of pre - school education, protection and discipline by parents.
Guidance and Counseling; Health and Safety; Home Economics
Dist - LAFIRE **Prod** - LAFIRE

Too Young to Say 15 MIN
16mm
Color
LC FIA56-1238
Demonstrates the use of the audiometer as a means of determining the threshold of hearing for the very young child.
Education; Health and Safety; Psychology
Dist - USC **Prod** - USC 1955

Too young, too far 25 MIN
VHS
Color (I J H)
Discusses myths and facts concerning pregnancy prevention. Examines problems teen parents face and encourages teen parents to stand behind their decisions when they are faced with opposition.
Guidance and Counseling; Health and Safety
Dist - CEPRO **Prod** - NEWIST 1989
BARR CEPRO

Tool - and - die maker 4.5 MIN
VHS / 16mm
Good work series
Color (H VOC G)
$40.00 purchase _ #BPN195802
Presents the occupation of a tool and die maker. Gives a profile of a young person who is either undergoing an apprenticeship or has recently completed training in this field. Takes the viewer on a tour of this person's workplace and explains the practical skills and training offered by employers and schools. Gives a better understanding of the demand for skilled workers today and the potential for personal growth.
Guidance and Counseling
Dist - RMIBHF **Prod** - RMIBHF 1981

Tool Bound Behavior 20 MIN
U-matic
Color (PRO)
Presents tool behavior as the first of five components of skill development within an apprenticeship model of occupational behavior. Defines all five components and applies them to the teaching - learning process. Narrated by Cynthia Heard.
Health and Safety; Psychology
Dist - AOTA **Prod** - AOTA 1977

The Tool Box I 30 MIN
VHS / U-matic
You Can Fixit Series
Color
Discusses various tools used in home repair.
Industrial and Technical Education
Dist - MDCPB **Prod** - WRJATV

The Tool Box II 30 MIN
VHS / U-matic
You Can Fixit Series
Color
Discusses various tools used in home repair.
Industrial and Technical Education
Dist - MDCPB **Prod** - WRJATV

Tool identification and finishing 30 MIN
VHS
Concrete series
Color (G H VOC)
$69.95 purchase _ #CEV00851V-T
Describes the importance of using the proper tools when finishing a concrete slab. Identifies each tool and explains how it is used. Includes information on edgers; jointers; finishing trowels; wood, bull, and magnesium floats; mason's and power trowels. Demonstrates small tricks of experienced concrete workers and how to create an exposed aggregate finish.
Industrial and Technical Education
Dist - CAMV

Tool Life - Measurement and Control 57 MIN
BETA / VHS / U-matic
Color
$400 purchase
Shows power measurements.
Industrial and Technical Education; Science
Dist - ASM **Prod** - ASM

The Tool Movie 12 MIN
U-matic / VHS / 16mm
Color (P I)
LC 76-700803
Presents a humorous history of the evolution of tools from the days of the caveman to the 1970's.
History - World; Social Science
Dist - AIMS **Prod** - JACOBL 1976

The Tool users 14 MIN
U-matic / VHS / 16mm
Animal behavior series
Color (H C A)
LC 76-703402
Shows how animals are tool users with examples of a weaver ant constructing a home, a finch pecking for food and a chimpanzee assembling and using a simple tool.
Science - Natural
Dist - NGS **Prod** - NGS 1975
AITECH

Tool using 23 MIN
U-matic / VHS / 16mm
Jane goodall - studies of the chimpanzee series
Color (H C A)
LC 76-703407
Shows how the adult male chimpanzee makes and uses tools and how the young prepare for these tasks in the way they play with objects, learning through observation and imitation. Includes views of chimpanzees using sticks and stones as weapons against baboons.
Science - Natural; Sociology
Dist - NGS **Prod** - NGS 1976
AITECH

Toolbox Ballet 8 MIN
U-matic
Color (P)
Shows various tools performing a ballet in which each tool's individual dance mimics its function.
Fine Arts
Dist - GA **Prod** - NBCTV

Tooling for composites 24 MIN
VHS / 16mm
Manufacturing insights series
Color (A IND)
$200.00, $190.00 purchase _ #VT288, #VT288U
Shows the latest techniques in composite tooling which save money and produce better parts.
Business and Economics; Industrial and Technical Education; Psychology
Dist - SME **Prod** - SME 1989

The Toolmaker's art 19 MIN
16mm
Color (J H VOC)
Shows how the tool, die and machining industry works and presents the professionals who make it run. Features an explanation of the career opportunities open to young people.
Business and Economics; Guidance and Counseling; Industrial and Technical Education; Psychology
Dist - MTP **Prod** - NATTDP

Toolmaker's vise - advanced
U-matic / VHS
Blueprint reading series
Color
Industrial and Technical Education
Dist - VTRI **Prod** - VTRI

Toolmaker's vise - advanced
U-matic / VHS
Blueprint reading - Spanish series
Color (SPANISH)
Industrial and Technical Education
Dist - VTRI **Prod** - VTRI

Tools
VHS
Do it Yourself Series
(H C A)
$39.95 purchase _ #RMDIY305V
Demonstrates the use of many tools in the home.
Home Economics
Dist - CAMV

Tools
VHS
$39.95 purchase _ #DI - 305
Portrays the use and care of hand tools. Describes the use and care of power tools.
Industrial and Technical Education
Dist - CAREER **Prod** - CAREER

Tools
VHS
Home Improvement Series
(H C G A IND)
$39.95 _ SH305
Discusses the use and care of hand tools and power tools.
Industrial and Technical Education
Dist - AAVIM **Prod** - AAVIM 1989

Tools 6 MIN
16mm
Safety and You Series
Color
Illustrates that the use of sophisticated tools requires special safety precautions.
Health and Safety
Dist - FILCOM **Prod** - FILCOM

Tools 44 MIN
VHS / 16mm
Do it Yourself Series
(G)
$39.95 purchase _ #DIY305
Covers the use and care of hand tools, including measuring, leveling, attaching, dismantling, finishing, safety and time saving tips. Includes use and care of power tools. Discusses cutting, drilling, assembling and finishing, and safety tips.
Home Economics
Dist - RMIBHF **Prod** - RMIBHF

Tools and Supplies
VHS / 35mm strip
Wiring a House Series
$85.00 purchase _ #DXWAH010 filmstrips, $85.00 purchase _ #DXWAH010V
Teaches about basic electrician's tools, wire and fittings, and temporary service.
Industrial and Technical Education
Dist - CAREER **Prod** - CAREER

Tools and tasks 29 MIN
VHS / 16mm
Villa alegre series
Color (P I J) (ENGLISH & SPANISH)
$46.00 rental _ #VILA - 128
Presents educational material in both Spanish and English.
Education
Dist - PBS

Tools for continual improvement - one and two series 139 MIN
VHS
Tools for continual improvement - one and two series
Color (COR)
$2400.00 purchase _ #ELI01, #ELI02
Presents eight titles including The Flowchart - picture of success, The Cause and effect diagram, Team meeting skills, Idea generating tools, Consensus decision making, Pareto analysis, Planning for data collection and Data collection methods. Teaches employee skills for improved performance. Includes trainer's notes, wall charts and reference cards. Available in healthcare and general business versions. Produced by Executive Learning, Inc.
Business and Economics; Psychology
Dist - EXTR

Tools for continual improvement - one and two series
Tools for continual improvement - one and two series 139 MIN
Dist - EXTR

Tools for continual improvement - one series 80 MIN
VHS
Tools for continual improvement - one series
Color (COR)
$1675.00 purchase _ #ELI01
Presents a five part series including The Flowchart - picture of success, The Cause and effect diagram, Team meeting skills, Idea generating tools and Consensus decision making. Trains employees in skills to improve performance.Includes trainer notes, wall charts and reference cards. Produced by Executive Learning, Inc.
Business and Economics; Psychology
Dist - EXTR

Tools for continual improvement series
The Flowchart - picture of success 12 MIN
Dist - EXTR

Tools for continual improvement - two series 59 MIN
VHS
Tools for continual improvement - two series
Color (COR)
$995.00 purchase _ #ELI02
Presents three programs including Pareto analysis, Planning for data collection and Data collection methods. Teaches employee skills for enhanced performance. Includes trainer's notes, wall charts and reference cards. Produced by Executive Learning, Inc.
Business and Economics
Dist - EXTR

Tools for job hunting 30 MIN
VHS
Kirby Stanat on jobs series
Color (H VOC)
Examines the tools that are necessary for successful job hunting. Covers subjects such as getting organized, resumes, appearance, grooming, researching the company, and unique tips for women and students. Includes a teacher's guide. Hosted by Kirby Stanat.
Guidance and Counseling; Psychology
Dist - CAMV **Prod** - CAMV
CAREER CAREER
GPN SUMITP
JISTW JISTW

Tools for Job Hunting 30 MIN
U-matic / VHS
Kirby Stanat on Job Series
(J H C PRO)
$180.00 _ #JW200V
Focuses on what one should know prior to setting out to find a job. Covers how to get organized, how to create a resume, how to make a good first impression, and other tips. Includes accompanying teacher's guide.
Business and Economics; Education; Guidance and Counseling; Psychology
Dist - CAMV **Prod** - CAMV

Tools for Research 40 MIN
U-matic / VHS / 16mm
Color
Raises the curtain on the research industry and its treatment of animals. Looks at who suffers and who profits. Attempts to interview researchers who were reluctant to talk on the topic of research treatment of animals.
Science
Dist - BULFRG **Prod** - LIBANI 1983

Tools for sketching 29 MIN
U-matic
Sketching techniques series; Lesson 23
Color (C A)
Discusses some common tools used in sketching. Explains advantages of some tools over others. Includes use of color and variety of media.
Fine Arts
Dist - CDTEL **Prod** - COAST

Tools for Teaching the Case Method 60 MIN
VHS / 16mm
Case Method Teaching in the Community College Series
Color (C)
$150.00 purchase, $45.00 rental _ #5200
Shows case method teaching in action, including interviews and activities with Harvard Business School and community college faculty.
Business and Economics; Education; Health and Safety; Psychology; Sociology
Dist - EDC **Prod** - EDC 1988

Tools for the Beginning Carpenter 60 MIN
BETA / VHS / 16mm
Color (IND G)
$39.95 purchase _ #VT1139
Explains the basic tools needed for the beginning carpenter's tool box, such as striking tools, measuring tools, cutting tools, fastening tools, and miscellaneous specialty tools. Taught by Pete Prlain.
Industrial and Technical Education
Dist - RMIBHF **Prod** - RMIBHF

Tools for the electrical trades 52 MIN
VHS / 35mm strip
(H VOC IND)
#819XV7
Introduces first year students and trainees to the various types and the proper use of hand tools used in the electrical industry. Includes wearing apparel & safety, basic hand tools, cutting tools, and specialty tools (4 tapes). Includes a study guide.
Education; Industrial and Technical Education
Dist - BERGL

Tools for thought 30 MIN
VHS / BETA
Computers and the mind series
Color (G)
$29.95 purchase _ #S175
Features Howard Rheingold, author of 'Tools for Thought - the History and Future of Mind - Expanding Technology,' who says that in the next ten years personal computers will be sufficiently powerful to realize the dreams of many innovators who write about 'fantasy amplifiers,' 'expert systems' and computerized villages. Part of a four - part series on computers and the mind.
Computer Science; History - United States; Industrial and Technical Education; Mathematics; Sociology
Dist - THINKA **Prod** - THINKA

Tools of ethnomusicology 27 MIN
16mm
B&W (H C)
Features a television program of non - western music.
Fine Arts
Dist - UCLA **Prod** - UCLA

Tools of exploitation 60 MIN
VHS / U-matic
Africans series; Pt 4
Color (G)
$45.00, $29.95 purchase
Traces the economic legacy of colonialism, the development of slavery and the European control of Africa's natural resources. Focuses on Belgium and Great Britain. Part of a nine - part series hosted by Dr Ali Mazrui, Cornell University and University of Michigan.
History - United States; History - World; Sociology
Dist - ANNCPB **Prod** - WETATV 1988
BBCENE

The Tools of ignorance 8 MIN
16mm
Color (G)
$15.00 rental
Pictures the battery as seen from the bleachers. Stages an aerial drama in four acts, with running commentary from the heavens.

Fine Arts; Physical Education and Recreation
Dist - CANCIN **Prod** - OSBONS 1983

Tools of ignorance 26 MIN
16mm
Color (G)
LC 72-702514
Presents Johnny Bench discussing his job as All - Star catcher of the Cincinnati Reds and clarifies how the 'men behind the plate' have stepped into the limelight in recent years, overcoming the stigma of the 'tools of ignorance,' an expression referring to the specialized gear worn by catchers.
Physical Education and Recreation
Dist - SFI **Prod** - SFI 1972

Tools of Job Hunting 30 MIN
VHS
Kirby Stanat on Jobs Series
$180.00 purchase _ #013 - 418
Discusses organization, resumes, appearance, grooming, researching the company, and tips for women and students.
Guidance and Counseling
Dist - CAREER **Prod** - CAREER

Tools of Job Hunting 30 MIN
U-matic / VHS
Kirby Stanat on Jobs Series
(C H A)
$180 _ JWGP8V
Covers preparatory steps to be used before beginning the job search.
Business and Economics; Education
Dist - JISTW **Prod** - JISTW

Tools of Job Hunting 30 MIN
VHS / U-matic
Kirby Stanat on Jobs Series
Color (H C A)
Emphasizes the things the job seeker should know, have and do before wading into the job market.
Guidance and Counseling; Psychology
Dist - GPN **Prod** - SUMITP 1983

Tools of Job Hunting 30 MIN
VHS / 16mm
Kirby Stanat on Jobs Series
Color (H)
$150.00 purchase _ #PAGP8V
Features tips on preparing a resume, gathering references and appropriate dress standards for job searchers. Examines the concerns of women who are reentering the job market.
Guidance and Counseling; Psychology
Dist - JISTW

The Tools of television 22 MIN
VHS
Color (J H C)
$59.00 purchase _ #TTOT
Shows what it's like to operate a TV camera. Looks at how TV stations and networks send news stories by satellite and examines how modern TV technology affect what viewers see. Explains the many kinds of equipment encountered at television stations. Explores TV cameras, remote microwave vans, satellites, transmitters and other vital links in the television chain.
Fine Arts
Dist - INSTRU

Tools of the trade 30 MIN
VHS
New faces on make - up series
Color (G A)
$24.95 purchase _ #PRO205V
Demonstrates how to use the different make - up tools, such as brushes, sponges, and applicators.
Home Economics
Dist - CAMV

Tools of the Trade 30 MIN
U-matic
Woodcarver's Workshop Series
Color
Industrial and Technical Education
Dist - PBS **Prod** - WOSUTV

Tools of the trade 30 MIN
VHS
Contenders series
Color (A)
PdS30 purchase
Examines science and the shifting goalposts of international competition. Part of a five-part series showing how scientific ideas have permeated almost every sporting event, bringing major advances in sports achievement. Follows some of the world's finest sportspeople in their struggle to succeed.
Physical Education and Recreation
Dist - BBCENE

Tools of writing 30 MIN
VHS / U-matic
Writing for work series; Pt 1
Color (T COR)
LC 81-706735
Focuses on teaching effective writing to office workers. Emphasizes the importance of being clear, correct, concise and complete. Hosted by Cicely Tyson.
Business and Economics; English Language
Dist - TIMLIF **Prod** - TIMLIF 1981

Tools that Shaped America
16mm
Color
Sketches the early history of the most basic tools, focusing on the grinding wheel. Discusses new types of grinding wheels and safety measures.
Health and Safety; History - United States; Industrial and Technical Education
Dist - GWI **Prod** - CINE

Toot, Whistle, Plunk and Boom 10 MIN
16mm / U-matic / VHS
Color (I)
LC 72-700157
Animated cartoons show origin and development of the four classes of musical instruments in a modern symphony - - horns, woodwinds, strings and percussion.
Fine Arts
Dist - CORF **Prod** - DISNEY 1959

Tooth and claw 60 MIN
VHS
Ark series; Episode 4
Color (G)
$290.00 purchase, $50.00 rental
Watches as a rebellious group at the Regent's Park Zoo in London calls a special meeting of the Zoological Society to carry out the takeover. Looks at the remaining overburdened zoo staff and the zoo's dropping standards. Meanwhile, the zoo's Director General awaits word of his future, alone in his office. Part of a series on the Zoo which has been told that, due to the market economy, it must now pay its own way. Records events at the Ark for over a year as a cost conscious management team moves in, slashing expenditures, including 90 people and 1200 animals - 40 percent of the zoo's stock. Founded in 1822, the zoo's scientific research has received world wide acclaim.
Business and Economics; Fine Arts; Science - Natural
Dist - FIRS **Prod** - DINEEN 1993

The Tooth and Gum Revue 18 MIN
VHS / 16mm / U-matic
Color (K P I)
$425, $300, $330 purchase _ #A401
Presents a musical message about teeth and gums. Shows viewers what teeth are made of - the crown, enamel, pulp, and the root. Gives viewers a three part harmony lesson on the techniques for teeth and gum care which are brushing, flossing, and rinsing. Teaches that bacteria feed on leftover food particles to form plaque which causes the gums to get red and swollen. Points out the damage that can be done to teeth and gums if plaque is left to grow. Explains how tooth and gum decay can be easily avoided.
Science - Natural
Dist - BARR **Prod** - BARR 1986

Tooth decay and gum disease 30 MIN
U-matic / VHS / BETA
Color; NTSC; PAL; SECAM (G)
PdS83
Presents a series of short dental health education programs which examine the cause, effect and prevention of the two most common diseases affecting teeth. Considers all age groups, from the newborn child to the elderly. Uses detailed computer graphics, clear close - up film and factual narrative to explain dental disease. Explains and demonstrates preventive techniques available for the improvement and maintenance of dental health.
Health and Safety; Science - Natural
Dist - VIEWTH

Tooth Fairy 8 MIN
VHS / U-matic
Giant First Start Series
Color (K P)
$29.95 purchase _ #VT008
Presents an adaptation of the story Tooth Fairy. Contains a 32 page hardcover book and a video.
English Language; Literature and Drama
Dist - TROLA

The Tooth Fairy is broke 20 MIN
VHS
Gentle giant series
Color (P I)
LC 90712920
Uses story to teach children universal truths. Thirteenth of 16 installments of series which uses stories from cultures throughout the world.
Health and Safety; Literature and Drama; Psychology
Dist - GPN

Tooth Fairy - Presto Change - O
VHS / 16mm
Video Read - Alongs Series
Color (K)
$8.88 purchase _ ISBN #5109 - 18651 - 3
Features animated stories and songs as lessons in children learning word skills. Available in a series of six similar videos.
Fine Arts; Literature and Drama
Dist - EDUCRT

Tooth - gnasher superflash
VHS
Reading rainbow series; No 63
Color; CC (K P)
$39.95 purchase
Portrays the Popsnorkles who decide they need a new car, and they can't believe their eyes when they test drive the amazing Tooth - Gnasher Superflash in a story by Daniel Pinkwater, narrated by Victoria Jackson. Reveals that LeVar is inspired to learn all the ins and outs of automobiles as he spends the day in a service station. Looks at what's in store for the future of automobiles in the Sunraycar, a solar - powered car. Part of a series offering a multicultural approach to generating reading enthusiasm with cross - curricular applications, hosted by LeVar Burton.
English Language; Industrial and Technical Education; Literature and Drama; Social Science; Sociology
Dist - GPN **Prod** - LNMDP

Tooth morphogenesis and maturation 15 MIN
U-matic / VHS
Color (C PRO)
$395.00 purchase, $80.00 rental _ #C861 - VI - 022
Helps students to develop a three - dimensional image of the teeth from the embryonic stage through maturity. Discusses hard tissue formation, root development and important epithelial - mesenchymal interactions. Presented by Dr Dennis O Overman.
Health and Safety; Science - Natural
Dist - HSCIC

The Tooth of the times 26 MIN
VHS
Ordinary people series
Color (G)
$190.00 purchase, $50.00 rental
Spends a day with Eddie, a fourth - generation farmer forced into bankruptcy by governmental changes in policies; Faan, a black laborer born and raised on the farm with Eddie; and Rudy, who is charged with auctioning away Eddie's life. Records the auction of Eddie's farm, along with all of his possessions, his herds, even his tools. An example of the widespread changes occurring in rural areas all over South Africa, which hurt farm laborers. Part of a series which chronicles an event in South Africa through the eyes of three or four 'ordinary' people, chosen to represent diverse backgrounds or dissimilar points of view. This current affairs series seeks to provide insight into the collective South African conscience.
Agriculture; Fine Arts; History - World
Dist - FIRS **Prod** - GAVSHO 1993

Tooth truth with Harv and Marv
U-matic / 16mm / VHS
Color (P)
LC 89-716028
Teaches the correct way to floss and brush teach. Looks at nutritious foods and smart snacks. Stresses the importance of good dental hygiene. Includes teacher's guide.
Health and Safety; Home Economics
Dist - HIGGIN **Prod** - HIGGIN 1989

Tooth Truth with Harv and Marv 11 MIN
16mm / U-matic / VHS
Color (P)
LC 76-702619
Show Harv and Marv as they visit a dentist's office and listen as Debbie and Jimmy learn the correct way to brush and floss their teeth and its importance to their future health.
Health and Safety
Dist - HIGGIN **Prod** - HIGGIN 1976

Toothbrushing - the Bass method 13 MIN
VHS / U-matic
Color (PRO C G)
$195.00 purchase _ #C870 - VI - 016
Introduces dental hygienists, dental assistants, nursing students and patients to the Bass method of toothbrushing. Presented by the Dental Education Center, Veterans Administration Medical Center, Washington, DC.
Health and Safety
Dist - HSCIC

Toothbrushing - the Bass Method 9 MIN
U-matic / VHS / 16mm
Color
Describes the Bass toothbrushing technique, emphasizing effective removal of bacterial plaque through frequent

toothbrushing. Demonstrates the technique on both a typodont and in the mouth of a patient. Shows changes in brush position and grip needed to reach all tooth surfaces.
Health and Safety
Dist - USNAC **Prod** - USVA 1981

Toothbrushing - the circular scrub method 13 MIN
VHS / U-matic
Color (PRO C G)
$195.00 purchase _ #C870 - VI - 017
Introduces dental hygienists, dental assistants, nursing students and patients to the circular scrub method of toothbrushing which is especially suited to the needs of the pediatric population. Presented by the Dental Education Center, Veterans Administration Medical Center, Washington, DC.
Health and Safety
Dist - HSCIC

Toothbrushing - the Circular Scrub Method 7 MIN
U-matic / VHS / 16mm
Color
Demonstrates effective removal of bacterial plaque through proper toothbrushing. Describes the circular scrub method using a soft multi - tufted toothbrush. Emphasizes changes in brush position and grip necessary for adequate cleaning of the various tooth surfaces.
Health and Safety
Dist - USNAC **Prod** - USVA 1981

Toothbrushing with Charlie Brown 5 MIN
16mm / VHS / BETA / U-matic
Color; PAL (P I)
PdS50, PdS58 purchase
Features Charlie Brown teaching Linus and Snoopy how to brush properly.
Health and Safety
Dist - EDPAT

The Toothpaste millionaire 15 MIN
VHS / U-matic
Book bird series
Color (I)
Tells a story about moneymaking that shows toothpaste sales is big business. From the book by Jean Merrill.
English Language; Literature and Drama
Dist - CTI **Prod** - CTI

Toothpicks 4 MIN
16mm
Mini Movies - Springboard for Learning - Unit 2, what do We Series
Color (P I)
LC 76-703095
Shows the many uses of the toothpick, from hors d'oeuvres to sculptures.
Fine Arts; Home Economics
Dist - MORLAT **Prod** - MORLAT 1975

Top 100 fishing tips 55 MIN
VHS
Color (G)
$29.95 purchase _ #0900
Presents 100 tips on freshwater fishing. Includes rod selection, baits, boats, reels, lures, lines, knots, depthfinders, casting errors, patterns, safety tips.
Physical Education and Recreation; Science - Natural
Dist - SEVVID

Top Axe 24 MIN
16mm
Color
LC 80-700929
Presents an account of the world's chopping and sawing championships.
Geography - World; Physical Education and Recreation
Dist - TASCOR **Prod** - TASCOR 1974

Top End 16 MIN
16mm
Color (H C A)
LC 73-709832
Studies four people who either own their own farms or work on the land in Australia's northern territory.
Agriculture; Geography - World; Social Science
Dist - AUIS **Prod** - ANAIB 1970

The Top five percent 55 MIN
VHS
Color (A PRO)
$85.50 purchase _ #585VU
Features Earl Nightingale in a presentation of the six steps necessary to join the top five percent of people in income, contribution to society, and overall happiness. Set includes a video, two audiocassettes and a progress guide.
Business and Economics; Psychology
Dist - NIGCON **Prod** - NIGCON

Top gun and beyond 58 MIN
U-matic / VHS
Nova series
Color (H C A)
$250.00 purchase _ #5271C
Talks about the fighter pilot's role in aerial combat.
Civics and Political Systems
Dist - CORF **Prod** - WGBHTV 1988

Top gun - the real story 35 MIN
VHS
Color (H C A)
$14.95 purchase
Takes an inside look at the Naval Fighter Weapons School, better known as 'Top Gun.' Documents the training that goes on there, and joins Navy fighter pilots as they fly assignments over Libya and the Indian Ocean.
Civics and Political Systems
Dist - PBS **Prod** - WNETTV

Top guns and toxic whales 52 MIN
VHS
Color (G)
$295.00 purchase, $95.00 rental
Challenges our traditional view of national security as being assured by elaborate armaments systems. Shows how environmental deterioration has now become the real threat to national and international security. Uses computer graphics to simulate a global environmental war room. Directed by Lawrence Moore.
Civics and Political Systems; Computer Science
Dist - CNEMAG

Top hat 99 MIN
VHS
B&W (G)
$19.95 purchase _ #S01390
Features Fred Astaire and Ginger Rogers in a musical about mistaken identities. Includes the Irving Berlin songs 'Top Hat, White Tie and Tails,' 'Cheek to Cheek,' and others.
Fine Arts
Dist - UILL **Prod** - RKOP
FI

Top Kid 52 MIN
U-matic / VHS
Winners from Down Under Series
Color (K)
$349.00, $249.00 purchase _ #AD - 1355
Reveals that Gary's good memory makes him the object of his classmates' jealousy until he becomes the star of a radio quiz program. Shows that Gary is faced with a moral dilemma when the program turns out to be rigged. Part of an eight - part series on children's winning over their circumstances produced by the Australian Children's Television Foundation.
Literature and Drama; Psychology
Dist - FOTH **Prod** - FOTH

Top of Europe 22 MIN
16mm
B&W
Illustrates the life of the Lapps on the north cape of Sweden.
Geography - World
Dist - AUDPLN **Prod** - ASI

Top of the Line 30 MIN
VHS / U-matic
Y E S Inc Series
Color (J H)
Helps young people learn to 'pay their dues' in order to achieve their aspirations. States that in addition to dreaming big dreams and getting excited about a bright future, one must also perform seemingly mundane but necessary tasks in a capable, committed and conscientious manner.
Guidance and Counseling; Psychology
Dist - GPN **Prod** - KCET 1983

Top of the trail 19 MIN
BETA / U-matic / VHS
Leopards, blankets and snow flakes - a 2 part documentary on the 'Apaloosa horse series
Color (I J H)
$29.95, $130.00 purchase _ #LSTF111
Explains the origins of the Appaloosa horse and its relationship to Native Americans. Takes a trail ride into the Rockies and explains each Biome - life zone - and the plants and animals that live there. Explains horse care on the trail. Part 1 of 2 parts produced by Nature Episodes.
Physical Education and Recreation; Science - Natural
Dist - FEDU

Top of the World - Taiga, Tundra and Ice Cap 20 MIN
16mm / U-matic / VHS
Captioned; Color (I J H)
Explores the remote areas of Canada, Siberia and Alaska. Shows how early inhabitants adapted to isolation and ponders effects of pollution and pipelines.
Geography - United States; Geography - World
Dist - LCOA **Prod** - LCOA 1972

The Top of the World - Taiga, Tundra and Ice Cap 19 MIN
U-matic / VHS / 16mm
Comparative Cultures and Geography Series
Color (I)
LC 72-701008
Shows the geographical characteristics and types of natural life to be found in the world's three northern - most regions, Canada, Siberia and Alaska. Suggests what the consequences might be should man seek to exploit the area's resources without sufficient concern for land and the balance of nature.
Geography - United States; Geography - World; Science - Natural; Social Science
Dist - LCOA **Prod** - LCOA 1972

Top secret 15 MIN
VHS
Books from cover to cover series
Color (P I G)
$25.00 purchase _ #BFCC - 109
Presents John Reynolds Gardiner's book 'Top Secret,' which centers around a nine - year - old boy named Allen who does his science project about human photosynthesis despite parental and teacher disapproval. Hosted by John Robbins.
Fine Arts; Literature and Drama
Dist - PBS **Prod** - WETATV 1988

Top Secret - a Friend's Cry for Help 30 MIN
VHS
Color (I)
LC 89700232
Helps establish guidelines to determine when a secret is too imporant to keep. Shows a teen who tells a friend she is thinking of suicide. The friend must decide whether to respect the request for confidence or get the help of a counselor.
Health and Safety; Psychology; Sociology
Dist - AIMS **Prod** - HRMC 1989

Topanga, Liberty and Mulholland Fires 20 MIN
16mm
Color
Shows footage of various fires in the Malibu area in Southern California in 1958. Without narration.
Health and Safety; Social Science
Dist - LAFIRE **Prod** - LAFIRE

Topaz 124 MIN
VHS
Color (G)
$59.95 purchase _ #S00910
Presents the Alfred Hitchcock Cold War tale of a high - ranking Soviet official who defects to the U S with classified information from the USSR. Stars Frederick Stafford, John Forsythe and John Vernon.
Fine Arts; Sociology
Dist - UILL

Topeka is a People Place 26 MIN
16mm
Color
LC 74-711543
Uses pictures, sound effects, music and occasional words to show various aspects that make Topeka, Kansas an enjoyable city in which to live.
Geography - United States
Dist - SWBELL **Prod** - SWBELL 1970

The Topic of cancer 56 MIN
VHS
Color (G)
$250.00 purchase
Follows comedian Andrew Denton's visit with young people who have cancer, bringing out their views that life goes on in spite of the difficulties surrounding the disease. Looks at chemotherapy's effects, remissions and relapses and other problems faced by cancer patients. Builds understanding for patients and their families and friends as well as for professionals.
Health and Safety
Dist - LANDMK

Topical Anesthesia for Endoscopic Examination of the Upper and Lower Airways 16 MIN
U-matic / VHS
Color (PRO)
Demonstrates the administration of topical anesthesia for an endoscopic examination by either the transnasal or transoral route. Emphasizes the material used, sequence of administration and precautions observed when using lidocaine.
Health and Safety; Science; Science - Natural
Dist - USNAC **Prod** - USVA

Topical anesthesia for endoscopic examination of upper and lower airways 15 MIN
VHS / 16mm

Endoscopy series; Bronchoscopy
(PRO)
$385.00 purchase _ #860VI057
Shows how to administer topical anesthesia for an endoscopic examination by either the transoral or transnasal route. Identifies areas requiring anesthesia and gives dosage limitations. Part of the Bronchoscopy Subseries.
Health and Safety
Dist - HSCIC **Prod** - HSCIC 1986

Topical Fluorides for Caries Prevention 10 MIN
16mm
Color (PRO)
LC 77-700088
Presents a story from bench to field of topical fluorides in caries prevention. Emphasizes fluoride mouth rinse and economy when used.
Health and Safety
Dist - USNAC **Prod** - NMAC 1975

Toplines 26 MIN
VHS
Clipping dairy cattle series; Vol 3
Color (G)
$49.95 purchase _ #6 - 099 - 103P
Discusses procedures for topline clipping of dairy cattle. Part 3 of a five - part series.
Agriculture
Dist - VEP **Prod** - VEP

Topographic anatomy of articular sites - Pt 1 - general and axial 20 MIN
U-matic / VHS / 16mm
Skeletal and topographic anatomy series
Color (C A)
Health and Safety; Science - Natural
Dist - TEF **Prod** - UTEXMH

Topographic anatomy of articular sites - Pt 2 - appendicular (upper extremity) 19 MIN
U-matic / VHS / 16mm
Skeletal and topographic anatomy series
Color (C A)
Health and Safety; Science - Natural
Dist - TEF **Prod** - UTEXMH

Topographic anatomy of articular sites - Pt 3 - appendicular (lower extremity) 20 MIN
16mm / U-matic / VHS
Skeletal and topographic anatomy series
Color (C A)
Health and Safety; Science - Natural
Dist - TEF **Prod** - UTEXMH

Topographic Anatomy of the Abdomen 18 MIN
16mm / U-matic / VHS
Skeletal and Topographic Anatomy Series
Color (C A)
Health and Safety; Science - Natural
Dist - TEF **Prod** - UTEXMH

Topographic Anatomy of the Back 20 MIN
U-matic / VHS / 16mm
Skeletal and Topographic Anatomy Series
Color (C A)
Health and Safety; Science - Natural
Dist - TEF **Prod** - UTEXMH

Topographic anatomy of the head and neck - Pt 1 - the neck 17 MIN
U-matic / VHS / 16mm
Skeletal and topographic anatomy series
Color (C A)
Health and Safety; Science - Natural
Dist - TEF **Prod** - UTEXMH

Topographic anatomy of the head and neck - Pt 2 - the face 12 MIN
U-matic / VHS / 16mm
Skeletal and topographic anatomy series
Color (C A)
Health and Safety; Science - Natural
Dist - TEF **Prod** - UTEXMH

Topographic anatomy of the head and neck - Pt 3 - the cranium 20 MIN
16mm / U-matic / VHS
Skeletal and topographic anatomy series
Color (C A)
Health and Safety; Science - Natural
Dist - TEF **Prod** - UTEXMH

Topographic anatomy of the head and neck - Pt 4 - the oral cavity 19 MIN
16mm / U-matic / VHS
Skeletal and topographic anatomy series
Color (C A)
Health and Safety; Science - Natural
Dist - TEF **Prod** - UTEXMH

Topographic anatomy of the lower extremity - Pt 1 - femoral, gluteal and popliteal regions 17 MIN
U-matic / VHS / 16mm
Skeletal and topographic anatomy series
Color (C A)
Health and Safety; Science - Natural
Dist - TEF **Prod** - UTEXMH

Topographic anatomy of the lower extremity - Pt 2 - knee, leg, ankle and foot 18 MIN
U-matic / VHS / 16mm
Skeletal and topographic anatomy series
Color (C A)
Health and Safety; Science - Natural
Dist - TEF **Prod** - UTEXMH

Topographic Anatomy of the Pelvis, Perineum and Inguinal Regions 18 MIN
16mm / U-matic / VHS
Skeletal and Topographic Anatomy Series
Color (C A)
Health and Safety; Science - Natural
Dist - TEF **Prod** - UTEXMH

Topographic anatomy of the thorax - Pt 1 - external features 19 MIN
U-matic / VHS / 16mm
Skeletal and topographic anatomy series
Color (C A)
Health and Safety; Science - Natural
Dist - TEF **Prod** - UTEXMH

Topographic anatomy of the thorax - Pt 2 - internal features 19 MIN
16mm / U-matic / VHS
Skeletal and topographic anatomy series
Color (C A)
Health and Safety; Science - Natural
Dist - TEF **Prod** - UTEXMH

Topographic Anatomy of the Upper and Lower Extremities - Nerve Injury 22 MIN
U-matic / VHS / 16mm
Skeletal and Topographic Anatomy Series
Color (C A)
Health and Safety; Science - Natural
Dist - TEF **Prod** - UTEXMH

Topographic anatomy of the upper extremity - Pt 2 - forearm, wrist and hand 15 MIN
U-matic / VHS / 16mm
Skeletal and topographic anatomy series
Color (C A)
Health and Safety; Science - Natural
Dist - TEF **Prod** - UTEXMH

Topographic Anatomy of the Upper Extremity, Shoulder, Axilla, Arm and Elbow 15 MIN
U-matic / VHS / 16mm
Skeletal and Topographic Anatomy Series
Color (C A)
Health and Safety; Science - Natural
Dist - TEF **Prod** - UTEXMH

Topographic and geological maps 51 MIN
VHS / U-matic
Basic and petroleum geology for non - geologists series; Structural
Color (IND)
Industrial and Technical Education; Science - Physical
Dist - GPCV **Prod** - PHILLP

Topographic maps 30 MIN
VHS
Color (J H)
$29.95 purchase _ #IV140
Reveals that topographic maps are graphic representations of selected human - made and natural features of a part of the Earth's surface plotted to a definite scale. Shows the location and shape of mountains, valleys and plains; the network of streams, rivers and the principle works of humans.
Geography - World
Dist - INSTRU

Topography, climate and vegetation 148 MIN
BETA / U-matic / VHS
Color (I J H)
$149.00 purchase _ #LSTF116
Includes three parts. Explains in the topography section that the Earth is full of bumps, scratches, wrinkles and folds that humans call mountains, valleys, oceans and canyons. Shows how the Earth's surface has evolved and the effects of unusual topographical features on human cultures. The climate section examines the factors that rule a region's climate and how habitats and cultures adapt to climate. The vegetation section looks at how the major vegetation regions - grasslands, rainforests - have affected human cultures. Shows how human culture is now affecting the Earth's vegetation, climate and topography.
Science - Natural; Science - Physical; Sociology
Dist - FEDU **Prod** - EDUCDE 1988

Topography - surface writing 37 MIN
16mm
Color (G)
$35.00 rental
Uses violence - physical, psychological and environmental - as the main theme without resorting to the conventional representation of violence as spectacle or drama. Attempts to show how integrated violence is in the very fabric of American lives. Produced by Jeffrey Skoller.
Fine Arts; History - United States; Sociology
Dist - CANCIN

The Topological constraints on analysis by Raoul H Bott 60 MIN
VHS
AMS - MAA joint lecture series
Color (C PRO)
$59.00 purchase _ #VIDBOTT - VB2
Focuses on two mathematical paradigms of this century - the maximal principle which Bott shows is 'quantified' by Morse theory, and the Brower Fixed Point Theorem. Connects the Brower theorem to the ideas of Lefschetz and to sheaf theory. Describes the completely new view that sheaf theory brought to cohomology. Discusses Hirzebruch's Riemann - Roch formula. Includes commentary on mathematicians Atiyah, Serre, Kodaira, Hirzebruch and a fanciful proof of the Riemenn - Roch theorem. Recorded in Providence.
Mathematics
Dist - AMSOC **Prod** - AMSOC 1988

Topology 30 MIN
16mm
MAA individual lecturers series
B&W (C)
Professor Raoul Bott introduces topology with contrasting notions of geometrical equivalence. Professor Marston Morse, with the aid of models and charts, describes the basic ideas of topological critical point theory.
Mathematics
Dist - MLA **Prod** - MAA 1966

Topology
16mm
B&W
Shows that by considering more general forms of transformation one can extend the congruence classes of Euclidean geometry to much wider equivalence classes.
Mathematics
Dist - OPENU **Prod** - OPENU

Topology - Closure
16mm
; Pt 4
B&W
Introduces the concept of a closed set in a topological space. Presents a construction for the closure of an arbitrary set in a space and relates the ideas of closure and continuity to each other.
Mathematics
Dist - OPENU **Prod** - OPENU

Topology - continuity
16mm
; Pt 2
B&W
Investigates the continuity of a specific function.
Mathematics
Dist - OPENU **Prod** - OPENU

Topology I 20 MIN
U-matic / VHS
Shapes of geometry series; Pt 1
Color (H)
LC 82-707387
Presents Beth McKenna and David Edmonds discussing 'rubber sheet geometry' and illustrating basic terms and definitions such as topological transformations and equivalent figures. Investigates some of the properties of the Moebius strip.
Mathematics
Dist - GPN **Prod** - WVIZTV 1982

Topology II 20 MIN
U-matic / VHS
Shapes of geometry series; Pt 2
Color (H)
LC 82-707388
Presents Beth McKenna and David Edmonds discussing the Klein bottle, Leonhard Euler and the Koenigsburg Bridge

problem. Deals with the topics of networks and Euler's theorem and the application of the theorem to the Platonic solids.
Mathematics
Dist - GPN **Prod** - WVIZTV 1982

Topology - Induced Topologies
16mm
; Pt 5
B&W
Considers a problem in topology involving the creation of a continuous map.
Mathematics
Dist - OPENU **Prod** - OPENU

Topology - introduction
16mm
; Pt 1
B&W
Offers an introduction to topology. Gives the four properties of a general distance function, or metric.
Mathematics
Dist - OPENU **Prod** - OPENU

Topology Series
Regular Homotopies in the Plane, Pt 1 16 MIN
Regular Homotopies in the Plane, Pt 2 19 MIN
Space Filling Curves 26 MIN
Turning a Sphere Inside Out 23 MIN
Dist - IFB

Topology short films series
The Butterfly catastrophe 5 MIN
Limit Curves and Curves of Infinite Length 14 MIN
Limit Surfaces and Space Filling Curves 11 MIN
Sierpinski's Curve Fills Space 5 MIN
Zooms on Self - Similar Figures 8 MIN
Dist - IFB

Topology - some historical concepts 22 MIN
16mm
Color
LC 74-700696
Uses diagrammatic animation in a presentation of some qualitative concepts of topology, including transformations, Jordan curve theorem, existence solutions and fixed points.
Mathematics
Dist - CLI **Prod** - CLI 1974

Topology - summary
16mm
B&W (C)
Summarizes topological concepts, giving particular emphasis to the Brouwer fixed point theorem.
Mathematics
Dist - OPENU **Prod** - OPENU

Topology - topological spaces
16mm
; Pt 3
B&W
Introduces the notion of a topological space and uses the framework of topological spaces to study continuous functions.
Mathematics
Dist - OPENU **Prod** - OPENU

Topology with Raoul Bott and Marston Morse 30 MIN
16mm
Mathematics today series
B&W (C)
LC FIA66-1279
Presents a discussion on topology with Raoul Bott and Marston Morse. Professor Bott uses models, charts and other devices to introduce the subject of topology. Professor Morse describes the basic ideas of topological critical point theory. John Mackenzie moderates.
Mathematics
Dist - MLA **Prod** - WNEDTV 1966

Topping Off the CN Tower 30 MIN
U-matic / VHS
Color
Illustrates the topping of the Canadian National Tower. Shows how the final 32 feet of the mast were put in place by helicopter, an unparalleled 'high wire' act.
Industrial and Technical Education
Dist - MPS **Prod** - AISC

Tops 8 MIN
U-matic / VHS / 16mm
Eames Film Collection Series
Color (J H C)
LC 74-700425
Reveals how tops are wound or prepared, how they are launched, how they spin, whirl and wobble and how they die.
Physical Education and Recreation; Science - Physical
Dist - EBEC **Prod** - EAMES 1973

Topsoil and Vegetation 9 MIN
U-matic / VHS / 16mm
Color (J)
Shows how topsoil is formed. Stresses that cultivable land is in short supply in the world and that the land needs to be treated more carefully.
Agriculture; Science - Natural
Dist - AIMS **Prod** - NORSK 1977

Topsy - Turvy 9 MIN
16mm
Look again series
Color (P I J)
$150.00, $195.00 purchase, $25.00 rental
Presents a film in the Look Again series, without dialogue. Builds upon and develops children's natural interest in their surroundings. Looks at a young boy's dream world where anything can happen and wonders about magic in the world of fantasy. Students in intermediate grades will want to discuss their own 'magic tricks.' Younger children can make hypotheses about why some events cannot really happen.
Psychology
Dist - BULFRG **Prod** - NFBC 1990

Topsy - turvy elephant 28 MIN
VHS
Elephant show series
Color (P I)
$95.00 purchase, $45.00 rental
Presents program 36 in the Sharon, Lois and Bram's Elephant Show series. Teaches reading readiness and social skills while engaging children in making music. Each program explores a new theme through adventure, fantasy, mystery and song with recording artists Sharon, Lois and Bram. Uses traditional materials which stress participation - action songs, sing - along songs, story songs, clapping songs, singing games, playground chants and folk songs from many different traditions. Includes teacher's guide co - authored by a music education specialist.
Fine Arts; Sociology
Dist - BULFRG **Prod** - CAMBFP 1991

Topsy turvy house 11 MIN
U-matic / VHS / 16mm
Color (P)
$270.00, $190.00 purchase _ #3506
Tells a story of a place where things go backward, such as pencils erasing, erasers writing, and beds making themselves. Discusses motivation in building vocabulary.
English Language
Dist - CORF **Prod** - CORF 1975

Tora - san goes to Vienna 109 MIN
VHS / 35mm
Color (G) (JAPANESE WITH ENGLISH SUBTITLES)
$300.00 rental
Offers the 41st chapter in the world's longest - running film series. Discovers Tora in Vienna with a suicidal businessman. Directed by Yoji Yamada.
Fine Arts
Dist - KINOIC

Tora, Tora, Tora 144 MIN
VHS / U-matic / BETA
Color (J H C A)
$129.00 purchase _ #05670 94
Presents the story of the Japanese attack on Pearl Harbor on December 7, 1941, as retold from both the Americans and Japanese viewpoints. Stars Jason Robards and E G Marshall.
Fine Arts; History - United States
Dist - GA **Prod** - GA 1970
ASPRSS
RMIBHF

The Torch and the Torso - Miguel Berrocal 14 MIN
16mm
B&W
LC FIA66-1368
Pictures the work of Spanish sculptor Miguel Berrocal. Shows him in his studio where he makes metal figures, using a panoply of elements and tools to produce extra ordinary forms which may be disassembled and re - assembled. Filmed in Spain.
Fine Arts
Dist - RADIM **Prod** - ENGLEJ 1966

The Torch has been passed - a history of the early '60s
VHS
Color (I J H)
$55.00 purchase _ #5488VD
Describes major events in the United States during the 1960s. Reveals how American confidence was high due to prosperity, and because the country had a young President with military and diplomatic power. Tells how the 1960s were also a time of turmoil and disenchantment, and a time when values were being questioned. Explores the roots of this important turning point in US history. Includes a resource guide.
Biography; Civics and Political Systems; History - United States; Sociology
Dist - KNOWUN

The Torch is Lit 26 MIN
16mm
Winston Churchill - the Valiant Years Series no 11
B&W
LC FI67-2117
Describes British losses in Libya and Egypt using documentary footage. Shows scenes of the fall of Tobruk, Churchill's meeting with Roosevelt in June of 1942, and of the landings by the allies in Algeria on November 8, 1942. Based on the book 'The Second World War,' by Winston S Churchill.
History - World
Dist - SG **Prod** - ABCTV 1961

The Torch is passed 30 MIN
VHS
Color (H C G)
$295.00 purchase, $55.00 rental
Examines the origins of the student movement of the 1960s. Tells the story of SLATE, the student political group founded at Berkeley, and looks at what the members are doing today. Gives insight into the McCarthy era and political activism on college campuses.
History - United States
Dist - FLMLIB

Torch Safety 13 MIN
U-matic / VHS
Steel Making Series
Color (IND)
Presents the safety procedures and equipment required for the safe operation of a torch.
Business and Economics; Health and Safety; Industrial and Technical Education
Dist - LEIKID **Prod** - LEIKID

Torch Welding 17 MIN
16mm
How to Weld Aluminum Series
B&W
Shows how to make a good torch weld and gives examples of torch welding aluminum forgings. Pictures castings and aluminum sheet and plate.
Industrial and Technical Education
Dist - USDIBM **Prod** - USDIBM 1946

Torchlight - Part IV
VHS
America the bountiful series
Color (G)
$89.95 purchase _ #6 - 402 - 004A
Focuses on the late 1800s as George Washington Carver arrives in Iowa and becomes one of America's great scientists. Reveals that farm prices are dropping and farmers are struggling as Henry Wallace uses the press to advance agricultural interests and reform the railroads, but many rural Americans begin to leave the farm for industrial cities. Part of a six - part series on the history of American agriculture hosted by Ed Begley, Jr.
Agriculture; Biography; History - United States; Sociology
Dist - VEP **Prod** - VEP 1993

Tordon - a Global Solution to a Global Problem 18 MIN
16mm
Color
Shows the use of tordon to rid croplands and pasturelands of weeds and shrubs.
Agriculture
Dist - DCC **Prod** - DCC

Torment 30 MIN
VHS
Cinematic eye series
Color (H)
$69.95 purchase, $40.00 rental
Considers the European movie 'Torment' within the context of its cultural, social and political milieu. Part 1 of a four - part series which reappraises classic European films as historic documents, aesthetic statements and as entertainment. Written and narrated by Benjamin Dunlap.
Fine Arts; History - World
Dist - SCETV **Prod** - SCETV 1977

The Torment of Joan of Arc 22 MIN
16mm / U-matic / VHS
You are There Series
Color (I J H)
LC 72-700118
Shows turbulent France during the 15th century and a young peasant girl, Joan of Arc, who is on trial for heresy and treason. Explains that by refusing to deny the charges against her, Joan faces the penalty of being burned at the stake.
Biography; Geography - World; History - World
Dist - PHENIX **Prod** - CBSTV 1972

Torn between two fathers 45 MIN
VHS
Color (J H C G)
$250.00 purchase, $75.00 rental
Tells of 15 - year - old Debbie's desire to live with her hearing - impaired stepfather and younger brother after her mother is killed in an automobile accident. Reveals that how her natural father asserts custody rights and moves her to another town. Shows how Debbie negotiates an agreement allowing her to choose where she will live after arranging a face - to - face meeting between her two fathers with the help of an independent - minded friend and a sympathetic attorney. live.
Sociology
Dist - CF **Prod** - CF 1989

Torn curtain 119 MIN
VHS
Color (G)
$49.95 purchase _ #S00911
Presents Alfred Hitchcock's tale about a defector who is really a double agent. Shows that the defector is embarrassed when his wife follows him into East Germany. Stars Paul Newman, Julie Andrews, Wolfgang Kieling, Ludwig Donath, Lila Kedrova, and others.
Fine Arts
Dist - UILL

Tornado 3 MIN
16mm
Color (G)
$5.00 rental
Utilizes different film stocks picked off the editing room floor to create a variety of images and light by Ar Garfield.
Fine Arts
Dist - CANCIN

Tornado 14 MIN
U-matic / VHS / 16mm
Your Chance to Live Series
Color (J H T)
Shows the nearly tragic event of a tornado that traps three young people. Presents the tornado's devastation of a nearby town.
Health and Safety; History - World; Science - Physical
Dist - CORF **Prod** - USDCPA 1972

Tornado - a Spotter's Guide 16 MIN
16mm
Color (A)
LC 78-700357
Explains methods of visually detecting and reporting severe storms and tornadoes.
Science; Science - Physical
Dist - USNAC **Prod** - USNWS 1977

Tornado Below 15 MIN
16mm
Rediscovery Series
Color
LC 75-702463
Explains how tornadoes are formed, gives their characteristics and tells of the destruction they cause. Relates this information to work being done in the laboratory to better understand the tornado and stresses the importance of information from early warning weather satellites.
History - World; Science; Science - Physical
Dist - USNAC **Prod** - NASA 1975

Tornado below
VHS
Color (I J H)
$29.95 purchase _ #IV184
Portrays a young female student pilot who almost gets caught in the path of a tornado on her first solo flight. Explains how tornadoes are formed, their characteristics and the destruction they cause. Discusses laboratory work being done to better understand tornadoes and the importance of information from early warning weather satellites in reducing casualties.
History - World; Science - Physical
Dist - INSTRU

Tornado Disaster Action 4 MIN
16mm
Color
Uses animation to illustrate the steps that can be taken to protect lives and property in areas under official tornado warning.
Health and Safety; Science - Physical; Sociology
Dist - AMRC **Prod** - AMRC 1968

Tornado preparedness
VHS
Color (I J H)
$29.95 purchase _ #IV190
Provides statistics on tornadoes and classifies them by intensity and watch - warning capability. Advocates community planning. Discusses the warning dissemination systems so that viewers can act quickly and make correct judgments - often the difference between life and death. Shows some of the larger, more destructive tornadoes and the damage they caused to schools and mobile homes.
History - World; Science - Physical
Dist - INSTRU **Prod** - USNWSD

Tornado Safety 10 MIN
16mm / VHS
Adventures of Safety Frog Series
Color (K P I)
$195.00, $240.00 purchase, $50.00 rental _ #9981
Teaches children safety procedures during a tornado.
Health and Safety; History - World
Dist - AIMS **Prod** - AIMS 1988

Tornadoes 29 MIN
Videoreel / VT2
Weather Series
Color
Features meteorologist Frank Sechrist showing where the tornado forms in the cumulonimbus cloud and illustrating the anatomy of the tornado. Explains the difference between tornadoes, water spouts and sand storms and describes the conditions necessary for a tornado to develop.
Science - Physical
Dist - PBS **Prod** - WHATV

Tornadoes - the entity 60 MIN
VHS
Color (J H C)
$32.95 purchase _ #113
Looks at the effects of 46 tornadoes over the past 40 years. Includes nine minutes of footage of the killer Andover, Kansas tornado of 1991. Illustrates baseball sized hail and the terrifying sound of the violent storm.
Science - Physical
Dist - INSTRU

Toro landscape irrigation series
Elements of residential design 21 MIN
Residential installation techniques 20 MIN
Dist - VEP

Toro technical skills series
Gives step - by - step instructions on the basics of installing an irrigation system. Teaches site layout, laying out heads, pipe installation, how to make pipe connections, valve installation, how to make riser assemblies, controller installation and how to set the heads.
Toro technical skills series 20 MIN
Dist - VEP

The Toronto passion play 55 MIN
VHS
Color (G C H)
$279.00 purchase _ #DL475
Recreates the spectacle, pageantry, and complexity of a large medieval production. Uses Ludus Coventriae as a basis, the only extant medieval cycle passion play that presents events in continuous action. Historical information is provided between scenes.
Fine Arts
Dist - INSIM

Toronto - the Queen City 14 MIN
16mm
Color
LC FIA68-1230
Surveys the city of Toronto and its tourist attractions.
Geography - World
Dist - MORLAT **Prod** - MORLAT 1968

Torques and Gyroscopes 30 MIN
U-matic / VHS / 16mm
Mechanical Universe Series
Color (C A)
Explains why a spinning top doesn't topple, how a torque acts on a spinning object causing the angular momentum to change but the object only precesses.
Science - Physical
Dist - FI **Prod** - ANNCPB

Torquing 11 MIN
16mm
Color (IND)
Demonstrates the utilization of torque in tightening threaded fasteners with emphasis on the use of washers and proper lubrication. Shows three methods of torquing and the recommended procedures for installing flanges or manway covers.
Industrial and Technical Education
Dist - MOKIN **Prod** - MOKIN

Torrential rains 27 MIN
16mm
Color (JAPANESE)
Explains that ruins of a legendary town Kusado - Sengen - Cho were found in the Ashida River bed in the western part of Fukuyama city. Points out that torrential rains destroyed this town several hundred years ago. Tells how factors causing torrential rains are being studied with the help of today's science and technology and that it may soon be possible to forecast such downpours.
Science - Physical
Dist - UNIJAP **Prod** - UNIJAP 1969

Torres - Garcia and the Universal Constructivism 30 MIN
VHS / U-matic / 16mm
Color (G) (SPANISH)
LC 75-700628; 75-700627
Discusses the life and works of Uruguayan painter Joaquin Torres - Garcia.
Fine Arts
Dist - MOMALA **Prod** - OOAS MOMALA 1975

Torse 55 MIN
16mm
Color (G)
Provides a complete archival record of the choreography of the dance, approximating the spectator's experience of viewing the work. Projects two synchronous films simultaneously.
Fine Arts
Dist - CUNDAN **Prod** - NYPL 1977

Tort Law 29 MIN
Videoreel / VT2
Just Generation Series
Color (H C A)
Focuses on tort law, the laws that deal with personal injury. Presents a skit by the Ace Trucking Company, which brings up the question of fault in an accident. Prompts a discussion of whether or not the idea of fault is a valid basis for settling such cases.
Civics and Political Systems; Sociology
Dist - PBS **Prod** - WITFTV 1972

Tort law - the legal regulation of mental health professionals - Tape 4
VHS
Law and persons with mental disability series
Color (C PRO G)
$95.00 purchase
Discusses cases brought on behalf of mentally disabled individuals against their treaters. Focuses on instances of sexual misconduct and improper medication, and cases in which mentally disabled persons are third parties. Considers some of the internal ambivalence in court decisions in this area. Weighs those areas of tort law where future impact litigation can be expected. Part of a six - part series featuring Michael I Perlin, JD on the law and persons with mental disability. Serves as a resource for attorneys practicing mental disability law. Advocates working with mentally disabled individuals, mental health professionals, hospital administrators and other care providers subject to legal regulation.
Civics and Political Systems; Psychology
Dist - BAXMED

Tortillas and Tacos 18 MIN
U-matic / VHS
Color (PRO)
Shows how to make tortillas and use them in preparing tacos.
Home Economics; Industrial and Technical Education
Dist - CULINA **Prod** - CULINA

The Tortoise and the Hare 30 MIN
VHS / U-matic
Reading Rainbow Series
Color (P)
Presents the classic story of The Tortoise And The Hare retold and illustrated by Janet Stevens and narrated by Gilda Radner. Shows host LeVar Burton in a paraphrase of the classic, competing in a bicycle race with top Hawaiian bicyclists, then deciding to tackle the tough Marine obstacle course, thus proving that 'winners' must try hard and do their best.
English Language; Literature and Drama; Physical Education and Recreation
Dist - GPN **Prod** - WNEDTV

Tortoise and the hare 9 MIN
16mm / U-matic / VHS
Color (P I) (FRENCH)
A cartoon telling the story of the persistent tortoise who wins a race with the over - confident hare. Illustrates the qualities of modesty and perseverance.
Guidance and Counseling; Literature and Drama
Dist - CORF **Prod** - DISNEY 1954

Tortoise and the Hare 15 MIN
16mm
Color
Features Grady Nutt giving a blow - by - blow account of the Identiapolis, which is the result of Harry Turtle challenging the boastful Jacques Rabbit to a race. Using tactics and patience Harry crosses the finish line first and proves that he too is worth something.
Guidance and Counseling; Religion and Philosophy
Dist - BROADM **Prod** - BROADM 1976

Torts practice - recent developments - 1992 150 MIN
Cassette
CEB 1992 recent developments programs series
Color (PRO)
$149.00, $89.00 purchase, $69.00 rental _ #TO-65234, #TO-55234, #TO-65234-63
Highlights and analyzes the most significant developments in torts practice for the past year, and offers practical tips from all perspectives - plaintiff, defense, personal injury, and business and commercial tort litigation. Includes handbook. Also available in 1991 version.
Civics and Political Systems
Dist - CCEB **Prod** - CCEB 1992

Torts - You as a Victim 29 MIN
U-matic
You and the Law Series Lesson 8
Color (C A)
Examines principles and applications of tort law that protect victims of injurious acts. Defines a tort. Enumerates freedoms or inherent rights of all individuals.
Civics and Political Systems
Dist - CDTEL **Prod** - COAST

Torts - You as Accused 29 MIN
U-matic
You and the Law Series Lesson 9
Color (C A)
Defines defenses available to a person accused of torts. Discusses how insurance can provide protection from financial loss for someone accused of wrongdoing.
Civics and Political Systems
Dist - CDTEL **Prod** - COAST

Tortuous mountain path 88 MIN
VHS
Color (G) (MANDARIN)
$45.00 purchase _ #1075B
Presents a movie produced in the People's Republic of China.
Fine Arts
Dist - CHTSUI

Torture 57 MIN
U-matic / VHS
Social Issue Series
Color (G)
$160.00, $110.00 purchase, $60.00, $40.00 rental
Documents torture graphically through news footage. Presents the personal testimonies of torture victims and activists opposed to it. Reveals that torture continues to be a tool of modern governments' efforts to control their peoples. Produced by Robert Byrd.
Civics and Political Systems; Sociology
Dist - IAFC

The Torture of Mothers 60 MIN
16mm
Color
Presents a documentary re - creation of the case known as the Harlem Six from the Harlem riot in the summer of 1964. Shows the inability of the mothers of the six to deal with the criminal justice system. Includes original tape recordings of the mothers' statements. Based on the book by Truman Nelson.
Civics and Political Systems; Sociology
Dist - BLKFMF **Prod** - BLKFMF

The Torture of mothers
VHS
Color (G)
$89.95 purchase
Portrays the events of 1964 in Harlem when a group of black youths overturned a vegetable stand. Reveals that what might have been an innocent prank turned into arrests and riots. Examines how African Americans are often powerless to defend themselves against police brutality and fabricated indictments. Uses the original statements of a mother to recreate the temper and fear in Harlem during the 1964 riots.
Civics and Political Systems; History - United States
Dist - ROLAND **Prod** - BLKFMF

Tortured dust 90 MIN
16mm
Color (G)
$135.00 rental
Meditates upon Miss MacIntosh, My Darling by Marquerite Young.
Fine Arts
Dist - CANCIN **Prod** - BRAKS 1984

The Tortured mind - Shakespeare workshop 1 60 MIN
VHS
Shakespeare workshop series
Color; PAL (J H C G)
PdS29.50 purchase
Gives an introduction to Shakespearean tragedy through an examination of key scenes from four of his plays. Shows how Shakespeare explores the minds of his characters Ophelia, Othello, Lady Macbeth and Lear. Offers insights into past and present interpretations and styles of presentation and acting. Part of a three - part series.
Fine Arts; Literature and Drama
Dist - EMFVL

Torvill and Dean - path to perfection 52 MIN
VHS
Color (G)
$19.95 purchase _ #S02093
Profiles the British skating pair of Jayne Torvill and Christopher Dean, who won a gold medal in the 1984 Olympics. Features excerpts from eight of their best performances.
Physical Education and Recreation
Dist - UILL

Tosca 123 MIN
VHS
Color (G) (ITALIAN WITH ENGLISH SUBTITLES)
$39.95 purchase _ #1213
Presents the Australian Opera production of 'Tosca' by Puccini, starring Eva Marton, John Shaw and Lamberto Furlan.
Fine Arts
Dist - KULTUR **Prod** - WNETTV
PBS

Tosca 120 MIN
VHS
Color (S) (ITALIAN)
$39.95 purchase _ #623 - 9406
Presents the Arena di Verona production of 'Tosca' by Puccini. Stars Eva Marton and Giacomo Aragall.
Fine Arts; Foreign Language; Geography - World
Dist - FI **Prod** - NVIDC 1986

Tosca 127 MIN
VHS
Metropolitan opera series
Color (G) (ITALIAN WITH ENGLISH SUBTITLES)
$29.95 purchase
Stars Hildegard Behrens, Placido Domingo, Cornell MacNeil, and Italo Tajo in a performance of 'Tosca' by Puccini. Conducted by Guiseppe Sinopoli. Includes a brochure with plot, historic notes, photographs, and production credits.
Fine Arts
Dist - PBS **Prod** - WNETTV 1985

Tosca 127 MIN
VHS
Color (S) (ITALIAN)
$29.95 purchase _ #384 - 9370
Presents 'Tosca' by Puccini in a Metropolitan Opera production directed by Franco Zeffirelli. Features Giuseppe Sinopoli as conductor, Hildegarde Behrens as lead and Placido Domingo.
Fine Arts; Foreign Language
Dist - FI **Prod** - PAR 1988

Toscanini - the Maestro 74 MIN
VHS
Color (S)
$39.95 purchase _ #055 - 9004
Presents rare footage of the Toscanini family, as well as conversations between the maestro and notables such as Serkin, Horowitz, Segovia and Menotti. Features throughout the NBC Symphony Orchestra, including the 1943 recording session of 'Hymn of Nations' by Verdi with Jan Peerce and the Westminster College Choir. Conductor Arturo Toscanini dominated the orchestral scene for more than 50 years.
Fine Arts
Dist - FI **Prod** - VAI 1988

Toscanini - the Maestro 60 MIN
U-matic / VHS
Color
Presents a musical portrait of Toscanini. Includes tapes of television performances and home movies. Examines the extent of his influence in music.
Fine Arts
Dist - FOTH **Prod** - ROPE

Toscanini - the Maestro and Verdi's Hymn of the Nations
VHS / U-matic
Color (G)
Presents rare home movies plus interviews with Bidu Sayao, Robert Merrill and others on the life of Toscanini. Includes Verdi's Hymn of the Nations featuring Jan Peerce.
Fine Arts
Dist - VAI **Prod** - VAI

Tosca's Kiss
U-matic / VHS
Color (G) (ITALIAN (ENGLISH SUBTITLES))
Presents a film by Daniel Schmid which looks at the current residents of Casa Verdi, the musician's retirement home founded by Verdi in 1902.
Fine Arts; Foreign Language
Dist - VAI **Prod** - VAI

Total Anomalies Pulmonary Venous Drainage 15 MIN
16mm
Color
LC FIA66-70
Demonstrates a method of complete repair of total anomalous pulmonary venous drainage. Shows step by step an operation performed on an eight - year - boy who had exertional dyspnea, cyanosis, clubbing of the nails and the typical mediastinal configuration.
Health and Safety
Dist - EATONL **Prod** - EATONL 1961

The Total athlete 30 MIN
VHS
Color (G)
$79.95 purchase _ #CCP0017V
Presents the concept of the 'total athlete' - a well - rounded person who participates in all areas of life. Covers subjects including success in academics at the college level, attitudes, communication skills, drugs, professional sports, and life after sports. Includes a student guide.
Physical Education and Recreation; Science - Natural
Dist - CAMV **Prod** - CAMV 1989

Total body massage 10 MIN
Videoreel / VT2
Janaki series
Color
Physical Education and Recreation
Dist - PBS **Prod** - WGBHTV

Total Body Workout 60 MIN
VHS
Color (G C A)
$19.95 purchase _ #KVC60006V ; $24.95 _ #WW300V
Uses aerobics and weight training in a cross training format.
Physical Education and Recreation
Dist - CAMV **Prod** - CAMV

Total Colectomy 27 MIN
16mm
Color
Shows the isolation of the distal ileum, the performance of an anal ileostomy, the excision of the two proximal stomata and the re - establishment of ileal continuity by anastomosis as an optional procedure if warranted by nutritional state and sphincter control.
Health and Safety; Science - Natural
Dist - USVA **Prod** - USVA 1957

Total Colectomy for Ulcerative Colitis in Corticosteroid Treated Patients 25 MIN
16mm
Color (PRO)
Illustrates one stage total colectomy with combined abdominoperineal resection for ulcerative colitis in a corticosteroid treated patient.
Health and Safety; Science
Dist - ACY **Prod** - ACYDGD 1961

Total coliform determination in drinking water - M F technique - membrane filtration procedure 21 MIN
BETA / VHS
Color
Discusses water purification, water reuse, and water and wastewater technology.
Health and Safety; Science; Social Science
Dist - RMIBHF **Prod** - RMIBHF

Total Coliform Determination in Drinking Water - Membrane Filtration Technique - Introduction 4 MIN
VHS / BETA
Color
Discusses water purification and drinking water, and provides an introduction to water analysis.
Health and Safety; Industrial and Technical Education; Social Science
Dist - RMIBHF **Prod** - RMIBHF

Total coliform determination in drinking water, membrane filtration technique, sample collection 10 MIN
BETA / VHS
Color
Discusses water purification, drinking water, and sample collection in water analysis.
Health and Safety; Industrial and Technical Education; Science; Social Science
Dist - RMIBHF **Prod** - RMIBHF

Total Communication 15 MIN
16mm
Western Maryland College Series
Color (C A)
LC 74-706283
Explains and demonstrates total communication. Shows a preschool class of deaf children and interviews parents of young deaf children.

Education; Guidance and Counseling; Psychology; Social Science
Dist - USNAC **Prod** - WMARYC 1973

A Total concept of youth ministry - Tape 1 30 MIN
VHS
Catching the rainbow videos series
Color (G A R)
$29.95 purchase, $10.00 rental _ #35 - 899200 - 1
Uses visual aids, music and mime to present a unique approach to youth ministry. Hosted by author and lecturer J David Stone.
Religion and Philosophy
Dist - APH **Prod** - ABINGP

The Total Environment Range 22 MIN
16mm
Color
LC 75-701738
Describes the mission and capabilities of the U S Navy's Pacific Missile Range Facility, Hawaiian area.
Civics and Political Systems; History - United States; Industrial and Technical Education
Dist - USNAC **Prod** - USN 1973

Total Fitness for Busy Professionals 56 MIN
VHS
Color (G)
$39.95 purchase _ #20144
Features Judy Greenan. Presents 35 minutes of safe - for - the - body aerobics, do - at - the - desk exercises and information about nutrition.
Health and Safety; Physical Education and Recreation; Psychology
Dist - CARTRP **Prod** - CARTRP

Total Fitness in 30 Minutes a Week 30 MIN
U-matic / VHS / 16mm
Color (H C A) (SPANISH)
LC 77-701117
Demonstrates how to develop a personal fitness program, regardless of age, weight, sex, occupation or present physical condition. Explains why exercise is essential to fitness. Adapted from the book Total Fitness In 30 Minutes A Week by Laurence E Morehouse.
Physical Education and Recreation
Dist - PFP **Prod** - PFP 1976

Total Gastrectomy in Ulcerogenic Tumor of the Pancreas 29 MIN
16mm
Color (PRO)
Presents a female patient harboring a malignant ulcerogenic tumor of the pancreas with intractable diarrhea of at least 10 years duration. Includes the effects on small bowel motility and their pertinent steps of total gastrectomy with an end to side esophagojejunostomy and jejuno - jejunostomy.
Health and Safety; Science
Dist - ACY **Prod** - ACYDGD 1963

Total Gastrectomy using the Abdominothoracic Approach 39 MIN
16mm
Color (PRO)
Explains that from the technical point of view, total gastrectomy performed through the ordinary abdominal incision may be exceedingly difficult. Demonstrates the superiority of the abdominothoracic approach.
Health and Safety; Science
Dist - ACY **Prod** - ACYDGD 1955

Total Gastrectomy with Jejunal Interposition 23 MIN
16mm
Color (PRO)
Presents a method whereby a segment of the proximal jejunum is employed to replace the stomach and reestablish continuity between the esophagus and duodenum. Demonstrates total gastrectomy performed in the treatment of malignant gastric neoplasms and accompanied by splenectomy and excision of the omentum.
Health and Safety; Science
Dist - ACY **Prod** - ACYDGD 1960

Total Golf Savings Strokes with Bruce Crampton 90 MIN
VHS
(H C A)
$49.95 purchase _ #UH1200V
Presents golf champion Bruce Crampton who discusses many aspects of golf including wedge and sand shots, driving and tee shots, grip, stroke, and more. Offers tips on improving performance.
Physical Education and Recreation
Dist - CAMV

Total Health 60 MIN
VHS / U-matic
Color
$300 rental
Discusses holistic medicine and its impact on church and society. Includes discussions with Norman Cousins, Joyce Brothers, Ray Stevens, C. Norman Shealy, and James Gordon.
Health and Safety
Dist - CCNCC **Prod** - CCNCC 1985

Total health 60 MIN
U-matic / VHS
Color (J A)
Gives a comprehensive look at a new form of medical practice called 'holistic medicine'. Looks at holistic centers across the nation where the body, mind and spirit are taken into consideration as religion and medicine combine to comfort both the young and the old.
Health and Safety
Dist - ECUFLM **Prod** - NBCNEW 1980

Total Hip Joint Replacement
U-matic / VHS
Color (ARABIC SPANISH)
Shows how the hip joint can degenerate to the point where total replacement is necessary. Describes the surgical procedures and therapy required along with the results that can be expected.
Foreign Language; Health and Safety; Science - Natural
Dist - MIFE **Prod** - MIFE

Total Hip Prostheses 48 MIN
VHS / U-matic
Color
Shows a total hip prostheses including pre - operation planning, surgical techniques and special techniques and complications. Explains the procedure in three parts.
Health and Safety
Dist - SPRVER **Prod** - SPRVER

Total Hip Prosthesis 34 MIN
16mm
Color
Shows the anatomical and mechanical design of binding - type total hip prosthesis made of titanium alloy. Explains that the prosthesis is combined of three parts.
Health and Safety; Science - Natural
Dist - UNIJAP **Prod** - UNIJAP 1971

Total hip replacement - patient education 24 MIN
VHS
Color (PRO C)
$250.00 purchase, $70.00 rental _ #4414
Provides information patients need before they have total hip replacement surgery. Begins with a discussion of the anatomy and physiology of the hip and hip joints. Explains the causes of hip degeneration. Includes a brief review of non - surgical ooptions. Focuses on four phases of hip replacement surgery - pre - operative covering hip evaluation and exercises the patient must do after surgery; discussion of actual surgery; post - op period covering the activities and precautions a patient can expect following surgery; rehabilitative phase showing patients how they need to handle everyday activities such as climbing stairs, and devices available to help them. Produced by the National Assn of Orthopaedic Nurses.
Health and Safety
Dist - AJN

Total Knee Replacement 9 MIN
VHS / U-matic
Color
Outlines the surgical knee replacement procedure, and pre and post operative care techniques to prospective patients.
Health and Safety
Dist - PRI **Prod** - PRI 1986

Total knee replacement - kickback to motion 28 MIN
VHS / U-matic
Color (PRO)
$275.00 purchase, $60.00 rental _ #7630S, #7630V
Focuses on postoperative nursing care following knee replacement. Includes patient education, monitoring activities, recognition and prevention of complications. Demonstrates progressive ambulation, exercise and types of prostheses used.
Health and Safety
Dist - AJN **Prod** - HOSSN 1986

Total knee replacement - patient education 23 MIN
VHS
Color (PRO C G)
$250.00 purchase, $70.00 rental _ #4423
Guides patients and their families through the phases of total knee replacement surgery. Uses easy - to - understand language to discuss the anatomy and functioning of a normal knee. Explains the problems that can result in decreased mobility, stiffness and pain. Looks at conservative treatment options. Covers in a detailed pre - operative phase what will happen to the patient and stresses the need for patient participation. Reviews the actual surgery, using clear pictures and gives patient information about the prosthesis. Explains discharge and the rehabilitation process. Produced by the National Assn of Orthopaedic Nurses.
Health and Safety
Dist - AJN

Total Laryngectomy 12 MIN
16mm
Color (PRO)
Explains the reasons for performing a total laryngectomy and considers the anesthesia used for this operation.
Health and Safety
Dist - LOMAM **Prod** - LOMAM

Total Laryngectomy 17 MIN
16mm
Color (PRO)
Explains that the operation of total laryngectomy is used for cancer of the intrinsic larynx, or true vocal cord, too advanced for treatment by radiation therapy or by a lesser surgical procedure.
Health and Safety; Science
Dist - ACY **Prod** - ACYDGD 1963

The Total Look 22 MIN
16mm
Color
Points out that many years ago, ceilings were recognized as one of the most important dimensions of interior design. Explains that now, through the design and development of modern materials, unique styling and simplified installation techniques, ceilings are once again being used to produce a total look in home decoration. Describes the new ceiling materials and shows how they can be used to add the comfort of sound conditioning, modern decoration, and trouble - free ceilings to new as well as older homes.
Guidance and Counseling; Home Economics
Dist - ACOC **Prod** - ACOC

Total Marketing 10 MIN
16mm / U-matic / VHS
Color (H C)
Covers all the aspects necessary to completely market a product. Points out that advertising is not sufficient alone or effective without top quality products, reasonable salesmanship, thorough distribution, proper pricing, attractive packaging and good in - store merchandising.
Business and Economics
Dist - MCFI **Prod** - NILCOM 1975

Total Ovariectomy and Adrenalectomy 17 MIN
16mm
Color (PRO)
Presents Dr Willard H Persons who points out that certain metastases from mammary cancer remain hormone dependent, and are benefited by castration. Advises that total ovariectomy and adrenalectomy should be restricted to women who have advanced carcinomatosis, subsequent to breast cancer, and who have failed to respond to all other known methods of treatment. Shows the more important technical aspects of adrenalectomy.
Health and Safety; Science
Dist - ACY **Prod** - ACYDGD 1959

Total Parenteral Nutrition - an Overview 13 MIN
U-matic / VHS
Color (PRO)
LC 80-730658
Defines total parenteral nutrition (TPN) and presents the goals of TPN therapy and its primary indications.
Health and Safety
Dist - MEDCOM **Prod** - MEDCOM

Total Parenteral Nutrition - Nursing Care - 1 the Protocol 10 MIN
VHS / U-matic
Color (PRO)
LC 80-730658
Explains the ongoing nursing care for the patient who is receiving total parenteral nutrition (TPN) therapy. Demonstrates nursing care performed every hour, including checking the rate of the infusion, checking the IV tubing and the dressing and observing the patient's behavior.
Health and Safety
Dist - MEDCOM **Prod** - MEDCOM

Total Parenteral Nutrition - Nursing Care the Administration Set 12 MIN
U-matic / 35mm strip
Color (PRO)
LC 80-730658;
Demonstrates the actions of the nurse in changing the dressing for the patient receiving total parenteral nutrition. Emphasizes aseptic technique.
Health and Safety
Dist - MEDCOM **Prod** - MEDCOM

Total Parenteral Nutrition, Part Two Complications of TPN 29 MIN
U-matic / VHS
Color (PRO)
Discusses the technical, metabolic and septic complications of total parenteral nutrition. Identifies signs and symptoms of the most common complications. Describes preventive steps and initial treatment and recommends equipment and supplies which can decrease the incidence of complications. Provides a thorough overview of possible problems and their solutions for the physician with primary responsibility for the monitoring and care of patients receiving parenteral nutrition.
Health and Safety
Dist - UMICHM **Prod** - UMICHM 1982

Total Parenteral Nutrition - Preparing the Patient 11 MIN
U-matic / VHS
Color (PRO)
LC 80-730658
Demonstrates ways in which the nurse teaches the patient about total parenteral nutrition (TPN) therapy. Illustrates examples of typical patient concerns about TPN.
Health and Safety
Dist - MEDCOM **Prod** - MEDCOM

Total Parenteral Nutrition, Pt 1 21 MIN
U-matic / VHS
Color (PRO)
Provides an introduction and overview of total parenteral nutrition (TPN) as a method of either primary or supportive therapy for adult patients. Discusses nutritional requirements during disease, specific indications for TPN therapy, catheter insertion and care. Provides specific information regarding TPN solutions and their administration.
Health and Safety; Social Science
Dist - UMICHM **Prod** - UMICHM 1980

Total Parotidectomy 22 MIN
U-matic / VHS
Head and Neck Series
Color
Health and Safety; Science - Natural
Dist - SVL **Prod** - SVL

Total Physical Fitness for Men 43 MIN
VHS / BETA
Color (A)
Presents a series of exercises that will lead to cardiovascular fitness, flexibility and strength.
Physical Education and Recreation
Dist - RMIBHF **Prod** - RMIBHF

Total product maintenance - maximizing productivity and quality 45 MIN
Slide / VHS
Color; CAV (IND A G)
$749.00 purchase _ #VTPM - 622, #STPM - 622
Shows how to achieve and maintain the highest level of plant equipment effectiveness by involving each worker in the day - to - day maintenance of the equipment used. Includes facilitator's guide. Produced by Japan Management Association.
Business and Economics; Psychology
Dist - PRODUC

Total productive maintenance - Maximizing productivity and quality 45 MIN
VHS / Slide
Color (IND C PRO)
$799.00 purchase _ #VTPM-40, #STPM-40
Explains the rationale and basic principles of TPM to supervisors, group leaders and workers in two parts. Covers five major developmental activities of TPM, how to improve equipment effectiveness and how to use P - M Analysis to solve complex problems.
Business and Economics; Industrial and Technical Education
Dist - PRODUC

Total Quality Control 30 MIN
U-matic / VHS
Business Nippon Series
Color (A)
LC 85-702165
Business and Economics; History - World
Dist - EBEC **Prod** - JAPCTV 1984

Total quality control Japanese style - from a top - management viewpoint 180 MIN
VHS
Color (PRO A G)
$1395.00 purchase
Features Jack Warne in an examination of Japanese style total quality control. Includes six videocassettes and 12 participant workbooks.
Business and Economics; Psychology
Dist - PRODUC **Prod** - PRODUC

Total quality leadership series
Continuous quality improvement 15 MIN
Empowered quality leaders 15 MIN
The Quality innovation process 15 MIN
Quality meetings 15 MIN
Quality problem solving 15 MIN
Quality tools 15 MIN
The Quest for quality 15 MIN
Self - managing quality teams 15 MIN
Statistical process controls for breakthrough 15 MIN
Statistical process controls for maintenance 15 MIN
Dist - BLNCTD

Total quality management in the law office - Ensuring quality service 50 MIN
VHS
Color (A PRO C)
$95.00 purchase _ #Y702
Explains the essential principles and benefits of TQM. Describes the basic steps to planning and implementing TQM programs.
Business and Economics; Civics and Political Systems
Dist - ALIABA **Prod** - CLETV 1992

Total quality management - more than just a training issue - Richard Y Chang 80 MIN
VHS
Color; PAL (C G PRO)
$89.95, $69.95 purchase _ #90AST - V - S9
Stresses that total quality management means that skills and awareness - building training lasts long term. Looks at proven strategies for designing, implementing and managing a TQM system. Shows how to assess organization readiness for such a system and how to integrate other human resource - HR - systems into a total training effort that emphasizes organizational commitment to excellence. Features the President of Richard Change Associates, Irvine CA.
Business and Economics; Psychology
Dist - MOBILE **Prod** - ASTD 1990

Total quality management series
Presents four videos featuring Dr Richard Chang. Helps front - line employees make necessary behavioral changes in creating a Total Quality Culture. Video titles are Building Commitment, Teaming Up, Applied Problem - Solving and Self - Directed Evaluation.
Total quality management series 96 MIN
Dist - EXTR **Prod** - DOUVIS 1990

Total quality management - Ten elements for implementation series 150 MIN
VHS
Total quality management - Ten elements for implementation series
Color (PRO IND A)
$2,495 purchase _ #GO02A - 02J
Outlines, through a ten - part series, helpful guidelines in the area of continous improvement. Includes extensive workshop materials. By Goal - QPC.
Business and Economics; Psychology
Dist - EXTR

Total quality management - what every law firm and corporate law department should know about TQM 180 MIN
VHS / Cassette
Color (PRO)
$295.00, $150.00 purchase, $150.00 rental _ #TQM1-000, #ATQM-000
Reveals that American companies have had to reexamine traditional ways of doing business as the result of intense world competition. Shows that many businesses have improved product quality, customer service and satisfaction through the adoption of quality programs known as 'Total Quality Management.' Introduces corporate counsel and private firm lawyers to the fundamental principles of TQM and their application and implementation in the legal world. Includes study guide.
Business and Economics; Civics and Political Systems; Education
Dist - AMBAR **Prod** - AMBAR 1993

Total quality: the bank's strategic tool for the 90s
VHS
Dream team series
Color (IND PRO)
$295.00 purchase, $150.00 rental _ #MAX03E
Introduces Nikki McCuistion in this part of an eight - part series on competitive banking. Includes a leader's guide. Produced by Marx Communication.
Business and Economics
Dist - EXTR

Total Rehabilitation of a Bilateral High Upper Extremity Amputee 30 MIN
16mm
Color
Shows how a bilateral double high - arm amputee can be restored to functional capacity.
Health and Safety
Dist - USVA **Prod** - USVA 1959

The Total self 90 MIN
VHS / BETA
Innerwork series
Color (G)
$49.95 purchase _ #W125
Proposes that individuals are not unitary beings, but consist of many autonomous sub - personalities and energy complexes. Considers that total self - understanding must include a detached awareness of both the primary and disowned parts of the self. Features Dr Hal Stone, author of 'Embracing Heaven and Earth.'
Health and Safety; Psychology
Dist - THINKA **Prod** - THINKA

Total Solids and Volatile Solids Determination in Wastewater 10 MIN
VHS / BETA
Color
Discusses sewage, sludge, water and wastewater technology.
Health and Safety; Industrial and Technical Education; Social Science
Dist - RMIBHF **Prod** - RMIBHF

Total Surgical Decompression of Late Intestinal Obstruction 29 MIN
16mm
Color (PRO)
Explains that in late obstruction of the small intestine, complete surgical decompression of the distended atonic gut from treitz' ligament to point of obstruction is essential to recovery. Illustrates a facile method to accomplish this.
Health and Safety; Science
Dist - ACY **Prod** - ACYDGD 1964

The Total teaching nursing home 15 MIN
VHS / U-matic
Color (IND G C)
$395.00 purchase, $80.00 rental _ #C901 - VI - 023
Helps nursing home staff to organize and direct a variety of educational activities for residents, staff and the outside community. Includes practical suggestions for forming partnerships with health professional schools, for conducting research in the nursing home and for community education. Presented by Michael Stotts, Northern Essex Community College, Center for Nursing Education, Haverhill, Massachussetts.
Education; Health and Safety; Physical Education and Recreation; Psychology
Dist - HSCIC

Total Thyroidectomy and Neck Dissection for Thyroid Cancer 24 MIN
16mm
Color (PRO)
Depicts a method of evaluation and the surgical treatment of well differentiated carcinoma of the thyroid in a child with bilateral lob involvement, cervical lymphnode metastases and tracheal invasion.
Health and Safety; Science
Dist - ACY **Prod** - ACYDGD 1968

Total War 26 MIN
16mm / U-matic / VHS
B&W (H C A)
LC 78-705155
Surveys the destructive elements of war as seen by the civilians who faced the brunt of Hitler's 'War of Terror.' Shows how war touches all of humanity and that total victory by blitzkrieg, as envisaged by Hitler, did nothing more than to wreck havoc and destruction on all involved.
Civics and Political Systems; History - World; Sociology
Dist - LCOA **Prod** - NFBC 1969

Total Wrist Joint Replacement 15 MIN
U-matic / VHS
Color
Demonstrates surgical techniques, results and possible complications in total wrist joint replacement.
Health and Safety
Dist - SPRVER **Prod** - SPRVER

The TOTE utilization process 41 MIN
VHS
Color; PAL; SECAM (G)
$70.00 purchase
Features Robert Dilts demonstrating the central organizing concept of TOTE, Test, Operate, Test, Exit. Shows how the TOTE concept can be utilized in behavior and experience to produced desired personal change. Intermediate level of NLP, neuro - linguistic programming.
Psychology
Dist - NLPCOM **Prod** - NLPCOM

Tots / Air Fare / Utilities
U-matic / VHS
Consumer Survival Series
Color
Presents tips on child care, air travel and utilities.
Home Economics; Social Science
Dist - MDCPB **Prod** - MDCPB

Tots / OTC Drugs / Banks
U-matic / VHS
Consumer Survival Series
Color
Presents tips on caring for children, over - the - counter drugs and banks.
Business and Economics; Health and Safety; Home Economics
Dist - MDCPB **Prod** - MDCPB

Touch 50 MIN
VHS
Healing arts series
Color; PAL (G)
PdS99 purchase
Examines the history of touch as a healing agent in human history. Delves into the uses of touch therapy as a possible therapeutic tool and its place in contemporary medicine. Part two of a nine - part series.
Health and Safety; Psychology
Dist - BBCENE

The Touch 122 MIN
U-matic / VHS
Color
Presents a drama in three acts about a deaf - blind man living on his own for the first time. Adapted from Butterflies Are Free by Leonard Gershe. On three tapes, one act each. Signed.
Guidance and Counseling; Literature and Drama; Psychology
Dist - GALCO **Prod** - HMTD 1977

Touch 33 MIN
VHS
Color (K P I)
$19.95 purchase _ #439 - V8
Provides a unique way for teachers, parents, and counselors to help elementary age children talk about sexual exploitation. Teaches basic prevention skills, and assures victims that they are never at fault. Hosted by Lindsay Wagner.
Guidance and Counseling; Health and Safety; Sociology
Dist - ETRASS **Prod** - ETRASS

Touch 32 MIN
U-matic / VHS / 16mm
Color (P I A)
Teaches children to recognize good touch and bad touch. Based on a play created by the Illusion Theater Company in conjunction with sexual abuse prevention experts.
Psychology; Sociology
Dist - CORF **Prod** - MEDVEN

Touch anchors and sliding anchors - Part Two 60 MIN
VHS
Healing patterns of Jesus of Nazareth series
Color; PAL; SECAM (G)
$60.00 purchase
Features Robert Dilts. Presents part two of a two - part series capturing Dilts' modeling of the healing patterns of Jesus Christ through his in - depth study of the New Testament. Intermediate level of NLP, neuro - linguistic programming. Produced by Western States Training Associates.
Health and Safety; Psychology; Religion and Philosophy
Dist - NLPCOM

Touch Clay, a Ceramic Experience 30 MIN
16mm
Creative Person Series
B&W (J)
Depicts natural objects that typify the things which inspire ceramist Dik Schwanke. Shows Schwanke working in his studio and pictures some of his pottery and sculpture. Accompanied by music by the 'SHAGS.'.
Fine Arts
Dist - IU **Prod** - NET 1967

Touch Football - the Game of Action 10 MIN
U-matic / VHS / 16mm
Color (J H C) (SPANISH)
LC 75-702214;
Shows high school athletes as they demonstrate techniques for good passing, receiving and punting as well as a variety of fast motion drills for the game of touch football.
Physical Education and Recreation
Dist - AIMS **Prod** - TFBCH 1972

A Touch of Finland 28 MIN
16mm
Color (C A)
Focuses on the natural and man - made attractions of Finland. Covers the scenic lake district, Finland's Summer Festivals, and many of Finland's product designs and shopping values.
Geography - World; History - World
Dist - WSTGLC **Prod** - WSTGLC

A Touch of Gold 28 MIN
16mm
Color
Tells the story of gold jewelry through the ages with historic re - enactments showing its use in the court of kings, as treasure acquired by the Conquistadores and its high - style uses in today's world of fashion.
Industrial and Technical Education
Dist - MTP **Prod** - MTP

A Touch of Hands 27 MIN
16mm / U-matic / VHS
Color
LC 78-701635
Follows the activities of an artist - teacher and a class of special education students in a rural elementary school as they prepare a puppet show.
Education; Fine Arts
Dist - STNFLD **Prod** - FRICEC 1978

Touch of Legend 50 MIN
16mm
Color
LC 76-700160
Presents a musical re - creation of the Trail of '98 featuring Ian and Sylvia Tyson. Shows how they follow the original Klondike Gold Rush route from Skagway, Alaska, to the Yukon Territory.
Fine Arts; History - United States
Dist - CHET **Prod** - CHET 1974

A Touch of Love 18 MIN
16mm
Color
LC 80-701489
Describes the Foster Grandparent Program.
Social Science; Sociology
Dist - ACTON **Prod** - ACTON 1980

A Touch of Magic 5 MIN
16mm
Color
Presents the Orange Bird exhibit at Disney World, Florida.
Psychology
Dist - FLADC **Prod** - FLADC

A Touch of Murder 60 MIN
16mm / U-matic / VHS
I, Claudius Series Number 1; No 1
Color (C A)
Tells how Livia, Claudius' grandmother, poisons Marcellus, Augustus' heir.
History - World
Dist - FI **Prod** - BBCTV 1977

A Touch of Paris 20 MIN
U-matic / VHS
Color (J)
LC 82-706787
Shows Paris, including its cafes, flower carts and markets and bakeries. Watches a bouillabaisse in the making and demonstrates how to make a light, fluffy omelet. Views artists at work in Montmartre and visits the Louvre and the Eiffel Tower.
Geography - World; History - World
Dist - AWSS **Prod** - AWSS 1981

A Touch of Royalty 26 MIN
16mm
Color (J) (SPANISH)
LC 74-700468; 74-700469
Recounts Roberto Clemente's brilliant career as a right fielder for the Pittsburgh Pirates, including anecdotes given by teammates, sports writers and Clemente's wife, Vera.
Biography; Physical Education and Recreation
Dist - SFI **Prod** - WWF 1973

Touch of Sensitivity 50 MIN
U-matic / VHS / 16mm
Color (H C A)
Demonstrates the importance of touching by showing that touch deprivation can lead to abnormal and violent behavior, to brain damage, heart disease and lack of resistance to infection. Presents evidence that premature babies do better lying on lambswool than on cotton sheets and that heart patients do better if they keep pets.
Science - Natural
Dist - FI **Prod** - BBCTV 1981

A Touch of Summer 28 MIN
16mm
Color
Presents the impressions of American teenagers after traveling the length and breadth of the country of Israel.
Geography - World; Social Science
Dist - ALDEN **Prod** - ALDEN

Touch the Earth 17 MIN
16mm
Color
LC 78-700316
Depicts the activities of three teenage curators at the Dayton Museum of Natural History. Includes interviews with the three in which they talk about their work and about the value of nature study in general.
Science - Natural
Dist - DAYMU **Prod** - DAYMU 1978

Touch the Earth
VHS / U-matic
Color
Provides a portrait of Native American existence. Tells the story of the Indians' loss of their way of life. Utilizes photographs of Edward S Curtis.
Social Science
Dist - CEPRO **Prod** - CEPRO

Touch the sky - precision flying with the Blue Angels 60 MIN
VHS
Color (H C A)
$39.95 purchase
Features Christopher Reeve in precision flying experiences with the Navy's Blue Angels aerobatic flying team.
Civics and Political Systems
Dist - PBS **Prod** - WNETTV

Touch the snow 30 MIN
VHS
Color (G A R)
$10.00 rental _ #36 - 80 - 2071
Presents a real - life situation in which a two - year - old child must cope with the death of her baby sister. Provides insights into the ways in which children deal with death in the family.
Guidance and Counseling; Psychology; Sociology
Dist - APH **Prod** - WHSPRO

Touch tone phone film 8 MIN
16mm
B&W (G)
$16.00 rental
Describers the slipping time between the dialed number and the hello at the other end. Produced by Bill Brand.
Fine Arts
Dist - CANCIN

Touch Wood, Pt 7 55 MIN
VHS
Hand and Eye Series - Vol IV; Vol IV; Pt 7
Color (S)
$99.00 purchase _ #386 - 9021
Melds together the past and the present in a celebration of handcrafted art. Traverses the globe to present the world's finest examples of sculpture, jewelry, glass, pottery, gardening, weaving and woodworking. Contemporary artisans demonstrate the ancient and innovative techniques they use to create their modern masterworks. Seven programs in four volumes. Part 7 looks at woodworking, from creating furniture to objects of art such as totems.
Fine Arts; Industrial and Technical Education
Dist - FI **Prod** - CANBC 1988

Touchdown 10 MIN
16mm
B&W
Studies the control tower of a modern airport contrasted with the public waiting rooms in the same airport. Explains the tension one might have expected in the tower is evident in the 'RELAXED' public spaces.
Industrial and Technical Education; Psychology; Social Science
Dist - UPENN **Prod** - UPENN 1971

Touchdown 27 MIN
16mm
Color
LC 79-701393
Tells how a college football player becomes paralyzed in a household accident. Follows the young man as he learns to cope with his disability and explores his changing relationship with his father who is unable to accept it.
Fine Arts; Psychology
Dist - RICHGO **Prod** - RICHGO 1979

Touches
VHS / U-matic
Color (T)
Discusses positive as well as problematic touches and encourages youngsters to confide in school personnel. Explains techniques for conducting satisfactory discussions with individual students and reporting suspected cases of abuse to proper authorities.
Education; Sociology
Dist - GA **Prod** - GA 1984

Touches - physical and sexual abuse of children 25 MIN
VHS
Color (T PRO)
$185.00 purchase _ #05500 - 126
Shows teachers how to use a sound filmstrip which helps youngsters to distinguish between positive and negative forms of touching, as well as reassuring youngsters about confiding in school personnel. Provides guidelines for using the filmstrip in the classroom and conducting discussions with individual students and for reporting suspected cases of abuse to the proper authorities. Produced by Harvey - Rydberg Associates.
Guidance and Counseling; Health and Safety; Sociology
Dist - GA

Touching 17 MIN
16mm
Color
Portrays a male who has a C - 6 spinal cord injury. Explains that he was injured seven years ago and has been with his partner for three years. Stresses that oral sexuality is the primary means of sexual expression open to persons with this type of lesion.
Guidance and Counseling; Psychology; Sociology
Dist - MMRC **Prod** - MMRC

Touching 20 MIN
16mm
All that I Am Series
B&W (C A)
Fine Arts; Guidance and Counseling
Dist - NWUFLM **Prod** - MPATI

Touching 35 MIN
16mm
Color
LC 75-701109
Features Dr Ashley Montagu discussing the key concepts of his book entitled Touching. Illustrates the importance of early tactile experiences and the use of touching in encounter therapy.
Guidance and Counseling; Science - Natural
Dist - PSYCHF **Prod** - PSYCHF 1975

Touching 16 MIN
U-matic / VHS
Color (C A)
Shows a male paraplegic and his partner of the last three years. Emphasizes oral sexuality as the primary means of sexual expression and pleasuring open to persons with this type of injury.
Health and Safety; Psychology
Dist - MMRC **Prod** - NATSF

Touching 19 MIN
16mm / VHS / U-matic
Color (H C G)
$60.00, $40.00 purchase, $35.00 rental _ #JVC - 690, #JHC - 690, #JRF - 690
Dramatizes the courtship of an Orthodox Jewish girl who falls in love with a unobservant Jewish boy and who questions the practrice of N'gia, the laws forbidding premarital contact between members of the opposite sex.
Guidance and Counseling; Psychology; Religion and Philosophy; Social Science; Sociology
Dist - ADL **Prod** - ADL 1991

T,O,U,C,H,I,N,G, 12 MIN
16mm
Color (C)
$336.00
Experimental film by Paul Sharits.
Fine Arts
Dist - AFA **Prod** - AFA 1968

Touching 14 MIN
16mm
Color
LC 78-711544
A young soldier on a one - day pass reaches out in desperation, finally finding an old friend, some genuine warmth and a temporary reprive from his Vietnam memories.
Fine Arts
Dist - USC **Prod** - USC 1970

Touching - Heart of Healing, Pt I
VHS / Cassette
(G)
$49.00, $18.00 purchase _ #U890001334
Discusses the experience and understanding of the ways in which individuals have been 'wounded' and shows how to nurture recovery. Produced by Access Group.
Health and Safety; Psychology; Religion and Philosophy
Dist - BKPEOP

Touching - Heart of Healing, Pt II
VHS / Cassette
(G)
$49.00, $18.00 purchase _ #U890001336, 1337
Discusses the experience and understanding of the ways in which individuals have been 'wounded' and shows how to nurture recovery. Produced by Access Group.
Health and Safety; Psychology; Religion and Philosophy
Dist - BKPEOP

The Touching Problem 8 MIN
16mm / U-matic / VHS
Color (A)
LC 83-700223
Looks at how adults can help children deal with sexual abuse by presenting the case history of a young girl's molestation by a male relative.
Sociology
Dist - CORF **Prod** - KVOSTV 1982

Touching the future - dialogues on education series
Adam Urbanski 29 MIN
Albert Shanker 29 MIN
Bob Hughes 29 MIN
Bruce Goldberg 29 MIN
Chris Held 28 MIN
Gary Watts 28 MIN
Harold Hodgkinson 29 MIN
Iris Carl 28 MIN
Jane M Healey 29 MIN
Joseph Prewitt - Diaz 29 MIN
Linda Darling - Hammond 29 MIN
Phillip Schlechty 29 MIN
William Kolberg 28 MIN
Dist - PSU

The Touching tree 38 MIN
VHS
Color (C A)
$295.00 purchase
Focuses on the behavioral disorder known as OCD - Obsessive - Compulsive Disorder. Shows the process of healing through professional help and through understanding and caring attention from others. Useful for mental health professionals and teachers in training. Produced by Awareness Films and funded by The OCD Foundation.
Health and Safety; Sociology
Dist - PFP

Touchpoints series
Offers a series of three videos with advice from Dr T Berry Brazelton about managing touchpoints, predictable times in the first years of life when bursts of rapid growth and learning occur. Recommends videos for new parents, so they can anticipate and recognize the touchpoints. Covers pregnancy through toddlerhood.
First month through the first year 45 MIN
One year through toddlerhood 45 MIN
Pregnancy, birth, and first weeks of life 45 MIN
Dist - CAMV

A touchy subject 16 MIN
VHS
Color (K P I)
$200.00 purchase _ #B002 - V8
Models practical ways for parents to talk to even their youngest children about sexual abuse. Shows parents how to effectively convey messages such as, your body is your own, you have a right to say no, and you can tell me if anyone makes you uncomfortable.
Guidance and Counseling; Health and Safety
Dist - ETRASS **Prod** - ETRASS

A Touchy subject 16 MIN
VHS
Color (C A PRO G)
$200.00 purchase
Offers simple accessible methods for talking to even the youngest children about protecting themselves from sexual abuse. Uses four short dramatic scenes to help parents teach children that they are special and important, that their body belongs to them, that they have the right to say 'no' if someone makes them feel uncomfortable, and that they can talk to their parents if anyone or anything bothers them.
Health and Safety; Social Science; Sociology
Dist - SELMED

Tough decisions - ethics issues in government contracting 59 MIN
VHS
Color (G)
$500.00 purchase, $150.00 rental _ #V1066 - 06
Promotes individuals' awareness of the ethical and possibly legal effects of their actions and decisions, particularly those relating to record - keeping, product quality, relations with competitors and proprietary information. Helps promote discussion of company ethics policies or the need for them. Video contains a two - part program on a single cassette. Includes discussion guide with the video.
Business and Economics
Dist - BARR **Prod** - ETHICS

The Tough decisions - how to make them 29 MIN
VHS
Color (J H)
$189.00 purchase _ #2249 - SK
Features guidance counselor Nancy Kellner in a presentation of a four - step process for decision making. Uses dramatic vignettes to illustrate the steps of the process. Identifies six behaviors that block decision making. Includes teacher's guide.
Psychology; Sociology
Dist - SUNCOM **Prod** - SUNCOM

Tough defense 60 MIN
VHS
Color (G)
$39.95 purchase _ #MXS230V
Presents former University of Washington basketball coach Marv Harshman demonstrating drills for developing defensive basketball skills. Covers both individual and team drills.
Physical Education and Recreation
Dist - CAMV **Prod** - CAMV 1987

Tough Defense - It'll Keep You in the Game 56 MIN
BETA / VHS
Men's Basketball Basics Series
Color
Demonstrates defensive play in men's basketball. Deals with both man - for - man and zone defensive strategy.
Physical Education and Recreation
Dist - MOHOMV **Prod** - MOHOMV

Tough guys 50 MIN
VHS
Color (G)
$19.95 purchase _ #NFL2019V
Profiles seven National Football League players whose careers exemplified toughness, including Dan Fouts, Jack Lambert, and Jim Taylor. Hosted by Chicago Bears coach Mike Ditka.
Literature and Drama; Physical Education and Recreation
Dist - CAMV

Tough Love 12 MIN
BETA / VHS / U-matic
(G)
$100.00 purchase
Comments on the philosophy of `Tough Love'. Many parents feel desperate because of their inability to influence the antisocial behavior of their children.
Sociology
Dist - CTV **Prod** - CTV 1981

Tough Love 30 MIN
16mm
Color (R)
Presents a story about love and faith behind prison walls.
Religion and Philosophy; Sociology
Dist - OUTRCH **Prod** - OUTRCH

Tough Love 30 MIN
16mm / VHS
Color (H A)
$39.95 video purchase, $39.00 film rental
Narrates how a young incorrigible is converted to the Christian faith in prison.
Religion and Philosophy
Dist - CAFM **Prod** - CAFM 1980

Tough - minded leadership 42 MIN
VHS
Color (H A T)
$35.00 purchase _ #WL200
Shows how to lead rather than just manage. Demonstrates creating motivation and building on strengths. Features Joe D Batten, author of the book 'Tough - Minded Leadership.'
Business and Economics; Guidance and Counseling
Dist - AAVIM

Tough - Minded Salesmanship - Ask for the Order and Get it 30 MIN
U-matic / VHS / 16mm
Tough - Minded Salesmanship Series
Color (H C)
LC 73-701078
Discusses five techniques for closing a sale and teaches how to take the fear out of asking for the order.
Business and Economics; Psychology
Dist - DARTNL **Prod** - DARTNL 1972

Tough - Minded Salesmanship Series
Ask for the order - and get it 30 MIN
Tough - Minded Salesmanship - Ask for the Order and Get it 30 MIN
Your price is right - sell it 30 MIN
Dist - DARTNL

The Tough new labor market of the 1990s - and what it takes to succeed 30 MIN

VHS
Color (J H C G)
$195.00 purchase _ #JWTNLMV
Offers an introduction to labor market trends. Presents the fastest growing jobs for the 90s. Reinforces the need for education and training while providing practical suggestions for career planning. Presents a list of the fastest growing jobs and what they have in common, as well as a contrasting list of rapidly declining occupations clearly depicted as low - skills, low - paying jobs that still require a high school education. Includes Work in the New Economy book.
Business and Economics; Guidance and Counseling
Dist - CAMV **Prod** - JISTW

Tough Old Gut 60 MIN
16mm
World at War Series
Color (H C A)
LC 76-701778
History - World; Sociology
Dist - USCAN **Prod** - THAMES 1975

Tough Old Gut - Italy, November 1942 - June 1944 52 MIN
U-matic / VHS / 16mm
World at War Series
Color (H C A)
States that Sicily was not the soft underbelly of the Mediterranean that Churchill imagined it to be. Shows that it was more like a tough old gut, but once the Anglo - American advance began to turn the tide it resulted in the conquest of the Axis forces between November 1942 and June 1944.
History - World
Dist - MEDIAG **Prod** - THAMES 1973

A Tough place to play 15 MIN
VHS / U-matic / 16mm
Color (I J H G)
$280.00, $330.00, $330.00 purchase, $45.00 rental
Depicts urbanization and poverty in a developing nation. Emphasizes social science concepts such as access to resources, migration, self - reliance and survival skills of urban dwellers.
Social Science; Sociology
Dist - NDIM **Prod** - UNICEF 1984

Tough, Pretty or Smart 29 MIN
16mm / U-matic / VHS
Color (J H G)
Portrays the Patoka Valley Boys, a six person string band, comprising one of America' old time and bluegrass musical groups. Through their own words, the 'Boys' proclaim their love for their music, a stark contrast to the technologically advanced jobs they all hold.
Fine Arts; Geography - United States
Dist - DOCEDR **Prod** - DOCEDR 1981

Tough, Pretty or Smart - a Portrait of the Patoka Valley Boys 29 MIN
16mm / U-matic / VHS
Color (I A)
Portrays old - time string band whose members span three generations. Presents and enhances old - time music in documentary form.
Fine Arts
Dist - KANLEW **Prod** - KANLEW 1981

Tough questions about sex
VHS
Color (J H R)
$49.99 purchase, $10.00 rental _ #35 - 83300 - 533
Features Christian youth speaker Dawson McAllister, speaking on sex and dating.
Religion and Philosophy
Dist - APH **Prod** - WORD

Tough Shots 29 MIN
U-matic / VHS
Photo Show Series
Color
Discusses picture taking problems and how to solve them. Includes how to shoot in rain and snow, how to take self - portraits and candid picture taking without being obvious.
Industrial and Technical Education
Dist - PBS **Prod** - WGBHTV 1981

Tough stuff workout 45 MIN
VHS
Color (G)
$24.95 purchase _ #JJ0019V
Introduces plyometrics, an advanced training system developed in the Soviet Union. Features Tracy Scoggins.
Physical Education and Recreation
Dist - CAMV

Tough talk - love, sex, dating 60 MIN
VHS
Color (J H R)
$29.00 purchase, $10.00 rental _ #35 - 80 - 2050
Features Haman Cross Jr in a stand - up comedy format. Focuses on Cross' thoughts about sex and dating and how they have changed since he was a teenager. Produced by Youth Encounter.
Health and Safety; Religion and Philosophy
Dist - APH **Prod** - CHLGRF

Tough times - finding the jobs 30 MIN
VHS
Tough times job strategies series
Color (H C G)
$69.95 purchase _ #CCP0129V
Explains how worldwide changes and trends affect the job market on a local, community level. Shows the importance of researching these effects on the community in which one is seeking employment and examining economic development strategies for their regions and states. Discusses the benefits of researching various industries to determine which are experiencing growth and which are declining. Encourages the acquisition of skills needed for entry level employment in the most promising job markets. Part of a two - part series.
Business and Economics; Guidance and Counseling
Dist - CAMV

Tough times job strategies series
Presents a two - part series on finding jobs and using an entry - level job as a stepping stone for career advancement. Includes the titles Finding the Jobs and Making the Most of Your Job.
Tough times - finding the jobs 30 MIN
Tough times - making the most of your job 30 MIN
Dist - CAMV

Tough times - making the most of your job 30 MIN
VHS
Tough times job strategies series
Color (H C G)
$69.95 purchase _ #CCP0130V
Teaches entry level employees the importance of making the most of their present jobs. Shows how jobs can be used to advance careers, either within or outside their companies. Stresses communication skills, flexibility, company knowledge and the willingness to take on extra responsibilities and learn new skills as stepping stones to career advance and job security. Part of a two - part series.
Business and Economics; Guidance and Counseling
Dist - CAMV

A Tough Winter 21 MIN
16mm
B&W
Presents a Little Rascals film featuring black comedian Stepin Fetchit.
Fine Arts
Dist - RMIBHF **Prod** - ROACH 1930

The Toughest Barrier 15 MIN
U-matic / VHS / 16mm
Color (J H C A)
$365.00, $250.00 purchase _ #81523
Shows that handicapped people can have normal lives as much as non - handicapped people.
Psychology
Dist - CORF

The Toughest Barrier 15 MIN
U-matic / VHS / 16mm
Color (J)
LC 81-701531
Presents a warm and personal encounter with four handicapped adults and shows how they live and respond to various social attitudes which bar them from job opportunities, marriage, and normal social and sexual relations.
Education; Psychology
Dist - CORF **Prod** - IOWA 1981

Toughest Game in Town 79 MIN
16mm
B&W (A)
LC 73-703226
Presents suggestions for social workers and community organizers regarding the struggles of a people's corporation. Shows how poor Chicanos of Santa Fe, New Mexico, come to grips with the powers that control their lives.
Sociology
Dist - BALLIS **Prod** - BALLIS

The Toughest Job You'll Ever Love 10 MIN 25 MIN
16mm
Color
LC 79-701707; 79-701708
Shows Peace Corps volunteers in Nepal, Colombia and Nigeria as they describe their experiences and explain what their service in the Peace Corps has meant to them.
Civics and Political Systems; Social Science
Dist - USNAC **Prod** - ACTON 1978

The Toughest Target 30 MIN
VHS / 16mm
World War II - G I Diary Series
(J H C)
$99.95 each, $995.00 series _ #11
Depicts the action and emotion that soldiers experienced during World War II, through their eyes and in their words. Narrated by Lloyd Bridges.
History - United States; History - World
Dist - AMBROS **Prod** - AMBROS 1980

The Toughest Target 30 MIN
U-matic / VHS
World War II - GI Diary Series
Color (H C A)
History - United States; History - World
Dist - TIMLIF **Prod** - TIMLIF 1980

Toujours En Retard Nicolas 13 MIN
16mm
En France Avec Nicolas Series Set I, Lesson 8; Set I; Lesson 8
B&W (J H)
LC 72-704502
Foreign Language
Dist - CHLTN **Prod** - PEREN 1968

Toujours En Retard Nicolas, Student Exercises 8 MIN
16mm
En France Avec Nicolas Series Set II, Lesson 8; Set II; Lesson 8
Color (J H)
LC 76-704503
Foreign Language
Dist - CHLTN **Prod** - PEREN 1968

Toula - the water spirit 80 MIN
VHS
Color (G) (FRENCH)
$120.00 rental
Portrays an ancient Fulani legend enacted by two villages in Nigeria. Reveals that agriculture in the West African Sahel, the ecological belt between the savannah grasslands and the Sahara Desert, is tied to fluctuations in rainfall. Shows that neither traditional nor modern means of dealing with disasters seem to be effective. Produced by Moustaphpa Allassane and Anna Soehring.
Agriculture; Geography - World; History - World
Dist - DOCEDR **Prod** - DOCEDR

Toulin's Model of Argument 16 MIN
VHS / U-matic
Communication Series
Color (H C A)
Teaches the basic components of an argument as well as the differences between an argument and an assertion. Covers the material used in composition, speech, communication and debate classes.
English Language
Dist - MSU **Prod** - MSU

Toulouse 7 MIN
U-matic / VHS / 16mm
Chroniques De France Series
Color (H C A) (FRENCH)
LC 81-700765
A French language motion picture. Presents Toulouse as a city of education and aviation.
Foreign Language; Geography - World
Dist - IFB **Prod** - ADPF 1980

Toulouse - Lautrec 52 MIN
VHS / U-matic
Great masters series
Color (J H G)
$225.00, $275.00 purchase, $60.00 rental
Records the life of the artist, born an aristocrat, who celebrated the social swirl of the cabaret, theaters and racetracks of Paris. Looks at his childhood disability and subsequent fascination with the world of physical action and his opus of art works that evoke the splendor and miseries of the unrestrained pursuit of urban pleasures. Covers the background and particulars of the lithographic process in detail. Documents key examples of his art in other media. Available in two parts for classroom use.
Fine Arts; Industrial and Technical Education
Dist - NDIM **Prod** - GREMAS 1993

Toulouse - Lautrec 60 MIN
VHS
Color (H C A)
$39.95 purchase _ #TOU-01
Explores the life of Henri Toulouse - Lautrec - 1864 - 1901 - artist and devotee of Parisian night life, which he painted with a sharp eye that saw beneath the gay surface to the corruption underneath. Reveals that Lautrec pioneered a style that shaped the future of graphic art, creating striking images by focusing on simple but dramatic shapes and using flat, pure colors.
Fine Arts
Dist - ARTSAM KNOWUN **Prod** - RMART LONWTV

Toulouse - Lautrec 29 MIN
U-matic
Meet the Masters Series
B&W
Examines the techniques Toulouse - Lautrec used as a commercial artist, illustrator and painter to capture the humanity of Bohemian life in Paris.
Fine Arts
Dist - UMITV **Prod** - UMITV 1966

Toulouse - Lautrec (1864 - 1901) 15 MIN
16mm
Color
Presents paintings of Toulouse - Lautrec, whose only weapon against self - mockery was a sharp eye for the degradations and harsh beauty of lives seemingly more glamorous than his own.
Fine Arts
Dist - ROLAND **Prod** - ROLAND

Tour En L'Air 50 MIN
16mm
Color (J)
LC 75-704382
Presents Canadian ballet dancers David and Anna Marie Holmes discussing the discipline of their art, the strains of living and working in the same ventures. Includes footage of the dancers in rehearsal and in performance around the world.
Fine Arts
Dist - NFBC **Prod** - NFBC 1974

Tour Louisiana Travel Series
Louisiana's Fabled Plantations 28 MIN
Dist - RAMSEY

Tour of the 14th Dalai Lama, Australia 240 MIN
VHS / BETA
Color; PAL (G)
PdS25 purchase
Captures highlights of His Holiness in Melbourne, Australia in May 1992. Includes a public talk attended by 21,000 people, planting a Bodhi Tree in the Peace Garden and Buddhist teachings. Two videotapes.
Fine Arts; Religion and Philosophy
Dist - MERIDT

A Tour of the Jack Daniel Distillery 18 MIN
16mm / U-matic
Color
Interweaves the history of the Jack Daniel Distillery with that of Lynchburg, Tennessee. Explains the four stages of whiskey production.
Business and Economics; History - United States
Dist - MTP **Prod** - DANDIS

Tour of the Louvre 53 MIN
VHS
Color (H C A)
$24.95 purchase
Tours the Louvre, the famous French art museum. Narrated by Charles Boyer.
Fine Arts
Dist - PBS **Prod** - WNETTV

A Tour of the Plant 22 MIN
16mm
Color
LC 78-700318
Shows how Johnson Outboards designs, tests and manufactures its outboard motors.
Business and Economics; Industrial and Technical Education; Social Science
Dist - SS **Prod** - JOMC 1978

A Tour of the Prado
BETA / VHS
Color
Presents a tour of the Prado in Madrid, spotlighting works by Titian, El Greco, Velasquez, Goya and Murillo.
Fine Arts; Geography - World
Dist - GA **Prod** - GA

Tour of the Thomas H Ince Studios 30 MIN
16mm
B&W (I)
LC 75-703861
Presents a tour of the Thomas H Ince Studios, featuring glimpses of famous stars of the early silent period, including Louise Glaum, Lloyd Huges, Lewis Stone and House Peters. Carries subtitles.
Fine Arts
Dist - RMIBHF **Prod** - FIRSTN 1922

A Tour of the Vatican Museums
BETA / VHS
Color
Views the riches of the Vatican, from Michelangelo's Sistine Chapel to paintings by Raphael, Martini, Lorenzetti and others.
Fine Arts; Geography - World; Religion and Philosophy
Dist - GA **Prod** - GA

Tourette Syndrome - the Sudden Intruder 46 MIN
16mm
Color
LC 78-701329
Documents the experiences of six individuals suffering from the primary and secondary effects of Tourette syndrome. Uses animation to describe the breakdown of motor control that results and the brain mechanisms that are affected.
Health and Safety; Psychology
Dist - UCLA **Prod** - UCLA 1978

Tourette Syndrome - the Sudden Intruder, Pt 1 23 MIN
16mm
Color
LC 78-701329
Documents the experiences of six individuals suffering from the primary and secondary effects of Tourette syndrome. Uses animation to describe the breakdown of motor control that results and the brain mechanisms that are affected.
Psychology; Science - Natural
Dist - UCLA **Prod** - UCLA 1978

Tourette Syndrome - the Sudden Intruder, Pt 2 23 MIN
16mm
Color
LC 78-701329
Documents the experiences of six individuals suffering from the primary and secondary effects of Tourette syndrome. Uses animation to describe the breakdown of motor control that results and the brain mechanisms that are affected.
Psychology; Science - Natural
Dist - UCLA **Prod** - UCLA 1978

Touring America's ghost towns
VHS
Color (G)
$29.95 purchase _ #TK044
Travels from Bodie, California which averaged a murder a day in the 'good old days' to Lake City, Colorado, the only town in the United States to convict a man of cannibalism in order to explore the haunting remains of the baddest towns in the old West.
Geography - United States; History - United States; Literature and Drama; Sociology
Dist - SIV

Touring Australia 70 MIN
VHS
Color (G)
$29.95 purchase _ #ST - QV2204
Travels to Australia, a continent, an island the size of North America, and a country with a population of 16 million people, home to immigrants from over 120 countries. Highlights Australia's major cities - Sydney, Canberra, Melbourne, Perth, Adelaide. Visits harbors, beaches, forests, red deserts, the untamed outback, Great Barrier Reef and Kakadiu National Park with its Aboriginal art.
Geography - World
Dist - INSTRU

Touring Austria 60 MIN
VHS
Color (G)
Tours countryside and cities of Austria. Available for free loan from the distributor.
Fine Arts; Geography - World
Dist - AUDPLN

Touring Civil War Battlefields 60 MIN
VHS
Color (G)
$29.95 purchase _ #12887
Travels to actual Civil War battlefields with reenactments of five engagements - Manassas, Gettysburg, Antietam, Fredricksburg and the Appomattox surrender.
History - United States
Dist - WCAT **Prod** - WCAT

Touring Civil War battlefields 60 MIN
VHS
Color (H C A)
$29.95 purchase
Tours the main battlefields of the Civil War. Visits Manassas, Antietam, Fredricksburg, Gettysburg, and Appomattox.
History - United States
Dist - PBS **Prod** - WNETTV

Touring Civil War battlefields 120 MIN
VHS
Color (J H C)
$39.95 purchase _ #QV2375V-S
Features 10,000 re-enactors to capture the heroism, pain, and tragedy of the battles of Ft Donelson, Shiloh, New Orleans, Manassas, 2nd Manassas, Antietam, Murfreesboro, Vicksburg, Gettysburg, Fredericksburg, Chickamauga, Chattanooga, Wilderness, and Atlanta. Expanded version of the 'Civil War Battlefields' videocassette. Narrated by James Whitmore. Two videocassettes.
Civics and Political Systems; History - United States
Dist - CAMV

Touring England 65 MIN
VHS
Color (G)
$29.95 purchase _ #ST - QV2219
Looks at the heritage of what was once the world's greatest empire. Travels from Buckingham Palace to Windsor Castle and tours the London Tower, the House of Parliament, Westminster Abbey, St Paul's, St James, the London of Jack the Ripper and Piccadilly Circus.
Geography - World; History - World
Dist - INSTRU

Touring France 60 MIN
VHS
Color (G)
$29.95 purchase _ #ST - QV2287
Views the largest Gothic cathedral in France in the town of Amiens. Visits Rouen, where Joan of Arc was burned at the stake; Giverny, home of Claude Monet; Reims, where champagne was created; and historic Strasbourg. Travels to the beaches of the French Riviera, the chateaux of the Loire Valley, the Eiffel Tower, Notre Dame, the Louvre and Paris, the abbey of Mont Saint - Michel in Brittany.
Geography - World; History - World
Dist - INSTRU

Touring Great Cities Series
Dublin 40 MIN
Edinburgh 40 MIN
London 40 MIN
Dist - FI

Touring Ireland 60 MIN
VHS
Color (G)
$29.95 purchase _ #ST - IV1806
Tours the Ring of Kerry, the ancient Aran Islands and the Rock of Cashel. Visits Blarney and Bunratty, the Giant's Causeway of Northern Ireland, Shannon, Kilarney, County Clare, County Cork, Galway, Connemarra and the hills of Silo.
Geography - World; History - World
Dist - INSTRU

Touring Italy 60 MIN
VHS
Color (G)
$29.95 purchase _ #ST - QV2271
Visits the home of the Roman Empire, the Vatican, Galileo, Christopher Columbus, da Vinci, Michelangelo, Casanova, Verdi and Caruso. Tours Naples and the Verona of Shakespeare, Renaissance Florence, and Rome, site of the Colosseum, the Forum, Piazza di Spagne and more.
Geography - World; History - World
Dist - INSTRU

Touring Korea 55 MIN
VHS
Color (G)
$29.95 purchase _ #ST - QV2213
Captures the drama, history and legends of Korea from Kyongju, the city of golden treasures of ancient kings, to Panmujon, the Korean War truce city.
Geography - World; History - World
Dist - INSTRU

Touring London, Paris, Rome 60 MIN
VHS
Color (G)
$29.95 purchase _ #ST - QV2281
Visits London to watch the changing of the Royal Guard at Buckingham Palace, tour the Tower Bridge and the halls of Westminster Abbey. Travels to Paris and the Arc de Triomphe, the Eiffel Tower, the Louvre, Notre Dame and more. Views the Pantheon, the Forum, the Colosseum, St Peter's, Trevi Fountain and Piazza di Spagne in Rome.
Geography - World; History - World
Dist - INSTRU

Touring Mexico 60 MIN
VHS
Color (G)
$29.95 purchase _ #ST - QV2216
Visits Mexico, a land with 70 million people, 18 million of them in Mexico City, the largest metropolis in the world. Explores the antiquities of the Aztecs and Mayas, the Yucatan, Mayan ruins at Uxmal, the city of Merida, Monte Alban in Oaxaca, the colossi of Tula and the Shrine of Guadalupe.
Geography - World; History - World
Dist - INSTRU

Touring New Zealand 70 MIN
VHS
Color (G)
$29.95 purchase _ #ST - QV2224
Chronicles a diverse culture blessed with unparalleled scenery and the geographical diversity of an entire continent. Visits Milfred Sound, Mitre Peak and Bowen Falls.
Geography - World
Dist - INSTRU

Touring on Two Wheels 20 MIN
U-matic / VHS
Color (J)
LC 82-706788
Discusses bicycle trips as a practical alternative to motor - powered excursions. Shows touring bikes, camping gear and packing tips. Includes information on tire changes, broken spokes, derailleurs and brake adjustments, along with the use of campgrounds vs the semiwilderness and rules of the road.
Physical Education and Recreation
Dist - AWSS **Prod** - AWSS 1981

Touring Paris Series
Arriving in Paris 20 MIN
Camping in France 20 MIN
Exploring Paris 20 MIN
French Restaurants 20 MIN
Parisian Sights and Shops 20 MIN
Dist - MEDIAG

Touring Red China - Teenage Impressions 9 MIN
16mm
Color (I J H)
Shows a group of Connecticut high school students on a tour of the People's Republic of China. Presents the reactions of the students to the Chinese culture.
Geography - World
Dist - MOKIN **Prod** - CBSTV 1979

Touring Scotland 65 MIN
VHS
Color (G)
$29.95 purchase _ #ST - QV2223
Travels from the Scottish border and Hadrian's Wall to the Abbeys and Gretna Green to Ayt. Tours Dumfries and Culzean Castle, the city of Glasgow, Gleneagles Turnberry and St Andrews shrine, and offers bagpipe concert in Edinburgh Castle.
Geography - World; History - World
Dist - INSTRU

Tourism 50 MIN
U-matic / 16mm
CTV Reports Series
Color; Mono (J H C A)
$350.00 purchase, $50.00 rental
Looks at the tourist industry in Canada including the problems facing it and a potential plan of action for the future.
Geography - World
Dist - CTV **Prod** - CTV 1977

Tourist 4 MIN
16mm
B&W; Color (G)
$25.00 rental
Proposes that the psychic desires of tourists permeate the architecture of seeing. Depicts the tourist look as ephemeral as the animation of this collage.
Fine Arts
Dist - CANCIN **Prod** - BARHAM 1985

Tourists in Heidelberg 5 MIN
U-matic / VHS / 16mm
European Studies - Germany Series
Color (H C A) (GERMAN)
LC 76-700763
Delineates the history and tourist attractions of Germany's oldest university city, Heidelberg.
Geography - World; History - World
Dist - IFB **Prod** - MFAFRG 1973

The Tournament 28 MIN
BETA / VHS
Color (G)
$29.95 purchase
Features Armor Collection curator Dr Helmut Nickel who discusses Medieval life and the comprehensive armory of the Metropolitan Museum of Art.
Civics and Political Systems; Fine Arts; History - World; Sociology
Dist - ARTSAM **Prod** - MMOA

Tourne Potatoes 5 MIN
U-matic / VHS
Color (PRO)
Shows how to carve potatoes into the shapes needed for noisette, rissole, fondante and chateau.
Home Economics; Industrial and Technical Education
Dist - CULINA **Prod** - CULINA

Tous les matins du monde - All the mornings of the world 114 MIN
35mm 16mm
Color (G)
$200.00 rental
Features a production based on the lives of the renowned 17th century royal musician Marin Marais and his mentor, the mysterious Monsieur de Sainte Colombe. Follows their lives in a quiet countryside mansion where Colombe, a widower, and his two beautiful daughters, play the viol and give occasional performances. When a young, brash man is accepted as the sole pupil of the testy Colombe, a tempestuous relationship between two brilliant artists begins. Produced by Jean - Louis Livi; directed by Alain Corneau; screenplay by Pascal Quignard and Alain Corneau. Stars Guillaume Depardieu. Based on the novel by Pascal Quignard.
Fine Arts; Psychology
Dist - OCTOBF

Tout Ecartille 6 MIN
16mm
Color (J)
LC 76-702150
Uses rapid, twirling, flashing images to create a poetic film allegory. Centers around a faceless man wearing a flowing, black magician's cape as he laughingly creates havoc wherever he visits.
Fine Arts
Dist - NFBC **Prod** - NFBC 1976

Tout Va Bien 95 MIN
16mm
Color (FRENCH)
Tells the story of a serious filmmaker, played by Yves Montand, who has lapsed into the easy money world of television commercials. Focuses also on Jane Fonda as an American reporter who makes a decision to quit establishment journalism.
Fine Arts; Foreign Language; Literature and Drama
Dist - NYFLMS **Prod** - NYFLMS 1972

A Toute betise 3 MIN
16mm
Color (G)
$15.00 rental
Generates a series of synthetic images through editing and printing techniques. Features a face - paced visual charade with a multitude of images such as a forest in downtown San Francisco, people in motion and music.
Fine Arts
Dist - CANCIN **Prod** - JONESE 1976

Toute La Bande - Episode 01 - Arrivee D'Elisabeth 15 MIN
16mm
Color (I J H)
Tells the story of Elisabeth from Orlay, who missed her hosts, the Ermonts, at the airport of Daker due to the Ermonts' late start and heavy traffic. Concludes with the happy get together of the guest and the host's entire family.
Foreign Language
Dist - SBS **Prod** - SBS 1970

Toute La Bande - Episode 02 - Jeudi 15 MIN
16mm
Color (I J H)
Explains that Elisabeth has chosen the carnations for Mrs Ermont's present through the suggestion of Mrs Ermont's son, Victor, who also received a record as a gift for his help.
Foreign Language
Dist - SBS **Prod** - SBS 1970

Toute La Bande - Episode 03 - Depart En Vacances 15 MIN
16mm
Color (I J H)
Follows the Ermonts to their vacation in Brittany. Includes a picnic near a river bank and the little fishing port where the Ermont's have their little summer home.
Foreign Language
Dist - SBS **Prod** - SBS 1970

Toute La Bande - Episode 04 - Vacances En Bretagne 15 MIN
16mm
Color (I J H)
Presents the Ermonts, their children, Caroline and Victor and their friends spending their wonderful vacation in Brittany. Includes window shopping, eating at the cafe and boat rides.
Foreign Language
Dist - SBS **Prod** - SBS 1970

Toute La Bande - Episode 05 - Aventure En Mer 15 MIN
16mm
Color (I J H)
Tells the adventure of Victor's and Jean - Louis' motorboat ride and how they returned safely with the help of a fisherman's family.
Foreign Language
Dist - SBS **Prod** - SBS 1970

Toute La Bande - Episode 06 - La Rentree 15 MIN
16mm
Color (I J H)
Tells the adventure of Caroline's and Victor's trip to a shop to buy their school supplies which brought Caroline's teacher's reprimands for wearing make - up.
Foreign Language
Dist - SBS **Prod** - SBS 1970

Toute La Bande - Episode 07 - Sur La Tour Eiffel 15 MIN
16mm
Color (I J H)
Presents a tour of the Eiffel Tower taken by Caroline, Victor and Elisabeth, who encounter a youth named Jacques, who becomes friends with the girls and a bore to Victor.
Foreign Language
Dist - SBS **Prod** - SBS 1970

Toute La Bande - Episode 08 - Feu Vert 15 MIN
16mm
Color (I J H)
Tells of the adventure of Caroline and Anne's motorbike ride to the Bois de Boulogne to meet Jacques, who was Caroline's boy friend, but soon got attracted to Anne.
Foreign Language
Dist - SBS **Prod** - SBS 1970

Toute La Bande - Episode 09 - Bricolage 15 MIN
16mm
Color (I J H)
Depicts how, through a visit to Caroline's and Victor's Uncle Paul to ask for his help, Jacques' intelligent interest in Uncle Paul's puttering activities results in the uncle treating him as a member of the family.
Foreign Language
Dist - SBS **Prod** - SBS 1970

Toute La Bande - Episode 10 - a Versailles 15 MIN
16mm
Color (I J H)
Presents a tour around Versailles taken by Caroline and Elisabeth. Includes the great ornamental fountains, gardens and Marie Antoinette's model farm.
Foreign Language
Dist - SBS **Prod** - SBS 1970

Toute La Bande - Episode 11 - Panne D'Essence 15 MIN
16mm
Color (I J H)
Features Victor, who took his father's car to the movie without his father's consent and is punished by having to spend his own money to fill up the tank and wash the car instead of watching his favorite soccer team on television.
Foreign Language
Dist - SBS **Prod** - SBS 1970

Toute La Bande - Episode 12 - Le Vieux Paris 15 MIN
16mm
Color (I J H)
Presents the adventures of Caroline, Elisabeth and Jacques as they travel through the Ile de la Cite and the Palace des vosges.
Foreign Language
Dist - SBS **Prod** - SBS 1970

Toute La Bande - Episode 13 - Bon Anniversaire 15 MIN
16mm
Color (I J H)
Describes how Victor uses his birthday gift of cash from his father to treat all his friends to an evening at a discotheque, which turns out to be a combination of birthday party, reunion and farewell - - for the next day the Ermonts and Elisabeth are going to the south of France.
Foreign Language
Dist - SBS **Prod** - SBS 1970

Toute la bande series
Arrivee D'Elisabeth - The Arrival of Elisabeth 15 MIN
Bon anniversaire - happy birthday 15 MIN
La Rentree - the Return to School 15 MIN
Le Vieux Paris 15 MIN
Sur La Tour Eiffel - on the Eiffel Tower 15 MIN
Vacances En Bretagne - Vacation in Brittany 15 MIN
A Versailles - at Versailles 15 MIN
Dist - SBS

TOW Modifications and Maintenance Lessons Learned 12 MIN
U-matic / VHS
Color
LC 81-706252
Illustrates modifications to the TOW weapon, showing both the old and newly - modified components, such as the launch tube, sight reticle light control, and changes affecting radio interference and missile simulation rounds. Emphasizes precautions to be observed by TOW crew members for boresighting and transporting the optical sight.
Civics and Political Systems
Dist - USNAC **Prod** - USA 1981

Toward 2001 22 MIN
16mm
Color
LC 78-700399
Presents experts from business, government and the academic community, who express their views about the electrical power needs of the United States and the options available to the electrical utility industry.
Business and Economics; Industrial and Technical Education; Social Science; Sociology
Dist - CONTR **Prod** - CONTR 1977

Toward a Broader Understanding of Ethnic Dance 30 MIN
VHS / U-matic
Third World Dance - Beyond the White Stream Series
Color
Fine Arts; Industrial and Technical Education; Sociology
Dist - ARCVID **Prod** - ARCVID

Toward a Caring Community 28 MIN
U-matic / VHS / 16mm
Color
Explores community attitudes toward mental patients by showing highlights of a workshop in which a cross section of New Jersey residents tackles the issues and problems of community care. Includes a historical review of attitudes toward the mentally ill and their treatment, a summary of the work of Dorothea Dix and commentary by an articulate representative of mental patients.
Health and Safety; Sociology
Dist - UCEMC **Prod** - NJDHS 1980

Toward a Governed World 27 MIN
Videoreel / U-matic / VHS
Color (G)
$95.00 purchase, $45.00 rental
Proposes that the abolition of war and injustice can only come about through the creation of a global democratic government. Features historical footage, graphics, and statements by well - known advocates of world government.
Civics and Political Systems; Social Science
Dist - EFVP **Prod** - EFVP 1988

Toward a livable city 28 MIN
VHS
Color (G)
$149.00 purchase _ #EX2345
Examines the development of Barcelona, Spain.
Fine Arts; Geography - World; Sociology
Dist - FOTH

Toward a more Common Language 27 MIN
16mm
Color
LC 74-705807
Presents a general overview of state education agencies, their growth, responsibilities, relationships to other state agencies, organization, functions and problems and the State Education Agency Handbook VII.
Education; Sociology
Dist - USNAC **Prod** - USOE 1973

Toward a New Brazil - a Cardinal and the People 24 MIN
U-matic / VHS
Color
$335.00 purchase
History - World; Religion and Philosophy
Dist - ABCLR **Prod** - ABCLR 1980

Toward a New Day - 1965 - 1980 58 MIN
16mm / U-matic / VHS
I Remember Harlem Series Part 4
Color (J)
LC 82-700482
History - United States
Dist - FOTH **Prod** - MILESW 1981

Toward a new paradigm of the unconscious 30 MIN
VHS / BETA
Roots of consciousness series
Color (G)
$29.95 purchase _ #S040
Features Dr Stanislav Grof, psychotherapist, who believes that in extraordinary circumstances the human mind is capable of accessing information from anywhere in time and space. Part of a four - part series on the roots of consciousness.
Psychology; Science - Natural; Science - Physical
Dist - THINKA **Prod** - THINKA

Toward Careers in Agriculture 21 MIN
16mm
Color
Delineates the importance of agriculture to primarily industrial states like Connecticut. Shows ways students train for jobs in modern agriculture through vocational agriculture programs in specialized high school curricula.
Agriculture; Education; Geography - United States; Guidance and Counseling; Psychology
Dist - USOE **Prod** - SGF 1967

Toward Freedom - 1940 - 1965 58 MIN
16mm / U-matic / VHS
I Remember Harlem Series Part 3
Color (J)
LC 82-700482
History - United States
Dist - FOTH **Prod** - MILESW 1981

Toward Immortality 50 MIN
16mm / U-matic / VHS
Color (H C A)
Discusses the explosion of information that has begun to reveal why people die and how they can remain young.
Health and Safety
Dist - CORF **Prod** - GANNET 1983

Toward Immortality 27 MIN
U-matic / VHS / 16mm
Color (A)
Focuses on studies in California and Texas proving that undernutrition without malnutrition, increasing food value while paring calories, not only prolongs the life of laboratory mammals, but also improves their health. Notes that nutritional adjustments teamed with regular exercise are one means of stalling the aging process. Compares the southeast U S with a comparable area in the northern Midwest where the soil and water are richer in minerals and trace elements. Visits laboratories, interviews researchers and looks at the aging. Suplements MTI's Stalking Immortality.
Health and Safety; Psychology; Social Science
Dist - CORF **Prod** - CORF

Toward intimacy - women with disabilities 60 MIN
VHS
Color (H C G)
$445.00 purchase, $75.00 rental
Portrays four women with disabilities and the fulfilling relationships they have established. Reveals their struggle for self esteem, search for love and sexual expression.
Guidance and Counseling; Health and Safety; Psychology; Sociology
Dist - FLMLIB **Prod** - NFBC 1993

Toward Jerusalem 28 MIN
VHS
Jewish music heritage library series
Color (G)
$39.95 purchase _ #796
Focuses on the dream of Jews from all corners of the world to come to Israel and the varied musical work of eight ethnic groups of instrumentalists and singers from around Israel who gather together in order to perform for and meet one another. Meets the musicians in their own surroundings as they prepare for their trip to Jerusalem. Israeli rock star Ehud Banai, who has made use of ethnic sounds in his own compositions, joins the musicians. Features musical ensembles from Persia, India, Iraq, Ethiopia, Bukhara, Kurdistan, Georgia - USSR, and Tajkhistan. Part of a series on Jewish music from around the world, featuring Martin Bookspan as narrator.
Fine Arts; Sociology
Dist - ERGOM **Prod** - IMHP

Toward Price - Based Reimbursement
U-matic / VHS
Revenues, Rates and Reimbursements Series
Color
Illustrates important reimbursement implications of medical care pricing. Shows the department - by - department roller coaster of margins within an institution.
Business and Economics; Health and Safety
Dist - TEACHM **Prod** - TEACHM

Toward Reconciliation - Part I and Part II 60 MIN
VHS / U-matic
Color
$300 rental
Examines, in part 1, the historical roots and current ecumenical situation between the Roman Catholic and Anglican churches in England. Includes interviews with Archbishop Robert Runcie and Cardinal George Basil Hume. Includes an analysis, in part 2, of the Pope's trip to Britain.
Religion and Philosophy
Dist - CCNCC **Prod** - CCNCC 1985

Toward the American dream 30 MIN
VHS
America in perspective - US history since 1877 series
Color (H C G)
$99.00 purchase _ #AIP - 19
Examines the civil rights movement of the early 1960s and analyzes the success of the movement as of 1965. Part of a 26 - part series.
Civics and Political Systems; History - United States
Dist - INSTRU **Prod** - DALCCD 1991

Toward the Global Family 20 MIN
16mm / U-matic / VHS
Communications Revolution Series
Color (H C A)
Addresses the impact of technology on business, industry, finance, the military and global relations.
Social Science; Sociology
Dist - CORF **Prod** - NVIDC

Toward the Least Restrictive Environment 27 MIN
16mm
Color
Presents teachers' views on the placement of handicapped students into classes with the nonhandicapped. Features one student expressing his feelings regarding attendance at a high school as compared with special school.
Education; Psychology
Dist - PDPI **Prod** - PDPI 1979

Toward the Sun 28 MIN
16mm
Color (H C A)
Looks at some of the research into tapping and storing the sun's energy for use in heating homes and providing power for industry. Visits a project in Nebraska where solar power is used in an irrigation scheme which delivers a thousand gallons a minute. Shows the Tower Power in Mexico which uses thousands of mirrors to concentrate the sun's rays so that they are able to burn through two - inch steel plates.
Social Science
Dist - FI **Prod** - CANBC

Toward the Unexplored 26 MIN
16mm
Color
LC 74-705809
Traces the history of Edwards Air Force Base, California, as an air proving ground and research center since the early days of aviation and documents experiments in rocketry.
History - United States; Industrial and Technical Education; Social Science
Dist - USNAC **Prod** - USAF 1967

Toward the year 2000 - can we survive the future
VHS
Color (J H C)
$197.00 purchase _ #00237 - 126
Presents two parts which discuss diverse views of the future. Features Alvin Toffler who is wary of accumulating technology, behavioral psychologist B F Skinner who suggests that human actions be engineered, historian Arnold Toynbee who deplores the long - term effects of television and computers, ecologist Barry Commoner who is convinced that it is his generation which must save the environment, and Charles Reich who sees revolution as inevitable. Includes teacher's guide and library kit.
Psychology; Science - Natural; Sociology
Dist - GA **Prod** - GA

Towards 4 MIN
16mm
Color (G)
$10.00 rental
Presents a variation of the filmmaker's other production entitled Bomen, redrawn here to imagine the bloody meet of two monologues. Features a collision of automobiles in place of conversation. A Michael Hoolboom production.
Fine Arts; Psychology
Dist - CANCIN

Towards a Better Society 12 MIN
16mm
B&W (H C A)
Presents the heart of a small Indian village built around a family facing the problem of social customs which are barriers to education and progress. Shows the change from old orthodox ways to new ones, which are paving the way to a better nation.
Social Science; Sociology
Dist - NEDINF **Prod** - INDIA

Towards a Modern Europe 30 MIN
U-matic / VHS / 16mm
Outline History of Europe Series
Color (H C A)
LC 79-701863
Outlines the movements and conditions that prepared Europe for modernity. Examines the Renaissance, the age of discovery, the rise of the mercantile class and the reign of Louis XIV.
History - World
Dist - IFB **Prod** - IFB 1975

Towards a New Community I - the Search for Alternatives 29 MIN
Videoreel / VT2
Black Experience Series
Color
History - United States; Social Science; Sociology
Dist - PBS **Prod** - WTTWTV

Towards a New Community II - the Experience of Blackness 29 MIN
Videoreel / VT2
Black Experience Series
Color
History - United States; Social Science; Sociology
Dist - PBS **Prod** - WTTWTV

Towards an Ultimate System 30 MIN
U-matic
Fast Forward Series
Color (H C)
Shows how information moves out instantly to consumers through computer, telephone and television technology.
Computer Science; Science
Dist - TVOTAR **Prod** - TVOTAR 1979

Towards an Understanding of Pain 16 MIN
16mm
Color (PRO)
Provides an overall review of current concepts of pain perception and their neurophysiological foundations.
Health and Safety
Dist - GEIGY **Prod** - GEIGY

Towards Baruya Manhood - Vol II 143 MIN
VHS
People in Change Series
Color (S)
$387.00 purchase _ #188 - 9058
Gives unique insights into the life of the Baruya tribe in the Easter Highlands of Papua New Guinea. Shows traditional Baaruya culture, liitle changed by European contact. Volume II of a two - part series which deals with traditional culture and how and why these cultures change. This series clearly demonstrates the impact of other cultures on the tradional way of life in Papua New Guinea. Three tapes.
Geography - World; History - World; Social Science; Sociology
Dist - FI **Prod** - FLMAUS 1988

Towards the future 60 MIN
VHS / BETA
Color; PAL (G)
PdS25, $50.00 purchase
Features a speech by the Venerable Sumedho Bhikkhu at the Amaravati Buddhist Centre, September and October 1986.
Fine Arts; Religion and Philosophy; Sociology
Dist - MERIDT

Towards Visual Learning
U-matic
Visual Learning Series Session 1
Color (T)
Defines the impact of television on society and comments on the implications of instructional television for education.
Education; Fine Arts; Industrial and Technical Education
Dist - NYSED **Prod** - NYSED

Towed in a hole 20 MIN
16mm
B&W (G)
Presents Laurel and Hardy as fish venders who decide to catch their own fish.
Fine Arts
Dist - KITPAR **Prod** - ROACH 1947

Tower 12 MIN
16mm
Color (G)
$15.00 rental
Studies a large water tower with overtones of mystery, play, the past and a presence. Reveals the essence of making a movie about a fixed object in final part which is 8mm blown up to 16. Produced by Darrell Forney.
Fine Arts
Dist - CANCIN

Tower and braid - a chronicle of Fort Snelling 19 MIN
VHS
Color (G)
$24.95 purchase _ #R50 - C
Relates the history of Minnesota's famous military outpost, Fort Snelling.
History - United States
Dist - MINHS

Tower of Babel 51 MIN
16mm / U-matic / VHS
Greatest Heroes of the Bible Series
Color (I)
Reveals that Amathar's original plan to build a tower to enable people to walk into the heavens and be with God is corrupted as he insists that his likeness be placed on the tower. Shows that because of Amathar's vanity God destroys the tower and gives people different languages. Stars Vince Edwards and Richard Basehart.
Religion and Philosophy
Dist - LUF **Prod** - LUF 1979

Tower of Fire 20 MIN
16mm
Unbroken Arrow Series
Color (P I)
Presents an adventure set in the time of the Saxons which tells how the Baron is building a watchtower which will overlook the forest and reveal the outlaws' movements. Describes how Robin is determined to destroy the tower.
Literature and Drama
Dist - LUF **Prod** - LUF 1977

Tower of London 31 MIN
VHS
Color (S)
$49.00 purchase _ #825 - 9330
Marks the first time television has been allowed to film the immensely entertaining Beefeater's Special - conducted tours in which the guards tell all about the gory fates of famous Tower 'guests' through the ages.
Civics and Political Systems; Fine Arts; Geography - World; History - World; Social Science; Sociology
Dist - FI **Prod** - BBCTV 1981

The Tower of London 45 MIN
VHS / BETA
Color (G)
$34.95 purchase _ #428
Chronicles the history, mysteries and legends of the Tower of London. Features actor Alec McCowen as host. Produced by Andrew Treagus Associates Productions Ltd.
Civics and Political Systems; Geography - World; History - World
Dist - IHF

The Tower of Washington 21 MIN
16mm
Color (J)
LC FIA65-490
Describes the construction of the Gloria in excelsis tower at the Washington Cathedral. Tells about the bells which were cast in England, pictures their installation and shows the ringing of the bells and carillon on the day of the dedication. Includes excerpts from Chief Justice Earl Warren's dedication message.
Fine Arts; Geography - United States; History - United States; Industrial and Technical Education
Dist - NCATHA **Prod** - NCATHA 1964

The Tower without ends 30 MIN
VHS
Metropolis series
Color; PAL (H C A)
PdS65 purchase
Traces the historical and technological evolution of components of a modern city. Focuses on the emergence of high rise buildings. Part one of a six part series.
Industrial and Technical Education; Sociology
Dist - BBCENE

The Towers 13 MIN
16mm
Color (P I)
Shows the building of the Watts Towers by an Italian immigrant, Simon Rodia.
Fine Arts; Geography - United States
Dist - CFS **Prod** - HALE 1965

Towers Without Infernos 15 MIN
16mm
Science in Action Series
Color (C)
Tells how today's highrise buildings pose unique problems to those involved in fire prevention, fire protection and fire suppression. Shows some of the latest methods and techniques developed to prevent and control future highrise fires.
Health and Safety; Industrial and Technical Education
Dist - COUNFI **Prod** - ALLFP

The Town 13 MIN
U-matic / VHS / 16mm
B&W
LC FIE52-784
Shows life in an American town, Madison, Indiana, and explains the Democratic characteristics of the social and civic life of the people.
Civics and Political Systems; Psychology; Social Science; Sociology
Dist - USNAC **Prod** - USOWI 1949

Town Against TB 30 MIN
16mm
Color
Discusses the planning, execution and results of a pilot community tuberculin testing program conducted in 1963 in Toms River, New Jersey. Presents a blueprint which can be followed by medical, health and civic groups in all communities planning disease detection and immunization programs.
Health and Safety; Sociology
Dist - LEDR **Prod** - ACYLLD 1964

Town Blody Hall 88 MIN
16mm / U-matic / VHS
Color
Features Norman Mailer vs Germaine Greer in the Great Debate on Women's Liberation at Town Hall, New York City in 1971. Other participants include Jill Johnston, Diana Trilling, Elizabeth Hartwick and Anatole Broyard. By Chris Hegdus and D A Pennebaker.
Sociology
Dist - PENNAS **Prod** - PENNAS

Town hall series
Documents the operation of government on a local level in Great Britain. Focuses on eight crises that the Lewisham borough council faces in a one - year period. Crises included are a projected overspending, dealings with financial advisors, housing problems within the borough, tension between council members, 'dirty squad' responsibilities, proposed cuts to social services, cuts in education and the establishment of a pole tax. Episodes are also available individually.
Town hall series 320 MIN
Dist - BBCENE

Town hall
Bad news 40 MIN
Caring 40 MIN
The crisis 50 MIN
Cuts 40 MIN
People power 40 MIN
Special needs 40 MIN
Threatening behaviour 40 MIN
Winners and losers 40 MIN
Dist - BBCENE

A Town in Old Mexico 10 MIN
16mm
Color
LC FIA52-675
Depicts 17th century architecture and beautiful gardens in the villages of Puebla, Oribaza and Fortin de las Floras.
Fine Arts; Geography - World; History - World
Dist - USOIAA **Prod** - UWF 1944

Town meeting - a process run amok - Thomas - Hill hearings 90 MIN
VHS
ABC News collection series
Color (G)
$29.98 purchase _ #6302316464
Features Ted Koppel who leads a discussion of the political and the media issues surrounding the Clarence Thomas - Anita Hill sexual harassment Senate hearings.
Civics and Political Systems
Dist - INSTRU CAMV **Prod** - ABCNEW 1991

Town meeting - Holy Land - Tuesday, April 26, 1988 30 MIN
VHS
Nightline series
Color (H C G)
$14.98 purchase _ #MP6166
Examines the political situation in the Middle East.
Fine Arts; History - World
Dist - INSTRU **Prod** - ABCNEW 1988

Town meeting - Pearl Harbor plus 50 90 MIN
VHS
ABC News collection series
Color (G)
$29.98 purchase _ #6302316472
Joins Ted Koppel with Japanese political, economic and business commentators in Tokyo and Americans in five United States cities to discuss Japanese - American relations.
Civics and Political Systems
Dist - INSTRU **Prod** - ABCNEW 1991

A Town meeting with Nelson Mandela 90 MIN
VHS
Color (J H C G)
$29.95 purchase _ #MH6100V
Contains the entire Ted Koppel interview with Nelson Mandela, 71 - year - old leader of the African National Congress, shortly after his release from South African prisons, February 11, 1990.
Civics and Political Systems; Guidance and Counseling
Dist - CAMV

The Town Mouse and the Country Mouse 14 MIN
16mm
B&W (P I)
Profiles the lives of field mice and house mice. Takes advantage of specially built nests that allow the filming of the mice carrying out their routine activities undisturbed.
Science - Natural
Dist - VIEWTH **Prod** - BBC

The Town Mouse and the Country Mouse 6 MIN
16mm
Color (P)
LC 81-701556
Presents an Aesop's fable about a field mouse who visits an elegant house mouse. Shows that although the house mouse has a more luxurious lifestyle, it is also more dangerous because there is a cat stalking him at all times.
Literature and Drama
Dist - BNCHMK **Prod** - NFBC 1981

Town Neighborhood - a General Description 15 MIN
U-matic / VHS
Neighborhoods series
Color (P)
Offers a general description of a town neighborhood.
Sociology
Dist - GPN **Prod** - NEITV 1981

Town Neighborhood - Good Neighbors Help each Other 15 MIN
VHS / U-matic
Neighborhoods Series
Color (P)
Explains how good neighbors help each other in towns.
Sociology
Dist - GPN **Prod** - NEITV 1981

Town Planning 15 MIN
U-matic / VHS / 16mm
B&W (H C A)
Illustrates the way the science of town planning can be directed toward the re - planning of a city that grew at random. Illustrates properly zoned business, residential and industrial areas.
Fine Arts; Psychology; Sociology
Dist - IFB **Prod** - NFBC 1958

The Town - Pt 4 20 MIN
VHS
Middle Ages Series
Color (I)
$79.00 purchase _ #825 - 9436
Incorporates source and historic material to recreate medieval life. Depicts the main social groups and captures the political climate of the time. Visits castles, cathedrals and battlegrounds, dramatizes pilgrimages and uprisings, uses close - up views of historical artifacts and architecture to bring the Middle Ages to life. Part 4 of five parts explores the establishment and history of a medieval town, along with the nature and work of the guild organizations.
Business and Economics; Geography - World; History - World; Social Science; Sociology
Dist - FI **Prod** - BBCTV 1987

The Town that Never was 20 MIN
16mm
Color
LC 81-700291
Recounts the history of Los Alamos, New Mexico, and the creation of the Los Alamos Scientific Laboratory in the 1940's.
Geography - United States
Dist - LASL **Prod** - LASL 1980

A Town that Washes its Water 13 MIN
16mm
Screen news digest series; Vol 13; Issue 1
Color (I)
LC 72-700578
Reports on a pioneer reclamation program that is turning sewage water into a valuable community asset.
Science - Natural; Social Science
Dist - HEARST **Prod** - HEARST 1970

Towns, Trade and Fairs 30 MIN
U-matic / Kit / VHS
Western Man and the Modern World in Video; Unit 2
Color (J H)
$1378.12 for the 25 part series purchase _ #C676 - 27347 - 5, $69.95, $72.00 purchase _ #MB - 510426 - 1, #MB - 510219 - 6
Shows the gradual transition from feudal agriculture to a modern money economy. Highlights the development of credit, banking, the rise of the middle class and the importance of towns.
Business and Economics; History - World
Dist - RH
SRA

Townscape - the language of place 20 MIN
VHS
Color (G)
Recreates on video the book 'Townscape' by architect and city planner Gordon Cullen. Develops a system which judges how cities and towns affect people. Produced by the Built Environment Communication Center of the University of Minnesota.
Fine Arts; Science - Natural; Sociology
Dist - IAFC

Towser and Goblin Gobble - Curiosity 5 MIN
16mm / U-matic / VHS
Towser Series
Color
Tells a story of Towser using a clever ploy to escape from Goblin Gobble.
Fine Arts; Psychology
Dist - JOU **Prod** - JOU

Towser and Sadie's Birthday - Imagination 5 MIN
16mm / U-matic / VHS
Towser Series
Color
Tells a story about wanting to give a friend a present.
Fine Arts; Psychology
Dist - JOU **Prod** - JOU

Towser and Sadie's Robot - Modern Conveniences 5 MIN
16mm / U-matic / VHS
Towser Series
Color
Shows the cat Towser being commanded by a robot.
Fine Arts; Industrial and Technical Education
Dist - JOU **Prod** - JOU

Towser and the Alien Invader Strategy 5 MIN
U-matic / VHS / 16mm
Towser Series
Color
Shows the cat Towser saving the king from an alien from the planet Nice.
Fine Arts
Dist - JOU **Prod** - JOU

Towser and the Black Hole - Listening to Sound Advice 5 MIN
U-matic / VHS / 16mm
Towser Series
Color
Shows the cat Towser lured to a Black Hole even though he was warned against entering it.
Fine Arts; Psychology
Dist - JOU **Prod** - JOU

Towser and the Black Knight - Courage 5 MIN
U-matic / VHS / 16mm
Towser Series
Color
Shows the cat Towser bravely challenging the Black Knight.
Fine Arts; Psychology
Dist - JOU **Prod** - JOU

Towser and the Conjuror - Confidence 5 MIN
16mm / U-matic / VHS
Towser Series
Color
Shows Towser restoring a magician's ability to perform by having faith in him.
Fine Arts; Psychology
Dist - JOU **Prod** - JOU

Towser and the Dentist - Quackery 5 MIN
U-matic / VHS / 16mm
Towser Series
Color
Tells of Towser's friends offering cures for his toothache. Shows the importance of good dental care.
Fine Arts; Health and Safety
Dist - JOU **Prod** - JOU

Towser and the Dinner Party - Deception 5 MIN
U-matic / VHS / 16mm
Towser Series
Color
Tells of Towser hiring a caterer to prepare a feast, when he'd promised to cook it himself.
Fine Arts; Psychology
Dist - JOU **Prod** - JOU

Towser and the Dragon - Giftgiving 5 MIN
16mm / U-matic / VHS
Towser Series
Color
Tells of the cat Towser trying to give away what he believes to be a useless dragon.
Fine Arts; Psychology
Dist - JOU **Prod** - JOU

Towser and the Flight - Faith 5 MIN
16mm / U-matic / VHS
The Towser Series
Color
Shows the cat Towser being able to fly like a bird as long as he believes in his ability to fly.
Fine Arts; Psychology
Dist - JOU **Prod** - JOU

Towser and the Funny Face - Punishments 5 MIN
U-matic / VHS / 16mm
Towser Series
Color
Shows Towser being punished by the wind for making funny faces and startling people.
Fine Arts; Psychology; Sociology
Dist - JOU **Prod** - JOU

Towser and the Haunted House - Fear 5 MIN
U-matic / VHS / 16mm
The Towser Series
Color
Shows Towser boasting that he's not afraid of a haunted house.
Fine Arts; Psychology; Sociology
Dist - JOU **Prod** - JOU

Towser and the Holiday - Adventure 5 MIN
U-matic / VHS / 16mm
Towser Series
Color
Tells of Towser taking a camping trip to cure his boredom.
Fine Arts; Physical Education and Recreation; Sociology
Dist - JOU **Prod** - JOU

Towser and the Lion (Bravery) 5 MIN
U-matic / VHS / 16mm
Towser Series
Color
Shows the cat Towser going after a lion.
Psychology
Dist - JOU **Prod** - JOU

Towser and the Magic Apple - Happiness 5 MIN
16mm / U-matic / VHS
Towser Series
Color
Tells of a magic apple which is supposed to give happiness.
Fine Arts; Psychology
Dist - JOU **Prod** - JOU

Towser and the Nosey Parker - Behavior 5 MIN
U-matic / VHS / 16mm
Towser Series
Color
Shows a creature who sniffs everything and causes a commotion.
Fine Arts; Psychology; Sociology
Dist - JOU **Prod** - JOU

Towser and the Secret - Ambition 5 MIN
U-matic / VHS / 16mm
Towser Series
Color
Tells of Towser trying to find out a butterfly's secret.
Fine Arts; Psychology
Dist - JOU **Prod** - JOU

Towser and the Slight Accident - Love 5 MIN
16mm / U-matic / VHS
Towser Series
Color
Tells of Towser trying science and magic to help his sore foot and finding help in an unexpected source.
Fine Arts; Psychology
Dist - JOU **Prod** - JOU

Towser and the Smile Machine - Appearances Can be Deceiving 5 MIN
U-matic / VHS / 16mm
Towser Series
Color
Tells of Towser visiting a doctor to get help with his smile.
Fine Arts; Psychology
Dist - JOU **Prod** - JOU

Towser and the Snow Man - Illusion 5 MIN
16mm / U-matic / VHS
Towser Series
Color
Tells of Towser making a snowman in the shape of a wizard.
Fine Arts
Dist - JOU **Prod** - JOU

Towser and the Space Shot - Judgment 5 MIN
U-matic / VHS / 16mm
Towser Series
Color
Tells of Towser showing good sense in declining to travel on a spacecraft going to the moon.
Fine Arts; Psychology; Science - Physical
Dist - JOU **Prod** - JOU

Towser and the Terrible Thing - Problem Solving 5 MIN
U-matic / VHS / 16mm
Towser Series
Color
Shows Towser devising an ingeneous solution to a terrible problem.
Fine Arts; Psychology
Dist - JOU **Prod** - JOU

Towser and the Water Rats - Bargaining 5 MIN
U-matic / VHS / 16mm
Towser Series
Color
Tells a story of two water rats who want to buy Towser's house.
Business and Economics; Fine Arts; Psychology
Dist - JOU **Prod** - JOU

Towser and the Wizard - Trickery 5 MIN
16mm / U-matic / VHS
Towser Series
Color
Tells of a wizard who pretends to lose his powers in order to take a holiday.
Fine Arts; Psychology
Dist - JOU **Prod** - JOU

Towser and Uncle Bosco - Practical Jokes 5 MIN
16mm / U-matic / VHS
Towser Series
Color
Tells of a practical joker who learns the error of his ways.
Fine Arts; Psychology
Dist - JOU **Prod** - JOU

Towser Series
Towser and Goblin Gobble - Curiosity 5 MIN
Towser and Sadie's Birthday - Imagination 5 MIN
Towser and Sadie's Robot - Modern Conveniences 5 MIN
Towser and the Alien Invader Strategy 5 MIN
Towser and the Black Hole - Listening to Sound Advice 5 MIN
Towser and the Black Knight - Courage 5 MIN
Towser and the Conjuror - Confidence 5 MIN
Towser and the Dentist - Quackery 5 MIN
Towser and the Dinner Party - Deception 5 MIN
Towser and the Dragon - Giftgiving 5 MIN
Towser and the Flight - Faith 5 MIN
Towser and the Funny Face - Punishments 5 MIN
Towser and the Haunted House - Fear 5 MIN
Towser and the Holiday - Adventure 5 MIN
Towser and the Lion (Bravery) 5 MIN
Towser and the Magic Apple - Happiness 5 MIN
Towser and the Nosey Parker - Behavior 5 MIN
Towser and the Secret - Ambition 5 MIN
Towser and the Slight Accident - Love 5 MIN
Towser and the Smile Machine - Appearances Can be Deceiving 5 MIN
Towser and the Snow Man - Illusion 5 MIN
Towser and the Space Shot - Judgment 5 MIN
Towser and the Terrible Thing - Problem Solving 5 MIN
Towser and the Water Rats - Bargaining 5 MIN
Towser and the Wizard - Trickery 5 MIN
Towser and Uncle Bosco - Practical Jokes 5 MIN
Dist - JOU

Toxic and Deficiency Diseases of the Central Nervous System and Neuromuscular Diseases. 20 MIN
VHS / 16mm
Neuropathology Laboratory Sessions Series
(C)
$385.00 purchase _ #860VI064
Outlines characteristics of toxic and deficiency diseases affecting the central nervous system and also examines neuromuscular diseases.
Health and Safety
Dist - HSCIC **Prod** - HSCIC 1986

Toxic chemicals - information is the best defense series
Developing a community right to know law - Pt 2 26 MIN
Dist - BULFRG

Toxic Chemicals - Information is the Best Defense
Who Needs to Know - Pt 1 26 MIN
Dist - BULFRG

Toxic Earth - the Need to Unite 18 MIN
U-matic
Color (A)
Describes the growing problem of toxic chemicals in the environment and the need to formulate solutions to the problem.
Health and Safety; Sociology
Dist - AFLCIO **Prod** - AFLCIO 1984

The Toxic Goldrush 26 MIN
U-matic / VHS
Color (C)
$249.00, $149.00 purchase _ #AD - 1871
Shows that cleaning up the environment has become a growth industry. Reveals that companies which dispose of hazardous materials are in great demand across the country. Questions whether these industries are really effective and poses other questions concerning toxic waste disposal.
Agriculture; Science - Natural; Sociology
Dist - FOTH **Prod** - FOTH

The Toxic Goldrush - 221 30 MIN
U-matic
Currents - 1985 - 86 Season Series
Color (A)
Concludes that toxic waste cleanup is a bonanza for those companies involved in it.
Social Science; Sociology
Dist - PBS **Prod** - WNETTV 1985

Toxic Hazards in Industry 23 MIN
16mm / U-matic / VHS
Color (IND)
Discusses the hazards of such toxic substances as silica, asbestos, lead, unrefined mineral oils, carbon dioxide, benzene and trichloroethylene. Deals with absorption routes and how the hazards may be kept within safe limits.
Health and Safety; Sociology
Dist - IFB **Prod** - MILLBK

The Toxic release inventory - meeting the challenge 19 MIN
VHS
Color (G IND)
$45.00 purchase _ #SHA17125
Reveals that, as part of the Emergency Planning and Community - Right - to - Know Act of 1986, manufacturing facilities must report annually on chemical releases. Discloses that the Toxics Release Inventory is a listing of over 300 chemicals that communities have a right - to - know when released into the air or water. Helps organizations to determine what is reportable and the procedures for reporting.
Health and Safety
Dist - USNAC **Prod** - EPA 1987

Toxic Substance Control Act - TSCA 21 MIN
BETA / U-matic / VHS
Color (G PRO)
$29.95, $130.00 purchase _ #LSTF119
Explains how the United States Environmental Protection Agency uses the TSCA - Toxic Substance Control Act - to regulate new and existing toxic substances.
Civics and Political Systems; Sociology
Dist - FEDU **Prod** - FEDU 1992

Toxic Waste 60 MIN
VHS
Perspectives in Science Series
Color (J)
$350.00 purchase, $75.00 rental
Discusses economic and societal implications of toxic waste and its potential dangers. Examines the technology to deal with toxic waste.
Business and Economics; Sociology
Dist - BULFRG **Prod** - NFBC 1990

Toxic Waste in America 25 MIN
U-matic / VHS
Color
Examines how people's lives have been destroyed after exposure to toxic wastes at Woodstock, New York. Depicts the residents of Seymour, Indiana, as they prevent a toxic waste dump from locating their community. Reviews the story of Hugh Kaufman, an official with the Environmental Protection Agency (EPA) who exposed EPA corruption.
Health and Safety; Social Science; Sociology
Dist - DCTVC **Prod** - DCTVC

Toxic waste in Cecil County, Maryland 28 MIN
U-matic / VHS / BETA
Color (G)
$29.95, $130.00 purchase _ #LSTF49
Documents the history of an abandoned toxic waste site and how it was cleaned up.
Sociology
Dist - FEDU **Prod** - USEPA 1984

Toxic wastes 36 MIN
VHS
Color (I J H)
$130.00 purchase _ #A5VH 1374
Presents two parts on toxic waste. Details the long history of toxic wastes in the biosphere, showing students that the past often had worse toxic waste problems than present day. Part 2 explains the scientific concepts needed to convert fear of toxic waste into intelligent action. Covers the nature of chemicals and radiation, the cycling of chemicals in the biosphere, food chains, and tolerance levels in organisms. Includes supplemental book.
Science - Natural; Science - Physical; Sociology
Dist - CLRVUE **Prod** - CLRVUE

Toxic wastes - future quest 33 MIN
VHS
Future quest series
Color (J H C)
$79.00 purchase _ #316
Features biochemist Bruce Ames, public health expert Elizabeth Whelan, radiation expert Bernard Cohen, asbestos biochemist William Barnes and environmental activist Jeremy Rifkin. Presents their conflicting views on toxic waste problems. Includes a guide. Part of ten parts.
Sociology
Dist - HAWHIL **Prod** - HAWHIL

Toxic wastes today 26 MIN
VHS
Color; CC (H C)
$79.00 purchase _ #916
Explains basic scientific concepts needed to understand toxic wastes, including the nature of chemicals, the biosphere, the cycling of chemicals in the biosphere, radiation, food chains and tolerence levels in organisms. Avoids scare talk and stresses the importance of research. Part 2 of the program Toxic Wastes. Includes a book of the same title from the Learning Power series.
Health and Safety; Science - Natural; Science - Physical; Sociology
Dist - HAWHIL **Prod** - HAWHIL 1994

Toxicological Review - Charles Kokoski, PhD 29 MIN
U-matic
Food and Nutrition Seminars for Health Professionals Series
Color (PRO)
LC 78-706167
Examines the link between additives and the microbiological contamination of food, malnutrition and environmental contamination.
Health and Safety; Social Science
Dist - USNAC **Prod** - USFDA 1976

Toxigenicity Test of C Diphteriae 13 MIN
16mm
Color
LC FIE63-111
Explains procedures of the in - vitro test and animal tests for the detection of toxigenic strains of corynebacterium diphtheriae. Shows preparation of materials and interpretation of results of the tests.
Health and Safety
Dist - USNAC **Prod** - USPHS 1962

Toxins and poisons 12 MIN
VHS
Chemical hazards identification and training series
Color (IND) (SPANISH)
$395.00 purchase, $100.00 rental _ #8293
Explains the serious effects of toxic substances on the human body and illustrates effective safety precautions when working with toxic and poisonous substances. Explains and complies with 'Right - to Know' laws protecting employees who work with or around hazardous chemicals. Enhances worker understanding of being informed about hazardous materials. Part of a six - part series that helps companies comply with federal - OSHA - and state Right - to - Know laws ensuring safe work environments for employees, and introduces the Material Safety Data Sheet - MSDS - chemical reference guide.
Health and Safety; Sociology
Dist - AIMS **Prod** - MARCOM 1991

Toxins in Our Lives 31 MIN
35mm strip / VHS
Color (J)
$84.00 purchase _ #PE - 540610 - 1, #PE - 540611 - X
Discusses the problem of toxic waste both as a small - scale everyday home issue and as a complex global question. Considers possible solutions. Filmstrip version includes two filmstrips, two cassettes and teacher's guide.

Science - Natural; Sociology
Dist - SRA **Prod** - SRA 1989

Toxins in Our Lives 30 MIN
VHS
Color (J)
$84.00 purchase _ #193 Y 1501
Introduces students to the threat of toxins in our world. Poses questions and asks what can be done to stem the growing volume of toxic waste. Presented in two parts.
Science - Physical
Dist - WARDS

Toxoplasmosis - an update 27 MIN
VHS / 16mm
(C PRO)
$385.00 purchase _ #870VI001; $395.00 purchase, $80.00 rental _ #C870 - VI - 001
Provides medical students and practicing physicians with a complete discussion of toxoplasmosis, the lifecycle of the texoplasma organism, the signs and symptoms of toxoplasma infection, and the effects of the infection during pregnancy and in the newborn. It also recommends methods of diagnosis, treatment, and prevention.
Health and Safety
Dist - HSCIC **Prod** - HSCIC 1987

The Toy tester 15 MIN
VHS / 16mm
Harriet's magic hats series; No IV
Color (P)
$175.00 purchase _ #207149
Presents thirteen new programs to familiarize children with more workers and their role in community life. Features Aunt Harriet's bottomless trunks of magic hats where Carrie has only to put on a particular hat to be whisked off to an investigation of the person's role represented by the hat. Reveals Ralph's concern over one of his creations not passing the toy tester's test, and Carrie's decision to visit Albert to learn about toy testing. Explains that a toy tester's job involves protecting small children from dangerous toys. Tells toy makers about safety rules, and conducts an examination of their products for safety features.
Fine Arts; Guidance and Counseling; Health and Safety; Psychology; Sociology
Dist - ACCESS **Prod** - ACCESS 1986

Toying with Reality 29 MIN
U-matic / VHS
Learning through Play Series
(H C A PRO)
$180.00 purchase
Discusses learning with toys and how children build skills from working with blocks.
Home Economics; Psychology; Sociology
Dist - UTORMC **Prod** - UTORMC 1980
AITECH TORMC

Toying with Reality 27 MIN
U-matic / VHS
Learning through Play - Programs Series Program 3
Color (C)
Describes how the right kinds of playthings can simulate growth and development in children, pointing out that too often toy selection is left to big business.
Psychology
Dist - UTORMC **Prod** - UTORMC 1976

Toyota families for learning program 10 MIN
VHS
Color (G)
$20.00 purchase
Focuses on family literacy programs, defining what they are and telling about the families in them. Discusses the Toyota Families for Learning Program in Louisiana.
English Language
Dist - NCFL

The Toyota Standard Four Speed Transmission Explained 70 MIN
VHS / 35mm strip
(H A IND)
Includes transmission principles, basic parts, operation, disassembly, and assembly (5 tapes). Includes a Study Guide.
Education; Industrial and Technical Education
Dist - BERGL

Toys 7 MIN
U-matic / VHS / 16mm
Color (H C A)
LC FIA68-1256
Examines the possible effects of modern war toys on children in a fantasy about a deadly battle fought by war toys in a Christmas store window.
Civics and Political Systems; Fine Arts; Literature and Drama; Psychology
Dist - MGHT **Prod** - NFBC 1966

Toys 30 MIN
U-matic / VHS
Antique Shop Series
Color
Presents guests who are experts in their respective fields who share tips on collecting and caring for antique toys.
Fine Arts
Dist - MDCPB **Prod** - WVPTTV

Toys and Games for Five Years and Older 14 MIN
Videoreel / VT2
Living Better I Series
Color
Home Economics; Psychology
Dist - PBS **Prod** - MAETEL

Toys and Games for Preschoolers 14 MIN
Videoreel / VT2
Living Better Series; No I
Color
Home Economics; Psychology
Dist - PBS **Prod** - MAETEL

Toys for all children 10 MIN
VHS
Color; Captioned (G)
$25.00 purchase
Presents a large variety of simple and complex toys and switches for children with disabilities. Includes selection guidelines and a resource guide.
Health and Safety
Dist - UATP **Prod** - UATP 1993

Toys for Infants 7 MIN
U-matic
Take Time Series
(A)
Demonstrates the influence of parents and others caring for pre - schoolers on the physical and emotional development of the child.
Health and Safety; Psychology; Sociology
Dist - ACCESS **Prod** - ACCESS 1976

Toys for Preschoolers 7 MIN
U-matic
Take Time Series
(A)
Demonstrates the influence of parents and others caring for pre - schoolers on the physical and emotional development of the child.
Health and Safety; Psychology; Sociology
Dist - ACCESS **Prod** - ACCESS 1976

Toys for Toddlers 7 MIN
U-matic
Take Time Series
(A)
Demonstrates the influence of parents and others caring for pre - schoolers on the physical and emotional development of the child.
Health and Safety; Psychology; Sociology
Dist - ACCESS **Prod** - ACCESS 1976

Toys from Nuremberg 5 MIN
U-matic / VHS / 16mm
European Studies - Germany Series
Color (H C A)
LC 76-700744
Shows the toy - producing center of Nuremberg where some operations are still carried out by hand.
Geography - World; Sociology
Dist - IFB **Prod** - MFAFRG 1973

Toys that grew up II series
The Bells 76 MIN
Cops, comics and girls - Pt 1 54 MIN
Cops, Comics and Girls, Pt 2 59 MIN
The Films of Ben Turpin 64 MIN
Foolish wives 91 MIN
The Heart of Texas Ryan 64 MIN
Judith of Bethulia 61 MIN
The Mad Whirl 71 MIN
The Magic Movies of Georges Malies 56 MIN
Mickey 61 MIN
The Shamrock and the Rose 68 MIN
Dist - PBS

Toys that grew up series
The Serials - Pt 1 64 MIN
The Serials - Pt 2 64 MIN
Dist - PBS

TPR - Temperature, Pulse and Respiration 18 MIN
16mm
Patients are People Series
Color (T)
Health and Safety
Dist - MLA **Prod** - CALVIN 1967

TQC and manufacturing - the customer, the process, the data 18 MIN
VHS
Color (PRO G A)
$495.00 purchase, $150.00 rental
Gives the example of Hewlett - Packard's integrated circuits division to point out the benefits of total quality control. Explains the need for commitment to quality from management and workers. Includes ten copies of the Pocket Guide to TQC.
Business and Economics; Psychology
Dist - EXTR **Prod** - EBEC
VLEARN

TQC and service - the customer, the process, the data 18 MIN
VHS
Color (A PRO IND)
$495.00 purchase, $150.00 rental
Shows how Total Quality Control reduced Hewlett - Packard's overdue receivables figures from 12 percent down to one percent. Reveals that TQC statistical process control demonstrated that the high rate had been due to company practices.
Business and Economics
Dist - VLEARN **Prod** - EBEC

TQC Introduction for Top Management 13 MIN
VHS
(PRO)
Introduces Total Quality Control, or TQC, and emphasizes the importance of implementing it. Features Dr Kaoru Ishikawa and Dr Noriaki Kano.
Business and Economics
Dist - TOYOVS **Prod** - JPC 1987

TQC series
Presents a two - part series on the managing and operating philosophy of Total Quality Control.
TQC series 36 MIN
Dist - VLEARN **Prod** - EBEC 1987

TQC - Service 18 MIN
VHS
Color (PRO G A)
$495.00 purchase, $150.00 rental
Gives the example of Hewlett - Packard's credit and collections department to point out the benefits of total quality control. Explains the importance of process control to maintaining quality in company activities. Includes ten copies of the Pocket Guide to TQC.
Business and Economics; Psychology
Dist - EXTR **Prod** - EBEC

TQC - the Customer, the Process and the Data
VHS
Color (G)
$495.00 purchase, $150.00 rental
Shows the use of Total Quality Control, TQC, in both manufacturing and service settings to serve internal and external customers.
Business and Economics; Psychology
Dist - VLEARN

TQM - a context for change 46 MIN
VHS
Educational horizons videos series
Color (C PRO)
$250.00 purchase, $100.00 rental _ #42 - 2515, #42 - 2515R
Stresses the need for nurses to be ready to take a leadership role in TQM programs. Explores ways of teaching management concepts in Part I. Reviews the total quality movement in health care. Includes a case study from Rush - Presbyterian Hospital - St Luke's Medical Center, where TQM is integrated throughout the complex and the affiliated Rush University College of Nursing. Business, health care, education experts and staff nurses discuss the powerful role of nursing in the TQM movement. Includes a study guide with discussion questions, related articles, bibliography and definitions of key terms. .3 CEUs - certification education units - per program. Part of a series overviewing contemporary nursing issues.
Business and Economics; Health and Safety
Dist - NLFN **Prod** - NLFN

TQM decision 18 MIN
VHS
Total quality management - Ten elements for implementation series
Color (PRO IND A)
$300.00 purchase _ #GO02B
Presents part two of a ten - part series which outlines a course of continuous improvement. Helps organizations, such as, educational institutions, manufacturing operations, hospitals and service industries. Includes extensive workshop materials. By Goal - QPC.
Business and Economics; Psychology
Dist - EXTR

TR and His Times 58 MIN
U-matic / VHS
Walk through the 20th Century with Bill Moyers Series
Color
LC 84-706735
Presents a portrait of Theodore Roosevelt and his America.
Biography; History - United States
Dist - PBS **Prod** - CORPEL 1983

Trabajamos como burros 30 MIN
VHS
Grammar music videos series
Color (G) (SPANISH)
$49.95 purchase _ #W1450
Uses comic dialogue and rhythmic music to help beginning language students practice verb forms and tenses. Covers ar, er, and ir verbs. Package includes video, audiocassette, exercise pages and teacher's guide.
Foreign Language
Dist - GPC

Trabajando Con Proporciones 12 MIN
16mm / U-matic / VHS
Color (J H) (SPANISH)
A Spanish - language version of the motion picture Proportion At Work. Introduces ratio and proportion as practical tools for solving problems by direct measurement.
Foreign Language; Mathematics
Dist - IFB **Prod** - VEF 1960

Trace and Breakpoint 30 MIN
VHS / U-matic
Hands - On with the 68000 Series
Color (IND)
Explains SHIFT and ROTATE instructions while using TUTOR commands. Shows differences in trace (T) and breakpoint (BR) commands.
Industrial and Technical Education; Mathematics; Sociology
Dist - COLOSU **Prod** - COLOSU

A Trace of Blood 13 MIN
16mm
Doctors at Work Series
B&W (H C A)
LC FIA65-1374
Describes the treatment of a bladder cancer after a physician discovers traces of blood in a patients urine. Shows details of the surgical procedure for a bladder resection.
Health and Safety
Dist - LAWREN **Prod** - CMA 1962

Tracer - Flo Movie 10 MIN
16mm
Color (C)
LC 76-701100
Shows the state of the art of the tracer - flo process. Illustrates the tracer - flo process leak tests, microelectronic hybrids, semiconductors and integrated circuits by forcing Krypton 85 into the packages and then running them through a counting station to detect emissions.
Industrial and Technical Education
Dist - JOYCE **Prod** - JOYCE 1975

Traces 63 MIN
16mm
Color; B&W (G)
$100.00 rental
Synthesizes two trains of cinematic thought - the imagist - poetic - abstract tradition and the conceptual - critical school - to create a formal yet lyrical work. Traces the story of light coursing through the world. A critique of media representations of life and light is inherent in the methodology. This is a composite production in which different kinds of representations, such as abstract, narrative, documentary, are set side by side. Moves through many different models of filmmaking. Contact Canyon Cinema for special projection notes.
Fine Arts
Dist - CANCIN **Prod** - RAYHER 1985

Tracheobronchial collapse in bronchitis 17 MIN
16mm
Color
Demonstrates the relationship between the degree of tracheobronchial collapse and the extent of pulmonary disease, as well as showing that it is related to a 'vicious cycle of chronic bronchitis.'
Health and Safety; Science - Natural
Dist - USVA **Prod** - USVA 1962

Tracheostomy 11 MIN
U-matic / VHS
Head and Neck Series
Color
Health and Safety; Science - Natural
Dist - SVL **Prod** - SVL

Tracheostomy 9 MIN
VHS / U-matic
Medical Skills Films Series
Color (PRO)
Health and Safety
Dist - WFP **Prod** - WFP

Tracheostomy and Mechanical Ventilation 20 MIN
16mm
Color (PRO)
Demonstrates the technique of mechanical support of ventilation including tracheostomy, respirators, blood gases, tracheal toilet, antibiotics and alternating tracheostomy cuff pressure site.
Health and Safety; Science
Dist - ACY **Prod** - ACYDGD 1968

Tracheostomy Care 25 MIN
16mm
Color (PRO)
Presents a description and demonstration of current techniques for deciding indication for tracheostomy, operative technique, choice of cannulae and postoperative nursing care.
Health and Safety; Science
Dist - ACY **Prod** - ACYDGD 1971

Tracheostomy care 28 MIN
VHS / U-matic
Color (PRO)
$275.00 purchase, $60.00 rental _ #9925S, #9925V
Teaches about tracheostomy procedures, indications for procedure, associated risks and potential complications. Gives clear, explicit instruction in using the various types of tracheostomy tubes and cuffs, with particular attention to a demonstration of suctioning and an explanation and demonstration of minimal - leak technique for cuff inflations. Highlights nursing care for all procedures described.
Health and Safety
Dist - AJN **Prod** - HOSSN 1986

Tracheotomy and Cricothyrotomy 23 MIN
16mm
Color
Companion to the film 'EMERGENCY AIRWAY.' Compares emergency methods for relieving obstructions in the upper and lower airways of dogs. Shows improvised devices, with stress on their hazards and crudity.
Health and Safety
Dist - PFI **Prod** - PFI 1960

Tracheotomy and Cricothyrotomy 27 MIN
VHS / U-matic
Color (PRO)
Describes tracheotomy and cricothyrotomy.
Health and Safety
Dist - WFP **Prod** - WFP

Traci and Ed - Birth 11
U-matic
Video birth library series
Color (J H G)
$100.00 purchase
Follows the childbirth experiences of Traci, 22, single, black, and having her second baby. Reveals that her boyfriend Ed and her mother are with her. Traci's labor is induced because she is overdue and having a large baby. Fetal heart rate deceleration occurs. After 14 hours of labor, the baby is still not descending so she delivers by cesarean. Illustrates an unscheduled cesarean with partner present. Part of a 15 - part series on childbirth education.
Health and Safety
Dist - POLYMR **Prod** - POLYMR

Tracing the Roots of Dance with Hanya Holm 30 MIN
VHS / U-matic
Shaping Today with Yesterday Series
Color
Fine Arts; Industrial and Technical Education
Dist - ARCVID **Prod** - ARCVID

Track and field 26 MIN
U-matic
Alberta elementary physical education series
Color (PRO)
Features individual coaching and the use of appropriate equipment.
Physical Education and Recreation
Dist - ACCESS **Prod** - ACCESS 1983

Track and Field - Conditioning the 400 Meter Runner and Intermediate Hurdler 20 MIN
U-matic / VHS / 16mm
Coach Bill Dillinger Track and Field Series
Color (J H C)
Explains special conditioning approaches for the 400 meter runner and intermediate hurdler. Breaks down each approach into elements of strength, flexibility, endurance and speed.
Physical Education and Recreation
Dist - ATHI **Prod** - ATHI 1981

Track and Field - Discus Technique 20 MIN
U-matic / VHS / 16mm
Coach Bill Dillinger Track and Field Series
Color (J H C)
Observes each phase of the discus throwing motion and shows drills for mastering each.
Physical Education and Recreation
Dist - ATHI **Prod** - ATHI 1981

Track and Field - Distance Conditioning 20 MIN
16mm / U-matic / VHS
Coach Bill Dillinger Track and Field Series
Color (J H C)
Illustrates Coach Bill Dillinger's guidelines and drills for competitive distance running.
Physical Education and Recreation
Dist - ATHI **Prod** - ATHI 1981

Track and Field - Distance Technique 20 MIN
16mm / U-matic / VHS
Coach Bill Dillinger Track and Field Series
Color (J H C)
Details aspects of top running form. Explains when to lay back and when to make a move.
Physical Education and Recreation
Dist - ATHI **Prod** - ATHI 1981

Track & Field Event Videos Series
Men's and Women's Javelin 30 MIN
Men's Discus Throw 30 MIN
Men's High Jump 30 MIN
Men's Long Jump 30 MIN
Men's Pole Vault 30 MIN
Men's Shot Put 30 MIN
Men's Sprints and Hurdles 30 MIN
Men's Triple Jump 30 MIN
Women's Jumps - High Jump, Long Jump, Triple Jump 30 MIN
Women's Sprints and Hurdles 30 MIN
Women's Throwing Events 30 MIN
Dist - TRACKN

Track and field for boys and girls - field events 16 MIN
16mm / U-matic / VHS
Color (I J H) (ARABIC)
LC 77-701289
Analyses five popular field events for boys and girls, defining terms and establishing correct techniques for each. Uses slow motion and freeze - frame photography to demonstrate the correct techniques for the high jump, pole vault, long jump, triple jump and shot put.
Physical Education and Recreation
Dist - AIMS **Prod** - ASSOCF 1976

Track and Field for Boys and Girls - Running Events 17 MIN
U-matic / VHS / 16mm
Color (I J H)
LC 77-701290
Uses slow - motion and freeze frames in demonstrating the fundamentals of starting and running sprints, distance races, hurdles and relays.
Physical Education and Recreation
Dist - AIMS **Prod** - ASSOCF 1976

Track and Field - Hammer Techniques 20 MIN
U-matic / VHS / 16mm
Coach Bill Dillinger Track and Field Series
Color (J H C)
Takes the beginner, novice and expert through the fundamentals and advanced techniques of the hammer throw.
Physical Education and Recreation
Dist - ATHI **Prod** - ATHI 1981

Track and Field - High Jump 20 MIN
U-matic / VHS / 16mm
Coach Bill Dillinger Track and Field Series
Color (J H C)
Presents Denis Whitby taking viewers through all jump events outlining areas for improvement.
Physical Education and Recreation
Dist - ATHI **Prod** - ATHI 1981

Track and Field - Hurdle Techniques 20 MIN
16mm / U-matic / VHS
Coach Bill Dillinger Track and Field Series
Color (J H C)
Demonstrates the proper form for high and intermediate hurdles as well as over and between hurdles.
Physical Education and Recreation
Dist - ATHI **Prod** - ATHI 1981

Track and Field - Javelin Techniques 20 MIN
16mm / U-matic / VHS
Coach Bill Dillinger Track and Field Series
Color (J H C)
Demonstrates the javelin throw and presents hints and drills to help gain proficiency.
Physical Education and Recreation
Dist - ATHI **Prod** - ATHI 1981

Track and Field - Jump Conditioning 20 MIN
16mm / U-matic / VHS
Coach Bill Dillinger Track and Field Series
Color (J H C)
Addresses how to develop explosiveness as well as other aspects of the long, triple and high jump.
Physical Education and Recreation
Dist - ATHI **Prod** - ATHI 1981

Track and Field - Pole Vault Conditioning 20 MIN
U-matic / VHS / 16mm
Coach Bill Dillinger Track and Field Series
Color (J H C)
Shows how the pole vault combines sprinter speed, shot - putter strength and acrobatic ability.
Physical Education and Recreation
Dist - ATHI **Prod** - ATHI 1981

Track and Field - Pole Vault Technique 20 MIN
U-matic / VHS / 16mm
Coach Bill Dillinger Track and Field Series
Color (J H C)
Presents all the aspects of pole vaulting using special technical effects.
Physical Education and Recreation
Dist - ATHI **Prod** - ATHI 1981

Track and Field - Relay Techniques 20 MIN
U-matic / VHS / 16mm
Coach Bill Dillinger Track and Field Series
Color (J H C)
Outlines the phases of the 400 - meter and mile relays showing the desirability of certain methods of exchanging the baton.
Physical Education and Recreation
Dist - ATHI **Prod** - ATHI 1981

Track and field series
Conditioning 33 MIN
Discus and shot put 39 MIN
High jump 23 MIN
Javelin 53 MIN
Long jump 23 MIN
Marathon challenge 60 MIN
Middle distance running 42 MIN
Sprints, hurdles and relays 48 MIN
Talent search 60 MIN
Dist - CAMV

Track and Field - Shot Put Technique 20 MIN
16mm / U-matic / VHS
Coach Bill Dillinger Track and Field Series
Color (J H C)
Illustrates the latest developments in shot - put techniques as exhibited by world class athletes.
Physical Education and Recreation
Dist - ATHI **Prod** - ATHI 1981

Track and Field Skills 16 MIN
16mm
Color (J H)
Presents an introduction to the high jump, broad or long jump, pole vault and shot put. Uses slow motion and frozen action to describe techniques. Depicts track and field event winners of the 1964 Olympics.
Physical Education and Recreation
Dist - SLFP **Prod** - SLFP 1966

Track and Field - Sprint Conditioning 20 MIN
U-matic / VHS / 16mm
Coach Bill Dillinger Track and Field Series
Color (J H C)
Demonstrates that conditioning for the 100 and 200 meters and high hurdles is divided into strength, flexibility and endurance. Includes special drills to improve performance.
Physical Education and Recreation
Dist - ATHI **Prod** - ATHI 1981

Track and Field - Sprint Techniques 20 MIN
U-matic / VHS / 16mm
Coach Bill Dillinger Track and Field Series
Color (J H C)
Shows how to develop leg speed, stride length and arm action in sprints. Covers block clearance, race patterns and drills to improve ability.
Physical Education and Recreation
Dist - ATHI **Prod** - ATHI 1981

Track & Field Technique Study Films Series
Men's Discus 4 MIN
Men's Glide Shot Put 4 MIN
Men's Hammer Throw 4 MIN
Men's High Jump 4 MIN
Men's Hurdle Races 4 MIN
Men's Hurdling Techniques 4 MIN
Men's Javelin 4 MIN
Men's Long Jump 4 MIN
Men's Middle and Long Distance Races 4 MIN
Men's Pole Vault 4 MIN
Men's Rotation Shot Put 4 MIN
Men's Sprint Races 4 MIN
Men's Sprinting Techniques 4 MIN
Men's Triple Jump 4 MIN
Women's Discus 4 MIN
Women's High Jump 4 MIN
Women's Hurdle Races 4 MIN
Women's Hurdling 4 MIN
Women's Javelin 4 MIN
Women's Long Jump 4 MIN
Women's Middle and Long Distance Races 4 MIN
Women's Shot Put 4 MIN
Women's Sprint Races 4 MIN
Women's Sprinting Techniques 4 MIN
Dist - TRACKN

Track and field techniques series
Presents a 13 - part series presenting field and track advice from champions. Includes Conditioning, Middle Distance Running, High Jump, Relay Running, Shot Put, Javelin, Discus, Sprinting, Hurdles, Pole Vault, Long Jump, Road Running and Hammer Throw. Features Daley Thompson, Sebastian Coe, Dwight Stones, David Hemery, Parry O'Brien, Miklos Nemeth, Al Oerter, Tommie Smith, Jan Johnson, Lynn Davis, Joan Benoit - Samuelson and Hal Connolly.
Conditioning 30 MIN
Discus 30 MIN
Hammer throw 30 MIN
High jump 30 MIN
Hurdles 30 MIN
Javelin 30 MIN
Long jump 30 MIN
Middle distance running 30 MIN
Pole vault 30 MIN
Relay running 30 MIN
Road running 30 MIN
Shot put 30 MIN
Sprinting 30 MIN
Dist - CAMV

Track and Field Today 28 MIN
16mm
Color (J H C)
LC 75-713516
This film takes an analytic view of this whole area of athletic competition in the interests of participants, officials, coaches coaches and spectators. Shows in close - up detail the basics of winning and record - setting performance - - by the rules.
Physical Education and Recreation
Dist - OSFS **Prod** - OSFS 1971

Track and Field - Triple Jump, Long Jump Techniques 20 MIN
16mm / U-matic / VHS
Coach Bill Dillinger Track and Field Series
Color (J H C)
Demonstrates how the long jump and triple jump are similar in technique. Details jump phases and specialty drills.
Physical Education and Recreation
Dist - ATHI **Prod** - ATHI 1981

Track and Field - Weight Events Conditioning 20 MIN
16mm / U-matic / VHS
Coach Bill Dillinger Track and Field Series
Color (J H C)
Emphasizes developing strength and channeling it into throwing action. Demonstrates proper weight lifting techniques.
Physical Education and Recreation
Dist - ATHI **Prod** - ATHI 1981

Track event series
VHS
NCAA instructional video series
Color (H C A)
$49.95 purchase _ #KAR2106V
Presents a two - part series on track events. Focuses on sprinting and hurdling techniques.
Physical Education and Recreation
Dist - CAMV **Prod** - NCAAF

Track library skills, series for grades 9 through adult 15 MIN
VHS / U-matic
Track library skills series
(J A)
#90518, #90528
Introduces Library Skills.
Education
Dist - FLIPLS **Prod** - FLIPLS

Track library skills series
Track library skills, series for grades 9 through adult 15 MIN
Dist - FLIPLS

Track - No 2 13 MIN
16mm
B&W
Presents tips from top college track men, including Bob Derrick, the record holder of 60 yard indoor hurdles and Hendrix Kruger, South African pole vaulter. Covers most of the track events, including shot put, discus, pole vault, broad jump and hurdles.
Physical Education and Recreation
Dist - SFI **Prod** - SFI

Track, no 1 - Wes Santee 13 MIN
16mm
B&W
Olympic star miler shows how to run the mile and tells what it takes to run a 4 - minute mile. Includes information on how to train, and get into condition for competition.
Physical Education and Recreation
Dist - SFI **Prod** - SFI

Track of the Consolidated Health Record 35 MIN
U-matic
Color
LC 79-707307
Traces the flow of consolidated health records through a typical Veterans Administration health care facility.
Health and Safety
Dist - USNAC **Prod** - USVA 1978

Track Stars - the Unseen Heroes of Movie Sound 8 MIN
U-matic / VHS / 16mm
Color (J)
LC 79-701025
Takes a behind - the - scenes look at the people who work at a motion picture sound studio and how they provide sound effects for movies and TV.
Fine Arts
Dist - LCOA **Prod** - FIARTS 1979

Track Two 90 MIN
16mm
Color
Describes the evolution of Toronto's gay community, focusing on the 1981 bathhouse raids that galvanized divergent gay interests into a powerful political force. Recreates the police raid and examines the political climate which led to the mass arrests.
Sociology
Dist - FIRS **Prod** - FIRS

Tracker 12 MIN
16mm
Color
LC 76-701388
Demonstrates the peacetime role of an eastern air squadron of the Canadian Armed Forces in maintaining daily surveillance of ocean areas adjacent to the Canadian coastline and of the eastern Arctic.
Civics and Political Systems; Geography - World
Dist - CDND **Prod** - CDND 1974
CFLMDC NFBC

Tracking in the Desert 15 MIN
VHS / U-matic
Encounter in the Desert Series
Color (I)
Shows the life of Bedouin nomads, and encounters with a snake, scorpion and rabbit.
Geography - World; Social Science; Sociology
Dist - CTI **Prod** - CTI

Tracking the Creative Process 30 MIN
VHS / 16mm
Focus on Watercolor Series
Color (C A)
$85.00, $75.00 purchase _ 21 - 13
Explains the progression of a painting, key shape, permanent pigments, displaying and preserving works.
Fine Arts
Dist - CDTEL **Prod** - COAST 1987

Tracking the Supertrains 57 MIN
U-matic / VHS
Nova Series
Color (H C A)
Discusses a joint Japanese - American project to put the Japanese 'bullet' train in service between Los Angeles and San Diego. Considers the developments in train system design that are making high - speed travel possible.
Social Science
Dist - TIMLIF **Prod** - WGBHTV 1982

Tracking Your Spending 15 MIN
U-matic
Color; Mono (H C)
Four families demonstrate 4 different methods of keeping financial records - the envelope method, the receipt method, the checkbook method, and the account method. Each family explains why their system works for them.
Business and Economics; Home Economics
Dist - UWISCA **Prod** - UWISCA 1984

Tracks 30 MIN
VHS
Color (A)
$525.00 purchase
Discusses progression of minor incidents to a serious accident, showing how patterns of behavior can be modified before a crisis. Emphasizes safety for operators of company - owned vehicles.
Business and Economics; Civics and Political Systems
Dist - COMFLM **Prod** - COMFLM

Tracks of the grizzly 27 MIN
VHS
Northwest wild series
Color (J H C A)
$89.95 purchase _ #P110974
Illustrates the differences between grizzly bears and other members of the bear family. Focuses on the behavior and habits of grizzlies with an emphasis on circumstances where they can be dangerous to humans. Features scientists as they track grizzlies in the six remaining high mountain habitats where the bears are found. Part of a series of seven programs.
Science - Natural
Dist - CF

Traction 25 MIN
VHS / 16mm
Licensed Practical Nursing Assistant Refresher Series
Color (C)
$75.00 purchase _ #270510
Helps nursing assistants make the transition back to their chosen career after an extended absence. Updates nursing techniques and procedures which have changed substantially in the last decade. Provides a practical demonstration of step - by - step nursing procedures. 'Traction' simplifies the complex health care practice of traction with a comprehensive overview. Covers the assembly, application and principles of three common traction treatments, Buck's traction, Bryant's traction and Pelvic traction.
Health and Safety; Science
Dist - ACCESS **Prod** - ACCESS 1989

Traction - checks and balances 28 MIN
VHS / U-matic
Color (PRO)
$275.00 purchase, $60.00 rental _ #7626S, #7626V
Depicts the various forms of traction, including manual, skin and skeletal traction. Details the purposes of traction, which include reduction of fractures and dislocations, reduction of muscle spasms, correction or prevention of deformity, increased comfort and the ability to rest. Demonstrates commonly applied forms of traction as well as key nursing observations, assessment techniques and interventions.
Health and Safety
Dist - AJN **Prod** - HOSSN 1986

Traction Series
Application of traction 30 MIN
Nursing Care for the Patient in Traction 30 MIN
Principles of Traction 20 MIN
Dist - FAIRGH

Tractor accidents - it's not gonna happen to me 24 MIN
VHS
Color (G) (SPANISH)
$95.00 purchase _ #6 - 084 - 001A, #6 - 084 - 200A
Offers safety rules for operating a tractor. Starts with Pre - operation Check which directs the examination of the spinner shield, shaft, tire, oil and fuel shut - off cable before operation. Transporting Tractors shows how to move tractors safely as cargo. Operation Check stresses removing hazards from the area to be worked, how to work hills and slopes safely, hitching details. Tractor Behavior and Accident Prevention focuses on the most common tractor mishaps and how they can be prevented. Emergency Response Procedures urges the training of all workers in first aid and outlines what to do in the event of an accident.
Agriculture; Health and Safety
Dist - VEP **Prod** - VEP

Tractor Safety 24 MIN
VHS
Color (G) (SPANISH)
$95.95 purchase _ #6 - 084 - 100P, #6 - 084 - 200P - Spanish
Stresses safety practices and knowledge of the tractor. Shows how to do a pre - operation check for examining the spinner shield, shaft, tires, oil and fuel shut - off cable before operation. Looks at transporting tractors, removing hazards from working areas, tractor safety on uneven terrain and the most common tractor mishaps and their avoidance. Includes emergency response procedures in the event of an accident.
Agriculture; Health and Safety
Dist - VEP **Prod** - VEP

Tractor safety
VHS
Color (H A T)
$35.00 purchase _ #KU101
Dramatizes three common tractor accidents. Demonstrates how novices and experienced tractor operators are likely to ignore safety precautions. Produced by Kubota Tractors. Includes their booklet 'The Ten Commandments of Tractor Safety.'
Agriculture; Health and Safety
Dist - AAVIM

Tractor safety on slopes 15 MIN
VHS
Color; PAL; NTSC (G)
PdS57, PdS67 purchase
Uses research by the Scottish Institute of Agricultural Engineering to emphasize the point that tractors and slopes are a dangerous combination. Includes models, diagrams and live action.
Health and Safety
Dist - CFLVIS

Tractors 24 MIN
U-matic / VHS
Agricultural Accidents and Rescue Series
Color
Covers the various options available for lifting a tractor off victim after a tractor overturn. Describes the many factors that can hinder rescue.
Agriculture; Health and Safety
Dist - PSU **Prod** - PSU

Tracy's Family Folk Festival 10 MIN
16mm
Color (G)
$20.00 rental
Offers an impression of the 1982 folk festival at the Tracy and Eloise Schwarz farm in Central Pennsylvania. Presents an elaborate collage which breaks up into a swarm of shapes derived from traditional Pennsylvania Dutch designs. Produced by Bill Brand.
Fine Arts
Dist - CANCIN

Trade 10 MIN
U-matic / VHS / 16mm
Economics for the Elementary Series
Color (P I)
LC 72-701683
Describes the complete trade cycle by tracing the route tomatoes take from grower to consumer, in the simplest possible terms. Provides an introduction to the economic cycle and the determination of prices.
Agriculture; Business and Economics
Dist - AIMS **Prod** - EVANSA 1971

Trade and Economics 30 MIN
U-matic
China After Mao Series
Color
Discusses methods by which China is trying to modernize her economy. Looks at problems associated with international business dealings with China.
Business and Economics; Civics and Political Systems; Geography - World
Dist - UMITV **Prod** - UMITV 1980

Trade deficit 30 MIN
U-matic
Adam Smith's money world series; 120
Color (A)
Attempts to demystify the world of money and break it down so that small as well as large businesses and it's people understand and adjust to new social and economic trends. Reports on the major economic stories and discoveries of the day.
Business and Economics
Dist - PBS **Prod** - WNETTV 1985

Trade - Offs and Future Trends 30 MIN
U-matic / VHS
Micros for Managers - Software Series
Color (IND)
Contrasts project implementations via random logic or microprocessors, with emphasis on software development costs. Explores high - level language versus assembly - language trade - offs. Concludes with future trends affecting software development.
Industrial and Technical Education; Mathematics; Sociology
Dist - COLOSU **Prod** - COLOSU

Trade - offs series
About Trade - offs 12 MIN
Dist - AITECH

Trade secrets - blue collar women speak out 23 MIN
VHS / U-matic
Color (G)
$225.00 purchase, $60.00 rental
Looks at four women working as an ironworker, welder, sprinklerfitter and electrician who reveal how their lives changed when they stepped into the traditionally male world of skilled crafts. Tells how they overcame physical and personal obstacles to find satisfaction in their trades, greater financial power and a new sense of identity as journeywomen.
Business and Economics; Sociology
Dist - WMEN **Prod** - STANT 1985

Trade Secrets - the Blue Collar Worker Speaks Out 9 MIN
VHS / 16mm
Color (C)
$250.00 purchase, $45.00, $65.00 rental
Focuses on women working in non - traditional jobs, including ironworkers, union carpenters, electricians and welders. Presents interviews with these women who discuss their function as role models, the physical demands of their work, and how they integrate work with their social lives. Produced by Stephanie Antalocy and Giora Gerzon.
Business and Economics; Sociology
Dist - WMENIF

Trade Show Selling Series
How not to Exhibit Yourself 30 MIN
It'll be OK on the Day 28 MIN
Dist - VISUCP

Trade Unions 43 MIN
16mm
Color (H C A) (GERMAN)
Reports on the everyday activities of a trade unionist, and explains the historic development of trade unionism in Germany.
Business and Economics; History - World
Dist - WSTGLC **Prod** - WSTGLC

Trade Unions - Putting You in the Picture 12 MIN
16mm
Color
LC 80-700845
Shows the historical development of trade unions in Australia and explains their basic functions. Stresses the importance of migrant workers becoming more involved in union activities.
Business and Economics; Geography - World; Sociology
Dist - TASCOR **Prod** - NSWF 1978

Trademarks - the Name Game 15 MIN
16mm / U-matic
Color
Uses the Eric Bass Puppets to explain the basic concepts of trademarks and brand names, including their function, history, selection, clearance and protection.
Business and Economics; Psychology
Dist - MTP **Prod** - MTP
USTRAD

Tradeoff in the Pacific - a Polynesian Island between Cash and Subsistence 27 MIN
16mm / U-matic / VHS
(H C G T A)
Presents a glimpse of the culture and values of the people of Bellona, one of the Solomon Islands, and the ways in which their traditional existence is threatened by outside commercial interests.
Business and Economics; Geography - World; Sociology
Dist - RTVA **Prod** - RTVA 1982

Trader Tom of the China Seas 180 MIN
35mm
Republic cliffhanger serials series
B&W (G)
Features a China Seas country which breeds revolution and threatens trade routes. Offers 12 episodes, 15 minutes each. Contact distributor for rental price.
Fine Arts
Dist - KITPAR **Prod** - REP 1954

Trader Vic's used cars 10 MIN
U-matic / VHS / 16mm
American character series
Color (J H C)
$49.00 purchase _ #3382; LC 76-701794
Presents a film portrait of Victor Snyder, a Southern California used car dealer. Portrays Trader Vic and talks frankly about his business and shares his secrets of success.
Business and Economics; Home Economics; Sociology
Dist - EBEC **Prod** - BRAVC 1976

The Traders - Pt 5 20 MIN
VHS
Middle Ages Series
Color (I)

$79.00 purchase _ #825 - 9437
Incorporates source and historic material to recreate medieval life. Depicts the main social groups and captures the political climate of the time. Visits castles, cathedrals and battlegrounds, dramatizes pilgrimages and uprisings, uses close - up views of historical artifacts and architecture to bring the Middle Ages to life. Part 5 of five parts explains the importance of the medieval wool trade and its financial operations and describes patterns of European trade.
Business and Economics; History - World; Social Science
Dist - FI **Prod** - BBCTV 1987

Tradesmen and Treasures - Gothic and Renaissance Nuremburg 55 MIN
VHS
Color (S) (ENGLISH AND GERMAN)
$39.95 purchase _ #412 - 9003
Documents the remarkable flowering of art and culture in Nuremburg during the 14th to 16th centuries. Traces the city's evolution from a trade center of the Holy Roman Empire to a complex Renaissance city. Filmed on location in Germany, period music, travelers' accounts and recreated scenes illuminate the artists, merchants and patrician families that brought Nuremburg to the forefront of European culture.
Geography - World; History - World; Sociology
Dist - FI **Prod** - MMOA 1987

Tradiciones Navidenas 56 MIN
U-matic / VHS
Color (C) (SPANISH)
$279.00, $179.00 purchase _ #AD - 2178
Uses the former Convent at the Desierto de los Leones as a backdrop for a traditional posada, the Christmas fiesta. Presents the songs, the pinata, litany, lights and candlelit walks through historic buildings. In Spanish.
Geography - World; History - World; Religion and Philosophy; Social Science
Dist - FOTH **Prod** - FOTH

Trading 57 MIN
16mm / U-matic / VHS
Heart of the Dragon Series Pt 12; Pt 12
Color (H C A)
Illustrates changing attitudes toward business in China by looking at individual enterprises. Examines recent experiments with free enterprise, leading to critical questions about whether trade with the outside world can be encouraged without Western influences undermining traditional values.
Business and Economics; Civics and Political Systems; History - World
Dist - TIMLIF **Prod** - ASH 1984

Trading 15 MIN
U-matic / VHS
Common Cents Series
Color (P)
Introduces the concept of trading, defines goods and services, and discusses barter and money as systems of exchange.
Business and Economics
Dist - AITECH **Prod** - KETCTV 1977

Trading, check method, story problems
VHS
Lola May's fundamental math series
Color (P)
$45.00 purchase _ #10262VG
Provides practice and instruction in trading, a process using models and then numbers. Teaches the check method which helps in adding when trading is involved. Comes with a teacher's guide and blackline masters. Part 12 of a 30 - part series.
Mathematics
Dist - UNL

Trading Places with the Difficult Customer 22.5 MIN
VHS / 16mm / U-matic
Color (H C G)
$525.00, $370.00, $400.00 _ #A530
Illustrates the skills of listening, empathizing, asking questions, offering options, agreeing on a solution, and following up when dealing with a difficult customer.
Business and Economics; Psychology; Social Science
Dist - BARR **Prod** - BARR 1988

Trading the Sun 20 MIN
U-matic / VHS / 16mm
One World Series
Color (J H)
Studies the importance of tourism to the economy of certain Caribbean islands, but also looks at the danger which outside patterns of behavior can have on local society.
Geography - World; History - World
Dist - FI **Prod** - BBCTV 1982

Tradition 20 MIN
16mm
Color (J)
LC 75-704034
Describes the making of moonshine in the Kentucky hills. Presents interviews with people involved in the distilling process.
Geography - United States; Sociology
Dist - APPAL **Prod** - APPAL 1974

Tradition and comtemporary Judaism series
Tradition and contemporary Judaism - joy and responsibility - a series
Dist - ADL

Tradition and contemporary Judaism - joy and responsibility - a series
Tradition and comtemporary Judaism series
Color
Explores Judaism in terms of knowledge of science and psychology. Features Rabbi David Hartman in a series of four lectures. Faith In The Age Of Technology; Interdependence - God And Man; Israel And The Renewal Of Judaism; Religious Laws As The Source Of Joy.
Religion and Philosophy
Dist - ADL **Prod** - ADL

Tradition and Contemporary Judaism - Joy and Responsibility Series Program 4
Israel and the Renewal of Judaism 28 MIN
Dist - ADL

Tradition and contemporary Judaism - prayer and the Jewish people series
The Shema - an affirmation of belief, love and trust 15 MIN
Dist - ADL

Tradition and revolution in French art - 1770 - 1880 24 MIN
VHS
Color (G)
PdS15.50 purchase _ #A4-300443
Provides an introduction to history painting in France from 1770 to 1880. Contrasts this high art with less heroic narrative paintings akin to comedy, the realist novel, or the historical novel. Includes works by David, Delacroix, and Courbet. Filmed in the Musee des Beaux-Arts in Lille.
Fine Arts
Dist - AVP **Prod** - NATLGL

A Tradition in Music 28 MIN
16mm
Color
LC 74-705812
Shows the U S Navy Band during rehearsals and recording sessions and shows the work involved in keeping the band in shape.
Fine Arts
Dist - USNAC **Prod** - USN 1969

A Tradition of Conscience 27 MIN
16mm
Color
LC FIA66-653
Pictures the operation of a major newspaper. Follows one day's editions of the St Louis Post Dispatch from the teletype machines to the street. Shows how the philosophy and historical background of the paper help shape the editing and reporting of today's events.
Psychology; Social Science
Dist - GUG **Prod** - PULTZR 1966

A Tradition of Justice 59 MIN
VHS / 16mm
Color (G)
$70.00 rental _ #TJST - 000
Examines the Magna Carta and the laws of democracy that formed from it.
Civics and Political Systems
Dist - PBS **Prod** - WETATV

The Tradition of performing arts in Japan 1990
VHS
Color (G C H)
$139.00 purchase _ #DL350
Overviews kabuki, bunraku and Noh theater from Japan, using excerpts from performances.
Fine Arts; History - World
Dist - INSIM

Tradition of Service 20 MIN
16mm
Color
LC 77-702160
Surveys the Chesapeake and Potomac Telephone Company's years of service from 1875 to 1975. Draws attention to the role of the company's employees in keeping the communication system working.
Business and Economics; Industrial and Technical Education; Sociology
Dist - CPTCO **Prod** - CPTCO 1977

Traditional Birthing - Maude Bryant 19 MIN
U-matic / VHS
Color (C PRO)
$385.00 purchase _ #841VI107
Conveys refreshing attitude towards using a midwife at birth of baby. Reflects on Maude Bryant who delivered over one hundred births in rural North Carolina.
Health and Safety
Dist - HSCIC **Prod** - HSCIC 1984

Traditional Chen style Taijiquan 60 MIN
VHS
Color (G)
$35.00 purchase _ #1104
Features Chen Peishan, 20th - generation successor of Chen family Taijiquan. Demonstrates the first routine, sword and Chen form power techniques, body dynamics, plus a step by step of the first routine.
Physical Education and Recreation
Dist - WAYF

Traditional dances of Indonesia series
Presents a 12 - part series which records traditional dances of Indonesia. Includes dances of Bali, Jogjakarta in Central Java, Surakarta in Central Java and West Sumatra. Contact distributor for description of individual films.

Dances of Bali - Baris Katekok Jago and Kebyar Duduk	20 MIN
Dances of Bali - Barong	32 MIN
Dances of Bali - Legong Kraton	20 MIN
Dances of Jogjakarta, Central Java - Bekasan Menak	19 MIN
Dances of Jogjakarta, Central Java - Langen Mandra Wanara	32 MIN
Dances of Jogjakarta, Central Java - Lawung Ageng	40 MIN
Dances of Surakarta, Central Java - Bedoyo Elo Elo	23 MIN
Dances of Surakarta, Central Java - Bedoyo Pangkur	23 MIN
Dances of Surakarta, Central Java - Menak Konchar	11 MIN
Dances of Surakarta, Central Java - Srimpi Anglir Mendung	19 MIN
Dances of Surakarta, Central Java - Srimpi Gondokusomo	19 MIN
Dances of West Sumatra - Tari Piring and Tari Alang	20 MIN

Dist - UCEMC **Prod** - HEICK

Traditional hand tools 32 MIN
VHS / 35mm strip
Color (G)
$85.00, $30.00 purchase
Describes some of the simple hand tools used by Kentucky pioneers. Reminds the viewer of the special skills and special lore that went with a pioneer economy. Features oldtime workmen who demonstrate the broad ax and frow, and a modern collector who demonstrates some items from his collection.
Fine Arts; History - United States
Dist - UWKY **Prod** - UWKY 1970

Traditional Handicrafts 15 MIN
16mm
How Yukong Moved the Mountains Series
Color (J A)
LC 80-700604
Examines traditional Chinese handicrafts as the craftsmen perform curio carving, glass bottle painting, ivory carving, dollmaking and other crafts.
Fine Arts; Geography - World; History - World
Dist - CINPER **Prod** - CAPI 1976

Traditional Japanese architecture 30 MIN
U-matic / VHS
Color (C)
$149.00 purchase _ #EX2090
Documents the Katsura Imperial Villa in Kyoto, Japan, which was built in the early 17th century. Examines its gardens and tea house as well as the main building and current processes of restoration.
Fine Arts; Geography - World; History - World; Industrial and Technical Education
Dist - FOTH **Prod** - FOTH

Traditional quilting 32 MIN
VHS / 35mm strip
Color (G)
$85.00, $30.00 purchase
Shows the patchwork quilt as an art form and a skill being revived in Kentucky. Uses samples of artistic quilting gathered from homes in western Kentucky and from the Kentucky Museum. Features traditional Kentucky quilters.
Fine Arts; History - United States; Home Economics
Dist - UWKY **Prod** - UWKY 1970

Traditional upholstery 25 MIN
VHS / U-matic
Better than new series
Color (H C A)
Demonstrates the remaking of a dining room chair from the canvas webbing upwards.

Fine Arts; Home Economics; Physical Education and Recreation
Dist - FI **Prod** - BBCTV

Traditional vs alternative, William C Rhodes vs Peter Knoblock 30 MIN
VHS
Video training workshops on child variance series
Color (T PRO)
$135.00 purchase _ #M1991
Presents discussion between William C Rhodes and Peter Knoblock representing traditional and alternative viewpoints on psychology respectively. Part of a six - part series produced by William C Morse and Judith M Smith.
Psychology; Sociology
Dist - CEXPCN **Prod** - CEXPCN

Traditions and the 20th Century 30 MIN
VHS
Global Links Series
Color (G)
$39.95 purchase _ #GLLI - 101
Examines six Third World countries. Questions how traditional culture can survive in the face of modernization and development.
Sociology
Dist - PBS **Prod** - WETATV 1987

Traffic 89 MIN
VHS
Color (G)
$24.95 _ #TRA130
Captures the absurdities of human behavior on the street and behind the wheel. Features Mr Hulot as an absentminded inventor transporting his ultramodern camper to Amsterdam for an auto show. Letterboxed version.
Fine Arts; Psychology; Sociology
Dist - HOMVIS **Prod** - JANUS 1971

Traffic Court 14 MIN
16mm / U-matic / VHS
Captioned; Color (J) (SPANISH)
LC 72-701041
Observes traffic court procedures in order to familiarize the viewer with the consequences of traffic violations.
Civics and Political Systems; Health and Safety; Psychology
Dist - AIMS **Prod** - CAHILL 1972

Traffic Direction and Control 20 MIN
U-matic / VHS / 16mm
Color
Presents a variety of traffic and pedestrian control situations including daytime, nighttime, inclement weather, traffic after major events and highway situations. Demonstrates the need for consistent traffic direction, hand signals and gestures, and correct use of the whistle, baton, flashlight, flares and reflectorized aids.
Civics and Political Systems; Health and Safety; Psychology; Social Science
Dist - CORF **Prod** - WORON

Traffic in rhythm logic 7 MIN
16mm
Color (G)
$20.00 rental
Assembles levels of movement, forms in repetition and brushstrokes of color in a film by Mark McGowan.
Fine Arts
Dist - CANCIN

Traffic in Souls 50 MIN
16mm
B&W
Takes a look at white slavery in New York during the early part of the 20th century.
Fine Arts; History - United States
Dist - REELIM **Prod** - UNKNWN 1913

Traffic jam 50 MIN
VHS
Inside story series
PAL; Color (H C A)
PdS99 purchase; Available only in the United Kingdom and Ireland
Discusses the improvements that are being made to the M1 motorway in the United Kingdom. Describes the setbacks that have delayed completion of the project. Part of the Inside Story series.
Industrial and Technical Education; Social Science
Dist - BBCENE

Traffic Law Observance and Enforcement 28 MIN
16mm
Sportsmanlike Driving Series no 10
B&W (H A)
LC FIA68-930
Discusses problems faced by law enforcement officials and the need for good traffic courts to protect the innocent and punish the guilty. Emphasizes the importance of continued observance of the laws.
Health and Safety
Dist - GPN **Prod** - AAA 1967

Traffic Laws 20 MIN
U-matic / 35mm strip
Color (J H)
Presents general rule of traffic. Emphasizes the laws of parking, speed, right - of - way, car positioning and passing that are recommended by the Uniform Vehicle Code. Covers laws that are common in most states.
Health and Safety; Industrial and Technical Education
Dist - BUMPA **Prod** - BUMPA

Traffic Laws made by Man 28 MIN
16mm
Sportsmanlike Driving Series no 8
B&W (H A)
LC FIA68-1080
Describes the role of the local community, the state, and the Federal government in the development of laws. Explains the organization of uniform traffic regulations through use of the uniform vehicle code and model traffic ordinances.
Health and Safety
Dist - GPN **Prod** - AAA 1967

Traffic Laws made by Nature 28 MIN
16mm
Sportsmanlike Driving Series no 7
B&W (H A)
LC FIA68-931
Demonstrates physical laws of friction, gravity, inertia, and impact which are involved in the operation of a motor vehicle.
Health and Safety
Dist - GPN **Prod** - AAA 1967

Traffic Safety 28 MIN
U-matic / VHS
Color (J A)
Features actor Robert Horton as he discusses the Alcohol Safety Action Program.
Health and Safety; Sociology
Dist - SUTHRB **Prod** - SUTHRB

Traffic Safety Advanced Driving - the Greater Adventure 26 MIN
16mm
Color
LC 74-705813
Dramatizes the relationship between traffic safety attitudes and society and points out the individual responsibilities to self and society.
Guidance and Counseling; Health and Safety; Psychology
Dist - USNAC **Prod** - USAF 1969

Traffic Safety, Vehicle Design and Equipment 28 MIN
16mm
Sportsmanlike Driving Series no 26
Color (H A)
LC FIA68-929
Discusses the use of safety equipment by the driver and passengers of a motor vehicle and the philosophy of safe driving.
Health and Safety
Dist - GPN **Prod** - AAA 1967

Traffic Stops - an Analysis of Officer Killed 13 MIN
VHS / 16mm
Color (PRO)
$295.00 purchase, $75.00 rental _ #8180
Discloses facts and reenactments of actual incidents of law enforcement officers killed while making traffic stops.
Civics and Political Systems
Dist - AIMS **Prod** - AIMS 1990

Traffic Trials - Heaven Won't Wait 19 MIN
16mm / U-matic / VHS
Color (J)
LC 81-700732
Tells how six drivers appear before a heavenly judge to review the driving errors that caused their deaths.
Health and Safety
Dist - AIMS **Prod** - CAHILL

Traffic Trigger Films Series
Behind the Wheel, Pt 1 8 MIN
Behind the Wheel, Pt 2 8 MIN
Driving while Intoxicated 28 MIN
Dist - PROART

Traffic Violation 30 MIN
U-matic / VHS
Behind the Wheel Series
Color (H)
Discusses the most frequent traffic violations which lead to accidents, such as speeding, drunk driving, tailgating, failure to yield the right of way, and mechanical defects of the car.
Health and Safety; Industrial and Technical Education; Psychology
Dist - GPN **Prod** - WCVETV 1983

Traffic Violation Stops 23 MIN
U-matic / VHS / 16mm
Legal Information for Law Enforcement Series
Color (PRO)
Uses four vignettes to dramatize the limitations on detention and investigation for a minor traffic violation. Shows when detention and search are justified.
Civics and Political Systems; Social Science
Dist - AIMS **Prod** - AIMS 1978

Traffic Watcher 14 MIN
16mm / U-matic / VHS
Color (P I)
LC 73-700623
Depicts a day in the life of Captain Dan, traffic helicopter pilot in Washington, DC, emphasizing his participation in the elementary school traffic safety program.
Health and Safety
Dist - EBEC **Prod** - WPLM 1972

The Traffic World 14 MIN
U-matic / VHS
Color
Explains the signs that control and the rules that regulate the traffic world.
Health and Safety; Social Science
Dist - PARPRO **Prod** - PARPRO

Tragada Bahavi - a Rural Theater Troupe of Gujarat 42 MIN
U-matic
Color
Follows a troupe of Bhavai performers through the Indian countryside. Shows preparations and negotiations with village sponsors. Illustrates an evening of a miracle play, comic skits, dances, juggling and a romantic drama.
Fine Arts; Geography - World; Sociology
Dist - DOCEDR **Prod** - DOCEDR

Tragedy at Tiananmen - the untold story 48 MIN
VHS / U-matic / BETA
China in revolution series
Color (H C A)
$250.00 purchase _ #JY - 6159C
Looks at Tiananmen Square in Beijing on the bloody night of June 3, 1989 when student support of China's new democratic movement was crushed. Interviews Chai Ling, Supreme commander of the Student Movement, and documents eyewitness accounts of foreign correspondents from many nations. Hosted by Ted Koppel. Part of a four - part series on revolutionary China.
Civics and Political Systems; Geography - World; History - World
Dist - CORF **Prod** - ABCVID 1989

The Tragedy of Addiction - the Trip Back 28 MIN
16mm
Color (H C A)
Contains a film report of one of many lectures to high school students by Florrie Fisher, who lost 23 years of her life to drug addiction. Miss Fisher spares her audience none of the tragic, sordid details of a drug addict's life. Hers is a rare talent to communicate with young men and women.
Health and Safety; Psychology
Dist - AVON **Prod** - UTEX

The Tragedy of Antony and Cleopatra 183 MIN
U-matic / VHS
Color (A)
$89.95 purchase _ #SO1592
Presents Shakespeare's classic love story of two of history's most famous personages.
Literature and Drama
Dist - KULTUR **Prod** - KULTUR 1985
UILL

The Tragedy of black suicide - Pt 2 29 MIN
U-matic / VHS
Color
History - United States; Sociology
Dist - SYLWAT **Prod** - RCOMTV 1981

Tragedy of Black Suicide, the, Pt 2 29 MIN
U-matic / VHS
Color
History - United States; Sociology
Dist - SYLWAT **Prod** - RCOMTV 1981

The Tragedy of Hamlet, Prince of Denmark 45 MIN
16mm
B&W (C A)
Presents the Gallaudet College Dramatics Club's performance of the Shakespeare classic. Signed.
Education; Guidance and Counseling; Literature and Drama; Psychology
Dist - GALCO **Prod** - GALCO 1958

The Tragedy of Hamlet - Prince of Denmark 22 MIN
U-matic / VHS / 16mm

Shakespeare in Rehearsal Series
Color (H C)
$495 purchase - 16 mm, $250 purchase - video _ #5791C
Depicts a rehearsal of Hamlet which includes the principal soliloquies. Provides insight into plot and character. Produced in association with Coronet by BBC, Milton Keynes.
Fine Arts
Dist - CORF

The Tragedy of Julius Caesar 35 MIN
VHS / U-matic
Shaw vs Shakespeare series
Color (C)
$89.00 purchase _ #47735
Portrays Donald Moffatt as George Bernard Shaw who criticizes Shakespeare's depiction of Caesar's death, its aftermath and Brutus' trauma thereafter. Illustrates Shaw's view of Shakespeare's tragedy Julius Caesar as 'the most splendidly written political melodrama that we possess.'.
Literature and Drama
Dist - EBEC

The Tragedy of King Lear
VHS
Color; PAL (J H C G)
PdS29.50 purchase
Tells Shakespeare's renowned story of familial deceit and murder. Captures the Elizabethan flavor of Shakespeare's own Globe productions by staging the play just as it was in the 16th century.
Fine Arts; Literature and Drama
Dist - EMFVL **Prod** - BARDPR

The Tragedy of King Lear 182 MIN
U-matic / VHS
Color (A)
Gives a new version of Shakespeare's classic story of a King who prematurely divides his kingdom.
Literature and Drama
Dist - KULTUR **Prod** - KULTUR 1985

The Tragedy of King Richard II 172 MIN
VHS
Color (G)
$89.95 purchase _ #S00550
Presents a film version of Shakespeare's tragedy 'Richard II.' Stars David Birney, Paul Shenar, John Devlin and William H Bassett. Features an artist's reproduction of the Globe Theater stage where the play was originally presented.
Fine Arts; Literature and Drama
Dist - UILL

The Tragedy of King Richard the Second 172 MIN
U-matic / VHS
Color (A)
Presents Shakespeare's classic story of a self centered, weak King.
Literature and Drama
Dist - KULTUR **Prod** - KULTUR 1985

The Tragedy of Macbeth 151 MIN
VHS
Color (G)
$89.95 purchase _ #S00551
Presents a film version of Shakespeare's tragedy 'Macbeth.' Stars Jeremy Brett, Piper Laurie, Simon MacCorkindale, and Barry Primus.
Fine Arts; Literature and Drama
Dist - UILL

The Tragedy of Macbeth 20 MIN
16mm / U-matic / VHS
Shakespeare in Rehearsal Series
Color (H C)
$495.00 purchase - 16 mm, $250.00 purchase - video _ #5792C
Talks about the development of Macbeth's character. Discusses how Shakespeare used actual events of his era to form parts of the tragedy. Produced in association with Coronet by BBC, Milton Keynes.
Fine Arts
Dist - CORF

The Tragedy of Macbeth 151 MIN
U-matic / VHS
Color (A)
Presents Shakespeare's classic story of murder, greed and intrigue over who shall be King.
Literature and Drama
Dist - KULTUR **Prod** - KULTUR 1985

The Tragedy of Othello 195 MIN
U-matic / VHS
Color (A)
Gives a new version of Shakespeare's classic story of jealousy.
Literature and Drama
Dist - KULTUR **Prod** - KULTUR 1985

The Tragedy of Othello, Moor of Venice 195 MIN
VHS
Color (G)
$89.95 purchase _ #S01594
Presents a film version of Shakespeare's tragedy 'Othello.' Stars William Marshall, Ron Moody, and Jenny Agutter.
Fine Arts; Literature and Drama
Dist - UILL

The Tragedy of Romeo and Juliet
VHS
Color; PAL (J H C G)
PdS29.50 purchase
Tells Shakespeare's tragic story of young love thwarted by a family feud. Captures the Elizabethan flavor of Shakespeare's own Globe productions by staging the play just as it was in the 16th century.
Fine Arts; Literature and Drama
Dist - EMFVL **Prod** - BARDPR

The Tragedy of the Commons 23 MIN
16mm / U-matic / VHS
Color (H)
LC 73-712844
Presents four sequences all related to overpopulation. Stresses the need for man to regulate population before nature, through disease or some type of violence, regulates the size of the population for man.
Sociology
Dist - PHENIX **Prod** - KINGSP 1971

Tragedy of the red salmon 24 MIN
U-matic / VHS / 16mm
Undersea world of Jacques Cousteau series
Color (G) (SPANISH)
$49.95 purchase _ #Q10614; LC 75-702736
A shortened version of Tragedy Of The Red Salmon. Shows Jacques Cousteau and his crew as they study the migration of the red sockeye salmon. Focuses on the salmons' journey from Fraser Lake in Alaska to the ocean and back again to the lake. Part of a series of 24 programs.
Science - Natural
Dist - CF **Prod** - METROM 1975

Tragedy or Triumph 28 MIN
16mm / U-matic / VHS
Color (J)
LC 75-702174
Explores the problems of hunger and food production in the modern world.
Geography - World; Health and Safety; Social Science
Dist - JOU **Prod** - UN 1975

The Tragic Comic 27 MIN
16mm
Color
Portrays an alcoholic comedian drinking his way through his TV performance. Intersperses his performance with appropriate statistics on alcohol.
Health and Safety; Psychology; Sociology
Dist - MTP **Prod** - SALVA

Tragic consequences - teenagers and guns 30 MIN
VHS
CC; Color (H) (SPANISH)
$99.00 purchase _ #10405VL
Features the story of a teen victim and a teen perpetrator of a shooting to show the effects of guns and violence. Uses interviews and scenes from the jail and the victim's therapy to teach lessons about the consequences of firearms and crime. Comes with a teacher's guide; student activities; discussion questions; and a set of blackline masters. A Spanish language version is available from catalog number 10406VG.
Sociology
Dist - UNL

The Tragic flaw - not in the stars but in ourselves 35 MIN
VHS
Color (J H)
$99.00 purchase _ #00266 - 026
Studies the tragic hero who, despite courage, intelligence and willpower, must act within human limitations. Examines the hero's imperfections and qualities of character. Illustrated with well - known literary characters such as Cervantes' Don Quixote and Fitzgerald's Gatsby. Includes teacher's guide and library kit.
Education; Literature and Drama
Dist - GA

The Tragic vision 30 MIN
U-matic / VHS
Art of being human series; Module 8
Color (C)
History - World; Literature and Drama; Religion and Philosophy
Dist - MDCC **Prod** - MDCC

The Tragicomedy of Marriage 10 MIN
16mm
B&W (A)
Presents a spoof of experimental films that use sexual symbolism. Deals with a man who is afraid of sex and wants a wife for domestic purposes only, and with a wife who is only interested in a sexual marriage and hates housework.
Fine Arts
Dist - CFS **Prod** - PIKE

Tragoedia 35 MIN
16mm
Color (G)
$1144.00 purchase, $74.00 rental
Discusses the derivation by Norman O Brown of the word tragedy from from the Greek for 'goat song.'
Fine Arts
Dist - CANCIN **Prod** - BRAKS 1976

The Trail Horse 22 MIN
16mm / U-matic / VHS
Color
Discusses the trail horse events including basic and advanced training methods which demonstrate what makes a good trail horse. Shows the origination of obstacles used in the class, utilizing actual trail ride sequences.
Physical Education and Recreation
Dist - AQHORS **Prod** - AQHORS

The Trail North 28 MIN
U-matic / VHS / 16mm
Color (H C A)
$425 purchase - 16 mm, $295 purchase - video, $55 rental
Recreates the journey of the ancestors of anthropologist Robert Alvarez which they made in coming north from Mexico several generations ago. Narrated by Martin Sheen. Produced by Paul Espinosa. Directed by Thomas Karlo.
Sociology
Dist - CNEMAG

Trail of Broken Treaties 26 MIN
U-matic / VHS / 16mm
Native Americans Series
Color
Describes the Indians as the most underprivileged ethnic group in the United States. Examines the past and present injustices and focuses on the attempts of Indian leaders to improve the situation.
Social Science; Sociology
Dist - CNEMAG **Prod** - BBCTV

Trail of death 27 MIN
VHS
Color (J H C G)
$39.95 purchase _ #WHP001V
Reveals that during the 19th century many Indian tribes were removed from the mid - west area of the United States and relocated west of the Mississippi River to Kansas and Oklahoma. Discloses that they were often subjected to physical and emotional suffering during the relocation. Focuses on the Menominee band of Potawatomi Indians who lived in north - central Indiana and were forcibly removed to Kansas, the Trail of Death, September 4 through November 4, 1838, when many Indians died and were buried in nameless graves along the way. Retraces the steps of the Potawatomi from Northern Indiana to Kansas in 1838.
Social Science
Dist - CAMV

The Trail of Tears 13 MIN
U-matic / VHS
America's Indians Series
Color (G)
$199.00, $99.00 purchase _ #AD - 974
Examines the seizure of Indian lands and the destruction of Indian culture. Part of a six - part series on America's Indians.
History - United States; History - World; Social Science; Sociology
Dist - FOTH **Prod** - FOTH

Trail of the Buffalo 9 MIN
U-matic / VHS / 16mm
Color (P I)
LC 83-700390
Describes the passing of the huge herds of buffalo that once roamed the prairies.
Science - Natural
Dist - EBEC **Prod** - JHNSTN 1983

Trail of the Ice Age Blues 29 MIN
U-matic / VHS / 16mm
Planet of Man Series
Color (J H C)
Describes the rise and decline of the Ice Age which occurred thousands of years ago. Speculates on the possibility of an ice age in the near future.
Geography - World; Science - Physical
Dist - FI **Prod** - OECA 1978

Trail of the Tarpon 14 MIN
16mm
Color
Shows Dave Newell fishing for Florida tarpon at Marco Island, Cape Sable and the Everglades.
Geography - United States; Physical Education and Recreation
Dist - FLADC **Prod** - FLADC

Trail Ride 20 MIN
16mm
Color (I J)
LC FIA65-1854
Shows how city boys visiting at the Blood Indian Reserve in Alberta ride herd, help brand calves and spend the night in tepees with the Blood Indians who have gathered for a sun dance.
Geography - World; Social Science
Dist - SF **Prod** - NFBC 1964

Trail series
Caring 20 MIN
Eating 20 MIN
Ending 20 MIN
Helping 20 MIN
Living 20 MIN
Measuring 20 MIN
Seeing 20 MIN
Sharing 20 MIN
Surviving 20 MIN
Dist - AITECH

A Trail to the West - by Louis L'Amour 60 MIN
VHS / U-matic
L'Amour Series
Stereo (K P I J H C G T A S R PRO IND)
Presents a western fiction.
Literature and Drama
Dist - BANTAP **Prod** - BANTAP

The Trail - Volume 5 49 MIN
VHS
Vietnam - the ten thousand day war series
Color (G)
$34.95 purchase _ #S00394
Covers the history of the Ho Chi Minh trail, which was the critical supply route for Viet Cong forces. Reveals that almost unending bombing by U S forces did not stop supply efforts. Interviews US soldiers on their reactions to fighting against guerilla tactics. Narrated by Richard Basehart.
History - United States
Dist - UILL

Trailblazer 20 MIN
16mm
Color
Presents the story of the first major pipeline to tap the vast natural gas reserves of the Rocky Mountain Overthrust area. Called Trailblazer, the 800 mile interstate system, built in 1982, extends from Whitney Canyon in Wyoming to Beatrice, Nebraska.
Business and Economics; Geography - United States; Social Science
Dist - MTP **Prod** - MIDCON

Trailblazers of Modern Dance 60 MIN
16mm / U-matic / VHS
Dance in America Series
Color (J)
LC 79-701683
Reviews the history of modern dance in America from the beginnings in the early 1900's to the appearance of Martha Graham in the early 1930's. Includes rare film footage of Doris Humphrey, Ruth St Denis, Anna Pavlova and what is believed to be Isadora Duncan, along with reconstructed performances of Duncan's Scriabin etudes, St Denis and Humphrey's Soaring and Ted Shawn's Polonaise.
Fine Arts
Dist - IU **Prod** - WNETTV 1977

Trailer for the angry god 2 MIN
16mm
Color (G)
$6.00 rental
Presents the trailer for the film The Angry God and is available free of charge when renting The Angry God.
Fine Arts
Dist - CANCIN **Prod** - DEGRAS 1973

The Train 7 MIN
U-matic / VHS
(G PRO)
$295.00 purchase, $75.00 rental, $25.00 preview
Illustrates the power of the mind. Reenacts the story of a man who is accidentally locked in a refrigerated boxcar and dies from the erroneous belief that there is no air, when in fact, the unit is dysfunctional. Features an epilogue discussing the power of thoughts.
Psychology
Dist - CREMED **Prod** - CREMED 1987
UTM

Train movie 6 MIN
16mm
B&W (G)
$7.00 rental
Pictures the Southern Pacific diesel locomotives preparing for their runs from San Francisco's China Basin. Records Muni subway running under Market Street and BART train speeding to Daly City. Music by Tangerine Dream.
Fine Arts
Dist - CANCIN

Train now departing, Part 1 87 MIN
VHS
Train now departing series
Color (G)
$29.95 purchase _ #TRA06
Presents part one of a two - part series on the preservation of steam locomotive and train history in Great Britain. Visits train museums and locomotives still in operation for steam enthusiasts.
History - World; Industrial and Technical Education; Social Science
Dist - HOMVIS **Prod** - BBCTV 1990

Train now departing, Part 2 86 MIN
VHS
Train now departing series
Color (G)
$29.95 purchase _ #TRA07
Presents part two of a two - part series on the preservation of steam locomotive and train history in Great Britain. Visits train museums and locomotives still in operation for steam enthusiasts.
History - World; Industrial and Technical Education; Social Science
Dist - HOMVIS **Prod** - BBCTV 1990

Train now departing series
Train now departing, Part 1 87 MIN
Train now departing, Part 2 86 MIN
Dist - HOMVIS

Train Ride to Grandfathers 3 MIN
16mm
Color (I) (AMERICAN SIGN)
LC 76-701707
Presents Florian Caliguiri relating to the deaf in American sign language his childhood experiences traveling by train to visit his grandfather.
Guidance and Counseling; Psychology
Dist - JOYCE **Prod** - JOYCE 1975

The Train Rolls on 33 MIN
16mm
B&W
LC 75-702768
Examines the work and career of Soviet filmmaker Alexander Medvedkin. Shows how Medvedkin moved camera crews into the interior of the Soviet Union in order to bring the cinema to the Russian masses.
Biography; Fine Arts; Foreign Language
Dist - NYFLMS **Prod** - MARKC 1975

Train the trainer - conducting one - on - one training 24 MIN
VHS
Train the trainer series
Color (H C A IND)
LC 90-716376
Trains those who are training employees in the hotel industry in the process of effective one - on - one training. Produced by Media Magic.
Business and Economics; Psychology
Dist - EIAHM

Train the trainer - leading group training 23 MIN
VHS
Train the trainer series
Color (H C A IND)
LC 90-716377
Trains those who are training employees in the hotel industry in the process of leading a group. Produced by Media Magic.
Business and Economics; Psychology
Dist - EIAHM

Train the trainer - preparing for training 17 MIN
VHS
Train the trainer series
Color (H C A IND)
LC 90-716380
Trains those who are training employees in the hotel industry how to prepare for the process. Produced by Media Magic.
Business and Economics; Psychology
Dist - EIAHM

Train the trainer series
Train the trainer - conducting one - on - one training 24 MIN
Train the trainer - leading group training 23 MIN
Train the trainer - preparing for training 17 MIN
Dist - EIAHM

The Train to happiness 57 MIN
VHS
Color (G)
$39.95 purchase _ #106
Focuses on the founding of the Jewish Shalom Theatre after the dissolution of the former Soviet Union. Reveals that the troupe travels the length and breadth of the region, bring Jewish culture to generations of Jews in the new found freedoms of the region. These same freedoms have also unleashed Pamyat and other virulently anti - Semitic groups, as well as other narrowly ethnocentric groups to flourish and spawn their evils of cultural narrowness. Examines the current status of Jews in Russia.
Fine Arts; Geography - World; Religion and Philosophy; Sociology
Dist - ERGOM

Train to heaven 86 MIN
VHS
Color; PAL (G)
PdS100 purchase
Illustrates the adventures of a 10 - year - old orphan in Ecuador, who believes the train to Quito, high up in the mountains, is the train to heaven and his parents. Features a Hans Lonnerheden production.
Sociology
Dist - BALFOR

Train your dog before your dog trains you 120 MIN
VHS
Color (G)
$49.95 purchase
Presents a comprehensive program for dog obedience and behavior training. Designed for all dogs regardless of age or breed. Covers subjects including housebreaking, destructiveness, wildness, aggressiveness, health, grooming, and more. Includes a leather training leash.
Physical Education and Recreation; Psychology; Science - Natural
Dist - PBS **Prod** - WNETTV

Trainable Mentally Handicapped 20 MIN
U-matic
One Giant Step - the Integration of Children with Special Needs 'Series
Color (PRO)
Focuses on mentally handicapped children who cannot achieve in the traditional academic sense but given instruction in living and vocational skills can function and live independently in society.
Education
Dist - ACCESS **Prod** - ACCESS 1983

The Trained Chinese tongue 20 MIN
16mm / VHS
Color (G)
$60.00, $75.00 rental, $225.00 purchase
Explores Chinese - American identity and the immigrant experience by taking the rituals of food and language as points of departure. Approaches a series of strangers - all immigrant women - in a Chinatown grocery store and then follows them home for dinner. As each one prepares the family dinner, the filmmaker opens a door into the important connections between food, language and culture.
Fine Arts; Foreign Language; History - United States; Home Economics; Sociology
Dist - WMEN **Prod** - WEN 1994

Trainer's package
CD-ROM
Color (IND PRO)
$299.00 purchase _ #35707
Allows the trainer to examine the student's locked and encrypted IMT Haz Mat Awareness Training Package test disk and to analyze the results of each test by learning objective. Enables the trainer to evaluate the student's strong and weak learning areas as shown by the test. Enables the trainer to encrypt the student's name onto the disk and print out test results. Requires Windows 3.1.
Health and Safety; Science - Physical; Social Science; Sociology
Dist - OKSU **Prod** - RJMMUL

Training
VHS
Dynamics of Fitness - the Body in Action Series
Color
Explains training techniques for achieving and maintaining physical fitness.
Physical Education and Recreation
Dist - IBIS **Prod** - IBIS

The Training 8 MIN
16mm / VHS
B&W (G)
$15.00 rental
Reenacts the behavior modification approach to toilet training. Satirizes the instructions in a popular book on the subject which the filmmaker, Elizabeth Sher, came across in her search to understand and solve this universal problem.

Fine Arts; Literature and Drama; Psychology
Dist - CANCIN

Training - a Bridge to the Future 30 MIN
VHS / U-matic
(H C A)
$65.00 purchase members, $85.00 purchase non - members, $35.00 rental
Provides audiences with predictions and opinions that may influence the decisions that they make in preparing for the future of their business or career.
Business and Economics; Education
Dist - ASTD **Prod** - ASTD

Training - a Major Responsibility 64 FRS
U-matic / VHS
New Supervisor Series
Color
Explains that training is an investment in time and that a supervisor's ability to get things done through others depends on the training others have received. Module four of the New Supervisor series.
Business and Economics; Psychology
Dist - RESEM **Prod** - RESEM

The Training Activity 69 FRS
VHS / U-matic
Pre - Supervisory Training Series Module 3
Color
Deals with both the 'how to' and the 'why' of training with emphasis on actual practice rather than theory.
Business and Economics; Psychology
Dist - RESEM **Prod** - RESEM

Training aids 23 MIN
16mm
Military instruction series; No. 3
B&W
LC FIE56-246
Describes the uses of simple and complex training aids including chalkboards, filmstrips, slides, transparencies, working models and motion pictures. Number 3 in the Military Instruction series.
Civics and Political Systems; Education
Dist - USNAC **Prod** - USA 1956

Training Aids - Classroom Utilization 15 MIN
16mm
B&W
LC FIE52-1290
Shows how a good navy instructor uses audio - visual aids to encourage student participation in class.
Civics and Political Systems; Education
Dist - USNAC **Prod** - USN 1950

Training Aids - Selection and Planning 16 MIN
16mm
B&W
LC FIE52-1289
Shows how a navy instructor selects motion pictures, charts and models to fit into his lesson and how he checks the aids, equipment and classroom prior to use.
Civics and Political Systems; Education
Dist - USNAC **Prod** - USN 1951

Training Aids - Slides, Large Drawings and Transparencies 18 MIN
16mm
Color
LC FIE52-1973
Explains the nature of the equipment and materials which are needed and the opportunities for preparing and using such training aids by naval instructors.
Psychology; Social Science
Dist - USNAC **Prod** - USNAC 1951

Training and customer service
VHS
Marketing electronic information series
Color (G C PRO)
$195.00 purchase
Shows how to combine sales presentations and training to make new sales and create new buyers. Part of an eight - part series on marketing electronic information.
Business and Economics; Psychology
Dist - DEJAVI **Prod** - DEJAVI

Training at the Peking Circus 16 MIN
16mm
How Yukong Moved the Mountains Series
Color (J A)
LC 80-700639
Provides a behind - the - scenes look at the Peking Circus, showing various performers rehearsing their acts. Concludes with an actual performance of the circus, showing the acts of the performers seen earlier in rehearsal.
Geography - World; History - World; Physical Education and Recreation
Dist - CINPER **Prod** - CAPI 1979

Training Decisions in a Microteaching Clinic 28 MIN
16mm
Color (T)
Discusses the various training procedures and issues which provide teachers with specific skills and wider range of instructional alternatives for their professional performance.
Education
Dist - EDUC **Prod** - EDUC

Training dogs the Woodhouse way series
The Advance, stand, sit and down 30 MIN
Dist - FI

Training Dogs the Woodhouse Way

Come when called	30 MIN
The Down	30 MIN
Nervous Dogs	30 MIN
Problem dogs	30 MIN
Puppies	30 MIN
The Right Start	30 MIN
Show handling	30 MIN
Sit and Stay	30 MIN
Walking to Heel	30 MIN

Dist - FI

Training for a Trade
VHS
Choosing Careers Series
(H C)
$59.00 _ CA109
Discusses post high school para - professional courses.
Business and Economics; Education
Dist - AAVIM **Prod** - AAVIM 1989

Training for child care providers series
Presents a seven - part series on caring for children of different ages, from infants to elementary school. Suggests activities to develop self - esteem in children. Includes a leader's guide and reproducible study materials for each part.

Enter toddling	20 MIN
Fun to be four	20 MIN
Infancy - the beginning	20 MIN
Now I'm five	20 MIN
The School - age connection	20 MIN
Terrific twos	20 MIN
Threes on the threshold	20 MIN
Training for child care providers series	140 MIN

Dist - CAMV

Training for track and field
VHS
Coaching men's field and track series
Color (H C G)
$59.95 purchase _ #TRS1259V
Features men's field and track coach Rick Sloan on training for competition. Explores thoroughly three distinct aspects of field and track - weight training, plyometrics and medicine ball routines. Allows coaches to select the training best suited to their particular program. Part of a nine - part series.
Physical Education and Recreation
Dist - CAMV

Training for Tracking 15 MIN
16mm
Dog Obedience Training Series
Color
LC 75-700107
Illustrates a variety of techniques used to train dogs for tracking.
Science - Natural
Dist - KLEINW **Prod** - KLEINW 1974

Training for upward mobility 70 FRS
VHS / U-matic
Supervisor and OJT series
Color
Defines upward mobility and shows why it is important to organizations. Gives three practical advantages of moving people upward within the organization, and the major reasons for failure of upward mobility training and ways to overcome them. Module four in the Supervisor and OJT series.
Business and Economics; Psychology
Dist - RESEM **Prod** - RESEM

Training for volleyball
VHS
Coaching boys' volleyball III series
Color (J H C G)
$49.95 purchase _ #TRS507V
Features Bill Neville, USA National Team coach. Focuses on training in volleyball. Part of a two - part series on volleyball coaching tactics and an eight - part series on boys' volleyball.
Physical Education and Recreation
Dist - CAMV

Training Greenhouse Workers to Handle Pesticides Safely
VHS
Color (IND VOC G) (SPANISH)
$89.95 purchase _ #6 - 064 - 103P, #6 - 064 - 203P
Looks at the four ways horticultural and agricultural workers might come into hazardous contact with pesticides. Examines handling, equipment, mixing, application, cleaning, clothing and safety gear and first aid.
Agriculture; Health and Safety; Psychology
Dist - VEP **Prod** - VEP

The Training manikin 10 MIN
16mm / U-matic / VHS
Emergency resuscitation series; No 4
Color (H C A)
LC FIA65-275
An instructor and his pupils demonstrate ways in which a manikin fabricated to resemble a human being may be used to train a class in exhaled air resuscitation and closed chest cardiac massage. Describes the care and maintenance of the manikin, as well as the hygienic precautions to be taken in order to safeguard users.
Education; Health and Safety
Dist - IFB **Prod** - BRITAD 1964

The Training Memorandum 12 MIN
U-matic / 8mm cartridge
Professional Management Program Series
Color (H C A)
LC 74-700230
Discusses the benefits of training to change attitudes of resistance and indifference. Takes a skeptical supervisor through a series of experiences which motivate him to see training in a new light. Illustrates examples of modern training methods and philosophy.
Business and Economics; Education; Psychology
Dist - NEM **Prod** - NEM 1973

Training Methods 15 MIN
16mm
Coaching Development Programme Series; No 9
Color
LC 76-701067
Discusses training methods for various sports.
Physical Education and Recreation
Dist - SARBOO **Prod** - SARBOO 1974

Training Module on Role Enactment in Children's Play Four
What Happens When You Go to the Hospital 12 MIN
Dist - CFDC

Training Module on Role Enactment in Children's Play Series One
Role Enactment in Children's Play - a Developmental Overview 29 MIN
Dist - CFDC

Training Module on Role Enactment in Children's Play Series Two
Concept Instancing of Role Enactment 12 MIN
Dist - CFDC

Training Module on Role Enactment in Children's Play Three
The Moat Monster 12 MIN
Dist - CFDC

Training needs assessment 20 MIN
VHS
Color (A PRO IND)
$495.00 purchase, $95.00 rental
Stresses the importance of training needs assessments for managers. Suggests that training needs assessments can help correct current performance deficiencies and anticipate future training needs.
Business and Economics; Psychology
Dist - VLEARN **Prod** - BBP

The Training of painters 28 MIN
VHS / U-matic / 16mm
Painter's world series
Color (H C A)
$595.00, $250.00 purchase _ #HP - 6093C
Shows how painters have been trained from the Renaissance to the present. Looks at the relationship between prevailing styles in art and corresponding art school doctrine. Visits the Slade School in London, Royal College of Art, Royal Academies of Art, Ecole des Beaux Arts in Paris, and the Rhode Island School of Design. Includes archival footage of Joseph Albers teaching at Yale Univesity. Part of a series on painters.
Fine Arts
Dist - CORF **Prod** - WGBHTV 1989

Training - One on One 16.25 MIN
VHS / U-matic / BETA
Supervisory Series
(PRO A)

$225 _ #1022
Gives a basic method for training beginning employees who otherwise will not receive training.
Education; Guidance and Counseling
Dist - CTT **Prod** - CTT

Training - one - on - one 17 MIN
VHS
Supervisory series
Color (PRO A G)
$225.00 purchase _ #BM122; $225.00 purchase _ #1022
Provides an effective format for training entry - level personnel who must be placed into the work force without benefit of a formal training program.
Business and Economics; Guidance and Counseling; Psychology
Dist - AAVIM CTT **Prod** - AAVIM CTT

Training Principles 15 MIN
VHS / 16mm
All Fit with Slim Goodbody Series
Color (P I)
$125.00 purchase, $25.00 rental
Emphasizes that personal improvement, not competition, is the most important part of fitness training.
Health and Safety; Physical Education and Recreation; Science - Natural
Dist - AITECH **Prod** - GDBODY 1987

The Training - Pt 2 22 MIN
BETA / VHS / U-matic
Fit for the final series
Color (G)
Health and Safety; Physical Education and Recreation
Dist - UCALG **Prod** - UCALG 1986

Training Resources and Techniques 28 MIN
U-matic / VHS
Color
Health and Safety
Dist - PRIMED **Prod** - PRIMED

Training resources and techniques 25 MIN
16mm
Counseling the mentally retarded series; No 3
Color (PRO)
LC 72-702013
Shows several training programs, facilities and procedures which vocational counselors employ in rehabilitation programs for retarded clients.
Education; Guidance and Counseling; Psychology
Dist - NMAC **Prod** - UKANS 1968

Training tape - caring for drug affected babies 20 MIN
VHS / U-matic
Cocaine - the domino effect series
Color (G)
$249.00 purchase _ #7425
Provides the most current methods for caring for babies born to mothers who abused drugs during pregnancy. Emphasizes the importance of early intervention and therapy to enable these youngsters to grow into healthy children and adults. Part of a six - series on the effect of cocaine in several social areas - the birth parents, foster care system, public schools, national finances, the medical and psychological professions, and the children of cocaine users.
Guidance and Counseling; Health and Safety; Psychology; Sociology
Dist - VISIVI **Prod** - VISIVI 1991

Training tape for caretakers of drug babies 20 MIN
VHS / U-matic
Original cocaine babies series
Color (G)
$199.00 purchase _ #7424
Instructs on ways to soothe, relax and comfort the drug addicted infant. Shows how to ensure bonding. Features social worker and foster parent Sherry Newcombe. Part two of two parts on cocaine babies.
Guidance and Counseling; Health and Safety; Psychology; Sociology
Dist - VISIVI **Prod** - VISIVI 1991

A Training tape for caretakers of drug babies 17 MIN
VHS
Color (PRO G)
$169.00 purchase
Looks at the devastating effect of cocaine and crack on children. Visits a hospital ward where the piercing cries of cocaine addicted babies are endlessly heard. Trains caretakers step - by - step how to soothe, relax and comfort drug addicted infants as they fight through the pain and frustration of withdrawal. Shows how to ensure bonding between baby and caretaker.
Health and Safety; Sociology
Dist - MEDIAI **Prod** - MEDIAI 1990

Training tape for living with FAS and FAE - independence, ages 12 to adult 32 MIN
VHS / U-matic
FAS series
Color (G)
$249.00 purchase _ #7496
Discusses the difficulty of adolescence for victims of fetal alcohol syndrome, FAS, and fetal alcohol effects, FAE. Emphasizes the value of early diagnosis, implementing specialized programs within existing budgets, and focusing on social and adaptive living skills. Part of a three - part series on the fetal alcohol syndrome.
Guidance and Counseling; Health and Safety; Psychology
Dist - VISIVI **Prod** - VISIVI 1991

Training tape for living with FAS and FAE - the early years, birth through age 12 32 MIN
VHS / U-matic
FAS series
Color (G)
$249.00 purchase _ #7495
Focuses on the effects of fetal alcohol syndrome, FAS, and fetal alcohol effects, FAE, on the early years of an individual. Teaches soothing techniques for the fussy baby and positive behavioral programming for the pre - adolescent. Part of a three - part series on the fetal alcohol syndrome.
Guidance and Counseling; Health and Safety; Psychology
Dist - VISIVI **Prod** - VISIVI 1991

Training the Advocate
VHS / U-matic
Color (PRO)
Designed as a basic trial skills training program. Includes trial demonstrations, critiques, interviews with the expert faculty and discussions of communications skills that can enhance an attorney's presentation in court.
Civics and Political Systems
Dist - ABACPE **Prod** - ABACPE

Training the advocate
VHS
Color (PRO C)
$1195.00 purchase _ #FVTTAOS
Trains new advocates. trial strategies and case development techniques. Includes six Doyle v Nita Power and Light case files, one 'Doyle v Nita Teacher's Manual,' one program planner's guide and 11 videocassettes.
Civics and Political Systems
Dist - NITA **Prod** - NITA 1983

Training the Advocate Series

Closing Arguments, Pt 1	57 MIN
Closing Arguments, Pt 2	29 MIN
Cross examination	55 MIN
Direct Examination	57 MIN
Expert Witness - Damages	58 MIN
Expert Witness - Liability	57 MIN
The Introduction and Use of Demonstrative Evidence	56 MIN
Jury Deliberation	43 MIN
Jury Selection	60 MIN
Laying the Foundation for Exhibits and Witnesses at Trial	49 MIN
Opening Statements	59 MIN

Dist - ABACPE

Training the advocate series

Closing arguments - Part I	56 MIN
Closing arguments - Part II	29 MIN
Cross examination	56 MIN
Expert witness - Damages	57 MIN
Expert witness - liability	57 MIN
Introduction and use of demonstrative evidence	56 MIN
Jury deliberation	43 MIN
Jury selection	60 MIN
Laying the foundation for exhibits and witnesses at trial	57 MIN
Opening statements	58 MIN

Dist - NITA

Training the advocate - the pretrial stage
VHS
Color (PRO C)
$1195.00 purchase _ #FVPTAOS
Teaches successful pretrial strategies and case development techniques. Includes six pretrial problem books, one 'Training the Advocate - the Pretrial Teacher's Manual,' one program planner's guide and 14 videocassettes.
Business and Economics; Civics and Political Systems
Dist - NITA **Prod** - NITA 1985

Training the advocate - the pretrial stage series 756 MIN
VHS
Training the advocate - the pretrial stage series
Color (C PRO)
$1,195.00 purchase, $700.00 rental _ #FVPTAOS
Presents lectures and demonstrations of the steps of the pretrial stage. Covers subjects including client interviews, discovery, depositions, negotiation of settlements, and motions. Fourteen - part series includes problem books, teacher's manual, and a planner's guide.
Civics and Political Systems
Dist - NITA **Prod** - NITA 1985

Training the Disadvantaged 11 MIN
U-matic / 35mm strip
Supervising the Disadvantaged Series Module 5
Color
Points out that the disadvantaged should be allowed to progress in meaningful tasks at a rate that will build up confidence and insure ultimate success on the job.
Business and Economics; Psychology
Dist - RESEM **Prod** - RESEM

Training the School Bus Driver 26 MIN
16mm
Color (A)
LC 76-703274
Presents a training film for school bus drivers which demonstrates safety, emergency procedures and the exacting nature of the work.
Health and Safety; Psychology
Dist - LAWREN **Prod** - PARKRD 1975

Training the trainer
U-matic / VHS / 16mm
Supervisory training office series
Color (A)
Shows how to prepare for the presentation of both the Supervisory Training (Office) series and the Supervisory Training (Industrial) series.
Business and Economics
Dist - CRMP **Prod** - CRMP 1983

Training the Trainer Series

Administering the training program	30 MIN
Developing and using lesson plans	30 MIN
Developing and writing training objectives	30 MIN
The Elements of effective training	30 MIN
Instructing to Facilitate Learning	30 MIN
Learning - How it Occurs	30 MIN
Measuring Instructional Effectiveness	30 MIN
Methods for Teaching Information	30 MIN
Methods for Teaching Skills	30 MIN
On - the - Job Training	30 MIN
Planning for Effective Training	30 MIN
Principles of Visual Training	30 MIN
Teaching Your First Class	30 MIN
Using Visual Aids Effectively	30 MIN

Dist - ITCORP

Training the Trainer Series

Administration and evaluation	50 MIN
Presentation	50 MIN
Research and Preparation	50 MIN

Dist - LEIKID

Training the Trainer Series

Defining training objectives - No 2	60 MIN
Evaluation and Reports - no 8	60 MIN
Lesson Plans - Part I - Designing Effective Training - no 3	60 MIN
Lesson Plans - Part II - Planning for Skills Training - no 4	60 MIN
Making it Stick - no 7	60 MIN
Presentation techniques - teaching in three domains - no 5	60 MIN
Selecting Goals - Deciding what to Train - no 1	60 MIN
Training with Video - no 6	60 MIN

Dist - VTRI

Training the Young Horse 27 MIN
U-matic / VHS / 16mm
Riding Training Series
Color (J)
LC 80-701072
Shows the step - by - step training of a young horse, from the handling and grooming of a foal through the introduction of complete tack and rider at age three to four years old. Covers leading, training on a lunge rein and in the basic paces, beginning jumping and the gradual addition of the tack. Emphasizes teaching the horse obedience, rhythm, and balance, with gradual introduction of the rider to the horse. Introduced by Princess Anne of Great Britain.
Physical Education and Recreation
Dist - IU **Prod** - BHORSE 1979

Training Tips 25 MIN
16mm
Color (H C A)
LC 76-701752
Presents a training aid for fire department officers.
Guidance and Counseling; Health and Safety
Dist - FILCOM **Prod** - LACFD 1964

Training with Video - no 6 60 MIN
U-matic
Training the Trainer Series
Color (PRO)
Presents training sessions for professional training personnel. Includes goal selection, design and presentation of training material and evaluation and reports.
Industrial and Technical Education
Dist - VTRI **Prod** - VTRI 1986

Training Your Dog 60 MIN
BETA
Color
Offers information on dog training, explaining how to turn a squirming ball of fluff into a respectable canine citizen.
Science - Natural
Dist - HOMET **Prod** - CINAS

Training Your Dog 61 MIN
VHS / 16mm
(G)
$39.95 purchase _ #VT1066
Shows the techniques of dog training, from early puppy work and breaking bad habits to the basic commands and activities like stick jumping and carrying. Taught by Mary Whiting, Director of the Canine College in Minneapolis, Minnesota and author of the book From Cradle to College.
Physical Education and Recreation; Science - Natural
Dist - RMIBHF **Prod** - RMIBHF

Training Your Retriever - Advanced
VHS / BETA
From the Sportsman's Video Collection Series
Color
Points out that at 22 weeks and older, it's time to train one's dog in multiple and blind retrieves, long distance retrieves, and to sharpen his obedience on and off lead. Results in a finished gun dog and lifelong companion. Includes hunting scenes to inspire one to work with dogs.
Physical Education and Recreation
Dist - CBSC **Prod** - CBSC

Training Your Retriever - Basic 55 MIN
BETA / VHS
From the Sportsman's Video Collection Series
Color
Shows step by step retriever training from ten - week - old pup to accomplished hunting partner. Tells how to teach your dog obedience, voice and whistle commands, as well as how to introduce him to water retrieves and birds. Includes actual hunting sequences.
Physical Education and Recreation
Dist - CBSC **Prod** - CBSC

Trains 30 MIN
U-matic
Today's Special Series
Color (K P)
Develops language arts skills in children. Programs are thematically designed around subjects of interest to youngsters. Action takes place in a department store where people, mannequins, puppets, comic characters and special guests present a light hearted approach to language arts.
Fine Arts; Literature and Drama; Psychology
Dist - TVOTAR **Prod** - TVOTAR 1985

Trains 5 MIN
16mm
Color
LC 76-703814
Depicts a historical journey on Canada's last operating steam engine.
Geography - World; Social Science
Dist - YORKU **Prod** - YORKU 1976

Trains 14 MIN
U-matic / 16mm / VHS
Goofy's field trips series
Color (P)
$425.00, $280.00 purchase _ #JC - 67243
Stars Goofy who takes two youngsters on a field trip to learn about trains. Shows them meeting an engineer, train attendant, conductor, head of on - board services, yard master and switchman. Observes the differences between freight and passenger trains and how a train runs. Visits the various kinds of passenger train cars, the switching yard, the distribution center and the dispatch center. Looks at the different kinds of cars on freight trains. Part of a series on transportation.
Social Science
Dist - CORF **Prod** - DISNEY 1989

Trains 15 MIN
16mm / U-matic / VHS
Color (I)
LC 73-700993
Presents a quick survey of railroads, past, present and future. Demonstrates influence of the railroad on our native American music. Portrays the excitement variety of railroad careers.
Fine Arts; Guidance and Counseling; Social Science
Dist - AIMS **Prod** - COMICO 1970

Trains 14 MIN
U-matic / VHS
Under the Yellow Balloon Series
Color (P)
Depicts Peggy after a train trip, describing the different cars on her train. Shows that the freight train she sees also has specialized cars.
Social Science
Dist - AITECH **Prod** - SCETV 1980

Trains - a First Film 11 MIN
U-matic / VHS / 16mm
Color (P I)
LC 72-703103
Shows passenger trains and freight trains, diesel engines and cars made for special purposes. Explains the jobs of the men who run the train. Shows how a train is made up in the railroad yard for its trip to the next city.
Social Science
Dist - PHENIX **Prod** - BEANMN 1969

Trains, planes, boats and cars 23 MIN
VHS
Bright sparks series
Color (P I)
$280.00 purchase
Looks at modern forms of transportation, including a covered racing bike and a hovercraft in motion. Examines new developments in car safety such as a behicle without a driver. Demonstrates all - terrain vehicles and visits the inventor of a wheel that can turn in two directions at the same time. Witnesses the fastest trains and planes known, the latest development in helicopters and considers the idea of a personal flying platform. Part of a 12 - part animated series on science and technology.
Industrial and Technical Education; Social Science
Dist - LANDMK **Prod** - LANDMK 1989

Trains, tracks and trestles series
Bench work and wiring 30 MIN
Gauges 30 MIN
Scenery 30 MIN
Structures 30 MIN
Dist - PBS

The Traitor within 11 MIN
16mm
Color (J H T I) (SPANISH)
Shows how cancer progresses within the human body if nothing is done about it when the first danger signal is given. Describes the danger signals and explains what to do about them.
Health and Safety
Dist - AMCS **Prod** - AMCS 1947

The Traitors 109 MIN
U-matic / VHS / 16mm
Color; Captioned (A) (SPANISH (ENGLISH SUBTITLES))
Portrays the life of trade union leader Roberto Barrera of Argentina and his opposition by militant leftist workers in this survey of Argentine history from the overthrow of Peron in 1955 to his return in 1973.
Fine Arts; History - World
Dist - CNEMAG **Prod** - TRIFCW 1973

Trajan's column 50 MIN
VHS
Trecanni video library series
Color (G)
$39.95 purchase
Studies Trajan's Column which was erected to celebrate the victorious military campaign of Emperor Trajan against the Dacians in 113 AD. Part of a four - part series on Italian culture produced by Treccani Publishers and RAI, Italian broadcast network.
Fine Arts; History - World
Dist - CREPRI

The Tramp 28 MIN
16mm
B&W (J H)
LC 72-711887
Portrays pathos and comedy in this first Chaplin classic. Shows Charlie as he rescues a girl from robbers, falls in love with her and gives her up when her fiancee arrives. Features Edna Purviance and Bud Jamison.
Fine Arts
Dist - RMIBHF **Prod** - ENY 1915
FI

Tramp Tramp Tramp 65 MIN
16mm
B&W (J)
Stars Harry Langdon as one of the last small time hand - made shoe manufacturers who are being put out of business by their mechanized competitors.
Business and Economics; Literature and Drama
Dist - TWYMAN **Prod** - MGM 1926

Trance and dance in Bali 22 MIN
16mm / VHS
Character formation in different cultures series
B&W (G C)
$440.00, $125.00 purchase, $15.50 rental _ #24636
Records a performance of the kris dance, a Balinese ceremonial dance which dramatizes the never - ending struggle between witch and dragon - the death - dealing and life - protecting - as it was performed in the village of Pagaoetan in 1937 - 1939. Shows dancers going into violent trance seizures and turning their krisses - daggers - against their breasts without injury. Consciosness is restored with incense and holy water. Balinese music forms a background for Dr Margaret Mead's narration. Part of a series produced by anthropologists Mead and Gregory Bateson documenting their 1930s studies on the relationship between culture and personality in Bali and New Guinea. Originally produced in 1951.
Fine Arts; Geography - World; History - World; Sociology
Dist - PSU **Prod** - MEAD 1991
NYU

The Tranporter's checklist 19 MIN
BETA / VHS / U-matic
Handling hazardous waste series
Color; PAL (IND G) (SPANISH ITALIAN)
$175.00 rental _ #HWH - 300
Illustrates the essentials of proper hazardous waste transportation. Reviews required equipment inspections. Demonstrates vehicle loading and placarding and emphasizes regulatory responsbilities. Includes leader's guide and 10 participant handouts. Part of a seven - part series which trains hazardous waste management workers. Available also in NTSC.
Business and Economics; Health and Safety; Psychology; Sociology
Dist - BNA **Prod** - BNA

Tranquilizers, a New Idea in Animal Feeds 15 MIN
16mm
B&W
LC FI68-659
Describes the work that is done by the Pfizer experimental farms in improving the economic and nutritive value of animal feeds through the use of tranquilizers. Demonstrates that when tranquilizers are added to feed, the animal not only improves emotionally, but gains in weight with less food consumption than before.
Agriculture
Dist - PFI **Prod** - PFI 1958

Trans Canada Highway 50.00 MIN
U-matic / 16mm / VHS
Color; Mono (J H C A)
$50.00
Recounts the events that led to the creation of the Trans Canada Highway. Rare historic film footage captures the earliest days of the highway construction and of the modern way of life in communities beside the longest highway in the world.
Geography - World; History - World
Dist - CTV **Prod** - CTV 1980
CFLMDC NFBC

Trans - Cervical Thymectomy 17 MIN
U-matic / VHS
Thoracic Series
Color
Health and Safety; Science - Natural
Dist - SVL **Prod** - SVL

Trans - It 7 MIN
16mm
B&W (G)
$10.00 rental
Features a Fred Safran production designed to turn off the mind, to relax and float the viewer downstream as the river of Columbus Avenue traffic flows to the hypnotic sound of a magic Indian flute.
Fine Arts; Health and Safety
Dist - CANCIN

Transabdominal Adrenalectomy for Encocrine Disease 26 MIN
16mm
Color (PRO)
Presents Edwin H Ellison, MD and George J Hamwi, MD, who point out that the anterior transabdominal approach permits preliminary exposure, and careful inspection of all adrenal tissue through one incision, before deciding on the definite operative procedure. Examines the principles of abdominal exposure, with special emphasis on mobilisation permitting a bilateral total or subtotal adrenalectomy. Includes a demonstration.
Health and Safety; Science
Dist - ACY **Prod** - ACYDGD 1957

Transabdominal Bilateral Adrenalectomy and Ovariectomy 18 MIN
16mm
Color (PRO)
Depicts a transabdominal approach to combined bilateral adrenalectomy and ovariectomy and describes its indications and advantages especially as related to disseminated mammary cancer.
Health and Safety; Science
Dist - ACY **Prod** - ACYDGD 1969

Transabdominal Bilateral Retroperitoneal Lymphadenectomy for Testis Tumors 15 MIN
16mm
Color (PRO)
LC 75-702240
Shows the diagnostic procedures and the operative procedure for the treatment of testicular tumors, stage I and II, which are non - seminomatous. Gives the results of over 65 patients having at least a 3 - year followup.
Health and Safety; Science; Science - Natural
Dist - EATONL **Prod** - EATONL 1974

Transabdominal Hysterectomy for Benign Disease 29 MIN
16mm
Color (PRO)
Explains that benign disease of the uterus if frequently complicated by significant involvement of other structures and that the surgical management of these complications is perhaps best undertaken by a general surgeon.
Health and Safety; Science
Dist - ACY **Prod** - ACYDGD 1958

Transabdominal Vagotomy, One Layer Pyloroplasty, Tube Gastrostomy 27 MIN
16mm
Color (PRO)
Shows techniques of vagotomy, utilizing traction on the stomach and upward retraction of the liver, one layer heineke - mikulicz pyloroplasty and tube gastrostomy.
Health and Safety; Science
Dist - ACY **Prod** - ACYDGD 1959

Transactional Analysis 31 MIN
16mm / U-matic / VHS
Behavior in Business Film Series
Color (H C A)
LC 75-700172
Shows how transactional analysis can be used by business management in order to understand why people act the way they do in organizations and to show what can be done to promote productive employee behavior and increased profits.
Business and Economics; Psychology
Dist - CRMP **Prod** - CRMP 1974
MGHT

Transactional Analysis - a Demonstration with Art 25 MIN
16mm
Color (A)
Indicates what therapy to use in the case of a client who is violently expressing anger. Points out, in this case, that behind the anger is the game If - It - Weren't - For - You.
Psychology
Dist - AACD **Prod** - AACD 1973

Transactional Analysis - a Demonstration with Elaine 33 MIN
16mm
Color (A)
Demonstates the game Why - Don't - You and the game Yes, But. Analyzes the therapeutic process. Demonstrates TA with a young woman who is engaging in self - defeating behavior.
Psychology
Dist - AACD **Prod** - AACD 1973

Transactional Analysis - a Demonstration with Pat 36 MIN
16mm
Color (A)
Demonstrates TA concept of the victim - persecutor - rescuer triangle with a client who has a marital problem. Becomes clear that the game being played is If It Weren't For Her. Analyzes what transpires.
Psychology
Dist - AACD **Prod** - AACD 1973

Transactional Analysis - Better Communications for Organizations 26 MIN
16mm / U-matic / VHS
Human Resources and Organizational Behavior Series
Color
Discusses transactional analysis and how it can be used to create a more productive corporate atmosphere. Features Dr Gilbert Levin who shows how to cut the edge on interpersonal conflicts that frequently inhibit effective management. Tells how corporations are using psychotherapy - oriented methods designed to teach awareness and communication skills. Includes a case study of TA, presenting role - playing sessions conducted with personnel at American Airlines.
Psychology
Dist - CNEMAG **Prod** - DOCUA

Transactional analysis - Part 1 20 MIN
BETA / VHS / U-matic
Communicating and interacting effectively series
Color (C PRO)
$150.00 purchase _ #137.6
Presents a video transfer from slide program which presents the two major constructs of transactional analysis and their application to health care - personality structure - describing the concepts of Child, Parent and Adult ego states; and interpersonal transactions - describing the dynamics of complementary, crossed and ulterior transactions. Part of a series on communicating and interacting effectively.
Psychology; Social Science
Dist - CONMED **Prod** - CONMED

Transactional analysis - Part 2 20 MIN
VHS / U-matic / BETA
Communicating and interacting effectively series
Color (C PRO)
$150.00 purchase _ #137.7
Presents a video transfer from slide program which presents and applies to a variety of health care situations the four transactional concepts of strokes, life positions, scripts and games. Emphasizes the importance of self - awareness and self - improvement in the caregivers as prerequisites to caring for and helping others. Part of a series on communicating and interacting effectively.
Psychology; Social Science
Dist - CONMED **Prod** - CONMED

Transactional Analysis Series
Meet Your Parent, Adult, Child 9 MIN
We're OK 9 MIN
Dist - PHENIX

Transactional Group Therapy with Muriel James 32 MIN
U-matic
Color
Dr Muriel James applies the principles of Transactional Analysis to group therapy. Demonstrates the power of an expert in the field.
Psychology
Dist - PSYCHF **Prod** - PSYCHF

Transactions
Videodisc
Financial FLASHFAX teller series
(H A)
$1995.00 purchase
Explains procedures for tellers in check cashing, deposits, withdrawals and various other types of transactions. Can be customized for a particular financial institution. Includes practice material, quizzes and tests.
Business and Economics
Dist - CMSL **Prod** - CMSL

Transactions 28 MIN
16mm
Learning to live series
Color (H C A)
Explains how two individual ego states hook into each other in conversation.
Psychology
Dist - ECUFLM **Prod** - UMCOM 1974

Transactions 30 MIN
VHS / U-matic
Learning to live series
Color (A)
Uses transactional analysis to deal with human relationship in conflict. Looks at how three ego states are involved when two people relate (transact). Discusses how people's ego states 'hook' one another's.
Psychology; Sociology
Dist - ECUFLM **Prod** - UMCOM 1974

Transactions - Letting Go and Taking Hold 29 MIN
U-matic / VHS / 16mm
Color (H C A) (SPANISH)
Examines the transitional process that is involved when an employee has to adapt to a new job.
Guidance and Counseling; Psychology
Dist - MGHT **Prod** - CRMP 1979

Transatlantic with Street 120 MIN
VHS
Color (G)
$49.95 purchase _ #0862
Sails the Atlantic Trade Wind Route from Ireland to the Caribbean. Gives practical illustrations of what ocean sailing is about.
Physical Education and Recreation
Dist - SEVVID

Transcendental meditation, yoga and reincarnation
VHS
Counterfeits series
Color (H C G A R)
$10.00 rental _ #36 - 82 - 2024
Explains the underlying Hindu philosophy of transcendental meditation, yoga and reincarnation. Implies that this philosophy is incompatible with Christianity. Suggests strategies for evangelism. Hosted by Ron Carlson. Produced by Cinema Associates and Film Educators.
Religion and Philosophy
Dist - APH

Transcending Illness 28 MIN
U-matic / VHS
Color
Presents a cancer patient talking about her disease and cure, beginning with her first knowledge of the operation, a mastectomy, her and her husband's reaction to the result, and the changes she made in her life to remain victorious over the cancer.
Health and Safety
Dist - HP **Prod** - HP

Transcending limitations 30 MIN
BETA / VHS
Transforming awareness series
Color (G)
$29.95 purchase _ #S120
Suggests that individuals limit themselves by attachment to old attitudes and outworn ideas. Features Dr James Fadiman, humanistic psychologist and author of 'Unlimit Your Life - Setting and Getting Goals,' who offers techniques for recognizing and discarding limiting attitudes and ideas. Part of a four - part series on transforming awareness.
Psychology
Dist - THINKA **Prod** - THINKA

Transcending the body senses, pt III 60 MIN
VHS
Nothing real can be threatened series
Color (G R)
$29.95 purchase _ #C042
Addresses the fundamental issue of fear which is at the root of most of the problems of humanity. Considers insecurity, anger, depression, blame, ambition and unfulfillment. Features spiritual teacher Tara Singh. Part three of a four - part workshop series on 'A Course in Miracles' by Dr Helen Shucman.
Health and Safety; Psychology; Religion and Philosophy
Dist - LIFEAP **Prod** - LIFEAP 1990

Transcochlear Approach to the Skull Base 30 MIN
U-matic / VHS
Color (PRO)
Demonstrates the approach to tumors of the skull base that arise medial to the internal auditory canal, or from the clivus. Involves a forward extension of the translabyrinthine opening, and the cochlea is removed with the facial nerve rerouted posteriorly. Shows that the forward limit of the dissection is the internal carotid artery.
Guidance and Counseling; Health and Safety; Science - Natural
Dist - HOUSEI **Prod** - HOUSEI

Transcochlear Removal of Congenital Cholesteatoma 56 MIN
VHS / U-matic
Color (PRO)
Presents a case history, a postoperative interview with the patient, and the procedure used in the removal of a large cholesteatoma using the transcochlear technique with microsurgical approach to lesion in the mastoid and inner ear.
Health and Safety; Science - Natural
Dist - HOUSEI **Prod** - HOUSEI

Transcontinental - 1865 - 1880 16 MIN
VHS / 16mm
Railroad series
Color (I J H G)
$280.00, $39.95 purchase
Reveals that building a railroad across the North American continent to the Pacific Ocean had been on people's minds almost from the beginning. Shows that President Lincoln signed the Pacific Railroad Act in 1862 but the Civil War delayed construction. After the war, money for the railroad was raised through land grants and the race was on. Tells the story of the Central Pacific and the Union Pacific line. Part of a series on American railroads.
History - United States; Social Science
Dist - KAWVAL **Prod** - KAWVAL

The Transcontinental Railroad 15 MIN
VHS / U-matic
Stories of America Series
Color (P)
Focuses on two Irish immigrants, father and son, who worked on the first transcontinental railroad.
History - United States
Dist - AITECH **Prod** - OHSDE 1976

Transcribed toxicosis 6 MIN
16mm
B&W (G)
$10.00 rental
Consists of the result of the filmmaker's experience with a psychological test that became a futuristic self - portrait.
Fine Arts; Psychology
Dist - CANCIN **Prod** - WENDTD 1974

Transcutaneous electrical nerve stimulation 12 MIN
VHS / U-matic
Special issues in pain control series
Color (PRO C)
$395.00 purchase, $80.00 rental _ #C901 - VI - 042
Presents information on TENS - transcutaneous electrical nerve stimulation - principles. Presented by Bethany Geldmaker, RN, Mark Lehman, PharmD, Brenda Jackson, PT, and Janet Kues, PT, Medical College of Virginia, Virginia Commonwealth University.
Health and Safety
Dist - HSCIC

Transcutaneous Electrical Nerve Stimulation 28 MIN
U-matic / VHS
Color (A)
Discusses the benefits and advantages of TENS therapy, components of the TENS unit, use of controls and adjustments, application and care of electrodes, batteries and cautions.
Health and Safety; Industrial and Technical Education; Psychology
Dist - USNAC **Prod** - VAMSLC 1984

Transduodenal Section of the Sphincter of Oddi for Pancreatitis 24 MIN
16mm
Color (PRO)
Presents Henry Doubilet, MD and John H Mulholland, Md, showing the technique and etiology of sphincterotomy and operative cholangiography, in the treatment of recurrent acute pancreatitis.
Health and Safety; Science
Dist - ACY **Prod** - ACYDGD 1952

Transesophageal echocardiography 8 MIN
VHS
Color (G)
$125.00 purchase, $70.00 rental _ #4363S, #4363V
Describes the procedure of transesophageal echocardiography in which the patient swallows a small transducer which places it in the esophagus, closer to the heart for better visualization and diagnosis. Helps reassure the patient and family by describing the procedure and possible results, using clear illustrations and comparing the procedure to familiar non - medical tests such as an automobile diagnostic. Discusses possible complications and explains and reviews common patient concerns. Produced by St Elizabeth Hospital Medical Center.
Health and Safety
Dist - AJN

Transfer 7 MIN
16mm
B&W
LC 76-703262
Shows a poetic fantasy depicting a streetcar gliding through the streets of Toronto, its interior full of the memories of all those people who once grasped its rails.
Geography - World; Social Science
Dist - CANFDC **Prod** - CANFDC 1974

Transfer and ambulation 30 MIN
16mm
Directions for education in nursing via technology series; Lesson 13
B&W (PRO)
LC 74-701787
Demonstrates how to assist a patient to ambulate and how to transfer a patient from bed to stretcher and using hemiplegic and pivot techniques, from bed to wheelchair.
Health and Safety
Dist - WSUM **Prod** - DENT 1974

Transfer from Bed to Wheelchair with Assistance 7 MIN
16mm
Color
LC 75-702148; FIE67-64
Shows a step - by - step procedure for transferring the hemiplegic patient from a low bed to a sitting position, then to a standing position, and finally to a wheel chair with the assistance of an attendant.
Health and Safety
Dist - USNAC **Prod** - USPHS 1965

Transfer Molding - Molding a Part with Inserts 10 MIN
16mm
Plastics Series; No 5
B&W
LC FIE52-297
Explains how transfer molding differs from compression molding. Shows how to mold a part by the transfer method and coordinate steps of the molding cycle.
Industrial and Technical Education
Dist - USNAC **Prod** - USOE 1945

The Transfer of power 29 MIN
16mm
Government story series; No 23
B&W (J H)
LC 79-707207
Explains how the office of the President of the United States changes hands and analyzes the problems involved in this change. Discusses the relative roles of both the outgoing and incoming presidents.
Biography; Civics and Political Systems
Dist - WESTLC **Prod** - WEBC 1968

Transfer of the wheelchair patient to and from the dental chair 6 MIN
U-matic / VHS
Color (C PRO)
$395.00 purchase, $80.00 rental _ #D861 - VI - 071
Demonstrates the proper method of transferring the wheelchair patient to and from the dental chair. Illustrates how to operate the parts of a wheelchair involved in patient transfers and how to prepare for and execute one - person and two - person transfers. Presented by Dr Thomas C Porter.
Health and Safety
Dist - HSCIC

Transfer RNA - the Genetic Messenger 10 MIN
U-matic
Protein Synthesis Series
Color (H C)
Explains the function of the three different types of RNA. The transfer RNA acts as a vehicle for the amino acids, ferrying them to the ribosome, where they link up with the messenger RNA molecules, forming a chain that becomes a protein.
Science; Science - Natural; Science - Physical
Dist - TVOTAR **Prod** - TVOTAR 1984

Transfer techniques 12 MIN
VHS
Color (C PRO G)
$395.00 purchase _ #R940 - VI - 005
Describes and demonstrates six transfer techniques to be used when moving patients, for use by two to three nursing staff working in tandem. Includes - two - person carry, two - person bear hug transfer, two - person assisted pivot, three - person pull sheet technique, the three - person carry and the mechanical lift.
Health and Safety
Dist - HSCIC **Prod** - BALLSU 1994

Transfer techniques - 22 11 MIN
VHS
Clinical nursing skills - nursing fundamentals - series
Color (C PRO G)
$395.00 purchase _ #R890 - VI - 056
Introduces basic, safe patient transfer techniques. Describes and demonstrates procedures for moving a patient up in bed, 'log - rolling,' dangling and moving the patient from bed to chair. Shows techniques for the three - person carry of a patient. Presents the proper methods for straightening a seated patient, as is proper placement of support pillows, rolls and bed elevation. Part of a 23 - part series on clinical nursing skills.
Health and Safety
Dist - HSCIC **Prod** - CUYAHO 1989

Transference and Countertransference 30 MIN
U-matic / VHS
Treatment of the Borderline Patient Series
Color
Discusses the major use of transference - countertransference feelings and associations to improve and sustain the relationship while understanding and respecting the stage of therapeutic symbiosis in the working through process of borderline patients.
Health and Safety; Psychology
Dist - HEMUL **Prod** - HEMUL

Transference Numbers - Hittorf Method, Moving Boundary Method in Solutions of One Binary 54 MIN
U-matic / VHS
Electrochemistry Series
Color
Teaches transference numbers - Hittorf Method, moving boundary method in solutions of one binary electrolyte, moving boundary with mixtures, complexes and 'true transference numbers.'
Science; Science - Physical
Dist - KALMIA **Prod** - KALMIA

Transference numbers - Hittorf method - transference numbers - moving boundary 54 MIN
U-matic / VHS
Electrochemistry - Pt I - introduction series
Color
Discusses transference numbers, Hittorf Method, numbers, moving boundary method in solutions of one binary electrolyte, transference numbers moving boundary with mixtures, complexes and 'true transference numbers.'.
Science; Science - Physical
Dist - MIOT **Prod** - MIOT

Transferring from Wheelchair to Bed - Affected Side of Patient Next to Bed 5 MIN
6 MIN
U-matic / 16mm
Color
LC 75-702150; 74-705815; 77-706091
Demonstrates the technique of transferring a patient from a wheelchair to a bed with his affected side next to his bed.
Health and Safety
Dist - USNAC **Prod** - USPHS 1966

Transferring from Wheelchair to Bed - Affected Side of Patient Next to Bed 6 MIN
VHS / U-matic / 8mm cartridge / Videoreel
Color
LC 75-702150; 74-705815; 77-706091
Explains with narration and close - up camera views the procedure that a patient uses to transfer himself from a wheelchair to a bed. Depicts locking wheelchair brakes, placement of feet and hands for standing, adjusting body position, raising from a sitting to a standing position and sitting down, and laying down and raising back up again to a sitting position in bed.
Health and Safety
Dist - PRIMED USPHS **Prod** - PRIMED USPHS 1966

Transferring from Wheelchair to Bed - Non - Affected Side of Patient Next to Bed 5 MIN
16mm
Color
LC 74-705814
Demonstrates a technique of transferring a patient from a wheelchair to a bed with the patient's non - affected side next to the bed.
Health and Safety
Dist - USNAC **Prod** - USPHS 1966

Transferring from Wheelchair to Bed with Maximal Assistance 4 MIN
16mm
Color
LC 74-705816
Demonstrates the safest and easiest way to transfer the patient who needs maximal assistance from wheelchair to bed.
Health and Safety
Dist - USNAC **Prod** - USPHS 1966

Transferring Pattern Markings 4 MIN
16mm
Clothing Construction Techniques Series
Color (J)
LC 77-701170
Illustrates alternate methods for transferring pattern markings, including tracing wheel and carbon paper, tailor's tacks and pins. Shows how to transfer needed markings from the wrong side to the right side of the fabric.
Home Economics
Dist - IOWASP **Prod** - IOWA 1976

Transferring the Patient with Arthritis 9 MIN
16mm
Color
LC 74-705818
Demonstrates the proper transfer of the patient with arthritis, a technique often neglected but which can contribute much to the comfort of the afflicted person.
Health and Safety
Dist - USNAC **Prod** - NMAC 1968

Transfers - a Key Rehabilitation 13 MIN
VHS / U-matic
Color
Health and Safety
Dist - UMDSM **Prod** - UMDSM

The Transfiguration 20 MIN
16mm
Living Bible Series
Color; B&W (J H T R)
Presents the biblical story of the Transfiguration. Tells of Jesus questioning His disciples about their knowledge of who He is. Peter confesses that Jesus is the Christ. Six

days later Jesus takes James, Peter and John to the mountain where He is transfigured before them. At the foot of the mountain Jesus heals an epileptic boy.
Religion and Philosophy
Dist - FAMF **Prod** - FAMF

Transformation and the body quartet 120 MIN
VHS / BETA
Color (G)
$69.95 purchase _ #Q254
Presents a four - part discussion about transformation and the body. Includes 'Consciousness and the Martial Arts' with George Leonard, 'Transforming the Human Body' with Michael Murphy, 'Spirit and Soma' with Stanley Keleman and 'The Body - Mind Connection' with Dr Eleanor Criswell.
Health and Safety; Physical Education and Recreation; Psychology; Religion and Philosophy; Science - Natural
Dist - THINKA **Prod** - THINKA

Transformation and the body series
Consciousness and the martial arts 30 MIN
The Mind - body connection 30 MIN
Spirit and soma 30 MIN
Transforming the human body 30 MIN
Dist - THINKA

The Transformation of Mabel Wells 12 MIN
16mm / U-matic / VHS
Color (K P I)
Follows the experiences of Mabel Wells, an elderly woman who recovers from an accident to find her room strewn with cards, flowers and gifts from well - wishers. Shows how these offerings stir childhood memories and transform the woman into a loving person.
Guidance and Counseling; Sociology
Dist - GA **Prod** - GA 1975

The Transformation of Persephone 11 MIN
16mm / VHS
Color (G)
$20.00 rental
Relates a flashback by Queen Persephone as she recalls her abduction, resistance, surrender, passion and transformation. Parallels the sexual history of women. Produced by Silvianna Goldsmith.
Fine Arts; Religion and Philosophy
Dist - CANCIN

The Transformation of Richard Nixon 29 MIN
Videoreel / VT2
Course of Our Times III Series
Color
Biography; Civics and Political Systems; History - United States
Dist - PBS **Prod** - WGBHTV

Transformation principles for inequations - Pt 1 31 MIN
16mm
Teaching high school mathematics - first course series; No 48
B&W (T)
Mathematics
Dist - MLA **Prod** - UICSM 1967

Transformation principles for inequations - Pt 2 28 MIN
16mm
Teaching high school mathematics - first course series; No 49
B&W (H)
Mathematics
Dist - MLA **Prod** - UICSM 1967

Transformations 20 MIN
VHS / U-matic
Color (J H G)
$225.00, $275.00 purchase, $50.00 rental
Invites the viewer to join a visual and philosophical journey into change and meaning. Uses nature a point of departure. Encourages discussion on a range of subjects, including themes and compositions.
Religion and Philosophy
Dist - NDIM **Prod** - BALFOR 1989

Transformations 15 MIN
U-matic
Math Makers One Series
Color (I)
Presents the math concepts of slides, turns, flips, rotation, motion of a grid, and diagonality.
Education; Mathematics
Dist - TVOTAR **Prod** - TVOTAR 1979

Transformations and Matrices 24 MIN
16mm / U-matic / VHS
Color
Asks which types of transformations of the plane can be represented by matrices.
Mathematics
Dist - MEDIAG **Prod** - OPENU

Transformations on a Soho street 27 MIN
16mm
B&W (G)
$20.00 rental
Breaks away from traditional documentaries by letting the subject inspire and determine both the form and structure and the visual approach or camera during filming. Records a happening in the Soho district of New York City. Produced by Bob Parent.
Fine Arts; Sociology
Dist - CANCIN

Transformer Maintenance 60 MIN
VHS
Transformers, Switchgear and Batteries Series
Color (PRO)
$600.00, $1500.00 purchase _ #EMTMT
Introduces transformer theory and connection schemes. Covers common types of transformers. Includes distribution - dry and wet - transformers, power and instrument transformers. Explains test procedures and safety precautions. Part of a four - part series on transformers, switchgear and batteries, which is part of a 29 unit set on electrical maintenance. Includes 10 textbooks and an instructor guide which provide four hours of instruction.
Education; Health and Safety; Industrial and Technical Education; Psychology
Dist - NUSTC **Prod** - NUSTC

Transformers 20 MIN
VHS / U-matic
Basic A C circuits - laboratory series
Color
Industrial and Technical Education
Dist - TXINLC **Prod** - TXINLC

Transformers 31 MIN
U-matic / VHS / 16mm
Color
LC 78-706203
Defines transformer action, step - up and step - down, turns ratio and coefficient of coupling. Illustrates the relationship between the magnitude of voltage and current in a transformer.
Industrial and Technical Education
Dist - USNAC **Prod** - USAF 1978

Transformers - no 5 60 MIN
U-matic
AC/DC Electronics Series
Color (PRO)
One of a series of electronic and electrical training sessions for electronics workers on direct and alternating current and how to work with each.
Industrial and Technical Education
Dist - VTRI **Prod** - VTRI 1986

Transformers series
Presents a three-part series which looks at teaching children with learning difficulties. Examines how deaf and blind children are taught in Zagorsk; details the teaching patterns devised by Prof Reuven Feuerstein for children in refugee camps; and discusses the theories of American philosopher Matthew Lipman.
The Butterflies of Zagorsk 60 MIN
Out of the wilderness 60 MIN
Socrates for six year olds 60 MIN
The Transformers series 180 MIN
Dist - BBCENE

Transformers, Switchgear and Batteries Series
Maintenance of High - Voltage Circuit Breakers and Switchgear - 4 kV and Over 60 MIN
Maintenance of Low - Voltage Circuit Breakers and Switchgear - Under 4 kV 60 MIN
Storage Batteries and Chargers 60 MIN
Transformer Maintenance 60 MIN
Dist - NUSTC

Transforming awareness quartet 120 MIN
BETA / VHS
Color (G)
$69.95 purchase _ #Q174
Presents a four - part discussion on transforming awareness. Includes 'Becoming More Fully Human' with Virginia Satir, 'Self - Observation' with Dr Charles Tart, 'Transcending Limitations' with Dr James Fadiman, and 'Metaphors of Transformation' with Dr Ralph Metzner.
Psychology; Religion and Philosophy
Dist - THINKA **Prod** - THINKA

Transforming awareness series
Becoming more fully human 30 MIN
Metaphors of transformation 30 MIN
Self - observation 30 MIN
Transcending limitations 30 MIN
Dist - THINKA

Transforming human nature 30 MIN
VHS / BETA
Personal and social change series
Color (G)
$29.95 purchase _ #S095
Expresses optimism that humanity is capable of rising to the challenge and learning to bring out that which is deepest and best within the self. Features George Leonard, author of 'Education and Ecstasy,' 'The Silent Pulse' and 'The Transformation.' Part of a four - part series on personal and social change.
Psychology; Religion and Philosophy
Dist - THINKA **Prod** - THINKA

Transforming stress into power 30 MIN
VHS
Color (A PRO)
$79.95 purchase _ #AH44212
Suggests that stress can be used in a positive way to increase productivity. Applies this principle to individual, team and corporate settings.
Health and Safety; Psychology
Dist - HTHED **Prod** - HTHED

Transforming the human body 30 MIN
BETA / VHS
Transformation and the body series
Color (G)
$29.95 purchase _ #S320
Describes how the physical evolution of an individual can be controlled through religious and athletic disciplines, biofeedback and medicine. Features Michael Murphy, founder of the Esalen Institute and author of 'The Psychic Side of Sports' and 'Golf in the Kingdom.' Part of a four - part series on transformation and the body.
Health and Safety; Physical Education and Recreation; Psychology; Religion and Philosophy; Science - Natural
Dist - THINKA **Prod** - THINKA

Transforming your songs - Video One 60 MIN
VHS
Guitar chord magic series
Color (G)
$49.95 purchase _ #VD - ART - MA01
Features Artie Traum who starts with three - note jazz chords, showing how the viewer can move them around the fingerboard and substitute them for ordinary major and minor chords. Shows how to build chords and develop an ear for choosing the right chords for a particular song. Illustrates these techniques in several blues and original songs. Part one of a two - part series on guitar chords. Includes chords.
Fine Arts
Dist - HOMETA **Prod** - HOMETA

Transfusing blood safely - a step - by - step guide for nurses 16 MIN
VHS
Color (PRO C)
$250.00 purchase, $70.00 rental _ #4368
Explains how to transfuse blood safely. Discusses blood and blood components, blood groups and Rh types, typing and crossmatching, blood products, equipment, managing the transfusion and recognizing and responding to reactions, and documenting events. Demonstrates step - by - step how to prepare and properly identify the patient, both adults and children, for blood transfusion and how to choose the correct equipment and rates of flow. Shows proper monitoring of the procedure and the need for thorough and accurate documentation.
Health and Safety; Science - Natural
Dist - AJN **Prod** - GCRBC

Transfusion of dialysis patients 20 MIN
VHS / U-matic
Contemporary problems in transfusion medicine series
Color (PRO C)
$395.00 purchase, $80.00 rental _ #C881 - VI - 055
Introduces medical students and first year residents to the case of one dialysis patient and to the factors associated with chronic transfusion. Discusses mechanisms of anemia in renal failure and the variety of symptomatic responses to anemia. Presents the hemodynamics resulting from lowered hemoglobin and subsequent changes in cardiac output. Outlines transfusion reactions and various types of resultant complications. Part of a three - part series on transfusion medicine presented by Dr James P Crowley.
Health and Safety; Science - Natural
Dist - HSCIC

Transient 24 MIN
16mm
Color
LC 76-703815
Deals with transient workers and their role on fruit - growing farms in South Okanagan, British Columbia.
Agriculture; Geography - World; Sociology
Dist - BCDA **Prod** - BCDA 1975

Transistor Amplifier Principles - Classification and Coupling 27 MIN
16mm
B&W
LC 75-702877
Explains the functions of voltage and current amplifiers. Illustrates the principles of several classes of bias levels and four types of couplings. Includes discussion of frequency range.
Industrial and Technical Education
Dist - USNAC **Prod** - USAF 1967

Transistor - Amplifiers
VHS
Industrial Electronics Training Program Series
$99.00 purchase _ #RPVCI7
Industrial and Technical Education
Dist - CAREER **Prod** - CAREER

Transistor amplifiers 60 MIN
VHS
Electronic systems and equipment series
Color (PRO)
$600.00 - $1500.00 purchase _ #ICTAM
Explains how transistor amplifiers work. Uses three typical transistor amplifier circuit configurations to teach about construction, bias and amplification characteristics. Part of a nineteen - part series on electronic systems and equipment, which is part of a 49 - unit set on instrumentation and control. Includes five workbooks and an instructor guide to support four hours of instruction.
Education; Industrial and Technical Education; Psychology
Dist - NUSTC **Prod** - NUSTC

Transistor amplifiers 17 MIN
U-matic / VHS
Introduction to solid state electronics series; Chapter 4
Color (IND) (SPANISH)
Develops three basic transistor amplifier configurations. Defines basic electronic terminology.
Education; Industrial and Technical Education
Dist - TAT **Prod** - TAT

Transistor - Amplifiers 25 MIN
VHS / 16mm
Electronics Series
(C A IND)
$99.00 purchase _ #VCI7
Gives common sense safety precautions for working with transistor amplifiers. Explains the function of transistors in RC coupling, transformer coupling, and DC coupling amplifying chains. Shows how to discriminate between standard and nonstandard class A biased transistor amplifiers, and to describe the function of class A, B, and C transistor amplifiers. Introduces oscillators and gives the viewer practice in identifying, measuring, and correcting the effects of negative oscillation. Utilizes an additional workbook.
Industrial and Technical Education
Dist - RMIBHF **Prod** - RMIBHF

Transistor FM Detector 35 MIN
16mm
B&W
LC 74-705819
Discusses the characteristics of a symmetrical transistor and reviews the phase relationship of voltage and current in a transformer. Explains the operation of the FM detector at the center frequency of the input and at frequencies above and below the center frequency. (Kinescope).
Industrial and Technical Education; Science - Physical
Dist - USNAC **Prod** - USAF

Transistor FM Oscillator 29 MIN
16mm
B&W
LC 74-705820
Compares the transistor FM oscillator and the reactance tube modulator. Explains the operation of the circuit, how the depletion region is established and how it can be used as a variable capacitance under a changing reverse bias. Shows how the voltage variable capacitor can be used in conjunction with an oscillator to make up a transistor FM oscillator. (Kinescope).
Industrial and Technical Education; Science - Physical
Dist - USNAC **Prod** - USAF

Transistor Operations
VHS / U-matic
Digital Techniques Series
Color
Industrial and Technical Education
Dist - HTHZEN **Prod** - HTHZEN

Transistor oscillators 60 MIN
VHS
Electronic systems and equipment series
Color (PRO)
$600.00, $1500.00 purchase _ #ICTOS
Covers basic operating principles of oscillators, how these principles specifically apply to different oscillators. Includes the Armstrong, Hartley, Colpitts and phase shift oscillators and multivibrators. Part of a nineteen - part series on electronic systems and equipment, which is part of a 49 - unit set on instrumentation and control. Includes five workbooks and an instructor guide to support four hours of instruction.
Education; Industrial and Technical Education; Psychology
Dist - NUSTC **Prod** - NUSTC

Transistor principles 60 MIN
VHS
Electronic systems and equipment series
Color (PRO)
$600.00, $1500.00 purchase _ #ICTPR
Considers the construction of N - P - N and P - N - P bipolar transistors. Explains how a transistor is properly biased and how current flow through through a properly biased transistor can be controlled. Part of a nineteen - part series on electronic systems and equipment, which is part of a 49 - unit set on instrumentation and control. Includes five workbooks and an instructor guide to support four hours of instruction.
Education; Industrial and Technical Education; Psychology
Dist - NUSTC **Prod** - NUSTC

Transistor push - pull amplifier 27 MIN
16mm / VHS / U-matic
B&W
LC 75-702878
Illustrates the principles and explains the advantages of the push - pull amplifier. Points out the functions and benefits of input transformer, discusses troubleshooting and explains two methods of achieving input.
Industrial and Technical Education
Dist - USNAC **Prod** - USAF 1967

Transistor Stabilization 19 MIN
U-matic / VHS / 16mm
B&W
Shows how a change in ambient temperature affects transistor stabilization and discusses its effect on circuit output. Explains thermistor characteristics and stabilization. Explains the function of forward and reverse biased temperature stabilization diodes.
Industrial and Technical Education; Science - Physical
Dist - USNAC **Prod** - USAF

Transistor Structure and Technology 38 MIN
16mm
Semiconductor Electronics Education Com - Mittee Films Series
Color (C)
LC 70-703368
Describes how the alloy junction transistor (PNP) is made, discusses the limitation of its speed and voltage characteristics and points out the characteristics of pnip and npnn types. Shows the fabrication of NPNN transistors. Includes a brief review of the power handling capability and heat dissipation.
Industrial and Technical Education; Science - Physical
Dist - EDC **Prod** - BELLTL 1967

Transistor Switches
VHS
Industrial Electronics Training Program Series
$99.00 purchase _ #RPVCI9
Industrial and Technical Education
Dist - CAREER **Prod** - CAREER

Transistor Switches 22 MIN
VHS / 16mm
Electronics Series
(C A IND)
$99.00 purchase _ #VCI9
Outlines the function of the transistor as a bistable switch with detailed explanations of the load line, maximum power line, cutoff state, full conduction state, saturation region, bistable switching transistor, and multivibrator circuits. Illustrates and explains the fabrication and funciton of logic gates and decoder circuits. Utilizes an additional workbook.
Industrial and Technical Education
Dist - RMIBHF **Prod** - RMIBHF

Transistor Tetrodes and Field Effect Transistors 14 MIN
16mm
B&W
LC 74-705821
Introduces transistor tetrodes and discusses their fundamental characteristics and elements. Introduces the field effect transistor and covers its basic characteristics. (Kinescope).
Industrial and Technical Education; Science - Physical
Dist - USNAC **Prod** - USAF

Transistor theory and testing silicon controlled rectifiers 60 MIN
U-matic / VHS
Electrical maintenance training series; Module 7 - Solid - state devices
Color (IND)
Industrial and Technical Education
Dist - LEIKID **Prod** - LEIKID

Transistor Triode Characteristics 26 MIN
16mm
B&W
LC 74-705822
Illustrates how to draw load lines from characteristic curves for CE and CB configurations. Defines alpha and beta as they pertain to transistors. Shows how to solve for actual current gain, voltage gain and power gain for CB configuration, using characteristic curves and load lines. (Kinescope).
Industrial and Technical Education; Science - Physical
Dist - USNAC **Prod** - USAF

Transistor Triodes 7 MIN
16mm
B&W
LC 74-705823
Explains derivation of the word 'transistor.' Identifies the elements of a PNP and an NPN transistor, by using block diagrams and discusses a method of remembering P and N type materials and the relative size of the transistor element. (Kinescope).
Industrial and Technical Education; Science - Physical
Dist - USNAC **Prod** - USAF

Transistor Triodes and Special Purpose Devices - Bias I 27 MIN
16mm
B&W
LC 74-705826
Discusses and illustrates forward and reverse bias of a PN junction and requires the student to draw a block diagram with forward bias and one with reverse bias. Shows how an NPN transistor is forward and reverse biased for efficient operation.
Industrial and Technical Education; Science - Physical
Dist - USNAC **Prod** - USAF

Transistor Triodes and Special Purpose Devices - Bias II 27 MIN
16mm
B&W
LC 74-705827
Discusses the depletion area at the junctions of a transistor, followed by an explanation of the effect of forward and reverse biasing on the majority and minority carriers in both. (Kinescope).
Industrial and Technical Education; Science - Physical
Dist - USNAC **Prod** - USAF

Transistor Triodes and Special Purpose Devices - Common - Base Configurations 29 MIN
16mm
B&W
LC 74-705829
Shows and discusses the schematic representation of a common - base transistor circuit, giving the identifying characteristics for a PNP and an NPN type. Explains the purpose of each component. (Kinescope).
Industrial and Technical Education; Science - Physical
Dist - USNAC **Prod** - USAF 1942

Transistor Triodes and Special Purpose Devices - Common - Collector Configuration 16 MIN
16mm
B&W
LC 74-705824
Provides information designed to enable the student to identify and state the purpose of various elements in NPN and PNP transistor common collector circuits.
Industrial and Technical Education; Science - Physical
Dist - USNAC **Prod** - USAF

Transistor Triodes and Special Purpose Devices - Operation 16 MIN
16mm
B&W
LC 74-705825
Illustrates the three configurations of transistor circuits and traces the current flow. Explains the amount of current in each part of a transistor circuit and the effect of an increase in total current in a transistor circuit.
Industrial and Technical Education; Science - Physical
Dist - USNAC **Prod** - USAF

Transistor Triodes - Construction 25 MIN
16mm
B&W
LC 75-702879
Explains the construction and functions of triode transistors. Shows the differences between PNP and NPN transistors and describes how emitter, collector and base operate in each type.
Industrial and Technical Education
Dist - USNAC **Prod** - USAF 1967

Transistorized Audio Amplifier 22 MIN
16mm
B&W
LC 75-702880
Explains the principles of the common base (in phase) and the common emitter (out of phase) audio amplifiers. Describes outlet characteristics and shows how to calculate voltage, power and current gain.
Industrial and Technical Education
Dist - USNAC **Prod** - USAF 1967

Transistorized Hartley Oscillator 40 MIN
16mm
B&W
LC 74-705831
Discusses the transistorized version of both the series and Shunt Hartley oscillators. Compares the two, emphasizing circuit identification, purpose of each component, direct current paths, feedback paths and the effects of varying feedback. (Kinescope).
Industrial and Technical Education; Science - Physical
Dist - USNAC **Prod** - USAF 1965

Transistorized Regulated Power Supply 24 MIN
16mm
B&W
LC 74-705832
Explains the advantages of a regulated supply, how regulation is accomplished using simplified schematics and the purpose of each control, as well as suggested operating procedure. (Kinescope).
Industrial and Technical Education; Science - Physical
Dist - USNAC **Prod** - USAF

Transistors 30 MIN
VHS / 16mm
Electronics Series
(C A IND)
$99.00 purchase _ #VCI6
Covers transistor features and functions. Illustrates the functions of common emitter PNP and NPN transistors. Shows the viewer how to identify beta and gain with respect to commone base, common emitter and common collector transistor circuits. Utilizes additional workbook.
Industrial and Technical Education
Dist - RMIBHF **Prod** - RMIBHF

Transistors 68 MIN
VHS / 35mm strip
(H A IND)
Introduces the fundamentals and operating theory of transistors. Includes operating principles, characteristics, basic amplifiers, and amplifier stages in cascade (4 tapes). Prerequisites required. Includes a Study Guide.
Education; Industrial and Technical Education
Dist - BERGL

Transistors
VHS
Industrial Electronics Training Program Series
$99.00 purchase _ #RPVCI6
Industrial and Technical Education
Dist - CAREER **Prod** - CAREER

Transistors - High Frequency Operations - Amplifiers and Oscillators 14 MIN
16mm
B&W
LC FIE60-55
Describes how transistors operate in high frequency amplifiers and in oscillator circuits. Shows the influence of transit effects in the base. Explains collector capacitance and base resistance on high frequency performance.
Industrial and Technical Education; Science - Physical
Dist - USNAC **Prod** - USN 1959

Transistors - How they Work, How they are made 60 MIN
Videoreel / VT1
Understanding Semiconductors Course Outline Series; No 7
Color (IND)
Describes how the holes and free electrons in an N - P - N transistor enable it to switch and vary a large 'working' current in response to a small 'control' current. Illustrates the manufacturing techniques used for all semiconductor products.
Industrial and Technical Education
Dist - TXINLC **Prod** - TXINLC

Transistors I
VHS / 35mm strip
Transistors I and II Series
$299.00 purchase _ #BX807 filmstrips, $269.00 purchase _ #BX807V VHS
Discusses the operating principles and characteristics of transistors. Discusses the basic amplifier and amplifier stages in cascade circuits which use transistors.
Industrial and Technical Education
Dist - CAREER **Prod** - CAREER

Transistors I and II
VHS / 35mm strip
Transistors I and II Series
$548.00 purchase _ #BX84 filmstrips, $538.00 purchase _ #BX84V VHS
Discusses the operating principles and characteristics of transistors. Discusses the basic amplifiers, amplifier stages in cascade, power amplifiers, single ended amplifiers, push - pull amplifiers, and complementary symmetry amplifiers which use transistors.
Industrial and Technical Education
Dist - CAREER **Prod** - CAREER

Transistors I and II Series
Transistors I
Transistors I and II
Transistors II
Dist - CAREER

Transistors II
VHS / 35mm strip
Transistors I and II Series
$299.00 purchase _ #BX808 filmstrips, $269.00 purchase _ #BX808V VHS
Discusses the theory and use of transistors in power amplifiers, single ended amplifiers, push - pull amplifiers, and complementary symmetry amplifiers.
Industrial and Technical Education
Dist - CAREER **Prod** - CAREER

Transistors - Low Frequency Amplifiers 15 MIN
16mm
B&W
LC FIE59-199
Shows how transistors are used to amplify low frequencies in common base, emitter and collector circuits.
Industrial and Technical Education
Dist - USNAC **Prod** - USN 1958

Transistors - Minority Carriers 10 MIN
16mm
B&W (H C A)
LC FIE58-350
Introduces the principle of minority carriers, shows how they produce a small reverse current under normal conditions and demonstrates the limitations imposed on transistor behavior by minority carriers when the transistor is heated or loaded.
Industrial and Technical Education; Science - Physical
Dist - USNAC **Prod** - NF 1958

Transistors - NPN Transistors - Pt 3 23 MIN
16mm
B&W (PRO)
LC 74-705834
Depicts construction and properties of NPN transistors. Shows how they function in basic transistor circuits and explains how current flow and amplification are achieved.
Industrial and Technical Education; Science - Physical
Dist - USNAC **Prod** - USA 1963

Transistors - P - N Junction Fundamentals 11 MIN
16mm
B&W
Explains the theory and mechanisms of semi - conductor diode and transistor action, and discusses the fundamental principles that apply to all transistors and junction rectifiers.
Industrial and Technical Education; Science - Physical
Dist - USNAC **Prod** - USN 1957

Transistors - PNP Transistors - Pt 4 26 MIN
16mm
B&W (PRO)
LC 74-705835
Explains the characteristics of PNP transistors and compares their capabilities and functioning to NPN types. Explains the flow of current through the circuit.
Industrial and Technical Education; Science - Physical
Dist - USNAC **Prod** - USA 1962

Transistors, Pt 8 - Repairing Transistor Circuits 28 MIN
16mm
B&W (PRO)
LC 74-705840
Presents equipment and techniques for repairing soldered joints, cracks and delaminated conductors. Shows how to test circuits and remove and replace lead and flush - mounted circuit components. (Kinescope).
Industrial and Technical Education; Science; Science - Physical
Dist - USNAC **Prod** - USA 1962

Transistors, Pt 5 - Transistor Amplifier and Oscillator Circuits 30 MIN
16mm
B&W (PRO)
LC 74-705837
Explains and illustrates features and operations of class A and B and tuned amplifier circuits and oscillator circuits. Includes the Armstrong and Hartley types. (Kinescope).
Industrial and Technical Education; Science - Physical
Dist - USNAC **Prod** - USA 1962

Transistors, Pt 1 - Introduction 17 MIN
16mm
B&W (PRO)
LC FIE63-88
Explains elements and operations of NPN and PNP transistors. Shows application and operation of high - medium - and low - powered transistors and describes their capabilities. (Kinescope).
Industrial and Technical Education; Science - Physical
Dist - USNAC **Prod** - USA 1962

Transistors, Pt 7 - Troubleshooting Transistor Circuits 31 MIN
16mm
B&W (PRO)
LC 74-705839
Shows how to check, search, localize and isolate malfunctions. Covers safety measures. (Kinescope).
Industrial and Technical Education; Science; Science - Physical
Dist - USNAC **Prod** - USA 1962

Transistors, Pt 6 - Transistors in Pulse Applications 39 MIN
16mm
B&W
LC 74-705838
Describes uses of transistors in pulse applications. Gives characteristics and application of three basic types of waveforms or pulses. Covers square, saw tooth and spiked pulses. Shows how transistors form various types of multivibrators. Gives features of A N D, N O R and N A N D gates. (Kinescope).
Industrial and Technical Education; Science - Physical
Dist - USNAC **Prod** - USA 1963

Transistors, Pt 2 - Semiconductors and Semiconductor Diodes 27 MIN
16mm
B&W (PRO)
LC 74-705833
Illustrates composition and properties of crystal diodes and depicts semiconductor materials used in their manufacture. (Kinescope).
Industrial and Technical Education; Science - Physical
Dist - USNAC **Prod** - USA 1962

Transistors, Semiconductor Diodes, Half Wave Rectifiers 17 MIN
VHS / U-matic
Introduction to Solid State Electronic Series; Chapter 2
Color (IND) (SPANISH)
LC 80-707260;
Education; Industrial and Technical Education
Dist - TAT **Prod** - TAT

Transistors - Servicing Techniques 14 MIN
16mm
B&W (H C A)
LC FIE61-131
Discusses common types of transistor failures such as opens, shorts, high leakage current, low gain and problems in localizing them. Demonstrates, with overshoulder camera views, the special techniques that must be used with transistorized equipment.
Industrial and Technical Education; Science - Physical
Dist - USNAC **Prod** - NF 1960

Transistors - Switching 14 MIN
U-matic
B&W
LC 79-707699
Provides examples of switching circuits in transistorized computers and explains briefly the concept of digital computation. Shows how transistors are used and how a simple transistor switch functions, illustrating ways in which the delaying effects of minority carrier storage are overcome. Issued in 1959 as a motion picture.
Industrial and Technical Education
Dist - USNAC **Prod** - USN 1979

Transistors - Switching 13 MIN
16mm
B&W (H C A)
LC FIE60-56
Shows examples of switching circuits in transistorized computers, explaining briefly the concept of digital computation and how transistors are used. Shows in more detail how a simple transistor switch works, with special attention to minority carrier storage in the base, showing how delaying effects of this storage are overcome.
Industrial and Technical Education; Science - Physical
Dist - USNAC **Prod** - NF 1959

Transistors - Triode Fundamentals 11 MIN
16mm
B&W
Shows that junction transistors, or triodes, consist of three sections with two P - N junctions separating them, and discusses the fundamentals of this arrangement as an amplifying device.
Industrial and Technical Education; Science - Physical
Dist - USNAC **Prod** - USN 1957

Transit Options for Small Communities 28 MIN
16mm
Color (A)
LC 78-700823
Focuses on four small communities and their efforts to solve their mass transportation problems.
Social Science; Sociology
Dist - USNAC **Prod** - USUMTA 1976

Transit to Black 13 MIN
16mm
B&W (C T)
A 'Modern Allegory' depicting the loneliness of a middle - aged man.
Guidance and Counseling; Psychology
Dist - NYU **Prod** - NYU 1962

Transition 29 MIN
16mm
Color
LC 79-700405
Documents the culture of northwest Montana's Flathead Valley from Indian days to the 1970's. Emphasizes changing lifestyles that will affect the valley's future social, economic and cultural changes.
Geography - United States; History - United States; Social Science; Sociology
Dist - FVCC **Prod** - FVCC 1979

Transition 7 MIN
16mm
Color
LC 77-702685
Uses experimental techniques to allow dance movements and visual treatments to take their own course.
Fine Arts
Dist - CANFDC **Prod** - HUNNL 1975

Transition - Double Offset, One Elevation - Sides of Openings Parallel 28 MIN
BETA / VHS
Exercise in Triangulating One - Piece Patterns Series
Color (IND)
Industrial and Technical Education; Psychology
Dist - RMIBHF **Prod** - RMIBHF

Transition Generation - a Third World Problem 20 MIN
VHS / U-matic
Color (J)
Points out the problems people the world over have in questioning traditional values while selecting only what is useful from western cultures. Highlights these problems by following three young people in their struggles to find a place in Afghanistan society. Shows an educated young man feeling out of place on return to his village, a son of a rich city man who cannot find a job and a liberated young woman who sees her place to be is in the home but does not wear a veil in public.
Geography - World; History - World; Social Science; Sociology
Dist - IFF **Prod** - IFF

Transition - One Elevation, Sides of Openings Parallel 29 MIN
BETA / VHS
Exercise in Triangulating One - Piece Patterns Series
Color (IND)
Industrial and Technical Education; Psychology
Dist - RMIBHF **Prod** - RMIBHF

Transition Package Series
Wipe Out Jargon 24 MIN
Dist - SEVDIM

Transition 'top up' or 'bottom up' or top down or bottom down - a series
Transition 'top up' or 'bottom up' or top down or bottom down - a series
Color (IND)
Demonstrates the full scale pattern development, working from a shop sketch or one - view drawing. Explains the application of the process of triangulation to develop the stretchout or true length of each of the four sides involved and how the seams may be 'chased around' once one of the sides is accurately developed. Square Or Rectangular Transition - Bottom Up, - ; Square Or Rectangular Transition - Top Up.
Industrial and Technical Education; Mathematics; Psychology
Dist - RMIBHF **Prod** - RMIBHF

Transition 'top up' or 'bottom up' or top down or bottom down - a series
Transition 'top up' or 'bottom up' or top down or bottom down - a series
Dist - RMIBHF

Transition 'Top Up' or 'Bottom Up' or Top Down or Bottom Down Series
Square or Rectangular Transition - Bottom Up, Double Offset, all Sides Slanting 30 MIN
Square or Rectangular Transition - Top Up, Double Offset, all Sides Slanting 43 MIN
Dist - RMIBHF

Transition Trek 5 MIN
U-matic / VHS
Write on, Set 2 Series
Color (J H)
Demonstrates making transitions between paragraphs.
English Language
Dist - CTI **Prod** - CTI

Transitional Elbow - Flat Top or Bottom, Change Cheek 28 MIN
VHS / BETA
Metal Fabrication - Transitional Elbows Series
Color (IND)
Industrial and Technical Education; Psychology
Dist - RMIBHF **Prod** - RMIBHF

Transitional Elbow - Flat Top or Bottom, same Size Cheeks 37 MIN
VHS / BETA
Metal Fabrication - Transitional Elbows Series
Color (IND)
Industrial and Technical Education; Psychology
Dist - RMIBHF **Prod** - RMIBHF

Transitional S - Offset (Flat Top or Bottom) 22 MIN
BETA / VHS
Color (IND)
Illustrates the layout for a transitional S - offset, using a mechanical method and involving the process of triangulation for the slanting cheek stretchout.
Industrial and Technical Education; Mathematics; Psychology
Dist - RMIBHF **Prod** - RMIBHF

Transitional S - Offset (Top or Bottom Up or Down) 19 MIN
BETA / VHS
Color (IND)
Explains the way the two cheeks are developed and the application of the stretchout of the cheeks to develop the wrappers for the throat or heel.
Industrial and Technical Education; Psychology
Dist - RMIBHF **Prod** - RMIBHF

Transitions 28 MIN
16mm / U-matic / VHS
Color (I)
LC 81-700777
Introduces three disabled adults whose goal is to be as independent as they can. Points out that their spunk and persistence is aided by families, governmental service agencies, and private organizations.
Psychology
Dist - PEREN **Prod** - SEPT 1981

Transitions 29 MIN
16mm / VHS
#107682 - 4 3/4
Examines the problems that can arise from the trauma of changing positions within an organization, and shows how it is possible to avoid allowing the problems to handicap an organization's productivity.
Business and Economics
Dist - MGHT

Transitions 10 MIN
16mm
Color (G)
$25.00 purchase
Depicts the disquieting sensations of being between, such as between falling asleep and being awake, between here and there, being and non - being. Evokes these images with a woman in white, layered with images and sound. Produced by Barbara Sternberg.
Fine Arts; Religion and Philosophy
Dist - CANCIN

Transitions and tensions 30 MIN
VHS
America in perspective - US history since 1877 series
Color (H C G)
$99.00 purchase _ #AIP - 12
Describes and analyzes the economic, social, cultural and political transitions and tensions characteristic of the 1920s. Part of a 26 - part series.
History - United States
Dist - INSTRU **Prod** - DALCCD 1991

Transitions - Caught at Midlife Series
Aging parents 30 MIN
Divorce 30 MIN
Empty Nest 30 MIN
Health and Mortality 30 MIN
Intimacy 30 MIN
Marriage 30 MIN
Parenting 30 MIN
Physical Changes 30 MIN
Widowhood 30 MIN
Dist - UMITV

Transitions - choices for mid - career changers 27 MIN
VHS
Color (A C G)
$89.00 purchase _ #1404
Gives solid advice for older and displaced workers on the job search process. Illustrates how to get started on the process, know one's skills, have a specific job objective and know how and when to look for a job. Reveals that it is normal to experience pain and loss when making a forced transition to another job.
Business and Economics; Guidance and Counseling; Health and Safety
Dist - NEWCAR

Transitions - Conversations with Wendell Castle 30 MIN
Videoreel / VT2
Synergism - Profiles, People Series
Color
Biography; Fine Arts
Dist - PBS **Prod** - WXXITV

Transitions for Older Workers 27 MIN
VHS / 16mm
Color (A)
$89.00 purchase _ NS101V
Depicts older and displaced workers who are left jobless. Offers advice on job search techniques, and provides guidelines for coping with emotions related to displacement and joblessness.
Guidance and Counseling; Psychology
Dist - JISTW

Transitions - Letting Go and Taking Hold 29 MIN
U-matic / VHS / 16mm
Color (H C A)
LC 79-700488
Examines the transitional process that is involved when an employee has to adapt to a new job.
Guidance and Counseling; Psychology
Dist - MGHT **Prod** - CRMP 1979

Transitions Series Program 101
Life Transitions 30 MIN
Dist - OHUTC

Transitions Series Program 104
An Introduction to Learning 29 MIN
Dist - OHUTC

Transitions series
Goals and risk taking 30 MIN
Dist - OHUTC

Translabyrinthine Approach - Removal of Acoustic Neuroma 22 MIN
16mm
Color (PRO)
LC FIA65-491
Uses animation and live action to show the surgical approach for the actual removal of an acoustic tumor. Discusses the problems as the surgery progresses and demonstrates how the tumor is separated from important structures and removed.
Health and Safety
Dist - EAR **Prod** - EAR 1964

Translabyrinthine Approach to the Internal Auditory Meatus and Posterior Fossa for Removal 15 MIN
16mm
Color (PRO)
Depicts the translabyrinthine approach to the cerebellopontine angle for the removal of acoustic neuromas. Describes the method of saving the facial nerve function and of avoiding injury to the anterior inferior cerebello artery.
Health and Safety
Dist - EAR **Prod** - EAR

Translating the code - protein synthesis 25 MIN
VHS
Color (J H C)
$170.00 purchase _ #A5VH 1268; $169.00 purchase _ #CG-876 - VS
Asks how DNA, which exists only in the nucleus of the cell, controls all of the forms and functions of the entire organism and how arrangements of only four bases in the DNA molecule carry all of the information for all of an

organism's features. Uses animated graphics to clarify the complex processes of genetic coding and protein synthesis. Helps to understand the central dogma of biology - one gene - one protein. Investigates notable exceptions to that rule - particularly Tonegawa's solution to the problem of antibody diversity.
Science - Natural
Dist - CLRVUE HRMC **Prod** - CLRVUE HRMC 1992

Translating theory into classroom practice series
Teacher decision making 26 MIN
Dist - SPF

Translating Theory into Classroom Practices Series
Motivation Theory for Teachers 28 MIN
Reinforcement Theory for Teachers 28 MIN
Retention Theory for Teachers 28 MIN
Dist - SPF

Translations 18 MIN
U-matic / VHS
Numerical Control/Computerized Numerical Control - Advanced Programming Series; Module 2
Color (IND)
Discusses program requirements for translation, translating a program to a new location and translating to the first point of origin.
Business and Economics; Industrial and Technical Education
Dist - LEIKID **Prod** - LEIKID

Translator Circuits 30 MIN
VHS / U-matic
Linear and Interface Circuits, Part II - Interface Integrated Circuits Series
Color (PRO)
Discusses application of integrated circuits that provide interface between one logic system of ECL, TTL or MOS to another logic system of a different type which may be ECL, TTL or MOS.
Industrial and Technical Education
Dist - TXINLC **Prod** - TXINLC

Translucent Appearances 22 MIN
16mm
Color; Silent (C)
$550.00 purchase
Experimental film by Barry Gerson.
Fine Arts
Dist - AFA **Prod** - AFA 1975

Transmagnifican Dambamuality 8 MIN
16mm
B&W
Portrays in slapstick manner a teenager's frenetic struggle for creative self - realization in the environment of a large family in a small apartment.
Fine Arts; Psychology; Sociology
Dist - BLKFMF **Prod** - GRAYRK

Transmetatarsal Amputation 25 MIN
16mm
Color (PRO)
Shows that the transmetatarsal amputation is a useful operation in some patients with ischemic lesions or diabetic gangrene of the toes. Discusses the indications for the transmetatarsal amputation and illustrates the step by step technique of the procedure.
Health and Safety; Science
Dist - ACY **Prod** - ACYDGD 1963

Transmission, Control and Storage of Power 15 MIN
VHS / 16mm
Exploring Technology Series
Color (I J)
$180.00 purchase, $25.00 rental
Shows a student - made version of a Hovercraft - and the four storage and transmission systems - mechanical, fluid, electrical and thermal.
Business and Economics; Industrial and Technical Education
Dist - AITECH **Prod** - AITECH 1990

Transmission, Control and Storage of Power - 3 13 MIN
VHS
Exploring Technology Education - Energy, Power and Transportation - Series
Color (I)
$180.00 purchase
Emphasizes the need for controlling, transmitting and storing power. Demonstrates the four storage and transmission systems - mechanical, fluid, electricla and thermal - by a model blimp and fighter planes on an aircraft carrier. Builds the technological literacy vital for current and future careers. Part of the Exploring Technology Series.
Education; Industrial and Technical Education; Social Science
Dist - AITECH **Prod** - AITECH 1990

Transmission, Drive Shaft and Differential 14 MIN
16mm
B&W
Explains how to check the transmission gear shift mechanism, drive shaft and differential and test their running condition.
Industrial and Technical Education
Dist - USNAC **Prod** - USOE

Transmission issues 31 MIN
VHS / U-matic
Distributed processor communication architecture series
Color
Industrial and Technical Education; Mathematics
Dist - MIOT **Prod** - MIOT

Transmission Lines 20 MIN
16mm
B&W
LC 74-705841
Discusses the types of transmission lines, such as the open two - wire line, the twin lead line, the twisted pair, flexible coaxial cable and rigid coaxial cable. Explains the major kinds of losses occurring in transmission lines. (Kinescope).
Industrial and Technical Education; Science - Physical
Dist - USNAC **Prod** - USAF 1964

Transmission of Information 13 MIN
16mm
B&W (C T)
LC 75-713855
Presents a test to discern the amount of information transmitted as a function of different stimulus dimensions. Shows students estimating width of diamonds, the variation in horizontal position of squares and the variation of the size of squares.
Psychology
Dist - PSUPCR **Prod** - NSF 1968

The Transmission of knowledge 30 MIN
BETA / VHS
Working on oneself series
Color (G)
$29.95 purchase _ #S066
Suggests that inner knowledge or spiritual wisdom cannot be communicated simply with words. Features Dr Claudio Naranjo, psychiatrist and prime mover in the human potential movement. Part of a four - part series on working on the self.
Psychology; Religion and Philosophy
Dist - THINKA **Prod** - THINKA

Transmission Security 19 MIN
16mm
B&W
LC FIE52-1103
Cautions radio operators against any action which might reveal a location or aid the enemy in any way. Points out the danger in sneaking out messages, sending unauthorized messages and cutting in.
Civics and Political Systems; Industrial and Technical Education; Social Science
Dist - USNAC **Prod** - USN 1948

Transmission - the Pipeline Company 19 MIN
U-matic / VHS
Introduction to the Natural Gas Industry Series; Pt 3
Color (IND)
Explains Gas transportation from the well to the distribution company. Covers pipeline construction, finance, legal requirements, gas control and operations.
Business and Economics; Psychology; Social Science
Dist - UTEXPE **Prod** - UTEXPE

Transmitter CFAC 26 MIN
16mm
Color
LC 76-701068
Shows what happens when a radio station decides to increase its broadcast power and relocate its transmitter site.
Fine Arts; Social Science
Dist - SAIT **Prod** - SAIT 1974

Transnational fiesta - 1992 61 MIN
VHS
Color (G) (ENGLISH QUECHUA & SPANISH W/ENG SUB)
Examines the multicultural and transnational experiences of Peruvian immigrants living in Washington, DC. Follows an elderly couple who agree to sponsor the costly five - day celebration of the festival honoring the Virgin of Carmen, which takes place every July in Cabanaconde, a peasant community in the southern Peruvian Andes. Expenses were shared with their seven children, who discuss the significance of this event as well as the prestige and spiritual solace it confers upon the sponsors. Films family members in traditional dress, dancing in the village plaza and observing the rituals that mesh Christianity with Incan beliefs. Produced and directed by Wilton Martinez and Paul H Gelles.
Fine Arts; Religion and Philosophy; Sociology
Dist - UCEMC

Transnational Manager as Cultural Change Agents
VHS / U-matic
Managing Cultural Differences Series
Color (IND)
Explains how the corporate representative abroad should be open to personal change and what skills are necessary to bring about positive systems change.
Business and Economics; Social Science; Sociology
Dist - GPCV **Prod** - GPCV

Transnational Managers as Intercultural Communicators
VHS / U-matic
Managing Cultural Differences Series
Color (IND)
Reviews concepts and challenges in cross - cultural communication and the interaction skills needed in a host culture, with an in - depth look at non - verbal communication.
Business and Economics; Social Science; Sociology
Dist - GPCV **Prod** - GPCV

The Transnationals 28 MIN
16mm / U-matic / VHS
Color (J)
Looks at the activities of multinational corporations, questioning whether they have an excessive influence on national economies.
Business and Economics; Social Science
Dist - LUF **Prod** - LUF 1979

Transonic flow and mixed equations by Cathleen S Morawetz 60 MIN
VHS
AMS - MAA joint lecture series
Color (PRO G)
$59.00 purchase _ #VIDMORAWETZ - VB2
Examines recent developments in the area of transonic flow and the associated differential equations. Begins with a short review of mixed equations - for many cases, including transonic flight, flow is governed partly by elliptic and partly by hyperbolic equations. Moves onto a discussion of compressible flow. Illustrates the phenomenon of shocks in transonic flow and describes computations made in the 1970s that showed that these shocks could be smoothed by design. Describes the DiPerna - Tartar - Murat method of compensated compactness and some new bounds that have been deduced for transonic flow. Recorded in Phoenix.
Mathematics
Dist - AMSOC **Prod** - AMSOC 1989

Transoral Introduction of the Flexible Bronchoscope 13 MIN
U-matic / VHS
Color (PRO)
LC 82-706314
Presents a systematic method for introducing the flexible bronchoscope. An oral endotracheal tube is used as an adjunct and helpful hints and actual endoscopic views are used to assist in its placement.
Health and Safety; Science; Science - Natural
Dist - USNAC **Prod** - VAMSLC 1982

Transoral Introduction of the Flexible Bronchoscope 12 MIN
VHS / 16mm
Endoscopy Series
(C)
$385.00 purchase _ #860VI055
Presents a method for transoral introduction of the flexible fiberoptic bronchoscope followed by insertin of an oral latex endotracheal tube. Part of the Bronchoscopy Series.
Health and Safety
Dist - HSCIC **Prod** - HSCIC 1986

Transorbital Lobotomy - Pt 1 12 MIN
16mm
B&W (PRO)
Traces the history of transorbital lobotomy, which is a modification of the recognized technique for prefrontal lobotomy. A demonstration of surgical procedures on cadaver preparations is presented and cadaver and clinical brains displaying transorbital operation are investigated. Depicts in full detail a bilateral operation employing electroshock anesthesia. Showings restricted.
Health and Safety; Psychology
Dist - PSUPCR **Prod** - PSUPCR 1949

Transorbital Lobotomy - Pt 2, Clinical Study of a Catatonic 9 MIN
16mm
B&W (C T)
Follows a 19 - year - old male catatonic before and after treatment by transorbital lobotomy. Shows that the patient

largely lost his anxious, delusional and hallucinated symptoms after therapy and found employment as a musician and as a salesman. Depicts the operation and recovery in still photography. Concludes with a gross dissection of frontal lobes after death, 11 months post - operatively.
Health and Safety
Dist - PSUPCR **Prod** - PSUPCR 1950

Transparency 11 MIN
16mm
Color (G)
$20.00 rental
Records and projects moving images which are the protagonists in the screen rectangle or field of action to produce cinematic ripplings and combustions for the audience's pleasure. Presents a film by Ernie Gehr.
Fine Arts
Dist - CANCIN

Transplant 30 MIN
VHS
Color (C A)
$295.00 purchase
Dramatizes issues related to transplantation and donation of human tissues. Follows the process from death through transplant recipients' checkups. Helps hospital staffs and the public prepare emotionally and personally to deal with the topic of transplantation.
Health and Safety
Dist - PFP **Prod** - BELLDA

Transplant 97 MIN
U-matic / VHS
Color (C A)
Tells of a workaholic businessman who suffers two heart attacks, which severely damage his heart. Depicts his fear when he is faced with the prospect of a risky heart transplant to save his life. Stars Kevin Dobson and Melinda Dillon.
Fine Arts; Health and Safety; Psychology
Dist - TIMLIF **Prod** - TIMLIF 1982

Transplant 17 MIN
U-matic / VHS / 16mm
Color (H C A)
LC 74-700506
Presents sequences on adopted children, migrant children in an alien culture and old people in a nursing home to illustrate how human beings, like plants, adjust to the shock of being transplanted.
Psychology; Sociology
Dist - AIMS **Prod** - GORKER 1974

The Transplant Experience 50 MIN
U-matic / VHS / 16mm
Nova Series
Color (H C A)
LC 78-700587
Documents a heart - transplant operation, including the rehabilitation process to help the patient's body accept the alien organ. Examines the ways in which a transplant affects the patient's life.
Health and Safety; Science - Natural
Dist - TIMLIF **Prod** - WGBHTV 1976

Transplantation of Sentiment 11 MIN
16mm
Color (C A)
LC 72-700400
Shows the way in which society makes individuals conform to its demands by telling the story of a milkman who is attacked by his milk tank and, after he receives help from no one, begins to deliver bombs instead of milk.
Literature and Drama; Psychology; Sociology
Dist - MMA **Prod** - MMA 1971

The Transplanted Brain 51 MIN
VHS
Color (S)
$149.00 purchase _ #825 - 9571
Examines surgical procedures which could change the lives of victims of strokes, paralyzing spinal injuries, Parkinson's disease and Alzheimer's disease. Considers that these new procedures raise critical questions of ethics because they involve transplanting brain cells from human fetuses. Interviews the doctors and scientists involved in the research and addresses the ethical issues surrounding the procedures.
Business and Economics; Health and Safety; Psychology; Religion and Philosophy; Science - Natural; Sociology
Dist - FI **Prod** - BBCTV 1988

Transplants - the immune system at risk 30 MIN
VHS
Color (J H C A)
$93.00 purchase _ #MB - 481119 - 3
Reveals how medical advances have made transplantation an almost standard medical practice. Shows that the immune system still often rejects donor organs, however.
Health and Safety; Science - Natural
Dist - SRA **Prod** - SRA

Transpo '72 28 MIN
16mm
Color
LC 73-701629
Highlights the activities at transpo '72 and describes the efforts of the Ford Motor Company to develop cleaner, safer automobiles.
Industrial and Technical Education; Social Science
Dist - FORDFL **Prod** - FMCMP 1972

Transpo 72 11 MIN
16mm
Color
LC 75-700701
Shows events at Transpo '72, held at Dulles International Airport in May, 1972.
Social Science
Dist - USNAC **Prod** - USDTFH 1972

Transport 6 MIN
16mm
Color (G)
$15.00 rental
Journeys with a man and woman who are lifted from the ground and carried through space then seen upside - down against the white sky. Views their relationship which is made entirely through the film editing as they never meet. Produced by Amy Greenfield.
Fine Arts
Dist - CANCIN

Transport Coefficients - Conductivity
VHS / U-matic
Plasma Process Technology Fundamentals Series
Color (IND)
States coefficients that describe mobility and conductivity are derived from the Boltzmann equation and compares to those previously obtained from the Langevin equation. Explains necessity for corrections to the simple Langevin calculation.
Industrial and Technical Education; Mathematics; Science - Physical
Dist - COLOSU **Prod** - COLOSU

Transport Coefficients - Mobility and Diffusion
VHS / U-matic
Plasma Process Technology Fundamentals Series
Color (IND)
Emphasizes comparison of mobility and diffusion fluxes. Compares Langevin equation results again with those derived from the Boltzmann equation. Discusses decreases in both electron and ion mobilities under high applied fields.
Industrial and Technical Education; Mathematics; Science - Physical
Dist - COLOSU **Prod** - COLOSU

Transport Game 10 MIN
16mm
Color
LC 80-700930
Illustrates Tasmania's transport system.
Geography - World; Social Science
Dist - TASCOR **Prod** - TASCOR 1978

Transport - Moving 20 MIN
VHS / U-matic
Video Career Library Series
(H C A)
$69.95 _ #CJ127V
Covers duties, conditions, salaries, and training connected with jobs in the transport and moving fields. Provides a view of employees in these types of occupation on the job, and gives information concerning the current market for such skills. Revised every two years.
Education; Guidance and Counseling; Industrial and Technical Education
Dist - CAMV **Prod** - CAMV

Transport networks in South Wales 10 MIN
VHS
Human geography series
Color; PAL (J H)
PdS29.50 purchase
Shows how the M4 corridor together with the sea, rail and air links are helping the economic growth of the region. Part of a three - part series focusing on aspects of the Human Geography component of Geography in National Curriculum (Attainment Target 4). Uses case studies in South Wales to illustrate typical changes and developments in transport and industry.
Geography - World; Social Science
Dist - EMFVL

Transport phenomena in solution - Conductance, transference, numbers - Pt 1 53 MIN
U-matic / VHS
Electrochemistry - Transport phenomena in solutions series; Pt IV
Color
Discusses transport phenomena in solution, including conductance, transference numbers, electrophoresis and electrokinetic phenomena.
Science; Science - Physical
Dist - MIOT KALMIA **Prod** - MIOT KALMIA

Transport phenomena in solution - Diffusion, viscosity, time of relaxation - Pt 2 49 MIN
U-matic / VHS
Electrochemistry - Transport phenomena in solutions series; Pt IV
Color
Discusses transport phenomena in solution, II, diffusion, viscosity, time of relaxation, non - aqueous solvents, ion pair formation, Walden's Rule and applications (especially titrations) of conductance.
Science; Science - Physical
Dist - MIOT KALMIA **Prod** - MIOT KALMIA

Transport system 29 MIN
U-matic
Radiographic processing series; Pt 8
Color (C)
LC 77-706077
Shows how radiographic processing time is controlled in the processor by the transport system. Discusses the relationship between the transport system and the subsystems for handling and moving the film, including components, functions and problems.
Health and Safety; Industrial and Technical Education; Science
Dist - USNAC **Prod** - USVA 1975

Transport systems in animals 17 MIN
U-matic / VHS / 16mm
Animal systems series
Color (J H C)
LC 78-713506
Explains that single - celled organisms transport materials by the streaming of cytoplasm and diffusion. Points out that the structure of hydra and planaria permit rapid exchange of gases, while larger animals have internal circulatory systems consisting of blood vessels and a pump or heart. Compares the heart structures and circulatory systems of various animals.
Science - Natural
Dist - IU VIEWTH **Prod** - IU GATEEF 1971

Transportation 30 MIN
U-matic
Fast Forward Series
Color (H C)
Explains the many ways in which computers are being used in air traffic control, traffic signals, information systems and other applications.
Computer Science; Science
Dist - TVOTAR **Prod** - TVOTAR 1979

Transportation 6 MIN
16mm / U-matic / VHS
Kingdom of Could be You Series
Color (K P I)
Guidance and Counseling
Dist - EBEC **Prod** - EBEC 1974

Transportation 8 MIN
U-matic / VHS / 16mm
First aid Rev - Ed series
Color
Details proper handling and transporting casualties, stressing careful examination and correct treatment before movement of the injured is attempted. Displays several types of stretchers, including the army type, stokes navala model, stretcher boards and the Bureau of Mines utility splint. Covers the most effective methods of carrying a patient without a stretcher, including one - man, two - man, and three - man lift and carry.
Health and Safety
Dist - USNAC **Prod** - USMESA 1981

Transportation 15 MIN
BETA / VHS / U-matic / 16mm
Your town II series
Color (K P)
$245.00, $68.00 purchase _ #C50738, #C51492
Shows how transportation systems link a community, move its goods and connect it with the rest of the world. Examines how a town's fianancial and social well - being depend greatly upon the efficiency and avilability of its transportation systems. Roadways, subways, even bicycle paths, enable citizens to commute to work, school, stores - in town and from state to state. Part of a five - part series on community services.
Social Science; Sociology
Dist - NGS **Prod** - NGS 1992

Transportation 10 MIN
VHS
Skills - occupational programs series
Color (H C)
$49.00 purchase, $15.00 rental _ #316620; LC 91-712447
Features a truck driver, a mover, an auto yard supervisor, a limousine chauffeur and a transit operator. Interviews several women in nontraditional occupations. Part of a series that features occupations in the skilled trades, in service industries and in business leading to careers in areas of demand and future growth. Includes teacher's guide with reproducible worksheets.
Guidance and Counseling; Psychology; Social Science
Dist - TVOTAR **Prod** - TVOTAR 1990

Transportation 28 MIN
U-matic / VHS
Personal Finance and Money Management Series
Color (C A)
Business and Economics; Civics and Political Systems
Dist - SCCON **Prod** - SCCON 1987

Transportation - a Basic Need 12 MIN
U-matic / VHS / 16mm
Color (P I)
LC 80-701170
Shows how transportation affects people's lives and how various types of vehicles are used to move people and things within a community.
Social Science
Dist - EBEC **Prod** - ODYSSP 1980

Transportation - a First Film on the Airport 11 MIN
16mm / U-matic / VHS
Color (P I) (FRENCH)
LC 72-700117
Examines the advantages and disadvantages derived by the community from a big city airport.
Social Science
Dist - PHENIX **Prod** - BEANMN 1972

Transportation - a Secret Agent Travels to Nutdale 15 MIN
U-matic
We Live Next Door Series
Color (K)
Continues the story of Nutdale with the arrival there of a secret agent.
Psychology; Social Science
Dist - TVOTAR **Prod** - TVOTAR 1981

Transportation and Communication - Air - Flight Service
VHS
Video Career Series
$29.95 purchase _ #MD170
Shows students going 'on the job' to learn the variety of skills required for this occupation and the special training or educational requirements. Discusses various hiring procedures and what is involved in joining a professional association or union.
Education; Guidance and Counseling
Dist - CAREER **Prod** - CAREER

Transportation and Communication - Air Transport - Ground Communications
VHS
Video Career Series
$29.95 purchase _ #MD171
Shows students going 'on the job' to learn the variety of skills required for this occupation and the special training or educational requirements. Discusses various hiring procedures and what is involved in joining a professional association or union.
Education; Guidance and Counseling
Dist - CAREER **Prod** - CAREER

Transportation and Communication in Underground Coal Mines 9 MIN
U-matic / VHS / 16mm
Color
Shows accidents involving the transportation of men and materials in a mine, with follow - ups showing what the safe procedure should have been. Explains and demonstrates underground mine communications systems.
Health and Safety; Industrial and Technical Education; Psychology; Social Science
Dist - USNAC **Prod** - USDL

Transportation and Communication - Materials Handling
VHS
Video Career Series
$29.95 purchase _ #MD174V
Shows students going 'on the job' to learn the variety of skills required for this occupation and the special training or educational requirements. Discusses various hiring procedures and what is involved in joining a professional association or union.
Education; Guidance and Counseling
Dist - CAREER **Prod** - CAREER

Transportation and feed mills - transfer points for disease 11 MIN
VHS / U-matic
Biosecurity and the poultry industry series
Color (IND)
$40.00, $80.00 purchase _ #TCA18199, #TCA18198
Covers biosecurity in the poultry industry as it relates to transportation and feed mills.
Agriculture; Health and Safety
Dist - USNAC **Prod** - USDA 1989

Transportation and Material Moving 20 MIN
VHS / 16mm
Video Career Library Series
Color (H C A PRO)
$79.95 purchase _ #WW117
Shows occupations in transportation and moving such as tractor - trailer truck drivers, heavy truck and bus drivers, airplane pilots and navigators, grader, dozer, scraper and forklift operators. Contains current occupational outlook and salary information.
Business and Economics; Guidance and Counseling
Dist - AAVIM **Prod** - AAVIM 1990

Transportation and travel - Parts 27 and 28 60 MIN
U-matic / VHS
French in action - part II series
Color (C) (FRENCH)
$45.00, $29.95 purchase
Illustrates expressing fear, insisting, talking about transportation, expressing admiration, making suggestions, pluperfect, conditional, conditional and imperfect, past conditional, compound tenses and past participles, agreement of past participles, expressions of time in Parts 27 and 28. Parts of a 52 - part series teaching the French language, all in French, written by Pierre Capretz, Director of the Language Laboratory at Yale.
Foreign Language; History - World
Dist - ANNCPB **Prod** - YALEU 1987

Transportation and travel - Parts 29 and 30 60 MIN
U-matic / VHS
French in action - part II series
Color (C) (FRENCH)
$45.00, $29.95 purchase
Illustrates expressing fear, insisting, talking about transportation, expressing admiration, making suggestions, pluperfect, conditional, conditional and imperfect, past conditional, compound tenses and past participles, agreement of past participles, expressions of time in Parts 29 and 30. Parts of a 52 - part series teaching the French language, all in French, written by Pierre Capretz, Director of the Language Laboratory at Yale.
Foreign Language; History - World
Dist - ANNCPB **Prod** - YALEU 1987

Transportation and travel - habitat - Parts 31 and 32 60 MIN
VHS / U-matic
French in action - part II series
Color (C) (FRENCH)
$45.00, $29.95 purchase
Illustrates talking about transportation, pluperfect, past conditional, compound tenses and past participles, agreement of past participles, expressions of time in Part 31. Demonstrates asking one's way, talking about housing, protesting, expressing satisfaction and dissatisfaction, imperfect, irregular imperatives, causative 'faire,' 'faire' versus 'rendre,' present participle in Part 32. Parts of a 52 - part series teaching the French language, all in French, written by Pierre Capretz, Director of the Language Laboratory at Yale.
Foreign Language; History - World
Dist - ANNCPB **Prod** - YALEU 1987

Transportation by Bus 10 MIN
U-matic / VHS / 16mm
Transportation Series
Color (K P I)
LC FIA67-5817
Two children go to the bus terminal where they buy tickets, check their baggage and board the bus. In the meantime the bus is being prepared for the journey.
Social Science
Dist - ALTSUL **Prod** - FILMSW 1968

Transportation by Freight Train 10 MIN
16mm / U-matic / VHS
Transportation Series
Color; Captioned (P I)
LC FIA67-5818
Shows special kinds of freight cars carrying different things that are used in everyday life. Also shows the engineer, conductor, flagman, dispatcher and other railroad personnel and equipment needed.
Social Science
Dist - ALTSUL **Prod** - FILMSW 1968

Transportation by Helicopter 11 MIN
16mm / U-matic / VHS
Transportation Series
Captioned; Color (K P I)
Shows how helicopters fly straight up, sideways, in one place and backwards. Illustrates how they are used in construction for lifting and stringing cable, in agriculture for pest and disease control, in emergency search and rescue missions, in transportation of passengers and light cargo and in carrying people and equipment to and from remote locations.
Social Science
Dist - ALTSUL **Prod** - FILMSW 1968

Transportation by Inland Waterways 10 MIN
U-matic / VHS / 16mm
Transportation Series
Color (P I)
LC FIA67-5819
Shows barges and boats of all kinds carrying people and cargo on lakes, rivers and canals. Animation illustrates how locks on inland waterways work. The functions of the coast guard patrolling inland waterways are shown.
Business and Economics; Geography - United States; Geography - World; Social Science
Dist - ALTSUL **Prod** - FILMSW 1968

Transportation - getting things from A to B - 3 20 MIN
VHS
Design and technology starters series
Color; PAL (J H)
PdS29.50 purchase
Begins with a search for worthwhile design possibilities within a particular real - world context. Suggests ways in which pupils might start thinking about certain artifacts, systems and environments, and how well they meet the needs and desires of different people who might use them. Part three of a seven - part series.
Fine Arts; Social Science; Sociology
Dist - EMFVL

Transportation in America - a history; Rev. 17 MIN
U-matic / VHS / 16mm
Color (J I)
$49.95 purchase _ #P10079; LC 83-700942
Chronicles the history of transportation in the United States, emphasizing the economic and social factors that demanded expanded tranportation options. Illustrates how transportation was modernized with the inventions of the steam and internal combustion engines. Considers tranportation for the future and ways to conserve resources. Animation.
Social Science
Dist - CF **Prod** - CF 1983

Transportation in America's History 19 MIN
16mm / U-matic / VHS
Color (P I J)
Traces the development of rail, auto and air travel from the American Revolution to the present day. Shows how the need to move people and their goods faster and farther led to the invention and the continuing improvement of transportation.
History - United States; Social Science
Dist - ALTSUL **Prod** - NORWIN 1984

Transportation in Neighborhoods 15 MIN
U-matic / VHS
Neighborhoods Series
Color (P)
Looks at transportation in neighborhoods.
Sociology
Dist - GPN **Prod** - NEITV 1981

Transportation is Moving 11 MIN
16mm / U-matic / VHS
Transportation Series
Color (K P I)
LC 74-708897
Features all modes of transportation with emphasis on moving people and goods. Stresses economics in fulfilling our daily needs.
Business and Economics; Social Science
Dist - ALTSUL **Prod** - FILMSW 1970

Transportation Maintenance 11 MIN
U-matic / VHS / 16mm
Transportation Series
Color (P I)
LC 72-704206
Shows mechanics demonstrating their skills to illustrate how effectively community transportation may function.

Industrial and Technical Education; Social Science
Dist - ALTSUL **Prod** - FILMSW 1969

Transportation - Master or Servant 56 MIN
16mm
Color (H C)
Debates whether society should continue to depend on the automobile or switch to public transportation methods.
Social Science; Sociology
Dist - SF **Prod** - SF 1973

Transportation - Mechanical Cluster 20 MIN
U-matic / VHS
Vocational Visions Series
Color
Discusses the requirements and duties for such jobs as auto mechanic, auto body worker, diesel mechanic and truck driver.
Guidance and Counseling; Psychology
Dist - GA **Prod** - GA

Transportation modes - airlines and special carriers 30 MIN
VHS
Business logistics series
Color (G C)
$200.00 purchase, $20.50 rental _ #34971
Examines transportation modes, in particular airlines and special carriers. Part of a 30 - part series on business logistics which deals with movement and storage of raw and finished products, and with managerial activities important for effective control of these operations. Interviews logistics managers of major US corporations and transportation companies. Uses on - site segments to demonstrate logistical carrier operations. Features program author Dr John Coyle.
Business and Economics; Social Science
Dist - PSU **Prod** - WPSXTV 1987

Transportation modes - motor carriers and water carriers 30 MIN
VHS
Business logistics series
Color (G C)
$200.00 purchase, $20.50 rental _ #34970
Examines transportation modes, in particular motor and water carriers. Part of a 30 - part series on business logistics which deals with movement and storage of raw and finished products, and with managerial activities important for effective control of these operations. Interviews logistics managers of major US corporations and transportation companies. Uses on - site segments to demonstrate logistical carrier operations. Features program author Dr John Coyle.
Business and Economics; Social Science
Dist - PSU **Prod** - WPSXTV 1987

Transportation modes - railroads and pipelines 30 MIN
VHS
Business logistics series
Color (G C)
$200.00 purchase, $20.50 rental _ #34969
Examines transportation modes, in particular railroads and pipelines. Part of a 30 - part series on business logistics which deals with movement and storage of raw and finished products, and with managerial activities important for effective control of these operations. Interviews logistics managers of major US corporations and transportation companies. Uses on - site segments to demonstrate logistical carrier operations. Features program author Dr John Coyle.
Business and Economics; Social Science
Dist - PSU **Prod** - WPSXTV 1987

The Transportation of Nuclear Materials 40 MIN
U-matic / VHS
Color (C)
$249.00, $149.00 purchase _ #AD - 1274
Documents a vast web of international nuclear shipments, deliberately mislabeled by shippers and knowingly covered up by government regulatory agencies in France and the US.
Business and Economics; Civics and Political Systems; Health and Safety; Religion and Philosophy; Social Science
Dist - FOTH **Prod** - FOTH

Transportation of the Injured 22 MIN
16mm
Color (PRO)
Explains that immediate care, safe and expeditious transportation of an injured person to a hospital is an important part of the overall management. Demonstrates recommended methods for a selected group of common injuries.
Health and Safety
Dist - ACY **Prod** - ACYDGD 1956

Transportation of the Injured 14 MIN
16mm
Medical Self - Help Series
Color (SPANISH)
LC 75-702552
Teaches the individual how to take care of his medical and health needs in time of disaster when medical assistance might not be readily available. Presents instructions on transportation of the injured.
Foreign Language; Health and Safety
Dist - USNAC **Prod** - USPHS 1965

Transportation of the Injured 15 MIN
U-matic
Trauma Series
Color (PRO)
Demonstrates methods for moving people from the scene of an injury to a hospital emergency room facility. Shows the three - man carry. Discusses specific types of injuries for immobilizing and positioning injured people prior to lifting and transporting. Gives special consideration to the person with a spinal cord injury.
Health and Safety
Dist - PRIMED **Prod** - PRIMED

Transportation of the injured 14 MIN
16mm
Medical self - help series
Color (SPANISH)
LC 74-705845; 75-702552
Shows how to use materials to be found in disaster areas to improvise means of moving injured persons. Describes precautions to prevent further injuries. To be used with the course 'Medical Self - Help Training.'
Health and Safety
Dist - USNAC **Prod** - USHHS USPHS 1965

Transportation of the Sick and Wounded 27 MIN
16mm
B&W
LC 74-705846
Deals with patient evacuation in the field by means of manual carries, animal carries and military vehicles and aircraft.
Civics and Political Systems; Health and Safety
Dist - USNAC **Prod** - USA 1964

The Transportation Revolution - Story of America's Growth 21 MIN
19 MIN
U-matic / 16mm / VHS
Color; Captioned (I J)
LC 76-708675
Highlights the history - making steps in road, rail and air transportation.
History - United States; Psychology; Social Science; Sociology
Dist - LCOA **Prod** - SCNDRI 1970

Transportation series

Transportation by Bus	10 MIN
Transportation by Freight Train	10 MIN
Transportation by Helicopter	11 MIN
Transportation by Inland Waterways	10 MIN
Transportation is Moving	11 MIN
Transportation Maintenance	11 MIN
Trucks and truck transportation	11 MIN

Dist - ALTSUL

Transportation strategies in a deregulated environment 30 MIN
VHS
Business logistics series
Color (G C)
$200.00 purchase, $20.50 rental _ #34976
Discusses transportation strategies in a deregulated environment. Part of a 30 - part series on business logistics which deals with movement and storage of raw and finished products, and with managerial activities important for effective control of these operations. Interviews logistics managers of major US corporations and transportation companies. Uses on - site segments to demonstrate logistical carrier operations. Features program author Dr John Coyle.
Business and Economics; Social Science
Dist - PSU **Prod** - WPSXTV 1987

Transportation Systems 15 MIN
VHS / 16mm
Exploring Technology Series
Color (I J)
$180.00 purchase, $25.00 rental
Presents transportation systems and discusses the history and growth of transportation technology.
Business and Economics; Social Science; Sociology
Dist - AITECH **Prod** - AITECH 1990

Transportation Systems - 4 13 MIN
VHS
Exploring Technology Education - Energy, Power and Transportation -`Series
Color (I)
$180.00 purchase
Presents different kinds of transportation systems and discusses the history and growth of transportation technology, analyzing them through the systems model. Builds the technological literacy vital for current and future careers. Part of the Exploring Technology Series.
Education; Industrial and Technical Education; Social Science
Dist - AITECH **Prod** - AITECH 1990

Transportation Systems Explained 120 MIN
VHS / 16mm
Color (H A)
$399.00 purchase _ T10
Presents the major types of transportaion. Explores highway, rail, pipeline and on site land systems. Describes outputs for land, air and marine systems.
Industrial and Technical Education; Social Science
Dist - BERGL **Prod** - BERGL 1988

Transportation - the Way Ahead 8 MIN
16mm
Color (A)
LC 77-703417
Describes various Energy Research and Development Administration programs aimed at developing new fuel sources for automobiles. Discusses research being conducted with methanol, isopropanol, denatured alcohol and other fuels not derived from petroleum.
Home Economics; Industrial and Technical Education; Science; Science - Natural; Social Science; Sociology
Dist - USNAC **Prod** - USERD 1977

Transportations 12 MIN
VHS / 16mm
B&W (A)
$50.00 rental
Presents an erotic lesbian film by Amanda Walliss.
Fine Arts; Sociology
Dist - WMEN

Transportation's Role in Disaster 15 MIN
16mm
Color
LC 74-706288
Describes the contribution of the National Defense Transportation Association, which has provided transportation services during major disasters over the last two decades.
History - World; Social Science
Dist - USNAC **Prod** - USOCD 1972

The Transporters checklist 15 MIN
VHS / U-matic / BETA
Hazardous waste training series
Color (IND G A)
$730.00 purchase, $175.00 rental _ #TRA004
Illustrates proper hazardous waste transportation. Reviews required equipment inspections, demonstrates vehicle loading and placarding. Emphasizes attention to regulatory responsibilities. Part of a comprehensive seven - part series on hazardous waste training.
Health and Safety; Psychology
Dist - ITF **Prod** - BNA

Transporting and Placing Quality Concrete 27 MIN
16mm
Color
LC 82-700034
A revised version of How To Transport, Place, Finish And Cure Quality Concrete. Demonstrates methods used for transporting concrete from the batch plant to the job and subsequent handling on the job site to convey, place and consolidate concrete into the forms. Emphasizes correct techniques for various types of structures and under varying conditions.
Industrial and Technical Education
Dist - PRTLND **Prod** - PRTLND 1976

Transporting and Refining 12 MIN
U-matic / VHS
Overview of the Petroleum Industry Series
Color (IND)
Shows how hydrocarbons produced from the well are collected and transported by pipeline, truck and tanker. Inspects fractionating and cracking towers and other refining operations.
Business and Economics; Industrial and Technical Education; Science - Physical; Social Science
Dist - GPCV **Prod** - GPCV

The Transporting of a Casualty 9 MIN
16mm / U-matic / VHS
First Aid Series
Color (A)
LC 80-701762
Describes casualty transportation methods which can be used by one person or by a team of two people. Provides information on the use of stretchers, special requirements for moving individuals with suspected spinal injuries and procedures for carrying an injured person in a confined space.

Health and Safety
Dist - IFB Prod - HBL 1977

Transporting the Patient for Surgery 18 MIN
16mm
Color (PRO)
Stresses basic operating room nursing principles as they apply to the transportation of the patient to and from the operating room.
Health and Safety; Science
Dist - ACY Prod - ACYDGD 1958

Transposition of the great arteries
Videodisc
Color (PRO C)
$1300.00 purchase _ #C901 - IV - 060
Presents a hypertext presentation on the Jatene operation adapted from classic articles. Includes graphic illustrations and a menu - accessed interactive video of the operation, with verbal discussion of the surgery during various video segments. Written by Dr Joel A Weinstein, Department of Surgery, Case Western Reserve University and developed by the Surgical Hypermedia Project, Cleveland Metropolitan General Hospital. Includes videodisc, courseware on floppies in 3.5 or 5.25 inch size, user's manual and study guide. Requires IBM InfoWindow Touch Display Monitor, IBM compatible with 20MB hard disk and a videodisc player. Ask distributor about other requirements.
Health and Safety
Dist - HSCIC

Transposition of the Index Finger for Amputated Thumb 12 MIN
16mm
Color (PRO)
Describes in detail the operative procedure for pollicization of the index finger.
Health and Safety; Science
Dist - ACY Prod - ACYDGD 1957

Transpubic Repair of Membranous Urethral Strictures 14 MIN
16mm
Color
LC 75-702257
Demonstrates the transpubic repair of membranous urethral strictures. Explains that the operation is only suitable for patients with traumatic strictures and should not be used for strictures due to previous gonorrheal infection.
Health and Safety; Science; Science - Natural
Dist - EATONL Prod - EATONL 1973

Transseptal Orchiopexy for Cryptorchidism 12 MIN
16mm
Color
LC FIA66-71
Dr H C Miller discusses three major surgical methods of correcting cryptorchidism in order to produce mature healthy sperm, to minimize trauma and to permit easier physical examination of the tests. Shows views of a typical transseptal operation and illustrates the technique used.
Health and Safety
Dist - EATONL Prod - EATONL 1965

Transsexuals - I Want to be Me 22 MIN
U-matic / VHS
Color
Reports on people who feel trapped in the body of the wrong sex. Includes interviews with transsexuals before and after sex - change surgery. Describes how their dilemma affected them, their families and friends.
Psychology; Sociology
Dist - WCCOTV Prod - WCCOTV 1974

Transthoracic Partial Gastrectomy 28 MIN
16mm
Color (PRO)
Shows intrathoracic esophageo - gastric anastomosis for carcinoma of the cardia.
Health and Safety; Science
Dist - ACY Prod - ACYDGD 1950

Transthoracic Repair of Sliding Hiatal Hernia 14 MIN
16mm
Color
Illustrates the mechanism and surgical repair of sliding hiatal hernia.
Health and Safety; Science - Natural
Dist - USVA Prod - USVA 1955

Transthoracic Repair of Sliding Hiatus Hernia with Reflux Esophagitis by the Mark 28 MIN
16mm
Color (PRO)
Presents the evaluation and repair of the herniated and incompetent gastroesophageal junction as developed by Belsey. Emphasizes the techniques important to achieve relief of symptoms and a low recurrence rate.
Health and Safety; Science
Dist - ACY Prod - ACYDGD 1970

The Transuranium Elements 58 MIN
16mm
B&W
LC FIE68-74
Dr Glenn T Seaborg describes the work leading to the discovery of all of the know transuranium elements, from element 93 through element 104. Discusses some practical applications of transuranium elements and the possibility of making newer, very heavy elements.
Science - Physical
Dist - USERD Prod - USNRC 1968

Transuranium elements 23 MIN
16mm / VHS
Chem study video - film series
Color (H C)
$368.00, $99.00 purchase, $33.00 rental _ #192 W 0910, #193 W 2042, #140 W 4178
Interviews four principal chemists in the discovery and identification of the transuranium elements. Includes Drs Glenn T Seaborg, Burris Cunningham, Stanley Thompson and Albert Ghiorso. Reviews methods and techniques for discovery and identification of transuranium elements. Part of a series for teaching chemistry to high school and college students.
Science - Physical
Dist - WARDS Prod - WARDS 1990

Transuranium Elements 23 MIN
16mm
CHEM Study Films Series
Color (H A)
Features four chemists from Lawrence Radiation Laboratory who were involved in the actual discovery and identification of the transuranium elements.
Science - Physical
Dist - MLA Prod - CHEMS 1962

Transurethral Prostatectomy - a Teaching Film 20 MIN
16mm
Color
Demonstrates the usefulness of the motion picture for teaching the procedure of transurethral prostatectomy. Acquaints the beginner with key points always encountered during transurethral prostatectomy.
Health and Safety; Science
Dist - EATONL Prod - EATONL 1966

Transurethral Resection of the Prostate (TURP) 10 MIN
U-matic / 35mm strip
Color
Helps the patient understand the closed prostate surgery technique using the resectoscope, pre - and post - procedures, the urinary catheter and necessary postoperative precautions.
Health and Safety; Science - Natural
Dist - MEDCOM Prod - MEDCOM

Transuterine resection of fibroids 15 MIN
VHS / U-matic
Color (PRO C)
$395.00 purchase, $80.00 rental _ #C881 - VI - 044
Introduces gynecologists and urologists to the team approach for the transuterine resection of fibroids. Reveals that the gynecologist establishes the diagnosis, arranges for admission and manages the patient post - operatively. At surgery, the urologist performs the surgery while the the gynecologist monitors by laparoscopy to make sure that intrauterine events remain intrauterine and that the glycene being used does not spill into the abdominal cavity. Presented by Drs Floyd A Fried and Jaroslaw Hulka.
Health and Safety
Dist - HSCIC

Transvesico - Capsular Prostatectomy - an Improved Technique 20 MIN
16mm
Color
LC FIA66-73
Demonstrates step - by - step the procedures followed in a prostatectomy using the transvesico - capsular technique. Combines the good features of both retropubic and suprapubic enucleation.
Health and Safety
Dist - EATONL Prod - EATONL 1960

Transvestism and Transsexualism 60 MIN
U-matic / VHS
Color
Discusses the causes, diagnosis and therapeutic management of transvestism and transsexualism, which are often erroneously linked to homosexuality. Presents evaluation factors important in differential diagnosis.
Health and Safety; Psychology; Sociology
Dist - HEMUL Prod - HEMUL

Tranzor Z - a Pilot is found 60 MIN
BETA / VHS
Color (G)
Presents a battle between Tranzor Z and Dr Doom, who is threatening to destroy the Earth.
Fine Arts
Dist - SONY Prod - UNKNWN

The Trap 25 MIN
16mm
Screen Test Series
Color; Silent (J H C G T A)
Religion and Philosophy
Dist - WHLION Prod - WHLION

Trap of Hate 30 MIN
16mm
Color (J)
LC 72-701642
Gives an account of the separation of a young man and his girlfriend which is caused when her parents learn that the boy's cousin has been in prison.
Guidance and Counseling; Psychology; Sociology
Dist - CPH Prod - CPH 1968

The Trap of Solid Gold 51 MIN
U-matic / VHS / 16mm
B&W (H C)
LC 70-707261
Shows the consequences of living beyond one's means, as exemplified in problems of a young executive who is caught in a trap of living beyond his income because of the status games of his company.
Business and Economics; Psychology; Social Science; Sociology
Dist - IFB Prod - ABCTV 1969

The Trapdoor 30 MIN
16mm
B&W
Tells how Jewish settlers in Newport, Rhode Island, came to understand the American principle of religious freedom. Describes how, expecting bigotry and intolerance, a secret tunnel and trapdoor for escaping from pogroms were built into the synagogue but were discovered to be unnecessary. (Kinescope).
Religion and Philosophy
Dist - NAAJS Prod - JTS 1954

Trapezoid Rule 20 MIN
VHS
Calculus Series
Color (H)
LC 90712920
Discusses trapezoid rule. The 45th of 57 installments of the Calculus Series.
English Language; Mathematics
Dist - GPN

Trapezoidal Sweep Generator - TSTR 33 MIN
16mm
B&W
LC 74-705848
Shows how the transistor trapezoidal sweep generator can be identified. Explains the purpose of the circuit components and develops a step - by - step analysis of the circuit's operation. (Kinescope).
Industrial and Technical Education; Science - Physical
Dist - USNAC Prod - USAF

Trapezoidal Sweep Generator - TV 19 MIN
16mm
B&W
LC 74-705849
Explains a typical radar indicator and television receiver, making specific reference to the type of deflection used in each system. Develops the required waveform necessary for electromagnetic deflection. (Kinescope).
Industrial and Technical Education
Dist - USNAC Prod - USAF

Trapline 18 MIN
16mm
Color (G)
$35.00 rental
Reflects independent Canadian filmmaking.
Fine Arts
Dist - CANCIN Prod - EPPEL 1976

Trapped 15 MIN
U-matic
Color (I)
Teaches writing skills while telling the story of Chris and his friends as they try to leave the planet Trialviron.
Education; English Language; Literature and Drama
Dist - TVOTAR Prod - TVOTAR 1982

Trapped (Rescue Work) 20 MIN
16mm
B&W
LC FIE55-45
Emphasizes the need for trained rescue workers and shows many of the risks, as well as the rewards, of rescue.

Health and Safety; Social Science
Dist - USNAC **Prod** - USDD 1962

Trapper Dan 15 MIN
16mm
Color
LC 75-703441
Spoofs silent movie serials.
Fine Arts; Literature and Drama
Dist - SFRASU **Prod** - SFRASU 1974

Trapping of Free Radicals at Low Temperatures 14 MIN
16mm
Color (J)
LC FIE61-147
Describes the behavior of free radicals as highly reactive molecular fragments. Explains their importance in high - temperature reactions and rocket flames.
Science - Physical
Dist - USNAC **Prod** - USNBOS 1960

Traps 43 MIN
U-matic / VHS
Petroleum Geology Series
Color (IND)
Industrial and Technical Education; Science - Physical
Dist - GPCV **Prod** - GPCV

Traps and Snares - Summer 11 MIN
16mm
Color (I J H)
Shows the construction and operation of traps and snares that can be used to obtain food in an emergency in the wilderness. The instructor in this film is an expert Indian trapper who regularly uses the traps and snares shown.
Psychology; Science - Natural; Social Science
Dist - SF **Prod** - SF 1968

Traps and Snares - Winter 12 MIN
16mm
Color (I J H)
Explains that Indian hunters still use ancient methods to trap wild game in the winter wilderness. Shows, how any person lost in the woods can use the same technique to catch small game.
Psychology; Science - Natural; Social Science
Dist - SF **Prod** - SF 1968

Traps - Anticlines 31 MIN
U-matic / VHS
Basic and Petroleum Geology for Non - Geologists - Traps Series; Traps
Color (IND)
Industrial and Technical Education; Science - Physical
Dist - GPCV **Prod** - PHILLP

Traps - Faulting 33 MIN
VHS / U-matic
Basic and Petroleum Geology for Non - Geologists - Traps Series; Traps
Color (IND)
Industrial and Technical Education; Science - Physical
Dist - GPCV **Prod** - PHILLP

Traps - Salt Domes 38 MIN
VHS / U-matic
Basic and Petroleum Geology for Non - Geologists - Traps Series; Traps
Color (IND)
Industrial and Technical Education; Science - Physical
Dist - GPCV **Prod** - PHILLP

Traps - Stratigraphic 44 MIN
U-matic / VHS
Basic and Petroleum Geology for Non - Geologists - Traps Series; Traps
Color (IND)
Industrial and Technical Education; Science - Physical
Dist - GPCV **Prod** - PHILLP

The Trash troll 13 MIN
VHS
Color (K P T)
$195.00 purchase, $45.00 rental
Introduces a gruff, environmentally - conscious gnome admonishing three children who carelessly litter his beach with a plastic six - pack ring. Visits a nearby marine hospital to show the kids the dangers that garbage presents to ocean inhabitants. When the kids return to the beach, they spread the word about beach litter. Produced by Stuart Perkin. Includes study guide.
Geography - World; Guidance and Counseling
Dist - BULFRG

Tratamiento Del Traumatismo Toracico 26 MIN
VHS / U-matic
Color (PRO) (SPANISH)
Discusses the more common surgical thoracic emergencies in the categories of penetrating and non - penetrating trauma. Presents the pathophysiology of thoracic trauma, the evaluation of patients with chest trauma, the initiation of appropriate therapy and some of the life - threatening injuries which may occur with little or no external evidence.
Foreign Language; Health and Safety
Dist - UMICHM **Prod** - UMICHM 1981

Trauer Um Einen Verlorenen Sohn 103 MIN
16mm
Color (GERMAN (ENGLISH SUBTITLES))
A German language film with English subtitles. Captures the pain and anguish of a family who follows their drug - addicted son through withdrawal, relapse, change to harder drugs and finally death.
Fine Arts; Foreign Language
Dist - WSTGLC **Prod** - WSTGLC

Trauma 50 MIN
VHS
QED series
Color; PAL (C H G)
PdS65 purchase
Explores arguments for and against the establishment of emergency care facilities in British hospitals. Looks at why some doctors oppose such reforms in health care.
Health and Safety
Dist - BBCENE

Trauma 41 MIN
U-matic
Forensic Medicine Teaching Programs Series
Color (PRO)
LC 78-706058
Discusses gunshot wounds, emphasizing those caused by hand guns or pistols.
Health and Safety
Dist - USNAC **Prod** - NMAC 1978

Trauma 43 MIN
U-matic / VHS
Attorneys' Guide to Medicine Series
Color (PRO)
Focuses on commonly litigated injuries caused by vehicular and industrial accidents. Explains priorities in treating multiple trauma.
Civics and Political Systems; Health and Safety
Dist - ABACPE **Prod** - PBI

Trauma and Shock 17 MIN
16mm / U-matic / VHS
Emergency First Aid Series
Color (J)
LC 80-701502
Dramatizes situations involving trauma and shock and shows how each victim should be treated.
Health and Safety
Dist - JOU **Prod** - MLIC 1980

Trauma Care - a Life at Stake 23 MIN
U-matic / VHS / 16mm
Color (J H C G T A)
$40 rental _ #9539
Gives instruction on what the average citizen can do to render emergency aid to a trauma victim before the arrival of health care professionals. Teaches lifesaving measures and educates the public on how to cope with the physical and emotional stress of trauma.
Health and Safety
Dist - AIMS **Prod** - AIMS 1977

Trauma Care - a Life at Stake 23 MIN
U-matic / VHS / 16mm
Color (J) (SPANISH ARABIC)
LC 78-700627
Uses reenactments of actual situations to illustrate how trauma can happen, how improper emergency assistance might be administered and how proper emergency care should be rendered to the victim before taking him to the hospital.
Foreign Language; Health and Safety
Dist - AIMS **Prod** - CAHILL 1977

Trauma care - a life at stake 23 MIN
VHS
Color (I J H G)
$49.95 purchase _ #AM9539
Features a nurse, a physician and a paramedic who give instruction on what the average citizen can do to render emergency aid to a trauma victim before the arrival of health care professionals. Teaches lifesaving measures and educates the public on how to cope with the physical and emotional stress of trauma.
Health and Safety; Psychology; Sociology
Dist - AAVIM **Prod** - AAVIM 1992

Trauma emergency 28 MIN
VHS
Color (C A)
$325.00 purchase
Provides training for first response personnel in recognizing trauma and beginning appropriate care. Covers trauma associated with vehicle accidents, wounds, burns and shock, with emphasis on patient assessment and communication and coordination with other caregivers. Useful for introductory and for continuing education training for ambulance, emergency medical, police, hospital, military and industrial personnel.
Health and Safety; Social Science
Dist - PFP

Trauma - It's an Emergency 25 MIN
VHS / U-matic
Killers Series
Color
Explores what is, and what isn't, being done for the 52 million Americans who are injured in accidents and violent crimes each year. Answers these questions by learning how they can prevent accidents and what they can do to save the lives of trauma victim.
Health and Safety; Sociology
Dist - MEDCOM **Prod** - MEDCOM

Trauma nursing - Part I 28 MIN
VHS
Trauma nursing series
Color (C PRO)
$285.00 purchase, $70.00 rental _ #6010S, #6010V
Presents part I of a two - part series on trauma nursing. Focuses on the primary survey and assessment of the trauma patient. Discusses immediate life - threatening conditions - A - Airway; B - Breathing - ventilation; C - Circulation; D - Disability; and E - Exposure. Illustrates how to assess, what injuries look like and methods of treatment. Considers psychological care of the patient. Follows the protocol of the American College of Surgeons Advanced Trauma Life Support which consists of the primary patient survey, resuscitation methods, secondary survey, definitive care, reevaluation of the patient and patient response to treatment. Produced by Health and Sciences Network.
Health and Safety
Dist - AJN

Trauma nursing - Part II 28 MIN
VHS
Trauma nursing series
Color (C PRO)
$285.00 purchase, $70.00 rental _ #6011S, #6011V
Presents part II of a two - part series on trauma nursing. Details the secondary survey in comprehensive injury identification. Discusses nurse role in head - to - toe assessment, monitoring, anticipation of diagnostic and therapeutic procedures. Demonstrates patient assessment and resuscitation, identifying injuries, initial treatment of potentially life - threatening injuries. Covers secondary survey tests, plan development for patient transfer, documentation. Follows protocol of the American College of Surgeons Advanced Trauma Life Support consisting of primary patient survey, resuscitation methods, secondary survey, definitive care, reevaluation of the patient and patient response to treatment. Produced by Health and Sciences Network.
Health and Safety
Dist - AJN

Trauma nursing series
Presents a two - part series on trauma nursing. Follows protocol of the American College of Surgeons Advanced Trauma Life Support consisting of primary patient survey, resuscitation methods, secondary survey, definitive care, reevaluation of the patient and patient response to treatment. Produced by Health and Sciences Network.
Trauma nursing - Part I 28 MIN
Trauma nursing - Part II 28 MIN
Dist - AJN

The Trauma of Treatment - a Patient's First Experience in Physical Therapy 15 MIN
16mm
Color (PRO)
LC 73-706384
Presents the story of a young man's first physical therapy experience after a motorcycle accident. Shows therapists evaluating and treating his brachial plexus injury with professional competence and outward warmth, but their failure to communicate effectively causes anxieties to build up.
Health and Safety; Psychology; Sociology
Dist - USC **Prod** - USC 1970

Trauma run - emergency response and reaction skills for children 19 MIN
VHS
Color (P I) (SPANISH)
$89.95 purchase _ #10375VG
Teaches children how to act quickly in an emergency as well as alleviating fears and misconceptions about hospitals, ambulances and emergency rooms. Presents the story of a bike accident and the proper procedures for helping an injured person. Focuses on knowing bike safety, first aid and basic life support. Includes a leader's guide and blackline masters.
Health and Safety; Psychology
Dist - UNL

Trauma Series
Bleeding and Bandaging 25 MIN
Fractures and Splinting 26 MIN
Shock 15 MIN
Transportation of the Injured 15 MIN
Dist - PRIMED

Trauma Stress Management 12 MIN
U-matic / VHS / 16mm
Stress Management System Series Film 2
Color (A)
Uses case histories to explore effective and ineffective techniques of stress management.
Psychology
Dist - CORF **Prod** - CORF 1983

Traumatic and Chemical Asphyxiation 55 MIN
16mm
Clinical Pathology - Forensic Medicine Outlines Series
B&W (PRO)
Discusses natural and traumatic causes of asphyxiation.
Psychology
Dist - NMAC **Prod** - NMAC 1970

Traumatic and Chemical Asphyxiation, Pt 1 28 MIN
16mm
Clinical Pathology - Forensic Medicine Outlines Series
B&W (PRO)
LC 74-705850
Discusses natural and traumatic causes of asphyxiation, such as strangulation, suffocation, drowning, inhalation of suffocating gases, pressure on the chest, strangulation due to food swallowing, carbon monoxide poisoning, glue sniffing and anesthetic gases. (Kinescope).
Science - Natural
Dist - USNAC **Prod** - NMAC 1970

Traumatic and Chemical Asphyxiation, Pt 2 28 MIN
16mm
Clinical Pathology - Forensic Medicine Outlines Series
B&W (PRO)
LC 74-705851
Discusses natural and traumatic causes of asphyxiation, such as strangulation, suffocation, drowning, inhalation of suffocating gases, pressure on the chest, strangulation due to food swallowing, carbon monoxide poisoning, glue sniffing and anesthetic gases. (Kinescope).
Science - Natural
Dist - USNAC **Prod** - NMAC 1970

Traumatic and Chemical Asphyxiation, Pt 2 27 MIN
U-matic
Forensic Medicine Series
Color (PRO)
Discusses natural and traumatic causes of asphyxiation. Includes strangulation, suffocation, drowning, inhalation of lethal gases, pressure on the chest, strangulation due to food swallowing, carbon monoxide poisoning, glue sniffing and anesthetic gases. Features Dr Milton Helpern, Chief Medical Examiner for the City of New York, presenting the material and its medical - legal aspects.
Civics and Political Systems; Health and Safety
Dist - PRIMED **Prod** - PRIMED

Traumatic Aneurysm of the Thoracic Aorta Resection and Direct Reanastomosis 22 MIN
16mm
Color (PRO)
Introduces a new concept in the surgical management of traumatic aneurysm of the thoracic aorta. Shows that the aneurysm was resected with the aid of left atrialfemoral artery by - pass, and the aorta reanastomosed without interposition of a graft.
Health and Safety; Science
Dist - ACY **Prod** - ACYDGD 1960

Traumatic brain injury - Tape 16 52 MIN
VHS
Legal Challenges in special education series
Color (G PRO A)
$90.00 purchase
Features Reed Martin, attorney, in the 16th part of a 17 - part series on legal challenges in special education. Focuses on traumatic brain injury. Includes print resource materials.
Civics and Political Systems; Education; Psychology
Dist - BAXMED

Traumatic Hernia of the Diaphragm 25 MIN
16mm
Color (PRO)
Demonstrates various pathological and clinical problems which have resulted from traumatic injuries of the diaphragm.
Health and Safety; Science
Dist - ACY **Prod** - ACYDGD 1956

Traumatic Injuries 156 MIN
U-matic
Forensic Medicine Teaching Programs Series no 7; No 7
Color (PRO)
LC 78-706059
Discusses traumatic injuries in terms of forensic pathology.
Health and Safety
Dist - USNAC **Prod** - NMAC 1978

Traumatic Injuries, Pt 1 39 MIN
U-matic
Forensic Medicine Teaching Programs Series no 7; No 7
Color (PRO)
LC 78-706059
Discusses various types of sharp force wounds, outlining procedures used to examine the wound victim and record information relating to weapons used and amount of force exerted.
Civics and Political Systems; Health and Safety
Dist - USNAC **Prod** - NMAC 1978

Traumatic Injuries, Pt 2 50 MIN
U-matic
Forensic Medicine Teaching Programs Series no 7; No 7
Color (PRO)
LC 78-706059
Deals with blunt force injuries, including head autopsy of a victim of such a wound.
Civics and Political Systems; Health and Safety
Dist - USNAC **Prod** - NMAC 1978

Traumatic Injuries, Pt 3 40 MIN
U-matic
Forensic Medicine Teaching Programs Series no 7; No 7
Color (PRO)
LC 78-706059
Focuses on injury from moving vehicles and thermal injuries.
Civics and Political Systems; Health and Safety
Dist - USNAC **Prod** - NMAC 1978

Traumatic Injuries, Pt 4 27 MIN
U-matic
Forensic Medicine Teaching Programs Series no 7; No 7
Color (PRO)
LC 78-706059
Examines different types of electrical deaths.
Civics and Political Systems; Health and Safety
Dist - USNAC **Prod** - NMAC 1978

Traumatic Instability of the Wrist 40 MIN
U-matic / VHS
Color (PRO)
Presents anatomic considerations, biomechanical bases, and the diagnostic clues to collapse deformities and instabilities following intracarpel fractures, dislocations and sprains of the wrist. Shows Dr Ronald L Linscheid treating illustrative cases.
Health and Safety
Dist - ASSH **Prod** - ASSH

Traumatic Oval Window Fistula 49 MIN
U-matic / VHS
Color (PRO)
Discusses the controversial and misunderstood subject of oval window fistula.
Guidance and Counseling; Health and Safety; Science - Natural
Dist - HOUSEI **Prod** - HOUSEI

Traumatic Transection of the Pancreas Complicated by Intervascular Hemolysis 11 MIN
U-matic / VHS
Color (PRO)
Shows traumatic transection of the pancreas complicated by intervascular hemolysis.
Health and Safety
Dist - WFP **Prod** - WFP

The Traumatically Brain Injured Patient - Acute Rehabilitative Aspects 36 MIN
VHS / 16mm
Medical Aspects of Disability - Course Lecture Series
Color (PRO)
$50.00, $65.00 purchase _ #8826
Presents one part of a course lecture series on the medical aspects of disability. Discusses the traumatically brain injured patient and aspects of his or her acute rehabilitation.
Health and Safety; Science - Natural
Dist - RICHGO **Prod** - RICHGO 1988

Travase Ulcer Care, Adjunctive Therapy 15 MIN
16mm
Color
LC 76-701069
Discusses adjunctive therapy for a travase ulcer.
Health and Safety
Dist - BAXLAB **Prod** - BAXLAB 1974

Travel 30 MIN
VHS
How do you do - learning English series
Color (H A)
#317706
Reveals that Chips wants to know all about Frankie's new bicycle and this leads to a discussion about other modes of transportation - bus, subway, car, train and airplane. Explains how to buy travel tickets. Part of a series that helps newcomers learn English or improve their ability. Includes viewer's guide with grammar explanations and vocabulary drills, worksheets and two audio cassettes.
English Language; Geography - United States
Dist - TVOTAR **Prod** - TVOTAR 1990

Travel 30 MIN
U-matic
Today's Special Series
Color (K P)
Develops language arts skills in children. Programs are thematically designed around subjects of interest to youngsters. Action takes place in a department store where people, mannequins, puppets, comic characters and special guests present a light hearted approach to language arts.
Fine Arts; Literature and Drama; Psychology
Dist - TVOTAR **Prod** - TVOTAR 1985

Travel and tourism 10 MIN
VHS
Skills - occupational programs series
Color (H C)
$49.00 purchase, $15.00 rental _ #316616; LC 91-712433
Features a fishing and hunting guide, a travel consultant, a tour guide, a tourism counsellor and an airline passenger agent. Part of a series that features occupations in the skilled trades, in service industries and in business leading to careers in areas of demand and future growth. Includes teacher's guide with reproducible worksheets.
Business and Economics; Guidance and Counseling; Psychology
Dist - TVOTAR **Prod** - TVOTAR 1990

Travel Barrier 19 MIN
16mm
B&W
LC 75-700703
Discusses the problems of the handicapped in using public transportation. Shows future plans to eliminate many of these problems and offers advice to the handicapped who use public facilities now.
Physical Education and Recreation; Psychology; Social Science
Dist - USNAC **Prod** - USDTFH 1970

Travel Movies - Travel Scandinavia 28 MIN
16mm
Color
Travels through Norway, Denmark and Sweden and shows the world's largest cross - country ski race. Views the culture, industry and recreational facilities in the area.
Geography - World
Dist - EKC **Prod** - EKC 1977

Travel Plans 7.40 MIN
VHS
Spanish Plus Series
(J H A) (SPANISH)
Examines the days of the week and modes of transportation in the Spanish language.
Foreign Language
Dist - AITECH **Prod** - LANGPL 1985

Travel Tales in Flowers 34 MIN
16mm
Color
LC FIA67-1210
Presents the Tournament of Roses held in Pasadena, California, on January 2, 1967. Includes views of the all - flower floats, bands and horses.
Geography - United States; Physical Education and Recreation; Social Science
Dist - TRA **Prod** - TRA 1967

Travel tips - a video travel guide to Alaska 60 MIN
VHS
Color (G)
$24.95 purchase _ #S01470
Presents a travel guide to Alaska. Includes tips on accommodations, packing, shopping, nightlife, historical and recreational sites, and much more. Hosted by Laura McKenzie.
Geography - United States; History - United States
Dist - UILL

Travel tips - a video travel guide to Athens 60 MIN
VHS
Color (G)
$24.95 purchase _ #S00715
Presents tips for people traveling to Athens. Discusses where to go, what to pack, where to stay, shopping, nightlife and more. Hosted by Laura McKenzie.

Geography - World; History - World; Sociology
Dist - UILL

Travel tips - a video travel guide to Australia 60 MIN
VHS
Color (G)
$24.95 purchase _ #S02094
Presents tips for people traveling to Australia. Discusses where to go, what to pack, where to stay, shopping, nightlife and more. Hosted by Laura McKenzie.
Geography - World; History - World
Dist - UILL

Travel tips - a video travel guide to Boston 60 MIN
VHS
Color (G)
$24.95 purchase _ #S01471
Presents a travel guide to Boston. Includes tips on accommodations, packing, shopping, nightlife, historical and recreational sites, and much more. Hosted by Laura McKenzie.
Geography - United States; History - United States
Dist - UILL

Travel tips - a video travel guide to Egypt 60 MIN
VHS
Color (G)
$24.95 purchase _ #S00716
Presents a travel guide to Egypt. Includes tips on accommodations, packing, shopping, nightlife, historical and recreational sites, and much more. Hosted by Laura McKenzie.
Geography - World; History - World
Dist - UILL

Travel tips - a video travel guide to Florida 60 MIN
VHS
Color (G)
$24.95 purchase _ #S02096
Presents tips for people traveling to Florida. Discusses where to go, what to pack, where to stay, shopping, nightlife and more. Hosted by Laura McKenzie.
Geography - United States; History - United States
Dist - UILL

Travel tips - a video travel guide to Hawaii 60 MIN
VHS
Color (G)
$24.95 purchase _ #S00717
Presents a travel guide to Hawaii. Includes tips on accommodations, packing, shopping, nightlife, historical and recreational sites, and much more. Hosted by Laura McKenzie.
Geography - United States; History - United States
Dist - UILL

Travel tips - a video travel guide to Hong Kong 60 MIN
VHS
Color (G)
$24.95 purchase _ #S01472
Presents a travel guide to Hong Kong. Includes tips on accommodations, packing, shopping, nightlife, historical and recreational sites, and much more. Hosted by Laura McKenzie.
Geography - World; History - World
Dist - UILL

Travel tips - a video travel guide to London 60 MIN
VHS
Color (G)
$24.95 purchase _ #S00719
Presents a travel guide to London. Includes tips on accommodations, packing, shopping, nightlife, historical and recreational sites, and much more. Hosted by Laura McKenzie.
Geography - World; History - World
Dist - UILL

Travel tips - a video travel guide to Los Angeles 60 MIN
VHS
Color (G)
$24.95 purchase _ #S00720
Presents a travel guide to Los Angeles. Includes tips on accommodations, packing, shopping, nightlife, historical and recreational sites, and much more. Hosted by Laura McKenzie.
Geography - United States; History - United States
Dist - UILL

Travel tips - a video travel guide to New York 60 MIN
VHS
Color (G)
$24.95 purchase _ #S01473
Presents a travel guide to New York City. Includes tips on accommodations, packing, shopping, nightlife, historical and recreational sites, and much more. Hosted by Laura McKenzie.
Geography - United States; History - United States; Sociology
Dist - UILL

Travel tips - a video travel guide to New Zealand 60 MIN
VHS
Color (G)
$24.95 purchase _ #S02097
Presents tips for people traveling to New Zealand. Discusses where to go, what to pack, where to stay, shopping, nightlife and more. Hosted by Laura McKenzie.
Geography - World; History - World
Dist - UILL

Travel tips - a video travel guide to Paris 60 MIN
VHS
Color (G)
$24.95 purchase _ #S00722
Presents a travel guide to Paris. Includes tips on accommodations, packing, shopping, nightlife, historical and recreational sites, and much more. Hosted by Laura McKenzie.
Geography - United States; Geography - World; History - World
Dist - UILL

Travel tips - a video travel guide to Rome 60 MIN
VHS
Color (G)
$24.95 purchase _ #S00723
Presents a travel guide to Rome. Includes tips on accommodations, packing, shopping, nightlife, historical and recreational sites, and much more. Hosted by Laura McKenzie.
Geography - World; History - World
Dist - UILL

Travel tips - a video travel guide to San Francisco 60 MIN
VHS
Color (G)
$24.95 purchase _ #S00724
Presents a travel guide to San Francisco. Includes tips on accommodations, packing, shopping, nightlife, historical and recreational sites, and much more. Hosted by Laura McKenzie.
Geography - United States; History - United States
Dist - UILL

Travel tips - a video travel guide to Spain 60 MIN
VHS
Color (G)
$24.95 purchase _ #S00725
Presents a travel guide to Spain. Includes tips on accommodations, packing, shopping, nightlife, historical and recreational sites, and much more. Hosted by Laura McKenzie.
Geography - World; History - World
Dist - UILL

Travel tips - a video travel guide to Switzerland 60 MIN
VHS
Color (G)
$24.95 purchase _ #S00726
Presents a travel guide to Switzerland. Includes tips on accommodations, packing, shopping, nightlife, historical and recreational sites, and much more. Hosted by Laura McKenzie.
Geography - World; History - World
Dist - UILL

Travel tips - a video travel guide to the Caribbean 60 MIN
VHS
Color (G)
$24.95 purchase _ #S02095
Presents tips for people traveling to the Caribbean. Discusses where to go, what to pack, where to stay, shopping, nightlife and more. Hosted by Laura McKenzie.
Geography - World; History - World
Dist - UILL

Travel tips - a video travel guide to western Canada 60 MIN
VHS
Color (G)
$24.95 purchase _ #S02098
Presents tips for people traveling to western Canada. Discusses where to go, what to pack, where to stay, shopping, nightlife and more. Hosted by Laura McKenzie.
Geography - World; History - World
Dist - UILL

Travel Tips from a Reluctant Traveler
16mm
Travel Tips from a Reluctant Traveler Series
Color; Stereo (H C G T A)
Shares scripturally based 'travel tips' for the journey of real life Christianity. Jeannette's stories have been visually interpreted to enhance the message of the film.
Religion and Philosophy
Dist - WHLION **Prod -** WHLION 1986

Travel tips from a reluctant traveler series
Don't take off the celebration attire
How to Celebrate in Flight
Is it Possible to Enjoy the Trip?
Life Lived in Celebration
Travel Tips from a Reluctant Traveler
Dist - WHLION

Travelbug Series
The Grand Canyon 13 MIN
Land of Mystery 13 MIN
Mountain Fun 13 MIN
Oregon Scenics 13 MIN
Dist - SFI

Traveler, traveler series
The Great Salt Lake - a vanishing sea 7 MIN
Dist - AUDPLN

Traveler's Cheques - a Safer Way 14 MIN
16mm
Color (H C A)
LC 81-701086
Takes a behind - the - scenes look at the design, printing and safeguarding of traveler's checks.
Business and Economics; Home Economics
Dist - KLEINW **Prod -** KLEINW 1981

Traveler's Tales 30 MIN
U-matic
Herodotus - Father of History Series
Color
Features classicist Dr Theodore Buttrey showing Herodotus retelling outlandish stories without evaluation as to their credibility.
History - World
Dist - UMITV **Prod -** UMITV 1980

Traveler's tales 60 MIN
16mm / U-matic / VHS
Cosmos series; Program 6
Color (J)
LC 81-701157
Shows scientists in the midst of conducting an exploratory mission to Jupiter, using the Voyager II spacecraft. Explains how data on the planet is transmitted and processed. Explores the nature of the Jovian system and contrasts 20th century space exploration with exploration in 17th century Holland. Based on the book Cosmos by Carl Sagan. Narrated by Carl Sagan.
History - World; Science - Physical
Dist - FI **Prod -** KCET 1980

Travelin' shoes 15 MIN
VHS / 16mm / U-matic
Inside-out series
Color
Presents the Billups family's mixed feelings of joy, remorse and anticipation as they prepare to move to Washington, DC.
Guidance and Counseling; Psychology; Sociology
Dist - AITECH

Traveling 15 MIN
VHS / U-matic
Safer You Series
Color (P I)
Tells what to take along when you travel by car, bus or airplane and what precautions you should take to make such a trip safer.
Health and Safety
Dist - GPN **Prod -** WCVETV 1984

Traveling - Consumer Reports - How to Spend Less and Enjoy more 60 MIN
VHS
(H C A)
$34.95 purchase _ #KA200V
Presents a consumer guide to traveling. Offers tips on travel agents, transportation, accommodations, equipment, and health and safety.
Geography - World; Health and Safety; Social Science
Dist - CAMV

Traveling Hopefully 28 MIN
U-matic / VHS / 16mm
Color (H C A)
Profiles Roger Baldwin, founder of the American Civil Liberties Union. Features Baldwin's conversations with Edward Kennedy, Arthur Schlesinger, Norman Lear and Gail Sheehy. Includes archive footage from the Scopes Trial, Klan marches and American Nazi demonstrations, all of which show the relevance of Baldwin's concerns.
Biography; Civics and Political Systems
Dist - FI **Prod -** FI 1981

Traveling Light 2 MIN
16mm
Presents Jane Aaron's film entry selected from the 1985 Whitney Biennial Film and Video Exhibition.
Fine Arts
Dist - AFA **Prod** - AFA

Traveling man 25 MIN
VHS
Pioneers of photography series
Color (A)
PdS65 purchase
Examines the work of Samuel Bourne, one of the best known British landscape photographers. Part of an eight-part series that examines the contributions made by pioneers in photography.
Fine Arts; Industrial and Technical Education
Dist - BBCENE

Traveller from an Antique Land 30 MIN
U-matic / VHS
Color
Explores and explains the Egyptians' meticulous attention to the preservation of the body after death. Includes a retinue of pathologists performing an autopsy to determine the origins of disease.
History - World; Sociology
Dist - JOU **Prod** - CANBC

Travellin Round 31 MIN
16mm
Color (J)
LC 76-701871
Details the adventures of three young Australians as they travel around Australia by landrover and motorbike, starting from Sydney, they travel to the Great Barrier Reef, Darwin, Perth and Adelaide and on the return route, one of them detours to the island State of Tasmania.
Geography - World
Dist - AUIS **Prod** - FLMAUS 1974

Travelling 50 MINS.
VHS
The private life of plants
Color; PAL (H G)
PdS99 purchase; not available in USA, Canada
Illustrates the ability certain plants have to move and colonize to promote their survival. Uses computer technology and time - lapse photography to highlight the process. Hosted by David Attenborough. First in the six - part series, The Private Life of Plants.
Science - Natural
Dist - BBCENE

Travelling Light 30 MIN
VHS / U-matic
What a Picture - the Complete Photography Course by John Hedgecoe 'Series Program 8
Color (H C A)
Features the ideas demonstrated in the first seven programs being put into action in Egypt. Shows holiday photography and its memories, surprises, disappointments and triumphs.
Industrial and Technical Education
Dist - FI

Travelling Together 7 MIN
U-matic / VHS
Looking for Series
Color (K P)
Allows children a personal glimpse at a variety of people mover systems, including buses, boats, planes and trains.
Industrial and Technical Education; Literature and Drama; Social Science
Dist - FILMID **Prod** - FILMID

Traveloguer collection series
Presents information about the historic past and the current status of a variety of European countries, including information about the cities and the countryside. Shows famous landmarks, out-of-the way sites, struggles and hardships, victories and championships, and the legends of the region. Uses live-action footage and historical clips to show the geography, history, and culture. Includes 16 60-minute programs on northern, western, eastern, and southern Europe.
Austria 60 MIN
Denmark 60 MIN
England 60 MIN
France 60 MIN
Greece 60 MIN
Norway 60 MIN
Russia 60 MIN
Scotland 60 MIN
Spain 60 MIN
Sweden 60 MIN
Switzerland 60 MIN
Traveloguer Eastern Europe series
Traveloguer Northern European series
Traveloguer Southern Europe series
Traveloguer Western Europe series
Dist - CAMV

Traveloguer collection series
Americans in Paris 60 MIN
Austrian odyssey 60 MIN
Bonny Scotland 60 MIN
Discovering Denmark 60 MIN
Eternal Greece 60 MIN
The Romance of Vienna 60 MIN
Romantic Germany 60 MIN
A Russian journey 60 MIN
Si, Spain 60 MIN
The Spirit of Sweden 60 MIN
This is Switzerland 60 MIN
Dist - SIV

Traveloguer Eastern Europe series
VHS
Traveloguer collection series
Color (I J H A)
$114.95 purchase _ #QC300SV-S
Presents information about the historic past and the current status of eastern Europe, including information about the cities and the countryside. Shows famous landmarks, out-of-the way sites, struggles and hardships, victories and championships, and the legends of the region. Uses live-action footage and historical clips to show the geography, history, and culture. Includes 4 60-minute programs on eastern Europe - Switzerland, Austria, Russia, and Germany.
Geography - World
Dist - CAMV

Traveloguer Eastern Europe series
Presents a four - part series that visits Eastern Europe - Switzerland, Austria, Russia, Germany - and their cities. Illustrates notable landmarks, special events in history and the legends that are part of of each country's culture.
Austria 60 MIN
Germany 60 MIN
Russia 60 MIN
Switzerland 60 MIN
Dist - CAMV

Traveloguer Northern Europe series
Presents a four - part series that visits Northern Europe - Norway, Sweden, Denmark, Holland - and their cities. Illustrates notable landmarks, special events in history and the legends that are part of of each country's culture.
Denmark 60 MIN
Holland 60 MIN
Norway 60 MIN
Sweden 60 MIN
Dist - CAMV

Traveloguer Northern European series
VHS
Traveloguer collection series
Color (I J H A)
$114.95 purchase _ #QC100SV-S
Presents information about the historic past and the current status of northern Europe, including information about the cities and the countryside. Shows famous landmarks, out-of-the way sites, struggles and hardships, victories and championships, and the legends of the region. Uses live-action footage and historical clips to show the geography, history, and culture. Includes 4 60-minute programs on northern Europe - Norway, Sweden, Denmark, and Holland.
Geography - World
Dist - CAMV

Traveloguer series
Bonjour France 55 MIN
The Charm of Holland 55 MIN
The Glory of England 55 MIN
Portugal and the Azores 55 MIN
Song of Ireland 55 MIN
The Wonder of Norway 55 MIN
Dist - SVIP

Traveloguer Southern Europe series
VHS
Traveloguer collection series
Color (I J H A)
$114.95 purchase _ #QC400SV-S
Presents information about the historic past and the current status of southern Europe, including information about the cities and the countryside. Shows famous landmarks, out-of-the way sites, struggles and hardships, victories and championships, and the legends of the region. Uses live-action footage and historical clips to show the geography, history, and culture. Includes 4 60-minute programs on southern Europe - Italy, Greece, Portugal, and Spain.
Geography - World
Dist - CAMV

Traveloguer Southern Europe series
Presents a four - part series that visits Southern Europe - Italy, Greece, Portugal, Spain - and their cities. Illustrates notable landmarks, special events in history and the legends that are part of of each country's culture.
Italy 60 MIN
Portugal 60 MIN
Spain 60 MIN
Dist - CAMV

Traveloguer Western Europe series
VHS
Traveloguer collection series
Color (I J H A)
$114.95 purchase _ #QC200SV-S
Presents information about the historic past and the current status of western Europe, including information about the cities and the countryside. Shows famous landmarks, out-of-the way sites, struggles and hardships, victories and championships, and the legends of the region. Uses live-action footage and historical clips to show the geography, history, and culture. Includes 4 60-minute programs on western Europe - England, Ireland, Scotland, and France.
Geography - World
Dist - CAMV

Traveloguer Western Europe series
Presents a four - part series that visits Western Europe - England, Ireland, Scotland, France - and their cities. Illustrates notable landmarks, special events in history and the legends that are part of of each country's culture.
England 60 MIN
France 60 MIN
Ireland 60 MIN
Scotland 60 MIN
Dist - CAMV

Travels 30 MIN
U-matic / VHS
Color
Deals with trips to the United States, Spain and Israel.
Fine Arts
Dist - KITCHN **Prod** - KITCHN

Travels in space and time
VHS
Cosmos series; Episode 8
Color (J H C)
$24.95 purchase _ #49 - 6638 - V
Studies how constellations change in space and time. Discusses Einstein, da Vinci, voyages to the stars and time travel. Episode eight of a 14 - part series featuring Carl Sagan.
History - World; Science - Physical
Dist - INSTRU

Travels in the combat zone 30 MIN
U-matic / VHS
Doris Chase concepts series
Color
Reveals a woman's view of the harsh and beautiful realities of city living and her travels through the eternal combat zone of cities and men.
Sociology
Dist - WMEN **Prod** - CHASED

Travels in Undiscovered Country 27 MIN
U-matic / VHS
Color
Discloses the experiences of people who have clinically died and been resuscitated. Points out the growing controversy in medical and religious circles about the validity of these experiences.
Health and Safety; Sociology
Dist - WCCOTV **Prod** - WCCOTV 1977

The Travels of St Paul 22 MIN
VHS
Color; PAL (J H)
PdS29
Visits the places that St Paul knew - his birthplace in Tarsus, Jerusalem and Damascus, Antioch on the Orontes, Cyprus, Iconium, Lystra, Hierapolis, Epheseus; Greece - Philippi, Thessalonika, Athens and Corinth. Ends the story at the Basilica of St Paul in Rome.
Religion and Philosophy
Dist - BHA

The Travels of Timothy Trent 10 MIN
16mm
Color (J)
LC 76-703440
Explains that safety packaging is a valuable tool that offers an additional margin of safety from accidental poisoning of children. Demonstrates this point by showing a child who cannot resist putting everything he can reach into his mouth.
Guidance and Counseling; Health and Safety; Home Economics
Dist - USNAC **Prod** - USCPSD 1976

A Travers Paris 12 MIN
16mm
Voix Et Images De France Series
Color (I) (FRENCH)
Pictures a French girl guiding a young foreigner through Paris.
Foreign Language
Dist - CHLTN **Prod** - PEREN 1962

Tray Set - Up for Various Examinations 12 MIN
VHS / BETA
Color
Explains how to set up for minor surgery, proctoscopic exams, and eye, ear, nose and throat exams.
Health and Safety
Dist - RMIBHF **Prod** - RMIBHF

Treacherous Paradise 23 MIN
VHS / U-matic
Color (K)
Explores a coral reef in the Pacific Ocean, Truk Lagoon. Shows the once desolate lagoon, now a dazzling kaleidoscope of marine life.
Geography - World; Science - Natural
Dist - NWLDPR **Prod** - NWLDPR

Tread Softly 27 MIN
Videoreel / VHS
Color
Portrays the relationship between an older and a younger woman. Reveals the difficulties and differences in their ages as well as their different identities as lesbian woman.
Sociology
Dist - WMEN **Prod** - WMEN

Tread softly 30 MIN
Videoreel / VT2
Designing home interiors series; Unit 14
Color (C A)
Examines standard and custom - made soft floor coverings. Filmed at a carpet manufacturing company.
Home Economics
Dist - CDTEL **Prod** - COAST

Treadle and Bobbin 9 MIN
16mm
Color (P)
Records the precision and rhythmic movements of a foot pedal - driven sewing machine. Follows its floral motifs, ornate scroll work and cast - iron arabesques.
Fine Arts
Dist - RADIM **Prod** - GALENT 1954

Treason of Benedict Arnold 22 MIN
U-matic / VHS / 16mm
Your are There Series
Color (I J H)
LC 72-701147
Documents the intrigues surrounding Benedict Arnold's treason in aiding the British to capture West Point, and the effects of his actions upon the course of the Revolutionary War.
Biography; History - United States
Dist - PHENIX **Prod** - CBSTV 1972

Treasure cay, the place to be 30 MIN
VHS
Scuba World series
Color (G)
$24.90 purchase _ #0456
Visits reefs which offer scenic photography.
Geography - World; Industrial and Technical Education; Physical Education and Recreation
Dist - SEVVID

Treasure City 15 MIN
16mm
Color
Explores the port city of Tampa, Florida.
Geography - United States
Dist - FLADC **Prod** - FLADC

Treasure from the Sea 4 MIN
16mm / U-matic / VHS
Color (C A)
Offers a comedic adventure on the high seas in search of buried treasure.
Literature and Drama
Dist - CORF **Prod** - GOLSH 1982

Treasure ho 15 MIN
VHS / U-matic
Dragons, wagons and wax - Set 1 series
Color (K P)
Demonstrates use of the lever and the inclined plane.
Science; Science - Physical
Dist - CTI **Prod** - CTI

Treasure Houses of Britain Series
Building for eternity - Pt 1 58 MIN
Palaces of Reason and Delight - Pt 2 58 MIN
Recapturing the Past - Pt 3 58 MIN
Dist - FI

Treasure hunt 28 MIN
VHS
Elephant show series
Color (P I)
$95.00 purchase, $45.00 rental
Presents program 26 in the Sharon, Lois and Bram's Elephant Show series. Teaches reading readiness and social skills while engaging children in making music. Each program explores a new theme through adventure, fantasy, mystery and song with recording artists Sharon, Lois and Bram. Uses traditional materials which stress participation - action songs, sing - along songs, story songs, clapping songs, singing games, playground chants and folk songs from many different traditions. Includes teacher's guide co - authored by a music education specialist.
Fine Arts; Sociology
Dist - BULFRG **Prod** - CAMBFP 1989

Treasure Hunt 20 MIN
16mm
Color (P I)
Reveals that when a treasure hunt is organized, the Graham children and Alice the chimp compete enthusiastically. Shows that when some of their opponents compete unfairly, the chimp mates show that they can come up with some tricks of their own.
Literature and Drama
Dist - LUF **Prod** - LUF 1978

A Treasure Hunt 15 MIN
VHS / U-matic
Under the Yellow Balloon Series
Color (P)
Reveals that finalists in a community treasure hunt have trouble if they don't know the cardinal directions or right from left.
Social Science
Dist - AITECH **Prod** - SCETV 1980

Treasure hunt - Animals move - Eight - legged engineer 30 MIN
VHS
Moody science adventures series
Color (R P I)
$14.95 purchase _ #6163 - 8
Searches the depths of the Earth for crystals. Shows how each animal has its own way of getting around. Focuses on spiders to examine their structures. Credits all of these activities to the creative aspects of the Christian deity. Part of a series.
Literature and Drama; Religion and Philosophy; Science - Physical
Dist - MOODY **Prod** - MOODY

The Treasure Hunt (Teamwork) 11 MIN
16mm / U-matic / VHS
Forest Town Fables Series
Color (K P)
LC 74-700395
Shows how the puppet friends of forest town learn the value of working together when they choose teams and go on a treasure hunt.
Guidance and Counseling; Literature and Drama
Dist - CORF **Prod** - CORF 1974

Treasure hunting 30 MIN
VHS
Scuba World series
Color (G)
$24.90 purchase _ #0434
Dives the Caribbean Sea and the Indian Ocean. Visits ships of the past and present and offers secrets and legends of treasures of the deep.
Physical Education and Recreation
Dist - SEVVID

Treasure Hunts 30 MIN
U-matic
Today's Special Series
Color (K P)
Develops language arts skills in children. Programs are thematically designed around subjects of interest to youngsters. Action takes place in a department store where people, mannequins, puppets, comic characters and special guests present a light hearted approach to language arts.
Fine Arts; Literature and Drama; Psychology
Dist - TVOTAR **Prod** - TVOTAR 1985

Treasure in the Pyramid 10 MIN
16mm / U-matic / VHS
Deadly Scent Series
Color (I J)
LC 75-703968
Uses puppets in order to tell an adventure story about an intrepid pair who foil the plans of a group of robbers seeking to take the treasure in a Mayan pyramid.
Literature and Drama
Dist - PHENIX **Prod** - SFSP 1974

A Treasure in the Sea - the Channel Islands National Park 24 MIN
16mm / U-matic / VHS
Color
Stresses the impact of man's presence on the fragile ecology of the Channel Islands off the coast of California. Encompasses their history, geology, biology and ethnology.
Geography - United States; History - United States; Science - Natural
Dist - USNAC **Prod** - USNPS

Treasure is trouble 50 MIN
VHS
Discoveries underwater series
Color; PAL (G)
PdS99 purchase
Presents the problems of historic shipwrecks and whether anyone should profit from salvage. Looks at the growing science of underwater archaeology and the issue of private gain from sites. Part one of an eight - part series.
History - United States; History - World
Dist - BBCENE

Treasure island 102 MIN
VHS
B&W (G)
$24.95 purchase _ #S00552
Presents the 1934 film version of the Robert Louis Stevenson tale. Stars Jackie Cooper, Wallace Beery and Lionel Barrymore. Directed by Victor Fleming.
Fine Arts; Literature and Drama
Dist - UILL

Treasure Island 15 MIN
16mm
Color
Presents the legendary Long John Silver, a venturesome pirate, exploring Treasure Island.
Geography - United States; History - United States
Dist - FLADC **Prod** - FLADC

Treasure Island 19 MIN
VHS / U-matic
Color
Explores the legend of Captain Kidd's great buried treasure in Nova Scotia, and describes the attempts to retrieve the booty.
Geography - World
Dist - JOU **Prod** - CANBC

Treasure island 120 MIN
VHS
Color (G A)
$79.95 purchase _ #TNO101AE
Features Charlton Heston as Long John Silver in a version of 'Treasure Island' by Robert Louis Stevenson. Originally broadcast on the TNT cable network.
Fine Arts; Literature and Drama
Dist - TMM **Prod** - TMM

Treasure island 28 MIN
VHS
Elephant show series
Color (P I)
$95.00 purchase, $45.00 rental
Presents program 28 in the Sharon, Lois and Bram's Elephant Show series. Teaches reading readiness and social skills while engaging children in making music. Each program explores a new theme through adventure, fantasy, mystery and song with recording artists Sharon, Lois and Bram. Uses traditional materials which stress participation - action songs, sing - along songs, story songs, clapping songs, singing games, playground chants and folk songs from many different traditions. Includes teacher's guide co - authored by a music education specialist.
Fine Arts; Sociology
Dist - BULFRG **Prod** - CAMBFP 1991

Treasure Island 40 MIN
16mm
Color (J H)
Tells the story of the gallant young Jim Hawkins pitted against the nefarious John Silver. Describes the plot summary and vivid character studies of the many intriguing personalities in this Stevenson's classic.
Literature and Drama
Dist - FI **Prod** - FI

Treasure Island 87 MIN
16mm / U-matic / VHS
Color
Presents the adventures of pirates and a one - legged rogue who led them to steal, only to have his own heart stolen by a boy's courage. Based on the novel 'TREASURE ISLAND' by Robert Louis Stevenson.
Fine Arts; Literature and Drama
Dist - FI **Prod** - DISNEY 1967

Treasure Island
Cassette / 16mm
Now Age Reading Programs, Set 1 Series
Color (I J)
$9.95 purchase _ #8F - PN681859
Brings a classic tale to young readers. The filmstrip set includes filmstrip, cassette, book, classroom materials and a poster. The read - along set includes an activity book and a cassette.
English Language; Literature and Drama
Dist - MAFEX

Treasure Island 30 MIN
U-matic / VHS / 16mm
Films as Literature, Series 1 Series
Color (J H)
Presents an excerpt from the film Treasure Island which reveals how young Jim Hawkins gets involved in a search for buried pirate treasure along with the greedy Long John Silver. Based on the novel Treasure Island by Robert Louis Stevenson.
Fine Arts; Literature and Drama
Dist - CORF **Prod** - DISNEY

Treasure Island 22 MIN
16mm / U-matic / VHS
Color (I J H)
Presents an animated version of the Stevenson classic, Treasure Island.
Literature and Drama
Dist - AIMS **Prod** - AIMS 1983

Treasure Island
U-matic / VHS
Color (J C I)
Presents an adaptation of Robert Louis Stevenson's pirate tale, Treasure Island. Stars Wallace Beery, Jackie Cooper and Lionel Barrymore.
Fine Arts; Literature and Drama
Dist - GA **Prod** - GA 1934

Treasure Island with Mr Magoo 52 MIN
16mm
Color (P I)
Fine Arts
Dist - FI **Prod** - FI

The Treasure of Alpheus Winterborn 35 MIN
U-matic / 16mm / VHS
Color (I J)
$595.00, $425.00, $395.00 purchase _ #C607
Adapts the mystery - adventure story 'The Treasure of Alpheus Winterborn,' by John Bellairs. Reveals that young Anthony Monday, worried over family money troubles, sets off on a a quest for the legendary hidden treasure of Alpheus Winterborn - but he is not alone.
Literature and Drama
Dist - BARR **Prod** - ASSELI 1990

The Treasure of the Grotoceans 16 MIN
16mm
Color (I J A)
Uses puppets to present an underwater fantasy about ecology and conservation. Shows two Grotoceans discovering all kinds of surprises awaiting them as they roam the sea in search of treasure.
Fine Arts; Science - Natural
Dist - NFBC **Prod** - NFBC 1980

Treasure of Tuscany series
The Cathedral and baptistry of Florence 24 MIN
Dist - RADIM

Treasure, People, Ships and Dreams - a Spanish Shipwreck on the Texas Coast 24 MIN
U-matic / VHS / Slide
Color; Mono (I J)
Presents a three part presentation about three Spanish ships which were wrecked on Padre Island while sailing to Spain in 1554. I. The Voyage, tells of travelers' and crew's reasons for being on board and trip conditions. II. Shipwreck, tells of travelers' struggles at sea and on land after shipwreck. III. The Past And The Present, discusses recovery and cleaning of artifacts from wreck site.
History - United States; Sociology
Dist - UTXITC **Prod** - UTXITC 1981

Treasure Search, Pt 1 - Diamonds in the Surf 28 MIN
VHS / U-matic
Color
LC 84-707119
Presents treasure hunters who use metal detectors to locate lost valuables in the shallow waters of Chesapeake Bay. Shows them recovering coins, jewelry and other collectibles and researching their value in books, newspaper and interviews. Explains how their hobby became a full - time occupation.
Business and Economics; Physical Education and Recreation
Dist - CREVID **Prod** - CREVID 1983

The Treasure Trail 15 MIN
U-matic
Two Plus You - Math Patrol One Series
Color (K P)
Presents the mathematical concepts of cardinal and ordinal aspects of the numbers from one to 10 and the concept of length.
Education; Mathematics
Dist - TVOTAR **Prod** - TVOTAR 1976

Treasured islands - Robert Louis Stevenson in the Pacific 56 MIN
VHS
Color (H C G)
$195.00 purchase, $40.00 rental _ #38184
Chronicles the last five years that Robert L Stevenson spent in the South Pacific. Provides a perceptive look at traditional Samoan culture and the early colonial history of Western Samoa. Produced by Prof Lowell Holmes, Dept of Anthropology, Wichita State University.
History - World; Literature and Drama; Sociology
Dist - UCEMC

Treasures 20 MIN
VHS
Color (G R)
$24.95 purchase _ #87EE0101
Portrays Mr Rich Man, who truly seeks to 'take it with him.' Shows that as Mr Rich Man goes along, he must rid himself of more and more of his possessions.
Guidance and Counseling; Literature and Drama; Religion and Philosophy
Dist - CPH **Prod** - CPH

Treasures 22 MIN
VHS
Color (J H C G A R)
$24.95 purchase, $10.00 rental _ #35 - 8101 - 19
Presents an allegorical story about stewardship. Profiles The Rich Man, who heads for the Kingdom Trail with all of his possessions. Shows that as The Rich Man goes along, he is forced to discard more and more of his possessions.
Religion and Philosophy
Dist - APH **Prod** - FAMF

Treasures from the Past 59 MIN
VHS / U-matic
Color (G)
Celebrates the arts of restoration and preservation as various works are rescued from oblivion, such as Leonardo's 'Last Supper', Curtis's 'Jenny', and more.
Fine Arts; History - World; Sociology
Dist - NGS **Prod** - NGS

Treasures in Snow 7 MIN
VHS / 16mm
Color (I J)
Explains that snow is a storehouse for water, a source of power for generating electricity and a source of recreation. Presents the concepts of evaporation and condensation. Shows the symmetrical perfection of individual snowflakes.
Science - Physical
Dist - MIS **Prod** - MIS 1955

The Treasures of Abu Simbel 3 MIN
16mm
Screen news digest series; Vol 6; Issue 10
B&W
LC FIA68-2083
Shows how the ancient statues and treasures of Abu Simbel in Egypt are threatened by the building of the Aswan Dam. Uses animation to describe the UNESCO plan to reassemble them on higher ground.
Geography - World; Science - Physical
Dist - HEARST **Prod** - HEARST 1964

Treasures of Canned Salmon 21 MIN
16mm
Color
Presents the story of canned salmon from the time it is caught through canning to use in soups, salads, main dishes and sandwiches.
Home Economics
Dist - MTP **Prod** - MTP

Treasures of France on Video Series
Chateaux de la Loire 55 MIN
Mont Saint Michel 55 MIN
Versailles 55 MIN
Dist - NORTNJ

Treasures of Germany 28 MIN
16mm
Color (C A)
Explores the art and architecture of the Federal Republic of Germany, and traces Germany's cultural history using the masterworks of different historical periods. Explains how skilled German artisans have interpreted the Central European spirit down through the ages.
Geography - World; History - World
Dist - WSTGLC **Prod** - WSTGLC

The Treasures of Jasna Gora - Skarby Jasnej Gory 60 MIN
VHS
Color (G A) (POLISH)
$29.95 purchase _ #V138, #V139
Visits Jana Gora, the Shrine of the Black Madonna in Czestochowa. Features the Chapel of Our Lady, the Basilica, the Treasury, the Arsenal and the Library. Also available with Polish narration.
Geography - World
Dist - POLART

The Treasures of King Tut 15 MIN
16mm
Color (I)
LC 78-700513
Surveys the art objects, gold and jewels found in King Tut's tomb.
Fine Arts; History - World
Dist - SRA **Prod** - SRA 1978

Treasures of Neptune - Klondike on the Ocean Floor 26 MIN
VHS / 16mm
Blue Revolution Series
Color (J)
$149.00 purchase, $75.00 rental _ #QD - 2291
Examines how the exploration of the sea made possible by new technology has led to both wealth and damaged marine ecosystems. The 11th of 16 installments of the Blue Revolution Series.
Science - Physical; Social Science
Dist - FOTH

Treasures of Pearl Island - Shells from Central America 21 MIN
U-matic / VHS / 16mm
Color (I H A)
MP=$475.00
Shows unusual shell life around the Pearl Archipelagoes. A variety of shell life is seen including a small cone shell which is able to kill larger predators.
Science - Natural
Dist - LANDMK **Prod** - LANDMK 1985

Treasures of Polish culture - Pomniki i skarby kultury narodowej 125 MIN
VHS
Color; B&W (J H C G) (POLISH)
$29.95 purchase _ #V295
Presents the second in a series designed for young people to show them examples of Polish culture. Contains six documents that were recorded from 1960 through 1985 about Polish castles. Shows Wawel Hill, Lazienki Park, Jasna Gora treasures, and Gniezno Cathedral.
Geography - World; Sociology
Dist - POLART

Treasures of San Marco 40 MIN
VHS / U-matic / 16mm
Color (C)
$89.95 purchase _ #EX133
Tours the Basilica of St Mark in Venice. Presents the art of the Basilica within the context of the cultures that forged Venice.
Fine Arts; Geography - World; History - World
Dist - FOTH **Prod** - FOTH

Treasures of the British crown 100 MIN
VHS
Color (H C G T A)
$39.95 purchase _ #S01448
Presents the British royal art collection, the largest private art collection in the world. Includes commentary from members of the royal family, as well as historical and artistic connections with the works. Hosted by Sir Huw Wheldon, former managing director of the BBC.
Civics and Political Systems; Fine Arts; History - World
Dist - UILL **Prod** - UILL

Treasures of the British Crown 98 MIN
VHS
Color (S)
$29.95 purchase _ #781 - 9010
Joins Sir Huw Wheldon for an inside look at the incomparable riches of the largest private art collection in the world. Features members of the Royal Family speaking of the collection, which includes works by most of the great masters of painting. Offers a privileged view of ceremonies and masterpieces not usually seen by the public inside the royal residences.
Civics and Political Systems; Fine Arts; Geography - World; History - World
Dist - FI **Prod** - BBCTV 1987

Treasures of the Earth 15 MIN
U-matic / VHS / 16mm
Rev.
Color (I J)
$49.95 purchase _ #Q10028; LC 74-703683
Describes the forces in the Earth's crust which cause deformations in rocks, thereby allowing concentration of minerals by various kinds of water action. Discusses coal formation and the accumulation of oil. Animation.
Science - Natural; Science - Physical
Dist - CF **Prod** - CF 1974

Treasures of the greenbelt 28 MIN
VHS
San Francisco Bay area - land and water series
Color (I J H C G)
$195.00 purchase, $40.00 rental _ #37989
Reveals that the nine counties surrounding San Francisco Bay hold some of the most beautiful and productive land in America - 4 million acres of parks and watersheds, farms and ranches, forests and vineyards - the 'Greenbelt' of the urban Bay Area. Explains the Greenbelt concept and its importance to the region ecologically and in terms of quality of life. Includes a real cowboy who works his cattle one hour from San Francisco, a master grapevine pruner in Napa Valley, the rare and endangered Mission Blue butterfly, antler - crashing tule elk in Point Reyes National Seashore. Hosted by San Francisco TV personality Jerry Graham. Produced by Chris Beaver and Judy Irving. Part of a two - part series.
Geography - United States
Dist - UCEMC

Treasures of the Gulf 50 MIN
U-matic / VHS
Color (H C A)
Looks at how the Persian Gulf has maintained its ecological balance of marine life and vast oil fields but is now threatened with devastation as the war between Iran and Iraq heats up with attacks on the oil wells and tankers.
Geography - World; Science - Natural
Dist - FI **Prod** - WNETTV

Treasures of the Holy Land - Ancient Art from the Israel Museum 30 MIN
VHS
Color (S)
$29.95 purchase _ #412 - 9062
Reviews a special exhibition of the Metropolitan Museum of Art representing more than ten thousand years' history of the Holy Land. Features Museum Director Philippe de Montebello who guides viewers through a rich sampling of artifacts mentioned in the Bible to the museum's crowning glory, two of the priceless Dead Sea Scrolls.
Fine Arts; History - World; Literature and Drama; Religion and Philosophy
Dist - FI **Prod** - MMOA 1986

Treasures of the Titanic
VHS
Color (H C A)
$29.95 purchase
Takes an underwater expedition to see the remains of the Titanic, which sank on its maiden voyage across the Atlantic in 1912, and the artifacts contained in the ship.
History - United States
Dist - PBS **Prod** - WNETTV

Treasures of the Titanic 60 MIN
VHS
Color (G)
$29.95 purchase _ #0818
Traces the history of the Titanic, from its construction through its sinking to its rediscovery with modern technology.
History - World; Physical Education and Recreation
Dist - SEVVID

Treasures of the Uffizi 28 MIN
16mm
Color (I J)
European art authority, Pietro Annigoni, comments on art works in the Uffizi, a one - time office building of Florence, Italy, used by the 15th century medici family who collected and preserved many paintings.
Fine Arts
Dist - MLA **Prod** - GALERY 1965

Treasures of Time - Oriental Art 15 MIN
16mm / U-matic / VHS
Color (I J H) (JAPANESE)
LC FIA65-395
Shows narrative scroll paintings, ceramic pottery, sculpture made of wood, Chinese furniture, ornaments, and porcelain Japanese screens. Relates these art works to their contemporary periods.
Fine Arts
Dist - IFB **Prod** - HORIZN 1963

Treasures of Time - Painting 15 MIN
U-matic / VHS / 16mm
Color (I J H)
LC FIA65-397
Surveys paintings from prehistoric times to the 20th century and relates them to their own times. Shows how pictures express, record, educate and beautify.
Fine Arts
Dist - IFB **Prod** - HORIZN 1963

Treasures of Time - Sculpture 15 MIN
U-matic / VHS / 16mm
Color (I J H)
LC FIA65-396
Depicts various statuary and shows how it reflects the culture and times of the nation where it was created. Briefly summarizes periods in sculpture from Greek to Renaissance times. Presents short descriptions of carving and modeling.
Fine Arts
Dist - IFB **Prod** - HORIZN 1963

Treasures of Tuscany Series

Basilica of San Lorenzo	24 MIN
The Basilica of Santa Croce	26 MIN
The Cantoria of Luca Della Robbia	15 MIN
The Davids of Florence	12 MIN
Florentine architecture of the Renaissance	27 MIN
The Francois Vase	18 MIN
Michelangelo - the Medici Chapel	22 MIN
Siena	22 MIN

Dist - RADIM

The Treasures of Tutankamun - an introduction to ancient Egypt 54 MIN
VHS
Color (J H)
$99.00 purchase _ #00352 - 026
Offers an opportunity to see the artifacts and learn about how they relate to the culture and religion of ancient Egypt. Reveals these pieces as dazzling examples of the cultural wealth and artistic brilliance of that society. Includes teacher's guide and library kit.
Education; Fine Arts; History - World
Dist - GA

The Treasures of Tutankhamen - an Introduction to Ancient Egypt
U-matic / VHS
Color
Relates the artifacts found in the tomb of Tutankhamen to the culture and religion of ancient Egypt. Photographs show the pieces as examples of the cultural wealth and artistic brilliance of ancient Egyptian society.
Fine Arts; Geography - World; History - World
Dist - GA **Prod** - GA

Treasures of Tutankhamum 5 MIN
16mm
Color
Shows the beauty and splendor of treasures from King Tutankhamun's tomb. Studies gold and alabaster objects, masterpieces of inlaid jewelry and other artifacts designed to glorify the king or to accompany him in the afterworld.
Fine Arts; History - World; Science - Physical
Dist - USNGA **Prod** - USNGA

The Treasures of Tutankhamun 29 MIN
VHS / 16mm
Color (G)
$55.00 rental _ #TTUT - 000
Features an essay on the traveling exhibit of artifacts from Tutankhamun's tomb. Examines the priceless objects and presents a re - enactment of the preparations made to bury King Tut.
Fine Arts
Dist - PBS **Prod** - WTTWTV

A Treasury of techniques - Video One 110 MIN
VHS
Branching out on bluegrass banjo series
Color (G)
$49.95 purchase _ #VD - WER - BO01
Features Pete - Dr Banjo - Wernick who presents hundreds of building blocks for creating licks, back - ups and solos. Teaches dozens of left - hand chord groups, versatile right - hand rolls, classic up - the - neck licks and variations, rhythm patterns and chord vamping for back - up, movable chord positions and more. Includes tablature. Part one of a two - part series.
Fine Arts
Dist - HOMETA **Prod** - HOMETA

Treat Wood Right 22 MIN
16mm
Color (H C A)
Discusses the advantages of using treated wood to control decay and insect pests. Presents the problems of decay which begin from the moment the tree is cut and depicts the operations of the wood preserving industry. Emphasizes the use of the wood preservative, pentachlorophenol.
Agriculture
Dist - DCC **Prod** - DCC 1952

Treaties 28 MIN
VHS
Color (G)
$55.00 purchase
Traces the concept and development of Indian treaties from early European philosophical thought down to 1990s Indian concerns over treaty rights. Dramatizes a speech that might have been made by Chief Seattle during a treaty session in 1855, featuring host John Kauffman, a Nez Perce actor.
Civics and Political Systems; Social Science
Dist - UPSTRE **Prod** - UPSTRE

Treaties made, Treaties Broken 18 MIN
16mm / U-matic / VHS
North American Indian Series Part 1
Color (H C A)
Explains that the treaty of Medicine Creek granted the Indians of Washington state the right to fish and hunt for As Long As The Grass Grows and Sun Comes Up In The East and points out that today the treaty is in dispute.
History - United States; Social Science
Dist - MGHT **Prod** - MGHT 1971

Treating and Preventing AIDS 20 MIN
VHS / 16mm
Color (PRO G)
$149.00, $249.00, purchase _ #AD - 1799
Explains how AIDS leaves its victim with no defenses against infection. Features a heterosexual drug user who describes life with AIDS as doctors seek delaying tactics, treating the infections to which victims are prone. Allows AIDS victims themselves to make clear recommendations, to those who still have a choice, to avoid shared needles and to make proper use of condoms and abstinence.
Health and Safety; Psychology; Sociology
Dist - FOTH **Prod** - FOTH 1990

Treating and Sulfur Recovery Operations 60 MIN
VHS
Process Unit Operations Series
Color (PRO)
$600.00 - $1500.00 purchase _ #ROTRO
Looks at the economical and environmental impacts of sulfur recovery. Covers the Claus and other processes. Includes ten textbooks and an instructor guide to support four hours of instruction.
Education; Industrial and Technical Education; Psychology
Dist - NUSTC **Prod** - NUSTC

Treating Blunt Trauma 15 MIN
U-matic / VHS
Color (C)
$249.00, $149.00 purchase _ #AD - 1477
Focuses on blunt trauma, especially trauma resulting from motor vehicle accidents. Reveals that such accidents present special problems because the injuries are usually multiple and severe. Explores the effects of such injuries, examination and emergency treatment.
Health and Safety; Psychology; Science - Natural
Dist - FOTH **Prod** - FOTH

Treating borderline personality disorder - the dialectical approach 35 MIN
VHS
Marsha M Linehan on borderline personality disorder series
Color (PRO)
$95.00 purchase _ #2840
Features Marsha M Linehan teaching patients in therapy sessions the use of the skills of mindfulness, distress tolerance, interpersonal effectiveness and emotional regulation. Depicts various stages of treatment using DBT or Dialectical Behavior Therapy, in which the use of skills training helps manage the extreme beliefs, actions and attitudes that form the criteria for BPD - borderline personality disorder. Illustrates how the principles of DBT can help reduce the frustration therapists often experience when treating BPD patients and views Dr Linehan with a team of therapists working through these problems. One of a two - part series on Dr Linehan's dialectical approach to BPD. Includes manual.
Psychology
Dist - GFORD

Treating Cocaine Addiction - Successfully, Pt 1 48 MIN
VHS
Color (A)
$225.00 purchase
Uses personal experiences of recovering addicts to illustrate guidelines for treatment of cocaine addicts. Includes suggestions on how to lead drug - free existence and addresses special concerns of freebasers. Part 2 is available on another tape and discusses how to avoid relapses with cocaine and other drugs.
Education; Guidance and Counseling; Health and Safety; Psychology; Sociology
Dist - HAZELB

Treating Cocaine Addiction - Successfully, Pt 2 45 MIN
VHS
Color (A)
$225.00 purchase _ #6967
Presents methods to help recovering addicts stay off cocaine and other drugs. Plans of action are given to handle cravings and avoid relapses. Part one of this program, available on another tape, deals with stopping cocaine use.

Education; Guidance and Counseling; Health and Safety; Psychology; Sociology
Dist - HAZELB

Treating cocaine addiction successfully series
From intake to abstinence - Part I 45 MIN
Preventing relapse - Part II 48 MIN
Dist - FMSP

Treating Crude - Oil Emulsions 27 MIN
U-matic / VHS
Color (IND)
Covers the key points in the handling and treatment of crude - oil emulsions.
Industrial and Technical Education; Social Science
Dist - UTEXPE **Prod** - UTEXPE 1981

Treating depression in the elderly 120 MIN
VHS
Virginia Geriatric Education Center Video Conference series
Color (G C PRO)
$149.00 purchase, $55.00 rental
Outlines diagnostic criteria for various forms of depression, giving recognizable signals of depression in patients for caregivers to be aware of. Discusses treatment methods and the importance of family responses to the patient.
Health and Safety
Dist - TNF **Prod** - VGEREC

Treating Erectile Problems 20 MIN
U-matic / VHS
Color (C A)
Part two of a two part series on erectile problems. Couple discusses anxiety related to sexual performance. Focuses on sexual fantasy and relaxation training.
Health and Safety; Psychology
Dist - MMRC **Prod** - MMRC

Treating Heart Attacks 10 MIN
U-matic / VHS
Color (H C A)
Describes how a portable monitor, originally created for the space program, is being used by paramedics treating heart attack victims.
Health and Safety
Dist - JOU **Prod** - UPI

Treating lung cancer 24 MIN
VHS
Color (G)
$149.00 purchase, $75.00 rental _ #UW3424
Reveals that lung cancer is seldom cured but it can be treated. Includes contributions from a pathologist, a radiographer, a pneumothoracic specialist, a surgeon and a radiologist. Covers the incidence, etiology, histology and natural history, clinical features, investigation and diagnosis, treatments, and palliation of lung cancer.
Health and Safety
Dist - FOTH

Treating medical emergencies 26 MIN
VHS
Color (G)
$149.00 purchase, $75.00 rental _ #UW2357
Covers electric shock, anaphylactic shock, poisoning, dog bites, automotive accidents and heart attacks. Highlights the dangers of high - velocity sports. Discusses what should and should not be done at the scene of an accident. Stresses that the primary factors in automobile accidents and injuries are the use of alcohol and the absence of seat belts.
Health and Safety
Dist - FOTH

Treating Penetrating Wounds 15 MIN
U-matic / VHS
Color (C)
$249.00, $149.00 purchase _ #AD - 1478
Deals with wounds caused by skin penetration which damages the underlying tissue. Considers knife wounds, gunshots, impalements.
Health and Safety; Physical Education and Recreation; Sociology
Dist - FOTH **Prod** - FOTH

Treating Phobias 19 MIN
U-matic / VHS
Color (G)
$249.00, $149.00 purchase _ #AD - 1326
Interviews an agoraphobic - one who is terrorized by public places - who talks about her first panic attack and the development of the phobia until she was totally housebound. Shows a therapy session and describes confrontation and the use of tranquilizers and beta - blockers.
Health and Safety; Psychology; Sociology
Dist - FOTH **Prod** - FOTH

Treating the casualties of the war with Iraq 30 MIN
VHS
America's defense monitor series; War with Iraq
Color (J H C G)
$29.95 purchase _ #ADM433V
Examines how military personnel injured in the war with Iraq were treated. Part of a six - part series examining the United States war with Iraq, 1990 - 1991.
Civics and Political Systems; History - United States; Sociology
Dist - CAMV

Treating the chemically dependent woman and her child 27 MIN
VHS
Women, drugs and the unborn child series
Color (C A)
$295.00 purchase
Presents part one of a two - part series focusing on the dangers of a pregnant woman's drinking and drug use to the unborn fetus. Discusses the patient - doctor relationship and the complications, effects on the child, and rehabilitative and psychological questions that arise.
Guidance and Counseling; Health and Safety; Psychology
Dist - PFP **Prod** - FOCPOI

Treating the enlarged prostate 13 MIN
VHS
Color (PRO A G)
$250.00 purchase _ #UR - 06
Reviews symptoms of an enlarged prostate and suggests Transurethral Resection for patients whose symptoms are causing problems. Uses animation to show surgery in a reassuring manner. Discusses possible complications and shows viewers what to expect during the hospital stay. Offers guidelines for the postoperative period at home. Developed in cooperation with and endorsed by the American Urological Association.
Science - Natural; Sociology
Dist - MIFE **Prod** - MIFE

Treating the Incestuous Family - the Parents 60 MIN
VHS
Color (C A)
$150.00 purchase, $100.00 rental
Uses role play, based on an actual case, of the family systems approach to treating incestuous parents.
Health and Safety; Sociology
Dist - CORNRS **Prod** - CORNRS 1987

Treating time effectively - the first session in brief therapy 50 MIN
VHS
Color (PRO)
$150.00 purchase _ #2984
Introduces time - effective therapeutic methods by Simon H Budman. Demonstrates in detail how to create a meaningful first session. Features a group of clinicians who respond to the case session and Dr Budman's presentation. Includes manual.
Psychology
Dist - GFORD

Treating urinary incontinence - a guide to behavioral methods 17 MIN
VHS
Color (C PRO G)
$99.00 purchase
Reviews the urinary system and defines urge and stress incontinence. Teaches pelvic muscle exercises and explains bladder training. Makes dietary recommendations. Instructs patients, nurses, aides, family care givers. Includes fact sheet, teacher's guide and broadcast rights documentation.
Health and Safety
Dist - FAMHEA **Prod** - FAMHEA 1994

Treating vaginismus 30 MIN
VHS
Color (C A)
$29.95 purchase
Portrays a couple who are dealing with the problems of vaginismus - painful spasm of the vagina. Proceeds to the office of a sex therapist who offers an anatomical explanation of vaginismus. Explains how dilators are to be used by the woman in the privacy of her home. Concludes with a scene of the couple engaged in sexual intercourse. Produced by Dr Mark Schoen.
Health and Safety; Sociology
Dist - FCSINT

Treating Vaginismus 19 MIN
VHS / U-matic
Color (C A)
LC 84-707244
Explains the condition vaginismus and describes its treatment through sex therapy.
Health and Safety; Psychology; Sociology
Dist - MMRC **Prod** - MMRC

Treatment 30 MIN
U-matic / VHS
Fundamentals of Alcohol Problems Series
Color (H C A)
Psychology; Sociology
Dist - GPN **Prod** - UMINN 1978

Treatment and education of autistic children in North Carolina series
Presents a two - part series on the TEACCH program of North Carolina by Dr Eric Schopler, UNC Medical School, University of North Carolina. Shows how older autistic children are integrated into school systems and introduces parents of autistic children to the TEACCH program.
TEACCH program for parents 45 MIN
TEACCH program for teachers 67 MIN
Dist - HSCIC

Treatment and management of opportunistic infections - 3 18 MIN
VHS
Coping with AIDS series
Color (H C G)
$250.00 purchase, $60.00 rental
Lists common opportunistic infections due to AIDS and how they can be treated or medically managed and how survival can be prolonged. States that AIDS doesn't have to mean the end of an intimate relationship and outlines precautions necessary to avoid transmitting the virus. Part of a five - part series for persons with AIDS and those involved with them, detailing medical and social aspects of living with AIDS. Resources are listed at the end of each program.
Health and Safety; Psychology
Dist - CF **Prod** - HOSSN 1989

Treatment and Recovery - Making Changes 30 MIN
U-matic
Action Options - Alcohol, Drugs and You Series
(H C A)
Shows programs and support groups for people dealing with dependency problems as well as the process involved in making successful changes.
Psychology; Sociology
Dist - ACCESS **Prod** - ACCESS 1986

Treatment and recovery - Tape 2 61 MIN
VHS
Methamphetamines - Haight - Ashbury training series
Color (G)
$250.00 purchase
Explores the process of detoxification, initial abstinence, sobriety and recovery. Examines the problems of drug hunger and shows how to engage a patient in recovery. Part two of a three - part series on methamphetamines.
Guidance and Counseling; Psychology
Dist - FMSP

Treatment Available to the Injured Dancer 30 MIN
VHS / U-matic
Dancers' Health Alert Series
Color
Fine Arts; Health and Safety
Dist - ARCVID **Prod** - ARCVID

Treatment by Married Co - Therapists of a Couple Moving toward Divorce 60 MIN
VHS / U-matic
Family and Group Therapy Series
Color
Features a severely dysfunctional couple which is helped to gain understanding of their marriage from past to present and given supportive guidance as they move toward a separation. Shows special efforts by therapists to stop the parents from using the children as pawns and scapegoats.
Psychology; Sociology
Dist - HEMUL **Prod** - HEMUL

Treatment decisions at the end of life 45 MIN
U-matic / VHS
Color (R C PRO)
$125.00 purchase, $25.00 rental _ #900, #901
Examines the real - life situations of Andy, David, Gail and Eugene to present the views and insights of prominent theologians and ethicists. Explains the major themes and principles of the Catholic tradition on respect for human life, the care of the sick and foregoing treatment.
Health and Safety; Religion and Philosophy
Dist - CATHHA **Prod** - CATHHA 1990

Treatment for a traumatic amputation 8 MIN
U-matic / VHS
EMT video - group one series
Color (PRO)
LC 84-706495
Gives a detailed sequence of steps for caring for complete and partial amputations, including application of a tourniquet and pressure dressing.
Health and Safety
Dist - USNAC **Prod** - USA 1979

Treatment for Alcoholics 28 MIN
U-matic / VHS
Color (J A)
Focuses on alcohol treatment such as modalites and 'Significant Others.'.
Health and Safety; Psychology; Sociology
Dist - SUTHRB **Prod** - SUTHRB

Treatment for an open chest wound 6 MIN
VHS / U-matic
EMT video - group one series
Color (PRO)
LC 84-706496
Shows treatment procedures for an open chest wound, including checking for other wounds, checking the airway, removing clothing and debris near the wound, sealing the wound, placing a sterile dressing over the material used to close a sucking wound, and applying and securing the bandage.
Health and Safety
Dist - USNAC **Prod** - USA 1983

Treatment for Recurrent Traumatic Pterygium 12 MIN
16mm
Color (PRO)
Illustrates two methods of treatment for recurrent traumatic pterygium, use of conjunctiva taken from the upper lid of the opposite eye and use of a mucous membrane graft.
Health and Safety; Science
Dist - ACY **Prod** - ACYDGD 1962

The Treatment is the Crisis - L - Dopa and Parkinson's Disease 31 MIN
16mm
Color (C A)
LC 73-703367
Documents the effects of the drug L - dopa on elderly patients suffering from Parkinson's disease. Shows the progress of several patients with the individuals and their families explaining the effects of the disease and its treatment.
Health and Safety; Psychology
Dist - ROLAND **Prod** - ROLAND 1972

Treatment modalities 38 MIN
VHS / U-matic / BETA
Substance abuse assessment and intervention series
Color (G C PRO)
$280.00 purchase _ #805.3
Shows the challenge of initiating treatment, including selecting the appropriate treatment facility - program and significant variables affecting these decisions. Illustrates family involvement in counseling and recovery, and describes the philosophy and effectiveness of 12 - step programs. Examines the importance of after - care and the acceptance that recovery is a life - long process and not a simple event. Part of a four - part series on assessment and intervention in substance abuse produced by M and M Productions.
Guidance and Counseling; Health and Safety; Psychology
Dist - CONMED

Treatment of Abdominal Penetrating Wounds in Civilian Practice 33 MIN
16mm
Color (PRO)
Explains that few injuries require greater surgical skill and resourcefulness for successful management than penetrating abdominal wounds. Depicts the method of managing these serious injuries in civilian practice.
Health and Safety
Dist - ACY **Prod** - ACYDGD 1961

Treatment of Abdominal Trauma 21 MIN
16mm
Color (PRO)
Shows the resuscitative and diagnostic approach in the management of patients with abdominal injury. Demonstrates diagnostic peritoneal lavage in patients with blunt abdominal injury. Shows operative findings in these patients.
Health and Safety
Dist - ACY **Prod** - ACYDGD 1969

Treatment of Acne 20 MIN
VHS / U-matic
Color (PRO)
Reviews several varieties of acne with respect to age of onset, areas of the body affected, endocrine system involvement and internal and external factors that may affect the condition. Reviews the characteristics of the four grades of acne vulgaris. Identifies therapeutic management alternatives for each grade of acne vulgaris and for each of the other types of acne presented.
Health and Safety
Dist - UMICHM **Prod** - UMICHM 1978

Treatment of an open abdominal wound 6 MIN
U-matic / VHS
EMT video - group one series
Color (PRO)
LC 84-706497
Shows treatment procedures for an open abdominal wound with exposed intestines, including removing restrictive clothing, and preparing, applying and securing a dressing to the wound.
Health and Safety
Dist - USNAC **Prod** - USA 1983

Treatment of Aneurysms of the Peripheral Arteries 11 MIN
16mm
Color
Discusses the treatment of arteriosclerotic and traumatic aneurysms of the femoral and popliteal arteries. Discusses two connected cases.
Health and Safety; Science - Natural
Dist - USVA **Prod** - USVA 1956

Treatment of anxiety, agitation and insomnia
VHS
Color (PRO)
#ATV - 368
Presents a free - loan program which trains medical professionals. Contact distributor for details.
Health and Safety; Psychology
Dist - WYAYLA **Prod** - WYAYLA

Treatment of Breast Cancer 14 MIN
VHS / 16mm
Understanding Breast Cancer Series
Color (H C A PRO)
$195.00 purchase, $75.00 rental _ #8069
Examines recent developments in the treatment of breast cancer.
Guidance and Counseling; Health and Safety
Dist - AIMS **Prod** - HOSSN 1988

Treatment of Carcinoma of the Stomach in Elderly Patients 28 MIN
16mm
Color (PRO)
Depicts the treatment of three patients with cancer of the stomach, 63, 69 and 75 years of age, who had advanced arteriosclerosis and coronary artery disease. Emphasizes preservation of adequate blood supply to the gastric remnant.
Health and Safety; Science
Dist - ACY **Prod** - ACYDGD 1962

The Treatment of Cardiac Arrhythmias by Drugs and Electricity 85 MIN
16mm
Boston Medical Reports Series
B&W (PRO)
LC 74-705855
Clarifies current usage of drugs and electrical devices for the control of cardiac arrhythmias.
Health and Safety; Science - Natural
Dist - NMAC **Prod** - NMAC 1968

The Treatment of Dysphonia 14 MIN
VHS / U-matic
Color (PRO)
LC FIA66-657
Demonstrates the use of silicone and teflon injections directly into a paralyzed vocal chord. Demonstrates usefulness of the method in the correction of dysphonia by before and after treatment voice recordings.
Dist - WFP **Prod** - WFP

Treatment of Hansen's Disease 17 MIN
U-matic
Color (PRO)
LC 79-706706
Discusses management of uncomplicated Hansen's disease or leprosy. Outlines basic drug choices, treatment regimes, efficacy measurements, drug resistance problems and research efforts.
Health and Safety
Dist - USNAC **Prod** - USPHS 1977

Treatment of heat injuries 9 MIN
VHS / U-matic
EMT video - group one series
Color (PRO)
LC 84-706498
Demonstrates procedures for identifying heat cramps, exhaustion, and stroke, with differentiation of symptoms for each and the emergency treatment to be given.
Health and Safety
Dist - USNAC **Prod** - USA 1983

Treatment of Infrabony Pocket with Three Osseous Walls 14 MIN
VHS / 8mm cartridge
Color (PRO)
Demonstrates the surgical management of an infrabony pocket involving the maxillary premolar. Shows how the periodontal ligament and bone marrow are used to provide two sources of repair tissue.
Health and Safety; Science
Dist - USNAC **Prod** - VA 1969

Treatment of Mental Disorders 20 MIN
16mm
B&W (C T)
Shows various aspects of a hospital for psychotics, such as interviews of patients and procedures of physical examination when they are admitted, methods of forced feeding with patients who refuse to eat, continuous baths for calming down excited patients, hot boxes and lamps for heat therapy, use of sedatives and narcotics, use of insulin and metrazol therapy on schizophrenics and other types, fever therapy, occupational therapy and recreational management.
Psychology
Dist - PSUPCR **Prod** - PSUPCR 1939

The Treatment of Pain 30 MIN
U-matic / VHS
Lifelines Series
Color
Discusses the medical treatment of pain.
Health and Safety
Dist - MDCPB **Prod** - UGATV

Treatment of Parkinsonism with Levodopa 14 MIN
16mm
Color
LC 75-702333
Depicts the features of the disease of Parkinsonism and discusses the historical and biochemical impact and relevance of levodopa. Illustrates the side effect of dyskinesia and some other major side effects of the medication.
Health and Safety; Science
Dist - EATONL **Prod** - EATONL 1971

Treatment of Patients in Chronic Renal Failure 24 MIN
16mm
Color (PRO)
Illustrates the treatment of patients with chronic renal insufficiency. Includes renal transplantation, institutional dialysis and home dialysis.
Health and Safety; Science
Dist - ACY **Prod** - ACYDGD 1968

Treatment of Simple Head Injuries 15 MIN
16mm
Color (PRO)
Emphasizes the meticulous care necessary in the examination and treatment of the simple head injury. Explains that proper early treatment of the simple head injury will prevent or anticipate the occurrence of serious results.
Health and Safety; Science
Dist - ACY **Prod** - ACYDGD 1954

Treatment of Strabismus 8 MIN
U-matic / VHS
Color
Reviews reasons for and principles of treatment of strabismus.
Science - Natural
Dist - MEDFAC **Prod** - MEDFAC 1974

Treatment of the Borderline Patient Series

The Cure - Playfulness and Other Signs of Progress	20 MIN
Definition of the borderline patient	27 MIN
Problems of the Therapeutic Symbiosis - Helplessness, Self - Doubt and Feelings of	16 MIN
Selecting Patients for Treatment	15 MIN
Separation Anxiety and Wishes to be Rid of Patients	15 MIN
Splitting the Transference - Group Treatment and Psychopharmacology	15 MIN
Strangleholds on the Therapist - Failure to Leave the Office, Phone Calls and Panic	16 MIN
Therapeutic techniques - Pt I - interpretations, silence and how silence is	30 MIN
Therapeutic techniques - Pt III - communications between therapist and patient -	24 MIN
Therapeutic Techniques, Pt II - 'Good Mothering'	15 MIN
Transference and Countertransference	30 MIN
Word Order, the Pause and the Importance of Meaning	15 MIN

Dist - HEMUL

Treatment of the HIV virus - 4 18 MIN
VHS
Coping with AIDS series
Color (H C G)
$250.00 purchase, $60.00 rental
Discusses AZT as a treatment which interrupts reproduction of the HIV virus. Explores other treatments currently under study - destran sulphate, DTC and others. Emphasizes the importance of attitude, the need for support groups and the need for persons with AIDS to take responsibility for their own treatment and lives. Part of a five - part series for persons with AIDS and those involved with them, detailing medical and social aspects of living with AIDS. Resources are listed at the end of each program.
Health and Safety
Dist - CF **Prod** - HOSSN 1989

Treatment of the Mutilating Hand Injury 60 MIN
VHS / U-matic
Color (PRO)
Presents a classification of the mutilating hand injuries with diagrams. Shows that photographs of representative cases taken before and after operation demonstrate unusual surgical technique.
Health and Safety
Dist - ASSH **Prod** - ASSH

Treatment of the ritually abused child 25 MIN
VHS
Color (A PRO)
$195.00 purchase, $50.00 rental _ #D - 221
Discusses sophisticated mind control techniques used by cult members and religious zealots which may leave youngsters fearful, confused and deeply traumatized. Includes therapy sessions and discussion by therapists.
Psychology; Religion and Philosophy
Dist - CAVLCD **Prod** - CAVLCD

Treatment options for early breast cancer 14 MIN
VHS
Color (G) (SPANISH)
$250.00 purchase
Offers a clear presentation of mastectomy, chemotherapy, radiation therapy and lumpectomy with radiation. Features cancer survivors who present a realistic picture and convey hope.
Health and Safety
Dist - LPRO **Prod** - LPRO

Treatment - Tape II 23 MIN
VHS
Proprioceptive neuromuscular facilitation - PNF - Evaluation and 'treatment in occupational therapy - hemiplegic patient in relative 'recovery series
Color (PRO)
$125.00 purchase
Trains occupational therapists and students who have knowledge of proprioceptive neuromuscular facilitation - PNF - in the treatment of a hemiplegic patient in relative recovery.
Health and Safety
Dist - RICHGO **Prod** - RICHGO 1990

Treatment Urgent 17 MIN
16mm
Doctors at Work Series
B&W (H C A)
LC FIA65-1371
A chronic condition of endometriosis is treated surgically with the removal of the uterus. Describes the doctor's method of handling the emotional reactions of the patient before the hysterectomy takes place and follows the doctor as he performs the surgery.
Health and Safety; Psychology; Science - Natural
Dist - LAWREN **Prod** - CMA 1962

The Treaty of 1868 29 MIN
VHS / U-matic / VT1
Treaty of 1868 series
Color (G)
$49.95 purchase, $35.00 rental
Focuses on the original treaties on the Black Hills of western South Dakota. Shows the radically different philosophies of the signers - the US government brought to the table its concepts of hierarchies, boundaries and diplomatic agreements implemented by a strong military and a complex legal system; the nomadic Lakota bringing no tradition of elected leadership, fixed boundaries or even land ownership - their world extended as far as the eye could see and the warriors could keep free of enemies. Explores the legal sophistication and political unity developed by the Lakotas in the struggle of the century after the Treaty. Part of a two - part series on the Treaty of 1868 featuring historic research and photographs and sometimes conflicting opinions.
History - United States; History - World; Social Science
Dist - NAMPBC **Prod** - NETCHE 1987

Treaty of 1868 series
Presents a two - part series on the Treaty of 1868 on the Black Hills featuring historic research and photographs and sometimes conflicting opinions. Offers commentary by Russell Means, American Indian Movement; Joe Assman, a white resident being sued for his land; Bill Welch, Black Hills Hotel owner; attorneys; spiritual leaders; and historians. Includes the titles The Treaty of 1868 and The Black Hills Claim.
The Black Hills claim 29 MIN
The Treaty of 1868 29 MIN
Dist - NAMPBC **Prod** - NETCHE 1987

Treaty with the Blackfoot 28 MIN
16mm
Color (G)
_ #106c 0177 345
Presents some of the history of the Blackfoot Indians from traders' exploitation to negotiations between the government of Canada.
History - World; Social Science
Dist - CFLMDC **Prod** - NFBC 1977

Trecanni video library series
Lorenzo Ghiberti - the gates of paradise 30 MIN
The Medici and Palazzo Vecchio - the Florentine Republic and ducal Florence 50 MIN
The Medici and the library - manuscripts and printed books in Renaissance Florence 50 MIN
Trajan's column 50 MIN
Dist - CREPRI

Treccani Italian Renaissance art series
Antonello Da Messina 30 MIN
Lorenzo Ghiberti - The Gates of Paradise 30 MIN
The Medici and Palazzo Vecchio - The Florentine republic and ducal Florence 60 MIN
The Medici and the library - Manuscripts and printed books in Renaissance Florence 30 MIN
Paolo Uccello Nel Chiostro Verde 30 MIN
Dist - ARTSAM

The trecento - Italian art and architecture in the fourteenth century 26 MIN
VHS
Color (G)
$29.95 purchase _ #ACE15V - F
Examines works by artists and architects of the thirteenth century throughout Italy. Includes views of works by Giotto and the Pisanos.
Fine Arts
Dist - CAMV

The Tree 11 MIN
VHS
Color; PAL (I J)
Portrays a young girl who seeks shade from the sun beneath a mature tree. Shows how she becomes aware of the birds and insects for whom the tree is a home. Under dead leaves, the soil is alive and an animated sequence shows the entry of minerals into the soil and their transport, in solution, into the tree. Illustrates how the tree and the life around it are essential to each other.
Science - Natural
Dist - VIEWTH **Prod** - VIEWTH

The tree; 2nd ed. 11 MIN
U-matic / VHS / 16mm
Color; Captioned (K P)
$59.95 purchase _ #Q10506; LC 77-703302
Describes the beauty of trees and their importance to birds, insects, other plants, animals and people. Introduces the concept that living things depend on each other. A Dimension Film.
Science - Natural
Dist - CF **Prod** - CF

The Tree - a Living Community 11 MIN
U-matic / VHS / 16mm
Color (I)
$59.95 purchase _ #Q10909
Adapted from the film, The Tree. Describes the importance of trees to birds, plants, animals, humans and non - living things. Introduces the concept of interdependence and utilizes live - action footage and animation.
Science - Natural
Dist - CF

A Tree, a Rock, a Cloud 19 MIN
U-matic / VHS / 16mm
Color (J)
LC 81-701240
Relates the meeting of a young newsboy and an old man at a restaurant where the old man explains his mysterious method for learning to love other people. Based on the short story A Tree, A Rock, A Cloud by Carson McCullers.
Fine Arts; Literature and Drama
Dist - PHENIX **Prod** - FLMPRS 1980

Tree again 4 MIN
16mm
Color (G)
$10.00 rental
Fine Arts
Dist - CANCIN **Prod** - KRENKU 1978

Tree and shrub care 21 MIN
VHS
Color (H A G T)
$225.00 purchase _ #BM118
Covers pruning techniques, fertilization, pest control and more. Shows full scale tree removal, shrub replacement and chain saw safety.
Agriculture; Health and Safety; Psychology; Science - Natural
Dist - AAVIM **Prod** - AAVIM

Tree and Shrub Care 20.3 MIN
BETA / VHS / U-matic
Basic Housekeeping Series
(PRO A)
$225 _ #1018
Summarizes methods for pruning fertilization, pest control, and others by using full size models and demonstrations.
Education; Guidance and Counseling
Dist - CTT **Prod** - CTT

Tree and Shrub Care 20.3 MIN
VHS / U-matic / BETA
Groundskeeping Series
(PRO A)
$225 _ #1018
Uses a full size model and demonstrations to illustrate methods in pruning, fertilization, and other tasks of tree and shrub care.
Education; Guidance and Counseling
Dist - CTT **Prod** - CTT

Tree and Shrub Planting 12 MIN
U-matic / VHS / 16mm
Garden Methods Series
Color (I)
LC 72-700803
Explains the care of trees and shrubs, methods of planting, care after planting, transplanting, site preparation and soil treatments.
Agriculture; Science - Natural
Dist - PEREN **Prod** - PEREN 1972

Tree Blossoms 12 MIN
U-matic / VHS / 16mm
Many Worlds of Nature Series
Color (I)
Shows that trees can be flowering plants of great beauty.
Science - Natural
Dist - CORF **Prod** - SCRESC

A Tree Community 18 MIN
U-matic / VHS / 16mm
Color
LC 80-700113
Presents an introduction to the ecological community consisting of a mature oak tree and the various animals and plants which use it as source of food and shelter. Follows the growth cycle of the tree through the seasons and examines the flow of energy from the Sun and the recycling of minerals from the soil.
Science - Natural
Dist - IFB **Prod** - SHMNKI 1979

The Tree diagram - Part 4 29 MIN
VHS
Memory jogger plus series
Color (PRO IND A)
$495.00 purchase _ #GO01D
Presents part four of a seven - part series featuring Michael Brassard. Uses an interactive format giving viewers hands - on experience with topic. By Goal - QPC. Includes extensive workshop materials.
Business and Economics; Psychology
Dist - EXTR

Tree environment (1) 50 MIN
U-matic / VHS
Computer languages series; Pt 1
Color
Gives definition of T - machine in LISP, as a modification of the S - machine in computer languages.
Industrial and Technical Education; Mathematics; Sociology
Dist - MIOT **Prod** - MIOT

Tree environment (2) 50 MIN
U-matic / VHS
Computer languages series; Pt 1
Color
Lectures on upward FUNARG problem, as evaluated by the T - machine and sketch of equivalence proof for tree machine and normal order algorithm.
Industrial and Technical Education; Mathematics; Sociology
Dist - MIOT **Prod** - MIOT

Tree Grading 28 MIN
16mm
Color
LC 75-700704
Discusses the procedures of tree grading.
Agriculture
Dist - USNAC **Prod** - USDA

A Tree Grows in Brooklyn 128 MIN
U-matic / VHS / 16mm
B&W
Presents the screen version of Betty Smith's semi - autobiographical novel of the struggle of a young girl for a meaningful life amid an environment of urban poverty.
Fine Arts
Dist - FI **Prod** - TWCF 1945

Tree Identification 45 MIN
VHS
Color (H C A PRO)
$79.95 purchase _ #CV601
Includes hardwood identification and timber - forage relationships.
Agriculture; Social Science
Dist - AAVIM **Prod** - AAVIM 1990

Tree Improvement and Genetics 26 MIN
U-matic / VHS / 16mm
Color (H C A)
Shows the forest geneticist using genetics as a guide to improve the quality of wood. Emphasizes statistical analysis. Illustrates grafting, rooting and controlled pollination. Uses time - lapse photography and animation to illustrate stages in tree growth.
Science - Natural
Dist - IFB **Prod** - SUCF 1966

A Tree is a Living Thing 11 MIN
U-matic / VHS / 16mm
Color (P) (SPANISH)
Shows how a tree's life cycle changes through the seasons, how a tree's age is determined and how a tree is nourished through photosynthesis.
Foreign Language; Science - Natural
Dist - EBEC **Prod** - EBEC

Tree Limit and the Alpine Tundra 20 MIN
VHS / U-matic
Color; Audible or Automated Advance (J H C)
$34.00 _ #52 - 3419
Discusses the world of the alpine tundra and the hardships that organisms encounter in living there. Covers tree limit and the factors which create alpine tundra. Video version of 35mm filmstrip program with live open and close.
Science - Natural
Dist - CBSC **Prod** - CBSC

The Tree Lives 30 MIN
16mm
B&W
LC FIA64-1181
Tells the story of Theodor Herzl, who, in his effort to secure Palestine as a homeland for the Jews, obtains an interview with the Kaiser in Palestine in the year 1898.
History - World
Dist - NAAJS **Prod** - JTS 1961

The Tree of iron 57 MIN
VHS
Color (G)
Documents archaeological work on African iron smelting on the western shores of Lake Victoria in Tanzania, East Africa, where Haya people have lived for centuries. Follows archaeologist Peter Schmidt whose 20 years of study have revealed ancient - more than 2000 - year - old - iron industrial sites and extensive oral traditions illustrating the role of iron in agriculture, political power and mythology. Observes the technical steps of African ironmaking and the degradation of the environment caused by this ancient technology. Produced by Peter O'Neill and Frank Muhly, Jr, with Peter Schmidt.
Business and Economics; Geography - World; History - World; Sociology
Dist - DOCEDR **Prod** - DOCEDR 1988

Tree of Knowledge 56 MIN
16mm
Color (C)
$1568.00
Experimental film by Larry Gottheim.
Fine Arts
Dist - AFA **Prod** - AFA 1980

Tree of Knowledge 27 MIN
16mm
Color (C G) (SPANISH (ENGLISH SUBTITLES))
Describes life in Huehuetla, a 90 per cent Totanac Indian village in eastern Mexico. Relates how Indian children are integrated into the Mexican national culture.
Geography - World; Literature and Drama; Social Science; Sociology
Dist - UTEX **Prod** - EARWRM 1982

The Tree of life 20 MIN
16mm / U-matic / VHS
Color (G)
$400.00, $225.00, $125.00 purchase
Documents the Volador ritual as performed by the Totonac Indians of Huehuetla, Puebla, Mexico. Brings alive the mythic dimension of ritual communal celebration in perhaps the oldest surving dance in the Western Hemisphere, dating back to 500 AD. It is accompanied by flute and drum music and narration taken from 15th - century Nahuatl poetry. Produced by Bruce Lane.
Religion and Philosophy; Social Science
Dist - FLOWER

Tree of Life 52 MIN
16mm
Color
LC 75-700487
Explores the meaning of Jewishness as it is seen in Israel.
History - World; Religion and Philosophy; Sociology
Dist - ALDEN **Prod** - UJA 1974

Tree of Life 26 MIN
16mm
Color
A short version of the film Tree Of Life. Presents a lyrical exploration of the unique meaning of Jewishness in the land of Israel, past and present. Narrated by Lord Laurence Olivier.
Geography - World; History - World; Sociology
Dist - ALDEN **Prod** - UJA

Tree of Life 20 MIN
VHS / 16mm
Color (J H C G)
Documents a 1500 year old ritual dance called "Los Voladores" (The Flyers) as done today by the Totanacs of the Sierra Norte de Puebla.
Fine Arts; Geography - World; History - World; Social Science
Dist - UTEX **Prod** - EARWRM 1978

The Tree of our forefathers 50 MIN
VHS
Developing stories II series
Color (G T)
$150.00 purchase, $75.00 rental
Looks at the flight of Mozambiquan refugees to neighboring countries during the 15 year civil war, in which one and a half million people fled, and their subsequent return when the war ended in 1993. Follows Alexandre Ferrao and his extended family as they toil home across a land emptied of people and littered with the war's scrap metal, recounting their experiences of years in exile. Presents first video in the second installment of the BBC series in which the BBC, with the guidance of Television Trust for the Environment, commissioned leading filmmakers from developing countries to create programs that deal with issues of people, population, and migration from the perspective of those directly affected by these crises. A film by Licinio Azevedo.
Fine Arts; Social Science; Sociology
Dist - BULFRG **Prod** - BBCENE 1994

Tree of survival 20 MIN
VHS / 16mm
Color (G)
$380.00, $220.00 purchase, $45.00 rental
Depicts the struggle of the people of the Sahel region of North Africa to halt desertification.
Agriculture; Geography - World; Science - Natural
Dist - FIRS **Prod** - UN 1984

Tree of Thorns 10 MIN
U-matic / VHS
Eye on Nature Series
Color (I J)
$250 purchase
Discusses the many animals who depend on the Acacia tree for food and shelter. Shows how the tree survives natural problems and destruction by animals. Produced by the BBC.
Science - Natural
Dist - CORF

Tree of Thorns 50 MIN
16mm / U-matic / VHS
Color (H C A)
Shows the importance of the Acacia tree in supporting the animal life of Africa.
Geography - World; Science - Natural
Dist - FI **Prod** - BBCTV 1981

The Tree of Wooden Clogs 185 MIN
16mm
Color (ITALIAN (ENGLISH SUBTITLES))
Describes incidents in the lives of four families sharecropping in Lombardy at the turn of the century. Directed by Ermanno Olmi. With English subtitles.
Fine Arts
Dist - NYFLMS **Prod** - UNKNWN 1978

Tree Portraits 21 MIN
U-matic / VHS / 16mm
Color (P I J H C)
LC FIA68-2886
Examines common trees of the United States. Shows the seasonal development and growth of oaks, elms, maples, pines and others. Explains how a tree is identified by its leaves, flowers, fruits, seeds and bark.
Science - Natural
Dist - IFB **Prod** - SUNYCF 1955

Tree Power 28 MIN
U-matic / VHS / 16mm
Color (A)
LC 80-701740
Offers information on converting to wood fuel as a major home energy source. Discusses equipment, costs and safety.
Home Economics; Social Science
Dist - BULFRG **Prod** - NFBC 1980

Tree stands - above all, safety first 16 MIN
VHS
Color (H A G)
$100.00 purchase _ #PP106
Shows bowhunters and rifle hunters how to avoid injury, paralysis and death through the use of safe practices when using a tree stand.
Health and Safety; Physical Education and Recreation
Dist - AAVIM **Prod** - AAVIM

The Tree that changed the world 46 MIN
VHS
Color (H C G)
$395.00 purchase, $65.00 rental
Shows how rubber, the botanical wonder that oozes out of a tree, has transformed modern life in just one century, through its application in the auto industry, medicine, engineering and technology. Visits a research station in Brazil where rubber forests are threatened by leaf blight, large plantations in Malaysia to follow a rubber tapper as he extracts liquid rubber from trees. Examines the industrial processing of rubber.
Social Science
Dist - FLMLIB **Prod** - CANBC 1990

The Tree that Grew Up 60 MIN
U-matic
Vista Series
Color (H C A)
Explores a new, experimental forestry business in hybrid poplars. Wood from this fast growing tree is being used for energy, cattle food and chip board.
Agriculture; Science
Dist - TVOTAR **Prod** - TVOTAR 1985

Treehouse 9 MIN
16mm / U-matic / VHS
Color (P I)
LC 72-711548
Questions whether or not man can live in the world without obliterating its beauty. Shows how a bulldozer operator strikes up a friendship with a young boy who has built a treehouse on the edge of a site the man has been assigned to clear. Ends with the driver unable to tell the boy why his tree, the last bit of greenery in a vast sea of tract homes, has to come down.
Science - Natural; Social Science
Dist - PHENIX **Prod** - KINGSP 1969

Treemonisha 86 MIN
VHS
Color (G)
$29.95 purchase _ #1240
Presents the only surviving opera composed by great ragtime composer Scott Joplin, 'Treemonisha.'.
Fine Arts
Dist - KULTUR

Trees 10 MIN
VHS
Take a look 2 series
Color (P)
$49.00 purchase, $15.00 rental _ #353804; LC 91-707967
Discusses the importance of trees and how all living things depend on each other. Part of a series that takes a hands - on approach to the principles of science.
Psychology; Science; Science - Natural
Dist - TVOTAR **Prod** - TVOTAR 1990

Trees 30 MIN
U-matic / VHS
Home Gardener with John Lenanton Series Lesson 17; Lesson 17
Color (C A)
Stresses that purchasing and planting a tree for the home garden is a major step. Discusses comparing the advantages and disadvantages of particular kinds of trees.
Agriculture
Dist - CDTEL **Prod** - COAST

Trees and our environment 16 MIN
U-matic / 16mm / VHS
Color (I J)
$350.00, $315.00 purchase
Follows Mike who gets a seedling, a small tree, from a nursery. Reveals that he intends to plant it and hopes that it will become a big tree. As the tree grows, Mike learns that trees play an important role in human life. The most important role is that of producing oxygen and absorbing pollutants. Looks at the dramatic decrease in world forests, particularly the rain forests along the Amazon River in South America.
Psychology; Science - Natural
Dist - HANDEL **Prod** - HANDEL 1990

Trees and People Need each Other 26 MIN
16mm
Color (H A)
Many urban forests have been in trouble in recent years. Dutch elm disease, other tree diseases, and insect pests, have all had a serious impact on the quality of urban life. Streets in many towns and cities are stripped of their greenery. This film tells how it could be otherwise.
Agriculture; Science - Natural; Sociology
Dist - UWISCA **Prod** - UWISCA 1980

Trees and their anatomy 16 MIN
VHS / U-matic / 16mm
Color (I J)
$350.00, $315.00 purchase
Examines the anatomy of trees. Looks at the root system, the five tissue layers of the trunk, and photosynthesis in leaves. Reveals that there are more than twenty thousand species of trees on earth. Encourages students to start leaf collections.
Science - Natural
Dist - HANDEL **Prod** - HANDEL 1990

Trees and their Care 29 MIN
U-matic / VHS / 16mm
Color (H C A)
LC FIA67-5548
Describes the principle phases in the care of shade trees, including transplanting, pruning, spraying, feeding and methods of repairing storm damage. Shows methods of detecting, identifying and treating tree diseases. Illustrates dormant and leaf spray methods to protect trees from destructive insects.
Agriculture; Science - Natural
Dist - IFB **Prod** - ISTREE 1964

Trees and their Importance 12 MIN
16mm / U-matic / VHS
Color; B&W (I)
LC FIA67-1247
Emphasizes conservation, the importance of trees as a renewable resource and their role in water and soil conservation. Uses animation to show life processes of a tree and how trees contribute to man's welfare.
Science - Natural
Dist - EBEC **Prod** - EBEC 1966

Trees - evergreens and deciduous 17 MIN
VHS
Color (I J)
$295.00 purchase, $50.00 rental _ #8382
Uses time - lapse photography to illustrate the similarities and differences between deciduous trees and perennial evergreens. Explains the amount of water required by each and the level of carbon dioxide each produces.
Science - Natural
Dist - AIMS **Prod** - GREATT 1991

Trees - How to Know Them 14 MIN
U-matic / VHS / 16mm
Color (I J H)
LC 79-707290
Presents the identifying features of trees as they change through the seasons and examines the bud and leaf scars of the deciduous broadleaved trees as well as the distinguishing features of their bark. Describes and compares the cones and needles of the narrow - leaved evergreens and shows emergence of new leaves and flowers as spring arrives.
Science - Natural
Dist - IFB **Prod** - IFB 1970

Trees - How We Identify Them 11 MIN
16mm / U-matic / VHS
Color (I J)
$270 purchase - 16 mm, $190 purchase - video _ #1083
Shows how to identify trees and explains the differences between deciduous and evergreen trees.
Science - Natural
Dist - CORF

Trees in the Wind 30 MIN
16mm
B&W
Relates an episode from the life of Chaim Soutine, who at 17, despite the traditional Jewish hostility of his family to art, decided to become an artist. (Kinescope).
Religion and Philosophy
Dist - NAAJS **Prod** - JTS 1956

Trees of life 30 MIN
VHS / U-matic
Forests of the world series
Color (J H G)
$270.00, $320.00 purchase, $60.00 rental
Focuses on forestry issues in Peru, Russia, Canada and the United States against a backdrop in Peru where the lack of trees has brought on killer floods and the erosion of top soil. Highlights conflicts in North America between efforts to save forest biomes and industrial development.
Geography - World; Science - Natural; Social Science
Dist - NDIM **Prod** - NRKTV 1993

Trees, shrubs, nuts and berries 60 MIN
VHS
Nature's pharmacy series
Color (H C G)
$29.95 purchase _ #MET157V
Helps identify useful trees and shrubs. Includes little known health tips and scientifically proven information, such as how apples lower serum cholesterol and control blood sugar levels, how blueberries block the penetration of cholesterol. Shows how to prepare 100 wild fruits, nuts and berries in healthful, delicious ways. Part of a three - part series on nature's pharmacy.
Health and Safety; Home Economics; Science - Natural
Dist - CAMV

Trees, the Biggest and the Oldest Living Things 19 MIN
U-matic / VHS / 16mm
Natural Phenomena Series
Color (J H)
Searches out some of the biggest and oldest trees to find out how they grow so big and what they tell us about man and his environment. Shows how information is gathered from trees and how that data is applied to other sciences.
Geography - United States; Science - Natural
Dist - JOU **Prod** - JOU 1982

Trees, the Endless Harvest 9 MIN
16mm
Color
Shows the scientific harvesting and regeneration techniques used by the forest industry to meet the increasing demand for timber.
Agriculture; Social Science
Dist - GPN **Prod** - REGIS

Trees - their Flowers and Seeds 11 MIN
U-matic / VHS / 16mm
Color (P I)
LC 79-703338
Shows a variety of tree flowers and their main parts, and explains how they produce fruits containing seeds for the next generation.
Science - Natural
Dist - CORF **Prod** - CORF 1969

Trees - their Importance to Man 14 MIN
16mm
Color (P I J H)
Depicts the many ways in which man benefits from the fruitless tree. Presents an overview of the importance of the tree to the development of America. Deals with conservation and manufacturing with emphasis on the practical use as well as the aesthetic value of trees.
Science - Natural
Dist - AVED **Prod** - AVED 1969

Treffpunkt - Osterreich 75 MIN
VHS
Color (S) (GERMAN)
$450.00 purchase _ #825 - 9539
Features Austrian youngsters, teenagers and adults speaking German in a variety of everyday situations. Develops comprehension of spoken German for second - third year students. Student Notes accompany the series.
Foreign Language; Geography - World; History - World
Dist - FI **Prod** - BBCTV 1988

Trek 14 MIN
U-matic
White Inferno Series
Color (H)
Shows the trip from the coastal base to Vostok in interior Antarctica and discusses the scientific methods used to measure the age and thickness of the polar ice.
Geography - World
Dist - TVOTAR **Prod** - TVOTAR 1971

Trek to Totality 28 MIN
16mm
Color
LC 80-701270
Uses historic photos, solar observatory footage and live expedition coverage in discussing the history of eclipse expeditions and solar physics. Examines the 1980 Los Alamos Scientific Lab Airborne expedition to Africa to see the 1980 solar eclipse.
Science - Physical
Dist - LASL **Prod** - LASL 1980

Trembling Cartoon Band 20 MIN
16mm
Color (K P I)
Presents animated designs made out of cut - outs, mache, flip cards and stuffed cloth.
Fine Arts; Literature and Drama
Dist - YELLOW **Prod** - YELLOW 1972

The Trembling Earth 30 MIN
16mm
Spectrum Series
B&W (J)
LC FIA68-1272
Explains earthquakes and the seismic studies of the Lamont Geological Observatory of Columbia University. Presents aerial views of two major faults and explains their relationship to earthquakes. Shows seismologists on an Alaskan expedition. Provides scenes of the 1964 Alaskan earthquake.
Science - Physical
Dist - IU **Prod** - NET 1968

Tremors in Guzman 30 MIN
VHS
Color (C G)
$195.00 purchase, $40.00 rental _ #37737
Visits Ciudad Guzman, a small Mexican city south of Guadalajara, to learn what everyday Mexicans think about the state of their country, its economy and its political leaders. Shows that many of the same problems fueling revolt elsewhere in Central America - corrupt government officials, uncontrolled inflation, economic depression and high unemployment - also exist in Mexico. Produced by John Hewitt and Sam Wonderly.
Geography - World
Dist - UCEMC

Trenchers - stay alert - stay alive 13 MIN
VHS
Color (G)
$95.00 purchase _ #6 - 201 - 200A
Takes a thorough look at safety methods and correct practices for trenching machinery operations. Emphasizes moment - to - moment safety awareness vital for safe trench work. Includes awareness training, pre - work inspections, loading and transporting, jobsite preparation, potential hazards, the danger zone and operator responsibility.
Agriculture; Health and Safety
Dist - VEP **Prod** - VEP

Trenching - a Grave Affair 15 MIN
VHS / 16mm
(A PRO)
$165.00 purchase _ #40.0150
Covers basic principles of trenching, such as proper entry and proper sloping. Explains the responsibilities of foremen and workers for safe working conditions.
Industrial and Technical Education; Social Science
Dist - UTEXPE **Prod** - UTEXPE 1982

Trenching - a Grave Affair 15 MIN
U-matic / VHS
Safety for Oilfield Contractors Series
Color
Covers basic trenching activities such as entering properly, sloping properly, dangerous horsing around with equipment and placing of equipment safely. Points out the responsibility of foreman and workers for safe working conditions.
Health and Safety
Dist - FLMWST **Prod** - FLMWST

Trends 27 MIN
U-matic / VHS / 16mm
Seventies Series
Color (J)
LC 81-700254
Examines developments in scientific and social affairs during the 1970s.
History - United States; History - World
Dist - JOU **Prod** - UPI 1980

Trends 14 MIN
16mm / U-matic / VHS
Color (J)
LC 79-701877
Focuses on the rights and responsibilities of the individual in a free society.
Civics and Political Systems; Sociology
Dist - MCFI **Prod** - NILCOM 1978

Trends 45 MIN
U-matic / VHS
Network Architectures - a Communications Revolution Series

Color
Explores the major trends that are leading towards the use of communications network architectures. Presents the layers that are used in network software and concentrates on the similarities between the different architectures.
Industrial and Technical Education; Social Science
Dist - DELTAK **Prod** - DELTAK

Trends 30 MIN
U-matic / VHS
Educational Alternatives for Handicapped Students Series
Color
Discusses individual differences, including handicapping conditions and explores what a handicap means for the student, the parent, the teacher and the school administrator. Provides historical perspective on the development of educational response to handicapped students and illustrates the current principles and procedural safeguards which have been incorporated into state and federal law (Education for All Handicapped Children Act).
Education; Psychology
Dist - NETCHE **Prod** - NETCHE 1977

Trends in Community Health Nursing 17 MIN
U-matic / VHS
Color (PRO)
Highlights the major historical developments in public health and compares them with current trends in community health organizations through utilization of historical photographs. Provides comparisons relating to focus of services, number and type of personnel, functions of community health nurses and mortality rate changes from 1910 - 1970.
Health and Safety
Dist - UMICHM **Prod** - UMICHM 1976

Trends in Information Technology 240 MIN
VHS / U-matic
(PRO A)
$1,590.00
Provides update on key developments in office data automation.
Business and Economics; Computer Science
Dist - VIDEOT **Prod** - VIDEOT 1988

Tres Riches Heures De L'Afrique Romaine 20 MIN
16mm
Color (H C A)
Uses architectural remains, sculpture and mosaics to suggest what the Roman period in Africa may have been like. Emphasizes mosaics showing mythological scenes as well as scenes of everyday life.
Fine Arts; History - World
Dist - FACSEA **Prod** - FACSEA

Trevino's tips for youngsters 40 MIN
VHS
Color (J H)
$29.95 purchase _ #PM12677V-P
Features golfer Lee Trevino demonstrating basics of golf for young people. Includes grip, stance, putting, chipping, sand trap play, and other techniques. Presented in segments.
Physical Education and Recreation
Dist - CAMV

Tri - Continental (Cuba) 10 MIN
16mm
Color
Depicts the spirit of the revolution in music and dance. Shows a short speech concluding the conference by Fidel of the 1966 cultural Congress of the peoples of Asia, Africa and Latin America held in Havana.
Biography; Civics and Political Systems
Dist - CANWRL **Prod** - CANWRL

Tri yoga video by Kali Ray 70 MIN
VHS
Color (G)
$29.95 purchase _ #V - TRIY
Presents an easy - to - learn form of yoga.
Physical Education and Recreation
Dist - WHOLEL

The Triad package
CD-ROM
(G)
$249.95 purchase
Includes 'The CIA World Factbook,' 'Dick's Some of the Earth's Planes' and 'Officer's Bookcase' CD - ROMs which focus on espionage, military aircraft history and military terminology.
Civics and Political Systems; Industrial and Technical Education; Sociology
Dist - QUANTA **Prod** - QUANTA

The Trial 118 MIN
VHS
Color (H C)
$49.00 purchase _ #05719 - 126
Stars Orson Welles and Anthony Perkins in a film adaptation of a story by Franz Kafka.
Fine Arts; Literature and Drama
Dist - GA **Prod** - GA

The Trial and Death of Socrates 25 MIN
16mm
B&W
LC FI68-660
Presents a drama. Before dying, Socrates defends his decision to live his philosophy and place the state above the individual. Depicts his trial at which he expostulates that the unexamined life is not worth living.
Literature and Drama; Religion and Philosophy
Dist - CBSTV **Prod** - CBSTV 1960

Trial and Error 18 MIN
16mm
Search for Solutions Series
Color (J)
LC 79-701465
Demonstrates how trial and errror is the basis for all learning, particularly in scientific investigation. Narrated by Stacy Keach.
Science
Dist - KAROL **Prod** - PLYBCK 1979

Trial Balance 27 MIN
16mm
Color (J H C)
LC 74-705858
Uses animation to show the scientific achievements of NASA's space programs. Emphasizes the knowledge that has been gained from studies of upper atmosphere physics, solar physics and planetology.
Science - Physical
Dist - NASA **Prod** - NASA 1965

Trial Balloons 6 MIN
16mm
Color
Presents Robert Breer's film entry selected from the 1985 Whitney Biennial Film and Video Exhibition.
Fine Arts
Dist - AFA **Prod** - AFA 1986

Trial balloons 6 MIN
16mm / VHS
B&W (G)
$20.00 rental
Offers a mix of rephotographed live action and animation using hand cut traveling mattes. Produced by Robert Breer.
Fine Arts
Dist - CANCIN

Trial Before Pilate 15 MIN
16mm
Living Bible Series
Color; B&W (J H T R)
Jesus is brought to pilate for judgment, but Pilate can find no fault with him and sends him to Herod. Jesus is retired to Pilate who turns him over to the mob to be crucified. The soldiers place a crown of thorns on his head as he is led away.
Religion and Philosophy
Dist - FAMF **Prod** - FAMF

Trial by Fire 29 MIN
U-matic / VHS / 16mm
Insight Series
Color; B&W (H C A)
LC FIA67-664
A dramatization about the attitudes of a much decorated combat pilot of proven loyalty and heroism who is serving with the United Nation's Air Force fighting against the aggression of totalitarian tyranny. When he refuses to obey the commands of his superior officer to carry out further bombing missions, he is faced with a general court martial, disgrace and an almost certain sentence of a coward's death by firing squad.
Psychology
Dist - PAULST **Prod** - PAULST 1966

Trial by interview 50 MIN
VHS
Doctors to be series
Color; PAL (C PRO)
PdS99 purchase
Covers the screening of applicants for enrollment at St Mary's Hospital Medical School in London. Includes the process of interviewing prospective students. First in the eight part series Doctors To Be which follows a group of medical students from their initial screening through their work as newly qualified doctors.
Health and Safety
Dist - BBCENE

The Trial - Der Prozess 270 MIN
16mm
Color; B&W (G) (GERMAN WITH ENGLISH SUBTITLES)
Details the six - year trial of the director and staff of Majdanek, the first Nazi extermination camp discovered by the Allies. Follows a 15 - year investigation into the murder of at least 250,000 people during Majdanek's three years in operation. Filming of the 1975 - 1981 Dusseldorf trial was forbidden, but director Eberhard Fechner interweaves testimonies from eyewitnesses to develop a complex, revealing interpretation of the trial. In three parts. Call for rental price.
Civics and Political Systems; Fine Arts; History - World; Religion and Philosophy
Dist - NCJEWF

Trial evidence - making and meeting objections
VHS
Color (C PRO)
$100.00 purchase, $50.00 rental _ #FVZ020S
Presents 50 vignettes of direct and cross examination, all of which contain possible points of evidentiary objection. Consists of two videocassettes and the book 'Trial Evidence - Making and Meeting Objections.'
Civics and Political Systems
Dist - NITA **Prod** - NITA 1987

Trial evidence skills series
Teaches how to recognize objectionable evidence, decide when to object to opposing evidence, and use persuasion in offering or objecting to evidence. Provides eight videotapes that are also available separately. Contact distributor for more information.
Trial evidence skills series 300 MIN
Dist - CCEB

Trial for rape 60 MIN
VHS / U-matic / 16mm
B&W (G) (ITALIAN (ENGLISH SUBTITLES))
$850.00, $275.00 purchase, $125.00, $75.00 rental
Records an actual rape trial which took place in Rome in 1978. Documents charges brought against three men by a young woman named Fiorella. Looks at sexist violence and a misogynist court system. Produced by M G Belmonti, A Carini, R Daupoulo, P DeMartis, A Miscuglio, and L Rotondo.
Civics and Political Systems; History - World; Sociology
Dist - WMEN

The Trial II and Adonis XIV 70 MIN
VHS
Glasnost film festival series
B&W; Color (H C G T A) (RUSSIAN (ENGLISH SUBTITLES))
$59.95 purchase, $35.00 rental
Presents two of the Soviet films shown at the Glasnost Film Festival. "The Trial" takes a look at the Stalinist trials of the 1930s and 1940s and the ways in which Soviet society reevaluated the Stalin cult of personality. Reveals the "Testament" of Bolshevik theoretician Nikolai Bukharin, who was executed by Stalin. "Adonis XIV" gives a parable of Soviet society, as a "Judas" goat leads sheep, cows and horses to the slaughterhouse.
Business and Economics; Civics and Political Systems; History - World; Sociology
Dist - EFVP

Trial masters forum series

Arguing damages	24 MIN
Arguing pain and suffering	27 MIN
Be who you are	84 MIN
Countering the defendant's annuity expert	33 MIN
Cross examination of medical experts	28 MIN
Damages for soft tissue and spinal injuries	33 MIN
Demonstrative evidence	28 MIN
Direct examination of plaintiff	25 MIN
Direct examination of treating physician	25 MIN
How to persuade the jury	3 HR 24 MIN
Opening statement	42 MIN
Summation	42 MIN

Dist - ATLA

Trial notebook 41 MIN
VHS
Advocacy lectures series
Color (C PRO)
$50.00 rental _ #LSX05
Presents lectures from various law school professors on principles of trial advocacy. Focuses on trial notebooks.
Civics and Political Systems
Dist - NITA **Prod** - NITA

Trial Notebook - a Lecture by James J Brosnahan 41 MIN
U-matic
Color (PRO)
LC 81-706219
Present James J Brosnahan explaining the use of a trial notebook.

Civics and Political Systems
Dist - ABACPE **Prod** - ABACPE 1979

Trial of a civil lawsuit series

Closing Arguments	50 MIN
Direct and cross - examination of defendant	48 MIN
Direct and cross - examination of plaintiff	35 MIN
Direct and cross - examination of plaintiff's doctor	40 MIN
Direct and cross - examination of plaintiff's engineer	52 MIN
Faculty Discussion with Jurors	16 MIN
Jury Deliberations	38 MIN
Plaintiff and Defendant Opening Statements	37 MIN

Dist - ABACPE

Trial of a civil - personal injury case series

Closing Arguments in a Personal Injury Case I	51 MIN
Closing Arguments in a Personal Injury Case II	30 MIN
Closing Arguments in a Personal Injury Case III	58 MIN
Comparative cross - examination of an economist in a personal injury case	53 MIN
Direct and comparative cross - examination of the defendant in a personal injury case	56 MIN
Direct Examination of an Economist in a Personal Injury Case	30 MIN
Jury Selection in a Personal Injury Case - a Demonstration	57 MIN

Dist - ABACPE

Trial of a criminal case series

Criminal trial series	431 MIN
Preliminary Hearing of a Criminal Case	161 MIN

Dist - ABACPE

Trial of a Criminal (Federal Narcotics Case Series

Closing Arguments in a Federal Narcotics Case	45 MIN
Comparative cross - examination of a government witness in a federal narcotics case	27 MIN
Comparative cross - examination of a witness with immunity in a federal narcotics case	50 MIN
Jury Selection in a Federal Narcotics Case - a Demonstration	58 MIN
Opening Statements in a Federal Narcotics Case	27 MIN

Dist - ABACPE

Trial of an Antitrust Bid - Rigging Case Series

Closing Arguments	76 MIN
The Examination of the Expert Witness	100 MIN
The Examination of the Government Witness	69 MIN

Dist - ABACPE

Trial of an antitrust case series

Closing Arguments in an Antitrust Case	122 MIN
Examination of defendant's national sales manager and expert economist in an antitrust case	215 MIN
Examination of plaintiff and plaintiff's expert economist in an antitrust case	224 MIN
Pretrial Conferences and Opening Statements in an Antitrust Case	170 MIN

Dist - ABACPE

Trial of an Equal Employment Opportunity Case
U-matic / VHS
Color (PRO)
Presents a simulated class - action employment discrimination case in which there has been a determination of liability. Focuses on the second stage of the proceedings where injunctive relief is formulated, back pay is litigated and attorneys' fees awarded.
Civics and Political Systems; Sociology
Dist - ABACPE **Prod** - ABACPE

Trial of an Extracontractural Damages Case 24 MIN
VHS / U-matic
Color
Helps attorneys prepare to pursue or defend extracontractural damage claims. Provides guide to theories, strategies and techniques effective in trials.
Civics and Political Systems
Dist - ABACPE **Prod** - ABACPE

The Trial of AVCO Ploughshares 75 MIN
VHS / 16mm
(G)
$45.00 purchase, $35.00 rental
Follows the trial of 13 political activists charged with trespass and malicious damage for hammering on computer systems and office equipment at AVCO Systems Division, a nuclear weapons components manufacturer.
Civics and Political Systems
Dist - EFVP **Prod** - EFVP 1987

The Trial of Leonard Peltier 16 MIN
U-matic / VHS
B&W (H C A)
Reports on the US Government's murder case against American Indian Movement Leader Leonard Peltier which drew many sympathetic Native Americans who criticized the Federal Government, both on the reservations and with the proceedings of Peltier's case.
Civics and Political Systems; Social Science
Dist - UCV **Prod** - UCV

The Trial of Standing Bear
U-matic / VT1 / VHS
Color (G)
$79.95 purchase, $50.00 rental
Reveals that in 1877 the United States government forcibly moved the Ponca Indian Nation from ancestral territory on the Niobrara River, nothern Nebraska, to Indian Territory in what is now Oklahoma. Discloses that this was US response to the confusion created when Ponca land was accidentally included in a government treaty with the Sioux. Tells the story of Standing Bear, arrested by the US Army after leading a small group of his people from Indian territory back to their homeland in northern Nebraska, in defiance of government orders. Standing Bear believed that the Poncas had been unfairly treated and were dying in the harsh realm of Indian Territory, and was fulfilling a promise to his dying son to return his body to Ponca territory.
History - United States; History - World; Social Science
Dist - NAMPBC **Prod** - NETV 1988

The Trial of Standing Bear 120 MIN
VHS
Color (H C)
$39.95 purchase _ #E306; LC 90-708221
Chronicles the struggle of Standing Bear for human rights in the concept that 'an Indian is a person within the meaning of the law' in the 1879 case of Standing Bear v Crook. Focuses on the arrest of Standing Bear, efforts of sympathetic citizens to assist him and the courtroom case that brought national attention to his struggle.
Civics and Political Systems; History - United States; Social Science; Sociology
Dist - GPN **Prod** - UNEBR 1988

The Trial of Susan B Anthony 22 MIN
16mm / U-matic / VHS
You are There Series
Color
Depicts the second day of legal proceedings in which Susan B Anthony is being prosecuted for voting.
Biography; Civics and Political Systems; History - United States
Dist - PHENIX **Prod** - CBSTV

The Trial of Tamara Russo - Pt 4 58 MIN
VHS
Comrades Series
Color (S)
$79.00 purchase _ #351 - 9025
Follows twelve Soviet citizens from different backgrounds to reveal what Soviet life is like for a cross section of the 270 million inhabitants in the vast country of fifteen republics. Features Frontline anchor Judy Woodruff who also interviews prominent experts on Soviet affairs. Part 4 of the twelve - part series sits in at the court of Lyubov Bubulich, a People's Judge who presides over all cases except those involving capital punishment or dissidents. Most of the cases dealt with in Bubulich's court involve theft, divorce or alcohol - related offenses.
Civics and Political Systems; Geography - World; Health and Safety; Sociology
Dist - FI **Prod** - WGBHTV 1988

The Trial of the AVCO ploughshares 60 MIN
VHS
Color (J H C G T A)
$45.00 purchase, $30.00 rental
Presents excerpts from a trial of anti - nuclear activists. Points out that civil disobedience does have legal consequences, and considers the activists' defense that "necessity" justified their actions. Produced by Julie Gustafson and John Reilly.
Civics and Political Systems; History - World; Sociology
Dist - EFVP

The Trial of Uriel 30 MIN
16mm
B&W
States that wisdom and scholarship are precious although they are insufficient by themselves. Dramatizes the moral with the story of a humble water carrier who, in spite of discouragement from learned men, is able to enter heaven. (Kinescope).
Religion and Philosophy
Dist - NAAJS **Prod** - JTS 1959

The Trial of Xavier Solorzano 90 MIN
VHS / U-matic
Color
Follows the proceedings of a real - life trial condensing over 60 hours of trial footage into a 90 - minute program. Narrated by Raymond Burr.
Civics and Political Systems; Sociology
Dist - PBS **Prod** - WTTWTV 1979

Trial practice series - volume 1 600 MIN
VHS
Trial practice series
Color (PRO)
$150.00, $450.00 purchase, $265.00 rental _ #CP-51243, #CP-61243
Teaches civil trial practice procedure in depth, covering voir dire, opening statements, direct examination, settlement, demonstrative evidence, courtroom strategy, proving damages, using expert witnesses, cross - examination, and final arguments in a series of ten audio or video programs. The series is accompanied by a handbook. Individual video programs are available separately in packages that include an outline and the series handbook. Contact distributor for more information.
Civics and Political Systems
Dist - CCEB

Trial practice series - volume 2 - advocacy and management in complex litigation 540 MIN
VHS
Trial practice series
Color (PRO)
$170.00, $450.00 purchase, $265.00 rental _ #CP-54155, #CP-64155
Teaches civil trial practice procedure in depth, with emphasis on management of cases involving several parties, several courts, or multiple causes. Focuses on preparation, development of a litigation plan, and special trial considerations for complicated legal matters. Includes a 312-page handbook.
Civics and Political Systems
Dist - CCEB

Trial practice series

Trial practice series - volume 1	600 MIN
Trial practice series - volume 2 - advocacy and management in complex litigation	540 MIN

Dist - CCEB

Trial presentation 45 MIN
VHS
Jeans on trial advocacy series
Color (C PRO)
$115.00 purchase, $50.00 rental _ #JJX02
Features law professor James Jeans in a lecture on basic trial advocacy. Covers strategies for trial presentation.
Civics and Political Systems
Dist - NITA **Prod** - NITA 1980

Trial Presentation 46 MIN
U-matic / VHS
James Jean Trial Advocacy Series
Color (PRO)
Civics and Political Systems
Dist - ABACPE **Prod** - ABACPE

The Trial - Process 108 MIN
VHS
(G A) (POLISH)
$29.95 purchase _ #V142
Presents a full - length documentary film about events which took place between 1949 and 1956, associated with the so - called General's Trial of General Stanislaw Tatar and others.
Civics and Political Systems; Fine Arts; History - World
Dist - POLART

Trial series
Provides an understanding of criminal trial proceedings in a series 'of five programs filmed by the BBC in the Scottish courts. Follows 'the individual trials of defendants accused of murder, robbery,'shoplifting, reckless driving, and attempted murder. Features the 'prosecutors and criminal defense lawyers as they work to garner a 'conviction or their client's freedom.

Daylight robbery	50 MIN
Loan path murder	50 MIN
One angry man	50 MIN
Sad, bad and mad	50 MIN
Stab in the dark	50 MIN

Dist - BBCENE

Trial skills illustrated - opening statements, closing arguments, direct and cross - examination 90 MIN
VHS
Color (PRO)
$149.00 purchase, $49.00 rental _ #CP-69105
Presents techniques to help legal students master fundamental skills of argument. Provides brief demonstrations of opening statements, direct examinations, cross examinations, and closing arguments. Includes a handbook.
Civics and Political Systems
Dist - CCEB

Trial strategies 50 MIN
VHS
Business litigation series
Color (C PRO)
$95.00 purchase, $71.25 rental _ #LBC06
Outlines appropriate trial strategies for business litigation cases.
Civics and Political Systems
Dist - NITA **Prod** - NITA 1987

Trial tactics - Adoption and implementation of a strategy 210 MIN
VHS
Color (A PRO C)
$52.20, $150.00 purchase _ #M656, #P180
Assists lawyers with the difficult tasks of strategic trial preparation and effective courtroom presentation.
Civics and Political Systems
Dist - ALIABA **Prod** - ALIABA 1986

Trial Techniques - a Products Liability Case Series

Closing Statements in a Products Liability Case	108 MIN
Direct and cross - examination of defendant's expert engineering witness in a products	168 MIN
Direct and cross - examination of plaintiff and plaintiff's witnesses in a products	157 MIN
Direct and cross - examination of plaintiff's expert engineering witness in a products	145 MIN
Direct and cross - examination of plaintiff's expert medical witness in a products	58 MIN
Opening Statements in a Products Liability Case	60 MIN

Dist - ABACPE

Trial Techniques in a Custody Case 74 MIN
VHS / U-matic
Preparing and Trying a Custody Case Series
Color (PRO)
Demonstrates the direct and cross - examination of an expert witness in a custody case. Discusses the role of both direct and cross - examination and effective preparation of an expert witness for examination.
Civics and Political Systems
Dist - ABACPE **Prod** - ABACPE

Trial Techniques with Professor Irving Younger, Pt 1 52 MIN
VHS / U-matic
NPI Video CLE Series Vol 4
Color (PRO)
LC 80-706565
Presents Professor Irving Younger discussing elements, techniques and strategies for trial - winning conduct by lawyers, including jury selection, opening statement and summation.
Civics and Political Systems
Dist - NPRI **Prod** - NPRI 1979

Trial Techniques with Professor Irving Younger, Pt 2 52 MIN
U-matic / VHS
NPI Video CLE Series Vol 4
Color (PRO)
LC 80-706565
Presents Professor Irving Younger discussing elements, techniques and strategies for trial - winning conduct by lawyers, including jury selection, opening statement and summation.
Civics and Political Systems
Dist - NPRI **Prod** - NPRI 1979

Trial Techniques with Professor Irving Younger, Pt 3 52 MIN
U-matic / VHS
NPI Video CLE Series Vol 4
Color (PRO)
LC 80-706565
Presents Professor Irving Younger discussing elements, techniques and strategies for trial - winning conduct by lawyers, including jury selection, opening statement and summation.
Civics and Political Systems
Dist - NPRI **Prod** - NPRI 1979

Trial Techniques with Professor Irving Younger, Pt 4 52 MIN
U-matic / VHS
NPI Video CLE Series Vol 4
Color (PRO)
LC 80-706565
Presents Professor Irving Younger discussing elements, techniques and strategies for trial - winning conduct by lawyers, including jury selection, opening statement and summation.
Civics and Political Systems
Dist - NPRI **Prod** - NPRI 1979

Trial Techniques with Professor Irving Younger, Pt 5 53 MIN
U-matic / VHS
NPI Video CLE Series Vol 4
Color (PRO)
LC 80-706565
Presents Professor Irving Younger discussing elements, techniques and strategies for trial - winning conduct by lawyers, including jury selection, opening statement and summation.
Civics and Political Systems
Dist - NPRI **Prod** - NPRI 1979

Trial Techniques with Professor Irving Younger, Pt 6 53 MIN
U-matic / VHS
NPI Video CLE Series Vol 4
Color (PRO)
LC 80-706565
Presents Professor Irving Younger discussing elements, techniques and strategies for trial - winning conduct by lawyers, including jury selection, opening statement and summation.
Civics and Political Systems
Dist - NPRI **Prod** - NPRI 1979

Trial Techniques with Professor Irving Younger, Pt 7 53 MIN
VHS / U-matic
NPI Video CLE Series Vol 4
Color (PRO)
LC 80-706565
Presents Professor Irving Younger discussing elements, techniques and strategies for trial - winning conduct by lawyers, including jury selection, opening statement and summation.
Civics and Political Systems
Dist - NPRI **Prod** - NPRI 1979

Trial Techniques with Professor Irving Younger, Pt 8 53 MIN
U-matic / VHS
NPI Video CLE Series Vol 4
Color (PRO)
LC 80-706565
Presents Professor Irving Younger discussing elements, techniques and strategies for trial - winning conduct by lawyers, including jury selection, opening statement and summation.
Civics and Political Systems
Dist - NPRI **Prod** - NPRI 1979

Trial - the City and County of Denver Vs Lauren R Watson Series

Trial - the First Day	90 MIN
Trial - the Fourth and Final Day	90 MIN
Trial - the Second Day	90 MIN
Trial - the Third Day	90 MIN

Dist - IU

Trial - the First Day 90 MIN
16mm / U-matic / VHS
Trial - the City and County of Denver Vs Lauren R Watson Series
B&W (H C A)
LC 71-709715
Discusses the trial of Lauren R Watson, a black man and known member of the Black Panther Party, who allegedly interfered with a police officer and resisted arrest. Tells how he and his lawyer doubted that he could receive a fair trial with an all - white middle - class jury. Discusses what is meant by a jury of one's peers.
Civics and Political Systems; History - United States; Psychology; Sociology
Dist - IU **Prod** - NET 1970

Trial - the Fourth and Final Day 90 MIN
U-matic / VHS / 16mm
Trial - the City and County of Denver Vs Lauren R Watson Series
B&W (H C A)
LC 72-709718
Shows the final day of the trial where both sides rest their case after closing arguments and instructions are given to the jury, which then spends two hours deliberating on the verdict. Interviews the judge, the arresting officer, both attorneys and the defendant. Conducts interviews with the jury members after the verdict is returned and tries to determine why they voted as they did.
Civics and Political Systems; History - United States; Psychology; Sociology
Dist - IU **Prod** - NET 1970

Trial - the Second Day 90 MIN
U-matic / VHS / 16mm
Trial - the City and County of Denver Vs Lauren R Watson Series
B&W (H C A)
LC 75-709716
Presents the prosecution's case against Lauren R Wat - son in the first day of the actual trial, including the examination and cross - examination of the arresting officer and a fellow patrolman, the only witnesses for the prosecution. Shows how the prosecution tries to prove that Watson resisted arrest and interfered with a police officer when he was apprehended for an al - leged traffic violation, whereas the defense attorney tries to show that Watson is innocent.
Civics and Political Systems; History - United States; Psychology; Sociology
Dist - IU **Prod** - NET 1970

Trial - the Third Day 90 MIN
16mm / U-matic / VHS
Trial - the City and County of Denver Vs Lauren R Watson Series
B&W (H C A)
LC 79-709717
Continues the trial with the prosecution resting its case and the defense making a motion for a judgment of acquittal and then presenting its witnesses. Tells how the interference charge is dropped for lack of evidence. Presents the defense trying to show that the defendant was being harassed and that he did not resist arrest. Uses post - trial interviews in stating that this trial has political as well as judicial significance and that class in justice must be eliminated.
Civics and Political Systems; History - United States; Psychology; Sociology
Dist - IU **Prod** - NET 1970

The Trials of Alger Hiss 165 MIN
16mm
Color
Documents the story of Alger Hiss, a State Department official who was accused in an espionage and perjury case which first brought then - Congressman Richard M Nixon to national prominence.
Biography; Civics and Political Systems; History - United States
Dist - DIRECT **Prod** - HISTOF 1980

The Trials of Eve 20 MIN
16mm
Color (G)
Addresses the complex issue of women and their place in society. Represents Eve as an artist's mannequin to transcend the barriers of race and culture. Produced by Gretchen Jordan - Bastow.
Fine Arts; Religion and Philosophy; Sociology
Dist - CANCIN

The Trials of Franz Kafka 15 MIN
U-matic / VHS / 16mm
B&W (H C A)
LC 73-701106
Explores the Trials of childhood, youth and tragic adulthood which Franz Kafka transformed into novels and stories. Helps in the understanding of modern man's anxiety and alienation.
Literature and Drama; Sociology
Dist - FOTH **Prod** - MANTLH 1969

Trials of life series
Presents a 12 - part series traveling with naturalist David Attenborough and his crew to exotic and dangerous places to observe the animal kingdom. Observes the different stages of the life cycle of animals and includes a bonus video, The Making of the Trials of Life, depicting the techniques used and the sometimes life - threatening risks taken to photograph the animals in the series.

Arriving	50 MIN
Continuing the line	50 MIN
Courting	50 MIN
Fighting	50 MIN
Finding food	50 MIN
Finding the way	50 MIN
Friends and rivals	50 MIN
Growing up	50 MIN
Homemaking	50 MIN
Hunting and escaping	50 MIN
Living together	50 MIN

Talking to strangers 50 MIN
Dist - CAMV Prod - TBSESI 1969

Trials of Richard - Ability Grouping 29 MIN
U-matic
As We See it Series
Color
Tells how a black student copes with life at a previously all - white school in Memphis, Tennessee. Explores how class assignments in an Evanston, Illinois, school, which are meant to separate students by academic ability, actually interfere with desegregation.
Education; Sociology
Dist - PBS Prod - WTTWTV

Triangle and Anchor - Chelsea Porcelain from the Williamsburg Collection 22 MIN
16mm
Color (A)
LC 78-701824; 78 - 701824
Traces the history of porcelain from China in the ninth century to Chelsea, England, in the mid - 18th century. Discusses the various factory marks used on Chelsea porcelain and shows the development from simple white tableware to elaborately colored and gilded dishes and figurines.
Fine Arts; Home Economics
Dist - CWMS Prod - CWMS 1978

The Triangle Factory Fire Scandal
BETA / VHS
Color
Describes the events leading up to the 1911 fire in New York where 146 women lost their lives. Starring Stephanie Zimbalist.
Geography - United States; History - United States; Social Science; Sociology
Dist - GA Prod - GA

The Triangle Fire Factory Scandal 98 MIN
16mm
Color
LC 79-700372
Presents a story based on the sweatshop fire of March 14, 1911, in which 146 female garment workers perished. Highlights the conflict between organized labor and management and the struggle for better working conditions.
History - United States; Sociology
Dist - LNDBRG Prod - LNDBRG 1979

Triangle Fire Factory Scandal - Pt 1 32 MIN
16mm
Color
LC 79-700372
Presents a story based on the sweatshop fire of March 14, 1911, in which 146 female garment workers perished. Highlights the conflict between organized labor and management and the struggle for better working conditions.
History - United States; Sociology
Dist - LNDBRG Prod - LNDBRG 1979

Triangle Fire Factory Scandal - Pt 2 33 MIN
16mm
Color
LC 79-700372
Presents a story based on the sweatshop fire of March 14, 1911, in which 146 female garment workers perished. Highlights the conflict between organized labor and management and the struggle for better working conditions.
History - United States; Sociology
Dist - LNDBRG Prod - LNDBRG 1979

Triangle Fire Factory Scandal - Pt 3 33 MIN
16mm
Color
LC 79-700372
Presents a story based on the sweatshop fire of March 14, 1911, in which 146 female garment workers perished. Highlights the conflict between organized labor and management and the struggle for better working conditions.
History - United States; Sociology
Dist - LNDBRG Prod - LNDBRG 1979

Triangle Island - British Columbia - Part 1 8 MIN
VHS
Natures kingdom series
Color (P I J)
$125.00 purchase
Visits the sea animal sanctuary on Triangle Island off British Columbia. Shows how sea lions raise their young. Part of a 26 - part series on animals showing the habitats and traits of various species.
Geography - World; Science - Natural
Dist - LANDMK Prod - LANDMK 1992

Triangle of Health - Arabic Series
Physical Fitness and Good Health 10 MIN
Dist - CORF

Triangle of Health - German Series
Physical Fitness and Good Health 10 MIN
Dist - CORF

Triangle of Health - Hungarian Series
Physical Fitness and Good Health 10 MIN
Dist - CORF

Triangle of Health Series
Physical Fitness and Good Health 10 MIN
The Social Side of Health 10 MIN
Steps toward Maturity and Health 10 MIN
Understanding Stresses and Strains 10 MIN
Dist - CORF

Triangle of Health - Spanish Series
Physical Fitness and Good Health 10 MIN
Dist - CORF

Triangle of Health - Swedish Series
Physical Fitness and Good Health 10 MIN
Dist - CORF

Triangle series
Congruent Triangles 7 MIN
Journey to the Center of a Triangle 9 MIN
Similar Triangles 8 MIN
Trio for three angles 7 MIN
Dist - IFB

Triangles
VHS
Now I see it geometry video series
Color (J H)
$79.00 _ #60248 - 026
Connects with students' lives and interests by linking lessons to everyday objects ranging from automobiles to ice cream cones, stereos to honeycombs. Includes reproducible worksheet book and answer key. Part of a nine - part series.
Education; Mathematics
Dist - GA

Triangles 15 MIN
VHS / U-matic
Math Matters Series Blue Module
Color (I J)
Identifies and defines equilateral, isosceles, scalene and right triangles.
Mathematics
Dist - AITECH Prod - STETVC 1975

Triangles - an Introduction 10 MIN
U-matic / VHS / 16mm
Color (P I)
LC FIA66-1432
Introduces the properties of the triangle, stressing the relationship between the size of the angles and the length of the opposite sides.
Mathematics
Dist - PHENIX Prod - BOUNDY 1966

Triangles - Part I 30 MIN
VHS
Geometry series
Color (H)
$125.00 purchase _ #7003
Presents the first part of two parts about triangles. Part of a 16 - part series on geometry.
Mathematics
Dist - LANDMK Prod - LANDMK

Triangles - Part II 30 MIN
VHS
Geometry series
Color (H)
$125.00 purchase _ #7004
Presents the second part of two parts about triangles. Part of a 16 - part series on geometry.
Mathematics
Dist - LANDMK Prod - LANDMK

Triangles, Pt 1 30 MIN
VHS
Mathematics Series
Color (J)
LC 90713155
Discusses triangles. The first of two parts. The 144th of 157 installments of the Mathematics Series.
Mathematics
Dist - GPN

Triangles, Pt 2 30 MIN
VHS
Mathematics Series
Color (J)
LC 90713155
Discusses triangles. The second of two parts. The 145th of 157 installments in the Mathematics Series.
Mathematics
Dist - GPN

Triangles - Sides and Angles 11 MIN
U-matic / VHS / 16mm
Color (P I)
LC FIA67-73
Demonstrates that the longest side of a triangle is opposite the largest angle, that the shortest side is opposite the smallest angle and that if two sides of a triangle are the same length, the angles opposite them will be the same size.
Mathematics
Dist - PHENIX Prod - BOUNDY 1966

Triangulos 7 MIN
U-matic / VHS / 16mm
Color (J H C) (SPANISH)
A Spanish - language version of the motion picture Trio For Three Angles. Presents animated angles which show the relationships between a triangle's different components. Shows separate sections of equilateral, isosceles and scalene triangles.
Foreign Language; Mathematics
Dist - IFB Prod - CORNW 1968

Tribal archives 13 MIN
U-matic / VHS
Color (PRO)
$19.95 purchase
Describes what an archive is, its value to the community and basic requirements for starting an archives program. Uses American Indian illustrations and examples. Produced by the Center for Museum Studies at the Smithsonian for use in museum training.
History - United States; Psychology; Social Science
Dist - SMITHS

Tribal Carvings from New Guinea 29 MIN
Videoreel / VT2
Museum Open House Series
Color
Fine Arts; Geography - World
Dist - PBS Prod - WGBHTV

Tribal eye series
Across the frontiers 55 MIN
Behind the Mask 52 MIN
The Crooked beak of heaven 52 MIN
Kingdom of Bronze 52 MIN
Man Blong Custom 52 MIN
The Sweat of the Sun 52 MIN
Woven Gardens 55 MIN
Dist - TIMLIF

Tribal Government 19 MIN
16mm
Color
LC 80-700418
Shows how effective tribal governments operate and what tribal members should expect from their government. Focuses on governmental processes and institutions, such as tribal councils, courts, and police.
Civics and Political Systems; Social Science
Dist - IDIL Prod - IDIL 1980

Tribal Groups of Central India - the Chota Maria, the Bhils 40 MIN
16mm
Central India - Lifeways, Ceremony, Dance Series no 1; No 1
Color (H C A)
LC 78-701749
Compares the daily lifestyles, ceremonial rites, and dance forms of the Chota Maria and Bhil tribes of central India.
Geography - World; Sociology
Dist - ITHCOL Prod - ITHCOL 1978

Tribal Self - Determination, Government and Culture 30 MIN
U-matic / VHS
Color
Looks at Fort Berthold, North Dakota, where three affiliated tribes of American Indians live. Examines the Tribal Council which consists of elected representatives from the tribes. Stresses their determination to develop their own standards and points out that they regard the running of the reservation as the same as running a state or business.
Social Science; Sociology
Dist - UWISC Prod - MINOND 1979

The Tribe and the Professor 44 MIN
VHS / U-matic
Color
Reconstructs the past of the Makah Indians past. Portrays their newly awakened awareness of their long and rich cultural heritage.
Social Science; Sociology
Dist - UWASHP Prod - UWASHP

The Tribe and the Professor - Ozette Archaeology 44 MIN
16mm

Color
Recounts the unearthing of a longhouse in Cape Alva, Washington, which had been used by Ozette Indians 500 years before. Illustrates the scientific processes involved in the restoration and preservation of more than 50,000 items found during the excavation including baskets, boxes, bowls, awls, harpoons, paddles and blankets.
History - United States; Science - Physical; Social Science
Dist - UWASHP **Prod** - KIRKRL 1978

A Tribe in the sea - Part I 26 MIN
VHS
Challenge of the seas series
Color (I J H)
$225.00 purchase
Records the daily lives of a school of dolphins. Follows a group for five years in the warm water of the Bahamas to the point of recognizing individuals and watching several young grow to maturity. Part of a 26 - part series on the oceans.
Science - Natural; Science - Physical
Dist - LANDMK **Prod** - LANDMK 1991

A Tribe in the sea - Part II 26 MIN
VHS
Challenge of the seas series
Color (I J H)
$225.00 purchase
Watches as a team of divers attempts to communicate with a school of dolphins in the Bahamas. Observes dolphins playing with sting rays and sharks. Part of a 26 - part series on the oceans.
Science - Natural; Science - Physical; Social Science
Dist - LANDMK **Prod** - LANDMK 1991

Tribe of the Turquoise Waters 13 MIN
16mm
Color (H)
Shows life in a small Indian village hidden in an almost inaccessible valley in a remote part of the Grand Canyon.
Geography - United States; Social Science; Sociology
Dist - MLA **Prod** - DAGP 1952

Tribes of the Eastern Plains 30 MIN
16mm
Great Plains Trilogy, 2 Series Nomad and Indians - Early Man on the 'Plains; Nomad and Indians - early man on the plains
B&W (J)
Describes the complicated political and social organizations of the Indian farming tribes and their profound religious beliefs. Traces their history from prehistoric times to the present.
Social Science; Sociology
Dist - UNL **Prod** - KUONTV 1954

Tribology 30 MIN
U-matic / VHS
Tribology 1 - Friction, Wear, and Lubrication Series
Color
Discusses the various topics that constitute the field of tribology and their interrelation.
Industrial and Technical Education
Dist - MIOT **Prod** - MIOT

Tribology 1 - Friction, Wear, and Lubrication Series
Abrasive wear 41 MIN
Adhesive particle size 36 MIN
Adhesive wear 43 MIN
Corrosive Wear 38 MIN
Friction 38 MIN
Lubrication (1) 43 MIN
Lubrication (2) 45 MIN
Stick - Slip 43 MIN
Surface Fatigue Wear 37 MIN
Tribology 30 MIN
Troubleshooting 38 MIN
Wear 32 MIN
Dist - MIOT

Tribology 2 - Advances in Friction, Wear , and Lubrication - Introduction 39 MIN
U-matic / VHS
Tribology 2 - Advances in Friction, Wear, and Lubrication Series
Color
Discusses the economic importance of tribology, the literature of the past few years, fatigue theories of adhesive wear and their status and recent trends in research and development.
Industrial and Technical Education
Dist - MIOT **Prod** - MIOT

Tribology 2 - Advances in Friction, Wear, and Lubrication Series
Abrasive wear and erosion 49 MIN
Adhesive wear 40 MIN
Experimental Techniques 41 MIN
Friction 42 MIN
Lubrication - the Automobile 44 MIN
Sliding Electric Contacts 48 MIN
Surface Energy Effects 43 MIN
Tribology 2 - Advances in Friction, Wear, and Lubrication - Introduction 39 MIN
Dist - MIOT

Tribulation 99 48 MIN
VHS
Color (G)
$35.00 purchase
Entertains with a pseudo - documentary on alien mutants, UFOs, and the Hollow Earth. Convolutes into a satire on US covert action in Latin America. Contains dense verbiage and pictorial montages. Based on factual research. Directed by Craig Baldwin.
Fine Arts; Literature and Drama
Dist - ALTFMW

Tribulations of a Chinese Gentleman 135 MIN
VHS
Color (G) (MANDARIN CHINESE (ENGLISH SUBTITLES))
$45.00 purchase _ #6020A
Presents a Mandarin Chinese language movie produced in the People's Republic of China.
Fine Arts; Geography - World; Literature and Drama
Dist - CHTSUI **Prod** - CHTSUI

Tribute 7 MIN
16mm
B&W (G)
$20.00 rental
Presents an affirmative view of life and death with images from the 1950s that serve as icons and metaphors for the most personal thoughts of most Americans. Features music by David Byrne.
Fine Arts
Dist - CANCIN **Prod** - FARWIL 1986

Tribute to a master 60 MIN
U-matic / VHS
Color (H C G)
$180.00 purchase, $35.00 rental _ #RC1269VU, #RC1269VH
Presents in concert eight celebrated American violinists. Includes Andres Cardenes, Miriam Fried, Herbert Greenberg, Jacques Israelievich, Raymond Kobler, William Preucie, Richard Roberts and Yuval Yaron - all students of Indiana University's violin master Josef Gingold - who came to perform in the special concert held in honor of Gingold's 75th birthday. Features music composed by Vivaldi, Bach and Spohr.
Fine Arts
Dist - IU **Prod** - WTIU 1986

Tribute to John Coltrane 57 MIN
VHS
Color (S)
$29.95 purchase _ #726 - 9008
Pays tribute to John Coltrane, one of jazz's brightest stars. Features Wayne Shorter, Dave Liebman, Richie Beirach, Eddie Gomez and Jack DeJohnette in session.
Fine Arts
Dist - FI **Prod** - VARJ 1989

A Tribute to Larry 24 MIN
16mm
Color
LC 79-701243
Deals with the story of a woman whose need for the man in her life is so strong that nothing can destroy her desire to believe in him.
Fine Arts
Dist - STAN **Prod** - STAN 1979

A Tribute to Malcolm X 15 MIN
16mm / U-matic / VHS
B&W (H C A)
LC 76-704231
Discusses the influence of Malcolm X upon the present black liberation movement. Includes an interview with his widow, Betty Shabbazz.
Civics and Political Systems; History - United States
Dist - IU **Prod** - NET 1969

A Tribute to Nam June Paik 28 MIN
U-matic / VHS
Color
Portrays a man who won't sit still. Reflects the philosophic and comic style of Nam June Paik.
Fine Arts
Dist - KITCHN **Prod** - KITCHN

Tribute to Poland 18 MIN
U-matic
Color
Features Father Terrence Mulkerin, Catholic Relief Services Coordinator for Refugees and Disasters, explaining how Catholic Relief Services food shipments to Poland are distributed throughout the country with the help of local parishes.
Geography - World; Health and Safety; Social Science; Sociology
Dist - MTP **Prod** - CATHRS

A Tribute to President Herbert Clark Hoover 11 MIN
16mm
B&W
LC 74-705859
Highlights President Hoover's ability as an organizer and views his humanitarian work as a food administrator in World Wars I and II. Cites his contribution to government reorganization as secretary of commerce and as an elder statesman and advisor to presidents.
Biography; History - United States
Dist - USNAC **Prod** - USDD 1964

Tribute to Sidney Bechet
VHS
Color (G)
$29.95 purchase _ #1279
Salutes soprano saxophonist Sidney Bechet. Features saxophonist Bob Wilbur and the Smithsonian Jazz Repertory Ensemble performing songs Bechet helped to popularize, such as 'Summertime' and 'Daydreams.'.
Fine Arts
Dist - KULTUR

Tribute to Svalbard 6 MIN
16mm
Color (G)
Free loan
Visits the Svalbard archipelago nestled between the Greenland Sea and the Barents Sea north of Norway, which consists of four large islands and a number of smaller ones. Reveals that the group has an area of 63,000 square kilometers, with glaciers covering 60 percent of the area. The largest island is Spitsbergen.
Geography - World; Science - Natural
Dist - NIS

Trichomonal Vaginitis 9 MIN
U-matic / VHS
Take Care of Yourself Series
Color
Focuses on the symptoms, medication and treatment for trichomonal vaginitis. Explains infection and the correct insertion of vaginal creams, tables and suppositories.
Health and Safety
Dist - UARIZ **Prod** - UARIZ

Trick and Fancy Roping 10 MIN
U-matic / VHS / 16mm
Color (I J H)
Explains techniques of rope handling and how to make rope for roping.
Physical Education and Recreation; Social Science
Dist - IFB **Prod** - IFB 1951

Trick or Drink 20 MIN
U-matic / VHS
Vanalyne Green Series
Color (G)
$250.00, $200.00 purchase, $50.00 rental
Recreates the childhood world of Vanalyne Green through crayon drawings, family albums, excerpts from her adolescent diary and her interpretation of subsequent events in her life - bulimia and relationships with men. Deals with the pain of growing up with alcoholic parents.
Fine Arts; Health and Safety; Literature and Drama; Psychology; Sociology
Dist - WMEN **Prod** - VANGRE 1985

Trick or Treat 8 MIN
U-matic / VHS / 16mm
Color
LC 72-700159
Presents a Halloween with Donald Duck to stress the idea that playing practical jokes can backfire and cause danger or injury to others.
Literature and Drama
Dist - CORF **Prod** - DISNEY 1968

Trick shots
VHS
Color (G)
$29.95 purchase _ #RV002
Features pool champions Jim Rempe, Loree Jon Jones, Earl Strickland, Sammy Jones, David Howard and Louie Roberts showing trick shots that go beyond the basics shown in the video 'Pool School' and the tournament techniques shown in 'Power Pool.'
Physical Education and Recreation
Dist - SIV

Trick Skiing 105 MIN
U-matic / VHS
Superstar Sports Tapes Series
Color
Covers equipment, boats, training and advanced trick runs in trick water skiing. Presents over 50 different tricks. Stars Cory Pickos.
Health and Safety; Physical Education and Recreation
Dist - TRASS **Prod** - TRASS

Tricks or powers - Part 4 30 MIN
VHS
Kid tricks series
Color (K P I R)
$19.99 purchase, $10.00 rental _ #35 - 891152 - 533
Features famed Christian magician Danny Korem, who uses simple tricks to illustrate Biblical and moral concepts. Exposes a current psychic as being a fraud, contrasting this to Jesus' miracles and resurrection.
Religion and Philosophy
Dist - APH **Prod** - WORD

The Trickster 15 MIN
VHS
Magic library series
Color (P)
LC 90-707945
Tells a story about a trickster. Raises children's awareness of a sense of story in order to enrich and motivate language, reading and writing skills. Includes teacher's guide. Part of a series.
Education; English Language
Dist - TVOTAR **Prod** - TVOTAR 1990

Trickster Tales 20 MIN
VHS / U-matic
Folk Book Series
Color (P)
LC 80-707186
Features folk tales centering around the trickster hero.
Literature and Drama
Dist - AITECH **Prod** - UWISC 1980

Tricky Alex 8 MIN
U-matic / VHS
Happy Time Adventure Series
Color (K P)
$29.95 purchase _ #VT006
Presents an adaptation of the book Tricky Alex. Contains a 32 page hardcover book and a video.
English Language; Literature and Drama
Dist - TROLA

Tricycle 30 MIN
U-matic
Best Kept Secrets Series
Color (H C A)
Reveals the history of a double agent in World War II. A Yugoslav agent for the Nazis with the code name of Tricycle was picked up by British Agents and turned into a conduit for misinformation back to Germany.
Civics and Political Systems; History - World
Dist - TVOTAR **Prod** - TVOTAR 1985

Trident 14 MIN
VHS
Color (S)
$49.00 purchase _ #322 - 9281
Examines the Trident, a nuclear - powered American submarine that carries 24 missiles, each with eight to ten warheads. Reveals that each warhead has a range of 4000 miles and is ten times more powerful than the bombs dropped on Hiroshima. This privileged view of life aboard the Trident discloses why these nearly invulnerable submarines are one of America's most expensive weapon systems.
Civics and Political Systems; Industrial and Technical Education; Science - Physical
Dist - FI **Prod** - NBCNEW 1987

A Tried faith - Tape 7 30 MIN
VHS
Acts of the Apostles series
Color (I J H C G A R)
$29.95 purchase, $10.00 rental _ #35 - 8368 - 1502
Presents stories of the early Christian church as described in the New Testament book of Acts. Covers the events of Paul and Barnabas' ministry in Antioch, the debate over circumcision, and the intervention of the zealot Zacharias.
Literature and Drama; Religion and Philosophy
Dist - APH **Prod** - BOSCO

Trier, Roman Imperial City 5 MIN
16mm / U-matic / VHS
European Studies - Germany Series
Color (H C A)
LC 76-700760
Explains the development of Trier under nearly 500 years of ancient Roman rule.
Geography - World; History - World
Dist - IFB **Prod** - MFAFRG 1973

Trier Und Frankfurt 4 MIN
16mm
Beginning German Films (German Series
Color
Foreign Language
Dist - CCNY **Prod** - MGHT

Trifles 22 MIN
U-matic / VHS / 16mm
Color (H C)
Narrates a low - key detective story based on Pulitzer Prize winning play by Susan Glaspell.
Fine Arts; Literature and Drama
Dist - CEPRO **Prod** - CEPRO

Trifles 21 MIN
16mm / U-matic / VHS
Color (J)
LC 79-700380
Tells how two women and three men attempt to solve the murder of a farmer. Based on the story Trifles by Susan Glaspell.
Fine Arts; Literature and Drama
Dist - PHENIX **Prod** - MORANM 1979

Trig functions 30 MIN
VHS
Calculus series
Color (C)
$125.00 purchase _ #6018
Explains trig functions. Part of a 56 - part series on calculus.
Mathematics
Dist - LANDMK **Prod** - LANDMK

Trig Functions and Derivatives
U-matic
Calculus Series
Color
Mathematics
Dist - MDCPB **Prod** - MDDE

The Trigger effect 52 MIN
U-matic / VHS / 16mm
Connections series; No 1
Color (H C A)
LC 79-700856
Explains how plowing, building, writing, taxation and astronomy began in Egypt. Illustrates 20th century man's dependence on complex technological networks, using the New York City blackout of 1965 as an example. Discusses the nation of Kuwait, which has moved from the technology of ancient Egypt to that of the modern world in a single generation.
History - World; Sociology
Dist - TIMLIF **Prod** - BBCTV 1979
AMBROS

Trigger Films on Aging 14 MIN
16mm
Color
LC 70-715305
Presents a discussion film on problems of the aged. Features five vignettes, each establishing a problem situation in the life of an elderly person which builds to an emotional climax and abruptly ends.
Psychology; Sociology
Dist - UMICH **Prod** - UMITV 1971

Trigger Foods 9 MIN
16mm / 8mm cartridge
Color (PRO A) (SPANISH)
Explains the relationship of carbohydrates to tooth decay. Tells how certain foods trigger the tooth decay process and points out the importance of avoiding these foods between meals. Suggests foods which are not harmful to the teeth.
Foreign Language; Health and Safety
Dist - PRORE **Prod** - PRORE

Trigger Squeeze, M1 Rifle 5 MIN
16mm
B&W
LC FIE55-362
Explains the correct method of squeezing the trigger of the MI rifle, including grasp of rifle, position of fingers, breathing, sight alignment and trigger squeeze.
Civics and Political Systems
Dist - USNAC **Prod** - USA 1955

Trigland - an Interactive Videodisk Minicourse
Videodisc
(J H A)
$250.00 purchase _ #VID5301 - 5
Features a one - semester mini - course on topics that include amplitude, phase, tangents and simple harmonic motion. Requires an Apple IIe or Apple IIGS computer with two disk drives, a Pioneer LD - V6000 series videodisc player and an Apple Super Serial Card. Contains a videodisc, 16 Apple 5.25" disks, and a support manual.
Computer Science; Mathematics
Dist - MECC **Prod** - MECC

Trigometric Equations 30 MIN
VHS
Mathematics Series
Color (J)
LC 90713155
Examines trigometric equations. The 104th of 157 installments of the Mathematics Series.
Mathematics
Dist - GPN

Trigometric Form, Demoivre's Theorum and Nth Roots of Complex Numbers 30 MIN
VHS
Mathematics Series
Color (J)
LC 90713155
Examines trigometric form, Demoivre's theorum and Nth roots of complex numbers. The 109th of 157 installments of the Mathematics Series.
Mathematics
Dist - GPN

Trigometric Functions of General Angles 30 MIN
VHS
Mathematics Series
Color (J)
LC 90713155
Discusses trigometric functions of general angles. The 96th of 157 installments of the Mathematics Series.
Mathematics
Dist - GPN

Trigometric Identities, Pt 1 30 MIN
VHS
Mathematics Series
Color (J)
LC 90713155
Examines trigometric identities. The first of three parts. The 100th of 157 installments in the Mathematics Series.
Mathematics
Dist - GPN

Trigometric Identities, Pt 2 30 MIN
VHS
Mathematics Series
Color (J)
LC 90713155
Examines trigometric identities. The second of three parts. The 101st of 157 installments of the Mathematics Series.
Mathematics
Dist - GPN

Trigometric Identities, Pt 3 30 MIN
VHS
Mathematics Series
Color (J)
LC 90713155
Examines trigometric identities. The third of three parts. The 102nd of 157 installments in the Mathematics Series.
Mathematics
Dist - GPN

Trigonal Ileal Anastomosis 14 MIN
16mm
Color
LC 75-702253
Demonstrates a method of joining the urinary tract to the isolated ileal conduit which prevents reflux of loop urine to the kidneys. Shows that this is accomplished by performing an anastomosis between the intact unmobilized trigone and the isolated ileal conduit.
Science
Dist - EATONL **Prod** - EATONL 1973

Trigonometric equations 30 MIN
VHS
Trigonometry series
Color (H)
$125.00 purchase _ #5011
Explains trigonometric equations. Part of a 16 - part series on trigonometry.
Mathematics
Dist - LANDMK **Prod** - LANDMK

Trigonometric form, DeMoivre's theorem and the roots of complex numbers 30 MIN
VHS
Trigonometry series
Color (H)
$125.00 purchase _ #5016
Explains trigonometric form, DeMoivre's theorem and the roots of complex numbers. Part of a 16 - part series on trigonometry.
Mathematics
Dist - LANDMK **Prod** - LANDMK

Trigonometric Functions 30 MIN
U-matic
Introduction to Mathematics Series
Color (C)
Mathematics
Dist - MDCPB **Prod** - MDCPB

Trigonometric functions of general angles 30 MIN
VHS
Trigonometry series
Color (H)

$125.00 purchase _ #5003
Explains trigonometric functions of general angles. Part of a 16 - part series on trigonometry.
Mathematics
Dist - LANDMK **Prod** - LANDMK

Trigonometric functions 1 - solving triangles 60 MIN
VHS
Concepts in mathematics series
Color; PAL (J H G)
PdS29.50 purchase
Illustrates trigonometric function by using computer animation. Presents methods of solving right - angled triangles using the sine, cosine and tangent ratios. Divided into six 10 minute sections covering trigonometric ratios; solving right - angled triangles; angles on the plane; the sine law; the cosine law; and applications of sine and cosine laws. Part of a four - part series.
Industrial and Technical Education; Mathematics
Dist - EMFVL **Prod** - TVOTAR

Trigonometric functions 2 - sinusoidal waves 60 MIN
VHS
Concepts in mathematics series
Color; PAL (J H G)
PdS29.50 purchase
Introduces sine, cosine and tangent functions through an examination of their graphs on the Cartesian plane. Examines the characteristics of amplitude and period to develop a general equation for sinusoidal waves. Divided into six 10 minute sections covering radian measure; the sine function; amplitude and period; cosine and tangent; sinusoidal waves; and applications of sinusoidal waves. Part of a four - part series.
Mathematics
Dist - EMFVL **Prod** - TVOTAR

Trigonometric identities - I 30 MIN
VHS
Trigonometry series
Color (H)
$125.00 purchase _ #5007
Presents the first of three parts which explain trigonometric identities. Part of a 16 - part series on trigonometry.
Mathematics
Dist - LANDMK **Prod** - LANDMK

Trigonometric identities - II 30 MIN
VHS
Trigonometry series
Color (H)
$125.00 purchase _ #5008
Presents the second of three parts which explain trigonometric identities. Part of a 16 - part series on trigonometry.
Mathematics
Dist - LANDMK **Prod** - LANDMK

Trigonometric identities - III 30 MIN
VHS
Trigonometry series
Color (H)
$125.00 purchase _ #5009
Presents the third of three parts which explain trigonometric identities. Part of a 16 - part series on trigonometry.
Mathematics
Dist - LANDMK **Prod** - LANDMK

Trigonometric integrals 30 MIN
VHS
Calculus series
Color (C)
$125.00 purchase _ #6039
Explains trigonometric integrals. Part of a 56 - part series on calculus.
Mathematics
Dist - LANDMK **Prod** - LANDMK

Trigonometric Limits
U-matic
Calculus Series
Color
Mathematics
Dist - MDCPB **Prod** - MDDE

Trigonometric Ratios as Periodic Functions 28 MIN
16mm
Trigonometry Series
B&W (H)
Shows the use of trigonometric functions in problems involving conic sections and periodic motion. Describes the generation of a circle, ellipse, parabola and hyperbola using sections of a cone. Pictures the graph of a sine curve.
Mathematics
Dist - MLA **Prod** - CALVIN 1959

Trigonometric substitutions 30 MIN
VHS
Calculus series
Color (C)
$125.00 purchase _ #6040
Explains trigonometric substitutions. Part of a 56 - part series on calculus.
Mathematics
Dist - LANDMK **Prod** - LANDMK

Trigonometry 15 MIN
U-matic
Graphing Mathematical Concepts Series
(H C A)
Uses computer generated graphics to show the relationships between physical objects and mathematical concepts, equations and their graphs. Relates theoretical concepts to things in the real world.
Computer Science; Mathematics
Dist - ACCESS **Prod** - ACCESS 1986

Trigonometry
VHS
Color (H)
$79.95 purchase _ #VAD011
Presents two videocassettes teaching trigonometry. Includes step - by - step instruction in graphs, applications, functions, equations and identities.
Mathematics
Dist - SIV

Trigonometry and Shadows 26 MIN
16mm
Trigonometry Series
B&W (H)
Reviews various applications of trigonometry, such as surveying, construction and navigation, and briefly describes the early history of trigonometry. Explains the significance of the ratio of lengths of the sides of a triangle and defines the sine of an angle.
Mathematics
Dist - MLA **Prod** - CALVIN 1959

Trigonometry Functions 30 MIN
VHS
Mathematics Series
Color (J)
LC 90713155
Explains trigonometry functions. The 127th of 157 installments of the Mathematics Series.
Mathematics
Dist - GPN

Trigonometry Measures the Earth 28 MIN
16mm
Trigonometry Series
B&W (H)
Shows how Eratosthenes, in Ancient Greece, used trigonometry and shadows cast by the sun to measure the circumference and diameter of the earth to an accuracy of two percent. Describes a method of finding the distance to the moon by trigonometry.
Mathematics; Science - Physical
Dist - MLA **Prod** - CALVIN 1959

Trigonometry of Large Angles 30 MIN
16mm
Trigonometry Series
B&W (H)
Explains that definitions of trigonometric functions in terms of R, X and Y apply to any large angle if the sign of the function is identified. Proves that trigonometric identities work in all four quadrants. Shows the reduction of functions of negative angles to functions of equivalent positive angles.
Mathematics
Dist - MLA **Prod** - CALVIN 1959

Trigonometry series
Presents a 16 - part series on trigonometry. Explains angles, degrees and radians, trigonometric functions, trigonometric identities, inverse trigonometric functions, equations, right triangle applications, laws of sines and cosines, polar coordinates, trigonometric form, DeMoivre's theorem and the roots of complex numbers.

Angles, degrees and radians	30 MIN
Evaluating trigonometric functions	30 MIN
Graphing trigonometric functions - I	30 MIN
Graphing trigonometric functions - II	30 MIN
Introduction to trigonometric functions	30 MIN
Inverse trig functions	30 MIN
Law of cosines	30 MIN
Law of sines	30 MIN
Polar coordinates	30 MIN
Right triangle applications	30 MIN
Trigonometric equations	30 MIN
Trigonometric form, DeMoivre's theorem and the roots of complex numbers	30 MIN
Trigonometric functions of general angles	30 MIN
Trigonometric identities - I	30 MIN
Trigonometric identities - II	30 MIN
Trigonometric identities - III	30 MIN

Dist - LANDMK **Prod** - LANDMK 1959

Trigonometry Series

Addition formulas and Demoivre's theorem	28 MIN
Cosecant, Secant and Cotangent	27 MIN
Double and half angle formulas	28 MIN
Eight fundamental trigonometric identities	28 MIN
Graphs of periodic functions	29 MIN
Interpolation in Trigonometric Tables	28 MIN
Introduction to Logarithms	28 MIN
Large Angles and Coordinate Axes	30 MIN
Law of Cosines	30 MIN
Law of Sines	30 MIN
Law of Tangents	28 MIN
Practical Use of Logarithms	30 MIN
Right triangles and trigonometric ratios	29 MIN
Tables of Trigonometric Ratios	29 MIN
Trigonometric Ratios as Periodic Functions	28 MIN
Trigonometry and Shadows	26 MIN
Trigonometry Measures the Earth	28 MIN
Trigonometry of Large Angles	30 MIN
Using Logarithm Tables	29 MIN
Using Sines, Cosines and Tangents	29 MIN
Working with Trigonometric Identities	29 MIN

Dist - MLA

Trikfilm III 4 MIN
16mm
Color (C)
$150.00
Presents an experimental film by George Griffin.
Fine Arts
Dist - AFA **Prod** - AFA 1973

Trildogy series
Offers a special package of all three in the Trildogy series - Up and Atom, Staid Poot and Ron Amok - dog party.

Ron amok - dog party	4 MIN
Staid poot	3 MIN
Up and atom	3 MIN

Dist - CANCIN **Prod** - WENDTD 1973

Trilingual Education - Birthday Party 15 MIN
U-matic
Trilingual Education Series
Color (J C) (ENGLISH, SPANISH AND AMERICAN SIGN)
Combines English, Spanish and sign language to teach conceptual signing. Allows the viewer to select either English or Spanish voice - over translations. There are fourteen lessons in the series, each presenting a different pragmatic situation. Each lesson describes the content of the situation.
Computer Science; Education; Foreign Language; Psychology
Dist - SDSC **Prod** - SDSC 1982

Trilingual Education - Doing Chores 13 MIN
U-matic
Trilingual Education Series
Color (J C) (ENGLISH, SPANISH AND AMERICAN SIGN)
Combines the Trilingual Education series with English, Spanish and sign language to teach conceptual signing. The dual audio track allows the viewer to select either English or Spanish voice - over translations. There are fourteen lessons in the series, each presenting a different pragmatic situation. Each lesson describes the content of the situation.
Computer Science; Education; Foreign Language; Psychology
Dist - SDSC **Prod** - SDSC 1982

Trilingual Education - Family Picnic 12 MIN
U-matic
Trilingual Education Series
Color (J C) (ENGLISH, SPANISH AND AMERICAN SIGN)
Combines the Trilingual Education series with English, Spanish and sign language to teach comceptual signing. The dual audio track allows the viewer to select either English or Spanish voice - over translations. There are fourteen lessons in the series, each presenting a different pragmatic situation. Each lesson describes the content of the situation.
Computer Science; Education; Foreign Language; Psychology
Dist - SDSC **Prod** - SDSC 1982

Trilingual Education - Helping at Home 10 MIN
U-matic
Trilingual Education Series
Color (J C) (ENGLISH, SPANISH AND AMERICAN SIGN)
Combines the Trilingual Education series with English, Spanish and sign language to teach conceptual signing. The dual audio track allows the viewer to select either English or Spanish voice - over translations. There are fourteen lessons in the series, each presenting a different pragmatic situation. Each lesson describes the content of the situation.

Computer Science; Education; Foreign Language; Psychology
Dist - SDSC Prod - SDSC 1982

Trilingual Education - I have a Headache 17 MIN
U-matic
Trilingual Education Series
Color (J C) (ENGLISH, SPANISH AND AMERICAN SIGN)
Combines The Trilingual Education series English, Spanish and sign language to teach conceptual signing. The dual audio track allows the viewer to select either English or Spanish voice - over translations. There are fourteen lessons in the series, each presenting a different pragmatic situation. Each lesson describes the content of the situation.
Computer Science; Education; Foreign Language; Psychology
Dist - SDSC Prod - SDSC 1982

Trilingual Education - Learning from Grandpa 13 MIN
U-matic
Trilingual Education Series
Color (J C) (ENGLISH, SPANISH AND AMERICAN SIGN)
Combines English, Spanish and sign language to teach conceptual signing. The dual audio track allows the viewer to select either English or Spanish voice - over translations. There are fourteen lessons in the series, each presenting a different pragmatic situation. Each lesson describes the content of the situation.
Computer Science; Education; Foreign Language; Psychology
Dist - SDSC Prod - SDSC 1982

Trilingual Education - Let's Go to School 11 MIN
U-matic
Trilingual Education Series
Color (J C) (ENGLISH, SPANISH AND AMERICAN SIGN)
Combines the Trilingual Education series with English, Spanish and sign language to teach conceptual signing. The dual audio track allows the viewer to select either English or Spanish voice - over translations. There are fourteen lessons in the series, each presenting a different pragmatic situation. Each lesson describes the content of the situation.
Computer Science; Education; Foreign Language; Psychology
Dist - SDSC Prod - SDSC 1982

Trilingual Education - Lunch at School 11 MIN
U-matic
Trilingual Education Series
Color (J C) (ENGLISH, SPANISH AND AMERICAN SIGN)
Combines English, Spanish and sign language to teach conceptual signing. The dual audio track allows the viewer to select either English or Spanish voice - over translations. There are fourteen lessons in the series, each presenting a different pragmatic situation. Each lesson describes the content of the situation.
Computer Science; Education; Foreign Language; Psychology
Dist - SDSC Prod - SDSC 1982

Trilingual Education - Making Friends 8 MIN
U-matic
Trilingual Education Series
Color (J C) (ENGLISH, SPANISH AND AMERICAN SIGN)
Combines English, Spanish and sign language to teach conceptual signing. The dual audio track allows the viewer to select either English or Spanish voice - over translations. There are fourteen lessons in the series, each presenting a different pragmatic situation. Each lesson describes the content of the situation.
Computer Science; Education; Foreign Language; Psychology
Dist - SDSC Prod - SDSC 1982

Trilingual Education - Mother's Helper 14 MIN
U-matic
Trilingual Education Series
Color (J C) (ENGLISH, SPANISH AND AMERICAN SIGN)
Combines the Trilingual Education series with English, Spanish and sign language to teach conceptual signing. The dual audio track allows the viewer to select either English or Spanish voice - over translations. There are fourteen lessons in the series, each presenting a different pragmatic situation. Each lesson describes the content of the situation.
Computer Science; Education; Foreign Language; Psychology
Dist - SDSC Prod - SDSC 1982

Trilingual Education Series
Trilingual education - birthday party 15 MIN
Trilingual Education - Doing Chores 13 MIN
Trilingual Education - Family Picnic 12 MIN
Trilingual Education - Helping at Home 10 MIN
Trilingual Education - I have a Headache 17 MIN
Trilingual Education - Learning from Grandpa 13 MIN
Trilingual Education - Let's Go to School 11 MIN
Trilingual Education - Lunch at School 11 MIN
Trilingual Education - Making Friends 8 MIN
Trilingual Education - Mother's Helper 14 MIN
Trilingual Education - Shopping for Groceries 17 MIN
Trilingual Education - Shopping for School 11 MIN
Trilingual Education - Snack Time 15 MIN
Trilingual Education - Time for Bed 12 MIN
Dist - SDSC

Trilingual Education - Shopping for Groceries 17 MIN
U-matic
Trilingual Education Series
Color (J C) (ENGLISH, SPANISH AND AMERICAN SIGN)
Combines the Trilingual Education series English, Spanish and sign language to teach conceptual signing. The dual audio track allows the viewer to select either English or Spanish voice - over translations. There are fourteen lessons in the series, each presenting a different pragmatic situation. Each lesson describes the content of the situation.
Computer Science; Education; Foreign Language; Psychology
Dist - SDSC Prod - SDSC 1982

Trilingual Education - Shopping for School 11 MIN
U-matic
Trilingual Education Series
Color (J C) (ENGLISH, SPANISH AND AMERICAN SIGN)
Combines the Trilingual Education series with English, Spanish and sign language to teach conceptual signing. The dual audio track allows the viewer to select either English or Spanish voice - over translations. There are fourteen lessons in the series, each presenting a different pragmatic situation. Each lesson describes the content of the situation.
Computer Science; Education; Foreign Language; Psychology
Dist - SDSC Prod - SDSC 1982

Trilingual Education - Snack Time 15 MIN
U-matic
Trilingual Education Series
Color (J C) (ENGLISH, SPANISH AND AMERICAN SIGN)
Combines English, Spanish and sign language to teach conceptual signing. The dual audio track allows the viewer to select either English or Spanish voice - over translations. There are fourteen lessons in the series, each presenting a different pragmatic situation. Each lesson describes the content of the situation.
Computer Science; Education; Foreign Language; Psychology
Dist - SDSC Prod - SDSC 1982

Trilingual Education - Time for Bed 12 MIN
U-matic
Trilingual Education Series
Color (J C) (ENGLISH, SPANISH AND AMERICAN SIGN)
Combines the Trilingual Education series English, Spanish and sign language to teach conceptual signing. The dual audio track allows the viewer to select either English or Spanish voice - over translations. There are fourteen lessons in the series, each presenting a different pragmatic situation. Each lesson describes the content of the situation.
Computer Science; Education; Foreign Language; Psychology
Dist - SDSC Prod - SDSC 1982

A Trillion Dollars for Defense 60 MIN
VHS / U-matic
Color (H C A)
Visits an arms fair where manufacturers exhibit their latest high technology weapons systems. Suggests that the emphasis on such expensive and complex weapons detracts from a leaner, simpler and tougher armed forces.
Civics and Political Systems
Dist - FI Prod - WNETTV 1982

Trilog - fisheries, the rhyme, the old 14 MIN
16mm
Color (G)
$40.00 rental
Plays with color, light and shadow. Flips from image to image with some surprises.
Fine Arts
Dist - CANCIN Prod - DOBERG 1977

Trilogy 10 MIN
16mm
B&W
LC 75-703245
Presents a visual expression of the complex love relationship among three people and the mental conflict it produces.
Fine Arts
Dist - USC Prod - USC 1969

Trilogy of War Series
Korea - the Coldest War 60 MIN
The War Years - 1931 - 1941 60 MIN
War Years After Pearl Harbor - 1941 - 1945 60 MIN
Dist - LUF

Trim Foot of Thrown Bowl 28 MIN
Videoreel / VT2
Wheels, Kilns and Clay Series
Color
Features Mrs Peterson describing certain ceramic processes for her classroom at the University of Southern California. Demonstrates how to trim the foot of a thrown bowl.
Fine Arts
Dist - PBS Prod - USC

Trim for speed 60 MIN
VHS
Color (G A)
$49.00 purchase _ #0929
Presents expert advice on how to trim sails for speed in sailboat racing. Features Hans Fogh, Tom McLaughlin, Tom Whidden and Gary Weisman.
Physical Education and Recreation
Dist - SEVVID

Trim Subdivisions 6 MIN
U-matic
Color; Silent (C)
$300.00
Presents an experimental film by Bob Snyder.
Fine Arts
Dist - AFA Prod - AFA 1981

Trimming and making cylinders 29 MIN
Videoreel / VT2
Exploring the crafts - pottery series
Color
Features Mrs Vivika Heino introducing and demonstrating basic techniques in trimming and making cylinders.
Fine Arts
Dist - PBS Prod - WENHTV

Trimming and Painting 30 MIN
BETA / VHS
This Old House, Pt 2 - Suburban '50s Series
Color
Provides a lesson on trimming windows and doors. Gives tips on preparing and painting interior walls.
Industrial and Technical Education; Sociology
Dist - CORF Prod - WGBHTV

Trimming and Shoeing the Normal Horse Foot 26 MIN
BETA / VHS
Color
Makes shoe and hoof maintenance simple. Covers the removing of clinches to filing.
Health and Safety; Physical Education and Recreation
Dist - EQVDL Prod - COLOSU

Trinity
VHS
Campus clips series
Color (H C A)
$29.95 purchase _ #CC0014V
Takes a video visit to the campus of Trinity College in Connecticut. Shows many of the distinctive features of the campus, and interviews students about their experiences. Provides information on the composition of the student body, professors, academics, social life, housing, and other subjects.
Education
Dist - CAMV

Trio 88 MIN
VHS
Color (G)
$39.95 purchase _ #S02194
Presents dramatizations of three W Somerset Maugham short stories - 'The Verger,' 'Mr Knowall,' and 'Sanatorium.' Stars Jean Simmons, Michael Rennie, Bill Travers, and many others.
Fine Arts; Literature and Drama
Dist - UILL

Trio 10 MIN
16mm / U-matic / VHS
Color (H C A)
LC 81-700669
Offers an animated social satire showing how a man, a dog and a cat live together. Explains that the dog does all the work while the lazy cat profits from every situation.
Fine Arts
Dist - IFB Prod - ZAGREB 1977

Trio - Easley Blackwood 29 MIN
Videoreel / VT2
Young Musical Artists Series
Color
Presents the music of the Easley Blackwood Trio.
Fine Arts
Dist - PBS **Prod** - WKARTV

Trio for three angles 7 MIN
U-matic / VHS / 16mm
Triangle series
Color (J H C)
LC FIA68-2885
Uses animated, free - swinging angles to help students discover the relationships of a triangle's different components. Shows separate sections of equilateral, isosceles and scalene tringles.
Mathematics
Dist - IFB **Prod** - CORNW 1968
IFB

Trio - magnificat, diamond and four elegies 30 MIN
16mm
Color (G)
$40.00 rental
Describes a subjective space in three films. Articulates the notion that the human body extends beyond the physical frame into the environment of light that surrounds it.
Fine Arts
Dist - CANCIN **Prod** - TARTAG 1979

The Triode - Amplification 14 MIN
16mm
B&W
LC FIE52-189
Discusses the diode and triode, electric fields, a triode amplifier circuit, amplification of DC voltage changes, alternating voltages, distortion, and amplification of audio frequency signals.
Industrial and Technical Education
Dist - USNAC **Prod** - SCE 1945

Triode Limiters 24 MIN
16mm
B&W
LC 74-705861
Discusses how limiting is accomplished using a triode tube. Describes the characteristics and operation of the cut - off limiter, the saturation limiter and the over - driver limiter and explains the effect on limiting when bias is changed. (Kinescope).
Industrial and Technical Education; Science - Physical
Dist - USNAC **Prod** - USAF

The Trip 5 MIN
U-matic / VHS / 16mm
Color (K P I)
LC 80-700855
Tells the story of a young boy who is lonely in his new neighborhood until he converts a shoebox into a magic diorama and sees his old friends trick - or - treating. Based on the story The Trip by Ezra Jack Keats.
Fine Arts; Literature and Drama
Dist - WWS **Prod** - WWS 1980

A trip in a hot air balloon 14 MIN
16mm / VHS
Terrific trips series
Color (K P)
$49.95 purchase _ #P11038
Travels with Yoyo the clown in a gentle, soaring ride in a colorful hot air balloon. Shows that it's hard work getting a balloon ready for flight and packing it up again, but the adventure is worth it. Part of an eight - part series on the community.
Physical Education and Recreation
Dist - CF **Prod** - LNMDP 1989

Trip into the hole
VHS / U-matic
Working offshore series
Color (IND)
Shows that Making Hole is an essential part of the oil industry. Includes preparation for the trip in, getting the new bit ready, making up the first drill collar connection, making up the rest of the collars, and two ways of making up the pipe, spinning chain and pipe spinner.
Business and Economics; Industrial and Technical Education; Social Science
Dist - GPCV **Prod** - GPCV

Trip out of the hole
U-matic / VHS
Working offshore series
Color (IND)
Details procedures for getting the drill pipe out of the hole. Includes preparing for wet pipe, safety preparations, breaking out the kelly and a stand of pipe and a stand of collars and preparing the new bit.
Business and Economics; Industrial and Technical Education; Social Science
Dist - GPCV **Prod** - GPCV

A trip to a magic show 14 MIN
16mm / VHS
Terrific trips series
Color (K P)
$49.95 purchase _ #P11043
Follows a small group of children to a magic show where magician George Gilbert performs magic tricks with bunnies, cards, scarves and other props. Part of an eight - part series on the community.
Physical Education and Recreation
Dist - CF **Prod** - LNMDP 1989

A Trip to awareness 30 MIN
16mm
Color (J G)
LC 76-702075
Examines Jain temples in India in order to show the differences between Jainism and Buddhism. Presents contemporary concepts of Jainism, including the Jain formula for self - realization, nonviolence and reverence for life.
Geography - World; Religion and Philosophy
Dist - HP **Prod** - HP 1976

A Trip to Modern China 26 MIN
U-matic / VHS / 16mm
Color (J)
Shows China from Peking to the fertile Yangtze River basin and on to the industrial - commercial city of Shang - Hai. Presents a comprehensive picture of the rural, communal and urban lives of the Chinese people. Considers both the benefits and the disadvantages of communism.
Civics and Political Systems; Geography - World; History - World; Sociology
Dist - PHENIX **Prod** - KINGSP 1973

A trip to the amusement park 14 MIN
VHS
Terrific trips series
Color (K P)
$49.95 purchase _ #P11039
Features a group of children who spend a day at Six Flags Over Georgia amusement park. Circles the sky with them on an airplane and parachute rides; steams through the park on an old train; chooses costumes for old - time photographs; and zigzags crazily on the rollercoaster. Part of an eight - part series on the community.
Physical Education and Recreation
Dist - CF **Prod** - LNMDP 1989

A trip to the aquarium 14 MIN
VHS
Terrific trips series
Color (K P)
$49.95 purchase
Presents Barry the Blowfish who narrates a watery glimpse of a big - city aquarium. Features a variety of sea creatures showing off their colors, shapes and unique talents. At feeding time, a diver brings lunch to eels, turtles, rays and an assortment of fish in an underwater viewing tank. Part of an eight - part series on the community.
Science - Natural
Dist - CF **Prod** - LNMDP 1989

A trip to the farm 14 MIN
16mm / VHS
Terrific trips series
Color (K P)
$49.95 purchase _ #P11041
Spends a day with Matt Weissmann and his family, who live on a dairy farm. Watches the family feed the hens, pigs and ducks; milk the cows; cut, bale and store hay. A milk truck comes and siphons milk for a commercial dairy. Reveals that even dogs and kittens have a home on the farm. Part of an eight - part series on the community.
Science - Natural; Sociology
Dist - CF **Prod** - LNMDP 1989

A trip to the firehouse 14 MIN
VHS
Terrific trips series
Color (K P)
$49.95 purchase _ #P11042
Features Jackie the Dalmation who narrates a visit to the firehouse. Presents firefighters inspecting and cleaning their equipment; relaxing over a game of checkers; and then racing into uniform and onto the trucks to fight a fire. Shows a small leaf fire which is quickly put out, leaving the firefighters time to rescue a cat. Part of an eight - part series on the community.
Social Science
Dist - CF **Prod** - LNMDP 1989

A Trip to the Forest 15 MIN
U-matic / VHS
Strawberry Square Series
Color (P)
Fine Arts
Dist - AITECH **Prod** - NEITV 1982

A Trip to the Hospital 15 MIN
VHS / U-matic
Pass it on Series
Color (K P)
Observes what takes place in all areas of a hospital and tells why people have to go there.
Education; Health and Safety
Dist - GPN **Prod** - WKNOTV 1983

Trip to the moon 9 MIN
16mm
B&W (H C)
Features an early film classic by France's George Melies, using trick photography in a film picturing travel in outer space. Includes scenes of dancers from the Theatre Du Chatelet and acrobats from the Folies - Bergere.
Fine Arts
Dist - FCE **Prod** - MELIES
CFS

A Trip to the Planets 15 MIN
16mm / U-matic / VHS
Color (I J) (SPANISH)
Illustrates an imaginary trip to the planets. Examines the structure, motion, size and imagined surface appearance of the planets. Explains how the Sun produces its enormous energy.
Foreign Language; Science - Physical
Dist - EBEC **Prod** - EBEC

A trip to the post office 14 MIN
16mm / VHS
Terrific trips series
Color (K P)
$49.95 purchase _ #P11044
Meets a talking letter and travels with it from the corner mailbox to Grandma's house. Takes a close - up look at the people and equipment of a modern post office and sees how a letter goes from pen to friend. Part of an eight - part series on the community.
Social Science
Dist - CF **Prod** - LNMDP 1989

A Trip to the Supermarket 7 MIN
U-matic
Take Time Series
(A)
Demonstrates the influence of parents and others caring for pre - schoolers on the physical and emotional development of the child.
Health and Safety; Psychology; Sociology
Dist - ACCESS **Prod** - ACCESS 1976

The Trip to the top 29 MIN
16mm
Government story series; No 11
B&W (J H)
LC 72-707208
Explains how seniority leads to power and affects the working Congress and points out how committee chairmen, having attained their positions through seniority, may block legislation that the majority of congressmen and their constituents want.
Civics and Political Systems
Dist - WESTLC **Prod** - WEBC 1968

A Trip to the University 14 MIN
Videoreel / VT2
Muffinland Series
Color
English Language; Literature and Drama
Dist - PBS **Prod** - WGTV

A trip to the zoo 14 MIN
VHS
Terrific trips series
Color (K P)
$49.95 purchase _ #P11045
Takes a close - up look at the exotic residents of a modern zoo. Features giraffes, orangutans, a newborn hippo and a baby Malaysian sun bear. Shows an elephant taking a bath and receiving a manicure. Part of an eight - part series on the community.
Psychology; Science - Natural; Social Science
Dist - CF **Prod** - LNMDP 1989

A Trip to Where 50 MIN
16mm
Color (H C A)
LC 74-705863
Dramatizes the impact of drug use on the lives and careers of three youthful sailors. Explains about methedrine, barbiturates and alcohol and centers on the abuse of marijuana and LSD.
Health and Safety
Dist - USNAC **Prod** - USN 1968

Tripes a La Mode 29 MIN
Videoreel / VT2
French Chef - French series

Color (FRENCH)
Features Julia Child of Haute Cuisine au Vin demonstrating how to prepare tripes a la mode. With captions.
Foreign Language; Home Economics
Dist - PBS **Prod** - WGBHTV

A Triple amputee steps out 14 MIN
16mm
Color
Illustrates specific instruction techniques to provide ambulation training for a triple amputee and shows the use of the Hosmer knee unit in the provisional limb, balance, gait training and transfer activities.
Health and Safety
Dist - USVA **Prod** - USVA 1963

Triple jump
VHS
Coaching women's track and field series
Color (H C G)
$59.95 purchase _ #TRS1106V
Features women's field and track coaches Bob Meyers and Meg Ritchie on the triple jump. Offers a comprehensive series of teaching progressions - Approach - proper sprint mechanics; Hop - tips on how to maximize horizontal distance; Step - how to make a smooth transition to the jump; Jump - take - off techniques clearly demonstrated in slow motion. Part of a nine - part series.
Physical Education and Recreation
Dist - CAMV

Triple jump
VHS
Coaching men's field and track series
Color (H C G)
$59.95 purchase _ #TRS1254V
Features men's field and track coach Rick Sloan on the triple jump. Reduces the most difficult event to the critical phases of the jump with each phase demonstrated in slow motion and stop action to enhance learning and retention. Part of a nine - part series.
Physical Education and Recreation
Dist - CAMV

The Triple Jump 11 MIN
U-matic / VHS / 16mm
Athletics Series
Color (H C A)
LC 80-700345
Uses slow - motion scenes to analyze key movements in the triple jump. Includes training for speed and distance, emphasizing the conditioning needed to avoid injury from shocks. Concludes with an actual competition involving four European athletes.
Physical Education and Recreation
Dist - IU **Prod** - GSAVL 1980

The Triple jump
VHS
NCAA instructional video series
Color (H C A)
$39.95 purchase _ #KAR2104V
Presents the second of a three - part series on field events. Focuses on the triple jump.
Physical Education and Recreation
Dist - CAMV **Prod** - NCAAF

Triple jump
VHS / U-matic
Frank Morris instructional videos series
Color (H C A)
Instructs athletes how to execute and improve performance of the Triple Jump. Approximately 60 minutes. Produced and narrated by coach Frank Morris.
Physical Education and Recreation
Dist - TRACKN **Prod** - TRACKN 1986

The Triple threat of genito - urinary disease - implications for improving quality of life 120 MIN
VHS
Virginia Geriatric Education Center Video Conference series
Color (G C PRO)
$149.00 purchase, $55.00 rental
Focuses on ways health care professionals can improve the lives of aging clients experiencing physical, social or psychological problems such as incontinence and sexual dysfunction that result from genito - urinary tract diseases.
Health and Safety
Dist - TNF **Prod** - VGEREC

The Triple vision 360 MIN
VHS / BETA
Color; PAL (G)
PdS6 purchase
Features His Eminence Sakya Trizin giving a general commentary to a widely studied text of Sachen Kunga Nyingpo, one of the five Great Masters of the Sakya lineage. Describes how it is known as the Triple Vision and is an introduction to the Lam - dre teachings - The Spiritual Path and its Fruits. These emphasize an approach found in the Hevajra Tantra where Triple Vision refers to the three views of the world - that of an ordinary being; of a practititioner with insight into reality; and the totally integrated view of a fully awakened master or Buddha. A series of three lectures recorded at Rigpa in London.
Fine Arts; Religion and Philosophy
Dist - MERIDT

Tripping 15 MIN
U-matic / VHS / 16mm
Rapping and tripping series
Color (J H S)
LC 70-706671
Demonstrates techniques of 'turning on' without drugs.
Psychology
Dist - ALTSUL **Prod** - ALTSUL 1970

Tripping on Two 25 MIN
16mm
Color (I)
Presents bicycle safety tips covering how to detect and avoid hazards, how to ride defensively, how to see and be seen and how to understand and obey the rules of the road.
Health and Safety
Dist - PROART **Prod** - PROART

Trippingly on the Tongue 30 MIN
U-matic
Speakeasy Series
(J H)
Demonstrates speaking activities that are in autobiographical, role playing, dramatic, impromptu, formal presentation and mock trial formats.
English Language
Dist - ACCESS **Prod** - ACCESS 1981

Triptych 12 MIN
16mm
B&W (G)
$25.00 rental
Reveals a self - portrait in three parts. Explores being seen, seeing and looking at oneself and what and how one sees. Produced by Charlotte Hill.
Fine Arts
Dist - CANCIN

Triptych 10 MIN
16mm
Color
Presents a visual adaptation of the dance Three Characters for a Passion Play. Portrays in Medieval imagery, the knowledge of inevitable betrayal, the act itself and the loneliness and self - acceptance following.
Fine Arts
Dist - FRAF **Prod** - FRAF

Triptych in four parts 12 MIN
16mm
Color (G)
$25.00 rental
Documents the 'Beat' movement from a personal inside perspective at North Beach, California. Begins with a portrait of artist John Reed, proceeds to southern Texas on a spiritual drug odyssey seeking religious epiphany through peyote, then returns to artist Wallace Berman's home in San Francisco. Poets Michael McClure and Phillip Lamantia are featured also.
Fine Arts
Dist - CANCIN **Prod** - JORDAL 1958

Trisha and Carmen 13 MIN
16mm / VHS
Color (H A)
$300.00 purchase, $55.00 rental
Presents a virtually non - verbal mosaic of preparations for a live performance of Lina Wertmuller's 1986 Carmen at the Teatro di San Carlo in Naples, with choreography by Trisha Brown. Juxtaposes views of Brown's rehearsal and the actual performance.
Fine Arts
Dist - AFA **Prod** - BARR 1988

The Trisha Brown Company 60 MIN
U-matic / VHS
Color
Features The Trisha Brown Company as it performs Splang and Line - Up. Presents an interview of Ms Brown by dance critic Deborah Jowitt. Includes performances by Trisha Brown, Elizabeth Garren, Lisa Kraus, Nina Lundborg, Wendy Perron and Mona Sulzman.
Fine Arts
Dist - EIF **Prod** - EIF

Triumph and defeat 30 MIN
16mm / U-matic / VHS
Living Christ series
Color
Shows Jesus casting the money changers out of the temple, the Last Supper and his trial and sentencing.
Religion and Philosophy
Dist - CAFM **Prod** - CAFM
ECUFLM

Triumph at Tokyo 35 MIN
16mm
Color
Presents highlights from the 18th Olympiad in Tokyo, Japan. Features young men and women who tell the meaning that Jesus Christ has given to their lives and to their faith in the disciplined world of the athlete.
Physical Education and Recreation; Religion and Philosophy
Dist - NINEFC **Prod** - WWP

Triumph in France 26 MIN
16mm
Winston Churchill - the Valiant Years Series no 20
B&W
LC FI67-2118
Describes with documentary footage the V - 1 bombings of London, the allied landings in southern France, the allied breakthrough in Normandy and the liberation of Paris. Based on the book 'THE SECOND WORLD WAR,' by Winston S Churchill.
History - World
Dist - SG **Prod** - ABCTV 1961

A Triumph of Love 20 MIN
VHS / U-matic
Color
$335.00 purchase
Sociology
Dist - ABCLR **Prod** - ABCLR 1983

The Triumph of Memory 30 MIN
VHS / 16mm
Color (G)
$49.95, $350.00 purchase _ #TROM - 000
Interviews four non - Jewish concentration camp survivors. Focuses on their experiences in the camps, noting different points of view. Emphasizes the testimony of all to the horrors of the Holocaust.
History - World
Dist - PBS **Prod** - GARDNR 1989

A Triumph of Modern Engineering - a Record of the Tokyo Monorail Line 24 MIN
16mm
Color
Explains that the monorail line was planned and constructed in order to relieve the congested traffic between Tokyo International Airport and the heart of the metropolis. Records the important sections of the line constructed by a Japanese construction company, applying the prefabricated tunnel methods, reverse circulation method, Dywidag method and others which require highly advanced techniques.
Geography - World; Industrial and Technical Education; Social Science
Dist - UNIJAP **Prod** - UNIJAP 1964

Triumph of the Cross (Martyr's Shrine, Midland) 60 MIN
BETA / VHS
Pope John Paul II - a Pilgrimage of Faith, Hope, and Love
(R G) (ITALIAN FRENCH)
$29.95 purchase, _ #VHS 5PV 130 _ #Beta 5PV 230 _ #VHS 5PV 103 Italian
Shows the visit of Pope John Paul II to the Martyr's Shrine in Midland, Canada in 1984.
History - World; Religion and Philosophy
Dist - CANBC

Triumph Of The Nomads Series
Focuses on the history of Australian Aborigines. Re - enacts tribal ceremonies, giving a view of Aboriginal culture and customs. Presents numerous examples of the Australian countryside. Three - part series is based on the book of the same name by Geoffrey Blainey.
The First invaders 60 MIN
Reign of the Wanderers 60 MIN
Sails of Doom 60 MIN
Dist - PBS **Prod** - NOMDFI

Triumph of the tyrant - Pt 2 60 MIN
VHS
USSR series
Color (J H G)
$250.00 purchase
Traces the rise of Stalin and his terrorist tactics in the times of the world wars. Looks at the beginnings of the Cold War and the background of the Berlin Airlift. Part of a series of three videos covering the rise and decline of the USSR. Videos are also available in a set.
History - World
Dist - LANDMK

Triumph of the West 650 MIN
VHS
Color; PAL (H C A)

PdS390 purchase; Not available in the United States
Features the rise of Western civilization and its continuing influence on the rest of the world in a series of 13 programs. Documents the progression of science, religion, exploration, politics and culture. Written and presented by British historian J M Roberts.
History - World; Sociology
Dist - BBCENE

Triumph of the West series
Age of exploration 50 MIN
Capitulations 50 MIN
Dangerous gifts 50 MIN
Decline of the West 50 MIN
East is red 50 MIN
East of Europe 50 MIN
Heart of the West 50 MIN
India - ironies of empire 50 MIN
Islam - world's debate 50 MIN
Monuments to progress 50 MIN
New direction 50 MIN
Dist - BBCENE

Triumph of the West Series
The Triumph of the West - Vol I 90 MIN
The Triumph of the West - Vol II 102 MIN
The Triumph of the West - Vol III 101 MIN
The Triumph of the West - Vol IV 101 MIN
The Triumph of the West - Vol V 101 MIN
The Triumph of the West - Vol VI 103 MIN
The Triumph of the West - Vol VII 57 MIN
Dist - FI

The Triumph of the West - Vol I 90 MIN
VHS
Triumph of the West Series
Color (S)
$99.00 purchase _ #825 - 9599, #825 - 9600
Features noted British historian John Roberts who explores the impact of Western civilization on the nations of the world. Tells a story of epic proportions, embracing leaders as diverse as Constantine, Charlemagne, Louis XIV, Karl Marx, Chairman Mao, Gandhi, Luther, Mohammed, and Jesus. Volume I of seven volumes has two parts. Part 1, 'Dangerous Gifts - The Continuing Impact Of Western Civilization,' examines how Western culture has changed the world. Part 2, 'A New Direction - Graeco - Roman And Judaic Roots,' considers the two myths that lie at the heart of the Western view of society.
History - World; Religion and Philosophy; Sociology
Dist - FI **Prod** - BBCTV 1987

The Triumph of the West - Vol II 102 MIN
VHS
Triumph of the West Series
Color (S)
$99.00 purchase _ #825 - 9601, #825 - 9602
Features noted British historian John Roberts who explores the impact of Western civilization on the nations of the world. Tells a story of epic proportions, embracing leaders as diverse as Constantine, Charlemagne, Louis XIV, Karl Marx, Chairman Mao, Gandhi, Luther, Mohammed, and Jesus. Volume II of seven volumes has two parts. Part 3, 'The Heart Of The West - The Fall and The Rise Of Christianity,' asks how Europe became the cradle of Western civilization and what role Christianity played in the shaping of Western culture. Part 4, 'The World's Debate - Interaction With Islam,' describes the sometimes fruitful, sometimes bitter interaction of Christian Europe and Islamic culture.
History - World; Religion and Philosophy; Sociology
Dist - FI **Prod** - BBCTV 1987

The Triumph of the West - Vol III 101 MIN
VHS
Triumph of the West Series
Color (S)
$99.00 purchase _ #825 - 9603, #825 - 9604
Features noted British historian John Roberts who explores the impact of Western civilization on the nations of the world. Tells a story of epic proportions, embracing leaders as diverse as Constantine, Charlemagne, Louis XIV, Karl Marx, Chairman Mao, Gandhi, Luther, Mohammed, and Jesus. Volume III of seven volumes has two parts. Part 5, 'East Of Europe - Russia And The East,' asks if Russia is part of the West. Russia developed an autocracy with its roots in Byzantium, then adopted Marxism, a philosophy with its origins in the European Enlightenment. Part 6, 'The Explorers - The Age Of Exploration,' follows European mastery of the seas - Henry the Navigator, Magellan, Vasco da Gama and Columbus and their impact on exotic cultures.
History - World; Sociology
Dist - FI **Prod** - BBCTV 1987

The Triumph of the West - Vol IV 101 MIN
VHS
Triumph of the West Series
Color (S)
$99.00 purchase _ #825 - 9605, #825 - 9606
Features noted British historian John Roberts who explores the impact of Western civilization on the nations of the world. Tells a story of epic proportions, embracing leaders as diverse as Constantine, Charlemagne, Louis XIV, Karl Marx, Chairman Mao, Gandhi, Luther, Mohammed, and Jesus. Volume IV of seven volumes has two parts. Part 7, 'New Worlds - Conquests and Settlements In The Americas,' considers the disastrous impact of European culture on the native populations of North and South America, as well as Africa. Part 8, 'An Age Of Light - The Enlightenment,' views the age of Newton, Voltaire, Rousseau and Jefferson, which coexisted with slavery, superstition and cruelty.
History - United States; History - World; Sociology
Dist - FI **Prod** - BBCTV 1987

The Triumph of the West - Vol V 101 MIN
VHS
Triumph of the West Series
Color (S)
$99.00 purchase _ #825 - 9607, #825 - 9608
Features noted British historian John Roberts who explores the impact of Western civilization on the nations of the world. Tells a story of epic proportions, embracing leaders as diverse as Constantine, Charlemagne, Louis XIV, Karl Marx, Chairman Mao, Gandhi, Luther, Mohammed, and Jesus. Volume V of seven volumes has two parts. Part 9, 'Monuments To Progress - The Industrial And Other Revolutions,' reveals that the Industrial Revolution sparked ideas like nationalism and socialism. Part 10, 'India - The Ironies Of Empire - Empire And India,' considers India, the Jewel of the British Empire and the irony of the Indian use of Western ideas to rebel against their English rulers.
History - United States; History - World; Sociology
Dist - FI **Prod** - BBCTV 1987

The Triumph of the West - Vol VI 103 MIN
VHS
Triumph of the West Series
Color (S)
$99.00 purchase _ #825 - 9609, #825 - 9610
Features noted British historian John Roberts who explores the impact of Western civilization on the nations of the world. Tells a story of epic proportions, embracing leaders as diverse as Constantine, Charlemagne, Louis XIV, Karl Marx, Chairman Mao, Gandhi, Luther, Mohammed, and Jesus. Volume VI of seven volumes has two parts. Part 11, 'The East Is Red - China,' considers that China, the oldest, largest, most self - confident culture to confront the West, crumbled in the modern age, having to choose between capitalism and communism, two ideas from the West. Part 12, 'The Decline Of The West - The Twentieth Century,' discusses the emergence of Japan as a superpower, leading to a loss of faith in Western civilization.
Civics and Political Systems; Geography - World; History - World; Sociology
Dist - FI **Prod** - BBCTV 1987

The Triumph of the West - Vol VII 57 MIN
VHS
Triumph of the West Series
Color (S)
$99.00 purchase _ #825 - 9611
Features noted British historian John Roberts who explores the impact of Western civilization on the nations of the world. Tells a story of epic proportions, embracing leaders as diverse as Constantine, Charlemagne, Louis XIV, Karl Marx, Chairman Mao, Gandhi, Luther, Mohammed, and Jesus. Volume VII of seven volumes has one part, Part 13, 'Capitulations - Western Civilization Today,' views the challenges to the reign of West culture - particularly the Islamic world.
History - World; Religion and Philosophy; Sociology
Dist - FI **Prod** - BBCTV 1987

Triumph of the West
Age of light 50 MIN
New Worlds 50 MIN
Dist - BBCENE

Triumph of the will 120 MIN
U-matic / VHS
B&W (GERMAN)
Focuses on the 1934 Nazi Party congress. Expresses one individual's impression of the Hitler movement. Conveys the complete dominance of one man's personality over an entire nation.
Foreign Language; History - World
Dist - IHF **Prod** - IHF

Triumph of the will 50 MIN
16mm
B&W
Presents the official record for the Sixth Nazi Party held at Nuremberg in September, 1934. Directed by Leni Riefenstahl.
Fine Arts; History - World; Sociology
Dist - REELIM **Prod** - RIEFSL 1934

Triumph of the will 80 MIN
VHS
B&W (G) (GERMAN (ENGLISH SUBTITLES))
$29.95 purchase _ #S00163
Presents a record of the 1934 Nazi Party Congress at Nuremberg, including a spectacular propaganda rally. Features military marches, armored divisions, and policy speeches by Hitler and the other major Nazi figures. Produced by Leni Riefenstahl.
Civics and Political Systems; History - World
Dist - UILL

Triumph of the will 110 MIN
16mm / U-matic / VHS
B&W (GERMAN)
Documents the Nazi's Sixth Party Congress in 1934 in Nuremberg. Shows Hitler appearing as a savior, speeches by Goebbels, Goering, Himmler and Hess, the marching, pomp and pageantry. Directed by Leni Riefenstahl.
Civics and Political Systems; Fine Arts; History - World; Sociology
Dist - PHENIX **Prod** - RIEFSL 1936

Triumph of the will (the arrival of Hitler) 12 MIN
16mm
Film study extracts series
B&W (J)
Presents an excerpt from the 1935 documentary Triumph Of The Will. Depicts Hitler's arrival at the party rally in Nuremberg. Directed by Leni Riefenstahl.
Fine Arts
Dist - FI **Prod** - RIEFSL

The Triumph of Thursday's Child
VHS
Color (G)
$29.95 purchase _ #0890
Documents the historic voyage of Warren Luhrs and his boat Thursday's Child, in early 1989, which beat a 135 year old passage record of sea travel from New York to San Francisco by way of Cape Horn.
Physical Education and Recreation
Dist - SEVVID

Triumphant 17 MIN
16mm
Color; B&W (J H T R)
Presents the story of Paul who preaches to all, even while a prisoner in Rome. Shows a mature triumphant Christian philosophy as demonstrated in the life of Paul.
Religion and Philosophy
Dist - FAMF **Prod** - BROADM 1957

Triumphant Symphony 15 MIN
16mm / U-matic / VHS
History Book Series
Color (G)
$195.00, $350.00 purchase, $45.00 rental
Covers the Industrial Revolution. Shows history as it has been lived and experienced by common people. Part of a nine - part series of animated episodes surveying the development of society from the Middle Ages to the present time from a grassroots perspective. Each title is 15 - 20 minutes in length.
Fine Arts; History - World; Social Science; Sociology
Dist - CNEMAG **Prod** - TRIFC 1974

The Triumphant Union and the Canadian Confederation (1863 - 1867) 58 MIN
16mm
Struggle for a Border
B&W (G H C)
_ #106B 0169 012
Studies the principles and practices of international relations and the subtle, many dimensional geometry of war and peace - Canada and the American Civil War, Canada, Britain, the North and the South, and a dangerous diplomatic game.
History - United States; History - World
Dist - CFLMDC **Prod** - NFBC 1969

Triune brain 30 MIN
16mm / VHS
Color (C A)
$395.00, $150.00 purchase, $25.00 rental _ #NC1755
Presents a detailed portrait of the human brain using models from antiquity through the more recently developed triune model, narrated by Paul McLean.
Psychology; Science - Natural
Dist - IU **Prod** - NFBC 1985

Trivia 15 MIN
16mm
Color (G)
$45.00 rental
Evaluates the Old World in the New World or rather a New World Aesthetic response to filmmaker Werner Herzog's Old World sentimental Romanticism of the New World.
Fine Arts
Dist - CANCIN **Prod** - DOBERG 1980

Trobriand Cricket - an Ingenious Response to Colonialism 54 MIN
U-matic / VHS / 16mm
Color
Documents the modifications made by the residents of the Trobriand Islands in Papua, New Guinea to the traditional British game of cricket. Shows how the islanders have changed the game into an outlet for mock warfare, community interchange, tribal rivalry, sexual innuendo and a lot of riotous fun.
History - World
Dist - UCEMC **Prod** - LEAKIL 1976

Trobriand Islanders of Papua New Guinea 52 MIN
VHS
Disappearing world series
Color (G C)
$99.00 purchase, $19.00 rental _ #51227
Examines the society of the Trobriand Islanders, showing the complex balance of male authority and female wealth as well as the magic and sorcery that pervade everyday life. Looks at two events in particular - distribution of a woman's wealth after death and a yam harvest. Features anthropologist Annette B Weiner. Part of a series working closely with anthropologists who lived for a year or more in societies whose social structures, beliefs and practices are threatened by the expansion of technocratic civilization.
Sociology
Dist - PSU **Prod** - GRANDA 1990

Trocar decompression in acute small bowel obstruction 21 MIN
16mm
Color
LC FIA67-667
Uses illustrations and surgical photography to describe the technique for small bowel decompression with the trocar.
Health and Safety
Dist - AMCSUR **Prod** - AVCORP 1966

Trogmoffy reading preparation series
Adventures of Trogmoffy - rescue on a strange planet 14 MIN
Adventures of Trogmoffy - Timmy and Margaret meet the orange creature 14 MIN
Dist - PHENIX

Troilus and Cressida 190 MIN
VHS / U-matic
Shakespeare's plays series
Color (H C A)
LC 82-707357
Presents William Shakespeare's play Troilus And Cressida about two lovers who mock love.
Literature and Drama
Dist - TIMLIF **Prod** - BBCTV 1982
INSIM
AMBROS

Troilus and Cressida - Shakespeare's most 'Modern' Play - Tragi - Comedy of Disillusionment 45 MIN
Videoreel / VT2
Shakespeare Series
B&W (C)
Literature and Drama
Dist - GPN **Prod** - CHITVC

Trois Themes 8 MIN
16mm
B&W
Presents later visions based on Moussorgsky's music, with slow - moving shadows on a sleepless night, an accelerated passage of drawings and sketches moving across the screen, and a third mood of conflict between material goods and artistic aims. Produced by Alexander Alexeieff and Claire Parker.
Fine Arts
Dist - STARRC **Prod** - STARRC 1980

A Trojan house 25 MIN
16mm
Color (G)
$40.00 rental
Views woman as the house. Interprets architectural structures as the structures of relationships where windows provide communication while the house preserves a sense of enclosure and isolation.
Fine Arts
Dist - CANCIN **Prod** - COUZS 1981

The Trojan War 13 MIN
VHS / 16mm
Greek and Roman Mythology in Ancient Art Series
Color (I)
LC 90708210
Examines the mythical origins of the Trojan War. Focuses on the abduction of Helen of Troy.
Fine Arts; History - World; Religion and Philosophy
Dist - BARR

The Trojan Women
U-matic / VHS
Classic Films - on - Video Series
Color (G C J)
$59 purchase _ #05821 - 85
Screens the film version of Euripides' tale concerning the fall of Troy. Stars Katherine Hepburn, Irene Pappas, and Vanessa Redgrave.
Fine Arts
Dist - CHUMAN

The Troll Music 15 MIN
VHS / U-matic
Magic Pages Series
Color (P)
Literature and Drama
Dist - AITECH **Prod** - KLVXTV 1976

Troll Troop 20 MIN
16mm
Color (P I)
Presents cut - offs and flip cards.
Fine Arts
Dist - YELLOW **Prod** - YELLOW 1973

The Trolls and the Christmas express 25 MIN
U-matic / VHS / 16mm
Color
$565.00, $250.00 purchase _ #4050
Describes what happens when six mischievous trolls try to ruin Christmas for all children, first by sabotaging Santa's toy production and then by keeping the reindeer up so that they are too tired to pull Santa's sleigh.
Fine Arts; Literature and Drama; Social Science
Dist - CORF **Prod** - CORF 1981

Trolls of Norway 15 MIN
16mm
Color (P I)
Uses short narrated sequences to introduce trolls, an element of Norway's folklore.
Literature and Drama
Dist - MMP **Prod** - MMP

Trollstenen 120 MIN
16mm
Color (G)
$175.00 rental
Presents a multilayered personal documentary of the filmmaker's parents and family in Sweden.
Literature and Drama; Sociology
Dist - CANCIN **Prod** - NELSOG 1976

Trombone 19 MIN
VHS / 16mm
Junior high music - instrumental series
Color (I)
$175.00, $200.00 purchase _ #288107
Features a host who introduces each program and offers a brief history of the instrument to be studied. Presents a master teacher, a professional musician with a philharmonic symphony, who demonstrates proper assembly, breathing and tone production, hand position, embouchure and articulation. A performance rounds out the program. 'Trombone' explains the proper handling and importance of the mouthpiece and slidelock, which are especially prone to damage. Demonstrates correct body position, breath control tonguing, hand position and embouchure tension. The necessity of determining pitch before playing is explained.
Fine Arts
Dist - ACCESS **Prod** - ACCESS 1988

Trombone for beginners 50 MIN
VHS
Maestro instructional series
Color (J H C G)
$29.95 purchase _ #BSPB24V
Supplements class lessons and reinforces private lessons on the trombone. Offers clear - cut examples and demonstrations on how to unpack and assemble the instrument, proper hand position and instrumental nomenclature. Discusses notes, breathing, posture, reading music and care and maintenance of the instrument. Includes booklet. Part of a ten - part series on musical instruments.
Fine Arts
Dist - CAMV

Tron 24 MIN
U-matic / VHS / 16mm
Color (J H)
Offers highlights from the motion picture Tron, which goes inside a computer where a real - life computer genius is pitted against electronic foes.
Fine Arts; Mathematics
Dist - CORF **Prod** - DISNEY 1983

The Troops 58 MIN
U-matic / VHS
Different Drummer - Blacks in the Military Series
Color (H C A)
LC 85-700750
Discusses the history of black military participation from World War II to Vietnam. Discusses President Truman's executive order of 1948 which suggested the end of segregation in the Armed Forces, and the achievement of full integration in the Vietnam War.
Civics and Political Systems; History - United States
Dist - FI **Prod** - WNETTV 1983

Trope 8 MIN
16mm
B&W
Provides an experimental approach in the treatment of four extremely conversational people at dinner. The film - maker combines time analysis with small talk in an amusing treatment of a common situation. Produced by a USC cinema student workshop.
Fine Arts; Guidance and Counseling; Psychology
Dist - USC **Prod** - USC 1965

The Trophy Case 26 MIN
16mm
Color (J)
LC 80-700051
Tells a story about a father who gives his all so his son can do and be all the things that he couldn't be when he was young. Shows how the father suddenly has to face the fact that his son has other goals and abilities in his life.
Fine Arts; Sociology
Dist - BYU **Prod** - BYU 1979

Trophy elk 15 MIN
16mm
Color
Shows hunters fashioning Indian game calls from native plants and downing the king of a buffalo herd with a single arrow.
Physical Education and Recreation
Dist - SFI **Prod** - SFI

Trophy tarpon 25 MIN
BETA / VHS
Color
Illustrates fishing for tarpon. Looks at a 130 - pound tarpon being caught, and shows information applicable anywhere for catching tarpon.
Physical Education and Recreation; Science - Natural
Dist - HOMEAF **Prod** - HOMEAF

Tropic Seacoast Survival 23 MIN
16mm
Color
LC 74-705864
Explains the teaching procedures and techniques to be followed for survival along tropical seacoasts.
Education; Social Science
Dist - USNAC **Prod** - USAF 1961

The Tropic seas 30 MIN
U-matic / VHS
Oceanus - the marine environment series; Lesson 25
Color
Focuses on the waters of the tropic zones. Contrasts the biological and physiological properties of the tropical seas. Examines the coral animal and reef ecosystem.
Science - Natural; Science - Physical
Dist - CDTEL **Prod** - SCCON
SCCON

The Tropic Seas 28 MIN
U-matic / VHS
Oceanus - the Marine Environment Series
Color (C A)
Science - Natural; Science - Physical
Dist - SCCON **Prod** - SCCON 1980

Tropical Botany Film Series
Flowering and fruiting of papaya 3 MIN
Fruiting of Coffee 3 MIN
Growth of Cassava - Manihot Utilissima 3 MIN
Dist - IOWA

Tropical Circulation 13 MIN
U-matic / VHS / 16mm
Color (I J H)
$49.95 purchase _ #Q10919
Uses animation to explain tropical weather patterns. Discusses global circulation of cold and warm air masses which bring about wet and dry seasons in the Tropics.
Science - Physical
Dist - CF **Prod** - IFFB 1984

Tropical Climate - Hawaii 30 MIN
VHS / BETA
Victory Garden Series
Color
Describes Hawaii's year - round growing climate where Chinese, Japanese, Vietnamese and other Asian - style crops thrive.

Agriculture; Physical Education and Recreation
Dist - CORF **Prod** - WGBHTV

Tropical creatures - Philippines - Part 8 8 MIN
VHS
Natures kingdom series
Color (P I J)
$125.00 purchase
Looks at cobras, calao birds, carnivorous spiders, cockatoos, green parrots and centipedes who share the jungle in the Philippines. Part of a 26 - part series on animals showing the habitats and traits of various species.
Geography - World; Science - Natural
Dist - LANDMK **Prod** - LANDMK 1992

Tropical depression 10 MIN
16mm
Color (G)
$15.00 rental
Deciphers the filmmaker's view of Florida and the way tourists and natives see it. Uses images from Florida to express this contradiction. Produced by Michele Fleming.
Fine Arts; Geography - United States
Dist - CANCIN

Tropical Harvest 17 MIN
U-matic / VHS / 16mm
Color (I J H)
LC FIA65-1542
Shows how a variety of plantation and natural crops of the tropics are grown. Emphasizes the effect of variation in altitude on climate.
Agriculture; Geography - World; Science - Physical
Dist - IFB **Prod** - IFB 1962

Tropical jungle 15 MIN
U-matic / VHS / 16mm
Color (I J)
$225.00 video purchase, $275.00 film purchase, $20.00 rental
Explores the sights, sounds, and conditions found in a Malayan jungle. Highlights unusual plants and animals. Shows a native hunting with a blowpipe.
Geography - World; Science - Natural
Dist - IFB **Prod** - DAVDW 1965

Tropical kingdom of Belize 60 MIN
VHS
Color; Captioned (G)
$29.95 purchase _ #S01474
Documents the diverse ecology of Belize, a tiny nation in Central America. Shows that the Belize wildlife includes mountain lions, jaguars, howler monkeys, hummingbirds and manatees.
Geography - World; Science - Natural
Dist - UILL **Prod** - NGS

Tropical kingdom of Belize 60 MIN
VHS
National Geographic video series
Color (G)
$29.95 purchase
Portrays the highly diverse natural environment of the Central American nation of Belize. Gives a close - up view of the many life forms.
Science - Natural
Dist - PBS **Prod** - WNETTV

Tropical Marshes 25 MIN
U-matic / VHS / 16mm
Untamed World Series
Color; Mono (J H C A)
$400.00 film, $250.00 video, $50.00 rental
Explores the tropical marshes of three continents to look at the rich animal and plant life of the dangerous swamplands. Visits North America, Africa, and Malaysia.
Geography - World; Science - Natural
Dist - CTV **Prod** - CTV 1973

Tropical Medicine 26 MIN
U-matic / VHS
Color (C)
$249.00, $149.00 purchase _ #AD - 1833
Visits the Tropical Disease Center at New York's Lenox Hill Hospital and laboratories where anti - parasitic vaccines and other treatments of tropical diseases are being developed.
Health and Safety; Science - Natural
Dist - FOTH **Prod** - FOTH

Tropical plants for the interiorscape series
Plant growth requirements - Volume III 23 MIN
Plant problem diagnosis - Volume IV 24 MIN
Plant selection and identification - Volume II 19 MIN
Principles of interior landscape design - Volume I 21 MIN
Dist - VEP

Tropical rain forest 13 MIN
VHS / U-matic / 16mm
Biomes series
Color (J H)
$350.00, $250.00 purchase _ #HP - 5945C
Examines the optimal environment in which life can succeed, the rain forest, home to an astonishing number of plant and animal species. Reveals that today rain forests are confined to areas near the equator - parts of Malaysia, Central America, the Amazon Basin, the Congo Basin and some tropical islands. Looks at the four distinct layers of the forest - Emergent, Canopy, Understory and Forest Floor. Part of a series on biomes produced by Partridge Films, Ltd.
Science - Natural
Dist - CORF

The Tropical rain forest 17 MIN
U-matic / VHS / 16mm
Biology - Spanish series; Ecosystems; Unit 2
Color (H) (SPANISH)
Examines the rich variety of animal and plant life in the humid environment of the tropical rain forest. Shows the layered structure of vegetation and describes conditions of temperature and rainfall.
Science - Natural
Dist - EBEC **Prod** - EBEC

The Tropical rainforest - diverse, delicate, disappearing 30 MIN
Slide / VHS
Color (G)
$25.00 purchase, $15.00, $20.00 rental
Explores the complex ecology of tropical rainforests. Highlights plant and animal species and indigenous peoples. Explores the causes and effects of forest destruction and suggests protective actions to be taken.
History - United States; Science - Natural
Dist - CMSMS **Prod** - SIERRA 1988

Tropicale 5 MIN
U-matic / 16mm / VHS
Color; Mono (G)
MV $85.00 _ MP $170.00 purchase, $50.00 rental
Visualizes the lush everglades and beach areas of southern Florida. Set to relaxing music.
Geography - United States
Dist - CTV **Prod** - MAKOF 1982

Tropici 87 MIN
16mm
B&W (PORTUGUESE (ENGLISH SUBTITLES) ITALIAN (ENGLISH SUBTITLES))
Tells of a poor Brazilian family forced to migrate to Sao Paulo in hopes of finding work. Describes encounters with the various people the family meets on its journey.
Fine Arts; Sociology
Dist - NYFLMS **Prod** - NYFLMS 1969

Tropism - Pt 1; 2nd ed. 15 MIN
U-matic
Search for science series; Unit VIII - Plants
Color (I)
Explains tropism as a vital process of plants.
Science - Natural
Dist - GPN **Prod** - WVIZTV

Tropism - Pt 2; 2nd ed. 15 MIN
U-matic
Search for science series; Unit VIII - Plants
Color (I)
Explains growth hormones and how they affect plant growth.
Science - Natural
Dist - GPN **Prod** - WVIZTV

Trotsky 58 MIN
VHS / 16mm
Color (J)
$179.00 purchase, $75.00 rental
Uses 1500 photos and filmclips to describe the role of Leon Trotsky in the creation of the Soviet Union. Examines how his leadership position changed during the course of the revolution and the establishment of the Soviet Union. Follows Trotsky's life up to his murder in Mexico.
Civics and Political Systems; History - World
Dist - FOTH

Trotta 95 MIN
16mm
Color (GERMAN (ENGLISH SUBTITLES))
Describes the downfall of the Austro - Hungarian monarchy up to the invasion of Hitler. Illustrates the non - political outlook of a resigned generation while politics are being determined by a new type of wealth - oriented aristocracy and while youth groups are attempting to realize their socialistic ideas through revolutionary protests.
Civics and Political Systems; History - World; Sociology
Dist - WSTGLC **Prod** - WSTGLC 1971

Trouble at Home - Learning to Cope
VHS / 35mm strip
$119.00 purchase _ #015 - 351 filmstrip, $139.00 purchase _ #015 -
Assists young people in understanding and coping with the fear, anger, and resentment they feel when trouble at home disrupts their lives. Instructs students how to identify the problem and gives methods of attaining peace of mind.
Guidance and Counseling; Sociology
Dist - CAREER **Prod** - CAREER

Trouble at home - learning to cope
VHS / U-matic
Color (I J)
Aids in understanding and coping with the fear, anger and resentment which occurs in a troubled home. Dramatizes such family problems as divorce, alcoholism, and unemployment. Describes methods of recognizing and accepting feeling. Outlines coping process.
Guidance and Counseling; Psychology; Sociology
Dist - SUNCOM **Prod** - SUNCOM

Trouble at number thirty - two - Paddington and the Christmas shopping - Christmas 17 MIN
U-matic / VHS / 16mm
Paddington bear series
Color (K P I)
LC 77-700667
Presents an animated adaptation of chapters 5 - 7 from the children's book More About Paddington by Michael Bond. Features a small, dark bear whose experiences with snow and Christmas shopping lead to many troubles.
Fine Arts; Literature and Drama
Dist - ALTSUL **Prod** - BONDM 1977

Trouble at Tonti Station 25 MIN
16mm
Color
LC 76-700481
Presents an actual account of civil defense teams in action. Shows how a train accident at Tonti Station in Illinois brought quick action from civil defense and volunteer forces in performing lifesaving and rescue missions.
Civics and Political Systems; History - United States; Sociology
Dist - USNAC **Prod** - USDCPA 1976

Trouble behind 56 MIN
16mm / VHS
Color (G)
$850.00, $250.00 purchase, $125.00, $75.00 rental
Uncovers the racist history of Corbin, Kentucky, home of Colonel Sanders Kentucky Fried Chicken. Reveals that during World War I, 200 blacks migrated to Corbin to fill jobs on the raiload. When whites returned from the war they found a changed community and on an October night in 1919, an armed mob rounded up the black workers, beat many, locked them into boxcars and 'railroaded' them out of the community. Part II explores the attitudes of present day residents and how they evade and deny their town's 'whites only' policy. Black residents of neighboring towns describe cross burnings, rock throwing and their fear of being in Corbin after dark - there is only one black family in Corbin. Produced by Robbie Henson.
History - United States; Sociology
Dist - CANWRL

Trouble beyond our shores 80 MIN
VHS
March of time - the great depression series
B&W (G)
$24.95 purchase _ #S02137
Presents newsreel excerpts covering the period from December 1935 to February 1936. Covers events including the Japanese occupation of China, competition in the Tennessee Valley between the TVA and private utilities, the beginning of dental anesthesia, and more. Part three of a six - part series.
History - United States
Dist - UILL

Trouble Brewing 60 MIN
U-matic / VHS
Sixty Minutes on Business Series
Color (G)
Business and Economics
Dist - VPHI **Prod** - VPHI 1984

Trouble Brewing - Adolph Coors Co
VHS / U-matic
Sixty Minutes on Business Series
Color
Presents one of ten segments selected from the realities of the business world, and chosen from key '60 Minutes' telecasts to provide insight into issues affecting business today. Includes sourcebook.
Business and Economics; Psychology
Dist - CBSFOX **Prod** - CBSFOX

Trouble down at Studleigh 30 MIN
U-matic / VHS
Wodehouse playhouse series

Color (C A)
Presents an adaptation of the short story Trouble Down At Studleigh by P G Wodehouse.
Literature and Drama
Dist - TIMLIF **Prod** - BBCTV 1980

Trouble for Lucy 14 MIN
U-matic / VHS
Readit Series
Color (P I)
LC 83-706832
Introduces the story of a young girl who travels with her family and puppy on the Oregon Trail in 1843. Shows that trouble comes when the girl leaves the wagon train in search of her puppy. Based on the book Trouble For Lucy by Carla Stevens.
English Language; Literature and Drama
Dist - AITECH **Prod** - POSIMP 1982

Trouble in Paradise 86 MIN
16mm
B&W
Features Herbert Marshall as the dashing Gaston Monescu, Miriam Hopkins as the Countess, and Kay Francis as the millionairess who takes them both under her wing. Directed by Ernst Lubitsch.
Fine Arts
Dist - TWYMAN **Prod** - PAR

Trouble in Space 8 MIN
VHS / U-matic
Giant First Start Series
Color (K P)
$29.95 purchase _ #VT009
Presents an adaptation of the book Trouble In Space. Contains a 32 page hardcover book and a video.
English Language; Literature and Drama
Dist - TROLA

Trouble in the family 90 MIN
16mm
America's crises series
B&W (H C A)
LC FIA66-1125
Shows how a therapist works with a family to get at the root of their problems. Dr Nathan W Ackerman, clinical professor of psychiatry at Columbia University, discusses family therapy with Harold Mayer.
Psychology; Sociology
Dist - IU **Prod** - NET 1965

Trouble in the firehouse 23 MIN
16mm
Color
Deals with a mayor's decision of a moratorium on new hiring. Poses questions about whether the Manning table is 'mandatory' or merely a 'goal.'
Business and Economics; Social Science
Dist - AARA **Prod** - AARA

Trouble in the Ghetto 25 MIN
16mm
Color
LC 74-702524
Examines the causes of the high rate of violent crime in Atlanta's ghetto.
Sociology
Dist - WAGATV **Prod** - WAGATV 1974

Trouble in Utopia 52 MIN
U-matic / VHS / 16mm
Shock of the New Series
Color (C A)
LC 80-700987
Describes the work of the German and Italian visionary architects. Tells how the Bauhaus and the functionalist faith started the worldwide spread of the glass - box style. Points out that the great myth of the architect as social legislator came to an end in the strange wasteland of Brasilia.
Fine Arts
Dist - TIMLIF **Prod** - BBCTV 1980

Trouble on Fashion Avenue 60 MIN
VHS / U-matic
Color (J)
LC 84-707173
Investigates the economic problems of the New York City garment industry, focusing on sweatshop conditions, the state of trade unions, the impact of imports and the role of organized crime.
Business and Economics; Home Economics
Dist - CNEMAG **Prod** - TVGDAP 1982

Trouble - Shooting an Electrocardiogram 11 MIN
VHS / BETA
Color
Explains how to eliminate artifacts.
Health and Safety
Dist - RMIBHF **Prod** - RMIBHF

Trouble shooting problems - fuel induction 17 MIN
16mm
B&W
LC FIE52-160
Illustrates how to locate trouble within the fuel system and how to correct over - heating, round running at idling speed and failure to develop full power.
Industrial and Technical Education
Dist - USNAC **Prod** - USOE 1945

Trouble Shooting Problems - Ignition 19 MIN
16mm
B&W
LC FIE52-250
Demonstrates how to locate trouble within the ignition system when an engine fails to start, when it runs roughly and when it fails to develop full power.
Industrial and Technical Education
Dist - USNAC **Prod** - USOE 1945

Trouble Shooting Problems - Mechanical and Lubrication 10 MIN
16mm
B&W
LC FIE52-147
Shows how to check symptoms and locate causes of an airplane engine's running rough, of low oil pressure and of high oil temperature.
Industrial and Technical Education
Dist - USNAC **Prod** - USOE 1945

Trouble - Shooting SCR Motor Controls 29 MIN
VHS / U-matic
Color (IND) (SPANISH)
Explains operation and repair of DC motor control systems. Provides opportunity to apply understanding of solid state electronics theory in a practical industrial context.
Education; Foreign Language; Industrial and Technical Education
Dist - TAT **Prod** - TAT

Trouble - Shooting with a Snap - Around Ammeter - Pilgrim 30 MIN
VHS / 16mm
Kirkwood Community College Auto Mechanics Series
(G PRO)
$111.00 purchase _ #KTI106
Shows how to trouble - shoot using a snap - around ammeter.
Industrial and Technical Education
Dist - RMIBHF **Prod** - RMIBHF

Trouble shooting your car 12 MIN
16mm
Automotive operation and maintenance - preventive maintenance series; No 5
B&W (H)
LC FIE52-348
Shows what a driver should do to locate and correct minor car troubles and how to recognize symptoms of impending trouble.
Industrial and Technical Education
Dist - USNAC **Prod** - USOE 1945

Trouble spot trimmer
VHS
(C A)
$24.95 _ #WW310V
Presents demonstrations of exercises that take the fat off of various trouble spots on the body.
Physical Education and Recreation
Dist - CAMV **Prod** - CAMV

Trouble stirring 13 MIN
U-matic / BETA / VHS
(H C A)
$100.00
Reports that Egypt is under increasing pressure from Moslem extremists to estabish a state based on traditional Islamic values.
Civics and Political Systems
Dist - CTV **Prod** - CTV 1986

The Trouble with Angels 112 MIN
16mm
Color (I J H C)
Stars Rosalind Russell as a Mother Superior who runs a convent school with considerable discipline and a sense of humor. Features Hayley Mills as a highspirited student determined to break every rule in the book just for the fun of it.
Fine Arts
Dist - TIMLIF **Prod** - CPC 1966

The Trouble with Harry 99 MIN
VHS
Color (G)
$59.95 purchase _ #S00912
Presents Alfred Hitchcock's black comedy about a Vermont community which clumsily tries to dispose of the body of a town resident found dead in the woods. Stars John Forsythe, Edmund Gwenn, and Shirley MacLaine in her first film role.
Fine Arts
Dist - UILL

The Trouble with Ice 10 MIN
16mm / U-matic / VHS
Color (I J H)
LC 72-701074
Teaches various rescue techniques to be used when aiding a person who has fallen through the ice.
Health and Safety
Dist - AIMS **Prod** - BSA 1971

The Trouble with Miss Switch 48 MIN
U-matic / VHS / 16mm
Color (I J)
LC 80-701785
Tells of two youngsters who face some bizarre and terrifying experiences as they try to save their teacher, who is a witch, from being banished by the evil head witch. Based on the book The Trouble With Miss Switch by Barbara Brooks Wallace. Originally shown as an ABC Weekend Special.
Literature and Drama; Sociology
Dist - CORF **Prod** - ABCLR 1980

The Trouble with Mother 24 MIN
U-matic / VHS
Young people's specials series
Color
Looks at a mother and daughter in conflict over the role of women in our changing society. Stars Sandy Dennis.
Sociology
Dist - MULTPP **Prod** - MULTPP

The Trouble with Rachel 30 MIN
VHS
Color (I)
Focuses on the relationship between school personnel, children and families in a context of common family stress and its effect on the child's school behavior.
Education; Guidance and Counseling; Psychology; Social Science; Sociology
Dist - WHITD **Prod** - WHITD 1986

The Trouble with sales training 8 MIN
VHS
Color (G)
$295.00 purchase, $100.00 rental _ #91F6110A
Features two top British comedians who illustrate why continuous training is important in sales.
Business and Economics; Psychology
Dist - DARTNL **Prod** - DARTNL

Trouble with Strangers 10 MIN
16mm / U-matic / VHS
Color (P)
LC 76-702161
Communicates through a child's eyes the problem of molestation. Shows the police rescuing a little girl and explaining how to avoid most situations involving such a danger.
Health and Safety
Dist - AIMS **Prod** - DAVP 1975

Trouble with the law 26 MIN
VHS
Challenge of the seas series
Color (I J H)
$225.00 purchase
Reveals that the American public has shown through law that they hold marine mammals in a special place. Shows that such laws are being subverted as evidenced by the deaths of thousands of dolphins and the killing of walrus for ivory. Documents the forbidden markets for sea mammals. Part of a 26 - part series on the oceans.
Science - Natural; Science - Physical
Dist - LANDMK **Prod** - LANDMK 1991

Trouble with the Law 16 MIN
16mm / U-matic / VHS
Searching for Values - a Film Anthology Series
Color (J)
LC 72-703092
Explains that a college student involved in an auto accident rejects the standard by which the court finds him guilty and decides that justice has not been served by the legal process.
Civics and Political Systems; Guidance and Counseling; Sociology
Dist - LCOA **Prod** - LCOA 1972

The Trouble with tobacco 12 MIN
VHS
CC; Color (I J)
$79.95 purchase _ #10409VG
Explains the advertising and facts about smoking and tobacco use. Presents the effects of smoking and the expense involved in maintaining a tobacco habit. Enumerates the chemicals and diseases connected to cigarettes, snuff and chewing tobacco. Includes a guide.
Health and Safety
Dist - UNL

The Trouble with Tommy 10 MIN
U-matic / VHS / 16mm

Color (P I)
Presents the topic of shoplifting from the child's viewpoint. Tells what happens when a child is encouraged to steal and is later caught.
Sociology
Dist - CORF **Prod** - CREATP

The Trouble with training 10 MIN
VHS
Color (A PRO IND)
$325.00 purchase, $125.00 rental
Stars Mel Smith as Bob Smedley, the 'average employee' who doesn't understand why training sessions are necessary. Shows that Smedley must learn he needs new skills.
Business and Economics; Guidance and Counseling; Psychology
Dist - VLEARN **Prod** - CRMF

Trouble with Travino 30 MIN
U-matic
Color (I J)
Shows the difference between fair and unfair and how to deal with disappointment.
Psychology; Sociology
Dist - TVOTAR **Prod** - TVOTAR 1986

The Trouble with Tuck 15 MIN
VHS
Books from cover to cover series
Color (P I G)
$25.00 purchase _ #BFCC - 110
Features a young girl who teaches her blind dog to follow and trust a guide dog. Shows how the girl's self - confidence is built as a result. Based on the book 'The Trouble with Tuck' by Theodore Taylor. Hosted by John Robbins.
Fine Arts; Literature and Drama
Dist - PBS **Prod** - WETATV 1988

Troubled Campers 16 MIN
16mm
Wediko Series
B&W (PRO)
LC 71-713199
Uses a composite of several episodes of spontaneous behavior to show various emotionally disturbed boys during a summer at a therapeutic camp.
Education; Psychology
Dist - DOCUFL **Prod** - MASON 1971

Troubled campers 18 MIN
U-matic / VHS
Wediko series - emotionally disturbed children at camp series
B&W (T)
Introduces some of the dimensions of emotional handicaps and encourages discussion about prevention, treatment, rehabilitation and education, especially as related to emotionally disturbed children campers.
Education; Psychology
Dist - DOCUFL **Prod** - DOCUFL

The Troubled cities 60 MIN
16mm
America's crises series
B&W (H C A)
LC FIA67-1843
Examines the attempts being made to solve problems brought about by the urban population explosion.
Psychology; Science - Natural; Sociology
Dist - IU **Prod** - NET 1966

The Troubled employee 25 MIN
16mm / U-matic / VHS
Color
Tells managers how to recognize workers with personal problems and what to do to return them to productivity.
Guidance and Counseling; Sociology
Dist - UNKNWN **Prod** - DARTNL

Troubled harvest 30 MIN
U-matic / VHS
Color (G)
$195.00 purchase, $50.00 rental
Examines the lives of women migrant workers from Mexico and Central America as they work in grape, strawberry and cherry harvests in California and the Pacific Northwest. Looks at the dangerous effects of pesticides on the health of these women and their children. Considers the destructive consequences of US immigration policies on the unity of their families. Features an interview with Dolores Huerta, co - founder of the United Farm Workers union.
Business and Economics; History - World; Social Science; Sociology
Dist - WMEN

Troubled joints 29 MIN
VHS / U-matic
Bodywatch series
Color (H C G)
$80.00 purchase _ #HH - 6005M
Reveals that although many people mistake arthritis as the inevitable consequence of age, thousands of young Americans are sufferers. Features an interview with baseball great and arthritis sufferer Mickey Mantle. Part of the Bodywatch series.
Health and Safety; Sociology
Dist - CORF **Prod** - WGBHTV 1989

Troubled Neighbors - Cuba and the United States 15 MIN
16mm
Screen news digest series; Vol 18; Issue 4
B&W (I)
LC 76-701849
Analyzes the changing nature of Cuban - American relations since Fidel Castro's seizure of power in 1959. Covers Castro's journey to power, nationalization of utility companies, the missile crisis and the significant differences which continue to exist between the two countries.
Civics and Political Systems; History - United States; History - World
Dist - HEARST **Prod** - HEARST 1975

Troubled paradise 58 MIN
VHS / U-matic / 16mm
Color (G)
$750.00, $295.00 purchase, $150.00, $75.00 rental
Celebrates the richness of Hawaiian culture and takes a compelling look at the social and political problems facing its indigenous population. Offers four stories about native Hawaiians fighting for the survival of their culture. Features performances by musicians and dancers and footage of recent volcanic eruptions. Produced and directed by Steven Ozaki.
History - United States; Sociology
Dist - CROCUR

Troubled waters 11 MIN
VHS
Color (G)
$19.95 purchase
Explains the unique dangers posed by nuclear weapons at sea. Includes commentary from a former Admiral of the US Navy as he explains how nuclear weapons on board ships have the potential to become a trigger, not a deterrent, for nuclear war. Presents statistics about naval nuclear accidents which reveal that the presence of nuclear weapons at sea threatens all life on the planet.
Civics and Political Systems; Science - Natural
Dist - GRNPCE **Prod** - GRNPCE 1989

Troubled Waters 55 MIN
BETA / VHS / U-matic
Color (J S C A G)
Shows Norwegian Americans and Chippewa Indian commerical fisherman in a time of crisis. Reveals Operation Gill Net, a massive undercover operation that entrapped the fisherman into selling illegal fish. Takes place in Wisconsin fishing villages of Bayfield and Red Cliff on the Chippewa Reservation.
Social Science
Dist - UCV

Troubled waters - plastic in the marine environment 29 MIN
VHS
Color (J H C G)
$195.00 purchase, $45.00 rental
Presents a clear and concise picture of the many ways that plastics can find a way into the oceans and of the danger this plastic poses to marine life. Looks at the actions being taken by concerned citizens, government agencies and industry associations to prevent and control the problem. Produced by Ernest Urvater and Beth Freishtat - EFP Services.
Fine Arts; Geography - World; Industrial and Technical Education; Science - Natural
Dist - BULFRG

Troublemakers 54 MIN
U-matic / VHS / 16mm
B&W
Documents the roots of political turmoil in the Sixties. Portrays efforts of former Students For A Democratic Society (SDS), including Tom Hayden, to organize people in the black community of Newark, NJ to work for social change.
Sociology
Dist - CNEMAG **Prod** - CNEMAG 1966

The Troubles 35 MIN
U-matic / VHS
Color
Examines the history and current issues of the 800 - year - old conflict between Protestants and Catholics in Ireland.
History - World; Religion and Philosophy
Dist - WCCOTV **Prod** - WCCOTV 1981

The Troubles - conquest 54 MIN
U-matic / VHS
Troubles series
Color (H C A)
Uses eminent historians, nineteenth - century photographs, motion picture film from the early twentieth century and folk memories to trace Irish history from the sixteenth century to the 1916 Easter Rising. Helps to explain what is happening today in Northern Ireland.
History - World
Dist - MEDIAG **Prod** - THAMES 1982

The Troubles - Deadlock 54 MIN
VHS / U-matic
Troubles Series
Color (H C A)
Presents the story of Bobby Sands, convicted member of the Irish Republican Army, who was serving a fourteen - year prison sentence for firearms charges when he was elected to Parliament. He was the thirteenth Irish nationalist to die from a hunger strike during the twentieth century as he protested his imprisonment on political grounds.
History - World
Dist - MEDIAG **Prod** - THAMES 1982

Troubles Going to Las Vegas 4 MIN
16mm
Color (J) (AMERICAN SIGN)
LC 76-701708
Relates in American sign language the catastrophe of a young deaf Chicano traveling to Las Vegas on vacation. Signed for the deaf by Ralph Gardenas.
Guidance and Counseling; Psychology
Dist - JOYCE **Prod** - JOYCE 1975

The Troubles - Intervention 54 MIN
VHS / U-matic
Troubles Series
Color (H C A)
Portrays the streets of Northern Ireland, occupied by the British Army, as they are normally. Shows the streets not erupting in smoke, but quiet, tense, and socially deprived in some areas.
History - World
Dist - MEDIAG **Prod** - THAMES 1982

The Troubles - partition 54 MIN
VHS / U-matic
Troubles series
Color (H C A)
Presents the history of Northern Ireland from 1920 to 1970, using newly - discovered archive film and eyewitness accounts. Features interviews with Glen Barr, who presents the loyalist perspective, and Michael Farrell presenting the Republican viewpoint.
History - World
Dist - MEDIAG **Prod** - THAMES 1982

The Troubles - Rebellion 54 MIN
U-matic / VHS
Troubles Series
Color (H C A)
Details Bloody Sunday, January 30, 1972, which signalled the collapse of the Northern Ireland Parliament at Stormont and the beginning of direct rule by Britain. Covers the period beginning in 1966 that led up to this historic event.
History - World
Dist - MEDIAG **Prod** - THAMES 1982

The Troubles - Rising 54 MIN
U-matic / VHS
Troubles Series
Color (H C A)
Describes how the British left 26 counties when Ireland was partitioned in 1921. The struggle of Irish nationalists began in the nineteenth century in the British Parliament and culminated in the country of Northern Ireland.
History - World
Dist - MEDIAG **Prod** - THAMES 1982

Troubles series
Presents six parts on the complex history of Ireland and the suffering the Irish people have had to endure. Includes the titles Conquest; Rising; Partition; Rellion; Intervention; and Deadlock. Contact distributor about availability outside the United Kingdom.
The Troubles series 374 MIN
Dist - ACADEM

Troubles Series
The Troubles - conquest 54 MIN
The Troubles - Deadlock 54 MIN
The Troubles - Intervention 54 MIN
The Troubles - partition 54 MIN
The Troubles - Rebellion 54 MIN
The Troubles - Rising 54 MIN
Dist - MEDIAG

Troubles with 'S' - the initial 'S' 30 MIN
Videoreel / VT2
Solutions in Communications Series
Color (T)
Education; English Language
Dist - SCCOE **Prod** - SCCOE

Troubleshooting 60 MIN
U-matic / VHS
Electrical maintenance training motors series; Module 2 - Motors
Color (IND)
Industrial and Technical Education
Dist - LEIKID **Prod** - LEIKID

Troubleshooting 38 MIN
VHS / U-matic
Tribology 1 - Friction, Wear, and Lubrication Series
Color
Teaches a systematic procedure for troubleshooting, including determining the characteristics and function of the failed part.
Industrial and Technical Education
Dist - MIOT **Prod** - MIOT

Troubleshooting
16mm / U-matic
Instrumentation Maintenance Series
Color (IND)
Explains troubleshooting of analog and digital control systems.
Mathematics
Dist - ISA **Prod** - ISA

Troubleshooting 30 MIN
VHS
A House for all seasons series
Color (G)
$49.95 purchase _ #AHFS - 201
Provides solutions to unusual energy - wasting problems. Considers how to deal with indoor moisture and air pollution. Features an architect's renovated house.
Home Economics; Science - Natural; Social Science; Sociology
Dist - PBS **Prod** - KRMATV 1985

Troubleshooting 30 MIN
VHS
Computing for the less terrified series
Color (A)
PdS65 purchase
Shows how a disastrous computer error may mean rebuilding an operation from scratch. Part of a seven-part series which aims to allay everyone's fear of the computer, whether experienced user or relative novice. Explores the numerous applications of the computer and illustrates some of the pitfalls.
Computer Science; Guidance and Counseling
Dist - BBCENE

Troubleshooting and Emergency Repair of AC Systems and Equipment 60 MIN
VHS
Electrical Maintenance Practices Series
Color (PRO)
$600.00, $1500.00 purchase _ #EMTAC
Focuses on AC systems and equipment troubleshooting. Shows what AC systems, subsystems, units and components are used, how to identify and locate grounds, shorts and opens and how to make simple repairs to AC equipment following safe procedures. Part of a six - part series on electrical maintenance practices, which is part of a 29 unit set on electrical maintenance. Includes 10 textbooks and an instructor guide which provide four hours of instruction.
Education; Health and Safety; Industrial and Technical Education; Psychology
Dist - NUSTC **Prod** - NUSTC

Troubleshooting and Emergency Repair of DC Systems and Equipment 60 MIN
VHS
Electrical Maintenance Practices Series
Color (PRO)
$600.00, $1500.00 purchase _ #EMTDC
Examines DC systems and equipment troubleshooting, with particular emphasis on industrial DC systems, subsystems, units and components in common use. Shows how to identify and locate grounds, shorts and opens and how to make simple repairs to DC equipment following safe procedures. Part of a six - part series on electrical maintenance practices, which is part of a 29 unit set on electrical maintenance. Includes 10 textbooks and an instructor guide which provide four hours of instruction.
Education; Health and Safety; Industrial and Technical Education; Psychology
Dist - NUSTC **Prod** - NUSTC

Troubleshooting and maintaining the IBM PC and compatibles 150 MIN
VHS
Self - teaching video learning package series
Color (G PRO)
$295.00 purchase _ #4TR57
Features Mark Minasi, author, editor and PC veteran who delivers a basic, step - by - step presentation showing how to find and eliminate the typical glitches that slow a computer down. Teaches installation, configuration, and repair. Takes a detailed look at circuit boards, hard and floppy disks, printers, and other essentials. Reveals how to solve memory errors and replace memory chips and isolate all types of hardware and software errors. Includes a fully - illustrated comprehensive workbook with extensive lists of BIOS upgrade vendors and recommended data recovery service companies, a specialized tool kit, and diagnostic program disk. Part of a series.
Computer Science
Dist - TECHIN

Troubleshooting automatic sprinkler systems 24 MIN
VHS
Color (G)
$89.95 purchase _ #6 - 051 - 101P
Teaches a systematic approach for quickly locating problems within an automatic sprinkler system. Examines the basic components of automatic sprinkler systems and how they relate to each other. Treats troubleshooting methodology moving from the most likely trouble spots to the least likely. Produced by the Toro Company.
Agriculture; Industrial and Technical Education
Dist - VEP

Troubleshooting Centrifugal Pumps 60 MIN
VHS / U-matic
Troubleshooting Series
Color
Covers troubleshooting centrifugal pumps. Outlines the conditions required for normal operation.
Education; Industrial and Technical Education
Dist - ITCORP **Prod** - ITCORP

Troubleshooting digital equipment 60 TO 90 MIN
VHS
Fundamentals of digital electronics module series
Color (PRO)
$600.00 - $1500.00 purchase _ #DETDE
Concentrates on troubleshooting techniques for digital equipment. Considers procedures for equipment not discussed previously. Includes safety precautions. Part of a twelve - part series on fundamentals of digital electronics. Includes five student guides, five workbooks and an instructor guide.
Computer Science; Health and Safety; Industrial and Technical Education; Psychology
Dist - NUSTC **Prod** - NUSTC

Troubleshooting digital sub - systems 30 MIN
VHS / U-matic
Digital sub - systems series
Color
Gives an approach for troubleshooting either for system check - out or for maintenance. Shows tour of digital test equipment.
Industrial and Technical Education; Mathematics; Sociology
Dist - TXINLC **Prod** - TXINLC

Troubleshooting distributed control systems - Pt 1 60 TO 90 MIN
VHS
Distributed control systems module series
Color (PRO)
$600.00 - $1500.00 purchase _ #DCTD1
Introduces distributed control system troubleshooting. Addresses the basic principles of system troubleshooting. Part of a fourteen - part series on distributed control systems. Includes five student guides, five textbooks and an instructor guide.
Computer Science; Education; Industrial and Technical Education; Psychology
Dist - NUSTC **Prod** - NUSTC

Troubleshooting distributed control systems - Pt 2 60 TO 90 MIN
VHS
Distributed control systems module series
Color (PRO)
$600.00 - $1500.00 purchase _ #DCTD2
Focuses on methods used to isolate common failures in a typical distributed control system. Presents an understanding of common techniques for troubleshooting distributed control systems which is applicable to all systems. Part of a fourteen - part series on distributed control systems. Includes five student guides, five textbooks and an instructor guide.
Computer Science; Education; Industrial and Technical Education; Psychology
Dist - NUSTC **Prod** - NUSTC

Troubleshooting Electrical Circuits 16 MIN
U-matic / VHS / 16mm
Color
Shows how to locate and repair shorted, grounded and open circuits.
Industrial and Technical Education; Science - Physical
Dist - USNAC **Prod** - USAF

Troubleshooting Electrical Components 40 MIN
VHS / 35mm strip
(H A IND)
#461XV7
Shows the proper procedures for servicing some basic electrical components in an automobile. Includes tools and equipment, troubleshooting techniques, and servicing electrical components (3 tapes). Prerequisite required. Includes a Study Guide.
Education; Industrial and Technical Education
Dist - BERGL

Troubleshooting electronic fuel injection 56 MIN
VHS
Color (H A)
$219.00 purchase _ #VMA09452V
Covers troubleshooting and service of Ford and General Motors electronic fuel injection systems. Consists of two videocassettes and a program guide.
Industrial and Technical Education
Dist - CAMV

Troubleshooting Field Device Malfunctions 30 MIN
U-matic / VHS
Programmable Controllers Series
Color
Deals with troubleshooting field device malfunctions. Stresses interpreting the program.
Industrial and Technical Education; Sociology
Dist - ITCORP **Prod** - ITCORP

Troubleshooting Hydraulic Systems Series
Presents a series of training videos that teaches the student how to identify, repair and prevent malfunctions in hydraulic systems.

Analyzing component faults	22 MIN
Applied troubleshooting	21 MIN
Contamination	18 MIN
Heat and Leakage	24 MIN
Troubleshooting hydraulic systems series	
Troubleshooting Techniques	20 MIN

Dist - TAT **Prod** - TAT

Troubleshooting Hydraulic Systems Series
Presents a series of training videos the help the student isolate a system fault quickly by systematically eliminating possible problems.

Analyzing component faults	22 MIN
Applied troubleshooting	21 MIN
Contamination	18 MIN
Heat and Leakage	24 MIN
Troubleshooting hydraulic systems series	
Troubleshooting Techniques	20 MIN

Dist - TAT **Prod** - TAT

Troubleshooting landscape equipment - power hand tools
VHS
Color (G)
$89.95 purchase _ #6 - 302 - 301S
Shows step - by - step job site troubleshooting and field repair methods for the most common problems with two - cycle engines used with line trimmers, power blowers, chain saws, hedge shears and other landscaping tools.
Agriculture
Dist - VEP **Prod** - VEP 1991

Troubleshooting Microcomputer I - O Devices 60 TO 90 MIN
VHS
Microcomputer I - O Devices Module Series
Color (PRO)
$600.00 - $1500.00 purchase _ #MCTMP
Discusses troubleshooting microcomputer systems. Moves onto troubleshooting system peripheral devices. Part of a six - part series on microcomputer I - O devices. Includes five student guides, five workbooks and an instructor guide.
Computer Science; Education; Industrial and Technical Education; Psychology
Dist - NUSTC **Prod** - NUSTC

Troubleshooting Microprocessors 60 TO 90 MIN
VHS
Microprocessors Module Series
Color (PRO)
$600.00 - $1500.00 purchase _ #MITMI
Overviews microprocessor operations. Discusses operation evaluation with both logic analyzers and signature

analyzers. Addresses both hardware and software approaches to microprocessor troubleshooting. Part of an eleven - part series on microprocessors. Includes five student guides, five workbooks and an instructor guide.
Computer Science; Education; Industrial and Technical Education; Psychology
Dist - NUSTC **Prod** - NUSTC

Troubleshooting Motors 21 MIN
VHS / 16mm
Maintaining & Troubleshooting Electric Motors Series
Color (H A)
$465.00 purchase, $110.00 rental
Demonstrates how to troubleshoot common motor failures, locate root causes and prevent potential failures.
Industrial and Technical Education
Dist - TAT **Prod** - TAT 1989

Troubleshooting P C Malfunctions 30 MIN
U-matic / VHS
Programmable Controllers Series
Color
Deals with troubleshooting P C Malfunctions. Points to CPU, I O, and power supply problems.
Industrial and Technical Education; Sociology
Dist - ITCORP **Prod** - ITCORP

Troubleshooting PCs - Pt 1 27 MIN
VHS / 16mm
Programmable Controllers (PLC's) Series
Color (H A)
$465.00 purchase, $110.00 rental
Describes the process for isolating problems. Covers documentation.
Computer Science; Industrial and Technical Education
Dist - TAT **Prod** - TAT 1984

Troubleshooting PCs - Pt 2 21 MIN
VHS / 16mm
Programmable Controllers (PLC's) Series
Color (H A)
$465.00 purchase, $110.00 rental
Describes the process for disabling and forcing coils. Shows proper troubleshooting methods and presents realistic situations.
Computer Science; Industrial and Technical Education
Dist - TAT **Prod** - TAT 1984

Troubleshooting pneumatic instrument systems 60 MIN
VHS
Pneumatic systems and equipment series
Color (PRO)
$600.00 - $1500.00 purchase _ #ICTPI
Presents the basics of troubleshooting pneumatic instrument systems. Part of an eleven - part series on pneumatic systems and equipment, which is part of a 49 - unit set on instrumentation and control. Includes five workbooks and an instructor guide to support four hours of instruction.
Education; Industrial and Technical Education; Mathematics; Psychology
Dist - NUSTC **Prod** - NUSTC

Troubleshooting Port Fuel Injection 90 MIN
VHS / 16mm
Color (H A)
$399.00 purchase _ A22
Introduces system maintenance, describes cleaning procedures, safe removal and troubleshooting of injectors.
Industrial and Technical Education
Dist - BERGL **Prod** - BERGL 1988

Troubleshooting Positive Displacement Pumps 60 MIN
U-matic / VHS
Troubleshooting Series
Color
Examines troubleshooting positive displacement pumps. Includes performing operational checks on suction components, speed control components and packing.
Education; Industrial and Technical Education
Dist - ITCORP **Prod** - ITCORP

Troubleshooting Programmable Controllers 60 TO 90 MIN
VHS
Programmable Controllers Module Series
Color (PRO)
$600.00 - $1500.00 purchase _ #PCPCM
Focuses on programmable controller troubleshooting procedures. Emphasizes board - level or module - level troubleshooting. Part of a seven - part series on programmable controllers. Includes five student guides, five workbooks and an instructor guide.
Computer Science; Education; Industrial and Technical Education; Psychology
Dist - NUSTC **Prod** - NUSTC

Troubleshooting Reciprocating Air Compressors 60 MIN
VHS / U-matic
Troubleshooting Series
Color
Investigates troubleshooting reciprocating air compressors, Describes conditions required for normal operation. Discusses performing operational checks.
Education; Industrial and Technical Education
Dist - ITCORP **Prod** - ITCORP

Troubleshooting Series
Principles of Mechanical Troubleshooting 60 MIN
Troubleshooting Centrifugal Pumps 60 MIN
Troubleshooting Positive Displacement Pumps 60 MIN
Troubleshooting Reciprocating Air Compressors 60 MIN
Dist - ITCORP

Troubleshooting Techniques 20 MIN
VHS / 16mm
Troubleshooting Hydraulic Systems Series
Color (H A)
$465.00 purchase, $110.00 rental
Helps the student isolate a system fault quickly by systematically eliminating possibile problems.
Industrial and Technical Education
Dist - TAT **Prod** - TAT 1986

Troubleshooting Techniques 30 MIN
U-matic / VHS
Programmable Controllers Series
Color
Delineates troubleshooting techniques. Stresses developing a logical approach.
Industrial and Technical Education; Sociology
Dist - ITCORP **Prod** - ITCORP

Troubleshooting the IBM PC
VHS / 35mm strip
$269.00 purchase filmstrip, $242.00 purchase video _ #016-747
Provides training on how to troubleshoot and repair the IBM PC.
Industrial and Technical Education
Dist - CAREER **Prod** - CAREER

Troubleshooting the IBM PC 64 MIN
VHS / 35mm strip
(G A IND)
#877XV7
Shows system components, using the diagnostics diskette, inside the system unit, testing the power supply (4 tapes). Study Guide included.
Computer Science; Industrial and Technical Education
Dist - BERGL

Troubleshooting the Ignition System
VHS
Troubleshooting the Ignition System - Testing and Service Series - 'three titles on eight VHS tapes -
$1,037.00 purchase _ #IEV045V
Explores methods for testing the primary circuit and ignition system. Portrays installing and timing the distributor.
Education; Industrial and Technical Education
Dist - CAREER **Prod** - CAREER

Troubleshooting the Ignition System - Testing and Service Series - three titles on eight VHS tapes -
Troubleshooting the Ignition System
Dist - CAREER

Troubleshooting the Ignition System - Testing and Service Series
Ignition Testing Procedures
Ignition Timing Procedures
Primary Circuit Testing
Dist - CAREER

Troubleshooting with the VAT - 40 72 MIN
VHS / 35mm strip
(H A IND)
#441XV7
Teaches how to perform troubleshooting operations on an automotive electrical system with the VAT - 40. Includes introduction and meter reading, performing system tests, testing battery performance, troubleshooting the starting system, and troubleshooting the charging system (5 tapes). Prerequisites required. Includes a Study Guide.
Education; Industrial and Technical Education
Dist - BERGL

Troublesome Pronouns - who and Whom 11 MIN
BETA / VHS
English and Speech Series
Color
English Language
Dist - RMIBHF **Prod** - RMIBHF

Troublesome Verbs - Lie and Lay, Sit and Set, Rise and Raise 11 MIN
BETA / VHS
English and Speech Series
Color
English Language
Dist - RMIBHF **Prod** - RMIBHF

The Troupe 112 MIN
VHS
Color (G) (HEBREW WITH ENGLISH SUBTITLES)
$79.95 purchase _ #549
Presents a musical comedy about 12 women and men who are members of an Israeli Army entertainment troupe in the period immediately after the Six Day War. Shows how they struggle with the stress of performing, competing for solo spots and falling in and out of love with each other. Stars Gidi Gov, Gali Atari, Meir Suissa and Tuvia Tzafir. Directed by Avi Nesher.
Fine Arts; History - World; Sociology
Dist - ERGOM **Prod** - ERGOM 1981

Troupers 84 MIN
16mm / VHS
Color (G)
$1215.00, $490.00 purchase, $125.00 rental
Entertains with the lively and irreverent San Francisco Mime Troupe, boisterous and fun but also keenly committed to social change. Looks at their history from their birth in the 1960s San Francisco counter - culture to playing in midwestern union halls and New York theaters.
Fine Arts
Dist - FIRS **Prod** - VIASIL 1985

A Trousseau to Treasure 29 MIN
Videoreel / VT2
Designing Women Series
Color
Home Economics
Dist - PBS **Prod** - WKYCTV

Trout Fishing in Tasmania 19 MIN
16mm
Color
LC 80-700931
Presents a guide on where fish are to be found in Tasmania.
Geography - World; Physical Education and Recreation; Science - Natural
Dist - TASCOR **Prod** - TASCOR 1976

A Trout stream in winter 18 MIN
VHS / 16mm
Color (G J H)
$310.00, $185.00 purchase, $16.50 rental _ #22591
Studies the reproductive behavior of brook trout, spawning of rainbow trout and dangers posed to stream ecology by low snowfall in a high snowpack area in the Sierra Nevada and by formation of frazil and anchor ice.
Science - Natural
Dist - PSU PSUPCR **Prod** - RBVH 1979

Trout systems 30 MIN
U-matic
Sport fishing series
Color (G)
Describes the conditions necessary for trout to thrive, including cold, fast flowing water.
Physical Education and Recreation; Science - Natural
Dist - TVOTAR **Prod** - TVOTAR 1985

The Trout that Stole the Rainbow 8 MIN
16mm
Color
Tells how the world loses all color when a selfish trout cannot resist the beauty of the rainbow and steals it. As punishment, the sun paints the trout in rainbow colors that can be enjoyed by all but Trout.
Literature and Drama
Dist - NFBC **Prod** - NFBC 1982

Trout USA 14 MIN
U-matic / VHS
Color
LC 80-797745
Studies the trout industry, discusses trout fishing as a sport, and tells how to prepare trout for the table.
Industrial and Technical Education; Physical Education and Recreation
Dist - USNAC **Prod** - USBCF 1980

Trowel trades 10 MIN
VHS
Skills - occupational programs series
Color (H A)
$49.00 purchase, $15.00 rental _ #316602; LC 91-708505
Looks at bricklayers and stonemasons, marble setters, plasterers and other skilled people employed in the trowel trades. Part of a series featuring occupations in the skilled trades, in service industries and in business leading to careers in areas of demand and future growth. Includes teacher's guide with reproducible wooksheets.
Guidance and Counseling; Psychology
Dist - TVOTAR **Prod** - TVOTAR 1990

Troy game 39 MIN
VHS
Color (S)
$39.95 purchase _ #086-9008
Mixes dance, aikido exercises and acrobatics to create Troy Game by choreographer Robert North. Features nine male dancers from the London Contemporary Dance Theatre performing this piece based on Brazilian macho competitions which are danced to percussion instrumentals that range from Brazilian folk songs to Shadow Boxing Solo by Bob Downes.
Fine Arts; Geography - World
Dist - FI **Prod** - IFPAL 1988

Troy - Patterson 30 MIN
16mm
IBC Championship Fights, Series 2 Series
B&W
Physical Education and Recreation
Dist - SFI **Prod** - SFI

TRS - 80 Model 4 operations
VHS
Computer operations series
$65 purchase _ #RM6312V
Introduces the configurations and operations of specific computers. Teaches the setup and "bootup" routines as well as load, save and run procedures.
Computer Science; Education
Dist - CAREER **Prod** - CAREER

Truce and Epilogue - Volume 5 120 MIN
VHS
Korean war series
Color; B&W (G)
$19.95 purchase _ #1649
Chronicles in two parts the truce which ended the Korean War and events following the war. Includes film footage from both North and South Korea and interviews with Korean, American and Russian military and political leaders who personally participated in the events. Part five of a five - part series on the Korean War. Produced by the Korean Broadcast System.
History - World
Dist - KULTUR

Truce in the Forest 38 MIN
16mm
Color
LC 78-700227
Tells the story of a German widow who extends her hospitality to both German and American soldiers on Christmas Eve, 1944.
History - United States; History - World; Literature and Drama; Psychology; Sociology
Dist - FAMF **Prod** - FAMF 1977

Truck - car safety TV spots 2 MIN
Videoreel / U-matic / VT1
Color (H G)
$15.00 purchase _ #332, #331
Presents a 30 second and 60 second TV PSA outlining how a car can safely share the road with a big truck. Features Mr Wizard.
Health and Safety; Industrial and Technical Education
Dist - AAAFTS **Prod** - AAAFTS 1987

A Truck Driver Named Gret 11 MIN
U-matic / VHS / 16mm
Color
Profiles a 38 - year - old wife, mother and delivery truck driver. Explores her motives and the varied attitudes of family members, storeowners and the people she encounters on the job. Explodes myths and stereotypes of women who choose non - traditional fields of work.
Sociology
Dist - CAROUF **Prod** - LEVKOF

Truck drivers only 15 MIN
16mm
Color; B&W
Covers key safety tips for the the prevention of truck accidents. Includes why accidents happen, how drivers can help prevent accidents, self discipline on the road, the truck's blind spot, vehicle safety checks, eye tests and health examinations.
Health and Safety; Industrial and Technical Education; Social Science
Dist - FO **Prod** - FO 1964

Truck driving - controlling skids 17 MIN
VHS
Color (H G)
$295.00 purchase, $75.00 rental _ #8312
Shows how to handle skids when driving a truck.
Health and Safety; Psychology
Dist - AIMS **Prod** - GND 1991

Truck Song 17 MIN
16mm / VHS
Color (I)
$335.00, $390.00 purchase, $50.00 rental _ #9927
Celebrates trucks and the life of truckers with a rhymed text evoking the rhythm of a truck's journey across country. Adapted from the book by Diane Siebert especially for intermediate children.
History - World; Social Science
Dist - AIMS **Prod** - WILETS 1988

Truck Song 13 MIN
16mm / VHS
Color (K P)
$245.00, $295.00 purchase, $50.00 rental _ #9991
Celebrates trucks and the life of truckers with a rhymed text evoking the rhythm of a truck's journey across country. Adapted from the book by Diane Siebert especially for kindergarten and primary children.
History - World; Social Science
Dist - AIMS **Prod** - WILETS 1988

Truck Stop 28 MIN
16mm / U-matic / VHS
Insight Series
Color; B&W (J) (SPANISH)
LC 73-701996
Tells of a tough young waitress who goes from man to man in her search for sexual identity until she is brought face to face with her own need for roots and emotional security. Shows that commitment and fidelity are signs of personal maturity.
Psychology; Religion and Philosophy
Dist - PAULST **Prod** - KIESER 1973

Truck, utility, 1/4 - ton M151A2 - characteristics and handling 18 MIN
16mm
Color
LC 80-701086
Offers pointers in the operation of the M151A2 utility truck and demonstrates its different uses.
Civics and Political Systems; Industrial and Technical Education; Social Science
Dist - USNAC **Prod** - USA 1971

Truckers for Christ 17 MIN
16mm
Color
LC 76-703823
Tells about a Canadian - based missionary group of truckers headquartered in Waterloo, Ontario, who own and operate mobile chapels that travel the truckstops and terminals of North America in order to provide religious services for truckers.
Geography - World; Religion and Philosophy
Dist - YORKU **Prod** - YORKU 1976

Truckin' - the road to Shreveport 12 MIN
16mm
B&W
LC 75-702999
Compares the comments and experiences of two truckers on a nonstop haul to Shreveport to those of another driver who hauled goods across the country in a horse and wagon more than a century ago.
History - United States; Social Science
Dist - DEPRTF **Prod** - TEMPLU 1974

Trucks and truck transportation 11 MIN
16mm / U-matic / VHS
Transportation series
Color (K P I)
LC FIA68-1675
Shows how vans, flat - bed trucks and tankers bring goods to the businesses and individuals in a community.
Business and Economics; Social Science
Dist - ALTSUL **Prod** - FILMSW 1968

Trucks in Our Neighborhood - a First Film 12 MIN
U-matic / VHS / 16mm
Color; B&W (P)
LC FIA68-392
Pictures the various trucks that might come to the neighborhood. Shows the trucks and the workers who drive them as they provide services, make deliveries and repairs and do the general work needed to keep a neighborhood running smoothly.
Social Science
Dist - PHENIX **Prod** - FA 1967

Trucs of the trade 70 MIN
VHS
Color (G)
$29.95 purchase _ #JJ0070V-H
Offers favorite trucs - French for 'tricks' - from 48 American chefs. Shows viewers how to make a perfect omlette, cook fish in paper, create the perfect hamburger, salvage burned rice, string-cut a cheesecake, tenderize meat, soften tortillas in a microwave, use plastic wrap as a sausage casing and many more helpful hints.
Home Economics
Dist - CAMV

Trudy Pitts 30 MIN
Videoreel / VT2
People in Jazz Series
Color (G)
$55.00 rental _ #PEIJ - 105
Presents the jazz music of Trudy Pitts. Features host Jim Rockwell interviewing the artist.
Fine Arts
Dist - PBS **Prod** - WTVSTV

True and false prophecy series
Amos 30 MIN
Ezekiel and another Isaiah 30 MIN
Hosea 30 MIN
Jeremiah 30 MIN
Jesus 30 MIN
Micah and Isaiah 30 MIN
Dist - ECUFLM

The True Art of Making Lasagna 7 MIN
16mm
Color (J) (AMERICAN SIGN)
LC 76-701709
Presents two cooks discussing in American sign language the subject of making lasagna and gives their individual recipes for making it. Signed for the deaf by Carolyn Larson and Florian Caliguiri.
Guidance and Counseling; Home Economics; Psychology
Dist - JOYCE **Prod** - JOYCE 1975

True blue 30 MIN
16mm
Footsteps series
Color
LC 79-701558
Illustrates why children put so much energy into play, what play means to them and what they learn from it. Shows what parents can do to encourage and support their children's play and how they can benefit from this aspect of growth.
Home Economics; Physical Education and Recreation; Sociology
Dist - USNAC **Prod** - USOE 1978

True blue and dreamy 17 MIN
16mm
B&W (G)
$35.00 rental
Relives the filmmaker's favorite dream.
Fine Arts; Psychology
Dist - CANCIN **Prod** - MCDOWE 1974

True Cross Fire 48 MIN
VHS / U-matic
Color
Presents a parody of docu - dramas that examines memory and information.
Fine Arts
Dist - KITCHN **Prod** - KITCHN

True, False 10 MIN
U-matic
Readalong One Series
Color (K P)
Introduces reading and spelling for preschoolers and children in grades 1 to 3 with animation, puppets, humor and music. Comes with teacher's guide and kit.
Education; English Language; Literature and Drama
Dist - TVOTAR **Prod** - TVOTAR 1975

True friends and devil's gate - Volume 12 45 MIN
VHS
Flying house series
Color (K P I R)
$11.99 purchase _ #35 - 8961 - 979
Uses an animated format to present events from the New Testament era, as three children, a professor and a robot travel in the 'Flying House' back to that time. 'True Friends' tells how Jesus healed a paralyzed person, while 'Devil's Gate' recalls the story of the raising of the widow's son.
Literature and Drama; Religion and Philosophy
Dist - APH **Prod** - TYHP

True Glory 85 MIN
U-matic / VHS / 16mm
B&W
Depicts the World War II campaign in Europe from D - day to V - E day. Directed by Garson Kanin and Carol Reed. Issued in 1945 as a motion picture.
History - United States; History - World
Dist - USNAC **Prod** - JAFPC 1979

True Glory, Pt 1 42 MIN
U-matic
B&W
LC 79-706287
Depicts the World War II campaign in Europe from D - day to V - E day. Directed by Garson Kanin and Carol Reed. Issued in 1945 as a motion picture.
Civics and Political Systems; History - United States
Dist - USNAC **Prod** - JAFPC 1979

True Glory, Pt 2 43 MIN
U-matic
B&W
LC 79-706287
Depicts the World War II campaign in Europe from D - day to V - E day. Directed by Garson Kanin and Carol Reed. Issued in 1945 as a motion picture.
Civics and Political Systems; History - United States
Dist - USNAC **Prod** - JAFPC 1979

True grit 128 MIN
VHS
Color (J H C)
$29.00 purchase _ #05933 - 126
Stars John Wayne as ornery US marshal Rooster Cogburn.
Fine Arts; Literature and Drama
Dist - GA **Prod** - GA

True Heart Susie 87 MIN
16mm
B&W
Tells how a plain girl sacrifices everything to send her love to college and how he pays her back by falling for a wicked city woman. Stars Lillian Gish. Directed by D W Griffith.
Fine Arts
Dist - REELIM **Prod** - UNKNWN 1919

True love - 58 10 MIN
VHS / U-matic
Life's little lessons - self - esteem 4 - 6 series
Color (I)
$129.00, $99.00 purchase _ #V687
Tells about handsome cowboy Clint Wilcox who drifts into town and in and out of relationships. Shows how he gets into trouble when he asks three different women for the same lunch date. Part of a 65 - part series on self - esteem.
Guidance and Counseling; Psychology
Dist - BARR **Prod** - CEPRO 1992

The True North 30 MIN
U-matic
North of Sixty Degrees - Destiny Uncertain Series
Color (H C)
Captures the variety of lands and people found north of sixty degrees and explores the region's basic geographical and demographic characteristics.
Geography - United States; Geography - World; History - World
Dist - TVOTAR **Prod** - TVOTAR 1985

A True prophet and flaming chariots - Volume 11 45 MIN
VHS
Superbook series
Color (K P I R)
$11.99 purchase _ #35 - 86616 - 979
Uses an animated format to tell the story of Chris and Joy and their time travels through Biblical places and events. 'A True Prophet' tells the story of Elijah, while 'Flaming Chariots' tells the story of Elisha.
Literature and Drama; Religion and Philosophy
Dist - APH **Prod** - TYHP

True Series
Defendant - Clarence Darrow 30 MIN
Dist - WB

A True Standard 12 MIN
16mm
Color (A)
LC FIE55-51
Shows how weights and measures are maintained at the international, national and state levels. Includes illustrations of careful testing procedures.
Mathematics; Science
Dist - USNBOS **Prod** - USNBOS 1954

A True Story about a not - So - Famous Person 57 MIN
16mm
Color (A)
LC 80-701528
Depicts the frustrations of an artist trying to market himself during the McCarthy Era of the 1950s. Illustrates the repercussions of the artist's situation through a dream set in the 1800s.
Fine Arts; History - United States
Dist - WARNKE **Prod** - WARNKE 1980

The True story of Ah Q 125 MIN
VHS
Color (G) (MANDARIN CHINESE)
$45.00 purchase _ #1023A
Presents a movie produced in the People's Republic Of China. Relates the tragedy of Ah Q, a farm laborer, written by Lu Hsun in 1921.
Fine Arts; Geography - World; Literature and Drama
Dist - CHTSUI **Prod** - CHTSUI

True Story of the Civil War 33 MIN
U-matic / VHS / 16mm
B&W (I)
Surveys the causes, battles, leaders and effects of the Civil War. Made up mostly of Matthew Brady's original wet plate photographs, newspaper cartoons and headlines. Raymond Massey narrates.
Fine Arts; History - United States; Industrial and Technical Education
Dist - MGHT **Prod** - CEP 1956

True story of the Roman arena 45 MIN
VHS
Timewatch series
Color; PAL (A)
PdS99 purchase; Not available in the United States or Canada
Reveals the world of the Roman amphitheatre, where cruelty became an art form and violence the essence of entertainment. Uses computer graphics to reconstruct grisly events. Goes back in time to face the modern dilemma of violence as mass entertainment.
History - World; Sociology
Dist - BBCENE

True Values 10 MIN
16mm
Color (P I)
Helps children to look beyond the immediate situation, to understand the responsibility inherent in mutual trust. Raises the question of true values, faced with the opportunity to exploit the moment, to cheat a parent or a friend.
Guidance and Counseling; Psychology; Sociology
Dist - SF **Prod** - SF 1970

True west 110 MIN
VHS
Color (H C A)
$59.95 purchase
Presents an American Playhouse performance of the Sam Shepard play True West. Tells the story of two brothers at odds with one another. Stars John Malkovich and Gary Sinise.
Literature and Drama
Dist - PBS **Prod** - WNETTV
UILL

True west 110 MIN
VHS
Color (J H C)
$89.00 purchase _ #04048 - 126
Stars John Malkovich in a Sam Shepard comedy - drama about an eccentric desperado who turns his brother's life upside down.
Fine Arts; Literature and Drama
Dist - GA **Prod** - GA

True you attitude 30 MIN
U-matic / VHS
Better business letters series; Lesson 5
Color
Looks at how to get the reader of a business letter to see the writer's viewpoint. Discusses the meaning of real courtesy.
Business and Economics; English Language
Dist - TELSTR **Prod** - TELSTR
DELTAK

The Truesteel affair 24 MIN
16mm / VHS
Color (PRO G COR)
$480.00 purchase, $100.00 - $50.00 rental
Looks at the dilemma faced by a young engineer whose loyalties to family, employer and fellow workers conflict with his professional judgement.
Business and Economics; Guidance and Counseling; Religion and Philosophy
Dist - FANPRO **Prod** - FANPRO 1989

Truing Balance Wheels 14 MIN
16mm
Light Mechanics Series
B&W
Shows how to recognize and correct a balance wheel which does not run true, including the use of calipers, bending the wheel, using a wrench and cleaning the balance wheel.
Industrial and Technical Education
Dist - USVA **Prod** - USVA 1949

Trulier Coolier 11 MIN
U-matic / VHS / 16mm
Poetry for Fun Series
Color (P I J)
$280, $195 purchase _ #76583
Shows the ways in which children perceive the world they live in. Includes poems by Shel Silverstein.
Literature and Drama; Psychology
Dist - CORF

Truly American Series
Amelia Earhart 20 MIN
Carl Sandburg 20 MIN
Dr Elizabeth and Teacher Mary 20 MIN
Dr Martin Luther King, Jr 20 MIN
Eleanor Roosevelt 20 MIN
Everyday Hero 20 MIN
The General and Honest Abe 20 MIN
The Girl in the Checkered Coat 20 MIN
Hannibal Boy 20 MIN
Harry Truman 20 MIN
Helen Keller 20 MIN
The Hero of San Juan Hill 20 MIN
I - Tan - Chan 20 MIN
Jackie Robinson 20 MIN
Jemmy and Dolley 20 MIN
Jim Thorpe 20 MIN
Langston Hughes 20 MIN
Louis Armstrong 20 MIN
Marian Anderson 20 MIN
Pioneer of Labor 20 MIN
Ragtime King 20 MIN
The Sage of Monticello and Old Hickory 20 MIN
The Slave who Wouldn't Give Up 20 MIN
Susan and Mrs Stanton 20 MIN
The Truth and Moses 20 MIN
The Two Benjamins 20 MIN
Walt Disney 20 MIN
Whitney Young 20 MIN
Will Rogers 20 MIN
Dist - GPN

The Truly Exceptional - Carol Johnston 16 MIN
U-matic / VHS / 16mm
Color (I J H) (GREEK FRENCH)
Features the story of Carol Johnston, born with one arm, who became a champion gymnast.
Foreign Language; Physical Education and Recreation; Psychology
Dist - CORF **Prod** - DISNEY 1979

Truly Exceptional People Series
Carol Johnston 15 MIN
Dan Haley 11 MIN
Tom and Virl Osmond 15 MIN
Dist - CORF

Truman - a Self Portrait 21 MIN
U-matic / VHS / 16mm
Color; B&W (H A)
Portrays the character of Harry S Truman. Presents historic footage and includes material from Truman's memoirs and public statements. Includes such historic events as VJ Day and the post - war era, the first nuclear weapons, the Berlin airlift, the Korean War and the MacArthur recall.
Biography; History - United States
Dist - USNAC **Prod** - SMITHS 1984

Truman and Containment 15 MIN
16mm / U-matic / VHS
American Foreign Policy Series
B&W (H C A)
Documents the growing tensions between the United States and the Soviet Union at the end of World War II. Identifies the origins of the Cold War and examines why the United States pursued a policy of containment in the post - war years.
Biography; Civics and Political Systems; History - United States
Dist - EBEC **Prod** - EBEC 1981

Truman and the Atomic Bomb 15 MIN
U-matic / VHS / 16mm
Truman Years Series
B&W (J H)
LC 73-703295
Discusses President Truman's decision to drop the first atom bomb on Japan.
Biography; Civics and Political Systems; History - United States; History - World
Dist - LCOA **Prod** - LCOA 1969

Truman and the Cold War 16 MIN
U-matic / VHS / 16mm
Truman Years Series
B&W (J H)
LC 70-703294
Discusses Truman's role in aiding European countries whose freedom was imperiled by the Soviet Union.
Biography; Civics and Political Systems; History - World
Dist - LCOA **Prod** - LCOA 1969

Truman and the Korean War 18 MIN
U-matic / VHS / 16mm
Truman years series
B&W (J H)
LC 76-703293
Discusses the involvement of the United States with Korea, the role of Truman in bringing the issue to the United Nations, his dismissal of MacArthur, and his role in ending the fighting.

Biography; Civics and Political Systems; History - United States; History - World
Dist - LCOA **Prod** - LCOA 1969

Truman and the Uses of Power 18 MIN
U-matic / VHS / 16mm
Truman Years Series
B&W (J H)
LC 72-703292
Presents a survey of the key aspects of the domestic policies of Truman following World War II.
Biography; Civics and Political Systems; Guidance and Counseling; Psychology
Dist - LCOA **Prod** - LCOA 1969

Truman Capote's the Glass House 91 MIN
16mm / U-matic / VHS
Color (J)
LC 74-703041
Documents author Truman Capote's experiences at Utah State Prison.
Fine Arts; Literature and Drama; Sociology
Dist - LCOA **Prod** - TOMENT 1974

The Truman Era 29 MIN
Videoreel / VT2
Course of Our Times II Series
Color
History - World
Dist - PBS **Prod** - WGBHTV

The Truman legacy 14 MIN
16mm
Screen news digest series; Vol 21; Issue 6
B&W
Presents a biographical study of the life and times of Harry S Truman, as well as the fateful decisions he made as President and their continuing influence on American domestic and foreign affairs.
Biography
Dist - AFA **Prod** - AFA 1979

Truman - Years of Decision 24 MIN
U-matic / VHS / 16mm
Leaders of the 20th century - portraits of power series
Color (H C A)
LC 80-700034
States that the presidency of Harry Truman was marked by great events and great decisions. Originally shown on the Canadian television program Portraits Of Power.
Biography; Civics and Political Systems; Guidance and Counseling; History - United States; Psychology
Dist - LCOA **Prod** - NIELSE 1980

Truman Years Series
Truman and the Atomic Bomb 15 MIN
Truman and the Cold War 16 MIN
Truman and the Korean War 18 MIN
Truman and the Uses of Power 18 MIN
Dist - LCOA

Trumpet 20 MIN
VHS / 16mm
Junior high music - instrumental series
Color (I)
$175.00, $200.00 purchase _ #288108
Features a host who introduces each program and offers a brief history of the instrument to be studied. Presents a master teacher, a professional musician with a philharmonic symphony, who demonstrates proper assembly, breathing and tone production, hand position, embouchure and articulation. A performance rounds out the program. 'Trumpet' demonstrates the correct embouchure, breath control and articulation techniques used in playing the soprano voice of the brass family.
Fine Arts
Dist - ACCESS **Prod** - ACCESS 1988

Trumpet Course 52 MIN
VHS
Color (G)
$29.95 purchase _ #1252
Presents 'Trumpet Course' for beginning through intermediate trumpeters. Features Clark Terry as instructor.
Agriculture; Fine Arts
Dist - KULTUR

Trumpet for beginners 50 MIN
VHS
Maestro instructional series
Color (J H C G)
$29.95 purchase _ #BSPT23V
Supplements class lessons and reinforces private lessons on the trumpet. Offers clear - cut examples and demonstrations on how to unpack and assemble the instrument, proper hand position and instrumental nomenclature. Discusses notes, breathing, posture, reading music and care and maintenance of the instrument. Includes booklet. Part of a ten - part series on musical instruments.
Fine Arts
Dist - CAMV

Trumpet garden 10 MIN
16mm
Color (G)
$18.00 rental
Employs juxtaposition of image and sound based on similar textures rather than temporal logic. Presents an emotional diary of the filmmaker's pregnancy. A woman in black explores the rituals of nature. Produced by Barbara Klutinis.
Fine Arts; Literature and Drama; Sociology
Dist - CANCIN

Trumpet, Horn and Trombone 11 MIN
16mm
Listening to Music Series
Color (P I J)
Introduces the trumpet, horn and trombone and shows basic techniques of producing sound from the instruments. Explains unique features of these instruments.
Fine Arts
Dist - VIEWTH **Prod** - GATEEF

Trumpet Kings 72 MIN
VHS
Color (S)
$39.95 purchase _ #055 - 9005
Draws on the jazz film collection of David Chertok to document the jazz heritage of Louis Armstrong, Red Allen, Miles Davis and Lester Bowie, among others. Sketches the development of the trumpet in jazz and shows great jazz musicians in their prime.
Fine Arts
Dist - FI **Prod** - VAI 1988

Trumpet Music of the Baroque 30 MIN
VHS / U-matic
Sounds they make Series
Color
Explains instrument construction and performance technique of the trumpet in the Baroque era. Defines and illustrates terms through the performance of works by Torelli, Purcell and other composers of the period. Gives an introduction to Baroque music.
Fine Arts
Dist - OHUTC **Prod** - OHUTC

The Trumpeter - The lovelorn giant - The tower of mice - Volume I 34 MIN
VHS
European folktales series
Color (G)
$99.00 purchase, $50.00 rental _ #8257
Presents the works of three Polish filmmakers who have reworked folktales from Poland into animated programs. Includes The Lovelorn Giant by Stanislaw Lenartowicz, The Trumpeter by Miroslav Kijowicz and The Tower of Mice by Daniel Szczechura. First volume of a six volume series of 18 European folktales produced by John Halas.
Fine Arts; Literature and Drama
Dist - AIMS **Prod** - EDPAT 1990

Trumpit 7 MIN
16mm
B&W (C A)
Presents a dadaistic comedy about frustrated love.
Psychology; Sociology
Dist - CFS **Prod** - CFS 1954

Truncal Vagotomy and Antrectomy for Duodenal Ulcer 33 MIN
U-matic / VHS
Gastrointestinal Series
Color
Health and Safety; Science - Natural
Dist - SVL **Prod** - SVL

Truncal vagotomy and pyloroplasty for obstructing duodenal ulcer 31 MIN
VHS / U-matic
Gastrointestinal series
Color
Health and Safety; Science - Natural
Dist - SVL **Prod** - SVL

Truncated Cone - Radial Line Method, Openings not Parallel 19 MIN
VHS / BETA
Metal Fabrication - Round Tapers Series
Color (IND)
Industrial and Technical Education; Psychology
Dist - RMIBHF **Prod** - RMIBHF

Trunkey on trauma 20 MIN
VHS
Color (C A)
$225.00 purchase
Presents a lecture by trauma expert Donald Trunkey on the background and key features of appropriate first - response medical care. Discusses the most useful and effective lifesaving procedures and the causes of trauma death. Focuses on techniques including endotracheal entubation and internal hemorrhage management. For emergency room personnel, first - response caregivers and medical and nursing students.
Health and Safety
Dist - PFP **Prod** - RENAN

Truss roof collapse 22 MIN
VHS
Collapse of burning buildings video series
Color (IND)
$140.00 purchase _ #35605
Presents one part of a five - part series that is a teaching companion for The Collapse Of Burning Buildings book, as well as to the IFSTA Building Construction manual. Provides information about lightweight and timber trusses and construction features. Discusses conflicting size - ups. Shows safe operating procedures. Produced by Fire Engineering Books & Videos.
Health and Safety; Science - Physical; Social Science
Dist - OKSU

Trussworthy 15 MIN
U-matic
Landscape of Geometry Series
Color (J)
Explains how triangles can be classified by the lengths of their sides or by their angles. Shows how engineers use triangular shaped supports to build bridges.
Education; Mathematics
Dist - TVOTAR **Prod** - TVOTAR 1982

Trust 2 MIN
16mm
Meditation Series
Color (I)
LC 80-700746
Explores the belief that in increasing the ability to trust, people experience life more fully.
Religion and Philosophy
Dist - IKONOG **Prod** - IKONOG 1975

Trust Brenda 30 MIN
U-matic / VHS / 16mm
Moving Right Along Series
Color (J H A)
Questions whether Brenda should follow her immigrant mother's traditional cultural values or assert her independence to gain her friends' acceptance. Reveals that her mother's accident helps them both realize that they each have needs that must be recognized.
Psychology; Sociology
Dist - CORF **Prod** - WQED 1983

Trust in Darkness 45 MIN
BETA / VHS
Psychological Growth and Spiritual Development Series
Color (G)
Psychology; Religion and Philosophy
Dist - DSP **Prod** - DSP

Trust in yourself - adult children of alcoholics 25 MIN
VHS / U-matic / BETA / 16mm
Color (G)
$475.00, $280.00 purchase _ #KC - 5200M
Documents what it means to be the adult child of an alcoholic. Enters the lives of five 'adult children' who struggle to overcome personal dilemmas and feelings of denial and confusion. Demonstrates the healing potential of group therapy and forgiveness. Features commentary by Robert J Ackerman, co - founder of the National Association of Children of Alcoholics. Produced by Chuck Olin Associates.
Health and Safety; Psychology; Sociology
Dist - CORF

Trust your instincts 24 MIN
VHS
Color (G)
$19.95 purchase _ #CEP010V-P
Presents information and techniques that could help protect women and others from dangerous situations. Alerts viewers to how to detect potential dangers, how to prevent them, and how to deal with them. Includes scenarios such as strangers on an elevator, forced entry into the home, and potential date rape.
Physical Education and Recreation; Sociology
Dist - CAMV

Trust Your Team 25 MIN
VHS / U-matic
(PRO)
$595.00 purchase, $125.00 rental
Illustrates the benefits of participation and teamwork. Presents training points on style, communication, involvement, commitment, trust, and responsibility. Also discusses developing objectives, monitoring performance, and sharing praise.
Business and Economics; Guidance and Counseling
Dist - CREMED **Prod** - CREMED 1987

Trust your team 28 MIN
VHS
Color (PRO A G)
$595.00 purchase, $125.00 rental
Dramatizes developing a participative management team. Explores the need for delegation of responsibilities in teamwork. Includes a leader's guide, sample workbook, reminder card and self - test. Additional materials are available separately.
Business and Economics; Psychology
Dist - EXTR **Prod** - EXTR
VLEARN

Trusts and trust busters 25 MIN
U-matic / VHS / 16mm
American history series
Color; B&W (J H)
LC FIA67-1328
Describes the power of the industrial giants at the turn of the century and relates how U S President Theodore Roosevelt helped to establish the principle that the government has the right to interfere in business.
Biography; Business and Economics; History - United States
Dist - MGHT **Prod** - MGHT 1967

Trut 18 MIN
16mm
B&W (SWEDISH)
Portrays the tyrant of the shore to be the Swedish sea hawk. Shows how it seizes and devours the eggs and chicks of other sea birds while they stand helpless.
Foreign Language; Geography - World
Dist - MOMA **Prod** - SUC 1944

Truth 60 MIN
U-matic / VHS
Six Great Ideas Series
Color (A)
LC 83-706819
Presents Bill Moyers and a panel who discuss the concept of truth with Mortimer J Adler. Explores and weighs the different notions of objective and subjective truth. Examines the idea that a truth is true for all men everywhere and for all time.
Religion and Philosophy
Dist - FI **Prod** - WNETTV 1982

Truth about AIDS Series
Part One - the Facts and Phobias 36.24 MIN
Questions Answered 36.24 MIN
Dist - SRA

The Truth about alcohol 30 MIN
VHS
Truth about...series
Color (I J H G)
$79.95 purchase _ #CCP0038V
Illustrates graphically the wide use and abuse of alcohol by both adults and teens. Examines its role as an important commodity in the economic system of the United States, as a deceptive escape from personal problems, its promotion in massive media campaigns and its role as a major contributing factor in the deaths of hundreds of thousands of drunk drivers. Exposes the contradictions of the drug while encouraging viewers to think about the implications - why do people drink, how much is too much, how can one deal with peer pressure, when does 'social drinking' stop and the self - deceptive web of alcoholism begin, the role of low self - esteem, self - doubt and insecurity in drinking. Part of a series.
Business and Economics; Guidance and Counseling; Health and Safety; Psychology
Dist - CAMV **Prod** - CAMV 1991

The Truth about Communism 30 MIN
VHS / U-matic
B&W
Features Ronald Reagan as host and narrator of a documentary about the communist threat to the free world with an introduction by Alexander Kerensky, the first premier of the provisional Russian Government in 1917. Traces the development of the Communist movement from birth, the Lenin years, its struggle for direction, the Stalin years (featuring a response by Trotsky attacking the Stalin purges) and the ascendancy of Nikita Khrushchev.
Civics and Political Systems; History - World
Dist - IHF **Prod** - IHF

The Truth about George 30 MIN
U-matic / VHS
Wodehouse Playhouse Series
Color (C A)
Presents an adaptation of the short story The Truth About George by P G Wodehouse.
Literature and Drama
Dist - TIMLIF **Prod** - BBCTV 1980

The Truth about Lies 60 MIN
VHS
Moyers - The Public Mind Series
Color; Captioned (G)
$59.95 purchase _ #MPUM - 104
Examines deception, both of self and of others. Pursues the question of how deception has affected major events such as Watergate, the Vietnam War and the Challenger shuttle disaster. Hosted by Bill Moyers.
Civics and Political Systems; Guidance and Counseling; Psychology; Religion and Philosophy
Dist - PBS

The Truth about lies - The tube is reality 60 MIN
VHS
Color (G)
$390.00 purchase, $75.00 rental
Examines American television and its commercialized entertainment which claims not to peddle politics or morals to its huge audience. Explores the networks' version of reality which is created to sell products they advertise and in turn honor the requests of advertisers who want conflict - free, optimistic and bland programming that won't raise anxieties or doubts about American life or values. Asks if such covert control represents the genuine American Dream or is it a fantasy of lies. Produced by Nicholas Fraser and Michael Jones.
Fine Arts; Sociology
Dist - FIRS

The Truth about smokeless tobacco
VHS
Color (I J H C G A PRO)
$79.50 purchase _ #AH46329
Discusses the medical hazards of smokeless tobacco. Focuses on the effects of smokeless tobacco on young people, as well as on peer pressure.
Health and Safety; Psychology; Science - Natural
Dist - HTHED **Prod** - HTHED

The Truth about teachers 47 MIN
VHS
Raising good kids in bad times series
Color (H C A)
$95.00 purchase
Illustrates problems among people and possible solutions, focusing on child - rearing methods. Provides material for educators and community leaders as well as young people. Written, produced and directed by Carol Fleisher.
Education; Guidance and Counseling; Health and Safety
Dist - PFP **Prod** - ASHAP

The Truth about tobacco 30 MIN
VHS
Truth about...series
Color (I J H G)
$79.95 purchase _ #CCP0039V
States that everyone knows the statistics that tobacco is the leading contributor to hundreds of thousands of deaths and debilitating illnesses. Asks why teens continue to take up smoking. Explores why they smoke, why smoking is hard to stop, why US society allows tobacco companies to promote a lethal drug utilizing state - of - the - art media persuasion techniques, and how tobacco is economically entrenched in the American system. Illustrates the negative consequences of smoking. Part of a series.
Business and Economics; Guidance and Counseling; Health and Safety; Psychology
Dist - CAMV **Prod** - CAMV 1991

Truth about...series
Presents a two - part series about alcohol and tobacco, The Truth about Alcohol, The Truth about Tobacco.
The Truth about alcohol 30 MIN
The Truth about tobacco 30 MIN
Dist - CAMV **Prod** - CAMV 1991

The Truth and Consequences - Drug and Alcohol Abuse
VHS / U-matic
Guidance, Health and Drug Prevention Series
(G J C)
$89 purchase _ #06862 - 851
Presents a wide variety of practical information and suggests resources, as well as solutions, for the problems of drug and alcohol abuse. Features Lee Dogoloff, Executive Director of the American Council for Drug Education, and Donald Ian Macdonald MD, Administrator of the National Drug Abuse and Mental Health Administration.
Guidance and Counseling; Health and Safety; Sociology
Dist - CHUMAN **Prod** - EDCC

The Truth and Moses 20 MIN
U-matic
Truly American Series
Color (I)
Describes the lives of Sojourner Truth and Harriet Tubman.
Biography; History - United States; History - World
Dist - GPN **Prod** - WVIZTV 1979

The Truth and the consequences - drug and alcohol abuse 28 MIN
VHS
Color (H)
$89.00 purchase _ #06862 - 126
Stresses the need for preventive measures in drug abuse. Discusses the effects of drugs, the influence of peer pressure and ways parents, teachers and the community can help young people develop healthy lifestyles.
Guidance and Counseling; Psychology; Sociology
Dist - GA **Prod** - GA

Truth for Ruth 4 MIN
16mm
B&W (G)
$15.00 rental
Plays with 'muffled, inaudible sound and no image to speak of.'
Fine Arts
Dist - CANCIN **Prod** - MCDOWE

Truth, Justice and the American Way 4 MIN
16mm
B&W
LC 75-703246
A comedy in which, during a cops and robbers chase, an odd assortment of characters are revealed to be other than what they had first appeared to be. Superman to the rescue. (A USC cinema student workshop production.).
Fine Arts; Literature and Drama
Dist - USC **Prod** - USC 1963

The Truth lies in the Rostock 78 MIN
VHS
Color (G)
$490.00 purchase, $100.00 rental
Looks at the racially charged attack on a hostel for Vietnamese refugees and guest workers that took place in August, 1992, at Rostock in the former East Germany. Uses material filmed from within the beseiged houses and interviews with the Vietnamese; police, who withdrew from the riot after a token appearance; bureaucrats; neo - Nazis; and town residents, 3000 of whom stood and clapped during the attack. Produced by Siobahn Cleary and Mark Saunders.
Civics and Political Systems; Fine Arts; Sociology
Dist - FIRS

The Truth of Fiction 18 MIN
U-matic / VHS / 16mm
Humanities Series
Color (J H)
LC 77-714097
Presents an introduction to the study of fiction.
Literature and Drama
Dist - MGHT **Prod** - MGHT 1971

Truth on trial - Part 8 60 MIN
VHS / U-matic
Ethics in America series
Color (G)
$45.00, $29.95 purchase
Features Supreme Court Justice Antonin Scalia, Judge Robert Merhige, attorneys Floyd Abrams and Stanley Chesley, philosopher John Smith of Yale and others. Asks if an attorney's first obligation is to the court, to the client or to the public. Part eight of a ten - part series on ethics in America, produced by Fred W Friendly.
Business and Economics; Civics and Political Systems; Religion and Philosophy; Sociology
Dist - ANNCPB **Prod** - COLMU 1989

Truth Serum 4 MIN
16mm
Color (H C A)
$15.00 rental
Combines eight discrete animation cycles with a soundtrack consisting of selected statements taken from a widely used true/false psychological test. Explores a way of telling stories from the subconscious. Produced by Brady Lewis.
Fine Arts; Psychology
Dist - CANCIN

The Truth shall make us free - inside the neo - Nazi network 51 MIN
VHS
Color (H C G)
$445.00 purchase, $75.00 rental
Follows freelance journalist Michael Schmidt who infiltrated the inner circle of German neo - Nazis who thought that the filmmaker would glorify their movement and its leader Michael Kuhnen. Documents racial and religious hatred being bred into a new generation - Nazi uniforms, sieg heil salutes, skin heads, mass rallies and secret plots. Violent anti - Semitism is fanned by the showing of old Nazi hate films such as The Eternal Jew. Reveals that revisionist historians who deny that the holocaust ever occured have close ties with the party, coining the slogan 'Wahrheit Macht Frei' - the truth shall make us free - to parody the 'Arbeit Macht Frei' which hung over the gates of concentration camps.
Civics and Political Systems; Geography - World; History - World
Dist - FLMLIB **Prod** - SWEDTV 1993

Truth Telling in the Health Professions 38 MIN
VHS / U-matic
Color (PRO)
Presents historical perspective of ethical dilemmas, dramatization of a case, and answers discussed within the framework of the professional code of ethics, the patient's right to know and the law.
Health and Safety
Dist - BUSARG **Prod** - BUSARG

Try a Little Tenderness 60 MIN
U-matic / VHS
Body in Question Series Program 2; Program 2
Color (H C A)
LC 81-706942
Points out that common symptoms can have many possible causes. Traces the long methodical and often humorous route which leads to a final diagnosis. Based on the book The Body In Question by Jonathan Miller. Narrated by Jonathan Miller.
Health and Safety; Science - Natural
Dist - FI **Prod** - BBCTV 1979

Try for Touch 18 MIN
16mm
B&W
Analyzes the nature of violence as seen in a group of sunday rugby players in Central Park. Interweaves the players, their audience and their reactions to and comments on 'body contact' and 'violence' in a view of people's reaction to blood, hurt and aggression.
Guidance and Counseling; Psychology; Sociology
Dist - UPENN **Prod** - UPENN 1970

Try it, They'll Like it 28 MIN
16mm
You Can do it - if Series
Color
LC 81-700093
Explains ways that parents can motivate their children. Stresses positive reinforcement of teachers' efforts.
Home Economics; Psychology
Dist - VANDER **Prod** - VANDER

Try it, You'll Like it 29 MIN
U-matic / VHS
Bean Sprouts Series
Color (P I)
Tells the story of a ten - year - old Chinese American boy who learns ways to move between traditional and contemporary lifestyles.
Sociology
Dist - GPN **Prod** - CTPROJ

Try to See it My Way 27 MIN
U-matic / VHS
Secretary and Management Relationship Series no 1
Color
Shows what has been going wrong in the administrative routines in an office partnership.
Business and Economics; Psychology
Dist - VISUCP **Prod** - VIDART

Tryin' to get home - a video history of African - American song 58 MIN
VHS
Color (G)
$49.95 purchase _ #HJ01V - F
Features musician and composer Kerrigan Black in a survey of the history of African American music, from spirituals to rap music. Includes 17 songs of 13 musical forms, photos and film footage with explanatory monologues.
Fine Arts; History - United States
Dist - CAMV

Trying Again 19 MIN
16mm
I Am, I Can, I will Level II Series
Color (K P S)
LC 80-700572
Presents Mr Rogers talking to a man with a hip defect to show that often people have to try again and again to do certain difficult things.
Guidance and Counseling; Psychology
Dist - HUBDSC **Prod** - FAMCOM 1979

Trying on Shoes and Boots to Get Ready for a Picnic 8 MIN
16mm
Crystal Tipps and Alistair Series
Color (K P)
LC 73-700456
Follows Crystal and Alistair as they try on many different styles of shoes and boots in preparation for a picnic with flutter and fancy.
Guidance and Counseling; Literature and Drama
Dist - VEDO **Prod** - BBCTV 1972

Trying Times - Crisis in Fertility 33 MIN
16mm / VHS
Color (G)
$265.00 purchase
Recognizes the emotional impact of infertility and demonstrates the importance of empathetic support from professionals.
Guidance and Counseling; Sociology
Dist - FANPRO **Prod** - FANPRO 1989

Trying to connect you 29 MIN
16mm / VHS / BETA / U-matic
Color; PAL (C PRO G)
PdS150, PdS158 purchase
Studies human communication and how breakdowns, or missed messages, occur between individuals. Suggests remedies for industry - management so that messages can be transmitted effectively.
Psychology; Social Science
Dist - EDPAT

Trying to find normal 17 MIN
VHS
Color (G)
$325.00 purchase, $75.00 rental _ #AV - 103; $325.00 purchase, $75.00 rental _ #8041
Features American artist Eric Fischl who talks about his mother's alcoholism and its effect upon his life and art. Portrays the many problems youngsters face while growing up with a parent who drinks too much. Includes a discussion guide by Dr Sheila B Blume.
Biography; Fine Arts; Guidance and Counseling; Health and Safety; Psychology; Sociology
Dist - COALF **Prod** - COALF
AIMS

Trying too hard to please others - 59 8 MIN
U-matic / VHS
Life's little lessons - self - esteem 4 - 6 series
Color (I)
$129.00, $99.00 purchase _ #V688
Tells about Clevous Rawlings who had the best recipe for bread in town, winning first prize at the local fair for years. Shows how the other bakers tricked him into trying their suggested changes instead of doing what he knew was right. Part of a 65 - part series on self - esteem.
Guidance and Counseling; Psychology
Dist - BARR **Prod** - CEPRO 1992

Tryout Performances - Pt 1 29 MIN
16mm
Job Instructor Training Series
B&W (IND)
LC 77-703324
Business and Economics; Psychology
Dist - EDSD **Prod** - EDSD

Tryout Performances - Pt 2 29 MIN
16mm
Job Instructor Training Series
B&W (IND)
LC 77-703324
Business and Economics; Psychology
Dist - EDSD **Prod** - EDSD

Tryout TV Series
Beginning Again - Widowers 29 MIN
Dist - WHATV

Tryst 13 MIN
16mm
Color (G)
$20.00 rental
Features a film by Allen Ross.
Fine Arts
Dist - CANCIN

The Tsar's Bride 97 MIN
VHS
B&W (G) (RUSSIAN (ENGLISH SUBTITLES))
$39.95 purchase _ #1287
Presents a Soviet movie version of the opera 'The Tsar's Bride' by Nikolai Rimsky - Korsakov, with singers and actors from the Bolshoi. Filmed in 1966.
Fine Arts
Dist - KULTUR **Prod** - KULTUR 1991

TSCA 8C Recording/Reporting Requirements 18 MIN
U-matic / VHS
Color (A)
Discusses requirements for the chemical industry in the reporting and retention of allegations of health effects and damage to the environment by a specific chemical.
Business and Economics; Civics and Political Systems; Science - Physical
Dist - USNAC **Prod** - USEPA 1983

Tschetan, Der Indianerjunge 96 MIN
16mm
Color
Focuses on Western American life in the middle of the last century. Portrays the history of a young Indian boy who, as an escapee of a liquidated tribe, finds his way to freedom with the help of a lonely shepherd. Produced in the mountains of upper Bavaria.
History - United States; Sociology
Dist - WSTGLC **Prod** - WSTGLC 1972

Tschibo 2 MIN
16mm
Color (G)
$10.00 rental
Fine Arts
Dist - CANCIN **Prod** - KRENKU 1977

Tsetse - the Fly that would be King 20 MIN
U-matic
Color
LC 80-707249
Looks at the impact of the tsetse fly in Africa and examines some of the scientific research directed at eradicating this scourge. Discusses American support of research that will benefit developing countries. Issued in 1979 as a motion picture.
Science - Natural; Sociology
Dist - USNAC **Prod** - USAID 1980
COMCOR

The Tsetse Trap 59 MIN
U-matic / VHS / 16mm
Nova Series
Color (H C A)
LC 79-701902
Discusses the problem of the tsetse fly, which causes bovine sleeping sickness and destroys potential food supplies for millions of people. Points out that despite 30 years of efforts aimed at controlling the insect, a 1,000 - mile wide belt of devastated lands across 35 African countries proves that no solution has been found.
Agriculture; Geography - World; Health and Safety; Science - Natural; Social Science; Sociology
Dist - TIMLIF **Prod** - WGBHTV 1978

The Tsetse trap 50 MIN
VHS
Horizon series
Color; PAL (C H A)
PdS99 purchase
Traces the attempts to destroy the tsetse fly in Africa. Discusses typanosome, which is the parasite that the fly carries. Provides footage of the transition from egg to caterpillar. Part of the Horizon series.
Agriculture; Fine Arts; Science - Natural
Dist - BBCENE

Tsiolkovski - the Space Age 24 MIN
VHS / 16mm
Color (I)
LC 90706268
Gives an account of Konstantin Tsiolkovski and his early research on space travel. Covers basic theories of space travel.
History - World; Industrial and Technical Education; Science - Physical
Dist - BARR

Tsunami
VHS
Color (I J H)
$29.95 purchase _ #IV186
Reveals that a tsunami is a tidal wave produced by an underwater earthquake. Looks at how the tidal wave is formed and the devastation that it can cause. Shows the worldwide warning system developed to warn residents in a tidal wave region.
History - World
Dist - INSTRU

Tsurphu - Home of the Karmapas
VHS / BETA
Color; PAL (G)
PdS20 purchase
Travels to the Tsurphu Monastery in Tibet where, for centuries, the Karma Kagyu lineage of Tibetan Buddhism and all 16 incarnations of the Karmapas lived. Offers a production by the Tsurphu Foundation.
Fine Arts; Religion and Philosophy
Dist - MERIDT

Tsvi Nussbaum - boy from Warsaw 50 MIN
VHS
Color (G)
$39.95 purchase _ #625
Focuses on a familiar photograph of a little boy, his arms raised in surrender as a Nazi soldier trains his machine gun on the little boy. Reveals what happened to the little boy, Tsvi C Nussbaum.
History - World
Dist - ERGOM

TT - 47UG Teletypewriter - General Principles and Operation 16 MIN
16mm
B&W
LC FIE54-285
Explains how teletypewriters are used in the navy's communications system and demonstrates for the operator the basic principles of operation, use of the various function keys and correct procedures for setting up messages and securing the machine.

Business and Economics; Civics and Political Systems; Industrial and Technical Education; Social Science
Dist - USNAC **Prod** - USN 1953

TT - 47UG Teletypewriter - Installation and Performance Tests 14 MIN
16mm
B&W
LC FIE54-286
Demonstrates the step - by - step procedure for unpacking, installation and assembly of the TT - 47ug teletypewriter.
Business and Economics; Civics and Political Systems; Industrial and Technical Education; Social Science
Dist - USNAC **Prod** - USN 1953

TT - 47UG Teletypewriter - Preventive Maintenance 6 MIN
16mm
B&W
LC FIE54-287
Explains the importance of frequent checks and stresses the preventive maintenance technique for the TT - 47ug teletypewriter. Shows cleaning, oiling and minor adjusting of the machine.
Business and Economics; Civics and Political Systems; Industrial and Technical Education; Social Science
Dist - USNAC **Prod** - USN 1953

TThe Write channel - Pt 13 15 MIN
U-matic / VHS
Color (P I)
Explains the use of commas and the conjunction 'and' in a series of phrases or clauses.
English Language
Dist - AITECH **Prod** - MAETEL 1979

TTL - ECL Logic Circuits
U-matic / VHS
Digital Techniques Video Training Course Series
Color
Industrial and Technical Education
Dist - VTRI HTHZEN **Prod** - VTRI HTHZEN

TTL Integrated Circuits 28 MIN
VHS / 16mm
Digital Electronics Series
Color (H A)
$465.00 purchase, $110.00 rental
Provides understanding of TTL integrated circuits.
Industrial and Technical Education
Dist - TAT **Prod** - TAT 1989

TTY - Telephone 30 MIN
VHS / U-matic
Say it with sign series; Pt 27
Color (H C A) (AMERICAN SIGN)
Presents Lawrence Solow and Sharon Neumann Solow introducing American Sign Language used by the hearing - impaired. Emphasizes signs having to to do with TTY and the telephone.
Education
Dist - FI **Prod** - KNBCTV 1982

Tu Es Dans La Maison 10 MIN
VHS / U-matic
Salut - French Language Lessons Series
Color
Focuses on home life and prepositions.
Foreign Language
Dist - BCNFL **Prod** - BCNFL 1984

The Tuareg 60 MIN
VHS
Disappearing world series
Color (G C)
$99.00 purchase, $19.00 rental _ #61403
Reveals that the Tuareg live in the heart of the Algerian desert. Discloses that life has changed drastically since slavery, the economic basis of their society, was abolished in 1962. Shows that the Tuareg carry on their traditions and customs to maintain prestige, but schools are teaching their children about the world outside the desert. Features anthropologist Jeremy Keenan. Part of a series working closely with anthropologists who lived for a year or more in societies whose social structures, beliefs and practices are threatened by the expansion of technocratic civilization.
Sociology
Dist - PSU **Prod** - GRANDA 1972

Tuareg 46 MIN
16mm
World Around Us Series
Color (A)
LC 79-701835
Documents the life of the Tauregs, a proud, nomadic people of Niger. Shows how a devastating drought has forced them to live in refugee camps, engage in manual labor, and accept aid from Catholic missionaries.
Geography - World; Sociology
Dist - ICARUS **Prod** - ICARUS 1979

Tuareg - Pt 1 23 MIN
16mm
World Around Us Series
Color (A)
LC 79-701835
Documents the life of the Tauregs, a proud, nomadic people of Niger. Shows how a devastating drought has forced them to live in refugee camps, engage in manual labor, and accept aid from Catholic missionaries.
Sociology
Dist - ICARUS **Prod** - ICARUS 1979

Tuareg - Pt 2 23 MIN
16mm
World Around Us Series
Color (A)
LC 79-701835
Documents the life of the Tauregs, a proud, nomadic people of Niger. Shows how a devastating drought has forced them to live in refugee camps, engage in manual labor, and accept aid from Catholic missionaries.
Sociology
Dist - ICARUS **Prod** - ICARUS 1979

Tuba 25 MIN
VHS / 16mm
Junior High Music - Instrumental Series
Color (I)
$175.00, $200.00 purchase _ #288109
Features a host who introduces each program and offers a brief history of the instrument to be studied. Presents a master teacher, a professional musician with a symphony philharmonic, who demonstrates proper assembly, breathing and tone production, hand position, embouchure and articulation. A performance rounds out the program. 'Tuba' describes correct posture and hand position and illustrates the necessity of accurate lip placement and articulation.
Fine Arts
Dist - ACCESS **Prod** - ACCESS 1988

Tuba for beginners 50 MIN
VHS
Maestro instructional series
Color (J H C G)
$29.95 purchase _ #BSPU25V
Supplements class lessons and reinforces private lessons on the tuba. Offers clear - cut examples and demonstrations on how to unpack and assemble the instrument, proper hand position and instrumental nomenclature. Discusses notes, breathing, posture, reading music and care and maintenance of the instrument. Includes booklet. Part of a ten - part series on musical instruments.
Fine Arts
Dist - CAMV

Tubal Ligation 58 MIN
U-matic / VHS
Color (SPANISH)
LC 78-730127
Describes how tubal ligation prevents pregnancy.
Guidance and Counseling; Sociology
Dist - MEDCOM **Prod** - MEDCOM

Tubal Ligation
U-matic / VHS
Color (SPANISH FRENCH)
Describes the various permanent surgical procedures of terminating fertility. Depicts various techniques.
Foreign Language; Health and Safety; Sociology
Dist - MIFE **Prod** - MIFE

Tubal Ligation 5 MIN
U-matic / VHS
Color (SPANISH)
LC 78-730127
Describes how tubal ligation prevents pregnancy.
Foreign Language; Guidance and Counseling; Sociology
Dist - MEDCOM **Prod** - MEDCOM

Tubal Ligation 9 MIN
U-matic / VHS
Color
Presents the physiology of tubal ligation and explains how it prevents pregnancy.
Health and Safety; Sociology
Dist - MEDFAC **Prod** - MEDFAC 1975

Tubal ligation reversal 45 MIN
VHS
Surgical procedures series
Color (G)
$149.00 purchase, $75.00 rental _ #UW5211
Focuses on Dr Gary Berger, tubal ligation reversal specialist at Chapel Hill, North Carolina, Fertility & Surgical Center, who performs a tubal ligation reversal. Part of a 17 - part series recording surgical procedures in detail, with specialists who explain the ailment, the anatomical function of the part of the body being operated on, and how successful surgery might improve the patient's quality of life, hosted by Dr Donna Willis.
Health and Safety
Dist - FOTH

Tubby Bunny 12 MIN
U-matic / VHS / 16mm
Tommy, Tubby, Tuffy Series
Color (P)
Introduces Tubby, a thoughtless, greedy bunny who escapes from the rabbit hutch into a world of danger. Presents two alternatives regarding his fate.
Literature and Drama; Science - Natural
Dist - LUF **Prod** - LUF 1979

Tubby the Tuba 9 MIN
16mm
Color (P I J)
Presents a cinematic adaptation of the children's story about a tuba who longs to play his own melody in the symphony orchestra.
Literature and Drama
Dist - CFS **Prod** - PALG

Tube and Shape Bending 14 MIN
16mm
How to Form Aluminum Series
B&W
LC FIE52-635
Explains hand bending, bending by power machines, cold and hot bending of aluminum.
Industrial and Technical Education
Dist - USDIBM **Prod** - USDIBM 1944

Tube Bending by Hand 15 MIN
16mm
B&W
LC FIE52-20
Explains why tubes must be bent for installation in airplanes. Demonstrates how to set up the tube bending machine for the job and how the various parts of the machine function.
Industrial and Technical Education
Dist - USNAC **Prod** - USOE 1943

Tube Repair 60 MIN
VHS / U-matic
Mechanical Equipment Maintenance, Module 10 - Boiler and Boiler 'Equipment Series
Color (IND)
Industrial and Technical Education
Dist - LEIKID **Prod** - LEIKID

Tube Tester Operation 9 MIN
16mm
Radio Technician Training Series
B&W
LC FIE52-928
Shows how to operate tube testers in determining conditions of various tubes as to internal shorts, cathode emissions and dynamic mutual conductance.
Industrial and Technical Education
Dist - USNAC **Prod** - USN 1947

Tuberculin affair 55 MIN
VHS
Microbes and men
Color; PAL (C PRO H)
PdS99 purchase; Not available in the United States
Describes how Koch announces that he has found a cure for tuberculosis before it has been adequately tested. Emphasizes the competitiveness among researchers of the time and the need for proper trials of new discoveries. Fifth in the six - part series Microbes and Men, which covers the history and development of modern medicine.
Health and Safety; Science
Dist - BBCENE

Tuberculin Skin Testing 14 MIN
16mm
Color (PRO)
LC 77-700079
Provides a general description of tuberculosis, the time span in which it can occur and the organs of the body it may affect if left untreated.
Health and Safety
Dist - USNAC **Prod** - USN 1976

Tuberculosis 10 MIN
U-matic / VHS / 16mm
Health for the Americas Series
Color
Explains the cause, symptoms and transmission of tuberculosis, and emphasizes that the disease is controllable and curable. Issued in 1946 as a motion picture.
Health and Safety
Dist - USNAC **Prod** - USOIAA 1980

Tuberculosis and the Primary Care Physician 17 MIN
U-matic / VHS

Color (PRO)
Reviews the pathogenesis of tuberculosis and provides guidelines to the primary care physician for prevention, treatment and management of the tuberculosis patient. Emphasizes particularly the circumstances under which the prevention or treatment of tuberculosis is indicated and the use of isoniazid in managing the tuberculosis patient.
Health and Safety
Dist - UMICHM **Prod** - UMICHM 1980

Tuberculosis Laboratory Procedures - Fluorescent Staining and Ziehl - Neelsen Staining 8 MIN
U-matic
Color
LC 78-706277
Demonstrates two methods of detecting the presence of acid - fast organisms in sputum. Issued in 1965 as a motion picture.
Science
Dist - USNAC **Prod** - USPHS 1978

Tuberculosis - the Disease and its Management
U-matic / VHS
Color (ARABIC SPANISH)
Explains the cause and development of tuberculosis, the mode of transmission, the precautions necessary to prevent spread and the essential role of medication in treating the disease.
Health and Safety; Science - Natural
Dist - MIFE **Prod** - MIFE

Tuberculosis - the forgotten plague 50 MIN
VHS
Color (G)
$149.00 purchase, $75.00 rental _ #UW5420
Traces the history of the re - emergence of TB. Follows patients on three continents and their doctors who are fighting TB. Discovers that, while high - tech scientific solutions may eventually help, immediate hopes of averting global catastrophe lie with community workers who encourage patients to take their drugs.
Health and Safety
Dist - FOTH

Tubes, tubes, tubes series
Presents a five - part series on feeding tubes and intravenous therapy. Includes the titles Enteral Feeding Tubes - Parts 1 and 2; Implantable Ports; Management of Total Parenteral Nutrition - Parts 1 and 2.

Enteral feeding - Part 1	18 MIN
Enteral feeding - Part 2	24 MIN
Implantable ports	25 MIN
Management of total parenteral nutrition - Part 1	25 MIN
Management of total parenteral nutrition - Part 2	24 MIN

Dist - CONMED

Tubex - Superscript R - Closed System Injections 14 MIN
16mm
Color (PRO)
LC 77-715453
An in - service training film for nurses which demonstrates the step - by - step procedures for loading, administering and disposing of tubex sterile cartridgeinjections.
Health and Safety; Science
Dist - WYLAB **Prod** - WYLAB 1971

Tubing and Piping 60 MIN
VHS / U-matic
Mechanical Equipment Maintenance, Module 7 - Piping Series
Color (IND)
Industrial and Technical Education
Dist - LEIKID **Prod** - LEIKID

Tubing Installations and Brazing 60 MIN
VHS / U-matic
Instrumentation Basics - Instrumentation Electrical and Mechanical 'Connections Series Tape 4; Instrumentation electrical and mechanical connections; Tape 4
Color (IND)
Industrial and Technical Education; Mathematics
Dist - ISA **Prod** - ISA

Tuck everlasting 15 MIN
VHS
Storybound series
Color (I)
#E375; LC 90-713287
Tells the story, 'Tuck Everlasting' by Natalie Babbitt, about an unusual family which drinks from a spring that bestows eternal life. Part of a 16 - part series designed to lead viewers to the library to find and finish the stories they encounter in the series.
English Language; Literature and Drama; Social Science
Dist - GPN **Prod** - CTI 1980
CTI

A Tudor interlude 125 MIN
VHS
Color; PAL (I)
PdS30 purchase
Presents five 25 - minute programs recreating Elizabethan times. Encompasses religious persecution, pageantry and intrigue, as well as a highly original theory on the early life of William Shakespeare. Includes three adventure dramas and two documentaries revealing when Papists were being ruthlessly sought out and a young man from Stratford was starting out in life. Portrays Shakespeare meeting the famous Jesuit fugitive priest and later saint, Edmund Campion. Includes teacher's booklet. Contact distributor about availability outside the United Kingdom.
History - World; Literature and Drama
Dist - ACADEM

The Tudors 60 MIN
U-matic / VHS / 16mm
Royal Heritage Series
Color (H C A)
Focuses on the palaces and castles built by the Tudor kings of England. Explores St James' Palace, Hampton Court and King's College Chapel at Cambridge, and discusses Henry VIII's personal firearms at the Tower.
Civics and Political Systems; History - World
Dist - FI **Prod** - BBCTV 1977

Tudors Series

The Beggars are Coming - Pt 4	20 MIN
The Great house - Pt 2	20 MIN
Mary, Queen of Scots - Pt 5	20 MIN
The Search for the Mary Rose - Pt 6	20 MIN
The Secrets of the Mary Rose - Pt 7	20 MIN
Ships and Seamen - Pt 1	20 MIN
The Vicars of Hessle - Pt 3	20 MIN

Dist - FI

The Tuesday Group 14 MIN
U-matic / VHS / 16mm
Color (PRO)
Documents a group session of severely emotionally and physically deteriorated elderly persons. Illustrates therapeutic group work techniques.
Health and Safety; Psychology; Sociology
Dist - FEIL **Prod** - FEIL

Tuesday, may 19th, 1981 12 MIN
16mm
Color
LC 78-700319
Describes five tragic accidents that may occur if safety regulations relating to chemical transportation are not observed.
Health and Safety; Social Science
Dist - UCC **Prod** - UCC 1977

Tuesday Night is the Loneliest Night of the Week 28 MIN
U-matic / VHS / 16mm
Insight Series
Color; B&W (H A)
LC 75-705453
A dramatization about the assistant editor of a woman's magazine and her affair with the public relations man for the magazine, who is married and the father of three children.
Fine Arts; Guidance and Counseling; Psychology; Sociology
Dist - PAULST **Prod** - PAULST 1969

Tuffy Puppy 9 MIN
U-matic / VHS / 16mm
Tommy, Tubby, Tuffy Series
Color (P)
Portrays what happens when Tuffy, a happy - go - lucky puppy, gets lost and cannot remember the instructions his mother gave him. Presents two alternatives regarding his fate.
Literature and Drama; Science - Natural
Dist - LUF **Prod** - LUF 1979

Tuffy, the Sea Teacher 28 MIN
16mm
Color
LC 74-706598
Presents a study of dolphins and other sea animals. Shows the methods of catching, training and testing dolphins and presents the results of some of these tests.
Science - Natural
Dist - USNAC **Prod** - USN 1972

Tuffy, the Turtle 11 MIN
U-matic / VHS / 16mm
Color (P)
$270.00, $190.00 purchase _ #1468; LC FIA65-329
Animals of the pond teased Tuffy, the turtle, because his shell made him slow and clumsy. A snail helps Tuffy realize that a hard shell can be very useful.
English Language; Science - Natural
Dist - CORF **Prod** - CORF 1965

Tuft of Flowers 7 MIN
16mm
Color (P I J H C)
A cinepoem visually interpreting the poem 'Tuft of Flowers' by Robert Frost.
Fine Arts; Literature and Drama
Dist - CFS **Prod** - CFS

Tufts
VHS
Campus clips series
Color (H C A)
$29.95 purchase _ #CC0058V
Takes a video visit to the campus of Tufts University in Massachusetts. Shows many of the distinctive features of the campus, and interviews students about their experiences. Provides information on the composition of the student body, professors, academics, social life, housing, and other subjects.
Education
Dist - CAMV

Tug of War 9 MIN
16mm
Yanomamo Series
Color (H C A)
Portrays South American Yanomamo Indian women and children playing tug - of - war.
Social Science; Sociology
Dist - DOCEDR **Prod** - DOCEDR 1975

Tug - of - war - Bushmen 6 MIN
16mm / VHS
San - Ju - Wasi series
Color (G)
$150.00, $100.00 purchase, $20.00 rental
Observe San boys in two teams who wrestle over a length of rubber hose. Part of a series by John Marshall about the Kung in Namibia and Botswana.
Geography - World; History - World; Sociology
Dist - DOCEDR **Prod** - DOCEDR

Tug of war - strategies for conflict resolution 20 MIN
VHS
Color (J H C)
$189.00 purchase _ #CG - 916 - VS
Portrays Seth, whose day is off to a bad start. Reveals that first Big Ben tries to pick a fight with him, then his girlfriend Kim is on his case because they both think that Seth went out with Ben's girlfriend. An on - camera host introduces conflict resolution strategies as Seth, Kim, Ben, and their friend Eddie try to resolve their disagreements. Presents a four - step process that anyone can use to deal with conflict.
Psychology; Social Science
Dist - HRMC **Prod** - HRMC

Tugboat Captain 14 MIN
U-matic / VHS / 16mm
Color (I J H)
LC 72-702521
Presents the work of tugboats in New York Harbor. Studies the life of the captain of one of these boats.
Geography - United States; Social Science
Dist - EBEC **Prod** - EBEC 1971

Tugboat Captain 14 MIN
U-matic / VHS
World of Work Series
Color (I J)
$59.00 purchase _ #3111
Presents the excitement and special requirements of being a tugboat captain in a look at a typical day of a New York harbor captain and his crew.
Social Science
Dist - EBEC

Tugboat Christina 20 MIN
16mm
B&W
Shows a day on the river in the life of a river tugboat, depicting the tugboat getting underway in the morning, working on the Delaware River, and returning to its berth in the evening. Portrays how each member of the crew contributes to the operation of the tugboat.
Social Science
Dist - UPENN **Prod** - UPENN 1962

Tugboat Mickey 8 MIN
U-matic / VHS / 16mm
Gang's all Here Series
Color
Depicts what happens when tugboat captain Mickey Mouse mistakes a radio drama episode for an actual sinking ship.
Fine Arts
Dist - CORF **Prod** - DISNEY

Tukiki and His Search for a Merry Christmas 25 MIN
U-matic / VHS / 16mm
Color (K P I J H C A)
$565, $250 purchase _ #4115
Introduces Tukiki, an Eskimo boy who is bewildered by the meaning of a colorful Christmas card blown in on the wind. Shows him getting no response from his busy friends and finally turning to the Northwind who blows him around the world where he is introduced to many Christmas customs.
Fine Arts; Literature and Drama; Social Science
Dist - CORF

Tuktoyaktuk - a Piece of the Action 29 MIN
U-matic
Like no Other Place Series
Color (J H)
Examines the effects of development in the Northwest Territories of Canada.
Geography - World; History - World
Dist - TVOTAR **Prod** - TVOTAR 1985

Tuktu and His Animal Friends 14 MIN
16mm / U-matic / VHS
Stories of Tuktu - a Children's Adventure Series
Color (K P I J)
LC 76-711293
Tells a story about Tuktu, a Netsilik Eskimo boy. Shows some of the smaller animals that live in the Arctic, including lemmings, weasels, ducks and kittiwakes. Describes some of the flowers of the Arctic.
Social Science; Sociology
Dist - FI **Prod** - NFBC 1969

Tuktu and His Eskimo Dogs 14 MIN
U-matic / VHS / 16mm
Stories of Tuktu - a Children's Adventure Series
Color (K P I J)
LC 70-711294
Tells a story about Tuktu, a Netsikik Eskimo boy. Shows how dogs are used by the Eskimo in winter and summer as pack animals and for hunting purposes.
Social Science; Sociology
Dist - FI **Prod** - NFBC 1969

Tuktu and His Nice New Clothes 14 MIN
U-matic / VHS / 16mm
Stories of Tuktu - a Children's Adventure Series
Color (K P I J)
LC 75-711302
Tells a story about Tuktu, a Netsilik Eskimo boy. Shows the cutting, stitching, and use of Arctic clothing, and points out the importance of sewing in an Eskimo household.
Social Science; Sociology
Dist - FI **Prod** - NFBC 1969

Tuktu and the Big Kayak 14 MIN
U-matic / VHS / 16mm
Stories of Tuktu - a Children's Adventure Series
Color (K P I J)
LC 73-711295
Tells a story about Tuktu, a Netsilik Eskimo boy. Shows the contruction of a kayak.
Social Science; Sociology
Dist - FI **Prod** - NFBC 1969

Tuktu and the Big Seal 14 MIN
16mm / U-matic / VHS
Stories of Tuktu - a Children's Adventure Series
Color (K P I J)
LC 77-711296
Tells a story about Tuktu, a Netsilik Eskimo boy. Show how eskimos carry out a seal hunt.
Social Science; Sociology
Dist - FI **Prod** - NFBC 1969

Tuktu and the Caribou Hunt 14 MIN
16mm / U-matic / VHS
Stories of Tuktu - a Children's Adventure Series
Color (K P I J)
LC 70-711297
Tells a story about Tuktu, a Netsilik Eskimo boy. Shows Eskimos hunting caribou from their kayaks when the animals cross the small lakes to reach new grazing ground.
Social Science; Sociology
Dist - FI **Prod** - NFBC 1969

Tuktu and the Clever Hands 14 MIN
U-matic / VHS / 16mm
Stories of Tuktu - a Children's Adventure Series
Color (K P I J)
LC 74-711298
Tells a story about Tuktu, a Netsilik Eskimo boy. Shows some of the things made by the Eskimos, and describes the use the Eskimos make of the few materials that are available in the harsh environment.
Social Science; Sociology
Dist - FI **Prod** - NFBC 1969

Tuktu and the Indoor Games 14 MIN
U-matic / VHS / 16mm
Stories of Tuktu - a Children's Adventure Series
Color (K P I J)
LC 78-711299
Tells a story about Tuktu, a Netsilik Eskimo boy. Describes some of the indoor games played by Eskimos.
Social Science; Sociology
Dist - FI **Prod** - NFBC 1969

Tuktu and the Magic Bow 14 MIN
U-matic / VHS / 16mm
Stories of Tuktu - a Children's Adventure Series
Color (K P I J)
LC 78-711300
Tells a story about Tuktu, a Netsilik Eskimo boy. Shows a bow being made, and Eskimos practicing their shooting skill, using snow men and snow bears as targets.
Social Science; Sociology
Dist - FI **Prod** - NFBC 1969

Tuktu and the Magic Spear 14 MIN
16mm / U-matic / VHS
Stories of Tuktu - a Children's Adventure Series
Color (K P I J)
LC 71-711301
Tells a story about Tuktu, a Netsilik Eskimo boy. Shows how the Eskimos fish through the ice during the winter and how they fish in the summer.
Social Science; Sociology
Dist - FI **Prod** - NFBC 1969

Tuktu and the Snow Palace 14 MIN
U-matic / VHS / 16mm
Stories of Tuktu - a Children's Adventure Series
Color (K P I J)
LC 79-711303
Tells a story about Tuktu, a Netsilik Eskimo boy. Shows Eskimos traveling to a new hunting ground to build igloos, including a giant igloo where feasting, dancing and games are held.
Social Science; Sociology
Dist - FI **Prod** - NFBC 1969

Tuktu and the Ten Thousand Fishes 14 MIN
U-matic / VHS / 16mm
Stories of Tuktu - a Children's Adventure Series
Color (K P I J)
LC 72-711304
Tells a story about Tuktu, a Netsilik Eskimo boy. Shows eskimos spear fishing and making fire with the Eskimo fire drill.
Social Science; Sociology
Dist - FI **Prod** - NFBC 1969

Tuktu and the Trials of Strength 14 MIN
U-matic / VHS / 16mm
Stories of Tuktu - a Children's Adventure Series
Color (K P I J)
LC 76-711305
Tells a story about Tuktu, a Netsilik Eskimo boy. Shows Eskimo hunters demonstrating and testing their strength in boxing, tug - of - war, and other strenuous activities. Includes scenes of the drum dance.
Social Science; Sociology
Dist - FI **Prod** - NFBC 1969

Tula to Tulum 27 MIN
16mm
Color
Features an interpretation of the archaeology of Mexico in the form of a trip.
Geography - World; Science - Physical
Dist - NYU **Prod** - NYU

Tulane
VHS
Campus clips series
Color (H C A)
$29.95 purchase _ #CC0033V
Takes a video visit to the campus of Tulane University in New Orleans. Shows many of the distinctive features of the campus, and interviews students about their experiences. Provides information on the composition of the student body, professors, academics, social life, housing, and other subjects.
Education
Dist - CAMV

Tule Technology - Northern Paiute Uses of Marsh Resources in Western Nevada 42 MIN
U-matic / VHS / 16mm
Color (H C G T A)
Shows that northern Paiute Indians have lived near the Stillwater marshes of western Nevada for generations. Called 'cattaileaters,' they depended for subsistence on fish, waterfowl, eggs, tule reeds, and cattails. The film focuses on Wuzzie George and members of her family constructing a duck egg bag, cattail house, duck decoy, and tule boat. The narration by Wuzzie's granddaughter and son includes reminiscences of many aspects of traditional Paiute life that have disappeared.
Fine Arts; Geography - United States; Social Science; Sociology
Dist - PSU **Prod** - PSU 1983
SIFP

Tulip doesn't feel safe 13 MIN
VHS
Color (K P I J)
$225.00 purchase
Presents an animated program for very young children to help them develop life skills to keep them safe in risky situations. Teaches children that they are not responsible for the bad behavior of the adults in their lives and provides resources that they can call on for help. Uses cartoon characters to de - personalize situations so that children can identify with the characters without feeling that they are betraying their parents or others.
Guidance and Counseling; Health and Safety; Social Science; Sociology
Dist - FMSP

Tulips and spring bulbs
VHS
Gardens of the world series
Color (H C G)
$24.95 purchase _ #GW02
Features host Audrey Hepburn and narrator Michael York. Looks at spring blossoms and their place in the history and art of the Netherlands. Part of a six - part series on gardens.
Agriculture; Science - Natural
Dist - SVIP **Prod** - AUVICA 1993

Tulsa 30 MIN
VHS
Classic short stories
Color (H)
#E362; LC 90-708404
Presents 'Tulsa' by Richard Wormser. Part of a series which combines Hollywood stars with short story masterpieces of the world to encourage appreciation of the short story.
Literature and Drama
Dist - GPN **Prod** - CTI 1988

Tulsa - Building a World Around You 17 MIN
16mm
Color
LC 79-701063
Creates a montage of local scenery and events reflecting an atmosphere unique to Tulsa, Oklahoma.
Geography - United States
Dist - TULSAS **Prod** - UTICA 1979

Tumacacori 14 MIN
16mm
Color (A) (SPANISH)
LC 78-700950
Emphasizes that English was a foreign language in the American Southwest during the era of Spanish dominance. Offers a picture of life at a typical Spanish mission church.
Foreign Language; Geography - United States; History - United States
Dist - USNAC **Prod** - USNPS 1977

Tumbles, Mumbles and Bumbles 13 MIN
16mm / U-matic / VHS
Color
Presents sports action which shows how everyone can learn from mistakes.
Physical Education and Recreation
Dist - PFP **Prod** - PFP 1983

Tumbleweed 14 MIN
U-matic / VHS / 16mm
Color
LC 72-702442
Follows a tumbleweed through the many encounters it has on the plains and in the cities of the Southwest.
Geography - United States; Science - Natural; Social Science
Dist - AIMS **Prod** - ACI 1972

Tumbleweeds 89 MIN
16mm
B&W
Tells the story of the newly - opened Cherokee Strip of the Old West. Portrays Don Carver, who is mistaken for a sooner who supposedly sneaks over the boundary line to make a claim sooner than the official starting time set by the government. Shows what happens when he is imprisoned and later escapes. Stars William S Hart and Lucien Littlefield. Directed by King Baggott.
Fine Arts
Dist - KILLIS **Prod** - UNKNWN 1925

Tumbling and Floor Exercise 12 MIN
U-matic / VHS / 16mm
Color (I J H C) (ARABIC SPANISH)

LC 74-706482;
Demonstrates proper techniques in various tumbling and floor exercise skills, from basic to intermediate difficulty.
Education; Physical Education and Recreation
Dist - AIMS **Prod** - ASSOCF 1970

Tumbling - Elementary for Boys and Girls 13 MIN
U-matic / VHS / 16mm
Color (P I) (SPANISH)
LC 74-700031;
Shows how tumbling can help a student develop body image, spatial awareness and symmetrical use of both sides of the body. Presents basic stumbling stunts in sequential manner for a beginning tumbling class.
Physical Education and Recreation
Dist - AIMS **Prod** - AIMS 1973

Tumbling for Cheerleaders 25 MIN
VHS / U-matic
Video for Cheerleading Series
Color
Physical Education and Recreation
Dist - ATHI **Prod** - ATHI

Tumbling I 15 MIN
VHS / U-matic
Leaps and Bounds Series no 8
Color (T)
Demonstrates how to explain to primary students the basics of tumbling, including rolls, principles for efficient rolling, balancing and safety, tumbling as part of a sequence, rolling and balancing in a sequence.
Physical Education and Recreation
Dist - AITECH

Tumbling II 15 MIN
VHS / U-matic
Leaps and Bounds Series no 9
Color (T)
Demonstrates how to explain to primary students the basics of tumbling, including warming up, rocking, back shoulder roll, backward roll, awareness of alignment, sequential movement of the spine and upside - down orientation.
Physical Education and Recreation
Dist - AITECH

Tumbling - Intermediate for Boys and Girls 17 MIN
U-matic / VHS / 16mm
Color (P I) (SPANISH)
LC 74-700032
Explains that in tumbling, the small and large muscles of the body are used to build flexibility, agility and endurance. Shows how bilateral development, coordination, self - confidence and attention span can be improved through continued participation in a tumbling program. Presents stunts starting with the forward roll and building toward the handspring.
Foreign Language; Physical Education and Recreation
Dist - AIMS **Prod** - AIMS 1973

Tumbling - Primary Skills 9 MIN
16mm / U-matic / VHS
Color (P)
LC 76-711120
Illustrates good form in the performance of basic tumbling skills which can be learned by the elementary student. Demonstrates the egg sit, egg roll, forward roll, backward roll, frog head stand and head stand. Emphasizes correct position of head, hands and feet and stresses safety procedures.
Physical Education and Recreation
Dist - PHENIX **Prod** - PART 1970

Tumbling - the Basic Skills 10 MIN
U-matic / VHS / 16mm
Color (J H)
LC 74-702723
Depicts the total body coordination effort utilized in performing tumbling stunts. Shows six young gymnasts executing shoulder, forward and backward rolls, cartwheels and head, neck, fronthand and backhand springs.
Physical Education and Recreation
Dist - AIMS **Prod** - OF 1974

Tumbling - the Forward Roll 11 MIN
16mm
Color (P I J)
LC FIA67-55
Explains the value of tumbling as a physical exercise activity. Shows how to perform the forward roll and demonstrates class activities using it.
Physical Education and Recreation
Dist - MMP **Prod** - MMP 1966

Tumbling 2 - Progression of Skills 11 MIN
16mm
Color (I J H)
LC 77-702997
Presents examples of training of elementary school children in performance of the backward roll, headstand, running handsprings, forward somersaults, backward handsprings, backward somersaults, cartwheels and roundoffs. Discusses how tumbling skills lend themselves to progressive development.
Physical Education and Recreation
Dist - MMP **Prod** - MMP 1968

Tumors of the Central Nervous System 21 MIN
VHS / 16mm
Neuropathology Laboratory Sessions Series
(C)
$385.00 purchase _ #850VI142
Introduces commoon tumors of the central nervous system. The tape outlines various tumor classifications and makes general observations.
Health and Safety
Dist - HSCIC **Prod** - HSCIC 1985

Tumors of the Eye, Current Outlook 28 MIN
16mm
Cancer Management Series
B&W (PRO)
Discusses several approaches to the problem of management of tumors of the eye, as presented during a 1969 meeting of the American Radium Society at Philadelphia, Pennsylvania.
Health and Safety; Science - Natural
Dist - NMAC **Prod** - AMCRAD 1969

Tumors of the Head and Neck 73 MIN
U-matic
Color (PRO)
LC 76-706121
Presents an anatomical review of the head and neck, outlines methods of examination and describes the various lesions which occur in this area. Discusses asymptomatic neck masses and considers cancer of the larynx.
Health and Safety
Dist - USNAC **Prod** - WARMP 1969

Tumors of the Head and Neck - Pt 1 24 MIN
U-matic
Color (PRO)
LC 76-706121
Presents an anatomical review of the head and neck, outlines methods of examination and describes the various lesions which occur in this area. Discusses asymptomatic neck masses and considers cancer of the larynx.
Health and Safety
Dist - USNAC **Prod** - WARMP 1969

Tumors of the Head and Neck - Pt 2 24 MIN
U-matic
Color (PRO)
LC 76-706121
Presents an anatomical review of the head and neck, outlines methods of examination and describes the various lesions which occur in this area. Discusses asymptomatic neck masses and considers cancer of the larynx.
Health and Safety
Dist - USNAC **Prod** - WARMP 1969

Tumors of the Head and Neck - Pt 3 25 MIN
U-matic
Color (PRO)
LC 76-706121
Presents an anatomical review of the head and neck, outlines methods of examination and describes the various lesions which occur in this area. Discusses asymptomatic neck masses and considers cancer of the larynx.
Health and Safety
Dist - USNAC **Prod** - WARMP 1969

Tumors of the Major Salivary Glands 16 MIN
16mm
Color (PRO)
Illustrates the differential diagnosis and management of tumors of the major salivary glands - parotid, submaxillary and sublingual. Lists the relative incidence of the various neoplastic lesions of these glands.
Health and Safety; Science
Dist - AMCS **Prod** - AMCS 1967

Tun Razak the New Head of Government 11 MIN
16mm
B&W
Records the transfer of leadership from Tunku Abdul Rahman to the new Prime Minister, Tun Abdul Razak. Covers the ceremonial swearing - in of Tun Razak and his cabinet.
Civics and Political Systems; Geography - World; History - World
Dist - PMFMUN **Prod** - FILEM 1970

Tundra 12 MIN
VHS / U-matic / 16mm
Biomes series
Color (J H)
$350.00, $250.00 purchase _ #HP - 5935C
Examines the tundra belt around the north polar regions of the world, which has less than five inches of precipitation each year, low temperatures all year long and a short growing season. Details the few, hardy species of plants and animals which live in the tundra and their special adaptations. Reveals that during the extremely short 'summer,' the tundra becomes a migratory home for a large number of short term visitors from the coniferous forests to the south. Part of a series on biomes produced by Partridge Films, Ltd.
Science - Natural
Dist - CORF

The Tundra 26 MIN
VHS / U-matic
Color (H C)
$43.95 purchase _ #52 3419A
Presents major types of tundra including the Arctic Tundra and its major subdivisions, and the temperate and tropical alpine regions. Looks at plant and animal adaptations to the brief growing season, cold, and aridity characteristics of the tundra biome. Introduces food webs of several communities. Video version of 35mm filmstrip program, with live open and close.
Science - Natural
Dist - CBSC **Prod** - BMEDIA

The Tundra - a land without trees 18 MIN
VHS
Color (J H)
$19.95 purchase _ #IV154
Explores the land above the treeline in the mountainous areas of Rocky Mountain National Park, Mt McKinley National Park in Alaska and Grand Teton National Park. Takes a close look at the delicate balance of life, the harsh conditions for plants and animals and the process of erosion at high elevations.
Geography - United States; Science - Natural
Dist - INSTRU **Prod** - INSTRU

The Tundra Ecosystem 15 MIN
VHS / 16mm
Ecosystems of the Great Land Series
Color (I H)
$125.00 purchase, $25.00 rental
Considers various adaptations made by plants and animals to the harsh tundra environment. Illustrates that damage to the tundra takes a long time to repair.
Geography - United States; Science - Natural
Dist - AITECH **Prod** - ALASDE 1985

The Tune 72 MIN
35mm / 16mm
Color (G)
Presents a feature - length animated production with ten original songs, each of which satirizes a different style of American popular music and a different technique in animation. Tells the story of Del, a struggling songwriter hoping for superstardom so can marry his sweetheart, Didi. When confronted by his boss with a deadline of 47 minutes for a smash hit, Del gets lost on a freeway overpass and ends up in a bizarre musical town full of ghoulish characters. Produced, directed and animated by Bill Plympton. Music by Maureen McElheron. Contact distributor for price.
Fine Arts; Literature and Drama; Psychology
Dist - OCTOBF

A Tune for Tippy 10 MIN
VHS / 16mm
Alcoholism in the home series
Color (K)
$125.00 purchase
Tells the story of Tippy, a young puppy whose father is an alcoholic. Describes the effect alcohol has on the body and explains that alcohol is a powerful drug which should never be used by children. Includes leader's guide.
Health and Safety; Psychology; Sociology
Dist - CHEF **Prod** - CHEF

Tune in Tomorrow 28 MIN
VHS / U-matic
Please Stand by - a History of Radio Series
(C A)
Fine Arts; History - United States; Psychology; Sociology
Dist - SCCON **Prod** - SCCON 1986

Tune up America - home video car repair series
Body and fender repair 80 MIN
Dist - AAVIM
CAMV

Tune Up America - Home Video Car Repair Series
Detailing 22 MIN
Oil Change, Filter and Lube 20 MIN
Replacing Exhaust Systems 22 MIN
Replacing Shocks and Struts 40 MIN
Tune Up and Maintenance 60 MIN
Dist - CAMV

Tune Up and Maintenance 60 MIN
VHS
Tune Up America - Home Video Car Repair Series
(A)
$29.95 _ #UMKHTR006V
Provides an instructional demonstration on tune up and maintenance that aids the viewer in carrying out these tasks himself.
Industrial and Technical Education
Dist - CAMV **Prod** - CAMV

Tune - Up and Maintenance 60 MIN
VHS
Color (G)
$19.95 _ TA101
Gives tune - up procedures for typical American cars by discussing and explaining each item. The film includes a full discussion of carburetors, points, plugs, fluid levels, ignition wires, filters, and much more.
Industrial and Technical Education
Dist - AAVIM **Prod** - AAVIM 1989

Tune - Up Principles and Procedures
VHS / 35mm strip
Automotive Technology Series
Color
$40.00 purchase _ #MX8007 filmstrip, $80.00 purchase _ #MX8007V VHS
Education; Industrial and Technical Education
Dist - CAREER **Prod** - CAREER

Tune - Up - Pt I 30 MIN
VHS / U-matic
Keep it Running Series
Color
Covers minor tune - ups on the ignition and fuel systems, identifies parts and discusses the need for periodic tune - ups.
Industrial and Technical Education
Dist - NETCHE **Prod** - NETCHE 1982

Tune - Up - Pt II 30 MIN
U-matic / VHS
Keep it Running Series
Color
Explains how to use a vacuum gauge and perform spark plug and distributor inspections and service.
Industrial and Technical Education
Dist - NETCHE **Prod** - NETCHE 1982

Tune - Up - Pt III 30 MIN
U-matic / VHS
Keep it Running Series
Color
Covers inspection and replacement of high - tension ignition wires and adjustment of points, ignition timing and carburetor.
Industrial and Technical Education
Dist - NETCHE **Prod** - NETCHE 1982

Tuned Base Oscillator 30 MIN
16mm
B&W
LC 74-705866
Compares the tuned base oscillator circuit and the grid oscillator. Points out how each of the four requirements for oscillation is met in the tuned base oscillator. Explains the checks for oscillation and the symptoms that would occur for each component failure. (Kinescope).
Industrial and Technical Education; Science - Physical
Dist - USNAC **Prod** - USAF

Tuned Centrifugal Pendulum 24 MIN
VHS / U-matic
Nonlinear Vibrations Series
B&W
Mathematics
Dist - MIOT **Prod** - MIOT

Tuned Circuits 28 MIN
16mm
B&W
LC FIE55-13
Explains the theories behind the electronics of tuned circuits and application of these theories to a practical radio receiver layout and a radio transmitter.
Industrial and Technical Education
Dist - USNAC **Prod** - USA 1954

Tuned Circuits - no 6 60 MIN
U-matic
AC/DC Electronics Series
Color (PRO)
One of a series of electronic and electrical training sessions for electronics workers on direct and alternating current and how to work with each.
Industrial and Technical Education
Dist - VTRI **Prod** - VTRI 1986

Tuned - in series
Commercials 15 MIN
Critical reviewing 15 MIN
Editing - music - special effects 15 MIN
Interviewing 15 MIN
Program types - stereotyping 15 MIN
Story elements 15 MIN
The Television studio 15 MIN
Viewing habits 15 MIN
Writing reviews 15 MIN
Dist - FI

Tuned Plate Oscillator 19 MIN
16mm
B&W
LC 74-705867
Develops and explains the major differences between an RF and an audio oscillator. Shows the purpose of each component in the schematic diagram.
Industrial and Technical Education; Science - Physical
Dist - USNAC **Prod** - USAF 1965

Tunes of glory 106 MIN
VHS
Color (G)
$29.95 purchase _ #TUN010
Features a drama about the pressures of military life. Features Alec Guinness as a gruff Scottish officer who refuses to relinquish his regiment to an aristocratic colonel. Directed by Ronald Neame.
Civics and Political Systems; Fine Arts
Dist - HOMVIS **Prod** - JANUS 1960

The Tunes of Language Intonation and Meaning 30 MIN
VHS / U-matic
Language and Meaning Series
Color (C)
English Language; Psychology
Dist - GPN **Prod** - WUSFTV 1983

Tung 5 MIN
VHS / 16mm
Color & B&W; Silent (G)
$11.00 rental; $224.00 purchase
Features an experimental film by Bruce Baillie.
Fine Arts
Dist - CANCIN **Prod** - BAILB 1966
AFA AFA

Tung hsieh hsi tu
VHS
Color (G)
$50.00 _ #27991
Features kung fu with Ch'ing - hsia Lin produced by Tai - pei.
Fine Arts; Physical Education and Recreation
Dist - PANASI

Tuning 25 MIN
VHS / U-matic
Rockschool Series
Color (J)
Explains types and gauge of guitar string and the problems of drum tuning, teaching that drum tuning is important for the authenticity of different styles.
Fine Arts
Dist - FI **Prod** - BBCTV

Tuning Pneumatic Control Systems 60 MIN
VHS
Pneumatic Systems and Equipment Series
Color (PRO)
$600.00 - $1500.00 purchase _ #ICTPC
Shows how to tune a controller with the guidance and assistance of an experienced instrument technician. Part of an eleven - part series on pneumatic systems and equipment, which is part of a 49 - unit set on instrumentation and control. Includes five workbooks and an instructor guide to support four hours of instruction.
Education; Industrial and Technical Education; Mathematics; Psychology
Dist - NUSTC **Prod** - NUSTC

Tunis '77 30 MIN
16mm
Color (FRENCH SPANISH GERMAN)
LC 78-700228
Documents the first World Youth Tournament in soccer for the Coca - Cola Cup.
Physical Education and Recreation
Dist - COCA **Prod** - COCA 1977

The Tunnel 25 MIN
16mm / VHS
Color (J)
LC 75-700488
Shows how a young man becomes enmeshed in a maze of conflicting authorities and personalities after he becomes involved in violence in a school.
Guidance and Counseling; Sociology
Dist - LRF **Prod** - LRF 1974

The Tunnel 36 MIN
VHS
Color (P I R)
$39.00 rental _ #36 - 84 - 2028
Tells how some children work together to find a lost show horse. Reveals that they form a special bond with some senior citizens during their search for the horse. Teaches the concepts that God has a plan for each person, that people should respect their peers, and that friendship is not dependent on age.
Literature and Drama; Religion and Philosophy
Dist - APH

Tunnel Diode Amplifier 18 MIN
U-matic / VHS / 16mm
B&W
Identifies the tunnel diode as an amplifier when it is operated within the negative resistance portion of its characteristic operating curve.
Industrial and Technical Education; Science - Physical
Dist - USNAC **Prod** - USAF 1983

Tunnels 19 MIN
VHS / 16mm
Color (I J H G)
$390.00, $49.95 purchase
Covers the history of tunnels from ancient Egypt and Rome to the present. Shows how modern tunnels are constructed.
Industrial and Technical Education
Dist - KAWVAL **Prod** - KAWVAL

Tunnels Under Chicago 16 MIN
16mm
Color
LC 81-701221
Explains the operations of the Robbins Company in designing, building and operating tunneling machines used in a sewer project in Chicago.
Industrial and Technical Education
Dist - AMMPCO **Prod** - ROBBNS 1981

Tupamaros 50 MIN
16mm / U-matic / VHS
Captioned; Color (A) (SPANISH (ENGLISH SUBTITLES))
Portrays Uruguay's National Liberation Movement, its origins, reasons for the guerilla struggle, and special tactics it employs.
Fine Arts; History - World
Dist - CNEMAG **Prod** - SBC 1972

Turandot 120 MIN
VHS
Color (S) (ITALIAN)
$39.95 purchase _ #623 - 9811
Stages 'Turandot' by Puccini in the open - air Arena di Verona. Stars Ghena Dimitrova and Nicola Martinucci.
Fine Arts; Foreign Language; Geography - World
Dist - FI **Prod** - NVIDC 1986

Turardot 120 MIN
U-matic / VHS
Color (A)
Presents a cruel Oriental princess who poses deadly riddles to those who love her, in Giacomo Puccini's opera, Turardot.
Fine Arts; Foreign Language
Dist - SRA **Prod** - SRA

Turbine 11 MIN
16mm / U-matic / VHS
Inventive Child Series
Color (P I)
Details that when Boy observes some natural occurrences that dramatize the power of wind and water, he creates devices to indicate wind direction and velocity, then experiments with ways to make waterpower turn the mill wheel he has invented. Demonstrates that water has weight and illustrates the principles of wind and water power.
History - World; Science - Physical
Dist - EBEC **Prod** - POLSKI 1983

Turbine and Useful Propeller 22 MIN
U-matic / VHS
Inventive Child Series
Color (P I J)
$89.00 purchase _ #1586
Shows that from observing nature natural power can be harnessed through the use of technology (1st part). Suggests that fantasizing can become constructive thinking by presenting advantageous uses of air pressure.
Industrial and Technical Education; Psychology
Dist - EBEC

Turbine Efficency - 1 30 TO 40 MIN
VHS
Heat Rate Improvement Series
Color (PRO)
$600.00 - $1500.00 purchase _ #HRO12
Discusses turbine blade design and efficiency in addition to the effects of solid particle erosion, silica buildup and packaging and seal problems on efficiency. Includes one textbook and instructor guide to support two hours of instruction.

Education; Industrial and Technical Education; Psychology
Dist - NUSTC Prod - NUSTC

Turbine Effiecncy - 2 30 TO 40 MIN
VHS
Heat Rate Improvement Series
Color (PRO)
$600.00 - $1500.00 purchase _ #HRO13
Covers efficient turbine startup and shutdown. Looks at the effects of main steam temperature changes, reheat temperature changes, main steam pressure changes and back pressure changes on turbine efficiency. Includes one textbook and instructor guide to support two hours of instruction.
Education; Industrial and Technical Education; Psychology
Dist - NUSTC **Prod** - NUSTC

Turbine Efficency - 3 30 TO 40 MIN
VHS
Heat Rate Improvement Series
Color (PRO)
$600.00 - $1500.00 purchase _ #HRO14
Focuses on three areas of turbine efficiency - the effects of attemperation on turbine heat rate, the efficient operation of turbine control valves and the effects of extraction steam problems on heat rate. Includes one textbook and instructor guide to support two hours of instruction.
Education; Industrial and Technical Education; Psychology
Dist - NUSTC **Prod** - NUSTC

Turbines - Pt 1
U-matic / VHS
Industrial Training, Module 4 - Power Production Series; Module 4 - Power production
Color (IND)
Covers principles, construction, oil system and gland seal system of turbines.
Industrial and Technical Education
Dist - LEIKID **Prod** - LEIKID

Turbines - Pt 2
U-matic / VHS
Industrial Training, Module 4 - Power Production Series; Module 4 - Power production
Color (IND)
Covers several aspects of turbines including back - pressure turbines and control equipment.
Industrial and Technical Education
Dist - LEIKID **Prod** - LEIKID

Turbines - Pt 3
U-matic / VHS
Industrial Training, Module 4 - Power Production Series; Module 4 - Power production
Color (IND)
Discusses the steam system, protection gear, supervisory equipment and turbine operation.
Industrial and Technical Education
Dist - LEIKID **Prod** - LEIKID

Turbocharger and supercharger service 24 MIN
VHS
Diesel engine video series
Color (G H)
$95.00 purchase _ #MG5216V-T
Describes the operation of a diesel engine with a particular emphasis on turbocharger and supercharger service. Explains in this videocassette how to spot and service troubles with a turbocharged diesel engine. Includes information on testing, removing, and installing turbochargers. Provides information on both gasoline and diesel engines for trucks and automobiles.
Education; Industrial and Technical Education
Dist - CAMV

The Turbocharger Explained 77 MIN
VHS / 35mm strip
(H A IND)
#488XV7
Shows operating principles, basic parts (pt 1 and 2), and problem diagnosis and service procedures (pt 1 and 2) (5 tapes). Includes a Study Guide.
Education; Industrial and Technical Education
Dist - BERGL

Turbocharger testing and service 30 MIN
VHS
Fuel delivery and induction systems series
Color (H A)
$219.00 purchase _ #VMA31363V
Discusses how to remove and test turbochargers. Includes two videocassettes and a program guide.
Industrial and Technical Education
Dist - CAMV

Turbocharger Testing and Service
VHS
$197.00 purchase _ #016 - 921
Portrays removal and bench testing, performing tests for axial and radial bearing clearances. Explains how to install a turbocharger unit and lubricate bearings.
Education; Industrial and Technical Education
Dist - CAREER **Prod** - CAREER

Turboprop - Turboshaft Engines - Introduction 13 MIN
16mm
Color
LC FIE60-57
Outlines the theory of operation of turboprop and turboshaft engines with comparison to the turbojet engine. Shows testing and assembly of engine components in manufacture and the maintenance and operation of the engines.
Business and Economics; Industrial and Technical Education; Science - Physical
Dist - USNAC **Prod** - USN 1959

The Turbulent end to a tragic war - America's final hours in Vietnam 60 MIN
VHS
Great TV news stories series
Color (I J H)
$24.98 purchase _ #MP1721
Covers April 4, 1975, when the last 2,000 Americans were evacuated from Saigon. Tells the story of those who fled and those who stayed behind to face the North Vietnamese army.
History - United States; Sociology
Dist - KNOWUN **Prod** - ABCNEW

The Turbulent term of Tyke Tyler 52 MIN
VHS
Book tower series
Color; PAL (I J)
PdS20 purchase
Adapts a book by Gene Kemp. Presents a comedy about an all - too - eventful final school term which almost ends in disaster. Part of a series reviewing new books and adapting them as drama serials. Contact distributor about availability outside the United Kingdom.
Education; Literature and Drama
Dist - ACADEM

Turckheim et sa Fete du Vin 30 MIN
VHS
Color (J H G) (FRENCH)
$39.95 purchase _ #W3493
Views life in the Alsatian village of Turckheim, covering both the people and the yearly festivals. Gives a closeup view of the wine - producing region. Includes a five - part video program that increases in difficulty and a transcript with exercise material.
Foreign Language
Dist - GPC

Turing Machines
16mm
B&W
Shows how a Turing machine will convert a unary to a ternary representation. Includes an analogy involving three rugby players with special jumpers and numbers on their backs.
Mathematics
Dist - OPENU **Prod** - OPENU

Turing Machines and Functions
16mm
B&W
Introduces the technique of arithmetization, which shows how to move just one step in a Turing machine using functions.
Mathematics
Dist - OPENU **Prod** - OPENU

Turing Machines and Post Systems
16mm
Color
Analyzes the logic of structure and computational aspects of language, arriving at the basic ingredients of the post system - alphabet axiom and production. Shows post systems as equivalent to Turing machines.
Mathematics
Dist - OPENU **Prod** - OPENU

Turkana conversations trilogy series
Presents three feature - length documentaries on the Turkana, relatively isolated seminomadic herders who live in the dry country of northwestern Kenya. Produced by David and Judith MacDougall. Includes the titles Lorang's Way, A Wife Among Wives and The Wedding Camels.
Lorang's Way 69 MIN
Wedding Camels, the 108 MIN
Wife among Wives, a 72 MIN
Dist - UCEMC

Turkey
VHS
Frugal gourmet - American classics series
Color (G)
$19.95 purchase _ #CCP829
Shows how to prepare turkey American style. Features Jeff Smith, the Frugal Gourmet. Part of the nine - part series, American Classics.
History - United States; Home Economics
Dist - CADESF **Prod** - CADESF

Turkey 29 MIN
Videoreel / VT2
International Cookbook Series
Color
Features home economist Joan Hood presenting a culinary tour of specialty dishes from around the world. Shows the preparation of Turkish dishes ranging from peasant cookery to continental cuisine.
Geography - World; Home Economics
Dist - PBS **Prod** - WMVSTV

Turkey 13 MIN
16mm
New Horizons Series
Color
Presents Istanbul, a skyline of spires and minarets and mosques. Features a lemonade vendor dispensing refreshment on the spot, samovars brewing tea and Turkish coffee.
Geography - World; Social Science; Sociology
Dist - PANWA **Prod** - TWCF

Turkey - between Europe and Asia 19 MIN
16mm / VHS
Color (I)
LC 90708915
Reviews Turkey's history and geography. Introduces Turkey's people and their culture.
Geography - World; History - World
Dist - BARR

Turkey Caller's Video 48 MIN
VHS / BETA
Color
Features Daniel Baker going through a seminar on wild turkey hunting and related activities.
Physical Education and Recreation; Science - Natural
Dist - HOMEAF **Prod** - HOMEAF

Turkey Calling and Hunting 82 MIN
BETA / VHS
Color
Provides a complete seminar on turkey hunting and calling, with tips on safety and hunting techniques.
Physical Education and Recreation; Science - Natural
Dist - HOMEAF **Prod** - HOMEAF

The Turkey Caper 24 MIN
U-matic / VHS / 16mm
Color
MP=$450.00
Follows cartoon characters Buttons and Rusty as they learn the story of Thanksgiving, the Pilgrims, and Indians while ending up in mischief.
Social Science
Dist - LANDMK **Prod** - LANDMK 1985

Turkey Hunting with Ben Rodgers Lee 30 MIN
BETA / VHS
Color
Presents Ben Lee and Bob McGuire instructing on the types of calls, hunting equipment, scouting and turkey signs. Shows an actual bowhunt for Alabama gobblers.
Physical Education and Recreation; Science - Natural
Dist - HOMEAF **Prod** - HOMEAF

Turkey in Transition 5 MIN
U-matic
See, Hear - the Middle East Series
Color (J)
Explores the turbulent history of Turkey as well as the steps taken toward modernization since the collapse of the Ottoman Empire.
Geography - World; History - World
Dist - TVOTAR **Prod** - TVOTAR 1980

Turkey operations - year round production 13 MIN
VHS / U-matic
Biosecurity and the poultry industry series
Color (IND)
$40.00, $95.00 purchase _ #TCA18207, #TCA18206
Covers the unique characteristics of biosecurity for turkey operations. Reveals that turkeys are sensitive to disease, require contact with people, and that range and wild turkeys must be raised separately.
Agriculture; Health and Safety
Dist - USNAC **Prod** - USDA 1989

The Turkey Shoot 27 MIN
U-matic / VHS / 16mm
Victory at Sea Series
B&W (J H)
Looks at the conquest and development of the Mariana Islands during World War II.
Civics and Political Systems; History - United States; History - World
Dist - LUF **Prod** - NBCTV

Turkey shoot - two if by sea, the battle for Leyte Gulf, return of the Allies and full fathom five 135 MIN
VHS

Victory at sea series
B&W (G)
$24.95 purchase _ #S01158
Contains five episodes from the Victory at Sea series, documenting the U S Navy battles of World War II. 'Turkey Shoot' features live footage of the battles for the Marianas Islands, including Guam, while 'Two If By Sea' covers the U S Army and Marines' assault and occupation of the Peleliu Islands in 1944. 'The Battle for Leyte Gulf' documents that key battle, while 'Return of the Allies' focuses on the 1941 situation in the Philippines. 'Full Fathom Five' explains the importance of shipping to Japan.
Civics and Political Systems; History - United States
Dist - UILL

The Turkish bath 30 MIN
VHS
Palette series
Color (G C)
$70.00 purchase, $12.50, rental _ #36408
Discloses that the last major painting, 1862, of Neoclassicist Jean - Domininque portrays 25 full - figured women relaxing in a Turkish bath - an exotic pretext for a sophisticated eroticism. Contains footage of art works depicting nude subjects. Part of a 13 - part series which examines great paintings by moving into their creative spaces and spending time with the characters and their surroundings. Uses special video effects to investigate artistic enigmas and studies material, technique, style and significance. Narrated by Marcel Cuvelier, directed by Alain Jaubert.
Fine Arts
Dist - PSU **Prod** - LOUVRE 1992

Turkiye 16 MIN
U-matic / VHS / 16mm
Color (I)
LC 77-703269
Presents a panorama of historical and modern sights in Turkey, including monuments, classical ruins, castles and temples.
Fine Arts; Geography - World; History - World
Dist - PFP **Prod** - TIO 1977

Turmoil in Communist China - the Troubles of Mao - Tse - Tung 16 MIN
16mm
Screen news digest series; Vol 9; Issue 10
B&W (J)
LC 73-700277
Tells the story of Mao Tse - Tung and presents the history of China since the founding of the Chinese Communist Party in 1921.
Civics and Political Systems; History - World
Dist - HEARST **Prod** - HEARST 1967

Turn a Handle, Flick a Switch; 2nd Rev. 14 MIN
16mm / U-matic / VHS
Color (I J)
$49.95 purchase _ #Q10017; LC 83-700648
Uses animation and a simple experiment to explain where water, gas and electricity come from and how they get to homes. Stresses conservation of water and power.
Science - Natural; Social Science
Dist - CF **Prod** - CF 1983

Turn a Handle, Flick a Switch 14 MIN
U-matic / VHS / 16mm
Color (P I)
$295 purchase - 16 mm, $220 purchase - video
Tells how water, gas, and electricity get into homes. Directed by Ben Shedd.
Science - Physical
Dist - CF

A Turn for the Best 26 MIN
16mm
Color (A)
Illustrates the use of labor - management committees to improve labor relations and alleviate problems concerning both parties. Sponsored by the Appalachian Regional Commission, this documentary demonstrates how Cumberland, MD, and Jamestown, NY reduced problems through use of such committees.
Business and Economics; Psychology
Dist - AFLCIO **Prod** - NPL 1982

Turn here sweet corn 58 MIN
VHS
Color (H C G)
$275.00 purchase, $85.00 rental
Presents a video essay about food, memory and the land - just before the shopping mall arrives. Looks at the loss of prime farmland to suburban sprawl. The Diffleys have been landowners in Minnesota for 150 years and are forced to sell their organic farm to developers. Their story is interwoven with a general contemplation of topics such as the relationship between producers and consumers of food, the eviction of a vibrant rural culture into the realm of memory and the future of the human food supply. Produced by Helen De Michiel. Also available in a shorter version.
Fine Arts; Health and Safety; Sociology
Dist - BULFRG

Turn here sweet corn - Short version 37 MIN
VHS
Color (H C G)
$195.00 purchase, $45.00 rental
Presents a video essay about food, memory and the land - just before the shopping mall arrives. Looks at the loss of prime farmland to suburban sprawl. The Diffleys have been landowners in Minnesota for 150 years and are forced to sell their organic farm to developers. Their story is interwoven with a general contemplation of topics such as the relationship between producers and consumers of food, the eviction of a vibrant rural culture into the realm of memory and the future of the human food supply. Produced by Helen De Michiel. Also available in a longer version.
Fine Arts; Health and Safety; Sociology
Dist - BULFRG

The Turn of the Century 60 MIN
U-matic / VHS
James Galway's Music in Time Series
Color (J)
Presents flutist James Galway discussing how music became more cosmopolitan around the turn of the century. Includes examples from The Mikado, Madame Butterfly, Strauss' Salome and Debussy's La Mer.
Fine Arts
Dist - FOTH **Prod** - POLTEL 1982

Turn of the Century 24 MIN
16mm
Color
Explores the effects of the massive influx of immigrants to America at the turn of the century, what we learned from the invasion of Cuba and the feelings and attitudes reflected in American sports, politics and business.
Civics and Political Systems; History - United States
Dist - REAF **Prod** - INTEXT

Turn of the Century 53 MIN
U-matic / VHS
Man and Music Series
Color (C)
$279.00, $179.00 purchase _ #AD - 2064
Focuses on Vienna during the closing days of the Austrian empire. Reveals that it was slow to accept modernism. Considers Mahler, Wolf, Freud, Klimt, Kokoschka, Richard Strauss and Arnold Schoenberg. Part of a 22 - part series that sets Western music into the historial and cultural context of its time.
Fine Arts; Geography - World; History - World
Dist - FOTH **Prod** - FOTH

Turn of the Century 30 MIN
U-matic / VHS / 16mm
Twentieth Century Series
B&W (J H)
Pictures the European world and way of life which was destroyed when the first world war shook the world and shows the personalities and forces which led up to the war.
History - World
Dist - MGHT **Prod** - CBSTV 1960

Turn - of - the - century America 16 MIN
VHS
Witness to history I series
Color (J H)
$49.00 purchase _ #06820 - 026
Gives a taste of the dramatic changes that took place in the first twenty years of the new century. Features immigrants at Ellis Island, scenes of Henry Ford inventing the 'horseless carriage,' and the development of assembly - line production. Part of a four - part series. Includes teacher's guide and library kit.
Education; Fine Arts; History - United States; Industrial and Technical Education
Dist - GA

Turn - of - the - Century America 14 MIN
16mm
Color
LC 79-700332
Examines a major exhibition of turn - of - the - century American art showing the period's pictorial arts. Discusses the rich complexity of forms, themes and techniques that reflect the diversity and vitality of the era.
Fine Arts
Dist - KAROL

Turn - of - the - century America 16 MIN
VHS
Color (J H)
$49.00 purchase _ #06820 - 026
Takes a look at the exciting, dramatic changes that took place in the first 20 years of the 20th century. Enters the United States with the immigrants of Ellis island and marvels at actual scenes of Henry Ford and the 'horseless carriage' and development of assembly - line production. Includes teachers' guide and library kit.
Business and Economics; History - United States; Social Science; Sociology
Dist - INSTRU

Turn Off Pollution 11 MIN
U-matic / VHS / 16mm
Color (P)
LC 73-712320
Stresses the importance of becoming involved in issues regarding pollution and taking steps to improve matters. Suggests steps elementary school children can take to curb the destruction of the environment.
Science - Natural; Social Science
Dist - EBEC **Prod** - EBEC 1971

Turn on, Light, Adjust Cutting Torch to a Neutral Flame, and Turn Off Oxyacetylene Cutting Equipment 8 MIN
Videoreel / VHS
Color (C A)
Shows equipment and materials and demonstrates procedures for turning on, lighting, adjusting and turning off the cutting torch. Emphasizes safety and distinguishing among the three types of flames.
Industrial and Technical Education
Dist - OSDVTE **Prod** - OSDVTE

Turn the Other Cheek 15 MIN
16mm
Our Children Series
Color; B&W (P I R)
Tells the story about a misunderstanding between some children and their parents which provides a practical illustration of Jesus' teaching to 'turn the other cheek.'
Guidance and Counseling; Psychology; Religion and Philosophy
Dist - FAMF **Prod** - FAMF

Turn to your gods dogs 17 MIN
16mm
B&W (G)
$35.00 rental
Combines re - edited soundtracks from old newsreels and new documentaries with their correct or incorrect image, forming a demented narrative dealing with the political machinations leading up to an amphibious assault on a nude beach. Says filmmaker Richard Beveridge, '...an homage to Bunuel and Fellini...a political satire.'
Fine Arts; Literature and Drama
Dist - CANCIN

Turn toward Identity 28 MIN
VHS / U-matic
Color (PRO)
LC 79-720267
Discusses the roles of patient, staff members and family in reestablishing the lost identity of a confused person. Describes specific techniques such as the use of clocks, calendars, personal possessions, sounds and colors. Emphasizes the importance of communicating expectations. Encourages the learner to have patience and perserverance when dealing with the confused individual and assurance that the rewards for patient as well as for the staff are well worth the wait.
Health and Safety; Psychology
Dist - MEDCOM **Prod** - MEDCOM

Turn your heart toward home series
Features Dr James Dobson and his wife Shirley in six presentations on issues affecting the family. Covers topics including the parental role in child - rearing, discipline, teenagers, societal values, painful childhoods and traditional values. Includes study guide, promotional materials and a copy of Dr Dobson's biography, 'Turning Hearts Towards Home.'
A Father looks back and power in parenting - Tape 1 120 MIN
Overcoming a painful childhood and the heritage - Tape 3 100 MIN
Power in parenting - the adolescent and the family under fire - Tape 2 98 MIN
Dist - APH **Prod** - WORD

Turn Yourself on 29 MIN
Videoreel / VT2
That's Life Series
Color
Guidance and Counseling
Dist - PBS **Prod** - KOAPTV

Turnabout - put yourself in the customer's shoes 30 MIN
VHS
Color (A PRO IND)
$485.00 purchase, $140.00 rental
Promotes a customer service attitude in employees by encouraging them to view things from the customer's point of view.

Business and Economics; Guidance and Counseling; Psychology
Dist - VLEARN **Prod** - DARTNL

Turnabout - Put Yourself in the Customer's Shoes 16 MIN
16mm / VHS
(PRO)
$140.00 rental
Presents an attitude awareness program that offers techniques for building a positive relationship with customers. Dramatizes how to handle customer service problems. Accompanied by a supplementary package of materials.
Business and Economics; Psychology
Dist - DARTNL

Turnaround 28 MIN
16mm
Color (H C A)
LC 76-703734
Documents the causes, events and results of the Homestead Steel Strike of 1892, which pitted the Amalgamated Association Of Iron And Steel Workers against the combined forces of the Carnegie Steel Company of Pennsylvania and a private army of Pinkerton agents.
Business and Economics; History - United States; Sociology
Dist - PSU **Prod** - WPSXTV 1976

Turnaround - a Story of Recovery 47 MIN
VHS / 16mm
(G PRO)
$75/3 Day VHS/3/4
Tells the story of Aurora House, a 6 - 12 week recovery program that helps women conquer their chemical dependencies. Features women at Aurora House discussing openly sensitive subjects, including abuse and prostitution. Shows how Aurora House helps them regain self - respect, autonomy, and control over their lives.
Health and Safety; Sociology
Dist - BAXMED **Prod** - NFBC 1989

Turnarounds - a pilot needle exchange program 9 MIN
VHS
Color (H C G)
$99.00 purchase, $40.00 rental
Documents a legal needle - exchange program in New Haven which is saving lives. Reveals that when the state of Connecticut passed a bill legalizing a needle - exchange program, the New Haven Health Department, supported by the Mayor and the Chief of Police began a pilot program. One thousand clients have enrolled and over 30,000 needles have been exchanged. Preliminary studies conducted by Yale University show that the rate of HIV transmission by participants was reduced by 33 percent without any associated increase in drug use. Produced by Susan Adler.
Health and Safety; Psychology
Dist - FLMLIB

Turned on 7 MIN
U-matic / VHS / 16mm
Color (P)
LC 73-706140
Shows dune buggies, surfing, snowmobiles, skiing, sailing and other sports as activities which emphasize the coordination and capabilities of the human body.
Physical Education and Recreation
Dist - PFP **Prod** - PFP 1969

Turned Round to See 11 MIN
16mm
Revelation Series
Color (H C A)
LC 71-711553
A dramatization about the experiences of a lonely and puzzled seventeen - year - old boy who wanders into a teenage discotheque. Expresses the fundamental belief that the revelation of Christ encompasses a revelation of self and that such a revelation leads an individual to reach out to others.
Guidance and Counseling; Psychology; Religion and Philosophy
Dist - FRACOC **Prod** - FRACOC 1970

Turner 40 MIN
VHS
Three painters 3 series
Color (A)
PdS65 purchase
Explores the work of the painter Turner, hosted by painter and critic Sir Lawrence Gowing. Based on the concept that Turner's work represents a distinct stage in the development of European painting between the Renaissance and the present day. Discusses the historical and social backgrounds against which the artist worked, but concentrates on examining a small number of canvases. Includes views of the places which particularly inspired the artist.
Fine Arts
Dist - BBCENE

Turner - 1775 - 1851 12 MIN
16mm
Color
Presents paintings by Turner that dramatized nature.
Fine Arts
Dist - ROLAND **Prod** - ROLAND

Turner - master of the sublime 55 MIN
VHS
Romantic versus Classic art series
Color (G)
PdS19.95 purchase _ #A4-ODY176
Examines the radical developments in Turner's style and the two different sides of his work - the public paintings and the private experimental pieces that were ridiculed by his contemporaries. Explores his use of color to create impact that influenced the next generation of artists, the Impressionists. One of a series of seven videos about the Romantic Rebellion in art in the second half of the 18th century written and narrated by art historian Kenneth Clark. Produced by Odyssey.
Fine Arts
Dist - AVP

Turning 20 MIN
VHS / U-matic
Math Topics - Trigonometry Series
Color (J H C)
Mathematics
Dist - FI **Prod** - BBCTV

Turning 16 series
Features an eight - part series exploring whether there is a global teenager. Examines the lives of six teens from different countries and explores major issues facing young people everywhere - including education, culture, sex and marriage, sports, religion, work and the future. Titles include Youth and the Global Village; The Story of Rosie; The Story of Idrissa; The Story of Eman; The Story of Pintinho; The Story of Puttinan; The Story of Sonam; and Youth and the Future. Includes guides. See individual titles for description and purchase - rental costs.

The Story of Eman	26 MIN
The Story of Idrissa	26 MIN
The Story of Pintinho	26 MIN
The Story of Puttinan	26 MIN
The Story of Rosie	26 MIN
The Story of Sonam	26 MIN
Youth and the future	26 MIN
Youth and the global village	26 MIN

Dist - BULFRG **Prod** - HARCOT

Turning a Cylinder between Centers 17 MIN
16mm
Precision Wood Machining Series Operations on the Wood Lathe
B&W
LC FIE52-44
Points out how to choose stock and mount it on a wood lathe for turning between centers. Demonstrates the use of a parting tool and skew chisel. Explains sand turning work.
Industrial and Technical Education
Dist - USNAC **Prod** - USOE 1944

Turning a Cylinder between Centers and Turning Work on a Face Plate 30 MIN
16mm
Precision Wood Machining Series Operations on the Wood Lathe
B&W
Points out how to choose stock and mount it on a wood lathe for turning between centers. Demonstrates the use of a parting tool and skew chisel. Explains sand turning work. Shows the various types of face plates. Explains how to attach the stock to the face plate, how to true up the wood, how to scribe the work for inside turning, how to use round nose and diamond point chisels and how to smoothe the recess bottom.
Industrial and Technical Education
Dist - USNAC **Prod** - USOE 1944

Turning a Radius
U-matic / VHS
Basic Engine Lathe Series
Color (SPANISH)
Industrial and Technical Education
Dist - VTRI **Prod** - VTRI

Turning a Sphere Inside Out 23 MIN
U-matic / VHS / 16mm
Topology Series
Color (C A)
LC 81-700612
Uses advanced computer animation to discuss the problem of turning a sphere inside out by passing the surface through itself without making any holes or creases. Illustrates the homotopy with a sequence of models, showing the crucial stages in the motion.
Mathematics
Dist - IFB **Prod** - EDS 1976

Turning a taper with the tailstock set over 17 MIN
16mm
Machine shop work series; Operations on the engine lathe; No 6
B&W
LC FIE51-537
Shows how to calculate tailstock offset for cutting tapers, how to offset the tailstock and how to turn a taper with the tailstock set over.
Industrial and Technical Education
Dist - USNAC **Prod** - USOE 1942

Turning and Review 29 MIN
U-matic / VHS
Cross Country Ski School Series
Color
Demonstrates the three most useful turns, the step, skating and the parallel turns, and gives a general review of all cross country skiing techniques.
Physical Education and Recreation
Dist - PBS **Prod** - VTETV 1981

Turning and transferring the patient - good body mechanics 13 MIN
U-matic / VHS
Color (PRO C)
$395.00 purchase, $80.00 rental _ #C911 - VI - 060
Helps nurses and nursing students to avoid injury and strain when they must turn or transfer a patient. Demonstrates proper body mechanics which utilize pulling, pushing and rolling and minimize lifting. Presents basic guidelines to use when moving patients. Demonstrates in detail ten types of turns and transfers. Presented by Judy M Grisell, RN, University of Texas, Health Science Center at Houston.
Health and Safety; Science - Natural
Dist - HSCIC

Turning Around 23 MIN
16mm
Color (H C A)
LC 75-702969
Shows how efforts by residents, local banks, government and private foundations are helping to reverse the pattern of urban decline in Cincinnati.
Geography - United States; Sociology
Dist - KAROL **Prod** - FDF 1975

Turning between centers 40 MIN
VHS / BETA
Machine shop - engine lathe series
Color (IND)
Industrial and Technical Education; Psychology
Dist - RMIBHF **Prod** - RMIBHF

Turning between Centers 18 MIN
VHS / U-matic
Introduction to Machine Technology, Module 2 Series; Module 2
Color (IND)
Focuses on aligning machine centers, drilling center holes and mounting the workpiece. Gives methods for straight turning and for taper turning.
Industrial and Technical Education
Dist - LEIKID **Prod** - LEIKID

Turning Brass with Hand Graver - Pt 1 14 MIN
16mm
Light Mechanics Series
B&W
Demonstrates how to use a graver in turning, facing and chamfering a brass dowel.
Industrial and Technical Education
Dist - USVA **Prod** - USVA 1949

Turning Brass with Hand Graver - Pt 2 11 MIN
16mm
Light Mechanics Series
B&W
Demonstrates how to use a graver in reducing diameter of brass wire and in squaring the shoulder.
Industrial and Technical Education
Dist - USVA **Prod** - USVA 1949

Turning Decisions into Programs 15 MIN
U-matic / VHS
Broadcasting Series
Color (J H)
Explores the decisions made in developing radio and television programming to serve the needs of the audience.
Fine Arts; Industrial and Technical Education; Social Science; Sociology
Dist - CTI **Prod** - CTI

Turning Dreams into Reality 29 MIN
VHS / U-matic
Color (H C A) (SPANISH (ENGLISH SUBTITLES))
$250 purchase, $50 rental
Profiles Fernando Birri, 'Father' of the New Latin American Cinema. Includes an interview with Birr, excerpts from his films, discussions with his coworkers and colleagues, and commentary by American film critic B Ruby Rich. Directed by Monica Melamid and Rafael Andreu.

Biography; Fine Arts
Dist - CNEMAG

Turning Fifty 43 MIN
U-matic
Color (G)
$450.00 purchase, $90.00, $80.00 rental
Considers menopause. Presented by Video Femmes.
Health and Safety; Sociology
Dist - WMENIF **Prod** - WMENIF 1986

Turning food into fuel 28 MIN
VHS
Human body - digestion - series
Color (J H G)
$89.95 purchase _ #UW4180
Follows the path of a sandwich from the plate into the mouth, through the various organs and processes of digestion, as far as the utilization of the food - derived energy in the cells. Part of a 39 - part series featuring computer animation, medical photography, electron micrography, full - color drawings and diagrams and three - dimensional working models to cover the workings of the human body from head to toe and inside out.
Home Economics; Science - Natural
Dist - FOTH

Turning 4 - new skills 51 MIN
VHS
Citizen 2000 child development series
Color (H C G)
$350.00 purchase, $65.00 rental
Visits Citizen 2000 children who became four years old in 1986. Reveals that they have emerged from toddlerhood to become independent, sociable, chatty and occasionally argumentative children. Looks at the children excercising their new skills in communication and imagination, their last year before they start full time school careers. Features Dr Judy Dunn, a developmental psychologist, and Prof David Crystal, a language specialist. Part of a series on child development which is following a group of children over a period of 18 years - from their birth in 1982 until they become adults in the year 2000. Produced by Dove Productions for Channel 4.
Health and Safety; Psychology; Social Science
Dist - FLMLIB **Prod** - CFTV 1993

Turning of the child 20 MIN
VHS / U-matic
We are one series
Color (G)
Shows the young child being prepared for the Turning of the Child Ceremony which marks the end of the infanthood and the beginning of the second stage or 'hill' of life. We see Inshat'sonwin take the child to the keepers sacred tent for the ceremony. The keeper is presented a fine quilled robe which Grandmother has made for the occasion. The Child enters the tent. At the conclusion of the ceremony, the young child now has her ni'kie name (Ml'wason) and a feast is held at the family lodge.
Social Science
Dist - NAMPBC **Prod** - NAMPBC 1986

Turning of the Tide 26 MIN
16mm
Winston Churchill - the Valiant Years Series no 16
B&W
LC FI67-2119
Uses documentary footage to describe the nightly bombing of German installations as the Allies began to achieve air supremacy and shows how the German U - boat menace was brought under control and how the stumbling blocks of Cassino and Anzio were overcome. Based on the book 'The Second World War,' by Winston S Churchill.
History - World
Dist - SG **Prod** - ABCTV 1961

Turning Off - Drugs and Peer Pressure
VHS / U-matic
Color (J H)
Explores peer pressure as a motivating factor in drug involvement. Dramatizes how peer pressure works. Provides assertive techniques in role - playing situations to help cope with peer pressure.
Health and Safety; Psychology; Sociology
Dist - SUNCOM **Prod** - SUNCOM

Turning over a new leaf 22 MIN
VHS / U-matic
Color (I)
$350.00 purchase _ #HH - 6161M
Adapts the Kids on the Block puppet program on drug and alcohol abuse prevention created by Barbara Aiello. Uses puppet characters to tell the story of a boy's return to his old neighborhood after his release from a drug rehabilitation program called 'A New Leaf.' Shows the emotions of a teenager faced with pressure to return to drugs. Illustrates the games and strategies used by drug dealers and how friends and parents can act as 'enablers' by ignoring or denying the problem.
Guidance and Counseling; Health and Safety; Psychology; Sociology
Dist - CORF **Prod** - CORF 1990

The Turning Point 29 MIN
U-matic / VT3
(G)
$95.00 purchase, $45.00 rental
Depicts a fictional conversation between a grandfather and grandchild. Shows how the world took its first major steps toward world peace and the elimination of poverty and injustice.
Literature and Drama; Sociology
Dist - EFVP **Prod** - EFVP 1988

Turning Point 24 MIN
16mm
B&W (H)
Shows the tension of the days leading to the overthrow of the Nazi empire and the massive effort to soften the defenses of Hitler's 'Fortress Europe,' then sweeps into the agony and triumph on the beaches of Normandy.
History - World
Dist - REAF **Prod** - REAF 1969

The Turning Point 24 MIN
16mm
Color
Discusses the care and cleanliness required for the production of small precision instrument ball bearings.
Business and Economics
Dist - GM **Prod** - GM

The Turning Point - 1941 to 1944 23 MIN
U-matic / VHS / 16mm
American Chronicles Series
Color (J H C G T A)
$75 rental _ #9817
Shows MacArthur lead the U S forces in the Pacific against Japan as Hitler declares war on America.
History - United States; History - World
Dist - AIMS **Prod** - AIMS 1986

The Turning Point in the Soviet Union 30 MIN
U-matic
Realities
Color (A)
Delves into the political, social, economic and cultural trends of the 1980s. Probes a wide range of contemporary concerns. Each segment includes a guest speaker who is an expert in the field under discussion.
Business and Economics; Civics and Political Systems; Social Science; Sociology
Dist - TVOTAR **Prod** - TVOTAR 1985

Turning Points 35 MIN
16mm / U-matic / VHS
Color
$630.00, $250.00 purchase _ #4061; LC 79-701604
Presents three women who have decided to pursue college and careers describing their daily lives and the impact of their decisions.
Sociology
Dist - CORF **Prod** - CCNY 1979

Turning Points 19 MIN
16mm
Color (H)
Uses 'Macbeth' as an example of a skillfilly structured dramatic work. Explains the structure of a play and how the action moves from one turning point to another.
Literature and Drama
Dist - SVE **Prod** - SINGER 1968

Turning Points in Life 145 MIN
U-matic
University of the Air Series
Color (J H C A)
$750.00 purchase, $250.00 rental
Examines some major life crises, such as entering the work force, adjusting to marriage and children and coming to grips with death. Program contains a series of five cassettes 29 minutes each.
Guidance and Counseling; Sociology
Dist - CTV **Prod** - CTV 1978

Turning points series
The Cable revolution 29 MIN
Crossroads - new treatment for alcoholics 29 MIN
A Flower under the bridge 29 MIN
The Free state of winston 29 MIN
Frozen hopes in Milwaukee 28 MIN
Here I am 29 MIN
Incident at Cass Lake 29 MIN
Is there a bike in the mix 29 MIN
The Next crisis - death in the mines 29 MIN
Nuclear reactions 28 MIN
Patients without doctors 29 MIN
Pigs no more 29 MIN
Public dducation - at whose expense 29 MIN
Rescue of a river 29 MIN
They laid it on the line 29 MIN
This guy Denenberg 29 MIN
Vanishing towns 29 MIN
Walk the first step 28 MIN
What's really comin' down 29 MIN
Dist - PBS

Turning points series
The Marshall plan and postwar Europe 35 MIN
Dist - SRA

Turning power into profit - the new entrepreneurs of electricity 30 MIN
U-matic
Adam Smith's money world 1986 - 1987 season series; 307
Color (A)
Attempts to demystify the world of money and break it down so that employees of a small business can understand and adjust to new social and economic trends. Reports on the major economic stories and discoveries of 1986 and 1987.
Business and Economics
Dist - PBS **Prod** - WNETTV 1987

Turning projects with Richard Raffan 90 MIN
VHS / BETA
Color (G A)
$39.95 _ #060065
Presents 12 of the projects from the book 'Turning Projects' by carpenter Richard Raffan.
Fine Arts; Home Economics; Industrial and Technical Education
Dist - TANTON **Prod** - TANTON

Turning Taper Work 12 MIN
16mm
B&W (H A)
LC FIE52-45
Explains centering cylindrical wood stock for spindle turning. Tells how and when to make clearance cuts. Shows how to establish the diameters of a taper, how to turn a single taper, how to establish diameters for turning two tapers from a single piece of material and how to turn them.
Industrial and Technical Education
Dist - USNAC **Prod** - UWF 1944

Turning the Tide Series
Presents 7 video programs, 26 minutes each, on the major environmental issues facing the Earth. Features David Bellamy, a British scientist, hosting the series in an entertaining, humorous and informative manner. Films include The Chips are Down; Running out of Steam; Growing Pains; Into Deep Water; The Great Gene Robbery; No Dam Good; and Bright Green. With purchase of the series, the companion volume 'Turning the Tide - Exploring the Options for Life on Earth,' is included.
Bright Green 26 MIN
The Great Gene robbery 28 MIN
Growing Pains 26 MIN
Into Deep Water 26 MIN
No Dam Good 28 MIN
Running Out of Steam 26 MIN
Dist - BULFRG **Prod** - TYNT 1944

Turning the tide series
The Chips are down 26 MIN
Dist - BULFRG
TYNT

Turning the toxic tide 27 MIN
VHS
Color (G T)
$195.00 purchase, $45.00 rental
Shows the true complexity of the job versus environment conflict. Examines the theory that a certain amount of environmental degradation is necessary to save valuable jobs - then asks what happens when that degradation threatens both the environment and other jobs. Looks at related water pollution problems encountered in Canada as well as the US. Produced by Bill Weaver and Shivon Robinsong - Across Borders Video. Includes study guide.
Business and Economics; Science - Natural; Sociology
Dist - BULFRG

Turning to dust - preserving our books 46 MIN
VHS
Color (H C G)
$395.00 purchase, $65.00 rental
Reveals that books and documents around the world are crumbling because the paper on which they are printed contains alum to prevent ink from bleeding and the alum is changing into sulfuric acid, making the paper brittle. Reviews ways of coping with deteriorating paper, such as boxing, filming and strengthening. Raises the crucial issues such as how to determine which books to save and how to prevent continued use of acidic paper when alternatives exist.
Education; Social Science
Dist - FLMLIB **Prod** - CANBC 1991

Turning to Giddings and Lewis 21 MIN
16mm
Color
LC 80-700224
Demonstrates a numerically - controlled lathe manufactured by the Giddings and Lewis Machine Tool Company.
Business and Economics
Dist - LOGPRO **Prod** - GIDLEW 1979

Turning 2 - out of babyhood 51 MIN
VHS
Citizen 2000 child development series
Color (H C G)
$350.00 purchase, $65.00 rental
Reveals that huge strides have been made by the Citizen 2000 children who are turning two years old. Shows that they have grown from sitting up and crawling to running and climbing. Speech has changed from monosyllables to complete sentences. Problems can be solved, instructions understood - and obeyed or flouted. Features Dr Judy Dunn, a developmental psychologist. Part of a series on child development which is following a group of children over a period of 18 years - from their birth in 1982 until they become adults in the year 2000. Produced by Dove Productions for Channel 4.
Health and Safety; Psychology
Dist - FLMLIB **Prod** - CFTV 1993

The Turning Wheel - Safety in Grinding Operations 16 MIN
U-matic / VHS / 16mm
Machine Tool Safety Series
Color (IND)
Health and Safety; Industrial and Technical Education
Dist - NATMTB **Prod** - NATMTB

Turning Wood with Richard Raffan 117 MIN
BETA / VHS
Color (H C A)
Uses a series of projects to teach the skills involved in centerwork and facework turning. Comes with booklet.
Industrial and Technical Education
Dist - TANTON **Prod** - TANTON

Turning work held on a fixture 21 MIN
16mm
Machine shop work series; Operations on the engine lathe; No 10
B&W (SPANISH)
LC FIE51-507
Shows how to mount an irregularly shaped casting which can't be held in a chuck, mount and center the fixture on a lathe, select and mount tools, and turn, face, bore, counterbore and ream surfaces of a valve bonnet.
Industrial and Technical Education
Dist - USNAC **Prod** - USOE 1944

Turning work held on a mandrel 20 MIN
16mm
Machine shop work series; Operations on the engine lathe; No 13
B&W (SPANISH)
LC FIE51-510
Describes the uses of the mandrel. Shows how to fit a mandrel into the workpiece, how to cut a bevel, how to use compound rest, how to calculate speed and feed, and how to set the controls.
Industrial and Technical Education
Dist - USNAC **Prod** - USOE 1943

Turning Work in a Chuck 15 MIN
16mm
B&W
LC FIE52-51
Explains how to mount work on a face plate, turn one face of the work, make a chuck for the opposite face and remove rechucked work from the chuck.
Industrial and Technical Education
Dist - USNAC **Prod** - USOE 1944

Turning Work in a Chuck and Face Turning a Collar 30 MIN
16mm
Precision Wood Machining Series Operations on the Wood Lathe
B&W
Examines the various types of face plates. Describes how to attach stock to a face plate, and how to true up and scribe the work. Explains the use of a chuck in machine work. Points out how to use round nose and diamond point chisels.
Industrial and Technical Education
Dist - USNAC **Prod** - USOE 1944

Turning Work of Two Diameters 14 MIN
16mm
Machine Shop Work Series
B&W
LC FIE51-515
Demonstrates the use of roughing, finishing, facing and radius tools.
Industrial and Technical Education
Dist - USNAC **Prod** - USOE 1941

Turning Work on a Face Plate 15 MIN
16mm
Precision Wood Machining Series Operations on the Wood Lathe
B&W
LC FIE52-50
Shows the various types of face plates. Explains how to attach the stock to the face plate, how to true up the wood, how to scribe the work for inside turning, how to use the round nose chisel and diamond point chisel and how to smoothe the recess bottom.
Industrial and Technical Education
Dist - USNAC **Prod** - USOE 1944

Turning work on two diameters 14 MIN
16mm / U-matic / VHS
Machine shop work series; Operations on the engine lathe; No 2
B&W
Shows how to use roughing, finishing, facing and radius tools. Demonstrates how to rough - turn and finish - turn a workpiece having two diameters, how to face a workpiece and how to machine a fillet. Issued in 1941 as a motion picture.
Industrial and Technical Education
Dist - USNAC **Prod** - USOE 1979

Turning your job into a business
VHS
Business Video Series
$89.95 purchase _ #RPDGP3V
Discusses the various steps to running a business.
Business and Economics
Dist - CAREER **Prod** - CAREER

Turning Your Job into a Business 30 MIN
VHS / 16mm
(PRO G)
$89.95 purchase _ #GDP3
Gives the testimony of three individuals who became their own bosses. Describes the steps in becoming your own boss. Hosted by Dick Goldberg.
Business and Economics
Dist - RMIBHF **Prod** - RMIBHF

Turns and Turnabouts 12 MIN
16mm
Color (H)
Shows how to adjust lane positions before a turn. Depicts how to make right and left turns from both two - way and one - way streets. Reveals the proper way of making a U - turn and Y - turn, and an alley or driveway turnabout.
Health and Safety
Dist - SF **Prod** - SF 1974

The Turret Lathe - an Introduction 17 MIN
16mm
Machine Shop Work Series
B&W
LC FIE51-597
Shows the function of the head, hexagon turret, square turret and bed, how to determine the sequence of operations, how to take a multiple cut, and how to combine cuts from the hexagon and square turrets.
Industrial and Technical Education
Dist - USNAC **Prod** - USOE 1945

Turret Lathe no 4 - Bar Turner Setup and Adjustment 18 MIN
VHS / BETA
Machine Shop - Turret Lathe Series
Color (IND)
Explains the function of the bar turner in machining accurate diameters and demonstrates set - up and adjustment.
Industrial and Technical Education; Psychology
Dist - RMIBHF **Prod** - RMIBHF

Turret Lathe no 1 - Familiarization 17 MIN
BETA / VHS
Machine Shop - Turret Lathe Series
Color (IND)
Introduces the controls and adjustments common to ram type turret lathes.
Industrial and Technical Education; Psychology
Dist - RMIBHF **Prod** - RMIBHF

Turret Lathe no 3 - Plunge Forming and Self - Opening Die Setups 12 MIN
BETA / VHS
Machine Shop - Turret Lathe Series
Color (IND)
Demonstrates the use of the form tool to machine several diameters at once. Explains the set - up and use of the 'Geometric' type self - opening die head.
Industrial and Technical Education; Psychology
Dist - RMIBHF **Prod** - RMIBHF

Turret Lathe no 2 - Drilling, Tapping, Knurling, Forming 21 MIN
BETA / VHS
Machine Shop - Turret Lathe Series
Color (IND)
Explains the sequence of operations for making a typical production part. Describes collet adjustment and the setting of turret and carriage stops. Includes an explanation of the releasing tap holder and knurling tool.
Industrial and Technical Education; Psychology
Dist - RMIBHF **Prod** - RMIBHF

The Turtle 11 MIN
U-matic / VHS / 16mm
Animal Families Series
(K P I J)
$225 purchase_#B407
Documents how a mother turtle lays her eggs on a beach.
Science - Natural
Dist - BARR **Prod** - BARR 1986

The Turtle 8 MIN
U-matic / VHS / 16mm
Little Dog Series
Color (K P)
Presents the story of Little Dog and his friend Kitten, helping a mother hen and her chicks. Tells how when one of the chicks keeps wandering away, they block the entrance with a rock but she keeps running away. Explains that the reason for this is that the rock is really a turtle.
Fine Arts; Literature and Drama
Dist - PHENIX **Prod** - ROMAF

Turtle 22 MIN
U-matic / VHS / 16mm
Animals, Animals, Animals Series
Color (P I)
Presents a marine biologist telling how he is helping to restore the numbers of endangered green turtles in Florida and a scientist who studies the habits of the California desert tortoise. Uses fable and song to tell of the docile nature of the turtle. Hosted by Hal Linden.
Science - Natural
Dist - MEDIAG **Prod** - ABCNEW 1977

The Turtle - Care of a Pet 8 MIN
U-matic / VHS / 16mm
Color (K P I) (SPANISH)
Shows the living habits of a pet turtle and the various activities involved in taking care of it. Shows how to feed the turtle, the proper living environment for the turtle and its characteristics.
Foreign Language; Guidance and Counseling; Psychology; Science - Natural
Dist - PHENIX **Prod** - BEANMN 1962

The Turtle People 26 MIN
16mm
Color
LC 74-700505
Presents a case study of the ecological and cultural changes that result from so - called development. Shows the Miskito Indians of Eastern Nicaragua who have depended on the sea turtle for food in the past and are now hunting the turtles to sell for cash.
Geography - World; Social Science; Sociology
Dist - BCFILM **Prod** - BCFILM 1973

Turtle shells 26 MIN
U-matic / VT1 / VHS
Color (G)
$49.95 purchase, $25.00 rental
Features Christine Hanneha, a Muscogee Creek Indian of Oklahoma, who demonstrates an ancient method of fashioning turtle shell leg rattles for women, talks about why she makes them, and gives step - by - step instructions, from the selection of turtle shells to the final fitting.
Social Science
Dist - NAMPBC **Prod** - CREEK

The Turtle story
VHS
Native American folk tales series
(G)
$79.00 purchase
Tells of a young boy who saves the world's last turtle from his wicked uncle.
Literature and Drama; Social Science
Dist - DANEHA **Prod** - DANEHA 1994

Turtle Talk 5 MIN
16mm
Color
Locates the luckiest turtle in the world at Silver Springs, Florida, where he describes his neighbors, friends and visitors.
Geography - United States; Science - Natural
Dist - FLADC **Prod** - FLADC

Turtles 15 MIN
VHS / U-matic
Up Close and Natural Series
Color (I P)
$125.00 purchase
Explains the habitats and lifestyles of turtles.
Agriculture; Education; Science - Natural; Social Science
Dist - AITECH **Prod** - NHPTV 1986

Turumba 94 MIN
16mm / U-matic / VHS
Color (G)
$1600.00, $600.00, $350.00 purchase
Focuses on a family in a tiny Philippine village. Reveals that they traditionally made papier - mache animals to sell during the Turumba religious festivities, but one year a department store buyer shows up in town and purchases all their stock. When she returns with an order for 500 more - this time with the word 'Oktoberfest' painted on them - the family's seasonal occupation becomes year round alienated labor. They can now purchase electric fans, TV sets and Beatle records, but increased production creates inflated needs and soon the entire village has gone to work on a jungle assembly line, turning out papier - mache mascots for the Munich Olympics, the fabric of traditional life torn asunder. Produced by Kidlat Tahimak.
History - World; Social Science
Dist - FLOWER

Tuscan Countryside 12 MIN
16mm / U-matic / VHS
B&W (I J H)
Studies peninsular Italy and stresses agriculture on the coastal plain and Apennine foothills.
Geography - World
Dist - IFB **Prod** - BHA 1954

Tuskegee Airmen's Story - 1941 - 1948 Series
The Black Eagles - a Picture Story 20 MIN
Tuskegee Airmen's Story - Pt 1 29 MIN
Tuskegee Airmen's Story - Pt 2 29 MIN
Tuskegee Airmen's Story - Pt 3 29 MIN
Tuskegee Airmen's Story - Pt 4 29 MIN
Dist - SYLWAT

Tuskegee Airmen's Story - Pt 1 29 MIN
U-matic / VHS
Tuskegee Airmen's Story - 1941 - 1948 Series
Color
History - United States
Dist - SYLWAT **Prod** - RCOMTV 1982

Tuskegee Airmen's Story - Pt 2 29 MIN
U-matic / VHS
Tuskegee Airmen's Story - 1941 - 1948 Series
Color
History - United States
Dist - SYLWAT **Prod** - RCOMTV 1982

Tuskegee Airmen's Story - Pt 3 29 MIN
U-matic / VHS
Tuskegee Airmen's Story - 1941 - 1948 Series
Color
History - United States
Dist - SYLWAT **Prod** - RCOMTV 1982

Tuskegee Airmen's Story - Pt 4 29 MIN
VHS / U-matic
Tuskegee Airmen's Story - 1941 - 1948 Series
Color
History - United States
Dist - SYLWAT **Prod** - RCOMTV 1982

Tut and Tuttle 97 MIN
VHS / U-matic
Color
Tells what happens when a disgraced junior high school student is magically transported back to ancient Egypt and becomes involved in the kidnapping of King Tutankhamen. Stars Chris Barnes, Hans Conreid and Vic Tayback.
Fine Arts
Dist - TIMLIF **Prod** - TIMLIF 1983

Tut - the Boy King 52 MIN
16mm / U-matic / VHS
Color (J H C)
Offers a view of 55 of the treasures from the tomb of Tutankhamun, including parchesi - like games the ten - year - old Pharoah used, his diminutive ebony and gold inlaid chair, statues and jewelry.
Fine Arts; History - World; Sociology
Dist - FI **Prod** - NBCTV 1977

Tut - the boy king 49 MIN
VHS
Color (G)
$39.95 purchase _ #S00562
Highlights the treasures found in the tomb of Egyptian King Tutankhamen. Documents the excavation and discovery of Tut's tomb in 1922.
History - World; Sociology
Dist - UILL

Tut - the boy king 60 MIN
VHS
Color (J H C G)
$29.95 purchase _ #MHV01V
Explores the mystery and romance surrounding the reign and burial of King Tutankhamen, who became king of Egypt at age nine, and died mysteriously ten years later. Views the artifacts buried with him for 3,000 years, including an alabaster flask containing a liquid still scented with pine.
History - World
Dist - CAMV

Tut, the Boy King - Pt 1 26 MIN
U-matic / VHS / 16mm
Color (H C A)
LC 77-703331
Features Orson Welles in an on - screen narration of a traveling exhibition of the Egyptian treasures taken from the tomb of King Tutankhamen. Filmed at the National Gallery of Art, Washington, DC.
History - World
Dist - FI **Prod** - NBCTV 1977

Tut, the Boy King - Pt 2 26 MIN
U-matic / VHS / 16mm
Color (H C A)
LC 77-703331
Features Orson Welles in an on - screen narration of a traveling exhibition of the Egyptian treasures taken from the tomb of King Tutankhamen. Filmed at the National Gallery of Art, Washington, DC.
History - World
Dist - FI **Prod** - NBCTV 1977

Tutankhamen - the Immortal Pharaoh 12 MIN
16mm / U-matic / VHS
Color (I J H C G T A)
$25 rental _ #4068
Provides an unparalleled view of the magnificent objects found in the tomb of King Tutankhamen.
History - World; Social Science; Sociology
Dist - AIMS **Prod** - AIMS 1968
UHOU

Tutankhamun - life and death series
Death 15 MIN
Dist - AITECH

Tutankhamun Live Forever 55 MIN
16mm
Color (J)
LC 83-700204
Explores the treasures of Tutankhamun, Egypt's boy king, as viewed in his tomb. Displays 55 magnificent treasures with details on the people of Egypt, its geography and its religion.
Civics and Political Systems; Fine Arts; History - World
Dist - IFEX **Prod** - FORWOP 1983

Tutankhamun Live Forever - Pt 1 27 MIN
16mm
Color (J)
LC 83-700204
Explores the treasures of Tutankhamun, Egypt's boy king, as viewed in his tomb. Displays 55 magnificent treasures with details on the people of Egypt, its geography and its religion.
History - World
Dist - IFEX **Prod** - FORWOP 1983

Tutankhamun Live Forever - Pt 2 28 MIN
16mm
Color (J)
LC 83-700204
Explores the treasures of Tutankhamun, Egypt's boy king, as viewed in his tomb. Displays 55 magnificent treasures with details on the people of Egypt, its geography and its religion.
History - World
Dist - IFEX **Prod** - FORWOP 1983

The Tutor 30 MIN
U-matic / VHS
Franco File Series
Color (I)
Dramatizes contemporary Franco - American life. Focuses on showing appreciation.
Sociology
Dist - GPN **Prod** - WENHTV

Tutorial Arabic video - Part 1
VHS
Color (K P I) (ARABIC)
$25.00 purchase _ #IES001
Teaches Arabic to young people, as well as Islamic culture. Part one of two parts.
Foreign Language; Literature and Drama; Religion and Philosophy
Dist - IBC

Tutorial Arabic video - Part 2
VHS
Color (K P I) (ARABIC)
$25.00 purchase _ #IES002
Teaches Arabic to young people, as well as Islamic culture. Part two of two parts.
Foreign Language; Literature and Drama; Religion and Philosophy
Dist - IBC

The Tutors of Fernald 35 MIN
16mm
B&W (C T)
LC 72-702443
Shows the activities of a remedial school at the University of California at Los Angeles in which Black and white pupils with similar learning disabilities but from differing socio - economic backgrounds tutor each other as part of their special education.
Education; Psychology; Sociology
Dist - SPF **Prod** - UCLA 1972

Tuxedo Junction 23 MIN
VHS / U-matic
Color (K)
Shows the Falkland Islands where 57 different species of birds live. Shows five species of penguins which make magic of the surrounding waters.
Science - Natural
Dist - NWLDPR **Prod** - NWLDPR

TV 3 MIN
16mm
B&W (G)
$10.00 rental
Represents the TV generation. Formulates the theory that the TV is alive and smarter than people think. Produced by Robert Daniel Flowers.
Fine Arts
Dist - CANCIN

TV 4 MIN
16mm
B&W (G)
$10.00 rental
Involves the audience in a conceptual and reflexive process of five short sequences.
Fine Arts
Dist - CANCIN **Prod** - KRENKU 1967

TV Ads - Our Mini - Myths 16 MIN
U-matic / VHS / 16mm
Color (H C A)
LC 77-703270
Presents 11 Clio Award - winning television commercials grouped according to their persuasive intent.
Business and Economics; Fine Arts; Industrial and Technical Education
Dist - PFP **Prod** - CESCFA 1977

TV and texte 50 MIN
VHS
Color (J H)
PdS60, PdS30 purchase _ #ML-145016
Presents news program clips from Germany to help students improve their grasp of the German language.
Computer Science; Foreign Language
Dist - AVP

TV and Thee 22 MIN
16mm
Color (R)
Considers the effect of television on family relationships and on an individual's relationship with God.
Fine Arts; Guidance and Counseling; Religion and Philosophy; Sociology
Dist - GF **Prod** - GF

TV, Behind the Screen 16 MIN
U-matic / VHS / 16mm
Color (P I)
LC 78-701971
Demonstrates how television shows are created by writers, editors and film crews. Focuses on special effects and dramatic productions and introduces various television jobs.
Fine Arts; Social Science
Dist - CF **Prod** - CF 1978

TV Commercials 3 MIN
16mm
B&W
$16.50 rental
Presents two animated examples of commericals for early television. Includes Muntaz TV and an Oklahoma Gas Company sequence.
Business and Economics; Industrial and Technical Education; Psychology; Social Science
Dist - CFS **Prod** - PFP 1952
CANCIN FISCHF

TV commercials - Mexican commercials 45 MIN
VHS
Color (G) (SPANISH)
$45.00 purchase _ #W1440
Focuses on the culture of the country as seen through television ads. Includes tapescript.
Business and Economics
Dist - GPC

TV commercials - Spain - Volume I 45 MIN
VHS
Color (G) (SPANISH)
$45.00 purchase _ #W1417
Focuses on the culture of the country as seen through television ads. Includes tapescript.
Business and Economics
Dist - GPC

TV commercials - Spain - Volume II 45 MIN
VHS
Color (G) (SPANISH)
$45.00 purchase _ #W1572
Focuses on the culture of the country as seen through television ads. Includes tapescript.
Business and Economics
Dist - GPC

TV commercials - Spain - Volumes I and II 45 MIN
VHS
Color (G) (SPANISH)
$82.90 purchase _ #W1573
Focuses on the culture of the country as seen through television ads. Includes two videos and tapescripts.
Business and Economics
Dist - GPC

TV Commercials Winners Reel 1983 - International Film and TV Festival of New York 55 MIN
U-matic
Color
Presents 1983's most creative and sales - effective television commercials, including a diversity of ideas and techniques representing a cross - section of current creative and marketing trends worldwide.
Business and Economics; Fine Arts
Dist - WSTGLC **Prod** - WSTGLC

TV current affairs reporting 48 MIN
VHS
Color (PRO G)
$149.00 purchase, $49.00 rental _ #741
Features the executive producers of four major Australian current affairs programs who discuss their approach to current affairs reporting. Offers their views of the qualities important in a good reporter, what makes an exciting television story. Emphasizes the importance of building a story around visual material rather than around a script. Produced by the Australian Film, Television and Radio School.
Fine Arts; Literature and Drama
Dist - FIRLIT

TV Engineer 15 MIN
16mm / U-matic / VHS
Career Awareness
(I)
$130 VC purchase, $240 film purchase, $25 VC rental, $30 film rental
Presents an empathetic approach to career planning, showing the personal as well as the professional qualities of television engineers. Highlights the importance of career education.
Guidance and Counseling
Dist - GPN

TV evangelists - Monday, March 23, 1987 and Tuesday, March 24, 1987 75 MIN
VHS
Nightline series
Color (H C G)
$14.98 purchase _ #MP6157
Examines the activities of American Protestant Christian television evangelists and their use of manipulatory practices to raise money.
Fine Arts; Religion and Philosophy
Dist - INSTRU **Prod** - ABCNEW 1987

TV for Better or Worse 29 MIN
VHS / 16mm
Color (G)
$55.00 rental _ #TFBW - 000
Examines the future of television as a medium. Features many television industry participants expressing their opinions on the issue.
Fine Arts; Sociology
Dist - PBS **Prod** - WCVETV

The TV gender gap 30 MIN
VHS
Inside story series
Color (G)
$50.00 purchase _ #INST - 411
Deals with women working in television news, considering the question of whether they are discriminated against. Focuses on the example of Christine Craft, who was fired by a Kansas City TV station on the advice of media consultants. Considers the possible reasons for Craft's firing. Hosted by Hodding Carter.
Fine Arts; Literature and Drama; Sociology
Dist - PBS

A TV Guide - Thinking about what We Watch 17 MIN
16mm / U-matic / VHS
Color (I J)
LC 78-701972
Questions the reality and values presented on television. Includes segments from television shows and commercials.
Business and Economics; Fine Arts; Guidance and Counseling; Social Science
Dist - CF **Prod** - CF 1978

TV Interview - with S Vanderbeek 13 MIN
16mm
Color
Presents an electric - collage via video - tape of an interview with Stan Vanderbeek.
Fine Arts; Industrial and Technical Education
Dist - VANBKS **Prod** - VANBKS

TV is for Learning 15 MIN
U-matic / VHS
Pass it on Series
Color (K P)
Discusses the different kinds of shows on TV and classifies real and make believe shows.
Education; Fine Arts
Dist - GPN **Prod** - WKNOTV 1983

The TV kid 15 MIN
U-matic / VHS
Book bird series
Color (I)
Tells of a lonely boy who gains a new understanding of himself and others after he is bitten by a rattlesnake. From the story by Betsy Byars.
English Language; Literature and Drama
Dist - CTI **Prod** - CTI

TV News 30 MIN
U-matic / VHS / 16mm
Media Probes Series
Color (H C A)
Examines how the drive for ratings has led to some dazzling newsroom packages. Introduces news consultant Frank Magid who advises local news operations on how to put pizzazz into their newscasts. Visits Phoenix, where a jet helicopter is expanding the concept of live coverage and Los Angeles, where a third - place station is challenging the local news competitors in a rating war. Narrated by John Cameron Swayze.
Fine Arts; Literature and Drama; Social Science
Dist - TIMLIF **Prod** - LAYLEM 1982

The TV news anchor 24 MIN
VHS
Color (H C)
$59.00 purchase _ #TTNA
Examines the many roles that local television anchors play - newscaster, field reporter, performer, local celebrity. Interviews successful local TV news anchors to show students how to prepare for this extremely competitive field. Offers tips on effective voice and on - camera skills from experienced news anchors. Presents a news update through the eyes of the newscaster, allowing a unique view of what it looks like from the other side of the camera.
Fine Arts
Dist - INSTRU

TV News - Measure of the Medium 16 MIN
16mm / U-matic / VHS
Color (I)
LC 79-714372
Demonstrates the complexities of broadcast journalism and portrays some of the factors that inhibit complete objective reporting.
Fine Arts; Industrial and Technical Education; Literature and Drama; Social Science
Dist - PHENIX **Prod** - SHANA 1971

TV News Reporter 15 MIN
16mm / U-matic / VHS
Career Awareness
(I)
$130 VC purchase, $240 film purchase, $25 VC rental $30 film rental
Presents an empathetic approach to career planning, showing the personal as well as the professional attributes of television news reporters. Highlights the importance of career education.
Guidance and Counseling
Dist - GPN

A TV news story and The Technique of television news 51 MIN
VHS
Color (J H C)
$59.00 purchase _ #ATNS
Presents two parts on a typical day in the live of a medium - sized market TV news reporter as captured by a network documentary crew. Portrays the pursuit of a lead story in Part 1. Part 2 views the same day from the perspective of examining the journalistic processes - writing, photography, editing - which get the lead story on the air. Offers students a spontaneous, entertaining and realistic view of what a local TV reporter really does. Includes a printed transcript of the reporter's finished story and newscast rundowns which may be reproduced for students.
Fine Arts; Literature and Drama
Dist - INSTRU

TV newsroom - news gathering 12 MIN
VHS
Color (PRO G)
$119.00 purchase, $39.00 rental _ #630
Follows the interlocking roles performed by the assignment editor, producers, news directors, reporters, writers and photographers as they shape decisions on what stories to cover and how to cover them. Watches investigative, political and medical reporters, a sports producer and the meteorologist all jockeying for time slots for their breaking stories as the executive producer balances shifting priorities throughout the day. Visits WHDH, CBS affiliate in Boston to observe a real day of news gathering and production. One of two parts on the TV newsroom. Produced by Sasha Norkin.
Fine Arts; Literature and Drama
Dist - FIRLIT

TV newsroom - news production 10 MIN
VHS
Color (PRO G)
$119.00 purchase, $39.00 rental _ #631
Shows that the director, technical director, floor manager and assistant director work under intense time pressure with tape editors, camera operators, audio mixers and engineers to bring in an evening newscast on time and to length. Watches the creation of graphics, production of a live remote, the use of robot cameras and color keying on the set. Stories are added, changed and dropped during the course of the newscast to meet shifting conditions. Visits WHDH, CBS affiliate in Boston to observe a real day of news gathering and production. One of two parts on the TV newsroom. Produced by Sasha Norkin.
Fine Arts; Literature and Drama
Dist - FIRLIT

TV on Trial 119 MIN
VHS / 16mm
Color (G)
$120.00 rental _ #TVOT - 000
Documents the trial of 15 - year - old Ronny Zamora for the murder of his 82 - year - old next - door neighbor. Presents the most significant moments of the nine - day trial. Includes a post - trial session with the judge and jury discussing the trial and the use of cameras in the courtroom. Features Dr George Gerbner, a communications expert, explaining why he is opposed to televising trials.
Civics and Political Systems; Fine Arts; Sociology
Dist - PBS **Prod** - WPBTTV

TV Series - Hal Cooper 20 MIN
VHS / 16mm
Action - a Day with the Directors Series
Color (H)
$39.95 purchase, $15.00 rental _ #86462
Reviews the list of shows directed by Hal Cooper that have made and held ratings - Mary Tyler Moore, All In The Family, Maude. Discusses how to get started in the business. Discusses laugh tracks and their uses, emphasizes the dependence of the directors on the talents of their teams. Cooper recommends a university degree, particularly for those interested in comedy, because of the theatrical base of comedy.
Fine Arts; Industrial and Technical Education; Literature and Drama; Psychology
Dist - UILL **Prod** - SSN 1987

TV Series - Marty Pasetta 19 MIN
VHS / 16mm
Action - a Day with the Directors Series
Color (H)

$39.95 purchase, $15.00 rental _ #86466
Features Marty Pasetta, director of the last sixteen Academy Award Shows, who discusses with interviewer Peter Brown the challenges of live broadcasts and of the difficulties of preparing for world broadcast in other time zones. Emphasizes that this is the bane of directing jobs, combining demands made by stage, screen and television on talent coordination without the convenience of the editing room. Pasetta considers worst moments and problems, such as imparting confidence to stars who are comfortable on a sound stage but have no live theatre experience.
Fine Arts; Industrial and Technical Education; Psychology
Dist - UILL **Prod** - SSN 1987

TV tutor calendar words
VHS
TV tutor series
Color (G)
$59.95 purchase _ #142 - 6
Builds recognition of words and teaches spelling of survival words. Uses a multisensory approach to teach days of the week, months, abbreviations, holidays and special days. Part of a series.
Education; English Language
Dist - LAULIT **Prod** - LAULIT

TV tutor number words
VHS
TV tutor series
Color (G)
$59.95 purchase _ #140 - X
Builds recognition of words and teaches spelling of survival words. Uses a multisensory approach to teach numerals and number words. Part of a series.
Education; English Language; Mathematics
Dist - LAULIT **Prod** - LAULIT

TV tutor series
TV tutor calendar words
TV tutor number words
TV tutor sight words 1
TV tutor sight words 2
Dist - LAULIT

TV tutor sight words 1
VHS
TV tutor series
Color (G)
$59.95 purchase _ #144 - 2
Builds recognition of words and teaches spelling of survival words. Uses a multisensory approach to teach 60 of the most frequently occurring English words. Part of a series.
Education; English Language
Dist - LAULIT **Prod** - LAULIT

TV tutor sight words 2
VHS
TV tutor series
Color (G)
$59.95 purchase _ #146 - 9
Builds recognition of words and teaches spelling of survival words. Uses a multisensory approach to teach 60 of the most frequently occurring English words. Part of a series.
Education; English Language
Dist - LAULIT **Prod** - LAULIT

TV und Texte 50 MIN
VHS
Color (G) (GERMAN)
$49.95 purchase _ #W7199
Presents narrations followed by news items from around Germany to highlight German society. Follows with written and oral exercises based on articles, with questions to check skill development. Includes an exercise and transcript text with the video.
Foreign Language
Dist - GPC

TV und texte 50 MIN
VHS
Color (J H)
PdS60, PdS30, PdS40 purchase _ CD-ROM single user, video, 5 or more disks each _ #ML-145016
Presents clips from German news programs to help students improve their grasp of the German language. Provides practice with either a CD-ROM or a videocassette and activity book. Features 12 media units on the video or the CD-ROM that include comments, key words and phrases, and transcripts. Encourages active use of the language in speaking and writing. Activity book may be purchased separately for PdS5.50.
Computer Science; Foreign Language
Dist - AVP

TV workouts
VHS
Converse basketball series; Vol 4
Color (G)
$29.95 purchase _ #AN003
Explains how to turn TV time into workout time with dozens of drills to improve strength, speed, and ability.
Physical Education and Recreation
Dist - SIV

Tviggy 13 MIN
16mm
Color (J)
Tells about the dreams of a young girl to become a famous fashion model.
Guidance and Counseling; Home Economics
Dist - SF **Prod** - SF

'Twas the Night Before Christmas 25 MIN
16mm / U-matic / VHS
Color (P I)
$555.00, $250.00 purchase _ #4378
Tells the story of how Santa Claus almost decides not to visit a town one Christmas because of a letter denying his existence. A Perspective film.
Literature and Drama; Social Science
Dist - PERSPF **Prod** - PERSPF 1982
CORF

Twee, Fiddle and Huff 12 MIN
VHS / 16mm
Color (P I G)
$325.00, $225.00 purchase, $75.00 rental _ #8232
Uses animation to show young children of alcoholics how to get help.
Guidance and Counseling; Health and Safety; Sociology
Dist - AIMS **Prod** - JOHNIN 1990

Tweedledum and Tweedledee - the party system and the major political parties 30 MIN
VHS
Remaking of Canada - Canadian government and politics in the 1990s 'series
Color (H C G)
$89.95 purchase _ #WLU - 508
Discusses the nature of party politics in Canada, the impact of television on party politics and the principles and policies of Canada's Liberals and Conservatives. Part of a 12 - part series incorporating interviews with Canadian politicians and hosted by Dr John Redekop.
Civics and Political Systems; History - World
Dist - INSTRU **Prod** - TELCOL 1992

Twelfth Anniversary Celebration 165 MIN
U-matic / VHS
Color
Celebrates the 12th Anniversary of Sri Gurudev's arrival in the United States. Recreates his arrival with a series of skits based on his biography.
Religion and Philosophy
Dist - IYOGA **Prod** - IYOGA

Twelfth night 165 MIN
VHS
Color; PAL (H)
PdS40 purchase
Presents the Shakespeare story of love, intrigues and mistaken identity in a production by The Renaissance Theatre Company, directed by Kenneth Branagh. Stars Richard Briers. Contact distributor about availability outside the United Kingdom.
Literature and Drama
Dist - ACADEM **Prod** - THAMES

Twelfth night 124 MIN
VHS / 16mm
BBC's Shakespeare series
(H A)
$249.95 purchase
Recounts Shakespeare's comedy Twelfth Night, which explores the many facets of human character.
Literature and Drama
Dist - AMBROS **Prod** - AMBROS 1980

Twelfth night 124 MIN
VHS
BBC Shakespeare series
Color (G C H)
$109.00 purchase _ #DL471
Fine Arts
Dist - INSIM **Prod** - BBC

Twelfth Night 124 MIN
U-matic / VHS
Shakespeare Plays Series
Color
LC 79-707320
Presents Shakespeare's play Twelfth Night, which describes the romantic infatuation of Orsino, the devoted loyalty of Viola, the selfless friendship of Antonio and the self - love of the ambitious steward Malvolio. Stars Alec McCowen, Trevor Peacock and Felicity Kendall.
Literature and Drama
Dist - TIMLIF **Prod** - BBCTV 1980

Twelfth Night 30 MIN
BETA / VHS / 16mm
Shakespeare - from Page to Stage Series
Color (J H A)
Presents key scenes from Shakespeare's plays bridged with on - camera commentary by one of the actors to reinforce the literary amd thematic aspects of the play. Includes written editions of the complete plays and study guides.
Literature and Drama
Dist - BCNFL **Prod** - CBCEN 1987

Twelfth Night - an Introduction 23 MIN
U-matic / VHS / 16mm
Shakespeare Series
Color (J)
LC 70-708560
Presents scenes of Shakespeare's play Twelfth Night. Attempts to preserve the continuity of the comedy and suggests its prevailing mood and rhythm, the tone and manner of expression of the characters and an idea of Elizabethan costuming.
Literature and Drama
Dist - PHENIX **Prod** - SEABEN 1969

Twelfth Rib Approach to the Kidney 15 MIN
16mm
Anatomy of the Flank Series
Color
LC 77-706141
Demonstrates surgical intervention. Uses medical illustrations and animation in conjunction with a complete operative procedure to deal with various types of renal pathology. Discusses all anatomical aspects.
Health and Safety; Science; Science - Natural
Dist - EATON **Prod** - EATONL 1970

Twelve 9 MIN
16mm
Color (G)
$20.00 rental
Presents the first three parts of a twelve part film exploring the history of imagery. Uses handpainted and scratched film, negative space, and elaborate optical printing techniques. By Beth Block.
Fine Arts
Dist - CANCIN

Twelve Angry Men 95 MIN
16mm
B&W
Depicts a jury room where the guilt or innocence of a ghetto youth is at stake. Stars Henry Fonda and Lee J Cobb. Directed by Sidney Lumet.
Fine Arts
Dist - UAE **Prod** - UAA 1957

Twelve angry men
Videodisc
Laserdisc learning series
Color; CAV (J H)
$40.00 purchase _ #8L206
Tells the story of a deadlocked jury and one man who makes the others listen to reason. Adapts a play by Reginald Rose. A teacher's guide is available separately.
Literature and Drama
Dist - BARR **Prod** - BARR 1992

Twelve angry men
VHS / U-matic
B&W (J H C A)
$79.00 purchase
Presents a historic courtroom drama. Stars Henry Fonda and Lee J Cobb.
Civics and Political Systems; Fine Arts
Dist - ASPRSS

Twelve Authorities Evaluate Fluoride 29 MIN
16mm
Color (PRO)
Presents a panel discussion composed of doctors and dentists evaluating the effective use of fluoride in the prevention of child tooth decay.
Health and Safety; Science - Natural
Dist - UPJOHN **Prod** - UPJOHN 1963

The Twelve characteristics of successful banks
VHS
Dream team series
Color (IND PRO)
$295.00 purchase, $150.00 rental _ #MAX03B
Introduces Kent Stickler in one of an eight - part series on competitive banking. Includes a leader's guide. Produced by Marx Communications.
Business and Economics
Dist - EXTR

The Twelve Days of Christmas 7 MIN
U-matic / VHS / 16mm
Color (P I)
LC 79-701878
Uses animation to illustrate the traditional Christmas song The Twelve Days Of Christmas.

Fine Arts; Social Science
Dist - MCFI **Prod** - UPA 1976

The Twelve Days of Christmas 5 MIN
U-matic / VHS / 16mm
Color (K P)
LC 72-700932
Presents the traditional song - accumulation of gifts given on the twelve days of Christmas.
Fine Arts; Religion and Philosophy
Dist - WWS **Prod** - WWS 1972

The Twelve days of Christmas - Greek Orthodox Christmas traditions and customs 28 MIN
VHS
Illuminations series
Color (G R)
#V - 1013
Explores Greek Orthodox Christmas customs and traditions. Interviews Greek, Cypriot and U S Orthodox Christians as they engage in their holiday celebrations. Features a Christmas celebration at an immigrant home.
Religion and Philosophy
Dist - GOTEL **Prod** - GOTEL 1988

The Twelve days of Christmas - the feast of Epiphany 28 MIN
VHS
Illuminations series
Color (G R)
#V - 1016
Gives the religious and ethnic significance of Epiphany. Includes footage from Greek Orthodox services and Archbishop Iakovos' water - blessing ceremony in Tarpon Springs, FL.
Religion and Philosophy
Dist - GOTEL **Prod** - GOTEL 1988

Twelve decades of concrete in American architecture series
The Architect's material - 1960's 23 MIN
The Long years of experiment - 1844 - 1920 16 MIN
The Material that can do almost anything, 1950 - 1964 21 MIN
New dimensions in concrete - through the 60's 16 MIN
The Search for a new architecture - 1920 - 1950 12 MIN
Dist - PRTLND

Twelve - Gauge, 4 - Foot Box and Pan Apron Brake 12 MIN
BETA / VHS
Color (IND)
Discusses the basic set - up and operation of a box and pan brake.
Industrial and Technical Education; Psychology
Dist - RMIBHF **Prod** - RMIBHF

The Twelve labours of Heracles
VHS / 35mm strip
Timeless tales - myths of ancient Greece; Set I
Color (I)
$39.95, $28.00 purchase
Recreates the myth of the twelve labors of Heracles. Part of a five - part series on Greek mythology.
English Language; History - World; Literature and Drama; Religion and Philosophy
Dist - PELLER

Twelve - lead EKG series 112 MIN
VHS / U-matic
Twelve - lead EKG series
Color (PRO)
$450.00 purchase _ #7280S
Presents a two - part series on the 12 - lead EKG. Explains how a 12 - lead EKG machine works and how to use single and multi - channel machines to obtain a 12 - lead EKG. Examines the progressive stages of an acute myocardial infarction and shows the characteristic changes each stage produces in the EKG.
Health and Safety
Dist - AJN **Prod** - HOSSN 1988

Twelve Like You 25 MIN
U-matic / VHS / 16mm
Color
Presents a discussion of career opportunities for women by women. Asks each woman to analyze and appraise her own assets and liabilities, and helps her find answers to crucial career questions.
Guidance and Counseling; Sociology
Dist - CCCD **Prod** - CCCD 1975

The Twelve Month Pregnancy 19 MIN
VHS / 16mm
Color (G)
$149.00, $249.00, purchase _ #AD - 1902
Makes a strong case for treating pregnancy as a process that begins months before conception. Explains that much of the critical development of the fetus occurs before a woman knows she is pregnant and that the health of the fetus is dependent on the health of the mother. Cautions about the risks to the fetus of the use of alcohol by the mother and describes possible effects of Valium, Accutane, and cocaine. Encourages the idea of a pre - conception exam.
Health and Safety; Psychology
Dist - FOTH **Prod** - FOTH 1990

The Twelve months 11 MIN
U-matic / VHS / 16mm
Favorite fairy tales and fables series
Color (P)
$280.00, $195.00 purchase _ #4143
Tells the story of a girl who meets the spirits of the twelve months.
Literature and Drama
Dist - CORF

The Twelve months 27 MIN
U-matic / VHS / 16mm
Storybook international series
Color
Presents a Hungarian tale of a girl who is sent out to do impossible tasks by her stepmother and stepsister. Shows how she is helped at these tasks by the twelve months of the year which she encounters. Reveals how the months freeze the stepmother and stepsister in a blizzard, freeing her to marry a farmer and find happiness.
Literature and Drama
Dist - JOU **Prod** - JOU 1982

Twelve O'Clock High 34 MIN
U-matic / VHS
B&W (H C A)
Offers a perceptive psychological study of an Air Force commander and his efforts to rebuild a bomber squadron whose shattered morale threatens the effectiveness of their crucial missions. Stars Gregory Peck. An abridged version of the motion picture 12 O'Clock High.
Business and Economics; Psychology
Dist - FI **Prod** - TWCF 1949

Twelve Recent Advances in Reproductive Physiology 29 MIN
16mm
Nine to Get Ready Series
B&W (C A)
Discusses recent research in reproductive physiology, biochemistry, endocrinology, genetics and clinical pathology.
Health and Safety; Science - Natural
Dist - UNEBR **Prod** - KUONTV 1965

A Twelve Step Plan to Citizen CPR Training 16 MIN
VHS / U-matic
Color
LC 81-707110
Lists the procedures that an organization can follow to implement a citizen cardiopulmonary resuscitation training program.
Health and Safety
Dist - USNAC **Prod** - NIH 1981

The Twelve Steps 45 MIN
16mm
Color
Describes Father Martin's personal observations of the Twelve Steps to an alcoholic cure.
Health and Safety; Psychology
Dist - KELLYP **Prod** - FMARTN

Twelve steps 35 MIN
VHS
(H C A)
$39.95 purchase _ #82008
Discusses the twelve - step approach to recovering from alcoholism, drug addiction, gambling, and overeating. Features scenery and music.
Guidance and Counseling; Health and Safety; Psychology
Dist - CMPCAR **Prod** - CMPCAR

The Twelve steps of AA 45 MIN
U-matic / Cassette
Color (G)
$495.00, $10.00 purchase
Comments on the most effective therapy for alcoholism.
Guidance and Counseling; Health and Safety; Psychology
Dist - KELLYP **Prod** - KELLYP

Twelve Steps the Video 35 MIN
16mm
Color (G)
Describes the Twelve Steps program which treats individuals with life - stress problems.
Health and Safety; Psychology; Sociology
Dist - UNKNWN

Twelve Steps - the Video
U-matic / VHS
Color (A)
$59.95, $39.95 purchase _ #4967, #4966
Explores chemical dependency as it relates to spirituality in the context of 12 - step recovery.
Education; Psychology
Dist - HAZELB

12 - string guitar techniques 90 MIN
VHS
Color (G)
$39.95 purchase _ #VD - HAP - TW01
Presents techniques for the 12 - string guitar in a wide range of styles for blues, rags, ballads and instrumentals taught by Happy Traum. Demonstrates fingerpicking ideas, powerful walking basses and rhythmic possibilities. Includes Alabama Bound, Good Morning Blues, In the Pines, House of the Rising Sun, Never Said a Mumblin' Word, Green Corn, Delia's Gone, Times Are Gettin' Hard, Bright Morning Stars and more. Addresses specific styles for the 12 - string guitar but songs and techniques are applicable to 6 - string instruments as well.
Fine Arts
Dist - HOMETA **Prod** - HOMETA

Twelve techniques for improving your skills as an instructor - Scott B Parry 100 MIN
VHS
Color; PAL (C G PRO)
$89.95, $69.95 purchase _ #84AST - V - W13
Introduces a dozen techniques for expanding an instructor's behavioral repertoire, enabling instructors to deal more effectively with common problems and opportunities arising when instructing groups. Uses the three - stage learning model, the adult - adult relationship of training and the stimulus - response - feedback links in the instructional chain. Includes handout. Features Scott B Parry, President, Training House, Princeton NJ.
Business and Economics; Education; Psychology
Dist - MOBILE **Prod** - ASTD 1984

Twelve Thousand Men 35 MIN
16mm
Color
_ #106C 0178 569N
Geography - World
Dist - CFLMDC **Prod** - NFBC 1978

Twelve to fourteen months 12 MIN
U-matic / VHS
Teaching infants and toddlers series; Pt 5
Color (H C A)
Shows how infants between the ages of twelve to fourteen months learn by seeing, hearing, imitation, spatial relationships, self - awareness, imagination, problem - solving and language.
Home Economics; Psychology
Dist - GPN **Prod** - BGSU 1978

Twelve - to - Fourteen Year Olds 16 MIN
VHS / U-matic
Child Sexual Abuse - an Ounce of Prevention Series
Color (J)
Features three young people debunking myths about sexual assault or rape. Illustrates the safety rules for preventing sexual abuse with examples of assertiveness, trusting one's feelings and telling others of experiences. Demonstrates how to walk, answer the door or phone and make a scene.
Health and Safety; Home Economics; Sociology
Dist - AITECH **Prod** - PPCIN

The Twenties 25 MIN
U-matic / VHS / 16mm
American History Series
Color (J H)
LC 71-702075
Analyzes the forces which arose after World War I and were at work in the twenties. Describes the conflict between those who accepted the complexity of the twentieth century and tried to cope with it, and those who rejected the new and tried to live according to past values.
History - World; Psychology; Sociology
Dist - MGHT **Prod** - PSP 1969

The Twenties 58 MIN
U-matic / VHS
Walk through the 20th Century with Bill Moyers Series
Color
Describes the 1920's as a decade in which old America was vanishing and a new urban nation was forming. Bill Moyers speaks with several Americans who lived through those years.
History - United States; History - World; Sociology
Dist - PBS **Prod** - CORPEL 1982

Twentieth Century 93 MIN
16mm
B&W (J)
Stars John Barrymore and Carole Lombard. Represents the height of Hollywood glamor during the Depression years of the thirties.
Fine Arts
Dist - TIMLIF **Prod** - CPC 1934

Twentieth Century American Art 27 MIN
VHS
Color (J)
$29.95 purchase _ #HV - 912
Uses the collection at the Whitney Museum of Art to overview modern and contemporary art in America. Starts with art at the turn of the century and continues through Abstract Expressionism, Pop Art and Minimalism.
Fine Arts
Dist - CRYSP **Prod** - CRYSP

Twentieth century American art 30 MIN
35mm strip / VHS
Color (J H C T A)
$93.00 purchase _ #MB - 909724 - 3, #MB - 909726 - X
Covers the development of 20th century American art. Suggests that a 1913 exhibition at a New York armory was responsible for opening the US to a wide variety of artistic styles, from Fauvism to Cubism to Expressionism.
Fine Arts
Dist - SRA **Prod** - SRA 1990

Twentieth Century American Art - Highlights of the Permanent Collection of the Whitney Museum of American Art 26 MIN
16mm
Color (H A)
$450.00 purchase, $55.00 rental
Documents 20th Century American Art exhibition at the Whitney Museum of American Art in 1982. Opens with a historical sequence leading to the founding by the museum in 1930 by Gertrude Vanderbilt Whitney. Goes on to a tour of the exhibition.
Fine Arts
Dist - AFA **Prod** - WMUS 1982

Twentieth century American art - highlights of the permanent collection - Pt 3 27 MIN
VHS
Whitney museum of American art series
Color (S)
$29.95 purchase _ #290 - 9006
Presents two of the biennial exhibitions of the Whitney Museum of American Art and traces the history of American art in the 20th century. Begins with American art at the turn of the century and continues through Abstract Expressionism, Pop Art and Minimalism. Part of a series.
Fine Arts
Dist - FI **Prod** - WMUS 1988

Twentieth Century Art 65 MIN
VHS
Color (I)
$29.95 purchase _ #HV - 668
Surveys twentieth century art from the Metropolitan Museum. Includes artists such as Bonnard, Picasso, Kandinsky, Matisse, Klee, O'Keefe, Pollock, de Kooning, Still, Motherwell, Avery, and Rauschenberg.
Fine Arts
Dist - CRYSP **Prod** - CRYSP

Twentieth Century Art at the Metropolitan Museum - the Wallace Wing 55 MIN
VHS
Color (S)
$39.95 purchase _ #412 - 9070
Displays selections from more than eight thousand works by American and European artists of the twentieth century in the Lila Acheson Wallace Wing at the Metropolitan Museum. Features the Met's director, Philippe de Montebello, who divides his tour into two parts - 1900 to 1940 includes works by Picasso, Kandinsky, Matisse, Klee and O'Keefe, 1940 to the present includes works by Pollock, de Kooning, Still, Avery and others.
Fine Arts; History - World
Dist - FI **Prod** - MMOA 1987

Twentieth Century Epidemic 30 MIN
U-matic / VHS
Color
Portrays diseases of the heart and blood vessels as the epidemic of the twentieth century. Stresses prevention of cardiovascular diseases through reduction of such high - risk factors such as overweight, fat - saturated diets, underexercise and cigarette smoking.
Health and Safety; Science - Natural
Dist - PRIMED **Prod** - PRIMED

Twentieth - century fiction - alienation and self - discovery
VHS
Color (J H C)
$197.00 purchase _ #00270 - 126
Examines the literary works of Sylvia Plath, Carson McCullers, Thomas Mann, Joseph Heller and James Baldwin to discuss the conflict of 20th - century fiction. Includes teacher's guide, library kit. In two parts.
Literature and Drama
Dist - GA **Prod** - GA

Twentieth Century History Series - Vol III
Cold War - confrontation - Pt 12 20 MIN
One Man's Revolution - Mao Tse - Tung - Pt 11 20 MIN
The Road to Berlin - Pt 9 20 MIN
Dist - FI

Twentieth Century History Series - Vol II
Britain Alone - Pt 6 20 MIN
Stalin and the Modernization of Russia - Pt 7 20 MIN
Why Appeasement - Pt 5 20 MIN
Dist - FI

Twentieth Century History Series - Vol I
Make Germany Pay - Pt 1 20 MIN
Roosevelt and the New Deal - Pt 4 20 MIN
Dist - FI

Twentieth Century History Series
Boom and bust 20 MIN
Boom and bust - Pt 2 20 MIN
Britain Alone 20 MIN
Cold War - confrontation 20 MIN
Hitler's Germany 1933 - 1936 20 MIN
India - the brightest jewel 20 MIN
Israel and the Arab States 20 MIN
Make Germany Pay 20 MIN
Mr Kennedy and Mr Krushchev 20 MIN
One Man's Revolution - Mao Tse - tung 20 MIN
Pearl Harbor to Hiroshima 20 MIN
The Road to Berlin 20 MIN
Roosevelt and the New Deal 20 MIN
Twentieth Century History - Vol I 80 MIN
Twentieth Century History - Vol II 80 MIN
Twentieth Century History - Vol III 80 MIN
Twentieth Century History - Vol IV 80 MIN
Why Appeasement 20 MIN
Dist - FI

Twentieth Century History - Vol I 80 MIN
VHS
Twentieth Century History Series
Color (S)
$129.00 purchase
Illuminates the events and issues which shaped our modern world. Uses archival footage, maps, drawings, feature film segments, paintings and posters to illustrate historic events. Volume I includes 4 parts, 'Make Germany Pay,' 'Boom And Bust,' 'Hitler's Germany 1933 - 36' and 'Roosevelt And The New Deal,' which look at the events leading up to World War II.
Civics and Political Systems; Geography - World; History - United States; History - World
Dist - FI **Prod** - BBCTV 1981

Twentieth Century History - Vol II 80 MIN
VHS
Twentieth Century History Series
Color (S)
$129.00 purchase
Illuminates the events and issues which shaped our modern world. Uses archival footage, maps, drawings, feature film segments, paintings and posters to illustrate historic events. Volume II includes 4 parts, 'Why Appeasement,' 'Britain Alone,' 'Stalin And The Modernization Of Russia' and 'Pearl Harbor To Hiroshima,' which consider the early part of World War II, including the entry of the US and Japan into the war, through the bombing of Hiroshima and Nagasaki.
Civics and Political Systems; History - United States; History - World
Dist - FI **Prod** - BBCTV 1981

Twentieth Century History - Vol III 80 MIN
VHS
Twentieth Century History Series
Color (S)
$129.00 purchase
Illuminates the events and issues which shaped our modern world. Uses archival footage, maps, drawings, feature film segments, paintings and posters to illustrate historic events. Volume III includes 4 parts, 'The Road To Berlin,' 'India - The Brightest Crown Jewel,' 'One Man's Revolution - Mao Tse - tung' and 'Cold War - Confrontation,' which consider the ending days of World War II and the period of time immediately after the war which ushered in the Cold War.
Business and Economics; Civics and Political Systems; History - United States; History - World; Sociology
Dist - FI **Prod** - BBCTV 1981

Twentieth Century History - Vol IV 80 MIN
VHS
Twentieth Century History Series
Color (S)
$129.00 purchase
Illuminates the events and issues which shaped our modern world. Uses archival footage, maps, drawings, feature film segments, paintings and posters to illustrate historic events. Volume IV includes 4 parts, 'Mr Kennedy And Mr Khrushchev,' 'China Since Mao,' 'Arabs And Israel Since 1947' and 'The Third World,' which consider the continuing cold war, China after the death of Mao, conflict in the Middle East after the creation of the state of Israel, and the emergence of the Third World and their struggles in self - government.
Geography - World; History - World; Religion and Philosophy
Dist - FI **Prod** - BBCTV 1987

The 20th century landscape 30 MIN
U-matic / Kit / VHS
Western Man and the modern world in video series
Color (J H C T A)
$1378.12 for 25 part series _ #C676 - 27342 - 5, $69.95 for individual
Discusses the pervasive impact of constant change in twentieth century society. Focuses on instantaneous communication, rapid transportation, automated data processing and the information explosion. Raises ethical and moral issues. Part of a 25 unit series.
Computer Science; History - World; Religion and Philosophy; Social Science; Sociology
Dist - RH

The 20th century landscape - Unit VII 30 MIN
35mm strip / VHS
Western Man and the modern world series
Color (J H C T A)
$72.00, $72.00 purchase _ #MB - 510378 - 8, #MB - 510291 - 9
Documents the almost constant change that characterizes modern industrial society. Focuses on the 'information explosion.'
Computer Science; History - World; Social Science; Sociology
Dist - SRA

Twentieth Century Poetry 1 20 MIN
U-matic / VHS
American Literature Series
Color (H C A)
LC 83-706206
Presents performers interpreting familiar poems by popular 20th century poets, including Carl Sandburg, Robert Frost and Edna St Vincent Millay.
Literature and Drama
Dist - AITECH **Prod** - AUBU 1983

Twentieth Century Poetry 2 20 MIN
U-matic / VHS
American Literature Series
Color (H C A)
LC 83-706207
Presents performers interpreting familiar poems by popular 20th century poets, including e e cummings, W H Auden and Theodore Roethke.
Literature and Drama
Dist - AITECH **Prod** - AUBU 1983

Twentieth Century River 29 MIN
16mm
Color
LC FIA66-789
Describes how a plan for the Potomac River Basin is drafted, showing the engineers, scientists, conservationists and other specialists at work. Probes such problems as flood, drought, pollution, sedimentation, development of recreation areas and aquiring lands for parks.
Geography - United States; Geography - World; Science - Natural
Dist - FINLYS **Prod** - FINLYS 1962

Twentieth Century Series
From Kaiser to Fuehrer 26 MIN
Minister of Hate - Josef Goebbels 27 MIN
Dist - CRMP

Twentieth Century Series
The Movies Learn to Talk 26 MIN
Dist - CRMP
MGHT

Twentieth Century Series
Dust Bowl 26 MIN
Turn of the Century 30 MIN
The Women Get the Vote 27 MIN
Dist - MGHT

The Twentieth Century - the Last of the Romantics - the Guitar - a Final Evocation - Pts 7 and 8 - Vol IV 60 MIN
VHS
Guitarra Series
Color (S)
$39.95 purchase _ #833 - 9073
Traces the evolution of the Spanish guitar from 1500 to the present day. Features world - renowned classical guitarist Julian Bream as host and musician. Volume IV of the four - volume series performs Torroba's 'Allegretto,' de Falla's 'Homenaje a Debussy' and 'Miller's Dance,' Turina's 'Fandaguillo,' and Ohana's 'Tiento' at locations in Granada, Barcelona and Cordova in Part 7. Bream plays Rodrigo's 'Concerto de Aranjuez' in the final program.
Fine Arts; Foreign Language; Geography - World; History - World
Dist - FI **Prod** - RMART 1986

Twentieth - First Century Series
Stranger than Science Fiction 27 MIN
Dist - MGHT

Twenty and Ten 15 MIN
VHS / U-matic
Readit Series
Color (P I)
LC 83-706831
Introduces the story about 20 school children who hide ten Jewish children from the Nazis occupying France during World War II. Shows that the children are safe only if the others can keep silent and not get caught taking them food at night. Based on the book Twenty And Ten by Claire Huchet Bishop.
English Language; Literature and Drama
Dist - AITECH **Prod** - POSIMP 1982

Twenty, Cubed 18 MIN
16mm
B&W
Explores a variety of ways of seeing. Attempts, through both visual and sound close - ups, to portray the world as it seems when one experiences it 'UP CLOSE.' Describes a day in the life of a young man who gets up, shaves, examines his image, goes to work, meets a client in a go - go bar, attends a party, finds a girl and looks too closely at his world.
Psychology; Sociology
Dist - UPENN **Prod** - UPENN 1967

28 - 46 29 MIN
VHS / 16mm
Color (G)
$55.00 rental _ #TEFS - 000
Features five video compositions accompanied by music. Shows how the unique video pieces are composed.
Fine Arts
Dist - PBS **Prod** - KCTSTV

Twenty - Eight Above - Below 10 MIN
U-matic / VHS / 16mm
Color (J)
LC 74-703030
Follows the events of the first underwater exploratory dive made in Arctic waters at Resolute Bay, Canada, by J B Mac Innis and astronaut Scott Carpenter in a specially designed Plexiglass diving bell.
Science; Science - Physical
Dist - IFB **Prod** - NFBC 1974

Twenty - Eight Grams of Prevention - Safety for Today's Laboratory 24 MIN
16mm
Color
LC 75-700489
Helps laboratory workers understand the need for safety regulations in the laboratory. Explains the need for safety regulations, training and proper safety equipment and protective clothing. Uses dramatic re - enactments in order to show the consequences of carelessness.
Health and Safety
Dist - FILCOM **Prod** - FISHSC 1975

Twenty - Eight Up 133 MIN
16mm
Color (G)
Presents an independent production by Michael Apted. Documents the lives of seven - year olds selected from a variety of economic and social backgrounds through interviewing them at ages 7, 14, 21 and 28. Creates a sociological document of postwar Britain and a portrait of growing up.
Fine Arts; Health and Safety; History - World; Psychology; Sociology
Dist - FIRS

The 25th anniversary party - it's got to be rough and sweet 160 MIN
VHS
Color; Stereo (A)
$19.98 purchase _ #ARV-402
Features 27 songs performed by a number of artists at Arhoolie's 25th anniversary party. Includes blues harpist Charlie Musslewhite; country singer Rose Maddox; a cajun band led by Michael Doucet of Beausoleil and Ann Savoy; and boogie and blues pianist Katie Webster with Juke Joint Johnny and the Hot Links. Features interviews and commentary with Arhoolie founder and president Chris Strachwitz.
Fine Arts
Dist - ARHOLE **Prod** - ARHOLE 1995

The Twenty - fifth defense
VHS
Color (G)
$29.80 purchase _ #0065
Documents the 1983 America's Cup Races with footage from official television coverage. Follows the elimination trials, the controversy over the Australian keel and the races. Uses some footage shot from the Goodyear balloon and features Richard Kiley as narrator.
Physical Education and Recreation
Dist - SEVVID

The Twenty First Annual World Eskimo Indian Olympics 27 MIN
VHS / U-matic
Color (H C A)
LC 83-706859
Excerpts participants' remarks at the 1982 World Eskimo Indian Olympics, observes their dedicated training and records the wholesome competition of the knuckle hop, greased pole walk, seal skinning contest and other events.
Social Science; Sociology
Dist - BLUMBS **Prod** - BLUMBS 1983

Twenty - First Century Series
Cities of the future 18 MIN
The First ten months of life - Pt 1 27 MIN
The First ten months of life - Pt 2 27 MIN
The Food revolution 17 MIN
The Four - Day week 17 MIN
From cradle to classroom 52 MIN
From cradle to classroom - Pt 1 25 MIN
From cradle to classroom - Pt 2 25 MIN
The Incredible voyage 26 MIN
Man - made Man 15 MIN
Miracle of the Mind 26 MIN
Stranger than Science Fiction 17 MIN
The Weird World of Robots 26 MIN
Dist - MGHT

Twenty - first century series
Atomic medicine 30 MIN
Bats, birds and bionics 30 MIN
Computer Revolution, the, Pt 1 30 MIN
Computer Revolution, the, Pt 2 30 MIN
The Four - Day week 30 MIN
The Laser - a Light Fantastic 30 MIN
Miracle of the Mind 30 MIN
Dist - MTP

The 25 best customer service ideas you can use today 44 MIN
VHS
Inc magazine customer service series
Color (A PRO COR)
$79.95 purchase _ #IBR30056V
Helps offices improve their relationship with their customers. Includes advice and tips from experts, top consultants, and CEOs. Includes color - coded segment breaks which enable the user to fast - forward or rewind to particular lessons. Deals with pushing the customer service envelope, innovations from leading customer - first companies and the lessons of a perfect cup of coffee. Part of a six - part series.
Business and Economics; Psychology
Dist - CAMV

Twenty - Five Feet from the Face 17 MIN
16mm
Color
LC 82-700703
Points out the leading causes of coal mine roof - fall accidents and outlines proper safety procedures for making a working place safe. Demonstrates various types of roof bolting equipment and roof control techniques. Emphasizes the workers learning and following the mine's approved roof - control plan, learning to recognize and properly evaluate roof conditions, and applying available roof control devices.
Health and Safety; Social Science
Dist - USNAC **Prod** - USDL 1982

25 Fireman's street 97 MIN
VHS
Color (G) (HUNGARIAN WITH ENGLISH SUBTITLES)
Portrays the post - war history of Hungary through the dreams, memories and nightmares of the inhabitants of an old house on the eve of its destruction. Directed by Istvan Szabo.
Fine Arts; History - World
Dist - KINOIC

25 - year - old gay man loses his virginity to a woman 22 MIN
VHS
Color (A)
$40.00 purchase
Explores the filmmaker's latent heterosexuality with porn star - performance artist Annie Sprinkle. Views Annie instructing in various aspects of heterosexuality and bodily functions, including the use of Tampax. A comedy produced by Phillip B Roth.
Fine Arts; Literature and Drama; Sociology
Dist - CANCIN

Twenty - five years of the presidency series 120 MIN
VHS
Twenty - five years of the presidency series
Color (G)
$89.95 purchase _ #YOPR - 000
Interviews several former White House chiefs of staff in two - part series. Explores the relationship between a President and his chief of staff. Part one focuses on crisis management, scrutinizing various historic moments. Part two emphasizes the day - to - day White House operations. Hosted by John Chancellor.
Civics and Political Systems; History - United States
Dist - PBS **Prod** - KPBS 1989

Twenty - five years of the presidency series
Twenty - five years of the presidency series 120 MIN
Dist - PBS

Twenty - Four Eyes 158 MIN
VHS
Japan Film Collection from SVS Series
B&W (G) (JAPANESE (ENGLISH SUBTITLES))
$59.95 purchase _ #K0676
Presents a movie produced in Japan. Features Keisuke Kinoshita as director. Stars Hideko Takamine.
Fine Arts; Geography - World
Dist - CHTSUI **Prod** - SONY

24 F P S 14 MIN
16mm
Color (G)
$56.00 rental
Explores the relationship of film projecting itself. Captures an image which was filmed and projected in the same movement of time which is 24 frames per second.
Fine Arts
Dist - CANCIN **Prod** - WONGAL 1977

24 frames per second 12 MIN
16mm
B&W (G)
$40.00 rental
Explores the relationship between sound and image. Resonates with symbolic meaning between opposites of black and white and silence and sound. A Takahiko Iimura production.
Fine Arts; Foreign Language
Dist - CANCIN

Twenty Four Heures Du Mans, 1982 19 MIN
16mm
Color (H)
Features Jim Busby and his experience behind the wheel of a BF Goodrich Comp T A Equipped Porsche Carrera Turbo.
Physical Education and Recreation
Dist - MTP **Prod** - GC

Twenty - four hours at Le Mans 50 MIN
VHS
Color (G)
$29.95 purchase _ #S01982
Presents an inside look at the famous Le Mans Grand Prix racing event, based on the experiences of an Australian racing driver who entered the event. Shows the extensive preparation beforehand, as well as excerpts from the race itself.
Business and Economics; Industrial and Technical Education; Physical Education and Recreation
Dist - UILL

Twenty - four techniques for closing the sale 65 MIN
VHS
Color (H C A)
$59.95 purchase _ #NGC568V
Features sales and management expert Brian Tracy, who explains the 24 most effective sales closing techniques. Suggests that these techniques can be applied to other interpersonal situations as well.
Business and Economics
Dist - CAMV **Prod** - WNETTV
PBS

Twenty hitting drills
VHS
You can teach hitting series
Color (J H C G)
$24.95 purchase _ #BIT011V - P
Illustrates 20 drills in batting through the collaborative teaching of a player, coach and teacher. Part of a three - part series on baseball and batting.
Physical Education and Recreation
Dist - CAMV

Twenty is Plenty 23 MIN
U-matic
Color (A)
LC 81-707317
Presents twenty suggestions from multiple - handicapped individuals on what persons beginning a career in rehabilitation should know, and gives a humorous look at special problems.
Guidance and Counseling; Health and Safety; Psychology
Dist - UCPNYC **Prod** - UCPNYC 1981

Twenty knots if by sea...55 if by land
VHS
Color (G)
$29.95 purchase _ #0817
Sails on the fast and foldable F - 27 sport cruiser. Follows an international yacht race from Newport, California, to Ensenada, Mexico. Travels down Baja California to cruise the Sea of Cortez.
Physical Education and Recreation
Dist - SEVVID

Twenty Mile Limit 12 MIN
16mm
Color
LC 80-700270
Discusses living toward the future and not in the past.
Psychology
Dist - HORNP **Prod** - HORNP 1980

Twenty Miles from Everything 16 MIN
16mm
Color
LC 79-701582
Focuses on six rural transportation systems and the various methods of conveyance which are employed. Illustrates how the people who rely on the availability of such systems would be severely restricted in their activities without them.
Social Science; Sociology
Dist - USNAC **Prod** - USFHAD 1979

Twenty million miles to earth 82 MIN
16mm
B&W (J)
Stars William Hopper and Joan Taylor. Shows a U S rocketship returning from Venus with a strange cargo from that planet. Introduces a miniature specimen of the Venus - beast which doubles in size every night to become a monster susceptible only to paralyzing electric shock.
Literature and Drama
Dist - TWYMAN **Prod** - CPC

Twenty minute workout 60 MIN
VHS
Color (G)
$19.95 purchase
Includes three complete aerobic workouts. Taught by Bess Motta.
Physical Education and Recreation
Dist - PBS **Prod** - WNETTV

Twenty Minutes 16 MIN
U-matic / VHS
Color
Explores techniques for conducting a reference interview with a library patron.
Education; Social Science; Sociology
Dist - LVN **Prod** - BCPL

29 - 'Merci, Merci' 30 MIN
16mm
B&W (C)
$504.00
Experimental film by Will Hindle.
Fine Arts
Dist - AFA **Prod** - AFA 1966

Twenty - Nine - Year - Old Men and Women Talk about their Sexuality 56 MIN
VHS / U-matic
Color
Explores the changing attitudes of society toward sexuality. Features two males and two females reviewing their sex education from 'playing doctor' as kids to attitudes, feelings, practices and problems related to the sexual revolution and the women's movement.
Psychology; Sociology
Dist - HEMUL **Prod** - HEMUL

Twenty - ninth biennial clergy - laity congress 28 MIN
VHS
Illuminations series
Color (G R)
#V - 1003
Documents the proceedings of the 1988 Greek Orthodox Archdiocesan Clergy - Laity Congress. Focuses on the issues presented at the Congress. Highlights participation from national and international leaders who attended.
Fine Arts; Religion and Philosophy
Dist - GOTEL **Prod** - GOTEL 1988

Twenty - One Days in the Life of an Egg 20 MIN
U-matic / VHS
Color (C)
$249.00, $149.00 purchase _ #AD - 1374
Uses special equipment which permits incubation of eggs without shells. Captures the complete process of development and growth and illustrates graphically the sequence and timetable in which ontogeny recapitulates phyllogeny.
Science - Natural
Dist - FOTH **Prod** - FOTH

The Twenty - One Days of Laura Wells 21 MIN
16mm
Color
LC 79-701170
Traces the odyssey of a young woman from the onset of an illness through her treatment and recovery in order to demonstrate the costs involved.
Health and Safety; Social Science
Dist - AETNA **Prod** - AETNA 1979

21 days to back pain relief
VHS
Color (G)
$129.00 purchase _ #BKV
Presents a set of three videos which discuss severe, moderate and mild back pain and exercises which help back pain sufferers get back to work. Includes step - by - step guide to the exercises. Produced by Dr Robert L Swezey, founder of the Arthritis and Back Pain Center in Santa Monica.
Health and Safety; Science - Natural
Dist - GPERFO

Twenty - One Going on 70 29 MIN
16mm
Color (R)
Shows how a young man developed a new belief in Christ after working with elderly people.
Guidance and Counseling; Religion and Philosophy; Sociology
Dist - OUTRCH **Prod** - OUTRCH

Twenty - One Hundred Year Old Tomb Excavated 30 MIN
16mm
Color
Records the discovery of a 2,100 - year - old tomb, recently unearthed in central China. Examines the body of a woman and the burial accessories recovered from the tomb.
History - World; Sociology
Dist - GROVE **Prod** - GROVE 1975

Twenty - One Inch Rotary Mower
VHS
Landscape Equipment Maintenance Series
Color (G) (SPANISH)
$65.00 purchase _ #6 - 075 - 100P, #6 - 075 - 200P - Spanish
Presents proper procedures on maintenance, safety and operation of the twenty - one rotary mower for landscaping. Part of a five - part series on landscaping.
Agriculture; Health and Safety
Dist - VEP **Prod** - VEP

The 21 - inch world 28 MIN
U-matic / BETA / VHS
Communication skills 2 - advanced series
Color (H C G)
101.95, $89.95 purchase _ #CA - 21
Reveals that television informs, entertains and persuades, that it is pervasive in United States society. Shows how understanding its capabilities and impact can assist the student in the development of critical attitudes toward television and how it affects personal lifestyle. Presents the various forms of television programming by type and function. Part of a 26 - part series.
Fine Arts; Social Science; Sociology
Dist - INSTRU

Twenty - One to Twenty - Nine Months 13 MIN
U-matic / VHS
Teaching Infants and Toddlers Series Pt 7
Color (H C A)
Shows how infants between the ages of 21 to 29 months learn through fine motor activities, gross motor activities, self - awareness, imagination, self - care, problem - solving and language.
Home Economics; Psychology
Dist - GPN **Prod** - BGSU 1978

Twenty questions 60 MIN
16mm
Color (G)
$100.00 rental
Interviews 19 people chosen at random, locked in a room for about eleven minutes. Asks various question ranging from 'What do you do when you find out your lover has AIDS,' to 'Why do you litter.' Directed by Gorman Bechard.
Fine Arts
Dist - CANCIN

The Twenty Questions 32 MIN
VHS / 16mm
Color (G)
$89.95, $29.95 purchase _ #6912, 6911
Combines the Johns Hopkins chemical dependency questionnaire with dramatizations of alcohol and other abusers finding answers which lead to getting help. Guides patients around the denial roadblock.
Guidance and Counseling; Health and Safety; Psychology
Dist - HAZELB **Prod** - MTVTM

Twenty questions about the Drug - Free Workplace Act - I 11 MIN
8mm cartridge / VHS / BETA / U-matic
Drug - free workplace series
Color; CC; PAL (IND G PRO)
$395.00 purchase, $175.00 rental _ #DFE - 100
Provides supervisors with an understanding of the Act and their role in enforcing the drug - free workplace policy. Covers the requirements of the Act, how to comply, who is covered, what to do if an employee is convicted, disciplinary sanctions, the role of alcohol under the Act, definitions of controlled substances, prescription drugs, rehabilitation programs and EAPs, where drug testing fits in and more. Part one of two parts.
Business and Economics; Guidance and Counseling; Psychology
Dist - BNA **Prod** - BNA

Twenty Seconds a Day - Coping with Diabetes 32 MIN
U-matic
Life with Diabetes Series
Color (PRO)
LC 81-707066
Presents interviews with a broad spectrum of diabetic patients to determine how they deal with their disease. Discusses diet regimen, scheduling, diabetic rebellion, feelings about death, long - term complications, patient education, compliance and scare tactics, the value of honesty, and the lack of sensitivity on the part of health professionals involved in caring for people with diabetes.
Health and Safety
Dist - UMICH **Prod** - UMICH 1980

Twenty Seven Hundred - 7200 Variable Venturi Carburetor 25 MIN
VHS / U-matic
Color
Discusses diagnosis, adjustment and operation of the Variable Venturi Carburetor. Provides propane enrichment idle mixture adjustment procedure. Contains modifications from 1977 - 82 as well as complete carburetor specifiations.
Industrial and Technical Education
Dist - FORDSP **Prod** - FORDSP

Twenty - Seventh Infantry Division 20 MIN
U-matic / VHS / 16mm
B&W (H A)
Presents the campaigns at Makin, Eniwetok, Saipan and Okinawa.
Civics and Political Systems; History - United States
Dist - USNAC **Prod** - USA 1953

26 Deutsche Kulturfilme
U-matic / VHS / 16mm
26 Deutsche Kulturfilme Series
Color (J H C A) (GERMAN)
Presents twenty - six German language programs. Acquaints the student of history and geography with various regions of Germany, past and present. Available with narration in German or English.
Geography - World
Dist - IFB **Prod** - FRGMFA 1982

26 Deutsche Kulturfilme Series
26 Deutsche Kulturfilme
Dist - IFB

Twenty six times in a row 24 MIN
U-matic / VHS / 16mm
Color (H C A)

LC 81-700010
Examines the strategies and techniques of marathon running and focuses on the winner of the 1976 Olympic Marathon in Montreal, Waldemar Cierpinski.
Physical Education and Recreation
Dist - FI **Prod** - NFBC 1980

Twenty - Sixth Infantry Division 16 MIN
16mm / U-matic / VHS
B&W (H A)
Presents scenes of the 26th Infantry Division combat operations in New Guinea, including actions at Maffin Bay, the amphibious landing at Sansapor to build an air base, and the assault landing at Lingayen Gulf, Luzon.
Civics and Political Systems; History - United States
Dist - USNAC **Prod** - USA 1952

The Twenty - Third Cease Fire 52 MIN
16mm
Color
Relates the story of the brief interlude during the Lebanese civil war, the twenty - third cease fire, and describes life in war - torn Beirut.
History - World; Sociology
Dist - ICARUS **Prod** - ICARUS

23rd Psalm branch - Part I 30 MIN
16mm
B&W (G)
$1047.00 purchase, $88.00 rental
Reclaims a meditation on peace.
Fine Arts; Religion and Philosophy
Dist - CANCIN **Prod** - BRAKS 1966

23rd Psalm branch - Part II 30 MIN
16mm
B&W (G)
$1075.00 purchase, $81.00 rental
Reclaims a mediation on peace.
Fine Arts; Religion and Philosophy
Dist - CANCIN **Prod** - BRAKS 1966

Twenty thousand leagues over the sea
VHS
Color (G A)
$39.90 purchase _ #0497
Tells the story of Guy Bernardin, one of the few competitors who finished both BOC Challenge Races - The Solo Round the World Sailing Races. Describes Bernardin's 1986 - 87 entry on his 60 footer designed for the race.
Geography - World; Physical Education and Recreation
Dist - SEVVID

Twenty Thousand Leagues Under the Sea 52 MIN
16mm / VHS
Children's Classics Series
Color (P)
$295.00 purchase
Recreates the classic '20,000 Leagues Under The Sea' by Jules Verne. Adapted by Richard Neubert. In two parts.
Fine Arts; Literature and Drama
Dist - LUF **Prod** - BROVID

Twenty Thousand Leagues Under the Sea 127 MIN
U-matic / VHS / 16mm
Color
Focuses on the Nautilus, the first man - made nuclear submarine, and its power - mad captain. Stars James Mason and Kirk Douglas.
Fine Arts; Literature and Drama
Dist - FI **Prod** - DISNEY 1954

Twenty Thousand Leagues Under the Sea
Cassette / 16mm
Now Age Reading Programs, Set 1 Series
Color (I J)
$9.95 purchase _ #8F - PN681808
Brings a classic tale to young readers. The filmstrip set includes filmstrip, cassette, book, classroom materials and a poster. The read - along set includes an activity book and a cassette.
English Language; Literature and Drama
Dist - MAFEX

Twenty thousand leagues under the sea 27 MIN
U-matic / VHS / 16mm
Films as literature series
Color
An edited version of the feature film 20,000 Leagues Under The Sea. Stars James Mason, Kirk Douglas, and Peter Lorre.
Fine Arts; Literature and Drama
Dist - CORF **Prod** - DISNEY

Twenty - Three Skidoo 10 MIN
16mm
B&W
Dramatizes the horror of the neutron bomb by showing a metropolis without a trace of human life, then focusing on a news teletype which has stopped halfway through its message reporting the explosion of the world's first neutron bomb.
Civics and Political Systems; Psychology; Sociology
Dist - NFBC **Prod** - NFBC 1964

Twenty - twenty foresight 45 MIN
VHS
Color (J H C G)
$189.00 purchase
Empowers women. Discusses the need for self - defense awareness and street smarts. Concerns the training of a young woman for preventing rape. Shows women that they have options and alternatives and that they can have power and control over their own personal safety.
Guidance and Counseling; Health and Safety; Physical Education and Recreation; Sociology
Dist - MEDIAI **Prod** - MEDIAI 1990

20 years of listening to America with Bill Moyers 90 MIN
VHS
Color (G)
$19.95 purchase _ #PBS359
Collects highlights of the journalistic career of Bill Moyers on PBS.
Fine Arts; History - United States; Literature and Drama
Dist - INSTRU **Prod** - PBS

Twice born 50 MIN
VHS
Horizon series
Color (A)
PdS99 purchase
Uses footage of fetal surgery to reveal that not all open womb surgery results in success - but the scientific possibilities are far reaching. Asks if scientists could do away with the mother and make pregnancy unnecessary. Airs the fierce moral debate surrounding pregnancy and associated issues.
Sociology
Dist - BBCENE

Twice five plus the wings of a bird 50 MIN
VHS
Horizon series
Color (A)
PdS99 purchase
Reveals that many mathematics educators are demanding a new approach in teaching methods which recognize that children are mathematical thinkers in their own right. Visits a school which encourages children to invent their own math problems to solve. Not available in the United States.
Mathematics
Dist - BBCENE

Twice pardoned 85 MIN
VHS
Color (J H C G A R)
$34.99 purchase _ #35 - 82 - 2025
Presents ex - convict Harold Morris with a message to young people. Emphasizes the importance of avoiding the bad influences that nearly destroyed his own life. Consists of two tapes. Produced by Focus on the Family.
Religion and Philosophy; Sociology
Dist - APH

The Twice promised land 47 MIN
BETA / VHS / U-matic
Color; Mono (H C A G)
$325.00 purchase, $65.00 Rental
Tells the story of the 'small peace' that exists among some Jews and Arabs in Israel. Focuses on the story of a small group of Jews and Arabs who have chosen the path of reconciliation and have accepted the fact that Jews and Arabs are destined to live together in Israel. Presents the everyday lives of the Jews and Arabs who make up Israeli society and who are working for peace in their common land.
History - World
Dist - CTV **Prod** - STWAY 1987

Twice Two 21 MIN
16mm
B&W
Features Laurel and Hardy as themselves and as their wives.
Fine Arts
Dist - RMIBHF **Prod** - ROACH 1933

Twice upon a time 15 MIN
U-matic / VHS
Color
Centers on a controversial study at the University of Minnesota which involves twins separated at birth and their reunion as adults.
Psychology; Sociology
Dist - WCCOTV **Prod** - WCCOTV 1980

Twice upon a time, or helping you helps me 30 MIN
VHS / U-matic
Coping with kids series
Color
Introduces parent and teacher discussion groups as a means of learning how to cope with kids.
Guidance and Counseling; Sociology
Dist - OHUTC **Prod** - OHUTC
FI MFFD

Twin engine powerboat handling 30 MIN
VHS
Color (G)
$24.95 purchase _ #0957
Covers the basic skills needed to operate twin engine powerboats. Includes safe docking and undocking techniques, basic handling and close quarters maneuvers, getting underway, tying alongside and dealing with the factors of wind and currents.
Physical Education and Recreation
Dist - SEVVID

Twin Power Scraper
16mm
Color
Shows the applications of the Twin Power Scraper in the earth moving job.
Industrial and Technical Education; Psychology
Dist - GM **Prod** - GM

Twin screw boathandling
VHS
Color (G)
$39.80 purchase _ #0056
Covers the basic skills needed to operate twin screw boats. Includes the use of controls, basic maneuvering, wind and currents, docking, emergency procedures. Shows how to maneuver with 'one engine out.'
Physical Education and Recreation
Dist - SEVVID

Twin strand continuous slab caster scheduling model
VHS
Color (C PRO G)
$150.00 purchase _ #87.03
Shows how a state - of - the - art twin strand continuous slab caster scheduling model, in use since 1983, utilizes implicit enumeration. Reveals that, through increased capacity and reduced production planning manpower, this Cleveland caster holds the monthly production record for all slab casters in North America, saving an estimated $1.95 million annually. LTV Steel Company - Cleveland Works. Richard E Box, Donald G Herbe.
Business and Economics; Industrial and Technical Education
Dist - INMASC

Twinkle, Twinkle, Little Star 29 MIN
U-matic
Music Shop Series
Color
Focuses on what children learn when they take music lessons.
Fine Arts
Dist - UMITV **Prod** - UMITV 1974

Twinkle, Twinkle, Little Star 25 MIN
U-matic
Not Another Science Show Series
Color (H C)
Explains building a backyard telescope and points out guidepost stars and constellations.
Science; Science - Physical
Dist - TVOTAR **Prod** - TVOTAR 1986

Twins 50 MIN
16mm
Color (A)
LC 80-701382
Tells how a pair of twins wake up to their 30th birthdays. Shows how one twin, a Chaplinesque bum, devises a plan to kill his brother while the other, a cop with a new bulletproof vest, becomes obsessed with his bowling ball.
Fine Arts
Dist - AHEARN **Prod** - AHEARN 1980

Twins - a case study 52 MIN
VHS
Color (H C G)
$445.00 purchase, $75.00 rental
Portrays 45 - year - old Yorkshire twins, Freda and Greta Chaplin, who are mirror images of one another. Reveals that they dress alike, speak in unison, share everything and are inseparable. Both twins have fixated on one man as a love object, and to gain the man's attention they harass him mercilessly. Asks if they are both psychotic or if one is just imitating the other. Produced by John Dollar for Volcano Films.
Psychology; Sociology
Dist - FLMLIB

Twins, Pt 1 25 MIN
16mm
Color (A)
LC 80-701382
Tells how a pair of twins wake up to their 30th birthdays. Shows how one twin, a Chaplinesque bum, devises a plan to kill his brother while the other, a cop with a new bulletproof vest, becomes obsessed with his bowling ball.
Fine Arts
Dist - AHEARN **Prod** - AHEARN 1980

Twins, Pt 2 25 MIN
16mm
Color (A)
LC 80-701382
Tells how a pair of twins wake up to their 30th birthdays. Shows how one twin, a Chaplinesque bum, devises a plan to kill his brother while the other, a cop with a new bulletproof vest, becomes obsessed with his bowling ball.
Fine Arts
Dist - AHEARN **Prod** - AHEARN 1980

Twinsburg, OH - some kind of weird twin thing 23 MIN
VHS / 16mm
Color (H C G)
$595.00, $295.00 purchase, $75.00, $55.00 rental
Looks at Twins Days in the small American town of Twinsburg, Ohio, when 2500 identically - dressed sets of twins congregate annually to celebrate their double identities. Includes marching bands, talent contests, carbon copy fashions and double helpings of food, twins in baby carriages and elderly twins on canes, intermarried twins and unmarried twins. Meets two self - styled anti - twins, the filmmaker and her identical sister. Reveals that they live 3000 miles apart, never dressed alike and have a history of conflict. Shares their struggle to balance the intimacy of a shared childhood with the adult need for individuality. Produced by Sue Marcoux.
Sociology
Dist - FLMLIB

Twist 78 MIN
35mm
Color; B&W (G)
Chronicles the evolution of rock and roll, from the time when moving one's hips marked you as a social degenerate, to a time when shaking your thing became the dance form that rocked the world. Combines rare and often hilarious archival footage with interviews. Produced and directed by Ron Mann; co - produced by Sue Len Quon. Features Chubby Checker, Hank Ballard, Joey Dee, Mama Lu Parks & the Parkettes, Dee Dee Sharp and Cholly Atkins. Contact distributor for price.
Fine Arts
Dist - OCTOBF

Twist Drill Procedure 16 MIN
VHS / U-matic
Color (PRO)
Focuses on diagnostic and therapeutic applications of the procedure. Reviews equipment, anatomical landmarks and a step - by - step analysis of the technique. Demonstrates procedure on trauma victims with interacerebral hemorrhage and chronic subdural hematoma.
Health and Safety; Psychology; Science - Natural
Dist - UWASH **Prod** - UWASH

Twist drills - Pt 5 7 MIN
16mm
B&W
LC FIE58-6
Explains the size designation of twist drills, their cutting action and how they are used and sharpened.
Industrial and Technical Education
Dist - USNAC **Prod** - USN 1954

The Twisted Cross 55 MIN
U-matic / VHS / 16mm
Project 20 Series
B&W (J)
Uses the story of Adolf Hitler and the Nazi movement to trace the rise and fall of a dictator. Includes scenes extracted from a captured German film.
Biography; Civics and Political Systems; History - World
Dist - MGHT **Prod** - NBCTV 1958

The Twisted cross 53 MIN
VHS
B&W (G)
$39.95 purchase _ #S00164
Portrays the rise and fall of Hitler and his Nazi ideology. Narrated by Alexander Scourby.
Civics and Political Systems; History - World
Dist - UILL

The Twisted cross - Pt 1 27 MIN
16mm / U-matic / VHS
Project 20 Series
B&W (J)
Uses the story of Adolf Hitler and the Nazi movement to trace the rise and fall of a dictator. Includes scenes extracted from a captured German film.
Civics and Political Systems
Dist - MGHT **Prod** - NBCTV 1958

The Twisted cross - Pt 2 28 MIN
16mm / U-matic / VHS
Project 20 Series
B&W (J)
Uses the story of Adolf Hitler and the Nazi movement to trace the rise and fall of a dictator. Includes scenes extracted from a captured German film.
Civics and Political Systems
Dist - MGHT **Prod** - NBCTV 1958

Twister 27 MIN
16mm
Color
LC 74-706413
Tells the story of how the city of Lubbock, Texas, responded when a tornado struck. Demonstrates the need for an emergency operating center to handle such disasters.
Geography - United States; Health and Safety; History - World; Sociology
Dist - USNAC **Prod** - USDCPA 1973

Twister and shout
VHS
McGee and me series; Episode 5
Color (P I R)
$19.95 purchase, $10.00 rental _ #35 - 84156 - 979
Features Nick and his animated friend McGee. Shows how a tornado gives Nick the opportunity to show others his faith in God's protection.
Literature and Drama; Religion and Philosophy
Dist - APH **Prod** - TYHP

The Twitch 13 MIN
16mm
Color (I)
LC 75-701939
Tells a story about a cat who sets out to find Utopia but finds instead a kingdom of brutal conformists ruled by a king with a nervous twitch.
Civics and Political Systems; Fine Arts; Guidance and Counseling; Sociology
Dist - SF **Prod** - NFBC 1976

2 - 60 - 48 Kopfe aus dem Szondi Test - 48 heads from the Zondi test 5 MIN
16mm
B&W (G)
$10.00 rental
Develops the notions of formal relationships between simple images.
Fine Arts; Industrial and Technical Education
Dist - CANCIN **Prod** - KRENKU 1960

Two against Cape Horn
VHS
Color (G)
$49.90 purchase _ #0496
Follows sailors Hal and Margaret Roth as they sail down the coast of Chile toward Cape Horn. Reveals that a storm drives them aground on a deserted Chilean island far from civilization. They manage to survive and repair their yacht.
Geography - World; Physical Education and Recreation
Dist - SEVVID

2 AM feeding 24 MIN
VHS / U-matic
Color (G H C)
$250.00 purchase, $100.00 rental
Interviews new mothers and fathers who speak openly and humorously about their early reactions to their babies and share valuable insights and advice about their coping strategies. Describes the physical and emotional roller coaster ride of the first few months of parenthood, the range of emotions that interrupt life as ususal and turn schedules upside down. Discusses breastfeeding; fatigue; crying and colic; mother's recovery; sexuality; fathering; single parenthood; role identification; and returning to work. Produced by Kristine Samuelson.
Sociology
Dist - BAXMED

Two American Audiences 40 MIN
16mm
B&W
Presents a discussion between Jean - Luc Godard and New York University students on filmmaking and politics, intercut with scenes from La Chinoise. By Mark Woodcock.
Civics and Political Systems; Fine Arts; Industrial and Technical Education
Dist - PENNAS **Prod** - PENNAS

Two bad daughters 12 MIN
VHS
Color (G)
$40.00 purchase
Posits play as subversive activity. Features a sabotage of the patriarchal institutions of psychoanalysis and sadomasochism through video image - processing. Made with Paula Levine.
Fine Arts; Psychology
Dist - CANCIN **Prod** - BARHAM 1988

Two Bagatelles 3 MIN
U-matic / VHS / 16mm
Color
Combines two films, 'ON THE LAWN' and 'IN THE BACKYARD.' Shows animated live actors dancing to waltzes and marches.
Fine Arts
Dist - IFB **Prod** - NFBC 1952

Two Baroque Churches in Germany 11 MIN
16mm / U-matic / VHS
Color (J H C)
LC 76-706839
Uses two churches, Vierzehnheiligen and Ottobeurer, as examples of mid - 18th century German Baroque style.
Fine Arts; Religion and Philosophy
Dist - PFP **Prod** - EAMES 1955

Two Become One 10 MIN
16mm
Family Life and Sex Education Series
Color (P I J)
Explains where sperm comes from, and how it reaches the egg. Uses live and animated photography to illustrate. Introduces the concept of female cycles and traces the changes in the uterus and the development of a fertilized egg in the female human.
Science - Natural
Dist - SF **Prod** - SF 1968

The Two Benjamins 20 MIN
U-matic
Truly American Series
Color (I)
Discusses the lives of Benjamin Franklin and Benjamin Banneker.
Biography; History - United States
Dist - GPN **Prod** - WVIZTV 1979

Two Black churches 21 MIN
U-matic
Color (C A)
Explores Black religious expression, ranging from old - time religious baptisms in rural Mississippi to an urban sanctified service in New Haven, Connecticut.
Geography - United States; History - United States; Religion and Philosophy
Dist - SOFOLK **Prod** - SOFOLK 1975

The Two brains 30 MIN
VHS
Mind - brain classroom series
Color (H)
$59.95 purchase _ #MDBR-102
Examines the characteristics of the two sides of the human brain.
Psychology
Dist - PBS **Prod** - WNETTV

The Two Brains 60 MIN
VHS / U-matic
Brain, Mind and Behavior Series
Color (C A)
Discusses the cortical hemispheres, the relation of thought and language, and sex differences of the human brain.
Psychology; Science - Natural
Dist - FI **Prod** - WNETTV

The Two brains 60 MIN
U-matic / VHS
Brain series
Color (G)
$45.00, $29.95 purchase
Looks at what happens if the right and the left brain do not communicate. Explores the cortical hemispheres, the relationship between thought and language, and sex differences through research work with split - brain patients. Part of an eight - part series on the brain.
Psychology; Science - Natural
Dist - ANNCPB **Prod** - WNETTV 1984

Two Breaths to 7 MIN
16mm
Color
LC 80-700972
Dramatizes the danger of working in oxygen - deficient areas. Describes procedures which are essential for the prevention of injuries and accidents.
Health and Safety
Dist - USNAC **Prod** - USDOE 1979

Two breaths to 7 MIN
16mm / VHS / BETA / U-matic
Color; PAL (IND VOC)
PdS125, PdS133 purchase; LC 80-700972
Stress the precautions needed to reduce the chances of injury caused by inhaling toxic chemicals. Features animation.
Health and Safety; Science - Physical
Dist - EDPAT **Prod** - USDOE
USNAC

The Two brothers 8 MIN
VHS / U-matic
Timeless tales series
Color (P I)
$110.00, $160.00 purchase, $60.00 rental
Tells the story of two brothers who decide to leave home to see the world. Examines greed, honesty and love.
Guidance and Counseling; Literature and Drama
Dist - NDIM **Prod** - TIMTAL 1993

Two Brothers in Greece 15 MIN
U-matic / VHS / 16mm
Man and His World Series
Color (P I J H C)
LC 76-705472
Looks at two Greek brothers, one who remains in the village of Peloponnesus to continue farming thus helping his brother financially as he goes to engineering school, while the other runs a tourist boat through the Greek Isles.
Agriculture; Geography - World; Social Science
Dist - FI **Prod** - FI 1969

Two by Forsyth Series
A Careful man 26 MIN
Privilege 26 MIN
Dist - FOTH

Two castles 3 MIN
16mm
B&W
Emphasizes the aggression and futility of war by featuring a determined knight. Pictures the knight persisting in his attacks on another, apparently vacant castle across the valley. Shows that the harder he tries, the less fruit his actions bear. Illustrates the backfiring of his missiles damaging his own fortress.
Literature and Drama; Sociology
Dist - VIEWFI **Prod** - JANUS 1963

2 cats and a dog - Vol 1 - 2 koty i pies - Cz 1 59 MIN
VHS
Color (K P) (POLISH)
$17.95 purchase _ #V158
Shows that two old enemies, a cat and a dog, always find a way to solve their differences.
Fine Arts; Literature and Drama
Dist - POLART

Two Cents' Worth Series
Buy, buy, buy - economic choice 15 MIN
Changes - Casuality (History) 13 MIN
Don't feed the animals - law enforcement - political science 15 MIN
I Need Somebody - Interdependence 15 MIN
It Belongs to You and Me - Cultural Change (Anthropology - Sociology) 14 MIN
It's not the same - Change (History) 15 MIN
Let's Get Together - Culture (Anthropology - Sociology) 15 MIN
Lost and found - Spatial Relationships (Geography) 14 MIN
Play fair - voluntary compliance - political science 15 MIN
We're in this Together - Scarcity and Economic Choice (Economics) 15 MIN
What I Like - Spatial Interaction (Geography) 15 MIN
Which Way - Mapping - Geography 14 MIN
Why Can't I - Laws 15 MIN
Work, Work, Work - Income 15 MIN
Your choice - decision - making - anthropology - sociology 15 MIN
Dist - AITECH

Two centuries of Black American art 26 MIN
16mm
Color (I J H C)
LC 77-700588
Traces the African influences in the first Black art in America, the widening range of work produced in the slave era, the early struggles for serious recognition in the 19th century and the cosmopolitan backgrounds and important work of modern Black American artists.
Fine Arts; History - United States
Dist - MTP **Prod** - PHILMO 1976
PFP MOSCAR

Two Centuries of Service 29 MIN
16mm
Color
LC 76-702735
Emphasizes people - to - people assistance programs, research, development, medical advances and humanitarian efforts which have led to many of the conveniences in the 20th century.
History - World; Sociology
Dist - USNAC **Prod** - USA 1975

Two Children - Contrasting Aspects of Personality Development 20 MIN
16mm
Film Studies on Integrated Development Series
B&W (C T)
Shows the different ways two children respond during the lying - in period, and the influence of activity type on development from birth to eight years.
Education; Psychology; Sociology
Dist - NYU **Prod** - FRIWOL 1942

Two Cities - London and New York 23 MIN
16mm / U-matic / VHS
Comparative Cultures and Geography Series
Color (P I) (SPANISH)
LC 73-701415
Presents a comparison of the quality of life and the approach to urban problems of two Western Englishspeaking international capitals - London and New York. Describes their differences in ethnic make - up, cultural traditions, physical layout, community organization, benefits and problems.
Geography - United States; Geography - World; Social Science; Sociology
Dist - LCOA **Prod** - LCOA 1973

Two Conversations with Jack Burnett 15 MIN
16mm
Color
Serves as a special addendum to Jack's Story for teachers, parents, adult leaders and interested students. Explores Jack Burnett's views on his life, the safety program he pioneered, his philosophy of driver education and why he believes his efforts are more effective in instilling in young drivers a sense of responsibility.
Industrial and Technical Education; Psychology
Dist - MTP **Prod** - AMINS

Two Cops 27 MIN
U-matic / VHS / 16mm
Color (H C A)
Takes a look at two police officers on the job.
Civics and Political Systems; Social Science
Dist - CORF **Prod** - BRAVC 1977

Two - Creeley and McClure 5 MIN
16mm
Color (G)
$10.00 rental, $144.00 purchase
Presents portraits of two poets, Robert Creeley and Michael McClure, in relation to one another.
Literature and Drama
Dist - CANCIN **Prod** - BRAKS 1965

The Two - Cycle Engine 4 MIN
16mm / U-matic / VHS
Power Mechanics Series
Color (J)
LC 70-703243
Presents basic information about the theory, maintenance, and tune - up of a 2 - cycle engine.
Industrial and Technical Education
Dist - CAROUF **Prod** - THIOKL 1969

Two - D and 3 - Art 15 MIN
U-matic
Is the Sky Always Blue Series
Color (P)
Fine Arts
Dist - GPN **Prod** - WDCNTV 1979

Two - D Shapes 15 MIN
U-matic
Math Makers Two Series
Color (I)
Presents the math concepts of regular and irregular polygons, parallel lines and parellelograms.
Education; Mathematics
Dist - TVOTAR **Prod** - TVOTAR 1980

Two Deaths of Adolph Hitler 52 MIN
U-matic / VHS
World at War Specials Series
Color (H C A)
States that how Hitler ended his life is a matter surrounded by mystery even today. His German followers say he shot himself in the head with a pistol, a defeated leader's traditional, honorable way to avoid capture rather than with the coward's method, poison.
History - World
Dist - MEDIAG **Prod** - THAMES 1974

Two Deserts - Sahara and Sonora 17 MIN
U-matic / VHS / 16mm
Color; Captioned (I J H) (SPANISH)
Offers a comparison of Africa's Sahara and America's Sonora deserts. Shows how they are totally different in the ways their heat, aridness, and soil affect the lives of their inhabitants, despite their physical similarities.
Fine Arts; Geography - World
Dist - LCOA **Prod** - LCOA 1971

Two - dimensional composition 15 MIN
VHS / 16mm
Art - I - facts series
Color (I)
$125.00 purchase, $25.00 rental
Explains basic principles of composition in two - dimensional art. Explores using balance, emphasis, repetition and rhythms to convey ideas and feelings.
Fine Arts
Dist - AITECH **Prod** - HDE 1986

Two - Dimensional Echocardiography 9 MIN
U-matic / VHS
Color (PRO)
Demonstrates techniques for taking echocardiograms and outlines various uses for the tests. Covers three case studies.
Health and Safety; Science - Natural
Dist - HSCIC **Prod** - HSCIC 1984

Two - Dimensional Graphics 17 MIN
VHS / U-matic
All about Computer Graphics Series
Color (J A)
Examines the possibilities of flat graphics in business, industry and the professions. Discusses simulations, CAD/CAM interactive programing, animation and more.
Industrial and Technical Education; Mathematics
Dist - SRA **Prod** - SRA

A Two - dollar room 3 MIN
16mm
Color (G)
$5.00 rental
Defines the Depression as both an emotional and a historical term by providing a jarring glimpse of the interior of a depression - era room in the present and future. Produced by Jerome Carolfi.
Fine Arts; History - United States; Psychology
Dist - CANCIN

Two dollars and a dream 56 MIN
16mm / VHS
Color (H C G)
$850.00, $495.00 purchase, $85.00 rental
Portrays Madam C J Walker, the child of slaves freed by the Civil War who became America's first self - made millionairess. Interweaves social, economic and political history to offer a view of black America from 1867 to the 1930s. Reveals that Mrs Walker's fortune was built on skin and hair care products. She parlayed a homemade beauty formula into a prosperous business, marketing her products from coast to coast, and her daughter, A'Leilia Walker, was an important patron of the Harlem Renaissance. Produced by Stanley Nelson.
Biography; History - United States; History - World; Sociology
Dist - FLMLIB

A Two Edged Sword 60 MIN
U-matic / VHS
Through the Genetic Maze Series
Color (H C G T A)
Examines Tay Sachs disease fatal genetic disorder more prevalent among those of Jewish descent from central and eastern Europe than among the general population. Discusses carrier tests, amniocentesis, care issues, abortion, and the need for parent support groups.
Health and Safety; Religion and Philosophy; Science; Science - Natural
Dist - PSU **Prod** - PSU 1982

Two English girls - Les Deux Anglaises 130 MIN
VHS
Color (G)
$39.95 _ #TWO050
Looks at rapture and torment of romantic love and the eternal triangle. Adapts the novel by Henri - Pierre Roche in which turn - of - the - century sisters are in love with the same man. Produced by Les Films du Carrosse.
Fine Arts; Psychology; Religion and Philosophy
Dist - HOMVIS

Two Faces of Group Leadership 30 MIN
U-matic / VHS
Color
Makes it clear that group therapy is only as good as their leaders and leaders are only as good as their leadership skills.
Psychology
Dist - PSYCHF **Prod** - PSYCHF

The Two faces of ozone 15 MIN
VHS
Color (J H)
$89.95 purchase _ #49 - 1189 - V; $89.95 purchase _ #10040VG
Covers both the positive and the negative effects of ozone on the Earth. Uses live action, computer graphics and interviews with scientists to explain the causes of the depletion of Earth's ozone shield. Presents the steps recommended by scientists to deal with the problem. Includes a teacher's guide and blackline masters.
Science - Physical
Dist - INSTRU UNL **Prod** - UNL 1992

Two factories - Japanese and American 22 MIN
U-matic / VHS / 16mm
Comparative cultures and geography series
Captioned; Color (J H) (SPANISH)
Compares the lives of the workers at the Sylvania plant in Batavia, New York, with those at the MatsuShita electronics complex in Osaka, Japan. Points out contrasts in the ways these two concerns relate to the people who work for them.
Business and Economics; Geography - World; Industrial and Technical Education
Dist - LCOA **Prod** - LCOA 1974

Two families - African and American 22 MIN
16mm / U-matic / VHS
Comparative cultures and geography series
Color (P I) (SPANISH)
LC 73-702234
Shows how the family, the basic unit and essential strength of all societies, can vary dramatically in form, function and philosophy. Depicts two family structures, one in central West Africa and one in New York City, and explores what may account for their differences.
Geography - World; Guidance and Counseling; Social Science; Sociology
Dist - LCOA **Prod** - LCOA 1974

Two farms - Hungary and Wisconsin 22 MIN
U-matic / VHS / 16mm
Comparative cultures and geography series
Color (P I) (SPANISH)
LC 73-702232
Contrasts farm life in Wisconsin and southeastern Hungary following one family in each rural area through a daily routine. Features members of the families commenting on how their farms operate and what they find satisfying in their lives.
Social Science; Sociology
Dist - LCOA **Prod** - LCOA 1973

Two Feet Under the Roof 5 MIN
16mm
B&W
LC 75-700490
An experimental film which contrasts the visual qualities and texture of a New York City rooftop with the movements of a pair of legs in a confined apartment.
Fine Arts; Industrial and Technical Education; Sociology
Dist - CRAR **Prod** - CRAR 1975

Two films by Bill Creston 105 MIN
VHS
B&W (G)
$100.00 purchase
Features Kelsy, a portrait of artist, madman and street entrepreneur Denham Arthur Oswald Kelsey, III and The Indiana Tapes, an intimate portrait of a back country Indiana preacher and his family.
Fine Arts
Dist - CANCIN

Two films by Mary Filippo 19 MIN
VHS
B&W (G)
$50.00 purchase
Includes Who do you Think you Are and Peace O'Mind. Features the filmmaker playing a woman addicted to smoking, who feels guilty creating a film on that trivial subject instead of a profound social statement. Peace O'Mind looks at feeling safe at home and isolated there from the world and its problems. Produced between 1983 - 1987.
Fine Arts; Health and Safety; Psychology; Sociology
Dist - CANCIN

Two films - Chick Strand 22 MIN
VHS
Color (G)
$50.00 purchase
Includes Artificial Paradise and By The Lake. See individual titles for description and availability for rental in 16mm format.
Fine Arts
Dist - CANCIN **Prod** - STRANC 1986

Two films I never made 4 MIN
16mm
B&W (A)
$10.00 rental
Provides an example of minimalist cinema.
Fine Arts
Dist - CANCIN **Prod** - DEGRAS 1973

Two films - Marjorie Keller 14 MIN
VHS
Color; Silent (G)
$60.00 purchase
Offers By 2's and 3's - Women, which puts together a perspective on the unhappy experience of traveling in cars, an activity aimless and unmemorable. Describes Six Windows as a moody record of the filmmaker's home by the sea in which a pan and dissolve make a window of a wall on film. Produced between 1976 - 1979.
Fine Arts; Geography - World
Dist - CANCIN

Two films - Odyssey and Filmmaker 16 MIN
VHS
Color (G)
$45.00 purchase
Features two productions made in 1986 - 1987 by Barry J Hershey. See individual titles for description and availability for rental in 16mm format.
Fine Arts
Dist - CANCIN

Two films - Preview and Notes after long silence 26 MIN
VHS
Color (G)
$35.00 purchase
See individual titles for description and availability for rental in 16mm format.
Fine Arts
Dist - CANCIN **Prod** - LEVINE 1989

Two for ballet 57 MIN
VHS
Color (T PRO)
$350.00 purchase, $95.00 rental
Tells the story of the prolific choreographer - composer team of Eric Hyrst and Webster Young. Examines the working relationship of the two, observes Hyrst's rehearsals with the dancers and features excerpts from several of the ballets. Directed by John Axline and Thomas Frantz.
Fine Arts
Dist - CNEMAG

Two for Fox, Two for Crow 16 MIN
16mm
Color
Features Elanco products, presenting the case for continued use of pesticides and other agricultural chemicals. Discusses statistics on the huge increases in crop yields made possible by the widespread use of pesticides and on the crop and livestock losses that would occur if the use of all agriculture chemicals were stopped. Tours Elanco's research laboratory, showing the procedures for testing the safety and effectiveness of new chemical products.
Agriculture; Health and Safety
Dist - MTP **Prod** - LILLY 1972

Two for Glory 30 MIN
16mm
Color (A)
LC 81-700400
Tells how a frustrated young man, unsatisfied with his life, executes a desperate attempt to achieve fame and success.
Fine Arts
Dist - MIKAS **Prod** - MIKAS 1980

Two for the road 12 MIN
U-matic
Matter of time series
(A)
Focuses on two retired friends who meet and share a lunch. Each has suffered the loss of a spouse and has had to cope with numerous changes in personal relationships, notably with their children.
Sociology
Dist - ACCESS **Prod** - ACCESS 1980

Two for the show 22 MIN
16mm
Color
Traces the two - year growing and production cycle of roses at the Jackson and Perkins Company Wasco, California fields, including planting, budding, cultivating, harvesting, grading, packing and shipping.
Agriculture; Science - Natural
Dist - JACPER **Prod** - JACPER

Two gentlemen of Verona 137 MIN
U-matic / VHS
BBC's Shakespeare series
Color (H C A)
Presents William Shakespeare's play Two Gentlemen Of Verona, in which two good friends both find themselves in love with Silvia, daughter of the Duke of Milan, who has promised her to another.
Literature and Drama
Dist - TIMLIF INSIM AMBROS **Prod** - BBCTV BBC AMBROS 1984

Two Girls Called Eve 18 MIN
16mm / U-matic / VHS
Color (I J H C)
LC 73-703060
Demonstrates the relationship of two young girls about the age of nine. Uses no narration to follow a summer seaside friendship which faces everyday challenges experienced by most children.
Guidance and Counseling; Psychology; Sociology
Dist - MCFI **Prod** - POLSKI 1973

Two Girls Downtown Iowa 10 MIN
16mm
B&W
Fine Arts
Dist - EIF **Prod** - EIF 1973

Two girls go hunting 50 MIN
VHS
Under the sun series - Hamar trilogy
Color (A)
PdS99 purchase
Examines the Hamar, an isolated people living in the dry scrubland of southwestern Ethiopia. Concentrates on the proud and outspoken Hamar women. Duka and Gardi are close friends, each betrothed to a man she has never met. Follows both in the customary preliminaries to their marriages.
Psychology
Dist - BBCENE

Two good business ideas that failed
VHS
Business video series
$89.95 purchase _ #RPDGP6V; $89.95 purchase _ #DGP6
Tells the stories of two entrepreneurs who had good ideas, ambition, and energy, buty still didn't make their businesses survive. Hosted by Dick Goldberg.
Business and Economics
Dist - CAREER RMIBHF **Prod** - CAREER RMIBHF

Two grasslands - Texas and Iran 21 MIN
16mm / U-matic / VHS
Comparative cultures and geography series
Color (K P I) (SPANISH)
LC 76-710028
Features the Edwards Plateau in Texas and the steppes of Iran as grasslands similar in rainfall pattern and sparsity of vegetation. Uses dramatic photography and spontaneous comments by individuals in each area to reveal the interrelationship between land, technology and culture.
Geography - United States; Geography - World; Science - Natural; Social Science; Sociology
Dist - LCOA **Prod** - LCOA 1971

Two Great Crusades
U-matic / VHS
Color
History - United States
Dist - MSTVIS **Prod** - MSTVIS

Two Great Crusades - 1930 - 1945
U-matic / VHS
(J H C A)
$79.00 purchase _ #04585 94
Dramatizes the unheralded efforts of many Americans on the homefront during World War II. Focuses on the New Deal.
Fine Arts; History - United States
Dist - ASPRSS

Two grilled fish 13 MIN
16mm / U-matic / VHS
Color (J)
Presents a Celebration of the indestructibility of life in which a pair of drifters discover a tiny island while sailing their raft.
Fine Arts
Dist - TEXFLM **Prod** - UWFKD

Two guys named Mike 24 MIN
VHS
Color (A PRO IND)
$520.00 purchase, $150.00 rental
Trains field service representatives in customer service. Stresses the idea that service calls should be used to reinforce previous sales, maintain current accounts, and develop future business.
Business and Economics; Guidance and Counseling; Psychology
Dist - VLEARN **Prod** - DARTNL

Two hands, ten fingers - hand safety 11 MIN
BETA / VHS / U-matic
Color (IND G)
$395.00 purchase _ #600 - 16
Motivates employees to protect their hands by using tools correctly and by exercising care in materials handling and plant operations.
Health and Safety; Industrial and Technical Education; Psychology
Dist - ITSC **Prod** - ITSC

The Two - Headed Dragon 16 MIN
16mm
Screen news digest series; Vol 14; Issue 3
B&W (J)
LC 72-702750
Examines the struggle between Chiang Kai - Shek, leader of Nationalist China, and Mao Tse - Tung, leader of Communist China, for control of the country. Discusses the decision of the United Nations to seat the People's Republic of China and to expel the Nationalist Chinese government.
Civics and Political Systems; Geography - World; History - World
Dist - HEARST **Prod** - HEARST 1971

Two Hundred 3 MIN
16mm
Color (H C A)
LC 77-700045
Explores the themes of historical and contemporary American culture.
History - United States; Sociology
Dist - USNAC **Prod** - USIA 1975

Two Hundred Fifty Thousand Ways to Destroy a Child's Life Without Leaving Home 15 MIN
16mm / U-matic / VHS
Color (J)
Shows how the accidental poisoning of infants and children can be avoided at each stage of their development.
Guidance and Counseling; Health and Safety; Sociology
Dist - MCFI **Prod** - CORHUM 1975

Two Hundred Miles 29 MIN
16mm
Color
LC 80-701870
Presents five experts discussing the Fisheries Conservation and Management Act of 1976, which extended the United States fishing jurisdiction to 200 miles off the coast.
Civics and Political Systems; Industrial and Technical Education
Dist - USNAC **Prod** - NOAA 1980

Two Hundred Ninety - Nine Foxtrot 11 MIN
16mm
Color
LC 80-700516
Shows the last flyable B - 29 superfortress as it flies from the Naval air facility at China Lake to the aircraft 'Boneyard' at Barstow, California.
Civics and Political Systems; Industrial and Technical Education
Dist - USNAC **Prod** - USN 1977

Two - Hundred One - Two - Hundred Three 20 MIN
16mm
B&W (H C A)
LC FIA68-373
Presents two occupants of neighboring hotel rooms, one an occidental male, the other an oriental female. Follows the private fantasies of each as they see the other in terms of the myths wrought by Hollywood movies.
Guidance and Counseling; Psychology; Sociology
Dist - CFS **Prod** - SHAHK 1970

278 12 MIN
16mm
Color (G)
$35.00 rental
Transfers colorized video tape to film of cars on Route 278 in Brooklyn. Presents the screen as an electronic canvas where color merges with speeding machines. Produced by Roy Colmer.
Fine Arts
Dist - CANCIN

Two Hundred Twenty Blues 18 MIN
16mm / U-matic / VHS
Color (J H)
LC 71-712289
Questions the value of integration in a system that is run by whites. Tells the story of Sonny, a Black high school athlete who is looking forward to an athletic scholarship to sponsor his education in architecture and shows how Larry, a new black militant student, challenges Sonny's security in a white system. Describes how Sonny's integrated life is now torn between Black and white.
Guidance and Counseling; History - United States; Psychology; Sociology
Dist - PHENIX **Prod** - KINGSP 1970

Two hundred years of Mozart 30 MIN
VHS
Color (J H C G)
$39.95 purchase _ #NOR200V
Offers footage filmed in Salzburg and Vienna which examines the legend of Mozart and his music through paintings, drawings and hand - written scores within the context of today's Austria. Evolves around the rehearsal and performance of The Marriage of Figaro by a cast of international students in the Schonbrunn Palace Theatre.
Fine Arts
Dist - CAMV

Two if by Sea 27 MIN
U-matic / VHS / 16mm
Victory at Sea Series
B&W (J H)
Shows highlights of the Battles for Peleliu and Angour during World War II.
Civics and Political Systems; History - United States; History - World
Dist - LUF **Prod** - NBCTV

Two journeys - Pt 4 50 MIN
VHS
Diary of a Maasai village series
Color (G)
$350.00 purchase, $50.00 rental
Contrasts the journey of the new wife of Miisia back to his village with that of Tipaia to sell cattle for Rerenko's legal fees. Part of a five-part series by Melissa Llelewyn - Davis, her diary of a 7- week visit to a single village in Kenya - Tanzania. Examines a village life centered around the senior man - the most important prophet and magician - the Laibon, who has 13 wives living in the village, a large number of children, 20 daughters-in-law and 30 grandchildren.
Geography - World; History - World; Sociology
Dist - DOCEDR **Prod** - BBCTV 1984
BBCENE

Two Laws of Algebra 4 MIN
U-matic / VHS / 16mm
Color
Presents the associative and distributive processes in algebra by using animation to manipulate formulas.
Mathematics
Dist - PFP **Prod** - EAMES 1973

The Two Legged Spaceship 15 MIN
U-matic / VHS / 16mm
(P I)
$25 rental _ #9622
Shows cigarettes, alcohol, and drugs as forms of personal pollution.
Guidance and Counseling; Health and Safety; Psychology; Sociology
Dist - AIMS **Prod** - AIMS 1972

The Two - legged spaceship 15 MIN
U-matic / VHS / 16mm
Color (P I)
LC 76-702167
Presents a lesson in which a group of elementary school students learn about cigarettes, alcohol and drugs as forms of personal pollution as destructive as the pollution of the earth, the space ship of all humankind.
Guidance and Counseling; Health and Safety; Psychology; Sociology
Dist - AIMS **Prod** - DAVP 1972
AIMS

Two Lies 25 MIN
16mm
B&W (G)
$275.00 purchase, $70.00 rental
Studies sexual and generational conflict as well as the search for identity in a world of hybrid cultures. Focuses on Doris Chu, a recently divorced Chinese - American and her two daughters. When Chu has cosmetic surgery to make her eyes rounder and more 'American,' the younger daughter Esther is unconcerned and much more interested in the American Indian culture she is studying in school. However, teenaged Mei calls her mother's eyes 'two lies.' The story climaxes when the family journeys to a desert resort for Mrs Chu's recuperation.
Foreign Language; Industrial and Technical Education; Sociology
Dist - WMEN **Prod** - PAMTOM 1989

Two Little Frosts 13 MIN
16mm / U-matic / VHS
Color
LC 81-700936
Presents an animated story about two frost creatures who assume that an old peasant will be an easy target. Shows how, despite all their attempts, the experienced woodsman goes on about his work.
Fine Arts
Dist - PHENIX **Prod** - TRNKAJ 1973

Two Little Owls 20 MIN
16mm
Color
Shares a nest - side vigil watching the everyday events, neighbors and growth of two young great horned owl chicks as their parents care for them.
Science - Natural
Dist - BERLET **Prod** - BERLET 1983

The Two little soldiers 15 MIN
VHS
Short story series
Color (J H C)
LC 90-713151
Examines the consequences of betrayal of love in The Two Little Soldiers by French writer Guy de Maupassant. Part of a series which introduces American and European short story writers and discusses the technical aspects of short story structure.
Literature and Drama
Dist - GPN **Prod** - CTI 1978
IU IITC

The Two Little Soldiers by Guy De Maupassant 15 MIN
16mm / U-matic / VHS
Short Story Series
Color (J)
LC 83-700053
Explores the consequences of friendship betrayed, emphasizing the despair which can occur when one partner directs exclusive attention toward a third person whose friendship the two once shared. Based on the short story Two Little Soldiers By Guy de Maupassant.
Literature and Drama
Dist - IU **Prod** - IITC 1982

The Two lives of William Byrd 58 MIN
VHS
Color (G)
$89.95 purchase _ #EX2921
Examines the double life of William Byrd as both the Anglican court composer and the composer of Catholic sacred music.
Biography; Fine Arts; History - World
Dist - FOTH

Two marches 9 MIN
16mm
Color (G)
$30.00 rental
Juxtaposes scenes shot at two national gay marches on Washington DC to reveal some of the major changes in the gay movement from 1979 to 1987. Illustrates how hope is replaced by frustration with the AIDS epidemic and mourning.
Fine Arts; Health and Safety; Sociology
Dist - CANCIN

Two Marys 30 MIN
VHS
Skirt through history
Color; PAL (H C A)
PdS65 purchase
Features the lives of Mary Prince, a slave born in 1788, and Mary, Lady Nugent, the wife of a slave owner in 1801. Utilizes their writings to provide a first - hand account of slavery from a woman's perspective. Sixth in a series of six programs featuring women's history through their writing.
History - World; Sociology
Dist - BBCENE

Two masks - one face 60 MIN
U-matic / VHS
Art of being human series
Color (H C A)
Religion and Philosophy
Dist - FI **Prod** - FI 1978

Two men and a wardrobe - the fat and the lean 35 MIN
U-matic / VHS
B&W (J H C)
Presents a fantasy - parable elucidating the problems of maintaining a private life in the world today, an example of absurdism without dialogue. Uses the relationship between a vulgar, filthy man and his browbeaten servant to attack government tyranny and absurdity. Told in terms of broad comedy.
Civics and Political Systems; Social Science; Sociology
Dist - IHF **Prod** - IHF

Two Mikes don't make a wright 79 MIN
35mm
Color (G)
Presents Two Mikes Don't Make A Wright, a collection of pithy, political and humorous short films. Contains Pets or Meat - The Return to Flint in which Michael Moore, director, comments on what's happened to him and his

hometown of Flint, Michigan; A Sense of History, directed by Mike Leigh, features writer - actor Jim Broadbent as the 23rd Earl of Leete, a patriarch whose influence on his family and those serving his estate is horrifyingly funny; and The Appointments Of Dennis Jenning, directed by Dean Parisot.
Fine Arts; Literature and Drama
Dist - OCTOBF

The Two - Minute Drill 17 MIN
16mm
Color
Presents Fran Tarkenton who explains how sales and support people can apply the time management techniques of a premiere quarterback. Uses football footage to stress that time is the most precious ally.
Psychology
Dist - PROTC **Prod** - PROTC 1979

Two Minutes 2 MIN
16mm
Color (J H C)
Presents the history of the state of Israel told vividly and dramatically in still photos.
History - World; Industrial and Technical Education
Dist - SLFP **Prod** - STNIZ 1969

Two Minutes - the History of Israel in Two Minutes 3 MIN
16mm
Color (I)
A kaleidoscopic, almost subliminal survey of the history of Israel from 1938 - 1971, using over 500 still photos.
Fine Arts; History - World
Dist - CFS **Prod** - CFS

Two motels - and a few other things 9 MIN
VHS
Color (G)
$12.50 rental
Explores the distinctly American concept of motels and why people go to them. Features facades and exeriors that impose themselves in epic style. Produced by Jerome Carolfi.
Fine Arts
Dist - CANCIN

Two mothers - Pt 3 50 MIN
VHS
Diary of a Masai village series
Color (G)
$350.00 purchase, $50.00 rental
Focuses on gender relationships. Reveals that the principal events for Masai women are a 'coming out ox' ritual and the birth of a child; for the men the birth of a calf is the central theme. Part of a five -part series by Melissa Llelewyn - Davis, her diary of a 7-week visit to a single village in Kenya - Tanzania. Examines a village life centered around the senior man - the most important prophet and magician - the Laibon, who has 13 wives living in the village, a large number of children, 20 daughters-in-law and 30 grandchildren.
Geography - World; Social Science; Sociology
Dist - DOCEDR **Prod** - BBCTV 1984
BBCENE

Two mountainlands - Alps and Andes 15 MIN
16mm / U-matic / VHS
Comparative cultures and geography series
Color (I P) (SPANISH)
LC 72-710027
Shows how the Alps and the Andes Mountains are both similar and different through comments of people of each region and through photography.
Geography - World; Science - Natural; Social Science
Dist - LCOA **Prod** - LCOA 1971

Two Mountainlands - Alps and Andes 15 MIN
16mm / U-matic / VHS
Captioned; Color (I J H) (SPANISH)
Compares two different lifestyles through unrehearsed comments of the people and searching photography of the Alps and the Andes.
Geography - World
Dist - LCOA **Prod** - LCOA 1971

Two of a time 8 MIN
VHS / U-matic
Color (A PRO)
$200.00 purchase, $60.00 rental _ #4308S, 4308V
Dramatizes the story of two people with cancer, a man and a boy, who meet while fishing. The boy discusses his family's feelings toward his disease and how they have withdrawn, and that he has taken on the responsibility of protecting them. The man, who has a more bitter viewpoint toward his illness, is struck by the young boy's optimism and changes his attitude. Fosters open communication in dealing with the issue of cancer.
Health and Safety
Dist - AJN **Prod** - UFLA 1982

Two of Hearts 60 MIN
U-matic / VHS
Rainbow Movie of the Week Series
Color (J A)
Presents the story of a young black girl in desperate need of a kidney transplant who learns upon meeting her long - absent mother that she is really bi - racial.
Sociology
Dist - GPN **Prod** - RAINTV 1981

Two on one with Gene Mills 60 MIN
VHS
Wrestling videos series
Color (H C A)
$39.95 purchase _ #DP003V
Features Gene Mills covering two - on - one wrestling skills. Includes live - action demonstration of these skills.
Physical Education and Recreation
Dist - CAMV

Two on their own 23 MIN
U-matic / VHS
Color (I J H)
Tells the story of two high school girls from the suburbs of Philadelphia who take a day trip to New York against their parents' wishes. The girls end up stranded and afraid.
Guidance and Counseling; Psychology; Sociology
Dist - NGS **Prod** - NGS

Two or Three Things I Know about Her 85 MIN
16mm
Color (FRENCH (ENGLISH SUBTITLES))
Describes a Parisian housewife who turns part - time prostitute to make ends meet. Directed by Jean - Luc Godard. With English subtitles.
Fine Arts; Foreign Language
Dist - NYFLMS **Prod** - UNKNWN 1966

Two Original Open - Heart Operations 25 MIN
16mm
Color (PRO)
Presents two open - heart operations. Shows the repair of a rupture at the base of the aorta into the left atrium and the removal of a billiard ball - sized myxomatous tumor from the left ventricle.
Health and Safety; Science; Science - Natural
Dist - UPJOHN **Prod** - UPJOHN 1959

2 page R 3 MIN
16mm
Color (G)
$5.00 rental
Entertains with a rotoscope animation of people and the everyday timeless things humans do. Features an Ar Garfield production with sound by Lauren Weinger.
Fine Arts
Dist - CANCIN

Two - part series on AIDS series
AIDS - a nursing perspective - Pt 1 28 MIN
Dist - AJN

The Two - pencil technique 29 MIN
U-matic
Sketching techniques series; Lesson 2
Color (C A)
Reviews elements of drawing and introduces the two pencil technique. Demonstrates use of color to give drawings a finished look.
Fine Arts
Dist - CDTEL **Prod** - COAST

The Two philosophies of Wittgenstein 45 MIN
VHS
Men of ideas series
Color; PAL (H C A)
PdS99 purchase; Not available in Canada.
Explains in simple terms the main developments in Western philosophy from the 19th century to the present day. Features a contemporary thinker discussing his ideas on Wittgenstein with Bryan Magee. Part five of a fifteen part series.
Psychology; Religion and Philosophy
Dist - BBCENE

Two photographers - Wynn Bullock and Imogen Cunningham 29 MIN
16mm / VHS
Color (G)
$25.00 rental, $29.00 purchase
Reveals a dialogue between these two internationally known photographers. Looks at their work while they discuss their backgrounds, personal philosophies and their art in their own environment.
Fine Arts; Industrial and Technical Education
Dist - CANCIN **Prod** - PADULA 1967

Two Plus Six Minus 1 18 MIN
16mm
Color
LC 74-702898
A revealing look into the lives of eight teenagers, two who meet their need for companionship, acceptance and peer recognition through wholesome fun and activities and six who depend upon alcoholic beverages for their kicks.
Guidance and Counseling; Health and Safety; Psychology; Sociology
Dist - MARTC **Prod** - MARTC 1973

Two plus you - math patrol one series
Are you ready for a game 15 MIN
A Balance for everything 15 MIN
Fair Exchange 15 MIN
The Great train contest 15 MIN
A Hard Day's Work 15 MIN
Hot or cold 15 MIN
Mr Bean's Special Day 15 MIN
Mr Beans's New Games 15 MIN
Rain, Rain, Go Away 15 MIN
The Secret Message 15 MIN
The Stick that Helped 15 MIN
The Teddy Bear who Wanted to Go Home 15 MIN
Ten has its Place 15 MIN
The Treasure Trail 15 MIN
A Very Fine Line 15 MIN
Dist - TVOTAR

2.5 minutes to eternity - emergency ward evacuation 21 MIN
16mm / VHS / BETA / U-matic
Color; PAL (PRO)
Offers a training film for hospital staff which examines the evacuation of a ward when fire breaks out, including staff routes. Looks at the time a rescuer can spend moving each patient.
Health and Safety; Social Science
Dist - EDPAT

Two Ports
16mm
B&W
Introduces two - port network theory.
Mathematics
Dist - OPENU **Prod** - OPENU

Two - Position and Proportional Control
Software / BETA
Basic Process Control Series
Color (PRO)
$600.00 - $1500.00 purchase _ #IDTWO
Examines controller identification, functions and modes. Considers two - position and proportional control and gain. Part of a six - part series on basic process control. Interactive training system includes course administrator guide, videodisc and computer software.
Industrial and Technical Education; Psychology
Dist - NUSTC **Prod** - NUSTC

Two puppet shows 9 MIN
16mm / U-matic / VHS
Color (P I J)
Presents two mechanical puppet shows filmed at the IBM exhibit of the New York World's Fair. Explains with humor various aspects of computer operation.
Industrial and Technical Education
Dist - PFP **Prod** - EAMES 1965

Two Rescuer CPR 15 MIN
16mm / U-matic / VHS
REACT - Review of Emergency Aid and CPR Training Series
Color (H C A)
Health and Safety
Dist - CORF **Prod** - CORF

Two - rescuer CPR 9 MIN
U-matic / VHS
Cardiopulmonary resuscitation series
Color (PRO A)
Explains three ways CPR procedures should be varied with two rescuers instead of one.
Health and Safety
Dist - HSCIC **Prod** - HSCIC 1984

The Two Rivers 60 MIN
16mm / VHS
Color (C)
$895.00, $560.00 purchase, $125.00 rental
Provides the political and cultural background which exists behind the continuing tensions in South Africa. Features the poet Rashaka Ratshitanga who narrates a journey across time to teach about South African native heritage from before European settlements to the present time. Ratshitanga then presents modern South Africa and travels from his village to the gold mines and skyscrapers of Johannesburgh to the black ghettos and the heart of new African culture.

Civics and Political Systems; Geography - World; History - World; Sociology
Dist - ICARUS

Two roads to the Pamirs 55 MIN
VHS
Silk road II series
Color (J H C A)
$29.95 purchase _ #CPM1059V-S
Presents a video produced by China Central Television to provide sights, sounds, and historic dramas of historic and inaccessible locations on the fabled Silk Road. Features the art, culture, and history that live on in artifacts and the daily lives of the residents. Part of a series.
Geography - World
Dist - CAMV

Two roads to the Pamirs - Volume 12 60 MIN
VHS
Silk road series
Color (G)
$29.95 purchase _ #CMP1014
Visits the Pamirs along the fabled Silk Road linking Europe and China and traveled by Marco Polo. Features a soundtrack by Kitaro. Part of a series.
Geography - World; History - World
Dist - CHTSUI

Two rode together 109 MIN
U-matic / VHS / 16mm
Color
Tells the story of a Texas marshal and an idealistic Army officer who try to rescue whites captured by Indians. Stars James Stewart and Richard Widmark. Directed by John Ford.
Fine Arts; Geography - United States; History - United States
Dist - TIMLIF **Prod** - CPC 1961

Two rolls 2 MIN
16mm
Color (G)
$5.00 rental
Presents two 25 - foot rolls of unslit 8mm color film, with color and contrasting, backwards and upside - down movements.
Dist - CANCIN **Prod** - VARELA 1978

Two routes west 30 MIN
U-matic / VHS
Hidden places - where history lives
(G)
Follows the Missouri River and the overland route west. Explores frontier sites including Hollenberg Station, Kansas, Independence Rock in Wyoming, and the wreck of the steamboat Bertrand. Features actor Philip Abbot as the series host.
History - United States
Dist - GPN **Prod** - NETV 1981

Two - sample design
VHS
Probability and statistics series
Color (H C)
$125.00 purchase _ #8057
Provides resource material about two - sample design for help in the study of probability and statistics. Presents a 60 - video series, each part 25 to 30 minutes long, that explains and reinforces concepts using definitions, theorems, examples and step - by - step solutions to tutor the student. Videos are also available in a set.
Mathematics
Dist - LANDMK

Two - Sample Inference
U-matic / VHS
Statistics for Managers Series
Color (IND)
Describes two - sample inference as way of making fair comparisons between one's own products, or a comparison with your product and the competition. Discusses paired and unpaired sample designs. Covers how to use these designs and how to calculate the statistics.
Business and Economics; Mathematics; Psychology
Dist - COLOSU **Prod** - COLOSU

Two - Sample Tests for Quantitative Data 30 MIN
U-matic / VHS
Engineering Statistics Series
Color (IND)
Includes F test for comparing two variances as well as two - sample independent t and paired t tests. Says paired t is used to compare before and after results. Discusses comparison of results from two production lines for comparing independent samples. Emphasizes proper distinction and usage of non - independent and independent sampling.
Industrial and Technical Education; Mathematics; Psychology
Dist - COLOSU **Prod** - COLOSU

Two seconds to midnight 90 MIN
VHS
Color; PAL (G)
PdS99 purchase; Not available in the United States, Canada or Puerto Rico
Presents the natural history of Earth, from its original formation through to the mid - 21st century. Examines the long - term cycles of the planet until the arrival of humankind. Shows how humans could make the Earth a much cleaner, healthier place. Uses a combination of film and video graphic techniques to illustrate the rapid rise of humans on the planet.
Science - Natural
Dist - BBCENE

Two See 15 MIN
16mm
Color
LC 77-705704
A montage of the various aspects of training guide dogs for the blind, showing a dog's development from the time it leaves the care of a young boy to its final training as a guide dog by the Pilot Dog Organization.
Science - Natural
Dist - OSUMPD **Prod** - PIDO 1969

Two self - made multi - millionairesses 30 MIN
VHS / 16mm
(PRO G)
$89.95 purchase _ #DGP15
Tells the stories of Lillian Vernon and Mary Kay Ash, two of the most successful businesswomen in America. Hosted by Dick Goldberg.
Business and Economics
Dist - RMIBHF **Prod** - RMIBHF

Two short stories from Saki 39 MIN
VHS
Color; CC (I J H)
$24.95 purchase _ #33438
Adapts two short stories by Saki. Includes The Open Window and A Child's Play.
Literature and Drama
Dist - KNOWUN

Two sides of an island 21 MIN
VHS / 16mm
Color (G)
$175.00 purchase, $45.00 rental
Introduces Maifredes, a 10 - year - old boy who romps with his dog on Muisne island in the Pacific Ocean. Documents the island's poverty perpetuated from one generation to the next. Explains that Maifredes, smart and curious, hopes to attend college some day.
Fine Arts; Geography - World; Social Science; Sociology
Dist - FIRS **Prod** - JENKIN 1993

Two sisters - Tsvey shvester 82 MIN
35mm
B&W (G) (YIDDISH WITH ENGLISH SUBTITLES)
Tells the story of Betty Glickstein as she from the Lower East Side to the Bronx to Brooklyn, from young adolescence to middle age. Traverses through the course of her life in which she obeys her mother's dying wish - to take care of her younger sister. A tale of family conflict, of promise and suffering, sacrifice and abandonment. Contact distributor for rental price.
Religion and Philosophy; Sociology
Dist - NCJEWF

Two sleeping lions 5 MIN
16mm
Otto the auto - pedestrian safety series
Color (K P)
$30.00 purchase _ #145
Features Otto the Auto who warns not to cross between parked cars. Part of a series on pedestrian safety. Complete series available on
Health and Safety
Dist - AAAFTS **Prod** - AAAFTS 1957

Two Societies - 1965 - 1968 60 MIN
VHS
Eyes On The Prize - Part II - Series
Color; Captioned (G)
$59.95 purchase _ #EYES - 202
Probes the efforts of Martin Luther King Jr. and the Southern Christian Leadership Conference to organize in Chicago, shows how the political machine of Mayor Richard Daley resisted their efforts. Demonstrates clashes between blacks and police officers in Detroit. Part of a series on the black civil rights movement.
Civics and Political Systems; History - United States; Sociology
Dist - PBS **Prod** - BSIDE 1990

Two Space 7.5 MIN
16mm
B&W; Sound (C)
$179.20
Experimental film by Larry Cuba.
Fine Arts
Dist - AFA **Prod** - AFA 1979

Two steps at a time 8 MIN
16mm
B&W
Studies a young woman whose rehabilitation from an accident which resulted in the loss of both legs and one arm is complicated by her new family responsibilities with a newborn.
Health and Safety; Sociology
Dist - USC **Prod** - USC 1981

Two Steps to Safety 10 MIN
16mm
Personal Side of Safety Series
B&W
Discusses knowing yourself and your job as requisites to safety.
Business and Economics; Health and Safety
Dist - NSC **Prod** - NSC

Two Stories for Christmas 30 MIN
16mm
Color (K P)
Presents the stories of Christopher Mouse and When the Littlest Camel Knelt, done in cartoon art form.
Literature and Drama; Religion and Philosophy
Dist - YALEDV **Prod** - YALEDV

Two successful trial attorneys 30 MIN
VHS / 16mm
(PRO G)
$89.95 purchase _ #DGP46
Discusses the joys and personal costs of being a trial attorney. Reveals the unique nature of the profession. Features Dick Goldberg as host.
Business and Economics; Civics and Political Systems
Dist - RMIBHF **Prod** - RMIBHF

Two supermen with Jim and Bill Scherr 60 MIN
VHS
Wrestling videos series
Color (H C A)
$39.95 purchase _ #DP015V
Features Jim and Bill Scherr covering basic wrestling skills. Includes live - action demonstration of these skills.
Physical Education and Recreation
Dist - CAMV

Two sword forms 120 MIN
VHS
Color (G)
$39.95 purchase _ #1126
Pictures a Yang style of sword fighting, learned from William Chen, with front and side views, step by step instruction and fighting applications. Continues with an intermediate sword form developed by host Robert Klein. Beginning fighting exercises included.
Physical Education and Recreation
Dist - WAYF

Two tales from India - The king who talked too much and The old she - goat 15 MIN
VHS
Gentle giant series
Color (K)
LC 90712405
Uses two stories from India to teach children universal truths. Features stories from cultures throughout the world. Fifth of 16 installments of The Gentle Giant Series.
Health and Safety; Literature and Drama; Psychology
Dist - GPN **Prod** - CTI 1988

Two tars 30 MIN
16mm
Laurel and Hardy festival series
B&W (G)
LC 73-713145
Features two GOBS on shore leave, a rented Model T roadster, two girls, a traffic jam and a mile-long string of vintage automobiles in this comedy starring Laurel and Hardy.
Fine Arts
Dist - RMIBHF **Prod** - ROACH 1928
KITPAR
NCFP

Two - Team Pelvic Exenteration 33 MIN
16mm
Color (PRO)
Demonstrates total pelvic exenteration carried out by two surgical teams operating simultaneously through the perineum and abdomen. Includes positioning the patient, the pelvic lymph node dissection, the perineal dissection, the en bloc mobilization of the pelvic viscera and the construction of an ileal urinary conduit.
Health and Safety; Science
Dist - ACY **Prod** - ACYDGD 1959

The Two - Tenths Percent Solution 6 MIN
16mm
Color (A)
Describes the benefits and procedures for conducting fluoride mouth rinse programs in schools.
Health and Safety
Dist - MTP **Prod** - NIH

The Two Thanksgiving Day gentlemen 15 MIN
VHS
Short story series
Color (J H)
#E373; LC 90-713149
Presents an ironic tale about two men tied to tradition in 'The Two Thanksgiving Day Gentlemen' by O. Henry. Part of a 16 - part series which introduces American short story writers and discusses the technical aspects of short story structure.
Literature and Drama
Dist - GPN **Prod** - CTI 1978

The Two Thanksgiving Day Gentlemen by O Henry 15 MIN
U-matic / VHS / 16mm
Short Story Series
Color (J)
LC 83-700051
Tells the story of a special Thanksgiving Day feast given each year by an old man tied to tradition for a seemingly less fortunate man. Based on the short story The Two Thanksgiving Day Gentlemen by O Henry.
Literature and Drama
Dist - IU **Prod** - IITC 1982

Two that stole the moon - O dwoch takich co ukradii ksiezyc 110 MIN
VHS
Color (K P) (POLISH)
$17.95 purchase _ #V156
Offers a four - part animated series about twin brothers who run away from home in search of Lazyland.
Fine Arts; Literature and Drama; Sociology
Dist - POLART

Two - thousand and one - a youth movement 28 MIN
VHS
Illuminations series
Color (G R)
#V - 1006
Focuses on the youth organizations and involvement in the Greek Orthodox Church. Profiles each of the three Orthodox youth organizations.
Education; Sociology
Dist - GOTEL **Prod** - GOTEL 1988

2616 3 MIN
16mm
B&W (G)
$3.00 rental
Embarks on a sentimental journey to the filmmaker's old house in a student ghetto in Austin, Texas.
Fine Arts
Dist - CANCIN

Two Thousand Years in One Generation 20 MIN
16mm / U-matic / VHS
Communications Revolution Series
Color (H C A)
Explores the impact of new technology on developing nations and responsibilities that come with it.
Social Science; Sociology
Dist - CORF **Prod** - NVIDC

Two, three, fasten your ski 18 MIN
U-matic
Color (P I J)
Profiles three amputee patients at Children's Hospital in Denver who are enrolled in the hospital rehabilitation program for amputee skiers. Outlines the learning process for the children and the role of the skiing challenges in their recovery.
Health and Safety; Physical Education and Recreation; Psychology
Dist - CRYSP **Prod** - LENATK
PHENIX OAKCRK

Two, Three Fasten Your Ski 17 MIN
16mm / U-matic / VHS
Color (I J H C)
LC 72-702444
Tells the story of three amputee patients at Children's Hospital in Denver who are enrolled in the hospital's rehabilitation Amputee Ski School.
Health and Safety; Psychology
Dist - PHENIX **Prod** - OAKCRK 1972

Two Tibetan Buddhist nunneries 30 MIN
VHS / BETA
Color; PAL (G)
PdS20 purchase
Reveals that nunneries were once an inherent part of Tibetan culture but, since 1959, the tradition has almost died out. Visits the only two nunneries in exile - Tilokpur, where the great Indian master Tilopa meditated, and Dharamsala, near the home of the Dalai Lama. Examines the status of nunneries today, their role in preserving the tradition for the future and ways that benefactors can help them attain financial stability.
Fine Arts; Religion and Philosophy
Dist - MERIDT

Two to Get Ready 30 MIN
16mm
Footsteps Series
Color
LC 79-701559
Examines the various emotions which both parents experience during pregnancy, suggesting ways to resolve these feelings and prepare for the birth of the child and the role of a parent.
Sociology
Dist - USNAC **Prod** - USOE 1978

Two to Get Ready - Prenatal Preparation 23 MIN
16mm / U-matic
Footsteps Series
Color
Deals with the ways parents - to - be prepare for the birth of a child. Focuses on psychological preparation.
Health and Safety; Sociology
Dist - PEREN **Prod** - PEREN

Two towns - Gubbio, Italy and Chillicothe , Ohio 22 MIN
U-matic / VHS / 16mm
Comparative cultures and geography series
Color (P I) (SPANISH)
LC 73-701414
Explains that the towns of Gubbio in Italy and Chillicothe in southeastern Ohio are both agricultural centers of about 30 thousand people. Describes the different value systems based on historical, cultural and geographical considerations that have created different life styles. Shows scenes of daily routines.
Agriculture; Geography - United States; Geography - World; Social Science; Sociology
Dist - LCOA **Prod** - LCOA 1973

The Two Traditions 50 MIN
U-matic / VHS
Royal Shakespeare Company Series
Color
Explains how Shakespeare's heightened language and modern naturalistic expectations must be brought into balance if Shakespeare is to be meaningful. Deals with how to understand Shakespeare's texts, which were written 200 years before motivation and characterization entered the critical vocabulary.
Literature and Drama
Dist - FOTH **Prod** - FOTH 1984

Two variance goodness of fit and independence
VHS
Probability and statistics series
Color (H C)
$125.00 purchase _ #8051
Provides resource material about goodness of fit and independence for help in the study of probability and statistics. Presents a 60 - video series, each part 25 to 30 minutes long, that explains and reinforces concepts using definitions, theorems, examples and step - by - step solutions to tutor the student. Videos are also available in a set.
Mathematics
Dist - LANDMK

Two Wagons - both Covered 20 MIN
16mm
B&W
Stars Will Rogers in a satire of a wagon train movie.
Fine Arts
Dist - REELIM **Prod** - UNKNWN 1923

Two - way analysis of variance I
VHS
Probability and statistics series
Color (H C)
$125.00 purchase _ #8054
Provides resource material about two - way variance analysis for help in the study of probability and statistics. Presents a 60 - video series, each part 25 to 30 minutes long, that explains and reinforces concepts using definitions, theorems, examples and step - by - step solutions to tutor the student. Videos are also available in a set.
Mathematics
Dist - LANDMK

Two - way analysis of variance II
VHS
Probability and statistics series
Color (H C)
$125.00 purchase _ #8055
Provides resource material about two - way variance analysis for help in the study of probability and statistics. Presents a 60 - video series, each part 25 to 30 minutes long, that explains and reinforces concepts using definitions, theorems, examples and step - by - step solutions to tutor the student. Videos are also available in a set.
Mathematics
Dist - LANDMK

Two way ticket 156 MIN
VHS
Color; PAL (I J)
PdS30 purchase
Presents a series of six programs of 26 minutes each focusing on six youngsters who live in areas ranging from a mountain in Peru to an oasis in the Sahara. Shows that, though setting and cultures could not be more different, children can be surprisingly alike. Contact distributor about availability outside the United Kingdom.
Social Science; Sociology
Dist - ACADEM

Two ways of justice - Pt 2 50 MIN
VHS
Diary of a Maasai village series
Color (G)
$350.00 purchase, $50.00 rental
Reveals that young men are ritually prohibited from eating grain. Discloses that several of them steal one of the Laibon's goats and then must make reparations. Part of a five-part series by Melissa Llelewyn - Davis, her diary of a 7-week visit to a single village in Kenya - Tanzania which examines a village life centered around the senior man - the most important prophet and magician - the Laibon, who has 13 wives living in the village, a large number of children, 20 daughters-in-law and 30 grandchildren.
Civics and Political Systems; Geography - World; History - World; Sociology
Dist - DOCEDR **Prod** - BBCTV 1984
BBCENE

Two - Wheeler 17 MIN
16mm
Color (I)
Looks at the world of bicycle racing by following a race from the exhilarating start to the pressure and frustration of the finish.
Physical Education and Recreation
Dist - CRYSP **Prod** - OAKCRK

Two Witches 1 MIN
VHS / U-matic
Color
Explains, in a television spot featuring two different witches, that we are what we eat.
Health and Safety; Home Economics
Dist - KIDSCO **Prod** - KIDSCO

Two works by Peter Rose - Digital speech and The Pressures of the text 30 MIN
VHS
Color (G)
$35.00 purchase
Features Digital Speech, which uses a traveler's anecdote, a perverse variant of a Zen parable, to explore language, thought and gesture. Plays with the nature of narrative and with ways of telling, performing and illustrating and uses nonsense language, scat singing and video rescan for comic comment. The Pressures of the Text integrates direct address, invented languages, ideographic subtitles, sign language and simultaneous translation to investigate the feel and form of sense, the shifting boundaries between meaning and meaninglessness. Parodies art and criticism. 1983 - 1984.
English Language; Fine Arts; Foreign Language; Psychology; Social Science; Sociology
Dist - CANCIN

Two worlds 30 MIN
U-matic
Color (J H)
Discusses the position and condition of Native Americans today. Focuses on attempts to integrate Indians into mainstream American life.
Social Science
Dist - ADL

Two Worlds 30 MIN
U-matic
Visions - Artists and the Creative Process Series
Color (H C A)
Features Canadian Northwest Coast Indian artists and a potlatch ceremony of the Kwakiutl people.
Fine Arts; History - World
Dist - TVOTAR **Prod** - TVOTAR 1983

The Two worlds of Angelita 73 MIN
U-matic
Color (I G) (SPANISH (ENGLISH SUBTITLES))
LC 84-706138
A Spanish language videocassette with English subtitles. Relates the odyssey of a Puerto Rican family through the eyes of the nine - year - old daughter.
Geography - United States
Dist - FIRS **Prod** - FIRS 1983

The Two Worlds of Hong Kong 24 MIN
U-matic / VHS / 16mm
Color (J)
LC 80-700236
Explores the clash between the cultures of the East and the West as exemplified by the lives of two Hong Kong families. Shows how changing values can affect traditional lifestyles and strain strong family ties. Explores the street markets, the religious shrines and Hong Kong's busy harbor.
Geography - World; Sociology
Dist - NGS **Prod** - NGS 1979

Two Worlds to Remember 40 MIN
16mm / U-matic / VHS
Color (H C A)
LC 81-700932
Presents two elderly women, a widowed actress and a divorcee, who share their transition from previously independent lives to a Jewish home for the aged. Follows them through the sensitive process of adjustment and their attempt to keep the two worlds of the past and present in balance.
Health and Safety; Sociology
Dist - PHENIX **Prod** - JNSNP 1978

Two worlds touch - a ten - year - old Mayan boy's world 24 MIN
VHS
Color (P I J G)
$29.95 purchase _ #TW101
Presents a documentary filmed in 1990 on the life of ten - year - old K'ayum - Singing God, a Mayan - Lacandones boy in Chiapas, Mexico. Reveals that when the Spaniards arrived in southern Mexico, the Lacandones fled to the safety and isolation of the rainforest. They now number less than 500 and live on a million acres of threatened land in Chiapas. Records the relationship between K'ayum and his grandfather, Chan - Kin Jorge, as they plant and gather in the forest, catch armadillos, fish and prepare food. Shows earthmovers and chainsaws - the 'advance' of a 'civilization' which threatens the traditional life of the Lacondones. Produced by Mark Hall.
Geography - World; Social Science; Sociology
Dist - ENVIMC

Two worlds - twenty years 29 MIN
16mm
B&W (J H G)
LC 74-705868
Compares two countries, Belgium and Czechoslovakia, each having a similar economy and a language problem. Shows how the two countries, devastated by war, have fared over the past 20 years, Belgium with a free economy under NATO and Czechoslovakia as a satellite of the USSR.
Business and Economics; Civics and Political Systems; Geography - World; History - World; Sociology
Dist - USNAC **Prod** - NATO

A Two - Year - Old Goes to Hospital; Abridged ed. 30 MIN
16mm
B&W
Features the abridged version of the film showing the behavior of a two - year - old during her eight day stay in a hospital ward as part of a study of the effects of maternal deprivation. Omits much of the research detail of the original to leave a pure narrative.
Health and Safety; Home Economics; Psychology; Sociology
Dist - NYU **Prod** - NYU
PSU ROBJJ

A Two - Year - Old Goes to Hospital 50 MIN
16mm
B&W
Shows the behavior of a two - year - old during a stay of eight days in a hospital ward as part of a study of the effects of maternal deprivation.
Health and Safety; Home Economics; Psychology; Sociology
Dist - NYU **Prod** - NYU

Two Years Before the Mast
Cassette / 16mm
Now Age Reading Programs, Set 3 Series
Color (I J)
$9.95 purchase _ #8F - PN682944
Brings literature to young readers. Filmstrip set includes filmstrip, cassette, corresponding book, classroom exercise materials and a poster. The read - along set includes student activity book, cassette and paperback.
English Language; Literature and Drama
Dist - MAFEX

Two Years or more 27 MIN
U-matic / VHS / 16mm
Color
LC 78-714345
Portrays the life of a prison inmate in both an old and a modern Canadian penitentiary.
Geography - World; Sociology
Dist - IFB **Prod** - NFBC 1970

Two Yosemites 10 MIN
VHS
Color (G)
$125.00 purchase, $10.00 rental
Reveals that in 1914 the scenic twin of Yosemite Valley, Hetch Hetchy, was flooded to provide electricity for San Francisco. Discloses that the waterfalls of both valleys originally plunged down to meadows, woodlands and clear streams but that those of Hetch Hetchy are now lost. Expresses regret that the natural resource was taken away from the public. Includes the artistic photography of David Brower which records the lost Yosemite.
History - United States; Industrial and Technical Education; Science - Natural
Dist - CMSMS **Prod** - SIERRA 1967

Two's Company - Three's a Crunch 49 MIN
VHS / U-matic / 16mm
Inquiry Series
Color; Mono (H C A)
MV $350.00 _ MP $600.00 purchase, $50.00 rental
Explores the issue of Canada's changing attitude toward its immigration policy.
History - World
Dist - CTV **Prod** - CTV

Twyla Tharp - Making Television Dance 58 MIN
U-matic / VHS / 16mm
Color (H C A)
LC 81-700805
Explores the relationship between the complex technology of television and the realm of dance. Highlights a new work entitled Country Dances, featuring Twyla Tharp, Tom Rawe, Jennifer Way, Shelley Washington and Christine Uchida. Includes Twyla Tharp and Mikhail Baryshnikov rehearsing a work entitled Once More Frank.
Fine Arts
Dist - PHENIX **Prod** - THARPT 1980

Twyla Tharp - making television dance - Pt 1 29 MIN
U-matic / VHS / 16mm
Color (H C A)
LC 81-700805
Explores the relationship between the complex technology of television and the realm of dance. Highlights a new work entitled Country Dances, featuring Twyla Tharp, Tom Rawe, Jennifer Way, Shelley Washington and Christine Uchida. Includes Twyla Tharp and Mikhail Baryshnikov rehearsing a work entitled Once More Frank.
Fine Arts
Dist - PHENIX **Prod** - THARPT 1980

Twyla Tharp - Making Television Dance, Pt 2 29 MIN
16mm / U-matic / VHS
Color (H C A)
LC 81-700805
Explores the relationship between the complex technology of television and the realm of dance. Highlights a new work entitled Country Dances, featuring Twyla Tharp, Tom Rawe, Jennifer Way, Shelley Washington and Christine Uchida. Includes Twyla Tharp and Mikhail Baryshnikov rehearsing a work entitled Once More Frank.
Fine Arts
Dist - PHENIX **Prod** - THARPT 1980

Txai macedo 50 MIN
VHS / 16mm
Color (G)
$390.00 purchase, $75.00 rental
Reveals the problems encountered by inhabitants of the Alto Jurua Reserve in the State of Acre in Brazil's Amazon Rain Forest. Profiles Antonio Macedo, who leads an alliance of Indian and White rubber tappers in a fight against rubber barons, land owners, drug lords and the legal system which protects them. Produced by Marcia Machado and Tal Danai.
Fine Arts; Social Science; Sociology
Dist - FIRS

Tycoon 85 MIN
U-matic / VHS / 16mm
Color (I J H C)
Stars John Wayne in a tale of romance and engineering in the Andes of South America, where an American engineer battles against mountain and river to build a railroad.
Geography - World; Literature and Drama
Dist - FI **Prod** - RKOP 1947

Tycoons series
Presents 13 videos that tell how internationally known millionaires began and developed their business interests, with some information about their personalities and interests. Includes videos on Lars - Erik Magnusson, Wolfgang Joop, Gordon Wu, Richard Branson, Dr Stanley Ho, Niki Lauda, Robert and Georgette Mosbacher, Philip Knight, Karl Lagerfeld, Malcolm Forbes, Dr Ivo Pitanguy, Anita Roddick and Robert Mondavi.

Anita Roddick - the Body Shop, London, England 47 MIN
Dr Ivo Pitanguy 47 MIN
Dr Stanley Ho - Hong Kong 47 MIN
Gordon Wu - hopewell holdings, Hong Kong 47 MIN
Karl Lagerfeld - fashion designer, Paris, France 47 MIN
Lars - Erik Magnusson - Larmag Investment Group, Amsterdam, Holland 47 MIN
Malcolm Forbes - Forbes Magazine, USA 47 MIN
Niki Lauda - Lauda Air, Vienna, Austria 47 MIN
Philip Knight - Nike, Oregon 47 MIN
Richard Branson 47 MIN
Robert and Georgette Mosbacher - USA 47 MIN
Robert Mondavi - Robert Mondavi Winery, USA 47 MIN
Wolfgang Joop - Joop, Hamburg, Germany 47 MIN
Dist - LANDMK

Tyger, Tyger Burning Bright Series
Limericks for Laughs 15 MIN
The Ordinary Can be Extraordinary 15 MIN
Weave a Web of Mystery 15 MIN
Dist - CTI

Tying the knot 26 MIN
16mm
Winston Churchill - the valiant years series; No 24
B&W
LC FI67-2120
Uses documentary footage to describe Churchill's meeting with Roosevelt aboard the USS Quincy in Alexandria Harbor, the first crossing of the Rhine at Remagen Bridge, British opposition to Eisenhower's plan to let the Russians enter Berlin and the death of Roosevelt. Based on the book The Second World War by Winston S Churchill.
Civics and Political Systems; History - World
Dist - SG **Prod** - ABCTV 1961

Tying Trout Flies 60 MIN
VHS / BETA
From the Sportsman's Video Collection Series
Color
Teaches techniques of tying dry flies, nymphs and streamers quickly and easily at one's own pace. Illustrates 90 percent of all trout fly tying techniques.
Physical Education and Recreation
Dist - CBSC **Prod** - CBSC

Tympani 30 MIN
U-matic / BETA / VHS
Color; Stereo (J H G)
Demonstrates Laura Dean's choreography, which uses complex rhythms and geometrical patterns to create dance works.
Fine Arts
Dist - UCV **Prod** - TCPT 1980

Tyner - Shared Parenting 25 MIN
U-matic
Color (C A)
LC 81-706226
Shows how a mother and father share the early rearing of their four - month - old child between themselves and an infant day - care center.
Home Economics; Sociology
Dist - CORNRS **Prod** - CUETV 1981

Type A personality and heart disease 30 MIN
U-matic / VHS
Here's to your health series
Color (C T)
Discusses the Type A personality. Suggests ways of controlling related behavior to minimize health risks.
Health and Safety; Psychology; Science - Natural
Dist - DALCCD **Prod** - DALCCD

Type I diabetes - one man's story as student, husband, father 40 MIN
VHS / U-matic
Color (G C)
$195.00 purchase _ #C900 - VI - 059
Discusses Type I - juvenile - onset - diabetes. Features Mike who describes his experiences with diabetes as a child, teenager, college student and parent. Covers family and peer relations, motivation factors and relations with healthcare professionals. Presented by Dr Norman Solar, Joan Feltovich and Linda McCall, RN, Springfield Diabetes and Endocrine Center and Southern Illinois School of Medicine.
Guidance and Counseling; Health and Safety
Dist - HSCIC

Type II Diabetes - a Stranger in Your Midst 24 MIN
VHS
Color (G PRO)
$195.00 purchase _ #N900VI042
Presents a man and a woman with Type II diabetes who discuss how the disease has affected their lives. Includes symptoms, treatment, diet, the aspect of family support, as well as how the two patients solved problems and made decisions about their condition. Considers that a person stricken with diabetes may not deal well with the situation because of past experience, the severity of the symptoms, the significance of the changes required in lifestyle, and the way the treatment plan is presented to the patient.
Health and Safety; Psychology; Science - Natural
Dist - HSCIC

Type it up series
Column centering 14 MIN
Help yourself learn the keyboard 10 MIN
How to get started 13 MIN
Learn the Typewriter Parts - Pt 1 10 MIN
Learn the Typewriter Parts - Pt 2 11 MIN
A Quick Review 10 MIN
Dist - ACCESS

Type on call from Adobe - 8 fonts
CD-ROM
Color (G A)
$229 .00 purchase _ #1751b
Offers the entire Adobe Type Library on CD - ROM. Delivers the fonts locked but can be unlocked with an access code purchased by telephone. Initial purchase includes disc, Adobe Type Manager - including 13 fonts - bitmaps - screen fonts to all the fonts included on the disc and access to eight typeface packages. For Macintosh Plus, SE and II computers. Requires at least one M of RAM, one floppy disk drive, and an Apple compatible CD - ROM drive.
Industrial and Technical Education
Dist - BEP

Type on call from Adobe - 2 fonts
CD-ROM
Color (G A)
$59.00 purchase _ #1751a
Offers the entire Adobe Type Library on CD - ROM. Delivers the fonts locked which can be unlocked with an access code purchased by telephone. Initial purchase includes disc, Adobe Type Manager - including 13 fonts - bitmaps - screen fonts to all the fonts included on the disc and access to two typeface packages. For Macintosh Plus, SE and II computers. Requires at least one M of RAM, one floppy disk drive, and an Apple compatible CD - ROM drive.
Industrial and Technical Education
Dist - BEP

Type Two Diabetes - a New Approach to Patient Management 31 MIN
U-matic / VHS
Color (PRO)
Demonstrates changes in insulin secretion and in insulin resistance that lead to the development of Type II or ketosis - resistant diabetes mellitus. Illustrates the interrelationships among changes in insulin resistance, insulin secretion and blood glucose concentration. Presents a short - term therapeutic intervention that will enhance the chances of preserving part of the patients' endogenous glucose regulatory system and long - term blood sugar control.
Health and Safety
Dist - UMICHM **Prod** - UMICHM 1983

Type Z - an alternative management style 95 MIN
BETA / 16mm
Color (A PRO)
Presents William G Ouchi, professor at UCLA Graduate School of Management, explaining his Type Z theory of management. Describes the American and Japanese approaches to management, puts them in their cultural contexts and discusses how American companies could profitably borrow techniques from the Japanese.
Business and Economics
Dist - CBSFOX **Prod** - CBSFOX

Types of Adjustments for Auto Door Glass 9 MIN
BETA / VHS / 16mm
Color (A PRO)
$58.50 purchase _ #KTI71
Presents types of adjustments for auto door glass. Demonstrates the componenents of mechanism and adjustment procedures.
Industrial and Technical Education
Dist - RMIBHF **Prod** - RMIBHF

Types of Breeding Programs, Low Cost Swine Breeding Units, and Breeding Management 19 MIN
U-matic / VHS
Color
Looks at alternative breeding programs for swine production and the requirements and advantages of implementing each method. Discusses the facilities and equipment needed for breeding, the management practices for newly - purchased stock and proper management during breeding.
Agriculture
Dist - HOBAR **Prod** - HOBAR

Types of Chemical Change 13 MIN
U-matic / VHS / 16mm
Introducing Chemistry Series
Color (J)
$325, $235 purchase _ #1667
Shows four different kinds of chemical reactions.
Science - Physical
Dist - CORF

Types of Controllers 30 MIN
U-matic / VHS
Digital Sub - Systems Series
Color
Shows in depth look at controller types from previous session design examples. Emphasizes hardware implementation.
Industrial and Technical Education; Mathematics; Sociology
Dist - TXINLC **Prod** - TXINLC

Types of Financial Aid 25 MIN
VHS / U-matic
(J H A)
$98.00 _ #CD6200V
Introduces the six main kinds of financial assistance, including grants, scholarships, part time employment, military assistance, loans, and personal and family funds. Includes accompanying reproducible worksheets.
Education
Dist - CAMV **Prod** - CAMV

Types of Financial Aid
BETA / VHS / U-matic
Paying for College Series
Color (H G)
#TAV 102
Covers the basics of financial aid, such as employment, loans, grants and scholarships. Comes with worksheets.
Business and Economics; Guidance and Counseling
Dist - CADESF **Prod** - CADESF 1988

Types of Floors 12 MIN
16mm / U-matic
Housekeeping Personnel Series
Color (IND)
LC 72-701689
Presents the types of floors commonly found in health care facilities, stressing the proper cleaning and maintenance of each type.
Health and Safety; Home Economics
Dist - COPI **Prod** - COPI 1972

Types of Inmates 31 MIN
16mm / U-matic / VHS
Penitentiary Staff Training Series
B&W (PRO)
LC FIA67-1172
A film for the Department of Justice. Categorizes prison inmates to show guards how the behaviour of an inmate relates to his crime.
Psychology; Sociology
Dist - IFB **Prod** - NFBC 1966

Types of maps 18 MIN
VHS
Geography tutor series
Color (J H C G)
$49.95 purchase _ #BM102V-S
Explains various types of maps and map projections and how they are used. Illustrates covered topics which are referenced through an on-screen digital timer. Includes teacher's guide and glossary. Part of a six - part series on geography.
Geography - World; Social Science
Dist - CAMV

Types of maps 20 MIN
U-matic
Map and globe skills series
Color (I J)
Shows professionals talking about the use of maps in their work. Describes possible advancements and developments in mapmaking.
Geography - World; Social Science
Dist - GPN **Prod** - WCVETV 1979

Types of maps and map projections 18 MIN
VHS
Geography tutor series
Color (J H)
$49.00 _ #60457 - 026
Features part of a six - part series on geography with illustrated terms, concepts and site studies to reinforce specific content. Includes teacher's guide.
Education; Geography - World
Dist - GA

Types of Paint Finishes 13 MIN
VHS / BETA / 16mm
Color (A PRO)
$68.50 purchase _ #AB164
Explains the difference between lacquer and enamel and the advantages and disadvantages of both. Describes the characteristics of enamels and lacquers.
Industrial and Technical Education
Dist - RMIBHF **Prod** - RMIBHF

Types of Shorelines 8 MIN
VHS
Color (C PRO)
$34.95 purchase _ #193 E 2078
Develops shorelines of submergence and depicts such featues as sea cliffs, estuaries, sea caves, stacks. Teacher's guide provided.
Science - Physical
Dist - WARDS

Types of shorelines 8 MIN
VHS
Geology stream table series
Color (H C)
$24.95 purchase _ #S9011
Discusses types of shorelines in a single - concept format, using models and NASA footage. Part of a 12 - part series on stream tables.
Geography - World; Science - Physical; Social Science
Dist - HUBDSC **Prod** - HUBDSC

Types of Suicide Adolescents, Pt 2 50 MIN
VHS
Teenage Suicide Series
Color (H)
LC 90712869
Considers teenage personality types who might attempt suicide. Describes environmental conditions which may contribute to attempted suicide. Presents concerns adolescents express about themselves and others. Related issues in education and psychology are examined. Part of a series.
Health and Safety; Psychology; Sociology
Dist - GPN

Typesetting 17 MIN
VHS
Color (H C)
$59.95 purchase _ #SE - 9
Covers five areas of typesetting - markup, typesetting, processing, proof reading and editing. Discusses the basics of pasteup, as well as information on point sizes, indents, runarounds, tabs, advance and reverse leading, character compensation, kerning, flash commands, set size, ruling program, search and replace function and more.
Industrial and Technical Education
Dist - INSTRU

Typewriter techniques 12 MIN
16mm
Color (J H)
Analyzes the action of electric typing as compared to manual typing and then describes the manipulative parts of the manual machine - the function and purpose of the space bar and the tabulator, setting the margin and responding to the bell. Closely analyzes the various functions of the back spacer, the carriage release, the line finder, the margin release and the variable button. Further demonstrations show the location of numbers and their operation.
Business and Economics; Industrial and Technical Education
Dist - SF **Prod** - SEF 1968

Typewriting (Pertaining to Stefan Brecht) 2 MIN
16mm
B&W; Silent; Sound (C)
$100.00
Experimental film by Stuart Sherman.
Fine Arts
Dist - AFA **Prod** - AFA 1982

Typewriting, Unit 2 - Skill Development Series
Skill Drills - Paragraph Centering, Block Centering, Spread Centering 30 MIN
Skill Drills - Vertical and Horizontal Centering, Typing all Capitals 30 MIN
Dist - GPN

Typhoid Mary 50 MIN
VHS
Timewatch series
Color; PAL (G)
PdS99; Available only in the U K and Eire
Reviews the case of New York cook Mary Mallon as a typhoid carrier and that case's role in provoking changes in the medical establishment's view on the transmission of diseases. Explores the contemporary relevance in light of the AIDS epidemic.
Health and Safety
Dist - BBCENE

Typical Appearance and Behavior of Newborns 20 MIN
VHS / U-matic
Color (H C A)
Gives parents basic information about the physical signs and behavior of newborns. Explains that some may seem unusual or abnormal, but are common.
Health and Safety; Home Economics
Dist - UARIZ **Prod** - UARIZ

Typical Frame Damage 6 MIN
VHS / 16mm
(A PRO)
$51.00 purchase _ #KTI90
Shows typical rear and front end damages. Examines yield point by yield point.
Industrial and Technical Education
Dist - RMIBHF **Prod** - RMIBHF

Typical Instrumentation Diagrams, Loop Diagrams 60 MIN
VHS / U-matic
Instrumentation Basics - Instrumentation Diagrams and Symbols Series'Tape 2; Instrumentation diagrams and symbols; Tape 2
Color (IND)
Industrial and Technical Education; Mathematics
Dist - ISA **Prod** - ISA

Typical Process Reactions 60 MIN
VHS
Basic Theory and Systems Series
Color (PRO)
$600.00 - $1500.00 purchase _ #RCTPR
Introduces the purposes of various reactions which occur in process systems. Discusses the concepts of inorganic reactions. Covers organic reactions such as alkylation, polymerization, halogenation and hydrogenation. Part of a twenty - four - part series on basic theory and systems. Includes ten textbooks and an instructor guide to support four hours of instruction.
Education; Industrial and Technical Education; Psychology; Science - Physical
Dist - NUSTC **Prod** - NUSTC

Typing a Resume 8 MIN
BETA / VHS
Color
Business and Economics; Guidance and Counseling
Dist - RMIBHF **Prod** - RMIBHF

Typing - Insurance Series

Insurance Abstracting	7 MIN
Insurance Typewriting - Auto Insurance	12 MIN
Insurance Typewriting - Fire Insurance	7 MIN
Insurance Typewriting - Health Insurance	7 MIN
Insurance Typewriting - Homeowner's Insurance	11 MIN
Insurance Typewriting - Inland Marine Insurance	10 MIN
Insurance Typewriting - Introduction	4 MIN
Insurance Typewriting - Life Insurance	10 MIN

Dist - RMIBHF

Typing - Legal Series

Legal Typing - a Lawyer Defines a Good Legal Secretary	11 MIN
Legal Typing - Course Introduction	17 MIN

Dist - RMIBHF

Typing - Medical Series

Medical Assistant's Transcribing	6 MIN
Medical Transcribing	8 MIN
Medical Typing - Consultation Report	4 MIN
Medical Typing - Discharge Summary or Clinical Resume	6 MIN
Medical Typing - Electroencephalogram	6 MIN
Medical Typing - Filing Rules	10 MIN
Medical Typing - History and Physical	12 MIN
Medical Typing - Introduction	6 MIN
Medical Typing - Laboratory	17 MIN
Medical Typing - Medical Records	12 MIN
Medical Typing - Operative Report	4 MIN
Medical Typing - Radiology	16 MIN
Problem - Oriented Medical Record	4 MIN

Dist - RMIBHF

Tyrannus Nix 12 MIN
16mm
Color (H C A)
Presents a case against Richard Nixon, narrated by American poet Lawrence Ferlinghetti. Describes Nixon as 'a computerized man, a war machine who betrays the American dream.'
Biography; Civics and Political Systems; Literature and Drama
Dist - NYFLMS **Prod** - NYFLMS

The Tyranny of control - discussion 30 MIN
U-matic / VHS / 16mm
Free to choose discussion series
Color (H C A)
Offers a debate among Dr Milton Friedman and others on government protection of domestic industry.
Business and Economics
Dist - EBEC **Prod** - EBEC 1983

The Tyranny of control - documentary 30 MIN
U-matic / VHS / 16mm
Free to choose documentary series
Color (H C A)
Presents case studies of both free and controlled societies which support Dr Milton Friedman's argument against protection of domestic industry.
Business and Economics
Dist - EBEC **Prod** - EBEC 1983

The Tyranny of the Majority - Pt 4 58 MIN
VHS
Struggle for Democracy Series
Color (S)
$49.00 purchase _ #039 - 9004
Explores the concept of democracy and how it works. Features Patrick Watson, author with Benjamin Barber of 'The Struggle For Democracy,' as host who travels to more than 30 countries around the world, examining issues such as rule of law, freedom of information, the tyranny of the majority and the relationship of economic prosperity to democracy. Part 4 examines majority - minority conflicts in three democratic societies - the United States, Australia, and Northern Ireland, and considers the words of Alexis de Tocqueville, the 'tyranny of the majority' poses the greatest threat to individual liberties.
Civics and Political Systems; Geography - World; History - United States; History - World; Sociology
Dist - FI **Prod** - DFL 1989

Tyrants will rise from my tomb 60 MIN
VHS / U-matic
Sweat of the sun tears of the moon series
Color (S C A)
$295.00 purchase
Focuses on Bolivia, where the prophetic words of the title were uttered by Simon Bolivar, the liberator of South America. Today, in 1986, Bolivia is politically unstable and still seeking an alternative to dictatorial government. Also covers politics in Chile, which is run by the military.
Geography - World; History - World
Dist - LANDMK **Prod** - LANDMK 1986

Tyrants will rise from my tomb - Bolivia 30 MIN
VHS / U-matic
Sweat of the sun tears of the moon series
Color (H C A)
$295.00 purchase
Focuses on Bolivia, where the prophetic words of the title were uttered by Simon Bolivar, the liberator of South America. Today, in the early 1980s, Bolivia is politically unstable and still seeking an alternative to dicatorial government. Edited classroom version.
Geography - World; History - World
Dist - LANDMK **Prod** - LANDMK 1983

Tyrants will rise from my tomb - Chile 30 MIN
VHS / U-matic
Sweat of the sun tears of the moon series
Color (H C A)
MV=$295.00
Shows that South American countries still share factors which encourage a 'strongman' type of leadership. Portrays Chilean politics, which in the early 1980s is run by the military. Edited classroom version.
Geography - World; History - World
Dist - LANDMK **Prod** - LANDMK 1983

Tyrone Guthrie 30 MIN
16mm
Creative Person Series
B&W (H C A)
Presents theatrical director Tyrone Guthrie, his ideas and methods of working. Shows him at home in Ireland, conducting a rehearsal in New York and talking with students at an American college. Guthrie discusses his general philosophy toward the theater as a medium.
Fine Arts; Literature and Drama
Dist - IU **Prod** - NET 1967

Ty's home - made band 20 MIN
VHS / BETA
Color
Tells the story of a traveling minstrel teaching a boy how to make music from home - made instruments. Based on the book by Mildred Pitts Walter.
Fine Arts; Literature and Drama
Dist - PHENIX **Prod** - PHENIX

Ty's one man band 30 MIN
U-matic / VHS
Reading rainbow series; No 15
Color (P)
Presents Lou Rawls narrating the story of a mysterious stranger who creates a one - man band out of odds and ends. Shows LeVar Burton discovering lots of different music and Ben Vereen dancing.
English Language; Fine Arts; Literature and Drama
Dist - GPN **Prod** - WNEDTV 1982

TZ 8.5 MIN
16mm
Color (C)
$325.00
Experimental film by Robert Breer.
Fine Arts
Dist - AFA **Prod** - AFA 1978

Tzvi Nussbaum - a boy from Warsaw 50 MIN
VHS
Color (G)
$39.95 purchase _ #625
Tells the story of the little boy who was photographed with his arms raised in surrender to a German soldier who has his machine gun aimed at him. Dr Tzvi Nussbaum, orphaned at age seven and presently a New York physician, narrates.
Civics and Political Systems; History - World; Sociology
Dist - ERGOM **Prod** - ERGOM

U

U-100 Insulin 12 MIN
U-matic / VHS
Color
Describes the U - 100 insulin. Points out the differences of U - 100 from other strengths of insulin.
Health and Safety
Dist - MEDFAC **Prod** - MEDFAC 1981

U Boats - the Wolf Pack 30 MIN
VHS
Color (G)
$14.98 purchase _ #TT8057
Presents footage and the story of the Nazi submarine attack force that sank hundreds of ships and invaded U.S. waters during World War II. Produced by Midwich Entertainment, Inc.
Civics and Political Systems; History - United States; History - World; Social Science
Dist - TWINTO **Prod** - TWINTO 1990

U Boats - the wolf pack 30 MIN
VHS
B&W/Color (G)
$100.00 rental
Tells of Nazi submarine attack force action during World War II. Includes footage of U - Boat construction. Depicts the claustrophobic life on board and actual attacks.
Civics and Political Systems; History - World
Dist - SEVVID

U - Boot Am Feind/Now it Can be Told 39 MIN
U-matic / VHS
B&W
Documents life on board a U - boat in the North Atlantic during World War II.
Civics and Political Systems; History - World
Dist - IHF **Prod** - IHF

U N I Shear 4 MIN
VHS / BETA
Color (IND)
Develops manipulative welding skills using industrial equipment, and demonstrates common types of weld joints used in welding fabrication and repair. Includes a student workbook.
Industrial and Technical Education; Psychology
Dist - RMIBHF **Prod** - RMIBHF

U N in Crisis - a Successor for U Thant 17 MIN
16mm
Screen news digest series; Vol 9; Issue 3
B&W (J)
LC 77-700278
Traces the history of the United Nations, and discusses the office of the secretary general.
Civics and Political Systems
Dist - HEARST **Prod** - HEARST 1966

U N Proceedings - Anti - Zionist Resolution 15 MIN
16mm
Color
Presents a condensation of the United Nations proceedings of November 10, 1975, on the Anti - Zionist Resolution, including selections of Ambassador Herzog and Ambassador Moynihan's speeches.
Civics and Political Systems; History - World
Dist - ALDEN **Prod** - UJA

Ubel 6 MIN
16mm
B&W (G)
$25.00 rental
Features five variations on an unfriendly - looking object.
Fine Arts
Dist - CANCIN FLMKCO **Prod** - SCHLEM 1991

Ubi est terram oobiae - Pt two 5 MIN
16mm
Oobieland series
Color (G)
$15.00 rental
Interviews the Princess of Oobieland in a television studio in New York City, where her responses are testimony to the closing of the gateways encountered in part one. Part two of a five - part series.
Fine Arts; Literature and Drama; Religion and Philosophy
Dist - CANCIN **Prod** - UNGRW 1969

Ubu Roi 60 MIN
VHS
Color (H C G)
$129.00 purchase _ #DL311
Presents an early example of modern, expressionistic drama in an anarchic political parody by Alfred Jarry which employs many non - realistic theatrical conventions. Includes a documentary section. Condensed version of the BBC production.
Fine Arts; Literature and Drama
Dist - INSIM

Ubu Roi 60 MIN
U-matic / VHS
Drama - play, performance, perception series; Conventions of the theatre
Color (H C A)
Discusses stylization, avantgardism, black theatre and realism in drama. Uses the play Ubu Roi as an example.
Fine Arts; Literature and Drama
Dist - FI **Prod** - BBCTV 1978

Uddeholm - a World Industry 31 MIN
16mm
B&W
Features Prince Wilhelm who pays a visit to Uddeholm's factory in the province of Varmland.
Business and Economics; Geography - World
Dist - AUDPLN **Prod** - ASI

UF6 from British Nuclear Fuels Limited 15 MIN
16mm
Color
Illustrates the large - scale facilities for the conversion of uranium ore concentrates to uranium hexafluoride at Springfields. Shows the complete process from the refining of uranium ore at the mine to the final transport of uranium hexafluoride to USAEC plants for enrichment.
Industrial and Technical Education; Science - Physical
Dist - UKAEA **Prod** - UKAEA 1971

Uffizi - Florence's treasure house of art 60 MIN
VHS / BETA
Color (G)
$29.95 purchase
Visits Uffizi Museum in Florence which houses works by Michelangelo, Leonardo da Vinci, Raphael. Shows the changes in thinking and architectural design which helped the Uffizi evolve in to Italy's leading museum. Produced by VPI - AC.
Fine Arts; History - World
Dist - ARTSAM

The UFO 5 MIN
U-matic / VHS
Write on, Set 1 Series
Color (J H)
Deals with avoiding jargon in writing.
English Language
Dist - CTI **Prod** - CTI

UFO series
Ascension of the demonoids 46 MIN
X - people 25 MIN
Dist - CANCIN

UFO - the Unsolved Mystery 75 MIN
VHS
Color (G)
$19.95 purchase _ #XVUFO
Examines numerous reports of UFO encounters from all over the world. Combines previously classified documents, photographs and film footage with on - site interviews of officials, scientists and civilians who claim to have witnessed UFOs or aliens.
Literature and Drama
Dist - GAINST

UFO - Unrestrained Flying Objects 15 MIN
16mm
Color
LC 79-700456
Features crash tests conducted at the General Motors proving grounds using instrumented dummies to show what happens in automobile collisions when restraints are used and when they are not used. Shows the correct way to wear seat belts and discusses other types of passive restraints.
Health and Safety; Industrial and Technical Education
Dist - GM **Prod** - GM 1978

UFO - Unrestrained Flying Objects 14 MIN
16mm
Color (H A)
LC 73-701439
Argues for universal and constant use of automobile seat belts. Describes their proper use and adjustment.
Health and Safety; Industrial and Technical Education
Dist - GM **Prod** - GM 1968

UFOs - are we alone 60 MIN
VHS
Nova video library series
Color; Captioned (G)
$29.95 purchase _ #S01844
Investigates claims, photographs, and film footage offered in support of the idea that UFOs exist. From the PBS series 'NOVA.'
History - World; Literature and Drama; Science - Physical
Dist - UILL PBS **Prod** - WNETTV

Uganda - guerrilla threat 22 MIN
VHS / U-matic
Color (H C A)
Tells how Uganda, after ousting Idi Amin, struggles as guerrilla fighters continue to attack. Examines the past, present and future of Uganda.
Geography - World; History - World
Dist - JOU **Prod** - JOU

Uganda - the right to life 28 MIN
VHS / U-matic
People matter series; Pt 6
Color (H C G)
$385.00, $355.00 purchase _ #V476
Profiles the recent history of Uganda, during which hundreds of thousands of people have been killed, mostly by police and troops. Discusses how tribal rivalry, colonial rule and the pattern of the brutalized becoming the brutalizers all contribute to a denial of human rights. Part five of a six - part series on human rights around the globe.
Civics and Political Systems; Geography - World; Sociology
Dist - BARR **Prod** - CEPRO 1989

Ugetsu 97 MIN
VHS
B&W (G)
$24.95 _ #UGE010
Presents a tale of ambition and passion. Follows two 16th - century peasants as they abandon their families to seek fame and fortune. Shows that in attaining their desires, both men destroy their lives and bring tragedy to their families. Directed by Kenji Mizoguchi. Digitally remastered with new translation.
Fine Arts; Sociology
Dist - HOMVIS **Prod** - JANUS 1953

The Ugly Dachshund 93 MIN
U-matic / VHS / 16mm
Color
Presents a romantic - comedy about a pair of newlyweds trying to cope with the unique personalities of five appealing dachshund puppies. Stars Dean Jones, Suzanne Pleshette and Charlie Ruggles.
Fine Arts
Dist - FI **Prod** - DISNEY 1966

The Ugly Duckling 8 MIN
U-matic / VHS / 16mm
Color (P I)
LC 72-700161
A baby duckling is shunned by his family because of his ugliness. He is rejected by all other birds and animals until a mother swan adopts him as one of her own. An animated cartoon.
English Language; Literature and Drama
Dist - CORF **Prod** - DISNEY 1955

The Ugly duckling 20 MIN
16mm
Color
Depicts the Hans Christian Andersen story of a baby swan and how he grew up to be a beautiful bird in spite of many hardships.
Literature and Drama
Dist - UNIJAP **Prod** - UNIJAP 1969

The Ugly Duckling 17 MIN
U-matic / VHS / 16mm
Color (P I)
$405, $250 purchase _ #4218
Tells the story of an 'ugly' duckling who becomes a swan. Puppet animated.
Literature and Drama
Dist - CORF

The Ugly duckling 11 MIN
U-matic / VHS / 16mm
Color (P I) (SPANISH)
Presents the Spanish language version of the film and videorecording The Ugly Duckling.
Literature and Drama
Dist - EBEC **Prod** - EBEC 1953

The Ugly Duckling 11 MIN
U-matic / VHS / 16mm
Classic Tales Retold Series
Color (P I)
LC 80-700042
Uses animation to tell the story of a homely duckling which grows up to be a beautiful swan. Based on the story The Ugly Duckling by Hans Christian Andersen.
Literature and Drama
Dist - PHENIX **Prod** - GREATT 1979

The Ugly duckling 7 MIN
U-matic / VHS / BETA
Classic fairy tales series
Color; PAL (P I)
PdS30, PdS38 purchase
Tells the story of an ugly duckling, rejected by the other ducks, who finds happiness when he grows up to be a swan. Features part of a six - part series containing the essence of the Brothers Grimm, Charles Perrault and Hans Anderson.
Literature and Drama
Dist - EDPAT **Prod** - HALAS 1992

The Ugly Duckling 35 MIN
VHS / 16mm
Children's Circle Video Series
Color (K)
$18.88 purchase _ #CCV009
Presents the classic children's story and The Stonecutter and The Swinegerd.
Literature and Drama
Dist - EDUCRT

The Ugly little boy 26 MIN
16mm / U-matic / VHS
Classics, dark and dangerous series
Color; Captioned (J) (SPANISH)
LC 76-703939
Presents the story by Isaac Asimov about a child brought back through time from the Neanderthal age by a group of scientists who ignore the human factor in their experiment.
Literature and Drama
Dist - LCOA **Prod** - LCOA 1977

Ujima - Modupe and the flood 5 MIN
U-matic / VHS / 16mm
Nguzo saba - folklore for children series
Color (K P I)
Illustrates how a farmer in West Africa notices a dam is about to burst and drown his neighbors in the valley below, and saves them by setting his own house on fire, and causing the villagers to rush up the hill to help him.
Guidance and Counseling; Sociology
Dist - BCNFL **Prod** - NGUZO 1979

Ujjaini 12 MIN
16mm
B&W (H C A)
Presents Ujjain, in Rajasthan, as a famous seat of learning in history. Discusses the Sanskirt poet Kalidas, who lived there, the famous observatory and the enlightened ruler, Vikramaditya.
Biography; History - World
Dist - NEDINF **Prod** - INDIA

UK dental care series
Contains Plaque - the facts; Plaque control - toothbrushing; Plaque control - flossing; and You have gingivitis. Offers the complete series of four programs on one video.
Plaque - the facts 7 MIN
Plaque control - flossing 7 MIN
Plaque control - toothbrushing 8 MIN
You have gingivitis - 4 8 MIN
Dist - EDPAT

Ukelele for kids series
Presents a two - part series featuring instructor Marcy Marxer and Ginger - a dog puppet. Teaches parts of the ukelele and how to hold and tune the instrument, as well as five basic chords in Video One. Introduces five new chords and a variety of strumming techniques in Video Two. Includes books and progress charts.
The Next ten lessons - Video Two 45 MIN
Play in ten easy lessons - Video One 55 MIN
Dist - HOMETA **Prod** - HOMETA

Ukiyo - E Prints 22 MIN
16mm
Color
Presents Ukiyo - e (pictures of the transient world) which reflect the life and sentiments of the commoners of the Edo period (17th - 19th centuries.).
Geography - World; History - World
Dist - UNIJAP **Prod** - UNIJAP 1969

Ukiyoe - the Fabulous World of Japanese Prints 30 MIN
16mm / U-matic / VHS
Japanese Woodblock Series
Color (H C A)
Describes the development of the first Japanese mass art, woodblock printing.
Fine Arts; Industrial and Technical Education
Dist - FI **Prod** - NHK 1973

Ukraine 29 MIN
Videoreel / VT2
International cookbook series
Color
Features home economist Joan Hood presenting a culinary tour of specialty dishes from around the world. Shows the preparation of Ukrainian dishes ranging from peasant cookery to continental cuisine.
Geography - World; Home Economics
Dist - PBS **Prod** - WMVSTV

Ukraine, ancient crossroads, modern dreams - Ukraina 55 MIN
VHS
Color (G A)
$24.95 purchase _ #V284
Features the fabled frescoes of Kiev's Cathedral of St. Sophia and the candlelit underground caves of the Perchersk Monastery. Visits with the artisans who craft intricate embroideries and 'pysanky' - painted Easter eggs. Discovers medieval castles, the vacation paradise of Crimea and the heartland city of Lviv.
Geography - World
Dist - POLART

Ukraine - lifting the yoke 50 MIN
VHS
Blood and belonging series
Color (A)
PdS99 purchase _ Available in UK only
Features host Michael Ignatieff taking a dramatic journey of discovery to examine nationalism in Ukraine. Visits the area in Ukraine where his great-grandfather owned land. He finds a land once devastated by famine and still haunted by memories of Stalin.
Civics and Political Systems; Geography - World; History - World
Dist - BBCENE

Ukrainian cooking 28 MIN
VHS / 16mm
World in your kitchen series
Color (G)
$90.00 purchase _ #BPN003782
Shows how to prepare Ukrainian borsch and holupchi - cabbage rolls - . Features Nadya Worobec and series hostess Anne Wanstall.
Home Economics
Dist - RMIBHF **Prod** - RMIBHF 1985
TVOTAR TVOTAR

Ukrainian Folktales Series
Animal tales - tails, horns and paws 30 MIN
Of Wits and Dimwits 30 MIN
Stories of the Fox 30 MIN
Dist - ACCESS

Ukrainian Shadow Puppets Series
The Bear who stole the Chinook 14 MIN
The Ghost Pipe 19 MIN
Nape and the Mice - Nape and the Rock 14 MIN
Scarface - Story of the Sundance 15 MIN
Wesakecha and the Flood 16 MIN
Wesakecha and the Geese - Wesakecha and the Chickadee 17 MIN
Why the Moose's Skin is Loose 16 MIN
Dist - ACCESS

Ula no Weo 26 MIN
16mm
Color
Shows how to learn the hula.
Geography - United States; Physical Education and Recreation
Dist - CINEPC **Prod** - CINEPC 1964

Ulcer at Work 26 MIN
U-matic / VHS / 16mm
B&W (A)
LC FIA65-378
Demonstrates how the peptic ulcer can create unhappiness and failure in man's working and personal life.
Health and Safety
Dist - IFB **Prod** - UOKLA 1959

Ulcer wars 50 MIN
VHS
Horizon series
Color (A)
PdS99 purchase _ Not available in Australia
Features Australian physician Barry Marshall who believes that peptic ulcers are caused by bacteria. States that, if the bacteria are killed the ulcer is cured - but ulcers are big business and the drug industry will not support Dr Marshall's views. The same bacteria may also be responsible for causing stomach cancer and heart disease - research is just beginnning to look at the possibilities.
Health and Safety
Dist - BBCENE

Ulcerative Colitis 30 MIN
16mm
Boston Medical Reports Series
B&W (PRO)
LC 74-705870
Examines the possible role of autoimmunity as a cause of ulcerative colitis. Reviews the use of immunosuppressive agents in its therapy. Presents details of the two main types of therapy - corticosteroids and colectomy.
Health and Safety; Science - Natural
Dist - NMAC **Prod** - NMAC 1966

Ulcerative Colitis
U-matic / VHS
Color
Differentiates between spastic colon, irritable bowel and ulcerative colitis. Details symptoms, treatment and possible surgery intervention where medication hasn't helped.
Health and Safety; Science - Natural
Dist - MIFE **Prod** - MIFE

Ulliisses 94 MIN
16mm
Color (G)
$150.00 rental
Features an independent film from Hamburg by Werner Nekes, who founded the Hamburg Cooperative in 1967 and has run the Hamburger Filmschau since then. Draws on The Odyssey by Homer, Ulysses by James Joyce and The Warp by Neil Oram.
Fine Arts; Literature and Drama
Dist - CANCIN

Ultimate achievers 7 MIN
VHS
Color (A PRO)
$250.00 purchase, $125.00 rental
Uses the example of Iron Man triathlon participants to point out the need for perseverance, dedication, and endurance in all things.
Business and Economics; Physical Education and Recreation; Psychology
Dist - VLEARN

The Ultimate Answer 28 MIN
U-matic / VHS
Color (J A)
Features actor Hugh O'Brian who shares his experiences with Dr. Albert Schweitzer.
Science; Sociology
Dist - SUTHRB **Prod** - SUTHRB

Ultimate beginner video series
Presents 11 parts offering self - paced, step - by - step lessons for beginning musicians. Allows students to stop and rewind videos as often as necessary for mastering fundamentals and progressing easily at their own pace. Includes Keyboard Basics 1 and 2 for Acoustical or Electric Piano; Drum Basics 1 and 2; Guitar Basics 1 for Electrical or Acoustical Guitar; Guitar Basics 2 for Electrical Guitar; Guitar Basics 2 for Acoustical Guitar; Bass Basics 1 and 2; Vocal Basics 1 and 2.
Bass basics - 1
Bass basics - 2
Drum basics - 1
Drum basics - 2
Guitar basics - for acoustical guitar - 2
Guitar basics - for electrical guitar - 2
Guitar basics - for electrical or acoustical guitar - 1
Keyboard basics - for acoustical or electric piano - 1
Keyboard basics - for acoustical or electric piano - 2
Vocal basics - 1
Vocal basics - 2
Dist - TILIED

The Ultimate challenge
VHS
Color (G A)
$49.90 purchase _ #0200
Reveals that only 10 crossed the finish line of the 17 starters who took part in the first solo yacht race around the world, the BOC Challenge Race. Follows the course from Newport, Rhode Island, to Capetown, South Africa, to Rio de Janeiro, Brazil, back to Newport.
Geography - World; Physical Education and Recreation
Dist - SEVVID

Ultimate Challenge 23 MIN
16mm
Color
Demonstrates how the B F Goodrich off - the - shelf street Radial T/A tires meet the challenge of the 14.1 mile race course at Nurburgring, Germany.
Physical Education and Recreation
Dist - MTP **Prod** - GC

The Ultimate Energy 28 MIN
16mm / U-matic / VHS
Color
Discusses the complex problems facing scientific researchers in their efforts to achieve fusion power. Outlines the theory of fusion power and describes experiments being conducted in the field. Includes interviews with physicists and visits to five fusion research laboratories.
Science; Science - Physical; Social Science
Dist - USNAC **Prod** - USERD 1976

Ultimate issues 120 MIN
VHS
Color (G R)
$19.95 purchase
Enables young people to confront false thinking in areas related to God, the Bible, Christ's claims and ultimate truth. Features teachings of R C Sproul. Includes guide.
Religion and Philosophy
Dist - GF

The Ultimate machine 30 MIN
16mm
Life around us Spanish series
Color (SPANISH)
LC 78-700059
Traces the development of the computer and examines its uses in industry, science and education.
Foreign Language; Mathematics; Science - Natural; Sociology
Dist - TIMLIF **Prod** - TIMLIF 1971

The Ultimate Machine 30 MIN
U-matic / VHS / 16mm
Life Around Us Series
Color (C A)
Studies the development and use of the computer.
Mathematics; Science - Natural; Science - Physical
Dist - TIMLIF **Prod** - TIMLIF 1971

The Ultimate Mystery 40 MIN
VHS / U-matic
Color
Presents Apollo 14 astronaut Edgar D Mitchell's contention that there is a oneness to all living things. Purports to contain scientific data supporting claims of mystics through the ages.
Religion and Philosophy
Dist - HP **Prod** - HP

The Ultimate Mystery 38 MIN
16mm
Films for a New Age Series
Color (J)
LC 73-702720
Presents scientific data supporting the claims of mystics through the ages that there is a oneness to all living things. Features Captain Edgar Mitchell, Apollo 14 astronaut.
Psychology; Religion and Philosophy
Dist - HP **Prod** - HP 1973

The Ultimate Outpost 29 MIN
U-matic / VHS
Vikings Series
Color
Examines how Erik the Red discovered and settled the island of Greenland, how Leif the Lucky discovered the areas known as Labrador and North Newfoundland and how the Vikings colonized Iceland.
History - World
Dist - PBS **Prod** - KTCATV 1980

Ultimate relaxation - freedom from stress
VHS
Color; Subliminal (G)
$29.95 purchase _ #MVSTR
Presents context for relaxation by incorporating subliminal visual and auditory messages into standard television viewing. Must be used with a MindVision processor, VCR and TV.
Psychology
Dist - GAINST **Prod** - GAINST

The Ultimate S A T Review 30 MIN
U-matic / VHS
(H T)
$49.95 _ #TH1014V
Presents an overview of the Scholastic Aptitude Test (SAT), and gives advice on understanding and answering each specific portion. Includes complete workbook.
Education
Dist - CAMV **Prod** - CAMV

The Ultimate Speed - an Exploration with High Energy Electrons 38 MIN
16mm
PSSC College Physics Films Series
B&W (H C)
LC FIA67-5924
Demonstrates the relationship between kinetic energy of electrons and their speed, using calorimetric means and time - of - flight techniques. Shows a result which agrees with the theory of special relativity. Features William Bertozzi of the Massachusetts Institute of Technology.
Science - Physical
Dist - MLA **Prod** - PSSC 1966

The Ultimate stretch and warrior workout 90 MIN
VHS
Color (G)
$29.95 purchase
Presents kundalini yoga with Ravi Singh as instructor. Begins with a 30 - minute breathing - stretching routine. Includes meditation and relaxation with musical accompaniment by Wahe Guru Kaur Khalso and Guru Prem Singh Khalsa.
Fine Arts; Physical Education and Recreation; Psychology; Religion and Philosophy
Dist - WLIONP **Prod** - WLIONP 1990

The Ultimate swan lake 126 MIN
VHS
Color (G)
$39.95 purchase _ #1162
Stars Natalia Bessmertnova in the dual role of Odette and Odile in the Bolshoi Ballet production of 'Swan Lake.' Costars Alexander Bogatyrev as Siegfried. Choreography by Yuri Grigorovich, with the Moscow Symphonic Orchestra.
Fine Arts; Physical Education and Recreation
Dist - KULTUR

Ultimate Tape on Whitetail 20 MIN
BETA / VHS
Color
Features Jackie Bushman showing some scouting techniques as well as hunting with the wind. Includes some mock scraping techniques.
Physical Education and Recreation; Science - Natural
Dist - HOMEAF **Prod** - HOMEAF

The Ultimate test animal 40 MIN
U-matic / VHS
Color (H C A)
$395 purchase, $55 rental
Examines the birth control injection Depo Provera and international controversy over its use. Raises questions about racism and sexism in health care, population control versus birth control, and how drugs are tested and marketed. Produced by Karen Branan and Bill Turnley.
Health and Safety; Psychology; Sociology
Dist - CNEMAG

The Ultimates 29 MIN
Videoreel / VT2
Our Street Series
Color
Sociology
Dist - PBS **Prod** - MDCPB

Ultra - Low Temperatures 12 MIN
VHS / 16mm
World of Extremes Series
Color (J)
$119.00 purchase, $75.00 rental _ #OD - 2408
Explains the kelvin scale. Uses the properties of liquid helium to illustrate super - fluidity. Explains the principle of superconductivity. The second of three installments of The World Of Extremes Series.
Science; Science - Physical
Dist - FOTH

Ultra - Monetary Success
VHS / Cassette
Color (G)
$19.95 purchase _ #VHS108 ; $24.95 purchase _ #C839
Uses hypnosis, sleep programming and subliminal programming to encourage the generation of wealth. Includes book.
Health and Safety; Psychology; Social Science; Sociology
Dist - VSPU **Prod** - VSPU

Ultra Sonic Method I 10 MIN
VHS / U-matic
Color (IND)
Describes the theory, equipment and procedures involved in basic ultrasonic testing. Demonstrates actual thickness measurement and flaw detection tests.
Industrial and Technical Education
Dist - MOKIN **Prod** - HTAVTI

Ultra - Strong Magnetic Fields 12 MIN
VHS / 16mm
World of Extremes Series
Color (J)
$119.00 purchase, $75.00 rental _ #OD - 2409
Depicts the division of magnets into smaller magnets. Shows how the Lorentz - force can bend electronic beams and other ways in which strong magnetic fields can affect the behavior of electrons. The final of three installments of The World Of Extremes Series.
Science; Science - Physical
Dist - FOTH

Ultra Structure of the Lower Motor Neurons and Muscle Fibers 32 MIN
U-matic
Intensive Course in Neuromuscular Diseases Series
Color (PRO)
LC 76-706123
Presents Dr Jerry E Mendell lecturing on the ultra structure of the lower motor neurons and muscle fibers.
Health and Safety; Science - Natural
Dist - USNAC **Prod** - NINDIS 1974

The Ultracentrifuge 51 MIN
U-matic / VHS
Colloids and surface chemistry - lyophilic colloids series
B&W
Science - Physical
Dist - MIOT **Prod** - MIOT
KALMIA KALMIA

Ultrasonic Aspiration Biopsy Technique 20 MIN
U-matic
Ultrasound in Diagnostic Medicine Series
Color (PRO)
LC 79-707580
Deals with the use of ultrasound as an aid in the biopsy of tissues and the aspiration of fluid. Describes how the use of ultrasound aspiration biopsy transducer avoids the undesirable consequence of other methods, such as inadvertent penetration of normal structures.
Health and Safety
Dist - USNAC **Prod** - NSF 1976

Ultrasonic Evaluation of Cerebral Trauma 20 MIN
U-matic
Ultrasound in Diagnostic Medicine Series
Color
LC 79-707581
Deals with the findings of echoencephalography in trauma with particular reference to cerebral contusion, hematoma formation and traumatic communicating hydrocephalus.
Health and Safety
Dist - USNAC **Prod** - NSF 1976

Ultrasonic Inspection 52 MIN
BETA / VHS / U-matic
Color
$400 purchase
Guidance and Counseling; Industrial and Technical Education; Psychology
Dist - ASM **Prod** - ASM

Ultrasonic Testing Applications 55 MIN
U-matic / BETA / VHS
Color
$400 purchase
Shows calibration standards and factors to consider when selecting the correct method.
Science - Physical
Dist - ASM **Prod** - ASM

Ultrasonic Testing Fundamentals 55 MIN
U-matic / BETA / VHS
Color
$400 purchase
Gives history and development and principles of wave propagation.
Science - Physical
Dist - ASM **Prod** - ASM

Ultrasonic Tomography of the Eye and Orbit 19 MIN
U-matic
Ultrasound in Diagnostic Medicine Series
Color (PRO)
LC 79-708120
Demonstrates the immersion technique using kinetic horizonal and vertical scans to produce a B - scans in real time to assist in diagnosing eye and orbit abnormalities.
Health and Safety; Science
Dist - USNAC **Prod** - USVA 1979

Ultrasonography of the Breast 35 MIN
U-matic
Color
Demonstrates how to use ultrasound equipment. Shows the results of effective and ineffective imagery.
Health and Safety
Dist - UTEXSC **Prod** - UTEXSC

Ultrasound - a Window to the Womb 15 MIN
VHS / 16mm
(C)
$385.00 purchase _ #870VI077
Explains the physics of ultrasound and shows how to perform the procedure. Defines the capabilities and limitations of ultrasonography.
Health and Safety
Dist - HSCIC **Prod** - HSCIC 1987

Ultrasound - a window to the womb 15 MIN
VHS / U-matic
Color (C PRO)
$395.00 purchase, $80.00 rental _ #C870 - VI - 077
Explains the physics of ultrasound and shows how to perform the procedure. Presents case studies to illustrate why ultrasound examinations are used during each of the trimesters of pregnancy. Defines the capabilities and limitations of ultrasonography. Presented by Charles B Cox, Vickie L Venne and Jan Mogoven.
Health and Safety
Dist - HSCIC

Ultrasound and the CT Scanner 15 MIN
U-matic / VHS
X - Ray Procedures in Layman's Terms Series
Color
Presents some of the latest advances in radiology. Shows how ultrasound utilizes sound waves that bounce off internal structures.
Health and Safety; Science
Dist - FAIRGH **Prod** - FAIRGH

Ultrasound in diagnostic medicine series

Abdominal ultrasound	17 MIN
Diagnostic Ultrasound in Emergency Room Medicine	20 MIN
Doppler ultrasonic evaluation of peripheral vascular disease	23 MIN
Echocardiography	23 MIN
Pediatric Ultrasonography	21 MIN
Retroperitoneal Ultrasonography	18 MIN
Ultrasonic Aspiration Biopsy Technique	20 MIN
Ultrasonic Evaluation of Cerebral Trauma	20 MIN
Ultrasonic Tomography of the Eye and Orbit	19 MIN

Dist - USNAC

Ultrasound in Obstetrics and Gynecology 20 MIN
U-matic
Color (PRO)
LC 79-708004
Discusses ultrasonography of the fetus. Considers number, location, normal and abnormal growth patterns, abnormalities of the fetus, the normal uterus and ovary, and findings related to contraceptive devices.
Health and Safety; Science
Dist - USNAC **Prod** - NSF 1977

Ultrasound in Renal Stone Surgery 15 MIN
VHS / U-matic
Color
Shows the surgical technique that allows intrarenal surgery without interruption of the renal arterial supply.
Health and Safety
Dist - SPRVER **Prod** - SPRVER

Ultrasound of the Breast 11 MIN
U-matic
Color
Discusses the use of ultrasound in the detection and diagnosis of breast disease.
Health and Safety
Dist - UTEXSC **Prod** - UTEXSC

Ultrasound - seeing with soundwaves 5 MIN
VHS
Color (C PRO G)
$175.00 purchase
Presents a brief overview of transabdominal and transvaginal sonography. Offers clear explanations, informative graphics and fascinating ultrasonic images to ensure patient interest.

Health and Safety
Dist - LPRO **Prod** - LPRO

Ulysses 2 SDS
VHS / 16mm
Mono; B&W; Color (C H A G)
$29.95 purchase
Presents a selection from Ulysses. Includes the following selections: Soliloquy Of Molly Bloom, Read By Siobhan McKenna, Soliloquy Of Leopold Bloom, Read By E G Marshall.
Literature and Drama
Dist - PBS **Prod** - WNETTV

Ulysses 104 MIN
U-matic / VHS / 16mm
Color
Based on the 'Odyssey' by Homer. Relates the adventures of Ulysses during his wanderings after the Trojan War. Stars Kirk Douglas and Anthony Quinn.
Fine Arts
Dist - FI **Prod** - PONTI 1955

Umbanda - the problem solver 52 MIN
VHS
Disappearing world series
Color (G C)
$99.00 purchase, $19.00 rental _ #51253
Focuses on umbanda, a religious cult based on a centuries - old African ritual taken to Latin America by slaves, that now has more than 20 million followers in Brazil. Reveals that umbanda blends elements of Roman Catholic ritual with belief in spirit possession. Contains graphic footage of a vast, weekend ceremony of worship, ritual dancing and hypnosis on the beach of Sao Paolo. Features anthropologist Peter Fry. Part of a series working closely with anthropologists who lived for a year or more in societies whose social structures, beliefs and practices are threatened by the expansion of technocratic civilization.
Religion and Philosophy; Sociology
Dist - PSU **Prod** - GRANDA 1977

Umberto D 90 MIN
VHS
B&W (G)
$29.95 purchase _ #UMB010
Focuses on a retired civil servant struggling to live on a meager pension. Uses non - actors and location shots to achieve documentary - like vignettes. A neorealist classic depicting society's indifference to poverty. Directed by Vittorio De Sica. Digitally remastered with new subtitles.
Fine Arts; Sociology
Dist - HOMVIS **Prod** - JANUS 1955

Umbilical hernia 11 MIN
U-matic / VHS
Hernia series
Color
Health and Safety; Science - Natural
Dist - SVL **Prod** - SVL

Umbra 5 MIN
16mm
B&W (G)
$10.00 rental
Introduces shadows to make the familiar foreign. Explores the human form. Produced by Wendy Blair.
Fine Arts
Dist - CANCIN

Umbra 18 MIN
16mm
Color (A)
LC 80-701383
Uses experimental techniques to show how film can be used as a filter between the filmmaker and the environment.
Fine Arts
Dist - SEIB **Prod** - SEIB 1980

Umbrella Jack 24 MIN
16mm / U-matic / VHS
Color (K)
$495.00, $349.00, $249.00 purchase _ #AD - 1130
Presents Umbrella Jack, the town eccentric, portrayed by John Carradine. Reveals that when Billy befriends him, he learns the reasons for the man's odd behavior.
Literature and Drama; Psychology; Sociology
Dist - FOTH **Prod** - FOTH

Umbrella Series
Afghan, caftan and friends 15 MIN
Doo - dads for Daddy 15 MIN
Everything under one lid 15 MIN
Guess what 15 MIN
How to Cheat at Bridge 15 MIN
Let's Think Fat 15 MIN
Liberated Tops 15 MIN
Little People Clothes 15 MIN
Manly Bacon, Unholey and Two - Minute Mousse 15 MIN
On the Seventh Day She Wore it 15 MIN
Open and Shut 15 MIN
Son of 15 MIN
Wrap it Up 15 MIN
Dist - PBS

Uminchu - The Old man and the east China sea 101 MIN
16mm / VHS
Color (G)
$1350.00, $490.00 purchase, $150.00 rental
Follows the travails of 82 - year - old Shigeru Itokazu, who goes to sea alone before dawn every morning in quest of marlin. Interviews the residents of tiny Yonakuni Island who tell stories of their battles with the sea and traditional way of life. Itokazu fishes with a hand held fishing line and spear, without the benefits of sonar or drift nets. His resolve and fierce pride are characteristic of his community. Produced by John Junkerman.
Fine Arts; Geography - World; Physical Education and Recreation; Social Science
Dist - FIRS

Umoja - tiger and the big wind 8 MIN
16mm / U-matic / VHS
Nguzo Saba folklore for children series
Color (K P I)
Relates how, during a long summer drought, the only available food and water was guarded by a large tiger who refused to share with other jungle creatures. Solves problem by showing how Brer Rabbit devised a plan to outwit the tiger so that all small creatures working together need never be hungry again.
History - World; Science - Natural
Dist - BCNFL **Prod** - NGUZO 1979

Umonhon - becoming a warrior 20 MIN
VHS
We are one series
(I)
$45.00 purchase
Presents the life and customs of the Omaha Indians of the central United States about 1820. Uses the viewpoint of a young tribal member. Aims to instill appreciation of the tribe's culture and values. Focuses on coming of age experiences with danger. Fifth in an eight part series.
Social Science
Dist - GPN **Prod** - NCGE

Umonhon - learning from others 20 MIN
VHS
We are one series
(I)
$45.00 purchase
Presents the life and customs of the Omaha Indian tribe of the central United States about 1820. Uses the viewpoint of a thirteen year old member of the tribe. Aims to instill appreciation of the tribe's culture and values. Focuses on a coming of age ceremony. Second in an eight part series.
Social Science
Dist - GPN **Prod** - NCGE

Umonhon - morning comes 20 MIN
VHS
We are one series
(I)
$45.00 purchase
Presents life and customs of the Omaha Indian tribe of the central United States about 1820. Uses the viewpoint of a thirteen year old member of the tribe. Aims to instill appreciation of the tribe's culture and values. First of an eight part series.
Social Science
Dist - GPN **Prod** - NCGE

Umonhon - preparing for the summer hunt 20 MIN
VHS
We are one series
(I)
$45.00 purchase
Presents the life and customs of the Omaha Indians of the central United States about 1820. Uses the viewpoint of a young tribal member. Aims to instill appreciation of the tribe's culture and values. Focuses on the importance of the summer hunt to the community. Sixth in an eight part series.
Social Science
Dist - GPN **Prod** - NCGE

Umonhon - storytelling 20 MIN
VHS
We are one series
(I)
$45.00 purchase
Presents the life and customs of the Omaha Indian tribe of the central United States about 1820. Uses the point of view of a thirteen year old member of the tribe. Aims to instill appreciation of the tribe's culture and beliefs. Focuses on the individual's growth through four stages from birth to death. Fourth in an eight part series.
Social Science
Dist - GPN **Prod** - NCGE

Umonhon - the buffalo hunt 20 MIN
VHS
We are one series
(I)
$45.00 purchase
Presents the life and customs of the Omaha Indians of the central United States about 1820. Uses the viewpoint of a young member of the tribe. Aims to instill appreciation of the tribe's culture and values. Focuses on ethics. Eighth of an eight part series.
Social Science
Dist - GPN **Prod** - NCGE

Umonhon - the dare 20 MIN
VHS
We are one series
(I)
$45.00 purchase
Presents the life and customs of the Omaha Indians of the central United States about 1820. Uses the viewpoint of a young tribal member. Aims to instill appreciation of the tribe's culture and values. Focuses on the community's respect for life. Seventh of an eight part series.
Social Science
Dist - GPN **Prod** - NCTE

Umonhon - turning of the child ceremony 20 MIN
VHS
We are one series
(I)
$45.00 purchase
Presents the life and customs of the Omaha Indian tribe of the central United States about 1820. Uses the viewpoint of a thirteen year old member of the tribe. Aims to instill appreciation of the tribe's culture and values. Focuses on social and religious implications of coming of age. Third in a three part series.
Social Science
Dist - GPN **Prod** - NCGE

UMP - the NAVAIR Way 30 MIN
16mm
Color
LC 75-700882
Shows how the U S Naval Air Systems Command deals with a person who joins the Upward Mobility Program (UMP.).
Civics and Political Systems; Guidance and Counseling
Dist - USNAC **Prod** - USN 1974

The Umpire Strikes Back - by Ron Luciano and David Fisher 60 MIN
U-matic / VHS
Stereo (G)
Tells stories from book.
History - United States; Literature and Drama; Physical Education and Recreation
Dist - BANTAP **Prod** - BANTAP

UMWA 1970 - a House Divided 14 MIN
U-matic
B&W
Contrasts United Mine Worker of America president Tony Boyle's speech at a miner's rally with those of the anti - Boyle faction.
Business and Economics; Social Science; Sociology
Dist - APPAL **Prod** - APPAL 1971

Un Amigo 40 MIN
16mm
Color (P I)
Fine Arts
Dist - FI **Prod** - FI

Un Asunto de familia 31 MIN
U-matic / VHS / 16mm
B&W (C A) (SPANISH)
LC 70-707237
Presents a trained family caseworker who is helping a family to understand its behavior problems. Shows viewers the techniques of interviewing and how to assist people in solving their own problems. A Spanish language film.
Psychology; Sociology
Dist - IFB **Prod** - FSAA 1966

Un Ballo in Maschera 150 MIN
VHS
Color (S) (ITALIAN)
$29.95 purchase _ #384 - 9362
Sets 'Un Ballo In Maschera' by Verdi in 18th - century Boston on the eve of the American Revolution. Features Luciano Pavarotti, Judith Blegen and Katia Ricciarelli in the leading cast of this production by the Metropolitan Opera.
Fine Arts; History - United States
Dist - FI **Prod** - PAR 1988

Un ballo in maschera 150 MIN
VHS
Metropolitan opera series

Color (G) (ITALIAN WITH ENGLISH SUBTITLES)
$29.95 purchase
Stars Luciano Pavarotti, Katia Ricciarelli, Judith Blegen, and Louis Quilico in a performance of 'Un Ballo In Maschera' by Verdi. Conducted by Guiseppe Patane. Includes a brochure with plot, historic notes, photographs, and production credits.
Fine Arts
Dist - PBS **Prod** - WNETTV 1980

Un Coeur en hiver - A Heart in winter 105
35mm / 16mm
Color (G)
$200.00 rental
Features a love story that examines friendship, unrequited love and betrayal. Stars Daniel Auteuil as Stephane, a man who protects himself from emotions and who uses his work as a source of denial, isolation and solitude. When his friend and business partner Maxime, played by Andre Dussolier, falls in love with Camille, routine is shattered. Produced by Jean - Louis Livi; directed by Claude Sautet; screenplay by Claude Sautet and Jacques Fieschi. Camille is played by Emmanuelle Beart.
Fine Arts; Psychology; Religion and Philosophy; Sociology
Dist - OCTOBF

Un Conte Africaine - Te Tareau De Bouki 8.5 MIN
U-matic / VHS
Color (H C) (FRENCH)
Uses personification to tell a typical African folk tale. Conveys the moral that tricksters are often tricked.
Literature and Drama
Dist - IFB **Prod** - HAMPU 1986

Un Conte Antillaise - Pe Tambou a 6.5 MIN
VHS / U-matic
Color (J H C) (FRENCH)
Presents the tale of Kinsonn the drummer. Reflects the warmth and color of creole culture in the French Antilles.
Geography - World; Literature and Drama
Dist - IFB **Prod** - HAMPU 1986

Un dia cualquiera 30 MIN
VHS
Color (G) (SPANISH)
$49.95 purchase _ #W1484
Focuses on both informal and organized activities such as sports, dances and celebrations. Enhances appreciation of Hispanic culture as evidenced by the activities. Provides vocabulary and phrase exercises, oral and written practice material and tests for intermediate - level language students.
Foreign Language
Dist - GPC

UN - Divided it Stands
U-matic / VHS
CNN Special Reports
(J H C)
$129.00 purchase purchase _ #31378 941
Explores the UN forty years after its birth. Explains how it works and how it does not work, its successes and failures in international finance and in feeding and educating the children of the world. Features UN Ambassador Vernon Walters who focuses on the U S's place in the UN.
Civics and Political Systems
Dist - ASPRSS **Prod** - TURNED

UN - Divided it Stands 30 MIN
VHS / U-matic
CNN Special Reports Series
(G J C)
$129 purchase _ #31378 - 851
Investigates the United Nations as a governing body of the world today. Focuses on the internal struggles that weaken its powers.
Civics and Political Systems
Dist - CHUMAN

Un Grand Verrier 20 MIN
16mm
B&W (FRENCH)
A French language film. Depicts the artist - artisan, Marinot, as he makes his original creations after hours in a glass factory. Uses little narration.
Foreign Language
Dist - FACSEA **Prod** - FACSEA

Un Homme Tranquille 7 MIN
16mm
Voix Et Images De France Series
B&W (I) (FRENCH)
The dialogue is exactly that of the humorous situation in the audio - visual lesson.
Foreign Language
Dist - CHLTN **Prod** - PEREN 1962

Un Hotel a Paris 11 MIN
16mm / U-matic / VHS
Sejour En France Series
Color (J H C) (FRENCH)
LC 74-709669
Presents the story of Penny who just arrived in Paris and is brought to her hotel by her friend, Michele. Shows how she is introduced to Mme Leriche, the owner, learns the vocabulary for the items in the hotel room and buys some postcards before she and Michele go to lunch. Uses dialogue in the first and second person to provide experience for understanding French.
Foreign Language
Dist - IFB **Prod** - IFB 1970

Un Hypermarche 19 MIN
U-matic / VHS / 16mm
La France Telle Qu'Elle Est Series
Color (H C)
Shows how to select and purchase goods, as well as asking directions, in a supermarket located outside the city of Angers. Describes the vast emporium which sells a huge variety of products and is an economical shopping place for both local residents and tourists.
Foreign Language; Geography - World
Dist - MEDIAG **Prod** - THAMES 1977

The UN is for You 14 MIN
U-matic / VHS / 16mm
Color (P I)
Introduces the United Nations and its functions.
Civics and Political Systems
Dist - LCOA **Prod** - UN 1984

Un Miracle 30 seconds
16mm
Color; Silent (C)
Presents an experimental film by Robert Breer.
Fine Arts
Dist - AFA **Prod** - AFA 1954

Un Petit examen 40 MIN
16mm
Color (G)
$50.00 rental
Narrates a story of reminiscence that also deals with loss. Delves into many digressions by a man reconciling himself with the death of his father by talking to his mother.
Fine Arts; Sociology
Dist - CANCIN **Prod** - WWDIXO 1975

Un Petit Navire 13 MIN
16mm
En Francaise, Set 2 Series
Color (J A)
Foreign Language
Dist - CHLTN **Prod** - PEREN 1969

Un Premier prix 25 MIN
VHS
Les jeunes entrepreneurs series
Color (I J H) (FRENCH)
$29.95 purchase _ #W3440
Tells of young teens who build a robot. Develops intermediate - level language students' listening, comprehending, reading, writing and speaking skills through exercises and follow - up activities based on the story. Comes with video and teacher's guide with class activity material.
Foreign Language
Dist - GPC

Un Problema De Algebra 11 MIN
16mm
Beginning Spanish Series no 1; No 1
B&W (J) (SPANISH)
See series title for annotation.
Foreign Language
Dist - AVED **Prod** - CBF 1960

Un Quebecois Retrouve 58 MIN
16mm
Color (FRENCH)
_ #106C 0280 008
Geography - World
Dist - CFLMDC **Prod** - NFBC 1980

Un Repas Chez Francis 11 MIN
16mm / U-matic / VHS
Sejour En France Series
Color (J H C) (FRENCH)
LC 76-709672
Features Penny and Michele who arrive so late for lunch that little choice of menu is left, but manage to enjoy a typical French meal of hor d'oeuvre, steak, fries and raspberries with whipped cream. Shows that the restaurateur enjoys serving them as much as they enjoy eating. Uses dialogue in the first and second person to provide experience for understanding French.
Foreign Language
Dist - IFB **Prod** - IFB 1970

Un - Stress
VHS
Color (G)
$19.95 purchase _ #VHS107
Uses hypnosis and subliminal suggestions.
Health and Safety; Psychology
Dist - VSPU **Prod** - VSPU

Un Viaje a Mexico 9 MIN
16mm
Project bilingual series
Color (K P I) (SPANISH)
LC 74-700386
Views Tony and Tina on vacation in Mexico, where they see some of the variety and vitality of that nation and learn that Mexican Americans can be proud of their ethnic and linguistic ties with Mexico.
Foreign Language; Geography - World
Dist - SUTHLA **Prod** - SANISD

Una Carta a Amy 7 MIN
16mm / U-matic / VHS
Color (K P) (SPANISH)
Tells the story of Peter who is having a birthday party and although he has asked all his friends in person, he decides to write out one special invitation to a girl. Shows what happens before he reaches the mailbox, leaving him very mixed - up and worried about whether or not she will come to the party. A Spanish - language version of the motion picture A Letter To Amy.
Literature and Drama
Dist - WWS **Prod** - WWS 1970

Una familia de peces 11 MIN
VHS / 16mm
Color (P I) (SPANISH)
Pictures the complete reproduction cycle of the blue acara fish. Includes the processes of preparing the nest, laying and fertilizing the eggs, incubation care, constructing the nursery, transporting hatchlings to nurseries and guarding the young. Emphasizes the close family relationship of the blue acaras. Spanish version of 'A Fish Family.'
Science - Natural
Dist - MIS **Prod** - MIS

Una Hacienda Chilena 11 MIN
U-matic / VHS / 16mm
Color (H C) (SPANISH)
Shows a rural property in Chile known as a 'FUNDO.' Spanish version of 'People of Chile.'
Agriculture; Geography - World; Social Science
Dist - IFB **Prod** - IFB 1961

Una Hacienda Mexicana 12 MIN
16mm / U-matic / VHS
Color (H C) (SPANISH)
Depicts the simple communal life of the hacienda. Spanish version of 'Hacienda Life in Old Mexico.'
Agriculture; Geography - World; Social Science
Dist - IFB **Prod** - IFB 1961

Una Vita in scatola - a life in a tin 7 MIN
16mm
Color (J H C)
LC 72-702041
An animated film without dialog which presents life as man's conformity to a succession of social norms in the midst of people who do not care.
Psychology; Sociology
Dist - UWFKD **Prod** - BOZETO 1972

The Unafraid 35 MIN
VHS
Color; B&W (G)
$29.95 purchase _ #206
Combines footage from 1947 when writer Meyer Levin recorded the journey of Jews trying to reach the shores of Palestine under the watchful eyes of the British. Reveals that these people fled Europe, trekked across snow covered mountains, boarded overcrowded ships and risked their lives. Levin returns 30 years later to discover what happened to these people.
Geography - World; History - World; Sociology
Dist - ERGOM **Prod** - ERGOM

The Unapproachable
16mm
Color
Features an aging, reclusive star whose privacy is unexpectedly interrupted by a young admirer.
Fine Arts
Dist - TLECUL **Prod** - TLECUL

Unarmed combat 90 MIN
VHS
Combat for the stage and screen series
Color (PRO C G)
$275.00 purchase, $90.00 rental _ #620
Presents safe techniques for punching, slapping, hair pulling, kneeing, kicking, gouging and headbashing for stage and screen. Features David Boushey as instructor and producer. Part of a three - part series on stage and screen combat.

Fine Arts
Dist - FIRLIT

Unbidden voices 32 MIN
U-matic / VHS
Color (G)
$225.00 purchase, $60.00 rental
Documents the life of Manjula Joshi, an Indian immigrant woman who works 12 hours a day making poori in a restaurant on Chicago's Devon Street. Interweaves Joshi's history with theoretical texts and images from Indian films to arrive at the 'truth' of the experience of East Indian women. Questions the role of women in traditional cultures, the undervaluation of women's labor and the experience of immigration. Produced by Prajna Paramita Parasher and Deb Ellis.
Business and Economics; Sociology
Dist - WMEN

Unbroken Arrow Series
Captured 21 MIN
The Crusaders 21 MIN
Fair Exchange 22 MIN
The Red Plague 21 MIN
The Spy 22 MIN
Tower of Fire 20 MIN
Dist - LUF

The Unbroken Line 30 MIN
16mm
Color
_ #106C 0179 670N
Geography - World
Dist - CFLMDC **Prod** - NFBC 1979

Unbroken Tradition - Jerry Brown Pottery 28 MIN
16mm / VHS
Color (G)
$475.00, $100.00 purchase _#JBAPVHS
Documents the life and work of Alabama potter Jerry Brown. Views Brown at work creating various types of pottery pieces.
Fine Arts; Geography - United States
Dist - APPAL

UNC - nuclear lake 17 MIN
VHS
Color (G)
$14.95 purchase
Tells the story of an experimental plutonium plant near Pawling, New York. Tours the closed plant and interviews two former workers about the plutonium spill that closed the facility. Reveals that there are plans to make part of the site an extension of the Appalachian Trail.
History - United States; Social Science; Sociology
Dist - WMMI **Prod** - WMMI

The Uncalculated Risk 26 MIN
U-matic / VHS / 16mm
Color (C A) (FRENCH)
LC 73-700188
Shows how to tell guesswork from fact, and how to minimize the risk of uncritical inferences. Describes how to distinguish inference from observation.
Business and Economics; Guidance and Counseling; Sociology
Dist - RTBL **Prod** - RTBL 1971

Uncensored Movies 17 MIN
16mm
B&W
Presents Will Rogers satirizing some of the famous stars and motion pictures of the 1920s including William S Hart, Tom Mix The Covered Wagon, Way Down East, Rudolph Valentino in The Sheik and a risque Cecil B DeMille bedroom scene.
Fine Arts
Dist - KILLIS **Prod** - UNKNWN 1923

Unchained goddess 54 MIN
VHS
Color (G)
$19.95 purchase _ #470227
Reissues a Frank Capra animation production on the Goddess of Weather and other cartoon characters who explain what weather really is. Discusses the importance of the sun in creating climate and how the poles and equator make wind. Uses animation and live - action footage to portray hurricanes, tornadoes and other atmospheric conditions.
Fine Arts; Science - Physical
Dist - INSTRU **Prod** - CAPRA

The Unchained Goddess 59 MIN
U-matic
Bell System Science Series
Color (J H)
Discusses weather, explaining what it is, what causes it, and what scientists are doing to predict and control it. Includes scenes of hurricanes, tornadoes and lightning.
Science - Physical
Dist - WAVE **Prod** - ATAT 1958

The Unchained goddess - Pt 1 30 MIN
16mm
Bell system science series
Color
Uses live action, animation and documentary film excerpts to tell the story of weather, explaining what it is, what causes it, and what scientists are doing to predict and control it. Includes scenes of hurricanes, tornadoes and lightning.
Science - Physical
Dist - WAVE **Prod** - ATAT 1958

The Unchained goddess - Pt 2 29 MIN
16mm
Bell system science series
Color
Uses live action, animation and documentary film excerpts to tell the story of weather, explaining what it is, what causes it, and what scientists are doing to predict and control it. Includes scenes of hurricanes, tornadoes and lightning.
Science - Physical
Dist - WAVE **Prod** - ATAT 1958

Uncle Ben 27 MIN
16mm
Color
LC 79-700333
Tells the story of a man who is an alcoholic but who overcomes his problems and cares for his orphaned niece and nephews.
Health and Safety; Psychology; Sociology
Dist - BYU **Prod** - BYU 1978

Uncle Homer, Big John and Mr Bass 25 MIN
16mm
Color
Presents two fishermen illustrating favorite casting and bass fishing techniques using Zebco tackle under all conditions in all types of water.
Physical Education and Recreation
Dist - KAROL **Prod** - BRNSWK

Uncle Jack's mimosa 24 MIN
U-matic / VHS
Dollar scholar series; Pt 10
Color (H)
LC 82-707408
Presents high school senior Jerry Malone discussing taxation and credit.
Business and Economics; Home Economics
Dist - GPN **Prod** - BCSBIT 1982

Uncle Jim's Dairy Farm 25 MIN
U-matic / VHS / 16mm
Color (I J)
Shows a different way of looking at rural life. Features the story of a city boy on the farm. Shows a family that succeeds by striving together.
Agriculture; Geography - United States; Social Science
Dist - MTOLP **Prod** - MTOLP 1975

Uncle Jim's dairy farm - a summer visit with Aunt Helen and Uncle Jim 22 MIN
16mm
Color
Tells of a boy named George who visits his cousin on a modern dairy farm. Shows him learning to care for calves, milk cows, manage the business, shop and prepare meals.
Agriculture
Dist - NDC **Prod** - NDC 1977

Uncle Monty's gone 14 MIN
U-matic / VHS / 16mm
Learning values with Fat Albert and the Cosby kids series; Set II
Color (P I)
Deals with the loss of a loved one, explaining the importance of carrying on. Stresses that mourning is important and that friends will give comfort and support.
Guidance and Counseling; Sociology
Dist - MGHT **Prod** - FLMTON 1977

Uncle Moses 87 MIN
VHS
Maurice Schwartz films series
B&W (G) (YIDDISH WITH ENGLISH SUBTITLES)
$59.95 purchase _ #753
Features Maurice Schwartz as a 'despot' who rules his Lower East Side sweatshop with a tight grip. Reveals that the tyrant falls in love with the daughter of one of his discontented workers. Features Judith Abarbanel and Zvee Scooler.
Literature and Drama; Sociology
Dist - ERGOM **Prod** - ERGOM 1932

Uncle Nick and the magic forest series
Happy day parade - Volume 2 30 MIN
Poco and friends - Volume 1 30 MIN
Dist - HFDANC

Uncle Sam Magoo 52 MIN
16mm / VHS / U-matic
Color (P I J)
LC 79-701808
A shortened version of the motion picture Uncle Sam Magoo. Uses cartoon character Mr Magoo to outline America's history from the founding of the New World to the landing on the moon.
Fine Arts
Dist - MCFI **Prod** - UPA

Uncle Sam Magoo - Pt 1 26 MIN
16mm / U-matic / VHS
Color (P I J)
LC 79-701808
Uses cartoon character Mr Magoo to outline America's history from the founding of the New World to the landing on the moon.
History - United States
Dist - MCFI **Prod** - UPA

Uncle Sam Magoo - Pt 2 26 MIN
U-matic / VHS / 16mm
Color (P I J)
LC 79-701808
Uses cartoon character Mr Magoo to outline America's history from the founding of the New World to the landing on the moon.
History - United States
Dist - MCFI **Prod** - UPA

Uncle Sam - the Man and the Legend 23 MIN
16mm
Color
LC 76-700203
Recounts the life and work of Sam Wilson, an American merchant who became the model for America's Uncle Sam. Shows the towns and countryside in which he worked during the early 19th century.
Biography; Business and Economics; History - United States
Dist - NAR **Prod** - NAR 1976

Uncle Sam, the observer 75 MIN
VHS
March of time - trouble abroad series
B&W (G)
$24.95 purchase _ #S02178
Uses newsreel excerpts to cover events from 1938 through 1939. Covers events including the battles at the Maginot Line, the Good Neighbor Policy, Mexican economic troubles, and Boy Scout activities. Part five of a six - part series.
History - United States; History - World
Dist - UILL

Uncle Smiley and the junkyard playground 13 MIN
U-matic / VHS / 16mm
Uncle Smiley series
Color (P I)
LC 72-701560
Portrays Uncle Smiley and the children converting a junk - strewn lot into a delightful play area, imaginatively turning much of the junk to use.
Guidance and Counseling; Health and Safety; Literature and Drama; Science - Natural
Dist - LCOA **Prod** - GMEFL 1972

Uncle Smiley follows the seasons 14 MIN
16mm / VHS / U-matic
Uncle Smiley series
Captioned; Color (P I)
LC 72-701563
Depicts the fascinating rhythm of nature, with children as an inextricable part. Shows how all four seasons, that 'rotate like a ferris wheel,' are interrelated.
Science - Natural; Science - Physical
Dist - LCOA **Prod** - GMEFL 1972

Uncle Smiley Goes Camping 16 MIN
16mm / U-matic / VHS
Uncle Smiley Series
Color (K P)
LC 72-701564
Shows children how to protect their environment by keeping it clean and safe.
Literature and Drama; Physical Education and Recreation; Science - Natural; Social Science
Dist - LCOA **Prod** - GMEFL 1972

Uncle Smiley Goes Planting 15 MIN
U-matic / VHS / 16mm
Uncle Smiley Series
Color (P I)
LC 72-701562
Shows Uncle Smiley and children planting trees in an area ravaged by forest fire, utilizeing modern reforestation techniques.
Guidance and Counseling; Literature and Drama; Science - Natural
Dist - LCOA **Prod** - GMEFL 1972

Uncle Smiley goes recycling 13 MIN
U-matic / VHS / 16mm
Uncle Smiley series
Color (K P)
LC 72-701561
Introduces the term 'Recycling' to children and provides information about different recycling possibilities.
Literature and Drama; Science - Natural; Social Science
Dist - LCOA **Prod** - GMEFL 1972

Uncle Smiley Goes to the Beach 13 MIN
U-matic / VHS / 16mm
Uncle Smiley Series
Color (P I)
LC 72-701559
Shows Uncle Smiley and his group playing where land and sea meet. Emphasizes the possibilities for either use or misuse of public beaches.
Guidance and Counseling; Literature and Drama; Science - Natural
Dist - LCOA **Prod** - GMEFL 1972

Uncle Smiley Goes Up the River 11 MIN
U-matic / VHS / 16mm
Uncle Smiley Series
Color (P I)
LC 72-701565
Portrays Uncle Smiley and his group joining in an actual community - action program to clean up a river and its banks.
Geography - United States; Guidance and Counseling; Literature and Drama; Science - Natural; Social Science; Sociology
Dist - LCOA **Prod** - GMEFL 1972

Uncle Smiley Series
Uncle Smiley and the junkyard playground 13 MIN
Uncle Smiley follows the seasons 14 MIN
Uncle Smiley Goes Camping 16 MIN
Uncle Smiley Goes Planting 15 MIN
Uncle Smiley goes recycling 13 MIN
Uncle Smiley Goes to the Beach 13 MIN
Uncle Smiley Goes Up the River 11 MIN
Dist - LCOA

Uncle Sugar's flying circus 3 MIN
16mm
Color (G)
$8.00 rental
Presents a film made without a camera, using hole punches, felt pens, film leader and images from Picasso's Guernica as commentary on the bombing of Cambodia in 1970.
Fine Arts; History - United States; Sociology
Dist - CANCIN **Prod** - BASSW 1970

Uncle Vanya 110 MIN
VHS / 16mm
Color (H C G)
$139.00 purchase _ #DL353; LC 74-701905
Adapts the play by Anton Chekhov as performed at the Chichester Drama Festival. Features Sir Laurence Olivier, Joan Plowright, Rosemary Harris and Michael Redgrave, directed by Stuart Burge in the film version.
Fine Arts; Literature and Drama
Dist - INSIM CANTOR **Prod** - BRENT 1962

Uncommon courtesy 15 MIN
VHS
Respect series
CC; Color (I)
$89.95 purchase _ #10415VG
Instructs children in the rules of common courtesy such as politeness, taking turns and sharing. Uses live - action, graphics, narration, and music to teach polite expressions and respect for the privacy and belongings of others. Comes with a teacher's guide and a set of blackline masters. Part one of a four - part series.
Guidance and Counseling; Home Economics
Dist - UNL

Uncommon Images 22 MIN
16mm
Color
LC 77-702162
Presents the work of black photographer James Van DerZee, who set up shop in Harlem at the beginning of the 20th century and for 60 years recorded the public and private life of the black community.
Fine Arts; History - United States
Dist - FLMLIB **Prod** - WNBCTV

An Uncommon Journey
BETA / VHS
Adult Years - Continuity and Change Series
Color
Deals with issues of leadership style, personality and group dynamics through the story of eight women who participated in a two - week wilderness experience.
Physical Education and Recreation; Psychology; Sociology
Dist - OHUTC **Prod** - OHUTC

An Uncommon Man 17 MIN
U-matic / VHS
Color
Illustrates an interview with former Governor James Longley of Maine, who is facing terminal cancer. Includes introduction and closing by Kirk Douglas and reveals a personal account of how one man dealt with life.
Health and Safety
Dist - AMCS **Prod** - AMCS 1982

Uncommon places - the architecture of Frank Lloyd Wright 60 MIN
U-matic / VHS
Color (G)
Examines the work of Frank Lloyd Wright and notes the influence of nature's geometric forms upon his designs. Includes Wright's recorded remarks, the comments of current residents of Wright homes, and the reminiscences of Wright's apprentices and of his wife, Olgivanna.
Fine Arts; Home Economics; Industrial and Technical Education; Mathematics
Dist - PBS UEUWIS **Prod** - WHATV 1985

The Uncommonplace 8 MIN
16mm
Color
LC 80-701054
Highlights the city of Norfolk, Virginia, including its festivals, museums and recreational attractions.
Geography - United States
Dist - KLEINW **Prod** - KLEINW 1979

The Uncompromising revolution 54 MIN
VHS
Color & B&W (G)
$295.00 purchase, $95.00 rental
Profiles the Cuban Revolution and Fidel Castro at political middle age. Finds Castro in the midst of a 'rectification' campaign aimed at getting the Revolution back on course. Castro reflects on his life and Cuba, details his thoughts on Communism and the so - called 'new man' modeled after Che Guevara, and mingles with Cuban citizens. Produced by Saul Landau.
Civics and Political Systems; Geography - World; History - World
Dist - CNEMAG

Unconformity 10 MIN
VHS
History in the rocks series
Color (H C)
$24.95 purchase _ #S9814
Discusses nonconforming stratification of sedimentary rock using single - concept format. Part of a ten - part series on rocks.
Science - Physical
Dist - HUBDSC **Prod** - HUBDSC

Unconquered 15 MIN
16mm
Color
Examines the Seminole Indians of Florida.
Geography - United States; History - United States; Social Science; Sociology
Dist - FLADC **Prod** - FLADC

The Unconscious Athlete - Conditions of the Head, Neck and Spine 30 MIN
U-matic
Sports Medicine in the 80's Series
Color (G)
Teaches the role of sports medicine as it relates to athlete, coach, trainer, team and school. Covers most kinds of injuries encountered in sports.
Health and Safety; Physical Education and Recreation
Dist - CEPRO **Prod** - CEPRO

Unconscious Cultural Clashes Series
Customs 30 MIN
Education vs education 30 MIN
Grand assumptions 30 MIN
Look Me in the Eye 30 MIN
Objective - Acculturation 30 MIN
Outlook 30 MIN
Dist - SCCOE

The Unconscious level - Section A 25 MIN
U-matic / VHS
Management by responsibility series
Color
Business and Economics; Psychology
Dist - DELTAK **Prod** - TRAINS

The Unconscious level - Section B 33 MIN
U-matic / VHS
Management by responsibility series
Color
Business and Economics; Psychology
Dist - DELTAK **Prod** - TRAINS

Unconscious London strata 22 MIN
16mm
Color (G)
$857.00 purchase, $50.00 rental
Photographs London in 1979. Explores the depths of unconscious reactions.
Fine Arts
Dist - CANCIN **Prod** - BRAKS 1982

Unconventional Gas Resources 29 MIN
16mm / U-matic / VHS
Color
Provides an overview of Department Of Energy, industry, state and national lab activities in the recovery of unconventional gas. Shows coring operations, test wells, production enhancement and how they relate to methane from coalbeds, geopressured acquifiers, eastern gas shales and western gas sands.
Industrial and Technical Education; Social Science
Dist - USNAC **Prod** - USDOE 1980

Uncounted Enemy - Unproven Conspiracy 29 MIN
U-matic / VHS
Inside Story Series
Color
Examines the 1982 CBS documentary, The Uncounted Enemy - A Vietnam Deception. Tells how it created great repercussions as it alleged that General William Westmoreland had been involved in a conspiracy to deceive both government leaders and the American public about enemy troop strength in Vietnam.
Fine Arts; History - United States; Sociology
Dist - PBS **Prod** - PBS 1981

Uncover Your Creativity 6 MIN
VHS / 16mm
Color (C A G)
$375.00 purchase, $150.00 rental _ #179
Offers six simple rules to help viewers uncover and use their creativity to solve personal and professional problems. Animated. Includes Leader's Guide.
Fine Arts; Literature and Drama; Psychology
Dist - SALENG **Prod** - REALVP 1985

Uncovering, remedying and reporting antitrust violations 176 MIN
U-matic / VHS
Preventive antitrust - corporate compliance program series
Color (PRO)
Uncovers antitrust problem and discusses appropriate compliance action. Explores obligations to report violations. Provides criteria for a corporation's determination of need to seek outside counsel and shows the method by which to choose such counsel.
Business and Economics; Civics and Political Systems
Dist - ABACPE **Prod** - ABACPE

Uncrating and assembly of the P - 47 thunderbolt airplane - dive bombing 60 MIN
U-matic / VHS
B&W
Illustrates step - by - step assembling of the P - 47 thunderbolt on the field without heavy lifting equipment. Depicts various dive - bombing techniques as Army Air Force training.
Civics and Political Systems; Industrial and Technical Education
Dist - IHF **Prod** - IHF

Und Der Regen Vewischt Jede Spur 100 MIN
16mm
Color (GERMAN (ENGLISH SUBTITLES))
Tells the story of a love destroyed by the death of the woman's former lover.
Sociology
Dist - WSTGLC **Prod** - WSTGLC 1972

Und Viel Zu Essen Nicht Vergessen 15 MIN
16mm / U-matic / VHS
Guten Tag Series no 20; No 20
B&W (H) (GERMAN)
LC 74-707333
Presents an episode in which the characters employ frequently used expressions and idioms in order to teach conversational German to beginners. Stresses the correct use of compound verbs, verbs written together with the infinitive, verbs with prepositions, and objectives with prepositions.
Foreign Language
Dist - IFB **Prod** - FRGMFA 1970

Und Weit Und Breit Keine Tankstelle 15 MIN
16mm / U-matic / VHS
Guten Tag Wie Geht's Series
Color (H C) (GERMAN)
Features Herr Hoffmann and his son trying to avoid heavy traffic on the Autobahn on Sunday. Pictures them travelling remote country roads which lead to total confusion.

Foreign Language
Dist - IFB **Prod** - BAYER 1973

Undala 28 MIN
U-matic / VHS / 16mm
Color (H C G T A)
Documents the varied rhythms and phases of human movement and life during undala, the hot, windy months preceding the monsoons, in a small Hindu village bordering the Thar Desert in northwest India. For farmers, it is a time of leisure and repair; for women, endless waterbearing; and for craftsmen, a time of little change in their daily routine. No narration. Original musical score of Hindustani classical and folk styles.
Fine Arts; Geography - World
Dist - PSU **Prod** - PSU 1967

The Undebt 5 MIN
U-matic / VHS
Color (H C A)
Presents comedy by the Brave New World Workshop of the Twin Cities.
Literature and Drama
Dist - UCV **Prod** - BRVNP

Undelivered - no such country 10 MIN
16mm
Color (A C)
$275.00 purchase, $20.00 rental
Documents the work required of US postal workers. Contrasts this with the image that is presented to customers on the exterior of the average small town post office. A Documentary by Ralph Arlyck.
Psychology; Social Science; Sociology
Dist - ARRA **Prod** - ARRA 1975

Undeniable evidence
VHS
Color (G)
$35.00 purchase _ #ARK001
Looks at England's strange crop circles to decide if they are evidence of alien landings or an elaborate hoax.
Science - Physical; Sociology
Dist - SIV

Under 30 series
Dimensions of Black 59 MIN
Dist - PBS

Under African skies series
Explores how African music reflects Africa's culture, religion, and politics. Seeks out the diverse music of Africa to find out where it comes from, what it means, and where it's going. Reviews music from Zimbabwe, Ethiopia, Mali, Algeria, and Zaire. A five-part series.
Algeria 60 MIN
Ethiopia 60 MIN
Mali 60 MIN
Zaire 60 MIN
Zimbabwe 60 MIN
Dist - BBCENE

Under Arrest 15 MIN
16mm / U-matic / VHS
Color (J H C)
LC 75-700988
Shows what happens when a young man, stopped by police because of his resemblance to a wanted murderer, resists arrest and assaults a police officer. Examines the rights and duties of the police and the citizen and explains the incident from both points of view.
Civics and Political Systems; Guidance and Counseling; Social Science
Dist - CORF **Prod** - NELCO 1974

Under cover 20 MIN
VHS / U-matic
Tomes and talismans series
(I J)
$145 purchase, $27 rental, $90 self dub
Uses a science fantasy format to define, illustrate and review basic library research concepts. Designed for sixth, seventh and eighth graders. Discusses the parts of a book. Third in a 13 part series.
Education; Social Science
Dist - GPN **Prod** - MISETV

Under fire
U-matic / VHS / BETA
Color (H C A)
$119.00 purchase _ #05955 94
Dramatizes the lives of correspondents caught up in intrique and violence amidst the 1979 Nicaraguan revolution. Stars Nick Nolte, Gene Hackamn, and Joanna Cassidy.
Fine Arts; History - World; Literature and Drama
Dist - ASPRSS **Prod** - GA
GA

Under Fives Series
Pre - Verbal Communication 16 MIN
Stress of Separation 16 MIN
Dist - FLMLIB

Under high skies 28 MIN
16mm
Color (H C A)
Describes Northern Germany and its trading towns, such as Bremen, Bremerhaven and Hamburg, whose close economic ties were forged with European and overseas partners. Presents three people and the circumstances peculiar to their lives - a fisherman from the North Sea coast, a coffee merchant in Hamburg and a farmer in East Frisia.
History - World
Dist - WSTGLC **Prod** - WSTGLC

Under milkwood 88 MIN
VHS
Color (H C)
$79.00 purchase _ #04586 - 126
Stars Richard Burton, Elizabeth Taylor and Peter O'Toole in a film adaptation of the radio play by Dylan Thomas. Describes life in the Welsh village of Llareggub.
Fine Arts; Literature and Drama
Dist - GA **Prod** - GA

Under One Roof 19 MIN
16mm
Color (A) (SPANISH)
Explains the benefits of a hospital Triage Clinic for communities with little medical care.
Health and Safety
Dist - FMSP **Prod** - FMSP 1977

Under One Roof 16 MIN
VHS / U-matic
Color (J A)
Documents the workings of a comprehensive ambulatory care center where all health care services are under one roof.
Health and Safety
Dist - SUTHRB **Prod** - SUTHRB

Under orders, under fire - Part 1 60 MIN
U-matic / VHS
Ethics in America series; 6
Color (G)
$45.00, $29.95 purchase; $8.00 rental _ #60867
Features Generals William Westmoreland, David Jones and Brent Scowcroft, correspondents Peter Jennings and Mike Wallace, and others. Questions the mility duty to follow orders and a general's obligation to protect soldiers. Part I of a two - part examination of military ethics, and part six of a ten - part series on ethics in America, produced by Fred W Friendly.
Civics and Political Systems; Religion and Philosophy; Sociology
Dist - ANNCPB **Prod** - COLMU 1989
PSU

Under orders, under fire - Part 2 60 MIN
VHS / U-matic
Ethics in America series; 7
Color (G)
$45.00, $29.95 purchase; $8.00 rental _ #60866
Features a debate between United States military generals and Chaplain Timothy Tatum of the US Army, the Rev J Bryan Hehir of the US Catholic Conference and others. Discusses the issues of confidentiality between the soldier and chaplain and military justice, an issue raised by the My Lai massacre. Part II of a two - part examination of military ethics and part seven of a ten - part series on ethics in America, produced by Fred W Friendly.
Civics and Political Systems; History - United States; Religion and Philosophy; Sociology
Dist - ANNCPB **Prod** - COLMU 1989
PSU

Under our skin - exploring racial and cultural differences 32 MIN
VHS
Color (I J H)
$189.00 purchase _ #CG - 906 - VS
Documents the creation and staging of a play by a diverse group of high school students who use music, dance and discussion to share their experiences and perceptions with the audience. Uses footage from workshops with the cast, live performances and post - performance classrooms discussion to address issues as stereotypes, discrimination, intervention techniques, classroom dynamics, cultural identity and cross - racial friendships.
Fine Arts; History - United States; Psychology; Social Science; Sociology
Dist - HRMC **Prod** - HRMC

Under Royal Patronage 28 MIN
16mm
B&W
LC 77-713144
A comedy about the clever ruse planned by a prince and his friend to avoid a state marriage.
Civics and Political Systems; Literature and Drama; Sociology
Dist - RMIBHF **Prod** - ENY

Under sail series
All hands on deck 30 MIN
Common courtesy 30 MIN
Every sailor's dream 30 MIN
Full Speed Ahead 30 MIN
Man Overboard 30 MIN
On the Open Sea 30 MIN
Right on Course 30 MIN
Set sail 30 MIN
Dist - CORF

Under sail with Robbie Doyle series
may sailing
Reading the wind
Rules of the sea
Sailing for new sailors
Sailing for paradise
Dist - SEVVID

Under - Secretary General of U N for the Office of Press Information 28 MIN
Videoreel / VHS
Marilyn's Manhattan Series
Color
Presents an interview with Under - Secretary - General of the United Nations for the Department of Press Information Genichi Akatani on the United Nations' place in the world. Hosted by Marilyn Perry.
Civics and Political Systems
Dist - PERRYM **Prod** - PERRYM

Under the arbor - a world premiere opera - as seen on PBS 112 MIN
VHS
Color (I)
$29.95 purchase_#1442
Presents a new American opera by Robert Greenleaf, with setting on banks of the Chattahoochee River in 1943. Tells the romance of a pair of young lovers taking the first steps toward sexual awakening.
Fine Arts
Dist - KULTUR

Under the Bethlehem Star 8 MIN
16mm
Christ, the Light of the World Series
Color (P)
A village shepherd family taking care of their sheep in the hills go into Bethlehem and find Joseph and Mary and the new - born Infant Jesus in a stable. Later, wise men from the East follow the sign of the star to the house where the young Child is found and offer their gifts to him.
Religion and Philosophy
Dist - FAMF **Prod** - FAMF

Under the Biltmore Clock 70 MIN
VHS / U-matic
Color (J H C A)
$125 purchase _ #5110C
Tells what happens when a woman falls for a wealthy young man and he hires actors to play the members of his 'eccentric' family. Based on the story 'Myra Meets His Family' by F. Scott Fitzgerald.
Literature and Drama
Dist - CORF

Under the Blue Umbrella Series
Alike but different 14 MIN
Beat the buzzer 14 MIN
Beth's new shoes 14 MIN
Family portraits 14 MIN
Grandmother's coming 14 MIN
It's a Grand Old Flag 14 MIN
It's Payday 14 MIN
It's Time to Go to Work 14 MIN
New York's My Town 14 MIN
Questions and Answers - Globes 13 MIN
Questions and Answers - Maps 14 MIN
St Matthews is My Home 14 MIN
Washington, DC - a Special City 14 MIN
Westville, 1850 14 MIN
What's Wrong 13 MIN
Yes, I Can 13 MIN
Dist - AITECH

Under the Bridge 117 MIN
VHS
Color (G) (MANDARIN CHINESE (ENGLISH SUBTITLES))
$45.00 purchase _ #1063A
Presents a Mandarin Chinese language movie produced in the People's Republic of China.
Fine Arts; Geography - World; Literature and Drama
Dist - CHTSUI **Prod** - CHTSUI

Under the Clouds of War 20 MIN
16mm / U-matic / VHS
March of Time Series
B&W (J)
Discusses the events leading up to World War II, including Mussolini's invasion of Ethiopia, Hitler's march into Austria and Neville Chamberlain's attempts to negotiate a peaceful settlement.

History - United States; History - World
Dist - TIMLIF **Prod** - TIMLIF 1974

Under the Covers - American Quilts 12 MIN
U-matic / VHS / 16mm
Color (H)
LC 76-702907
Focuses on the historical importance and homespun vitality of American quilts while showing different patterns, stitches, colors and shapes.
Fine Arts; Home Economics
Dist - PFP **Prod** - PFP 1976

Under the gun - democracy in Guatemala 40 MIN
16mm / VHS
Color (G)
$685.00, $325.00 purchase, $85.00 rental
Looks at Guatemala's statistics - after 30 years of military rule 100,000 people are dead, another 40,000 have 'disappeared,' and hundreds of thousands are exiled, widowed or orphaned. Examines the veracity of the United States' State Department's announcement that the election of Vinicio Cerezo marked the return of democracy. Focuses on the issues of military vs civilian control, land and the rural economy, and the status of human rights practices in the country. Produced by Pat Goudvis and Robert Richter.
Civics and Political Systems; Fine Arts
Dist - FIRS

Under the Hood 35 MIN
U-matic / VHS / 16mm
Color
Demonstrates how to make regular inspections of tires, shock absorbers, the brake system and the exhaust system. Shows how to identify problems early and describe the problems accurately to a mechanic.
Industrial and Technical Education
Dist - BULFRG **Prod** - ODECA

Under the hood and around your car 27 MIN
VHS
Color (H C G)
$29.95 purchase _ #SPR101V; $14.95 purchase _ #HT19
Offers step - by - step instructions on engine maintenance and the physical upkeep of a car. Provides easily referenced sections on changing engine oil, brake fluid, power steering fluid, windshield washer solvent, transmission fluid, coolant - antifreeze, air filters, batteries and drive belts. Discusses lamp inspection, tire inspection, changing windshield wipers, spray lubricants, shock absorber inspection and appearance preservation. Stresses safety practices.
Home Economics; Industrial and Technical Education
Dist - CAMV
SVIP

Under the influence 27 MIN
16mm / U-matic
Color (J H C)
LC 77-701382
Documents the 1975 tests designed to discover exactly how impaired the average driver is at .10 percent blood alcohol concentration. Compares drivers' ability to negotiate a driving course sober and after five to six drinks.
Health and Safety; Industrial and Technical Education; Sociology
Dist - IA **Prod** - NHTSA 1976
USNAC USDTFH

Under the Influence 26 MIN
16mm
Color (H C A)
LC 77-701382
Shows the results of experiments conducted to determine whether .1 percent alcohol in the bloodstream impairs an individual's driving abilities.
Health and Safety; Sociology
Dist - SUTHRB **Prod** - RAMFLM 1977

Under the Influence 25 MIN
16mm / VHS
Color (J H C PRO)
$295.00, $395.00 purchase, $75.00 rental _ #9770
Documents that drivers consistently overestimate the amount of alcohol they can drink and still drive safely.
Health and Safety; Industrial and Technical Education
Dist - AIMS **Prod** - AIMS 1977

Under the influence II - a decade later 27 MIN
VHS
Color (J H) (SPANISH)
$395.00 purchase
Presents the results of a two - day drinking and driving experiment. Shows that safe driving is significantly impaired by even .05 blood - alcohol content, and most definitely at .10. Made in cooperation with the California Highway Patrol.
Guidance and Counseling; Health and Safety; Sociology
Dist - FMSP **Prod** - FMSP 1994

Under the influence - pt 2 30 MIN
VHS
At the wheel - edited version - series
Color (S)
$79.00 purchase _ #101 - 9209
Examines the complexity of the problem of drunk driving. Portrays an actual murder trial held after a motorist driving under the influence of alcohol caused a fatal accident. Edited version.
Health and Safety; Industrial and Technical Education; Psychology; Sociology
Dist - FI **Prod** - NFBC 1988

Under the influence - Pt 3 50 MIN
16mm / VHS
At the wheel - unedited version - series
Color (S)
$750.00, $79.00 purchase _ #101 - 9108
Investigates a matter of increasing public concern, death and destruction on our roads and highways. Examines four aspects of the problem of drunk driving in a four part series. Portrays an actual murder trial held after a motorist driving under the influence of alcohol caused a fatal accident. Unedited version.
Health and Safety; Industrial and Technical Education; Psychology; Sociology
Dist - FI **Prod** - NFBC 1987

Under the Israeli thumb - dispossession of Palestinians 20 MIN
U-matic / VHS
Color
$335.00 purchase
History - World; Sociology
Dist - ABCLR **Prod** - ABCLR 1982

Under the knife 30 MIN
VHS
Business matters series
Color (A)
PdS65 purchase
Looks at management styles at the Beth Israel Hospital in Boston - as Britain's National Health Service experiences upheaval with the creation of independent trusts. Questions what the London's Royal Free Hospital can learn from the United States.
Health and Safety
Dist - BBCENE

Under the Law, Pt 2 Series
Bad guys - good guys 25 MIN
The Matter of David J 16 MIN
Three Days in the County Jail 19 MIN
Vandals 17 MIN
Dist - CORF

Under the law series
Arrest and Seize 17 MIN
The Hitchhike 17 MIN
Muggers 15 MIN
The Plea 15 MIN
The Ripoff 15 MIN
Dist - CORF

Under the Men's Tree 15 MIN
U-matic / VHS / 16mm
B&W (H C A)
LC 74-703380
Shows life in a Jie cattle camp in the Karamoja district of northern Uganda. Focuses on a group of men as they cut cowhide rope, tell stories and sleep.
Agriculture; Geography - World; Sociology
Dist - UCEMC **Prod** - MCDGAL 1973

Under the rainbow - a school girl in India helps kids 28 MIN
VHS
Color (J H G)
$295.00 purchase, $55.00 rental
Focuses on 15 - year - old Jacinta Gomes who is teaching street children the basics of reading and writing. Reveals that Gomes and her classmates, as part of the Rainbow Program, teach on the rooftop of their school because their students cannot adjust to traditional instruction. Directed by Marc Cayer.
Education; English Language; Geography - World; Sociology
Dist - FLMLIB

Under the Sun 15 MIN
16mm
Color (G)
_ #106C 0182 571
Shows what research has been done for alternate energy sources in Canada. Shows how solar energy is being used through private and public initiatives and promotes a greater understanding of solar energy.
Geography - World; Social Science
Dist - CFLMDC **Prod** - NFBC 1982

Under the sun series - Hamar trilogy 150 MIN
VHS
Under the sun series - Hamar trilogy
Color (A)
PdS150 purchase
Examines the Hamar, an isolated people living in the dry scrubland of south-western Ethiopia. Concentrates on the proud and outspoken Hamar women.
Psychology
Dist - BBCENE

Under the sun series
Cat and the mouse 50 MIN
Dragon bride 50 MIN
Guardians of the flute 50 MIN
Under the sun series
Women of the yellow earth 50 MIN
Dist - BBCENE

Under the Thumb 50 MIN
16mm / U-matic
Assignment Maclear Series
Color; Mono (J H C A)
$500.00 film, $350.00 video, $50.00 rental
Presents a look into three cities whose governments were seized by a hostile force and then reformed. Looks at the attitude of the peoples in Athens, Budapest, and Singapore following the takeovers.
Civics and Political Systems; Sociology
Dist - CTV **Prod** - CTV 1977

Under the volcano 112 MIN
VHS
Color (H C)
$97.00 purchase _ #04587 - 126
Portrays a desperate, alcoholic ex - British consulate who mulls over his life in Mexico during the 'Day of the Dead' ceremonies in 1939.
Literature and Drama
Dist - GA **Prod** - GA

Under the Yellow Balloon Series
Buying a house 13 MIN
Daddy's gone 14 MIN
Errands for Mama 14 MIN
Flying 14 MIN
I'm Adopted 14 MIN
It's My Job 14 MIN
Making a Newspaper 13 MIN
My New Home 14 MIN
The Phone Isn't Working 14 MIN
Ships A'Sail 14 MIN
Trains 14 MIN
A Treasure Hunt 15 MIN
We're Spending Too Much Money 12 MIN
What Should I Buy 14 MIN
Where are We 14 MIN
Working in Washington 13 MIN
Dist - AITECH

Under the Yum Yum Tree 110 MIN
U-matic / VHS / 16mm
Color (J)
Stars Jack Lemmon as a whimsical philanderer dedicated to the pursuit of beautiful and desirous females.
Literature and Drama
Dist - FI **Prod** - CPC 1963

Under wraps 19 MIN
VHS
Color (A)
$525.00 purchase
Discusses the importance of protecting business information from unauthorized outsiders and insiders. Demonstrates how written and non - written information is vulnerable and what can be done to secure it.
Business and Economics; Computer Science; Education
Dist - COMFLM **Prod** - COMFLM

Underachievement syndrome - causes, prevention and cures
VHS
Giftedness - research and practice series
Color (T)
$49.95 purchase
Looks at the pressures to achieve from home and school on gifted children which may produce the opposite result. Focuses on the characteristics and causes of underachievement in gifted children as well as the prevention and cure. Presented by Dr Sylvia Rimm of Educational Assessment Service Inc. Part of a six - part series on gifted children.
Education; Psychology
Dist - UCALG **Prod** - UCALG 1991

Undercurrents 12 MIN
16mm
B&W w/color tint (H C A)
$35.00 rental
Journeys through underwater landscapes, superimposed over time altered urban scenes. Utilizes heavily filtered light and shadows and multiple exposures to create a

surrealistic, dreamy effect. Produced by Jon Behrens with original music by Rubato.
Fine Arts; Geography - World
Dist - CANCIN

Undercurrents 12 MIN
U-matic / VHS / 16mm
Color (J)
LC 73-703443
Presents impressions of the blue - green depths of the Mexican seas, showing fish swaying like orchestral members tuning up, crabs dancing and a giant manta ray waltzing with the camera.
Industrial and Technical Education; Science - Natural
Dist - PHENIX **Prod** - PHENIX 1973

Underdeveloped and overexposed - putting your self - esteem in focus 30 MIN
VHS
Color (I J H)
$79.95 purchase _ #CCP120V
Acquaints young adults with the problems caused by low self - esteem and teaches techniques for creating a more positive self - image. Shows what self - esteem is, how it is formed and the difficulties created by low self - esteem. Follows three high school students who are struggling with their own self - image and teaches techniques for combating low self - esteem and exercises for turning negative feelings into positive attributes. Includes Feel Better About You workbook.
Guidance and Counseling; Health and Safety; Psychology
Dist - CAMV **Prod** - CAMV 1993

Underexposed - the temple of the fetus 72 MIN
VHS
Color (G)
$75.00 rental, $275.00 purchase
Combines drama and documentary to probe into high - tech baby - making. Tracks the history of the treatment of women's sexual and reproductive systems as 'diseased,' requiring the intervention of medical institutions to 'save' them from their own bodies. Looks at the social and political contexts of contemporary reproductive technologies. Produced by Kathy High.
Fine Arts; Science - Natural; Sociology
Dist - WMEN

Underglaze and Overglaze Decor 28 MIN
Videoreel / VT2
Wheels, Kilns and Clay Series
Color
Features Mrs Peterson describing certain ceramic processes for her classroom at the University of Southern California. Illustrates underglaze and overglaze decor.
Fine Arts
Dist - PBS **Prod** - USC

Undergraduate Medical Education 78 MIN
U-matic
Color
LC 77-706034
Presents a discussion on undergraduate medical education by Dr John A Cooper given at the Colloquium on the Bicentennial of Medicine in the United States. Based on the paper Undergraduate Medical Education by John A Cooper in the book Advances In American Medicine - Essays At The Bicentennial.
Education; Health and Safety; Science
Dist - USNAC **Prod** - NMAC 1976

Undergraduate medical education - Pt 1 39 MIN
U-matic
Color
LC 77-706034
Presents a discussion on undergraduate medical education by Dr John A Cooper given at the Colloquium on the Bicentennial of Medicine in the United States. Based on the paper Undergraduate Medical Education by John A Cooper in the book Advances In American Medicine - Essays At The Bicentennial.
Health and Safety
Dist - USNAC **Prod** - NMAC 1976

Undergraduate medical education - Pt 2 39 MIN
U-matic
Color
LC 77-706034
Presents a discussion on undergraduate medical education by Dr John A Cooper given at the Colloquium on the Bicentennial of Medicine in the United States. Based on the paper Undergraduate Medical Education by John A Cooper in the book Advances In American Medicine - Essays At The Bicentennial.
Health and Safety
Dist - USNAC **Prod** - NMAC 1976

Underground 5 MIN
16mm
B&W (H C A)
Presents a cinematic examination of subway paranoia presented in a series of still photographs interspersed with scenes of a moving subway train.
Industrial and Technical Education; Literature and Drama
Dist - UWFKD **Prod** - UWFKD

Underground 88 MIN
16mm
Color
Documents the political activism of the 1960's and 1970's, focusing on the Weather Underground Organization.
Civics and Political Systems; History - United States; Sociology
Dist - FIRS **Prod** - FIRS

Underground centenary 18 MIN
16mm / U-matic / VHS
B&W (I J H)
Traces the development of the London Underground from 1850 to the present day. Shows how London continues to improve the underground which is so important to its economic and social needs.
Geography - World; Psychology; Science - Natural; Social Science; Sociology
Dist - IFB **Prod** - BTF 1963

Underground Coal Mine Blasting 19 MIN
16mm
Color
LC 76-701543
Points out the importance of using explosives as a kind of industrial force to remove coal from the Earth. Describes some of the more common hazards encountered when working with explosives, detonators and related equipment.
Industrial and Technical Education; Social Science
Dist - USNAC **Prod** - USMESA 1975

Underground explosion 6 MIN
16mm
Color (G)
$15.00 rental
Features Paul and Limpe Fuchs, Amom Duul II, Valie Export and Peter Weibel with music by Heinz Hein.
Fine Arts
Dist - CANCIN **Prod** - KRENKU 1969

Underground film 29 MIN
Videoreel / VT2
Synergism - in today's world series
Color
Explores the phenomenon of the underground film movement. Follows Chick Strand as she films on location, edits in her studio garret and philosophizes on the art of fimmaking. Visits the office of Genesis Films in Los Angeles, a company formed by young filmmakers to distribute their films. Includes a visit to a midnight showing of underground films at the Unicorn Theatre in La Jolla.
Fine Arts; Industrial and Technical Education
Dist - PBS **Prod** - KPBS

Underground Haulage Hazards 12 MIN
U-matic / VHS / 16mm
Color (IND)
Presents an overview of factors that can contribute to accidents involving haulage vehicles in underground mines and shows methods of prevention.
Health and Safety; Psychology; Social Science
Dist - USNAC **Prod** - USDL 1983

Underground Housing 22 MIN
U-matic / VHS
Color
Visits several existing underground homes in Minnesota, a new trend in energy saving which saves up to 70 per cent in energy bills.
Social Science; Sociology
Dist - WCCOTV **Prod** - WCCOTV 1978

The Underground Movie 14 MIN
16mm
Color (K P I)
LC 77-703381
Introduces the basic composition of the Earth's interior by presenting an animated story about a journey through the center of of the Earth.
Science - Physical
Dist - BESTF **Prod** - NFBC 1972

Underground Nuclear Weapons Testing 29 MIN
16mm
Color (H C)
LC FIE67-133
Shows how underground tests of nuclear weapons are planned and conducted at the Nevada test site in a manner designed to contain radioactivity within the ground and to comply with the limited Test Ban Treaty, while providing the diagnostic information needed. Explains various types of nuclear tests and the use of various test areas and their facilities.
Civics and Political Systems; Science - Physical
Dist - USNAC **Prod** - NOO 1967

The Underground Railroad 15 MIN
U-matic / VHS
Stories of America Series
Color (P)
Focuses on the contribution of one young boy to the Underground Railroad.
History - United States
Dist - AITECH **Prod** - OHSDE 1976

Underground water 21 MIN
VHS
Color (J H C)
$39.95 purchase _ #IV114
Explores water trapped in between grains of rock underground. Investigates wells, water flow, hydrology, artesian wells and the water table.
Science - Physical
Dist - INSTRU

Underground Waters 19 MIN
16mm
Color
Portrays the water cycle, action of rainwater on rocks, caverns, underground streams and hot springs.
Science - Natural; Science - Physical
Dist - BELMNE **Prod** - BELMNE 1958

Underhand Throw and Catch 15 MIN
VHS / U-matic
Leaps and Bounds Series no 12
Color (T)
Explains how to teach primary students the underhand roll, how to catch a rolling ball, rolling at stationary and moving targets, the underhand self - toss, the throw for force and the throw for accuracy.
Physical Education and Recreation
Dist - AITECH

Underlining and Stay Stitching 29 MIN
Videoreel / VT2
Sewing Skills - Tailoring Series
Color
Features Mrs Ruth Hickman demonstrating how to underline and stay stitch.
Home Economics
Dist - PBS **Prod** - KRMATV

Underlining, italics, hyphenation, quotations - tricks of the trade 18 MIN
VHS
Language construction company series
Color (H C G)
$50.00 purchase _ #LCC - 14
Assists students in improving their written and spoken English grammar skills. Bases all programs on a 'construction theme.' Includes review tests as an integral part of each lesson. Students may stop, start and repeat any part of the lesson. Visual cues are given for review purposes. Part of a 15 - part series.
English Language
Dist - INSTRU

Underlining techniques 5 MIN
16mm
Clothing construction techniques series
Color (J)
LC 77-701174
Describes uses of underlinings and shows how to attach the underlining fabric to the fashion fabric. Illustrates techniques of stitching darts and hemming when an underlining is used.
Home Economics
Dist - IOWASP **Prod** - IOWA 1976

Underlying concepts in the proof of the Bieberbach conjecture 60 MIN
VHS
ICM Plenary addresses series
Color (PRO G)
$49.00 purchase _ #VIDDEBRANGES - VB2
Presents Louis de Branges who discusses the underlying concepts in the proof of the Bieberbach conjecture.
Mathematics
Dist - AMSOC **Prod** - AMSOC

The Underlying threat 48 MIN
VHS
Color (J H C G)
$285.00 purchase, $75.00 rental
Offers a penetrating look at the poisoning of Earth's underground water supplies and the devastating consequences for people whose drinking water comes from beneath the Earth. Examines how four families and two communities in Canada and the United States responded to the discovery of toxic chemicals in their water. A film by Kevin Matthews.
Fine Arts; Science - Natural
Dist - BULFRG **Prod** - NFBC 1990

Undermining the Great Depression 25 MIN
VHS / U-matic
Color
Narrates the story of a small Oregon town's unique means of survival during the Great Depression, gold mining in their own backyards. Presents five oldtimers recalling stories of the period.
Business and Economics; History - United States; Industrial and Technical Education; Social Science
Dist - MEDIPR **Prod** - MEDIPR 1981

Underscan 8 MIN
U-matic
B&W
Chronicles the daily events in the aging woman's life, including the gradual deterioration of both her body and her house.
Health and Safety; Sociology
Dist - WMEN **Prod** - WMEN

Underscoring 10 MIN
16mm
Color (R)
Describes the work of the film composer. The film follows one musical segment from its inception through its incorporation into the film Beyond the Night.
Fine Arts
Dist - UF **Prod** - UF

The Undersea adventures of Pickle and Bill 24 MIN
VHS / U-matic
Young people's specials series
Color
Follows two teenagers on a zoological expedition to Jamaica.
Geography - World; Sociology
Dist - MULTPP **Prod** - MULTPP

Undersea Explorer 14 MIN
16mm
Color
LC 74-705871
Tells about the operating techniques and features common to Navy and commercial submersibles. Shows methods used to avoid them.
Civics and Political Systems; Health and Safety; Science - Physical
Dist - USNAC **Prod** - USN 1971

Undersea oases - the science of hardbottoms 15 MIN
VHS
Color (J H G)
$19.95 purchase _ #UO101
Plunges to the continental shelf between North Carolina and Florida for a view of the perplexing rocky outcrops called hardbottoms. Reveals that the crumbling ledges of these rocky cliffs are surrounded by sandy flats and topped by algal meadows that attract an array of marine life. Discloses that the amount of life along these hard bottoms is more abundant than on other parts of the continental shelf, a phenomena not yet explained by scientists. Produced by Marine Grafics and University of North Carolina Sea Grant College Program. Includes a fact sheet listing organisms appearing in the video, scientists, equipment and suggested further reading.
Science - Natural; Science - Physical
Dist - ENVIMC

The Undersea stranglers 22 MIN
U-matic / VHS
America at war series
Color (H C A)
$79.00 purchase _ #HP - 6286C
Traces the history of submarines in warfare. Considers that today's nuclear subs are far more deadly, harder to detect and contain enough power to win a war. Part of a series produced by Lou Reda Productions, Inc.
Civics and Political Systems; History - United States; Sociology
Dist - CORF

Undersea world of Jacques Cousteau series
Utilizes undersea photography to document the adventures of the sea in a series of 24 programs. Features shortened versions of the original programs.

Beneath the frozen world	23 MIN
Blizzard at Hope Bay	52 MIN
Coral divers of Corsica	52 MIN
Coral jungle	52 MIN
Desert whales	52 MIN
The dragons of Galapagos	23 MIN
The Dragons of the Galapagos	52 MIN
Fish that swallowed Jonah	52 MIN
500 million years beneath the sea	24 MIN
Five hundred million years beneath the sea	24 MIN
The Flight of penguins	24.5 MIN
The Flight of the penguins	25 MIN
The green sea turtle	21 MIN
Hippo	52 MIN
Lagoon of Lost Ships	52 MIN
Legend of Lake Titicaca	22 MIN
Life at the End of the World	52 MIN
Mysteries of the Hidden Reefs	22 MIN
The night of the squid	22 MIN
Octopus, octopus	22 MIN
The return of the sea elephants	20 MIN
The sea birds of Isabela	23 MIN
Seals	22 MIN
Search in the Deep	52 MIN
Secret of the Sunken Caves	52 MIN
Sharks	24 MIN
The singing whales	24 MIN
Sleeping Sharks of Yucatan	52 MIN
The smile of the walrus	22 MIN
A sound of dolphins	22 MIN
South to Fire and Ice - Cousteau in the Antarctic	53 MIN
Sunken treasure	21 MIN
Those incredible diving machines	22 MIN
Tragedy of the red salmon	24 MIN
The Unexpected Voyage	52 MIN
The unsinkable sea otter	25 MIN
The water planet	19 MIN
Whales	23 MIN

Dist - CF

Undersea world of Jacques Cousteau series
The Dragon of Galapagos
Dist - EDPAT

Underseas 16 MIN
16mm / U-matic / VHS
Advance of Science Series
Color (J H C A)
$385, $250 purchase _ #3816
Shows the history of undersea exploration, including the ideas, people, and inventions, that have helped advance science.
Science - Physical
Dist - CORF

Understand and be understood - success through communication 60 MIN
VHS
Life skills video series
Color (I J H)
$34.95 purchase _ #LF801V
Shows ways to communicate that can have a significant effect on success at home and school. Teaches strategies on how to get ideas across and build strong, positive relationships. Illustrates a formula for communicating to create understanding and improve rapport with parents, teachers and peers. Includes booklet. Part of a two - part series on life skills.
Psychology; Social Science
Dist - CAMV

Understanding 57 MIN
U-matic / VHS / 16mm
Heart of the dragon series; 9
Color (H C A)
Reveals that modern Chinese scientists and technologists are trying to catch up after the disruptions of the Cultural Revolution. Shows that in today's China, modern science and ancient belief exist side by side.
Geography - World; History - World; Science
Dist - TIMLIF AMBROS **Prod** - ASH AMBROS 1984

Understanding a material safety data sheet - Module 9 14 MIN
VHS / U-matic / BETA
Chemsafe series
Color; PAL (IND G) (SPANISH DUTCH ITALIAN)
$175.00 rental _ #CSF - 900; $546.00 purchase, $150.00 rental _ #MAY105
Presents a users guide to Material Safety Data Sheets - MSDS. Explains common scientific terms to assist employees in understanding the health and physical hazards of chemicals. Explains each part of the MSDS in easy - to - remember format. Part of a comprehensive nine - part series on chemical safety in the workplace. Includes leader's guide and 10 workbooks which are available in English only.
Business and Economics; Health and Safety; Psychology; Science - Physical
Dist - BNA ITF **Prod** - BNA

Understanding Abstraction in Art 20 MIN
U-matic
Color
LC 79-706379
Explains aspects of abstract art, showing how technique influences style and pointing out the relationship between mood, color, and communication.
Fine Arts
Dist - SRA **Prod** - SRA 1979

Understanding addiction 28 MIN
VHS
Color (H C)
$395.00 purchase
Explores myths of addiction, children of alcoholics, genetic predisposition, triggering factors, addictions other than alcohol and drugs, guidelines for the non - addict, cross addiction and stages of recovery. Features Roberta Meyer.
Guidance and Counseling; Health and Safety; Psychology
Dist - FMSP **Prod** - FMSP

Understanding Adolescence 22 MIN
U-matic / 16mm
Color (J H A)
Emphasizes communication between parents and teenagers. Deals with the pressures that affect adolescents and adults. Shows the importance of teens and adults understanding each other's perspectives.
Psychology; Sociology
Dist - PEREN **Prod** - SCCL

Understanding adolescents 156 MIN
VHS
Color; PAL (G)
PdS40 purchase
Presents six 26 - minute programs examining in detail the problems facing adolescents today such as sex, drugs, family tensions, peer pressure and expectations. Features Anna Ford as presenter. Contact distributor about availability outside the United Kingdom.
Guidance and Counseling; Health and Safety; Sociology
Dist - ACADEM

Understanding advance directives 26 MIN
VHS
Color (C A PRO)
$195.00 purchase
Clarifies legal requirements for health care workers with respect to a patient's directions concerning treatment when the patient can no longer communicate with them. For staff training. Produced by J W Gregg Meister of Interlink Video Productions Inc.
Health and Safety
Dist - PFP

Understanding Aggression 29 MIN
16mm
Color (J)
LC 72-702515
Combines artwork depicting man's aggressive behavior throughout the centuries with live - action sequences in order to examine the problem of the possible destruction of mankind by means of man's own aggressive tendencies. Psychologist Roger Ulrich discusses his theories of aggression and demonstrates some of his findings with actual animal experiments that reveal various causes of aggression.
Guidance and Counseling; Psychology; Sociology
Dist - PHM **Prod** - APPLE 1971

Understanding AIDS
VHS
Color (I J H)
$98.00 purchase _ #CCV500
Encourages young adults to think seriously about the responsibilities of sexuality and the importance of personal health decisions. Examines high risk groups, methods of transmission, methods of safer sex. Interviews AIDS patients to encourage compassion and highlight the reality of the disease.
Health and Safety; Sociology
Dist - CADESF **Prod** - CADESF

Understanding AIDS
VHS
Color (H C)
$49.95 purchase _ #193 W 0122
Gives basic scientific information on AIDS - acquired immune deficiency syndrome - and dispels common myths. Discusses contraceptive methods which can be used to avoid infection. Emphasizes that abstinence is the preferred method for teenagers.
Health and Safety; Sociology
Dist - WARDS **Prod** - WARDS

Understanding AIDS - what teens need to know 19 MIN
VHS
Color (J H)
$149.00 purchase _ #2224 - SK
Features AIDS experts in a discussion of the facts about the disease. Explains why teenagers are at risk, the role of alcohol and drugs in compromising good decision - making, and covers behaviors that can reduce or eliminate the risk of AIDS. Presents the perspectives of teenagers. Includes teacher's guide.
Health and Safety; Psychology; Sociology
Dist - SUNCOM **Prod** - SUNCOM

Understanding alcohol use and abuse 12 MIN
U-matic / BETA / 16mm / VHS
Color (I J H) (FRENCH THAI)
$320.00, $240.00 purchase _ #JR - 67542; LC 79-700890
Communicates the dangers of using alcohol to young people. Demonstrates how alcohol disrupts mental and emotional responses and explains the clinical effects of alcohol on the body.
Guidance and Counseling; Health and Safety; Psychology; Sociology
Dist - CORF **Prod** - DISNEY 1980

Understanding Allergies
VHS / U-matic
Color (SPANISH ARABIC)
Discusses how allergies can take many forms, the action of histamines, the various diagnostic procedures available and the recommended management procedures including desensitization shots.
Foreign Language; Health and Safety
Dist - MIFE **Prod** - MIFE

Understanding American Fianance - the Commodities and Stock Markets
U-matic / VHS / 35mm strip
(J H C)
$139.00 purchase _ #31296 94
Explores the history, importance, amd potential future development of the American financial investment institutions, the commodities and stock markets. Explains the complexities of the commodities market, including the difference between spot sales and future sales, and the nature of trading limits and time limits. Investigates the workings of the stock market, including its relationships with other exchanges and its effect on the national economy. In 3 parts.
Business and Economics
Dist - ASPRSS **Prod** - ASPRSS

Understanding and appreciating poetry 30 MIN
35mm strip / VHS
Color (J H C A)
$93.00, $93.00 purchase _ #MB - 513005 - X, #MB - 512729 - 6
Presents an in - depth examination of the genre of poetry. Covers the basics of poetic form and how words are used to evoke the reader's response. Includes excerpts from classical and contemporary poems.
Literature and Drama
Dist - SRA **Prod** - SRA

Understanding and Dealing with Sexual Variations
VHS / U-matic
Continuing Medical Education - Basic Sexology Series
Color (PRO)
Health and Safety; Psychology
Dist - MMRC **Prod** - TIASHS

Understanding and Dealing with Student Attitudes and Behavior 30 MIN
16mm
Teaching Role Series
Color; B&W (C T)
LC 73-703326
Teaches the nursing instructor various principles, tools and methods of teaching. Deals with student attitudes, how they relate to behavior and tells how both can be changed.
Education
Dist - TELSTR **Prod** - MVNE 1968

Understanding and implementing ISO 9000 52 MIN
VHS
Color (PRO IND A)
$595.00 purchase, $225.00 rental _ #HSA01
Provides teaching on becoming certified in ISO 9000 standards. Helps managers learn steps that comply with the standards - tailoring requirements to their company, preparing for a certification audit, maintaining certification - using case study examples. Features Eric Linnell. By H Silver and Assoc. Includes charts and reference material.
Business and Economics
Dist - EXTR

Understanding and Overcoming Emotional Upset
VHS / U-matic
Color
Shows how to change irrational self - talk and how to translate rational thinking into behavioral change.
Guidance and Counseling; Health and Safety
Dist - IRL **Prod** - IRL

Understanding and resolving conflicts 23 MIN
VHS
Color (I J)
$95 purchase _ #10240VL
Shows avoidance and conflict in common situations for young people. Uses step - by - step demonstrations to illustrate methods of dealing with confrontations. Teaches collaboration, communication skills, mutual respect, and active listening. Comes with a teacher's guide, acitivities, script, and eight blackline masters.
Guidance and Counseling; Psychology; Social Science
Dist - UNL

Understanding and treating incontinence series
Presents a seven - part series on incontinence presented by J C Brocklehurst and Bernadette M Ryan - Wooley. Includes the titles Urinary Incontinence - Causes, Investigations and Treatment Options; Urinary Incontinence - Principles of Management for the General Practitioner; Pelvic Floor Re - Education; Promoting Urinary Continence - Who and How; Faecal Incontinence; Urethral Catheterization - Intermittant and Continuous; Aids and Appliances Used for the Management of Incontinence.

Aids and appliances used for the management of incontinence	33 MIN
Faecal incontinence	19 MIN
Pelvic floor muscle re - education	24 MIN
Promoting urinary continence - who and how	21 MIN
Understanding and treating incontinence series	177 MIN
Urethral catheterization - intermittent and continuous	35 MIN
Urinary incontinence - causes, investigations and treatment options	18 MIN
Urinary incontinence - principles of management for the general practitioner	27 MIN

Dist - HSCIC

Understanding and treating the rape victim 60 MIN
VHS
Color (PRO C)
$285.00 purchase, $70.00 rental _ #6526
Presents guidelines on managing the rape victim admitted to an emergency unit. Emphasizes the role of nursing professionals in treating and documenting injuries sustained in the attack, collecting evidence of recent sexual intercourse and assessing the victinm's degree of acute stress reaction or rape trauma syndrome. Discusses appropriate psychosocial interventions a nurse may need to take to help the victim after he or she leaves the hospital. Provides vital information on helping victims of rape - treating and properly documenting injuries, providing emotional support during the emergency unit assessment and to see that the rape victim seeks further counseling and is aware of community resources. In two parts.
Health and Safety; Sociology
Dist - AJN **Prod** - HESCTV

Understanding and using decimals 130 MIN
VHS
Computational skills in mathematics series
Color (J H)
$99.00 _ #07902 - 026
Covers all essental elements of the decimal system. Begins with the basic skills of reading and writing decimals to comparing, adding, subtracting, multiplying, rounding and dividing decimals, along with changing fractions into decimal form. Part of a four - part series. Includes teacher's guide and library kit.
Education; Mathematics
Dist - GA

Understanding and using Fractions
VHS / U-matic
Color (J)
Uses real - life problems to demonstrate operations performed on fractions, from finding equivalent fractions to renaming improper fractions, and multiplication and division of fractions and mixed numbers.
Mathematics
Dist - GA **Prod** - GA

Understanding and using fractions 190 MIN
VHS
Computational skills in mathematics series
Color (J H)
$99.00 _ #07994 - 026
Uses real - life problems to lead students through the operations performed on fractions. Covers all areas, from finding equivalent fractions to multiplication and division of fractions and mixed numbers. Part of a four - part series. Includes teacher's guide and library kit.
Education; Mathematics
Dist - GA

Understanding and using percents 145 MIN
VHS
Computational skills in mathematics series
Color (J H)
$99.00 _ #07903 - 026
Teaches students how to change percentages into decimals and fractions, and, at upper levels, they explore a range of practical applications of percent. Looks at discounts, commissions and interest to demonstrate that the mastery of percent is a crucial consumer skill. Part of a four - part series. Includes teacher's guide and library kit.
Education; Mathematics
Dist - GA

Understanding and using whole numbers 161 MIN
VHS
Computational skills in mathematics series
Color (J H)
$99.00 _ #07901 - 026
Helps students master basic arithmetic skills. Covers all areas, from place value, simple addition and subtraction, to multiplication and long division. Part of a four - part series. Includes teacher's guide and library kit.
Education; Mathematics
Dist - GA

Understanding angina pectoris 12 MIN
VHS / U-matic
Color
LC 77-730406
Describes angina pectoris, what it is and why it happens. Uses terse narration and full - color visuals to present the relationship between physical and emotional stress and angina.
Health and Safety; Science - Natural
Dist - MEDCOM **Prod** - MEDCOM

Understanding animals 26 MIN
VHS
Wonderstruck presents series
Color (I J)
$99.95 purchase _ #Q11171
Explores the relationships of understanding between animals and humans. Features a woman who trains capuchin monkeys to assist physically - challenged people and a man who studies monitor lizards. Part of a series of 11 programs produced by the British Broadcasting Corporation and hosted by Bob McDonald.
Psychology; Science - Natural
Dist - CF

Understanding Animals - Pt 3 30 MIN
VHS
Wonderstruck Presents Series
Color (I)
$99.00 purchase _ #386 - 9057
Organizes science programs thematically for classroom use. Features Bob McDonald as host who makes learning fun with amazing science information and engaging activities. Part 3 of the eight part series asks how well humans and animals understand each other in segments about monitor lizards, imprinting a beaver, polar bears, dog - sledding teams and monkeys helping the disabled.
Psychology; Science - Natural; Science - Physical
Dist - FI **Prod** - CANBC 1989

Understanding arthritis series

Understanding osteoarthritis	19 MIN
Understanding rheumatoid arthritis	22 MIN

Dist - FANPRO

Understanding asbestos in the workplace 8 MIN
U-matic / BETA / VHS
Color (IND G)
$295.00 purchase _ #820 - 36
Gives factual information to employees whose workplace will undergo asbestos removal.
Health and Safety; Industrial and Technical Education; Psychology
Dist - ITSC **Prod** - ITSC

Understanding Asthma 14 MIN
VHS / U-matic
Color
Describes the clinical characteristics of asthma. Presents the physiological facts about asthma. Explains the role of allergy, emotion, and family history in asthma.
Health and Safety
Dist - MEDFAC **Prod** - MEDFAC 1980

Understanding autism 19 MIN
VHS
Color (G)
$195.00 purchase, $100.00 rental _ #CA - 100
Features therapists, teachers and parents of children with autism who discuss the nature and symptoms of this lifelong disability which can occur in between 5 and 15 of every 10,000 births. Outlines a treatment program based on behavior modification principles which can be used in schools or at home. Produced by NewsCart Productions.
Health and Safety; Psychology
Dist - FANPRO

Understanding babysitting 11 MIN
16mm
Babysitter series; Unit 1
Color (J)
LC 80-700509
Shows how to seek and accept work as a babysitter in a business - like way, how to create a good first impression on a job and how to establish a trusting relationship with parents and children.

Guidance and Counseling; Home Economics
Dist - FILCOM **Prod** - SOCOM 1979

Understanding barriers
U-matic / 16mm
Art of negotiating series; Module 7
Color (A)
Shows how to overcome barriers to successful negotiations, communicate effectively, learn how to listen, prepare through role playing, psychodrama, conferences, brainstorming and other methods.
Business and Economics; Psychology
Dist - BNA **Prod** - BNA 1983

Understanding Behavior in Organizations - How I Feel is what I do 26 MIN
16mm / U-matic / VHS
Human Resources and Organizational Behavior Series
Color
Demonstrates that a knowledge of human behavior can help in designing more effective organizations. Presents Dr Harry Levinson who explains significant concepts in psychoanalytic theory in terms of their applicability to corporate settings. Defines certain human needs which organizations must understand and fulfill in order to better design jobs and foster employee commitment.
Psychology
Dist - CNEMAG **Prod** - DOCUA

Understanding Blood Sugar 21 MIN
U-matic / VHS / 16mm
Color (A)
Explains the body's use of sugar and the pathophysiology of diabetes. Describes how blood sugar acts during the course of a day. Includes information on causes, treatment and prevention of ketoacidosis and low blood sugar as well as guidelines for meals, exercise and insulin.
Health and Safety; Science - Natural
Dist - PRORE **Prod** - PRORE

Understanding borderline personality disorder - the dialectical approach 35 MIN
VHS
Marsha M Linehan on borderline personality disorder series
Color (PRO C)
$95.00 purchase _ #2567
Features Marsha M Linehan providing a thorough overview of her therapy approach, Dialectical Behavior Therapy - DBT - for treating borderline personality disorder. Looks at the clinical features of BPD based on DSM - IV criteria. Describes the underlying causes of the disorder. Defines her approach which is rooted in behavior therapy and incorporates elements of psychodynamic thinking as well as Eastern philosophy. Created for therapists. One of a two - part series on Dr Lineman's dialectical approach to BPD. Includes manual.
Psychology
Dist - GFORD

Understanding borderline personality disorder - the dialectical approach and Treating borderline personality - the nd Treating borderline personality - the ialectical approach 70 MIN
VHS
Marsha M Linehan on borderline personality disorder series
Color (PRO)
$175.00 purchase _ #LINVD
Features Marsha M Linehan explaining her treatment approach to BPD - borderline personality disorder, using Dialectical Behavior Therapy or DBT. Gives a thorough overview in a straightforward introduction for therapists in 'Understanding BPD.' Treating BPD teaches skills training for therapists to help manage the extreme beliefs, actions and attitudes that form the criteria for BPD. Offers a special package of both programs, each 35 minutes in length and using actual case sessions and graphics. Includes manuals.
Psychology
Dist - GFORD

Understanding Breast Cancer Series
Diagnosis of breast cancer 14 MIN
Life after breast cancer 15 MIN
Lumpectomy 11 MIN
Mastectomy 14 MIN
The Nature of breast cancer 10 MIN
Treatment of breast cancer 14 MIN
Who gets breast cancer 12 MIN
Dist - AIMS

Understanding business finance series
The balance sheet barrier 30 MIN
Dist - EXTR
VISUCP

Understanding Business Finance Series
The Control of working capital 25 MIN
Cost, Profit, and Break - Even 21 MIN
Depreciation and inflation 18 MIN
Dist - VISUCP

Understanding Business Graphics Series
Computer Graphics in Business 30 MIN
Graphics applications 30 MIN
Graphics systems 30 MIN
Dist - DELTAK

Understanding Buyer Behavior 60 MIN
U-matic / VHS
Strategic Selling - a Thinking Person's Guide Series Pt 2
Color (A)
Shows how to interpret a buyer's behavior, which invariably provides clues to the identification of his or her need. Emphasizes listening actively, observing nonverbal behavior, questioning effectively and paraphrasing effectively.
Business and Economics
Dist - TIMLIF **Prod** - TIMLIF 1984

Understanding CAD - CAM video series
VHS
Understanding CAD - CAM video series
Color (G H VOC C PRO)
$219.95 purchase _ #MGUCCSV-T
Describes the basics of CAD - CAM through a three part video series that includes detailed information on how the computer programs work. Defines what they are and what they do, the software requirements, the capabilities of the program, how CAD drawing is done, how CAM is integrated with other programs, and the background of the programs.
Computer Science
Dist - CAMV

Understanding CAD - CAM video series
Understanding CAD - CAM video series
Dist - CAMV

Understanding Cancer Series
The Patients' story 46 MIN
The Road to recovery 50 MIN
The Search for a cause 50 MIN
Dist - LANDMK

Understanding cardiac catheterization 6 MIN
VHS
Color (C PRO G)
$250.00 purchase
Presents a reassuring explanation of the procedure, illustrated with angiographic images and cath lab scenes.
Health and Safety
Dist - LPRO **Prod** - LPRO

Understanding chemical labels 12 MIN
VHS / U-matic
Color (IND A)
LC 90-708107
Shows how to locate chemical labels and understand the information on them. Produced by Business and Legal Reports.
Health and Safety; Industrial and Technical Education; Psychology; Science - Physical; Sociology
Dist - IFB

Understanding Chemotherapy
U-matic / VHS
Color
Presents information essential to the new chemotherapy patient. Uses computer graphics and animation to describe how cancer grows within the body and how chemotherapy works in treating cancer cells.
Health and Safety
Dist - GRANVW **Prod** - GRANVW

Understanding chess
VHS
Color (G)
$39.95 purchase
Teaches chess strategies. Features Bruce Pandolfini.
Physical Education and Recreation
Dist - CHESSR **Prod** - CHESSR 1991

Understanding chest tube drainage systems 28 MIN
VHS / U-matic
Color (PRO)
$275.00 purchase, $60.00 rental _ #7315S, #7315V
Reviews the physiology of respiration. Explains indications for the use of chest tubes. Provides closeup demonstrations involving the operation of 1, 2 and 3 bottle systems. Presents disposable systems such as Pleur - evac and high vacuum systems such as the Emerson pump. Looks at troubleshooting and nursing management during insertion and system maintenance.
Health and Safety
Dist - AJN **Prod** - HOSSN 1984

Understanding children 30 MIN
VHS
Active parenting series
Color (J H G)
$99.00 purchase _ #05537 - 126
Looks at the psychology of a child. Visits a variety of homes and families to observe parent and child dynamics. Includes excerpts from group discussions to critique parent and child interactions and to help spot common mistakes in parenting. Part of a six - part series on parenting.
Health and Safety; Social Science; Sociology
Dist - GA **Prod** - GA

Understanding Children's Drawings 11 MIN
16mm
B&W (J H C)
Follows a child's progress from primitive scribblings, through a recognition of form and design, to the emergence of a story - telling picture.
Fine Arts; Psychology
Dist - RADIM **Prod** - BOXAVR 1949

Understanding children's play 12 MIN
16mm
Studies of normal personality - development series
B&W (C T)
Shows how adults can understand and help children through observation of their use of toys and play materials. A variety of materials made available in a nursery school room, including blocks, poster paints, crayons, clay, and watercolors are presented.
Education; Psychology; Sociology
Dist - NYU **Prod** - ZACHRY 1948

Understanding Cities Series
The American urban experience 27 MIN
The City of the future 27 MIN
John Nash and London 27 MIN
Paris - Living Space 27 MIN
Rome - Impact of an Idea 27 MIN
Dist - FI

Understanding common breast problems 12 MIN
VHS
Color (G PRO C)
$200.00 purchase _ #OB - 64
Portrays two women experiencing the common problems of breast tenderness, benign tumors and cysts and nipple discharges. Discusses the treatments involved, breast self examination techniques and the role of mammography.
Health and Safety; Sociology
Dist - MIFE **Prod** - MIFE

Understanding computers
VHS / U-matic
Audio visual library of computer education series
Color
Describes in non - technical terms exactly what computers can and can't do. Shows why computers are more suitable for some applications than others. Emphasises the programmer's responsibility for efficient utilization of the computer.
Business and Economics; Mathematics
Dist - PRISPR **Prod** - PRISPR

Understanding congregational change 20 MIN
VHS
Congregational planning series
Color (G A R)
$39.95 purchase, $10.00 rental _ #35 - 875 - 2076
Suggests positive ways of dealing with change within a church congregation. Hosted by Dr Margaret Wold. Produced by Seraphim.
Religion and Philosophy
Dist - APH

Understanding contemporary American realist painting 40 MIN
35mm strip / VHS
Color (J H C T A)
$93.00 purchase _ #MB - 513003 - 3, #MB - 512455 - 6
Features numerous examples of paintings by contemporary American artists. Focuses on the artistic concept of realism, which depends on the artist's visual perception. Includes paintings by Close, Eddy, Leslie, Beal, Estes, Fish, Pearlstein, and others.
Fine Arts
Dist - SRA **Prod** - SRA

Understanding Cultural Differences
U-matic / VHS
Managing Cultural Differences Series
Color (IND)
Examines concepts of culture in general and ways of analyzing a culture, providing a model with benchmarks or identifying characteristics of any culture.
Business and Economics; Social Science; Sociology
Dist - GPCV **Prod** - GPCV

Understanding Data Base 30 MIN
U-matic / VHS
End User's Guide to Data Base Series
Color
Provides an overview of data base technology and the jargon that describes it. Explains the basic terms and principles of data base technology and describes the end user's essential role in data base evolution.
Business and Economics; Industrial and Technical Education
Dist - DELTAK **Prod** - DELTAK

Understanding Decimals 13 MIN
U-matic
Basic Math Skills Series Adding, Subtracting, Multiplying Decimals; Adding - subtracting - multiplying decimals
Color
Mathematics
Dist - TELSTR **Prod** - TELSTR

Understanding Desktop Publishing 45 MIN
VHS
(C A PRO)
$49.00 purcahse _ #CHE100V
Explains all aspects of desktop publishing on the MacIntosh system. Explains how to merge drawings, figures and graphics, type styles, and color screenings, how to set columns and more. Discusses many MacIntosh software packages.
Computer Science
Dist - CAMV

Understanding diabetes
VHS
Color (J H C G A)
$79.50 purchase _ #AH46311
Deals with diabetes. Suggests that while diabetes is incurable, it can be prevented in many cases. Discusses the medical complications most common to diabetics.
Health and Safety; Science - Natural
Dist - HTHED **Prod** - HTHED

Understanding Diabetes Series

Good nutrition and the diabetic	24 MIN
Insulin, Insulin Administration and Hypoglycemic Agents	18 MIN
Personal Care Considerations of the Diabetic	22 MIN
The Roadmap to Control	17 MIN

Dist - FAIRGH

Understanding digital electronics
VHS
Color (H A)
$289.00 purchase _ #BXE13XSV
Deals with concepts of digital electronics. Consists of four videocassettes and a study guide.
Industrial and Technical Education
Dist - CAMV

Understanding digital electronics 60 MIN
VHS / 16mm
Color (H A)
$259.00 purchase _ E13
Examines the AND function, explores OR and NOT functions from switching networks and developes XOR and XNOR from combinations of primary logic gates.
Industrial and Technical Education
Dist - BERGL CAREER **Prod** - BERGL CAREER 1987

Understanding Dinnerware 15 MIN
16mm
Color (J)
LC 80-701055
Shows two little girls who startle their parents by shopping for their own fine china. Discusses stoneware, earthenware, porcelain and progressive china.
Home Economics
Dist - KLEINW **Prod** - KLEINW 1977

Understanding Dos Passos' USA 30 MIN
VHS
Modern American Literature Eminent Scholar - Teachers Video Series
Color (C)
$95.00 purchase
Features Professor Townsend Luddington as he explains Dos Passos' novel trilogy's political thesis, its technical innovations and its prophetic and satiric vision of American culture. The second of 35 installments of the Modern American Literature Eminent Scholar - Teacher Video Series.
Literature and Drama
Dist - OMNIGR

Understanding DP/OA Integration 45 MIN
U-matic / VHS
Integrating DP and Office Automation Series
Color
Looks at some of the successful systems that have integrated data processing functions with office automation to create total information management systems, the process by which integration was achieved and the important issue of human involvement in system integration.
Business and Economics; Industrial and Technical Education; Psychology
Dist - DELTAK **Prod** - DELTAK

Understanding Dreiser's Sister Carrie 30 MIN
VHS
Modern American Literature Eminent Scholar - Teachers Video Series
Color (C)
$95.00 purchase
Expresses the viewpoint that Dreiser's novel Sister Carrie is the ultimate expression of his philosophy that environment and heredity are the primary forces that determine human conduct. The fourth of thirty - four installments of the Modern American Literature Eminent Scholar - Teacher Video Series.
Literature and Drama; Religion and Philosophy
Dist - OMNIGR

Understanding EEOC - Pt 1
VHS / 16mm
(PRO G)
$80.00 purchase _ #EEO1
Introduces the possibility of discrimination problems. Presents dramatizations of actual discrimination cases.
Business and Economics; Sociology
Dist - RMIBHF **Prod** - RMIBHF

Understanding EEOC - Pt 2
VHS / 16mm
(PRO G)
$80.00 purchase _ #EEO2
Outlines the major provisions of equal employment laws. Overviews the basics of compliance and shows how to protect against unnecessary litigation.
Business and Economics; Sociology
Dist - RMIBHF **Prod** - RMIBHF

Understanding EEOC - Pt 3
VHS / 16mm
(PRO G)
$80.00 purchase _ #EEO3
Answers the most frequently asked questions about equal employment laws.
Business and Economics; Sociology
Dist - RMIBHF **Prod** - RMIBHF

Understanding Eliot's the Waste Land 30 MIN
VHS
Modern American Literature Eminent Scholar - Teachers Video Series
Color (C)
$95.00 purchase
Focuses on Ezra Pound's role as virtual collaborator in the making of the poem and explores its methods through an examination of key motifs and passages. The 20th of 34 installments of the Modern American Literature Eminent Scholar - Teacher Video Series.
Literature and Drama
Dist - OMNIGR

Understanding - Entendimiento 28 MIN
VHS / 16mm
Sonrisas Series
Color (T P) (SPANISH)
Shows the children helping community members.
Sociology
Dist - PBS

Understanding extra - sensory perception 30 MIN
BETA / VHS
Exploring parapsychology series
Color (G)
$29.95 purchase _ #S270
Discusses factors which facilitate ESP performance in the laboratory and in the world. Examines feedback learning strategies and methods for shielding the body from electromagnetic and geomagnetic influences. Features Dr Charles Tart, author of 'Psi - Studies in the Scientific Realm' and 'Learning to Use Extrasensory Perception.' Part of a four - part series on exploring parapsychology.
Psychology; Religion and Philosophy
Dist - THINKA **Prod** - THINKA

Understanding families 156 MIN
VHS
Color; PAL (G)
PdS40 purchase
Presents six 26 - minute programs. Seeks to increase understanding of family relationships and problems. Contact distributor about availability outside the United Kingdom.
Psychology; Social Science; Sociology
Dist - ACADEM

Understanding fast pitch pitching 28 MIN
VHS
VIP softball series
Color (G)
$29.95 purchase _ #ASAT05V
Covers the basics of fast pitch softball pitching. Features Cindy Bristow teaching and demonstrating appropriate skills. Taught by Bobby Simpson, Cindy Bristow and Buzzy Keller.
Physical Education and Recreation
Dist - CAMV **Prod** - CAMV

Understanding feelings 26 MIN
16mm / VHS
Facts, feelings and wonder of life - the teenage years series
Color (I J H PRO)
$295.00, $450.00 purchase, $50.00 rental _ #9975
Considers peer pressure, the different standards for males and females, the importance of self - esteem and the effects of `locker room talk.'
Guidance and Counseling; Health and Safety; Psychology; Sociology
Dist - AIMS **Prod** - PVGP 1988

Understanding financial statements 57 MIN
VHS
Color (PRO IND A)
$695.00 purchase _ #VIM07
Helps explain, through the expertise of Prof Marc Bertoneche, the function of various types of financial statements. Educates managers who are not financial specialists.
Business and Economics
Dist - EXTR

Understanding Fitzgerald's the Great Gatsby 30 MIN
VHS
Modern American Literature Eminent Scholar - Teachers Video Series
Color (C)
$95.00 purchase
Explicates Fitzgerald's solution to the problems of citation structure by means of a first person, secondary character as the narrator, who could control the intentionally fragmented chronology of the novel. The eighth of thirty - four installments of the Modern American Literature Eminent Scholar - Teacher Video Series.
Literature and Drama
Dist - OMNIGR

Understanding Footnotes 20 MIN
VHS / 16mm
Study, Research, Library Skills Series
Color (J)
Teaches how to read and write foonotes using the different formats.
Education; English Language
Dist - COMEX **Prod** - COMEX 1987

Understanding Frustration and its Effects 29 MIN
16mm
Controlling Turnover and Absenteeism Series
B&W
LC 76-703321
Business and Economics; Psychology
Dist - EDSD **Prod** - EDSD

Understanding genetics 37 MIN
VHS
Color (J H)
$125 purchase _ #10315VG
Provides an introduction to genetics and modern molecular gene theory. Combines the classical and contemporary scientific approaches to the study of inheritance. Comes with an interactive video quiz, teacher's guide and ten blackline masters.
Science - Natural
Dist - UNL

Understanding geography using globes and 35 MIN
maps - Volume 1
VHS
Visions of adventure series
Color (P)
$24.95 purchase _ #GE01
Explains latitude and longitude, magnetic and natural poles, globes and time zones. Explores different kinds of political, geographical and topological maps. Part of an eight - part series on geography.
Geography - World
Dist - SVIP

Understanding globes
VHS
Using maps, globes, graphs, tables, charts and diagrams series
Color (I J H)

$49.50 purchase _ #UL1023VJ
Covers basic globe skills. Presents part of a five - part series on interpreting data from pictorial and other graphic representations.
Geography - World
Dist - KNOWUN

Understanding Greenhouse Flammability 18 MIN
16mm
Color
Describes a three - year research project done at Colorado State University using controlled burnings of an actual greenhouse covered with rigid and film plastics. Discusses types of covers and structures, employee safety, alarm systems and sprinkler systems.
Agriculture; Health and Safety
Dist - COLOSU **Prod** - COLOSU 1977

Understanding group psychotherapy series
Presents a three - part series on group psychotherapy produced by the Brooks Cole Publishing Co, featuring Dr Irvin D Yalom, Prof of Psychiatry, Stanford University School of Medicine. Includes the titles Outpatients, Inpatients, and Yalom - an Interview.
Inpatients 100 MIN
Outpatients 100 MIN
Yalom - an interview 40 MIN
Dist - UCEMC

Understanding hearing loss 15 MIN
VHS
Color (G)
$149.00 purchase, $75.00 rental _ #UW4362
Explains sound, hearing, hearing loss and the relationship between listening to speech and different kinds of hearing loss. Includes a realistic simulation of what speech sounds like with different kinds of hearing loss, and useful hints on improving communication.
Fine Arts; Social Science
Dist - FOTH

Understanding Hemingway's a Farewell to Arms 30 MIN
VHS
Modern American Literature Eminent Scholar - Teachers Video Series
Color (C)
$95.00 purchase
Separates the autobiographical from the fictional in an analysis of the novel's backgrounds and composition. Features Professor Michael S Reynolds. The tenth of thirty - four installments of the Modern American Literature Eminent Scholar - Teacher Video Series.
Literature and Drama
Dist - OMNIGR

Understanding hidden meanings in conversation 33 MIN
U-matic / 16mm / VHS
Art of negotiating series; Module 10
Color (A)
Shows how conversations reveal more than is intended and demonstrates ear - opening methods and experiences. Describes meta - talk and gestures with attitudes and relationships.
Business and Economics; Psychology
Dist - BNA DELTAK **Prod** - BNA DELTAK 1983

Understanding high blood pressure 10 MIN
VHS
Color (G)
#FSR - 495
Presents a free - loan program which presents the causes of high blood pressure and its treatments. Reveals that there is no exact answer as to the reason for high blood pressure, but it is believed that heredity, intake of salt, obesity and stress may be contributing factors. Explains the benefits of lowering blood pressure and discusses treatments.
Health and Safety
Dist - WYAYLA **Prod** - WYAYLA

Understanding His Illness 29 MIN
16mm / U-matic / VHS
Stroke Patient Comes Home Series
B&W (A)
Describes the nature and effects of a stroke, followed by patient interview and discussion by internist, psychologist and psychiatrist of the physiological and psychological worlds of the patient.
Health and Safety; Psychology
Dist - IFB **Prod** - RCCHA 1966

Understanding His Problems 29 MIN
U-matic / VHS / 16mm
Stroke Patient Comes Home Series
B&W (A)
Uses filmed examples and discussion by psychologist and psychiatrist, to probe the stroke patient's speech and communication problems, his motivation to work toward recovery and the family's expected reactions and role in assisting his recovery.
Health and Safety; Psychology
Dist - IFB **Prod** - RCCHA 1966

Understanding home health care video
VHS
Health care consumerism system series
Color (G)
$179.00 purchase _ #WMV15
Explains the what, why, who and how of successful home health care. Explores the different roles of the most common home health care providers. Helps viewers to become wise, efficient users of such services. Part of a ten - part series.
Home Economics
Dist - GPERFO **Prod** - GPERFO

Understanding how you think - Pt one 29.42
VHS
Critical thinking
Color (J H C)
LC 88-700273
Aids students in appreciation of key points on thinking careers. Uses examples and exercises to instruct students.
Business and Economics
Dist - SRA **Prod** - SRA 1986

Understanding human behavior - an introduction to psychology - a series
Understanding human behavior - an introduction to psychology - a series
Color (C A)
Reinforces visually the concepts in the telecourse text. Gives the viewer a better understanding of the classic experiments in psychology. Applies basic concepts of psychology to all age groups and to everyday situations. Includes Abnormal Psychology; Altered States Of Consciousness; Applied Psychology; Brain, The; Cognitive Development; Conditioning; Consciousness And Sleep; Emotional Development; Functions Of The Brain; Genetic Psychology; Human Psychology; Interpersonal Attraction; Memory; Motivation And Hunger; Operant Conditioning; Pain And Hypnosis; Personality Tests; Personality Theory; Persuasion.
Psychology
Dist - CDTEL **Prod** - COAST

Understanding Human Behavior - an Introduction to Psychology Series Lesson 1
Human Psychology 29 MIN
Dist - CDTEL

Understanding Human Behavior - an Introduction to Psychology Series Lesson 2
The Brain (Understanding Human Behavior) 29 MIN
Dist - CDTEL

Understanding Human Behavior - an Introduction to Psychology Series Lesson 3
Consciousness and Sleep 29 MIN
Dist - CDTEL

Understanding Human Behavior - an Introduction to Psychology Series Lesson 5
Functions of the Brain 29 MIN
Dist - CDTEL

Understanding Human Behavior - an Introduction to Psychology Series Lesson 6
Sensory Psychology 29 MIN
Dist - CDTEL

Understanding Human Behavior - an Introduction to Psychology Series Lesson 7
Taste, Smell, Hearing 29 MIN
Dist - CDTEL

Understanding Human Behavior - an Introduction to Psychology Series Lesson 9
Sensory Deprivation and Controlled Sensory Stimulation 29 MIN
Dist - CDTEL

Understanding Human Behavior - an Introduction to Psychology Series Lesson 11
Subliminal Perception 29 MIN
Dist - CDTEL

Understanding Human Behavior - an Introduction to Psychology Series Lesson 12
Motivation and Hunger 29 MIN
Dist - CDTEL

Understanding Human Behavior - an Introduction to Psychology Series Lesson 13
Sexual Motivation 29 MIN
Dist - CDTEL

Understanding Human Behavior - an Introduction to Psychology Series Lesson 14
Stress 29 MIN
Dist - CDTEL

Understanding Human Behavior - an Introduction to Psychology Series Lesson 20
Emotional Development 29 MIN
Dist - CDTEL

Understanding Human Behavior - an Introduction to Psychology Series Lesson 22
Personality Theory 29 MIN
Dist - CDTEL

Understanding Human Behavior - an Introduction to Psychology Series Lesson 23
Personality Tests 29 MIN
Dist - CDTEL

Understanding Human Behavior - an Introduction to Psychology Series Lesson 27
Interpersonal Attraction 29 MIN
Dist - CDTEL

Understanding Human Behavior - an Introduction to Psychology Series Lesson 29
Persuasion 29 MIN
Dist - CDTEL

Understanding human behavior - an introduction to psychology series
Abnormal psychology - Lesson 24 29 MIN
Altered states of consciousness 29 MIN
Applied psychology 29 MIN
Cognitive development 29 MIN
Genetic psychology and physical development 29 MIN
Psychotherapy I 29 MIN
Psychotherapy II 29 MIN
Social Groups 29 MIN
Vision 29 MIN
Visual Perception 29 MIN
Dist - CDTEL

Understanding Human Reproduction
U-matic / VHS
Color (J H)
Designed as a foundation for sex education. Gives students a thorough understanding of human reproduction. Describes human reproductive systems. Explains conception. Follows fetal development. Concludes with labor and delivery and the bonding of parents and child.
Guidance and Counseling; Health and Safety; Psychology; Science - Natural
Dist - SUNCOM **Prod** - SUNCOM

Understanding industrial hygiene 18 MIN
VHS / U-matic
Foreman's accident prevention series
Color (IND)
Introduces supervisors to industrial hygiene (IH) basics. Shows three ways toxic substances can enter the body, how to test worker's exposure and how to protect against radiation and other IH problems.
Health and Safety
Dist - GPCV **Prod** - GPCV

Understanding Infertility 10 MIN
U-matic / VHS / 16mm
Color (PRO)
Explains how a pregnancy occurs and how any dysfunction in the process may lead to infertility. Discusses causes and treatments for infertility for both men and women.
Health and Safety; Science - Natural
Dist - PRORE **Prod** - PRORE

Understanding insulin 15 MIN
VHS
AADE patient education video series
Color; CC (G C PRO)
$175.00 purchase _ #DB - 25
Explains how insulin helps control blood sugar for adult diabetics who need to take insulin. Covers types of insulin and their action times. Part of an eight - part series produced in cooperation with the American Association of Diabetes Educators. Contact distributor for special purchase price on multiple orders.
Health and Safety; Science - Natural
Dist - MIFE

Understanding Labor 11 MIN
U-matic / VHS / 16mm
Prepared Childbirth and Parenting Series
Color
Describes what labor is, the stages of labor and how to recognize true labor from false labor.
Health and Safety
Dist - JOU **Prod** - JOU 1979

Understanding Labor and Delivery 20 MIN
16mm

Color
LC 79-701020
Explains the stages of labor and delivery using charts and film of actual childbirths. Illustrates various medical techniques to help familiarize the viewer with the procedures that might be used in a hospital setting.
Health and Safety
Dist - AMCOG **Prod** - AMCOG 1978

Understanding Law
U-matic / VHS
Color (J H)
Describes what happens when kids break the law. Discusses legal responsibilities of parents, children and schools. Includes a complete court case of young people arrested for drug use.
Civics and Political Systems; Psychology; Sociology
Dist - EDUACT **Prod** - EDUACT

Understanding learning disabilities, the F.A.T. City Workshop series
How difficult can this be? A learning disabilities workshop 70 MIN
Dist - PBS

Understanding Leukemia 10 MIN
BETA / VHS / U-matic
Living with Leukemia Series
(G)
Provides patients and families with information about leukemia and how it affects people.
Health and Safety
Dist - UTXAH **Prod** - UTXAH 1985

Understanding Lightning and Thunder 20 MIN
16mm
Color (J H)
LC 79-701647
Discusses the safety rules relating to lightning and thunder.
Health and Safety
Dist - ECI **Prod** - REDDB 1977

Understanding Luther's catechism 83 MIN
VHS
Color (J H C G A R)
$29.95 purchase, $10.00 rental _ #4 - 810090
Presents the concepts of Luther's Small Catechism for varying audiences - pastors, parents, teenagers and adult converts. Includes leader's guide.
Religion and Philosophy
Dist - APH **Prod** - APH

Understanding maternal grief series
Presents a five - part series produced by Margaret Nicol, an Australian clinical psycologist specializing in the effects of reproductive loss on women's physical and mental health. Includes the titles Loss of a Baby - Death of a Dream; Infertility and Adoption; Miscarrige and Stillbirth; Neonatal Death; The Birth of a Handicapped Child.
The Birth of a handicapped baby 39 MIN
Infertility and adoption 24 MIN
Loss of baby - death of a dream 45 MIN
Miscarriage and stillbirth 51 MIN
Neonatal death 46 MIN
Dist - UCEMC

Understanding matter and energy 18 MIN
U-matic / VHS / 16mm
Color (J H C)
LC 79-706896
Explains the three forms of matter - liquid, solid and gas - and the different forms of energy - chemical, mechanical, heat, light, electrical, atomic and radiant. Uses animation to clarify the molecular action of the three forms of matter.
Science - Physical
Dist - IFB **Prod** - VEF 1960

Understanding menstruation
VHS
Color (H C G PRO)
$79.50 purchase _ #AH46321
Covers the process of menstruation in women.
Health and Safety; Science - Natural
Dist - HTHED **Prod** - HTHED

Understanding mental health care video
VHS
Health care consumerism system series
Color (G)
$179.00 purchase _ #WMV13
Discloses that good mental health means increased productivity. Presents the 14 signs for recognizing when an employee needs help. Includes an important section, Helping Your Kids. Part of a ten - part series.
Health and Safety; Home Economics
Dist - GPERFO **Prod** - GPERFO

Understanding Microprocessors Series Pt 7
Sixty - Eight Hundred Instruction Set , Pt 1 60 MIN
Dist - UAZMIC

Understanding Microprocessors Series Pt 8
Sixty - Eight Hundred Instruction Set , Pt 2 60 MIN
Dist - UAZMIC

Understanding Modern Art Series
Cubism 6 MIN
Expressionism 7 MIN
Impressionism 7 MIN
Non - Objective Art 8 MIN
Surrealism 7 MIN
Dist - PHENIX

Understanding modern ethical standards series
Analyzes the American Bar Association's Model Rules of Professional Conduct. Covers subjects including client confidentiality, conflict of interest and zeal of representation. Applies ABA standards to both attorneys and paralegals. Three - part series includes a two - volume set of books, 'Understanding Modern Ethical Standards.'
Conflict of interest 24 MIN
Limits on the zeal of representation 25 MIN
Protection of client confidences 38 MIN
Dist - NITA **Prod** - NITA

Understanding mythology 30 MIN
BETA / VHS
Roots of consciousness series
Color (G)
$29.95 purchase _ #S075
Features Joseph Campbell who argues against the literal interpretation of ancient myth. Claims that modern science provides the raw materials for future myths which can serve to unite all of humanity as one biological and spiritual unit. Part of a four - part series on the roots of consciousness.
History - World; Religion and Philosophy; Sociology
Dist - THINKA **Prod** - THINKA

Understanding on - Line Systems 20 MIN
U-matic / VHS
On - Line Systems Concepts for Users Series
Color
Stresses the growing importance of end - user participation in the application development process, provides the user with a functional description of on - line systems and makes the distinction between on - line access to computing resources and traditional batch processing.
Business and Economics; Industrial and Technical Education
Dist - DELTAK **Prod** - DELTAK

Understanding Orthopedic Evaluation - Diagnostic Tests 30 MIN
U-matic
Color; Mono
X - rays, myelograms, and other diagnostic tests are discussed and illustrated. Limitations of each tests and other options to explore.
Health and Safety
Dist - PROEDS **Prod** - PROEDS 1986

Understanding orthopedic evaluation - history and physical exam 31 MIN
U-matic
Color; Mono
Demonstrative approach to orthopedic evaluation. An approach that translates 'medicalese.' What orthopods look for and why. How to use the information to better represent clients.
Health and Safety
Dist - PROEDS **Prod** - PROEDS 1986

Understanding osteoarthritis 19 MIN
VHS
Understanding arthritis series
Color (G)
$125.00 purchase _ #CE - 124
Summarizes and explains the nature and course of the disease osteoarthritis. Outlines treatments and addresses unproven and folk remedies. Underscores the importance of self - management and support groups. Shows how medication, occupational and physiotherapy, nutrition and exercise can relieve pain, increase mobility and improve the quality of life. Interviews medical and allied health professionals, as well as people living with arthritis. Produced by James Brodie.
Health and Safety
Dist - FANPRO

Understanding our Earth - glaciers 11
VHS
Color; PAL (H)
Shows the similarities and differences between the three main types of glaciers by using examples drawn from the United States and a number of other countries. Contrasts North American examples with the more commonly studied European examples. Looks at the processes which contribute to glacial growth and the effects of glaciation on landscapes.
Geography - World; Science - Physical
Dist - VIEWTH **Prod** - VIEWTH

Understanding Our Earth - Glaciers 11 MIN
16mm / U-matic / VHS
Understanding Our Earth Series
Color (I J)
LC 77-700864
Presents glaciers from Alaska, the United States, Canada and Europe to show the different kinds and to explain how they are formed. Examines the formation of icebergs and the significance and impact of glaciers during the ice age. Shows evidences of glaciation in glacier lakes in the Rocky Mountains, soil in the Midwest, glacial drift in New England and the Matterhorn peak in the Swiss Alps.
Geography - World; Science - Physical
Dist - CORF **Prod** - CORF 1977

Understanding Our Earth - How its Surface Changes 12 MIN
U-matic / VHS / 16mm
Understanding Our Earth Series
Color (I J)
LC 77-701127
Investigates the forces which cause changes in the earth's surface, such as wind, water, glaciers, rivers, volcanoes and human activities.
Science - Natural; Science - Physical
Dist - CORF **Prod** - CORF 1977

Understanding Our Earth - Rocks and Minerals 12 MIN
16mm / U-matic / VHS
Understanding Our Earth Series
Color (I J)
LC 77-701128
Describes the three classes of rocks, their formations and uses.
Science - Physical
Dist - CORF **Prod** - CORF 1977

Understanding Our Earth Series
Glaciers 11 MIN
How its surface changes 12 MIN
Rocks and Minerals 12 MIN
Soil 12 MIN
Understanding Our Earth - Glaciers 11 MIN
Understanding Our Earth - How its Surface Changes 12 MIN
Understanding Our Earth - Rocks and Minerals 12 MIN
Understanding Our Earth - Soil 12 MIN
Dist - CORF

Understanding Our Earth - Soil 12 MIN
U-matic / VHS / 16mm
Understanding Our Earth Series
Color (I J)
LC 77-700863
Explains the soil profile, which consists of topsoil, subsoil, mantle rock and bedrock. Presents a breakdown of the elements of soil and describes the process of soil making, whereby rocks are broken down by erosion and decaying matter changes into humus. Covers the types of soil throughout the United States and the importance of conservation.
Agriculture; Science - Natural; Science - Physical
Dist - CORF **Prod** - CORF 1977

Understanding our losses 60 MIN
VHS
Passages - A National course of healing and hope for teens, their 'parents, friends and caregivers series
Color (R G)
$49.95 purchase _ #PASS1
Addresses how teens understand and experience loss through death. Features Dr Patrick Del Zoppo. Part of three parts.
Guidance and Counseling; Religion and Philosophy; Sociology
Dist - CTNA **Prod** - CTNA

Understanding our world series
Understanding our world, Unit II - geography we should know - a series
Dist - GPN

Understanding our world, Unit I - tools we use series
All kinds of maps 20 MIN
Globes are useful 20 MIN
Modern Mapmakers 20 MIN
Reading a Map 20 MIN
World Streets and Avenues 20 MIN
Dist - GPN

Understanding our world, Unit II - geography we should know - a series
Understanding our world series
Color (I)
Islands Of Japan; Land Below The Sea; Life On The Great Plains; Mountainous Land; Oceans Surround Us; Trailing A River; What Is A Desert.

Geography - World
Dist - GPN **Prod** - KRMATV

Understanding Our World, Unit II - Geography We Should Know Series
Mountainous Land 20 MIN
Oceans Surround Us 20 MIN
What is a Desert 20 MIN
Dist - GPN

Understanding Our World, Unit III - Living in Other Lands Series
Australian contrast 20 MIN
High in the Andes 20 MIN
Impressions in East Africa 20 MIN
Dist - GPN

Understanding ovarian cancer 13 MIN
VHS
Color (C PRO G)
$250.00 purchase
Presents a clear overview of ovarian cancer and currently recommended treatment methods. Uses statements by cancer survivors to enhance the effectiveness of the program.
Health and Safety; Sociology
Dist - LPRO **Prod** - LPRO

Understanding Percent 10 MIN
U-matic
Basic Math Skills Series Per Cent; Per cent
Color
Mathematics
Dist - TELSTR **Prod** - TELSTR

Understanding Personality and Behavior 23 MIN
U-matic / VHS
Color
Demonstrates how a better understanding of basic human needs can help supervisors deal successfully with troubled employees.
Business and Economics; Psychology; Sociology
Dist - AMA **Prod** - AMA

Understanding Place Value 15 MIN
U-matic / 35mm strip
Color (I P)
Explains that Kaylin learns the hard way how the place value of a number changes when another number is put to its right - she ends up with too many cookies and too many ads. Includes an animated segment in which Zero teaches Numberville about place value.
Mathematics
Dist - VMI **Prod** - VMI

Understanding preterm labor 17 MIN
VHS
Color (H G)
$295.00 purchase, $40.00 rental
Reveals that preterm labor is the leading cause of infant mortality and long - term developmental handicaps. Discloses that the number of premature births can be significantly reduced by educating patients in the early detection of preterm labor. Identifies major risk factors and explains the early warning signs and symptoms of preterm labor. Illustrates uterine contractions and cervical changes, discusses tocolytics and bedrest treatments and addresses the dangers of delivering prematurely. Emphasizes early detection and encourages open communication with health care professionals.
Health and Safety
Dist - POLYMR

Understanding printing terminology - prepress procedures 20 MIN
VHS
Color (H C A)
$129.00 purchase _ #60395 - 027
Teaches students the technical side of prepress procedures. Gives a general overview and acquaints the viewer with terminology by following a six - color printing job through the stages of prepress planning and preparation. Includes sample forms for estimating, scheduling, specifications and pagination, a glossary and a proportional scale.
Industrial and Technical Education
Dist - GA **Prod** - GA

Understanding profound knowledge - Volume XIV 25 MIN
VHS
Deming library series
Color (PRO A G)
$595.00 purchase, $150.00 rental; $595.00 purchase, $150.00 rental
Presents Dr. Edwards Deming as he explains principles of quality achievement. Discusses his definition of profound knowledge that managers need for decision - making. Part of a sixteen - volume series.
Business and Economics; Psychology
Dist - EXTR **Prod** - FI
VLEARN

Understanding psychological trauma 61 MIN
U-matic / VHS
Color (C A PRO)
$595.00 purchase, $125.00 rental
Treats the effects on survivors of such traumatic events as homicide, suicide, social violence, disaster, and war. Notes that individuals most likely to suffer post - traumatic stress reactions are frequently neither recognized nor treated. Presents first - person accounts of survivors of severely traumatizing experiences. Features commentary from several expert clinicians in the area of post - traumatic stress. Includes Part I, Learning from Survivors, and Part II, Healing and Recovery.
Guidance and Counseling; Psychology
Dist - BAXMED

Understanding Radiation Therapy
VHS / U-matic
Color
Presents information essential to the new radiation therapy patient. Uses computer graphics and animation to describe how cancer grows within the body and how radiation therapy works in treating cancer cells.
Health and Safety
Dist - GRANVW **Prod** - GRANVW

Understanding reengineering 85 MIN
VHS
Reengineering the corporation - Dr Michael Hammer series
Color (G C PRO)
$950.00 purchase
Delves into the six characteristics that distinguish reengineering from other business improvement plans. Features Dr Michael Hammer, coauthor of Reengineering the Corporation - a Manifesto for Business Revolution. Includes a videocassette, audiocassette, leader's and viewer's guide and a discussion guide. Part one of a two - part series.
Business and Economics; Psychology
Dist - FI **Prod** - HAMMIC 1995

Understanding Relations
16mm
B&W
Illustrates general concepts of relation and equivalence relation.
Mathematics
Dist - OPENU **Prod** - OPENU

Understanding rheumatoid arthritis 22 MIN
VHS
Understanding arthritis series
Color (G)
$125.00 purchase _ #CE - 123
Summarizes and explains the nature and course of the disease rheumatoid arthritis. Outlines treatments and addresses unproven and folk remedies. Underscores the importance of self - management and support groups. Shows how medication, occupational and physiotherapy, nutrition and exercise can relieve pain, increase mobility and improve the quality of life. Interviews medical and allied health professionals, as well as people living with arthritis. Produced by James Brodie.
Health and Safety
Dist - FANPRO

Understanding robotics video series
Robots - an important place in American industry
Robots - designed to meet almost any need
Robots - putting them to work
Dist - CAMV

Understanding science series
Classification of living things 15 MIN
Ecosystems 15 MIN
Energy 15 MIN
Matter 15 MIN
Scientific problem solving 15 MIN
Weather systems 15 MIN
Dist - GA

Understanding science series
Classification of living things - Volume 4 18 MIN
Ecosystems - Volume 5 18 MIN
Energy - Volume 3 18 MIN
Matter - Volume 2 18 MIN
Scientific problem solving - Volume 1 18 MIN
Weather systems - Volume 6 18 MIN
Dist - SVIP

Understanding science video series
Presents a six - part series on science. Includes Classification of Living Things; Scientific Problem Solving; Matter; Energy; Ecosystems; and Weather Systems.
Classification of living things 22 MIN
Ecosystems 22 MIN
Energy 22 MIN
Matter 22 MIN
Scientific problem solving 22 MIN
Weather systems 22 MIN
Dist - KNOWUN

Understanding Semiconductors Course Outline Series no 01
What Electricity Does in Every Electric System 60 MIN
Dist - TXINLC

Understanding semiconductors course outline series - No 02
Basic circuit functions in the system 60 MIN
Dist - TXINLC

Understanding Semiconductors Course Outline Series no 03
How Circuits make Decisions 60 MIN
Dist - TXINLC

Understanding Semiconductors Course Outline Series no 08
P - N - P Transistor and Transistor Specifications 60 MIN
Dist - TXINLC

Understanding Semiconductors Course Outline Series no 10
Introduction to Integrated Circuits 60 MIN
Dist - TXINLC

Understanding Semiconductors Course Outline Series no 12
MOS and Linear Integrated Circuits 60 MIN
Dist - TXINLC

Understanding semiconductors course outline series
Digital integrated circuits 60 MIN
Diode performance and specifications 60 MIN
Diodes - what they do and how they work 60 MIN
Relating semiconductors to systems 60 MIN
Thyristors and optoelectronics 60 MIN
Transistors - How they Work, How they are made 60 MIN
Dist - TXINLC

Understanding Sexuality 30 MIN
16mm / U-matic / VHS
Look at Me Series
Color (C A)
Explains how parents can answer children's questions about sex. Points out that an understanding of sexuality does not stop with biology, but involves a social awareness of male and female roles. Narrated by Phil Donahue.
Guidance and Counseling; Health and Safety; Home Economics; Psychology; Sociology
Dist - FI **Prod** - WTTWTV 1980

Understanding Shakespeare 59 MIN
35mm strip / VHS
Color (J H C A)
$186.00, $186.00 purchase _ #MB - 481115 - 0, #MB - 512725 - 3
Presents a four - part examination of William Shakespeare and his many plays. 'A Life in the Theater' focuses on Shakespeare's professional life, while the theater of the Elizabethan Age is the subject of 'Shakespeare in Performance - The Globe...The World.' 'Comedy, Fantasy, Romance' covers Shakespeare's unique comedic vision, and 'The Tragic Theme' examines the concepts of tragedy and the tragic hero.
Fine Arts; Literature and Drama
Dist - SRA **Prod** - SRA

Understanding Shakespeare - His Sources 20 MIN
U-matic / VHS / 16mm
Color (J H)
Shows how Shakespeare's plays grew out of the many elements available to him. Focuses on Shakespeare at home, school, great houses of the nobility, and in London mixing with the Roughes elements. Depicts Shakespeare searching libraries, watching plays of rival authors and visiting the Commedia del Arte. Presents excerpts from big plays whose origins can be traced to the sources previously described.
Fine Arts; Literature and Drama
Dist - VIEWTH **Prod** - GATEEF

Understanding Shakespeare - His Sources 19 MIN
16mm / U-matic / VHS
Shakespeare Series
Color (J H C)
$465, $250 purchase _ #1012; LC 79-714983
Presents excerpts from four plays of Shakespeare to show how he enhanced his sources with imagination, knowledge of human nature and command of language.
Fine Arts; Literature and Drama
Dist - CORF **Prod** - GATEEF 1971

Understanding Shakespeare - His Stagecraft 25 MIN
U-matic / VHS / 16mm
Shakespeare Series
Color (J H C)
$555, $250 purchase _ #1997
Shows stagings from several of Shakespeare's plays.
Fine Arts; Literature and Drama
Dist - CORF

Understanding Shakespeare - His Stagecraft 25 MIN
U-matic / VHS / 16mm
Color (J H)
Shows how the physical features of the Elizabethan stage influenced the work of William Shakespeare. Reenacts how 16th century strolling players found Stratford innyards as the most adaptable setting for their plays. Brings a full size replica of the Globe Theatre stage to life showing the bookholder, actors, props and costumes. Illustrates how Shakespeare used the features of the stage to represent balconies, city walls or town gates.
Fine Arts; Literature and Drama
Dist - VIEWTH **Prod** - GATEEF

Understanding Shakespeare - His Stagecraft 25 MIN
U-matic / VHS / 16mm
Shakespeare series
Color (J H C)
LC 72-714984
Uses stagings of episodes from four plays by Shakespeare to show how the theaters of Elizabethan England affected the way in which the plays were written.
Fine Arts; Literature and Drama
Dist - CORF **Prod** - GATEEF 1971

Understanding Shakespeare Series
Comedy, Fantasy, Romance 58.18 MIN
Part Four - the Tragic Theme 58.18 MIN
Part One - a Life in the Theater 58.18 MIN
Shakespeare in Performance - the Globe - the World 58.18 MIN
Dist - SRA

Understanding Shakespeare - The Tragedies series
Hamlet 90 MIN
MacBeth 90 MIN
Othello 90 MIN
Romeo and Juliet 90 MIN
Dist - SVIP

Understanding Shakespeare's Othello 40 MIN
VHS
Modern American Literature Eminent Scholar - Teachers Video Series
Color (C)
$95.00 purchase
Features Professor George Williams of Duke University discussing Shakespeare's drama Othello. The 33rd of 33 installments of the Modern American Literature Eminent Scholar - Teachers Video Series.
Literature and Drama
Dist - OMNIGR

Understanding Shakespeare's Romeo and Juliet 40 MIN
VHS
Modern american literature eminent scholar - teachers video series
Color (C)
$95.00 purchase
Features Professor George Williams of Duke University discussing Shakespeare's drama Romeo and Juliet. The 32nd of 34 installments of the Modern American Literature Eminent Scholar - Teachers Video Series.
Literature and Drama
Dist - OMNIGR

The Understanding Soccer Movie 18 MIN
16mm
Color (J)
LC 76-700210
Uses game action, planned action and animation to capture the excitement of soccer and to show the basic rules governing play.
Physical Education and Recreation
Dist - FILMSM **Prod** - GRADYM 1975

Understanding Software 15 - 30 MIN
U-matic / Kit / VHS
Business Computing...Cut Down to Size
(G A)
Introduces undergraduate and graduate business students to the applications of computer capabilities to business. Focuses on types, sources, and application of software. Fourth in a five part series.
Computer Science
Dist - GPN

Understanding space and time series
As Surely as Columbus saw America 28 MIN
At the frontier 28 MIN
Conflict Brought to Light 28 MIN
E equals mc squared 28 MIN
Ground Control to Mr Galileo 28 MIN
An Isolated Fact 28 MIN
Marking Time 28 MIN
Measuring Shadows - the Universe Today 28 MIN
A Note of Uncertainty - the Universe Tomorrow 28 MIN
Pushed to the Limit 28 MIN
Royal Road 28 MIN
Shades of Black 28 MIN
Vanished Brilliance - the Universe Yesterday 28 MIN
Dist - UCEMC

Understanding Steinbeck's Grapes of Wrath 30 MIN
VHS
Modern American Literature Eminent Scholar - Teachers Video Series
Color (C)
$95.00 purchase
Clarifies the ideological backgrounds, composition and literary merits of Steinbeck's masterpiece, demonstrating its still powerful union of political matter and artistic excellence. The 12th of 34 installments of the Modern American Literature Eminent Scholar - Teacher Video Series.
Literature and Drama
Dist - OMNIGR

Understanding Stress 12 MIN
VHS / 16mm
Stress - Unwinding the Spring Series
Color (H C A PRO)
$195.00 purchase, $75.00 rental _ #8073
Analyses stress.
Health and Safety; Psychology
Dist - AIMS **Prod** - HOSSN 1988

Understanding Stress - the Marginal Manager 30 MIN
VHS / U-matic
Stress Intelligence - an Approach to Stress Management Series
Color
Psychology
Dist - DELTAK **Prod** - DELTAK

Understanding Stresses and Strains 10 MIN
U-matic / VHS / 16mm
Triangle of Health Series
Color (I J) (ARABIC GERMAN HUNGARIAN SPANISH SWEDISH)
LC FIA68-2684
Discusses the mental side of the health triangle, with emphasis on the pressures and worries of everyday life which can damage man's health.
Guidance and Counseling; Health and Safety; Psychology
Dist - CORF **Prod** - DISNEY 1968

Understanding stroke 13 MIN
VHS
Color (G)
$250.00 purchase, $70.00 rental _ #4345S, #4345V
Explains to the family and caregiver of a stroke victim what a stroke is, its possible effects, causes, treatments and warning signs. Emphasizes how family members are affected and how they cope when a relative has a stroke. Describes briefly the brain and the functions of each hemisphere. Explains risk factors and controllable factors such as high blood pressure. Highlights early warning signs of a stroke and the importance of family support.
Health and Safety; Sociology
Dist - AJN

Understanding student behavior - or I've got 30 ET's in my classroom 30 MIN
VHS
First - year teacher series
Color (T)
$69.95 purchase, $45.00 rental
Discusses the unique challenges and rewards that first - year school teachers face. Serves as the eleventh episode of a 12 - part telecourse. Features discussions between first - year teachers and Winthrop College professor Glen Walter on understanding student behavior.
Education; Psychology
Dist - SCETV **Prod** - SCETV 1988

Understanding Surrealism - Painters of the Dream Series
Automation and Dream Painting 18 MIN
Part One - Dada and the Surrealist Revolution 18 MIN
Dist - SRA

Understanding the American Economy
VHS
Color
Discusses capitalism, the price system, GNP, inflation, business cycle, unemployment, corporations, public sector and private sector.
Business and Economics; Civics and Political Systems
Dist - HRMC **Prod** - HRMC

Understanding the art of the Renaissance - Ideas and ideals 27 MIN
35mm strip / VHS
Color (J H C T A)
$93.00 purchase _ #MB - 481097 - 9, #MB - 512391 - 6
Considers the ideas and ideals behind Renaissance art. Focuses on the intellectual, social, religious, and economic developments that paved the way. Features the artwork of Michelangelo, Da Vinci and Raphael.
Fine Arts; History - World; Religion and Philosophy
Dist - SRA **Prod** - SRA

Understanding the Art of the Renaissance - Ideas and Ideals - Part One 14 MIN
VHS
Color (J H C)
LC 88-700279
Looks at the painting, sculpture and architecture created during the Renaissance period, with special focus on students' appreciation of the art of that era.
Fine Arts; History - World
Dist - SRA **Prod** - SRA 1986

Understanding the Art of the Renaissance - Ideas and Ideals - Part Two 14 MIN
VHS
Color (J H C)
LC 88-700279
Looks at the painting, sculpture and architecture created during the Renaissance Period, with special focus on students' appreciation for the art of that era.
Fine Arts; History - World
Dist - SRA **Prod** - SRA 1986

Understanding the Assignment 30 MIN
U-matic / VHS
Introduction to Technical and Business Communication Series
Color (H C A)
Business and Economics; English Language
Dist - GPN **Prod** - UMINN 1983

Understanding the atom - 02 - nuclear reactions 29 MIN
16mm
B&W
LC FIE64-7
Discusses neutron capture processes, fission by neutrons, calculations involving activation of gold in a nuclear reaction and detection of minute quantities.
Industrial and Technical Education; Science - Physical
Dist - USERD **Prod** - USNRC

Understanding the atom - 1970s - series
Properties of radiation 30 MIN
Radiation and matter 44 MIN
Radioisotopes in biology and agriculture 26 MIN
Dist - USNAC

Understanding the atom - 1980s - series
Nuclear reactions 30 MIN
Radiation detection by ionization 30 MIN
Radiation detection by scintillation 30 MIN
Radioisotoper applications in medicine 26 MIN
Dist - USNAC

Understanding the atom - No. 01 - Alpha, beta and gamma 44 MIN
16mm
Color
Discusses the origin and nature of alpha, beta and gamma radiation, the methods of describing atoms and the energy level concept. Introduces the potential energy wheel model of the nucleus. Illustrates alpha ray emission and energy levels in the nucleus.
Science - Physical
Dist - USNAC **Prod** - USNRC

Understanding the atom - No 03 - properties of radiation 30 MIN
16mm
B&W (H C A)
Discusses laws of radioactive decay, standard deviation in counts, energy distribution of alpha and beta - emitters, absorption curves, self - absorption and scattering.
Industrial and Technical Education; Science - Physical
Dist - USERD **Prod** - USNRC 1962

Understanding the atom - No 03 - radiation and matter 44 MIN
16mm
B&W (H C A)
LC FIE64-3
Considers the interaction of radiation with matter and develops the various processes by which alpha, beta and gamma radiation give up energy to their surroundings. Explains the relation between energy of a particle and the number of ion pairs formed. Discusses gamma and the four possibilities of gamma ray absorption.
Science - Physical
Dist - USERD **Prod** - USNRC 1962

Understanding the atom - No 05 - radiation detection by ionization 30 MIN
16mm
B&W (H C A)
LC FIE64-4
Discusses principles of ionization detectors. Provides examples of suitable instruments and a detailed discussion of the geiger counter.
Science; Science - Physical
Dist - USERD **Prod** - USNRC 1962

Understanding the atom - No 06 - radiation detection by scintillation 30 MIN
16mm
B&W (H C A)
LC FIE64-5
Discusses the reaction of gamma - radiation with matter, the scintillation process, solid and liquid scintillator detection devices and the operation of a pulse - height analyzer.
Science; Science - Physical
Dist - USERD **Prod** - USNRC 1962

Understanding the atom - No 07 - radiological safety 30 MIN
16mm
B&W (H C A)
LC FIE64-8
Discusses background radiation, action of larger doses, units of measurement, maximum permissible limits, maximum concentration of radioisotopes, reduction of radiation hazard and safety techniques.
Health and Safety; Science; Science - Physical
Dist - USERD **Prod** - USNRC 1963

Understanding the atom - No 08 - Radioisotope applications in industry 26 MIN
16mm
B&W (C)
LC FIE64-151
Presents a lecture demonstration by Paul C Aebersold, Director of Isotope Development at the Atomic Energy Commission. Discusses the various industrial uses of radioisotopes in the tire plants and steel mills, in the petroleum and chemical industries and in food plants.
Business and Economics; Science - Physical
Dist - USNAC **Prod** - USNRC 1964

Understanding the atom - No 09 - radioisotope in biology and agriculture 26 MIN
16mm
B&W (C)
LC FIE65-44
Dr Howard Curtis of Brookhaven National Laboratory discusses the importance of radioisotopic tracers in the determination of the structure and role of nucleic acids and other cellular components. He describes plant breeding projects and the various theories of aging which have been tested and other examples of the importance of radiation to molecular biology.
Agriculture; Science - Natural; Science - Physical
Dist - USNAC **Prod** - USNRC 1964

Understanding the atom - No 11 - the Atom in physical science 26 MIN
16mm
B&W (C)
LC FIE65-46
Dr Glenn T Seaborg, chairman of the Atomic Energy Commission, outlines briefly the types of experiments which were used in production of transuranium elements. He describes various sources employed in producing the new elements and discusses applications of the atom to other chemical problems and use of special techniques. Dr Seaborg stresses the need for scientists and the importance of good scientific training in schools.
Science - Physical
Dist - USNAC **Prod** - USNRC 1964

Understanding the atom - No 10 - radioisotope applications in medicine 26 MIN
16mm
B&W (C)
LC FIE65-45
Dr John Cooper of Northwestern University traces the development of the use of radioisotopes and radiation in the field of medicine from the early work by Hervesy to present. He describes the areas of medical research, diagnosis and therapy in which radioisotopes and radiation are being used and explains how radioisotopes are used for the treatment of various diseases.
Health and Safety; Science - Physical
Dist - USNAC **Prod** - USNRC 1964

Understanding the Back and Neck - Anatomy 47 MIN
U-matic
Color; Mono
The contents and container of the spinal column and spinal cord. Clinical and diagnostic testing procedures for the neck and back. The basics of back and neck examinations.
Civics and Political Systems; Science - Natural
Dist - PROEDS **Prod** - PROEDS 1985

Understanding the Back and Neck - Intervertebral Disc 47 MIN
U-matic
Color; Mono
A review of the intervertebral disc including an explanation of regional differences between the cervical and lumbar areas, biomechanics of the spine, physical and neurological exams, special studies & treatments.
Civics and Political Systems; Health and Safety
Dist - PROEDS **Prod** - PROEDS 1985

Understanding the back and neck - sprain, strain and cord injury 53 MIN
U-matic
Color; Mono
Examines strain versus sprain and cord injuries. Demonstrates diagnosis and evaluation of an injury. Covers treatment and rehabilitation.
Civics and Political Systems; Health and Safety
Dist - PROEDS **Prod** - PROEDS 1985

Understanding the balance sheet 26 MIN
VHS
Color (H C A PRO)
$89.00 purchase _ #S01439
Defines and describes important accounting concepts. Shows how they are used to determine a company's financial condition. Closes with a quiz to review the concepts learned.
Business and Economics
Dist - UILL

Understanding the Basics 34 MIN
VHS / U-matic
Computers in Legal Research Series
Color (PRO)
Gives a general overview of legal research, then focuses upon computer research. Provides demonstrations on Lexis and Westlaw systems.
Industrial and Technical Education; Mathematics; Sociology
Dist - ABACPE **Prod** - ABACPE

Understanding the business of world and stocks 58 MIN
VHS / BETA / 16mm
Color (G)
$39.95 purchase _ #VT1072
Introduces common and preferred stocks. Gives an overview of business structure and practice, securities terminology, and stockholder rights. Conveys the background necessary for approaching the stock market intelligently without giving counsel on what investments to make.
Business and Economics; Home Economics
Dist - RMIBHF **Prod** - RMIBHF

Understanding the Business World and Stocks 58 MIN
VHS / U-matic
Your Money Series
(H C A)
$29.95 _ #MX1201V
Introduces the viewer to preliminary concepts concerning common and preferred stocks. Gives an overview of the business world, and prepares students to approach the stock market.
Business and Economics
Dist - CAMV **Prod** - CAMV

Understanding the Business World and Stocks 58 MIN
BETA / VHS
Investing Series
Color
Explains Common and preferred stocks. Discusses securities terminology. Provides an overview of business structure and practice.
Business and Economics
Dist - MOHOMV **Prod** - MOHOMV

Understanding the Cardiac Workup 18 MIN
U-matic / VHS
Color
LC 77-730598
Explains what the cardiac workup is and discusses its role in preventing and minimizing heart problems. Describes electrocardiograms, blood tests and X - ray procedures that may be required during a cardiac workup.
Science; Science - Natural
Dist - MEDCOM **Prod** - MEDCOM

Understanding the cell 20 MIN
VHS
Introduction to the cell structure series
Color (J H)
$105.00 purchase _ #UL115003B
Presents a two - part program which overviews the basic facts of cell structure and function. Covers the definition of a cell, the internal structure of a cell, how cells multiply and how they are organized. Includes two videos, a teacher's guide and duplicating masters. Part of a three - part series on the cell.
Science - Natural
Dist - KNOWUN

Understanding the courts - Anatomy of a criminal case and Anatomy of a civil case 40 MIN
VHS
Color (G)
$25.00 purchase
Presents two programs on the court system. Explains the criminal and civil justice systems. Highlights the use of constitutional principles to shape judicial processes and dramatizes courtroom proceedings.
Civics and Political Systems
Dist - AMBAR **Prod** - AMBAR

Understanding the Deaf 21 MIN
16mm / U-matic / VHS
Color (J)
LC 77-700592
Records instructional methods used with the deaf. Presents many of the obstacles which deaf children must overcome in their education.
Education; Guidance and Counseling; Psychology
Dist - PEREN **Prod** - PORTAM 1977

Understanding the Expectation Effect 30 MIN
U-matic / VHS
Interaction - Human Concerns in the Schools Series
Color (T)
Explains the expectation effect in an educational setting.
Education
Dist - MDCPB **Prod** - MDDE

Understanding the FCC Regulations on Radio Frequency Interference 65 MIN
U-matic
Color (PRO)
Teaches businesses how to comply with FCC regulation Part 15, Subpart J to ensure that computing devices, peripherals, or digital products do not create radio frequency emissions.
Computer Science; Industrial and Technical Education
Dist - VENCMP **Prod** - VENCMP 1986

Understanding the female body 15 MIN
VHS
Living with your body series
Color (P I)
$69.00 purchase _ #MC311
Discusses female genitalia and menstruation.
Health and Safety; Psychology; Sociology
Dist - AAVIM **Prod** - AAVIM 1992

Understanding the Japanese 30 MIN
16mm
Color
Describes how the Japanese view romance, love and marriage by interviewing six foreign residents of Japan.
Geography - World; History - World; Sociology
Dist - MTP **Prod** - MTP

Understanding the Listening Process 11 MIN
U-matic / VHS
Listening - the Forgotten Skill Series
Color
English Language; Psychology
Dist - DELTAK **Prod** - DELTAK

Understanding the male body 15 MIN
VHS
Living with your body series
Color (P I)
$69.00 purchase _ #MC310
Discusses the development of male genitalia.
Health and Safety; Psychology; Sociology
Dist - AAVIM **Prod** - AAVIM 1992

Understanding the Metric System 8 MIN
16mm
Measurement Series
Color (J)
LC 78-700703
Shows the importance of understanding the metric system, particularly for laboratory work. Explains the metric system and how it is related to systems of ten.
Mathematics
Dist - PSU **Prod** - PSU 1972

Understanding the physical Earth - 3 60 MIN
VHS
Land, location and culture - a geographical synthesis series
Color (J H C)
$89.95 purchase _ #WLU103
Initiates a three - part look at the physical world from an earth - science perspective. Opens with a discussion of the notion of systems as a way to facilitate understanding of the complex physical world. The major portion of the programs takes the systems notion and applies it first to the ecosystem and then to the lithosphere. Explores in the first case the energetics of ecosystems through the example of a meadow. Discusses and illustrates in the second case, the processes giving rise to the erosion, transportation and deposition of soil materials, including the contribution of people to the soil erosion problem. Part of a 12 - part series.
Agriculture; Geography - World; Science - Natural; Science - Physical
Dist - INSTRU

Understanding the Pill 9 MIN
16mm / U-matic / VHS
Color (A)
Examines oral contraceptives and how they work. Gives directions for use, posible complications and limitations and signs and symptoms to be reported.
Health and Safety; Sociology
Dist - PRORE **Prod** - PRORE

Understanding the Science Behind Food Preservation 15 MIN
16mm / U-matic / VHS
Color (C A)
LC 81-700685
Explains the scientific reasons for bacterial growth causing spoilage in canned food.
Home Economics
Dist - CORNRS **Prod** - CUETV 1976

Understanding the Sentry Fire Extinguisher 10 MIN
VHS
Color (IND)
Teaches the proper use of fire extinguishers to employees and emphasizes safety awareness.
Health and Safety
Dist - ANSUL **Prod** - ANSUL

Understanding the TENS Unit 15 MIN
VHS
Color (PRO)
$395.00 purchase _ #N900VI050
Explores the use of the Transcutaneous Electrical Nerve Stimulation - TENS - unit. Discusses its history and its use as a method of electrotherapy in the control of chronic pain.
Health and Safety; Psychology; Science - Natural
Dist - HSCIC

Understanding the Totality 55 MIN
VHS / U-matic
Color
Presents Margaret Rood on understanding the totality of physical therapy.
Health and Safety
Dist - UMDSM **Prod** - UMDSM

Understanding the Turbocharger
VHS / 35mm strip
Color
$219.00 purchase _ #016 - 902 filmstrips, $219.00 purchase _ #016 -
Uses narration to teach step by step procedures for troubleshooting a turbocharger, disassembling the unit, rebuilding the center housing and rotating assembly, and final inspection and assembly.
Education; Industrial and Technical Education
Dist - CAREER **Prod** - CAREER

Understanding the turbocharger 56 MIN
VHS
Color (H A)
$229.00 purchase _ #VMA09424V
Takes a comprehensive look at the turbocharger. Covers troubleshooting, disassembly, rebuilding, and final inspection and assembly. Consists of two videocassettes and a program guide.
Industrial and Technical Education
Dist - CAMV

Understanding the Whitetail Rut 27 MIN
VHS / BETA
Color
Shows whitetail scraping, scent marking and breeding behaviors. Features bucks fighting over an estrous doe and buck/doe copulations.
Physical Education and Recreation; Science - Natural
Dist - HOMEAF **Prod** - HOMEAF

Understanding the Working Back 20 MIN
16mm / VHS
Color (H)
$475.00, $395.00 purchase
Describes back injury prevention and back injury care with an emphasis on understanding the back and self - responsibility. Features Dr. Leonard Ring.
Health and Safety; Science - Natural
Dist - FLMWST

Understanding the Working Back 20 MIN
16mm / VHS
Color (A IND)
$545.00, $495.00 purchase _ #30.0137, #40.0137
Presents basic back care techniques. Illustrates ways to prevent back injuries by considering posture, lifting procedures and using good judgment.
Business and Economics; Health and Safety; Psychology; Science - Natural
Dist - UTEXPE

Understanding the working back 20 MIN
BETA / VHS / U-matic
Color (IND G A)
$463.00 purchase, $125.00 rental _ #UND007
Illustrates the mechanics of back movement and the consequences of incorrect lifting habits. Features Leonard King, authority on back injury and ergonomics.
Health and Safety; Science - Natural
Dist - ITF **Prod** - CREMED 1991

Understanding Thomas Wolfe's Look Homeward, Angel 30 MIN
VHS
Modern American Literature Eminent Scholar - Teachers Video Series
Color (C)
$95.00 purchase
Describes Wolfe's first novel as autobiographical, told with emotional fervor and rhetorical high style. The 16th of 34 installments of the Modern American Literature Eminent Scholar - Teacher Video Series.
Literature and Drama
Dist - OMNIGR

Understanding Title III - emergency planning and community right to know 15 MIN
U-matic / BETA / VHS
Color (IND G)
$295.00 purchase _ #827 - 01
Overviews the major provisions of Title III of the Superfund Amendments and Reauthorization Act - SARA. Covers federal government, local and business responsibilities under Title III. Discusses emergency response procedures, interacting with state and community citizen groups, disseminating chemical hazard information to surrounding communities and proper reporting procedures.
Health and Safety; Industrial and Technical Education; Psychology; Sociology
Dist - ITSC **Prod** - ITSC

Understanding toddlers 156 MIN
VHS
Color; PAL (G)
PdS40 purchase
Presents six 26 - minute programs. Helps parents understand themselves and their young children. Contact distributor about availability outside the United Kingdom.
Psychology; Sociology
Dist - ACADEM

Understanding Topographic Maps 14 MIN
U-matic / VHS / 16mm
Color (J H)
LC 79-706766
Describes how a topographic map is made, demonstrates the meaning of contour lines and explains the uses of the topographic map.
Science - Physical
Dist - MEDIAG **Prod** - WILEYJ 1970

Understanding under 12s 156 MIN
VHS
Color; PAL (G)
PdS40 purchase
Presents six 26 - minute programs helping parents to undertand what makes children tick including their thoughts, emotions, feelings, fears, worries, excitements and joys. Features Anna Ford as presenter. Contact distributor about availability outside the United Kingdom.
Health and Safety; Psychology; Sociology
Dist - ACADEM

Understanding Urine Testing 30 MIN
U-matic / VHS / 16mm
Color (A)
Informs about glucose metabolism, ketone formation and renal thresholds. Shows types of urine test materials, which tests to use, when to test and exceptions to normal test routines. Describes equipment, procedures and results. Reviews storage and handling, and the effects of diet, medication and physical condition.
Health and Safety
Dist - PRORE **Prod** - PRORE

Understanding Wall Street 110 MIN
VHS
Color (J H C G)
$49.95 purchase _ #LIB054V
Explains what a share of stock is and how prices are determined. Traces the colorful history of Wall Street, the role of the investment banker, how to identify the 'best' companies, read an annual report, financial statements and the financial pages.
Business and Economics
Dist - CAMV

Understanding Weather and Climate
VHS / U-matic
Color (H)
Examines the major factors that affect weather, various types of weather phenomena, the vocabulary of weather observation and the instruments used to trace weather patterns.
Science - Physical
Dist - GA **Prod** - GA

Understanding Wharton's House of Mirth 30 MIN
VHS
Modern American Literature Eminent Scholar - Teachers Video Series
Color (C)
$95.00 purchase
Examines the composition and themes of Wharton's most devastating critique of high society in New York during the Gilded Age. The 14th of 34 installments of the Modern American Literature Eminent Scholar - Teacher Video Series.
Literature and Drama; Sociology
Dist - OMNIGR

Understanding what We Value 30 MIN
VHS / U-matic
Interaction - Human Concerns in the Schools Series
Color (T)
Looks at the role of values in a school setting.
Education
Dist - MDCPB **Prod** - MDDE

Understanding who you are - the personality video series 150 MIN
VHS
Understanding who you are - the personality video series
Color (J H)
$725.00 purchase _ #HEC200
Presents a ten - part series on personality types and how personality affects the teenage years. Covers self - esteem and self perception, family issues, peer pressure, tolerance for differences, the effects of personality on work and values, dating, personal conflict and success in school.
Education; Psychology; Social Science; Sociology
Dist - CADESF **Prod** - CADESF 1990

Understanding who you are - the personality video series
Self - esteem - I would be perfect if only I didn't have this zit 15 MIN
Dist - CADESF
UNL

Understanding William Faulkner's as I Lay Dying 30 MIN
VHS
Modern American Literature Eminent Scholar - Teachers Video Series
Color (C)
$95.00 purchase
Explains how Faulkner surprises and challenges the reader by his use of mulitiple points of view and unusual mixtures of style. Features Professor Cleanth Brooks. Sixth of thirty - five installments of the Modern American Literature Eminent Scholar - Teacher Video Series.
Literature and Drama
Dist - OMNIGR

Understanding worker's comp video
VHS
Health care consumerism system series
Color (G)
$179.00 purchase _ #WMV12
Explains the facts about worker's compensation. Assists employees in becoming aware of their rights and responsibilities. Encourages open communication between employees and managers. Part of a ten - part series.

Guidance and Counseling; Home Economics
Dist - GPERFO **Prod** - GPERFO

Understanding world geography - using maps and globes 30 MIN
VHS
Color (H)
$89.00 purchase _ #60312 - 025
Covers the history of maps and the development of techniques to render maps and globes more accurately. Examines different kinds of globes, latitude and longitude, and political, geographical and topographical maps. Shows how to use maps and globes.
Geography - World; Social Science
Dist - GA **Prod** - GA 1992

Understanding Your Anesthesia 8 MIN
U-matic / VHS / 16mm
Color (PRO) (SPANISH)
Describes anesthesiology as a medical specialty developed to control pain, and helps reduce the fear and apprehension associated with surgical experiences.
Health and Safety
Dist - PRORE **Prod** - PRORE

Understanding your preterm infant - baby behavior 22 MIN
VHS
Color (H C A PRO) (SPANISH)
$200.00 purchase, $50.00 rental
Instructs parents of newborn infants on baby behaviors. Covers behavioral cues and signals, strengths and sensitivities, and ways to improve health care and home life for the baby.
Health and Safety; Psychology
Dist - UARIZ **Prod** - UARIZ

Understanding your preterm infant - the NICU 10 MIN
VHS
Color (H C A PRO) (SPANISH)
$100.00 purchase, $50.00 rental
Instructs parents of premature or ill term babies on the Neonatal Intensive Care Unit.
Health and Safety
Dist - UARIZ **Prod** - UARIZ

Understanding Your Safety Responsibility 14 MIN
U-matic / VHS
Foreman's Accident Prevention Series
Color (IND)
Gives seven rules to observe in order to attain the company's accident prevention goals while ensuring the safety of the entire work crew.
Health and Safety
Dist - GPCV **Prod** - GPCV

Understanding yourself and your body series
Birth process
Female anatomy and physiology
Male anatomy and physiology
Puberty
Dist - AAVIM

Understated or overrated 29 MIN
VHS
Fitness for life series
Color (G)
$170.00 purchase, $17.50 rental _ #35451
Examines the state of fitness and wellness in society and overviews the rest of the series. Features Davies Bahr, instructor in exercise and sport science at Penn State. Part of a six - part series.
Physical Education and Recreation
Dist - PSU **Prod** - WPSXTV 1988

The Understudy 26 MIN
16mm
Color
LC 76-701490
Tells the story of a tangled love relationship which spans 30 years.
Fine Arts; Guidance and Counseling
Dist - ONCA **Prod** - ONCA 1975

Undertow 9 MIN
16mm
Color (H C)
Features a symbolic fantasy of a young woman's conflict between sexual desires and religious training.
Fine Arts; Guidance and Counseling; Sociology
Dist - CFS **Prod** - JORDAL

Undertow 7 MIN
16mm
Color (G)
$15.00 rental
Paints a portrait of a bathing woman who gradually merges with her environment. Experiments with editing and erotic images to portray a sensual dance. Produced by Varda Hardy.
Fine Arts
Dist - CANCIN

Undertow 15 MIN
VHS
Color (G)
$15.00 rental, $200.00, $50.00 purchase
Tells the story of Mike and his impressionistic relationships with women.
Fine Arts; Psychology; Sociology
Dist - CANCIN **Prod** - KNWLDB 1980

Undertow 12 MIN
16mm
Color (G)
$24.00 rental
Explores a middle - aged man's emotional chaos and descent into self - destruction. Contrasts his point of view with the cold facts of the police report. Based on a real incident and filmed at San Francisco, Florida beaches and the desert of Death Valley. Produced by Virgina Giritlian.
Fine Arts
Dist - CANCIN

Undertow and Count Me Gone 20 MIN
VHS / U-matic
Matter of Fiction Series
Color (J H)
Presents Undertow by Finn Haverold, set in Norway. Tells of a young boy's idolatry for an older boy who has stolen a sailboat. Narrates from Count Me Gone by Annable and Edgar Johnson, set in an American city. Describes how a boy becomes disillusioned after his brother uses him as a scapegoat to cover his own inadequacies. (Broadcast quality).
Literature and Drama
Dist - AITECH **Prod** - WETATV

Underwater 15 MIN
U-matic / VHS
Let's Draw Series
Color (P)
Fine Arts
Dist - AITECH **Prod** - OCPS 1976

Underwater 25 MIN
16mm / U-matic / VHS
Untamed World Series
Color; Mono (J H C A)
$400.00 film, $250.00 video, $50.00 rental
Unveils the underwater world of the Red Sea and features its majestic coral reef.
Geography - World; Science - Natural
Dist - CTV **Prod** - CTV 1973

Underwater 30 MIN
16mm / VHS
Color (H G)
$60.00, $75.00 rental, $250.00 purchase
Tells a coming - of - age story about a young girl who is haunted by memories of an incestuous incident which makes her shy and introverted, living vicariously through the secret joys and pains of another similarly troubled girl. Deals with young women, sexuality and sexual abuse with a lyrical visual beauty.
Fine Arts; Psychology; Sociology
Dist - WMEN **Prod** - LAMATT 1994

Underwater Animals 15 MIN
U-matic / VHS
Draw Along Series
(K P)
$125.00 purchase
Details the drawing of a diver, a shark, whales and an octopus.
Fine Arts
Dist - AITECH **Prod** - AITECH 1986

Underwater Flight of the Tufted Puffin 9 MIN
16mm / U-matic / VHS
Aspects of Animal Behavior Series
Color
Shows the surface and underwater locomotion of the tufted puffin, a marine bird that swims underwater by means of synchronous movements of partially flexed wings. Analyzes the development of thrust by the wings and the use of the feet, tail and bill for steering and maneuvering.
Science - Natural
Dist - UCEMC **Prod** - UCLA 1979

Underwater I 25 MIN
16mm / U-matic / VHS
Untamed World Series
Color; Mono (J H C A)
$400.00 film, $250.00 video, $50.00 rental
Presents the Coral Sea and its impressive array of colorful great polyps. This is the first of a two part underwater study and features Dr. Sebastian Holzberg and Dr. Hans Walter Fricke.
Geography - World; Science - Natural
Dist - CTV **Prod** - CTV 1969

Underwater II 25 MIN
16mm / U-matic / VHS
Untamed World Series
Color; Mono (J H C A)
$400.00 film, $250.00 video, $50.00 rental
Features the underwater world as a film crew travels the oceans observing the incredible marine life from a skin diver's perspective.
Geography - World; Science - Natural
Dist - CTV **Prod** - CTV 1970

Underwater kids 28 MIN
VHS
Color (I J H C A)
$19.95 purchase _ #UK101
Joins a group of divers ages 12 to 16 from a coastal North Carolina town on an expedition to explore Key Largo's coral reef, the only living coral reef found along the continental United States. Produced by Marine Grafics.
Geography - United States; Geography - World; Physical Education and Recreation
Dist - ENVIMC

Underwater Louisbourg 12 MIN
16mm
Color
LC 75-703442
Follows a group of divers as they explore shipwrecks in the harbor off the shore of the Louisbourg fortress in Nova Scotia.
Geography - World; Physical Education and Recreation; Sociology
Dist - NSDTI **Prod** - NSDTI 1972

Underwater photography made easy 60 MIN
VHS
Color (H C)
$29.95 purchase _ #D514
Features scuba diver and videographer Robert 'Tuna' Townsend who instructs on underwater photography. Includes a guidebook.
Industrial and Technical Education
Dist - INSTRU

Underwater Sound - Basic Principles 21 MIN
16mm
Color
LC 74-705872
Illustrates the basic principles of the behavior of sound under water. Shows the effects of absorption, scattering, bottom loss and sound refraction on sound transmissions in the sea.
Science - Physical
Dist - USNAC **Prod** - USN 1969

Underwater worlds - 103 29 MIN
VHS
FROG series 1; Series 1; 103
Color (P I J)
$100.00 purchase
Offers the third program by Friends of Research and Odd Gadgets. Lifts science off the textbook page into the real world to show how enjoyable and challenging science can be. In this episode, the Froggers compare an aquarium and scuba diving. Special focus on how fish and humans obtain oxygen while underwater, swim bladders for buoyancy and filtration systems. Produced by Greg Rist.
Science - Physical
Dist - BULFRG **Prod** - OWLTV 1993

Undescended Testis 15 MIN
VHS / U-matic
Pediatric Series
Color
Health and Safety
Dist - SVL **Prod** - SVL

Undetermined Coefficients 29 MIN
VHS / U-matic
Calculus of Differential Equations Series
B&W
Mathematics
Dist - MIOT **Prod** - MIOT

The Undifferentiated Lump 10 MIN
16mm / U-matic / VHS
Color (H C A)
LC 75-703835
Illustrates the application of behavioral shaping techniques and demonstrates the art of differential reinforcement by showing how a professor molded the verbal behavior of a young man who was remiss in his studies. Tells how the student was then able to pass the examination.
Psychology; Sociology
Dist - STNFLD **Prod** - STNFLD 1973

Une Femme Douce 87 MIN
16mm
Color (FRENCH)
Uses a series of flashbacks to tell the story of a young wife who commits suicide. Follows her husband's reconstruction of the past as he sits by her bed.

Fine Arts; Foreign Language; Sociology
Dist - NYFLMS **Prod** - NYFLMS 1969

Une Journee Dans Les Reserves Africaines 23 MIN
16mm
Color (I) (FRENCH)
Views African wildlife reservations.
Foreign Language; Geography - World; Science - Natural
Dist - FACSEA **Prod** - FACSEA

Une Nuit Sur Le Mont Chauve 8 MIN
16mm
B&W
Presents the first film made on the pinboard, an animation classic illustrating the music of Moussorgsky's tone poem, Night On Bald Mountain, and creates a fantasy world of witches, demons, and skeletons. By Alexander Alexeiff and Claire Parker.
Fine Arts
Dist - STARRC **Prod** - STARRC 1933

Une Ombre Du Passe 15 MIN
U-matic / VHS / 16mm
La Maree Et Ses Secrets Series
Color (C A)
Foreign Language
Dist - FI **Prod** - FI

Une Simple Histoire 60 MIN
16mm
B&W (FRENCH)
Focuses on a young woman who moves to Paris with her daughter to look for work and shelter. Finds her after nine days, without a job and without a home, until she moves in with an older woman.
Fine Arts; Foreign Language; Sociology
Dist - NYFLMS **Prod** - NYFLMS 1957

Une Vile De Province 19 MIN
U-matic / VHS / 16mm
La France Telle Qu'Elle Est Series
Color (H C)
Describes a visit to a small market town, purchasing hardware and medicine in shops whose description ends in ' - erie' on the market square of the town of Bauge, located in the Loire Valley.
Foreign Language; Geography - World
Dist - MEDIAG **Prod** - THAMES 1977

Une Visite a Leon Trotsky, par Andre Breton 30 MIN
16mm
B&W (G)
$60.00 rental
Uses the encounter between the French surrealist Breton and exiled Soviet revolutionary Trotsky in 1938 to explore problems in separating the personal from the political and how the media affects that. Deals with the impossibility of an objective reality. Produced by Linda Tadic.
Civics and Political Systems; Sociology
Dist - CANCIN

Unearthing the Past 26 MIN
U-matic / VHS
Color (G)
$249.00, $149.00 purchase _ #AD - 1814
Discusses some of the new horizons in archaeology with Dr Anna Roosevelt, curator of South and Middle American archaeology at the Museum of the American Indian. Reveals that the technology and techniques are applicable to classical archaeology.
History - World; Science - Physical; Sociology
Dist - FOTH **Prod** - FOTH

Uneasy allies - Volume 4 49 MIN
VHS
Vietnam - the ten thousand day war series
Color (G)
$34.95 purchase _ #S00396
Suggests that the US presence in South Vietnam had a negative impact overall. Focuses on how the American influence was felt in Saigon. Features Premier Ky's assessment that US forces should fight to win because they lacked staying power, mutual understanding, and largely ignored their South Vietnamese counterparts. Narrated by Richard Basehart.
History - United States
Dist - UILL

Uneasy neighbors 35 MIN
VHS
Color (H C G A)
$250.00 purchase, $50.00 rental _ #38066
Investigates the growing tensions between residents of migrant worker camps and affluent homeowners in northern San Diego county, one of the wealthiest and fastest - growing areas in the nation. Shows that migrant workers live in camps where conditions are worse than in much of the Third World. Produced by Paul Espinosa for KPBS - TV, San Diego.
Sociology
Dist - UCEMC

The Unelected 60 MIN
VHS
Power Game Series
Color; Captioned (G)
$59.95 purchase _ #TPGE - 103
Considers the role that media, interest groups and lobbyists have on public policy in Washington, D.C. Focuses on the activities of the American Association of Retired Persons and the American - Israel Public Affairs Committee. Hosted by Hedrick Smith.
Civics and Political Systems; Literature and Drama; Sociology
Dist - PBS **Prod** - MPTPB 1988

Unemployment, inflation and national output 30 MIN
VHS
Introductory economics series
Color; PAL (J H C G)
PdS29.50 purchase
Looks at how cycles in our economy develop by explaining how unemployment, inflation and gross domestic product are measured. Introduces aggregate supply and demand. Features Ellen Roseman and Professor John Palmer describing three methods. Part of a four - part series.
Business and Economics
Dist - EMFVL **Prod** - TVOTAR

Unemployment portrayal 4 MIN
16mm
Color (G)
$10.00 rental
Fine Arts
Dist - CANCIN **Prod** - LEVINE 1983

UNESCO 28 MIN
Videoreel / VHS
International Byline Series
Color
Interviews Mr Doudou Diene, director of UNESCO liason office at the United Nations in New York. Presents slides and film clips on UNESCO's achievements. Hosted by Marilyn Perry.
Civics and Political Systems; Geography - World
Dist - PERRYM **Prod** - PERRYM

Uneven Parallel Bars for Girls 13 MIN
16mm / VHS / U-matic
Color (J H C) (ARABIC SPANISH)
LC 76-714078
Demonstrates beginning, intermediate and advanced skills on the uneven parallel bars for girls. Portrays spotting techniques and combined movements in sequence.
Physical Education and Recreation
Dist - AIMS **Prod** - AIMS 1971

The Uneven Seesaw - Sexual Abuse of Children 20 MIN
VHS / U-matic
Color (C A)
Speaks to people who were victims of sexual abuse and incest as children. Discusses the roots of our public policies. Details the state's intervention in incest cases.
Psychology; Sociology
Dist - MMRC **Prod** - MMRC

Uneventful Day 29 MIN
16mm / U-matic / VHS
Planet of Man Series
Color (H C)
LC 76-703569
Discusses the process of weathering that produces the variety and beauty of our planet's geological formations.
Agriculture; Geography - World; Science - Physical
Dist - FI **Prod** - OECA 1976

The Unexpected 53 MIN
U-matic / VHS / 16mm
Jack London's Tales of the Klondike Series
Color (H C A)
Relates what happens when a gold miner runs amok in his camp, killing two other miners. Depicts the informal trial which takes place, affording the Indian guides a chance to ponder the curious ways of white man's justice. Based on the short story The Unexpected by Jack London.
Literature and Drama
Dist - EBEC **Prod** - NORWK 1982

The Unexpected 20 MIN
16mm
Color
LC 75-703123
Examines some of Xerox Corporation's television commercials and tells how they came to be. Describes the growth of Xerox as it relates to the television advertising medium.
Business and Economics; Fine Arts; Industrial and Technical Education; Psychology
Dist - WSTGLC **Prod** - XEROX 1975

The Unexpected universe - 3
VHS
Space age series
Color (G)
$24.95 purchase _ #SPA080
Reveals that, for years, telescopes offered humans a very serene view of the heavens. Discloses that when scientists began using rockets to rise above the atmosphere of the Earth, human perceptions were shattered with revelations of colliding galaxies, exploding stars and a universe that was unimaginably violent and chaotic and, for the first time, humans got a glimpse of how large the universe is - as their vision improved, their imagination has soared. Features Patrick Stewart as host. Part three of a six - part series.
History - World; Science - Physical
Dist - INSTRU **Prod** - NAOS

The Unexpected Voyage 52 MIN
16mm / U-matic / VHS
Undersea World of Jacques Cousteau Series
Color
Records the behavior of two seals who develop an amiable relationship with Jacques Cousteau's oceanographers.
Psychology; Science - Natural
Dist - CF **Prod** - METROM 1970

An Unexplained Injury 31 MIN
16mm
Color (A)
Looks at a case of child abuse, emphasizing the factors in the backgrounds of the parents which make them act this way.
Psychology; Sociology
Dist - LAWREN **Prod** - UTORMC

The Unfair Advantage 45 MIN
VHS
(H C A)
$39.95 purchase _ #82347
Presents Tom Millers Unfair Advantage System which teaches individuals how to reduce the magnitude of their emotional reactions to daily situations.
Psychology
Dist - CMPCAR

Unfair Exchange 27 MIN
16mm / U-matic / VHS
Five Billion People Series
Color
Investigates the economic relationship between developed and underdeveloped countries. Examines the situation in which underdeveloped countries export raw materials and import finished products, explaining the relationship between buyer and seller, and how prices are fixed on the international market.
Business and Economics
Dist - CNEMAG **Prod** - LEFSP

Unfinished Business 27 MIN
16mm / U-matic / VHS
Insight Series
Color (H C A)
Demonstrates how a father's illness makes his son realize how much he needs him. Stars Jack Bannon and Bill Quinn.
Guidance and Counseling; Psychology; Religion and Philosophy; Sociology
Dist - PAULST **Prod** - PAULST

Unfinished business 58 MIN
VHS / U-matic
Japanese American experience in World War II series
Color (G)
$250.00 purchase, $75.00 rental
Tells the stories of three Japanese Americans, Fred Korematsu, Gordon Hirabayashi and Minoru Yasui, who refused to be interned and were imprisoned for violating Executive Order 9066. Reveals efforts by the three men to reopen their cases and overturn their convictions. Produced and directed by Steven Okazaki.
History - United States; Sociology
Dist - CROCUR

Unfinished Diary 55 MIN
16mm / VHS
Color (G) (SPANISH (ENGLISH SUBTITLES))
$295.00 purchase, $125.00, $100.00 rental
Examines the differing perceptions of the world as experienced by women and by men. Focuses on the experiences of Chilean emigre Marilu Mallet in Canada, where she explores the profound cultural silences she experiences as an artist, an exile, a woman.
Fine Arts; History - United States; Psychology; Sociology
Dist - WMEN **Prod** - MARMA 1986

Unfinished Miracles - the Story of Agricultural Research 29 MIN
16mm
Color (J H C A)
Discloses the work of scientists at the nation's Agricultural Experiment Stations.

Agriculture
Dist - UILL **Prod** - UILL 1975

An Unfinished piece for player piano 100 MIN
16mm / 35mm
Color (G) (RUSSIAN WITH ENGLISH SUBTITLES)
$250.00, $300.00 rental
Adapts loosely the play Plantonov by Anton Chekhov. Portrays a gathering of friends on a summer day. Directed by Nikita Mikhalkov.
Fine Arts; Literature and Drama
Dist - KINOIC **Prod** - CORINT 1977

Unfinished Symphony 15 MIN
16mm
Color
LC 78-701577
Presents an appeal for funds to protect endangered species around the world.
Science - Natural
Dist - WWF **Prod** - WWF 1978

An unfinished symphony 30 MIN
VHS
Gospel of Mark series
Color (J H C G A R)
$39.95 purchase, $10.00 rental _ #35 - 821 - 2076
Features New Testament scholar Dr Donald Juel in a historical and cultural consideration of the Gospel of Mark. Produced by Seraphim.
Literature and Drama; Religion and Philosophy
Dist - APH

The Unfinished Task 72 MIN
16mm
B&W (A)
LC 72-701651
A story of the conflict which arises between a materialistic father and his spiritually minded son when the son follows his vocation as a foreign missionary. Traces the father's realization of the importance and urgency of his son's calling.
Guidance and Counseling; Psychology; Religion and Philosophy; Sociology
Dist - CPH **Prod** - CPH 1956

Unfolding 16 MIN
VHS / 16mm
B&W (A)
$100.00 purchase, $25.00 rental
Presents heterosexual lovemaking as poetic expression. Produced by Coni Beeson.
Fine Arts
Dist - CANCIN

Unfolding 17 MIN
16mm
B&W
Suggests universal awareness, including aloneness, fantasies, searching, touching and loving. Blends ocean, hills, sun, woman and man to portray subterranean feelings. Emphasizes a value - oriented view of sexuality, and expresses the woman's point of view.
Guidance and Counseling; Psychology; Sociology
Dist - MMRC **Prod** - MMRC

Unforeseen Problems 30 MIN
BETA / VHS
This Old House, Pt 1 - the Dorchester Series
Color
Uncovers some problems in a house about to be renovated, from the roof to the plumbing.
Industrial and Technical Education; Sociology
Dist - CORF **Prod** - WGBHTV

The Unforgettable pen pal - a story about prejudice and discrimination 28 MIN
VHS
Human race club series
Color (P I)
$59.00 purchase _ #RB871
Uses animation to portray pen pals A J and Joey, who share an interest in basketball. Reveals that when they finally meet at a professional basketball game, they encounter prejudice where they least expect it. Teaches about the negative effects of prejudice and the importance of forming opinions about others intelligently. Part of a series teaching essential living skills.
Guidance and Counseling; Psychology; Sociology
Dist - REVID **Prod** - REVID 1990

The Unfortunate bride - Di umgliklekhe kale - Broken hearts 68 MIN
35mm
Silent; B&W (G) (YIDDISH AND ENGLISH INTERTITLES)
Captures New York through a new immigrant's eyes. Presents a tragic love story framed by the wisdom of the Torah which opens and closes the film. Portrays a writer, Benjamin Rezanov, who is forced to emigrate from Czarist Russia and leave his wife behind. Adjusting to a new land, he dedicates himself to working and learning English, despite continual reversals. Believing his wife dead, he marries a cantor's daughter and is shunned by her hypocritical family. When he receives news that his first wife is still alive, he rushes back to Russia, only to find her dead. He never manages to return again to America and Ruth, the cantor's daughter, dies of a broken heart. Contact distributor for rental fee. Reissue of Broken Hearts, USA, 1926.
Literature and Drama; Religion and Philosophy; Sociology
Dist - NCJEWF

UNFPA 28 MIN
Videoreel / VHS
International Byline Series
Color
Interviews Mr Rafael M Salas, Executive Director of the United Nations Fund for Population Activities. Illustrates the goals and program activities of UNFPA through a film. Hosted by Marilyn Perry.
Civics and Political Systems; Geography - World
Dist - PERRYM **Prod** - PERRYM

Unfried Clams 29 MIN
Videoreel / VT2
Observing Eye Series
Color
Science - Natural; Sociology
Dist - PBS **Prod** - WGBHTV

Unfriendly Flora and Fauna 15 MIN
U-matic / VHS / 16mm
Color (J)
LC 81-700051
Offers an overview of plants and animals that are harmful to humans, including jimsonweed, poison ivy and oak, nightshade, mushrooms, snakes, spiders, scorpion and wasps.
Health and Safety; Science - Natural
Dist - CORF **Prod** - CENTRO 1980

Ung - Young 28 MIN
16mm
B&W (DANISH)
Presents a round table conference among youngsters. Discusses young people's attitude to the fear of the atomic bomb, modern requirements as regards education and specialization, choice of a career and the pleasure taken in one's work, young people's need for a place of their own and their view of sexual life.
Foreign Language; Psychology
Dist - STATNS **Prod** - STATNS 1965

Ungava char
VHS
Color (G)
$29.90 purchase _ #0384
Travels to Ungava Bay in the sub - Arctic region of northern Quebec province. Features 65 foot vertical tides, the highest in the world, and the evasive action of the elusive char fish.
Geography - World; Physical Education and Recreation; Science - Natural
Dist - SEVVID

The Ungrateful Land 27 MIN
16mm
Color
_ #106C 0172 104N
Geography - World
Dist - CFLMDC **Prod** - NFBC 1972

Unheard voices 16 MIN
VHS
Color (J H C G T A)
$55.00 purchase, $30.00 rental
Portrays the children of El Salvador, where a civil war has raged for more than a decade. Reveals that many Salvadoran children live in orphanages or refugee camps, and even more are poor. Suggests that all are negatively affected by the war. Produced by Ray Gatchalian and Nancy Juliber.
Civics and Political Systems; Geography - World; History - World
Dist - EFVP

UNICEF 28 MIN
Videoreel / VHS
International Byline Series
Color
Interviews H R H Prince Talal Bin Abdul Aziz Al Saud of Saudi Arabia as he discusses the United Nations Children's Fund and his activities as the Fund's special envoy. Includes a film clip on UNICEF.
Civics and Political Systems; Geography - World
Dist - PERRYM **Prod** - PERRYM

UNICEF Christmas Show 28 MIN
Videoreel / VHS
International Byline Series
Color
Features Celeste Holm as she brings a Christmas message at the beginning of the show. Interviews the Executive Director of UNICEF. Presents a film clip on children from different parts of the world.
Civics and Political Systems; Geography - World
Dist - PERRYM **Prod** - PERRYM

UNICEF - The First forty years 28 MIN
VHS / U-matic / 16mm
Color (I J H G)
$280.00, $330.00, $495.00 purchase, $65.00 rental
Traces the evolution of UNICEF's commitments to children throughout the world in the last four decades. Provides an historical perspective to an agency whose work was recognized with a Nobel Prize for Peace.
Civics and Political Systems; Sociology
Dist - NDIM **Prod** - UNICEF 1986

Unicorn 20 MIN
16mm
Color (G)
$35.00 rental
Explores myth as geographic time and the unicorn as a symbol of transformation. Illustrates the unicorn as a magical imaginary beast and its effect on a small boy and young man. Shot in the USA and Europe. Produced by Donna Cameron.
Fine Arts
Dist - CANCIN

The Unicorn 13 MIN
16mm
Color
LC 79-700735
Presents a view from aboard the Unicorn, one of the ships in the Operation Sail 1976 Parade of Sail from Greenwich, Connecticut, to Graves End Bay.
Geography - United States; Physical Education and Recreation
Dist - MCGUST **Prod** - MCGUST 1976

Unicorn Tales Series

Alex and the wonderful doowah lamp	23 MIN
Big apple birthday	23 MIN
Carnival circus	23 MIN
The Magic Hat	23 MIN
The Magic Pony Ride	23 MIN
The Magnificent Major	23 MIN
The Maltese Unicorn	23 MIN
The Stowaway	23 MIN

Dist - MGHT

Unicycle - Looking at My World 15 MIN
U-matic / VHS / 16mm
Color (I J H)
LC 76-700929
Raises the question of establishing personal values and goals with an account of the thoughts a young man has about himself, older people and life in general, while riding his unicycle.
Guidance and Counseling
Dist - BARR **Prod** - BARR 1976

The Unicycle Race 8 MIN
16mm / VHS
Color (P I)
LC 80-701156
Presents an animated story about a unicycle race in which the good pair of legs triumphs over the dastardly plots of the evil red pair of legs.
Fine Arts
Dist - LRF **Prod** - SWARR 1980

Unidentified flying objects 51 MIN
16mm
Color (G)
$80.00 rental
Tells the story of an alien who falls in love and fathers a child, then gets confused and leaves for his own world. Continues with the explosion of the planet which splits in two and turns to stone. An avant garde travelogue by the dean of Hungarian experimentalists, Andras Szirtes.
Fine Arts; Literature and Drama
Dist - CANCIN

Unification of a Double Uterus 16 MIN
16mm
Color (PRO)
Presents a case of a double uterus. Describes the clinical problem history, laboratory findings and management. Illustrates the operative technique with the end results.
Health and Safety; Science
Dist - ACY **Prod** - ACYDGD 1969

Uniform and function 50 MIN
VHS
Look series
Color (A)
PdS99 purchase _ Unavailable in the USA
Reveals the selling of personal identity through logos. Strips away the glitz and glamor of the fashion business to look behind the scenes. Explores the mystique of the designer label and debates the meaning of style. Reveals the mysteries of material and unveils the interdependence between the fashion industry, the media, financiers, and the consumer. Part of a six-part series.

Home Economics
Dist - BBCENE

Uniform Annual Cash Flow Method 30 MIN
VHS / U-matic
Engineering Econony Series
Color (IND) (JAPANESE)
Introduces the evaluation method which converts all cash flows to a time adjusted equivalent annual amount. Illustrates economic evaluation of solar energy for residential heating as an example problem.
Business and Economics
Dist - COLOSU **Prod** - COLOSU

Uniform Guidelines on Employee Selection Procedures 48 MIN
U-matic / VHS
Color
LC 79-707988
Provides a general overview of the purpose and scope of the uniform guidelines on employee selection procedures. Contains a discussion of these guidelines by staff of the Office of Personnel Management.
Psychology
Dist - USNAC **Prod** - USOPMA 1979

The Uniform hazardous waste manifest 13 MIN
VHS / U-matic / BETA
Handling hazardous waste series
Color; PAL (IND G) (SPANISH)
$175.00 rental _ #HWH - 400
Focuses on the central tracking document essential in management of hazardous waste - from creation to disposal. Explains step - by - step the manifest and its importance to the process of hazardous waste management. Includes leader's guide and 10 participant handouts. Part of a seven - part series which trains hazardous waste management workers.
Business and Economics; Health and Safety; Psychology; Sociology
Dist - BNA **Prod** - BNA

Uniform hazardous waste manifest 15 MIN
VHS / U-matic / BETA
Hazardous waste training series
Color (IND G A)
$730.00 purchase, $175.00 rental _ #UNI003
Focuses on the central tracking document essential in hazardous waste management from beginning to end. Explains the uniform hazardous waste manifest through a step - by - step process and emphasizes its importance in documenting hazardous waste. Part of a comprehensive seven - part series on hazardous waste training.
Health and Safety; Psychology
Dist - ITF **Prod** - BNA

Uniforms, Weapons and Equipment - Pt 14 30 MIN
VHS
And Then There were Thirteen Series
Color (H)
$69.95 purchase
Considers the uniforms, weapons and equipment that accompanied warfare in the late 18th century. Uses footage shot on battleground locations. Describes command personalities, weapons and uniforms. Part 14 of a twenty - part series on Southern theaters of war during the American Revolution.
Civics and Political Systems; History - United States; Home Economics; Physical Education and Recreation
Dist - SCETV **Prod** - SCETV 1982

Unijunction Sawtooth Generator 29 MIN
16mm
B&W
LC 74-705873
Explains the physical and electrical operating characteristics of the unijunction transistor, and identifies the sawtooth generator circuit using a unijunction transistor, and explains the purpose of each component. (Kinescope).
Industrial and Technical Education
Dist - USNAC **Prod** - USAF

Unijunction Transistor and Tunnel Diode 9 MIN
16mm
B&W
LC 74-705874
Introduces the unijunction transistor and tunnel diode. Discusses their fundamental characteristics and identifies component parts. (Kinescope).
Industrial and Technical Education
Dist - USNAC **Prod** - USAF

Unilateral Hypertrophy of Mandibular Condyle 4 MIN
16mm
Color (PRO)
Examines unilateral hypertrophy of mandibular condyle, a condition with no known cause.
Health and Safety
Dist - LOMAM **Prod** - LOMAM

The Uninvited Guest 23 MIN
U-matic / VHS / 16mm
Color
Presents the rules for fire prevention, control and escape as they apply to work areas, especially in hotels. Explains the fire prevention responsibilities of watchmen, maids, housekeepers, kitchen staff and management.
Health and Safety
Dist - IFB **Prod** - WALGRV

The Uninvited - the Homeless of Phoenix 24 MIN
VHS / U-matic
Color
$335.00 purchase
Sociology
Dist - ABCLR **Prod** - ABCLR 1983

Union 15 MIN
16mm
Color
Shows how the oil workers in Northern California struck and how they asked the students at San Francisco State and University of California to join the union in the struggle, January 1969.
Business and Economics; Geography - United States; Sociology
Dist - CANWRL **Prod** - CANWRL 1969

Union at Work 28 MIN
16mm
Color (A)
Gives an overview of the AFSCME union which represents 100,000 city workers.
Business and Economics; Sociology
Dist - AFLCIO **Prod** - AFLCIO 1970

The Union Besieged - 1861 - 1862 22 MIN
16mm
Color (J H)
Presents Lincoln facing the tasks of hastily assembling a strong army and choosing a general, General Mc Clellan. Explains how hostility toward Lincoln and the ensuing battle of wills deeply affected the events of the early Civil War.
History - United States
Dist - FI **Prod** - WOLPER 1974

Union democracy 30 MIN
16mm / U-matic / VHS
Color (IND G)
$295.00, $225.00 purchase, $120.00 rental
Uses historical footage and and typical elections under the Wagner and Landrum - Griffin acts to show how both laws work. Interviews movement participants such as Victor Reuther and Chip Yablonski. Evaluates current American labor laws. A companion to Unions in Crisis.
Business and Economics; Civics and Political Systems; Social Science
Dist - ROLAND **Prod** - MRMKF

The Union has Filed a Petition for Election 180 MIN
U-matic
How to Keep Your Company Union Free Series
Color (A)
Tells management how to win a unionizing election, selling a non - union policy to employees, avoiding a hearing.
Business and Economics
Dist - VENCMP **Prod** - VENCMP 1986

The Union Meeting - Rules of Order 13 MIN
U-matic
Color (A)
Sets forth some of the basic rules governing parliamentary procedure including motions and amendments to the motion.
Business and Economics; Sociology
Dist - AFLCIO **Prod** - CANLAB 1983

Union of opposites - new directions - Parts 25 and 26 60 MIN
VHS / U-matic
Discovering psychology series
Color (C)
$45.00, $29.95 purchase
Presents parts 25 and 26 of the 26 - part Discovering Psychology series. Presents a yin - yang model of complementary opposites to help understand the basic principles thought to govern human nature and animal behavior. Features prominent psychologists who discuss the future of psychology and new directions in research, theory and application. Two thirty - minute programs hosted by Professor Philip Zimbardo of Stanford University.
Psychology
Dist - ANNCPB **Prod** - WGBHTV 1989

The Union Steward and You 15 MIN
16mm
Color
LC 74-705875
Shows the relationship between a first line supervisor and a union steward in solving problems.

Business and Economics; Sociology
Dist - USNAC **Prod** - USN 1969

Union Theological Seminary 18 MIN
16mm
Color
LC 74-700491
Presents an impressionistic montage about life and work at Union Theological Seminary.
Religion and Philosophy
Dist - UTS **Prod** - UTS 1973

The Union Triumphant - 1863 - 1865 30 MIN
16mm
Color (J H)
Presents the defeat and withdrawal at Gettysburg of General Robert E Lee's Confederate Army constituting the turning point of America's Civil War. Analyzes the war from a 19th - century civilian viewpoint, evaluating the desertions, riots and public disenchantment with an unwinnable war. Concludes with the collapse of the Confederacy.
History - United States; Sociology
Dist - FI **Prod** - WOLPER 1974

Unions - Awareness and Organizing Tactics
U-matic / VHS
Meeting the Union Challenge Series
Color (IND)
Shows how unions work to turn the work force against the company. Discusses union tactics, peer pressure, how unions infiltrate a company and gain access to personal data of employees, the business approach of unions and how they work to gain influence in the work place.
Business and Economics
Dist - GPCV **Prod** - GPCV

Unions in crisis 30 MIN
U-matic / VHS
Color (IND G)
$225.00 purchase, $120.00 rental
Reveals that union membership has declined from one - third of the United States labor force to less than one - sixth. Uses historical footage and interviews with Victor Reuther, Ron Carey, Joseph Rauh and young union activists to consider reasons for the decline and ways to reverse it. Written and directed by Henry Bass.
Business and Economics; Social Science
Dist - ROLAND **Prod** - MRMKF

Unions - Strategies for Prevention
VHS / U-matic
Meeting the Union Challenge Series
Color (IND)
Shows what can and cannot be done to defeat organizing campaigns. Shows that supervisors must know the law, facts about company policies and benefits, and how to detect early signs of union activity.
Business and Economics
Dist - GPCV **Prod** - GPCV

Unique Beginnings 30 MIN
U-matic / VHS / 16mm
Color (A)
LC 81-701482
Focuses on mothers and fathers who watch hopefully as doctors struggle to save their children's lives. Examines medical ethics and responsibilities, the quality of life, the rights of the disabled, familial love and the death of very young babies.
Health and Safety; Home Economics
Dist - PEREN **Prod** - AMERFF 1982

Unique Me 29 MIN
VHS / 16mm
Villa Alegre Series
Color (P T)
$46.00 rental _ #VILA - 121
Presents educational material in both Spanish and English.
Education; Psychology
Dist - PBS

Uniroyal World Junior Curling Championship, 1976 17 MIN
16mm
Color
LC 77-702692
Covers the 1976 Uniroyal World Junior Curling Championship held in Aviemore, Scotland.
Physical Education and Recreation
Dist - CHET **Prod** - UNIRYL 1976

Unisphere - Biggest World on Earth 14 MIN
16mm
Color (H C A)
LC FI67-45
Discusses concepts of design behind the unisphere of the U S Steel Corporation, and its construction at the New York World's Fair.
Fine Arts; Industrial and Technical Education; Physical Education and Recreation
Dist - USSC **Prod** - USSC 1964

Unit 1
VHS / 35mm strip
Building Construction - Interior Series
$85.00 purchase _ #017 - 251 filmstrip, $85.00 purchase _ #017 - 256
Talks about roughing - in plumbing, heating and cooling systems, and running electrical wire.
Industrial and Technical Education; Sociology
Dist - CAREER **Prod** - CAREER

Unit 2
VHS / 35mm strip
Building Construction - Interior Series
$85.00 purchase _ #017 - 270 filmstrip, $85.00 purchase _ #017 - 275
Discusses insulation, putting up drywall, and finishing drywall.
Industrial and Technical Education
Dist - CAREER **Prod** - CAREER

Unit 3
VHS / 35mm strip
Building Construction - Interior Series
$85.00 purchase _ #017 - 294 filmstrip, $85.00 purchase _ #017 - 299
Discusses trim, underlayment and hardwood floors, and vinyl tile floors.
Industrial and Technical Education
Dist - CAREER **Prod** - CAREER

Unit 4 - Antiquing 40 MIN
VHS / U-matic
Decorative Painting Series
Color
Shows through various methods the valued qualities of worn, distressed and aged appearances for many surfaces. Illustrates how badly cracked walls, ceilings and woodwork can be treated with fine to heavy patinas and plastic mixtures are antiqued.
Fine Arts
Dist - EXARC **Prod** - EXARC

Unit Method - Pupil Centered - Pt 3 - Wise 48 MIN
16mm
B&W (C)
An unrehearsed class session where the teacher does not know what subject the class will choose to study until the decision is made during the class period.
Education
Dist - PSU **Prod** - PSU 1962

Unit 1 - Chrysler System
VHS / 35mm strip
Electronic Ignition System Series
$85.00 purchase _ #017 - 331 filmstrip, $85.00 purchase _ #017 - 336
Provides instruction about electronic ignition systems.
Education; Industrial and Technical Education
Dist - CAREER **Prod** - CAREER

Unit 1 - Glazing Methods 75 MIN
U-matic / VHS
Decorative Painting Series
Color
Shows the application of translucent treatments for raised and flat surfaces. Illustrates different techniques to add 'broken color' effects for an elegant look over single color finishes.
Fine Arts
Dist - EXARC **Prod** - EXARC

Unit Pricing 15 MIN
VHS / U-matic
Math Matters Series Green Module
Color (I J)
Shows how a robot housekeeper is sent to the factory for an adjustment in his circuitry which will equip him to do comparison shopping.
Mathematics
Dist - AITECH **Prod** - KRLNTV 1975

Unit record applications 45 MIN
Videoreel / VT2
Data processing - introduction to data processing series; Unit 1
B&W
Business and Economics; Computer Science
Dist - GPN **Prod** - GPN

Unit removal and installation of the cylinder power assembly of the General Motor's series 35 MIN
16mm
Color (IND)
LC 78-700006
Uses a General Motors' series 645 diesel engine to illustrate the step - by - step removal and installation of a cylinder power assembly on a diesel engine.
Industrial and Technical Education
Dist - VCI **Prod** - VCI 1974

Unit 3 - GM System
VHS / 35mm strip
Electronic Ignition System Series
$85.00 purchase _ #017 - 374 filmstrip, $85.00 purchase _ #017 - 379
Provides instruction about electronic ignition systems.
Education; Industrial and Technical Education
Dist - CAREER **Prod** - CAREER

Unit 3 - Graining 43 MIN
VHS / U-matic
Decorative Painting Series
Color
Shows how to simulate choice woodgrain used where wood brings warmth and charm of nature. May be used attractively on painted woodwork, steel and painted doors, kitchen cabinets and furniture.
Fine Arts
Dist - EXARC **Prod** - EXARC

Unit 2 - Ford System
VHS / 35mm strip
Electronic Ignition System Series
$85.00 purchase _ #017 - 350 filmstrip, $85.00 purchase _ #017 - 355
Provides instruction about electronic ignition systems.
Education; Industrial and Technical Education
Dist - CAREER **Prod** - CAREER

Unit 2 - Marbleizing 53 MIN
VHS / U-matic
Decorative Painting Series
Color
Describes marbleizing as an initiative or 'faux' type of painting used on surfaces where the real thing is desired, impractical or too expensive. Brings refinement in the classic manner to rooms where baseboards, door frames, mantels, table tops and such are treated with a 'personal touch' rendering.
Fine Arts
Dist - EXARC **Prod** - EXARC

United Airlines station manpower planning system
VHS
Color (C PRO G)
$150.00 purchase _ #85.06
Focuses on the United Airlines system for scheduling shift work at its reservations offices and airports which uses integer and linear programming and network optimization techniques and encompasses the entire scheduling process from forecasting of requirements to printing employee schedule choices. Reveals that the system has produced direct labor cost savings of over $6 million annually while earning rave reviews from United's upper management, operating managers and affected employees. United Airlines. Judson E Byrn, Thomas J Holloran.
Business and Economics; Social Science
Dist - INMASC

United and divided 25 MIN
VHS
Jerusalem - of heaven and earth series
Color (H C G)
$99.00 purchase
Contrasts the lives of two women in Jerusalem, one Jewish and one Arab, to picture the separation between the two peoples who have a stake in the future of the city. Part of a set of eight videos that view Jerusalem from various angles. Videos are also available separately.
Geography - World
Dist - LANDMK

United Graphics Communication System 8 MIN
U-matic / VHS
Color
LC 80-707597
Provides an overview of the Veterans Administration guidelines for a unified graphics communications system as developed by Malcolm Grear Designers.
Industrial and Technical Education
Dist - USNAC **Prod** - VAHSL 1980

United Kingdom 30 MIN
VHS
Essential history of Europe
Color; PAL (H C A)
PdS65 purchase; Not available in Denmark
Presents the culture and history of the United Kingdom from an insider's perspective. Ninth in a series of 12 programs featuring the history of European Community member countries.
Geography - World; History - World
Dist - BBCENE

United Mine Workers of America, 1970 - a House Divided 14 MIN
16mm
Color
LC 79-700977
Contrasts statements made by Tony Boyle, president of the United Mine Workers of America, with those of the anti - Boyle faction. Includes scenes of dissident miners and exposes the weaknesses of the union under his leadership two years before the rank and file rejected him.
Business and Economics; Social Science
Dist - APPAL **Prod** - APPAL 1971

The United Nations 31 MIN
VHS
Color (J H)
$79.95 purchase _ #CCP0051V-S
Helps students become involved with the United Nations organization, structure, and purpose. Covers most aspects of the UN, from its history and status as an international forum, to more traditional explanations of the political divisions between the developed and developing worlds. Explains the inner workings of the UN, and explains how the organization has changed as the result of the end of the Cold War. Produced independently of the UN, this is an impartial overview of its strengths and weaknesses.
Civics and Political Systems; History - World
Dist - CAMV

United Nations Chief of Protocol 28 MIN
Videoreel / VHS
Marilyn's Manhattan Series
Color
Focuses on the position of Chief of Protocol at the United Nations. Includes an interview with Ambassador Pedro De Churruca, United Nations protocol chief. Hosted by Marilyn Perry.
Civics and Political Systems
Dist - PERRYM **Prod** - PERRYM

United Nations Christmas Show 28 MIN
Videoreel / VHS
International Byline Series
Color
Features interviews with United Nations officials. Includes dramatic presentations and a choir from the UN.
Civics and Political Systems; Geography - World
Dist - PERRYM **Prod** - PERRYM

United Nations Disaster Relief Organization 28 MIN
Videoreel / VHS
International Byline Series
Color
Interviews Mr Faruk Berkol, Under - Secretary - General and UNDRO Coordinator. Discusses UNDRO programs regarding a series of major disasters that had occurred around the world. Focuses on how UNDRO promotes disaster preparedness. Includes an informative film on world disasters.
Civics and Political Systems; Geography - World
Dist - PERRYM **Prod** - PERRYM

United Nations for a better future 23 MIN
VHS
Color (G)
$175.00 purchase, $50.00 rental
Details United Nations' impact on world affairs by examining the roles of its six principle organs - the General Assembly; the Security Council; the Secretariat; the Trusteeship Council; the International Court of Justice; and the Economic and Social Council. Demonstrates how the UN's increasingly active role in international affairs is helping to bring peace and equality to all people on the earth. Directed by Niels von Kohl.
Civics and Political Systems; Fine Arts
Dist - FIRS **Prod** - UN 1991

United Nations Fund for Population Activities 28 MIN
Videoreel / VHS
International Byline Series
Color
Interviews Dr Rafael M Salas, Under - Secretary - General of the United Nations and Executive Director of UNFPA. Covers the census in China, UNFPA's neutral approach to population policies, major contribution by United Nations member nations to UNFPA and the International Population Conference to be held in Mexico City in August of 1984. Includes a film clip on Sri Lanka.
Civics and Political Systems; Geography - World
Dist - PERRYM **Prod** - PERRYM

United Nations High Commission for Refugees 28 MIN
Videoreel / VHS
International Byline Series
Color
Interviews Mr Paul Hartling, United Nations High Commissioner for Refugees, who discusses the world refugee problem. Includes a film clip. Hosted by Marilyn Perry.
Civics and Political Systems; Geography - World
Dist - PERRYM **Prod** - PERRYM

United Nations International Post Office 28 MIN
Videoreel / VHS
International Byline Series
Color
Interviews with officials from the United Nations. Focuses on the U N Post Office. Includes a film clip on U N stamps and a new post office in Austria.
Civics and Political Systems; Geography - World
Dist - PERRYM **Prod** - PERRYM

The United Nations - its more than you think 31 MIN
VHS / Videodisc
Color (J H G)
$199.00, $79.95 purchase _ #CCP0051Z, #CCP0051V
Covers most aspects of the United Nations, from its history and status as an international zone in the center of New York City to more traditional explanations of the political divisions between developed and developing worlds. Features people closely involved with the UN explain its inner workings, discussing tensions in the UN Security Council and the balance of power between nations. Stresses the role of the UN in the Gulf War and shows the organization at a turning point. Covers specialized agencies such as UNICEF.
Civics and Political Systems
Dist - CAMV **Prod** - CAMV 1991

United Nations Peace - Keeping 28 MIN
Videoreel / VHS
International Byline Series
Color
Interviews George Sherry, United Nations Director for Special Political Affairs. Presents a film segment on peace - keeping. Hosted by Marilyn Perry.
Civics and Political Systems; Geography - World
Dist - PERRYM **Prod** - PERRYM

United Nations Relief Works Agency 28 MIN
Videoreel / VHS
International Byline Series
Color
Interviews Commissioner General Olof Olof Rydbeck. Discusses the problems of rebuilding the towns and cities in Lebanon. Examines some of the building projects and looks at the education of women.
Business and Economics; Civics and Political Systems; Geography - World
Dist - PERRYM **Prod** - PERRYM

United Nations School 28 MIN
Videoreel / VHS
International Byline Series
Color
Interviews Mr Helmut Debatin, Chairman of the Board of Trustees for the United Nations School, Mrs Sylvia Fuhrman, Special Representative of the Secretary - General for the United Nations International School, and Mr Robert Belle - Isle, Director of the United Nations International School. Hosted by Marilyn Perry.
Civics and Political Systems; Geography - World
Dist - PERRYM **Prod** - PERRYM

United Nations Stamp Show on Environment 28 MIN
Videoreel / VHS
International Byline Series
Color
Interviews Mr Clayton C Timbrell, Assistant Secretary General, Office of General Services of the United Nations, and Mr Noel Brown, Director and Special Assistant to the Executive Director of UNEP. Discusses the United Nations stamp on environment. Includes a film clip on water resources.
Civics and Political Systems; Geography - World
Dist - PERRYM **Prod** - PERRYM

The United States 25 MIN
BETA / VHS / U-matic / 16mm
Democratic forms of government series
Color (H G)
$390.00, $110.00 purchase _ #C50795, #C51511
Examines the basic principles that shape the government of the United States. Visits the underground vault where the United States Constitution and the Declaration of Independence are preserved. Follows a current issue to learn how people make their voices heard at both the national and local levels. Looks at the powers of the three branches of the national government. Part of a five - part series on democratic forms of government.
Civics and Political Systems
Dist - NGS **Prod** - NGS 1992

United States 1902 - 1914 26 MIN
VHS / 16mm
What do those old films mean series; Pt 2
Color (G)
Parallels the development of American films with the emergence of different audiences, including immigrant groups. Uses film excerpts and newsreels, photographic documents and original music. Series directed by film historian Noel Burch.
Fine Arts; History - United States; Sociology
Dist - FLMWST

The United States Air Force in Vietnam 28 MIN
VHS / U-matic
Color
Shows Air Force activities and operations in Southeast Asia beginning in 1964. Depicts personnel and equipment buildup, includes footage of chemical, psychological and tactical warfare.
Civics and Political Systems; History - United States; History - World
Dist - USAF **Prod** - USAF

United States and China Relations 13 MIN
16mm
Screen news digest series; Vol 21; Issue 8
Color
Traces the events that led to the normalization of diplomatic relations between the USA and China.
History - United States; History - World
Dist - AFA **Prod** - AFA 1978

United States and the Philippines - in our image series 180 MIN
VHS / U-matic
United States and the Philippines - in our image series
Color; Captioned (G)
$150.00, $210.00 purchase _ #TPHI - 000C
Explores the influence of the United States on the Philippines. Surveys the history of the Philippines from 1898 to the present. Three - part series interviews leading Philippine figures such as Ferdinand Marcos and Corazon Aquino.
Civics and Political Systems; Geography - World; History - United States; History - World
Dist - PBS **Prod** - KCET 1989

United States and the Philippines - in our image series
United States and the Philippines - in our image series 180 MIN
Dist - PBS

The United States and the Soviet Union - looking to the future 28 MIN
VHS
Public agenda foundation series
Color (H C G)
$250.00 purchase, $55.00 rental
Explores briefly the recent history of United States - Soviet relations. Presents four alternative 'futures' which could be pursued. Observes the debating of the pros and cons of each alternative by 12 students. Produced by Jeffrey Tuchman for the Public Agenda Foundation and the Center for Foreign Policy Development at Brown University.
Civics and Political Systems; Geography - World; Sociology
Dist - FLMLIB

The United States and Western Europe 29 MIN
16mm
B&W (H C)
LC 76-707513
Shows informal conversations with four policy - level officers of the State Department on U S Relations with Western Europe, mentioning NATO in the mid 1960s, moves for European unity, the Common Market, and France and her allies.
Civics and Political Systems; History - World
Dist - USNAC **Prod** - USDS 1966

The United States Army Combat Developments Command - Vision to Victory 32 MIN
16mm
Color
LC 74-706292
Describes the mission and organization of the U S Army Combat Developments Command, focusing on tools and techniques used to develop new concepts and equipment for the Army of the future.
Civics and Political Systems; Sociology
Dist - USNAC **Prod** - USA 1969

United States Arriving 28 MIN
16mm
Color
LC 74-705876
Follows the visit in June, 1963, of John F Kennedy, late President of the United States, to the first fleet, Point Mugu, Nots, China Lake and the Marine Corps depot, San Diego. Presents the historical relationship between the President's fleet visit and the history and traditions of the sea service.
Biography; Civics and Political Systems
Dist - USNAC **Prod** - USN 1963

The United States as a great power 60 MIN
VHS
Europe and America in the modern age - 1776 to the present series
Color (H C PRO)
$95.00 purchase
Presents a lecture by David M Kennedy. Focuses on a critical period in European and American history and on leaders of the time. Part of a 20 - part series that looks at the last two centuries in Europe and America. Series presents lectures by David M Kennedy and James Sheehan of Stanford University on such figures as Adam Smith, Marx, Lincoln, Washington, Jefferson, Freud, Margaret Sanger, Susan B Anthony and Jane Adams and their impact on the events of their day. For history resource material and continuing education courses.
Civics and Political Systems; History - United States; History - World
Dist - LANDMK

The United States Becomes a World Power 25 MIN
16mm / U-matic / VHS
American History Series
Color; B&W (J H)
LC FIA67-1331
Analyzes events which led up to the Spanish - American War. Shows the social, economic and historical forces that caused the United States to become a world power and to play an active role in world affairs.
Business and Economics; Civics and Political Systems; History - United States; History - World
Dist - MGHT **Prod** - MGHT 1967

The United States Congress - of, by and for the People 26 MIN
U-matic / VHS / 16mm
Color (J H C)
LC 72-703420
Follows two congressmen through two days of work as legislators, committee members, investigators, case workers, communicators and politicians. Examines the philosophy that has led to the evolution of Congress to its present state. Describes the specific functions of the Houses of Congress and their activities.
Civics and Political Systems
Dist - EBEC **Prod** - EBEC 1972

The United States Constitution 30 MIN
VHS / U-matic
American Government Series; 1
Color (C)
Traces the events which led to the Constitutional Convention. Reviews the different ideologies represented and offers some conclusions about the political differences and the ways they were or were not resolved.
Civics and Political Systems
Dist - DALCCD **Prod** - DALCCD

United States Constitution series
Checks and balances in the Federal Government 30 MIN
Constitutional Government - the Rule of Law in a Free Society 30 MIN
Equal protection of the laws 30 MIN
Federalism - balance of power between national and state government 30 MIN
Freedom of Speech 30 MIN
Dist - AITECH

United States Contitution Series
The Constitution and the Economy 30 MIN
Dist - AITECH

The United States Disciplinary Barracks - Our Mission, Your Future 37 MIN
16mm
Color
LC 74-705877
Shows the facilities and operation of the U S Disciplinary Barracks in Ft Leavenworth, Kansas, including training, rehabilitation programs and levels of confinement.
Civics and Political Systems; Education; Health and Safety
Dist - USNAC **Prod** - USA 1972

United States Elections - How We Vote 14 MIN
U-matic / VHS / 16mm
Color (I J)
Shows how a person registers and how he votes, both on ballots and voting machines. Presents preparation for the election and the counting of the votes, including electronic tabulations. Helps to prepare a student to exercise his right to vote and will acquaint him with a process that protects the rights of both voters and candidates.
Civics and Political Systems
Dist - PHENIX **Prod** - WILETS 1971

United States European Command 20 MIN
16mm
Color (A)
LC 78-700951
Stresses the importance of the U S European Command. Defines the role and mission of the American Armed Forces and explains its responsibility to the NATO alliance.

Civics and Political Systems; History - United States; History - World
Dist - USNAC Prod - USDD 1974

United States Expansion - California 16 MIN
U-matic / VHS / 16mm
United States Expansion Series
Color (I J H C)
LC 74-700698
Uses graphic materials and historical quotations to narrate the history of California, from its discovery by Spanish explorers to its admission to the United States.
History - United States
Dist - CORF **Prod** - CORF 1969

United States Expansion - Florida 13 MIN
16mm / U-matic / VHS
United States Expansion Series
Color (J H C)
Recounts the history of Florida from its discovery until its acquisition by the United States. Discusses the role of Andrew Jackson in combating the lawlessness and bringing about the annexation of Florida.
History - United States
Dist - CORF **Prod** - CORF 1956

United States Expansion - Louisiana Purchase 13 MIN
U-matic / VHS / 16mm
United States Expansion Series
Color (J H C)
LC 77-701876
Examines the national and international issues and events which led to Thomas Jefferson's decision to purchase the Louisiana Territory.
Civics and Political Systems; History - United States; History - World
Dist - CORF **Prod** - CORF 1977

United States Expansion - Northwest Territory 13 MIN
U-matic / VHS / 16mm
United States Expansion Series
Color (J H C)
Re - creates events leading to the opening of the Northwest territory. Depicts the work of the Ohio Company of Associates, the ordinances which governed the territory, and the pattern of statehood being formed.
Geography - United States; History - United States
Dist - CORF **Prod** - CORF 1958

United States Expansion - Oregon Country 13 MIN
U-matic / VHS / 16mm
United States Expansion Series
Color
LC 77-701884
Discusses the Lewis and Clarke expedition, stressing how it helped the United States establish claim to the Northwest and opened the way to settlers along the Oregon trail.
History - United States
Dist - CORF **Prod** - CORF 1977

United States Expansion - Overseas 14 MIN
16mm / U-matic / VHS
United States Expansion Series
Color (J H C)
Describes how the United States began expanding its territories beyond North American limits in the late 1800s. Outlines the U S involvement with Hawaii, Cuba, Puerto Rico, the Philippines, the Panama Canal and the Virgin Islands.
History - United States; History - World
Dist - CORF **Prod** - CORF 1977

United States expansion series
California and the Southwest 15 MIN
Florida and the Southeast 19 MIN
The Growth of a nation 21 MIN
Louisiana Territory 15 MIN
The Northwest territory 20 MIN
Oregon Territory 15 MIN
Texas 15 MIN
United States Expansion - California 16 MIN
United States Expansion - Florida 13 MIN
United States Expansion - Louisiana Purchase 13 MIN
United States Expansion - Northwest Territory 13 MIN
United States Expansion - Oregon Country 13 MIN
United States Expansion - Overseas 14 MIN
United States Expansion - Settling the West - 1853 - 1890 13 MIN
United States Expansion - Texas and the Far Southwest 16 MIN
Dist - CORF

United States Expansion - Settling the West - 1853 - 1890 13 MIN
U-matic / VHS / 16mm
United States Expansion Series
Color (J H C)
Explains that in the period between 1853 and 1890 the largest frontier region of the west was settled. Uses dramatized re - enactments to trace this settlement of the area which extended westward from Iowa to Missouri to the mountain ranges of California and Oregon.
Geography - United States; History - United States
Dist - CORF **Prod** - CORF 1960

United States Expansion - Texas and the Far Southwest 16 MIN
16mm / U-matic / VHS
United States Expansion Series
Color (J H C)
LC 77-701877
Chronicles the events leading up to the acquisition of Texas and the far southwest by the United States.
History - United States
Dist - CORF **Prod** - CORF 1977

The United States - Geography of a Nation 25 MIN
16mm / VHS
Color (I)
$525.00, $395.00 purchase, $60.00 rental
Explores the various sections of the nation and its geographical features, including mountains, plains, coastlines, rivers, uninhabited marshlands, and empty deserts. Shows how geography influences the way people live and work, how they dress, and the games they play.
Geography - United States; Social Science
Dist - HIGGIN **Prod** - HIGGIN 1987

United States geography series 255 MIN
VHS / U-matic / 16mm / BETA
United States geograpphy series
Color (I J)
$913.50, $711.00 purchase _ #C50110, #C51232
Presents a ten - part series on United States geography. Includes the titles The Mid - Atlantic States, Alaska and Hawaii, The Great Lakes States, The Mountain States, The Pacific Coast States, The Heartland, The Southwest, New England, The Lower South, The Upper South.
Geography - United States
Dist - NGS **Prod** - NGS 1983

United States Geography Series
Alaska and Hawaii 25 MIN
The Great Lakes states 25 MIN
The Heartland 25 MIN
The Lower South 25 MIN
The Mid - Atlantic States 27 MIN
The Mountain States 25 MIN
New England 23 MIN
The Pacific Coast States 25 MIN
The Southwest 25 MIN
The Upper south 25 MIN
Dist - NGS

United States geograpphy series
United States geography series 255 MIN
Dist - NGS

The United States in the 20th Century - 1900 - 1912 12 MIN
U-matic / VHS / 16mm
United States in the 20th Century Series
B&W (J H C)
LC 74-702685
Highlights U S history under the Roosevelt and Taft administrations and the election of Woodrow Wilson.
Biography; Civics and Political Systems; History - United States
Dist - CORF **Prod** - CORF 1974

The United States in the 20th Century - 1912 - 1920 12 MIN
16mm / U-matic / VHS
United States in the 20th Century Series
B&W (J H C)
LC 74-702686
Highlights U S history during Woodrow Wilson's administration, through the outbreak of World War I and the rejection of the League of Nations.
History - United States
Dist - CORF **Prod** - CORF 1974

The United States in the 20th Century - 1920 - 1932 19 MIN
16mm / U-matic / VHS
United States in the 20th Century Series
B&W (J H C)
LC FIA67-116
Highlights the conservative era of the 20th century, beginning with Wilson's return from the Versailles Conference and ending with the Great Depression and new liberalism under the New Deal.
Business and Economics; Civics and Political Systems; History - United States
Dist - CORF **Prod** - CORF 1967

The United States in the 20th Century - 1932 - 1940 21 MIN
U-matic / VHS / 16mm
United States in the 20th Century Series
B&W (J H C)
LC FIA67-117
Presents the history of the U S from the inauguration of Franklin D Roosevelt to the eve of World War II, including the Great Depression and New Deal legislation designed to overcome it. Emphasizes events that had lasting effects on the nation, such as the Tennessee Valley Authority, the strengthening of organized labor and the growing power of the Federal government.
Business and Economics; Civics and Political Systems; History - United States
Dist - CORF **Prod** - CORF 1967

United States in the 20th Century Series
1912 to 1920 12 MIN
1920 to 1932 18 MIN
1932 to 1940 21 MIN
1900 to 1912 12 MIN
The United States in the 20th Century - 1900 - 1912 12 MIN
The United States in the 20th Century - 1912 - 1920 12 MIN
The United States in the 20th Century - 1920 - 1932 19 MIN
The United States in the 20th Century - 1932 - 1940 21 MIN
Dist - CORF

The United States in World War I 15 MIN
VHS
Witness to history I series
Color (J H)
$49.00 purchase _ #06821 - 026
Features vignettes to show how 'war fever' raged at home as Americans pitched in to support their boys overseas. Takes the viewer into the trenches of Europe and to the conflict over the League of Nations. Part of a four - part series. Includes teacher's guide and library kit.
Education; Fine Arts; History - United States
Dist - GA

The United States in World War I 15 MIN
VHS
Color (J H)
$49.00 purchase _ #06821 - 026
Portrays the 'war fever' of the United States as Americans pitched in to support their 'boys' overseas. Travels to the trenches of Europe and discusses the conflict over the League of Nations. Includes teachers' guide and library kit.
History - United States; Sociology
Dist - INSTRU

United States Involvement in Central America 22 MIN
U-matic / VHS / 35mm strip
(J H C)
Explores the dilemmas faced by the U S in its dealings with communist leaning Latin American countries such as El Salvador and Nicaragua. Discusses the ethics of financial aid. In 2 parts.
Civics and Political Systems
Dist - ASPRSS **Prod** - ASPRSS
INSTRU
GA

The United States Military Academy Cadet Mess 21 MIN
VHS / U-matic
Color (PRO)
Tours the cadet mess at West Point and discusses the planning and organizational skills needed to feed 4000 people quickly and efficiently.
Civics and Political Systems; Home Economics; Industrial and Technical Education
Dist - CULINA **Prod** - CULINA

United States Olympic Committee - the Struggle and Triumph 25 MIN
U-matic
Color
LC 81-706236
Describes the work of the US Olympic Committee and its purpose and programs. Highlights the committee's achievements as told through the experiences of athletes.
Physical Education and Recreation
Dist - USOC **Prod** - USOC 1980

The United States Post Office 6 MIN
16mm / U-matic / VHS
Color (P)
LC 70-712846
Takes a look at the system and procedures of the U S post office.
Social Science
Dist - PHENIX **Prod** - PHENIX 1970

The United States Presidents - Personality and Politics 60 MIN
VHS
Color (J H)
Takes a unique approach to the Presidency, examining how a President's personality reflects the mood of his times and the dreams and hopes of the voters. Examines how a President's personal outlook affects his handling of domestic and foreign problems, plus shapes the events and mood of his time.
Civics and Political Systems; Social Science
Dist - HRMC **Prod** - HRMC 1985

United States - Soviet Relations
VHS
Color
Looks at the central themes and dynamics which have shaped U S - Soviet relations throughout history and continue to affect foreign policy today.
Civics and Political Systems
Dist - HRMC **Prod** - HRMC

The United States Strike Command 20 MIN
16mm
Color
LC 74-706293
Examines the role of the United States Strike Command, America's composite back - up force of action - ready strength ready to deal with any type of crisis.
Civics and Political Systems
Dist - USNAC **Prod** - USDD 1967

The United States Supreme Court - Guardian of the Constitution 24 MIN
U-matic / VHS / 16mm
Color (J H C)
LC 73-701888
Highlights the history and landmark cases of the U S Supreme Court from its beginnings in 1789 to the 1970s. Presents Judge Luther Youngdahl explaining the uniqueness of the Supreme Court, Professor Gerald Guther discussing the power of judicial review and Senator Hubert Humphrey analyzing the role of the Court as protector of rights.
Civics and Political Systems; History - United States
Dist - EBEC **Prod** - CONCPT 1973

The United States Teams 45 MIN
16mm
Color
LC 80-700310
Demonstrates the impact that private industry can have on amateur athletics, using the example of the Miller Brewing Company's support of U S national teams in boxing, track and field, cycling and skiing.
Business and Economics; Physical Education and Recreation
Dist - MBC **Prod** - MBC 1980

The United States Teams - Pt 1 22 MIN
16mm
Color
LC 80-700310
Demonstrates the impact that private industry can have on amateur athletics, using the example of the Miller Brewing Company's support of U S national teams in boxing, track and field, cycling and skiing.
Physical Education and Recreation
Dist - MBC **Prod** - MBC 1980

The United States Teams - Pt 2 23 MIN
16mm
Color
LC 80-700310
Demonstrates the impact that private industry can have on amateur athletics, using the example of the Miller Brewing Company's support of U S national teams in boxing, track and field, cycling and skiing.
Physical Education and Recreation
Dist - MBC **Prod** - MBC 1980

United States - the great American desert 15 MIN
VHS
Great deserts of the world series
Color; PAL (H)
Looks at the four true and distinct North American deserts within the Great American Desert extending west of the Mississippi. Shows how the diversion of mountain streams and the damming of the Colorado River have created a wealth of fertile oases and spurred the growth of major communities. However, competition for water, a population explosion and controversial land uses have led to concern over the future of these deserts. Part of a six - part series on deserts of the world.
Agriculture; Geography - United States; Geography - World; Science - Natural; Social Science
Dist - VIEWTH **Prod** - VIEWTH

United States - the Great American Desert 15 MIN
U-matic / VHS / 16mm
Great Deserts of the World Series
Color (I J H)
$400 purchase - 16 mm, $250 purchase - video _ #5295C
Talks about the deserts of North America.
Geography - World
Dist - CORF

United States V Aaron Burr 76 MIN
16mm
Equal Justice Under Law Series
Color (H C)
LC 78-700004
Presents a dramatization of the U S Supreme Court trial of Aaron Burr for treason. Highlights the legal issues involved.
Biography; Civics and Political Systems; History - United States
Dist - USNAC **Prod** - USJUDC 1977

Unititled 30 MIN
16mm
Color; Silent (C)
Experimental film by Ernie Gahr.
Fine Arts
Dist - AFA **Prod** - AFA 1981

The Unitive Way 45 MIN
VHS / BETA
Psychological Growth and Spiritual Development Series
Color (G)
Psychology; Religion and Philosophy
Dist - DSP **Prod** - DSP

Units of Electrical Measurement 30 MIN
U-matic / VHS
Basic Electricity, DC Series
Color (IND)
Introduces the language of electricity and basic vocabulary including ohms, volts, amperes, watts. Introduces Ohm's Law as basis for all electrical calculations.
Industrial and Technical Education; Science - Physical
Dist - AVIMA **Prod** - AVIMA

Unity 30 MIN
U-matic / VHS
Writing for a Reason Series
Color (C)
English Language
Dist - DALCCD **Prod** - DALCCD

The Unity of man and nature 90 MIN
BETA / VHS
Innerwork series
Color (G)
$49.95 purchase _ #W063
Contrasts the native American way of life in harmony with nature with the Western concept of man as dominator over nature. Features Rolling Thunder, Cherokee and intertribal medicine man.
Health and Safety; Religion and Philosophy; Social Science
Dist - THINKA **Prod** - THINKA

Unity of Personality - Expressive Behavior 18 MIN
16mm
B&W (C T)
Shows the consistency of expressive movements of five individuals with very different personalities. Includes gestures, facial movements (also split portraits), handwriting responses to stimulus words and questions, handling objects, athletic activities and walking gaits. Demonstrations show similarities of expressive behavior characteristics, which relate to the Unity of personality. P
Psychology
Dist - PSUPCR **Prod** - PSUPCR 1946

A Unity of Variety - Part 3 21 MIN
16mm / U-matic / VHS
Picasso - a Painter's Diary Series
Color (H C A)
$430, $250 purchase _ #4183
Focuses on the works of Picasso and includes interviews with his close friends. A Perspective film.
Fine Arts
Dist - CORF

Unity - Program 8 15 MIN
U-matic
Artscape Series
Color (I)
Shows children leaving a magic land after passing a test about art and art materials.
Fine Arts
Dist - TVOTAR **Prod** - TVOTAR 1983

Universal Blood and Body Fluid Precautions - an Approach to Patient Care 25 MIN
VHS
Color (PRO)
$395.00 purchase _ #N900VI017
Provides guidelines to reduce the risk of transmission of HIV, hepatitis B and other blood - borne infections. Provides statistics on prevalence and risk groups. Emphasizes the need to consider the blood and body fluids of any individual as potentially infectious. Procedures are given for the handling and disposal of used equipment and instruments, collection of specimens, personal hygiene, laundry and garbage disposal and the wearing of protective clothing.
Health and Safety; Science
Dist - HSCIC

Universal Christ 60 MIN
U-matic / VHS
Color
Presents Sri Gurudev speaking on the Universal Christ present in Yoga.
Religion and Philosophy
Dist - IYOGA **Prod** - IYOGA

The Universal declaration of human rights 20 MIN
VHS
Color (G A) (SPANISH FRENCH ARABIC)
$25.00 purchase
Gathers 41 talented animators to bring the 30 articles of the Universal Declaration of Human Rights to life. Features Jeff Bridges and Debra Winger as narrators of the English version. Produced by Prudence Fenton.
Civics and Political Systems; History - United States
Dist - AMNSTY

Universal Gravitation 31 MIN
16mm
PSSC Physics Films Series
B&W (H C A)
Derives the law of universal gravitation by imagining a solar system of one star and one planet. The kinematics and dynamics of planetary motion are demonstrated with models. Satellite orbits are displayed using a digital computer.
Science - Physical
Dist - MLA **Prod** - PSSC 1961

The Universal mind of Bill Evans 45 MIN
VHS
B&W (G)
$29.95 purchase
Jazzes universal with artist Bill Evans.
Fine Arts
Dist - KINOIC **Prod** - RHPSDY

The Universal organism 30 MIN
BETA / VHS
New pathways in science series
Color (G)
$29.95 purchase _ #S496
Challenges the so - called 'laws of nature' which are categorized as habits and instincts rather than immutable and inviolable principles. Features Dr Rupert Sheldrake, biologist and author of 'A New Science of Life,' who believes that creation may be viewed as a living organism rather than a machine with God as the great mechanic. Part of a four - part series on new pathways in science.
Religion and Philosophy; Science; Science - Natural
Dist - THINKA **Prod** - THINKA

Universal precautions - AIDS and hepatitis B prevention for health care workers 25 MIN
VHS
Color (C PRO)
$315.00 purchase, $70.00 rental _ #4334S, #4334V
Presents five parts which identify the sources and methods of transmission of the HIV and Hepatitis B viruses in the workplace. Explains universal precautions as they relate to all health care workers. Describes protective equipment and safe work practices. Includes workbook. Reviewed by OSHA, the CDC and APIC.
Health and Safety
Dist - AJN **Prod** - MEDCOM

Universal precautions - AIDS and hepatitis B prevention for home health care 31 MIN
VHS
Color (PRO C)
$195.00 purchase, $70.00 rental _ #4341
Identifies the sources and methods of transmission of HIV and HBV in the workplace. Explains universal precautions in relation to home healthcare workers, describing not only protective equipment available but safe work practices as well. Includes workbook.
Health and Safety
Dist - AJN **Prod** - MEDCOM

Universal precautions - AIDS and hepatitis B prevention for long term care 32 MIN
VHS

Color (C PRO)
$195.00 purchase, $70.00 rental _ #4342S, #4342V
Focuses on long term care workers to present five parts which identify the sources and methods of transmission of the HIV and Hepatitis B viruses in the workplace. Explains universal precautions as they relate to all health care workers. Describes protective equipment and safe work practices. Includes workbook. Reviewed by OSHA, the CDC and APIC.
Health and Safety
Dist - AJN **Prod** - MEDCOM 1993

Universal precautions - specimen handling and laboratory testing 17 MIN
VHS
Color (IND)
$495.00 purchase, $95.00 rental _ #801 - 21
Explains how laboratory personnel can follow universal precautions by handling all human tissue and body fluids as if contaminated. Covers pathogen types, routes of entry, barrier concepts and protective measures, disposal, personal hygiene and emergency situations.
Health and Safety; Psychology
Dist - ITSC **Prod** - ITSC

Universal Product Code - Train Travel - Appliance Repairs
VHS / U-matic
Consumer Survival Series
Color
Discusses the universal product code, train travel and appliance repairs.
Home Economics; Social Science
Dist - MDCPB **Prod** - MDCPB

Universal Proximal Femur Prosthesis 20 MIN
VHS / U-matic
Prothesis Films Series
Color (PRO)
Health and Safety
Dist - WFP **Prod** - WFP

Universal responsibility in a nuclear age 30 MIN
VHS / BETA
Color; PAL (G)
PdS15, $30.00 purchase
Features a program recorded from His Holiness the Dalai Lama of Tibet's 1988 visit to England. Includes His impassioned speech on the necessity of developing universal responsibility - what he terms 'the universal religion' - in order for humanity to survive in the nuclear age. Recorded at the Global Conference of Spiritual and Parliamentary Leaders on Human Survival in Oxford, England, April, 1988.
Fine Arts; Religion and Philosophy
Dist - MERIDT **Prod** - MERIDT 1988

Universal Rhythms 11 MIN
16mm
Color
LC 79-700334
Tells that harmony and motion are evident in all realms of the cosmic order. Explains that the smallest subatomic particle provides an array of motion that is comparable to movement of celestial bodies. Concludes that natural rhythms are an important link in exploring the phenomenon of periodic motion on various scales of time and space.
Science - Physical
Dist - EDMEDC **Prod** - ESPZAM 1979

Universal studios 30 MIN
VHS
Color (H C G)
$19.95 purchase _ #T/C476018
Visits a motion picture studio to show how pieces of the giant 'movie production' puzzle fit together.
Fine Arts; Industrial and Technical Education
Dist - INSTRU

Universal Themes in Fiction 30 MIN
U-matic / VHS
Communicating through Literature Series
Color (C)
Literature and Drama
Dist - DALCCD **Prod** - DALCCD

Universal Vehicle 11 MIN
U-matic / VHS / 16mm
Inventive Child Series
Color (P I)
Shows Boy and Grandpa experimenting with devices that will help them maneuver their wagon. Shows them creating steering and breaking mechanisms to keep it under control and constructing special wheels and paddles to transport their vehicle over water.
History - World; Science - Physical
Dist - EBEC **Prod** - POLSKI 1983

The Universal video yearbook reference library - 1942 - 1967 1560 MIN
VHS
Color (H C G)
$1295.00 purchase
Offers 26 one - hour videos which chronicle events in the years 1942 - 1967. Includes a viewing guide for each video and a topical index for the total collection. Includes a bonus of The War Years - 1931 - 1941.
History - World
Dist - LUF **Prod** - LUF 1991

The Universe 60 MIN
VHS
Color (G)
$64.95 purchase _ #S02042
Reviews the current state of knowledge about the universe.
History - World; Religion and Philosophy; Science - Physical
Dist - UILL

Universe
VHS / U-matic
Color
Science - Physical
Dist - MSTVIS **Prod** - MSTVIS

The Universe 18 MIN
VHS
Color; CC (H C)
$79.00 purchase _ #701
Takes a dramatic trip through the universe to help students understand planets, stars, galaxies and the place of human intelligence in the cosmos. Includes a guide. Part 1 of the program Spaceship Earth.
Science - Physical
Dist - HAWHIL **Prod** - HAWHIL 1994

Universe 27 MIN
VHS
Color (I J H G)
$59.00 purchase _ #SS160
Explores almost inconceivable extremes of size and time - from vast galaxies to subatomic particles; from cosmic events which occurred billions of years ago to microscopic events occurring now and lasting a billionth of a second.
Mathematics
Dist - INSTRU

Universe 30 MIN
VHS
Color (G)
Features former 'Star Trek' star William Shatner in a tour of the solar system. Discusses subjects including the theories behind black holes, pulsars, and other space phenomena.
Science - Physical
Dist - PBS **Prod** - WNETTV
CBSC
SCTRES
UILL

The Universe - Beyond the Solar System 18 MIN
U-matic / VHS / 16mm
Color (I J H A) (SPANISH)
A Spanish language version of the film and videorecording The Universe - Beyond The Solar System.
Science - Physical
Dist - EBEC **Prod** - EBEC 1978

The Universe - Flight to the Stars 20 MIN
U-matic / VHS / 16mm
Color (I J H) (SPANISH NORWEGIAN)
LC 79-703539
Creative and modern camera techniques and up to date footage are used to convey basic concepts pertaining to the universe.
Science - Physical
Dist - AIMS **Prod** - CAHILL 1969

The Universe from Palomar 30 MIN
16mm
Spectrum Series
B&W (H C A)
LC FIA68-242
Presents a history of the Hale telescope at Mount Palomar and the contributions its use has made to our knowledge of the universe. Shows the construction and transportation of the 200 inch mirror. Illustrates recent discoveries with photographs taken through the telescope.
Science; Science - Physical
Dist - IU **Prod** - NET 1967

The Universe from Palomar 29 MIN
16mm
Color
Tells the story of the 200 - inch Hale telescope. Provides a tour of the observatory at Mount Palomar. Describes the design of the Hale telescope, taking the viewer through the pouring, grinding, polishing, transportation and installation phases of the giant mirror. Describes the research conducted by the astronomers, including some photographs of distant stars and galaxies.
Science; Science - Physical
Dist - CIT **Prod** - CIT

The Universe - Man's Changing Perceptions 29 MIN
16mm
Color (J)
LC 76-702106
Takes a look at cosmological ideas from different cultures and shows the evolution these ideas have undergone. Demonstrates the way in which information gathered by astronomers today has influenced present understanding of the universe.
History - World; Religion and Philosophy; Science - Physical
Dist - PRESTH **Prod** - PRESTH 1976

Universe on a Scratchpad 29 MIN
16mm
B&W (J H T)
LC FIE67-126
A candid study of a modern astro - physicist and his methods of studying the solar system and universe. Shows the facilities of the NASA Goddard Institute for Space Studies, New York.
Science; Science - Physical
Dist - NASA **Prod** - NASA 1967

A University in the City 16 MIN
16mm
College Profile Film Series
Color (J)
LC 77-711470
Shows how life at an urban university is influenced by, and inseparable from, its environment. Shows students and faculty discussing the advantages and disadvantages of city surroundings. Filmed at New York University.
Education; Guidance and Counseling; Psychology
Dist - VISEDC **Prod** - VISEDC 1971

University of Akron
VHS
Campus clips series
Color (H C A)
$29.95 purchase _ #CC0089V
Takes a video visit to the campus of the University of Akron in Ohio. Shows many of the distinctive features of the campus, and interviews students about their experiences. Provides information on the composition of the student body, professors, academics, social life, housing, and other subjects.
Education
Dist - CAMV

University of Alabama
VHS
Campus clips series
Color (H C A)
$29.95 purchase _ #CC0001V
Takes a video visit to the campus of the University of Alabama. Shows many of the distinctive features of the campus, and interviews students about their experiences. Provides information on the composition of the student body, professors, academics, social life, housing, and other subjects.
Education
Dist - CAMV

University of Arizona
VHS
Campus clips series
Color (H C A)
$29.95 purchase _ #CC0005V
Takes a video visit to the campus of the University of Arizona. Shows many of the distinctive features of the campus, and interviews students about their experiences. Provides information on the composition of the student body, professors, academics, social life, housing, and other subjects.
Education
Dist - CAMV

University of Arizona - Towards New Frontiers 24 MIN
16mm
Color (H A)
Views the rapidly expanidng campus of the University of Arizona and looks into the activities of some of the scientifists who have brought distinction to the university in the fields of astronomy, optics, lunar and planetary studies, environmental research and medicine.
Education; Health and Safety; Science
Dist - UARIZ **Prod** - UARIZ 1971

University of California 15 MIN
16mm
Color (H)
Encourages junior and senior high students to consider one of the multi media programs at the University of California.
Education; Sociology
Dist - MTP **Prod** - UCDFT

University of California - Berkeley
VHS
Campus clips series
Color (H C A)
$29.95 purchase _ #CC0006V
Takes a video visit to the campus of the University of California - Berkeley. Shows many of the distinctive features of the campus, and interviews students about their experiences. Provides information on the composition of the student body, professors, academics, social life, housing, and other subjects.
Education
Dist - CAMV

University of California - Los Angeles
VHS
Campus clips series
Color (H C A)
$29.95 purchase _ #CC0012V
Takes a video visit to the campus of the University of California - Los Angeles. Shows many of the distinctive features of the campus, and interviews students about their experiences. Provides information on the composition of the student body, professors, academics, social life, housing, and other subjects.
Education
Dist - CAMV

University of Chicago Round Table Series
Abortion reform 29 MIN
Advertising in consumer affairs 29 MIN
Cinema 70 29 MIN
The FCC - television and the 70's 29 MIN
The Honest Politicans Guide to Crime Control 29 MIN
The Inner City and Mass Communications 29 MIN
Oh Theatre, Pt 1 29 MIN
Oh Theatre, Pt 2 29 MIN
The Pill, Population and Family Planning 29 MIN
The Politics of hunger in America 29 MIN
The Revival of Victorianism 29 MIN
Urban Universities and their Responsibilities 29 MIN
What has Happened to Political Machines 29 MIN
Dist - PBS

University of Cincinnati
VHS
Campus clips series
Color (H C A)
$29.95 purchase _ #CC0090V
Takes a video visit to the campus of the University of Cincinnati in Ohio. Shows many of the distinctive features of the campus, and interviews students about their experiences. Provides information on the composition of the student body, professors, academics, social life, housing, and other subjects.
Education
Dist - CAMV

University of Connecticut
VHS
Campus clips series
Color (H C A)
$29.95 purchase _ #CC0015V
Takes a video visit to the campus of the University of Connecticut. Shows many of the distinctive features of the campus, and interviews students about their experiences. Provides information on the composition of the student body, professors, academics, social life, housing, and other subjects.
Education
Dist - CAMV

University of Delaware
VHS
Campus clips series
Color (H C A)
$29.95 purchase _ #CC0018V
Takes a video visit to the campus of the University of Delaware. Shows many of the distinctive features of the campus, and interviews students about their experiences. Provides information on the composition of the student body, professors, academics, social life, housing, and other subjects.
Education
Dist - CAMV

University of Georgia
VHS
Campus clips series
Color (H C A)
$29.95 purchase _ #CC0026V
Takes a video visit to the campus of the University of Georgia. Shows many of the distinctive features of the campus, and interviews students about their experiences. Provides information on the composition of the student body, professors, academics, social life, housing, and other subjects.
Education
Dist - CAMV

University of Illinois Arithemtic Project Series
Which Rule Wins 28 MIN
Dist - AGAPR

University of Illinois Arithmetic Project Series
Three A'S, Three B'S and One C 48 MIN
Dist - AGAPR

University of Maine - Orono
VHS
Campus clips series
Color (H C A)
$29.95 purchase _ #CC0038V
Takes a video visit to the campus of the University of Maine - Orono. Shows many of the distinctive features of the campus, and interviews students about their experiences. Provides information on the composition of the student body, professors, academics, social life, housing, and other subjects.
Education
Dist - CAMV

University of Maryland
VHS
Campus clips series
Color (H C A)
$29.95 purchase _ #CC0041V
Takes a video visit to the campus of the University of Maryland. Shows many of the distinctive features of the campus, and interviews students about their experiences. Provides information on the composition of the student body, professors, academics, social life, housing, and other subjects.
Education
Dist - CAMV

University of Massachusetts - Amherst
VHS
Campus clips series
Color (H C A)
$29.95 purchase _ #CC0059V
Takes a video visit to the campus of the University of Massachusetts - Amherst. Shows many of the distinctive features of the campus, and interviews students about their experiences. Provides information on the composition of the student body, professors, academics, social life, housing, and other subjects.
Education
Dist - CAMV

University of Mexico 3 MIN
16mm
Of all Things Series
Color (P I)
Presents the University of Mexico.
Geography - World
Dist - AVED **Prod** - BAILYL

University of Miami
VHS
Campus clips series
Color (H C A)
$29.95 purchase _ #CC0022V
Takes a video visit to the campus of the University of Miami in Florida. Shows many of the distinctive features of the campus, and interviews students about their experiences. Provides information on the composition of the student body, professors, academics, social life, housing, and other subjects.
Education
Dist - CAMV

University of Michigan
VHS
Campus clips series
Color (H C A)
$29.95 purchase _ #CC0064V
Takes a video visit to the campus of the University of Michigan. Shows many of the distinctive features of the campus, and interviews students about their experiences. Provides information on the composition of the student body, professors, academics, social life, housing, and other subjects.
Education
Dist - CAMV

University of Michigan Media Library - Clinical Commentary Series MI 48103
Imaging of the Heart using Radionuclide Scanning 19 MIN
Dist - UMICH

University of Michigan Media Library - clinical commentary series
Antibiotic - associated colitis 21 MIN
Antimicrobial resistance - molecular basis and clinical appreciation 25 MIN
Hepatic arterial chemotherapy for cancer in the liver 15 MIN
Hypothalamic Amenorrhea - Etiology and Management 28 MIN
Obesity - Effective Management 27 MIN
Oxygenation Assessment of the Critically Ill Patient 30 MIN
Dist - UMICH

University of New Hampshire
VHS
Campus clips series
Color (H C A)
$29.95 purchase _ #CC0066V
Takes a video visit to the campus of the University of New Hampshire. Shows many of the distinctive features of the campus, and interviews students about their experiences. Provides information on the composition of the student body, professors, academics, social life, housing, and other subjects.
Education
Dist - CAMV

University of North Carolina - Chapel Hill
VHS
Campus clips series
Color (H C A)
$29.95 purchase _ #CC0082V
Takes a video visit to the campus of the University of North Carolina - Chapel Hill. Shows many of the distinctive features of the campus, and interviews students about their experiences. Provides information on the composition of the student body, professors, academics, social life, housing, and other subjects.
Education
Dist - CAMV

University of North Carolina - Greensboro
VHS
Campus clips series
Color (H C A)
$29.95 purchase _ #CC0083V
Takes a video visit to the campus of the University of North Carolina - Greensboro. Shows many of the distinctive features of the campus, and interviews students about their experiences. Provides information on the composition of the student body, professors, academics, social life, housing, and other subjects.
Education
Dist - CAMV

University of Pennsylvania
VHS
Campus clips series
Color (H C A)
$29.95 purchase _ #CC0094V
Takes a video visit to the campus of the University of Pennsylvania, also known as 'Penn.' Shows many of the distinctive features of the campus, and interviews students about their experiences. Provides information on the composition of the student body, professors, academics, social life, housing, and other subjects.
Education
Dist - CAMV

University of Rhode Island
VHS
Campus clips series
Color (H C A)
$29.95 purchase _ #CC0100V
Takes a video visit to the campus of the University of Rhode Island. Shows many of the distinctive features of the campus, and interviews students about their experiences. Provides information on the composition of the student body, professors, academics, social life, housing, and other subjects.
Education
Dist - CAMV

University of Richmond
VHS
Campus clips series
Color (H C A)
$29.95 purchase _ #CC0113V
Takes a video visit to the campus of the University of Richmond in Virginia. Shows many of the distinctive features of the campus, and interviews students about their experiences. Provides information on the composition of the student body, professors, academics, social life, housing, and other subjects.
Education
Dist - CAMV

University of San Diego
VHS
Campus clips series
Color (H C A)
$29.95 purchase _ #CC0009V
Takes a video visit to the campus of the University of San Diego. Shows many of the distinctive features of the campus, and interviews students about their experiences. Provides information on the composition of the student body, professors, academics, social life, housing, and other subjects.

Education
Dist - CAMV

University of San Francisco
VHS
Campus clips series
Color (H C A)
$29.95 purchase _ #CC0010V
Takes a video visit to the campus of the University of San Francisco. Shows many of the distinctive features of the campus, and interviews students about their experiences. Provides information on the composition of the student body, professors, academics, social life, housing, and other subjects.
Education
Dist - CAMV

University of Southern California
VHS
Campus clips series
Color (H C A)
$29.95 purchase _ #CC0011V
Takes a video visit to the campus of the University of Southern California. Shows many of the distinctive features of the campus, and interviews students about their experiences. Provides information on the composition of the student body, professors, academics, social life, housing, and other subjects.
Education
Dist - CAMV

University of Southern Maine
VHS
Campus clips series
Color (H C A)
$29.95 purchase _ #CC0039V
Takes a video visit to the campus of the University of Southern Maine. Shows many of the distinctive features of the campus, and interviews students about their experiences. Provides information on the composition of the student body, professors, academics, social life, housing, and other subjects.
Education
Dist - CAMV

University of the Air Series
Abstract with meaning 145 MIN
Africa - historical perspectives on a troubled continent 145 MIN
Ancient technology 145 MIN
Anglo - Saxon England 145 MIN
Archeology of British Columbia 145 MIN
Architect and writer 145 MIN
The Brain 145 MIN
Buddhism and the modern world 145 MIN
Cancer chemotherapy 145 MIN
Celestial navigation 145 MIN
Cell division 145 MIN
Classical mythology 145 MIN
The Complete actor 145 MIN
The Crusade 145 MIN
Dance - the Enduring Art of India 145 MIN
Effective supervision 145 MIN
English in Action 145 MIN
The Experience of Literature 145 MIN
Experimental Parapsychology 145 MIN
Founders of living faith 145 MIN
From conception to neurosi 145 MIN
Great trials in history 145 MIN
Heritage Kingston 145 MIN
Human Settlements 145 MIN
The Incredible eyewitness 145 MIN
The Language of Cells 145 MIN
The Law and the Family 145 MIN
Lessons from life sciences 145 MIN
Love in the Western World 145 MIN
Man and Resources 145 MIN
Man Shapes His World 145 MIN
The Many Faces of Renaissance Man 145 MIN
Microwaves and the Future 145 MIN
Money and Interest 145 MIN
National Party Conventions 145 MIN
The Nature of Children's Books 145 MIN
Nutrition and Health 145 MIN
The Oceans 145 MIN
On the Fringes of Science 145 MIN
The Origin and Evolution of Life 145 MIN
Painting - Landscape into Landscape 145 MIN
Personality of the West 145 MIN
Pillars of Modern Drama 145 MIN
Prejudice and Racism 145 MIN
Preventive Marriage Counselling 145 MIN
The Psychology of Aging, Dying and Death 145 MIN
The Puzzle of Pain 145 MIN
Science and archeology 145 MIN
Science fiction - the Promethean imagination 145 MIN
Shakespeare's Theatres 145 MIN
Sing We and Chant it 145 MIN
Sleep and Dream Research 145 MIN
So You Want to make a Buck? 145 MIN
The Spanish Enigma 145 MIN
Sport and Physical Activity in Society 145 MIN
Stress and Modern Life 145 MIN
Those Miracle Drugs 145 MIN
Turning Points in Life 145 MIN
The Use and Abuse of Statistics 145 MIN
Violence and Society 145 MIN
War - the most Dangerous Game 145 MIN
Western Canada - a Region within a Federation 145 MIN
Wilderness, Education and Skills 145 MIN
Women in History 145 MIN
Dist - CTV

University of the Air
Music for the Piano 145 MIN
Dist - CTV

University of Vermont
VHS
Campus clips series
Color (H C A)
$29.95 purchase _ #CC0101V
Takes a video visit to the campus of the University of Vermont. Shows many of the distinctive features of the campus, and interviews students about their experiences. Provides information on the composition of the student body, professors, academics, social life, housing, and other subjects.
Education
Dist - CAMV

University of Virginia
VHS
Campus clips series
Color (H C A)
$29.95 purchase _ #CC0106V
Takes a video visit to the campus of the University of Virginia. Shows many of the distinctive features of the campus, and interviews students about their experiences. Provides information on the composition of the student body, professors, academics, social life, housing, and other subjects.
Education
Dist - CAMV

University of Wisconsin - Madison
VHS
Campus clips series
Color (H C A)
$29.95 purchase _ #CC0104V
Takes a video visit to the campus of the University of Wisconsin - Madison. Shows many of the distinctive features of the campus, and interviews students about their experiences. Provides information on the composition of the student body, professors, academics, social life, housing, and other subjects.
Education
Dist - CAMV

University of Wisconsin School of Social Work Promotional Tape 15 MIN
U-matic / VHS
Color
Describes the University of Wisconsin School of Social Work. Gives glimpses of classes and the building while describing the school and its programs.
Sociology
Dist - UWISC **Prod** - UWISC 1977

Univerzum 5 MIN
16mm / U-matic / VHS
Color (H C A)
LC 81-700613
Tells how a hero is born and how he explores the depths of the universe. Shows how he returns unnoticed in another time and place, after his moment has passed.
Fine Arts
Dist - IFB **Prod** - ZAGREB 1977

UNIX Administration
VHS / U-matic
UNIX and 'C'Language Training - a Full Curriculum Series
Color
Industrial and Technical Education; Mathematics; Sociology
Dist - COMTEG **Prod** - COMTEG

UNIX - an Executive Perspective 30 MIN
U-matic / VHS
Color
Describes the UNIX system, its features, applications and operation. Assists users in understanding the total environment in which they are working.
Business and Economics; Industrial and Technical Education; Mathematics; Sociology
Dist - COMTEG **Prod** - COMTEG

UNIX and 'C' language training - a full curriculum series
Advanced 'C' programming under UNIX
Berkeley UNIX fundamentals and 'csh' shell
C Language programming
Shell as a command language
Shell programming
Dist - COMTEG

UNIX and 'C'Language Training - a Full Curriculum Series
UNIX Administration
UNIX Fundamentals for Non - Programmers
UNIX Fundamentals for Programmers
UNIX Internals
UNIX Overview
Using Advanced UNIX Commands
Dist - COMTEG

UNIX Fundamentals for Non - Programmers
U-matic / VHS
UNIX and 'C'Language Training - a Full Curriculum Series
Color
Industrial and Technical Education; Mathematics; Sociology
Dist - COMTEG **Prod** - COMTEG

UNIX Fundamentals for Programmers
VHS / U-matic
UNIX and 'C'Language Training - a Full Curriculum Series
Color
Industrial and Technical Education; Mathematics; Sociology
Dist - COMTEG **Prod** - COMTEG

UNIX fundamentals series
Advanced 'ed'
Advanced 'ed' (continued)
Command lines
Commands
Communicating with other users
Communicating with the system
Directory Commands
Ed
Ed - continued
File access permissions
File name generation
Files
I/O
More Commands
Pathnames
Dist - COMTEG

UNIX Internals
U-matic / VHS
UNIX and 'C'Language Training - a Full Curriculum Series
Color
Industrial and Technical Education; Mathematics; Sociology
Dist - COMTEG **Prod** - COMTEG

UNIX Overview
U-matic / VHS
UNIX and 'C'Language Training - a Full Curriculum Series
Color
Industrial and Technical Education; Mathematics; Sociology
Dist - COMTEG **Prod** - COMTEG

UNIX Overview Series Unit 1
An Introduction
Dist - COMTEG

UNIX Overview Series Unit 5
Programmer's Workbench
Dist - COMTEG

UNIX Overview Series Unit 6
Security and 'C' Language
Dist - COMTEG

UNIX overview series
Commands
Files, data bases, data communications
The Shell
Dist - COMTEG

UNIX series
File manipulation 30 MIN
Files and directories, Part I 30 MIN
Files and directories, Part II 30 MIN
Process control 30 MIN
Shell files - Pt I 30 MIN
Shell files - Pt II 30 MIN
Text editor - Part I 30 MIN
Text editor - Part II 30 MIN
Wild Characters, Patterns, Pipes and Tees 30 MIN
Dist - COLOSU

UNIX system administration
VHS / U-matic
Color (H C G)
$1404.00, $1170.00 purchase _ #09 - USA
Trains users of Unix - based systems who have had some experience managing Unix - Posix systems. Overviews administrative functions, review of major Unix internal features and processes, initializing and configuring files and subsystem administration. Includes six videocassettes, an administrator's guide and a student guide. Published by Computer Technology Group.
Computer Science
Dist - VIDEOT

UNIX SYSTEM executive perspective 45 MIN
U-matic / VHS
(A PRO)
$195.00
Addresses frequently asked questions about UNIX.
Computer Science
Dist - VIDEOT **Prod** - VIDEOT 1988

UNIX SYSTEM Fundamentals 420 MIN
VHS / U-matic
(A PRO)
$2.925.00
Introduces fundamentals of UNIX.
Computer Science
Dist - VIDEOT **Prod** - VIDEOT 1988

UNIX SYSTEM Overview 180 MIN
U-matic / VHS
(A PRO)
$1,170.00
Introduces UNIX to new users.
Computer Science
Dist - VIDEOT **Prod** - VIDEOT 1988

UNIX system quick start
U-matic / VHS
Color (H C G)
$1404.00, $1170.00 purchase _ #09 - USQ
Trains new users of Unix - based systems. Overviews essential concepts and commands. Includes 6 videocassettes, an administrator's guide and a student guide. Published by Computer Technology Group.
Computer Science
Dist - VIDEOT

UNIX SYSTEM Shell 360 MIN
VHS / U-matic
(A PRO)
$2,730.00
Addresses Bourne Shell aspects that increase productivity of UNIX.
Computer Science
Dist - VIDEOT **Prod** - VIDEOT 1988

UNIX SYSTEM V Internals 240 MIN
U-matic / VHS
(A PRO)
$1,560.00
Covers basic operating system algorithms.
Computer Science
Dist - VIDEOT **Prod** - VIDEOT 1988

UNIX - the Videotape 6 MIN
U-matic / VHS
(PRO A)
$295 Purchase, $100 Rental 5 days, $35 Preview 3 days
Outlines introductory methods for using the UNIX system.
Business and Economics; Mathematics
Dist - ADVANM **Prod** - ADVANM

UNIX Vi Editor 120 MIN
VHS / U-matic
(A PRO)
$780.00
Addresses fundamental concepts and commands for Vi Editor.
Computer Science
Dist - VIDEOT **Prod** - VIDEOT 1988

Unknown Chaplin - 1918 - 1931 52 MIN
16mm / U-matic / VHS
Unknown Chaplin Series
Color (H C A)
Tells how Chaplin did not release his first film, How To Make Movies, which was a tour of the studio he built in 1917 as a new independent filmmaker. Includes footage and interviews about such films as The Kid, The Gold Rush and City Lights.
Fine Arts
Dist - MEDIAG **Prod** - THAMES 1983

Unknown Chaplin - a Documentary Trilogy 3 MIN
U-matic / VHS
Color
Presents previously unknown footage of Charlie Chaplin in three 52 minute documentaries.
Fine Arts
Dist - SUCBUF **Prod** - THAMES

Unknown Chaplin Series
Unknown Chaplin - 1918 - 1931 52 MIN
Unknown Chaplin - the Mutual Period, 1916 - 1917 52 MIN
Unknown Chaplin - Unshown Chaplin 52 MIN
Dist - MEDIAG

Unknown Chaplin - the Mutual Period, 1916 - 1917 52 MIN
U-matic / VHS / 16mm
Unknown Chaplin Series
Color (H C A)
Uncovers the progression of Chaplin's pioneer ideas, using fragments of his films, mostly outtakes and uncut rushes which are assembled in slate order.
Fine Arts
Dist - MEDIAG **Prod** - THAMES 1983

Unknown Chaplin - Unshown Chaplin 52 MIN
16mm / U-matic / VHS
Unknown Chaplin Series
Color (H C A)
Features a wealth of background footage screened from movies Chaplin made for fun, films he abandoned and sequences he cut from such films as City Lights and Modern Times. Shows his dance of the rolls from The Gold Rush.
Fine Arts
Dist - MEDIAG **Prod** - THAMES 1983

Unknown Eiffel 28 MIN
VHS / 16mm
Color (S) (ENGLISH AND FRENCH)
$460.00, $49.00 purchase _ #311 - 9001
Celebrates the 100th anniversary of the Eiffel Tower with a look at Alexandre - Gustave Eiffel, one of the great engineering geniuses of all time. Reveals that he left a legacy of landmarks throughout the world, as well making innumerable contributions to design and construction.
Agriculture; Fine Arts; Geography - World; History - World; Industrial and Technical Education
Dist - FI **Prod** - LENAC 1987

The Unknown Eiffel 28 MIN
U-matic / VHS / 16mm
Color
LC 75-703124
Explores the engineering genius and accomplishments of Gustave Eiffel.
Biography; Industrial and Technical Education
Dist - FI **Prod** - BCI 1975

Unknown Force 50 MIN
16mm
Unknown Powers Series
Color
LC 78-701406
Explores and demonstrates psychic and occult phenomena, including prana, ki - power, psychokinesis and Kirlian photography.
Sociology
Dist - ITFP **Prod** - ITFP 1978

Unknown force - Pt 1 25 MIN
16mm
Unknown powers series
Color
LC 78-701406
Explores and demonstrates psychic and occult phenomena, including prana, ki - power, psychokinesis and Kirlian photography.
Psychology
Dist - ITFP **Prod** - ITFP 1978

Unknown force - Pt 2 25 MIN
16mm
Unknown powers series
Color
LC 78-701406
Explores and demonstrates psychic and occult phenomena, including prana, ki - power, psychokinesis and Kirlian photography.
Psychology
Dist - ITFP **Prod** - ITFP 1978

Unknown Genius - the Savant Syndrome 16 MIN
U-matic / VHS
Color (H C A)
LC 84-706149
Introduces three people who have extraordinary mental talents despite being mentally retarded. Includes a gifted sculptor, a man who can tell what day of the week a given date will fall and a blind cerebral palsy victim who can play any piece of music after hearing it only once. Originally shown on the CBS program 60 Minutes.
Education; Psychology
Dist - LAWREN **Prod** - CBSTV 1984

Unknown Land 28 MIN
16mm
Color (J)
LC 73-702260
Covers the development of Australia's Northwest. Explains that once isolated and largely unexplored, the sparsely populated land is now being opened up by major development projects.
Geography - World
Dist - AUIS **Prod** - ANAIB 1972

Unknown Powers Series
Unknown Force 50 MIN
Unknown force - Pt 1 25 MIN
Unknown force - Pt 2 25 MIN
Dist - ITFP

Unknown Reasons 6 MIN
16mm
Color (H C A)
Combines animation and live - action as inks, colors and pens are taken over by the conscious, exploding in a wild fury of color and nightmarish designs.
Fine Arts; Industrial and Technical Education
Dist - UWFKD **Prod** - UWFKD

Unknown - Risk Stop 34 MIN
VHS
Crime to Court Procedural Specials Series
Color (PRO)
$99.00 purchase
Reveals that officers have been killed making 'routine stops.' Describes procedures to be used when making these stops. Trains law enforcement personnel. Part of an ongoing series to look in depth at topics presented in 'Crime To Court.' Produced in cooperation with the South Carolina Criminal Justice Academy and the National Sheriff's Association.
Civics and Political Systems; Psychology; Social Science; Sociology
Dist - SCETV **Prod** - SCETV

Unknown secrets - Art and the Rosenberg era 30 MIN
VHS
Color (G)
$50.00 purchase
Features the nationwide touring exhibition of the same name. Presents visual works by artists like Picasso and Sue Coe and readings of Arthur Miller and Adrienne Rich - all responding to the fate of Julius and Ethel Rosenberg, the only Americans sentenced to death for espionage by a public jury. Begins by setting the historical context for the responses of artists to the questionable verdict of this case. Explores the outpouring of artwork through interviews and the documentation of the exhibit. Produced by Rosenberg Era Art Productions - Green Mountain Post Films.
Fine Arts; Religion and Philosophy
Dist - NCJEWF

The Unknown soldier 58 MIN
VHS
Color (G)
$69.95 purchase _ #S01509
Features profiles of the six US World War II soldiers declared to be permanently missing in action. Uses combat footage, personal letters, mementoes and interviews with family members and fellow servicemen to present intimate looks at these men.
Biography; History - United States
Dist - UILL

The Unknown Soldier 57 MIN
VHS
Color (S)
$19.95 purchase _ #313 - 9004
Gives tribute to the 'American soldier known but to God.' Features Jason Robards, actor and decorated World War II veteran, as host. Six representative profiles of World War II casualties are presented, using combat footage, personal letters, mementos and candid interviews with family, friends and fellow soldiers.
Civics and Political Systems; History - United States; History - World; Sociology
Dist - FI

Unknown Soldiers 58 MIN
VHS / U-matic
Different Drummer - Blacks in the Military Series
Color (H C A)
LC 85-700749
Discusses the growth of importance of black soldiers through the Indian Wars and the Spanish - American War to World War I.
Civics and Political Systems; History - United States
Dist - FI **Prod** - WNETTV 1983

The Unknown Thirty - Six Seconds - Aircraft Accident Investigation 35 MIN
16mm
Color

LC 74-705878
Describes the organization and mission of the Aircraft Accident Investigation board. Depicts its painstaking inspection of plane wreckage to determine possible electrical, mechanical, structural or hydraulic failure.
Civics and Political Systems; Health and Safety; Industrial and Technical Education; Social Science
Dist - USNAC **Prod** - USAF 1968

Unknowns
Software / Videodisc / Kit
Annenberg - CPB Project Interactive Science Instruction Videodisc
(H)
$495 purchase
Enables high school students to conduct simulated chemistry experiments to isolate unknowns without coping with the constraints of time, temperature and luck.
Education; Science
Dist - GPN

Unless they are sent
VHS
Color (A R)
$12.50 purchase _ #S11767
Describes the role that laypersons have in promoting seminary education for the Lutheran Church - Missouri Synod.
Guidance and Counseling; Literature and Drama; Religion and Philosophy
Dist - CPH **Prod** - LUMIS

Unlikely Addicts - Middle Class Women 29 MIN
U-matic
Woman Series
Color
Discusses private and public addicts. Explains that some women are private addicts who attempt to keep their problem secret and who usually become dependent on alcohol and/or barbiturates.
Health and Safety; Psychology; Sociology
Dist - PBS **Prod** - WNEDTV

Unlikely Star 8 MIN
U-matic / VHS / 16mm
B&W (J)
LC 81-701033
Relates what happens when a shy young man is swallowed up by a camera and begins an odyssey into the world of celluloid that almost ends on the cutting room floor. Shows the man finally making his escape during the film's premiere when he leaps straight out from the screen.
Fine Arts; Literature and Drama
Dist - PHENIX **Prod** - PHENIX 1980

Unlock Your Imagination 15 MIN
U-matic
You Can Write Anything Series
Color (P I)
Teaches writing techniques through Amanda who is told that writers can use their imagination to make up any person, place or thing.
Education; English Language
Dist - TVOTAR **Prod** - TVOTAR 1984

Unlocking the creative self 23 MIN
35mm strip / VHS
Color (J H C A)
$93.00, $93.00 purchase _ #MB - 494790 - 7, #MB - 512846 - 2
Utilizes the act of drawing to develop the critical skills of both sides of the brain. Shows that the goal is to strengthen the creative self.
Fine Arts; Literature and Drama
Dist - SRA **Prod** - SRA

Unlocking the Creative Self Series
Dare to Use it 22.35 MIN
Part One - the Key! 22.35 MIN
Dist - SRA

Unlocking the Mystery 20 MIN
U-matic / VHS
Color
$335.00 purchase
Health and Safety; Psychology
Dist - ABCLR **Prod** - ABCLR 1983

Unlocking your body - regaining youth through somatic awareness 90 MIN
BETA / VHS
Innerwork series
Color (G)
$49.95 purchase _ #W307
Features Thomas Hanna who believes that many of the effects of aging - aching muscles and joints, poor posture, stiffness and weakness - are unnecessary and reversible. Considers the issue of sensory - motor amnesia whch can be corrected through a conscious awareness of the body. Explains how to establish such a consciousness.
Health and Safety; Physical Education and Recreation; Psychology; Science - Natural; Sociology
Dist - THINKA **Prod** - THINKA

Unlucky boy, Green mountain, Cinderella barber
U-matic / VHS / BETA
European folktale series
Color; PAL (P I)
PdS180, PdS188 purchase
Features folktales from Czechoslovakia, Sweden and Italy. Presents a series of 6 programs of 18 titles from 12 countries around the world. 3 animated programs per cassette.
Fine Arts; Literature and Drama
Dist - EDPAT **Prod** - HALAS

Unmarried Mother Interview - Peters - Browning 68 MIN
16mm
Studies in Interviewing Series
B&W
Consists of four studies supplied on four reels each about 17 minutes in length. See series title for further description.
Guidance and Counseling
Dist - USC **Prod** - USC 1965

Unmarried mother interview - Peters - Browning - Pt 1 17 MIN
16mm
Studies in interviewing series
B&W
Guidance and Counseling
Dist - USC **Prod** - USC 1965

Unmarried mother interview - Peters - Browning - Pt 2 17 MIN
16mm
Studies in interviewing series
B&W
Guidance and Counseling
Dist - USC **Prod** - USC 1965

Unmarried mother interview - Peters - Browning - Pt 3 17 MIN
16mm
Studies in interviewing series
B&W
Consists of four studies supplied on four reels each about 17 minutes in length. See series title for further description.
Guidance and Counseling
Dist - USC **Prod** - USC 1965

Unmarried mother interview - Peters - Browning - Pt 4 17 MIN
16mm
Studies in interviewing series
B&W
Consists of four studies supplied on four reels each about 17 minutes in length. See series title for further description.
Guidance and Counseling
Dist - USC **Prod** - USC 1965

Unmeasured prelude for Kerry Laitala 3 MIN
16mm
B&W (G)
$20.00 rental
Features multiple camera passes of baroque statuary with a soundtrack of dripping water and a Louis Couperin prelude highly distorted. Focuses on Kerry Laitala's Chattertonesque photographic self - portrait.
Fine Arts
Dist - CANCIN FLMKCO **Prod** - SCHLEM 1992

Unmixed Mixed Numbers 30 MIN
U-matic / VHS
Adult Math Series
Color (A)
Shows adult math students how mixed numbers fit into the number system and how to handle them.
Education; Mathematics
Dist - KYTV **Prod** - KYTV 1984

Unnecessary surgery - physicians react 29 MIN
U-matic
Woman series
Color
Presents two doctors discussing reports of widespread unnecessary surgery in the United States. Points out that elective and unconfirmed surgeries are gray areas of medical statistics and stresses the need for clear definitions of what is and is not necessary.
Health and Safety
Dist - PBS **Prod** - WNEDTV

Unordnung Und Fruehes Lied 86 MIN
16mm
Color (GERMAN (ENGLISH SUBTITLES))
Focuses on the family of Professor Cornelius, who seems unable to cope with the political and social upheavals of the early 1920s, and who seeks escape in the past and in his love for his five - year - old daughter. Based on a short story by Thomas Mann.
Foreign Language; History - World; Sociology
Dist - WSTGLC **Prod** - WSTGLC 1977

Unorganized manager - Part III - lamentations 20 MIN
VHS
Unorganized manager series
Color (A PRO IND)
$790.00 purchase, $220.00 rental
Presents the third of a four - part series that takes an often humorous look at how managers can organize themselves and others. Features Richard Lewis, the harried manager who finds himself advised by St Peter, played by John Cleese of 'Monty Python' fame. Shows that Richard blames his staff for doing poorly at assigned tasks, but St Peter shows him that such an approach makes for real failure.
Business and Economics; Guidance and Counseling; Psychology
Dist - VLEARN **Prod** - VIDART

Unorganized manager - Part IV - revelations 29 MIN
VHS
Unorganized manager series
Color (A PRO IND)
$790.00 purchase, $220.00 rental
Presents the final episode of a four - part series that takes an often humorous look at how managers can organize themselves and others. Features Richard Lewis, the harried manager who finds himself advised by St Peter, played by John Cleese of 'Monty Python' fame. Shows how St Peter teaches Richard that a manager must clarify responsibilities, set standards, and agree on targets.
Business and Economics; Guidance and Counseling; Psychology
Dist - VLEARN **Prod** - VIDART

The Unorganized manager - Pt 1 - Damnation 24 MIN
U-matic / VHS
Color (A)
Presents in a humorous vein important principles of good business management. Follows a bumbling manager through a typical day, a coronary and a confrontation with St. Peter, who shows him the errors of his ways.
Business and Economics
Dist - XICOM **Prod** - XICOM 1983

The Unorganized manager - Pt 2 - Salvation 27 MIN
U-matic / VHS
Color (A)
Presents in a humorous vein important principles of good business management. Shows a bumbling manager who, with guidance from St. Peter, mends his ways and miraculously improves his business techniques.
Business and Economics
Dist - XICOM **Prod** - XICOM 1983

Unorganized Manager Series
Lamentations - Pt 3 20 MIN
Revelations - Pt 4 29 MIN
Dist - VIDART

Unorganized Manager Series
Damnation, Pt 1 26 MIN
Salvation, Pt II 26 MIN
Dist - VISUCP

Unorganized manager series
Presents a four - part series that takes an often humorous look at how managers can organize themselves and others. Features Richard Lewis, the harried manager who finds himself advised by St Peter, played by John Cleese of 'Monty Python' fame.
Unorganized manager - Part III - lamentations 20 MIN
Unorganized manager - Part IV - revelations 29 MIN
Dist - VLEARN **Prod** - VIDART 1983

The Unorganized salesperson - Parts I and II
VHS
Color (A PRO)
$1,344.00 purchase, $374.00 rental
Suggests that there are two types of salespersons - those who see themselves as managers and those who believe they are just sellers. Covers managerial and organizational skills that may be of use to salespersons. Consists of two videocassettes.
Business and Economics; Psychology
Dist - VLEARN **Prod** - VIDART

Unorganized Salesperson Series
Valuing Your Customers - Pt 1 25 MIN
Valuing Yourself - Pt 2 23 MIN
Dist - VIDART

Unpack Your Adjectives 43 FRS
U-matic / VHS
Grammar Rock Series
Color (P I)
LC 76-730873
Presents a little girl and her pet turtle unpacking adjectives from her backpack after a camping trip in order to describe the people, places and things she saw on the trip.
English Language
Dist - GA **Prod** - ABCTV 1976

Unpeopled Space 3 MIN
16mm / U-matic
B&W (G)
$75.00, $105.00 purchase, $50.00, $30.00 rental
Uses slow motion and stark solarization to evoke a somber, isolated mood as it concentrates on one person in an otherwise unpeopled seascape. Created by Kim Blain.
Fine Arts; Psychology
Dist - WMENIF **Prod** - WMENIF 1987

The Unplanned 20 MIN
16mm
Color (H C A)
LC 73-700554
Uses dramatized incidents to warn industrial workers against unsafe acts which often cause serious industrial accidents. Emphasizes safety procedures which help avoid crippling and costly mishaps.
Health and Safety; Industrial and Technical Education
Dist - NFBC **Prod** - NFBC 1971

Unpleasant Feelings 7 MIN
16mm
Project Bilingual Series
Color (K P) (SPANISH)
LC 73-700625
Helps young Mexican - American children understand that feelings of fear, disappointment and loneliness are natural and universal. Includes narration in Spanish and English.
Foreign Language; Psychology
Dist - SUTHLA **Prod** - SANISD 1973

Unpleasantness at Bludleigh Court 30 MIN
U-matic / VHS
Wodehouse Playhouse Series
Color (C A)
Presents an adaptation of the short story Unpleasantness At Bludleigh Court by P G Wodehouse.
Literature and Drama
Dist - TIMLIF **Prod** - BBCTV 1980

The Unquiet dead - an introduction to spirit depossession therapy 90 MIN
BETA / VHS
Innerwork series
Color (G)
$49.95 purchase _ #W415
Features psychologist Edith Fiore who describes how, working with her clients, she has come to diagnose and treat cases of apparent spirit possession. Demonstrates an actual spiritual depossession technique, a method entirely different from the classical notion of 'exorcism.'
Psychology; Religion and Philosophy; Sociology
Dist - THINKA **Prod** - THINKA

The Unquiet death of Eli Creekmore 55 MIN
VHS
Color (H C G)
$445.00 purchase, $75.00 rental
Examines the death of 3 - year - old Eli Creekmore, who was beaten to death by his father when he couldn't stop crying. Reveals that his abuse had been reported by his grandmother to Child Protective Services, his teacher and the doctor who treated his previous injuries and, although removed from his home briefly, he was returned because the mandate of the agency was to keep families together whenever possible.
Sociology
Dist - FLMLIB **Prod** - KCTSTV 1988

The Unquiet library 45 MIN
VHS
Color (G)
$49.95 purchase _ #UNQL - 000
Presents the musical side of the Library of Congress. Shows how the Library preserves musical scores and manuscripts, as well as sponsoring performance artists. Reveals that the Library has a Juilliard String Quartet in residence.
Fine Arts; Social Science
Dist - PBS **Prod** - WETATV 1985

The Unreasonable Man 60 MIN
16mm
Color
Takes a look at today's bureaucratic institutions and how they affect the quality of man's life.
Civics and Political Systems; Psychology; Sociology
Dist - KQEDTV **Prod** - KQEDTV

Unreasonable Searches and Seizures 50 MIN
VHS / U-matic
Criminal Procedure and the Trial Advocate Series
Color (PRO)
Provides a review of the fourth amendment proscription against unreasonable searches and seizures, an analysis of the exceptions to the exclusionary rule and a discussion of issues of standing to assert the defense.
Civics and Political Systems; Sociology
Dist - ABACPE **Prod** - ABACPE

Unreliable sources - the media and drugs 29 MIN
VHS
America's drug forum second season series
Color (G)
$19.95 purchase _ #220
Asks if the media is giving straight facts about drugs and the drug war. Takes a close look at media coverage of drug issues. Features Jefferson Morley, freelance writer for The New Republic and The Nation, Dr Robert Lichter, director, Center for Media and Public Affairs.
History - United States; Psychology; Sociology
Dist - DRUGPF **Prod** - DRUGPF 1992

An Unremarkable Birth 52 MIN
16mm
Color (H C A)
Presents parents and doctors discussing less traditional methods of childbirth. Records the prepared birth of a baby and the interaction of the mother and father.
Health and Safety; Sociology
Dist - NFBC **Prod** - NFBC 1978

Unremitting Tenderness 9 MIN
16mm / U-matic / VHS
Color (H C A)
LC 81-700908
Presents an experimental film showing the execution, transformation and rearrangement of dance sequences.
Fine Arts; Industrial and Technical Education
Dist - PHENIX **Prod** - ELDERB 1977

The Unresponsive Articulation Problem - Child Apraxia 98 MIN
U-matic / VHS
Color
Discusses problem definition and terminology, types, diagnosis and clinical management. Includes clinical demonstrations.
Education; Psychology
Dist - PUAVC **Prod** - PUAVC

The Unrooted 33 MIN
16mm
Color
Presents the story of Salvation Army refugee and relief operations, filmed on location in Africa and Asia.
Sociology
Dist - MTP **Prod** - SALVA

Unruly cells 30 MIN
VHS
Perspectives - health and medicine - series
Color; PAL; NTSC (G)
PdS90, PdS105 purchase
Looks at an operation being perfected at the Christie Hospital in Manchester, England, to replace the bone marrow of leukemia sufferers.
Health and Safety
Dist - CFLVIS **Prod** - LONTVS

UNRWA 28 MIN
Videoreel / VHS
International Byline Series
Color
Interviews Mr Olof Rydbeck, Commissioner General of the United Nations Relief and Works Agency for Palestine refugees in the Near East. Discusses the problems and achievements of the agency during its long history. Presents clips of films about refugees.
Civics and Political Systems; Geography - World
Dist - PERRYM **Prod** - PERRYM

The UN's blue helmets 29 MIN
VHS
America's defense monitor series
Color (J H C G T A)
$25.00 purchase
Explores the past and present - day role of United Nations peacekeeping forces. Interviews former UN Under - Secretary General Brian Urquhart and other past and present UN officials on the forces' role in keeping the peace. Produced by Sandy Gottlieb.
History - World; Sociology
Dist - EFVP **Prod** - CDINFO 1990

Unseen courage 23 MIN
VHS
Color (COR)
$350.00 purchase, $155.00 five - day rental, $25.00 three - day preview _ #USC
Inspires employees to strive to reach their goals through discussion of personal challenges, concentration on what lies ahead, and use of resources at hand. Helps viewers elevate self - confidence, accomplish what they try, and attain new levels of success. Includes a Leader's Guide. Available for three - day preview and five - day rental, as well as for lease or purchase.
Business and Economics; Psychology
Dist - ADVANM

The Unseen enemy 9 MIN
16mm / VHS / BETA / U-matic
Color; PAL (PRO IND)
PdS115, PdS123 purchase
Shows how safe, basic food handling methods are necessary to prevent contamination by bacteria. Looks at how unhygenic handling of cooked meat results in food poisoning.
Industrial and Technical Education
Dist - EDPAT

The Unseen World 54 MIN
16mm / U-matic / VHS
Color (H C)
LC 71-708742
Uses photomicrography, rocket - mounted cameras and other photographic techniques to reveal the microscopic world of cells and ocean animals, as well as the nature of light and the planets of the solar system.
Industrial and Technical Education
Dist - MGHT **Prod** - ABCTV 1970

The Unseen world - Pt 1 - How small is small 17 MIN
U-matic / VHS / 16mm
Color (H C)
LC 71-708742
Uses photomicrography to reveal the microscopic world of plant cells and protozoa. Shows the surface of aspirin and human hair as viewed through light - receiving and electronic instruments.
Science - Natural; Science - Physical
Dist - MGHT **Prod** - ABCTV 1970

The Unseen world - Pt 3 - Oceans of space 17 MIN
U-matic / VHS / 16mm
Color (H C)
LC 71-708742
Reveals those vast areas of the world that are hidden by barriers of water and air. Explores the seaweed forests of the ocean bottom as well as the ocean of atmosphere to the stars and far - off galaxies.
Science - Natural; Science - Physical
Dist - MGHT **Prod** - ABCTV 1970

The Unseen world - Pt 2 - The time between 14 MIN
U-matic / VHS / 16mm
Color (H C)
LC 71-708742
Uses time lapse and slow motion photography to reveal the flick of a toad's tongue as it snares an insect, a drop of water as it splashes onto a liquid surface to form a perfect crown, the vibrations of a lightbulb filament as it approaches its glow point and blooming flowers and twisting vines in animated and accelerated motion.
Science - Natural; Science - Physical
Dist - MGHT **Prod** - ABCTV 1970

Unsere Afrikareise 13 MIN
16mm
Color (G)
$48.00 rental
Presents a meticulous production by Peter Kubelka which took five years to make.
Fine Arts
Dist - CANCIN

Unsere Strasse 20 MIN
16mm / U-matic / VHS
B&W (J H C) (GERMAN)
Deals with the problems of persuading the city council of a German town to vote funds for the construction of a street in a section where new houses have been built.
Foreign Language
Dist - IFB **Prod** - IFB 1964

The Unsinkable Bette Davis 26 MIN
16mm
B&W
LC FI68-288
Describes major events in the life and career of Bette Davis. Illustrates her acting versatility by showing scenes from several of her films.
Biography; Fine Arts
Dist - WOLPER **Prod** - WOLPER 1963

The unsinkable sea otter 25 MIN
U-matic / VHS / 16mm

Undersea world of Jacques Cousteau series
Color (G)
$49.95 purchase _ #Q10615; LC 75-702737
A shortened version of The Unksinkable Sea Otter. Follows Jacques Cousteau and his divers as they study the underwater life of the sea otter and examine the conditions essential for its survival. Describes reasons why the sea otter almost became extinct and examines problems caused by man and pollution. Part of a series of 24 programs.
Science - Natural
Dist - CF **Prod** - METROM 1975

Unsolved problems - three dimensions - Film 2 21 MIN
16mm
Maa general mathematics series
Color
Presents problems in three dimensions which mathematicians cannot solve.
Mathematics
Dist - MLA **Prod** - MAA

Unsolved problems - two dimensions - Film 1 22 MIN
16mm
Maa general mathematics series
Color
Presents a number of geometric problems which mathematicians cannot solve.
Mathematics
Dist - MLA **Prod** - MAA

Unspeakable acts 30 MIN
VHS
Open space series
Color; PAL (A)
PdS50 purchase
Investigates the research into female sexual abuse and female rape. Observes victims as they tell about sexual abuse by mothers; possible motivations and the area of sexual abuse in long - term lesbian relationships. This video is verbally rather than visually explicit. Researcher Frances Allam narrates.
Sociology
Dist - BBCENE

The Unspoken Message and the Interview 15 MIN
U-matic / VHS
Communication at Work Series
Color (H)
Stresses the importance of non - verbal cues in a job interview.
Guidance and Counseling; Psychology
Dist - AITECH **Prod** - OHSDE 1979

Unstable Angina - New Observations in Management 45 MIN
VHS / U-matic
Color (PRO)
Reviews definition, prognosis, pathophysiology and therapy of unstable angina. Discusses angiographic findings and the role of spasm, platelet dynamics, prostoglandins and their inhibitors, histamine, opioids and calcium flux. Closes with Dr Bertram Pitt's discussion of therapy in light of newer pathophysiologic interpretations.
Health and Safety
Dist - AMCARD **Prod** - AMCARD

Unstable angina pectoris - pathogenesis and management - Volume 3
VHS / 8mm cartridge
Cardiology video journal series
Color (PRO)
#FSR - 509
Presents a free - loan program, part of a series on cardiology, which trains medical professionals. Contact distributor for details.
Health and Safety
Dist - WYAYLA **Prod** - WYAYLA

Unsteady Steadiness 10 MIN
U-matic
Chemical Equilibrium Series
Color (H C)
Explores the direction of chemical reactions by seeking completion of both endothermic and exothermic reactions. Illustrated examples lead to a comparison of steady state and closed systems and to an apparently stopped reaction, equilibrium.
Science; Science - Physical
Dist - TVOTAR **Prod** - TVOTAR 1984

The Unsterile field - an O R challenge 21 MIN
16mm
Color (PRO)
Involves the entire operating room with the exception of the 'sterile' field. Covers problems such as filters, air exchange rate, humidity and conductive floors as well as the responsibility for mechanical performance of major equipment.
Health and Safety; Science
Dist - ACY **Prod** - ACYDGD 1966

Unstrap me 77 MIN
16mm
Color (G)
$80.00 rental
Features Kuchar's longest movie in color. Ventures to Cape Cod, New Jersey and Florida drinking with Walter Gutman, producer.
Fine Arts; Geography - United States; Psychology
Dist - CANCIN **Prod** - KUCHAR 1968

The Unsung soldiers - Volume 13 48 MIN
VHS
Vietnam - the ten thousand day war series
Color (G)
$34.95 purchase _ #S00685
Interviews Vietnam veterans on their readjustment to society. Suggests that many came home with psychological scars, not just physical ones. Narrated by Richard Basehart.
History - United States
Dist - UILL

Unsuspected 16 MIN
16mm
B&W
Illustrates facts about the discovery of unsuspected cases of tuberculosis. Shows how community health agencies assist in the rehabilitation of patients and in aiding families of tubercular patients to solve their problems.
Health and Safety; Sociology
Dist - AMLUNG **Prod** - NTBA 1962

Untamed Frontier Series

African eagles	25 MIN
African predators	25 MIN
The Canadian marsh	25 MIN
Elba	25 MIN
Eleanora Falcon	25 MIN
Eskimo Point	25 MIN
Indian ocean	25 MIN
Kenya Safari	25 MIN
Marmots	25 MIN
Puffins	25 MIN
The Seasons - autumn	25 MIN
The Seasons - Spring	25 MIN
The Seasons - summer	25 MIN
The Seasons - Winter	25 MIN
The Seychelles	25 MIN
Snow Geese	25 MIN
Waterholes	25 MIN

Dist - CTV

Untamed olympics 26 MIN
16mm
Audubon wildlife theatre series
Color (I)
Explains that Olympic National Park's 1400 square miles, in the extreme northwestern corner of the United States, extends across a dramatically changing landscape and includes 50 miles of rugged Pacific shoreline, rainforests and jagged granite peaks. Shows more than 50 species of plant and animal life from this area.
Geography - United States; Geography - World; Science - Natural
Dist - AVEXP **Prod** - AVEXP

Untamed world series series

Japan	25 MIN
Man and Environment	25 MIN
Marquiritare	25 MIN
Morocco	25 MIN
New Guinea	25 MIN
Nomads of Africa	25 MIN
Nuba	25 MIN
Nuguria	25 MIN
The Orissa Dombs	25 MIN
People of Africa	25 MIN
People of the Waters	25 MIN
Pygmies	25 MIN
The Sherpas	25 MIN
South American Tribes	25 MIN
Thailand	25 MIN
Yanomama I	25 MIN

Dist - CTV

Untamed World Series

African elephants	25 MIN
African parks	25 MIN
African plains	25 MIN
African wild life	25 MIN
The Alps	25 MIN
American parks	
Animal behaviour	25 MIN
Animal rodeo	25 MIN
Animals that work for men	25 MIN
Antarctica I	25 MIN
Antarctica II	25 MIN
Antelopes	25 MIN
The Arctic	25 MIN
The Arctic and man	25 MIN
Armand and Michaela and the animals	25 MIN
Asia	25 MIN
Asia Minor	25 MIN
Australia	25 MIN
Australia I	25 MIN
Australia II	25 MIN
Australia III	25 MIN
The Beach	25 MIN
Bighorn sheep	25 MIN
Birds - how they get around	25 MIN
Birds of different feathers	25 MIN
Birds of prey	25 MIN
British Columbia	25 MIN
Carnivores	25 MIN
Ceremonies of Man	25 MIN
Ceremonies of Man - Part II	25 MIN
Chimpanzees I	25 MIN
Chimpanzees II	25 MIN
Colour	25 MIN
Communication	25 MIN
Communications	25 MIN
Conservation	25 MIN
Continental Survivors	25 MIN
Cordilleras	25 MIN
Cranes	25 MIN
Creatures of the waters	25 MIN
A Day in Africa	25 MIN
A Day in the Park	25 MIN
Deserts	25 MIN
Dogon I	25 MIN
Dogon II	25 MIN
Dragons	25 MIN
Elephant	25 MIN
European Forests	25 MIN
Farne Islands	25 MIN
Florida Everglades	25 MIN
Florida Everglades II	25 MIN
Forest dwellers	25 MIN
Galapagos - the sea	25 MIN
Galapagos II - the land	25 MIN
Gazelles	25 MIN
Getting the Job Done	25 MIN
Giants	25 MIN
The Great barrier reef	25 MIN
The Great Rift Valley	25 MIN
Grebes and geese	25 MIN
The Grey Goose	25 MIN
Guillemots	25 MIN
Guinea	25 MIN
Herbivores	25 MIN
Hong Kong on Borrowed Time	25 MIN
Iceland I	25 MIN
India	25 MIN
Insects	25 MIN
Insects - a Success Story	25 MIN
Insects II	25 MIN
Island Survivors	25 MIN
The Jungle	25 MIN
Kalahari	25 MIN
Kangaroos	25 MIN
Lions	25 MIN
Madagascar I	25 MIN
Madagascar II	25 MIN
Magazine I - Birds, Beasts, and Breathing Fish	25 MIN
Magazine II - Bats, Birds, and Bigger Beasts	25 MIN
Malaysia	25 MIN
Mangrove Swamps	25 MIN
Marsupials	25 MIN
Mating Dances	25 MIN
Methods	25 MIN
The Midgets	25 MIN
Nakuru	25 MIN
New England	25 MIN
The New Generation	25 MIN
Ngorongoro Crater	25 MIN
The Nile	25 MIN
Operation Gwamba	25 MIN
Operation Noah	25 MIN
Other Cats	25 mniutes
Pachyderms	25 MIN
Pacific Coast	25 MIN
Parklands	25 MIN
Penguins	25 mniutes
Pets	25 MIN
Poland	25 MIN
Polar Bears	25 MIN
The Prairies	25 MIN
Predators and Scavengers	25 MIN
Primates	25 MIN
Rituals of man	25 MIN
The Rockies	25 MIN
The Rocky Mountains	25 MIN
Safari	25 MIN
Scandinavia	25 MIN
Sea Islands	25 MIN

The Search for Gertie 25 MIN
Serengeti 25 MIN
Snakes 25 MIN
Sockeye Salmon 25 MIN
South America 25 MIN
South American Coast 25 MIN
Storks 25 MIN
Survival 25 MIN
Tropical Marshes 25 MIN
Underwater 25 MIN
Underwater I 25 MIN
Underwater II 25 MIN
Water 25 MIN
Water and Life 25 MIN
Waterbirds 25 MIN
Waterfowl 25 MIN
Waterhole 25 MIN
Wheels in Africa 25 MIN
The World of Birds 25 MIN
The World of Insects 25 MIN
Yanomama II 25 MIN
Yugoslavia 25 MIN
Dist - CTV

Untamed world
Afghanistan 25 MIN
Arts and Crafts 25 MIN
Handicrafts 25 MIN
Dist - CTV

Unter Denkmalschutz 97 MIN
16mm
B&W (GERMAN)
Documents the history of an old house in Frankfurt and of its inhabitants.
Foreign Language; History - United States; History - World; Sociology
Dist - WSTGLC **Prod** - WSTGLC 1975

Unter Heissem Himmel 102 MIN
16mm
B&W (GERMAN (ENGLISH SUBTITLES))
Tells an adventure story of a non - commissioned skipper who becomes involved in a scheme to ship arms out of the country illegally, and who is able to take initiative to prevent the worst from happening after he realizes the seriousness of the situation.
Fine Arts; Foreign Language
Dist - WSTGLC **Prod** - WSTGLC 1936

Until I die 30 MIN
VHS / U-matic / 16mm
Color (PRO)
$350.00, $250.00 purchase, $60.00 rental _ #3688SF, #3688S, #3688F, #3688V
Features Dr Elisabeth Kubler - Ross. Explains her work with terminally ill patients. Examines the five stages - denial, anger, bargaining, depression and acceptance. Illustrates Kubler's methods through an interview with a sixty - year - old cancer patient.
Health and Safety; Psychology; Sociology
Dist - AJN **Prod** - WTTWTV 1970

Until I Die 29 MIN
Videoreel / VT2
Synergism - in Today's World Series
Color
Health and Safety; Psychology; Sociology
Dist - PBS **Prod** - WTTWTV

Until I Die 30 MIN
16mm
Color
Presents Dr Elizabeth Kubler - Ross and her work with terminal patients. Examines her concept of the patients' reaction to an unfavorable diagnosis as a five - state process of grieving, including denial, anger, bargaining, depression and acceptance.
Guidance and Counseling; Health and Safety; Psychology; Sociology
Dist - AMCS **Prod** - AMCS 1972

Until I Get Caught 20 MIN
U-matic / VHS / 16mm
Color (H A)
Discusses why more action has not been taken to stop the combination of drinking and driving. Includes interviews with a district attorney, Swedish drivers, members of a New York community action group and relatives of victims killed in DWI - related accidents.
Education; Health and Safety; Psychology; Sociology
Dist - USNAC **Prod** - NHTSA 1980

Until I get caught 27 MIN
16mm
Color; PAL (H C A)
LC 80-700225
Explores the psychological attitudes of drunk drivers, victims, judges, jurors and police. Contrasts the drunk driving problem in the United States with that of Sweden, where the problem is much less severe.
Health and Safety; Sociology
Dist - MTP **Prod** - NYSLG 1980
EDPAT

Until I get caught 28 MIN
U-matic / VHS / 16mm
Color
$75 rental _ #9771
Discusses interviewees' feelings about driving under the influence and how alcohol related incidents have affected their lives.
Health and Safety; Psychology; Sociology
Dist - AIMS **Prod** - AIMS 1984

Until I Get Caught - Excerpts 20 MIN
16mm / U-matic / VHS
Color (H A)
Discusses the issue of DWI in America. Features interviews with survivors of victims killed by drunken drivers. Discusses the problem and potential solutions.
Health and Safety; Psychology; Sociology
Dist - USNAC **Prod** - USDTFH 1980

Until it is Safe to Return 46 MIN
Videoreel / U-matic / VT3
(G)
$125.00 purchase, $50.00 rental; $35.00 purchase, $25.00 rental
Features an account of an El Salvadoran woman and her child as they find sanctuary in Ithaca, New York. Documents the commitment of public officials as Ithaca became the fifth U S city to declare itself a Sanctuary for Central American refugees.
Civics and Political Systems; Geography - World; Social Science; Sociology
Dist - EFVP **Prod** - EFVP 1985

Until she talks 44 MIN
16mm
Color
LC 81-700437
Relates the true story of a young woman who chooses not to answer questions which were asked illegally by a grand jury. Reveals the legal process which put her in jail.
Civics and Political Systems
Dist - FIRS **Prod** - ALASSP 1981

Until she talks - Pt 1 22 MIN
16mm
Color
LC 81-700437
Relates the true story of a young woman who chooses not to answer questions which were asked illegally by a grand jury. Reveals the legal process which put her in jail.
Civics and Political Systems
Dist - FIRS **Prod** - ALASSP 1981

Until she talks - Pt 2 22 MIN
16mm
Color
LC 81-700437
Relates the true story of a young woman who chooses not to answer questions which were asked illegally by a grand jury. Reveals the legal process which put her in jail.
Civics and Political Systems
Dist - FIRS **Prod** - ALASSP 1981

Until We Say Good - Bye 62 MIN
16mm
Color
LC 81-700493
Explores the hospice concept in its most successful forms in three English and American facilities.
Sociology
Dist - WJLATV **Prod** - WJLATV 1981

Until we say good - bye - Pt 1 31 MIN
16mm
Color
LC 81-700493
Explores the hospice concept in its most successful forms in three English and American facilities.
Sociology
Dist - WJLATV **Prod** - WJLATV 1981

Until we say good - bye - Pt 2 31 MIN
16mm
Color
LC 81-700493
Explores the hospice concept in its most successful forms in three English and American facilities.
Sociology
Dist - WJLATV **Prod** - WJLATV 1981

Untitled 8 MIN
16mm
Color; Silent (C)
$350.00
Experimental film by Peter Gidal.
Fine Arts
Dist - AFA **Prod** - AFA 1978

Untitled 4 MIN
16mm
B&W
Experimental treatment of a savage attack upon a girl. Staccato drum beats play in counterpoint to the highly formalized imagery. (A USC Cinema Student Workshop production.).
Fine Arts; Psychology; Sociology
Dist - USC **Prod** - USC 1965

Untitled 3 MIN
16mm
Color (G)
$25.00 rental
Looks at gay desire and the fantasy of desire in a John Sabo production.
Fine Arts; Sociology
Dist - CANCIN

Untitled 3 MIN
16mm
Color (A)
Presents a hand colored silent experimental film by Diana Barrie which is an abstract combining strict control with chance effects of the action of chemicals on the emulsion.
Fine Arts
Dist - STARRC **Prod** - STARRC 1980

Untitled 3 MIN
16mm
B&W; Color (G)
$20.00 rental ; $15.00 rental
Presents a film by William English.
Fine Arts
Dist - CANCIN

Untitled - 1977 5 MIN
16mm
Color (G)
$10.00 rental
Zeroes in on snowflakes, with a slow pulling of focus, falling in front of a pond, a field and a brick wall. Presents a film by Ernie Gehr.
Fine Arts
Dist - CANCIN

Untitled 1987 7 MIN
16mm / VHS
Color (G)
$18.00 rental, $20.00 purchase
Challenges common perceptions of reality and, through cinematic means, suggests a deeper reality. Explores the mystic's vision of oneness of all using camera, music, movement, color and light. Produced by Barry J Hershey.
Fine Arts
Dist - CANCIN

Untitled Film 18 MIN
16mm
B&W
Presents a documentary about a group of Tibetans living in a community in New Jersey. Shows them at prayers, eating, playing with a tape recorder, and going out for hamburgers. Intercuts the workings of a Hamburger King Restaurant with the analysis of Tibetan religious practices.
Geography - United States; Guidance and Counseling; Religion and Philosophy; Social Science; Sociology
Dist - UPENN **Prod** - UPENN 1970

Untitled Film - a Search for Ecological Balance 38 MIN
16mm
Color
LC 74-705706
Presents the views of an internationally - known ecologist, Eugene P Odum, who believes it necessary to consider a master plan for the total environment in order to maintain an ecological balance.
Science - Natural
Dist - RADIM **Prod** - OIPFLM 1969

Untitled - for Marilyn 11 MIN
16mm
Color (G)
$24.00 rental
Features a hand - painted film. Interweaves a hypnagogic four - part thought process with scratched words in thanks to and praise of God.
Fine Arts
Dist - CANCIN **Prod** - BRAKS 1992

The Untitled frenzy of history 45 MIN
16mm
Color (G)
$90.00 rental
Consists of a series of short pieces both interrelated and somewhat independent resonating with each other as well as standing on their own. Looks at memory and recuperation, language and the body. Made between 1970 - 1984.
Fine Arts; Psychology
Dist - CANCIN **Prod** - SONDHE 1984

Untitled - hands 5 MIN
16mm
B&W (G)
$10.00 rental
Utilizes hands as the object of study. Creates its own loud silent soundtrack by implementing repeated visual rhythms.
Fine Arts
Dist - CANCIN **Prod** - FORTDE 1980

Untitled - Part One - 1981 29 MIN
16mm
Color (G)
$50.00 rental
Reveals brief close - ups of people on the street shot from a high but intimate angle. Shows fragments of feet, heads, hands and elbows against the backdrop of an old sidewalk. Produced by Ernie Gehr.
Fine Arts
Dist - CANCIN

The Untitled Population Film 12 MIN
16mm
Color (I J)
LC 76-703651
Uses animation in presenting the complex problem facing national governments and international agencies of finding useful work for growing populations and for those already without jobs, while meeting the needs of economic growth.
Business and Economics; Guidance and Counseling; Social Science; Sociology
Dist - SF **Prod** - INLAOR 1976

Untitled - three parts 7 MIN
16mm
B&W (G)
$14.00 rental
Introduces a concerto for three solo voices. Consists of three parts - the Party, Canines and The Nude.
Fine Arts
Dist - CANCIN **Prod** - FORTDE 1980

Unto us a child is born 5 MIN
16mm
Color
LC FIA68-855
Uses pictures and animation synchronized with measures from the 'For Unto Us a Child is Born' chorus of 'The Messiah' to augment the expression of the music in terms of time structure, ideas and the underlying emotional intent.
Fine Arts; Religion and Philosophy
Dist - USC **Prod** - USC 1968

Unusual 10 MIN
U-matic
Readalong Three Series
Color (P)
Provides reading instruction for third grade students. Uses animation, humor, music, repetition and audience participation. Comes with teacher's guide and kit.
Education; English Language; Literature and Drama
Dist - TVOTAR **Prod** - TVOTAR 1977

The Unusual situation 30 MIN
U-matic / VHS
Hearing screening series
Color
Deals with the problems of the multiple handicapped child, who requires special testing and special programs in education.
Guidance and Counseling; Health and Safety; Science - Natural
Dist - NETCHE **Prod** - NETCHE 1971

Unwanted Aliens 11 MIN
16mm
Color
LC FIE63-219
Shows foreign insects that could be introduced into the United States in a plant - pest detection training film.
Agriculture; Science - Natural
Dist - USNAC **Prod** - USDA 1961

Unwanted - do not enter 60 MIN
VHS
Americans, too - black experiences in rural America series
Color (J H C G)
$70.00 purchase, $12.50 rental _ #61559
Follows the efforts of Williamsport, Pennsylvania, to adjust to and organize an influx of recovering drug and alcohol addicts from urban areas. Part of a six - part series visiting widely scattered geographic areas of Pennsylvania to interview and understand the rural black community.
Geography - United States; Health and Safety; History - United States; Psychology
Dist - PSU **Prod** - OCONEL 1992

Unwasted Stories 75 MIN
U-matic / VHS
Social Issue Series
Color (G)
$200.00, $140.00 purchase, $75.00, $50.00 rental
Considers Minnesota waste issues. Endeavors to address the complexities of the difficult and multi - dimensional waste issue. Centers on many current Minnesota subjects, including an impending downtown Minneapolis garbage incinerator. Produced by Kathleen Laughlin.
Psychology; Sociology
Dist - IAFC

Unwasted stories - approaching Minnesota waste issues 75 MIN
VHS / U-matic
Color (H C G)
$200.00, $140.00 purchase, $75.00, $50.00 rental
Portrays citizen activists who oppose the construction of a solid waste incinerator in downtown Minneapolis. Stresses recycling, resource recovery, composting and the obligation of every citizen to reduce the amount of waste produced and to be sure that wastes are disposed of in an environmentally friendly way.
Geography - United States; Science - Natural; Sociology
Dist - IAFC **Prod** - IAFC 1988

Unwed Mothers in Today's World 29 MIN
U-matic
Color (H C A)
Features four young women discussing their experiences as unwed mothers. Emphasizes the need for sensitive counseling and sound pre - natal care.
Health and Safety
Dist - LAWREN **Prod** - LAWREN

The Unwelcome Guest 20 MIN
16mm
Color
LC 78-700443
Shows how comprehensive prevention and treatment programs for helminth diseases can improve the quality of life in many nations. Discusses the commitment of Pfizer International to do research in the field of parasitic diseases.
Health and Safety
Dist - PFIZRL **Prod** - PFIZRL 1977

Up 15 MIN
U-matic / VHS / 16mm
Color (I)
Presents an allegorical hang gliding adventure of a young man and an eagle. Includes aerial maneuvers and soaring sequences, which lead to a thought provoking conclusion. From the producers of the film, Solo.
Physical Education and Recreation
Dist - PFP **Prod** - PFP

Up a gum tree with David Bellamy series
Travels around Australia and looks at the flora and fauna of the continent. Employs David Bellamy as a tour guide.
Fire down below 30 MIN
The great barriers 30 MIN
The landscape architects 30 MIN
Not so much a desert... more a way of life 30 MIN
Dist - BBCENE

Up a new rope - a talk about AIDS and recovery 15 MIN
VHS
AIDS and addiction series
Color (G)
$50.00 purchase
Portrays the connection between the use of IV drugs and AIDS through concrete and candid delivery of information by recovered drug users, outreach workers and others who work closely with the addicted. Cautions against high risk behavior, demonstrates methods of protection and encourages viewers to reach out for recovery. Part of a three - part series designed to be used in treatment or support group settings with IV drug addicts, prostitutes and persons living with AIDS.
Guidance and Counseling; Health and Safety; Psychology; Sociology
Dist - NEWIST **Prod** - NEWIST

Up a Tree 8 MIN
U-matic / VHS / 16mm
Three Decades of Donald Duck Series
Color (P I)
Shows how lumberjack Donald Duck runs into trouble when he tries to chop down the tree home of two chipmunks.
Fine Arts
Dist - CORF **Prod** - DISNEY

Up a tree with David Bellamy series
Present from Gondwanaland 30 MIN
Dist - BBCENE

Up against the wall Miss America 7 MIN
16mm
Color
Details the attempt of women's liberation groups to disrupt the annual pageant and make boardwalk and contestant spectators more aware of the contest with its image of the 'mindless womanhood.'
Sociology
Dist - CANWRL **Prod** - CANWRL 1968

Up and atom 3 MIN
16mm
Trildogy series
Color (G)
$8.00 rental
Features a comedy and part of the Trildogy with music by Fletcher Henderson to be shown with Staid Poot.
Fine Arts; Literature and Drama
Dist - CANCIN **Prod** - WENDTD 1970

Up and Away 30 MIN
U-matic
Polka Dot Door Series
Color (K)
Presents a variety show for pre - school children. Includes songs, mime, stories, film sequences, talk, dance and fantasy figures. Each show emphasizes a particular theme such as numbers, feelings, exploring, music or time. Comes with parent teacher guide.
Fine Arts; Literature and Drama
Dist - TVOTAR **Prod** - TVOTAR 1985

Up and Coming
Presents a realistic view of a black family's move into an integrated neighborhood. The 15 30 - minute programs deal with the family's conflicts, problems and adjustments.
Up and Coming 30 MIN
Dist - GPN **Prod** - KQEDTV 1985

Up and Down 8 MIN
U-matic / VHS / 16mm
Color (P I)
LC 74-713572
Relates the directions up and down to the student's observations of the energy of moving things.
Science - Physical
Dist - PHENIX **Prod** - PHENIX 1971

Up and Down, in and Out, Big and Little 30 MIN
VHS / 16mm
Science, Health and Math Series
Color (P)
$39.95 purchase _ #CL7903
Introduces basic concepts concerning size and volume.
Science; Science - Natural
Dist - EDUCRT

Up and down the slopes 30 MIN
VHS / U-matic
Alpine ski school series
Color
Presents instruction in downhill skiing techniques. Illustrates traveling around the mountain and introduces the christie or controlled skid.
Physical Education and Recreation
Dist - PBS **Prod** - PBS 1983

Up and down the waterfront 8 MIN
16mm
B&W (G)
$35.00 rental
Films crates and boxes unloading in the morning, lonely men sitting on half - broken docks in the afternoon, sailor bars at night with one poor bum actually getting the heave - ho, a mighty waterhose washing it all away.
Fine Arts
Dist - CANCIN **Prod** - BURCKR 1946

Up and running - 4 30 MIN
VHS
Venturing...the entrepreneurial challenge series
Color (G)
$14.95 purchase
Shows that getting a company up and running never goes according to plan. Describes inevitable mistakes and shows how to recover from them. Part four of a 13 - part series on the steps involved in starting and developing an entrepreneurial company. Viewers' guide available separately. Sponsored under a grant from the Farmers Home Administration to help small and rural businesses.
Business and Economics; Psychology
Dist - VTETV **Prod** - VTETV 1992

Up and running - Part One 45 MIN
VHS
Workplace ready - job skills for the 21st century series
Color (J H)
$189.00 purchase _ #FG - 985 - VS
Presents four sessions which set the stage for understanding how skills apply in the workplace. Introduces students to the world of business in Session One. Session Two visits a rollerblade company in Madison, Wisconsin. Session Three focuses on advancing through increasing and refining work skills. Session Four emphasizes the importance of skills showing that three foundation skills - listening, sociability and problem solving - are important job skills. Includes a

teacher's resource guide with reproducible worksheets and homework assignments. Part One of a four - part series.
Business and Economics; English Language; Guidance and Counseling; Psychology
Dist - HRMC **Prod** - HRMC 1994

Up close and in person
VHS
Career process series
Color (H A)
$84.95 purchase _ #ES1220V
Presents tips for job interviews. Shows how to answer typical interview questions and write a follow - up letter.
Psychology
Dist - CAMV **Prod** - CAMV 1987

Up Close and in Person
VHS / 35mm strip
$43.50 purchase _ #XY862 filmstrip, $84.95 purchase _ #XY812 for VHS
Portrays the job interview from both sides of the desk. Emphasizes how to convince the employer that you are the right person for the job.
Business and Economics; Guidance and Counseling
Dist - CAREER **Prod** - CAREER

Up Close and Natural Series

Animals without backbones	15 MIN
Fish	15 MIN
Frogs, toads and salamanders	15 MIN
In the Field	15 MIN
Insects	15 MIN
Introduction - Up Close and Natural Series	
Life in the Winter Forest	15 MIN
Mammals	15 MIN
Marsh and Swamp	15 MIN
Outside Your Door	15 MIN
The Pond	15 MIN
Snakes	15 MIN
Turtles	15 MIN
What is a Bird?	15 MIN
Winter at Squam Lake	15 MIN

Dist - AITECH

Up, down, all around - directional relationships 10 MIN
U-matic / VHS / 16mm
Math readiness series
Color (P)
$255, $180 purchase _ #3643
Shows the differences between up and down, left and right, and front and back. Illustrates spatial directions by discussing the construction of a house.
Mathematics
Dist - CORF

Up, Down, and all Around 15 MIN
VHS / U-matic
Mrs Cabobble"s Caboose
(P)
Designed to teach primary grade students basic music concepts. Highlights melody, rhythm, harmony and the different families of musical instruments. Features Mrs. Fran Powell.
Fine Arts
Dist - GPN **Prod** - WDCNTV 1986

Up, Down and Sideways 15 MIN
U-matic
Landscape of Geometry Series
Color (J)
Looks at the geometry of falling, balance and construction with emphasis on the importance of the right angle.
Education; Mathematics
Dist - TVOTAR **Prod** - TVOTAR 1982

Up for the cup 15 MIN
16mm
Magnificent 6 and 1/2 series
Color (P I J)
Explains that unable to obtain tickets for the football final the 'Six and a Half' gang decide to build a viewing platform.
Fine Arts
Dist - LUF **Prod** - CHILDF 1972

Up from the underground 60 MIN
VHS
History of rock 'n' roll series
Color (G)
$19.99 purchase _ #0 - 7907 - 2434 - 0NK
Observes the birth of MTV, rap and alternative rock. Presents clips of breakthrough videos - Michael Jackson - Billy Jean; Dire Straits - Money for Nothing; Eurythmics - Sweet Dreams; Madonna - Secrets. Includes hits by Run - DMC, Red Hot Chili Peppers, REM, Smashing Pumpkins and more. Part of a ten - part series unfolding the history of rock music. May contain mature subject matter and explicit song lyrics.
Fine Arts
Dist - TILIED

Up Front 28 MIN
16mm
Color (J)
LC 75-715510
Presents young people who discuss drugs and drug dependency, the underlying problems of drug abuse and some possible effective solutions.
Guidance and Counseling; Health and Safety; Psychology; Sociology
Dist - IA **Prod** - LACOS 1971

Up Front 27 MIN
VHS / U-matic
Color
Presents a rehabilitated drug user talking to a group of young people about drugs and drug dependency. Introduces a variety of treatment facilities and points out underlying problems that lead youth to drug misuse.
Psychology; Sociology
Dist - IA **Prod** - LACFU

Up in flames and live
VHS / U-matic
Color (IND)
Shows how race car drivers walk away from fiery accidents by wearing Nomex clothing. Explains how most burn fatalities are a result of clothes igniting, and how this special clothing decreases burn - related deaths.
Health and Safety; Industrial and Technical Education
Dist - GPCV **Prod** - GPCV

Up in Smoke 38 MIN
U-matic / VHS
Color (J H C)
LC 82-706874
Presents the history of smoking in Western society, explains the chemical makeup of tobacco and gives a description of its damaging effects on the body. Enumerates the social and personal influences on someone who is trying to decide whether or not to smoke. Provides information about how to stop smoking.
Health and Safety; Psychology
Dist - GA **Prod** - GA 1982

Up in smoke - how smoking affects your health 57 MIN
VHS
Color (J H)
$129.00 purchase _ #06791 - 026
Investigates why people smoke and how difficult it is to stop. Considers the psychological reasons why teenagers start smoking such as the need to be accepted, to appear mature, to rebel against authority. Describes the effects of nicotine on the body and ends with suggestions for methods of quitting. Includes teacher's guide and library kit.
Health and Safety; Sociology
Dist - GA

Up in the Air 43 MIN
U-matic / VHS / 16mm
Color (P I)
Portrays Victorian children improvising a balloon to escape their boarding school. Features a chase across the country.
Literature and Drama
Dist - LUF **Prod** - LUF

Up in the Air 29 MIN
Videoreel / VT2
Observing Eye Series
Color
Science - Physical; Sociology
Dist - PBS **Prod** - WGBHTV

Up is Down 6 MIN
16mm / U-matic / VHS
Color (H C)
LC 71-709494
Presents through animation a direct treatment of some of the most central themes of intolerance, conformity and the generation gap.
Psychology; Sociology
Dist - PFP **Prod** - GOLDES 1970

Up is not the Only Way 24 MIN
U-matic / 16mm / VHS
Color (H C)
$525, $370, $400 _ #A534; LC 88-710220;
Shows viewers that promotion is only one of six options available for career enhancement. Discusses six career moves that one can make for greater job satisfaction. Discusses vertical or promotion, lateral, moving out/relocation, realignment or moving down, exploratory, and job enrichment.
Guidance and Counseling
Dist - BARR **Prod** - BARR 1988

Up one day, down the next - why do I feel the way I do 56 MIN
VHS
Color (J H)
$129.00 purchase _ #60115 - 026
Illustrates a wide range of feelings that most people share such as feelings that help us survive, feelings that are warning signals and feelings that make life worthwhile. Encourages students to communicate their emotions and examine different ways of expressing them. Includes teacher's guide and library kit.
Guidance and Counseling; Psychology
Dist - GA

Up Pill, Down Pill 24 MIN
U-matic / VHS / 16mm
Color (I)
LC 73-711149
Presents an open - ended film that explores different lifestyles in which the central figures find disappointments and frustrations and make decisions which all young people will have to make for themselves.
Guidance and Counseling; Health and Safety; Sociology
Dist - PHENIX **Prod** - MITCHG 1970

Up the Airy Mountain - Songs from Famous Children's Poems 45 MIN
U-matic / VHS
(P I)
Contains 24 two part songs and the words of a much loved children's poem set to brand new music. Teacher source book supplies writer music in two versions - piano scores and reproducible vocal parts for students. Background notes about poems and poets. Reinforces basic music reading, vocal and expressive skills.
Fine Arts
Dist - WALCHJ **Prod** - WALCHJ 1987

Up the block one Sunday 13 MIN
16mm
Color (G)
$30.00 rental
Says critic Andrej Zdravic, 'Blau, an experienced photographer, shows us here that he's a real jazz - man of the camera...' Film by Dick Blau.
Fine Arts
Dist - CANCIN

Up the Corporate Ladder 60 MIN
U-matic / VHS
Road to Achievement Series
Captioned (J H C)
$34.95 _ #KA1220V
Deals with intermediate career objectives, such as salary negotiation, financing, management and others.
Business and Economics
Dist - CAMV **Prod** - CAMV

Up the Creek 15 MIN
16mm
Time Out Series
Color
LC 81-701203
Focuses on a man whose wife has left him after he violently attacked her. Explore the isolation he feels as he confronts loss and legal consequences of his behavior.
Sociology
Dist - ODNP **Prod** - ODNP 1982

Up the creek 14 MIN
16mm
Magnificent 6 and 1/2 series
Color (P I J)
Explains that the 'Six and a Half' gang are so desperate to become boat owners that they offer their services free of charge to the owner of a local boatyard in exchange for his promise of a boat.
Fine Arts
Dist - LUF **Prod** - CHILDF 1972

Up the down stream 12 MIN
U-matic
Color (K A)
Documents the natural cycle of the king salmon as well as how humans help with hatcheries, fish ladders and transplanting.
Geography - United States; Science - Natural
Dist - CALDWR **Prod** - CSDWR

Up the Dressing Ladder - Steps to Independence 26 MIN
U-matic
Color
LC 76-706124
Demonstrates how young multiple - handicapped children can be helped to independence, including instruction in their development of skills in holding, pulling, pushing, finding and opening.
Health and Safety; Psychology
Dist - USNAC **Prod** - USBEH 1974

Up the Ladder Down 10 MIN
U-matic / VHS / 16mm
Color (J H A)

LC 76-702163
Presents three vignettes dealing with marijuana, barbiturates, cocaine and heroin, showing the consequences of drug abuse.
Health and Safety; Psychology; Sociology
Dist - AIMS **Prod** - DAVP 1976

Up the organization 30 MIN
U-matic / VHS / 16mm
Color
LC 77-702186
Presents author and businessman Robert Townsend, who discusses his views on topics such as chief executives, personnel departments, management consultants, computers, public relations departments and business success.
Business and Economics
Dist - FI **Prod** - BBCTV 1973

Up the Power Curve 10 MIN
16mm
Color (J)
LC 77-700513
Demonstrates the practicality of energy conservation and the important role it has in helping solve America's energy problems. Covers a wide variety of energy - saving ideas and points out the significant dollar savings that can be achieved when these ideas are put into practice.
Science - Natural; Social Science
Dist - USNAC **Prod** - USFEAP 1976

Up Tight - L a is Burning 20 MIN
16mm
Color (C A)
Presents a psychedelic comment on the attitudes and problems of the now generation.
Psychology; Sociology
Dist - CFS **Prod** - CFS 1968

Up to Code 18 MIN
U-matic / VHS / 16mm
Color
LC 79-701214
Explores the attitudinal problems encountered by many firemen when called upon to do inspections of public facilities. Discusses ways of improving attitudes and demonstrates training devices for making thorough inspections.
Health and Safety; Psychology; Social Science
Dist - PFP **Prod** - PFP 1979

Up to Date with the Catholic Church
BETA / VHS
Up to Date with the Catholic Church Series
Color
Presents a fresh look at Catholicism with Archbishop John Whealon. Comes with study guide.
Religion and Philosophy
Dist - DSP **Prod** - DSP

Up to Date with the Catholic Church Series
Developing a life of personal prayer - living a sacramental life 60 MIN
Up to Date with the Catholic Church
Why be a Roman Catholic - the Importance of Magisterium for Catholic Living 30 MIN
Why Believe in God - Why Accept Jesus as Your Lord 60 MIN
Dist - DSP

Up to the Moon 11 MIN
U-matic / VHS / 16mm
Reading and Word Play Series
Color (P)
Presents an imaginative word romp with children and a gorilla on merry - go - rounds, carousels, tettertotters, swings and slides to reinforce the words up, down, walk, run, boy, girl and stop.
English Language
Dist - AIMS **Prod** - PEDF 1976

Up to the Sequoias 8 MIN
16mm
Color (J)
Shows that the sequoias on the western slopes of the Sierra Nevadas in California are some of the world's oldest living things, including trees as tall as 200 feet and some 3,000 years of age. Captures the great beauty of the region with natural sounds and close - ups of various species of birds.
Geography - United States; Science - Natural
Dist - AVEXP **Prod** - AVEXP 1968

Up to you 28 MIN
U-matic / BETA / VHS
Communication skills 2 - advanced series
Color (H C G)
$101.95, $89.95 purchase _ #CA - 02
Identifies the differences betwen 'intra' and 'inter' when applied to levels of communication. Lists six levels of human functioning and gives examples of each. Defines intra - personal, inter - personal, intra - group, inter - group, intra - cultural and inter - cultural communication. Part of a 26 - part series.
Social Science
Dist - INSTRU

Up, Up and Afraid 29 MIN
16mm / U-matic / VHS
Color
Explains that for many people the fear of flying is a very real disease. Documents the many programs which help people overcome this fear.
Psychology
Dist - JOU **Prod** - CANBC

Up, Up, and Away 25 MIN
U-matic
Not Another Science Show Series
Color (H C)
Explores the mechanics of flight and the factors involved in the successful flight of airplanes, birds and insects.
Science; Science - Physical
Dist - TVOTAR **Prod** - TVOTAR 1986

UPA Carnival - No 1 20 MIN
16mm / U-matic / VHS
Color
Includes the cartoon features 'Follow Me,' 'The Invisible Mustache of Raoul Dufy' and 'The Matador and Troubador.'
Literature and Drama
Dist - FI **Prod** - UPA

UPA Carnival - No 2 20 MIN
U-matic / VHS / 16mm
Color
Includes the cartoon features 'Fight on for Old,' 'The Merry Go Round in the Jungle,' 'Aquarium' and 'Ballet Lesson.'
Literature and Drama
Dist - FI **Prod** - UPA

UPA Carnival - No 3 20 MIN
U-matic / VHS / 16mm
Color
Includes the cartoon features 'Peewee the Kiwi Bird,' 'The Two Musicians,' 'Turned Around Clown' and 'Der Team from Zwischendorf.'
Literature and Drama
Dist - FI **Prod** - UPA

UPA Carnival - No 4 20 MIN
U-matic / VHS / 16mm
Color
Includes the cartoon features 'Marvo the Magician,' 'The Unenchanted Princess,' 'The Freezee Yum Story,' 'The Little Boy Who Ran Away' and 'Mr Charmely Greets a Lady.'
Literature and Drama
Dist - FI **Prod** - UPA

UPA Carnival - No 5 20 MIN
16mm / U-matic / VHS
Color
Includes the cartoon features 'The Average Giraffe,' 'Be Quiet, Kind and Gentle,' 'The Day of the Fox' and 'The Outlaws.'
Literature and Drama
Dist - FI **Prod** - UPA

UPA Carnival - No 6 20 MIN
U-matic / VHS / 16mm
Color
Includes the cartoon features 'Good Ole Country Music,' 'One Wonderful Girl,' 'The Lost Duchess' and 'The Last Doubloon.'
Literature and Drama
Dist - FI **Prod** - UPA

UPA Carnival - No 7 20 MIN
U-matic / VHS / 16mm
Color
Includes the cartoon features 'Mr Tingley's Tangle,' 'Punch and Judy' and 'Meet the Inventor, Samuel F B Morse.'
Literature and Drama
Dist - FI **Prod** - UPA

UPA Carnival - No 8 20 MIN
U-matic / VHS / 16mm
Color
Includes the cartoon features 'The Lion Hunt,' 'The Trial of Zelda Belle' and 'The Five Cent Nickel.'
Literature and Drama
Dist - FI **Prod** - UPA

UPA Carnival - No 9 20 MIN
16mm / U-matic / VHS
Color
Includes the cartoon features 'Martians Come Back,' 'Two by Two,' 'We Saw Sea Serpents' and 'Winter Sports.'
Literature and Drama
Dist - FI **Prod** - UPA

UPA Carnival - No 10 20 MIN
16mm / U-matic / VHS
Color
Includes the cartoon features 'Lion on the Loose,' 'Just Believe in Make Believe' and 'The Magic Fiddle.'
Literature and Drama
Dist - FI **Prod** - UPA

UPA Carnival - No 11 20 MIN
16mm / U-matic / VHS
Color
Presents cartoon features, including 'A Little Journey,' 'Old MacDonald,' 'The Election,' 'Don Coyote and Chico and Alouette.'
Literature and Drama
Dist - FI **Prod** - UPA

UPA Carnival - No 14 20 MIN
U-matic / VHS / 16mm
Color
Presents cartoon features, including 'Persistent Mr Fulton,' 'Alphabet Song,' 'Mr Buzzard' and 'The Armored Car.'
Literature and Drama
Dist - FI **Prod** - UPA

Update - Adult Learning and the New Technologies 120 MIN
VHS / 16mm
Color (G)
$70.00 rental _ #MIKE - 001
Views a teleconference on the role the new telecommunications technologies play in adult education.
Education; Fine Arts
Dist - PBS **Prod** - PBS

Update Appliances Meetings Series
Chicago 5 MIN
U S Air Force Academy 4 MIN
Dist - SRCIPP

Update Brazil 15 MIN
VHS / 16mm
Color (G)
$225.00 purchase, $50.00 rental
Looks at Brazil's innovative solution to violence against women in cultures where the criminal justice systems are largely staffed by men with little understanding and sympathy for the victims of these crimes. Considers Brazil's establishment of police stations completely run and operated by plainclothed but armed women who offer legal assistance and emotional support to victims of violence. Produced by Nancy Marcotte and Colette Loumede.
Civics and Political Systems; Guidance and Counseling; Social Science; Sociology
Dist - WMEN **Prod** - MARLOU 1986

Update - defence 15 MIN
VHS
Field trips series
Color (I J)
$34.95 purchase _ #E337; LC 90-708567
Goes behind the scenes at a state museum in Maine to find out how conservators put together their research about life on a Revolutionary privateer. Part of a series which provides visual opportunities for children to 'visit' a variety of locations and activities as if they were on a field trip.
Education; Fine Arts; History - United States
Dist - GPN **Prod** - MPBN 1983

Update - Diet, Nutrition and Cancer 52 MIN
VHS / 16mm
(C)
$385.00 purchase _ #850VI048
Reports recent findings on the relationship between nutrition and prevention of cancer and the growth of existing cancers.
Health and Safety
Dist - HSCIC **Prod** - HSCIC

Update Europe Series
Belgium's old industrial area 22 MIN
French Farmer 22 MIN
A Long Way Home 22 MIN
Norwegian Oil 25 MIN
Southern Italy 23 MIN
Dist - CORF

Update - hypertension 90061 37 MIN
U-matic
Color (PRO)
Discusses history, examination and laboratory evaluation of the hypertensive patient. Includes pharmacology and clinical guidelines.
Health and Safety; Science - Natural
Dist - AYERST **Prod** - AYERST

Update on hypnosis in psychiatry 60 MIN
U-matic / VHS
Hypnosis series

Color
Demonstrates how the hypnotic trance is an alerting rather than a sleep experience as Dr Herbert Spiegel clarifies major misconceptions about hypnosis and uses his method of self hypnosis to treat a patient with chronic head pain. Presents Dr Spiegel's theoretical views and his clinical technique of assessing a patient.
Health and Safety; Psychology
Dist - HEMUL **Prod** - HEMUL

Update on silent myocardial ischemia - Volume 10
VHS / 8mm cartridge
Cardiology video journal series
Color (PRO)
#FSR - 499
Presents a free - loan program, part of a series on cardiology, which trains medical professionals. Contact distributor for details.
Health and Safety
Dist - WYAYLA **Prod** - WYAYLA

Update on the homosexualities 60 MIN
U-matic / VHS
Color
Presents findings from the world's most comprehensive research on Homosexualities - A Study Of Diversity - which debunk many cultural sterotypes and myths related to homosexuals preying on children, being violence - prone, forfeiting their masculinity or feminity, or that they are pathological transvestites and transsexuals.
Health and Safety; Psychology; Sociology
Dist - HEMUL **Prod** - HEMUL

Update - the high cost of health care 30 MIN
U-matic
Adam Smith's money world series; 113
Color (A)
Attempts to demystify the world of money and break it down so that employees of a small business can understand and adjust to new social and economic trends. Reports on the major economic stories and discoveries of the day.
Business and Economics
Dist - PBS **Prod** - WNETTV 1985

Update - Topics of Current Concern Series
The Dance Critic's Role 30 MIN
Dancers' Changing Attitudes 30 MIN
Politics and the arts 30 MIN
Running a Dance Company 30 MIN
Dist - ARCVID

Updated Beef Cookery 15 MIN
U-matic / VHS
Color (IND)
Demonstrates importance of meat department personnel in having a complete knowledge of beef cookery. Covers six basic methods of beef cookery.
Business and Economics; Home Economics
Dist - NLSAMB **Prod** - NLSAMB

Upgrading and repairing your computer 57 MIN
VHS
Color (J H C G)
$29.95 purchase _ #MYR20001V
Shows how simple it is to upgrade a PC. Reveals that IBM - compatible computers are designed around a handful of plug - in modular components. Discloses that anyone who can use a screwdriver and has an hour to watch this video can gain the knowledge and confidence to replace computer components in just minutes. Covers removing the cover, video board, floppy drive, hard drive, power supply, modem, memory - motherboard and many other components.
Computer Science
Dist - CAMV

Upgrading and troubleshooting your PC 45 MIN
VHS
Computer training series
Color (G)
$24.95 purchase _ #CI02
Shows how to diagnose and repair a personal computer to cut repair bills and down time. Reveals how to extend a system's life or improve its performance with add - on or new components. Part of a six - part series explaining PCs and software. Includes booklet. Produced by M - USA.
Computer Science
Dist - SVIP

Upgrading Performance of Existing Bridge Rail Systems 18 MIN
U-matic / VHS / 16mm
Color (IND)
Discusses retrofit concepts for upgrading various types of deficient bridge rails to provide an improved vehicle - barrier interface.
Health and Safety; Industrial and Technical Education; Social Science
Dist - USNAC **Prod** - USDTFH 1983

Upgrading to DOS 5 60 MIN
VHS
PC video training for DOS series
Color (J H C G)
$29.95 purchase _ #GVS104V
Teaches students how to use DOS - Disk Operating System - without the confusion and frustration of a software training manual. Uses an interactive system which allows students to watch the video and practice at the same time at their computers. Shows how to upgrade to DOS 5. Demonstrates starting DOS 5 shell, working with files, creating directories, disk utilities, online help, and macros in Part 4 of a four - part series on DOS.
Computer Science
Dist - CAMV

Upgrading to DOS 5.0 58 MIN
VHS
Video professor operating systems series
Color (J H C G)
$29.95 purchase _ #VP151V
Shows how to upgrade a DOS sytem to DOS 5.0. Allows viewer to see the keyboard and the monitor simultaneously so that students can see the result of every keystroke. Part of a seven - part series on operating systems.
Computer Science
Dist - CAMV

Upgrading your kitchen 60 MIN
U-matic / VHS
Ortho's video series
Color (A)
$24.95 _ #OR105
Shows demonstrations of kitchen repairs and remodeling that the viewer can perform himself, such as installing new countertops, floors, lighting and others.
Industrial and Technical Education
Dist - AAVIM **Prod** - AAVIM

The Uphill Ride - a Shoplifting Fable 13 MIN
16mm
Color (P I)
LC 75-701610
Shows what happens when two boys decide to shoplift two new tires for their bikes. Shows that shoplifting can only have bad consequences.
Guidance and Counseling; Sociology
Dist - LAWREN **Prod** - GBHDTR 1974

Upholstering a dining room chair - box welted style, fabric to frame style 60 MIN
VHS / 16mm
(G)
$39.95 purchase _ #VT1036
Shows the proper way to upholster two different types of dining room chairs. Explains how to take off the old upholstering and how to measure, cut and attach the new upholstering. Taught by Bonnie Enault.
Home Economics
Dist - RMIBHF MOHOMV **Prod** - RMIBHF MOHOMV

Upholstering a Dining Room Chair - Standard Wraparound Seat Style 60 MIN
BETA / VHS
Color
Demonstrates how to upholster the standard wraparound seat style dining room chair. Shows a variety of fabrics and gives step - by - step instruction.
Home Economics
Dist - MOHOMV **Prod** - MOHOMV

Upjohn Company 19 MIN
16mm
Color
LC 73-700626
Traces the history of the Upjohn Company and provides an overall look at the operations of the company. Follows the development of a new medicine from discovery to usage.
Business and Economics; Health and Safety
Dist - UPJOHN **Prod** - UPJOHN 1972

Upjohn vanguard of medicine series
Anaerobic infections 20 MIN
Clinical applications of lasers 19 MIN
Cold - light endoscopy 21 MIN
Lillehei on Stagnant Shock 21 MIN
Locomotion of cancer cells in vivo compared with normal cells 21 MIN
Medical Potential of Lasers 21 MIN
Myocardial Revascularization - Vineberg Procedure 20 MIN
The Obsolete Menopause 18 MIN
Preparatory techniques for gravlee jet washer endometrial specimens 17 MIN
Pulmonary Complications in Shock 17 MIN
Technique of Intra - Articular and Peri - Articular Injection 20 MIN
Visceral Organ Transplants 30 MIN
X - Ray, Ultrasound and Thermography in Diagnosis 22 MIN
Dist - UPJOHN

Upon a coral reef - Belize, Hawaii, Sea of Cortez 30 MIN
VHS
Scuba World series
Color (G)
$24.90 purchase _ #0449
Visits a variety of reefs and the creatures who live there. Includes the reefs near Belize and Hawaii and in the Sea of Cortez.
Geography - World; Physical Education and Recreation
Dist - SEVVID

Upper Airway Infections 19 MIN
VHS / U-matic
Pediatric Emergency Management Series
Color
Discusses upper airway infections in children, including diagnosis, examination and management decisions and techniques.
Health and Safety
Dist - VTRI **Prod** - VTRI

The Upper Back 29 MIN
Videoreel / VT2
Maggie and the Beautiful Machine - Backs Series
Color
Physical Education and Recreation
Dist - PBS **Prod** - WGBHTV

Upper body beautiful 30 MIN
VHS
Esquire great body series
Color (H C A)
$19.99 purchase _ #EQGB03V
Presents the third of a nine - part exercise series oriented to women. Combines stretches and exercises designed for the upper body. Developed by Deborah Crocker.
Physical Education and Recreation; Science - Natural
Dist - CAMV

Upper Brainstem - Diencephalon and Midbrain Structures Bordering the Third Ventricle 29 MIN
U-matic
Dissection of the Brain Series
Color (C)
Demonstrates the divisions of the diencephalon along with the structures which can be seen related to the third ventricle.
Health and Safety; Science - Natural
Dist - UOKLAH **Prod** - UOKLAH 1978

The Upper Digestive Tract - Eating to Live 26 MIN
16mm / U-matic / VHS
Living Body - an Introduction to Human Biology Series
Color
Looks at appetite and hunger, and observes the actions of a salivary gland, the swallowing reflex, and the powerful churning of the stomach as food is broken down and processed.
Science - Natural
Dist - FOTH **Prod** - FOTH 1985

Upper elementary grades - Tape 3 23 MIN
VHS
Making meaning - integrated language arts series
Color (C A PRO)
$295.00 purchase, $125.00 rental _ #614 - 231X01
Emphasizes a whole - language approach to teaching reading, writing, speaking and listening skills in the classroom. Shows classes using whole - language principles in guided reading, journal keeping, oral presentations and other classroom activities emphasizing language arts skills. Includes teacher's guide and text.
Education; English Language
Dist - AFSCD

Upper Extremities Functional Range of Motion Series
Elbow, Forearm, and Wrist 11 MIN
Hand Measurement 9 MIN
Shoulder Joint 12 MIN
Dist - HSCIC

Upper Extremity - Clavicle 20 MIN
U-matic / VHS
Osteopathic Examination and Manipulation Series
Color (PRO)
Emphasizes some general considerations relating shoulder problems to the support features of spinal regions and the rib cage. Demonstrates application of direct principles in both articulatory and muscle energy techniques for manipulation in acromioclavicular and sternoclavicular dysfunctions.
Health and Safety; Science - Natural
Dist - MSU **Prod** - MSU

Upper Extremity Muscle Testing 30 MIN
U-matic / VHS
Color; Mono (C A)
Illustrates motion testing of the scapula, shoulder, elbow, forearm, wrist and hand. Discusses how to evaluate against gravity and when gravity is eliminated.
Health and Safety
Dist - BUSARG **Prod** - ANDSRC 1985

Upper Extremity Nerve Blocks 14 MIN
U-matic / VHS
Anesthesiology Clerkship Series
Color (PRO)
Covers the selection of candidates for upper extremity regional anesthesia. Describes the anatomy of the axillary area, with special emphasis upon locating the bronchial plexus. Describes and demonstrates the administration of an axillary block. Shows indications for and techniques of intravenous regional administration.
Health and Safety
Dist - UMICHM **Prod** - UMICHM 1982

Upper extremity prosthetic options for kids below elbow 25 MIN
VHS
Color (G PRO)
$35.00 purchase
Teaches parents and health care professionals about prosthetic options for children with congenital deficiencies or amputations.
Health and Safety; Sociology
Dist - RICHGO **Prod** - RICHGO 1992

Upper extremity prosthetic principles - Pt 1 23 MIN
16mm
Color
Presents highlights of prescription, fabrication, fitting and harnessing, including the criteria for acceptance of artificial arms. Emphasizes the importance of teamwork, shows preprosthetic and prosthetic training activities and describes modern devices and appliances.
Health and Safety
Dist - USVA **Prod** - USVA 1952

Upper extremity prosthetic principles - Pt 2 29 MIN
16mm
Color
LC FIE56-35
Shows examples of research efforts resulting in a body of prosthetic principles leading to better artificial arms. Describes the functions lost at different levels of amputation and of the principles involved in their prosthetic restoration.
Health and Safety
Dist - USVA **Prod** - USVA 1955

Upper Gastrointestinal Examination 12 MIN
U-matic / VHS
Color (PRO)
Gives basic information about upper GI exam. Defines terms the patient needs to know. Explains what happens during and after exam.
Health and Safety; Science - Natural
Dist - HSCIC **Prod** - HSCIC 1983

Upper GI
U-matic / VHS
X - Ray Procedures in Layman's Terms Series
Color
Health and Safety; Science
Dist - FAIRGH **Prod** - FAIRGH

Upper GI Endoscopy
VHS / U-matic
Color (SPANISH ARABIC)
Describes how the endoscopic procedure is used to identify and diagnose common problems in the upper digestive tract.
Foreign Language; Science - Natural
Dist - MIFE **Prod** - MIFE

The Upper Mississippi - Mark Twain's river 55 MIN
VHS
On the waterways series
Color (G H)
$29.95 purchase _ #OW04
Travels with the crew of the Driftwood to follow the Mississippi from its origin as a stream in the backwoods of Minnesota. Narrated by Jason Robards. Part of a 13 - part series on the history, geography, culture and ecology of North American waterways.
Social Science
Dist - SVIP

Upper Reaches 29 MIN
VHS / 16mm
A Different Understanding Series
Color (G)
$90.00 purchase _ #BPN178003
Presents Terry, a teenage boy whose parents are divorced. Shows how he views his parents and the demands their divorce places on him.
Sociology
Dist - RMIBHF **Prod** - RMIBHF

Upper Reaches 30 MIN
U-matic
A Different Understanding Series
Color (PRO)
Reveals the problems of a boy whose parents are divorced and the demands of his lonely mother and his guilt ridden father.
Sociology
Dist - TVOTAR **Prod** - TVOTAR 1985

The Upper Room 15 MIN
16mm
Living Bible Series
Color; B&W (I)
Jesus washes the disciples' feet after the paschal meal in the upper room. He announces that one of them will betray him. Jesus takes the bread and the wine, passes them to the disciples and offers the benediction.
Religion and Philosophy
Dist - FAMF **Prod** - FAMF

An upper room and a garden and Jesus' trial - Part 5 60 MIN
VHS
Jesus the Christ series
Color (I J H C G A R)
$14.95 purchase _ #35 - 87575 - 2086
Presents accounts of Jesus' life from the Living Bible. 'An Upper Room and a Garden' centers around Jesus' prediction that one of the disciples would betray him, while 'Jesus' Trial' considers the implications of Jesus as 'King of the Jews.'
Literature and Drama; Religion and Philosophy
Dist - APH **Prod** - VANGU

The Upper south 25 MIN
U-matic / VHS / 16mm
United States geography series
Color (I J)
Visits the states of North Carolina, Virginia, West Virginia, Kentucky and Tennessee - an area that is rich in history and mines coal, harnesses rivers, raises horses and weaves textiles.
Geography - United States
Dist - NGS **Prod** - NGS 1983

Uppers, downers, all arounders - Part 1 30 MIN
VHS
Color (J H C G A) (SPANISH)
$79.95 purchase _ #AH45504
Describes how and why psychoactive drugs affect the brain. Gives an overview of the types of drugs. Examines levels of drug - seeking behavior. Available in Spanish - language version only.
Guidance and Counseling; Health and Safety; Psychology; Sociology
Dist - HTHED **Prod** - HTHED

Uppers, downers, all arounders - Part 2 30 MIN
VHS
Color (J H C G A) (SPANISH)
$79.95 purchase _ #AH45505
Portrays the most commonly used psychoactive drugs. Describes how the drugs are absorbed and metabolized. Available in Spanish - language version only.
Guidance and Counseling; Health and Safety; Psychology; Sociology
Dist - HTHED **Prod** - HTHED

Uppers, downers, all arounders - Pt 1 - the effects 30 MIN
16mm
Color
Examines how and why the physical and emotional centers of the brain are affected by psychoactive drugs. Gives a general classification of the drugs, which are stimulants, depressants and psychedelics. Looks at the various levels of drug seeking behavior. Safety Psychology.
Health and Safety; Psychology; Sociology
Dist - CNMD **Prod** - CNMD 1984

Uppers, downers, all arounders series
Presents two parts on psychoactive drugs. Includes the titles The Effects and The Drugs.

The Drugs - Part II	30 MIN
The Effects - Part I	30 MIN
Uppers, downers, all arounders series	60 MIN

Dist - FMSP

The Upperville Show 9 MIN
16mm / U-matic
American Traditional Culture Series
Color (P A)
LC 70-712026
Presents a documentary of the oldest horse show in America in Upperville, Virginia. Views pedigreed people and thoroughbred horses in a spring festival.
Geography - United States; Physical Education and Recreation
Dist - DAVT **Prod** - DAVT 1971

Upright man - Pt 26 30 MIN
16mm
Life on Earth series; Vol VII
Color (J)
$495.00 purchase _ #865 - 9047
Blends scientific data with breathtaking wildlife photography to tell the story of the development of life. Features wildlife expert David Attenborough as host. Part 26 of 27 parts is entitled 'Upright Man.'
Science; Science - Natural; Science - Physical
Dist - FI **Prod** - BBCTV 1981

The Uprising 96 MIN
VHS / 35mm / 16mm
Color (G) (SPANISH WITH ENGLISH SUBTITLES)
$200.00, $250.00 rental
Portrays Augustin, a soldier in Somoza's national guard in Nicaragua, who slowly turns to the revolutionary cause. Probes the forces contributing to individual and social change.
History - World
Dist - KINOIC

The Uprooted 48 MIN
16mm
Roots series; 07
Color (J)
Tells how Kizzy's happiness at being in love with handsome young Noah is shattered when Noah is captured during an escape attempt and implicates her as well. Shows Kizzy and Noah being sold to the evil Tom Moore, who later rapes Kizzy, and depicts Kizzy's pledge that she will have a son who will grow up and exact vengeance on her new owner.
Fine Arts; History - United States
Dist - FI **Prod** - WOLPER

The Uprooted 33 MIN
U-matic
Color
Presents the story of the Salvation Army refugee and relief operations in Uganda, Zambia, Thailand and Hong Kong. Filmed on location.
Civics and Political Systems; Sociology
Dist - MTP **Prod** - SALVA

Uprooted - a Japanese - American family's experience 29 MIN
16mm / VHS
B&W (G)
$375.00, $35.00 purchase
Uses family album photographs and home movie footage, preserving the original shooting style and providing a visual context for the chronology of the internment of a Japanese - American family in a concentration camp during World War II. Includes scenes of the family's prosperous California lifestyle prior to World War II, including their citrus nursery business, film footage of concentration camp activities, the return train trip and the family's destroyed property. Interviews one member of the family over 30 years later.
History - United States; Sociology
Dist - SUMAI **Prod** - RUNDS 1976

Uprooted - children in foster care 29 MIN
VHS / 16mm
A Different understanding series
Color (G)
$90.00 purchase _ #BPN178011
Examines the issues involved when a child must be removed from his or her natural parents. Includes interviews with foster children, a natural mother, foster parents, and experts.
Sociology
Dist - RMIBHF **Prod** - RMIBHF
TVOTAR TVOTAR

The Ups and Downs of Highs and Lows 29 MIN
Videoreel / VT2
Weather Series
Color
Features meteorologist Frank Sechrist explaining that the forces which affect weather are pressure gradient force, Coriolis effect and friction. Includes a look at a synoptic weather chart, isobars and the weatherman when he is drawing all those highs and lows.
Science - Physical
Dist - PBS **Prod** - WHATV

Ups and downs of pH 16 MIN
BETA / VHS / U-matic
Acid base balance series
Color (C PRO)
$280.00 purchase _ #605.1
Uses animation, graphics and clinical footage to explain principles of acids, bases and buffers. Discusses the topics of ionization of water into hydrogen and hydroxyl ions, the definition of acid, base and neutral, the pH scale and its interpretation, pH limits for survival, cell shifts with other cations and buffer systems, bicarbonate in particular. Produced by Golden West College.

Health and Safety
Dist - CONMED

Ups - Downs 24 MIN
16mm / U-matic / VHS
Drug Abuse Education Series
Color (J H C)
Defines uppers and downers as types of drugs and tells about their effects and available cures.
Health and Safety; Sociology
Dist - EBEC **Prod** - CONCPT 1971

Upstairs downstairs 60 MIN
VHS
Learning in America series
Color; Captioned (G)
$49.95 purchase _ #LEIA - 102
Shows that some experts believe the American educational system is becoming divided into well - funded and poorly - funded schools. Suggests that children born into poverty are more likely to fail. Examines programs that are attempting to change matters. Hosted by Roger Mudd.
Education
Dist - PBS **Prod** - WETATV 1989

Upstairs, Downstairs at the Times 25 MIN
BETA / 16mm / VHS
Color
LC 77-702531
Profiles Lord Roy Thompson of Fleet, who entered a newspaper office at age 50 and aspires to become a billionaire through the acquisition of hundreds of companies and some 192 newspapers, including the London Times.
Biography; Social Science
Dist - CTV **Prod** - CTV 1976

The Upstairs Room
35mm strip / VHS / Cassette
Newbery Award - Winners Series
Color (I)
$66.00, $14.00 purchase
English Language; Literature and Drama
Dist - PELLER

The Upstairs Room 15 MIN
U-matic / VHS
Best of Cover to Cover 2 Series
Color (I)
Literature and Drama
Dist - WETATV **Prod** - WETATV

Upstream, downstream - River Wye, Wales 24 MIN
VHS / 16mm
Amateur naturalist series
Color (I J H C G)
$495.00, $195.00 purchase
Journeys down the River Wye in Wales to discover a wealth of tiny invertebrates, water birds and polecats and to learn the right way to collect live fish for observation. Encounters pike, mink and otter downstream. Part of a 13 - part series featuring a naturalist and a zoologist, Gerald and Lee Durrell, on field trips to different habitats.
Geography - World; Science - Natural
Dist - LANDMK **Prod** - LANDMK 1988

Uptake and Distribution of Inhalation Anesthetic Agents 23 MIN
VHS / U-matic
Anesthesiology Clerkship Series
Color (PRO)
Describes the pharmacodynamics of administration of inhalation anesthetic agents. Covers factors influencing the alveolar anesthetic tension. Discusses the influence of the anesthetic system and various physiologic abnormalities on the development of the anesthetic state.
Health and Safety
Dist - UMICHM **Prod** - UMICHM 1982

Upton Sinclair 30 MIN
16mm
Sum and Substance Series
B&W (H)
LC FIA67-5102
Upton Sinclair, author, socialist and reformer, expresses his desire for social justice and recalls his efforts to achieve industrial democracy, stressing his contact with the Henry Ford Empire. (Kinescope).
Biography; Civics and Political Systems; Literature and Drama
Dist - MLA **Prod** - MLA 1964

The Upturned Face 9 MIN
16mm / U-matic / VHS
Color
LC 73-702387
Presents an adaptation of the short story 'THE UPTURNED FACE' by Stephen Crane which treats death with relentless honesty, protesting angrily against dying.
Literature and Drama; Sociology
Dist - PFP **Prod** - CHGLNG 1973

Upwardly Mobile 14 MIN
VHS / U-matic
Color
Explores the effects of architecture and construction on urban living. Uses visual information juxtaposed against an operatic soundtrack. An experimental film.
Fine Arts; Sociology
Dist - MEDIPR **Prod** - MEDIPR 1982

The Upwelling Phenomenon 15 MIN
16mm
Science in Action Series
Color (C)
Deals with studies of upwelling, an ocean process that covers only a thousandth of the sea surface, yet provides more than half of mankind's seafood.
Science; Science - Natural; Science - Physical
Dist - COUNFI **Prod** - ALLFP

Upwind sailing
VHS
Color (G A)
$48.00 purchase _ #0733
Teaches upwind sailing techniques for intermediate to advanced racers. Includes sail trim, shifting gears, and tacking. Includes graphics. Produced by J - World.
Physical Education and Recreation
Dist - SEVVID

Uranium 48 MIN
16mm / VHS
Color (H C G)
$750.00, $285.00 purchase, $75.00 rental
Takes a devastating look at the consequences of uranium mining. Shows how the toxic and radioactive waste of mining produces long - term environmental hazards for miners and indigenous populations whose lands have an abundance of uranium. Exposes how societal need for resources causes the trampling of native people's rights without regard for their traditional economic and spiritual way of life. Filmed in Canada by Magnus Isacsson and narrated by Buffy Sainte - Marie.
Fine Arts; Social Science
Dist - CANCIN **Prod** - NFBC 1991

The Uranium Factor - the Safety for Miners of Nuclear Fuel 48 MIN
VHS
Color
From the ABC TV program, Close Up.
Health and Safety
Dist - ABCLR **Prod** - ABCLR 1980

Uranus 29 MIN
VHS
Color (J)
$29.95 purchase _ #ES 8340
Explores Uranus, the planet which remained a mystery for centuries at the outer reaches of the solar system. Uses data from Voyager 2 to reveal a world with a surface temperature of 300 degrees below zero and surrounded by a halo of ultra - violet light. Looks at the geology, weather, moons and magnetic fields.
History - World; Industrial and Technical Education; Science - Physical
Dist - SCTRES **Prod** - SCTRES

Uranus, Neptune, and Pluto 29 MIN
U-matic
Project Universe - Astronomy Series Lesson 12
Color (C A)
Recounts circumstances leading to discovery of Uranus, Neptune and Pluto. Describes general physical characteristics of Uranus and Neptune.
Science - Physical
Dist - CDTEL **Prod** - COAST

Urashima Taro 12 MIN
VHS / U-matic / 16mm
Color (K P I)
$260.00, $210.00, $180.00 purchase _ #B340
Adapts in animated form an ancient Japanese folk tale. Tells of Urashima Taro, a poor, young but kindhearted fisherman. After he saves a small sea turtle's life he is taken to a kingdom under the sea. He visits for three days and is given a small box - which he is told never to open. When Urashima returns home, he finds that he has been gone for 300 years. Thinking the box may hold an answer, he opens it and suddenly becomes a very old man.
Fine Arts; Geography - World; Literature and Drama
Dist - BARR **Prod** - OKEYA 1982

Urban Alternatives 19 MIN
U-matic / VHS / 16mm
Color (J)
LC 73-701802
Explores examples of what has been done to solve some of our urban problems and make our cities an environment for people to use and enjoy. Features planners who work as urban environmentalists who discuss the alternatives and their philosophy of what a city can and should be.
Science - Natural; Social Science; Sociology
Dist - BARR **Prod** - BARR 1973

The Urban Campus 28 MIN
16mm
Color
Presents University of Pittsburgh Chancellor Wesley Posvar discussing the role of the university in a large metropolitan area with several faculty members. Interviews two students who discuss the role of higher education in their lives.
Education
Dist - UPITTS **Prod** - UPITTS 1973

Urban Change and Conflict Series
City centre developments - who decides 45 MIN
The Historic Legacy - Capital and Urbanization 45 MIN
Housing and the Market 45 MIN
Images of Cities 45 MIN
Industrial Dereliction 45 MIN
People into Politics 45 MIN
State Intervention in Cities 45 MIN
Urban - Rural Relationships 45 MIN
Dist - ACCESS

Urban Combat 50 MIN
16mm / U-matic
Assignment Maclear Series
Color; Mono (J H C A)
$500.00 film, $350.00 video, $50.00 rental
Features a look into the investigative techniques used in homocide cases as well as a report on gun control in the urban centers of America and its possible effects on Canadians and their crime management.
Sociology
Dist - CTV **Prod** - CTV 1977

Urban Crisis Series
Bomb threat - plan, don't panic 15 MIN
The Bunco boys - and how to beat them 21 MIN
Cool plates - hot car 19 MIN
Highfire - Plan for Survival 19 MIN
Instant Arson - Testing Fire Bombs and Incendiaries 12 MIN
Kidnap - Executive Style 25 MIN
My Dad's a Cop 18 MIN
Senior Power and How to Use it 19 MIN
Vehicle Under Attack - Officer Survival of Incendiary Ambush 15 MIN
Dist - BROSEB

Urban Development, Urban Climate 15 MIN
16mm
Color (H C A)
Discusses how the city managers of Stuttgart improved airflow and temperature for residents, with low - budget do - it - yourself methods including how to reduce heat from city parking lots to building codes which increase the flow of cool air through the city.
History - World; Sociology
Dist - WSTGLC **Prod** - WSTGLC

The Urban dilemma 30 MIN
VHS
Global links series
Color (G)
$39.95 purchase _ #GLLI - 106
Discusses the problems of overpopulation in Third World cities such as Shanghai, China and Sao Paulo, Brazil. Reveals that overpopulation places heavy strains on public services. Explores possible solutions.
Social Science; Sociology
Dist - PBS **Prod** - WETATV 1987

Urban ecology 24 MIN
VHS
Color (G C)
$149.00 purchase _ #EX2344
Examines the changing urban ecology of Abidjan, the capital of the Ivory Coast.
Fine Arts; History - World; Science - Natural; Sociology
Dist - FOTH

Urban Ecology - Garbage Disposal 7 MIN
U-matic / VHS / 16mm
Color (I J)
LC 76-713133
Explains that trash forms blemishes on the landscape and that Americans must constantly look for ways to reduce the total amount of trash.
Science - Natural
Dist - PHENIX **Prod** - COLLRD 1971

The Urban Experience 29 MIN
Videoreel / VT2
Black Experience Series
Color
History - United States; Sociology
Dist - PBS **Prod** - WTTWTV

Urban focus series
Ask my name 15 MIN
Generations 30 MIN
An Imaginary they 22 MIN

My City 22 MIN
Dist - MLA

Urban Impact on Weather and Climate 16 MIN
U-matic / VHS / 16mm
Captioned; Color (J)
Shows how weather and climate can be affected by the concentration of large buildings in urban environments.
Science - Physical; Sociology
Dist - LCOA **Prod** - LCOA 1972

Urban Impact on Weather and Climate 16 MIN
U-matic / VHS / 16mm
Environmental Sciences Series
Color (J H)
LC 73-710054
Presents a range of recent meteorological findings on the effects cities have on weather and climate causes and suggests possible solutions.
Science - Physical; Sociology
Dist - LCOA **Prod** - LCOA 1971

Urban Indians 20 MIN
U-matic / VHS
Color
Explores the problems of American Indians living in cities. Reveals the disorientation and confusion which may be experienced by Indians who leave the reservation. Portrays a member of the Oglala Sioux tribe as he struggles to overcome the drug and alcohol abuse which had comforted him.
Social Science; Sociology
Dist - DCTVC **Prod** - DCTVC

Urban landscape 25 MIN
VHS
Exploring photography series
Color (A)
PdS65 purchase
Describes how photographers record the environment in which people live. Includes interviews with Chris Killip and Joel Meyerwitz. Explores the creative possibilities of still photography. Covers the major topics of interest to any photographer. Part of a six-part series hosted by Bryn Campbell.
Fine Arts; Industrial and Technical Education
Dist - BBCENE

Urban Life in Modern China 7 MIN
VHS / 35mm strip / U-matic
Modern China Series
Color; Sound
$25 each color sound filmstrip, $115 filmstrip series, $115 five
Explores the changes taking place in China, especially in Shanghai and Beijing. Focuses on daily urban life, and highlights the kinds of goods and services available and the balance between government and private enterprise.
Geography - World; History - World; Sociology
Dist - IFB

The Urban Maes Amputation for Peripheral Vascular Disease 12 MIN
16mm
Color
Demonstrates the advantages in the Urban Maes technique of below - the - knee amputation in diseases of compromised circulation. Shows the operative technique from initial incision to final stump closure and the healed stump with range of motion some weeks later. Presents several other patients who have been handled in a similar manner, with views of their stumps, ambulatory on pylon temporary and final prosthesis.
Health and Safety; Science - Natural
Dist - USVA **Prod** - USVA 1956

Urban Patterns 16 MIN
16mm
Color (H C A)
Traces the development of urban systems, past and present, and examines the dominance of a city over its surrounding area.
Geography - World; Sociology
Dist - SF **Prod** - ANAIB 1971

Urban Peasants 60 MIN
16mm
B&W (C)
$1124.00
Experimental film by Ken Jacobs.
Fine Arts
Dist - AFA **Prod** - AFA 1976

Urban phytonarian
CD-ROM
(G A PRO)
$149.00 purchase _ #1943
Offers an electronic, multimedia database on trees, turf, flowers, shrubs and other flora that flourish in urban environments. For IBM PC and compatibles. Requires 640K RAM, DOS Version 3.1 or greater, one floppy disk drive - a hard drive is recommended, one empty expansion slot, and an IBM compatible CD - ROM drive.
Agriculture
Dist - BEP

The Urban phytonian handbook
CD-ROM
(G PRO)
$149.00 purchase
Reprints on CD - ROM 'The Urban Phytonian Handbook' published by the University of Wisconsin - Extension Service. Covers over 100 plant disorders in black - and - white and VGA color images. Includes categories such as pesticides, soil insects, diseases, weeds, veterbrate pests.
Agriculture; Science - Natural
Dist - QUANTA **Prod** - QUANTA

Urban Problems 30 MIN
U-matic / VHS
Focus on Society Series
Color (C)
Discusses historical and contemporary urban problems and issues.
Sociology
Dist - DALCCD **Prod** - DALCCD

Urban Renewal in Scotland and Canada - Regions - 1 30 MIN
VHS
Common Issues in World Regions Series
Color (J)
$180.00 purchase
Looks at families in Glasgow, Scotland, and Toronto, Ontario, adjusting to changes caused by urban renewal. Develops international understanding and geographic literacy for today's students growing up in a global community.
Geography - World; Sociology
Dist - AITECH **Prod** - AITECH 1991

Urban - Rural Relationships 45 MIN
U-matic
Urban Change and Conflict Series
Color (H C A)
Explores the regional context of cities and how they relate to the land and examines the surrounding rural communities for contrast and comparison.
Sociology
Dist - ACCESS **Prod** - BBCTV 1983

Urban Sprawl 22 MIN
16mm
Color
Points out that urban sprawl is no accident and describes the great economic pressures that cause today's zoning system to break down. Explains that what is needed is a new system which can protect natural resources and yet produce quality urban communities free from blight.
Business and Economics; Science - Natural; Sociology
Dist - FINLYS **Prod** - FINLYS

Urban Sprawl Vs Planned Growth 22 MIN
16mm
Color (J)
LC 71-702627
Shows how new techniques of planning can promote orderly growth and development, thereby counteracting the natural tendency of urban sprawl which ultimately creates blighted communities. Includes scenes of the upper east branch of Brandywine Creek near Philadelphia, Pennsylvania.
Psychology; Sociology
Dist - FINLYS **Prod** - FINLYS 1968

The Urban Structure 30 MIN
VHS / U-matic
Designing the Environment Series
Color
Explores the problems facing the architect as he designs the urban community of the future.
Fine Arts; Science - Natural; Sociology
Dist - NETCHE **Prod** - NETCHE 1971

Urban studies series
Aspects of central place 20 MIN
Central City 20 MIN
The developing city 20 MIN
Dist - FOTH

Urban Turf
VHS
Is Anyone Listening - a Documentary Series
$89.95 purchase _ #ULUT
Uses interviews with gang members to analyze the street gang problem and investigates alternatives and solutions.
Psychology; Sociology
Dist - CAREER **Prod** - CAREER

Urban turf - a focus on street gangs 26 MIN
VHS
Color (J H)
$95.00 purchase _ #133VG
Documents the street gangs and problems in Chicago, Milwaukee, Los Angeles and Philadelphia. Interviews typical gang members to help the viewers understand why teens get involved with gangs. Shows how gangs have become a family for many adolescents, and may lead to crime and drugs. Offers alternatives and possible solutions as a basis for discussion. Includes a leader's guide.
Sociology
Dist - UNL

Urban Universities and their Responsibilities 29 MIN
Videoreel / VT2
University of Chicago Round Table Series
Color
Education; Sociology
Dist - PBS **Prod** - WTTWTV

Urban Wilderness 30 MIN
U-matic
Sport Fishing Series
Color (G)
Visits some Algonquin Park lakes in quest of brook trout and smallmouth bass.
Physical Education and Recreation
Dist - TVOTAR **Prod** - TVOTAR 1985

The Urbanite 22 MIN
U-matic
Color (A)
Discusses the urban experience and the need for local political and planning control. Cites advantages of heterogeneity, cultural diversity and the variety of social worlds that exist in urban environment.
Social Science; Sociology
Dist - SLDTRS **Prod** - SLDTRS 1980

Urbicide - A Sarajevo diary 50 MIN
VHS
Color (G)
$390.00 purchase, $75.00 rental
Reveals that the bloody Bosnian war runs much deeper than an ethnic conflict between Muslims, Serbs and Croats. Explains that the combatants are besieged supporters of an integrated and multicultural society set against groups that espouse ethnic nationalisms and the racism and fascism such nationalism manfests. Gives a personal account of Bill Tribe, a Sarajevo refugee, former professor and translator, as he returns to the city. Illustrates Sarajevo's devastation and its human toll as he wanders among ravaged landmarks and into the homes of various people, whose stories reveal that the city is under attack because its existence is a threat to the modern day fascists who act under the pretense of ethnic nationalism. Produced by Dom Rotheroe.
Civics and Political Systems; Fine Arts; History - World; Sociology
Dist - FIRS

Urbs Mea 11 MIN
16mm
Color (H) (LATIN)
LC FIA65-292
A classical Latin language film. Adapted from 'Roman Life in Ancient Pompeii.' Describes the economic, social, political and cultural life of the Romans who lived in ancient Pompeii. Shows scenes of the ruins of Pompeii, destroyed by Vesuvius. Tours the streets, homes, shops, temples and theatre of Pompeii.
Foreign Language
Dist - SUTHLA **Prod** - SUTHLA 1963

Ureter Bladder Uretra 26 MIN
VHS / 16mm
Histology review series; Unit XI
(C)
$330.00 purchase _ #821VI051
Covers the major structural and functional characteristics of the ureter, urinary bladder, and uretra. Identifies the major histological features of the urinary passageways. Characterizes the process involved in urine transport. Part 2 of the Urinary System Unit.
Health and Safety
Dist - HSCIC **Prod** - HSCIC 1983

The Ureter in Colon Surgery 19 MIN
16mm
Color (PRO)
Explains that exposure and identification of the ureter is the only sure way of preventing injury to it during resection of the colon. Demonstrates the exposure and preservation of the ureter in surgery of the colon.
Health and Safety; Science
Dist - ACY **Prod** - ACYDGD 1959

Ureteral Injury 35 MIN
16mm
Color (PRO)
Demonstrates the operative management of surgical ureteral injuries. Demonstrates techniques for use during operation, convalescence or in a remotely post - operative period.

Health and Safety; Science
Dist - ACY Prod - ACYDGD 1960

Ureteral Peristaltic Activity 21 MIN
16mm
Color
LC 71-705708
Demonstrates peristaltic activity in the ureter of both humans and dogs. Shows unobstructed and obstructed urine flow in the ureter and the inability of the ureter to transport urine against gravity.
Science - Natural
Dist - EATONL **Prod** - EATONL 1969

Ureteral Re - Implantation and Bladder Neck Revision 20 MIN
16mm
Color (PRO)
LC FIA66-76
Demonstrates the surgical procedure for ureteral reimplantation and bladder neck revision as it is performed transvesically. Includes a detailed step - by - step illustration of technique and prognosis and demonstrates ureteral reflux by cineradiography.
Health and Safety
Dist - EATON **Prod** - EATON 1962

Uretero - Arachnoid Anastomosis in Treatment of Hydrocephalus 18 MIN
16mm
Color (PRO)
Shows the operative technique for shunting spinal fluid from the lumbar sub - arachnoid space into the ureter by means of a plastic catheter in the treatment of hydrocephalus.
Health and Safety; Science
Dist - ACY **Prod** - ACYDGD 1950

Uretero - Ileo - Neocystostomy 15 MIN
16mm
Color
Demonstrates criteria for using a segment of the ileum as a replacement of the ureter and discusses the operative technique in two patients. Includes follow - up sequences.
Health and Safety; Science
Dist - EATONL **Prod** - EATONL 1964

Uretero - Ileo - Urethral Anastomosis - a Bladder Substitute 18 MIN
16mm
Color
Explains that uretero - ileo - urethral anastomosis is a method of urinary diversion which may be used following total cystectomy, that this technique substitutes a segment of ileum for the normal bladder and that to this ileum are anastomosed both ureters and urethra, allowing both urinary continence and relatively normal voiding through the normal channel.
Health and Safety; Science - Natural
Dist - USVA **Prod** - USVA 1959

Uretero - Ureteral Anastamosis 20 MIN
16mm
Surgical Correction of Hydronephrosis, Pt 2 - Dismembering 'Procedures Series
Color
Explains that, at the time of birth, this patient was found to have a mass in the right flank and a positive diagnosis of a marked hydronephrosis in a solitary kidney was made by the introduction of x - ray media through a silastic tube that was introduced into the umbilical vein. Shows that the side - to - side anastomosis was the procedure of choice and was extremely successful.
Science
Dist - EATONL **Prod** - EATONL 1968

Uretero - Ureteral Anastomosis 20 MIN
16mm
Color (PRO)
LC FIA68-856
Dr W R Smart discusses uretero - ureteral anastomosis and its nature, ethiology and surgical repair.
Health and Safety; Science - Natural
Dist - EATONL **Prod** - EATONL 1968

Ureteroscopic management of difficult ureteral calculi 18 MIN
VHS / U-matic
Color (PRO C)
$395.00 purchase, $80.00 rental _ #C891 - VI - 027
Uses videotape filmed through a ureteroscope in two clinical cases to demonstrate the procedure for ureteroscopic extraction of kidney stones. Reveals that the two cases - steinstrasse and impacted stones - are examples of types in which ureteroscopic extraction is the treatment of choice. Presented by Dr Jeffry L Huffman.
Health and Safety; Science - Natural
Dist - HSCIC

Ureterosigmoidostomy and Closure of Exstrophy of the Urinary Bladder 20 MIN
16mm
Color (PRO)
LC 75-702239
Shows the authors' technique of open transcolonic ureterosigmoidostomy for urinary diversion performed on a five - year - old boy with typical exstrophy of the urinary bladder and associated epispadias as well as a large right inguinal hernia.
Health and Safety; Science; Science - Natural
Dist - EATONL **Prod** - EATONL 1974

Urethral Catherization of Male and Female 17 MIN
16mm
Color (PRO)
LC FIA66-77
Discusses the various purposes for, and methods of urethral catheterization and the various types of catheters. Illustrates the exact procedures for catheterization in both the male and female patient.
Health and Safety
Dist - EATON **Prod** - EATON 1964

Urethral Catheterization 22 MIN
16mm
Color (PRO)
Explains that urethral catheterization represents the major hospital - borne infection. Demonstrates catheterization in its relationship to anatomy and bacteriology. Shows how these techniques can significantly reduce the incidence of infection.
Health and Safety; Science
Dist - ACY **Prod** - ACYDGD 1969

Urethral Catheterization 9 MIN
U-matic / VHS
Medical Skills Films Series
Color (PRO)
Health and Safety
Dist - WFP **Prod** - WFP

Urethral catheterization - intermittent and continuous 35 MIN
VHS / U-matic
Understanding and treating incontinence series
Color (PRO C)
$395.00 purchase, $80.00 rental _ #C891 - VI - 009
Presents indications for urinary catheterization and differentiation between continuous indwelling and intermittent catheterization. Covers type of patient, techniques, equipment, risks and benefits, typical microorganisms causing infection and methods for avoiding or resolving complications. Uses several case studies - a 50 - year - old woman with MS for 12 years who desires intermittant catheterization, a 78 - year - old woman with dementia who requires an indwelling catheter which will stay in place for four weeks at a time. Demonstrates catheterization in a male patient. Part of a seven - part series on incontinence presented by J C Brocklehurst and Bernadette M Ryan - Wooley.
Health and Safety; Science - Natural
Dist - HSCIC

Urethral Meatoplasty 10 MIN
16mm
Color
LC 75-702299
Illustrates an operative procedure used to permanently enlarge the urethral meatus in over 800 female patients. Discusses the symptoms associated with urethral disease based on statistics from questionnaires returned by 500 post - operative patients.
Health and Safety; Science
Dist - EATONL **Prod** - EATONL 1964

Urethral Strictures 49 MIN
16mm
Visits in Urology Series
Color (PRO)
LC 75-702669
Presents through a lecture, preoperative and postoperative review and operative techniques, the author's concept in the diagnosis and treatment of urethral strictures.
Health and Safety; Science; Science - Natural
Dist - EATONL **Prod** - EATONL 1975

Urethral Suspension using Stainless Steel Staples 20 MIN
16mm
Color
LC 75-702289
Describes a simple method of urethral suspension for urinary stress incontinence. Shows how, using the vaginal approach, the fibrous tissue on each side of the upper urethra is stapled to the posterior pubic bone, thus elevating the bladder neck. Explains that this operation has been most frequently performed for recurrent urinary stress incontinence and has been well - tolerated by the patients.
Science
Dist - EATONL **Prod** - EATONL 1969

Urethrolysis in Girls and Urethroplasty in Women 15 MIN
16mm
Color
LC 75-702290
Explains that urethroplasty is a surgical procedure in correction of a stricture of the distal segment of the urethra by lysis in girls and excision of posterior periurethral corrective tissues in women. Shows the external and internal sphincters and their relationship to the distal urethral segment. Presents surgical technique and case histories.
Science
Dist - EATONL **Prod** - EATONL 1969

Urethroplasty - Repair of the Recurrent Penile Fistula 10 MIN
16mm
Color
LC 75-702280
Presents a two - stage procedure to compensate for the excessive scarring and poor local vascular supply that follows a primary or secondary repair of a recurrent fistula of the anterior urethra. Presents a graphic illustration of the technique which utilizes the basic principles of the Cecil and Denis - Browne recommendations.
Science
Dist - EATONL **Prod** - EATONL 1969

Ureto - Ileo - Neocyctostomy 15 MIN
16mm
Color (PRO)
LC FIA66-75
Defines the rationale for using segment of the ileum as a replacement for the ureter. Demonstrates the surgical procedure in 62 year - old female patient with a bilateral ureteral occlusion due to late radiation changes with no evidence of residual carcinoma of the cervix.
Health and Safety
Dist - EATON **Prod** - EATON 1962

Urge to Build 27 MIN
16mm
Color (H C A)
Tells about ordinary people who have decided to take the risk of planning and building their own homes.
Industrial and Technical Education; Social Science; Sociology
Dist - DIRECT **Prod** - HOOVJ 1981

The Urgency
VHS
Color (H C A R)
$12.50 purchase _ #S11768
Discusses the pastoral ministry of the Lutheran Church - Missouri Synod. Targeted to LCMS men who are considering the pastoral ministry as a career.
Guidance and Counseling; Religion and Philosophy
Dist - CPH **Prod** - LUMIS

Urgent Message 5 MIN
16mm
Color
LC 74-702772
Shows stockpiles of weapons in order to promote an anti - bomb message.
Civics and Political Systems; Sociology
Dist - CANFDC **Prod** - UTORMC 1973

Urgent Messages 22 MIN
U-matic / VHS / 16mm
Color (H C A)
Dispels the myths and taboos surrounding teenage suicide. Introduced by Patty Duke - Astin, this film makes the point that the two leading causes of adolescent deaths, auto accidents and suicide, may be one and the same.
Sociology
Dist - MEDIAG **Prod** - LASREM 1983

Urinalysis 8 MIN
U-matic / BETA / VHS
Basic CLinical Laboratory Procedure Series
Color; Mono (C A)
Demonstrates proper equipment, procedures, attention to critical details and efficient, accurate methods for proper collection of specimens.
Health and Safety; Science
Dist - UIOWA **Prod** - UIOWA 1985

Urinalysis - Chemical Examination of the Urine 12 MIN
VHS / BETA
Color
Explains how to perform the chemical analysis of urine.
Health and Safety; Science - Natural
Dist - RMIBHF **Prod** - RMIBHF

Urinalysis - Microscopic Examination of the Urine 9 MIN
VHS / BETA
Color

Explains how to perform the microscopic analysis of urine.
Health and Safety; Science - Natural
Dist - RMIBHF **Prod** - RMIBHF

Urinalysis - Physical Examination of the Urine 10 MIN
BETA / VHS
Color
Explains how to perform the physical analysis of urine.
Health and Safety; Science - Natural
Dist - RMIBHF **Prod** - RMIBHF

Urinary Calculi 14 MIN
VHS / 16mm / U-matic
Color (PRO A) (SPANISH)
Provides a comprehensive picture of causes, effects and treatment of urinary stones. Illustrates anatomy, physiology and mechanics of stone formation. Outlines diagnosis, medical and surgical therapy and long term care.
Health and Safety; Science - Natural
Dist - PRORE **Prod** - PRORE

Urinary Catheter Procedures
U-matic / VHS
Infection Control III Series
Color
Describes some commonly performed urinary catheter procedures that have proven ineffective in reducing infections and are thus no longer recommended. Illustrates measures that do reduce infection during catherization.
Health and Safety
Dist - CONMED **Prod** - CONMED

Urinary Catheterization
Videodisc
Color (C)
$350.00 purchase _ #2880
Presents proper catheterization techniques for both male and female patients. Shows nursing assistants and nursing and medical students how to prepare the patient and the tray. Can be played on SONY LDP 1000, 1000A or 2000 series players with Level II capability. Includes user's manual.
Health and Safety; Psychology; Science
Dist - ACCESS **Prod** - ACCESS 1987

Urinary Catheterization 15 MIN
U-matic / VHS
Color (PRO)
Presents the fundamental facts about catheterization. Demonstrates equipment needed.
Health and Safety; Science - Natural
Dist - MEDFAC **Prod** - MEDFAC 1976

Urinary incontence in women
VHS
Mosby cameo series; Volume 6
Color (C PRO G)
$150.00 purchase
Features nurse researcher Dr Thelma J Wells and her work. Part of a series featuring the work of outstanding nurse researchers.
Health and Safety; Sociology
Dist - MOSBY **Prod** - SITHTA

Urinary incontinence - causes, investigations and treatment options 18 MIN
U-matic / VHS
Understanding and treating incontinence series
Color (PRO C)
$395.00 purchase, $80.00 rental _ #C891 - VI - 004
Defines urinary incontinence and explains the physiological, psychological and environmental causes of the condition. Explains that incontinence is a symptom, not a disease. Presents the initial diagnostic approach involving the basic clinical methods of history - taking, examination and simple tests such as mid - stream urine. Discusses trials of therapy to initiate if the first approach is unsuccessful. Suggests referral to urological, gynecological or geriatric clinics for urodynamic assessment if the condition persists. Part of a seven - part series on incontinence presented by J C Brocklehurst and Bernadette M Ryan - Wooley.
Health and Safety; Science - Natural
Dist - HSCIC

Urinary incontinence in elderly women 20 MIN
VHS / U-matic
Color (PRO C)
$395.00 purchase, $80.00 rental _ #C920 - VI - 048
Describes ways of helping people, especially women, manage their urinary incontinence. Looks at incontinence supplies and reviews issues of concern for health professionals. Discusses types of incontinence and its treatment. Presented by Dr Ruth Mooney and Kevin Bishop, University of Florida, Geriatric Education Center.
Health and Safety
Dist - HSCIC

Urinary incontinence in women 13 MIN
VHS
Color; CC (G C PRO)
$175.00 purchase _ #OB - 134
Stresses types and treatments of the condition. Covers symptoms, tests, medications and behavioral techniques to control the bladder. Contact distributor for purchase price on multiple orders.
Health and Safety; Sociology
Dist - MIFE **Prod** - MIFE 1995

Urinary incontinence - principles of management for the general practitioner 27 MIN
VHS / U-matic
Understanding and treating incontinence series
Color (PRO C)
$395.00 purchase, $80.00 rental _ #C891 - VI - 005
Presents four case studies. Begins with the presentation of each patient's problem to the physician. Continues through therapy and ultimate resolution of each patient's problem. Includes a nine - year - old boy who wets the bed, managing stress incontinence in a young mother with two small children, a 64 - year - old man with numerous urinary complaints and a 76 - year - old woman with urgency and urge incontinence. Part of a seven - part series on incontinence presented by J C Brocklehurst and Bernadette M Ryan - Wooley.
Health and Safety; Science - Natural
Dist - HSCIC

Urinary Retention 19 MIN
VHS / U-matic
Emergency Management - the First 30 Minutes, Vol II Series
Color
Discusses urinary retention, including causes. Demonstrates techniques of evacuating the bladder, alternative approaches and precautions.
Health and Safety; Science
Dist - VTRI **Prod** - VTRI

Urinary Stress Incontinence - Urethroscopy as an Aid to Surgical Treatment 20 MIN
VHS / U-matic
Color (PRO)
Demonstrates through surgery how to correct urinary stress incontinence with the aid of the cystometer and the urethroscope.
Health and Safety
Dist - WFP **Prod** - WFP

The Urinary System 14 MIN
BETA / VHS
Color
Discusses the anatomy of the urinary tract and the purposes of urinalysis.
Health and Safety; Science - Natural
Dist - RMIBHF **Prod** - RMIBHF

Urinary System - Pt 1 - Kidney 39 MIN
U-matic / VHS
Histology review series
Color (PRO)
Describes the role, components, and functions of the kidney. Identifies the processes of urine formation, reabsorption, and secretion.
Health and Safety; Science - Natural
Dist - HSCIC **Prod** - HSCIC

Urinary System - Pt 2 - Ureter Bladder, Urethra 26 MIN
U-matic / VHS
Histology review series
Color (PRO)
Covers the major structural and functional characteristics of the ureter, urinary bladder, and urethra. Identifies the major histological features of the urinary passageways. Characterizes the process involved in urine transport.
Health and Safety; Science - Natural
Dist - HSCIC **Prod** - HSCIC

Urinary Tract I 13 MIN
U-matic
Microanatomy Laboratory Orientation Series
Color (C)
Shows the microarchitecture of the uriniferous tubule, demonstrating in sequence the renal corpuscle, proximal convoluted tubule, loop of Henle, distal convoluted tubules and the principal collecting ducts ending with the ducts of Bellini.
Health and Safety; Science - Natural
Dist - UOKLAH **Prod** - UOKLAH 1986

Urinary Tract II 12 MIN
U-matic
Microanatomy Laboratory Orientation Series
Color (C)
Shows all portions of the urinary tract with the exception of the kidney proper.
Health and Safety; Science - Natural
Dist - UOKLAH **Prod** - UOKLAH 198

Urinary Tract Infection 21 MI
U-matic / VHS
Color (PRO)
Presents the magnitude of nosacomial urinary tract infectio and identifies susceptible population groups. Stresses the diagnosis, treatment and prevention of urinary tract infection.
Health and Safety
Dist - UMICHM **Prod** - UMICHM 197

Urinary Tract Infection 17 MI
16mm / 8mm cartridge
Color (PRO A) (SPANISH)
Presents facts and fallacies about urinary tract infections. Describes medical treatments and long - term care.
Health and Safety; Science - Natural
Dist - PRORE **Prod** - PRORE

Urinary Tract Infection (UTI) 10 MI
U-matic / VHS
Color
Describes common causes of UTI and necessary medical intervention. Emphasizes therapeutic techniques such as site baths, ingesting extra fluids and the critical need to take appropriate medication.
Health and Safety; Science - Natural
Dist - MEDCOM **Prod** - MEDCOM

Urinary tract infections 16 MIN
U-matic / VHS
Breaking the chain of nosocomial infections series
Color (C PRO)
$395.00 purchase, $80.00 rental _ #C930 - VI - 005
Helps medical students, nurses, doctors and other hospital and nursing home staff to reduce the risk factors that cause urinary tract infections. Demonstrates techiques and suggests types of drug therapy to lessen the chances of infection. Part of a five - part series on nosocomial infections presented by Crescent Counties Foundation for Medical Care.
Health and Safety; Science - Natural
Dist - HSCIC

Urinary Tract Infections 32 MIN
8mm cartridge / 16mm
Color
LC 75-702274
Presents a comprehensive approach to help recognize, diagnose and appropriately treat individuals with urinary infections. Features a working classification along with definite suggestions as to a therapeutic approach and follow - up.
Health and Safety; Science; Science - Natural
Dist - EATONL **Prod** - EATONL 1971

Urinary Tract Infections 7 MIN
U-matic / VHS
Take Care of Yourself Series
Color
Focuses on the causes, symptoms and treatment for urinary tract infections. Uses illustrations to describe the area of possible infection. Encourages the patient to take responsibility for self care.
Health and Safety
Dist - UARIZ **Prod** - UARIZ

Urinary Tract Infections in Girls 20 MIN
16mm
Color (PRO)
LC FIA66-703
Presents recommended diagnosis and treatment procedures of urinary tract infections in young girls, as performed at the University of Minnesota of Medicine.
Health and Safety
Dist - EATON **Prod** - EATON 1966

The Urinary Tract - Water 26 MIN
16mm / U-matic / VHS
Living Body - an Introduction to Human Biology Series
Color
Explains the function of water in the body and discusses the system for keeping it in balance. Covers drinking, sweating and breathing, and analyzes the urinary tract, focusing on the functioning of the kidneys.
Science - Natural
Dist - FOTH **Prod** - FOTH 1985

Urine Collection 15 MIN
16mm
Color
LC 75-702243
Depicts the proper techniques of obtaining valid urine specimens in adult males and females and in children.
Health and Safety; Science; Science - Natural
Dist - EATONL **Prod** - EATONL 1972

Urine elimination assessment and intervention series
Presents a four - part series on urinary elimination. Includes the titles Aterations in Patterns of Urinary Elimination - Assessment; Alterations in Patterns of Urinary Elimination - Dysuria; Alterations in Patterns of Urinary Elimination - Temporary Retention; Incontinence - Independent Interventions and Indwelling Catheter.
Alterations in patterns of urinary elimination - assessment 27 MIN
Alterations in patterns of urinary elimination - dysuria 17 MIN
Alterations in patterns of urinary elimination - temporary retention 20 MIN
Incontinence, independent interventions and indwelling catheter 28 MIN
Urine elimination assessment and intervention series 92 MIN
Dist - CONMED **Prod** - UWISCM 1972

Urlaub Zur Beerdigung 112 MIN
16mm
Color
Conveys the awkward situation Juergen finds himself in when he is granted one day's leave from prison to attend his mother's funeral, and the unbridgeable gap between the normal citizens and this 'criminal.'.
Sociology
Dist - WSTGLC **Prod** - WSTGLC 1977

Urologic Nursing Care of Patients with Spinal Cord Lesions, Pt 2 24 MIN
Slide / VHS / 16mm
Nursing Management in Neurogenic Bladder Series
Color (PRO)
$70.00, $110.00, $130.00 purchase, $30.00, $35.00 rental _ #8016
Presents information on neurogenic bladder conditions. Focuses on urologic nursing care of patients with spinal cord lesions. Presents the work of Y C Wu, MD, R King, MS, RN, and W Griggs, MSN, RN. Slide program includes 78 slides and audiocassette. Video and slides accompanied with study guide package.
Health and Safety; Science - Natural
Dist - RICHGO **Prod** - RICHGO 1980

The Urological Examination 27 MIN
16mm
Color (PRO)
LC FIA66-78
Points out the continuing importance of the clinical urological examination in providing the initial diagnosis upon which laboratory studies are based. Provides a step - by - step demonstration and explaination of each phase of Dr Boyarsky's technique.
Health and Safety
Dist - EATON **Prod** - EATON 1965

Urological Nursing Series
Male Catheterization, Pt 1 9 MIN
Male Catheterization, Pt 2 11 MIN
Dist - TRNAID

Urology Series
Cystoscopy - equipment and procedure 30 MIN
Pre - Vasectomy Family Consultation 13 MIN
Sounding for Urethral Strictures 25 MIN
Vascetomy Operative Procedure 28 MIN
Dist - MSU

Urostomy Care at Home 13 MIN
VHS / U-matic
Color
LC 79-730905
Reviews important aspects of self - care, and encourages patient's confidence in his/her ability to manage the urostomy appliance. Notes program can be shown to patient prior to surgery in some cases but otherwise before discharge from the hospital.
Health and Safety; Science - Natural
Dist - MEDCOM **Prod** - MEDCOM

Ursae Majoris 9 MIN
U-matic / VHS / BETA
Color; PAL (G H C)
PdS30, PdS38 purchase
Science - Physical
Dist - EDPAT

Uruguay - Shark Fishing 14 MIN
VHS / U-matic
Color (H C A)
Presents a story of a group of men who established a small fishing village when their farms failed to yield adequate food for their families. Tells how they were successful and are able to offer hope for a better way of life for their families.
Geography - World; History - World
Dist - JOU **Prod** - JOU

Us 20 MIN
16mm
Cellar Door Cine Mites Series
Color (I)
LC 74-701552
Fine Arts
Dist - CELLAR **Prod** - CELLAR 1972

US Air Force 15 MIN
U-matic / 16mm / VHS
Career Awareness
(I)
$130 VC purchase, $240 film purchase, $25 VC rental, $30 film rental
Presents an empathetic approach to career planning, showing the personal as well as professional qualities of US Air Force personnel. Highlights the importance of career education.
Guidance and Counseling
Dist - GPN

US and Canada 30 MIN
U-matic
Realities
Color (A)
Delves into the political, social, economic and cultural trends of the 1980s. Probes a wide range of contemporary concerns. Each segment includes a guest speaker who is an expert in the field under discussion.
Business and Economics; Civics and Political Systems; Social Science; Sociology
Dist - TVOTAR **Prod** - TVOTAR 1985

Us and Changes 28 MIN
16mm
Earthkeeping Series
Color (P I J)
LC 73-703399
Examines changes in the environment that have caused serious problems brought about by industry, growth and technology. Shows such ways to initiate and effect changes to alleviate the environmental crisis as recycling centers, land - use planning, pollution devices and alternatives to the automobile.
Science - Natural
Dist - IU **Prod** - WTTWTV 1973

U S A volleyball 60 MIN
VHS
Color (H C A)
$89.95 purchase _ #SWP001V
Features the U S men's Olympic volleyball team covering the basics of volleyball. Explains and demonstrates skills including the ready position, serving, passes, the dig, the spike, and blocks.
Physical Education and Recreation
Dist - CAMV

U S Adventure 10 MIN
16mm
Color (H)
Captures the feel of today's Army and its people. Includes climbing, driving, jumping and moving on land, through water and in the air.
Civics and Political Systems; Guidance and Counseling
Dist - MTP **Prod** - USARC

U S Air Force Academy 4 MIN
16mm
Update Appliances Meetings Series
Color
LC 75-703012
Tours the U S Air Force Academy. Designed to instill employees of Sears, Roebuck and Company with pride in America.
Business and Economics; Education
Dist - SRCIPP **Prod** - SEARS 1975

U S and China 29 MIN
U-matic
Conversations with Allen Whiting Series
Color
Assesses the relationship between the United States and China.
Civics and Political Systems; Geography - World
Dist - UMITV **Prod** - UMITV 1979

The U S and the Middle East - Dangerous Drift 30 MIN
VHS
World Beat - Great Decisions In Foreign Policy Series
Color (G)
$39.95 purchase _ #WDBT - 102
Emphasizes the Palestinian situation, with particular emphasis paid to emotional issues among Arabs and Israelis. Considers the role of grassroots politics.
Civics and Political Systems; History - World
Dist - PBS **Prod** - WETATV 1988

The U S Armed Forces Bicentennial Band and Chorus 59 MIN
VHS / 16mm
Color (G)
$70.00 rental _ #BICB - 000
Features a concert of American music played by the Army, Navy, Air Force and Marine Corps.
Fine Arts
Dist - PBS **Prod** - WQLN

U S Army Air Force Report 50 MIN
U-matic / VHS
B&W
Introduces the first Army Air Force report made to be shown to the public. Contains air - combat footage from all theaters of war taken from 1941 through 1944.
Civics and Political Systems; History - United States
Dist - IHF **Prod** - IHF

U S Champions, Pt 1 29 MIN
Videoreel / VT2
Grand Master Chess Series
Color
Physical Education and Recreation
Dist - PBS **Prod** - KQEDTV

U S Champions, Pt 2 29 MIN
Videoreel / VT2
Grand Master Chess Series
Color
Physical Education and Recreation
Dist - PBS **Prod** - KQEDTV

U S China Relations 30 MIN
U-matic
China After Mao Series
Color
Reflects on transitions and motives upon which America's relationship with China is based.
Civics and Political Systems; Geography - World
Dist - UMITV **Prod** - UMITV 1980

U S choice 11 MIN
16mm
Color (G)
$24.00 rental
Wonders what happens when calling one's mother on the phone and instead it turns out to be 'your ex - wife, Jesus Christ, Lolita, Yourself, Bull Dike, Bowling Queen, Two Georgia Red Worms on their Wedding Night.'
Fine Arts; Psychology; Social Science
Dist - CANCIN **Prod** - WONGAL 1968

U S chronicle series
At the gate alone 29 MIN
Dist - WVIATV

U S Cities - Growth and Development 19 MIN
16mm / U-matic / VHS
Color (J H)
Examines the forces that shape American cities and how they determine a city's future growth or decline.
Geography - United States; Sociology
Dist - EBEC **Prod** - JAYD 1984

U S Culture 30 MIN
U-matic / VHS
Focus on Society Series
Color (C)
Studies pleasure as a value and its impact upon American life in areas such as economics, family and community.
Sociology
Dist - DALCCD **Prod** - DALCCD

U S Foreign Policy - Projecting U S Influence 30 MIN
VHS
World Beat - Great Decisions In Foreign Policy Series
Color (G)
$39.95 purchase _ #WDBT - 108
Examines the limits of power and influence that powerful nations can exercise. Focuses on the example of U S policy toward Nicaragua.
Civics and Political Systems; History - World
Dist - PBS **Prod** - WETATV 1988

U S geography series
The agricultural Midwest 15 MIN
The Manufacturing Midwest 15 MIN
The Middle Atlantic Region 17 MIN
New England 15 MIN
The Pacific Northwest 18 MIN
The South Atlantic Region 15 MIN
The South Central Region 15 MIN
The Southwest 17 MIN
Dist - MGHT

U S government in action series
Presents a six - part series on the various branches of the US government and how they work together. Emphasizes the concept of checks and balances. Uses archival and modern graphics.
U S government in action series 108 MIN
Dist - SRA **Prod** - SRA 1988

U S Grant - I Remember Appomattox 17 MIN
U-matic / VHS / 16mm
Color (I)
LC 76-701785
Dramatizes Ulysses S Grant's reminisces about Lee's surrender at Appomattox, Civil War battles, his boyhood days, love of horses and his West Point years.
Biography; History - United States
Dist - CORF **Prod** - CORF 1976

U S Intervention in Latin America 15 MIN
VHS
Witness to History Series
Color (J H)
$49.00 purchase _ #60154
Describes how the Monroe Doctrine and the Rosevelt Corollary influenced the Americas in the nineteenth and early twentieth centuries.
History - United States; History - World
Dist - GA **Prod** - GA 1989

The U S is - People 15 MIN
U-matic / VHS / 16mm
Color (I)
LC 79-701709
Explores the variety of national origins, places, lifestyles and occupations of the people of the United States. Shows how these have changed since the nation's beginning and points out certain American traits and beliefs.
History - United States; Sociology
Dist - PHENIX **Prod** - MLTES 1979

The U S is - Resources 14 MIN
U-matic / VHS / 16mm
Color (I) (SWEDISH)
LC 79-700584
Surveys the United States reserves of natural resources and points out that a high productivity of raw materials, goods and energy results from the availability of these resources. Emphasizes the importance of using the remaining resources wisely.
Foreign Language; Geography - United States; Science - Natural; Social Science
Dist - PHENIX **Prod** - MLTES 1979

U S Marine Corps Bicentennial Television Spot 2 MIN
16mm
Color (H C A)
LC 77-700080
Illustrates patriotic scenery with the American National Anthem played by the Marine Corps Band.
Civics and Political Systems; Fine Arts
Dist - USNAC **Prod** - USMC 1976

U S Men's Championships
VHS / U-matic
Color
Physical Education and Recreation
Dist - MSTVIS **Prod** - MSTVIS

U S Naval Observatory 18 MIN
16mm
Color
LC 74-705869
Shows how astronomers and mathematicians determine time, predict and publish the positions of the sun, moon, stars and planets for navigation and scientific purposes in addition to doing fundamental astronomical research.
Civics and Political Systems; Industrial and Technical Education; Mathematics; Science; Science - Physical
Dist - USNAC **Prod** - USN 1970

The U S Naval Test Pilot School 13 MIN
16mm
Color
LC FIE63-57
Follows a test pilot through the school at the Patuxent River Naval Air Station, showing the school's academic and flying curricula.
Civics and Political Systems; Guidance and Counseling; Industrial and Technical Education; Psychology
Dist - USNAC **Prod** - USN 1959

U S Navy Armored Life Jacket 7 MIN
16mm
B&W
LC FIE52-1272
Demonstrates how a bullet - proof fabric material called Doran can be used to protect Navy personnel against small arms fire.
Civics and Political Systems; Home Economics
Dist - USNAC **Prod** - USN 1945

U S Neutrality, 1914 - 1917 17 MIN
16mm / U-matic / VHS
World War I Series
B&W (H C)
LC FIA67-1963
Shows events that forced the United States into World War I, the loss of trade with Germany, suspected sabotage and the sinking of ships.
Civics and Political Systems; History - United States; History - World
Dist - FI **Prod** - CBSTV 1967

U S Office of Personnel Management 20 MIN
U-matic / VHS
Clues to Career Opportunities for Liberal Arts Graduates Series
Color (C A)
LC 80-706239
A revised version of the 1978 videotape Federal Civil Service. Explains application procedures for obtaining a job in the U S government. Discusses the Professional Administrative Career Examination, hiring policies, advancement opportunities, the locations of jobs, and the lifestyles of employees.
Civics and Political Systems; Psychology
Dist - IU **Prod** - IU 1979

The U S Open - Trevino at Merion 30 MIN
16mm
Color (J)
LC 72-703184
Presents highlights of the 1971 U S Open, held at the Merion Golf Course in Philadelphia.
Geography - United States; Physical Education and Recreation
Dist - SFI **Prod** - USGOLF 1972

U S Presidential Elections 1928 - 1968 Series
Presidential Campaign of 1952 9 MIN
Presidential Campaign of 1956 9 MIN
Presidential Election of 1928 7 MIN
Presidential Election of 1960 16 MIN
Presidential Election of 1964 10 MIN
Presidential Election of 1968 9 MIN
Dist - KRAUS

U S Regions - Contrasts of Land and People 26 MIN
16mm / U-matic / VHS
Color (I J H)
Describes and illustrates traditional regions of the United States. Shows how regional differences result from a combination of differences in physical environment and human history.
Geography - United States
Dist - EBEC **Prod** - EBEC 1986

U S Social Classes 30 MIN
U-matic / VHS
Focus on Society Series
Color (C)
Discusses two social classes, their values, behavior patterns and activities.
Sociology
Dist - DALCCD **Prod** - DALCCD

U S - Soviet Joint Space Mission 15 MIN
16mm
Color
LC 76-700488
Presents a pictorial report on the events leading up to the historic Apollo - Soyuz mission.
Civics and Political Systems; History - United States; History - World; Science; Science - Physical
Dist - USNAC **Prod** - NASA 1976

U S - Soviet Relations - Potsdam to Vietnam 27 MIN
U-matic / VHS
Color (H C A)
Provides background on the relationships existing between the United States and Russia from the close of World War II to 1972. Focuses on the Cold War, the Korean conflict, the introduction of detente, and Vietnam.
Civics and Political Systems; History - United States; History - World
Dist - JOU **Prod** - UPI

The U S - Soviet Space Mission 26 MIN
U-matic / VHS
Color
Documents the American - Russian space linkup in 1975. Explains that this was an historic moment not only in space technology but in United States - Soviet relations.
History - World; Industrial and Technical Education; Science - Physical
Dist - JOU **Prod** - UPI

U S Specialty Cities - Manufacturing Cities 26 MIN
16mm
Color (H C A)
LC 76-700295
Identifies and examines cities in the United States which specialize in manufacturing. Considers the historic, geographic, economic and social factors surrounding these cities and takes a look at their future viability.
Business and Economics; Geography - United States; Geography - World; Social Science; Sociology
Dist - IU **Prod** - IU 1975

U S Staff Report no 1 30 MIN
U-matic / VHS
B&W
Presents U S Staff Reports from July, 1944, including Monsoons In Burma and Armies Near Gothic Line.
History - United States; History - World
Dist - IHF **Prod** - IHF

U S Staff Report no 2 30 MIN
U-matic / VHS
B&W
Presents U S Staff Reports from 1944 including Chinese Round Out Training In Yunan and Allies take Elba.
History - United States; History - World
Dist - IHF **Prod** - IHF

U S Staff Report no 3 30 MIN
VHS / U-matic
B&W
Presents U S Staff Reports from Nov - Dec, 1944, including Japs Saipan Base and Activities in East China.
History - United States; History - World
Dist - IHF **Prod** - IHF

U S Staff Report no 4 30 MIN
VHS / U-matic
B&W
Presents U S Staff Reports from 1944 including 5th Army Enters Pisa and Activities in Burma - Aircraft Evacuating Wounded.
History - United States; History - World
Dist - IHF **Prod** - IHF

U S Sweat 15 MIN
U-matic / VHS
Color
Presents a montage of American landscape as seen from an automobile. Intercuts alarming events, places and sounds that interpret what is seen.
Fine Arts
Dist - KITCHN **Prod** - KITCHN

U S Trade and Global Markets - Can the U S Compete 30 MIN
VHS
World Beat - Great Decisions In Foreign Policy Series
Color (G)
$39.95 purchase _ #WDBT - 101
Describes how trade deficits and restrictive trade policies of other nations have hurt the U S role in the international marketplace. Examines proposals to curb the trade deficit.
Business and Economics; Civics and Political Systems
Dist - PBS **Prod** - WETATV 1988

U S Vs USSR - Who's Ahead 28 MIN
16mm / U-matic / VHS
Issues in the News Series
Color (J H C)
Strives to answer the question of which of the superpowers is militarily strongest. Interviews such experts as former director of the CIA William Colby, Admiral Hyman Rickover, General Homer Boushey (USAF), former director of Missiles Development at Wright Patterson AFB, and General William Fairbourn (USMC), former director of Operations and Planning for the Joint Chiefs of Staff.
Civics and Political Systems
Dist - CNEMAG **Prod** - FUNPC 1984

U S War Department Report - July 1943 - the Battle of Industry 55 MIN
VHS / U-matic
B&W
Illustrates, through captured Japanese and German footage, the importance of industrial production. Includes a complete film segment from a German newsreel showing the Mussolini rescue.
History - United States; History - World
Dist - IHF **Prod** - IHF

U S Women's Championships
U-matic / VHS
Color
Physical Education and Recreation
Dist - MSTVIS **Prod** - MSTVIS

U S/Europe Economic Conflict 25 MIN
U-matic / VHS
Color (H C A)
Discusses the fact that as the international economy continues to experience recession the relations between the United States and Europe have experienced stresses with respect to trade, import/export and licensing. Explores the political and diplomatic implications of these controversies.
Civics and Political Systems; Geography - World; Social Science
Dist - JOU **Prod** - JOU

US atlas
CD-ROM
(G)
$109.00 purchase _ #2232
Brings the entire North American continent to computer screen. Covers geography, education, crime, travel, and the economy of each state of the United States, as well as the population, climate, latitude, longitude, local time, area codes, and zip codes of major cities. Prints maps and text, and graphs map data. IBM PC and compatibles require at least 640K of RAM, DOS 3.1 or greater, one floppy disk drive - hard disk recommended, one empty expansion slot, an IBM compatible CD - ROM drive, and an EGA or VGA monitor.

Geography - United States; Geography - World; Literature and Drama
Dist - BEP Prod - BEP

US atlas 3.0 multimedia
CD-ROM
Color (J H C G)
$74.95 purchase _ #BO13R5CD, #BO30R5CD
Presents a practical combination of fact book, almanac and atlas which allows access to full - color maps and a huge database. Includes data entry, notepad, map trails, map makers and other features.
Geography - United States
Dist - CAMV

US campaign against the death penalty 28 MIN
VHS
Color (G A)
$20.00 purchase
Explains why capital punishment should be unconditionally abolished in the United States. Shows that the death penalty in the US is arbitrary, racially discriminatory and a violation of human rights. Produced and directed by Paul Stern.
Civics and Political Systems; Sociology
Dist - AMNSTY

US cavalry horsemanship training series
Horsemanship - aids and gaits 38 MIN
Horsemanship - care of the animal in the field 31 MIN
Horsemanship - how to saddle and bridle 22 MIN
Horsemanship - jumping and cross country 32 MIN
Horsemanship - mounting and dismounting 30 MIN
Horsemanship - suppling exercises 16 MIN
Dist - EQVDL

US civics
CD-ROM
(G)
$99.00 purchase
Contains a full - text database of important historical and relevant, recent national events, sample history tests, biographies, conflicts, government structure and reference manuals based on the US Immigration and Naturalization Service 'Federal Citizenship Texts.' Includes the publications 'A Reference Manual for Citizenship Instructors, 'Citizenship Education and Naturalization Information,' 'United States History 1600 - 1987 Level I and II,' 'US Government Structure I and II.' Available in MS - DOS and MAC format.
Civics and Political Systems; History - United States; Social Science
Dist - QUANTA Prod - QUANTA

US civics disc
CD-ROM
(T)
$125.00 purchase _ #1933p
Helps instructors and others who assist people in becoming US citizens. Includes information from the Department of Justice, Immigration and Naturalization Services, and a wide variety of other official sources. For IBM PCs and compatibles. Requires at least 640K RAM, DOS Version 3.1 or greater, one floppy disk drive - a hard drive is recommended, one empty expansion slot, and an IBM compatible CD - ROM drive.
Civics and Political Systems; Sociology
Dist - BEP

US civics disc - Mac
CD-ROM
(T)
$125.00 purchase _ #2856m
Informs instructors and those who assist people becoming US citizens. Includes information from the Department of Justice, Immigration and Naturalization Services, and a wide variety of other official sources. For Macintosh Plus, SE and II computers. Requires at least one M of RAM, one floppy disk drive, and an Apple compatible CD - ROM drive.
Civics and Political Systems; Sociology
Dist - BEP

The US Coast Guard
VHS
Color (G)
$19.95 purchase _ #0014
Presents three parts on the United States Coast Guard. Describes the history of the guard in The First 200 Years. Tells about guard activities, its present day work and tasks in At the Ready. Explains the guard involvement in the war on drugs in Zero Tolerance.
Civics and Political Systems; History - United States
Dist - SEVVID Prod - USCG

US customary system
VHS
Basic mathematical skills series
Color (I J H)
$125.00 purchase _ #1022
Teaches the concepts of the US system of weights and measures. Presents part of a series that provides 27 videos, each between 25 and 30 minutes long, that explain and reinforce basic mathematical concepts. Tutors the student through definitions, theorems, step - by - step solutions and examples. Videos are also available in a set.
Mathematics
Dist - LANDMK

US Economic Growth - what is the Gross National Product 30 MIN
U-matic / VHS
Economics USA Series
Color (C)
Business and Economics
Dist - ANNCPB Prod - WEFA

US government in action series
The Cabinet 18 MIN
The House of representatives 18 MIN
The Presidency 18 MIN
The Regulatory agencies 18 MIN
The Senate 18 MIN
The Supreme court 18 MIN
Dist - SRA

US Government seals
CD-ROM
(G)
$69.95 purchase
Presents 588 federal identifying images for official use only in the TIFF format. Offers images scanned at 300 dots - per - inch for crisp resolution. Available in MS - DOS and MAC format.
Civics and Political Systems; Computer Science; Industrial and Technical Education
Dist - QUANTA Prod - QUANTA

US history on CD - ROM
CD-ROM
(G)
$395.00 purchase _ #3001
Contains the full text of 107 books relating to US history. Includes over 1000 VGA photos, maps and tables of historical events as well. Users can browse or search by word, event, book, picture, or article. For IBM PCs and compatibles, requires 604K RAM, DOS 3.1 or later, one floppy disk drive - hard disk recommended, one empty expansion slot, an IBM compatible CD - ROM drive, and a VGA monitor. For Macintosh Classic, Plus, SE or II computers, requires 1MB RAM, one floppy disk drive, and an Apple compatible CD - ROM drive. Network editions available.
History - United States
Dist - BEP

US invades Panama - Tuesday, December 19, 1989 60 MIN
VHS
Nightline series
Color (H C G)
$14.98 purchase _ #MP6177
Focuses on the 1989 invasion of Panama.
Fine Arts; Sociology
Dist - INSTRU Prod - ABCNEW 1989

US Military leaders of World War II 21 MIN
VHS
Color (I J H G)
$49.95 purchase _ #3033D
Offers biographies of United States military generals Douglas MacArthur, William 'Bull' Halsey, George Marshall, Omar Bradley, Claire Chennault and George Patton. Features Bob Considine as host.
Biography; History - United States
Dist - INSTRU

US patents - ASIST
CD-ROM
(PRO)
$395.00 purchase _ #2264
Provides help and other background information on US patents. Includes at least two updates per year. One of three discs developed by the US Patent and Trademark Office Documentation Organization. Complete set suggested. For IBM PCs and compatibles. Requires 640K RAM, DOS Version 3.1 or greater, one floppy disk drive - a hard drive is recommended, one empty expansion slot, and an IBM compatible CD - ROM drive.
Business and Economics; History - United States
Dist - BEP

US patents - bibliographic
CD-ROM
(PRO)
$395.00 purchase _ #2262
Contains bibliographic information for all patents. Includes at least two updates per year. One of three discs developed by the US Patent and Trademark Office Documentation Organization. Complete set suggested. For IBM PCs and compatibles. Requires at least 640K RAM, DOS Version 3.1 or greater, one floppy disk drive - a hard drive is recommended, one empty expansion slot, and an IBM compatible CD - ROM drive.
Business and Economics; History - United States
Dist - BEP

US patents - classification
CD-ROM
(PRO)
$395.00 purchase _ #2263
Offers the Manual of Classification and classification information. Includes at least two updates per year. One of three discs developed by the US Patent and Trademark Office Documentation Organization. Complete set suggested. For IBM PCs and compatibles. Requires 640K RAM, DOS Version 3.1 or greater, one floppy disk drive - a hard drive is recommended, one empty expansion slot, and an IBM compatible CD - ROM drive.
Business and Economics; History - United States
Dist - BEP

US Power squadron's boating course 80 MIN
VHS
Color (G A)
$39.95 purchase _ #0137
Teaches boating skills for sailboats and motorboats. Covers all the material normally taught in six weekly United States Power Squadron classes.
Physical Education and Recreation
Dist - SEVVID

US Powerboat championships
VHS
Color (G)
$24.95 purchase _ #0869
Travels to Laughlin, Nevada to view the United States Powerboat Championships.
Physical Education and Recreation
Dist - SEVVID

US President Ronald Reagan 16 MIN
35mm strip / VHS
In our time series
Color (J H C T A)
$81.00, $48.00 purchase _ #MB - 540370 - 6, #MB - 509124 - 0
Profiles Ronald Reagan and his presidency. Traces his roots, his acting and political careers, the origins of his conservative ideology, and more. Reveals that his ultimate impact is still being debated.
Biography; Fine Arts; History - United States
Dist - SRA Prod - SRA 1989

US presidents - Mac
CD-ROM
(G A)
$125.00 purchase _ #2857m
Contains biographies and statistics of the 41 presidents of the US. Includes First Lady Statistics and 256 color VGA and Super VGA images of all 41 presidents. For Macintosh Plus, SE and II computers. Requires at least one M of RAM, one floppy disk drive, and an Apple compatible CD - ROM drive.
Civics and Political Systems
Dist - BEP

US presidents - PC
CD-ROM
(G A)
$125.00 purchase _ #2857p
Contains biographies and statistics of the 41 presidents of the US. Includes First Lady statistics and 256 color VGA and Super VGA images of all 41 presidents. For IBM PCs and compatibles. Requires 640K RAM, DOS Version 3.1 or greater, one floppy disk drive - a hard drive is recommended, one empty expansion slot, and an IBM compatible CD - ROM drive.
Civics and Political Systems
Dist - BEP

US Sweat 15 MIN
U-matic
Color (C)
$250.00
Experimental Film by Shalom Gorewitz.
Fine Arts
Dist - AFA Prod - AFA 1982

US Virgin Islands, St Thomas, St John and St Croix
VHS
Color (G)
$19.80 purchase _ #0882
Relaxes in the warm waters of Megan's Bay on St Thomas. Enters a fishing paradise in the Puerto Rican Trench. Cruises in a submarine.

Geography - World; Physical Education and Recreation
Dist - SEVVID

US vs Nixon 20 MIN
VHS
Supreme Court decisions that changed the nation series
Color (J H)
$69.00 _ #60106 - 026
Delves into the decision held that the President cannot withhold evidence in a criminal investigation. Presents part of an eight - part series providing comprehensive history and legal background to landmark rulings and demonstrates their impact on American life. Includes teacher's guide and library kit.
Biography; Civics and Political Systems; Education
Dist - GA
INSTRU

USA 47 MIN
16mm
Color
Presents a tour of the United States which shows it to be a land of many lands. Stresses the blending of varied cultural values into one nation by interspersing scenes of historical and geographical landmarks with those of people at work and play.
History - United States; Sociology
Dist - PANWA **Prod** - PANWA 1957

USA 50 MIN
BETA / VHS / U-matic
Road to war series
Color (J H C)
$250.00 purchase _ #JY - 5837C
Shows that the United States watched old European rivalries rekindle after World War I and tried to avoid involvement. Reveals that the US distrusted European imperialism and faced a massive economic depression on the homefront. America favored changes in the balance of power but failed to use its potential strength to stabilize the international system. Part of an eight - part series on the history of World War II using a country - by - country perspective.
Civics and Political Systems; History - United States; History - World
Dist - CORF **Prod** - BBCTV 1989

The USA 20 MIN
16mm
Color
LC 70-711558
A music and image tour of the United States, utilizing modern cutting and camera techniques to reveal the quality and character of the people. Includes sequences on New York, California, the Rocky Mountains and the Southwest.
Fine Arts; Geography - United States; Industrial and Technical Education; Sociology
Dist - PANWA **Prod** - PANWA 1971

USA fact book - Mac
CD-ROM
Color (G A)
$125.00 purchase _ #1947m
Offers an electronic almanac of the US and its territories. Includes details on state geography, vital statistics, government, politics, economics, communications, and transportation. For Macintosh Plus, SE and II computers. Requires at least one M of RAM, one floppy disk drive, and an Apple compatible CD - ROM drive.
History - United States; Literature and Drama
Dist - BEP

USA fact book - PC
CD-ROM
(G A)
$125.00 purchase _ #1947p
Offers an electronic almanac of the US and its territories. Includes details on state geography, vital statistics, government, politics, economics, communications and transportation. For IBM PCs and compatibles. Requires 640K RAM, DOS Version 3.1 or greater, one floppy disk drive - hard disk drive recommended, one empty expansion slot, and an IBM compatible CD - ROM drive.
History - United States; Literature and Drama
Dist - BEP

USA Film 17 MIN
U-matic / VHS / 16mm
Color (H C A)
LC 81-700937
Offers a view of America by using time - lapse photography to compress a cross - country trip.
Geography - United States
Dist - PHENIX **Prod** - PHENIX 1977

USA - Seeds of Change 30 MIN
16mm
Population Problem Series; No 6
B&W (H C A)
LC FIA67-1519
Analyzes United States population trends from colonial days to the present. Focuses particularly on the baby boom era, the increasing number of senior citizens and the present and future problems to be faced in housing, rising crime, overcrowded school, unemployment and poverty.
Psychology; Science - Natural; Sociology
Dist - IU **Prod** - NET 1967

USA Series

Artists - Barnett Newman	28 MIN
Artists - Claes Oldenburg	30 MIN
Artists - Frank Stella and Larry Poons - the New Abstraction	30 MIN
Artists - Jack Tworkov	29 MIN
Artists - Jasper Johns	29 MIN
Artists - Jim Dine	29 MIN
Artists - Robert Rauschenberg	29 MIN
Artists - the New Abstraction - Morris Louis and Kenneth Noland	30 MIN
Composers - the American tradition	30 MIN
The Novel - 1914 - 1942 - the Loss of Innocence	30 MIN
The Novel - Ralph Ellison on Work in Progress	30 MIN
The Novel - Saul Bellow - the World of the Dangling Man	29 MIN
The Novel - the Nonfiction Novel - a Visit with Truman Capote	30 MIN
The Novel - Vladimir Nabokov	30 MIN
Photography - Dorothea Lange - the Closer for Me	30 MIN
Photography - Dorothea Lange - Under the Trees	30 MIN
Photography - the Daybooks of Edward Weston - How Young I was	30 MIN
Photography - the Daybooks of Edward Weston - the Strongest Way of Seeing	30 MIN
Poetry - Brother Antonius and Michael Mc Clure	30 MIN
Poetry - Denise Levertov and Charles Olson	30 MIN
Poetry - Frank O'Hara and Ed Sanders	30 MIN
Poetry - Louis Zukofsky	30 MIN
Poetry - Philip Whalen and Gary Snyder	30 MIN
Poetry - Richard Wilbur and Robert Lowell	30 MIN
Poetry - Robert Creeley	30 MIN
Poetry - Robert Duncan and John Wieners	30 MIN
Poetry - William Carlos Williams	30 MIN
Writers - John Updike	30 MIN
Writers - Philip Roth	30 MIN
Writers - Science Fiction	30 MIN

Dist - IU

USA - USSR Youth Summit - Program 1 60 MIN
U-matic / VHS
USA - USSR Youth Summit Series
Color (G)
$60.00, $80.00 purchase _ #USRY - 101H, #USRY - 101U
Documents the state of education and music in the Soviet Union. Focuses on the differences and similarities of American and Soviet teenagers. Includes a question and answer session before a studio audience.
Education; Health and Safety; History - World
Dist - PBS

USA - USSR Youth Summit - Program 2 60 MIN
U-matic / VHS
USA - USSR Youth Summit Series
Color (G)
$60.00, $80.00 purchase _ #USRY - 102H, #USRY - 102U
Explores the fashions, foods and family life of the Soviet Union. Includes a question and answer session before a studio audience.
Education; Health and Safety; History - World
Dist - PBS

USA - USSR Youth Summit - Program 3, Spacebridge Teleconference 90 MIN
U-matic / VHS
USA - USSR Youth Summit Series
Color (G)
$90.00, $110.00 purchase _ #USRY - 103H, #USRY - 103U
Features a satellite teleconference connecting American and Soviet teenagers. Hosted by Cable News Network correspondent Stuart Loory and Soviet news commentator Vladimir Pozner.
Education; Health and Safety; History - World; Psychology; Sociology
Dist - PBS

USA - USSR youth summit series 210 MIN
VHS / U-matic
USA - USSR youth summit series
Color (G)
$170.00, $215.00 purchase _ #USRY - 000H, #USRY - 000U
Presents a three - part series on the lives of Soviet teenagers. Program 1 considers education and music in the Soviet Union. Program 2 looks at family life, fashion and food. Program 3 is a satellite simulcast linking Soviet and American teenagers.
Education; Health and Safety; History - World; Psychology; Sociology
Dist - PBS

USA wars - Civil War - Mac
CD-ROM
(G A)
$129.00 purchase _ #2842m
Examine the war that tore apart the US from 1860 to 1865. Covers biographies, statistics, chronology, equipment, campaigns, battles, foreign involvement, bibliography, political figures, and photographs. Includes homespun music of the Civil War era. For Macintosh Plus, SE and II Computers. Requires at least one M of RAM, one floppy disk drive, and an Apple compatible CD - ROM drive.
History - United States
Dist - BEP

USA wars - Civil War - PC
CD-ROM
(G A)
$129.00 purchase _ #2842p
Examines the war that tore apart the US from 1860 to 1865. Covers biographies, statistics, chronology, equipment, campaigns, battles, foreign involvement, bibliography, political figures, and photographs. Includes homespun music of the Civil War era. For IBM PCs and compatibles. Requires 640K RAM, DOS Version 3.1 or greater, one floppy disk drive - a hard disk drive is recommended, one empty expansion slot, and an IBM compatible CD - ROM drive.
History - United States
Dist - BEP

USA Wars - Korea - Mac
CD-ROM
Color (G A)
$125.00 purchase _ #2856m
Covers US involvement in the Korean conflict of the 1950s. Includes biographies, campaigns and the role played by UN forces. For Macintosh Plus, SE and II computers. Requires at least one M of RAM, one floppy disk drive, and an Apple compatible CD - ROM drive.
History - United States
Dist - BEP

USA wars - Korea - PC
CD-ROM
(G A)
$125.00 purchase _ #2856p
Covers US involvement in the Korean conflict of the 1950s. Includes biographies, campaigns, and the role played by UN forces. For IBM PCs and compatibles. Requires 640K RAM, DOS Version 3.1 or greater, one floppy disk drive - a hard drive is recommended, one empty expansion slot, and an IBM compatible CD - ROM drive.
History - United States
Dist - BEP

USA wars - Vietnam
CD-ROM
(G)
$99.00 purchase
Presents a historical retrospective database which encompasses American involvement in Southeast Asia from 1946 to 1976. Allows searches on words and phrases accompanied by viewing of color and - or black - and - white images related to the text. Includes biographies, statistics, order of battle, equipment, missions, bibliography, chronologies, glossaries and the Wall - national Vietnam Memorial listing. Available in MS - DOS and MAC format.
History - United States; Sociology
Dist - QUANTA **Prod** - QUANTA

USA wars - Vietnam - Mac
CD-ROM
Color (G A)
$125.00 purchase _ #1941m
Encompasses American involvement in Southeast Asia from 1946 to 1976. Includes the complete record from The Wall, along with marching orders, biographies and other Vietnam - related statistics. For Macintosh Plus, SE and II computers. Requires at least one M of RAM, one floppy disk drive, and an Apple compatible CD - ROM drive.
History - United States
Dist - BEP

USA wars - Vietnam - PC
CD-ROM
(G A)

$125.00 purchase _ #1941p
Encompasses American involvement in Southeast Asia from 1946 to 1976. Includes the complete record from The Wall, along with marching orders, biographies and other Vietnam - related statistics. For IBM PC and compatibles. Requires 640K RAM, DOS Version 3.1 or greater, one floppy disk drive - a hard drive is recommended, one empty expansion slot, and an IBM compatible CD - ROM drive.
History - United States
Dist - BEP

Us - Them 32 MIN
VHS / 16mm
(G)
$275.00 purchase, $100.00, $50.00 rental
Explores three close relationships between physically challenged and non - physically challenged people.
Health and Safety; Sociology
Dist - FANPRO **Prod** - FANPRO 1989

A Usable Past 60 MIN
U-matic / VHS
Smithsonian World Series
Color (J)
Shows Alnwick Castle, whose 296 rooms have been occupied for 700 years by one of England's oldest and wealthiest families. Visits the Royal Scottish Museum in Edinburgh. Tours an estate outside London. Examines the ways institutions and individuals affect the past and the present.
History - World; Sociology
Dist - WETATV **Prod** - WETATV

USAC Champions 30 MIN
16mm
B&W
Shows exciting highlights from the USAC champions.
Physical Education and Recreation
Dist - SFI **Prod** - SFI

USAF Aerospace 10th Anniversary 7 MIN
16mm
Color
LC 74-706294
Traces the history of man's efforts to explore outer space. Discusses the overall significance of the space challenge and its present and future effect on man.
History - World; Science; Science - Physical
Dist - USNAC **Prod** - USAF 1957

USAF Flight Test School 19 MIN
16mm
Color (H C)
LC FIE58-281
Describes the entrance requirements and curriculum of USAF Flight Test School at Edwards Air Force Base, California. Discusses the courses on aircraft performance data and on maneuver ability of the aircraft control system.
Civics and Political Systems
Dist - USNAC **Prod** - USDD 1957

The USAF Maintenance Management Improvement Program 20 MIN
16mm
B&W (A)
LC FIE59-234
Shows the processing of an emergency maintenance request at a typical air base to demonstrate how the maintenance management improvement program stretches the Air Force dollar and its buying power.
Civics and Political Systems
Dist - USNAC **Prod** - USDD 1958

USARPAC 29 MIN
16mm
Big Picture Series
Color
LC 74-706299
Shows the missions of American soldiers in the Far East.
Civics and Political Systems; History - United States; History - World; Sociology
Dist - USNAC **Prod** - USA 1968

USArt - the Gift of Ourselves 28 MIN
16mm
Color
Presents a survey of the arts in the United States for the past 200 years.
Fine Arts; History - United States
Dist - MTP **Prod** - SEARS 1975

Use and Abuse of Diagnostic Measures in Emergencies 15 MIN
U-matic / VHS
Color (PRO)
Considers in brief detail central venous pressure monitoring, arterial blood gas analysis and selective arteriography.
Health and Safety; Science - Natural
Dist - PRIMED **Prod** - PRIMED

Use and Abuse of Force 20 MIN
16mm / U-matic / VHS
Color
Explores the whole phenomenon of violence in American history and the changing attitudes toward police use of force. Emphasizes that current attitudes demand an officer to use only the minimum amount of force necessary to accomplish a goal.
Civics and Political Systems; Social Science; Sociology
Dist - CORF **Prod** - WORON

The Use and Abuse of Intermittent Positive Pressure Breathing 9 MIN
VHS / U-matic
Color (PRO)
Provides information for determining when I.P.P.B. is indicated. Discusses the necessary elements in a standard prescription for I.P.P.B. including frequency, duration, pressure and medication.
Health and Safety; Science - Natural
Dist - UMICHM **Prod** - UMICHM 1974

Use and Abuse of Interrogatories 120 MIN
U-matic / VHS / Cassette
(PRO)
Focuses on the use of interrogatories in the legal process. Covers tactical considerations, permissible interrogatories, objections, protective orders, motions to compel, drafting considerations in personal injury, contract, and business tort cases and using interrogatories and responses at trial.
Civics and Political Systems
Dist - CCEB **Prod** - CCEB
ABACPE

The Use and Abuse of Statistics 145 MIN
U-matic
University of the Air Series
Color (J H C A)
$750.00 purchase, $250.00 rental
Examines the different methods and techniques used in collecting, analyzing and interpreting statistical information. Program contains a series of five cassettes 29 minutes each.
Mathematics; Sociology
Dist - CTV **Prod** - CTV 1978

Use and application of Lotus 1 - 2 - 3
VHS
Color (G PRO)
$49.95 purchase _ #590 - 67
Teaches the basics of creating a spreadsheet, using all the power and shortcuts built into Lotus. Shows how to copy and move data, use print - control, margins, titles, headers and automatic page numbering to create complete reports.
Computer Science
Dist - MEMIND

Use and application of MS - DOS
VHS
Color (G PRO)
$49.95 purchase _ #589 - 67
Shows how to change drives, format diskettes, work with internal and external DOS commands, copy files, create and change AUTOEXEC.BAT, creating Batch files and use - switches.
Computer Science
Dist - MEMIND

Use and application of WordPerfect
VHS
Color (G PRO)
$49.95 purchase _ #586 - 67
Shows how to set up, install and produce professional documents using WordPerfect.
Computer Science
Dist - MEMIND

Use and Care of Axes and Knives 10 MIN
16mm
Survival in the Wilderness Series
Color (I)
LC FIA67-1423
Shows how to select the right type of axe or knife for doing different tasks and demonstrates the correct use of each tool.
Health and Safety; Physical Education and Recreation
Dist - SF **Prod** - MORLAT 1967

Use and Care of Basic Tools 26 MIN
VHS / U-matic
Color (A PRO IND) (SPANISH)
$150.00 purchase _ #16.1367, $160.00 purchase _ #56.1367
Gives a general introduction to the types of hand tools used on rigs and leases. Tells how to properly use and care for the tools.
Health and Safety; Industrial and Technical Education
Dist - UTEXPE **Prod** - UTEXPE 1973

Use and Care of Books 13 MIN
U-matic / VHS / 16mm
School Citizenship Series
Color (P I)
Introduces books of various kinds, including library books and textbooks. Emphasizes the correct ways of using, handling and protecting books.
Education; Guidance and Counseling; Literature and Drama; Social Science
Dist - CORF **Prod** - CENTRO 1979

Use and care of books 13 MIN
VHS
Color; PAL (P I J H)
Demonstrates through animation how to use and care for books from school, the library and home. Shows children how to locate information in the library and use a book's index and table of contents. Looks at protective covers for books, the correct way to turn pages and mark places in a volume, and procedures for carrying books outside in wet weather.
Education; English Language; Literature and Drama; Social Science
Dist - VIEWTH

Use and Care of Fiber Rope 20 MIN
16mm
B&W
LC FIE52-1202
Explains how to care for, inspect and use fiber ropes. Compares sisal, manila and jute and shows methods of splicing and eyeing.
Civics and Political Systems; Physical Education and Recreation; Social Science
Dist - USNAC **Prod** - USN 1948

Use and Care of the Air Regulator 6 MIN
VHS / 16mm
Kirkwood Community College Auto Mechanics Series
(G PRO)
$51.00 purchase _ #KTI55
Instructs on the use and care of the air regulator.
Industrial and Technical Education
Dist - RMIBHF **Prod** - RMIBHF

Use and Care of the Micrometer 19 MIN
VHS / 16mm
Machine Shop Series
(IND)
$84.00 purchase _ #MS5
Shows the use and care of the micrometer. Gives safety tips.
Industrial and Technical Education
Dist - RMIBHF **Prod** - RMIBHF

Use and Care of Wire Rope 18 MIN
16mm
B&W
LC FIE52-1219
Describes the construction, use and protective qualities of wire rope. Stresses the importance of careful handling to avoid kinks and explains seizing, the eye splice, frieze fitting and the thimble.
Industrial and Technical Education; Physical Education and Recreation; Social Science
Dist - USNAC **Prod** - USN 1948

Use and Maintenance of the Air System 8 MIN
VHS / 16mm
Kirkwood Community College Auto Mechanics Series
(G PRO)
$56.00 purchase _ #KTI91
Covers general use and care of the compressor, transformer and lines and the basic manifold design.
Industrial and Technical Education
Dist - RMIBHF **Prod** - RMIBHF

Use it in Good Health, Charlie 27 MIN
U-matic / VHS / 16mm
Color (J H A)
Probes problems of retirement and of the life of senior citizens. Offers suggestions for creating positive attitudes toward aging.
Sociology
Dist - AIMS **Prod** - CLYDVS 1983

Use of a Boning Rod 4 MIN
16mm
Color
LC 76-701072
Shows the importance of a boning rod in maintaining proper depth when laying a pipe.
Industrial and Technical Education
Dist - SAIT **Prod** - SAIT 1973

Use of a Torque Wrench 4 MIN
U-matic / VHS / 16mm
Power Mechanics Series
Color (H A)
LC 71-703249
Presents basic information about the use of a torque wrench.

Industrial and Technical Education
Dist - CAROUF **Prod** - THIOKL 1969

Use of a Voltmeter 38 MIN
BETA / 16mm
B&W
LC 79-707534
Demonstrates a procedure for setting up the multimeter (PSM - 6) for use as a voltmeter. Shows how to connect the instrument into a DC circuit and how to adjust and read the meter for different values of voltage. Issued in 1970 as a motion picture.
Industrial and Technical Education
Dist - USNAC **Prod** - USAF 1979

The Use of Activity in the Evaluation and Treatment Process
U-matic / VHS
Color
Shows an occupational therapist working with a group of patients in a psychiatric setting. Demonstrates the use of magazine collage as an evaluation and treatment modality. Provides several scenarios which can be used to illustrate patient pathology as well as interpersonal dynamics.
Health and Safety
Dist - UWASH **Prod** - UWASH

Use of Air Impact Cutter 6 MIN
BETA / VHS / 16mm
Color (A PRO)
$51.00 purchase _ #KAB10
Covers application and use of a Sioux air impact cutter with upper and edging bits.
Industrial and Technical Education
Dist - RMIBHF **Prod** - RMIBHF

Use of Ammeter 30 MIN
16mm
B&W
LC 74-705882
Demonstrates the procedure for setting up the multimeter for use as an ammeter. Shows the method of adjusting the meter to read values in the range of milliamperes to amperes, and how to connect the meter into a DC circuit to measure. (Kinescope).
Health and Safety; Industrial and Technical Education; Science - Physical
Dist - USNAC **Prod** - USAF

Use of an in - Line Air File 16 MIN
BETA / VHS / 16mm
Color (A PRO)
$76.00 purchase _ #KTI57
Demonstrates the use of an in - line air file.
Industrial and Technical Education
Dist - RMIBHF **Prod** - RMIBHF

Use of Anticoagulants in Rodent Control 11 MIN
16mm
Color (H C)
LC FIE61-18
Describes the use of various anticoagulants to kill rodents, advantages of these poisons, preparation of various baits, placement of the poisons to provide the most effective results, and precautionary measures.
Health and Safety; Home Economics
Dist - USNAC **Prod** - USPHS 1961

Use of Basic Layout Tools 7 MIN
BETA / VHS
Metal Fabrication - Hand Tool Identification, Demonstration and 'Applications Series
Color (IND)
Industrial and Technical Education; Psychology
Dist - RMIBHF **Prod** - RMIBHF

Use of Bridging and Tracking to Overcome Apparent Resistance 17 MIN
VHS / U-matic
Multimodal Therapy Series
Color
Teaches how to use bridging to change focus of therapy so client is able to understand therapist's message, explains how to use tracking to determine client's responses.
Psychology
Dist - RESPRC **Prod** - RESPRC

Use of Chemical Agents 22 MIN
16mm / U-matic / VHS
Color
Discusses the use of various chemical agents including inert gas, tear gas or irritant gas. Examines situations in which chemical agents can be effectively used. Describes the four basic delivery systems.
Civics and Political Systems; Social Science
Dist - CORF **Prod** - WORON

Use of Computers in Complex Litigation Series
Are computerized litigation support systems discoverable 104 MIN
Computer Evidence Law 135 MIN
Computerized Litigation Support Systems 231 MIN
Deposition of a computer expert 46 MIN
Using the Computer and Preventing its Abuse 67 MIN
Dist - ABACPE

Use of Condoms 21 MIN
16mm / VHS
Color (J H)
$395.00, $480.00 purchase, $75.00 rental _ #9935, #9935LD
Discusses candidly the use of condoms in the prevention of AIDS. Designed for teenagers.
Health and Safety; Sociology
Dist - AIMS **Prod** - RAINBO 1988

Use of Curare as a Diagnostic Test of Myasthenia Gravis 20 MIN
16mm
B&W (C T)
Follows three normal individuals who have been subjected to curarization to produce artificial symptoms of myasthenia gravis. Five patients with varying degrees of true myasthenia gravis who were given from 1/10 to 1/40 of a normal dose of curare, developed marked exaggeration of the symptoms. This suggests that small doses of crare can be used as a diagnostic test in cases of myasthenia gravis.
Health and Safety; Psychology
Dist - PSUPCR **Prod** - PSUPCR 1944

Use of Disclaimers in Postmortem Planning 54 MIN
VHS / U-matic
Postmortem Tax Planning After ERTA Series
Color (PRO)
Provides a survey of the use of disclaimers in postmortem planning. Discusses severable property and pecuniary or fractional disclaimers.
Civics and Political Systems; Social Science
Dist - ABACPE **Prod** - ABACPE

Use of Dividing Head and Rotary Table
VHS / U-matic
Milling and Tool Sharpening Series
Color (SPANISH)
Industrial and Technical Education
Dist - VTRI **Prod** - VTRI

Use of Face Milling Cutters on the Horizontal Mill
U-matic / VHS
Milling and Tool Sharpening Series
Color (SPANISH)
Industrial and Technical Education
Dist - VTRI **Prod** - VTRI

Use of foam
U-matic / VHS
Marine firefighting series; Pt 4
Color (IND) (KOREAN ITALIAN)
Demonstrates how easily foam extinguishes a diesel fire, explains how foam works, different types available, fixed and portable systems and proper technique.
Health and Safety; Social Science
Dist - GPCV **Prod** - GPCV

Use of Fossils and the Geological Time Scale 43 MIN
VHS / U-matic
Basic Geology Series
Color (IND)
Science - Physical
Dist - GPCV **Prod** - GPCV

Use of Frame Gauges 9 MIN
VHS / BETA / 16mm
Color (A PRO)
$58.50 purchase _ #KTI89
Explains and demonstrates chain and strap drop type frame gauges. Demonstrates with Guy Chart and Buske.
Industrial and Technical Education
Dist - RMIBHF **Prod** - RMIBHF

Use of Fully Crimpable Connectors and Crimping Tools 26 MIN
BETA
Color
LC 79-707531
Demonstrates the use of crimping tools for replacing broken or bent pins in coaxial cable plugs. Shows how to remove defective connectors, strip wire, and crimp and install new pins. Issued in 1967 as a motion picture.
Industrial and Technical Education
Dist - USNAC **Prod** - USAF 1979

Use of General Surgical Facilities by the Dental Service 25 MIN
16mm
Color
LC 74-706302
Familiarizes the clinical dentist with general operating room procedures.
Health and Safety
Dist - USNAC **Prod** - USVA 1962

The Use of Handcuffs 8 MIN
16mm
Color (H C)
LC 75-701987
Helps police officers become familiar with the correct way to search and handcuff a suspect. Uses dramatizations to show what happens when incorrect techniques are used.
Civics and Political Systems; Social Science; Sociology
Dist - MCCRNE **Prod** - MCCRNE 1975

Use of laboratory tests in the diagnosis of liver disease 15 MIN
VHS / U-matic
Color (PRO C)
$395.00 purchase, $80.00 rental _ #C880 - VI - 027
Introduces medical students to laboratory tests used in the diagnosis of liver disease. Groups the tests according to the following clinical conditions - hepato - cellular injury, protein synthesis and cholestasis. Explicates each group of tests for efficacy in four clinical categories - extrahepatic biliary obstruction, viral hepatitis, alcohol liver disease and space - occupying lesions. Describes morphological details and discusses etiological findings. Presented by Dr Gerald J Kost.
Health and Safety
Dist - HSCIC

The Use of landscapes in a sketch 29 MIN
U-matic
Sketching techniques series; Lesson 11
Color (C A)
Studies how to draw landscapes. Illustrates that the shape of the land can be as important as the growth of the land. Shows the relationship between buildings and a landscape.
Fine Arts
Dist - CDTEL **Prod** - COAST

The Use of Layout Tools in Machine Technology
U-matic / VHS
Basic Machine Technology Series
Color (SPANISH)
Industrial and Technical Education
Dist - VTRI **Prod** - VTRI

The Use of Layout Tools in Machine Technology 15 MIN
VHS / U-matic
Machining and the Operation of Machine Tools, Module 1 - Basic 'Machine Technology Series
Color (IND)
Industrial and Technical Education
Dist - LEIKID **Prod** - LEIKID

Use of mathematical decomposition to optimize investments in gas production and distribution
VHS
Color (C PRO G)
$150.00 purchase _ #86.05
Focuses on a system developed at SANTOS to plan capital investment in new reservoirs, pipelines and processing to maximize the net present value of profits. Reveals that the approach starts with an LP, with standard reports providing comprehensive information on reservoir performance and cash flow. The system is the company's official and main planning aid, with savings estimated to be $1 - 3 million in total annual capital costs. SANTOS Ltd. E L Dougherty, E Lombardino, P Hutchison, P A Goode.
Business and Economics
Dist - INMASC

The Use of Measuring Tools in Machine Technology 15 MIN
VHS / U-matic
Machining and the Operation of Machine Tools, Module 1 - Basic 'Machine Technology Series
Color (IND)
Industrial and Technical Education
Dist - LEIKID **Prod** - LEIKID

The Use of Measuring Tools in Machine Technology
VHS / U-matic
Basic Machine Technology Series
Color (SPANISH)
Industrial and Technical Education; Mathematics
Dist - VTRI **Prod** - VTRI

Use of Metal Conditioners with Lead and Plastic Fill 15 MIN
VHS / BETA / 16mm

Color (A PRO)
$73.50 purchase _ #KTI30
Shows the advantages and limitations of etching liquids.
Industrial and Technical Education
Dist - RMIBHF **Prod** - RMIBHF

Use of Motivation in Building a Championship Football Program 27 MIN
VHS / U-matic
Joe Paterno - 'Winning Football' Series
Color (C A)
$49.00 purchase _ #3763
Presents successful techniques for developing the leadership qualities that inspire enthusiasm and loyalty in team members and describes how to earn the respect of the players. Conducted by Joe Paterno, head coach of the Penn State football team.
Physical Education and Recreation
Dist - EBEC

Use of Ohmmeter 37 MIN
16mm
B&W
LC 74-705883
Demonstrates the procedure for setting up the PSM - 6 multimeter for use as an ohmmeter, how to adjust the range selector switch for the most accurate reading of a resistor, how to zero the meter and how to connect the instrument to read the ohmic values of resistors. (Kinescope).
Industrial and Technical Education; Science - Physical
Dist - USNAC **Prod** - USAF

Use of Oscilloscope 21 MIN
U-matic / VHS / 16mm
B&W
Shows waveshapes, amplitudes and phase relationships on an oscilloscope screen. Shows the general operation of the oscilloscope and how to use it to find frequency and amplitude.
Industrial and Technical Education; Mathematics; Science - Physical
Dist - USNAC **Prod** - USAF

Use of PCR, dot blot for dried stain and hair analysis, and polymerase chain reaction 99 MIN
VHS
DNA technology in forensic science series
Color (A PRO)
$50.00 purchase _ #TCA17409
Presents two lectures on DNA technology in forensic science. Covers subjects including polymerase chain reaction technology, the relationship of in vitro PCR to cell division, and how Cetus developed the PCR.
Science - Natural; Sociology
Dist - USNAC **Prod** - FBI 1988

Use of Plain and Side Milling Cutters on the Horizontal Milling Machine
U-matic / VHS
Milling and Tool Sharpening Series
Color
Industrial and Technical Education
Dist - VTRI **Prod** - VTRI

Use of Plain and Side Milling Cutters on the Horizontal Milling Machine 15 MIN
U-matic / VHS
Machine Technology IV - Milling Series
Color
Industrial and Technical Education
Dist - CAMB **Prod** - CAMB

The Use of Plantar Skin in Correcting a Severe Finger Contracture 15 MIN
16mm
Color
LC 75-702320
Shows in detail the release of a 90 degree flexion contracture at the proximal interphalangeal joint in the long finger. Illustrates immediate and long term post - operative results.
Health and Safety; Science
Dist - EATONL **Prod** - EATONL 1970

The Use of plastic sealants in preventive dentistry 13 MIN
U-matic / VHS
Color (PRO)
Uses typodont models to demonstrate the use of sealants to eradicate deep fissures and grooves in posterior teeth. Shows the use of two sealants, one using ultraviolet light to bring about polymerization and the other using a chemical catalyst to convert the monomer.
Health and Safety; Science
Dist - USNAC **Prod** - VADTC 1978

The Use of PNF in the Treatment of an Adult with Limb - Girdle Muscular Dystrophy 38 MIN
VHS / U-matic
B&W
Demonstrates the various combinations of PNF strengthening techniques and patterns applied within a motor developmental framework.
Health and Safety
Dist - BUSARG **Prod** - BUSARG

Use of Positive Reinforcement 49 MIN
U-matic / VHS
Learning and Liking it Series
Color (T)
Presents six humanistic uses of reinforcement. Demonstrates some of the uses.
Education; Psychology
Dist - MSU **Prod** - MSU

Use of Postioning and Adaptive Equipment in Management of Disorders of Posture and Tone
U-matic / VHS
Color
Demonstrates positioning and adaptive equipment used for children and adults with physical disabilities. Includes positioning in sidelying, prone, sitting and standing.
Health and Safety; Psychology
Dist - VALHAL **Prod** - VALHAL

Use of Pressure - Indicating Paste during the Delivery of Dentures 15 MIN
16mm
Color
LC 75-702157; 74-705885
Shows use of pressure - indicating pastes for developing better - fitting dentures. Shows use of these materials when delivering newly - made dentures to the patient.
Health and Safety; Science
Dist - USNAC **Prod** - USVA 1970

The Use of questions to structure the negotiation 24 MIN
U-matic / VHS
Art of negotiating series
Color
Business and Economics; Psychology
Dist - DELTAK **Prod** - DELTAK

Use of Resonant Sections 22 MIN
BETA
B&W
LC 79-707533
Shows the use of resonant sections of transmission lines as circuit elements. Develops the lecher line oscillator and explains how a shortened quarter wavelength section of transmission line can be used as a parallel resonant circuit. Issued in 1970 as a motion picture.
Industrial and Technical Education
Dist - USNAC **Prod** - USAF 1979

The Use of Sealants in Preventive Dentistry 13 MIN
16mm
Color (PRO)
LC 79-700990
Uses typodont models to demonstrate the use of sealants to eradicate deep fissures and grooves in posterior teeth. Shows the use of two sealants, one using ultraviolet light to bring about polymerization and the other using a chemical catalyst to convert the monomer.
Health and Safety
Dist - USNAC **Prod** - VADTC 1978

Use of Sickle Scalers 21 MIN
U-matic
Scaling Techniques Series; No 5
Color (PRO)
LC 77-706010
Demonstrates how to use straight and hooked sickle scalers on anterior teeth and contra - angle scalers on posterior teeth in removal of calculus from the supragingival area.
Health and Safety; Science; Science - Natural
Dist - USNAC **Prod** - UTENN 1976

Use of Side Rails 22 MIN
16mm / U-matic
Nurse's Aide, Orderly and Attendant Series
Color (H C A)
LC 75-704831
Demonstrates the need for side rails and explains how to use them safely and effectively. Shows how to handle complaints and requests of the patients.
Guidance and Counseling; Health and Safety
Dist - COPI **Prod** - COPI 1969

Use of Soldering Coppers 8 MIN
U-matic / VHS / 16mm
B&W
Describes the techniques of soft soldering in a sequence of operations, including proper selection and tinning of the copper, correct heating, cleaning and flexing the surfaces to be soldered and the method of transferring sufficient heat from the copper.
Industrial and Technical Education
Dist - USNAC **Prod** - USN 1954

Use of Space and Equipment, Pt 1 30 MIN
U-matic
Day Care Series
Color (A)
Education; Home Economics
Dist - MDCPB **Prod** - MDCPB

Use of Space and Equipment, Pt 2 30 MIN
U-matic
Day Care Series
Color (A)
Education; Home Economics
Dist - MDCPB **Prod** - MDCPB

The Use of Split Thickness Skin Grafts in Contractures of the Elbow 10 MIN
16mm
Color
LC 75-702319
Demonstrates the development of a very severe soft tissue, muscular and capsular contracture at the elbow in a burned patient. Illustrates the functional and cosmetic results obtained by this procedure.
Health and Safety; Science
Dist - EATONL **Prod** - EATONL 1967

Use of Surgical Instruments 19 MIN
16mm
Color (PRO)
Defines the various instruments and their functions in the surgical procedures. Describes a variety of basic surgical maneuvers common to practically all operations, such as cutting, dissecting, grasping with tissue forceps, clamping with hemostats, retracting and suturing.
Health and Safety; Science
Dist - ACY **Prod** - ACYDGD 1967

The Use of Synthetic Knitted Mesh in Hernia Repair 27 MIN
16mm
Color (PRO)
Explains that knitted mesh made of either nylon or dacron has been used for the past two years for the repair of recurrent hernias in selected patients. Illustrates the technique of the use of this material in two patients.
Health and Safety; Science
Dist - ACY **Prod** - ACYDGD 1958

Use of the Baton - the Lamb Method 22 MIN
U-matic / VHS / 16mm
Color (PRO)
LC 77-700939
Teaches service baton self - defense techniques based on the system developed by Arthur Lamb of the Boston Police Department.
Civics and Political Systems
Dist - CORF **Prod** - HAR 1977

Use of the Computer as a Tool 15 MIN
VHS
Micro Moppets Series
Color (I)
Fine Arts; Industrial and Technical Education; Mathematics; Psychology
Dist - GPN **Prod** - RITVC

Use of the Condom Appliance for the Incontiment Patient 9 MIN
16mm
Color
LC 74-705886
Presents in detail the assembly and application of the condom appliance, which provides a means whereby the incontinent male patient can be kept dry without the use of an indwelling catheter.
Health and Safety
Dist - USNAC **Prod** - USPHS 1966

Use of the Condom Catheter for Incontinence 10 MIN
VHS / U-matic
Color
LC 82-706232
Describes cleansing and skin preparation, use of adhesive liner and application of condom. Discusses solutions for problems with fit and skin irritation, and describes leg bag and night bag.
Health and Safety; Science; Science - Natural
Dist - USNAC **Prod** - VAMCMM 1981

Use of the Explorer 15 MIN
U-matic
Scaling Techniques Series; No 4
Color (PRO)
LC 77-706012
Demonstrates how to use an explorer stroke in the detection of calculus and caries and in examination of the texture, contour and character of tooth surfaces.

Health and Safety; Science; Science - Natural
Dist - USNAC **Prod** - UTENN 1976

Use of the Face Milling Cutter on the Horizontal Mill 15 MIN
U-matic / VHS
Machining and the Operation of Machine Tools, Module 4 - Milling and Tool Series
Color (IND)
Industrial and Technical Education
Dist - LEIKID **Prod** - LEIKID

Use of the Gracey Curet no 07 - 08 21 MIN
U-matic
Scaling Techniques Series; No 6
Color (PRO)
LC 77-706013
Demonstrates how to use the gracey curet no. 07 - 08 in subgingival scaling and root planing. Discusses curettage which is not generally practiced by hygiene students.
Health and Safety; Science; Science - Natural
Dist - USNAC **Prod** - UTENN 1976

Use of the Gracey Curet no 11 - 12 13 MIN
U-matic
Scaling Techniques Series; No 7
Color (PRO)
LC 77-706014
Demonstrates how to use the gracey curet no. 11 - 12 in scaling mesial surfaces of posterior teeth.
Health and Safety; Science; Science - Natural
Dist - USNAC **Prod** - UTENN 1976

Use of the Gracey Curet no 13 - 14 12 MIN
U-matic
Scaling Techniques Series; No 8
Color (PRO)
LC 77-706015
Demonstrates how to use the gracey curet no. 13 - 14 in scaling distal surfaces of posterior teeth.
Health and Safety; Science; Science - Natural
Dist - USNAC **Prod** - UTENN 1976

Use of the Malleable Mesh in the Reduction and Fixation of Jaw Fractures 11 MIN
16mm
Color
LC 75-702159; 74-705888
Demonstrates the adaptation and fixation of the mesh, used when teeth need secondary support, on a mannequin and in the operating room.
Health and Safety; Science; Science - Natural
Dist - USNAC **Prod** - USVA 1969

Use of the normal value algorithm 50 MIN
U-matic / VHS
Computer languages series; Pt 1
Color
Introduces evaluations using the nv algorithm, free and bound variables, conditionals, logic values.
Industrial and Technical Education; Mathematics; Sociology
Dist - MIOT **Prod** - MIOT

Use of the oscilloscope 30 MIN
U-matic / VHS
Automotive oscilloscope series; Lesson 2
Color (IND)
Outlines some of the precautions and procedures to observe for successful diagnosis. Continues test procedure, covering cylinder timing, coil and condenser testing and dwell variation. Explains test procedures for secondary resistance.
Industrial and Technical Education
Dist - LEIKID **Prod** - LEIKID

Use of the Periodontal Probe 11 MIN
U-matic
Scaling Techniques Series; No 9
Color (PRO)
LC 77-706023
Demonstrates how to use the periodontal probe instrument in examining the shape and dimensions of the gingival sulcus and periodontal pockets.
Health and Safety; Science
Dist - USNAC **Prod** - UTENN 1976

Use of the Pneumatic Otoscope 12 MIN
16mm
Color
LC 80-700353
Demonstrates the use of the pneumatic otoscope and shows views of the human ear through the otoscope while describing conditions observed.
Health and Safety
Dist - USNAC **Prod** - NMAC 1978

Use of the Polygraph in Investigations 26 MIN
16mm
B&W
LC 74-706303
Describes the use of the polygraph in investigations.
Civics and Political Systems; Sociology
Dist - USNAC **Prod** - USA 1967

Use of the Problem in Teaching 28 MIN
16mm
B&W
LC FIE58-329
An air university instructor employs a clever method of impressing his students with the principles and techniques of using the problem as an effective teaching aid.
Education
Dist - USNAC **Prod** - USAF 1958

Use of the Resistance Spot Welder 13 MIN
BETA / VHS
Color (A PRO)
$68.00 purchase _ #AB124
Deals with auto body repair.
Industrial and Technical Education
Dist - RMIBHF **Prod** - RMIBHF

The Use of the Revocable Trust in Estate Planning 150 MIN
U-matic / VHS
Color (PRO)
Discusses the pros and cons of using a revocable intervivos trust. Considers tax consequences, community property and choice of trustee.
Civics and Political Systems
Dist - ABACPE **Prod** - ABACPE

Use of the Scribble Technique in Art Therapy as a Psychiatric Treatment Adjunct 60 MIN
U-matic / VHS
Art Therapy Series
Color
Demonstrates the scribble technique with a woman in her 30s as a tool to elicit repressed material and free associations for working - through. Shows how the patient is helped to make her own connections through questions rather than interpretations. Presents the step - by - step use of the scribble technique and its use as a psychotherapeutic adjunct in clincal practice.
Fine Arts; Health and Safety; Psychology
Dist - HEMUL **Prod** - HEMUL

Use of the Short Baton 20 MIN
16mm / U-matic / VHS
Color
Discusses the use of the short baton by police officers. Presents the baton as an acceptable, publicly - approved, second - level weapon. Stresses the need for such equipment in the police arsenal.
Civics and Political Systems; Psychology; Social Science; Sociology
Dist - CORF **Prod** - WORON

Use of the Triple Beam Balance 11 MIN
U-matic / VHS / 16mm
Basic Laboratory Techniques in Chemistry Series
Color (H C)
Shows correct tecnnique in weighing out specified amounts of solids and a specified volume of a liquid. Emphasizes careful handling of the balance and materials and accuracy in reading the weights obtained.
Science
Dist - LUF **Prod** - SCHLAT

Use of the Wire Feed Welder 18 MIN
BETA / VHS / 16mm
Color (A PRO)
$81.00 purchase _ #AB125
Discusses the use of the wire feed welder.
Industrial and Technical Education
Dist - RMIBHF **Prod** - RMIBHF

Use of Thickness Gauges 10 MIN
16mm / U-matic / VHS
Power Mechanics Series
Color (H C)
LC 70-703251
Presents basic information about the use of thickness gauges.
Industrial and Technical Education
Dist - CAROUF **Prod** - THIOKL 1969

Use of Time 25 MIN
VHS / 16mm
Color (G)
$165.00 purchase, $40.00 rental _ #5804H, 5805H, 0400J, 0416J
Examines four major time zones of life - work time, sleep time, life maintenance time and leisure time. Considers how chemical abuse affects each zone. Features Dr Damian McElrath.
Guidance and Counseling; Health and Safety; Mathematics; Psychology
Dist - HAZELB **Prod** - HAZELB

Use of Turning Frames 25 MIN
16mm
B&W
LC 74-705890
Teaches nursing personnel the clinical requirement for and proper use of turning frames.
Health and Safety
Dist - USNAC **Prod** - USA 1966

Use of Visitation Logs in Permanency Planning 15 MIN
VHS / U-matic
Color
Demonstrates the use of visitation logs in the coordination of visit planning and the enhancement of the working relationship of the social practitioner, natural parent and foster parent.
Sociology
Dist - UWISC **Prod** - UWISC 1981

Use of Your Portable Auto Syringe Pump 26 MIN
U-matic
Color
Demonstrates how to use the auto syringe pump.
Health and Safety
Dist - UTEXSC **Prod** - UTEXSC

Use Your Ears 9 MIN
16mm / U-matic / VHS
Color (P I)
LC 74-703502
Promotes an understanding and appreciation for the variety of sounds in everyday life, such as the sound of the police whistle, the roar of the ocean and the sound of rock and roll music.
Science - Physical
Dist - BARR **Prod** - BARR 1974

Use Your Eyes 10 MIN
16mm / U-matic / VHS
Color (P I)
LC 73-702958
Shows young people exploring and discovering the wonders of a meadow and their own backyard, the details of common household items and the many elements that make up their environment. Uses close - up photography.
English Language; Guidance and Counseling; Psychology; Science - Natural
Dist - BARR **Prod** - BARR 1973

Use Your Imagination 4 MIN
VHS / 16mm / U-matic
Most Important Person - Creative Expression Series
Color (K P I)
Emphasizes the use of imagination as a tool. Presents the imagination as a tool to making things happen and to keep from being bored.
Psychology
Dist - EBEC **Prod** - EBEC 1972

Use Your Voice to Sing 15 MIN
U-matic / VHS
Music and Me Series
Color (P I)
Discusses various aspects of singing.
Fine Arts
Dist - AITECH **Prod** - WDCNTV 1979

Used Cars - How to Find Them and Buy Them
VHS / U-matic
Color
Teaches the skills of finding and evaluating used cars. Includes information on financing and insurance.
Home Economics; Industrial and Technical Education
Dist - EDUACT **Prod** - EDUACT

Used Innocence 95 MIN
16mm
Color (G)
Presents an independent production by James Benning. Offers a portrait of a pretty woman wrongly imprisoned.
Civics and Political Systems; Fine Arts; Sociology
Dist - FIRS
ICARUS

Useful Knots for Boatmen 25 MIN
16mm
Color
LC 74-705892
Discusses knots most commonly used by boatmen and gives instructions for tieing and whipping.
Physical Education and Recreation; Social Science
Dist - USNAC **Prod** - USCG 1972

Useful Propeller 11 MIN
U-matic / VHS / 16mm
Inventive Child Series
Color (P I)
Reveals that during a hot spell, Boy fantasizes about ways to cool off, first designing a fan, then experimenting with homemade devices that make use of airpower to create suction. Shows that in the process he creates a vacuum cleaner. Develops the concept of using air pressure and vacuums to do various kinds of work.

History - World; Science - Physical
Dist - EBEC **Prod** - POLSKI 1983

The Useless Jug 20 MIN
16mm
Animatoons Series
Color (K P)
LC FIA68-1531
Relates the story of an unruly and ill - tempered jug that didn't become useful until it was broken into many pieces.
Literature and Drama
Dist - RADTV **Prod** - ANTONS 1968

The Useless Jug - Pt 1 10 MIN
16mm
Animatoons Series
Color (K P)
LC FIA67-5491
Tells the story of a jugmaker who accidentally creates a giant jug that has a mind of its own and refuses to let itself be used.
Fine Arts
Dist - RADTV **Prod** - ANTONS 1968

The Useless Jug - Pt 2 10 MIN
16mm
Animatoons Series
Color (K P)
LC FIA67-5492
Describes how a jugmaker and his wife try to sell their useless, ill - tempered jug.
Fine Arts
Dist - RADTV **Prod** - ANTONS 1968

The Useless Jug - Pt 3 10 MIN
16mm
Animatoons Series
Color (K P)
LC FIA67-5493
Shows how a donkey breaks a giant useless jug and an old woman finally makes the jug useful by filling its shards with water for her duckling.
Fine Arts
Dist - RADTV **Prod** - ANTONS 1968

USEPA culturing and toxicity test methods for marine and estuarine effluents - red algal, sheepshead effluents - red algal, sheepshead d minnow and sea urchin 74 MIN
U-matic / VHS / BETA
Color (G PRO)
$60.00 purchase _ #LSTF22
Explains measurement of chronic toxicity of marine and estuarine waters by studying toxic effects on various flora and fauna.
Science - Natural
Dist - FEDU **Prod** - USEPA 1990

The User and the Database 25 MIN
U-matic / VHS / 16mm
Color
Depicts the role of a database for the control and scheduling of materials, one of five databases used by a construction firm. Shows the problem of getting access to data in the field as opposed to trained personnel using equipment withing computing facilities.
Business and Economics; Mathematics
Dist - MEDIAG **Prod** - OPENU 1980

User - Defined Data Types 30 MIN
U-matic / VHS
Pascal, Pt 1 - Beginning Pascal Series
Color (H C A)
LC 81-706049
Introduces user - defined enumerated data type in Pascal. Shows examples involving assignment, loop control, CASE selectors and IF - THEN. Discusses input/output limitations, and built - in functions SUCC, PRED for manipulating enumerated data elements.
Industrial and Technical Education; Mathematics; Sociology
Dist - COLOSU **Prod** - COLOSU 1980

User - Directed Information Systems Series
Changing Technology and the Role of the User 20 MIN
Managing and using the Data Resource 20 MIN
Network Concepts for Users 20 MIN
Dist - DELTAK

User Needs and Industrial Innovation 42 MIN
VHS / U-matic
Management of Technological Innovation Series
Color
Discusses how to transfer an accurate understanding of user need to the manufacturer.
Business and Economics; Industrial and Technical Education
Dist - MIOT **Prod** - MIOT

User responsibilities in information management series
Communicating with MIS 45 MIN
Participating in Implementation 45 MIN
Planning and Selecting High Payoff Applications 45 MIN
Supporting Ongoing Operations 45 MIN
Dist - DELTAK

Users - Losers 20 MIN
16mm / U-matic / VHS
Color (I J)
LC 76-702159
Tells about a boy in junior high school who tries to find acceptance at school by taking marijuana and pills. Shows an older boy, a former user, giving him the facts about narcotics and drug abuse.
Health and Safety; Psychology; Sociology
Dist - AIMS **Prod** - DAVP 1971

Uses of Blood 27 MIN
U-matic / VHS / 16mm
Perspective Series
Color (C A)
Discusses the many types of research done on blood donated to Britain's National Blood Transfusion Service.
Science; Science - Natural
Dist - STNFLD **Prod** - LONTVS

Uses of Control Charts 50 MIN
VHS / U-matic
Deming Video Tapes - Quality, Productivity and the Competitive 'Series
Color
Business and Economics
Dist - SME **Prod** - MIOT

Uses of Control Charts/Advantages of Achieving Statistical Control
U-matic / VHS
Deming Videotapes - Quality, Productivity, and Competitive Series
Color
Business and Economics
Dist - MIOT **Prod** - MIOT

Uses of Energy 29 MIN
VHS / 16mm
Villa Alegre Series
Color (P T)
$46.00 rental _ #VILA - 140
Presents educational material in both Spanish and English.
Education; Science - Physical
Dist - PBS

The Uses of Media 26 MIN
U-matic / VHS
Color (C)
$249.00, $149.00 purchase _ #AD - 1920
Profiles Tony Schwartz, advertising and political media producer to show how he uses media to influence people to vote for his sponsor. Explores subliminal messages.
Business and Economics; Computer Science; Fine Arts; Psychology; Sociology
Dist - FOTH **Prod** - FOTH

Uses of Motivation in Building a Championship Football Program 27 MIN
16mm / U-matic / VHS
Joe Paterno - Coaching Winning Football Series
Color (T)
Presents coach Joe Paterno explaining how to build a sound football program around empathy with students, parents, faculty and community. Demonstrates how to best utilize assistant coaches and how to motivate student athletes by developing pride, morale and loyalty.
Physical Education and Recreation
Dist - EBEC **Prod** - UNIDIM 1982

Uses of Music Series
Mexican - American Culture - its Heritage 18 MIN
Music - from Popular to Concert Stage 15 MIN
Dist - CGWEST

Uses of Penicillins - Old and New 40 MIN
16mm
Boston Medical Reports Series
B&W (PRO)
LC 74-705893
Describes one observer's experiences with methicillin, oxacillin, ampicillin and cephalosporin. Discusses the use of penicillin G in gram - negative injections.
Health and Safety; Science - Natural
Dist - NMAC **Prod** - NMAC 1964

Uses of Resonant Sections 22 MIN
16mm
B&W
LC 74-705894
Shows the use of resonant sections of transmission lines and circuit elements. Develops the Lecher line oscillator and explains how a shorted quarter wavelength section of transmission line can be used as a parallel resonant circuit. (Kinescope).
Industrial and Technical Education; Science - Physical
Dist - USNAC **Prod** - USAF

Uses of the Electromagnet 9 MIN
U-matic / VHS
Introductory Concepts in Physics - Electricity Series
Color (C)
$229.00, $129.00 purchase _ #AD - 1177
Presents a series of experiments which explain why a current passed through a wire fails to attract some nearby nails. Includes other aspects of electromagnetism.
Science - Physical
Dist - FOTH **Prod** - FOTH

Uses of the Mouthparts of the Orthoptera during Feeding 8 MIN
16mm
B&W (H C A)
LC FIA65-429
Uses close - ups and slow motion to show the mouthparts at work. Illustrates and explains the forms and functions of the mouthparts.
Science - Natural
Dist - WSUM **Prod** - WSUM 1960

Usher's Syndrome - Retinitis Pigmentosa and Deafness 20 MIN
16mm / U-matic / VHS
Color (PRO)
Discusses progressive blindness with congenital hearing impairment, ways of diagnosing the condition, the importance of genetic counseling. Captioned or uncaptioned.
Guidance and Counseling; Psychology
Dist - GALCO **Prod** - GALCO 1978

Usiku - an African folk tale 6 MIN
VHS
Color (P I J G)
$99.00 purchase, $40.00 rental
Recreates an African ritual to honor ancestors using string puppets. Captures the ebb and flow of life in a jungle fishing village where the boats go out each morning and return at night. Tells of a special evening when a celebration begins with dancing and singing to the music of drums and marimbas. As the dawn breaks, the mysterious ghosts of the village's ancestors emerge from the jungle mist.
History - United States; Literature and Drama; Religion and Philosophy
Dist - FLMLIB

Using a 12 - lead EKG to document acute myocardial infarction 56 MIN
VHS / U-matic
Twelve - lead EKG series
Color (PRO)
$275.00 purchase, $60.00 rental _ #7808S, #7808V
Explains the progressive stages of an acute myocardial infarction - MI - and shows the characteristic changes each stage produces in the EKG. Helps nurses identify the site of the MI by the presence of these changes in specific leads. Illustrates actual 12 - lead EKGs that show wave form changes in various sites. Part of a two - part series on 12 - lead EKG.
Health and Safety
Dist - AJN **Prod** - HOSSN 1988

Using a boring bar between centers - work held on carriage 22 MIN
16mm
Machine shop work series; Operations on the engine lathe; No 16
B&W (H)
LC FIE51-528
Shows how to set up, mount, adjust and use a boring bar between centers of the lathe, how to clamp an irregular workpiece on a lathe carriage and how to align the workpiece center with the lathe centerline.
Industrial and Technical Education
Dist - USNAC **Prod** - USOE 1944

Using a Boring Head 22 MIN
BETA / VHS
Machine Shop - Milling Machine Series
Color (IND)
Industrial and Technical Education; Psychology
Dist - RMIBHF **Prod** - RMIBHF

Using a Card Catalog 20 MIN
VHS / 16mm
Study, Research, Library Skills Series
Color (J)
Presents a lesson on using the card catalog.
Education
Dist - COMEX **Prod** - COMEX 1987

Using a Compass 10 MIN
16mm
Survival in the Wilderness Series
Color (I)
LC FIA67-1425
Shows types of compasses and how to use the compass with a map. Explains how to follow a bearing, to estimate distance by tally and to use the pace system.
Health and Safety; Mathematics; Social Science
Dist - SF **Prod** - MORLAT 1967

Using a compound microscope
VHS
Science laboratory technique series
Color (J H)
$79.95 purchase _ #193 W 2203
Illustrates step - by - step procedures for operating a compound microscope. Part of a series on laboratory technique, including proper use and handling of equipment, preparation of materials and recording observations. Includes a supplementary teaching guide.
Science
Dist - WARDS **Prod** - WARDS

Using a Computer 30 MIN
U-matic / VHS
Working with the Computer Series
Color
Describes the basic components that make up computer systems. Explains these components and their inter - relationships in simple terms. Examines a variety of computer systems at work in the business world.
Industrial and Technical Education; Mathematics; Psychology
Dist - DELTAK **Prod** - DELTAK

Using a computer I graph
16mm
Color (G)
$90.00 rental
Collects shorter works whose content ranges from appropriation to computer graphics. Looks at the relationship of abstract systems to gender; gender plays itself out in a number of ways. Includes some short sequences dealing with memories of 1960.
Computer Science; Fine Arts
Dist - CANCIN **Prod** - SONDHE 1985

Using a Data Base 30 MIN
U-matic / VHS
End User's Guide to Data Base Series
Color
Describes technological advances that have and will continue to change data base use and stresses the advantages of this technology.
Business and Economics; Industrial and Technical Education
Dist - DELTAK **Prod** - DELTAK

Using a follower rest 21 MIN
16mm
Machine shop work series; Operations on the engine lathe; No 15
B&W (H)
LC FIE51-529
Illustrates the use of a follower rest in the turning of a long shaft into two diameters.
Industrial and Technical Education
Dist - USNAC **Prod** - USOE 1943

Using a Hand Punch 6 MIN
BETA / VHS
Color (IND)
Presents the operation and set - up for changing punches and dies in a hand punch.
Industrial and Technical Education; Psychology
Dist - RMIBHF **Prod** - RMIBHF

Using a Mathematics Laboratory Approach 15 MIN
16mm
Project on Interpreting Mathematics Education Research Series
Color
LC 74-705986
Acquaints teachers with the laboratory approach by describing what labs are, why they are used, how they are organized and the kinds of activities that are valuable in the mathematics laboratory.
Education; Mathematics
Dist - USNAC **Prod** - USOE 1970

Using a Pop Rivet Tool 9 MIN
VHS / BETA
Color (IND)
Shows the basic operation of the pop rivet gun (blind rivet).
Industrial and Technical Education; Psychology
Dist - RMIBHF **Prod** - RMIBHF

Using a Portable Spray Gun 26 MIN
16mm
B&W
LC FIE52-91
Explains how the pressure tank operates, and shows how to clean portable spray guns, adjust the paint, spray and air controls stroke while painting and use the suction type spray gun.
Industrial and Technical Education
Dist - USNAC **Prod** - USOE 1945

Using a pre - fabricated post in the restoration of an endodontically treated tooth 21 MIN
U-matic / VHS
Color (C PRO)
$395.00 purchase, $80.00 rental _ #D891 - VI - 036
Demonstrates step - by - step procedures necessary in the use of a pre - fabricated post technique for the restoration of a mutilated and endodontically treated tooth. Demonstrates post selection, tooth canal reaming and sizing, post fittings and post cementation. Presented by Dr F Dean S Arnault and the Office of Instructional Development in conjunction with the Dept of Occlusion and Fixed Prosthodontics.
Health and Safety
Dist - HSCIC

Using a Shell End Mill 21 MIN
16mm
Machine Shop Work Series Operations on the Vertical Milling Machine,'no 1
B&W (H)
LC FIE51-570
Tells how the vertical milling machine differs from others. Shows how to make a flat surface with a shell end mill and how to use the sliding head. Explains speed and feed and how to calculate them.
Industrial and Technical Education
Dist - USNAC **Prod** - USOE 1943

Using a Spectrophotometer 7 MIN
U-matic / VHS / 16mm
Basic Laboratory Techniques Series
Color (C)
LC 79-700103
Presents a demonstration of the use of the spectrophotometer, an electronic laboratory instrument used for measuring the concentration and absorbency of chemical compounds.
Science; Science - Physical
Dist - IU **Prod** - IU 1978

Using a steady rest 25 MIN
16mm
Machine shop work series; Operations on the engine lathe; No 14
B&W (H)
LC FIE51-511
Describes the steady rest and its uses. Shows how to spot the work for the location of the steady rest, how to mount the steady rest on the lathe and how to adjust the jaws of the rest to the work.
Industrial and Technical Education
Dist - USNAC **Prod** - USOE 1943

Using a steady rest when boring 21 MIN
16mm
Machine shop work series; Operations on the engine lathe; No 17
B&W (H)
LC FIE51-512
Shows how to mount a long casting on a lathe faceplate, how to turn a true bearing spot for supporting the workpiece with a steady rest and how to perform boring, turning and forming operations when work is supported by a steady rest.
Industrial and Technical Education
Dist - USNAC **Prod** - USOE 1944

Using addition facts
VHS
Lola May's fundamental math series
Color (P)
$45.00 purchase _ #10266VG
Practices mental addition of two and three one - digit numbers in and around a square. Uses addition problems to teach mental arithmetic and find the total value of different pictures. Comes with a teacher's guide and blackline masters. Part 16 of a 30 - part series.
Mathematics
Dist - UNL

Using Advanced UNIX Commands
U-matic / VHS
UNIX and 'C'Language Training - a Full Curriculum Series
Color
Industrial and Technical Education; Mathematics; Sociology
Dist - COMTEG **Prod** - COMTEG

Using an Analytical Balance Model H - 30 12 MIN
BETA / VHS
Color
Discusses wastewater reclamation, water and wastewater technology.
Health and Safety; Industrial and Technical Education; Science; Social Science
Dist - RMIBHF **Prod** - RMIBHF

Using an optimization software package to lower overall electric production costs
VHS
Color (C PRO G)
$150.00 purchase _ #90.02
Focuses on Southern Company Services which, since 1982, has used a dynamic - programming optimization package to formulate daily operating strategy and to compare actual pool dispatch against ideal strategy. Reveals that the system, based on the Wescouger optimization program and designed by ABB, also utilizes branch - and - bound techniques resulting in a saving of $140 million over seven years. Southern Co Services Inc. K D Le, J T Day, C K Yin, J S Griffith, S R Erwin, J T Wood.
Business and Economics; Computer Science; Social Science
Dist - INMASC

Using an otoscope 18 MIN
BETA / VHS / U-matic
Pediatrics - physical care series
Color (C PRO)
$150.00 purchase _ #147.6
Presents a video transfer of a slide program which describes the anatomy of the outer and inner ear to parents as well as to health care providers. Illustrates the procedures for viewing these structures with the otoscope and describes both normal and abnormal findings. Part of a series on physical care in pediatric nursing.
Health and Safety; Science - Natural
Dist - CONMED **Prod** - CONMED

Using and Caring for Art Materials 11 MIN
16mm / U-matic / VHS
School Citizenship Series
Color (P I)
LC 73-701683
Illustrates safe use and proper care of paints, brushes, paper, paste, glue, scissors, clay and crayons.
Fine Arts; Guidance and Counseling
Dist - CORF **Prod** - CENTEF 1973

Using and Evaluating Materials - 3 13 MIN
VHS
Exploring Technology Education - Manufacturing - Series
Color (I)
$180.00 purchase
Emphasizes the importance of the right choice of material for each project and discusses the properties of wood, metals, earth materials - brick, ceramics, plastics and composites. Builds the technological literacy vital for current and future careers. Part of the Exploring Technology Series.
Business and Economics; Education; Industrial and Technical Education; Social Science
Dist - AITECH **Prod** - AITECH 1990

Using and Maintaining SCBAs 30 MIN
VHS
Firefighter II - III Video Series
Color (G PRO)
$145.00 purchase _ #35237
Uses an in - depth demonstration to show the operation and maintenance of open circuit and closed circuit breathing apparatus systems. Covers emergency procedures, air conservation and buddy breathing.
Health and Safety; Psychology; Social Science
Dist - OKSU **Prod** - OKSU

Using Application Programs 240 - 360 MIN
Videodisc
(A PRO)
$990.00 purchase
Covers application programs and their use on personal computers. User learns how to create and use batch files.
Computer Science
Dist - VIDEOT **Prod** - VIDEOT 1988

Using `C' and `G' 15 MIN
VHS / 16mm
Reading Way Series
Color (P)
$125.00 purchase, $25.00 rental
Shows Mrs. Read explaining that `g' and `c' have two different pronunciations and are used in a variety of words at the Readmore Bookstore.
English Language
Dist - AITECH **Prod** - WXXITV 1988

Using California trusts - planning, implementing, administering, and terminating 315 MIN
VHS
Color (PRO)
$97.00, $175.00 purchase, $69.00 rental _ #ES-54150, #ES-64150
Provides detailed information about setting up trusts under California law. Explains planning for a trust, deciding between a revocable and an irrevocable trust, how a trust differs from other ownership arrangements, how a trust can be funded, how a trust affects tax consequences, and how to modify, revoke or terminate a trust. Includes a handbook with either the audio or the video program.
Civics and Political Systems
Dist - CCEB

Using Centimeters, Meters, and Kilometers 10 MIN
U-matic / VHS / 16mm
Let's Measure Series
Color (P)
$265, $185 purchase _ #3684
Compares measuring things with centimeters, meters, and kilometers.
Mathematics
Dist - CORF

Using Cleco Fasteners 5 MIN
BETA / VHS
Color (IND)
Discusses the application of the Cleco fastener for holding a fitting or fabrication together, prior to permanent riveting.
Industrial and Technical Education; Psychology
Dist - RMIBHF **Prod** - RMIBHF

Using Community Resources 29 MIN
VHS / U-matic
Focus on Children Series
Color (C A)
LC 81-707446
Presents a teacher, who also serves as a volunteer community leader, discussing and showing examples of a range of human and institutional resources available to parents at the community level to help children and the family as a whole.
Psychology; Sociology
Dist - IU **Prod** - IU 1981

Using Computer Simulations in Social Science, Science and Math 21 MIN
U-matic / VHS
New Technology in Education Series
Color (J)
Discusses the use of computer simulations in education, including a simulation on the lobbying process, a simulation of an automobile engine and a biology simulation on genetics.
Education; Industrial and Technical Education
Dist - USNAC **Prod** - USDOE 1983

Using computers in the practice of law 60 MIN
VHS
Color (A PRO C)
$95.00 purchase _ #Y704
Surveys a variety of functional applications to encourage lawyers to make the switch from pen and paper to an automated desktop.
Civics and Political Systems; Computer Science
Dist - ALIABA **Prod** - CLETV 1993

Using Crayons 15 MIN
VHS / U-matic
Draw Along Series
(J H)
$125.00 purchase
Demonstrates ways to use crayons for different lines and tones.
Fine Arts
Dist - AITECH **Prod** - AITECH 1986

Using credit wisely 20 MIN
VHS
Credit series
Color (A H C)
$79.95 purchase _ #CCP0162V-D
Addresses first - time home buyers' concerns by taking viewers through the nine - step process of buying a home - from research to closing costs. Helps viewers to take advantage of the many resources available. Part of a three-part series on credit.
Business and Economics
Dist - CAMV

Using Credit Wisely 25 MIN
VHS / U-matic
Money Smart - a Guide to Personal Finance Series
Color (H C A)
Outlines types and sources of credit, means to evaluate loans, ways to cut interest costs and steps to developing a good credit record.
Business and Economics; Education; Home Economics
Dist - BCNFL **Prod** - SOMFIL 1985

Using credit wisely - mortgage and equity loans 30 MIN
VHS
Credit series
Color (H C A)
$79.95 purchase _ #CCP0162V
Addresses first - time home buyers' concerns by taking viewers through the 9 - step process of buying a home - research, determining a buyer's wants, finding a real estate agent, making an offer, signing a contract, applying for financing, processing the loan, insurance and closing costs. Learning about these steps can help the viewer avoid the problems and pitfalls in purchasing a house through proper research and planning in advance.
Business and Economics
Dist - CAMV

Using Cuisenaire Rods Series no 3
Multiplication 1, using the Cuisenaire Rods 9 MIN
Dist - MMP

Using DBase II
U-matic / VHS
Compututor series
Color
Demonstrates the use and application of the Ashton/Tate dBase II, a popular relational database program.
Industrial and Technical Education; Mathematics
Dist - EMBASY **Prod** - CHASCI

Using DBASE II - Apple IIe, IIc 60 MIN
VHS / 16mm
(G PRO)
$79.95 purchase _ #TM5
Presents various uses of dBASE II - Apple IIe, IIc, from database recordkeeping to writing a program for a printed report.
Computer Science
Dist - RMIBHF **Prod** - RMIBHF

Using DBase III - IBM - PC 116 MIN
VHS / Software / U-matic
Compututor series
(J H)
$69.95 _ #C676 - 27469 - 2N
Provides step by step video training in computer literacy. Explains how to use dBase III with the IBM personal computer. Helps interpret the user's manual and aids in mastering the most widely used programs.
Computer Science
Dist - RH

Using DBASE III - IBM PC and Compatibles 60 MIN
VHS / 16mm
(G PRO)
$79.95 purchase _ #TM6
Teaches various uses of using dBASE III - IBM PC and compatibles, from database recordkeeping to writing a program for a printed report.
Computer Science
Dist - RMIBHF **Prod** - RMIBHF

Using DBASE III Plus - Executive Edition 120 - 180 MIN
U-matic / VHS
(A PRO)
$195.00 purchase, $270.00 purchase
Provides explanation of system installation procedures, design and creation of databases. Includes instructional diskettes and audiotapes.
Computer Science
Dist - VIDEOT **Prod** - VIDEOT 1988

Using DBASE III Plus - IBM PC and Compatibles 60 MIN
VHS / 16mm
(G PRO)
$79.95 purchase _ #TM7
Covers extended applications of the dBASE III program upgrade.
Computer Science
Dist - RMIBHF **Prod** - RMIBHF

Using DBASE III Plus Learning System 220 MIN
VHS / U-matic
(A PRO)
$495.00 purchase, $595.00 purchase
Covers comprehensive training on computers and dBASE including data entry, data management and how to generate reports and labels.
Computer Science
Dist - VIDEOT **Prod** - VIDEOT 1988

Using Decimals
VHS / U-matic
Color (I J A)
Introduces the use of decimals. Focuses on mathematical procedures with decimals.
Mathematics
Dist - EDUACT **Prod** - EDUACT

Using Degrees of Comparison 14.28 MIN
U-matic / VHS
Grammar Mechanic
(I J)
Designed to help intermediate students apply the rules of grammar. Focuses on the function in language of the degrees of comparison.. Highlights analytical skills. Thirteenth in a 16 part series.
English Language
Dist - GPN **Prod** - WDCNTV

Using demonstrative evidence and visual aids 55 MIN
Cassette
Winning the business jury trial series
Color (PRO)
$125.00, $30.00 purchase, $50.00 rental _ #BUS1-008, #ABUS-008
Provides sophisticated trial skills training for the business litigator. Demonstrates business cases including lender liability, securities fraud and antitrust. Explains how to use demonstrative evidence and visual aids, giving the viewer an analytical framework in which to view subsequent demonstrations and discussions. Gives an insider's look at nationally recognized business litigators as they plan their strategies. Includes a psychologist who specializes in persuasive communication strategies and decision - making processes providing analysis based on empirical research and juror interviews. Includes study guide.
Business and Economics; Civics and Political Systems
Dist - AMBAR **Prod** - AMBAR 1992

Using Diagnosis in a Mathematics Classroom 15 MIN
16mm
Project on Interpreting Mathematics Education Research Series
Color
LC 74-705987
Points out that mathematics instruction can be improved by effectively diagnosing pupil needs. Shows the use of interview inventories and a diagnostic instrument.
Education; Guidance and Counseling; Mathematics
Dist - USNAC **Prod** - USOE 1970

Using Discovery Techniques 30 MIN
U-matic / VHS
Creating a Learning Environment Series
Color
Education; Guidance and Counseling
Dist - NETCHE **Prod** - NETCHE 1975

Using Documentary and Demonstrative Evidence Effectively 120 MIN
U-matic / VHS / Cassette
Color; Mono (PRO)
Describes the principal types of documentary and demonstrative evidence in trial law. Explains how to lay a proper foundation for the admission of documentary and demonstrative evidence.
Civics and Political Systems
Dist - CCEB **Prod** - CCEB

Using DOS 5.0 with a hard drive, advanced
VHS
DOS series
Color (G)
$39.95 purchase _ #VIA039
Teaches the advanced use of DOS 5.0 with a hard drive.
Computer Science
Dist - SIV

Using Dual Trace Oscilloscopes 120 MIN
VHS / 16mm
Color (H A)
$399.00 purchase _ E20
Explains the function of the oscilloscope, introduces X/Y setting, measures DC - AC voltage and shows proper steps for dual trace operation.
Industrial and Technical Education
Dist - BERGL **Prod** - BERGL 1990

Using Electrical Test Equipment 60 MIN
VHS
Electrical Maintenance Practices Series
Color (PRO)
$600.00, $1500.00 purchase _ #EMUET
Provides a basic understanding of of the purpose and operation of voltage testers, multimeters, clamp - on ammeters and megohmmeters. Addresses safety concerns. Part of a six - part series on electrical maintenance practices, which is part of a 29 unit set on electrical maintenance. Includes 10 textbooks and an instructor guide which provide four hours of instruction.

Health and Safety; Industrial and Technical Education; Psychology; Science - Physical
Dist - NUSTC **Prod** - NUSTC

Using Electricity 20 MIN
VHS / U-matic
Engineering Crafts Series
Color (H C A)
Industrial and Technical Education
Dist - FI **Prod** - BBCTV 1981

Using electronic test equipment - 1 60 MIN
VHS
Electronic systems and equipment series
Color (PRO)
$600.00 - $1500.00 purchase _ #ICUE1
Discusses how meters are used to measure DC current, DC voltage, AC voltage and resistance. Shows how to measure electrical properties with a volt - ohm - milliammeter, a vacuum tube volt - ohmmeter, a field - effect transistor volt - ohm - milliammeter and a digital multimeter. Part of a nineteen - part series on electronic systems and equipment, which is part of a 49 - unit set on instrumentation and control. Includes five workbooks and an instructor guide to support four hours of instruction.
Education; Industrial and Technical Education; Psychology
Dist - NUSTC **Prod** - NUSTC

Using electronic test equipment - 2 60 MIN
VHS
Electronic systems and equipment series
Color (PRO)
$600.00 - $1500.00 purchase _ #ICUE2
Shows how to operate an oscilloscope. Part of a nineteen - part series on electronic systems and equipment, which is part of a 49 - unit set on instrumentation and control. Includes five workbooks and an instructor guide to support four hours of instruction.
Education; Industrial and Technical Education; Psychology
Dist - NUSTC **Prod** - NUSTC

Using electronic test equipment - 3 60 MIN
VHS
Electronic systems and equipment series
Color (PRO)
$600.00 - $1500.00 purchase _ #ICUE3
Describes the operation of a Wheatstone bridge circuit and explains how this circuit relates to the use of a resistance decade box which checks an RTD monitoring system. Part of a nineteen - part series on electronic systems and equipment, which is part of a 49 - unit set on instrumentation and control. Includes five workbooks and an instructor guide to support four hours of instruction.
Education; Industrial and Technical Education; Psychology
Dist - NUSTC **Prod** - NUSTC

Using Enable 120 MIN
VHS / U-matic
(A PRO)
$495.00, $595.00 purchase
Teaches introductory level facilities of Enable such as windows, creating and manipulating worksheets, word processing and graphics.
Computer Science
Dist - VIDEOT **Prod** - VIDEOT 1988

Using equivalent fractions to compute sums 8 MIN
VHS
Children's encyclopedia of mathematics - using fractions to add and 'subtract series
Color (I J)
$49.95 purchase _ #8218
Computes sums with equivalent fractions. Part of a five - part series on adding and subtracting with fractions.
Mathematics
Dist - AIMS **Prod** - DAVFMS 1991

Using evidence 45 MIN
U-matic / VHS
Artificial intelligence series; Fundamental concepts, Pt 1
Color (PRO)
Deals with strategy versus tactics, improving situation evaluation, linear evaluation, and nonlinear evaluation.
Mathematics
Dist - MIOT **Prod** - MIOT

Using filters, creative techniques and photographing people - Volume 3 45 MIN
VHS
Color (H C)
$29.95 purchase _ #KV - 127
Contains information on how filters can improve picture taking. Shows how filters create new pictures of everyday objects. Discusses how to add softness, blur, star - bursts, rainbows and mind - boggling multi - image effects to pictures. Part two shows how to photograph people. Teaches how to light a face and creative techniques in composing and lighting.
Industrial and Technical Education
Dist - INSTRU

Using financial experts in business litigation series
Gives a broad perspective on the use of financial experts in business litigation cases. Features business litigation attorneys and financial experts in a joint analysis of an imaginary case. Nine - part series includes case files, teacher's manual and a planner's guide.

Closing arguments	55 MIN
Cross examination of the defendant's financial expert	45 MIN
Cross examination of the plaintiff's financial expert	59 MIN
Deposing the financial expert	59 MIN
Direct examination of the defendant's financial expert	54 MIN
Direct examinations of the plaintiff's financial expert	55 MIN
Preparing the financial expert for deposition	59 MIN
Using financial experts in case analysis and planning	51 MIN
Using financial experts in negotiation and settlement	42 MIN

Dist - NITA **Prod** - NITA

Using financial experts in case analysis and planning 51 MIN
VHS
Using financial experts in business litigation series
Color (C PRO)
$195.00 purchase, $95.00 rental _ #Z0401
Gives a broad perspective on the use of financial experts in business litigation cases. Features business litigation attorneys and financial experts in a joint analysis of an imaginary case. Shows how financial experts may be used in case analysis and planning.
Business and Economics; Civics and Political Systems
Dist - NITA **Prod** - NITA 1988

Using financial experts in negotiation and settlement 42 MIN
VHS
Using financial experts in business litigation series
Color (C PRO)
$195.00 purchase, $95.00 rental _ #Z0404
Gives a broad perspective on the use of financial experts in business litigation cases. Features business litigation attorneys and financial experts in a joint analysis of an imaginary case. Presents guidelines for using financial experts in negotiation and settlement.
Business and Economics; Civics and Political Systems
Dist - NITA **Prod** - NITA 1988

Using Fire Extinguishers 11 MIN
U-matic / 35mm strip
Color (PRO)
LC 80-731001;
Explains fundamental principles of fighting fires and illustrates specific techniques in using fire extingusihers effectively.
Health and Safety
Dist - MEDCOM **Prod** - MEDCOM

Using flash 30 MIN
VHS
Color (G)
$24.95 purchase _ #S00941
Describes how to use automatic or manual flash equipment most effectively.
Industrial and Technical Education
Dist - UILL **Prod** - EKC

Using focus groups to identify attitudes towards a case 58 MIN
VHS
Art of advocacy - selecting and persuading the jury series
Color (C PRO)
$95.00 purchase, $71.25 rental _ #Z0308
Describes how focus groups may be utilized to identify potential jurors' attitudes towards a case.
Civics and Political Systems
Dist - NITA **Prod** - NITA 1988

Using Fractional and Rational Exponents 28 MIN
16mm
Intermediate Algebra Series
B&W (H)
Presents properties of real numbers with fractional and rational exponents. Shows methods of manipulating numbers and gives example of an exponential equation.
Mathematics
Dist - MLA **Prod** - CALVIN 1959

Using fractions to add and subtract series
Presents a five - part series teaching the use of fractions to add and subtract developed by the National Council of Teachers of Mathematics. Includes the titles 'Machine - Adding with Fractions,' 'Fraction Singers - Equivalence Classes in Addition,' 'Coal Miners - Adding with Mixed Numbers,' 'Gems - Subtracting Fractions' and 'Stones - Subtracting Mixed Numbers.'

Coal miners - adding with mixed numbers	9 MIN
Fraction singers - equivalence classes in addition	8 MIN
Gems - subtracting fractions	11 MIN
Machine - adding with fractions	10 MIN
Stones - subtracting mixed numbers	9 MIN

Dist - AIMS **Prod** - DAVFMS 1959

Using Fusible Interfacing 3 MIN
16mm
Clothing Construction Techniques Series
Color (J)
LC 77-701173
Shows how interfacing is attached to the garment by the use of steam, heat and pressure. Illustrates cutting, attaching and special effects with fusible interfacing.
Home Economics
Dist - IOWASP **Prod** - IOWA 1976

Using Gift Paper 15 MIN
Videoreel / VT2
Living Better I Series
Color
Fine Arts; Home Economics
Dist - PBS **Prod** - MAETEL

Using Glazing Putty 8 MIN
BETA / VHS / 16mm
Color (A PRO)
$54.75 purchase _ #AB157
Defines glazing putty and discusses when it should be used. Shows application and sanding procedures.
Industrial and Technical Education
Dist - RMIBHF **Prod** - RMIBHF

Using Government Agencies 15 MIN
U-matic / VHS
By the People Series
Color (H)
Shows how citizens can use government agencies.
Civics and Political Systems; Social Science
Dist - CTI **Prod** - CTI

Using Grams and Kilograms 10 MIN
16mm / U-matic / VHS
Let's Measure Series
Color (P)
$265, $185 purchase _ #3683
Discusses weight measurement using the metric system.
Mathematics
Dist - CORF

Using Hand Stitches 3 MIN
16mm
Clothing Construction Techniques Series
Color (J)
LC 77-701180
Demonstrates hand stitches and discusses where each might be used. Shows the blind or slip stitch, catch stitch, lock stitch and buttonhole stitch.
Home Economics
Dist - IOWASP **Prod** - IOWA 1976

Using Home Appliances Safely 18 MIN
VHS / U-matic
Home Safety and Security Series
Color (A)
Provides tips on safe use small portable appliances, emphasizing kitchen ones. Includes guidelines on purchasing appliances and a checklist for their safe use and maintenance.
Health and Safety
Dist - IFB **Prod** - ALLAMI 1986

Using Human Resources 29 MIN
U-matic / VHS / 16mm
Teaching Children to Read Series
Color (C T)
Suggests ways of maximizing outside adult involvement in the classroom. Shows how parent volunteers, community volunteers, teachers, aides and older students may be used.
Education
Dist - FI **Prod** - MFFD 1975

Using industrial robots 30 MIN
VHS / U-matic
Manufacturing automation - a key to productivity series
Color
Examines the important aspects of the industrial robot and discusses how it is being used in manufacturing today.
Business and Economics; Industrial and Technical Education
Dist - DELTAK **Prod** - DELTAK

Using Industrial Statistics
U-matic / VHS
Organizational Quality Improvement Series
Color
Deals with industrial statistics. Shows how to use a multi - vary chart, a scatter diagram and a component search pattern.

Business and Economics; Psychology
Dist - BNA **Prod** - BNA

Using 'L' Blends 15 MIN
VHS / 16mm
Reading Way Series
Color (P)
$125.00 purchase, $25.00 rental
Shows Tim learning the sounds 'fl', 'bl', 'cl' blends and using them in a variety of words at the Readmore Bookstore.
English Language
Dist - AITECH **Prod** - WXXITV 1988

Using Legal Assistance 15 MIN
U-matic / VHS
By the People Series
Color (H)
Tells how to use professional legal help. Shows how to take a case to Small Claims Court.
Civics and Political Systems; Social Science
Dist - CTI **Prod** - CTI

Using lines 16 MIN
VHS
Art - i - facts series; Pt 1
Color (I)
$125.00 purchase
Discovers lines as one of several basic tools to be used in expressing ideas and feelings visually. Shows how illustrators use lines to convey the emotion and action of a story. Part of the Art - I - Facts Series to give third and fourth graders a foundation in the visual arts.
Fine Arts; Geography - United States; History - United States
Dist - AITECH **Prod** - HDE 1986

Using Logarithm Tables 29 MIN
16mm
Trigonometry Series
B&W (H)
Shows how to find the mantissa of a logarithm and a number, given its logarithm from a three place table. Illustrates interpolation and inverse interpolation in log tables. The log of a trigonometric value is found in a table and the use of a slide rule is discussed.
Mathematics
Dist - MLA **Prod** - CALVIN 1959

Using Logarithms in Problems 31 MIN
16mm
Advanced Algebra Series
B&W (H)
Defines the logarithm of a number. Shows the use of logarithms for solving problems involving powers, ratios and roots of numbers.
Mathematics
Dist - MLA **Prod** - CALVIN 1960

Using Logarithms to Solve Equations 28 MIN
16mm
Intermediate Algebra Series
B&W (H)
Shows how to find the mantissa and antilog from logarithm tables. Includes the use of linear interpolation. Closes with examples of how to use logarithms to multiply, divide and find the roots of numbers.
Mathematics
Dist - MLA **Prod** - CALVIN 1959

Using Loran series
Apelco 6300, RayNav 520 60 MIN
Apelco 6500 60 MIN
Apelco DXL 6000, Ratheon RayNav 550 60 MIN
Impulse 2830 60 MIN
Micrologic - Explorer - Voyager 60 MIN
Micrologic 5500 - 5000 - 3000 60 MIN
Micrologic 7500 - 8000 60 MIN
Northstar 9000 60 MIN
Ray Jefferson L999 60 MIN
Raytheon RayNav 570, Apelco 6100, 6600 60 MIN
Ross 200 60 MIN
Searanger - ASB 2001, LCN 100, ALN 200 60 MIN
Dist - SEVVID

Using Lotus 1 - 2 - 3 - IBM PC 100 MIN
VHS / Software / U-matic
Compututor series
(J H)
$69.95 _ #C676 - 27470 - 6N
Provides step by step video training in computer literacy. Explains how to use Lotus 1 - 2 - 3 with the IBM personal computer. Helps interpret the user's manual and aids in mastering the most widely used programs.
Computer Science
Dist - RH

Using Lotus 1 - 2 - 3 - IBM PC and Compatibles 60 MIN
VHS / 16mm
(G PRO)
$79.95 purchase _ #TM8
Covers all basic spreadsheet and Macro programming capabilities of Lotus, and the use of integrated databases.
Computer Science
Dist - RMIBHF **Prod** - RMIBHF

Using Managerial Techniques on the Job
VHS / U-matic
Team Building for Administrative Support Staff Series
Color
Deals with four key skills, including using the checklist, keeping supervisor informed, doing complete staff work and getting cooperation from others.
Business and Economics; Psychology
Dist - AMA **Prod** - AMA

Using maps
VHS
Using maps, globes, graphs, tables, charts and diagrams series
Color (I J H)
$49.50 purchase _ #UL1043VJ
Shows how to interpret data in maps. Presents part of a five - part series on basic globe skills and understanding data from pictorial and other graphic representations.
Geography - World
Dist - KNOWUN

Using maps and globes - understanding world geography 30 MIN
VHS
Color (J H C G)
$29.95 purchase _ #VMU001V
Examines the history of maps and globes, latitude and longitude, time zones and types of maps such as political, geographical, topographical.
Geography - World; Social Science
Dist - CAMV

Using maps, globes, graphs, tables, charts and diagrams series
Presents a five - part series on basic globe skills and understanding data in maps, tables, charts and other graphic representations. Includes Understanding Globes; Maps and What They Tell Us; Using Maps; Reading Graphs; Tables, Charts and Diagrams; and a teacher's guide with a set of duplicating masters.
Maps and what they tell us
Reading graphs
Tables, charts and diagrams
Understanding globes
Using maps
Dist - KNOWUN

Using Maps - Measuring Distance 11 MIN
16mm / U-matic / VHS
Color; B&W (P I J) (SPANISH)
Defines what a map is and shows several different ways of measuring distance. Explains what a map scale is and illustrates how it is used to measure distance on a map. Includes brief glimpses of professional map makers at their work.
Social Science
Dist - EBEC **Prod** - EBEC 1962

Using Maps Together 12 MIN
16mm / U-matic / VHS
Map Skills Series
Color (I J)
$350 purchase - 16 mm, $250 purchase - video _ #5195C
Shows how to use several maps to obtain the information on an area. Talks about colors, lines, and symbols. Produced by Christianson Productions, Inc.
Social Science
Dist - CORF

Using marine electronics
VHS
Color (G A)
$49.80 purchase _ #0262
Explains Loran, radar, Sat - Nav, ADF, Fathometer for navigating on water.
Physical Education and Recreation
Dist - SEVVID

Using Marine Electronics 30 MIN
BETA / VHS
Color
Shows many types of electronic marine equipment, including the video recorders, Loran - C Systems, and depth Sounders.
Physical Education and Recreation; Science - Natural
Dist - HOMEAF **Prod** - HOMEAF

Using Materials 15 MIN
16mm / U-matic / VHS
Craft, Design and Technology Series
Color (I J)
Explains that the family of materials known as plastics (both thermoplastic and thermosetting) can be manipulated and molded through extrusion. This is a process in which granules melt into a fluid that is shaped by pressure through dies and cooled for permanence, as well as through injection molding.
Business and Economics; Sociology
Dist - MEDIAG **Prod** - THAMES 1983

Using Materials 20 MIN
VHS / U-matic
Engineering Crafts Series
Color (H C A)
Industrial and Technical Education
Dist - FI **Prod** - BBCTV 1981

Using Math in Everyday Situations
U-matic / VHS
Third R - Teaching Basic Mathematics Skills Series
Color (T)
Focuses on ways mathematics can be used in real situations. Discusses everyday use of computational skills, problem - solving strategies, geometric concepts and other basic skill areas.
Education; Mathematics
Dist - EDCORP **Prod** - EPCO

Using math on the job
VHS
Color (H C A)
$295.00 purchase _ #JR150V
Examines common business math problems and shows how to solve them. Includes 10 workbooks, 20 color transparencies, and a teacher's guide.
Business and Economics
Dist - CAMV

Using Microcomputers - an Introduction 3 MIN
VHS / U-matic
Microcomputers at School Series Program One
Color
Introduces various applications of microcomputers in school setting.
Business and Economics; Mathematics
Dist - EDCORP **Prod** - EPCO

Using Milliliters and Liters 12 MIN
U-matic / VHS / 16mm
Let's Measure Series
Color (P)
$305, $215 purchase _ #3682
Shows how to use milliliters and liters, illustrating the concept by comparing it to making a brew.
Mathematics
Dist - CORF

Using Modern Libraries Video Programs 20 MIN
VHS
(H)
#87359
Education
Dist - FLIPLS **Prod** - FLIPLS

Using Money Wisely 18 MIN
16mm / U-matic / VHS
Color (H C)
LC 71-713645
Presents three typical families with money problems who represent a cross section of economic levels. Shows these families as they encounter, and reach solutions to their money management difficulties.
Business and Economics; Home Economics
Dist - JOU **Prod** - CUNA 1970

Using MultiPlan Series
Introduction to the Worksheet
Setting Up a Worksheet
Storing, Retrieving, Printing and Advanced Features
Dist - COMTEG

Using Networking and Bar Charting in Project Scheduling 30 MIN
VHS / U-matic
Project Management Series
Color
Shows how to use networking and bar charting in project scheduling. Includes calculating critical path and slack time.
Business and Economics; Psychology
Dist - ITCORP **Prod** - ITCORP

Using Networking and Bar Charting in Project Scheduling 30 MIN
VHS / 16mm
Project Management Series
Color (PRO)
$400.00 purchase, $100.00 rental
Includes Scheduling Techniques, Network Notation Techniques and Symbols, Network Diagramming, Time Estimates, Calculating Critical Path and Slack Time and Bar Chart Symbols and Notations. Part of a six - part series on project management.
Business and Economics; Industrial and Technical Education; Psychology
Dist - ISA **Prod** - ISA

Using new life insurance products in estate planning 50 MIN
VHS
Color (A PRO C)
$95.00 purchase _ #Y147
Examines a variety of life insurance products and techniques that can enhance the creation of an effective and tax - conscious estate plan. Covers topics such as the use of survivorship life insurance policies, first - to - die policies, the exchange of single life insurance policies for joint policies and the exchange of joint policies for single policies.
Business and Economics; Civics and Political Systems
Dist - ALIABA **Prod** - CLETV 1991

Using Norton Utilities, advanced
VHS
Color (G)
$39.95 purchase _ #VIA037
Teaches advanced use of Norton Utilities.
Computer Science
Dist - SIV

Using on - Line Systems 20 MIN
VHS / U-matic
On - Line Systems Concepts for Users Series
Color
Describes some of the things on - line systems can do for the end user, discusses on - line systems from the user's viewpoint and shows how users can work effectively with system designers. Shows how the manager of a large data processing organization was able to transfer more computer power into the hands of the users and discusses how on - line systems can cause basic changes in corporate procedures.
Business and Economics; Industrial and Technical Education
Dist - DELTAK **Prod** - DELTAK

Using Oracle SQL Plus 120 MIN
U-matic / VHS
(A PRO)
$495.00 purchase, $595.00 purchase
Inlcudes overviews, creating tables, data entry, data query, and modifications as well as report generation. Includes instructional diskettes.
Computer Science
Dist - VIDEOT **Prod** - VIDEOT 1988

Using Others to Save Time 10 MIN
U-matic / 35mm strip
Management of Time Series Module 3
Color
Stresses that delegation will work and will save time and in the process will develop others' abilities. Emphasizes that training is a key to saving time.
Business and Economics; Psychology
Dist - RESEM **Prod** - RESEM

Using oxyacetylene welding to replace damaged sheet metal series
Fitting, welding and metal finishing - Part Three 29 MIN
Inspection of the damage - Part One 15 MIN
Removal of rust and metal treatment - Part Two 11 MIN
Dist - AAVIM

Using PC Tools, deluxe
VHS
Color (G)
$39.95 purchase _ #VIA020
Teaches the use of PC Tools.
Computer Science
Dist - SIV

Using people - 60 11 MIN
U-matic / VHS
Life's little lessons - self - esteem 4 - 6 series
Color (I)
$129.00, $99.00 purchase _ #V689
Tells about small and mousy Horace who wore thick, horn - rimmed glasses, and Rhonda, his dream girl, asked him to take her to the dance. Reveals that Rhonda was only using him so she could be with someone else. Part of a 65 - part series on self - esteem.
Guidance and Counseling; Psychology
Dist - BARR **Prod** - CEPRO 1992

Using Persona in Poetry 15 MIN
Videoreel / VHS
Color (I)
Introduces the writing of poetry. Presents two performers/teachers who interpret several poems for a group of young children.
Literature and Drama
Dist - WHITD **Prod** - WHITD

Using personal computers
Videodisc
(H A)
$2395.00
Introduces individuals with little or no experience to IBM Personal Computers and compatibles, emphasizing practical applications to business. Provides practice in using the computer by simulating various applications.
Business and Economics; Computer Science; Education
Dist - CMSL **Prod** - CMSL

Using Personal Protective Equipment 24 MIN
VHS / U-matic
Foreman's Accident Prevention Series
Color (IND)
Provides a detailed review of the personal protection equipment available to workers, how and why each is used, plus the foreman's responsibility.
Health and Safety
Dist - GPCV **Prod** - GPCV

Using Political Resources 15 MIN
U-matic / VHS
By the People Series
Color (H)
Suggests some resources of value in influencing political decisions.
Civics and Political Systems; Social Science
Dist - CTI **Prod** - CTI

Using Positive Discipline (Industry)
16mm / U-matic / VHS
Supervisory Training (Industry Series
Color (A)
Discusses how to use positive discipline in an industrial setting.
Business and Economics
Dist - CRMP **Prod** - CRMP 1983

Using Positive Discipline (Office)
U-matic / VHS / 16mm
Supervisory Training (Office Series
Color (A)
Discusses how to use positive discipline in an office setting.
Business and Economics
Dist - CRMP **Prod** - CRMP 1983

Using Positive Exponents 15 MIN
VHS
Power of Algebra Series
Color (J)
LC 90712872
Uses computer animation and interviews with professionals who use algebra to explain using positive exponents. The fifth of 10 installments of The Power Of Algebra Series.
Mathematics
Dist - GPN

Using power of 1-2-3 Windows
VHS
Lotus video series
Color (G)
$49.95 purchase _ #LPVO006V
Familiarizes viewers with the ins and outs of Lotus 1-2-3. Provides information for both beginners and experts, using illustrations and analogies. Notes creators of series are sole authorized developers of video training for Lotus 1-2-3 software. Details commands and functions of software program. Focuses on using 1-2-3 Windows.
Computer Science
Dist - CAMV

Using R with A and O 15 MIN
VHS / 16mm
Reading Way Series
Color (P)
$125.00 purchase, $25.00 rental
Shows Tim working on "ar" and "or" words at the Readmore Bookstore.
English Language
Dist - AITECH **Prod** - WXXITV 1988

Using R with E, I and U 15 MIN
VHS / 16mm
Reading Way Series
Color (P)
$125.00 purchase, $25.00 rental
Shows Mrs. Read and Tim discussing the "er" partner and the similar sound of "ir".
English Language
Dist - AITECH **Prod** - WXXITV 1988

Using reinforcement techniques to manage patient behavior 30 MIN
16mm
Nursing - cues behavior consequences series; No 3
B&W
LC 76-700928
Describes techniques of managing consequences of patient behavior in bringing about desired patient or student behavior.
Health and Safety; Psychology
Dist - UNEBR **Prod** - NTCN 1973

Using resources wisely 35 MIN
VHS
Color (R G)
$19.95 purchase _ #9323 - 8
Features Christian financial expert Larry Burkett who discusses giving, tithing and investments.
Business and Economics; Religion and Philosophy
Dist - MOODY **Prod** - MOODY 1994

Using Respiratory Protection 29 MIN
VHS / U-matic
Foreman's Accident Prevention Series
Color (IND)
Provides detailed instructions for putting on, testing and maintaining respirators and other hose - line and self - contained breathing apparatus used in industry.
Health and Safety
Dist - GPCV **Prod** - GPCV

Using Satellite - Based Communications 30 MIN
VHS / U-matic
Color
From The Communications Satellite Systems Series. Outlines the services offered by companies marketing satellite communications systems. Discusses user responsibilities and requirements.
Industrial and Technical Education; Science - Physical; Social Science
Dist - DELTAK **Prod** - DELTAK

Using Short `A' and `I' 15 MIN
VHS / 16mm
Reading Way Series
Color (P)
$125.00 purchase, $25.00 rental
Looks at Tim substituting "a" and "i" vowels for each other to change the meaning of words.
English Language
Dist - AITECH **Prod** - WXXITV 1988

Using Short E Patterns 15 MIN
VHS / 16mm
Reading Way Series
Color (P)
$125.00 purchase, $25.00 rental
Shows that short "e" is used in many words at Readmore Bookstore. Discusses the difference between "ry" and "ny".
English Language
Dist - AITECH **Prod** - WXXITV 1988

Using Short O and U 15 MIN
VHS / 16mm
Reading Way Series
Color (P)
$125.00 purchase, $25.00 rental
Shows Tim making new words by changing the vowels "o" and "u" for each other.
English Language
Dist - AITECH **Prod** - WXXITV 1988

Using Silent E 15 MIN
VHS / 16mm
Reading Way Series
Color (P)
$125.00 purchase, $25.00 rental
Shows Mrs Read and Tim discussing silent "e" and its effect on other vowels.
English Language
Dist - AITECH **Prod** - WXXITV 1988

Using Simple Machines 14 MIN
16mm
Color (P I)
Illustrates various kinds of simple machines such as levers, pulleys, and inclined planes, describes their functions, and shows their practical uses in the context of everyday life.
Science - Physical
Dist - CORF **Prod** - DISNEY 1986

Using Sines, Cosines and Tangents 29 MIN
16mm
Trigonometry Series
B&W (H)
Reviews the definitions of the sine, cosine and tangent functions. Shows how to approach a trigonometric problem. Defines the unit circle and uses it to develop simple trigonometric identities and to show that the functions are not linear.
Mathematics
Dist - MLA **Prod** - CALVIN 1959

Using Standard Units 13 MIN
U-matic / VHS / 16mm
Let's Measure Series
Color (P)
$305, $215 purchase _ #3070
Shows the standard units using for measuring height and weight.
Mathematics
Dist - CORF

Using standardized recipes 9 MIN
16mm / U-matic / VHS
Professional food preparation and service program series
Color (J) (FRENCH GERMAN SPANISH)
LC 73-702731
Shows how to properly interpret and use standardized commercial recipes with utilization of several different types of recipes.
Health and Safety; Home Economics; Industrial and Technical Education
Dist - NEM **Prod** - NEM 1971

Using Stimuli to Influence Behavior 29 MIN
16mm
Controlling Turnover and Absenteeism Series
B&W
LC 76-703321
Business and Economics; Psychology
Dist - EDSD **Prod** - EDSD

Using subtraction facts
VHS
Lola May's fundamental math series
Color (P)
$45.00 purchase _ #10269VG
Teaches how to solve subtraction facts. Focuses on the 'hill method' and the 'dot method' as means of solving subtraction problems. Comes with a teacher's guide and blackline masters. Part 19 of a 30 - part series.
Mathematics
Dist - UNL

Using surveying instruments series
The Dumpy level - the tilting level - Cassette 1 23 MIN
The Theodolite on site - Cassette 2 45 MIN
Dist - EMFVL

Using swing bass 29 MIN
U-matic
Beginning piano - an adult approach series; Lesson 26
Color (H A)
Introduces B - flat major scale. Reviews pieces from previous programs. Begins an approach to choosing chromatic chords in playing by ear.
Fine Arts
Dist - CDTEL **Prod** - COAST

Using System Diagrams 60 MIN
VHS
Systems Operations Series
Color (PRO)
$600.00 - $1500.00 purchase _ #OTUSD
Illustrates the various types of system diagrams used in industrial facilities. Describes how flow diagrams, P&IDs and electrical one - line diagrams can help operators perform various tasks. Part of a seventeen - part series on systems operations. Includes ten textbooks and an instructor guide to support four hours of instruction.
Industrial and Technical Education; Psychology
Dist - NUSTC **Prod** - NUSTC

Using Teaching Materials 12 MIN
U-matic / 35mm strip
ElementsOf Effective Teaching Series
Color
Helps instructors establish guidelines for use and dissemination of handouts, student guides, notebooks and other teaching materials.
Business and Economics; Education
Dist - RESEM **Prod** - RESEM

Using Technology 29 MIN
VHS / 16mm
Breaking the Unseen Barrier Series
Color (C)
$180.00, $240.00 purchase _ #269708
Demonstrates through dramatic vignettes effective teaching strategies to help students with learning disabilities reach their full potential. Offers insight into integrating learning disabled students into the classroom. 'Using Technology' considers Rahinder, Andrew and Dale, secondary school students with learning disabilities who could all be helped, using various technologies. However, their teacher may be reluctant to give any student an 'unfair advantage' or the technology may be too expensive. Shows the potential of technologies and how students can best be helped in a regular classroom as the three characters work to improve their situation.
Education; Mathematics; Psychology
Dist - AITECH **Prod** - ACCESS 1988

Using the analytical balance 9 MIN
VHS
Chemistry master apprentice series
Color (H C)
$49.95 purchase _ #49 - 7218 - V
Demonstrates the use of the single pan analytical balance to weigh an object to the nearest 0.1 mg. Illustrates the use of tongs and paper strips to handle the object. Emphasizes common errors made by beginning balance users that could result in damage to the balance or incorrect readings. Part of the Chemistry Master Apprentice series.
Science; Science - Physical
Dist - INSTRU **Prod** - CORNRS

Using the Analytical Balance - Mettler 9 MIN
U-matic / VHS
Chemistry - master - apprentice series; Program 16
Color (C A)
LC 82-706033
Demonstrates the use of the Mettler single pan analytical balance Model H6 to weigh an object to the nearest 0.1 mg. Emphasizes the common errrors made by beginning balance users that could result in damage to the balance or incorrect readings.
Health and Safety; Science; Science - Physical
Dist - CORNRS **Prod** - CUETV 1981

Using the Balance and Spring Scales 20 MIN
VHS / BETA
Color (G PRO)
$59.00 purchase _ #QF13
Demonstrates the differences between the balance and spring scales, and discusses various methods of scaling, using both the balance and spring scales.
Home Economics
Dist - RMIBHF **Prod** - RMIBHF

Using the Bennett Machine 6 MIN
16mm
ICARE Training Series
Color
LC 75-704051
Shows a mock classroom session on the use of the Bennett machine, which is used in respiratory therapy.
Health and Safety
Dist - USNAC **Prod** - BHME 1975

Using the Bunsen Burner and Working with Glass 11 MIN
U-matic / VHS / 16mm
Basic Laboratory Techniques in Chemistry Series
Color (H C)
Demonstrates basic techniques used in working with glass tubing.
Science
Dist - LUF **Prod** - SCHLAT

Using the Clues 30 MIN
U-matic / VHS
Play Bridge Series
Color (A)
Physical Education and Recreation
Dist - KYTV **Prod** - KYTV 1983

Using the Computer and Preventing its Abuse 67 MIN
VHS / U-matic
Use of Computers in Complex Litigation Series
Color (PRO)
Explores ways an attorney can use a computer to enhance a law practice. Examines the type of statistical analysis a computer expert can provide for litigation and ways to effectively present computer - generated data in a trial.
Civics and Political Systems; Industrial and Technical Education; Sociology
Dist - ABACPE **Prod** - ABACPE

Using the Computer Terminal - Pt 1
16mm
B&W
Explains how to use a computer terminal. Discusses installation, connection to the computer, and logging on.
Mathematics
Dist - OPENU **Prod** - OPENU

Using the Computer Terminal - Pt 2
16mm
B&W
Explains how to use a computer terminal. Discusses installation, connection to the computer, and logging on.
Mathematics
Dist - OPENU **Prod** - OPENU

Using the Computer to Develop Writing Abilities 27 MIN
U-matic / VHS
New Technology in Education Series
Color (J)
Discusses what has been learned about the writing process and how the computer can be used as a tool to simplify and stimulate this process in children.
Education; Industrial and Technical Education
Dist - USNAC **Prod** - USDOE 1983

Using the Cutoff Tool on the Lathe
U-matic / VHS
Intermediate Engine Lathe Operation Series
Color (SPANISH)
Industrial and Technical Education
Dist - VTRI **Prod** - VTRI

Using the Disc and Drum Micrometer 27 MIN
VHS / 16mm
Automotive Tech Series
(G PRO)
$103.50 purchase
Gives step - by - step instructions on using the disc and drum micrometer.
Industrial and Technical Education
Dist - RMIBHF **Prod** - RMIBHF

Using the Encyclopedia 20 MIN
VHS / 16mm
Study Research Library Skills Series
Color (J)
Gives a lesson on how to use the encyclopedia.
Education
Dist - COMEX **Prod** - COMEX 1987

Using the Evidence Code in Civil Cases 120 MIN
U-matic / VHS / Cassette
Color; Mono (PRO)
Focuses on rules of evidence. Discusses how to deal comprehensively with hearsay and objections to hearsay. Looks at statements under Evidence Code Sections 1200 and 1250, business records, best evidence rule and authentication, computer printouts, use of evidence by experts and spontaneous exclamations.
Civics and Political Systems
Dist - CCEB **Prod** - CCEB

Using the four - jaw chuck 13 MIN
BETA / VHS
Machine shop - engine lathe series
Color (IND)
Industrial and Technical Education; Psychology
Dist - RMIBHF **Prod** - RMIBHF

Using the Gravity Displacement Steam Autoclave in the Biomedical Laboratory 29 MIN
U-matic / VHS
Color
LC 84-706402
Demonstrates aseptic and safe procedures for preparing, processing and handling materials undergoing steam sterilization and decontamination.
Health and Safety; Science
Dist - USNAC **Prod** - USHHS 1983

Using the gravity displacement steam autoclave in the biomedical laboratory 29 MIN
VHS
Color (C PRO G)
$395.00 purchase _ #R861 - VI - 045
Demonstrates techniques and procedures for preparing, processing and handling materials undergoing steam sterilization and decontamination. Produced at the School of Public Health, Univ of Minnesota, Minneapolis.
Health and Safety; Science
Dist - HSCIC

Using the Index Head 29 MIN
VHS / BETA
Machine Shop - Milling Machine Series
Color (IND)
Industrial and Technical Education; Psychology
Dist - RMIBHF **Prod** - RMIBHF

Using the Journal, Pt 1 50 MIN
U-matic / VHS
Process - Centered Composition Series
Color (T)
LC 79-706298
Focuses on the introduction and use of a journal project. Discusses a variety of journal - writing assignments.
English Language; Literature and Drama
Dist - IU **Prod** - IU 1977

Using the Journal, Pt 2 44 MIN
VHS / U-matic
Process - Centered Composition Series
Color (T)
LC 79-706298
Focuses on the introduction and use of a journal project. Discusses a variety of journal - writing assignments.
English Language; Literature and Drama
Dist - IU **Prod** - IU 1977

Using the Library 20 MIN
U-matic / VHS
Art of Learning Series
Color (H A)
Tells of resources available in the college library and how to use them. Shows how to look up a book by subject, author or title by locating it in a card catalog, on microfiche, or on a computer. Describes how to locate articles in the Reader's Guide and The New York Times Index. Deals with the reserve book area, nonprint materials and additional indexes.
Education; Literature and Drama; Social Science
Dist - GPN **Prod** - WCVETV 1984

Using the library 28 MIN
U-matic / BETA / VHS
Communication skills 2 - advanced series
Color (H C G)
$101.95, $89.95 purchase _ #CA - 17
Shows how to develop a reseach paper, using the library for gathering and organizing information. Suggests the steps necessary to make effective use of the library. Discusses the outline stage of paper preparation and suggestions on the rough draft and final writing. Part of a 26 - part series.
English Language; Social Science
Dist - INSTRU

Using the Metric System Every Day 20 MIN
U-matic
Metric System Series
Color (J)
Emphasizes that the metric system is used increasingly in daily life.
Mathematics
Dist - GPN **Prod** - MAETEL 1975

Using the New ADA Exchange System for Meal Planning 12 MIN
VHS / U-matic
Color
Reviews the principles of exchange diet. Reviews each exchange list with discussion and examples. Demonstrates how a diet can be created from the various lists.
Health and Safety
Dist - MEDFAC **Prod** - MEDFAC 1979

Using the Normal Distribution 20 MIN
U-matic / VHS
Statistics for Technicians Series
Color (IND)
Discusses calculation of areas under the normal curve and how applied to find percent of defective parts for a production operation. Shows comparisons for processes in and out of control, and applications for setting the mean of the process and for setting guarantees.
Business and Economics; Mathematics; Psychology
Dist - COLOSU **Prod** - COLOSU

Using the Parts of a Book 20 MIN
VHS / 16mm
Study Research Library Skills Series
Color (J)
Presents a lesson on how to use the different parts of a book.
Education
Dist - COMEX **Prod** - COMEX 1987

Using the power of Allways
VHS
Lotus video series
Color (J H C G)
$49.95 purchase _ #LPVO001V
Familiarizes viewers with the ins and outs of Lotus 1-2-3. Provides information for both beginners and experts, using illustrations and analogies. Notes creators of series are sole authorized developers of video training for Lotus 1-2-3 software. Details commands and functions of software program. Focuses on using Allways.
Computer Science
Dist - CAMV

Using the power of Ami Pro
VHS
Lotus video series
Color (J H C G)
$49.95 purchase _ #LPVO008V
Teaches the key features of Lotus - Ami Pro software. Involves beginning to advanced users in the learning process with simple illustrations and colorful analogies. Shows how Lotus software reacts to commands as students follow along at their keyboards. Part of an eight - part series on Lotus.
Computer Science
Dist - CAMV

Using the power of 1 - 2 - 3 Windows
VHS
Lotus video series
Color (J H C G)
$49.95 purchase _ #LPVO006V; $49.95 purchase _ #LP004
Teaches the key features of Lotus - 1 - 2 - 3 Windows software. Involves beginning to advanced users in the learning process with simple illustrations and colorful analogies. Shows how Lotus software reacts to commands as students follow along at their keyboards. Part of an eight - part series on Lotus.
Computer Science
Dist - CAMV
SIV

Using the power of WYSIWYG
VHS
Lotus video series
Color (J H C G)
$49.95 purchase _ #LPVO004V; $49.95 purchase _ #LP003
Teaches the key features of Lotus - WYSIWYG software. Involves beginning to advanced users in the learning process with simple illustrations and colorful analogies. Shows how Lotus software reacts to commands as students follow along at their keyboards. Part of an eight - part series on Lotus.
Computer Science
Dist - CAMV
SIV

Using the Readers Guide to Periodical Literature 20 MIN
VHS / 16mm
Study Research Library Skills Series
Color (J)
Teaches how to use the readers guide to periodical literature.
Education
Dist - COMEX **Prod** - COMEX 1987

Using the shaper to make drawers 14 MIN
VHS
Color (J H A T)
$49.95 purchase _ #AM1453
Shows how to make a drawer with a lip front. Demonstrates how to measure and use a scrap sample for testing set ups. Explains procedures for shaping ends and edges of the front, calculating depth of cut for joints, cutting the joint and using the tenoning jig.
Industrial and Technical Education
Dist - AAVIM **Prod** - AAVIM 1992

Using the Shaper to make Drawers 14 MIN
16mm / U-matic / VHS
Wood Shop - Safety and Operations Series
Color (J) (SPANISH)
LC 75-705173;
Demonstrates through the use of close - up photography the basic operations involved in using the shaper to make drawers.
Industrial and Technical Education
Dist - AIMS **Prod** - EPRI 1970

Using the shaper to make panel doors 16 MIN
VHS
Color (J H A T)
$49.95 purchase _ #AM1454
Demonstrates step - by - step procedures for shaping and jointing stiles and rails for making panel doors. Shows how to measure, cut sample stiles and rails to test set ups, and how to use a pattern and hold the jig to shape stock. Illustrates reversing the cutter and cutter rotation for grain change and the use of a variety of cutters.
Industrial and Technical Education
Dist - AAVIM **Prod** - AAVIM 1992

Using the shaper to make panel doors 16 MIN
U-matic / VHS / 16mm
Wood shop - safety and operations series
Color (J) (SPANISH)
Shows step - by - step procedures for shaping and jointing stiles and rails, including how to measure, how to cut sample stiles and rails to test set - ups and using a pattern and a holding jig to shape the stock.
Industrial and Technical Education
Dist - AIMS **Prod** - EPRI 1970

Using the shaper to make raised panels for doors 9 MIN
16mm / U-matic / VHS
Wood shop - safety and operations series
Color (J) (SPANISH)
Provides step - by - step instructions for producing raised panels. Explains use of tall fence and shows how to make a trial run on a practice piece. Explains how to determine the exact shape of an irregular end so that it will fit the rail.
Health and Safety; Industrial and Technical Education
Dist - AIMS **Prod** - EPRI 1971

Using the shaper to make raised panels for doors 9 MIN
VHS
Color (J H A T)
$49.95 purchase _ #AM1455
Presents step - by - step instructions for producing raised panel doors. Explains how to use a tall fence, make a trial run on a practice piece and how to solve major problems in the making of raised panel doors. Uses the rails and stiles created in 'Using the Shaper to Make Panel Doors.'
Industrial and Technical Education
Dist - AAVIM **Prod** - AAVIM 1992

Using the Spirometer 25 MIN
VHS / U-matic
Color (PRO)
Explains and demonstrates the use of the spirometer, a device for measuring lung volumes and capacities.
Health and Safety; Science - Natural
Dist - HSCIC **Prod** - HSCIC 1981

Using the steady rest and follower rest on the lathe
VHS / U-matic
Intermediate engine lathe operation series
Color (SPANISH)
Industrial and Technical Education
Dist - VTRI **Prod** - VTRI

Using the Steady Rest and Follower Rest to Machine on the Lathe 15 MIN
U-matic / VHS
Machining and the Operation of Machine Tools, Module 3 - 'Intermediate Engine Lathe Series
Color (IND)
Industrial and Technical Education
Dist - LEIKID **Prod** - LEIKID

Using the three - jaw chuck 26 MIN
BETA / VHS
Machine shop - engine lathe series
Color (IND)
Industrial and Technical Education; Psychology
Dist - RMIBHF **Prod** - RMIBHF

Using the tool post grinder on the lathe
VHS / U-matic
Intermediate engine lathe operation series
Color (SPANISH)
Foreign Language; Industrial and Technical Education
Dist - VTRI **Prod** - VTRI

Using the Toolpost Grinder on the Lathe 15 MIN
U-matic / VHS
Machining and the Operation of Machine Tools, Module 3 - 'Intermediate Engine Lathe series
Color (IND)
Industrial and Technical Education
Dist - LEIKID **Prod** - LEIKID

Using the Training Day 12 MIN
U-matic / 35mm strip
Elements of Effective Teaching Series
Color
Helps instructors plan the best use of classroom time. Emphasizes that it is important to know when various teaching techniques are most effective.
Business and Economics; Education
Dist - RESEM **Prod** - RESEM

Using the Verse 50 MIN
VHS / U-matic
Royal Shakespeare Company Series
Color
Discusses blank verse, why it is better for drama than other verse forms and how it should be read. Shows actors trying out different stresses and discovering how Shakespeare uses antithesis, short lines, end - stopped lines and pauses in the middle of a line. Uses examples from Henry V, The Winter's Tale, The Merchant Of Venice and King John.
Literature and Drama
Dist - FOTH **Prod** - FOTH 1984

Using the Writer's Tools
U-matic / VHS
Write Course - an Introduction to College Composition Series
Color (C)
Focuses on editing, proofreading and the books which can help with these tasks. Gives instructions in using common reference books.
Education; English Language
Dist - DALCCD **Prod** - DALCCD

Using the Writer's Tools 30 MIN
U-matic / VHS
Write Course - an Introduction to College Composition Series
Color (C A)
LC 85-700990
Focuses on editing, proofreading and books which can be of help with these tasks. Includes specific, practical instructions on using common reference books.
English Language; Literature and Drama
Dist - FI **Prod** - FI 1984

Using Time Management 19 MIN
U-matic / VHS
Time Management for Managers and Professionals Series
Color
Business and Economics; Psychology
Dist - DELTAK **Prod** - DELTAK

Using transition time wisely
VHS
Strategies for classroom management series
Color (T PRO)
$100.00 purchase _ #V4 - 3
Features Pam Wolfe who teaches strategies for increasing instructional learning time. Part of a four - part series on research - based techniques for improving student attitude and behavior. Includes demonstrations by actual teachers in their classrooms and a leader's guide.

Business and Economics; Education
Dist - NSDC **Prod** - NSDC

Using Trial Objections 120 MIN
U-matic / VHS
Color (PRO)
Presents six dramatizations of situations commonly met during trial of a contract case and a tort case. Features expert trial practitioners and a trial judge as they analyze the situations. Fcuses on objections to the introduction of evidence, in light of the questions of law and tactical considerations.
Civics and Political Systems
Dist - CCEB **Prod** - CCEB

Using Values Clarification 30 MIN
U-matic / VHS / 16mm
Dealing with Classroom Problems Series
Color (A)
LC 76-703578
Shows Dr Sidney Simon as he conducts a workshop in values clarification for teachers and counselors. Includes scenes of high school classes participating in values clarification exercises and interviews with students, teachers and counselors who testify to the success of this process in helping people cope with life's problems.
Education; Guidance and Counseling
Dist - FI **Prod** - BELLDA 1976

Using Verbs Correctly 14 MIN
U-matic / VHS
Grammar Mechanic
(I J)
Designed to help the intermediate student apply the rules of grammar. Focuses on common problems with verb usage. Eighth in a 16 part series.
English Language
Dist - GPN **Prod** - WDCNTV

Using Visicalc
U-matic / VHS
Compututor series
Color
Shows the viewer all the basic properties and applications of the Visicalc, the electronic spreadsheet. Uses the actual screen displays on video that will be seen later on the computer.
Industrial and Technical Education; Mathematics
Dist - EMBASY **Prod** - CHASCI

Using VISICALC 60 MIN
VHS / 16mm
(G PRO)
$79.95 purchase _ #TM9
Shows how to install the VISICALC Software, set up a spreadsheet and automatic calculations, plus more. Aims presentation for users of APPLE IIe, IIc, or IBM and Compatibles.
Computer Science
Dist - RMIBHF **Prod** - RMIBHF

Using VisiCalc - Apple IIe 95 MIN
VHS / Software / U-matic
Compututor series
(J H)
$69.95 _ #C676 - 27472 - 2N
Provides step by step video training in computer literacy. Explains how to use VisiCalc with the Apple IIe. Helps interpret the user's manual and aids in mastering the most widely used programs.
Computer Science
Dist - RH

Using VisiCalc - IBM - PC 99 MIN
VHS / Software / U-matic
Compututor series
(J H)
$69.95 _ #C676 - 27467 - 6N
Provides step by step video training in computer literacy. Explains how to use the IBM personal computer with VisiCalc. Helps interpret the user's manual and aids in mastering the most widely used programs.
Computer Science
Dist - RH

Using VisiCalc - TRS - 80, IV 97 MIN
VHS / Software / U-matic
Compututor series
(J H)
$69.95 _ #C676 - 27476 - 5N
Provides step by step video training in computer literacy. Explains how to use VisiCalc with the TRS - 80, IV. Helps interpret the user's manual and aids in mastering the most widely used programs.
Computer Science
Dist - RH

Using Visual Aids Effectively 30 MIN
VHS / U-matic
Training the Trainer Series
Color (T)
Discusses visual aids for class use. Deals with Computers and videodisc.
Education; Psychology
Dist - ITCORP **Prod** - ITCORP

Using Visual Aids in Training 14 MIN
16mm
B&W (T)
LC FIE52-84
Depicts an instructor's use of a training motion picture, a coordinated filmstrip and a manual in teaching his class the use of the micrometer.
Civics and Political Systems; Education
Dist - USNAC **Prod** - USOE 1944

Using Volunteers in the Class 14 MIN
VHS / 16mm
English as a Second Language Series
Color (A PRO)
$165.00 purchase _ #290311
Demonstrates key teaching methods for English as a Second Language - ESL teachers. Features a teacher - presenter who introduces and provides a brief commentary on the techniques, then demonstrates the application of the technique to the students. 'Using Volunteers In The Class' offers tips on how a teacher should monitor and direct volunteer activities, such as field trips, remedial sessions and large group settings.
Education; English Language; Mathematics; Social Science
Dist - ACCESS **Prod** - ACCESS 1989

Using Water Wisely 20 MIN
16mm
Color (PRO)
Charts a series of tests on the use of fog on various types of structural fires. Shows how exposures are covered and how fires are extinguished with minimum amounts of water.
Health and Safety; Social Science
Dist - LAFIRE **Prod** - LAFIRE

Using Windows 103 MIN
VHS
First step for AutoCAD LT series
Color (G H VOC C PRO)
$49.95 purchase _ #AVT201V-T
Provides instruction on operating AutoCAD LT and Release 12 for Windows for all level of user. Focuses on using AutoCAD within the Windows system - equipment and software; starting Windows; basic functions; Program Manager; getting help; File Manager; using a mouse; and Control Panel.
Computer Science
Dist - CAMV

Using Wolkswriter 3 - IBM PC and Compatibles 60 MIN
VHS / 16mm
(G PRO)
$79.95 purchase _ #TM11
Shows how to use Wolkswriter 3, from installing the program to all the features available through creating style sheets and performing text merge.
Computer Science
Dist - RMIBHF **Prod** - RMIBHF

Using Words 15 MIN
U-matic
You Can Write Anything Series
Color (P I)
Teaches writing techniques through Amanda who is told about the importance of careful word usage, the value of a thesaurus, the use of alliteration and the power of descriptive passages.
Education; English Language
Dist - TVOTAR **Prod** - TVOTAR 1984

Using Wordstar 60 MIN
VHS / 16mm
(G PRO)
$79.95 purchase _ #TM10
Teaches the major features of the wordstar program. Covers cursor movement, word wrap, margins and tabs, formatting copy, charts, and more. Designed for users of APPLE IIe, IIc, and the IBM PC and compatibles.
Computer Science
Dist - RMIBHF **Prod** - RMIBHF

Using WordStar
U-matic / VHS
Compututor series
Color
Shows the use and application of the Micropro International WordStar, a popular word processing program.
Industrial and Technical Education; Mathematics
Dist - EMBASY **Prod** - CHASCI

Using WordStar - Apple IIe 112 MIN
VHS / Software / U-matic
Compututor series
(J H)
$69.95 _ #C676 - 27473 - 0N
Provides step - by - step video training in computer literacy. Explains how to use WordStar with the Apple IIe personal computer. Helps interpret the user's manual and aids in mastering the most widely used programs.
Computer Science
Dist - RH

Using WordStar - IBM - PC 100 MIN
VHS / Software
Compututor series
(J H)
$69.95 _ #C676 - 27468 - 4N
Provides step - by - step video training in computer literacy. Explains how to use WordStar with the IBM personal computer. Helps interpret the user's manual and aids in mastering the most widely used programs.
Computer Science
Dist - RH

Using Your Apple IIe 100 MIN
VHS / 16mm
(G PRO)
$79.95 purchase _ #TM3
Teaches the beginner about using the Apple IIe. Covers assembly, printer options, choosing software, and some basic programming language.
Computer Science
Dist - RMIBHF **Prod** - RMIBHF

Using Your Commodore C - 128 100 MIN
VHS / 16mm
(G PRO)
$79.95 purchase _ #TM4
Shows how to use the Commodore C - 128. Covers setup, operation, software selection, some basic programming language, and some system commands.
Computer Science
Dist - RMIBHF **Prod** - RMIBHF

Using Your Creative Brain 42 MIN
VHS
Color (J)
$89.95 purchase _ #HV - 676
Shows how to access the hidden potential of the mind. Presents two parts which explore the left brain - right brain, each with specific tasks and powers, and the mind and perception.
Fine Arts; Psychology
Dist - CRYSP **Prod** - CRYSP

Using your creative brain 43 MIN
35mm strip / VHS
Color (J H C A)
$99.00, $93.00 purchase _ #MB - 512850 - 0, #MB - 512852 - 7
Discusses the different capabilities of the left and right sides of the human brain. Focuses on research which has sought to maximize the effectiveness of the brain in creative thinking. Suggests that perceptions are often an obstacle to thought.
Fine Arts; Psychology
Dist - SRA **Prod** - SRA

Using Your Creative Brain Series
Left Brain - Right Brain - Part One 43.06 MIN
The Mind and Perception - Part Two 42.06 MIN
Dist - SRA

Using your head - 61 11 MIN
VHS / U-matic
Life's little lessons - self - esteem 4 - 6 series
Color (I)
$129.00, $99.00 purchase _ #V690
Tells about Stanley who was extremely absent - minded. Reveals that his wife was planning a party for Stanley's boss and one by one the guests called and cancelled, including his boss, but Stanley didn't think to tell Elda until the night of the party. Part of a 65 - part series on self - esteem.
Guidance and Counseling; Psychology
Dist - BARR **Prod** - CEPRO 1992

Using Your IBM PC 100 MIN
VHS / 16mm
(G PRO)
$79.95 purchase _ #TM2
Trains on the use and operation of the IBM - PC compatibles. Includes training on assembling the equipment, printer options, choosing software and some basic programming language.
Computer Science
Dist - RMIBHF **Prod** - RMIBHF

Using Your Library 18 MIN
U-matic
Color
LC 79-706405
Introduces the great variety of materials found in libraries, including books, magazines, art, sound recordings and films. Explains the Dewey Decimal System and shows how to use the card catalog and reference books.

Social Science
Dist - SRA **Prod** - SRA 1979

Using your library to write a research paper series
Presents a four - part series which walks viewers through the process, offering tips, tricks and insights that make the research and writing process fast and more productive. Includes the titles Selecting and Defining a Topic; Finding Sources of Information; Taking Notes and Organizing Your Ideas; and Writing the Paper.
Finding sources of information
Selecting and defining a topic
Taking notes and organizing your ideas
Using your library to write a research paper series
Writing the paper
Dist - CAMV

Using your machine
U-matic / VHS
Compututor series
Color
Gives a brief overview of computer literacy. Discusses equipment hook - up, the keyboard, major operating commands and working with printers. Shows how to write a 'BASIC' program.
Industrial and Technical Education; Mathematics
Dist - EMBASY RH **Prod** - CHASCI

Using Your Machine 90 MIN
U-matic / VHS / Cassette
(A PRO)
$195.00 purchase, $250.00 purchase
Gives an overview of how spreadsheets, databases, and word processing programs opoerate. Provides instructions for assembly of various parts of computer systems.
Computer Science
Dist - VIDEOT **Prod** - VIDEOT 1988

Using your machine - Apple IIe 100 MIN
VHS / Software / U-matic
Compututor series
(J H)
$69.95 _ #C676 - 27471 - 4N
Provides step - by - step video training in computer literacy. Explains the Apple IIe personal computer. Helps interpret the user's manual and aids in mastering the most widely used programs.
Computer Science
Dist - RH

Using Your Machine for the IBM PC 90 MIN
VHS
(C A PRO)
$95.00 purchase _ #TM200V
Discusses many topics concerning the use of the IBM PC, including history and orientation on terms, assembly of the IBM, system features, DOS operation, major commands, software applications, and more.
Computer Science
Dist - CAMV

Using your machine - TRS - 80, IV 92 MIN
VHS / Software / U-matic
Compututor series
(J H)
$69.95 _ #C676 - 27475 - 7N
Provides step - by - step video training in computer literacy. Explains the TRS - 80, IV personal computer. Helps interpret the user's manual and aids in mastering the most widely used programs.
Computer Science
Dist - RH

Using your medicines wisely 31 MIN
16mm
Color (A S R PRO IND)
Demonstrates the proper use of medications and discusses ways to work with your doctor and pharmacist for good health. Comes with information booklet.
Health and Safety
Dist - AARP **Prod** - AARP 1979

Using your safety zone - protecting your back 4 MIN
VHS
Color (G)
$145.00 purchase _ #4028 - HDLQ
Uses real - life work situations to teach safe lifting skills and reduce costly on - the - job accidents and injuries. Introduces the concept of the Safety Zone, which teaches how to lift and move materials safely within natural body limits. Also available as part of Safety Zone - Safe Lifting Program.
Health and Safety; Science - Natural
Dist - KRAMES **Prod** - KRAMES

Uso Correcto De Escaleras 10 MIN
U-matic / VHS / 16mm
Color (IND) (SPANISH)
A Spanish - language version of the motion picture Ladders And Lineman. Points out how accidents can be avoided when using a ladder. Stresses the importance of selecting the right ladder for the job, especially when electricity is involved.
Foreign Language; Guidance and Counseling; Health and Safety; Home Economics; Industrial and Technical Education
Dist - IFB **Prod** - EUSA 1974

Uso De Los Triangulos Semejantes 11 MIN
U-matic / VHS / 16mm
Color (J H C) (SPANISH)
A Spanish - language version of the motion picture Similar Triangles In Use. Presents the practical value of knowing that corresponding sides of similar triangles are proportional. Shows the use of the surveyor's quadrant and sextant.
Foreign Language; Mathematics
Dist - IFB **Prod** - IFB 1962

USO - Thirty Years of Service 28 MIN
16mm
Big Picture Series
Color
LC 75-701214
Takes a look at the United Service Organizations today, from San Francisco to Boston and Southeast Asia to Italy. Narrated by Bob Hope.
Civics and Political Systems; Geography - World; History - United States; Sociology
Dist - USNAC **Prod** - USA 1971

USO - Wherever they Go 28 MIN
16mm
Color (H A)
LC FIE67-113
A documentary account of the history and activity of the USO. Shows the entertainer, the stars and the gags, from Jolson to Hope, that have entertained service men, and the various other USO activities during its 25 years of service.
Civics and Political Systems; Physical Education and Recreation; Sociology
Dist - USNAC **Prod** - USDD 1966

USS Arizona - the life and death of a lady 47 MIN
VHS
Color (J H C G)
$29.95 purchase _ #ARM200V
Portrays the history of the USS Arizona, which remains in Pearl Harbor in memory of December 7, 1941. Offers footage of the ship's launch in 1915 and follows its history with photographs and interviews with still - living crew members from the 20s, 30s and 40s who describe life aboard the Arizona. Includes underwater footage of the ship today - a rusty, growth - covered hulk at the bottom of Pearl Harbor with nearly 1000 American seamen entombed aboard. Introduces the Japanese dive bomber who actually dropped the first bomb on the Arizona, visits the teahouse where the key Japanese spy sat daily plotting ship positions prior to the attack, the temple where, unknown to the public, Japanese veterans of the attack hold a memorial service each year.
History - United States; Sociology
Dist - CAMV

USS Forrestal (CVA - 59) 21 MIN
16mm
B&W (J H)
LC FIE56-337
A documentary on the construction of a modern aircraft carrier. Shows building phases from keel laying to sea trials and final commissioning.
Civics and Political Systems; Industrial and Technical Education; Social Science
Dist - USNAC **Prod** - USN 1955

USS Forrestal - CVA - 59 / the American Dreadnought 50 MIN
VHS / U-matic
Color
Documents the construction of a U S aircraft carrier from the laying of the keel to actual sea trials and final commissions. Shows the USS New Jersey being recommissioned to join the fleet for service in Vietnam.
Civics and Political Systems; History - United States; History - World; Industrial and Technical Education
Dist - IHF **Prod** - IHF

USS Line Pipe 9 MIN
16mm
Pipe and Tubing Series
Color
Business and Economics; Industrial and Technical Education
Dist - USSC **Prod** - USSC

USS Mechanical and Pressure Tubing 10 MIN
16mm
Pipe and Tubing Series
Color
Business and Economics; Industrial and Technical Education
Dist - USSC **Prod** - USSC

USS Nautilus - Operation Sunshine 14 MIN
16mm
Color
LC FIE60-60
Shows events leading up to and the actual polar passage of the nuclear submarine USS Nautilus. Concludes with the triumphant arrival of SSN - 571 in New York.
Civics and Political Systems; Geography - World; Social Science
Dist - USNAC **Prod** - USN 1959

USS Nautilus - Operation Sunshine 17 MIN
U-matic
Color
Describes the events leading up to and during the actual polar passage of the USS Nautilus.
Geography - World; Social Science
Dist - USNAC **Prod** - USNAC 1972

USS Nautilus - Operation Sunshine 45 MIN
U-matic / VHS
Color
Documents the historic trip under the polar ice cap by the world's first nuclear submarine.
Civics and Political Systems
Dist - IHF **Prod** - IHF

USS Oil Country Goods 11 MIN
16mm
Pipe and Tubing Series
Color
Business and Economics; Geography - United States; Home Economics; Social Science
Dist - USSC **Prod** - USSC

USS Standard Pipe 9 MIN
16mm
Pipe and Tubing Series
Color
Business and Economics; Industrial and Technical Education
Dist - USSC **Prod** - USSC

USS Steel Sheets 21 MIN
16mm
Color
Indicates that the techniques for producing steel sheets have changed considerably in the past few years and that today production is faster, bigger and more precise.
Business and Economics; Industrial and Technical Education
Dist - USSC **Prod** - USSC

USS Structural Tubing 11 MIN
16mm
Pipe and Tubing Series
Color
Business and Economics; Industrial and Technical Education
Dist - USSC **Prod** - USSC

USSA 14 MIN
16mm
Color; B&W (G)
$35.00 rental
Attempts to combine both the USA and the USSR and create a situation in which geopolitics loses its bearings. Features Moscow, New York and Berlin. Super 8 blown up to 16mm.
Civics and Political Systems; Fine Arts
Dist - CANCIN **Prod** - OSTROV 1985

USSR 50 MIN
BETA / VHS / U-matic
Road to war series
Color (J H C)
$250.00 purchase _ #JY - 5838C
Recalls August 24, 1939, when an astonished world watched Communist Russia sign a nonagression pact with Nazi Germany. Reveals that Stalin had brutally industrialized and collectivized the Soviet republics during the 1930s at a cost of millions of lives, and was still the largest military power in the world. Stalin saw no reason to place this power at the disposal of 'decadent imperialism' - but Hitler's victory over France and Poland left the USSR shocked and vulnerable. Part of an eight - part series on the history of World War II using a country - by - country perspective.
Civics and Political Systems; History - World
Dist - CORF **Prod** - BBCTV 1989

USSR 1926 - 1930
VHS / 16mm
What do those old films mean series; Pt 5
Color (G)
Details the changes in Soviet life that resulted from the revolution, including a new role for women. Uses film excerpts and newsreels, photographic documents and original music. Series directed by film historian Noel Burch.
Fine Arts; History - World; Sociology
Dist - FLMWST

USSR series
Provides a series of three videos covering the history of the USSR, from the time of the tsars to the fall of the Union. Looks at the development of the communist government through archival footage. Includes part 1, Stolen Revolution covering the Bolshevik revolution; part 2, Triumph of the Tyrant, covering Stalin's rule and the Berlin Airlift; and part 3, Illusion, Decline and Fall, covering the end of the Cold War and the breaking up of the Soviet state. Each part is available separately.
Illusion, decline and fall - Pt 3 — 60 MIN
Stolen revolution - Pt 1 — 60 MIN
Triumph of the tyrant - Pt 2 — 60 MIN
Dist - LANDMK

The USSR - The People speak in the 1990s — 26 MIN
VHS / U-matic / 16mm
Color (J H G)
$280.00, $330.00 purchase, $50.00 rental
Pans the broad range of opinions and social realities that permeate the Soviet Union in the 1990s. Places economic and political changes against the dramatic backdrop of a nation inexorably changing, with all the risks and unrest that accompany such upheaval. Suggested companion to Russia - The People Speak.
Civics and Political Systems; History - World
Dist - NDIM **Prod** - DEVYAT 1991

Ustinov's Russia — 12 MIN
BETA / VHS / U-matic
(G H C)
$100.00
Explores personal observations of actor Peter Ustinov. Ustinov argues that if world peace is to be obtained we must look beyond the rhetoric of the Cold War and attempt to understand the complexity of the Russian character.
Civics and Political Systems
Dist - CTV **Prod** - CTV 1985

Utah — 60 MIN
VHS
Portrait of America series
Color (J H C G)
$99.95 purchase _ #AMB44V
Visits Utah. Offers extensive research into the state's history. Films key locations and presents segments on its history, government, education, folklore, science, journalism, sociology, industry, agriculture and business. Shows what is unique about Utah and what is distinctive about its regional culture and how it got to be that way. Includes teacher study guides. Part of a 50 - part series.
Geography - United States; History - United States
Dist - CAMV

Utah - Another Time Another Place — 27 MIN
16mm
Color
LC 79-700335
Provides a glimpse into the heritage, culture and history of Utah. Surveys its recreational and scenic opportunities.
Geography - United States; History - United States; Physical Education and Recreation
Dist - UTAPC **Prod** - UTAPC 1978

Utah Assistive Technology Foundation — 6 MIN
VHS
Color; Captioned (G)
$15.00 purchase
Shows why technology is necessary for independent living, productivity and inclusion. Discusses the foundation.
Health and Safety
Dist - UATP **Prod** - UATP 1993

Utah, England, Taiwan, Russia, Panama — 27 MIN
16mm
Big Blue Marble - Children Around the World Series Program G; Program G
Color (P I)
LC 76-700646
Portrays a Navajo Indian from Utah, an 11 - year - old Panamanian fisherman and an English animal trainer. Presents a Russian folk tale about a boy named Igor who sells magic horses to the Czar.
Geography - United States; Geography - World; Literature and Drama; Social Science
Dist - VITT **Prod** - ALVEN 1975

Utamaro and His Five Women — 95 MIN
16mm
B&W (JAPANESE)
Plunges the viewer into the underground world of Japan in the late 1700's, a world of brothels, drinking parties, marketplaces, intertangled love affairs and violent outbreaks of passion. Explores this period through the eyes of a placid painter, Utamaro.
Fine Arts; Foreign Language; History - World
Dist - NYFLMS **Prod** - NYFLMS 1946

Uterine Aspiration in the First Trimester — 27 MIN
VHS / U-matic
Color (PRO)
Describes step - by - step uterine aspiration by means of flexible cannulas and syringe as well as by vacuum operated suction curettage.
Health and Safety
Dist - WFP **Prod** - WFP

Uterine bleeding series
Endometrial hyperplasia — 8 MIN
Endometriosis — 8 MIN
Fibroids — 8 MIN
Uterine bleeding - the causes — 9 MIN
Dist - MIFE

Uterine bleeding - the causes — 9 MIN
VHS
Uterine bleeding series
Color (G PRO C)
$150.00 purchase _ #SN - 339
Reveals that abnormal uterine bleeding can be a sign of impending miscarriage, tubal pregnancy, fibroids, cancer or endometrial hyperplasia. Discloses that most commonly, it indicates a disturbance in the hormones that control menstruation. In this case an endometrial biopsy is used to sample uterine tissue for hormone analysis. Explains the steps involved in a D and C - dilatation and curettage - procedure to confirm or eliminate the possibility of cancer. Part of a four - part series on uterine bleeding.
Health and Safety; Sociology
Dist - MIFE **Prod** - HOSSN

Uterine Cancer - Diagnosis and Management, Pt 1 — 20 MIN
16mm
Color (PRO)
Deals with cancer of the cervix. Demonstrates the technique of pelvic examination including cytology. Discusses etiology, symptoms, diagnosis and cone biopsy. Presents principles of treatment and end results at various stages.
Health and Safety
Dist - AMCS **Prod** - AMCS 1967

Uterine Cancer - Diagnosis and Management, Pt 2 — 12 MIN
16mm
Color (PRO)
Deals with cancer of the endometrium. Presents symptoms and methods of biopsy. Demonstrates therapy, surgery and discusses indications for postoperative radiation.
Health and Safety; Science
Dist - AMCS **Prod** - AMCS 1967

Uterine Cancer - the Problem of Early Diagnosis — 21 MIN
16mm
Color (PRO)
Illustrates the practicability of reducing deaths, from cancer of the uterus and cervix by adherence in general office practice to the routine pelvic examination of all adult women.
Health and Safety; Science
Dist - AMCS **Prod** - AMCS 1952

Uterine fibroids - what you should know — 11 MIN
VHS
Color (G C PRO)
$175.00 purchase _ #OB - 127
Answers the many questions patients have about this common condition. Explains what fibroids are, how they are diagnosed, and what symptoms may occur. Describes treatment options. Contact distributor for purchase price on multiple orders.
Health and Safety; Sociology
Dist - MIFE **Prod** - MIFE

Utilities Equipment Operator — 15 MIN
VHS / 16mm
(H C A)
$24.95 purchase _ #CS175
Describes the skills involved in a career as a utilities equipment operator. Features interviews with people working in this field.
Guidance and Counseling
Dist - RMIBHF **Prod** - RMIBHF

Utility Dog Obedience — 15 MIN
16mm
Dog Obedience Training Series
Color
LC 75-700106
Illustrates a variety of techniques for developing utility dog obedience.
Science - Natural
Dist - KLEINW **Prod** - KLEINW 1974

Utility Equipment Operator — 15 MIN
BETA / VHS / U-matic
Career Success Series
(H C A)
$29.95 _ #MX175
Portrays the occupation of utility equipment operator by reviewing its required abilities and interviewing people employed in this job. Tells of the anxieties and rewards involved in pursuing a career as a utility equipment operator.
Education; Guidance and Counseling; Industrial and Technical Education
Dist - CAMV **Prod** - CAMV

A Utility fuel inventory model
VHS
Color (C PRO G)
$150.00 purchase _ #88.02
Focuses on the utility fuel inventory model - UFIM - a modeling system currently in use among over 50 utilities to set fuel inventory strategy. Reveals that a recent random survey attributed to UFIM over $1 million per utility per year in savings. Demonstrated present value savings for at least one utility are over $100 million. UFIM was the only analysis type project recognized by Electric Power Research Institute as producing the highest benefits to member utilities. Electric Power Research Inst. Hung - po Chao, Stephen W Chapel, Peter A Morris, M James Sandling, Richard B Fancher, Michael A Kohn.
Business and Economics; Social Science
Dist - INMASC

Utility Functions with more than Two Attributes — 42 MIN
VHS / U-matic
Decision Analysis Series
Color
Industrial and Technical Education; Mathematics
Dist - MIOT **Prod** - MIOT

Utility Systems
U-matic / VHS
Drafting - Piping Familiarization Series
Color (IND)
Industrial and Technical Education
Dist - GPCV **Prod** - GPCV

Utility Workers — 11 MIN
16mm / U-matic / VHS
Community Helpers Series
Color (P I)
$280, $195 purchase _ #79520
Shows the operation of a water treatment plant, the installation of power lines, and an electrical generating plant.
Industrial and Technical Education
Dist - CORF

Utilization of retraction cord for gingival tissue management — 12 MIN
VHS / U-matic
Color (PRO C)
$395.00 purchase, $80.00 rental _ #C901 - VI - 032
Demonstrates procedures for gingival tissue retraction during the impression phase of restorative treatment. Discusses the use of the procedure in order to allow for the temporary lateral displacement of the sulcular tissue and to help control seepage of fluid into the sulcus so that an accurate registration of the preparation finish line is ensured. Presented by Drs Kathy L O'Keefe and H Philip Pierpont, the University of Texas Health Science Center at Houston.
Health and Safety
Dist - HSCIC

Utilizing computers to facilitate language in preschool children with Down syndrome — 8 MIN
VHS
Color (G C PRO)
$40.00 purchase
Demonstrates the use of computers to facilitate language for preschool children with Down syndrome. Illustrates special adaptive equipment, featuring a speech and language pathologist working with 3 and 4 - year old children using various software programs.
Computer Science; Education; Foreign Language; Health and Safety
Dist - ADWNSS **Prod** - ADWNSS

Utilizing Effective Communication 30 MIN
16mm
Nursing - R Plus M Equals C, Relationship Plus Meaning Equals 'Communication Series
B&W (C A)
LC 74-700215
Reviews and reinforces basic course themes and applies the general communication theory to specific suggestions for improving communication skills.
Health and Safety; Psychology
Dist - NTCN **Prod** - NTCN 1971

Utilizing effective disciplinary action 10 MIN
VHS
Color (A PRO IND)
$495.00 purchase, $130.00 rental
Presents a six - step program for discipline of employees suspected of substance abuse. Teaches approaches to handling the employee's denial, resistance, and aggression. Suggests that offering professional help is an effective way to get the employee to accept the discipline and seek help.
Business and Economics; Guidance and Counseling; Psychology; Sociology
Dist - VLEARN **Prod** - AIMS

Utilizing Effective Disciplinary Action - Video 3 10 MIN
VHS / 16mm
Handling a Suspected Substance Abuse Problem Series
Color (PRO)
$495.00 purchase, $130.00 rental, $35.00 preview
Instructs supervisors on disciplining their sustance abusing employees. Shows how to respond to resistance, agression, and denial and how to actively help the rehabilitation of the employee. Includes a leader's guide.
Business and Economics; Guidance and Counseling; Psychology
Dist - UTM **Prod** - UTM

Utilizing Fresh Water Resources - the Columbia River 14 MIN
16mm
Color (J)
LC FIA68-3079
Shows how the utilization of the Columbia River for hydroelectric power, irrigation, transportation, industry and recreation constitutes a prime example of proper long - range planning with natural resources.
Geography - United States; Science - Natural
Dist - NWFLMP **Prod** - NWFLMP 1968

Utopias 26 MIN
U-matic / VHS / 16mm
Today's History Series
Color (H C)
States that the earliest Utopias date back to the 16th century and that they were seeking an ideal society. Presents the political and philosophical ideas of Utopias, and tells of some that worked.
Civics and Political Systems; History - United States; History - World
Dist - JOU **Prod** - JOU 1984

Utopias 15 MIN
U-matic / VHS
America past series
(J H)
$125.00 purchase
Introduces the origin and development of utopian communities and movements.
History - United States
Dist - AITECH **Prod** - KRMATV 1987

Utu 104 MIN
VHS / 35mm / 16mm
Color (G)
$250.00, $300.00 rental
Presents the kaleidoscopic memories of a Maori chieftain about to be executed by European settlers in the late 19th century. Reveals that, having witnessed the massacre of his village by colonial troops, the warrior vows revenge and wages a hopeless war against the well - armed white settlers. Contains scenes of graphic violence. Directed by Geoff Murphy.
Fine Arts; History - World
Dist - KINOIC

UXB 30 MIN
16mm
B&W (H C)
LC FI67-134
Examines the experiences and emotions of two members of a British bomb disposal unit as they dismantle a series of unexploded bombs dropped by the Nazis in World War II.
Civics and Political Systems; History - World
Dist - WB **Prod** - GE 1962

V

V 3 MIN
16mm
The Roman numeral series
Color (G)
$132.00 purchase, $12.00 rental
Presents the fifth of a series of abstract, non - objective, non - representational films.
Fine Arts
Dist - CANCIN **Prod** - BRAKS 1980

V-2 / German V-2 Rocket Tests 29 MIN
U-matic / VHS
B&W
Documents postwar V - 2 rocket tests in the New Mexico desert.
Civics and Political Systems; Industrial and Technical Education
Dist - IHF **Prod** - IHF

V - Belt Drive Installation and Maintenance 19 MIN
VHS
Power Transmission Series II - Selection, Application and 'Maintenance Series
Color (A)
$265.00 purchase, $50.00 rental _ #57972
Covers advantages, types, selection, storage and installation of V - belts. Explains the identification and numbering system, based on cross section and outside lengths. Discusses both classical and narrow series, and RMA tolerances. Demonstrates cleaning and aligning sheaves and checking for wear. Describes QD bushings and their installation, care and removal.
Industrial and Technical Education
Dist - UILL **Prod** - MAJEC 1986

V - Belt Drive Selection 16 MIN
VHS
Power Transmission Series II - Selection, Application and 'Maintenance Series
Color (A)
$265.00 purchase, $50.00 rental _ #57975
Elaborates on the numbering system for both classical and narrow series V - belt drives, explaining the four elements which determine the capacity of a belt to transmit power. Explains how to read charts which show horsepower capacity, length correction values, and arc - length correction factors. Lists seven types of information needed for the proper selection of a V - belt.
Industrial and Technical Education
Dist - UILL **Prod** - MAJEC 1986

V - Belts 23 MIN
U-matic / VHS
Color (IND) (SPANISH)
Discusses basic concept and components of V - Belts. Details advantages and disadvantages.
Education; Industrial and Technical Education
Dist - TAT **Prod** - TAT

V - Belts and Sheaves 22 MIN
VHS
Power Transmission Series I - PT Products Series
Color (A)
$225.00 purchase, $50.00 rental _ #57962
Describes basic V - belt construction, including backing, tensile cord, and cover. Includes FHP belts, multiple (classical and narrow), raw edge cog, banded, double angle, open end, and adjustable link. Explains numbering of standard series, and how to select the type you need from the numbers. Also covers sheave styles, sizes, and mounting options.
Industrial and Technical Education
Dist - UILL **Prod** - MAJEC 1986

V - Belts and V - Belt Drives 19 MIN
U-matic / VHS / 16mm
Mechanical Power Transmission Series
Color (IND)
Portrays the V - belt principle as it developed from the wedge. Demonstrates their use on automobiles, machines and appliances while explaining the involvement of such forces as tension, friction and arc of contact.
Industrial and Technical Education
Dist - LUF **Prod** - LUF 1977

V - belts proper care 15 MIN
U-matic / VHS
Marshall maintenance training programs series; Tape 39
Color (IND)
Covers installation and maintenance of V - belts and the importance of proper care. Teaches how to inspect, tension, align, store and replace V - belts.
Industrial and Technical Education
Dist - LEIKID **Prod** - LEIKID

V - Butt Joint 3 MIN
VHS / BETA
Welding Training (Comprehensive - Metal Inert Gas (M I G Welding 'Series
Color (IND)
Industrial and Technical Education; Psychology
Dist - RMIBHF **Prod** - RMIBHF

V - Butt Joint Horizontal 2 MIN
BETA / VHS
Welding Training (Comprehensive - Metal Inert Gas (M I G Welding 'Series
Color (IND)
Industrial and Technical Education; Psychology
Dist - RMIBHF **Prod** - RMIBHF

V - butt joint multi - pass 13 MIN
BETA / VHS
Welding training - comprehensive - basic shielded metal arc welding series
Color (IND)
Industrial and Technical Education; Psychology
Dist - RMIBHF **Prod** - RMIBHF

V D Prevention 11 MIN
VHS / U-matic / 16mm
Color (SPANISH)
Outlines methods of prevention and care necessary to stop infection. Discusses cleansing measures, prophylactics, preventive medications and regular VD checkups. Host - narrated by TV actress Adrienne Barbeau.
Health and Safety
Dist - AMEDFL **Prod** - ASHA

V D Quiz 25 MIN
U-matic / VHS
Color (H A) (SPANISH)
Contains the most up - to - date facts, options for treatment, solutions to the pandemic of sexually transmissible diseases. Uses quiz format to encourage audience participation. Documents gonorrhea, NGU, herpes, syphillis and other venereal diseases.
Foreign Language; Health and Safety
Dist - AMEDFL **Prod** - ASHA

V for victory series
The Battle of the Bulge and the Drive to the Rhine 45 MIN
D - Day and the Battle for France 45 MIN
The Eagle triumphant 45 MIN
Iwo Jima, Okinawa and the push on Japan 45 MIN
Pearl Harbor to Midway 45 MIN
Women at war 45 MIN
Dist - KNOWUN

V for Vigilante 12 MIN
16mm
Color (J)
Presents the story of the Mach 2 A3J vigilante 'A5. Includes dramatic scenes of structural 'torture' testing, escape seat system firings and flight action at Columbus, Palmdale and aboard carriers.
Social Science
Dist - RCKWL **Prod** - NAA

V groove open root - 1 - G position 15 MIN
U-matic / VHS
Arc welding training series
Color (IND)
Industrial and Technical Education
Dist - AVIMA **Prod** - AVIMA

V groove with backer - 4 - G position 15 MIN
U-matic / VHS
Arc welding training series
Color (IND)
Industrial and Technical Education
Dist - AVIMA **Prod** - AVIMA

V groove with backer - 1 - G position 15 MIN
VHS / U-matic
Arc welding training series
Color (IND)
Industrial and Technical Education
Dist - AVIMA **Prod** - AVIMA

V groove with backer - 3 - G position 15 MIN
VHS / U-matic
Arc welding training series
Color (IND)
Industrial and Technical Education
Dist - AVIMA **Prod** - AVIMA

V groove with backer - 2 - G position 15 MIN
VHS / U-matic
Arc welding training series
Color (IND)
Industrial and Technical Education
Dist - AVIMA **Prod** - AVIMA

V is for Voluntary Childlessness 8 MIN
16mm
ABC's of Canadian Life Series
Color
Looks at reasons for having or not having children, pointing out that while, for some couples, childlessness is liberating, one - third of a million babies are born in Canada each year.

Geography - World; Sociology
Dist - UTORMC **Prod** - UTORMC

V, M, N 15 MIN
U-matic / VHS
Cursive writing series
Color (P)
Presents techniques of handwriting, focusing on the lower case letters v, m and n.
English Language
Dist - GPN **Prod** - WHROTV 1984

V, Y, Z, Q 15 MIN
VHS / U-matic
Cursive writing series
Color (P)
Presents techniques of handwriting, focusing on the capital letters V, Y, Z and Q.
English Language
Dist - GPN **Prod** - WHROTV 1984

VA Nursing - the Challenge is Yours 9 MIN
VHS / U-matic
Color (PRO)
Discusses the variety of nursing career opportunities in the Veterans Administration Nursing Service. States that the individual is responsible for managing his or her own career goals, objectives and timetable, although resources are available to enhance planning, goal setting and achievement.
Civics and Political Systems; Guidance and Counseling; Health and Safety
Dist - USNAC **Prod** - VAMSLC

VA Ration Allowance as a Management Tool 55 MIN
U-matic
Color (PRO)
LC 77-706085
Defines terms used by the U S Veterans Administration in the operation and management of hospital food services. Features dietician Carol B Rooney explaining how food ration allowances should be applied in planning food purchases and how menu planning guides should be individualized in terms of the health care facilities and clientele.
Guidance and Counseling; Health and Safety; Industrial and Technical Education
Dist - USNAC **Prod** - USVA 1976

Va - rice - ity - a New Look at Rice 15 MIN
16mm
Color
Illustrates the growth, production and harvesting of rice. Presents recipes and highlights rice production as a significant American industry.
Agriculture; Home Economics
Dist - MTP **Prod** - RICMD

Vacances En Bretagne - Vacation in Brittany 15 MIN
16mm
Toute la bande series; No 4
Color (H) (FRENCH)
LC 78-715480
A French language film. Presents the Ermonts, their children, Caroline and Victor and their friends spending their wonderful vacation in Brittany. Includes window shopping, eating at the cafe and boat rides.
Foreign Language
Dist - SBS **Prod** - SBS 1970

Vacant Lot 21 MIN
16mm / U-matic / VHS
Living Science Series
Color (J H C)
LC FIA67-5549
Shows the various forms of life to be found on a vacant lot in a region near upper Michigan. Pictures plant and insect life and shows adaptation and interdependence of various forms of life.
Science - Natural
Dist - IFB **Prod** - CRAF 1961

Vacation 3.05 MIN
U-matic / VHS
Photo Tips Series
Color (J H A)
Establishes technique for photographing vacations including the sites as well as family and freinds.
Fine Arts; Industrial and Technical Education
Dist - AITECH **Prod** - TURR 1986

Vacation planning 30 MIN
VHS / U-matic
Consumer survival series; Recreation
Color
Presents tips on vacation planning.
Home Economics; Physical Education and Recreation
Dist - MDCPB **Prod** - MDCPB

Vacation Safety
16mm
Color; B&W
Gives tips on having vacation fun without 'overdoing it' or becoming involved in an accident.
Health and Safety; Physical Education and Recreation
Dist - NSC **Prod** - NSC

Vacationing 30 MIN
U-matic / VHS
Say it with sign series; Pt 32
Color (H C A) (AMERICAN SIGN)
Presents Lawrence Solow and Sharon Neumann Solow introducing American Sign Language used by the hearing - impaired. Emphasizes signs having to do with vacationing.
Education
Dist - FI **Prod** - KNBCTV 1982

Vacations 30 MIN
U-matic
Today's Special Series
Color (K P)
Develops language arts skills in children. Programs are thematically designed around subjects of interest to youngsters. Action takes place in a department store where people, mannequins, puppets, comic characters and special guests present a light hearted approach to language arts.
Fine Arts; Literature and Drama; Psychology
Dist - TVOTAR **Prod** - TVOTAR 1985

Vaccine on trial 60 MIN
U-matic / VHS
Quest for the killers series
Color
Deals with the mobilization of New York's gay community to help research and test a vaccine against hepatitis B, the prime cause of fatal liver cancer.
Health and Safety
Dist - PBS **Prod** - PBS

Vaccines and Preventive Medicine 26 MIN
U-matic / VHS
Color (C)
$249.00, $149.00 purchase _ #AD - 1804
Looks at how recombinant DNA technology has spawned the development of new vaccines. Examines work with the vaccinia virus at the University of Maryland Medical School Center for Vaccine Development. Explains some of the controversies about the production and use of vaccines.
Health and Safety; Psychology; Science; Science - Natural
Dist - FOTH **Prod** - FOTH

Vaclav Havel - leadership in Eastern Europe - 2 51 MIN
VHS
Eastern Europe - breaking with the past series
Color (H C G)
$50.00 purchase
Portrays Vaclav Havel of Czechoslovakia in two parts. Interviews Havel and other dissidents in The Other Europe, 1988. Presents Audience, a recent production of Havel's play which was banned for 16 years. Ends with Balance, an animated look at balance of power and the nature of greed. Part two of 13 parts.
Civics and Political Systems; History - World
Dist - GVIEW **Prod** - GVIEW 1990

Vacuum filtration 9 MIN
VHS
Chemistry master apprentice series
Color (H C)
$49.95 purchase _ #49 - 7209 - V
Demonstrates the use of a Buchner funnel and vacuum filtration apparatus to perform a qualitative separation. Part of the Chemistry Master Apprentice series.
Science; Science - Physical
Dist - INSTRU **Prod** - CORNRS

Vacuum Filtration in Gravimetric Analysis 12 MIN
U-matic / VHS
Chemistry - master - apprentice series; Program 102
Color (C A)
LC 82-706049
Shows how to use vacuum filtration to collect a precipitate (nickel dimethlglyoximate) in a porcelain crucible with a porous bottom. Demonstrates the techniques of quantitative transfer, decanting, washing, and testing the wash solution.
Health and Safety; Science; Science - Physical
Dist - CORNRS **Prod** - CUETV 1981

Vacuum investing 25 MIN
VHS / U-matic
Color (C PRO)
$395.00 purchase, $80.00 rental _ #D911 - VI - 010
Demonstrates how to sprue and vacuum invest a wax pattern. Uses a model number 29 tooth to show the steps for attaching a wax sprue to a wax pattern, prepare the base former and casting ring and vacuum investing. Presented by Drs Stephen M Collard and Magda S Eldiwany.
Health and Safety
Dist - HSCIC

Vacuum Pump, Air Ejector, Strainer, and Trap Operations 60 MIN
VHS / U-matic
Equipment Operation Training Program Series
Color (IND)
Describes the operations of a vacuum pump, air ejector, strainer and trap.
Industrial and Technical Education
Dist - ITCORP **Prod** - ITCORP

Vacuum tubes and circuits 60 MIN
VHS
Electronic systems and equipment series
Color (PRO)
$600.00 - $1500.00 purchase _ #ICVTC
Explains how different types of vacuum tubes operate, how tubes are biased, how amplification is achieved in single - stage and two - stage vacuum tube circuits and how schematic symbols and conventions are used to represent vacuum tubes and circuits. Part of a nineteen - part series on electronic systems and equipment, which is part of a 49 - unit set on instrumentation and control. Includes five workbooks and an instructor guide to support four hours of instruction.
Education; Industrial and Technical Education; Psychology
Dist - NUSTC **Prod** - NUSTC

Vacuum Tubes - Bias in Triodes 18 MIN
16mm
B&W
LC 74-705898
Explains the term bias. Discusses fixed bias and shows the schematic of a fixed bias network. Identifies the components and gives their purpose. Traces an AC signal through the circuit. Kinescope).
Industrial and Technical Education
Dist - USNAC **Prod** - USAF

Vacuum Tubes - Electron Theory and the Diode Tube 16 MIN
16mm
B&W (J H)
LC FIE52-1486
The three functions of the vacuum tube in radio are explained.
Industrial and Technical Education; Science - Physical
Dist - USNAC **Prod** - USOE 1944

Vacuum Tubes - Triode and Multi - Purpose Tubes 14 MIN
16mm
B&W (H)
LC FIE59-176
Describes the triode tube as evolved from the diode tube, its structure and capacities and the circuits in which the tube functions. Indicates the functions of the grid, the grid bias, the screen and suppression grids and the multi - purpose tubes.
Science - Physical
Dist - USNAC **Prod** - USA 1942

Vacuum Tubes - Triodes - Cathode Self Bias 17 MIN
16mm
B&W
LC 74-705899
Defines cathode self bias and shows an amplifier circuit schematic with cathode bias. Identifies the components, gives the function of the components, traces the charge and discharge paths of CK, and defines degeneration. (Kinescope).
Industrial and Technical Education; Science - Physical
Dist - USNAC **Prod** - USAF

Vacuum Tubes - Triodes - Grid Leak Bias 27 MIN
16mm
B&W
LC 74-705900
Shows a grid - leak bias network, identifies the components that comprise the circuit and explains how the network functions. Traces the charge and discharge paths of CG and the AC signal through the circuit. (Kinescope).
Industrial and Technical Education
Dist - USNAC **Prod** - USAF

Vadya Vrinda 26 MIN
16mm
B&W (H C A)
Introduces Indian music and explains the roles of the various musical instruments in the Indian orchestra.
Fine Arts
Dist - NEDINF **Prod** - INDIA

The Vagabond 25 MIN
U-matic / VHS / 16mm
Charlie Chaplin Comedy Theater Series
B&W (I)
Features Charlie Chaplin as the pathetic little tramp who rescues a girl after she has been kidnapped by gypsies. Shows how he grows to love her, but she proves to be the inspiration for a famous artist and Charlie seems doomed to the lonely life of a hobo once more until the girl, in her gratitude, insists that he stay with her.
Fine Arts
Dist - FI **Prod** - MUFLM

Vagabond 105 MIN
16mm / 35mm
Color (G) (FRENCH WITH ENGLISH SUBTITLES)
$300.00, $400.00 rental
Focuses on the wanderings of a young woman who abandons a secure but limiting lifestyle for the freedom of the open road. Stars Sandrine Bonnaire as Mona. Directed by Agnes Varda.
Fine Arts; Sociology
Dist - KINOIC **Prod** - IFEX 1986

Vaginal birth after Cesarean - VBAC 12 MIN
VHS
Color; CC (G C PRO) (SPANISH)
$175.00 purchase _ #OB - 139
Explains the benefits of VBAC and encourages women who are suitable candidates to strongly consider this option. Features testimonials from women who chose vaginal delivery after prior Cesarean. Contact distributor for purchase price on multiple orders.
Health and Safety
Dist - MIFE **Prod** - MIFE 1995

Vaginal Hysterectomy 36 MIN
16mm
Color (PRO)
Shows the technique of vaginal hysterectomy used in the area Department of Obstetrics and Gynaecology at Oxford. Illustrates transfixion and double ligation of the pedicles following the use of clamps, together with high support of the vaginal vault, plus high anterior and posterior fascial colporrhaphy.
Health and Safety; Science
Dist - ACY **Prod** - ACYDGD 1957

Vaginal hysterectomy 10 MIN
VHS
5 - part gynecological series
Color (G)
$100.00 purchase, $40.00 rental _ #5306S, #5306V
Illustrates graphically how weakened pelvic supports cause uterine prolapse, cystocele rectocele and enterocele. Explains what to expect from the procedure of vaginal hysterectomy. Part of a five - part series on gynecology.
Health and Safety
Dist - AJN **Prod** - VMED

Vaginal Hysterectomy, a Simplified Technique 28 MIN
16mm
Color (PRO)
Shows a simplified technique for the performance of vaginal hysterectomy when removal of the uterus without repair of the vagina is indicated. Explains that using this technique, hysterectomy can be accomplished vaginally in many instances in which the abdominal approach might have been done formerly.
Health and Safety; Science
Dist - ACY **Prod** - ACYDGD 1963

Vaginal Hysterectomy and Repair
VHS / U-matic
Color
Describes how physical complications resulting from childbirth often require surgical attention including vaginal hysterectomy. Discusses the problems of a prolapse, retocele and cystocele.
Health and Safety
Dist - MIFE **Prod** - MIFE

Vaginal Hysterectomy for the Enlarged Uterus 11 MIN
16mm
Color (PRO)
LC 73-701952
Demonstrates for three cases of benign myomatous uteri a simple, safe method of reducing the size of the uterus to facilitate its vaginal delivery, showing in detail each step of the procedure. Discusses indications and advantages of the vaginal approach to hysterectomy.
Health and Safety; Science - Natural
Dist - SQUIBB **Prod** - KAISP 1968

Vaginal Hysterectomy, Pathology Laboratory and Operation for Post -Operative Hemorrhage 37 MIN
U-matic / VHS
Gynecologic Series
Color
Health and Safety
Dist - SVL **Prod** - SVL

Vaginitis 14 MIN
U-matic / VHS / 16mm
Color (PRO)
Discusses the major sources of vaginitis, its signs, symptoms, treatment and prevention.
Health and Safety
Dist - PRORE **Prod** - PRORE

Vaginitis 12 MIN
16mm / U-matic / VHS
Color (H C A)
LC 79-701612
Describes the causes and symptoms of vaginitis, introduces frequently - prescribed medications and demonstrates their use, and suggests ways of maintaining vaginal hygiene.
Health and Safety
Dist - PEREN **Prod** - CROMIE 1979

Vaginitis 12 MIN
16mm / 8mm cartridge
Captioned; Color (H C A)
Explains three types of vaginal infections and tells how they are diagnosed and treated.
Health and Safety; Science - Natural
Dist - PEREN **Prod** - CROMIE

Vaginitis and abnormal GYN discharges 9 MIN
VHS
Color (G PRO C)
$200.00 purchase _ #OB - 82
Contains information on gynecological discharges which originate in the vagina, uterus, fallopian tubes, ovaries or cervix. Discusses the possible causes of each and the usual treatment. Explains how women often experience discharge when taking antibiotics and that this is caused by a resultant yeast imbalance.
Health and Safety; Sociology
Dist - MIFE **Prod** - MIFE

Vagotomy and Antrectomy for Duodenal Ulcer 23 MIN
16mm
Color (PRO)
Illustrates the technical features of both selective gastric vagotomy and truncal vagotomy combined with antral resection in definitive treatment of duodenal ulcer disease.
Health and Safety; Science
Dist - ACY **Prod** - ACYDGD 1965

Vagotomy and Pyloroplasty 27 MIN
16mm
Color (PRO)
Discusses finney pyloroplasty, including its historical background. Demonstrates the operative techniques currently used.
Health and Safety; Science
Dist - ACY **Prod** - ACYDGD 1967

Vagotomy and Pyloroplasty for Bleeding and for Perforated Duodenal Ulcer 25 MIN
16mm
Color (PRO)
Explains that vagotomy not only provides effective control of duodenal ulcer disease but also induces amazingly rapid healing of duodenal ulceration. Points out that pyloroplasty inherently provides a simple method for excision of perforated or bleeding anterior duodenal ulcer.
Health and Safety; Science
Dist - ACY **Prod** - ACYDGD 1963

Vagotomy and Pyloroplasty for Duodenal Ulcer 22 MIN
16mm
Color (PRO)
Explains that vagotomy and pyloroplasty has proven to be an effective and simple method for dealing with duodenal ulcer. Shows operative technique, the operation being carried out through the abdomen.
Health and Safety; Science
Dist - ACY **Prod** - ACYDGD 1965

Vagotomy, Choice of Drainage Sites 24 MIN
16mm
Color (PRO)
Covers tests for completeness of vagotomy, consideration with regard to choice of gastroenterostomy, pyloroplasty or subtotal gastrectomy and technique of vagotomy and gastroenterostomy.
Health and Safety; Science
Dist - ACY **Prod** - ACYDGD 1965

Vagotomy, Pyloroplasty, and Supra - Antral Segmental Gastrectomy for Duodenal Ulcer 34 MIN
16mm
Color (PRO)
Presents a procedure calculated to control the ulcerogenic mechanisms with maximal conservation of gastrointestinal function. Shows that adequate acid reduction is accomplished by vagotomy and subtotal resection of the acid - producing area of the stomach.
Health and Safety; Science
Dist - ACY **Prod** - ACYDGD 1956

V A I - video math review for the A C T 110 MIN
VHS
V A I - video reviews series
Color (H)
$29.00 purchase _ #04593 - 126
Reviews mathematics in preparation for the ACT exam. Features an experienced instructor who analyzes questions, gives test - taking techniques, time - saving hints, multiple choice strategies and creative ways to approach questions.
Education; Mathematics; Psychology
Dist - GA **Prod** - GA

VAI - video math review for the GED 120 MIN
VHS
VAI - video reviews series
Color (H A)
$29.00 purchase _ #04590 - 126
Reviews mathematics in preparation for the GED exam. Features an experienced instructor who analyzes questions, gives test - taking techniques, time - saving hints, multiple choice strategies and creative ways to approach questions.
Education; Mathematics; Psychology
Dist - GA **Prod** - GA

VAI - video math review for the GMAT 120 MIN
VHS
VAI - video reviews series
Color (C A)
$29.00 purchase _ #04604 - 126
Reviews mathematics in preparation for the GMAT exam. Features an experienced instructor who analyzes questions, gives test - taking techniques, time - saving hints, multiple choice strategies and creative ways to approach questions.
Education; Mathematics; Psychology
Dist - GA **Prod** - GA

VAI - video math review for the GRE 120 MIN
VHS
VAI - video reviews series
Color (C A)
$29.00 purchase _ #04688 - 126
Reviews mathematics in preparation for the GRE exam. Features an experienced instructor who analyzes questions, gives test - taking techniques, time - saving hints, multiple choice strategies and creative ways to approach questions.
Education; Mathematics; Psychology
Dist - GA **Prod** - GA

VAI - video review for the Armed Forces exam 120 MIN
VHS
VAI - video reviews series
Color (H)
$29.00 purchase _ #04594 - 126
Shows how to prepare for the Armed Forces exam. Features an experienced instructor who analyzes questions, gives test - taking techniques, time - saving hints, multiple choice strategies and creative ways to approach questions.
Civics and Political Systems; Education; Psychology
Dist - GA **Prod** - GA

VAI - video review for the police officer exam 120 MIN
VHS
VAI - video reviews series
Color (H A)
$29.00 purchase _ #04598 - 126
Offers instruction in preparation for the police officer exam. Features an experienced instructor who analyzes questions, gives test - taking techniques, time - saving hints, multiple choice strategies and creative ways to approach questions.
Civics and Political Systems; Education; Psychology
Dist - GA **Prod** - GA

VAI - video reviews series

V A I - video math review for the A C T	110 MIN
VAI - video math review for the GED	120 MIN
VAI - video math review for the GMAT	120 MIN
VAI - video math review for the GRE	120 MIN
VAI - video review for the Armed Forces exam	120 MIN
VAI - video review for the police officer exam	120 MIN
V A I - video verbal review for the A	105 MIN

C T
VAI - video verbal review for the GED 120 MIN
VAI - video verbal review for the GMAT 120 MIN
VAI - video verbal review for the GRE 120 MIN
Dist - GA

V A I - video verbal review for the A C T 105 MIN
VHS
V A I - video reviews series
Color (H)
$29.00 purchase _ #04600 - 126
Looks at verbal skills in preparation for the ACT exam. Features an experienced instructor who analyzes questions, gives test - taking techniques, time - saving hints, multiple choice strategies and creative ways to approach questions.
Education; English Language; Psychology; Social Science
Dist - GA **Prod** - GA

VAI - video verbal review for the GED 120 MIN
VHS
VAI - video reviews series
Color (H A)
$29.00 purchase _ #04583 - 126
Looks at verbal skills in preparation for the GED exam. Features an experienced instructor who analyzes questions, gives test - taking techniques, time - saving hints, multiple choice strategies and creative ways to approach questions.
Education; English Language; Psychology; Social Science
Dist - GA **Prod** - GA

VAI - video verbal review for the GMAT 120 MIN
VHS
VAI - video reviews series
Color (C A)
$29.00 purchase _ #04596 - 126
Looks at verbal skills in preparation for the GMAT exam. Features an experienced instructor who analyzes questions, gives test - taking techniques, time - saving hints, multiple choice strategies and creative ways to approach questions.
Education; English Language; Psychology; Social Science
Dist - GA **Prod** - GA

VAI - video verbal review for the GRE 120 MIN
VHS
VAI - video reviews series
Color (C A)
$29.00 purchase _ #04597 - 126
Looks at verbal skills in preparation for the GRE exam. Features an experienced instructor who analyzes questions, gives test - taking techniques, time - saving hints, multiple choice strategies and creative ways to approach questions.
Education; English Language; Psychology; Social Science
Dist - GA **Prod** - GA

Vain glory 32 MIN
VHS
Color (J H C G A R)
$39.99 purchase, $10.00 rental _ #35 - 83541 - 533
Interviews Tony Cox, former husband of Yoko Ono, on his experiences with the 'cult' known as 'The Walk' and on how he eventually became a Christian.
Religion and Philosophy
Dist - APH **Prod** - WORD

Val D'Herens - an Alpine Community in Change 21 MIN
16mm
Color (H C G)
Discusses the changing exploitation of environmental resources in Southern Switzerland.
Geography - World; Social Science
Dist - VIEWTH **Prod** - VIEWTH

The Vale of Kashmir 30 MIN
U-matic / VHS
Journey into the Himalayas Series
Color (J S C A)
MV=$195.00
Looks behind the tourist facade to find the lifestyle of the real Kashmir.
Geography - World; History - World
Dist - LANDMK **Prod** - LANDMK 1986

Valencia diary 108 MIN
VHS / 16mm
B&W (G)
$490.00 purchase, $125.00 rental
Draws out universal themes as it records life in a Philippine village at a time when the atmosphere is charged with the tension of an impending Presidential election. Depicts the barrio Sinayawan on Mindanao Island, a rice growing community. Central characters are a couple who came to the barrio after losing a farm; a charasmatic village priest; Imelda and Fernando Marcos stumping; Cory Aquina, a surprise challenger. Delivers sociological insights and the couple offer commentary on unfolding events in the context of their own experiences.
Civics and Political Systems; Fine Arts; Geography - World; History - World
Dist - FIRS **Prod** - KILDEA 1992

Valentin De Las Sierras 10 MIN
16mm
Color (C)
$392.00
Experimental film by Bruce Baillie.
Fine Arts
Dist - AFA **Prod** - AFA 1967

Valentine 97 MIN
VHS / U-matic
Color (H C A)
Tells what happens when a pair of 70 - year - olds in a retirement village embark on a high - spirited affair. Reveals that when the man finds that the woman has a terminal illness, he whisks her off on a romantic odyssey of fun and excitement. Stars Jack Albertson and Mary Martin.
Fine Arts; Health and Safety; Sociology
Dist - TIMLIF **Prod** - TIMLIF 1982

A Valentine for Nelson 5 MIN
16mm
Color (G)
$15.00 rental
Pays homage to love and relationships and the ups and downs of living together. Intends every shot to be a metaphor. Produced by Jim Hubbard.
Religion and Philosophy; Sociology
Dist - CANCIN

The Valentine Lane Family Practice 29 MIN
U-matic / VHS / 16mm
Color
Looks at an approach to health care which emphasizes the treatment of the family, as well as comprehensive individual care.
Health and Safety
Dist - CNEMAG **Prod** - DOCUA

Valentine wishes 15 MIN
U-matic / VHS
Music machine series
Color (P)
Demonstrates the ABA form and simple rhythms in music. Uses a Valentine theme.
Fine Arts
Dist - GPN **Prod** - GPN

Valentine's Day 11 MIN
VHS
Color (K P I)
$69.95 purchase _ #10101VG
Presents facts, traditions and legends of St Valentine's Day. Traces the holiday's roots to the Roman Empire. Contains riddles, poems and activities for children. Includes a guide.
Civics and Political Systems; Religion and Philosophy
Dist - UNL

Valentine's Day 15 MIN
U-matic
Celebrate Series
Color (P)
Biography; Civics and Political Systems; Social Science
Dist - GPN **Prod** - KUONTV 1978

Valentine's Day Grump 8 MIN
VHS / U-matic
Giant First Start Series
Color (K P)
$29.95 purchase _ #VV004
Presents an adaptation of Valentine's Day Grump. Contains a 32 page hardcover book and a video.
English Language; Literature and Drama
Dist - TROLA

Valentine's Second Chance 24 MIN
16mm / U-matic / VHS
Color (I J)
LC 78-701060
Presents the story of a ten - year - old boy who helps to reform the legendary safecracker Jimmy Valentine.
Guidance and Counseling; Literature and Drama; Sociology
Dist - CORF **Prod** - ABCTV 1977

The Valentino Mystique 28 MIN
16mm
History of the Motion Picture Series
B&W
Shows Rudolph Valentino's early childhood in Italy, the fateful move to New York, and the coincidences and performances that made him a cult. Includes excerpts from such Valentino films as Passion's Playground, Alimony, An Adventuress, Stolen Moments, Eyes Of Youth, The Sheik and Blood And Sand.
Fine Arts
Dist - KILLIS **Prod** - KILLIS 1972

Valerie 15 MIN
16mm / U-matic / VHS
Color (J)
LC 76-702498
Explores some of the ideas and work of Valerie Maynard, sculptor.
Biography; Fine Arts
Dist - PHENIX **Prod** - PHENIX 1975

Valerie, a Woman, an Artist, a Philosophy of Life 15 MIN
U-matic / 16mm
Color
Documents the life and work of black sculptor Valerie Maynard. Shows her in her studio and her home in Harlem discussing her life as an artist.
Fine Arts; Sociology
Dist - BLKFMF **Prod** - BLKFMF

Valerie Bettis and Pauline Koner 30 MIN
VHS / U-matic
Eye on Dance - Dance on TV and Film Series
Color
Looks at the earliest days of dance on television.
Fine Arts
Dist - ARCVID **Prod** - ARCVID

Valerie's Stained Glass Window 25 MIN
U-matic / VHS / 16mm
World Cultures and Youth Series
Color (I J A)
LC 81-700058
Introduces Valerie, a French girl who would like to create beautiful stained glass windows. Shows her choosing a design, selecting the colors and glass, and assembling the window.
Fine Arts; Geography - World; Sociology
Dist - CORF **Prod** - SUNRIS 1980

Valery and Galina Panov 15 MIN
16mm
Color
Illustrates the struggle endured by Valery and Galina Panov, the former Russian ballet stars, before they were allowed to emigrate to Israel.
Civics and Political Systems; History - World; Sociology
Dist - ALDEN **Prod** - NBCTV

Valiant Hans 16 MIN
U-matic / VHS / 16mm
Color (P I)
LC 73-701730
Presents an animated puppet film based on a fairy tale by the Brothers Grimm. Tells the story of Hans, a vagabond, who rescues the king's daughter from the forest where she is harassed by ghosts.
Literature and Drama
Dist - IU **Prod** - NET 1970

Validating Pricing Strategies
U-matic / VHS
Revenues, Rates and Reimbursements Series
Color
Introduces pricing strategies which help hospitals cope with predictable payment problems.
Business and Economics; Health and Safety
Dist - TEACHM **Prod** - TEACHM

Valium 18 MIN
16mm / U-matic / VHS
Color (J)
LC 78-701871
Presents a report about the extensive use and abuse of the drug Valium.
Health and Safety; Psychology
Dist - CAROUF **Prod** - CBSTV 1977

Valium 7 MIN
U-matic / 35mm strip
Color
Covers all the precautions your patient taking valium needs to know.
Health and Safety
Dist - MEDCOM **Prod** - MEDCOM

The Valley 15 MIN
U-matic / VT1 / VHS
Walking with Grandfather series
Color (G)
$39.95 purchase, $35.00 rental
Tells of Sun Cloud who wants to marry the very beautiful and vain Snowflower who tells him to bring her a Rainbow Rose in order to win her love. Shows that he does because of a kind maiden in the garden. When he returns, Snowflower scorns him and tells him to cut his hair, symbol of his manliness. He does and she ridicules him and refuses to marry him. He returns to the garden and falls in love with the kind maiden, realizing that a kind heart is better than outer beauty. She turns into the Daughter of the Sun and they return to the village, where the extraordinary beauty of the kind maiden turns the jealous Snowflower into a bitter, lonely old woman. Part of a series on storytelling by elders produced by Phil Lucas Productions, Inc.

Guidance and Counseling; Literature and Drama; Social Science
Dist - NAMPBC

The Valley 28 MIN
16mm
Color (J)
Explains that some pollution - sensitive organisms such as Asiatic clams and caddis fly larvae are returning to the Ohio River where they had previously been unable to live. Shows this as living proof that the river is getting cleaner.
Geography - United States; Geography - World; Science - Natural
Dist - FINLYS **Prod** - FINLYS

Valley 30 MIN
VHS
Perspective - the environment - series
Color; PAL; NTSC (G)
PdS90, PdS105 purchase
Visits a place where farmer, fisherman, biologist and conservationist coexist happily.
Science - Natural
Dist - CFLVIS **Prod** - LONTVS

Valley Deep - Mountain High 23 MIN
16mm
Color (J)
LC 72-709229
Shows the attractions for skiers, bushwalkers and others of the Kosciusko National Park in the snowy mountains of Australia.
Geography - World; Physical Education and Recreation
Dist - AUIS **Prod** - ANAIB 1969

Valley fever 20 MIN
16mm
Color (G)
$40.00 rental
Questions how people perceive things. Depicts a man and woman who carry on a disjunctive conversation, superficially about how illness affects perception, actually about their inability to perceive the world from any but a personal viewpoint. Produced by Stephanie Beroes.
Fine Arts
Dist - CANCIN

Valley Fever 60 MIN
U-matic / VHS
Color (PRO)
LC 81-706303
Presents bacteriologic and medical aspects of coccidioidomycosis as well as new treatment methods.
Health and Safety
Dist - USNAC **Prod** - USVA 1980

Valley Forge 24 MIN
U-matic / VHS / 16mm
Color (I)
LC 75-704249
Re - creates the Continental Army's historic stay at Valley Forge and conveys the loyalty, dedication and fortitude of soldiers who defended the cause of American independence. Contrasts the hunger, sickness and cold endured by the patriots with the comfortable conditions enjoyed by the redcoats during the same time.
History - United States
Dist - AIMS **Prod** - FFVF 1975

Valley Forge - no Food, no Soldier 13 MIN
U-matic / VHS / 16mm
Color (I)
LC 70-713449
Uses the authentic words of Revolutionary War soldiers to recreate the ordeal of the harsh, crucial winter of 1778. Filmed in Valley Forge National Park.
Geography - United States; History - United States
Dist - CORF **Prod** - NYT 1971

Valley Forge - the battle for survival 16 MIN
U-matic / VHS / 16mm
Americana series; No 6
Color (J H)
Presents Valley Forge, the decisive chapter of the Revolutionary War, as seen through the eyes of a young man who was there. Shows him marching along with the other exhausted men stumbling through the snow into Valley Forge and helping in the construction of the fortifications to protect the army from British attack. Expresses the hope he feels that other men will be prepared to defend America whenever liberty is threatened.
Civics and Political Systems; History - United States
Dist - HANDEL **Prod** - HANDEL 1969

Valley Forge - the young spy 24 MIN
VHS / U-matic
Young people's specials series
Color
Dramatizes an account of a young tory farm boy's mission to spy on George Washington's camp. Focuses on the power of the ideals that inspired the men of the Revolution.
Fine Arts; History - United States; Sociology
Dist - MULTPP **Prod** - MULTPP

Valley Furniture 30 MIN
VHS / U-matic
Antique Shop Series
Color
Presents guests who are experts in their respective fields who share tips on collecting and caring for antique valley furniture.
Fine Arts
Dist - MDCPB **Prod** - WVPTTV

Valley Glaciers 20 MIN
VHS
Color (J)
$139.00 purchase _ #5235V
Examines the characteristics of contemporary valley glaciers in the Swiss Alps, including a cirque glacier. Shows the significance of banding or layering, ice - falls, crevasses and ogives and how to calculate water loss through the use of simple tools.
Geography - World; Science - Physical
Dist - SCTRES **Prod** - SCTRES

Valley of Heart's Delight - Pt 5 28 MIN
VHS
Only One Earth Series
Color (S)
$79.00 purchase _ #227 - 9005
Explores and demystifies the links between environment and development and illustrates the detrimental clashes between economics and ecology in the first three programs. Presents positive examples of how development can be achieved without harming the environment in the last eight half - hour programs. Part 5 of eleven shows residents of Silicon Valley working to eliminate the water pollution and consequent birth defects the 'clean' computer chip industry brought with it.
Geography - United States; Mathematics; Science - Natural; Science - Physical; Social Science
Dist - FI **Prod** - BBCTV 1987

Valley of the giants 30 MIN
VHS
Classic short stories
Color (H)
#E362; LC 90-708402
Presents 'Valley of the Giants' by Kenneth Earl. Part of a series which combines Hollywood stars with short story masterpieces of the world to encourage appreciation of the short story.
Literature and Drama
Dist - GPN **Prod** - CTI 1988

Valley of the Kings 30 MIN
16mm / VHS
Ancient Lives Series
Color (H)
Depicts the lives of a tomb craftsman and a tomb architect. Examines their clothes, their money, their tools, their furniture, their kitchen utensils and their food. Also examines the Egyptian belief that the individual was divided into body, soul and image. The second of eight parts of the Ancient Lives Series.
Fine Arts; History - World; Sociology
Dist - PSU
FOTH

Valley of the Tennessee 29 MIN
16mm / U-matic / VHS
Color
Shows the need for conservation in the Tennessee River Valley, the origin of the TVA, the building of the dams and the influence of the TVA on the lives of the people in the Valley.
History - United States; Science - Natural; Social Science
Dist - USNAC **Prod** - USOWI 1979

Valley Town 27 MIN
16mm
B&W (J H C)
A study of workers displaced by automatic machinery. Traces the history of a typical American steel town of the 1920's and 30's through a boom, the depression and the war.
Business and Economics; Psychology; Social Science; Sociology
Dist - NYU **Prod** - NYU 1940

Valse triste 5 MIN
16mm
B&W (G)
$300.00 purchase
Travels to 1940s Kansas in an autobiographical journey of the filmmaker's boyhood.
Fine Arts; Geography - United States; Literature and Drama
Dist - CANCIN **Prod** - CONNER 1979

Value and purpose in science 30 MIN
BETA / VHS
Science and the spirit series
Color (G)
$29.95 purchase _ #S112
Reveals that consciousness, rather than being a property which 'emerges' at higher orders of complexity, is a basic principle intrinsic to every level of creation. Features Arthur M Young, inventor of the Bell Helicopter and author of 'The Reflexive Universe,' 'The Geometry of Meaning' and 'Which Way Out.' Part of a four - part series on science and the spirit.
Guidance and Counseling; Religion and Philosophy
Dist - THINKA **Prod** - THINKA

Value and Value Keys 15 MIN
VHS / 16mm
Drawing with Paul Ringler Series
Color (I H)
$125.00 purchase, $25.00 rental
Develops guidelines for recognizing and using tones from dark to light and contrast in visual design.
Fine Arts; Industrial and Technical Education
Dist - AITECH **Prod** - OETVA 1988

Value billing - does it work
Cassette
Color (PRO)
$295.00, $150.00 purchase, $150.00 rental _ #VAL1-00F, #AVAL-000
Answers the key questions - will there be a major change in the way legal fees are determined; what can law firms do to succeed under these new arrangements; who will shape the changes; which innovations have been successful and which have not; why do some clients get more value for their legal dollar; are clients moving towards fewer firms and longer term relationships; do clients know how to create the right economic incentives; what are the lasting implications for the attorney - client relationship.
Business and Economics; Civics and Political Systems
Dist - AMBAR **Prod** - AMBAR 1994

Value clarification 30 MIN
16mm
Project STRETCH Series; Module 3
Color (T)
LC 80-700610
Demonstrates a practical application of value clarification with a high school class.
Biography; Education; Psychology
Dist - HUBDSC **Prod** - METCO 1980

Value Clarification and Decision Making 30 MIN
U-matic / VHS
Creating a Learning Environment Series
Color
Education; Guidance and Counseling
Dist - NETCHE **Prod** - NETCHE 1975

Value Engineering 24 MIN
16mm
B&W
LC 74-706304
Evaluates the impact of value engineering programs on cost performance. Discusses the need for incentives, savings, subcontractor participation and contractor support.
Business and Economics; Industrial and Technical Education; Psychology
Dist - USNAC **Prod** - USAF 1965

Value Engineering - more Ships for Less Money 13 MIN
16mm
Color
LC FIE58-12
Shows how the U S Navy value engineering program works and explains its key techniques.
Industrial and Technical Education; Psychology
Dist - USNAC **Prod** - USN 1957

Value Engineering - the Hundred Million Dollar Story 28 MIN
16mm
Color
LC FIE64-61
Tells the story of the latest Air Force economy concept - a savings of millions of dollars in aircraft and missile cost.
Civics and Political Systems; Industrial and Technical Education
Dist - USNAC **Prod** - USAF 1963

The Value of Being a Friend 15 MIN
VHS / 16mm
Color (I)
LC 90712985
Teaches children about the importance of having friends and being a friend. Indicates characteristics of a friend. Includes teacher's guide.
Psychology
Dist - HIGGIN

The Value of Being Friends
16mm / VHS
Values Series
Color (P)
Identifies, through a series of vignettes and music, some of the characteristics of friendship. Illustrates the value of being friends.
Guidance and Counseling; Health and Safety; Psychology
Dist - HIGGIN **Prod** - HIGGIN 1990

The Value of being responsible 19
16mm / VHS
Values series
Color (P)
$425.00, $380.00 purchase, $60.00 rental
Shows the value of being responsible through Balderdash, a character who has become a ghost of his former irresponsible self, as he visits Wendy on Halloween.
Health and Safety; Psychology
Dist - HIGGIN **Prod** - HIGGIN 1990

Value of Digits 15 MIN
U-matic
Studio M Series
Color (P)
Explains how to express each digit in a two - or three - digit number as a single numeral. Tells how to write two numerals from two digits and six numerals from three digits. Describes how to order a list of numerals from lowest to highest.
Mathematics
Dist - GPN **Prod** - WCETTV 1979

The Value of Ongoing Direct Mail 30 MIN
VHS / U-matic
Business of Direct Mail Series
Color
Explains the value of ongoing direct mailing.
Business and Economics
Dist - KYTV **Prod** - KYTV 1983

The Value of Teamwork 15
16mm / VHS
Values Series
Color (P)
$355.00, $320.00 purchase, $50.00 rental
Shows young Max, with the help of his talking dog, Einstein, that a cooperative attitude at school, home, and at play is very important. Emphasizes the value of teamwork.
Health and Safety; Psychology
Dist - HIGGIN **Prod** - HIGGIN 1990

The Value of Telling the Truth
16mm / VHS
Values Series
Color (P)
Demonstrates the consequences of telling a lie, as young Bryce sees unexpected results from his behavior. Illustrates the value of telling the truth.
Health and Safety; Psychology
Dist - HIGGIN **Prod** - HIGGIN 1990

Values 20 MIN
VHS / 16mm
Color (H)
$98.00 purchase _ #CC17V
Defines what values are and relates them to choosing a career. Explores values in a classroom discussion between students and their teacher.
Guidance and Counseling; Psychology
Dist - JISTW

Values 30 MIN
VHS
Personal development video series
Color (J H)
Features four students who discuss values, motivations and life priorities. Describes broad categories of values and illustrates the students playing the values auction. Each student begins with $1000 and must decide which values to spend it on. If the student bids but doesn't win the value, the money bid is lost. Emphasizes the concepts that each one holds a number of values which sometimes must be prioritized and that values may change over time. Includes reproducible worksheets. Part of a five - part series using dramatization and humor to show young people how to adjust and cope with a number of problems virtually everyone faces in making the transition to adulthood.
Guidance and Counseling; Health and Safety; Psychology
Dist - NEWCAR
CAMV

Values 45 MIN
VHS
Color (G)
$250.00, $10.00 purchase
Discusses principles to live by as alternatives to drugs and alcohol.
Guidance and Counseling; Health and Safety; Psychology
Dist - KELLYP **Prod** - KELLYP

Values 30 MIN
VHS / U-matic
Economics exchange series; Program 6
Color (T)
LC 82-706418
Presents Dr Willard M Kniep of Arizona State University instructing teachers in the strategies and skills of teaching children economics and consumer education concepts. Focuses on the topic of values by explaining it and then demonstrating specific approaches that teachers can use in their classrooms.
Business and Economics; Education; Home Economics
Dist - GPN **Prod** - KAETTV 1981

Values 30 MIN
VHS
Making a living work series
Color (G A)
Features Richard Bolles, author of the job seekers' and changers' book, 'What Color Is Your Parachute?' Focuses on the importance of values clarification in life and work.
Business and Economics; Psychology
Dist - CAMV
CAREER
JISTW

Values and Attitudes 27 MIN
Videoreel / VHS
One Strong Link Series
B&W
Guidance and Counseling; Social Science
Dist - CORNRS **Prod** - CUETV 1971

Values and choices - a 7th and 8th grade abstinence program 120 MIN
VHS
Color (I J H)
$450.00 purchase _ #434 - V8
Presents a multimedia sexuality education program developed by experts in adolescent pregnancy prevention. Teaches 7th and 8th graders about all aspects of sexuality. Discusses seven values - equality, self - control, respect, responsibility, honesty, promise - keeping, and fairness. Covers sexual attraction, basic values, sexual abstinence, puberty, dating, sexual pressures, decision making, STDs, pregnancy and birth, teenage parenting, acquaintance rape, and incest. Includes 159 - page Teacher's Guide and 48 - page Guide for Parents. Video and guides also available separately.
Guidance and Counseling; Health and Safety; Psychology; Sociology
Dist - ETRASS **Prod** - ETRASS

Values and Conflicts Series
Homosexuality and Lesbianism - Gay or Straight, is There a Choice 26 MIN
Dist - CNEMAG

Values and ethics - situations for discussion 12 MIN
VHS
Color; CC (G PRO)
$595.00 purchase, $145.00 rental
Offers 12 short, dramatized 'What Would You Do' vignettes, each followed by a short video break to allow for group discussion. Discusses the difference between ethical and unethical business practices and the use of a three - step process to decide if each situation is ethical. Includes training leader's guide.
Business and Economics
Dist - AMEDIA **Prod** - AMEDIA 1993

Values and Goals - a Way to Go 29 MIN
U-matic / VHS / 16mm
Color (H C A) (SPANISH)
LC 72-703125
Presents the story of youth preparing to meet the world on their own terms, by their own definitions, in their own ways.
Foreign Language; Guidance and Counseling; Psychology; Sociology
Dist - AIMS **Prod** - COP 1972

Values - Being Friends 9 MIN
U-matic / VHS / 16mm
Values Series
Color (I) (SPANISH)
LC 78-711615
Teaches the meaning of friendship. Shows that people may disagree but still remain friends. Emphasizes trust and helping each other.
Guidance and Counseling
Dist - PHENIX **Prod** - COLLRD 1969

Values clarification 16 MIN
BETA / VHS / U-matic
Ethics, values and health care series
Color (C PRO)
$150.00 purchase _ #132.2
Presents a video transfer from slide program featuring Diann Uustal, RN, authority on values clarification and nursing practice, who presents the theory along with the seven steps in the valuing process. Discusses seveal complex issues of an ethical nature around which caregivers need to clarify their values. Part of a series on ethics, values and health care.
Guidance and Counseling; Health and Safety; Religion and Philosophy
Dist - CONMED **Prod** - CONMED

Values Clarification in the Classroom 29 MIN
U-matic / VHS / 16mm
Color (T)
Shows Values Clarification teaching styles being used in an eighth grade classroom in Illinois. Includes experts who discuss how to raise issues, stimulate thinking and be nonjudgmental with positions held by students.
Education
Dist - FI **Prod** - MFFD

Values - Cooperation 11 MIN
U-matic / VHS / 16mm
Values Series
Color (SPANISH)
LC 78-711616
Applies the adage 'No man is an island unto himself,' emphasizing that no one is too young to learn this. Views Rod, Julian and John playing together, picturing them in action as they get things done and have lots of fun by cooperating with each other. Stresses the value of cooperation, whether at work, play or school.
Foreign Language; Guidance and Counseling; Psychology
Dist - PHENIX **Prod** - COLLRD

Values, Decisions, Success 15 MIN
VHS / 35mm strip
$43.50 purchase _ #XY855 filmstrip, $84.95 purchase _ #XY805 VHS
Demonstrates the role that values play in getting and keeping a job. Discusses dependability, cooperation, honesty, initiative, willingness to learn, and following directions.
Guidance and Counseling
Dist - CAREER **Prod** - CAREER

Values, decisions, success
VHS
Career process series
Color (H A)
$84.95 purchase _ #ES1150V
Suggests that strong values - such as honesty, loyalty, initiative, and reliability - are essential to job performance.
Psychology
Dist - CAMV

Values, Decisions, Success 15 MIN
VHS / 16mm
Color (H C A PRO)
$84.95 purchase _ #CA128
Shows ambition, cheerfulness, cleanliness, cooperation, dependability, honesty and other values as leading to job success.
Business and Economics; Guidance and Counseling
Dist - AAVIM **Prod** - AAVIM 1990

Values, Decisions, Success 14 MIN
VHS / U-matic
(H C A)
$98 _ #EA4V
Presents basic values required to obtain and maintain a successful career. Offers the option of viewer participation in some segments.
Business and Economics; Education
Dist - JISTW **Prod** - JISTW

Values for Grades K - Three Series
The Hideout 15 MIN
Lost Puppy 14 MIN
Dist - CF

Values in America 24 MIN
U-matic / VHS
Color (J H)
Introduces values as a basis for the choices people make in their lives with emphasis on the divergence of American life.
Sociology
Dist - CEPRO **Prod** - CEPRO

Values - Playing Fair 10 MIN
16mm / U-matic / VHS
Values Series
Color (SPANISH)
LC 75-711617
Presents a class round table discussion which allows students to decide for themselves what 'playing fair' really means. Identifies various social interactions to.
Foreign Language; Guidance and Counseling; Psychology
Dist - PHENIX **Prod** - COLLRD 1969

Values series
The Value of Being Friends
The Value of being responsible 19
The Value of Teamwork 15

The Value of Telling the Truth
Dist - HIGGIN

Values Series
Values - Being Friends 9 MIN
Values - Cooperation 11 MIN
Values - Playing Fair 10 MIN
Values - Telling the Truth 10 MIN
Values - the Right Thing to do 9 MIN
Values - Understanding Others 8 MIN
Values - Understanding Ourselves 9 MIN
Dist - PHENIX

Values - Telling the Truth 10 MIN
U-matic / VHS / 16mm
Values Series
Color (P I) (SPANISH)
LC 79-711618
Illustrates specific values as three boys walk home from school together. Explains that the boys pick up some stones which are left over from the cement mixer and hit Mrs Jensen's window. Concludes with Rod and Julian running away, but John stays and tells the truth.
Foreign Language; Guidance and Counseling
Dist - PHENIX **Prod** - COLLRD 1969

Values - the Right Thing to do 9 MIN
16mm / U-matic / VHS
Values Series
Color (I) (SPANISH)
LC 78-709268
Presents a dilemma in which Terry and his friends accidentally cause a pile of lumber to fall on an old man, whose yard they are playing in. Shows Terry trying to decide whether to run away with the rest of his friends, or stay and help the man - in which case he may be blamed for the incident.
Guidance and Counseling
Dist - PHENIX **Prod** - COLLRD 1970

Values - Understanding Others 8 MIN
U-matic / VHS / 16mm
Values Series
Color (SPANISH SWEDISH)
LC 74-710562;
Suggests how one can learn to understand other people better. Stresses that when one tries to understand how other people feel, an attitude of caring about them is created.
Foreign Language; Guidance and Counseling; Psychology
Dist - PHENIX **Prod** - COLLRD 1970

Values - Understanding Ourselves 9 MIN
U-matic / VHS / 16mm
Values Series
Color (I) (SPANISH)
LC 72-711619
Uses a story of three boys to present the concept that everybody has an idea of the kind of person he is. Explains that sometimes it seems like it would be more fun to be someone else but each person, if he could really chose, would rather be himself.
Foreign Language; Guidance and Counseling; Psychology
Dist - PHENIX **Prod** - COLLRD 1969

Valuing Assets 30 MIN
U-matic / VHS
Accounting Series; Pt 6
Color (C)
Discusses valuing assets as it applies to accounting.
Business and Economics; Guidance and Counseling
Dist - GPN **Prod** - UMA 1980

Valuing diversity series
Presents a seven - part series on diversity in the workplace. Argues that diversity can be a strength if properly handled. Dramatizes situations leading to conflict and poor performance, showing how they can be better handled.
Champions of diversity - valuing diversity - Part VI 30 MIN
Communicating across cultures - valuing diversity - Part III 30 MIN
Diversity at work - valuing diversity - Part II 30 MIN
Managing differences - valuing diversity - Part I 30 MIN
Profiles in change - valuing diversity - Part VII 60 MIN
Supervising differences - valuing diversity - Part V 30 MIN
You make the difference - valuing diversity - Part IV 30 MIN
Dist - VLEARN

Valuing Your Customers - Pt 1 25 MIN
VHS / 16mm
Unorganized Salesperson Series
Color (A PRO)
$790.00 purchase, $220.00 rental
Shows how to use time management and organization to improve sales. Features John Cleese as a hot - shot salesperson. Part 1 of a two - part series on sales management.
Business and Economics; Psychology
Dist - VIDART **Prod** - VIDART 1990

Valuing Yourself - Pt 2 23 MIN
VHS / 16mm
Unorganized Salesperson Series
Color (A PRO)
$790.00 purchase, $220.00 rental
Shows how to manage self - behavior to present a professional image and interact more effectively with clients. Features John Cleese as a hot - shot salesperson. Part 2 of a two - part series on sales management.
Business and Economics; Psychology
Dist - VIDART **Prod** - VIDART 1990

Valve Amintenance - Reciprocating Compressors 60 MIN
U-matic / VHS
Mechanical Equipment Maintenance, Module 9 - Air Compressors Series
Color (IND)
Industrial and Technical Education
Dist - LEIKID **Prod** - LEIKID

Valve Maintenance - 1 60 MIN
VHS
Piping and Valves Series
Color (PRO)
$600.00, $1500.00 purchase _ #GMVM1
Describes the full range of valves and their components. Explains the functions and uses of each type of valve. Part of a six - part series on piping and valves, which is part of a set on general and mechanical maintenance. Includes 10 textbooks and an instructor guide which provide four hours of instruction.
Education; Health and Safety; Industrial and Technical Education; Psychology
Dist - NUSTC **Prod** - NUSTC

Valve Maintenance - 2 60 MIN
VHS
Piping and Valves Series
Color (PRO)
$600.00, $1500.00 purchase _ #GMVM2
Presents the basic of valve maintenance - damage inspection, maintenance problems and malfuction identification and overhaul techniques. Part of a six - part series on piping and valves, which is part of a set on general and mechanical maintenance. Includes 10 textbooks and an instructor guide which provide four hours of instruction.
Education; Health and Safety; Industrial and Technical Education; Psychology
Dist - NUSTC **Prod** - NUSTC

Valve Operation 60 MIN
VHS / U-matic
Equipment Operation Training Program Series
Color (IND)
Illustrates valve functions and operations. Explains how to identify and properly operate rising and non - rising gate valve stem designs.
Education; Industrial and Technical Education; Psychology
Dist - LEIKID **Prod** - LEIKID

Valve Operations 60 MIN
U-matic / VHS
Equipment Operation Training Program Series
Color (IND)
Identifies valve parts and functions. Describes manual and automatic valve operation. Demonstrates safety practices and valve inspections.
Industrial and Technical Education
Dist - ITCORP **Prod** - ITCORP

Valve Spacing and Pressuring 19 MIN
U-matic / VHS / 16mm
Gas Lift Series
Color (IND)
Business and Economics; Industrial and Technical Education; Social Science
Dist - UTEXPE **Prod** - EXXON

Valve Stem, Tip Grinding and Champhering on Sioux Valve Grinder 12 MIN
VHS / 16mm
Auto Mechanics Series
(G PRO)
$66.00 purchase _ #AM32
Shows how to use the Sioux valve grinder on valve stems, tip grinding and champhering.
Industrial and Technical Education
Dist - RMIBHF **Prod** - RMIBHF

Valve Timing the 4 - Cycle Engine 8 MIN
U-matic / VHS / 16mm
Power Mechanics Series
Color (H A)
LC 78-703248
Presents basic information about timing the valves in the 4 - cycle engine.
Industrial and Technical Education
Dist - CAROUF **Prod** - THIOKL 1969

Valve Train Engine Repair
VHS / 35mm strip
Automotive Technology Series
Color
$40.00 purchase _ #MX8003 filmstrip, $80.00 purchase _ #MX8003V VHS
Industrial and Technical Education; Psychology
Dist - CAREER **Prod** - CAREER

Valves 20 MIN
VHS / U-matic
Color (IND)
Discusses plug valves using disassembled valves. Explains pressure drop and water hammer.
Education; Industrial and Technical Education
Dist - TAT **Prod** - TAT

Valves
VHS / U-matic
Drafting - Piping Familiarization Series
Color (IND)
Industrial and Technical Education
Dist - GPCV **Prod** - GPCV

Valves 240 MIN
U-matic / VHS
Mechanical Equipment Maintenance Series
Color (IND) (SPANISH)
Describes various types of valves.
Industrial and Technical Education
Dist - ITCORP **Prod** - ITCORP

Valves - 1 60 MIN
VHS
Equipment operations series
Color (PRO)
$600.00 - $1500.00 purchase _ #OTVA1
Centers on the purpose and use of various types of valves used in industrial processes. Covers gate, globe, needle, plug, ball, butterfly, diaphragm, pinch, check and safety - relief. Part of a twenty - part series on equipment operation. Includes ten textbooks and an instructor guide to support four hours of instruction.
Health and Safety; Industrial and Technical Education; Psychology
Dist - NUSTC **Prod** - NUSTC

Valves - 2 60 MIN
VHS
Equipment operations series
Color (PRO)
$600.00 - $1500.00 purchase _ #OTVA2
Focuses on valve actuators. Details the components and operators of pneumatic, hydraulic, solenoid and motor driven actuators. Part of a twenty - part series on equipment operation. Includes ten textbooks and an instructor guide to support four hours of instruction.
Health and Safety; Industrial and Technical Education; Psychology
Dist - NUSTC **Prod** - NUSTC

Valves and cylinder heads 23 MIN
VHS
Diesel engine maintenance video series
Color (G H)
$19.95 purchase _ #CEV00841V-T
Defines preventive maintenance for diesel engine owners and focuses on the valves and cylinder heads and the possible reasions for equipment failure. Discusses the importance of maintenence on the `setting of the fly wheel, torquing the head bolts and adjusting valve clearance.'
Education; Industrial and Technical Education
Dist - CAMV

Valvular Incompetence and Varicose Veins 18 MIN
16mm
Color (PRO)
Explores the fundamental pathogenesis and the importance of valvular incompetence in the production of varicose veins.
Health and Safety; Science - Natural
Dist - SCITIF **Prod** - AL 1966

Valvulotomy for Valvular Pulmonic Stenosis 27 MIN
16mm
Color (PRO)
Explains that by brief interruption of the flow of blood into the heart under moderate hypothermia, incision can be placed

in the pulmonary artery and under direct vision, complete relief of valvular obstruction in congenital pulmonic stenosis may be accomplished in a simple and precise manner.
Health and Safety; Science
Dist - ACY **Prod** - ACYDGD 1955

Vamos a Colombia 11 MIN
U-matic / VHS / 16mm
Color (H C) (SPANISH)
LC 70-704294
A Spanish version of 'REPUBLIC OF COLUMBIA.' Shows location of the country in relationship to New York. Describes the geographical regions, principal cities and major products of Columbia.
Foreign Language
Dist - IFB **Prod** - PAU 1956

Vamos a Comer - Let's Eat 15 MIN
U-matic / VHS
Saludos
(P I G) (ENGLISH AND SPANISH)
$130 purchase, $25 rental, $75 self dub
Designed to introduce Spanish to the English speaking student at primary through intermediate levels. Fifteenth in a 25 part series.
Foreign Language
Dist - GPN

Vamos a Cuba 12 MIN
16mm / U-matic / VHS
Color (J H C) (SPANISH)
LC FIA65-276
Spanish version of 'VISIT TO CUBA.' Describes aspects of Cuban life - - modern cities, historical landmarks, natural vegetation, important crops, schools, cathedrals and public buildings.
Foreign Language
Dist - IFB **Prod** - IFB 1961

Vamos a Dibujar - Let's Draw 15 MIN
U-matic / VHS
Saludos
(P I G) (ENGLISH AND SPANISH)
$130 purchase, $25 rental, $75 self dub
Designed to introduce Spanish to the English speaking student at primary through intermediate levels. Twenty fourth in a 25 part series.
Foreign Language
Dist - GPN

Vamos a Guatemala 22 MIN
16mm / U-matic / VHS
Color; B&W (H C) (SPANISH)
Spanish version of 'REPUBLIC OF GUATEMALA.' Shows modern life in Guatemala and indicates high points of Guatemalan history.
Foreign Language
Dist - IFB **Prod** - IFB 1957

Vamos a Repasar II - Let's Review II 15 MIN
VHS / U-matic
Saludos
(P I G) (ENGLISH AND SPANISH)
$130 purchase, $25 rental, $75 self dub
Designed to introduce Spanish to the English speaking student at primary through intermediate levels. Sixteenth in a 25 part series.
Foreign Language
Dist - GPN

Vamos a Repasar III - Let's Review III 15 MIN
VHS / U-matic
Saludos
(P I G) (ENGLISH AND SPANISH)
$130 purchase, $25 rental, $75 self dub
Designed to introduce Spanish to the English speaking student at primary through intermediate levels. Twenty third in a 25 part series.
Foreign Language
Dist - GPN

Vamos a Repasar - Let's Review 15 MIN
VHS / U-matic
Saludos
(P I G) (ENGLISH AND SPANISH)
$130 purchase, $25 rental, $75 self dub
Designed to introduce Spanish to the English speaking student at primary through intermediate levels. Eighth in a 25 part series.
Foreign Language
Dist - GPN

Vamos Al Campo - Let's Go to the Country 15 MIN
U-matic / VHS
Saludos
(P I G) (ENGLISH AND SPANISH)
$130 purchase, $25 rental, $75 self dub
Designed to introduce Spanish to the English speaking student at primary through intermediate levels. Twenty fifth in a 25 part series.
Foreign Language
Dist - GPN

Vamos Al Cine - 13 15 MIN
VHS
Amigos Series
Color (K) (SPANISH)
$125.00 purchase
Enables teachers with no knowledge of Spanish to introduce basic words to children in kindergarten through second grade. Uses simple concepts and music and features Perro Pepe, a six - foot orange dog, and Senorita Fernandez as instructors. Promotes awareness of and appreciation for Hispanic culture and sparks interest in the geography of Spanish - speaking countries. Part 13 is entitled 'Vamos Al Cine.'.
Foreign Language; Geography - World
Dist - AITECH

Vamos Al Peru, Pt 1, El Peru 10 MIN
U-matic / VHS / 16mm
Color (H C) (SPANISH)
A Spanish language film. Shows Peru as a whole, then each region, major cities and their people.
History - World
Dist - IFB **Prod** - IFB 1957

Vamos Al Peru, Pt 2, Lima 10 MIN
U-matic / VHS / 16mm
Color (H C) (SPANISH)
A Spanish language film. Shows the location of Lima and its port city, Callao. Describes the historical background of the city, chief buildings and other points of interest.
History - World
Dist - IFB **Prod** - IFB 1957

Vampira - the passion of 22 MIN
16mm
Color (A)
$30.00 rental
Exudes a lushness with heavy muted colors and a variety of lighted set - ups. Transforms masturbation in a ritual and auto - eroticism into a religion with a study of a woman enjoying her body. A Carl Linder production.
Fine Arts; Psychology; Sociology
Dist - CANCIN

Vampire 25 MIN
U-matic / VHS / 16mm
Color (H C A)
Covers the physiology of the vampire bat and demonstrates that they often form complex relationships and can display great gentleness.
Science - Natural
Dist - FI **Prod** - BBCTV 1981

Vampire 10 MIN
U-matic / VHS
Eye on nature series
Color (I J)
$250.00 purchase _ #HP - 5853C
Looks at vampire bats, nature's only order of flying mammals. Reveals that the bats prey primarily upon farm and other animals for their meals of blood. Part of the Eye on Nature series.
Science - Natural
Dist - CORF **Prod** - BBCTV 1989

Vampires, devilbirds and spirits 50 MIN
VHS
Natural world series
Color; PAL (H C A)
PdS99 purchase; Not available in the United States
Travels to the twin islands of Trinidad and Tobago to view the wildlife. Explores the swamps, seacliffs, forests, caves and mud - volcanos to uncover the variety of animals living there. Shows how these animals contribute to the cultural life of the islands.
Science - Natural
Dist - BBCENE

Vampires in Havana 80 MIN
16mm / U-matic / 35mm strip / VHS
Color (H C A) (SPANISH (ENGLISH SUBTITLES))
Parodies horror and gangster movies. Talks about a professor's invention of 'Vampisol' which allows vampires to survive in sunlight. Directed by Juan Padron.
Fine Arts
Dist - CNEMAG

Vamps 17 MIN
16mm
Color (J H C)
LC 72-702091
Follows volunteer firemen in West Islip, New York, through their day - to - day struggle to fight and prevent fires, and through their many other community service and rescue activities.
Health and Safety; Sociology
Dist - RVINOP **Prod** - FVINO 1972

Vampyr 75 MIN
VHS
B&W (G)
$29.95 purchase
Offers a nightmarish fantasy about a man who tries to rescue the soul of a vampire - bitten woman. Directed by Carl Theodor Dreyer.
Fine Arts; Literature and Drama
Dist - KINOIC

Vampyre 77 MIN
16mm
Color
Tells a story of an ancient castle haunted by vampires and the man who tries to overcome their seemingly supernatural powers of evil.
Religion and Philosophy
Dist - FCE **Prod** - UNKNWN

The Van Der Pol Equation 31 MIN
U-matic / VHS
Nonlinear Vibrations Series
B&W
Mathematics
Dist - MIOT **Prod** - MIOT

Van Der Waals Forces 29 MIN
U-matic / VHS
Colloid and Surface Chemistry - Lyophobic Colloids Series
Color
Science; Science - Physical
Dist - KALMIA **Prod** - KALMIA

Van Der Waals Forces (Cont'd), Influence of a Medium, Retardation, Lifshitz Method, 39 MIN
VHS / U-matic
Colloid and Surface Chemistry - Lyophobic Colloids Series
Color
Discusses Van der Waals forces, influence of a medium, retardation, Lifshitz method and experiments.
Science; Science - Physical
Dist - KALMIA **Prod** - KALMIA

Van Der Waals Forces, Influences of a Medium, Retardation, Lifshitz Method , Experiments 39 MIN
U-matic / VHS
Colloid and Surface Chemistry - Lyophobic Colloids Series
B&W (PRO)
Science - Physical
Dist - MIOT **Prod** - MIOT

Van Eyck - Father of Flemish Painting 27 MIN
U-matic / VHS / 16mm
Color (H C A)
Studies the personal style of the 15th - century Flemish artist, Jan Van Eyck.
Biography; Fine Arts
Dist - IFB **Prod** - IFB 1974

Van Gogh 30 MIN
VHS
Tom Keating on painters series
Color (J H C G)
$195.00 purchase
Focuses on the painter van Gogh. Features Tom Keating who recreates the painting of van Gogh exactly as the artist did the original work and gives biographical information. Part of a six - part series on painters.
Fine Arts
Dist - LANDMK **Prod** - LANDMK 1987

Van Gogh 6 MIN
16mm / U-matic / VHS
Color (P I)
LC 79-706591
Tells the story of Vincent van Gogh through the presentation of his major works as well as through the re - creation of settings and events in the painter's life.
Fine Arts
Dist - PHENIX **Prod** - CAIR 1969

Van Gogh 57 MIN
VHS
Color (I)
$39.95 purchase _ #HV - 663
Presents a portrait of van Gogh in Arles. Focuses on his art and dispels many of the myths surrounding the Post - Impressionist painter.
Fine Arts; History - World
Dist - CRYSP **Prod** - CRYSP

Van Gogh - a museum for Vincent 32 MIN
VHS
Color; Hi-fi; Dolby stereo (G)

$29.95 purchase _ #1306
Focuses on the collection of Van Gogh paintings in the Rijksmuseum Vincent Van Gogh in Amsterdam. Assesses Van Gogh's role in the Post - Impressionist movement and examines his visual style and technique.
Fine Arts
Dist - KULTUR **Prod** - KULTUR 1991

Van Gogh - a Self Portrait 55 MIN
16mm / U-matic / VHS
Color (J)
LC FIA68-1957
Presents the art of Vincent van Gogh and shows the places, the people and the objects affecting his tragic life.
Fine Arts
Dist - MGHT **Prod** - NBCTV 1968

Van Gogh - a Self Portrait, Pt 1 26 MIN
16mm / U-matic / VHS
Color (J)
Presents the art of Vincent van Gogh and shows the places, the people and the objects affecting his tragic life.
Fine Arts
Dist - MGHT **Prod** - NBCTV 1968

Van Gogh - a Self Portrait, Pt 2 29 MIN
U-matic / VHS / 16mm
Color (J)
Presents the art of Vincent van Gogh and shows the places, the people and the objects affecting his tragic life.
Fine Arts
Dist - MGHT **Prod** - NBCTV 1968

Van Gogh at work 22 MIN
VHS
Color (I J H)
$104.00 purchase _ #87 - 009732
Offers an enhanced video program which portrays van Gogh on location in the countryside around Arles. Watches the artist set up his easel and begin a canvas, translating the vista into a whirling and soaring brushwork. Explores his state of mind and its echoing in his turbulent shapes.
Fine Arts
Dist - SRA **Prod** - SRA 1990

Van Pooling 15 MIN
16mm / U-matic / VHS
Color
Presents an overview of the three major types of van pooling - employer sponsored, third party sponsored and individually owned and operated. Discusses the benefits of van pooling.
Health and Safety; Social Science
Dist - USNAC **Prod** - USDOE

Vanadium - a Transition Element 22 MIN
16mm
CHEM Study Films Series
Color (H)
LC FIA63-1058
Explores vanadium as a typical transition element. The different oxidation states of vanadium and their colors are observed and then identified by means of a quantitative titration of vanadium (II) solution with cerium (IV) solution. Discusses the changes in vanadium in terms of ion size and charge density.
Science - Physical
Dist - MLA **Prod** - CHEMS 1962
WARDS

Vanalyne Green Series
A Spy in the House that Ruth Built 29 MIN
Trick or Drink 20 MIN
Dist - WMEN

Vancouver, B C 29 MIN
16mm / U-matic / VHS
Color (H C A)
Takes one on a tour of Vancouver, B C, the site of the 1986 World Exposition.
Geography - World; Sociology
Dist - LCOA **Prod** - SPCTRA 1985

Vancouver - Pacific Gateway to Canada 12 MIN
16mm
Color (J H)
Describes life in Vancouver. Highlights the city's climate, its many sites, its beaches, its parks and its theaters, sports events and quiet spots of greenery.
Geography - World
Dist - MORLAT **Prod** - MORLAT

Vancouver - the world in a city 30 MIN
VHS
Color (G)
$29.95 purchase _ #S01981
Tours Vancouver, Canada. Focuses on the city's hosting of Expo '86, but also shows many other city attractions as well.
Geography - World; History - World; Sociology
Dist - UILL

Vandalism 11 MIN
U-matic / VHS
Cop Talk Series
Color (I J)
Illustrates the causes of acquisitive vandalism, tactical vandalism, vindictive vandalism and play vandalism. Points out the enormous costs to society of this 'small - time offense.'.
Sociology
Dist - AITECH **Prod** - UTSBE 1981

Vandalism - 62 9 MIN
VHS / U-matic
Life's little lessons - self - esteem 4 - 6 series
Color (I)
$129.00, $99.00 purchase _ #V691
Portrays Marty who vandalizes the garden of an elderly couple because he is convinced that they are very rich. Reveals that when he discovers that they were dependent upon the garden for their food, he rallies neighbors to help the couple out and admits that he destroyed the garden. Part of a 65 - part series on self - esteem.
Guidance and Counseling; Psychology; Sociology
Dist - BARR **Prod** - CEPRO 1992

Vandalism - Crime or Prank 5 MIN
16mm / U-matic / VHS
Color (J H C)
Explores the question of whether vandalism is a crime or a prank, and whether or not an adult who witnesses such an act and recognizes one of the participants has an obligation to report the matter to either the police or the boy's parents.
Civics and Political Systems; Education; Guidance and Counseling; Psychology; Sociology
Dist - IFB **Prod** - HORIZN 1964

The Vandalism Film - Only You Can Stop it 12 MIN
16mm / U-matic / VHS
Color (P)
LC 76-702634
Tells the story of vandalism through a character known as Sneaky, a thoughtless fellow who shows no concern for the feelings, rights or privileges of others. Emphasizes cooperation and positive action that will halt destructive behavior.
Guidance and Counseling; Health and Safety; Sociology
Dist - BARR **Prod** - SAIF 1976

Vandalism is not funny 45 MIN
VHS
Color (J H)
$69.95 purchase _ #ST - CF1000
Focuses on the causes and damages of vandalism. Shows how student reporters on a class assignment investigate vandalism in their Connecticut community and discover that it is a serious issue costing the United States more than $5 billion annually. Shows how students, staff and community can generate positive action to reduce vandalism in schools, neighborhoods and communities.
Sociology
Dist - INSTRU

Vandalism - it is a Big Deal 20 MIN
16mm / U-matic / VHS
Color (J)
Presents a documentary investigation into the causes, extent and consequences of vandalism. Asks audiences to examine their own attitudes as parents, potential parents and community members to this ever increasing social problem. Shows steps to be taken to control the problem.
Guidance and Counseling; Sociology
Dist - BCNFL **Prod** - BORTF 1983

Vandalism - It's a Dog's Life 12 MIN
U-matic / VHS / 16mm
Color (P I J)
LC 80-701679
Uses animation to show how a child becomes a vandal. Tells how a person's irresponsible behavior can lead to vandalizing, asks what makes a person continue to vandalize, and points out that damaging someone's property affects the instigator as well as other people.
Sociology
Dist - PHENIX **Prod** - CHRISP 1980
ADL

A Vandalism Story - the Clubhouse 10 MIN
16mm
Color (P I)
LC 74-702790
Tells the story of four young boys who have made a small clubhouse. Follows the boys to a local school where they yield to peer - group pressure and throw rocks through a classroom window. Shows that three of the boys are not caught by the police and return to their clubhouse, where they are shocked to find that it too, has been vandalized.
Guidance and Counseling; Psychology; Social Science; Sociology
Dist - MCDOCR **Prod** - MCDOCR 1973

Vandalism - the Mark of Immaturity 12 MIN
U-matic / VHS / 16mm
Color (I J H)
LC 78-700628
Shows typical scenes of vandalism and the problems they cause others and examines why children destroy property.
Sociology
Dist - AIMS **Prod** - CAHILL 1977

Vandalism - what and Why 12 MIN
U-matic / VHS / 16mm
Color (I J H)
LC 73-702689
Features a racially mixed group of youngsters, ages 11 to 16, discussing vandalism and what it means to them. Includes interviews with school principals, park directors and a district attorney's specialist on vandalism.
Education; Sociology
Dist - ALTSUL **Prod** - MASB 1973

Vandalism - Why 11 MIN
16mm / VHS
Color (I J)
$225.00, $205.00 purchase, $50.00 rental
Asks why recreation areas, parks, and schools are prime targets for vandals when these places should be considered important to us. Shows that vandalism is one of the worst forms of destruction because it is deliberate and is often the result of immature behavior, peer pressure, or misdirected feelings of anger. Emphasizes the constructive ways in which young people can direct their energies toward improving their surroundings.
Sociology
Dist - HIGGIN **Prod** - HIGGIN 1972

The Vandals 25 MIN
U-matic
Color (H C)
Describes the after - effects and the social causes of vandalism.
Sociology
Dist - GA **Prod** - ABCTV

Vandals 17 MIN
U-matic / VHS / 16mm
Under the Law, Pt 2 Series
Color (I J H C)
LC 75-703577
Tells a story about a teenage boy and girl who vandalize a construction site and their school and are caught by the police. Shows how the juvenile justice system might deal with this typical case of vandalism.
Civics and Political Systems; Sociology
Dist - CORF **Prod** - USNEI 1975

Vandenberg - Aerospace Air Force Base 14 MIN
16mm
Color (A)
LC FIE61-62
Reviews six years of progress in aerospace operations at Vandenberg Air Force Base, home of USAF'S first ballistic missile division. Depicts the training required for crews that man the missile bases.
Civics and Political Systems
Dist - USNAC **Prod** - USDD 1961

Vangrams no 1 5 MIN
16mm
Color
Deals with an invention in camera - less film making, exposing raw film to a flashlight.
Fine Arts; Industrial and Technical Education
Dist - VANBKS **Prod** - VANBKS

Vanished Brilliance - the Universe Yesterday 28 MIN
16mm / U-matic / VHS
Understanding Space and Time Series
Color
Discusses the big bang and what it must have been like.
Science - Physical
Dist - UCEMC **Prod** - BBCTV 1980

Vanished Vikings, the, Pt 1 - Eric the Red 15 MIN
U-matic / VHS / 16mm
Color (I J H C)
LC 73-700987
Traces Eric the Red's travels using sagas as well as archaeological evidence to tell the story of how their settlements ceased to exist.
Geography - World; History - World; Literature and Drama
Dist - JOU **Prod** - ALTSUL 1973

Vanished Vikings, the, Pt 2 - Where Did they Go 15 MIN
U-matic / VHS / 16mm
Color (I J H C)
LC 73-700988
Introduces the leading theories about the Viking disappearances and follows leading scholars as they explain their different points of view.

Geography - World; History - World; Literature and Drama
Dist - JOU **Prod** - ALTSUL 1973

Vanishing Cornwall 54 MIN
16mm
Color (I)
LC FIA68-490
Discusses the history, legends and people of Cornwall, England.
Geography - World
Dist - SF **Prod** - DOUBLE 1968

Vanishing Hawaii 5 MIN
16mm
Color (K P I J)
Touches upon the customs and lifestyle of Hawaii in the past which are rapidly disappearing.
Geography - United States; History - United States; Sociology
Dist - CINEPC **Prod** - TAHARA 1978

The Vanishing lands - the story of sea level rise 30 MIN
VHS
Color (J H G)
$24.95 purchase _ #VL101
Reveals that 18,000 years ago at the end of the last ice age, the slow warming of the Earth began and the water level began to rise. Looks at Chesapeake Bay, which reached its current shape 3,000 years ago. While in the last century sea level rise has accelerated, the waters of the Bay appear to have risen at a rate twice the worldwide average. Features Stephen Leatherman, Laboratory for Coastal Research, University of Maryland at College Park, who states that Bay levels are rising because the land surrounding it is sinking, due to long - term geologic changes and the withdrawal of groundwater for agricultural and other uses. Produced by the Laboratory.
Geography - United States; History - United States; Science - Physical
Dist - ENVIMC

Vanishing Point - Painting and Sculpture of Nancy Camden Witt 10 MIN
16mm
Virginia Artists Series
Color
LC 78-701331
Looks at the paintings and sculpture of surrealist Nancy Camden Witt.
Fine Arts
Dist - SCHDRC **Prod** - SCHDRC 1978

Vanishing Prairie Norwegian Series
Pioneer Trails, Indian Lore and Bird Life of the Plains 14 MIN
Dist - CORF

Vanishing Prairie Portuguese Series
Pioneer Trails, Indian Lore and Bird Life of the Plains 14 MIN
Dist - CORF

Vanishing Prairie Series
The Buffalo - majestic symbol of the American plains 12 MIN
Pioneer Trails, Indian Lore and Bird Life of the Plains 14 MIN
Small animals of the plains 15 MIN
Dist - CORF

Vanishing Prairie
Large Animals that Once Roamed the Plains 12 MIN
Dist - CORF

Vanishing rain forests 6 MIN
VHS
Color (P I J H)
$20.00 purchase
Provides information on tropical rain forests and the importance of caring for and preserving rain forest ecosystems. Uses rap music to carry the message. Includes student booklet, teacher's manual and two posters.
Science - Natural; Science - Physical
Dist - WOWILF **Prod** - WOWILF 1988

The Vanishing schoolmate 20 MIN
VHS
Goosehill gang adventure series
Color (K P I R)
Features the five members of the Goosehill Gang in adventures with a Christian message. Shows how the gang learns what it means to be a Good Samaritan when they help a schoolmate.
Guidance and Counseling; Literature and Drama; Religion and Philosophy
Dist - CPH **Prod** - CPH
APH

The Vanishing sea 26 MIN
16mm
Audubon wildlife theatre series
Color (P)
LC 79-709410
Bob Davidson presents scenes from Utah, where the Salt Lake country touches farmlands, wetlands and industrial areas. Features many sequences, including the western grebe's mating display, family life at a muskrat hut and pelicans with their young. Shows the people of the valley, struggling to retain their quality of life by protecting the valley's wilderness.
Geography - United States; Science - Natural
Dist - AVEXP **Prod** - KEGPL 1969

The Vanishing Stream 22 MIN
16mm
Color; B&W (I J H C G T A)
Report of the condition of streams in Idaho. Conducted by the Idaho Department of Fish and Game. Presents one of the great dilemmas of the day on the subject of man and his environment.
Agriculture; Geography - United States; Science - Natural; Social Science
Dist - FO **Prod** - FO 1971

Vanishing towns 29 MIN
Videoreel / VT2
Turning points series
Color
Looks at the fate of the small town in America through an examination of three South Carolina towns. Includes Ft Motte, Ellenton and Cokesbury.
Geography - United States; Sociology
Dist - PBS **Prod** - SCETV

The Vanishing Tribe 17 MIN
16mm
Color (H C A)
Discusses the economic, religious and social life of the Todas, who live in the 'BLUE MOUNTAINS' of South India. Explains that they are a fast dwindling tribe with a fabulous past. Highlights their customs and beliefs.
History - World; Social Science; Sociology
Dist - NEDINF **Prod** - INDIA

Vapor Compression Cycle Designs and Refrigerants 60 MIN
VHS / U-matic
Air Conditioning and Refrigeration - - Training Series
Color (IND)
Focuses on design variations and operating principles of evaporators, compressors, condensers, metering devices. Shows refrigrants, including qualities and types and auxiliary equipment.
Education; Industrial and Technical Education
Dist - ITCORP **Prod** - ITCORP

Vapor Pressure 10 MIN
U-matic
Chemistry 102 - Chemistry for Engineers - Series
Color (C)
Cites incidents and accidents which arise from volatility of flammable substances. Describes temperature dependence of vapor pressure. Shows how to figure heat of sublimation and discusses partial pressure with relative humidity as an example.
Industrial and Technical Education; Science - Physical
Dist - UILL **Prod** - UILL 1981

Vapor Pressure - Boiling Points and Distillation 13 MIN
VHS
Color (H)
$245.00 purchase
Introduces vapor pressure through a real life situation - filling the gas tank in a car. Utilizes a manometer to show that pressure is exerted by the vapor of a liquid. Observes that a maximum vapor pressure is achieved after a period of time.
Science; Science - Physical
Dist - LUF **Prod** - LUF 1989

Vapor Pressure, Boiling Points and Distillation 13 MIN
VHS
Chemistry - from Theory to Application Series
Color (H)
$190.00 purchase
Demonstrates that in pure liquid substances the boiling point is determined by a combination of a particular saturated vapor pressure with a particular temperature. Illustrates this point through a series of experiments with decane and octance, both petroleum derivatives.
Science; Science - Physical
Dist - LUF **Prod** - LUF 1989

Vapor Pressure of Solutions 13 MIN
U-matic
Chemistry 102 - Chemistry for Engineers - Series
Color (C)
Discusses how solute and solvent affect each other's vapor pressure. Demonstrates Henry's Law with carbonated beverages and Raolut's Law with a bell jar and burets.
Industrial and Technical Education; Science - Physical
Dist - UILL **Prod** - UILL 1981

Vapor Recovery Units - an Introduction 19 MIN
U-matic / VHS
Color (IND)
Explains how a vapor recovery system works. Discusses the basic parts of a vapor recovery unit. Gives information on basic maintenance of the system.
Industrial and Technical Education; Social Science
Dist - UTEXPE **Prod** - UTEXPE 1981

Vaquero 15 MIN
16mm
Color (I J H) (SPANISH)
LC 76-700859
Shows the history of the Mexican cowboy and his influence upon American history. Explains that the dress, language and skills of the 'great American cowboy' are Mexican and Spanish in origin. Includes scenes of the modern vaquero, using skills that are nearly 500 years old, such as branding and roping.
Foreign Language; History - United States; Social Science
Dist - GARET **Prod** - GARET 1974

The Varanger - Dora Weems Incident 4 MIN
16mm
B&W
LC FIE52-945
Describes the collision of the Varanger and the Dora Weems and the causes of the accident.
Civics and Political Systems; Health and Safety; History - United States; Social Science
Dist - USNAC **Prod** - USN 1943

Varia, Pt 1 29 MIN
Videoreel / VT2
Grand Master Chess Series
Color
Physical Education and Recreation
Dist - PBS **Prod** - KQEDTV

Varia, Pt 2 29 MIN
Videoreel / VT2
Grand Master Chess Series
Color
Physical Education and Recreation
Dist - PBS **Prod** - KQEDTV

Varia, Pt 3 29 MIN
Videoreel / VT2
Grand Master Chess Series
Color
Physical Education and Recreation
Dist - PBS **Prod** - KQEDTV

Variable Area Light Control in X - Ray Duplication 5 MIN
16mm
Color (PRO)
LC 77-706053
Demonstrates X - ray duplication equipment and techniques used for improving X - ray by variable light control using a custom - made light box.
Health and Safety; Science
Dist - USNAC **Prod** - NMAC 1977

Variable Sampling (MIL - STD - 414) 30 MIN
VHS / U-matic
Quality Control Series
Color
Describes the history and application of a popular variable sampling plan.
Business and Economics; Industrial and Technical Education
Dist - MIOT **Prod** - MIOT

Variable Speed Drives 19 MIN
VHS
Power Transmission Series I - PT Products Series
Color (A)
$225.00 purchase, $50.00 rental _ #57959
Describes open - belted and enclosed mechanical (non - electric) variable speed drives, explaining their function as changing the speed ratio. Lists various types of configurations, suggesting appropriate applications for each, with rationale. Describes numbering systems.
Industrial and Technical Education
Dist - UILL **Prod** - MAJEC 1986

Variable Speeds 13 MIN
U-matic / VHS / 16mm
Reading Self - Improvement Series
Color (I J H)
$315, $220 purchase _ #3541
Shows how reading speed can assist in comprehension of ideas.
English Language
Dist - CORF

Variable volume hydraulic pumps 60 MIN
VHS / U-matic
Hydraulic systems series
Color
Discusses fixed volume and variable volume pumps. Highlights horsepower reduction and electrical checks.
Industrial and Technical Education
Dist - ITCORP **Prod** - ITCORP

Variables and Keyboard Input
VHS / U-matic
PASCAL - a Modern Programming Language Series
Color
Introduces declaration of variables - Real, Integer and String. Includes READLN and formatted output.
Industrial and Technical Education; Mathematics
Dist - EDUACT **Prod** - EDUACT

Variables in Financial Statements 15 MIN
U-matic / VHS
Finance for Nonfinancial Managers Series
Color
Business and Economics
Dist - DELTAK **Prod** - DELTAK

Variables - input statement 30 MIN
VHS / U-matic
Programming for microcomputers series; Units 7 and 8
Color (J)
LC 83-707125
Explains variables and introduces 'let' or assignment statements, using both numeric and string variables. Discusses the importance of variable names, legal and illegal names and the reserved words which cannot be used as variable names. Introduces input statements and shows how to use more than one variable in an input statement. Emphasizes the importance of considering the user's response and providing clear instructions. Shows programs with good and poor instructions and explains how to combine print and input statements.
Mathematics
Dist - IU **Prod** - IU 1983

Variance and standard deviation
VHS
Probability and statistics series
Color (H C)
$125.00 purchase _ #8007
Provides resource material about the meaning of standard deviation and variance for help in the study of probability and statistics. Presents a 60 - video series, each part 25 to 30 minutes long, that explains and reinforces concepts using definitions, theorems, examples and step - by - step solutions to tutor the student. Videos are also available in a set.
Mathematics
Dist - LANDMK

Variance of random variables
VHS
Probability and statistics series
Color (H C)
$125.00 purchase _ #8020
Provides resource material about random variables and variance for help in the study of probability and statistics. Presents a 60 - video series, each part 25 to 30 minutes long, that explains and reinforces concepts using definitions, theorems, examples and step - by - step solutions to tutor the student. Videos are also available in a set.
Mathematics
Dist - LANDMK

Variant Vowels - Au, Ou and Aw 15 MIN
VHS / 16mm
Reading Way Series
Color (P)
$125.00 purchase, $25.00 rental
Compares the "ou", "aw" and "au" sounds.
English Language
Dist - AITECH **Prod** - WXXITV 1988

Variant Vowels - Ay and Ow 15 MIN
VHS / 16mm
Reading Way Series
Color (P)
$125.00 purchase, $25.00 rental
Shows Mrs. Read building "ay" words in the computer. Tim finds "ow" in words. He thinks of "y", "ly", and "ful" words.
English Language
Dist - AITECH **Prod** - WXXITV 1988

Variation 15 MIN
VHS / Software / U-matic
Genetics Series
Color (J H)
$125.00 purchase,$95.00 software purchase
Depicts genetic building blocks and cell division through use of Microphotography and graphics. Examines the units that arrange the genetic code on the DNA molecule.
Industrial and Technical Education; Science - Natural
Dist - AITECH **Prod** - WETN 1985

Variation - a Lesson in Reading 26 MIN
16mm
Intermediate Algebra Series
B&W (H)
Presents mathematical expressions for simple proportionalities found in the natural world - - current varying with voltage, volume of a sphere varying with the cube of the radius and volume of gas at constant temperature varying inversely with pressure.
Mathematics
Dist - MLA **Prod** - CALVIN 1959

Variation - the foundation of run charts and control charts 30 MIN
VHS
Color (G C PRO)
$495.00 purchase
Defines variation in a way that employees can understand. Offers extensive support materials to show how to use run charts, control charts and other strategies for improving quality. Includes videocassette, trainer's notes, participant notes, reference cards and wall chart.
Business and Economics
Dist - FI **Prod** - EXECUT 1995

Variations and Conclusion of New Dance 7 MIN
16mm
Color (J)
LC 78-701823
Presents the concluding section of Doris Humphrey's modern dance work entitled New Dance, as reconstructed in 1972 by the Repertory Company of the American Dance Festival at Connecticut College from the choreography originally done by Doris Humphrey in 1935.
Fine Arts
Dist - UR **Prod** - ADFEST 1978

Variations in Normal Behavior - Brazelton Neonatal Behavioral Assessment Scale 20 MIN
Videoreel / VHS
Brazelton Neonatal Behavioral Assessment Scale Films Series
B&W
Explains that the Neonatal Scale demonstrates three infant capabilities including the ability to start a response to disturbing events, the ability to alert and orient and the ability to control states of arousal. Contrasts performance of different infants to the same stimuli.
Psychology
Dist - EDC **Prod** - EDC

Variations of Parameters 24 MIN
U-matic / VHS
Calculus of Differential Equations Series
B&W
Mathematics
Dist - MIOT **Prod** - MIOT

Variations on a Cellophane Wrapper 8 MIN
16mm
Color (J)
LC 72-702588
Employs a film loop technique to produce a variety of visual images.
English Language; Home Economics; Industrial and Technical Education
Dist - CANFDC **Prod** - RIMMER 1972

Variations on a Landscape - Land and Values in Ohio 25 MIN
16mm
Color
Identifies the issues concerning land use in Ohio. Includes environmentalist, localist and local/regional partnership views.
History - United States
Dist - HRC **Prod** - OHC

Variations on a Seven Second Loop - Painting 6 MIN
16mm
B&W
Uses of an optical printer to show the variations involving step - printing, repetitions and optical manipulations.
Fine Arts
Dist - FMCOOP **Prod** - SPINLB 1970

Variations on a theme 37 MIN
VHS
Color (G)
$40.00 purchase
Features a series of in - camera edited shorts from 1988 - 1990. Includes - Just Passing; The Big D; Icontact; and Crossings. Just Passing looks at the memorabilia saved by a loving wife in order to posses the spirit and remnants of affection of a dead husband. In Crossings, the body of a deer on asphalt as apathetic cars rip past is a statement on our world where humane treatment refers to how quickly we kill. In Icontact, the icon is a soft porn photo and worship is attention. Big D is a diary of an afternoon spent in an anatomy lab and examines our attitudes on mortality.
Fine Arts; Sociology
Dist - CANCIN **Prod** - BRIMUS

Variations V 50 MIN
16mm
B&W (G)
Presents an experimental dance and music work which incorporates electronic equipment as an important part of the concept.
Fine Arts
Dist - CUNDAN **Prod** - NORRUN 1966

Varicose Veins 28 MIN
16mm
Color (PRO)
Presents the basic aspects of physiological background for the treatment of varicose veins. Demonstrates basic safeguards and the critical points of technical value.
Health and Safety; Science
Dist - ACY **Prod** - ACYDGD 1969

Varietal Meats
U-matic
Matter of taste series; Lesson 13
Color (H A)
Discusses the organ meats of the animal. Shows how varietals can be the basis for flavorful and nutritious meals.
Home Economics
Dist - CDTEL **Prod** - COAST

Varieties of Energy 29 MIN
VHS / 16mm
Villa Alegre Series
Color (P T)
$46.00 rental _ #VILA - 160
Presents educational material in both Spanish and English.
Education; Science - Physical
Dist - PBS

Variety 97 MIN
35mm / 16mm / VHS
Color (G)
$250.00, $300.00 rental
Portrays a New York woman desperate for work who takes a job as a ticket seller at an adult movie theater. Reveals that, after endless nights in the claustrophobic booth, Christine accepts the advances of a shady businessman and gradually becomes obsessed with his secrets. She becomes increasingly entangled in a milieu of pornography, leading to a confrontation with the businessman and an ambiguous finale. Examines feminism and pornography. Directed by Bette Gordon.
Fine Arts; Sociology
Dist - KINOIC

Variety 29 MIN
Videoreel / VT2
Making Things Grow III Series
Color
Agriculture
Dist - PBS **Prod** - WGBHTV

Variety 27 MIN
16mm
History of the Motion Picture Series
B&W (H C)
Presents this drama of human passions, which is set against a circus and vaudeville background and which contains revolutionary photographic techniques that once affected filmaking. Stars Emil Jannings.
Fine Arts
Dist - KILLIS **Prod** - SF 1960

Variety lights 93 MIN
VHS
B&W (G)
$29.95 purchase _ #VAR020
Follows a motley band of traveling entertainers as a beautiful woman joins them and beguiles the group's manager, breaks the heart of his mistress and moves on to a bigger career.
Fine Arts; Psychology
Dist - HOMVIS **Prod** - JANUS 1950

Variety Meats 14 MIN
Videoreel / VT2
Living Better II Series
Color
Introduces good tasting and low cost menus using variety meats. Discusses why variety meats are economical and how to select and store them.
Home Economics
Dist - PBS **Prod** - MAETEL

Variety Meats 28 MIN
VHS / 16mm
What's Cooking Series
Color (G)
$55.00 rental _ #WHAC - 108
Home Economics
Dist - PBS **Prod** - WHYY

Variety of Glaze Effects - Introduction to Glaze Melts 28 MIN
Videoreel / VT2
Wheels, Kilns and Clay Series
Color
Features Mrs Peterson describing certain ceramic processes for her classroom at the University of Southern California. Explains a variety of glaze effects and an introduction to glaze melts.
Fine Arts
Dist - PBS **Prod** - USC

Variety Saw (Trim) 43 MIN
U-matic / VHS
Furniture Manufacturing Series
Color (IND)
Focuses on skill - building in operations associated with ripping, cross - cutting, grooving, mitre cutting and dadoing.
Industrial and Technical Education
Dist - LEIKID **Prod** - LEIKID

Variety's video directory plus
CD-ROM
(G)
$189.00 purchase _ #2361
Contains information on over 70,000 videos issued on VHS, Beta, 8mm, and video disc. Produced by Bowker Electronic Publishing. Includes over 43,000 educational and documentary films in addition to the theatrical releases. Users can search by title, keyword, awards, subject, date, MPAA rating, performer, director, price, genre, language, etc. Videos can be ordered with Variety's software. Subscription option with quarterly updates also available. For IBM PCs and compatibles, requires 604K RAM, DOS 3.1 or later, one floppy disk drive - hard disk recommended, one empty expansion slot, and an IBM compatible CD - ROM drive.
Fine Arts
Dist - BEP

Various Career Development Tracks 19 MIN
U-matic
Executive Development and Training Issues - Government and Industry Series; Part 3
Color (PRO)
LC 77-700636
Presents a panel discussion on various ladders and tracks for executive development. Features participants from the United States Civil Service, Social Security Administration and the Martin Marietta Corporation, who agree that evaluation and objectives are difficult but essential in executive training and development.
Business and Economics; Civics and Political Systems; Guidance and Counseling
Dist - USNAC **Prod** - USCSC 1976

Various Methods of Fixation for the Control of Fractured Jaws 45 MIN
16mm
Color
LC FIE58-285
Describes the known methods for the reduction of fractured jaw bones, including various traction methods of moving the bones and the constant fixation of splinting of bones.
Health and Safety; Science - Natural
Dist - USVA **Prod** - USVA 1958

Varley 16 MIN
16mm
Color
_ #106C 0153 015N
Geography - World
Dist - CFLMDC **Prod** - NFBC 1953

Varnette's World - a Study of a Young Artist 26 MIN
16mm
Color
LC 79-701244
Presents Varnette Honeywood, a painter who honors her ancestral heritage while searching for alternative skills to earn a living.
Fine Arts
Dist - BLUCAP **Prod** - BLUCAP 1979

Varnishing made easy
VHS
Color (G A)
$24.95 purchase _ #0794
Shows how to refinish exterior marine wood. Illustrates the techniques and equipment.
Physical Education and Recreation
Dist - SEVVID

Varsity Show 80 MIN
16mm
B&W (J)
Stars Dick Powell and Priscilla and Rosemary Lane. Presents the dance numbers created and staged by Busby Berkeley. Includes the musical numbers Have You Got Any Castles, Baby, Old King Cole, Moonlight On The Campus and Love Is In The Air Tonight.
Fine Arts
Dist - UAE **Prod** - WB 1937

Vartan Gregorian 30 MIN
VHS
World of ideas with Bill Moyers - Season I - series
Color (G)
$39.95 purchase _ #BMWI - 146
Interviews Dr Vartan Gregorian, former president of the New York Public Library. Discusses Gregorian's views on the importance of libraries, learning and the growing amount of information available. Hosted by Bill Moyers.
Education; Social Science
Dist - PBS

Varying Structure of the Simple Sentence 14.27 MIN
VHS / U-matic
Grammar Mechanic
(I J)
Designed to help the intermediate student apply the rules of grammar. Focuses on strategies for varying the structure of simple sentences. Fifteenth in a 16 part series.
English Language
Dist - GPN **Prod** - WDCNTV

Vasarely (Born 1908) 9 MIN
16mm
B&W
Presents one of the masters of the optical illusion, Vassarely, who uses in his drawings the theme that we no longer simply believe what we see or simply see what we believe.
Fine Arts
Dist - ROLAND **Prod** - ROLAND

Vascetomy Operative Procedure 28 MIN
U-matic / VHS
Urology Series
Color (PRO)
Health and Safety; Science - Natural
Dist - MSU **Prod** - MSU

Vascular anatomical chart
VHS
(J H C G A)
$36.50 purchase _ #AH70203
Portrays the anatomy of the vascular system from a variety of angles. Available with mounting rods or framed.
Health and Safety; Science - Natural
Dist - HTHED **Prod** - HTHED

Vascular Complications of the Thoracic Outlet Syndrome 22 MIN
16mm
Color (PRO)
LC 78-700323
Explains diagnosis and treatment of thoracic outlet syndrome using drawings to illustrate anatomy and pathophysiology. Presents X - rays and angiograms to demonstrate pathology in three patients. Shows supraclavicular approach with resection of a portion of the clavicle correcting the syndrome and its vascular complications.
Health and Safety
Dist - SQUIBB **Prod** - KAISP 1978

Vascular series
Abdominal aortic endarterectomy 33 MIN
Aortic aneurysm review and two aortic aneurysm procedures 60 MIN
Carotid endarterectomy 18 MIN
Distal splenorenal shunt 16 MIN
Emergency Embolectomy 8 MIN
Emergency mesocaval shunt 25 MIN
Femoro - popliteal bypass 15 MIN
Hyperalimentation I - Percutaneous Insertion / Hyperalimentation II - Operative 12 MIN
Insertion of Subclavian Catheter for Intravenous Hyperalimentation 15 MIN
Dist - SVL

Vascular System 34 MIN
VHS / 16mm
Histology review series; Unit VII
(C)
$330.00 purchase _ #821VI041
Presents an overview of the functional parts of the circulatory system, emphasizing those structures involved in transporting blood to and from the heart. Various types of vessels and their adaptive evolution to perform specific functions are also discussed. Part 1 of the Circulation Unit.
Health and Safety
Dist - HSCIC **Prod** - HSCIC 1983

Vasectomia 20 MIN
U-matic
Are you listening series
Color (J H C)
LC 80-707407
Presents a group of Colombian men discussing why they had vasectomies.
Sociology
Dist - STURTM **Prod** - STURTM 1972

Vasectomy 17 MIN
U-matic / VHS / 16mm
Color (C A) (SPANISH)
LC 75-715529
Uses animation to describe the male reproductive system and vasectomy surgery. Interviews men and their wives to explain their reasons for having a vasectomy and their feelings, fears and satisfactions.
Psychology; Science - Natural
Dist - CF **Prod** - CF 1972

Vasectomy
VHS / U-matic
Color (SPANISH)
Shows how a vasectomy eliminates the risk of pregnancy and discusses the surgical procedures involved.
Health and Safety
Dist - MIFE **Prod** - MIFE

Vasectomy 15 MIN
U-matic / 8mm cartridge / VHS / 16mm
Color (A PRO) (SPANISH)
Explains how a vasectomy prevents conception and helps alleviate fears about loss of masculinity and sexual prowess. Includes detailed instructions for post - operative care.
Health and Safety; Science - Natural; Sociology
Dist - PRORE **Prod** - PRORE

Vasectomy 18 MIN
16mm
B&W (H C A)
Uses live action and animated diagrams to show how doctors should proceed with vasectomy operations.
Health and Safety
Dist - NEDINF **Prod** - INDIA

Vasectomy 5 MIN
U-matic / VHS
Color
Emphasizes permanency, reminds patient of physical and psychological implications. Describes how surgery interrupts seminal flow to prevent impregnation and reassures patient concerning future sexual performance.
Guidance and Counseling; Sociology
Dist - MEDCOM **Prod** - MEDCOM

Vasectomy 9 MIN
VHS / U-matic
Color
Describes normal male anatomy. Explains how a vasectomy works. Discusses possible complications.
Science - Natural; Sociology
Dist - MEDFAC **Prod** - MEDFAC 1972

Vasectomy - Male Sterilization 29 MIN
Videoreel / VT2
B&W
Explains a vasectomy, a simple operation to sterilize the male. Considers both the physical and possible psychological effects of this procedure.
Health and Safety; Psychology; Sociology
Dist - PBS **Prod** - KQEDTV

Vasectomy Patient Counseling 10 MIN
16mm
Color
LC 75-702256
Shows a simulated interview between the physician and a couple seeking information concerning vasectomy.
Science
Dist - EATONL **Prod** - EATONL 1973

Vasectomy Procedures 10 MIN
16mm
Color
LC 75-702255
Shows all currently employed techniques of performing vasectomy.
Science
Dist - EATONL **Prod** - EATONL 1973

Vasectomy reversal 45 MIN
VHS
Surgical procedures series
Color (G)
$149.00 purchase, $75.00 rental _ #UW5210
Focuses on Dr Cullie Carson who works with a high - powered microscope to reconnect the 6mm tube through which sperm travel. Part of a 17 - part series recording surgical procedures in detail, with specialists who explain the ailment, the anatomical function of the part of the body being operated on, and how successful surgery might improve the patient's quality of life, hosted by Dr Donna Willis.

Health and Safety
Dist - FOTH

Vasectomy Techniques 16 MIN
U-matic / VHS
Color
Views each step in performing a vasectomy.
Health and Safety; Sociology
Dist - PRIMED **Prod** - PRIMED

Vasectomy - tubal ligation 45 MIN
VHS
Surgical procedures series
Color (G)
$149.00 purchase, $75.00 rental _ #UW5209
Reveals that either vasectomy or laparscopic tubal ligation is presently the most reliable form of birth control. Shows that each operation takes approximately 20 minutes to perform and, in both cases, patients can return home on the same day. The major choice a couple must make is - which partner is the better - suited to undergo a surgical procedure. Part of a 17 - part series recording surgical procedures in detail, with specialists who explain the ailment, the anatomical function of the part of the body being operated on, and how successful surgery might improve the patient's quality of life, hosted by Dr Donna Willis.
Health and Safety
Dist - FOTH

Vasillis of Athens 15 MIN
U-matic / VHS
Other families, other friends series; Red module; Greece
Color (P)
Pictures the ancient Palace of Knossis on Crete and modern Athens in Greece.
Geography - World; Social Science
Dist - AITECH **Prod** - WVIZTV 1971

Vassa 106 MIN
16mm / 35mm
Color (G) (RUSSIAN WITH ENGLISH SUBTITLES)
$250.00, $300.00 rental
Portrays a matriarch's attempts to manipulate her family with the same psychological techniques she uses to regulate her business enterprises. Directed by Gleb Panfilov.
Fine Arts; Sociology
Dist - KINOIC **Prod** - IFEX 1983

Vassily Kandinsky 60 MIN
VHS
Color (H C A)
$39.95
Discusses the works of Russian artist Vassily Kandinsky. Shows a retrospective of his works at the Paris Centre Pompidou. Illustrates his emotional use of color and form in his abstract expression.
Fine Arts
Dist - ARTSAM **Prod** - RMART

The Vatican 54 MIN
U-matic / VHS / 16mm
Color (H C A)
Provides a tour of the Vatican, a review of its history, a display of some of its art treasures, an explanation of the Swiss Guard tradition and an audience with the late Pope John.
Fine Arts; Geography - World; Religion and Philosophy; Sociology
Dist - MGHT **Prod** - ABCTV 1963

The Vatican 18 MIN
VHS / U-matic
Color
Examines the functions and governmental structure of the Vatican.
Geography - World; Religion and Philosophy
Dist - JOU **Prod** - UPI

Vatican City 20 MIN
VHS / U-matic
Color (J)
LC 82-706789
Visits Vatican City, including St Peter's Basilica, the Sistine Chapel and the papal residence. Shows the mausoleums, Borgia apartment and the Swiss guards.
Geography - World; History - World
Dist - AWSS **Prod** - AWSS 1980

Vatican control of WHO population policy 34 MIN
VHS
Color (G)
$19.00 purchase
Interviews Prof Milton P Siegel, Assistant Director General of the World Health Organization, regarding the controlling influence of the Vatican on the formulation of WHO policy. Examines the deplorable record of WHO in family planning during the 44 - year history of the organization. Shows how predominantly Roman Catholic nations lobbied against the discussion of population growth and birth control as a health issue within WHO.
Civics and Political Systems; Health and Safety; Social Science
Dist - CRPS **Prod** - CRPS 1992

Vatican - Fortress of Christianity 29 MIN
VHS / 16mm
Countries and Peoples Series
Color (H C G)
$90.00 purchase _ #BPN128130
Traces the historical development of the Catholic religion in Europe and the World, and the establishment of the Vatican as the spiritual center of Christianity. Features St Peter's Basilica and other example of Roman architecture.
Geography - World; History - World
Dist - RMIBHF **Prod** - RMIBHF

Vatican - Fortress of Christianity 30 MIN
U-matic
Countries and Peoples Series
Color (H C)
Traces the historical development of the Catholic religion and the establishment of the Vatican as the spiritual centre of Catholicism.
Geography - World; History - World; Religion and Philosophy
Dist - TVOTAR **Prod** - TVOTAR 1982

The Vatican museums - 2 53 MIN
VHS / BETA
Grand museum series
Color (G)
$29.95 purchase
Visits the Vatican museums. Offers close - up views of paintings with informative narrative rich in artistic and historic detail. Includes a chronological list of the works and artists shown. Part two of a three - parts series on famous art museums produced by Vistar.
Fine Arts
Dist - ARTSAM

The Vatican - Pt 1 24 MIN
16mm / U-matic / VHS
Color (H C A)
Provides a tour of the Vatican, a review of its history, a display of some of its art treasures, an explanation of the Swiss guard tradition and an audience with the late Pope John.
Religion and Philosophy
Dist - MGHT **Prod** - ABCTV 1963

The Vatican - Pt 2 30 MIN
16mm / U-matic / VHS
Color (H C A)
Provides a tour of the Vatican, a review of its history, a display of some of its art treasures, an explanation of the Swiss Guard tradition and an audience with the late Pope John.
Religion and Philosophy
Dist - MGHT **Prod** - ABCTV 1963

Vatican world 90 MIN
VHS / 16mm
Color (G)
$35.00 rental, $14.95 purchase
Features the future world of the Vatican with a very young Pope and his power - hungry assistant. Follows the events as the Pope learns to use a marketing expert to help improve the Church's image, such as a billboard campaign 'I Can't Believe I Ate The Whole Body of Christ.' The Pope eventually becomes a born - again marketeer. Produced by Tom Ciesielka and directed by Chicago filmmaker Tom Palazzolo.
Business and Economics; Fine Arts; Literature and Drama; Religion and Philosophy
Dist - CANCIN

Vaucherin 32 MIN
16mm
B&W (C A) (FRENCH (ENGLISH SUBTITLES))
Follows a man, alone among his books, as he meticulously tidies up his room and prepares to depart for a journey. Includes English subtitles.
Foreign Language
Dist - UWFKD **Prod** - UWFKD

Vaudeville Jazz 30 MIN
U-matic / VHS
Stage at a Time
(K P I)
$180 VC purchase, $30 VC five day rental, $110 self dub
Uses theater to teach students self awareness, values and ethics. Focuses on the changing relationship between a girl and her aging grandfather, highlighting the uncertainty of life. Fourth in a series of four.
Psychology; Sociology
Dist - GPN **Prod** - WUFT 1983

Vault 12 MIN
U-matic / VHS
Color
Traces the relationship between a woman pole vaulter - concert cellist and a cowboy - abstract painter. Presented by Bruce and Norman Yonemoto.
Fine Arts
Dist - ARTINC **Prod** - ARTINC

Vault 12 MIN
VHS
Color
Presents Bruce and Norman Yonemotos' video entry selected from the 1985 Whitney Biennial Film and Video Exhibition.
Fine Arts
Dist - AFA **Prod** - AFA 1986

Vault Clinic on Tape 30 MIN
U-matic / VHS
Color (H C A)
Presents technique and training in the pole vault by Abilene Christian coach Don Hood. Illustrates his specialized drills and training methods. Features film footage of some of the world's best vaulters, including Olson, Bubka, Dial, Vigneron, Tully, and others.
Physical Education and Recreation
Dist - TRACKN **Prod** - TRACKN 1986

Vaux - Le Vicomte, France 26 MIN
16mm / U-matic / VHS
Place in Europe Series
Color (H C A)
Used as a model for many imitators, Vaux was built as a country house by the treasurer of France, whose team of artists was commanded by King Louis XIV to build Versailles. La Fontaine's poem about the house is read.
Geography - World
Dist - MEDIAG **Prod** - THAMES 1975

VCR time machine 120 MIN
VHS
Color (H C A)
$24.95 purchase
Provides a guide to using the video cassette recorder more successfully. Focuses on the VCR counter numbers and their meaning, but considers other subjects as well.
Industrial and Technical Education
Dist - PBS **Prod** - WNETTV

VD - a New Focus 16 MIN
VHS / 16mm / U-matic
Color (J H C) (SPANISH)
Features young people from locations throughout America who present the problems themselves and outline the answers for treating venereal disease. Describes the medical facts, the myths and the attitudes of young people that often prevent prompt treatment of VD.
Foreign Language; Health and Safety
Dist - AMEDFL **Prod** - AMEDFL

VD - a New Focus 15 MIN
U-matic / VHS / 16mm
Color
LC 79-712989
Presents an entire picture of the VD problem, giving medical facts, and probing the myths and attitudes of young people concerning VD that often prevent prompt treatment.
Education; Health and Safety
Dist - AMEDFL **Prod** - DUNLF 1971

VD - a New(Er) Focus 20 MIN
U-matic / VHS
Color (J H)
Refers to a revised edition of 'VD - A New Focus,' which includes all of the most serious new and increasing sexually transmissible diseases. Shows symptoms and treatment, including information on herpes, one of the most serious new diseases, and is host - narrated by James Brotin and Joseph Campanella.
Foreign Language; Health and Safety
Dist - AMEDFL **Prod** - ASHA

VD - a Newer Focus 20 MIN
16mm
Color (J H)
LC 77-702447
A revised version of the 1971 motion picture VD - A New Focus. Surveys the historical prevalence of sexually transmissible diseases and enumerates the symptoms of gonorrhea, nongonococcal urethritis, herpes simplex Z and syphillis.
Health and Safety
Dist - AMEDFL **Prod** - AMEDFL 1977
EDPAT

VD - Attack Plan 16 MIN
U-matic / VHS / 16mm
Color (J H) (FRENCH HUNGARIAN SWEDISH SPANISH POLISH PORTUGUESE)
LC 73-700962
Presents a veteran germ in the contagion corps who outlines how syphilis and gonorrhea can attack man. Points out the steps which man can follow to defeat the two diseases but emphasizes the myth that keeps uninformed humans from seeking treatment.
Health and Safety; Sociology
Dist - CORF **Prod** - DISNEY 1973

VD - it is Your Problem 14 MIN
VHS / U-matic
Pregnancy Prevention and Sex Hygiene Series
Color
LC 85-700100
Deals with misinformation, facts and the dangers of untreated gonorrhea and syphilis. Stresses the need for early medical care.
Health and Safety
Dist - USNAC **Prod** - USA 1983

VD - more Bugs, more Problems - Rev AIDS Section; Rev. 20 MIN
16mm / VHS
Color (J A) (SPANISH)
$440.00, $390.00 purchase, $60.00 rental
Explains how to recognize symptoms of, and guard against, chlamydia, AIDS, and herpes, along with other sexually transmitted diseases (STDs). Stresses that care for your own health and the health of others is a personal responsibility. Also available in Spanish.
Health and Safety
Dist - HIGGIN **Prod** - HIGGIN 1989

VD - Old Bugs, New Problems 20 MIN
U-matic / VHS / 16mm
Color (J)
LC 77-703319
Acquaints the viewer with the various types of sexually transmitted diseases.
Health and Safety
Dist - HIGGIN **Prod** - HIGGIN 1978

VD - One, Two 14 MIN
16mm
Color
LC 74-706599
States that the tracking of the source of venereal infection is as important as medical treatment. Shows why an individual infected with VD must not only seek proper medical treatment, but also cooperate with the VD contact interviewer.
Health and Safety; Sociology
Dist - USNAC **Prod** - USN 1973

VD - play it safe 14 MIN
VHS
Color (H A)
Presents a series of short, snappy musical vignettes to explain the facts of sexually transmitted diseases. Discusses how these diseases are contracted, the symptoms, where to get treatment. Deals with herpes, syphilis and gonorrhea. Preview is recommended prior to presentation to any audience.
Health and Safety; Sociology
Dist - VIEWTH **Prod** - VIEWTH

VD - Play it Safe 14 MIN
16mm / U-matic / VHS
Color (J)
LC 80-700782
Uses a series of vignettes to explain the communicability and disease process of sexually transmitted diseases, including gonorrhea, syphilis and genital herpes. Shows how these diseases can be prevented and treated.
Health and Safety
Dist - CORF **Prod** - GORKER 1980

VD - Prevent it 10 MIN
16mm / U-matic / VHS
Color (H A)
Explains that of all communicable diseases, VD is the easiest to prevent. Discusses the ways of preventing the spread of venereal disease by using soap and water, urinating after contact, using a bacteria douche, properly employing a condom, using germ - killing medications and attending periodic physical examinations.
Health and Safety
Dist - HIGGIN **Prod** - HIGGIN 1978

VD Questions, VD Answers 15 MIN
16mm / U-matic / VHS
Color
LC 72-700790
Describes how VD is contracted and what to do about prevention and treatment.
Health and Safety
Dist - PHENIX **Prod** - PHENIX 1972

VD - See Your Doctor 22 MIN
16mm
Family Life Education and Human Growth Series
Color (J)
LC FIA67-16
Describes the causes, symptoms and dangers of venereal disease and emphasizes the importance of obtaining prompt medical treatment.
Guidance and Counseling; Health and Safety; Sociology
Dist - SF **Prod** - MORLAT 1966

VD - Self - Awareness Project Series Module 2
Next Time 12 MIN
Dist - FMD

VD - Self - Awareness Project Series Module 3
Number 23 10 MIN
Dist - FMD

VD Self - Awareness Project Series
VD - who Needs it 24 MIN
Dist - AAHPER

VD - the Love Bug 15 MIN
U-matic / VHS / 16mm
Color (J H C)
LC 80-701786
Identifies the symptoms of venereal disease, tells how to avoid it and what to do if it is contracted, and discusses herpes simplex II. Emphasizes the importance of tracing VD carriers and the need for developing responsible attitudes about sexual relations.
Health and Safety
Dist - CORF **Prod** - WABCTV 1979

VD - Truths and Consequences 28 MIN
16mm
Color (I)
LC 73-702777
Presents the prevailing myths and misinformation that have conspired to make venereal disease the epidemic it is today. Features four leading medical authorities covering their special field of practice.
Health and Safety
Dist - MTVTM **Prod** - AVANTI 1973

VD - Very Communicable Diseases 19 MIN
16mm / U-matic / VHS
Color (J)
LC 73-701068
Presents the how's, why's, wherefore's and ramifications of venereal disease, syphilis and gonorrhea. Includes preventive measures.
Guidance and Counseling; Health and Safety; Sociology
Dist - AIMS **Prod** - CAHILL 1972

VD - who Needs it 24 MIN
16mm
VD Self - Awareness Project Series
Color (J H C)
LC 75-702842
Presents facts about venereal disease.
Guidance and Counseling; Health and Safety
Dist - AAHPER **Prod** - AAHPER 1974

VDRL Tests for Syphilis 22 MIN
16mm
B&W (PRO)
LC FIE59-246
Describes the preparation of the basic antigen emulsion. Shows the procedures for the spinal fluid test and for the slide and tube flocculation tests for serum. For professional use only.
Health and Safety
Dist - USNAC **Prod** - USPHS 1959

VDT - the human connection 12 MIN
16mm / VHS / BETA / U-matic
Color; PAL (IND PRO)
PdS150, PdS158 purchase
Assesses the health and safety - related problems of workers who use video display terminals. Gives simple and straightforward suggestions dealing with problems such as eye strain, stress, and back and muscle aches, along with placement of the work station, lighting, keyboard, screen and chair. Includes manual and employee handbook.
Health and Safety
Dist - EDPAT **Prod** - CLMI 1988

VEBA's 30 MIN
VHS / U-matic
Tax Reform Act of 1984 Series
Color (PRO)
Business and Economics; Civics and Political Systems; Social Science
Dist - ALIABA **Prod** - ALIABA

Vector component computations 30 MIN
VHS
Calculus series
Color (C)
$125.00 purchase _ #6055
Explains vector component computations. Part of a 56 - part series on calculus.
Mathematics
Dist - LANDMK **Prod** - LANDMK

Vector cross product 30 MIN
VHS
Calculus series
Color (C)
$125.00 purchase _ #6056
Explains vector cross product. Part of a 56 - part series on calculus.
Mathematics
Dist - LANDMK **Prod** - LANDMK

Vector Functions of a Scalar Variable 38 MIN
U-matic / VHS
Calculus of several Variables - Vector - - Calculus Series; Vector calculus
B&W
Mathematics
Dist - MIOT **Prod** - MIOT

Vector Kinematics 16 MIN
16mm
PSSC Physics Films Series
B&W (C)
Introduces velocity and acceleration vectors and shows them simultaneously for various two - dimensional motions including circular and simple harmonic.
Science - Physical
Dist - MLA **Prod** - PSSC 1962

Vector Q 9 MIN
16mm
Color
LC 78-711560
A young hero who is taking his heroine into the autumn forest discovers that he is inextricably ensnared in physics, mathematics and nature.
Mathematics; Science - Natural; Science - Physical
Dist - UMD **Prod** - UMD 1971

Vector Spaces
16mm
B&W
Defines geometric vectors and introduces the idea of a basis. Demonstrates how real vector spaces can be regarded as sets of ordered strings of numbers. Indicates the power of the vector space concept.
Mathematics
Dist - OPENU **Prod** - OPENU

Vector Spaces 31 MIN
U-matic / VHS
Calculus of Linear Algebra Series
B&W
Mathematics
Dist - MIOT **Prod** - MIOT

Vectors 60 MIN
VHS
Concepts in mathematics series
Color; PAL (J H G)
PdS29.50 purchase
Investigates and develops the definition of vectors. Uses three - dimensional computer animation to show practical applications of vector theory. Illustrates magnitude and direction, force and velocity. Divided into six 10 minute sections titled follow that arrow; finding the resultant; ordered pairs; resolving without grids; force; and applying forces. Part of a four - part series.
Industrial and Technical Education; Mathematics
Dist - EMFVL **Prod** - TVOTAR

Vectors 30 MIN
16mm / U-matic / VHS
Mechanical Universe Series
Color (C A)
Deals with vectors which describe quantities such as displacement and velocity, expressing the laws of physics in the same way for all coordinate systems.
Science - Physical
Dist - FI **Prod** - ANNCPB

Vectors 12 MIN
U-matic / VHS / 16mm
Radio Technician Training Series
B&W (C)
LC FIE52-929
Explains vectors, changes in angle or magnitude, how vectors are plotted and how the resultant is found.
Industrial and Technical Education
Dist - USNAC **Prod** - USN 1945

Vectors 30 MIN
VHS
Calculus series
Color (C)
$125.00 purchase _ #6053
Explains vectors. Part of a 56 - part series on calculus.
Mathematics
Dist - LANDMK **Prod** - LANDMK

Vectors and projectiles - 3 47 MIN
VHS
Conceptual physics alive series
Color (H C)
$45.00 purchase
Explains vector addition and vector resolution, using examples such as airplanes flying in the wind and projectile motion. Looks at the concept of the independence of horizontal and vertical motion. Part 3 of a 35 - part series adapted from the college and high school textbook Conceptual Physics by Professor Paul Hewitt.
Science - Physical
Dist - MMENTE **Prod** - HEWITP 1992

Vectors in Polar Coordinates 27 MIN
U-matic / VHS
Calculus of several Variables - Vector - - Calculus Series; Vector calculus
B&W
Mathematics
Dist - MIOT **Prod** - MIOT

Vectors - Newton's laws - Parts 5 and 6 60 MIN
VHS / U-matic
Mechanical universe...and beyond - Part I series
Color (G)
$45.00, $29.95 purchase
Reveals that physics must explain not only why and how much, but also where and which way in Part 5. Portrays Newton who laid down the laws of force, mass and acceleration in Part 6. Parts of a 52 - part series on the mechanics of the universe.
Science; Science - Physical
Dist - ANNCPB **Prod** - SCCON 1985

VEE - a National Emergency 11 MIN
16mm
Color (SPANISH)
LC 74-705904; 76-703680
Describes action to control the deadly horse sleeping sickness, Venezuelan equine encephalomyelitis. Depicts mass vaccination, quarantine and aerial spraying to suppress mosquitoes.
Agriculture; Health and Safety
Dist - USNAC **Prod** - USDA 1972

Vee Butt Joint 12 MIN
BETA / VHS
Welding Training Comprehensive - Oxy - Acetylene Welding Series
Color (IND)
Industrial and Technical Education; Psychology
Dist - RMIBHF **Prod** - RMIBHF

Veg Lover's Cookbook III 80 MIN
U-matic / VHS
Vegetable Lover's Video Cookbook Series
(C A)
$44.00 _ #VC300V
Features Bert Greene, authority on food and author of the book Greene On Greens, as he discusses effective methods for cooking vegetables, as well as demonstrating his own recipes himself, such as Blazing Brussel Sprouts.
Home Economics; Industrial and Technical Education
Dist - CAMV **Prod** - CAMV

Veg Lover's Video Cookbook I 80 MIN
U-matic / VHS
Vegetable Lover's Video Cookbook Series
(C A)
$44.00 _ #VC100V
Features Bert Greene, authority on food, and author of the book Greene On Greens, as he introduces a comprehensive guide to cooking vegetables, and demonstrates various recipes himself, such as Groccoli Pesto and others.
Home Economics; Industrial and Technical Education
Dist - CAMV **Prod** - CAMV

Vegetable and Fruit Prints 15 MIN
U-matic
Is the Sky Always Blue Series
Color (P)
Fine Arts
Dist - GPN **Prod** - WDCNTV 1979

Vegetable Art 1 25 MIN
VHS / U-matic
Color (PRO)
Demonstrates carving techniques for making vegetables resemble flowers, including tulips from radishes and a rose from a turnip.
Home Economics; Industrial and Technical Education
Dist - CULINA **Prod** - CULINA

Vegetable Art 2 12 MIN
VHS / U-matic
Color (PRO)
Presents more advanced vegetable carving techniques - the chain, the fish net and the basketweave, using potatoes, rutabagas and daikon radishes.
Home Economics; Industrial and Technical Education
Dist - CULINA **Prod** - CULINA

Vegetable Art 3 12 MIN
U-matic / VHS
Color (PRO)
Teaches techniques for making an exotic bouquet from common vegetables. Makes daisies from turnips, carrots and scallions, orchids from cabbages, carrots and scallions, and Hawaiian flowers from beets, carrots and young corn.
Home Economics; Industrial and Technical Education
Dist - CULINA **Prod** - CULINA

Vegetable Art 4 9 MIN
U-matic / VHS
Color (PRO)
Shows how to make a rose from a celery knob, a lily and a crocus from a red onion, butterflies from zucchini, and a rose from slices of a beet, turnip or rutabaga.
Home Economics; Industrial and Technical Education
Dist - CULINA **Prod** - CULINA

Vegetable Art 5 13 MIN
U-matic / VHS
Color (PRO)
Concentrates on the proper angling of the knife for precision and speed of production. A rose is carved from a beet and other exotic flowers from carrots.
Home Economics; Industrial and Technical Education
Dist - CULINA **Prod** - CULINA

Vegetable Cuts
U-matic / VHS
Vegetable Cutting Series
Color
Home Economics; Industrial and Technical Education
Dist - CULINA **Prod** - CULINA

Vegetable Cuts - Dicing
U-matic / VHS
Vegetable Cutting Series
Color
Home Economics; Industrial and Technical Education
Dist - CULINA **Prod** - CULINA

Vegetable Cutting Series
Mise En Place
Vegetable Cuts
Vegetable Cuts - Dicing
Dist - CULINA

Vegetable Flowers 10 MIN
VHS / U-matic
Color (PRO)
Shows how to make flowers from scallions, tomatoes, radishes and potatoes, and how to arrange them attractively.
Home Economics; Industrial and Technical Education
Dist - CULINA **Prod** - CULINA

Vegetable Gardening 55 MIN
VHS / BETA / 16mm
Color (G)
$39.95 purchase _ #VT1026
Discusses vegetable gardening. Covers the proper way to prepare the soil, which tools to use, the best way to water, how to fertilize, how to control garden pests and diseases, and when to plant and harvest. Taught by Ed Hume.
Agriculture; Social Science
Dist - RMIBHF **Prod** - RMIBHF

Vegetable Gardening 15 MIN
16mm / U-matic / VHS
Garden Methods Series
Color (I)
LC 72-700802
Explains planning, seed selection, tools, preparing the garden plot, row marking, spacing, thinning, cultivating, fertilization, pest control, harvesting and rotation of crops.
Agriculture
Dist - PEREN **Prod** - DSC 1972

Vegetable Industry 3 MIN
16mm
Of all Things Series
Color (P I)
Discusses the vegetable industry.
Business and Economics; Social Science
Dist - AVED **Prod** - BAILYL

Vegetable Lover's Video Cookbook Series
Veg Lover's Cookbook III 80 MIN
Veg Lover's Video Cookbook I 80 MIN
Dist - CAMV

Vegetable Preparation 6 MIN
U-matic / VHS
Color (PRO)
Shows how to simplify preparation of vegetables for use as crudites or in other dishes. Demonstrates the proper cleaning and handling of cauliflower, broccoli, mushrooms and potatoes, and shows how they should be cut.
Home Economics; Industrial and Technical Education
Dist - CULINA **Prod** - CULINA

Vegetable preparation 10 MIN
U-matic / VHS / 16mm
Professional food preparation and service program series
Color (J)
LC 74-700408
Shows how to maintain color, taste, texture and nutrition in preparing vegetables. Demonstrates proper procedures for boiling and other cooking methods including steaming, sauteeing, deep fat frying and others. Exposes errors of overcooking, use of excessive water, delays, bad planning and harmful additives. Encourages creativity in sauces.
Industrial and Technical Education
Dist - NEM **Prod** - NEM 1972

Vegetable Processor 15 MIN
U-matic
Harriet's Magic Hats II Series
(P I J)
Shows a food processing factory receive corn on the cob and process it.
Guidance and Counseling
Dist - ACCESS **Prod** - ACCESS 1983

Vegetables 30 MIN
VHS / 16mm
Matter of taste series
Color (C A)
$85.00, $75.00 purchase _ 14 - 05
Focuses on steam, deep - and stir - fry cookery using vegetables.
Home Economics; Social Science
Dist - CDTEL **Prod** - COAST 1984

Vegetables 28 MIN
VHS / 16mm
What's Cooking Series
Color (G)
$55.00 rental _ #WHAC - 111
Home Economics
Dist - PBS **Prod** - WHYY

Vegetables
VHS
Way to Cook - Julia Child Series
$29.95 purchase _ #5 INCH 45 RPM RECORD741V
Features Julia Child demonstrating how to prepare a variety of vegetables.
Home Economics; Industrial and Technical Education
Dist - CAREER **Prod** - CAREER

Vegetables 45 MIN
VHS
Le Cordon Bleu cooking series
Color (H C G)
$24.95 purchase _ #LCB001V
Details, with close - up footage, techniques and practical methods needed to prepare a fabulous assortment of vegetable dishes. Features the world - renowned chefs of Le Cordon Bleu's teaching staff. Part of an eight - part series.
Home Economics
Dist - CAMV

Vegetables 60 MIN
U-matic / VHS
Way to Cook with Julia Child
(C A)
$34.95 _ #KN300V
Features popular American cooking teacher Julia Child as she demonstrates various recipes that use vegetables.
Home Economics; Industrial and Technical Education
Dist - CAMV **Prod** - CAMV

Vegetables and Fruits
VHS / 35mm strip
Food Preparation Series
$185.00 purchase _ #PX1142 filmstrip, $185.00 purchase _ #PX1142V
Provides a background in handling and processing foods as students learn how to classify fruits and vegetables. Tells how classification determines storage, preparation and cooking. Portrays how to wash, clean, peel, chop, mince and dice. Tells how to prepare fresh, frozen, dried and canned food.
Health and Safety; Home Economics; Industrial and Technical Education; Social Science
Dist - CAREER **Prod** - CAREER

Vegetables and Fruits
VHS
Food Preparation
$169 purchase _ #PX1142V
Teaches how to classify fruits and vegetables and how this classification determines storage, preparation and cooking. Demonstrates how to wash, clean, peel, chop, mince and dice. Describes preparation methods for fresh, frozen, dried and canned food.
Health and Safety; Home Economics; Social Science
Dist - CAREER **Prod** - CAREER

Vegetables - from Garden to Table 18 MIN
16mm / U-matic / VHS
Color (J)
LC 81-701385
Demonstrates a variety of ways to cook vegetables, including baking, boiling, steaming, stir frying, and deep fat frying. Shows how to select vegetables and how to prepare them to be eaten raw.
Home Economics
Dist - CORF **Prod** - CENTRO 1981

Vegetables, Pt 1 29 MIN
Videoreel / VT2
Cookin' Cajun Series
Color
Features gourmet - humorist Justin Wilson showing ways to cook vegetables with various ingredients.
Geography - United States; Home Economics
Dist - PBS **Prod** - MAETEL

Vegetables, Pt 2 29 MIN
Videoreel / VT2
Cookin' Cajun Series
Color
Features gourmet - humorist Justin Wilson showing ways to cook vegetables with various ingredients.
Geography - United States; Home Economics
Dist - PBS **Prod** - MAETEL

Vegetables Vegetables 3 MIN
Videoreel / VT2
Beatrice Trum Hunter's Natural Foods Series
Color
Suggests storing and preparing fresh vegetables with care. Demonstrates how to cook them briefly and suggests combining left - over vegetables with sour cream or yogurt for a good cold salad or blending them to make a cold soup.
Home Economics; Social Science
Dist - PBS **Prod** - WGBH

Vegetarian protein 30 MIN
VHS
Color (J H C G)
$79.95 purchase _ #PSV100V
Teaches students who are contemplating or practicing a vegetarian diet and life - style how to plan a diet containing adequate protein for a growing body. Focuses on the interests and needs of teens. Discusses the different types of vegetarians and explains the functions of each food group within a vegetarian diet. Examines the social implications of alternative dietary practices, teaches associated vocabulary and describes the relationship of food and metabolism. Includes teacher's manual and reproducible exercise masters.
Health and Safety; Home Economics; Social Science
Dist - CAMV

The Vegetarian World 29 MIN
16mm / U-matic / VHS
Color
Looks at the history and practice of the vegetarian lifestyle and presents archival footage of such famous vegetarians as Count Leo Tolstoy, George Bernard Shaw and Mahatma Gandhi. Traces the development of vegetarianism from its Eastern beginnings to the sophisticated vegetarian restaurants of Europe and North America. Narrated by William Shatner.
Health and Safety; Social Science
Dist - BULFRG **Prod** - KSFILM 1983

Vegetarianism - Food for Thought 25 MIN
U-matic / VHS
Color
Reports on the nutritional values of meatless diets and analyzes the reasons why people choose vegetarian diets. Shows how their regimen can save money at the market.
Health and Safety; Home Economics
Dist - MEDCOM **Prod** - MEDCOM

Vegetarianism in a Nutshell 14 MIN
VHS / U-matic
Color (J)
Provides the answers to why people become vegetarians, the different types of vegetarian diets, the nutritional implications, how to plan a vegetarian diet, and the dietary precautions.
Health and Safety; Psychology; Social Science
Dist - POAPLE **Prod** - POAPLE

Vegetation and Soil 15 MIN
U-matic
North America - Growth of a Continent Series
Color (J H)
Explores the close relationships between climate, soil, vegetation and humans. North America's natural and vegetation regions are described.
Geography - United States; Geography - World
Dist - TVOTAR **Prod** - TVOTAR 1980

Veggie lovers cookbook I 80 MIN
VHS
Color (H C G)
$39.95 purchase _ #VC100V
Features food authority Bert Greene who presents an informative guide to vegetable cookery while demonstrating a generous collection of recipes. Part one of two parts.
Home Economics
Dist - CAMV

Veggie lovers cookbook II 80 MIN
VHS
Color (H C G)
$39.95 purchase _ #VC300V
Features food authority Bert Greene who presents an informative guide to vegetable cookery while demonstrating a generous collection of recipes. Part two of two parts.
Home Economics
Dist - CAMV

Vehicle Interaction 21 MIN
U-matic / VHS
Right Way Series
Color
Tells how to apply mental and physical skills to negotiating intersections.
Health and Safety
Dist - PBS **Prod** - SCETV 1982

Vehicle Maintenance and Fluid Services 40 MIN
VHS
Color (H C A PRO)
$89.00 purchase _ #MC100; $95.00 purchase _ #MG5121V
Covers all of the basic inspections and service operations needed to keep a car running safely and dependably. Serves the needs of service station attendants, driver ed and 'powder puff' courses.
Industrial and Technical Education
Dist - AAVIM **Prod** - AAVIM 1990
CAMV

The Vehicle Maintenance Story 14 MIN
16mm
Color
LC 74-705905
Points out the value of good vehicle maintenance and the effort made by the post office to establish proper maintenance procedures.
Industrial and Technical Education; Social Science
Dist - USNAC **Prod** - USPOST

Vehicle Safety and Maintenance Checks 30 MIN
U-matic / VHS
Keep it Running Series
Color
Covers the procedures for performing an extensive vehicle safety and maintenance check.
Industrial and Technical Education
Dist - NETCHE **Prod** - NETCHE 1982

Vehicle Stop Tactics, Pt 1 20 MIN
U-matic / VHS / 16mm
Color
LC 81-700381
Shows safety procedures to be used when approaching a vehicle that has been required to pull off the road. Shows the safest position for the officer while writing a citation, use of emergency lights, occupant removal and arrest procedures.
Civics and Political Systems
Dist - CORF **Prod** - BRAVO

Vehicle Stop Tactics, Pt 2 20 MIN
16mm / U-matic / VHS
Color
LC 81-700381
Shows safety procedures to be used when approaching a vehicle that has been required to pull off the road. Shows the safest position for the officer while writing a citation, use of emergency lights, occupant removal and arrest procedures.
Civics and Political Systems
Dist - CORF **Prod** - BRAVO

Vehicle Under Attack - Officer Survival of Incendiary Ambush 15 MIN
16mm
Urban Crisis Series
Color
Discusses police ambush and the survival of incendiary attack. Alerts law enforcement to the possibility of firebomb ambush against their vehicles. Outlines procedures, methods and tactics recommended to combat this terrorist attack.
Civics and Political Systems; Health and Safety; Sociology
Dist - BROSEB **Prod** - CPECOF

Vehicles 10 MIN
VHS
Stop, look, listen series
Color; PAL (P I J)
Watches children counting passing traffic. Observes buses, a car transporter, oil tanker, milk truck, concrete mixer and various other vehicles. Shows that some vehicles have a picture outside indicating what they are carrying. Part of a series of films which start from some everyday observation and show more of what is happening, how and why. Builds vocabulary and encourages children to be more observant.
English Language; Social Science
Dist - VIEWTH

Vehicles 29 MIN
U-matic
Sketching techniques series; Lesson 27
Color (C A)
Concentrates on designing several kinds of vehicles, such as cars, skateboards and wagons. Explains some of the reasoning involved in the design of vehicles.
Fine Arts
Dist - CDTEL **Prod** - COAST

Vehicles 30 MIN
VHS / U-matic
Say it with sign series; Pt 28
Color (H C A) (AMERICAN SIGN)
Presents Lawrence Solow and Sharon Neumann Solow introducing American Sign Language used by the hearing - impaired. Emphasizes signs having to to do with vehicles.
Education
Dist - FI **Prod** - KNBCTV 1982

Vehicular Trauma 22 MIN
VHS / 16mm
(C)
$385.00 purchase _ #8671VI034
Illustrates, through actual scenes of automotive testing with dummies, how injuries can differ depending on the kind of impact.
Health and Safety
Dist - HSCIC **Prod** - HSCIC

A Veiled Revolution 26 MIN
16mm / U-matic / VHS
Women in the Middle East Series
Color
Discusses the reasons why Egypt, which was once among the most liberal of Middle Eastern countries in regards to women's rights, is now experiencing a return to traditional Islamic women's roles.
History - World; Religion and Philosophy; Sociology
Dist - ICARUS **Prod** - ICARUS 1982

Veins - the way to the heart 28 MIN
VHS
Human body - the heart and circulation - series
Color (J H G)
$89.95 purchase _ #UW4163
Shows how the veins and the lymph vessels return the waste - laden blood to the heart again and the potentially serious results if this return flow is disturbed. Illustrates various ways of dealing with the problem of varicose veins. Part of a 39 - part series featuring computer animation, medical photography, electron micrography, full - color drawings and diagrams and three - dimensional working models to cover the workings of the human body from head to toe and inside out.
Science - Natural
Dist - FOTH

Vejen 22 MIN
U-matic / VHS / 16mm
Color (J H A)
LC 77-713869
Presents Eastern principles of stoicism, meditation and impermanence by following a young Buddhist priest and his acolyte on their daily rounds.
Religion and Philosophy
Dist - CAROUF **Prod** - PHTC 1971

Vejen (the Path) 21 MIN
16mm
Color (DANISH)
A Danish language film. Describes the Buddhist religion with shots of Rangoon.
Foreign Language; Religion and Philosophy
Dist - STATNS **Prod** - STATNS 1969

Vela Program - Satellite Detection System 15 MIN
16mm
Color (H C A)
LC FIA65-495
Explains the purpose of the Vela Program. Describes the problems involved in developing satellites for detecting nuclear radiation. Illustrates the manufacturing and testing of detection systems and anticipates future developments of the Satellite Detection Program.
Civics and Political Systems; Science - Physical
Dist - USNAC **Prod** - USNRC 1964

Velars and Glottals 10 MIN
VHS / BETA
Speech Reading Materials Series
Color (A)
English Language
Dist - RMIBHF **Prod** - RMIBHF

Velasquez - Las Meninas 9 MIN
16mm / U-matic
Through Artists' Eyes Series
Color (H A)

$225.00 purchase, $45.00 rental
Views the work of Velasquez through the eyes of contemporary art historian Avigdor Arikha.
Fine Arts; Industrial and Technical Education
Dist - AFA **Prod** - ASDA 1986

Velazquez 15 MIN
U-matic / VHS / 16mm
Color (H C)
Shows major works of the artist at the Prado Museum.
Fine Arts
Dist - IFB **Prod** - IFB 1955

Velazquez 50 MIN
VHS / 16mm
Color (C H)
$159.00 purchase _ #EX2215
Portrays Spanish painter Velazquez. Documents his life and work and his friendship with King Philip IV, chronicled in his painting.
Fine Arts; History - World
Dist - FOTH

The Veldt 23 MIN
16mm / U-matic / VHS
Color (J)
LC 79-701715
Describes a futuristic house which can do housework, cook, and entertain. Tells how its occupants are increasingly disturbed by the images and sounds of the African veldt which appear on the playroom walls. Based on the short story The Veldt by Ray Bradbury.
Literature and Drama
Dist - BARR **Prod** - WILETS 1979

Velnio Nuotaka 78 MIN
VHS / U-matic
Color (LITHUANIAN)
A Lithuanian language version of the film The Devil's Bride.
Fine Arts; Foreign Language
Dist - IHF **Prod** - IHF

Velocity, Acceleration, Related Rates 20 MIN
VHS
Calculus Series
Color (H)
LC 90712920
Discusses velocity, acceleration and related rates. The 20th of 57 installments in the Calclulus Series.
Mathematics
Dist - GPN

Velocity and Rates
U-matic
Calculus Series
Color
Mathematics
Dist - MDCPB **Prod** - MDDE

Velocity and time - mass, momentum, energy - Parts 43 and 44 60 MIN
VHS / U-matic
Mechanical universe...and beyond - Part II series
Color (G)
$45.00, $29.95 purchase
Portrays Albert Einstein who was motivated to perfect the central ideas of physics, resulting in a new understanding of the meaning of space and time in Part 43. Reveals that the new meaning of space and time made it necessary to formulate a new mechanics - E = mc squared - in Part 44. Parts of a 52 - part series on the mechanics of the universe.
Science; Science - Physical
Dist - ANNCPB **Prod** - SCCON 1985

Velocity Distribution of Atoms in a Beam 16 MIN
16mm
College Physics Film Program Series
B&W (H C)
LC FIA68-1445
Describes an experiment determing the velocity distribution of the atoms in a beam of potassium atoms.
Science; Science - Physical
Dist - MLA **Prod** - UEVA 1968

Velocity Meters
Software / BETA
Fluid Flow Measurement Series
Color (PRO)
$600.00 - $1500.00 purchase _ #IDVEM
Focuses on velocity meters. Presents the difference between flow rate and velocity. Describes how several devices can be used to measure flow rate. Part of a four - part series on fluid flow measurement. Interactive training system includes course administrator guide, videodisc and computer software.
Industrial and Technical Education; Mathematics; Psychology
Dist - NUSTC **Prod** - NUSTC

The Velocity of gamma rays 16 MIN
VHS
Color; PAL (H)
Supports the Nuffield 'A' Level Physics Course to show that gamma radiation is electromagnetic. Demonstrates in an experiment that the velocity of gamma rays is the same as that of light or radio waves. The velocity of gamma rays, produced by bombarding a metal plate with cyclotron - generated deuterons, is measured directly in nanoseconds using a detector, amplifier and scaler.
Science - Physical
Dist - VIEWTH **Prod** - MULLRD

Velopharyngeal Function 20 MIN
U-matic
Color (J C)
Demonstrates velopharyngeal activity in two patients who have had surgical removal of a carcinoma located in the maxillary sinus and adjacent tissues. In one patient the entire hard palate was excised, but all musculature was left intact. The second patient had a portion of the hard palate removed but soft palate musculature was not disturbed. In both patients, the eye was removed, permitting a superior view of velopharyngeal activity during speech. The focus of the videotape is on the velopharyngeal mechanism during speech.
English Language; Health and Safety; Psychology
Dist - SDSC **Prod** - SDSC 1984

Velvet Roll Separator 3 MIN
16mm
Principles of Seed Processing Series
Color (H C A)
LC 77-701160
Combines animation and live action to illustrate the mechanism for separating smooth and rough seeds to separate containers. Shows the manner and degree of separation of a sample of mixed seed.
Agriculture; Science - Natural
Dist - IOWA **Prod** - EVERSL 1975

The Velveteen Rabbit 19 MIN
16mm
Color
LC 75-700164
Tells a story about nursery magic which causes a toy bunny to become real.
Literature and Drama
Dist - LSBPRO **Prod** - LSBPRO 1974

The Velveteen rabbit 30 MIN
VHS
Color (K P I J)
Presents an animated version of the Margery Williams story 'The Velveteen Rabbit.' Narrated by Meryl Streep. Music by George Winston.
Fine Arts; Literature and Drama
Dist - UILL
PELLER

The Velveteen rabbit 15 MIN
VHS
Color (K P I R)
$10.00 rental _ #36 - 84 - 1439
Shows how the Velveteen Rabbit learns to be 'real' through making friends. Suggests that humans become 'real' through their relationships as well.
Literature and Drama; Religion and Philosophy
Dist - APH **Prod** - BBF

Vena Cava Bonchovascular Triad 16 MIN
U-matic / VHS
Color (PRO)
Shows the vena cava bronchovascular triad.
Health and Safety
Dist - WFP **Prod** - WFP

Venceremitos 20 MIN
16mm
B&W (H C A)
$50 rental
Features interviews with American children at International Pioneer Camp at Varadero beach in Cuba, who spend three weeks with children from all over the world. Directed by Octavio Cortazar.
Sociology
Dist - CNEMAG

Venceremos 20 MIN
16mm
B&W
LC 74-702317
Examines the gap between the rich and poor sectors of Chilean society and presents a sequence on the 1970 elections in Chile.
Civics and Political Systems; Geography - World; Sociology
Dist - TRIFC **Prod** - CHASKP 1970

Vendons ces meubles 13 MIN
16mm
Les Francais chez vous series
B&W (I J H)
Foreign Language
Dist - CHLTN **Prod** - PEREN 1967

Vendor Certification and Rating 33 MIN
U-matic / VHS
Quality Control Series
Color
Describes plans used by manufacturing companies to evaluate the capabilities of vendors to produce product in conformance to delivery dates and quality requirements.
Business and Economics; Industrial and Technical Education
Dist - MIOT **Prod** - MIOT

Venecia Kaputt 1 MIN
16mm
B&W (G)
$10.00 rental
Utilizes scratching on film to erase an image of Venice in a production that lasts only six seconds long.
Fine Arts
Dist - CANCIN **Prod** - KRENKU 1968

Venereal Disease - the Hidden Epidemic 23 MIN
16mm / U-matic / VHS
Color (J H)
LC 72-702868
Traces the history of venereal diseases and attitudes toward them. Examines the two major venereal diseases - gonorrhea and syphilis. Describes the symptoms and demonstrates their cycles of appearance and disappearance. Identifies the early signs of syphilis and gonorrhea and tells of the importance of getting competent medical help promptly. Emphasizes prevention and what should be done to prevent the spread of venereal disease.
Health and Safety
Dist - EBEC **Prod** - EBEC 1972

Venereal disease - the hidden epidemic 30 MIN
U-matic / VHS
Family portrait - a study of contemporary lifestyles series
Color (C A)
Focuses on the recent rise in venereal diseases. Covers symptoms, tests, treatment and prevention.
Health and Safety
Dist - CDTEL **Prod** - SCCON

Venereal Disease - the Hidden Epidemic 23 MIN
U-matic / 8mm cartridge
Color (J H C) (SPANISH)
Provides a history of venereal diseases and attitudes toward them. Presents a clinical analysis of gonorrhea and syphilis, and illustrates how cases are diagnosed.
Foreign Language; Health and Safety
Dist - EBEC **Prod** - EBEC

Venereal Disease - Why do We Still have it 20 MIN
U-matic / VHS / 16mm
Color (J H A)
Introduces issues of personal values, behavior and personal decision - making as they apply to sexual behavior and the threat of catching a venereal disease. Demonstrated that penicillin and antibiotics can kill the bacteria that cause gonorrhea and syphillis. Shows how VD spreads, what the symptoms are and what the long - term effects of the untreated conditions can be.
Health and Safety; Sociology
Dist - PEREN **Prod** - WFP

The Venetian Twins 60 MIN
U-matic / VHS
Drama - play, performance, perception series; Dramatis personae
Color (H C A)
Explores methods of character development. Uses the play The Venetian Twins as an example.
Literature and Drama
Dist - FI **Prod** - BBCTV 1978

The Venetian twins 60 MIN
VHS
Color (H C G)
$119.00 purchase _ #DL309
Presents a wild, fast - paced farce of mistaken identity, with mixed pairs of lovers, blustering soldiers and clever servants by Carlo Goldini, based on commedia dell'arte stock characters. Includes a general discussion of commedia.
Fine Arts; History - World; Literature and Drama
Dist - INSIM **Prod** - BBC 1977

Venezia Museo All'Aperto 13 MIN
16mm / U-matic / VHS
Color (H C A) (ITALIAN)
An Italian - language version of the motion picture Venice. Features the city of Venice where boats, bridges, canals and campaniles are as prolific as sidewalks, streets and stoplights in other cities. Tours the city, including the Doge's Palace and the Piazza of St Mark's.
Foreign Language; Geography - World
Dist - IFB **Prod** - CINEVI 1975

Venezuela 25 MIN
U-matic / VHS
Color (H C A)
Documents the developing economy of Venezuela, which has been strengthened by oil sales, and discusses the accompanying problems.
Geography - World
Dist - JOU **Prod** - UPI

Venezuela 14 MIN
16mm / U-matic / VHS
Man and His World Series
Color (I J H)
LC 79-711291
Discusses Venezuela today as an extreme contrast between rich and poor. Depicts the struggle to nationalize the oil industry and shows the development of a varied industrial structure which has created more jobs and better living standards.
Business and Economics; Geography - World; Sociology
Dist - FI **Prod** - FI 1970

Venezuela - Children of the Island 26 MIN
U-matic / VHS
Growing Up Young Series
Color
Documents the life of a 13 - year - old barracuda fisherman on an island off the coast of Venezuela.
Geography - World; Sociology
Dist - FOTH **Prod** - FOTH

Venezuela - Children of the Street 26 MIN
VHS / U-matic
Growing Up Young Series
Color
Documents the life of a 12 - year - old newspaper vendor in Caracas, Venezuela.
Geography - World; Sociology
Dist - FOTH **Prod** - FOTH

Venezuela - Oil Builds a Nation 17 MIN
U-matic / VHS / 16mm
Color (I J H)
LC 72-703419
Portrays the rapid growth, industrialization and wealth of Venezuela, with emphasis upon the importance of the vast oil resources recently discovered. Studies the problems that this rapid growth has caused. Examines future of Latin America's first modern industrial nation.
Business and Economics; Geography - World; Social Science; Sociology
Dist - EBEC **Prod** - EBEC 1972

Venezuela - Petroleum Powered Economy 30 MIN
U-matic
Countries and Peoples Series
Color (H C)
Examines Venezuela from its colonial past to its present oil wealth.
Geography - World; History - World
Dist - TVOTAR **Prod** - TVOTAR 1982

Venezuela - Petroleum Powered Economy 29 MIN
VHS / 16mm
Countries and Peoples Series
Color (H C G)
$90.00 purchase _ #BPN128136
Discusses Venezuela's beginnings as a backwater Spanish colony and its progress to an independent. oil - producing nation. Talks about how it is enjoying a new level of commercial, industrial, and artistic growth, but its rural villages are being deserted.
Geography - World; History - World
Dist - RMIBHF **Prod** - RMIBHF

Venezuela - South American diving 30 MIN
VHS
Scuba World series
Color (G)
$24.90 purchase _ #0440
Visits the Caribbean diving areas off Venezuela. Examines soft coral which have grown to tremendous sizes. Experiences some wild and wooly diving.
Geography - World; Physical Education and Recreation
Dist - SEVVID

Venezuelan Adventure 30 MIN
16mm
Color (I)
LC 74-702022
Shows views of Caracas and interior Venezuela, and of the fishing and tiger hunting activities of General James H Doolittle and his companions.
Geography - World
Dist - MCDO **Prod** - DAC 1966

Venezuelan Equine Encephalitis - Epidemic in Colombia 16 MIN
16mm
Color (H C) (SPANISH)
LC 74-705908; 74-705906
Documents two simultaneous outbreaks of Venezuelan equine encephalitis affecting both equines and humans in Colombia, South America.
Foreign Language
Dist - USNAC **Prod** - USPHS 1968

Venezuelan prairie 26 MIN
16mm
Audubon wildlife theatre series
Color (P A)
LC 71-710209
Studies the savannah country of Central Venezuela, showing the blue - faced night herons, the scarlet ibis, vividly colored tropical birds and howler monkeys.
Geography - World; Science - Natural
Dist - AVEXP **Prod** - KEGPL 1970

Vengeance is Mine 140 MIN
VHS
Japan Film Collection from SVS Series
Color (G) (JAPANESE (ENGLISH SUBTITLES))
$59.95 purchase _ #K0678
Presents a movie produced in Japan. Features Shohei Imamura as director. Stars Ken Ogata, Muyumi Ogawa and Rentaro Mikuni.
Fine Arts; Geography - World
Dist - CHTSUI **Prod** - SONY

Vengeance is Mine 29 MIN
16mm
Color
LC 73-701034
Shows Les Merrill, a young black man, released from prison after spending three years for a crime he did not commit. Pictures him returning to the ghetto neighborhood in which he spent his boyhood, determined to find who framed him and seek vengeance. Presents his girl friend, Edith, trying to convince Les that vengeance belongs to God, and that Christians have faith that evil must be overcome with good.
Guidance and Counseling
Dist - FAMF **Prod** - FAMF 1971

Vengeance is mine 128 MIN
35mm / 16mm / VHS
Color (G) (JAPANESE WITH ENGLISH SUBTITLES)
$250.00, $300.00 rental
Portrays a pathological rapist - killer, based on a true story, fleeing a nationwide dragnet. Reveals that the killer, portrayed by Ken Ogata, finds temporary refuge in the home of a young woman. Directed by Shohei Imamura.
Fine Arts
Dist - KINOIC

Vengo a Ayudarla (I Come to Help You) Program Number 3 20 MIN
VHS / U-matic
Spanish for Health Professionals Series
Color (PRO)
Presents vocabulary pertaining to time - seasons, months, days, hours. Gives language commonly used in blood tests, x - ray exams and new patient orientation.
Foreign Language; Health and Safety
Dist - HSCIC **Prod** - HSCIC 1982

Veni - Puncture 9 MIN
U-matic / VHS
Medical Skills Films Series
Color (PRO)
Health and Safety
Dist - WFP **Prod** - WFP

Veni, Vidi, Vici 15 MIN
16mm
B&W (J H)
Discusses Caesar's campaigns in Gaul and his conquest of what is now France, Germany and Switzerland. Shows how skillfully used 'MODERN' methods of warfare against heroic warriors with primitive weapons.
History - World
Dist - FCE **Prod** - FCE 1961

Venice 13 MIN
16mm / U-matic / VHS
Color (H C A)
Features the city of Venice where boats, bridges, canals and campaniles are as prolific as sidewalks, streets and stoplights in other cities. Tours the city, including the Doge's Palace and the Piazza of St Mark's.
Geography - World
Dist - IFB **Prod** - CINEVI 1975

Venice, Etude, no 1 10 MIN
16mm
Color
Unites the color and motion of Venice. Juxtaposes the horizontal and frontal dimensions to introduce a third plane and create a total visual experience.
Geography - World
Dist - RADIM **Prod** - HUGOI

The Venice gondola pageant 30 MIN
VHS
World of festivals series
Color (J H C G)
$195.00 purchase
Travels to Venice, Italy, and the Regata Storica, a water pageant featuring standing oarsmen in period costumes reenacting a pirate raid. Includes races, parades of craft, concerts and exhibitions. Part of a 12 - part series on European festivals.
Geography - World; Social Science
Dist - LANDMK **Prod** - LANDMK 1988

Venice - the Sinking City 11 MIN
VHS / U-matic
Color (H C A)
Documents the damage caused by persistent flooding in Venice. Examines the work being done to prevent further disasters.
Geography - World
Dist - JOU **Prod** - UPI

Venice - Themes and Variations 20 MIN
16mm
Color (J)
Depicts life in Venice from the 14th century to the 20th century. Shows the works of such artists as Bellini, Guardi, Canaletto, Carpaccio, Whistler and Saul Steinberg.
Fine Arts; Geography - World; History - World
Dist - RADIM **Prod** - IVORYJ 1957

Venipuncture 9 MIN
U-matic / VHS
Color
Explains the principle of vein puncture. Demonstrates proper technique for obtaining venous sample.
Health and Safety; Science - Natural
Dist - MEDFAC **Prod** - MEDFAC 1978

Venipuncture 16 MIN
U-matic / VHS
Color (PRO)
Describes the various equipment and techniques for performing venipunctures including methods appropriate for drawing blood samples and for starting intravenous infusions. Discusses possible complications and their resolutions.
Health and Safety; Science
Dist - UMICHM **Prod** - UMICHM 1975

Venipuncture 10 MIN
U-matic
Emergency Techniques Series
Color (PRO)
Discusses venipuncture, a method of entering a vein for the purpose of injecting fluid or withdrawing blood. Demonstrates the procedure on a simulated arm and also in a clinical situation.
Health and Safety; Science
Dist - PRIMED **Prod** - PRIMED

Venipuncture 10 MIN
BETA / VHS / U-matic
Basic Clinical Laboratory Procedure Series
Color; Mono (C A)
Demonstratres the proper equipment, procedures, attention to critical details and efficient, accurate methods for proper collection of specimens.
Health and Safety; Science
Dist - UIOWA **Prod** - UIOWA 1985

Venipuncture and arterial puncture techniques 27 MIN
U-matic / VHS
Color (PRO C)
$395.00 purchase, $80.00 rental _ #C870 - VI - 021
Introduces nursing and medical students to the techniques of proper blood specimen collecting and handling. Describes in detail equipment and procedures required to perform both venipuncture and arterial puncture techniques. Discusses the roles of medical specialists in a blood collection laboratory and common patient complications such as fainting, difficult veins and sampling from an IV site. Presented by Carol Laputz, RN, Marsha Prater, Debra A M Buchele, RN, and Dr Roland Folse.
Health and Safety; Science; Science - Natural
Dist - HSCIC

Venipuncture for the purpose of obtaining a 20 MIN
blood specimen
VHS / U-matic
Color (C PRO)
$395.00 purchase, $80.00 rental _ #C851 - VI - 025
Covers selecting and preparing the materials and the site, performing the venipuncture, and methods of obtaining blood specimens and promoting coagulation. Presented by Dr Robert Potts.
Health and Safety; Science; Science - Natural
Dist - HSCIC

Venipuncture skills 27 MIN
VHS / U-matic
Color (PRO)
$250.00 purchase, $60.00 rental _ #4248S, #4248V
Provides clear and basic coverage of venipuncture skills for practicing and student nurses. Reviews the purposes, anatomical locations, dilation methods and equipment necessary for a venipuncture. Demonstrates catheter insertion for a continuous IV solution and a heparin lock. Illustrates venipuncture for drawing blood.
Health and Safety
Dist - AJN **Prod** - ICNE 1989

Venipuncture technique 22 MIN
BETA / VHS / U-matic
Medications administration and absorption series
Color (C PRO)
$280.00 purchase _ #613.5
Describes the various types of needles available and indications for use. Details in depth the procedures for insertion of various needles and catheters. Discusses complications from the insertion, the infusion and medications. Presents precautions to prevent such complications. Produced by the College of Nursing, Brigham Young University. Part of a six - part series on medications administration and absorption including five video programs and supporting software simulation.
Health and Safety
Dist - CONMED

Venison Sauce Piquante 29 MIN
Videoreel / VT2
Cookin' Cajun Series
Color
Features gourmet - humorist Justin Wilson showing ways to cook venison with various ingredients.
Geography - United States; Home Economics
Dist - PBS **Prod** - MAETEL

Venom 26 MIN
VHS / U-matic
Survival in nature series
Color (J H)
$275.00, $325.00 purchase, $50.00 rental
Informs that animals were using chemical weapons for both defensive and offensive maneuvers long before humankind. Distinguishes between 'poisonous' and 'venomous.' Features a wide range of potentially lethal creatures, from snakes and scorpions to poison dart frogs, salamanders and lionfish.
Science - Natural
Dist - NDIM **Prod** - SURVAN 1990

Venous Cannulation 6 MIN
VHS / U-matic
Color (PRO)
Presents three types of indwelling line assemblies preferred sites for cannulation, and a step - by - step analysis of the procedure.
Health and Safety; Psychology; Science - Natural
Dist - UWASH **Prod** - UWASH

Venous Cutdown 9 MIN
16mm
Medical Skills Library Series
Color
LC 73-702390
Demonstrates an approved medical procedure when entry into the circulatory system is necessary and percutaneous techniques are inadequate or inadvisable. Shows the preparation of the patient, reviews the necessary equipment and portrays the procedure in close - up detail.
Health and Safety; Science
Dist - SUTHLA **Prod** - ACEPHY 1972

Venous peripheral vascular disease 30 MIN
16mm
Directions for education in nursing via technology series
Color (PRO)
LC 77-703463
A revised version of the motion picture Nursing Responsibility In The Care Of The Patient With Venous Peripheral Vascular Disease. Discusses nursing care of the patient with venous peripheral vascular disease.
Health and Safety
Dist - WSUM **Prod** - DENT 1977

Ventilation 25 MIN
16mm
B&W (PRO)
LC 72-700754
Details the use of tools and the importance of their operations in rescue. Illustrates laddering and ventilating to accomplish the control and extinguishing of fires.
Health and Safety
Dist - FILCOM **Prod** - LACFD 1950

Ventilation 30 MIN
VHS
Firefighter I Video Series
Color (PRO G)
$115.00 purchase _ #35064
Covers principles of ventilation in fire suppression. Shows how to safely cut holes in roofs and floors, break glass and protect against backdraft explosion. Includes an instruction guide for review. Part of a video series on Firefighter I training codes to be used with complementing IFSTA manuals.
Health and Safety; Psychology; Social Science
Dist - OKSU **Prod** - OKSU

Ventilation 27 MIN
16mm
Color (PRO)
A training film showing basic ventilation practices to use in instructing recruit fire fighters. Shows use of forcible entry equipment, proper use of hose streams for ventilating and theory of fire spread. Includes practical demonstration and blackboard discussion of ventilating techniques.
Health and Safety; Science - Physical
Dist - FILCOM **Prod** - NFPA

Ventilation 30 MIN
U-matic / VHS
Color
Presents live footage covering the principles of ventilation in fire suppression. Shows how to cut holes in roofs and floors, break glass and protect against backdraft explosion.
Health and Safety; Science - Physical; Social Science
Dist - OKSU **Prod** - OKSU

Ventilation 56 MIN
U-matic / VHS
Color (PRO)
Shows effective fire emergency ventilation techniques for old apartments with extremely high occupancy. Describes ventilation training for use in old, multi - storied dwellings.
Health and Safety; Social Science
Dist - FILCOM **Prod** - LACFD

Ventilation 14 MIN
U-matic / Kit / VHS
Color (A IND)
$425 purchase, $60 one week rental
Explains what ventilation is, how to tell if a ventilation system is effective, and discusses the importance of maintenance. Describes basic design principles necessary to good ventilation. Divided into five parts.
Health and Safety
Dist - IFB

Ventilation procedures 17 MIN
VHS
Firefighter I series
Color (IND)
$130.00 purchase _ #35642
Presents one part of a 19 - part series that is the teaching companion for IFSTA's Essentials of Fire Fighting manual. Demonstrates procedures for performing six types of ventilation and the tools required. Shows the cause and effect of backdraft explosions and how to avoid backdraft in ventilation procedures. Presents procedures for negative - pressure and positive - pressure forced ventilation. Based on Chapter 7.
Health and Safety; Science - Physical; Social Science
Dist - OKSU **Prod** - ACCTRA

Ventilation Techniques in Lightweight Roofs 46 MIN
VHS / U-matic
Color (PRO)
Shows ventilation of lightweight roofs under fire conditions. Gives special tips for handling fires at large commercial installations, where unbraced plywood is often a problem for roof ventilation.
Health and Safety; Social Science
Dist - FILCOM **Prod** - LACFD

The Ventilator assisted patient preparing for home 25 MIN
U-matic / VHS
Color (PRO C)
$395.00 purchase, $80.00 rental _ #C910 - VI - 021
Offers a program to provide program coordinators, patient educators and other caregivers with a better understanding of the Ventilator Assisted Patient Education Program - VAPEP. Includes 400 page manual and a videocassette which provides a detailed look at VAPEP's six phases. Presented by Tony Hilton, RN, Loma Linda University Medical Center, California.
Business and Economics; Health and Safety; Science - Natural
Dist - HSCIC

Ventricular Aneurysm 15 MIN
VHS / U-matic
Color (PRO)
Shows ventricular aneurysm.
Health and Safety
Dist - WFP **Prod** - WFP

Ventricular Aneurysm Following Myocardial Infarction - Surgical Excision 12 MIN
16mm
Color (PRO)
LC FIA66-79
Shows step by step a method of surgical repair of massive left ventricular aneurysm on a 50 - year - old laborer who suffered a severe anterior myocardial infarction approximately three months prior to his admission.
Health and Safety
Dist - EATONL **Prod** - EATONL 1961

Ventricular Arrhythmias 39 MIN
U-matic
EKG Interpretation and Assessment Series
Color (PRO)
Teaches the criteria for the identification of common arrhythmias originating in the ventricles.
Science; Science - Natural
Dist - CSUS **Prod** - CSUS 1984

Ventricular arrhythmias in patients with congestive heart failure - mechanisms and therapeutic options - Volume 15
VHS / 8mm cartridge
Cardiology video journal series
Color (PRO)
#QDX - 22
Presents a free - loan program, part of a series on cardiology, which trains medical professionals. Contact distributor for details.
Health and Safety
Dist - WYAYLA **Prod** - WYAYLA

Ventricular Conduction Defects
VHS / U-matic
Interpretation of the Twelve Lead Electrocardiogram Series
Color (PRO)
Describes the anatomy of the ventricular conduction system. Shows how to determine the presence or absence of following elecrocardiographic abnormalities, alone or in combination, right bundle branch block, left bundle branch blocks left posterior hemiblock, and left anterior hemiblock.
Health and Safety; Science - Natural
Dist - BRA **Prod** - BRA

Ventricular Conduction Disturbances 53 MIN
VHS / U-matic
Electrocardiogram Series
Color (PRO)
Discusses right and left bundle branch blocks. Illustrates hemiblocks and the trifascicular system.
Health and Safety; Science; Science - Natural
Dist - HSCIC **Prod** - HSCIC 1982

Ventricular Defibrillation 9 MIN
U-matic / VHS
Medical Skills Films Series
Color (PRO)
Health and Safety
Dist - WFP **Prod** - WFP

Ventricular dysrhythmias and AV blocks - Part 3 28 MIN
VHS / U-matic
Basic dysrhythmia interpretation
Color (PRO)
$275.00 purchase, $60.00 rental _ #7541S, #7541V
Presents ventricular dysrhythmias and AV blocks, emphasizing rhythm recognition, patient assessment, associated nursing diagnoses and medical and nursing interventions. Part of three - parts on basic dysrhythmia interpretation.
Health and Safety
Dist - AJN **Prod** - HOSSN 1986

The Ventricular System 15 MIN
U-matic / VHS
Neurobiology Series
Color (PRO)
Using brain specimens and diagrams, identifies the parts of the brain's ventricular system. Discusses the flow of cerebrospinal fluid within the ventricles and related pathology when applicable.
Health and Safety; Science - Natural
Dist - HSCIC **Prod** - HSCIC

Ventura 1.1 introduction 68 MIN
VHS
Desktop publishing series
Color (J H C G)
$29.95 purchase _ #VP118V
Introduces concepts in Ventura 1.1. Allows viewer to see keyboard and monitor simultaneously so that students can see the result of every keystroke. Part of two parts on desktop publishing.

Computer Science
Dist - CAMV

Ventura, Charlene - a Leader of Women 30 MIN
U-matic
Decision Makers Series
Color
Presents Charlene Ventura, a leader of the feminist movement in Cincinnati. Discusses the movement and problems it faces.
Biography; History - World; Sociology
Dist - HRC **Prod** - OHC

Ventura Professional Extension
VHS
Color (G)
$199.95 purchase _ #VPE
Provides video PC software training in the Ventura Professional Extension. Includes training guide.
Computer Science
Dist - HALASI **Prod** - HALASI

Ventura Publisher 360 MIN
U-matic / VHS
(A PRO)
$395.00 purchase, $495.00 purchase
Covers basic and advanced functions of popular desktop publishing package. Teaches paragraph tagging, text editing and framing among other topics.
Computer Science
Dist - VIDEOT **Prod** - VIDEOT 1988

Ventura Publisher
VHS
Color (G)
$179.95 purchase _ #VP
Provides video PC software training in the Ventura Publisher. Includes training guide.
Computer Science
Dist - HALASI **Prod** - HALASI

Ventura publisher 2.0 - basic to intermediate
VHS / U-matic
Color (H C G)
$295.00, $295.00 purchase _ #02 - XVP
Covers the basic and sophisticated functions of the Ventura desktop publishing package. Teaches paragraph tagging, text editing and framing, graphic framing, drawing headers and footers, tabs and the full complement of printing operations. Includes videotape, guide and diskette. Published by VideoTutor.
Computer Science
Dist - VIDEOT

Ventura Techniques
VHS
Color (G)
$179.95 purchase _ #VPT
Provides video PC software training in Ventura Techniques. Includes training guide.
Computer Science
Dist - HALASI **Prod** - HALASI

Venture Doubly Blessed 28 MIN
16mm
Color (R)
LC 73-701573
Describes the Lay Institute for Evangelism, a program sponsored by the Campus Crusade for Christ. Reports on the program's success in evangelization in Haiti.
Religion and Philosophy
Dist - CCFC **Prod** - CCFC 1972

Venture into Nature 28 MIN
16mm
Color
LC 75-703252
Guides the viewer through scenes which show the beauty of nature, only to discover distressing scenes of the destruction of the natural environment. Designed to promote awareness of the environmental crises.
Guidance and Counseling; Science - Natural
Dist - MORALL **Prod** - MORALL 1974

Venture Read - Alongs Series
Building a new nation - venture read - alongs 55 MIN
Creatures that walk, swim or fly - venture read - alongs 66 MIN
Discovering the Past - Venture Read - Alongs 99 MIN
Famous Americans - venture read - alongs 88 MIN
Famous men and women - venture read - alongs 88 MIN
Geography - Venture Read - Alongs 99 MIN
Government of the people - venture read - alongs 55 MIN
Green and Growing - Venture Read - Alongs 66 MIN
Indians of America - Venture Read - Alongs 66 MIN
Keeping in Touch - Venture Read - Alongs 66 MIN
Let's Explore Our World - Venture Read - Alongs 99 MIN
Progress! Technology on the Move Set - Venture Read - Alongs 66 MIN
Space Station - Venture Read - Alongs 77 MIN
The World We Live in - Venture Read - Alongs 110 MIN
Dist - TROLA

The Venturer 30 MIN
U-matic / VHS / 16mm
Case Studies in Small Business Series
Color (C A)
Business and Economics
Dist - GPN **Prod** - UMA 1979

Venturing - Old and New Firms 54 MIN
VHS / U-matic
Technology, Innovation, and Industrial Development Series
Color
Business and Economics
Dist - MIOT **Prod** - MIOT

Venturing Out 15 MIN
U-matic
Through the Language Barrier Series
Color (PRO)
Focuses on the challenge that parents face to help their children understand various social activities and functions.
English Language; Psychology
Dist - ACCESS **Prod** - ACCESS 1980

Venturing - the entrepreneurial challenge series
Getting started - 2 30 MIN
The personal side - 12 30 MIN
Dist - VTETV

Venturing...the entrepreneurial challenge series
Presents a 13 - part series on the steps involved in starting and developing an entrepreneurial company. Includes the titles The Fire Within, Getting Started, Finding Financing, Up and Running, Marketing and Sales, Market and Product Expansion, Financing Growth, Managing Growth, The Human Challenge, Managing Adversity, Agricultural Entrepreneurs, The Personal Side, The Innovators. Viewers' guide available separately. Sponsored under a grant from the Farmers Home Administration to help small and rural businesses.
Agricultural entrepreneurs - 11 30 MIN
Financing growth - 7 30 MIN
Finding financing - 3 30 MIN
The Fire within - 1 30 MIN
The Human challenge - 9 30 MIN
The Innovators - 13 30 MIN
Managing adversity - 10 30 MIN
Managing growth - 8 30 MIN
Market and product expansion - 6 30 MIN
Marketing and sales - 5 30 MIN
Up and running - 4 30 MIN
Dist - VTETV **Prod** - VTETV 1980

Venus 31 MIN
16mm
Color (G)
$80.00 rental
Presents the myth of Venus - Aphrodite - Ishtar.
Fine Arts
Dist - CANCIN **Prod** - DEGRAS 1969

Venus and Mars and Company - the Art of Pompeii 45 MIN
Videoreel / VT2
Humanities Series Unit II - the World of Myth and Legend
Color
Literature and Drama
Dist - GPN **Prod** - WTTWTV

Venus and the Cat 10 MIN
16mm
Color (H C A) (ITALIAN)
LC 72-702042
Presents an animated version of the Aesop fable about a lonely man and a cat which Venus sends him as a gift.
Foreign Language; Literature and Drama
Dist - RADIM **Prod** - ZAGREB 1971

Vera 87 MIN
35mm / 16mm / VHS
Color (G) (PORTUGUESE WITH ENGLISH SUBTITLES)
$250.00, $300.00 rental
Portrays Vera, an 18 - year - old girl who has grown up in a home for unwanted children. Reveals that when she leaves the home, she believes that she is a man trapped in the body of a woman. Tormented by her sexual confusion, she meets Clara, a beautiful, independent woman who has had trouble with men. They fall in love - until Vera's possessiveness threatens their relationship and further confuses her feelings. Directed by Sergio Toledo.
Fine Arts; Sociology
Dist - KINOIC

Vera and the Law - toward a more Effective System of Justice 39 MIN
16mm
Color (H C A)
LC 75-702970
Examines the programs of the Vera Institute of Justice in working to reform the criminal justice system.
Civics and Political Systems; Sociology
Dist - KAROL **Prod** - FDF 1975

Vera Cruz 11 MIN
16mm
Color (I)
Depicts Fortin de las Flores, the peak of Orizaba and the beach of Mocambo. Shows the flower markets from which gardenias, camelias and orchids are shipped to all parts of the world.
Geography - World
Dist - AVED **Prod** - BARONA 1958

Vera Paints Ibiza in the Sun 20 MIN
16mm / U-matic / VHS
Color (J)
LC 73-700627
Visits the island of Ibiza off the coast of Spain with American textile designer, Vera Newmann. Shows how her sketch becomes a design for a textile print and how artists, technicians, chemists and craftsmen transmit Vera's design onto fabric.
Business and Economics; Fine Arts; Home Economics
Dist - LUF **Prod** - SCHLAT 1973

Verb mood and voice and problems verbs 18 MIN
VHS
Language construction company series
Color (H C G)
$50.00 purchase _ #LCC - 8
Assists students in improving their written and spoken English grammar skills. Bases all programs on a 'construction theme.' Includes review tests as an integral part of each lesson. Students may stop, start and repeat any part of the lesson. Visual cues are given for review purposes. Part of a 15 - part series.
English Language
Dist - INSTRU

Verb tenses - time matters 18 MIN
VHS
Language construction company series
Color (H C G)
$50.00 purchase _ #LCC - 7
Assists students in improving their written and spoken English grammar skills. Bases all programs on a 'construction theme.' Includes review tests as an integral part of each lesson. Students may stop, start and repeat any part of the lesson. Visual cues are given for review purposes. Part of a 15 - part series.
English Language
Dist - INSTRU

Verb - That's Where the Action is 3 MIN
U-matic / VHS
Grammar Rock Series
Color (P)
Shows how a little boy learns about the characteristics of verbs from a 'verb' playing the part of a super - hero.
English Language
Dist - GA **Prod** - ABCTV 1974

Verb 'to Be,' the - 2 30 MIN
VHS
English 101 - Ingles 101 Series
Color (H)
$125.00 purchase
Presents a series of thirty 30 - minute programs in basic English for native speakers of Spanish. Focuses on a specific topic in order to emphasize a particular grammatical point or set of idioms. English is used from the beginning as the primary language of instruction but Spanish translations are included to ensure understanding. Part 2 deals with present tense, past tense and idiomatic expressions.
English Language; Foreign Language
Dist - AITECH **Prod** - UPRICO 1988

Verb 'to Be,' the - Contractions and Negatives - 4 30 MIN
VHS
English 101 - Ingles 101 Series
Color (H)
$125.00 purchase
Presents a series of thirty 30 - minute programs in basic English for native speakers of Spanish. Focuses on a specific topic in order to emphasize a particular

grammatical point or set of idioms. English is used from the beginning as the primary language of instruction but Spanish translations are included to ensure understanding. Part 4 considers contractions, contractions with question words, negative sentences, negative contractions.
English Language; Foreign Language
Dist - AITECH **Prod** - UPRICO 1988

Verb 'to Be,' the - Interrogative Sentences - 3 30 MIN
VHS
English 101 - Ingles 101 Series
Color (H)
$125.00 purchase
Presents a series of thirty 30 - minute programs in basic English for native speakers of Spanish. Focuses on a specific topic in order to emphasize a particular grammatical point or set of idioms. English is used from the beginning as the primary language of instruction but Spanish translations are included to ensure understanding. Part 3 deals with the subject of the verb, simple yes - no questions, information questions, question intonation.
English Language; Foreign Language
Dist - AITECH **Prod** - UPRICO 1988

Verbal Ability, Analogies, Antonyms, Sentence Completion, Lesson 2
VHS / U-matic
GRE/Graduate Record Examination Series
Color (H A)
Education; English Language
Dist - COMEX **Prod** - COMEX

Verbal and Nonverbal Congruence 12 MIN
Videoreel / VT2
Interpersonal Competence, Unit 02 - Communication Series; Unit 2 - Communication
Color (C A)
Features a humanistic psychologist who, by analysis and examples, discusses verbal and nonverbal congruence in relation to effective communication.
Psychology
Dist - TELSTR **Prod** - MVNE 1973

Verbal Communication 28 MIN
U-matic / VHS / 16mm
Color (H C A) (SPANISH)
LC 82-700361;
Presents some of the reasons why effective communication is difficult, such as the ambiguity of language itself, the indirectness of speech and one's inner conflicts. Introduces processes which can be used to communicate more effectively by defusing arguments precipitated by inner conflict, by listening instead of just hearing and by using feedback to provide a two - way channel that both people can use to build on each other's ideas.
English Language
Dist - CRMP **Prod** - CRMP 1981
MGHT

Verbal communication in the trial 50 MIN
VHS
Effective communication in the courtroom series
Color (C PRO)
$100.00 purchase _ #ZCX01
Features University of Nevada professor Gordon Zimmerman in a discussion of courtroom verbal communication.
Civics and Political Systems; English Language
Dist - NITA **Prod** - NITA 1982

Verbal Communication in the Trial 50 MIN
VHS / U-matic
Effective Communication in the Courtroom Series
Color (PRO)
Covers matters common to all trial advocates, including avoidance of complicated language and finding the proper pace, volume and projection. Gives suggestions for solving problems that often interfere with effective communication.
Civics and Political Systems; Psychology; Social Science
Dist - ABACPE **Prod** - ABACPE

Verbal Communication - the Power of Words 30 MIN
16mm / U-matic / VHS
Color (H C A)
LC 81-706765
Uses animation, humorous vignettes and dramatized slices of organizational life to illustrate the four critical parts of every verbal exchange - the speaker, the language used, the atmosphere and the listener.
Psychology
Dist - CRMP **Prod** - CRMP 1981

Verbal Interventions for Violent Behaavior - Words, Away from Violence 37 MIN
VHS / 16mm
(C)
$385.00 purchase _ #861VI049
Teaches the nurse to recognize potentially violent patients and develop verbal intervention skills to deal with them.
Health and Safety
Dist - HSCIC **Prod** - HSCIC 1989

Verbal Judo 25 MIN
U-matic / VHS
Color (C)
$375 purchase _ #9861
Presents three training modules, each on their own videocassette. Leads officers through a variety of situations in which verbal skills are needed.
English Language; Guidance and Counseling; Psychology
Dist - AIMS **Prod** - AIMS 1985

Verbal judo series
Diffusing aggressive behavior 25 MIN
Words as Force Option 25 MIN
Working with the Public 25 MIN
Dist - AIMS

Verbal problems and introduction to trigonometry 43 MIN
VHS
Algebra series
Color (G)
$29.95 purchase _ #6892
Uses careful explanations and repeated examples to teach algebra. Fifth in a series of five videos.
Mathematics
Dist - ESPNTV **Prod** - ESPNTV

Verbal problems and introduction to trigonometry - Part 5 43 MIN
VHS
Math tutor series
Color (G)
$29.95 purchase
Uses live action and computer graphics to help in the review of verbal problems and an introduction to trigonometry.
Mathematics
Dist - PBS **Prod** - WNETTV

Verbal reasoning - analogies
VHS
Test taking - SAT I series
Color (H A)
$49.95 purchase _ #VA847V-G
Helps students study for the SAT scholastic aptitude test. Uses a test-taking instructor to guide viewer. Outlines what to expect on the test, how to prepare, and tips to getting a higher score. Each program 120-160 minutes in length. Part of a five-part series.
Education; English Language
Dist - CAMV

Verbal reasoning - critical reading
VHS
Test taking - SAT I series
Color (H A)
$49.95 purchase _ #VA839V-G
Helps students study for the SAT scholastic aptitude test. Uses a test-taking instructor to guide viewer. Outlines what to expect on the test, how to prepare, and tips to getting a higher score. Each program 120-160 minutes in length. Part of a five-part series.
Education; English Language
Dist - CAMV

Verbal reasoning - sentence completions
VHS
Test taking - SAT I series
Color (H A)
$49.95 purchase _ #VA855V-G
Helps students study for the SAT scholastic aptitude test. Uses a test-taking instructor to guide viewer. Outlines what to expect on the test, how to prepare, and tips to getting a higher score. Each program 120-160 minutes in length. Part of a five-part series.
Education; English Language
Dist - CAMV

Verbal review for the A C T
VHS / U-matic
Standardized video exam review series
(H C T)
$39.95 _ #VA220V
Shows effective strategies to use in taking the ACT exam. Includes study guide.
Education
Dist - CAMV **Prod** - CAMV

Verbal review for the A C T 120 MIN
VHS
Test preparation video series
Color (H G A)
$39.95 purchase _ #VAI112
Features experienced teachers who guide students through verbal review courses for the ACT. Includes tips, 'insider' test taking strategies and confidence building hints. Stresses problem solving.
Education; English Language; Psychology
Dist - CADESF **Prod** - CADESF

Verbal review for the G R E
VHS
Standardized video exam review series
Color (H C A)
$39.95 purchase _ #VA620V
Presents a video review of verbal skills for the G R E graduate school admissions test. Includes a study guide.
Education
Dist - CAMV

Verbal Review for the GED 120 MINUTES
VHS / 16mm
Test Preparation Video Series
Color (H)
$39.95 _ VAI 102
Reviews verbal skills for GED test takers. Testing strategies and problem solving techniques are given.
Education; Psychology
Dist - CADESF **Prod** - CADESF

Verbal review for the GMAT
U-matic / VHS
Standardized video exam review series
(H T)
$39.95 _ #VA720V
Shows effective strategies to use in taking the GMAT. Includes study guide.
Education
Dist - CAMV **Prod** - CAMV

Verbal review for the S A T - P S A T
U-matic / VHS
Standardized video exam review series
(H C A)
$39.95 _ #VA120V
Shows effective strategies to use when taking the SAT and PSAT exams. Includes study guide.
Education
Dist - CAMV **Prod** - CAMV

Verbal Review for the SAT - PSAT 120 MINUTES
VHS / 16mm
Test Preparation Video Series
Color (H)
$39.95 _ VAI 106
Reviews verbal skills for SAT and PSAT test takers. Testing strategies and problem solving techniques are given.
Education; Psychology
Dist - CADESF **Prod** - CADESF

Verbal Review, Tape 1 45 MIN
VHS / U-matic
S A T / A C T Examination Video Review Series
Color (H A)
Introduces the verbal section of the Scholoastic Aptitude Test. Covers vocabulary, contextual clues and word analysis questions found on the SAT/ACT exam.
Education; English Language
Dist - COMEX **Prod** - COMEX

Verbal Review, Tape 2 45 MIN
U-matic / VHS
S A T / A C T Examination Video Review Series
Color (H A)
Focuses on a review of etymology, synonyms and antonyms in preparation for taking the SAT/ACT exam.
Education; English Language
Dist - COMEX **Prod** - COMEX

Verbal Review, Tape 3 45 MIN
U-matic / VHS
S A T / A C T Examination Video Review Series
Color (H A)
Focuses on analogies as presented in the SAT/ACT examination.
Education; English Language
Dist - COMEX **Prod** - COMEX

Verbal Review, Tape 4 45 MIN
VHS / U-matic
S A T / A C T Examination Video Review Series
Color (H A)
Focuses on sentence completion and reading skills as presented in the SAT/ACT exam.
Education; English Language
Dist - COMEX **Prod** - COMEX

Verbal Review, Tape 5 45 MIN
U-matic / VHS
S A T / A C T Examination Video Review Series
Color (H A)
Focuses on reading speed and finding the main ideas as they apply to the SAT/ACT exam.
Education; English Language
Dist - COMEX **Prod** - COMEX

Verbal Review, Tape 6 45 MIN
U-matic / VHS
S A T / A C T Examination Video Review Series
Color (H A)
Focuses on how to approach a reading comprehension question on the SAT/ACT examination.
Education; English Language
Dist - COMEX **Prod** - COMEX

Verbal Review, Tape 7 45 MIN
VHS / U-matic
S A T / A C T Examination Video Review Series
Color (H A)
Focuses on levels of usage, subject - verb agreement and parts of speech as tested on the SAT/ACT examination.
Education; English Language
Dist - COMEX **Prod** - COMEX

Verbal Review, Tape 8 45 MIN
VHS / U-matic
S A T / A C T Examination Video Review Series
Color (H A)
Focuses on irregular verbs and word pairs. Includes sample questions from the SAT/ACT examination.
Education; English Language
Dist - COMEX **Prod** - COMEX

Verbalizing generalizations in the classroom 20 MIN
16mm
Teaching high school mathematics - first course series; No 25
B&W (T)
Mathematics
Dist - MLA **Prod** - UICSM 1967

Verbs 15 MIN
VHS
Planet Pylon Series
Color (I)
LC 90712897
Uses character Commander Wordstalker from the Space Station Readstar to develop language arts skills. Studies verbs. Includes a worksheet the student can work on with help from series characters. Intended for third grade audience.
Education; English Language
Dist - GPN

Verbs 8 MIN
16mm / U-matic / VHS
Basic Grammar Series
Color (I)
LC 81-700755
Examines the functions of verbs within simple English sentences.
English Language
Dist - AIMS **Prod** - LEVYL 1981

Verbs and Adverbs 9 MIN
16mm / U-matic / VHS
Wizard of Words Series
Color (P I)
Points out verbs and illustrates ways in which adding adverbs makes the verbs more expressive.
English Language
Dist - MGHT **Prod** - MGHT 1976

Verbs - Being, Action, Linking 11 MIN
VHS / BETA
English and Speech Series
Color
English Language
Dist - RMIBHF **Prod** - RMIBHF

Verbs - being and doing 18 MIN
VHS
Language construction company series
Color (H C G)
$50.00 purchase _ #LCC - 6
Assists students in improving their written and spoken English grammar skills. Bases all programs on a 'construction theme.' Includes review tests as an integral part of each lesson. Students may stop, start and repeat any part of the lesson. Visual cues are given for review purposes. Part of a 15 - part series.
English Language
Dist - INSTRU

Verbs in Sentences 14 MIN
U-matic / VHS / 16mm
Grammar Skills Series
Color (P I)
LC 81-700387
Shows how a verb is an action word that performs important jobs in sentences. Discusses their forms, their relation to nouns and their uses.
English Language
Dist - JOU **Prod** - GLDWER 1981

Verdi - La Traviata
VHS
Color (G)
$49.98 purchase _ #SON48353V - F
Presents Verdi's opera as produced at La Scala and led by Riccardo Muti. Stars Tiziana Fabbricini. Includes two videocassettes.
Fine Arts
Dist - CAMV

Verdi - Otello 121 MIN
VHS
Color (G)
$39.95 purchase _ #VU1405V - F
Presents Verdi's tragic opera involving Othello, Desdemona and Iago as produced by Felsenstein and sung in German.
Fine Arts
Dist - CAMV

Verdi - Rigoletto 90 MIN
VHS
Color (G)
$39.95 purchase _ #VU1403V - F
Presents Verdi's opera telling the story of a hunchbacked jester and his daughter. Sung in Italian with dialog dubbed in English. Features Gobbi and Del Monaco.
Fine Arts
Dist - CAMV

Verdict for Tomorrow 28 MIN
16mm
Color; B&W (H C A)
An account of the Eichmann trial, based on footage gathered during the Eichmann trial in Jerusalem, utilizes the trial as a reminder of Nazism and of persecution of the Jews rather than as a dated legal presentation. Narrated by Lowell Thomas.
Civics and Political Systems; Psychology; Religion and Philosophy; Sociology
Dist - ADL

Verdi's Rigoletto at Verona 115 MIN
VHS / U-matic
Color
Fine Arts
Dist - MSTVIS **Prod** - MSTVIS

Verdi's Rigoletto at Verona 115 MIN
VHS
Color (G) (ITALIAN)
$74.95 purchase
Presents a production of 'Rigoletto' by Verdi, presented at the Roman amphitheater in Verona, Italy.
Fine Arts
Dist - PBS **Prod** - WNETTV

Verdun 29 MIN
16mm
Legacy Series
B&W (J)
LC 74-707211
Shows scenes of the battle of Verdun, describing the German plan of attack and explaining the long - lasting effect the battle had on the French nation.
History - World
Dist - IU **Prod** - NET 1965

Vergette Making a Pot 9 MIN
16mm / U-matic / VHS
Color (J H C)
LC FIA67-675
Portrays the artistry of the potter and shows him at work, throwing, trimming, glazing and firing.
Fine Arts
Dist - AIMS **Prod** - SILLU 1966

Vergissmeinnicht 104 MIN
16mm
Color (GERMAN (ENGLISH SUBTITLES))
Follows the love affairs of a woman in Italy.
Foreign Language; Sociology
Dist - WSTGLC **Prod** - WSTGLC 1958

Verlorenes Leben 90 MIN
16mm
B&W (GERMAN (ENGLISH SUBTITLES))
A German language motion picture with English subtitles. Focuses on the question of justice, guilt and atonement. Portrays the 'lost life' of two individuals, one being executed for the crime he committed, the other having to live with an everlasting feeling of guilt for his part in the conviction.
Civics and Political Systems; Foreign Language; Sociology
Dist - WSTGLC **Prod** - WSTGLC 1977

Vermeer 40 MIN
VHS
Three painters 2 series
Color (A)
PdS65 purchase _ Available only in the UK
Explores the work of the painter Vermeer, hosted by painter and critic Sir Lawrence Gowing. Based on the concept that Vermeer's work represents a distinct stage in the development of European painting between the Renaissance and the present day. Discusses the historical and social backgrounds against which the artist worked, but concentrates on examining a small number of canvases. Includes views of the places which particularly inspired the artist.
Fine Arts
Dist - BBCENE

Vermeer - Woman Holding a Balance 13 MIN
16mm / U-matic
Through Artists' Eyes Series
Color (H A)
$275.00 purchase, $50.00 rental
Views the work of Vermeer through the eyes of contemporary art historian Avigdor Arikha.
Industrial and Technical Education
Dist - AFA **Prod** - ASDA 1986

Vermilion Editions - Right to print 55 MIN
VHS / U-matic
Color (H C A)
$49.95, $150.00
Highlights the work of Vermilion Editions and master printer Steven Andersen in the creative process involved in bringing art to paper. Shows painters Sam Gilliam and T L Solien working with the printers and interviews Harmony Hammond, Red Grooms and Arakawa about their experiences.
Fine Arts; Industrial and Technical Education
Dist - ARTSAM

Vermilonectomy 7 MIN
16mm
Color (PRO)
LC 74-705910
Demonstrates an operation to correct a recurring lesion on the lower lip by removing the lip mucosa.
Health and Safety; Science
Dist - USNAC **Prod** - USA 1973

Vermont 60 MIN
VHS
Portrait of America series
Color (J H C G)
$99.95 purchase _ #AMB45V
Visits Vermont. Offers extensive research into the state's history. Films key locations and presents segments on its history, government, education, folklore, science, journalism, sociology, industry, agriculture and business. Shows what is unique about Vermont and what is distinctive about its regional culture and how it got to be that way. Includes teacher study guides. Part of a 50 - part series.
Geography - United States; History - United States
Dist - CAMV

Vernier Caliper 13 MIN
U-matic / VHS
Metalworking - Precision Measuring Series
Color (A)
Shows main parts of, how to read in both inches and metric, take inside and outside measurements, and how to test measurements with a vernier caliper.
Industrial and Technical Education
Dist - VISIN **Prod** - VISIN

Vernier Height Gage 13 MIN
VHS / U-matic
Metalworking - Precision Measuring Series
Color (A)
Shows main parts of Vernier height gage, Vernier principle, how to read it in both inches and metric, its use for layout and inspection, and the test on reading.
Industrial and Technical Education
Dist - VISIN **Prod** - VISIN

Vernier Scale and Vernier Caliper 15 MIN
VHS / U-matic
Machining and the Operation of Machine Tools, Module 1 - Basic 'Machine technology Series
Color (IND)
Includes inside, outside and dial calipers.
Industrial and Technical Education
Dist - LEIKID **Prod** - LEIKID

Vernier Scale and Vernier Caliper
U-matic / VHS
Basic Machine Technology Series
Color (SPANISH)
Industrial and Technical Education; Mathematics
Dist - VTRI **Prod** - VTRI

Vernier Scale and Vernier Caliper (Inside, Outside, and Dial Calipers) 15 MIN
U-matic / VHS
Machine Technology II - Engine Lathe Accessories Series
Color
Health and Safety; Industrial and Technical Education
Dist - CAMB **Prod** - CAMB

Veronica 27 MIN
16mm
Jason Films Portrait Series
Color (J H C)
LC 75-705709
A cinema verite portrait of Veronica Glover, a black teenager who is president of her predominately white high school in New Haven, Conn, showing her inner struggle to maintain her identity under stress.
Guidance and Counseling; History - United States; Psychology; Sociology
Dist - JASON **Prod** - JASON 1970

Veronica 14 MIN
U-matic / VHS / 16mm
Color (I J) (POLISH)
Introduces Veronica, a girl of Polish descent who lives in a multiethnic neighborhood in Toronto, Canada. Shows her learning traditional Polish dances at school and maintaining a strong affection for her native roots.
History - World; Sociology
Dist - MEDIAG **Prod** - NFBC 1978

Veronica 4 Rose 45 MIN
16mm / VHS
Color (G)
$195.00 purchase, $125.00, $90.00 rental
Features teenage girls from Newcastle, Liverpool and London, England, who talk about what it means to be young and lesbian in a culture obsessed with wedding bells and white dresses. Shows that these teens share the same problems as others in their age group - dealing with a newfound sexuality, their parents, peer pressure and school.
Fine Arts; Psychology; Sociology
Dist - WMEN **Prod** - MELCH 1985

Vers Des Temps Nouveaux - toward New Times 52 MIN
16mm
Le Temp Des Cathedrales Series
Color
Explores the importance of a realistic view of death, cadavers and funeral ceremonies during the middle ages in Western Europe.
History - World; Religion and Philosophy
Dist - FACSEA **Prod** - FACSEA 1979

Vers Notre Deuxieme Siecle 30 MIN
16mm
Color (H C) (FRENCH)
A French version of 'THE QUALITY OF A NATION.' Celebrates Canada's 100th anniversary of confederation.
Foreign Language
Dist - CFI **Prod** - CRAF

VersaCAD explained
VHS
Color (H A)
$479.00 purchase _ #BXD20XSV; $479.00 purchase _ #D20
Presents a comprehensive guide to VersaCAD software. Considers subjects including object construction, modify and inquiry options, working parameters, and more. Consists of six videocassettes and a study guide.
Computer Science; Industrial and Technical Education
Dist - CAMV
BERGL

Versailles 55 MIN
VHS
Treasures of France on Video Series
Color (G)
$34.50 purchase _ #V72171
Displays the beauty and unique character of the famed palace of French kings.
Geography - World
Dist - NORTNJ

A Versailles - at Versailles 15 MIN
16mm
Toute la bande series; No 10
Color (H) (FRENCH)
LC 79-715491
A French language film. Presents a tour around Versailles taken by Caroline and Elisabeth. Includes the great ornamental fountains, gardens and Marie Antoinette's model farm.
Foreign Language
Dist - SBS **Prod** - SBS 1970

Versailles - Le Petit Trianon and Louis XV 26 MIN
U-matic / VHS
Castles of france series
Color (C) (FRENCH (ENGLISH SUBTITLES))
$249.00, $149.00 purchase _ #AD - 1508
Focuses on Le Petit Trianon, built in 1751 by Louis XV. Reveals that Louis XVI later gave the castle and its gardens to Marie Antoinette. Part of a six - part series on castles of France. In French with English subtitles.
Civics and Political Systems; Fine Arts; Foreign Language; Geography - World; History - World
Dist - FOTH **Prod** - FOTH

Versailles - the Lost Peace 26 MIN
16mm / U-matic / VHS
Between the Wars Series
Color (H C)
Shows how President Woodrow Wilson's idealistic hopes for world peace clashed at Versailles with the harsh old - world 'real - politik' of Europe, which wanted to punish Germany. Explains that the resultant punitive treaty sowed the seeds of World War II.
Civics and Political Systems; History - United States; History - World
Dist - FI **Prod** - LNDBRG 1978

Versailles - the lost peace and return to isolationism - Volume 1
VHS
Between the wars - 1918 - 1941 series
Color (H C A)
$19.95 purchase
Reviews part of the history of the years between World War I and World War II. Focuses on the events of Versailles and the growth of isolationism worldwide. Includes newsreels, soundtracks, and archival footage of the period. Hosted and narrated by Eric Sevareid.
History - World
Dist - PBS **Prod** - WNETTV

The Versatile machine 25 MIN
U-matic / VHS / 16mm
Making the most of the micro series; Episode 1
Color (H C A)
Introduces Richard Gomme, a victim of cerebral palsy whose life has been transformed by the addition of a microcomputer to his home. Describes all the things he is able to do despite the severity of his handicap.
Mathematics
Dist - FI **Prod** - BBCTV 1983

Versatility and the Variety of Weaves Possible with the Four - Harness Loom are 29 MIN
U-matic
Your Weekly Weaver Series
Color
Demonstrates the variety of weaves possible with the four - harness loom.
Fine Arts
Dist - PBS **Prod** - GAEDTN

Verse Person Singular 60 MIN
U-matic / VHS
Color (H C A)
LC 84-706096
Presents Richard Kiley performing some of his favorite first - person poems, including those by Lewis Carroll and some by Edgar Allen Poe.
Literature and Drama
Dist - FI **Prod** - FI 1984

Vertebral artery surgery series
Carotid distal vertebral artery bypass for carotid occlusion 10 MIN
Dist - BFLODY

Vertebrate series
Birds 14 MIN
Fish 14 MIN
Reptiles 14 MIN
Dist - CORF
VIEWTH

Vertebrate series
Amphibians 14 MIN
Mammals 14 MIN
Dist - VIEWTH

Vertebrates 15 MIN
VHS / 16mm
Challenge Series
Color (I)
$125.00 purchase, $25.00 rental
Reviews the characteristics of the five groups of vertebrate animals. Explains the concept of heredity.
Science; Science - Natural; Sociology
Dist - AITECH **Prod** - WDCNTV 1987

Vertebrates and Invertebrates in the Sea 20 MIN
Videoreel / VT2
Science Room Series
B&W (I)
Science - Natural; Science - Physical
Dist - GPN **Prod** - MCETV

Vertebrates - Escaping Enemies, Protection and Adaptations 20 MIN
Videoreel / VT2
Exploring with Science, Unit III - Animals Series
Color (I)
Science - Natural
Dist - GPN **Prod** - MPATI

Vertebrates - fish 15 MIN
U-matic / VHS
Discovering series; Unit 1 - Vertebrate animals
Color
LC 79-706333
Discusses the classification of various kinds of fish, explaining that scientists group animals according to characteristics such as appearance, behavior and habitat.
Science - Natural
Dist - AITECH **Prod** - WDCNTV 1978

Vertebrates - Securing Food, Food Getting and Adaptations 20 MIN
Videoreel / VT2
Exploring with Science, Unit III - Animals Series
Color (I)
Science - Natural
Dist - GPN **Prod** - MPATI

Vertebrates series
Amphibians 14 MIN
Mammals 14 MIN
Dist - CORF

The Vertebrates - this was the Beginning, Pt 2 11 MIN
U-matic / VHS / 16mm
Color (J H C)
Provides a visual catalog in which vertebrates are grouped according to common characteristics and evolutionary sequence.
Science - Natural
Dist - IFB **Prod** - NFBC

Vertical and Horizontal Asymptotes 30 MIN
VHS
Mathematics Series
Color (J)
LC 90713155
Discusses vertical and horizontal asymptotes. The 86th of 157 installments of the Mathematics Series.
Mathematics
Dist - GPN

Vertical and horizontal asymptotes 30 MIN
VHS
College algebra series
Color (C)
$125.00 purchase _ #4024
Explains vertical and horizontal asymptotes. Part of a 31 - part series on college algebra.
Mathematics
Dist - LANDMK **Prod** - LANDMK

Vertical and Overhead Butt Welds with Filler Rod
VHS / U-matic
Oxyacetylene Welding - Spanish Series
Color (SPANISH)
Foreign Language; Industrial and Technical Education
Dist - VTRI **Prod** - VTRI

Vertical and Overhead Welding 10 MIN
U-matic / VHS / 16mm
Welding Series
Color
LC 74-701450
Demonstrates mig welding techniques. Shows how to make vertical fillet and prepared butt welds and overhead fillet and prepared butt welds.
Industrial and Technical Education
Dist - FI **Prod** - UCC 1972

Vertical Bandsaws - Parts and Accessories
U-matic / VHS
Basic Machine Technology Series
Color (SPANISH)
Industrial and Technical Education
Dist - VTRI **Prod** - VTRI

Vertical down fillet 6 MIN
BETA / VHS
Welding training - comprehensive - basic shielded metal arc welding series
Color (IND)
Industrial and Technical Education; Psychology
Dist - RMIBHF **Prod** - RMIBHF

Vertical File 20 MIN
U-matic
Access Series
Color (T)
LC 76-706263
Presents information about the purposes and structure of the vertical file with emphasis on the type of materials to include in the file, their purpose and access to them.
Education
Dist - USNAC **Prod** - UDEN 1976

Vertical fillet weld E7018 electrode 9 MIN
BETA / VHS
Arc welding and M I G welding series
Color (IND)
Industrial and Technical Education; Psychology
Dist - RMIBHF **Prod** - RMIBHF

Vertical Flap Ureteropelvioplasty 20 MIN
16mm
Surgical Correction of Hydronephrosis, Pt 1 - Non - Dismembering 'Procedures Series
Color
LC 75-702259
Depicts a patient with a very definite extrarenal type of hydronephrosis. Explains that the pelvis was not atonic and maintained an active musculature and that the obstruction was at the ureteropelvic juncture. Describes the surgical indications for this operation.
Science
Dist - EATONL **Prod** - EATONL 1968

The Vertical Milling Machine Explained 81 MIN
VHS / 35mm strip
(H A IND)
#512XV7
Introduces the parts, accessories and operations of the Bridgeport series one vertical milling machine. Includes basic parts, setting up, accessories and work samples, the rotary table explained, additional accessories, and the digital readout system (6 tapes). Prerequisites required. Includes a Study Guide.
Education; Industrial and Technical Education; Sociology
Dist - BERGL

Vertical practices - half slave, half free 44 MIN
U-matic / VHS
Antitrust and economics series
Color (PRO)
Discusses the economics of vertical restraints, including resale price maintenance.
Business and Economics
Dist - ABACPE **Prod** - ABACPE

Vertical Relation of Occlusion by the Patient's Neuromuscular Perception 14 MIN
16mm
Color (PRO)
LC 77-700477
Shows how the vertical dimension is recorded with intraoral hearing plates using the patient's memory pattern and neuromuscular perception. Follows procedures for recognizing mandibular positions which are both too high and too low, from which extreme alterations in height are made and an occlusal vertical position compatible with the neuromuscular physiology is arrived at.
Psychology; Science
Dist - USNAC **Prod** - USVA 1977

Vertical Roll 20 MIN
VHS / U-matic
B&W
Presents repetitive, spatially and rhythmically disorienting movement of the rolling video signal.
Fine Arts
Dist - KITCHN **Prod** - KITCHN

Vertical up butt weld 8 MIN
VHS / BETA
Welding training - comprehensive - advanced shielded metal arc welding series
Color (IND)
Industrial and Technical Education; Psychology
Dist - RMIBHF **Prod** - RMIBHF

Vertical up fillet weld 8 MIN
BETA / VHS
Welding training - comprehensive - advanced shielded metal arc welding series
Color (IND)
Industrial and Technical Education; Psychology
Dist - RMIBHF **Prod** - RMIBHF

Vertical Vowels and Lingua - Dentals 10 MIN
BETA / VHS
Speech Reading Materials Series
Color (A)
English Language
Dist - RMIBHF **Prod** - RMIBHF

Vertigo 12 MIN
VHS
Color (PRO A)
$250.00 purchase _ #OT - 13
Explains the problem of vertigo for patients and their families. Explains symptoms, causes, evaluation, medical and surgical treatment options and risks. Uses state - of - the - art animation to depict the anatomy. For use in the practicing otolaryngologist's office and helpful to hospital patient educators or clinical staff.
Science - Natural
Dist - MIFE **Prod** - MIFE 1992

Vertigo 128 MIN
VHS
Color (G)
$59.95 purchase _ #S00913
Presents Alfred Hitchcock's tale of a San Francisco retired police officer who is afraid of heights. Shows how the man falls in love with a woman he is hired to shadow. Stars James Stewart, Kim Novak, and Barbara Bel Geddes.
Fine Arts
Dist - UILL

Vertigo - a Question of Balance
U-matic / VHS
Color (ARABIC)
Differentiates true vertigo from other forms of dizziness. Explains how it is almost always a result of some inner ear disorder. Discusses the different causes of vertigo.
Science - Natural
Dist - MIFE **Prod** - MIFE

Vertigo - Differential Diagnosis 25 MIN
16mm
B&W (PRO)
LC FIA68-858
Demonstrates procedures for performing an examination of the patient with vertigo. Shows the onset of vertigo with symptoms of dizziness, loss of balance, and tinnitus. Demonstrates the Romberg and Gait tests for balance and the optokinetic, positional, and caloric tests for the measurement of nystagmus.
Health and Safety
Dist - AMEDA **Prod** - SKF 1959

Very Basic Economics 18 MIN
16mm / U-matic / VHS
Color (H C A)
Presents a basic economics lesson regarding supply and demand, specialization, division of labor, competition, price mechanism, GNP, and inflation.
Business and Economics
Dist - AIMS **Prod** - SAIF 1986

A Very Delicate Matter 30 MIN
16mm / VHS / U-matic
Color (H A)
LC 82-700158; 83-700994
Tells the story of two teenagers whose close relationship is threatened when one contracts venereal disease and fails to inform the other. Stresses the need for infected persons to act responsibly by notifying others with whom they have had sexual contact.
Health and Safety; Sociology
Dist - LCOA **Prod** - HGATE 1982

Very Enterprising Women 15 MIN
U-matic / VHS / 16mm
Color
Shows women who have started their own businesses and succeeded. Presents interviews in which the women reveal what they feel is necessary to make it in the business world.
Business and Economics; Sociology
Dist - USNAC **Prod** - SBA 1980

The Very Eye of Night 15 MIN
16mm
Color
Highlights a celestial cinematic ballet filmed entirely in the negative.
Fine Arts
Dist - GROVE **Prod** - GROVE

A Very Fine Line 15 MIN
U-matic
Two Plus You - Math Patrol One Series
Color (K P)
Presents the mathematical concepts of sorting and classifying of such common two dimensional objects as squares, triangles and circles showing how these are faces of related three dimensional objects.
Education; Mathematics
Dist - TVOTAR **Prod** - TVOTAR 1976

The Very First Easter 12 MIN
16mm
Color
Presents a little boy telling his dog Sniffy about the events of the first Easter, how Jesus and his disciples came to Jerusalem to celebrate the Passover, the happy processional into the city, driving the merchants and the vendors out of the Temple, the Last Supper, praying in the garden, the arrest and crucifixion, the empty tomb, and Jesus forgiving Peter and telling his disciples to share the good news of God's love with all men.
Guidance and Counseling
Dist - FAMF **Prod** - FAMF 1972

The Very first Milo Moose Day celebration 26 MIN
VHS
Color (K P I)
Tells the story of Milo the Moose, who aspires to be able to fly, just like Santa Claus' reindeer. Shows how Milo's Grammy encourages him to try, and how Milo literally stumbles on success.
Fine Arts; Literature and Drama; Religion and Philosophy
Dist - SCETV **Prod** - SCETV 1980

Very Good Friends 29 MIN
U-matic / VHS / 16mm
Color (J)
LC 77-702003
Tells the story of 13 - year - old Kate, whose younger sister is killed in a sudden accident. Describes how Kate learns to cope with the loss. Based on the book Beat The Turtle Dove by Constance Green. An ABC Afterschool Special.
Guidance and Counseling; Sociology
Dist - LCOA **Prod** - TAHSEM 1977

Very High Pressures 12 MIN
VHS / 16mm
World of Extremes Series
Color (J)
$119.00 purchase, $75.00 rental _ #OD - 2407
Demonstrates how high pressure can be used to alter the atomic structure of carbon atoms and how under sufficient pressure all materials can be turned into metals. The first of three installments of The World Of Extremes Series.
Science; Science - Physical
Dist - FOTH

A Very Important Person 29 MIN
16mm
Giving Birth and Independence Series
Color (H C A)
LC 81-701611
Presents a dramatization about a couple whose son is disabled due to a brain injury suffered in an accident. Tells how they are fearful and unprepared to work with educators in making an individualized education plan until they turn to more experienced parents for help.
Education; Home Economics; Sociology
Dist - LAWREN **Prod** - JRLLL 1981

A Very Merry Cricket 26 MIN
U-matic / VHS
Color
Presents the story a musical cricket, who takes advantage of a power failure to transform discord into peace and harmony after a Christmas in New York City has turned into bedlam.
Literature and Drama; Social Science
Dist - GA **Prod** - GA

A Very Perfect Woman 10 MIN
16mm
Color
Presents the story of a beautiful woman who cannot face her husband after she has breast removal surgery.
Psychology; Sociology
Dist - LUTTEL **Prod** - LUTTEL 1979

A Very Public Private Affair 50 MIN
16mm / U-matic / VHS
Yesterday's Witness in America Series
Color (H C A)
LC 83-700363
Relates the love affair between millionaire publisher William Randolph Hearst and showgirl Marion Davies. Explains that Hearst leaves his family and sets up a home with her at San Simeon, an extravagant castle he built in California. Presents film stars, writers and journalists who recollect the affair.
History - United States; Literature and Drama
Dist - TIMLIF **Prod** - BBCTV 1982

The Very quick job search 30 MIN
VHS
Color (H G) (SPANISH)
$129.00 purchase _ #C3VJSVA, #C3VJCAPA, #C3VJSCSPA
Covers the major techniques required for an effective job search. Offers practical tips on networking, finding job leads, organizing time, etc. Available in open - captioned versions.
Business and Economics; Guidance and Counseling
Dist - CFKRCM **Prod** - CFKRCM

The Very quick job search video 35 MIN
VHS
Color (H C G)
$129.95 purchase _ #JW0476V
Covers the major techniques for an effective job search. Uses methodology based on job seeking processes developed by Mark Farr. Ties together interviews with job seekers and employers to teach job seekers essential strategies. Discusses workforce trends, employer interviews, limitations of traditional job search methods, networking, telephone techniques, the importance of a job objective and how to organize time to get two interviews each day.
Business and Economics; Guidance and Counseling
Dist - CAMV **Prod** - JISTW 1992

The very Remarkable Yamato Family, Pt 1 59 MIN
U-matic / VHS / 16mm
Very Remarkable Yamato Series
Color (H C A)
LC 77-700772
Presents a report on the economic and social structure of Japan, as reviewed on location by journalist Bill Moyers and Professor Takashi Inagaki. Includes an examination of the work ethic and the need to identify with a group, the home and its structure, disappearing family farms and the fishing industry. Deals with protests over the policies of huge industries, overcrowding and pollution.
Business and Economics; Geography - World; History - World; Sociology
Dist - IU **Prod** - WNETTV 1977

The very Remarkable Yamato Family, Pt 2 59 MIN
U-matic / VHS / 16mm
Very Remarkable Yamato Series
Color (H C A)
LC 77-700772
Presents a documentary on the social and political structure of modern Japan, as reviewed on location by journalist Bill Moyers and Professor Takashi Inagaki. Includes reports on the change in family structure, individualized education, the fading image of the Emperor, women's liberation and the growing interdependence of Japan and other nations.
Civics and Political Systems; Education; Geography - World; History - World; Sociology
Dist - IU **Prod** - WNETTV 1977

Very Remarkable Yamato Series
Very Remarkable Yamato Family, the Pt 1 59 MIN
Very Remarkable Yamato Family, the Pt 2 59 MIN
Dist - IU

A Very special dance
16mm
Dance experience series
Color (A G T S)
$28.95 rental _ #243 - 26404
Shows teachers, students, administrators, and concerned parents how students with handicaps can be creative and can communicate with others through dance. Motivates and inspires audiences through the work of dance educator Anne Riordan with mentally handicapped young adults. Developed in cooperation with NBC - TV of Salt Lake City. Demonstrates the conceptual roots and motivations of modern dance. Produced by the Athletic Institute. Conceived and choreographed by Lynda Davis with Nancy Smith Fichter as a consultant.
Fine Arts; Physical Education and Recreation
Dist - AAHPER **Prod** - AAHPER 1975

A Very Special Dance 20 MIN
16mm
Color
Focuses on the work of Anne Riordan, a dance educator of mentally and physically handicapped young adults.
Education; Physical Education and Recreation
Dist - NDI **Prod** - KUTV 1978

A Very Special Day 15 MIN
U-matic
Celebrate Series
Color (P)
Social Science
Dist - GPN **Prod** - KUONTV 1978

A Very Special Education 20 MIN
U-matic / VHS
Color
$335.00 purchase
Presents an ABC TV program on rural schools.
Education; Social Science; Sociology
Dist - ABCLR **Prod** - ABCLR 1984

A Very Special Girl 26 MIN
16mm
Color
LC 76-702736
Presents the story of Denise Anne Miller, a high school junior who won the Navy's highest award at the annual International Science and Engineering Fair. Shows her trip to the Nobel Prize ceremonies in Stockholm where she received her award from Admiral M D Van Orden, Chief of Naval Research.
Education; Guidance and Counseling; Science
Dist - USNAC **Prod** - USN 1975

A Very Special Man 20 MIN
16mm
Color
LC 74-706313
Shows the importance of electronics to the Navy and opportunities available for recruits in advanced electronics.
Civics and Political Systems; Industrial and Technical Education
Dist - USNAC **Prod** - USN 1968

A Very Special Place 14 MIN
16mm
Color
Presents Anita Bryant and her husband fishing in the Florida Keys, near Marathon, in pursuit of tarpon.
Physical Education and Recreation
Dist - FLADC **Prod** - FLADC

A Very Special Place 23 MIN
16mm
Color
LC 81-700650
Provides an opportunity to observe the value of Assateague Island National Seashore, a barrier island existing in a very fragile environment. Discusses the ecological aspects of the island.
Science - Natural
Dist - USNAC **Prod** - USNPS 1980

A Very Special Village 30 MIN
16mm
B&W (H A)
Relates the story of Shaar Menashe, a village in Israel, inhabited only by people over 65. (Kinescope).
Religion and Philosophy
Dist - NAAJS **Prod** - JTS 1956

The Very, very best Christmas present of all 10 MIN
VHS
Color (K P R)
$19.95 purchase, $10.00 rental _ #35 - 84 - 8579
Uses an animated format to present the story of a little boy who tells his dog, Sniffy, about the very first Christmas.
Literature and Drama; Religion and Philosophy
Dist - APH **Prod** - VIDOUT

The Very, Very, Very Best Christmas Present of all 10 MIN
16mm
Color
Deals with a little boy who tells his dog the story of the first Christmas. The very, very, very best Christmas present of all, explains the little boy is the gift of God's son.
Religion and Philosophy
Dist - FAMF **Prod** - SWAMD

The Very Worst Monster 4 MIN
U-matic / VHS
Color; Mono (K P I)
Presents when Billy Monster was born, and conflicts between his sister and his parents.
English Language; Guidance and Counseling; Literature and Drama; Sociology
Dist - WWS **Prod** - WWS 1985

Vesak 20 MIN
U-matic
Color (H C A)
Documents the Buddhist Festival of Light which celebrates the day Buddha was born, attained enlightenment and the day he entered Nirvana.
Religion and Philosophy; Sociology
Dist - HANMNY **Prod** - HANMNY 1971

Vesicle Diverticulatum 14 MIN
16mm
Color (PRO)
Presents the surgical procedures for incision of the bladder, evacuating contents of the diverticulatum, mucosa stripping and drainage procedure, and final suturing.
Health and Safety
Dist - LOMAM **Prod** - LOMAM

Vesicular Exanthema 16 MIN
16mm
Color
LC FIE54-401
Tells the story of the outbreak of vesicular exanthema in 1952, its rapid spread and measures taken to control it. Shows disease symptoms and depicts differential diagnostic field tests.
Agriculture; Health and Safety
Dist - USNAC **Prod** - USDA 1954

Vespucciland the great and free 3 MIN
16mm
Color (G)
$35.00 rental
Presents a Rock Ross production of a celebration of 'Abandon in the ParallelNation.'
Fine Arts
Dist - CANCIN

Vessel Entry 12 MIN
VHS / U-matic
Take Ten for Safety Series
Color (IND)
Illustrates the safety procedures that should be followed when entering any vessel or enclosed space.
Health and Safety; Industrial and Technical Education
Dist - CORF **Prod** - OLINC

Vessel entry 17 MIN
VHS / U-matic / BETA
Color; PAL (IND G) (PORTUGUESE)
$175.00 rental _ #AEB - 112
Reveals that working safely in any type of vessel - from tanks to hopper cars to pits - requires special precautions. Presents seven steps to assure worker safety - isolating the vessel, emptying and purging it, ventilation, air testing, using the proper protective equipment, being prepared to deal with emergencies and using the 'buddy' system. Includes leader's guide and 10 workbooks.
Health and Safety; Psychology; Science - Natural
Dist - BNA **Prod** - BNA

Vessel of wrath 30 MIN
VHS
Classic short stories
Color (H)
#E362; LC 90-708398
Presents 'Vessel of Wrath' by W Somerset Maugham. Part of a series which combines Hollywood stars with short story masterpieces of the world to encourage appreciation of the short story.
Literature and Drama
Dist - GPN **Prod** - CTI 1988

Vessels and Nerves of the Superficial Face 12 MIN
U-matic / VHS / 16mm
Guides to Dissection Series
Color (C A)
Focuses on the head and neck. Demonstrates the dissection of the vessels and nerves of the superficial face.
Health and Safety; Science - Natural
Dist - TEF **Prod** - UCLA

Vessels of the spirit - pots and people in North Cameroon 50 MIN
VHS
Color (G) (FRENCH)
$275.00 purchase _ #6812VE, #6812VF
Reveals that pots are people and people are pots to the inhabitants of the Mandara highlands of North Cameroon. Documents unusual techniques of manufacture of utilitarian and figurated sacred pottery among the Mafa, Sirak and Hide peoples. Shows how pots are assimilated to people by their decoration and in their capacity to contain spirits, including those of gods and ancestors.
Fine Arts; History - United States; History - World; Religion and Philosophy; Sociology
Dist - UCALG **Prod** - UCALG 1990

The Vestal theatre 11 MIN
16mm
Color (G)
$20.00 rental
Captures the lobby of a movie theatre from behind the candy counter. Documents movie goers who could see the camera clearly. Produced by Helene Kaplan.
Fine Arts
Dist - CANCIN

Vestibule - in 3 episodes 24 MIN
VHS
B&W; Color (G)
$45.00 rental, $25.00 purchase
Ruminates on a familiar city place - space filled with histories, fantasies and the everyday in a Ken Kobland production.
Fine Arts
Dist - CANCIN

Vestibuloplasty with Epithelial Inlays 19 MIN
VHS / U-matic
Color (PRO)
LC 81-706310
Shows a modified skin grafting technique for a mandibular labial vestibuloplasty and lowering of the floor of the mouth using epithelial inlays.
Health and Safety; Science
Dist - USNAC **Prod** - VADTC 1980

The Veteran Becomes a Farmer 28 MIN
16mm
B&W
LC FIE52-316
Discusses how individuals and groups in a farm community cooperate in giving help and counsel to a veteran wishing to become a farmer.
Agriculture; Social Science
Dist - USNAC **Prod** - USOE 1946

Veterans Administration Extended Care Environments - Past, Present, Future 14 MIN
U-matic
Color (A)
LC 78-706082
Traces the history of extended medical care services and facilities in the Veterans Administration.
Guidance and Counseling; Health and Safety
Dist - USNAC **Prod** - USVA 1977

Veterans Administration - may I Help You 29 MIN
16mm
Color (A)
LC 78-700824
Highlights the activities and functions of the Veterans Administration through visits with some of its employees.
Civics and Political Systems; Guidance and Counseling; Sociology
Dist - USNAC **Prod** - USVA 1977

Veteran's Day 15 MIN
U-matic
Celebrate Series
Color (P)
Civics and Political Systems; Social Science
Dist - GPN **Prod** - KUONTV 1978

Veterinarian 30 MIN
BETA / VHS
American Professionals Series
Color
Features Dr Nora Matthews, a Cornell graduate and veterinarian who treats large and small animals in upper New York State. Describes how she helps local farmers take care of their cattle, along with her daily job of treating domestic pets.
Guidance and Counseling; Health and Safety
Dist - RMIBHF **Prod** - WTBS

Veterinarian 15 MIN
U-matic
Harriet's Magic Hats I Series
(P I J)
Teaches that a veterinarian is a doctor for animals who can treat them for various injuries and diseases as well as offer information on how to care for pets.
Guidance and Counseling
Dist - ACCESS **Prod** - ACCESS 1980

Veterinarian 15 MIN
16mm / U-matic / VHS
Career Awareness
(I)
$130 VC purchase, $240 film purchase, $25 VC rental, $30 film rental
Presents an empathetic approach to career planning, showing the personal as well as the professional attributes of veterinarians. Highlights the importance of career education.
Guidance and Counseling; Health and Safety
Dist - GPN

A Veterinarian Looks at Functional Type 22 MIN
16mm
Color (PRO)
Uses bone and marrow specimens and live animals to demonstrate the economic importance of functional type with regard to dairy cattle.
Agriculture
Dist - HFAA **Prod** - HFAA

The Veterinarian Serves the Community 11 MIN
16mm / U-matic / VHS
Color (K P I)
LC FIA67-5820
Introduces children to the community health services provided for their pets by the veterinarian. Shows care of all types of animals, the function and personnel of an animal hospital along with their humanitarianism.
Guidance and Counseling; Health and Safety; Science - Natural; Social Science; Sociology
Dist - ALTSUL **Prod** - FILMSW 1968

Veterinarian Serves the Community, the Captioned Version) 11 MIN
U-matic / VHS / 16mm
Color (K P I)
LC FIA67-5820
Introduces children to the community health services provided for their pets by the veterinarian. Shows care of all types of animals, the function and personnel of an animal hospital along with their humanitarianism.
Guidance and Counseling; Health and Safety; Science - Natural; Social Science; Sociology
Dist - ALTSUL **Prod** - FILMSW 1968

Veterinary medicine career encounters 28 MIN
VHS
Career encounters video series
Color (J H)
Offers a documentary on careers in the field of veterinary medicine. Visits workplaces and hears professionals explain what they do, how they got where they are and why they find the work so rewarding. Emphasizes human diversity in the professions. Dispels myths, misconceptions and stereotypes and offers practical information about the requirements for entering the field. Part of a 13 - part series.
Business and Economics; Guidance and Counseling; Science
Dist - NEWCAR
CAMV

The Vever affair 60 MIN
VHS
Smithsonian world series
Color (G)
$49.95 purchase _ #SMIW - 405
Tells the story of the Vever Collection of Persian and Indian paintings. Shows that the collection disappeared in France during World War II, and describes the commotion that resulted when the works reappeared some 40 years later. Suggests that the collection is one of the most significant acquisitions ever made by the Smithsonian.
Fine Arts
Dist - PBS **Prod** - WETATV

VHF made easy 24 MIN
VHS
Color (G A)
$19.95 purchase _ #0921
Discusses the use of VHF - very high frequency - communication on the seas. Covers channel selections, 'Mayday,' ship - to - ship, ship - to - shore, dealing with the marine radio operator and license applications.
Industrial and Technical Education; Physical Education and Recreation; Social Science
Dist - SEVVID

VI 13 MIN
16mm
The Roman numeral series
Color (G)
$391.00 purchase, $19.00 rental
Presents the sixth of a series of abstract, non - objective, non - representational, etc, films.
Fine Arts
Dist - CANCIN **Prod** - BRAKS 1980

VI - Portrait of a Silent Star 30 MIN
VHS / 16mm
Color (G)
$250.00 purchase, $50.00 rental
Profiles prominent American silent films star Viola Dana who began her career with the Edison Company in 1910 and starred in more than 100 productions before her retirement in 1929. Discusses her work as a child actress on the stage, films with her first husband, director John Collins, comedians Buster Keaton and Roscoe 'Fatty' Arbuckle, and her work with Frank Capra. Roddy MacDowall narrates.
Fine Arts
Dist - CNEMAG **Prod** - CNEMAG 1986

Via Dolorosa (1648 - 1705) 14 MIN
16mm
B&W
Shows 25 small chapels in lush meadows by a tranquil river, each one housing a life - size scene sculpted from Christ's Passion.
Fine Arts
Dist - ROLAND **Prod** - ROLAND

Via Dolorosa - The Sorrowful way 10 MIN
VHS / 16mm
Maya series
Color (G)
$210.00, $125.00 purchase, $20.00 rental
Records Good Friday in the colonial town of Antigua, Guatemala. Reveals that the 'sorrowful way' of this day is created by a path of colored sawdust and flower petals. Several hundred people take turns carrying a huge mahogany bier and Indians from the surrounding countryside come to observe townspeople garbed in Biblical and Roman military costumes. Contrasts the solemnity of the Via Dolorosa with the livliness of Indian festivities such as Tajimoltik. Part of a series by Georges Payrastre and Claudine Viallon.
Geography - World; Religion and Philosophy; Social Science
Dist - DOCEDR **Prod** - DOCEDR 1978

Via rio 7 MIN
16mm
Color (G)
$20.00 rental
Tumbles through a series of relationships woven around one woman's narration of her parents' marriage - narrated while sitting naked and pregnant in a garden. Intersperses the stories with scenes that feed the complex nature of human interaction. Produced by Dana Plays.
Fine Arts; Psychology; Sociology
Dist - CANCIN

Viajando Por Mexico Y Espana Series

Centinelas Del Silencio	19 MIN
Pueblo Andaluz	14 MIN
Viaje Por El Norte De Espana	15 MIN
Viaje Por El Sud De Espana	17 MIN

Dist - EBEC

Viaje Por El Norte De Espana 15 MIN
16mm / VHS / U-matic
Viajando Por Mexico Y Espana Series
Color; B&W (H C) (SPANISH)
LC FIA68-1611
A Spanish language film. Presents an overview of the topography, industry and way of life in northern Spain. To be used after lesson 20 of level II, 'Emilio en Espana.'.
Foreign Language; Geography - World
Dist - EBEC **Prod** - EBEC 1966

Viaje Por El Sud De Espana 17 MIN
U-matic / VHS / 16mm
Viajando Por Mexico Y Espana Series
Color (H C) (SPANISH)
LC FIA67-1251
A Spanish language film. Describes the life and culture of southern Spain. Presents scenes of Madrid, Toledo and Merida, with brief scenes of Andalucia and the Levante areas. To be used after lesson 10 of level II, 'Emilio en Espana.'.
Foreign Language; Geography - World
Dist - EBEC **Prod** - EBEC 1966

Vibe - Vanellus Vanellus (Lapwing) 4 MIN
16mm
Color
Presents a description of the lapwing in his natural surroundings, accompanied by sound effects.
Science - Natural
Dist - STATNS **Prod** - STATNS 1965

Vibrant Mirror of the Sun 10 MIN
U-matic / VHS
Color (SPANISH English)
Discusses one kinetic work of Venezuelan artist Alejandro Otero Rodriguez.
Fine Arts; Foreign Language
Dist - MOMALA **Prod** - MOMALA

Vibrant Strings, Pt 1 16 MIN
VHS / U-matic
Musical Instruments Series
Color
Fine Arts
Dist - GPN **Prod** - WWVUTV

Vibrant Strings, Pt 2 19 MIN
VHS / U-matic
Musical Instruments Series
Color
Fine Arts
Dist - GPN **Prod** - WWVUTV

Vibration 29 MIN
16mm
Color
Shows how destructive power brought about by vibrations can be prevented and even utilized for man's benefits. Depicts the mechanisms of vibrations caused by friction.
Science - Physical
Dist - UNIJAP **Prod** - UNIJAP 1971

Vibration Analysis 60 MIN
U-matic / VHS
Mechanical Equipment Maintenance (Spanish Series
Color (IND) (SPANISH)
Deals with vibration analysis. Includes measurement, evaluation and correction.
Foreign Language; Industrial and Technical Education
Dist - ITCORP **Prod** - ITCORP

Vibration Analysis 60 MIN
VHS / U-matic
Mechanical Equipment Maintenance Series
Color (IND)
Goes into proper meausurement, evaluation and correction of excessive vibration.
Industrial and Technical Education
Dist - ITCORP **Prod** - ITCORP

Vibration of Molecules 11 MIN
16mm
Color (H C)
Illustrates the motion of a molecule, the number of normal modes of a molecule, the relation between symmetry and the normal modes of vibration of methane, and the quantization of vibrational energy.
Science - Physical
Dist - SUTHLA **Prod** - SUTHLA 1959

Vibration of Molecules 12 MIN
16mm
CHEM Study Films Series
Color (H)
Shows the relationship between the structure of a molecule and its vibrational motions. Indicates the effect of molecular collision or absorption of light on molecular vibrations.
Science - Physical
Dist - MLA **Prod** - CHEMS 1959

Vibration Problems in the Design of Shipboard Electronic Equipment 19 MIN
16mm
B&W
LC FIE57-162
Demonstrates how breakage can occur when equipment chassis are not protected against vibration and shock. Shows ways in which vibration can be eliminated by the use of bands, screws and braces placed in different ways on a chassis.
Industrial and Technical Education
Dist - USNAC **Prod** - USN 1956

Vibration syndrome 35 MIN
U-matic / VHS
Color (PRO C)
$395.00 purchase, $80.00 rental _ #C881 - VI - 032
Looks at the etiology, assessment and treatment of conditions resulting from hand - arm vibration. Reveals that the force generated by hand - held tools used in a variety of jobs in the shipbuilding, mining, foundry, forest and construction industries can cause vasopastic, neuromuscular and arthritic disorders of the hand and upper limbs. Presented by Ray Sinclair.
Health and Safety; Science - Natural
Dist - HSCIC

Vibration Syndrome, Pt 1 27 MIN
U-matic / VHS
Color (PRO)
LC 84-706456
Discusses the etiology, symptomology, assessment and treatment of Vibration Syndrome. Includes a brief introduction to the physics of vibration and an examination of different assessment techniques.
Health and Safety; Science - Physical
Dist - USNAC **Prod** - USPHS 1981

Vibrations 14 MIN
U-matic / VHS / 16mm
Color; B&W (I J)
LC 74-705913
Defines vibration and demonstrates how vibrations are produced and the relationship between sound and vibration. Focuses on the natural frequency of the vibrations of some objects.
Science - Physical
Dist - EBEC **Prod** - EBEC 1961

Vibrations 60 MIN
VHS / U-matic
Color
Shows Swami Satchidananda speaking on Vibrations.
Religion and Philosophy
Dist - IYOGA **Prod** - IYOGA

Vibrations and Oscillations 29 MIN
VHS / 16mm
Villa Alegre Series
Color (P T)
$46.00 rental _ #VILA - 120
Presents educational material in both Spanish and English.
Education; Science - Physical
Dist - PBS

Vibrations and Pagan Rites 60 MIN
U-matic / VHS
James Galway's Music in Time Series
Color (J)
LC 83-706265
Presents flutist James Galway demonstrating how ageless and universal is the human impulse to make music and how logical and natural has been the development of Western music.
Fine Arts
Dist - FOTH **Prod** - POLTEL 1982

Vibrations and sound I - 26 47 MIN
VHS
Conceptual physics alive series
Color (H C)
$45.00 purchase
Contrasts transverse and longitudinal waves. Explains and demonstrates interference. Explains shock waves and the sonic boom. Part 26 of a 35 - part series adapted from the college and high school textbook Conceptual Physics by Professor Paul Hewitt.
Science - Physical
Dist - MMENTE **Prod** - HEWITP 1992

Vibrations and sound II - 27 43 MIN
VHS
Conceptual physics alive series
Color (H C)
$45.00 purchase
Explains the reflection, refraction and speed of sound. Offers a discussion of forced vibrations and resonance which leads into historic footage of the 1940 collapse of the Tacoma Narrows Bridge. Part 27 of a 35 - part series adapted from the college and high school textbook Conceptual Physics by Professor Paul Hewitt.
Science - Physical
Dist - MMENTE **Prod** - HEWITP 1992

Vibrations of Music 24 MIN
VHS / U-matic
Discovering Physics Series
Color (H C)
Uses the vibrating strings and sound board of a violin as an illustration of the physics of sound production that results in music. Reviews other instruments to show the roles of strings, air columns, plates, and membranes in the production of sound as well as music.
Fine Arts; Science - Physical
Dist - MEDIAG **Prod** - BBCTV 1983

Vibrato 10 MIN
16mm
Color
LC 75-700492
Uses camera movement, multiple images and synchronized music to transform nature into a statement of beauty. Without narration.
Industrial and Technical Education
Dist - INPAC **Prod** - OAC 1975

Vic 13 MIN
16mm
Color
LC 76-700163
Dramatizes the problems of a caretaker who has to vacate the building which has played a major part in his life.
Guidance and Counseling
Dist - SFRASU **Prod** - SFRASU 1974

Vic and Tad - a Moving Portrait 30 MIN
Videoreel / VT2
Color
Portrays Vic and Tad Simpson and their years of struggle to exist and endure within the framework of changing society. Shows how they adjusted to the fast pace of modern culture.
Sociology
Dist - PBS **Prod** - KVIETV

Vic Braden's tennis for the future series
Features Vic Braden in a thirteen - part tennis clinic. Instructs in topics including conditioning, techniques, strategy and sports psychology.

Approach shot, spin and service return	29 MIN
The Backhand	29 MIN
Conditioning	29 MIN
Lob and drop shot	29 MIN
Most Frequently Asked Tennis Questions	29 MIN
The Overhead	29 MIN
Playing Doubles	29 MIN
Psychology	29 MIN
The Serve	29 MIN
Singles Strategy, Pt 1	29 MIN
Singles Strategy, Pt 2	29 MIN
Tennis Philosophy and the Forehand Stroke	29 MIN
The Volley	29 MIN

Dist - PBS **Prod** - WGBHTV

The Vicars of Hessle - Pt 3 20 MIN
VHS
Tudors Series
Color (I)
$79.00 purchase _ #825 - 9423
Paints a detailed and historically accurate picture of the Tudor period, 1485 - 1603, in British history. Examines historical trends over a broad time period or concentrates on one aspect of the era. The dramatizations are based on source material and the locations are authentic. Part 3 of seven parts discusses the religious uncertainties and changes which occurred under the Tudors.
History - World; Religion and Philosophy; Sociology
Dist - FI **Prod** - BBCTV 1987

Vicious Cycle - the Pre Menstrual Syndrome 20 MIN
VHS
Color
From an ABC TV program.
Health and Safety
Dist - ABCLR **Prod** - ABCLR 1982

Vicious Cycles 7 MIN
U-matic / VHS / 16mm
Color (I)
LC 70-708975
A student - produced film which spoofs commercial motorcycle movies.
Fine Arts
Dist - PFP **Prod** - CFS 1969

Vicki 10 MIN
16mm
B&W (J)
LC 76-701872
Tells about a girl who was born with no arms but learned to use her feet with remarkable skill through the patient training of her mother. Presents how she attended regular schools throughout her education and is now employed and engaged to be married.
Health and Safety; Psychology
Dist - AUIS **Prod** - AUSDSS 1975

The Victim 15 MIN
16mm
Cargo Security Series
Color (A)
LC 78-700825
Presents a dramatized railcar theft. Explains the ramifications to the railroad, the shipper, the manufacturer and ultimately the consumer.
Social Science; Sociology
Dist - USNAC **Prod** - USDT 1978

Victim 20 MIN
16mm
Color
LC 80-700487
Tells how a young student helps a girl who is being attacked, only to be accused of the crime himself and sent to jail.
Sociology
Dist - USC **Prod** - USC 1979

A Victim of Gravity 3 MIN
U-matic / VHS
Science Rock Series
Color (P I)
Explains the concept of gravity, describing the experiments of Galileo and Sir Isaac Newton.
Science; Science - Physical
Dist - GA **Prod** - ABCTV 1978

Victim of the brain - based on the book Godel, Escher, Bach 90 MIN
VHS / U-matic
Color (H C G)
$325.00, $295.00 purchase _ #V545
Looks at the book 'Godel, Escher, Bach' by Douglas Hofstadter which proposes an entirely new model of the brain and the thinking process, from material bio - chemical facts up to the most abstract level of 'consciousness' and 'self.' Interviews Hofstadter. Uses animation to explain his philosophy. Looks at whether it might be possible to design machines which can think independently.
Mathematics; Psychology; Science - Natural
Dist - BARR **Prod** - CEPRO 1991

Victim to Victimizer - Breaking the Cycle of Male Sexual Abuse 24 MIN
VHS / 16mm / U-matic
Color (H C G)
$515, $360, $390 _ #A435
Reveals that almost all male child molesters are themselves molestation victims. Suggests that one of the best ways to prevent child abuse is to identify and counsel young men such as these. Describes the necessity for a program to treat molested children who are themselves potential offenders.
Psychology; Sociology
Dist - BARR **Prod** - BARR 1986

Victims 24 MIN
VHS / U-matic
Color (A)
LC 82-706396
Examines the effects of, and some means of countering, parents' violent disciplinary action toward their children. Narrated by Christina Crawford.
Sociology
Dist - WINTNC **Prod** - WINTNC 1981

Victims at birth 58 MIN
VHS
Color (J H C G)
$295.00 purchase, $60.00 rental _ 37910
Reveals that the number of babies born premature, with low birthweight and with other life - threatening health problems is overwhelming the resources of American hospitals. Takes an in - depth look at the causes and examines its effects on society as a whole. Explores three trends behind the rising infant mortality rate and the

tremendous increase in babies born needing immediate intensive care - denial of prenatal care to poor expectant mothers, the growing rate of drug and alcohol abuse among pregnant women and the surge in teenagers giving birth. Produced by Matthew Eisen.
Health and Safety; Sociology
Dist - UCEMC

Victims of Crime - Once is Enough 29 MIN
U-matic / VHS
Inside Story Series
Color
Discusses whether the press should identify a crime victim's name and address. Burglary and rape victims are interviewed.
Fine Arts; Literature and Drama; Social Science; Sociology
Dist - PBS **Prod** - PBS 1981

Victims of the Sea 18 MIN
16mm
Color
LC 77-700593
Dramatizes the efforts made to rescue a diver trapped underwater. Shows the cooperation of the U S Coast Guard and the Los Angeles County lifeguards in the rescue operations.
Civics and Political Systems; Health and Safety
Dist - USC **Prod** - USC 1976

Victims' Rights - 112 30 MIN
U-matic
Currents - 1984 - 85 Season Series
Color (A)
Reveals the growing social and legislative push in the area of victim's rights and how effective they have been.
Civics and Political Systems; Social Science; Sociology
Dist - PBS **Prod** - WNETTV 1985

Victims - their Circumstances, Management and Legal Issues 30 MIN
VHS / U-matic
Management and Treatment of the Violent Patient Series
Color
Discusses the context and factors in violent patient incidents. Illustrates victims as 'provocateurs' versus 'helpless', self - destructive factors and denial.
Health and Safety; Psychology
Dist - HEMUL **Prod** - HEMUL

Victor
Color (K P I J H G)
Deals with the challenge facing American families in which English is a second language.
Literature and Drama; Psychology
Dist - BARR **Prod** - BARR 1988

Victor 11 MIN
16mm
Color
LC 80-700311
Presents the story of a young migrant farmworker and his struggle to maintain his share of the family workload while trying to continue his education.
Agriculture; Sociology
Dist - CHOSAN **Prod** - CHOSAN 1979

Victor Borge birthday gala
VHS
Victor Borge series
Color (G)
$29.95 purchase _ #GU014
Presents live performances of pianist - comedian Victor Borge.
Fine Arts; Literature and Drama
Dist - SIV

Victor Borge in London 50 MIN
VHS
Color (G)
$19.95 purchase_#1302
Presents Victor Borge performing his best-loved classic bits at the London Palladium. Includes hilarious variations on Beethoven, Chopin, Liszt, Schubert and Strauss, and his version of Tchaikovsky's Piano Concerto No.1.
Fine Arts; Literature and Drama
Dist - KULTUR

Victor Borge on Stage Video 120 MIN
VHS
Color (G)
$49.95 purchase _ #12835
Presents Victor Borge taped live in performance in Minneapolis in 1986. Includes 'Aria From Rigor Mortis By Joe Green,' 'Birthday Improvisations,' 'Inflationary Language,' 'Phonetic Punctuation.'.
Fine Arts; Literature and Drama
Dist - WCAT **Prod** - WCAT

Victor Borge series
The Best of Victor Borge - Act I
The Best of Victor Borge - Act I and II
Victor Borge birthday gala
Dist - SIV

Victor Hernandez Cruz - 12 - 11 - 81 30 MIN
VHS / Cassette
Poetry Center reading series
Color (G)
$15.00, $45.00 purchase, $15.00 rental _ #465 - 395
Features the Puerto Rican American poet reading from his works, including a series on real and imagined herbs, at the Poetry Center, San Francisco State University, with an introduction by Tom Mandel.
Literature and Drama
Dist - POETRY **Prod** - POETRY 1981

Victor Hernandez Cruz - 4 - 17 - 89 58 MIN
VHS / Cassette
Lannan Literary series
Color (G)
$15.00, $19.95 purchase, $15.00 rental _ #900
Features the Puerto Rican American poet reading from his book ByLingualWholes and Rhythm, Content, and Flavor. Includes an interview by Lewis MacAdams. Part of a series of literary videotapes presenting major poets and writers from around the globe reading and talking about their work; readings were sponsored by The Lannan Foundation of Los Angeles, a private contemporary arts organization.
Literature and Drama
Dist - POETRY **Prod** - METEZT 1989

Victor Hernandez Cruz - 3 - 3 - 76 28 MIN
VHS / Cassette
Poetry Center reading series
Color (G)
$15.00, $45.00 purchase, $15.00 rental _ #172 - 133B
Features the Puerto Rican American poet reading from his works at the Poetry Center, San Francisco State University, with an introduction by Lewis MacAdams.
Literature and Drama
Dist - POETRY **Prod** - POETRY 1976

Victor Hernandez Cruz - 3 - 3 - 83 35 MIN
VHS / Cassette
Poetry Center reading series
Color (G)
$15.00, $45.00 purchase, $15.00 rental _ #526 - 446
Features the Puerto Rican American poet reading from his works at the Poetry Center, San Francisco State University. Includes a discussion of his visit to Puerto Rico.
Geography - United States; Literature and Drama
Dist - POETRY **Prod** - POETRY 1983

Victor Hugo (1802 - 1885) 13 MIN
16mm
B&W
Presents a collection of Victor Hugo's unknown drawings, many only postage stamp size and others as large as oil paintings. Filmed at the Victor Hugo House in Paris.
Fine Arts
Dist - ROLAND **Prod** - ROLAND 1964

Victor Hugo - Les Miserables 228 MIN
U-matic / VHS
Color (C) (FRENCH)
$399.00, $249.00 purchase _ #AD - 1619
Presents 'Les Miserables' by Victor Hugo in French.
Foreign Language; History - World; Literature and Drama
Dist - FOTH **Prod** - FOTH

Victor Kiam - a case study in leadership and motivation 32 MIN
VHS
Color (A PRO IND)
$475.00 purchase, $150.00 rental
Interviews Remington Razors owner Victor Kiam on his philosophy of success. Covers topics including motivation, productivity, and how Kiam rebuilt the company. Includes five workbooks with self - assessment exercises.
Business and Economics; Guidance and Counseling; Psychology
Dist - VLEARN

Victor Pasmore 30 MIN
VHS
Seven artists series
Color (A)
PdS65 purchase _ Unavailable in Europe
Focuses on some of the main features of 20th-century art by exploring the work of Victor Pasmore. The development of art in this century has resulted in a multiplicity and profusion of styles. Pasmore is placed in his own social and geographical environment. Follows the creation of an art object begun and completed under the camera's eye.
Fine Arts
Dist - BBCENE

Victor Sjostrom 65 MIN
VHS
Color; B&W (G)
$29.95 purchase
Portrays the life of Swedish actor and film director Victor Sjostrom. Directed by Gosta Werner.
Fine Arts
Dist - KINOIC

Victoria and Albert 60 MIN
U-matic / VHS / 16mm
Royal Heritage Series
Color (H C A)
Describes the family life of Queen Victoria and Prince Albert, using Buckingham Palace as the background. Shows Osborne, an early example of pre - fabrication, the design and construction of the Crystal Palace and the mausoleum at Frogmore.
Civics and Political Systems; History - World
Dist - FI **Prod** - BBCTV 1977

Victoria Falls - the Smoke that Thunders 11 MIN
U-matic / VHS / 16mm
Color (J H)
Locates Victoria Falls on the Zambesi River in South Africa. Shows parts of Rhodesia and the country surrounding the falls with its abundant wild life.
Geography - World; History - United States
Dist - MCFI **Prod** - HOE 1958

Victoria, Queen and Empress 60 MIN
16mm / U-matic / VHS
Royal Heritage Series
Color (H C A)
Focuses on Queen Victoria's homes in Scotland and on the Isle of Wight and her additions to the royal collections, including paintings of India.
Civics and Political Systems; History - World
Dist - FI **Prod** - BBCTV 1977

Victoria Regina 76 MIN
VHS / U-matic
Color
Presents Laurence Houseman's play Victoria Regina about the fabled Queen Victoria, providing a human portrait of this queen, so troubled in her personal life and so austere in public. Stars Julie Harris, James Donald and Basil Rathbone.
Fine Arts; Literature and Drama
Dist - FOTH **Prod** - FOTH 1984

The Victorian Age
U-matic / VHS
Color (H)
Gives literary and historical insights into key Victorian themes. Examines Victorian thought and tradition through the eyes of the writers and poets of the day, particularly Dickens. On - location photography and Victorian art are included.
Civics and Political Systems; History - World
Dist - GA **Prod** - GA

The Victorian Age - Dickens and His World
VHS / Slide / 35mm strip / U-matic
English Literature Series
(G C J)
$109, $139, $189 purchase _ #06214 - 85
Examines key Victorian historical events, and portrays Charles Dickens as the central driving force in Victorian literature. Presents the whole range of Victorian thought and tradition through readings of poetry and prose.
Literature and Drama
Dist - CHUMAN **Prod** - GA

Victorian Cape May - a visit to a town out of time 25 MIN
VHS
Color (G)
$29.95 purchase
Presents the highlights of Cape May, New Jersey, a town known for its historic Victorian architecture. Shows that the town, besides having more than 600 19th century buildings, is also known for its beach, fine restaurants, shops, and historical events. Includes a directory of goods and services and a map.
Geography - United States
Dist - PBS **Prod** - WNETTV

The Victorian era 24 MIN
VHS
Color (J H C G)
$150.00 purchase
Reveals that the Victorian era was one of the most creative and inventive periods in American history. Examines the rapid change of an era in the Industrial Age. Focuses on the architecture of the era.
Fine Arts; History - United States
Dist - LANDMK **Prod** - LANDMK 1988

The Victorian era 30 MIN
VHS
Color (I J H C)
LC 90-700003
Looks at the social, economic and political changes in Great Britain during the reign of Queen Victoria.
Civics and Political Systems; History - World
Dist - EAV **Prod** - EAV 1990

Victorian Flower Paintings 7 MIN
16mm
Color (C A)
LC 70-711175
Presents a filmed folio of dated flower paintings which symbolically portray an unknown person passing through a temporary phase of schizophrenic illness.
Fine Arts; Psychology
Dist - NYU **Prod** - IPSY 1968

Victorian masterpiece 50 MIN
VHS
The great palace: the story of parliament
Color; PAL (C H)
PdS99 purchase
Highlights the architecture of Royal Westminster. Explores its Gothic style and unique features. Third in the eight - part series The Great Palace: The Story of Parliament, which documents the significance of the institution.
Civics and Political Systems; History - World
Dist - BBCENE

Victorian Poetry 28 MIN
U-matic / VHS
Survey of English Verse Series
Color (C)
$249.00, $149.00 purchase _ #AD - 1304
Surveys Victorian poetry. Includes selections from Tennyson, Emily Bronte, Christina Rosetti, Browning, Matthew Arnold and Swinburne.
Fine Arts; Literature and Drama
Dist - FOTH **Prod** - FOTH

Victorian Tapestry Workshop 9 MIN
16mm
Color
LC 80-700877
Traces the making of a tapestry by a leading Australian artist.
Fine Arts
Dist - TASCOR **Prod** - VICCOR 1979

Victorian times in Britain 16 MIN
U-matic / VHS / BETA
Color; NTSC; PAL; SECAM (I J)
PdS58
Illustrates domestic and industrial life in Victorian Britain at all levels of society. Contrasts the opulence of the upper classes with the stark poverty of 'the other England.' Shows the part played by steam power in the expansion of railways, the great iron foundries, the textile mills of the north and the hard work expected of children in those times. Concludes with a look at the many great public buildings ofthe time and some of the engineering achievements which made Victorian England 'The Workshop of the World.'
History - World; Social Science
Dist - VIEWTH

Victories - three women triumph over breast disease 23 MIN
VHS
Color (H C G)
$195.00 purchase, $40.00 rental _ #37988
Discloses that one out ten American women will have breast cancer in her lifetime. Portrays three women who have fought their disease with courage and her are proud of their victories. Motivates women to taken an active role in their health care and stresses the importance of early detection of breast disease. Produced by Mary Beth Moorad.
Health and Safety; Sociology
Dist - UCEMC

The Victors 152 MIN
16mm
Color (H C A)
Stars Vincent Edwards, Albert Finney and George Hamilton as part of the men and women who find themselves trapped and changed by the tragedy of war.
Fine Arts; Literature and Drama; Sociology
Dist - TWYMAN **Prod** - CPC

Victor's Egg - O - Mat 10 MIN
U-matic / VHS / 16mm
Meet Professor Balthazar Series
Color (K P I J H C)
Uses animation to show how Professor Balthazar helps his friends who have problems with solutions that are ostensibly magical but actually use the spiritual resources the friends already have.
Guidance and Counseling; Religion and Philosophy
Dist - ZAGREB **Prod** - IFB 1986

Victors of the dry land 58 MIN
VHS / U-matic
Life on Earth series; Program 7
Color (J)
LC 82-706679
Describes the characteristics that made reptiles the first successful inhabitants of dry land and shows examples of this astonishingly diverse family. Discusses the evolution of dinosaurs and the reasons for their sudden extinction.
Science - Natural
Dist - FI **Prod** - BBCTV 1981

Victory at Sea 79 MIN
U-matic / VHS / 16mm
B&W (J A)
LC FIA66-1839
Presents significant events of World War II, including London under fire, the Pearl Harbor attack, the battle of Guadalcanal, Italian and French campaigns and the destruction of Japanese resistance in the Pacific. Musical score by Richard Rogers.
Civics and Political Systems; History - World
Dist - FI **Prod** - NBCTV 1966
ASPRSS
UILL

Victory at Sea
VHS / U-matic
Color (J C I)
Presents a condensation of the TV series portraying exploits of the United States Navy in World War II. Score by Richard Rodgers.
Fine Arts; History - United States
Dist - GA **Prod** - GA

Victory at sea boxed set series
Contains 26 episodes from the Victory at Sea series, documenting the US Navy battles of World War II. Covers events including Pearl Harbor, Normandy, Guadalcanal, and the bombing of Hiroshima and Nagasaki. Consists of six tapes.
Victory at sea boxed set series 720 MIN
Dist - UILL

Victory at Sea, Pt 1 26 MIN
U-matic / VHS / 16mm
B&W
Presents significant events of World War II, including London under fire, the Pearl Harbor attack, the battle of Guadalcanal, Italian and French campaigns and the destruction of Japanese resistance in the Pacific. Musical score by Richard Rogers.
History - United States
Dist - FI **Prod** - NBCTV

Victory at Sea, Pt 2 26 MIN
16mm / U-matic / VHS
B&W
Presents significant events of World War II, including London under fire, the Pearl Harbor attack, the battle of Guadalcanal, Italian and French campaigns and the destruction of Japanese resistance in the Pacific. Musical score by Richard Rogers.
History - United States
Dist - FI **Prod** - NBCTV

Victory at Sea, Pt 3 26 MIN
16mm / U-matic / VHS
B&W
Presents significant events of World War II, including London under fire, the Pearl Harbor attack, the battle of Guadalcanal, Italian and French campaigns and the destruction of Japanese resistance in the Pacific. Musical score by Richard Rogers.
History - United States
Dist - FI **Prod** - NBCTV

Victory at sea - series 13 - 16 120 MIN
VHS
Victory at sea series
Color (H C A)
$24.95 purchase
Presents episodes 13 through 16 of the 'Victory At Sea' series, which covered the American and Allied naval efforts during World War II. Includes the episodes 'Melanesian Nightmare,' 'Roman Renaissance,' 'D - Day - Normandy,' and 'Killers And The Killed.'
History - United States
Dist - PBS **Prod** - WNETTV

Victory at sea, series 13 - 16, Volume 4 26 MIN
VHS
Victory at sea series
Color (G)
$24.80 purchase _ #0163
Profiles the New Guinea campaign, Sicily and the Italian campaign, D - Day, Normandy, victory in the Atlantic in 1943 - 1945. Volume 4 of a 6 volume series on sea battles in World War II.
Civics and Political Systems; Geography - World; History - United States; History - World; Physical Education and Recreation
Dist - SEVVID **Prod** - NBCTV

Victory at sea - series 17 - 21 120 MIN
VHS
Victory at sea series
Color (H C A)
$24.95 purchase
Presents episodes 17 through 21 of the 'Victory At Sea' series, which covered the American and Allied naval efforts during World War II. Includes the episodes 'The Turkey Shoot,' 'Two If By Sea,' 'The Battle For Leyte Gulf 'Return Of The Allies,' and 'Full Fathom Five.'
History - United States
Dist - PBS **Prod** - WNETTV

Victory at sea, series 17 - 21, Volume 5 26 MIN
VHS
Victory at sea series
Color (G)
$24.80 purchase _ #0164
Profiles the conquest of the Marianas, Paleliu and Angaur, the battle for Leyte Gulf, liberation of the Philippines, United States submarines in 1941 - 1945. Volume 5 of a 6 volume series on sea battles in World War II.
Civics and Political Systems; History - United States; History - World; Physical Education and Recreation
Dist - SEVVID **Prod** - NBCTV

Victory at sea - series 22 - 26 120 MIN
VHS
Victory at sea series
Color (H C A)
$24.95 purchase
Presents episodes 22 through 26 of the 'Victory At Sea' series, which covered the American and Allied naval efforts during World War II. Includes the episodes 'The Fate Of Europe,' 'Target Suribachi,' 'The Road To Mandalay,' 'Suicide For Glory,' and 'Design For Peace.'
History - United States
Dist - PBS **Prod** - WNETTV

Victory at sea, series 22 - 26, Volume 6 26 MIN
VHS
Victory at sea series
Color (G)
$24.80 purchase _ #0165
Profiles the Black Sea, the South of France, surrender, Iwo Jima, China, Burma, India and the Indian Ocean, Okinawa, the surrender of Japan and aftermath of the war. Volume 6 of a 6 volume series on sea battles in World War II.
Civics and Political Systems; Geography - World; History - United States; History - World; Physical Education and Recreation
Dist - SEVVID **Prod** - NBCTV

Victory at sea - series 5 - 8 120 MIN
VHS
Victory at sea series
Color (H C A)
$24.95 purchase
Presents episodes five through eight of the 'Victory At Sea' series, which covered the American and Allied naval efforts during World War II. Includes the episodes 'Mediterranean Mosaic,' 'Guadalcanal,' 'Rings Around Rabaul,' and 'Mare Nostrum.'
History - United States
Dist - PBS **Prod** - WNETTV

Victory at sea, series 5 - 8, Volume 2 26 MIN
VHS
Victory at sea series
Color (G)
$24.80 purchase _ #0161
Profiles Gibraltar and the Allied and enemy fleets, Malta, Guadalcanal, the struggle for the Solomon Islands, command of the Mediterranean in 1940 - 1942. Volume 2 of a 6 volume series on sea battles in World War II.
Civics and Political Systems; Geography - World; History - United States; History - World; Physical Education and Recreation
Dist - SEVVID **Prod** - NBCTV

Victory at sea - series 9 - 12 120 MIN
VHS
Victory at sea series
Color (H C A)
$24.95 purchase
Presents episodes nine through 12 of the 'Victory At Sea' series, which covered the American and Allied naval efforts during World War II. Includes the episodes 'Sea And Sand,' 'Beneath The Southern Cross,' 'Magnetic North,' and 'The Conquest Of Micronesia.'
History - United States
Dist - PBS **Prod** - WNETTV

Victory at sea, series 9 - 12, Volume 3 26 MIN
VHS
Victory at sea series
Color (G)
$24.80 purchase _ #0162
Profiles the invasion of North Africa in 1942 - 1943, the war in the South Atlantic and from Murmansk to Alaska in the Pacific, and carrier warfare in the Gilbert and Marshall Islands in the Pacific. Volume 3 of a 6 volume series on sea battles in World War II.

Civics and Political Systems; Geography - World; History - United States; History - World; Physical Education and Recreation
Dist - SEVVID **Prod** - NBCTV

Victory at sea, series 1 - 26, Volumes 1 - 6 156 MIN
VHS
Victory at sea series
Color (G)
$145.00 purchase _ #0166
Presents a 6 volume series on sea battles in World War II. Covers the theaters on the Atlantic, Pacific and Indian Oceans and on the Mediterranean and Black Seas.
Civics and Political Systems; Geography - World; History - United States; History - World; Physical Education and Recreation
Dist - SEVVID **Prod** - NBCTV

Victory at sea - series 1 - 4 120 MIN
VHS
Victory at sea series
Color (H C A)
$24.95 purchase
Presents the first four episodes of the 'Victory At Sea' series, which covered the American and Allied naval efforts during World War II. Includes the episodes 'Design For War,' 'The Pacific Boils Over,' 'Sealing The Breach,' and 'Midway Is East.'
History - United States
Dist - PBS **Prod** - WNETTV

Victory at sea, series 1 - 4, Volume 1 26 MIN
VHS
Victory at sea series
Color (G)
$24.80 purchase _ #0160
Profiles the battle of the Atlantic, 1939 - 1941, Pearl Harbor, antisubmarine warfare in 1941 - 1943, Japanese victories and the battle of Midway. Volume 1 of a 6 volume series on sea battles in World War II.
Civics and Political Systems; History - United States; History - World; Physical Education and Recreation
Dist - SEVVID **Prod** - NBCTV

Victory at Sea series
The Battle for Leyte Gulf 27 MIN
Beneath the Southern Cross 27 MIN
The Conquest of Micronesia 27 MIN
D - Day 27 MIN
Design for peace 27 MIN
Design for war 27 MIN
The Fate of Europe 27 MIN
Full Fathom Five 27 MIN
Guadalcanal 27 MIN
Killers and the Killed 27 MIN
Magnetic North 27 MIN
Mare Nostrum 27 MIN
Mediterranean Mosaic 27 MIN
Melanesian Nightmare 27 MIN
Midway is East 27 MIN
The Pacific Boils Over 27 MIN
Return of the Allies 27 MIN
Rings Around Rabaul 27 MIN
The Road to Mandalay 27 MIN
Roman Renaissance 27 MIN
Sea and Sand 27 MIN
Sealing the Breach 27 MIN
Suicide for Glory 27 MIN
Target Suribachi 27 MIN
The Turkey Shoot 27 MIN
Two if by Sea 27 MIN
Dist - LUF

Victory at sea series
Presents a six - volume collection of all the episodes of the 'Victory At Sea' series. Tells the story of the American and Allied naval operations in both the Pacific and Atlantic oceans during World War II.
Victory at sea - series 13 - 16 120 MIN
Victory at sea - series 17 - 21 120 MIN
Victory at sea - series 22 - 26 120 MIN
Victory at sea - series 5 - 8 120 MIN
Victory at sea - series 9 - 12 120 MIN
Victory at sea - series 1 - 4 120 MIN
Dist - PBS **Prod** - WNETTV

Victory at sea series
Victory at sea, series 13 - 16, Volume 4 26 MIN
Victory at sea, series 17 - 21, Volume 5 26 MIN
Victory at sea, series 22 - 26, Volume 6 26 MIN
Victory at sea, series 5 - 8, Volume 2 26 MIN
Victory at sea, series 9 - 12, Volume 3 26 MIN
Victory at sea, series 1 - 26, Volumes 1 - 6 156 MIN
Victory at sea, series 1 - 4, Volume 1 26 MIN
Dist - SEVVID

Victory at sea series
Design for war, the Pacific boils over, Sealing the breach and Midway is east 108 MIN
The Fate of Europe, target Suribachi, the road to Mandalay, suicide for glory and design for peace 135 MIN
Mediterranean mosaic, Guadalcanal, rings around Rabaul and mare nostrum 108 MIN
Melanesian nightmare, D - day, Roman renaissance and killers and the killed 108 MIN
Sea and sand - Beneath the Southern Cross - Magnetic north - Conquest of Micronesia 108 MIN
Turkey shoot - two if by sea, the battle for Leyte Gulf, return of the Allies and full fathom five 135 MIN
Dist - UILL

Victory at Yorktown 12 MIN
16mm
Color
LC 77-703160
Depicts the day - long ritual of surrender, counterpointing the scenes of triumph for the Americans and French and agony for the British as reflections regarding the significance of Yorktown then and now.
History - United States
Dist - USNAC **Prod** - USNPS 1975

Victory at Yorktown 30 MIN
U-matic / VHS
American story - the beginning to 1877 series
Color (C)
History - United States
Dist - DALCCD **Prod** - DALCCD

The Victory Division - 24th Infantry 17 MIN
16mm / U-matic / VHS
B&W (H A)
Discusses the role of the 24th Infantry in the Pacific during the war.
Civics and Political Systems; History - United States
Dist - USNAC **Prod** - USA 1950

The Victory garden 60 MIN
VHS
Color (A)
$24.95 purchase _ #S01376
Features master gardeners Bob Thompson and Jim Wilson in a presentation of gardening tips for both novice and expert alike.
Agriculture
Dist - UILL **Prod** - PBS

Victory garden 60 MIN
VHS
Color (G)
$19.95 purchase
Instructs in the planning, planting and maintaining of a vegetable garden. Takes viewers through a whole year, month by month. Hosted by Bob Thomson and Jim Wilson.
Agriculture
Dist - PBS **Prod** - WNETTV

Victory Garden Recipes 90 MIN
VHS / U-matic
(C A)
$29.95 _ #RH300V
Features Marian Marsh, author of the book, The Victory Garden Cookbook, as she demonstrates various vegetable recipes. Includes recipe book with 70 recipes and instructions.
Home Economics; Industrial and Technical Education
Dist - CAMV **Prod** - CAMV

Victory garden series
All - American roses 30 MIN
Bounty for the table 30 MIN
Cutting a bouquet 30 MIN
Flowers in bloom 30 MIN
Good and plenty 30 MIN
Green Thumb Needed 30 MIN
Harvest of Things to Come 30 MIN
Herbs, cantaloupes, watermelon 30 MIN
Horticulture Exhibit 30 MIN
In Full Bloom 30 MIN
Landscape Artistry 30 MIN
Magnolia Gardens - Charleston 30 MIN
Native Hawaiian Plants 30 MIN
Oriental Vegetables 30 MIN
Patio Gardening 30 MIN
Peak Harvest 30 MIN
Pick of the Crop 30 MIN
Pick the Winner 30 MIN
Preparation for Spring 30 MIN
Spring Lawn Care 30 MIN
A Star is Grown 30 MIN
Summer Vegetables 30 MIN
Tips from the Pros 30 MIN
Tropical Climate - Hawaii 30 MIN
Walker Gardens - Honolulu 30 MIN
Warm - Season Gardens 30 MIN
Dist - CORF

Victory in the Pacific 330 MIN
VHS
Color; CC (G)
$79.95 purchase _ #VITP
Uses original World War II film to portray the most memorable battles in the Pacific Theater. Includes Pearl Harbor and Corregidor, the Battle of Midway, battles in the Solomons, New Britain and New Guinea, the victories in Iwo Jima and Okinawa and surrender ceremonies in Tokyo Bay.
History - United States; Sociology
Dist - APRESS **Prod** - READ

The Victory of Father Karl 30 MIN
VHS / BETA
B&W
Tells of the life and death of Karl Leisner who was ordained a priest in the Nazi concentration camp Dachau.
Biography; History - World; Religion and Philosophy
Dist - DSP **Prod** - DSP

A Victory of spirit 60 MIN
VHS
Color (I J H)
$149.00 purchase _ #GW - 118 - VS
Presents a documentary featuring two young North Carolina Special Olympic athletes. Features Maria Shriver as narrator. Shows the reality of mental retardation and the everyday challenges and victories that these athletes experience. Follows tennis player J C Mingo of Charlotte and swimmer D C Mitchell of Jacksonville in all aspects of their lives as they prepare for the International Summer Special Olympic Games. Produced by the North Carolina Special Olympics.
Health and Safety; Psychology
Dist - HRMC

Victory Variations 10 MIN
16mm
Color
LC 77-702697
Documents the reconstruction of the Victory Burlesque in Toronto.
Geography - World; Industrial and Technical Education; Sociology
Dist - CANFDC **Prod** - CANFDC 1976

Vicus 18 MIN
16mm
Color (J H C) (SPANISH)
LC 75-700290
Displays pre - Columbian ceramics and jewelry of the vicus culture in Peru.
Fine Arts; Foreign Language
Dist - MOMALA **Prod** - OOAS 1970

Vida - for Latina women 18 MIN
VHS
AIDSFILMS series
Color (A G) (SPANISH)
$65.00 purchase
Illustrates the powerful role women can play in supporting each other's changes in sexual behavior and attitutes towards people with AIDS. Tells of Elsie, a single Latina mother, who struggles with her apprehension about contracting AIDS and her fear of losing her new partner, Luis. When Elsie learns that her neighbor Bianca is sick with AIDS, she realizes that she, too, may be at risk of HIV infection. Elsie is able to ask Luis to use condoms, and when he refuses, Elsie leaves him. After taking this important step to protect herself, Elsie is able to reach out compassionately to her sick neighbor. Includes discussion guide in English and Spanish.
Health and Safety; Psychology; Sociology
Dist - SELMED

Vidal in Venice - Part 1 55 MIN
VHS
Color (G)
$29.95 purchase _ #S02281
Presents the first part of a two - part historical overview of and a modern - day visit to Venice. Covers the Palace of the Doges and political developments. Hosted by author Gore Vidal.
Geography - World; History - World; Sociology
Dist - UILL

Vidal in Venice - Part 2 55 MIN
VHS
Color (G)
$29.95 purchase _ #S02282
Presents the second part of a two - part historical overview of and a modern - day visit to Venice. Covers the cultural and artistic heritage of the city. Hosted by author Gore Vidal.
Geography - World; History - World; Sociology
Dist - UILL

Vidalia McCloud - a Family Story 28 MIN
VHS / 16mm
Color (H C A)
$325.00, $275.00
Presents a portrait of a family of African - Americans in a migrant town in central Florida. Vidalia, a single mother of three, works as a fruit picker and short - order cook and at times collects welfare. The program has the flavor of a family album, exposing the many sides of Vidalia - her humor, warmth, anger, depression and hope.
History - United States; Sociology
Dist - CAROUF **Prod** - THMACK 1986

Vidas en peligro 15 MIN
U-matic / VHS / 16mm
Emergency resuscitation - Spanish series
Color (C A) (SPANISH)
A Spanish - language version of the motion picture Seconds Count. Emphasizes the need for speed in applying emergency resuscitation by the mouth - to - mouth method using incidents stemming from drowning and asphyxia.
Foreign Language; Health and Safety
Dist - IFB **Prod** - UKMD

Vidas Secas 115 MIN
16mm
B&W (PORTUGUESE (ENGLISH SUBTITLES))
Describes two years in the life of a ranch family struggling to eke out an existence in 1940's Brazil. Directed by Nelson Pereira dos Santos.
Fine Arts; Foreign Language
Dist - NYFLMS **Prod** - UNKNWN 1963

Videano - beginning keyboard - Phase One 37 MIN
VHS
Color (J H C G)
$39.95 purchase _ #TPP100V
Teaches the basics of keyboard geography and correct keyboard posture. Part one of two parts.
Fine Arts
Dist - CAMV

Videano - beginning keyboard - Phase Two 60 MIN
VHS
Color (J H C G)
$39.95 purchase _ #TPP100V
Teaches correct rhythms and music reading. Guides through intervals, transposing pieces and self - accompaniment. Part two of two parts.
Fine Arts
Dist - CAMV

Video - a practical guide and more series
Camera techniques for video 30 MIN
Directing Non - Professional Talent 30 MIN
Editing and special effects 30 MIN
Format analysis and writing for videotape 30 MIN
Lighting Application for Video 30 MIN
Mobile Videotape Production 30 MIN
Operation and Maintenance of a Video System 30 MIN
Preparation and use of graphics 30 MIN
Producing a Videotape 30 MIN
Sets and Locations for Videotape 30 MIN
Sound Application for Video 30 MIN
What's Wrong - Troubleshooting a Video System 30 MIN
Dist - VIPUB

Video Amplifier 25 MIN
16mm
B&W
LC 74-705914
Describes the frequency range and states the function of each component of the video amplifier. Explains methods used to obtain low and high frequency response. (Kinescope).
Industrial and Technical Education; Science - Physical
Dist - USNAC **Prod** - USAF

Video and if Amplifiers 30 MIN
U-matic / VHS
Linear and Interface Integrated Circuits, Part I - Linear Integrated Circuits Series
Color (PRO)
Discusses definition and application of wide - bandwidth amplifiers for video use and selective bandwidth amplifiers for intermediate - frequency amplifiers use. Discusses typical applications.
Industrial and Technical Education
Dist - TXINLC **Prod** - TXINLC

Video and learning 29 MIN
VHS
Color; CC (G)
$20.00 purchase _ #VIDE
Discusses the value of learning from videos and suggests that school libraries use videos as an educational resource.
Education
Dist - APRESS **Prod** - APRESS

Video aquarium 60 MIN
VHS
Color (G)
$19.95 purchase
Presents a video aquarium featuring an assortment of exotic marine fish.
Science - Natural
Dist - PBS **Prod** - WNETTV

Video as an organizing tool 36 MIN
16mm / VHS
Color (G IND)
$5.00 rental
Provides examples of the type of video programming used by various unions in organizing campaigns. Features a 'worker to worker' video experiment used by the Steelworkers and IUD in an organizing drive in Carrollton, Georgia.
Business and Economics; Fine Arts; Industrial and Technical Education; Social Science
Dist - AFLCIO **Prod** - LIPA 1985

The Video basics of kitchen safety and organization
VHS
Video basics of kitchen safety and organization series
Color (H IND)
$129.95 purchase _ #CDKIT110SV-H
Presents information about general kitchen safety techniques, kitchen arrangement, proper storage in a kitchen - including holding temperatures and shelf life, cleaning, sanitizing and food borne illnesses.
Health and Safety; Home Economics; Industrial and Technical Education
Dist - CAMV

Video basics of kitchen safety and organization series
Cleaning the kitchen - things my parents never told me 10 MIN
The Video basics of kitchen safety and organization
Dist - CAMV

Video basics of kitchen safety and organization
General kitchen safety - keeping a clear floor and a clear head 10 MIN
Kitchen organization - I think it's here somewhere 10 MIN
Safe food storage - I thought it would last forever 10 MIN
Dist - CAMV

The Video basics of word processing 15 MIN
VHS
Job skills for career success series
Color (H C G)
$79.00 purchase _ #CDSBED106V
Introduces the basic skills and key terms associated with word processing. Presents numerous on - screen examples with follow - along dialogue from real work settings. Part of a ten - part series which explores basic job skills necessary for a successful career. Includes student guide.
Business and Economics; Guidance and Counseling; Psychology
Dist - CAMV

Video Biblical illustrator series
Listen - to the butterfly
The Potter
The Vine and the branches
Dist - APH

Video birth library series
Presents 15 programs on varying childbirth experiences. Illustrates childbirth by teen and young mothers, over - 35 mothers, with midwives attending, by black, Hispanic or single mothers, vaginal births after cesareans, the birth of twins, cesarean sections, induced labor, the use of epidurals, birth with siblings present, and the use of the Jacuzzi or showers to relax women in labor.
Andrea - birth 14
Ann and Shelley - birth 15
Chantell and Junior - Birth 6
Donna and Joey - birth 1
Evie and Larry - Birth 9
Harriet and Jim - Birth 17
Kathy and Joe - Birth 13
Laurie and Pete - Birth 4
Lisa and Billy - Birth 8
Lori and Mike - Birth 2
Lucy and Pete - Birth 12
Mirna and Mario - Birth 3
Sandy and Rick - Birth 7
Terri - Birth 16
Traci and Ed - Birth 11
Dist - POLYMR **Prod** - POLYMR 1991

Video boardsailing clinic
VHS
Color (G)
$100.00 rental _ #0084
Presents Olympic coach Major Hall and medalist Scott Steele in a clinic on boardsailing technique, designed for boardsailors who know the basics.
Physical Education and Recreation
Dist - SEVVID

Video Career Library Series
Administration and management 30 MIN
Clerical and admistrative support 21 MIN
Construction 36 MIN
Education 26 MIN
Engineering and related occupations 45 MIN
Literary and Performing Arts 40 MIN
Marketing and Sales 21 MIN
Mechanical Fields 22 MIN
Medicine and Related Fields 30 MIN
Physical and Life Sciences 26 MIN
Production I 28 MIN
Production II 32 MIN
Repair Fields 23 MIN
Social Sciences 26 MIN
Technical Occupations 33 MIN
Transportation and Material Moving 20 MIN
Dist - AAVIM

Video Career Library Series
Allied health fields 42 MIN
Public and Personal Services 35 MIN
Dist - AAVIM
CAMV

Video career library series
Administration - management 30 MIN
Clerical - administrative support 26 MIN
Construction 36 MIN
Education 30 MIN
Engineering - Related Occupations 45 MIN
Literary - Performing Arts 40 MIN
Marketing and Sales 21 MIN
Mechanical Fields 22 MIN
Medicine and Related Fields 30 MIN
Physical and Life Sciences 26 MIN
Production I 28 MIN
Production II 32 MIN
Repair Fields 23 MIN
Social Sciences
Technical Occupations 33 MIN
Transport - Moving 20 MIN
Dist - CAMV

Video career library series
Presents 18 videos showing 165 occupations. Describes job duties; working conditions; wages and salaries; job outlook; and training and education required. Includes Physicians and Health Practioners; Allied Health I; Administration and Management; Engineering and Related Occupations; Physical and Life Sciences; Social Sciences; Education; Literary and Performing Arts; Technical Occupations; Marketing and Sales; Clerical and Adminstratiive Support; Public and Personal Services; Mechanical Fields; Repair Fields; Construction; Production I and II; Transportation and Material Moving.
Physicians and health practitioners 30 MIN
Video career library series 542 MIN
Dist - NEWCAR

Video Career Series
Applied sciences - architecture
Applied sciences - civil engineering
Applied sciences - community planning
Applied sciences - computer programming and systems analysis
Applied sciences - electrical and electronic engineering
Applied sciences - forestry sciences
Construction - Carpentry
Construction - Insulating and Roofing Occupations
Construction - Pipefitting and Plumbing
Education - elementary and secondary education
Education - post secondary education
Fine Arts - Music
Fine Arts - Photography
Fine Arts - Visual Arts
Fine Arts - Writing and Journalism
Management and Commerce - Accounting
Management and Commerce - Business and Data Processing Machine Operations
Management and Commerce - Clerk - Bank, Insurance and Commerce
Management and Commerce - Financial Business Services
Management and Commerce -

Management and Private Enterprise
Management and Commerce - Sales and Commodities
Management and Commerce - Secretarial Services
Medical Sciences - Dentistry
Medical Sciences - Medicine
Medical Sciences - Optometry
Medical Sciences - Pharmacy
Private and Public Service - Cosmetic and Personal Services
Private and Public Service - Fire Prevention and Firefighting
Private and Public Service - Nursing and Paramedical
Private and Public Service - Retailing and Merchandising
Social Sciences - Household Economics
Social Sciences - Library and Archival Science
Social Sciences - Psychology
Social Sciences - Social Work
Sports - Professional Sports
Sports - Sports - Attendants and Support Service
Technical Occupations - Dental Hygienics
Technical Occupations - Drafting
Technical Occupations - Graphic Arts
Technical Occupations - Mechanics
Technical Occupations - Medical Laboratory Technology
Technical Occupations - Performing Arts Technologies
Technical Occupations - Photographic Processing
Technical Occupations - Printing
Technical Occupations - Radio and Television Production
Technical Occupations - Utilities Equipment Operation
Transportation and Communication - Air - Flight Service
Transportation and Communication - Air Transport - Ground Communications
Transportation and Communication - Materials Handling
Dist - CAREER

Video chess mentor series
The Lottery video
Pro - chess - Volumes 1 & 2 240 MIN
Pro chess - Volume 1 120 MIN
Pro chess - Volume 2 120 MIN
Dist - SIV

Video cooking library series
Presents a 22 - part series on cookery using step - by - step demonstrations. Covers everything needed from ingredients to equipment, with clear explanations of cooking techniques. Includes recipes. Covers bread, Italian, Mexican, Middle Eastern, American cuisine, meals and dishes for special occasions.
Basic Mexican cuisine
Basic Middle Eastern cuisine
Candles, champagne and romance
Delicious dishes to go
Fun meals for kids
Hearty New England dinners
Holiday cookies and treats
Holiday gifts from your kitchen
Magnificent recipes for brunch
Microwave miracles
Mouthwatering meatless meals
Salads supreme
Sensational soups
Southern desserts - delights
Dist - CAMV

Video cooking library series
The Basic bread baker
Basic Italian cuisine
Basic New Orleans cuisine
Meals for Two
One Dish Meals
Pasta, Pasta, Pasta
Seven simple chicken dishes
Thanksgiving Dinner
Dist - KARTES

Video Cooking Series
Madeleine Kamman Cooks 90 MIN
Dist - BAFBRG

Video cruising Florida's waterways
VHS
Color (G)
$29.95 purchase _ #0815
Reveals that Florida has uncountable miles of inland water easily accessible from salt water by cruising boats.
Geography - United States; Physical Education and Recreation
Dist - SEVVID

Video - cued structural drills series
Basic verbs - Video 7
Causatives - Video 2
Honorifics 1 - Video 5
Honorifics 2 - Video 6
Passives - Video 1
Time - Nagara - Video 4
Time - Tokoro - Video 3
Dist - CHTSUI

Video dance and The Video dance lectures 79 MIN
VHS
Film, video and TV production series
Color (H C G)
$179.00 purchase _ #776
Offers technical advice on videotaping dance performance and dance lectures in two programs on separate tapes.
Fine Arts; Industrial and Technical Education
Dist - INSTRU

Video Diary of a Madman or My Day Reflects My Mood 83 MIN
U-matic / VHS
Color
Focuses on confession. Presented by Michel Auder and Michael Zwack.
Fine Arts
Dist - ARTINC **Prod** - ARTINC

Video Dictionary of Classical Ballet 270 MIN
VHS
Color (G)
$99.95 purchase _ #1100
Provides an index to over 800 variations in international Russian, French and Cecchetti ballet styles, all numbered and correspondingly indicated in an accompanying booklet. Shows many of the movements in slow motion with multiple camera angles and narrative description. Accuracy of all the movements has been certified by Georgina Parkinson, Ballet Mistress, ABT. Features Merrill Ashley, Denise Jackson, Kevin Mckenzie and Georgina Parkinson.
Fine Arts; Physical Education and Recreation
Dist - KULTUR

The Video Display Terminal and You 16 MIN
VHS / 16mm
Color (PRO)
$550.00 purchase, $110.00 rental, $30.00 preview
Teaches employees the use of video display terminals. Explains counteracting negative effects of video terminals on the well - being of an employee. Discusses ergonomic principles - good posture, proper seating, eye strain, vision breaks and exercises. Includes a handbook.
Computer Science; Guidance and Counseling; Mathematics; Psychology
Dist - UTM **Prod** - UTM

Video display terminals 10 MIN
U-matic / BETA / VHS
Color (IND G)
$295.00 purchase _ #840 - 05
Trains video display terminal - VDT - operators in techniques to minimize the physical problems that can develop as a result of operating a VDT. Presents solutions to problems of visual fatigue, neck, upper back and shoulder pain, plus studies on radiation levels emitted by VDTs.
Business and Economics; Health and Safety; Psychology
Dist - ITSC **Prod** - ITSC

Video display terminals 16 MIN
VHS
Color (IND) (SPANISH)
$395.00 purchase, $95.00 rental _ #CVP04
Teaches computer personnel techniques to reduce the stress of repetitive motions, glare, poor posture and eyestrain. Includes 10 employee handbooks.
Health and Safety
Dist - EXTR **Prod** - COASTL

Video DOS 60 MIN
VHS / U-matic
(A PRO)
$49.95 purchase, $125.00 purchase
Generic PC DOS training program. Provides complete training for MS and PC DOS commands and functions using hard disks or floppies. Covers all versions of DOS 2.1 and higher.
Computer Science
Dist - VIDEOT **Prod** - VIDEOT 1988

Video DOS - IBM PC 60 MIN
VHS / 16mm
(G PRO)
$39.95 purchase _ #TM1
Trains the user for general use of MS - PC DOS 2.1 or above. Begins with the concept of default drives, then goes through many of the DOS capabilities.
Computer Science
Dist - RMIBHF **Prod** - RMIBHF

Video encyclopedia of psychoactive drugs series
Presents a 10 - part series on psychoactive drugs. Includes the titles Alcohol - Alcoholism; Teenage Drinking; Amphetamines; Barbituates; Cocaine and Crack; Heroin; Marijuana; Nicotine; Prescription Narcotics; Teen Depression and Suicide.
Alcohol - alcoholism 30 MIN
Amphetamines 30 MIN
Barbituates 30 MIN
Cocaine and crack 30 MIN
Heroin 30 MIN
Marijuana 30 MIN
Nicotine 30 MIN
Prescription narcotics 30 MIN
Teen depression and suicide 30 MIN
Teenage drinking 30 MIN
Dist - CAMV

Video encyclopedia of space series
The Applications of space technology 28 MIN
The Earth in perspective 28 MIN
First steps in space exploration 28 MIN
Flight to the moon 28 MIN
The History of Space Technology 28 MIN
Introduction to the Solar System 28 MIN
Living and Working in Space 28 MIN
Living in Space 28 MIN
Origins of the Universe 28 MIN
The Shuttle in close - up 28 MIN
The Space Shuttle 28 MIN
Dist - FOTH

Video Exam Over Sterile Techniques for Oral Surgery and Periodontal Surgery 13 MIN
BETA / VHS
Color (PRO)
Complete title reads Video Exam Over Sterile Techniques For Oral Surgery And Periodontal Surgery Procedures. Provides an examination covering sterile techniques for oral surgery and periodontal surgery procedures.
Education; Fine Arts; Health and Safety
Dist - RMIBHF **Prod** - RMIBHF

Video eyes - video ears 25 MIN
16mm
Color (G)
$40.00 rental
Discusses the production, editing and distribution of sounds and images on video. Pushes the viewer into thinking about a better use of modern video technology such as changing daily lives. In Montreal, Canada, people from all walks of life learned to produce a video at the Videographe center. Produced by Leonard Henny.
Fine Arts
Dist - CANCIN

Video Feedback as a Treatment Modality for Persons with Low Back Pain 19 MIN
U-matic
Color (PRO)
Describes the use of videotape as a diagnostic and treatment modality for low back pain.
Health and Safety; Psychology
Dist - RICHGO **Prod** - RICHGO

Video Field Trips
Cotton Production 35 MIN
The Greenhouse 30 MIN
Leather Production 23 MIN
Lumber Production 35 MIN
The Winery 21 MIN
Dist - VEP

Video for Cheerleading Series
Cheerleading jumps 25 MIN
Conditioning for Cheerleaders 25 MIN
Partner Stunts for Cheerleading 25 MIN
Tumbling for Cheerleaders 25 MIN
Dist - ATHI

Video from Russia 45 MIN
VHS
Color (G)
$29.95 purchase _ #S02015
Presents an American film crew's interviews with Soviet citizens of all ages. Considers the Soviets' views of war, work, rock music, and more. Filmed in six Soviet cities.
Geography - World; History - World; Sociology
Dist - UILL

Video from Russia
U-matic / VHS
(J H C A)

$49.00 purchase _ #03758 941
Presents candid interviews with Russian people in the Soviet Union by an American film crew.
Fine Arts; History - World
Dist - ASPRSS

The Video GOE - artistic 45 MIN
VHS
Color (G)
$69.95 purchase _ #CCP100V-F
Guides people interested in careers in the arts. Looks at aspects in this career field, including aptitude, skills, education and training, work activities, and work situations such a career entails. Interviews a film maker and producer, a clothing designer, painter, symphony conductor, disc jockey, jazz musician, dance instructor, live radio producer, and a professional make-up artist. Readily integrated into most career guidance programs. Includes special introductory tape.
Business and Economics; Fine Arts; Guidance and Counseling
Dist - CAMV

Video guide to basic photography 90 MIN
VHS
On assignment - the video guide for photography series
Color (J H C G)
$29.95 purchase _ #MED100V VHS
Contains three chapters covering how a camera works, lighting, flash, shooting and finding pictures. Part of an eight - part series hosted by nationally known photographer Brian D Ratty.
Fine Arts; Industrial and Technical Education
Dist - CAMV

Video guide to basic videography
VHS
Color (H C)
$29.95 purchase _ #265A
Takes the mystery out of shooting effective, entertaining videos. Offers three half - hour chapters for easy viewing. Features Brian D Ratty, photographer, as host.
Industrial and Technical Education
Dist - INSTRU

The Video guide to cruising the Chesapeake Bay
VHS
Color (G)
$49.90 purchase _ #0742
Takes the C and D Canal to Solomons Island, the Patuxent River. Visits Annapolis, Baltimore, St Michaels, Oxford, Havre de Grace and other cruising spots and anchorages.
Geography - United States; Physical Education and Recreation
Dist - SEVVID

Video Guide to Interviewing Series
Interview Preparation 30 MIN
Dist - CAMV
CAREER

Video guide to interviewing series
Handling difficult questions 30 MIN
Dist - CAMV
CAREER
JISTW

Video Guide to Interviewing Series
Discusses the various parts of a job interview.
Video Guide to Interviewing Series 30 MIN
Dist - CAREER **Prod -** CAREER

Video Guide to Interviewing Series
Four Stages of Interviewing 30 MIN
Dist - JISTW

Video Guide to Inteviewing Series
Interviewing Preparation 30 MIN
Dist - JISTW

Video guide to occupational exploration - the video GOE series 455 MIN
VHS
Video guide to occupational exploration - the video GOE series
Color (J H C G)
$749.00 purchase _ #CCP15SV
Presents a 14-part series exploring occupational clusters. Includes Artistic, Scientific, Plants and Animals, Protective, Mechanical I and II, Industrial, Business Detail, Selling, Accomodating, Humanitarian, Leading and Influencing I and II, Physical Performing.
Business and Economics; Guidance and Counseling
Dist - CAMV **Prod -** CAMV 1991

A Video guide to professional conduct - Part I - Overview 50 MIN
VHS
Color (C PRO A)
$95.00 purchase _ #P243
Provides a succinct summary of the ABA Model Rules of Professional Conduct as amended and adapted in a majority of states, which are included with the videotape. Illustrates and explains the complexities and importance of these rules and their application.
Business and Economics; Civics and Political Systems
Dist - ALIABA **Prod -** CLETV 1988

A Video guide to professional conduct - Part II - Civil litigation 50 MIN
VHS
Color (C PRO A)
$95.00 purchase _ #P239
Gives instructive discussion on the professional ethics issues confronted by attorneys in preparing and trying civil lawsuits. Includes the ABA Model Rules of Professional Conduct.
Business and Economics; Civics and Political Systems
Dist - ALIABA **Prod -** CLETV 1988

A Video guide to professional conduct - Part III - Corporate representation 50 MIN
VHS
Color (C PRO A)
$95.00 purchase _ #P240
Examines the ethical dilemmas that persistently confront attorneys who counsel corporations. Includes the ABA Model Rules of Professional Conduct.
Business and Economics; Civics and Political Systems
Dist - ALIABA **Prod -** CLETV 1988

A Video guide to professional conduct - Part IV - Conflict of interest 50 MIN
VHS
Color (C PRO A)
$95.00 purchase _ #P238
Explains the many and often complex issues that arise when attorneys and law firms represent clients with conflicting interests. Includes the ABA Model Rules of Professional Conduct.
Business and Economics; Civics and Political Systems
Dist - ALIABA **Prod -** CLETV 1988

A Video guide to quilting
VHS
Color (H A G)
$35.00 purchase _ #ZZ100
Looks at quilt construction and artistry. Covers design, fabric, templates, marking and cutting materials, piecing - hand and machine, sandwiching and framing, quilting and binding.
Fine Arts; Home Economics
Dist - AAVIM **Prod -** AAVIM

Video guide to the Virgin Islands
VHS
Color (G)
$39.80 purchase _ #0232
Visits the United States and British Virgin Islands. Looks at St Croix, St John, St Thomas, Anegada, Jost Van Dyke, Norman, Peter, Tortola, Virgin Gorda.
Geography - World; Physical Education and Recreation
Dist - SEVVID

Video guide to videography 90 MIN
VHS
On assignment - the video guide for photography series
Color (J H C G)
$29.95 purchase _ #MED104V VHS
Explains how the viewer can become involved in video photography and how to make filming entertaining and colorful. Part of an eight - part series hosted by nationally known photographer Brian D Ratty.
Industrial and Technical Education
Dist - CAMV

Video health series
Presents a four - part series on health. Includes Feeling Good with Arthritis, Say Goodbye to High Blood Pressure, Coming of Age, and Cardiac Comeback.
Cardiac comeback
Dist - CAMV

Video history of the Civil War - the battle of Gettysburg 40 MIN
VHS
Color (H C A)
$29.95 purchase
Combines original photos, eyewitness accounts, and a live reenactment to recreate the Battle of Gettysburg. Reviews the battles at McPherson's Ridge, Seminary Hill, Devil's Den, and other key sites.
History - United States
Dist - PBS **Prod -** WNETTV

Video home inventory guide 20 MIN
VHS
Color (G)
$19.95 purchase _ #VIDH
Shows how to organize each room and the basic information to read into the camera. Features a Black Rabbit production video.
Business and Economics; Civics and Political Systems; Home Economics
Dist - NOLO

Video immersion method 780 MIN
VHS
Color (G) (FRENCH SPANISH GERMAN)
$295.00 purchase
Offers 13 hours of instruction in French, Spanish or German on seven videocassettes. Includes 14 supplementary audiocassettes and 3 course books.
Foreign Language
Dist - LLAB **Prod -** LLAB 1991

Video in combination with live dance performance 30 MIN
U-matic / VHS
Dance on television and film series
Color
Fine Arts
Dist - ARCVID **Prod -** ARCVID

Video in the ESL Class 30 MIN
VHS
Color (T)
$99.50 purchase _ #SV7260
Demonstrates ten techniques to help teachers use video in the classroom, with guidelines for adapting the program to fit individual needs. Includes text by Susan Stempleski and Barry Tomalin.
English Language; Fine Arts
Dist - NORTNJ **Prod -** BBC

The Video Job Search Tool Kit
U-matic / BETA / VHS
Color (G)
#TKV 102
Identifies the major shifts directing the current job market. Teaches the six major job search steps. Comes with worksheets.
Guidance and Counseling
Dist - CADESF **Prod -** CADESF 1987

Video Job Search Tool Kit 30 MIN
VHS / U-matic
(J H C)
$98.00 _ #CD600V
Gives specific information on techniques and steps to use in looking for a job. Covers many aspects of job search, such as writing a resume, creating a cover letter, conducting an interview and others. Includes accompanying reproducible work sheets.
Business and Economics; Guidance and Counseling; Psychology
Dist - CAMV **Prod -** CAMV

Video Job Search Tool Kit
U-matic / VHS
$98.00 purchase _ #VP50V
Discusses six major job search steps. Compares techniques that the job applicant uses in identifying potential employers with the tactics employers use to locate qualified job applicants.
Guidance and Counseling
Dist - CAREER **Prod -** CAREER

Video journal II - From Grandma's house to Bar Mitzvah 60 MIN
VHS
B&W (G)
$100.00 purchase
Presents an autobiography by Bill Creston. Covers ages six to thirteen. Features scenes and narrative shot on location and ends with a video transfer of the actual 16mm film footage of the artist's elaborate wartime Bar Mitzvah.
Fine Arts; Literature and Drama; Religion and Philosophy; Sociology
Dist - CANCIN

The Video Keys to Job Success
VHS / BETA / U-matic
(G)
#KJV 101
Explores how to be successful when working with a boss, working with others, and working with an organization. Comes with worksheets.
Guidance and Counseling
Dist - CADESF **Prod -** CADESF

The Video keys to school success series
Presents a five part series on school success. Includes the titles Why Follow the Rules, Study Preparation for School Success, Study Skills for School Success, Getting Along With Teachers, Following Directions for School Success.
The Video keys to school success series 124 MIN
Dist - CADESF **Prod -** CADESF
CAMV

Video keys to school success series
Following directions for school success
Getting along with teachers
Study preparation for school success
Why follow the rules
Dist - CAMV

Video learning library series
How to light for videography 30 MIN
How to record sound for video 30 MIN
How to shoot a wedding 30 MIN
How to shoot home video - the basics 30 MIN
How to shoot sports action 30 MIN
Dist - PBS

Video lectures of Hamza Yusuf series
Muhammad - pbuh - the honest
Opposition to Islam yesterday and today
Dist - SOUVIS

Video lectures of Khurram Murad series
Dawa for us and against us
The Prophet and the people around Him
Saving our children in America
Dist - SOUVIS

Video lectures of Yusuf Islam series
Diseases of the heart and its solution in Islam
Education and Muslim youth
Following Muhammad in the Valley of Makkah
From darkness to light
Reaching out with Islam
Yusuf Islam on the Seerah of Prophet Muhammad
Dist - SOUVIS

Video Math Review for the A C T
U-matic / VHS
$35.95 purchase _ #VI104
Provides step by step solutions, multiple choice strategies, important concepts, and time saving hints in a review for the mathematic American Collegiate Test - ACT - .
Education
Dist - CAREER **Prod** - CAREER

Video math review for the SAT - PSAT 105 MIN
VHS
Color (J H)
$29.95 purchase _ #S01009
Features a math teacher who reviews algebra, geometry and arithmetic problems typical of those appearing on the SAT and PSAT college tests. Covers test formats and time - saving testing skills.
Education; Mathematics; Psychology
Dist - UILL

Video music composer library series
The Video music composer library, vol 1
The Video music composer library, vol 2
The Video music composer library, vol 3
Dist - SONYIN

The Video music composer library, vol 1
VHS / U-matic
Video music composer library series
Color (G)
$295.00 purchase
Records songs in segments - verses, bridges, choruses, endings - and cues to graphics on the video screen. Uses the graphics to easily connect musical segments to create complete compositions. Records some musical instruments on channel 1 and others on channel 2. Includes a 30 - page manual with easy to read song index section and a full page of information for each song in the library. A simple step - by - step tutorial illustrates an actual editing exercise using the library. Purchase price is entitlement to unlimited use of the music. Part of a three - volume composer library.
Fine Arts; Industrial and Technical Education
Dist - SONYIN **Prod** - SONYIN

The Video music composer library, vol 2
U-matic / VHS
Video music composer library series
Color (G)
$295.00 purchase
Records songs in segments - verses, bridges, choruses, endings - and cues to graphics on the video screen. Uses the graphics to easily connect musical segments to create complete compositions. Records some musical instruments on channel 1 and others on channel 2. Includes a 30 - page manual with easy to read song index section and a full page of information for each song in the library. A simple step - by - step tutorial illustrates an actual editing exercise using the library. Purchase price is entitlement to unlimited use of the music. Part of a three - volume composer library.
Fine Arts; Industrial and Technical Education
Dist - SONYIN **Prod** - SONYIN

The Video music composer library, vol 3
VHS / U-matic
Video music composer library series
Color (G)
$295.00 purchase
Records songs in segments - verses, bridges, choruses, endings - and cues to graphics on the video screen. Uses the graphics to easily connect musical segments to create complete compositions. Records some musical instruments on channel 1 and others on channel 2. Includes a 30 - page manual with easy to read song index section and a full page of information for each song in the library. A simple step - by - step tutorial illustrates an actual editing exercise using the library. Purchase price is entitlement to unlimited use of the music. Part of a three - volume composer library.
Fine Arts; Industrial and Technical Education
Dist - SONYIN **Prod** - SONYIN

Video music lesson series
Presents a 16 - part series offering step - by - step musical instruction. Features studio musicians, composers, arrangers and educators who lend hands - on instruction about tuning instruments, chord progressions, timing and finger exercises, common note combinations, instrument set - up, special sound techniques. Includes examples of chord and scale theory, examples for technical improvement and songs to teach the principles of the instruments. Includes booklets and titles on guitar chords, rock and roll guitar, fingerpicking country blues guitar, bluegrass banjo, dobro, electric bass, jazz saxophone, country fiddle, blues piano, country piano, accordion, blues harmonica, hammered dulcimer, drum set, steel guitar, songwriting.
Basic bluegrass banjo 60 MIN
Basic guitar chords and accompaniment 60 MIN
Basic jazz saxophone 60 MIN
Blues piano 60 MIN
Blues style harmonica made easy 60 MIN
Country fiddle 60 MIN
Country piano 60 MIN
Dobro 60 MIN
Electric bass 60 MIN
Fingerpicking country blues for guitar 60 MIN
Learn the hammered dulcimer 60 MIN
Pedal steel guitar 60 MIN
Play the accordion 60 MIN
Playing the drum set 60 MIN
Rock and roll guitar 60 MIN
The Songwriter's video guide 60 MIN
Video music lesson series 960MIN
Dist - CAMV

Video package I - Dominic Angerame 29 MIN
VHS
Color & B&W (G)
$35.00 purchase
Presents a set of three productions made between 1982 - 1983. Includes A Ticket Home; I'd Rather Be In Paris; and Honeymoon in Reno. Also available separately in 16mm format. See individual titles for description.
Fine Arts; Geography - United States; Psychology; Sociology
Dist - CANCIN FLMKCO **Prod** - ANGERA

Video package II - Dominic Angerame 25 MIN
VHS
B&W (G)
$35.00 purchase
Presents a set of three productions made between 1984 - 1985. Includes Voyeuristic Tendencies; Phone - Film Portraits; and Hit The Turnpike. Also available separately in 16mm format. See individual titles for description.
Fine Arts; Psychology; Sociology
Dist - CANCIN FLMKCO **Prod** - ANGERA

Video package III - Dominic Angerame 28 MIN
VHS
Color & B&W (G)
$35.00 purchase
Presents a set of six productions made between 1975 - 1982. Includes Scratches, Inc.; El Train Film; A Film; Art Institutionalized - SFAI 1980; Freedom's Skyway; and The Mystery Of Life - As Discovered In Los Angeles. Also available separately in 16mm format. See individual titles for description.
Fine Arts; Geography - United States; Literature and Drama; Mathematics
Dist - CANCIN FLMKCO **Prod** - ANGERA

Video Pioneers 32 MIN
VHS / U-matic
Color
Sketches five New York artists - Vito Acconci, Richard Serra, Willoughby Sharp, Keith Sonnier and William Wegman.
Fine Arts
Dist - ARTINC **Prod** - ARTINC

Video Portrait - Antonio Muntadas 27 MIN
VHS / U-matic
Color
Features an interview with videomaker Antonio Muntadas. Presented by the Long Beach Museum of Art.
Fine Arts
Dist - ARTINC **Prod** - ARTINC

Video Portrait - John Cage 60 MIN
U-matic / VHS
Color
Portrays musician John Cage.
Fine Arts
Dist - KITCHN **Prod** - KITCHN

Video Portrait - Nancy Buchanan 25 MIN
U-matic / VHS
Color
Features an interview with videomaker Nancy Buchanan. Presented by the Long Beach Museum of Art.
Fine Arts
Dist - ARTINC **Prod** - ARTINC

Video Portraits - Max Almy, Dara Birnbaum, David Em, Gary Hill, Bill Viola 37 MIN
U-matic / VHS
Color
Portraits videomakers who discuss their work. Presented by the Long Beach Museum of Art.
Fine Arts
Dist - ARTINC **Prod** - ARTINC

Video post production 28 MIN
VHS
Color (PRO G)
$149.00 purchase, $49.00 rental _ #714
Overviews video post - production basics. Discusses pre - production planning, the efficient use of time code and user bits, structuring the off - line edit to make the on - line edit fast and economical, digital effects, audio sweetening, digital audio and mixed format film - tape procedures. Produced by the Australian Film, Television and Radio School.
Industrial and Technical Education
Dist - FIRLIT

The Video post production survival kit 210 MIN
VHS
Color (G)
$445.00 purchase
Contains an extensive glossary of terms. Teaches shortcut words and common post - production language to enable communications with production engineers. Examines each piece of equipment in a typical post house and explains its purpose and capabilities. Interviews post - production engineers to reveal the tricks of the trade, time - saving, money - saving preparation techniques. Includes a workbook and a list of questions to use when shopping for a facility.
Fine Arts; Industrial and Technical Education; Social Science
Dist - SONYIN **Prod** - SONYIN

Video professor IBM series
Presents a 49-part series on IBM-compatible computer applications which allows the viewer to see keyboard and monitor simultaneously so that students can see the result of every keystroke. Includes seven parts on DOS, 17 parts on word processing, nine parts on spreadsheets, six parts on dBase applications, two parts on desktop publishing and eight parts on Windows applications.
Video professor IBM series 2739 MIN
Dist - CAMV

Video professor Macintosh series
Presents a six-part series on Macintosh graphics which makes the most complex operations of a computer program easy to understand. Uses advanced production techniques which allow viewer to see keyboard and monitor simultaneously. Allows students to learn at their own pace, rewinding or pausing for any section they don't fully understand.
Excel 2.01 introduction
Know your Mac, Mac SE, Mac Plus
Microsoft Word 3.01 introduction
Microsoft Works 2.0 - word processor
Pagemaker 2.0a introduction
Pagemaker 2.0a level II
Dist - CAMV

Video professor - operating systems
VHS
Video professor series
Color (H C A)
Combines the magic of video with computer graphics and animation to make the most complex operations of a computer program easy to understand. Allows viewers to see the keyboard and the monitor simultaneously, so students see the result of every keystroke. Offers Intro to DOS 5.0; Intro to DOS 6.0 and 6.2; DOS 6.0 and 6.2 Level II; DOS 6.0 and 6.2 Level III; and Windows 3.1 Intro. Each title available separately for $29.95.
Computer Science
Dist - CAMV

Video professor operating systems series
DOS introduction 42 MIN
DOS level II 36 MIN
DOS level III 52 MIN
Introduction to DOS 5.0 60 MIN
Introduction to DOS 6.0 60 MIN
OS - 2 for DOS users - introduction 46 MIN
Upgrading to DOS 5.0 58 MIN
Dist - CAMV

Video professor series
Video professor - operating systems
Video professor - spreadsheet MS - DOS
Video professor - Windows applications
Dist - CAMV

Video professor - spreadsheet MS - DOS
VHS
Video professor series
Color (H C A)
Combines the magic of video with computer graphics and animation to make the most complex operations of a computer program easy to understand. Allows viewers to see the keyboard and the monitor simultaneously, so students see the result of every keystroke. Offers Lotus Introduction and Lotus 2.2 and 3.0 Intro. Each title available separately for $29.95.
Computer Science
Dist - CAMV

Video professor - Windows applications
VHS
Video professor series
Color (H C A)
$29.95 purchase
Combines the magic of video with computer graphics and animation to make the most complex operations of a computer program easy to understand. Allows viewers to see the keyboard and the monitor simultaneously, so students see the result of every keystroke. Offers Access 2.0; Word 6.0 Intro; Word 6.0 Level II; Word 6.0 Level III; Excel 5.0 Intro; Lotus 1.1 Intro; Lotus 1.1 Level II; Lotus 1.1 Level III; Lotus 4.0 Intro; Lotus 5.0 Level I; Pagemaker 5.0; WordPerfect 5.1 Intro; WordPerfect 6.0 Intro; WordPerfect 6.0 Level II; WordPerfect 6.0 Level III. Each program available separately for $29.95.
Computer Science
Dist - CAMV

Video professor's Lotus 123 series
Presents a three - part series which uses slow, clear narration and graphics to go step - by - step through each operation in an introduction to Lotus 123. Includes an introduction; Level II; Level III.
Introduction to Lotus 123 45 MIN
Lotus 123 - Level II 74 MIN
Lotus 123 - Level III 50 MIN
Dist - ESPNTV **Prod** - ESPNTV

Video professor's WordPerfect series
Presents a three - part series which uses slow, clear narration and graphics to go step - by - step through each operation in an introduction to WordPerfect.
Introduction to WordPerfect 38 MIN
WordPerfect - Level II 56 MIN
WordPerfect - Level III 57 MIN
Dist - ESPNTV **Prod** - ESPNTV

Video Read - Alongs Series
Balloonia - magic shoelaces
Drip Drop - Play Ball, Kate
Home for a dinosaur - The Monster under my bed
Maxwell Mouse - Great Bunny Race
Tooth Fairy - Presto Change - O
What Time is it - Trouble in Space
Dist - EDUCRT

Video Recorders / Food Processors / Cancer
U-matic / VHS
Consumer Survival Series
Color
Discusses the purchase of video recorders and food processors and the treatment of cancer.
Health and Safety; Home Economics
Dist - MDCPB **Prod** - MDCPB

Video Reflections Series
Body beautiful 30 MIN
Creativity 30 MIN
Dissolving fear and worry 30 MIN
Improved Memory and Concentration 30 MIN
Natural Healing Forces 30 MIN
Self - Image, Self - Confidence 30 MIN
Stop Smoking 30 MIN
Stress Reduction 30 MIN
Wealth and Prosperity 30 MIN
Weight Loss 30 MIN
Dist - GAINST

Video Replay in Group Psychotherapy 50 MIN
VHS / U-matic
Family and Group Therapy Series
Color
Demonstrates through instant feedback the multiple - level inconsistent and contradictory verbal and non - verbal communications which stimulate insight and working through. Allows a look at a woman who faces and is helped to work through psycho - sexual fixated material which she has not been consciously aware.
Health and Safety; Psychology
Dist - HEMUL **Prod** - HEMUL

The Video Resume Writer
U-matic / VHS
(J H C)
$98.00 _ #DC400V
Uses full motion and a medievil scenario to illustrate different sections of a resume and how they should be prepared. Topics covered include the header, the career objective, the content body and others.
Business and Economics; Education; Guidance and Counseling; Psychology
Dist - CAMV **Prod** - CAMV

The Video Resume Writer
VHS / BETA / U-matic
Color (G)
#RRV 101
Provides the basics for resume writing by using numerous examples. Discusses resume sections and how to best package marketable job skills. Comes with worksheets.
Guidance and Counseling
Dist - CADESF **Prod** - CADESF 1987

Video Review for the GED
VHS / U-matic
$59.95 purchase _ #VI107
Provides two tapes for reviewing writing skills, social studies, science, reading skills, and mathematics to prepare for the General Equivalency Diploma - GED - .
Education
Dist - CAREER **Prod** - CAREER

Video sampler 30 MIN
VHS
Color (G R)
$2.50 purchase _ #S12368
Presents excerpts from 10 mission - oriented videos produced by the Lutheran Church - Missouri Synod's Board for Communication Services.
Guidance and Counseling; Literature and Drama; Religion and Philosophy
Dist - CPH **Prod** - LUMIS

The Video S A T Review 120 MIN
U-matic / VHS
$69.95 purchase _ #EE69807V
Provides an instructional prgram which contains exercises to help students improve their Scholastic Aptitude Test - SAT - scores.
Education
Dist - CAREER **Prod** - CAREER

The Video SAT Review 120 MIN
U-matic / Kit / VHS
(H)
Sharpens students' college entrance examination skills. Covers math and verbal sections and teaches anxiety reduction techniques. Includes a sample SAT type test and suggestions for parents in coaching their students. Includes booklets and practice test.
Education
Dist - RH
DIAPRO

Video series
Videomaker - Volume 1, no 1 60 MIN
Dist - INSTRU

The Video SOS - help for parents 65 MIN
VHS
Color (G PRO)
$150.00 purchase _ #PAR100V
Teaches child management skills and concepts such as rewarding good behavior, social rewards, activity rewards, material rewards, point rewards, Grandma's rule, active ignoring, scolding, natural consequences, logical consequences, time - out, behavior penalty, punishment, giving instructions, reflective listening, building self - esteem, being a good role model, rules to follow and four errors to avoid. Includes leader's guide, reproducible handouts and a handbook for parents and professionals.
Guidance and Counseling; Health and Safety; Sociology
Dist - CAMV **Prod** - PARENT 1991

Video story starters - a writer's workshop 120 MIN
VHS
Color (I J H)
$225.00 purchase _ #GW - 128 - VS
Helps young students write their own fiction stories. Provides classroom focus on two distinct areas of writing - the free - wheeling creative process and the rigors of editorial organization. Includes two videos - The Story - Starters and The Writer's Workshop documentary portraying a real writing class learning concepts such as plot structure, imagery, dramatic resolution and the importance of editing and rewriting materials. Includes an extensive teacher's resource book and 30 student writing journals.
English Language; Fine Arts
Dist - HRMC

A Video Supreme Court review of the 1988 - 1989 term - Part B - Labor and employment law opinions 50 MIN
VHS
Color (C PRO A)
$95.00 purchase _ #Y113
Discusses the US Supreme Court rulings of the past term that deal with employee drug testing, equal employment, Title VII, affirmative action and unions and management.
Civics and Political Systems; Social Science
Dist - ALIABA **Prod** - CLETV 1989

A Video Supreme Court review of the 1989 - 1990 term - Civil practice and procedure opinions 50 MIN
VHS
Color (A PRO C)
$95.00 purchase _ #Y131
Examines the 1989 - 1990 High Court opinions that impact on attorneys' fees, subject matter and personal jurisdiction, jury trials, evidence and the Federal Rules of Civil Procedure.
Civics and Political Systems
Dist - ALIABA **Prod** - CLETV 1990

A Video Supreme Court review of the 1989 - 1990 term - Commercial law opinions 50 MIN
VHS
Color (C PRO A)
$95.00 purchase _ #Y132
Covers decisions made in the areas of business, taxation, banking, securities and antitrust law.
Business and Economics; Civics and Political Systems
Dist - ALIABA **Prod** - CLETV 1990

A Video Supreme Court review of the 1989 - 1990 term - First Amendment free - expression opinions 50 MIN
VHS
Color (A PRO C)
$95.00 purchase _ #Y133
Reviews the practical implications of the 1989 - 1990 decisions of the US Supreme Court in the areas of libel, free speech, affirmative action and employment discrimination.
Civics and Political Systems
Dist - ALIABA **Prod** - CLETV 1990

A Video Supreme Court review of the 1989 - 1990 term - Labor and employment law opinions 50 MIN
VHS
Color (C PRO A)
$95.00 purchase _ #Y134
Discusses the US Supreme Court rulings of the past term that deal with unions and management, employment compensation, employment records, 42 USC Section 1983 and employer rights.
Civics and Political Systems; Social Science
Dist - ALIABA **Prod** - CLETV 1990

Video techniques - on - location lighting 40 MIN
VHS / U-matic / BETA
Color (G PRO)
$125.00 purchase _ #A542 - Me
Describes the basic of on - location lighting. Discusses the importance of contrast, selection of lighting fixtures, shooting with available light, principles of key, back and fill lights, using tools such as frames, screens and umbrellas. Features Ralph Metzer.
Fine Arts; Industrial and Technical Education
Dist - KIPI **Prod** - KIPI 1985

The Video toolbox - how to make a video program 70 MIN
VHS
Color (G)
$49.95 purchase
Illustrates video production from A to Z. Shows in detail how to develop a concept, the principles behind screenwriting, how to plan the shoot, the role of the director, the basics of screen language, shot coverage and the key concepts of editing. Interweaves graphics, animation, practical advice and technical tips with two case studies, a documentary and a 'road movie,' and follow - up activities are suggested at the end of each segment.
Industrial and Technical Education
Dist - FIRLIT **Prod** - AFTRS 1994

Video tours history series
Henry Ford Museum and Greenfield Village 30 MIN
Dist - SVIP

Video Training for Educators Series
The Assaultive student - Vol III 30 MIN
The Disruptive Adolescent - Vol II 30 MIN
The Disruptive Child - Vol 1 30 MIN
Dist - NCPI

Video training workshops on child variance series
Presents a six - part series produced by William C Morse and Judith M Smith. Offers behavior sequences and five tapes of discussion between educators and psychologists representing differing viewpoints. Examines psychodynamic, behavioral, biophysical, sociological, ecological, traditonal and alternative therapies.
Behavioral vs biophysical, James McConnell vs Aaron Smith 30 MIN
Ecological vs behavioral, Jacob Kounin vs Frank Hewitt 30 MIN
Psychodynamic vs behaviorial, Jane Kessler vs Richard Whelan 30 MIN
Sociological vs psychodynamic - Edgar Epps vs Nicholas Long 30 MIN
Tape of 15 behavior sequences 30 MIN
Traditional vs alternative, William C Rhodes vs Peter Knoblock 30 MIN
Dist - CEXPCN **Prod** - CEXPCN 1994

Video trilogy series
Consists of three short films, 'A Picture of Sin,' 'A Picture of Rebirth,' and 'A Picture of Celebration.' Includes leader's guide. Produced by Paul Keller and Stan Kloth.
A picture of celebration - Video 3
A picture of rebirth - Video 2
A picture of sin - Video 1
Dist - APH

Video tutor basic math series
Presents a seven - part series on basic mathematics. Includes Percents, Decimals, Fractions, Pre - Algebra, Basic Word Problems, Basic Number Concepts and Basic Geometry.
Basic geometry 62 MIN
Basic number concepts 46 MIN
Decimals 60 MIN
Fractions 98 MIN
Percents 98 MIN
Pre - algebra 95 MIN
Dist - CAMV

Video tutor basic math series
Basic word problems 63 MIN
Dist - CAMV
UILL

Video Verbal Review for the A C T
U-matic / VHS
$35.95 purchase _ #VI105
Examines creative test taking techniques, multiple choice strategies, time - saving suggestions, and rules and hints.
Education
Dist - CAREER **Prod** - CAREER

Video verbal review for the SAT - PSAT 105 MIN
VHS
Color (J H)
$29.95 purchase _ #S01010
Covers antonyms, analogies, sentence completions amd reading comprehension, all of which appear on SAT and PSAT college tests. Stresses the importance of using logic and reasoning in taking the verbal tests.
Education; English Language; Psychology
Dist - UILL

Video visits series
Presents a 38-part series visiting cities, countries, islands, kingdoms, states and provinces in Europe, Asia, the Mediterranean area and Africa, Central and South America, the South Pacific and North America. Teaches about the people, culture and history of specific locations in all these areas. Visits historic buildings, monuments and landmarks. Examines the physical topography of locations.
Portugal - land of discovery 60 MIN
Video visits series 2280 MIN
Dist - CAMV

Video voodoo 30 MIN
VHS
Color (G)
$25.00 purchase
Entertains with a collection of shorts and excerpts by The Residents. Features their retrospective of visual works from the Museum of Modern Art in New York. Covers 1975 - 1980. Presents It's A Man's Man's Man's World; Earth vs Flying Saucers; One - Minute Movies; Hello Skinny; excerpt from the Moleshow - Sack Your Lips; excerpt from Vileness Fats - Eloise; The Third Reich and Roll; and Songs for Swinging Larvae. Produced by Ralph Records, The Residents' recording label.
Fine Arts; Industrial and Technical Education
Dist - CANCIN

Video voyages - cruising Puerto Rico and the Dominican Republic 43 MIN
VHS
Color (G)
$39.95 purchase _ #0924
Visits the second and third largest islands in the Caribbean, Puerto Rico and the Dominican Republic. Gives information about harbors, facilities and services for cruisers.
Geography - United States; Geography - World; Physical Education and Recreation
Dist - SEVVID

Video Wars
U-matic / VHS
$29.95 purchase
Points out that at the International Video Game Championship, the winner can save the world. OR, destroy it.
Computer Science
Dist - BESTF **Prod** - BESTF

The Video Wine Guide 90 MIN
U-matic / VHS
Color (A)
LC 83-706676
Introduces wine by visiting winemaking regions of Italy, France, Germany, California and New York State. Hosted by Dick Cavett, who demystifies the sommelier and ordering wine in a restaurant. Concludes with investing in wine, setting up a wine cellar, pronouncing wine names and selecting a cork puller.
Home Economics
Dist - SERPRO **Prod** - SERPRO 1982

Video Workshops Series - Nine Titles on Nine VHS Tapes -
Video Workshops Set
Dist - CAREER

Video workshops series
Bowl turning
Carve a ball - and - claw foot
Carving techniques and projects
Dovetail a Drawer
Making Mortise and Tenon Joints
Radial Arm Saw Joinery
Router Jigs and Techniques
Small shop tips and techniques
Wood Finishing
Dist - CAREER

Video Workshops Set
VHS
Video Workshops Series - Nine Titles on Nine VHS Tapes -
$309.55 purchase _ #FW001
Master craftsmen provide demonstrations of their techniques for doing various woodworking projects.
Education; Industrial and Technical Education
Dist - CAREER **Prod** - CAREER

Videoclinical Series Series
Milisen - Articulation Testing 37 MIN
Dist - WMUDIC

Videoconferencing 48 MIN
VHS / U-matic / BETA
Color (G A)
$5.00 rental
Shows step - by - step how to use the method of videoconferencing as a workplace tool. Interviews two union representatives who have used the technology.
Business and Economics; Social Science
Dist - AFLCIO **Prod** - LIPA 1983

Videocycle Exercise Programs - Grand Teton Tour 60 MIN
BETA / VHS
Color (I)
Describes the programs as a 'perfect cure' for cycling boredom blues. Provides videotaped bicycle tour along America's most scenic routes, complete with the occasional passing of cars and the motion of biking. Like being there. Has three 18 minute, self paced segments, each with warm up workout and cool down. Has periodic pulse checks and a tour coach to monitor progress.
Physical Education and Recreation
Dist - CBSC **Prod** - CBSC

Videocycle Exercise Programs - Yellowstone Tour 60 MIN
BETA / VHS
Color (I)
Describes the programs as a 'perfect cure' for cycling boredom blues. Provides a videotaped bicycle tour among America's most scenic routes, complete with the occasional passing of cars and the motion of biking. Like being there. Has three 18 minute, self paced segments, each with warm up work and cool down. Has periodic pulse checks and a tour coach to monitor progress.
Physical Education and Recreation
Dist - CBSC **Prod** - CBSC

Videodance project series
Suite fantaisiste 9 MIN
Dist - ARCVID

Videodance Project, Vol 1 Series
Etude in Free 8 MIN
Dist - ARCVID

Videodance Project - Volume One Series
Etude in Free 9 MIN
Herald's round 8 MIN
Dist - ARCVID

The Videodisc encyclopedia of medical images
Videodisc
Color (G C PRO)
$795.00 purchase _ #UW3243
Contains more than 12,000 images in high quality photographs and illustrations selected by medical experts. Includes a complete index on floppy disk and in print, as well as Slideshow, a software program that makes it easy to create a custom presentation in minutes. Trains healthcare professionals, teachers, students and medical resource center personnel. Contact distributor about requirements.
Health and Safety
Dist - FOTH

Videodiscs in Education - Minnesota, the Cutting Edge 26 MIN
VHS / 16mm
(T)
$50.00 purchase _ #VID5202
Explains the capabilities, uses and advantages of videodiscs and considers how they should be used in schools. Provides instruction for educators wondering how videodiscs can enhance classroom learning.
Computer Science; Education
Dist - MECC **Prod** - MECC

VideoFrance series
Optiques - la vie quotidienne 60 MIN
Panorama de la France 60 MIN
Profils des Francais 60 MIN
Dist - NTCPUB

Videograms 14 MIN
U-matic
B&W (C)
$100.00
Experimental film by Gary Hill.
Fine Arts
Dist - AFA **Prod** - AFA 1981

A Videoguide to dis - ability awareness 25 MIN
VHS
Color (G)
Features President Bill Clinton who opens and closes a program on the Americans with Disabilities Act. Explores the impact of personal attitudes and public awareness on the goals of the ADA. Visits McDonald's Corporation, Orion Pictures, K mart and Levi Strauss & Co. Shows how to communicate with people with specific disabilities such as vision, hearing, physical and developmental. Offers guidelines on appropriate language, expressions and terminology. Distinguishes myths from facts about people with disabilities by revealing important facts about people with disabilities while dispelling many widely - held misconceptions.
Health and Safety
Dist - IDEABA **Prod** - IDEABA 1993
FANPRO

The Videoguide to Stamp Collecting 50 MIN
VHS
Color (G)
Uses M A S H star Gary Burghoff to explain stamp collecting. Available for free loan from the distributor.
Business and Economics; Fine Arts; Physical Education and Recreation
Dist - AUDPLN

Videomaker - Volume 1, no 1 60 MIN
VHS
Video series
Color (H C G)
$29.95 purchase _ #T/C519651
Includes lighting tips, making documentaries, capturing news stories, and more. Discusses the tools and techniques of the professionals.
Fine Arts; Industrial and Technical Education
Dist - INSTRU

VideoPassport French 60 MIN
VHS
Color (G A) (ENGLISH AND FRENCH)
$39.95 purchase
Features native speakers taped on location to emphasize communication skills such as asking directions, ordering meals and shopping while using the French language. Videotape is augmented by a comprehensive user's manual with grammar instructions and an audiocassette of the videoscript. Prepared by Brian Hill and Catherine Carpenter.
Foreign Language; Geography - World; History - World
Dist - NTCPUB **Prod** - NTCPUB

VideoPassport Spanish 60 MIN
VHS
Color (G A) (ENGLISH AND SPANISH)
$39.95 purchase
Features native Spanish speakers taped on location to emphasize communication skills such as asking directions, ordering meals and shopping while using the language. Videotape is augmented by a comprehensive user's manual with grammar instructions and an audiocassette of the videoscript. Prepared by Brian Hill and Pili Batley - Matlas.
Foreign Language; Geography - World; History - World
Dist - NTCPUB **Prod** - NTCPUB

Videosearch behavior skill model series
Developing ideas 16 MIN
Giving recognition 12 MIN
Handling Conflicts 18 MIN
Providing Feedback 19 MIN
Dist - DELTAK

Videosearch Employment Interview Series
The Employment Interview - a Case Study 60 MIN
Making the Interview Work - Five Ways to Improve Interviewing 25 MIN
What's Wrong with the Interview 20 MIN
Dist - DELTAK

Videosearch Performance Appraisal (Case Studies Series
Engineering 40 MIN
Finance / Control 30 MIN
Manufacturing 30 MIN
Sales - marketing 30 MIN
Dist - DELTAK

Videotape - Disc - or 30 MIN
U-matic / VHS
On and about Instruction Series
Color (T)
Examines new and emerging technologies in teaching methods.
Education
Dist - GPN **Prod** - VADE 1983

Videotape for a woman and man 34 MIN
VHS
Color & B&W (G A)
$70.00 purchase
Features a dance production directed, choreographed and performed by Amy Greenfield. Makes an absorbing inquiry into male - female relationships. Examines the possible physical and emotional encounters between men and women. Features dancer Ben Dolphin with Greenfield.
Fine Arts; Psychology
Dist - CANCIN

Videotape of 1986 Abraham Joshua Heschel award
VHS
Color (R G)
$30.00 purchase, $15.00 rental
Records the presentation of the 1986 Abraham Joshua Heschel award to Rabbi Bruce Cohen. Includes Elie Weisel and Susannah Heschel as speakers. Transcript of the ceremony available separately.
Religion and Philosophy; Sociology
Dist - JPEACE **Prod** - JPEACE 1986

Videotaped Case Vignettes 60 MIN
VHS
Complete DSM - III - R Training Program Series
(PRO)
$200 Videotape
Presents several vignettes for practice and self - evaluation in applying the APA's DSM - III - R diagnostic system. Disorders covered include Major Depression, Borderline Personality Disorder Schizophrenia, Childhood Onset Pervasive Developmental Disorder, and Presenile Dementia. Case histories and findings are included. Based on real cases and altered to fit DSM - III - R criteria for each disorder.
Psychology
Dist - BRUMAZ **Prod** - BRUMAZ 1989

Videoteca - Spanish programme 100 MIN
VHS
Color; PAL (H) (ENGLISH & SPANISH)
PdS40 purchase
Presents five programs of 20 minutes each illustrating different aspects of everyday life in Spain for students and tourists. Covers cooking, writing postcards, asking for information and arranging accommodations. Contact distributor about availability outside the United Kingdom.
Foreign Language; Geography - World
Dist - ACADEM

Videothek - German programme 100 MIN
VHS
Color; PAL (H) (ENGLISH & GERMAN)
PdS40 purchase
Presents five programs of 20 minutes each designed to develop listening and speaking skills in German. Enlarges active and passive speaking vocabularies and develops understanding of the German people, country and language. Uses scenes from everyday life to illustrate the similarities and differences between people living in Britain and in Germany. Contact distributor about availability outside the United Kingdom.
Foreign Language; Geography - World
Dist - ACADEM

Videotheque - Niveau superieur 200 MIN
VHS
Color; PAL (H) (ENGLISH & FRENCH)
PdS55 purchase
Presents ten programs of 20 minutes each recorded on location in France. Covers a different aspect of everyday life in France in each program, illustrated by sequences filmed in Caen, Normandy. Provides a language model and texts for comprehension, using authentic material to stimulate student interest in the language. Contact distributor about availability outside the United Kingdom.
Foreign Language; Geography - World
Dist - ACADEM

VideoTours history series
American Museum of Natural History 30 MIN
Audubon zoo 30 MIN
Biltmore estate 30 MIN
Boston Freedom Trail 30 MIN
Busch Gardens 30 MIN
Colonial Williamsburg 30 MIN
Columbus zoo 30 MIN
Monterey Bay Aquarium 30 MIN
Newport mansions 30 MIN
Old Salem 30 MIN
Old Sturbridge Village 30 MIN
Old Surbridge Village - growing up in New England 30 MIN
Plimoth plantation 30 MIN
San Diego Zoo 30 MIN
Dist - SVIP

Vidisco's video preparation for the S A T - math 115 MIN
VHS
Color (H)
$29.95 purchase
Presents a review of mathematics skills for students planning to take the Scholastic Aptitude Test. Uses fast - paced, familiar television situations and characterizations to capture the student's attention. Offers test - taking techniques, time - saving hints, multiple - choice strategies, and more. Includes study guide.
Education
Dist - PBS **Prod** - WNETTV

Vidisco's video preparation for the S A T - verbal 115 MIN
VHS
Color (H)
$29.95 purchase
Presents a review of verbal skills for students planning to take the Scholastic Aptitude Test. Uses fast - paced, familiar television situations and characterizations to capture the student's attention. Offers test - taking techniques, time - saving hints, multiple - choice strategies, and more. Includes study guide.
Education
Dist - PBS **Prod** - WNETTV

Vielleicht Versuchen Wir's Einmal Mit Studenten 15 MIN
U-matic / VHS / 16mm
Guten Tag Wie Geht's Series
Color (H C) (GERMAN)
Features Siggi, a music student, joining Gunther's construction crew and surprising everyone.
Foreign Language
Dist - IFB **Prod** - BAYER 1970

Vienna 30 MIN
VHS
Color (G)
$29.95 purchase _ #S02030
Tours Vienna. Features the coffee houses, pastry shops, cathedrals, museums, and other sites. Includes musical excerpts from Mozart, Beethoven, and Strauss, all of whom lived in Vienna at one time or another.
Geography - World
Dist - UILL

Vienna 25 MIN
VHS
Color (G)
Visits Vienna. Available for free loan from the distributor.
Fine Arts; Geography - World
Dist - AUDPLN

Vienna 60 MIN
VHS / U-matic
James Galway's Music in Time Series
Color (J)
LC 83-706263
Presents flutist James Galway discussing the work of Mozart and Schubert, and Sir Peter Hall examining Mozart's operas.
Fine Arts
Dist - FOTH **Prod** - POLTEL 1982

Vienna 1900 53 MIN
VHS
Color (G)
$39.95 purchase _ #VIE02
Portrays a society lost in the pleasures of the glittering empire of Vienna at the turn of the century. Reveals that iconoclastic thinkers in that society, such as Schoenberg, Mahler, Klimt, Schiele, Freud and Kraus, were to be part of a revolution which would change the world forever.
History - World; Sociology
Dist - HOMVIS **Prod** - RMART 1990

Vienna is different - 50 years after the Anschluss 75 MIN
VHS
Color (H C G)
$495.00 purchase, $80.00 rental
Depicts Austrians addressing a past that has been suppressed and denied. Films in cafes, the street, public demonstrations and cabaret performances to show how many Austrians still evade and excuse their nation's collaboration with the Nazis. Portrays aristocrats, neo - Nazis, Jews, people on the street and Kurt Waldheim. Reveals that Hitler boasted that he learned his anti - Semitism in the streets of Vienna. Produced by Susan Korda and David Leitner.
Geography - World; History - World
Dist - FLMLIB

Vienna - Stripping the Facade 25 MIN
U-matic / VHS / 16mm
Rise of Modernism in Music Series
Color (A)
LC 82-700636
Portrays Vienna in the early 20th century to show what gave rise to the atonal, innovative music of Arnold Schoenberg and other modern Viennese composers. Explores the political and cultural environments which helped to shape Schoenberg's music, including achievements in the arts, architecture and literature.
Fine Arts
Dist - MEDIAG **Prod** - BBCTV 1982

The Vienna Tribunal 48 MIN
VHS
Color (G)
$60.00 rental, $195.00 purchase
Highlights moving personal testimonies at the Global Tribunal on Violations of Women's Rights, held in conjunction with the United Nations World Conference on Human Rights in Vienna in 1993. Reveals why women's rights need to be seen as human rights. Not simply a documentation of past events, but also a thought - provoking analysis of the abuses women suffer the world over.
Civics and Political Systems; Fine Arts; History - World; Sociology
Dist - WMEN **Prod** - ROGGER 1994

Viennese waltz 60 MIN
VHS
Kathy Blake dance studios - let's learn how to dance series
Color (G A)
$39.95 purchase
Features dance instructors Kathy Blake and Gene Russo, who instruct viewers on the basics of the Viennese waltz. First of three parts.
Fine Arts
Dist - PBS **Prod** - WNETTV

Viennese waltz II 60 MIN
VHS
Kathy Blake dance studios - let's learn how to dance series
Color (G A)
$39.95 purchase
Features dance instructors Kathy Blake and Gene Russo, who instruct viewers on the basics of the Viennese waltz. Second of three parts.
Fine Arts
Dist - PBS **Prod** - WNETTV

Viennese waltz III 60 MIN
VHS
Kathy Blake dance studios - let's learn how to dance series
Color (G A)
$39.95 purchase
Features dance instructors Kathy Blake and Gene Russo, who instruct viewers on the basics of the Viennese waltz. Third of three parts.
Fine Arts
Dist - PBS **Prod** - WNETTV

Vierundzwanzig Stunden Aus Dem Leben Einer Frau 80 MIN
16mm
B&W (GERMAN (ENGLISH SUBTITLES))
Tells the story of Helga Wanroh, a widow who moves to the Riviera, where chance brings her together with a compulsive gambler who has already tried to rid himself of his addiction and is now convinced that the only way out is death. Ends with the two sharing hope for a new beginning.
Fine Arts; Foreign Language
Dist - WSTGLC **Prod** - WSTGLC 1931

Viet - flakes 11 MIN
VHS
B&W w/color tint (G)
$25.00 purchase
Composes an obsessive collection of Vietnam atrocity images collected from foreign magazine and newspapers over a five - year period. Uses various experimental techniques, such as taping magnifying glass onto a 16mm Bolex in order to physically 'travel' within the photographs. Produced by Carolee Schneemann.
Fine Arts; History - United States; Industrial and Technical Education; Sociology
Dist - CANCIN

Viet Nam Report - Focus on Indonesia 20 MIN
16mm
Screen news digest series; Vol 7; Issue 8
B&W
Describes the deepening crisis in Viet Nam as the Viet Cong step up their bombings and raids, and the United States retaliates with air assaults in the north. Discusses the geography and history of Indonesia, and describes her withdrawal from the United Nations.
Geography - World; History - World
Dist - HEARST **Prod** - HEARST 1965

Viet Nam - Why - a Timely Report 15 MIN
16mm
Screen news digest series; Vol 7; Issue 1
B&W (J A)
LC FIA68-2101
Traces the history of Viet Nam from its reconstruction after the French Indo - China war to the events of the summer of 1964.
History - World
Dist - HEARST **Prod** - HEARST 1964

Vietnam 30 MIN
VHS / 16mm
Say Brother National Edition Series
Color (G)
$55.00 rental _ #SBRO - 102
Sociology
Dist - PBS **Prod** - WGBHTV

Vietnam 25 MIN
VHS / U-matic / 16mm / BETA
Changing faces of communism series
Color (J H G)
$390.00, $110.00 purchase _ #C50544, #C51392
Examines the efforts of the communist leaders of Vietnam to apply Marxist - Leninist principles to traditional Asian culture. Shows the adjustments to the communist system that must be made to improve the economy. Part of a three - part series on the changing status of communism.
Civics and Political Systems; Geography - World; History - World
Dist - NGS **Prod** - NGS 1990

Vietnam 54 MIN
VHS
Color (J H C G)
$29.95 purchase _ #IVN1336V - S
Travels the Red River Delta to the broad boulevards of Hanoi. Looks at the legacy of Ho Chi Minh in his home and mausoleum. Celebrates the Hun King Festival marking Vietnam's founding. Examines the history of the Vietnam War and witnesses the rebuilding of Vietnam. Journeys to Confucian and Buddhist shrines and caves in Da Nang's Marble Mountain. Explores the Huyen Khong Cave, a field hospital during the 'American War.' Watches the performance of water puppets, a cast of frog catchers, fairies and mythical monsters.
History - United States
Dist - CAMV

Vietnam 101 14 MIN
U-matic / VHS
Color (G)
$249.00, $149.00 purchase _ #AD - 1732
Presents a segment from '60 Minutes' designed to provoke discussion about the war in Vietnam.
History - United States; History - World; Sociology
Dist - FOTH **Prod** - FOTH

Vietnam - 1955 to 1975 52 MIN
VHS
Century of warfare series
Color (G)
$19.99 purchase _ #0 - 7835 - 8426 - 1NK
Looks at the 20 - year conflict in Vietnam. Covers strategy, tactics, personalities, campaigns, victories and defeats. Part of a 20 - part series on 20th - century warfare.
Civics and Political Systems; History - World; Sociology
Dist - TILIED

Vietnam - a case study for critical thinking 52 MIN
VHS
Color (J H C G)
$129.95 purchase _ #CLE0199V
Describes the Vietnam war from two points of view. Features Historian Smith who holds that the United States was wrong to be engaged in affairs in Vietnam either as an advisor or active combatant. Historian Jones argues that the US was justifiably engaged and should have perservered to victory. Focuses on persuasion tactics used in the opposing presentations, including music, tone of voice, visual sequences, treatment of issues and selection of evidence. Includes worksheets for duplication offering 15 varied exercises, 41 photocopy masters and a teacher's guide.
Civics and Political Systems; History - United States; Psychology; Sociology
Dist - CAMV

Vietnam - a rising dragon 29 MIN
VHS
Color (J H)
$195.00 purchase
Focuses on changes occurring in Vietnam as the country develops its industrial base and becomes a rice and oil exporter. Looks at governmental reforms and economic expansion.
Geography - World
Dist - LANDMK

Vietnam - a television history series 780 MIN
VHS
Vietnam - a television history series
Color (H C A)
$99.95 purchase
Presents a 13 - part series covering the history of the Vietnam War. Covers the major events, from the 1945 rebellion against France to the fall of Saigon in 1975. Consists of seven videocassettes.
History - United States
Dist - PBS **Prod** - WNETTV

Vietnam - a television history series 780 MIN
VHS
Vietnam - a television history series
Color (G)
$195.65 purchase _ #S01535
Consists of 13 programs examining the US involvement in Vietnam. Covers the relevant history from 1946, when Vietnam was still a French colony, to 1975 and the fall of Saigon.
History - United States
Dist - UILL **Prod** - PBS

Vietnam - a television history series
America takes charge, 1965 - 1967 60 MIN
America's Mandarin, 1954 - 1963 60 MIN
The End of the Tunnel, 1973 - 1975 60 MIN
The First Vietnam War, 1946 - 1954 60 MIN
Homefront USA 60 MIN
LBJ Goes to War, 1964 - 1965 60 MIN
Legacies - episode 13 60 MIN
No Neutral Ground - Cambodia and Laos 60 MIN
Peace is at Hand 60 MIN
The Roots of War 60 MIN
Tet, 1968 60 MIN
Vietnamizing the War, 1969 - 1973 60 MIN
With America's Enemy, 1954 - 1967 60 MIN
Dist - FI

Vietnam - After the Fire 106 MIN
VHS / 16mm
Color (G)
$395.00 purchase, $100.00 rental; LC 89715752
Examines Vietnam and the extensive damage done to its environment and people by the war. Reveals that more bombs were dropped on Vietnam then were used during World War II, leaving over 26 million craters and an unknown number of unexploded bombs which continue to kill or maim thousands of Vietnamese each year. The extensive use of Agent Orange destroyed vast areas of the country's ecosystem and is still present in people's bodies. Deformed babies continue to be born and many women are at risk for cancer of the womb.
Health and Safety; History - United States; History - World; Sociology
Dist - CNEMAG **Prod** - CNEMAG 1988

Vietnam - an American Journey 85 MIN
U-matic / VHS / 16mm
Color (H C A)
Surveys Vietnam since the end of the war by traveling from Hanoi to Saigon and interviewing survivors, visiting orphanages and rehabilitation centers. Includes an interview with a My Lai massacre survivor.
History - United States
Dist - FI **Prod** - MCBRID 1979
FIRS

Vietnam - an Historical Document 56 MIN
U-matic / VHS / 16mm
Color (C)
LC 76-700552
Uses television videotape news reports to trace the history of American involvement in Vietnam from the early 1950's to the fall of South Vietnam in 1973. Narrated by Walter Cronkite.
History - United States; History - World
Dist - CAROUF **Prod** - CBSTV 1976

Vietnam and Southeast Asia 20 MIN
16mm
B&W (SPANISH)
Explains that while the U S government's direct involvement in the Vietnam war is now ten years old, the forgotten war in neighboring Laos continues. Uses an introduction in Spanish to show that our government's presence is being fought by a united front of the Laotian people.
Civics and Political Systems; Sociology
Dist - CANWRL **Prod** - CANWRL

Vietnam - chronicle of a war 88 MIN
VHS
Color; B&W (G)
$49.95 purchase _ #S00348
Uses footage from the CBS News archives to review events of the Vietnam War. Attempts to give a total perspective of US involvement, from the defeat of the French to the lasting effects of the war on Americans. Includes commentary from CBS News personnel Walter Cronkite, Dan Rather, Morley Safer, Eric Severeid and others.
History - United States
Dist - UILL **Prod** - CBSTV 1981
IHF
ASPRSS
GA

Vietnam Crucible 29 MIN
16mm
Big Picture Series
Color
LC 74-706314
Reports on the American soldier's activities in Vietnam, presenting both the military and civilian situation.
Civics and Political Systems; History - United States; History - World; Sociology
Dist - USNAC **Prod** - USA 1968

Vietnam Epilogue - the End of the Tunnel 15 MIN
16mm
Screen news digest series; Vol 15; Issue 7
Color (I)
LC 73-701273
Presents a chronology of United States involvement in Indo - China from the fall of Dien Bien Phu in 1954 to the Vietnam cease - fire agreement in 1973.

Civics and Political Systems; Geography - World; History - United States; History - World
Dist - HEARST **Prod** - HEARST 1973

Vietnam - Five Years After the War 11 MIN
U-matic / VHS
Color (H C A)
Examines society and government in Vietnam during the late 1970's.
History - World
Dist - JOU **Prod** - UPI

Vietnam - good morning Uncle Sam 40 MIN
VHS
Business matters series
Color (A)
PdS65 purchase
Reveals that, almost 20 years after Vietnam defeated the military might of the United States, it is on the brink of yet another victory - in commerce. States that Western businesses are lining up to organize joint ventures, even though the country is still under a United States trade embargo and American businessmen have to pose as Canadian tourists for entry into Vietnam to compete with Europeans and Japanese.
Business and Economics; Civics and Political Systems
Dist - BBCENE

Vietnam home movies series
Presents a four - part series which features actual footage shot by soldiers during their tour of duty in Vietnam. Tells the story of one soldier in his own words, the combat missions, his friends, his joy after a successful rescue, the devastation after an enemy raid, the sounds of war. Offers footage aboard a UH1 Huey helicopter gunship, a pass dodging sniper fire from the Viet Cong, looking down the rocket sight on a search and destroy mission. Includes Demailo - Smiling Tigers; Powell - Gunslingers; White - Outpost Legionnaire; Overton - Rife Company.

Demailo - smiling tigers 30 MIN
Overton - rifle company 30 MIN
Powell - gunslingers 30 MIN
White - outpost legionnaire 30 MIN
Dist - CAMV

Vietnam - Images of War 26 MIN
VHS / U-matic
Color (H C A)
Presents a montage of scenes which made headline news coverage during the 15 years of the Vietnam War.
History - United States; History - World
Dist - JOU **Prod** - UPI

Vietnam, Land of Fire 25 MIN
16mm
B&W (FRENCH)
Shows the American invasion of Vietnam and attack on the civilian population. Shows the use of naplam, gas and toxic chemicals. Views bombings of schools and leprosaria. Filmed in North and South Vietnam.
Civics and Political Systems; Foreign Language; Geography - World
Dist - CANWRL **Prod** - UNKNWN 1967

Vietnam Legacy 50 MIN
16mm / U-matic
Assignment Maclear Series
Color; Mono (J H C A)
$500.00 film, $350.00 video, $50.00 rental
Explores the CIA sponsored program 'Operation Phoenix' and also looks at the Vietnam veterans who need counceling and what forms of help are available for them.
Health and Safety; History - World
Dist - CTV **Prod** - CTV 1977

Vietnam - Lessons of a Lost War 50 MIN
VHS / U-matic
Color (H C A)
Examines the facts and myths about the longest and most controversial war in American history. Presents facts, interpretations and film about the war's most controversial moments.
History - United States
Dist - FI **Prod** - NBCNEW

Vietnam Memorial 52 MIN
VHS / U-matic
Color (H C A)
LC 84-707630
Documents the gathering of Vietnam War Veterans and families in Washington on Veteran's Day, 1982, at which time they expressed their frustrations over bureaucracy, agent orange and public indifference.
Guidance and Counseling; History - United States; Sociology
Dist - YRKWIL **Prod** - YRKWIL 1983

Vietnam Memorial 58 MIN
VHS / BETA
Frontline Series
Color
Describes the events of November 1982 when more than 150,000 people came to Washington DC to participate in the National Salute to Vietnam Veterans. Captures the celebration and emotion of the five - day tribute, which ended with a parade honoring the returning veterans and the dedication of the Vietnam Memorial.
History - United States; History - World
Dist - PBS **Prod** - DOCCON

Vietnam Newsreel Review - 1967 50 MIN
VHS / U-matic
Color
Presents highlights of USAF military action in Vietnam in 1967 photographed by combat cameramen of the 600th Photo Squadron. Includes visits to Air Force bases by General McConnell, F - 105 strikes on targets in North Vietnam, B - 57 ground - support bombing, Super Sabres in action, supply drops to Khe Sanh, air - traffic controllers at Danang air base, a medical evacuation to the United States, Air Force chaplains at Cam Ranh air base and Operation ATL Buro airlift sorties.
Civics and Political Systems; History - United States
Dist - IHF **Prod** - IHF

Vietnam Perspective 32 MIN
U-matic / VHS / 16mm
Color (I J H C)
Presents an objective chronology of foreign involvement in Southeast Asia. Highlights America's participation in the VietnamWar.
History - United States; History - World
Dist - EBEC **Prod** - EBEC 1985

Vietnam - Picking Up the Pieces 60 MIN
16mm
Color
LC 79-706203
Takes a tour of Vietnam two years after the liberation. Reveals a nation in the throes of change, seeking to heal the social and economic wounds of war. Looks at government programs aimed at social improvement.
Geography - World; History - World
Dist - DCTVC **Prod** - DCTVC 1978

Vietnam Report 22 MIN
VHS / U-matic
Color
Offers reports of Soviet correspondents on U S bombing raids over North Vietnam and the effects they are having on the people.
History - World
Dist - IHF **Prod** - IHF

Vietnam Report - Guardians at the Gate 12 MIN
16mm
Screen news digest series; Vol 8; Issue 1
B&W (J)
LC 70-700508
Examines the history and the nature of the commitment of the United States to South Vietnam.
Civics and Political Systems; History - United States
Dist - HEARST **Prod** - HEARST 1965

Vietnam Requiem 58 MIN
16mm
Color (H C A)
Interviews five Vietnam veterans, all decorated war heroes who are now serving prison sentences. Relays the horrors of war and the unhappiness and bitterness felt by these heroes returning home from an unpopular war.
History - United States
Dist - DIRECT UILL **Prod** - KORTY 1983

Vietnam Rewritten 26 MIN
U-matic / VHS
Color (G)
$249.00, $149.00 purchase _ #AD - 1710
Examines the changes in America's perception of the Vietnam War. Discusses the nature of historical revision. Includes comments by Frances Fitzgerald and Stanley Karnow.
History - United States; History - World; Sociology
Dist - FOTH **Prod** - FOTH

Vietnam Rewritten - 123 30 MIN
U-matic
Currents - 1984 - 85 Season Series
Color (A)
Takes another look at the American incursion in Southeast Asia and the effects it had on the soldiers who fought there and the nation as a whole.
History - United States; Social Science
Dist - PBS **Prod** - WNETTV 1985

Vietnam stories 35 MIN
VHS
Color (J H C G)
$89.95 purchase, $45.00 rental _ #TTP140
Features an oral history documentary made in collaboration with high school students about the Vietnam War. Presents 11th grade students interviewing both Vietnam combat veterans who fought in the war and draft resisters who went to jail fighting against it. The veterans give a riveting personal account of their experiences and talk candidly with the students about how ill - prepared they were for the realities of combat, along with the difficulties of returning home to civilian life. The war resisters discuss why they refused to fight and describe facing the consequences of imprisonment - raising fundamental questions about an individual's right to dissent in a democracy.
Fine Arts; Guidance and Counseling; History - United States; History - World
Dist - TURTID

Vietnam - the 10,000 day war series 637 MIN
VHS
Vietnam - the 10,000 day war series
Color (H C A)
$149.70 purchase
Presents a six - volume boxed set of all episodes from the 'Vietnam - The 10,000 Day War' series. Reviews the history of the war from the various perspectives of the policy makers, commanders and soldiers.
History - United States
Dist - PBS **Prod** - WNETTV

Vietnam - the Bombing 59 MIN
VHS / U-matic
Color
Tells the story of pilots, bombardiers and navigators and the air war over North Vietnam through interviews filmed between actual combat missions.
History - United States; History - World
Dist - IHF **Prod** - IHF

Vietnam - the Enemy 18 MIN
U-matic / VHS
Color (G)
$249.00, $149.00 purchase _ #AD - 2057
Travels back to Saigon - now Ho Chi Minh City - with a group of Vietnam War veterans seeking to come to terms with their own past and to heal old wounds. Interviews some of those who had been the enemy - students who marched from their university in Hanoi to the battle front, a woman doctor who was part of the American Embassy circle, and also a high - ranking spy. They speak of sacrifice, fear and anguish, the certainty that they acted honorably and the absence of rancor toward America.
History - United States; History - World; Sociology
Dist - FOTH **Prod** - FOTH

Vietnam - the news story 60 MIN
VHS
Color (J H C G)
$29.95 purchase _ #SVCI5002V
Presents five parts on the history of the Vietnam War. Includes D - Day in Vietnam - the first 3500 American combat troops sent to Vietnam by President Kennedy to prevent the 'domino - like' spread of communism; Taking on the Vietcong - over 500,000 American troops clash with 'Charlie' in a helicopter war; The Tide Turns - North Vietnamese and Vietcong suicide squads of the Tet Offensive and the bodycount after the Battle for Hue; War in the Air - the US switches from B52 bombings to the use of 20 million gallons of Agent Orange to destroy the 'invisible' enemy; Yanks Go Home - military operations cease and the Hanoi Hilton, home to American POWs, is revealed. Contains uncut news footage of the war.
Civics and Political Systems; History - United States; Literature and Drama; Sociology
Dist - CAMV

Vietnam - the secret agent 56 MIN
VHS
Color (G)
$29.95 purchase _ #S01510
Examines the use of the toxic defoliant Agent Orange during the Vietnam War. Features archival footage and interviews with Vietnam veterans, scientists and Dow Chemical personnel.
History - United States; Sociology
Dist - UILL

Vietnam - the ten thousand day war series
America in Vietnam - Volume 1 49 MIN
Days of decision - Volume 3 49 MIN
Dien Bien Phu - Volume 2 49 MIN
Firepower - Volume 6 49 MIN
Frontline America - Volume 8 48 MIN
Peace - Volume 11 48 MIN
Siege 48 MIN
Soldiering on - Volume 9 48 MIN
Surrender - Volume 12 48 MIN
The Trail - Volume 5 49 MIN
Uneasy allies - Volume 4 49 MIN
The Unsung soldiers - Volume 13 48 MIN

The Village war - Volume 10 48 MIN
Dist - UILL

Vietnam - the war at home 100 MIN
VHS
Color (G)
$29.95 purchase _ #S01512
Explores the anti - Vietnam War movement, focusing on Wisconsin student radicals.
History - United States; Religion and Philosophy; Sociology
Dist - UILL

Vietnam - the War that Divided America
U-matic / VHS / 35mm strip
(J H C)
Focuses on how the Vietnam war affected the American people, including political demonstrations and the difficult adjustments of veterans. Uses journalistic photography to document actual battles, the My Lai massacre, the American evacuation of Saigon, and the horrors of the refugee camps. Shows how the war continues to affect the conscience and foreign policy of America. In 4 parts.
History - United States; Sociology
Dist - ASPRSS **Prod** - ASPRSS
GA

Vietnam - time of the locust 55 MIN
VHS
Color (G)
$29.95 purchase _ #S01511
Presents an anti - Vietnam war documentary. Also includes two government - sponsored films, 'The Battle' and 'A Day in Vietnam,' which is narrated by Jack Webb.
History - United States
Dist - UILL

Vietnam Today 18 MIN
16mm / U-matic / VHS
Color (I J H C)
LC 75-702216
Presents an overview of South Vietnam's people, heritage and progress. Points out South Vietnam's three distinct geographic areas, introduces families that live in each one and shows the traditions, challenges and changes that are part of Vietnamese life.
Geography - World; Social Science; Sociology
Dist - AIMS **Prod** - SIERAW 1975

Vietnam Under Communism 60 MIN
VHS
Frontline Series
Color; Captioned (G)
$150.00 purchase _ #FRON - 302K
Reveals the state of affairs in Vietnam a decade after the end of the Vietnam War. Shows that living conditions for many Vietnamese are improving, but war damage is still evident. Cites statistics showing that more than 1.5 million Vietnamese have left the country or seek to do so. Surveys the creation of collective farming units, small businesses and other economic developments.
History - World
Dist - PBS **Prod** - DOCCON 1985

Vietnam Vets 29 MIN
VHS / 16mm
Washington Connection Series
Color (G)
$55.00 rental _ #WACO - 109
Civics and Political Systems; History - World; Social Science
Dist - PBS **Prod** - NPACT

Vietnam vets - dissidents for peace 29 MIN
VHS / 16mm
Color (H C G)
$550.00, $295.00 purchase, $55.00 rental
Shows veterans who experienced the devastation of the Vietnam War protesting US involvement in Central America. Includes footage of Vietnam veteran Brian Wilson trying to stop a munitions train by protesting on the train tracks. The navy train doesn't stop and Wilson's legs are severed - Wilson is back a few weeks later, inspiring others with his heroism. Produced by Ying Ying Wu.
Civics and Political Systems; History - World
Dist - FLMLIB

Vietnam Vets - Over Here 25 MIN
VHS / U-matic
Color
Points out that the Vietnam War is a fading memory, but its veterans remain a troubling presence.
Guidance and Counseling; History - United States
Dist - WCCOTV **Prod** - WCCOTV 1977

The Vietnamese - a refugee journey 8 MIN
VHS
Columbus legacy series
Color (J H C G)
$40.00 purchase, $11.00 rental _ #12338
Uses war footage, photographs and interviews to depict the homeland circumstances of Vietnamese refugees, their processing at Ft Indiantown Gap, and their subsequent adjustment to life in the United States. Part of a 15 - part series commemorating the 500th anniversary of Columbus' journeys to the Americas - journeys that brought together a constantly evolving collection of different ethnic groups and examining the contributions of 15 distinct groups who imprinted their heritage on the day - to - day life of Pennsylvania.
History - United States; Sociology
Dist - PSU **Prod** - WPSXTV 1992

Vietnamese Buddhism in America 14 MIN
U-matic
Asians in America Series
Color (C H)
Focuses on Dr. Thich Thien - An, head of the Vietnamese Buddhist Church in America, and illustrates the form of Buddhism practiced by his disciples, both Vietnamese and American.
History - United States; History - World; Religion and Philosophy; Sociology
Dist - CEPRO **Prod** - CEPRO

Vietnamese Cultures and Customs 110 MIN
U-matic / VHS
Color
Shows a direct lecture by a U S professor on Vietnamese cultures and customs with emphasis on politics and war.
History - United States; History - World; Sociology
Dist - IHF **Prod** - IHF

Vietnamese Refugees in America 14 MIN
U-matic
Asians in America Series
Color (C H)
Describes the difficulty of the refugees' experiences, the process of integrating them into American culture, and the importance of appreciating the contributions they are making to this nation of immigrants.
History - United States; History - World; Religion and Philosophy; Sociology
Dist - CEPRO **Prod** - CEPRO

Vietnamese Series
Speak to Me - Level 1 159 MIN
Speak to Me - Level 2 159 MIN
Speak to Me - Level 3 159 MIN
Dist - NORTNJ

Vietnamizing the War, 1969 - 1973 60 MIN
U-matic / VHS / 16mm
Vietnam - a television history series; Episode 8
Color (H C A)
Describes how the U S began disinvolving itself from the war by training the South Vietnamese army to fight the battles. States that the withdrawal of U S troops resulted in hardship for the Vietnamese as the flow of goods and dollars diminished. Recalls that in the 1972 spring offensive, nearly all the casualties were Vietnamese.
History - United States; History - World
Dist - FI **Prod** - WGBHTV 1983

View and do Film, no 1 20 MIN
16mm
B&W
Features three separate creative movement exercises for the elementary school student that he can watch, then get up and practice himself.
Education; Physical Education and Recreation
Dist - SLFP **Prod** - SLFP

View and do Series
Inmate Behavior
Officer - Inmate Relationship
Officer as a Source of Change
Security, Custody and Control
Dist - SCETV

View and Write
VHS / 16mm
(I)
$60.00 purchase _ #VID5201
Demonstrates how to prewrite, draft and edit on a computer. Provides material on tape for student writing exercises.
English Language
Dist - MECC **Prod** - MECC 1989

VIEW, BLOCK and PLOT Commands 98 MIN
VHS
Autocad basics series
Color (G H VOC C PRO)
$49.95 purchase _ #AVT105V-T
Demonstrates the intricacies of the AutoCAD program by explaining its more complex functions, SPACE; MSPACE; UCS; UCSION; VPOINT; VIEW; VIEWPORTS; BLOCK; WBLOCK; INSERT; MINSERT; XREF; PLOT; PRPLOR; and Editing blocks. Explains the basics of workspace, paperspace, modelspace, and metaview.
Computer Science
Dist - CAMV

View from Another World 16 MIN
16mm
Color (C T)
LC 78-701612
Uses a futuristic setting to highlight the problems of the mentally retarded and the attitudes of the public toward them. Explains the normalization or deinstitutionalization principle.
Education; Health and Safety; Psychology
Dist - UKANS

View from Below 33 MIN
16mm
Color
LC 80-700865
Describes the environment of an Australian deep coal mine.
Geography - World; Industrial and Technical Education; Social Science
Dist - TASCOR **Prod** - IMPACT 1978

The View from Mount Vernon 28 MIN
16mm
Government story series; No 31
B&W (J H)
LC 71-707213
A discussion with Dr Samuel Beer of Harvard University regarding the changes which have taken place in the presidency and the presidents of history who brought about those changes.
Biography
Dist - WESTLC **Prod** - WEBC 1968

View from My Room is Great series
Lenni Workman 25 MIN
Dist - QUEENU

View from My Room is Great, the
Eugenia Zundel 25 MIN
Dist - QUEENU

The View from my room is great
Andre Bieler 25 MIN
J C Heywood 25 MIN
R E Buff 25 MIN
Dist - QUEENU

View from My Window is Great series
Juan Gever 25 MIN
Mary Rawlyk 25 MIN
Dist - QUEENU

The View from Outside 3 MIN
16mm
Color
LC 74-706315
Shows a father giving his Marine son a 'VIEW FROM THE OUTSIDE' of Marine Corps life.
Civics and Political Systems
Dist - USNAC **Prod** - USMC 1966

The View from the Edge 52 MIN
U-matic / VHS / 16mm
Shock of the New Series
Color (C A)
LC 80-700989
Explains that Expressionism was ruined as an esthetic possibility by the horrors of World War II, when photography of the war surpassed any distortions of the body an artist could imagine. Tells how some artists struggled but lost in their attempts to maintain a mythic - religious imagery in the face of increasing secularization of 20th century life.
Fine Arts
Dist - TIMLIF **Prod** - BBCTV 1980

A View from the Inside 30 MIN
16mm
Color (PRO)
LC 79-700996
Presents excerpts from therapy sessions in which the psychotherapist helps a patient relive her traumatic memories of child abuse.
Psychology; Sociology
Dist - FMSP **Prod** - FMSP 1978

A View from the mountains - the Oskar Reinhart Foundation 20 MIN
VHS
Color (G)
PdS15.50 purchase _ #A4-300489
Presents the local collection of the Oskar Reinhart Foundation in Winterthur, Switzerland, and explores its capacity to celebrate the unique point of view created by the mountains surrounding the Swiss. Includes works by Wolf, Bocklin, and Hodler; Romantic artists Runge and Friedrich; and the Austrian Waldmuller. Records the natural landscape of Switzerland.
Fine Arts
Dist - AVP **Prod** - NATLGL

A View from the Standpipe - John Falter's World 30 MIN
U-matic / VHS
(G)
Examines the work and background of Nebraska artist and illustrator John Falter. Focuses on Falter's magazine illustrations and later historical painting.
Fine Arts
Dist - GPN Prod - NETV 1987

View from the Top 3 MIN
16mm
Color
Presents a closeup of an uncircumcised penis from manual masturbation to ejaculation.
Guidance and Counseling; Psychology; Sociology
Dist - MMRC Prod - MMRC

The View from the Top 60 MIN
U-matic / VHS
Managing the Data Base Environment Series
Color
Stresses that successful development of a data base environment requires two types of 'views from the top,' cooperation, support and control from top management and an overall understanding of the organization's operations and resources.
Business and Economics; Industrial and Technical Education
Dist - DELTAK Prod - DELTAK

View from the Top 11 MIN
16mm
Color (PRO)
LC 77-702740
Describes the functions and capabilities of the airborne warning and control system. Explains why the system is necessary to the American national defense, how it operates and how it might be used in combat situations.
Civics and Political Systems; Industrial and Technical Education; Sociology
Dist - USNAC Prod - USAF 1977

The View from within, Pt 1 30 MIN
VHS
Japan 2000 Series
Color (C) (ENGLISH AND JAPANESE)
LC 90712870
Looks at the changing role of women in Japanese society, Japan's aging population and its ecomomic restructuring and regional development. Presents a Japanese perspective. Part of a series.
Foreign Language; Geography - World; Psychology
Dist - GPN

View of a vanishing frontier 58 MIN
VHS / BETA
Color (G)
$29.95 purchase
Retraces the historic journey of Prince Maximillian zu Wied, a German aristocrat, and the Swiss artist Karl Bodner to the American West during 1832 - 1834. Uses Bodmer's drawings and watercolors of the Plains Indians, location photography and journal readings to recreate their journey.
Fine Arts; History - United States
Dist - ARTSAM Prod - MMOA

A View of America from the 23rd Century 21 MIN
U-matic / VHS / 16mm
Public Broadcast Laboratory Series
Color; B&W (H C A)
LC 75-704657
Presents John W Gardner, former Secretary of Health, Education and Welfare, who dramatizes how present American institutions might look when viewed from the perspective of the 23rd century. Shows man increasingly raging against his institutions because most have been designed to resist rather than to facilitate change. Discusses the belief that if the future does not hold destruction for our institutions they must be able to change and would - be reformers must use reason rather than destruction to achieve this end.
Civics and Political Systems; History - United States; Psychology; Social Science; Sociology
Dist - IU Prod - NET 1969

A View of the Sky 28 MIN
U-matic / VHS / 16mm
Color
Explores various theories of the origin and order of the solar system, from Copernicus through Einstein, with a brief look at modern scientific exploration of space.
Science - Physical
Dist - USNAC Prod - NASA

View of the Sky 28 MIN
16mm
Conquest of Space Series
Color (J)
LC FIE67-125
Explains the historical theories of the solar system and the universe. Includes theories of Copernicus, Galileo, Newton, Einstein and others. Uses symbolic photography to illustrate these concepts and poses the question of how today's youth will envision the universe. Shows some ways in which NASA has gained new knowledge of other planets.
Science; Science - Physical
Dist - NASA Prod - NASA 1967

The View of the Water - 13 20 TO 25 MIN
VHS
If You Paint, You See more Series
Color (I)
Shows that water can be deep or shallow, clear or muddy, storm - tossed or calm. Reveals children using a variety of media to capture these variations.
Education; Fine Arts
Dist - AITECH

Viewing and Critiquing a Counseling Session 20 MIN
U-matic / VHS
B&W
Shows an initial interview followed by a demonstration of the social worker watching the interview and processing her internal frame of reference.
Guidance and Counseling; Sociology
Dist - UWISC Prod - COLSTT 1982

Viewing habits 15 MIN
U-matic / VHS
Tuned - in series; Lesson 1
Color (J H)
Shows a class beginning their study of television by keeping a log of what they watch. Discusses some of their reasons for watching television and the complaints they have about their parents' TV watching rules.
Fine Arts; Sociology
Dist - FI Prod - WNETTV 1982

Viewing Points and Point of View 29 MIN
VHS / 16mm
Encounters Series
Color (I)
$200.00 purchase _ #269205
Presents a ten - part series on art. Introduces art concepts, encourages students to visually explore their world and the world of art, and demonstrates art techniques such as drawing, printmaking, photography, clay and wire sculpture, painting and fabric arts to motivate art expression. 'Viewing Points And Point Of View' reveals that the world can be viewed from many angles. Discovers that the viewing point from which objects are observed affects their own point of view or reaction to the object.
Fine Arts; Psychology
Dist - ACCESS Prod - ACCESS 1988

Viewing the news 28 MIN
U-matic / BETA / VHS
Communication skills 2 - advanced series
Color (H C G)
101.95, $89.95 purchase _ #CA-22
Assists the viewer in developing a greater awareness of television news and critical evaluation of news program contents and treatment. Discusses the effect of television news on viewers. Presents arguments for and against control of news agencies. Covers the importance of the relationship between news and human activity. Part of a 26 - part series.
Fine Arts; Social Science; Sociology
Dist - INSTRU

Viewmaster 3 MIN
16mm
Color (G)
$15.00 rental
Pays homage to Eadweard Muybridge's pre - cinema studies of humans and animals in motion. Features a cycle of eight drawings in a variety of styles and media. Produced by George Griffin.
Fine Arts
Dist - CANCIN

Viewpoint 26 MIN
16mm
Color
LC 74-705917
Tells the story of the national forests through Bob Bray, who played Forest Ranger Corey Stuart on the Lassie TV series. Includes many striking scenes from national forests in different sections of the country.
Geography - United States; Science - Natural; Social Science
Dist - USNAC Prod - USDA 1967

Views of a Decorticate Dog 10 MIN
16mm
B&W (C T)
Demonstrates the abnormal responses of a decorticate dog - - postural and locomotional anomalies, tendency to continue locomotion once under way, lack of adaptative response to obstacles placed in its path, lack of initiative in food - getting, 'SHAM RAGE' elicited by trivial stimuli, intense resistence to impressed movements and degree of susceptibility to simple conditioning.
Psychology; Science - Natural
Dist - PSUPCR Prod - PSUPCR 1934

Views of a Vanishing Frontier 55 MIN
VHS
Color (S)
$39.95 purchase _ #412 - 9072
Recreates the historic journey of Prince Maximilian zu Wied, a German aristocrat, and Swiss artist Karl Bodmer to the American West during 1832 to 1834. Uses Bodmer's watercolors and drawings of the Plains Indians and the landscape, together with the illustrated journals of Prince Maximilian and location photography to provide an accurate picture of the frontier at a pivotal stage.
Fine Arts; Geography - United States; History - United States; History - World; Literature and Drama
Dist - FI Prod - MMOA 1988

Views of the Council on Economic Development 18 MIN
VHS / U-matic
Technology, Innovation, and Industrial Development Series
Color
Business and Economics
Dist - MIOT Prod - MIOT

Vigil 90 MIN
16mm / 35mm
Color (G)
$250.00, $300.00 rental
Tells the story of a 12 - year - old girl who sees her father fall to his death near their isolated farm. Reveals that when her mother hires a poacher as a farmhand, tension among the three rises as the girl recognizes the threat posed by the man who seems to be replacing her father. Directed by Vincent Ward.
Fine Arts; Literature and Drama; Sociology
Dist - KINOIC

Vignette series - chairs 10 MIN
16mm
Vignette series
B&W (T)
LC 70-707932
Observes three - and four - year - olds learning, playing and talking in classroom situations. Filmed at Cambridge Neighborhood Head Start Center, Cambridge, Massachusetts.
Education; Psychology; Sociology
Dist - EDC Prod - EDC 1969

Vignette Series

Chairs	9 MIN
Injections	10 MIN
Marble Game	12 MIN
Seven day itch	7 MIN
Vignette series - chairs	10 MIN
Wall Washing	12 MIN
Waterplay, Pt 1	12 MIN

Dist - EDC

Vignettes Series

Being real	11 MIN
Close Feelings	11 MIN
Me, Myself	12 MIN
Rapport	12 MIN
Walls and Windows	12 MIN

Dist - MEDIAG

Vignettes Series

Daily Bread	12 MIN
Free to Obey	12 MIN
Images of God	12 MIN
Images of Jesus	12 MIN
Images of the Church	12 MIN
Kinships	11 MIN
A Place to Stand	11 MIN
The Price of Life	12 MIN
Priorities	12 MIN
The Search for faith	12 MIN

Dist - PAULST

VII 5 MIN
16mm
The Roman numeral series
Color (G)
$196.00 purchase, $17.00 rental
Presents the seventh of a series of abstract, non - objective, non - representational, etc, films.
Fine Arts
Dist - CANCIN Prod - BRAKS 1980

VIII 4 MIN
16mm
The Roman numeral series
Color (G)
$161.00 purchase, $10.00 rental
Presents the eighth in a series of abstract, non - objective, non - representational, etc, films.
Fine Arts
Dist - CANCIN **Prod** - BRAKS 1980

Viking 29 MIN
16mm
Color
LC 76-703708
Presents a comprehensive look at the preparations for the Viking - Mars landing scheduled for July 4, 1976. Describes the beginning of the search for life on the Martian surface and looks at other experiments. Focuses on scientists connected with the Viking mission and explores the problems, solutions, concerns, anxieties and aspirations leading to the event.
Industrial and Technical Education; Science; Science - Physical
Dist - USNAC **Prod** - NASA 1976

Viking on Mars 16 MIN
VHS
Color (J H C)
$14.95 purchase _ #NA067
History - World; Science - Physical
Dist - INSTRU **Prod** - NASA

Viking sacrifice in Shetland 30 MIN
VHS
World of festivals series
Color (J H C G)
$195.00 purchase
Marches in darkness through the streets in Scotland's Shetland Islands, to observe 1,000 burning torches and 100 Vikings in full glory. Follows the procession to a Viking galley, and after the Norsemen's anthem, the torches are thrown into the galley. Part of a 12 - part series on European festivals.
Geography - World; Social Science
Dist - LANDMK **Prod** - LANDMK 1988

Viking ships 10 MIN
VHS
Color; PAL (P I J H)
Photographs the sailing of a replica Viking ship with a crew in authentic costume. Uses diagrams, drawings, photos and models to illustrate the principle features of a Viking ship. Includes maps showing the main routes taken by the Vikings and the controversial 'Vinland Map.'
Geography - World; History - World; Physical Education and Recreation; Social Science
Dist - VIEWTH

The Viking Ships of Roskilde 14 MIN
16mm
Color
Reports on the excavations made after the ships from the Viking period were found underwater in a channel in Roskilde Fjord. Explains the many problems technicians and scientists had to solve before the fragments of the wrecks could be removed for conservation.
History - World; Science - Physical
Dist - AUDPLN **Prod** - RDCG

Viking Women Don't Care 13 MIN
16mm
Color
LC 75-703248
Two hippies with a car load of marihuana meet a runaway bank robber in a car containing a dead body. Their confrontation satarizes the portrayal of violence in films.
Fine Arts; Psychology; Sociology
Dist - USC **Prod** - USC 1968

The Vikings 28 MIN
U-matic / VHS
Once upon a Time - Man Series
Color (P I)
MV=$99.00
Follows the range of the Viking expeditions from the seventh to the ninth centuries. Animated.
History - World
Dist - LANDMK **Prod** - LANDMK 1981

Vikings and Normans 52 MIN
VHS
Europe in the Middle Ages series
Color (H) (ENGLISH AND FRENCH)
$16.50 rental _ #51032
Presents the Vikings as farmers and warriors possessing strong clan loyalties and as explorers and traders with the Far East. Discusses the discovery by Vikings of America 500 years before Columbus. Follows the history of the Normans' battles with the Moors. Looks at Norman architecture, their adoption of the French language, their conquest of England in 1066, and the Magna Carta.
Fine Arts; Foreign Language; History - World
Dist - PSU

Vikings and Normans 37 MIN
U-matic / VHS
Europe in the Middle Ages series
Color (G)
$299.00, $199.00 purchase _ #AD - 1960
Looks at Viking seafaring and exploration. Considers Viking influences in England and Scotland, Viking trade with Far East 300 years before Marco Polo and the discovery of America 500 years before Columbus. Covers the Normans and their establishment of the Norman Kingdom of Sicily, the Norman conquest of England in 1066 and the Magna Carta and its effects. Part of a seven - part series on Europe in the Middle Ages.
History - World
Dist - FOTH **Prod** - FOTH

The Vikings and their Explorations 11 MIN
U-matic / VHS / 16mm
Color (I J H)
Considers how the Viking warriors of the ninth and tenth centuries influenced the history of many nations. Discusses Leif Ericson's discovery of the North American continent. Presents a dramatization showing the homelife, manners and dress of Norsemen.
History - World
Dist - CORF **Prod** - CORF 1958

The Vikings - September 25, 1066 30 MIN
VHS / 16mm
Timeline Video Series
Color (J)
$69.95 purchase _ #ZF301VTM
Chronicles Viking or Norse conquests from Byzantium to Britain. Reports that the forces of Viking King Harald Hardradi have fallen to the Saxons. Indicates that in the south William the Conqueror is waiting to invade Saxon England, an event that alters the course of English and American history. Part of a series.
History - World
Dist - ZENGER **Prod** - MPTPB 1989

Vikings Series
Bitter is the Wind 29 MIN
Bolt from the blue 29 MIN
Empire of the Northern Seas 29 MIN
England at Bay 29 MIN
From the fury of the northmen 29 MIN
Halfdan was Here 29 MIN
Hammer of the North 29 MIN
Here King Harold is killed 29 MIN
An Island Called Thule 29 MIN
The Ultimate Outpost 29 MIN
Dist - PBS

Vikings to the East 10 MIN
16mm
Color
Portrays the Swedish Viking period, from 800 - 1000 A D.
Geography - World; History - World
Dist - AUDPLN **Prod** - ASI 1963

Villa Alegre Series
Measuring Up 30 MIN
Dist - MDCPB

Villa alegre series
Alone - together 29 MIN
Animals 29 MIN
Animals and people 29 MIN
Balance of nature 29 MIN
The Breadbasket 29 MIN
Brooms, Brushes and Scrubbing 29 MIN
Change of Direction 29 MIN
Collisions and bouncing 29 MIN
Community, people and places 29 MIN
Containers and Packaging 29 MIN
Control and measurement of energy 29 MIN
Cycles 29 MIN
Done by the sun 29 MIN
Elaboration 29 MIN
Face of objects 29 MIN
Family 29 MIN
Fasteners 29 MIN
Flowing 29 MIN
Food derivatives 29 MIN
Friends 29 MIN
From farm to market 29 MIN
From plant, animal to table 29 MIN
From shadow to silence 29 MIN
Fuels 29 MIN
Garbage 29 MIN
Hands as Tools 29 MIN
Houses 29 MIN
Ingredients of Toys 29 MIN
Light and Sound Tools 29 MIN
Making Choices 29 MIN
Mealtime 29 MIN
Movement no 1 29 MIN
Movement no 2 29 MIN
Music, Music, Music 29 MIN
My Feelings 29 MIN
My Interests 29 MIN
Neighbors 29 MIN
Oceans 29 MIN
Paper 29 MIN
Pebbles, Rocks and Bigger Chunks 29 MIN
People and Environment 29 MIN
Physical Me 29 MIN
Plants 29 MIN
Plants and people 29 MIN
School 29 MIN
Skeletons and Frameworks 29 MIN
Skills 29 MIN
Social Responsibility 29 MIN
Sources and Uses of Light and Sound 29 MIN
The Tabular Tube 29 MIN
Textiles 29 MIN
Tools and tasks 29 MIN
Unique Me 29 MIN
Uses of Energy 29 MIN
Varieties of Energy 29 MIN
Vibrations and Oscillations 29 MIN
Water 29 MIN
Water and Food 29 MIN
Weather 29 MIN
What Part of the Plant 29 MIN
What Powers Them 29 MIN
The Wheels of Toys 29 MIN
Where Does it Grow 29 MIN
You are what You Eat 29 MIN
Dist - PBS

Villa El Salvador - a Desert Dream 50 MIN
VHS / 16mm
Documentaries by Adobe Foundations Series
Color (G)
$295.00 purchase, $80.00 rental; LC 89715576
Tells the story of Peru's Villa El Salvador, one of Latin America's best organized squatter settlements. Chronicles its history from its establishment in the early 1970s in the middle of a desert prairie south of Lima and built from scratch by its residents. Today the city has over 300,000 inhabitants, dozens of schools, markets and recreation and a 97 percent literacy rate.
Geography - World; Science - Natural; Sociology
Dist - CNEMAG **Prod** - ADOF 1989

Villa - Lobos, the Guitar, and Julian Byzantine 26 MIN
U-matic / VHS / 16mm
Musical Triangle Series
Color (J)
Tells how Brazilian composer Villa - Lobos (1884 - 1959) was inspired by Brazilian folk and popular music to write pieces he called Choros, as well as symphonies, operas, concertos, chamber music and songs. Features professional musician Julian Byzantine playing Villa - Lobos music on the guitar and commenting on his life.
Fine Arts
Dist - MEDIAG **Prod** - THAMES 1975

The Village 11 MIN
16mm / U-matic / VHS
Pioneer Living Series
Color (I J H)
$280, $195 purchase _ #3133
Talks about the different activities and trades in a village in the early 1800s.
History - United States; Sociology
Dist - CORF

The Village 70 MIN
U-matic / VHS / 16mm
B&W (H C A) (GAELIC (ENGLISH SUBTITLES))
Presents an intimate study of the slowpaced diurnal round of activity in Dunguin, County Kerry, one of the last Gaelic - speaking communities in Ireland. Depicts a peasant society at a time when acculturation by urban tourists was beginning.
Foreign Language; Geography - World; Sociology
Dist - UCEMC **Prod** - UCLA 1969

Village 10 MIN
VHS
Stop, look, listen series
Color; PAL (P I J)
Visits a village. Watches the thatcher, saddler, blacksmith and wood carver at work. Observes that buses are few, the streets are neither lit nor paved, but the inhabitants prefer the slower pace to life in town. Part of a series of films which start from some everyday observation and show more of what is happening, how and why. Builds vocabulary and encourages children to be more observant.
English Language; Geography - World; Social Science; Sociology
Dist - VIEWTH

The Village green 17 MIN
BETA / U-matic / VHS
Color (G)
$29.95, $130.00 purchase _ #LSTF55
Documents the successful and self sustaining recycling center of the environmental action coalition in New York City.
Science - Natural
Dist - FEDU **Prod** - USEPA 1975

A Village in Baltimore 58 MIN
16mm
Look at Greek - American Women Series
Color
LC 81-700503
Presents a documentary set in Baltimore's Greektown, focusing on assimilation of four Greek women into American society. Explores such issues as traditions, marriage, professional goals and views on American society.
Sociology
Dist - MOSESD **Prod** - MOSESD 1981

Village in Baltimore, a, Pt 1 29 MIN
16mm
Look at Greek - American Women Series
Color
LC 81-700503
Presents a documentary set in Baltimore's Greektown, focusing on assimilation of four Greek women into American society. Explores such issues as traditions, marriage, professional goals and views on American society.
Sociology
Dist - MOSESD **Prod** - MOSESD 1981

Village in Baltimore, a, Pt 2 29 MIN
16mm
Look at Greek - American Women Series
Color
LC 81-700503
Presents a documentary set in Baltimore's Greektown, focusing on assimilation of four Greek women into American society. Explores such issues as traditions, marriage, professional goals and views on American society.
Sociology
Dist - MOSESD **Prod** - MOSESD 1981

A Village in Russia - Verkola 29 MIN
VHS / U-matic
Color (J H)
$280.00, $330.00 purchase, $50.00 rental
Focuses on the inhabitants and commerce of a Russian village today. Points out that the Russian village has been a vital aspect of Russian culture and that as late as 1920, 80 percent of the population lived in villages. Considers the role of traditional village life and the changes that are taking place in Soviet society.
Fine Arts; Geography - World; Social Science
Dist - NDIM **Prod** - DEVYAT 1987

Village life 12 MIN
U-matic / 16mm / VHS / BETA
Indians of the Orinoco - the Makiritare tribe series
Color (G H C)
Introduces the variety of activities in the Makiritare village of Kononama. Features women spinning cotton, taking care of their families, bathing in the river, children painting and drawing and men wrestling and throwing spears. Without narration. Part of an eight - part series on the Makiritare Indians of Venezuela.
Fine Arts; Social Science; Sociology
Dist - IFF **Prod** - IFF 1972
EDPAT

Village life 15 MIN
U-matic / VHS / BETA
Pacific Island life series
Color; PAL (G H C)
PdS40, PdS48 purchase
Looks at village life on a South Pacific atoll. Includes children playing on swings and frolicking in a lagoon; carving a canoe and building a new home. No narration. Part of a five - part series on life in the Pacific islands.
Fine Arts; Geography - World; Social Science; Sociology
Dist - EDPAT **Prod** - IFF

Village Life 15 MIN
16mm
Pacific Island Life Series
Color
Presents a nonnarrated look at village life on a South Pacific atoll, including children playing on swings and frolicking in a lagoon, carving a canoe and building a new home.
Geography - World; Sociology
Dist - IFF **Prod** - IFF

Village Life Series
The Best kept secret - Western Samoa 16 MIN
Bill, Peggy, Royal and friends - london horses (London) 29 MIN
El Pueblo (Spain) 24 MIN
On Seven Hills they Built a City - Rome 26 MIN
Samoa I Sisifo (Western Samoa) 26 MIN
Ten times empty - Greece) 21 MIN
Tonga Royal - Tonga 20 MIN
Village of the Rain Forest (Nigeria) 23 MIN
Dist - JOU

The Village of the Craftsman 24 MIN
16mm
Ancient Lives Series
Color (H)
Depicts life in a village of craftsmen over 3000 years ago in the Valley of the Kings on the west bank of the Nile. Features Egyptologist John Romer explaining the work of craftmen on the tombs of the pharoahs. First of eight parts of the Ancient Lives Series.
Fine Arts; History - World; Sociology
Dist - PSU
FOTH

Village of the Rain Forest (Nigeria) 23 MIN
16mm / U-matic / VHS
Village Life Series
Color (H C A)
Describes life in a Nigerian farming village.
Geography - World; Sociology
Dist - JOU **Prod** - JOU 1983

The Village of the Round and Square Houses 12 MIN
16mm / VHS
Color (K P I)
$120.00, $235.00 purchase, $25.00 rental _ #VC326V, #MP326
Presents the story from the book The Village Of The Round And Square Houses by Ann Grifalconi, which tells of a village where the men live in square houses and the women live in round houses.
Geography - World; Health and Safety; Literature and Drama; Psychology
Dist - WWS **Prod** - WWS 1989

Village School 18 MIN
16mm
B&W (P I T)
LC 70-712803
Shows a primary school classroom in rural Kenya, where African children learn science in new ways by using local materials and modern methods.
Education; Geography - World
Dist - EDC **Prod** - EDC 1970

The Village singer 15 MIN
VHS
Short story series
Color (J H)
#E373; LC 90-713142
Presents a story of conflict within a 19th - century New England church congregation in 'The Village Singer' by Mary Wilkins Freeman. Part of a 16 - part series which introduces American short story writers and discusses the technical aspects of short story structure.
Literature and Drama; Religion and Philosophy
Dist - GPN **Prod** - CTI 1978

The Village Singer by Mary Wilkins Freeman 15 MIN
16mm / U-matic / VHS
Short Story Series
Color (J)
LC 83-700044
Tells of the impassioned revenge of a village church vocalist directed against her successor and the congregation, and the ultimate reconciliation of all involved. Based on the short story The Village Singer by Mary Wilkins Freeman.
Literature and Drama
Dist - IU **Prod** - IITC 1982

The Village that Refused to Die 56 MIN
U-matic / VHS
B&W
Relates the story of a group of Chinese refugees who set up a village in South Vietnam.
History - United States; History - World
Dist - IHF **Prod** - IHF

The Village, the Village, the Village 36 MIN
16mm / U-matic / VHS
Color (H C A)
LC 77-701012
Shows how the growth of Greenwich Village in New York City has paralleled the growth of America's cities. Relates the changes that Greenwich Village has undergone to those which have taken place in America's culture and society.
Geography - United States; Sociology
Dist - PHENIX **Prod** - COHENJ 1977

Village Theater in Senegal - Queen Ndate and the French Conquest 14 MIN
16mm / U-matic / VHS
Color (H C A)
Presents actors, members of a rural youth association in northwestern Senegal, performing a play about the French conquest of their region in the 19th century.
Fine Arts; History - World
Dist - IU **Prod** - IU 1983

The Village war - Volume 10 48 MIN
VHS
Vietnam - the ten thousand day war series
Color (G)
$34.95 purchase _ #S00687
Focuses on the struggle between US and North Vietnamese forces for control of the Vietnamese villages. Suggests that the Communists had an easier time of it, as they were able to blend in easily with the villagers. Interviews former CIA director William Colby, who claims that three US presidents ignored US intelligence assessments of Vietnam, leading to key errors in US strategy. Narrated by Richard Basehart.
Biography; History - United States
Dist - UILL

The Village Watchman 17 MIN
16mm / U-matic / VHS
Color (J)
LC 75-702523
Studies the ancient, disappearing culture of the Vlachs of the Balkan peninsula. Depicts their work habits and their arts and crafts. Describes the seasonal migration of all villagers, with the exception of the watchman, to the lowland grazing areas.
Geography - World; Sociology
Dist - CAROUF **Prod** - PASHA 1975

Village women in Egypt 30 MIN
U-matic
Are you listening series
Color (J H C)
LC 80-707408
Presents a group of rural, tradition - bound Egyptian women talking about sex roles, family life, customs, and birth control. Reveals the conflict between traditional values and the opportunities that are becoming available to them and their children.
Geography - World; Sociology
Dist - STURTM **Prod** - STURTM

Villagers of the Sierra de Gredos 52 MIN
VHS
Disappearing world series
Color (G C)
$99.00 purchase, $19.00 rental _ #51228
Visits the village of Navalguijo, located high in the Sierra de Gredos Mountains of central Spain. Follows the descent of the villagers with their herds to the valleys below, where the cattle graze from February to June, a seasonal migration that makes these people one of the last transhumant societies of Europe. Features anthropologist William Kavanagh. Part of a series working closely with anthropologists who lived for a year or more in societies whose social structures, beliefs and practices are threatened by the expansion of technocratic civilization.
Sociology
Dist - PSU **Prod** - GRANDA 1989

Villages in the clouds 20 MIN
BETA / VHS / U-matic
Soviet Union series
Color (H C A)
$250.00 purchase _ #JY - 5866C
Visits the Soviet Republic of Georgia in the highest mountains in Europe. Reveals that Georgia is a relatively isolated land of plenty where much of the produce and livestock is privately owned. Part of a five - part series on the diverse lifestyles and regions of the USSR.
Business and Economics; Civics and Political Systems; Geography - World; History - World
Dist - CORF **Prod** - BBCTV 1989

Villages in the Sky 13 MIN
16mm
Color (I J)
Shows life in the high mesa villages of the Hopis. Women are shown making baskets and pottery and baking bread in outdoor adobe ovens. Portions of some of the dances conclude the film.
Social Science; Sociology
Dist - MLA **Prod** - DAGP 1952

Villanova
VHS
Campus clips series
Color (H C A)
$29.95 purchase _ #CC0095V
Takes a video visit to the campus of Villanova University in Pennsylvania. Shows many of the distinctive features of the campus, and interviews students about their

experiences. Provides information on the composition of the student body, professors, academics, social life, housing, and other subjects.
Education
Dist - CAMV

Villard De Honnecourt, Builder of Cathedrals (1230 - 1235) 15 MIN
16mm
Color
Presents a notebook of Villard de Honnecourt's life from 1230 to 1235 A D. Shows the engineer as an artist and as one of the great cathedral builders of the 12th century.
Fine Arts
Dist - ROLAND **Prod** - ROLAND

A Vilna legend - Dem rebns koyekh 60 MIN
16mm
B&W (G) (YIDDISH WITH ENGLISH SUBTITLES)
Features a classic tale of frustrated love and destiny in which a yeshiva student and an orphan girl are deeply in love yet face eternal separation, even though their parents promised them to each other before birth. Dramatizes the prophet Elijah's miraculous intervention, which allows their parents to fulfill their vow and the lovers to be united. A reissue of Tkies kaf, Poland, 1924. Contact distributor for rental fee.
Religion and Philosophy; Sociology
Dist - NCJEWF

Vimbuza - Chilopa 55 MIN
VHS
Color (G C)
$200.00 purchase, $19.00 rental _ #61295
Shows healing ceremonies among the Tumbuka of Malawi who attribute illness - vimbuza - to spirit possession. Documents nightlong rituals of singing, clapping and drumming during full moon, culminating in an animal sacrifice - chilopa - at dawn. Portrays the interaction of patients, healers and village community and includes an interview with a patient. Produced by Drs Rupert and Ulrike Poeschl.
Health and Safety; Religion and Philosophy; Sociology
Dist - PSU

Vincent - Painter of Light in Paris - 2 30 MIN
VHS
Vincent Van Gogh Series
Color (I)
$150.00 purchase
Dramatizes the life and work of Vincent van Gogh, 1853 - 1890. Shows the influence of French Impressionist Pissaro on van Gogh in Paris where his comrades included Lautrec, Cezanne, Bernard and Gauguin in part 2. Van Gogh trains himself in what he called 'gymnastic exercises with color,' and experiments with the minimalistic style of Japanese prints. Bold strong colors are characteristic of this phase.
Fine Arts; Geography - World; History - World
Dist - AITECH

Vincent - Painter of Peasant Scenes - 1 30 MIN
VHS
Vincent Van Gogh Series
Color (I)
$150.00 purchase
Dramatizes the life and work of Vincent van Gogh, 1853 - 1890. Presents his early career which began at age 16 in the Hague where he worked as a clerk in his uncle's art shop in part 1. Millet inspired his interest in the peasant genre of art. Van Gogh served briefly as a lay minister among the miners of the Borinage in Belgium before he decided at the age of 27 to study art with Anton Mauve of the Hague School. 'The Potato Eaters,' 1885, reflects this phase of van Gogh's artistic development.
Fine Arts
Dist - AITECH

Vincent - Sun Painter in France - 3 30 MIN
VHS
Vincent Van Gogh Series
Color (I)
$150.00 purchase
Dramatizes the life and work of Vincent van Gogh, 1853 - 1890. Continues van Gogh's odyssey starting with 1988 when he moved to Arles in southern France in part 3. There and in Saint - Remy and Auvers he created his most important works, alternately reflecting his depressed and violent states which were attributed to epilepsy. Portrays the violent severing of his friendship with Gauguin during which van Gogh threatens Gauguin, then cuts off his own ear. He retreats to Auvers where he ends his life by shooting himself in July, 1890.
Fine Arts; Geography - World; History - World
Dist - AITECH

Vincent Sweeney, MD and Jane Donner, PhD - How Far Can We Go a Family's Question 60 MIN
U-matic / VHS
Perceptions, Pt a - Interventions in Family Therapy Series
Color (PRO)
Focuses on the facilitation of clear communication between a father and his eldest adolescent daughter.
Guidance and Counseling; Psychology; Sociology
Dist - BOSFAM **Prod** - BOSFAM

Vincent Sweeney, MD, Jane Donner, PhD, Center for the Study of Human Systems, Chevy Chase, MD 60 MIN
U-matic / VHS
Perceptions, Pt B - Dialogues with Family Therapists Series
Color (PRO)
Emphasizes the fact that two differentiated individuals make an effective co - therapy team.
Guidance and Counseling; Psychology; Sociology
Dist - BOSFAM **Prod** - BOSFAM

Vincent Van Gogh 30 MIN
VHS / U-matic
Color (J A)
Presents various views of historians on the personal and professional life of Van Gogh, a world - famous Dutch painter.
Fine Arts
Dist - SUTHRB **Prod** - SUTHRB

Vincent Van Gogh 25 MIN
16mm
Color (J)
Interweaves the paintings of Van Gogh with selections from his letters to his brother Theo. Shows many of the locales associated with Van Gogh, such as the Borinage and Arles.
Biography; Fine Arts
Dist - CORF **Prod** - HULSKR 1959

Vincent Van Gogh - his art and life 26 MIN
35mm strip / VHS
Color (J H C T A)
$93.00 purchase _ #MB - 481089 - 8, #MB - 512477 - 7
Portrays the life and work of artist Vincent Van Gogh. Reveals that Van Gogh only sold one of his paintings during his lifetime, and that he painted the majority of his more than 800 paintings within a decade.
Fine Arts
Dist - SRA **Prod** - SRA

Vincent Van Gogh - Portrait of a Painter 26 MIN
U-matic
Color
Describes the life and paintings of the Dutch artist Vincent Van Gogh. Emphasizes his sources of inspiration in nature. Includes paintings and drawings from many countries.
Fine Arts; Geography - World
Dist - MTP **Prod** - ROYNET

Vincent Van Gogh Series
Vincent - Painter of Light in Paris - 2 30 MIN
Vincent - Painter of Peasant Scenes - 1 30 MIN
Vincent - Sun Painter in France - 3 30 MIN
Dist - AITECH

The Vine and the branches
VHS
Video Biblical illustrator series
Color (H C G A R)
$24.99 purchase, $10.00 rental _ #35 - 83599 - 533
Explores the Biblical concept of 'abiding in the vine' of Christ.
Literature and Drama; Religion and Philosophy
Dist - APH **Prod** - WORD

Vines and Other Parasites 28 MIN
U-matic / VHS
Life of Plants Series
Color (C)
$249.00, $149.00 purchase _ #AD - 1676
Looks at mistletoe as an ingenious parasite. Shows how its life cycle is finely attuned to the life of its host tree and various bird species. Its seeds are glued to host branch by some, ingested but not digested by others, broadcast and then pruned while the host tree lures the vine with its sap, then produces tannin to kill or stunt the vine's growth. Part of a series on plants.
Science - Natural
Dist - FOTH **Prod** - FOTH

Vineyard IV 3 MIN
16mm
B&W; Color (G)
$1.00 rental
Represents the concept of a camera flowing because it is free to move through space. Also available from the Carpenter Center for Visual Arts, Harvard University.
Fine Arts
Dist - CANCIN **Prod** - FULTON

The Vineyard race 30 MIN
VHS
Color (G)
$29.80 purchase _ #0233
Records the 50th anniversary of the Long Island Sound distance sailing race.
Physical Education and Recreation
Dist - SEVVID

Vinland Mystery 29 MIN
16mm
Color
_ #106C 0184 030
Geography - World
Dist - CFLMDC **Prod** - NFBC 1984

Vinoba Bhave - Walking Revolution 39 MIN
U-matic / VHS / 16mm
Color (C)
LC 72-707291
Presents a picture of Gandhi's principles in practice today, especially through the work of his disciple and successor and his Bhoodan movement to revive Indian village life. Shows a group of boys educated according to Gandhi's theories as they go into villages after graduation to teach others what they have learned.
Geography - World; History - World; Psychology; Religion and Philosophy; Sociology
Dist - IFB **Prod** - PILGRM 1970

The Vintage 7 MIN
16mm
Color (I)
LC 74-703292
Shows one of Australia's major wine producing areas, the Barossa Valley in south Australia. Shows the harvesting of grapes and other stages in the production of wine.
Agriculture; Geography - World
Dist - AUIS **Prod** - ANAIB 1973

Vintage Cars 3 MIN
16mm
Of all Things Series
Color (P I)
Shows vintage cars.
Industrial and Technical Education; Physical Education and Recreation
Dist - AVED **Prod** - BAILYL

Vintage Cartoon Holiday Color
U-matic / VHS
Color
Presents many animated cartoons made by major studios.
Fine Arts
Dist - IHF **Prod** - IHF

Vintage Hitchcock 29 MIN
U-matic / VHS / 16mm
Art of film series
Color
Examines the directorial style of Alfred Hitchcock, from his first film until his appearance in America. Includes sequences from Young And Innocent, The Lodger, Blackmail, Rich And Strange, The Man Who Knew Too Much, Sabotage, The Lady Vanishes and The 39 Steps. Narrated by Douglas Fairbanks, Jr.
Fine Arts
Dist - CORF **Prod** - JANUS 1979

Vinyl chloride 9 MIN
BETA / VHS / U-matic
Hazard communication series
Color (IND G)
$295.00 purchase _ #830 - 03
Informs employees of the dangers of exposure to vinyl chloride gas while working with polyvinyl chloride resins and latex. Discusses the characteristics of vinyl chloride and preventive measures. Covers OSHA exposure limits. Part of a series on hazard communication.
Health and Safety; Industrial and Technical Education; Psychology
Dist - ITSC **Prod** - ITSC

Vinyl Floors 60 MIN
VHS
$39.95 purchase _ #DI - 304
Portrays how to install vinyl sheeting, including making a paper template and cutting and installing the vinyl for both perimeter bond and full spread adhesive floorings. Provides instruction in installing self adhesive floorings and vinyl floor tiles including planning, layout, cutting border tiles and curves.
Industrial and Technical Education
Dist - CAREER **Prod** - CAREER

Vinyl Floors 45 MIN
VHS / 16mm
Do it Yourself Series
(G)
Shows how to install sheet vinyl, including making a paper template and cutting and installing the vinyl for both perimeter bond and full spread adhesive floorings. Covers installing self adhesive vinyl floor tiles, including planning, layout, cutting border tiles and curves, tips, tools, and materials.

Home Economics
Dist - RMIBHF Prod - RMIBHF
CAMV

Vinyl floors 30 MIN
VHS
Home improvement video series
Color (G)
$39.95 purchase _ #223
Discusses vinyl floors. Explains installing sheet vinyl, including making a paper template and cutting and installing the vinyl for both perimeter bond and full spread adhesive floorings, installing self adhesive floor tile, including planning, layout, cutting border tile amd curves. tools and materials.
Home Economics
Dist - DIYVC Prod - DIYVC

Vinyl Floors
VHS
Home Improvement Series
(H C G A IND)
$39.95 _ SH304
Shows installing sheet vinyl including making a paper template and cutting and installing the vinyl for both perimeter bond and full spread adhesive floorings. The film also shows installing self adhesive floorings.
Industrial and Technical Education
Dist - AAVIM Prod - AAVIM 1989

Vinyl Top Repair 18 MIN
BETA / VHS / 16mm
Color (A PRO)
$81.00 purchase _ #KTI42
Covers heat gun vinyl method of repair on small tears.
Industrial and Technical Education
Dist - RMIBHF Prod - RMIBHF

Viola 28 MIN
U-matic / VHS / 16mm
Color (J)
LC 81-700294
Follows the steps in creating stringed instruments, showing how an ordinary tree becomes a shining viola.
Fine Arts
Dist - BCNFL Prod - BCNFL 1980

Viola 29 MIN
U-matic / VHS / 16mm
Color (J)
Shows master craftsman Otto Erdesz creating violas considered by professional musicians as the finest made today. Follows the process from selection of the wood, through the art of its construction, to its performance in concert.
Fine Arts
Dist - BCNFL Prod - NGUZO 1981

Viola for beginners 50 MIN
VHS
Maestro instructional series
Color (J H C G)
$29.95 purchase _ #BSPA21V
Supplements class lessons and reinforces private lessons on the viola. Offers clear - cut examples and demonstrations on how to unpack and assemble the instrument, proper hand position and instrumental nomenclature. Discusses notes, breathing, posture, reading music and care and maintenance of the instrument. Includes booklet. Part of a ten - part series on musical instruments.
Fine Arts
Dist - CAMV

Viola Und Sebastian 90 MIN
16mm
Color (GERMAN (ENGLISH SUBTITLES))
A free adaptation of William Shakespeare's comedy Twelfth Night.
Foreign Language; Literature and Drama
Dist - WSTGLC Prod - WSTGLC 1973

A Violation of trust 27 MIN
VHS
Color (A)
$525.00 purchase
Dramatizes how a salesperson's promotion increases pressure to produce and encourages discussions with competitors, leading to the temptation to violate antitrust laws. Shows how Justice Department investigations reveal a conspiracy that results in criminal penalties.
Business and Economics; Civics and Political Systems; Education
Dist - COMFLM Prod - COMFLM

Violence Against Women 60 MIN
U-matic
Perspectives on Women
Color (A)
Focuses on women in the economy, women and physical well being and how men and women are working to improve women's status in society.
Sociology
Dist - ACCESS Prod - ACCESS 1986

Violence and Physical Restraint 9 MIN
U-matic / VHS
Crisis Intervention Series
Color (PRO)
Shows police working with emergency medical technicians in physically restraining a psychotic. A continuation of Psychosis - A Family Intervention.
Health and Safety; Psychology; Sociology
Dist - GPN Prod - SBG 1983

Violence and Society 145 MIN
U-matic
University of the Air Series
Color (J H C A)
$750.00 purchase. $250.00 rental
Discusses what types of behaviour constitute aggression and then talks on theories of human aggression. Program contains a series of five cassettes 29 minutes each.
Health and Safety; Psychology; Sociology
Dist - CTV Prod - CTV 1977

Violence and the Law 30 MIN
U-matic / VHS
Ethics in America Series
Color (H C A)
Shows former U S Attorney General Ramsey Clark and law professor - author Ernest Van Den Haag debating the effectiveness of the American system of law and justice. Highlights the question of whether the system is too lenient or severe with the criminal.
Civics and Political Systems; Religion and Philosophy; Sociology
Dist - AMHUMA Prod - AMHUMA

Violence and Vandalism 15 MIN
16mm
Color (J H C)
LC 70-713579
Explores the problems and proposes some answers to the issue of vandalism. Points out gravity of the matter through up - to - date facts and location sites from California to New York.
Social Science; Sociology
Dist - AMEDFL Prod - AMEDFL 1971

Violence and Vandalism
16mm
Color (I)
LC 71-713579
Explains the causes of vandalism, why American cities spend millions a year clearing up the destruction caused by violence and vandalism and the alternatives to young people who feel they must destroy to be heard.
Guidance and Counseling; Sociology
Dist - AMEDFL Prod - DUNLF 1971

Violence at noon 99 MIN
VHS / 16mm
B&W (G) (JAPANESE WITH ENGLISH SUBTITLES)
$250.00 rental
Reveals that after the failure of a collective farm, the husband of an idealistic socialist schoolteacher goes berserk and becomes a sex criminal and murderer.
Fine Arts; Literature and Drama; Sociology
Dist - KINOIC
CHTSUI

Violence has no Enemies 15 MIN
16mm
B&W
LC 77-702164
Tells the story of three teenagers who become victims of violence in New York City.
Fine Arts
Dist - WISOT Prod - WISOT 1977

Violence in Black American Life 60 MIN
U-matic / VHS
Blacks, Blues, Black Series
Color
Sociology
Dist - PBS Prod - KQEDTV

Violence in the emergency room 60 MIN
VHS
Color (PRO C)
$285.00 purchase, $70.00 rental _ #6522
Identifies the causes of abusive - aggressive behavior and explains the factors that may escalate and de - escalate an abusive - aggressive situation. Describes intervention strategies for the management of the violent patient. Covers the impact of abusive - aggressive action in the hospital setting, as well as the legal aspects of violent patient management - in terms of documentation and restraints. In two parts.
Health and Safety; Sociology
Dist - AJN Prod - HESCTV

Violence in the family 30 MIN
VHS / U-matic
Family portrait - a study of contemporary lifestyles series; Lesson 21
Color (C A)
Compares natural family conflict or agression to abnormal physical violence. Investigates the socioeconomic roots of family violence. Examines the problem of abused children.
Sociology
Dist - CDTEL Prod - SCCON

Violence in the Family 44 MIN
VHS
Color (H)
Examines causes, characteristics, and possible solutions of family violence.
Guidance and Counseling; Health and Safety; Sociology
Dist - IBIS Prod - IBIS 1978

Violence in the Family 44 MIN
VHS
Color (J H C)
LC 85-703940
Examines the causes, characteristics, and possible solutions to family violence.
Sociology
Dist - HRMC Prod - HRMC

Violence in the Family
VHS / 35mm strip
$159.00 purchase _ #HR636 filmstrip, $159.00 purchase _ #HR636V VHS
Examines the causes, characteristics and possible solutions to family violence. Discusses the effects of family violence on individuals and society as a whole.
Sociology
Dist - CAREER Prod - CAREER

Violence in the Home - Living in Fear 30 MIN
VHS / 16mm
Color (H A PRO)
$275.00 purchase, $75.00 rental _ #8120
Features men and women in treatment whose lives were damaged by domestic violence. Discusses immediate and long term help available for people in those circumstances.
Health and Safety; Psychology; Sociology
Dist - AIMS Prod - AIMS 1989

Violence - Just for Fun 15 MIN
16mm / U-matic / VHS
Searching for Values - a Film Anthology Series
Color (J)
LC 72-703147
Shows how Roman spectators applaud the destruction of human lives for entertainment, easily accepting violence as an enjoyable facet of 'CIVILIZED LIFE.'.
Guidance and Counseling; History - World; Psychology; Religion and Philosophy; Sociology
Dist - LCOA Prod - LCOA 1972

Violence prevention 30 MIN
VHS
Club connect series
Color (J G H)
$59.95 purchase _ #CCNC-909-WC95
Describes how teenagers are combatting street violence in their neighborhoods by offering their peers anti-violence counseling. Includes interviews with teenagers that discuss the friends that they have they have lost to street violence.
Sociology
Dist - PBS Prod - WTVSTV 1994

Violence prevention curriculum - Dramatic video combinations for grades 4 - 5
VHS
Color (I)
$355.00 purchase _ #230 - 208
Combines the Second Step Violence Prevention Curriculum for grades 4 - 5 with the Facing Up Violence Prevention Dramatic Classroom Video for grades 2 - 7. Teaches children about interpersonal violence, empathy, problem solving and anger management. Issues such as gang involvement, bullying and peer pressure are addressed. Videos may be purchased separately.
Sociology
Dist - SICACC Prod - SICACC

Violence prevention curriculum - Dramatic video combinations for grades 6 - 8
VHS
Color (I J)
$405.00 purchase _ #330 - 208
Combines the Second Step Violence Prevention Curriculum for grades 6 - 8 with the Facing Up Violence Prevention Dramatic Classroom Video for grades 2 - 7. Teaches children about interpersonal violence, empathy, problem solving and anger management. Issues such as gang involvement, bullying and peer pressure are addressed. Videos may be purchased separately.
Sociology
Dist - SICACC Prod - SICACC

Violence Prevention Curriculum for Adolescents 60 MIN
VHS / 16mm
Teenage Health Teaching Modules Program Series
Color (H)
$150.00 purchase, $60.00 rental _ #5300
Addresses the growing problems of violence and homicide among young people. Helps teachers prepare to use the curriculum effectively by reviewing each session.
Psychology; Religion and Philosophy; Sociology
Dist - EDC **Prod** - EDC 1988

Violence prevention curriculum - Training video combinations for grades 1 - 3
VHS
Color (P PRO)
$325.00 purchase _ #130 - 611
Combines the Second Step Violence Prevention Curriculum for grades 1 - 3 with the Staff Training Video for Second Step for preschool - grade 5. Teaches young children about interpersonal violence, empathy, problem solving and anger management. Issues such as gang involvement, bullying and peer pressure are addressed. Trains educators in how best to present Second Step lessons and implement the program on a school - wide basis. Videos may be purchased separately.
Sociology
Dist - SICACC **Prod** - SICACC

Violence prevention curriculum - Training video combinations for preschool - kindergarten
VHS
Color (K PRO)
$315.00 purchase _ #30 - 611
Combines the Second Step Violence Prevention Curriculum for preschool - kindergarten with the Staff Training Video for Second Step for preschool - grade 5. Teaches young children about interpersonal violence, empathy, problem solving and anger management. Issues such as gang involvement, bullying and peer pressure are addressed. Trains educators in how best to present Second Step lessons and implement the program on a school - wide basis. Videos may be purchased separately.
Sociology
Dist - SICACC **Prod** - SICACC

Violence prevention - inside out 62 MIN
VHS
CC; Color (J H)
$135 purchase _ #10043VL
Examines the feelings leading to violence and the experience of violence in home, school, and society in general. Uses narration, interviews, and dramatization to aid in understanding, preventing and coping with violence. Consists of three thematic parts on one video, a resource guide and 10 blackline masters.
Guidance and Counseling; Sociology
Dist - UNL

Violence prevention - inside out 45 MIN
VHS
Color (J H)
$125.00 purchase
Explores violence - how it starts, how it affects individuals, how to prevent it at home, at school and in the community. Interviews young men in juvenile detention centers, treatment programs, in school and on the streets to offer a comprehensive view of the cycle of violence as it manifests itself in a variety of situations - domestic, sexual, gang - related and institutional.
Sociology
Dist - FMSP

Violence prevention package 58 MIN
VHS
Practical parenting series
CC; Color (A T J)
$170 purchase _ #300VL
Contains two 29 - minute programs that deal with issues of violence at home and in junior high schools. Addresses the concerns and methods available for parents, teachers and administrators to cope with violence. Focuses on conflict avoidance, peer mediation and problem solving. Comes with two facilitator's guides and two sets of blackline masters.
Education; Psychology; Sociology
Dist - UNL

Violence prevention - what every parent should know 29 MIN
VHS
Practical parenting series
CC; Color (A F)
$99 purchase _ #302VL
Defines how children view violence and intervention tactics that can be used by parents in the home. Presents crisis avoidance, conflict resolution and problem solving. Comes with a facilitator's guide and a set of blackline masters.
Psychology; Sociology
Dist - UNL

Violence prevention - what middle school teachers and students should know 29 MIN
VHS
Practical parenting series
CC; Color (T J)
$99 purchase _ #301VL
Presents teachers and administrators with three strategies to cope with increasing levels of violence and hostility in junior high schools. Focuses on early intervention, diffusing a hostile situation, and peer mediation. Uses dramatic scenarios and concludes with tips on improving middle school atmospheres. Comes with a facilitator's guide and a set of blackline masters.
Education; Sociology
Dist - UNL

Violence - reducing your risk 28 MIN
VHS
Color; CC (IND)
$625.00 purchase, $165.00 rental _ #VTC03
Introduces experts in personal safety and law enforcement with methods on avoiding violent situations and planning escape or defense if necessary.
Business and Economics; Guidance and Counseling; Health and Safety; Social Science; Sociology
Dist - EXTR **Prod** - VTCENS

Violence Sonata, no 2 45 MIN
16mm
Color
Explores a non - verbal essay on the unconscious forces of violence in a hope for the conscious understanding of man's future to adapt or die.
Psychology; Religion and Philosophy; Sociology
Dist - VANBKS **Prod** - VANBKS

Violence - the Tragic Legacy 29 MIN
Videoreel / VT2
Black Experience Series
Color
History - United States; Sociology
Dist - PBS **Prod** - WTTWTV

Violence - where have all the children gone 30 MIN
VHS
Teen - aiders video series
Color (I J H G)
$149.95 purchase _ #NIMBS3V
Dramatizes how violence sometimes results from unresolved problems. Demonstrates how to help identify causes of teen violence through awareness. Utilizes roleplay and audience participation while demonstrating problem solving techniques. Includes a workbook. Part of a four - part series on teen issues.
Psychology; Sociology
Dist - CAMV

Violence - where have all the children gone 26 MIN
VHS
Color (I J H)
$149.00 purchase _ #NC100
Dramatizes how violence sometimes results from unresolved problems. Utilizes role playing and audience participation to demonstrate problem - solving techniques.
Sociology
Dist - AAVIM **Prod** - AAVIM

Violence - will it Ever End 19 MIN
U-matic / VHS / 16mm
Color
Points out that every day the threat of violence becomes more real. Features Rollo May, psychiatrist and author of Power and Innocence, who discusses the phenomenon that our society has become obsessed by violence and a feeling of hopelessness. Depicts researchers at Yale University's School of Medicine who are studying methods of brain regulation by remote control.
Psychology; Science; Sociology
Dist - CNEMAG **Prod** - DOCUA

Violent Behavior
U-matic / VHS
Bedside Emergencies Series
Color
Presents five characteristics common to individuals who exhibit violent behavior. Discusses the function of the behavioral disorder team during physical intervention.
Health and Safety
Dist - CONMED **Prod** - CONMED

The Violent Earth 52 MIN
U-matic / VHS / 16mm
Color
LC 76-703413
Shows French volcanologist Haroun Tazieff conducting a tour of Mt Etna in Sicily and Nyiragongo in Zaire during periods of volcanic eruption.
Geography - World; Science - Physical
Dist - NGS **Prod** - NGS 1973

The Violent mind 60 MIN
VHS
Mind Series
Color; Captioned (G)
$59.95 purchase _ #MIND - 108
Discusses the implications of recent research which indicates that violent behavior may have biological and environmental causes. Suggests that changes in anatomy and brain chemistry may create violent tendencies. Explores how concepts such as free will and guilt are affected.
Psychology
Dist - PBS **Prod** - WNETTV 1988

Violent storms 14 MIN
VHS
Atmospheric science series
Color; PAL (H)
Uses cinematography and time - lapse photography to portray the thunderstorm. Stresses that the great destructiveness of hurricanes and tornadoes makes early warning systems imperative. Part of a series of eight parts which teaches about the Earth's atmosphere.
Science - Physical
Dist - VIEWTH **Prod** - VIEWTH
CORF

The Violent Universe 148 MIN
U-matic / VHS / 16mm
Public Broadcast Laboratory Series
B&W (H C)
LC 72-703008
A comprehensive report of astronomical theories, research and discoveries. Visits thirty astronomers at their observatories throughout the world as they discuss pulsars, infra - red galaxies, red giants, white dwarfs, cosmic rays and redshift. Includes a motion picture view of a quasar.
Science - Physical
Dist - IU **Prod** - NET 1969

Violent Youth - the Un - Met Challenge 23 MIN
U-matic / VHS / 16mm
Color (PRO)
LC 75-703772
Presents various approaches to dealing with juvenile crime by examining the cases of three serious offenders who are confined to a maximum security facility for boys in Goshen, New York. Gives views of a director of an institution for serious juvenile offenders, a family court judge and a chief of police.
Sociology
Dist - CORF **Prod** - ALTANA 1975

Violette 123 MIN
16mm
Color (FRENCH (ENGLISH SUBTITLES))
Focuses on an 18 - year - old French girl who poisons her parents. Directed by Claude Chabrol.
Fine Arts; Foreign Language
Dist - NYFLMS **Prod** - UNKNWN 1978

The Violin 24 MIN
U-matic / 16mm / VHS
Color (J H A P) (SPANISH)
LC 73-700227
Tells story of a young boy and an old musician who leaves his violin with the boy.
Fine Arts; Guidance and Counseling; Literature and Drama; Sociology
Dist - LCOA **Prod** - LCOA 1973

The Violin and the Viola 25 MIN
U-matic
Instruments of the Orchestra and their Techniques Series
Color
Fine Arts
Dist - UWASHP **Prod** - UWASHP

Violin - Door 13 MIN
16mm
B&W
LC 77-702631
A character study of a deaf - mute who comes upon the farmhouse of a lonely, but over - bearing young woman.
Fine Arts; Psychology; Sociology
Dist - FMCOOP **Prod** - SHOWN 1969

Violin for beginners 50 MIN
VHS
Maestro instructional series
Color (J H C G)
$29.95 purchase _ #BSPN20V
Supplements class lessons and reinforces private lessons on the violin. Offers clear - cut examples and demonstrations on how to unpack and assemble the instrument, proper hand position and instrumental nomenclature. Discusses notes, breathing, posture, reading music and care and maintenance of the instrument. Includes booklet. Part of a ten - part series on musical instruments.

Fine Arts
Dist - CAMV

The Violin Maker (in Praise of Hands) 12 MIN
U-matic / VHS / 16mm
Color (I J H)
LC 72-700789
Pictures, without narration, an aged craftsman at work fashioning a violin from what appears to be firewood. Shows that the old man's work reflects patience, attention to detail, a respect for both materials and tools and pride.
Fine Arts; Guidance and Counseling
Dist - PHENIX **Prod** - ZAGREB 1972

Violin Making in Colonial America 30 MIN
16mm
Color
LC 77-700006
Shows the many stages involved in making a violin with the tools and methods of 18th century craftsmen.
Fine Arts; Industrial and Technical Education
Dist - CWMS **Prod** - CWMS 1976

Violin making - unit C 36 MIN
VHS
Furniture, soft furnishing and musical instruments technology - 'teaching and learning process series; Unit C
Color; PAL (J H IND)
PdS29.50 purchase
Part of a four - part series which observes teaching and learning in a variety of workshop situations.
Fine Arts
Dist - EMFVL

Violincello 60 MIN
U-matic / VHS
(G)
Chronicles the work of Nebraska violin, viola and cello maker David Wiebe. Begins with selecting wood for the instrument and follows the steps in its creation. Features cello pieces by Bach and Schumann and backgrounds from Oregon's Crater Lake region.
Fine Arts
Dist - UNKNWN **Prod** - NETV 1982

VIP softball series
Presents a seven - part series on softball. Includes the titles Beginning Fast Pitch Pitching; Advanced Fast Pitch Pitching; Defensive Fundamentals and Drills; Fast Pitch Strategy, Team Defense and Sliding; Slow Pitch Strategy, Team Defense and Sliding; Coaching Fast Pitch Softball; Coaching Slow Pitch Softball.

Advanced fast pitch pitching 60 MIN
Baserunning basics and drills 25 MIN
Beginning fast pitch pitching 60 MIN
Coaching fast pitch softball 75 MIN
Coaching slow pitch softball 75 MIN
Defensive fundamentals and drills 60 MIN
Fast pitch strategy, team defense and sliding 60 MIN
Fundamentals of hitting 33 MIN
Hitting drills 25 MIN
Practice organization 32 MIN
Principles of coaching 20 MIN
Slow pitch strategy, team defense and sliding 60 MIN
Teaching throwing - the skills and drills 20 MIN
Understanding fast pitch pitching 28 MIN
Dist - CAMV

Vir Amat 15 MIN
16mm
Color
Portrays two men who have been living together for over a year, sharing their sexual pattern. Begins in the kitchen with dinner and subsequent dishwashing, and moves into the living room. Shows them kissing and caressing each other. Concludes with them engaging in oral - genital activity and mutual masturbation to orgasm.
Guidance and Counseling; Psychology; Sociology
Dist - MMRC **Prod** - MMRC

Viracocha 30 MIN
16mm
Faces of Change - Bolivia Series
Color
Shows how Indians of pure and mixed blood interact in the Andean highlands within a near - subsistence economic system. Shows how market days and fiestas provide opportunities for the Spanish - speaking mestizos to assert their traditional social dominance over the native Indians.
Geography - World; Social Science; Sociology
Dist - WHEELK **Prod** - AUFS

Virgin Machine 86 MIN
16mm
B&W (C)
Presents an independent production by Monica Treut. Explores the shifting sexual orientation of a young female journalist who searches for romantic love in Hamburg and San Francisco.
Fine Arts; Psychology; Sociology
Dist - FIRS
ICARUS

The Virgin of Guadalupe 111 MIN
16mm
B&W
Portrays the vision of the virgin of Guadalupe which converted the Indian worshippers from their Aztec gods.
Religion and Philosophy; Social Science
Dist - TRANSW **Prod** - CATHFC

The Virgin of Zapopan
VHS
Color (J H G) (SPANISH)
$44.95 purchase _ #MCV5047, #MCV5048
Presents a program on the culture of Mexico.
Geography - World
Dist - MADERA **Prod** - MADERA

The Virgin spring 88 MIN
VHS
B&W (G)
$39.95 purchase _ #VIR030
Adapts a medieval legend in which a devout young girl is raped by herders, causing her father to become consumed by a violent need for vengeance. Exposes a society on the cusp between mysticism and Christianity and explores the power of reconciliation.
Fine Arts; Psychology; Religion and Philosophy; Sociology
Dist - HOMVIS **Prod** - JANUS 1959

Virgin wives
VHS
Frontiers series
Color; PAL (G)
PdS20 purchase
Reveals that non - consummation of marriage is much more common than either the general public or the medical profession imagines. Shows that it is a distressing problem crossing culture, community and class. Includes support material. Part of a series examining how developments at the frontiers of science, technology and psychology have had a major impact on a range of health and medical issues. Contact distributor about availability outside the United Kindgom.
Psychology; Sociology
Dist - ACADEM

Virginia 60 MIN
VHS
Portrait of America series
Color (J H C G)
$99.95 purchase _ #AMB46V
Visits Virginia. Offers extensive research into the state's history. Films key locations and presents segments on its history, government, education, folklore, science, journalism, sociology, industry, agriculture and business. Shows what is unique about Virginia and what is distinctive about its regional culture and how it got to be that way. Includes teacher study guides. Part of a 50 - part series.
Geography - United States; History - United States
Dist - CAMV
TBSESI

Virginia 20 MIN
16mm
B&W
Introduces Virginia, an elderly woman with a hearing handicap, who is presented in an oppresive interview situation on a darkened sound stage responding to muffled inquiries from a condescending young man. Shows her patience and gentleness triumphing over her interrogator.
Health and Safety; Psychology
Dist - DIRECT **Prod** - MARBLO 1975

Virginia Artists Series
Vanishing Point - Painting and Sculpture of Nancy Camden Witt 10 MIN
Dist - SCHDRC

Virginia Blacks - a History, Pt 1 20 MIN
U-matic / VHS
B&W
History - United States
Dist - SYLWAT **Prod** - RCOMTV 1978

Virginia Blacks - a History, Pt 2 21 MIN
U-matic / VHS
B&W
History - United States
Dist - SYLWAT **Prod** - RCOMTV 1978

Virginia City 54 MIN
VHS / 16mm
Color (G)
$70.00 rental _ #VRGC - 000
Tours Virginia City, Nevada, a once - prosperous silver mining town. Features modern - day residents discussing their city's tourism industry.
History - United States; Social Science
Dist - PBS **Prod** - KLVXTV

Virginia de Araujo - 12 - 5 - 79 30 MIN
VHS / Cassette
Poetry Center reading series
Color (G)
$15.00, $45.00 purchase, $15.00 rental _ #366 - 306
Features the Hispanic American writer translating Carlos Drummond de Andrade at a reading of translations of three 20th - century Latin American poets at the Poetry Center, San Francisco State University, with an introduction by Tom Mandel.
Literature and Drama
Dist - POETRY **Prod** - POETRY 1979

Virginia Geriatric Education Center Video Conference series
Aging and developmental disabilities - issues of concern to families 120 MIN
Alcoholism and substance abuse in older adults 120 MIN
Case management for older adults - new issues, new venues 120 MIN
The Challenge of Alzheimer's disease - advances in etiology, diagnosis and management 120 MIN
Drug use and misuse in the elderly 120 MIN
Ethical choices along the continuum of care 120 MIN
Ethnic diversity - barrier or benefit in health care of the elderly 120 MIN
Falls in late life - problems and prevention 120 MIN
Functional assessment of the older adult 120 MIN
Health promotion and wellness in older adults 120 MIN
Healthful living environments for older adults 120 MIN
Managing urinary incontinence in older adults 120 MIN
The Physiological and psychological challenge - osteoporosis 120 MIN
Promoting the independence of older adults through the use of assistive devices 120 MIN
Sensory changes in the elderly 120 MIN
Sexuality in later life 120 MIN
Stroke rehabilitation - health care options for elderly patients 120 MIN
Suicide and abuse - the vulnerable elderly 120 MIN
Treating depression in the elderly 120 MIN
The Triple threat of genito - urinary disease - implications for improving quality of life 120 MIN
Dist - TNF

The Virginia Hill Story 77 MIN
16mm / U-matic / VHS
Color (H C A)
Looks at the life of Virginia Hill and her life with underground figures. Stars Dyan Cannon.
Fine Arts; Sociology
Dist - LUF **Prod** - LUF 1976

Virginia law everyone should know series
Accidents and liability, juvenile law, and criminal law 30 MIN
Domestic relations, contracts and consumer transactions, accidents and liability 30 MIN
Domestic relations, contracts and estate planning 30 MIN
Dist - SYLWAT

Virginia plantations - Mount Vernon, Monticello, and other great houses of old Virginia 30 MIN
VHS
Color (G)
$19.95 purchase _ #S02187
Tours and gives the significance of the historic plantations of Virginia. Features footage of plantation gardens with people in period costumes. Focuses on Mount Vernon, Monticello and Shirley Plantation.
Fine Arts; History - United States
Dist - UILL

Virginia Satir - families and relationships series 502 MIN
VHS
Virginia Satir - families and relationships series
Color; PAL; SECAM (G)
$476.00 purchase
Presents Virginia Satir in a 10 - part series on families and relationships. Shows Satir interacting with families and individuals, creating tableaus and role - plays that illustrate ineffective and effective communication styles, how to change viewpoints and perceptions and get beyond old roles and personal history to honest and direct

feeling communication. Includes the titles Family Relations, Endings and Beginnings, Forgiving Parents, Self - Worth, Empowering Communication, Divorced Parents and Children, Blended Families. All levels of NLP, neuro - linguistic programming.
Psychology; Social Science; Sociology
Dist - NLPCOM **Prod** - NLPCOM

Virginia Satir, MSW - Sisters and Parents - a Family Finds Options 60 MIN
U-matic / VHS
Perceptions, Pt a - Interventions in Family Therapy Series
Color (PRO)
Uses simple action techniques to demonstrate problem - solving in a family. Features Virginia Satir helping two sisters and their parents define their relationships.
Guidance and Counseling; Psychology; Sociology
Dist - BOSFAM **Prod** - BOSFAM

Virginia Silver 30 MIN
U-matic / VHS
Antique Shop Series
Color
Presents guests who are experts in their respective fields who share tips on collecting and caring for antique Virginia silver.
Fine Arts
Dist - MDCPB **Prod** - WVPTTV

Virginia Woolf 58 MIN
VHS
Modern World - Ten Great Writers Series
Color (H)
$13.00 rental _ #60963
Examines Virginia Woolf's narrative method and experimental techniques in her works 'Mrs Dalloway,' 'To The Lighthouse,' 'Orlando' and 'The Waves.' Studies ten important modernist European writers by placing them against turn - of - the century settings, dramatizing their own experiences and looking at their principal works in a ten part series.
Literature and Drama
Dist - PSU **Prod** - FI

Virginia Woolf 30 MIN
VHS
Famous Authors Series
Color (H)
$11.50 rental _ #35512
Follows Virginia Woolf's life from her childhood in London, her marriage to Leonard Woolf, her struggle with mental illness, and ends at her suicide. An installment in the Famous Authors Series, which examines important English writers in the context of their times.
English Language; Literature and Drama; Sociology
Dist - PSU **Prod** - EBEC
EBEC

Virginia Woolf - the Moment Whole 10 MIN
16mm / U-matic / VHS
Color (H C A)
LC 72-702447
Introduces the philosophy and literary style of the 20th - century writer, Virginia Woolf, by presenting visuals of the milieu in which she worked complemented by selections from 'A ROOM OF ONE'S OWN' and 'THE WAVES,' read and portrayed by Marian Seldes.
Literature and Drama; Religion and Philosophy
Dist - AIMS **Prod** - NET 1972

Virginia's Civil War parks 55 MIN
VHS
National park series
Color (J H C G)
$34.95 purchase _ #FHFS90V
Visits famous Civil War battlefields, from the first major confrontation at Bull Run to the final surrender at Appomattox Courthouse. Part of a five - part series on United States' national parks.
Geography - United States; History - United States
Dist - CAMV

Virginia's Fishing Industry 12 MIN
16mm
Color (I)
Shows the importance of the fishing industry in the Chesapeake Bay. Depicts methods of catching fish.
Business and Economics; Geography - United States; Geography - World
Dist - VADE **Prod** - VADE 1956

Virgins 28 MIN
VHS / 16mm
Color (G)
$149.00, $249.00, purchase _ #AD - 1240
Reports that virginity seems to be alive and well, partly as a backlash against two decades of sexual freedom, and partly because of fear of disease. Examines the reasons why people choose to remain virgins until marriage.
Health and Safety; Psychology
Dist - FOTH **Prod** - FOTH 1990

Virgo I 14 MIN
16mm
Color (I)
Presents a poetic cinepoem about a young man's escape from the noise of the city to the serene environment of Big Sur.
Fine Arts; Sociology
Dist - CFS **Prod** - CFS 1969

Virile Games 14 MIN
16mm
Color (G)
Presents an independent production by Jan Svankmajer. Creates a soccer match played by the freewheeling rules of Svankmajer, where 'taking out a man' is more important than scoring a goal. Also available in 35mm film format.
Business and Economics; Fine Arts; Industrial and Technical Education; Physical Education and Recreation; Sociology
Dist - FIRS

Viro's Reel 30 MIN
U-matic / VHS
Color
Presented by Howard Freid.
Fine Arts
Dist - KITCHN **Prod** - KITCHN

Virtual reality - an introduction to the technology and its applications 120 MIN
VHS
Color (G)
$30.00 purchase
Profiles and explains various types of VR - virtual reality - systems currently in use or in development. Draws from the Introduction to Virtual Reality workshop at the New York Virtual Reality Expo - November, 1993 - produced by Louis M Brill and Otto von Ruggins. Includes speakers such as Dr Bernie Roehl on technical aspects, and Don Morris on cab simulators, with additional presentations by David Smith, Steve Glenn, Louis M Brill and Myron Krueger.
Computer Science
Dist - MCAS

Virtual reality in medicine 30 MIN
VHS
Color (G)
$89.95 purchase _ #UW3049
Shows how surgeons in training are using virtual reality to learn complicated procedures before ever working on a live patient. Looks at plastic surgeons reconstructing faces on a computer and how drug designers are coming up with cancer medications.
Computer Science; Health and Safety
Dist - FOTH

Virtual reality - reality and the truth 52 MIN
VHS
Color (H G)
$250.00 purchase
Presents in two parts a discussion of reality, seeming reality and truth. Looks at how our senses interpret the world around us in part 1, Reality and Truth. Part 2, Beyond Our Dimension, shows the effects of altered senses on the perception of reality. Explains the meaning of 'virtual reality' and how it is applied in medicine, industry and communications.
Computer Science
Dist - LANDMK

Virtual Valerie
CD-ROM
(A)
$95.00 purchase _ #2811
Takes a tour with Valerie through the seamier side of 'adult' games. Offers color animation and interaction features. Adult only. For Macintosh Plus, SE and II computers. Requires at least one M of RAM, one floppy disk drive, and an Apple compatible CD - ROM drive.
Computer Science; Sociology
Dist - BEP

Virtue Rewarded - Henry Fielding's Joseph Andrews 45 MIN
U-matic / VHS
Survey of English Literature I Series
Color
Dramatizes selected incidents from Henry Fielding's novel Joseph Andrews.
Literature and Drama
Dist - MDCPB **Prod** - MDCPB

Virus 25 MIN
VHS
Color; CC (H A)
$110.00 purchase - #A51618
Uses computer images and animation to dramatize how viruses invade the body. Points out the danger of viral epidemics, emphasizing the modern HIV threat. Includes a teacher's guide.
Science - Natural
Dist - NGS **Prod** - NGS 1994

A Virus Knows no Morals 82 MIN
16mm
Color (G)
Presents an independent production by Rosa von Praunheim. Offers a savagely funny, irreverent, but serious burlesque on the AIDS crisis.
Health and Safety
Dist - FIRS

Virus - prevention, detection, recovery 22 MIN
VHS
Color (A)
$525.00 purchase
Defines computer viruses and explains how they function to spread and to damage data. Explains steps to prevent or to minimize the effects of viruses, and to avoid further contamination of data. Applies particularly to PC and LAN setups. Includes one user's reinforcement guide. Additional copies are available separately.
Business and Economics; Civics and Political Systems; Computer Science; Education
Dist - COMFLM **Prod** - COMFLM

Viruses 15 MIN
VHS
Biology live series
Color (I J) (SPANISH)
$129.00 purchase _ #GW - 5074 - VS, #GW - 5074 - SP
Reviews the different shapes of viruses. Reveals how viruses can invade and damage cells. Part of a 13 - part series on biology which uses high resolution animation, live - action photography and interesting narrative to teach a core curriculum in biological science.
Science - Natural
Dist - HRMC

Viruses
VHS
Basic science series
Color (J H) (ENGLISH AND SPANISH)
$39.95 purchase _ #MCV5015
Focuses on viruses, presenting only basic concepts. Includes teacher's guide and review questions. Combines computer animation and the use of 'sheltered language' to help students acquire content vocabulary, become comfortable with scientific language and achieve success in science curriculum. Part of a series on basic science concepts.
Science; Science - Natural
Dist - MADERA **Prod** - MADERA

Viruses 16 MIN
VHS
Color; PAL (H)
Examines the range of virus morphology and two modes of virus action. Discusses virus replication within cells.
Agriculture; Health and Safety; Science - Natural
Dist - VIEWTH

Viruses 12 MIN
VHS
Color (J H)
$130.00 purchase _ #A5VH 1610
Describes the various shapes and structures of viruses. Emphasizes the importance of nucleic acid. Shows how viruses enter plant and animal cells and illustrates, in detailed animation, how the virus that causes AIDS destroys white blood cells and impairs the body's ability to fight infection. Discusses the ability of bacteriophages to invade bacteria, causing them to produce disease - causing toxins.
Health and Safety; Science - Natural
Dist - CLRVUE **Prod** - CLRVUE 1992

Viruses 15 MIN
VHS / 16mm
Inhabitants of the planet Earth series
Color (H C)
$240.00, $180.00 purchase, $25.00 rental _ #194 W 2055, #193 W 2011, #140 W 2055
Shows the range of virus morphology and two modes of virus action - the direct takeover of the host cell as seen in the T4 bacteriophage, and the subtle phenomenon of virus insertion, whereby the viral nucleic acid 'snips' its way into the host cell's DNA and replicates along with the host's genes at each cell divison. Shows culturing methods and the effects of viruses on plant tissue. Part of a series on microorganisms.
Science - Natural
Dist - WARDS **Prod** - WARDS

Viruses 13 MIN
16mm / U-matic / VHS
Color (J H)
$325, $235 purchase _ #3817
Examines the nature of viruses and talks about viral research.
Science - Natural
Dist - CORF

Viruses and Cancer 37 MIN
U-matic / VHS
Color
Considers the properties of the oncogenic viruses, the biological events which occur after viral infection of individual cells grown in cell culture, and the evidence that viruses may play a role in certain human cancers. Video version of 35mm filmstrip program, with live open and close.
Health and Safety
Dist - CBSC **Prod** - BMEDIA

Viruses - the Mysterious Enemy 39 MIN
VHS
Color (I)
LC 85-703881
Describes viruses, their discovery, their structure, how they operate and how they can evolve, and examines some virus - caused diseases.
Health and Safety
Dist - HRMC **Prod** - HRMC

Viruses - the Mysterious Enemy 38 MIN
VHS
Color
Discloses the most recent research to describe viruses.
Health and Safety; Science - Natural
Dist - IBIS **Prod** - IBIS 1982

Vis - a - Vid 13 MIN
VHS
Color (G)
Composes three vignettes dealing with an individual's inhumanity to himself or herself. Features Cold Java, in which a man, contemplating a cup of coffee, is suspended between drinking and abstaining, engagement and alienation; Disconnected views a woman who, after a menacing phone call from her boyfriend, wanders the streets of Los Angeles feeling estranged from her surroundings; and in Fast Lane a young boy devours a hamburger while offering precocious commentary regarding the nihilistic nature of American mass - producing, mass - consuming society.
Fine Arts
Dist - GAMBOA **Prod** - GAMBOA 1991

Visages De La Ville Lumiere 22 MIN
U-matic / VHS / 16mm
Accent Aigu Series
B&W (H C) (FRENCH)
Shows scenes of Paris.
Foreign Language
Dist - IFB **Prod** - FFC 1956

The Visas that saved lives 115 MIN
VHS
Color (G) (JAPANESE W/ENGLISH SUBTITLES)
$49.95 purchase _ #648
Portrays Chiune Sugihara, Japan's consul - general in Lithuania in 1940, who awoke very early one summer morning to the sound of a low rumble outside. Reveals that he found over 200 people filling the crowded street outside the consulate and immediately hid his wife and children, fearing for their safety. Sugihara soon realized that those outside were Jews hoping to get visas that would take them out of the country to freedom. While American consuls throughout the neutral world were instructed not to grant such visas, Sugihara took it upon himself to do just that, working day and night issuing an estimated 1600 visas. Tells the story of a man who sacrificed his own career to save an estimated 2,000 to 6,000 lives.
History - World
Dist - ERGOM

Visceral Angiography 22 MIN
16mm
Color (PRO)
Discusses the proper technique and catheters for performing visceral angiography.
Health and Safety; Science
Dist - CORDIS **Prod** - CORDIS

Visceral Organ Transplants 30 MIN
16mm
Upjohn Vanguard of Medicine Series
Color (PRO)
LC FIA66-673
Reports developments in the field of medicine and discusses three major problems involving surgery, immunology and supply.
Health and Safety
Dist - UPJOHN **Prod** - UPJOHN 1966

Visceral Reflexes and Taste - Visceral Motor and Sensory Components 18 MIN
16mm / U-matic / VHS
Anatomical Basis of Brain Function Series
Color (PRO)
Science - Natural
Dist - TEF **Prod** - AVCORP

Viscosity 30 MIN
VHS / U-matic
Kinetic Karnival of Jearl Walker Pt 4
Color (H)
LC 83-706118
Presents physics professor Jearl Walker offering graphic and unusual demonstrations exemplifying the principles of the viscosity of fluids.
Science - Physical
Dist - GPN **Prod** - WVIZTV 1982

Vises, Clamps, Pliers, Screwdrivers, Wrenches 60 MIN
U-matic / VHS
Mechanical Maintenance Basics, Module a - Hand Tools Series
Color (IND)
Industrial and Technical Education
Dist - LEIKID **Prod** - LEIKID

Vishnu's Maya 30 MIN
U-matic / VHS / 16mm
Color (H C A)
LC 78-700464
Explores the beauty of India and examines classical Hindu culture.
Geography - World; Religion and Philosophy; Sociology
Dist - PHENIX **Prod** - SARASW 1977

Visibility - Moderate 40 MIN
VHS / U-matic
Color
Presents a parody of a vacation film through Ireland. Touches upon several Irish issues, such as the sentimental mythologizing of the national past.
Fine Arts
Dist - KITCHN **Prod** - KITCHN

Visible absorption spectrophotometry - absorbance - Part I 12 MIN
VHS
Chemistry master apprentice series
Color (H C)
$49.95 purchase _ #49 - 7216 - V
Demonstrates the use of the spectrophotometer and the techniques required for the quantitative and reproducible measurement of the absorbance of a solution. Part of the Chemistry Master Apprentice series.
Science; Science - Physical
Dist - INSTRU **Prod** - CORNRS

Visible absorption spectrophotometry - concentration - Part II 8 MIN
VHS
Chemistry master apprentice series
Color (H C)
$49.95 purchase _ #49 - 7217 - V
Supports Part I. Shows how the spectrophotometer is used to measure directly the concentration of a solution using the concentration mode and the factor set button. Assumes familiarity with the operations presented in Part I. Part of the Chemistry Master Apprentice series.
Science; Science - Physical
Dist - INSTRU **Prod** - CORNRS

Visible Absorption Spectrophotometry - Pt 1 - Absorbance 30 MIN
U-matic / VHS
Chemistry - master - apprentice series; Program 14
Color (C A)
LC 82-706045
Demonstrates the use of the Bausch and Lomb Spectronic 21 spectrophotometer and the techniques required for the quantitative and reproducible measurement of the absorbance of a solution.
Health and Safety; Science; Science - Physical
Dist - CORNRS **Prod** - CUETV 1981

Visible Absorption Spectrophotometry - Pt 2 - Concentration 9 MIN
U-matic / VHS
Chemistry - master - apprentice series; Program 15
Color (C A)
LC 82-706078
Uses the Spectronic 21 to directly measure the concentration of a solution using the concentration mode and the factor set button. Assumes that the viewer is familiar with the operations presented in Part 1, Program 14.
Health and Safety; Science; Science - Physical
Dist - CORNRS **Prod** - CUETV 1981

The Visible compendium 15 MIN
16mm
Color (G)
$35.00 rental
Attempts, through animation, to engage the mind with unknown possibilities. Constructs unnamed meanings and fragments of light which is the essence of photography. The soundtrack employs strange sounds and some music.
Fine Arts
Dist - CANCIN **Prod** - JORDAL 1991

Visible harm 41 MIN
VHS
Color (G)
$225.00 purchase
Draws from studies by Dr Catherine Itzin to argue that trade in pornography is detrimental to society's view of women and children and promotes abusive and violent behavior.
Sociology
Dist - LANDMK

Visible inventories series
Visible inventory nine - pattern of events 12 MIN
Visible inventory six - motel dissolve 15 MIN
Dist - CANCIN

Visible inventory nine - pattern of events 12 MIN
16mm
Visible inventories series
Color (G)
$35.00 rental
Creates a non - fiction narrative which relays the second thoughts of individuals meeting by accident in public places. Forms the soundtrack from tones which grow and change unpredictably - not single notes on a page.
Fine Arts
Dist - CANCIN **Prod** - LIPZIN 1981

Visible inventory six - motel dissolve 15 MIN
16mm
Visible inventories series
Color (G)
$40.00 rental
Surveys the interiors of motel rooms in which the filmmaker stayed during transcontinental auto trips. Counterpoints printed word, spoken text and photographs to give the viewer alternate options of reading, viewing and listening. Soundtrack consists of two Gertrude Stein texts.
Fine Arts; Geography - World
Dist - CANCIN **Prod** - LIPZIN 1978

Visible man 5 MIN
16mm
Color (G)
$22.00 rental
Confronts the imbalance between society's technoculture and its consumer product slavery. Utilizes processed vignettes to depict a world devoid of morality. Produced by Jerome Cook.
Fine Arts
Dist - CANCIN

Visicalc
U-matic / VHS
Color
Illustrates the overall concept of an electronic spreadsheet and the basic model - building tools of VisiCalc. Offers an introduction to the 'what if' game, split screens, inserting and deleting rows and variety of formatting options.
Industrial and Technical Education; Mathematics
Dist - ANDRST **Prod** - LANSFD

Vision 16 MIN
16mm / Slide
Learning about the Human Body Series
B&W; Color (G J H C I)
$18.95 purchase; LC 77-731249
Demonstrates the work of optical science with emphasis on the need for accurate vision. Examines the parts of the eye and common eye defects, and shows the optical glass laboratory.
Religion and Philosophy
Dist - UNL **Prod** - MORLAT 1976

Vision 29 MIN
U-matic
Understanding Human Behavior - an Introduction to Psychology Series
Color (C A)
Defines and explains vision in terms of the parts of the eye and the characteristics of light waves. Discusses handicap of blindness.
Psychology
Dist - CDTEL **Prod** - COAST

Vision 4 MIN
16mm
Color (G)
$10.00 rental
Explores handmade images by bleaching and dyeing to achieve shapes and patterns. Looks at 150 feet of selected squares and circles. Inspired by Mondrian. Second in the Direct - on - Film series by Dirk De Bruyn.
Fine Arts
Dist - CANCIN

Vision and Movement 60 MIN
VHS / U-matic
Brain, Mind and Behavior Series

Color (C A)
Discusses how we perceive the world and move within it.
Psychology; Science - Natural
Dist - FI **Prod** - WNETTV

Vision and movement - Part 2 60 MIN
VHS / U-matic
Brain series
Color (G)
$45.00, $29.95 purchase
Illustrates the neurological miracle of coordinating vision and movement. Features Olympic diver Greg Louganis and the work of Nobel Prize - winners David Hubel and Torsten Wiesel on the visual cortex. Part two of an eight - part series on the brain.
Psychology; Science - Natural
Dist - ANNCPB **Prod** - WNETTV 1984

Vision dance 60 MIN
VHS
Color (G)
$115.00 purchase
Presents a dance theater piece based on Ihanbla Waktoglag Wacipi from the Lakota Sioux Nation. Includes SOLARIS members and traditional dancers and drummers from the Lakota Sioux Nation. Shot on location in South Dakota on Rosebud and Pine Ridge Reservations, and in the Black Hills and the Badlands. Presents 13 Lakota Plains Dances.
Social Science
Dist - SOLARS

Vision exercises 54 MIN
VHS
Color (G T PRO)
$49.95 purchase _ #70034
Presents 12 vision exercises designed for adults who are learning to read. Develops perceptual and visual - motor skills related to successful classroom learning that may not have been acquired earlier in life. Creator Dr Joel N Zaba has studied the links between classroom, vision, learning, and social - emotional problems.
Education; English Language
Dist - LITERA

The Vision for change 13 MIN
VHS
System of change series
Color (PRO G A)
$465.00 purchase, $130.00 rental
Outlines seven steps for developing the concept of needed change and encouraging participation in the reorganization. Helps leaders share the vision with others. Part of Change Excellence, Unit 1.
Business and Economics; Guidance and Counseling; Psychology
Dist - EXTR **Prod** - CCCD

Vision for Tomorrow 22 MIN
16mm
Color (PRO)
LC 82-700341
Shows new surgical and pharmaceutical procedures in opthalmology. Features experts in the field from Switzerland, France and the United States.
Health and Safety
Dist - MESHDO **Prod** - MESHDO 1982

Vision in meditation No 4 - D H Lawrence 19 MIN
16mm
Color (G)
$656.00 purchase, $45.00 rental
Offers homage to D H Lawrence.
Fine Arts
Dist - CANCIN **Prod** - BRAKS

Vision in meditation No 3 - Plato's cave 18 MIN
16mm
Color (G)
$673.00 purchase, $45.00 rental
Presents an experimental film by Stan Brakhage. Meditates on Plato's cave, set to the three movements of Memory Suite by Rick Corrigan.
Fine Arts
Dist - CANCIN **Prod** - BRAKS 1990

Vision in meditation No 2 - Mesa Verde 17 MIN
16mm
Color (G)
$656.00 purchase, $45.00 rental
Examines the Mysteries of the ruins at Mesa Verde.
Fine Arts
Dist - CANCIN **Prod** - BRAKS 1989

Vision in Military Aviation - Sense of Sight 25 MIN
16mm
Color
LC 74-705919
Describes anatomy and physiology of the eye, including structure of the retina and functions of the rods and cones for light discrimination, dark - adaption and techniques for the relaying of rod vision. Describes how different forces and chemicals affect the eye.
Civics and Political Systems; Psychology; Science - Natural
Dist - USNAC **Prod** - USN 1962

A Vision in the Desert 28 MIN
VHS / 16mm
Color (G)
Portrays ballet master and teacher Vassili Sulich. Recounts Sulich's struggles to obtain support and respect for his classical dance troupe, which is composed of professional Las Vegas show dancers.
Fine Arts
Dist - PBS **Prod** - KLVXTV
KLVXTV

The Vision is Electric 13 MIN
16mm
Color
LC 79-700338
Looks at the employees and activities of Mc Graw - Edison Company, a manufacturer of electrical products.
Business and Economics
Dist - MCEDCO **Prod** - MCEDCO 1978

Vision loss - focus on feelings 20 MIN
U-matic / VHS / BETA
Color; NTSC; PAL; SECAM (G)
PdS95
Reveals that on the average, humans who have reached 65 years of age have also lost a third of their usable vision. Discloses that vision loss is perhaps second only to cancer as a source of fear and apprehension. Features seven people with different eye problems who discuss their common fears and concerns and reveal how they have faced their vision loss and maintained their quality of life.
Health and Safety
Dist - VIEWTH
ORACLE

Vision of Chaim Weizmann 21 MIN
16mm
B&W
Presents a biography of Israel's first president, incorporating the story of Zionism and the re - establishment of the Jewish people in their land.
Biography; History - World; Religion and Philosophy
Dist - ALDEN **Prod** - ALDEN

The Vision of Dr Koch 22 MIN
16mm / U-matic / VHS
You are There Series
Color (I J H)
LC 72-700115
Presents Dr Robert Koch, a German bacteriologist, who was the first man to prove that a single germ can cause a specific disease. Re - enacts a dramatic incident which was at first interpreted as proof that his theories were invalid, but which later led to development of vaccines and other life - saving discoveries.
Biography; Health and Safety; Science; Science - Natural
Dist - PHENIX **Prod** - CBSTV 1972

The Vision of Galileo 28 MIN
U-matic / VHS
Color (I J H)
Examines the findings of Galileo, the father of modern astronomy and physics.
Biography; Science
Dist - JOU **Prod** - CANBC

A Vision of independence 25 MIN
VHS
Color (G)
Describes for family members of persons with low vision the major types of functional vision loss - blurred vision, central field loss, peripheral field loss. Explains to family members what they can do to assist the person with low vision in experimenting with lighting, color and contrast. Explores other modifications in the home that will increase independence. Produced by Ann Hubbard and Gale Watson.
Health and Safety
Dist - ATREF

Vision of Juazeiro 19 MIN
U-matic / VHS / 16mm
Color (A) (PORTUGUESE (ENGLISH SUBTITLES))
Documents the transformation of a small town in northeastern Brazil into a religious shrine under the guidance of Father Cicero, a religious and political leader in the region. Analyzes the perpetuation of his teachings through the religious festivities of pilgrims, and examines commercial and political aspects of the event. Portuguese dialog with English subtitles.
Fine Arts; History - World
Dist - CNEMAG **Prod** - CNEMAG

The Vision of Stephan Crane 28 MIN
VHS
Color (J H)
$99.00 purchase _ #06221 - 026
Relates Crane's life to his works, applying his experiences as a journalist and correspondent, his romantic involvement with Cora Taylor, friendships with other literary figures and preoccupation with fatalism. Includes an extended photo - illustrated reading from The Red Badge of Courage, along with a teacher's guide and library kit.
Education; Literature and Drama
Dist - GA

The Vision of the blind 46 MIN
VHS
Color (H C G)
$395.00 purchase, $65.00 rental
Reveals that new psychological insights are giving researchers a clearer understanding of how the brain of a blind person adapts to provide a unique vision of the unseen environment. Theorizes that when a person cannot see, the visual cortex actively processes input from the four remaining senses. This new understanding of how the blind 'see,' advanced teaching techniques and electronic aids are helping the blind become more active in the world. Introduces several blind artists who have found ways to express their image of the unseen world.
Fine Arts; Guidance and Counseling
Dist - FLMLIB **Prod** - CANBC 1990

Vision of the fire tree
16mm
Color (G)
$155.00 purchase, $15.00 rental
Seeks, like a fire in the mind, the tree metaphorically referred to by D H Lawrence in reference to the human race.
Fine Arts
Dist - CANCIN **Prod** - BRAKS 1991

Vision screening in preschool and school age children 35 MIN
VHS
Color (PRO)
$275.00 purchase _ #6849
Describes the principles and strategies of vision screening of preschool and school age children. Reviews history - taking, critical points in screening procedures and the choice of appropriate tests. Includes three vignettes of health nurses working with children of various ages and their parents. Demonstrates effective communication with a child from another culture.
Health and Safety
Dist - UCALG **Prod** - UCALG 1986

The Vision - Strip Audio - Visual Classroom 14 MIN
U-matic / VHS / 16mm
B&W (C A)
Examines desirable modern classroom construction in terms of economy of construction, pupil health and teaching efficiency.
Education
Dist - IFB **Prod** - WITICH 1959

Vision - Structure of the Eye 8 MIN
16mm
B&W (J H C G)
Shows the structure of the eye. Explains how the eye works using the familiar analogy of the camera. Discusses near and far sightedness and the corrective glasses required for each problem.
Science - Natural
Dist - VIEWTH **Prod** - GBI

Vision video series
World of C++ 120 MIN
Dist - BORLND

Vision videos series
World of ObjectWindows for Turbo Pascal 120 MIN
Dist - BORLND

Vision with Spatial Inversion 18 MIN
16mm
B&W (C T)
Follows a complete repetition of the classical experiment in which the subject wears inverting spectacles continuously for several weeks. Shows that initial difficulties in orientation, walking, eating, writing and card sorting gradually dissipate as the subject becomes accustomed to the 'UPSIDE DOWN WORLD.'.
Psychology
Dist - PSUPCR **Prod** - PSUPCR 1951

Vision workout 180 MIN
VHS
Color (G)
$99.00 purchase _ #P16
Consists of an easy to follow six - week program of eye exercises that teaches how to improve vision. Contains two videos, booklets and special training equipment to enhance fifty years of study in vision therapy.

Health and Safety
Dist - HP

Vision workout - strengthen your eyesight naturally 180 MIN
VHS
Color (G)
$89.00 purchase _ #V - VWO
Presents a home training program for enhancing vision naturally, holistically and effectively. Claims to work for common vision ailments such as near sightedness, far sightedness, astigmatism, lazy eye, double vision and more. Includes two videocassettes, an eye examination chart to measure progress and special training charts and equipment.
Psychology
Dist - WHOLEL

The Visionaries 30 MIN
U-matic / VHS
Art America series
Color (H C A)
$43.00 purchase
Deals with American painting in the Romantic style. Part of a 20-part series on art in America.
Fine Arts
Dist - CTI **Prod** - CTI
GPN

Visionaries series
Presents a four - part series about innovative ideas on intelligence, genetics, evolution, agriculture and economics. Profiles Jeremy Rifkin - Foundation on Economic Trends, Chilean economist Manfred Max - Neef, Professor James Lovelock - Gaia hypothesis, and Bill Mollison - permaculture.
Barefoot economist 52 MIN
Declaration of a heretic 52 MIN
In Grave danger of falling food 52 MIN
The Man who named the world 52 MIN
Dist - LANDMK **Prod** - LANDMK

Visionary experience or psychosis 30 MIN
VHS / BETA
Spiritual psychology quartet series
Color (G)
$29.95 purchase _ #S060
Features Jungian psychotherapist Dr John Weir Perry, author of 'The Heart of History' and 'The Far Side of Madness,' who suggests that psychiatric labeling and the use of anti - psychotic drugs serve to stifle the valuable integration of life's mythic dimensions. Part of a series on spiritual psychology.
Psychology; Religion and Philosophy
Dist - THINKA **Prod** - THINKA

Visionary voices - Women on power 22 MIN
VHS
Color (G)
$50.00 rental, $195.00 purchase
Features a multi - racial group of women activists, artists and healers reading excerpts from their interviews in a book of the same name. Deals with healthy uses of power. A Penny Rosenwasser and Lisa Rudman production.
Sociology
Dist - WMEN

Visions and Revisions 15 MIN
U-matic
Process of Reading Series
Color
Examines ways in which a single text can yield a variety of readings. How a text is read depends on what the reader wants to get out of it.
English Language; Literature and Drama
Dist - TVOTAR **Prod** - TVOTAR 1976

Visions - Artists and the Creative Process Series
Challenging Directions 30 MIN
Definitions of space 30 MIN
The Endless Vista 30 MIN
A Form of magic 30 MIN
The Human Link 30 MIN
An Introduction 60 MIN
Magnetism of Place 30 MIN
The Need to Explore 30 MIN
A Passionate Harmony 30 MIN
The Riddle of Reality 30 MIN
Simple Treasures 30 MIN
The Spirit Visible 30 MIN
Two Worlds 30 MIN
Dist - TVOTAR

Visions in meditation No 1 20 MIN
16mm
Color (G)
$656.00 purchase, $45.00 rental
Uses Gertrude Stein's 'Stanzas in Meditation' as a guide in editing a meditative series of images of landscapes and human symbolism 'indicative of that field - of - consciousness within which humanity survives thoughtfully.'
Fine Arts
Dist - CANCIN **Prod** - BRAKS 1989

Visions of a city 8 MIN
16mm
Sepia (G)
$20.00 rental
Stars poet Michael McClure who emerges from the reflecting imagery of glass shops, car windows, bottles, mirrors, etc. Portrays McClure and the city of San Francisco in 1957. Edited in 1978. Music by William Moraldo.
Fine Arts
Dist - CANCIN **Prod** - JORDAL 1978

Visions of adventure series
Australia and New Zealand - Volume 3 35 MIN
Canada 35 MIN
The North central US - Volume 2c 35 MIN
The Northeastern US - Volume 2a 35 MIN
The Seven seas 35 MIN
The Southern US - Volume 2b 35 MIN
Understanding geography using globes and maps - Volume 1 35 MIN
The Western US - Volume 2d 35 MIN
Dist - SVIP

Visions of Cinema 24 MIN
U-matic / VHS
Documentaries on Art Series
Color (G)
$160.00, $110.00 purchase, $60.00, $40.00 rental
Portrays Joseph Mankewicz, Jonathan Demme and Jean - Luc Godard, each stylistically different, each seeing the movies as an arena for critical discourse and discussion. Features Deanna Kamiel who interviews and produces the documentary.
Fine Arts; Industrial and Technical Education
Dist - IAFC

Visions of Eight 105 MIN
16mm / VHS
Color (J)
LC 78-701091
Presents eight aspects of the 1972 Olympic games in Munich, Germany. Looks at the pole - vault, decathlon, 100 - meter dash, losing athletes, marathon runners, women contestants, weight - lifters and the tension of the moments before the starting gun.
Fine Arts; Physical Education and Recreation
Dist - CINEMV **Prod** - WOLPER 1973
UILL

Visions of Greece 30 MIN
VHS
Color (G)
$14.95 purchase
Presents a guide to what to see and do when visiting Greece. Focuses on the city of Athens, but also gives tour and cruise options for the various classical and archaeological sites, as well as the most popular islands. Includes a tour directory and discount coupon.
Geography - World
Dist - PBS **Prod** - WNETTV

Visions of Home 30 MIN
VHS / U-matic
Documentaries on Art Series
Color (G)
$160.00, $110.00 purchase, $60.00, $40.00 rental
Considers the importance of place in determining cultural, individual and artistic identity. Captures the spirit of the Midwest in three short segments. Includes a portrait of Mickey's restaurant, one of the country's last Dining Cars, as well as interviews of poet Patricia Hampl and writer Paul Gruchow. Produced by Deanna Kamiel.
Fine Arts; Psychology; Sociology
Dist - IAFC

Visions of hope - the near death experience 40 MIN
VHS / BETA
Color; PAL (G)
PdS25, $50.00 purchase
Explores the individual experiences of six people who had been clinically certified as dead. Contains professional comments from doctors and theologians along with the visionary experiences of the six, which transformed their lives and removed all fear of death. Produced by The Michaelmas Trust.
Fine Arts; Health and Safety; Sociology
Dist - MERIDT

Visions of Light - Gothic Stained Glass (1200 - 1300 a D) 15 MIN
16mm
Color
Presents Gothic stained glass from the Middle Ages dating from 1200 to 1300 A D.
Fine Arts; History - World
Dist - ROLAND **Prod** - ROLAND

Visions of light - the art of cinematography 90 MIN
35mm / 16mm
Color; B&W (G)
Interviews 26 leading directors of photography who discuss their influences and relate anecodotes about their work. Contains 125 clips chronicling the changing role of the cinematographer. Traces cinematography from its beginnings from before Griffith, through the influences of sound technology, color, Citizen Kane, film noir, CinemaScope into contemporary film making.
Fine Arts
Dist - KINOIC **Prod** - AMERFI 1992

Visions of paradise series
The Angel that stands by me - Minnie Evan's painting 29 MIN
Grandma's bottle village - the art of Tressa Prisbrey 28 MIN
Hundred and Two Mature, the Art of Harry Lieberman 29 MIN
The Monument of Chief Rolling Mountain Thunder 29 MIN
Dist - SARLGT

Visions of Russia - a granddaughter returns 29 MIN
VHS
Jewish life around the world series
Color (G)
$34.95 purchase _ #118
Follows young American college studnet Sharon Cohen to the Soviet Union. Takes a look at life in the Soviet and Soviet Jewry under 'glasnost.'
Geography - World; History - World; Sociology
Dist - ERGOM **Prod** - ERGOM

Visions of the deep 60 MIN
VHS
Nova video library
Color (G)
$29.95 purchase
Takes a tour of the underwater sea world. Photography by underwater photographer Al Giddings. From the PBS series 'NOVA.'
Geography - World
Dist - PBS **Prod** - WNETTV

Visions of the deep 60 MIN
VHS
Color; Captioned (G)
$29.95 purchase _ #S01845
Features the underwater filmwork of Al Giddings, whose previous work has included the underwater scenes from the movies 'For Your Eyes Only' and 'The Deep.' Part of the PBS series 'NOVA.'
Fine Arts; Industrial and Technical Education
Dist - UILL **Prod** - PBS

Visions of the reef
VHS
Color (G)
$29.90 purchase _ #0739
Joins underwater photographer Al Giddings in an underwater exploration of the oceans.
Industrial and Technical Education; Science - Natural; Science - Physical
Dist - SEVVID

Visions of the Spirit 58 MIN
16mm / VHS
Color (G)
$295.00 purchase, $125.00, $75.00 rental
Portrays Pulitzer Prize winner Alice Walker. Films Walker's California home, her Georgia hometown and the film set of 'The Color Purple.' Shows Walker as a mother, daughter, philospher, activist, as well as a writer. Interviews the writer, her family and Black feminist literary scholar Barbara Christian. Produced by Elena Featherston.
History - United States; Literature and Drama; Sociology
Dist - WMEN **Prod** - ELF 1989

Visions of war and peace - Part 13 60 MIN
VHS / U-matic
War and peace in the nuclear age series
Color (G)
$45.00, $29.95 purchase
Explores the magnitude and power of current nuclear arsenals. Addresses five critical issues of the nuclear age - the superpower relationship, nuclear deterrence in Europe, defenses against nuclear weapons, arms control and proliferation. Part thirteen of a thirteen - part series on war and peace in the nuclear age.
Civics and Political Systems; History - World
Dist - ANNCPB **Prod** - WGBHTV 1989

Visions - the Critical Eye Series

The Divine state	29 MIN
Eye openers	29 MIN
Gateway to Reality	29 MIN
Great expectations	29 MIN
Is it in to be Out	29 MIN
Mainstreams and Cross Currents	29 MIN
The Massive Mirror	29 MIN
The Minefield	29 MIN
The New and the Old	29 MIN
Who Says It's Great	29 MIN

Dist - TVOTAR

Visions unlimited 60 MIN
BETA / U-matic / VHS
Color (G)
$59.95, $39.95 purchase
Contains three exhibitions of Visionary, Social and Classical Surrealism featuring over 140 San Francisco Bay Area painters and sculptors. Represents 20 contemporary women visionaries in the Emergence exhibition, Collins Gallery, 1984. 100 Vows of the Sun includes over 100 artists shown at the Southern Exposure Gallery, 1985, and is introduced by art historian Michael S Bell. The Dream Show, Collins Gallery, 1985, exhibits visionary surrealism inspired by actual dreams. Produced by Seers Institute.
Fine Arts
Dist - ARTSAM

Visions video series

Learn programming today with Turbo Pascal	90 MIN
World of database management	29 MIN
World of objects	20 MIN
World of ObjectVision	85 MIN
World of ObjectWindows for C++	120 MIN

Dist - BORLND

The Visit 30 MIN
U-matic
Color (I J)
Reveals the conflicting emotions children have when they find out their father is planning to remarry a woman with two children.
Psychology; Sociology
Dist - TVOTAR **Prod** - TVOTAR 1986

A Visit from Captain Cook 16 MIN
U-matic / VHS / 16mm
Color (I)
LC 82-700430
Presents a re - enactment of Captain James Cook's stopovers on Vancouver Island's west coast during his search for the elusive 'Northwest Passage' to the Orient. Shows the importance of Captain Cook's voyages in opening up the seas to commerce and world trade. Describes the Nootke Indians and their habitats at the time of Captain Cook's visit.
Geography - World; Social Science
Dist - CRMP **Prod** - NFBC 1982

A Visit from Saint Nicholas 4 MIN
U-matic / VHS / 16mm
Color (P I J H C A)
$145, $100 purchase _ #490
Tells the story of the midnight visit of Saint Nicholas. Animated.
Literature and Drama; Social Science
Dist - CORF

A Visit from St Nicholas 4 MIN
16mm / U-matic / VHS
Color (P I J H)
An animated story about the midnight visit of St Nicholas and his reindeer.
Literature and Drama; Religion and Philosophy
Dist - CORF **Prod** - CORF 1949

Visit through Saturday 14 MIN
16mm
B&W
Features a narrative dealing with the father - son relationship. Reveals a young boy's eagerness to discover the world.
Sociology
Dist - NYU **Prod** - NYU

A Visit to a Container Port 12 MIN
U-matic / VHS / 16mm
Visit to Series
Color (P I)
Presents a visit to a container port, showing the special machines that move containers around the terminal and onto the ship.
Social Science
Dist - JOU **Prod** - JOU 1983

A Visit to a County Fair 11 MIN
16mm / U-matic / VHS
Visit to Series
Color (P I)
LC 80-700255
Shows the sights, sounds and excitement of a country fair.
Social Science
Dist - JOU **Prod** - ALTSUL 1979

A Visit to a Dairy Farm 12 MIN
16mm / U-matic / VHS
Visit to Series
Color (P I)
Introduces a dairy farm, showing a district agricultural show and a milk factory where milk is churned into butter, made into cheese and powdered.
Agriculture
Dist - JOU **Prod** - JOU 1983

A Visit to a Honey Bee Farm 10 MIN
U-matic / VHS / 16mm
Visit to Series
Color (P I)
LC 77-703374
Presents Gary, the beekeeper, who takes two young children on a tour of the honey bee farm. Shows the bees gathering the nectar from the blossoms and returning with it to the hive. Describes the process of collecting the honey.
Agriculture; Social Science
Dist - JOU **Prod** - JOU 1977

A Visit to a limestone quarry 19 MIN
VHS / 35mm strip
Field trips series
Color (I J H)
$39.95, $39.05 purchase _ #551VB03, #551FSTB03
Presents a multimedia kit that visits a limestone quarry in northwest Ohio. Investigates the workings in an active quarry. Explores crystal formations, sedimentation of limestone and dolomite, calcite, marcasete, fluorite and dolomite. Investigates the formation of pyrite and solution cavities and small caves. Includes a videotape or filmstrip, samples kit and topographic map exercises. Part of a series.
Geography - United States; Science - Physical
Dist - INSTRU

A Visit to a Maple Sugar Farm - Sugarbush 11 MIN
16mm / U-matic / VHS
Visit to Series
Color (P)
LC 75-704276
Shows how maple syrup is made.
Agriculture
Dist - JOU **Prod** - JOU 1975

A Visit to a Movie Studio 14 MIN
U-matic / VHS / 16mm
Visit to Series
Color (P I)
LC 80-700256
Explores the world of motion pictures by focusing on the roles of actors, directors, producers, cameramen, editors and others involved in moviemaking.
Fine Arts
Dist - JOU **Prod** - ALTSUL 1979

A Visit to a Nature Center 12 MIN
U-matic / VHS / 16mm
Visit to Series
Color (P I)
LC 79-700316
Focuses on a group of children as they visit a nature center and learn about the plant and animal life of the region.
Science - Natural
Dist - JOU **Prod** - ALTSUL 1978

A Visit to a Pond 9 MIN
U-matic / VHS / 16mm
Visit to Series
Color (K P I)
LC 75-704277
Shows various kinds of plants and animals found in and around a pond.
Science - Natural
Dist - JOU **Prod** - JOU 1975

Visit to a Pond 9 MIN
16mm / U-matic / VHS
Captioned; Color (K P I)
Shows various kinds of plants and animals found in and around a pond.
Science - Natural
Dist - JOU **Prod** - JOU 1975

Visit to a Russian School 5 MIN
16mm
Screen news digest series; Vol 3; Issue 4
B&W
Takes viewers into a Russian school to see and hear how third grade pupils learn English.
Education; English Language; Geography - World
Dist - HEARST **Prod** - HEARST 1960

A Visit to a Sheep Farm 12 MIN
U-matic / VHS / 16mm
Visit to Series
Color (P I)
Shows two children visiting their uncle's sheep farm and learning about the shearing of sheep and how the wool is sold.
Agriculture; Social Science
Dist - JOU **Prod** - JOU 1982

A Visit to a Theatre 14 MIN
U-matic / VHS / 16mm
Visit to Series
Color (P I)
LC 79-700317
Takes a look at the work involved in staging a play by visiting a theater and following a production from the weeks of preparation through the opening night.
Fine Arts
Dist - JOU **Prod** - ALTSUL 1978

A Visit to a Wild Bird Island 9 MIN
16mm / U-matic / VHS
Visit to Series
Color (P I)
LC 78-700842
Follows a naturalist and his brothers on a visit to an island to study aquatic birds. Observes tiny chicks cut their way out of the confinement of eggs and adult birds build their nests, catch fish and return to their nests to feed the young.
Science - Natural
Dist - JOU **Prod** - JOU 1978

A Visit to an Airport 12 MIN
U-matic / VHS / 16mm
Visit to Series
Color (P I)
Presents two children as they take a tour of an airport. Shows the kitchens, the maintenance hanger and the control tower. Describes a flight simulator where pilots are trained and discusses the care and coordination which combine to keep planes flying safely.
Social Science
Dist - JOU **Prod** - JOU 1983

A Visit to Apple Cider Country 16 MIN
U-matic / VHS / 16mm
Visit to Series
Color (P I)
LC 77-703188
Shows how apple cider is made as a young city boy visits a unique, self - sustaining farm and examines the process of picking, cleaning, crushing and pressing the apples and pasteurizing and bottling the cider.
Agriculture; Home Economics; Social Science
Dist - JOU **Prod** - NELVNA 1977

Visit to Aruba 15 MIN
U-matic / VHS
Other families, other friends series; Blue module; Aruba
Color (P)
Pictures white sand beaches and a sunken ship viewed through a glass - bottomed boat in Aruba.
Geography - World; Social Science
Dist - AITECH **Prod** - WVIZTV 1971

A Visit to Bryce Canyon, Utah 18 MIN
VHS / 35mm strip
Field trips series
Color (I J H)
$39.95, $39.05 purchase _ #551VB04, #551FSTB04
Presents a multimedia kit that visits Bryce Canyon, Utah, noted for its spectacular weathering and erosion. Investigates chemical and mechanical weathering transportation of sediments and the deposition of rock materials. Includes a videocassette or filmstrip, samples kit and topographic map. Part of a series.
Geography - United States; Science - Physical
Dist - INSTRU

A Visit to Craters of the Moon National Monument 20 MIN
VHS / 35mm strip
Field trips series
Color (I J H)
$39.95, $38.50 purchase _ #551VB06, #551FSTB06
Presents a multimedia kit that visits Craters of the Moon National Monument in Idaho. Explores the unusual landscape of lava flows and cinder cones. Includes a videocassette or filmstrip, samples kit and topographic map. Part of a series.
Geography - United States; Science - Physical
Dist - INSTRU

Visit to Cuba 12 MIN
16mm / U-matic / VHS
Color (I J H)
Studies aspects of Cuban life - - the nation's agriculture, physical appearance and climate, schools and public buildings, major cities and historic points of interest about the country.

Geography - World
Dist - IFB **Prod** - IFB 1960

A Visit to Dinosaur National Monument 22 MIN
VHS / 35mm strip
Field trips series
Color (I J H)
$39.95, $28.80 purchase _ #551VB08, #551FSTB08
Presents a multimedia kit that visits Dinosaur National Monument. Explores 'diggings' with fossil specialists. Discusses dionosaurs and theories about why they became extinct. Include a videocassette or filmstrip, samples kit and topographic map. Part of a series.
Geography - United States; Science - Natural; Science - Physical
Dist - INSTRU

A Visit to EPCOT Center 20 MIN
U-matic / VHS / 16mm
Color
Tours EPCOT center in Florida, which has exhibits of various world cultures and the world of the future.
Geography - United States; Physical Education and Recreation
Dist - CORF **Prod** - DISNEY 1982

A Visit to Fra Mauro 14 MIN
16mm
Screen news digest series; Vol 13; Issue 7
B&W (I)
LC 72-700571
Documents, from blast - off to splashdown, the flight of Apollo 14.
History - World; Science - Physical
Dist - HEARST **Prod** - HEARST 1971

A Visit to Grand Teton National Park 27 MIN
VHS / 35mm strip
Field trips series
Color (I J H)
$39.95, $38.30 purchase _ #551VB01, #551FSTB01
Presents a multimedia kit that studies fault - block mountains, the effects of glaciers on mountains, moraines and glacial features and teaches topographic map skills. Includes a videotape or filmstrip, samples kit and topographic maps. Part of a series.
Geography - United States; Science - Physical
Dist - INSTRU

The Visit to Indiana 10 MIN
16mm
Color (J H C A)
LC 72-702288
Intercuts a conversation between an Indiana boy and his uncle with flashes of the boy's homelife and his family.
Geography - United States; Guidance and Counseling; Sociology
Dist - CANCIN **Prod** - CANCIN 1970

A Visit to Lassen Volcanic National Park 22 MIN
VHS / 35mm strip
Field trips series
Color (I J H)
$39.95, $38.70 purchase _ #551VB05, #551FSTB05
Presents a multimedia kit that visits Lassen Volcanic National Park in northern California, site of a fairly recent volcanic eruption. Reveals that the area is still active. Explores the work of magma chambers and geysers. Looks at some of the rapid changes resulting from volcanism. Includes a videocassette or filmstrip, samples kit and topographic map. Part of a series.
Geography - United States; Science - Physical
Dist - INSTRU

Visit to Puerto Rico 17 MIN
U-matic / VHS / 16mm
Color (I J H)
Surveys Puerto Rico's location, population, racial heritage, geography, topography, major cities, chief crops and farming methods.
Geography - World
Dist - IFB **Prod** - IFB 1962

A Visit to Rocky Mountain National Park 32 MIN
VHS / 35mm strip
Field trips series
Color (I J H)
$39.95, $38.85 purchase _ #551VB02, #551FSTB02
Presents a multimedia kit that visits Rocky Mountain National Park, just 50 miles from Denver, Colorado. Studies mountain building, the effect of glaciers on mountains, the work of running water, mass wasting and volcanic activity in the park. Includes a videotape or filmstrip, samples kit with rocks and topographic maps. Part of a series.
Geography - United States; Science - Physical
Dist - INSTRU

Visit to Series
Let's Go Out Together 13 MIN
A Visit to a Container Port 12 MIN
A Visit to a County Fair 11 MIN
A Visit to a Dairy Farm 12 MIN
A Visit to a Honey Bee Farm 10 MIN
A Visit to a Maple Sugar Farm - Sugarbush 11 MIN
A Visit to a Movie Studio 14 MIN
A Visit to a Nature Center 12 MIN
A Visit to a Pond 9 MIN
A Visit to a Sheep Farm 12 MIN
A Visit to a Theatre 14 MIN
A Visit to a Wild Bird Island 9 MIN
A Visit to an Airport 12 MIN
A Visit to Apple Cider Country 16 MIN
A Visit to Snow Country 9 MIN
A Visit to Wild Rice Country 10 MIN
A Visit with Farmer Joe 13 MIN
A Visit with the Animal Doctors 11 MIN
A Visit with the Goldminers 14 MIN
A Visit with the Ranchers 16 MIN
Dist - JOU

A Visit to Snow Country 9 MIN
U-matic / VHS / 16mm
Visit to Series
Color (P I)
LC 78-700841
Follows a young boy and his parents on a cross - country ski tour through snow - covered forests. Points out a wide variety of forest animals and shows how they survive during the winter.
Science - Natural
Dist - JOU **Prod** - JOU 1978

A Visit to St Helens 20 MIN
U-matic / VHS
Nature Episodes Series
Color
Tells the story of the eruption of Mount St Helens.
Geography - United States; Geography - World; Science - Physical
Dist - EDIMGE **Prod** - EDIMGE

A visit to St. Helens - volcano in Washington state 21 MIN
BETA / U-matic / VHS
Color (I J H)
$29.95, $130.00 purchase _ #LSTF87
Looks at the recovery of the area around the volcanic eruption of Mt St Helens. Shows mud slides, sink holes, the effect of minerals on water and the recovery of thousands of damaged trees. Includes teachers' guide. Produced by Nature Episodes, US Forest Service at Vancouver, Oregon State University, Portland State University.
Geography - United States; Geography - World
Dist - FEDU

A Visit to Sunset Crater National Monument 22 MIN
VHS
Color (J H)
$29.95 purchase _ #IV - 128
Travels to Sunset Crater National Monument located near Flagstaff, Arizona. Reveals that the cinder cone volcano erupted almost 900 years ago but lava flows and ash make the onlooker think that the eruption took place recently. Examines the cinder core volcano which is very different from Hawaiian types - Kilauea and Mauna Loa - or the composite types - Mt St Helens.
Geography - United States; Geography - World; Science - Physical
Dist - INSTRU

Visit to the Bank - Paddington's Patch - in and Out of Trouble - Paddington at the Tower 22 MIN
16mm / U-matic / VHS
Paddington Bear, Series; 2
Color (K P I)
LC 80-700957
Describes Paddington's adventures at a bank. Tells how he cultivates a garden patch and tests a hammock, with alarming results. Discusses his outing to the Tower Of London. Based on the books Paddington Abroad, Paddington's Garden, Paddington At The Tower and Paddington Takes The Test by Michael Bond.
Literature and Drama
Dist - ALTSUL **Prod** - BONDM 1980

Visit to the Dentist - Paddington Recommended 11 MIN
U-matic / VHS / 16mm
Paddington Bear, Series; 1
Color (K P I)
LC 77-700669
Presents an animated adaptation of chapters 1 and 6 from the children's book Paddington Takes The Air by Michael Bond. Tells about a small, dark bear whose visits to the dentist and a fashionable restaurant result in surprises and unexpected rewards.
Fine Arts; Literature and Drama
Dist - ALTSUL **Prod** - BONDM 1977

A Visit to the Doctor 30 MIN
BETA / VHS
Mister Rogers - Conceptual Behavior Series
Color (P I J)
Introduces viewers to a routine pediatric examination through visits with a young sister and brother during a regular check - up. Features Mister Rogers.
Guidance and Counseling; Health and Safety; Psychology
Dist - BRENTM **Prod** - BRENTM

A Visit to the Emergency Department 30 MIN
BETA / VHS
Mister Rogers - Health and Safety Series
Color (P I J) (SPANISH)
Visits the main areas of a hospital emergency room, such as x - ray, suture and waiting room. Shows and explains common procedures and equipment. Features Mister Rogers.
Health and Safety
Dist - BRENTM **Prod** - BRENTM

A Visit to the Emergency Department 15 MIN
U-matic / VHS
Let's Talk about the Hospital Series
Color (P) (SPANISH)
Visits a hospital emergency department, Triage, X ray, Suture and the Waiting Room, while showing and explaining some of the common procedures and equipment. Features television's Mister Rogers.
Health and Safety; Psychology
Dist - FAMCOM **Prod** - FAMCOM

A Visit to the John Birch Society 27 MIN
16mm
Color (A)
LC 73-700816
Presents G Edward Griffin who guides a tour of the facilities of the John Birch Society, showing the headquarters in Belmont, Massachusetts and regional offices in San Marino, California. Tells about its publishing house, two magazines, four hundred book stores and reading rooms, its nationwide speakers bureau and youth program. Focuses on membership activities across the country and provides a brief bio graphical information about the founder of the organization, Robert Welch.
Civics and Political Systems
Dist - AMMED **Prod** - AMMED 1972

The Visit to the Sepulcher 30 MIN
16mm
Color
Relates the Gospel story of the first Easter, including the appearance of the Archangel to the Maries at Christ's sepulcher, their discovery that the tomb is empty, the race of Peter and John to join the Maries.
Religion and Philosophy
Dist - TW **Prod** - TW

Visit to the World of Sholom Aleichem, a Pt 1 30 MIN
16mm
B&W
LC FIA64-1182
Features Maurice Samuel and Mark Van Doren who discuss shtetl life as reflected in the works of Sholom Aleichem, his role as the representative of that world and one of the characters which he created - - Tevya, the dairyman. Includes the reading of illustrative selections from Maurice Samuel's 'THE WORLD OF SHOLOM ALEICHEM.'.
Literature and Drama
Dist - NAAJS **Prod** - JTS 1960

Visit to the World of Sholom Aleichem, a Pt 2 30 MIN
16mm
B&W
LC FIA64-1183
Features Maurice Samuel and Mark Van Doren who discusses Manachem Mendel, a character created by Sholom Aleichem, and the significance of the sabbath in the world of Sholom Aleichem, as well as the stories, 'THE SEAT OF THE EASTERN WALL' and 'THE JUDGEMENT OF REB YOZIFEL.' Includes selected readings from the two stories.
Literature and Drama
Dist - NAAJS **Prod** - JTS 1960

Visit to the World of the Muffins, Pt 1 14 MIN
Videoreel / VT2
Muffinland Series
Color
English Language; Literature and Drama
Dist - PBS **Prod** - WGTV

Visit to the World of the Muffins, Pt 2 14 MIN
Videoreel / VT2
Muffinland Series
Color

English Language; Literature and Drama
Dist - PBS **Prod** - WGTV

A Visit to the zoo 15 MIN
U-matic / VHS
Animals and such series; Module green - animals and plants
Color (I J)
Gives detailed information about zoo dwellers and endangered species.
Science - Natural
Dist - AITECH **Prod** - WHROTV 1972

A Visit to Tuskegee 10 MIN
16mm
Color
Highlights the various activities and work of the VA Negro Hospital at Tuskegee. Points out that the institution has done particularly noteworthy work in malaria therapy and group therapy programs.
Social Science; Sociology
Dist - USVA **Prod** - USVA

A Visit to Wild Rice Country 10 MIN
16mm / U-matic / VHS
Visit to Series
Color (P I)
LC 76-700107
Shows the harvesting and preparation techniques of wild rice and provides insight into the Great Lakes region. Includes a visit with the Chippewa Indians which shows that harvesting techniques have changed very little in a thousand years.
Geography - United States; Social Science
Dist - JOU **Prod** - JOU 1975

A Visit to William Blake's Inn
VHS / 35mm strip
ALA Notable Children's Filmstrips Series
Color (K)
$35.00 purchase
Presents a children's story. Part of the American Library Association series.
English Language; Literature and Drama
Dist - PELLER

A Visit to Yosemite National Park 17 MIN
VHS / 35mm strip
Field trips series
Color (I J H)
$39.95, $38.30 purchase _ #551VB07, #551FSTB07
Presents a multimedia kit that visits Yosemite National Park in California. Explores the workings of glaciers in the making of U - shaped valleys, hanging valleys and moraines. Include a videocassette or filmstrip, samples kit and topographic map. Part of a series.
Geography - United States; Science - Physical
Dist - INSTRU

A Visit with a Jean Ayres 30 MIN
U-matic
Color (PRO)
Presents an interview with Dr A Jean Ayres about her background in occupational therapy and research. Includes a tour of her clinic and a discussion of the therapeutic equipment used there.
Health and Safety
Dist - AOTA **Prod** - AOTA 1978

A Visit with Amory and Hunter Lovins 14 MIN
VHS / U-matic
Color (J H A)
Features energy experts Amory and Hunter Lovins showing that nobody has to reduce their standard of living in order to be environmentally responsible. Views their lavishly handsome, environmentally responsible new home that demonstrates their continued support for the sane use of renewable energy.
Business and Economics; History - World; Home Economics; Science - Physical; Social Science
Dist - BULFRG **Prod** - CBSTV 1985

Visit with Beatrice Wade, a, Pt 1 30 MIN
U-matic
Visual History Series
Color (PRO)
Begins an interview with Beatrice Wade, occupational therapist.
Health and Safety
Dist - AOTA **Prod** - AOTA 1979

Visit with Beatrice Wade, a, Pt 2 30 MIN
U-matic
Visual History Series
Color (PRO)
Concludes an interview with Beatrice Wade, occupational therapist.
Health and Safety
Dist - AOTA **Prod** - AOTA 1979

A Visit with Bill Peet 14 MIN
VHS / U-matic
Color (P)
LC 83-706382
Capsulizes selected stories written by children's book author and illustrator Bill Peet and recollects their inspirations. Looks at examples of his ink - and - colored pencil drawings.
Biography; Fine Arts; Literature and Drama
Dist - HMC **Prod** - HMC 1983

A Visit with Clare Spackman 30 MIN
U-matic
Visual History Series
Color (PRO)
Presents an interview with Clare Spackman, occupational therapist.
Health and Safety
Dist - AOTA **Prod** - AOTA 1979

A Visit with David Macaulay 25 MIN
VHS / U-matic
Color
LC 83-706383
Visits the studio of book illustrator and architect David Macaulay to learn how he constructs his pen - and - ink drawings. Talks about his educational and professional background.
Biography; Fine Arts; Industrial and Technical Education; Literature and Drama
Dist - HMC **Prod** - HMC 1983

A Visit with Don Juan in Hell 22 MIN
U-matic / VHS / 16mm
Color (H C A)
LC 75-704158
Explores the success of George Bernard Shaw's play, Don Juan in Hell. Traces the author's life with photographs and live footage and presents comments by actors and actresses concerning the play.
Biography; Literature and Drama
Dist - MCFI **Prod** - KROWN 1975

Visit with Dr Sidney Licht - Pt 1 30 MIN
U-matic
Visual History Series
Color (PRO)
Begins an interview with Dr Sidney Licht, occupational therapist.
Health and Safety
Dist - AOTA **Prod** - AOTA 1979

Visit with Dr Sidney Licht - Pt 2 30 MIN
U-matic
Visual History Series
Color (PRO)
Concludes an interview with Dr Sidney Licht, occupational therapist.
Health and Safety
Dist - AOTA **Prod** - AOTA 1979

A Visit with Farmer Joe 13 MIN
U-matic / VHS / 16mm
Visit to Series
Color (P I)
LC 75-702175
Introduces children to the world of farm animals and their products.
Science - Natural; Social Science
Dist - JOU **Prod** - BERLET 1975

A Visit with Helen Willard 30 MIN
U-matic
Visual History Series
Color (PRO)
Presents an interview with Helen Willard, occupational therapist.
Health and Safety
Dist - AOTA **Prod** - AOTA 1979

A Visit with Isaac Stern 30 MIN
16mm
B&W
Interviews Isaac Stern, concert violinist. Explores his attitudes about the United States, the American tradition, Israel and the world in general and his feelings toward his artistry and his sense of social responsibility. (Kinescope).
Biography; Religion and Philosophy
Dist - NAAJS **Prod** - JTS 1962

A Visit with J I Rodale 15 MIN
16mm / U-matic / VHS
Color (J)
LC 72-702478
J I Rodale, pioneer organic farmer, talks about his ideas on organic farming, health and ecology.
Agriculture; Health and Safety; Home Economics; Science - Natural
Dist - BULFRG **Prod** - RPFD 1972

A Visit with Leland Jacobs 12 MIN
16mm
Access to Learning Series
Color
LC 79-711563
Documents a visit with a third grade class by teacher and writer Dr Leland Jacobs. Shows the expressions and reactions of the children as they listen to Dr Jacobs.
Psychology; Sociology
Dist - OSUMPD **Prod** - OSUMPD 1970

A Visit with Lois Duncan 18 MIN
BETA / VHS
Color
Presents Lois Duncan, author of young adult suspense novels. Highlights her writing process.
Literature and Drama
Dist - RDAENT **Prod** - RDAENT

A Visit with the Animal Doctors 11 MIN
16mm / U-matic / VHS
Visit to Series
Color (P I)
LC 81-700244
Looks at the work of veterinarians.
Health and Safety; Science
Dist - JOU **Prod** - JOU 1980

A Visit with the Goldminers 14 MIN
U-matic / VHS / 16mm
Visit to Series
Color (P I)
Shows two children as they learn about gold mines when they visit their uncle in Alaska. Describes the different methods of mining gold and provides information on placer mines as well as underground mines. Visits operational mines, showing how they work and how the gold is processed.
Geography - United States; Social Science
Dist - JOU **Prod** - JOU 1983

A Visit with the Ranchers 16 MIN
16mm / U-matic / VHS
Visit to Series
Color (P I)
Follows a husband and wife team of cowpunchers through a typical day on the range. Demonstrates the skills of shoeing, riding and roping as well as the veterinary skills necessary for the day - to - day care of a herd of cattle.
Agriculture; Social Science; Sociology
Dist - JOU **Prod** - JOU 1978

A Visit with Winter 30 MIN
U-matic
Magic Ring I Series
(K P)
Shows the children trying to describe snow and ending up on a visit to Old Man Winter.
Education; Literature and Drama
Dist - ACCESS **Prod** - ACCESS 1984

Visitatio sepulchri 28 MIN
VHS
Color (C A) (LATIN)
$129.00 purchase _ #DF211
Presents a 12th - century music - drama filmed in period costume on the location of the play's presumed origin, a medieval abbey. Relates the Gospel story of the first Easter.
Literature and Drama
Dist - INSIM

Visite en France 105 MIN
VHS
Color (I J H) (FRENCH)
$49.95 purchase _ #W3463
Presents 15 - minute segments based on practical situations such as traveling and socializing to encourage practice of conversational French. Simulates travel to several areas in France to build cultural awareness and understanding. Includes video and booklet with script and language notes.
Foreign Language
Dist - GPC

Visite en France - Pt 1 45 MIN
VHS
Color (T G)
PdS19.95 purchase _ #ML-SKA026
Provides teachers of elementary French a supplement to their classroom lessons. Part of a two-part set that goes on to cover intermediate French. Produced by Skan Productions.
Foreign Language
Dist - AVP

Visite en France - Pt 2 45 MIN
VHS
Color (T G)
PdS19.95 purchase _ #ML-SKA027
Provides teachers of intermediate French a supplement to their classroom lessons. Part of a two-part set that begins with elementary French in Visits en France - Part 1.
Foreign Language
Dist - AVP

Visitemos a Puerto Rico 17 MIN
16mm / U-matic / VHS
Color (H C) (SPANISH)
Spanish version of 'VISIT TO PUERTO RICO.' Shows how Puerto Rico has benefited from the island's development program. Explains the changes which have occurred on farms, in villages, industry, education and public health.
Foreign Language
Dist - IFB **Prod** - IFB 1962

Visiting artists series
Grant Johannesen 55 MIN
Zara Nelsova 54 MIN
Dist - PBS

Visiting for health 8 MIN
U-matic / VHS / BETA
Color; NTSC; PAL; SECAM (H C G)
PdS83
Describes the role of visiting healthcare personnel as being liaisons between the many medical services available and the mothers and children. Stresses the monitoring of child development. Informs nurses considering health visiting as a career and prospective mothers who want information on the part a Health Visitor plays in the health of mothers and their children.
Health and Safety; Psychology
Dist - VIEWTH

The Visiting Teacher - a School Social Worker 19 MIN
16mm
B&W (T)
Tells the story of the visiting teacher by showing how she works with three children who have problems that encompass the school, home and community.
Education; Psychology; Sociology
Dist - VADE **Prod** - VADE 1964

Visiting the Doctor 4 MIN
16mm / U-matic / VHS
Most Important Person - Health and Your Body Series
Color (K P I)
Presents a visit to the doctor's office, where James and his pet frog learn that the doctor can do many things and be a friend as well.
Guidance and Counseling; Health and Safety; Science - Natural
Dist - EBEC **Prod** - EBEC 1972

The Visitor 33 MIN
VHS
Color (J H C G A R)
$29.95 purchase, $10.00 rental _ #35 - 811 - 8516
Shows how an unexpected guest helps Martin find God's grace amid his daily difficulties. Based on the Leo Tolstoy short story 'Where Love Is.'
Religion and Philosophy
Dist - APH **Prod** - VISVID

The Visitor 22 MIN
16mm / VHS
Color (J H A)
$395.00, $545.00 purchase, $50.00 rental _ #9790, #9790LD
Focuses on human greed and treachery. Uses 'The Visitor', a short story by Ray Bradbury as a base. Special effects. Produced by Buz Alexander.
Literature and Drama
Dist - AIMS

A Visitor for Christmas 30 MIN
16mm
Color; B&W (P)
LC FIA67-5760
Aunt Hattie, an unexpected houseguest of the Thompson family during the Christmas season, decides to leave their home when she overhears an uncomplimentary telephone conversation. On her departure, the Thompsons realize they have been acting contrary to the real meaning of Christmas.
Religion and Philosophy
Dist - FAMF **Prod** - FAMF 1967

Visitor from America 30 MIN
16mm
B&W
Relates the story of an American Jew's return on Passover to the old country to find a wife who will keep his home in the traditional way. Tells how he falls in love with the matchmaker's daughter but is opposed by her father, and how the rabbi adjudicates. (Kinescope).
Religion and Philosophy
Dist - NAAJS **Prod** - JTS 1954

A Visitor's guide to London 45 MIN
VHS
Color; PAL (G)
Introduces the capital city of Great Britain. Starts at Hampstead Heath, the highest point in the city, and tours the sights of the city.
Geography - World; History - World
Dist - VIEWTH

Visitors Only 30 MIN
16mm
Color (R)
Tells the story of Paul Rose, a hard - working family man who learns to see the value of regular church attendance.
Guidance and Counseling; Religion and Philosophy
Dist - GF **Prod** - GF

Visits in Urology Series
Ectopic ureterocele 42 MIN
Selected Surgical Approaches to Testis, Bladder, and Prostatic Cancers 38 MIN
Selected Surgical Approaches to Testis, Bladder, and Prostatic Cancers, Pt 1 19 MIN
Surgery for Vesicular Ureteral Reflux 57 MIN
Surgery for Vesicular Ureteral Reflux - Pt 1 28 MIN
Surgery for Vesicular Ureteral Reflux - Pt 2 29 MIN
Surgery of Upper Urinary Tract Stone Disease 39 MIN
Urethral Strictures 49 MIN
Dist - EATONL

Visits with God - two first hand accounts of near death experiences 25 MIN
16mm
Color (G)
Explores the possibility of life after death through two cases based on the model established by Dr Raymond Moody in his book, Life After Life. Features two women who recall in detail their own near death experiences during critical medical procedures. Produced by Richard Brick.
Fine Arts
Dist - CANCIN
PHENIX

Vislumbres De Madrid Y Toledo 17 MIN
U-matic / VHS / 16mm
Color (H C) (SPANISH)
LC FIA67-5705
Views physical and artistic aspects of two Castilian cities, Madrid and Toledo.
Foreign Language
Dist - IFB **Prod** - IFB 1963

Vista series
The Back attack 60 MIN
Don't play dead 60 MIN
Dream Cities 60 MIN
Fueling the Future 60 MIN
Hear Today, Gone Tomorrow 60 MIN
Power Play 60 MIN
The Tree that Grew Up 60 MIN
We've been There 60 MIN
Dist - TVOTAR

Vistas De Andalucia 10 MIN
U-matic / VHS / 16mm
Color; B&W (H C) (SPANISH)
LC FIA65-277
Shows scenes of Arcos, Cadiz and Cordoba.
Foreign Language
Dist - IFB **Prod** - IFB 1957

Visual Aids 26 MIN
16mm
Color (C A)
Illustrates a variety of conventional audiovisual equipment and techniques, including examples of good utilization practices. Shows the use of the chalk board, magnetic board, models, remote control slide and filmstrip projectors, the opaque projector and various graphic devices.
Education
Dist - MLA **Prod** - USN 1968

Visual Alchemy 8 MIN
16mm
Color
LC 75-704352
Presents a variety of images and holographic projections in space.
Fine Arts
Dist - CANFDC **Prod** - CANFDC 1973

Visual and Liquid Penetrant Inspection 38 MIN
U-matic / BETA / VHS
Color
$400 purchase
Guidance and Counseling; Industrial and Technical Education; Psychology
Dist - ASM **Prod** - ASM

Visual Arts 15 MIN
VHS / U-matic
Arts Express Series
Color (K P I J)
Fine Arts
Dist - KYTV **Prod** - KYTV 1983

The Visual Arts 18 MIN
U-matic / VHS / 16mm
Humanities Series
Color (J H C)
LC 72-714121
Presents an introduction to art.
Fine Arts
Dist - MGHT **Prod** - MGHT 1971

Visual Arts and Design 15 MIN
VHS / 16mm
(H C A)
$24.95 purchase _ #CS313
Describes the skills necessary for a career in visual arts and design. Features interviews with people working in this field.
Guidance and Counseling
Dist - RMIBHF **Prod** - RMIBHF

Visual arts and design 15 MIN
VHS
Career success series
Color (H C A)
$29.95 purchase _ #MX313
Presents an introduction to visual arts and design careers. Covers the necessary skills, and interviews people in these careers on the rewards and stresses involved.
Education; Fine Arts
Dist - CAMV

Visual Arts - Design 15 MIN
BETA / VHS / U-matic
Career Success Series
(H C A)
$29.95 _ #MX313
Portrays occupations in visual arts and design by reviewing their required abilities and interviewing people employed in these fields. Tells of the anxieties and rewards involved in pursuing a career as an artist or designer.
Education; Fine Arts; Guidance and Counseling; Industrial and Technical Education
Dist - CAMV **Prod** - CAMV

Visual Arts for the Physically Challenged Person 25 MIN
VHS
Color (C)
$150.00 purchase
Shows how physically challenged students can, with a little assistance, achieve self - expression through the visual arts. Demonstrates practical adaptations of equipment, activities and teaching methods which allow handicapped children to become active participants in classroom art activities. Features Dr Betty Ross - Thomson, supervisor of physically handicapped programs for the Wisconsin Department of Public Instruction, who introduces the Education for All Handicapped Children Act of 1975 and its implications for integrating disabled children into regular classrooms.
Business and Economics; Education; Fine Arts; Mathematics; Psychology
Dist - AITECH

Visual Arts, the, Pt 1 30 MIN
U-matic / VHS
Japan - the Living Tradition Series
Color (H C A)
Examines the visual arts as practiced in Japan.
Fine Arts; History - World
Dist - GPN **Prod** - UMA 1976

Visual Arts, the, Pt 2 30 MIN
U-matic / VHS
Japan - the Living Tradition Series
Color (H C A)
Examines the visual arts as practiced in Japan.
Fine Arts; History - World
Dist - GPN **Prod** - UMA 1976

Visual Awareness 15 MIN
U-matic
Children and the Visual Arts Series
Color (PRO)
Introduces the primary elements of visual arts; line texture, color and shape. Shows how they all play an important role in daily life.
Education; Fine Arts
Dist - ACCESS **Prod** - ACCESS 1983

Visual Awareness Series
Building lines 4 MIN
The Role of the Wheel 7 MIN
Shapes a La Cart 8 MIN
Dist - IFB

Visual Clues that Help to Determine Whether a Vowel Sound will be Long or Short 20 MIN
U-matic / VHS
Getting the Word Series Unit III; Unit III

Color (J H)
Presents visual clues that help to determine whether a vowel sound will be long or short, emphasizing vowel pairs.
English Language
Dist - AITECH **Prod** - SCETV 1974

Visual Day Signals 14 MIN
16mm
B&W
LC FIE52-939
Shows international day signals for ships not under command, inland day signals and various other signals.
Civics and Political Systems; Health and Safety; Social Science
Dist - USNAC **Prod** - USN 1943

Visual Detection of Driving while Intoxicated 10 MIN
U-matic / VHS / 16mm
Color (H A)
Illustrates 20 of the most common indicators of DWI, including drifting, weaving, erratic braking and turning, and driving off the roadway. Intended for police officers.
Education; Health and Safety; Psychology; Social Science; Sociology
Dist - USNAC **Prod** - NHTSA 1980

Visual display of data
VHS
Probability and statistics series
Color (H C)
$125.00 purchase _ #8003
Provides resource material about display of data for help in the study of probability and statistics. Presents a 60 - video series, each part 25 to 30 minutes long, that explains and reinforces concepts using definitions, theorems, examples and step - by - step solutions to tutor the student. Videos are also available in a set.
Mathematics
Dist - LANDMK

Visual display units series
The Key position 8 MIN
Safe stations 18 MIN
Dist - CFLVIS

Visual Distress Signals 10 MIN
U-matic / VHS
Color (A)
Discusses the 1980 US Coast Guard visual distress signal law and requirements, safe handling, and types of visual distress signals.
Civics and Political Systems; Health and Safety
Dist - USNAC **Prod** - USCG 1981

Visual documents 29 MIN
VHS
Photographic vision series
Color (G)
$49.95 purchase _ #RM116V-F
Examines aesthetic and emotional responses to the visual art of photography. Presents the technical aspects of photography clearly and simply, including principles of the camera and techniques for controlling exposure, the use of various kinds of lighting, selection of appropriate lenses and film and basic darkroom techniques. Focuses on the world of photographers and photography - its history and evolution, its uses for personal development and expression, and the impact of photography on the world. Part of a 20-part series examining all aspects of the field of photography.
Fine Arts; Industrial and Technical Education
Dist - CAMV

Visual Documents 30 MIN
U-matic / VHS
Photographic Vision - all about Photography Series
Color
Industrial and Technical Education
Dist - CDTEL **Prod** - COAST

Visual Effects for TV - the Battlefield 30 MIN
U-matic / VHS
BBC TV Production Training Course Series
Color (C)
$279.00, $179.00 purchase _ #AD - 2082
Follows the three - day build - up to a major battle scene. Reveals that although the final sequence ran only a few minutes and was shot in a single day, the scene involved over a hundred extras, a team of visual effects designers and dozens of others. Part of a twelve - part series on TV production by the BBC.
Fine Arts; Geography - World; Industrial and Technical Education
Dist - FOTH **Prod** - FOTH

Visual Effects - Wizardry on Film 29 MIN
U-matic / VHS / 16mm
Color (J H C A)
Uses Mel Brooks' History Of The World, Part 1 as a backdrop to show the work of visual effects genius Albert Whitlock. Shows how Whitlock superimposes ancient Rome on a California backlot.
Fine Arts
Dist - CF **Prod** - CF 1984

Visual essays - Origins of film series 65 MIN
16mm
Visual essays - Origins of film series
Color; B&W (G)
$100.00 rental
Presents essays on film - image history. Attempts to reconstruct the vision of cinematic creation that occurred in the minds of cinema's 'primitives,' since together they comprise a critical - structural investigation of silent cinema. Includes Lumiere's Train; Melies Catalog, which presents the mythic iconography of Melies' work in a grab - bag of magician's surprises; Sequels in Transfigured Time; Ghost: Image; For Artaud, an essay on expressionism and the tradition of Gothic horror; and Storming the Winter Palace, the last essay on Eisenstein, montage and the dialectics of film form - content. Individual titles not available separately except for Lumiere's Train; Sequels in Transfigured Time; and Ghost: Image.
Fine Arts
Dist - CANCIN **Prod** - RAZUTI 1984

Visual essays - Origins of film series
Visual essays - Origins of film series 65 MIN
Dist - CANCIN

Visual essays series
Sequels in transfigured time 12 MIN
Dist - CANCIN

Visual Form Discrimination in the Cat 11 MIN
16mm
B&W (C T)
Cats are trained to respond positively to a triangle card in the windows of two or more food boxes. Cats trained in 'PAIRED' stimulus situation 4two boxes) transfer readily to 'UNPAIRED' situations (three or four boxes) and those trained with three or four boxes transfer to two boxes. Triangle choice remains even when stimulus sizes and figure - ground relationships are varied.
Psychology; Science - Natural
Dist - PSUPCR **Prod** - PSUPCR 1933

Visual Glossary - How Stories from the Bible are Shown in Medieval and Byzantine Art 22 MIN
VHS / Kit / 35mm strip
Color (J H A)
$67.00=MV, $42.00=FS
Explores the vital role that religious art played in medieval life. Explains how paintings, mosaics, sculpture, and stained glass windows provided the illterate public with visual tools for learning lessons from the Bible.
Fine Arts; History - World
Dist - ALARP **Prod** - ALARP 1987

Visual guide to physical examination - 2nd ed series
Breast and Axillae 12 MIN
Cardiovascular - neck vessels and heart 16 MIN
Cardiovascular - peripheral vascular 11 MIN
Eyes, ears, and nose 18 MIN
Female genitalia, anus and rectum 20 MIN
Male Genitalia, Anus and Hernias 12 MIN
Musculoskeletal 17 MIN
Thorax and lungs 18 MIN
Dist - LIP

Visual guide to physical examination series
Abdomen 11 MIN
Head, face, mouth, and neck 11 MIN
Dist - LIP

Visual Guide to Physical Examination
Neurologic - Cranial Nerves and Sensory System 22 MIN
Neurologic - Motor System and Reflexes 18 MIN
Dist - LIP

A Visual Heritage 30 MIN
U-matic / VHS
Photographic Vision - all about Photography Series
Color
Industrial and Technical Education
Dist - CDTEL **Prod** - COAST

A Visual heritage 29 MIN
VHS
Photographic vision series
Color (G)
$49.95 purchase _ #RM102V-F
Offers a history of photography. Presents the technical aspects of photography clearly and simply, including principles of the camera and techniques for controlling exposure, the use of various kinds of lighting, selection of appropriate lenses and film and basic darkroom techniques. Focuses on the world of photographers and photography - its history and evolution, its uses for personal development and expression, and the impact of photography on the world. Part of a 20-part series examining all aspects of the field of photography.
Industrial and Technical Education
Dist - CAMV

Visual History Series
Visit with Beatrice Wade, a, Pt 1 30 MIN
Visit with Beatrice Wade, a, Pt 2 30 MIN
A Visit with Clare Spackman 30 MIN
Visit with Dr Sidney Licht - Pt 1 30 MIN
Visit with Dr Sidney Licht - Pt 2 30 MIN
A Visit with Helen Willard 30 MIN
Dist - AOTA

Visual Impairement, Pt 1 19 MIN
VHS / U-matic
Color (PRO)
Describes an organized approach for the primary care physician to take in diagnosing abnormalities of the cornea, anterior chamber, lens, vitreous cavity and retina. Discusses decreased visual acuity due to uncorrected refractive errors.
Health and Safety; Science - Natural
Dist - UMICHM **Prod** - UMICHM 1976

Visual Impairment, Pt 2 15 MIN
VHS / U-matic
Color (PRO)
Considers disorders occurring between the retina and brain. Discusses diagnosis of senile macular melanoma and chorioretinitis. Details causes of, and diagnostic procedures to detect, disorders of the optic nerve, including glaucoma, extraocular disorders and optic atrophy.
Health and Safety; Science - Natural
Dist - UMICHM **Prod** - UMICHM 1976

Visual Learning Series Session 1
Towards Visual Learning
Dist - NYSED

Visual Learning Series Session 3
Television in the Classroom
Dist - NYSED

Visual Learning Series Session 4
The Mechanics of Television
Dist - NYSED

Visual Learning Series Session 5
Program Acquisition
Dist - NYSED

Visual learning series
The Many faces of television
Dist - NYSED

Visual literacy series
Body talking 36 MIN
The Movie movie 36 MIN
A Sense of touch and A sense of sound 36 MIN
Speaking objectly 36 MIN
Dist - EMFVL

Visual literacy series
Sequence and story 5 MIN
Dist - ILEA
MOKIN

Visual merchandising 30 MIN
VHS
Color (J H C G)
$79.95 purchase _ #CCP0137V
Shows how good visual presentation focuses customer attention and helps in deciding what to buy. Illustrates how to analyze the essential elements in crating the right ambiance for merchandise. Includes - the creation or change of a store's identity both from the inside and through windows; techniques for using space, line and lighting; how to utilize colors; the showmanship created by using current events and holiday themes. Teaches about the skills and interests necessary to become a visual merchandiser and about the wide range of career options available.
Business and Economics; Guidance and Counseling
Dist - CAMV **Prod** - CAMV 1993

Visual Perception 29 MIN
U-matic
Understanding Human Behavior - an Introduction to Psychology Series
Color (C A)
Tells problems of man who first received sight through an operation at age 50. Shows that visual stimulation is not the same as perception and that the brain needs both innate and learned clues for interpretation.
Psychology; Science - Natural
Dist - CDTEL **Prod** - COAST

Visual Perception 18 MIN
16mm
Color
Presents a display of what things appear to be when carefully laid out to be something else.
Psychology
Dist - THIOKL **Prod** - THIOKL 1960

Visual Perception and Failure to Learn 20 MIN
16mm / U-matic / VHS
Color; B&W (T) (SPANISH)
LC FIA66-1796
Depicts difficulties in learning for children who have disabilities in visual perception. Demonstrates the Marianne Frostig Test and outlines a training program.
Education; Foreign Language; Psychology
Dist - AIMS **Prod** - HORNE 1970

Visual perception in driving 21 MIN
16mm / VHS
Color (H G)
$100.00, $35.00 purchase _ #295, #490
Presents two parts on visual perception in driving. Discusses eye habits and training the use of eyes in scanning and searching the road ahead in 'Eye Habits - Part One'. 'Identification - Part Two' demonstrates that visual perception in driving is more than just seeing. Shows how traffic experience helps in interpreting what is seen and how to react. Both films are on a single tape in video format.
Health and Safety; Industrial and Technical Education; Science - Natural
Dist - AAAFTS **Prod** - OSUPD 1981

Visual Perception Training in the Regular Classroom 23 MIN
U-matic / VHS / 16mm
B&W (T) (SPANISH)
LC 78-708898
Demonstrates integration of training in visual perception with training in language and regular curriculum of pre - school and primary grade levels.
Education
Dist - AIMS **Prod** - HORNE 1970

Visual Stretches 10 MIN
Videoreel / VT2
Janaki Series
Color
Physical Education and Recreation
Dist - PBS **Prod** - WGBHTV

Visual System - the Globe 16 MIN
16mm / U-matic / VHS
Anatomy of the Human Eye Series
Color (PRO)
LC 74-702442
Discusses the location, relations and functions of the structures that comprise the eyeball, including the corneoscleral coat, uveal tract, retina, lens, zonula, accommodation mechanism, posterior and anterior segments and aqueous circulation.
Science - Natural
Dist - TEF **Prod** - BAYCMO 1972

Visual System - the Visual Pathway 13 MIN
16mm / U-matic / VHS
Anatomy of the Human Eye Series
Color (PRO)
LC 74-702443
Explains the path of visual impulses from the globe to the visual cortex, with discussion, in turn of the retina, optic nerve, optic tracts and chiasm and optic radiations.
Science - Natural
Dist - TEF **Prod** - BAYCMO 1972

Visual variations on Noguchi 4 MIN
16mm
B&W (G)
$25.00 rental
Captures the sculptures of the famous Japanese - American artist, Isamu Noguchi. Uses a hand - held camera combined with ususual editing and an experimental score by Lucille Dlugozewski.
Fine Arts
Dist - CANCIN

Visualing road 20 MIN
VHS / U-matic
Efficient reading - instructional tapes series; Tape 2
Color
Discusses setting goals to become an all - purpose reader.
English Language
Dist - TELSTR **Prod** - TELSTR

Visualizacion De Un Objeto 9 MIN
U-matic
B&W (SPANISH)
LC 79-707560
Explains how a blueprint is developed by pointing out how dimensions are shown by different views and how special information is indicated.
Foreign Language; Industrial and Technical Education
Dist - USNAC **Prod** - USOE 1979

Visualization - a Key to Reading 25 MIN
16mm
Color (C A)
LC 72-700947
Presents procedures for testing and developing the skill of visualization.
Education; English Language; Psychology
Dist - SOUND **Prod** - SOUND 1972

Visualizing an Object 9 MIN
16mm
Machine Shop Work Series Fundamentals of Blueprint Reading series
B&W (SPANISH)
LC 74-705922
Tells how a blueprint is developed, how dimensions are shown by different views and how various kinds of information are indicated on a blueprint.
Industrial and Technical Education
Dist - USNAC **Prod** - USOE 1945

Visualizing what you paint 19 MIN
VHS
Art is ... video series
Color (G)
$29.95 purchase _ #CPC887V - F
Motivates visualizing how positive - negative shapes and light - to - dark painting techniques or using toned backgrounds would add to a planned work. Discusses the use of watercolor methods, composition, color, visual impact and media combinations for creative experimentation. Part of a five - part series. Videos are also available in a set.
Fine Arts
Dist - CAMV

The Visually Handicapped in the Mainstream 14 MIN
16mm
Exceptional Learners Series
Color (T S)
LC 79-700716
Shows how teachers can help visually handicapped children learn skills necessary for mobility and independence.
Education; Psychology
Dist - MERILC **Prod** - MERILC 1978

Visually Impaired 20 MIN
U-matic
One Giant Step - the Integration of Children with Special Needs 'Series
Color (PRO)
Reveals that the visually impaired child should progress through the regular curriculum according to personal ability and special skills.
Education
Dist - ACCESS **Prod** - ACCESS 1983

The Visually Impaired 30 MIN
U-matic / VHS
Promises to Keep Series
Color (T)
Offers an educational definition of visual impairment and identifies the common behavioral signs which may suggest visual impairment and the special material, equipment and instructional procedures which will assist the visually impaired child.
Education
Dist - LUF **Prod** - VPI 1979

Vita Futurista - Italian Futurism 1909 - 44 52 MIN
16mm / VHS
Color (H A)
$1200.00 purchase, $100.00 rental
Traces the evolution of Futurism in Italy from 1909 to 1944, focusing on its founder and leader, Italian poet Filippo Tommaso Marinetti. Includes archival footage of such artists as Umberto Boccioni, Carlo Carra, and Gino Severini, interviews with their families and colleagues, and views of futurist works shown at the 1986 exhibition held at the Palazzo Grossi in Venice.
Fine Arts; History - World
Dist - AFA **Prod** - ACGB 1988

Vita Stone Working with Indians 60 MIN
VHS / U-matic
B&W
Presents Vita Stone, a Caucasian who has been working with Indians in Wisconsin for 20 years as she talks with Ada Deer's graduate students about being Caucasian and working with Indians.
Social Science
Dist - UWISC **Prod** - UWISC 1978

The Vital Connection
U-matic / VHS
Body Human Series
Color
Shows a voyage of discovery into the inner space of the human brain, a visual revelation of the workings of the clusters of vital connections that manage conscious and automatic actions and reactions. Depicts tragic consequences of function breakdown and courage of doctors and patients to restore 'the vital connection'.
Health and Safety; Industrial and Technical Education
Dist - MEDCOM **Prod** - MEDCOM

The Vital Connection 17 MIN
16mm
Color (H C A)
LC 79-700610
Presents a pictorial discussion of the economic contributions made by small - scale farming and possible steps to encourage agriculture.
Agriculture
Dist - FENWCK **Prod** - FENWCK 1978

Vital Facts - Reading Material Safety Data Sheets 21 MIN
VHS / 16mm
Haz - Comp Solution Series
Color (PRO)
$350.00 purchase, $125.00 rental, $40.00 preview
Presents information needed for compliance with OSHA's Hazard Communication Standard. Explains how to read material safety data sheets. Available individually or as part of a complete program. Includes support materials.
Business and Economics; Computer Science; Guidance and Counseling; Health and Safety; Psychology; Sociology
Dist - UTM **Prod** - UTM

The Vital Force 16 MIN
16mm
Color
Describes in simple terms how the Chicago Board of Trade functions, what a futures market is and the role the futures market plays in the world's economy.
Business and Economics
Dist - MTP **Prod** - CBT

The Vital force 30 MIN
VHS
Perspectives - health and medicine - series
Color; PAL; NTSC (G)
PdS90, PdS105 purchase
Reveals that a greater understanding of the nervous system - millions of nerves carrying millions of electrical impulses - enables doctors to repair it when it breaks down.
Health and Safety; Science - Natural
Dist - CFLVIS **Prod** - LONTVS

Vital interests 15 MIN
16mm
B&W (G)
$30.00 rental
Condenses the news of two years into a single strange newscast, from the past on into a bizarre 'future consisting of real stories from the recent past. Produced by Beth Block.
Fine Arts
Dist - CANCIN

Vital Key to a Better Future for Man 10 MIN
16mm
Color
Examines the phosphate - producing area of Florida and explains its importance to the existence of human and animal life.
Geography - United States; Industrial and Technical Education; Science - Natural
Dist - FLADC **Prod** - FLADC

The Vital Land 15 MIN
16mm
B&W (H C A)
Documents the glorious past, the scenic splendor and the modern achievements of the state of Punjab.
Geography - World; History - World
Dist - NEDINF **Prod** - INDIA

The Vital Link 15 MIN
VHS / U-matic
Color (J A) (SPANISH)
Portrays how emergency medical services are designed to handle many different kinds of medical crises.
Foreign Language; Health and Safety
Dist - SUTHRB **Prod** - SUTHRB

The Vital Link 29 MIN
16mm
Color (H A)
LC FIE67-129
Presents an overview of the world - wide tracking and data acquisition networks which the National Aeronautics and Space Administration uses to communicate between earth and manned and unmanned spacecraft.
Psychology; Science - Physical; Social Science
Dist - NASA **Prod** - NASA 1967

The Vital Link 17 MIN
VHS
Color (J H)
Investigates questions concerning the development and location of communications systems, using examples of road, rail, sea and air transport on a European scale.
Social Science
Dist - VIEWTH **Prod** - VIEWTH

The Vital Link 27 MIN
16mm
Color
LC 77-700064
Discusses the Parent Advisory Council of Turtle Mountain Community School in Belcourt, North Dakota. Shows how it performs its duties and meets its reponsibilities in connection with programs funded by the federal government under Title I.
Education; Social Science; Sociology
Dist - BAILYL **Prod** - USBIA 1976

The Vital Link 15 MIN
16mm
Color (J)
LC 77-700431
Details emergency procedures to use in various situations and suggests who to contact for help.
Health and Safety; Social Science; Sociology
Dist - IA **Prod** - LAC 1976

Vital link series
Looking for love - teenage parents 30 MIN
Dist - CAREER
EDCC
GA

Vital Link Series
Sense of Responsibiity - How it Grows 27 MIN
Dist - CORNRS
EDCC

Vital Link Series
Decision making for careers
Family and the disabled child 29 MIN
Newcomer in School - Adventure or Agony
Parent - Teacher Conference
Parents and the Young Teen - a Delicate Balance
Pre - school readiness - foundation for learning
Signals of Change - the Junior High Child
Signals of Change - the Senior High Child
Single Parent Family
Testing - What's it all about?
Today's Family - Adjusting to Change
Dist - EDCC

The Vital Moment 30 MIN
VHS / U-matic
What a Picture - the Complete Photography Course by John Hedgecoe 'Series
Color (H C A)
Explains importance of precision and timing in action photography using examples from wrestling, white - water canoeing and a motorcycle stunt team.
Industrial and Technical Education
Dist - FI

A Vital Network 10 MIN
VHS / U-matic
Color
Discusses the importance of proper telephone communication in a hospital and demonstrates proper techniques.
Health and Safety; Social Science
Dist - AHOA **Prod** - AHOA 1982

The Vital Ocean 29 MIN
16mm
Color
LC 74-705924
Describes the current strength of the NATO navies in the Atlantic and explains the task of SCALANT (Supreme Allied Command Atlantic) at Norfolk, Virginia, where officers from six NATO countries work together to coordinate defense plans in the North Atlantic area.
Civics and Political Systems
Dist - USNAC **Prod** - NATO

A Vital poison 50 MIN
VHS
Horizon series
Color (H C A)
PdS99 purchase
Explains that nitrous oxide, though a poisonous gas that comes from car exhaust and is involved in the process that produces acid rain, is necessary for many human body processes. Details how the body manufactures the gas and uses it to perform such tasks as fighting cancer and controlling blood pressure.
Science - Natural
Dist - BBCENE

The Vital Sea 14 MIN
16mm
Color
LC 74-706600
States that the U S Navy ensures free use of the sea as a means of transportation, a place for recreation and a source of food and natural resources.
Civics and Political Systems; Geography - World; Science - Physical; Social Science
Dist - USNAC **Prod** - USN 1973

A Vital Service 10 MIN
U-matic / VHS / 16mm
Color
Introduces the Volunteer Income Tax Assistance (VITA) program, an IRS - sponsored program to train volunteers to assist low - income, non - English speaking and handicapped taxpayers with their income tax forms.
Business and Economics; Civics and Political Systems; Social Science
Dist - USNAC **Prod** - USIRS

Vital signs 14 MIN
U-matic / VHS
Emergency medical training series; Lesson 20
Color (IND)
Teaches recognition and evaluation of vital and diagnostic signs. Emphasizes need for association of signs to arrive at a diagnosis.
Health and Safety; Industrial and Technical Education
Dist - LEIKID **Prod** - LEIKID

Vital signs 9 MIN
16mm
B&W; Color (G)
$35.00 rental
Employs images and text to intertwine Western constructions of death with Hammer's personal interaction wtih a skeleton, clips of Renais' Hiroshima, Mon Amour, and scenes from a hospital's intensive care unit.
Fine Arts; Sociology
Dist - CANCIN **Prod** - BARHAM 1991

Vital signs - 23 15 MIN
VHS
Clinical nursing skills - nursing fundamentals - series
Color (C PRO G)
$395.00 purchase _ #R890 - VI - 053
Reveals that changes in body function are often reflected in body temperature, pulse, blood pressure and respiratory rate and are early indicators of body condition change. Presents procedures and techniques for assessing and measuring these vital signs. Provides the means for gathering accurate data on body temperature and pulse rate - choices of sites, as well as conditions influencing those choices. Describes and demonstrates methods for assessing respiratory function and taking blood pressure readings. Part of a 23 - part series on clinical nursing skills.
Health and Safety
Dist - HSCIC **Prod** - CUYAHO 1989

Vital Signs and their Interrelation - Body Temperature, Pulse, Respiration, Blood Pressure 32 MIN
16mm
Nursing Series
B&W
LC FIE52-412
Discusses the physiology and inter - relationships of the respiratory, heat regulatory and circulatory systems. Shows how to find and record the vital signs - temperature, pulse, respiration and blood pressure.
Health and Safety
Dist - USNAC **Prod** - USOE 1945

Vital Signs - Blood Pressure 20 MIN
8mm cartridge / 16mm
Nurse's Aide, Orderly and Attendant Series
Color (H C A IND)
LC 80-701068
Discusses the terminology, equipment and techniques associated with measuring blood pressure.
Health and Safety
Dist - COPI **Prod** - COPI 1976

Vital signs - how to take them 14 MIN
U-matic / VHS
Emergency medical training series
Color
Points out which are vital and diagnostic signs, the normal range for each vital sign, how a sphygomomanometer operates to measure blood pressue level and how to use vital sign information to aid diagnosis of victim.
Health and Safety
Dist - VTRI **Prod** - VTRI

Vital Signs, Pt 1 - Cardinal Symptoms 21 MIN
16mm
B&W
LC FIE56-384
Explains temperature, pulse, respiration and blood pressure by means of live action and animation, art work and sound effects. Tells how these vital signs present a picture of the condition of the body.
Health and Safety; Science; Science - Natural
Dist - USNAC **Prod** - USN 1956

Vital Signs, Pt 3 - Taking Blood Pressure 11 MIN
16mm
B&W
LC FIE56-386
Explains and demonstrates the principles of taking systolic and diastolic pressures and the procedures followed with patients. Uses sound effects to show the significant changes in pulse tone.
Health and Safety; Science; Science - Natural
Dist - USNAC **Prod** - USN 1956

Vital Signs, Pt 2 - Taking Temperature, Pulse and Respiration 20 MIN
16mm
B&W
LC FIE56-385
Demonstrates the techniques of taking temperature, pulse and respiration of patients with a variety of conditions. Shows equipment needed and includes sanitary procedures and charting.
Health and Safety; Science; Science - Natural
Dist - USNAC **Prod** - USN 1956

Vital Signs - Temperature 20 MIN
8mm cartridge / 16mm
Nurse's Aide, Orderly and Attendant Series
Color (H C A IND)
LC 80-701070
Shows mercury thermometers and the steps to be taken in obtaining and recording temperature readings. Discusses indications for choosing oral, axillary or rectal thermometers.
Health and Safety
Dist - COPI **Prod** - COPI 1976

Vital signs - the good health resource
CD-ROM
(H C G)
$95.00 purchase _ #TCR123CDM - P, #TCR123CD2 - P
Teaches about health problems, important ways to reduce health risks. Tracks personal data and finds community organizations to help with heath needs. Includes information from The American Heart Association, National Cancer Institute, American Lung Association, President's Council on Physical Fitness and others. Lists general categories of people - children, women, the aging and others, categories of emergency response. Includes a telphone book of health organizations and home learning activities, a glossary of medical terms. Covers over 2000 topics. Available for both Macintosh and Windows.
Health and Safety; Physical Education and Recreation
Dist - CAMV

Vital signs - the good health resource
CD-ROM
Color (G)
Enables the location of desired information in health through categories arranged according to age and gender. Contains utilities and tools for assessing health risk and recording health information, tutorials and learning activities. Available for both Apple Mcintosh and IBM compatibles with Windows 3.0.
Health and Safety; Physical Education and Recreation
Dist - TXCAV **Prod** - TXCAV

Vital Signs - Understanding Hazardous Materials Labels 19 MIN
VHS / 16mm
Haz - Comp Solution Series
Color (PRO)
$350.00 purchase, $125.00 rental, $40.00 preview
Presents information needed for compliance with OSHA's Hazard Communication Standard. Explains hazardous material labels. Available individually or as part of a complete program. Includes support material.
Business and Economics; Computer Science; Guidance and Counseling; Health and Safety; Psychology; Sociology
Dist - UTM **Prod** - UTM

Vital Statistics of a Citizen Simply Obtained 40 MIN
U-matic / VHS
B&W
Presented by Martha Rosler.
Fine Arts
Dist - KITCHN **Prod** - KITCHN

Vital Statistics of a Citizen Simply Obtained 40 MIN
U-matic
Color (C)
$300.00 purchase, $40.00, $55.00 rental
Examines, in non - documentary form, the objectification of women and others in a technological and bureaucratic society. Probes how women come to see themselves as objects and how human values become subordinate to principles of control. Uses symbolic action to reveal the crimes against women. Produced by Martha Rosler.
Fine Arts; Industrial and Technical Education; Psychology; Sociology
Dist - WMENIF

Vital Waterway - the Suez Canal 14 MIN
16mm
Screen news digest series; Vol 18; Issue 3
Color (I)
LC 76-701848
Examines the past and present history of the Suez Canal and its role in the Middle East. Covers the construction and history of the canal, political issues which resulted in the closing of the canal and its subsequent re - opening in 1975.
Civics and Political Systems; Geography - World; History - United States; History - World
Dist - HEARST **Prod** - HEARST 1975

Vital Xingyiquan - Volume 2 90 MIN
VHS
Color (G)
$49.95 purchase _ #1140
Presents basic forms for the five elements, and extended teaching of Ann Shenn Pau, an important partner sparring sequence. Covers Xingyi theory, 5 conditioning exercises employing 5 elements fist training, and 12 qigong training exercises. Shows some of the form and sequence for the 12 animals. With Master Shouyu Liang and Sam Masich. Intended as a teaching tape, with slow motion, closeups, freeze frames, different angles, repetition, and explanation of important details.
Physical Education and Recreation
Dist - WAYF

Vital Xingyiquan - Volume I 70 MIN
VHS
Color (G)
$49.95 purchase _ #1139
Introduces an internal martial art. Presents solo and partner exercises, basic stances and movements, and partner conditioning exercises. Includes basic and advanced linking forms, San Shau Pau and 5 elements restraining routine. With Master Shouyu Liang and Sam Masich. Intended as a teaching tape, with slow motion, closeups, freeze frames, different angles, repetition, and explanation of important details.
Physical Education and Recreation
Dist - WAYF

Vital Xingyiquan - Volumes 1 and 2 160 MIN
VHS
Color (G)
$85.00 purchase
Offers two parts which introduce an internal martial art and present the basic forms for the five elements, and extended teaching of Ann Shenn Pau - Peaceful Body Cannon - an important partner sparring sequence. Features Master Shouyu Liang and Sam Masich. Includes slow motion, closeups, freeze frames, different angles, repetition, and explanation of important details.
Physical Education and Recreation
Dist - WAYF

The Vitalogram 19 MIN
VHS / 16mm
Procedures for the Family Physician Series
(C)
$385.00 purchase _ #850VI013
Explains the vitalogram and defines terms used in its interpretation. Teaches the calculations used to figure peak flow and tracings of individuals with normal breathing capacity, an airway obstruction, or a diminished total capacity.
Health and Safety
Dist - HSCIC **Prod** - HSCIC 1985

Vitamin basics
VHS / 35mm strip
Color (G A)
$79.00, $69.00 purchase _ #LS55V, #LS55F
Presents the facts about vitamins. Reveals what vitamins are needed and how best to get them. Covers vitamin supplements, their benefits and risks. Reveals that storing and preparing foods can remove much of the vitamin content. Includes student support materials.
Health and Safety; Psychology; Social Science
Dist - CAMV

Vitamin Basics
VHS / 35mm strip
$69.00 purchase _ #LSVB filmstrip, $79.00 purchase _ #LSVBV VHS
Discusses the importance of vitamins and what a lack of vitamins can do to the body.
Health and Safety; Social Science
Dist - CAREER **Prod** - CAREER

Vitamin Deficiencies in Chickens and Turkeys 23 MIN
16mm
Color
Presents various symptoms exhibited by chickens and turkey which are deficient in vitamins A, D, E, K, riboflavin, biotin and folicin.
Agriculture; Health and Safety
Dist - COLOSU **Prod** - COLOSU 1975

Vitamins 30 MIN
VHS
Nutrition in action series
Color (C T)
$200.00 purchase, $20.50 rental _ #34730
Highlights essential vitamins and the functions they perform. Details vitamins A and C. Part of a ten - part series preparing K - 6 educators to teach nutrition, each program covering a specific nutritional topic and demonstrating creative classroom activities for teaching the concepts. Includes self - help manual.
Education; Health and Safety; Social Science
Dist - PSU **Prod** - WPSXTV 1987

Vitamins 30 MIN
U-matic / VHS
Food for Life Series
Color
Home Economics; Social Science
Dist - MSU **Prod** - MSU

Vitamins - 1 33 MIN
VHS
Introductory principles of nutrition series
Color (C A PRO)
$70.00 purchase, $16.00 rental _ #34080
Presents the first part of two parts on vitamins. Part of a 20 - part series on nutrition. Emphasizes controversial nutritional issues and the principle instructional objectives.
Health and Safety; Social Science
Dist - PSU **Prod** - WPSXTV 1978

Vitamins - 2 48 MIN
VHS
Introductory principles of nutrition series
Color (C A PRO)
$70.00 purchase, $16.00 rental _ #50703
Presents the second part of two parts on vitamins. Part of a 20 - part series on nutrition. Emphasizes controversial nutritional issues and the principle instructional objectives.
Health and Safety; Social Science
Dist - PSU **Prod** - WPSXTV 1978

Vitamins and nutrition for a healthier life 30 MIN
VHS
Healthy habits video series
Color (G)
$29.95 purchase _ #DVC2766V
Teaches about the vitamins that are needed on a daily basis. Discusses foods containing necessary vitamins and the role of vitamins in preventing cancer and heart disease. Part of a series on nutrition and health.
Health and Safety; Home Economics; Social Science
Dist - CAMV

Vitamins and some Deficiency Diseases 35 MIN
16mm
Color (PRO)
Presents vitamins A, C, D, E, K and the vitamin B complex. Demonstrates deficiencies in experimental animals, including cheilosis, scurvy, rickets, pellagra and vitamin K deficiency. Shows color rerroductions of early ocular changes due to vitamin A and riboflavin deficiencies as seen through the slit lamp and of motor disturbances in pigs suffering from pyridoxine and panothenic acid deficiencies.
Health and Safety; Science
Dist - LEDR **Prod** - ACYLLD 1955

Vitamins from Food 20 MIN
U-matic / VHS / 16mm
Nutrition Education Series
Color (I J)
LC FIA68-3278
Depicts the discovery of vitamins, beginning in 1840 with Dr Lind's treatment of sailors suffering from scurvy. Tells how Dr Rijkman accidentally found a cure for beriberi, fifty years later. Uses animation to show how vitamins work with enzymes to break down food.
Health and Safety; Home Economics; Science - Natural; Social Science
Dist - PEREN **Prod** - WFP 1968

Vitamins / Vocational Schools / Homes
U-matic / VHS
Consumer Survival Series
Color
Provides tips on selecting vocational schools and buying vitamins and homes.
Business and Economics; Education; Health and Safety; Home Economics
Dist - MDCPB **Prod** - MDCPB

Vitamins - what do they do 22 MIN
16mm / U-matic / VHS
Color (J)
LC 79-700132
Defines vitamins and explains how they work in the human body. Debunks myths about vitamins and points out the dangers of taking excessive amounts of vitamin supplements.
Health and Safety
Dist - HIGGIN **Prod** - HIGGIN 1979

Vito Acconci 55 MIN
VHS / U-matic
Color
Features an interview with Vito Acconci. Presented by Kate Horsfield and Lyn Blumenthal.
Fine Arts
Dist - ARTINC **Prod** - ARTINC

Vito Acconci - Association Area 30 MIN
VHS / U-matic
B&W
Focuses on duality.
Fine Arts
Dist - ARTINC **Prod** - ARTINC

Vito Acconci - Claim Excerpts 30 MIN
U-matic / VHS
B&W
Features duality.
Fine Arts
Dist - ARTINC **Prod** - ARTINC

Vito Acconci - Face - Off 30 MIN
U-matic / VHS
B&W
Highlights duality.
Fine Arts
Dist - ARTINC **Prod** - ARTINC

Vito Acconci - Open Book 10 MIN
U-matic / VHS
B&W
Considers duality.
Fine Arts
Dist - ARTINC **Prod** - ARTINC

Vito Acconci - Pryings 20 MIN
VHS / U-matic
B&W
Presents a silent picture. Deals with duality.
Fine Arts
Dist - ARTINC **Prod** - ARTINC

Vito Acconci - the Red Tapes 140 MIN
U-matic / VHS
B&W
Explores duality.
Fine Arts
Dist - ARTINC **Prod** - ARTINC

Vito Acconci - Turn - on 20 MIN
U-matic / VHS
B&W
Addresses duality.
Fine Arts
Dist - ARTINC **Prod** - ARTINC

Vitrectomy 6 MIN
VHS
5 - part retina series
Color (G)
$75.00 purchase, $40.00 rental _ #5315S, #5315V
Shows the reasons for surgery to remove the vitreous fluid - hemorrhage in the vitreous, complex retinal detachment, retinal membrane removal, trauma - and what to expect before, during and after surgery. Part a five - part series on the retina.
Health and Safety; Science - Natural
Dist - AJN **Prod** - VMED

Vitrectomy - After Perforating Injury with Intraocular Foreign Body 10 MIN
16mm
Color
LC 73-702391
Shows the surgical technique for vitrectomy through the pars plana. Demonstrates how the vitreous infusion suction cutter with fiber optics illumination is used to remove a non - magnet intraocular foreign body. Points out that fiber optics illumination is used as the only illumination source for the operative procedure and the photography.
Health and Safety; Science
Dist - UMIAMI **Prod** - UMIAMI 1973

Viva La Causa 12 MIN
16mm
Color
Provides a record of the making of a mural in Chicago's Chicano community and traces the mural movement back to murals done in Mexico.
Fine Arts; Sociology
Dist - KART **Prod** - KART 1974

Viva la difference - women and nutrition 17 MIN
VHS
Color (G)
$79.95 purchase _ #NHV700V-P
Provides information about nutrition choices as they relate to iron stores, dieting, PMS, osteoporosis, birth control, heart disease, and menopause. Offers women the opportunity to understand their body's nutrition needs as it experiences uniquely female changes.
Home Economics; Social Science
Dist - CAMV

Viva Las Vegas 20 MIN
VHS / U-matic
Color (J)
LC 82-706791
Takes viewers to Las Vegas to see the big hotels, gambling casinos and some of the city's finest entertainment.
Geography - United States; History - United States; Physical Education and Recreation
Dist - AWSS **Prod** - AWSS 1980

Viva Mexico - a Cultural Portrait 25 MIN
16mm / U-matic / VHS
Color (I)
Presents a cultural portrait of Mexico, including artists at work, village life, traditional Indian dances, customs, art and architecture dating back to pre - Columbian times, archeology and fiestas.
Fine Arts; Geography - World; Sociology
Dist - MGHT **Prod** - MGHT 1971

Viva San Fermin - the Bulls of Pamplona 48 MIN
U-matic / VHS
Color (H C A)
LC 84-706104
Uses the importance of bullfighting to explain the Spanish concepts of machismo, honor and immortality.
History - World
Dist - FOTH **Prod** - BOWENI 1984

Vivaldi, the Flute and James Galway 26 MIN
U-matic / VHS / 16mm
Musical Triangle Series
Color (J)
Presents Italian composer Antonio Vivaldi (1675 - 1743), who standardized the concerto grosso as a three - movement musical form and enhanced the virtuoso element in solo passages. Features professional musician James Galway playing some of Vivaldi's music on the flute.
Fine Arts
Dist - MEDIAG **Prod** - THAMES 1975

Vivaldi - the Four Seasons 51 MIN
U-matic / VHS
Color (C)
$249.00, $149.00 purchase _ #AD - 1236
Presents 'The Four Seasons' by Vivaldi. Features Yehudi Menuhin as soloist and narrator of Vivaldi's poems. Peter Norris conducts the Orchestra of the Yehudi Menuhin Violin School.
Fine Arts
Dist - FOTH **Prod** - FOTH

Vivaldi - The Four Seasons - Israel Philharmonic Orchestra conducted by Zubin Mehta 50 MIN
VHS
Huberman Festival series
Color (G)
$19.95 purchase_#1347
Begins with violinist Isaac Stern playing Spring from Vivaldi's The Four Seasons. Continues this work with Pinchas Zukerman performing Summer, Shlomo Mintz playing Autumn and Itzhak Perlman concluding with Winter.
Fine Arts
Dist - KULTUR

Vive Le Quebec 14 MIN
16mm
Color (FRENCH)
A French - language film which presents the many faces of Quebec, from the silent grandeur of her territory to the hustle - bustle of her city streets.
Foreign Language; Geography - World
Dist - MTP **Prod** - QDTFG

Vive Le Tour 19 MIN
16mm
Color
Depicts the marathon Tour de France bicycle race held each July, describing the speed, the collisions, the uproar, and the exploitation. Directed by Louis Malle.
Physical Education and Recreation
Dist - NYFLMS **Prod** - UNKNWN 1962

Vivian and Ten second film 3 MIN
16mm
B&W (G)
$15.00 rental
Features two productions from 1964 - 1965. Portrays Vivian Kurtz entombed in a glass display case at a 1964 show of Conner's artwork in San Francisco, and cut to the tune of Conway Twitty's version of 'Mona Lisa.' Ten Second Film acts as a television commercial designed for the 1965 New York Film Festival.
Fine Arts
Dist - CANCIN **Prod** - CONNER

A Vivid awareness of the consequences of prolonged and intense stress 60 MIN
VHS
Stress and the caregiver - Are we driving each other mad - series
Color (R G)
$49.95 purchase _ #SCGR3
Reveals that stress in the lives of Americans is causing immense suffering in the form of painful emotional and physical disease. Discloses that most stress is borne unnecessarily and can be prevented if one is willing to gain some self - knowledge and make changes in attitudes, beliefs and approaches to life. Presents the principles of emotional, physical and mental health that can be applied to daily situations. Features Father James Gill, MD, SJ, who examines ways of distinguishing the painful and disturbing emotions of anger, resentment, loss, anxiety and fear and replacing them with a healthy and energizing way of life. Part of four parts.
Guidance and Counseling; Health and Safety; Psychology; Religion and Philosophy
Dist - CTNA **Prod** - CTNA

Vivika Heino, Potter 30 MIN
Videoreel / VT2
World of the American Craftsman Series
Color
Fine Arts
Dist - PBS **Prod** - WENHTV

The Vixen and the hare, The Unlucky boy The Lady of the apple - Volume II 38 MIN
VHS
European folktales series
Color (G)
$99.00 purchase, $50.00 rental _ #8258
Presents folk stories from the Soviet Union and Czechoslovakia brought to life by three of those countries' animators. Includes 'The Vixen and the Hare' by Yuri Norstein of the Soviet Union, 'The Lady of the Apple' by Bretislav Pojar of Czechoslovakia and 'The Unlucky Boy' by Czech animator Jiri Brdecka. Second volume of a six volume series of 18 European folktales produced by John Halas.
Fine Arts; Literature and Drama
Dist - AIMS **Prod** - EDPAT 1990

Vizcaya Museum gardens 30 MIN
VHS
Color (G)
$29.95 purchase
Visits Vizcaya, an Italian Renaissance - style villa built by industrial James Deering. Reveals that the villa is now a museum of European decorative arts.
Agriculture; Fine Arts
Dist - ARTSAM **Prod** - HOLDAY

Vladimir Horowitz - the last romantic 89 MIN
VHS
Color (G)
$39.95 purchase _ #S01458
Features pianist Vladimir Horowitz in a performance of works from Bach, Mozart, Rachmaninoff and other composers. Interviews Horowitz and his wife.
Fine Arts
Dist - UILL

Vladimir Lenin 13 MIN
U-matic / VHS
Color (G)
$229.00, $129.00 purchase _ #AD - 1860
Recounts the life of Vladimir Lenin. Presents an outline of Marxist Socialism and the historic social and economic conditions which brought it into existence.
Biography; Civics and Political Systems; History - World
Dist - FOTH **Prod** - FOTH

Vladimir Mayakovsky 22 MIN
16mm / U-matic / VHS
Color (C)
$485.00, $289.00, $189.00 purchase _ #AD - 738
Portrays Vladimir Mayakovsky, a poet destroyed by conflict between artistic integrity and the demands of the Russian Revolution. Examines his influential body of work.
Biography; Foreign Language; History - World; Literature and Drama
Dist - FOTH **Prod** - FOTH

Vladimir Nabokov - LOLITA 29 MIN
Videoreel / VT2
One to One Series
Color
Presents readings from the novel LOLITA by Vladimir Nabokov.
Literature and Drama
Dist - PBS **Prod** - WETATV

VLED devices - process and fabrication 30 MIN
U-matic / VHS
Optoelectronics series; Pt II - Optoelectronic displays
Color (PRO)
Gives brief summary of technology for slice processing and fabrication of visible optoelectronic devices to aid in application of these devices.
Industrial and Technical Education
Dist - TXINLC **Prod** - TXINLC

VLSI Logic Design 39 MIN
U-matic / VHS
Color (PRO)
Uses classroom format to videotape one 1 - hour and one 1 1/2 hour lecture weekly for 13 weeks and 39 cassettes. Covers introduction to VLSI CAD, design hierarchy, design rules, symbolic layout language, design methodologies, logic implementation and design tools.
Industrial and Technical Education; Mathematics
Dist - AMCEE **Prod** - USCCE

VMCJ 15 MIN
16mm
Color
LC 74-706601
Presents the story of a photographic aerial reconnaissance squadron in combat.
Civics and Political Systems; History - United States; Industrial and Technical Education; Sociology
Dist - USNAC **Prod** - USN 1970

VO - ID 7 MIN
16mm
B&W (G) (FRENCH AND ENGLISH)
$25.00 rental
Places side by side two texts, one in French and the other in English, with two cassette soundtracks discussing sexuality on one side and philosophy on the other. Forms bilingual puns between the two visual texts, mocking the seriousness of the Discourse. By Yann Beauvais. Dual screen format requires two projectors.
Fine Arts
Dist - CANCIN

Vocabulary and Word Analogies 120 MIN
U-matic / VHS
SAT Exam Preparation Series
Color
Education; English Language
Dist - KRLSOF **Prod** - KRLSOF 1985

The Vocabulary of Art 29 MIN
Videoreel / VT2
Museum Open House Series
Color
Fine Arts; Sociology
Dist - PBS **Prod** - WGBHTV

Vocabulary road 20 MIN
U-matic / VHS
Efficient reading - instructional tapes series; Tape 3
Color
Focuses on working with vocabulary to read better and understand more.
English Language
Dist - TELSTR **Prod** - TELSTR

Vocabulary Skills Series
Word Wise - Antonyms 12 MIN
Word Wise - Compound Words 10 MIN
Word Wise - Homographs 12 MIN
Word Wise - Homonyms 11 MIN
Word Wise - Prefixes 11 MIN
Word Wise - Root Words 12 MIN
Word Wise - Suffixes 12 MIN
Word Wise - Synonyms 13 MIN
Word Wise - Word Families 9 MIN
Dist - PHENIX

Vocal basics - 1
VHS
Ultimate beginner video series
Color (G)
$9.95 purchase _ #0 - 8972 - 4813 - 9NK
Offers self - paced, step - by - step lessons for vocalists. Allows students to stop and rewind videos as often as necessary for mastering fundamentals and progressing easily at their own pace. Part one of two parts and part of a series of musical instruction.
Fine Arts
Dist - TILIED

Vocal basics - 2
VHS
Ultimate beginner video series
Color (G)
$12.95 purchase _ #0 - 8972 - 4819 - 8NK
Offers self - paced, step - by - step lessons for vocalists. Allows students to stop and rewind videos as often as necessary for mastering fundamentals and progressing easily at their own pace. Part two of two parts and part of a series of musical instruction.
Fine Arts
Dist - TILIED

Vocal cord repair 45 MIN
VHS
Surgical procedures series
Color (C PRO G)
$149.00 purchase, $75.00 rental _ #UW4580
Focuses on Dr Robert Ossof who has done vocal cord repair work with recording artists Larry Gatlin and Wynonna Judd at the Vanderbilt Voice Center, Nashville, Tennessee. Watches as Ossof removes cysts from the vocal cords of Tammy Leigh Heart, a 33 - year - old aspiring country music singer. Reveals that the procedures and tools he uses include video visualization, which enables patients to view their own vocal cords through a scope - camera. Part of a 17 - part series recording surgical procedures in detail, with specialists who explain the ailment, the anatomical function of the part of the body being operated on, how successful surgery might improve the patient's quality of life. Hosted by Dr Donna Willis.
Fine Arts; Health and Safety
Dist - FOTH

Vocal harmony workshop - singing bluegrass and gospel songs 60 MIN
VHS
Color (G)
$29.95 purchase _ #VD - NAS - VC01
Guides singers through arrangements of the Nashville Bluegrass Band, from basic duets through three, four and five - part harmonies. Demonstrates old - time country, bluegrass and gospel songs. Features special guests, The Fairfield Four. Includes the songs My Native Home, Back Tracking, Who's That Knockin', To Be His Child, Prodigal Son, Two Wings, I've Got a Newborn Soul, as well as music and lyrics.
Fine Arts
Dist - HOMETA **Prod -** HOMETA 1994

Vocal Nodules 10 MIN
VHS / U-matic
Children's Medical Series
Color (P I)
Shows that vocal nodules can be confusing to a child because it may seem to be a punishment for shouting or getting angry. Illustrates what vocal nodules actually are and helps children find substitutes for shouting and alternative way of expressing anger.
Health and Safety
Dist - CORF **Prod -** HFDT 1982

Vocal Quality Counts 30 MIN
U-matic / VHS
Your Speaking Image Series
(C A PRO)
$180.00 purchase
Explores the tone quality that is most effective in holding other's attention and how that speech pattern may be achieved even by women with a high, soft voice.
English Language
Dist - AITECH **Prod -** WHATV 1986

Vocal Quality Counts 180 MIN
U-matic / VHS
Speaking Image - When Women Talk Business Series
Color (H C A)
Business and Economics; Education; Psychology; Sociology
Dist - UEUWIS **Prod -** UEUWIS 1984

Vocal Quality Counts 30 MIN
U-matic / VHS
Your Speaking Image - When Women Talk Business Series
Color
English Language; Psychology
Dist - DELTAK **Prod -** WHATV

Vocal style and performance - developing your vocal and performing style 90 MIN
VHS
Color (G)
$39.95 purchase _ #VD - MUL - VC01
Features vocalist Maria Muldaur who gives practical advice and helpful tips for anyone who wants to get up on stage and sing. Illustrates Muldaur's personal vocal warmup exercises on an accompanying audiocassette, plus tips on phrasing, building a song for dramatic impact, the importance of proper breathing and other tricks of the trade.
Fine Arts
Dist - HOMETA **Prod -** HOMETA

The Vocal workout 78 MIN
VHS
Color (H C G A R)
$19.95 purchase, $10.00 rental _ #35 - 84000 - 1518
Teaches techniques for improving both singing and speaking voices. Emphasizes the importance of good posture, breathing and vocal warm - ups. Hosted by Chris and Carole Beatty.
Fine Arts
Dist - APH **Prod -** SPAPRO

The Vocalist's guide to fitness, health and musicianship 105 MIN
VHS
Color (G)
$39.95 purchase _ #VD - JUL - VC01
Features Julie Lyonn Lieberman with special guests Katie Agresta, Jeannie Deva, Maitland Peters and Michael Schwartz. Covers breath support, control and vocal stamina. Discusses the causes of vocal dysfunction, injury, tension, hoarseness, and other problems. Offers relaxation, healing and movement techniques for vocalists from three top vocal experts and a physical fitness trainer.
Fine Arts
Dist - HOMETA **Prod -** HOMETA

Vocalization and Speech in Chimpanzees 12 MIN
16mm
B&W (C A)
Shows typical chimpanzee vocalizations and demonstrates that vocal responses can be conditioned. Portrays in detail the training of a female to whisper 'MAMA,' 'PAPA' and 'CUP.'.
English Language; Psychology
Dist - PSUPCR **Prod -** HAYESS 1950

Vocation 7 MIN
16mm / VHS
Color (G)
$25.00 rental
Voices a short hymn to the horned god Pan, who embodies the creative energies of human male sexuality. Available for purchase in video format with Remembrance for $50.00.
Fine Arts; Sociology
Dist - CANCIN **Prod -** TARTAG 1981

Vocation Training Inventory and Exploration Survey - Voc - Ties -
VHS / Slide / 35mm strip / U-matic
$495.00 purchase _ #PM400
Assesses a student's interest in school based training programs.
Education; Guidance and Counseling
Dist - CAREER **Prod -** CAREER

Vocational and career planning series
Career planning steps
Plans for Success
The Quiz master
Dist - CADESF

Vocational and Career Planning Series
Explores the four major steps of constructing a vocational and career plan which are self discovery, exploration, career preparation, and career participation.
Career planning steps
Plans for Success
Quiz Master
Dist - CAREER **Prod -** CAREER

Vocational and Career Planning Series
Presents a series to aid the viewer in planning and achieving career goals.
Career planning steps 19 MIN
Plans for Success 18 MIN
The Quiz Master
Dist - JISTW

Vocational and Career Planning Video Series
Keys to Job Success 24 MIN
Dist - CADESF
CAMV
CAREER
JISTW

Vocational and Career Planning Video Series
Career planning steps 25 MIN
Plans for Success 25 MIN
The Quiz Master
Dist - CAMV

Vocational Interviewing Series
Getting ready for the interview 30 MIN
Succeeding in the Interview 30 MIN
Dist - CADESF

Vocational Interviewing Series
Getting Ready for the Interview 30 MIN
Dist - CAMV

Vocational interviewing series
Succeeding in your interview 30 MIN
Dist - CAMV
JISTW

Vocational interviewing series
Getting ready for the interview 30 MIN
Dist - JISTW

Vocational interviewing series
Presents a two - part series using examples of individuals interviewing for vocational jobs - printer, auto - body repair, computer repair technician, secretarial. Includes the titles Getting Ready for the Interview and Succeeding in Your Interview, both available separately.
Vocational interviewing series 60 MIN
Dist - NEWCAR

Vocational inventory video 30 MIN
VHS
(J H G)
Provides three critical functions relative to vocational training. Shows students what vocational training is all about, helps determine a student's vocational preferences and promotes the concept of sex equity by showing students in non - traditional roles. Describes 15 common training programs available in most vocational schools. Includes guide, 200 reproducible answer sheets, Exploring Careers book, instructor's guide and workbook.
Business and Economics; Education; Guidance and Counseling
Dist - CAMV
CFKRCM

Vocational Opportunities in High School 14 MIN
U-matic / VHS / 16mm
Color (J H)
LC 73-700795
Offers practical suggestions in the area of vocational education for high school students. Includes a broad sampling of vocational shops and classes and points out the advantages of early exposure to different trades and fields of employment.
Education; Guidance and Counseling; Psychology
Dist - EBEC **Prod -** RUSIRV 1973

Vocational Rehabilitation and the Individual with Head Trauma 51 MIN
VHS / 16mm
Medical Aspects of Disability - Course Lecture Series
Color (PRO)
$50.00, $65.00 purchase _ #8826
Presents one part of a course lecture series on the medical aspects of disability. Discusses vocational rehabilitation of an individual with head trauma.
Guidance and Counseling; Health and Safety; Science - Natural
Dist - RICHGO **Prod -** RICHGO 1988

Vocational Skillfilms - Machine Shop Skills Series
Introduction to Grinding Machines 14 MIN
Introduction to horizontal milling machines 14 MIN
Introduction to the Engine Lathe 14 MIN
Introduction to Vertical Milling Machines
Mounting and Dressing of Grinding Wheels 14 MIN
Taper Turning 14 MIN
Dist - RTBL

Vocational Skillfilms - Woodworking Skills Series
Joining Wood with Nails 14 MIN
Joining Wood with Screws 14 MIN
Measuring, Marking and Sawing Wood 14 MIN
Dist - RTBL

Vocational Time Vs Management Time 20 MIN
U-matic / VHS
Time Management for Managers and Professionals Series
Color
Business and Economics; Psychology
Dist - DELTAK **Prod -** DELTAK

Vocational visions - automobile mechanic 16 MIN
VHS
Color (H A)
$39.95 purchase _ #CCP1110V
Surveys the career possibilities available in automobile mechanics. Covers the skills, employment opportunities, duties, earnings, benefits, and more. Interviews people in the profession.
Industrial and Technical Education; Psychology
Dist - CAMV

Vocational visions career series
Presents a ten - part series which examines the potential of various occupations. Interviews people who have careers in each occupation. Answers questions about the educational requirements and necessary skills for the occupation, as well as its career opportunities, salary range and outlook for the future. Examines the occupations of paralegal, letter carrier, physical therapist, insurance agent, chef, potter, national park ranger, florist, band director, and auto mechanic.
Auto mechanics

Band director
Chef
Florist
Insurance agent
Letter carriers
National park ranger
Paralegal
Physical therapist
Potter
Dist - CADESF **Prod** - CADESF

Vocational visions series
Agricultural cluster 20 MIN
Business - office cluster 30 MIN
Communications cluster 10 MIN
Construction Cluster 15 MIN
Health - Related Cluster 25 MIN
Personal Service Cluster 20 MIN
Repair Cluster 15 MIN
Technical - Manufacturing cluster 1 20 MIN
Technical - Manufacturing cluster 2 25 MIN
Transportation - Mechanical Cluster 20 MIN
Dist - GA

Vocations in Agriculture 15 MIN
16mm / U-matic / VHS
Color (J H)
LC FIA65-1159
Explores opportunities, requirements and rewards of specific careers in agriculture. Emphasizes need for specialized college training.
Agriculture; Guidance and Counseling; Psychology
Dist - JOU **Prod** - JOU 1965

Vogues of 1938 113 MIN
16mm
B&W
Tells the story of the head of a famous fashion house who has two problems - financing his wife's acting ambitions and helping a socialite escape an arranged marriage.
Fine Arts
Dist - TLECUL **Prod** - TLECUL

Voice 20 MIN
16mm
All that I Am Series
B&W (C A)
Fine Arts; Guidance and Counseling
Dist - NWUFLM **Prod** - MPATI

Voice at Work 29 MIN
U-matic
Pike on Language Series
Color
Explains how langauge and behavior work together. Shows how the different regions of sound - producing anatomy are responsible for the quality, tone and pitch of the words we hear.
English Language; Psychology
Dist - UMITV **Prod** - UMITV 1977

The Voice Box 4 MIN
16mm / U-matic / VHS
Most Important Person - Health and Your Body Series
Color (K P I)
Depicts a side show barker's efforts to sell the children a 'WONDROUS' voice box. Follows as Fumble intervenes to explain that everyone already has a voice box and it works better than any that can be purchased.
Guidance and Counseling; Health and Safety; Science - Natural
Dist - EBEC **Prod** - EBEC 1972

A Voice Cries Out 29 MIN
16mm
Legacy Series
B&W (J)
LC 75-707214
Pictures the sculpture and architecture of Florence, Italy. Reviews the history of the Medici family. Exposes the forces which encouraged and undermined the greatness of Florence. Discusses the Pazzi conspiracy and the influence of a Dominican monk, Savanarola.
Fine Arts
Dist - IU **Prod** - NET 1965

A Voice from the Past 30 MIN
VHS / U-matic
Wodehouse Playhouse Series
Color (C A)
Presents an adaptation of the short story A Voice From The Past by P G Wodehouse.
Literature and Drama
Dist - TIMLIF **Prod** - BBCTV 1980

Voice in Exile 29.75 MIN
U-matic / VHS / 16mm
Color (J H C G)
$575, $400, $430 _ #C434
Discusses the struggle to overcome one's legitimate and unfounded fears - fears which inhibit us, often with disastrous results.
Guidance and Counseling; Literature and Drama; Psychology
Dist - BARR **Prod** - BARR 1986

The Voice in the Bells 28 MIN
16mm
Color (P I J)
Presents the 1972 open house day at Washington Cathedral as seen through the eyes of a 12 - year - old boy. Includes views of the cathedral's windows, carvings, tower and bells.
Geography - United States
Dist - NCATHA **Prod** - NCATHA 1972

Voice in the City 28 MIN
16mm
B&W (H C A)
LC 72-703116
Presents a look at district number 37 station, a county and municipal union in New York City.
Civics and Political Systems; Social Science; Sociology
Dist - PFLMAS **Prod** - PFLMAS 1969

A Voice in the Wilderness 28 MIN
U-matic / VHS
Please Stand by - a History of Radio Series
(C A)
Fine Arts; History - United States; Psychology; Sociology
Dist - SCCON **Prod** - SCCON 1986

A Voice in the Wilderness 40 MIN
16mm
B&W (P)
Dramatizes the story of John the Baptist beginning with his birth and his early life in the desert as preparation for his ministry as forerunner to Christ.
Religion and Philosophy
Dist - CAFM **Prod** - CAFM

The Voice of Britannia 53 MIN
U-matic / VHS
Man and Music Series
Color (C)
$279.00, $179.00 purchase _ #AD - 1771
Focuses on Georgian London. Looks at Handel's 'Messiah' and the composers Arne and Boyce. Part of a 22 - part series that sets Western music into the historial and cultural context of its time.
Fine Arts; Geography - World; History - World
Dist - FOTH **Prod** - FOTH

The Voice of Cape Cod 12 MIN
U-matic / VHS
Color (J A)
Portrays turn - of - the - century Massachusetts and the occasion of the first transatlantic wireless radio transmission. Discusses the 'Father of Radio,' Guglielmo Marconi, and traces the development of radio from its beginnings to ship - to - shore and plane - to - ground transmission. Uses archival footage, vintage photos and period music.
History - United States; Industrial and Technical Education; Social Science
Dist - USNAC **Prod** - USNPS 1984

Voice of La Raza 54 MIN
U-matic / VHS / 16mm
Color
LC 73-701126
Presents a documentary report from El Barrios of Spanish speaking America dealing with job and cultural discrimination against Spanish surnamed Americans.
Business and Economics; Sociology
Dist - GREAVW **Prod** - EQEMOP 1970

Voice of the customer - Part 3 13 MIN
VHS
Breakthrough improvement in quality series; Pt 3
Color (PRO IND A)
$495.00 purchase, $175.00 rental _ #GP133C
Presents part three of a five - part series developed by Florida Power and Light's - Qualtec Quality Service. Pictures the principles that make up policy management and gives organizations a resource to help achieve and keep a competitive advantage.
Business and Economics
Dist - EXTR **Prod** - GPERFO

The Voice of the Desert 22 MIN
U-matic / VHS / 16mm
Color (I)
LC FIA66-1506
Pictures the plants and animals of the desert community in Arizona. Joseph Wood Krutch narrates. Adapted from an NBC news production.
Geography - United States; Science - Natural
Dist - MGHT **Prod** - NBCTV 1964

Voice of the Fugitive 28 MIN
16mm / U-matic / VHS
Adventures in History Series
Color (I J H)
Depicts a group of slaves seeking freedom in Canada in 1851. Tells how Henry Bibb's newspaper, The Voice Of The Fugitive, inspired their quest for freedom.
Fine Arts; History - United States; Literature and Drama
Dist - FI **Prod** - NFBC 1978

Voice of the Plains - John G Neihardt 60 MIN
U-matic / VHS
(G)
Examines the life and works of Nebraska author and poet John G Neihardt. Uses biographic material, interviews with family and colleagues, readings from Neihardt's work, and film footage. Features clips from Neihardt's appearance on the Dick Cavett Show.
Literature and Drama
Dist - GPN **Prod** - NETV

Voice of the whale 54 MIN
VHS
Color (G)
$24.95 purchase
Focuses on jazz artist George Crumb.
Fine Arts
Dist - KINOIC **Prod** - RHPSDY

The Voice of those who are not Here 45 MIN
16mm
Color
Introduces several people who have experienced detention and torture at the hands of the special police of nations throughout the world.
Civics and Political Systems
Dist - FLMLIB **Prod** - RASKER 1982

The Voice of youth 28 MIN
U-matic / 16mm / VHS
Color (G)
$250.00, $49.95, $29.95 purchase, $40.00 rental _ #ZPF - 750, #ZVC - 750, #ZHC - 750, #ZRP - 750
Focuses on the young people of Israel growing up on collective farms, in border villages and in the cities. Ranges from the shores of the Sea of Galilee and the Lebanese border to the streets and parks of Jerusalem.
Geography - World; Sociology
Dist - ADL **Prod** - ADL

Voice - the universal instrument 32 MIN
VHS
Color (J H C G)
Starts from the premise that everyone can sing. Follows several students who learn how to develop their singing voices and how to achieve their own styles of communicating through singing. Explores varied approaches to singing - including a performance by Bobby McFarrin, the physical and social benefits of voice training, the voice mechanism and how to protect it, breathing, interpretation, techniques and career opportunities related to singing. Includes teacher's guide.
English Language; Fine Arts; Guidance and Counseling
Dist - CAMV
EAV

A Voice to be Heard 51 MIN
16mm
Color (H C A)
LC 75-702396
Traces the election of members of the National Aboriginal Consultative Committee in Australia. Shows how the committee was formed to give aborigines a more direct voice in the government of Australia.
Civics and Political Systems; Geography - World
Dist - AUIS **Prod** - FLMAUS 1975

Voice workout for the actor 33 MIN
VHS
Color (PRO G)
$99.00 purchase, $39.00 rental _ #615
Provides the actor with a complete voice and body warm - up. Includes full - body relaxation and stretching followed by exercises for pitch and resonance, clarity and dynamic vocal control. Features voice expert Susan Leigh and includes a manual, bone props and vocal health tips. Produced by the Theater Arts Video Library.
English Language; Fine Arts
Dist - FIRLIT

Voice workout for the actor - Volume 1 33 MIN
VHS
Color (G C H)
$129.00 purchase _ #DL253
Combines exercises from yoga and T'ai Chi with some from the Linklater and Skinner systems to provide student actors with a complete vocal and physical warmup. Teaches relaxation and stretching, face preparation, pitch and resonance work, and tongue twisters. With Susan Leigh of the La Jolla Playhouse.
English Language; Fine Arts
Dist - INSIM

Voice workout for the actor - Volume 2 40 MIN
VHS
Color (G C H)
$129.00 purchase _ #DL263
Combines exercises from yoga and T'ai Chi with some from the Linklater and Skinner systems to provide student actors with a complete vocal and physical warmup. Uses physical exercises and visualization techniques to examine the connection between mind, body, and breath. With Susan Leigh of the La Jolla Playhouse.
English Language; Fine Arts
Dist - INSIM

Voice Your Choice 10 MIN
U-matic / VHS
Book, Look and Listen Series
Color (K P)
Points out that some methods of solving social problems are more positive than other methods.
English Language; Literature and Drama
Dist - AITECH **Prod** - MDDE 1977

The Voiceless 30 MIN
U-matic
Medical - Legal Issues Series
(A)
Explores the legal gray areas of minors, the mentally ill and those with disabilities who cannot exercise their right to accept or refuse medical treatment.
Civics and Political Systems; Health and Safety; Sociology
Dist - ACCESS **Prod** - ACCESS 1983

Voices and visions series
Presents a thirteen - part series on the lives and works of modern American poets. Includes Elizabeth Bishop, Hart Crane, Emily Dickinson, T S Eliot, Robert Frost, Langston Hughes, Robert Lowell, Marianne Moore, Sylvia Plath, Ezra Pound, Wallace Stevens, Walt Whitman and William Carlos Williams.
Elizabeth Bishop - Part 1 60 MIN
Emily Dickinson - Part 3 60 MIN
Ezra Pound - Part 10 60 MIN
Langston Hughes - Part 6 60 MIN
Marianne Moore - Part 8 60 MIN
Robert Frost - Part 5 60 MIN
Robert Lowell - Part 7 60 MIN
Sylvia Plath - Part 9 60 MIN
T S Eliot - Part 4 60 MIN
William Carlos Williams - Part 13 60 MIN
Dist - ANNCPB **Prod** - NYCVH 1983

Voices and Visions Series
Hart Crane - Part 2 60 MIN
Wallace Stevens 60 MIN
Walt Whitman 60 MIN
Dist - ANNCPB
PSU

Voices and Visions Series
Elizabeth Bishop 60 MIN
Emily Dickinson 60 MIN
Ezra Pound 60 MIN
Langston Hughes 60 MIN
Marianne Moore 60 MIN
Robert Frost 60 MIN
Robert Lowell 60 MIN
Sylvia Plath 60 MIN
T S Eliot 60 MIN
William Carlos Williams 60 MIN
Dist - PSU

Voices, Faces, Brown 28 MIN
16mm
Color
LC 79-700339
Records the events in a typical academic year at Brown University.
Education
Dist - BROWNU **Prod** - BROWNU 1978

Voices from Gaza 51 MIN
VHS / 16mm
Color (G)
$390.00 purchase
Presents a picture of conditions along the Gaza strip. Tells the story of the Israeli occupation through the eyes of the refugees themselves.
Geography - World; History - World; Social Science; Sociology
Dist - ICARUS

Voices from Sepharad series
Commemorates 500 years of Sephardi culture in exile. Examines Sephardic Jewry from its roots in the Iberian soil that simultaneously supported Jewish, Islamic and Christian cultures. Filmed on location at historic sites in Eastern and Western Europe, North Africa, the Middle East and the Americas, this series documents and celebrates the persistence and flexibility of the Sephardim. Features artists performing secular and sacred music. Looks at the preservation of poetry, music and folklore of 15th - century Spain and new works created within that tradition. Three videotapes; seven chapters at 52 minutes each; and companion book. A Television Espanola production. Written and directed by Solly Wolodarsky. Produced by Jose Luis Gracia.
Voices from Sepharad series 364 MIN
Dist - NCJEWF

Voices from the ice - Alaska 20 MIN
VHS
Color (I J H)
$29.95 purchase _ #49 - 6158 - V
Travels to the rugged Chugach National Forest and Portage Glacier areas which are still dominated by active glaciers, providing a constantly changing atmosphere for plant and animal communities.
Geography - United States; Geography - World
Dist - INSTRU

Voices from within 20 MIN
16mm / U-matic / VHS
Color
Examines the problems of long - term women prisoners at Bedford Hills Correction Facility. Captures the feelings and emotions, loneliness and desperation of the inmates. Discusses the effects of being separated from their families for many years.
Sociology
Dist - CNEMAG **Prod** - PACSFM 1977

Voices in Society Series
How to Talk with Your Teenager about VD 28 MIN
Dist - WSTGLC

Voices in the chora 28 MIN
16mm
Color (G)
$40.00 purchase
Gives voice to desire and fear in the current 'Era of Decimation through AIDS.' Uses images drawn from a Gay Pride procession in Chicago 1991. A Zack Stiglicz production.
Psychology; Sociology
Dist - CANCIN

Voices in the dark 156 MIN
VHS
Color; PAL (G)
PdS40 purchase
Presents six 26 - minute programs about the two million British children who are growing up with parents who are divorced or separated. Explores the experience of divorce through the eyes of a child who is witnessing her parents' conflicts. Reveals that the marriage of Jean and David is disintegrating and Carol, their 13 - year - old daughter, is caught in the crossfire. When David finally decides to move out, both parents are too preoccupied with their own conflicts to offer Carol any explanation or support. She has to handle the emotional stress alone. Contact distributor about availability outside the United Kingdom.
Sociology
Dist - ACADEM

Voices in the Park 30 MIN
U-matic
Read all about it - One Series
Color (I)
Teaches reading and writing skills as it continues a story in which Chris's friend Lynn interviews a company of actors and Mr Walker tells about a mysterious house fire decades ago.
Education; English Language; Literature and Drama
Dist - TVOTAR **Prod** - TVOTAR 1982

Voices in verses 15 MIN
U-matic / VHS
Return to the magic library series
Color (P I)
#362409; LC 91-706860
Features a poetry book that comes to life and shows the puppet characters how exciting poetry can be. Part of a series using puppet mice and live storytellers to encourages students to read the featured story and respond with questions and comments. Includes teacher's guide and five readers.
Literature and Drama; Social Science
Dist - TVOTAR **Prod** - TVOTAR 1990

Voices of a Union 20 MIN
16mm
Color (A)
Presents the profile of a union showing the many kinds of work union members do and the role unions play in grievance procedures, bargaining and education.
Business and Economics; Psychology
Dist - AFLCIO **Prod** - BCTWIU 1982

Voices of Blue and Grey - the Civil War
VHS / U-matic
Color (H)
Depicts the Civil War era, its people, issues, battles and regional feelings.
History - United States
Dist - GA **Prod** - GA

Voices of dance series
Alexandra Danilova and Frederic Franklin 30 MIN
Change of Attitudes within the Ballet Community from the 1930's 30 MIN
Influences of Bauhaus and Russian Constructivism on Dance 30 MIN
Interpreting Choreographers from the 50's and 60's 30 MIN
Dist - ARCVID

Voices of Israel 18 MIN
16mm
Color
LC 80-701440
Uses three generations of a family to explore Israel's past, present and future, emphasizing the nation's economic needs. Examines the cost of peace as well as the cost of settling new immigrants and establishing programs to meet the needs of the disadvantaged, aged and handicapped.
Geography - World; History - World
Dist - VISION **Prod** - UJA 1979

Voices of Latin America 60 MIN
VHS
Smithsonian World Series
Color (G)
$49.95 purchase _ #SMIW - 302
Profiles five Latin American authors, including Jose Marti and Jorge Luis Borges. Suggests that their writings tell much about Latin America and its cultures.
History - World; Literature and Drama
Dist - PBS **Prod** - WETATV

Voices of Leningrad 59 MIN
VHS / U-matic / 16mm / BETA
Color (G)
$400.00, $90.00 purchase _ #C50693, #C51460
Focuses on Leningrad during the changes sweeping the Soviet Union. Meets a young ballerina, a rock guitarist, factory workers and 'citizen diplomats'.
Geography - World; Sociology
Dist - NGS **Prod** - NGS 1990

Voices of lupus 28 MIN
VHS
Color (G)
$149.00 purchase, $75.00 rental _ #UW3361
Shows how women with lupus can help themselves through peer group support and better communication with their physicians and families. Interviews patients and physicians to demonstrate strategies for helping people with lupus and their families as theycope with the unpredictable illness.
Health and Safety; Sociology
Dist - FOTH

Voices of memory 60 MIN
VHS
Moyers - The Power of the word series
Color; Captioned (G)
$59.95 purchase _ #MOPW - 104
Interviews poets Gerald Stern and Li - Young Lee. Features their work in readings at Glassboro State College in New Jersey. Presents Stern and Lee's observations on how their poetry has been influenced by their respective Jewish and Chinese heritages. Hosted by Bill Moyers.
English Language; Literature and Drama
Dist - PBS

Voices of power 47 MIN
U-matic / VHS
Color (H C G)
$170.00 purchase, $35.00 rental _ #CC3516VU, #CC3516VH
Examines the process of recovery from the crime of rape. Presents the stories of several assault victims and dramatizes a support group setting of four victims, two counselors and their interactions. Produced by Nancy Brooks and Chris Lamar.
Psychology; Sociology
Dist - IU

Voices of the 30s
CD-ROM
Color (J H C G)
$129.00 purchase _ #6511 - HH
Links and indexes the images, sounds and texts of the 1930s in the United States. Includes over 300 classroom activities on topics such as land use, government programs and the role that the arts played in shaping society. Includes quick reference card and teacher's guide. Designed by Patricia Hanlon, Robert Campbel and Abbe Don. Macintosh.
History - United States
Dist - SUNCOM

The Voices of the Cave 12 MIN
U-matic / VHS / 16mm

Color (J A)
Presents the history of Mammoth Cave in Kentucky from exploration by Indians of the Adena culture more than 4,000 years ago to its use as a mine, a hospital for tubercular patients and an underground church. Includes dramatic re - creations.
Geography - United States; History - United States
Dist - USNAC **Prod** - USNPS 1984

Voices of the land 21 MIN
VHS
Color (J H C G)
$195.00 purchase, $40.00 rental
Discusses the spiritual connection to land and to nature. Interviews a Southern Ute elder in Colorado, native Hawaiians protesting geothermal energy development in the rainforest home of the goddess Pele, and Dave Foreman, co - founder of Earth First. Produced by Christopher McLeod.
Fine Arts; Science - Natural; Social Science
Dist - BULFRG

Voices of the morning 15 MIN
VHS
Color; B&W (G)
$125.00 purchase, $50.00 rental
Uses layered images and text to examine familial and societal restrictions placed on South Asian women. Meditates on women's roles as defined by orthodox Islamic laws. Directed by Meena Nanji.
Religion and Philosophy; Sociology
Dist - CROCUR

Voices of the New Age 60 MIN
BETA
Color (G)
LC 89716216
Informs and educates about change.
Fine Arts; Religion and Philosophy
Dist - AIMS **Prod** - HP 1989

Voices of the Voiceless 58 MIN
U-matic / VT3 / VHS
(G)
$125.00 purchase, $50.00 rental
Portrays the struggles of the half a million El Salvadoran refugees who were forced to flee their homeland to live in the United States. Chronicles the U S - supported war that has resulted in the death of over 44,000 Salvadorans.
Geography - World; Sociology
Dist - EFVP **Prod** - EFVP 1987

Voices on the River 22 MIN
16mm
Color
LC 78-700331
Documents the history of the Minnesota River and highlights the town of St Peter, through authentic graphics, commentary and music, and interviews with two elderly local residents.
Geography - United States; History - United States
Dist - MASONG **Prod** - MASONG 1976

Voices on the road back - a program about drugs 15 MIN
U-matic / VHS
Color (J H)
$250.00 purchase _ #JC - 67283
Interviews teenagers who began using drugs at an early age. Shows the effects that addiction can have on family life, school, self - confidence and physical well - being. Emphasizes the importance of making the right decisions and choosing the right values at an early age. Stresses that addicts do not belong to any particular race, social status, neighborhood or sex.
Guidance and Counseling; Health and Safety; Psychology; Sociology
Dist - CORF **Prod** - DISNEY 1990

Voices that count 20 MIN
VHS / 16mm
Color (G IND)
$5.00 rental
Explains the basics of what unions do. Features workers such as actor Jack Lemmon and employers who talk about the advantages of a union workplace.
Business and Economics; Social Science
Dist - AFLCIO **Prod** - UMINN 1989

Voici Des Fruits 18 MIN
16mm
En Francais, set 1 series
Color (J A)
Foreign Language
Dist - CHLTN **Prod** - PEREN 1969

Voiding Dysfunction and Urinary Tract Infection 15 MIN
16mm
Color
LC 75-702286
Presents actual cinefluoroscopic studies and pressure measurements obtained from patients with persistent urinary tract infection or with distal urethral stenosis. Defines the aberrations in voiding mechanisms. Describes spasm of the striated external sphincter as a functionally obstructive mechanism which can initiate or perpetuate the infection.
Health and Safety; Science; Science - Natural
Dist - EATONL **Prod** - EATONL 1970

Voigt fitness series
Presents a five - part exercise series which features Karen Voigt as instructor. Includes Great Weighted Workout, Power Packed Workout, Firm Arms and Abs, Lean Legs and Buns, and Pure and Simple Stretch.

Firm arms and abs	40 MIN
Great weighted workout	85 MIN
Lean legs and buns	45 MIN
Power packed workout	60 MIN
Pure and simple stretch	35 MIN

Dist - CAMV

Voila Gilbert, le voila 13 MIN
16mm
Les Francais chez vous series
B&W (I J H)
Foreign Language
Dist - CHLTN **Prod** - PEREN 1967

Voix Et Images De France Series

Au jardin public	8 MIN
Images De La Campagne	8 MIN
Images Du Travail	6 MIN
Je Marchais	11 MIN
La Petite Ferme	12 MIN
Le Marche	11 MIN
Le Telephone	6 MIN
Partons En Vacances	6 MIN
A Travers Paris	12 MIN
Un Homme Tranquille	7 MIN

Dist - CHLTN

Volatiles 10 MIN
16mm / U-matic / VHS
Drug Information Series
Color
Discusses the characteristics of volatiles. Identifies the signs of use and abuse, the pharmacological and behavioral effects, and the short - and long - term dangers.
Health and Safety
Dist - CORF **Prod** - MITCHG 1982

Volcanic Eruptions of Hawaii 5 MIN
16mm
Color (G)
Shows eruptions of the Hawaiian volcanos Kilauea, Kapoho and Mauna Kea.
Geography - United States; Geography - World; History - United States
Dist - CINEPC **Prod** - TAHARA 1987

Volcanic Eruptions, Pt 1 27 MIN
16mm
B&W (C A)
Outlines means by which volcanoes are classified and illustrates volcanoes through film clips, stills and diagrams.
Science - Physical
Dist - UTEX **Prod** - UTEX 1960

Volcanic Eruptions, Pt 2 26 MIN
16mm
B&W (C A)
Illustrates the volcanian type of eruption as characterized by Paricutin and Vesuvius. Pictures the Peleean Volcano typified by Me Pelee and the lava dome of Sitkin Island. Summarizes various other kinds of volcanic eruptions.
Science - Physical
Dist - UTEX **Prod** - UTEX 1960

Volcanic Landscapes, Pt 1 29 MIN
16mm
Color
LC 74-702801
Presents an examination of volcanic processes and landforms using examples from the rich landscapes of the Pacific Northwest. Suggests a source for magma and follows it to the surfaces. Studies lava flows and introduces the effect of gas - charged magma on an eruption. Views the many products and landforms produced by violent Vulcanism.
Geography - World; Science - Physical
Dist - MMP **Prod** - MMP 1973

Volcanic Landscapes, Pt 2 29 MIN
16mm
Color (J)
LC 74-702802
Uses views of the volcanic landscapes of the Pacific Northwest in order to study special types of volcanic activity and landforms and to relate volcanism to such things as groundwater and hydrothermal activity. Shows the inevitable end of volcanoes through destruction by weathering and erosion.
Geography - United States; Geography - World; Science - Physical
Dist - MMP **Prod** - MMP 1974

Volcanic Processes and Deposits 51 MIN
VHS / U-matic
Basic and Petroleum Geology for Non - Geologists - Earth's Interior '- - Series; Earth's interior
Color (IND)
Industrial and Technical Education; Science - Physical
Dist - GPCV **Prod** - PHILLP

Volcano 58 MIN
U-matic / VHS
Nova Series
Color (H C A)
$250 purchase _ #5263C
Shows scientific research to invent a technique that will help predict when and how explosively a volcano will erupt. Produced by WGBH Boston.
Science - Physical
Dist - CORF

Volcano
VHS / 35mm strip
ALA Notable Children's Filmstrips Series
Color (K)
$35.00 purchase
Presents a children's story. Part of the American Library Association series.
English Language; Literature and Drama
Dist - PELLER

Volcano 29 MIN
U-matic / VHS
Color (C)
$249.00, $149.00 purchase _ #AD - 957
Shows a volcanic eruption in progress. Illustrates the force, heat and apparent unpredictability of lava flow, fire, windstorm and destruction.
Geography - World; History - United States; History - World; Science - Physical
Dist - FOTH **Prod** - FOTH

Volcano 29 MIN
Videoreel / VT2
Color
Shows Volcano, West Virginia in 1875 when it was reaping the benefits of the Alleghenies oil boom and possessed its own railroad line, department store and opera house. Explains that the Volcano of today is three oil tanks and a wooden shed on a dirt road.
Geography - United States; History - United States; Sociology
Dist - PBS **Prod** - WWVUTV

Volcano 59 MIN
BETA / VHS
Color (G)
$24.20 purchase _ #C51411
Geography - World; Science - Physical
Dist - NGS **Prod** - NGS

Volcano Hazards in the U S 30 MIN
VHS / U-matic
Color
Science - Physical
Dist - SYLWAT **Prod** - RCOMTV 1982

Volcano in the Azores 8 MIN
16mm
Color (J)
Pictures the 1957 eruption on Fayal Island. Uses animation to explain gases, viscous lava and eruption.
Science - Physical
Dist - WSUM **Prod** - WSUM 1962

Volcano Surtsey 26 MIN
16mm
Color
Shows the cycle of a volcanic eruption near Iceland on November 14, 1963. Discusses the formation of a shield volcano.
Geography - World; Science - Physical
Dist - GIS **Prod** - NSN 1965

Volcano - the Birth of a Mountain 24 MIN
16mm / U-matic / VHS
Color (J) (SPANISH)
A Spanish language version of the film and videorecording Volcano - The Birth Of A Mountain.
Foreign Language; Geography - United States; Science - Physical
Dist - EBEC **Prod** - EBEC 1977

Volcano - the eruption of Mt St Helens
VHS
Color (J H C G)
$29.98 purchase _ #MH1719V
Covers the tragedies, the heroics and the survivors of the eruption of Mt St Helens.
Geography - World; History - United States
Dist - CAMV

Volcano watchers 50 MIN
VHS
Natural world series
Color; PAL (H C A)
PdS99 purchase; Not available in the United States
Documents the work of Maurice and Katia Krafft, who travel around the world to film erupting volcanos. Includes footage of the Hawaiian eruption in 1984.
Science - Physical
Dist - BBCENE

Volcanoes 15 MIN
VHS
Color (J)
$125.00 purchase _ #5221V
Studies basaltic and andesitic volcanism. Contrasts eruption scenes of Hawaiian volcanoes with their massive flows of dark, viscous lava to the explosive nature of Mt St Helens and its ash clouds derived from water - rich magma. Explains hot spot and subduction zone volcanism and their relationships to broader tectonic theory.
Geography - World; Science - Physical
Dist - SCTRES **Prod** - SCTRES

Volcanoes 10 MIN
U-matic / VHS / 16mm
Earth Series
Color (J H)
$255, $180 purchase _ #3020
Shows how volcanic eruptions affect the earth's crust.
Science - Natural; Science - Physical
Dist - CORF

Volcanoes 28 MIN
U-matic / VHS
Earth Explored Series
Color
Explores Mount St Helens, Surtsey and Heimay, which provide an explosive backdrop for the examination of igneous activities and the creation of landforms.
Geography - World; Science - Physical
Dist - PBS **Prod** - BBCTV

Volcanoes 21 MIN
VHS
Color (J H C)
$39.95 purchase _ #IV124
Investigates the mechanisms of a volcano, types of volcanoes and why and how they erupt. Uses animation to explain what is taking place underground and introduces the student to volcanic terms such as magma, batholith, sills, dikes, cinder cones, composite cones, shield volcanoes and pahoehoe lavas.
Geography - World
Dist - INSTRU

Volcanoes 30 MIN
VHS / U-matic
Earth, Sea and Sky Series
Color (C)
Demonstrates the main types of volcanoes. Explores the possibility of production and avoidance of volcanic eruptions.
Science - Physical
Dist - DALCCD **Prod** - DALCCD

Volcanoes, Earthquakes and Other Earth Movements 17 MIN
16mm / U-matic / VHS
Natural Phenomena Series
Color (J)
LC 81-700631
Studies the phenomenon of plate tectonics, showing how this science can help in predicting future disasters.
History - World; Science - Physical
Dist - JOU **Prod** - JOU 1981

Volcanoes - Exploring the Restless Earth 18 MIN
16mm / U-matic / VHS
Earth Science Program Series
Color (J)
LC 73-703116
Presents scenes of the volcanic activity that formed two new islands off the coast of Iceland in the 1960s. Examines three other volcanoes and views a fourth volcano which document the destructive power of the volcanic process.
Geography - World; Science - Physical
Dist - EBEC **Prod** - EBEC 1973

The Volcanoes of Hawaii 30 MIN
VHS
Color (J H C)
$19.95 purchase _ #VH101
Shows the many moods of Mauna Loa and Kilauea volcanoes of Hawaii. Includes footage from three separate eruptions from 1979 to 1989.
Geography - United States; Geography - World
Dist - INSTRU

Volcanoes of the Kenya Rift 28 MIN
VHS / U-matic
Plate Tectonics Series
Color (H C)
$250 purchase
Discusses volcanic activity in the Kenya Rift Valley of Africa. Explains how these geologic features coincide with the rift valley system. A BBC Television production for the Open University.
Science - Physical
Dist - CORF

Volcanoes of the United States 20 MIN
VHS
Color (J)
$56.50 purchase _ #ES 8130
Visits regions of the US where volcanic activity has been most concentrated. Includes footage of Kilauea and Mauna Loa in Hawaii, Mt St Helens and Mt Shasta in Washington and California, Mt Mazama and Katmai in Alaska.
Geography - United States; Geography - World; Science; Science - Physical
Dist - SCTRES **Prod** - SCTRES

Volcanoes of the United States 20 MIN
VHS
Basic concepts in physical geology video series
Color (J H)
$53.95 purchase _ #193 Y 0187
Visits regions of the United States where volcanic activity has been most concentrated. Examines the mechanisms behind volcanic processes and the different types of eruptions. Includes scenes from Kilauea and Mauna Loa in Hawaii, Mt St Helen's in Washington, Mt Shasta in California and Mt Mazama and Mt Katmai in Alaska. Part of a ten - part series on physical geology.
Geography - World; Science - Physical
Dist - WARDS **Prod** - WARDS 1990

Volcanoes - Our restless Earth 45 MIN
VHS
Color (J H C)
$69.95 purchase _ #IV - 123
Answers the question, what is a volcano. Looks at different types of volcanoes - cinder cone, composite, shield and lava domes - and other volcanic features - plugs, necks, maars and cryptovolcanic structures. Examines types of volcanic eruption, submarine volcanoes, geysers, fumeroles and hot springs, where volcanoes can be found, the plate - tectonic theory, extra - terrestrial volcanoes, volcano monitoring and research and how volcanoes affect people.
Geography - World
Dist - INSTRU

Volcanoes - understanding the hazards 20 MIN
VHS
Color (J H)
$64.95 purchase _ #GW - 5124 - VS
Examines the processes that lead to one of nature's most terrifying phenomena - the eruption of volcanoes. Uses recent live footage to illustrate the hazards that volcanoes pose to humans who may live nearby.
Geography - World; History - World
Dist - HRMC **Prod** - SCTRES

Volcanoes - understanding the hazards 20 MIN
Videodisc / VHS
Earth sciences video library series
Color (J H)
$99.95, $69.95 purchase _ #ES8530; $99.95, $69.95 purchase _ #Q18532
Shows the most recent examples of Earth's most dramatic agents of geologic change. Part of a series which takes a contemporary look at Planet Earth, its natural resources and the human impact on the global environment.
Geography - World; Science - Physical
Dist - INSTRU
CF

Volcanoes - Vulcan's Forge 18 MIN
U-matic / VHS
Natural Science Specials Series Module Blue
Color (I)
Explores the development of volcanic eruptions, shows island chains formed by volcanic activity and demonstrates uses for volcanic materials.
Geography - World; Science - Physical
Dist - AITECH **Prod** - COPFC 1973

The Volga 59 MIN
U-matic / VHS / 16mm
Color
Travels along the Volga River, showing the sights of interest and visiting with the people who populate its shores. Includes visits to Lenin's birthplace, a state farm and a caviar processing plant.
Geography - World
Dist - NGS **Prod** - NGS 1977

The Volga 54 MIN
U-matic / VHS / 16mm
Color (J)
LC 81-706935
Presents the heartland of the Soviet Union and visits the villages and cities along the banks of the Volga River. Discusses economic, social and political aspects of the country and explains the Soviet system.
Business and Economics; Civics and Political Systems; Geography - World
Dist - CRMP **Prod** - CBSTV 1981

Volga, the, Pt 1 27 MIN
16mm / U-matic / VHS
Color (J)
LC 81-706935
Presents the heartland of the Soviet Union and visits the villages and cities along the banks of the Volga River. Discusses economic, social and political aspects of the country and explains the Soviet system.
Geography - World
Dist - CRMP **Prod** - CBSTV 1981
MGHT

Volga, the, Pt 2 27 MIN
U-matic / VHS / 16mm
Color (J)
LC 81-706935
Presents the heartland of the Soviet Union and visits the villages and cities along the banks of the Volga River. Discusses economic, social and political aspects of the country and explains the Soviet system.
Geography - World
Dist - CRMP **Prod** - CBSTV 1981
MGHT

Volksfeste 4 MIN
16mm
Beginning German Films (German Series
Color
Foreign Language
Dist - CCNY **Prod** - MGHT

Volkswagen Beetle 25 MIN
VHS
Design classics 1 series
Color (A)
PdS65 purchase _ Available world wide
Uses archive film, period commercials, and interviews with key figures to examine the contribution to design made by some of the most successful products marketed in the 20th century. Part of a six-part series.
Business and Economics; Fine Arts
Dist - BBCENE

The Volley
VHS
NCAA instructional video series
Color (H C A)
$39.95 purchase _ #KAR2302V
Presents the second of a four - part series on tennis. Focuses on the volley.
Physical Education and Recreation
Dist - CAMV **Prod** - NCAAF

The Volley 29 MIN
VHS / U-matic
Vic Braden's Tennis for the Future Series
Color
Physical Education and Recreation
Dist - PBS **Prod** - WGBHTV 1981

The Volley 30 MIN
VHS
Tennis talk series
Color (J H A)
$24.95 purchase _ #PRO009V
Features tennis instructor Dennis Van der Meer teaching about volleying.
Physical Education and Recreation
Dist - CAMV

Volleyball - a Sport Come of Age 23 MIN
U-matic / VHS / 16mm
Color (H C A) (SPANISH)
LC 76-700963
Explains the origins of volleyball and why it has become so popular.
Physical Education and Recreation
Dist - AIMS **Prod** - LEWSBS 1975

Volleyball - Dig it 13 MIN
U-matic / VHS / 16mm
Color (J H C)
LC 75-700206
Features Kathy Gregory, volleyball expert, who discusses the skills of playing volleyball as demonstrated by a number of outstanding women players. Illustrates techniques for skillful serving, the underhand pass, recovery from the net, the set up and the spike.
Physical Education and Recreation
Dist - PHENIX **Prod** - PHENIX 1975

Volleyball Fundamentals 17 MIN
U-matic / VHS / 16mm
Color (I J)
LC 80-700447
Introduces the rules and techniques of volleyball. Includes court - positioning strategies.
Physical Education and Recreation
Dist - AIMS **Prod** - ASSOCF 1979

Volleyball - Skills and Practice 12 MIN
U-matic / VHS / 16mm
Color; B&W (I J H) (SPANISH)
LC FIA67-1426
Uses normal and slow motion to show six specific volleyball skills and to explain the proper techniques to perfect each skill.
Physical Education and Recreation
Dist - PHENIX **Prod** - FA 1967

Volleyball - the Winning Points 17 MIN
16mm
National Federation Sports Films Series
Color
LC 79-701268
Explains the rules and correct officiating procedures as written by the National Federation Volleyball Rules Committee. Demonstrates such points as pre - match responsibilities of officials, player alignment, and illegal spikes.
Physical Education and Recreation
Dist - NFSHSA **Prod** - NFSHSA 1979

Volleyball, the Winning Points 17 MIN
U-matic / VHS
Color
LC 79-707713
Designed to provide an understanding of the rules and officiating procedures used in volleyball by focusing on such topics as play alignment, legal and illegal hits and illegal spikes.
Physical Education and Recreation
Dist - NFSHSA **Prod** - NFSHSA 1978

Volt Ohmmeter Operation 12 MIN
16mm / U-matic / VHS
Radio Technician Training Series
B&W
Shows how to operate a volt ohmmeter in order to measure ohms and volts. Issued in 1944 as a motion picture.
Industrial and Technical Education
Dist - USNAC **Prod** - USN 1978

Volta Lake 9 MIN
16mm
Color
LC 74-701047
Describes and shows the effects caused by Lake Volta, a large manmade body of water, on the food production of the country of Ghana.
Geography - World; Social Science
Dist - EDC **Prod** - EDC 1973

Voltage 15 MIN
U-matic / VHS
Introductory Concepts in Physics - Magnetism and Electricity Series
Color (C)
$229.00, $129.00 purchase _ #AD - 1185
Explores the relationship between electric current and voltage through experiments which measure electric current sent at different voltages through nichrome wire with a fixed resistance and plotting the results on a graph.
Science - Physical
Dist - FOTH **Prod** - FOTH

Voltage control equipment
VHS / U-matic
Distribution system operation series; Topic 9
Color (IND)
Focuses on voltage control. Demonstrates why voltage variations occur and what corrective action can be taken. Includes standards, voltage profile and regulation, network boosters and transformer traps.
Industrial and Technical Education
Dist - LEIKID **Prod** - LEIKID

Voltage, current and resistance 30 MIN
VHS / U-matic
Basic electricity and D C circuits series
Color
Analyzes voltage, current and resistance. Explains schematic diagrams. Covers resistance of a conductor, resistor color codes and voltage ratings.
Industrial and Technical Education; Science - Physical; Social Science
Dist - TXINLC **Prod** - TXINLC

Voltage Dividers 21 MIN
16mm
B&W
LC 74-705926
Explains and demonstrates how voltages are developed at the taps with respect to ground. Explains ground both as a reference point and current path. (Kinescope).
Industrial and Technical Education; Science - Physical
Dist - USNAC **Prod** - USAF

Voltage dividers and power 30 MIN
U-matic / VHS
Basic electricity and D C circuits series
Color
Provides additional analysis involving Ohm's Law and circuit reduction techniques. Describes basic concepts for designing voltage divider circuits with plus or minus outputs. Expands basic formulas for calculating power distribution in circuits involving voltage dividers.
Industrial and Technical Education; Science - Physical; Social Science
Dist - TXINLC **Prod** - TXINLC

Voltage dividers with parallel branch circuits 15 MIN
VHS / U-matic
Basic electricity and D C circuits - laboratory series
Color
Industrial and Technical Education; Science - Physical; Social Science
Dist - TXINLC **Prod** - TXINLC

Voltage Doubler 30 MIN
16mm
B&W
LC 74-705927
Develops, through analogy and demonstration, the theory of a voltage doubler circuit. Traces the charge and discharge paths for the capacitors, computes peak output voltage and ripple frequency and relates malfunctions in a voltage doubler circuit to the symptoms. (Kinescope).
Industrial and Technical Education; Science - Physical
Dist - USNAC **Prod** - USAF

Voltage Doublers - Transistorized 20 MIN
16mm
B&W
LC 75-703703
Illustrates the principles of voltage doubler circuits, discusses troubleshooting procedures and shows the functions of capacitors.
Industrial and Technical Education
Dist - USNAC **Prod** - USAF 1967

Voltage, energy and force - the electric battery - Parts 31 and 32 60 MIN
VHS / U-matic
Mechanical universe...and beyond - Part II series
Color (G)
$45.00, $29.95 purchase
Looks at the nature of electricity - when it is dangerous or benign, spectacular or useful - in Part 31. Portrays Alessandro Volta who invented the electric battery using the internal properties of different metals in Part 32. Parts of a 52 - part series on the mechanics of the universe.
Science; Science - Physical
Dist - ANNCPB **Prod** - SCCON 1985

Voltage - no 2 60 MIN
U-matic
AC/DC Electronics Series
Color (PRO)
One of a series of electronic and electrical training sessions for electronics workers on direct and alternating current and how to work with each.
Industrial and Technical Education
Dist - VTRI **Prod** - VTRI 1986

Voltage Regulator Applications 30 MIN
U-matic / VHS
Linear and Interface Circuits, Part II - Interface Integrated 'Circuits Series
Color (PRO)
Defines range of application of integrated circuit regulators to various voltage and current conditions. Defines and demonstrates coefficients contributing to output voltage change.
Industrial and Technical Education
Dist - TXINLC **Prod** - TXINLC

Voltage Regulators 15 MIN
16mm
B&W
LC 74-705928
Discusses the operation, use, representation and characteristic curve of zener diodes. Shows the schematic of a circuit with a zener diode and discusses its operation or function in the circuit. (Kinescope).
Industrial and Technical Education; Science - Physical
Dist - USNAC **Prod** - USAF

Voltage Regulators - Solid State 22 MIN
16mm
B&W
LC 75-703705
Describes the principles of transistorized electronic voltage regulators. Uses schematics to show how current is controlled. Discusses differences between breakdown and zener diodes and illustrates their functions.
Industrial and Technical Education
Dist - USNAC **Prod** - USAF 1967

Voltaic Cell, Dry Cell and Storage Battery 18 MIN
16mm / U-matic / VHS
Color
Explains the principles of a voltaic cell, a dry cell and a storage battery.
Industrial and Technical Education; Science - Physical
Dist - USNAC **Prod** - USA

Voltaire - Candide 112 MIN
U-matic / VHS
Color (C) (FRENCH)
$399.00, $249.00 purchase _ #AD - 1488
Presents 'Candide' by Voltaire in French.
Foreign Language; History - World; Literature and Drama; Sociology
Dist - FOTH **Prod** - FOTH

Volterra's Fishes 37 MIN
U-matic / VHS
Nonlinear Vibrations Series
B&W
Mathematics
Dist - MIOT **Prod** - MIOT

The Voltmeter and its use 15 MIN
VHS / U-matic
Basic electricity and D C circuits - laboratory series
Color
Industrial and Technical Education; Science - Physical; Social Science
Dist - TXINLC **Prod** - TXINLC

Volume 15 MIN
U-matic
Mathways series
Color (I J)
LC 80-706452
Uses special visuals in explaining how to measure the volume of a prism, a cylinder and a cone.
Mathematics
Dist - AITECH **Prod** - STSU 1979

Volume 15 MIN
U-matic
Math makers two series
Color (I)
Presents the math concepts of the relationship of volume to area, using cubes to find volume and a formula for the volume of a rectangular prism.
Education; Mathematics
Dist - TVOTAR **Prod** - TVOTAR 1980

Volume 27 MIN
U-matic / VHS
Metric education video tapes for pre and inservice teachers (K - 8) series
Color
Defines volume and capacity. Compares the metric system of measuring volume to the customary system. Discusses why the litre is used for measuring volume.
Mathematics
Dist - PUAVC **Prod** - PUAVC

Volume 1
VHS
Mastering jujutsu series
Color (G)
$49.95 purchase _ #PNT007
Presents the first of a 3 - part jujutsu series taught by 8th Dan Master Shizuya Sato. Demonstrates fundamentals such as breakfalls, stances, strikes, throwing and joint locks.
Physical Education and Recreation; Psychology
Dist - SIV

Volume 2
VHS
Mastering jujutsu series
Color (G)
$49.95 purchase _ #PNT008
Presents the second of a 3 - part jujutsu series taught by 8th Dan Master Shizuya Sato. Demonstrates advanced techniques including choke holds, advanced throwing and defenses against gun and knife attacks.
Physical Education and Recreation; Psychology
Dist - SIV

Volume 3
VHS
Mastering jujutsu series
Color (G)

$49.95 purchase _ #PNT009
Presents the third of a 3 - part jujutsu series taught by 8th Dan Master Shizuya Sato. Demonstrates highly advanced throws, joint locks, chokes, more knife and gun skills, seated self - defense and more.
Physical Education and Recreation; Psychology
Dist - SIV

Volume and vensity 5 MIN
U-matic
Eureka series
Color (J)
Explains that volume refers to the amount of space an object envelops and that density refers to the amount of mass that is compacted into a given volume.
Science; Science - Physical
Dist - TVOTAR **Prod** - TVOTAR 1980

Volume by shells 9 MIN
16mm
MAA calculus series
Color (H C)
LC FIA67-679
Expresses the volume of a solid of revolution as a definite integral using the method of cylindrical shells. An animated film narrated by George Leger.
Mathematics
Dist - MLA **Prod** - MAA 1966

Volume (discs, washers)
U-matic
Calculus series
Color
Mathematics
Dist - MDCPB **Prod** - MDDE

Volume I 15 MIN
VHS / U-matic
Math matters series
Color (I J)
Uses a detective format in a story centering around the investigation of a construction company, where the basics of volume must be learned in order to compute cubic yards of dirt and cubic yards of concrete.
Mathematics
Dist - AITECH **Prod** - KRLNTV 1975

Volume I - Fitness for Sport, Strength Training, Coaching Young Athletes 50 MIN
U-matic / VHS
Athletics - Track & Field - Series
Color (J H C A)
Features Britain's top athletes demonstrating the basics of athletic education.
Physical Education and Recreation
Dist - TRACKN **Prod** - TRACKN 1985

Volume II 15 MIN
U-matic / VHS
Math matters series
Color (I J)
Presents characters computing the volume of cylinders, pyramids and cones.
Mathematics
Dist - AITECH **Prod** - KRLNTV 1975

Volume II - Sprints, Relays, Hurdles, Middle Distances 50 MIN
U-matic / VHS
Athletics - Track & Field - Series
Color (J H C A)
Features Britain's top athletes demonstrating the basics of sprints, relays, hurdles, and middle distances.
Physical Education and Recreation
Dist - TRACKN **Prod** - TRACKN 1985

Volume III - Long Jump, Triple Jump, High Jump, Javelin 50 MIN
VHS / U-matic
Athletics - Track & Field - Series
Color (J H C A)
Features Britain's top athletes demonstrating the basics of long jump, triple hump, high hump, and javelin events.
Physical Education and Recreation
Dist - TRACKN **Prod** - TRACKN 1985

Volume IV - Shot Put, Pole Vault, Hammer, Discus 50 MIN
VHS / U-matic
Athletics - Track & Field - Series
Color (J H C A)
Features Britain's top athletes demonstrating the basics of shot put, pole vault, hammer, and discus events.
Physical Education and Recreation
Dist - TRACKN **Prod** - TRACKN 1985

Volume (known cross - section)
U-matic
Calculus series
Color
Mathematics
Dist - MDCPB **Prod** - MDDE

Volume of a solid of revolution 8 MIN
16mm
MAA calculus series
Color (H C)
LC FIA66-674
Presents the disc method for expressing the volume of a solid of revolution as a definite integral. An animated film narrated by George Leger.
Mathematics
Dist - MLA **Prod** - MAA 1965

Volume 1 - Introduction to Landscape Design 22 MIN
VHS
Landscape Design Series
Color (H C A IND)
LC 88-700131
Introduces the viewer to landscape design by comparing designing and landscaping architecture.
Agriculture; Fine Arts
Dist - CSPC **Prod** - CSPC 1987

Volume Problems 30 MIN
VHS
Mathematics Series
Color (J)
LC 90713155
Discusses volume problems. The 138th of 157 installments of the Mathematics Series.
Mathematics
Dist - GPN

Volume problems 30 MIN
VHS
Calculus series
Color (C)
$125.00 purchase _ #6029
Explains volume problems. Part of a 56 - part series on calculus.
Mathematics
Dist - LANDMK **Prod** - LANDMK

Volume (shells)
U-matic
Calculus series
Color
Mathematics
Dist - MDCPB **Prod** - MDDE

The Volumetric flask - I 8 MIN
VHS
Chemistry master apprentice series
Color (H C)
$49.95 purchase _ #49 - 7213 - V
Demonstrates the use of the volumetric flask in preparation of a solution of known concentration. Part of the Chemistry Master Apprentice series.
Science; Science - Physical
Dist - INSTRU **Prod** - CORNRS

The Volumetric flask - II 15 MIN
VHS
Chemistry master apprentice series
Color (H C)
$49.95 purchase _ #49 - 7214 - V
Presents a more detailed version of Part I. Demonstrates the use of the volumetric flask in preparation of a solution of known concentration. Explains the markings on the flask. Stresses the importance of temperature effects and the importance of cleanliness. Shows the preparation of solutions from solids of low solubility. Part of the Chemistry Master Apprentice series.
Science; Science - Physical
Dist - INSTRU **Prod** - CORNRS

Voluntary Control of Hair Raising with Associated Autonomic Phenomena 8 MIN
16mm
B&W (C T)
The authors of this film discovered a man able to erect hair on the surface of the skin 'VOLUNTARILY.' Pictures show the elevation of hair on the arm and leg, accompanying 'GOOSEFLESH,' a small amount of dilation of pupils, changes in respiration as recorded by a pneumograph, changes in the electroencephalographic record from pre - motor brain areas and other autonomic behavior.
Psychology
Dist - PSUPCR **Prod** - PSUPCR 1938

The Voluntary sector and charities 30 MIN
VHS
Inside Britain 2 series
Color; PAL; NTSC (G) (BULGARIAN CZECH HUNGARIAN SPANISH POLISH ROMANIAN RUSSIAN SLOVAK UKRAINIAN ENGLISH WITH ARABIC SUBTITLES LITHUANIAN)
PdS65 purchase
Shows how voluntary organizations and charities make a vital contribution to society. Follows the work of community self - help groups and larger charities such as Friends of the Earth.
Sociology
Dist - CFLVIS **Prod** - LEESOC 1992

Voluntary Tubal Sterilization 14 MIN
VHS / 16mm / 8mm cartridge
Color (A) (SPANISH)
Explains how tubal sterilization prevents conception, discussing laparoscopy and ligation methods.
Foreign Language; Health and Safety; Sociology
Dist - PRORE **Prod** - PRORE

Volunteer Experience - a Patient's Perspective 15 MIN
U-matic
Color
Presents a number of patients' perspectives on the volunteer's role and the experience of being a patient at the University of Texas M D Anderson Hospital.
Health and Safety; Social Science
Dist - UTEXSC **Prod** - UTEXSC

Volunteer Firefighters - the Unique Breed 18 MIN
16mm
Color (A)
LC 79-701574
Traces the history of volunteer firefighting from colonial times to the 1970's. Shows volunteers receiving training and presents the comments of firefighters regarding their reasons for volunteering, their duties and their emotions.
Social Science
Dist - FILCOM **Prod** - LHPRO 1979

The Volunteer Fireman 19 MIN
16mm
Color
LC FIE63-220
Shows techniques of using hand tools and back pack pumps to suppress wood fires. Includes the important work of mopping up, cleaning and storing tools, reporting and prevention follow - up.
Health and Safety; Social Science
Dist - USNAC **Prod** - USDA 1962

Volunteer Story 22 MIN
U-matic / VHS
Color (J A)
Explains the role of volunteers and how they serve people.
Health and Safety; Social Science
Dist - SUTHRB **Prod** - SUTHRB

Volunteer to Live 30 MIN
16mm
Color
Shows how some churches are working with the elderly to encourage self - help projects and offer opportunities for the elderly to help others.
Health and Safety; Religion and Philosophy; Sociology
Dist - CCNCC **Prod** - CBSTV

Volunteerism 29 MIN
U-matic / VHS
On and about Instruction Series
Color (T)
Visits city schools to show how a volunteer program can be designed.
Education; Social Science
Dist - GPN **Prod** - VADE 1983

Volunteers 25 MIN
U-matic / VHS
Color
Explores a few of the hundreds of ways that people from 14 to 100 can volunteer their services in medicine and health.
Health and Safety; Social Science
Dist - MEDCOM **Prod** - MEDCOM

Volunteers 8 MIN
16mm
Color
LC 80-700401
Demonstrates the structure and function of a volunteer fire company. Shows volunteers at work at when they are called to answer a false alarm.
Social Science
Dist - FSHRA **Prod** - FSHRA 1980

Volunteers in the Library 20 MIN
U-matic
Access Series
Color (T)
LC 76-706264
Discusses five steps a library can take to develop an organized volunteer program. Touches on solutions to possible problems that could arise when using volunteers.
Education; Social Science
Dist - USNAC **Prod** - UDEN 1976

Volunteers in Vocational Education - Four Urban Programs 29 MIN
16mm / U-matic / VHS
Color
Presents comments from community leaders from four areas about their local volunteer vocational education programs. Discusses applicable vocations, community support, recruitment techniques and student goal - setting and accomplishment.
Education; Guidance and Counseling; Psychology; Social Science
Dist - USNAC **Prod** - USDED 1982

Volvox - Structure, Reproduction and Differentation in V Carteri - Hk 9 and 10 25 MIN
U-matic / VHS / 16mm
Color (H C A)
LC 71-707560
Depicts the details of cellular differentiation and its control in a simple multicellular organism. Shows the form and sturcture of volvox carteri, a green, spheroidal alga and the development of asexual, male and female embryos.
Science - Natural
Dist - IU **Prod** - IU 1970

Volvulus of the Sigmoid Colon 30 MIN
16mm
Color (PRO)
Outlines the important features, the etiology, diagnosis and surgical management of volvulus of the sigmoid. Presents X - ray films of typical cases.
Health and Safety; Science
Dist - ACY **Prod** - ACYDGD 1954

Vom Mittelgebirge Bis Zu Den Alpen 10 MIN
16mm / U-matic / VHS
German Teaching Series
Color (H C) (GERMAN)
LC 73-702965
Visits Munchen, Bavaria, and the Alps of Germany. Views the agriculture of the region which is still done as it was 100 years ago.
Foreign Language
Dist - IFB **Prod** - IFB 1972

Vom Schwarzwald Bis Koln 10 MIN
16mm / VHS / U-matic
German Teaching Series
Color (H C) (GERMAN)
LC 73-702964
Describes the Black Forest, Heidelberg and the Rhine, the Moselle vineyards, and the Ruhr Valley.
Foreign Language
Dist - IFB **Prod** - IFB 1972

Von Bodense in Die Schweiz 4 MIN
16mm
Beginning German Films - German Series
Color
Foreign Language
Dist - CCNY **Prod** - MGHT

Von Der Nordseekuste Bis Berlin 9 MIN
16mm / U-matic / VHS
German Teaching Series
Color (GERMAN)
LC 73-702966
Explains that the occupations of the Berlin region are fishing, cattle raising and farming.
Foreign Language
Dist - IFB **Prod** - IFB 1972

Von Weimar Nach Rom, 1775 - 1789
16mm
Johann Wolfgang V Goethe Series, Pt 2
Color (GERMAN)
Follows the maturing Goethe during his years in Weimar and Rome and his development into a great classical writer. Explores how his unfulfilled love for Frau von Stein and his travels through Italy contributed to this development.
Foreign Language; Literature and Drama
Dist - WSTGLC **Prod** - WSTGLC 1982

Voodoo and the Church in Haiti 40 MIN
VHS
Color (H C G)
$370.00 purchase, $45.00 rental _ #37868
Reveals that despite centuries of vigilant opposition from the Roman Catholic Church, Voodoo has flourished in Haiti. Dispels the sensationalist stereotypes surrounding Voodoo. Shows that Voodoo is a complex system of beliefs which have developed over time from West African origins. Introduces the culture, history, sociology and politics of the first black republic in the New World. Produced by Andrea Leland and Bob Richards.
Geography - World; Religion and Philosophy
Dist - UCEMC

Vor Sonnenaufgang 104 MIN
16mm
Color (GERMAN (ENGLISH SUBTITLES))
Tells the story of the young social democrat politician Albert Loth, who studies conditions in a Silesian village that has become rich as coal is found in the region. Continues as he meets an old friend from student days, who, along with his wife, has become rich and also a drunk, and whose daughter Helene eventually falls in love with Loth. Concludes with Loth leaving Helene because she is the daughter of alcoholics, and with Helene taking her own life.
Fine Arts; Foreign Language
Dist - WSTGLC **Prod** - WSTGLC 1976

Vormittagsspuk 7 MIN
16mm
B&W
Presents Hans Richter's witty, cinegenic mini - classic on the universal theme of the objects' revolt, an excellent introduction to avant - garde film. Produced 1927 - 28.
Fine Arts
Dist - STARRC **Prod** - STARRC

Vortex 87 MIN
16mm
Color (G)
Presents an independent production by Beth B And Scott Billingsley. Looks at corporate paranoia and political corruption with Lydia Lunch.
Business and Economics; Civics and Political Systems; Literature and Drama
Dist - FIRS

Vortex, and, Rotation 27 MIN
VHS
Color (S)
$129.00 purchase _ #386 - 9034
Presents two programs. Introduces the concept of the vortex, one of nature's primary patterns of movement, which can be seen around the eye of a storm, in space as stardust is sucked into a black hole, and in the cream mixing in with coffee. With colorful visuals, 'Rotation' examines the principles of circular motion - in tops, potter's wheels, dancer's pirouettes, Frisbees and the earth.
History - World; Religion and Philosophy; Science - Physical
Dist - FI **Prod** - CANBC 1988

Vostok 14 MIN
U-matic
White Inferno Series
Color (H)
Shows the arrival of the expedition at Vostok in interior Antarctica and its siginificance for the crew members.
Geography - World
Dist - TVOTAR **Prod** - TVOTAR 1971

Vote for Ira 11 MIN
16mm
Color
LC 76-700439
Presents a documentary comedy which follows the exploits of Ira Bernstein, an idealistic yet inept young man running for the State Assembly of New York in 1972, reliving his past through the insights of his father.
Civics and Political Systems; Literature and Drama
Dist - POSTMN **Prod** - POSTMN 1975

The Vote - Organizing the Rural South 30 MIN
16mm
Black History, Section 20 - Freedom Movement Series; Section 20 - Freedom movement
B&W (H C A)
LC 70-704110
Joanne Grant discusses the evolution of the civil rights movement in the 1960's and the growth of the concept of Black Power. She explains that this period of resistance reached its peak when thousands of Blacks all over the South began to organize around the vote, which symbolized the ulimate in attaining political power.
Civics and Political Systems; History - United States
Dist - HRAW **Prod** - WCBSTV 1969

Vote Power 20 MIN
16mm / U-matic / VHS
Color (H C)
LC 73-700935
Deals with the right to vote of the 18 - year - old individual, explaining that it can make change possible. Shows such people as Julian Bond, representative from Georgia and an 18 - year - old mayor in California in order to encourage young people to register and vote.
Civics and Political Systems
Dist - AMEDFL **Prod** - AMEDFL 1973

Voter files on compact disc
CD-ROM
(G)
$5000.00 purchase _ #2861
Provides access to information on registered voters in 18 states - Alaska, California, Colorado, Delaware, Hawaii, Illinois, Iowa, Kentucky, Louisiana, Maryland, Minnesota, New Jersey, New York, North Carolina, Ohio, Rhode Island, South Carolina and Texas. Gives the telephone number, address, party membership, and voting history. Files can be exported to Lotus, dBase, and other programs. For IBM PCs and compatibles, requires 604K RAM, DOS 3.1 or later, one floppy disk drive - hard disk recommended, one empty expansion slot, and an IBM compatible CD - ROM drive.
Civics and Political Systems
Dist - BEP

Votes for women - the 1913 US Senate testimony 17 MIN
BETA / Cassette / U-matic / VHS
Women's history and literature media series
Color (P I J H G)
$95.00 purchase, $40.00 rental
Portrays the 1913 US Senate testimony conscerning whether or not women should be allowed to vote. Features testimony against women's suffrage by Kate Douglas Wiggin, author of Rebecca of Sunnybrook, who argued, 'It is even more difficult to be an inspiring woman than a good citizen and an honest voter,' and testimony against Wiggin's romantic and sentimental arguments by Belle Case La Follette. Part of a series about women's history and literature created by Jocelyn Rile. Resource guide available separately.
Civics and Political Systems; History - United States; History - World
Dist - HEROWN **Prod** - HEROWN 1991

Voting 15 MIN
VHS / U-matic
By the People Series
Color (H)
Demonstrates voting procedures. Looks at voting for candidates and voting on issues.
Civics and Political Systems; Social Science
Dist - CTI **Prod** - CTI

The Voting Machine 20 MIN
U-matic / VHS
Rights and Responsibilities Series
Color (J H)
Shows a young person registering to vote and using an electronic voting machine. Includes a question - and - answer session between students, a professor of political science, and the chairpersons of the local Democratic and Republic parties.
Civics and Political Systems; Social Science
Dist - AITECH **Prod** - WHROTV 1975

Vous, encore vous 13 MIN
16mm
Les Francais chez vous series
B&W (I J H)
Foreign Language
Dist - CHLTN **Prod** - PEREN 1967

A Vous La France 360 MIN
VHS
Color (S) (FRENCH)
$1110.00 purchase _ #825 - 9015
Journeys to some of the most scenic areas of France to listen to the language as spoken by natives. Helps students to pick up key words and phrases while conversations reinforce basic language skills. Fifteen 25 - minute programs.
Foreign Language; Geography - World; History - World
Dist - FI **Prod** - BBCTV 1985

A Vous La France - French Culture Today - the Documentary Sequences
VHS
Color (S) (FRENCH)
$499.00 purchase
Covers everything from the modern high - tech city of Grenoble to the largest fishing village on the Mediterranean, to the sunny wine - producing region of Languedoc. Tours Pezanas, currently being restored to its medieval splendor, and the nearby abbey of Valemagne. Edited from the full - length 'A Vous La France' series.
Foreign Language; Geography - World; History - World
Dist - FI **Prod** - BBCTV 1989

The Vowel a 13 MIN
16mm / U-matic / VHS
Reading Skills, Set 1 - 2nd Ed Series
Color (P)
Deals with the short and long sounds of the letter a, emphasizing the effects of the final e, the ai combination, and the ay combination at the end of a word. Presents exercises using the concepts that have been explained.
English Language
Dist - JOU **Prod** - JOU 1983

Vowel Combinations - what are Letters for 11 MIN
U-matic / VHS / 16mm

Color (P I)
Shows how vowels work in the English language. Uses a story of two characters who visit a ranch and a fair to find as many vowel combinations as they can.
English Language
Dist - PHENIX **Prod** - PHENIX 1983

Vowel Digraphs 15 MIN
VHS / 16mm
Reading Way Series
Color (P)
$125.00 purchase, $25.00 rental
Shows that 'ea' and 'ee' make the same vowel sound. 'Ai' and 'oa' are read in a variety of words.
English Language
Dist - AITECH **Prod** - WXXITV 1988

Vowel Diphthongs 15 MIN
VHS / 16mm
Reading Way Series
Color (P)
$125.00 purchase, $25.00 rental
Shows Mrs. Read and Tim writing 'oo' and 'ew' words.
English Language
Dist - AITECH **Prod** - WXXITV 1988

Vowel E, the 13 MIN
16mm / U-matic / VHS
Reading Skills, Set 1 (2nd Ed Series
Color (P)
Shows the major patterns of letters which give the vowel e its long and short sounds, e followed by only a consonant, e followed by a consonant and final e. Covers ee together in the middle of a word, ee and ea at the end of a word and e at the end of a word not followed by a consonant.
English Language
Dist - JOU **Prod** - JOU 1983

Vowel I, the 13 MIN
U-matic / VHS / 16mm
Reading Skills, Set 1 (2nd Ed Series
Color (P)
Deals with the long and short sounds of the letter i, emphasizing the effect of the final e, the ght combination, and the final y acting like the letter i. Presents exercises using the concepts that have been explained.
English Language
Dist - JOU **Prod** - JOU 1983

Vowel O, the 13 MIN
U-matic / VHS / 16mm
Reading Skills, Set 1 (2nd Ed Series
Color (P)
Shows the major patterns of letters which give the vowel o its long and short sounds, o followed by a consonant and then a final e, o followed by a consonant only, and the vowel digraph oa together. Covers o alone at the end of a word, oe at the end of a word, and the ough combination.
English Language
Dist - JOU **Prod** - JOU 1983

Vowel pairs 15 MIN
U-matic / Kit / VHS
Space station readstar series
(P)
$130 purchase, $25 rental, $75 self dub
Teaches phonics in a series designed to supplement second grade reading programs. Focuses on vowel pairs. Seventh in a 25 part series.
English Language
Dist - GPN

Vowel U, the 13 MIN
U-matic / VHS / 16mm
Reading Skills, Set 1 (2nd Ed Series
Color (P)
Shows the major patterns of letters which give the vowel u its long and short sounds, u followed by a consonant and then a final e, u followed only by a consonant, and the vowel digraph ew either in the middle or at the end of a word. Covers the vowel digraph oo either in the middle or at the end of a word, and ue at the end of a word. Presents exercises using the concepts that have been explained.
English Language
Dist - JOU **Prod** - JOU 1983

Vowels and glides 26 MIN
U-matic
Articulatory movements in the production of English speech sounds series; Pt 2
Color (PRO)
LC 78-706044
Uses live - action photography of the movements of the laryngeal and articulatory structures to illustrate the production of vowels and their movements with glide sounds. Shows the importance of resonance as a factor in speech intelligibility through samples of connected speech.
English Language
Dist - USNAC **Prod** - USVA 1978

Vowels and their Sounds 12 MIN
U-matic / VHS / 16mm
Reading Skills, Set 1 (2nd Ed Series
Color (P)
Focuses on short and long vowel sounds and presents the steps of understanding sound - letter association. Includes scenes of children in suggested follow - up activities.
English Language
Dist - JOU **Prod** - JOU 1983

Vowels - what are Letters for 13 MIN
16mm / U-matic / VHS
Color (P I)
Teaches long and short vowel sounds. Shows each letter with pictures of words using the letter in the initial position.
English Language
Dist - PHENIX **Prod** - BEANMN

Vox Pop - the Voice of the People 30 MIN
16mm
Color
LC 80-701576
Tells how a man is chosen as the symbol of Australian apathy and how his life undergoes upheaval as a result.
Fine Arts
Dist - TASCOR **Prod** - TASCOR 1979

Voyage of Charles Darwin Series
Can any mountains, any continent, withstand such waste 52 MIN
In the Distant Future, Light will be Thrown on the Origin of Man, and His History 52 MIN
Dist - HRC

Voyage of Discovery 14 MIN
16mm
Color (A)
LC 77-703133
Uses paintings to describe the discovery of the California coast by 16th century Spanish explorer Juan Rodriquez Cabrillo.
History - United States; History - World
Dist - USNAC **Prod** - USNPS 1969

Voyage of Dreams 27 MIN
16mm / U-matic
Color
Documents the story of the Haitian boat people.
History - United States; History - World; Sociology
Dist - BLKFMF **Prod** - BLKFMF

Voyage of Dreams 30 MIN
U-matic / VHS / 16mm
Captioned; Color (A) (CREOLE (ENGLISH SUBTITLES))
Discusses the story of the Haitian boat people. Creole dialog with English subtitles.
History - World
Dist - CNEMAG **Prod** - CNEMAG 1983

The Voyage of Eros
VHS
Color (G)
$100.00 rental _ #0762
Takes a Pacific voyage with the yacht Eros. Starts with the preparations for the voyage, witnesses the cruise from departure and travels to Honolulu, Hawaii.
Geography - United States; Physical Education and Recreation
Dist - SEVVID

The Voyage of Odysseus 27 MIN
16mm / U-matic / VHS
Color (J)
LC 82-700556
Features Julie Harris who, as the voice of a muse, retells the voyage section of Homer's classic tale The Odyssey.
Literature and Drama; Religion and Philosophy
Dist - CF **Prod** - CF 1982

Voyage of SS Columbia - Just Short of a Miracle 22 MIN
16mm / U-matic / VHS
Color (J)
Looks at the development of the space shutttle Columbia and follows it on to the launch pad and into orbit with astronauts Crippen and Young. Documents the activities during the first flight through to its successful landing at Andrews Air Force Base.
Science; Science - Physical
Dist - CORF **Prod** - ABCNEW 1981

Voyage of the Elisha Kane 15 MIN
16mm
Color
LC 70-705710
Follows an ocean expedition exploring the mid - Atlantic ridge and the sea floor to explain how marine geologists explore land masses beneath the sea.
Science - Natural; Science - Physical
Dist - USNPC **Prod** - USNO 1969

Voyage of the Great Southern Ark 139 MIN
VHS
Color (S)
$39.95 purchase _ #408 - 9000
Journeys through the history of Australia and its inhabitants, from 4.2 billion years ago to modern times. Pt 1, 'Dust Of The Southern Cross,' covers the formation of the Australian landmass, the genesis and early evolution of life, and the continent's drift from the Equator to the Arctic to the Antarctic. Pt 2, 'The Invaders Of Gondwana,' follows Australia's drift to Africa, India, North China and South America over 400 million years, when it was populated by the 'living fossils' that still inhabit Australia. Pt 3, 'Behold The Dreamer,' recalls the appearance of humans on the Australian landscape, travels to every corner of the continent in search of the unique flora and fauna, and looks at humankind's effect.
Geography - World; History - World; Science - Physical
Dist - FI

The Voyage of the Manatee 18 MIN
VHS / 16mm
Color (I)
$425.00, $385.00 purchase, $45.00 rental _ #C - 524; LC 89706231
Tells the story of Nyri, who loves boats and the idea of sailing, but is kept from accomplishing her desires by her parents who fear that a thirteen - year - old girl with cerebral palsy cannot stand up to the dangers. Produced by Ken Nelson.
Health and Safety; Literature and Drama; Physical Education and Recreation; Psychology
Dist - ALTSUL

Voyage of the San Carlos 18 MIN
U-matic
Color (I A)
Documents the activities of the San Carlos, a water quality monitoring vessel, as it gathers information along the Sacramento - San Joaquin Delta.
Geography - United States; Science - Natural; Social Science; Sociology
Dist - CALDWR **Prod** - CSDWR

The Voyage of the St Louis 52 MIN
VHS
Color & B&W (G)
$90.00 purchase
Tells the story of the German luxury liner, the St Louis, which sailed from Hamburg to Cuba carrying 917 Jewish refugees in the summer of 1939. Reveals that their visas were revoked upon arrival in Cuba and for 30 days they wandered the seas as they were refused haven by every country in the Americas. International publicity forced them back to Germany when, two days before landing, the passengers were accepted by Holland, France, England and Belgium. Four months later the war began and nearly three quarters of the passengers perished in the Nazi death camps. Directed by Maziar Bahari. English, German, French with English subtitles.
Fine Arts; History - World; Religion and Philosophy
Dist - NCJEWF

Voyage on the Bounty 30 MIN
VHS
Color (G)
$29.95 purchase _ #0777
Travels on a replica of the 18th century Bounty, the HMAV Bounty, built in 1978. Sails from Sydney, Australia, to Freemantle across the Great Australian Bight.
Physical Education and Recreation
Dist - SEVVID

Voyage Optique 8 MIN
16mm
B&W (H C)
LC 75-703251
A humorous collage of abstract and concrete images set to lively music.
Fine Arts
Dist - USC **Prod** - USC 1965

A Voyage through the cosmos 20 MIN
16mm / U-matic / VHS
Cosmos series; Edited version
Color (J H C)
Presents a journey from a far - off region of the universe, traveling through galaxies and the planets to Earth. Features Dr Carl Sagan.
Science - Physical
Dist - FI **Prod** - SAGANC 1980

Voyage to Next 10 MIN
16mm / U-matic / VHS
Color (H C A)
Presents an animated plea for world cooperation and understanding, featuring Maureen Stapleton as Mother Earth and Dizzy Gillespie as Father Time.
Fine Arts; Literature and Drama; Sociology
Dist - PFP **Prod** - HUBLEY

Voyage to save the whales 30 MIN
VHS
Color (G)
$19.95 purchase
Documents the first campaigns of Greenpeace to halt whale hunting by the Soviet whaling fleet in 1975. Includes dramatic footage of Greenpeace activists placing themselves in the path of harpoons.
Geography - World; Science - Natural
Dist - GRNPCE **Prod** - GRNPCE 1978

A Voyage to Spitzbergen - 2 53 MIN
VHS
War Baby cruising series
Color (G A)
$39.90 purchase _ #0490
Sails from Europe's northernmost town, Hammerfest, Norway, across the Barents Sea to Bear Island. Travels from there to the mountains and glaciers of Spitzbergen. Part of a series.
Geography - World; Physical Education and Recreation
Dist - SEVVID

Voyage to the Arctic 25 MIN
VHS
Color (G)
$29.95 purchase _ #S01846
Retraces British explorer George Vancouver's voyage along the northwest coast of North America, from Puget Sound to the Gulf of Alaska.
Geography - World; History - World; Science - Natural
Dist - UILL

Voyage to the Arctic 25 MIN
U-matic / VHS / 16mm
Natural Environment Series
Color (I)
LC 77-703488
Explores the ecological regions from British Columbia to Alaska from the vantage point of a cruise ship. Examines the land and water environments and their interrelationships.
Science - Natural
Dist - JOU **Prod** - WILFGP 1977

Voyage to the Enchanted Isles, Pt 1 27 MIN
U-matic / VHS / 16mm
Color (I J H)
LC 78-702634
Visits the Galapagos Islands, where Charles Darwin, During a five - week stay in 1835, obtained the first insights for his famous theory on the origin of the species. Reviews the theories of evolution and adaptation of species of plants and animals and the hereditary transmissions of variations in successive generations of plant and animal life.
Science - Natural
Dist - PHENIX **Prod** - CBSTV 1969

Voyage to the Enchanted Isles, Pt 2 27 MIN
16mm / U-matic / VHS
Color (I J H)
LC 78-702634
Visits the Galapagos Islands, where Charles Darwin, during a five - week stay in 1835, obtained the first insights for his famous theory on the origin of the species. Reviews the theories of evolution and adaptation of species of plants and animals and the hereditary transmissions of variations in successive generations of plant and animal life.
Science - Natural
Dist - PHENIX **Prod** - CBSTV 1969

Voyage to the Ends of the Earth 29 MIN
VHS / 16mm
Color (G)
$55.00 rental _ #VTEE - 000
Examines the work of Norwegian explorer and scientist Fridtjof Nansen, who set out in 1893 to study the North Pole. Traces Nansen's adventure from beginning to end.
Biography
Dist - PBS **Prod** - WETATV

Voyage to the Galapagos 21 MIN
16mm / U-matic / VHS
Color (I J H C)
Takes one on a journey to the Galapagos Islands of Ecuador. Showsthe diverse flora and fauna, together with various wildlife. Musical accompaniment provided in film.
Geography - World; Science - Natural
Dist - EBEC **Prod** - EBEC 1985

Voyage to the Galapagos 21 MIN
U-matic / VHS
Phenomenal World Series
Color (J C)
$129.00 purchase _ #3974
Presents the Galapagos Islands, a chain of sixteen islands about 600 miles west of Ecuador, and many different types of its inhabitants including the blue - footed booby, the clown of the bird world.
Geography - World; Science - Natural
Dist - EBEC

Voyage to the moon 10 MIN
VHS
Junior space scientist series
CC; Color (P I)
$55.00 purchase _ #10362VG
Shows the moon through the eyes of astronauts who first explored it. Explores concepts such as the phases of the moon, gravity and lunar exploration. Comes with a teacher's guide and blackline masters. Part two of a three - part series.
History - World; Science - Physical
Dist - UNL

Voyage to the Ocean of Storms 11 MIN
16mm
Color (I)
Depicts the Apollo 12 mission, including scenes of the astronauts aboard the 'YANKEE CLIPPER' and the 'INTREPID' and the moon walks of Conrad and Bean. Portrays the placement of the Apollo Lunar Experiments Package (ALSEP) on the lunar surface and the recovery of equipment from the Surveyor Three unmanned spacecraft.
History - World; Industrial and Technical Education; Science - Physical
Dist - RCKWL **Prod** - NAA

Voyage to the planets - volume 1 - Mac
CD-ROM
(G A)
$180.00 purchase _ #2491m
Offers the first of three CD - ROMS full of images from Mars, Jupiter, Neptune, and other planets. Contains images of Jupiter, Saturn, and Uranus and its moons. For Macintosh Plus, SE and II computers. Requires at least one M of RAM, one floppy disk drive, and and Apple compatible CD - Rom drive.
Geography - World; Science - Physical
Dist - BEP

Voyage to the planets - volume 1 - PC
CD-ROM
(G A)
$120.00 purchase _ #2491p
Offers the first of three CD - ROMS full of images from Mars, Jupiter, Neptune, and other planets. Contains images of Jupiter, Saturn, and Uranus and its moons. For IBM PCs and compatibles. Requires 640K RAM, DOS Version 3.1 or greater, one floppy disk drive - hard disk drive recommended, one empty expansion slot, and an IBM compatible CD - ROM drive.
Geography - World; Science - Physical
Dist - BEP

Voyage to the planets - volume 3 - Mac
CD-ROM
(G A)
$180.00 purchase _ #2493m
Offers the third of three CD - ROMS full of images from Mars, Jupiter, Neptune, and other planets. Contains images of Neptune and its moons. For Macintosh Plus, SE and II computers. Requires at least one M of RAM, one floppy disk drive, and and Apple compatible CD - Rom drive.
Geography - World; Science - Physical
Dist - BEP

Voyage to the planets - volume 3 - PC
CD-ROM
(G A)
$120.00 purchase _ #2493p
Offers the third of three CD - ROMS full of images from Mars, Jupiter, Neptune, and other planets. Contains images of Neptune and its moons. For IBM PCs and compatibles. Requires at least 640K RAM, DOS Version 3.1 or greater, one floppy disk drive - a hard disk drive is recommended, one empty expansion slot, and an IBM compatible CD - ROM drive.
Geography - World; Science - Physical
Dist - BEP

Voyage to the planets - volume 2 - Mac
CD-ROM
(G A)
$180.00 purchase _ #2492m
Offers the second of three CD - ROMS full of images from Mars, Jupiter, Neptune, and other planets. Contains images of Mars. For Macintosh Plus, SE and II computers. Requires at least one M of RAM, one floppy disk drive, and and Apple compatible CD - Rom drive.
Geography - World; Science - Physical
Dist - BEP

Voyage to the planets - volume 2 - PC
CD-ROM
(G A)
$120.00 purchase _ #2492p
Offers the second of three CD - ROMS full of images from Mars, Jupiter, Neptune, and other planets. Contains images of Mars. For IBM PC and compatibles. Requires 640K RAM, DOS Version 3.1 or greater, one floppy disk drive - a hard disk drive is recommended, one empty expansion slot, and an IBM compatible CD - ROM drive.
Geography - World; Science - Physical
Dist - BEP

Voyage to Understanding 59 MIN
VHS / BETA
Color (J)
LC 84-707098
Tells the story of 11 young adults, age 14 to 19, who set out to sail around the world in a refurbished schooner, a voyage which became an unparalleled adventure in seamanship, maturation and friendship recalled four years later to the accompaniment of movies shot on board.
Geography - World; Physical Education and Recreation; Sociology
Dist - GLNASS **Prod** - GPEF
OFFSHR
SEVVID

Voyager 20 MIN
16mm / U-matic / VHS
Color (H A)
Presents the flight of the Voyager and the first close - up photos of Jupiter and Saturn and their moons.
Industrial and Technical Education; Science - Physical
Dist - USNAC **Prod** - NASA 1982

Voyager - a retrospective summary 28 MIN
VHS
Color (J H C)
$14.95 purchase _ #NA206
Looks back at the Voyager space Satellites I and II and their voyages in and around the solar system of Earth. Takes an in - depth look at Jupiter's spot, Saturn's rings and the gaseous world of Neptune. Includes the Solar System Visualization Program. Includes actual pictures sent back by Voyager computer enhanced to the point where actual craters and geysers can be seen on the most distant moons.
History - World; Science - Physical
Dist - INSTRU **Prod** - NASA

Voyager - Angels - Smoky's journal - Vigo and Broadway 26 MIN
VHS
Color (G)
$15.00 purchase
Features four productions by Phil Costa Cummins, made between 1985 - 1989. Includes Voyager, which combines images of objects in his mother's living room with family photos and soft light refractions to suggest the contemplative nature of thought - memory; Angels, reveals fears, laments and remembrances silently told in romantic images on the classic Kodachrome 8mm; Smoky's Journal, is a silent diary film shot while living in a rural area; and Vigo and Broadway articulates the conflict between man and nature, in the style of a cinepoem. Titles available as a package only.
Fine Arts; Psychology; Sociology
Dist - CANCIN

The Voyager discoveries 15 MIN
VHS
Color (J H C)
$14.95 purchase _ #NA068
History - World; Science - Physical
Dist - INSTRU **Prod** - NASA

Voyager 2 - encounters Neptune and Triton 5 MIN
VHS
Color (J H C)
$14.95 purchase _ #NA073
History - World; Science - Physical
Dist - INSTRU **Prod** - NASA

Voyager 2 - Neptune's annual movements 28 MIN
VHS
Color (J H C)
$14.95 purchase _ #NA074
History - World; Science - Physical
Dist - INSTRU **Prod** - NASA

Voyages - journey of the Magi 25 MIN
BETA / VHS
Color (G)
$29.95 purchase
Recreates the actual route taken by the Wise Men of the Bible. Places the event in both its cultural and archeological contexts. Visits historic sites, looks at coins and artifacts from the period. Features archeologist Karl Katz as narrator.
Fine Arts; History - World
Dist - ARTSAM **Prod** - MMOA

Voyages of Charles Darwin series
I Felt Myself Brought within Reach of that Great Fact - that Mystery of Mysteries 52 MIN
Suppose that all animals and all plants are represented by the branches of a tree 52 MIN
Dist - HRC
TIMLIF

Voyages of charles darwin series
Can any mountain, any continent, withstand such waste 52 MIN
How Wide was the Distance between Savage and Civilized Man 52 MIN
I was considered a very ordinary boy 52 MIN
In the Distant Future, Light will be Thrown on the Origin of Man and His History 52 MIN
My Mind was a Chaos of Delight 52 MIN
Dist - TIMLIF

Voyages of Ulysses and Aeneas 37 MIN
VHS
Color (J H C)
LC 89-700176
Examines the works of Homer and Vergil, and their heroic treatment of the voyages of Ulysses and Aeneas.
History - World; Religion and Philosophy
Dist - EAV **Prod** - EAV 1989

The Voyageurs 20 MIN
16mm
Color (J H A)
LC FIA65-1149
Documents the big business of fur - traders who drove their freighter canoes through the waterways of the wilderness. Shows how the often - hazardous trips of the voyageurs were cheered by their songs.
Business and Economics; History - World
Dist - NFBC **Prod** - NFBC 1965

Voyeur 7 MIN
16mm
Color (G)
$15.00 rental
Toys with the illusionistic space and time from a window perspective. Allows events to occur naturally in combination with events, juxtaposed for contrast and comparison. Produced by Caroline Savage - Lee.
Fine Arts; Science - Physical
Dist - CANCIN

VR video festival highlights 30 MIN
VHS
Color (G)
$30.00 purchase
Presents virtual reality - VR - as a unique communications process. Introduces many pioneering scientific, business and entertainment applications of interactive and immersive computer graphics simulations.
Computer Science
Dist - MCAS

Vrindavan, Land of Krishna 23 MIN
16mm
Color
Depicts the lifestyles and religious observances of the inhabitants and pilgrims of Vrindavan, India, site of Lord Krishna's appearance. Features the history, art and architecture of the city and the devotion of the people who inhabit it.
Religion and Philosophy
Dist - BHAKTI **Prod** - ISKCON 1980

Vroom 25 MIN
U-matic
Not Another Science Show Series
Color (H C)
Looks at the working of the internal combustion engine and the properties of different types of fuel.
Industrial and Technical Education; Science
Dist - TVOTAR **Prod** - TVOTAR 1986

Vroom at the Top 28 MIN
16mm
Color
Examines the racing adventures of ex - driver Roger Penske and his team's efforts in the Indianapolis 500, Monaco Grand Prix and the World 600 stock car race.
Physical Education and Recreation
Dist - MTP **Prod** - SEARS

Vrooom 17 MIN
16mm / U-matic / VHS
Color (J)
LC 74-703227
Uses a variety of cinematic devices, including stop - action, slow motion and split screen techniques in order to show some of the fun and excitement of competition drag racing.
Physical Education and Recreation
Dist - PFP **Prod** - NHRA 1974

VTR - CRT 30 MIN
VHS
Color (G)
$50.00 purchase
Collects comic pantomime skits with high tech tricks. Includes Multiple Identity Marathon; Just a Day in the Life; and Gullible's Travels.
Fine Arts
Dist - CANCIN **Prod** - DEWITT 1976

VTR - Downtown Community Television 30 MIN
VHS / U-matic
Color
Gives examples of how to use video as a tool for community organizing. Includes excerpts of tapes on health education, use of mobile units, workshops, community service programs and others.
Health and Safety; Industrial and Technical Education; Social Science
Dist - DCTVC **Prod** - DCTVC 1975

Vulnerabilities of the premature infant 12 MIN
VHS / U-matic
Color (PRO C)
$395.00 purchase, $80.00 rental _ #C821 - VI - 024
Acquaints medical and nursing students with the major problems associated with premature birth. Familiarizes students with the timely medical attention essential to remove as much risk to the child as possible. Presented by Dr Ernest N Kraybill.
Health and Safety
Dist - HSCIC

Vulnerable to Attack 28 MIN
16mm
Color (H C A)
LC 75-701988
Helps women learn various tactics for self - defense. Discusses physical defense, locking hardware, doors and safety strategy on streets.
Health and Safety; Sociology
Dist - MCCRNE **Prod** - MCCRNE 1975

Vulva Self - Examination 30 MIN
U-matic
Color
Demonstrates how to perform a self - examination of the vulva.
Health and Safety
Dist - UTEXSC **Prod** - UTEXSC

Vulvovaginal Problems
U-matic / VHS
Color
Presents the common problems of the vulva and vagina. Discusses concepts in differential diagnosis and management of nonvenereal and venereal infections. Stresses recognition of masquerading or underlying neoplasia.
Health and Safety
Dist - AMEDA **Prod** - AMEDA

W

W A Mozart 26 MIN
U-matic / VHS / 16mm
Great Composers Series
Color (J)
Features soloist Nina Milkina with the London Mozart Players for a performance of the Ninth Piano Concerto.
Fine Arts
Dist - IFB **Prod** - SEABEN 1974

W B Yeats 65 MIN
VHS / U-matic
Color (H C)
$325.00, $295.00 purchase _ #V562
Explores six poems written by W B Yeats between 1910 and 1939. Includes 'No Second Troy,' 'September 1913,' 'The Fisherman,' 'Sailing to Byzantium,' 'Among Schoolchildren' and 'The Circus Animals' Desertion.' Uses a combination of dramatic readings, period art, live - action imagery and commentary by host Daragh Brehan.
History - World; Literature and Drama
Dist - BARR **Prod** - CEPRO 1991

W C Fields Comedy Series
Much Ado about Golf 9 MIN
Dist - RMIBHF

W C Fields festival series
The Barber shop 21 MIN
Dist - FI

W C Fields Mosaic 45 MIN
16mm
B&W
Highlights sequences from W C Field's Paramount and Universal feature films, including The Great Mc Goryl, Big Thumb, If I Had A Million, Circus Slickers and Hurry Hurry.
Fine Arts; Literature and Drama
Dist - CFS **Prod** - CFS 1975

W C Handy 14 MIN
16mm / U-matic / VHS
Color (J)
LC FIA68-861
Traces the cultural contribution of an outstanding Negro composer, W C Handy. Reflects the political, economic and sociological conditions of the American scene during the period 1890 - 1950. Shows the influences which directed William Christopher Handy's career.
Biography; Fine Arts; History - United States
Dist - PHENIX **Prod** - VIGNET 196

W E B DuBois 30 MIN
VHS
Black Americans of achievement collection II series
Color (J H C G)
$49.95 purchase _ #LVCD6617V - S
Provides interesting and concise information on scholar and activist W E B DuBois. Part of a 10 - part series on African - Americans.
History - United States
Dist - CAMV

W H Auden 30 MIN
VHS
Writers of today series
B&W (G)
$125.00 purchase, $50.00 rental
Features Auden talking about the declining role of the poet in modern times and explaining that the problem lies in the grand scale on which current events occur. Quotes him defining a poet as 'If one is stimulated by arbitrary restrictions, that person may be a poet.' Part of a series of dialogues between drama and literary critic Walter Kerr and a well - known male writer speaking about contemporary literature and society at the time of his own writing peaks.
Fine Arts; Literature and Drama
Dist - FIRS

W H Bill McGovern 30 MIN
U-matic
Not One of the Crowd Series
Color
Profiles a 77 year old deaf man who talks about the independent life he's led working, bringing up six children and being president of the Toronto Association for the Deaf. Available in a closed captioned version.
Guidance and Counseling; Psychology
Dist - TVOTAR **Prod** - TVOTAR 1981

W is for Wife Abuse 8 MIN
16mm
ABC's of Canadian Life Series
Color
Sets the issue of wife abuse in historical context, asking why there are so few convictions for this offense and what can be done about this problem.
Geography - World; Sociology
Dist - UTORMC **Prod** - UTORMC

W J Knox 30 MIN
VHS
Eminent chemists videotapes series
Color (H C G)
$60.00 purchase _ #VT - 029
Meets chemist W J Knox. Part of a series glimpsing into the history of chemistry and offering insights into the successes, trials and tribulations of some of the most distinguished names in the world of chemistry.
Science
Dist - AMCHEM

W Lincoln Hawkins 30 MIN
VHS
Eminent chemists videotapes series
Color (H C G)
$60.00 purchase _ #VT - 019
Meets chemist W Lincoln Hawkins. Part of a series glimpsing into the history of chemistry and offering insights into the successes, trials and tribulations of some of the most distinguished names in the world of chemistry.
Science
Dist - AMCHEM

W O Baker 30 MIN
VHS
Eminent chemists videotapes series
Color (H C G)
$60.00 purchase _ #VT - 027
Meets chemist W O Baker. Part of a series viewing the history of chemistry and offering insights into the successes, trials and tribulations of some of the most distinguished scientists in the world of chemistry.
Science
Dist - AMCHEM

W O Mitchell - Novelist in Hiding 58 MIN
16mm
Color (G)
_ #106C 0180 022
Shows W O Mitchell as writer, teacher, father, husband and on stage entertainer. Talks about himself, his work, and about the prairies which effected him and his writing. Passages are read from Mitchell's works.
Biography; Literature and Drama
Dist - CFLMDC **Prod** - NFBC 1980

W O W - women of the world 11 MIN
U-matic / VHS / 16mm
Color
LC 75-703618
Features an animated film without narration which presents a playfully earnest history of the world from the feminist viewpoint. Emphasizes the evolution of women's role in civilization.
History - World; Sociology
Dist - PFP **Prod** - WCCH 1975

An W plus B 8 MIN
16mm
Color (G)
$15.00 rental
Fine Arts
Dist - CANCIN **Prod** - KRENKU 1976

W, R, S 15 MIN
U-matic / VHS
Cursive writing series
Color (P)
Presents techniques of handwriting, focusing on the lower case letters w, r and s.
English Language
Dist - GPN **Prod** - WHROTV 1984

W S Mervin 29 MIN
U-matic
Poets Talking Series
Color
Literature and Drama
Dist - UMITV **Prod** - UMITV 1975

W Somerset Maugham 60 MIN
U-matic / VHS
Man of Letters Series
Color
Presents Malcolm Muggeridge discussing W Somerset Maugham. Includes the views of people who knew him and deals with what his works said about him.
Literature and Drama
Dist - MDCPB **Prod** - SCETV

The Wackiest Ship in the Army 99 MIN
U-matic / VHS / 16mm
Color (J)
Stars Jack Lemmon and Ricky Nelson in the saga of the most fouled - up crew ever.
Fine Arts
Dist - FI **Prod** - CPC 1961

The Wacky Machine 24 MIN
16mm / U-matic / VHS
Color (I)
Tells how Homer Price gets his hands on Uncle Ulysses' new doughnut machine, causing it to mass produce an endless supply of doughnuts. Describes the commotion when Mrs Chambers loses her diamond ring in the batter. Originally shown on the television series ABC Weekend Specials.
Fine Arts; Literature and Drama
Dist - CORF **Prod** - ABCTV 1976

The Waddingtons - Beaulieu House 29 MIN
U-matic
Dana Wynter in Ireland Series
Color
Presents Dana Wynter interviewing Nesbit and Sydney Waddington, tenth generation owners of Beaulieu House, one of Ireland's most beautiful estates.
Biography; Geography - World
Dist - PBS **Prod** - GRIAN

Wade Hampton 30 MIN
U-matic
Not One of the Crowd Series
Color
Profiles a polio victim who requires crutches to walk. He discusses the problems of the physically disabled as well as his success as a stockbroker and family man.
Psychology
Dist - TVOTAR **Prod** - TVOTAR 1981

Waffen - SS
VHS
War on Land and Sea Series
Color (G)
$29.95 purchase _ #1611
Shows the hidden war of World War II. Experiences the war from the point of view of the soldiers, pilots, sailors, leaders and home - front patriots. Includes archival footage from Britain and the Eastern Bloc countries. 'Waffen - SS' describes the German land troops of World War II.
Civics and Political Systems; History - United States; History - World; Sociology
Dist - KULTUR

Waffles 11 MIN
VHS
Color (P I)
$275.00, $205.00 purchase, $60.00 rental
Offers a fanciful children's story to inspire creative writing. Portrays a girl who falls asleep and dreams of making waffles. When she runs out of eggs she goes to a neighboring farm and gets a chicken; when she runs out of milk she brings back a cow. With all ingredients assembled she makes waffles for herself, her dog, the cow and the chicken. Upon awakening she finds her family in the kitchen - eating waffles.
English Language; Fine Arts; Literature and Drama
Dist - CF **Prod** - SCHIND 1986

Wages and Production 18 MIN
U-matic / VHS / 16mm
People on Market Street Series
Color (H A)
LC 77-702442
Applies demand and supply principles to labor. Shows how wage rates affect the kinds and amounts of labor services offered and the amount demanded. Presents some factors affecting wage rates.
Business and Economics; Social Science
Dist - CORF **Prod** - FNDREE 1977

Wages of fear 148 MIN
35mm / 16mm / VHS
B&W (G) (FRENCH WITH ENGLISH SUBTITLES)
Offers the complete version of the movie directed by Henri - Georges Clouzot. Tells of four down and out men in a small Latin American town who agree to transport two truckloads of unstable nitroglycerine over treacherous backroads to an oil fire. The drivers encounter a series of increasingly brutal setbacks and, as their chances of survival dwindle, are compelled to perform actrs of suicidal bravery. Stars Yves Montand.
Fine Arts; Sociology
Dist - KINOIC HOMVIS **Prod** - JANUS 1953

Wages of Sin 50 MIN
U-matic / 16mm
Assignment Maclear Series
Color; Mono (J H C A)
$500.00 film, $350.00 video, $50.00 rental
Discusses the possible legalization of some popular illegal activities, such as prostitution, gambling, and drugs. Looks at the pros and cons as well as how the government may stand to profit from the legalization.
Sociology
Dist - CTV **Prod** - CTV 1977

Waging a Campaign and Winning an Election 20 MIN
16mm
Government and Public Affairs Films Series
B&W (H A)
Robert Humphreys, former campaign director, Republican National Committee, shows how campaign strategy is developed.
Civics and Political Systems
Dist - MLA **Prod** - RSC 1960

Waging peace 90 MIN
VHS
CNN special reports series
Color (G A)
$29.95 purchase _ #TCO114OE
Examines the concept of peacemaking as it is being practiced around the world. Focuses on ongoing conflicts in Europe, El Salvador, Ireland, Israel and Africa. Explains and evaluates conflict resolution techniques. Hosted by Mark Walton.
Civics and Political Systems; History - World
Dist - TMM **Prod** - TMM

Wagner - Concert in Leipzig 90 MIN
VHS
Color (G)
$19.95 purchase _ #1243
Presents a concert of Wagner, including excerpts from 'Tristan And Isolde' and 'The Meistersinger.' Features Kurt Masur conducting the Leipzig Grandhaus Orchestra.
Fine Arts
Dist - KULTUR

Wagner Electric Corporation 12 MIN
16mm
Color
LC 77-701458
Offers a look at the Wagner Electric Corporation in order to show the flexibility of new management to the needs of the marketplace.
Business and Economics
Dist - WAGNER **Prod** - WAGNER 1976

Wagner ring cycle series

Das Rheingold	150 MIN
Die Walkure	245 MIN
Gotterdammerung	266 MIN
Siegfried	253 MIN

Dist - FOTH

Wagner - the Complete Epic 540 MIN
VHS
Color (G)
$124.95 purchase _ #1140
Presents a nine hour unedited biography of Richard Wagner. Stars Richard Burton in his final major film role. Costars Vanessa Redgrave, Sir Laurence Olivier, Sir John Gielgud and Sir Ralph Richardson. Includes the musical interpretation of Sir Georg Solti.
Fine Arts; Geography - World
Dist - KULTUR

Wagner - the Ring Cycle
VHS
Color (C) (GERMAN)
$599.00 purchase _ #AD - 740
Presents 'Das Rheingold,' 'Die Walkure,' 'Siegfried' and 'Gotterdammerung' by Wagner. Features the Bayreuth Festival production, staged by Patrice Cherau, conducted by Pierre Boulez, with Donald McIntyre, Gwyneth Jones and Herman Becht.
Fine Arts
Dist - FOTH **Prod** - FOTH

Wagonmaster 86 MIN
VHS
B&W; CC (G)
$19.95 purchase _ #6128
Tells about two roaming cowhands who join a Mormon wagon train heading for the Utah frontier. Stars Ben Johnson, Joanne Dru, Harry Carey, Jr, Ward Bond, Jane Dawell and James Arness. Directed by John Ford.
Fine Arts; Literature and Drama
Dist - APRESS

Wagons west 20 MIN
16mm / U-matic / VHS
Americana series
Color
Traces the history of the crossing of America by using a 90 - mile, 8 - day tourist excursion in covered wagons to compare and contrast the experiences on the contemporary wagon train with those of the pioneers.
History - United States
Dist - HANDEL **Prod** - HANDEL 1977

Wagons West 14 MIN
16mm
B&W (H)
Re - enacts the journey of a mule - drawn covered wagon train over the Oregon Trail, from Missouri to Oregon.
History - United States
Dist - HF **Prod** - NYLI 1960

The Wahgi - eater of men 57 MIN
VHS
River journeys series
Color (H C G)
$285.00 purchase, $75.00 rental
Travels with Christina Dodwell who looks for adventure on two of New Guinea's rivers. Reveals that on the Sepik she goes alligator hunting and is included in a 'skin cutting' ceremony, rite of passage in which adolescent males are ritually scarred with razor blades. Dodwell then joins a rafting expedition attempting to make the first descent of the ferocious Wahgi River, the 'Eater of Men.' Part of a seven - part series on world rivers.
Geography - World
Dist - CF **Prod** - BBCTV 1985

Wai Dan Chi Kung - The eight pieces of brocade 60 MIN
VHS
Color (G)
$45.00 purchase _ #1158
Teaches a fundamental external ch'i kung exercise that is said to be easy to do and balances the ch'i in the body. Involves both sitting and standing postures for beginners. With Dr Yang Jwing - ming.
Physical Education and Recreation
Dist - WAYF

Waiapi body painting and ornaments 18 MIN
U-matic / VHS
Waiapi Indians of Brazil series
Color (C G)
$105.00 purchase, $20.00 rental _ #CC3782VU, #CC3782VH
Documents Waiapi body ornamentation. Shows how they use urucu, a red pigment spread without pattern across body surfaces, or genipapo, a black pigment carefully painted in fixed patterns. Shows how feathers, glass beads and flowers are used to adorn and celebrate various aspects of Waiapi culture. Part of a five - part series on the Waiapi Indians of Brazil. Produced by Victor Fuks.
Fine Arts; Geography - World; Social Science; Sociology
Dist - IU

Waiapi Indians of Brazil series

Caxiri or manioc beer	19 MIN
Music, dance and festival among the Waiapi Indians of Brazil	39 MIN

Waiapi body painting and ornaments 18 MIN
Waiapi instrumental music 58 MIN
Waiapi slash and burn cultivation 22 MIN
Dist - IU

Waiapi instrumental music 58 MIN
VHS / U-matic
Waiapi Indians of Brazil series
Color (C G)
$180.00 purchase, $35.00 rental _ #CC3783VU, #CC3783VH
Examines a variety of wind instruments and the contexts in which they are used. Demonstrates several flutes, including so'o kangwera, played solo, and pira ra'anga, played in ensemble and shown accompanying the dance of a fish festival. Explains several 'trumpets' and reed instruments, the nhima poku and jawarun ra'anga. Reveals that the Waiapi make gender distinctions in music - women can sing, but only the men play the instruments. Part of a five - part series on the Waiapi Indians of Brazil. Produced by Victor Fuks.
Fine Arts; Geography - World; Social Science; Sociology
Dist - IU

Waiapi slash and burn cultivation 22 MIN
VHS / U-matic
Waiapi Indians of Brazil series
Color (C G)
$150.00 purchase, $25.00 rental _ #CC3780VU, #CC3780VH
Examines the slash and burn cultivation techniques used by the Waiapi Indians of Brazil. Part of a five - part series on the Waiapi. Produced by Victor Fuks.
Agriculture; Geography - World; Social Science; Sociology
Dist - IU

The Waika and Makiritare - Food Gathering 11 MIN
16mm
Indians of the Orinoco Series
Color (J)
Geography - World; Social Science; Sociology
Dist - IFF **Prod** - BRYAN 1972

The Waika and Makiritare - Journey to the Makiritare 9 MIN
16mm
Indians of the Orinoco Series
Color (J)
LC 72-703353
Geography - World; Social Science; Sociology
Dist - IFF **Prod** - BRYAN 1972

The Waist Land - Eating Disorders 23 MIN
U-matic / VHS / 16mm
Color (C A)
Explores the social and psychological forces behind the rapid rise of bulimia and anorexia, two eating disorders.
Health and Safety; Psychology
Dist - CORF **Prod** - GANNET

The Waist Land - Why Diets Don't Work 23 MIN
16mm / U-matic / VHS
Color (C A)
Explores the dangerous obsession with slimness and gives tips on safe, healthy diets.
Health and Safety; Psychology
Dist - CORF **Prod** - GANNET

Wait 7 MIN
16mm
Color (G)
$15.00 rental
Offers a companion film to Morning. Reveals, through rhythms of light, something happening on a mental level between two people sitting in a room. Produced by Ernie Gehr.
Fine Arts
Dist - CANCIN

The Wait 18 MIN
16mm
B&W
LC 75-700092
Presents an experimental film which presents the violent story of a confrontation between a bounty hunter and four outlaws.
Industrial and Technical Education; Literature and Drama
Dist - WESTRN **Prod** - WESTRN 1974

Wait - and - Weight Method - Worksheet, Calculations and Procedures 24 MIN
U-matic / VHS
Color (IND)
Describes filling out a kill sheet, calculations needed and using a chart to figure pump kill rate for the wait - and - weight well - killing method.
Industrial and Technical Education; Social Science
Dist - UTEXPE **Prod** - UTEXPE 1978

Wait of the world 87 MIN
VHS
Color (G R) (SPANISH)
$69.95 purchase _ #268VSV
Follows T J, Brian and Karen, all writers for a Christian magazine, as they cover mission stories in various locations. Shows how the three become involved in the lives of the people they are writing about.
Guidance and Counseling; Literature and Drama; Religion and Philosophy
Dist - GF

Wait 'til Trish sees this - Video II 30 MIN
U-matic / VHS / BETA
Sexual harassment pure and simple series
Color; CC; PAL (PRO G IND)
$695.00 purchase
Presents options available for resolving sexual harassment situations. Shows how harassment victims can confront or report the incident to a supervisor or human resource person. Outlines different corrective actions in vignettes to serve as a useful deterrent for would - be harassers. Supports a 30 - minute to two - hour training session. Part two of two parts on preventing costly sexual harassment complaints and lawsuits in manufacturing and service industries.
Business and Economics; Psychology; Social Science; Sociology
Dist - BNA **Prod** - BNA 1994

Wait 'till we're sixty five 60 MIN
Videoreel / VHS
Color (J)
Presents a documentary that examines the aging process, the value of the elderly in our society and the importance of developing realistic attitudes about the problems of growing old. Narrated by Steve Allen and featuring interviews with Roy Rogers, Dale Evans, Molly Picon and Representative Claude Pepper.
Health and Safety; Sociology
Dist - ECUFLM **Prod** - NBCNEW 1981

Wait Until Dark 108 MIN
16mm / U-matic / VHS
Color (J)
Stars Audrey Hepburn. Tells of how three clever and diabolical thugs insinuate themselves into the apartment of a recently blinded young woman in search of a shipment of smuggled heroin.
Fine Arts
Dist - FI **Prod** - WB 1968

Wait your turn 25 MIN
VHS
Big comfy couch series
Color (K P)
$14.99 purchase _ #0 - 7835 - 8313 - 3NK
Shows that interrupting is not a good thing to do when a clown is talking on the phone. Reveals that Loonette and Molly discover ways to have their say and wait their turn. Stimulates physical, mental and emotional growth. Shows youngsters how to deal with typical feelings and fears. Offers movement games and activities for developing coordination and motor skills. Builds positive attitudes toward books and reading. Part of a series.
English Language; Guidance and Counseling; Literature and Drama
Dist - TILIED **Prod** - PBS 1995

Waiter 5 MIN
U-matic
Good work series
Color (H)
Provides useful, up to date information on various occupations to aid high school students in career selection. Available in five series of ten jobs each.
Education; Guidance and Counseling; Health and Safety; Social Science
Dist - TVOTAR **Prod** - TVOTAR 1981

Waiter 4.5 MIN
VHS / 16mm
Good works 5 series
Color (A PRO)
$40.00 purchase _ #BPN238004
Presents the occupation of a waiter. Gives a profile of a young person who is either undergoing an apprenticeship or has recently completed training in this field. Takes the viewer on a tour of this person's workplace and explains the practical skills and training offered by employers and schools. Gives a better understanding of the demand for skilled workers today and the potential for personal growth.
Guidance and Counseling
Dist - RMIBHF **Prod** - RMIBHF

Waiters and waitresses - basic responsibilities 15 MIN
U-matic / VHS / 16mm
Professional food preparation and service programs series
Color
Covers every important responsibility of food servers, including effective preparation, welcoming the guest, order taking and proper serving. Discusses the importance of good grooming and personal hygiene. Stresses menu knowledge and gives helpful tips on suggestive selling and checking back with guests.
Industrial and Technical Education
Dist - NEM **Prod** - NEM 1983

The Waiter's Ball 13 MIN
16mm
B&W
Presents Fatty Arbuckle and Al St John in a madcap exhibition of slapstick comedy.
Fine Arts
Dist - KILLIS **Prod** - UNKNWN 1914

Waiting 7 MIN
16mm
Audio visual research briefs series
Color
LC 75-702441
Describes the social, mental and physical problems of a woman suffering from kidney disease. Explains the problem of finding and keeping a job along with her many hours on a kidney machine and her eventual vocational rehabilitation.
Health and Safety; Psychology; Science - Natural; Sociology
Dist - USNAC **Prod** - USRSA 1974

Waiting for a Shearwater 17 MIN
16mm
Color
LC 80-700932
Shows the work of National Park rangers in keeping a balance between nature and man.
Geography - World; Science - Natural
Dist - TASCOR **Prod** - TASCOR 1979

Waiting for Beckett 86 MIN
VHS
Color (H C G)
Profiles the life of Irish playwright Samuel Beckett. Includes footage from performances of his plays, historical footage, interviews and excerpts from Beckett's private correspondence. Interviews Mary Manning, the only surviving family friend who grew up with Beckett, and villagers of Roussillon in the south of France, who recall when Beckett was a member of the French Resistance and was forced to remain in the village in hiding. Features actors Steve Martin and Bill Irwin performing and discussing their personal responses to Beckett's work, as well as archival footage of Burgess Meredith and Zero Mostel in the first television production of Waiting for Godot, along with performances by others. Available for purchase with Peephole Art for $99.95.
Fine Arts; Literature and Drama
Dist - GLOBAL **Prod** - GLOBAL

Waiting for Cambodia 60 MIN
VHS
Color (G)
$59.95 purchase _ #WTCM - 000
Surveys the problem of Cambodian refugees, who have fled their country but cannot legally immigrate elsewhere. Suggests that political considerations have prevented a solution, and reviews the political and strategic history of Cambodia.
History - World; Sociology
Dist - PBS **Prod** - WHYY 1988

Waiting for Fidel 58 MIN
16mm
Color (H C A)
LC 76-701075
Portrays three government and communications experts as they await a promised interview with Fidel Castro. Shows them discussing socialism and their experiences in Cuba.
Civics and Political Systems; Fine Arts; Geography - World; History - World
Dist - NFBC **Prod** - NFBC 1974

Waiting for Fidel, Pt 1 29 MIN
16mm
Color (H C A)
LC 76-701075
Documents a trip to Cuba by former Premier of Newfoundland Joey Smallwood.
Geography - World
Dist - NFBC **Prod** - NFBC 1974

Waiting for Fidel, Pt 2 29 MIN
16mm
Color (H C A)
LC 76-701075
Documents a trip to Cuba by former Premier of Newfoundland Joey Smallwood.
Geography - World
Dist - NFBC **Prod** - NFBC 1974

Waiting for Godot 102 MIN
16mm
B&W (H C A)
LC 72-700444
Presents Samuel Beckett's two - act tragicomedy.
Literature and Drama
Dist - GROVE **Prod** - GROVE 1971

Waiting for Harry 57 MIN
VHS / 16mm
Color (C G)
$950.00, $295.00 purchase, $60.00 rental _ #10727, #37467
Illustrates many of the problems faced by contemporary Australian Aborigines in practicing their ancient rituals, as well as the dilemmas faced by a sympathetic anthropologist who must decide whether to observe or become involved in the events studied.
Geography - World; History - World; Religion and Philosophy; Sociology
Dist - UCEMC **Prod** - AUSIAS 1981

Waiting for Love 80 MIN
16mm
Color (H C A) (RUSSIAN (ENGLISH SUBTITLES))
LC 83-700205
Presents a light - hearted romance about Rita, who plans to marry a mechanic named Gavrilov. Relates that waiting for Gavrilov at the registry, Rita is involved in a number of comical situations.
Fine Arts; Foreign Language
Dist - IFEX **Prod** - MOSFLM 1983

Waiting for Love, Pt 1 40 MIN
16mm
Color (H C A) (RUSSIAN (ENGLISH SUBTITLES))
LC 83-700205
A Russian language film with English subtitles. Presents a light - hearted romance about Rita, who plans to marry a mechanic named Gavrilov. Relates that waiting for Gavrilov at the registry, Rita is involved in a number of comical situations.
Fine Arts
Dist - IFEX **Prod** - MOSFLM 1983

Waiting for Love, Pt 2 40 MIN
16mm
Color (H C A) (RUSSIAN (ENGLISH SUBTITLES))
LC 83-700205
A Russian language film with English subtitles. Presents a light - hearted romance about Rita, who plans to marry a mechanic named Gavrilov. Relates that waiting for Gavrilov at the registry, Rita is involved in a number of comical situations.
Fine Arts
Dist - IFEX **Prod** - MOSFLM 1983

Waiting for Madonna 10 MIN
VHS
Magnum eye series
Color (G)
$125.00 purchase, $30.00 rental
Explores the life of the paparazzi, freelance photographers who single - mindedly track down celebrities in hopes of a candid shot - effectively turning voyeurism into an art form and big business. Follows Dave Hogan, an English paparazzo, from crowded costume balls, to airport runways at dawn, to backdoors of hotels. Records the photographer's daily life with all its waiting, momentary thrills and innumerable disappointments. Culminates with a tense chase of the elusive pop star, Madonna. Taps into our society's obsession with fame. Directed by Peter Marlow. Part of a series by photographers from the Magnum Photo Agency.
Fine Arts; Industrial and Technical Education; Sociology
Dist - FIRS **Prod** - MIYAKE 1993

Waiting for the caribou 30 MIN
VHS / 16mm
Color (G)
$280.00 purchase, $55.00 rental
Shows what goes on behind the headlines of emergency relief to disaster victims and the people delivering these goods to devastated regions. Tells the story of a warehouse worker in Maputo, Mozambique, who travels for the first time into the war - torn countryside where millions have fled their homes. Examines the many exasperating tribulations often retarding these well - intentioned missions of mercy. Film by Peter Entell; produced by the United Nations Disaster Relief Office.
Civics and Political Systems; Fine Arts; History - World
Dist - FIRS

Waiting for the Go 4 MIN
16mm
Color
LC 76-701391
Presents one man's dilemma while standing at a stoplight.
Fine Arts
Dist - YORKU **Prod** - YORKU 1975

Waiting for the Invasion - U S Citizens in Nicaragua 27 MIN
16mm
Color
Presents the human side of the complex drama unfolding in Nicaragua, and approaches the situation from a novel perspective, by exploring the lives and work of the U S community residing in Managua.
Geography - World; History - World
Dist - ICARUS **Prod** - ICARUS

Waiting for the Wind 10 MIN
VHS / U-matic
Color
Evokes the terror of a world completely out of personal control. Presents a tornado - like catastrophe.
Fine Arts
Dist - KITCHN **Prod** - KITCHN

The Waiting Game - Control or Confrontation 20 MIN
VHS / U-matic
Missiles of October - a Case Study in Decision Making Series
Color
Business and Economics; Civics and Political Systems; History - World
Dist - DELTAK **Prod** - LCOA

The Waiting Generation 25 MIN
U-matic / BETA / VHS
Our Man in China Series
Color; Mono (H C A)
$200.00 purchase, $50.00 rental
Reflects on the fate of young people in modern China.Points out that there are not enough jobs for most young people unless they have well placed friends or a relative who is close to retirement. Video includes interveiws with a leadind movie actress and a shipyard worker.
Geography - World; History - World; Sociology
Dist - CTV **Prod** - CTV 1982

Waiting in the Wings 60 MIN
16mm / U-matic / VHS
I, Claudius Series Number 3; No 3
Color (C A)
Describes how the bloody competition for the Roman throne intensifies and a favorable portent ushers young Claudius into the scene.
History - World
Dist - FI **Prod** - BBCTV 1977

Waiting Months, the 13 MIN
U-matic / VHS
Color
Explains normal pregnancy. Describes physical changes. Gives some of the reasons for careful medical supervision during pregnancy.
Health and Safety
Dist - MEDFAC **Prod** - MEDFAC 1981

Waiting on Tables at Sea 14 MIN
16mm
Color
LC 77-700707
Provides guidelines for food service personnel aboard ships at sea, including the importance of their relationship with passengers, personal cleanliness, preparations before the meal, conduct and cleanup after the meal.
Guidance and Counseling; Industrial and Technical Education; Sociology
Dist - USNAC **Prod** - USN 1955

The Waiting Room 29 MIN
16mm / U-matic / VHS
Color (H C A)
Provides a discussion of the pros and cons of abortion set at an abortion clinic on the day of a Right - To - Life demonstration. Deals with how the women feel about abortions and how it affects their family and themselves.
Health and Safety; Sociology
Dist - CAROUF **Prod** - LOUISL

The Waiting Room 28 MIN
16mm
Color
LC 79-701310
Traces the experiences of a man who is unknowingly suffering from a duodenal ulcer and does not seek medical attention until his personal and physical problems reach an advanced stage. Shows the advanced technology and treatment available for ulcers.
Health and Safety
Dist - VISION **Prod** - SKF 1979

Waiting tables 20 MIN
VHS
Color (H C G)
$250.00 purchase, $45.00 rental
Takes a lighthearted look at waitressing and raises serious questions about women's labor issues. Reveals that waitressing is non - unionized and underpaid because the workers are mostly women. Meets waitresses who enjoy their work but worry because they have no job security, health and disabilty insurance and are subject to age discrimination. Offers an entertaining Lily Tomlin routine and the experiences of Gloria Steinem as a Playboy bunny. Produced by Linda Chapman, Pam LeBlanc and Freddi Stevens Jacobi.
Sociology
Dist - FLMLIB

Waiting to work 20 MIN
VHS
Works series
Color; PAL (G)
PdS50 purchase
Follows the efforts of engineers as they face the challenge of setting up mechanisms which work when, and only when, they are needed. Shows engineers in a creative light as they apply their knowledge and skills to the problems of machinery timing. Part one of a six - part series.
Industrial and Technical Education
Dist - BBCENE

Waitress Wanted 9 MIN
16mm
Color
LC 80-700403
Looks at an older man who is possessed by his love for a young woman. Tells how he confronts her with his passion and she rejects him.
Fine Arts
Dist - CYRUS **Prod** - CYRUS 1979

The Wake 14 MIN
16mm
Color (G)
$25.00 rental
Portrays the wide range of emotions dealing with grief. Represents a sense of emptiness evolving from landscapes that graphically and poetically evoke the theme of loss. A Carolyn McLuskie production.
Fine Arts; Health and Safety; Sociology
Dist - CANCIN

Wake Forest
VHS
Campus clips series
Color (H C A)
$29.95 purchase _ #CC0084V
Takes a video visit to the campus of Wake Forest University in North Carolina. Shows many of the distinctive features of the campus, and interviews students about their experiences. Provides information on the composition of the student body, professors, academics, social life, housing, and other subjects.
Education
Dist - CAMV

Wake of '38 59 MIN
VHS / 16mm
Color (G)
$70.00 rental _ #WAKE - 000
Documents the great hurricane and tidal wave of 1938.
Geography - United States; History - United States
Dist - PBS

The Wake - Up Call 19 MIN
16mm / VHS
Color; B&W (H C R)
$650.00 film, $69.95 and $49.95 video purchase
Tells the story of a reclusive photographer who wakes to find a Bible - quoting intruder in his apartment. Scene provokes an energetic dialogue about righteousness and personal responsibility and focuses on fundamental theological issues.
Religion and Philosophy
Dist - OTAR **Prod** - OTAR 1990

Wake Up, Charlie Churchman 20 MIN
16mm
B&W
Shows that, in a harrowing dream, Charlie finds himself attending God's funeral. Pictures him stealing back to the cemetery to examine the casket, and finding it empty. Concludes with Charlie's realization that it is not God who is dead, but apathetic, lethargic churchmen.
Guidance and Counseling; Religion and Philosophy
Dist - FAMF **Prod** - FAMF

Wake up, Freddy 21 MIN
VHS
Color (P I J T)
$195.00 purchase, $40.00 rental
Follows the path energy takes to get to Freddy's house and to power his alarm clock. Looks at the origins of water and how it travels through pipes and processing stations all the way to Freddy's shower head. Provides a whimsical introduction to where resources come from and where waste goes, with a bouncy soundtrack. Produced by Christopher O'Donnell. Includes study guide.

Social Science
Dist - BULFRG

Wake Up Mes Bons Amis - Pays Sans Bon Sens 117 MIN
16mm
B&W
_ #106B 0170 082N
Geography - World
Dist - CFLMDC **Prod** - NFBC 1970

Wake up to sleep 30 MIN
VHS
Bodymatters series
Color (H C A)
PdS65 purchase
Explains the body's need for rest and sleep. Part of a series of 26 30-minute videos on various systems of the human body.
Health and Safety; Psychology; Science - Natural
Dist - BBCENE

Wake Up You Sleepyhead 30 MIN
VHS / 16mm
Color (P)
$14.44 purchase _ #V5084
Present songs and movements for waking children up.
Fine Arts; Psychology
Dist - EDUCRT

Waking from coma 51 MIN
VHS
Color (G)
$149.00 purchase, $75.00 rental _ #UW5350
Shows how a British hospital is pioneering a program of coma arousal therapy designed to give some PVS patients a chance for a better life. Looks at three young men in their twenties who have spent months in a twilight world between life and death. The three are at different stages of arousal and the program illustrates how long and arduous the process is. Discloses that the therapy is controversial - provoking passionate debate about whether treating severely brain - injured people is worthwhile for the patients, their families and those who must bear the financial burden.
Health and Safety; Psychology
Dist - FOTH

Waking up 30 MIN
VHS / BETA
Personal and spiritual development series
Color (G)
$29.95 purchase _ #S020
Suggests that the normal waking state of human consciousness can be likened to being asleep in comparison to other states of awareness which could be attained. Features Dr Charles Tart, psychologist and author of 'Altered States of Consciousness' and 'Waking Up.' Part of a four - part series on personal and spiritual development.
Health and Safety; Psychology
Dist - THINKA **Prod** - THINKA

Waking Up from Dope 40 MIN
VHS
(J H C A)
$69.95 purchase _ #AE100V
Discusses the effects of marijuana, cigarettes, mushrooms, alcohol, andgel dust and heroin and the satisfaction that can come from rejecting the use of these substances. Hosted by former drug addict and rock star Jevon Thompson.
Guidance and Counseling; Health and Safety; Psychology; Sociology
Dist - CAMV **Prod** - CAMV

Waking Up to Rape 35 MIN
16mm / VHS
Color (G)
$500.00, $250.00 purchase, $65.00 rental
Examines the trauma of rape, the long - term psychological effects, societal attitudes about sexual assault and the problem of racism in the criminal justice system. Describes the rape experiences of three survivors - Black, Chicana and White. Discusses acquaintance rape, incest and rape by a stranger. Interviews women police officers, counselors and self - defense instructors. Offers support for those coping with sexual assault experiences. Produced by Meri Weingarten.
Health and Safety; Psychology; Sociology
Dist - WMEN **Prod** - MERI 1985

Walbiri Fire Ceremony 21 MIN
U-matic / VHS / 16mm
Australian Institute of Aboriginal Studies Series
Color
Documents a spectacular Aboriginal ceremony, a communal ritual of penance that serves to settle disputes within the community. Shows how it culminates in a nighttime ordeal in which some of the participants are humiliated and engage in self - flagellation with burning bundles of twigs.
History - World
Dist - UCEMC **Prod** - AUSIAS 1979

Walcott - Marciano 30 MIN
16mm
IBC Championship Fights, Series 1 Series
B&W
Physical Education and Recreation
Dist - SFI **Prod** - SFI

Walden 10 MIN
U-matic / VHS / 16mm
Color (H C)
LC 81-700401
Presents images which illustrate passages from Thoreau's book Walden.
Literature and Drama
Dist - ICARUS **Prod** - LAFCAR 1980

Waldenville I 38 MIN
16mm
Out of Conflict - Accord Series
Color
LC 78-701086
Shows the unfolding of a collective bargaining negotiation to the point of deadlock and the subsequent realization that some type of neutral third party intervention is required.
Business and Economics
Dist - USNAC **Prod** - USDL 1978

Waldenville I 36 MIN
16mm / VHS
Color (G IND)
$5.00 rental
Presents a realistic picture of collective bargaining between and public employee union and city officials. Concentrates on the mechanics of bargaining - how proposals and counter proposals are made and responded to, how agreements on various issues are reached at the bargaining table. Part one of two parts.
Business and Economics; Psychology; Social Science
Dist - AFLCIO **Prod** - USDL 1978

Waldenville II 28 MIN
16mm / VHS
Color (G IND)
$5.00 rental
Begins with the final scenes of the collective bargaining film to show how the mediation process works to help reach an agreement when bargaining is deadlocked. Ends short of total agreement. Part two of two parts.
Business and Economics; Psychology; Social Science
Dist - AFLCIO **Prod** - USDL 1978

Waldenville II 31 MIN
16mm
Out of Conflict - Accord Series
Color
LC 78-701082
Shows the mediation process and the way in which the mediation works to assist the parties in reaching an agreement.
Business and Economics
Dist - USNAC **Prod** - USDL 1978

Waldenville III 36 MIN
16mm
Out of Conflict - Accord Series
Color
LC 81-700660
Presents a dramatization of collective bargaining negotiations ending in a deadlock, showing how fact finding is used as another means of reaching accord.
Business and Economics
Dist - USNAC **Prod** - USDL 1980

Waldenville jogger 39 MIN
16mm / VHS
Color (G IND)
$5.00 rental
Looks at the case of a young man who works as a technician at the city hospital and is charged with violating attendance rules by jogging during working hours. Shows both the city and the employee preparing and presenting their cases to the arbitrator. Produced by the Department of Labor, Public Employees Division.
Business and Economics; Psychology; Social Science
Dist - AFLCIO

Waldenville Jogger 39 MIN
16mm
Out of Conflict - Accord Series
Color
LC 78-700773
Shows the arbitration of a grievance which results when a city attempts to enforce attendance rules for workers at a municipal hospital. Depicts preparation for the hearing and presentation of the case to the arbitrator.
Business and Economics
Dist - USNAC **Prod** - USDL 1980

Waldo's Hat 30 MIN
U-matic
Today's Special Series
Color (K P)
Develops language arts skills in children. Programs are thematically designed around subjects of interest to youngsters. Action takes place in a department store where people, mannequins, puppets, comic characters and special guests present a light hearted approach to language arts.
Fine Arts; Literature and Drama; Psychology
Dist - TVOTAR **Prod** - TVOTAR 1985

Wales and the Midlands - Pt 2 105 MIN
VHS
Great Houses of Britain Series
Color (S)
$29.95 purchase _ #057 - 9002
Joins art historian Viscount Norwich for a tour of twelve of Britain's great houses and castles. Teaches about British architecture, views the exquisite contents of the houses and surveys the magnificent grounds from a helicopter. Interviews the owners and caretakes - a fascinating cast of characters which includes a water - skiing marquis and an especially articulate kitchen maid. Part 2 glimpses at 'downstair' life as revealed by a former maid at Chirk Castle, tours Haddon Hall, a thirteenth century dwelling in Derbyshire, and Ragley Hall, a famous house saved from destruction.
Fine Arts; Geography - World; History - World; Sociology
Dist - FI

Wales and the Welsh Borderlands 21 MIN
U-matic / VHS / 16mm
Color (I J H)
LC 76-707292
Points out the physical character, agriculture and industry of Wales and the borderlands, surveys the types of industry in different regions and contrasts the changing pattern of industry in South Wales with the almost unchanging agriculture and scenic grandeur.
Agriculture; Business and Economics; Geography - World; Science - Natural; Science - Physical; Social Science
Dist - IFB **Prod** - BHA 1969

Wales - Heritage of a Nation 25 MIN
VHS
Color (S)
$19.95 purchase _ #423 - 9003
Features as narrator the late Richard Burton who provides the commentary for this colorful portrait of his native land. Views the startlingly beautiful Welsh landscape of mountains and valleys, peaceful lakes, dramatic cliffs, as well as Roman forts, thirteenth century castles, ancient abbeys, relics of the early industrial age and the home of poet Dylan Thomas.
Fine Arts; Geography - World; History - World
Dist - FI

The Wales of Dylan Thomas 15 MIN
U-matic / VHS
Color (C)
$249.00, $149.00 purchase _ #AD - 1707
Combines the images of the words of Dylan Thomas and his native habitat, Wales.
Fine Arts; Geography - World; Literature and Drama
Dist - FOTH **Prod** - FOTH

Walk 20 MIN
16mm
Color (G)
$30.00 rental
Documents the marking out of suburban space by following walking feet. Progresses to a preoccupation with the dancing shadow of the camera. Footage contains golden colors and solarization effects. Produced by Dirk De Bruyn.
Fine Arts
Dist - CANCIN

Walk 8 MIN
16mm / U-matic / VHS
Color
LC 74-702592
Uses clay figures and animation by means of modeling in presenting a story of a busy mother who sends her husband and son for a walk and the boy is carried away by a balloon on a string.
Fine Arts; Literature and Drama
Dist - PHENIX **Prod** - CFET 1974

Walk a Country Mile 29 MIN
VHS / 16mm
Color (G)
$55.00 rental _ #WALK - 000
Examines the lifestyles and difficulties of poor residents in rural New Jersey.
Geography - United States; Social Science; Sociology
Dist - PBS **Prod** - NJPBA

Walk Around Inspection 15 MIN
16mm
Color (IND)
Follows an OSHA inspector as he walks around a plant and a construction site checking noise levels, air pollution and guard rails. Discusses the role of a safety committee.
Civics and Political Systems; Health and Safety
Dist - AFLCIO **Prod** - USDL 1972

Walk Awhile in My Shoes 27 MIN
16mm
Color (J)
LC 76-702151
Explores the problems of architectural barriers and poorly designed transportation systems which make it difficult for handicapped people to get around.
Education; Fine Arts; Industrial and Technical Education; Psychology; Social Science
Dist - NFBC **Prod** - NFBC 1974

Walk Before You Run - the Developmental Stages of Thinking 29 MIN
VHS / 16mm
Color (C PRO)
$250.00 purchase _ #292001
Demonstrates through a dramatization how students differ in their development and thinking skills at different ages. Emphasizes that educators cannot assume that children think, perceive and learn as adults do.
Education; Psychology
Dist - ACCESS **Prod** - ACCESS 1989

Walk, Don't Run 114 MIN
16mm / U-matic / VHS
Color (H C A)
Stars Cary Grant, Samantha Eggar and Jim Hutton in an escapade set in Tokyo, where the Olympic Games had created a considerable housing shortage.
Fine Arts
Dist - FI **Prod** - CPC 1966

Walk - Don't Walk 10 MIN
16mm
Color (P I)
Discusses pedestrian safety practices for everyday situations. Includes crossing streets, the use of traffic signs and signals and becoming aware of possible dangers.
Health and Safety
Dist - VADE **Prod** - VADE 1975

A Walk in the Forest 28 MIN
16mm
Color (G)
_ #106C 0176 094
Illustrates the adaptability of wild life through the seasonal changes in the British Columbia forests and stresses man's responsibility for the renewal of the forest.
Geography - World; Science - Natural
Dist - CFLMDC **Prod** - NFBC 1976

A Walk in the Forest 28 MIN
U-matic / VHS / 16mm
Color (K) (FRENCH GERMAN)
LC 76-700722
Presents a documentary film on the ecological interdependence of all living things in the fir rainforests of the Pacific slope. Shows how animals, seasons, rain, fire and man work in concert.
Science - Natural
Dist - PFP **Prod** - PFP 1976

A Walk in the rainforest 11 MIN
VHS
Color (P I J)
$195.00 purchase, $25.00 rental
Takes a tour of the rainforest guided by eight - year - old Jason Harding of Belize, Central America. Points out the rich diversity of life there and the desirability of saving such important places. In the Chan Chich Wildlife Reserve, children see the beauty of the environment, with mahogany trees, toucans, monkeys and leaf - cutter ants. With study guide.
Fine Arts; Geography - World; Science - Natural
Dist - BULFRG **Prod** - YNF 1990

Walk in their Shoes - Parent - Child Communication 24 MIN
16mm
Color (J)
LC 75-700063
Tells the story of how a brother and sister find out what it is like to carry some of the responsibilities their parents have. Shows how they find that being responsible for someone's life is not easy, especially where there is opposition.
Guidance and Counseling; Psychology
Dist - BYU **Prod** - BYU 1968

Walk on the Moon 15 MIN
16mm
Screen news digest series; Vol 12; Issue 1
Color (J)
LC 77-710004
Historic documentary on the exploration of space from the pioneering flights of Dr Goodard to the lunar landing of Apollo 11.
History - United States; Science - Physical; Social Science
Dist - HEARST **Prod** - HEARST

Walk on the moon, walk with the Son 60 MIN
VHS
Color (J H C G A R)
$29.95 purchase, $10.00 rental _ #35 - 96 - 8936
Presents the personal testimony of astronaut Charlie Duke. Shows that Duke considers his Christian spiritual journey of far greater importance than his having walked on the Moon. Produced by Bridgestone.
Religion and Philosophy
Dist - APH

Walk Safe, Young America 16 MIN
16mm / U-matic / VHS
Color (K P I)
LC 76-701847
Presents June Lockhart as a school crossing guard pointing out pedestrian safety rules, including ways to observe traffic signs, the need to stay in crosswalks and avoid rushing into the street and the practicality of entering and leaving cars on the sidewalk side.
Guidance and Counseling; Health and Safety
Dist - PFP **Prod** - STNLYL 1976

Walk Safely 13 MIN
16mm
Color (I)
LC 83-700512
Points out the causes of walking accidents and shows correct crossing procedure.
Health and Safety
Dist - FIESTF **Prod** - FIESTF 1983

Walk the first step 28 MIN
Videoreel / VT2
Turning points series
Color
Examines the problem of unemployment among minority groups and the success of Los Angeles' Mexican - American Opportunity Foundation (MAOF) in finding jobs for the unemployable.
Sociology
Dist - PBS **Prod** - KCET

Walk this path of hope - Al - Anon in institutions 11 MIN
VHS
Color (G)
$25.00 purchase _ #AV - 19
Shares the experiences of Al - Anon members involved in institutions services.
Guidance and Counseling; Health and Safety; Psychology
Dist - ALANON **Prod** - ALANON

A Walk through the 20th century - the democrat and the dictator 58 MIN
VHS
Color & B&W (G)
$19.95 purchase _ #PBS117
Features Bill Moyers who examines the parallels between Franklin Delano Roosevelt - FDR - and Adolf Hitler.
Biography; History - United States; History - World
Dist - INSTRU **Prod** - PBS

Walk through the 20th Century with Bill Moyers Series
Reviews many of the most significant events of the 20th century. Considers issues such as the world wars, the growth of mass communications, politics, science and advertising. Uses archival film, newsreel and televsion footage. Nineteen - part series is hosted by Bill Moyers.

America on the road 58 MIN
The Arming of the Earth 58 MIN
Change, Change 55 MIN
Come to the fairs 58 MIN
The Democrat and the dictator 58 MIN
The Helping hand 55 MIN
The Image makers 58 MIN
Marshall, Texas - Marshall, Texas 90 MIN
Out of the Depths - the Miners' Story 55 MIN
Postwar hopes, cold war fears 58 MIN
Presidents and Politics with Richard Strout 58 MIN
The Reel world of news 58 MIN
The Second American Revolution - Pt 1 58 MIN
The Second American Revolution - Pt 2 58 MIN
The Thirty - Second President 55 MIN
TR and His Times 58 MIN
The Twenties 58 MIN
World War II - the Propaganda Battle 58 MIN
Dist - PBS **Prod** - CORPEL

Walk through the 20th century with Bill Moyers
I I Rabi - Man of the century 58 MIN
Dist - PBS

A Walk Up the Hill 29 MIN
16mm
Color
LC 74-700482
Discusses the subject of euthanasia from a Christian perspective by depicting the problems a family faces when one of its members suffers a paralyzing stroke.
Health and Safety; Psychology; Religion and Philosophy; Sociology
Dist - FAMF **Prod** - FAMF 1974

Walk with Me 28 MIN
U-matic / 16mm
Color
Deals with how children learn about sexuality from their parents. Interviews three different families. Includes a single mother, adopted children and a black family.
Health and Safety; Psychology; Sociology
Dist - PEREN **Prod** - PPGCL

Walk with the people 28 MIN
VHS
Color (G)
$14.95 purchase
Presents discussion among lay and clergical missionaries about why they chose to serve among African, Asian and Latin American peoples.
Religion and Philosophy
Dist - MARYFA

Walk Without Fear 20 MIN
U-matic / VHS / 16mm
Color (H C A)
Presents Chief of Police Tom Harris who addresses a local citizens' group on the growing problem of crime and the fear it breeds. Offers a number of precautionary measures which women can take to increase their peace of mind while decreasing the likelihood of their becoming a crime statistic.
Sociology
Dist - AIMS **Prod** - DAVP 1970

Walk Your Way to Weight Control
16mm
World of Medicine Series
Color
LC 75-704354
Uses pedometers in order to illustrate the value of activity in weight reduction and control.
Physical Education and Recreation
Dist - INFORP **Prod** - INFORP 1974

Walkabout 25 MIN
16mm
Color (J)
LC 76-700576
Shows the ancient way of life of the Aboriginals of central Australia. Includes scenes of men decorating their bodies for ceremony, the ritual of a kangaroo dance, the cooking of a kangaroo, and Aboriginal art in a cave in Ayers Rock.
Fine Arts; Foreign Language; Geography - World; Sociology
Dist - AUIS **Prod** - FLMAUS 1975

Walker Evans - His Time, His Presence, His Silence 22 MIN
16mm
B&W (A)
LC 73-701261
Presents an accumulation of individual photographic prints taken by Walker Evans.
Fine Arts; Industrial and Technical Education
Dist - RADIM **Prod** - RADIM 1970

Walker Gardens - Honolulu 30 MIN
BETA / VHS
Victory Garden Series
Color
Explores the Walker Gardens in Honolulu and tours a Japanese - style garden. Gives tips on planting beans and celery.
Agriculture; Physical Education and Recreation
Dist - CORF **Prod** - WGBHTV

Walker Weed, Wood Worker 30 MIN
Videoreel / VT2
World of the American Craftsman Series
Color
Fine Arts
Dist - PBS **Prod** - WENHTV

Walkin' on a Cloud 52 MIN
16mm
Color
LC 80-700404
Tells the story of a young comedian and his mentor, an aging and forgotten vaudevillian whose alcohol problem has ruined his life.
Fine Arts
Dist - MIDSUN **Prod** - MIDSUN 1980

Walkin' on a Cloud, Pt 1 26 MIN
16mm
Color
LC 80-700404
Tells the story of a young comedian and his mentor, an aging and forgotten vaudevillian whose alcohol problem has ruined his life.
Fine Arts
Dist - MIDSUN **Prod** - MIDSUN 1980

Walkin' on a Cloud, Pt 2 26 MIN
16mm
Color
LC 80-700404
Tells the story of a young comedian and his mentor, an aging and forgotten vaudevillian whose alcohol problem has ruined his life.
Fine Arts
Dist - MIDSUN **Prod** - MIDSUN 1980

Walking 5 MIN
16mm / U-matic / VHS
Color (J)
LC 73-708748
Uses animation without narration to depict the joys of walking. Shows that the manner of walking reflects the character of the individual.
Fine Arts; Health and Safety; Literature and Drama; Physical Education and Recreation
Dist - LCOA **Prod** - NFBC 1970

Walking Dance for Any Number 8 MIN
16mm
Color
Shows variations on a walking theme. Includes four films to be shown sinultaneously. Dance films by Elaine Summers.
Fine Arts
Dist - EIF **Prod** - EIF

Walking fit 27 MIN
VHS
Color (G)
$29.95 purchase _ #SFV100V
Features top - ranked racewalker Ann Peel who shows why walking is the perfect exercise. Discusses walking shoes, proper walking technique, setting up a fitness program, warm - up and cool - down exercises, avoiding injury and pain, walking as a competitive sport, tour walking and hiking and sticking to one's goals.
Physical Education and Recreation
Dist - CAMV

Walking for Physical Fitness 11 MIN
U-matic / VHS / 16mm
Color (H C A) (ARABIC)
LC 79-700887; 79-700881
Explains that walking is one of the healthiest forms of exercise and that it can tone muscles, stimulate the heart and lungs, burn excess calories and improve mental outlook.
Foreign Language; Physical Education and Recreation
Dist - AIMS **Prod** - AF 1978

Walking Home from School 11 MIN
16mm / U-matic / VHS
Color (P)
Follows children on an assignment in which they must look at things very closely while walking home from school. Stresses safety in crossing streets and driveways.
Guidance and Counseling; Health and Safety
Dist - AIMS **Prod** - AIMS 1970

Walking Home from School 13 MIN
16mm / U-matic / VHS
Color (K P) (SPANISH)
LC 78-706483
Stresses the concept of observing things around you and emphasizes safety.
Foreign Language; Health and Safety
Dist - AIMS **Prod** - ASSOCF 1970

Walking in a Sacred Manner - North American Indians and the Natural World 23 MIN
U-matic / VHS / 16mm
Color (J)
LC 82-701187
Explores the profound respect and appreciation of the Indians for the natural world and its importance to the physical, spiritual and psychological well - being of man. Presents photographs taken by Edward S Curtis between 1896 and 1930 combined with authentic Indian songs and commentary.
Social Science
Dist - IFB **Prod** - CROSSS 1982

Walking in God's story - Part 2
VHS
Keith Miller - new wine series
Color (H C G A R)
$10.00 rental _ #36 - 87402 - 533
Proposes the theory that living one's faith can provide good opportunities for evangelism. Based on the Keith Miller book 'A Taste of New Wine.'
Religion and Philosophy
Dist - APH **Prod** - WORD

Walking in the Wilderness 20 MIN
U-matic / VHS
Color (J)
LC 82-706792
Discusses walking trips as a practical alternative to motor - powered holidays. Describes pack types, shoes, clothing, food and camping gear. Includes information on pack loading, map reading, route finding, altitudes and dangerous wildlife and plants.
Physical Education and Recreation
Dist - AWSS **Prod** - AWSS 1981

Walking on a Miracle 14 MIN
16mm
Color
Covers the design and construction of the water treatment plant at Deer Creek Lake in Ohio.
Geography - United States; Industrial and Technical Education; Sociology
Dist - MTP **Prod** - USAE

Walking on Air 55 MIN
VHS
WonderWorks Series
Color (P)
$29.95 purchase _ #766 - 9005
Tells the story of a wheelchair - bound boy who fights to realize his dream of walking in space. Stars Lynn Redgrave, Jordan Marder. Based on the book by Ray Bradbury. Part of the WonderWorks Series which centers on themes involving rites of passage that occur during the growing - up years from seven to sixteen. Features young people as protagonists and portrays strong adult role models.
Fine Arts; Literature and Drama; Psychology
Dist - FI **Prod** - PBS 1990

Walking on the Moon 30 MIN
VHS / 16mm
Conquest of Space Series
Color (G)
Describes the first walk on the moon and explores its implications.
History - World
Dist - FLMWST

Walking Safe 10 MIN
16mm / U-matic / VHS
Color (K P)
LC 78-701255
Offers pedestrian safety tips.
Health and Safety
Dist - MEDIAG **Prod** - MEDIAG 1978

Walking Safely to School 18 MIN
16mm
Color (P I)
LC 74-702804
Covers basic principles of pedestrian safety, showing both correct and incorrect examples. Follows a boy who has learned safety rules from his policeman father as he goes about helping children at school to learn safe walking habits.
Guidance and Counseling; Health and Safety
Dist - MMP **Prod** - MMP 1974

Walking Tall 125 MIN
16mm
Color (H A)
Presents the true story of a vigilante farmer - sheriff who meets violence with violence and becomes a hero. Stars Joe Don Baker.
Fine Arts
Dist - TIMLIF **Prod** - CROSBY 1973

Walking Tall, Final Chapter 112 MIN
16mm
Color (H A)
Presents the sequel to Walking Tall and Walking Tall Part II. Stars Bo Svenson.
Fine Arts
Dist - TIMLIF **Prod** - CROSBY 1977

Walking Tall Part II 110 MIN
16mm
Color (H A)
Presents the sequel to Walking Tall. Stars Bo Svenson.
Fine Arts
Dist - TIMLIF **Prod** - CROSBY 1976

Walking the tightrope 30 MIN
VHS
How do you manage series
Color (A)
PdS65 purchase
Shows how to find the balance between work and home and why one cannot give 100 percent to both. Examines time management; the difference between positive pressure and negative stress; learning how to say 'no.' Part of a six part series featuring Dr John Nicholson, a business psychologist who specializes in helping people to develop new attitudes and ways of thinking to improve both job performance and satisfaction.
Business and Economics; Psychology
Dist - BBCENE

Walking the tundra 5 MIN
16mm
Color & B&W (G)
$15.00 rental
Employs a variety of experimental techniques to create a collage that draws upon the history of American Avant Garde. Captures a moment in thought, using modern methods of transporation metaphorically and ending with footsteps to complete a circle. Produced by Jeremy Coleman.
Fine Arts
Dist - CANCIN

Walking through the fear - women and substance abuse 28 MIN
VHS
Color (G)
$149.00 purchase, $75.00 rental _ #UW5149
Reveals that increasing numbers of women are addicted to alcohol and drugs, yet only one in five people in treatment centers is a woman. Investigates the problems women face when they seek help in overcoming addictions. Four women talk about what their lives were like before they sought help and how life changed after recovery.
Guidance and Counseling; Health and Safety; Psychology
Dist - FOTH

Walking through the Fire 143 MIN
U-matic / VHS
Color (H C A)
LC 80-706890
Chronicles Laurel Lee's real - life struggle with Hodgkin's disease.
Fine Arts; Health and Safety
Dist - TIMLIF **Prod** - TIMLIF 1980

Walking to Heel 30 MIN
U-matic / VHS
Training Dogs the Woodhouse Way
Color (H C A)
Shows Barbara Woodhouse's method of teaching a dog to walk to heel.
Home Economics; Science - Natural
Dist - FI **Prod** - BBCTV 1982

Walking with Grandfather series
Presents a six - part series on storytelling in order to pass on cultural values by elders, produced by Phil Lucas Productions, Inc. Includes The Arrival, The Woods, The Mountain, The Valley, The Stream, The Gift.

The Arrival	15 MIN
The Gift	15 MIN
The Mountain	15 MIN
The Stream	15 MIN
The Valley	15 MIN
Walking with Grandfather series	87 MIN
The Woods	15 MIN

Dist - NAMPBC

Walking with Jesus 30 MIN
VHS
Stories to remember series
Color (K P I R)
$14.98 purchase _ #35 - 87 - 2063
Uses animation and puppetry to present Biblical stories. Covers the stories of Jesus' birth, Jesus' baptism, the miracle of the possessed man, the healing of a sick woman, Peter walking on water, and the withering of the fig tree. Produced by Kids International.
Literature and Drama; Religion and Philosophy
Dist - APH

Walking with the Buddha 30 MIN
VHS
Maryknoll video magazine presents series
Color (G)
$14.95 purchase
Provides a look at the faith and practices of Buddhism and its emphasis on compassion for others. Focuses on the life of Buddha and the influence of his life on followers.
Religion and Philosophy
Dist - MARYFA

Walking with Zuma (in Our Zoo) 14 MIN
16mm
B&W (P I)
Tells a story about a visit to the zoo with Zuma - - an orangutan designed to stimulate creative expressions.
Fine Arts
Dist - AVED **Prod** - AVED 1969

Walking Workout
VHS
(C A)
$24.95 _ #WW320V
Presents a workout that utilizes walking.
Physical Education and Recreation
Dist - CAMV **Prod** - CAMV

The Walkout that never was 30 MIN
VHS / U-matic
La Esquina series
Color (H C A)
Presents a story centering on a protested school closing. Uses the story to try to reduce the minority isolation of Mexican - American students by showing the teenager as an individual, as a member of a unique cultural group and as a member of a larger complex society.
Sociology
Dist - GPN **Prod** - SWEDL 1976

Walkover 77 MIN
16mm
B&W (POLISH)
Follows the up - and - down life of a boxing hustler, fighting in amateur matches for beginners, throughout Poland. Underscores the feelings of alienation suffered by young people in modern society.
Fine Arts; Foreign Language; Sociology
Dist - NYFLMS **Prod** - NYFLMS 1965

The Wall 20 MIN
16mm
B&W
Discusses radio - activity and exposes the meaning of the wall erected between East and West Berlin by the communist East Germany government in 1961.
Civics and Political Systems; Geography - World
Dist - HEARST **Prod** - HEARST 1962

The Wall 117 MIN
VHS / 35mm
Color (G) (TURKISH WITH ENGLISH SUBTITLES)
$300.00 rental
Uses prison life as a metaphor for life in the director's native Turkey. Focuses on the child inmates of a Turkish prison. Directed by Yilmaz Guney.
Fine Arts; Literature and Drama; Sociology
Dist - KINOIC

Wall 1 MIN
16mm
Color (PORTUGUESE SPANISH)
LC 76-703355
Uses animation to show the importance of cooperation in realizing better living conditions.
Fine Arts; Guidance and Counseling; Industrial and Technical Education
Dist - USCC **Prod** - CHD 1976

The Wall - 82
VHS
Reading rainbow series
Color; CC (K P)
$39.95 purchase
Visits the Vietnam Veteran's Memorial with LeVar, inspired by the story by Eve Bunting. Meets Maya Lin, the young architect who designed the monument. Looks at Mount Rushmore and a mural dedicated to Louis Armstrong and expands the concept of walls as a way to pay tribute. Part of a series offering a multicultural approach to generating reading enthusiasm with cross - curricular applications, hosted by LeVar Burton.
English Language; History - United States; Literature and Drama
Dist - GPN **Prod** - LNMDP

Wall collapse 17 MIN
VHS
Collapse of burning buildings video series
Color (IND)
$140.00 purchase _ #35603
Presents one part of a five - part series that is a teaching companion for the Collapse of Burning Buildings book, as well as to the IFSTA Building Construction manual. Shows the different kinds of walls, the three ways they collapse, and how far they fall. Illustrates how to establish a danger zone. Demonstrates the proper use of hose streams, flanking, and the responsibilities of officers and firefighters. Produced by Fire Engineering Books & Videos.
Health and Safety; Science - Physical; Social Science
Dist - OKSU

Wall Framing 26 MIN
U-matic / VHS
Garages Series
$39.95 purchase _ #DI - 131
Talks about designing and planning the garage, how to layout and frame the walls, and explains the tools, materials, safety, and codes used.
Industrial and Technical Education
Dist - CAREER **Prod** - CAREER

Wall Hangings 10 MIN
U-matic
Get it together series
Color (P I)
Teaches children how to make wall hangings from twigs, yarn and cloth.
Fine Arts
Dist - TVOTAR **Prod** - TVOTAR 1978

Wall Hangings 60 MIN
VHS / BETA / 16mm
Color (G)
$49.00 purchase _ #FA1003
Shows how to utilize brooms, fans, frying pans, wicker baskets, mats, and other objects in making wall hanging designs. Taught by Pat Quigley.
Fine Arts; Home Economics
Dist - RMIBHF **Prod** - RMIBHF

A Wall in Jerusalem 95 MIN
16mm
Silent; B&W (G)
$85.00 rental; $59.95 purchase _ #211
Traces the history of modern Jewish nationalism. Follows the struggles of the Zionist movement from Herzl's time through the Six Day War. Documents the many faces of antisemitism in European prosecutions; Arab opposition and terroism; Nazi genocide; British intransigence; and world indifference. Touches on the conflicting aspirations of the Jews themselves, as well as their arduous and joyful struggle to build and rebuild the land of Israel. Uses seventy years worth of historical footage. Narrated by Richard Burton. Directed by Frederic Rossif.
Fine Arts; History - World; Religion and Philosophy; Sociology
Dist - NCJEWF
ERGOM

Wall of denial 47 MIN
VHS
Color (G)
$325.00 purchase
Educates 'hard to reach' individuals about the largest stumbling block to recovery from addictive disorders - denial. Emphasizes the three manifestations of the denial process as it affects the addict's thinking, feelings and behavior. Features multicultural speakers who candidly share experiences in their own language to inform and inspire those with drug or alcohol problems. Places special emphasis on reaching incarcerated individuals, the homeless and other institutionalized persons so they may break down their own wall of denial.
Guidance and Counseling; Health and Safety; Psychology
Dist - FMSP

Wall Repairs and Remodeling - Drywall and Spackle, Wainscotings 30 MIN
BETA / VHS
Wally's Workshop Series
Color
Home Economics; Industrial and Technical Education
Dist - KARTES **Prod** - KARTES

The Wall Street Connection 40 MIN
16mm / U-matic / VHS
Color (J H C A)
Investigates the 'casinoization' of Wall Street on the long term capital formation needs of the American economy.
Business and Economics; Social Science
Dist - CANWRL **Prod** - CANWRL 1984

Wall Street Inside Trading 24 MIN
VHS / U-matic
Color
$335.00 purchase
Business and Economics
Dist - ABCLR **Prod** - ABCLR 1984

Wall Street - Money, Greed and Power 51 MIN
VHS
Color (S)
$79.00 purchase _ #322 - 9287
Looks at conditions on today's stock market, focusing special attention on the insider - trading scandals that recently rocked Wall Street. Features NBC News anchor Tom Brokaw. Also includes reports from Chief Economic Correspondent Mike Jensen, Maria Shriver, Peter Kent and Lucky Severson.
Business and Economics; Civics and Political Systems; Psychology; Religion and Philosophy; Sociology
Dist - FI **Prod** - NBCNEW 1987

Wall tiling - Part 1 - Unit J - Cassette 16 50 MIN
VHS
Building crafts - the teaching and learning process series
Color; PAL (J H IND)
PdS29.50 purchase
Features part of an 18 - part series which observes teaching and learning in a variety of workshop situations. Includes such skills as plumbing, brickwork, carpentry, painting and decorating.
Industrial and Technical Education
Dist - EMFVL

Wall tiling - the students' attempts - Part 2 - Unit J - Cassette 17 55 MIN
VHS
Building crafts - the teaching and learning process series
Color; PAL (J H IND)
PdS29.50 purchase
Features part of an 18 - part series which observes teaching and learning in a variety of workshop situations. Includes such skills as plumbing, brickwork, carpentry, painting and decorating.
Industrial and Technical Education
Dist - EMFVL

Wall to wall 30 MIN
Videoreel / VT2
Designing home interiors series; Unit 21
Color (C A)
Stresses combining and coordinating a variety of wall treatments. Presents the views of designer Russell Phinder on importance of a coordinated look throughout an environment.
Home Economics
Dist - CDTEL **Prod** - COAST

Wall to Wall Selling 20 MIN
16mm
Color
Features Orson Bean speaking to distributors of Schenley Products. Emphasizes special packaging and display techniques used during holiday seasons. Points out that wall - to - wall display of these products increases sales.
Business and Economics; Psychology
Dist - CCNY **Prod** - SCIND

Wall to wall series
Examines the vast range of dwelling places and buildings which can be found in the United Kingdom and abroad, and charts their history and evolution. Looks at the different building materials used through the centuries and compares and contrasts British buildings with similar structures found abroad.

Back to Earth	30 MIN
Concrete realities	30 MIN
Forging ahead	30 MIN
On the rocks	30 MIN
Out of the wood	30 MIN
Safe as houses	30 MIN
Wall to wall series	180 MIN

Dist - BBCENE

Wall Washing 12 MIN
16mm
Vignette Series
B&W (T)
LC 77-707934
Observes closely a group of pre - school children at Hilltop Head Start Center washing the walls and windows of their store - front school.
Education; Guidance and Counseling; Psychology; Sociology
Dist - EDC **Prod** - EDS 1968

The Wall within 49 MIN
VHS
Color (C G PRO)
$330.00 purchase, $25.50 rental _ #51234
Interviews Vietnam War veterans suffering from post - traumatic stress disorder, a little - understood illness that afflicts one of three individuals who served in that conflict. Examines the manifestations of PTSD, including suicide, drug and alcohol abuse, family dysfunction and withdrawal from family. Features correspondent Dan Rather. Produced by Paul and Holly Fine.
History - United States; Psychology
Dist - PSU **Prod** - CBSTV 1988

The Wall (Zid) 4 MIN
U-matic / VHS / 16mm
Color
Presents an example of the animation coming from the Yugoslavian studios. Presents a commentary on the people user, the one who watches while others innocently do the work.
Fine Arts; Industrial and Technical Education; Psychology; Sociology
Dist - IFB **Prod** - ZAGREB 1966

The Wallace Brand - Ranching by a Black Texas Family 11 MIN
U-matic / VHS / Slide
Color; Mono (I J H)
Shows a visit with a black rancher whose grandfather began ranching in West Texas.
Education; History - United States; Sociology
Dist - UTXITC **Prod** - UTXITC 1978

The Wallace Brand - Ranching by a Black Texas Family 10 MIN
U-matic / VHS / Slide
Hispanic Studies, Ranching and Farming Series
Color; Mono (I J H)
History - United States; Sociology
Dist - UTXITC **Prod** - UTXITC 1973

Wallace Stevens 60 MIN
VHS / 16mm
Voices and Visions Series
Color (H)
$8.00 rental _ #60737; $45.00, $29.95 purchase
Profiles businessman, insurance lawyer, and poet Wallace Stevens (1879 - 1955), who explored the question of where and how modern people find meaning in a world bereft of belief. The answer for Stevens was in poetry and the imagination, and in the power to transform reality. Helen Vendler, Mark Strand, James Merrill, Joan Richardson, and Harold Bloom discuss Stevens' lush and provocative poetry, and explore both the whimsical and dark sides of his vision.
Literature and Drama
Dist - PSU **Prod** - NYCVH 1988
ANNCPB

Wallboard Series
Finishing and Repairing 30 MIN
Installing 40 MIN
Planning and Estimating 20 MIN
Taping and Topcoating 25 MIN
Dist - COFTAB

Wallenstein, Parts L and 2 250 MIN
16mm
B&W (GERMAN)
Characterizes commander - in - chief Wallenstein, who wants to lead the Emperor to peace by going over to the enemy, but waits too long, not noticing the mutual intrigue. Shows his treason and murder. A film version of Schiller's trilogy.
Foreign Language; Literature and Drama
Dist - WSTGLC **Prod** - WSTGLC 1962

Walleye I 60 MIN
VHS / BETA
Color
Presents the weed walleye of Lake Erie. Teaches methods of catching trophy walleye and walleye of Lake Sakakawea.
Physical Education and Recreation; Science - Natural
Dist - HOMEAF **Prod** - HOMEAF

Walleye II 60 MIN
VHS / BETA
Color
Presents the walleye of the Great Lakes region and his unique pattern.
Physical Education and Recreation; Science - Natural
Dist - HOMEAF **Prod** - HOMEAF

The Wallflower 5 MIN
VHS
Color (G)
$100.00 purchase, $40.00, $30.00 rental
Depicts through claymation a shy, introverted personality attempting to communicate in a social setting. Created by Gita Saxena.
Fine Arts; Psychology; Sociology
Dist - WMENIF **Prod** - WMENIF 1989

Wallflower 25 MIN
16mm
B&W (H C A)
Tells the story of a young man, feeling undesirable and unwanted, who decides that if he becomes a rock star he will find love and friends.
Guidance and Counseling
Dist - UWFKD **Prod** - UWFKD

Wallflower Order 59 MIN
VHS / U-matic
Color
Presents a feminist women's dance theatre which incorporates theatre, music, comedy, martial arts and sign language into their work to create multi - dimensional performance pieces of strong impact.
Fine Arts; Sociology
Dist - WMENIF **Prod** - WMENIF

Wallpaper 23 MIN
VHS / 16mm
Do it Yourself Series
(G)
$39.95 purchase _ #DIY112
Shows how to prepare and repair walls for wallpapering. Gives tips on wallpaper planning and hanging. Illustrates how to do inside and outside corners, doors and window openings, and shows some common mistakes and time saving tips.
Home Economics
Dist - RMIBHF **Prod** - RMIBHF

Wallpaper - Hanging Wallpaper, Steaming and Removing Wall Paper 30 MIN
BETA / VHS
Wally's Workshop Series
Color
Home Economics
Dist - KARTES **Prod** - KARTES

Wallpaper Like a Pro 55 MIN
VHS
Color (G)
$19.95 purchase _ #6115
Home Economics; Sociology
Dist - SYBVIS **Prod** - HOMES

Walls 11 MIN
U-matic / VHS / 16mm
Critical Moments in Teaching Series
Color (C T)
Presents a sensitive young teacher who has tried to expose his high school class to the type of independent study it will be expected to do in college. Explains that all the students have failed to pursue the assignments on their own. Focuses on the ways in which the teacher can make them respond.
Education; Guidance and Counseling; Psychology
Dist - PHENIX **Prod** - HRAW 1969

Walls 45 MIN
VHS
Color (A)
$19.95 purchase _ #S00433
Covers home improvement projects for walls. Includes drywalls, preparation for wallpaper or paint, paneling, trim and more.
Home Economics; Industrial and Technical Education
Dist - UILL

Walls 27 MIN
VHS
Ceramic Tile Series
$39.95 purchase _ #DI - 216
Discusses the problems, solutions, and techniques for installing ceramic tile on walls.
Industrial and Technical Education
Dist - CAREER **Prod** - CAREER

Walls and Bonds 12 MIN
16mm
Hand Operations - Woodworking Series
Color
LC 75-704355
Demonstrates different kinds of wood bonds.
Industrial and Technical Education
Dist - SF **Prod** - MORLAT 1974

Walls and Walls 10 MIN
U-matic / VHS / 16mm
Color; Captioned (J) (FRENCH)
LC 73-703089
Traces the evolution of wall building through the ages. Discusses walls represented by prejudice and stereotypes.
Psychology; Sociology
Dist - ALTSUL **Prod** - NORMBP 1973

Walls and Windows 30 MIN
U-matic
Energy Efficient Housing Series
(A)
Demonstrates how to insulate an attic kneewall and a sloped ceiling.
Industrial and Technical Education; Social Science
Dist - ACCESS **Prod** - SASKM 1983

Walls and Windows 12 MIN
16mm / U-matic / VHS
Vignettes Series
Color (J)
LC 73-701777
Explores values in parent - teenager communications.
Psychology; Sociology
Dist - MEDIAG **Prod** - PAULST 1973

Walls Below the Pavement 30 MIN
U-matic / VHS
Color (J H C)
Shows the course of an archaeological excavation in downtown Kingston, Ontario, of Fort Frontenac, a 1673 French outpost. Introduces basic archaeological procedures.
Sociology
Dist - QUEENU **Prod** - QUAF 1985

Walls - Framing and Removal 30 MIN
VHS
$39.95 purchase _ #DI - 135
Describes the techniques needed to frame and remove a window. Discusses how to frame a wall with window and door openings and how to remove a wall to open up a room.
Industrial and Technical Education
Dist - CAREER **Prod** - CAREER

Walls - framing and removal 30 MIN
VHS
Home improvement video series
Color (G)
$39.95 purchase _ #219
Shows how to frame a wall with window and door openings. Demonstrates removing a wall to open up a room.
Home Economics
Dist - DIYVC **Prod** - DIYVC

Walls - Framing and Removal
VHS
Home Improvement Series
(H C G A IND)
$39.95 _ SH135
Shows how to frame a wall with window and door openings as well as how to remove a wall and open a room.
Industrial and Technical Education
Dist - AAVIM **Prod** - AAVIM 1989

Walls - Framing and Removing 30 MIN
VHS / 16mm
Do it Yourself Series
(G)
$39.95 purchase _ #DIY135; #RMDIY135V
Shows how to frame a wall with window and door openings. Includes how to remove a wall to open up a door.
Home Economics
Dist - RMIBHF **Prod** - RMIBHF
CAMV

Walls of Skinn 20 MIN
16mm
B&W
Examines 'LONELINESS' through the world of an autistic child of 11 who has spent the last seven years in a mental institution. Examines loneliness and hopelessness, as well as those who help the helpless.
Health and Safety; Psychology
Dist - UPENN **Prod** - UPENN 1964

The Walls of Time 25 MIN
16mm / U-matic / VHS
Color (J)
LC 72-702171
Documents the history of Biblical translations in English, from Wyclif to today's new version, the Living Bible.
Literature and Drama
Dist - PFP **Prod** - PFP 1972

Walls We Build 30 MIN
16mm
B&W (A)
LC FIA65-1618
Uses a dramatization about the self - centered members of a family to point out the need for the members of a Christian family to share interests and problems.
Psychology; Religion and Philosophy; Sociology
Dist - CPH **Prod** - CPH 1964

Walls - Wood Paneling, Wood Paneling Over Masonry, Wainscotings, Room Dividers, 90 MIN
VHS / BETA
Best of Wally's Workshop Series
Color
Explains do - it - yourself procedures for the homeowner. Title continues ... Drywall And Spackle, Shelving.
Home Economics; Industrial and Technical Education
Dist - KARTES **Prod** - KARTES

Wally Butts - a Great Georgian 30 MIN
16mm
Great Georgians Series
Color
Looks at the career of Wally Butts, the famous coach, from his birth in Milledgeville to his death on December 17, 1973. Includes such notables as Ed Sullivan and Bear Bryant. Shows footage of the famous Tarkenton to Herron pass that won the SEC Championship in 1959 and also of the 9 - 0 win over UCLA in the Rose Bowl. Narrated by TV celebrity and Georgia graduate Monte Markham.
Biography; Physical Education and Recreation
Dist - WGTV **Prod** - WGTV 1974

Wally's workshop series
Alarms and safes - installing burglar alarms, installing wall safe 30 MIN
Antiques, kits and faking - antique kits , 'faking' antiques 30 MIN
Bathroom remodeling - ceramic tiling, bathtub enclosure 30 MIN
Bathroom repairs - toilet repair, copper plumbing 30 MIN
Beamed and suspended ceilings 30 MIN
Building room dividers and shelving 30 MIN
Ceiling ladders and fireplaces - ceiling ladder, installing fireplaces 30 MIN
Decorated and tiled ceilings - decorated ceilings, acoustic tile ceilings 30 MIN

Decoupage, framing and matting - how to decoupage, picture framing and matting	30 MIN
Hardwood Floors - Installing Hardwood Floors, Refinishing Hardwood Floors	30 MIN
Household repairs	30 MIN
Kitchen Remodeling - Kitchen Cabinets, Counter Tops	30 MIN
Lamps and Electrical Outlets - Lamps and Chandeliers, Adding Electrical Outlets	30 MIN
Locks and garage door openers - installing door locks, garage door opener	30 MIN
Maintenance and Exterior Repairs - Household Maintenance, Exterior Repairs	30 MIN
Murals and China Repairs - Wallpaper Murals, Gold Leaf and China Repairs	30 MIN
Painting and Staining - Spray and Roller Painting, Staining Wood	30 MIN
Paneling - Wood Paneling, Wood Paneling Over Masonry	30 MIN
Parquet Floors and Carpet Installations	30 MIN
Refinishing antiques - refinishing antiques, varnish - refinishing antiques, paint	30 MIN
Slate and Vinyl Floors - Slate Floors , Tile Floors	30 MIN
Wall Repairs and Remodeling - Drywall and Spackle, Wainscotings	30 MIN
Wallpaper - Hanging Wallpaper, Steaming and Removing Wall Paper	30 MIN
Weatherizing - Fiberglass Insulation, Weatherstripping	30 MIN

Dist - KARTES

The Walrus and the Carpenter 6 MIN
16mm / U-matic / VHS
Color
LC 79-701121
Uses animation to represent Lewis Carroll's whimsical poem in which the walrus and the carpenter entice a family of oysters to join them in their journey along the beach.
Fine Arts; Literature and Drama
Dist - LUF **Prod** - SPAMA 1978

Walt Disney 20 MIN
U-matic
Truly American Series
Color (I)
Biography; Fine Arts
Dist - GPN **Prod** - WVIZTV 1979

Walt Disney Archives Series

The Big bad wolf	9 MIN
Pecos Bill	17 MIN
The Walt Disney Story	23 MIN

Dist - CORF

The Walt Disney creativity strategy 41 MIN
VHS
Color; PAL; SECAM (G)
$70.00 purchase
Features Robert Dilts. Models the strategy of Walt Disney to find out how Disney solved the problem of criticism as an obstacle to creative, original thinking. Reveals that Disney sequenced his creative processes into three functional stages - Dreamer, Realist and Critic, and carefully sorted these three functions in to different rooms. Shows how this combination of sequencing and spatial sorting fosters creative thinking. Intermediate level of NLP, neuro - linguistic programming.
Fine Arts; Psychology
Dist - NLPCOM **Prod** - NLPCOM

The Walt Disney Story 23 MIN
16mm
Walt Disney Archives Series
Color (G)
Shows Walt Disney's remarkable life story that has been enjoyed by millions of guests at Disneyland and Walt Disney World. Insights into this famous animation master's life are given through his family photo album, interviews, documentary footage and excerpts from Disney movies.
Biography; Fine Arts
Dist - CORF **Prod** - DISNEY 1986

Walt Disney's Fantasia video 120 MIN
VHS
Color (G H A)
$24.95 purchase _ #19629
Presents the Walt Disney movie 'Fantasia.'
Fine Arts
Dist - WCAT **Prod** - WCAT

Walt Michael's hammer dulcimer series
Presents a two - part series featuring Walt Michael. Teaches a variety tunes on Video One, then breaks them down and describes the techniques for playing them smoothly and proficiently. Draws on tunes from Ireland, Scotland, northern England and the Shetland Islands in Video Two and slows the tunes down and takes them apart for the learning player. Include music.

Celtic tunes for hammer dulcimer - Video Two	60 MIN
Hammer dulcimer tunes and techniques - Video One	80 MIN
Walt Michael's hammer dulcimer series	140 MIN

Dist - HOMETA **Prod** - HOMETA

Walt Whitman 12 MIN
U-matic / VHS
Color (C)
$229.00, $129.00 purchase _ #AD - 1752
Portrays Walt Whitman who created an American poetic language to democratize poetic expression.
English Language; Fine Arts; Literature and Drama
Dist - FOTH **Prod** - FOTH

Walt Whitman 30 MIN
VHS
Famous authors series
Color (J H G)
$225.00 purchase
Looks at the life and career of the American poet through selections from his works. Uses the music and events of his time, including his stints as an editor, teacher, government clerk and nurse of wounded Civil War soldiers. Part of a series of videos about 24 major American and British authors. Videos are also available in a set.
History - United States; Literature and Drama
Dist - LANDMK

Walt Whitman 60 MIN
VHS / 16mm
Voices and Visions Series
Color (H)
Portrays the poetry of Walt Whitman, focusing on the sources of his inspiration and style. Galway Kinnell, Allen Ginsberg, Justin Kaplan, and Harold Bloom read from 'Leaves of Grass' and discuss the language, themes, music, and visionary power of this seminal work.
Literature and Drama
Dist - PSU
ANNCPB

Walt Whitman 10 MIN
U-matic / VHS / 16mm
Poetry by Americans Series
Color (J H C)
LC 72-702684
Presents both the poet and his poetry in American style by outlining the life and character of Whitman.
Biography; Literature and Drama
Dist - AIMS **Prod** - EVANSA 1972

Walt Whitman - Endlessly Rocking 21 MIN
VHS / U-matic
Color (J H C)
Provides a contemporary and humorous approach to the study of Walt Whitman's poetry.
Literature and Drama
Dist - CEPRO **Prod** - CEPRO 1986

Walt Whitman - Poet for a New Age 29 MIN
16mm / U-matic / VHS
Humanities - Poetry Series
Color (J H C)
LC 72-715417
Presents a sensitive study of poet Walt Whitman - his beliefs and his conflicts with contemporaries.
Biography; Literature and Drama
Dist - EBEC **Prod** - EBEC 1971

Walt Whitman - sweet bird of freedom 29 MIN
VHS / U-matic
Color (H C)
$325.00, $295.00 purchase _ #V168
Features Dallas McKennon in a portrayal of American poet Walt Whitman. Provides insights into Whitman's poetic style and shows how he felt about his world and his poetry. Produced by Turtle on the Move Productions.
Literature and Drama
Dist - BARR

Walt Whitman's Civil War 15 MIN
16mm / VHS
Color (J H C)
$235.00, $79.00 purchase
Uses the poetry of Walt Whitman and eyewitness prose accounts of the war to present the power of Whitman's style and his despair at the tragedy of war. Includes archival photographs and live reenactments.
History - United States; Literature and Drama; Sociology
Dist - CF

Walt Whitman's 'Leaves of Grass' 21 MIN
16mm
Color (J)
LC FIA66-1201
Presents the story of Walt Whitman's life, told in his own words, both prose and verse. Shows places where he lived and worked. Describes the influences which led to his writing 'LEAVES OF GRASS.'.
Biography; Literature and Drama
Dist - LINE **Prod** - LINE 1965

Walter Cronkite Presentation Excellence Video
$1450.00 purchase, $350.00 rental _ ACB - 151
Hosted by Walter Cronkite, this takes you step by step through the process of presentation - understanding your audience, defining the purpose of your presentation, and what you can expect your audience to think about or to do after the presentation.
Fine Arts
Dist - BLNCTD **Prod** - BLNCTD

Walter Cronkite Remembers and the Battle of the Bulge 60 MIN
VHS / BETA
World War II with Walter Cronkite Series
B&W
Shows Walter Cronkite reminiscing with his colleague, CBS News correspondent Charles Kuralt, about his experiences on the battlefield and in combat planes above it. Follows with the epic Battle Of The Bulge, a vicious struggle between American and German troops, which shows turned out to be the beginning of the end for the Third Reich. Concludes with a preview of future video cassettes in the series.
Civics and Political Systems; History - United States; History - World
Dist - CBSVL **Prod** - CBSTV

Walter Cronkite's Universe Series

Disappearance of the Great Rainforest	12 MIN

Dist - MOKIN

Walter Fish - a Modern Adult Parable 5 MIN
16mm
Color (J)
LC 75-703013
Uses animation to present the story of a fish who finds himself on the beach and tries to get help to get back into the water. Features an interpretation of the Biblical parable of the Good Samaritan.
Guidance and Counseling; Literature and Drama; Religion and Philosophy
Dist - ALBA **Prod** - ALBA 1971

Walter Gropius - His New World Home 12 MIN
16mm
Color (H C A)
LC 75-703768
Discusses the art and architecture of Walter Gropius, founder of the Bauhaus School. Examines the architectural innovations incorporated into Gropius's home built in Lincoln, Massachusetts in 1937.
Biography; Fine Arts
Dist - HOWRD **Prod** - HOWRD 1974

Walter Kerr on Theater 26 MIN
U-matic / VHS / 16mm
Color (H C A)
LC 70-708179
Demonstrates the joy, magic and power of the theater. Provides insight into the unique characteristics of live drama by contrasting excerpts from outstanding plays with film. Shows the range of forms and ideas possible in live theater.
Fine Arts; Literature and Drama
Dist - LCOA **Prod** - IQFILM 1970
INSIM

Walter Payton - winning in life 55 MIN
VHS
Color (J H A)
$29.95 purchase _ #NGC567V; $19.95 purchase _ #S01794
Features former Chicago Bears star Walter Payton and his insights on success and failure in all areas of life. Includes highlights of some of Payton's most spectacular NFL successes, as well as Payton discussing how he handles defeat. Interviews his wife Connie, former teammates, and Coach Mike Ditka about their relationships with Payton.
Physical Education and Recreation; Science - Natural
Dist - CAMV
UILL

Walter, the Lazy Mouse 10 MIN
16mm
Color (K P I)
LC 74-702679
Presents Walter, the lazy mouse who learns independently to provide for himself and to teach others.
Guidance and Counseling
Dist - SF **Prod** - SF 1972

Walter Verkehr - Violinist and David Renner - Pianist 29 MIN
Videoreel / VT2
Young Musical Artists Series
Color
Presents the music of violinist Walter Verkehr and pianist David Renner.
Fine Arts
Dist - PBS **Prod** - WKARTV

Waltz
VHS
Arthur Murray dance lessons series
Color (G)
$19.95 purchase _ #MC052
Offers lessons in classic ballroom dancing from instructors in Arthur Murray studios, focusing on the waltz. Part of a 12 - part series on various ballroom dancing styles.
Fine Arts; Physical Education and Recreation; Sociology
Dist - SIV

Waltz 60 MIN
VHS
Kathy Blake dance studios - let's learn how to dance series
Color (G A)
$39.95 purchase
Features dance instructors Kathy Blake and Gene Russo, who instruct viewers on the basics of the Waltz. First of three parts.
Fine Arts
Dist - PBS **Prod** - WNETTV

The Waltz City 53 MIN
U-matic / VHS
Man and Music Series
Color (C)
$279.00, $179.00 purchase _ #AD - 2063
Focuses on Vienna during the closing days of the Austrian empire. Looks at the waltzes of Strauss and composers Johannes Brahms, Richard Wagner and Anton Bruckner. Contains a segment with Brahms speaking and playing a few chords on the piano to inaugarate Mr. Edison's new phonograph machine. Part of a 22 - part series that sets Western music into the historial and cultural context of its time.
Fine Arts; Geography - World; History - World
Dist - FOTH **Prod** - FOTH

Waltz II 60 MIN
VHS
Kathy Blake dance studios - let's learn how to dance series
Color (G A)
$39.95 purchase
Features dance instructors Kathy Blake and Gene Russo, who instruct viewers on the basics of the Waltz. Second of three parts.
Fine Arts
Dist - PBS **Prod** - WNETTV

Waltz III 60 MIN
VHS
Kathy Blake dance studios - let's learn how to dance series
Color (G A)
$39.95 purchase
Features dance instructors Kathy Blake and Gene Russo, who instruct viewers on the basics of the Waltz. Third of three parts.
Fine Arts
Dist - PBS **Prod** - WNETTV

A Waltz through the Hills 110 MIN
VHS
WonderWorks Series
Color (P)
$29.95 purchase _ #766 - 9001
Tells the story of two orphans who make a dangerous journey through the wilds of the Australian outback. Stars Dan O'Herlihy, Ernie Dingo. Based on the book by G M Glaskin. Part of the WonderWorks Series which centers on themes involving rites of passage that occur during the growing - up years from seven to sixteen. Features young people as protagonists and portrays strong adult role models.
Fine Arts; Geography - World; Literature and Drama; Psychology
Dist - FI **Prod** - PBS 1990

Waltzing Matilda 8 MIN
16mm / VHS
Color (P I J H A)
$150.00, $195.00 purchase, $30.00 rental _ #8014
Shows a chorus of animated clay animals of the Australian Bush singing the famous Australian folk song `Waltzing Matilda'. Full story of the song is enacted.
Geography - World; Literature and Drama
Dist - AIMS **Prod** - EDMI 1988

Walzerkrieg 93 MIN
16mm
B&W (GERMAN)
Depicts the friendship of Viennese waltz composers Lanner and Strauss, which is tested when the maestros have to compete against each other in London and Vienna.
Fine Arts; Foreign Language
Dist - WSTGLC **Prod** - WSTGLC 1933

The Wampanoags of Gay Head 30 MIN
U-matic
People of the First Light Series
Color
Social Science; Sociology
Dist - GPN **Prod** - WGBYTV 1977

The Wampanoags of Gay Head - Community Spirit and Island Life 29 MIN
VHS / U-matic
People of the First Light Series
Color (G)
Shows how three generations of Wampanoag Indians live and maintain traditional values and keep community spirit alive on the Island of Martha's Vineyard. The people of Gay Head depend on the sea for their livelihood. They use the colorful clay found in the Gay Head cliffs to make unusual pottery. Both these aspects of the Wampanoag lifestyle make the Gay Head people unique in their attempt to blend traditions with their present way of life.
Social Science
Dist - NAMPBC **Prod** - NAMPBC 1979

Wanda Coleman - 4 - 14 - 85 64 MIN
VHS / Cassette
Color (G)
$15.00, $45.00 purchase, $15.00 rental _ #648 - 538
Features the writer participating in a continuation of A Dickinson Colloquium at the Women Working in Literature conference at the Poetry Center, San Francisco State University.
Literature and Drama; Sociology
Dist - POETRY **Prod** - POETRY 1985

Wanda Coleman - 10 - 14 - 82 40 MIN
VHS / Cassette
Poetry Center reading series
Color (G)
$15.00, $45.00 purchase, $15.00 rental _ #503 - 425
Features the writer reading selections of her works at the Poetry Center, San Francisco State University.
Literature and Drama
Dist - POETRY **Prod** - POETRY 1982

Wanda Gag 1893 - 1946 - a Minnesota Childhood 10 MIN
VHS / U-matic
Color (K P I)
LC 84-730301
Depicts childhood of artist and author Wanda Gag. Portrays her artistic development and how she came to write her well - known children's book Millions Of Cats. Includes photographs of Gag's home and illustrations from her books.
Biography; Fine Arts; Literature and Drama
Dist - HERPRO **Prod** - HERPRO 1984

Wanderer and the Swan 99 MIN
VHS
Color (G) (MANDARIN CHINESE)
$45.00 purchase _ #6022A
Presents a movie produced in the People's Republic Of China.
Fine Arts; Geography - World; Literature and Drama
Dist - CHTSUI **Prod** - CHTSUI

The Wanderers - Paths of Planets 10 MIN
U-matic / VHS / 16mm
Color (J H) (GREEK)
LC 73-705711
Traces the development of man's understanding of the planets and describes the observations of early Greek astronomers. Includes a discussion of Kepler's laws and the later significance of Newton's work. Includes questions and vocabulary.
Science - Physical
Dist - PHENIX **Prod** - PHENIX 1969

The Wandering Continents - a Study of Rock Magnetism 21 MIN
16mm
B&W (J H C G)
Shows how a study of the residual magnetism in certain old rocks suggests that the magnetic poles have moved extensively in past ages. Discusses this theory.
Geography - World; Science - Physical
Dist - VIEWTH **Prod** - GATEEF

The Wandering Dunes 15 MIN
16mm / U-matic / VHS
Color
Discusses the creation, growth and movement of coastal and desert dunes. Details plant and animal life in the dunes.
Science - Natural
Dist - STANF **Prod** - STANF

The Wandering Jew AKA The Life of Theodore Herzl 59 MIN
16mm
B&W (G) (SILENT WITH ENGLISH INTERTITLES)
$85.00 rental
Presents a biography of the founder of modern Zionism. Depicts Herzl learning in his youth about Jewish persecution throughout the ages. Illustrated with melodramatic scenes of Judah Hamaccabee, King David, Bar Kochba, and the Spanish Inquisition. Looks at Herzl's development of the theory of political Zionism as the only solution to antisemitism. Produced by Foxy Penser, directed by Otto Kreisler. 91 - minute English version available.
Fine Arts; Religion and Philosophy
Dist - NCJEWF

Wandering through Winter 50 MIN
16mm / U-matic / VHS
Four Seasons Series
Color
LC 72-702731
Uses close - ups of animals in their natural habitats to picture winter and the changes it brings to the country. Shows winter as a time of migration and hibernation, a constantly recurring drama of nature.
Science - Natural
Dist - CNEMAG **Prod** - HOBLEI 1970

Wandering through Winter, Pt 1 24 MIN
U-matic / VHS / 16mm
We Need each Other Series
Color
Uses close - ups of animals in their natural habitats to picture winter and the changes it brings to the country. Shows winter as a time of migration and hibernation, a constantly recurring drama of nature.
Science - Natural
Dist - CNEMAG **Prod** - HOBLEI 1970

Wandering through Winter, Pt 2 26 MIN
U-matic / VHS / 16mm
We Need each Other Series
Color
Uses close - ups of animals in their natural habitats to picture winter and the changes it brings to the country. Shows winter as a time of migration and hibernation, a constantly recurring drama of nature.
Science - Natural
Dist - CNEMAG **Prod** - HOBLEI 1970

Wandlungen 27 MIN
16mm
Color
Presents excerpts from various German films of the late 1960s.
Fine Arts
Dist - WSTGLC **Prod** - WSTGLC 1969

Wang Word Processor on the Wang PC 60 MIN
U-matic / VHS
(A PRO)
$495.00, $595.00
Covers introduction to word processing.
Computer Science
Dist - VIDEOT **Prod** - VIDEOT 1988

Wang Word Processor Training 145 MIN
VHS / U-matic
(A PRO)
$1,295, $1,395.00
Trains operators with five lessons supported by diskette and guide.
Computer Science
Dist - VIDEOT **Prod** - VIDEOT 1988

Wang zhao jun 348 MIN
VHS
Color (G) (CHINESE)
$150.00 purchase _ #5105
Presents a film from the People's Republic of China. Includes five videocassettes.
Geography - World; Literature and Drama
Dist - CHTSUI

Wanna See ASL Stories 105 MIN
VHS / U-matic
Color (S)
Presents stories in sign language at all levels. Provides signed stories together with written questions and signed answers. On three tapes. Signed.
Education; Guidance and Counseling; Psychology
Dist - GALCO **Prod** - GALCO 1979

The Wannabes 30 MIN
VHS
Over the edge series
Color; PAL (G A)
PdS50 purchase; Available only in the U K and Eire
Looks at two men who share a common desire - to have an amputation and thereby become disabled. Portrays the unfolding of the emotion and drive behind their obsession as the two men from different backgrounds and countries turn to each other for support.
Health and Safety; Psychology
Dist - BBCENE

The Wannsee conference 85 MIN
VHS
Color (G)
$19.95 _ #WAN020
Depicts the meeting of key representatives of the SS, the Nazi Party and the government bureaucracy to discuss The Final Solution, systematic extermination of eleven million Jews, while meeting secretly for a luxurious buffet luncheon in a house in Wannsee, a quiet Berlin suburb. Uses actual notes from the conference, along with letters and testimony of Adolf Eichmann at his 1961 trial in Israel. Directed by Heinz Schirk. Produced by INFAFILM Gmbh Munich.
Fine Arts; History - World
Dist - HOMVIS

The Wannsee Conference 85 MIN
16mm / VHS
Color (S) (GERMAN (ENGLISH SUBTITLES))
$89.00 purchase _ #893 - 9002
Recreates events of January 20, 1942, when key Nazis met in Wannsee, a suburb of Berlin, to discuss 'The Final Solution.' Tells how they discussed methods for exterminating eleven million people as they had a luncheon.
Foreign Language; Geography - World; History - United States; History - World; Sociology
Dist - FI **Prod** - FI 1988

The Wannsee conference 87 MIN
VHS
Color (G)
$39.95 purchase _ #635
Recreates dramatically the meeting of high ranking Nazi civil servants and SS officers, who gathered in utter secrecy for 85 minutes in a villa in the elegant Berlin suburb of Wannsee on January 20, 1942. Reveals that their sole purpose was to discuss the logistical and technical implementations of what has come to be called 'The Final Solution to the Jewish Problem.' Producer Korytowski carefully researched the minutes of the conference to recreate the conference.
History - World
Dist - ERGOM

Wanted - a Million teachers 60 MIN
VHS
Learning in America series
Color; Captioned (G)
$49.95 purchase _ #LEIA - 104
Focuses on the American teacher. Shows that they are a target of many reform efforts. Reveals that fewer people are entering teaching despite a growing need for qualified teachers. Examines problems facing teachers, including 'burnout,' low pay, low morale and heavy administrative duties. Hosted by Roger Mudd.
Education
Dist - PBS **Prod** - WETATV 1989

Wanted - Babies 20 MIN
U-matic / VHS
Color
Explores adoption and alternatives to adoption, including surrogate mothers and 'grey market' adoptions.
Sociology
Dist - WCCOTV **Prod** - WCCOTV 1982

Wanted - Baby to Adopt 26 MIN
U-matic / VHS
Color (G)
$249.00, $149.00 purchase _ #AD - 1939
Considers the legal but controversial process of private adoption which flourishes because parents seeking to adopt greatly outnumber adoptable healthy white American infants. Shows how contacts are made between pregnant women and prospective parents and the emotional and financial risks in such transactions. Raises ethical, legal, emotional and sociological questions about adoption.
Civics and Political Systems; Health and Safety; Sociology
Dist - FOTH **Prod** - FOTH

Wants and Needs 15 MIN
VHS / U-matic
Pennywise Series no 1
Color (P)
LC 82-706004
Uses the format of a television program to demonstrate the basic economic concept of wants and needs and the differences between them. Explains how people want and need both goods and services.
Business and Economics
Dist - GPN **Prod** - MAETEL 1980

Wapoose the Rabbit 15 MIN
VHS / U-matic
Tales of Wesakechak Series
Color (G)
Portrayed once as a very handsome rabbit with wide, strong shoulders. He attracted the attention of two girl rabbits who each wish to be his wife. But Wapoose can't choose between them and seeks Weshakechak's help to make a decision.
Social Science; Sociology
Dist - NAMPBC **Prod** - NAMPBC 1984

The War 52 MIN
16mm
Roots series; 10
Color (J)
Tells how Chicken George returns to his family as a free man but soon leaves, promising to return with enough money to free them all. Shows how the family befriends a young white couple who have lost their farm to the ravages of the Civil War.
Fine Arts; History - United States
Dist - FI **Prod** - WOLPER

The War 11 MIN
16mm
Color (G)
$25.00 rental
Contrasts love and beauty, hate and horror. Sketches a love story between an Oriental boy and Caucasian girl, a fight for a knife between a Negro man and a white man, scenes of war. Music by Dylan.
Fine Arts; History - United States; Sociology
Dist - CANCIN **Prod** - DEGRAS 1969

War abroad, depression at home 71 MIN
VHS
March of time - trouble abroad series
B&W (G)
$24.95 purchase _ #S02174
Uses newsreel excerpts to cover events from June through December of 1937. Covers events including troubles with the spoils system, Hawaiian lobbying for US citizenship, the white - fringed beetle and dust bowl's negative impact on agriculture, unrest in Poland, Spain and China, and more. Part one of a six - part series.
History - United States; History - World
Dist - UILL

War and Advice 20 MIN
16mm
B&W (H C)
LC 70-707549
Depicts the role of the special U S forces who serve as observers and instructors for Vietnamese troops. Shows how American aid and influence reach into military, political and economic areas.
Civics and Political Systems
Dist - USNAC **Prod** - USDD 1964

War and empire 30 MIN
VHS
America in perspective - US history since 1877 series
Color (H C G)
$99.00 purchase _ #AIP - 7
Analyzes the causes and consequences of the Spanish - American War, as well as the costs and benefits of establishing an overseas empire. Part of a 26 - part series.
Civics and Political Systems; History - United States
Dist - INSTRU **Prod** - DALCCD 1991

War and hope 32 MIN
U-matic / 16mm / VHS
Across five Aprils series
Color (J H G)
$595.00, $250.00 purchase _ #HH - 5975L
Adapts 'Across Five Aprils' by Irene Hunt. Portrays the difficult social issues and the intense emotional conflicts of an Illinois family whose sons have taken opposite sides in the American Civil War. Part one of a two - part series.
History - United States; Literature and Drama; Sociology
Dist - CORF **Prod** - LCA 1990

War and labor woes 107 MIN
VHS
March of time - the great depression series
B&W (G)
$24.95 purchase _ #S02138
Presents newsreel excerpts covering the period from April to August of 1936. Covers events including the World's Fair at Dallas, the development of the house trailer, Austrian bankruptcy, growing railroad competition, and more. Part four of a six - part series.
History - United States
Dist - UILL

War and Peace 29 MIN
U-matic / VHS / 16mm
Footsteps Series
Color (A)
Explores problems of sibling rivalry through the dramatization of a situation in the fictional Marshall family, in which Sonny tries to make peace between two squabbling stepdaughters. Includes a brief introduction and commentary by real - life families and child development experts.
Psychology; Sociology
Dist - USNAC **Prod** - USDED 1980

War and peace 403 MIN
VHS
Color (G) (RUSSIAN WITH ENGLISH SUBTITLES)
$99.95 purchase _ #1339
Presents the original Russian - language film of Tolstoy's War and Peace, directed by Sergei Bondarchuk.
Literature and Drama
Dist - KULTUR **Prod** - KULTUR 1993

War and Peace 2 MIN
VHS / BETA
Color
Presents a two - cassette set of the 1956 adaptation of Leo Tolstoy's novel WAR AND PEACE. Stars Audrey Hepburn and Henry Fonda.
Fine Arts; Literature and Drama
Dist - GA **Prod** - GA

War and Peace 60 MIN
U-matic / VHS
James Galway's Music in Time Series
Color (J)
Presents flutist James Galway discussing how music between the two World Wars reflected history. Includes examples from Stravinsky's Rite Of Spring, Gershwin's An American In Paris and Brecht's The Beggar's Opera.
Fine Arts
Dist - FOTH **Prod** - POLTEL 1982

War and peace in the nuclear age series
Presents a thirteen - part series on war and peace in the nuclear age. Traces the development and history of nuclear weaponry from World War II through the Cold War, the proliferation of nuclear power in developing countries, to present time.
At the brink - Part 5 60 MIN
A Bigger bang for the buck - Part 3 60 MIN
Carter's new world - Part 9 60 MIN
Dawn - Part 1 60 MIN
The Education of Robert McNamara 60 MIN
Europe goes nuclear - Part 4 60 MIN
Haves and have - nots - Part 8 60 MIN
Missile experimental - Part 11 60 MIN
One step forward - Part 7 60 MIN
Reagan's shield - Part 12 60 MIN
Visions of war and peace - Part 13 60 MIN
The Weapon of choice - Part 2 60 MIN
Zero hour - Part 10 60 MIN
Dist - ANNCPB **Prod** - WGBHTV 1982

War and Violence 52 MIN
U-matic / VHS
Human Animal Series
Color (G)
$279.00, $179.00 purchase _ #AD - 1133
Considers that poverty and violence seem to go hand in hand. Looks at inner - city Boston, Maryland and Oakland, California, where a young Hispanic speaks of the machismo that underlies gang violence. Examines Ireland, the Middle East and South Africa where violence is fueled by religion, nationalism and - or race. Part of a series by Phil Donahue on the Human Animal.
Civics and Political Systems; Religion and Philosophy; Sociology
Dist - FOTH **Prod** - FOTH

The War at Home 100 MIN
16mm
Color
Chronicles the anti - war movement in the United States during the 1960's and documents how American foreign policy and American values at home were challenged and changed.
Civics and Political Systems; History - United States; Sociology
Dist - FIRS **Prod** - FIRS

The War at sea 1939 - 45 52 MIN
VHS
Century of warfare series
Color (G)

$19.99 purchase _ #0 - 7835 - 8414 - 8NK
Looks at sea warfare in World War II, 1939 - 1945. Covers strategy, tactics, weapons, personalities, battles and campaigns, victories and defeats. Part of a 20 - part series on 20th - century warfare.
Civics and Political Systems; History - World; Sociology
Dist - TILIED

War Baby cruising series
Beyond the Arctic Circle - 1 — 60 MIN
A Voyage to Spitzbergen - 2 — 53 MIN
War Baby sails to the Faroes and St Kilda - 3
Dist - SEVVID

War Baby sails to the Faroes and St Kilda - 3
VHS
War Baby cruising series
Color (G A)
$39.90 purchase _ #0491
Explores the Faroe Islands and their capital Torshaven. Sails to Stornaway in the outer Hebrides and makes smooth passage to St Kilda. Part of a series.
Geography - World; Physical Education and Recreation
Dist - SEVVID

The War between the classes — 32 MIN
VHS
Color (J H R)
$10.00 rental _ #36 - 87 - 854
Describes the 'Color Game,' an experiment which examines attitudes toward racism and class differences.
Religion and Philosophy; Sociology
Dist - APH **Prod** - CORF

War between the States
VHS / U-matic
Color
History - United States
Dist - MSTVIS **Prod** - MSTVIS

The War between the Tates — 90 MIN
VHS / U-matic
Color (H C A)
LC 80-706891
Reveals how the marriage of a supposedly happy couple falls apart when the husband has an affair with one of his students. Shows the ironies and complexities of the marital relationship as the children, spouses and lover adjust to their new lives. Stars Richard Crenna and Elizabeth Ashley.
Fine Arts; Sociology
Dist - TIMLIF **Prod** - TIMLIF 1980

War chronicles series
Presents an eight - part series on World War II, focusing on the most critical battles of the war.
The Battle of Germany - Volume 8 — 35 MIN
The Battle of the Bulge - Volume 7 — 35 MIN
The Beachhead at Anzio - Volume 3 — 35 MIN
The Bomber offensive - air war in Europe - Volume 6 — 35 MIN
D - Day - the Normandy invasion - Volume 4 — 35 MIN
The Greatest conflict - Volume 1 — 35 MIN
North Africa, the desert war - Volume 2 — 35 MIN
Pursuit to the Rhine - Volume 5 — 35 MIN
Dist - UILL

The War Chronicles, Vols 1 and 2
VHS / BETA
Color
Presents a two - cassette set chronicling World War II, including authentic footage shot by combat cameramen. Narrated by Patrick O'Neal.
Fine Arts; History - United States; Industrial and Technical Education
Dist - GA **Prod** - GA

War comes to America — 67 MIN
VHS
B&W (G)
$100.00 rental _ #0972; $39.95 purchase _ #S00349
Mixes footage of peaceful streets in the United States with war footage as Americans listen to war reports on the radio. Ends with Pearl Harbor and President Roosevelt's declaration of war. Produced in 1944.
History - United States; Sociology
Dist - SEVVID
UILL

War Comes to America — 67 MIN
16mm
Why We Fight Series
B&W (H)
LC FIE52-1713
Reviews the history of the United States from 1931 to 1941, explaining the events which led up to the entry of the United States into World War II. Describes the characteristics, habits and beliefs of the Americans.
History - United States; History - World
Dist - USNAC **Prod** - USWD 1945

War Comes to America, Pt 1 — 33 MIN
U-matic
Why We Fight Series
B&W
LC 79-706470
Reviews the history of the United States and describes the characteristics, habits and beliefs of the American people. Explains the events from 1931 to 1941 that caused the United States to enter World War II. Issued in 1945 as a motion picture.
History - United States
Dist - USNAC **Prod** - USOWI 1979

War Comes to America, Pt 2 — 34 MIN
U-matic
Why We Fight Series
B&W
LC 79-706470
Reviews the history of the United States and describes the characteristics, habits and beliefs of the American people. Explains the events from 1931 to 1941 that caused the United States to enter World War II. Issued in 1945 as a motion picture.
History - United States
Dist - USNAC **Prod** - USOWI 1979

War Comes to Pearl Harbor — 26 MIN
U-matic / VHS / 16mm
Between the Wars Series
Color (H C)
Examines American diplomacy in 1941, describing the events which led to the bombing of Pearl Harbor.
Civics and Political Systems; History - United States; History - World
Dist - FI **Prod** - LNDBRG 1978

War Department Film Communique no 1 — 30 MIN
VHS / U-matic
B&W
Presents War Department Film Communiques from 1943 including Fifth Army in Italy and With the Australians in New Guinea - Australian Footage.
History - United States; History - World
Dist - IHF **Prod** - IHF

War Department Film Communique no 2 — 45 MIN
U-matic / VHS
B&W
Offers War Department Film Communiques including Hitting The Beach in Italy and Dogfight - P47s In Combat on W Front.
History - United States; History - World
Dist - IHF **Prod** - IHF

War Department Film Communique no 3 — 30 MIN
U-matic / VHS
B&W
Offers War Department Film Communiques from 1944 including Capture Of Toulon And Marseilles and Operation In France And Belgium.
History - United States; History - World
Dist - IHF **Prod** - IHF

War for Empire — 30 MIN
VHS / U-matic
American story - the beginning to 1877 series
Color (C)
History - United States
Dist - DALCCD **Prod** - DALCCD

The War for independence - a military history — 24 MIN
VHS
Color (J H C G)
$49.00 purchase _ #SOC122V
Outlines the often slow sequence of important military events in the Revolutionary War, beginning with the first at Lexington. Shows early British victories at Boston, New York and Philadelphia, as well as unsuccessful British attempts to divide the colonies. Highlights the defeat of Burgoyne in the frontier of New York, the entry of the French against the British, the encampment at Valley Forge, the treason of Benedict Arnold at West Point, the American capture of the British outpost at Detroit, guerilla warfare in the Carolinas and the surrender of Cornwallis at Yorktown. Includes teacher's guide.
History - United States; Sociology
Dist - CAMV

The War Game — 49 MIN
16mm / U-matic / VHS
B&W (H C A)
LC 76-701418
Enacts the carnage and destruction that would result from a thermonuclear war between the Soviet Union and England in a fictional sequence. Raises questions about the societal logic that permits the existence of thermonuclear weapons. Produced in 1966 in England.
Sociology
Dist - FI **Prod** - BFI 1976

The War Game — 47 MIN
U-matic / VHS
B&W
Shows what could happen in Great Britain if it were under nuclear attack and the after - effects its survivors would suffer in a post - nuclear - war world.
Civics and Political Systems
Dist - IHF **Prod** - IHF

War Game, the, Pt 1 — 24 MIN
16mm / U-matic / VHS
B&W (H C A)
LC 76-701418
Enacts the carnage and destruction that would result from a thermonuclear war between the Soviet Union and England in a fictional sequence. Raises questions about the societal logic that permits the existence of thermonuclear weapons. Produced in 1966 in England.
Fine Arts; Sociology
Dist - FI **Prod** - BFI 1976

War Game, the, Pt 2 — 25 MIN
U-matic / VHS / 16mm
B&W (H C A)
LC 76-701418
Enacts the carnage and destruction that would result from a thermonuclear war between the Soviet Union and England in a fictional sequence. Raises questions about the societal logic that permits the existence of thermonuclear weapons. Produced in 1966 in England.
Fine Arts; Sociology
Dist - FI **Prod** - BFI 1976

War Generation - Beirut — 50 MIN
VHS / 16mm
Color (G) (ARABIC (ENGLISH SUBTITLES))
$350.00 purchase, $80.00 rental; LC 89715655
Looks at the effect of the conflict in Beirut, Lebanon, on the lives of its children and young people. Interview Lebanese youths from various backgrounds.
Health and Safety; History - World; Religion and Philosophy; Sociology
Dist - CNEMAG **Prod** - CNEMAG 1988

War - Gods of the Deep — 85 MIN
U-matic / VHS / 16mm
Color (I J H C)
Stars Vincent Price as the 'CAPTAIN,' cruel and ruthless ruler of Lyonesse, the golden city submerged beneath the sea.
Fine Arts; Literature and Drama
Dist - FI **Prod** - AIP 1965

War - Heads — 15 MIN
16mm
Color & B&W (G)
$40.00 rental
Features a dark, militaristic satire in four parts - Commercial, Stealth, Funeral and Ritual. Composes found images originating on video and re - photographed with high - contrast color and B&W film. Produced by Robert Daniel Flowers.
Civics and Political Systems; Fine Arts; Literature and Drama; Sociology
Dist - CANCIN

The War in El Cedro — 50 MIN
VHS
Color (J H C G T A)
$39.95 purchase, $25.00 rental
Profiles U S combat veterans as they travel to Nicaragua to help in whatever ways they can. Produced by Don North.
Geography - World; History - World
Dist - EFVP

The War in El Cedro - American Veterans in Nicaragua — 50 MIN
Videoreel / U-matic / VT3
(G)
$95.00 purchase, $45.00 rental
Follows ten American veterans of World War II, Korea, and Vietnam as they travel to the village of El Cedro to help rebuild a health clinic destroyed by the Contras. Illustrates how the veterans come to terms with their conflicts about patriotism and American foreign policy.
Civics and Political Systems; Geography - World; History - World; Sociology
Dist - EFVP **Prod** - EFVP 1987

War in the Gulf - answering children's questions — 75 MIN
VHS
Color (G)
$19.98 purchase _ #UPC 30306 - 6439 - 3
Joins host Peter Jennings, ABC News correspondents in the United States and Middle East, Operation Desert Storm military personnel and other experts, who explain the complex issues of war to children and their parents. Includes taped segments focusing on aspects of the Gulf War.
Sociology
Dist - INSTRU **Prod** - ABCNEW

War in the Middle East - 1946 - 1989 52 MIN
VHS
Century of warfare series
Color (G)
$19.99 purchase _ #0 - 7835 - 8427 - XNK
Examines the conflicts in the Middle East from 1946 to 1989. Covers strategy, tactics, personalities, campaigns, victories and defeats. Part of a 20 - part series on 20th - century warfare.
Civics and Political Systems; History - World; Sociology
Dist - TILIED

War in Vietnam series
Chu Chi guerrilla village 20 MIN
Dist - CANWRL

War is hell 29 MIN
16mm
B&W (G)
$60.00 rental
Provides no description other than directed by Robert Nelso and William Allan.
Fine Arts
Dist - CANCIN **Prod** - NELSOR 1968

The War is Over 28 MIN
16mm / U-matic / VHS
Adventures in History Series
Color (I J H)
Portrays the men aboard a returning troop ship in 1919, showing the re - adjustment and self - examination they are going through.
Fine Arts; History - United States; History - World
Dist - FI **Prod** - NFBC 1978

War Lab 30 MIN
VHS / 16mm
Color (G)
$250.00 purchase, $50.00 rental
Looks at the development of bombs and other weapons of mass destruction since World War II. Reveals that modern wars increasingly involve civilian populations. Civilian casualties during World War I were only 5 percent, World War II - 45 percent, Vietnam - 70 percent. Begins with the bombing of Hiroshima and Nagasaki to chronicle the development of anti - personnel weaponry.
History - United States; History - World; Sociology
Dist - CNEMAG **Prod** - CNEMAG 1987

The War Lover 105 MIN
U-matic / VHS / 16mm
B&W (C A)
Stars Steve McQueen and Robert Wagner in the story of a war hero whose talent for annihilation becomes an obsession. Based on the novel THE WAR LOVER by John Hersey.
Fine Arts
Dist - FI **Prod** - CPC 1962

War machine 50 MIN
VHS
White heat series
Color; PAL (G)
PdS99 purchase; Not available in the United States or Canada
Questions the positive opinions about weapons technology and the political assumption that sophisticated weaponry is a necessity. Examines thoughts on military technology and its progression through history. Part seven of an eight - part series.
Civics and Political Systems; Sociology
Dist - BBCENE

The War of 1812 (1783 - 1818) 58 MIN
16mm
Struggle for a Border
B&W (G H C)
_ #106B 0167 108
Presents the Canadian - British - American struggle for the Ohio valley, the War of 1812 and its contribution to American and Canadian nationalism, and some looks at the myths of war.
History - United States; History - World
Dist - CFLMDC **Prod** - NFBC 1967

War of 1812, the 14 MIN
16mm / U-matic / VHS
Color (I J H)
Reveals that when the British begin impressing American seamen, Congress declares war in 1812. Shows that stunning American land and naval victories help end the war while spurring American industry, stimulating national pride and shaping relations with Canada.
History - United States
Dist - CORF **Prod** - CORF 1982

War of Independence 1775 - 1783 24 MIN
U-matic
B&W
Presents through still pictures the general movements of the Continental Army and Navy from 1775 - 1783. Describes the founding Of the Navy, the battle of Valcour Island, the patriot John Paul Jones and Washington's strategy of Yorktown.
Biography; Civics and Political Systems; History - United States
Dist - USNAC **Prod** - USNAC 1972

War of the eagles - Eastern Front - 1914 18 52 MIN
VHS
Century of warfare series
Color (G)
$19.99 purchase _ #0 - 7835 - 8431 - 8NK
Looks at the field of war on the Eastern Front during World War I, 1914 - 1918. Covers strategy, tactics, weapons, personalities, battles and campaigns, victories and defeats. Part of a 20 - part series on 20th - century warfare.
Civics and Political Systems; History - World; Sociology
Dist - TILIED

The War of the Eggs 27 MIN
16mm / U-matic / VHS
Insight Series
Color; B&W (H C A) (SPANISH)
LC 78-713916
A dramatization about an unhappy young couple who vent their hostilities on their two - year - old son.
Foreign Language; Guidance and Counseling; Psychology; Sociology
Dist - PAULST **Prod** - PAULST 1971

The War of the Eggs 27 MIN
16mm / U-matic / VHS
Color (H C A)
LC 78-713916
A dramatization about an unhappy young couple who vent their hostilities on their two - year - old son.
Guidance and Counseling; Psychology; Sociology
Dist - MEDIAG **Prod** - PAULST 1971

War of the gods 66 MIN
VHS
Disappearing world series
Color (G C)
$99.00 purchase, $19.00 rental _ #51229
Reveals that for thousands of years the Maku and Barasana Indians have lived in the deep forests of northwest Amazonia, but now the traditions of the past are giving way to the forces of Christianity as Catholic missionaries and American evangelists compete to convert the Indians. Features anthropologists Peter Silverwood - Cope and Stephen and Christine Hugh - Jones. Part of a series working closely with anthropologists who lived for a year or more in societies whose social structures, beliefs and practices are threatened by the expansion of technocratic civilization.
History - World; Religion and Philosophy; Sociology
Dist - PSU **Prod** - GRANDA 1971

War of the words 27 MIN
VHS / U-matic
Color (H G)
$195.00, $245.00 purchase, $50.00 rental
Covers the volatile issues of 'political correctness' and multi - culturalism. Looks at the resulting polarization in academic departments and universities throughout the country in recent years. Produced by Television and Film Productions.
Civics and Political Systems; Fine Arts
Dist - NDIM

The War of the Worlds 20 MIN
16mm
American Film Genre - the Science Fiction Film Series
Color (J)
LC 75-702629
Presents a melodrama about the invasion of a rural California town by seemingly invulnerable Martians. Tells of the battle between the invaders and the residents and of the invaders from the earth's bacteria.
Fine Arts; Literature and Drama
Dist - FI **Prod** - TWCF 1975

War of the Worlds
BETA / VHS
Color
Presents H G Wells' story of the invasion of Earth by Martians, starring Gene Barry.
Fine Arts; Literature and Drama
Dist - GA **Prod** - GA

The War of the Worlds
Cassette / 16mm
Now Age Reading Programs, Set 2 Series
Color (I J)
$9.95 purchase _ #8F - PN681980
Brings a classic tale to young readers. Filmstrip set includes filmstrip, cassette, corresponding book, classroom exercise materials and a poster. The read - along set includes student activity book, cassette and paperback.
English Language; Literature and Drama
Dist - MAFEX

War on land and sea series
Presents four videocassettes on World War II. Includes the titles Churchill's War; Dunkirk - the Battle for France; Waffen - SS; D - Day.
War on land and sea series 240 MIN
Dist - CAMV **Prod** - KULTUR

War on Land and Sea Series
Churchill's war
D - Day
Dunkirk
Waffen - SS
Dist - KULTUR

War on lesbians 32 MIN
VHS
Color (G)
$60.00 rental, $250.00 purchase
Provides a witty critique of the invisibility of positive images of lesbians. Satirizes talk show television and radio self - help programs. Features supposed experts on sexuality who espouse the many, often ill - informed, theories presented to explain homosexuality. Intercut with the drama are actual recordings of a radio talkback therapist and documentary interviews with lesbians. Reveals how far many of the myths about lesbians are from the truth. By Jane Cottis.
Fine Arts; Literature and Drama
Dist - WMEN

War, peace and America 91 MIN
VHS
March of time - trouble abroad series
B&W (G)
$24.95 purchase _ #S02179
Uses newsreel excerpts to cover events in the US and abroad from March through August of 1939. Covers events including the battles between Italy and France and between Japan and China, the World's Fair, problems in the US South's economy, and more. Final part of a six - part series.
History - United States; History - World
Dist - UILL

War powers and covert action - Part 2 60 MIN
VHS / U-matic
Constitution - that delicate balance series
Color (G)
$45.00, $29.95 purchase
Presents a panel with former President Gerald Ford, former CIA Deputy Director Bobby Inman, former Secretary of State Edmund Muskie and others. Debates whether the President, as commander - in - chief, can declare war without restraint from Congress. Part of a thirteen - part series on the US Constitution created by journalist Fred Friendly.
Civics and Political Systems; Sociology
Dist - ANNCPB **Prod** - WNETTV 1984

War powers - who decides 20 MIN
VHS
Color (J H C T A)
$81.00 purchase _ #MB - 540340 - 4
Discusses the conflict over war powers between the Congress and the President. Covers subjects including separation of powers, checks and balances, and the differences between hostilities and war. Focuses on the Persian Gulf war as an example of the conflict. Includes activities package.
Civics and Political Systems; Sociology
Dist - SRA **Prod** - SRA 1989

The War room 93 MIN
35mm / 16mm
Color (G)
$200.00 rental
Views the inner workings of Bill Clinton's campaign through the eyes of senior strategist James Carville and communications director George Stephanopoulos. Features intimate and exclusive footage that allows the viewer to experience the triumph of election night from inside, and come away with a new understanding of the political process, the dynamics of a modern campaign, and the passion behind it. Produced by R J Cutler, Wendy Ettinger and Frazer Pennebaker.
Civics and Political Systems; Fine Arts
Dist - OCTOBF

War series
Anybody's son will do 60 MIN
The Deadly Game of Nations 60 MIN
Goodbye war 60 MIN
Keeping the Old Game Alive 60 MIN
Notes on Nuclear War 60 MIN
The Profession of Arms 60 MIN
The Road to total war 60 MIN
Dist - FI

War Shadows 25 MIN
U-matic / VHS
Color
Explores the Viet Nam war experiences of Paul Reutershan, his contact with Agent Orange, and subsequent illness

and death. Reutershan was the first to bring the plight of veterans exposed to this defoliant to national attention before he died of cancer at 28 years of age.
Science - Natural; Sociology
Dist - GMPF **Prod** - GMPF

War songs 12 MIN
VHS
Films for music for film series
Color; B&W (G)
$50.00, $60.00 rental
Presents one of a series of films by Lawrence Brose that reconsider the interactive dynamic of sound and image in film. Presents war footage illustrating 5 poems by Paul Schmidt, with a musical score by Mark Bennett.
Fine Arts; Sociology
Dist - CANCIN

A War Story 82 MIN
16mm
Color (H C A)
Dramatizes life in a Japanese prisoner - of - war camp during World War II. Interweaves scenes from inside the camp with footage of the fall of Singapore and interviews survivors of the camp.
History - World
Dist - NFBC **Prod** - NFBC 1981

War, Taxes and the Almighty Dollar 30 MIN
VHS / 16mm
Color (G)
$100.00 purchase _ #TAXESVH
Discusses the effects of defense spending on the U S economy. Considers the causes and effects of Pentagon spending practices. Documents the impact of foreign debt and trade deficits on farming and manufacturing. Depicts a tax resister who explains why he does not pay federal income tax.
Business and Economics; Education; History - United States; Sociology
Dist - APPAL

War - the most Dangerous Game 145 MIN
U-matic
University of the Air Series
Color (J H C A)
$750.00 purchase, $250.00 rental
Surveys five battles and the long term effects of victory and defeat. Program contains a series of five cassettes 29 minutes each.
History - World; Sociology
Dist - CTV **Prod** - CTV 1976

The War which Never Happened 28 MIN
16mm
Color
Explores one of today's most pressing issues, the commitment of Europe to the Alliance and to its own defense.
Civics and Political Systems; Sociology
Dist - MTP **Prod** - MTP

War with Mexico 30 MIN
VHS / U-matic
American story - the beginning to 1877 series
Color (C)
History - United States
Dist - DALCCD **Prod** - DALCCD

The War with Mexico - 1846 - 1848 26 MIN
VHS
Color (J H C G)
$49.00 purchase _ #SOC7164V
Overviews one of the most controversial wars in United States history. Explains the factors which led to the decisions for war, the far - reaching impact of the war and the internal differences within each country. Shows the goals and objectives of both sides to point out the weaknesses and strengths in both Mexican and United States forces. Includes teacher's guide.
History - United States; Sociology
Dist - CAMV

The War within 60 MIN
U-matic / VHS
Color (C A)
Portrays the personal lives of six highly decorated Vietnam War veterans. Shows them as patients at the Vietnam Veterans Treatment Center in Menlo Park, California, reliving the nightmares of Vietnam by talking about them.
History - United States; Psychology; Sociology
Dist - FI **Prod** - KRONTV

War Without Winners II 29 MIN
U-matic / VHS / 16mm
Color
Intertwines interviews with celebrities, scientists and layman on the dangers of nuclear war. Features excerpts from a historically unprecedented nuclear effects roundtable discussion between leading American and Soviet physicians. Narrated by Paul Newman.
Sociology
Dist - FI **Prod** - CDINFO 1983

War work, housework and growing discontent - 1942 - 1952 - Program 4 15 MIN
VHS
Women in American life series
B&W (H C G)
$110.00 purchase _ #EHC - 657
Explores the daily life experiences of women, their work lives and involvement with social issues during World War II through the early 1950s. Includes women from a wide variety of geographic, ethnic and racial populations. Includes historic photographs. Part four of a four - part series.
History - United States; History - World
Dist - ADL **Prod** - ADL 1991

The War years 10 MIN
VHS
American Revolution series
Color (J H)
$59.00 purchase _ #MF - 3770; $265.00, $185.00 purchase _ #3770
Studies the major phases of the American Revolution from the shots fired at Concord, 1775, to Yorktown in 1781. Examines the role of George Washington and his leadership.
Biography; History - United States
Dist - INSTRU **Prod** - CORF
CORF

The War Years - 1931 - 1941 60 MIN
VHS
Trilogy of War Series
Color (G)
$99.00 purchase
Documents German, Japanese and Italian aggression around the globe. Culminates in the attack on Pearl Harbor and US entry into World War II. Part of a three - part series, the Trilogy of War.
History - United States; History - World; Sociology
Dist - LUF **Prod** - LUF

War Years After Pearl Harbor - 1941 - 1945 60 MIN
VHS
Trilogy of War Series
Color (G)
$99.00 purchase
Presents edited Allied and enemy films of World War II. Shows Japan overrunning the Pacific, the Allies turning the tide at the battle of Midway, Hitler and the Holocaust, the invasion of France, the collapse of the Third Reich and the Pacific theater. Part of a three - part series, the Trilogy of War.
History - United States; History - World; Sociology
Dist - LUF **Prod** - LUF

The War Years - Fabulous 1939, Then Global Conflict 35 MIN
U-matic / VHS / 16mm
Life Goes to the Movies Series Part 2
Color
LC 77-701542
Discusses the great studio magnates and some of the film masterpieces that made 1939 Hollywood's most glorious year. Enumerates the film industry's later contributions to the World War II effort, including propaganda films, the creation of symbolic heroes and the stars' entertainment of the troops.
Fine Arts
Dist - TIMLIF **Prod** - TIMLIF 1976

Warbirds (WWII Fighters and Bombers) 20 MIN
U-matic / VHS
Color (J)
LC 82-706793
Discusses such famous World War II fighters and bombers as the Mustang, Corsair and Flying Fortress. Notes that nearly 40 years after rolling off wartime assembly lines, these fighters and bombers are still flying.
History - United States; Industrial and Technical Education
Dist - AWSS **Prod** - AWSS 1981

Wardrobe 14 MIN
U-matic / VHS / 16mm
Good Grooming Series
Color (H C)
Discusses propriety of dress to occasion, suitability of accessories, camouflaging overweight and underweight tendencies by style selection, and the importance of posture.
Guidance and Counseling; Home Economics
Dist - IFB **Prod** - IFB 1961

Wardrobe in a Weekend 30 MIN
VHS
Quick and Easy Sewing Series
(H C A)
$19.95 purchase _ #CH410V
Demonstrates how to sew six interchangeable separates.
Home Economics
Dist - CAMV

The Warehouse in logistics systems 30 MIN
VHS
Business logistics series
Color (G C)
$200.00 purchase, $20.50 rental _ #34965
Examines the role of the warehouse in logistical systems. Part of a 30 - part series on business logistics which deals with movement and storage of raw and finished products, and with managerial activities important for effective control of these operations. Interviews logistics managers of major US corporations and transportation companies. Uses on - site segments to demonstrate logistical carrier operations. Features program author Dr John Coyle.
Business and Economics
Dist - PSU **Prod** - WPSXTV 1987

Warehouse operations 30 MIN
VHS
Business logistics series
Color (G C)
$200.00 purchase, $20.50 rental _ #34966
Examines warehouse operations. Part of a 30 - part series on business logistics which deals with movement and storage of raw and finished products, and with managerial activities important for effective control of these operations. Interviews logistics managers of major US corporations and transportation companies. Uses on - site segments to demonstrate logistical carrier operations. Features program author Dr John Coyle.
Business and Economics
Dist - PSU **Prod** - WPSXTV 1987

Warehouse safety series
Be warehouse safe 22 MIN
Handling with care 12 MIN
Dist - CFLVIS

Warehousing 10 MIN
VHS
Skills - occupational programs series
Color (H A)
$49.00 purchase, $15.00 rental _ #316611; LC 91-712291
Describes the roles played by a receiver, a lift - truck operator, an order filler and a shipper in a large material - handling operation. Explains why math skills, computer knowledge and writing skills are necessary in warehouse environments. Part of a series featuring occupations in the skilled trades, in service industries and in business leading to careers in areas of demand and future growth. Includes teacher's guide with reproducible wooksheets.
Guidance and Counseling; Psychology
Dist - TVOTAR **Prod** - TVOTAR 1990

Warfare prayer
VHS
Color (R)
$29.99 purchase _ #SPCN 85116.00612
Focuses on aggressively invoking God for power and protection and the growth of churches. Features Peter Wagner who illustrates Biblical ways to make the prayer life of Christians - both individually and as leaders of corporations - more targeted and fruitful. Includes two videos.
Religion and Philosophy
Dist - GOSPEL **Prod** - GOSPEL

Warlords of Atlantis 96 MIN
16mm
Color
Describes how a father - and - son team plumb the ocean's depth to search for the lost continent of Atlantis.
Fine Arts
Dist - TWYMAN **Prod** - CPC 1978

Warm - Blooded and Cold - Blooded Animals 14 MIN
U-matic / VHS / 16mm
Color (I J)
LC 79-711492
Utilizes experiments to demonstrate how environment affects the temperature of cold - blooded animals and how body coverings help warm - blooded animals keep a more constant temperature.
Science - Natural
Dist - CORF **Prod** - CORF 1971

The Warm Coat 14 MIN
16mm
Color
LC 72-704659
A documentary account of the airlifting of sea otters from the Bering Sea to Alaskan coves, an environment which will offer the animals a better chance to thrive and multiply.
Geography - United States; Geography - World; Science - Natural
Dist - USNAC **Prod** - USNRC 1969

A Warm place inside 29 MIN
VHS
This is the life series
Color (G R)

$24.95 purchase
Tells the story of a pastor and his wife who offer shelter to the street people of their city. Produced by the International Lutheran Laymen's League.
Guidance and Counseling; Literature and Drama; Religion and Philosophy
Dist - CPH **Prod** - LUMIS

Warm - Season Gardens 30 MIN
BETA / VHS
Victory Garden Series
Color
Shows how to start a warm - season garden. Gives tips on growing in containers. Discusses dimension and intent of a main season bed.
Agriculture; Physical Education and Recreation
Dist - CORF **Prod** - WGBHTV

Warm - Up and Conditioning 30 MIN
U-matic / VHS
Health and Well - Being of Dancers Series
Color
Fine Arts; Health and Safety; Physical Education and Recreation
Dist - ARCVID **Prod** - ARCVID

Warm Up and Cool Down 15 MIN
VHS / 16mm
All Fit with Slim Goodbody Series
Color (P I)
$125.00 purchase, $25.00 rental
Explains the need for warming up before vigorous exercise and cooling down after exercise.
Health and Safety; Physical Education and Recreation; Science - Natural
Dist - AITECH **Prod** - GDBODY 1987

Warming Warning 52 MIN
16mm / U-matic / VHS
Color (H C)
Analyzes a major environmental threat - the warming of the earth's climate due to increased burning of fossil fuels. Explains how the carbon dioxide content of the earth's atmosphere acts like the glass in a greenhouse resulting in warming of the global climate.
Geography - World; Science - Physical
Dist - MEDIAG **Prod** - THAMES 1985

Warner Brothers trio - 1 21 MIN
35mm
Warner Brothers Trios series
Color (G)
Features a trio of cartoons. Includes Knighty Knight Bugs, Scarlet Pumpernickel, and To Beep or Not to Beep. First in a series of three. Contact distributor for rental price.
Fine Arts
Dist - KITPAR **Prod** - WB

Warner Brothers trio - 2 21 MIN
35mm
Warner Brothers Trios series
Color (G)
Features a trio of cartoons. Includes Bear Feat, Cheese Chasers, and What's Opera Doc. Second in a series of three. Contact distributor for rental price.
Fine Arts
Dist - KITPAR **Prod** - WB

Warner Brothers trio - 3 21 MIN
35mm
Warner Brothers Trios series
Color (G)
Features a trio of cartoons. Includes Mississippi Hare, Mousewreckers, and Rabbit of Seville. Third in a series of three. Contact distributor for rental price.
Fine Arts
Dist - KITPAR **Prod** - WB

Warner Brothers Trios series
Warner Brothers trio - 1 21 MIN
Warner Brothers trio - 2 21 MIN
Warner Brothers trio - 3 21 MIN
Dist - KITPAR

Warner - Pathe newsreel series
Gadgets galore 11 MIN
Say it with spills 11 MIN
Too much speed 11 MIN
Dist - KITPAR

Warning Arrhythmias 22 MIN
16mm
Intensive Coronary Care Multimedia Learning System (ICC/MMLS Series
Color (PRO)
LC 73-701773
Discusses the concept of warning arrhythmias, including a discussion of specific warning arrhythmias. Describes types, electrocardiographic patterns and treatment. Covers heart block (A - V block).
Health and Safety
Dist - SUTHLA **Prod** - SUTHLA 1969

The Warning Arrhythmias 22 MIN
16mm
Multimedia Instructional System for Coronary Care Unit Nurses Series
Color
LC 74-705016
Discusses the warning arrhythmias which are the precursors of more serious arrhythmias and uses animation to explain the anatomical and electrocardiographic aspects.
Health and Safety; Science - Natural
Dist - SUTHLA **Prod** - HOFLAR 1969

Warning - Breathing may be Hazardous to Your Health 25 MIN
U-matic / VHS
Color
Shows just how bad pollution really is, who is responsible and what can be done about it. Interviews Dr Joseph Boyle, specialist in internal medicine and disease of the chest and lungs, and a former member of the California State Air Resource Board, on the timely topic of pollution and its threat to mankind.
Health and Safety; Science - Natural
Dist - MEDCOM **Prod** - MEDCOM

Warning - Earthquake 24 MIN
U-matic / VHS / 16mm
Wide World of Adventure Series
Color (I J)
LC 77-701912
Presents scenes from actual earthquakes. Shows workers trying to help the injured and unharmed survivors rummaging through the debris and total destruction that surrounds them. Illustrates the devastating effects of the earthquake. Gives insights into survivors' feelings through interviews.
History - World
Dist - EBEC **Prod** - AVATLI 1976

Warning from Outer Space 11 MIN
16mm
Color (P I)
Space explorers find that 'OLD - FASHIONED EARTHPEOPLE' are still smoking - - a habit that Z - Men made a Zeta Crime 96 million earth years ago.
Health and Safety
Dist - PROART **Prod** - PROART

Warning - it Could Happen to You 14 MIN
16mm
Color (J H C A)
Provides medical, biomechanical and statistical information on the full range of injuries for such sports as gymnastics, wrestling, basketball, baseball and most other school sports. Includes interviews with injured student athletes and medical experts about the effects ofpermanent injury.
Health and Safety; Physical Education and Recreation
Dist - ATHI **Prod** - ATHI

Warning signs 27 MIN
VHS
Color (A) (JAPANESE)
$525.00 purchase
Explains the six requirements for an effective warning label and demonstrates applying the requirements to product design. Promotes awareness of product liability from product conception through manufacture.
Business and Economics; Civics and Political Systems; Education
Dist - COMFLM **Prod** - COMFLM

Warnock's children 45 MIN
VHS
Education special
Color (A)
PdS65 purchase
Features Baroness Warnock who examines the education of children with special needs 12 years after the 1981 Education Act was passed. Visits several schools in Birmingham and Oxfordshire to see if the implementation of the Act is helping or hindering the education of the estimated 20 percent of Great Britain's children who have special needs.
Education
Dist - BBCENE

Warpaint and wigs 29 MIN
U-matic / VT1 / VHS
Images of Indians series
Color (G)
$49.95 purchase, $35.00 rental
Shows how the portrayal of American Indians as the Noble Savage and the Savage Savage has affected their self - image. Criticizes Hollywood because the impact of film images on Native Americans has been enormous and damaging. Observes that Hollywood makes money portraying Indians being killed, and calls for positive, realistic portrayals of Native people in the past and in the present. By Robert Hagopian and Phil Lucas. Will Sampson narrates. Part of a five - part series on images of Indians.

Fine Arts; Religion and Philosophy; Social Science; Sociology
Dist - NAMPBC **Prod** - KCTSTV

The Warpath 13 MIN
U-matic / VHS
America's Indians Series
Color (G)
$199.00, $99.00 purchase _ #AD - 975
Looks at warfare between native Indians and American whites who usurped their fertile lands and the riches of the west. Part of a six - part series on America's Indians.
History - United States; History - World; Social Science; Sociology
Dist - FOTH **Prod** - FOTH

Warren 2 MIN
16mm
Color (G)
$5.00 rental
Explores a young man's soul crying out for help. Presents poetic cell animation inspired by the works of Susan Pitt. Produced by Paul Heilemann.
Fine Arts
Dist - CANCIN

Warren Miller's learn to ski better 90 MIN
VHS
Color (G)
$19.95 purchase
Presents an instructional video teaching the basics of skiing. Covers performance, conditioning, equipment, and mind - body awareness. Hosted by Warren Miller.
Physical Education and Recreation
Dist - PBS **Prod** - WNETTV

Warring and Roaring
VHS / U-matic
Color (J H C A)
$79.00 purchase _ #05963 94
Dramatizes early twentieth century America, from the start of World War I to the Wall Street crash of 1929.
Fine Arts; History - United States
Dist - ASPRSS

Warring and Roaring
VHS / U-matic
Color
History - United States
Dist - MSTVIS **Prod** - MSTVIS

Warring factions 50 MIN
VHS
Fire in the blood series
Color (A)
PdS99 purchase
Looks at the Spain that has evolved since Franco's death, especially in light of the 1992 Olympic Games in Barcelona, EXPO in Seville, and the quintentenary of Columbus' landing in the Americas. Deals with the Basque country, separatism, and terrorism.
Geography - World; History - World
Dist - BBCENE

Warrior 52 MIN
VHS / U-matic
World at War Specials Series
Color (H C A)
Examines the universal experience of men who kill in time of war - preparing for it, participating in it, and reflecting on it afterward - demonstrating that no man who has experienced combat is ever quite the same again.
History - World; Sociology
Dist - MEDIAG **Prod** - THAMES 1974

Warrior marks 54 MIN
VHS / 16mm
Color (G)
$85.00, $150.00 rental, $295.00 purchase
Looks at female genital mutilation which affects one hundred million of the world's women. Unlocks some of the cultural and political complexities surrounding this issue. Interviews women from Senegal, the Gambia, Burkino Faso, the United States and England who are concerned with and affected by genital mutilation. Features Alice Walker, Pulitzer Prize - winning author, as executive producer and who offers her own personal reflections on the subject.
Fine Arts; Sociology
Dist - WMEN **Prod** - PARMAR 1993

Warriors 58 MIN
VHS / U-matic
Native American Topics Series
Color (G)
$160.00, $110.00 purchase, $60.00, $40.00 rental
Honors Native American veterans of the Vietnam war and sheds light on a number of cultural issues about the Indian tradition of warriors. Raises questions about the place of Indian warriors within the context of American society. Created by Deb Wallwork.
History - World; Social Science
Dist - IAFC

Warriors at Peace 13 MIN
16mm
Color (I J)
Presents life among the once warlike Apaches in Arizona. Shows their wealth in stock, art of basketry and the tribal tradition of the pollen blessing ceremony.
Social Science; Sociology
Dist - MLA **Prod** - DAGP 1953

Warriors of the Wind 52 MIN
16mm
Color
LC 81-701396
Looks at the Hamamatsu Kite Festival which has been held in Japan for over 400 years.
History - World; Social Science
Dist - SHAWBR **Prod** - SHAWBR 1981

Wars in peace - 1946 to the present 52 MIN
VHS
Century of warfare series
Color (G)
$19.99 purchase _ #0 - 7835 - 8425 - 3NK
Examines the latest trend of the 20th century, peacetime wars. Covers strategy, tactics, personalities, campaigns, victories and defeats. Part of a 20 - part series on 20th - century warfare.
Civics and Political Systems; History - World; Sociology
Dist - TILIED

The Wars of religion - the rise of the trading cities - Parts 29 and 30 60 MIN
U-matic / VHS
Western tradition - part II series
Color (G)
$45.00, $29.95 purchase
Presents two thirty - minute programs tracing the history of ideas, events and institutions which have shaped modern societies hosted by Eugen Weber. Follows more than a century of war and quarreling between Roman Catholics and Protestants which tore Europe apart in part 29. Part 30 examines the few wise cities of Europe who learned that religious tolerance increased their stability and prosperity. Parts 29 and 30 of a 52 - part series on the Western tradition.
Geography - World; Religion and Philosophy; Sociology
Dist - ANNCPB **Prod** - WGBH 1989

The Warsaw File 30 MIN
VHS
Inside Story Series
Color (G)
$50.00 purchase _ #INST - 310
Focuses on Poland and its citizens' desire for change from Communism. Reveals the problems American media correspondents face in covering Polish events. Hosted by Hodding Carter.
Civics and Political Systems; History - World
Dist - PBS

The Warsaw File 29 MIN
U-matic / VHS
Ifside Story Series
Color
Focuses on the continuing story of Poland and the daily problems which American correspondents face as they try to cover Polish events.
Fine Arts; Geography - World; Literature and Drama; Social Science; Sociology
Dist - PBS **Prod** - PBS 1981

The Warsaw ghetto uprising 23 MIN
VHS
Color (G)
$39.00 purchase
Commemorates the Warsaw Ghetto Uprising taking place in April, 50 years ago. Utilizes archival film footage, authentic still photographs, along with actual testimonies of survivors of the ghetto to help viewers understand that chapter in Jewish history. Begins with the Nazi invasion of Poland, and leads step - by - step through the deportations, life in the ghetto, the formation of a reistance organization, and finally, the Warsaw Ghetto Uprising. Produced by the Ghetto Fighters' House Museum, located at Kibbutz Lohamei Hagetaot in Israel.
History - World; Religion and Philosophy; Sociology
Dist - ERGOM

Warsaw, Poland 3 MIN
16mm
Of all Things Series
Color (P I)
Discusses the city of Warsaw in Poland.
Geography - World
Dist - AVED **Prod** - BAILYL

Warsaw uprising chronicle - Kroniki powstania Warszawskiego 45 MIN
VHS
B&W (G A) (POLISH)
$29.95 purchase _ #V145
Presents a unique documentary from the 1944 Warsaw Uprising against Nazi occupation, restored from films confiscated and badly mutilated by communist censors.
Civics and Political Systems; Fine Arts; History - World
Dist - POLART

The Warship, a Society at Sea 53 MIN
16mm
Color
LC 78-701580
Examines a ship as a model for social organization.
Sociology
Dist - VPI **Prod** - VPI 1978

Warship, a Society at Sea, the, Pt 1 26 MIN
16mm
Color
LC 78-701580
Examines a ship as a model for social organization.
Social Science; Sociology
Dist - VPI **Prod** - VPI 1978

Warship, a Society at Sea, the, Pt 2 27 MIN
16mm
Color
LC 78-701580
Examines a ship as a model for social organization.
Social Science; Sociology
Dist - VPI **Prod** - VPI 1978

Warthog - Part 5 8 MIN
VHS
Safari TV series
Color (P I)
$125.00 purchase
Studies the daily life of the warthog. Part of a 13 - part series on African animals.
Geography - World; Science - Natural
Dist - LANDMK **Prod** - LANDMK 1993

Wartime combat - Volume VI
VHS
British documentary movement series
B&W (G)
$29.95 purchase
Presents two classic documentaries from the General Post Office in Great Britain - GPO. Contains 'Desert Victory', 1943, by Major David MacDonald, directed by Capt Roy Boulting, and 'Cameramen at War', 1945. Volume six of seven volumes on the British Documentary movement founded by John Grierson.
Fine Arts; History - World
Dist - KINOIC

Wartime homefront - Volume IV
VHS
British documentary movement series
B&W (G)
$29.95 purchase
Presents two classic documentaries from the General Post Office in Great Britain - GPO. Contains 'London Can Take It', 1940, and 'Fires Were Started', 1943, by Humphrey Jennings. Volume four of seven volumes on the British Documentary movement founded by John Grierson.
Fine Arts; History - World
Dist - KINOIC

Wartime in Washington 30 MIN
U-matic / VHS
Color (J)
Tells the story of life in the nation's capital during World War II. Includes archival footage and interviews of residents.
History - United States
Dist - WETATV **Prod** - WETATV

Wartime moments - Volume V
VHS
British documentary movement series
B&W (G)
$29.95 purchase
Presents three classic documentaries from the General Post Office in Great Britain - GPO. Contains 'Listen to Britain', 1942, 'Target for Tonight', 1941, and 'A Diary for Timothy', 1945, by Humphrey Jennings. Volume five of seven volumes on the British Documentary movement founded by John Grierson.
Fine Arts; History - World
Dist - KINOIC

Wartime romance 93 MIN
35mm / 16mm
Color (G) (RUSSIAN WITH ENGLISH SUBTITLES)
$250.00, $300.00 rental
Portrays the bittersweet love affair of an army private and a nurse and their reunion at the end of World War II. Directed by Pyotr Todorowsky.
Fine Arts
Dist - KINOIC **Prod** - IFEX 1984

Warts, Songs and Jokes 30 MIN
U-matic
Folklore - U S a Series
B&W
Discusses why jokes, songs and folk cures are a part of American folklore. Uses special staging and recordings.
Literature and Drama
Dist - UMITV **Prod** - UMITV 1967

Warty, the Toad 13 MIN
U-matic / VHS / 16mm
Color (P)
LC 73-702901
Presents the story of Warty, the toad, who is vain about his ugliness until he learns that there are more important things than looks.
Literature and Drama
Dist - CORF **Prod** - CORF 1973

Warty, the toad 13 MIN
VHS
Color (P)
Presents an animated version of 'Warty, the Toad.' Tells about a toad who is vain about his ugliness and feels sorry for animals who aren't as ugly. When the butterfly, turtle, grasshopper and frog save him from a hognose snake, Warty learns that there are more important things than how one looks.
Fine Arts; Literature and Drama
Dist - VIEWTH **Prod** - VIEWTH

Warum Lauft Herr R Amok 102 MIN
16mm
B&W (GERMAN (ENGLISH SUBTITLES))
A German language motion picture available with or without English subtitles. Depicts an apparently normal man who returns from work one evening and is irrationally and inexplicably compelled to kill his wife and child and a visiting neighbor, and finally himself. Directed by R. W. Fassbinder.
Foreign Language; Psychology; Sociology
Dist - WSTGLC **Prod** - WSTGLC 1970

Was 13 MIN
16mm
B&W; Color (G)
$20.00 rental
Concerns sexuality and the mother. Combines a collage of diary fragments, a landscape and a surreal ad of a Ford Mustang concealing two lovers. Exemplifies Michael Hoolboom's avant - garde film traditions.
Fine Arts
Dist - CANCIN

Was Ich Bin, Sind Meine Filme 99 MIN
16mm
Color (GERMAN (ENGLISH SUBTITLES))
Focuses on the dreams, childhood, adventures, obsessions, and movies of director Werner Herzog. Gives special attention to his surrealistic visions.
Biography; Fine Arts; Foreign Language
Dist - WSTGLC **Prod** - WSTGLC 1978

Was Ist Los 15 MIN
U-matic / VHS / 16mm
Guten Tag Series no 10; No 10
B&W (H) (GERMAN)
LC 77-707323
A German Language Film. Presents an episode in which the characters employ frequently used expressions and idioms in order to teach conversational German to beginners, stresses the correct use of aum baden gehen, participles with the ending ge, perfect verb forms without a prefix, personal verb forms with ihr, impersonal expressions with es, and the preposition in.
Foreign Language
Dist - IFB **Prod** - FRGMFA 1970

Was it Something I Said 13 MIN
16mm / U-matic / VHS
Color (C A)
Illustrates that employees at all levels are responsible for classified information.
Business and Economics; Psychology
Dist - CORF **Prod** - GLI

Was it Worth Reading 14 MIN
16mm
Patheways to Reading Series
B&W (I J)
Discusses criteria for evaluating what is read. Presents several paragraphs to be read and judged. Lists questions on which to base the evaluation.
English Language; Literature and Drama
Dist - AVED **Prod** - CBF 1958

Was Man Nicht Kann, Muss Man Eben Lernen 15 MIN
16mm / U-matic / VHS
Guten Tag Wie Geht's Series
Color (H C) (GERMAN)
Features Gunther and Francois spending their vacation skiing in Inzell and enjoying the festivities of Fastnacht.
Foreign Language
Dist - IFB **Prod** - BAYER 1973

Was Tut Man in Dem Fall 15 MIN
U-matic / VHS / 16mm
Guten Tag Series
B&W (H) (GERMAN)
LC 75-707336
Presents an episode in which the characters employ frequently used expressions and idioms in order to teach conversational German to beginners. Stresses the correct use of gerade with the predicate, verbs with prepositions, the pronoun etwas, and the prepositions am, bei, fur and zu.
Foreign Language
Dist - IFB **Prod** - FRGMFA 1970

Wash it 6 MIN
16mm / VHS
Color (G)
$12.00 rental
Entertains with Low Riders getting squeaky clean at the drive - through to the spicy salsa sounds of Los Agitadores featuring Steve Mitchell in a Elizabeth Sher production.
Fine Arts; Sociology
Dist - CANCIN

Wash Techniques of Painting 25 MIN
VHS / U-matic
Paint Series Program 6
Color (H C A)
Fine Arts
Dist - FI **Prod** - BBCTV

The Washing Feel Good Movie 6 MIN
U-matic / VHS / 16mm
Color (P)
$130 purchase - 16 mm, $79 purchase - video
Discusses cleanliness and hygiene from a child's point of view. A Paul Fillinger Film.
Health and Safety
Dist - CF

The Washing Feel Good Movie 6 MIN
U-matic / VHS / 16mm
Feel Good - Primary Health Series
Color (K P)
LC 74-702237
Portrays children experiencing the pleasures of getting dirty and the pleasure of being clean.
Health and Safety
Dist - CF **Prod** - CF 1974

Washing of a river 30 MIN
VHS
Perspective - the environment - series
Color; PAL; NTSC (G)
PdS90, PdS105 purchase
Reveals that the expertise that cleaned the Thames River system is being applied to the Ganges in India.
Geography - World; Science - Natural
Dist - CFLVIS **Prod** - LONTVS

Washington 60 MIN
VHS
Portrait of America series
Color (J H C G)
$99.95 purchase _ #AMB47V
Visits the state of Washington. Offers extensive research into the state's history. Films key locations and presents segments on its history, government, education, folklore, science, journalism, sociology, industry, agriculture and business. Shows what is unique about Washington and what is distinctive about its regional culture and how it got to be that way. Includes teacher study guides. Part of a 50 - part series.
Geography - United States; History - United States
Dist - CAMV

Washington 15 MIN
U-matic
Celebrate Series
Color (P)
Social Science
Dist - GPN **Prod** - KUONTV 1978

Washington, City of the World 14 MIN
U-matic / VHS / 16mm
Color (I J H)
LC FIA65-501
Pictures Washington, D C, showing federal buildings, national monuments and offices of the representatives of governments of other nations.
Geography - United States; Social Science
Dist - PHENIX **Prod** - PART 1965

The Washington colorists 37 MIN
VHS
Color (G)
$49.95 purchase _ #WCOL - 000
Features the artwork of the Washington Colorists, six Washington, D C painters who emphasized color as the key element of their work. Interviews some of the artists, critics and experts.
Fine Arts
Dist - PBS **Prod** - WETATV 1986

Washington Connection Series

Busing	29 MIN
Disaster Relief	29 MIN
Energy	29 MIN
Food costs - bread	29 MIN
Generic Vs Brand Name Drugs	29 MIN
Housing	29 MIN
I R S	29 MIN
Impeachment Primer	29 MIN
Land Use	29 MIN
LEAA	29 MIN
Lobbying	29 MIN
Occupational Health	29 MIN
The People Ask James Cardwell - Commissioner of Social Security	29 MIN
The People Ask William Simon	29 MIN
Postal Service	29 MIN
The Press	29 MIN
State of the Union	29 MIN
Vietnam Vets	29 MIN
Washington Walk Around	29 MIN
Watergate Morality	29 MIN

Dist - PBS

Washington, D C - Symbol of Freedom 16 MIN
16mm
Color (I J H)
Takes the viewer on a guided tour of our nation's capital. Includes the White House and such buildings and monuments as the Library of Congress, Washington Monument and the Smithsonian Institution.
Geography - United States; History - United States
Dist - BECKLY **Prod** - BECKLY

Washington, DC 20 MIN
U-matic / VHS / 16mm
Color (I)
Tours Washington DC, the nation's capital. Shows Pierre L'Enfant's original plan and how it has been changed over the years. Emphasizes the importance of political activity to the city.
Geography - United States; History - United States
Dist - NGS **Prod** - NGS 1983

Washington, DC 3 MIN
16mm
Of all Things Series
Color (P I)
Discusses Washington, DC.
Geography - United States
Dist - AVED **Prod** - BAILYL

Washington DC 55 MIN
VHS
Color (G)
$29.95 purchase _ #S01647
Tours Washington DC. Includes visits to the Smithsonian Institution, the Library of Congress, the White House, and more.
Civics and Political Systems; Geography - United States; Social Science; Sociology
Dist - UILL

Washington, DC - a Special City 14 MIN
U-matic / VHS
Under the Blue Umbrella Series
Color (P)
Tells how Michael shows his friend Stephanie the historic sites of Washington, DC.
Geography - United States
Dist - AITECH **Prod** - SCETV 1977

Washington, DC, Fancy Free 22 MIN
16mm
Color
LC 77-703421
Presents a montage of the opportunities for the visitor to Washington, DC.
Geography - United States
Dist - USNAC **Prod** - USNPS 1976

Washington DC - Heartland of a Nation
16mm / VHS
Color (I)
#C - 536
Introduces the ideals which went into the planning for the city of Washington DC, the grand design that evolved and the years of neglect and fitful construction that followed. Profiles some of the characters who stood at the center of events, and examines specific buildings. Produced by Ken Nelson.
Civics and Political Systems; Fine Arts; Geography - United States; History - United States
Dist - ALTSUL

Washington DC - L'Enfant's Dream, Our Heritage 21 MIN
16mm / U-matic / VHS
Color (I J H)
Presents the story of Pierre Charles L'Enfant, the architect of Washington, DC. Tells how he planned the city and the history of the capitol. Describes how L'Enfant died in poverty never knowing that his dream was realised and that Washington today is the way he planned it.
Geography - United States; History - United States
Dist - HANDEL **Prod** - HANDEL 1984

The Washington DC public talk 60 MIN
VHS / BETA
Color; PAL (G)
PdS20 purchase
Features the Dalai Lama's moving discourse on the purpose of compassion in the modern world.
Fine Arts; Religion and Philosophy
Dist - MERIDT

Washington Irving 18 MIN
U-matic / VHS / 16mm
B&W (J H)
Significant episodes in the life of the first American to receive prominent recognition in the world of literature. Describes his travels and life abroad, highlighting the incidents on which hinged the writing of his best known literary works.
Biography; Literature and Drama
Dist - EBEC **Prod** - EBEC 1949

Washington Irving
VHS / 35mm strip
Meet the Classic Authors Series
Color (I)
$39.95, $28.00 purchase
Portrays Washington Irving. Part of a series on authors.
English Language; Literature and Drama
Dist - PELLER

Washington monuments 30 MIN
VHS
Color (G)
$19.95 purchase _ #S02191
Presents the history and significance of many of Washington DC's most celebrated monuments and buildings. Features more than a dozen of the city's monuments, along with several museums, the Library of Congress, the Capitol, and more.
Geography - United States
Dist - UILL

Washington - Time of Triumph (1781 - 1783) 22 MIN
16mm
Color (H C)
Shows how Washington's Revolutionary Army defeats General Cornwallis' Army. Portrays how Washington, after the surrender, refused absolute power in order that democracy might work.
Civics and Political Systems; History - United States
Dist - FI **Prod** - WOLPER 1974

Washington to Moscow Peacewalk - the Road to Global Sanity 15 MIN
U-matic / VHS
Color
Presents the beginning of the Nuclear Freeze Campaign.
Sociology
Dist - GMPF **Prod** - GMPF

The Washington Trail 25 MIN
U-matic / VHS / 16mm
Color (H T)
Traces the ancestral roots of George Washington, providing an important chapter in history as well as a valuable lesson in genealogical investigation.
Biography
Dist - EBEC **Prod** - TFVPRO 1983

The Washington visit 30 MIN
VHS / BETA
Color; PAL (G)
PdS18, $36.00 purchase
Focuses on His Holiness, the Dalai Lama, and his visit to Washington, DC in April, 1991. Highlights his historic address to members of the United States Congress at the Capitol Rotunda.
Civics and Political Systems; Fine Arts; Religion and Philosophy
Dist - MERIDT **Prod** - MERIDT 1991

Washington Walk Around 29 MIN
VHS / 16mm
Washington Connection Series
Color (G)
$55.00 rental _ #WACO - 101
Civics and Political Systems; Social Science
Dist - PBS **Prod** - NPACT

Washington - Years of Trial (1754 - 1781) 32 MIN
16mm

Color (H C)
Provides a more human understanding of the complex personality of Washington by stripping away much of the legendary character of the man.
Biography
Dist - FI **Prod** - WOLPER 1974

Washington's Farewell 15 MIN
U-matic / VHS / 16mm
Great American Patriotic Speeches Series
Color (J H C)
LC 73-701831
Presents better - known portions of George Washington's Farewell Address. Illustrates the political context of the period through the use of original artwork and period graphics. Features William Shatner.
Biography
Dist - AIMS **Prod** - EVANSA 1973

Washington's influence peddlers - is America up for sale 30 MIN
U-matic
Adam Smith's money world 1985 - 1986 season series; 237
Color (A)
Attempts to demystify the world of money and break it down so that small as well as large businesses and it's people understand and adjust to new social and economic trends. Reports on the major economic stories and discoveries of 1985 and 1986.
Business and Economics
Dist - PBS **Prod** - WNETTV 1986

Washinton, DC 23 MIN
16mm / U-matic / VHS
Color (I J H)
Reveals that from a Potomac River Swampland site, Washington, DC has become a triumph of urban engineering and architectural elegance which has continued to expand and develop for nearly two centuries.
Geography - United States
Dist - EBEC **Prod** - EBEC 1984

The Wasp 11 MIN
VHS / 16mm / U-matic
Animal Families Series
Color (K P I K P I)
$225 purchase_#B411
Describes and shows in great detail how worker wasps build their hives, tend to the colony's nursery, and protect the hive. Outlines the life cycles of a worker wasp from egg to grub or larva, to metamorphosis and, finally, adult. Explains the amazing phenomenon of the firefly's tail. Shows how a firefly develops from an egg layed in a shallow stream, to larva, to pupa and, finally, to an adult firefly.
Science - Natural
Dist - BARR **Prod** - BARR 1986

The Wasp nest 20 MIN
VHS / 16mm
San - Ju - Wasi series
Color (G)
$380.00, $200.00 purchase, $35.00, $25.00 rental
Observes the gathering activities of San women. Reveals that men distribute the game they kill and maintain a network of community obligation, but women provide primarily for their family. A group of women gather oley berries and sha roots, and the younger women bait a nest of wasps. Part of a series by John Marshall about the Kung in Namibia and Botswana.
Geography - World; History - World; Social Science; Sociology
Dist - DOCEDR **Prod** - DOCEDR

Wasps - Paper Makers of the Summer 10 MIN
16mm / U-matic / VHS
Real World of Insects Series
Captioned; Color (P I) (SPANISH)
LC 73-701797
Explains that about two thousand years ago, the Chinese discovered how to make paper from wood pulp. Describes how insects have been making paper from wood pulp for about 20 million years and using it to build their homes. Examines various kinds of nests and views the growth stages of the wasps.
Science - Natural
Dist - LCOA **Prod** - PEGASO 1973

Wasser Fur Canitoga 98 MIN
U-matic / VHS
B&W (GERMAN)
Portrays a drunken railroad engineer mistakenly accused of sabotaging a water conveyance for the remote town of Canitoga. Shows how he continues to work against the whiskey smugglers responsible and finally redeems himself by rescuing water - line workmen from a dynamite charge. Set in the Canadian wilderness, with music by Peter Kreuder. No subtitles.
Fine Arts; Geography - World
Dist - IHF **Prod** - IHF

Wasser Fur Canitoga 120 MIN
16mm
B&W (GERMAN (ENGLISH SUBTITLES))
Presents an adventure film about the construction of an aqueduct in Canada.
Fine Arts; Foreign Language
Dist - WSTGLC **Prod** - WSTGLC 1939

Waste 10 MIN
U-matic
Take a Look Series
Color (P I)
Shows how recycling of garbage is valuable and how decay is part of the life cycle.
Science; Science - Natural
Dist - TVOTAR **Prod** - TVOTAR 1986

Waste and global pollution 21 MIN
VHS
Life science - science in focus series
Color (J H)
$395.00 purchase, $40.00 rental
Urges students to consider how much garbage and waste their families discard each week. Asks if disposal of such garbage is only a local problem. Observes bacterial growth in a closed system petri dish. Asks why growth stops and shows that toxic wastes are responsible. Asks if the earth is a closed system. Examines water flowing to the sea at intervals to test for pollution. Observes major causes of pollution and suggests solutions through prevention and recycling. Part of a five - part series on science.
Science - Natural; Sociology
Dist - BNCHMK **Prod** - BNCHMK 1990

Waste Disposal by Hydraulic Fracturing 11 MIN
16mm
Color
LC 74-705933
Depicts the development, at Oak Ridge National Laboratory, of a process for the disposal of intermediate level radioactive wastes in underground bedded shale formations.
Industrial and Technical Education; Science; Science - Physical
Dist - USNAC **Prod** - USNRC 1966

Waste handling practices in the health care industry 22 MIN
BETA / VHS / U-matic
Hazard communication - live - action video series
Color (IND G PRO)
$295.00 purchase _ #810 - 01
Introduces basic facts about proper waste handling procedures. Emphasizes the correct procedures for handling and disposal of each of the five major waste streams within a hospital environment - chemical, infectious, pharmaceutical, radioactive and general. Stresses the importance of maintaining proper segregation of each waste stream. Part of a series on hazard communication.
Health and Safety; Psychology
Dist - ITSC **Prod** - ITSC

Waste Heat Management - Energy Utilization for Profit 26 MIN
16mm
Color (A)
LC 76-704013
Shows how waste heat from various industrial processes can be captured and reused to help cut industrial fuel bills and thereby increase profits while, at the same time, helping to conserve the nation's energy supply. Includes several waste heat recovery systems and techniques. Discusses how waste heat management programs have permitted industry spokesmen to maintain productivity with less fuel.
Business and Economics; Industrial and Technical Education; Science - Natural; Science - Physical
Dist - USNAC **Prod** - USOECE 1976

Waste Management 30 MIN
VHS / 16mm
Interactions Series
Color (H T PRO)
$180.00 purchase, $35.00 rental
Describes how technology has helped to create our waste disposal problem and how technology may help us solve it by reducing the amount and changing the nature of its contents. Emphasizes that this will require a change in attitudes and lifestyles.
Business and Economics; Science - Natural; Sociology
Dist - AITECH **Prod** - WHATV 1989

Waste Management - 1 29 MIN
VHS
Interactions in Science and Society - Student Programs series
Color (H T)
$125.00 purchase
Considers that technology has contributed to the world's waste disposal problem and may also help to solve it. Stresses that it will be necessary to change attitudes and lifestyles in order to reduce waste and recycle more. Part 1 of a 12-part series on interacting technological and societal issues. Includes teacher in- service. Computer component available which enhances decision - making skills.
Science - Natural
Dist - AITECH **Prod** - WHATV 1990

Waste Management, Buildings and Equipment 36 MIN
VHS
Dairy Production And Management Series
Color (G)
$95.00 purchase _ #6 - 096 - 305P
Discusses manure storage, shelter for cattle and forage cropping equipment. Part of a five - part series on dairy management.
Agriculture; Business and Economics
Dist - VEP **Prod** - VEP

Waste not 15 MIN
Videoreel / VT2
Making Things Work Series
Color
Home Economics
Dist - PBS **Prod** - WGBHTV

Waste not - reducing hazardous waste 35 MIN
VHS
Color (G)
$395.00 purchase, $60.00 rental
Examines waste management in the industrial world. Draws a distinction between pollution control and pollution prevention. Shows the inefficiency of pollution control and how such a method is subject to breakdown, such as failing landfill methods. Discusses production process changes, materials substitution, plant operation modifications and recycling as part of pollution prevention. Profiles industries and companies with pollution prevention policies. Discusses the role of federal agencies - Office of Technology Assessment, Environmental Protection Agency - in waste management.
Business and Economics; Science - Natural; Sociology
Dist - UMBPRO **Prod** - UMBPRO 1988

Waste not, Want not 25 MIN
U-matic
Not Another Science Show Series
Color (H C)
Looks at re - use, refuse and recycle and how they can reduce the mountains of garbage we create.
Science; Science - Natural
Dist - TVOTAR **Prod** - TVOTAR 1986

Waste, penalty of affluence 18 MIN
16mm / VHS / BETA / U-matic
Color; PAL (G)
Outlines the environmental hazards of improper disposal of household, commercial and industrial waste. Includes new technologies such as the production of fodder from animal wastes.
Social Science
Dist - EDPAT
IFB

Waste - Recycling the World 22 MIN
U-matic / VHS / 16mm
Color
States that North America with six percent of the world's population consumes 50 percent of the world's production. Indicates that the rest goes to pollution. Suggests that many valuable elements can be reused rather than thrown away or wasted.
Science - Natural
Dist - CNEMAG **Prod** - DOCUA 1971

Waste Storage 14 MIN
U-matic / VHS
Color
Presents terminology used in describing waste storage systems for dairy cattle. Identifies types of wastestorage systems and the equipment needed for various types of systems.
Agriculture
Dist - HOBAR **Prod** - HOBAR

Waste to energy series
Explains how to go about setting up a waste - to - energy recycling system in your community. divided into 2 parts - 1. 'Questions to Consider' covers questions which should be asked in deciding whether incineration could work in your community. 2. 'Planning the Project' - people with experience in waste - to - energy projects the planning process.
Waste to energy series 21 MIN
Dist - UWISCA **Prod** - UEUWIS

Waste trade in Poland 16 MIN
VHS
Color (G)
$19.95 purchase
Reveals that when Poland began opening its borders to Western investment and trade it did not expect trade in hazardous waste. Discloses that, according to the Polish Environmental Department, 46,000 tons of foreign industrials wastes entered Poland in just two years. Tells of an entire town becoming so enraged by a local incinerator burning foreign toxic wastes that they destroyed it. Offers testimonies of Polish environmentalists, government officials and local citizens to illustrate a growing awareness and opposition to the illicit trade.
Business and Economics; Geography - World; Science - Natural; Sociology
Dist - GRNPCE **Prod** - GRNPCE 1990

Waste watchers - how to handle hazardous waste at the generator 22 MIN
8mm cartridge / VHS / BETA / U-matic
Color; CC; PAL (IND G)
$495.00 purchase, $175.00 rental _ #WWG - 000
Trains employees who handle hazardous waste at the generator facility. Provides RCRA training for all workers at hazardous waste generating facilities. Trains workers in proper waste handling procedures. Motivates employees to follow procedures, understand the benefits of safe and proper handling and control and reduce hazardous waste. Makes employees aware of their duties and obligations under Federal and State regulations. Includes a trainer's manual and ten employee manuals.
Health and Safety; Psychology; Sociology
Dist - BNA **Prod** - BNA 1994

Waste water 12 MIN
VHS / U-matic
Water environment series
Color (J H)
$195.00, $245.00 purchase, $50.00 rental
Introduces students to stages of the waste water treatment process and teaches what must be done to make sludge safe for disposal. Suggests that individuals can take a personal role in protecting the finite supply of clean water.
Science - Natural
Dist - NDIM **Prod** - WAENFE 1988

Wasted 27 MIN
VHS
Color (J)
$79.00 purchase _ #323 - 9089
Profiles teens who have lived through substance abuse. Considers the families who must cope with the painful situation. Parents and children confront their problems together and make decisions for change, providing effective models for the communication that is essential in curtailing drug addiction.
Guidance and Counseling; Health and Safety; Psychology; Sociology
Dist - FI **Prod** - NBCNEW 1986

Wasted - a True Story 22 MIN
16mm
Color
Conveys a clear health message that adamantly discourages illicit drug use.
Health and Safety; Psychology; Sociology
Dist - MTP **Prod** - ACOE

Wasted - a True Story 24 MIN
U-matic / VHS / 16mm
Color (I)
Describes how substance abuse affects not only the user, but the whole family as well. Presents a drug abuser and his sister who discuss the hurt, bewilderment and anger of family members as the abuser exhibited violent behavior toward them and a total lack of self - respect.
Sociology
Dist - CORF **Prod** - RINGE 1983

A Wasted breath - kids on inhalants 20 MIN
VHS
Color (I J)
$150.00 purchase
Alerts children to the dangers of inhalant abuse. Discusses physical and emotional damage, positive and negative peer pressure. Interviews youngsters in recovery. Observes a peer counseling group and a lecture by a drug education specialist.
Guidance and Counseling; Psychology; Sociology
Dist - MEDPRJ **Prod** - MEDPRJ 1992

The Wasted Years 28 MIN
16mm
Color (J H C)
Compares the penal system philosophies of Austria which has moved away from traditional closed institutions, Hungary which is experimenting with labor camps where minor offenders are not exposed to professional criminals and Denmark where open prison camps resemble holiday villages.
Civics and Political Systems; History - World; Sociology
Dist - SF **Prod** - SF 1975

The Wasted years - the depressions 30 MIN
35mm strip / VHS
Western man and the modern world series
Color (J H C T A)
Documents the worldwide economic woes that followed the 1929 Wall Street stock market crash. Focuses on how Germany's economic troubles may have paved the way for Nazism.
Business and Economics; Civics and Political Systems; History - United States; History - World
Dist - SRA
RH

Wasteland - Wealth Out of Waste 27 MIN
16mm
Color
States that America's affluent society has cluttered its open spaces, fouled its streams and rivers, polluted its air, and has squandered minerals that are needed to support an expanding population and a growing economy. Discusses these problems and the steps being taken by government and the private sector to solve them.
Science - Natural; Sociology
Dist - USDIBM **Prod** - USDIBM

The Wastes of War - Pt 3 55 MIN
VHS
First Eden Series
Color (S)
$129.00 purchase _ #825 - 9504
Presents a spectacular portrait of the Mediterranean Sea and the variety of plants and animals that call the region home. Features David Attenborough as narrator. Part 3 of four parts visits Italy, the Mideast and Spain to explore changes in the natural environment from the 4th century BC to the 16th century AD. Considers horses and the fall of the Roman Empire, fleas and the Black Plague, and pasturing merino sheep.
Agriculture; Geography - World; Health and Safety; History - World; Science - Natural; Sociology
Dist - FI **Prod** - BBCTV 1988

Wastewater equipment lockout procedures 14 MIN
VHS
Color (G A PRO)
$59.99 purchase _ #V1800GA
Shows correct methods to lockout or tagout energy source lines at a wastewater treatment plant, with special attention given to particular problems.
Health and Safety; Industrial and Technical Education
Dist - WAENFE

Wastewater Management - Options for Unsewered Areas 25 MIN
16mm / U-matic / VHS
Color (A)
Shows various options for sewage treatment used in areas where centralized treatment is too expensive and the septic tank/soil absorption system doesn't work.
Sociology
Dist - USNAC **Prod** - UWISC 1982

Wastewater treatment H2O TV
VHS
Color (I J H)
$59.00 purchase _ #Z1215GA
Examines how wastewater is treated, focusing on water quality topics including pollution. Features Dino Sorrus, an animated character, with computer graphics. Package includes one videocassette, one teacher's guide and 20 student workbooks. Additional materials are also available.
Industrial and Technical Education
Dist - WAENFE

Wasting Away - Identifying Anorexia and Bulimia 25 MIN
VHS / 16mm
Wasting Away - Identifying Anorexia and Bulimia Series
Color (I H A)
$180.00 purchase, $35.00 rental
Depicts a high school girl responding to the pressures of society and the stresses in her life by starving her body.
Guidance and Counseling; Health and Safety; Psychology; Social Science; Sociology
Dist - AITECH **Prod** - NWGTN 1987

Wasting Away - Identifying Anorexia and Bulimia Series
Wasting Away - Identifying Anorexia and Bulimia 25 MIN
Dist - AITECH

Wasting Away - Understanding Anorexia Nervosa and Bulimia
VHS / U-matic
Color
Uses a selection of vignettes to characterize typical anorectic and bulimic behavior. Emphasizes the psychological side of the disorders, pointing out the combinations of adolescent stresses, personality types and family/social situations that can precipitate problems.
Guidance and Counseling; Health and Safety; Psychology
Dist - GA **Prod** - GA 1984

The Wasting of a wetland 23 MIN
VHS
Color; Captioned (J H C G)
$195.00 purchase, $40.00 rental
Looks at the abuse of wetlands - by filling, draining and polluting - which is rapidly destroying habitats for plants and animals, eliminating feeding stations along the flyways of migratory birds and damaging fresh water supplies across the country. Features the Everglades of south Florida, the most critically endangered of all National Parks. Produced by Daniel Elias.
Fine Arts; Science - Natural
Dist - BULFRG

Wasting the Alps 50 MIN
VHS
Horizon series
Color; PAL (G)
PdS99 purchase
Investigates the fragile mountain environment of the Alps and threats by tourism, pollution and acid rain. Visits Austria, France and Switzerland to observe efforts being made to check the decline of the environment.
Geography - World; Sociology
Dist - BBCENE

Wasting time - 29 9 MIN
VHS / U-matic
Life's little lessons - self - esteem K - 3 - series
Color (K P)
$129.00, $99.00 _ #V628
Portrays Sergeant Sydney Bloomfield who mastered time wasting so well that by the time he got up, it was time for bed. Reveals how Sydney's life changed forever when the Colonel made a surprise visit. Part of a 30 - part series on self - esteem.
Guidance and Counseling; Psychology
Dist - BARR **Prod** - CEPRO 1992

Watardori - birds of passage 37 MIN
VHS / U-matic
Color (G)
$125.00 purchase, $50.00 rental
Commemorates the Issei - first generation Japanese Americans. Features three Issei who describe a collective history through their personal memories. Mr Nakamura paints the canvas of their lives with lush imagery of sea and land. Mr Miura, a fisherman and wanderer, came to the United States because he wanted 'to see the world.' Mrs Sumi tells of the creation of the prosperous Imperial Valley farmlands despite the Alien Land Law. Directed by Robert A Nakamura.
History - United States; Sociology
Dist - CROCUR **Prod** - VISCOM 1976

Watch it 15 MIN
VHS / U-matic
It's Your Move Series
Color (J)
Discusses various bicycle riding hazards and offers safety tips.
Health and Safety
Dist - AITECH **Prod** - WETN 1977

The Watch on Health 14 MIN
16mm
Color
LC FIE67-518
Cites major challenges faced by the U S Public Health Service in a program for preventing disease and for attacking the major illnesses of mankind. Depicts career opportunities in health fields. Emphasizes the significance of health activities to national life.
Guidance and Counseling; Health and Safety
Dist - USNAC **Prod** - USPHS 1966

Watch Out 5 MIN
U-matic
Color (G)
$200.00 purchase, $50.00, $35.00 rental
Traces the life of an Australian Aboriginal dancer. Presented by Janet Bell.
Fine Arts; Geography - World; Sociology
Dist - WMENIF **Prod** - WMENIF 1988

Watch Out 15 MIN
U-matic / VHS
All about You Series
Color (P)
Indicates that children have a personal responsibility for taking care of themselves. Reviews, in a humorous manner, various safety rules.
Health and Safety
Dist - AITECH **Prod** - WGBHTV 1975

Watch out 15 MIN
VHS
Color (P I J)
Takes a look at the risks people take in everyday life, either through ignorance or carelessness. Encourages safety awareness in children.
Health and Safety
Dist - VIEWTH **Prod** - VIEWTH

Watch out for assault - staying safe and secure 13 MIN
VHS
Color; CC (IND PRO)
$250.00 purchase, $95.00 rental _ #BBP224
Alerts employess to personal safety dangers on and off the job. Includes a leader's guide.
Business and Economics; Guidance and Counseling; Health and Safety; Social Science; Sociology
Dist - EXTR **Prod** - BBP

Watch out for Big Freddy
VHS
Bippity boppity bunch series
Color (K P I R)
$14.95 purchase _ #35 - 822 - 8579
Teaches the importance of loving one's enemies. Shows how Buddy gets a black eye from a bully.
Literature and Drama; Religion and Philosophy
Dist - APH **Prod** - FAMF

Watch Out for My Plant 14 MIN
U-matic / 16mm
Color (I) (SPANISH)
Tells the story of an inner - city boy trying to grow a flower in a small patch of dirt between his house and the sidewalk.
Foreign Language; Science - Natural
Dist - BARR **Prod** - BARR

Watch Out for Witchweed 14 MIN
16mm
Color
LC FIE63-222
Shows what is being done to control the spread of the parasitic plant witchweed and what methods of eradication have already been developed.
Agriculture; Science - Natural
Dist - USNAC **Prod** - USDA 1963

Watch that Space Series
Confined Space Hazards in Factories 16 MIN
Confined Space Hazards in Shipbuilding 16 MIN
Confined Space Hazards in the Construction Industry 16 MIN
Dist - AMEDFL

Watch the doors please 10 MIN
16mm
Color (G)
$15.00 rental
Documents one of the major works of Daniel Buren in situ, 'Watch the Doors Please,' which was exhibited at the Art Institute of Chicago from 1980 - 1982. Shows how Buren utilized commuter trains passing in front of a large window of the museum by covering the central doors of all the trains with his customary vertical stripes thereby highlighting the singular fact that the Art Institute extends over a railroad line. Produced by Rob Savage. Narrative text by Anne Rorimer and music by A Meyer and F Miniere.
Fine Arts; Social Science
Dist - CANCIN

Watch the stars come out - 29
VHS
Reading rainbow series
Color; CC (K P)
$39.95 purchase
Explores with LeVar the plight of the many courageous immigrants who came to America filled with homes and dreams as they landed on Ellis Island, inspired by the featured book. Comes face - to - face with Lady Liberty herself and shows why and how she has been restored. Part of a series offering a multicultural approach to generating reading enthusiasm with cross - curricular applications, hosted by LeVar Burton.
English Language; Literature and Drama; Sociology
Dist - GPN **Prod** - LNMDP

Watch their backs 18 MIN
VHS
Manual handling series
Color; PAL (IND G)
PdS95 purchase
Informs supervisors and other managerial professionals of their responsibilities under the currect legislation of the EC directive on manual handling. Highlights correct procedures for safe lifting. Part of a two - part series to assist businesses in conforming with new EC directives. Includes a booklet and checklist.
Business and Economics; Health and Safety; Psychology
Dist - CFLVIS **Prod** - SCHWOP 1994

Watch Word - Caution
16mm
Community Protection and Crime Prevention Series
Color (J)
LC 72-701744
Presents policewoman Pat Pocher describing crimes of personal assault against females, showing how to avoid the situations entirely and how to deal with them if they occur.
Guidance and Counseling; Health and Safety; Sociology
Dist - SUMHIL **Prod** - SUMHIL 1972

Watch your back 14 MIN
VHS
Manual handling series
Color; PAL (IND G)
PdS95 purchase
Instructs new trainees as well as reminds long - term employees on how to lift correctly and on proper techniques for variable loads. Stresses the importance of preventing back injuries and avoiding resulting work loss and expense. Part of a two - part series to assist businesses in conforming with new EC directives. Includes a booklet and checklist.
Business and Economics; Health and Safety; Psychology
Dist - CFLVIS **Prod** - SCHWOP 1994

Watch your back - backstrain amongst chainsaw operators 13 MIN
VHS
Color; PAL; NTSC (G)
PdS57, PdS67 purchase
Identifies the causes and effects of back strain from chain saw use and associated timber - handling activities. Describes bad practices and shows correct techniques to avoid back injury.
Health and Safety
Dist - CFLVIS

Watch Your Language Series
Animals 15 MIN
Computers 15 MIN
Environment 15 MIN
Families 15 MIN
Fashion 15 MIN
Film 15 MIN
Fitness 15 MIN
Food 15 MIN
Medicine 15 MIN
News 15 MIN
Peer Pressure 15 MIN
Relationships 15 MIN
Space 15 MIN
Sports 15 MIN
Work 15 MIN
Dist - AITECH

Watch your mouth series
Anybody out there with their ears on 29 MIN
Assembly 29 MIN
Bringing it all home 29 MIN
Caftan caper 29 MIN
Chicago Red and the mugger, Part 1 29 MIN
Chicago Red and the mugger, Part 2 29 MIN
The Derriere pain 29 MIN
First days, Pt 1 29 MIN
The Great debate 29 MIN
The Handsomest boy 29 MIN
Hostages, Pt 1 29 MIN
Hostages, Pt 2 29 MIN
The Informer 29 MIN
A Lesson in love 29 MIN
Los Gallos combativos 29 MIN
Mary and Melvin 29 MIN
New blues 29 MIN
On being 17, bright and unable to read 29 MIN
The Ounce 29 MIN
The Outcast 29 MIN
Shew - be - do - Wop - Wah - Wah 29 MIN
The Star 29 MIN
The Student prince 29 MIN
Tangled web, Pt 1 29 MIN
Tangled web, Pt 2 29 MIN
Dist - PBS

Watch your step 5 MIN
16mm / VHS / BETA / U-matic
Color; PAL (IND)
PdS110, PdS118 purchase
Illustrates the need for care, practice and planning in the prevention of falls in the industrial workplace.
Health and Safety
Dist - EDPAT **Prod** - TASCOR

Watch Your Step 11 MIN
16mm
Color (A)
LC FIA52-845
Presents safe practices for railroad employees through examples of yard practices, riding cars, boarding trains, alighting from moving equipment, throwing switches, setting and releasing hand brakes and working in machine shops.
Health and Safety; Industrial and Technical Education; Social Science
Dist - STAFER **Prod** - STAFER

Watch Your Step 6 MIN
16mm
Color
LC 80-700933
Discusses industrial safety and focuses on falls in the workplace.
Health and Safety
Dist - TASCOR **Prod** - TASCOR 1968

Watchamacallit - the Mystery Machine 30 MIN
U-matic
Magic Ring II Series
(K P)
Continues the aim of the first series to bring added freshness to the commonplace and assist children to discover more about the many things in their world. Each program starts with the familiar, goes to the less familiar, then the new, and ends by blending new and old information.
Education; Literature and Drama
Dist - ACCESS **Prod** - ACCESS 1986

Watchdogs of the treasury 29 MIN
16mm
Government story series; No 13
B&W (J H)
LC 79-707215
Discusses the relative roles of the Appropriations Committee of the House and the Senate and explains how they control government spending. Points out that appropriations are a potential source of conflict between the President and the Congress.
Civics and Political Systems
Dist - WESTLC **Prod** - WEBC 1968

Watcher in the Woods 25 MIN
U-matic / VHS / 16mm
Film as Literature, Series 5 Series; Series 5
Color (I J H)
Reveals that after her family moves into an old English estate, a girl is told by the caretaker of the disappearance of another young girl. Shows how the girl pieces together the solution to the mystery. Based on the novel THE WATCHER IN THE WOODS by Florence Engle Randall.
Literature and Drama
Dist - CORF **Prod** - DISNEY 1983

Watchia 15 MIN
U-matic / VHS
Other families, other friends series; Green module; Quebec
Color (P)
Pictures family life on Cape Jones in Quebec.
Geography - World; Social Science; Sociology
Dist - AITECH **Prod** - WVIZTV 1971

Watching a Woodcarver 12 MIN
16mm / U-matic / VHS
Color (I)
LC 82-700630
Shows the joys of woodcarving by showing a man creating a mallard duck decoy from a block of wood. Provides a brief history of the purpose and variety of decoys.
Fine Arts; Industrial and Technical Education; Physical Education and Recreation
Dist - IFB **Prod** - BERLET 1982

Watching Animals 12 MIN
U-matic / VHS / 16mm
Color (I)
LC 78-700729
Shows various kinds of animal behavior and how scientists learn about animals.
Psychology
Dist - NGS **Prod** - NGS 1978

Watching birds 26 MIN
VHS
Wonderstruck presents series
Color (I J)
$99.95 purchase _#Q11172; $99.00 purchase _ #386 - 9058
Investigates the many different ways in which birds have adapted to changing environments. Provides information on how to make hummingbird food and features the penguins of Cachagua Island off the coast of Chile. Part of an 11 part series produced by the Canadian Broadcasting Corporation and hosted by Bob McDonald.
Science; Science - Natural
Dist - CF FI **Prod** - CANBC 1995

Watching the whales 29 MIN
VHS
Color (G)
$29.95 purchase
Presents extensive footage of whales and dolphins in their natural settings. Features no accompanying narration or music, with only the natural sounds of the ocean and the animals.

Science - Natural
Dist - PBS **Prod** - WNETTV

Watching too much TV - 63 11 MIN
U-matic / VHS
Life's little lessons - self - esteem 4 - 6 series
Color (I)
$129.00, $99.00 purchase _ #V692
Portrays Wilbur Moffat who watched too much TV. Reveals that it happened gradually but before he knew it he was filling his mind with junk food for the brain and getting very depressed. Shows how he cured his problem. Part of a 65 - part series on self - esteem.
Fine Arts; Guidance and Counseling; Psychology
Dist - BARR **Prod** - CEPRO 1992

Watching Wildlife 26 MIN
16mm
Color
LC 83-700332
Looks at the various locales at which people can see wildlife, from a national park to a backyard animal feeder.
Geography - United States; Science - Natural
Dist - STOUFP **Prod** - STOUFP 1982

Watchkins adventure music video 30 MIN
VHS
Color (K P I)
$29.95 purchase _ #EE106
Teaches young children wholesome social skills - how to live, how to like themselves, how to treat others. Includes songs which emphasize self - control, cooperation, perseverance, courtesy, loyalty and friendship, dependability, that everyone is special. Complements self - esteem programs.
Fine Arts; Health and Safety; Psychology
Dist - AAVIM **Prod** - AAVIM

Watchword - Caution 27 MIN
U-matic / VHS / 16mm
Color (J)
LC 75-700388
Presents policewoman Pat Parker who employs dramatized incidents to show how young girls and women can avoid crimes of personal assault.
Health and Safety; Sociology
Dist - AIMS **Prod** - SUMHIL 1974

Water 60 MIN
VHS
Perspectives in Science Series
Color (J)
$350.00 purchase, $75.00 rental
Considers water both as a basic requisite of life and as a danger because of polluted sources. Discusses water treatment technology.
Business and Economics; Science - Natural; Science - Physical; Social Science; Sociology
Dist - BULFRG **Prod** - NFBC 1990

Water 10 MIN
U-matic / 16mm / VHS
Primary science series
Color (P I)
LC 91-705317
Explains that animals, plants and people need water to live. Looks at the different forms of water. Includes two teacher's guides. Part of a series on primary science produced by Fred Ladd.
Science; Science - Natural; Science - Physical; Social Science
Dist - BARR

Water 11 MIN
16mm
Color (H)
Stresses the importance of water to all forms of life and how humanity is wasting it.
Science - Natural; Social Science; Sociology
Dist - DYP **Prod** - UNEP

Water 25 MIN
VHS
Ask Oscar series
Color (P I)
$250.00 purchase
Reveals amazing facts about water. Asks where it comes from, what happens when it gets very hot or very cold, why some things float and others sink. Looks at condensation, evaporation, buoyancy, floatation and the water cycle of sea, clouds, rain and rivers. Features Oscar the Mole. Part of a three - part series on basic science.
Science - Physical
Dist - LANDMK **Prod** - LANDMK 1990

Water 14 MIN
U-matic / VHS / 16mm
Color (J)
LC 77-703189
Discusses the possibility of a worldwide water shortage crisis and suggests solutions.
Geography - World; Science - Natural; Social Science; Sociology
Dist - JOU **Prod** - JOU 1977

Water 12 MIN
16mm / U-matic / VHS
Early Childhood Education Series
Color (C)
Demonstrates how children playing with water can have satisfying mathematical and emotional experiences as they feel water of various temperatures and depths.
Education; Psychology
Dist - MEDIAG **Prod** - MEDIAG 1976

Water 29 MIN
VHS / 16mm
Villa Alegre Series
Color (P T)
$46.00 rental _ #VILA - 117
Presents educational material in both Spanish and English.
Education; Social Science
Dist - PBS

Water 8 MIN
16mm
Color (I J H)
Shows how water shapes the lives of people everywhere.
Science - Natural; Social Science; Sociology
Dist - IFF **Prod** - IFF

Water 30 MIN
VHS
A House for all seasons series
Color (G)
$49.95 purchase _ #AHFS - 211
Emphasizes water - saving techniques from colonial times to the present. Focuses on water - saving showerheads and toilets, as well as low - maintenance landscaping.
Home Economics; Science - Natural; Social Science; Sociology
Dist - PBS **Prod** - KRMATV 1985

Water 30 MIN
U-matic
Today's Special Series
Color (K P)
Develops language arts skills in children. Programs are thematically designed around subjects of interest to youngsters. Action takes place in a department store where people, mannequins, puppets, comic characters and special guests present a light hearted approach to language arts.
Fine Arts; Literature and Drama; Psychology
Dist - TVOTAR **Prod** - TVOTAR 1985

Water 25 MIN
U-matic / VHS / 16mm
Untamed World Series
Color; Mono (J H C A)
$400.00 film, $250.00 video, $50.00 rental
Focuses on water habitats and the animal life that abounds within. Looks at the components, locations, and importance of water to all life forms.
Geography - World; Science - Natural
Dist - CTV **Prod** - CTV 1971

Water 30 MIN
VHS / 16mm
Interactions Series
Color (H A PRO)
$180.00 purchase, $35.00 rental
Examines water problems in various parts of the United States. Addresses the frequent conflict between the environment and industrial and societal needs.
Science - Natural; Social Science; Sociology
Dist - AITECH **Prod** - WHATV 1986

Water - 11 29 MIN
VHS
Interactions in Science and Society - Student Programs series
Color (H T)
$125.00 purchase
Scrutinizes the situation in the Southwest United States where much of the water is too salty for drinking or irrigation and water purification is too expensive. Reveals that scientists are trying to develop salt - tolerant plants and that the water needs of Los Angeles may rob surrounding areas of water supplies. Part 11 of a 12-part series on interacting technological and societal issues. Includes teacher in-service. Computer component available which enhances decision - making skills.
Agriculture; Social Science
Dist - AITECH **Prod** - WHATV 1990

Water - 11 10 MIN
U-matic / 16mm / VHS
Primary science series
Color (K P I)
$265.00, $215.00, $185.00 purchase _ #B592
Defines the different forms of water, solid, liquid and gas. Uses simple experiments to show how water changes from one form to another. Discusses condensation and evaporation. Part of an 11 - part series on primary science.
Science - Natural; Science - Physical; Social Science
Dist - BARR **Prod** - GREATT 1990

Water - 30 15 MIN
VHS
Draw man series
Color (I)
$125.00 purchase
Illustrates the nuances of drawing scenes with water as a feature. Features Paul Ringler, the 'Draw Man,' as instructor. Part of 'The Draw Man' Series.
Fine Arts
Dist - AITECH **Prod** - KOKHTV 1975

Water - a Clear and Present Danger 26 MIN
U-matic / VHS / 16mm
Color (H C A)
Looks at the medical implications of serious ground water contamination. Shows that despite efforts to regulate it, 700 man - made chemicals have been found in drinking water, some of which are harmful.
Science - Natural; Sociology
Dist - CORF **Prod** - ABCNEW 1983

Water - a Cutting Edge with Time 28 MIN
U-matic / VHS
Earth Explored Series
Color
Deals with the science of hydrology, which comes to life on a field trip to the canyonlands of Utah and a raft ride down the Arkansas River.
Science - Physical
Dist - PBS **Prod** - BBCTV

Water - a First Film 9 MIN
16mm / U-matic / VHS
Color (P I)
LC FIA68-2116
Discusses the role played by water in the processes of life. Shows that where there is little water the land is desert. Points out that water is used to drink, to cook, to water lawns and to fight fires with.
Psychology; Science - Natural; Science - Physical; Social Science
Dist - PHENIX **Prod** - FA 1968

Water - a miraculous substance 20 MIN
VHS
Biology of water series
Color (J H)
$90.00 purchase _ #A5VH 1338; $89.00 purchase _ #1963VG
Examines the unique physical and chemical properties of water. Presents molecular structure, solvent capabilities, change of physical state, surface tension, heat capacity and latent heat. Looks at the role of water in the origin of life and explains how it came to play an essential part as an internal medium for cells. Examines the various ways water acts as an external medium for aquatic life. Part of a four - part series on the role of water.
Science - Natural; Science - Physical
Dist - CLRVUE **Prod** - CLRVUE
UNL

Water - a treasure in trouble 14 MIN
VHS
Color (I)
$295.00 purchase
Teaches about water, that it is vital to every living thing, a primary building block for skin, bones and blood, and necessary for the growth of all animal and plant life. Shows why water is one of the Earth's greatest treasures, how pollutions threatens the water supply of the Earth and what humans can do to safeguard sources of pure water.
Science - Natural; Science - Physical
Dist - PFP **Prod** - MOODY

Water Affects the Weather 15 MIN
VHS / U-matic
Why Series
Color (P I)
Discusses how water affects the weather.
Science - Physical
Dist - AITECH **Prod** - WDCNTV 1976

Water Against Wildfire 16 MIN
16mm
Color
LC 80-700846
Shows how bush fires in Australia and in all parts of the world create havoc not only in the human environment but also in the delicate balance of the natural world.
Geography - World; Health and Safety; Science - Natural
Dist - TASCOR **Prod** - VICCOR 1978

Water Analysis 32 MIN
U-matic / VHS
Color
Covers the Most Probable Numbers (MPN) and membrane filter methods for determing coloforms in finished drinking water. Includes details of each step and interpretation of MPN tables.
Science; Science - Natural; Science - Physical
Dist - AVMM **Prod** - AMSM

Water and Dust Leak Repair 10.5 MIN
BETA / VHS
Color (A PRO)
$62.00 purchase _ #AB131
Deals with auto body repair.
Industrial and Technical Education
Dist - RMIBHF **Prod** - RMIBHF

Water and Energy 17 MIN
U-matic
Chemistry 102 - Chemistry for Engineers - Series
Color (C)
Describes some of the unusual physical properties of water and discusses them in terms of hydrogen bonding. The heating curve of water is drawn and the consequent energy changes of the water are described.
Industrial and Technical Education; Science - Physical
Dist - UILL **Prod** - UILL 1980

Water and fire
VHS / U-matic
Marine firefighting series; Pt 3
Color (IND) (ITALIAN KOREAN)
Demonstrates effectiveness of water for cooling a diesel oil fire. Details use of water for control purposes, hoseline team setups, proper techniques, different equipment available and hoseline tests.
Foreign Language; Health and Safety; Social Science
Dist - GPCV **Prod** - GPCV

Water and Food 29 MIN
VHS / 16mm
Villa Alegre Series
Color (P T)
$46.00 rental _ #VILA - 149
Presents educational material in both Spanish and English.
Education; Social Science
Dist - PBS

Water and hunger 28 MIN
VHS
Color (G)
$14.95 purchase
Combines three short videos - Water, The Face of Hunger, and Faces of the Third World - to point out the illness and starvation that result from poverty and lack of sanitation throughout the world.
Fine Arts; Social Science; Sociology
Dist - MARYFA

Water and Life 25 MIN
U-matic / VHS / 16mm
Untamed World Series
Color; Mono (J H C A)
$400.00 film, $250.00 video, $50.00 rental
Discusses the plains of East Africa and the critical importance of water to animals that live there. Presents a filmed study of the struggle of the animal life to survive frequent droughts and disappearing watering places.
Geography - World; Science - Natural
Dist - CTV **Prod** - CTV 1969

Water and Life - a Delicate Balance 13 MIN
U-matic / VHS
Color (C)
$239.00, $139.00 purchase _ #AD - 1139
Shows the role of water in the human body, the cycles of water, industrial water consumption and pollution. Considers ways of increasing water supplies and reminds the viewer that water is not necessarily a renewable resource.
Science - Natural
Dist - FOTH **Prod** - FOTH

Water and Life on Earth 11 MIN
16mm
Color (I J H)
Explains the accepted theory of how water was first formed and how it is still being formed from hydrogen and oxygen. Shows the water cycle, types of clouds and methods of getting water to dry areas.
Science - Natural; Science - Physical
Dist - AVED **Prod** - CBF 1963

Water and Plant Growth, Set 2 25 FRS
VHS / Slide / Cassette
Western Fertilizer Handbook Series
Color (G)
$32.95, $40.00, $8.50 purchase _ #1 - 580 - 602P, #1 - 580 - 202P, #1 - 580 - 532P
Looks at water and its role in plant growth. Part of a fourteen - part series based on the Western Fertilizer Handbook.
Agriculture; Social Science
Dist - VEP **Prod** - VEP

Water and Plant Life 28 MIN
U-matic / VHS
Life of Plants Series
Color (C)
$249.00, $149.00 purchase _ #AD - 1674
Examines the water cycle in plants - clouds, rain, plants, transpiration, clouds. Shows types of adaptation to insufficient water or problems of water storage - extended shallow root networks, specialized seed pods, bulbs, leaf shape, water preservation in freezing temperatures, as well as adaptations to heat and the special adaptations of cacti and succulents. Part of a series on plants.
Science - Natural; Social Science
Dist - FOTH **Prod** - FOTH

Water and power 57 MIN
16mm
Color (H C A)
$150.00 rental
Offers a metaphorical look at the exchange of energy between two places. Focuses on the cyclical motion of the planets and tides with the implied rotation of the camera on its axis and the repetitive actions of the performers. Includes quotations from older movies and their soundtracks. Produced by Pat O'Neill.
Social Science; Sociology
Dist - CANCIN

Water and Rain 15 MIN
U-matic / VHS
Let Me See Series no 6
Color (P)
Presents examples of evaporation and Myrtle shows how water recycles, while Pocus tells the story of a water droplet, and Hocus and Myrtle prepare to create a cloud.
Science - Physical
Dist - AITECH **Prod** - WETN 1982

Water and Spirit - a Meditation on Baptism 5 MIN
16mm
Color (I)
LC 73-702537
Presents a collection of visual images of the absence, presence and use of water in man's life. Moves from the desert to the sea, capturing dry winds, mountain streams and verdant pasture.
Religion and Philosophy; Science - Natural
Dist - FRACOC **Prod** - FRACOC 1973

Water and the weather 11 MIN
VHS
Color; PAL (P I)
PdS29.50 purchase
Presents the role of water in determining the weather. Introduces basic weather terms.
Science; Science - Physical
Dist - EMFVL **Prod** - STANF

Water and weather - Volume 2
VHS
Tell me why series
Color (P I J)
$19.80 purchase _ #0149
Shows how weather happens. Describes storms and cyclones, wind. Tells why the ocean is salty and what fog is. Part one of a two - part series on the Earth.
Science - Natural; Science - Physical
Dist - SEVVID **Prod** - WNETTV
PBS

Water and what it Does 11 MIN
U-matic / VHS / 16mm
Color; B&W (P) (SPANISH)
Shows that water is composed of tiny, constantly moving particles, and that it exists in three states - solid, liquid and gas. Demonstrates dissolving, evaporation, condensation, freezing and expansion.
Science - Physical
Dist - EBEC **Prod** - EBEC 1962

Water animals of the Cascades 12 MIN
VHS
Animal profile series
Color (P I)
$59.95 purchase _ #RB8116
Studies beavers, otters, ducks, dippers, frogs, toads, newts and rainbow trout, animals described in the food chain of a Cascade lake or pond. Teaches the importance of each animal in maintaining an environment that allows all of the animals to survive. Part of a series on animals which looks at examples from the mammal, snake and bird classes, filmed in their natural habitat.
Science - Natural
Dist - REVID **Prod** - REVID 1990

Water Babies 48 MIN
VHS
Color (S)
$24.95 purchase _ #807 - 9001
Takes a fascinating look at a possible explanation for human behavior that has been largely ignored in the scientific circles. Suggests that a period of aquatic adaptation followed by a return to the land was the decisive factor in human evolution.
Psychology; Science - Natural; Sociology
Dist - FI

Water - base muds 29 MIN
U-matic / VHS / Slide
Rotary drilling fluids series; 02
Color (IND) (SPANISH)
Covers each phase of water - base muds. Gives the purpose and control of each.
Business and Economics; Foreign Language; Industrial and Technical Education; Social Science
Dist - UTEXPE **Prod** - UTEXPE

Water Bikes 24 MIN
16mm
Color (P I)
Tells of the Chiffy Kids plan to win new bikes by winning a cross - country bicycle race aboard their old ones. Shows them outwitting a shady bicycle shop owner.
Literature and Drama
Dist - LUF **Prod** - LUF 1979

Water Birds 6 MIN
16mm
Birds of America, 1, their Songs and Sounds Series no 3; No 3
Color (P I)
Describes the characteristics of the loon, tern, heron and ring - billed gull. Discusses their habitat and breeding and migration habits. Captures the songs and calls of the birds. Uses only natural sound.
Science - Natural
Dist - GIB **Prod** - GIB 1966

Water Birds 32 MIN
U-matic / VHS / 16mm
Color (I J H) (PORTUGUESE SPANISH AFRIKAANS DUTCH FRENCH DANISH GERMAN ITALIAN)
LC 79-714975
Glimpses the behavior of seaside and marshland birds. Features a musical bird ballet.
Foreign Language; Science - Natural
Dist - CORF **Prod** - DISNEY 1957

Water Birds - Loon, Tern, Heron, Ring - Billed Gull
16mm
Color (P A)
LC FIA67-2098
Looks at the habits and behavior of several species on the shoreline of a wilderness lake. Features the mournful cry of the loon, the graceful flight of the tern, the shrill sounds of gulls and the heron in solitude.
Science - Natural
Dist - AVEXP **Prod** - GIB

Water Birds of the Inland 14 MIN
16mm
Color (J)
Examines bird life around a lake in inland Australia.
Geography - World; Science - Natural
Dist - AUIS **Prod** - ANAIB 1964

Water, birth, planet Earth series
Water, birth, planet Earth - the land 27 MIN
Dist - CORF
VIEWTH

Water, birth, planet Earth series
Water, birth, planet Earth - the sea 22 MIN
Dist - VIEWTH

Water, birth, planet Earth - the land 27 MIN
VHS
Water, birth, planet Earth series
Color; PAL (H G)
Considers how plants and animals emerged from the seas to thrive and develop on dry land. Focuses on how living things adapted to their new environment and the new dangers they faced.
Science - Natural; Science - Physical
Dist - VIEWTH
CORF

Water, birth, planet Earth - the sea 22 MIN
VHS
Water, birth, planet Earth series
Color; PAL (H G)
Traces back to the beginnings of Earth, from the formation of its atmosphere to the rains which leached minerals out of the land and deposited them in the seas. Uses underwater photography to depict a variety of environments to which plants and animals have adapted in order to survive.
Science - Natural; Science - Physical
Dist - VIEWTH

Water Bugs 30 MIN
16mm
Classic Christie Comedies Series
B&W
Literature and Drama
Dist - SFI **Prod** - SFI

Water California Style 16 MIN
U-matic
Color (I)
Traces the 200 - year history of water development in California. Covers water management policies, conservation, reclamation techniques and the process of planning for California's needs through the year 2000.
Geography - United States; History - United States; Industrial and Technical Education; Science - Natural; Social Science
Dist - CALDWR **Prod** - CSDWR

Water Chemistry and Chemical Handling Practices 60 MIN
U-matic / VHS
Equipment Operation Training Program Series
Color (IND)
Deals with treatment of boiler and cooling water systems. Identifies chemicals used in water treatment. Discusses safety gear and protective clothing.
Industrial and Technical Education
Dist - ITCORP **Prod** - ITCORP

The Water circle 3 MIN
16mm
Color (G)
$10.00 rental
Presents an homage to Lao - Tzu, set to music by Corelli. Offers an image of a continuous flow of light on water.
Fine Arts; Religion and Philosophy
Dist - CANCIN **Prod** - BROUGH 1975

Water circus - Part 1 22 MIN
VHS
Complete protozoans series
Color (J H)
$110.00 purchase _ #A2VH 4711
Offers basic information about the most primitive form of animal life - protozoans. Covers collecting samples, preparing slides, types of locomotion and identification of the amoeba, paramecium, peranema and volvox. Part one of a three - part series on protozoans.
Science - Natural
Dist - CLRVUE **Prod** - CLRVUE

Water Color 14 MIN
VHS
Rediscovery Art Media Series
Color
$69.95 purchase _ #4168
Shown are the wide range of technical and expressive possibilities inherent in watercolor painting. Demonstrated are the two most important and distinctive characteristics of the medium fluidity and transparency.
Fine Arts
Dist - AIMS **Prod** - AIMS

Water Color Basics 60 MIN
VHS / BETA
Color
Explains supplies, drawings, composition and washes. Demonstrates the unique characteristics of watercolor.
Fine Arts
Dist - HOMEAF **Prod** - HOMEAF

Water color techniques 30 MIN
VHS
Learning to paint with Carolyn Berry series
Color (H G)
$49.95 purchase
Offers an easy to follow, step - by - step method for creating a finished painting or drawing from a blank canvas. Features part of an eight - part series covering everything from arranging or selecting your subjects to an explanation of the material needed and the specific techniques to be applied. Professional art instructor Carolyn Berry designed this series for students, hobbyists, amateur painters and professionals seeking new tips. Produced by Artists Video and directed by Christian Surette; 1991 - 1994. Video jackets available.
Fine Arts
Dist - CNEMAG

Water Colors
Cassette / VHS / CD
Color (G)
$19.95, $14.98, $9.98 purchase
Combines photography of ice caps, waterfalls, Yellowstone geysers and the shorelines of Alaska with music by Peter Bardens.
Fine Arts; Industrial and Technical Education; Science - Natural; Social Science
Dist - MIRMP **Prod** - MIRMP 1991

Water - Coming and Going 20 MIN
16mm
Science Twenty Series
Color (I)
LC 70-704164
Demonstrates evaporation, condensation and precipitation of water by a series of simple, clear experiments which necessitate responses from the student, performs various experiments to explain the stages of the natural cycle of water. Shows actual examples of the water cycle in nature, including streams, clouds, fog, snow, rain and oceans. Includes multiple choice questions.
Science - Physical
Dist - SF **Prod** - PRISM 1970

The Water Crisis 57 MIN
U-matic / VHS / 16mm
Nova Series
Color (H C A)
LC 81-700872
Describes water problems currently being experienced by communities from the Adirondack Mountains to the American West Coast and explains that water scarcity will be the next ecology issue.
Science - Natural; Social Science
Dist - TIMLIF **Prod** - WGBHTV 1981

The Water cycle 11 MIN
VHS / U-matic
Weather wise series
Color (J H)
$120.00, $170.00 purchase, $50.00 rental
Covers the different processes in the water cycle precipitation, evaporationand condensation. Discusses each process and explains the possible elements in each one.
Science - Physical
Dist - NDIM **Prod** - LAWRN 1990

The Water cycle 11 MIN
VHS / U-matic
Color (P I J)
$225.00, $195.00 purchase _ #V219
Teaches about the water cycle - the evaporation of water, the formation of water vapor into clouds, rainfall. Shows how rainwater becomes groundwater, how water is used by plants to transport food, by humans in factories and cities. Discusses the danger of water pollution and unwise water management. Produced by FWU.
Science - Natural; Science - Physical; Social Science
Dist - BARR

The Water Cycle 6 MIN
U-matic
Color (K P I)
Traces the journey of water from rivers to the ocean, to clouds, rain and snow, and finally back to lakes, rivers and underground storage areas. Simplifies the water cycle so children can understand it.
Science - Natural
Dist - CALDWR **Prod** - CSDWR

The Water cycle 11 MIN
VHS
Color (I J)
$79.95 purchase _ #10039VG
Explains the relative scarcity of fresh water and the importance of the water cycle. Uses location footage and computer graphics to show the complete hydrologic cycle and the effects of water pollution. Comes with a teacher's guide, discussion questions and blackline masters.
Science - Natural; Science - Physical
Dist - UNL

The Water Cycle and Erosion 15 MIN
VHS
Color (J)
$125.00 purchase _ #5271V
Opens with the origin of the atmosphere. Traces the path of water from the oceans through evaporation, condensation and precipitation over the land to its eventual return to the ocean. Explores the action of running water and its effects and chemical weathering.
Geography - World; Science - Physical
Dist - SCTRES **Prod** - SCTRES

Water Cycle, the 14 MIN
U-matic / VHS / 16mm
Color (P I) (SPANISH)
LC 80-700712
Illustrates the importance of the vast exchange of water between land, the atmosphere and the sea. Examines in detail the processes of evaporation and condensation and the effects of the water cycle on the climate and the land.
Science - Natural; Science - Physical
Dist - EBEC **Prod** - EBEC 1980

Water Distribution Systems 30 MIN
VHS
Firefighter II - III Video Series
Color (G PRO)
$145.00 purchase _ #35243
Identifies the primary components of water systems, including source, movement and distribution. Trains firefighters.
Health and Safety; Industrial and Technical Education; Psychology; Science - Physical; Social Science
Dist - OKSU **Prod** - OKSU

The Water Dwellers 15 MIN
16mm
Color (H C A)
LC FIA68-2246
Studies the people who live, work or holiday along the foreshores of Broken Bay, 25 miles north of Sydney, Australia.
Geography - World
Dist - AUIS **Prod** - ANAIB 1968

Water Environment Federation Annual Conference Videotapes series
Paper - anaerobic pretreatment of combined domestic - industrial wastewater
Paper - considerations in the selection and design of high solids centrifuges
Paper - control of deicing fluids at the new Denver - CO - international airport
Paper - cycling for compliance
Paper - field application of the Clarifier Research Technical Committee's protocol for evaluating secondary clarifier performance
Paper - local pretreatment limits - implementation allocation strategies
Paper - sewer rehabilitation using trenchless technology on mainlines and service laterals
Paper - sliplining large diameter sewers
Paper - state - of - the - art evaluation of high cake solids centrifuge technology for municipal wastewater solids dewatering
Paper - status of on - site bioremediation for site restoration by the US Army Corps of Engineers
Paper - summary of water reuse regulations and guidelines in the US
Paper - the implementation of EPA's technical sludge regulations - 40 CFR part 503
Paper - vacuum wastewater collection - 10 years later - still a practical solution
Dist - WAENFE

Water environment series
Presents a four - part series in which each program focuses on a specific concern of water quality and the environment. Includes Ground Water; Conservation - Saving Water; Waste Water; and Surface Water. Each program is 10 - 12 minutes in length with comprehensive teacher and student guides. Programs available for separate purchase or rental.
Conservation - saving water 11 MIN
Ground water 10 MIN
Surface water 12 MIN
Waste water 12 MIN
Dist - NDIM **Prod** - WAENFE 1968

Water farmers 29 MIN
VHS / 16mm
Taste of China series
Color (J H C G)
$580.00, $225.00 purchase, $45.00 rental _ #1176, #37089
Visits the Yangzi River delta region south of Shanghai which is known as the water country. Reveals that hundreds of miles of canals link towns and villages and serve as 'liquid highways' for wedding boats, traveling vendors and foot - powered rowboats. Shows that near the city of Shaoxing, water has completely shaped the local farmers' way of life and that their lives exemplify the traditional harmonious relationship between the Chinese and their environment. Part of a four - part series on traditional Chinese cuisine.
Geography - World; History - World; Home Economics
Dist - UCEMC **Prod** - YUNGLI 1984

Water - Fluid for Life 16 MIN
16mm / U-matic / VHS
Color (J H)
$375.00 purchase - 16 mm, $250.00 purchase - video _ #3851
Shows water's role in the survival and emergence of life on earth.
Science - Natural; Social Science
Dist - CORF **Prod** - CORF 1978

Water follies 7 MIN
BETA / U-matic / VHS

Color (G)
$29.95, $130.00 purchase _ #LSTF5
Presents an animated feature that provokes thoughts about the need to conserve water and ways of doing so.
Science - Natural; Social Science
Dist - FEDU **Prod** - USEPA 1980

Water for a City 24 MIN
VHS / 16mm
Earth's Physical Resources Series
Color (S)
$200.00 purchase _ #236209
Presents a global view of the earth's resource potential. Features footage filmed in Britain, Europe and North America. 'Water For A City' illustrates the concept of water as a renewable resource through a filmed look at how the City of Nottingham obtains water from the aquifers by storing run - off and drawing from the river. The problems inherent in maintaining a hydrological cycle are illustrated through an examination of the aquifer, the reservoirs and river and distribution and reclamation methods.
Geography - World; Industrial and Technical Education; Science - Natural; Science - Physical; Social Science
Dist - ACCESS **Prod** - BBCTV 1984

Water for a City 13 MIN
16mm
Color (J)
LC 72-702251
Shows the scale and complexity of the system to store and supply water for a large Australian city.
Geography - World; Science - Natural; Social Science; Sociology
Dist - AUIS **Prod** - ANAIB 1972

Water for a Thirsty World 15 MIN
16mm
Science in Action Series
Color (C)
Tells that man's enormous demands and polluting habits threaten his limited fresh water supply which is less that one percent of all the water on earth. Explains that currently there are 1000 desalting plants in operation, producing 1,800,000,000 liters of fresh water a day. Investigates new ways of mapping ground water deposits, the more than 95 percent of fresh water that lies underground.
Science; Science - Natural; Science - Physical; Sociology
Dist - COUNFI **Prod** - ALLFP

Water for Farming 5 MIN
U-matic
Color (K P I)
Describes agricultural water uses and how farmers conserve water.
Agriculture; Science - Natural
Dist - CALDWR **Prod** - CSDWR

Water for Industry 5 MIN
U-matic
Color (K P I)
Shows cleaning and recycling of industrial water as methods for using water more efficiently. Uses foods as example of industrial process water use.
Business and Economics; Industrial and Technical Education; Science - Natural; Social Science
Dist - CALDWR **Prod** - CSDWR

Water for Jordan 26 MIN
U-matic / VHS / 16mm
Color (H C)
Uses animated photography to show how water can be located and stored in the desert. Traces the geology, vegetation and patterns of rainfall in Jordan Valley and explains the development of the Jordan Valley Water Project.
Geography - World; Science - Physical
Dist - MEDIAG **Prod** - BBCTV 1985

Water for Jordan 27 MIN
VHS / 16mm
Earth's Physical Resources Series
Color (S)
$200.00 purchase _ #236210
Presents a global view of the earth's resource potential. Features footage filmed in Britain, Europe and North America. Demonstrates the diversity and magnitude of water management problems in the southwestern United States. Discusses evaporation, the scale of capital required and the sedimentation of the reservoirs and channels. Large - scale irrigation is also investigated.
Agriculture; Geography - United States; Industrial and Technical Education; Science - Natural; Science - Physical; Social Science
Dist - ACCESS **Prod** - BBCTV 1984

Water for Life 15 MIN
16mm
Color
Shows the natural sources of water and demonstrates the two main systems of desalination - multi - stage flash evaporation and electrodialysis. Discusses dual - purpose plants to produce power from a nuclear reactor and at the same time to produce water, as well as the possible allocation of the costs of such a plant to water and to electricity.
Geography - United States; Industrial and Technical Education; Science - Natural; Science - Physical; Social Science; Sociology
Dist - UKAEA **Prod** - UKAEA 1967

Water for the City 11 MIN
U-matic / VHS / 16mm
Color; B&W (P I) (SPANISH)
LC FIA67-2142
Shows that water needed by people in a city begins as rain and snow that forms rivers, lakes and underground water basins. Depicts ways this water is purified and brought into homes in the city.
Science - Natural; Social Science
Dist - PHENIX **Prod** - FA 1967

Water for Tonoumasse 28 MIN
VHS
Color (H C G)
$295.00 purchase, $55.00 rental
Observes how women and men worked together in the village of Tonoumasse to obtain safe water for the village through the drilling of a well. Shows that the men of the village learned that women were capable of making decisions, handling money and learning the mechanics of keeping the well's pump in working order. The women, by taking responsibility, have transformed their daily life because they no longer have to walk eight hours for water that is very often contaminated, allowing them to take better care of their children and have more time to grow food. Produced by Gary Beitel.
Geography - World; Social Science; Sociology
Dist - FLMLIB **Prod** - NFBC 1988

Water fowl 27 MIN
U-matic / VHS / BETA
Stationary ark series
Color; PAL (G H C)
PdS50, PdS58 purchase
Discusses the recreation of humankind, nature and wildlife in part of a 12 - part series. Features Gerald Durrell. Filmed on location in Jersey, England.
Science - Natural
Dist - EDPAT

Water - Friend or Enemy 10 MIN
16mm
Color
Shows safe and unsafe water supplies in rural areas, sinking of wells, seepage problems, dangers and sources of contamination.
Science - Natural; Social Science
Dist - USNAC **Prod** - DISNEY 1946

Water - Friend or Enemy 9 MIN
16mm
Color
Discusses the pollution of springs and wells, how this may be prevented and how well - water may be made safe to drink.
Health and Safety; Science - Natural; Social Science
Dist - USIS **Prod** - USIS 1944

Water - Friend or Foe 23 MIN
U-matic / VHS / 16mm
Color (I) (ARABIC)
Presents a series of dramatic episodes set in a variety of situations involving still and moving water. Describes basic safety rules of how to avoid accidents and how to rescue oneself and others in case of emergencies.
Health and Safety
Dist - PFP **Prod** - PFP 1973

Water - Friend or Foe 23 MIN
U-matic / VHS / 16mm
Color (I) (ARABIC)
An Arabic language version of the film, Water - Friend Or Foe. Demonstrates how to prevent accidents in or around water, and how to act when accidents occur. Includes step - by - step information on what to do in common water emergencies, involving swimming, boating, fishing, and scuba diving, or being near a pond or swimming pool.
Foreign Language; Health and Safety
Dist - PFP **Prod** - PFP

Water from Another Time 29 MIN
16mm / U-matic / VHS
Color (J H G)
Profiles three elderly residents of Orange County, Indiana.
Fine Arts; Sociology
Dist - DOCEDR **Prod** - DOCEDR 1982

Water from Another Time 16 MIN
U-matic / VHS / 16mm
Color (H C A)
Emphasizes the contributions of senior citizens to society. Features three elderly individuals in Orange County, Indiana.
Health and Safety; Social Science
Dist - KANLEW **Prod** - KANLEW 1982

Water in the air 81 MIN
VHS
Color (I J H)
$200.00 purchase _ #A5VH 1148
Presents five programs on the water cycle and its relationship to weather. Includes Evaporation - Where Does the Water Go; Condensation - the Other Side of the Story; The Water Cycle - Completing the Picture; Humidity - the Degree of Moisture; Humdidity - Measurement and Application.
Science - Physical
Dist - CLRVUE **Prod** - CLRVUE

Water in the Atmosphere 25 MIN
VHS
Active Atmosphere Series
Color (J)
$79.00 purchase _ #2241V
Shows how water in the atmosphere plays an important role in weather. Considers vapor, clouds, rain, atmosphere, and the water cycle. Part of an eight - part series on the atmosphere and the weather it creates. Includes a comprehensive study guide.
Science - Physical
Dist - SCTRES **Prod** - SCTRES

Water in the Desert - the Imperial Valley 52 FRS
VHS / U-matic
Color (J H C)
$43.95 purchase _ #52 3495
Uses full color photographs to show how irrigation water from the Colorado River was brought to the dry Imperial Valley of Southern California, turning desert into lush farmland, but causing extensive floods and creating the Salton Sea in the process. Video version of 35mm filmstrip program, with live open and close.
Agriculture; Science - Natural
Dist - CBSC **Prod** - CBSC

Water Insects 14 MIN
16mm / U-matic / VHS
Insect Series
Color (J H)
LC 80-700680
Shows how some insects have adapted to an aquatic environment. Discusses insects that live on the surface of the water, insects that live beneath the water but return to the surface for air, and insect larvae and nymphs that obtain oxygen from the water.
Science - Natural
Dist - IFB **Prod** - BHA 1977

Water is So Clear that a Blind Man Could See 30 MIN
16mm / U-matic / VHS
Our Vanishing Wilderness Series no 7
Color (J H)
LC 75-710660
Describes the plight of the Taos Indians and their home in the Blue Lake area of New Mexico, which is threatened by lumber companies. Explains that the Indian has not exploited ecology because he considers all life sacred and uses only what is necessary to him.
Science - Natural; Social Science
Dist - IU **Prod** - NET 1970

Water is Wet 20 MIN
16mm
Metooshow Series
Color (K A)
LC 77-705712
Encourages singing, working with paper and colors, making up stories and acting them out, thinking and talking about things and a feeling of having done well. Suggests that the best way to bring children enjoyment is through a parent or teacher who shows enjoyment in these activities.
Literature and Drama; Science - Physical
Dist - TPTP **Prod** - TPTP 1970

Water its many Voices 20 MIN
16mm
Color
Shows ways to conserve water supply.
Science - Natural
Dist - IDEALF **Prod** - ALLISC

Water - Land 17 MIN
U-matic / VHS / 16mm
Color
Presents the polder, land reclaimed from the sea, in the Lake Yssel area in The Netherlands, now known as South Flevoland.
Geography - World
Dist - IFB **Prod** - NETHIS
EDPAT

Water - Lenses 12 MIN
U-matic / VHS

Introductory Concepts in Physics - Light Series
Color (C)
$229.00, $129.00 purchase _ #AD - 1212
Shows, through everyday examples, that we live in a world of convex lenses. Illustrates how water produces an image.
Science - Physical
Dist - FOTH **Prod** - FOTH

Water Life to a City 24 MIN
16mm
Color
LC 76-701392
Deals with the problems of water resources of Victoria, British Columbia.
Geography - World; Social Science; Sociology
Dist - WILFGP **Prod** - WILFGP 1975

Water - Lifeblood of the West 13 MIN
16mm
Color (I J)
LC FIA59-31
Stresses the importance of water in building the West and shows the many ways that western rivers have been harnessed by reclamation projects.
Geography - United States; History - United States; Science - Natural
Dist - MLA **Prod** - DAGP 1958

Water Masses of the Ocean 45 MIN
16mm
Color (J H)
LC 72-700686
Studies the locations and dynamic movements of the major water masses of the oceans.
Science - Physical
Dist - USNAC **Prod** - USN 1967

Water Means Life 5 MIN
16mm
Color
Portrays the need for safe water for persons overseas who often die from the constant consumption of contaminated water.
Business and Economics; Social Science; Sociology
Dist - CARE **Prod** - CARE

Water Means Life 19 MIN
16mm
Color (ITALIAN FRENCH GERMAN SPANISH)
LC 80-700178
Discusses the worldwide problems caused by unsafe drinking water and explains what UNICEF is doing to alleviate these problems.
Foreign Language; Science - Natural; Sociology
Dist - UNICEF **Prod** - UNICEF 1979

Water Media Techniques - Acrylic and Casein 45 MIN
VHS
Water Media Techniques Series
Color (J)
$39.95 purchase _ #VC - - 768
Demonstrates the special properties and handling characteristics of acrylic and casein paints. Shows how to create transparent and opaque washes in both mediums and use the two mediums together. Part of a two - part series on water media techniques by Stephen Quiller.
Fine Arts
Dist - CRYSP **Prod** - CRYSP

Water Media Techniques Series
Water Media Techniques - Acrylic and Casein 45 MIN
Water Media Techniques - Watercolor and Gouache 45 MIN
Dist - CRYSP

Water Media Techniques - Watercolor and Gouache 45 MIN
VHS
Water Media Techniques Series
Color (J)
$39.95 purchase _ #VC - - 767
Shows how to use watercolor and gouache media. Illustrates equipment, papers and materials used for special effects. Part of a two - part series on water media techniques by Stephen Quiller.
Fine Arts
Dist - CRYSP **Prod** - CRYSP

Water - more Precious than Oil 58 MIN
VHS / U-matic
Color
LC 82-706843
Examines the use and abuse of water around the world. Shows how water resources must be managed on small, as well as large scales and shows the consequences for those who are unwilling or unable to manage their water resources.
Science - Natural; Social Science
Dist - PBS **Prod** - KTCATV 1980

The Water Movie 8 MIN
U-matic / VHS / 16mm
Color (J)
LC 76-700272
A visual study which presents closeup shots of the surface of a body of water moving at varying speeds, with different colored patterns created by holding objects over the water. Alternates music by William Russell with excerpts from Mozart's horn duos.
Fine Arts
Dist - AIMS **Prod** - ACI 1975

Water - Nebraska's Heritage 29 MIN
16mm
Nebraska Water Resources Series
Color (H C A)
LC 74-700161
Describes the use of water in Nebraska and the extent of the supply. Illustrates the relative amounts of water used for homes, industry and agriculture. Locates geographically the sources of ground water and surface water in the state by extensive use of aerial photography.
Geography - United States; Science - Natural
Dist - UNL **Prod** - UNEBR 1971

The Water of Ayole 28 MIN
VHS / U-matic / 16mm
Color (J H C G)
$450.00, $90.00, $80.00 purchase, $65.00, $25.00 rental
Visits Togo, West Africa, to explore the problems of developing countries in providing safe and accessible drinking water to rural and urban populations. Focuses on Dracunculiasis, infection with guinea worm, endemic to 19 African countries where up to 120 million people are at risk of infection, and India and Pakistan, where 20 million people are at risk. Reveals that 1000 children die each day from the disease and five percent of the population is permanently disabled as a result of the disease.
Geography - World; Social Science
Dist - UNDPI **Prod** - UNDPI 1988

Water of Life 25 MIN
16mm / VHS
Big Ice Series
Color (H)
$990.00, $390.00 purchase
Depicts the oceans surrounding Antarctica as containing an enormous food supply. Investigates whether they can be harvested without destruction.
Geography - World; Industrial and Technical Education; Science - Natural
Dist - FLMWST

The Water of words - a cultural ecology of a small island in Eastern Indonesia 30 MIN
16mm / VHS
Color (G)
$550.00, $275.00 purchase, $55.00, $35.00 rental
Studies the utilization of lontar, a borassus palm on the Indonesian island of Roti. Shows techniques for tapping and cooking the palm's juice and its transformation into syrup, beer and gin - 'the water of words'. Includes mythic poetry from the clan leader and ritual specialists which recounts the origin of the lontar from the sea. By James Fox, Timothy Asch and Patsy Asch.
Geography - World; History - World; Religion and Philosophy
Dist - DOCEDR **Prod** - DOCEDR

Water - Old Problems, New Approaches 30 MIN
U-matic / VHS / 16mm
World We Live in Series
Color (I J H)
LC 70-700244
Tells the story of water shortage problems and how scientists are combatting them.
Science; Science - Natural
Dist - MGHT **Prod** - TIMELI 1968

The Water People 25 MIN
16mm
Eye of the Beholder Series
Color
LC 75-701945
Profiles the water people of Southeast Asia in Hong Kong, Macao and Thailand.
Geography - World; Sociology
Dist - VIACOM **Prod** - RCPDF 1972

The Water Planet 30 MIN
VHS / U-matic
Oceanus - the Marine Environment Series Lesson 1
Color (C A)
Discusses the earth as a water planet, with over seventy - one percent of the earth covered by water. Explores modern theories of the origins of life.
Science - Natural; Science - Physical
Dist - CDTEL **Prod** - SCCON SCCON

The water planet 19 MIN
16mm / U-matic / VHS
Undersea world of Jacques Cousteau series
Color (G)
$49.95 purchase _ #Q10616; LC 72-710106
A shortened version of The Water Planet. Describes aspects of life aboard an underwater exploration ship. Shows the unending manual and mental labor and illustrates the dangers with which underwater photographers must contend.
Science - Natural; Science - Physical
Dist - CF **Prod** - METROM 1970

Water Play 7 MIN
U-matic
Take Time Series
(A)
Demonstrates the influence of parents and others caring for pre - schoolers on the physical and emotional development of the child.
Health and Safety; Psychology; Sociology
Dist - ACCESS **Prod** - ACCESS 1976

Water Play for Teaching Young Children 17 MIN
16mm
Color
Shows the value of water as a natural resource in the preschool, with children from toddler age up to age five and in settings as different as a college laboratory nursery school and an inner city day care center. Illustrates how water can provide a deeply satisfying sensory experience as well as an educational medium. Demonstrates how the staff can control and direct the use of water so that it is constructive.
Education; Psychology
Dist - NYU **Prod** - VASSAR

Water Pollution 30 MIN
U-matic / VHS
Living Environment Series
Color (C)
Deals with water pollutants, their sources and their effects on wildlife and on people, as well as potential technological and economic solutions.
Science - Natural
Dist - DALCCD **Prod** - DALCCD

Water Pollution 10 MIN
16mm
Color (P I J)
Encourages student concern about the abuse of natural resources, tracing the causes and results of water pollution. Shows how clear water becomes contaminated and useless as garbage, sewage, insecticides and industrial wastes flow into rivers, lakes and streams. Points out that science alone cannot fight the battle against pollution.
Science - Natural
Dist - SF **Prod** - SF 1970

Water pollution - a first film 12 MIN
U-matic / VHS / BETA
Color; NTSC; PAL; SECAM (I J H)
PdS58
Reveals that most forms of life require pure, clean water. Discloses that water that becomes polluted is unsafe and can destroy life. Describes the water cycle and the roles of humans to illustrate the problems and dangers of pollution. Adds important information about aquifers and their role in the reprocessing of polluted water. Shows specific causes and results of pollution, and possible methods of pollution control.
Science - Natural; Social Science
Dist - VIEWTH

Water Pollution - a First Film 8 MIN
16mm / U-matic / VHS
Color (P I) (FRENCH NORWEGIAN)
LC 75-712385
Follows a single stream from its origin to its end in order to reveal the many different sources of pollution. Points out that individuals as well as groups can help clean up our water sources.
Science - Natural
Dist - PHENIX **Prod** - BEANMN 1971

Water Pollution - Can We Keep Our Water Clean 16 MIN
U-matic / VHS / 16mm
Captioned; Color (I J)
LC 73-712694
Shows six major sources of pollution and the ways in which each contributes to the contamination of our waterways. Includes examples such as trash and garbage from individuals, fertilizers, chemicals and manure from farms, waste and oil from boats, industrial wastes and detergent effluents from factories, thermal pollution from nuclear plants and city sewage.
Science - Natural; Sociology
Dist - JOU **Prod** - WER 1971

Water Pollution in Norway and the United States - Human - Environmental Interaction - 7 30 MIN
VHS
Common Issues in World Regions Series
Color (J)
$180.00 purchase
Looks at families in Porsgrunn, Norway, and Smith Island, Maryland, who find their livelihood threatened by environmental degradation. Develops international understanding and geographic literacy for today's students growing up in a global community.
Geography - United States; Geography - World; Sociology
Dist - AITECH **Prod** - AITECH 1991

Water polo
VHS
N C A A instructional video series
Color (H C A)
$39.95 purchase _ #KAR2902V
Presents an instructional program on water polo.
Physical Education and Recreation
Dist - CAMV **Prod** - NCAAF

Water Power 15 MIN
16mm
Color
LC 73-702066
Presents scenes of traditional Ghana followed by scenes of people of Ghana changing their landscape and their way of life through technology. Witnesses the effects of the Volta Dam on Ghana.
Geography - World; Industrial and Technical Education; Sociology
Dist - EDC **Prod** - EDC 1973

Water Power 25 MIN
U-matic / VHS / 16mm
Color (J)
LC 82-700653
Looks at the history of water power using archival footage and old photographs.
Social Science
Dist - BULFRG **Prod** - LIVNGN 1982

Water Power 23 MIN
U-matic / VHS / 16mm
Color (I)
Declares that man is once more turning to water as a source of energy, including the harnessing of tidal power for water - driven generators.
Social Science
Dist - LUF **Prod** - LUF 1981

Water Power 24 MIN
16mm / U-matic / VHS
Color (J H)
Shows how water wheels operated and their past importance. Examines new ways of exploiting water power and explores waves, tides and torrents as potential sources of power.
Industrial and Technical Education
Dist - VIEWTH **Prod** - GATEEF

Water Pressure 3 MIN
VHS / 16mm
Color (PRO)
$245.00 purchase, $125.00 rental, $30.00 preview
Uses puppets to humorously comment on business meetings. Intended for use during businesss meetings to introduce a break.
Business and Economics; Psychology
Dist - UTM **Prod** - UTM

Water Purification, Introduction 100 MIN
16mm
Color
LC FIE54-157
Emphasizes the importance of disinfecting water. Explains the various sources of water and the steps required to provide a safe water supply.
Health and Safety; Industrial and Technical Education; Science - Natural
Dist - USNAC **Prod** - USN 1953

Water Rescue 13 MIN
U-matic
Rescue Procedures Series
Color (PRO)
Demonstrates the technique for rescuing a drowning person and swimming with him to shore, and for transporting him by means of the four - man carry to a beach area where he is positioned for mouth - to - mouth resuscitation. Shows the rescue procedure for lifting a drowning victim from the water into a rowboat, a canoe or onto a surfboard.
Health and Safety; Physical Education and Recreation
Dist - PRIMED **Prod** - PRIMED

Water rescue 35 MIN
VHS
Color (IND)
$150.00 purchase _ #35468
Identifies the major hazards of water rescue. Specifies needed equipment and personal protective clothing. Demonstrates safe water rescue procedures for lakes, rivers, and floods.
Health and Safety; Science - Physical; Social Science
Dist - OKSU **Prod** - MEDIRE

Water Resourcefulness 20 MIN
16mm
Color (I)
LC FIA67-684
Describes the accelerated water resources program of New York State. Explains how state coordination is required to provide an aggressive water conservation program consisting of federal, state and local elements. Explains examples of water resourcefulness, such as stream impoundment, drainage improvement and a wetlands preservations project.
Agriculture; Science - Natural
Dist - FINLYS **Prod** - NYSCD 1966

Water Resources 30 MIN
U-matic / VHS
Living Environment Series
Color (C)
Probes the issues of the circulation of water through the ecosystem, the contamination of water, desalination and flood control for solutions in water management.
Science - Natural
Dist - DALCCD **Prod** - DALCCD

Water resources
CD-ROM
(PRO)
$575.00 purchase _ #1711
Contains the entire two years worth of SWRA monthly publications which includes over 200,000 citations, thousands of abstracts, and the WRSIC Thesaurus. For IBM PCs and compatibles. Requires at least 640K RAM, DOS Version 3.1 or greater, one floppy disk drive - a hard drive is recommended, one empty expansion slot, and an IBM compatible CD - ROM drive.
Literature and Drama; Social Science
Dist - BEP

Water Roundup 15 MIN
U-matic
Color (I)
Explores the California State Water Project, its many facilities and the benefits it provides Californians.
Geography - United States; Industrial and Technical Education; Science - Natural; Social Science
Dist - CALDWR **Prod** - CSDWR

Water Runs Downhill 13 MIN
U-matic / VHS / 16mm
Scientific Fact and Fun Series
Color (P I)
LC 80-700716
Presents observations and inferences about clouds, rain and running streams. Defines the terms erosion, evaporation and water cycle.
Science - Physical
Dist - JOU **Prod** - GLDWER 1980

Water Safety 15 MIN
U-matic
Calling all Safety Scouts Series
Color (K P)
Teaches children the importance of life jackets, precautions for safe swimming, rescue breathing and proper boat equipment.
Health and Safety
Dist - TVOTAR **Prod** - TVOTAR 1983

Water safety - 64 7 MIN
VHS / U-matic
Life's little lessons - self - esteem 4 - 6 series
Color (I)
$129.00, $99.00 purchase _ #V693
Reveals that real friends never dare people to do something harmful. Shows that youngsters have to be smart enough to walk away from a dare and that when playing around water, safety comes first. Part of a 65 - part series on self - esteem.
Guidance and Counseling; Health and Safety; Psychology
Dist - BARR **Prod** - CEPRO 1992

Water Safety - an Introduction 10 MIN
U-matic / VHS / 16mm
Color
LC 74-702533
Illustrates a variety of ways to avoid water accidents, the right and wrong ways of helping oneself and someone else in trouble in the water and some survival floating techniques.
Health and Safety
Dist - PHENIX **Prod** - DELEAU 1974

Water Safety - It's Elementary 12 MIN
U-matic / VHS / 16mm
Color (P I)
LC 75-700972
Attempts to promote swimming safety for young children by providing suggestions for both swimmers and nonswimmers on how to combine fun with safety.
Health and Safety
Dist - AIMS **Prod** - CAHILL 1974

Water Safety - the Basics 17 MIN
U-matic / VHS / 16mm
Color (I J H C A)
$395.00, $250.00 purchase _ #76574
Discusses safety rules to observe while swimming, boating, and performing rescues.
Health and Safety
Dist - CORF **Prod** - CENTRO 1979

Water - Seal Chest Drainage 30 MIN
U-matic / VHS
Color
Presents a program on water - seal chest drainage. Begins with a basic review of the anatomy and physiology of the respiratory system, then explains water - seal drainage systems.
Health and Safety; Science - Natural
Dist - AJN **Prod** - AJN

Water Service 11 MIN
16mm
B&W
Illustrates the scientific and engineering methods used in the collection, storage, purification and distribution of water supplies.
Business and Economics; Industrial and Technical Education; Science - Natural
Dist - USIS **Prod** - USIS 1945

Water Service Installation using a Mueller B Drilling and Tapping Machine 23 MIN
VHS / BETA
Color
Discusses water pipes, water supply engineering apparatus and supplies.
Health and Safety; Industrial and Technical Education; Social Science
Dist - RMIBHF **Prod** - RMIBHF

Water Skiing 30 MIN
VHS / BETA
Color
Demonstrates proper form and technique for water skiing, on one ski or two.
Physical Education and Recreation
Dist - MOHOMV **Prod** - MOHOMV

Water Skiing, Acapulco 3 MIN
16mm
Of all Things Series
Color (P I)
Shows water skiing in Acapulco, Mexico.
Geography - World; Physical Education and Recreation
Dist - AVED **Prod** - BAILYL

Water skiing on four wheels 13 MIN
VHS / 16mm
Color (H G)
$65.00, $30.00 purchase _ #300, #495
Discusses the phenomenon of hydroplaning by cars on wet pavement and steps drivers must take to maintain control when driving under such conditions.
Health and Safety; Industrial and Technical Education
Dist - AAAFTS **Prod** - AAAFTS 1978

Water - Solute Balance 29 MIN
16mm
Clinical Pathology Series
B&W (PRO)
Discusses total body changes in water, protein and sodium.
Health and Safety; Science - Natural
Dist - USNAC **Prod** - NMAC

Water Spider 10 MIN
16mm
Color (P I J H)
Shows the life cycle of the water spider, an arachnid that has adapted to life under water by carrying an air bubble with it.
Science - Natural
Dist - VIEWTH **Prod** - GATEEF

Water supplies 20 MIN
VHS
Firefighter II series
Color (IND)
$130.00 purchase _ #35658
Presents one part of a 14 - part series that is the teaching companion for IFSTA's Essentials of Fire Fighting manual. Identifies and describes the components of a water system. Explains the operation of different types of

hydrants, and how certain conditions can reduce the effectiveness of a hydrant. Based on Chapter 9.
Health and Safety; Science - Physical; Social Science
Dist - OKSU **Prod** - ACCTRA

Water Supply 20 MIN
16mm
B&W
Describes the means by which water is collected, purified and distributed to users.
Business and Economics; Science - Natural; Social Science
Dist - USIS **Prod** - USIS 1951

Water Supply and Sanitation in Development Series
People and Problems 28 MIN
Problems and solutions 42 MIN
Solutions and People 26 MIN
Dist - IU

Water Supply Videos 90 MIN
VHS
Color (PRO G)
$375.00 purchase _ #35415
Presents a three - part series of videos on water supply and tanker operations. Examines construction, pre - fire planning and planning and resources for rural areas.
Health and Safety; Psychology; Social Science
Dist - OKSU **Prod** - OKSU

Water supply - Wodociag 66 MIN
VHS
Color (P I J) (POLISH)
$17.95 purchase _ #V171
Presents seven different animated stories for children.
Fine Arts; Literature and Drama
Dist - POLART

Water - the Common Necessity 9 MIN
VHS / 16mm
Color
LC 75-704198
Explains the water cycle and lists ways that water is essential to life. Raises the problem of conservation of this natural resource and points out little - known information about uses of water.
Science - Natural; Social Science
Dist - MIS **Prod** - MIS 1975

Water - the Effluent Society 22 MIN
16mm / U-matic / VHS
Color (J)
Predicts that in the near future, sustaining the life of one human being will require three million gallons of fresh water every year. Studies the availability of water and the pollution control measures necessary to maintain a constant supply of clean, fresh water.
Science - Natural
Dist - CNEMAG **Prod** - DOCUA 1971

Water - the eternal cycle 15 MIN
VHS / 16mm
Color (I J)
$350.00, $315.00 purchase
Stresses the importance of water to life. Looks at the different forms water takes and the historical importance of water to population centers - both human and animal.
Science - Natural; Social Science
Dist - HANDEL **Prod** - HANDEL 1990

Water, the Plain Wonder 9 MIN
16mm
Color
Deals with the importance of water as a natural resource. Shows that many Americans take it for granted even at a time when problems such as pollution and drought have begun to threaten water supplies.
Social Science
Dist - GPN **Prod** - REGIS

Water - the timeless compound 25 MIN
U-matic / VHS / BETA
Color; PAL (G H C)
PdS60, PdS68 purchase
Features a dramatic production about water and the power it possesses, from tidal waves to frozen water disasters.
History - World; Science - Physical
Dist - EDPAT

Water transport 15 MIN
VHS
Color; PAL (P I)
PdS25.00 purchase
Explores the changes in shipping over the last 100 years and identifies today's types, such as a modern car ferry.
Geography - World; Social Science
Dist - EMFVL **Prod** - LOOLEA

Water Treatment
U-matic / VHS
Industrial Training, Module 2 - Boiler Fundamentals Series; Module 2 - Boiler fundamentals
Color (IND)
Covers several aspects of water treatment such as clarifier, softener, zeolite base exchange and demineralizer.
Industrial and Technical Education
Dist - LEIKID **Prod** - LEIKID

Water Treatment - 1 60 MIN
VHS
Systems Operations Series
Color (PRO)
$600.00 - $1500.00 purchase _ #OTWT1
Introduces the process of water treatment. Describes the causes and effects of corrosion and scale buildup and the functions of typical water treatment systems. Part of a seventeen - part series on systems operations. Includes ten textbooks and an instructor guide to support four hours of instruction.
Industrial and Technical Education; Psychology
Dist - NUSTC **Prod** - NUSTC

Water Treatment - 2 60 MIN
VHS
Systems Operations Series
Color (PRO)
$600.00 - $1500.00 purchase _ #OTWT2
Focuses on the operation of water treatment systems and operator responsibilities for water treatment. Describes system and equipment operation and general operation duties in a wastewater and water recycling system. Part of a seventeen - part series on systems operations. Includes ten textbooks and an instructor guide to support four hours of instruction.
Health and Safety; Industrial and Technical Education; Psychology
Dist - NUSTC **Prod** - NUSTC

The Water Treatment Engineer 15 MIN
U-matic
Harriet's Magic Hats III Series
(P I J)
Shows the steps involved in treating water to make sure it is safe to drink.
Guidance and Counseling
Dist - ACCESS **Prod** - ACCESS 1985

Water treatment in hemodialysis 30 MIN
VHS / U-matic
Hemodialysis series
Color (C PRO)
$395.00 purchase, $80.00 rental _ #C911 - VI - 041
Provides a comprehensive overview of the process of water treatment in hemodialysis. Reviews the contaminants commonly found in tap water and their possible health hazards. Looks in detail at each component in a water treatment facility. Demonstrates the importance of water treatment for patient care and the necessity for a well - trained, diligent staff to carry it out. Part of a four - part series on hemodialysis presented by the Health Industry Manufacturers Association, Food and Drug Administration, Renal Physicians' Association and American Nephrology Nurses' Association.
Health and Safety; Science - Natural; Science - Physical
Dist - HSCIC

Water Treatment Plant
VHS / U-matic
Field Trips in Environmental Geology - Technical and Mechanical 'Concerns Series
Color
Visits the Akron city water treatment plant on Lake Rockwell, Portage County, Ohio. Examines the natural steam collection system and storage reservoirs. Traces the purification process from raw water to customer delivery and looks at the chemical testing procedures and EPA requirements.
Science - Natural; Science - Physical
Dist - KENTSU **Prod** - KENTSU

Water Tricks 13 MIN
16mm
Exploring Childhood Series
Color (J)
LC 76-701899
Presents Paul, a student, planning and carrying out an activity at a water - table. Shows how he makes use of the children's interest to show them tricks with siphons and pumps and then evaluates the activity in a discussion with his class.
Education; Psychology; Sociology
Dist - EDC **Prod** - EDC 1975

Water walkers 10 MIN
VHS / U-matic
Eye on nature series
Color (I J)
$250.00 purchase _ #HP - 5851C
Looks at insects like pondskaters, water boatmen, springtails and water measurers and how they walk upon water and exist upon the surfaces of ponds. Reveals how these creatures mate, detect prey and protect themselves from severe weather. Part of the Eye on Nature series.
Science - Natural
Dist - CORF **Prod** - BBCTV 1989

Water Walkers 25 MIN
U-matic / VHS / 16mm
Color (H C A)
LC 82-701113
Explores the miniature and unsuspected world of creatures living on the surface of ponds and streams. Shows the water surface and its inhabitants, including pondskaters, swamp spiders, whirligigs and water boatmen.
Science - Natural
Dist - FI **Prod** - BBCTV 1981

Water wars series
Examines water as a powerful element and the focus of many of the world's political and social conflicts. Includes discussions on water as a valuable resource; as a fatal poison; and as the cause of religious hostility.
The Giver of life 50 MIN
Good as gold 50 MIN
To the last drop 50 MIN
Dist - BBCENE

Water wars - the battle of Mono Lake 39 MIN
VHS
Color (H C G)
$195.00 purchase, $45.00 rental _ #37082
Examines the controversies surrounding the diversion of fresh water to the city of Los Angeles from river flowing into California's Mono Lake. Profiles the ecosystem of the rapidly falling lake and shows how the battle over its water pits vested property rights against a growing belief that natural resource management must place a high priority on environmental preservation.
Geography - United States; History - United States; Science - Natural
Dist - UCEMC **Prod** - TAYWOH 1984

Water, water everywhere 23 MIN
VHS
Bright sparks series
Color (P I)
$280.00 purchase
Travels around the world to examine the importance of water. Looks at the use of water and attitudes towards its conservation. Examines solutions to water shortages, polluted drinking water and flooding. Part of a 12 - part animated series on science and technology.
Science - Natural; Social Science
Dist - LANDMK **Prod** - LANDMK 1989

Water, Water Everywhere 15 MIN
16mm
Color (IND) (SPANISH)
LC 77-702469
Defines cross - connections in water systems and discusses specific cases of illness which resulted from cross - connections. Describes remedial measures, such as air gaps, double check valves and vacuum breakers.
Industrial and Technical Education; Science - Natural; Sociology
Dist - CS **Prod** - LASL 1977
LASL

Water - what Happens to it 15 MIN
U-matic / VHS
Hands on, Grade 5 - Our Environment Series
Color (I)
Discusses various aspects of water.
Social Science
Dist - AITECH **Prod** - WHROTV 1975

Water - Why it is, what it is 11 MIN
VHS / 16mm
Color (I J H)
Suggests that water is one of our earth's most valuable resources and that it helps shape the earth, moderates its weather and preserves life.
Science - Natural; Social Science
Dist - MIS **Prod** - MIS

Water workout 60 MIN
VHS
Color (G)
$49.95 purchase
Features 1984 Olympic gold medalist Candy Costie in an aerobic water workout program. Teaches a series of routines designed for people of all ages. Includes an accompanying audio cassette to use at poolside.
Physical Education and Recreation
Dist - PBS **Prod** - WNETTV

Waterbed 6 MIN
16mm
Color (G)
$15.00 rental
Travels down the Niagara River rapids. Holds the basic premise to all of the filmmaker's endeavors - to infuse the viewer with a life force or shot of energy that enters the bones and whirls up the spirits.
Fine Arts
Dist - CANCIN **Prod** - ZDRAVI 1974

Waterbirds 25 MIN
VHS
Nature watch series
Color (P I J H C)
$49.00 purchase _ #320220; LC 89-715863
Looks at waterbirds. Part of a series that explores the curious and uncommon characteristics of a variety of mammals, insects, birds and sea creatures.
Science - Natural
Dist - TVOTAR **Prod** - TVOTAR 1988

Waterbirds 25 MIN
16mm / U-matic / VHS
Untamed World Series
Color; Mono (J H C A)
$400.00 film, $250.00 video, $50.00 rental
Looks at Europe's great river marshes, the deltas of the Rhone and the Danube examining the birdlife that is specialized to these wet regions.
Geography - World; Science - Natural
Dist - CTV **Prod** - CTV 1973

Waterbirds - Volume 2 60 MIN
VHS
Audubon society videoguides to the birds of North America series
Color (G)
$29.95 purchase
Combines live footage and color photography in an Audubon Society bird watching program. Focuses on waterbirds. Uses bird sights and sounds, visual graphics, and maps to aid in the identification of bird types. Narrated by Michael Godfrey.
Science - Natural
Dist - PBS **Prod** - WNETTV

Waterborne 10 MIN
VHS / U-matic / 16mm
Color (I J H G)
$145.00, $195.00, $245.00 purchase, $40.00 rental
Features a visual essay on the mesmerism of water with original piano music of George Winston. Meditates on the statement by Loren Eiseley 'If there is magic on this planet, it is contained in water.' Produced by Don Briggs.
Religion and Philosophy
Dist - NDIM

The Waterclock Crisis 28 MIN
16mm
Color
LC 79-701397
Depicts the freshwater cycle in the State of Florida, documents cases of the misuse of water, presents testimony from water experts, and shows the positive contributions of various interest groups in remedying the freshwater problem.
Geography - United States; Science - Natural; Social Science
Dist - INTMCC **Prod** - INTMCC 1979

Watercolor 14 MIN
16mm / U-matic / VHS
Rediscovery - Art Media - Spanish Series
Color (I) (SPANISH)
Presents the wide range of technical and expressive possibilities inherent in watercolor painting. Shows the use of the simplest materials as well as the more costly and professional items.
Fine Arts; Foreign Language
Dist - AIMS **Prod** - ACI 1967

Watercolor 15 MIN
U-matic / VHS
Expressions
(I J)
#130 purchase, $25 rental, $75 self dub
Designed to interest fifth through ninth graders in art. Emphasizes creativity and experimentation. Features watercolorist Susan Hansen demonstrating technique. Sixth in an 18 part series.
Fine Arts
Dist - GPN

Watercolor 14 MIN
16mm / U-matic / VHS
Rediscovery - Art Media - French Series
Color (I)
Presents the wide range of technical and expressive possibilities inherent in watercolor painting. Shows the use of the simplest materials as well as the more costly and professional items.
Fine Arts; Foreign Language
Dist - AIMS **Prod** - ACI 1967

Watercolor 30 MIN
U-matic
Media and Methods of the Artist Series
Color (H C A)
Demonstrates how an artist approaches the difficult medium of watercolors.
Fine Arts
Dist - TVOTAR **Prod** - TVOTAR 1971

Watercolor 15 MIN
U-matic / VHS / 16mm
Rediscovery - Art Media Series
Color (I)
LC FIA67-1523
Illustrates the characteristics of watercolor as a painting medium and the many ways in which it may be used from simple pan colors to a wide palette of tube colors. Emphasizes the importance of personal vision in the development of an individual style.
Fine Arts
Dist - AIMS **Prod** - ACI 1967

Watercolor 1 60 MIN
BETA / VHS
Color
Looks at the moods that can be created with watercolors, using a waterfall and a rustic lighthouse to demonstrate.
Fine Arts
Dist - HOMEAF **Prod** - HOMEAF

Watercolor 2 60 MIN
BETA / VHS
Color
Illustrates what can be accomplished with watercolors. Demonstrates with variety of pictures and patterns.
Fine Arts
Dist - HOMEAF **Prod** - HOMEAF

Watercolor and collage 50 MIN
VHS
Color (J H C G)
$39.95 purchase _ #CPC783V
Illustrates how collage is applied with watercolor to create small abstract paintings. Demonstrates a watercolor and collage landscape painting from conception to finished work. Features Gerald Brommer who teaches a five - step creation process - paint, collage, paint again, recollage and paint again.
Fine Arts
Dist - CAMV

Watercolor fast and loose 60 MIN
VHS / BETA
Color (G)
$29.95 purchase
Observes watercolorist Ron Ranson who demonstrates some fast, loose and fun painting. Creates five outdoor scenes using only seven colors and three brushes. Produced by North Light.
Fine Arts
Dist - ARTSAM

Watercolor in action - responding to nature 60 MIN
VHS
Watercolor painting with artist Gerald F Brommer series
Color (G A)
$39.95 purchase _ #CP - 780
Shares the watercolor techniques of author, educator and artist Gerald Brommer. Shows how to capture the mood and feeling of a landscape. Focuses on a lighthouse in combination with rocks, cypress trees, the ocean and shoreline. Finishes the painting in the studio, enhancing the details and values.
Fine Arts
Dist - CRYSP **Prod** - CRYSP 1991

Watercolor methods 18 MIN
VHS
Art is ... video series
Color (G)
$29.95 purchase _ #CPC884V - F
Provides demonstrations of wet - on - wet, controlled wash and drybrush techniques using a variety of papers and materials to create watercolor paintings, with a landscape done as an example. Discusses the use of watercolor methods, composition, color, visual impact and media combinations for creative experimentation. Part of a five - part series. Videos are also available in a set.
Fine Arts
Dist - CAMV

Watercolor Painting - Abstract Designs from Nature with Edward Betts 19 MIN
16mm / U-matic / VHS
Watercolor Painting Series
Color
LC 73-700684
Watches Edward Betts as he makes several pencil drawings at a quarry. Shows how he develops one of his drawings into an acrylic watercolor in his studio.
Fine Arts
Dist - CORF **Prod** - PERSPF 1973

Watercolor painting basics 60 MIN
VHS
Color (H C G T A)
$29.95 purchase _ #S00115
Teaches the basics of watercolor painting. Covers topics including supplies, drawing, composition, and washes. Emphasizes the unique characteristics of watercolors.
Fine Arts
Dist - UILL **Prod** - UILL

Watercolor Painting - Imaginative Designs with Alex Ross 20 MIN
U-matic / VHS / 16mm
Watercolor Painting Series
Color
Presents Alex Ross demonstrating how he creates arresting patterns of vivid color and how he uses acrylic paint on a textured media board.
Fine Arts
Dist - CORF **Prod** - PERSPF 1973

Watercolor painting - Part 1 - waterfall and lighthouse 60 MIN
VHS
Color (G)
$29.95 purchase _ #S00116
Demonstrates watercolor painting techniques as applied to two paintings, one of a waterfall and another of a lighthouse.
Fine Arts
Dist - UILL

Watercolor Painting Series
Watercolor Painting - Abstract Designs from Nature with Edward Betts 19 MIN
Watercolor Painting - Imaginative Designs with Alex Ross 20 MIN
Dist - CORF

Watercolor painting with artist Gerald F Brommer series
Presents two lessons which share the watercolor techniques of author, educator and artist Gerald Brommer. Discusses location painting and finishing up paintings in the studio.
Exploring watercolor - from location to studio 60 MIN
Watercolor in action - responding to nature 60 MIN
Dist - CRYSP **Prod** - CRYSP

Watercolor pure and simple 60 MIN
BETA / VHS
Color (G)
$29.95 purchase
Observes watercolorist Ron Ranson who demonstrates ideas and techniques for beginning artists. Illustrates wet - into - wet techniques, color mixing and correcting composition faults. Produced by North Light.
Fine Arts
Dist - ARTSAM

Watercolor Society, The/Lou Harrison 30 MIN
U-matic / VHS
Kaleidoscope Series
Color
Fine Arts
Dist - SCCOE **Prod** - KTEHTV

Watercolor Symbols - Rocks, Puddles and Weeds 55 MIN
VHS
Tony Couch Watercolor Series
Color (I)
$39.95 purchase _ #VC - - 728
Demonstrates watercolor symbols for painting rocks, puddles and weeds and the 'spatter' technique. Part of a four - part series on watercolor techniques by Tony Couch.
Fine Arts
Dist - CRYSP **Prod** - CRYSP

Watercolor Symbols - Trees and Water 55 MIN
VHS
Tony Couch Watercolor Series
Color (I)
$39.95 purchase _ #VC - - 727
Demonstrates watercolor symbols for painting trees and water and the 'spatter' technique. Part of a four - part series on watercolor techniques by Tony Couch.
Fine Arts
Dist - CRYSP **Prod** - CRYSP

Watercolors in Action 12 MIN
U-matic / VHS / 16mm
Color (J)
Explains the method used by many contemporary watercolorists. Focuses on the method of holding the brush and the effect of its skillful manipulation on paper. Explains mixing tints, use of dry brush, neutralizing a color, laying dark values over light and obtaining color perspective and depth.
Fine Arts
Dist - IFB **Prod** - IFB 1953

Watercolour painting with Jason Partner
VHS
Color (G)

PdS19.95 purchase _ #A4-ARG18
Demonstrates mixing and wash techniques of watercolor paintiing, and teaches how to show perspective, atmosphere, and texture through the application of color and water. Features Jason Partner, who demonstrates how to paint a coastal scene in the classic English style.
Fine Arts
Dist - AVP **Prod** - ARGUS

Water/Contemplating 12 MIN
16mm
Color; Silent (C)
$400.00
Experimental film by Barry Gerson.
Fine Arts
Dist - AFA **Prod** - AFA 1976

Watercress 13 MIN
16mm
Color (A)
$20.00 rental
Offers episodes in alternative lifestyles. Produced by Coni Beeson.
Fine Arts
Dist - CANCIN

Watercress line 14 MIN
VHS
Color (H C G)
Records the campaign to save the Mid - Hants Railway in Great Britain. Shows the line as it once was, the struggle to raise money to purchase the line and the work that culminated in the ceremonial reopening.
Geography - World; Social Science
Dist - VIEWTH **Prod** - VIEWTH

Waterfall 3 MIN
VHS / 16mm
Color (G)
$5.00 rental
Uses found film and stock footage altered by printing, home development and solarization to invoke a feeling of flow and movement to Japanese Koto music.
Fine Arts
Dist - CANCIN **Prod** - STRANC 1967

Waterfalls 9 MIN
VHS
Color (C PRO)
$34.95 purchase _ #193 E 2079
Demonstrates waterfall formation and development, including migration, undercutting and erosion. Teacher's guide provided.
Science - Physical
Dist - WARDS

Waterfalls 10 MIN
VHS
Geology stream table series
Color (H C)
$24.95 purchase _ #S9012
Treats waterfalls in a single - concept format, using models and NASA footage. Part of a 12 - part series on stream tables.
Geography - World; Science - Physical; Social Science
Dist - HUBDSC **Prod** - HUBDSC

Waterfowl 25 MIN
U-matic / VHS / 16mm
Untamed World Series
Color; Mono (J H C A)
$400.00 film, $250.00 video, $50.00 rental
Probes the ways of one group of waterfowl called 'anatidae' which is the family consisting of ducks, geese, and swans.
Geography - World; Science - Natural
Dist - CTV **Prod** - CTV 1972

Waterfowl wilderness 26 MIN
16mm
Audubon wildlife theatre series
Color (I)
Follows the enormous migration flights of waterfowl, battling their way through storms and over mountain ranges, to their nesting place in Canada. Shows each phase of their life from ritualistic courting to the mating and raising of the young.
Geography - World; Science - Natural
Dist - AVEXP **Prod** - AVEXP

Watergate 14 MIN
VHS
Color (J H)
$99.00 purchase _ #08569 - 026
Utilizes authentic footage and interviews that follow events from the break - in to the resignation of Richard Milhous Nixon as President of the United States. Discusses the implications of the downfall of an American president. Includes teacher's guide and library kit.
Biography; Civics and Political Systems; Education; Fine Arts; History - United States
Dist - GA

Watergate
U-matic / VHS / 35mm strip
(J H C)
$97.00 purchase _ #08569 94
Goes behind the scenes for a chronological analysis of Watergate and the events which led up to Nixon's resignation. Highlights the roles of Ehrlichman, Halderman, and John Dean. Features historical photographs and interviews. In 2 parts.
History - United States
Dist - ASPRSS **Prod** - ASPRSS

Watergate - a Constitutional Crisis 30 MIN
U-matic / VHS
American Government Series; 1
Color (C)
Examines the struggle that brought into conflict all three branches of the government. Considers the questions of voting articles of impeachment, and the court states anew that not even the President is above the law.
Civics and Political Systems
Dist - DALCCD **Prod** - DALCCD

The Watergate Affair 29 MIN
U-matic / VHS
Color
Documents the Watergate scandal, which touched the highest offices in the land, caused the resignation of a President, and pushed the call for a new code of conduct and ethics by public officials.
Civics and Political Systems; History - United States
Dist - JOU **Prod** - UPI

The Watergate Hearings 120 MIN
VHS
Summer Of Judgement Series
Color (G)
$90.00 purchase _ #SUJG - 101
Provides an outline of the major events of the Watergate scandal. Includes excerpts from Congressional hearings. Hosted by Charles McDowell. Part one of a two - part series.
Biography; Civics and Political Systems; History - United States
Dist - PBS **Prod** - WETATV 1983

Watergate Morality 29 MIN
VHS / 16mm
Washington Connection Series
Color (G)
$55.00 rental _ #WACO - 120
Civics and Political Systems; Social Science
Dist - PBS **Prod** - NPACT

Watergate series
Covers the Watergate Affair in a series of five programs. Focuses on the events that led up to Richard Nixon's resignation in 1974 and features the the investigators of the Watergate Affair and those convicted of Watergate crimes.

Break in 50 MIN
Cover up 50 MIN
Impeachment 50 MIN
Massacre 50 MIN
Scapegoat 50 MIN
Dist - BBCENE

Watergate - the real story 90 MIN
VHS
Color (J H)
$21.95 purchase _ #7031V
Gives an account of the crime that toppled a United States President and changed the course of American history. Includes interviews with key Watergate figures and newly uncovered information. Mike Wallace hosts.
Biography; Civics and Political Systems; History - United States
Dist - KNOWUN **Prod** - KNOWUN 1993

Waterground 16 MIN
16mm
Color (H C A)
LC 78-700773
Looks at the owner of a family - operated, water - powered gristmill in North Carolina. Shows his skepticism of technological advancements as he comments about mass - production and laments the passing of an era when the small farmer could thrive.
Agriculture; Geography - United States; Sociology
Dist - APPAL **Prod** - APPAL 1977

The Waterhole 9 MIN
16mm / VHS
Color (I J H A)
$195.00, $160.00 purchase, $30.00 rental _ #8042
Documents the dependency of life on its environment - in this case a waterhole in the desert of Central Australia.
Science - Natural
Dist - AIMS **Prod** - EDMI 1984

Waterhole 25 MIN
U-matic / VHS / 16mm
Untamed World Series
Color; Mono (J H C A)
$400.00 film, $250.00 video, $50.00 rental
Looks at the cooperative nature of animals who share the common threat of roaming, hunting predatory creatures. The waterhole is their source of sustenance and security.
Geography - World; Science - Natural
Dist - CTV **Prod** - CTV 1970

The Waterhole 9 MIN
VHS / U-matic
Color
Depicts a day, dawn - to - dusk, at a water hole in Central Australia. Reveals changing moods as sun, wind and time trigger changes in animal life visiting the water hole.
Geography - World; History - World; Science - Natural
Dist - EDMI **Prod** - AFTS 1984

Waterholes 25 MIN
16mm / U-matic / VHS
Untamed Frontier Series
Color; Mono (J H C A)
$400.00 film, $250.00 video, $50.00 rental
Gives an account of the origin, life cycle and importance of waterholes in east Africa.
Geography - World; Science - Natural
Dist - CTV **Prod** - CTV 1975

Watering 30 MIN
U-matic / VHS
Home Gardener with John Lenanton Series Lesson 12; Lesson 12
Color (C A)
Discusses the varieties of watering techniques. Explains water movement and soil penetration.
Agriculture
Dist - CDTEL **Prod** - COAST

Watering Houseplants 30 MIN
U-matic / VHS
Even You Can Grow Houseplants Series
Color
Discusses the watering requirements of houseplants.
Agriculture
Dist - MDCPB **Prod** - WGTV

Waterloo Farmers 28 MIN
U-matic / VHS / 16mm
Color (J)
LC 83-700185
Juxtaposes the old and new order Mennonites. Shows their differing beliefs in their methods of farming, with the old order using nonmechanized methods and the new order using modern, mechanized methods. Asks whether a compromise will have to be reached between the two groups.
Agriculture; Sociology
Dist - BULFRG **Prod** - NFBC 1976

Watermelon Etching and Melon Carving 7 MIN
VHS / U-matic
Color (PRO)
Shows how to make a template to trace a pattern on a watermelon and fill the etching with cream cheese for contrast. Shows how to use masking tape as a guide for uniform zig - zag melon cuts.
Home Economics; Industrial and Technical Education
Dist - CULINA **Prod** - CULINA

Watermelon Man 97 MIN
16mm
Color
Tells how a bigoted white suburbanite turns black overnight. Stars Godfrey Cambridge.
Fine Arts
Dist - TWYMAN **Prod** - CPC 1970

The Watermelon Man
BETA / VHS
Color
Presents a poignant comedy about a white bigot who turns permanently black, starring Godfrey Cambridge and Estelle Parsons.
Fine Arts; Sociology
Dist - GA **Prod** - GA

Watermelons - equivalent fractions 10 MIN
VHS / 16mm
Meeting fractions series
Color (I J H G)
$195.00, $125.00 purchase, $50.00 rental _ #8214
Looks at watermelon magically cut by an invisible hand demonstrating the segmenting of the whole into equivalent parts. Part of a series developed by the National Council of Teachers of Mathematics.
Mathematics
Dist - AIMS **Prod** - DAVFMS 1990

Watermen and Lighthouses of the Chesapeake Bay 13 MIN
VHS / U-matic
Color (I J)
Serves as a supplement to a geography unit in eastern coastal states. Explains how fish and shellfish of Chesapeake Bay are caught and transported.
Geography - United States; Science - Natural
Dist - ENJOY **Prod** - ENJOY 1981

Waterplay 30 MIN
U-matic / VHS
Learning through Play Series
Color (H C A)
Discusses waterplay. Presents five illustrations, including bathtub play and water table play.
Psychology
Dist - UTORMC **Prod** - UTORMC 1980

Waterplay, Pt 1 12 MIN
16mm
Vignette Series
B&W (T)
Shows boys playing with water and such materials as funnels, basters, hoses and siphons at hilltop head start center.
Education; Guidance and Counseling; Psychology; Sociology
Dist - EDC **Prod** - EDS 1970

A Waterproof Arboreal Frog 10 MIN
U-matic / VHS / 16mm
Aspects of Animal Behavior Series
Color (H C A)
Discusses Phyllomedusa sauvagei, a South American tree frog which lives under conditions of heat and prolonged drought by virtue of a tolerance of high temperatures, excretion of solid nitrogenous waste and a waterproof coating of wax on its skin.
Science - Natural
Dist - UCEMC **Prod** - UCLA 1976

Waterproofing the Basement 30 MIN
BETA / VHS
This Old House, Pt 2 - Suburban '50s Series
Color
Demonstrates waterproofing a basement and installing a wood stove, a free - standing chimney, windows and doors.
Industrial and Technical Education; Sociology
Dist - CORF **Prod** - WGBHTV

Water's Edge, the, Pt 1 - the Unseen World 28 MIN
16mm
Nature of Things Series
Color (C)
LC 78-701670
Focuses on the interrelationships of animal and vegetable life that exist in a freshwater pond.
Science - Natural
Dist - FLMLIB **Prod** - CANBC 1978

Water's Edge, the, Pt 2 - the Silent Explosion 28 MIN
16mm
Nature of Things Series
Color (C)
LC 78-701671
Studies the creatures that have been lying dormant all winter in and around a freshwater pond.
Science - Natural
Dist - FLMLIB **Prod** - CANBC 1978

Waters from the Mountain 20 MIN
16mm
Color
LC 74-705934
Shows water supply forecasting and snow surveys. Emphasizes the need for such information and how it is used by all segments of society in the West. Traces water from snowmelt on the mountain to corps and other uses in the valley.
Science - Natural; Science - Physical
Dist - USNAC **Prod** - USSCS 1964

The Waters of the Earth 30 MIN
U-matic / VHS
Oceanus - the Marine Environment Series Lesson 4
Color
Describes the remarkable properties of water. Discusses the physical conditions of the sea in terms of salinity, temperature, density and pressure. Looks at water - sampling instruments and techniques used on modern research vessels.
Science - Physical
Dist - CDTEL **Prod** - SCCON
SCCON

Waters of Yosemite 9 MIN
U-matic / VHS / 16mm
Wilderness Series
Color (I A)
LC FIA67-687
Presents a poetic interpretation of running water.
Geography - United States; Science - Natural
Dist - PHENIX **Prod** - PFP 1967

Water's Way 7 MIN
U-matic / VHS / 16mm
Color (P I)
Presents an introduction to our greatest natural resource, water. Features a little boy and a water drop who guides the boy through the basic story of water.
Science - Natural; Social Science
Dist - PHENIX **Prod** - ROMAF 1983

Watershed management series
Managing riparian areas on forest lands 28 MIN
Dist - OSUSF

Waterskier's Guide to Excellence 30 MIN
VHS
(H C A)
$39.95 purchase _ #BM200V
Discusses how to improve slalom water skiing techniques. describes slalom rules, cutting, body positioning, changing speed, and turns.
Physical Education and Recreation
Dist - CAMV **Prod** - CAMV
SEVVID

Waterskiing for Kids 30 MIN
VHS / U-matic
Superstar Sports Tapes Series
Color
Discusses equipment, techniques and dock practice useful for teaching waterskiing to children. Includes signals, safety and crossing the wake. Stars Mike Suyderhoud.
Health and Safety; Physical Education and Recreation
Dist - TRASS **Prod** - TRASS

Waterskiing Fundmentals 40 MIN
VHS
(H C A)
$29.95 purchase _ #MXS229V
Explains proper technique and form in waterskiing. Discusses slalom skiing, maneuvering, body angles, jumping, and more.
Physical Education and Recreation
Dist - CAMV

Waterskiing with Brett Wing
VHS
Color (G)
$39.80 purchase _ #0397
Teaches all facets of waterskiing. Features Brett Wing.
Physical Education and Recreation
Dist - SEVVID

Watersmith 32 MIN
16mm
Color (C)
$504.00
Experimental film by Will Hindle.
Fine Arts
Dist - AFA **Prod** - AFA 1969

Watersong 13 MIN
16mm
Color
LC 77-701459
Considers the possibilities for vacationing in Missouri by showing the availability and abundance of lakes, rivers and streams within the state.
Geography - United States
Dist - MODT **Prod** - MODT 1977

Waterstart
VHS
Color (G)
$39.90 purchase _ #0734
Uses innovative methodology and systems in teaching boardsailing to allow the learner to proceed at an individual pace.
Physical Education and Recreation
Dist - SEVVID

Watertime 5 MIN
16mm
Color
LC 77-702701
Presents an animated film portraying the excitement and invigoration of sailing, kayaking, canoeing and swimming.
Fine Arts; Industrial and Technical Education; Physical Education and Recreation
Dist - CANFDC **Prod** - GORDND

Waterwheel Village 14 MIN
16mm / U-matic / VHS
Color (P I)
LC 77-700726
Consists of a story of two brothers who are delighted with their discovery of a miniature water wheel village until they learn that it was built by a girl. Emphasizes cooperation and respect for the ability of others regardless of sex.
Guidance and Counseling; Literature and Drama; Sociology
Dist - ALTSUL **Prod** - ATPPRO 1977

Waterworks 30 MIN
VHS
Bodymatters series
Color (H C A)
PdS65 purchase
Explains how the body makes use of water. Part of a series of 26 30-minute videos on various systems of the human body.
Science - Natural
Dist - BBCENE

Waterworx - a clear day and no memories 6 MIN
16mm
Color (G)
$30.00 rental
Uses Wallace Stevens' ironic and enigmatic poem, A Clear Day and No Memories, to address the phenomenon of the waterworks in the Beaches area of Toronto. Fuses the poem and imagery so that the film provides an effective reading of it. Hancox believes the waterworks is not merely a filtration plant but serves as a kind of temporal metaphor.
Fine Arts; Literature and Drama
Dist - CANCIN **Prod** - HANCXR 1982

Watts made Out of Thread 26 MIN
U-matic / VHS / 16mm
Insight Series
Color; B&W (J H A) (SPANISH)
LC 70-702640
A theological comedy of redemption in which a guiltridden ghetto exploiter meets a Negro Christ while dying.
Psychology; Religion and Philosophy
Dist - PAULST **Prod** - PAULST 1968

Watts made Out of Thread 29 MIN
VHS / U-matic
Color (J A) (SPANISH)
Dramatizes the story of Eddie who learns a lesson from God about honesty and admission of guilt.
Fine Arts; Religion and Philosophy
Dist - SUTHRB **Prod** - SUTHRB

Watts Tower Theatre Workshop 28 MIN
Videoreel / VT2
Synergism - in Today's World Series
Color
Fine Arts; Sociology
Dist - PBS **Prod** - KCET

Watts Towers Theatre Workshop 28 MIN
16mm
Color (H C A)
LC 70-703297
Examines the Watts Towers Theater Workshop which consists of black teenagers from the Los Angeles Watts ghetto, and explains that its purpose is to show entertainment by, for and about people living in the ghetto.
Fine Arts; History - United States; Psychology; Social Science
Dist - IU **Prod** - KCET 1969

Wattsie 11 MIN
16mm
Color (H C)
Focuses on the difficulties encountered by a conscientious assistant principal who is working under a likable but inefficient administrator.
Education
Dist - OSUMPD **Prod** - OSUMPD 1961

Watunna 24 MIN
16mm / VHS
Color (H C G)
$500.00.00, $295.00 purchase, $45.00 rental _ #11396, #37907
Uses animation to depict five stories from the creation myths of the Yekuana Indians inhabiting the rainforests of Venezuela. Explores the genesis of evil, night, sexuality, fire and food using metamorphosing designs drawn in part from ancient Yekuana art. Produced and animated by Stacey Steers.
Geography - World; Religion and Philosophy; Social Science; Sociology
Dist - UCEMC

The Wave 46 MIN
16mm / VHS
Color (J)
$750.00, $79.00 purchase _ #817 - 9001
Recreates the classroom experiment in which a high school teacher formed his own 'Reich' to deomonstrate why the German people could so willingly embrace Nazism. Raises critical questions regarding individualism and conformity. Asks how peer pressure usurps individual rights, and when dedication to a group crosses the line from loyalty to fanaticism.
Education; Mathematics; Psychology; Sociology
Dist - FI **Prod** - EMBASY 1984
EMBASY

The Wave - a Japanese Folk Tale 9 MIN
U-matic / VHS / 16mm
Color (P I)
LC FIA68-2117
Presents the Japanese tale of how a grandfather saved the lives of the villagers from drowning by luring them to the mountain top.
English Language; Literature and Drama
Dist - PHENIX **Prod** - FA 1968

The Wave - ecstatic dance for body and soul 35 MIN
VHS
Color (G)
$24.95 purchase _ #V - WAVE
Features Gabrielle Roth who reveals five powerful universal rhythms to be used for relaxation, breathing, meditation and surrendering into one's own ritual trance - dance.
Religion and Philosophy
Dist - PACSPI

Wave Jumping 6 MIN
VHS / 16mm
Color
Shows boardsailing in Hawaii. Includes music.
Fine Arts; Geography - United States; Geography - World; Physical Education and Recreation
Dist - OFFSHR **Prod** - OFFSHR

The Wave - Mechanical Model 10 MIN
U-matic
Structure of the Atom Series
Color (H C)
Eplains the behaviour of multi - electron atoms and multi - atom compounds by establishing the wave - mechanical model of atomic structure.
Science; Science - Physical
Dist - TVOTAR **Prod** - TVOTAR 1984

The Wave Model 10 MIN
U-matic
Wave Particle Duality Series
Color (H C)
Examines the developments of Huygen's wave model of light behaviour, Young's theory of light interference and Foucault's observations on the speed of light.
Science; Science - Physical
Dist - TVOTAR **Prod** - TVOTAR 1984

Wave motion 11 MIN
VHS
Color; PAL (P I J H)
Investigates what a wave is, how to see a wave and how to think about the concept. Shows simple examples. Observes wave phenomenon from various viewpoints - time waves, space waves and propagating waves. Uses pendulums to help understand the concept of the sea wave.
Science - Physical
Dist - VIEWTH **Prod** - VIEWTH

Wave Motion - Diffraction 8 MIN
U-matic / VHS / 16mm
B&W (C)
LC 70-712275
Demonstrates diffraction patterns formed when ripples spread beyond the barriers placed to limit wave fronts, and the related patterns formed when narrow apertures and obstacles are placed in the path of a beam of light. True images are obtained by applying the Schlieren technique to the optical system of the ripple tank. Included are views of optical diffraction patterns.
Science - Physical
Dist - IFB **Prod** - GATEEF 1971

Wave Motion - Interference 7 MIN
U-matic / VHS / 16mm
B&W (H C)
LC 73-712276
Illustrates a true image of wave patterns through the use of a ripple tank and employing the Schlieren technique. Explains the principles underlying Thomas Young's interference experiment.
Science - Physical
Dist - IFB **Prod** - GATEEF 1971

A Wave of awakening 23 MIN
VHS / U-matic / 16mm
Color (H)
$240.00, $290.00 purchase, $50.00 rental
Features high school students from North America sharing their concerns, hopes and positive actions for a healthy environment. Pictures positive role models and committment to the Earth. Produced by Media Network Society.
Science - Natural
Dist - NDIM

Wave - Particle Duality 22 MIN
U-matic / VHS / 16mm
Color (H C)
LC 77-700599
Traces the development of the two contrasting theories of light which led to the discovery of the wave - like properties of matter. First released in England.
Science - Physical
Dist - IFB **Prod** - EFVA 1974

Wave - particle duality 60 MIN
VHS
Concepts in science - physics series
Color; PAL (J H)
PdS29.50 purchase
Traces the development of the various theories on the behavior of light, from the concepts of the early Greeks to the proven models of today. Contains six ten - minute concepts - The Particle Model; The Wave Model; The Electromagnetic Model; The Quantum Idea; Photons; and Matter Waves. Part of a five - part series.
Science; Science - Physical
Dist - EMFVL **Prod** - TVOTAR

Wave Particle Duality Series

The Electromagnetic Model	10 MIN
Matter Waves	10 MIN
The Particle Model	10 MIN
Photons	10 MIN
The Quantum Idea	10 MIN
The Wave Model	10 MIN

Dist - TVOTAR

Wave - Powered Desalination 13 MIN
U-matic / VHS / 16mm
One Second Before Sunrise - Search for Solutions, Program 1 Series
Color (J)
$110.00, $85.00 purchase, $25.00 rental
Depicts Dr Michael Pleass' low - cost desalination device, which uses wave power. Suggests that the device could be used by coastline communities for creating supplies of cheap, clean drinking water.
Geography - World; Industrial and Technical Education; Science - Natural; Science - Physical; Social Science
Dist - BULFRG **Prod** - HCOM 1990

Wave Soldering, Rework and Resource Training 150 MIN
U-matic
Electronics Manufacturing - Components, Assembly and Soldering 'Series
Color (IND)
Discusses wave and drag soldering, pre - and post - cleaning operations, inspection and rework, and resource training, including training certified operators, workmanship standards and safety.
Business and Economics; Industrial and Technical Education
Dist - INTECS **Prod** - INTECS

Wave Velocities, Despersion, and the Omega - Beta Diagram 28 MIN
Videoreel / VHS
B&W
Considers traveling waves and the way they propagate through transmission systems. Can be used in connection with lectures on phase velocity, group velocity, backward waves and dispersion. Concentrates on visualization of the concepts through animation and experiment.
Science - Physical
Dist - EDC **Prod** - NCEEF

Wave Velocities, Dispersion and the Omega - Beta Diagram 28 MIN
16mm
National Committee for Electrical Engineering Film Series
B&W (IND)
LC 74-703369
Presents Theodore van Duzer who discusses traveling waves and the way in which they propagate through transmission systems, emphasizing visualization of the concepts through animation and experiment.
Industrial and Technical Education; Science - Physical
Dist - EDC **Prod** - EDS 1969

Waveguide Fabrication Techniques, Pt 1 46 MIN
U-matic / VHS
Integrated Optics Series
Color (C)
Discusses methods for fabricating waveguides in passive (non - light emitting) materials such as deposited thin films, ion bombardment, and ion migration, and waveguide fabrication in semiconductors such as heteroepitaxial growth of gallum aluminum arsenide.
Science - Physical
Dist - UDEL **Prod** - UDEL

Waveguide Fabrication Techniques, Pt 2 44 MIN
U-matic / VHS
Integrated Optics Series
Color (C)
Discusses proton bombarded waveguides in semiconductors, electro - optic waveguides, and methods of defining the shape of channel waveguides.
Science - Physical
Dist - UDEL **Prod** - UDEL

Waveguide Plumbing 26 MIN
16mm
B&W
LC 74-705935
Covers the 90 degree E and H band in rectangular waveguides by explaining the effect on the fields within the guide. Discusses twists, flexible waveguide and improper bends. (Kinescope).
Industrial and Technical Education
Dist - USNAC **Prod** - USAF

Waveguide to Waveguide Couplers and Modulators 40 MIN
VHS / U-matic
Integrated Optics Series
Color (C)
Describes the use of closely spaced dual channel waveguides as directional couplers and electro - optic switches and modulators. Theoretical models are compared with experimental results.
Science - Physical
Dist - UDEL **Prod** - UDEL

Waveguides 29 MIN
16mm
B&W
LC 74-705936
Explains the inadequacy of transmission lines, other than waveguides, at microwave frequencies. Stresses factors determining the power handling capability and the frequency handling capability of waveguides. (Kinescope).
Industrial and Technical Education; Science - Physical
Dist - USNAC **Prod** - USAF

Wavelength 45 MIN
16mm
Color (C)
$1400.00
Experimental film by Michael Snow.
Fine Arts
Dist - AFA **Prod** - AFA 1967

Wavelines I 11 MIN
16mm
Color
LC 79-700345
Presents four visual - musical compositions produced with a Moog synthesizer, an oscilloscope and acoustic sounds.
Fine Arts
Dist - MAGMUS **Prod** - MAGMUS 1978

Wavelines II 8 MIN
16mm
Color
LC 80-700269
Contains three visual - musical compositions, produced visually with a Moog synthesizer connected to a filmed oscilloscope and musically with synthesizers and acoustic instruments.
Fine Arts
Dist - WEID **Prod** - WEID 1979

Waves 25 MIN
U-matic / VHS
Oceanography series
Color (H C)
$250.00 purchase _ #HP - 5741C
Covers two significant oceanographic issues - how wave energy propagates across oceans and what happens when waves hit shore and dissipate their energy. Shows what kind of scientific devices are used to measure wave height and speed, what offshore changes are caused by tides rather than waves, and how data is collected to determine wave configurations and water velocity. Part of a series on oceanography.
Science - Physical
Dist - CORF **Prod** - BBCTV 1989

Waves 26 MIN
16mm / U-matic / VHS
Color (I)
LC 77-703385
Presents the sights and sounds of the sea in recording the moods of the ocean and its coastal shallows.
Geography - World; Science - Natural; Science - Physical
Dist - IFB **Prod** - BBCTV 1977

Waves 30 MIN
16mm / U-matic / VHS
Mechanical Universe Series
Color (C A)
Shows how Newton, with an analysis of simple harmonic motion and a stroke of genius, extended mechanics to the propagation of sound.

Science - Physical
Dist - FI **Prod** - ANNCPB

Waves and Energy 11 MIN
U-matic / VHS / 16mm
Color (I J) (SPANISH ARABIC)
Shows how sound, radio, light and heat waves are made and their characteristics. Shows how waves carry energy from one plane to another and how waves are reflected.
Science - Physical
Dist - EBEC **Prod** - EBEC 1961

Waves, coastlines and beaches 18 MIN
VHS
Color (J H C)
$39.95 purchase _ #IV107
Visits rugged coastlines, barrier islands, spits, tombolos, wave cut terraces, sea stacks, beaches to study the geologic processes where ocean meets land. Uses graphics and animation to go below the surface of the water to show what happens offshore under water.
Science - Natural; Science - Physical
Dist - INSTRU

Waves in Fluids 33 MIN
16mm / U-matic / VHS
Fluid Mechanics Series
Color (H C)
Demonstrates concepts in one - dimensional wave motion using a water channel, a flume and shock tubes. Covers particle motion in small amplitude waves, steepening and breaking of compression waves, surge waves and hydraulic jumps, sound waves and shock waves, shock diffractin and shock heating.
Science - Physical
Dist - EBEC **Prod** - NCFMF 1966

Waves of Change 29 MIN
U-matic
Pike on Language Series
Color
Discusses the belief that language changes through 'waves' which flow and merge.
English Language
Dist - UMITV **Prod** - UMITV 1977

Waves of Change / Culture of the Individual 34 MIN
VHS / U-matic
Focus on Change Series
Color
Sociology
Dist - DELTAK **Prod** - TVOTAR

Waves of Revolution 30 MIN
16mm
B&W
Presents an underground record of an historic Indian populist movement, the anti - government Bihar Movement in India, which was led by Shri Jayaprakash Narayan (JP), from March, 1974, to March, 1975.
Civics and Political Systems; Geography - World; History - World
Dist - ICARUS **Prod** - ICARUS 1976

Waves, Vibrations and Atoms 10 MIN
U-matic
Chemistry Videotapes Series
Color
Deomstrates fundamentals of wave behavior. Relates standing wave on a guitar, drum and bell to atomic orbitals.
Science - Physical
Dist - UMITV **Prod** - UMITV

Wavesailing women
VHS
Color (G)
$29.80 purchase _ #0102
Illustrates wave jumping by boardsailors in Hawaii. Features Rhoda Smith, Karla Weber and 14 other women.
Physical Education and Recreation
Dist - SEVVID

Waveshaping Networks 34 MIN
16mm
B&W
LC 74-705937
Shows how to determine the amount of capacitor charge applied to an RC network. Discusses differentiated and integrated waves. Gives definitions for short, medium and long time constant circuits and shows how the waveforms for each circuit can be recognized. (Kinescope).
Industrial and Technical Education; Science - Physical
Dist - USNAC **Prod** - USAF

Wax and Grease Silicone Removal 8 MIN
VHS / 16mm
(A PRO)
$54.75 purchase _ #AB158
Discusses the reasons for using wax, grease, and silicone removing solvent. Shows application procedures.
Industrial and Technical Education
Dist - RMIBHF **Prod** - RMIBHF

Wax experiments 3 MIN
16mm
Color tint (G)
$16.50 rental
Represents the different ways Fischinger used sliced wax from a sequence of pure wax imagery to positive and negative imagery and thin line animation superimposed over a wax background.
Fine Arts
Dist - CANCIN **Prod** - FISCHF 1923

WAX - Or the discovery of television among the bees 85 MIN
VHS / 16mm
Color (G)
$490.00 purchase, $125.00 rental
Presents the bizarre fictional story of Jacob Maker, weapons - guidance designer and committed beekeeper, whose bees drill a hole in his head and insert a television. Continues with Jacob entering an hallucinatory alternative reality due to the television's supernatural images that control his will. The first full length film broadcast over the Internet. Produced by David Blair.
Computer Science; Literature and Drama; Sociology
Dist - FIRS
BALFOR

Waxing and Trail Sense 29 MIN
VHS / U-matic
Cross Country Ski School Series
Color
LC 82-706435
Examines the art and theory behind waxing cross country skis and provides information and tips about clothing, equipment, trail safety and how to prepare for a cross country ski trip.
Physical Education and Recreation
Dist - PBS **Prod** - VTETV 1981

The Waxing of Complete Dentures 56 MIN
U-matic
Color (C)
Compares the anatomic features of a dentate dental cast and edenate dental cast. It demonstrates the technical procedures for accomplishing the proper anatomic features of the complete denture wax up.
Health and Safety; Science - Natural
Dist - UOKLAH **Prod** - UOKLAH 1982

Waxing Technique for Resin - Veneered Fixed Bridges 36 MIN
16mm
Color
LC 76-701545
Covers anterior and posterior copying construction.
Science
Dist - USNAC **Prod** - USVA 1975

Waxworks 15 MIN
16mm
Color (P I)
Reveals that when the Graham children and Alice the chimp visit the wax museum, they have an opportunity to foil a robbery.
Literature and Drama
Dist - LUF **Prod** - LUF 1978

Way back home 81 MIN
VHS
B&W (G)
$19.95 purchase
Features characters from a 1932 radio show in Down East comedy situations with humorist Seth Parker - Phillips Lord.
Fine Arts; History - United States; Literature and Drama
Dist - NEFILM

A Way back - redefining masculinity 21 MIN
BETA / VHS / U-matic
Men in crisis series
Color (G)
$280.00 purchase _ #803.5
Portrays one man's painful journey through addiction and recovery and on to important but difficult choices that pointed him toward improved self - esteem, wholeness and integration. Emphasizes the importance of men's process groups and their role in providing a safe setting for feedback and new behaviors. Part of a five - part series on men in crisis.
Health and Safety; Psychology; Sociology
Dist - CONMED

Way Down East 119 MIN
16mm
B&W
Portrays the story of Anna, a country girl tricked into a fake marriage by a city playboy who deserts her when she becomes pregnant. Shows her being ostracized for being an unwed mother and being forced to take refuge as a servant girl, yet finding ultimate happiness with a young man who has befriended her. Stars Lillian Gish. Directed by D W Griffith.
Fine Arts
Dist - KILLIS **Prod** - GFITH 1920
KINOIC
REELIM

Way down east (the rescue) 14 MIN
16mm
Film study extracts series
B&W (J)
Presents an excerpt from the 1920 motion picture Way Down East. Tells how Anna gets lost in a blizzard and is swept perilously close to the edge of a waterfall. Directed by D W Griffith.
Fine Arts
Dist - FI **Prod** - UNKNWN

A Way for Diana 14 MIN
16mm
Color
LC 79-715511
Presents a reading motivation program which shows a city girl discovering new worlds through reading in the library.
English Language; Guidance and Counseling
Dist - MALIBU **Prod** - MALIBU 1972

The Way I Remember it 15 MIN
VHS / U-matic
Reading for a Reason Series no 7
Color (J)
LC 83-706578
Uses a dramatic approach to reading and understanding expository texts. Illustrates strategies for studying texts in preparing for written tests, including underlining main ideas, taking notes, visualizing, asking questions, paraphrasing, discussing and reviewing.
Education; English Language
Dist - AITECH **Prod** - WETN 1983

The Way I See it 8 MIN
16mm
Color
Uses animation to point out the differences in how people perceive, focusing on the themes of reading readiness, art and working together. Follows an artist and a house painter as they struggle through a see - saw battle in which each attempts to do the other's job better.
Guidance and Counseling; Psychology; Sociology
Dist - ECI **Prod** - ECI

The Way I See it 29 MIN
16mm
Color
Offers the pictorial views of four experienced photographers as they photograph their favorite subjects including people, backyard subjects, the action of sports and the beauty of the landscape.
Industrial and Technical Education
Dist - EKC **Prod** - EKC 1983
UILL

The Way I See it 23 MIN
16mm / U-matic / 8mm cartridge
Color; B&W (H C) (DUTCH)
Presents a discussion about the influence of perceptual differences on supervisor - subordinate relations and job performance.
Business and Economics; Foreign Language; Psychology
Dist - RTBL **Prod** - RTBL 1965

The Way it Can be 23 MIN
16mm
Color
Describes the work of the Learning Research and Development Center of the University of Pittsburgh in the field of adaptive education which strives to shape schools to fit their students rather than shaping children to fit the schools.
Education; History - United States
Dist - UPITTS **Prod** - UPITTS 1975

The Way it is 27 MIN
16mm
Color
LC 77-700328
Depicts a typical day at McGill University, showing undergraduate students, researchers and part - time students engaged in their studies and other activities.
Education
Dist - MCGILU **Prod** - MCGILU 1976

The Way it is - After the Divorce 24 MIN
U-matic / VHS / 16mm
Color (I)
Shows how a family deals with divorce, focusing on the 12 - year - old daughter who relates her experiences and feelings.
Guidance and Counseling; Sociology
Dist - CF **Prod** - NFBC 1983

Way it is series
Apartment and house rental 29 MIN
The Family Budget 29 MIN
Food purchasing 29 MIN

Furniture buying 29 MIN
Home Buying 29 MIN
Home Remodeling 30 MIN
New and used Cars 29 MIN
The Small Loan 29 MIN
Dist - PBS

The Way it was - angling in Newfoundland , 1938 - 1940
VHS
Color (G)
$29.90 purchase _ #0392
Recalls fishing days in the province of Newfoundland, Canada, circa 1938 - 1940.
Geography - World; Physical Education and Recreation; Science - Natural
Dist - SEVVID

The Way Men Behave 30 MIN
U-matic
Herodotus - Father of History Series
Color
Features Dr Theodore Buttrey, classicist professor, as he explores the myth and reality in Herodotus' world.
History - World
Dist - UMITV **Prod** - UMITV 1980

Way of Escape 25 MIN
16mm
Color (C A)
Tells the story of Charles, a young man from mainland China, who chose Christianity instead of communism.
Guidance and Counseling; Religion and Philosophy
Dist - CBFMS **Prod** - CBFMS

A Way of Life 23 MIN
16mm
Color
LC 75-703619
Presents a collage of scenes and action revealing the history and character of Wabash College in Crawfordsville, Indiana.
Education; Geography - United States
Dist - STEEGP **Prod** - WABCOL 1975

A Way of Life 20 MIN
U-matic / VHS / 16mm
Color
Uses dramatic vignettes to realize safety is a way of life. Shows easily overlooked but potentially dangerous situations in automobiles, in the kitchen, canoeing, ashtrays and corrective measures to be used.
Health and Safety
Dist - BCNFL **Prod** - OHMPS 1983

Way of life series
The Colombian way of life 24 MIN
Dist - AIMS

The Way of music 60 MIN
U-matic / VHS
Art of being human series
Color (H C A)
Discusses different aspects of music.
Fine Arts
Dist - FI **Prod** - FI 1978

The Way of Our Fathers 33 MIN
16mm / U-matic / VHS
Color (J)
LC 73-700282
Presents members of several northern California Indian tribes, who depict unique elements of a way of life as it flourished before the imposition of a foreign culture. Explores effects of conventional white - oriented educational programs, such as destruction of Indian self - concepts and loss of cultural heritage and identity. Features native American teachers who discuss historical methods of Indian education and ways that both methods and content might be incorporated in the mainstream of American education.
Geography - United States; Psychology; Social Science; Sociology
Dist - UCEMC **Prod** - HUMBLT 1972

A Way of seeing 20 MIN
VHS / U-matic
Catalyst series
Color (I J H)
$260.00, $310.00 purchase, $50.00 rental
Defines force in physical terms and explores how forces are central to understanding how humans live and how different cultures may have different ways of explaining and interpreting various phenomena. Uses the solar system as a vehicle for exploring people's views; atomic structure and the importance of electromagnetic fields help explain the attraction of opposites.
Science - Physical; Sociology
Dist - NDIM **Prod** - ABCTV 1991

The Way of T'ai Chi Ch'uan - gentle exercise for health and inner peace 60 MIN
VHS
Color (G)
$49.95 purchase
Presents a complete t'ai chi ch'uan exercise program from ancient China. Features Lana Spraker as instructor backed by music from the Findhorn Foundation.
Fine Arts; Physical Education and Recreation; Psychology; Religion and Philosophy
Dist - TAIPRO **Prod** - TAIPRO 1988

The Way of the artist 60 MIN
VHS / U-matic
Art of being human series
Color (H C A)
Discusses man as an artistic being.
Fine Arts
Dist - FI **Prod** - FI 1978

The Way of the Dinosaur 7 MIN
16mm / U-matic / VHS
Color (I)
Explores the history of energy sources. Asks whether we are going the way of the dinosaur.
Social Science
Dist - LUF **Prod** - LUF

Way of the humanist 30 MIN
U-matic / VHS
Art of being human series; Module 1
Color (C)
History - World; Literature and Drama; Religion and Philosophy
Dist - MDCC **Prod** - MDCC

Way of the Nomad - Australia's Desert Aboriginals 28 MIN
VHS / U-matic
Color (J)
Shows documentary footage, recently released from a museum, made in 1963 from an expedition to remote desert areas of Central Australia. Shows how well adapted aboriginals were to survive in such an arid environment, how they were able to find adequate food and water where white explorers and prospectors perished. Views tool making, food gathering and cooking, and notes that great time and care are taken in the shaping of transportable, multipurpose utensils from tough desert trees.
Geography - World; History - World; Sociology
Dist - EDMI **Prod** - EDMI 1984

The Way of the shaman 30 MIN
BETA / VHS
Living traditions series
Color (G)
$29.95 purchase _ #S059
Reveals that the shaman learns to interact with the spirits of the lower world and the higher world in order to intercede on behalf of humans in the 'middle world.' Features Dr Michael Harner, author of 'The Jivaro,' 'Hallucinogens and Shamanism' and 'The Way of the Shaman.' Part of a series on living traditions.
Health and Safety; Religion and Philosophy; Social Science
Dist - THINKA **Prod** - THINKA

The Way of the wicked 15 MIN
U-matic / 16mm / VHS
Color (G)
$500.00, $250.00 purchase, $50.00 rental
Comments on the restrictive roles of women within the Roman Catholic Church. Dramatizes a women - Church skirmish in which two women rush to rescue a young girl from her first communion accompanied by 'action' music. Produced by Christine Vachon.
Religion and Philosophy; Sociology
Dist - WMEN

The Way of the Willow 30 MIN
16mm / U-matic / VHS
Color (J)
Explores the trauma, trials and tribulations of a family of Vietnamese boat people and their sponsoring family in adjusting to each other and to a whole new way of life. Concludes with a crisis which draws the two families together and establishes communications.
History - United States; Literature and Drama; Social Science; Sociology
Dist - BCNFL **Prod** - CATLSF 1982

The Way of the wind 112 MIN
VHS
Color (G A)
$39.80 purchase _ #0277
Tells about a successful businessman who walked away from almost everything he owned, boarded his boat with his camera and went on a 30,000 mile voyage.
Literature and Drama; Physical Education and Recreation
Dist - SEVVID

Way of the woman artist - interviews with strong creators series 720 MIN
VHS
Way of the woman artist series
Color (G)
$269.75 purchase
Presents a six - part series on women artists in South Florida which interviews the artists and discusses their artistic development. Features 24 artists.
Fine Arts; History - United States
Dist - WOCAU **Prod** - WOCAU

Way of the woman artist series
Way of the woman artist - interviews with strong creators series 720 MIN
The Way of the woman artist - Tape 1 120 MIN
The Way of the woman artist - Tape 2 120 MIN
The Way of the woman artist - Tape 3 120 MIN
The Way of the woman artist - Tape 4 120 MIN
The Way of the woman artist - Tape 5 120 MIN
The Way of the woman artist - Tape 6 120 MIN
Dist - WOCAU

The Way of the woman artist - Tape 1 120 MIN
VHS
Way of the woman artist series
Color (G)
$49.95 purchase
Interviews four South Florida women painters and looks at examples of their work. Features Terri Anne Fandler - A Painter Observed, The Shadow Within; Pam Neuman, painter - sculptor - A Mixed Female Heritage, The Kinetic Heart; Vera Walker - A Painter's Allegorical Progress Towards Radiant Energy; and Carol Cornelison - Carol Cornelison - Building from Fragments of Personal Experience. Part one of a six - part series on women artists in South Florida which interviews the artists and discusses their artistic development.
Fine Arts; History - United States
Dist - WOCAU **Prod** - WOCAU

The Way of the woman artist - Tape 2 120 MIN
VHS
Way of the woman artist series
Color (G)
$49.95 purchase
Interviews four South Florida women artists and looks at examples of their work. Features Patricia Riveron Lee - painter - An Artist Records Her Environment; Freda Tschumy - sculptor - A Sculptor Looks Beyond the Surface; Amalia Padilla - Gregg - painter - A Kaleidoscope of Color and Symbols; and Alice Lewis - painter - Movement and Balance in Paint. Part two of a six - part series on women artists in South Florida which interviews the artists and discusses their artistic development.
Fine Arts; History - United States
Dist - WOCAU **Prod** - WOCAU

The Way of the woman artist - Tape 3 120 MIN
VHS
Way of the woman artist series
Color (G)
$49.95 purchase
Interviews four South Florida women artists and looks at examples of their work. Features Peggy Hering - painter - A Spiritual Flowering in the Tropics; Maria Martinez - Canas - photographer - Mixed Media Site Photography; Arlene Luckower - painter - A Color Journey in Paint - From the Intimate to the Expansive; and Zaydee Martinez - watercolor - A Personal Encounter with Watercolor Still Life. Part three of a six - part series on women artists in South Florida which interviews the artists and discusses their artistic development.
Fine Arts; History - United States
Dist - WOCAU **Prod** - WOCAU

The Way of the woman artist - Tape 4 120 MIN
VHS
Way of the woman artist series
Color (G)
$49.95 purchase
Interviews four South Florida women artists and looks at examples of their work. Features Betty Kjelson - paper - Painting with Paper Pulp in the Subtropics; Leslie Klein - pastel - installation - A Mystical Light Permeating Time and Space; Maggie Davis - painter - Alchemical Transformations with the Energized Mark; and Ellen Jacobs - glass - silversmith - Glassblowing Sculptor and Silversmith. Part four of a six - part series on women artists in South Florida which interviews the artists and discusses their artistic development.
Fine Arts; History - United States
Dist - WOCAU **Prod** - WOCAU

The Way of the woman artist - Tape 5 120 MIN
VHS
Way of the woman artist series
Color (G)
$49.95 purchase
Interviews four South Florida women artists and looks at examples of their work. Features Rona Harris - painter - A Warm and Cool Palette; Marilyn Catlow - fused glass -

Fused Glass; Karen Rifas - sculptor - A Sculptor Manipulates Structure; and Judith Hoch - painter - The Vision from Within. Part five of a six - part series on women artists in South Florida which interviews the artists and discusses their artistic development.
Fine Arts; History - United States
Dist - WOCAU **Prod** - WOCAU

The Way of the woman artist - Tape 6 120 MIN
VHS
Way of the woman artist series
Color (G)
$49.95 purchase
Interviews four South Florida women artists and looks at examples of their work. Features Jeanne Janson - mixed media - collage - White Glue and the Inner Voice - Visual Poetry Collage; Barbara Farrell - painter - Building Layers of Colors, Lines and Texture; Yehudas Levitan - painter - A Painter's Odyssey; and Sofia Fillmore Taylor - painter - Dreams and Symbols. Part six of a six - part series on women artists in South Florida which interviews the artists and discusses their artistic development.
Fine Arts; History - United States
Dist - WOCAU **Prod** - WOCAU

The Way of the World 60 MIN
U-matic / VHS
Drama - play, performance, perception series; Conventions of the theatre
Color (H C A)
Discusses stylization, avantgardism, black theatre and realism in drama. Uses the play The Way Of The World as an example.
Fine Arts; Literature and Drama
Dist - FI **Prod** - BBCTV 1978

The Way of the world 60 MIN
VHS
Color (H C G)
$129.00 purchase _ #DL310
Presents a BBC production of the play by William Congreve, containing shortened versions of acts II, III, IV and V and eliminating confusing subplots.
Fine Arts; History - World; Literature and Drama
Dist - INSIM **Prod** - BBC

The Way of the world 313 MIN
VHS
Color; PAL (H)
PdS55 purchase
Presents a set of five plays from one of England's high ages of comedy, the years following the restoration of Charles II, from 1660. Includes The Way of the World by William Congreve; The Confederacy of Wives by Sir John Vanbrugh; The Virtuoso by Thomas Shadwell; A Journey to London by Vanbrugh; and The Bellamira by Sir Charles Sedley. Contact distributor about availability outside the United Kingdom.
Literature and Drama
Dist - ACADEM

A Way Out 32 MIN
16mm
Color (PRO)
Examines the Boston State Hospital Community Residential Treatment Program for chronic mental patients. Focuses on the belief that many chronic mental patients can live useful, meaningful lives in supervised settings outside the hospital.
Health and Safety; Psychology
Dist - SQUIBB **Prod** - SQUIBB

Way - out architecture 44 MIN
VHS
Color (C G)
$149.00 purchase _ #EX2272
Features some 'unusual' homes designed by Americans.
Fine Arts; Sociology
Dist - FOTH

Way Out of the Wilderness 29 MIN
U-matic
B&W
Shows the care of retarded children at the Plymouth State Home and Training Center, where a home atmosphere is provided in preparing the children for return to the outside world. Describes what is being done to help blind and motor - handicapped children find 'a way out of the wilderness.'.
Guidance and Counseling; Health and Safety; Psychology
Dist - USNAC **Prod** - USNAC 1972

Way Out West 66 MIN
16mm 60 MIN
B&W (I A)
Features Laurel and Hardy as two desert prospectors who blunder their way through a series of misadventures in the West of the 1890's.
Fine Arts
Dist - RMIBHF **Prod** - ROACH 1937

The Way - Out World of Fred Feldman 48 MIN
16mm
Color (A)
LC 78-702642
Describes the work of a helicopter pilot - traffic reporter. Shows reporter Fred Feldman as he reports on traffic, enjoys the beauty and grandeur of New York City from his low - flying helicopter and engages in radio repartee with his anchor man, John Gambling.
Guidance and Counseling; Psychology; Sociology
Dist - RKOGEN **Prod** - CFILMC 1968

The Way she lives 99 MIN
VHS
Color (G) (CHINESE)
$45.00 purchase _ #6048C
Presents a film from the People's Republic of China by Wang Anyi.
Geography - World; Literature and Drama
Dist - CHTSUI

Way south series
Fernandina to Miami - Volume 2
Norfolk - Fernandina - Volume 1
Dist - SEVVID

The Way they Live There - a Ghanaian Fishing Village 19 MIN
U-matic / VHS / 16mm
Way they Live There Series
Color (I J H)
Shows everyday life in a small fishing village in Ghana as a young girl spends the day shopping in the village market, preparing the family meal, playing on the beach and sharing the excitement of the return of the fishing fleet.
Geography - World; Sociology
Dist - LUF **Prod** - LUF 1980

The Way they Live There - a Ghanian Fishing Village 17 MIN
VHS / U-matic
Color (J H)
Shows everyday life in a small fishing village on the coast of Ghana. Features the village market, children playing on a beach, return of fishing boats and dancing and singing.
Geography - World; Sociology
Dist - VIEWTH **Prod** - VIEWTH

The Way they Live There - an Egyptian Village 18 MIN
16mm / U-matic / VHS
Way they Live There Series
Color (I J H)
Characterizes life in a village in the Nile delta in Egypt where survival depends on local crops and livestock. Shows that the social life of the children follows centuries - old traditions.
Geography - World; Sociology
Dist - LUF **Prod** - LUF 1980

The Way they live there - an Egyptian village 17 MIN
VHS
Color; PAL (H)
Looks at life in an Egyptian village at the edge of the Nile delta. Visits one of the wealthier households. Examines the crops and animals of that area in Egypt and observes the lives of boys and girls - the boys spend much of their time in play while girls are introduced to the work which will occupy them as adults.
Geography - World; History - World; Sociology
Dist - VIEWTH **Prod** - VIEWTH

The Way they Live There - Poland 19 MIN
U-matic / VHS / 16mm
Way they Live There Series
Color (I J H)
Introduces the Popielarz family of Poland who live in an inexpensive, but small, state - owned apartment in Poland. Shows that although three - quarters of Mr Popielarz's income goes for food, his wife is part of a minority of non - working mothers.
Geography - World; Sociology
Dist - LUF **Prod** - LUF 1980

The Way they live there - Poland 18 MIN
VHS
Color; PAL (H)
Observes a Polish shipyard worker and his family. Demonstrates some of the differences and similarities between Poland and Western Europe.
Geography - World; History - World; Home Economics
Dist - VIEWTH **Prod** - VIEWTH

Way they Live There Series
The Way they Live There - a Ghanaian Fishing Village 19 MIN
The Way they Live There - an Egyptian Village 18 MIN
The Way they Live There - Poland 19 MIN
Dist - LUF

The Way Things Burn 16 MIN
16mm
Color (JAPANESE)
A Japanese Language Film. Divides flame into three parts, the bright, the dark and the blue part. Points out that a flame consumes oxygen when it burns and lets out steam, carbon - dioxide, light and heat.
Foreign Language; Science - Physical
Dist - UNIJAP **Prod** - UNIJAP 1969

The Way Things Go 30 MIN
VHS / 16mm
Color (G)
$280.00 purchase
Records a performance of a deconstructing art piece by German artists David Weiss and Peter Fischli.
Fine Arts
Dist - ICARUS

Way Things Work Series
How a Chimney Works 9 MIN
How a Photograph is made 8 MIN
How a Saw Cuts 6 MIN
How a Screw Works 7 MIN
How Batteries Work 7 MIN
How Candles Work 9 MIN
How gears work 8 MIN
How lenses work 8 MIN
How levers work 5 MIN
How light changes color 9 MIN
How Pins Float on Water 8 MIN
How Planes Fly 6 MIN
How Ships Float 8 MIN
How Speedometers Work 8 MIN
How Telephones Work 7 MIN
How Television Works 6 MIN
How to float on steam 5 MIN
How to make pictures move 8 MIN
How to measure time 7 MIN
How to Recognize Plant Fingerprints 7 MIN
What Happens When Water Freezes 5 MIN
What is a Wedge 4 MIN
What is Air Pressure 6 MIN
What is Safety Glass 10 MIN
What is Water Pressure 6 MIN
What Magnets do 7 MIN
Why Every Action has a Reaction 5 MIN
Why it Rains 6 MIN
Why Lightbulbs Glow 6 MIN
Why Lightning is Dangerous 7 MIN
Dist - FOTH

The way to Baba 54 MIN
VHS / U-matic
Color (G)
LC 90-707508
Records life in the ashram of Sai Baba. Interviews his followers.
Religion and Philosophy
Dist - HP **Prod** - HP 1990

A Way to Bridge the Distance 25 MIN
VHS / U-matic
Color
LC 81-707241
Explores different strategies for delivering health information to rural villages, including two - way radio, mass media campaigns, satellite - linked diagnostic assistance and social marketing.
Health and Safety; Sociology
Dist - USNAC **Prod** - USAID 1980

The Way to Cook - Julia Child
VHS
Way to Cook - Julia Child (Series of Six Titles)
$179 purchase _ #5 INCH 45 RPM RECORD700V
Features Julia Child showing how to prepare a variety of dishes. Uses a combination of hands - on techniques and practical tips.
Education; Home Economics
Dist - CAREER **Prod** - CAREER

Way to Cook - Julia Child (Series of Six Titles)
The Way to Cook - Julia Child
Dist - CAREER

Way to Cook - Julia Child Series
First Courses and Desserts
Meat
Soups, Salads, and Breads
Vegetables
Dist - CAREER

Way to cook with Julia Child series
First courses and desserts 60 MIN
Dist - CAMV

Way to cook with Julia Child series
Fish and eggs 60 MIN
Dist - CAMV
CAREER

Way to Cook with Julia Child
Meat 60 MIN
Soups, Salads and Bread 60 MIN
Vegetables 60 MIN
Dist - CAMV

Way to cook with Julia Child
Poultry 60 MIN
Dist - CAMV
CAREER

The Way to Go 28 MIN
16mm
Color (A)
LC 73-700996
Combines good cinematography of scenery, parks, camp sites and families with a montage of on - site comments by park officials, owners of camp sites and more elaborate recreational facilities and individuals who are sold on camping as a frequent recreation or as a way of life.
Physical Education and Recreation; Sociology
Dist - SFI **Prod** - RVI 1972

The Way to Shadow Garden 12 MIN
16mm
B&W; Silent (C)
$257.60
Experimental film by Stan Brakhage.
Fine Arts
Dist - AFA **Prod** - AFA 1954

Way to the Capital 15 MIN
16mm
Color
LC 74-706604
Discusses a youth physical fitness program.
Physical Education and Recreation; Sociology
Dist - USNAC **Prod** - USN 1972

Way we fight series
The Battle of Russia 67 MIN
The Battle of Russia, Pt 1 33 MIN
The Battle of Russia, Pt 2 34 MIN
Dist - USNAC

Way We Know - the Value of Theory in Linguistic Study 29 MIN
U-matic
Pike on Language Series
Color
Focuses on Kenneth Pike's theory of Tagmemics which is based on a series of components and concepts that help explain how words are arranged.
English Language
Dist - UMITV **Prod** - UMITV 1977

The Way We Live 25 MIN
U-matic / VHS
Color (H A)
Shows how a town and its residents contribute to keeping the crime rate low. Features interviews with residents and municipal officials in the black town of Lawnside, New Jersey.
Sociology
Dist - CORNRS **Prod** - CUETV

The Way We Live 29 MIN
16mm
Color (J)
Presents four examples of urban living in the Federal Republic of Germany. Discusses government - subsidized housing programs which have been successful in reconstructing apartments and houses.
History - World; Sociology
Dist - WSTGLC **Prod** - WSTGLC

The Way we wear 60 MIN
VHS
Smithsonian world series
Color (G)
$49.95 purchase _ #SMIW - 403
Uses the Smithsonian's costume collection to trace American fashion mores from the 18th century to the present. Focuses on contemporary fashion and its meaning.
Home Economics; Psychology; Sociology
Dist - PBS **Prod** - WETATV

The Way We were 118 MIN
16mm
Color (H C)
Tells the romantic story of an upper - crust WASP novelist and a Jewish bluestocking girl. Stars Barbara Streisand and Robert Redford. Directed by Sydney Pollack.
Fine Arts
Dist - TIMLIF **Prod** - CPC 1973

Way", "Which 3 MIN
16mm
Color (G)
$5.00 rental
Illustrates the idea that no man is born into the world whose work is not born with him and there is always work and tools to work withal for those who will. Offers a film by Ar Garfield.
Fine Arts
Dist - CANCIN

The Way you were 7 MIN
VHS / 16mm
Color (G) (SPANISH)
$325.00, $300.00 purchase, $75.00 rental
Points out that creativity is essential to success and happiness. Shows in action the imagination, natural creativity, self - assurance and lack of conformity of the young. Teaches the importance of learning to think and try like a child. Features David Wayne as narrator.
Fine Arts; Psychology
Dist - CCCD **Prod** - CCCD
VLEARN

Wayne Cilento and Jud Alper 30 MIN
U-matic / VHS
Eye on Dance - Dance on TV and Film Series
Color
Focuses on dancing in commercials.
Fine Arts
Dist - ARCVID **Prod** - ARCVID

Wayne Fielding - Human Skeleton 17 MIN
U-matic / VHS
Color
Constructs a world through various transitions.
Fine Arts
Dist - ARTINC **Prod** - ARTINC

Wayne Fielding - Motion Sickness 6 MIN
VHS / U-matic
Color
Includes black and white shots.
Fine Arts
Dist - ARTINC **Prod** - ARTINC

Wayne Gretzky above and beyond
VHS
Color (G)
$24.95 purchase _ #FFW003
Chronicles the life and career of hockey star Wayne Gretzky.
Physical Education and Recreation
Dist - SIV

Wayne Thiebaud and Peter Voulkos 30 MIN
16mm
Creative Person Series
Color (H C T)
LC FIA68-67
Contrasts the paintings and philosophy of pop artist Wayne Thiebaud with the abstract bronze sculpture of Peter Voulkos. Shows Thiebaud at work in his studio and teaching in the classroom and Boulkos working in his foundry studio. Both artists discuss their philosophy and ideas concerning teaching.
Fine Arts
Dist - IU **Prod** - NET 1968

Wayne's Decision 6 MIN
16mm
Responsible Caring Series
Color (J)
LC 81-701350
Deals with some of the complex and painful issues faced by teenage fathers.
Health and Safety; Psychology
Dist - MEMAPP **Prod** - MEMAPP 1980

The Ways and the means 29 MIN
16mm
Government story series; No 12
B&W (J H)
LC 72-707216
Discusses the role of Congress in raising the revenues required to run the federal government and explains the unique role of the House Ways and Means Committee in this process.
Civics and Political Systems
Dist - WESTLC **Prod** - WEBC 1968

The Ways at Wallace and Sons
VHS / BETA
Color
Relates story of the wood construction of the ill - fated schooner John F Leavitt which went down on its maiden voyage.
Geography - World; Physical Education and Recreation; Social Science
Dist - MYSTIC **Prod** - MAYDYF 1979

Ways in the Night 98 MIN
16mm
Color (GERMAN (ENGLISH SUBTITLES))
Tells about the relationship between a German Army officer and a Polish countess during World War II. Includes English subtitles.
Fine Arts; Foreign Language
Dist - TLECUL **Prod** - TLECUL

Ways of Assessing Reading Progress 29 MIN
16mm / U-matic / VHS
Teaching Children to Read Series
Color (C A)
Illustrates alternative means of assessing reading skills that can benefit students parents, teachers and administrators.
Education; English Language
Dist - FI **Prod** - MFFD 1976

Ways of Dealing with Conflict in Organizations 27 MIN
16mm / U-matic / VHS
Management Development Series
B&W (H C A)
LC 71-700263
Herbert Shepard, professor of behavioral sciences, Case Institute of Technology, analyzes three alternative methods of resolving conflict - - suppression, bargaining and problem - solving.
Business and Economics; Psychology
Dist - UCEMC **Prod** - UCLA 1962

Ways of decreasing or eliminating the unnecessary stresses in your life 60 MIN
VHS
Stress and the caregiver - are we driving each other mad series
Color (R G)
$49.95 purchase _ #SCGR4
Reveals that stress in the lives of Americans is causing immense suffering in the form of painful emotional and physical disease. Discloses that most stress is borne unnecessarily and can be prevented if one is willing to gain some self - knowledge and make changes in attitudes, beliefs and approaches to life. Presents the principles of emotional, physical and mental health that can be applied to daily situations. Features Father James Gill, MD, SJ, who examines ways of distinguishing the painful and disturbing emotions of anger, resentment, loss, anxiety and fear and replacing them with a healthy and energizing way of life. Part of four parts.
Guidance and Counseling; Health and Safety; Psychology; Religion and Philosophy
Dist - CTNA **Prod** - CTNA

Ways of faith 50 MIN
U-matic / VHS
Arabs - a living history series
Color (H C A)
MV=$495.00
Follows a group that journeyed to the central Sudan to seek guidance and blessings from an elderly religious Sheikh.
Geography - World; History - World; Religion and Philosophy
Dist - LANDMK **Prod** - LANDMK 1986

Ways of Hearing Series
Hearing Impairment - an Overview 16 MIN
Language through Sight and Sound 18 MIN
Listening for Language 22 MIN
Dist - BCNFL

Ways of Looking at Children's Art 7 MIN
U-matic
Take Time Series
(A)
Demonstrates the influence of parents and others caring for pre - schoolers on the physical and emotional development of the child.
Health and Safety; Psychology; Sociology
Dist - ACCESS **Prod** - ACCESS 1976

The Ways of Nature 22 MIN
16mm
Color
LC 76-702306
Describes antibiotic processes and their effects on the environment.
Science - Natural
Dist - MTP **Prod** - LILLY 1976

Ways of Our Fathers 40 MIN
U-matic / VHS / 16mm
Color
Focuses on improving the educational experiences of Indian children. Advocates that Indian culture is an essential part of a child's school experience and must become an integral part of school curriculum. Features elders and youths in song, dance and traditional oral history.
Social Science
Dist - SHENFP **Prod** - SHENFP

Ways of Seeing Series
Camera and printing 25 MIN
Fine Arts and Commerce 25 MIN
Painting and Possessions 25 MIN
Women and Art 25 MIN
Dist - FI

Ways of the law series
Civil law - what really happened 19 MIN
Contract - Consumer law - be assertive 19 MIN

Criminal procedure - time for not thinking 19 MIN
Due Process - Student Rights and Responsibilities 19 MIN
Environmental law 19 MIN
Family law - domestic relations 19 MIN
Family law - juvenile justice 19 MIN
Introduction and overview of law series 19 MIN
Law Enforcement - Patrol Officers 19 MIN
Law Enforcement - the Citizen's Role 19 MIN
Our Legal System 19 MIN
Reasons for Law - Le Cafe Politic 19 MIN
Sources of Law 19 MIN
Substantive Criminal Law - Happy Here 19 MIN
Wills and Estates 19 MIN
Dist - GPN

The Ways of the Wind 24 MIN
U-matic / VHS
Color (I A)
LC 82-707158
Features young sailboat skipper Bruce Klein telling why he was attacted to the sport and talking of the challenges and pleasures that maintain his interest in it. Shows him instructing novices at a yacht club, maneuvering his craft through a squall and winning a race on Long Island Sound.
Physical Education and Recreation
Dist - DENOPX **Prod** - DENONN 1982

Ways of the Wind 23 MIN
U-matic / VHS / 16mm
Color (J)
Features champion sailor Bruce Klein, a junior instructor at the Sea Cliff Yacht Club. Describes how he teaches youngsters to read cloud movements and the dark spots on the water where the stronger winds blow.
Physical Education and Recreation
Dist - MOKIN **Prod** - DENONN 1983

The Ways of Wallace and Sons - the Bank Dory 58 MIN
VHS
Color (G)
$29.95 purchase _ #SS - A2B
Shows New England shipwrights constructing the first coasting schooner built in many years, the ill - fated John F Leavitt which went down on its first voyage. Looks at shipbuilding from keel laying to launching day. Includes a program on the bank dory, featuring historic footage of the dory at work and under construction in Lunenburg, Nova Scotia.
Geography - World; Industrial and Technical Education; Physical Education and Recreation
Dist - MYSTIC **Prod** - MYSTIC

Ways of water 46 MIN
U-matic / VHS
Color (C A)
$225.00, $195.00 purchase _ #V695
Examines how water in its gaseous, liquid and solid forms shapes the Earth. Shows how animal life relies on water.
Science - Natural; Science - Physical; Social Science
Dist - BARR **Prod** - CEPRO 1991

The Ways of Water 13 MIN
16mm / U-matic / VHS
Earth Science Program Series
Color (I J)
LC 76-712999
Examines undisturbed nature, explaining the different forms of water as ice, streams, dew, mist, rain, clouds and the sea. Shows the relationship between water and the forests, insects, fish, birds and other elements.
Science - Physical
Dist - EBEC **Prod** - EBEC 1971

Ways to Solve a Problem 15 MIN
U-matic / VHS
Out and about Series
Color (P)
Reveals that when Molly accidentally smears paint on her brother's shirt, she is upset especially because she wore it without permission. Shows that with Sam's encouragement, she thinks of several possible solutions and finally decides to tell her mother and ask her to help wash the shirt.
Guidance and Counseling
Dist - AITECH **Prod** - STSU 1984

Ways to Weigh Less 25 MIN
VHS / U-matic
Color
Evaluates various techniques for weight reduction, including jaw wiring, hypnosis, acupuncture, crash dieting, intestinal surgery and behavior modification.
Health and Safety; Psychology
Dist - MEDCOM **Prod** - MEDCOM

Ways with Coal 20 MIN
U-matic / VHS
Chemistry in Action Series
Color (C)
$249.00, $149.00 purchase _ #AD - 1276
Looks at processes to combust coal more efficiently and to reduce pollution. Considers coke manufacture and gasification of coal, both processes yielding useful chemical raw materials.
Industrial and Technical Education; Science - Physical
Dist - FOTH **Prod** - FOTH

Ways with Pork 14 MIN
Videoreel / VT2
Living Better II Series
Color
Identifies economical pork cuts in the retail market. Gives tips on selecting good quality pork and storing it properly. Includes recipes featuring pork.
Home Economics
Dist - PBS **Prod** - MAETEL

WCAUTV eye on series
Camden - a suitable case for treatment 30 MIN
Dist - WCAUTV

WCB's Wide World of Rescue 8 MIN
16mm / VHS
(A IND)
$375.00, $360.00 purchase _ #30.0143 #40.0143
Utilizes techniques from television sportscasting to demonstrate a rescue of people exposed to hydrogen sulfide. Shows errors in rescue techniques through replays and comments by an announcer and colorman.
Health and Safety; Industrial and Technical Education
Dist - UTEXPE

WCB's Wide World of Rescue 10 MIN
VHS / U-matic
Hydrogen Sulphide Safety Series,
Color
Adapts the techniques of modern televison sportcasting to analyze the errors committed in an attempt to rescue several hydrogen sulphide victims.
Health and Safety
Dist - FLMWST **Prod** - FLMWST

WCB'S Wide World of Rescue 10 MIN
16mm
H2S Training Series
Color
LC 77-700325
Portrays a rescue operation conducted for hydrogen sulfide victims. Shows commentators who analyze the errors committed during the procedures and discuss the reasons why rescue attempts succeed or fail.
Health and Safety; Industrial and Technical Education
Dist - FLMWST **Prod** - AWHSC 1977

WCCO - TV on the Move - a Look to the Future 30 MIN
U-matic / VHS
Color
Tours the new broadcast facilities of WCCO - TV on the day of the move to the 'new building.' Previews the news room and air control post - production unit, the satellite system and other highlights of the building that was six years in planning and construction.
Fine Arts; Industrial and Technical Education; Sociology
Dist - WCCOTV **Prod** - WCCOTV

WCCO - TV on the Move - a Salute to the Past 30 MIN
VHS / U-matic
Color
Explores the past 36 years of Channel 4's history. Looks at the people and technology of WCCO's past on the eve of the move to the 'new building.'.
Fine Arts; Industrial and Technical Education; Sociology
Dist - WCCOTV **Prod** - WCCOTV

We 29 MIN
16mm 15 MIN
Color
LC 74-705939; 74-705938
Presents key findings of the 1970 census including the enormous growth of our suburbs, the continued historic movement of the population from rural to urban areas and the movement of the population towards the nation's coasts.
Sociology
Dist - USNAC **Prod** - USBC 1973

We all came to America 53 MIN
VHS
Color (G)
$30.95 purchase _ #S00891
Examines the reasons most immigrants have come to the United States - slavery, economic gain, religious persecution, famine and wars. Shows that many attempts have been made to restrict immigration. Narrated by Theodore Bikel.
Civics and Political Systems; History - United States; Sociology
Dist - UILL

We all Came to America 21 MIN
16mm / VHS / U-matic
American Documents Series
Color (H C A)
Uses archival film and photographs to document the story of people who immigrated to America.
History - United States; Sociology
Dist - LUF **Prod** - LUF 1977

We all get wet when it rains
VHS
Color (K P)
$79.00 purchase _ #ME2014A
Teaches students that everyone is 'differently abled' - that they are more like their classmates than unlike them, regardless of physical and mental abilities. Includes teachers' guide.
Education; Health and Safety; Psychology
Dist - CFKRCM **Prod** - CFKRCM

We all have our reasons 30 MIN
U-matic / 16mm / VHS
Color (G)
$500.00, $225.00 purchase, $60.00 rental
Explores the reasons why women become alcoholics and abusers of other substances. Looks at the process of recovery from a feminist perspective.
Guidance and Counseling; Health and Safety; Sociology
Dist - WMEN **Prod** - IRIS
IRIS

We all live downstream 30 MIN
VHS
Color (G)
$29.95 purchase
Journeys down the Mississippi River on the Greenpeace research ship Beluga. Explores the effects of toxic pollution on the Mississippi River. Reveals that Minneapolis has issued advisories against eating fish from the Mississippi, that people in Louisiana have been poisoned with toxic chemicals. Features music by Nancy Griffith and Mississippi John Jackson.
Geography - United States; Science - Natural; Sociology
Dist - GRNPCE **Prod** - GRNPCE 1990

We are a River Flowing 28 MIN
BETA / VHS / U-matic
Color; Stereo (S C A G)
Compares the effects of the British occupation of Northern Ireland to the American occupation of the Dakota Nation in Pine Ridge, South Dakota. Depicted through the eyes of an orphan of political turmoil in Northern Ireland who visits the Pine Ridge Reservation.
Social Science
Dist - UCV

We are all Arab Jews in Israel 120 MIN
16mm
Color
Documents the far - reaching tensions between European and Oriental Jews in Israel. Directed by Igaal Niddam.
Fine Arts; Geography - World; Sociology
Dist - NYFLMS **Prod** - UNKNWN 1977

We are all One People 45 MIN
16mm / VHS / U-matic
Color
LC 80-701563; 80-700668
A shortened version of the motion picture We Are All One People. Tells how four American students travel to Israel to meet their pen pals. Tells how they participate in the customs and traditions of the people.
Geography - World; Sociology
Dist - ALTSUL **Prod** - GABOR 1981

We are at the Controls 17 MIN
16mm
Color
LC 78-700444
Identifies some causes and effects of oil pollution and appeals for individual commitment to pollution prevention.
Sociology
Dist - PROCCO **Prod** - API 1977

We are Driven 58 MIN
VHS / BETA
Frontline Series
Color
Takes a probing and penetrating look into the 'darker side' of Japanese management techniques. Profiles Nissan Motors and their new anti - union auto plant in Tennessee.
Business and Economics
Dist - PBS **Prod** - DOCCON

We are Family 29 MIN
U-matic / VHS
Color
Reveals the present state of the Hispanic community in the Twin Cities area. Looks at Hispanics and their culture, social services, economic development, education and participation in local government.
Geography - United States; Sociology
Dist - WCCOTV **Prod** - WCCOTV 1982

We are family - An Adoption story 24 MIN
VHS / U-matic
Color (J H G)
$270.00, $320.00 purchase, $60.00 rental
Presents one dramatic case study of an adoption process that includes the birth mother and father and their families and the adoptive parents. Provides a discussion generator for families or individuals facing an unplanned pregnancy and the possible scenarios that may occur when going through an adoption procedure. Produced by the Boys and Girls Aid Society.
Sociology
Dist - NDIM

We are family - parenting and foster parenting in gay families 57 MIN
VHS
Color (H C G)
$445.00 purchase, $75.00 rental
Looks at what life is really like in homosexual families, with a focus on parenting and the well being of the children. Meets three different families - one foster, one biological and one adoptive. Two gay fathers tell of their efforts to create a secure environment for their 16 - year - old foster son who was on the road to delinquency. In another household, two lesbian mothers have helped their adopted 11 - year - old son to overcome the emotional trauma of disability and early neglect. Two daughters in the third family tell have they have accepted their father's homosexuality. Produced in Aimee Sands.
Sociology
Dist - FLMLIB **Prod** - WGBHTV 1987

We are Guatemalans 28 MIN
VHS
Color (G)
$14.95 purchase _ #102
Reveals that there are 17 million refugees in the world and the number is growing daily due to war, repression and 'ethnic cleansing.' Shows how, in 1994, a group of 2,000 Guatemalans reversed this trend. After 12 years of exile in Mexican refugee camps, they returned to their homeland in the Ixcan jungle region of Guatemala. Their homecoming is not over yet - many still call the returnees 'the enemy,' and a base of the feared Guatemalan army is only a few miles away. Joins the refugees in their camps in Mexico and follows them to their homeland. Centers on the people of one town, Cuarto Pueblo, where an army massacre forced survivors to flee to Mexico.
History - World
Dist - MARYFA **Prod** - MARYFA 1994

We are hablando 14 MIN
VHS
Color (G)
Offers a multi - layered examination of personal, artistic and global censorship. Features Cuban - American artist Roly Chang Barrero recounting two occasions when his work was censored and Roberto Rodriguez's experiences with discrimination as a gay man. Intertwines testimony with videotext concerning the sexual - ethnic identity of the videomaker, culturally informed footage of a Latino celebration and the media - censored broadcasts of the Gulf War. Produced and directed by Raul Ferrera - Balanquet.
Fine Arts; Sociology
Dist - LATINO

We are not Alone - Myths and Realities of Woman Abuse 53 MIN
U-matic / VHS
Color
Presents an introduction to the history, sanctioning, facts and figures related to woman abuse. Confronts the reality of battered women by the grass - root response of the movement and the gains that have been made.
Sociology
Dist - UWISC **Prod** - DACABW 1982

We are Nothing Without the People - Pt 4 26 MIN
VHS
Human Face of Indonesia Series, the
Color (S)
$99.00 purchase _ #118 - 9038
Focuses on the lives of five very different Indonesians. Presents an enthralling and informative picture of the life and culture of Indonesia by putting their personal stories into the broader context of the modern country. Part 4 of five parts considers Brigadier General Dr Ben Mboi, the governor of Nusa Tenggara Timur. He and his wife discuss their medical work for one of the poorest provinces and talk about the role of the military in Indoesia today.
Geography - World; Health and Safety; History - World; Sociology
Dist - FI **Prod** - FLMAUS 1987

We are of the Soil 23 MIN
16mm / VHS
Color (H C A)
Examines our use of soil in relationship to the heritage of the prairies which the Indians and early settlers knew. Contrasts our increased emphasis on crop production with the exploitation of our natural soil resources.
Agriculture
Dist - IOWA **Prod** - IOWA 1977

We are One 13 MIN
U-matic / VHS / 16mm
Color (J)
LC 80-701495
Presents three handicapped young adults describing the difficulties that often occur when handicapped and non - handicapped individuals interact. Stresses the need for better communication.
Psychology
Dist - JOU **Prod** - LINCS 1980

We are one
VHS / U-matic
We are one series
Color (G)
Shows the life and culture of a Native American family in early 19th century Nebraska. Helps to show the life, richness and complexity of Native American culture, in particular, the Omaha culture. Focuses on a 13 year old and his younger sister, and on the daily rituals and rites of passage that make up their world.
Social Science
Dist - NAMPBC **Prod** - NAMPBC 1986

We are One 10 MIN
16mm
Color
Features visuals by leading Israeli artist Pinchas Shaar and music by Issachar Miron as it dramatizes the 1975 United Jewish Appeal campaign slogan We Are One. Narrated by Melvyn Douglas.
Fine Arts; Sociology
Dist - ALDEN **Prod** - UJA

We are one series

Banbrytare - by the sweat of thy brow	20 MIN
Banbrytare - getting established	20 MIN
Banbrytare - getting to Nebraska	20 MIN
Banbrytare - heritage	20 MIN
Banbrytare - survival of the fittest	20 MIN
Banbrytare - the big decision	20 MIN
Banbrytare - those good old golden rule days	20 MIN
The Big decision	15 MIN
By the sweat of thy brow	15 MIN
The Crisis	15 MIN
Getting established	15 MIN
Getting to Nebraska	15 MIN
Heritage	15 MIN
Los Peregrinos modernos - give me your poor	20 MIN
Los Peregrinos modernos - give me your tired	20 MIN
Los Peregrinos modernos - I lift my lamp beside the golden door	20 MIN
Los Peregrinos modernos - send these to me	20 MIN
Los Peregrinos modernos - the homeless	20 MIN
Los Peregrinos modernos - the huddled masses	20 MIN
Los Peregrinos modernos - the wretched refuse	20 MIN
Los Peregrinos modernos - yearning to breathe free	20 MIN
Those good old golden rule days	15 MIN
Umonhon - becoming a warrior	20 MIN
Umonhon - learning from others	20 MIN
Umonhon - morning comes	20 MIN
Umonhon - preparing for the summer hunt	20 MIN
Umonhon - storytelling	20 MIN
Umonhon - the buffalo hunt	20 MIN
Umonhon - the dare	20 MIN
Umonhon - turning of the child ceremony	20 MIN

Dist - GPN

We are one series

Becoming a warrior	20 MIN
The Buffalo hunt	20 MIN
The Dare	20 MIN
Learning from others	20 MIN
Morning comes	20 MIN
Preparing for the summer hunt	20 MIN
Storytelling	20 MIN
Turning of the child	20 MIN
We are one	

Dist - NAMPBC

We are one - the DNA connection 50 MIN
VHS
Cracking the code series
Color (A PRO C)
PdS99 purchase _ Unavailable in USA
Questions how close we are to pigs and worms. Examines DNA's role in determining this. Part of a series written and presented by David Suzuki.
Science - Natural
Dist - BBCENE

We are Ourselves 15 MIN
U-matic / VHS
Color (C A)
Shows two thoughtful and independent women who have followed their individual desires to seek a fulfilling and creative lifestyle together.
Health and Safety; Psychology; Sociology
Dist - MMRC **Prod** - NATSF

We are the American Hospital Volunteers 6 MIN
VHS / U-matic
Color
Reveals how to recruit new hospital volunteers and motivate current volunteers by expressing pride in their volunteer activities.
Health and Safety; Social Science
Dist - AHOA **Prod** - ASDVS

We are the Church Together
16mm
Color
Shows volunteers interacting with mentally impaired persons within the context of a religious education program.
Education; Psychology; Religion and Philosophy
Dist - TNF **Prod** - TNF

We are the Palestinian people 55 MIN
16mm
B&W (G)
$30.00 rental
Chronicles the history of the Palestinians' cause, from the refugee camps they have lived in for over 30 years, to building a movement to regain their homeland from the Zionists. Reveals the symbiotic relationship between the Zionist movement and larger imperialist powers. Represents revolutionary filmmakers in the 1960s whose work provides a window to that period.
Fine Arts; History - World; Sociology
Dist - CANCIN **Prod** - SINGLE 1973

We are the Parcel People 31 MIN
U-matic
Color
Presents the story of the United Parcel Service from its beginnings in Seattle in 1907 through the present day. Emphasizes the company's fast, reliable service.
Business and Economics
Dist - MTP **Prod** - UPS

We are the Sierra Club 14 MIN
Slide / VHS
Color (G)
$25.00, $85.00 purchase, $15.00, $20.00 rental
Overviews the history of the Sierra Club, its conservation efforts and outing programs, with emphasis on opportunities for member participation.
Physical Education and Recreation; Science - Natural; Sociology
Dist - CMSMS **Prod** - SIERRA 1985

We are these people 15 MIN
VHS / 16mm
Color (G)
$350.00 purchase, $45.00 rental
Features Will Sampson. Fosters an appreciation for the richness of Native American cultures. Reinforces the traditional values of friendship, sharing and respect for all people.
Guidance and Counseling; Social Science
Dist - SHENFP **Prod** - SHENFP

We are Universal 23 MIN
U-matic / 16mm
B&W
Documents the art of black Americans. Shows art organizations, performances and interviews with black artists. Includes such artists as Quincy Jones, Freddie Hubbard, Nikki Giovanni and Betty Carter.
Fine Arts; Sociology
Dist - BLKFMF **Prod** - BLKFMF

We are Water 27 MIN
16mm
Montana - as Science Sees it Series
Color
LC 77-702168
Discusses problems in the use and abuse of Montana's water resources. Offers a look at the state's waterways.
Geography - United States
Dist - CONICO **Prod** - CONICO 1977

We Belong to the Land 30 MIN
U-matic / VHS / 16mm
Color
Shows an Indian youth spending some time with his friend Joe 'Giron, an Apache and professional range manager. Reaffirms the relationship between the Indian and the land. Explores lifestyles in natural resource careers, such as forestry, game management, range management and related fields.
Guidance and Counseling; Social Science
Dist - SHENFP **Prod** - SHENFP

We both have to change - a commentary 30 MIN
VHS
Color (A PRO IND)
$450.00 purchase, $150.00 rental
Addresses stereotypes and cultural differences between whites and African - Americans. Suggests that these factors stronly affect work relationships, and that better communication can help.
Business and Economics; English Language; Guidance and Counseling; Psychology; Social Science; Sociology
Dist - VLEARN

We Build, We Fight 22 MIN
16mm
Color
LC 74-706316
Tells about the Seabees from their first days of World War II to their construction and counterinsurgency activities in Vietnam. Narrated by the founder, Admiral Ben Morrell.
Civics and Political Systems; History - United States; History - World; Industrial and Technical Education
Dist - USNAC **Prod** - USN 1969

We Call Them Chaplain 11 MIN
16mm
B&W
LC 74-706317
Explains to new recruits the role of the U S Army chaplain.
Civics and Political Systems; Religion and Philosophy; Sociology
Dist - USNAC **Prod** - USA 1967

We Call Them Killers 16 MIN
16mm
Color (I J H C)
LC 74-703670
Presents a close - up study of two killer whales. Features Dr Paul Spong who tells of his work with the whales, which involves trying to establish interspecies relationship and communication.
Science; Science - Natural
Dist - NFBC **Prod** - NFBC

We Call Them Killers 16 MIN
16mm
Color (G)
_ #106C 0172 106
Observes two killer whales at Victoria Sealand of the Pacific aquarium in British Columbia displaying a sense of fun and rapport with their trainers who attempt inter species communication. Shows musician Paul Horn who captivates one whale with the sounds of his flute.
Science - Natural
Dist - CFLMDC **Prod** - NFBC 1972

We Came from the Valley 28 MIN
16mm
Color (H C)
LC 72-701861
Shows how a large aerospace firm trained and put to work in its Dallas plant several hundred unskilled Mexican - American workers from the Rio Grande Valley.
Business and Economics; Industrial and Technical Education; Sociology
Dist - VOAERO **Prod** - VOAERO 1971

We Can Change the World 60 MIN
VHS / 16mm
Making Sense of the Sixties Series
Color (G)
$59.95 purchase _ #MSIX - N903
Chronicles the years 1960 to 1964 when the civil rights movement and President John F Kennedy inspired idealism in college students. Explores the Cuban missile crisis, the assassination of Kennedy and the 1963 March on Washington. Part of a six - part series on the Sixties.
Biography; Civics and Political Systems; History - United States
Dist - PBS **Prod** - WETATV 1990

We Can Decide 60 MIN
VHS / U-matic
Through the Genetic Maze Series
Color (H C G T A)
Traces the development of aminiocentesis, an examination of the amniotic fluid and the cells of the developing fetus it contains, which is used to detect such genetic defects as Down's syndrome and Tay Sachs disease. Explores ethical issues, such as abortion, that can arise as a result of this test.
Health and Safety; Religion and Philosophy; Science; Science - Natural
Dist - PSU **Prod** - PSU 1982

We can do it 14 MIN
VHS
Color (K P I J) (SPANISH)
$250.00 purchase, $70.00 rental _ #4355S, #4359S, #4355V, #4359V
Teaches children techniques for dealing with cancer treatment. Uses clips from televison shows, movies and sports programs along with cartoons and upbeat music. Interviews children of different ages and backgrounds undergoing cancer treatment who speak about their experiences, along with the things they do to make the tests and treatment less stressful. Describes relaxation techniques such as distraction, imagery and muscle relaxation. Encourages children to communicate feelings, wants and needs. Produced by the University of Texas MD Anderson Cancer Center.
Health and Safety
Dist - AJN

We Can do it 4 MIN
16mm / U-matic / VHS
Most Important Person - Attitudes Series
Color (K P I) (SPANISH)
Suggests that children try alternatives to arrive at solutions.
Guidance and Counseling
Dist - EBEC **Prod** - EBEC 1972

We can do it together 13 MIN
VHS
AFB shoestring video series
Color (G PRO T)
$19.95 purchase
Illustrates a transdisciplinary team orientation and mobility program for students with severe visual and multiple impairments which was developed by the special education unit of the New York City Board of Education. Shows the communication systems used to teach mobility skills. For mobility instructors, administrators, special education teachers, therapists, and parents. Discussion guide included.
Guidance and Counseling; Health and Safety
Dist - AFB **Prod** - AFB

We Can do it Too 15 MIN
U-matic / VHS
Strawberry Square Series
Color (P)
Fine Arts
Dist - AITECH **Prod** - NEITV 1982

We Can Help 15 MIN
VHS / U-matic
Color
Demonstrates step - by - step procedures for documenting the declining work performance of white collar, executive - level employees and the intervention and referral process.
Business and Economics
Dist - WHITEG **Prod** - WHITEG

We can help 2000 18 MIN
VHS
Color (H G IND PRO)
$350.00 purchase
Updates the original program produced in 1982. Demonstrates step - by - step procedures for documenting declining work performance in employees and the process of intervention and referral for treatment of substance abuse. Discusses Employee Assistance Programs - EAP.
Business and Economics; Guidance and Counseling; Health and Safety; Psychology
Dist - FMSP

We Can Help Series

Barb - breaking the cycle of child abuse	20 MIN
The Interview	35 MIN
Investigating Cases of Child Abuse and Neglect	28 MIN
The Medical Witness	35 MIN
Presenting the case	32 MIN
Second Chance	13 MIN
Sexual abuse - the family	30 MIN
Working Together	30 MIN

Dist - USNAC

We can keep you forever 75 MIN
VHS
Color (J H C G)
$29.95 purchase _ #KU1655V - S
Speculates that many of the Missing in Action in Vietnam and Laos are still alive - and still being held prisoner. Features a group of senior American and British journalists who, after a year long investigation all over the world, reveal what is already known to American intelligence.
Civics and Political Systems; History - United States
Dist - CAMV **Prod** - KULTUR 1992

We can make a difference 16 MIN
VHS
Color (K P I J H C A)
$55.00 purchase, $30.00 rental
Interviews hundreds of children ages 4 through 18 on their knowledge of environmental issues and their perspectives on whether young people can make a difference. Produced by 12 high school students at the Oak Meadow School.
Geography - World; Science - Natural
Dist - EFVP

We Can Turn the Tide 22 MIN
16mm
Color
Reports on the benefits for the general economy of increased exports of farm commodities.
Agriculture; Business and Economics
Dist - MTP **Prod** - MTP

We Can Work it Out 29 MIN
U-matic / VHS
Secretary and Management Relationship Series no 2
Color
Business and Economics; Psychology
Dist - VISUCP **Prod** - VIDART

We can work it out - conflict resolution 11 MIN
VHS
Color (K P)
$95 purchase No. 2455-YZ
Teaches young students age-appropriate strategies for resolving conflicts. Demonstrates that asking questions, listening, and thinking alternative ways of doing things can provide satisfying solutions. Includes 11-minute video, 9 student worksheets and teacher's guide.
Education; Psychology
Dist - SUNCOM **Prod** - SUNCOM

We Can't Go on Like this 32 MIN
16mm / U-matic / VHS
Color (H A)
As triggers for discussion, presents vignettes portraying smokers who have recently quit or those who are considering it. Exposes the rationalizations that can become pitfalls.
Health and Safety; Psychology
Dist - USNAC **Prod** - NHLI 1981

We can't go on like this 20 MIN
VHS / U-matic
Color (PRO C G)
$195.00 purchase _ #C881 - VI - 027
Presents seven short vignettes to promote discussions about the problems and rewards of smoking cessation. Presented by Edmond Levy, Thomas Flavin, Dr Gary Lauger and Donna Rains.
Health and Safety; Psychology
Dist - HSCIC

We Can't Sleep
VHS / 35mm strip
ALA Notable Children's Filmstrips Series
Color (K)
$33.00 purchase
Presents a children's story. Part of the American Library Association series.
English Language; Literature and Drama
Dist - PELLER

We Care Series

- Brushing the patient's teeth - care of dentures - mouth care for the unconscious - Pt 3
- Combing the patient's hair - how to give a shampoo - shaving the male patient - Pt 4
- Diabetes and older patient - urine testing for diabetic control - the Daily Treatment - Pt 6 daily treatment - Pt 6
- Handwashing Techniques / Vital Signs / Catheter Care - Pt 9
- How to Clean a Patient's Room / How to Clean a Patient's Bathroom / How to Clean a Room - Pt 8
- How to give a partial bed bath - hand and foot care - how to make the occupied bed - pt 5
- Principles of Body Mechanics / Moving the Patient in Bed / Assisting the Patient Out of bed - Pt 3
- Sanitation for food service workers - housekeeping and safety in the - Pt 7
- You make the difference - food handling and you - safety in housekeeping - pt 1

Dist - VTRI

We Did it 27 MIN
16mm
Color
LC 79-700346
Shows the construction of the Volkswagen of America plant, the first automobile assembly plant of a foreign manufacturer in the United States. Describes the international cooperation involved in this endeavor.
Business and Economics; Industrial and Technical Education
Dist - KAROL **Prod** - VWA 1978

We Didn't Want it to Happen this Way 30 MIN
16mm
Color (A)
Interviews workers in the Zenith Corporation after the corporation announced that they were moving production to Mexico and Taiwan. Portrays the experiences of the workers and concludes that our foreign trade policies fail to protect the welfare of American workers.
Business and Economics; Sociology
Dist - AFLCIO **Prod** - IAM 1979

We Dig Coal - a Portrait of Three Women 58 MIN
16mm / U-matic / VHS
Color (A)
LC 82-700362
Portrays Marilyn McCusker, Bernice Dombroski and Mary Louise Carson and their struggle to be hired as miners in the face of opposition from their families, the community and their male coworkers.
Social Science; Sociology
Dist - CNEMAG **Prod** - SACVP 1981

We Discover Fractions 11 MIN
U-matic / VHS / 16mm
Color (P I)
$270, $190 purchase _ #1995
Discusses the reasons that fractions are used and explains the meaning of denominator and numerator.
Mathematics
Dist - CORF

We Discover the Encyclopedia 11 MIN
U-matic / VHS / 16mm
Color (I)
LC 76-712345
Shows children how to use the encyclopedia. Covers key word selection, alphabetical topic arrangement, guide words, sub - topic headings, pictures, charts, maps and diagrams.
Literature and Drama
Dist - CORF **Prod** - CORF 1971

We do, We do 11 MIN
16mm
Marriage Series
Color (H C)
LC 72-700512
Uses a fantasized approach to explore the last minute warnings which barrage a teenage bride and groom. Pictures the young couple as they argue before a skeptical teenage jury, presenting their reasons for early marriage.
Guidance and Counseling; Psychology; Sociology
Dist - FRACOC **Prod** - FRACOC 1970

We Don't Want to Live on Our Knees 20 MIN
VHS / U-matic
History in Action Series
Color
Describes the Russian invasion of Czechoslavakia in August of 1968.
History - World
Dist - FOTH **Prod** - FOTH 1984

We Drivers 13 MIN
16mm
Color (H C A)
Scenes from a helicopter show safe driving techniques. Driving pitfalls and their remedies are also depicted.
Health and Safety
Dist - GM **Prod** - GM 1965

We Explore Ocean Life 11 MIN
U-matic / VHS / 16mm
We Explore Series
Color (P I)
Explores the coral reef and the ocean floor showing sea anemones, squids and jellyfish. Explains their dependence upon one another, how they get their food and how they protect themselves.
Science - Natural
Dist - CORF **Prod** - CORF 1962

We Explore Series
We Explore Ocean Life 11 MIN
We Explore the Beach 12 MIN
We Explore the Desert 10 MIN
We Explore the Marsh 11 MIN
Dist - CORF

We Explore the Beach 12 MIN
U-matic / VHS / 16mm
We Explore Series
Color (P I)
$295.00, $210.00 purchase _ #3724
Shows the many organisms that live on the seashore.
Science - Natural
Dist - CORF **Prod** - CORF 1977

We Explore the Desert 10 MIN
16mm / U-matic / VHS
We Explore Series
Color (P I)
On an afternoon visit to the desert, Steve and Cathy observe desert plants and how they are adapted to the desert conditions. In the desert museum, they learn about nocturnal animals. These animals are also shown in their natural habitat as night comes to the desert.
Geography - United States; Science - Natural
Dist - CORF **Prod** - CORF 1967

We Explore the Marsh 11 MIN
U-matic / VHS / 16mm
We Explore Series
Color (P I)
LC 74-700049
Introduces the concept of marshes as wet lands. Shows some characteristic marsh plants and animals and points out some of their adaptations and interrelationships.
Science - Natural
Dist - CORF **Prod** - CORF 1973

We Get Married Twice 22 MIN
16mm
Color (J)
LC 74-700649
Tells of a couple who first celebrated their marriage with an informal gathering of friends at their lake front cottage where the rites were performed in the living room and then had a traditional Jewish ceremony, held in order to satisfy their parents, relatives and friends who did not attend the first.
Religion and Philosophy; Sociology
Dist - WEINSM **Prod** - WEINSM 1973

We Grew a Frog 13 MIN
16mm / U-matic / VHS
Color (P I)
LC 72-702127
Presents the elementary school science classroom activity of growing frogs from eggs in an aquarium. Explains the development of the eggs and the different stages of the growing process. Includes changes seen as the gills appear and disappear, the development of the back legs, loss of the tail and the development of the front legs.
Science; Science - Natural
Dist - IFB **Prod** - BHA 1971

We Hand the Torch to You 29 MIN
16mm
Color
LC 76-711573
A study of the Billy Graham Crusade in Europe, April 1970, which used the first - of - its - kind largest closed circuit TV with simultaneous translations to carry to 39 cities.
Religion and Philosophy; Social Science
Dist - WWPI **Prod** - WWPI 1970

We have a Dream 35 MIN
U-matic / VHS
Color
Follows three people who achieve their dreams despite severe odds. Includes stories of two handicapped persons overcoming disabilities and an adoptee locating his mother.
Health and Safety; Sociology
Dist - DCTVC **Prod** - DCTVC

We have an Addict in the House 30 MIN
U-matic / VHS / 16mm
Color (J)
LC 73-701394
Uses drug abuse to provide some insight into the psychosocial causes of alienation among young adults. Provides a situation wherein the participants can explore individual and group attitudes about drugs and about intra - family relationships.
Health and Safety; Psychology; Sociology
Dist - PFP **Prod** - COMFON 1973

We have Come of Age 13 MIN
16mm
Color (A)
Recognizes that those who helped build the nation and create its wealth are often the victims of gross neglect in their old age. Introduces retired persons to the National Council of Senior Citizens.
Business and Economics; Health and Safety; Sociology
Dist - AFLCIO **Prod** - NCSCIT 1973

We have Met the Enemy and He is Us 13 MIN
16mm
Color (J)
Takes a look at the problem of environmental pollution through the use of animation. Introduces the cartoon character, Pogo, who, with his friends, sets forth to find out who is responsible for pollution in the Okefenokee Swamp.
Science - Natural
Dist - CGWEST **Prod** - KELLYW

We have to be Able to do it Ourselves 27 MIN
16mm
Color
LC 72-700162
Provides a basic overview of the activities of a community design center through the voices of people from poor and minority inner - city communities, and of personnel working in local centers to provide architectural and planning services to these communities. Explores the work of community design centers in Cleveland, New Orleans, San Francisco and Philadelphia.
Social Science; Sociology
Dist - AIA **Prod** - AIA 1972

We hold these 12 MIN
16mm
Color; Silent (H C A)
Inquire for rental price
Features slightly recognizable patterns of fish and animal biology, plant and flower shapes, and human anatomy which are interwoven with pastel cubes and other geometries. Combines a sense of hair and mucous membranes with the electric "x-ray" sense of bones. Builds on the interplay between black and white sections and multi-colored sections until there is some sense of merging the two toward an end. Produced by Stan Brakhage.
Fine Arts; Science - Natural
Dist - CANCIN

We Hold these Truths 28 MIN
16mm
Color (J H A)
Presents a young Negro soldier, who after visiting freedom's shrines in Washington is depressed by slum conditions into which his people are forced by race segregation, but who takes new hope from a visit to East Harlem Protestant Parish.
Guidance and Counseling; Sociology
Dist - YALEDV **Prod** - YALEDV

We Hold these Truths 29 MIN
16mm
Color
LC 74-700484
Helps stimulate interest in the three themes of the American revolution bicentennial celebrations - heritage, horizon and festival. Shows how each of these themes is reflected in activities as varied as a health delivery system and an Afro - American Center for the Performing Arts in Boston.
Civics and Political Systems; Fine Arts; Physical Education and Recreation; Social Science
Dist - AMRBC **Prod** - AMRBC 1974

We Hold these Truths 15 MIN
16mm / U-matic / VHS
Color (I)
LC 75-703683
Considers the ideas and ideals expressed in the Declaration of Independence.
Civics and Political Systems; History - United States
Dist - AIMS **Prod** - PAR 1975

We interrupt this program 55 MIN
VHS
Color & B&W (G)
$19.98 purchase _ #UPC 30306 - 6057 - 3
Focuses on extraordinary news events - the assassination of Martin Luther King, Jr, April 4, 1968; the hijacking of TWA Flight 847, June 14, 1985; the San Francisco earthquake, October 17, 1989.
History - United States; Literature and Drama
Dist - INSTRU **Prod** - ABCNEW

We jive like this 52 MIN
VHS
Color (H C G)
$295.00 purchase, $75.00 rental
Reveals that in the South African townships created for the blacks - over 8 million people - there are no theaters, that the arts are not taught in black schools. Shows the spirit and energy of dance, poetry, theater and music of the townships as practiced in streets, backyards, garages and empty school rooms. Produced by Cinecontact - Kinoki Production for the Arts Council.
Geography - World; History - World
Dist - FLMLIB

We know where you live 58 MIN
U-matic / VHS

Nova series
Color (H C A)
$250.00 purchase _ #HP - 6377C
Looks at the growing marketing phenomenon of direct mail by direct marketers who hold extensive computer information on almost every household in the United States. Delves into the methods companies use to collect consumer data and build mailing lists, and the major criticisms the industry is facing. Part of the Nova series.
Business and Economics; Home Economics; Psychology
Dist - CORF **Prod** - WGBHTV 1990

We Know who We are 28 MIN
16mm
Color (H C A)
LC 77-703472
Presents case studies of three blind people who have overcome their disabilities through participation in a program offered by the Iowa Commission for the Blind, Orientation Center.
Geography - United States; Guidance and Counseling; Psychology
Dist - NFB **Prod** - NFB 1977

We Learn about the Telephone II 26 MIN
16mm
Color (P I)
Presents two elementary school teachers taking a group of ten third graders of different ethnic backgrounds to the telephone company exhibit at the Museum of Science and Industry. Shows how they meet Mr Richards who guides them through the exhibits and answers their questions as the children learn basic skills in using the telephone, including how to find numbers in the phone book.
Education
Dist - WAVE **Prod** - ATAT 1981

We Learn about the World 50 MIN
VHS
Learning Library Series
Color (K P I) (SPANISH)
Depicts the stories of other children who explore the world around them and learn from their daily experiences. Shapes, colors, sizes, etc. are visually explored.
Literature and Drama
Dist - BENNUP **Prod** - VIDKNW

We live next door series
Communications - getting the message 15 MIN
Earning and spending 15 MIN
Fire in Nutdale 15 MIN
Food comes to the neighborhood 15 MIN
Hospitals and helpers 15 MIN
Keeping the Neighborhood Clean 15 MIN
Meet the Neighborhood 15 MIN
The Neighborhood Works Together 15 MIN
Rules and Laws 15 MIN
Transportation - a Secret Agent Travels to Nutdale 15 MIN
Dist - TVOTAR

We lost control - illegal software duplication 16 MIN
VHS
Color (A)
$525.00 purchase
Explains the penalties for unauthorized software copying and what each person can do to protect the company and him or herself. Details provisions of licensing agreements and the Copyright Protection Act.
Business and Economics; Civics and Political Systems; Computer Science; Education
Dist - COMFLM **Prod** - COMFLM

We Love You Nasty 47 MIN
16mm
Color
LC 82-700137
Presents a film portrait of tennis star Ilie Nastase which has been set to music.
Biography; Physical Education and Recreation
Dist - PHILMO **Prod** - PHILMO 1981

We Love You Nasty, Pt 1 24 MIN
16mm
Color
LC 82-700137
Presents a film portrait of tennis star Ilie Nastase which has been set to music.
Physical Education and Recreation
Dist - PHILMO **Prod** - PHILMO 1981

We Love You Nasty, Pt 2 23 MIN
16mm
Color
LC 82-700137
Presents a film portrait of tennis star Ilie Nastase which has been set to music.
Physical Education and Recreation
Dist - PHILMO **Prod** - PHILMO 1981

We make anything 15 MIN
16mm / U-matic / VHS
American legacy series
Color (I)
Presents John Rugg showing the mass production of bicycles and automobiles to show the importance of the assembly line in American manufacturing. Highlights the ingredients and techniques of making iron and steel. Discusses the innovations of Henry Ford and Thomas Edison.
Business and Economics; History - United States
Dist - AITECH **Prod** - KRMATV 1983

We make Things 20 MIN
U-matic
Exploring Our Nation Series
Color (I)
Shows steel, automobiles, and apple pies being made. Defines technology, machinery, mass production, property, capital, labor and management.
Business and Economics; Social Science; Sociology
Dist - GPN **Prod** - KRMATV 1975

We Need each Other Series
Wandering through Winter, Pt 1 24 MIN
Wandering through Winter, Pt 2 26 MIN
Dist - CNEMAG

We Never Left Home 31 MIN
16mm
Color
LC 76-702214
Deals with the American South And Southern Living magazine. Includes scenes of various cities, resort areas and landscapes, showing how the magazine interacts with and serves its readers from Texas to the Southeast.
Geography - United States; Literature and Drama
Dist - PROFAC **Prod** - PROFAC 1976

We never talked about my drinking 58 MIN
VHS
Color (G)
$295.00 purchase, $100.00 rental
Features Dr Enoch Gordis and other specialists who comment on the extent of the misuse of alcohol in the United States - in most hospitals as high as 30 percent of illnesses treated have a substantial relation to alcohol intake, in VA hospitals as high as 50 percent. Reveals that patients are treated for liver problems, cirrhosis, heart disease and trauma, but are rarely confronted with their alcoholism in spite of the fact that alcoholism is not difficult to identify. Points out that health professionals are given very little education on alcoholism and too few hospitals have functioning employee assistance programs. Discusses the symptoms of alcoholism and reiterates the point that intervention is cheaper than hospitalization.
Health and Safety
Dist - BAXMED **Prod** - CPT 1993

We Owe Them that Much 20 MIN
16mm
Color
Deals with the mental and physical defects in rubella babies and the efforts to treat them. Supports an Oklahoma Medical Society effort to immunize a majority of Oklahoma children against rubella. Points out the results of the campaign.
Health and Safety; Home Economics; Psychology; Sociology
Dist - WKYTV **Prod** - WKYTV

We proceeded on... - the expedition of Lewis and Clark - 1804 - 1806 32 MIN
16mm / VHS
Color (I J H G)
$550.00, $89.00 purchase
Uses on - location footage, dramatic reenactments, journal excerpts and maps to document the 8000 mile journey into the American West by Meriwether Lewis and William Clark.
Geography - United States; History - United States
Dist - KAWVAL **Prod** - KAWVAL 1992

We Remember Amber Valley 25 MIN
16mm / VHS
Color (J)
$415.00, $95.00 purchase
Tells the story of Amber Valley, Canada's northernmost black community. Reveals that it was settled by black Americans in the early 1900s and became known throughout Northern Alberta for its baseball team. The community declined during the 1950s.
Geography - World; History - World; Social Science; Sociology
Dist - FLMWST

We remember - the space shuttle pioneers - 1981 - 1986 60 MIN
VHS
Color (G)
$29.95 purchase _ #S01939
Presents a tribute to the first U S space shuttle missions, from 1981 to 1986. Gives highlights of the 25 space shuttle flights that took place over that five - year period.
History - United States; History - World; Industrial and Technical Education
Dist - UILL

We See Them through 21 MIN
U-matic / VHS / 16mm
B&W (A)
Shows what Rhode Island is doing to integrate a broad co - ordinated network of services to bring new health and hope to young rheumatic patients.
Health and Safety; Psychology
Dist - IFB **Prod** - IFB 1948

We Seek no Wider War 6 MIN
16mm
Screen news digest series; Vol 7; Issue 8
B&W
Shows how America's involvement in Vietnam deepened in 1965 with further Viet Cong attacks and U S retaliation. Defense Secretary Mc Namara emphasizes that the U S does not desire to broaden the conflict.
Civics and Political Systems; History - World
Dist - HEARST **Prod** - HEARST 1965

We shall march again 8 MIN
16mm
B&W (G)
$10.00 rental
Depicts the 1965 Vietnam Day Peace March, remembered for the Hell's Angels' attack. Provides an historical perspective on the period.
Fine Arts; History - United States; Sociology
Dist - CANCIN **Prod** - LIPTNL 1965

We shall overcome 58 MIN
VHS
Color (G)
$250.00 purchase, $75.00 rental
Traces the sources of the song We Shall Overcome from an isolated woodframe church on the tidal islands of South Carolina through a 1945 tobacco strike in Charleston and its discovery by Peter Seeger and Guy Carawan who taught the song to young activists of the Civil Rights Movement. Features Harry Belafonte as narrator, footage of the SNCC Freedom Singers, Julian Bond, Andrew Young, folksingers Peter, Paul and Mary, and Joan Baez at the 1963 March on Washington. Produced by Jim Brown, Ginger Brown, Harold Leventhal and George Stoney.
Civics and Political Systems; Fine Arts; History - United States
Dist - CANWRL

We shall overcome - a history of the civil rights movement 20 MIN
VHS
Color (I J H)
$55.00 purchase _ #5464VD
Uses historic and modern photographs to tell the complete story of the struggle of African Americans for full equality. Reviews the years of slavery, reconstruction, and 'Jim Crow' segregation. Focuses on the dramatic events of the 1950s and 1960s. Assesses the impact of the still unfinished revolution on American life.
Civics and Political Systems; History - United States; Sociology
Dist - KNOWUN **Prod** - KNOWUN 1989

We sing for safety 30 MIN
VHS
Color (H A T K P)
$29.95 purchase _ #MK800
Presents seven original songs and safety reminders. Features Bill McClellan and singing children.
Education; Fine Arts; Health and Safety
Dist - AAVIM **Prod** - AAVIM 1992

We Sing more than We Cry 16 MIN
16mm
Color
_ #106C 0175 007N
Geography - World
Dist - CFLMDC **Prod** - NFBC 1975

We Speak Spanish 28 MIN
VHS / 16mm
Que Pasa, U S a Series
Color (G)
$46.00 rental _ #QUEP - 105
Social Science; Sociology
Dist - PBS **Prod** - WPBTTV

We the Addicts, Pt I 60 MIN
U-matic / VHS
B&W
Offers comments and opinions by drug and alcohol addicts at Wisconsin's Waupun State Prison on how they started using drugs and on the lack of rehabilitation programs in and out of prison.

Sociology
Dist - UWISC **Prod** - UWISC 1971

We the Addicts, Pt II 60 MIN
VHS / U-matic
B&W
Offers discussion by drug and alcohol addicts at Wisconsin's Waupun State Prison on the effects of drugs on one's personality and inconsistencies in the criminal court system in sentencing for drug related and non - drug related crimes.
Sociology
Dist - UWISC **Prod** - UWISC 1971

We, the Japanese People 25 MIN
16mm
B&W
LC FIE52-2115
Shows some of the democratic changes the Japanese people have adopted since 1945.
Civics and Political Systems; History - World
Dist - USNAC **Prod** - USA 1952

We the People 15 MIN
VHS / U-matic
It's all Up to You Series
Color (I J)
Looks at national governments and their functions.
Civics and Political Systems
Dist - AITECH **Prod** - COOPED 1978

We the People - a Freshman Comes to Washington / the Two Houses of Congress, Pt 1 30 MIN
VHS / U-matic
Congress - We the People Series
Color
Introduces Congress through the eyes of a newly - elected representative.
Civics and Political Systems
Dist - FI **Prod** - WETATV 1984

We, the People - Careers in Public Service 13 MIN
16mm
Working Worlds Series
Color (I J H)
LC 75-701544
Deals with career opportunities within government. Examines all levels of government and stresses that careers are available for people with all kinds of educational backgrounds and skills. Divides public service careers into legislation, law enforcement and the courts, transportation, social services, commercial regulation and international affairs.
Guidance and Counseling; Psychology
Dist - FFORIN **Prod** - OLYMPS 1974

We the People Series
Free to Believe 56 MIN
Law and Order 56 MIN
What Price Equality 56 MIN
Who's in Charge 56 MIN
Dist - FOTH

We, the People - Story of Our Federal Government 20 MIN
16mm
Screen news digest series; Vol 10; Issue 6
Color (H)
LC FIA68-1821
Examines the federal government and explains how it has worked for almost two hundred years to serve 'WE, THE PEOPLE.'.
Civics and Political Systems
Dist - HEARST **Prod** - HEARST 1968

We the people - The Growth of the Constitution 13 MIN
VHS / U-matic
Constitution series
Color (I J H)
$280.00, $330.00 purchase, $50.00 rental
Depicts courageous people who defended or challenged Constitutional law. Employs dramatic reenactment, live action and archival footage that includes a family that opposed secessionist efforts leading to the Civil War, the Women's Suffrage movement in the early 1900s and the Civil Rights movement of the 1960s.
Civics and Political Systems; History - United States
Dist - NDIM **Prod** - VIDDIA 1992

We, the People - the Story of Our Federal Government 28 MIN
16mm
B&W (H)
LC 74-706320
Portrays the organization and responsibilities of the legislative, executive and judicial branches of the U S government as it is run by and for the people.
Civics and Political Systems
Dist - USNAC **Prod** - USDD 1967

We Tiptoed Around Whispering 30 MIN
16mm
Western Maryland College Series
Color (A)
LC 74-706319
Presents a dramatization and documentary on what parents of deaf children experience from the birth of their child until the deafness is diagnosed.
Guidance and Counseling; Psychology; Sociology
Dist - USNAC **Prod** - USBEH 1973

We Use Mammography 1 MIN
U-matic / VHS
Color
Shows a radiologist stressing the safety of low dose x - rays and their effectiveness in detecting breast cancer, some - times before a lump can be felt. Concludes with message that 'Today, a tiny breast cancer is almost always curable.'.
Health and Safety
Dist - AMCS **Prod** - AMCS 1979

We Use the Number Line 11 MIN
16mm / U-matic / VHS
Color (P)
LC 70-706796
Introduces the number line as a useful way to represent numbers and understand addition and subtraction.
Mathematics
Dist - CORF **Prod** - CORF 1970

We were German Jews 58 MIN
VHS / U-matic
Color
Grapples with the torment of living with the legacy of the Holocaust. Shows a surviving couple confronting their past by returning to where they lived before the onslaught that claimed most of their relatives.
History - World; Sociology
Dist - BLACKW **Prod** - BLACKW

We were Just Too Young 30 MIN
U-matic / VHS / 16mm
Color
LC 79-701122
Looks at teenage parents whose lives have been burdened by bad decisions and unrealistic expectations. Focuses on the problems of unemployment, lack of education, demands of child care and lack of freedom.
Guidance and Counseling; Health and Safety; Psychology; Sociology
Dist - CORF **Prod** - MITCHG 1979

We were marked with a big 'A' 44 MIN
VHS
Color (G)
$24.95 purchase _ #25012
Features three homosexual Holocaust survivors who provide testimony in a German video with English subtitles. Tells of duplicity, arrest, humiliation, beatings, castration and survival in work camps. The title comes from the the yellow cloth imprinted with the letter 'A' that homosexuals were forced to wear prior to the use of pink triangles. Produced by Mediengruppe Schwabing Film Production.
Civics and Political Systems; History - World; Sociology
Dist - USHMC

We were Separate People 29 MIN
U-matic
A Different Understanding Series
Color (PRO)
Gives a follow up seven years later on four people who attended a McGill University summer program for adolescents with learning disabilities.
Psychology
Dist - TVOTAR **Prod** - TVOTAR 1985

We were Separate People 29 MIN
VHS / 16mm
A Different Understanding Series
Color (G)
$90.00 purchase _ #BPN230607
Discusses the experiences four young people with leaarning disabilities had in the 7 years after attending a McGill University summer program for learning disabled adolescents. Talks about their plans for the future. Features black and white footage from the original programs and comments by its director, Dr Renee Steven.
Education; Psychology
Dist - RMIBHF **Prod** - RMIBHF

We were So Beloved 145 MIN
16mm
Color (G)
Presents an independent production by Manny Kirchheimer. Documents the excape by Jews to New York City's Washington Heights.
Fine Arts; Geography - United States; History - United States; Sociology
Dist - FIRS

We were the Ones who Decided 28 MIN
16mm
Color
LC 77-702704
Investigates reconstruction efforts in Niger and Mali which have received encouragement from churches and organizations. Shows how both projects are affecting the lives of nomadic herdsmen who were hardest hit by the 1973 drought conditions.
Geography - World; Social Science; Sociology
Dist - RTVA **Prod** - RTVA 1976

We were there 30 MIN
VHS
Color & B&W (G)
$29.99 purchase
Depicts victims of Nazi concentration camps and their view of Jewish United States soldiers who liberated them.
History - World
Dist - DANEHA **Prod** - DANEHA 1994

We were There - but not for Conquest 28 MIN
16mm
Color
Tells the story of the U S Army Corps of Engineers in peace and war from its inception in 1775. Highlights their many contributions.
Civics and Political Systems; Industrial and Technical Education
Dist - MTP **Prod** - USAE

We who grieve 60 MIN
VHS
Pastoral bereavement counseling series
Color (R G)
$49.95 purchase _ #PSBC1
Helps participants to understand the dynamics of grief and 'tasks' necessary to journey from grief to healing. Develops the personal, technical and pastoral skills necessary to assist the griever. Shows how to design and lead an effective bereavement ministry team. Features Dr Patrick Del Zoppo. Part of eight parts of a complete training program in ministry to the bereaved. Workbook available separately.
Guidance and Counseling; Health and Safety; Religion and Philosophy; Sociology
Dist - CTNA **Prod** - CTNA

We will Freeze in the Dark 42 MIN
U-matic / VHS / 16mm
Color (H C A)
LC 77-701996
Shows examples of how conservation, when spurred by self - interest or economic incentive, can help solve the energy dilemma in the United States.
Business and Economics; Science - Natural
Dist - MGHT **Prod** - CAPCC 1977

We will not be Beaten 40 MIN
U-matic
B&W
Recounts experiences of battered women and shelter staff members. Demonstrates the incredibly difficult dilemmas that countless women face as a result of society's neglect and the economic straight - jacket in which women with children find themselves.
Sociology
Dist - WMENIF **Prod** - TRANSH

We will not do Nothing 20 MIN
16mm
Color
LC 73-702067
Contrasts the effective results achieved by a branch of the League of Women Voters in San Francisco concerning the passage of a school bond issue with the frustrated attempts of a women's organization which is neither well organized nor politically involved.
Civics and Political Systems; Sociology
Dist - SFLWV **Prod** - SFLWV 1973

We won't leave you 17 MIN
16mm / VHS
Documentaries for learning series
Color (C G PRO)
$310.00, $60.00 purchase, $29.00 rental _ #24272
Shows how the presence of family members can reduce the psychological stress of a child's hospital experience. Focuses on the use of the hospital's one - day surgery unit for a hernia operation on a five - year - old girl. Part of a series produced for use by health care professionals and educators.
Health and Safety; Psychology; Sociology
Dist - PSU **Prod** - MASON 1975

We would see Jesus 120 MIN
VHS
Color (J H C G A R)
$59.95 purchase _ #35 - 8401 - 2087
Provides a six - session look at the last week of Jesus' life, as seen from the perspective of John of Zebedee, Peter, and Mary the sister of Lazarus. Features footage of the

Holy Land. Includes a student workbook. Produced by Kerr and Associates.
Literature and Drama; Religion and Philosophy
Dist - APH

The Weakest link 13 MIN
BETA / VHS / U-matic
Color (IND G)
$395.00 purchase _ #600 - 24
Details the physical stress factors that can cause carpal tunnel syndrome, tendinitis, bursitis and similar repetitive motion disorders. Discusses the symptoms and physical effects of carpal tunnel syndrome, the importance of prompt medical attention. Demonstrates appropriate work practices and exercises designed to prevent repetitive motion disorders.
Business and Economics; Health and Safety; Psychology
Dist - ITSC **Prod** - ITSC

The Weakest Link 18 MIN
16mm / U-matic / VHS
Color
Demonstrates safe lifting procedures for crane operators.
Health and Safety
Dist - IFB **Prod** - MILLBK

The Weakest Link - Guarding Against Head and Neck Injuries 12 MIN
16mm / U-matic / VHS
Football Injury Prevention Series
Color (I J H)
Deals with the importance of properly - fitted, approved football helmets and the requirement that players understand and abide by regulations against dangerous practices, such as spearing, butt blocking and face mask tackling. Explains and demonstrates correct blocking and tackling techniques.
Physical Education and Recreation
Dist - ATHI **Prod** - ATHI

Weaknesses of the Flesh 22 MIN
U-matic
Intensive Course in Neuromuscular Diseases Series
Color (PRO)
LC 76-706129
Presents Dr Michael H Brooke describing the effects of neuromuscular diseases on human bodily functions such as walking and sitting.
Health and Safety; Science - Natural
Dist - USNAC **Prod** - NINDIS 1974

Wealth and poverty 8 MIN
16mm
Color & B&W (G)
$15.00 rental
Features sarcastic commentary on the theories about the work ethic of conservative economist George Gilder. Points out that unfortunately his ideas were influential to Ronald Reagan's budget advisors. Produced by Linda Tadic.
Business and Economics; Civics and Political Systems; Fine Arts
Dist - CANCIN

Wealth and Prosperity 30 MIN
VHS
Video Reflections Series
Color (G)
$29.95 purchase _ #VPRS
Combines images of nature with music and soothing environmental sounds. Uses visual and auditory subliminal messages to promote enhancement of financial success.
Psychology; Social Science; Sociology
Dist - GAINST **Prod** - GAINST

Wealth, make it Come to You - for Men and for Women by Audio Activation, Inc 60 MIN
U-matic / VHS
Self Help Subliminal Series
Stereo
Shows relaxation techniques, affirmations, subliminal messages of images of affluence and luxury.
Psychology
Dist - BANTAP **Prod** - BANTAP

Wealth Out of Wilderness 24 MIN
16mm
B&W (I J)
Pictures the development of the major uses of California's land since the first Indian settlers.
Agriculture; Geography - United States; History - United States
Dist - MLA **Prod** - ABCTV 1963

The Weapon of choice - Part 2 60 MIN
U-matic / VHS
War and peace in the nuclear age series
Color (G)
$45.00, $29.95 purchase
Explores the growing reliance of the superpowers on nuclear weaponry against the backdrop of the Cold War, the development of the hydrogen bomb and the war in Korea. Part two of a thirteen - part series on war and peace in the nuclear age.
Civics and Political Systems; History - United States; History - World; Sociology
Dist - ANNCPB **Prod** - WGBHTV 1989

Weaponeers of the Deep 28 MIN
16mm
Color
LC 74-705940
Acquaints members of selected civic organizations and personnel at Navy Recruit Training Centers with the educational and career opportunities of serving as an FBM weaponeer in the Polaris Submarine Fleet.
Civics and Political Systems
Dist - USNAC **Prod** - USN 1967

Weapons Controller - Key to Effective Air Defense 22 MIN
16mm
Color
LC 74-706321
Portrays the global role of weapons controller and describes career opportunities in this field.
Civics and Political Systems; Guidance and Counseling; History - United States; Industrial and Technical Education; Psychology
Dist - USNAC **Prod** - USAF 1968

Weapons in Space - National Teleconference on Space - Based Missile Defense 28 MIN
U-matic / VHS
Color
Analyzes the feasibility and consequences of space - based defenses. Presents four distinguished Americans who comment on these questions in a condensed version of the nationally televised two hour teleconference on space weapons in April 1984. Includes the seven - minute program Weapons in Space - An Overview.
Civics and Political Systems; Sociology
Dist - EFVP **Prod** - EFVP

Weapons in the workplace 40 MIN
VHS
Color (T PRO C G)
$425.00 purchase
Teaches staff proactive strategies which can be put into place at a facility immediately. Gives realistic, effective measures to take to reduce the risk of a weapons incident. Shows how to respond safely, if an incident should occur, during the critical time between when a weapon is first introduced and when professional law enforcement personnel arrive. Covers incidents when people are threatened with assault with everyday objects never intended to be used as weapons. Illustrates how to arrange space to avoid being trapped by a violent individual, strategic visualizations to boost confidence and save lives, negotiation over weapons, safety tips when traveling, relying on instincts, early intervention techniques, safety assessments. Reference manual.
Social Science; Sociology
Dist - NCPI **Prod** - NCPI 1995

Weapons of the Infantry 21 MIN
16mm
Color (PRO)
LC 77-700753
Shows characteristics, employment, capabilities and limitations of weapons used in the Infantry. Covers M14, M14A1 and M16A1 rifles, the M79 grenade launcher, M60 and .50 caliber machineguns, the M72 rocket, the 3.5 rocket launcher, 90 mm and 106 mm recoiless rifles, 81 mm and 4.2 - inch mortars and the .50 caliber spotting gun.
Civics and Political Systems
Dist - USNAC **Prod** - USA 1968

Weapons of the Spirit 90 MIN
16mm
Color (G)
Presents an independent production by Pierre Sauvage. Tells the story of Le Chambon, a small French village which successfully defied the Nazis during World War II. Recalls that 5000 peasants and villagers gave refuge to 5000 Jews under the nose of Vichy French collaborators. Also available in 35mm film format.
History - World; Religion and Philosophy; Sociology
Dist - FIRS
ICARUS

Weapons of the spirit 30 MIN
VHS / U-matic / BETA
Color (I J H G)
$60.00, $50.00 purchase
Follows filmmaker Pierre Sauvage to the village Le Chambonsur - Lignon in south - central France. Reveals that the 5,000 residents of the village during World War II saved 5,000 Jews from the Nazis. Examines the issue of moral choice during difficult times. Includes discussion guide.
Civics and Political Systems; Guidance and Counseling; History - World; Sociology
Dist - ADL **Prod** - ADL

The Weapons of war - Book 3 98 MIN
VHS
Vietnam - the 10,000 day war series
Color (H C A)
$24.95 purchase
Presents Book Three of the 'Vietnam - The 10,000 Day War series. Surveys the weapons used in the war.
History - United States
Dist - PBS **Prod** - WNETTV

Weapons Ranges 40 MIN
U-matic / VHS
Color
Shows the Strategic Air Command crews participating in actual firing exercises. Shows bombing, strafing, rocketry, shooting at air - tow targets and drones.
Civics and Political Systems
Dist - IHF **Prod** - IHF

Weapons Safety 7 MIN
U-matic / VHS
Color
LC 81-707115
Demonstrates operation, malfunctions and methods of clearing malfunctions of the UZI submachine gun and the Remington model 870 shotgun.
Civics and Political Systems
Dist - USNAC **Prod** - USSS 1981

Weapons Safety, Pt 5 - the M203 Grenade Launcher 10 MIN
16mm
Color
LC 80-701847
Demonstrates safety precautions to be used when firing the M203 grenade launcher mounted on an M16 rifle. Shows minimum firing range and illustrates how to identify the correct ammunition.
Civics and Political Systems
Dist - USNAC **Prod** - USA 1973

Weapons Safety, Pt 6 - the M18A1 Claymore Mine 13 MIN
16mm
Color
LC 80-701848
Demonstrates safety precautions to be used when laying, arming, firing and disarming the Claymore antipersonnel mine.
Civics and Political Systems
Dist - USNAC **Prod** - USA 1973

Wear 32 MIN
U-matic / VHS
Tribology 1 - Friction, Wear, and Lubrication Series
Color
Discusses wear, its definition, its place both as a cause of loss of usefulness and a process with many uses.
Industrial and Technical Education
Dist - MIOT **Prod** - MIOT

Wear and Care of Soft Contact Lenses
U-matic / VHS
Color
Details the methods for cleaning, disinfecting and storing soft contact lenses.
Science - Natural
Dist - MIFE **Prod** - MIFE

Wearable art
VHS
Color (G A)
$24.95 purchase _ #NN500V
Teaches the techniques of creating wearable art in sewing.
Home Economics
Dist - CAMV

Wearable art from California - K Lee Manuel 27 MIN
VHS
Wearable art from California series
Color (H C G)
$195.00 purchase, $35.00 rental _ #37347
Features the unique painted leather garments and accessories that incorporate painted feathers and feather imagery by K Lee Manuel. Explores the sources of her imagery and her evolution over the past 15 years as one of the pioneers of the wearable art movement. Part of a series produced by Instructional Media, University of

California, Davis, for Prof Jo Ann Stabb, Dept of Environmental Design.
Fine Arts; Home Economics
Dist - UCEMC

Wearable Art from California Series
Gaza Bowen - Shoemaker 29 MIN
Jean Cacicedo 25 MIN
Katherine Westphal 27 MIN
Dist - UCD

Wearable art from California series
Ellen Hauptli/Candace Kling 45 MIN
Dist - UCDEXT

Wearable art from California series
Presents a five - part series produced by Instructional Media, University of California, Davis, for Prof Jo Ann Stabb, Dept of Environmental Design. Includes the artists Ellen Hauptli - Candace Kling; Gaza Bowen - Shoemaker; Katherine Westphal; Jean Cacicedo; and K Lee Manuel.
Wearable art from California - K Lee Manuel 27 MIN
Dist - UCEMC

Wearing a Cast 30 MIN
BETA / VHS
Mister Rogers - Health and Safety Series
Color (P I J) (SPANISH)
Shows how casts are applied and removed. Shows children how they can do many things for themselves even while wearing a cast. Features Mister Rogers.
Health and Safety
Dist - BRENTM **Prod** - BRENTM

Wearing a Cast 17 MIN
VHS / U-matic
Let's Talk about the Hospital Series
Color (P) (SPANISH)
Features Mister Rogers in a program which shows how casts are applied and removed and how children can do many things for themselves even while wearing a cast.
Foreign Language; Health and Safety; Psychology; Science - Natural
Dist - FAMCOM **Prod** - FAMCOM

Wearing Extended Wear - Soft Contact Lenses 11 MIN
VHS / U-matic
Color
Introduces the patient to the basic principles and benefits of extended wear lenses. Discusses proper technique of application, removal, hygiene and care.
Health and Safety; Science - Natural
Dist - MEDCOM **Prod** - MEDCOM

Wearing Soft Contact Lenses - Chemical Disinfection 8 MIN
U-matic / VHS
Color
Discusses application, removal, proper hygiene and care of soft lenses.
Health and Safety; Science - Natural
Dist - MEDCOM **Prod** - MEDCOM

Wearing Soft Contact Lenses - Heat Disinfection 8 MIN
U-matic / VHS
Color
Discusses application, removal, proper hygiene and care of soft lenses.
Health and Safety; Science - Natural
Dist - MEDCOM **Prod** - MEDCOM

Wearout Failure 30 MIN
VHS / U-matic
Reliability Engineering Series
Color (IND)
Describes use of the normal distribution for modelling wearout failure. Presents example of how to estimate the economic time to do preventative maintenance.
Industrial and Technical Education
Dist - COLOSU **Prod** - COLOSU

Wearout Failure - Examples 30 MIN
U-matic / VHS
Reliability Engineering Series
Color (IND)
Contains worked - out examples of wearout failure problems to supplement previous lecture.
Industrial and Technical Education
Dist - COLOSU **Prod** - COLOSU

A Weary Pilgrimage 29 MIN
U-matic
Country of Old Men Series
Color
Discusses the aging theory proposed by David Gutman of the Psychology Department at the University of Michigan.
Sociology
Dist - UMITV **Prod** - UMITV 1974

Weather 3 MIN
U-matic / VHS
Science Rock Series
Color (I)
Explains how tornados, thunderstorms and other climatic wonders happen.
Science - Physical
Dist - GA **Prod** - ABCTV

Weather 20 MIN
16mm
Color (H C A)
$400 purchase, $50 rental
Examines the science of weather forecasting and efforts to improve forecasting and control weather.
Science - Physical
Dist - CNEMAG **Prod** - DOCUA 1988

Weather 15 MIN
VHS / U-matic
Matter and Motion Series Module Brown; Module brown
Color (I)
Considers how the weather influences one's life.
Science - Physical; Sociology
Dist - AITECH **Prod** - WHROTV 1973

Weather 29 MIN
VHS / 16mm
Villa Alegre Series
Color (P T)
$46.00 rental _ #VILA - 152
Presents educational material in both Spanish and English.
Education; Science - Physical
Dist - PBS

Weather 30 MIN
VHS
How do you do - learning English series
Color (H A)
#317715
Shows that stormy weather prompts CHIPS to find out about weather forecasting, weather terms and weather maps. Explains some colloquial expressions for different types of weather. Visits a weather office. Part of a series that helps newcomers learn English or improve their ability. Includes viewer's guide with grammar explanations and vocabulary drills, worksheets and two audio cassettes.
English Language; Science - Physical
Dist - TVOTAR **Prod** - TVOTAR 1990

Weather - a film for beginners 14 MIN
VHS
Color; PAL (P I)
PdS29.50 purchase
Uses simple experiments to observe the role of the Sun in creating changes in the weather. Illustrates various concepts with animated graphics.
Science; Science - Physical
Dist - EMFVL **Prod** - ALTSUL

Weather - Air in Action Series
Fronts and Storms 11 MIN
Pressure and Humidity 10 MIN
Temperature and Wind 8 MIN
Dist - AIMS

Weather and climate
VHS
Color (P I J)
$88.00 purchase _ #0185
Shows how a wind is born, why a raindrop falls and where animals go in wintertime.
Science - Natural; Science - Physical
Dist - SEVVID

Weather and Climate 25 MIN
U-matic / VHS
Weather and Climate Series
Color (K P I)
Contains 1 videocassette.
Science; Science - Physical
Dist - TROLA **Prod** - TROLA 1987

Weather and climate 18 MIN
VHS
Geography tutor series
Color (J H)
$49.00 _ #60460 - 026
Features part of an six - part series on geography packed with illustrated terms, concepts and site studies to reinforce specific content. Includes teacher's guide.
Education; Geography - World; Science - Physical
Dist - GA

Weather and climate 18 MIN
VHS
Geography tutor series
Color (J H C G)
$49.95 purchase _ #BM105V-S
Explains weather patterns, how they are formed and climate changes around the world. Illustrates covered topics which are referenced through an on-screen digital timer. Includes teacher's guide and glossary. Part of a six-part series on geography.
Geography - World; Science - Physical
Dist - CAMV

Weather and Climate Series
Weather and Climate 25 MIN
Dist - TROLA

Weather and Radar 17 MIN
16mm
Aerology Series
B&W
LC FI54-159
Illustrates some of the operational values to be gained by using radar in locating and identifying weather disturbances, including cold fronts, warm fronts, thunderstorms, typhoons and hurricanes. Shows characteristic echo patterns on the planned positionindicator scope.
Industrial and Technical Education; Social Science
Dist - USNAC **Prod** - USN 1954

Weather Building 10 MIN
16mm
Color
LC 77-702705
Presents an experimental film depicting three - dimensional planes through positive - negative images, illuminated surfaces and video images.
Fine Arts; Industrial and Technical Education
Dist - CANFDC **Prod** - MCLARR 1976

Weather by Numbers 30 MIN
16mm / U-matic / VHS
Experiment Series
Color (J)
Shows how Dr Joseph Smagorinsky and his colleagues at the Environmental Science Services Administration experiment with mathematical equations and computers for predicting the weather.
Mathematics; Science - Physical
Dist - IU **Prod** - NET 1966

Weather - Come Rain, Come Shine 22 MIN
16mm / U-matic / VHS
Color (I)
LC 83-700362
Discusses the global weather machine involving the interaction of sun, air and water. Shows old and new weather forecasting tools, including anemometers, barometers and satellites.
Science - Physical
Dist - NGS **Prod** - NGS 1983

Weather Does its Thing 28 MIN
U-matic / VHS / 16mm
Color (J H C)
LC 74-701767
Shows the ways in which scientists and meteorologists are probing the past for clues to previous climates and are using the information they find to help them make long - term climatic predictions.
Science; Science - Physical
Dist - JOU **Prod** - UN 1974

Weather dynamics
Videodisc
Color; CAV (I J)
$189.00 purchase _ #8L223
Features a scientist from the National Center for Atmospheric Research who conducts simple experiments to illustrate various factors influencing weather. Teaches about cloud formation, temperature inversion, the formation of tornadoes, what drives weather systems and the Coriolus effect. Barcoded for instant random access.
Science - Physical
Dist - BARR **Prod** - BARR 1991

Weather Dynamics 20 MIN
VHS / 16mm
Color (I)
LC 90707575
Demonstrates basic principles of weather dynamics. Shows how these dynamics affect weather both globally and locally.
Science - Physical
Dist - BARR

The Weather Eye 13 MIN
16mm
Color (H C)
LC 78-700857
Describes the design, development, and fabrication of Snap - 19, a small, long - lived, radioisotope - fueled nuclear generator designed to be the auxiliary power for the nimbus weather satellite.
Industrial and Technical Education; Science - Physical
Dist - USNAC **Prod** - USNRC 1969

Weather Eye 29 MIN
16mm
Color
LC 75-700885
Describes the duties of an aerographer's mate assigned to a duty station with the U S Naval Weather Service.
Guidance and Counseling; Science; Science - Physical
Dist - USNAC **Prod** - USN 1974

Weather Eye for Safety 20 MIN
U-matic / VHS
Color (IND)
Explains the procedures and equipment unique to a petroleum and petroleum product tanker. Includes special smoking restrictions, cargo hazards, compartment precautions and slip, trip and fall hazards.
Business and Economics; Health and Safety; Industrial and Technical Education; Social Science
Dist - UTEXPE **Prod** - TEXACO

Weather for Beginners 10 MIN
U-matic / VHS / 16mm
Color (P)
Demonstrates concepts of weather, such as why air above land gets warmer than air above water, what causes winds, how clouds form and why it rains.
Science - Physical
Dist - CORF **Prod** - CORF 1964

The Weather Forecaster 15 MIN
U-matic
Harriet's Magic Hats III Series
(P I J)
Shows that forecasters predict weather using information such as wind direction, cloud cover and temperature.
Guidance and Counseling
Dist - ACCESS **Prod** - ACCESS 1985

Weather Forecasting 22 MIN
U-matic / VHS / 16mm
Earth Science Program Series
Color (I J)
Examines the history of weather forecasting and shows the kinds of instruments and techniques used to forecast the weather.
Science - Physical
Dist - EBEC **Prod** - EBEC 1975

Weather fronts and precipitation 9 MIN
VHS
Meteorology series
Color (J H)
$34.95 purchase _ #193 W 0061
Explores weather fronts and the meteorological phenomena that they cause. Part of a six - part single concept series which uses NASA footage to complement experimental devices and laboratory set - ups to demonstrate basic meteorological principles.
Science - Physical
Dist - WARDS **Prod** - WARDS

Weather I 30 MIN
U-matic / VHS
Say it with sign series; Pt 6
Color (H C A) (AMERICAN SIGN)
Presents Lawrence Solow and Sharon Neumann Solow introducing American Sign Language used by the hearing - impaired. Emphasizes signs that have to do with the weather.
Education
Dist - FI **Prod** - KNBCTV 1982

Weather II 30 MIN
VHS / U-matic
Say it with sign series; Pt 7
Color (H C A) (AMERICAN SIGN)
Presents Lawrence Solow and Sharon Neumann Solow introducing American Sign Language used by the hearing - impaired. Emphasizes signs that have to do with the weather.
Education
Dist - FI **Prod** - KNBCTV 1982

Weather is Out 15 MIN
U-matic / VHS
Other families, other friends series; Green module; Quebec
Color (P)
Shows the Cree culture on Cape Jones in Quebec.
Geography - World; Social Science
Dist - AITECH **Prod** - WVIZTV 1971

The Weather Machine, Pt 1 59 MIN
16mm / U-matic / VHS
Color (H C A)
LC 76-703948
Discusses various methods of observing climatic changes, such as examining ice layers, following global weather patterns by satellite, computer - assisted forecasting, weather modification and weather research.
Science; Science - Physical
Dist - IU **Prod** - EDUCBC 1977

The Weather Machine, Pt 2 58 MIN
16mm / U-matic / VHS
Color (H C A)
LC 76-703948
Offers examples of change in global climate, including major and minor ice ages, changes in the jet stream's flow, changing solar radiation, increasing levels of carbon dioxide, droughts and inconsistent rainfall patterns.
Science - Physical
Dist - IU **Prod** - EDUCBC 1977

The Weather Map 12 MIN
16mm
Color (J H)
LC FIA68-2247
Presents an explanation and interpretation of the weather map.
Science - Physical; Social Science
Dist - AUIS **Prod** - ANAIB 1968

The Weather People 15 MIN
VHS / 16mm
Color (K)
LC 89715690
Explains how a television weather report is created. Outlines the different weather - related jobs and their duties.
Fine Arts; Science - Physical
Dist - BARR

Weather Science - Pierrot and Lightning and Thunder 5 MIN
U-matic / VHS / 16mm
Weather Science Series
Color (P)
Introduces a cartoon character named Pierrot and his friends, who explain the causes of thunderstorms, thunder and lightning.
Science - Physical
Dist - CORF **Prod** - CORF 1979

Weather Science - Pierrot and Rain and Snow 7 MIN
U-matic / VHS / 16mm
Weather Science Series
Color (P)
Introduces a cartoon character named Pierrot and his friends, who explain the water cycle and the causes of clouds, rain and snow.
Science - Physical
Dist - CORF **Prod** - CORF 1979

Weather Science - Pierrot and the Rainbow 6 MIN
U-matic / VHS / 16mm
Weather Science Series
Color (P)
Introduces a cartoon character named Pierrot and his friends, who explain how a rainbow is formed.
Science - Physical
Dist - CORF **Prod** - CORF 1979

Weather Science - Pierrot and the Sun 6 MIN
16mm / U-matic / VHS
Weather Science Series
Color (P)
Introduces a cartoon character named Pierrot and his friends, who explain the characteristics of the sun and its effect on the earth.
Science - Physical
Dist - CORF **Prod** - CORF 1979

Weather Science - Pierrot and the Wind 4 MIN
U-matic / VHS / 16mm
Weather Science Series
Color (P)
Introduces a cartoon character named Pierrot and his friends, who explain how the sun, the moving earth, mountains and bodies of water affect the movement of winds.
Science - Physical
Dist - CORF **Prod** - CORF 1979

Weather Science Series
Pierrot and Lightning and Thunder 5 MIN
Pierrot and Rain and Snow 7 MIN
Pierrot and the Rainbow 6 MIN
Pierrot and the Sun 6 MIN
Pierrot and the Wind 4 MIN
Weather Science - Pierrot and Lightning and Thunder 5 MIN
Weather Science - Pierrot and Rain and Snow 7 MIN
Weather Science - Pierrot and the Rainbow 6 MIN
Weather Science - Pierrot and the Sun 6 MIN
Weather Science - Pierrot and the Wind 4 MIN
Dist - CORF

Weather series
Climate - the summing up 29 MIN
The Core of the matter 29 MIN
The Formation of clouds 29 MIN
Hurricanes 28 MIN
Jet Streams 29 MIN
Rainmaking 29 MIN
The Thunderstorm 29 MIN
Tornadoes 29 MIN
The Ups and Downs of Highs and Lows 29 MIN
What's Behind the Front 30 MIN
Dist - PBS

Weather systems 15 MIN
VHS
Understanding science series
Color (J H)
$39.00 purchase _ #60491 - 026
Part of a series that presents difficult scientific concepts in an easy - to - understand format designed with natural stopping points so the instructor can choose when to stop for classroom discussion.
Science - Physical
Dist - GA **Prod** - GA 1993

Weather systems 22 MIN
VHS
Understanding science video series
Color (I J H)
$39.95 purchase _ #KUS206
Covers weather patterns, atmospheric factors that cause weather, heat transfer and wind patterns and more. Presents part of a six - part series on science.
Science - Physical
Dist - KNOWUN

Weather Systems in Motion 14 MIN
U-matic / VHS / 16mm
Atmospheric Science Series
Color (I J H C)
$400, $250 purchase _ #4624C
Discusses how weather systems form and how their movements causes alternating storms and fair weather.
Science - Physical
Dist - CORF **Prod** - VIEWTH 1986
VIEWTH

Weather systems - Volume 6 18 MIN
VHS
Understanding science series
Color (I J)
$39.95 purchase _ #SC06
Presents experiments and demonstrations that can be easily repeated in the classroom. Includes a teacher's guide. Part of a six - part series explaining difficult scientific ideas in an informal way.
Science; Science - Physical
Dist - SVIP

Weather - the water cycle; 2nd ed. 15 MIN
U-matic
Search for science series; Unit VI - Air and weather
Color (I)
Shows that through the same volume of various elements, the same cyclical processes occur over and over with regard to vaporization and condensation.
Science - Physical
Dist - GPN **Prod** - WVIZTV

Weather Warfare 18 MIN
U-matic / VHS
Color (H C A)
Discusses the potential of weather modification as an act of aggression.
Civics and Political Systems; Science - Physical
Dist - JOU **Prod** - CANBC

The Weather Watchers 15 MIN
16mm
Color
LC 78-700256
Traces the development of tools used to understand weather conditions. Shows a tornado tracking mission which gathers data from aircraft satellites and radar. Shows how the data is then coordinated and analyzed by NASA scientists using computer readouts and visual images to achieve long - range severe weather forecasting.
Industrial and Technical Education; Science - Physical
Dist - USNAC **Prod** - NASA 1977

The Weather Watchers 30 MIN
U-matic / VHS / 16mm
World We Live in Series
Color (I J H)
LC 74-700245
Tells the story of the baffling problems of weather watching and the possibility of eventual weather control.
Science - Physical
Dist - MGHT **Prod** - TIMELI 1968

Weather - who Votes for Rain 22 MIN
U-matic / 16mm / VHS

Color
Explains how researchers are attempting to remove some of the guesswork from weather forecasting. Looks at the possibility that man might one day be able to control the weather.
Science; Science - Physical
Dist - CNEMAG **Prod** - DOCUA

Weather - Why it Changes 10 MIN
U-matic / VHS / 16mm
Color (I J)
Presents a simple and clear explanation of how and why changes in weather occur. Locates the air masses which govern major weather changes in North America, and shows what happens when these masses interact, forming cold fronts, warm fronts and occluded fronts.
Science - Physical
Dist - CORF **Prod** - CORF 1958

Weather wise series
Helps students understand the weather and how it affects human life. Features separate teaching modules. In three parts - The Water Cycle; An Ocean of Air; and Forecasting the Weather.
Forecasting the weather 12 MIN
An Ocean of air 10 MIN
The Water cycle 11 MIN
Dist - NDIM **Prod** - LAWRN 1958

Weathering and erosion 20 MIN
VHS
Basic concepts in physical geology video series
Color (J H)
$53.95 purchase _ #193 Y 0184
Explores the processes of weathering and erosion and the landforms they create. Looks at natural forces and their effect on the Earth's surface. Part of a ten - part series on physical geology.
Agriculture; Science - Physical
Dist - WARDS **Prod** - WARDS 1990

Weathering and erosion 20 MIN
Videodisc / VHS
Earth science library series
Color (J H)
$99.95, $69.95 purchase _ #Q18620
Explores the earth, its natural resources and the human impact on our global environment. Investigates how wind, gravity, temperature and chemical reactions break down rock formations to form soils, river deposits and dunes. Utilizes computer graphics and includes a teacher's guide; videodisc guides are barcoded for access of still frames and independent segmented lessons.
Agriculture; Science - Physical
Dist - CF

Weathering and Erosion 20 MIN
VHS
Color (J)
$56.50 purchase _ #ES 8140
Illustrates the breakdown of rock formations to form soils, river deposits and dunes. Looks at wind, water, gravity, temperature and chemical reactions as a part of the process. Depicts the landforms created. Includes teacher's guide.
Science; Science - Physical
Dist - SCTRES **Prod** - SCTRES

Weathering, Erosion, and Unconformities 48 MIN
U-matic / VHS
Basic Geology Series
Color (IND)
Industrial and Technical Education; Science - Physical
Dist - GPCV **Prod** - GPCV

Weathering Processes 31 MIN
U-matic / VHS
Basic and Petroleum Geology for Non - geologists - Fundamentals and '- - Series; Fundamentals
Color (IND)
Industrial and Technical Education; Science - Physical
Dist - GPCV **Prod** - PHILLP

Weatherization 46 MIN
VHS / 16mm
Do it Yourself Series
(G)
$39.95 purchase _ #DIY307
Discusses weatherstripping and caulking doors, replacing the door threshold, and home weatherization audit. Includes weatherizing windows, caulking foundation cracks, insulating hot water heaters, and energy conservation projects.
Home Economics
Dist - RMIBHF **Prod** - RMIBHF

Weatherization
VHS
Home Improvement Series
(H C G A IND)
$39.95 _ SH307
Shows weatherstripping, caulking doors, replacing door thresholds, weatherization of windows, caulking foundation cracks, insulating hot water heaters, and other energy conservation projects.
Education; Home Economics; Industrial and Technical Education
Dist - AAVIM **Prod** - AAVIM 1989
CAMV

Weatherization 47 MIN
VHS
Insulation, Weatherization, Drywall Series
$39.95 purchase _ #DI - 307
Discusses weatherstripping and caulking doors, replacing door thresholds, and home weatherization audit, weatherizing windows, caulking foundation cracks, insulating hot water heaters, and energy conservation projects.
Industrial and Technical Education
Dist - CAREER **Prod** - CAREER

Weatherize Your Home 19 MIN
U-matic / VHS / 16mm
Home Repairs Series
Color (J H C A)
$460, $250 purchase _ #80537
Shows how to improve the energy efficiency of a home.
Home Economics
Dist - CORF

Weatherize Your Home 19 MIN
16mm / U-matic / VHS
Home Repairs Series
Color (J)
LC 80-701533
Provides step - by - step instructions on insulating floors, ceilings, attics, water heaters, ductwork and windows in the interest of conserving energy.
Home Economics; Social Science
Dist - CORF **Prod** - BRMFDK 1980

Weatherizing - Fiberglass Insulation, Weatherstripping 30 MIN
BETA / VHS
Wally's Workshop Series
Color
Industrial and Technical Education
Dist - KARTES **Prod** - KARTES

Weatherly or not 17 MIN
16mm
Color
Depicts Joe Weatherly on his way to winning the 1960 Rebel Stock Car Race at the Darlington, North Carolina Raceway.
Physical Education and Recreation
Dist - DCC **Prod** - DCC

The Weatherman - a Scientist 10 MIN
16mm / U-matic / VHS
Color (I)
LC 77-711107
Discusses the special training required of a weatherman. Points out that most weathermen are college graduates whose training helps them understand the factors that contribute to weather changes and to be able to use a wide variety of tools to measure these factors. Tells how weathermen gather data from all over the world and prepare weather maps that help them forecast weather changes.
Science; Science - Physical; Social Science
Dist - PHENIX **Prod** - EVANS 1970

The Weatherman - Community Helper 10 MIN
U-matic / VHS / 16mm
Color (P I)
LC 78-711150
Describes the role the weatherman plays in the community. Describes how scientists called meteorologists use special instruments and knowledge to measure, record and predict weather. Tells how they help the farmer to know about growing conditions, the ship captain to decide the wisest course for his ship and people in all walks of life to know how to plan their day.
Science - Physical
Dist - PHENIX **Prod** - EVANSA 1970

Weatherproofing 30 MIN
U-matic / VHS
Consumer survival series; Homes
Color
Presents tips on weatherproofing.
Home Economics
Dist - MDCPB **Prod** - MDCPB

Weatherproofing Baca County 6 MIN
16mm
B&W
LC FIE63-225
Depicts man's fight against drought, dust and disaster in the Great Plains. Shows how farmers and ranchers in Baca County, Colorado, through low level weed killing flights by airplanes and stubble mulching operations on the ground, protect the land against the erosive force of the wind and conserve each drop of moisture.
Agriculture; Civics and Political Systems; Geography - United States; Science - Natural; Science - Physical
Dist - USNAC **Prod** - USDA 1963

Weave a Web of Mystery 15 MIN
U-matic / VHS
Tyger, Tyger Burning Bright Series
Color (I)
Deals with writing a mystery story.
English Language; Literature and Drama
Dist - CTI **Prod** - CTI

Weave and spin 13 MIN
VHS
Natural history series
Color (I J H)
$80.00 purchase _ #A5VH 1108
Studies the evolution of spider behavior through following the development of the orb web from nursery webs, sheet webs, funnel webs and cob webs. Illustrates the details of web - spinning as well as the methods used to catch prey. Part of a series on natural history.
Science - Natural
Dist - CLRVUE **Prod** - CLRVUE

Weave beads 13 MIN
U-matic / VHS
Electric arc welding series; Chap 7
Color (IND)
Education; Industrial and Technical Education
Dist - TAT **Prod** - TAT

Weave with paper 15 MIN
Videoreel / VT2
Art corner series
B&W (P)
Develops an awareness of woven fabrics by discovering the principles of weaving through paper weaving.
Fine Arts
Dist - GPN **Prod** - CVETVC

The Weaver 15 MIN
VHS
Field trips series
Color (I J)
$34.95 purchase _ #E337; LC 90-708569
Explores modern hand weaving. Looks at the machinery involved, the materials used in the craft and the techniques employed. Part of a series which provides visual opportunities for children to 'visit' a variety of locations and activities as if they were on a field trip.
Education; Fine Arts; Home Economics
Dist - GPN **Prod** - MPBN 1983

Weavers of the West 13 MIN
16mm
Color (I J)
The complete story of the making of the Navaho rug with some insight into the lives, habits and ceremonies of the tribe. Filmed in the Navaho country in northern Arizona and New Mexico.
Fine Arts; Social Science; Sociology
Dist - MLA **Prod** - DAGP 1954

The Weavers - Wasn't that a Time 78 MIN
U-matic / VHS / 16mm
Color
Presents the reunion of the germinal folk singing group The Weavers at Carnegie Hall in 1980. Traces the group's history, including their blacklisting during the McCarthy era.
Fine Arts
Dist - FI **Prod** - FI 1982

Weaves 12 MIN
U-matic / VHS / 16mm
Color (J H C)
Shows various weaving processes. Depicts a weaver at her handloom and the preparation for an exhibit.
Fine Arts; Home Economics
Dist - IFB **Prod** - SETHNA 1965

Weaving 14 MIN
U-matic / VHS / 16mm
Color (I) (AFRIKAANS)
Demonstrates the basic principle of interlocking fibers used in weaving, then presents a variety of weaving methods.
Fine Arts; Foreign Language
Dist - AIMS **Prod** - ACI 1969

Weaving 29 MIN
Videoreel / VT2
Commonwealth Series
Color
Fine Arts; History - United States
Dist - PBS **Prod** - WITFTV

Weaving 15 MIN
U-matic / VHS / 16mm
Rediscovery - Art Media Series

Color (I)
LC 79-704579
Illustrates the basic principle of weaving threads into cloth. Shows how even simple looms may be used creatively to produce a wide variety of effects.
Fine Arts; Home Economics
Dist - AIMS **Prod** - ACI 1969

Weaving
VHS / U-matic
ITMA 1983 Review Series
Color
Industrial and Technical Education
Dist - NCSU **Prod** - NCSU

Weaving 14 MIN
U-matic / VHS / 16mm
Rediscovery - Art Media - Spanish Series
Color (I) (SPANISH)
Demonstrates the basic principle of interlocking fibers used in weaving, then presents a variety of weaving methods.
Fine Arts; Foreign Language
Dist - AIMS **Prod** - ACI 1969

Weaving 14 MIN
VHS
Rediscovery Art Media Series
Color
$69.95 purchase _ #4468
Presents a variety of methods that can be executed with the simplest kind of equipment.
Fine Arts
Dist - AIMS **Prod** - AIMS

Weaving 14 MIN
16mm / U-matic / VHS
Rediscovery - Art Media - French Series
Color (I)
Demonstrates the basic principle of interlocking fibers used in weaving, then presents a variety of weaving methods.
Fine Arts; Foreign Language
Dist - AIMS **Prod** - ACI 1969

Weaving Cloth - Pushto 9 MIN
U-matic / VHS
Mountain Peoples of Central Asia - Afghanistan Series
Color
Geography - World; History - World; Industrial and Technical Education
Dist - IFF **Prod** - IFF

Weaving Cloth - Pushtu 9 MIN
16mm
Mountain Peoples of Central Asia Series
Color
Shows how the art of weaving is fostered by Pushtu tribal wives in central Asia. Shows how the weaving done on looms dating back to the days of Genghis Khan is imperative to the tribes survival.
History - World; Sociology
Dist - IFF **Prod** - IFF

Weaving complexes - 7 94 MIN
VHS
Creating therapeutic change series
Color; PAL; SECAM (G)
$95.00 purchase
Features Richard Bandler in the seventh part of a seven - part series on creating therapeutic change using advanced NLP, neuro - linguistic programming. Reveals that just solving problems often isn't enough and that time distinctions can be used to interlace beliefs, feeling states and 'chains' into complexes that generatively reorganize fundamental attitudes throughout a person's life. Recommended that tapes be viewed in order. Bandler sometimes uses profanity for emphasis, which may offend some people.
Health and Safety; Psychology
Dist - NLPCOM **Prod** - NLPCOM

Weaving Series
Simple Looms 13 MIN
Dist - CORF

Weaving the Future - Women of Guatemala 28 MIN
VHS / 16mm
Color (G)
$225.00 purchase, $60.00 rental
Presents a film by and about Guatemalan women. Reveals that Guatemala, one of the smallest and poorest nations in Central America, has been devastated by political upheaval and economic instability. Produced by Capuca and Tiempo Nuevo, a collective of Guatemalan independent filmmakers in exile in Mexico.
Civics and Political Systems; Fine Arts; Geography - World; Sociology
Dist - WMEN **Prod** - CATINU 1988

Weaving with Looms You Can make 16 MIN
16mm / U-matic / VHS
Textile Design Series
Color (J)
LC 73-703446
Features artist Nancy Belfer giving demonstrations of the techniques of weaving with cardboard, branch, backstrap and frame looms to make multicolored and textured materials.
Fine Arts
Dist - AIMS **Prod** - TETKOW 1973

Weaving Without a Loom 55 TO 60 MIN
VHS
Morris Craft Series
(A)
$29.95 _ #MX415V
Features Lee Maher, renowned craft designer, as he demonstrates various weaving craft ideas that do not utilize a loom.
Fine Arts
Dist - CAMV

The Web 15 MIN
U-matic / VHS
Strawberry Square II - Take Time Series
Color (P)
Fine Arts
Dist - AITECH **Prod** - NEITV 1984

The Web 10 MIN
16mm
Color (G)
$20.00 rental
Delves into film as mischief - making and childlike wickedness.
Fine Arts
Dist - CANCIN **Prod** - KELLEM 1977

A Web not a ladder 24 MIN
VHS
Color (H C G)
$225.00 purchase
Features six women in business talking about difficulties they overcame when they started their businesses. Deals with obtaining loans, establishing ethical practices and setting goals while beginning a hairdressing shop, craft store, renovation contracting business, health care facility, hotel and restaurant, and a trainer - consulting operation.
Business and Economics
Dist - LANDMK

The Web of life 16 MIN
VHS
Color; CC (H C)
$79.00 purchase _ #906
Outlines concepts used by ecologists today to study modern ecosystems. Discusses food chains, food webs, cycling of elements and more. Part 2 of the program Ecosystems. Includes a book of the same title from the Learning Power series.
Science - Natural
Dist - HAWHIL **Prod** - HAWHIL 1994

Web of life 60 MIN
VHS
Smithsonian world series
Color (G)
$49.95 purchase _ #SMIW - 404
Explores the scientific advances and ethical dilemmas related to genetics. Interviews scientists, historians, social scientists and philosophers.
Science - Natural; Sociology
Dist - PBS **Prod** - WETATV

Web of Life, Endless Chain 28 MIN
16mm / U-matic / VHS
Color
Combines music and sound effects with footage of desert flora and fauna to show the interacting and interdependent chains of life in a desert ecosystem. Issued in 1972 as a motion picture.
Science - Natural
Dist - USNAC **Prod** - BEET 1979

The Web of Taxes 20 MIN
16mm
Government and Public Affairs Films Series
B&W (H A)
W B Boyer, vice president and treasurer, Republic Steel Corporation, covers the problem of individual and corporate taxes and their effects on incentives and investments.
Business and Economics; Civics and Political Systems
Dist - MLA **Prod** - RSC 1960

Webbing Your Idea 15 MIN
U-matic / VHS
Fins, Feathers and Fur
Color (P)
Features a pet shop for teaching writing to second and third graders. This program shows how to organize an idea web to organize information.
English Language; Psychology
Dist - AITECH **Prod** - WXXITV 1986

Webbing Your Thought 15 MIN
VHS / U-matic
Fins, Feathers and Fur Series
(P)
$125.00 purchase
Focuses on the construction of an 'idea web' and its significance for children attempting to organize their thoughts in writing.
Education; English Language
Dist - AITECH **Prod** - WXXITV 1986

Webs and Other Wonders
VHS / U-matic
Science and Nature Series
Color (G C J)
$197 purchase _ #06867 - 851
Surveys the invisible world of spiders and their kin.
Science - Natural
Dist - CHUMAN **Prod** - OSF 1988

Webster Groves Revisited 53 MIN
U-matic / VHS / 16mm
B&W (J)
LC 72-707894
An experimental documentary which shows the effect of the telecast of the film, '16 IN WEBSTER GROVES' in February 1966 upon the Missouri Community of Webster Groves, an affluent suburb of St Louis. Includes interviews with citizens of Webster groves who express their views about the telecast which discussed the 16 - year - old youth of the community.
Geography - United States; Psychology; Social Science; Sociology
Dist - CAROUF **Prod** - CBSTV 1967

Webster Groves Revisited, Pt 1 27 MIN
U-matic / VHS / 16mm
Color (H C A)
Shows the effect of the telecast of the film , '16 IN WEBSTER GROVES' in February, 1966, upon the Missouri community of Webster Groves, an affluent suburb of St Louis. Includes interviews with citizens of Webster Groves who express their views about the telecast which discussed the 16 - year - old youths of the community.
Sociology
Dist - CAROUF **Prod** - CBSTV

Webster Groves Revisited, Pt 2 26 MIN
U-matic / VHS / 16mm
Color (H C A)
Shows the effect of the telecast of the film , '16 IN WEBSTER GROVES' in February, 1966, upon the Missouri community of Webster Groves, an affluent suburb of St Louis. Includes interviews with citizens of Webster Groves who express their views about the telecast which discussed the 16 - year - old youths of the community.
Sociology
Dist - CAROUF **Prod** - CBSTV

Webster's 9th dictionary with sound
CD-ROM
(G A)
$189.00 purchase _ #1782
Contains everything in the print edition of Webster's Ninth New Collegiate Dictionary, plus enhancements possible only in an electronic edition - point and click access to cross references, optional 18 point display, and sound. For Macintosh Plus, SE and II computers. Requires at least one M of RAM, one floppy disk drive, and an Apple compatible CD - ROM drive.
English Language; Literature and Drama
Dist - BEP

A Wedding 26 MIN
16mm
B&W (G)
$35.00 rental
Follows filmmaker Allen Ross' friend from high school as he prepares to get married. Views the bachelor party, getting dressed for the wedding, the wedding rehearsal. The editing creates a circular structure of these events in an attempt to reveal an empty, hollow, going - through - the - motions approach to the ceremony to please the parents.
Fine Arts; Sociology
Dist - CANCIN

The Wedding
VHS
Marriage, Family Living and Counseling Series
(C G)
$59.00_CA228
Discusses weddings and the realities therein.
Guidance and Counseling
Dist - AAVIM **Prod** - AAVIM 1989

Wedding and Anniversary Flowers 56 MIN
VHS / 16mm
Flower Arranging Series
Color (G)

$69.95 purchase _ #AD102
Demonstrates flower arranging for weddings and anniversaries, featuring traditional as well as modern designs, plus how to make roses out of dollar bills.
Agriculture; Home Economics
Dist - AAVIM **Prod** - AAVIM 1990

Wedding Bells 15 MIN
16mm
Color (P I)
Tells how the Graham children and Alice the chimp are almost run over on the way to a wedding and stumble into a plan to steal the wedding gifts. Reveals how Alice devises an ingenious plan to stave off disaster and alert the guests.
Literature and Drama
Dist - LUF **Prod** - LUF 1977

Wedding cake construction 30 MIN
VHS / 16mm
Art of decorating cakes series
(G)
$49.00 purchase _ #BCD19
Instructs in the art of cake decorating. Shows how to bake wedding cakes of various sizes, and how to ice and construct a wedding cake. Taught by master cake decorator Leon Simmons.
Home Economics; Industrial and Technical Education
Dist - RMIBHF **Prod** - RMIBHF

Wedding cake designs 30 MIN
VHS / 16mm
Art of decorating cakes series
(G)
$49.00 purchase _ #BCD20
Instructs in the art of cake decorating. Shows how to assemble the cakes to size and design, after decorating. Taught by Leon Simmons, master cake decorator.
Home Economics; Industrial and Technical Education
Dist - RMIBHF **Prod** - RMIBHF

Wedding Camels, the 108 MIN
U-matic / VHS / 16mm
Turkana Conversations Trilogy Series
Color (TURKANA (ENGLISH SUBTITLES))
Shows how bridal negotiations are carried out in the Turkana culture of northwestern Kenya. Depicts a suitor for the hand of the chief's daughter who must negotiate how many camels to give her father without appearing foolish or depleting his camel herd. Presented in Turkana with English subtitles.
Foreign Language; History - World
Dist - UCEMC **Prod** - MCDGAL 1980

Wedding day dancing 90 MIN
VHS
Color (G)
$29.95 purchase _ #STE000
Prepares couples for confident dancing on their wedding day. Features Chris Riley and easy routines for mastering the waltz, foxtrot, jitterbug, triple swing and more. Offers over 100 love songs and 50 big band tunes.
Fine Arts; Sociology
Dist - SIV

Wedding finery 60 MIN
VHS
Color (G A)
$29.95 purchase _ #VDC146V
Teaches how to create bridal headwear, including veils, poufs and bows. Presents step - by - step instructions for creating the floral cluster, wreath, headband, sidesweep, and a bridal hat.
Home Economics
Dist - CAMV

Wedding in a Persian Village 11 MIN
16mm
Color (I)
LC 76-706445
Depicts traditional marriage ceremonies of remote regions of Iran, where weddings are community events.
Geography - World; Psychology; Social Science; Sociology
Dist - NYU **Prod** - NYU 1963

Wedding in Galilee 113 MIN
35mm / 16mm / VHS
Color (G) (HEBREW AND ARABIC)
$300.00, $350.00 rental
Portrays an Arab village chief elder who wants his son to be married in the traditional manner - a wedding that lasts from sundown until dawn, but the town is under Israeli curfew. Reveals that the leader goes to ask the military governor's permission to celebrate a traditional wedding and receives it - under the condition that he and his fellow officers are invited as guests of honor. Directed by Michel Khleifi. With English subtitles.
Geography - World; Sociology
Dist - KINOIC

A Wedding in the Family 22 MIN
16mm
Color
LC 78-700257
Presents a documentary on a family during the week before the wedding of one of the children. Focuses on issues relating to marriage, sex roles, career expectations and life choices.
Sociology
Dist - NEWDAY **Prod** - FRANCO 1977

The Wedding of Princess Margrethe 32 MIN
16mm
Color
Covers the events preceding the wedding on June 10, 1967, of Princess Margrethe to Prince Henrick.
History - World; Religion and Philosophy; Sociology
Dist - AUDPLN **Prod** - RDCG

The Wedding Reception - the Grand Pas De Deux 15 MIN
16mm
Rudolf Nureyev's Film of Don Quixote Series
Color
LC 78-701881
Fine Arts
Dist - SF **Prod** - WRO 1978

The Wedding - Wesele 103 MIN
VHS
Color (G A) (POLISH WITH ENGLISH SUBTITLES)
$39.95 purchase _ #V085
Presents a moving drama of Polish destiny based on a popular nationalistic play by Stanisaw Wyspianski. Pictures the wedding of a peasant's daughter to a poet. Directed by Andrzej Wajda.
Fine Arts; Sociology
Dist - POLART

Weddings 30 MIN
U-matic / VHS
Consumer survival series; Personal planning
Color
Presents tips on planning weddings.
Home Economics; Sociology
Dist - MDCPB **Prod** - MDCPB

Weddings 5.35 MIN
VHS / U-matic
Photo Tips Series
Color (J H A)
Prevents tips for the bridal party in choosing a photographer for the wedding.
Fine Arts; Industrial and Technical Education; Sociology
Dist - AITECH **Prod** - TURR 1986

Wedge - a Simple Machine 15 MIN
U-matic / VHS
Why Series
Color (P I)
Discusses the characteristics of the wedge.
Science - Physical
Dist - AITECH **Prod** - WDCNTV 1976

Wedging the Clay and Making a Pitch Pot 28 MIN
Videoreel / VT2
Wheels, Kilns and Clay Series
Color
Features Mrs Peterson describing certain ceramic processes for her classroom at the University of Southern California. Demonstrates how to wedge the clay and make a pitch pot.
Fine Arts
Dist - PBS **Prod** - USC

Wedgwood 30 MIN
U-matic
Antiques series
Color
Fine Arts
Dist - PBS **Prod** - NHMNET

Wediko Series - Emotionally Disturbed - - Children at Camp Series
Boys in Confict 72 MIN
Troubled campers 18 MIN
Dist - DOCUFL

Wediko Series
Bruce 26 MIN
Troubled Campers 16 MIN
Dist - DOCUFL

Wediko series
Johnny 32 MIN
Dist - DOCUFL
PSU

Wediko series
An Adolescent group - social springboard for personal growth 33 MIN
At the edge of a desert - renegotiating a contract 29 MIN
Beach interview 27 MIN
Boys in conflict 74 MIN
Bruce 26 MIN
Can you love two moms - talking with older adopted children 29 MIN
Chrysalis '86 - the development of a therapeutic group 32 MIN
Randy 27 MIN
Reunion as a therapeutic strategy - a teenage adoptee encounters his birth mother 35 MIN
A Tape for Sam 15 MIN
Why should I stay - crisis intervention with a resistant teenager 26 MIN
Dist - PSU

Wedlock house - an intercourse 11 MIN
16mm
Color (A)
$14.00 rental, $345.00 purchase
Says Cinema 16, 'The first months of marriage, with moments of mutual awareness, frightening understandings, lovemaking.'
Fine Arts; Sociology
Dist - CANCIN **Prod** - BRAKS 1959

Wee beasties - the protozoa 30 MIN
U-matic / VHS / BETA
Color (T)
$39.95 purchase _ #5102
Teaches teachers of junior high students and up how to teach concepts in biology. Begins at the edge of a pond and moves into a laboratory to show microscopic shots of live protozoa. Uses live footage and stop - action pictures to capture the structure and function of each of the four major phyla represented by amoeba, paramecium, euglena and plasmodium. Discusses the relationship of protozoa with humans. Illustrates sexual and asexual reproduction.
Science - Natural
Dist - INSTRU

Wee Geese 7 MIN
16mm / U-matic / VHS
Color (K P I)
LC FIA65-1125
Shows the life and habits of the young Canada goose. Pictures a typical day in the life of the goslings and the adventures of one gosling who goes exploring.
Science - Natural
Dist - AIMS **Prod** - ACI 1964

Wee Gillis 19 MIN
U-matic / VHS / 16mm
Color (P I)
Presents the story of Wee Gillis, who spends a year in the Lowlands of Scotland herding cattle with his mother's relatives and then a year in the Highlands stalking stags with his father's relatives. Tells how he finds his calling as a bagpipe player. Based on the book Wee Gillis by Munro Leaf and Robert Lawson.
Literature and Drama
Dist - CF **Prod** - CF 1985

Wee Sing in Sillyville Video
VHS
Wee Sing Video Series
(K)
$19.95, $23.95 purchase _ #2761 - 9, #2792 - 9
Presents a children's music program. Available with soundtrack audiocassette.
Fine Arts
Dist - PRSTSL

Wee Sing the Best Christmas Ever
VHS
Wee Sing Video Series
(K)
$19.95, $23.95 purchase _ #2848 - 8, #2882 - 8
Presents a children's music program. Available with soundtrack audiocassette.
Fine Arts
Dist - PRSTSL

Wee sing together 60 MIN
VHS
Color (K P I T)
$21.95 purchase _ #S01558
Presents a fantasy video with sing - along songs for children. Features live action and special effects. Includes songbook.
Fine Arts; Literature and Drama
Dist - UILL

Wee sing together - grandpa's magical toys 60 MIN
VHS
Color (K P I)
$21.95 purchase
Combines live action and sing - along songs in telling the story of a little boy's visit to his grandfather's amazing toy collection. Includes more than 20 songs, such as 'Hokey Pokey' and 'The Farmer In the Dell.'

Fine Arts
Dist - PBS **Prod** - WNETTV

Wee sing together - King Cole's party 60 MIN
VHS
Color (K P I)
$21.95 purchase
Combines live action and sing - along songs in a format that allows children to sing and play along with nursery rhyme characters - among them, Jack and Jill, Little Boy Blue, Mary and her Little Lamb, and others. Teaches that gifts from the heart are the most special.
Fine Arts
Dist - PBS **Prod** - WNETTV

Wee Sing Together Video
BETA / VHS
Wee Sing Video Series
(K)
$19.95, $23.95 purchase _ #1444 - 4, #1223 - 9
Presents a children's music program. Available with soundtrack audiocassette.
Fine Arts
Dist - PRSTSL

Wee sing together - Volume 1 60 MIN
VHS
Color (K P I)
$21.95 purchase
Presents Volume 1 of 'Wee Sing Together,' a sing - along program for children. Features live action, special effects, and a collection of songs to sing along with. Includes a songbook.
Fine Arts
Dist - PBS **Prod** - WNETTV

Wee sing video series
Grandpa's magical toys video
King Cole's Party Video
Wee Sing in Sillyville Video
Wee Sing the Best Christmas Ever
Wee Sing Together Video
Dist - PRSTSL

Weeding the garden 14 MIN
VHS / 16mm
Yanomamo series
Color (G)
$270.00, $140.00 purchase, $30.00, $25.00 rental
Portrays Dedeheiwa the shaman who weeds his manioc garden and clears the leaves around his plaintains. Shows the shaman, tired and sore, resting while he is massaged and groomed by his wife and numerous children, with whom he plays affectionately. Part of a series on the Yanomamo Indians of Venezuela by Timothy Asch and Napoleon Chagnon.
Geography - World; Social Science; Sociology
Dist - DOCEDR **Prod** - DOCEDR 1974

Weegee's New York 20 MIN
16mm
Color (H C A)
LC FIA67-1837
Presents a tour of New York, emphasizing the life and tempo of the metropolis and combining documentary and experimental photographic techniques.
Fine Arts; Geography - United States
Dist - GROVE **Prod** - WEEGEE 1953

A Week Full of Saturdays 17 MIN
16mm
Color (A)
LC 79-700061
Discusses the financial, residential and recreational factors of retirement. Shows the daily routines of various retired people and presents their views on retirement.
Guidance and Counseling; Health and Safety; Social Science; Sociology
Dist - FLMLIB **Prod** - ALTERC 1979

A Week in the Life of a Chinese Student 20 MIN
U-matic / VHS / 16mm
Color (I J H C G T A)
$50 rental _ #9852
Describes lifestyle and typical week in life of students in these foreign countries.
Geography - World; History - World
Dist - AIMS **Prod** - SAIF 1986

A Week in the Life of a Chinese Student 20 MIN
16mm / VHS
Color (I J H A)
$380.00, $460.00 purchase, $50.00 rental _ #9852
Features young students of the fourth class of grade one in the Number Two Junior Middle School of Beijing. Includes an early reading session, math and English lessons, physical exercise amd a snack break.
Education; Geography - World
Dist - AIMS **Prod** - AIMS 1986

A Week in the Life of a Mexican Student 24 MIN
U-matic / VHS / 16mm
Color (I J H C G T A)
$50 rental _ #9847
Describes lifestyle and typical week in life of students in these foreign countries.
Geography - World; History - World
Dist - AIMS **Prod** - SAIF 1986

A Week in the Life of a Mexican Student 24 MIN
16mm / VHS
Color (I J H A) (SPANISH)
$395.00, $495.00 purchase, $50.00 rental _ #9847
Overviews a week in the life of a fourteen - year - old high school student, Xavier Sierra. Shows Xavier working in a tortilla factory every morning before school in order to earn money for his schooling. Follows him through English, history and chemistry classes, at work and with his friends and family. Also available in two Spanish versions, one for second and third year Spanish students and one for Spanish speakers.
Education; Geography - World
Dist - AIMS **Prod** - SANDE 1986

A Week of remembrance - the dedication of the United States Holocaust Memorial Museum 45 MIN
VHS
Color (G)
$14.95 purchase _ #25009
Captures the highlights of the ceremonies that accompanied the dedication of the Museum - the interfaith service at the National Cathedral, the annual Days of Remembrance ceremony at the United States Capitol, and the tribute to liberators and rescuers at Arlington National Cemetery.
History - World
Dist - USHMC **Prod** - USHMC

A Week of sweet water 40 MIN
VHS
Color (G)
$350.00 purchase, $50.00 rental
Portrays Minata and Bouremia, a couple from the village of Somiaga in Upper Volta, who re - enact their story. Reveals that during 1973 - 1974 over 200,000 people slowly starved to death in the Sahel region of West Africa along the southern edge of the Sahara, because of drought and famine. Depicts the complex decision - making process which men must endure to provide for their families, which women must face as they decide for the futures of of their children and communities must consider in developing land for the greatest benefit. By Peter Adamson. Co - produced by the BBC.
Geography - World; History - World
Dist - DOCEDR **Prod** - UNICEF

The Week that shook the world - the Soviet coup 65 MIN
VHS
ABC News collection series
Color (G)
$29.98 purchase _ #6302316553
Chronicles ABC News coverage of the attempted coup in the Soviet Union from August 19 - 25, 1991.
History - World
Dist - INSTRU **Prod** - ABCNEW 1991

Weekend 60 MIN
VHS / U-matic
Rainbow Movie of the Week Series
Color (J A)
Reveals that the ostensibly liberal attitudes of a middle - class Anglo couple are challenged when their teenaged children invite two black school friends for the weekend.
Sociology
Dist - GPN **Prod** - RAINTV 1981

The Weekend 16 MIN
16mm
Marriage Series
Color (H C)
LC 70-711574
Presents an estranged couple, who stranded together in a motel room, learn about the communication breakdown in their marriage and their need to rediscover personal identity and affirmation in the marriage relationship.
Guidance and Counseling; Psychology; Sociology
Dist - FRACOC **Prod** - FRACOC 1970

Weekend 12 MIN
16mm
Color (G)
$20.00 rental
Features a production from Yugoslavia in which the problems and conflicts in the relationships between old and young are posed allegorically. Reveals a senile invalid old man who is taken by his daughter, her husband and child to a country picnic, leaving behind the hot, crowded apartment where they all live. As the peaceful day ends, Grandfather is left sitting in the meadow, helpless in his favorite chair, along with many other grandparents similarly abandoned there by their families.
Fine Arts; Health and Safety; Literature and Drama; Sociology
Dist - NCJEWF

The Weekend Athletes 48 MIN
16mm
Color (H C A)
LC 77-703382
Examines the physical fitness movement in the United States. Presents interviews with medical authorities on the values of jogging and other exercises and points out the dangers in getting too much exercise too fast.
Physical Education and Recreation
Dist - BESTF **Prod** - ABCTV 197

Weekend in Vermont 157 MIN
U-matic / VHS / 16mm
Age of Uncertainty Series
Color (H C A)
LC 77-701494
Focuses on the prospects of democratic capitalism and the industrial West. Based on the book The Age Of Uncertainty by John Kenneth Galbraith.
Business and Economics
Dist - FI **Prod** - BBCL 1977

Weekend in Vermont, Pt 1 26 MIN
U-matic / VHS / 16mm
Age of Uncertainty Series
Color (H C A)
LC 77-701494
Focuses on the prospects of democratic capitalism and the industrial West. Based on the book The Age Of Uncertainty by John Kenneth Galbraith.
Business and Economics; Civics and Political Systems
Dist - FI **Prod** - BBCL 1977

Weekend in Vermont, Pt 2 26 MIN
U-matic / VHS / 16mm
Age of Uncertainty Series
Color (H C A)
LC 77-701494
Focuses on the prospects of democratic capitalism and the industrial West. Based on the book The Age Of Uncertainty by John Kenneth Galbraith.
Business and Economics; Civics and Political Systems
Dist - FI **Prod** - BBCL 1977

Weekend in Vermont, Pt 3 26 MIN
U-matic / VHS / 16mm
Age of Uncertainty Series
Color (H C A)
LC 77-701494
Focuses on the prospects of democratic capitalism and the industrial West. Based on the book The Age Of Uncertainty by John Kenneth Galbraith.
Business and Economics; Civics and Political Systems
Dist - FI **Prod** - BBCL 1977

Weekend in Vermont, Pt 4 26 MIN
16mm / U-matic / VHS
Age of Uncertainty Series
Color (H C A)
LC 77-701494
Focuses on the prospects of democratic capitalism and the industrial West. Based on the book The Age Of Uncertainty by John Kenneth Galbraith.
Business and Economics; Civics and Political Systems
Dist - FI **Prod** - BBCL 1977

Weekend in Vermont, Pt 5 26 MIN
16mm / U-matic / VHS
Age of Uncertainty Series
Color (H C A)
LC 77-701494
Focuses on the prospects of democratic capitalism and the industrial West. Based on the book The Age Of Uncertainty by John Kenneth Galbraith.
Business and Economics; Civics and Political Systems
Dist - FI **Prod** - BBCL 1977

Weekend in Vermont, Pt 6 27 MIN
U-matic / VHS / 16mm
Age of Uncertainty Series
Color (H C A)
LC 77-701494
Focuses on the prospects of democratic capitalism and the industrial West. Based on the book The Age Of Uncertainty by John Kenneth Galbraith.
Business and Economics; Civics and Political Systems
Dist - FI **Prod** - BBCL 1977

Weekend of Champions 29 MIN
16mm
Color
Films the efforts of various athletes during the Weekend of Champions in Dallas.
Physical Education and Recreation
Dist - FELLCA **Prod** - FELLCA 1969

Weekend Pass 35 MIN
16mm
B&W (H C A)
Presents a short story about a shy sailor's weekend pass in Los Angeles.

Literature and Drama
Dist - CFS **Prod** - CFS 1963

Weekend Sports - Fun, not Injuries 25 MIN
VHS / U-matic
Color
Features sports doctor Robert Kerlan, MD (LA Rams, Lakers, and Kings), joining tennis pro Charlie Passarel, a ski instructor, a motorcycle patrolman, and host Mario Machado for free lessons and safety tips on tennis, skiing and motorcycling.
Health and Safety; Physical Education and Recreation
Dist - MEDCOM **Prod** - MEDCOM

Weeknight inspiration 60 MIN
VHS
Too busy to cook series
Color (H C G)
$29.95 purchase _ #KA1010V
Shows how to prepare two simple but very stylish meals fast. Includes recipe cards. Part of a four - part series from Bon Appetite magazine showing time - saving techniques for preparing delicious, quick and creative meals.
Home Economics
Dist - CAMV

The Weenie worm or the fat innkeeper 11 MIN
16mm
Color (G)
$15.00 rental
Shares the filmmaker's discovery and subsequent fascination with weenie worms at a marine biology lab.
Fine Arts; Science - Natural
Dist - CANCIN **Prod** - WILEYJ 1972

Weep no more, My Lady 24 MIN
U-matic / VHS / 16mm
Color (I J)
LC 79-700654
Presents an animated adventure story about a 13 - year - old boy who takes in a stray dog that brings him joy and teaches him a poignant lesson in what it takes to become a man. Based on the short story Weep No More, My Lady by James Street. Originally shown on the television series ABC Weekend Specials.
Literature and Drama
Dist - CORF **Prod** - ABC 1979

Weeping film 2 MIN
16mm
B&W (G)
$15.00 rental
Features a scratch film.
Fine Arts
Dist - CANCIN **Prod** - SCHLEM 1991
FLMKCO

Weetamoe
BETA / VHS
B&W
Shows a seldom seen look at sailing aboard a J Boat - sail and boat handling and match racing in R I waters in 1934.
Geography - World; Physical Education and Recreation; Social Science
Dist - MYSTIC **Prod** - MYSTIC 1984

Wei cheng 500 MIN
VHS
Color (G) (CHINESE)
$150.00 purchase _ #5158
Presents a film from the People's Republic of China. Includes five videocassettes.
Geography - World; Literature and Drama
Dist - CHTSUI

The Weibull Distribution and its Reliability and Maintainability Engineering Applications for Engineers and Managers 360 MIN
U-matic / VHS
Weibull Distribution and its Reliability and Maintainability 'Engineering Applications for Reliability Engineers and Managers 'Series
Color
Provides an overview of the very valuable Weibull Distribution.
Industrial and Technical Education
Dist - UAZMIC **Prod** - UAZMIC 1986

Weibull Distribution and its Reliability and Maintainability Engineering Applications for Reliability Engineers and Managers Series
The Weibull Distribution and its Reliability and Maintainability Engineering Applications for Reliability Engineers and Managers 360 MIN
Dist - UAZMIC

Weibull Failure Model 30 MIN
U-matic / VHS
Reliability Engineering Series
Color (IND)
Describes use of the Weibull Distribution to model failures. Plots an example on Weibull probability paper, and estimates of failure mode and characteristic life are read from the plot.
Industrial and Technical Education
Dist - COLOSU **Prod** - COLOSU

Weibull Probability Paper - Example 30 MIN
VHS / U-matic
Reliability Engineering Series
Color (IND)
Contains worked - out example using Weibull probability paper to predict the characteristic life and shaping parameter for a set of sample data.
Industrial and Technical Education
Dist - COLOSU **Prod** - COLOSU

Weighing and Measuring 10 MIN
16mm
Color (I J H)
Discusses the common English system of weighing and introduces the metric system.
Mathematics
Dist - SF **Prod** - SF 1970

Weighing Techniques 9 MIN
16mm / U-matic / VHS
Biological Techniques Series
Color (H C)
Shows techniques and principles of handling basic laboratory scales, including the hand scale, the triple beam balance, the analytical balance and others.
Science; Science - Natural
Dist - IFB **Prod** - THORNE 1961

Weighing the Choices - Positive Approaches to Nutrition 20 MIN
16mm
Color
Offers positive, practical choices for breakfast, lunch and dinner.
Health and Safety; Social Science
Dist - SPEF **Prod** - SPEF 1981

The Weight 60 MIN
16mm
Color
Depicts high school seniors struggling with questions of love, honor and friendship, alcohol, cruelty and war.
Guidance and Counseling; Psychology; Religion and Philosophy
Dist - CAFM **Prod** - CAFM

Weight Control 9 MIN
U-matic / VHS
Color
Explains calories and calorie requirement. Discusses fats, protein and carbohydrates. Outlines basic principles of weight reduction.
Health and Safety; Social Science
Dist - MEDFAC **Prod** - MEDFAC 1981

Weight Control 30 MIN
U-matic / VHS
Food for Life Series
Color
Home Economics; Social Science
Dist - MSU **Prod** - MSU

Weight Control 13 MIN
16mm / U-matic / VHS
Nutrition Series
Color (J) (SPANISH)
LC 81-701110
Deals with the causes of obesity, how to prevent it and how to develop a lifetime program of safe and effective weight control. Notes that being overweight can shorten one's life and lead to problems such as heart disease, diabetes and high blood pressure.
Health and Safety
Dist - JOU **Prod** - PRORE 1975

Weight Control / Real Estate Investments / Advertising
U-matic / VHS
Consumer Survival Series
Color
Discusses various aspects of weight control, real estate investments and advertising.
Business and Economics; Health and Safety; Home Economics
Dist - MDCPB **Prod** - MDCPB

Weight Events Conditioning
VHS / U-matic
From the Bill Dellinger's Championship Track and Field Videotape 'Training Library Series.
Color (H C)
Emphasizes strength development and channeling strength into throwing action. Recommends proper weight lifting technique and specialized drills for incorporating strength into throwing plus overall conditioning.
Physical Education and Recreation
Dist - CBSC **Prod** - CBSC

Weight Loss 30 MIN
VHS
Video Reflections Series
Color (G)
$29.95 purchase _ #VWT
Combines images of nature with music and soothing environmental sounds. Uses visual and auditory subliminal messages for enhancing weight control.
Health and Safety; Physical Education and Recreation; Psychology
Dist - GAINST **Prod** - GAINST

Weight Loss 30 MIN
VHS / Cassette
B&W (G)
$12.95 purchase _ #U890001412; $12.50 purchase _ #RX124
Combines relaxation techniques, a daily visualization and subliminal affirmations to enhance weight loss.
Health and Safety; Psychology; Religion and Philosophy
Dist - VSPU **Prod** - VSPU

Weight loss, diet and exercise - 3 13 MIN
VHS
Postpartum period series
Color (J H C G PRO)
$250.00 purchase, $60.00 rental
Discusses weight loss, diet and exercise for women after giving birth. Informs women recovering from childbirth, their partners, childbirth educators and obstetrical staff. Features new parents in real situations. Hosted by Dr Linda Reid. Part of a five - part series.
Health and Safety; Physical Education and Recreation
Dist - CF **Prod** - HOSSN 1989

Weight management
VHS
Personal action system series
Color (G)
$149.00 purchase _ #V203
Teaches employees about the benefits of weight management. Part of a 13 - part series to educate employees on the importance of health.
Health and Safety; Physical Education and Recreation; Psychology
Dist - GPERFO

Weight management package
VHS
Personal action for better health series
Color (A IND)
$299.00 purchase _ #AH45405
Reveals techniques for managing body weight. Covers exercise, nutrition, energy needs, and the importance of recognizing emotions, attitudes and norms. Includes 125 booklets and three posters.
Health and Safety
Dist - HTHED **Prod** - HTHED

Weight, Nutrition and Exercise during Pregnancy 8 MIN
U-matic / VHS / 16mm
Prepared Childbirth and Parenting Series
Color
Examines what foods a woman should eat while she is pregnant, how much weight gain is normal and safe, and what physical activities she can continue safely. Provides suggestions to improve physical comfort.
Health and Safety
Dist - JOU **Prod** - JOU 1976

Weight, Nutrition and Exercise during Pregnancy 13 MIN
16mm / U-matic / VHS
Color
Explores the physiological changes which take place during pregnancy and why these changes increase a woman's nutritional and fitness needs. Emphasized is the importance of a balanced diet and discussed are concerns about weight gain. Demonstrates specific exercises and stresses that being fit optimizes a woman's sense of well - being during pregnancy.
Health and Safety
Dist - PRI **Prod** - PRI 1986

Weight, Pressure, Combinations 17 MIN
16mm / U-matic / VHS
From the Measuring Things Series
Color; Captioned (I J)
Explained in relation to gravity and mass. Scales are shown from those that can measure minute quantities up to others that are used to weigh heavy trucks. The principle of leverage is demonstrated. Pressure is related to weight. The barometer indicates air pressure which changes with altitude. Sometimes measurements are used in combinations - miles per hour, time and temperature, calories and horsepower.

Mathematics; Science
Dist - HANDEL **Prod** - HANDEL 1985

Weight training series
Presents a three - part series on weight training. 'Barbell And Dumbbell Training' demonstrates 25 free - weight exercises that can be performed in the home. 'Ladies Weight Training' and 'Mens Weight Training' offer workouts targeted to beginners. Each tape presents two different workouts to choose from.
Barbell and dumbbell training 60 MIN
Ladies weight training 60 MIN
Mens weight training 60 MIN
Dist - CAMV **Prod** - CAMV 1985

Weight Vs Mass 5 MIN
U-matic
Eureka Series
Color (J)
Explains the difference between weight and mass and shows how only mass is the same on the moon and on earth.
Science; Science - Physical
Dist - TVOTAR **Prod** - TVOTAR 1980

Weight Watchers magazine guide to a healthy lifestyle 60 MIN
VHS
Color; Captioned (G)
$39.95 purchase _ #S00332
Features Lynn Redgrave in a discussion of exercise, fitness, diet tips, low - calorie recipes and beauty makeovers.
Health and Safety; Physical Education and Recreation; Social Science
Dist - UILL **Prod** - GA
GA

Weight Watchers magazine guide to dining and cooking 56 MIN
VHS
Color; Captioned (A)
$29.95 purchase _ #S00696
Features Lynn Redgrave and Weight Watchers experts in a guide to dining out and home cooking for people wanting to lose weight. Presents meals that are designed not to ruin a diet.
Health and Safety; Home Economics; Physical Education and Recreation; Social Science
Dist - UILL

Weighting techniques 16 MIN
VHS
Color (J H)
$145.00 purchase _ #A5VH 1007
Illustrates important weighing techniques. Details procedures for using different types of single and double pan balances. Outlines specific techniques for reading scales, recording measurements, weighing liquids and measuring specific quantities.
Mathematics; Science
Dist - CLRVUE **Prod** - CLRVUE

Weightlifters 11 MIN
16mm
B&W
LC 77-702707
Documents lifestyles in a high - pressure urban environment.
Sociology
Dist - CANFDC **Prod** - PEAMIL 1972

Weightlifting 5 MIN
16mm / VHS
Sports Lego Series
Color (K)
$220.00, $165.00 purchase
Uses animation with Lego toys to introduce weightlifting. Uses music but hasno narration.
Fine Arts; Physical Education and Recreation
Dist - FLMWST

Weightlifting training and conditioning
VHS
To your health series
Color (G)
$29.95 purchase _ #IV - 027
Presents a basic weightlifting program to strengthen and condition the body.
Physical Education and Recreation; Science - Natural
Dist - INCRSE **Prod** - INCRSE

The Weimar Republic 29 MIN
Videoreel / VT2
Course of Our Times I Series
Color
History - World
Dist - PBS **Prod** - WGBHTV

Wein Bridge Oscillator 21 MIN
16mm
B&W
LC 74-705941
Explains the theory of operation of the Wein bridge vacuum tube oscillator and states the purpose of each component. Explains the action when the size of the frequency determining components is changed and gives the formula for finding the operating frequency. (Kinescope).
Industrial and Technical Education; Science - Physical
Dist - USNAC **Prod** - USAF

The Weir - Falcon Saga 30 MIN
16mm
Color; Silent (C)
$907.20
Experimental film by Stan Brakhage.
Fine Arts
Dist - AFA **Prod** - AFA 1970

Weird Bird 10 MIN
U-matic / VHS
Color (K P I J H)
Uses animation to show a weird bird using his imagination to help him live in a society that demands conformity.
Fine Arts; Sociology
Dist - SUTHRB **Prod** - SUTHRB

The Weird Number - Rational Numbers 13 MIN
U-matic / VHS / 16mm
Exploring Mathematics Series
Color (P)
LC 70-713196
Presents an amusing introduction of rational numbers to a community of natural numbers. The weird number, 2/3, steals a piece of cake and then leads the Major and the baker on a merry chase. He escapes and 4/6 comes forth to explain to the integers of system of rational numbers and the concept of equivalent fractions.
Mathematics
Dist - GA **Prod** - DAVFMS 1970

The Weird World of Robots 26 MIN
U-matic / VHS / 16mm
Twenty - First Century Series
Color (H C)
LC 72-700128
Describes two types of robots - - the simulators, which mimic human performance and the augmentors, which assist in human performance. Shows examples of several robots in action in industry and science.
Psychology; Sociology
Dist - MGHT **Prod** - CBSTV 1968

The Weird World of Robots 18 MIN
U-matic / VHS / 16mm
Twenty - First Century Series
Color (J)
LC 75-702570
Edited version of the 1968 motion picture of the same title. Describes two types of robots, the simulators which mimic human performance and the augmentors which assist in human performance. Shows examples of several robots in action in industry and science.
Industrial and Technical Education; Social Science; Sociology
Dist - MGHT **Prod** - CBSTV 1975

Weirded Out and Blown Away 43 MIN
U-matic / VHS / 16mm
Color (H C A)
$595 purchase - 16 mm, $395 purchase - video, $70 rental
Explores the public's attitudes toward physical disability and challenges misconceptions about the disabled. Features interviews with five career people who are disabled. Directed by Sharon Greytak.
Health and Safety; Sociology
Dist - CNEMAG

Welcome 28 MIN
VHS / U-matic
Old Friends - New Friends Series
Color
Consists of home movies sent by viewers to Old Friends - New Friends. Also features recollections of host Fred Rogers' own childhood and grandfather.
Guidance and Counseling; Sociology
Dist - PBS **Prod** - FAMCOM 1981

Welcome aboard 25 MIN
VHS
Color (PRO IND A)
Illustrates the consequences of being negligent or haphazard when introducing new members of the management team to their co - workers, physical surroundings and their specific functions.
Business and Economics; Guidance and Counseling; Psychology
Dist - CRMF **Prod** - CRMF 1990

Welcome Aboard 21 MIN
16mm / U-matic / 8mm cartridge / VHS
Color (SPANISH FRENCH NORWEGIAN)
LC 72-701782
Emphasizes the importance of new employee orientation, of helping him get a good start and helping him to achieve maximum productivity quickly, in order to prevent excessive turnover.
Business and Economics; Foreign Language; Guidance and Counseling; Psychology
Dist - RTBL **Prod** - RTBL 1972

Welcome Aboard 23 MIN
VHS / U-matic
Captioned; Color (T)
Gives practical suggestions to teachers for modifying techniques to include deaf students. In classes. Signed.
Education; Guidance and Counseling; Psychology
Dist - GALCO **Prod** - GALCO

Welcome Aboard 11 MIN
U-matic / VHS / 16mm
Color (P I)
LC 76-703933
Stresses the importance of children's good behavior and the practice of safety habits while riding the school bus. Illustrates disruptive behavior and the safety hazards involved.
Guidance and Counseling; Health and Safety; Social Science
Dist - AIMS **Prod** - SEGALW 1976

Welcome Back, Norman 7 MIN
16mm / U-matic / VHS
Color
Depicts a humorous tale about what befalls a weary traveler in an airport parking lot.
Fine Arts; Literature and Drama
Dist - CORF **Prod** - CORF

Welcome Back to School 30 MIN
16mm
Aide - Ing in Education Series
Color (T)
Introduces viewers to the educational changes that have taken place in schools so that students will learn more. Emphasizes the professional responsibility for decision - making by the adults in the classroom.
Education; Psychology
Dist - SPF **Prod** - SPF

Welcome change 40 MIN
VHS
John Bull business series
Color (A)
PdS65 purchase
Redefines workplace attitudes and management structures. Part of a six-part series on British business culture.
Business and Economics
Dist - BBCENE

Welcome customer series
Have a nice stay - Pt 1 25 MIN
Dist - VIDART
XICOM

Welcome Home 29 MIN
16mm / U-matic / VHS
Color (H C A)
Declares that alienation is one of the main causes of juvenile delinquency and one of the most severe problems in rehabilitating young offenders.
Sociology
Dist - MEDIAG **Prod** - PAULST 1976

Welcome Home 27 MIN
U-matic / VHS / 16mm
Color; B&W (J)
Depicts a teenager who finally realizes that love, not aggressiveness, defines a man.
Fine Arts
Dist - MEDIAG **Prod** - PAULST

Welcome Home, Stranger 14 MIN
VHS / U-matic
Going International Series
Color (A)
LC 84-706120
Explains to Americans living abroad the personal reactions experienced upon returning to the United States and adjusting to American culture.
Geography - World; Social Science
Dist - COPGRG **Prod** - COPGRG 1983

Welcome Mr President 68 MIN
16mm
B&W
Depicts President Kennedy's visit to Ireland.
Biography; Geography - World
Dist - CONSUI **Prod** - CONSUI

Welcome the stranger 20 MIN
VHS
Color (K P I R)

$14.95 purchase, $10.00 rental _ #35 - 8131 - 19
Features Nanny and Isaiah envisioning what it was like at the first Christmas. Shows them meeting Mary, Joseph, Jesus and the shepherds. Based on the Christmas carol 'What Child is This?'
Literature and Drama; Religion and Philosophy
Dist - APH **Prod** - CPH

Welcome the stranger 20 MIN
VHS
Color (K P I R)
$14.95 purchase _ #87EE0131
Presents two homeless children, who are on their way to see the newborn Savior. Describes their experience of learning that Jesus' love is for all people. Based on the carol 'What Child Is This?'
Fine Arts; Guidance and Counseling; Literature and Drama; Religion and Philosophy
Dist - CPH **Prod** - CPH

Welcome to a Hindu wedding 9 MIN
U-matic / VHS / BETA
Color; NTSC; PAL; SECAM (J H)
PdS58
Features Sunita Gulati who tells the story of a Hindu wedding in Shrewsbury. Shows a Brahmin priest conducting the service in Sanskrit, and explains the significance of the sacred fire, the joining of hands, the exchange of gifts and garlands. The day ends with Bhangra music at the reception.
Religion and Philosophy; Sociology
Dist - VIEWTH

Welcome to Bangkok 16 MIN
16mm
Color (P)
Visits Bangkok, the capital of Thailand. Includes scenes of the city, temples, schools and people.
Geography - World; Social Science
Dist - WSUM **Prod** - WSUM 1960

Welcome to Britain 20 MIN
VHS
Color (S)
$19.95 purchase _ #423 - 9001
Begins and ends amid the streets of London. Visits in between the universities of Cambridge and Oxford - cathedrals such as Canterbury, York and Salisbury - Edinburgh and the Scottish Highlands - the Lake District and the mountains and castles of Wales - Stratford - Upon - Avon and tranquil Cotswold Hills - and Devon and South Coast resorts.
Fine Arts; Geography - World; History - World
Dist - FI

Welcome to Happy Valley 50 MIN
VHS
Everyman series
Color; PAL (C A H)
PdS99 purchase
Explores the controversy surrounding the antidepressant drug prozac, looking at how it affects the body and why some consider it dangerous.
Psychology
Dist - BBCENE

Welcome to high school 12 MIN
VHS
Color (J H)
$79.95 purchase _ #10213VL
Presents the high school environment to students who are about to make the transition from junior high school. Gives advice from teachers and high school students on classes, social life and activities. Includes a teacher's guide, student activities and discussion questions.
Education; Psychology
Dist - UNL

Welcome to Kennedy Space Center 9 MIN
16mm
Color
Highlights a spaceport tour at the Kennedy Space Center in Florida.
Geography - United States; Industrial and Technical Education; Science - Physical
Dist - FLADC **Prod** - FLADC

Welcome to Management
VHS / 16mm
Management Skill Development Series
(PRO)
$89.95 purchase _ #MDS1
Teaches the principles of management.
Business and Economics
Dist - RMIBHF **Prod** - RMIBHF

Welcome to Miami, Cubanos 28 MIN
16mm / U-matic / VHS
Color (I J H)
LC 81-700959
Shows how Mike, a high school student, has difficulty facing his Cuban heritage but must confront it and finally accept it when his cousin and his family stay at his house during their period of resettling in America.
Guidance and Counseling; Sociology
Dist - LCOA **Prod** - LCOA 1981

Welcome to my world 35 MIN
U-matic / VHS
Color (PRO C G)
$195.00 purchase _ #C890 - VI - 075
Visits the world of Anne Shuell - a quadriplegic wife and mother who has had multiple sclerosis since 1970. Shares her experiences about learning to cope with her crippling disability. Discusses the changing role of the handicapped individual and how this changing role affects family and friends, the support systems that are needed, the emotional ups - and - downs, the relationship between the patient and healthcare professionals, techniques for developing a positive life philosophy. Presented by Anne Shuell, Dr James A Anderson and Betsy Farkas.
Health and Safety
Dist - HSCIC

Welcome to normal 19 MIN
VHS
Works of Sadie Benning series
Color (A)
$200.00 purchase, $50.00 rental
Focuses on an irrepressible young girl who hams it up for the camera. Comments on caged desire and injustice. Part of a autobiographical series produced by Sadie Benning.
Fine Arts; Literature and Drama; Religion and Philosophy
Dist - WMEN

Welcome to Our Drug Free Workplace 13 MIN
VHS / 16mm
Color (A IND)
LC 91705370
Instructs workers about the hazards of specific drugs and the requirements of the Drug Free Workplace Act.
Education; Psychology; Sociology
Dist - IFB

Welcome to Our Party 5 MIN
16mm
Adventures in the High Grass Series
Color (K P I)
LC 74-702126
Portrays an insect community in puppet animation. Depicts a spirit of dance and celebration of nature.
Guidance and Counseling; Literature and Drama; Science - Natural
Dist - MMA **Prod** - MMA 1972

Welcome to our wetlands 13 MIN
VHS / U-matic
Color (P I)
$270.00, $320.00 purchase, $50.00 rental
Provides an introductory primer on what constitutes a wetland and the different kinds of wetlands. Instructs youngsters on how they can help keep a clean environment. Produced by Linda Reagan - King County.
Fine Arts; Science - Natural
Dist - NDIM

Welcome to outerspace 23 MIN
VHS
Color (J H C)
$14.95 purchase _ #NA070
History - World; Science - Physical
Dist - INSTRU **Prod** - NASA

Welcome to Parenthood 16 MIN
16mm
Color
Discusses the rewards and sacrifices of parenthood, presenting three young couples who describe the abrupt change in their lives after having children.
Sociology
Dist - FLMLIB **Prod** - FLMLIB

Welcome to Spivey's Corner, N C 17 MIN
U-matic / VHS / 16mm
Color (I J H C A)
$370, $250 purchase _ #4026
Describes regional America, focussing on farmers, and country people.
Sociology
Dist - CORF

Welcome to Spivey's Corner, N C 17 MIN
U-matic / VHS / 16mm
Color
LC 79-701452
Describes life in Spivey's Corner, North Carolina, home of the National Hollerin' Contest. Interviews past hollerin' champions to explain the history and significance of this folk art.
Geography - United States; Sociology
Dist - CORF **Prod** - PERSPF 1978

Welcome to the Colloquium on the Bicentennial of Medicine in the United States 59 MIN
U-matic
Color
LC 77-706051
Introduces the two - day Colloquium on the Bicentennial of Medicine in the United States. Highlights historical influences on American medicine and discusses the interplay of forces that contributed to an increase in federal support of biomedical research in the United States.
Health and Safety; Science
Dist - USNAC **Prod** - NMAC 1976

Welcome to the Future - Computers in the Classroom 28 MIN
16mm / U-matic / VHS
Dealing with Social Problems in the Classroom Series
Color (T)
Introduces computer literacy in the educational field including programming languages, pre - recorded software and the variety of ways computers can be used in schools. Illustrate how teachers and students can become computer literate.
Education; Mathematics
Dist - FI **Prod** - MFFD 1983

Welcome to the Hospital Corps 17 MIN
16mm
Color
LC 74-706605
Shows technical specialities for which hospital corps members may apply during their Navy careers and describes the training received at hospital corps schools and duty stations.
Civics and Political Systems; Guidance and Counseling; Health and Safety; Psychology
Dist - USNAC **Prod** - USN 1972

Welcome to the real world 50 MIN
VHS
Doctors to be series
Color; PAL (C PRO)
PdS99 purchase
Covers work on the wards and in casualty for ten medical students at St Mary's Hospital Medical School in London. Shows the situations students encounter during their first days working with patients. Third in the series Doctors To Be which follows a group of medical students from their initial screening through their work as newly qualified doctors.
Health and Safety
Dist - BBCENE

Welcome to the Third Grade 12 MIN
U-matic / VHS / 16mm
Critical Moments in Teaching Series
Color (C T)
Presents Jerry, who despite all his effort, must repeat the third grade. Explains that Mrs Gibson who has tutored him all year is leaving the school. Focuses on Jerry's new teacher and how she will handle this critical situation.
Education; Psychology
Dist - PHENIX **Prod** - HRAW 1970

Welcome to the Universe 53 MIN
VHS
Color (P I J)
$129.00 purchase _ #800
Teaches the basics of the major science in six parts. Includes the titles Astronomy - Hello Out There; Ecology - Our Home on Earth; Biology - To Be Alive; Cell Biology - An Ocean Inside; Chemistry - The Traveling Atoms; Physics and Poetry - Once Upon a Time, and a guide.
Science; Science - Natural; Science - Physical
Dist - HAWHIL **Prod** - HAWHIL

Welcome to the USA 13 MIN
16mm
Color (C A)
Follows immigration procedures from debarking at JFK Airport through immigrations, customs, to getting into Manhattan or making a connection to another airline.
History - United States; Social Science; Sociology
Dist - MCDO **Prod** - MCDO 1970

Welcome to the Working Worlds 17 MIN
16mm
Working Worlds Series
Color (I J)
Introduces the student to the concept of occupational clusters as a means of career exploration. Presents each of the 13 clusters in terms of its interrelated contribution to society as a whole.
Guidance and Counseling; Psychology; Sociology
Dist - COUNFI **Prod** - OLYMPS

Welcome to the World of Work 17 MIN
16mm

Color
LC 74-706322
Demonstrates the value of the summer work program in the Navy. Shows how supervisory training, orientation and meaningful work assignments are important to the program.
Business and Economics; Civics and Political Systems; Psychology
Dist - USNAC **Prod** - USN 1970

Welcoming New Neighbors 15 MIN
VHS / U-matic
Neighborhoods Series
Color (P)
Shows how to welcome new neighbors.
Sociology
Dist - GPN **Prod** - NEITV 1981

Welcoming Visitors 15 MIN
U-matic / VHS
Encounter in the Desert Series
Color (I)
Deals with hospitality among Bedouin nomads.
Geography - World; Social Science; Sociology
Dist - CTI **Prod** - CTI

Weld Defects - Causes and Corrections 60 MIN
U-matic / VHS
Welding Training Series
Color (IND)
Covers weld defects and nondestructive testing.
Education; Industrial and Technical Education
Dist - ITCORP **Prod** - ITCORP

Weld in Safety 23 MIN
U-matic / VHS / 16mm
Color (IND)
LC 81-700752
Demonstrates safety measures for using gas welding or cutting equipment.
Health and Safety; Industrial and Technical Education
Dist - IFB **Prod** - STFD 1980

Weld Joint Preparation and Temperature Control 42 MIN
BETA / VHS / U-matic
Color
$400 purchase
Guidance and Counseling; Industrial and Technical Education; Psychology
Dist - ASM **Prod** - ASM

Weld test coupon preparation - plate and pipe 38 MIN
VHS
Color (G H VOC IND)
$89.95 purchase _ #CEV00853V-T
Describes the correct procedures for preparing weld test coupons. Explains how to prepare a three-eighths inch plate for a weld test and includes beveling the plate, using a tract torch; filling beveled edges to form approximately one-sixteenth inch landing; and tacking the plates together utilizing a spacing tool to attain a gap between the coupons of approximately one-sixteenth inch. Also provides similar information for an eight inch diameter pipe.
Education; Industrial and Technical Education
Dist - CAMV

Welder 15 MIN
U-matic
Harriet's Magic Hats I Series
(P I J)
Shows a welder reading blueprints and using a gas welding system to build a sled.
Guidance and Counseling
Dist - ACCESS **Prod** - ACCESS 1980

Welder Certification 19 MIN
BETA / VHS
Color (IND)
Explains and demonstrates the theory of welding, grinding, cutting and bending of weld test plates, using procedures in accordance with the American Welding Society for use of E6010 and E7018 electrodes.
Industrial and Technical Education; Psychology
Dist - RMIBHF **Prod** - RMIBHF

Welder - fitter 5 MIN
VHS / 16mm
Good works 2 series
Color (A PRO)
$40.00 purchase _ #BPN205604
Presents the occupation of a welder - fitter. Gives a profile of a young person who is either undergoing an apprenticeship or has recently completed training in this field. Takes the viewer on a tour of this person's workplace and explains the practical skills and training offered by employers and schools. Gives a better understanding of the demand for skilled workers today and the potential for personal growth.
Guidance and Counseling
Dist - RMIBHF **Prod** - RMIBHF

Welder - fitter 5 MIN
U-matic
Good work series
Color (H)
Provides useful, up to date information on various occupations to aid high school students in career selection. Available in five series of ten jobs each.
Education; Guidance and Counseling; Industrial and Technical Education
Dist - TVOTAR **Prod** - TVOTAR 1981

Welding 13 MIN
16mm
Metalwork - Hand Tools Series
Color (H C A)
Welding equipment - - setting up, lighting, shutting down, making a puddle, running a bead, adding fillerbrazing and cutting.
Industrial and Technical Education
Dist - SF **Prod** - MORLAT 1967

Welding 15 MIN
VHS / U-matic
Manufacturing Materials and Processes Series
Color
Covers steps in welding, types of welding and welding defects.
Industrial and Technical Education
Dist - WFVTAE **Prod** - GE

Welding 19 MIN
U-matic
Occupations Series
B&W (J H)
Shows how an apprentice to a fabrication welder was trained for the job at an occupational school.
Guidance and Counseling
Dist - TVOTAR **Prod** - TVOTAR 1985

Welding
VHS
Career connections video series
Color (J H C G)
$39.95 purchase _ #CCP0202V
Examines career options in welding. Looks at educational requirements, skills needed, safety considerations, advancement opportunities and related occupations. Interviews workers and shows on - the - job footage to overview the work. The last segment provides a brief summary of how to use the Occupational Outlook Handbook - OOH and the Dictionary of Occupational Titles - DOT. Part of a six - part series on occupations.
Business and Economics; Guidance and Counseling; Industrial and Technical Education
Dist - CAMV **Prod** - CAMV 1993

Welding Aluminum with Inert Gas Tungsten Arc
U-matic / VHS
MIG and TIG Welding - Spanish Series
Color (SPANISH)
Foreign Language; Industrial and Technical Education
Dist - VTRI **Prod** - VTRI

Welding Aluminum with MIG and TIG 28 MIN
16mm
Color (J)
LC 76-702321
Highlights the importance of joint design cleaning and proper adjustment of welding equipment with MIG (metal inert gas) and TIG (tungsten inert gas). Includes slow motion footage of MIG and TIG.
Industrial and Technical Education
Dist - REYMC **Prod** - REYMC 1968

Welding and Cutting Processes I 48 MIN
BETA / VHS / U-matic
Color
$400 purchase
Guidance and Counseling; Industrial and Technical Education; Psychology
Dist - ASM **Prod** - ASM

Welding and Cutting Processes II 44 MIN
U-matic / BETA / VHS
Color
$400 purchase
Contains two tapes.
Guidance and Counseling; Industrial and Technical Education; Psychology
Dist - ASM **Prod** - ASM

Welding Bandsaw Blades 22 MIN
BETA / VHS
Machine Shop - Bandsaw Series
Color (IND)
Industrial and Technical Education; Psychology
Dist - RMIBHF **Prod** - RMIBHF

Welding by Tape 8 MIN
16mm
Color
Shows an installation used for developing automatically - controlled welding.
Industrial and Technical Education
Dist - UKAEA **Prod** - UKAEA 1964

Welding cast iron in flat position with electric arc, hard facing surfaces
U-matic / VHS
Shielded metal arc welding - Spanish series
Color (SPANISH)
Discusses welding cast iron in flat position and hard facing surfaces with electric arc.
Foreign Language; Industrial and Technical Education
Dist - VTRI **Prod** - VTRI

Welding Equipment, Accessories and Shop Safety
VHS / U-matic
Oxyacetylene Welding - Spanish Series
Color (SPANISH)
Foreign Language; Health and Safety; Industrial and Technical Education
Dist - VTRI **Prod** - VTRI

Welding Explained - Oxyacetylene Fusion 58 MIN
VHS / 35mm strip
Color (H A IND)
#902XV7
Explains the equipment and procedures of oxyacetylene fusion welding applications. Includes basic nomenclature, preparing the unit for welding, lighting and adjusting the welding flame, fusion welding - basic application, and fusion welding - varying applications (5 tapes). Prerequisites required. Includes a Study Guide.
Education; Industrial and Technical Education
Dist - BERGL

Welding Explained - Oxyacetylene Non Fusion 58 MIN
VHS / 35mm strip
Color (H A IND)
#901XV7
Introduces the basic equipment and procedures of oxyacetylene non - fusion welding applications. Includes basic nomenclature, preparing the unit for welding, lighting and adjusting the welding flame, basic application, and varying applications (5 tapes). Prerequisite required. Includes a Study Guide.
Education; Industrial and Technical Education
Dist - BERGL

Welding - health hazards 22 MIN
U-matic / BETA / VHS
Hazard communication series
Color (IND G)
$395.00 purchase _ #820 - 09
Trains employees in the health hazards associated with welding, cutting and brazing. Identifies the sources and primary routes of entry, protective measures and basic first aid procedures. Part of a series on hazard communication.
Health and Safety; Industrial and Technical Education; Psychology
Dist - ITSC **Prod** - ITSC

Welding I - Basic Oxy - Acetylene Welding Series
Setup of the Combination Torch and Cutting of Sheet Metal, Sheet Plate 15 MIN
Dist - CAMB

Welding III - TIG and MIG (Industry Welding Series
Making T - Joint, Lap Joint and Outside Corner Welds all Positions with Aluminum, Steel 15 MIN
Selection of Electrode, Gas, Cups and Filler Rod for Gas Tungsten Arc (Tig) Welding 15 MIN
Dist - CAMB

Welding inspection and quality control series
Eddy current inspection, acoustic emissions, proof tests and leak tests
Dist - AMCEE

Welding Inspector 42 MIN
U-matic / BETA / VHS
Color
$400 purchase
Guidance and Counseling; Industrial and Technical Education
Dist - ASM **Prod** - ASM

Welding Machine Set - Up and Operation Miller 35 Wire Feed 9 MIN
BETA / VHS
Color (IND)
Explains the set - up for a Miller 35 wire feed welder.
Industrial and Technical Education; Psychology
Dist - RMIBHF **Prod** - RMIBHF

Welding - Metal Inert Gas Techniques 13 MIN
16mm
Welding Series
Color (H C A)
LC 72-701843
Explains the theory of MIG welding. Shows details of the equipment used and the functions of the various units, including power supplies. Demonstrates operating procedures in the making of butt and fillet welds with various metals.
Industrial and Technical Education
Dist - SF **Prod** - MORLAT 1969

Welding Metallurgy 64 MIN
BETA / VHS / U-matic
Color
$400 purchase
Contains two tapes.
Guidance and Counseling; Industrial and Technical Education; Psychology
Dist - ASM **Prod** - ASM

Welding Mild Steel with Inert Gas Tungsten Arc
VHS / U-matic
MIG and TIG Welding - Spanish Series
Color (SPANISH)
Foreign Language; Industrial and Technical Education
Dist - VTRI **Prod** - VTRI

Welding of Carbon Steel Pipe 37 MIN
U-matic / VHS
Advanced Welding Series
Color (IND)
Provides training to performance qualify to ASME code requirements using SMAW for all positions on pressure piping and vessels.
Education; Industrial and Technical Education
Dist - TAT **Prod** - TAT

Welding of low alloy steel pipe 34 MIN
U-matic / VHS
Advanced arc welding series
Color (IND)
Discusses code requirements for welding low - alloy steel pipe. Develops and proves manipulative skills through testing.
Education; Industrial and Technical Education
Dist - TAT **Prod** - TAT

Welding of stainless steel pipe 20 MIN
VHS / U-matic
Advanced arc welding series
Color (IND)
Covers welding with 18 percent chrome and 8 percent nickel stainless steel pipe.
Education; Industrial and Technical Education
Dist - TAT **Prod** - TAT

Welding - physical hazards 11 MIN
U-matic / BETA / VHS
Hazard communication series
Color (IND G)
$395.00 purchase _ #820 - 08
Describes the various types of physical hazards associated with welding, including noise, fire and burns, electrical and ultraviolet radiation, as well as protective measures. Explains emergency first aid and fire procedures. Part of a series on hazard communication.
Health and Safety; Industrial and Technical Education; Psychology
Dist - ITSC **Prod** - ITSC

Welding - Pipe Welding Techniques 13 MIN
16mm
Welding Series
Color (J A)
LC 72-701844
Shows in detail the preparation of joints for arc welding and proper use of the body in making a weld. Demonstrates all the aspects of downhill and uphill welding and roll and vertical welding. Gives examples of pipe welding in industry and checking with X - rays.
Industrial and Technical Education
Dist - SF **Prod** - SF 1969

Welding Procedure and Welding Operator Qualifications 51 MIN
BETA / VHS / U-matic
Color
$400 purchase
Guidance and Counseling; Industrial and Technical Education; Psychology
Dist - ASM **Prod** - ASM

Welding Procedures Series Oxyacetylene Welding, no 1
Oxy - Acetylene Welding - Light Metal 21 MIN
Dist - USNAC

Welding Procedures Series Oxygen Cutting, no 1
Manual Cutting to a Line - Freehand 21 MIN
Dist - USNAC

Welding Procedures Series Oxygen Cutting
Manual Cutting a Bevel - Freehand 13 MIN
Manual Cutting a Shape - Freehand Guided 16 MIN
Dist - USNAC

Welding Procedures Series Testing, no 1
The Guided Bend Test 17 MIN
Dist - USNAC

Welding Safety 27 MIN
VHS / 35mm strip
(H A IND)
#515XV7
Explains the safe use and storage of gas and electric welding equipment and safety in the welding shop. Includes exyacetylene welding and electric arc welding (2 tapes). Includes a Study Guide.
Education; Health and Safety; Industrial and Technical Education
Dist - BERGL

Welding Safety with Oxyacetylene and Arc Welding
VHS / 35mm strip
Skills Related Safety Series
$96.00 purchase _ #TX3C1 filmstrips, $186.00 purchase _ #TX3C1V VHS
Teaches about welding safety with oxacetylene and arc welding equipment. Includes shop and specific requirements of arc and oxyacetylene welding.
Health and Safety
Dist - CAREER **Prod** - CAREER

Welding Series
Brazing and Braze Welding
Careers in Welding
Electric Welding Safety and Setup
Introduction to Electric Welding
Introduction to Oxyacetylene
MIG Welding
Oxyacetylene Safety and Setup
TIG Welding
Dist - CAREER

Welding series
The Air - acetylene flame 10 MIN
Flame cutting 11 MIN
Flame grooving 10 MIN
Flat and horizontal welding 12 MIN
Fusion welding 11 MIN
Fusion welding of light gauge steel 10 MIN
Hard Facing 10 MIN
Heliarc (TIG) welding introduction to manual heliarc welding 8 MIN
Heliarc welding of carbon steel pipes 10 MIN
Oxy - Acetylene Welding and Cutting - Braze Welding 13 MIN
Setting up for welding 12 MIN
Vertical and Overhead Welding 10 MIN
Dist - FI

Welding Series
Introduction to Arc Welding 60 MIN
Introduction to Gas Welding 60 MIN
Practical Shop Metallurgy 60 MIN
Dist - NUSTC

Welding Series
Welding - Metal Inert Gas Techniques 13 MIN
Welding - Pipe Welding Techniques 13 MIN
Dist - SF

Welding Stainless Steel with Inert Gas Tungsten Arc
U-matic / VHS
MIG and TIG Welding - Spanish Series
Color (SPANISH)
Foreign Language; Industrial and Technical Education
Dist - VTRI **Prod** - VTRI

Welding techniques 25 MIN
VHS
Technical studies series
Color (A PRO IND)
PdS50 purchase
Shows how welding techniques are applied to manufacturing. Part of a series designed to take students out of the classroom setting and into the world of engineering.
Business and Economics; Industrial and Technical Education
Dist - BBCENE

Welding tips and techniques 13 MIN
U-matic / VHS
Electric arc welding series; Chap 9
Color (IND)
Education; Industrial and Technical Education
Dist - TAT **Prod** - TAT

Welding training - advanced shielded metal arc welding series
All position fillet test 18 MIN
Dist - RMIBHF

Welding training - comprehensive - advanced shielded metal arc welding series
Arc air cutting 4 MIN
Overhead fillet weld 8 MIN
Overhead v - butt weld 9 MIN
Vertical up butt weld 8 MIN
Vertical up fillet weld 8 MIN
Dist - RMIBHF

Welding training - comprehensive - basic shielded metal arc welding series
Arc welding safety 10 MIN
Electrode identification 11 MIN
Lap joint 4 MIN
Square butt joint single - pass 6 MIN
T joint 12 MIN
T joint - multi - pass weave 6 MIN
T joint - 3 - pass stringer 7 MIN
V - butt joint multi - pass 13 MIN
Vertical down fillet 6 MIN
Dist - RMIBHF

Welding training comprehensive - basic shielded wetal arc welding series
Butt joint whip 6 MIN
Dist - RMIBHF

Welding Training (Comprehensive - Metal Inert Gas (M I G Welding Series
Introduction to G M a W 10 MIN
Lap Joint V - Down 2 MIN
Single Pass Fillet 3 MIN
Single Pass Fillet (Vertical Down) 2 MIN
Square Butt Joint 2 MIN
Square Butt Joint Flat 2 MIN
V - Butt Joint 3 MIN
V - Butt Joint Horizontal 2 MIN
Dist - RMIBHF

Welding Training - Comprehensive - Metal Inert Gas - M I G Welding Series
Fillet weld horizontal - aluminum 5 MIN
Fillet weld overhead 2 MIN
Introduction to Flux - Cored - G M A W 9 MIN
Multi - Pass Fillet 4 MIN
Multi - Pass Fillet Flat - Steel 5 MIN
Multi - Pass Fillet V - Up 3 MIN
Square Butt Joint Flat Aluminum 2 MIN
Dist - RMIBHF

Welding training - comprehensive - oxy - acetylene welding series
Bevel machine cutting 4 MIN
Cast Iron V - Butt Bronze 11 MIN
Inside Corner Joint 8 MIN
Lap Weld 7 MIN
Open Corner Joint 5 MIN
Oxy - Acetylene Equipment Set - Up and Safety 33 MIN
Square Butt Backhand 7 MIN
Stringer Bead 7 MIN
T joint aluminum braze 5 MIN
Dist - RMIBHF

Welding Training Comprehensive - - - Oxy - Acetylene Welding Series
Cast iron fusion weld 8 MIN
Hole Cutting Manual 3 MIN
Ninety Degree Machine Cutting 4 MIN
Square Butt Aluminum 5 MIN
Square Butt Bronze 6 MIN
Square Butt Horizontal 6 MIN
Square Butt Joint Filler Rod 6 MIN
Square Butt Silver Braze 4 MIN
Square Butt Vertical - Up 6 MIN
Vee Butt Joint 12 MIN
Dist - RMIBHF

Welding training comprehensive series
Plate cutting manual 8 MIN
Dist - RMIBHF

Welding Training (Comprehensive - Tungsten Inert Gas (T I G Welding Series
Inside Corner Joint A1 4 MIN
Introduction to T I G Welding 19 MIN
Lap Weld A1 3 MIN
Dist - RMIBHF

Welding Training Comprehensive - Tungsten Inert Gas T I G Welding Series
Square Butt A1 2 MIN
Square Butt Joint Aluminum with Fixture 4 MIN
Square Butt Joint Stainless 4 MIN

Square Butt Joint Stainless Vertical - Up 2 MIN
Square Butt Stainless with Fixture 4 MIN
Dist - RMIBHF

Welding Training Series
Brazing and Braze Welding 60 MIN
Cutting - plasma arc and carbon arc 60 MIN
General Techniques and Safety Practices 60 MIN
Joint Design and Symbols 60 MIN
Oxygen - Fuel Gas Cutting 60 MIN
Principles and Metallurgy 60 MIN
Principles and Techniques of MIG 60 MIN
Principles of TIG 60 MIN
Shielded Metal - Arc Structural and Pipe Welding 60 MIN
Shielded Metal - Arc Welding Principles 60 MIN
TIG structural and pipe welding 60 MIN
Weld Defects - Causes and Corrections 60 MIN
Dist - ITCORP

Welding training series
Pipe welding - qualifying for all positions 20 MIN
Symbols for welding 18 MIN
Dist - ITSC

Welding training series
Corner joint A1 open 3 MIN
Corner weld stainless 2 MIN
Cutting gauge materials manual 4 MIN
Horizontal lap weld 5 MIN
Horizontal V - Butt Weld 11 MIN
Dist - RMIBHF

Weldment Imperfections and Discontinuities 51 MIN
U-matic / BETA / VHS
Color
$400 purchase
Guidance and Counseling; Industrial and Technical Education; Psychology
Dist - ASM **Prod** - ASM

Welfare 167 MIN
16mm / U-matic / VHS
B&W (J)
LC 75-703460
Describes the daily activities of a large welfare center, focusing on problems with which staff and clients must deal.
Social Science; Sociology
Dist - ZIPRAH **Prod** - WELFI 1975

Welfare and the Fatherless Family 15 MIN
U-matic / VHS / 16mm
Color
LC 73-702675
Shows how the poor families restructure themselves to obtain welfare benefits. Tells the history of day care centers and their inadequacies.
Sociology
Dist - CAROUF **Prod** - CBSTV 1973

The Welfare Dilemma 30 MIN
VHS / U-matic
Ethics in America Series
Color (H C A)
Presents Sar A Levitan, professor of economics, and Marvin Bloom, professor of social work, exploring the strengths and weaknesses of many welfare programs. Examines whether the government is financially overextended, whether the people who really need welfare programs benefit, and what improvements are needed.
Religion and Philosophy; Sociology
Dist - AMHUMA **Prod** - AMHUMA

Welfare mothers 28 MIN
U-matic
Are you listening series
Color (J)
LC 80-707154
Presents women welfare recipients describing the problems of the welfare system.
Sociology
Dist - STURTM **Prod** - STURTM 1971

The Welfare Revolt 60 MIN
16mm
Net Journal Series
B&W (H C A)
LC FIA68-504
Documents complaints of welfare recipients and their attempts to change the system by organizing local unions. Discusses the unions' goals and describes the federal government's emphasis on training programs. Shows protest marches in Cleveland and Washington, D C.
Civics and Political Systems; History - United States; Psychology; Sociology
Dist - IU **Prod** - NET 1968

The Well 18 MIN
U-matic / VHS
Color (IND)
States the methods by which a well is drilled, produced and abandoned.
Business and Economics; Industrial and Technical Education; Social Science
Dist - UTEXPE **Prod** - UTEXPE

The Well 8 MIN
VHS / U-matic
Timeless tales series
Color (P I)
$110.00, $160.00 purchase, $60.00 rental
Tells the tale of an old woman's two daughters, one a step - daughter. Presents a lesson in hard work, which can reap rewards, versus laziness, which goes unrewarded.
Guidance and Counseling; Literature and Drama
Dist - NDIM **Prod** - TIMTAL 1993

Well - baby check - ups - from infant to tot
VHS
Color (G)
$59.95 purchase _ #CCP0221V
Presents information for new parents about typical procedures doctors and other healthcare professionals follow during well-baby check-ups. Explains recommended schedule of visits, evaluations, questions to expect during the visits, and questions to ask. Provides schedule of timings for tests such as blood tests, eye screenings, hearing tests. Contains scenes with young children.
Health and Safety
Dist - CAMV

Well-baby check-ups - from infant to tot
VHS
Color (A)
$59.95 purchase _ #CCP0221V-D
Focuses on information for new parents. Describes the normal procedures doctors and other healthcare professionals follow during a typical well-baby check-up. Advises parents on scheduling visits, types of tests that will be performed on their child, kinds of questions doctors will ask new parents, and more. Uses on-screen graphics, narration, interviews.
Health and Safety; Sociology
Dist - CAMV

The Well Being of the Organization 59 FRS
VHS / U-matic
Organization Development Series Module 1
Color
Covers some of the symptoms of unhealthy organizations and how they get that way. Illustrates the point that office development can help solve specific organizational deficiences.
Business and Economics; Psychology
Dist - RESEM **Prod** - RESEM

We'll bury you 73 MIN
16mm
B&W (G)
$75.00 rental
Features a documentation of Communism from Marx through the Cold War. Views rare film clips, many from Russian newsreels and captured footage. By J W Thomas with narration by William Woodsons.
Civics and Political Systems; Fine Arts
Dist - KITPAR

Well Completion 40 MIN
U-matic / VHS
Basic and Petroleum Geology for Non - Geologists - Drilling and - - 'Series; Drilling
Color (IND)
Industrial and Technical Education; Science - Physical
Dist - GPCV **Prod** - PHILLP

Well Completions 22 MIN
U-matic / Slide / VHS / 16mm
Color (IND A PRO)
$140.00 purchase _ #11.1257, $150.00 purchase _ #51.1257
Covers the planning of completions, production - method options, and workover options.
Industrial and Technical Education; Social Science
Dist - UTEXPE **Prod** - UTEXPE 1972

Well Control Operations - Instructions on Blowout Prevention Equipment for Rotary 27 MIN
VHS / U-matic
Color (IND)
Gives instructions on the purpose, operation and general maintenance of the annular blowout prevention, diverter system ram - type preventer, accumulator system, drill string inside BOP, drill string safety valve, kelly cock and adjustable choke. Designed for use by rotary helpers and derrickmen.
Health and Safety; Industrial and Technical Education; Social Science
Dist - UTEXPE **Prod** - UTEXPE 197

Well Control Operations - Instructions on Drilling Fluids for Derrickmen 20 MI
U-matic / VHS
Color (A PRO IND)
$150.00 purchase _ #11.1017, $160.00 purchase _ #51.1017
Gives general instructions on drilling fluids with emphasis o density, viscosity, fluid loss, salinity, gas cutting and general procedures for increasing mud density.
Health and Safety; Industrial and Technical Education; Social Science
Dist - UTEXPE **Prod** - UTEXPE 198

Well Control Operations - Instructions on General Well - Killing Procedures for Derrickmen 25 MI
VHS / U-matic
Color (A PRO IND)
$150.00 purchase _ #11.1019, $160.00 purchase _ #51.1019
Provides general instructions in the procedures for killing a well that has kicked, including the driller's method and the wait - and - weight method.
Health and Safety; Industrial and Technical Education; Social Science
Dist - UTEXPE **Prod** - UTEXPE 198

Well Control Operations - Instructions on OCS Training Requirements for Rotary Helpers 6 MI
U-matic / VHS
Color (IND)
Covers governmental regulations that are pertinent to work of rotary helpers and derrickmen on offshore drilling areas of the continental shelf of the United States.
Business and Economics; Industrial and Technical Education
Dist - UTEXPE **Prod** - UTEXPE 1979

Well Control Operations - Instructions on OCS Training Requirements for Rotary Helpers and Derrickmen 6 MIN
Slide / VHS / 16mm
(A PRO)
$100.00 purchase _ #11.1018, $110.00 purchase _ #51.1018
Covers governmental regulations that are pertinent to the work of rotary helpers and derrickmen on offshore drilling areas of the continental shelf of the U S.
Health and Safety; Industrial and Technical Education; Social Science
Dist - UTEXPE **Prod** - UTEXPE 1979

Well Control Operations - Instructions on Warning Signs of Kicks for Rotary Helpers 23 MIN
U-matic / VHS
Color (IND)
Gives instructions on the more obvious warning signs of a kick. Includes a gain in pit volume, increase in mud return rate, hole not taking the proper amount of mud, and trip, connection and background gas changes. Designed for use by derrickmen as well as rotary helpers.
Industrial and Technical Education; Social Science
Dist - UTEXPE **Prod** - UTEXPE 1979

Well Control Operations - Instructions on Warning Signs of Kicks for Rotary Helpers and Derrickmen 23 MIN
Slide / VHS / 16mm
(A PRO)
$150.00 purchase _ #11.1016, $160.00 purchase _ #51.1016
Gives instructions on the more obvious warning signs of a kick including a gain in pit volume, increase in mud return rate, hole not taking the proper amount of mud, well flowing with pump shut down, and more.
Health and Safety; Industrial and Technical Education; Social Science
Dist - UTEXPE **Prod** - UTEXPE 1979

The Well dressed man's guide to the five classic tie knots 15 MIN
VHS
Color (G)
$19.95 purchase _ #VIF05V-B
Teaches men five ways to knot a tie so that they can project confidence and style. Outlines how to tie the four-in-hand, the full Windsor, the half Windsor, the Shelby, and the bow tie. Notes that ties are a crucial part of a working man's wardrobe and help define his image to potential clients and customers.
Home Economics
Dist - CAMV

The Well - Flowing, Dead and Unloading 13 MIN
16mm / U-matic / VHS
Gas Lift Series
Color (IND)
Business and Economics; Industrial and Technical Education; Social Science
Dist - UTEXPE **Prod** - EXXON

Well, if You Ask Me 4 MIN
VHS / 16mm / U-matic / BETA
Working Together Series
Color; Stereo
Presents the difficulties of eliciting opinions from within a group.
English Language; Sociology
Dist - SEVDIM **Prod** - SEVDIM 1983

A Well in West Virginia 15 MIN
16mm
Color
LC 74-702680
Illustrates the work and excitement of drilling for natural gas. Shows how geologists and engineers employing principles which are useful in the science class, locate the site, drill to the proper depth and penetrate through earth and rock to the gas deposits.
Geography - United States; Science - Physical; Social Science
Dist - FINLYS **Prod** - AGA 1974

Well Logging 40 MIN
U-matic / VHS
Petroleum Geology Series
Color (IND)
Industrial and Technical Education; Science - Physical
Dist - GPCV **Prod** - GPCV

Well Logging - Answers from Beneath the Ground 23 MIN
VHS / 16mm / U-matic
Color (A PRO IND)
$325.00 purchase _ #30.0112, $300.00 purchase _ #50.0112
Explains the various well logging instruments. Describes the methods, uses and techniques of well logging.
Health and Safety; Industrial and Technical Education; Social Science
Dist - UTEXPE **Prod** - UTEXPE 1978

Well Logging Fundamentals 25 MIN
VHS / U-matic
Color (IND)
Looks at electrical, acoustic and radioactivity logging.
Industrial and Technical Education; Social Science
Dist - UTEXPE **Prod** - UTEXPE 1974

Well Logging Interpretation 58 MIN
VHS / U-matic
Basic and Petroleum Geology for Non - Geologists - Reservoirs and - '- Series; Reservoirs
Color (IND)
Industrial and Technical Education; Science - Physical
Dist - GPCV **Prod** - PHILLP

Well Logging Mechanics 40 MIN
U-matic / VHS
Basic and Petroleum Geology for Non - Geologists - Reservoirs and - '- Series; Reservoirs
Color (IND)
Industrial and Technical Education; Science - Physical
Dist - GPCV **Prod** - PHILLP

Well Model and Lift 11 MIN
U-matic / VHS / 16mm
Gas Lift Series
Color (IND)
Business and Economics; Industrial and Technical Education; Social Science
Dist - UTEXPE **Prod** - EXXON

The Well of the World's End 27 MIN
U-matic / VHS / 16mm
Storybook International Series
Color
Presents the Scottish tale of a girl who is sent by her stepmother to get water from a well using a sieve. Relates that she is helped at this task by a frog who then makes many demands. Reveals that the frog then turns into a handsome prince whom she marries.
Guidance and Counseling; Literature and Drama
Dist - JOU **Prod** - JOU 1982

We'll See Tomorrow 10 MIN
U-matic / VHS / 16mm
Color; Captioned (I J A)
LC 72-715433
Depicts those shop hazards that can cause serious eye injury, including intense light or heat, splattered liquid, flying sparks and chips of wood, cement or metal. Demonstrates the eye safety devices that can prevent these injuries from happening.
Health and Safety; Industrial and Technical Education
Dist - JOU **Prod** - ALTSUL 1971

A Well - Spent Life 44 MIN
16mm
Color (H A)
$500.00 purchase, $65.00 rental
Interviews the late Texas singer Maurice Lipscomb who lived as a poverty - stricken sharecropper before he made his first recording in 1960.
Fine Arts
Dist - AFA **Prod** - BLNKL 1971

Well, We are Alive 30 MIN
U-matic
B&W
Explores the attitudes of family, friends and society toward older people. Focuses on such issues as living on a fixed income, coping with the social services maze, physical and mental difficulties, self - image and societal emphasis on women.
Health and Safety; Sociology
Dist - WMEN **Prod** - WMEN

Well, well, well with Slim Goodbody series

Choosing food wisely	15 MIN
Cleanliness	15 MIN
The Doctor - patient team	15 MIN
Exercise	15 MIN
First Aid and Medicine	15 MIN
Food for energy and growth	15 MIN
The Healthy Community	15 MIN
Indoor Safety	15 MIN
Mental Health	15 MIN
Outside Safety	15 MIN
The Senses	15 MIN
Sleep, Stress and Relaxation	15 MIN

Dist - AITECH

Well Worth it 10 MIN
VHS / 16mm
Color (PRO)
$295.00 purchase, $75.00 rental, $35.00 preview
Teaches employees how to use the health care system to reduce costs both for the employee and the company.
Guidance and Counseling; Health and Safety; Psychology
Dist - UTM **Prod** - UTM

The Welland Canal - Merritt's Folly 28 MIN
16mm
Color (G)
_ #106C 0181 129
Describes William Hamilton Merritt who built the Welland Canal between Lake Erie and Lake Ontario which has been and continues to be a vital link in the St Lawrence Seaway system.
Biography; History - World; Social Science
Dist - CFLMDC **Prod** - NFBC 1981

Wellesley
VHS
Campus clips series
Color (H C A)
$29.95 purchase _ #CC0061V
Takes a video visit to the campus of Wellesley College in Massachusetts. Shows many of the distinctive features of the campus, and interviews students about their experiences. Provides information on the composition of the student body, professors, academics, social life, housing, and other subjects.
Education
Dist - CAMV

Wellhead Operations 23 MIN
U-matic / VHS
Color (IND)
Introduces gas field operators to routing wellhead operations such as turning the well on or off and performing daily maintenance checks. Includes instructions on how to identify and correct common well head malfunctions such as freezes in the production line, tubing, or wellhead and fluid build - up in the wellbore.
Industrial and Technical Education; Social Science
Dist - UTEXPE **Prod** - UTEXPE 1981

Wellman - Lord / Allied Chemical Flue Gas Desulfurization Process 13 MIN
16mm
Color
LC 78-701896
Describes the flue gas desulfurization system being demonstrated by the Environmental Protection Agency and Northern Indiana Public Services Company. Provides an overview of the sulfur dioxide problem and examines the equipment and chemistry involved in the process.
Sociology
Dist - USNAC **Prod** - USEPA 1978

Wellmet House 30 MIN
16mm
To Save Tomorrow Series
B&W (H C A)
Explains that the objective is not to gain conforming behavior but to help patients relate to other people in natural and unstructured ways and for the patients this means finding individual ways of expressing themselves.
Psychology
Dist - IU **Prod** - NET

Wellness
VHS
Personal action system series
Color (G)
$149.00 purchase _ #V213
Teaches employees about wellness concepts. Part of a 13 - part series to educate employees on the importance of health.
Health and Safety; Physical Education and Recreation; Psychology
Dist - GPERFO

Wellness in the Workplace 24 MIN
U-matic / VHS / 16mm
Color (PRO)
Demonstrates how to strengthen a prime resource - people. Features corporation executives who evaluate how employee wellness has affected company productivity and morale.
Health and Safety; Physical Education and Recreation; Psychology
Dist - PRORE **Prod** - PRORE

Wellness - Investing in Your Health 28 MIN
U-matic / VHS
What it Means to be Healthy Series
Color
Health and Safety
Dist - SYLWAT **Prod** - RCOMTV 1982

Wellness, It's not Magic 15 MIN
U-matic / VHS
Color (K P)
LC 81-707650
Uses puppets to explain to the overweight Wicked Witch of the Woods the importance of nutrition and exercise. Shows the four basic foods and the fun of exercising.
Health and Safety; Home Economics; Physical Education and Recreation
Dist - KIDSCO **Prod** - KIDSCO 1981

Wellness - It's not Magic 15 MIN
16mm / VHS
Kid's Corner Series
Color (P I)
$150.00, $315.00 purchase, $30.00 rental _ #9784
Uses an updated version of Hansel and Gretel to teach youngsters the importance of good health. While jogging in the woods, Hansel and Gretel are tempted by the old witch to eat sweets. They teach the witch about proper nutrition, she changes her ways and becomes a shining example of good health and good will.
Health and Safety; Psychology
Dist - AIMS **Prod** - AIMS 1984

The Wellness Lifestyle 30 MIN
U-matic / VHS / 16mm
Planning for Wellness System Series
Color (H C A)
Presents information to help in assessing a person's health attitudes. Demonstrates a variety of techniques for handling everyday sources of stress, maintaining good working conditions and assuring proper nutrition.
Health and Safety; Psychology; Social Science
Dist - CORF **Prod** - ABCVID 1983

Wellness programs work - the benefits of working well 50 MIN
VHS
Color (A PRO)
$129.00 purchase _ #S01540
Stresses the importance of a positive managerial style to encouraging good employee health. Covers various risk factors and their costs. Points out four negative managerial styles. Presentations by Dr Mark Tager and Marjorie Blanchard, with a summary interview by Michael Harbert.
Business and Economics; Guidance and Counseling; Physical Education and Recreation; Psychology
Dist - UILL

The Wellness Revolution 28 MIN
16mm
Color
Discusses the importance of choosing healthful lifestyles. Includes professional tips on stress management techniques, nutrition, exercises for all stages of life, available support groups and various other physical activities.
Health and Safety; Physical Education and Recreation; Psychology; Social Science
Dist - MTP **Prod** - JHI

Wellness video 3 MIN
VHS
Meeting opener motivation videos series

Color (G)
$89.00 purchase _ #MV5
Presents an inspiration video which incorporates breakthrough cinematography, stirring music and powerful lyrics to create a mood that enhances the impact of the desired message.
Business and Economics; Health and Safety; Psychology
Dist - GPERFO

Wells and Wellhead Equipment 18 MIN
U-matic / VHS
Color (IND)
Introduces the well to field operators and other entry - level personnel. Teaches the basic principles of petroleum formation and accumulation, drilling and recovery procedures, casing installation and the function and assembly of a typical wellhead.
Industrial and Technical Education; Social Science
Dist - UTEXPE **Prod** - UTEXPE 1981

Wells, Ida B 30 MIN
U-matic
American Women - Echoes and Dreams Series
Color
Dramatizes the life of Ida B Wells, a black American who fought for the rights of blacks and women.
Biography; History - United States; History - World; Sociology
Dist - HRC **Prod** - OHC

The Wellspring of prayer 30 MIN
VHS
Color (G A R)
$39.95 purchase, $10.00 rental _ #35 - 84 - 2076
Portrays the late Ruth Youngdahl, who offers her thoughts about prayer. Produced by Seraphim.
Religion and Philosophy
Dist - APH

Wellsprings 59 MIN
16mm
Color
LC 76-702914
Features a documentary on the importance of coastal wetlands to marine ecology as exemplified by the mangrove swamps of Florida. Shows the human side of oceanographic research with studies of scientists documenting the need to preserve coastal estuaries.
Science; Science - Natural; Science - Physical; Sociology
Dist - WPBTTV **Prod** - WPBTTV 1976

Welsh Cupboard 30 MIN
VHS / 16mm
Build Your Own Series
Color (H C A PRO)
$15.00 purchase _ #TA215
Features construction of a welsh cupboard, a wood paneling project.
Industrial and Technical Education
Dist - AAVIM **Prod** - AAVIM 1990

The Welsh - music from the mines 8 MIN
VHS
Columbus legacy series
Color (J H C G)
$40.00 purchase, $11.00 rental _ #12329
Reveals that vertical harmony began in Wales in the 14th century, according to conductor Carlton Jones Lake. Discloses that Welsh miners taught each other to sing using their hands. Lake conducts members of the Minersville Congregational Church, as well as other Welsh descendants in traditional hymn singing. Part of a 15 - part series commemorating the 500th anniversary of Columbus' journeys to the Americas - journeys that brought together a constantly evolving collection of different ethnic groups and examining the contributions of 15 distinct groups who imprinted their heritage on the day - to - day life of Pennsylvania.
Fine Arts; History - United States; Sociology
Dist - PSU **Prod** - WPSXTV 1992

Wendell Berry 29 MIN
U-matic
Poets Talking Series
Color
Literature and Drama
Dist - UMITV **Prod** - UMITV 1975

Wendell Berry - 3 - 3 - 77 43 MIN
VHS / Cassette
Poetry Center reading series
Color (G)
$15.00, $45.00 purchase _ #245 - 197
Features the writer reading his works at the Poetry Center, San Francisco State University.
Literature and Drama
Dist - POETRY **Prod** - POETRY 1977

Wendell Willkie 26 MIN
16mm
Biography Series
B&W (H A)
Uses rare actuality footage to portray the personal life and history - making deeds of Wendell Willkie.
Biography; Civics and Political Systems; History - United States
Dist - SF **Prod** - WOLPER 1965

Wendy 3 MIN
16mm
B&W (G)
$5.00 rental
Features four turned - on photographers putting each other on. Presents a Paul Ryan production with music by Bob Dylan.
Fine Arts
Dist - CANCIN

Wendy and the whine 30 MIN
VHS
Color (K P I R)
$14.95 purchase, $10.00 rental _ #35 - 8251 - 19
Uses music and animation to present the message that God can help overcome any habit.
Fine Arts; Religion and Philosophy
Dist - APH **Prod** - FAMF

Wendy and the whine 20 MIN
VHS
Color (K P I R)
$14.95 purchase _ #87EE0251
Uses an animated format to tell the story of Wendy, a little girl who has a problem with whining. Shows how she overcomes this problem with God's help.
Fine Arts; Guidance and Counseling; Literature and Drama; Religion and Philosophy
Dist - CPH **Prod** - CPH

Wendy's Christmas Card 11 MIN
U-matic / VHS / 16mm
Color (P I J)
LC 75-700063
Shows the step - by - step process of making a Christmas card, including the origination of the idea, the sketching of design, choosing the colors, printing, folding and boxing.
Business and Economics; Fine Arts; Religion and Philosophy
Dist - IFB **Prod** - IFB 1956

We're all Beautiful Here 15 MIN
16mm
Color (J)
LC 80-701056
Presents information on acne, showing young members of Acne Anonymous chanting, singing and shouting about acne and how it can be controlled.
Health and Safety
Dist - KLEINW **Prod** - KLEINW 1976

We're all in the Driver's Seat 15 MIN
U-matic / VHS / 16mm
Color
Studies the American school bus experience. Reveals facts about safety, cost, convenience and comfort.
Health and Safety; Social Science
Dist - KLEINW **Prod** - KLEINW

We're Counting on You 30 MIN
U-matic / VHS
Professional Skills for Secretaries Series Pt 1
Color (A)
LC 81-707648
Discusses the role of the modern secretary, how they fit into the corporate structure, and how their jobs interact with those of their bosses.
Business and Economics; Guidance and Counseling
Dist - TIMLIF **Prod** - TIMLIF 1981

We're Doing OK 5 MIN
16mm
Color
LC 78-701508
Tells about a young career woman who is anxious about her aging mother living in a deteriorating neighborhood. Shows how she discovers that the neighborhood has a vitality and sense of caring which she had not been aware of at first.
Health and Safety; Sociology
Dist - FRAF **Prod** - FRAF 1978

We're Fighting Back 93 MIN
VHS / BETA
Color (P A)
Features story of New York City youths trying to fight crime in their neighborhood.
Fine Arts; Sociology
Dist - LCOA **Prod** - LCOA

We're Here Now - Prostitution 35 MIN
U-matic / VHS
Color
Presents seven women who talk openly about their former lives in prostitution. Discusses their struggle to return to the mainstream of society and the pressures that caused them to become prostitutes.
Sociology
Dist - FLMLIB **Prod** - WIEKD 1984

We're in the People Business 18 MIN
16mm
Golden Triangle Teller Training Film Series
Color (IND)
LC 76-700452
Presents 15 how - to - do - it bank teller - customer vignettes on how to win customers and influence deposits.
Business and Economics; Guidance and Counseling
Dist - PART **Prod** - PART

We're in this Together - Scarcity and Economic Choice (Economics) 15 MIN
VHS / U-matic
Two Cents' Worth Series
Color (P)
Reveals that when Kathy brags about walking home from school to save energy and money, her mother and brother point out how she doesn't always practice what she preaches.
Business and Economics
Dist - AITECH **Prod** - WHATV 1976

We're no Heroes 27 MIN
16mm
Color
LC 77-700433
Follows representative units of the Fire Department of the District of Columbia as they answer a variety of fire calls. Exemplifies the courage and dedication of members of the country's most dangerous profession.
Geography - United States; Guidance and Counseling; Social Science
Dist - WMALTV **Prod** - WMALTV 1976

We're not Afraid Anymore 27 MIN
16mm
Color
LC 74-702900
Presents a documentary on homosexuality. Includes interviews with homosexual men and women, an attorney and a psychologist. Shows scenes of various activities of homosexuals such as church activities, a parade and protest demonstrations.
Guidance and Counseling; Psychology; Sociology
Dist - PARNAS **Prod** - PARNAS 1974

We're not Candy 1 MIN
U-matic / VHS
Color
Features a quartet of pills singing a television spot describing their worries that a child might think they're candy and eat them.
Health and Safety; Home Economics
Dist - KIDSCO **Prod** - KIDSCO

We're not Drinkable 1 MIN
U-matic / VHS
Color (SPANISH)
A Spanish language version of the television spot for children which explains that bottles usually found under the sink are poison.
Health and Safety; Home Economics
Dist - KIDSCO **Prod** - KIDSCO

We're not Leaving 15 MIN
U-matic
Color (A)
Describes the two - year strike by steelworkers and 12 other unions against Phelps Dodge Copper Company.
Business and Economics; Psychology
Dist - AFLCIO **Prod** - USTLW 1985

We're not Stupid 15 MIN
VHS / 16mm
Breaking the Unseen Barrier Series
Color (C) (TUPI)
$180.00, $240.00 purchase _ #269701
Demonstrates through dramatic vignettes effective teaching strategies to help students with learning disabilities reach their full potential. Offers insight into integrating learning disabled students into the classroom. 'We're Not Stupid' takes an emotional journey into the lives of children and adults with learning disabilities.
Education; Mathematics; Psychology
Dist - AITECH **Prod** - ACCESS 1988

We're Number One Series
Racial Relationships 29 MIN
Sports and Business 29 MIN
Dist - AMERLC

We're OK 9 MIN
U-matic / VHS / 16mm
Transactional Analysis Series
Color (J) (DUTCH SWEDISH)
Uses animation to present the transactional analysis theory which explains how each individual adopts a

psychological life position. States that effective interpersonal relationships result from the viewpoint that each person is an equal, expressed by the motto 'I'm OK, you're OK.'.
Foreign Language; Psychology
Dist - PHENIX **Prod** - PHENIX 1975

We're on the same team, remember 21 MIN
VHS
Color (PRO A G)
$675.00 purchase, $175.00 rental
Illustrates the importance of individual responsibility to company success. Describes a business in which everything went wrong because of lack of attention. Encourages more effective communication and participation by employees. Includes a leader's guide.
Business and Economics; Psychology
Dist - EXTR **Prod** - CRMP

We're on the same team, remember 25 MIN
VHS
Color (PRO IND A)
Presents a dramatization about some seemingly unimportant service - oriented details that go wrong within an organization, ruining its credibility and destroying customer relations.
Business and Economics; Guidance and Counseling
Dist - CRMF **Prod** - CRMF 1990

We're on the same Time, Remember 21 MIN
16mm / U-matic / VHS
Color
A revised version of the videocassette Who Killed The Sale. Illustrates how an important business deal can be lost due to ineffective communication, careless talk and lack of organization.
Business and Economics; Psychology
Dist - RTBL **Prod** - RANKAV 1984

We're on Your Side 24 MIN
16mm
Color
LC 75-702761
Documents methods of oil recovery from presumably exhausted oil fields by using new methods which are within environmental tolerances.
Industrial and Technical Education; Science - Natural; Social Science
Dist - GETTY **Prod** - GETTY 1974

We're Spending Too Much Money 12 MIN
U-matic / VHS
Under the Yellow Balloon Series
Color (P)
Eavesdrops as the Anthony family discusses how all family members have bought more than they need and can afford. Shows that all agree to spend less and help make a family budget.
Guidance and Counseling; Home Economics; Sociology
Dist - AITECH **Prod** - SCETV 1980

We're Taking Off 12 MIN
16mm
Color
LC 80-700506
Celebrates the 25th anniversary of Honeywell's entry into the computer field by highlighting landmarks in the company's history.
Business and Economics
Dist - HONIS **Prod** - HONIS 1980

We're the boyz - Reservation of education
VHS
Color (G)
$19.95 purchase
Features Robby Bee and the Boyz from the Rez performing songs from their Native Rap Recording produced by NAIRD.
Fine Arts; Social Science
Dist - SOAR

Were You There Series

The Black West	28 MIN
The Cotton Club	28 MIN
The Facts of life	28 MIN
Oscar Micheaux, Film Pioneer	28 MIN
Portrait of two artists	29 MIN
Sports Profile	29 MIN
When the Animals Talked	28 MIN

Dist - BCNFL

Werner Herzog eats his shoe 20 MIN
16mm / U-matic / VHS
Color (G)
$425.00, $250.00, $150.00 purchase
Pictures German filmmaker Werner Herzog honoring a vow he made to Errol Morris that he - Herzog - would eat his shoe if Morris ever actually made one of the films he was forever talking about. Reveals that Morris was stung to action and directed Gates of Heaven, a film about a pet cemetery. Herzog returned to Berkeley to consume one of his desert boots at the UC theater where Blank and Maureen Gosling document the event.
Fine Arts
Dist - FLOWER **Prod** - BLNKL 1979

Wernher Von Braun 26 MIN
16mm
History Makers of the 20th Century Series
B&W (I J H)
Uses rare actuality footage to portray the personal life and history - making deeds of Wernher von Braun.
Biography; History - United States; Science
Dist - SF **Prod** - WOLPER 1965

Wertheim - Meigs Hysterectomy with Pelvic Lymphadectomy 29 MIN
16mm
Color (PRO)
Points out that this operation is the optimum choice in surgery for cancer of cervix in stages one and two - A. Stresses an extensive dissection of the para - cervical and para - vaginal tissues.
Health and Safety; Science
Dist - ACY **Prod** - ACYDGD 1970

Werther 107 MIN
VHS
Color (G) (FRENCH (ENGLISH SUBTITLES))
$44.95 purchase _ #V72156
Presents a 1986 production of an opera by Jules Massenet based on a novella by Goethe. Features Peter Dvorsky, Brigitte Fassbaender and Magdalena Vasary as directed by Peter Weigl.
Fine Arts; Foreign Language
Dist - NORTNJ

Werther - Alfredo Kraus 60 MIN
VHS
My favorite opera series
Color (G)
$24.95 purchase_#1373
Presents Alfredo Kraus' interpretation of the title role in Jules Massenet's opera Werther. Shares also Kraus' knowledge and insights into the opera. Takes place at Teatro Sao Carlo in Lisbon, Portugal.
Fine Arts
Dist - KULTUR

Wes Montgomery 30 MIN
Videoreel / VT2
People in Jazz Series
Color (G)
$55.00 rental _ #PEIJ - 101
Presents the jazz music of Wes Montgomery. Features host Jim Rockwell interviewing the artist.
Fine Arts
Dist - PBS **Prod** - WTVSTV

The WES Story 14 MIN
16mm
Color
LC 75-700594
Shows how the Waterways Experiment Station in Mississippi grew from a small hydraulic laboratory to become the principal and most diverse research, testing and development center for Corps of Engineers research in the field of civil engineering.
History - United States; Industrial and Technical Education
Dist - USNAC **Prod** - USAE 1969

Wesakecha and the Flood 16 MIN
VHS / 16mm
Ukrainian Shadow Puppets Series
Color (I) (ENGLISH AND UKRAINIAN)
$175.00 purchase _ #277101
Introduces some of the cultural heritage of the Cree and Blackfoot people of Alberta, Canada, through a Ukrainian bilingual program to reach the Ukrainian commmunity. Contains a unique blend of myths and legends and original music and artwork commissioned from Cree and Blackfoot artists with Ukrainian silhouette puppets. 'Wesakecha And The Flood' tells the story of a Cree culture hero, a trickster, who is given the job of supervising the earth. He becomes lazy and chaos reigns. The Great Spirit sends a flood to wash the world clean and Wesakecha tries to rebuild the world with the only other survivors - Otter, Beaver and Muskrat. Includes a booklet with Ukrainian language transcripts.
Geography - World; History - World; Literature and Drama; Religion and Philosophy; Social Science; Sociology
Dist - ACCESS **Prod** - ACCESS 1987

Wesakecha and the Geese - Wesakecha and the Chickadee 17 MIN
VHS / 16mm
Ukrainian Shadow Puppets Series
Color (I) (ENGLISH AND UKRAINIAN)
$175.00 purchase _ #277104
Introduces some of the cultural heritage of the Cree and Blackfoot people of Alberta, Canada, through a Ukrainian bilingual program to reach the Ukrainian commmunity. Contains a unique blend of myths and legends and original music and artwork commissioned from Cree and Blackfoot artists with Ukrainian silhouette puppets. 'Wesakecha And The Geese - Wesakecha And The Chickadee' recounts the trickster cycle of Wesakecha who is always 'up to something.' He convinces a flock of geese to give him wings so he can fly in one story, and tricks Chickadee into engaging in some misadventures in the other. Includes a booklet with Ukrainian language transcripts.
Geography - World; History - World; Literature and Drama; Religion and Philosophy; Social Science; Sociology
Dist - ACCESS **Prod** - ACCESS 1987

Wesakechak and the First Indian People 15 MIN
VHS / U-matic
Tales of Wesakechak Series
Color (G)
Shows Wesakechak didn't like his name. He felt he deserved a more powerful name like Bear or Eagle. He asks the Creator to give him and the other creatures new names. The Creator agrees to have a naming ceremony the following day, and Wesakechak's troubles begin.
Social Science
Dist - NAMPBC **Prod** - NAMPBC 1984

Wesakechak and the Medicine 15 MIN
VHS / U-matic
Tales of Wesakechak Series
Color (G)
Shows Wesakechak hear chickadees sing. He discovers they have some medicine berries, and tricks the birds into giving him some. Although he's given careful instructions, Wesakechak abuses the power of the medicine berries and gets himself into trouble.
Social Science
Dist - NAMPBC **Prod** - NAMPBC 1984

Wesakechak and the Whiskey Jack 15 MIN
VHS / U-matic
Tales of Wesakechak Series
Color (G)
Indicates long ago Whiskey Jack was called Kweekweeseu. He thought he was ugly, so he hid in the forest and grew very lonely. One day he asks Wesakechak for help. Unfortunately things do not work out for KweeKweeseu the way that he hopes.
Literature and Drama; Social Science
Dist - NAMPBC **Prod** - NAMPBC 1984

Wesley, Charles 29 MIN
U-matic
Like it is Series
Color
Discusses the past, present and future of Wilberforce University and Central State University.
Sociology
Dist - HRC **Prod** - OHC

Wesley Hall - a special life 28 MIN
VHS
Color (G C PRO)
$245.00 purchase, $55.00 rental
Looks at a nursing home pilot project to care for Alzheimer's patients set up by the University of Michigan and the Chelsea United Methodist nursing home. Shows how the 'untreatable' patients are encouraged to participate in everyday tasks, recreation and volunteer activities.
Health and Safety; Sociology
Dist - TNF

Wesleyan
VHS
Campus clips series
Color (H C A)
$29.95 purchase _ #CC0017V
Takes a video visit to the campus of Wesleyan University in Connecticut. Shows many of the distinctive features of the campus, and interviews students about their experiences. Provides information on the composition of the student body, professors, academics, social life, housing, and other subjects.
Education
Dist - CAMV

West 17 MIN
VHS / 16mm
Color (I J H G)
$295.00, $49.95 purchase
Chronicles the expansion of the American frontier from the Atlantic to the Pacific coast. Emphasizes the four trails that opened the 'West' to trade and settlement - the Santa Fe Trail, the Oregon Trail, the California Trail, the Mormon Trail.
Geography - United States; History - United States; Religion and Philosophy
Dist - KAWVAL **Prod** - KAWVAL

West 8 MIN
16mm
Color (G)
$15.00 purchase
Introduces part one of a trilogy chronicling a journey to Alaska.
Fine Arts; Geography - United States; Geography - World
Dist - CANCIN **Prod** - STREEM 1985

West Africa - Two Life Styles 18 MIN
U-matic / VHS / 16mm
Color (I J H)
LC 75-708743
Compares and contrasts the life styles, occupations, recreational activities and family life of two Africans by following their daily lives.
Geography - World; History - United States; History - World; Psychology; Social Science; Sociology
Dist - PHENIX **Prod** - GARJA 1970

The West African Heritage 30 MIN
U-matic / VHS
From Jumpstreet Series
Color (J H)
Looks at the West African heritage in Black music by recounting the contributions of such artists as Alhaji Bai Konte, Dembo Konte, Hugh Masakela and the Wo'se Dance Theater.
Fine Arts; History - United States; Sociology
Dist - GPN **Prod** - WETATV 1979

West African Instruments 17 MIN
VHS / U-matic
Musical Instruments Series
Color
Fine Arts
Dist - GPN **Prod** - WWVUTV

West African Panorama 25 MIN
U-matic
Color
Presents a tour through the countries of Nigeria, the People's Republic of Benin, Togo and Ghana. Shows African culture and lifestyle.
Geography - World; History - United States; History - World
Dist - BLKFMF **Prod** - BLKFMF

The West and the Wider World, 1500 - 1800 26 MIN
16mm / U-matic / VHS
World - a Television History Series
Color (J H C)
MP=$475
Shows the first circumnavigation of the globe by Ferdinand Magellan which marked the start of European domination of the world. The shift in power from the Mediterranean to west and northwestern Europe led to the great empires of Spain and Portugal. Follows the gradual increase of Dutch trade and power and the English developments in marine science and technology which were the start of the British Empire.
History - World
Dist - LANDMK **Prod** - NETGOL 1985

The West and the Wider World - 1500 - 1800 26 MIN
VHS / 16mm / U-matic
World - a Television History Series
Color (J H C)
MP=$475.00
Shows the first circumnavigation of the globe by Ferdinand Magellan which marked the start of European domination of the world. The shift in power from the Mediterranean to west and northwestern Europe led to the great empires of Spain and Portugal. Follows the gradual increase of Dutch trade and power and the English developments in marine science and technology which were the start of the British Empire.
History - World
Dist - LANDMK **Prod** - NETGOL 1985

The West and the wider world - 1500 - 1800 30 MIN
VHS
World - A Television history series
Color (C A T)
$55.00 rental
Covers developments in the West in the period from 1500 to 1800. Based on "The Times Atlas of World History." Serves as part 18 of a 26 - part telecourse. Available only to institutions of higher education.
History - World; Sociology
Dist - SCETV **Prod** - SCETV 1986

West Berlin - a Show of Faith 5 MIN
16mm
Screen news digest series; Vol 4; Issue 2
B&W
Presents Vice President Johnson's trip to West Berlin as a message of American support to West Berlin. Shows America's determination to remain there as exemplified by the fifteen hundred U S troops that have made their way through communist East Germany to West Berlin.
Civics and Political Systems; Geography - World
Dist - HEARST **Prod** - HEARST 1961

West Coast Logging, Vancouver Island, 1939 10 MIN
16mm
B&W
LC 76-703335
Presents a documentary produced in 1939 which shows a west coast logging operation.
Agriculture; Geography - World; Social Science
Dist - BCPM **Prod** - BCPM 1975

West coast swing
VHS
Sodanceabit dance and fitness video series
Color (H C A)
$39.95 purchase _ #SDB003V
Presents an aerobic workout program based on the West Coast Swing. Uses slow motion, step - by - step instructional techniques.
Physical Education and Recreation
Dist - CAMV

West coast swing 60 MIN
VHS
Kathy Blake dance studios - let's learn how to dance series
Color (G A)
$39.95 purchase
Features dance instructors Kathy Blake and Gene Russo, who instruct viewers on the basics of West Coast swing.
Fine Arts
Dist - PBS **Prod** - WNETTV

West coast swing 76 MIN
VHS
Step into fitness - sodanceabit series
Color (G A)
$39.95 purchase
Features dance instructors Phil Martin and Betty Griffith Railey, who teach the West Coast swing to encourage dancing for fitness. Includes step - by - step instruction, slow motion and close - up patterns, and dance - along sessions.
Physical Education and Recreation
Dist - PBS **Prod** - WNETTV

West Germany 18 MIN
U-matic / VHS
Families of the World Series, Pt 1; Pt 1
Color (I)
$172.00 purchase _ #51068
Follows the daily life of a West German family.
Geography - World; Sociology
Dist - NGS

West Germany 27 MIN
U-matic / VHS
Nations of the World Series
Color (I J H A)
Teaches the viewers about Germany's birth after World War II and about the economic miracle that transformed a devastated Germany into one of the world's most powerful industrial states. Visits major cities, including West Berlin, and travels from the lowlands of the north coast to the Bavarian Alps.
Geography - World
Dist - NGS **Prod** - NGS

West Germany After Adenauer 29 MIN
Videoreel / VT2
Course of Our Times II Series
Color
History - World
Dist - PBS **Prod** - WGBHTV

West Germany - New Government 18 MIN
VHS / U-matic
Color (H C A)
Documents the events in West Germany that led to the no - confidence vote for the coalition government of Helmut Schmidt. Provides a brief history of post World War II Germany's political parties and their maneuvers and speculation in starting new coalitions.
Civics and Political Systems; Geography - World
Dist - JOU **Prod** - JOU

West is west 80 MIN
35mm
Color; PAL (G)
Follows the misadventures of Vikram, a hopeful immigrant to the United States from Bombay, who is set adrift in San Francisco when his sponsors leave the country. Features fun cross - cultural discoveries, dodging of immigration officials, a bungled burglary, a streetside wedding and a romantic ending. Directed by David Rathod for Rathod Partners. Contact distributor for price and availability outside the United Kingdom.
History - United States; Literature and Drama
Dist - BALFOR

The West - Land of many Faces 13 MIN
U-matic / VHS
Natural Science Specials Series Module Blue
Color (I)
Focuses on the topography, beauty and geologic history of the five physiographic provinces that make up America's western uplands.
Geography - United States; Science - Physical
Dist - AITECH **Prod** - COPFC 1973

West meets East - in Japan 37 MIN
VHS
Color (C PRO G)
$300.00 purchase _ #880
Introduces Japanese social and business etiquette to Western executives. Illustrates public behavior, etiquette in Japanese interiors, gender roles in the Japanese business world, dealing with disagreement. Produced by West Meets East Productions.
Business and Economics; Civics and Political Systems; Geography - World; Home Economics; Psychology; Sociology
Dist - INCUL

The West of Charles Russell 53 MIN
U-matic / VHS / 16mm
Color (I)
LC 76-709061
Discusses the art of Charles Russell, commentator and painter of the Western era. Shows how Russell caught and preserved the spirit of the West that really was, saw the West from an Indian's point of view and expressed the crushing of the beauty of the primitive land by the white settlers. Uses historic stills, films and actual Russell paintings to illustrate the ideas and personality of the artist.
Fine Arts; History - United States; Social Science
Dist - FI **Prod** - NBCNEW 1970

West of Charles Russell, the, Pt 1 27 MIN
16mm / U-matic / VHS
Color (I)
LC 76-709061
Discusses the art of Charles Russell, commentator and painter of the Western era. Shows how Russell caught and preserved the spirit of the West that really was, saw the West from an Indian's point of view and expressed the crushing of the beauty of the primitive land by the white settlers. Uses historic stills, films and actual Russell paintings to illustrate the ideas and personality of the artist.
Fine Arts
Dist - FI **Prod** - NBCNEW 1970

West of Charles Russell, the, Pt 2 27 MIN
U-matic / VHS / 16mm
Color (I)
LC 76-709061
Discusses the art of Charles Russell, commentator and painter of the Western era. Shows how Russell caught and preserved the spirit of the West that really was, saw the West from an Indian's point of view and expressed the crushing of the beauty of the primitive land by the white settlers. Uses historic stills, films and actual Russell paintings to illustrate the ideas and personality of the artist.
Fine Arts
Dist - FI **Prod** - NBCTV 1970

West of Hester Street 58 MIN
VHS / U-matic
Color (J)
LC 84-707130
Documents Jewish history during the 'Galveston Movement' at the turn of the century when Jewish immigrants were encouraged to settle in Texas. Combines theatrical interpretations and actual historical footage.
History - United States; Sociology
Dist - MEDPRJ **Prod** - MEDPRJ 1984

West of the Imagination Series
Enduring Dreams 52 MIN
The Golden land 52 MIN
Images of Glory 52 MIN
Play the Legend 52 MIN
The Romantic Horizon 52 MIN
The Wild Riders 52 MIN
Dist - FOTH

West Point on the Hudson 17 MIN
U-matic / VHS / 16mm
Re - discovering America Series
Color (I J H)
LC 74-702697
Documents the importance of West Point during the Revolutionary War and emphasizes the Academy's contribution to the development of the United States. Narrated by William Shatner.
Civics and Political Systems; Education; History - United States
Dist - AIMS **Prod** - COP 1974

West Point Winter Knee Squad 17 MIN
16mm
Color
LC 75-703075
Outlines a recovery plan designed to repair knee injuries, based on a program at the U S Military Academy to rehabilitate injured athletes to full competitive status. Traces progress of athletes who have undergone knee operations, from early orthopedic exercises with special equipment to full scale mobility tests under simulated game conditions. Emphasizes minimizing the incidence of recurring injuries.
Health and Safety; Physical Education and Recreation; Science - Natural
Dist - USNAC **Prod** - USA 1974

West Series
The New Boys 27 MIN
Dist - WOMBAT

West Side Story 155 MIN
16mm
Color
Presents a modern - day version of Romeo and Juliet against a backdrop of New York street gangs. Stars Richard Beymer and Natalie Wood.
Fine Arts
Dist - UAE **Prod** - UAA 1961

West side story 151 MIN
VHS
Color (G)
$29.95 purchase _ #S00288
Presents the film version of the Broadway musical, which updates the Romeo and Juliet story to the 1950s in New York City's West Side. Stars Natalie Wood and Richard Beymer. Directed by Robert Wise and Jerome Robbins. Musical score by Leonard Bernstein and Stephen Sondheim.
Fine Arts
Dist - UILL

West Side Story
U-matic / VHS
Color (J C I)
Presents the musical, West Side Story, about gang rivalry and dommed love.
Fine Arts
Dist - GA **Prod** - GA

The West that never was 58 MIN
VHS
Color (G)
$29.95 purchase _ #IV - 515
Explores the American film genre of westerns. Reveals that there have been more than 4000 films made about the American West. Looks at western stars like Tom Mix, William S Hart, Ken Maynard, Hoot Gibson, Buck Jones, Tim McCoy, Tex Ritter, Gene Autry, Roy Rogers, and archetypal giants like Randolph Scott and John Wayne. Features Tony Thomas as writer and narrator.
Fine Arts; Geography - United States; History - United States; Literature and Drama
Dist - INCRSE **Prod** - INCRSE

West to Santa Fe - Vol 1 40 MIN
VHS
Color (J H)
$29.95 purchase _ #OAQ320V-S
Provides a visual tour of one of America's most fabled routes - The Santa Fe Trail. Takes the viewer from Missouri to New Mexico, from historic sites to trail crossings, to forts and museums.
Geography - United States; History - United States
Dist - CAMV

West to Santa Fe - Vol 2 40 MIN
VHS
Color (J H)
$29.95 purchase _ #OAP325V-S
Provides a visual tour of one of America's most fabled routes - The Santa Fe Trail. Tells the fascinating stories behind forts ranging from large military posts to remote outposts on this Missouri - New Mexico route.
Geography - United States; History - United States
Dist - CAMV

West Virginia 60 MIN
VHS
Portrait of America series
Color (J H C G)
$99.95 purchase _ #AMB48V
Visits West Virginia. Offers extensive research into the state's history. Films key locations and presents segments on its history, government, education, folklore, science, journalism, sociology, industry, agriculture and business. Shows what is unique about West Virginia and what is distinctive about its regional culture and how it got to be that way. Includes teacher study guides. Part of a 50 - part series.
Geography - United States; History - United States
Dist - CAMV

West Virginia State Folk Festival 59 MIN
Videoreel / VT2
Color
Explains that every June in Glenville, West Virginia, a state festival is held. Traces the state's heritage of traditional Appalachian music. Includes fiddlers Ira Mullins, Lee Triplett, Delbert Hughes and Melvin Wine, fiddle and banjo contests, after - dark square dancing in the streets and a variety of performances in the Glenville State College auditorium.
Fine Arts; Geography - United States; Sociology
Dist - PBS **Prod** - WWVUTV

Westcoaster 18 MIN
16mm
Color
LC 80-700924
Charts the course of the Blue Water Classic yachting competition in Australia down the west coast of Tasmania from Melbourne.
Geography - World; Physical Education and Recreation
Dist - TASCOR **Prod** - TASCOR 1976

Western 3 MIN
16mm
Color (G)
$10.00 rental
Fine Arts
Dist - CANCIN **Prod** - KRENKU 1970

Western Australia - out west down under 48 MIN
VHS
Jacques Cousteau II series
Color; CC (G)
$19.95 purchase _ #3055
Features Jean - Michel Cousteau and the team of windship Alcyone who venture into the waters off western Australia. Examines the healthy and protected marine life resulting from good management, ecological balance and planning for the future. Part of a six - part series by Cousteau.
Geography - World; Science - Natural
Dist - APRESS

Western birds and flowers
VHS
Our natural heritage series
Color (K P)
$19.95 purchase _ #HSV4031
Presents two programs. Includes Waterbirds of the Western Flybys and Wildflowers of the West.
Geography - United States
Dist - INSTRU

The Western Buddhist teachers' conference 960 MIN
Cassette
Color; PAL (G)
PdS125, $250.00, PdS75, $150.00 purchase
Records a group of teachers representing different traditions from several countries who met with His Holiness the Dalai Lama in March 1993 for a four - day conference concerning the transmission and development of Dharma in the West. Includes discussions on ethics, sexism, psychotherapy, monasticism, authenticity and more. Individual 2 hour sessions available for $20.00 audio and $40.00 video.
Education; Fine Arts; Religion and Philosophy
Dist - MERIDT

Western Canada - a Region within a Federation 145 MIN
U-matic
University of the Air Series
Color (J H C A)
$750.00 purchase, $250.00 rental
Explains the discovery and adoption of the western half of Canada. Program contains a series of five cassettes 29 minutes each.
Geography - World; History - World
Dist - CTV **Prod** - CTV 1978

Western civilization - majesty and madness series
The Bible - a literary heritage 27 MIN
The Middle Ages - a wanderer's guide to life and letters 27 MIN
Romanticism - the revolt of the spirit 24 MIN
Dist - CORF

Western Civilization - Majesty and Madness Series
Charlemagne - Holy Barbarian 26 MIN
The Crusades - saints and sinners 26 MIN
Elizabeth - the Queen who Shaped an Age 26 MIN
The French Revolution - the Bastille 21 MIN
The French Revolution - the Terror 19 MIN
Freud - the hidden nature of man 29 MIN
Galileo - the challenge of reason 26 MIN
The Greeks - in Search of Meaning 25 MIN
A Matter of Conscience - Henry VIII and Thomas more 30 MIN
Medieval England - the Peasants' Revolt 31 MIN
Napoleon - the End of a Dictator 26 MIN
Napoleon - the Making of a Dictator 27 MIN
The Puritan revolution - Cromwell and the rise of parliamentary democracy 33 MIN
The Romans - Life, Laughter and Law 22 MIN
Dist - LCOA

Western diary '75 17 MIN
16mm
Color (G)
$40.00 rental
Captures moments of awareness of contrasting textures, forms and color as seen spontaneously during the filmmaker's walks with his camera. Creates patterns of people walking by while rich densities of color - contrasts are placed adjacent to each other. Filmed in Colorado, Los Angeles and San Francisco.Produced by Howard Guttenplan.
Fine Arts
Dist - CANCIN

The Western dry lands 20 MIN
U-matic / 16mm / VHS / BETA
Physical geography of North America series
Color (P I J H)
$315.00, $90.00 purchase _ #C50480, #C51361
Explores the rugged intermontane west which spreads through much of western United States and Mexico. Examines high plateaus, deep gorges and deserts that are characteristic of the region. Looks at wildlife from wild horses and coyotes to sidewinders. Part of a five - part series on the physical geography of North America.
Geography - United States; Geography - World
Dist - NGS **Prod** - NGS 1989

Western Europe - a Community of Nations 21 MIN
16mm / U-matic
Color (I J H)
Looks at the nations of western Europe since World War II. Examines the ways in which these nations form a community.
Geography - World; History - World
Dist - PHENIX **Prod** - SVEK

Western Europe - an Introduction 20 MIN
16mm / U-matic / VHS
Color (I J)
Provides an overview of the 15 nations of Western Europe. Shows Europeans creating out of their historic differences a competitive, technological society that finds unifying bonds in the Common Market and the European Parliament.
Business and Economics; History - World
Dist - CORF **Prod** - CORF 1982

Western Europe - an Overview 25 MIN
16mm / VHS
Color; Captioned (P)
$550.00, $495.00 purchase, $60.00 rental _ #C - 509; LC 87708351
Overviews the nations which comprise Western Europe. Emphasizes the geographic, economic and cultural forces which converged at the time of the Renaissance and led to Western Europe's rise to world prominence. Animated map sequences show the ancient empires of Greece and Rome flowing into the Holy Roman Empire, through intermediary stages into the modern nation - states. Available in captioned version on videocassette only. Produced by Ken Nelson.
Geography - World; History - World
Dist - ALTSUL

Western Europe - between the Superpowers 30 MIN
VHS
World Beat - Great Decisions In Foreign Policy
Color (G)
$39.95 purchase _ #WDBT - 106
Analyzes the effects of American - Soviet arms agreements on the nations of Western Europe. Questions whether these agreements have changed the way Western Europe deals with the two superpowers.
Civics and Political Systems; History - World
Dist - PBS **Prod** - WETATV 1988

Western fertilizer handbook series
Presents a fourteen - part series based on the Western Fertilizer Handbook available in slide sets, videocassette transfers and audiocassettes. Examines soils, plant growth, fertilizers, organic fertilizers, soil testing, fertilizer application, environmental considerations and laws regulating the use of fertilizers.
Amending physical properties of soils - Set 14 17 FRS
Benefits of fertilizers to the environment - Set 12 14 FRS
Correcting Problem Soils with Amendments, Set 7 18 FRS

Essential Plant Nutrients, Set 4 — 56 FRS
Fertilizers - a source of plant nutrients — 29 FRS
Formulation, storage and handling, Set 6 — 26 FRS
Growing Plants in Solution Culture, Set 11 — 12 FRS
Methods of Applying Fertilizer, Set 10 — 22 FRS
Principles of plant growth - Set 3 — 24 FRS
Soil - a medium for plant growth - Set 1 — 39 FRS
Soil and Tissue Testing - Set 9 — 26 FRS
Soil Organic Material - Set 8 — 17 FRS
Water and Plant Growth, Set 2 — 25 FRS
Western Laws Relating to Fertilizing Materials, Set 13 — 12 FRS
Dist - VEP **Prod** - VEP 1988

Western flickers 50 MIN
VHS
B&W (G)
$29.95 purchase
Features a mock documentary about a silent - era film studio that churned out westerns, or 'oaters' as they were sometimes called, for two decades. Delves into the most colorful story in the studio's history, when, in 1909, an ex - Texas bounty hunter asked the studio to film his pursuit, and hopefully the capture, of The Cactus Kid, a notorious outlaw. The adventure was to be filmed and released as 'the greatest western ever made.' Produced by R J Thomas.
Fine Arts
Dist - CANCIN

Western Great Lakes 60 MIN
VHS
AAA travel series
Color (G)
$24.95 purchase _ #NA05
Explores the Western Great Lakes.
Geography - United States; Geography - World
Dist - SVIP

The Western Guilt and the Third World 30 MIN
U-matic
Realities
Color (A)
Delves into the political, social, economic and cultural trends of the 1980s. Probes a wide range of contemporary concerns. Each segment includes a guest speaker who is an expert in the field under discussion.
Business and Economics; Civics and Political Systems; Social Science; Sociology
Dist - TVOTAR **Prod** - TVOTAR 1985

The Western Gulf Coast - from the border to the bayou 55 MIN
VHS
On the waterways series
Color (G H)
$29.95 purchase _ #OW02
Travels with the crew of the Driftwood from Mexico to Louisiana through a region of contrasts - from cowboys to Cajuns. Narrated by Jason Robards. Part of a 13 - part series on the history, geography, culture and ecology of North American waterways.
Social Science
Dist - SVIP

Western History 8 MIN
16mm
Color (G)
$18.00 rental, $328.00 purchase
Says Brakhage, 'A thumbnail History of the Western World, all centered around the basketball court.'
Fine Arts
Dist - CANCIN **Prod** - BRAKS 1971

Western Horsemanship 28 MIN
U-matic / VHS / 16mm
Color
Features Clark Bradley and Richard Shrake explaining their theory of horsemanship and illustrating individual patterns and maneuvers in both normal and slow motion.
Physical Education and Recreation
Dist - AQHORS **Prod** - AQHORS 1979

Western Laws Relating to Fertilizing Materials, Set 13 12 FRS
VHS / Slide / Cassette
Western Fertilizer Handbook Series
Color (G)
$16.95, $40.00, $8.50 purchase _ #1 - 580 - 613P, #1 - 580 - 213P, #1 - 580 - 543P
Looks at laws in the westerns state of the US governing the use of fertilizers. Part of a fourteen - part series based on the Western Fertilizer Handbook.
Agriculture; Civics and Political Systems; Science - Natural
Dist - VEP **Prod** - VEP

Western man and the modern world in video series
City under fire - London — 30 MIN
The English Revolution — 45 MIN
The Enlightenment and the age of Louis XIV
Fascism - the rise of Hitler — 45 MIN
Greece — 45 MIN
The 20th century landscape — 30 MIN
Dist - RH

Western Man and the Modern World in Video
Aftric - tribalism to independence — 30 MIN
The Ancient river civilizations
The Cold War — 45 MIN
Czarist Russia - the Russian Revolution — 30 MIN
Early Russia — 30 MIN
Exploration and discovery — 30 MIN
The French Revolution and Napoleon — 45 MIN
The Industrial Revolution — 30 MIN
Latin America — 30 MIN
The Medieval Monument — 30 MIN
The Oriental Mind and the Modern World — 45 MIN
The Renaissance — 45 MIN
Rome — 45 MIN
Science, technology and man — 30 MIN
World War I — 45 MIN
Dist - RH

Western man and the modern world in video
Prelude to World War I — 45 MIN
Towns, Trade and Fairs — 30 MIN
Dist - RH
SRA

Western man and the modern world series - Unit III
The French revolution and Napoleon — 45 MIN
Dist - SRA

Western man and the modern world series - Unit II
Exploration and discovery — 30 MIN
The Medieval movement — 30 MIN
The Renaissance — 45 MIN
Dist - SRA

Western man and the modern world series - Unit I
The Ancient river civilizations — 45 MIN
Rome — 45 MIN
Dist - SRA

Western man and the modern world series - Unit VIII
Latin America — 30 MIN
The Oriental mind and the modern world — 45 MIN
Dist - SRA

Western man and the modern world series - Unit VII
The Cold war — 45 MIN
Dist - SRA

Western man and the modern world series - Unit V
The Industrial revolution — 30 MIN
World War I — 45 MIN
Dist - SRA

Western man and the modern world series
The Wasted years - the depressions — 30 MIN
Years of revolt and revolution — 30 MIN
Dist - RH
SRA

Western man and the modern world series
City under fire - London — 30 MIN
Czarist Russia - the Russian Revolution — 30 MIN
Early Russia — 30 MIN
The English Revolution — 45 MIN
The Enlightenment and the age of Louis XIV — 30 MIN
Fascism - rise of Hitler — 45 MIN
Greece — 45 MIN
Science, technology and man — 30 MIN
The 20th century landscape - Unit VII — 30 MIN
Dist - SRA

Western Maryland College Series
Listen — 30 MIN
Total Communication — 15 MIN
We Tiptoed Around Whispering — 30 MIN
Dist - USNAC

Western Medicine Meets East 26 MIN
U-matic / VHS
Color (C)
$249.00, $149.00 purchase _ #AD - 1909
Examines the use of acupuncture and other traditional Eastern medical techniques. Shows it being used as anesthetics during surgery and as treatment for various ailments such as arthritis and backache.
Geography - World; Health and Safety; Science - Natural
Dist - FOTH **Prod** - FOTH

Western movement series
The Dam job — 8 MIN
Fugue — 5 MIN
Jesus Christ made Seattle under protest — 15 MIN
The Jim Petty place — 12 MIN
Western movements - four films — 43 MIN
Dist - CANCIN

Western movements - four films 43 MIN
U-matic / 16mm / VHS
Western movement series
B&W (G)
$75.00 rental, $39.95 purchase
Forms a contemplative journey from urban complexity to rural solitude set on the western edge of North America. Includes The Dam Job; Fugue; Jesus Christ made Seattle Under Protest; and The Jim Petty Place. Offers one continuous program of four films or as four separate films. A Jeff Stookey production.
Geography - World; Sociology
Dist - CANCIN

Western Pleasure 22 MIN
VHS
Practice Horse Judging Set Z - 1 Series
Color (H C A PRO)
$69.95 purchase _ #CV801
Contains two classes in practice horse judging - western pleasure class. Features John Pipkin of Texas Tech U who places and critiques each class.
Agriculture; Physical Education and Recreation
Dist - AAVIM **Prod** - AAVIM 1990

Western Pleasure - Advanced 30 MIN
BETA / VHS
Western Training Series
Color
Covers the fine points of training a pleasure horse.
Physical Education and Recreation
Dist - EQVDL **Prod** - EQVDL

Western Pleasure - Basics 30 MIN
VHS / BETA
Western Training Series
Color
Reveals how to make pleasure horses move in a relaxed, smooth manner.
Physical Education and Recreation
Dist - EQVDL **Prod** - EQVDL

Western Riding 35 MIN
VHS
Practice Horse Judging Set Z - 1 Series
Color (H C A PRO)
$69.95 purchase _ #CV803
Contains two classes in practice horse judging - western riding class. Features John Pipkin of Texas Tech U who places and critiques each class.
Agriculture; Physical Education and Recreation
Dist - AAVIM **Prod** - AAVIM 1990

Western Riding Clinic 30 MIN
BETA / VHS
Western Training Series
Color
Covers training and showing horses.
Physical Education and Recreation
Dist - EQVDL **Prod** - EQVDL

Western Samoa - I Can Get Another Wife but I Can't Get Parents - Pt 6 28 MIN
VHS
Human Face of the Pacific Series, the
Color (S)
$79.00 purchase _ #118 - 9006
Looks behind the romance and mystery of the islands of the South Seas to reveal the islands as they really are - a heterogeneous group of countries and colonies struggling to meet the challenges of the modern world while trying to preserve their cultural identities. Part 6 of six parts looks at Western Samoa, whose population continues to emigrate to New Zealand, despite independence. Focuses on a young Samoan couple who must join the exodus and leave their close - knit families.
Geography - World; Guidance and Counseling; History - World; Sociology
Dist - FI **Prod** - FLMAUS 1987

Western Show 24 MIN
U-matic / VHS
Color
Features bluegrass fiddling and singing, glass blowing, fencing, baton twirling and tap dancing during a visit to state high school rodeo. Shows a young boy who babysits lion cubs.
Fine Arts; Physical Education and Recreation; Sociology
Dist - WCCOTV **Prod** - WCCOTV 1981

Western tradition - part I series
Alexander the Great - the Hellenistic Age - Pts 7 and 8 — 60 MIN

The Byzantine Empire - the fall of Byzantine — 60 MIN
Common life in the Middle Ages - cities and cathedrals of the Middle Ages - Parts 21 and 22 — 60 MIN
The Dark Ages - the age of Charlemagne - Parts 17 and 18 — 60 MIN
The Dawn of history - the ancient Egyptians - Parts 1 and 2 — 60 MIN
The Decline of Rome - the fall of Rome - Parts 13 and 14 — 60 MIN
Early Christianity - the rise of the Church - Parts 11 and 12 — 60 MIN
The Late Middle Ages - the national monarchies - Parts 23 and 24 — 60 MIN
Mesopotamia - from bronze to iron - Parts 3 and 4 — 60 MIN
The Middle Ages - the feudal order - Parts 19 and 20 — 60 MIN
The Renaissance and the age of discovery - the Renaissance and the New World - Parts 25 and 26 — 60 MIN
Dist - ANNCPB

Western tradition - part II series
The Age of absolutism - absolutism and the social contract - Parts 31 and 32 — 60 MIN
The American Revolution - the American Republic - Parts 37 and 38 — 60 MIN
The Cold war - Europe and the third world - Parts 49 and 50 — 60 MIN
The Death of the old regime - the French Revolution - Pts 39 and 40 — 60 MIN
The Enlightened despots - the Enlightenment - Pts 33 and 34 — 60 MIN
The Enlightenment and society - the modern philosophers - Pts 35 and 36 — 60 MIN
The First World War and the rise of Fascism - the second World War - Parts 47 and 48 — 60 MIN
The Industrial revolution - the industrial world - Parts 41 and 42 — 60 MIN
A New public - fin de siecle - Parts 45 and 46 — 60 MIN
The Reformation - the rise of the middle class — 60 MIN
Revolution and romantics - the age of the nation - states - Parts 43 and 44 — 60 MIN
The Technological revolution - toward the future - Parts 51 and 52 — 60 MIN
The Wars of religion - the rise of the trading cities - Parts 29 and 30 — 60 MIN
Dist - ANNCPB

Western tradition - Pt I series
The Rise of Greek civilization - Greek thought — 60 MIN
Dist - ANNCPB

The Western tradition series - Part II — 780 MIN
VHS / U-matic
The Western tradition series
Color (G)
$500.00, $350.00 purchase
Presents 26 thirty - minute programs on the Western tradition which surveys the history of Western civilization from the Protestant Revolution spawned by Martin Luther to the present time.
Geography - World; History - World; Religion and Philosophy; Sociology
Dist - ANNCPB **Prod** - WGBH 1989

The Western tradition series - Pt I — 780 MIN
VHS / U-matic
The Western tradition series
Color (G)
$500.00, $350.00 purchase
Presents 26 thirty - minute programs on the Western tradition which surveys the history of Western civilization from its dawning to the discovery of the American continents.
Geography - World; History - World; Sociology
Dist - ANNCPB **Prod** - WGBH 1989

The Western tradition series
Presents 52 thirty - minute programs on the Western tradition which surveys the history of Western civilization from its dawning to the present time.
The Rise of Rome and The Roman Empire — 60 MIN
The Western tradition series - Part II — 780 MIN
The Western tradition series - Pt I — 780 MIN
Dist - ANNCPB **Prod** - WGBH 1989

Western tradition series
The American Revolution — 30 MIN
The First World War and the rise of fascism — 30 MIN
The French Revolution — 30 MIN
The Industrial revolution — 30 MIN
The Middle ages — 30 MIN
The Rise of Greek civilization — 30 MIN
The Roman empire — 30 MIN
The Second World War — 30 MIN
Dist - EMFVL

Western training series
Bareback bronc clinic — 30 MIN
Bull riding clinic — 30 MIN
Bull riding clinic - advanced — 30 MIN
Colt training — 30 MIN
Colt training clinic — 29 MIN
Cow Cutting - Advanced — 30 MIN
Cow Cutting Clinic — 30 MIN
Girl rodeo events — 30 MIN
Hackamore Magic — 30 MIN
Halter Showmanship - Fitting — 30 MIN
Halter Showmanship - How to Show — 30 MIN
Saddle Bronc Clinic — 30 MIN
Shaffle Bit Horsemanship — 30 MIN
Steer Wrestling Clinic — 30 MIN
Team Roping Clinic — 30 MIN
Western Pleasure - Advanced — 30 MIN
Western Pleasure - Basics — 30 MIN
Western Riding Clinic — 30 MIN
Dist - EQVDL

The Western United States - 4 — 30 MIN
VHS
50 States, 50 capitals - geography of the USA series
Color (H)
$89.00 purchase _ #60316 - 025
Discusses in detail the states included in the western region of the United States. Includes locations, industries, agriculture, capitals, populations, sizes and areas, climates and points of interest. Part one of four parts on US geography.
Geography - United States
Dist - GA **Prod** - GA 1992

The Western US - Volume 2d — 35 MIN
VHS
Visions of adventure series
Color (P)
$24.95 purchase _ #GE05
Focuses on the United States West. Part of an eight - part series on geography.
Geography - United States
Dist - SVIP

The Western World and its Reaction to Genocide — 29 MIN
Videoreel / VT2
Course of Our Times I Series
Color
History - World
Dist - PBS **Prod** - WGBHTV

Westfield Infants School — 10 MIN
16mm
B&W (T)
LC 75-701396
Follows an integrated day in a British infant school. Shows ways in which an experienced teacher works with her children.
Education
Dist - EDC **Prod** - EDC 1974

Westinghouse in Alphabetical Order — 12 MIN
16mm / U-matic / VHS
Color
Pictures products of the Westinghouse company in alphabetical order.
Business and Economics
Dist - PFP **Prod** - EAMES 1965

Westminster Abbey — 55 MIN
VHS
Color (G)
$29.95 purchase _ #WES01
Visits Westminster Abbey in London, the most famous Anglican church in the world, which traces its history back to Edward the Confessor in the year 1050. Views documents and parts of the Abbey never seen by the public.
Fine Arts; History - World; Religion and Philosophy
Dist - HOMVIS **Prod** - BBCTV 1990

Weston Woods - Set 02 series
Georgie — 6 MIN
Dist - WWS

Westport Point — 30 MIN
VHS
John Stobart's WorldScape series
Color (A G)
$19.95 purchase _ #STO - 13
Shows how Stobart uses the charming community on the Massachusettes - Rhode Island border to demonstrate perspective and simple composition. Follows artist John Stobart as he travels the globe, painting directly from life, and demonstrates the simplicity of the method that has made him the foremost living maritime artist. Demonstrates Stobart's classical maritime style in numerous evocative settings around the world. Part of a series on painting outdoors.
Fine Arts
Dist - ARTSAM **Prod** - WORLDS

A Westside Story — 27 MIN
16mm
Color (H C A)
Features Chancellor Charles E Young and former Chancellor Franklin D Murphy narrating this chronicle of the fifty year history of UCLA.
Guidance and Counseling; Social Science
Dist - UCLA **Prod** - UCLA

Westville, 1850 — 14 MIN
U-matic / VHS
Under the Blue Umbrella Series
Color (P)
Introduces family life in the 1850's, focusing on how families made the most of the things they needed.
History - United States; Sociology
Dist - AITECH **Prod** - SCETV 1977

Westward Coal — 14 MIN
16mm
Color
Discusses the history of coal mining in the west and new technological advances in the industry, including all aspects of western surface mining.
Industrial and Technical Education; Social Science
Dist - MTP **Prod** - AMAX

Westward Expansion
VHS / U-matic
Color (H)
Details the century - long progress to the Pacific and relates the 'pioneer spirit' to current American attitudes and beliefs. Considers the infatuation with frontier mythology.
History - United States
Dist - GA **Prod** - GA

Westward Expansion — 25 MIN
U-matic / VHS / 16mm
American History Series
Color (J H)
LC 79-702077
Traces westward expansion in America from the Atlantic to the Pacific, and discusses the effect of the frontier on the American personality.
History - United States
Dist - MGHT **Prod** - PSP 1969

Westward expansion - the pioneer challenge — 17 MIN
VHS
Color (P I J)
$89.00 purchase _ #RB882
Examines the westward expansion of the United States. Reveals that during the Revolutionary War Thomas Jefferson and George Washington dreamed of mapping the territory to the west of the thirteen colonies. Looks at the important role of geography.
Geography - United States; History - United States
Dist - REVID **Prod** - REVID 1990

Westward Ho — 15 MIN
VHS / U-matic
Draw Man Series
Color (I J)
Applies many drawing lessons to a western scene. Includes objects, figures, animals, picture design, costume and drama.
Fine Arts
Dist - AITECH **Prod** - OCPS 1975

The Westward Movement - 5 - the Gold Rush — 23 MIN
16mm / U-matic / VHS
Color; B&W (I J H)
Relates how the discovery of gold at Sutter's Mill changed the history of California and the nation. Filmed in the Mother Lode country of California and Columbia Historic State Park.
History - United States
Dist - EBEC **Prod** - EBEC 1965

Westward wagons — 24 MIN
U-matic / VHS
Young people's specials series
Color
Tells the story of a ten - year - old boy and his family as they cross the plains in 1870.
Fine Arts; History - United States; Sociology
Dist - MULTPP **Prod** - MULTPP

Wet — 5 MIN
VHS / 16mm
Color (G)
$15.00 rental
Examines the sensual aspects of film. Uses color, light and motion to create a subtle visual experience around the

solitary figure of a woman swimming. A Chel White production. Also available in video format in a group package entitled Five Films by Chel White.
Fine Arts
Dist - CANCIN

A Wet and wild frog trap - 107 29 MIN
VHS
FROG series 1; Series 1; 107
Color (P I J)
$100.00 purchase
Offers the seventh program by Friends of Research and Odd Gadgets. Lifts science off the textbook page into the real world to show how enjoyable and challenging science can be. In this episode, the Froggers learn about pumps, water wheels and flush valves, from water fights to building a Rube Goldberg - type water trap. Special focus on municipal water supply systems and waste treatment plants. Produced by Greg Rist.
Industrial and Technical Education; Science - Physical
Dist - BULFRG **Prod** - OWLTV 1993

The Wet Bush 6 MIN
16mm
Color
LC 80-700935
Shows the variety of geographic areas in which gum trees grow.
Science - Natural
Dist - TASCOR **Prod** - TASCOR 1976

Wet Culture Rice 17 MIN
16mm
Faces of Change - Taiwan Series
Color
Demonstrates how Taiwan's rice farmers rely less on mechanization than on human labor to produce and harvest two crops during the annual agricultural cycle.
Agriculture; Geography - World
Dist - WHEELK **Prod** - AUFS

Wet Earth and Warm People 59 MIN
16mm
Color (J H C)
LC 72-703038
Presents a view of life in Indonesia.
Geography - World; Social Science; Sociology
Dist - NFBC **Prod** - NFBC 1971

The Wet Look 15 MIN
16mm
Environmental Series - Landsat - Satellite for all Seasons Series
Color (PRO)
LC 76-704015
Explores how the Landsat satellite helps resolve water resource problems with its remote sensing capabilities. Shows how the satellite helps hydrologists control floods and water supplies by monitoring flood plains, snow packs and potentially dangerous manmade lakes. Demonstrates its use in flood assessment and pollution control.
History - World; Science - Natural; Science - Physical
Dist - USNAC **Prod** - USGSFC 1976

A Wet Tale 11 MIN
16mm / U-matic / VHS
Color (K P I)
Features an animated adventure of a small drop of water. Emphasizes the recycling of water on earth.
Fine Arts; Science - Natural
Dist - PHENIX **Prod** - KRATKY

Wet vacs, upright vacs and carpet - scrubbers
VHS
Equipment maintenance series
Color (H A G T)
$225.00 purchase _ #BM137
Shows how to keep wet and upright vacuums, carpet - scrubbers and other cleaning equipment out of the repair shop and on the job. Part of a series on equipment maintenance.
Home Economics; Industrial and Technical Education; Psychology
Dist - AAVIM **Prod** - AAVIM 1992

Wetland wilderness - The Camargue, France 24 MIN
VHS / 16mm
Amateur naturalist series
Color (I J H C G)
$495.00, $195.00 purchase
Shows how, in the wide open landscape, various techniques are used to watch and track all the thriving creatures of the area - birds, mammals and wild herds of white horses. Observes many different birds in the marsh and salt water lagoons. Part of a 13 - part series featuring a naturalist and a zoologist, Gerald and Lee Durrell, on field trips to different habitats.
Geography - World; Science - Natural
Dist - LANDMK **Prod** - LANDMK 1988

Wetlands 30 MIN
VHS
Perspective 10 series
Color; PAL; NTSC (G)
PdS90, PdS105 purchase
Discloses that bogs, marshes, swamps and estuaries are all wetlands. Reveals that, historically, they have been deemed to be unimportant and, therefore, systematically polluted or destroyed. In fact, these lands have enormous economic significance as a source of employment, are agriculturally rich and serve as the finest organic filter of society's effluent. Protecting wetlands protects the human race.
Science - Natural
Dist - CFLVIS **Prod** - LONTVS 1993

The Wetlands 58 MIN
VHS
Conserving America series
Color (J H C G A)
$29.95 purchase
Portrays concerned Americans who are working to conserve U S swamps and marshes. Reveals that 300,000 acres of wetlands disappear annually. Shows how habitats are being created for wetland wildlife. Includes a workbook.
Geography - World; Science - Natural; Social Science
Dist - EFVP **Prod** - WQED

The Wetlands 13 MIN
VHS / Videodisc / 16mm
Color (I J H)
$325.00, $245.00 purchase, $75.00 rental _ #8234
Shows that wetlands - coastal marshes, river estuaries, man - made ponds, 'prairie potholes' - support many kinds of vegetation and are no longer considered waste areas. Points out the ecological importance of wetlands and what can be done to protect them.
Science - Natural
Dist - AIMS **Prod** - BEANMN 1990

Wetlands ecology - estuaries 23 MIN
VHS / U-matic
Color (H C)
$325.00, $295.00 purchase _ #V541
Explores the ecology of the land between oceans and fresh waters, estuaries. Reveals that no other wetland has such a diversity of life. Photographs the estuaries of Washington state. Features John Huston as narrator and music by Scott Cossu.
Science - Natural; Science - Physical; Social Science
Dist - BARR **Prod** - CEPRO 1991

Wetlands, marshes and swamps 15 MIN
VHS
Color (J H C)
$29.95 purchase _ #IVWCM94
Explores the watery world of the wetlands. Examines the origins of the regions, the plant and animal life within them and why marshes are important to the food chain and to humans. Visits the Florida Everglades and tours the 'River of Grass.' Discusses various types of wetlands such as bogs and marshes, the many natural habitats these areas provide and reveals the role of wetlands in filtering water pollution.
Geography - United States; Science - Natural
Dist - INSTRU

Wetlands - Our Natural Partners in Wastewater Management 39 MIN
16mm
Color
LC 81-700661
Documents research in Michigan and Florida, where wetlands are being used for advanced wastewater treatment. Deals with the financial and environmental advantages of this type of treatment over dry land treatment.
Sociology
Dist - USNAC **Prod** - NSF 1980

The Wetlands Problem 25 MIN
U-matic / VHS
Color (J H C)
Shows the wetlands of Australia which, like Florida's Everglades, support an abundance of wildlife, including some of economic importance to man. Notes how the aborigines lived in harmony with the wetlands for centuries, but now the situation and ecology are changing by dam construction, swamp draining and clearing of wetland forests.
Geography - World; Science - Natural
Dist - EDMI **Prod** - EDMI 1978

Wetlands regained 15 MIN
VHS
Color (G)
$19.95 purchase _ #BOR - 10
Explains the San Joaquin Basin Action Plan which improves the plight of wetlands in the Central Valley of California.
Geography - United States; Science - Natural
Dist - INSTRU **Prod** - USBR

Wetten Ist Ehrensache 15 MIN
16mm / U-matic / VHS
Guten Tag Wie Geht's Series
Color (H C) (GERMAN)
A German language film. Features Gabi on a rickshaw ride after viewing the six - day bicycle races.
Foreign Language
Dist - IFB **Prod** - BAYER 1973

We've been There 60 MIN
U-matic
Vista Series
Color (H C A)
Examines the growing self help movement that offers support, encouragement and understanding to those in need.
Psychology; Science
Dist - TVOTAR **Prod** - TVOTAR 1985

We've Come of Age 12 MIN
16mm
Color
LC 74-700266
Uses the story of an old man's efforts to urge his generation to join him in celebrating age and life in order to promote the work of the National Council of Senior Citizens.
Health and Safety; Social Science; Sociology
Dist - NCSCIT **Prod** - NCSCIT 1973

We've got rhythm 30 MIN
16mm
Cuba - a view from inside series
B&W (G)
$400.00 purchase, $50.00 rental
Interviews elderly local musicians who trace the history of Cuban music and its basic instruments. Features part of a 17 - part series of shorts by and about Cuban women. Directed by Sara Gomez. Illustrated catalog available. Contact distributor for programming advice and discount package rental fees.
Fine Arts
Dist - CNEMAG

We've got you covered - chemical protective clothing - Los tenemos cubierto - ropa protectora de emos cubierto - ropa protectora de stancias quimicas 16 MIN
U-matic / BETA / VHS
Hazard communication - live - action video series
Color (IND G) (SPANISH)
$495.00 purchase _ #826 - 02, #826 - 08
Trains on the importance of wearing and maintaining chemical protective clothing. Gives detailed instructions of donning, using, removing and storing chemical protective clothing. Covers heat stress and decontamination procedures. Part of a series on hazard communication.
Business and Economics; Health and Safety; Industrial and Technical Education; Psychology
Dist - ITSC **Prod** - ITSC

Whadizzit - How to Identify the Auto 10 MIN
BETA / VHS
Color (A PRO)
$61.00 purchase _ #KTI92
Explains how to decipher the serial and identification plates on American cars.
Industrial and Technical Education
Dist - RMIBHF **Prod** - RMIBHF

The Whale 7 MIN
16mm
B&W; Color (G)
$20.00 rental
Documents an event in the fall of 1970 in which a dead sperm whale washed up on a deserted Oregon beach and officials ordered the disposal of the carcass, choosing to blow it up with a half - ton of dynamite. Reflects mindset of the times as America was planning then to bomb Cambodia. Produced by Ron Finne with music courtesy of the humpback whales.
Fine Arts
Dist - CANCIN

The Whale hunters of Lamalera 52 MIN
VHS
Disappearing world series
Color (G C)
$99.00 purchase, $19.00 rental _ #51254
Reveals that the Lamaholot live in the village of Lamalera on an island in Indonesia and that, armed only with forged iron harpoons, they hunt the sperm whale from May to October, ten hours a day, six days a week. Discloses that the Lamaholot way of life is threatened by the scarcity of their prey and people are leaving the island to find more profitable work elsewhere. Features anthropologist Robert Barnes. Part of a series working closely with anthropologists who lived for a year or more in societies whose social structures, beliefs and practices are threatened by the expansion of technocratic civilization.

Sociology
Dist - PSU **Prod** - GRANDA 1988

Whale Hunters of San Miguel 15 MIN
U-matic / VHS
Color (H C A)
Examines the whaling industry of San Miguel and presents the pros and cons of this ancient endeavor.
Industrial and Technical Education
Dist - JOU **Prod** - UPI

A Whale of a Friend 15 MIN
U-matic / VHS
Explorers Unlimited Series
Color (P I)
Shows trainers working with dolphins and with the whale Shamu at Sea World of Ohio.
Science - Natural
Dist - AITECH **Prod** - WVIZTV 1971

Whale Rescue 58 MIN
U-matic / VHS
Nova Series
Color (H C A)
$250 purchase _ #5279C
Discusses the beaching of whales and methods of handling whale strandings. Produced by WGBH Boston.
Science - Natural
Dist - CORF

Whale Song 60 MIN
VHS / U-matic / 16mm / BETA
Last Frontier Series
Color; Mono (G)
MV $225.00 _ MP $550.00
Features the song of the humpback whale. Could there still be a chance to bring this gentle animal back from the brink of extinction.
Science - Natural
Dist - CTV **Prod** - MAKOF 1985

Whale Watch 57 MIN
U-matic / VHS / 16mm
Nova Series
Color (H C A)
Observes the whales and their activities in the lagoons off the coast of central Mexico and introduces the methods used in studying and filming their behavior.
Science - Natural
Dist - TIMLIF **Prod** - WGBHTV 1982

Whale watch 60 MIN
VHS
Nova video library
Color (G)
$29.95 purchase
Documents the annual migration of the North American Gray whales from Southern California to the Bering Strait of Alaska. From the PBS series 'NOVA.'
Science - Natural
Dist - PBS **Prod** - WNETTV

Whales 24 MIN
Videodisc
Color (P I J)
Presents information about whales, using still and motion pictures, narration and on - screen text. Can be used as a 24 - minute presentation, as four individual six - minute lessons or as a text - and - image data base.
Science - Natural
Dist - NGS **Prod** - NGS

Whales 60 MIN
VHS
National Audubon Society specials series
Color; Captioned (G)
$49.95 purchase _ #NTAS - 303
Shows that while whale products were once very much in demand, synthetic equivalents have led to a decline in whale hunting. Focuses on efforts to protect whales from remaining threats. Also produced by Turner Broadcasting and WETA - TV. Narrated by talk - show host Johnny Carson.
Science - Natural
Dist - PBS **Prod** - NAS 1988

Whales 60 MIN
VHS
Color (G)
$29.98 purchase _ #0804
Films whales swimming, spouting and breaching. Shows a baby sperm whale nursing, the breeding of the North Atlantic right whale and underwater footage of sperm whales. Johnny Carson narrates.
Science - Natural
Dist - SEVVID **Prod** - NAS

Whales 23 MIN
U-matic / VHS / 16mm
Undersea world of Jacques Cousteau series
Color (G)
$49.95 purchase _ #Q10617
Utilizes undersea footage to explore the whales of the Indian Ocean. Part of a series of 24 programs.
Science - Natural; Science - Physical
Dist - CF

Whales and Whalermen 22 MIN
U-matic / VHS / 16mm
Color (I)
Follows a whaling expedition out of Durban into the Indian Ocean. Shows the killing of three whales - - a sperm, a finback and a sei. Gives details of the economic importance of whaling.
Business and Economics; Psychology; Science - Natural; Social Science
Dist - MCFI **Prod** - HOE 1967

The Whales are Waiting 28 MIN
16mm
Color (G)
_ #106C 0176 016
Presents the dilemma of the whale, its value to certain industries and as a source of food, weighed against the growing possibility of its extinction.
Science - Natural; Social Science
Dist - CFLMDC **Prod** - NFBC 1976

Whales - Close Encounters of a Deep Kind 23 MIN
VHS / U-matic
Color (K)
Shows the intelligent humpback whale which must run the gauntlet of pirate whaling ships and killer whales to reach feeding waters.
Science - Natural
Dist - NWLDPR **Prod** - NWLDPR

Whales, Dolphins and Men 52 MIN
U-matic / VHS / 16mm
Color (H C A)
LC 78-700097
Examines and explains the extraordinary intelligence and behavior of dolphins, the smallest and most numerous members of the whale family.
Psychology; Science - Natural
Dist - FI **Prod** - BBCTV 1973

Whales of August 98 MIN
VHS
Color (G)
$89.95 purchase _ #S02105
Stars Lillian Gish, Bette Davis, Ann Sothern, and Vincent Price in an examination of the different ways people come to terms with aging.
Fine Arts; Health and Safety; History - United States
Dist - UILL

The Whales that came back 26 MIN
VHS
Challenge of the seas series
Color (I J H)
$225.00 purchase
Reveals that although gray whales were almost hunted to extinction, they have returned to their pre - hunting population. Discloses that annually they conduct the longest mammalian migratin on Earth, ending up in the lagoons of Baja, California. Now that they are not hunted, they exhibit extraordinary friendliness to humans, even sticking their heads into small boats for a pet. Part of a 26 - part series on the oceans.
Science - Natural; Science - Physical
Dist - LANDMK **Prod** - LANDMK 1991

The Whales that Wouldn't Die
U-matic / VHS
Color
Looks at the Pacific gray whale and its rebound from near extinction. Shows Laguna Ojo de Liebre, a calving lagoon in Baja California. Uses rare whaling footage and interviews to describe two decimations of the population, specifically the Scammon expedition and modern factory ships.
Industrial and Technical Education; Science - Natural; Social Science
Dist - KPBS **Prod** - KPBS

The Whales that Wouldn't Die 28 MIN
U-matic / VHS / 16mm
Color (I)
LC 81-700214
Uses close - up photography to depict the migration activities of the gray whale, which can ingest a ton of food a day and swim at a steady three - to - five knots a day for over 4,000 miles.
Science - Natural
Dist - CRMP **Prod** - KPBS 1981

The Whales that Wouldn't Die 30 MIN
U-matic
Color (J C)
Shows award - winning film on the remarkable history of the Pacific gray whale, a sea - going mammal which has come back from the brink of extinction and enjoys relative prosperity at the present time. Narrated by Jack Lord.
Science - Natural
Dist - SDSC **Prod** - SDSC 1984

Whales Weep not 26 MIN
16mm / U-matic / VHS
Color (H C A)
Looks at the underwater world of the sperm whale and the blue whale. Depicts turn - of - the - century whaling.
Psychology; Science - Natural
Dist - CORF **Prod** - CORF

Whalesong 29 MIN
16mm / VHS
(J A)
$50.00 rental
Documents a unique experience featuring the Vancouver Symphony Orchestra, the Vancouver Bach Choir, opera singers and three killer whales. Also available in a one hour version.
Fine Arts; Science - Natural
Dist - BULFRG

Whalesong 50 MIN
16mm / U-matic / VHS
Color; Stereo (J)
$775.00, $300.00 purchase, $80.00 rental; $550.00, $275.00 purchase, $50.00 rental
Presents a concert at the Vancouver Aquarium with the Vancouver Symphony Orchestra and the Vancouver Bach Choir. Features opera singers Judith Forst and Mark Pedrotti. The aquarium's killer whales perform behind the musicians during the concert. Hour version available.
Fine Arts; Science - Natural
Dist - BULFRG **Prod** - RHOMBS 1989

Whaling Voyage 23 MIN
16mm
B&W
LC 74-701048
Shows the preparation and the voyage of a whaling ship working under sail, killing and rendering a large whale.
Business and Economics; Social Science
Dist - EDC **Prod** - EDC 1973

Wharton executive development video series
Business ethics 58 MIN
Managing People 52 MIN
Marketing Strategy 51 MIN
Dist - KANSKE

Wharton School of Business Executive Development Video Series
Finance and Accounting 55 MIN
Dist - KANSKE
SYBVIS

Wharton School of Business Executive Development Video Series
Marketing Strategy 51 MIN
Dist - SYBVIS

What 7 MIN
16mm
B&W (G)
$10.50 rental
Depicts a bar room drama. Uses clay animation. Produced by Michael Connor.
Fine Arts
Dist - CANCIN

What 60 MIN
VHS / U-matic
Color (H A)
Examines various aspects of being deaf and shows how creative signing can be.
Guidance and Counseling; Literature and Drama; Psychology
Dist - GALCO **Prod** - GALCO 1982

What 80 Million Women Want 55 MIN
16mm
B&W (J H C)
LC 76-700213
Also known under the title, Eighty Million Women Want. Uses a drama featuring Emmeline Pankhurst to present the cause of women suffrage. With subtitles.
Civics and Political Systems; Sociology
Dist - FCE **Prod** - FCE 1974

What a magnet does - Part 1 10 MIN
VHS
Magnets series
Color; PAL (P I J)
Introduces the basic concepts of permanent magnets. Part one of a five - part series on magnets.
Science - Physical
Dist - VIEWTH **Prod** - VIEWTH

What a mouthful 30 MIN
VHS
Bodymatters series
Color (H C A)
PdS65 purchase
Discusses teeth and their effect on health. Part of a series of 26 30-minute videos on various systems of the human body.

Science - Natural
Dist - BBCENE

What a Picture - the Complete Photography Course by John Hedgecoe Series Program 1
Making a Picture 30 MIN
Dist - FI

What a Picture - the Complete Photography Course by John Hedgecoe Series Program 3
Lighting and Composition 30 MIN
Dist - FI

What a Picture - the Complete Photography Course by John Hedgecoe Series Program 6
Perspectives of Space 30 MIN
Dist - FI

What a Picture - the Complete Photography Course by John Hedgecoe Series Program 7
Imagination and Technique 30 MIN
Dist - FI

What a Picture - the Complete Photography Course by John Hedgecoe Series Program 8
Travelling Light 30 MIN
Dist - FI

What a Picture - the Complete Photography Course by John Hedgecoe Series
Landscape and Light 30 MIN
The Vital Moment 30 MIN
Dist - FI

What a State You're in 15 MIN
U-matic / VHS
It's all Up to You Series
Color (I J)
Concentrates on the in - between jurisdiction of state governments.
Civics and Political Systems
Dist - AITECH **Prod** - COOPED 1978

What a Way to Go - an Extravaganza in the Making 26 MIN
16mm
B&W (IND)
LC FI68-311
Views production problems of the set of 'WHAT A WAY TO GO.' Shows the writers, actors, costume designer and crew rehearsing and shooting.
Fine Arts
Dist - WOLPER **Prod** - WOLPER 1964

What a Way to make a Living 30 MIN
U-matic / VHS
Color
Provides biographies of a break dancer, a boxer, a fast - draw marksman and a turkey caller, four peculiar American success stories.
Biography; Sociology
Dist - DCTVC **Prod** - DCTVC

What a Way to Run an Airline 12 MIN
U-matic / VHS / 16mm
Color (C A)
Uses the success story of People Express Airlines to offer a new perspective on employee involvement in business operations.
Business and Economics
Dist - CORF **Prod** - ABCTV

What a Way to Start a Day 15 MIN
16mm
Color (C A)
LC 72-701862
A motivational film using dramatized incidents to alert workers about the importance of safety regulations on their jobs.
Business and Economics; Guidance and Counseling; Health and Safety
Dist - VOAERO **Prod** - VOAERO 1971

What about gangs series
Provides an overview of gangs and gang - related activities to young adolescents and teachers. Discusses suggestions for curbing gang membership and helping present gang members. Contains two videos - one for students and one for teacher education. Includes teacher's guides.
Program 1 - Gangs - decisions and options 18 MIN
Program 2 - Recognizing, containing and eliminating gangs - strategies for educators 40 MIN
What about gangs series 58 MIN
Dist - UNL

What about grace and miracles
VHS
Questions of faith III series
Color (J H C G A R)
$10.00 rental _ #36 - 85 - 217
Explores the concepts of grace and miracles. Features the perspectives of a wide variety of contemporary Christian and Jewish thinkers.
Religion and Philosophy
Dist - APH **Prod** - ECUFLM

What about love 60 MIN
VHS
Mister Rogers' home videos series
Color; Captioned (K P)
$14.95 purchase _ #HV103
Stars Mister Rogers who reminds everyone that it's the people one loves most who can make one the angriest - and the happiest. Part of a series featuring favorite Mister Rogers Neighborhood programs.
Guidance and Counseling; Health and Safety; Psychology
Dist - FAMCOM **Prod** - FAMCOM 1990

What about me 17 MIN
VHS / U-matic
Color (K P I)
$280.00, $330.00 purchase, $50.00 rental
Helps children cope with the psychiatric hospitalization of a sibling. Addresses the emotional and practical implications this can have on the children and family unit. Produced by McLean Hospital Corporation.
Psychology; Sociology
Dist - NDIM

What about Mom and Dad 60 MIN
VHS / 16mm
Color (A G)
$300.00 purchase, $190.00, $95.00 rental
Explores the difficult decisions that must be made by those who care for elderly spouses or parents.
Health and Safety; Sociology
Dist - FANPRO **Prod** - FANPRO 1989

What about Mom and Dad 58 MIN
U-matic / VHS
Frontline Series
Color
Deals with the problems of families facing difficult emotional and financial choices in caring for older parents whose savings have been eaten up by nursing home care, with federal programs for medical costs covering less than expected.
Business and Economics; Health and Safety; Sociology
Dist - PBS **Prod** - DOCCON

What about Pot 20 MIN
U-matic / VHS / 16mm
Color (I)
LC 76-702165
Takes the viewer into the drug subculture. Shows how the marijuana problem develops, illustrates the differing impact of marijuana in the ghetto and in suburbia and presents a cross - section of the ideas, fears and myths that still obscure the real nature of the marijuana question. Explores the role, if any, that marijuana should have in society.
Guidance and Counseling; Psychology; Sociology
Dist - AIMS **Prod** - DAVP 1972

What about Reading Systems 29 MIN
16mm / U-matic / VHS
Teaching Children to Read Series
Color (C A)
Discusses the values and pitfalls of packaged reading systems.
Education; English Language
Dist - FI **Prod** - MFFD 1976

What about Thad 9 MIN
16mm
Color (H C A)
LC 76-700917
Considers the emotional problems of a young, lonely boy who is growing up without needed attention or acceptance from parents, teacher or friends. Allows the viewer to make judgments about ways to help the child's problems.
Education; Psychology; Sociology
Dist - BYU **Prod** - BYU 1970

What about the Russians 28 MIN
16mm
(G)
$350.00 purchase, $50.00 rental
Features fourteen top experts answering questions about the nuclear arms race, a nuclear weapons treaty and national security.
Civics and Political Systems; Geography - World
Dist - EFVP **Prod** - EFVP 1984

What about the workers - 1880 - 1918 - Part 1 18 MIN
VHS
Color; PAL (H C G)
Presents a history of the British Trade Union Movement in two parts. Discusses the Labour Movement in the period between 1880 - 1918. Uses prints, photographs and excerpts from historical newsreels to trace modern trade unionism.
Business and Economics; History - World; Social Science; Sociology
Dist - VIEWTH

What about the workers - 1918 - 1945 - Part 2 19 MIN
VHS
Color; PAL (H C G)
Presents a history of the British Trade Union Movement in two parts. Discusses the Labour Movement in the period between 1918 - 1945. Uses prints, photographs and excerpts from historical newsreels to trace modern trade unionism.
Business and Economics; History - World; Social Science; Sociology
Dist - VIEWTH

What about the Workers Series
A Discussion on the Government White Paper 24 MIN
Dist - MEDIAG

What about Timber 20 MIN
U-matic
Exploring Our Nation Series
Color (I)
Views the giant fir trees of Washington. Describes a timber company which believes that restoration of the forest is as important as the cutting, sorting and milling operations.
Agriculture; Science - Natural
Dist - GPN **Prod** - KRMATV 1975

What about Tomorrow 20 MIN
U-matic / VHS / 16mm
Color
LC 80-700847
Explores the world of basic scientific research into such areas as fluorocarbons and the ozone layer, earthquake prediction, food production and laser chemistry.
Agriculture; Science - Physical
Dist - IU **Prod** - NSF 1978

What about Winter Driving 11 MIN
16mm
Color
LC 75-703076
Illustrates safe techniques for winter driving maintenance and for starting, stopping and driving on snow - covered and ice - covered highways. Presents information on the pulling ability and stopping distances obtained with different tires.
Health and Safety; Psychology
Dist - NSC **Prod** - USDTFH 1974

What Affects Your Hearing 50 MIN
16mm
B&W (PRO)
Demonstrates how hearing can be temporarily or permanently damaged by noise. Shows a stapedectomy and the diagnosis and correction of hearing loss due to stiffening or calcification of the tiny bones in the middle ear.
Health and Safety; Science - Natural
Dist - LAWREN **Prod** - CMA

What am I doing here 30 MIN
VHS
Open space series
Color; PAL (H C A)
PdS50 purchase
Features a nursing home project in which a theatre company assists the residents in the production of a musical play. Examines the residents' feelings about aging and explores ways to improve the quality of life for those residing in institutions. Part of the Open Space series.
Health and Safety; Sociology
Dist - BBCENE

What am I good at 15 MIN
VHS
Career planning series
Color (H C)
$39.00 purchase _ #BPN207002; LC 89-715839
Encourages self - discovery before making a career choice. Shows Jamie and Susan taking aptitude tests. Includes teacher's guide. Part of a six - part series.
Guidance and Counseling; Psychology; Sociology
Dist - TVOTAR **Prod** - TVOTAR 1989

What Am I Supposed to do 12 MIN
VHS / 16mm
Sexual Harassment - Shades of Gray Series
Color (PRO)
$500.00 purchase, $50.00 rental
Explains the responsibilities of employees at all levels to stop sexual harassment. Part of a training program to stop sexual harassment in the workplace.
Business and Economics; Civics and Political Systems; Guidance and Counseling; Psychology; Sociology
Dist - UTM **Prod** - UTM

What America does right series
Presents two parts drawing from the book What America Does Right by Bob Waterman. Shows how three companies are building work forces for tomorrow with strategies such as horizontal management, cross - functional teams and reengineering. Offers two corporate examples showing why organizational arrangement is a most powerful strategic tool.
Management turned upside down - Volume I 30 MIN
Organization is strategic - Volume II 30 MIN
Dist - FI **Prod** - ENMED

What an Idea 15 MIN
VHS
Art's place series
Color (K P)
$49.00 purchase, $15.00 rental _ #295811
Reveals that Art is having trouble coming up with an idea for the Art and Science Fair, so Mirror conjures up his old friend Leonardo da Vinci, who offers some advice. Explores computer - generated images. Reveals why Mona Lisa smiles the way she does. Part of a series that combines songs, stories, animation, puppets and live actors to convey the pleasure of artistic expression. Includes an illustrated teacher's guide.
Computer Science; Fine Arts
Dist - TVOTAR **Prod** - TVOTAR 1989

The What and why of co - dependency 22 MIN
VHS / U-matic / BETA
Co - dependency series
Color (G)
$280.00 purchase _ #801.1
Uses mime and family vignettes to overview the history of co - dependency. Describes current thinking about the disorder and discusses its origins, including family traits such as faulty communication, inadequate boundaries and abuse. Part of a five - part series on co - dependency.
Guidance and Counseling; Health and Safety; Psychology; Sociology
Dist - CONMED

The What and why of nursing diagnosis 14 MIN
BETA / VHS / U-matic
Nursing diagnosis and care planning series
Color (C PRO)
$150.00 purchase _ #144.1
Presents a video transfer from slide program which defines nursing diagnosis and justifies its use. Introduces two important facets of nursing diagnosis - the accepted NANDA list of diagnoses and the PES format. Includes a review of the nursing process. Confronts common concerns and confusions and is of value in change strategy. Part of a series on nursing diagnosis and care planning.
Health and Safety
Dist - CONMED **Prod** - CONMED

What animals eat 15 MIN
VHS / U-matic
Animals and such series; Module red - life processes
Color (I J)
Examines the feeding processes of animals, including parasites.
Science - Natural
Dist - AITECH **Prod** - WHROTV 1972

What are Ecosystems? 61 MIN
U-matic / VHS
What are Ecosystems Series
Color (I)
Contains 1 videocassette.
Science; Science - Natural
Dist - TROLA **Prod** - TROLA 1987

What are Ecosystems Series
What are Ecosystems? 61 MIN
Dist - TROLA

What are Families for 15 MIN
VHS / U-matic
All about You Series
Color (P)
Introduces the idea that there are many different kinds of family structures in society. Suggests that members of a family depend on each other and work together to help each other.
Guidance and Counseling
Dist - AITECH **Prod** - WGBHTV 1975

What are fractions - Program 1 29 MIN
VHS
Fraction action series
Color (I J H)
$175.00 purchase _ #CG - 919 - VS
Introduces fraction strips and shows how they can be used to compare fractions. Shows students how to generate a series of equivalent fractions and use it to compare different fractions and solve other real - world problems. Presents ways of dividing groups of discrete units, volumes and areas into parts. Includes teacher's activity book, overhead transparencies, student worksheets, transparent fraction strips and geoboards. Part of a two - part series.
Mathematics
Dist - HRMC **Prod** - HRMC

What are Friends for 47 MIN
U-matic / VHS / 16mm
Teenage Years Series
Color (I J)
LC 80-700634
Tells how a 12 - year - old girl learns to adjust to her parents' divorce. Originally shown on the television show ABC Afterschool Specials.
Fine Arts; Sociology
Dist - TIMLIF **Prod** - TAHSEM 1980

What are Letters for - Consonant Blends and Combinations 13 MIN
U-matic / VHS / 16mm
Color (P)
English Language
Dist - PHENIX **Prod** - PHENIX 1983

What are Letters for - Initial Consonants 12 MIN
16mm / U-matic / VHS
Reading Motivation Series
Color (P)
LC 73-703306
Presents words selected from commonly used vocabulary lists and primary readers which are used orally and visually superimposed over action. Makes it clear that language and reading are fun and useful.
English Language
Dist - PHENIX **Prod** - PHENIX 1973

What are Letters for - Vowel Combinations 11 MIN
16mm / U-matic / VHS
Color (P I)
LC 84-707087
Presents a combination of visuals and graphic demonstrations of the various vowel combinations to help children understand the ways vowels work in English.
English Language
Dist - PHENIX **Prod** - BEANMN 1983

What are Letters for - Vowels 12 MIN
U-matic / VHS / 16mm
Reading Motivation Series
Color (P)
LC 73-703305
Presents words selected from commonly used vocabulary lists and primary readers which are used orally and visually superimposed over action. Makes it clear that language and reading are fun and useful.
English Language
Dist - PHENIX **Prod** - PHENIX 1973

What are Numbers 15 MIN
U-matic
Mathematical Relationship Series
Color (I)
Illustrates the probable development and evolution of our Hindu - Arabic number system.
Education; Mathematics
Dist - TVOTAR **Prod** - TVOTAR 1982

What are Slips 12 MIN
VHS / 16mm
Roughneck Training Series
(A PRO)
$175.00 purchase _ #40.0524
Shows the floor hand that although slips are simple, rugged, and dependable devices, proper procedures should be followed when using them.
Industrial and Technical Education; Social Science
Dist - UTEXPE **Prod** - UTEXPE 1983

What are Stars made of 16 MIN
16mm / U-matic / VHS
Color (I J H C)
Portrays an astronomer at the Mount Wilson and Palomar observatories who investigates a question about the chemistry of the stars.
Science - Physical
Dist - IFB **Prod** - VEF 1960

What are the moral dilemmas
VHS
Questions of faith III series
Color (J H C G A R)
$10.00 rental _ #36 - 83 - 217
Deals with moral issues. Invites viewers to determine what is the most pressing moral issue for them. Features perspectives from a wide variety of contemporary Jewish and Christian thinkers.
Religion and Philosophy
Dist - APH **Prod** - ECUFLM

What are they 30 MIN
U-matic / VHS
Management for the '90s - Quality Circles Series
Color
Business and Economics; Psychology
Dist - DELTAK **Prod** - TELSTR

What are Values 9 MIN
16mm / U-matic / VHS
Color (I J)
LC 77-700852
Discusses the meaning of values, explains how people learn them and describes a method for making difficult value decisions.
Guidance and Counseling
Dist - PHENIX **Prod** - PHENIX 1977

What are We Doing Here 12 MIN
VHS / 16mm
Sexual Harassment - Shades of Gray Series
Color (PRO)
$500.00 purchase, $50.00 rental
Discusses in depth the problem of sexual harassment in the workplace. Part of a training program aimed to control sexual harassment in an organization.
Business and Economics; Civics and Political Systems; Guidance and Counseling; Psychology; Sociology
Dist - UTM **Prod** - UTM

What are You made of 15 MIN
U-matic / VHS
All about You Series
Color (P)
Explains that one's body is comprised of cells and the that it grows by adding more cells. Discusses the different functions of cells.
Science - Natural
Dist - AITECH **Prod** - WGBHTV 1975

What are you really eating 28 MIN
35mm strip / VHS
Color (J H C A)
$93.00, $93.00 purchase _ #MB - 540637 - 3, #MB - 540639 - X
Encourages viewers to read food labels and find out just what they are eating. Presents the pros and cons of various ingredients commonly used in food.
Health and Safety; Social Science
Dist - SRA **Prod** - SRA 1988

What are you thinking, daddy 1 MIN
16mm
Color (G)
$4.00 rental
Protests the Vietnam war in a production by Fred Wellington.
Dist - CANCIN

What are You, Woman 25 MIN
U-matic / VHS / 16mm
Color
LC 77-701518
Presents four segments, including Medea - An Aftermath, Chinese Lament, I Am A Woman Growing Old and I Wear History On My Back, each dealing with an aspect of woman's experience from a different cultural perspective.
Sociology
Dist - PHENIX **Prod** - WITTEN 1977

What Black Americans Should Know about Cancer 30 MIN
VHS / U-matic
Color
Health and Safety; History - United States
Dist - SYLWAT **Prod** - RCOMTV 1982

What Business Lawyers Need to Know about the Law of Evidence 120 MIN
U-matic / VHS / Cassette
Color; Mono (PRO)
Focuses on the actions law clients can take to avoid evidentiary pitfalls. Explains procedures for maintaining attorneys' files, client business records and ohter documents, and for protecting privileged information and information subject to the freedom of information acts.
Business and Economics; Civics and Political Systems
Dist - CCEB **Prod** - CCEB

What Buys more 15 MIN
U-matic
Math Factory, Module VI - Money Series
Color (P)
Applies simple number sentences to money problems and introduces adding with three addends.
Business and Economics
Dist - GPN **Prod** - MAETEL 1973

What Can a Guy do 15 MIN
U-matic / VHS / 16mm
Color
Discusses attitudes young men have toward birth control. Portrays high school couples and individuals in difficult

circumstances, such as an unplanned pregnancy and the inability of a girlfriend to take the pill.
Health and Safety; Sociology
Dist - CNEMAG **Prod** - HEDUC

What Can a Guy do? 15 MIN
U-matic
Color (J H)
LC 81-707098
Uses vignettes and on - the - street interviews in offering a sampling of male attitudes and knowledge about birth control. Designed to motivate the viewer to learn the facts about sex and pregnancy from suggested reliable sources.
Health and Safety; Sociology
Dist - SERIUS **Prod** - SERIUS 1980

What Can Birds do 15 MIN
U-matic
Tell Me what You See Series
Color (P)
Studies a baby chick and a duckling to show how birds are uniquely suited for their needs.
Science - Natural
Dist - GPN **Prod** - WVIZTV

What Can Go Wrong? 20 MIN
U-matic / Kit / VHS
Growing Up
(J)
Discusses the risks of irresponsible sexual behavior. Focuses on the health risks attendant on teen pregnancy, explains sexually transmitted diseases. Sixth in a six part series.
Science - Natural; Sociology
Dist - GPN

What can I do? 80 MIN
16mm
Color (H C A)
$100.00 rental
Tells the story of an elderly woman in New York City who has a group of dinner guests over one evening to whom she tells of the difficulties of her life and her family relationships. Produced by Wheeler Dixon.
Guidance and Counseling; Sociology
Dist - CANCIN

What Can I do 22 MIN
U-matic / VHS / 16mm
Color (J)
LC 75-700617
Tells how the average American citizen can influence ongoing social change through personal, political and social action. Includes explanations of the use of media, the impact of effective letters and the power of a single vote.
Civics and Political Systems; Guidance and Counseling; Social Science; Sociology
Dist - BARR **Prod** - CALLFM 1975

What can I do 80 MIN
16mm
Color (G)
$100.00 rental
Views an old woman who gathers a group of paid dinner guests in her New York apartment for an evening of dinner and drinks and attempts to beguile them into staying the night, in the manner of Scheherezade. Explores the reciprocal discourse between spectator, image and performer. As the evening progresses, she not only looks directly at the viewers, the audience, but also at the five guests, who directly return her gaze in a series of precise eye - matches. Intercut with her monologue are extreme close - ups of the listeners, smoking, pouring coffee, etc, while blocks of written text from her diatribe are presented in long scrolling sections against the flow of the narrative.
Fine Arts; Home Economics; Psychology
Dist - CANCIN **Prod** - WWDIXO 1993

What can I do today - adults 45 MIN
VHS
What can I do today series
Color (C A)
$295.00 purchase
Shows adults in frank discussion of their experiences as substance abusers and in recovery, mentioning job situations, social stresses and withdrawal among the difficulties faced by the individuals.
Guidance and Counseling; Health and Safety; Psychology
Dist - PFP **Prod** - CLEARP

What can I do today - family 43 MIN
VHS
What can I do today series
Color (C A H)
$295.00 purchase
Presents family members, spouses, adult children and others talking about their experiences living with substance abusers. Covers what life is like under those conditions and how one can successfully deal with the problems.
Guidance and Counseling; Health and Safety; Psychology
Dist - PFP **Prod** - CLEARP

What can I do today series
What can I do today - adults 45 MIN
What can I do today - family 43 MIN
What can I do today - teens 30 MIN
Dist - PFP

What can I do today - teens 30 MIN
VHS
What can I do today series
Color (J H)
$295.00 purchase
Presents several teenagers who are recovering from substance abuse discussing their abusive habits and how they regained sobriety. Shows only young people, from different backgrounds and social levels.
Guidance and Counseling; Health and Safety; Psychology
Dist - PFP **Prod** - CLEARP

What Can I do When I Feel Bad 30 MIN
VHS
Color (J)
LC 89700231
Explores teenagers' feelings of low self - esteem and their search for solutions. Presents two parts, 'State Of Mind' and 'Flying High.'.
Guidance and Counseling; Health and Safety; Psychology
Dist - AIMS **Prod** - HRMC 1989

What Can I Tell You - a Portrait of Three Generations of Women 55 MIN
16mm
Within America Series
Color (J)
LC 79-701570
Focuses on three generations of women from an Italian - American family, who offer anecdotes and personal perspectives on their self - images and family relationships. Covers topics such as marriage, children, working and independence.
Sociology
Dist - CEPRO **Prod** - CEPRO 1979

What Can I Tell You - a Portrait of Three Generations of Women, Pt 1 27 MIN
16mm
Within America Series
Color (J)
LC 79-701570
Focuses on three generations of women from an Italian - American family, who offer anecdotes and personal perspectives on their self - images and family relationships. Covers topics such as marriage, children, working and independence.
Sociology
Dist - CEPRO **Prod** - CEPRO 1979

What Can I Tell You - a Portrait of Three Generations of Women, Pt 2 28 MIN
U-matic / VHS / 16mm
Color (J H C A)
LC 79-701570
Focuses on three generations of women from an Italian - American family, who offer anecdotes and personal perspectives on their self - images and family relationships. Covers topics such as marriage, children, working and independence.
Sociology
Dist - CEPRO **Prod** - CEPRO 1979

What Can My Child Hear 30 MIN
16mm / U-matic / VHS
Color (C A)
Explains the testing process, and describes and evaluates hearing aids.
Education; Guidance and Counseling
Dist - PFP **Prod** - YASNYP

What Can You do 26 MIN
16mm
Color
LC 74-706606
States that more young people from Spanish - speaking communities must aspire to careers as physicians, dentists, nurses, other health professionals and health technicians. Includes recent graduates describing how they overcame obstacles and started a career.
Guidance and Counseling; Health and Safety; Psychology; Science; Sociology
Dist - USNAC **Prod** - USHHS 1974

What Can You do 28 MIN
16mm
Color (J H A)
Examines the problem of the lack of Spanish - speaking Americans in the health care fields. Presents interviews with Spanish - Americans discussing how they overcame financial obstacles, family problems and their own personal doubts.
Guidance and Counseling; Health and Safety; Sociology
Dist - MTP **Prod** - USHHS

What Can You Find 12 MIN
16mm
Color (K P)
LC FIA67-2264
Notes differences in size, shape, feel and color of similar creatures and natural objects. Illustrates seasonal change.
Science - Natural
Dist - LOH **Prod** - LOH 1966

What Can You Learn from an Aardvark? 30 MIN
U-matic / VHS
Zoolab Series
Color (J H)
$180.00 purchase
Explains the benefits of animal research including the genetic theories that allow a species to thrive.
Science - Natural
Dist - AITECH **Prod** - WCETTV 1985

What Can You Show Me 29 MIN
VHS / U-matic
Bean Sprouts Series
Color (P I)
Tells the story of a shy but talented Chinese American boy drawn out of his shell through a class project involving puppets.
Education; Guidance and Counseling; Sociology
Dist - GPN **Prod** - CTPROJ

What Causes Current Flow - EMF 3 MIN
16mm
Basic Electricity Series
B&W
LC FIE56-56
Shows an outside force converted into electrical force of attraction. Points out that in a circuit the electrical forces of attraction and repulsion taken together are called electromotive force (EMF).
Industrial and Technical Education; Science - Physical
Dist - USNAC **Prod** - USN 1954

What Changes Prices 10 MIN
U-matic
Calling Captain Consumer Series
Color (P I J)
Shows a man who makes leather belts thinking he can be his own boss making and selling objects.
Business and Economics; Home Economics
Dist - TVOTAR **Prod** - TVOTAR 1985

What clients need to know about the Public Accommodations Provisions of the ADA 50 MIN
VHS
Color (A PRO C)
$95.00 purchase _ #Y158
Examines the statutory provisions of Title III of the ADA and offers practical advice to lawyers and their business clients on complying with the Act's sweeping accessibility requirements.
Business and Economics; Civics and Political Systems; Health and Safety
Dist - ALIABA **Prod** - CLETV 1992

What color are you 15 MIN
16mm
Color (P I J)
$30.00 rental _ #PRF - 754
Presents simply stated scientific explanations for the differences in human racial characteristics. Follows three children who spend a day at the zoo marveling at the diversity in the animal world. Uses animation to illustrate mutations and adaptations which made it possible for people and animals to adapt to their environment.
Science - Natural
Dist - ADL **Prod** - ADL

What Color are You 15 MIN
U-matic / VHS / 16mm
Color (I)
LC FIA68-483
Explains why there are different races, in answer to children's questions about race. Discusses pigmentation and mutations. Describes why scientists believe all human beings derived from one common ancestor.
Guidance and Counseling; History - United States; Psychology; Science - Natural; Sociology
Dist - EBEC **Prod** - EBEC 1967

What Color is Skin 9 MIN
U-matic / VHS / 16mm
Who We are Series
Color (K P I)
LC 77-701120
Shows variations of skin coloring in the human race and explains how heredity determines skin color.

Guidance and Counseling; Science - Natural; Sociology
Dist - PFP Prod - KORTY 1977

What Color is the Wind 27 MIN
16mm
Color (C A)
LC 74-700294
Tells the story of twin boys, three years old, one of whom was born blind. Tells how their parents, with some professional help, are determined that the blind boy shall compete and have an opportunity no less than that of his twin brother in the sighted world.
Education; Guidance and Counseling; Psychology; Sociology
Dist - ALGRAN Prod - ALGRAN 1968

What Comes Out of the Blast Furnace 8 MIN
U-matic / VHS / 16mm
Chemistry of Iron Making Series
B&W (J H C)
Shows how molten iron is removed from the furnace, cooled into pigs or cast and how slag and gases are handled, processed and used.
Business and Economics; Science - Physical
Dist - IFB Prod - IFB 1956

What Controls Current Flow - Resistance 4 MIN
16mm
Basic Electricity Series
B&W (H)
Shows the symbol for resistance to current flow, the atomic basis for resistance in materials, and the effect of the use of a resistor in a circuit.
Industrial and Technical Education; Science - Physical
Dist - USNAC Prod - USN 1954

What Could I Say? 18 MIN
U-matic / VHS
Color
Presents 20 vignettes which illustrate common situations that require assertive responses, weds professional validity with wit, charm and style.
Business and Economics; Guidance and Counseling; Psychology; Sociology
Dist - RESPRC Prod - RESPRC

What Could I Say - an Assertion Training Stimulus Program 18 MIN
16mm
Color
Presents 20 vignettes which illustrate common situations that require assertive responses. Includes social, sexual, work, marital, family and consumer problems.
Business and Economics; Psychology
Dist - RESPRC Prod - RESPRC

What Could You do with a Nickel 26 MIN
16mm
Color
Tells the story of two hundred black and hispanic women in the south Bronx who formed the first domestic workers union in the history of the United States.
Business and Economics; Sociology
Dist - FIRS Prod - FIRS

What courts are requiring in the IEP - Tape 9 78 MIN
VHS
Legal challenges in special education series
Color (G)
$90.00 purchase
Reviews the constitutional basis for the IEP plan and discusses areas in which courts have recently struck down IEPs, including involvement of appropriate personnel, covering all required elements at the meeting, providing for related services, discussing methodology, insuring appropriate evaluation and planning for graduation. Features Reed Martin, JD. Includes resource materials. Part of a 12 - part series on Public Law 94 - 142.
Civics and Political Systems; Education
Dist - BAXMED

What dads need to know about fathering - Part 2 60 MIN
VHS
Focus on the family series
Color (G A R)
$24.99 purchase, $10.00 rental _ #35 - 83579 - 533
Presents Dr James Dobson in a discussion of what fathers should know about parenting.
Guidance and Counseling; Sociology
Dist - APH Prod - WORD

What Did You do in School Today 35 MIN
16mm
Color (T)
LC 73-703425
Explores child - centered schooling in English informal schools. Illustrates the development of curiosity and involvement with learning among children from working - class areas and describes the school's relationships with the community and parents.
Education
Dist - AGAPR Prod - AGAPR 1973

What did you learn at school today 38 MIN
U-matic / VHS / BETA
Color; PAL (T PRO)
PdS70, PdS78 purchase
Features six Leicestershire schools - primary, high and upper - and their philosophy of education which states that the most valuable education is self - education and the best discipline is self - discipline. Shows children and young students learning and developing in their own ways without self - consciousness, or any sense of apology for what they are doing. Views the importance Leicestershire places upon creativity, self - expression and personal relationships, along with a vigorous pursuit of academic learning. Produced by James Archibald and Associates.
Education; Fine Arts
Dist - EDPAT

What Did You Learn in School Today 48 MIN
16mm
B&W (H C A)
Examines, through narration by newswoman Joan Murray, the 'open - classroom,' an alternative method being used in schools in England and the United States. Interviews Lady Bridget Plowden, whose report on education altered many English classrooms. Visits North Dakota, a state changing entirely to the 'open - classroom', the Grape School in Watts, Los Angeles and a teacher - training workshop in Connecticut. Focuses on the idea of 'satellite' or 'mini' high schools in order to show changes going on in suburban schools.
Education
Dist - IU Prod - WNETTV 1972

What did you read - from the pathways to reading series 15 MIN
16mm
The Pathways to reading series
B&W (I J H)
Discusses the importance of comprehension in reading. Emphasizes words, main ideas and details. Compares reading to travel. Shows how both require knowing where you're going and what you're looking for.
English Language
Dist - AVED Prod - CBF 1958

What Did You Say in School Today 23 MIN
16mm
Color
LC 77-700434
Tells what is being done to help children overcome barriers to fluent speech. Portrays two speech pathologists at work in a public school, dealing with a variety of speech problems presented by children from four to 16 years of age.
Education; English Language; Psychology
Dist - PCHENT Prod - PCHENT 1977

What Did You Say - Oral Communications 15 MIN
U-matic / VHS / 16mm
Color (I J)
LC 82-701178
Dramatizes the problem of poor oral communication skills and presents systematic techniques for improving oral communication skills.
English Language
Dist - ALTSUL Prod - VITASC

What Difference Does it make? 13 MIN
U-matic / Slide
Production - Minded Management Series Module 4
Color
Offers a series of dramatized incidents to show how little things do make a difference. Uses a light approach to the serious matter of minutes, hours and days that are lost because of inattention to little things.
Business and Economics; Psychology
Dist - RESEM Prod - RESEM

What do Flowers do - a First Film 11 MIN
16mm / U-matic / VHS
Color (P I J)
LC 74-705714
Describes parts of the flower, how seeds develop and how germination and growth take place.
Science - Natural
Dist - PHENIX Prod - BEANMN 1969

What do Flowers do - a First Film 11 MIN
16mm / U-matic / VHS
Color (P) (SPANISH)
LC 74-705714
Describes parts of the flower, how seeds develop and how germination and growth take place.
Foreign Language
Dist - PHENIX Prod - BEANMN 1958

What do I do Now 30 MIN
U-matic / VHS / 16mm
Children and Deafness Series
Color (C A)
Presents options for testing and treatment, education, and systems of communication.
Education; Guidance and Counseling; Psychology
Dist - PFP Prod - YASNYP

What do I do When I See a Fire? 13 MIN
VHS / U-matic
Color
Deomonstrates proper responses and reactions in case of a fire. Emphasizes learning the fire department phone number, how to report a fire and the importance of getting out fast. Narrated by Sparky the Fire Dog and features puppet characters.
Health and Safety; Social Science
Dist - NFPA Prod - NFPA

What do I Know about Benny 10 MIN
U-matic / VHS / 16mm
Critical Moments in Teaching Series
Color (C A)
LC FIA68-2463
Illustrates the difficulties a teacher may face in her evaluation of a student's ability and in her explanation of the evaluation to that student's parents. Discusses problems of reconciling parent's expectations and the student's apparent ability to perform.
Education; Psychology
Dist - PHENIX Prod - CALVIN 1968

What do I Receive for My Money 9 MIN
16mm
Color (P I J)
Discusses how to find value for money, how much money a person needs, the difference between need and want, comparison shopping and bargain buying.
Business and Economics; Education; Home Economics; Social Science
Dist - SF Prod - SF

What do investment bankers do and why do they make so much money 30 MIN
U-matic
Adam Smith's money world 1985 - 1986 season series; 243
Color (A)
Attempts to demystify the world of money and break it down so that small as well as large businesses and it's people understand and adjust to new social and economic trends. Reports on the major economic stories and discoveries of 1985 and 1986.
Business and Economics
Dist - PBS Prod - WNETTV 1986

What do Plants do - a First Film 11 MIN
U-matic / VHS / 16mm
Color (P I)
Points out that plants are important parts of our world, that they produce food for plants and animals, return oxygen to the air and are adapted to live almost everywhere. Tells how plants are living things that use food, grow, are sensitive and move. Shows how we use plants to make clothes and to keep us warm.
Science - Natural
Dist - PHENIX Prod - BEANMN 1971

What do Seeds do - a First Film 11 MIN
U-matic / VHS / 16mm
Color (P I J)
LC 70-710608
Shows the relative size and development of various seeds.
Science - Natural
Dist - PHENIX Prod - BEANMN 1970

What do Seeds Need to Sprout 11 MIN
16mm / U-matic / VHS
Color (P)
LC 73-701235
Reveals the need for three things in order for a seed to germinate - the right temperature, water and air.
Science - Natural
Dist - CORF Prod - CORF 1973

What do they do - Part 3 30 MIN
VHS
Teaching early reading series
Color (K P I)
#E376; LC 90-712991
Provides a broad spectrum of teaching methods and materials for teaching beginning reading skills. Presents the concept that word recognition emerges from a child's total learning experience. Part 3 of a six - part series on teaching early reading.
Education; English Language; Social Science
Dist - GPN Prod - CTI 1978

What do they do - Word Recognition 30 MIN
U-matic / VHS

Teaching Early Reading Series
Color (T)
Education; English Language
Dist - CTI Prod - CTI

What do they Eat 5 MIN
U-matic / VHS / 16mm
Wonder Walks Series
Color (P I)
LC 72-713439
Illustrates food chains and food webs commonly found in nature.
Science - Natural
Dist - EBEC Prod - EBEC 1971

What do those old films mean series
Denmark 1910 - 1912 26 MIN
France 1904 - 1922
Germany 1925 - 1932
Great Britain 1900 - 1912 26 MIN
United States 1902 - 1914 26 MIN
USSR 1926 - 1930
Dist - FLMWST

What do We - Cans 4 MIN
16mm / U-matic / VHS
Mini Movies, Unit 2 - what do We do Series
Color (I J)
Shows cans of different sizes, shapes, openings and contents taking on new dimensions as they become an instrument, a vase, a game or a telephone. Explores these and other possibilities so that children will want to try their own imaginative, creative ways of using this throw - away product.
Fine Arts
Dist - CORF Prod - MORLAT 1976

What do We - Chocolate 4 MIN
U-matic / VHS / 16mm
Mini Movies, Unit 2 - what do We do Series
Color (I J)
Traces the chocolate bar's origins back to cocoa beans. Shows how curiosity aroused by an all - time children's favorite, the chocolate bar, results in an intriguing visit to a chocolate factory and an increased awareness of chocolate in the diet.
Agriculture; Health and Safety; Home Economics; Social Science
Dist - CORF Prod - MORLAT 1976

What do We do Now 30 MIN
16mm
Color
LC 77-700435
Shows the difficulties faced by families in finding the right services for a handicapped child. Presents the Regional Referral System, operative in California and elsewhere, where families can learn about the needs of the handicapped and get help in meeting those needs.
Education; Psychology; Sociology
Dist - RSF Prod - RSF 1976

What do We do Now - the Need for Direction 29 MIN
16mm
Color (S)
LC 77-700866
Discusses the problems and frustrations facing the parents of a handicapped child as they try to secure proper services for the child. Introduces Direction, a program for the handicapped in California which assesses a handicapped child's special needs and matches those needs with locally available services.
Education; Psychology; Sociology
Dist - USNAC Prod - USBEH 1975

What do We Know about the Metric System 20 MIN
U-matic
Metric System Series
Color (J)
Reviews the first nine lessons of the Metric System series.
Mathematics
Dist - GPN Prod - MAETEL 1975

What do We Mean by Meaning 30 MIN
VHS / U-matic
Language and Meaning Series
Color (C)
English Language; Psychology
Dist - GPN Prod - WUSFTV 1983

What do We Mean - Culture 20 MIN
U-matic
Exploring Our Nation Series
Color (I)
Investigates the American way of life as a product of diverse cultural elements.
Sociology
Dist - GPN Prod - KRMATV 1975

What do we series
Mini movies - springboard for learning - Unit 2, what do we - a series
Dist - MORLAT

What do You do When You See a Blind Person 14 MIN
16mm
Color (H C A)
LC 72-700146
Presents a light touch approach to the right and wrong ways of dealing with blind people in various situations.
Guidance and Counseling; Sociology
Dist - AFB Prod - AFB 1971

What do You do When You See a Blind Person 13 MIN
16mm / U-matic / VHS
Color (I)
Shows the proper way to aid the blind.
Guidance and Counseling; Health and Safety; Psychology
Dist - PHENIX Prod - AFB

What do You do while You Wait 11 MIN
U-matic / VHS / 16mm
Color (I J)
LC 73-701909
Points out that waiting is something everyone has to do some time in their life. Shows children waiting for different things and what you can do while you wait if you use your imagination.
Guidance and Counseling; Psychology
Dist - EBEC Prod - EBEC 1973

What do You do with a Kid Like that 29 MIN
U-matic
A Different Understanding Series
Color (PRO)
Dramatizes the story of a boy with a reading disability whose father thinks he is bad and other students think he is lazy and stupid before his problem is recognized.
Psychology
Dist - TVOTAR Prod - TVOTAR 1985

What do You do with a Kid Like that 28.5 MIN
VHS / 16mm
A Different Understanding Series
Color (G)
$90.00 purchase _ #BPN164101
Tells the story of Tony, a 15 year old boy whose teacher discovers that he has a reading disability, rather than is just a `stupid' or `bad' kid.
Education; Psychology
Dist - RMIBHF Prod - RMIBHF

What do You Know about Carpet 22 MIN
16mm
Color
Presents information and advice from an expert on selecting carpet for the home, including tips on fibers, construction, color and style.
Guidance and Counseling; Home Economics
Dist - ACOC Prod - ACOC

What do You Know about Your Teeth? 25 MIN
VHS / U-matic
Color
Gives a multiple - choice and true - false fun - for - all quiz on dental health. Shows Dr David Gaynor answering and explaining important facts about dental hygience, for instance, what it means when gums bleed. Discusses fluoridation of water supply as well.
Health and Safety; Science - Natural
Dist - MEDCOM Prod - MEDCOM

What do You Mean 4 MIN
U-matic / VHS / 16mm
Most Important Person - Getting Along with Others Series
Color (K P I)
Describes Bobby's thinking as he learns that when his parents have had a 'HARD DAY,' he must treat them with more understanding.
Guidance and Counseling; Psychology
Dist - EBEC Prod - EBEC 1972

What do You Mean 30 MIN
U-matic / VHS
Principles of Human Communication Series
Color (H C A)
Explains how words derive their meanings and the relationship between the culture and the meanings of words.
English Language; Psychology
Dist - GPN Prod - UMINN 1983

What do you mean by faith
VHS
Questions of faith III series
Color (J H C G A R)
$10.00 rental _ #36 - 80 - 217
Explores the significance of faith. Attempts to differentiate between faith and belief. Features a wide variety of contemporary Jewish and Christian thinkers.
Religion and Philosophy
Dist - APH Prod - ECUFLM

What do You People Want 30 MIN
16mm
Color
Presents an angry indictment of white oppression made by the Black Liberation Movement at a number of meetings during the turbulent events of the Black Panther party's history in 1968.
Sociology
Dist - IMPACT Prod - IMPACT 1968

What do you really want for your children 60 MIN
VHS
Color (A)
$49.95 purchase _ #S01795
Features Dr Wayne Dyer in a discussion of how parents can help their children develop their talents and abilities.
Psychology; Sociology
Dist - UILL

What do You Say Now 8 MIN
16mm
Color (C A)
LC 80-701592
Presents vignettes of children making statements which would elicit an adult response. Offers practice in communication and child management skills.
Home Economics; Psychology
Dist - PSUPCR Prod - PSUPCR 1980

What do You See? 6 MIN
U-matic / VHS
Color
Tells hospital personnel, through the thoughts of an elderly woman, how it feels to be a patient and how hospital staff affect patient care.
Health and Safety; Psychology
Dist - AHOA Prod - AHOA 1980

What do You See Now 22 MIN
16mm
Color (T)
Adds or subtracts colorful felt shapes from a board, challenging the child to remember which has appeared or disappeared. Designed to teach visual discrimination of color, shape and size and for reinforcing basic shapes.
Psychology
Dist - SF Prod - SF 1970

What do You See Now, Pt 1 11 MIN
16mm
Color (K P I)
Shows different ideas about addition and subtraction - addition - circle, square, triangle, subtraction - circle, square, triangle, addition - rectangle, diamond, cross, subtraction - rectangle, diamond and cross.
Mathematics
Dist - SF Prod - SF

What do You See Now, Pt 2 11 MIN
16mm
Color (K P I)
Shows different ideas about addition and subtraction - addition - circle, square, triangle, subtraction - circle, square, triangle, addition - rectangle, diamond, cross, subtraction - rectangle, diamond and cross.
Mathematics
Dist - SF Prod - SF

What do You See, Nurse 12 MIN
U-matic / VHS / 16mm
Color (I)
LC 80-701595
Presents an elderly woman in a nursing home who says that people should look beyond the wrinkles and pain of old age and recognize the beauty and richness of her life.
Health and Safety; Sociology
Dist - CORF Prod - GORKER 1980

What do you see when you see a blind person 14 MIN
VHS
Color (G S T)
$69.95 purchase
Takes a humorous look at myths and misconceptions about blind and visually impaired people. Follows the adventures - and misadventures - of Phil as he learns that common courtesy and common sense conquers all.
Guidance and Counseling; Health and Safety; Home Economics
Dist - AFB Prod - AFB

What do you tell a phone
VHS
Amazing advantages for kids series
Color (T K P)
$19.95 purchase _ #AMZ002V-K
Teaches children proper phone etiquette and what to do when they answer the door. Expands the concept of manners to explain how to treat guests and also includes

safety lessons about dealing with strangers on the phone or at the door. Presented entirely by children. One of a three-part series that teaches manners and social skills.
Health and Safety; History - World; Psychology
Dist - CAMV

What do You Think 15 MIN
U-matic
Keys to the Office Series
Color (H)
Gives advice on how to make sound decisions in career choices and business.
Business and Economics
Dist - TVOTAR **Prod** - TVOTAR 1986

What do You Think 10 MIN
16mm / U-matic / VHS
Color (C A)
Uses animation and live - action to leave no doubt that flower power is flourishing in Tokyo.
Geography - World; Psychology
Dist - TEXFLM **Prod** - UWFKD

What do You Think? 34 MIN
16mm / U-matic / VHS
Color (A C T)
$60 rental _ #4473
Demonstrates three major stages of cognitive development in children from four to eleven.
Guidance and Counseling; Psychology
Dist - AIMS **Prod** - AIMS 1971

What do You Think You Want to be 4 MIN
U-matic / VHS / 16mm
Most Important Person - Identity Series
Color (K P I)
Features fumble singing 'YOU CAN BE ANYTHING YOU WANT TO BE.' Observes the children visualizing the many things there are to be as an adult.
Guidance and Counseling
Dist - EBEC **Prod** - EBEC 1972

What do You Think You Want to be 4 MIN
U-matic / VHS / 16mm
Most Important Person - Identity (Spanish Series
Color (K P) (SPANISH)
Foreign Language; Guidance and Counseling
Dist - EBEC **Prod** - EBEC

What do You Trust? 25 MIN
U-matic / VHS
Introduction to Philosophy Series
Color (C)
Religion and Philosophy
Dist - UDEL **Prod** - UDEL

What do You Want 27 MIN
16mm
Color (H C A)
LC 73-700182
Points out that people with dedication can create opportunities to promote growth in towns that are dying. Explores things that some people are doing to keep their towns alive. Shows how a group of concerned local people from various walks of life come together, and begin exploring what they could do to put their community back on its feet.
Guidance and Counseling; Social Science; Sociology
Dist - BANDEL **Prod** - BANDEL 1972

What does it mean to be human
VHS
Color (J H C)
$197.00 purchase _ #00284 - 126
Helps students analyze and appreciate basic human characteristics. Focuses on the physical and mental traits of individuals, the fundamental patterns of society, and the special qualities of civilization. Uses three simple societies as models to explain that humans are social and that their societies share certain basic characteristics. Includes teacher's guide and library kit. Three parts.
Psychology; Sociology
Dist - GA **Prod** - GA

What Does Music do 20 MIN
16mm
Music of America Series
Color (I)
Points out that there is no category of music that is basically good or bad, but that all of the varieties of music can be well or poorly presented. Implies that the child should not make a blanket condemnation of any type of music, but should try and judge each selection on its own merits.
Fine Arts
Dist - GPN **Prod** - KQEDTV

What Does Our Flag Mean 11 MIN
16mm / U-matic / VHS
Color (P I)
Explains, through the story of a family that become naturalized American citizens, the meaning of the American flag, how it has changed through the years, how it is displayed and how one shows respect for it.
Civics and Political Systems
Dist - CORF **Prod** - CORF 1967

What Does the Future Hold 30 MIN
16mm
What Series
(H H C G T A)
Religion and Philosophy
Dist - WHLION **Prod** - WHLION

What Does the Law Say 12 MIN
VHS / 16mm
Sexual Harassment - Shades of Gray Series
Color (PRO)
$500.00 purchase, $50.00 rental
Explains laws governing sexual harassment in the workplace. Presents a US Supreme Court case and examines EEOC guidelines. Part of a training program to stop sexual harassment in the workplace.
Business and Economics; Civics and Political Systems; Guidance and Counseling; Psychology; Sociology
Dist - UTM **Prod** - UTM

What Electricity Does in Every Electric System 60 MIN
Videoreel / VT1
Understanding Semiconductors Course Outline Series no 01
Color (IND)
Describes the elements of electricity, such as current and voltage, and what electricity does in every electric system.
Industrial and Technical Education
Dist - TXINLC **Prod** - TXINLC

What Employers Want 25 MIN
VHS / 16mm
Job Search - How to Find and Keep a Job Series
(H)
$69.00 _ #PA111V
Lists the skills and qualities employers say the seek in employees. Provides tips for meeting these expectations.
Guidance and Counseling
Dist - JISTW

What Employers Want - Program 11 22 MIN
VHS / 16mm
Job Search - How to Find and Keep a Job
Color (H C A PRO)
$720.00 purchase _ #SD100
Tells what employers expect and want in skills and qualities of employees. Available only as part of the complete series. Part 11 of 12 parts.
Business and Economics; Guidance and Counseling
Dist - AAVIM **Prod** - AAVIM 1990

What Energy Means 15 MIN
16mm / U-matic / VHS
Color (P I)
Discusses the various forms of energy, the ways in which energy can be converted from one form to another, the difference between fuel and energy and the need to conserve fuels.
Social Science
Dist - NGS **Prod** - NGS 1982

What Ever Happened to Baby Jane 132 MIN
16mm / U-matic / VHS
B&W (H C A)
Stars Bette Davis and Joan Crawford as two once - idolized and wealthy females now living as virtual recluses.
Literature and Drama
Dist - FI **Prod** - WB 1962

What ever happened to the American dream 55 MIN
VHS
Color (R G)
$19.95 purchase _ #7177 - 3
Adapts the book by conservative Christian financial expert Larry Burkett and features commentary by John Ankerberg and other conservative Christian personalities in politics, business and science.
Civics and Political Systems; Guidance and Counseling; Religion and Philosophy
Dist - MOODY **Prod** - MOODY 1994

What every baby knows 60 MIN
VHS
Color (J H)
$9.00 purchase _ #04627 - 126
Features pediatrician Dr T Berry Brazelton. Gives practical advice on how to handle emergency situations, how to set limits for children and explains the meaning of temper tantrums.
Health and Safety; Psychology
Dist - GA **Prod** - GA

What every business litigator needs to know about federal criminal investigations 220 MIN
Cassette
Color (PRO)
$295.00, $150.00 purchase, $150.00 rental _ #FCI1-00F, #AFCI-000
Examines the major strategic, procedural and ethical issues which affect the corporate litigator during a governmental criminal investigation. Provides legal and practical suggestions for the civil litigator, in - house corporate counsel, or general practitioner who may represent a corporation, director, officer or employee affected by a federal criminal investigation. Covers a wide range of administrative, procedural and substantive issues, including principles of corporate criminal liability, internal investigations, subpoenas and search warrants, protecting clients from indictment, and negotiations with the prosecution. Includes a study guide.
Business and Economics; Civics and Political Systems
Dist - AMBAR **Prod** - AMBAR 1989

What Every Child Should Know 30 MIN
BETA / VHS
Color
Discusses the basic lessons of chilhood that make useful common knowledge.
Fine Arts; Literature and Drama
Dist - HOMEAF **Prod** - HOMEAF

What every lawyer needs to know about drafting documents for closely - held corporations 210 MIN
VHS
Color (C PRO A)
$67.50, $150.00 purchase _ #M708, P217
Follows a hypothetical client from start - up to buy - out. Briefs lawyers on how to draft clear and accurate documents, including reviewing the planning considerations in capitalization, private placement, control and voting issues. Highlights the pitfalls and problems involved in drafting subscription agreements, voting trusts, shareholder management agreements and share - transfers - buy - out agreements.
Business and Economics; Civics and Political Systems
Dist - ALIABA **Prod** - ALIABA 1988

What every litigator should know about mediation 210 MIN
VHS / Cassette
Color (PRO)
$295.00, $75.00 purchase, $150.00 rental _ #WEL1-000, #AWEL-000
Provides a practical guide for litigators. Includes discussion and demonstrations addressing what mediation is and when you should use it; how to prepare your client and yourself for mediation; and how to represent your client during mediation.
Civics and Political Systems
Dist - AMBAR **Prod** - AMBAR 1993

What every woman should know about a man ... from a man's point of view - of course 45 MIN
VHS
Color (G)
$19.95 purchase
Interviews 17 men of different backgrounds who have their own views and ideas about relationships in the 1990s. Contains a message for all women today who want to establish a relationship or who are presently in a relationship and need answers. By Morris Productions.
Fine Arts; Psychology; Sociology
Dist - CANCIN

What everybody should know about toxicology 21 MIN
BETA / VHS / U-matic
British video programs series
Color; PAL (IND G)
$595.00 purchase _ #550 - 01
Trains employees in the United Kingdom. Explains the fundamental concepts of toxicology in laymen's terms so that workers can understand and act upon the health and safety information contained on product labels and safety data sheets. Covers routes of entry, acute and chronic health effects and the dose - response relationship.
Health and Safety; Industrial and Technical Education; Psychology
Dist - ITSC **Prod** - ITSC

What Everyone Should Know about Fabrics
VHS / 35mm strip
$69.00 purchase _ #LSKAF filmstrip, $79.00 purchase _ #LSKAFV VHS
Teaches basic information about the fabrics we wear, sit on, sleep on, and use everyday. Points out the difference between natural and synthetic fibers, and discusses how to choose the best fabric for one's needs.
Home Economics
Dist - CAREER **Prod** - CAREER

What everyone should know about toxicology 20 MIN
U-matic / BETA / VHS
Hazard communication - live - action video series
Color (IND G)
$495.00 purchase _ #825 - 05
Familiarizes employees with basic toxicological terms so that they can understand information on product labels and Material Safety Data Sheets - MSDSs - and take precautionary measures to safeguard health in the workplace and at home. Illustrates terms such as toxicity, dose - response, routes of entry, acute and chronic, units of measurement for potential health hazards and exposure limits. Discusses categories of chemicals such as irritants, corrosives, skin and respiratory sensitizers, target organ poisons, neurotoxins, anesthetics, reproductive toxins and carcinogens. Part of a series on hazard communication.
Health and Safety; Industrial and Technical Education; Psychology
Dist - ITSC **Prod** - ITSC 1990

What Goes into the Blast Furnace 15 MIN
16mm / U-matic / VHS
Chemistry of Iron Making Series
B&W (J H C)
Shows the preparation and handling of ore, coke, limestone and air.
Business and Economics; Science - Physical
Dist - IFB **Prod** - IFB 1956

What Goes Up 12 MIN
VHS / U-matic
Color
Presents a program beautifully photographed at Lake Compounce, Connecticut, for cardiovascular patients.
Health and Safety
Dist - PRIMED **Prod** - PRIMED

What good are rocks 12 MIN
VHS / U-matic / 16mm
Wonder world of science series
Color (P)
$320.00, $250.00 purchase _ #HP - 5707C
Stars Wondercat who stumbles on a rock and wonders what good they are. Considers why rockhounds like to collect rocks. Uses a magnifying glass to compare rock colors, patterns and textures and to group them. Shows that minerals make each rock different and that rocks and the minerals extracted from them both have important uses. Part of the Wonder World of Science series. Produced by Bill Walker Productions.
Science - Physical; Social Science
Dist - CORF

What Good are Woods 15 MIN
VHS / 16mm
Forever Wild Series
Color (I)
$125.00 purchase, $25.00 rental
Examines the value of forests from a variety of social perspectives - aesthetic, economic and environmental.
Agriculture; Geography - United States; Science - Natural
Dist - AITECH **Prod** - WCFETV 1985

What Good is a Warbler 13 MIN
16mm
Color (P)
LC 75-703299
Uses the intimate family life of an endangered bird, the golden - cheeked warbler, to show what may happen when humans alter the environment. Explores the warbler's home and special needs revealing its intricate relations with other elements of the natural world. Points out that each living thing plays a role and has a value in the natural cycle.
Science - Natural
Dist - ADAMSF **Prod** - ADAMSF 1975

What Guys Want 16 MIN
U-matic / VHS
Color (J H A)
Presents teenagers of diverse ethnic, racial and economic backgrounds expressing their attitudes and feelings about maleness and their male sexual behavior.
Health and Safety; Sociology
Dist - POLYMR **Prod** - POLYMR

What Hands Can do 10 MIN
16mm
Color (P I)
LC 72-702566
Portrays children's hands performing all the roles in a three act play that tells of the endless variety of uses for hands.
Fine Arts
Dist - SF **Prod** - SF 1967

What Happened to Harry - Back Siphonage 20 MIN
16mm
Color (H C)
Utilizes a comic sketch of 'HAPPY - GO - LUCKY' Harry to show dangers of back siphonage and cross - connections in plumbing systems.
Industrial and Technical Education
Dist - OSUMPD **Prod** - OSUMPD 1963

What Happened to Mooretown 19 MIN
16mm
B&W
Presents a high disease incidence neighborhood in Shreveport, Louisiana, which takes action to correct its communicable disease problem through programs involving improved housing, sewage disposal and vector control and general environmental sanitation.
Health and Safety
Dist - NMAC **Prod** - DUART

What Happened to My Paycheck 16 MIN
16mm
Color (H C A)
LC 81-700639
Tells the story of a high school student who is upset when he receives less pay than he expected because of withholding taxes. Shows how to prepare tax forms and offers a tour of an Internal Revenue Service Office where tax forms are processed.
Business and Economics; Home Economics
Dist - USNAC **Prod** - USIRS 1980

What happens in Hamlet 30 MIN
VHS
Color (G C H)
$119.00 purchase _ #DL502
Analyzes three interlocking stories in 'Hamlet' - the ghost story, the detective story, and the revenge story. Probes major characters and movements.
Fine Arts; Literature and Drama
Dist - INSIM

What Happens in Our High Schools 29 MIN
U-matic / VHS / 16mm
Dealing with Classroom Problems Series
Color (T)
Examines the essence of secondary education and looks optimistically to its futuro. Includes experimential learning approaches and a visit to a unique school - within - a - school program.
Education
Dist - FI **Prod** - MFFD 1976

What Happens Inside 10 MIN
16mm
Family Life and Sex Education Series
Color (K P I)
Uses animation and live action to record the growth of a fertilized mammal egg. Explains the meaning of the terms 'GESTATION,' 'UMBILICUS' and 'PLACENTA.' Shows the birth of a litter of kittens. Draws comparisons between the care of a mother cat for her kittens and of a human mother for her children. Describes the first four months of the development of a human baby inside the mother.
Science - Natural
Dist - SF **Prod** - SF 1968

What Happens Next 18 MIN
U-matic / VHS / 16mm
Color (IND)
LC 81-701629
Dramatizes four industrial accidents and explores what should be done to protect the injured and those persons on the shop floor. Demonstrates the correct and incorrect responses to each accident.
Health and Safety
Dist - IFB **Prod** - MILLBK 1981

What Happens Next - Code 4 16 MIN
16mm
B&W (PRO)
LC FIA67-690
Portrays human and technical factors to be considered in organizing and training a hospital resuscitation team. Shows a program in action at the Palo Alto Hospital in California.
Health and Safety
Dist - AMEDA **Prod** - SKF 1965

What happens next - living through childhood
VHS
Color; PAL (G)
Helps parents come to terms with the diagnosis of cancer in their child.
Health and Safety; Sociology
Dist - VIEWTH

What happens next - living through childhood cancer 16 MIN
U-matic / VHS / BETA
Color; NTSC; PAL; SECAM (G)
PdS83
Gives a positive, hopeful message to the parents of a child recently diagnosed with cancer. Talks to other parents who have gone through the same experience and gives a broad explanation of treatment and the equipment used. Shows children in various stages of therapy and those who have benefitted from treatment. Trains nurses and support staff involved with childhood cancer and helps staff to develop an understanding of patient needs and parent fears and emphasizes that successful therapy requires cooperation among all staff involved.
Health and Safety
Dist - VIEWTH

What Happens When Air is Heated and Cooled 15 MIN
VHS / U-matic
Why Series
Color (P I)
Discusses what happens when air is heated and cooled.
Science - Physical
Dist - AITECH **Prod** - WDCNTV 1976

What Happens When it Works / no more Lunchsacks for Me 29 MIN
U-matic
As We See it Series
Color
Tells how students in Stockton, California, spearheaded a successful city - wide effort to prepare for desegregation. Dramatizes a free school lunch program in Wichita, Kansas, and shows how it affected desegregation.
Sociology
Dist - PBS **Prod** - WTTWTV

What Happens When Water Freezes 5 MIN
U-matic / VHS
Way Things Work Series
Color (K)
$149.95, $49.95 purchase _ #AD - 1663
Reveals that water expands when it freezes. Uses Bob Symes' freezer to prove this fact. Part of a thirty - part series on the way things work hosted by Bob Symes.
Science; Science - Physical
Dist - FOTH **Prod** - FOTH

What Happens When You Go to the Hospital 12 MIN
16mm
Training Module on Role Enactment in Children's Play Four
Color (A)
LC 76-700937
Shows young children enacting a child's recent hospitalization. Shows the roles of patient, doctor, nurse and parents, with occasional role reversal and sharing, as assumed by children and facilitates study and discussion for students and practitioners in child development, child psychology and other related disciplines.
Education; Health and Safety; Psychology
Dist - CFDC **Prod** - UPITTS 1974

What Happens When You're Sick 17 MIN
16mm / U-matic / VHS
Color (P I)
LC 81-700170
Describes Dennis's tour through Symptom Headquarters by Selena the Symptom Sender. Explains such symptoms as fever, sneezing, upset stomach, diarrhea, bleeding, swelling and pain.
Health and Safety; Science - Natural
Dist - HIGGIN **Prod** - HIGGIN 1981

What Harvest for the Reaper 59 MIN
16mm
Net Journal Series
B&W (H C)
LC FIA68-1479
Documents the experiences of a group of farmworkers who became trapped in a system that kept them perpetually in debt. Shows methods of recruitment, labor camps on Long Island and the types of work involved. Presents the opinions of growers and processors and refutes their views.
Agriculture; Business and Economics; Psychology; Sociology
Dist - IU **Prod** - NET 1968

What has Happened to Political Machines 29 MIN
Videoreel / VT2
University of Chicago Round Table Series
Color
Civics and Political Systems
Dist - PBS **Prod** - WTTWTV

What have we learned 15 MIN
Videoreel / VT2
Art corner series
B&W (P)
Reviews materials and make suggestions for using some of them during the summer.

Fine Arts
Dist - GPN **Prod** - CVETVC

What have we learnt 30 MIN
VHS
Computing for the terrified series
Color (A)
PdS65 purchase
Asks where computers take society from here. Part of a seven-part series which introduces some of the growing range of computer applications in the home, office and industry, aimed at those returning to work.
Computer Science; Guidance and Counseling
Dist - BBCENE

What have You Done for Yourself Lately? 15 MIN
U-matic / VHS
Color
Shows employees how to zero in on the priority tasks where maximum results can be achieved, helps them develop job enrichment programs for themselves and provides self - development techniques that ensure continued personal growth.
Psychology
Dist - EFM **Prod** - EFM

What have You Done for Yourself Lately 20 MIN
U-matic / VHS
Color
Provides self - development techniques for use in achieving one's full potential. Includes a leader's guide.
Psychology
Dist - DELTAK **Prod** - DELTAK

What have You Done with My Country 50 MIN
16mm
Color (J H C)
Looks at Australia through the eyes of the Aboriginal, contrasting 200 years of white settlement with over 30,000 years of black occupation of the land.
Geography - World; History - World; Sociology
Dist - CINETF **Prod** - CINETF 1970

What have You Got to Lose 30 MIN
U-matic / VHS / 16mm
Powerhouse Series
Color (I J)
Shows how the Powerhouse Kids learn there are no shortcuts to losing weight.
Health and Safety; Social Science
Dist - GA **Prod** - EFCVA 1982

What Holds You Up 15 MIN
VHS / U-matic
All about You Series
Color (P)
Describes the framework of bones inside the human body. Explains that the skeleton gives the human body its shape and support and protects the vital organs.
Science - Natural
Dist - AITECH **Prod** - WGBHTV 1975

What Hope for the Children 50 MIN
U-matic / 16mm
Assignment Maclear Series
Color; Mono (J H C A)
$500.00 film, $350.00 video, $50.00 rental
Considers the efforts of governmental and private organizations of Canada in the attempt to suffering children at home and abroad.
Geography - World; Sociology
Dist - CTV **Prod** - CTV 1977

What Hurts - Emotional Abuse 14.45 MIN
U-matic / VHS
Color; Mono (J)
LC 88-713721
Gives children a view of the effects of emotional abuse while explaining to them how and why they should seek relief from it.
Sociology
Dist - ALTSUL **Prod** - ALTSUL 1988

What I Like - Spatial Interaction (Geography) 15 MIN
VHS / U-matic
Two Cents' Worth Series
Color (P)
Reveals that as Deron travels from his city home to his uncle's farm, he notices how the landscapes, buildings, vehicles and activities change along the way.
Geography - United States
Dist - AITECH **Prod** - WHATV 1976

What if 3 MIN
U-matic / VHS / 16mm
Magic Moments, Unit 1 - Let's Talk Series
Color (K P I)
LC 77-705921
Presents four situations that are often difficult to cope with when they occur in real life, so that appropriate responses can be worked out in advance, or if these situations have already been met, to show why people respond the way they do. Includes a situation where a girl finds a wallet and a boy's ice cream cone is knocked out of his hand.
English Language; Guidance and Counseling
Dist - EBEC **Prod** - EBEC 1969

What if 8 MIN
35mm
Eastern European animation series
Color (G)
Features a spoof on wishful thinking. Presents a Czech non - narrative production. Part of a four - part series. Contact distributor for rental price.
Fine Arts; Literature and Drama
Dist - KITPAR

What if 13 MIN
VHS
Space education series
Color (J H G T A)
$49.00 purchase, $15.00 rental _ #335702; LC 91-706537
Helps viewers understand what would happen if everyday physical processes, such as convection, sedimentation and surface tension, were unaffected by gravity. Part of a series providing teachers and students with information regarding the latest experimentation with weightlessness. Includes teacher's guide.
Science; Science - Physical
Dist - TVOTAR **Prod** - TVOTAR 1989

What if and lost sheep - Volume 9 45 MIN
VHS
Flying house series
Color (K P I R)
$11.99 purchase _ #35 - 8958 - 979
Uses an animated format to present events from the New Testament era, as three children, a professor and a robot travel in the 'Flying House' back to that time. 'What If' reviews the parables of the talents and the house on the rock, while 'Lost Sheep' is based on the parable of the lost sheep.
Literature and Drama; Religion and Philosophy
Dist - APH **Prod** - TYHP

What if I 5 MIN
BETA / VHS / U-matic
Color; Stereo (S C A G)
Reflects the human struggle to break free of individual isolation and achieve a balance with our environments and others through an exhibition of dance and music.
Fine Arts
Dist - UCV

What if the Patient has AIDS 20 MIN
VHS / U-matic
Color (PRO)
Discusses AIDS for nurses and other professional and technical health workers who come into contact with AIDS patients. Includes 25 information booklets.
Health and Safety; Sociology
Dist - USNAC **Prod** - USPHS 1984

What if You Couldn't Read 29 MIN
16mm
Color (H C A)
LC 78-702011
Focuses on an illiterate fur trader who, after 40 years of being unable to read and write, has begun learning these skills with the help of a tutor. Shows how the ability to read has changed his marriage and entire life.
English Language; Guidance and Counseling
Dist - FLMLIB **Prod** - TODD 1978

What in the world is the World Council of Churches 21 MIN
VHS
Color (J)
Presents a history of the World Council of Churches from 1928 to 1982. Highlights major themes which are representative of the issues of the future. Includes worship, encounter, sharing, solidarity and expectation.
Religion and Philosophy
Dist - ECUFLM **Prod** - FLEMIP 1982

What in the World's Come Over You 15 MIN
U-matic / VHS
It's all Up to You Series
Color (I J)
Analyzes historical events as they influence present societies and act as clues to future ones.
History - United States
Dist - AITECH **Prod** - COOPED 1978

What is a Bird 17 MIN
U-matic / VHS / 16mm
Biology (Spanish Series Unit 7 - Animal Classification and 'Physiology; Unit 7 - Animal classification and physiology
Color (H) (SPANISH)
Describes how the body structures of birds are adapted for flight and how birds are able to live in a wide variety of environments. Illustrates the behavior patterns of birds and the evolutionary relationships between birds and reptiles.
Foreign Language; Science - Natural
Dist - EBEC **Prod** - EBEC

What is a Bird? 15 MIN
U-matic / VHS
Up Close and Natural Series
Color (I P)
$125.00 purchase
Explores the various species of birds and the world they inhabit.
Agriculture; Science - Natural; Social Science
Dist - AITECH **Prod** - NHPTV 1986

What is a Cat 14 MIN
U-matic / VHS / 16mm
Color; Captioned (K P I J H)
LC 72-702097
Presents the history of the domestic cat, tracing the animal as a house pet and as a symbol of mystery and worship from ancient Egypt to the present day.
Science - Natural
Dist - ALTSUL **Prod** - NILCOM 1972

What is a Christian 30 MIN
16mm
B&W (H C A R)
LC 72-701662
A story concerning a hesitant Christian who is sent to four men about Christ and answers their question 'WHAT IS A CHRISTIAN.'.
Guidance and Counseling; Religion and Philosophy
Dist - CPH **Prod** - CPH 1956

What is a Church? 10 MIN
U-matic / VHS / 16mm
Color (P I)
$25 rental _ #9740
Explains the social and educational role of churches, synagogues, and mosques in the community.
Religion and Philosophy; Social Science; Sociology
Dist - AIMS **Prod** - AIMS 1972

What is a Computer? 18 MIN
VHS / U-matic
Color (A)
Introduces the viewer to the basic workings of the computer. Explains the connections between the central processors and the peripherals, including the printer, disk drives and video consol.
Business and Economics; Industrial and Technical Education
Dist - XICOM **Prod** - XICOM

What is a Computer 18 MIN
16mm
Everybody's Guide to the Computer Series Part 1; Pt 1
Color (A)
Looks at the the processor and peripherals in a computer. Explains the concepts of input, output and storage.
Mathematics
Dist - VISUCP **Prod** - VISUCP 1980

What is a Computer 19 MIN
U-matic / VHS / 16mm
Color (H)
LC 73-712292
Dispels some of the mysteries about how a computer operates. Contains a brief introduction to the binary system of numeration which leads to a description of how numbers are punched into cards, converted into pulses and stored magnetically in the computer memory. Describes and explains terms such as alphanumerics, program and flow chart. Shows the main functions of the computer - - calculating, controlling and storing information.
Mathematics
Dist - EBEC **Prod** - EBEC 1971

What is a Computer? 30 MIN
VHS / U-matic
Working with the Computer Series
Color
Presents a nontechnical introduction to the nature of computers and the kinds of tasks they perform. Uses analogies from everyday life to explain technical concepts. Discusses a number of fears and misconceptions about computers.
Industrial and Technical Education; Mathematics; Psychology
Dist - DELTAK **Prod** - DELTAK

What is a Computer Program? 17 MIN
VHS / U-matic
Color (A)
Explains what a computer program is and details the differences between a programmer and a systems analyst. Discusses the significance of flow charts, programming specifications and programming languages.

Business and Economics; Industrial and Technical Education
Dist - XICOM Prod - XICOM

What is a Computer Program 17 MIN
16mm
Everybody's Guide to the Computer Series Part 3; Pt 3
Color (A)
Explains the mysteries of the computer program and the programmer.
Mathematics
Dist - VISUCP Prod - VISUCP 1980

What is a Course in Miracles and the certain are perfectly calm 60 MIN
VHS
Color (G R)
$29.95 purchase _ #C037
Features spiritual teacher Tara Singh speaking on 'A Course in Miracles' written by Dr Helen Shucman.
Psychology; Religion and Philosophy
Dist - LIFEAP Prod - LIFEAP

What is a Desert 20 MIN
U-matic
Understanding Our World, Unit II - Geography We Should Know Series
Color (I)
Presents a 1500 - mile photographic safari through the great American Desert from the great Sand Dunes National Monument to Monument Valley.
Geography - United States; Geography - World; Science - Natural
Dist - GPN Prod - KRMATV

What is a Desert 13 MIN
U-matic / VHS / 16mm
(French (from the Living Desert (French Series
Color (I J H)
Shows how geographic and weather factors such as winds, mountains and temperature create deserts.
Foreign Language; Geography - United States; Science - Natural
Dist - CORF Prod - DISNEY

What is a Desert 13 MIN
16mm / U-matic / VHS
Color (I J H) (ARABIC)
Shows how geographic and weather factors such as winds, mountains and temperature create deserts.
Foreign Language; Geography - World; Science - Natural
Dist - CORF Prod - DISNEY 1974

What is a Family 7 MIN
U-matic / VHS / 16mm
Learning to Look Series
Color (P)
Uses animation and puppets to show that different combinations of people make a family, including single people.
English Language; Guidance and Counseling; Psychology
Dist - MGHT Prod - MGHT 1973

What is a Fish 22 MIN
16mm / U-matic / VHS
Biology (Spanish Series Unit 7 - Animal Classification and 'Physiology; Unit 7 - Animal classification and physiology
Color (H) (SPANISH)
Outlines the major types of fishes. Shows the anatomy of a typical fish and demonstrates behavior patterns in various species of fishes.
Foreign Language; Science - Natural
Dist - EBEC Prod - EBEC

What is a flower 15 MIN
VHS
Kingdom of plants series
Color; PAL (K P)
Uses animation to show the parts of a flower. Depicts how a flower's structure encourages pollination. Presents close - up views of insects gathering nectar and pollen. Considers that birds and bats as well as wind and water transport pollen. Part of a series on the Kingdom of plants.
Science - Natural
Dist - VIEWTH

What is a Food? 30 MIN
U-matic / VHS
Food for Life Series
Color
Home Economics; Social Science
Dist - MSU Prod - MSU

What is a Friend 4 MIN
16mm / U-matic / VHS
Most Important Person - Getting Along with Others Series
Color (K P I)
Explores friendship and what friends can do for each other.
Guidance and Counseling; Psychology
Dist - EBEC Prod - EBEC 1972

What is a Friend 13 MIN
16mm / U-matic / VHS
Learning Values with Fat Albert and the Cosby Kids, Set I Series
Color (K P I)
Tells the story of Begging Benny, Fat Albert's cousin, who gives the impression that he is an all - right guy, generous, giving and always thinking of others before himself. Reveals that this isn't the case, that Benny is out strictly for himself. Shows that Benny doesn't gain acceptance by the kids until there's a lot of soul searching. Concludes with Benny realizing that he must be honest and fair with others, if he wants them to treat him the same way.
Guidance and Counseling; Sociology
Dist - MGHT Prod - FLMTON 1975

What is a gene 20 MIN
VHS
Color; CC (H C)
$79.00 purchase _ #910
Outlines in simple terms the basic picture held today of what a gene is and how it works. Teaches about the genetic code, cloning, cell physiology, DNA, RNA, recombinant DNA and more. Part 2 of the program The Gene. Includes a book of the same title from the Learning Power series.
Science - Natural
Dist - HAWHIL Prod - HAWHIL 1994

What is a Good Drawing (Neolithic - 1970 a D) 17 MIN
16mm
Color
Examines the draughtman's magic over many centuries to decide what makes a drawing good, no matter what the style. Covers from the Neolothic period to 1970.
Fine Arts
Dist - ROLAND Prod - ROLAND

What is a Hero 14 MIN
U-matic / VHS / 16mm
Color (P I)
Shows how heroes can provide inspiration and guidance for young people. Looks at different kinds of heroes and the purposes they serve.
Guidance and Counseling
Dist - PHENIX Prod - PHENIX

What is a Jew to You 50 MIN
VHS / 16mm
Color (S)
$1300.00, $79.00 purchase _ #188 - 9027
Explores the question, 'What does it mean to be Jewish today?' Reveals some of the paradoxes and uncertainties that are part of the Jewish heritage. Directed by Aviva Ziegler.
Geography - World; History - World; Psychology; Religion and Philosophy; Sociology
Dist - FI Prod - FLMAUS 1987

What is a leaf 15 MIN
BETA / VHS / U-matic / 16mm
Kingdom of plants series
Color (P I)
$245.50, $68.00 purchase _ #C50675, #C51454
Shows how leaves vary in shape, size and color, and perform the vital functions of manufacturing food for the plant and releasing oxygen through the process of photsynthesis. Uses animation to show how light energy, water and carbon dioxide are combined in leaves during photosynthesis. Teaches about the leaves of deciduous and evergreen trees. Part of a five - part series on the plant kingdom.
Science - Natural
Dist - NGS Prod - NGS 1991

What is a leaf 15 MIN
VHS
Kingdom of plants series
Color; PAL (K P)
Examines the variations in shape, size and color of leaves. Considers the vital functions of leaves in manufacturing food for the plant and releasing oxygen through the process of photosynthesis. Uses animation to show how light energy, water and carbon dioxide are combined in leaves during photosynthesis. Teaches about deciduous and evergreen trees. Part of a series on the Kingdom of plants.
Science - Natural
Dist - VIEWTH

What is a Limit
16mm
B&W
Explains that mathematical analysis in founded on the concept of a limit. Discusses the ideas behind a limit.
Mathematics
Dist - OPENU Prod - OPENU

What is a Lutheran
VHS
Color (G R)
$19.95 purchase _ #87EE1014
Discusses Lutheran origins, history and doctrines. Emphasizes Lutheranism in its American forms.
Guidance and Counseling; Literature and Drama; Religion and Philosophy
Dist - CPH Prod - CPH

What is a Machine 15 MIN
VHS / U-matic
Why Series
Color (P I)
Discusses the characteristics of a machine.
Science - Physical
Dist - AITECH Prod - WDCNTV 1976

What is a Magazine made of 20 MIN
16mm
Color
Shows how the Family Circle magazine comes into being each month. Depicts how the editorial features are created and how the magazine is assembled.
Literature and Drama; Social Science
Dist - CCNY Prod - FAMLYC

What is a Mammal 14 MIN
16mm / U-matic / VHS
Biology (Spanish Series Unit 7 - Animal Classification and 'Physiology; Unit 7 - Animal classification and physiology
Color (H) (SPANISH)
Demonstrates the basic structural and behavioral characteristics of mammals and describes their successful adaptation to a wide variety of ecological niches. Discusses the evolution of mammals and shows their distribution.
Foreign Language; Science - Natural
Dist - EBEC Prod - EBEC

What is a Microprocessor? 30 MIN
VHS / U-matic
Programming Microprocessors Series
Color (IND)
Presents in four videotapes simplest architecture to get by, save costs and reduce design time. Depicts minimum hardware configuration. Demonstrates simple tasks by example.
Industrial and Technical Education; Mathematics; Sociology
Dist - COLOSU Prod - COLOSU

What is a Mountain 23 MIN
16mm
Color (I J)
LC FIE68-19
Presents a study of Mount Rainier, including its geology, life and history.
Geography - United States; Science - Physical
Dist - USNAC Prod - USNPS 1967

What is a Painting / Realism
U-matic / VHS
Metropolitan Museum Seminars in Art Series
Color
Introduces the principles of art appreciation and explains technique, composition and personal expression. Traces realism in painting from Van Eyck to Hopper.
Fine Arts
Dist - GA Prod - GA

What is a Physician Assistant 30 MIN
U-matic / VHS
Color
Guidance and Counseling
Dist - SYLWAT Prod - RCOMTV 1984

What is a plant 15 MIN
VHS / U-matic / 16mm / BETA
Kingdom of plants series
Color (P I)
$245.50, $68.00 purchase _ #C50672, #C51453
Examines the different parts of a plant - roots, stems and leaves - and outlines their functions. Uses animation to reveal the food - making process of photosynthesis. Examines the plant life cycle to show how pollination enables flowers to produce seeds for the next generation of plants. Explores different kinds of plants, from simple algae and mosses to the tall trees of a tropical rain forest and their habitats. Part of a five - part series on the plant kingdom.
Science - Natural
Dist - NGS Prod - NGS 1991

What is a plant 15 MIN
VHS
Kingdom of plants series
Color; PAL (K P)
Examines the different parts of a plant. Outlines the functions of roots, stems and leaves. Uses animation to reveal the foodmaking process of photosynthesis. Illustrates the life - cycle of a plant and explores the different types of plants and their habitats. Part of a series on the Kingdom of plants.

Science - Natural
Dist - VIEWTH

What is a Policeman 12 MIN
16mm
Color (I J)
LC 70-701675
Discusses, for young people, the role of the policeman in society. Points out that a policeman is like other men, but that his uniform and badge make him stand out as a man who enforces the law. Explains who makes the laws, how changing times have created changes in the laws and what would happen if there were no laws.
Civics and Political Systems; Social Science
Dist - AVED **Prod** - GOLDSF 1969

What is a print 25 MIN
VHS / U-matic
Artist in print series
Color (H C A)
Explains the various categories of 'print' available on the market to potential buyers, what is original and what is a reproduction. Demonstrates the making of a Turner print by the Tate Gallery in London.
Fine Arts
Dist - FI **Prod** - BBCTV

What is a Reptile 18 MIN
U-matic / VHS / 16mm
Biology Series Unit 7 - Animal Classification and Physiology; Unit 7 - Animal classification and physiology
Color; B&W (H)
Describes four orders of reptiles and discusses their physical characteristics, reproductive processes and evolutionary development. Discusses reasons for the reptile's successful evolution and survival.
Science - Natural
Dist - EBEC **Prod** - EBEC 1961

What is a Reptile 18 MIN
U-matic / VHS / 16mm
Biology - Spanish Series Unit 7 - Animal Classification and Physiology; Unit 7 - Animal classification and physiology
Color (H) (SPANISH)
Points out representatives of each of the four orders of reptiles. Describes their physical characteristics, reproductive processes and evolutionary development.
Foreign Language; Science - Natural
Dist - EBEC **Prod** - EBEC

What is a seed 15 MIN
BETA / VHS / U-matic / 16mm
Kingdom of plants series
Color (P I)
$245.50, $68.00 purchase _ #C50669, #C51452
Reveals that seeds can be larger than a fist or no bigger than a speck of dust. Shows that a seed is the beginning and end of a plant's life cycle. Illustrates the different ways in which seeds are dispersed. Uses time - lapse photography of seed germination to reveal how new generations of plants are born. Part of a five - part series on the plant kingdom.
Science - Natural
Dist - NGS **Prod** - NGS 1991

What is a seed 15 MIN
VHS
Kingdom of plants series
Color; PAL (K P)
Examines the wide variety in size and shape of seeds. Shows how seeds are dispersed. Presents a time - lapse sequence of seed germiation. Part of a series on the Kingdom of plants.
Science - Natural
Dist - VIEWTH

What is a Set, Pt 1 14 MIN
16mm
MAA Elementary Arithmetic Series
Color (P T)
Uses a variety of concrete illustrations to develop the concept of a set. Introduces and illustrates braces to indicate a set, elements of a set, capital letters as names of sets and lower case letters for members of a set.
Mathematics
Dist - MLA **Prod** - MAA 1967

What is a Set, Pt 2 7 MIN
16mm
MAA Elementary Arithmetic Series
Color (P T)
Uses animation to introduce the set - builder notation for a set, the concept of a subset, the notion of an empty set, the use of Venn diagrams for sets and the intuitive idea of the intersection of two sets.
Mathematics
Dist - MLA **Prod** - MAA 1967

What is a Short Story 14 MIN
16mm / U-matic / VHS
Humanities - Short Story Classics Series
Color (J H)
LC 80-701810
Illustrates the art of the short story form, including plot, theme, motivation, characterization, mood and style. Features commentary by Clifton Fadiman.
Fine Arts; Literature and Drama
Dist - EBEC **Prod** - EBEC 1980

What is a short story - a discussion by Clifton Fadiman 14 MIN
VHS
Color (J H)
$99.00 purchase _ #47834 - 026
Illustrates the art of the short story form. Focuses on plot, theme, motivation, characterization, mood and style. Includes teacher's guide.
Education; Literature and Drama
Dist - GA **Prod** - EBEC

What is a Simple Sentence? 14.27 MIN
U-matic / VHS
Grammar Mechanic
(I J)
Designed to help intermediate students apply the rules of grammar. Introduces students to the simple sentence. Shows how to correct run on sentences and sentence fragments. Uses dramatization. First in a sixteen part series.
English Language
Dist - GPN **Prod** - WDCNTV

What is a String Quartet 15 MIN
U-matic / VHS
Chamber Music - the String Quartet Series
Color (I J H)
Fine Arts
Dist - AITECH **Prod** - NETCHE 1977

What is a teacher 30 MIN
VHS
Effective teacher telecourse series
Color (T)
$69.95 purchase, $50.00 rental
Discusses the characteristics of a teacher. Hosted by Dr Loren Anderson.
Education; Psychology
Dist - SCETV **Prod** - SCETV 1987

What is a Teenager 30 MIN
16mm
Dial C - 12 - 18 for Family Understanding Series
B&W (J)
LC 74-700168
Attempts to dispel some of the misconceptions about adolescence and to introduce an understanding of this stage of physical and psychological development.
Guidance and Counseling; Psychology; Sociology
Dist - UNEBR **Prod** - UNL 1970

What is a Texan 8 MIN
U-matic / VHS / Slide
Color; Mono (J H)
Overview of the ethnic diversity of early Texas settlers. Sketches of interesting individuals who helped settle and shape the state.
Education; History - United States
Dist - UTXITC **Prod** - UTXITC 1970

What is a Tree 7 MIN
U-matic / VHS / 16mm
Color (P I)
Pictures the natural beauty of trees during the seasons and follows a young boy's developing appreciation for the value of trees.
Science - Natural
Dist - AIMS **Prod** - PRECFI 1965

What is a Wedge 4 MIN
U-matic / VHS
Way Things Work Series
Color (K)
$149.95, $49.95 purchase _ #AD - 1639
Shows that wedges exert force in two directions - forward and up. Demonstrates the difference between thin wedges and thick wedges. Part of a thirty - part series on the way things work hosted by Bob Symes.
Science; Science - Physical
Dist - FOTH **Prod** - FOTH

What is a Word Processor 24 MIN
16mm
Color (A)
Presents John Cleese explaining the capabilities of word processors. Demonstrates the processor's ease of storage, correction, formatting, reorganizing and printing documents.
Business and Economics; Mathematics
Dist - VISUCP **Prod** - VISUCP 1983

What is a Word Processor? 24 MIN
U-matic / VHS
Color
Demonstrates the ease of storage, correction, formatting, reorganizing and printing documents of a word processor.
Mathematics
Dist - VISUCP **Prod** - VIDART

What is a Word Processor? 28 MIN
VHS / U-matic
Color (A)
Explains and demonstrates, using humorous illustrations, how a word processor works and what it can do to improve work flow. Focuses on allaying fears of the machine.
Business and Economics; Industrial and Technical Education
Dist - XICOM **Prod** - XICOM

What is AIDS 16 MIN
VHS
Color (P I J H)
Describes how the AIDS virus damages the human immune system in easy to understand terms. Shows how to prevent AIDS infection and dispells many of the myths surrounding the disease.
Health and Safety; Sociology
Dist - VIEWTH **Prod** - VIEWTH

What is AIDS - 1 19 MIN
VHS
Coping with AIDS series
Color (H C G)
$250.00 purchase, $60.00 rental
Reviews how the HIV virus disables the immune system, rendering people with AIDS susceptible to opportunistic infections. Discusses symptoms which may signal the onset of AIDS and outlines some common coping strategies. Part of a five - part series for persons with AIDS and those involved with them, detailing medical and social aspects of living with AIDS. Resources are listed at the end of each program.
Health and Safety
Dist - CF **Prod** - HOSSN 1989

What is Air 15 MIN
VHS / U-matic
Why Series
Color (P I)
Discusses the characteristics of air.
Science - Physical
Dist - AITECH **Prod** - WDCNTV 1976

What is Air Pressure 6 MIN
U-matic / VHS
Way Things Work Series
Color (K)
$149.95, $49.95 purchase _ #AD - 1661
Reveals the power of air pressure through a simple experiment with an ordinary tin can which is heated and then sealed tight. Part of a thirty - part series on the way things work hosted by Bob Symes.
Science; Science - Physical
Dist - FOTH **Prod** - FOTH

What is America 72 MIN
U-matic / VHS
Milton Friedman Speaking Series Lecture 1
Color (C)
LC 79-708059
Features economist Milton Friedman reviewing the problems and accomplishments of America. Notes that restoration of the free market is the only way the country can regain its prestige and influence.
Business and Economics; History - United States
Dist - HBJ **Prod** - HBJ 1980

What is America, Pt 1 36 MIN
U-matic / VHS
Milton Friedman Speaking Series Lecture 1
Color (C)
LC 79-708059
Features economist Milton Friedman reviewing the problems and accomplishments of America. Notes that restoration of the free market is the only way the country can regain its prestige and influence.
Business and Economics
Dist - HBJ **Prod** - HBJ 1980

What is America, Pt 2 36 MIN
VHS / U-matic
Milton Friedman Speaking Series Lecture 1
Color (C)
LC 79-708059
Features economist Milton Friedman reviewing the problems and accomplishments of America. Notes that restoration of the free market is the only way the country can regain its prestige and influence.
Business and Economics
Dist - HBJ **Prod** - HBJ 1980

What is American Music 54 MIN
U-matic / VHS / 16mm
Young People's Concerts Series
B&W (I)
LC FIA67-218
Features Leonard Bernstein, who traces the development of American music as the basis of a school of composition, presents orchestral selections to illustrate various periods and analyzes the elements that characterize American concert music. Features Gershwin, Schuman, Harris, Thompson and Copland.
Fine Arts
Dist - MGHT **Prod** - CBSTV 1967

What is American Music, Pt 1 27 MIN
U-matic / VHS / 16mm
Young People's Concerts Series
B&W (I J H)
Features Leonard Bernstein, who traces the development of American music as the basis of a school of composition, presents orchestral selections to illustrate various periods and analyzes the elements that characterize American concert music. Features Gershwin, Schuman, Harris, Thompson and Copland.
Fine Arts
Dist - MGHT **Prod** - CBSTV 1967

What is American Music, Pt 2 27 MIN
U-matic / VHS / 16mm
Young People's Concerts Series
B&W (I J H)
Features Leonard Bernstein, who traces the development of American music as the basis of a school of composition, presents orchestral selections to illustrate various periods and analyzes the elements that characterize American concert music. Features Gershwin, Schuman, Harris, Thompson and Copland.
Fine Arts
Dist - MGHT **Prod** - CBSTV 1967

What is an Actuary 29 MIN
VHS / U-matic
Color
Guidance and Counseling
Dist - SYLWAT **Prod** - RCOMTV 1983

What Is an American, Pt 1 10 MIN
16mm / VHS / U-matic
Who We are Series
Color (P I)
LC 79-701215; 79-707039
Uses animation and live action to portray America's diverse heritage and to explain the concepts of culture and immigration. Shows how individual ethnic groups have enriched the American experience, using the Puerto Rican and American Indian cultures as examples.
Civics and Political Systems; Social Science; Sociology
Dist - PFP **Prod** - COLOSP 1979

What is an American, Pt 2 12 MIN
16mm / VHS / U-matic
Who We are Series
Color (P I)
LC 79-701215; 79-707039
Uses animation and live action to portray America's diverse heritage and to explain the concepts of culture and immigration. Shows how individual ethnic groups have enriched the American experience, using the Puerto Rican and American Indian cultures as examples.
Civics and Political Systems; Social Science; Sociology
Dist - PFP **Prod** - COLOSP 1979

What is an Amphibian 11 MIN
U-matic / VHS / 16mm
Biology (Spanish Series Unit 7 - Animal Classification and 'Physiology); Unit 7 - Animal classification and physiology
Color (H) (SPANISH)
Examines the body and life cycle of the amphibian. Presents the development of an amphibian from egg to maturity and traces the origin and evolution of the amphibian.
Foreign Language; Science - Natural
Dist - EBEC **Prod** - EBEC

What is an atom 16 MIN
VHS
Color; CC (H C)
$79.00 purchase _ #901
Helps students to understand what an atom is and its role in modern scientific concepts. Discusses the periodic table of elements, protons, electrons, neutrons, alpha particles, molecular structure, carbon chemistry, DNA. Part 2 of the program The Atom. Includes a book of the same title from the Learning Power series.
Science - Physical
Dist - HAWHIL **Prod** - HAWHIL 1994

What is an eclipse 11 MIN
U-matic / VHS / BETA
Color; NTSC; PAL; SECAM (J H)
PdS58
Uses animation and three - dimensional models to illustrate how the motion of the Moon around the Earth causes both solar and lunar eclipses. Shows how an eclipse of the Sun occurs when the moon passes between the Earth and the Sun, an eclipse of the Moon occurs when the Moon passes into the shadow of the Earth. Explains why lunar and solar eclipses don't occur each month. Uses time - lapse and telescopic motion pictures of both lunar and solar eclipses. Illustrates new astronomical telescopes and discusses what these new telescopes have disovered about eclipses and the sun.
Science - Physical
Dist - VIEWTH

What is an Eclipse 11 MIN
16mm / U-matic / VHS
Color (I J H C) (SPANISH)
Uses animation and three - dimensional models to show how the motion of the Moon around the Earth causes both solar and lunar eclipses.
Foreign Language
Dist - PHENIX **Prod** - FA 1965

What is an Element 2 MIN
16mm
Color
Uses animation to define the elements and their physical and chemical properties.
Science - Physical
Dist - CUYAHO **Prod** - CUYAHO 1967

What is an Integral 61 MIN
16mm
Maa Individual Lecturers Series Collegiate
Color (H C T)
Professor Edwin Hewitt proves five properties that characterize the Riemann integral. He defines averages and describes the Riesz - representation theorem, giving the construction of the weight function necessary to make the average a Stieltjes integral.
Mathematics
Dist - MLA **Prod** - MAA 1965

What is an Integral, Pt 1, Integrals are Averages 29 MIN
16mm
MAA Individual Lecturers Series
Color (H C T)
Professor Edwin Hewitt proves five properties that characterize the Riemann integral.
Mathematics
Dist - MLA **Prod** - MAA 1965

What is an Integral, Pt 2, Averages are Integrals 29 MIN
16mm
MAA Individual Lecturers Series
Color (H C T)
Professor Edwin Hewitt defines averages and describes the Riesz - representation theorem, giving the construction of the weight function necessary to make the average a Stieltjes integral.
Mathematics
Dist - MLA **Prod** - MAA 1965

What is Area 20 MIN
16mm
MAA Calculus Series
Color (H C)
Defines the area of a given region as the common limit of the areas of inner and outer polygonal approximations. Uses the circle to illustrate that this definition is consistent with previous notions. An animated film narrated by Charles E Rickart.
Mathematics
Dist - MLA **Prod** - MAA 1967

What is Arthritis?
U-matic / VHS
Color
Defines arthritis along with its symptoms.
Health and Safety
Dist - MIFE **Prod** - MIFE

What is Autumn 7 MIN
16mm
Science Series
Color (K P I)
The meaning of autumn for people, animals and plants.
Science - Natural
Dist - SF **Prod** - MORLAT 1967

What is benchmarking? 16 MIN
VHS
Color (IND)
$495.00 purchase, $150.00 rental _ #VC015
Explores the benchmarking process through case studies from Xerox and Toyota of Australia. Includes a leader's guide. Produced by Video Communicators.
Business and Economics
Dist - EXTR

What is biosecurity 11 MIN
U-matic / VHS
Biosecurity and the poultry industry series
Color (IND)
$40.00, $95.00 purchase _ #TCA18193, #TCA18192
Presents an overview of biosecurity.
Agriculture; Health and Safety
Dist - USNAC **Prod** - USDA 1989

What is camera ready copy 21 MIN
VHS
Color (H C)
$79.95 purchase _ #SE - 11
Shows customers the relationship between mechanicals and the negatives and plates and how they can have a great deal of control over the quality, schedule and cost of printing.
Business and Economics; Industrial and Technical Education
Dist - INSTRU

What is Cancer 21 MIN
16mm
Color (PRO)
Explains the biology of cancer. Emphasizes the role of the nurse in early diagnosis and rehabilitation of patients who have undergone treatment. Combines scenes from operating room and clinic with animation showing how cancer begins, spreads and can be treated.
Health and Safety
Dist - AMCS **Prod** - AMCS 1962

What is Capitalism?
U-matic / VHS / 35mm strip
Political Ideologies of the Twentieth Century - Understanding the 'Isms Series
(J H C)
$109.00 purchase=FS, $139.00 purchase=MV _ 06110 94
Examines the evolution of capitalist thought from the theory of Adam Smith through such concepts as the ownership of private capital and the operation of a free market based on supply and demand. Features historical photography. In 2 parts.
Business and Economics
Dist - ASPRSS **Prod** - GA

What is Cerebral Palsy 20 MIN
16mm
Color (A)
Diagrams the nature of cerebral palsy and how the brain injury affects the individual.
Health and Safety; Psychology; Science - Natural
Dist - UCPA **Prod** - UCPA 1948

What is 'channeling' 30 MIN
VHS / BETA
Channels and channeling series
Color (G)
$29.95 purchase _ #S370
Explores the phenomenon known as spirit communication, trance mediumship or 'channeling.' Features Dr Arthur Hastings, psychologist. Part of a four - part series on channels and channeling.
Psychology; Religion and Philosophy
Dist - THINKA **Prod** - THINKA

What is chemistry 24 MIN
VHS
Chemistry 101 series
Color (C A)
$50.00 purchase _ #S01196
Presents a basic introduction to chemistry, as taught in the introductory freshman - level class at the University of Illinois. Utilizes both lectures and demonstrations to illustrate the various concepts.
Science; Science - Physical
Dist - UILL **Prod** - UILL

What is Christmas 10 MIN
16mm / U-matic / VHS
Color (K P I) (SPANISH)
LC 74-702052;
Presents the story of the Nativity as seen through the eyes of a young boy and his puppy.
Religion and Philosophy
Dist - AIMS **Prod** - FLEMRP 1972

What is Clay 28 MIN
Videoreel / VT2
Wheels, Kilns and Clay Series
Color
Features Mrs Peterson describing certain ceramic processes for her classroom at the University of Southern California. Includes the art of working with clay.
Fine Arts
Dist - PBS **Prod** - USC

What is Communication? 15 MIN
U-matic / VHS
Arts Express Series
Color (K P I J)
Fine Arts
Dist - KYTV **Prod** - KYTV 1983

What is Communication 30 MIN
16mm
Dial C - 12 - 18 for Family Understanding Series
B&W (J)
LC 74-700169
Defines the communication process and illustrates ways in which adolescents communicate with themselves, their peers, their parents and other adults.
Guidance and Counseling; Psychology; Sociology
Dist - UNEBR **Prod** - UNEBR 1970

What is Communism?
U-matic / VHS / 35mm strip
Political Idelogies of the Twentieth Century - Understanding the 'Isms.
(J H C)
$109.00 purchase=FS, $139.00 purchase=MV _ #06108 94
Reviews the history and leaders of Soviet communism. Presents alternate models in Yugoslavia and Cuba. Considers the international response to Soviet repression of opposing and liberalizing movements in Hungary and Czechoslavakia. Examines the hisitory of Chinese communism and explores the Maoist philosophy. In 2 parts.
Civics and Political Systems
Dist - ASPRSS **Prod** - GA

What is Conditioning 35 MIN
16mm
Color
Illustrates the importance of planning an overall conditioning program tailored to specific individual needs. Considers the cardio - pulmonary and neuro - muscular systems, body flexibility and weight control.
Physical Education and Recreation
Dist - MTP **Prod** - SC 1982

What is Configuration Managment 60 MIN
BETA / VHS
Manufacturing Series
(IND)
Teaches the purposes of configuration management, its costs and benefits and identifies the functional areas it affects.
Business and Economics
Dist - COMSRV **Prod** - COMSRV 1986

What is corporate video 28 MIN
VHS
Color (H C)
$39.95 purchase _ #IVMCCV
Shows how more and more companies and agencies are using videos to get out their messages. Examines this new application of video. Defines what is meant by corporate video by experts in the field. Illustrates many applications and examples of how video media is used by various types of organizations.
Business and Economics; Social Science
Dist - INSTRU

What is Corrosion 25 MIN
VHS / U-matic
Oil Field Corrosion Series
Color (IND)
Gives basic corrosion terminology and explains the mechanism of corrosion.
Business and Economics; Industrial and Technical Education; Social Science
Dist - UTEXPE **Prod** - UTEXPE

What is diabetes 12 MIN
VHS
Color (PRO A)
$250.00 purchase _ #DB - 20
Uses animation to depict the action of insulin and glucose in the body and shows how the process is disrupted when diabetes develops. Explores the roles of nutrition, exercise and medication in controlling the condition. Teaches viewers about skin and food care, eye care and the importance of reducing risk factors of cardiovascular disease.
Health and Safety
Dist - MIFE **Prod** - MIFE 1991

What is Dimension
16mm
B&W
Discusses vector spaces and shows how to express 'dimension' of geometric space in terms of 'vector space language.'.
Mathematics
Dist - OPENU **Prod** - OPENU

What is Discipline 30 MIN
U-matic
Parent Puzzle Series
(A)
Demonstrates the difference between punishment, often a negative means of altering behavior, and discipline, teaching new positive behavior.
Psychology; Sociology
Dist - ACCESS **Prod** - ACCESS 1982

What is Discipline, Anyway 29 MIN
16mm / U-matic / VHS
Human Relations and School Discipline Series
Color (C)
Provides answers to the question, 'WHAT IS DISCIPLINE, ANYWAY,' which reveals a montage of viewpoints around the central theme of school discipline, what it is and how to achieve it within a framework of realistic, enforceable rules. Differentiates between discipline and punishment.
Education; Sociology
Dist - FI **Prod** - MFFD

What is Disease 11 MIN
U-matic / VHS / 16mm
Health for the Americas Series
Color
Explains that disease can be caused by tiny creatures so small that they cannot be seen without a microscope, and suggests ways to protect oneself against disease. Issued in 1946 as a motion picture.
Health and Safety
Dist - USNAC **Prod** - USOIAA 1980

What is Disease - Unseen Enemy 11 MIN
16mm
Health for the Americas Series
Color (SPANISH)
LC FIE52-541
Uses animation to show how germs and microbes cause sickness and outlines simple preventive measures.
Health and Safety
Dist - USNAC **Prod** - USIA 1945

What is Dizziness and Why Does it Happen? 60 MIN
U-matic / VHS
Dizziness and Related Balance Disorders Series
Color
Health and Safety
Dist - GSHDME **Prod** - GSHDME

What is Easter 11 MIN
U-matic / VHS / 16mm
Color (P I) (SPANISH)
Tells the story of the first Easter as a fairy tale.
Religion and Philosophy; Social Science
Dist - AIMS **Prod** - COUNTR 1976

What is Ecology 21 MIN
16mm / U-matic / VHS
Color (H) (SPANISH)
A Spanish language version of the film and videorecording What Is Ecology.
Foreign Language; Science - Natural
Dist - EBEC **Prod** - EBEC 1977

What is Ecology 21 MIN
16mm / U-matic / VHS
Color (H)
Illustrates basic terms in the science of ecology. Features specific ecosystems and explores the ways in which plant and animal species are related to each other.
Science - Natural
Dist - EBEC **Prod** - EBEC 1978

What is Economics?
U-matic / VHS / 35mm strip
Introducing the Social Sciences Series
(J H C)
$109.00 purchase=FS, $139.00=MV _ 06103 94
Demonstrates the scientific nature and purposes of economics. Outlines the major types of economic systems and explores the mechanisms, assumptions and values of the American economic system. Demonstrates how values and priorities shape the decisions which direct the economy. In 2 parts.
Business and Economics; Guidance and Counseling
Dist - ASPRSS **Prod** - GA

What is Economics about 45 MIN
U-matic / VHS
Economic Perspectives Series
Color
Gives an overview of the topics which are studied in economics.
Business and Economics
Dist - MDCPB **Prod** - MDCPB

What is EDP Auditing 30 MIN
VHS / U-matic
Auditing EDP Systems Series
Color
Explains the need for Electronic Data Processing (EDP) auditing and outines the role of the EDP auditor. Discusses the relatinship of the EDP auditing function to the organization with particular emphasis on the relationship to data processing.
Industrial and Technical Education; Psychology
Dist - DELTAK **Prod** - DELTAK

What is Electric Current 14 MIN
U-matic / VHS / 16mm
Color (I J)
Shows how electric current works. Demonstrations and charts are used to show that electric charges flow as electric current.
Science - Physical
Dist - EBEC **Prod** - EBEC 1961

What is Electricity 5 MIN
U-matic / VHS / 16mm
Basic Electricity Series
Color (H C A)
Discusses electrons, protons, charges, free electrons, conducting and non - conducting materials and electron flow.
Science - Physical
Dist - IFB **Prod** - STFD 1979

What is Emphysema? 14 MIN
VHS / U-matic
Color (SPANISH FRENCH)
LC 71-7391224; 71-739124
Describes the causes of emphysema, especially the effects of smoking on the lungs and brochi. Emphasizes the need to alter life style to control the disease.
Foreign Language; Health and Safety; Science - Natural
Dist - MEDCOM **Prod** - MEDCOM

What is Ethics? 30 MIN
VHS / U-matic
Ethics in America Series
Color (H C A)
Defines ethics in the broad sense and discusses ethical applications in contemporary terms. A video presentation of Sidney Hooks, author of Reform And Social Justice.
Religion and Philosophy
Dist - AMHUMA **Prod** - AMHUMA

What is Family Day Care 28.5 MIN
VHS / 16mm
B&W (C A H)
$90.00 - $125.00 purchase, $16.00 rental
Examines family day care homes. Discusses the rewards and problems involved.
Sociology
Dist - CORNRS **Prod** - CORNRS 1972

What is Family Day Care 28 MIN
U-matic / VHS / 16mm
B&W
Examines family day care homes in Ithaca, New York. Shows that the quality of care does not depend upon the luxury of the setting, but rather on the talent and dedication of women serving in the day care mother role.
Home Economics; Sociology
Dist - CORNRS **Prod** - CUETV 1972

What is Fascism?
U-matic / VHS / 35mm strip
Political Ideologies of the Twentieth Century - Understanding the 'Isms Series
(J H C) (LATIN)
$109.00 purchase=FS, $139.00 purchase=MV _ #06147 94
Outlines the basic features of fascism and compares World War II European dictatorship to the beliefs held by the U S Fascists and to the policies of certain Latin American governments. Explores conditions in Europe leading to the rise of Mussolini and Hitler and examines the ideology of the American Nazi party. In 2 parts.
Civics and Political Systems
Dist - ASPRSS **Prod** - GA

What is Fitness
VHS
Dynamics of Fitness - the Body in Action Series
Color
Reviews the components of physical fitness and explains the benefits of fitness.
Health and Safety; Physical Education and Recreation
Dist - IBIS **Prod** - IBIS

What is Fitness Exercise 11 MIN
16mm / U-matic / VHS
Fitness and Me Series
Color (P)
Presents the tale of a good sorceress who teaches a scrawny knight the value of physical fitness for his general health and for his knightly pursuits. Tells how he learns about the five elements of physical fitness.
Physical Education and Recreation
Dist - CORF **Prod** - DISNEY

What is geology 20 MIN
VHS
Color (J H)
$19.95 purchase _ #IV101
Overviews the science of geology. Looks at paleontology, mineralogy, geomorphology, glaciology, volcanism, petrology, movement in the Earth's crust and geologic time.
Science - Physical
Dist - INSTRU

What is Gestalt 24 MIN
U-matic / VHS / 16mm
Gestalt Series
Color (H C)
LC 79-706494
Dr Frederick Perls explains the basic principles of Gestalt therapy to a group of people with one person becoming the subject for an introduction to 'AWARENESS TRAINING.'.
Guidance and Counseling; Psychology
Dist - FI **Prod** - PMI 1969

What is God Like 30 MIN
16mm
What Series
(J H C G T A)
Religion and Philosophy
Dist - WHLION **Prod** - WHLION

What is God Like, and what Does the Future Hold 30 MIN
16mm
What Series
(J H C G T A)
Designed to encourage individuals to evaluate their faith and share their beliefs with others in the group. Filmed on three separate continents, where people were asked, 'what is God like?'.
Religion and Philosophy
Dist - WHLION **Prod** - WHLION

What is God like - what does the future hold 30 MIN
VHS
Color (J H C G A R)
$19.99 purchase, $10.00 rental _ #35 - 867137 - 533
Interviews people from three continents on their views of God and the future. Produced by White Lion.
Religion and Philosophy
Dist - APH

What is Going on Up There? 28 MIN
16mm
Color (G)
_ #106C 0180 534
Asks what Americans know about their neighbor in the north. Touches bilingualism, national unity, economic relationship with the U S combining animation and live action. Interviews well known Canadian writers, eonomists, philosophers and men and women on the street.
Geography - World; Sociology
Dist - CFLMDC **Prod** - NFBC 1980

What is Good Writing Series
Thinking made Visible 70 MIN
Dist - USNAC

What is Harness Racing 15 MIN
BETA / VHS
Color
Introduces harness racing. Compare gaits of trotters and pacers.
Physical Education and Recreation
Dist - EQVDL **Prod** - USTROT

What is Humanism? 30 MIN
VHS / U-matic
Moral Values in Contemporary Society Series
Color (J)
Features Corliss Lamont, author of Voice In The Wilderness, defining humanism.
Religion and Philosophy; Sociology
Dist - AMHUMA **Prod** - AMHUMA

What is Inflation 13 MIN
U-matic / VHS / 16mm
Color (J)
LC 75-702972
Defines the concept of inflation and the options open to government in dealing with it. Reconstructs the political, social and natural factors which have given rise to the new phenomemon of stagflation.
Business and Economics; Civics and Political Systems; Social Science
Dist - PHENIX **Prod** - ABCNEW 1975

What is ISO 9000, and why do I care 33 MIN
VHS
Color (PRO IND A)
$450.00 purchase, $95.00 rental _ #BBP142
Demonstrates how two companies became ISO certified. Explains to managers what the ISO 9000 standards are, the beginning and nature of the certification process, and how the standards can help their organization improve their profitability and quality. Includes Companion Leader's Guide.
Business and Economics
Dist - EXTR **Prod** - BBP

What is it Out There 20 MIN
16mm
Color
Presents play - test instruments which test and record the response of infants to their environment. Discusses applications for helping handicapped children enrich their experiences.
Health and Safety; Psychology
Dist - CWRU **Prod** - CWRU 1967

What is Justice 29 MIN
VHS / 16mm
A Different Understanding Series
Color (G)
$90.00 purchase _ #BPN178017
Explores the juvenile system. Compares the judges' and experts' views of the issues with the perceptions of a young criminal offender in training school. Shows the effects of the training school envronment on the identity and development of the antisocial teenager. Taken from the program `Sharp And Terrible Eyes'.
Sociology
Dist - RMIBHF **Prod** - RMIBHF

What is Justice 29 MIN
U-matic
A Different Understanding Series
Color (PRO)
Explores the juvenile justice system with interviews of a young offender in training school and of judges and experts in the field.
Civics and Political Systems
Dist - TVOTAR **Prod** - TVOTAR 1985

What is Kundalini 30 MIN
VHS / BETA
Meditative experience series
Color (G)
$29.95 purchase _ #S062
Describes in detail the changes in the brain and nervous system which can result from intensive spiritual disciplines. Discusses Kundalini, which refers to energy coiled at the base of the spine which can rise up to the brain. Features Dr Lee Sannella, author of 'Kundalini - Psychosis or Transcendence.' Part of a four - part series on the meditative experience.
Religion and Philosophy; Science - Natural
Dist - THINKA **Prod** - THINKA

What is Leadership? 14 MIN
U-matic / VHS
Man Management and Rig Management Series Lesson 2
Color (IND)
Defines leadership and describes its value in the workplace. Highlights the importance of leadership in improved productivity and the relationship of leadership to effective management.
Business and Economics; Psychology
Dist - UTEXPE **Prod** - UTEXPE 1983

What is life 13 MIN
VHS
Color (J H)
$130.00 purchase _ #A5VH 1606
Asks if the question, 'What is life,' is possible to answer. Considers the characteristics of living things and shows how Francesco Redi - 1627 - 1698 - and Louis Pasteur - 1822 - 1895, using the scientific method of hypothesis, experimentation and conclusion, disproved the theory of the spontaneous generation of organisms. Examines the prevailing theory of how life arose and the experiment scientists constructed to show how life may have begun.
Science - Natural
Dist - CLRVUE **Prod** - CLRVUE 1992

What is life 11 MIN
VHS
Basic biology series
Color (I J)
$79.95 purchase _ #10044VG
Addresses the question of what it is that separates living things from the nonliving. Looks at life in a biological sense, from cells to life cycles. Comes with a teacher's guide, student activities, discussion questions, and six blackline masters.
Science - Natural
Dist - UNL

What is life 15 MIN
VHS
Biology live series
Color (I J) (SPANISH)
$129.00 purchase _ #GW - 5073 - VS, #GW - 5073 - SP
Describes the seven characteristics of living things in part of a 13 - part series on biology which uses high resolution animation, live - action photography and interesting narrative to teach a core curriculum in biological science.
Science - Natural
Dist - HRMC

What is Love 29 MIN
16mm
Real Revolution - Talks by Krishnamurti Series
B&W
LC 73-703036
Features Indian spiritual leader Krishnamurti who discusses how we can try to discover what love is. States that in order to find the meaning of love the mind must be sensitive, energetic and free of all desire and pleasure.
Guidance and Counseling; Religion and Philosophy
Dist - IU **Prod** - KQEDTV 1968

What is Love 30 MIN
BETA / VHS
Mister Rogers - Conceptual Behavior Series
Color (P I J)
Helps children understand the many facets of love. Uses an example to show that people who make each other angry can still love each other very much. Features Mister Rogers.
Guidance and Counseling; Psychology
Dist - BRENTM **Prod** - BRENTM

What is M B O 13 MIN
VHS / U-matic
Practical M B O Series
Color
Business and Economics; Education; Psychology
Dist - DELTAK **Prod** - DELTAK

What is Managing? 72 FRS
VHS / U-matic
Improving Managerial Skills Series
Color
Lists the essential managerial skills, such as.perception, decision - making communicating, organizing and planning what they really mean and how to tell if they are being done well.
Business and Economics; Psychology
Dist - RESEM **Prod** - RESEM

What is Managment? 23 MIN
U-matic / VHS
Man Management and Rig Management Series Lesson 1
Color (IND)
Demonstrates the value of basic management skills such as planning, coordinating and instructing. Discusses who is responsible for developing these skills and how their absence usually results in inefficiency.
Business and Economics; Psychology
Dist - UTEXPE **Prod** - UTEXPE 1983

What is Marketing 15 MIN
16mm / U-matic / VHS
Captioned; Color
Uses animation to tell the story of Edwin, the first Iron Age marketing manager. Shows him unearthing the principles of a sound marketing operation.
Business and Economics
Dist - RTBL **Prod** - RANKAV

What is marketing electronic information - and hot trends
VHS
Marketing electronic information series
Color (G C PRO)
$195.00 purchase
Shows how to market electronic information on the INTERNET. Discusses the six hottest trends in software marketing. Part of an eight - part series on marketing electronic information.
Business and Economics
Dist - DEJAVI **Prod** - DEJAVI

What is Mathematics and How do We Teach it 45 MIN
16mm
MAA Individual Lecturers Series
B&W (H C T)
LC FIA66-1277
Presents a panel discussion among top research mathematicians on the relation of counting circuits to group theory and other abstract mathematics. Covers the changing role of mathematics.
Mathematics
Dist - MLA **Prod** - MAA 1966

What is Mathematics and How do We Teach it, Pt 1 22 MIN
16mm
Mathematics Today Series
B&W (H C T)
Presents a panel idscussion among top research mathematicians on the relation of counting circuits to group theory and other abstract mathematics. Covers the changing role of mathematics.
Mathematics
Dist - MLA **Prod** - MAA 1966

What is Mathematics and How do We Teach it, Pt 2 23 MIN
16mm
Mathematics Today Series

B&W (H C T)
Presents a panel idscussion among top research mathematicians on the relation of counting circuits to group theory and other abstract mathematics. Covers the changing role of mathematics.
Mathematics
Dist - MLA **Prod** - MAA 1966

What is Measurement - Standards 10 MIN
16mm
Color (K P I J)
Discusses the need for units of measurement, how our present system of units came into being and the desireability of a standard universal system like the metric system.
Mathematics
Dist - SF **Prod** - SF 1970

What is Measurement - Standards 11 MIN
U-matic
Color (I J)
Offers a history of measurement in the western world. Explains why the metric system is the only system capable of simplifying international trade and communication.
Mathematics
Dist - SF **Prod** - SF 1974

What is medication - Module I 13 MIN
VHS / U-matic
Supervision of self administration of medication series
Color (PRO C)
$395.00 purchase, $80.00 rental _ #C920 - VI - 017
Defines medication for staff working with developmentally delayed clients. Stresses that the effectiveness of medication depends upon the right medication being used in the right manner. Cautions that medications can harm as well as heal and that they should be used and stored with care. Reviews the forms of medication, describes prescription and over - the - counter medications, defines generic drugs and examines the uses and abuses of medications. Part of a five - part series presented by the Richmond State School Staff Development, Texas Dept of Mental Health and Mental Retardation.
Health and Safety; Psychology
Dist - HSCIC

What is Money 11 MIN
16mm
Consumer Education Series
Color (P I J)
LC 72-702565
Discusses the history of money from barter to dollar bills, how money is earned, the meaning of the parents' pay, how far a dollar goes and the real value of money.
Business and Economics; Education; Home Economics; Social Science
Dist - SF **Prod** - SF 1970

What is music 58 MIN
VHS / U-matic
Nova series
Color (H C A)
$250.00 purchase _ #HP - 6175C
Investigates the nature of music. Explores music as the interplay of many things - the imagination of the composer, the skill of the instrument maker, the talent of the musician, the frequencies and modulation of sound waves, the sense of hearing and the brain's interpretation of what it hears. Part of the Nova series.
Fine Arts; Psychology
Dist - CORF **Prod** - WGBHTV 1989

What is New 52 MIN
U-matic / VHS / 16mm
Magic of Dance Series
Color (J)
Looks at the work of great dance pioneers, from the Commedia dell'Arte in 17th century Italy to Martha Graham in 20th century America.
Fine Arts
Dist - TIMLIF **Prod** - BBCTV 1980

What is news 14 MIN
VHS / U-matic
Inside television news series
Color (J H C)
$125.00, $175.00 purchase, $40.00 rental
Defines the parameters of what constitutes news, the differences between information delivery in television and newspapers, between opinion and fact, local and national news orientation.
Fine Arts; Literature and Drama; Social Science
Dist - NDIM **Prod** - LETHRV 1989

What is Normal 30 MIN
VHS / 16mm
Psychology - the Study of Human Behavior Series
Color (C A)
$99.95, $89.95 purchase _ 24 - 20
Explains the distinction between normal and abnormal.
Psychology
Dist - CDTEL **Prod** - COAST 1990

What is Nothing 9 MIN
U-matic / VHS / 16mm
Color (K P I)
LC 73-701550
Explores the concept of multiple meanings and shades of meaning of a common word. Follows two young boys as they explore many ways to use the word 'NOTHING' as they search for its meaning in the dictionary and during their everyday activities.
English Language
Dist - BARR **Prod** - BARR 1973

What is Organization Development? 61 FRS
VHS / U-matic
Organization Development Series Module 3
Color
Examines the role of the third party as the person who gets things said that others are afraid to say, brings people together and sees to it that actions are not only planned but carried out.
Business and Economics; Psychology
Dist - RESEM **Prod** - RESEM

What is past is prologue 30 MIN
U-matic / VHS
America - the second century series
Color (C H)
$34.95 purchase
Offers an analysis of prospects for the United States.
History - United States
Dist - DALCCD **Prod** - DALCCD
GPN

What is Philosophy 19 MIN
16mm / U-matic / VHS
Color (H C)
LC 76-702251
Presents an overview of philosophy as a discipline of inquiry and a process of reasoning. Made in Australia.
Religion and Philosophy
Dist - WOMBAT **Prod** - FLMAUS 1976

What is Physical Fitness 10 MIN
U-matic
Body Works Series
Color (P I J H)
Explains that physical fitness is a combination of flexibility, endurance and strength.
Physical Education and Recreation; Social Science
Dist - TVOTAR **Prod** - TVOTAR 1979

What is Physical Fitness 11 MIN
U-matic / VHS / 16mm
Fitness for Living Series
Color (J H)
Demonstrates the elements that constitute physical fitness, including cardio - respiratory endurance, muscle strength, muscle endurance, flexibility and body composition.
Physical Education and Recreation
Dist - CORF **Prod** - DISNEY 1982

What is Poetry 30 MIN
U-matic / VHS
Engle and Poetry Series
Color
Discusses poetry as an everyday language used to communicate emotion, mood and experience.
Literature and Drama
Dist - NETCHE **Prod** - NETCHE 1971

What is Poetry 10 MIN
U-matic / VHS / 16mm
Color (I J H)
Compares and contrasts a news report and a poem about one event, an auto wreck. Shows how the poet makes his poem an emotional experience.
Literature and Drama
Dist - PHENIX **Prod** - FA 1963

What is preterm labor 8 MIN
VHS / U-matic
Color (PRO C G)
$195.00 purchase _ #C870 - VI - 059
Presents for patient educators and patients the characteristics of women who are at greater risk of experiencing preterm labor, the physical signs that indicate preterm labor, steps that can be taken to prevent preterm labor and dispells common myths about preterm labor. Presented by RNs Mary C Brucker and Laura Mueller.
Health and Safety
Dist - HSCIC

What is probability - random variables - Parts 15 and 16 60 MIN
VHS / U-matic
Against all odds - inside statistics series
Color (C)
$45.00, $29.95 purchase
Presents parts 15 and 16 of 26 thirty - minute programs on statistics hosted by Dr Teresa Amabile of Brandeis University. Looks at the long - range relative frequency of an event. Distinguishes between deterministic and random phenomena. Shows how statisticians compute the probability of unusual events, with looks at independence, the multiplication rule for independent events, and discrete and continuous random variables. Produced by the Consortium for Mathematics and Its Applications - COMAP - and the American Statistical Association and American Society of Quality Control.
Mathematics; Psychology
Dist - ANNCPB

What is Psychology? 30 MIN
VHS / U-matic
Psychology of Human Relations Series
Color
Presents an overview, and the nature and scope of the field of Psychology. Examines the various perspectives from which psychologists look at behavior.
Psychology
Dist - WFVTAE **Prod** - MATC

What is Psychology 20 MIN
16mm / U-matic / VHS
Color (H C A)
LC 76-700574
Surveys the subject of psychology for high school students. Made in Australia.
Guidance and Counseling; Psychology
Dist - WOMBAT **Prod** - FLMAUS 1975

What is Psychology 30 MIN
VHS / 16mm
Psychology - the Study of Human Behavior Series
Color (C A)
$99.95, $89.95 purchase _ 24 - 01
Describes the nature of psychology and what its practitioners do.
Psychology
Dist - CDTEL **Prod** - COAST 1990

What is public relations 28 MIN
VHS
Color (H C)
$39.95 purchase _ #IVMCPR
Reveals that one of the fastest growing areas of mass communication is public relations. Overviews the field. Meets practitioners, including corporate, hospital, non - profit and government organizations. Defines the concept of public relations and shows the everyday applications of the field.
Business and Economics; Guidance and Counseling
Dist - INSTRU

What is Quality? 30 MIN
U-matic / VHS
Quality Planning Series
Color
Discusses the interrelationships among quality of design, quality of conformance to design and quality of performance.
Business and Economics; Industrial and Technical Education
Dist - MIOT **Prod** - MIOT

What is quality 18 MIN
VHS
Color (PRO A G)
$495.00 purchase, $100.00 rental
Defines quality as viewed by businessmen, employees, and young people. Examines the steps involved in achieving excellence.
Business and Economics; Psychology
Dist - EXTR **Prod** - EBEC

What is Safety Glass 10 MIN
U-matic / VHS
Way Things Work Series
Color (K)
$169.95, $69.95 purchase _ #AD - 1655
Looks at safety glass which is used for car windshields. Considers that it shatters into tiny crystals when it breaks. Part of a thirty - part series on the way things work hosted by Bob Symes.
Psychology; Science
Dist - FOTH **Prod** - FOTH

What is Salesmanship? 10 MIN
U-matic / 35mm strip
Basic Sales Series
Color
Introduces the idea that selling can be broken down into identifiable steps, each of which, when learned, can improve selling success.
Business and Economics; Psychology
Dist - RESEM **Prod** - RESEM

What is scarcity 17 MIN
VHS / U-matic
Real world economic series
Color (J H)
$240.00, $290.00 purchase, $60.00 rental
Includes material on natural resources, needs and wants, economic scarcity, free goods, resource use, factors of production, consumer and producer goods, rationing by vouchers and examples of opportunity cost.
Business and Economics; Geography - World
Dist - NDIM **Prod** - REALWO 1993

What is Schizophrenia
VHS
Schizophrenia - Removing the Veil Series
Color
Examines the symptoms of schizophrenia. Dispels common myths. Presents major diagnostic categories. Includes examples of the paranoid, the disorganized and the catatonic types.
Health and Safety; Psychology
Dist - IBIS **Prod** - IBIS

What is science 29 MIN
VHS / U-matic / 16mm
Color (J H G)
$250.00, $330.00, $545.00 purchase, $50.00 rental
Features an eclectic sampling of the different fields in science and scientific methodology. Helps students and non - specialists appreciate how scientists conduct research and why science is important to the development and survival of humankind.
History - World; Science
Dist - NDIM **Prod** - UNESCO 1985

What is science - an exploration of scientific methods and values today 17 MIN
VHS
Color (I J H C)
$59.00 purchase _ #915
Introduces the nature of science and scientists. Includes the book Scientific Methods and Values.
Science
Dist - HAWHIL **Prod** - HAWHIL

What is Sexual Harassment 12 MIN
VHS / 16mm
Sexual Harassment - Shades of Gray Series
Color (PRO)
$500.00 purchase, $50.00 rental
Defines the behavior patterns of sexual harassment. Encourages employees to think about discrimination and to modify their own behavior.
Business and Economics; Civics and Political Systems; Guidance and Counseling; Psychology; Sociology
Dist - UTM **Prod** - UTM

What is sexuality? 30 MIN
U-matic / VHS
Contemporary health issues series; Lesson 5
Color (C A)
Focuses on sexuality. Gives particular attention to an analysis of culturally induced sex differences, including social and cultural role expectations and male and female sexual taboos.
Psychology; Sociology
Dist - CDTEL **Prod** - SCCON

What is Socialism?
VHS / 35mm strip / U-matic
Political Ideologies of the Twentieth Century - Understanding the 'Isms Series
(J H C)
$109.00=FS, $139.00=MV _ #06111 94
Defines Socialism as the replacement of private ownership and profit by a planned economy, based on cooperative activity and nationalization of production. Examines the impact of 'scientific' socialism on preWWI thought and postwar Russia. In 2 parts.
Civics and Political Systems
Dist - ASPRSS **Prod** - GA

What is Socialism
VHS / U-matic
Color (H)
Traces the formation and application of socialism. Examines the impact of 'scientific' socialism on pre - World War I thought and postwar Russia, and explores the schism between parliamentary and revolutionary socialists.
Civics and Political Systems
Dist - GA **Prod** - GA

What is Sociology?
U-matic / VHS / 35mm strip
Introducing the Social Sciences Series
(J H C)
$139.00 purchase=FS, $159.00 purchase=MV _ 06118 94
Dramatizes the techniques sociologists use to study human social systems and group relationships. Applies these concepts to predict the outcome of a local election. Features case studies. In 3 parts.
Sociology
Dist - ASPRSS **Prod** - GA

What is Sound 15 MIN
U-matic / VHS
Why Series
Color (P I)
Discusses the characteristics of sound.
Science - Physical
Dist - AITECH **Prod** - WDCNTV 1976

What is Space 10 MIN
U-matic / VHS / 16mm
Color (I J) (SPANISH)
Portrays a flight by helicopter and a rocket trip through outer space in order to convey the tremendous extent of space.
Foreign Language; Science - Physical
Dist - EBEC **Prod** - EBEC

What is Spina Bifida 22 MIN
16mm
Color
Presents an introduction to the physically disabling neurological disease, spina bifida. Depicts its clinical manifestation, surgical and medical treatments possible, therapeutic exercise to prevent limb stiffness and the fitting and use of orthosis.
Health and Safety; Psychology
Dist - NYU **Prod** - VASSAR

What is Spring 7 MIN
16mm
Science Series
Color (P I J)
The meaning of spring for people, animals and plants.
Science - Natural
Dist - SF **Prod** - MORLAT 1967

What is statistics - picturing distributions - Parts 1 and 2 60 MIN
VHS / U-matic
Against all odds - inside statistics series
Color (C)
$45.00, $29.95 purchase
Presents parts 1 and 2 of 26 thirty - minute programs on statistics hosted by Dr Teresa Amabile of Brandeis University. Shows how the study of statistics has evolved and how it is used to understand large bodies of information. Demonstrates the construction of stemplots and histograms and the importance of pattern deviation. Produced by the Consortium for Mathematics and Its Applications - COMAP - and the American Statistical Association and American Society of Quality Control.
Mathematics; Psychology
Dist - ANNCPB

What is strategic planning 15 MIN
VHS
Color (IND PRO)
$495.00 purchase, $150.00 rental _ #VC014
Incorporates two case studies, one from a commercial organization and one from the public sector, in a run - down on the five steps in the strategic planning process. Includes a leader's guide. Produced by Video Communicators.
Business and Economics
Dist - EXTR

What is Summer 7 MIN
16mm
Science Series
Color (P I J)
The meaning of summer for people, animals and plants.
Science - Natural
Dist - SF **Prod** - MORLAT 1967

What is the Brightest Star? 11 MIN
U-matic / VHS / 16mm
Wonder World of Science Series
Color (P)
$320 purchase - 16 mm, $250 purchase - video _ #4913C
Shows the difference between planets and stars and tells why the sun can't be seen at night.
Science - Physical
Dist - CORF

What is the brightest star 11 MIN
VHS
Wonder world of science series
Color; PAL (P)
Follows Wondercat, an animated, curious kitten, who tries to find the brightest star in a beautiful night sky. Illustrates the difference between a planet and and a star, and shows why the brightest star, the sun, can't be seen at night. Looks at sunlight, shadows, day and night. Part of a series which encourages youngsters to explore the limitless wonders of the world of science through careful observation, thoughtful comparisons and well - supported conclusions.
Science - Physical
Dist - VIEWTH **Prod** - VIEWTH

What is the Church 30 MIN
16mm
Color; B&W
Features leaders of a local church meeting to study results of a community survey, and explore ways to minister effectively. Shows controversy developing over what the real business of the church is. Portrays the son of one of the men coming home for semester break, and bringing a college roomate, who is campus newspaper editor. Concludes with him writing an article focusing attention on the purpose of the church.
Guidance and Counseling; Religion and Philosophy
Dist - FAMF **Prod** - FAMF

What is the Law 30 MIN
VHS / 16mm
You and the Law Series
Color (C A)
$85.00, $75.00 purchase _ 11 - 01
Presents a broad overview of our legal system.
Civics and Political Systems
Dist - CDTEL **Prod** - COAST 1981

What is the limit 23 MIN
VHS
Color (G)
$15.00 rental
Surveys the environmental problems created by modern industry and agriculture. Points to rapid population growth as a factor responsible for threatening the prosperity of all people and warns of a population crash if births continue to rise and the Earth's carrying capacity is exceeded. Concludes with a discussion of the responsibilities of developed coutries, focusing in particular on current US policies on family planning.
Business and Economics; Health and Safety; Science - Natural; Social Science; Sociology
Dist - CMSMS **Prod** - NAS 1987

What is the Metric System 20 MIN
U-matic
Metric System Series
Color (J)
Explains the use of meters, liters and grams. Discusses decimal systems and precision in measurement.
Mathematics
Dist - GPN **Prod** - MAETEL 1975

What is the most Important Priority of a Teacher 28 MIN
16mm
You Can do it - if Series
Color
LC 81-700094
An updated version of the 1975 motion picture Up With Teachers. Focuses on the 'essence' of teaching and tells how teachers can rededicate themselves to the challenge at hand.
Education
Dist - VANDER **Prod** - VANDER 1980

What is the Nature of Reading Comprehension Series Instruction Today - 30 MIN
U-matic / VHS
Teaching Reading Comprehension Series
Color (T PRO)
$180.00 purchase,$50.00 rental
Focuses on the state of reading comprehension in the classroom today. Suggests some new solutions and strategies.
Education; English Language
Dist - AITECH **Prod** - WETN 1986

What is the Teacher/Student Role 30 MIN
VHS / U-matic
Basic Education - Teaching the Adult Series
Color (T)
Examines the proper teacher/student role in adult education.
Education
Dist - MDCPB **Prod** - MDDE

What is this Thing Called Food 52 MIN
U-matic / VHS / 16mm
Consumer Reports Series
Color (H C A)
LC 77-701506
Examines the use of chemicals in today's food supply, with narration by Betty Furness. Shows how new food technology has served the consumer and points out a growing concern among scientists as to the possible effects of chemical additives on the human body.
Health and Safety; Home Economics; Social Science
Dist - FI **Prod** - NBCTV 1976

What is Total Quality Control 27 MIN
VHS
Seven Steps to TQC Promotion Series
(PRO) (JAPANESE)
 # C101
Explains the nature and philosophy of total quality control, or TQC, as it has developed in Japan. Notes different social

backgrounds that exist in Japan and the West. Features Dr Kaoru Ishikawa.
Business and Economics
Dist - TOYOVS **Prod** - TOYOVS 1987

What is water 22 MIN
VHS
Color (J H)
$29.95 purchase _ #IV159
Examines the chemical and physical processes of water. Looks at chemical bonding, heat capacity, surface tension as well as the origin of water on Earth.
Science - Physical; Social Science
Dist - INSTRU **Prod** - INSTRU

What is Water Pressure 6 MIN
U-matic / VHS
Way Things Work Series
Color (K)
$149.95, $49.95 purchase _ #AD - 1664
Explains the principle of water pressure. Demonstrates that the amount of presure depends upon the depth of the water, not the quantity. Part of a thirty - part series on the way things work hosted by Bob Symes.
Science; Science - Physical
Dist - FOTH **Prod** - FOTH

What is Weather 15 MIN
U-matic / VHS
Why Series
Color (P I)
Discusses the causes of various weather conditions.
Science - Physical
Dist - AITECH **Prod** - WDCNTV 1976

What is Winter 8 MIN
16mm
Science Series
Color (P I J)
The meaning of winter for people, animals and plants.
Science - Natural
Dist - SF **Prod** - MORLAT 1967

What is Work 20 MIN
16mm
Color (C T)
LC FIA68-61
Explores the theories and concepts formulated by Dr Elliot Jacques on work measurement to determine their relevance to good labor and management relations.
Business and Economics
Dist - SIUFP **Prod** - SIUFP 1966

What is Wrong with the Welfare State 87 MIN
VHS / U-matic
Milton Friedman Speaking Series Lecture 5
Color (C)
LC 79-708064
Presents economist Milton Friedman exploring the welfare state and discussing why it doesn't work. Concludes that voluntary cooperation and giving are preferable to welfare.
Business and Economics; Sociology
Dist - HBJ **Prod** - HBJ 1980

What is Wrong with the Welfare State, Pt 1 43 MIN
U-matic / VHS
Milton Friedman Speaking Series Lecture 5
Color (C)
LC 79-708064
Presents economist Milton Friedman exploring the welfare state and discussing why it doesn't work. Concludes that voluntary cooperation and giving are preferable to welfare.
Business and Economics; Sociology
Dist - HBJ **Prod** - HBJ 1980

What is Wrong with the Welfare State, Pt 2 44 MIN
U-matic / VHS
Milton Friedman Speaking Series Lecture 5
Color (C)
LC 79-708064
Presents economist Milton Friedman exploring the welfare state and discussing why it doesn't work. Concludes that voluntary cooperation and giving are preferable to welfare.
Business and Economics; Sociology
Dist - HBJ **Prod** - HBJ 1980

What is your coping style and what you can do about it 34 MIN
VHS
Color (J H C)
$189.00 purchase _ #CG - 915 - VS
Explains that genetic differences in temperament and personality manifest themselves in the way that individuals react to stress. Reveals that some cope by running away from problems, others by confrontation and others may involve themselves in drugs and unconscious defense mechanisms such as denial and rationalization. Shows several dramatic vignettes which demonstrate unproductive coping - drugs, avoidance, confrontation and submission. Dramatizes principles of healthy coping - compromise, self - talk, relabelling, find the winning alternative and desensitization to stress.
Guidance and Counseling; Health and Safety; Psychology
Dist - HRMC **Prod** - HRMC

What is Your Health Hazard Risk? 45 MIN
VHS
Color (J H)
Presents students' answers to a health quiz with facts about their race, sex, and age to provide important health guidelines. Program includes 25 copies of The Nutrition, Health, and Activity Profile questionnaire by Dr Robert Marshall that can be completed by students and, for a fee, receive an appraisal from Pacific Research Systems.
Health and Safety
Dist - IBIS **Prod** - IBIS 1981

What is Your Health Hazard Risk? 45 MIN
VHS
Color (J H)
Students answers to a health quiz can be tallied with facts about their race, sex, and age to provide important health guidelines. Includes 25 copies of the questionnaire, The Nutrition, Health, and Activity profile by Dr Robert Marshall. Students can complete the test and, for a fee, receive an appraisal from Pacific Research Systems.
Health and Safety
Dist - HRMC **Prod** - HRMC 1981

What is Your Patient Medication Profile? 4 MIN
U-matic / Slide
Color
Explains importance of patient profiles and emphasizes the pharmacist's role in protecting patients from potential problems.
Health and Safety
Dist - MEDCOM **Prod** - MEDCOM

What it Means to be Healthy Series
Wellness - Investing in Your Health 28 MIN
Dist - SYLWAT

What it Takes to be a Real Salesman 30 MIN
U-matic / VHS / 16mm
B&W (PRO)
Shows salesmen how to develop the right attitude, how to overcome discouragement and frustration, how to meet every day, every call, every problem with confidence and faith. Explains that without maintaining a 'WILL TO WIN' attitude, a salesman can never produce the volume of sales that really is within his capacity.
Business and Economics; Psychology; Social Science; Sociology
Dist - DARTNL **Prod** - DARTNL

What it takes to live an extraordinary life
VHS
Individual success series
Color (G)
$29.95 purchase _ #CF010
Features Tim Piering who inspires individuals to be the best they can be.
Business and Economics; Psychology
Dist - SIV

What it was all about 28 MIN
U-matic / BETA / VHS
Communication skills 2 - advanced series
Color (H C G)
101.95, $89.95 purchase _ #CA - 26
Reviews all the programs in the series. Touches upon key concepts of communication in each program. Part of a 26 - part series.
Fine Arts; Literature and Drama; Social Science; Sociology
Dist - INSTRU

What Johnny Can't Read 13 MIN
16mm / U-matic / VHS
Color (H C A)
LC 80-701652
Focuses on a Texas housewife who has spent 18 years studying the content of textbooks and whose opinions have influenced curriculum publishing. Presents her answer to charges that she is promoting censorship. Narrated by Mike Wallace. Originally shown on the CBS television series 60 Minutes.
Education; Literature and Drama; Sociology
Dist - CAROUF **Prod** - CBSTV 1980

What Keeps You Alive 15 MIN
U-matic / VHS
All about You Series
Color (P)
Reviews the necessities of human life. Includes food, air, water, sleep, exercise, rest, love and stimulation.
Health and Safety; Science - Natural; Social Science
Dist - AITECH **Prod** - WGBHTV 1975

What Kind of Peer Pressure are You into, Vol 3 22 MIN
VHS / 16mm
Friend Like Patty Series
Color (G)
$95.00 purchase
Focuses upon positive messages to teenage girls. Examines the issue of peer pressure upon young women. Part of an eight - part series, 'A Friend Like Patty,' featuring Patty Ellis.
Health and Safety; Psychology; Sociology
Dist - PROSOR

What liberty and justice means; 2nd ed. 17 MIN
U-matic / VHS / 16mm
Color (I J)
$49.95 purchase _ #P10504; LC 78-701975
Introduces the concepts of liberty and justice and illustrates how these principles affect daily life in America. Considers how the principles of freedom and fairness are much the same for people at work, on a playground, or in the history of America. A Dimension Film.
Civics and Political Systems; Guidance and Counseling; Sociology
Dist - CF **Prod** - DF 1978

What Magnets do 7 MIN
U-matic / VHS
Way Things Work Series
Color (K)
$159.95, $59.95 purchase _ #AD - 1666
Shows what happens to a compass needle if a wire with an electric current is placed next to the compass. Proves that the principle works backwards as well. Part of a thirty - part series on the way things work hosted by Bob Symes.
Science; Science - Physical
Dist - FOTH **Prod** - FOTH

What makes a Catholic health care facility Catholic 46 MIN
VHS / U-matic
Color (R G)
$100.00 purchase, $50.00 rental _ #942, #943, #944
Features Archbishop Daniel E Pilarczyk who addresses issues in Catholic health care and explores the specific purpose and identity of Catholic healthcare facilities.
Guidance and Counseling; Health and Safety; Religion and Philosophy
Dist - CATHHA

What Makes a Good Father 60 MIN
VHS / 16mm
Color (G)
$70.00 rental _ #WMGF - 000
Profiles three fathers and looks at the joys and problems of fatherhood.
Sociology
Dist - PBS **Prod** - WGBHTV

What Makes a Good Negotiation 25 MIN
U-matic / VHS / 16mm
Negotiating Successfully Series Part 1
Color (A)
LC 76-702385
Presents a lecture by Chester L Karrass defining negotiation and giving basic principles. Shows the four steps of a sample negotiation.
Business and Economics; Guidance and Counseling
Dist - TIMLIF **Prod** - TIMLIF 1975

What Makes a Modern Army 28 MIN
16mm
Big Picture Series
Color
LC 75-703706
Discusses the training and support the soldier receives to enable him to implement the four responsibilities of the modern army, namely mission, motivation, modernization and management.
Civics and Political Systems
Dist - USNAC **Prod** - USA 1970

What Makes Amos Famous 30 MIN
VHS / 16mm
Marketing Series
Color (C A)
$130.00, $120.00 purchase _15 - 12
Features the channel strategy of a cookie company.
Business and Economics
Dist - CDTEL **Prod** - COAST 1989

What Makes Art 26 MIN
16mm
Color (J H C A)
LC 78-700712
Surveys the activities carried on by the department of fine art at Pennsylvania State University. Studio work includes painting, etching and woodcutting, photography, graphic design, sculpture, pottery and ceramic sculpture. Describes critiques of student work.
Fine Arts; Industrial and Technical Education
Dist - PSU **Prod** - PSU 1970

What Makes Clouds 19 MIN
U-matic / VHS / 16mm
Earth Science Program Series

Color; B&W (I J H) (SPANISH)
LC FIA65-436
Notes that fog and clouds are composed of droplets of water. Conducts an experiment with condensation producing fog in a bottle and concludes with an investigation of how condensation occurs in nature.
Science - Physical
Dist - EBEC **Prod** - EBEC 1965

What Makes Clouds 19 MIN
U-matic / VHS / 16mm
Color (I J H) (SPANISH)
Notes that fog and clouds are composed of droplets of water. Conducts an experiment with condensation producing fog in a bottle and concludes with an investigation of how condensation occurs in nature.
Foreign Language; Science - Physical
Dist - EBEC **Prod** - EBEC 1965

What Makes Him Run 12 MIN
16mm
Color
Presents scenes of quarter horse racing.
Physical Education and Recreation
Dist - AQHORS **Prod** - AQHORS

What Makes Him Run 23 MIN
16mm / U-matic / VHS
Color
LC 80-701272
Illustrates the economical and cultural impact of quarter horse racing upon the general public, as well as upon specific geographical areas. Includes footage from major tracks around the country.
Physical Education and Recreation
Dist - AQHORS **Prod** - AQHORS 1980

What Makes Japan Work 11 MIN
16mm
Color
Presents three Japanese workers who demonstrate an attitude that definitely influences the quality of their work. Includes an interview with Alan Watts, the West's leading interpreter of Eastern thought, who explains what it is like to live in the now.
Business and Economics; History - World
Dist - HP **Prod** - HP

What Makes Juries Listen 540 MIN
VHS
Color (PRO)
$250.00 purchase _ #09156
Covers every aspect of the trial process, from voir dire to final argument. Includes six audiocassettes and a written guide. Based on the Sonya Hamlin book of the same title, the set offers her perspective on the dynamics of a trial and the lawyer's role in it.
Civics and Political Systems
Dist - PH **Prod** - NITA 1989

What Makes Me Different 9 MIN
16mm / U-matic / VHS
Who We are Series
Color (K P I)
LC 77-701121
Demonstrates and explains differences in accents, smells and types of hair. Uses the senses of hearing, smell and sight to study human physical characteristics and differences.
Guidance and Counseling; Sociology
Dist - PFP **Prod** - KORTY 1977

What Makes Millie Run 16 MIN
16mm
Color (J H)
Presents a film on aerobics for women, featuring Mildred Cooper, author of the book Aerobics For Women. Designed to motivate women to become physically fit.
Guidance and Counseling; Health and Safety; Physical Education and Recreation; Sociology
Dist - BYU **Prod** - BYU 1977

What Makes Muscle Pull - the Structural Basis of Contraction 9 MIN
U-matic / VHS / 16mm
Physiology Series
Color
Uses animation to clarify the relation of muscle structure to muscle function and the protein assembly to the energy flow.
Science - Natural
Dist - MEDIAG **Prod** - WILEYJ 1972

What Makes Music 24 MIN
16mm
Color (J)
LC 78-700713
Surveys the activities carried on by the department of music at Pennsylvania State University. Shows an orchestra in rehearsal, classes at work, demonstrations of individual instruments by students and choral rehearsals.
Fine Arts
Dist - PSUPCR **Prod** - PSU 1970

What Makes Rabbit Run 29 MIN
U-matic / VHS
Color (H C A)
Presents a biography of John Updike, Pulitzer Prize winning author.
Biography; Literature and Drama
Dist - CEPRO **Prod** - BBCTV 1986

What Makes Rain 22 MIN
16mm / U-matic / VHS
Earth Science Program Series
Color (J H)
LC 75-703973
Considers the nature and causes of rainfall. Examines cloud formation, traces the origin of raindrops, hail, sleet and snow and shows what happens in areas where rain does not fall.
Science - Physical
Dist - EBEC **Prod** - EBEC 1975

What makes the weather
U-matic / VHS
Exploring weather, climate and seasons series
Color (P I J)
$239.00, $219.00 purchase
Examines the factors which affect weather. Part of a six - part series on meteorology.
Science - Physical
Dist - GA **Prod** - GA 1988

What Makes the Wind Blow 16 MIN
16mm / U-matic / VHS
Color (I A) (SPANISH)
A Spanish language version of the film and videorecording What Makes The Wind Blow.
Foreign Language; Science - Physical
Dist - EBEC **Prod** - EBEC 1965

What Makes Theatre 29 MIN
16mm
Color (J)
LC 78-700714
Surveys the activities carried on by the department of theatre arts at Pennsylvania State University. Shows classroom demonstrations to develop expressive abilities and improve voice quality. Visits small group workshops and includes scenes from dress and technical rehearsals.
English Language; Fine Arts; Literature and Drama
Dist - PSUPCR **Prod** - PSU 1970

What Makes Them Run 21 MIN
16mm / U-matic / VHS
Color (J)
LC 81-700670
Explores the increasing popularity of the sport of orienteering, described as a car rally on foot. Looks at the International Orienteering Meet in Sweden.
Physical Education and Recreation
Dist - IFB **Prod** - SILVAC 1975

What Makes Them Run 22 MIN
16mm
Color
LC 77-702711
Shows the world championship meets for orienteering held in Sweden in the summer of 1973.
Geography - World; Physical Education and Recreation
Dist - CRAF **Prod** - SILIND 1974

What Makes Us Tick 24 MIN
U-matic / VHS
Color (G)
$249.00, $149.00 purchase _ #AD - 2033
Explores the relationship between genes and the environment in the formation of human personality. Shows that an increasingly important part is being conceded to genetics in the nature - nurture controversy.
Psychology; Science - Natural; Sociology
Dist - FOTH **Prod** - FOTH

What Makes Weather 14 MIN
16mm / U-matic / VHS
Earth Science Program Series
Color (I J)
LC 81-700071
Uses satellite footage, animation and time - lapse photography to show the working forces that produce weather. Examines the movement of winds and air masses, and shows some of the visual clues to weather change.
Science - Physical
Dist - EBEC **Prod** - EBEC 1981

What makes work meaningful 30 MIN
BETA / VHS
Optimal performance series
Color (G)
$29.95 purchase _ #S202
Suggests that individuals can find as much meaning, commitment and passion in work as in other areas of life. Features Dr Dennis T Jaffe, past president of the Association for Humanistic Psychology and author of 'Take This Job and Love It.' Part of a four - part series on optimal performance.
Business and Economics; Guidance and Counseling; Psychology
Dist - THINKA **Prod** - THINKA

What Man Shall Live and not See Death 57 MIN
16mm / U-matic / VHS
Color (J)
Studies the subject of death and how Americans deal with it. Provides insight into a profound and universal experience.
Psychology; Sociology
Dist - FI **Prod** - WNBCTV 1971

What Man Shall Live and not See Death, Pt 1 30 MIN
U-matic / VHS / 16mm
Color (J)
Studies the subject of death, and how Americans deal with it. Provides insight into a profound and universal experience.
Sociology
Dist - FI **Prod** - WNBCTV 1971

What Man Shall Live and not See Death, Pt 2 27 MIN
U-matic / VHS / 16mm
Color (J)
Studies the subject of death, and how Americans deal with it. Provides insight into a profound and universal experience.
Sociology
Dist - FI **Prod** - WNBCTV 1971

What Mary Jo Shared 15 MIN
VHS / U-matic
Picture Book Park Series Blue Module; Blue module
Color (P)
Presents the children's story What Mary Jo Shared by Janice Udry.
Literature and Drama
Dist - AITECH **Prod** - WVIZTV 1974

What Mary Jo Shared 13 MIN
16mm / U-matic / VHS
Color (P)
LC 81-701063
Tells the story of a little girl who overcomes her shyness and shares something unusual with her classmates. Based on the book What Mary Jo Shared by Janice May Udry.
Guidance and Counseling; Literature and Drama
Dist - PHENIX **Prod** - WILETS 1981

What Mary Jo Shared / Sam, Bangs, and Moonshine 28 MIN
BETA / VHS
Color
Tells about a girl who needs to find something special to bring to a sharing session at school. Based on the book by Janice May Udry. Tells of a girl who makes up a tall story that causes trouble. Based on the book by Evaline Ness.
Literature and Drama
Dist - PHENIX **Prod** - PHENIX

What Mary Jo Wanted 15 MIN
U-matic / VHS / 16mm
Color (K P)
LC 82-700742
Captures the story about a little girl who gets her wish to have a puppy and a chance to show that she can take care of it on her own, even though it isn't always easy. Based on the book of the same name by Janice May Udry.
Literature and Drama
Dist - BARR **Prod** - WILETS 1982

What Memphis needs 6 MIN
16mm
Color (G)
$16.00 rental, $25.00 purchase
Contrasts the black and white cultures of Memphis, Tennessee. Refers to a poem written in a poetry workshop led by Ethridge Knight. Music by Harmonikeys and Roosevelt Briggs.
Civics and Political Systems; Fine Arts; History - United States; Literature and Drama; Sociology
Dist - CANCIN **Prod** - KRASIL 1991

What motivates human behavior? 30 MIN
U-matic / VHS
Contemporary health issues series; Lesson 2
Color (C A)
Considers the various theories about the determinants of personality and explores four principal theories of motivation. Shows how positive feedbacks is used to train a bear to perform a specific behavior.
Psychology; Sociology
Dist - CDTEL **Prod** - SCCON

What Motivates Man to Work? 57 FRS
U-matic / VHS
Job Enrichment Series
Color
Offers suggestions for examining jobs and seeing what can be done to make them more motivating.
Psychology
Dist - RESEM **Prod** - RESEM

What must I do to be Saved 17 MIN
16mm
Book of Acts Series
Color; B&W (J H T R)
Presents the story of Paul who receives a call to help in Macedonia. Leads viewer into an experience of salvation through faith in Christ.
Religion and Philosophy
Dist - FAMF **Prod** - BROADM 1957

What My Parents Didn't Tell Me 25 MIN
U-matic / VHS
Color (J H C A)
Features a group of teenagers discussing their book, Changing Bodies, Changing Minds, which deals with the problems of puberty and sexual awareness. Discusses the learning of sex from peers and the difficulties in sharing the sexual awakening with their parents.
Health and Safety; Psychology; Sociology
Dist - GERBER **Prod** - SIRS

What Next
16mm
B&W
Presents views on the probable developments in computers and computing.
Mathematics
Dist - OPENU **Prod** - OPENU

What Next 30 MIN
VHS / U-matic
Bits and Bytes Series Pt 12; Pt 12
Color (A)
Reviews the main topics presented in the Bits And Bytes Series and speculates on the future of the computer in schools, workplaces and homes.
Mathematics
Dist - TIMLIF **Prod** - TVOTAR 1984

What next 15 MIN
VHS
Color (P I J)
Deals with the development of children during puberty. Discusses social and emotional relationships and how one becomes increasingly more responsible for one's one behavior as one grows older.
Guidance and Counseling; Health and Safety; Psychology; Sociology
Dist - VIEWTH **Prod** - VIEWTH

What no Exit 4 MIN
16mm
Color
LC 78-701333
Presents a texture study of pain, pathos and privacy on the frontier of urban America.
Fine Arts
Dist - KNIGN **Prod** - KNIGN 1978

What - no friction 11 MIN
VHS
Color; PAL (P I J)
Describes the problems caused by friction and the various means devised for reducing friction when undesirable. Shows two young boys encountering friction when they try to drag a heavy crate of books over the road. Dramatizes what the world would be like without friction, then helps the boys by mysteriously presenting various devices to help reduce friction.
Agriculture; Science - Physical
Dist - VIEWTH **Prod** - VIEWTH

What Now? 12 MIN
VHS / U-matic
Entering a Nursing Home Series
Color
Shows specific ways to help families during nursing home placement, including the use of family support groups, one - to - one counseling and supportive clergy.
Health and Safety; Psychology; Sociology
Dist - AJN **Prod** - SITH

What Now 29 MIN
U-matic
Decision Makers Series
Color
Evaluates the Decision Makers Series. Describes characteristics and goals of leaders.
Biography; Civics and Political Systems
Dist - HRC **Prod** - OHC

What Now - Deciding What's Right 48 MIN
VHS / 16mm
Color (K)
$119.95 purchase
Designed to encourage children to look at their alternatives and to weigh the possible consequences of their actions before reaching a decision or taking an action, and to promote participation in class discussion. Combines four units also available separately - Good Intentions (about responsibility), Why Pay (shoplifting), Just One Look (cheating), and Start The Party (disobeying).
Education; Religion and Philosophy
Dist - JANUP **Prod** - JANUP

What Now - Deciding What's Right Series
Good intentions 12 MIN
Just One Look 12 MIN
Start the Party 12 MIN
Why Pay 12 MIN
Dist - JANUP

What Now Skipper 19 MIN
16mm
Color
LC 74-705946
Depicts the recommended procedures for selecting, maintaining and using marine fire extinguishers. Familiarizes the boating public with the federal requirements for fire extinguishers and their proper use on the pleasure boat.
Health and Safety
Dist - USNAC **Prod** - USCG 1972

What on earth 15 MIN
U-matic / VHS
Dragons, wagons and wax - Set 2 series
Color (K P)
Discusses solids, liquids and gasses.
Science; Science - Physical
Dist - CTI **Prod** - CTI

What on Earth 14 MIN
U-matic / VHS / 16mm
Safe at Home Series
Color (P I)
MV=$99.00
Teaches children about poison labels, that pills are not candy and that irons are hot stuff.
Health and Safety
Dist - LANDMK **Prod** - LANDMK 1984

What on Earth 10 MIN
16mm / U-matic / VHS
Color (I J A)
LC FIA68-1261
Presents an animated cartoon about Martians who visit earth and are confused about whether the prevailing and most intelligent form of life on earth is man or the automobile.
Industrial and Technical Education; Literature and Drama
Dist - MGHT **Prod** - NFBC 1966

What on earth series
Science and the sea - Pt 2 30 MIN
Dist - GPN

What one child can do - U S and Soviet youth make peace 29 MIN
U-matic / VT3
(I)
$75.00 purchase, $45.00 rental
Tells how a group of 48 American youths travelled on their own initiative to Leningrad and Moscow to meet with Soviet children. Shows how the children bridged their cultural differences.
Geography - World; Sociology
Dist - EFVP **Prod** - EFVP 1988

What parents and kids need to know about AIDS 30 MIN
VHS
Color (G A R)
$89.95 purchase, $10.00 rental _ #35 - 82 - 69
Presents the basic facts about AIDS. Intended primarily for parents to learn about, and educate their children on, AIDS.
Health and Safety
Dist - APH

What Parents Should Know about Drugs 55 MIN
16mm / U-matic / VHS
Color (C A)
Discusses basic facts that every parent should know about drugs by interviewing medical experts, psychiatrists, leaders of parent action groups and former young drug users. Examines new findings about the dangers of drugs and traces the four dangers of the drug - use cycle. Tells parents what signs to look for in their children which indicate drug use, what to do if their children are on drugs and where to find help.
Health and Safety; Sociology
Dist - CORF **Prod** - ABCTV 1981

What Part of the Plant 29 MIN
VHS / 16mm
Villa Alegre Series
Color (P T)
$46.00 rental _ #VILA - 119
Presents educational material in both Spanish and English.
Education; Science - Natural
Dist - PBS

What people are calling PMS 28 MIN
U-matic / VHS
Color (G)
$295.00 purchase, $100.00 rental
Challenges the commonly held notion that women experiencing premenstrual changes are ill or out of control. Affirms a positive view of this phase. Helps to broaden women's awareness and understanding of their bodies. Features several women who describe with humor and honesty the spectrum of emotional and physical changes undergone during the premenstrual phase. Discusses the largely negative images perpetuated by society about premenstrual women. Presents straightforward information about the menstural cycle. Discloses that diet and exercise can be a factor in premenstrual syndrome, but women whose symptoms are severe should consult a medical professional.
Sociology
Dist - BAXMED **Prod** - NFBC

What Persuades Whom 30 MIN
VHS / U-matic
Introduction to Technical and Business Communication Series
Color (H C A)
Business and Economics; English Language
Dist - GPN **Prod** - UMINN 1983

What Plants Need for Growth 11 MIN
U-matic / VHS / 16mm
Color (P) (SPANISH)
Uses simple laboratory experiments to illustrate the basic needs of plants for water, light, minerals, air and warmth. Shows how plants react to favorable and unfavorable conditions.
Foreign Language; Science - Natural
Dist - EBEC **Prod** - EBEC

What Powers Them 29 MIN
VHS / 16mm
Villa Alegre Series
Color (P T)
$46.00 rental _ #VILA - 150
Presents educational material in both Spanish and English.
Education
Dist - PBS

What practitioners need to know to negotiate offers in compromise with the IRS 50 MIN
VHS
Color (C PRO A)
$95.00 purchase _ #Y157
Looks at the IRS code, section 7122, in which the IRS is authorized to cut deals with taxpayers owing back taxes. Describes the procedures for submitting an offer and explains ways to maximize clients' chances of obtaining workable settlements.
Civics and Political Systems
Dist - ALIABA **Prod** - CLETV 1992

What Price Clean Air 57 MIN
U-matic / VHS
Color
Discusses the price the American public could pay in terms of poor health and environmental damage if existing standards of the Clean Air Act are relaxed. Reveals that the auto and steel industries and Reagan administration officials charge that costs of meeting pollution standards increase industry depression and unemployment while public health and environmental groups maintain that high - sulfur coal and auto emissions cause acid rain and the deaths of thousands of lakes and streams.
Health and Safety; Sociology
Dist - PMI **Prod** - PMI

What Price Coal 60 MIN
U-matic
Nova Series
Color
Examines the 1969 Coal Mine Health and Safety Act and illustrates the problems that still remain in the 1970's, especially the fact that mines are unsafe. Explores the cost in human terms for energy.
Industrial and Technical Education; Social Science
Dist - PBS **Prod** - WGBHTV 1977

What Price Confidence 28 MIN
16mm
Big Picture Series

Color
LC 75-703707
Describes how the U S Army test and Evaluation Command ensures that equipment is free from defects and that it will function in any climate and on any terrain.
Civics and Political Systems
Dist - USNAC **Prod** - USA 1970

What Price Equality 56 MIN
U-matic / VHS
We the People Series
Color (G)
$279.00, $179.00 purchase _ #AD - 1422
Focuses on Yonkers, New York, where, more than a century after ratification of the Fourteenth Amendment, a federal court ruled that the city and school district violated the Constitution by intentionally discriminating against minorities in housing and schools. Reveals that 'we the people' meant something quite different to the framers of the Constitution than to us today - 200 years ago slaves were property and women were not even mentioned. Part of a four - part series on the American Constitution.
Civics and Political Systems; Education; Sociology
Dist - FOTH **Prod** - FOTH

What Price Gas 20 MIN
U-matic / VHS
Color
$335.00 purchase
From the ABC TV program, 20 20. Presents a program on natural gas deregulation.
Civics and Political Systems; Science - Physical
Dist - ABCLR **Prod** - ABCLR 1978

What Price Glory 122 MIN
16mm
B&W
Introduces Captain Flagg and Sergeant Quirt, who battle each other as vigorously as they do an opposing army, especially over the lovely but fickle Charmaine. Stars Victor McLaglen and directed by Raoul Walsh.
Fine Arts
Dist - KILLIS **Prod** - UNKNWN 1926

What price miracles 29 MIN
VHS
Color (G)
$50.00 purchase, $21.50 rental _ #34117
Points out that high - technology health care does much to ease suffering and prolong life, but at enormous financial costs. Raises basic questions about who lives and who dies.
Health and Safety
Dist - PSU **Prod** - KTCATV 1980

What Price Steak 60 MIN
U-matic / VHS
Color (H A)
Presents the economic implications of meat production, including use of grain and international demand for grain and meat. Mentions grain embargos and their effect upon producers and consumers.
Agriculture; Home Economics
Dist - CORNRS **Prod** - CUETV 1981

What Price Water 35 MIN
16mm
Color
Details the extensive research and development program on a number of techniques which are enabling Britain to maintain her position as a leading exporter of desalination plants.
Industrial and Technical Education; Science - Natural; Sociology
Dist - UKAEA **Prod** - UKAEA 1970

What Ramon Did 30 MIN
16mm / VHS
Color (J H A)
$395.00, $545.00 purchase, $75.00 rental _ #8130
Tells how intravenous drug user Ramon returns from jail and finds his neighbors and friends afraid that he might have AIDS. Shows how Ramon's high risk behavior becomes a catalyst for an examination and a change of lifestyle.
Guidance and Counseling; Health and Safety; Psychology
Dist - AIMS **Prod** - HYFP 1989

What Really Happened at the East Los Angeles Chicano Riot 15 MIN
16mm
Color (I)
Presents a documentary exposing the subtle biases of supposedly objective news reporting.
Psychology; Sociology
Dist - CFS **Prod** - CFS 1971

What remains for the future 29 MIN
VHS / U-matic
Color (H C)
$325.00, $295.00 purchase _ #V542
Presents the history and ecology of the Pacific Northwest. Shows the many plants and animals which inhabit the area. Features coastal and mountain environments and the impact of recent human development on this area.
Geography - United States; Science - Natural
Dist - BARR **Prod** - CEPRO 1991

What Right has a Child 15 MIN
16mm / U-matic / VHS
Color (I)
LC 70-704156
Uses children's art from all over the world with commentary by the children as they talk about each of the clauses of the Universal Declaration of the Rights of the Child and what they mean to them.
Civics and Political Systems; Fine Arts
Dist - MGHT **Prod** - UN 1969

What Series
What Does the Future Hold 30 MIN
What is God Like 30 MIN
What is God Like, and what Does the Future Hold 30 MIN
Dist - WHLION

What Shall I be 8 MIN
U-matic / VHS / 16mm
Color (P I)
LC 72-701506
Explores the fun and excitement of different occupations as the viewer follows the little hero who imagines himself in different situations.
Guidance and Counseling
Dist - CORF **Prod** - CORF 1972

What Shall We do about Claudius 60 MIN
16mm / U-matic / VHS
I, Claudius Series Number 4; No 4
Color (C A)
Tells how Tiberius steps closer to power, his shadow falling on the clownish Claudius.
History - World
Dist - FI **Prod** - BBCTV 1977

What Shall We do about Mother 49 MIN
U-matic / VHS / 16mm
Color (H C A)
LC 80-701952
Looks at the conflicts and guilt suffered by two families as they seek ways to care for their aging parents.
Health and Safety; Sociology
Dist - CAROUF **Prod** - CBSTV 1980

What should a guy do 29 MIN
VHS / U-matic
Color (J H)
$425.00, $395.00 purchase _ #V469
Discusses male sexual responsibility and teenaged fathers.
Guidance and Counseling; Health and Safety; Psychology; Sociology
Dist - BARR **Prod** - CEPRO 1988

What Should I be When I Grow Up 30 MIN
VHS / 16mm
Science, Health and Math Series
Color (P)
$39.95 purchase _ #CL7905
Introduces basic concepts concerning careers.
Psychology
Dist - EDUCRT

What Should I Buy 14 MIN
VHS / U-matic
Under the Yellow Balloon Series
Color (P)
Reveals that Karen learns about wants and needs when she spends the $20 she receives for her birthday.
Business and Economics; Home Economics
Dist - AITECH **Prod** - SCETV 1980

What should I do series
The Fight 6 MIN
The Game 6 MIN
The Lunch money 6 MIN
The New girl 6 MIN
The Pproject 6 MIN
Dist - CORF

What should we do in school today 22 MIN
VHS
Public agenda foundation series
Color (H C G)
$250.00 purchase, $55.00 rental
Explores pressing issues facing educators today - the content of curriculum, the extent of discipline, evaluating teachers and keeping kids from dropping out. Visits four schools trying to deal with those issues in new and sometimes controversial ways. Visits a principle in Philadelphia who has dropped 'frills' such as art and music to focus on 'basics.' Shows how a violence - ridden inner city school has been transformed through a strict - some say too strict - discipline program. Looks at a teacher evaluation and merit - pay project. Produced and directed by Jeffrey Tuchman.
Education; Sociology
Dist - FLMLIB **Prod** - MAYSLS 1992

What should you do? Deciding what's right 27 MIN
VHS
Color (I)
$149 purchase No. 2422-YZ
Explores the issues of honesty, fairness and responsibility with children grades 4-6. Using short scenarios, allows students to decide what is right. Includes 27-minute video and teacher's guide.
Education; Religion and Philosophy
Dist - ETHICS **Prod** - SUNCOM

What Should Your Business Plan Contain? 22 MIN
U-matic / VHS / 16mm
Starting a Business Series
Color (H C A)
Notes how certain sections of business plan are essential to include, and illustrates steps to be followed in developing since effective plans reduce risks and increase potential.
Business and Economics
Dist - BCNFL **Prod** - SOMFIL 1983

What Soviet Children are Saying about Nuclear War 22 MIN
16mm / U-matic / VHS
Color
Interviews Soviet children on the subject of nuclear war. Shows a group of American doctors visiting two Soviet Pioneer camps.
Civics and Political Systems; Geography - World; Sociology
Dist - EFVP **Prod** - EFVP

What tadoo 18 MIN
U-matic / VHS / 16mm
Anti - victimization series
Color (P)
Looks at the ways strangers entice children. Provides four basic rules for protection - say no, get away, tell someone and sometimes, yell.
Civics and Political Systems; Health and Safety; Sociology
Dist - CORF **Prod** - CORF

What tadoo 18 MIN
U-matic / Videodisc / 16mm / VHS
Color (P I)
$370.00, $330.00 purchase _ #JR - 4647M
Takes a fantasy trip with a young boy to the 'Land of Lessons' where Perfessor Sir Hillary Von Carp and two frogs named What and Tadoo teach him how to protect himself from strangers. Stresses four basic rules - Say No, Get Away, Tell Someone and Sometimes, Yell.
Health and Safety; Sociology
Dist - CORF **Prod** - MITCHG 1984

What tadoo with fear 18 MIN
U-matic / Videodisc / 16mm / VHS
Color (P I)
$385.00, $330.00 purchase _ #JR - 5173M
Tells about Samantha and two wise frogs named What and Tadoo who advise her what to do about a 'deal' she made with her babysitter. Uses song and puppetry to show Samantha that by taking action and sharing troubling secrets with her mother, she can stop fear from getting the best of her.
Guidance and Counseling; Health and Safety; Sociology
Dist - CORF **Prod** - MITCHG 1988

What the Chinese See 20 MIN
U-matic / VHS
$335.00 purchase
Fine Arts; Geography - World
Dist - ABCLR **Prod** - ABCLR 1983

What the Computer Can do for You - Part I
VHS / Software / Kit / U-matic
New Horizons Series
(PRO)
$1595 series purchase
Examines a group of direct instruction computer applications, drill and practice, educational games, demonstrations and simulations.
Computer Science
Dist - AITECH **Prod** - ALASDE 1986

What the Computer Can do for You - Part II
VHS / Software / Kit / U-matic
New Horizons Series
(PRO)
$1595 series purchase
Presents two other groups of instructional uses for computers, including instructional support applications and instructional resource management applications.
Computer Science
Dist - AITECH **Prod** - ALASDE 1986

What the decorticate pigeon can do 4 MIN
16mm
Dukes physiology film series
Color (C)

LC 75-710198
Demonstrates the various reflexes which arise in the brainstem, spinal cord, and cerebellum, using a pigeon which lacks the cerebral cortex.
Science - Natural
Dist - IOWA **Prod** - IOWA 1971

What the Earth was Like 15 MIN
U-matic / VHS
Why Series
Color (P I)
Discusses what the earth was like in the past.
Science - Physical
Dist - AITECH **Prod** - WDCNTV 1976

What the Four Wise Monkeys Had to Say 3 MIN
Videoreel / VT2
Color
Presents computer animation of shapes, colors and movements against a background of the song What The Four Wise Monkeys Had To Say, bringing a message about such everyday events as smoking, overeating, driving and the need to keep an inner equilibrium.
Health and Safety
Dist - AMPFRI **Prod** - AMPFRI

What the glaciers did to Ohio 30 MIN
VHS
Color (J H C)
$29.95 purchase _ #IVOH05
Reveals that glaciers moving over Ohio have probably had more influence on the present appearance of the state than any other force. Discloses that continental glaciers thousands of feet thick scoured the northern section of Ohio like a giant bulldozer. As they melted they deposited mud, silt and sand which became the fertile soil of the state's rich farmland. Investigates how the ice age came to Ohio, where various glaciers reached as well as some of the physical features left behind when the ice melted. Introduces the study of glaciology.
Geography - United States; Geography - World; History - United States; Science - Physical
Dist - INSTRU

What the Hell's Going on Up There 28 MIN
16mm
Color
_ #106C 0179 628N
Geography - World
Dist - CFLMDC **Prod** - NFBC 1979

What the Market will Bear 30 MIN
VHS / 16mm
Marketing Series
Color (C A)
$130.00, $120.00 purchase _ 15 - 23
Focuses on cost, expenses, profit, and consumer attitudes.
Business and Economics
Dist - CDTEL **Prod** - COAST 1989

What the Nose Knows 26 MIN
U-matic / VHS
Color (G)
$249.00, $149.00 purchase _ #AD - 1880
Visits the Monell Chemical Senses Center in Philadelphia where scientists are discovering the relationships between smell and behavior. Examines how animal species, including humans, use odor to communicate messages about reproduction. Scrutinizes synthetic aroma chemicals which produce odors ranging from flowers to new cars to sun - dried laundry.
Psychology; Science - Natural; Sociology
Dist - FOTH **Prod** - FOTH

What the Well Dressed Harness Horse Should Wear and Why 10 MIN
BETA / VHS
Color
Explains how to dress trotters and pacers. Describes their jogging gear, points to the differences between jogging carts and sulkies.
Physical Education and Recreation
Dist - EQVDL **Prod** - USTROT

What the World Dishes Out 15 MIN
16mm / VHS
Color (PRO)
$295.00, $420.00 purchase, $75.00 rental, $50.00 preview
Discusses aspects of work - related stress. Explains job related problems which can induce stress including lack of creativity, sex role conflicts, work overload, job changes, boredom, lack of control. Shows how some businesses are working to help employees reduce stress.
Education; Guidance and Counseling; Psychology; Sociology
Dist - UTM **Prod** - UTM

What the World Dishes Out 15 MIN
U-matic / VHS / 16mm
Managing Stress Series
Color (H C A)
Outlines some types of stressors that evoke a health - threatening response. Includes loss of self - esteem, boredom, role conflicts, excessive responsibility, lack of control and work overload. Shows specific techniques for temporarily relieving stress, such as deep breathing or meditation and gives suggestions for warding off stressors through cognitive restructuring.
Guidance and Counseling; Psychology
Dist - CENTEF **Prod** - CENTRO 1984
CORF

What they Don't Know Can Hurt 13 MIN
16mm
Safety and the Foreman Series
B&W (A)
Discusses the need of knowing the right way of doing a job and for keeping a watchful eye open to correct the workers when a task is being done improperly.
Business and Economics; Health and Safety
Dist - NSC **Prod** - SARRA 1956

What they Don't Teach You at Harvard Business School
U-matic / VHS
Color
Presents Mark McCormack's best selling book emphasizing 'Street Smarts' as something not taught at Harvard's business school in a training format for employees. Shows how to read people, following McCormack's tips on selling and negotiating to help employees become more confident, more productive in any business encounter.
Business and Economics; Education; Psychology
Dist - CBSFOX **Prod** - CBSFOX

What they Don't Teach You at Harvard Business School - Street Smarts 48 MIN
VHS / U-matic
Color (G)
Teaches insights and perceptions that give employees the edge on selling and negotiating.
Business and Economics; Psychology
Dist - VPHI **Prod** - VPHI 1985

What they mean when they say... 10 MIN
16mm / VHS
Color (G IND)
$5.00 rental
Helps voters to become more discerning when they listen to political campaign speeches. Features political writer Mark Shields who looks at the hidden messages behind such over - used buzz words as competiveness and free trade.
Civics and Political Systems; Sociology
Dist - AFLCIO **Prod** - LIPA 1986

What they still don't teach you at Harvard Business School 60 MIN
VHS
Color (J H C G)
$29.95 purchase _ #NAC11007V
Features Mark McCormack, founder and CEO of International Management Group. Shows how 'applied people sense' turns one into a street - smart executive. Divides into eight easy - to - use chapters, including the ten commandments of street smarts, how to be a supersalesperson, what makes a world - class negotiator, personal positioning, time management, getting organized, doing business on the road and how to follows one's own advice.
Business and Economics
Dist - CAMV **Prod** - NIGCON

What this Country Needs 30 MIN
U-matic / VHS / 16mm
Color (H C A)
LC 81-701597
Looks at the declining growth rate of U S productivity and notes that the human factor is a major cause. Presents a panel of experts who discusses the problem, focusing on worker - management relationships, the implications of changing worker attitudes and the need for management to provide motivation.
Business and Economics; Psychology
Dist - FI **Prod** - WTTWTV 1981

What Time is it 11 MIN
16mm / U-matic / VHS
Color (P)
$280, $195 purchase _ #3415
Discusses how to tell time using hours, minutes, half hours, and quarter hours.
Mathematics
Dist - CORF

What Time is it 8 MIN
U-matic / VHS
Giant First Start Series
Color (K P)
$29.95 purchase _ #VW010
Presents an adaptation of the book What Time Is It. Contains a 32 page hardcover book and a video.
English Language; Literature and Drama
Dist - TROLA

What Time is it in Tokyo 14 MIN
U-matic / VHS / 16mm
Color (I J) (SPANISH)
LC 76-715434
Uses the principles pertaining to the rotation of the earth and its position in relation to the sun to develop a step - by - stop logical understanding of why there are time differences around the world and how man has worked out ways of coping with them.
Foreign Language; Mathematics; Science - Physical
Dist - JOU **Prod** - WER 1971

What Time is it - Trouble in Space
VHS / 16mm
Video Read - Alongs Series
Color (K)
$8.88 purchase _ ISBN #5109 - 18603 - 3
Features animated stories and songs as lessons in children learning word skills. Available in a series of six similar videos.
Fine Arts; Literature and Drama
Dist - EDUCRT

What Time is the Next Swan 9 MIN
16mm / U-matic / VHS
Color (I)
LC 76-701935
Features Sarah Caldwell and the Boston Opera Company, following them through a rehearsal of an actual production.
Fine Arts
Dist - PHENIX

What Time is Your Body 23 MIN
U-matic / VHS / 16mm
Color (H C A)
LC 77-701963
Demonstrates that the human body is a natural clock run by an internal timing mechanism known as circadium rhythm. Contains footage of long - term isolation experiments performed on humans to ascertain their circadium rhythm.
Health and Safety; Psychology; Science - Natural
Dist - FI **Prod** - BBCTV 1975

What to Appraise 53 FRS
VHS / U-matic
Performance Appraisal Series Module 2
Color
Stresses the importance of knowing how employees perform and describes a means of evaluating what is important in a job and how to translate this into a usable form.
Business and Economics; Psychology
Dist - RESEM **Prod** - RESEM

What to be 18 MIN
16mm
Color
Presents the story of Richard, a chicano high school senior, who is having an internal struggle about his future. Explains that he is coping with the common feeling that college might not, after all, be necessary for his future development.
Guidance and Counseling; Psychology; Sociology
Dist - USC **Prod** - ELCC

What to do at an Accident 25 MIN
U-matic / VHS
Killers Series
Color
Shows program host Mario Machado rendering aid at a realistically recreated auto accident. Uses emergency ward doctor, policeman and fireman explaining the proper steps to be taken at the scene of an accident and demonstrating first - aid techniques.
Health and Safety
Dist - MEDCOM **Prod** - MEDCOM

What to do at home 16 MIN
U-matic / 16mm / VHS
Mickey's safety club series
Color (P)
$425.00, $280.00 purchase _ #JC - 67186
Teaches about home safety. Demonstrates important home safety information - fire safety procedures, emergency telephone numbers, how to fix safe snacks, how to correctly answer the phone and door when home alone and how to call for help in an emergency. Part of the Mickey's Safety Club series.
Health and Safety; Sociology
Dist - CORF **Prod** - DISNEY 1989

What to do Instead of a Performance Appraisal 23 MIN
VHS / 16mm
Deming User's Manual Series

(PRO)
$150.00 rental
Explains how to replace damaging performance appraisals with successful methods for giving feedback and direction to employees, selecting people for promotion, and determining salaries. Guide included.
Business and Economics; Psychology
Dist - FI **Prod** - CCMPR 1989

What to do Instead of Managing by Objective 23 MIN
VHS / 16mm
Deming User's Manual Series
(PRO)
$150.00 rental
Examines the issue of management by objective, and the uses and limitations of numerical data. Explains how to plan and achieve improvement without using management by objective. In two parts. Guide included.
Business and Economics; Psychology
Dist - FI **Prod** - CCMPR 1990

What to do on the Three - Day Weekend 25 MIN
16mm
Color
LC 75-713382
Shows a vast collection of ways in which to spend three - day weekends, including being towed underwater behind a boat and performing a double somersault on skis. Includes views of the Grand Tetons in the clouds.
Geography - United States; Physical Education and Recreation
Dist - GROENG **Prod** - JMOTOR 1970

What to do Series
What to do When You Need a Banker 18 MIN
What to do When You Need a Doctor 20 MIN
What to do When You Need a Lawyer 21 MIN
What to do When You Need a Real Estate Agent 21 MIN
What to do When You Need an Insurance Agent 19 MIN
Dist - CORF

What to do 'till the wrecker comes series
The Big secret - what's under the hood 29 MIN
The Great expressway rip - off 29 MIN
How to Amuse Yourself on a Saturday Afternoon 28 MIN
I'm Late for Work and the Car Won't Start 28 MIN
Yes, You Can Change a Flat 29 MIN
Dist - PBS

What to do When Someone Chokes 15 MIN
U-matic / VHS
Color
Presents simple and easy - to - follow instructions and demonstrates the various ways to handle a choking victim, whether conscious or unconscious.
Health and Safety
Dist - FILCOM **Prod** - KGPROD 1983

What to do when you are due - a comprehensive guide to prenatal care
VHS
Color (J H C G)
$79.95 purchase _ #CCP0122V
Answers commonly asked questions from mothers - to - be and discusses the importance of healthy habits before, during and after pregnancy. Discusses the physical and emotional changes that occur during pregnancy and what can be done to minimize their effects. Features nutritionists, physicians and prenatal educators who explain the importance of good nutrition and exercise.
Sociology
Dist - CAMV **Prod** - CAMV 1993

What to do When You Need a Banker 18 MIN
U-matic / VHS / 16mm
What to do Series
Color (J)
LC 80-701609
Shows what happens when two young people inadvertently overdraw their checking account. Explains how to choose the correct bank and make use of all banking services.
Business and Economics; Home Economics
Dist - CORF **Prod** - CORF 1980

What to do When You Need a Doctor 20 MIN
U-matic / VHS / 16mm
What to do Series
Color (J)
LC 80-701606
Tells how a young woman learns how to cope with the medical system after she has an accident. Explains how to find a doctor and discusses fees and services.
Health and Safety; Home Economics
Dist - CORF **Prod** - CORF 1980

What to do When You Need a Lawyer 21 MIN
U-matic / VHS / 16mm
What to do Series
Color (J)
LC 80-701607
Shows what happens when legal services are needed, telling how to find and hire a lawyer, use small claims courts, and seek out alternatives for legal assistance.
Civics and Political Systems; Home Economics
Dist - CORF **Prod** - CORF 1980

What to do When You Need a Real Estate Agent 21 MIN
16mm / U-matic / VHS
What to do Series
Color (J)
LC 80-701608
Shows a young couple finding a real estate agent and learning the process of purchasing a home.
Business and Economics; Home Economics
Dist - CORF **Prod** - CORF 1980

What to do When You Need an Insurance Agent 19 MIN
16mm / U-matic / VHS
What to do Series
Color (J)
LC 80-701610
Describes how to buy insurance, select an agent, and file a claim.
Business and Economics; Home Economics
Dist - CORF **Prod** - CORF 1980

What to do with your money if you have to leave the country fast 30 MIN
U-matic
Adam Smith's money world 1985 - 1986 season series; 229
Color (A)
Attempts to demystify the world of money and break it down so that small as well as large businesses and it's people understand and adjust to new social and economic trends. Reports on the major economic stories and discoveries of 1985 and 1986.
Business and Economics
Dist - PBS **Prod** - WNETTV 1986

What to make of a wall 30 MIN
Videoreel / VT2
Designing home interiors series; Unit 19
Color (C A)
Introduces the importance of walls as background areas. Shows many uses of paint and wood to create interesting wall treatments.
Home Economics
Dist - CDTEL **Prod** - COAST

What was I supposed to do - 3 30 MIN
16mm / VHS / BETA / U-matic
Parenting the child who is handicapped series
Color; PAL (G PRO T)
PdS150, PdS158 purchase
Focuses on the emotional and psychological aspects of bearing and raising a handicapped child. Presents part of a three - part series.
Health and Safety; Sociology
Dist - EDPAT

What We are 17 MIN
16mm
Color
LC 80-700078
Looks at employees of Eastman Chemical Products at work and at leisure in the communities where the plants are located.
Business and Economics
Dist - ECP **Prod** - ECP 1979

What We have 32 MIN
16mm
Color
Follows the growing relationship between a grandmother and a rebellious youth at the Teaching - Learning Communities of the Ann Arbor, Michigan, Public Schools where both elderly and young people benefit from contact with each other.
Education; Health and Safety
Dist - UMICH **Prod** - UMICH

What we know 30 MIN
VHS
Effective teacher telecourse series
Color (T)
$69.95 purchase, $50.00 rental
Reviews the concepts and strategies taught in the series. Hosted by Dr Loren Anderson.
Education; Psychology
Dist - SCETV **Prod** - SCETV 1987

What We Need to Know to Conquer Addiction 31 MIN
VHS
Back to Reality Series
Color (G)
$565.00 purchase, $70.00 rental _ #9686, 0646J
Follows a family as it begins to confront the issue of addiction of one of its members. Part one of a three - part series which features Hugh Downs as narrator. Available in 3/4 inch video format by special request.
Guidance and Counseling; Health and Safety; Psychology
Dist - HAZELB **Prod** - JOHNIN

What Went Wrong 20 MIN
VHS / U-matic
Color
Provides managers and supervisors with skills to identify problems and their impact on the organization. Goes on to provide the know - how to make the appropriate decisions to solve the problems. Leader's Guide available to extend course for three hours of training.
Business and Economics; Psychology
Dist - CREMED **Prod** - CREMED

What went wrong - turning mistakes into gold
BETA / VHS / U-matic
Color (G IND)
$495.00 purchase, $95.00 rental _ #QHG0
Shows supervisors how to create an open atmosphere for uncovering mistakes, finding the patterns which are causing mistakes, changing such patterns and looking at such problems as opportunities for growth.
Business and Economics; Psychology
Dist - BBP **Prod** - BBP 1990

What, Where and When - the Story of the U S Army Supply and Maintenance Command 27 MIN
16mm
Color
LC 74-705947
Describes the dual mission of the U S Army Supply and Maintenance Command to deliver supplies to the soldier and to perform fifth echelon maintenance of Army equipment.
Civics and Political Systems; Industrial and Technical Education
Dist - USNAC **Prod** - USA 1966

What will I be 30 MIN
U-matic
Color
Examines the problems of sexism in education and its effects on children. Discusses how two teachers have been deeply involved in changing sexism in education in British Columbia.
History - World; Sociology
Dist - WMENIF **Prod** - WMENIF

What will I be Tomorrow 14 MIN
U-matic / VHS / 16mm
Just One Child Series
Color (I J)
Depicts the changing life of a thirteen year old son of proud, cattle - herding Masai parents in Kenya. Shows how he spends his day herding, watering, feeding, and milking the cows owned by his father, who has two wives and eight children, all living in a settlement of dried dung huts. Defines how new ways are testing traditional culture and making growing up more difficult.
Geography - World; Psychology; Sociology
Dist - BCNFL **Prod** - REYEXP 1983

What will I do with My Time 26 MIN
16mm
Color
LC 77-700595
Presents a series of portraits of men and women from different socio - economic and geographic backgrounds as they engage in a wide variety of professional and non - professional careers.
Guidance and Counseling
Dist - MTP **Prod** - NYLI 1976

What will the Weather be 11 MIN
16mm / U-matic / VHS
Color (P I J)
LC FIA68-2739
Reviews the general nature of the atmosphere. Introduces those air conditions in which measureable changes occur - - temperature, pressure, wind direction and velocity and humidity. Explains the basis for local weather reports and forecasts.
Science; Science - Physical
Dist - ALTSUL **Prod** - FILMSW 1968

What will the Weather be 25 MIN
VHS
Active Atmosphere Series
Color (J)
$79.00 purchase _ #2250V
Illustrates forecasting techniques. Explains the responsibilities of the National Weather Service.

Examines the monitoring of severe weather conditions. Considers the different types of clouds associated with certain types of weather. Part of an eight - part series on the atmosphere and the weather it creates. Includes a comprehensive study guide.
Science - Physical
Dist - SCTRES **Prod** - SCTRES

What will We do on Saturday 20 MIN
16mm
Inherit the Earth Series
Color (I)
Explains that our decreasing workday, coupled with increasing affluence, is resulting in more and more leisure time for the majority of our society. Points out that this new found leisure is creating some serious psychological and environmental problems. Stresses the fact that our society can no longer stress vocational - oriented education alone, it must also begin to educate for the use of leisure as well.
Education; Sociology
Dist - GPN **Prod** - KQEDTV

What will Your New Venture Demand 20 MIN
U-matic / VHS / 16mm
Starting a Business Series
Color (H C A)
Challenges those planning careers to examine their strengths and interests and assess what role is best.
Business and Economics; Guidance and Counseling
Dist - BCNFL **Prod** - SOMFIL 1983

What wives wish their husbands knew about women - Part 4 90 MIN
VHS
Focus on the family series
Color (G A R)
$24.99 purchase, $10.00 rental _ #35 - 83581 - 533
Presents Dr James Dobson in a discussion of what wives wish their husbands knew about women.
Sociology
Dist - APH **Prod** - WORD

What would Happen if 9 MIN
16mm
Color
LC 70-706883
Illustrates what would happen if everyone stole things. Stimulates oral language skills.
English Language; Psychology; Sociology
Dist - MLA **Prod** - MLA 1969

What would You do 8 MIN
16mm
Color (P I)
LC 73-700632
Depicts two children at play, one black, one white. Poses problematical situations requiring active student participation and assessment of basic human values.
Guidance and Counseling; Sociology
Dist - ATLAP **Prod** - ATLAP 1973

What would You do 24 MIN
VHS / 16mm
Color (K)
$109.95 purchase
Encourages children to think about what's right and what's wrong. Combines four units previously available separately as fimstrips or enhanced videos: Finders, Keepers (about stealing), To Tell Or Not To Tell (tattling), The Easy Way Out (cheating), and I Wish I Hadn't Said That (lying).
Education; Religion and Philosophy
Dist - JANUP **Prod** - JANUP

What would You do 20 MIN
16mm / U-matic / VHS
Color
Presents six open - ended vignettes representing typical situations police officers might encounter in dealing with the mentally retarded.
Civics and Political Systems; Education; Psychology; Social Science
Dist - CORF **Prod** - UKANS 1979

What would you do - a video and curriculum for grades K - 2 11 MIN
VHS
Color (K P)
$95.00 purchase
Presents three short interactive segments to help students develop decision - making and problem - solving skills related to the avoidance of substance abuse. Uses short vignettes to discuss medication, alcohol and the use of youngsters in drug trafficking. Produced by the Bank Street College of Education.
Guidance and Counseling; Health and Safety; Psychology
Dist - SELMED

What would You do - Banking 11 MIN
U-matic / VHS
(PRO)
$325.00 purchase, $85.00 rental
Presents possible awkward customer service situations, with the opportunity for the trainer to discuss solutions and company policies with the viewers.
Business and Economics
Dist - CREMED **Prod** - CREMED 1987

What would you do - banking version 10 MIN
VHS
Color (A PRO IND)
$325.00 purchase, $85.00 rental
Presents dramatic vignettes which portray common bank customer problems. Allows viewers to discuss how to resolve each situation.
Business and Economics; Guidance and Counseling; Psychology
Dist - VLEARN **Prod** - AIMS

What would You do - Banks 11 MIN
VHS / 16mm
Color (PRO)
$325.00 purchase, $85.00 rental, $30.00 preview
Presents dramatizations which teach the bank employee how to handle situations in which a customer has a problem and wants an exception to company policy.
Business and Economics; Psychology
Dist - UTM **Prod** - UTM

What would You do if a Robber Stuck a Gun in Your Ribs 40 MIN
U-matic / VHS / 16mm
National Crime and Violence Test Series
Color
Uses a question and answer session to explain what should be done during a robbery attempt.
Guidance and Counseling; Sociology
Dist - CORF **Prod** - CORF

What would You do - Retail 10 MIN
U-matic / VHS
(PRO)
$35.00 purchase, $85.00 rental
Presents difficult customer service situations and allows the viewer to give feedback. Trainers have the opportunity to present company policy and regulations for the various situations.
Business and Economics
Dist - CREMED **Prod** - CREMED 1987

What would you do - retail version 10 MIN
VHS
Color (A PRO IND)
$325.00 purchase, $85.00 rental
Presents 14 dramatic vignettes which portray common retail customer problems. Allows viewers to discuss how to resolve each situation.
Business and Economics; Guidance and Counseling; Psychology
Dist - VLEARN **Prod** - AIMS

What would You do Series
Behavior - Drugs in the Home - the Stranger 3 MIN
Dist - MSTRMD

What would You Really do if Accosted by a Rapist 40 MIN
16mm / U-matic / VHS
National Crime and Violence Test Series
Color
Uses a question and answer session to explain what to do if accosted by a rapist.
Guidance and Counseling; Sociology
Dist - CORF **Prod** - CORF

What you are is... 150 MIN
VHS / 16mm / U-matic
Color (G PRO A)
$2195.00, $995.00 purchase, $300.00, $250.00 rental
Combines What You Are Is Where You Were When and its sequel, What You Are Is Not What You Have to Be, both by Morris Massey. Exposes the value programming influences of the past and present. Explores present day conflict between the younger and older generations. Stresses the need to accept responsibility for creating positive change first within the self and in those around us. Includes leader's manual and participant's workbook.
Business and Economics; Guidance and Counseling; Psychology; Sociology
Dist - MAGVID **Prod** - MAGVID 1984

What you are is 150 MIN
VHS / U-matic
Massey series
Color (G)
$1095.00, $995.00 purchase, $250.00 rental
Discusses the generational imprinting, modeling and socialization of individuals which forms their value systems. Considers how to communicate and interact with people from diverse backgrounds. Features Dr Morris Massey. Part two of a four - part series.
Business and Economics; History - United States; Psychology; Social Science
Dist - VPHI **Prod** - VPHI 1984

What You are is 60 MIN
16mm / U-matic / VHS
Color (C A)
Presents Dr Morris Massey making observations on each generation in terms of social, political and moral events, and attitudes that affected their lives while growing up. Relates these underlying influences to the way we work, play and worship.
Psychology
Dist - FI **Prod** - CBSTV 1983

What you are is not what you have to be - Part B 69 MIN
U-matic / VHS
Massey triad series
Color (G PRO A)
$875.00 purchase, $200.00 rental
Presents an exploration of the development of value systems. Stresses the need for self - understanding in order to work with others more efficiently. Looks at intergenerational conflict. Part two of a three - part series. Features Morris Massey.
Business and Economics; Guidance and Counseling; Psychology; Sociology
Dist - MAGVID **Prod** - MAGVID 1986

What You are is , Pt 1 30 MIN
BETA / 16mm
Massey Tapes Series
Color (A)
Presents Dr Morris Massey explaining how value systems are formed and how one can change his own and those of other people. Emphasizes improving communications.
Guidance and Counseling; Psychology
Dist - CBSFOX **Prod** - CBSFOX

What You are is , Pt 2 60 MIN
BETA / 16mm
Massey Tapes Series
Color (A)
Presents Dr Morris Massey explaining how value systems are formed and how one can change his own and those of other people. Emphasizes improving communications.
Guidance and Counseling; Psychology
Dist - CBSFOX **Prod** - CBSFOX

What You are is , Pt 3 30 MIN
BETA / 16mm
Massey Tapes Series
Color (A)
Presents Dr Morris Massey explaining how value systems are formed and how one can change his own and those of other people. Emphasizes improving communications.
Guidance and Counseling; Psychology
Dist - CBSFOX **Prod** - CBSFOX

What You are is what You Choose - So Don't Screw it Up 85 MIN
VHS / 16mm
Color (PRO)
Explores motivation. Reinforces training agendas on ethics, empowerment, teams and leadership.
Business and Economics; Guidance and Counseling; Psychology
Dist - VICOM **Prod** - VICOM 1990
MAGVID

What you are is what you were when - Part A 64 MIN
VHS / U-matic
Massey triad series
Color (G PRO A)
$875.00 purchase, $200.00 rental
Presents an exploration of the development of value systems. Stresses the need for self - understanding in order to work with others more efficiently. Looks at intergenerational conflict. Part one of a three - part series. Features Morris Massey.
Business and Economics; Guidance and Counseling; Psychology; Sociology
Dist - MAGVID **Prod** - MAGVID 1986

What You are is Where You See 75 MIN
16mm / BETA
Massey Tapes Series
Color (A)
Shows Dr Morris Massey describing how to prepare for a better future by adopting a more flexible and realistic point of view. Focuses on positive change.
Guidance and Counseling; Psychology
Dist - CBSFOX **Prod** - CBSFOX
VPHI
MAGVID

What you are is where you see 75 MIN
VHS / U-matic
Massey series
Color (G)

$1095.00, $995.00 purchase, $250.00 rental
Discusses the generational imprinting, modeling and socialization of individuals which forms their value systems. Considers how to communicate and interact with people from diverse backgrounds. Features Dr Morris Massey. Part four of a four - part series.
Business and Economics; History - United States; Psychology; Social Science
Dist - VPHI **Prod** - VPHI 1984

What You are is Where You were When 90 MIN
16mm / BETA
Massey Tapes Series
Color (A)
Features Dr Morris Massey explaining how persons' individual value systems are formed through their early life experiences. Discusses imprinting, modeling and socialization.
Psychology
Dist - CBSFOX **Prod** - CBSFOX
VPHI

What you are is where you were when 90 MIN
VHS / 16mm / U-matic
Color (G PRO A)
$1295.00, $695.00 purchase, $250.00, $200.00 rental
Presents Morris Massey and his orginal probe into the value - progamming years of the development of an individual. Stimulates self - understanding and understanding of others who are different from the self.
Business and Economics; Guidance and Counseling; Psychology
Dist - MAGVID **Prod** - MAGVID 1976

What You are Is'nt Necessarily what You will be 60 MIN
16mm / BETA
Massey Tapes Series
Color (A)
Shows Dr Morris Massey profiling two generations of Americans, traditionalists and rejectionists. Explains how the two groups attained their distinct value systems and offers a basis for bridging the generation gap.
Psychology
Dist - CBSFOX **Prod** - CBSFOX

What You are Isn't Necessarily what You will be 60 MIN
U-matic / VHS / 16mm
Color (C A)
Presents Dr Morris Massey profiling two unique generations within American society, the traditionalists and the rejectionists. Defines the two groups and their approaches to solving problems.
Psychology
Dist - FI **Prod** - MAGVID 1980

What You Bring on Yourself 15 MIN
16mm / VHS
Color (PRO)
$295.00, $420.00 purchase, $75.00 rental, $50.00 preview
Discusses how employees with Type A behavior patterns affect the work environment. Teaches managers how to help reduce the stress of compulsive employees through positive reinforcement.
Business and Economics; Guidance and Counseling; Psychology; Sociology
Dist - UTM **Prod** - UTM

What You Bring on Yourself 15 MIN
16mm / U-matic / VHS
Managing Stress Series
Color (H C A)
Shows the effect of personality on stress and shows the importance of professional help.
Psychology
Dist - CORF
CENTEF

What You Can do 30 MIN
VHS / U-matic
CHD and You Series
Color
Suggests ways of combatting the nine problems that may indicate a predisposition to CHD. Examines the interrelationships among obesity, exercise and elevated levels of serum cholesterol and triglyceride.
Health and Safety
Dist - NETCHE **Prod** - NETCHE 1976

What You Don't Know Can Hurt You
U-matic / VHS
Color
Shows the importance for older patients in understanding their health problems and the treatments and medicines being prescribed to them.
Health and Safety
Dist - GRANVW **Prod** - GRANVW

What you don't know can hurt you - toxicology 16 MIN
BETA / VHS / U-matic
Hazard communication series
Color (IND G)
$395.00 purchase _ #600 - 12
Informs employees of the potentially harmful effects of chemicals. Examines the nature of toxic effects, the dose - response relationship, routes of entry. Describes various acute and chronic effects. Part of a series on hazard communication.
Health and Safety; Industrial and Technical Education; Psychology
Dist - ITSC **Prod** - ITSC

What You Don't Know Can Kill You - Sexually Transmitted Diseases and AIDS 54 MIN
VHS
Color (J H)
$209.00 purchase _ #60122
Defines sexually transmitted diseases, breaking them into three categories - viral infections, bacterial infection, and diseases caused by organisms like protozoans and fungi.
Guidance and Counseling; Health and Safety
Dist - GA **Prod** - GA 1989

What You Don't Know - Learning about Hazardous Materials
U-matic / 16mm
Color (A)
Stresses joint effort by company, supervisor and workers to make the work environment safe from hazardous substance exposure.
Health and Safety
Dist - BNA **Prod** - BNA 1983

What You Just Did 29 MIN
U-matic / VHS
Color (I)
Presents visually hypnotic sequences of movement interspersed with dancers talking about improvisation, being male, touching, the give - and - take of 'contact dance' and dance as art - sport.
Fine Arts; Physical Education and Recreation
Dist - UCV **Prod** - UCV

What you must know about drugs - Volume 1 and Volume 2 31 MIN
VHS
Color (I J)
$128.00 purchase
Presents safety rules about the use of prescription drugs in Volume 1. Discusses the effects of alcohol upon the body and fetal alcohol syndrome in Volume 2. Introduces the concept of addition. Suggests follow - up activities.
Guidance and Counseling; Health and Safety; Psychology
Dist - BRODAT **Prod** - SRA 1987

What you need to know about asbestos abatement projects 14 MIN
8mm cartridge / VHS / BETA / U-matic
Color; PAL (IND G PRO)
$295.00 purchase, $175.00 rental _ #ACT - 100
Shows what workers need to know to prevent their exposure during an asbestos abatement project as well as to alleviate needless worry. Presents the history and use of asbestos, shows why asbestos is dangerous and discusses symptoms of exposure. Identifies diseases caused by asbestos and highlights the actions taken to protect employees during abatement. Describes methods used to identify, remove or cover asbestos. Examines warning signs, marks and labels and details what must be done if an employee's job requires entry to the abatement are and more. Includes leader's guide and ten workbooks.
Health and Safety
Dist - BNA

What you need to know about the new taxpayer Bill of Rights 210 MIN
VHS
Color (C PRO A)
$67.20, $200.00 purchase _ #M738, #P244
Presents a comprehensive and practical explanation of this set of provisions created by the Technical and Miscellaneous Revenue Act of 1988.
Civics and Political Systems
Dist - ALIABA **Prod** - ALIABA 1989

What you never knew about sex 25 MIN
VHS / U-matic
Developmental biology series
Color (H C)
$250.00 purchase _ #HP - 5982C
Looks at the factors which influence sexual differentiation. Examines species which use one, two or more mechanisms to create a balanced supply of female and male individuals. Shows that humans, like many reptiles, employ chromosomal sex determinants. Reveals how meiosis gives rise to equal numbers of female and male offspring. Part of a four - part series on biology which addresses regeneration, internal and external structures, cellular communication, gender influences, growth and stability of form.
Science; Science - Natural
Dist - CORF **Prod** - BBCTV 1990

What you say is what you get 13 MIN
VHS
Let's get along - conflict skills training series
Color (P I)
$69.95 purchase _ #10382VG
Teaches the importance of tone of voice and using positive or negative words. Features Gary Wick, ventriloquist and comedian, as he shows kids conflict skills. Includes a reproducible teacher's guide. Part of a four - part series.
Psychology; Social Science
Dist - UNL

What You Should Know about Your Pension Plan 28 MIN
U-matic / VHS / 16mm
Color
Features a public affairs program in talk show format that discusses pension plans and the problems that occur with receiving benefits, and what to do about them.
Social Science; Sociology
Dist - USNAC **Prod** - USDL

What You Take for Granted 75 MIN
16mm / VHS
Color (G)
$950.00, $250.00 purchase, $150.00, $100.00 rental
Looks at women's experiences in jobs traditionally held by men. Explores the tentative friendship between Anna, a feisty, tough talking truckdriver, and Diana, an upper middle class doctor. Weaves in fictionalized interviews of four other non - traditionally employed women to intercut narrative and documentary.
Business and Economics; Fine Arts; Sociology
Dist - WMEN **Prod** - MICI 1983

Whatabout Series
Measuring in Science 14 MIN
Observing in Science 14 MIN
Dist - AITECH

What'Cha Gonna do 11 MIN
U-matic / 16mm
Color
Shows some simple and effective ways that children use to protect themselves from abduction. Dramatizes situations in which youngsters are approached by strangers.
Health and Safety; Sociology
Dist - PEREN **Prod** - PEREN

Whatcha Gonna do Series
Getting Ready 15 MIN
Dist - EBEC

Whatever Happened to Baby Jane 132 MIN
16mm
B&W
Focuses on two aging actresses who live as recluses in their old mansion. Tells what happens when one woman (Joan Crawford) decides to sell the house and put her sister (Bette Davis) in an old people's home.
Fine Arts
Dist - TWYMAN **Prod** - WB 1962

Whatever Happened to Childhood? 45 MIN
U-matic / VHS / 16mm
Color (H C A)
$495 purchase - 16 mm, $320 purchase - video
Discusses the complex problems of today's children, such as drug use, sexual and criminal behavior, and family breakdowns. Produced by Churchill Films and Chris - Craft Television Productions.
Sociology
Dist - CF

Whatever Happened to Childhood 46 MIN
16mm / U-matic / VHS
Color (H C T)
Explains how the concept of childhood is being obliterated by early drug usage, a changing sexual morality and an indifference to criminal behavior.
Health and Safety; Sociology
Dist - CF **Prod** - KCOPTV 1984

Whatever Happened to El Salvador 52 MIN
VHS / U-matic
Color (H C A)
Examines the situation in El Salvador since the elections held March 28, 1982. Includes exclusive interviews with members of the U S Special Forces training government troops, who specifically deny that they have been involved in the fighting.
History - World
Dist - FI **Prod** - NBCNEW 1982

Whatever Happened to Green Valley 55 MIN
16mm
Color (H C A)
LC 75-702397
Presents a view of Green Valley, a large government - sponsored housing project outside of Sydney, Australia,

from the vantage point of its residents. Attempts to counteract unfavorable publicity and criticism from sectors of the mass media.
Geography - World; Sociology
Dist - AUIS **Prod** - FLMAUS 1975

Whatever Happened to Honesty 13 MIN
U-matic / VHS / 16mm
Color (I A)
LC 77-700046
Investigates the problem of theft and its effect on the American way of life.
Sociology
Dist - HIGGIN **Prod** - HIGGIN 1977

Whatever Happened to Lori Jean Lloyd 28 MIN
16mm / U-matic / VHS
Dealing with Social Problems in the Classroom Series
Color (J)
LC 81-700336
Presents a view of the life of runaway children along the back alleys of Hollywood and along New York's infamous Minnesota Strip, where they become victims of drugs, sexual exploitation, disease, fear, loneliness, deprivation and death.
Psychology; Sociology
Dist - FI **Prod** - BELLDA 1980

Whatever Happened to Marx 26 MIN
U-matic / VHS / 16mm
Today's History Series
Color (H C)
Presents the influence of Karl Marx in the Russian Revolution of 1917 and its effect on the Third World.
Civics and Political Systems; History - United States; History - World
Dist - JOU **Prod** - JOU 1984

Whatever Happened to Mike 12 MIN
16mm
Color (H C A)
LC 79-700078
Tells how a young man who had a reading problem in school learned to overcome it and became a skilled worker. A sequel to the motion picture If A Boy Can't Learn.
English Language; Psychology
Dist - LAWREN **Prod** - LAWREN 1979

Whatever happened to the human race series
Features Dr Francis Schaeffer and former U S Surgeon General Dr C Everett Koop in a highly critical view of abortion, euthanasia and infanticide. Suggests that these practices reflect a decline in respect for human life, and that Christianity provides the only answer to these and other moral questions. Includes five episodes on three tapes, as well as a study guide. Produced by FSV.
Whatever happened to the human race series 250 MIN
Dist - GF

Whatever Your New Year's Resolutions 1 MIN
U-matic
Color
Does a take - off on the Rosie's Diner paper towel commercials. Deals with new year's resolutions.
Sociology
Dist - LVN **Prod** - MDPL

What'll I do if 10 MIN
16mm
Golden Triangle Teller Training Film Series
Color (H C A)
LC 75-701989
Helps bank tellers and others who handle money in dealing with a robbery situation. Stresses three simple rules which are do exactly what the robber says, make no suspicious moves while the robber is watching and get a good description of the robber.
Business and Economics; Health and Safety; Sociology
Dist - PART **Prod** - PART 1975

What'll it do for Me 22 MIN
16mm
Color
Demonstrates the usefulness of the UNIVAC computer, stressing capability, versatility and performance of the UNIVAC 9000 series.
Mathematics
Dist - UNIVAC **Prod** - SPGYRO 1970

What'll we do with the waste when we're through 13 MIN
VHS
Color (I J H)
$30.00 purchase _ #A5VH 1384; $25.00 purchase _ #1155RG, #115504G
Addresses concerns about the transportation and disposal of high - level nuclear waste. Describes nuclear energy, how it is used and shows ways to properly store the waste. Although produced by the American Nuclear Society, it does present many facts about nuclear waste and explains current disposal methods.
Science - Physical; Social Science; Sociology
Dist - CLRVUE
UNL

What'll You do if 12 MIN
16mm
You and Your Car Series
B&W (J)
Illustrates in a group of emergency situations such conditions as the brakes failing, the accelerator sticking, the car going off the pavement and the car skidding. Describes some of the dangers to be alert for in routine driving.
Health and Safety; Social Science
Dist - PART **Prod** - PART 1964

What's a Balanced Diet 28 MIN
16mm
Food for Youth Series
Color
LC 76-701598
Defines the four basic food groups, namely fruits and vegetables, breads and cereals, milk and milk products and meat, poultry and fish. Discusses how much of each group children need. Explains meat alternatives and gives the latest USDA recommendations for type A school lunches.
Health and Safety; Home Economics; Social Science
Dist - USNAC **Prod** - USFNS 1974

What's a Balanced Diet 15 MIN
U-matic / VHS
Great American Eating Machine - You Series Pt 4; Pt 4
Color (P)
LC 83-706108
Explains a balanced diet and emphasizes the importance of food choices. Features situations where children can exercise some choice over the foods they eat, namely, in the school cafeteria and at snack time.
Health and Safety; Social Science
Dist - GPN **Prod** - NJPTV 1982

What's a Cop 25 MIN
U-matic / VHS / 16mm
Law Enforcement Education Series
Color
LC 73-702206
Describes opinions held by the public about the police tells of problems faced by the police in doing their job.
Civics and Political Systems; Social Science; Sociology
Dist - CORF **Prod** - WORON 1973

What's a Coward - a Drama 15 MIN
16mm
Guidance - Emotions Series
Color
LC 74-703612
Shows how a young boy copes with the fears and uncertainties associated with moving from a small town to the inner city.
Guidance and Counseling
Dist - MORLAT **Prod** - MORLAT 1973

What's a Good Book - Selecting Books for Children 27 MIN
U-matic / VHS / 16mm
Color (C A)
LC 82-701203
Presents librarians, authors and college professors who address the question of what constitutes a good book for children citing literary quality, incidents linking plot with life and a book's ability to fulfill a particular purpose.
Education; Literature and Drama
Dist - WWS **Prod** - PULIDO 1982

What's a good story - Noah's ark 20 MIN
VHS / U-matic
Long ago and far away series
Color (I)
$250.00 purchase _ #HP - 6092C
Uses animation by Peter Spier to discover parallels between the world of Noah and the present time. Teaches about the problems of living together on Planet Earth. Narrated by James Earl Jones. Part of the Long Ago and Far Away Series.
Fine Arts; Literature and Drama
Dist - CORF **Prod** - WGBHTV 1990

What's a Heaven for 18 MIN
16mm
Color
LC FIE68-18
A college art presentation about Booker T Washington's life and effect on America.
Biography; History - United States
Dist - USNAC **Prod** - USNPS 1966

What's a heaven for - 6
VHS
Space age series
Color (G)
$24.95 purchase _ #SPA110
Shows how space exploration has contributed to international political change, including helping to bring about the end of the Cold War, hastening the end of the Soviet Union. Reveals that space telecommunications may also have an important role to play in helping developing countries. Features Patrick Stewart as host. Part six of a six - part series.
Civics and Political Systems; History - World; Science - Physical; Sociology
Dist - INSTRU **Prod** - NAOS

What's a Natural Resource 17 MIN
16mm / VHS
Color (P)
$345.00, $310.00 purchase, $50.00 rental
Illustrates the meaning of the term 'natural resource' as a park ranger helps a group of children on a picnic. The ranger explains the sources of water, oil, wood, metals, soil, even air. Emphasizes the difference between renewable and non - renewable resources.
Geography - World; Science - Physical; Social Science
Dist - HIGGIN **Prod** - HIGGIN 1987

What's a Nice Girl Like You Doing in a Place Like this 11 MIN
16mm
B&W (C)
Presents a narrative about a young man with an hallucination. Satirizes the use of the cliche.
English Language
Dist - NYU **Prod** - NYU 1965

What's a nice girl like you doing in a place like this 9 MIN
16mm
B&W (G)
Presents an early film by Martin Scorsese. Portrays a young writer who grows increasingly obsessed with a framed photograph hanging on his wall.
Fine Arts; History - United States
Dist - KINOIC

What's a nice guy like you doing in local TV news 30 MIN
VHS
Inside story series
Color (G)
$50.00 purchase _ #INST - 418
Interviews CBS' Charles Kuralt and three local news anchors in an examination of local news coverage. Considers whether sensationalism sells in local news. Explores how these anchors have managed to stay in such a competitive profession. Hosted by Hodding Carter.
Literature and Drama; Social Science
Dist - PBS

What's a parent to do 52 MIN
VHS
Color (G)
$29.95 purchase _ #MH6182V
Demonstrates ways to develop emotionally healthy babies. Starts in the delivery room and uses humor to present techniques and advice for meeting the biggest challenges of parenting. Shows how to establish a close and loving relationship with infants, what to do and not to do when a baby won't sleep through the night, how to handle the 'terrible twos,' temper tantrums and other difficult stages in child development. Features John Stossel as host, and child development experts, parents, babies and toddlers.
Guidance and Counseling; Health and Safety; Sociology
Dist - CAMV **Prod** - ABCNEW 1992

What's a parent to do - Teenage suicide 21 MIN
VHS / U-matic / 16mm
Color (J H G)
$285.00, $335.00 purchase, $50.00 rental
Studies a community and school system dealing with the problem of teenage suicide. Presents parents, teachers and administrators voicing their concerns and approaches to dealing with this growing problem. Produced by MLA Productions.
Psychology; Social Science; Sociology
Dist - NDIM

What's a Party for? 60 MIN
VHS / U-matic
Bill Moyers' Journal Series
Color
Looks at the decline of political parties.
Civics and Political Systems
Dist - PBS **Prod** - WNETTV 1976

What's Alive 11 MIN
U-matic / VHS / 16mm
Color (P I)
LC FIA67-5854
Illustrates with pictures of animals, plants, machines and chemicals how living and non - living things are alike and different. Shows that only a thing that can move, respond, change fuel into energy, reproduce and grow can be said to be alive.

Science - Natural; Science - Physical
Dist - PHENIX **Prod** - FA 1961

What's an abra without a cadabra 15 MIN
U-matic / 16mm / VHS
Language arts through imagination series
Color (P I)
$400.00, $280.00 purchase _ #JC - 67699
Uses live action, animation and clips from classic Disney movies to portray the magical transportation of Kim and her brother Justin to Figonia when they recite the magic words in a mysterious magic kit. Reveals that they meet the whimsical dragon Figment who tells them he doesn't know the magical words to return them home. Explores the world of words - antonyms, homonyms, synonyms and rhymes - and the 'magic of the mind' as the two youngsters try to discover the word keys that will reverse their fanciful journey and send them home.
English Language; Psychology
Dist - CORF **Prod** - DISNEY 1989

What's an Animal - a First Film 17 MIN
U-matic / 16mm
Color (P I)
Describes the characteristics of the eight most common groups of animals. Shows the variety of animals and points out that all backboned animals make up only one of the eight groups.
Science - Natural
Dist - PHENIX **Prod** - BEANMN 1984

What's an Ergonomic 15 MIN
16mm / U-matic / VHS
Color (H A)
Studies ergonomics, the science that seeks to adapt work or working conditions to suit the worker. Features high - tech furnishings used by the computer society.
Industrial and Technical Education; Mathematics; Science - Physical; Sociology
Dist - KLEINW **Prod** - KLEINW

What's Behind Behavior? 65 FRS
VHS / U-matic
Human Side of Management Series
Color
Explains the many influences that shape a person's behavior.
Business and Economics; Psychology
Dist - RESEM **Prod** - RESEM

What's Behind the Front 30 MIN
Videoreel / VT2
Weather Series
Color
Features meteorologist Frank Sechrist explaining how one low can cause different types of weather in different parts of the country. Relates the pressure, winds, temperature and clouds of the low to the weather.
Science - Physical
Dist - PBS **Prod** - WHATV

What's Bugging Him 14 MIN
U-matic
A Different Understanding Series
Color (PRO)
Follows Kevin, an abused child, who has been placed in a foster home as he learns that he must take responsibility for his role in the family and cooperate with the authorities and his parents.
Psychology; Sociology
Dist - TVOTAR **Prod** - TVOTAR 1985

What's Bugging Him 14 MIN
VHS / 16mm
A Different Understanding Series
Color (G)
$60.00 purchase _ #BPN185901
Shares the experiences of an abused child placed in a foster home for his own safety. Shows how he learns to take responsibility for his role in the family and cooperate with the authorities and his parents.
Sociology
Dist - RMIBHF **Prod** - RMIBHF

What's Communism all about 25 MIN
U-matic / VHS / 16mm
CBS News Special Report for Young People Series
Color (J)
Compares capitalism and communism in the 20th century and examines the history of the communist movement.
Civics and Political Systems
Dist - CAROUF **Prod** - CBSTV 1973

What's Cookin' 30 MIN
16mm
Footsteps Series
Color
LC 79-701560
Focuses on how young children acquire their food likes and dislikes, their feelings about food and their patterns of eating. Provides some basic information about nutrition and explains how parents can help their children develop good eating habits.
Health and Safety; Home Economics; Social Science; Sociology
Dist - USNAC **Prod** - USOE 1978

What's cooking 10 MIN
16mm / VHS / BETA / U-matic
Color; PAL (PRO T G)
PdS120, PdS128 purchase
Teaches how to improve hygiene in food handling and preparation in the home. Includes proper refrigeration, observation of shelf life, blown cans and more. Subject matter is treated in a light - hearted way.
Home Economics
Dist - EDPAT **Prod** - TASCOR 1983

What's Cooking 15 MIN
U-matic / VHS / 16mm
Color (P I J)
LC 79-701692
Shows how five children of Chinese - American, Mexican - American, Italian - American, Afro - American and Anglo ancestry help their families prepare traditional meals. Tells how each culture has different ways of meeting nutritional needs.
Home Economics; Social Science; Sociology
Dist - CF **Prod** - CF 1979

What's Cooking - Nutrition 23 MIN
U-matic / 16mm
Footsteps Series
Color
Deals with developing good eating habits in young children. Discusses attitudes toward eating, children's likes and dislikes, and some basic nutritional information.
Health and Safety; Psychology; Social Science
Dist - PEREN **Prod** - PEREN

What's Cooking Series

Breakfast	28 MIN
Chicken	28 MIN
Eggs	28 MIN
Fish	28 MIN
Inexpensive Meals	28 MIN
International Dinner	28 MIN
Low Calorie	28 MIN
One Pot Meals	28 MIN
Pancakes	28 MIN
Quick skillet	28 MIN
Snacks and Appetizers	28 MIN
Variety Meats	28 MIN
Vegetables	28 MIN

Dist - PBS

What's eating you - a guide to sensible dieting 30 MIN
VHS
Color (I J H C G)
$79.95 purchase _ #CCP0090V
Examines how historical and cultural perspectives of what is beautiful and attractive have changed over the years. Takes an in - depth look at how the body works and what it needs to make it function most efficiently. Covers what approaches to losing weight really work and which ones don't. Discusses the dangers of overeating and fasting and examines how nutritional requirements differ between teenagers and adults. Shows that a healthy diet, exercise and a positive self - image are the keys to looking and feeling great. Includes student manual.
Health and Safety; Home Economics; Physical Education and Recreation; Social Science
Dist - CAMV **Prod** - CAMV 1992

What's Expected of Me? 30 MIN
U-matic
B&W
Focuses on one year in the life of a girl named Renee. Documents the change from the 'kid's world' of sixth grade to the more grown up life of a New York City junior high school.
Psychology; Sociology
Dist - WMEN **Prod** - WMEN

What's for Breakfast 4 MIN
16mm / U-matic / VHS
Most Important Person - Nutrition Series
Color (K P I)
Presents the nutritious and energy - producing foods to start the day with.
Guidance and Counseling; Health and Safety; Home Economics; Social Science
Dist - EBEC **Prod** - EBEC 1972

What's for Breakfast 10 MIN
U-matic
Body Works Series
Color (P I J H)
Presents recipes, exercises and Mother Goose rhymes in honor of the morning meal.
Physical Education and Recreation; Social Science
Dist - TVOTAR **Prod** - TVOTAR 1979

What's going on around here 15 MIN
U-matic / VHS
Dragons, wagons and wax - Set 2 series
Color (K P)
Deals with the relationship between plant and animal communities and their environment.
Science; Science - Natural
Dist - CTI **Prod** - CTI

What's Going on with Women 30 MIN
U-matic
Decison Makers Series
Color
Discusses the diversity of beliefs in the women's movement and where future feminist leaders will come from.
Civics and Political Systems; History - World; Sociology
Dist - HRC **Prod** - OHC

What's Good for GM 55 MIN
U-matic / VHS / 16mm
Color
Offers a dramatic case study of the cost of corporate control over the vital process of urban economic development. Shows how the city of Detroit destroyed it's Poletown neighborhood in the hope of retaining a few thousand industrial jobs. Shows unions and citizen groupsexploring ways to insure that their investment in reindustrialization pays off in a more stable employment base.
Business and Economics; Sociology
Dist - CANWRL **Prod** - CBSTV 1981

What's Good for Me 15 MIN
U-matic / VHS
Great American Eating Machine - You Series Pt 3; Pt 3
Color (P)
LC 83-706107
Explains the body's need for a variety of foods and nutrients. Presents Mother Hubbard telling about the functions and sources of carbohydrates, fats, proteins, vitamins and minerals.
Health and Safety; Social Science
Dist - GPN **Prod** - NJPTV 1982

What's good for the shareholder - Volume II 27 MIN
VHS / U-matic / BETA
Into the boardroom series
Color (C A G)
$870.00 purchase, $240.00 rental
Cautions investors not to confuse rising share price with rising shareholder value. Offers formulas for evaluating a company's potential. Produced jointly by The Economist and Video Arts.
Business and Economics
Dist - VIDART **Prod** - VIDART 1993

What's good health 15 MIN
VHS
Drug wise series
(I)
$40 purchase, $25 rental, $75 self dub
Discusses the individual as a whole person made up of physical, social, mental, spiritual and emotional parts.
Health and Safety; Psychology; Sociology
Dist - GPN **Prod** - NCGE 1984 - 1985

What's good health 15 MIN
U-matic / VHS
Drug wise series; Module 1
Color (I)
Introduces the concept of the individual as a `whole person' who is made up of many parts, physical, social, mental, emotional and spiritual.
Health and Safety
Dist - GPN **Prod** - WDCNTV

What's Good to Eat 18 MIN
U-matic / 16mm
Color (P I J) (SPANISH)
Shows how the body uses nutrients and how the food groups provide necessary nutrients.
Health and Safety; Social Science
Dist - PEREN **Prod** - WFP

What's Half, What's a Fourth 15 MIN
U-matic
Math Factory, Module V - Fractions Series
Color (P)
Introduces the concepts of one - half and one - fourth.
Mathematics
Dist - GPN **Prod** - MAETEL 1973

What's Happened Since 'Fire' 13 MIN
U-matic / VHS / 16mm
Color (J)
Offers an update of the ABC television special Close - Up On Fire. Discusses the manufacture of flammable plastic cribs, new methods of testing urethane, and the problems of high - rise building fires.
Health and Safety
Dist - PHENIX **Prod** - SANDEM 1976

What's Happened Since Fire 13 MIN
16mm / U-matic / VHS
Color (H C A)
LC 76-702515
Based on the television special Fire in the ABC series Closeup. Includes the controversial test burning of a baby's crib made of polystyrene and interviews with the president of the American Plastics Association. Reports the progress and need for consumer fire safety protection.
Health and Safety; Home Economics; Industrial and Technical Education
Dist - PHENIX **Prod** - PHENIX 1976

What's happening to me 30 MIN
VHS
Color; Captioned (I J H)
$19.95 purchase _ #S01456
Uses an animated format to address the changes and concerns of puberty.
Health and Safety; Psychology; Sociology
Dist - UILL

What's Happening to Television 60 MIN
16mm
At Issue Series
B&W (H C A)
Presents a critical view of the program material which is being shown by commercial and educational TV. Includes comments by network executives, news commentators, writers, the Nielson Company President and the FCC chairman. Discusses the viewer's responsibility.
Education; Guidance and Counseling; Psychology; Social Science; Sociology
Dist - IU **Prod** - NET 1966

What's his name and the stopped clock 30 MIN
VHS
Davey and Goliath series
Color (P I R)
$19.95 purchase, $10.00 rental _ #4 - 8835
Presents two 15 - minute 'Davey and Goliath' episodes. 'What's His Name?' shows how Davey deals with being wrongly blamed for vandalism. 'The Stopped Clock' explores how a nightmare of an empty world makes Davey appreciate his friends and family. Produced by the Evangelical Lutheran Church in America.
Literature and Drama; Religion and Philosophy
Dist - APH

What's Impeachment all about 15 MIN
U-matic / VHS / 16mm
CBS News Special Report for Young People Series
Color
Shows that the Founding Fathers conceived of the idea of impeachment because they were well experienced with tyrannical monarchs they couldn't get rid of. Reviews where and when the impeachment clause has been implemented.
Civics and Political Systems
Dist - CAROUF **Prod** - CAROUF

What's important to you 15 MIN
VHS / U-matic
Drug wise series; Module 1
Color (I)
Stimulates viewers to think about personal values and beliefs.
Health and Safety
Dist - GPN **Prod** - WDCNTV

What's in a Book 9 MIN
16mm
Pathways to Reading Series
B&W (I J H)
Describes the parts of a book - - title page, table of contents, index, preface, foreword, introduction, chapters, footnotes, appendix, bibliography and glossary. Illustrates the design and art production involved in making a book.
English Language; Guidance and Counseling; Literature and Drama; Psychology
Dist - AVED **Prod** - CBF 1958

What's in a Frame 29 MIN
VHS / U-matic
Photo Show Series
Color
Explains the concepts of framing and composition and how you can use the depth - of - field control to get a good photograph.
Industrial and Technical Education
Dist - PBS **Prod** - WGBHTV 1981

What's in a Horn
U-matic / VHS / 16mm
Color (I)
Shows that a horn works by using valves to change pitch instead of using many horns of different tube size.
Fine Arts
Dist - EBEC **Prod** - EBEC 1983

What's in a Play 17 MIN
U-matic / VHS / 16mm
Color (J)
LC FIA67-5854
Analyzes a simple example of dramatic action - - a conflict between a salesman and a customer - - to show the structure of a play. Points out the three parts - a beginning, a climax and an ending.
English Language; Fine Arts; Literature and Drama
Dist - PHENIX **Prod** - FA 1967

What's in a Rainbow 13 MIN
U-matic / VHS / 16mm
Scientific Fact and Fun Series
Color (P I)
LC 80-701503
Explains how to observe a rainbow. Discusses the techniques of building a scientific model.
Science
Dist - JOU **Prod** - GLDWER 1980

What's in a Shadow 13 MIN
U-matic / VHS / 16mm
Scientific Fact and Fun Series
Color (P I)
LC 80-700260
Relates the shadow to the idea of the Sun's position at different times of day. Shows how a knowledge of that position helps in finding directions.
Science - Physical
Dist - JOU **Prod** - GLDWER 1979

What's in a Spider Web 13 MIN
16mm / U-matic / VHS
Scientific Fact and Fun Series
Color (P I)
LC 82-700386
Shows how a spider uses its web to capture its food, how it lays eggs and raises a family.
Science - Natural
Dist - JOU **Prod** - GLDWER 1981

What's in a Story 12 MIN
U-matic / VHS / 16mm
Color (I J)
LC 78-700924
Tells how pleasure and knowledge can be increased by discovering the different messages a story presents.
English Language; Literature and Drama
Dist - PHENIX **Prod** - PHENIX 1977

What's in an Egg 13 MIN
16mm / U-matic / VHS
Scientific Fact and Fun Series
Color (P I)
Shows how various animals including fish, amphibians, reptiles and insects begin life within an egg.
Science - Natural
Dist - JOU **Prod** - GLDWER 1982

What's in it for Me 29 MIN
16mm / U-matic / VHS
Career Job Opportunity Film Series
Color
LC 79-707888
Tells how the Manpower Development and Training Act skills program helps a young man gain the ability and self - respect needed to get a job. Issued in 1967 as a motion picture.
Guidance and Counseling
Dist - USNAC **Prod** - USDLMA 1979

What's in it for Me 27 MIN
U-matic / VHS
Food for Youth Series
Color (J H A)
Industrial and Technical Education; Social Science; Sociology
Dist - CORNRS **Prod** - CUETV 1975

What's in it for Me 28 MIN
16mm / U-matic / VHS
B&W (H C A)
LC 74-706323
Follows a young man through his experiences with the Job Corps where he begins as an unskilled laborer with many frustrations. Shows him as he goes through the Youth Opportunity Center to become skilled and employable.
Sociology
Dist - USNAC **Prod** - USDLMA 1967

What's in it for Me - the Nutrients 28 MIN
16mm
Food for Youth Series
Color
LC 76-701599
Discusses the six classes of nutrients, namely protein, fats, carbohydrates, vitamins, minerals and water. Shows why each is important to the body, making specific reference to USDA guidelines for school lunches.
Health and Safety; Home Economics; Social Science
Dist - USNAC **Prod** - USFNS 1974

What's in it for you? 30 MIN
VHS / U-matic
Appraisals in action series; Ses 1
Color
Covers the why of a systematic and ongoing performance appraisal system. Shows how appraisal systems provide organizations with meaningful data for manpower planning and development.
Business and Economics; Guidance and Counseling; Psychology
Dist - DELTAK **Prod** - PRODEV

What's in that Dish 28 MIN
U-matic / VHS
Color (C)
$249.00, $149.00 purchase _ #AD - 1588
Asks if eating is hazardous to health. Considers salmonella in chicken dishes, leafy greens sprayed with carcinogens. Features Phil Donahue and Ralph Nader.
Health and Safety; Psychology; Social Science; Sociology
Dist - FOTH **Prod** - FOTH

What's in the box 30 MIN
VHS
Join in series
Color (K P)
#362307
Shows that Zack has won the role of a skater in a play and Nikki is helping him with it, but they have a hard time concentrating because they are so curious about a large box that is waiting for Jacob. Discusses curiosity in a story, 'Don't Open That Door.' Part of a series about three artist - performers who share studio space in a converted warehouse.
Fine Arts; Literature and Drama
Dist - TVOTAR **Prod** - TVOTAR 1989

What's in the Box? 30 MIN
U-matic / VHS
Eager to Learn Series
Color (T)
Education; Psychology
Dist - KTEHTV **Prod** - KTEHTV

What's in the Course - 1 30 MIN
VHS
English 101 - Ingles 101 Series
Color (H)
$125.00 purchase
Presents a series of thirty 30 - minute programs in basic English for native speakers of Spanish. Focuses on a specific topic in order to emphasize a particular grammatical point or set of idioms. English is used from the beginning as the primary language of instruction but Spanish translations are included to ensure understanding. Part 1 introduces the course.
English Language; Foreign Language
Dist - AITECH **Prod** - UPRICO 1988

What's inside a seed 12 MIN
VHS / U-matic / 16mm
Wonder world of science series
Color (P)
$320.00, $250.00 purchase _ #HP - 5763C
Stars Wondercat who discovers a baby plant inside a bean seed with help from a magnifying glass. Uses time - lapse photography to observe how roots of baby plants grow downward while stems grow upward. Shows what plants need to grow, how flowers form and that flowers make fruit - and that seeds which make more baby plants are in the fruit. Part of the Wonder World of Science series. Produced by Bill Walker Productions.
Science - Natural
Dist - CORF

What's inside these shorts 50 MIN
VHS
Color (G)
$45.00 purchase
Features Juggling, a hilarious and manic short about the pressure of combining motherhood with work, starring Sue White, of the Mutants; Beat It, an exercise in frustration; The Training, as serious as any potty - training film can be; Check Up, where radically cropped frames reveal the mechanics of feminine hygiene at its clinical coolest; and a sweet look at pre - pubescent lust.
Fine Arts; Literature and Drama; Sociology
Dist - CANCIN **Prod** - SHEREL

What's Inside Your Body, Volume 2 30 MIN
VHS / 16mm
Science, Health and Math Series
Color (P)
$39.95 purchase _ #CL7911
Introduces basic concepts of human anatomy.
Home Economics; Science - Natural
Dist - EDUCRT

What's Inside Your Body, Volume I 30 MIN
VHS / 16mm
Science, Health and Math Series

Color (P)
$39.95 purchase _ #CL7910
Introduces basic concepts of human anatomy.
Home Economics; Science - Natural
Dist - EDUCRT

What's it all about 28 MIN
U-matic / BETA / VHS
Communication skills 2 - advanced series
Color (H C G)
$101.95, $89.95 purchase _ #CA - 01
Overviews the major units of study for the 26 programs of the series. Defines the elements of the communication process - source, channel, receiver, encode and decode. Coordinates elements of the series in to a learning package.
Social Science
Dist - INSTRU

What's it all about 12 MIN
16mm
Color (H C)
Presents a factual look at the economic consequences of competition. Shows what happens when an important product line is nearly eliminated because it no longer can compete in the market place.
Business and Economics
Dist - GM **Prod** - GM

What's it all about, Harry 29 MIN
16mm
Color (IND)
LC 73-700531
Follows a young telephone installer as he takes his kid brother along on his saturday errands. Shows how they give ratings to the kinds of service they receive and in turn are rated on the craft jobs done the day before.
Guidance and Counseling; Industrial and Technical Education; Social Science
Dist - PART **Prod** - ILBELL 1970

What's it all about - hazard communication - De que se trata todo esto 11 MIN
BETA / VHS / U-matic
Hazard communication - live - action video series
Color (IND G) (SPANISH)
$495.00 purchase _ #820 - 01, #820 - 16
Introduces the OSHA Hazard Communication standard requirements for chemical hazard evaluations, warning labels, Material Safety Data Sheets - MSDSs, written hazard communication plans and work area specific training. Part of a series on hazard communication.
Health and Safety; Industrial and Technical Education; Psychology
Dist - ITSC **Prod** - ITSC

What's it all about - warehouse hazard communication training package 16 MIN
VHS
Color (IND)
$395.00 purchase, $95.00 rental _ #820 - 43
Simplifies compliance with OSHA Hazard Communication Standard for warehouse operations. Includes leader's guide, ten study booklets, two posters.
Health and Safety; Psychology
Dist - ITSC **Prod** - ITSC

What's it all about - WP - 1 11 MIN
U-matic
Word Processing Series
(PRO)
$235.00 purchase
Defines word processing and its role in the workplace.
Business and Economics
Dist - MONAD **Prod** - MONAD

What's killing the children 58 MIN
U-matic / VHS
Nova series
Color (H C A)
$250.00 purchase _ #HP - 6378C
Investigates a mysterious disease which killed ten children between the ages of 3 months and 7 years in the rural town of Pomissao in south Brazil in 1984. Reveals that, initially, investigators from the Centers for Disease Control could not identify the disease. Follows the efforts of EIS officer David Fleming who used techniques of epidemiology to identify a new and deadly disease, Brazilian purpuric fever. Part of the Nova series.
Geography - World; Health and Safety
Dist - CORF **Prod** - WGBHTV 1990

What's left is the wind 4 MIN
16mm
Color (G)
$20.00 rental
Meditates on a poetic elegy about the dissolution of memory - not as concrete recall of the past, but as a reconstruction of a fading image that is transformed through time.
Fine Arts; Psychology
Dist - CANCIN **Prod** - PIERCE 1988

What's mine, is mine, is mine - Volume 2 40 MIN
VHS
Circle square series
Color (J H R)
$11.99 purchase _ #35 - 86753 - 979
Explores, from a Biblical perspective, the question of why people should give in a 'gimme' world.
Religion and Philosophy
Dist - APH **Prod** - TYHP

What's Missing - Missing Addends 20 MIN
U-matic
Let's Figure it Out Series
B&W (P)
Mathematics
Dist - NYSED **Prod** - WNYE 1968

What's My Score 20 MIN
16mm
B&W
Demonstrates the ability of paraplegics to show their qualifications and proficiency to handle jobs in competition with nonhandicapped veterans. Shows the basic steps in training a paraplegic to get around and assist himself and features other veterans with various handicaps actually on the job.
Health and Safety
Dist - USVA **Prod** - USVA 1947

What's New in Cancer Research 20 MIN
VHS
Color
From the ABC TV program, 20 20.
Health and Safety
Dist - ABCLR **Prod** - ABCLR 1983

What's New in Cancer Research 20 MIN
VHS / U-matic
$335.00 purchase
Health and Safety; Sociology
Dist - ABCLR **Prod** - ABCLR 1982

Whats New in Diabetes Care? 15 MIN
VHS / U-matic
Color (S)
Provides patients with information about new advancements and current research in the field of diabetes. Discusses blood glucose monitoring, insulin pumps, new oral antidiabetes medications, islet cell and pancreatic transplantation, and the use of new techniques to identify and possibly prevent Type 1 insulin dependent diabetes in certain high risk individuals. Explains how these new advancements may have an impact on the patient with diabetes in the years to come.
Health and Safety
Dist - UMICHM **Prod** - UMICHM 1984

What's New in Solid Waste Management 37 MIN
16mm
Color (J A)
LC 70-714060
Describes new techniques in solid waste management and shows how demonstration grants provide guidance for public works officials throughout America.
Science - Natural
Dist - FINLYS **Prod** - USEPA 1970

What's New Series
A Special Kind of Morning 28 MIN
Dist - IU

What's Nutrition 29 MIN
16mm
Food for Youth Series
Color
LC 76-701600
Presents a brief history of nutrition, emphasizing the importance of forming food habits for a lifetime. Stresses attitudes toward food, nutrition and eating and shows how they affect the job of the school food service worker.
Health and Safety; Home Economics; Social Science
Dist - USNAC **Prod** - USFNS 1974

What's Nutrition 28 MIN
U-matic / VHS
Food for Youth Series
Color (J H A)
Industrial and Technical Education; Social Science; Sociology
Dist - CORNRS **Prod** - CUETV 1975

What's Out There - Exploring the Solar System 15 MIN
VHS
Color (J)
$89.00 purchase _ #1222V
Explores the solar system starting with early ideas about the universe to the dawning of the space age. Studies the ideas of Ptolemy, Galileo, Copernicus and Newton. Shows how knowledge is being constantly broadened and updated through new technology.
Industrial and Technical Education; Religion and Philosophy; Science - Physical
Dist - SCTRES **Prod** - SCTRES

What's out there - exploring the solar system 15 MIN
VHS
Color (P I)
$89.00 purchase _ #RB812
Traces the history of the study of astonomy. Examines the concepts of Ptolemy, Galileo, Copernicus and Newton. Explores new space technology - advanced telescopes and other tools, and discoveries by spacecraft. Emphasizes that knowledge of space is constantly being broadened and updated.
History - World; Science - Physical
Dist - REVID **Prod** - REVID

What's out tonight is lost 8 MIN
16mm
Color (G)
$25.00 rental
Adopts its title from a poem by Edna St Vincent Millay to produce an elegaic production sifting through the unrecoverable. Acts like a reflecting pool where everything breaks up - a home is swallowed in the brume, light barely penetrates and the yellow school bus delivers us into new clouds.
Fine Arts; Psychology
Dist - CANCIN **Prod** - SOLOMO 1983

What's quality got to do with it 27 MIN
VHS
Color (A PRO IND)
$645.00 purchase, $155.00 rental
Outlines a process of quality improvement for all companies. Reveals that the first step in this process is to identify customer expectations and strive to meet them consistently.
Business and Economics
Dist - VLEARN **Prod** - RTBL

What's really comin' down 29 MIN
Videoreel / VT2
Turning points series
Color
Focuses on teenager's views of life in suburbia, USA.
Sociology
Dist - PBS **Prod** - NJPBA

What's religion got to do with sex
VHS
Questions of faith III series
Color (J H C G A R)
$10.00 rental _ #36 - 82 - 217
Explores the traditional Judeo - Christian perspectives of sexuality. Focuses on nontraditional relationships such as homosexuality. Considers how the church and synagogue can respond meaningfully to people in such relationships. Features the perspectives of a wide variety of contemporary Jewish and Christian thinkers.
Religion and Philosophy; Sociology
Dist - APH **Prod** - ECUFLM

What's Riding Hood without the Wolf 10 MIN
16mm / VHS
Creative writing series
Color (I)
$315.00, $235.00 purchase, $60.00 rental
Discusses plot - the protagonist, the goal of the protagonist and obstacles to attainment of the goal. Part of a four - part series set in a classroom with a small demonstration group of students and a teacher of creative writing. Projector stops are provided to encourage viewer participation in creative thinking and writing paralleling that done by the group onscreen. Directed by Bud Freeman.
English Language; Fine Arts; Literature and Drama
Dist - CF

What's right for me - making good decisions 20 MIN
VHS
Behavior - values - middle school survival kit series
Color (I J)
$99.00 purchase _ #RB8192
Portrays a group of young people working on a school project, but one person has not done his part. Reveals that in trying to solve the dilemma, the teens discover six steps to follow. Part of a three - part series on behavior and values.
Guidance and Counseling; Psychology; Sociology
Dist - REVID **Prod** - REVID 1993

What's right for Mom and baby 8 MIN
VHS
Having a baby series
Color (H G PRO)
$195.00 purchase _ #E910 - VI - 036
Discusses the benefits of breast - feeding, formula feeding or a combination of both. Helps parents to decide which is best for them and their baby. Part of a six - part series on all aspects of birth, from prenatal to postnatal care of the mother and care of the newborn infant.

Health and Safety; Social Science; Sociology
Dist - HSCIC Prod - UTXHSH 1991

What's right, what's wrong - you decide 23 MIN
35mm strip / VHS
Color (I J)
$145.00, $129.00 purchase _ #2195 - SK, #2176 - SK
Dramatizes moral decisions that pre - adolescents must make. Considers questions of friendship, fairness, responsibility, and honesty. Includes teacher's guide.
Education; Guidance and Counseling; Religion and Philosophy
Dist - SUNCOM Prod - JACSTO

What's Say 14 MIN
16mm / U-matic / VHS
Learning Values with Fat Albert and the Cosby Kids, Set II Series
Color (P I)
Stresses that attention to health problems is important for physical and emotional well - being and urges consultation with professionals when their advice can solve a problem.
Guidance and Counseling; Health and Safety
Dist - MGHT Prod - FLMTON 1977

What's school got to do with it 30 MIN
VHS
Color (J H)
$189.00 purchase _ #GW - 126 - VS
Helps students to appreciate the relevance of school experience to future success and happiness. Features real students who talk about their career aspirations and their views on education. Includes profiles of accomplished professionals working in the same field that the students aspire to pursue. Features an auto mechanic, an athletic trainer for the New York Giants, and a master chef, as well as other professionals. Includes teacher's resource book and newspapers.
Education; Guidance and Counseling
Dist - HRMC

What's So Great about Books 14 MIN
16mm
Color
LC 78-700231
Deals with parents reading with their children from infancy throughout the school years to help children develop language skills, appreciate good literature and develop creative thinking.
English Language; Literature and Drama; Psychology; Sociology
Dist - ORPULI Prod - ORPULI 1977

What's So Important about a Wheel 10 MIN
16mm / U-matic / VHS
Color (P)
LC 72-700771
Examines the many different varieties of wheels in use in our society. Traces the history of the wheel and its subsequent development from a simple wooden cart to the modern automobile, locomotive and jet aircraft.
Science - Physical; Social Science
Dist - JOU Prod - ALTSUL 1972

What's So Special about Computers? 33 MIN
VHS / U-matic
Color
Illustrates many of the reasons for project failure, using the story of a company which is on the brink of financial ruin because a data processing project designed to steamline its distribution system failed to achieve its goals.
Business and Economics; Mathematics
Dist - VISUCP Prod - VISUCP

What's So Special about Paper 29 MIN
16mm
Color (J H)
Reveals a great range of jobs, for people with almost any educational background, and shows how the paper industry is involved in such socially important work as forest conservation and water purification.
Business and Economics; Education; Guidance and Counseling; Science - Natural
Dist - MTP Prod - AMERPI

What's that you said - hearing conservation 13 MIN
U-matic / BETA / VHS
British video programs series
Color; PAL (IND G)
$595.00 purchase _ #520 - 24
Trains employees in the United Kingdom. Examines the duties and responsibilities of the worker as set forth in the recently enacted United Kingdom Noise at Work Regulation. Explains the function of the ear, how hearing can be permanently damaged by repeated exposure to loud noise, methods employed to control workplace noise and the function of hearing protection devices.
Health and Safety; Industrial and Technical Education; Psychology; Science - Natural; Sociology
Dist - ITSC Prod - ITSC

What's the Best Business for You? 16 MIN
U-matic / VHS / 16mm
Starting a Business Series
Color (H C A)
Provides tools for the aspiring entrepreneur in assessing a business idea, including personal considerations, possible growth, income and market share.
Business and Economics
Dist - BCNFL Prod - SOMFIL 1982

What's the Best Word 15 MIN
VHS / U-matic
In Other Words Series Giving Meaning to Messages, Pt 7; Giving meaning to messages; Pt 7
Color (J)
Explains the importance of using the right word to convey information by telling the story of Rita who should have described the student body fund as low and not bankrupt. Shows Scott helping Jeff look up just the right word to describe his feelings for Sally Ann.
English Language
Dist - AITECH Prod - AITECH 1983

What's the Big Idea, Ben Franklin 15 MIN
VHS / U-matic
Through the Pages Series no 7
Color (P)
LC 82-707375
Presents librarian Phyllis Syracuse reading from the children's biography What's The Big Idea, Ben Franklin by Jean Fritz. Discusses candle and soap making.
English Language
Dist - GPN Prod - WVIZTV 1982

What's the biggest living thing 11 MIN
VHS
Wonder world of science series
Color; PAL (P)
Follows Wondercat, an animated, curious kitten, who is impressed with size of elephants and giraffes in a zoo and wonders what the biggest living thing is. Shows that whales are the biggest animals but the biggest living thing is a tree. Part of a series which encourages youngsters to explore the limitless wonders of the world of science through careful observation, thoughtful comparisons and well - supported conclusions.
Mathematics; Science - Natural
Dist - VIEWTH Prod - VIEWTH

What's the danger - drug effects and hazards 30 MIN
VHS / U-matic
Contemporary health issues series; Lesson 17
Color (C A)
Focuses on what is known and not known about the effects of drugs. Includes the relationships between drugs and crime, drugs and creativity and drug overdose and death.
Health and Safety; Psychology; Sociology
Dist - CDTEL Prod - SCCON

What's the Difference Being Different? 19 MIN
VHS / U-matic
Color
Shows students and teachers participating in activities which increase feelings of self - worth and understanding of others.
Psychology; Sociology
Dist - RESPRC Prod - RESPRC

What's the Energy Crisis all about 25 MIN
U-matic / VHS / 16mm
CBS News Special Report for Young People Series
Color
Presents a mock - up of a typical American home to show how the American nation is now habituated to plug - in power rather than old - fashioned elbow power. Shows experiments in solar, thermonuclear and geothermal systems which must be expanded and developed to provide sufficient energy supplies. Explains how Americans can help in energy conservation.
Guidance and Counseling; Science - Natural; Social Science
Dist - CAROUF Prod - CBSTV

What's the Good of a Test 12 MIN
U-matic / VHS / 16mm
Color; B&W (P I)
LC FIA66-785
Describes how to use tests, what tests measure and how to prepare for and take a test. Explains and illustrates composition or essay questions, objective questions and standardized tests.
Education; Guidance and Counseling; Psychology
Dist - JOU Prod - JOU 1965

What's the Idea? 15 MIN
U-matic / VHS
Writer's Realm Series
Color (I)
$125.00 purchase
Introduces techniques for choosing a subject in order to improve creative writing skills.
English Language; Literature and Drama; Social Science
Dist - AITECH Prod - MDINTV 1987

What's the Presidency all about 25 MIN
U-matic / VHS / 16mm
CBS News Special Report for Young People Series
Color (P I J H C)
LC 73-703129
Shows the office of the Presidency from George Washington to Richard Nixon, with its tremendous growth and responsibilities. Deals with the system of checks and balances.
Business and Economics; Civics and Political Systems
Dist - CAROUF Prod - CBSTV 1973

What's the Rule - Concepts from Algebra 20 MIN
U-matic
Let's Figure it Out Series
B&W (P)
Mathematics
Dist - NYSED Prod - WNYE 1968

What's the score - text analysis for the actor 85 MIN
VHS
Color (PRO G)
$179.00 purchase, $49.00 rental _ #614
Features Dr Arthur Wagner who presents a system for text analysis in two segments. Examines each action of the text in terms of immediate and overall objectives, then relates each to personal experience. The analysis is logged into a columnar 'score' facing the text. The second segment presents methodology for examining character dynamics and interactions based largely on transactional analysis. Uses scenes from A Streetcar Named Desire and other plays. Produced by the Theater Arts Video Library.
Fine Arts
Dist - FIRLIT
CAMV

What's the Sense 25 MIN
U-matic
Not Another Science Show Series
Color (H C)
Looks at each of the five senses and explains how the brain produces a composite picture from the information it receives from the senses.
Science; Science - Natural
Dist - TVOTAR Prod - TVOTAR 1986

What's the Solution
16mm
B&W
Examines whether or not a system of simultaneous equations has a solution, and, if it has, whether or not it is unique.
Mathematics
Dist - OPENU Prod - OPENU

What's the Weather - Pt 1 22 MIN
VHS
Active Atmosphere Series
Color (J)
$79.00 purchase _ #2211V
Explains weather analysis and the components of weather maps, including station models, isolines, pressure centers and fronts. Shows how to prepare weather maps. Part of an eight - part series on the atmosphere and the weather it creates. Includes a comprehensive study guide.
Science - Physical
Dist - SCTRES Prod - SCTRES

What's the Weather - Pt 2 20 MIN
VHS
Active Atmosphere Series
Color (J)
$79.00 purchase _ #2212V
Presents additional tools of weather analysis such as upper air maps. Explains radar and satellites, data collection, pressure levels, contours and lines of constant height. Part of an eight - part series on the atmosphere and the weather it creates. Includes a comprehensive study guide.
Science - Physical
Dist - SCTRES Prod - SCTRES

What's this 2 MIN
16mm
Color (G)
$5.00 rental
Makes an ecological statement of sorts.
Fine Arts; Science - Natural
Dist - CANCIN Prod - MERRIT 1973

What's to Understand 4 MIN
16mm
Responsible Caring Series
Color (J)
LC 81-701351
Shows two young teenagers bitterly struggling with the apprehensions and peer pressures associated with sexuality.

Health and Safety; Psychology
Dist - MEMAPP Prod - MEMAPP 1980

What's Under My Bed 10 MIN
U-matic / VHS
(K P)
Shows Mary Ann and Louie tell Grandpa that there was something scary under their beds. But then Grandpa told them about what had been under his bed when he was their age. In the process of comforting and reassuring, Grandpa, Mary Ann and Louie found that they were ready for some ice cream, and a good night's sleep.
English Language; Literature and Drama; Psychology; Sociology
Dist - WWS Prod - WWS 1984

What's Under Your Hood 11 MIN
U-matic / VHS / 16mm
Color (H C A) (SPANISH)
Uses model engine, animation and simple narration to answer questions about the major automobile parts and how and why they do function.
Health and Safety; Industrial and Technical Education; Science - Physical
Dist - AIMS Prod - PANTON 1973

What's Up Josh 54 MIN
16mm
Color (R)
Relates the story of Tom, a student with inner conflicts who is helped by Josh Mc Dowell, Campus Crusade college representative.
Guidance and Counseling; Religion and Philosophy
Dist - GF Prod - GF

What's Up Tiger Lily 80 MIN
16mm
Color
Features a Japanese spy movie re - dubbed with Woody Allen's dialogue.
Fine Arts
Dist - TWYMAN Prod - UNKNWN 1966

What's worth learning 30 MIN
VHS
Effective teacher telecourse series
Color (T)
$69.95 purchase, $50.00 rental
Discusses goals for learning. Hosted by Dr Loren Anderson.
Education; Psychology
Dist - SCETV Prod - SCETV 1987

What's Wrong 13 MIN
VHS / U-matic
Under the Blue Umbrella Series
Color (P)
Shows how Sally questions the need for rules when she breaks one at school and her mother breaks a traffic law. Explains how she has a dream about a world without rules.
Guidance and Counseling
Dist - AITECH Prod - SCETV 1977

What's Wrong - Troubleshooting a Video System 30 MIN
VHS / U-matic
Video - a Practical Guide and more Series
Color
Diagnoses many production problems and their solution through a process of observation, isolation, definition, correction and returning.
Fine Arts; Industrial and Technical Education
Dist - VIPUB Prod - VIPUB

What's wrong with beer 20 MIN
VHS
Color (P I J)
$149.00 purchase _ #CG - 958 - VS
Uses dramatic vignettes and frank information to help elementary school students sort out fact from fiction when it comes to beer. Shows how beer affects the body and brain and explores ways of dealing with social pressure to engage in drinking. Delivers a strong 'no' to use of beer and models refusal skills.
Guidance and Counseling; Health and Safety; Psychology
Dist - HRMC Prod - HRMC 1992

What's wrong with beer 25 MIN
VHS
Color (I J H)
$169.00 purchase _ #B072 - V8
Takes a critical look at what beer really is - a potentially addictive and destructive drug. Details the psychological and physiological effects of drinking on young bodies. Contrasts the facts about beer with the myths generated by advertising and popular culture. Models positive behaviors for enjoying life without drugs. Includes discussion guide.
Guidance and Counseling; Health and Safety; Psychology
Dist - ETRASS Prod - ETRASS

What's wrong with ME 25 MIN
VHS
Where there's life series
Color; PAL (G)
PdS25 purchase
Focuses on Myalgic Encephalomyelitis - ME - also known as the yuppie disease. Reveals that, currently, 150,000 people claim to suffer its symptoms which are mainly exhaustion and fatigue. According to some doctors there's nothing wrong with most of the sufferers that a good night's sleep wouldn't cure. Tries to define the point at which the stress of modern life stops and illness starts. A very controversial topic within the medical community. Features Dr Miriam Stoppard as host in a series of shows making sense of science and treating controversial subjects in an informed way. Contact distributor about availability outside the United Kingdom.
Health and Safety; Psychology
Dist - ACADEM

What's Wrong with Me 16 MIN
U-matic / VHS / 16mm
Learning Laws - Respect for Yourself, Others and the Law Series
Color (I)
Introduces Eddie, a victim of child abuse who is removed from his home environment and taken to a home for abused youngsters. Shows him gradually learning that the abuse he experienced was not his fault.
Sociology
Dist - CORF Prod - DISNEY 1982

What's wrong with my child 25 MIN
BETA / VHS / U-matic
Color (G)
$295.00 purchase _ #KC - 6282M
Focuses on the lifetime of damage that fetal alcohol syndrome inflicts on grown children and young adults. Examines the lives of several of these children and reveals the tragic reactions of their unsuspecting adoptive parents who are puzzled by children unable to learn, who cannot remember and misbehave without fear or remorse. Features Hugh Downs and Barbara Walters as hosts.
Health and Safety; Psychology; Sociology
Dist - CORF Prod - ABCNEW 1991
PBS

What's Wrong with the Interview 20 MIN
U-matic / VHS
Videosearch Employment Interview Series
Color
Business and Economics; Fine Arts; Guidance and Counseling; Psychology
Dist - DELTAK Prod - DELTAK

What's Wrong with this Building 28 MIN
16mm / VHS
Color (G)
$425.00, $250.00 purchase, $55.00 rental
Documents the history of the building of the Whitney Museum of Modern Art in 1966. Reveals that in 1981 the Board of the Whitney chose American architect Michael Graves to design an addition to the building designed by Marcel Breuer. When Graves presented his designs in 1985, they generated a great deal of controvery and have gone through several revisions. Examines the problems encountered by the Whitney in choosing to add to a landmark building. Discusses Modernist and Post - Modernist styles, architecture as an art.
Fine Arts
Dist - CNEMAG Prod - CNEMAG 1989

What's wrong with this picture 11 MIN
16mm
Color; B&W (G)
$25.00 rental
Begins with an old instructional clip about being a 'good citizen' then features a color reconstruction of the old black and white by filmmaker Owen Land. Abounds in absurdities in both image and sound.
Fine Arts; Literature and Drama
Dist - CANCIN

What's wrong with this picture
BETA / VHS / 16mm
Color (T G)
$150.00, $25.00 purchase
Encourages dialogue between school principles and their community resources. Presents the critical issues of school safety - school - related crime and violence, drug abuse and suicide.
Guidance and Counseling; Health and Safety; Social Science; Sociology
Dist - NSSC Prod - NSSC 1990

What's Wrong with this Picture? Parts I and II 12.5 MIN
16mm
Color; B&W (C)
$476.00
Experimental film by George Landow (aka Owen Land).
Fine Arts
Dist - AFA Prod - AFA 1972

What's wrong with vandalism 11 MIN
VHS
Taking responsibility series
Color (P)
Uses animation to show how to manage destructive feelings. Teaches children how to empathize with the victims of vandalism to show that vandalism always hurts someone. Shows children how to resist peer pressure to vandalize and to influence their friends by deciding against property destruction. Part of a series teaching health, safety and responsibility to youngsters.
Sociology
Dist - VIEWTH Prod - VIEWTH
CORF

What's Your Authority 11 MIN
U-matic / VHS / 16mm
Color (I J) (SPANISH)
LC 72-700987
Examines the nature of authority and prepares the child to cope with the authorities he will encounter at home, at school and in society.
Guidance and Counseling; Social Science
Dist - EBEC Prod - EBEC 1971

What's Your Bag 16 MIN
U-matic / VHS / 16mm
Color (H C)
LC 75-703682
Presents eight students evaluating their interests and abilities. Relates their interests and abilities to a variety of occupations within the scientific, mechanical, clerical and computational levels. Explains that these levels are found in unskilled, skilled, semiprofessional and professional occupations.
Education; Guidance and Counseling; Psychology
Dist - AIMS Prod - MCCRNE 1975

What's Your Excuse 7 MIN
U-matic / VHS / 16mm
Color (H C A)
LC 76-702138
Shows people giving excuses for their indiscretion with alcohol. Explains that it is a human quality that characterizes bad judgment with a frail excuse.
Guidance and Counseling; Health and Safety; Psychology; Sociology
Dist - AIMS Prod - AIMS 1974

What's Your Fuel 15 MIN
U-matic / VHS
All about You Series
Color (P)
Explains that just as a toy steam engine needs fuel to operate so does the human body. Illustrates how food is digested. (Broadcast quality).
Psychology; Science - Natural; Social Science
Dist - AITECH Prod - NITC 1975

What's your poison 30 MIN
VHS
Bodymatters series
Color (H C A)
PdS65 purchase
Explains how alcohol affects the body. Part of a series of 26 30-minute videos on various systems of the human body.
Health and Safety; Psychology; Science - Natural
Dist - BBCENE

The Whatsit and the Zoo 30 MIN
U-matic
Magic Ring I Series
(K P)
Shows children on a visit to the zoo to study the habits and needs of animals.
Education; Literature and Drama
Dist - ACCESS Prod - ACCESS 1984

Whatsoever You do 8 MIN
U-matic / VHS / 16mm
Color
Dramatizes the plight and history of primitive people in the United States and East Africa who suffer from disease and famine. Shows the boundless faith, hope and humor which exist in people of all races and color.
Religion and Philosophy; Sociology
Dist - PAULST Prod - PAULST

Whazzat 10 MIN
16mm / U-matic / VHS
Color (P)
LC 75-701428
Presents an adaptation of the East Indian folktale about six blind men who come upon an elephant and attempt to describe it. Stresses the moral that cooperating with others can achieve more than working alone.
Literature and Drama
Dist - EBEC Prod - EBEC 1975

Wheat 22 MIN
16mm / U-matic / VHS

Color
Describes wheat, from the planting of seed to the baking of bread.
Agriculture
Dist - KAWVAL **Prod** - KAWVAL

Wheat - a New Breed 25 MIN
16mm / U-matic / VHS
Genetics Series
Color (C)
$550 purchase - 16 mm, $250 purchase - video _ #5046C
Talks about experiments in producing new crop varieties. Discusses the successes and problems of the wheat breeders of Great Britain and the United States. Produced by the BBC for the Open University.
Agriculture
Dist - CORF

Wheat Cycle 16 MIN
16mm
Faces of Change - Afghanistan Series
Color
Examines farming in Afghanistan, showing the cycle of activities from the sowing to the harvesting of the wheat.
Geography - World; Sociology
Dist - WHEELK **Prod** - AUFS

Wheat - from Field to Flour 11 MIN
U-matic / VHS / 16mm
Color (I J H)
LC 73-702569
Views the cereal crop that constitutes a basic food for almost half the people in the world. Shows the world's major wheat producing regions, then focuses on the greatest wheat producing area of them all, the central United States.
Agriculture; Geography - World; Social Science
Dist - CORF **Prod** - CENTRO 1973
VIEWTH

Wheat - its Growth, Transportation and Marketing 28 MIN
16mm
How Does Your Garden Grow Series
Color (I)
Documents the history of wheat, including planting, growing and harvesting techniques, testing and grading and selling at the Kansas City Board of Trade. Shows the storage problems and elaborate railroad operations involved in moving the harvest.
Agriculture
Dist - STAFER **Prod** - OTT 1955

Wheat - the daily chapati 15 MIN
VHS
Fruits of the earth series
Color (G)
$175.00 purchase
Looks at positive and negative effects of the green revolution as seen in the Punjab state of India. Considers what is necessary to produce more wheat with fewer undesired effects. Part of a series of 15 videos that describe everyday conditions in regions throughout the earth and look at plants available for environmentally sound, economically productive development.
Home Economics; Science - Natural
Dist - LANDMK

Wheat Today, what Tomorrow 32 MIN
VHS / 16mm
(P A)
$50.00 rental
Investigates the disaster facing dryland farming in Western Australia. Shows that farmers are indebted to bankers whose 'profit first' ethic exploits the land. Narrated by David Bellamy.
Agriculture; Science - Natural; Social Science
Dist - BULFRG

Wheat Weaving 85 MIN
BETA / VHS
Color
Shows the selection and preparation of natural wheat for weaving purposes. Describes seasonal projects utilizing wheat weaving.
Fine Arts
Dist - HOMEAF **Prod** - HOMEAF

Wheat, White, and Cinnamon Bread 87 MIN
Videoreel / VHS
Baking Bread Series
Color
Demonstrates the basics of bread baking.
Home Economics
Dist - ANVICO **Prod** - ANVICO

Wheaton
VHS
Campus clips series
Color (H C A)
$29.95 purchase _ #CC0062V
Takes a video visit to the campus of Wheaton College in Massachusetts. Shows many of the distinctive features of the campus, and interviews students about their experiences. Provides information on the composition of the student body, professors, academics, social life, housing, and other subjects.
Education
Dist - CAMV

The Wheatstone bridge 15 MIN
U-matic / VHS
Basic electricity and D C circuits - laboratory series
Color
Industrial and Technical Education; Science - Physical; Social Science
Dist - TXINLC **Prod** - TXINLC

Wheeeels, no 1 5 MIN
16mm
Color
Explores the highways and by - ways of America.
Geography - United States; Social Science; Sociology
Dist - VANBKS **Prod** - VANBKS 1959

Wheeeels, no 2 5 MIN
16mm
Color
Presents a fantasy farce on the car of everyday life. Depicts everything as a vehicle.
Literature and Drama; Social Science; Sociology
Dist - VANBKS **Prod** - VANBKS 1959

Wheel alignment theory and adjustment 27 MIN
VHS
Color (H G IND)
$109.00 purchase _ #60518 - 027
Uses three - dimensional computer animation to make wheel alignment principles easy to visualize. Features live action footage of actual components and gives examples of tire wear patterns to bring the viewer into the auto repair center.
Education; Industrial and Technical Education
Dist - GA

The Wheel and Axle 11 MIN
16mm
Color (P I J)
Describes the wheel and axle and develops the concepts of force, work and mechanical advantage.
Science - Physical
Dist - VIEWTH **Prod** - CENCO

The Wheel and Axle - a Simple Machine 15 MIN
VHS / U-matic
Why Series
Color (P I)
Discusses the characteristics of the wheel and axle.
Science - Physical
Dist - AITECH **Prod** - WDCNTV 1976

Wheel and Axle - an Introduction 10 MIN
U-matic / VHS / 16mm
Color (I J)
LC 78-712383
Explores machines of many sizes and shapes that are part of our lives. Points out that all these machines are either simple machines or combinations of simple machines. Presents experiments with different wheel and axle combinations to reveal number patterns that help us understand how simple machines work.
Science - Physical
Dist - PHENIX **Prod** - PHENIX 1971

Wheel Bearing and Seal Servicing 18 MIN
VHS / 16mm
Automotive Tech Series
(G PRO)
$81.50 purchase
Shows how to service wheel bearings and seals.
Industrial and Technical Education
Dist - RMIBHF **Prod** - RMIBHF

Wheel Bearing Service 27 MIN
VHS / 16mm
Automotive Tech Series
(G PRO)
$104.50 purchase
Gives step - by - step instructions on servicing wheel bearings.
Industrial and Technical Education
Dist - RMIBHF **Prod** - RMIBHF

Wheel Bearings and Lubrication 30 MIN
VHS / U-matic
Keep it Running Series
Color
Explains how to lubricate the suspension and steering systems and how to inspect and service wheel bearings.
Industrial and Technical Education
Dist - NETCHE **Prod** - NETCHE 1982

A Wheel is Round 8 MIN
16mm / U-matic / VHS
Starting to Read Series
Color (K P)
Introduces the youngest readers and pre - readers to words and concepts, including pictures and songs.
English Language
Dist - AIMS **Prod** - BURGHS 1971

The Wheel of fortune 52 MIN
U-matic / VHS / 16mm
Connections series; No 5
Color (H C A)
LC 79-700860
Traces the connection between astrology, ancient Greek medical manuscripts, the need for precise measuring devices, and the invention of such things as the telescope, forged steel, and interchangeable machine parts.
History - World; Sociology
Dist - TIMLIF **Prod** - BBCTV 1979
AMBROS

The Wheel of life - a Buddhist map to enlightenment 53 MIN
VHS
Color (G)
$34.95 purchase _ #5140
Discusses the Buddhist Wheel of Life as a symbolic representation of the path to enlightenment. Shows how various artists have depicted the Wheel of Life and how the symbolism can be interpreted, drawing from Kundalini teachings, Christian tradition and the Bhagavad Gita. Features Swami Sivananda Radha.
Fine Arts; Literature and Drama; Religion and Philosophy
Dist - TIMEB **Prod** - TIMEB 1991

Wheel on the Chimney 7 MIN
16mm / U-matic / VHS
Color (K P)
LC 70-702901
Uses pictures, words and music from the book by Margaret Wise Brown, to tell the story of how a stork nest on cartwheels fastened to the chimneys of European farmhouses.
Literature and Drama
Dist - WWS **Prod** - WWS 1969

Wheel Puller 15 MIN
U-matic / VHS
Blueprint Reading for Machinists Series
Color (IND)
Continues introduction to blueprint reading. Shows how to lay out a workpiece from a print and how to plan an effective machining sequence.
Industrial and Technical Education
Dist - LEIKID **Prod** - LEIKID

Wheel Puller (Intermediate)
VHS / U-matic
Blueprint Reading Series
Color (SPANISH)
Industrial and Technical Education
Dist - VTRI **Prod** - VTRI

Wheel thrown pottery 30 MIN
VHS
ArtSmart pottery series
Color (J H C G)
$49.95 purchase _ #IBX01010V
Offers a start - to - finish demonstration of wheel throwing, including trimming, handle attachment, bisquing, glazing and firing. Includes booklet. Part of a four - part series on pottery.
Fine Arts
Dist - CAMV

Wheel Thrown Pottery 30 MIN
VHS
ArtSmart Series
Color (C)
LC 90708435
Depicts processes and techinques of wheel thrown pottery in a manner that allows students to make immediate use of those processes and techniques. The first of ten installments of the ArtSmart Series.
Fine Arts
Dist - GPN **Prod** - UNKNWN 1990

Wheelbarrow Man 22 MIN
16mm
B&W (C A)
An allegorical tale of a soldier who finds himself in purgatory and how his soul searches for an answer to what it means to die a hero.
Guidance and Counseling; Psychology
Dist - UWFKD **Prod** - USC

Wheelchair Group 21 MIN
VHS / U-matic
Color
Demonstrates upper torso and relaxation exercises that can be done by physically handicapped persons in their wheelchairs.

Psychology; Sociology
Dist - UWISC **Prod** - LASSWC 1979

Wheelchair inspection and cleaning 7 MIN
VHS / U-matic
Wheelchair video series
Color (PRO C)
$395.00 purchase, $80.00 rental _ #C920 - VI - 012
Describes the basic types of wheelchairs. Demonstrates how to inspect and clean them. Part of a three - part series presented by Richmond State School Staff Development and K Duffy Sharlach, Texas Dept of Mental Health and Mental Retardation.
Health and Safety
Dist - HSCIC

Wheelchair positioning and transfer 12 MIN
U-matic / VHS
Wheelchair video series
Color (PRO C)
$395.00 purchase, $80.00 rental _ #C920 - VI - 014
Reveals that correctly positioning a person in a wheelchair is extremely important. Emphasizes that incorrect positioning or being in the same position too long can cause tissue damage and bed sores. Taking a person out of their wheelchair and changing positions from time to time is also important. Demonstrates techniques for correctly positioning patients in wheelchairs and safely transferring them. Illustrates one and two - person transfers between wheelchair and bed, wheelchair and chair and wheelchair and mat or floor. Part of a three - part series presented by Richmond State School Staff Development and K Duffy Sharlach, Texas Dept of Mental Health and Mental Retardation.
Health and Safety
Dist - HSCIC

Wheelchair Transfer 29 MIN
U-matic
Wheelchair Transfers Series
Color (PRO)
Covers common wheelchair transfers used in the clinical care of patients. Includes a convalescent patient a weak patient and a hemiplegic patient. Demonstrates the hydraulic lifter.
Health and Safety
Dist - PRIMED **Prod** - PRIMED

Wheelchair Transfers for the Paraplegic 7 MIN
8mm cartridge / 16mm
Color
LC 75-702161; 74-705948
Explains and demonstrates three transfer techniques for the paraplegic patient - - frontwards, sidewards with removable armrests on the wheelchair and sidewards without removable armrests. Demonstrates spotting techniques for the therapist.
Health and Safety; Science - Natural
Dist - USNAC **Prod** - USPHS 1966

Wheelchair Transfers Series
Arm pulling - pushing transfer 19 MIN
Swivel Bar Transfer for Quadriplegia 11 MIN
Wheelchair Transfer 29 MIN
Dist - PRIMED

Wheelchair Transport 20 MIN
16mm
Nurse's Aid, Orderly and Attendant Series
Color
LC 79-704832
Shows how to operate a wheelchair and transport a patient safely.
Guidance and Counseling; Health and Safety
Dist - COPI **Prod** - COPI 1969

Wheelchair use and safety 11 MIN
VHS / U-matic
Wheelchair video series
Color (PRO C)
$395.00 purchase, $80.00 rental _ #C920 - VI - 013
Demonstrates the proper techniques for safely transporting patients in all types of wheelchairs. Includes a description of the Foam in Place, Mull Holland, Jay Seat and Back wheelchairs. Discusses general safety guidelines and demonstrates safe wheelchair transportation technique while going through a doorway, up and down a curb and into a van. Part of a three - part series presented by Richmond State School Staff Development and K Duffy Sharlach, Texas Dept of Mental Health and Mental Retardation.
Health and Safety
Dist - HSCIC

Wheelchair video series
Presents three parts on wheelchairs. Includes the titles Wheelchair Inspection and Cleaning, Wheelchair Use and Safety and Wheelchair Positioning and Transfer. Presented by Richmond State School Staff Development and K Duffy Sharlach, Texas Dept of Mental Health and Mental Retardation.
Wheelchair inspection and cleaning 7 MIN
Wheelchair positioning and transfer 12 MIN
Wheelchair use and safety 11 MIN
Wheelchair video series 28 MIN
Dist - HSCIC

Wheeled Fire Power 6 MIN
U-matic / VHS
Color (IND)
Demonstrates the varied uses of the Ansul brand model 350 - D wheeled fire extinguisher.
Health and Safety
Dist - ANSUL **Prod** - ANSUL 1980

Wheeler quick art
CD-ROM
(G)
$249.00 purchase
Presents a 300 megabyte CD - ROM with over 2,200 clip art images in the TIFF format. Offers images scanned at 300 dots - per - inch for crisp resolution. Available in MS - DOS and MAC format.
Computer Science; Industrial and Technical Education
Dist - QUANTA **Prod** - QUANTA

Wheeler quick art - Mac
CD-ROM
(G)
$245.00 purchase _ #1935m
Includes over 2200 images in the TIFF format at 300 dpi. Provides access to cartoons, drawings, and border designs that can used in desktop publishing. Includes a Hypercard stack to view images. No royalty or subscription charges. For Macintosh Classic, Plus, SE and II computers, requires 1MB RAM, one floppy disk drive, and an Apple compatible CD - ROM drive.
Computer Science
Dist - BEP

Wheeler quick art - PC
CD-ROM
(G)
$245.00 purchase _ #1935p
Includes over 2200 images in the TIFF format at 300 dpi. Provides access to cartoons, drawings, and border designs that can used in desktop publishing. No royalty or subscription charges. For IBM PCs and compatibles, requires 604K RAM, DOS 3.1 or later, one floppy disk drive - hard disk recommended, one empty expansion slot, and an IBM compatible CD - ROM drive.
Computer Science
Dist - BEP

Wheelies 29 MIN
16mm
Earthkeeping Series
Color (P I J)
LC 73-703397
Asks young people to examine their already forming attitudes toward the automobile - a major air pollutor as well as the source of many amusements. Uses animated characters to explain how the natural environment is unable to clean air that has been heavily polluted by automobiles. Presents bicycling and walking as inexpensive and nonpolluting forms of transportation.
Science - Natural; Social Science
Dist - IU **Prod** - WTTWTV 1973

Wheelin' Steel 28 MIN
VHS / U-matic
Color
Captures the action and emotion of the 25th National Wheelchair Games, five days of intense competition in track, field, weight - lifting, swimming, archery, table tennis and slalom.
Health and Safety; Psychology
Dist - UWASHP **Prod** - UWASHP

Wheeling free 52 MIN
VHS
Color (H C G)
$445.00 purchase, $75.00 rental
Follows paraplegic Jeff Heath on a travel adventure through Central America. Observes the beautiful landscape and tough politics of this diverse group of countries through Heath's eyes as he in his wheelchair plunges into crowded Indian markets, navigates steep pyramids of Mayan ruins, investigates teeming jungles and coral reefs. Heath travels by local bus, stays in fleabag hotels and calls upon the courtesy of strangers when access is too difficult. He also meets with disabled activists along the way and tours a computer workshop staffed and run by the 'disabled.' Directed by Judy Ditter and Kim Batterham for Stormbringer Films.
Geography - World; Health and Safety; Sociology
Dist - FLMLIB

Wheels 30 MIN
VHS
Perspectives - transport and communication - series
Color; PAL; NTSC (G)
PdS90, PdS105 purchase
Looks at the testing of automotive developments in the rough five day RAC - Lombard Rally.
Industrial and Technical Education; Physical Education and Recreation
Dist - CFLVIS **Prod** - LONTVS

Wheels 30 MIN
U-matic
Today's Special Series
Color (K P)
Develops language arts skills in children. Programs are thematically designed around subjects of interest to youngsters. Action takes place in a department store where people, mannequins, puppets, comic characters and special guests present a light hearted approach to language arts.
Fine Arts; Literature and Drama; Psychology
Dist - TVOTAR **Prod** - TVOTAR 1985

Wheels 15 MIN
16mm
Color
LC 76-703168
Features a boy who wishes for a car and gets his wish, but then finds he is too young for it.
Geography - World; Guidance and Counseling; Psychology
Dist - CIHIB **Prod** - CIHIB 1976

Wheels and Axles 12 MIN
U-matic / VHS / 16mm
Simple Machines Series
Color (I J)
$315, $215 purchase _ #4484
Shows how wheels and axles make certain kinds of work easier.
History - World
Dist - CORF

Wheels and Things - Linear Measurement 20 MIN
U-matic
Let's Figure it Out Series
B&W (P)
Mathematics
Dist - NYSED **Prod** - WNYE 1968

Wheels and Tires 12 MIN
16mm
Color (J A)
Presents information about wheels and tires, including tire construction, wheels and hubs, front wheel parts, care of tires and changing a tire.
Industrial and Technical Education
Dist - SF **Prod** - SF 1968

Wheels and Tires 30 MIN
U-matic / VHS
Keep it Running Series
Color
Describes the functions of the various parts of the suspension and steering systems. Discusses the different types of tires and demonstrates preventive service and maintenance checks on tires.
Industrial and Technical Education
Dist - NETCHE **Prod** - NETCHE 1982

Wheels, Belts and Gears 11 MIN
16mm
Color (P I J)
Shows how one wheel can be made to turn another. Shows methods for doing this. Shows that when a smaller wheel or gear turns a larger one, there is a gain in force, but a loss in speed. Develops the concept of mechanical advantage and ways of finding it.
Science - Physical
Dist - VIEWTH **Prod** - CENCO

Wheels in Africa 25 MIN
16mm / U-matic / VHS
Untamed World Series
Color; Mono (J H C A)
$400.00 film, $250.00 video, $50.00 rental
Follows a truck safari from the Nile river to the center of the African continent to examine the land and its people.
Geography - World; History - World; Science - Natural
Dist - CTV **Prod** - CTV 1973

Wheels, Kilns and Clay Series
Ancient techniques in clay 28 MIN
Artist Potters make a Living Today 28 MIN
Beginning to Throw - the Bowl 28 MIN
Beginning to Throw - the Cylinder 28 MIN
Bottles, a modification of the basic cylinder 28 MIN
Building pot forms by coil methods 28 MIN
Building with clay slabs 28 MIN
Casting and pressing in molds 28 MIN
Centering and Opening the Ball 28 MIN
Ceramic Terms and Concepts 28 MIN
Clay batches for plastic clay slips 28 MIN
Clay forms in ancient cultures 28 MIN
Clay wall treatments 28 MIN
Cliff Steward, guest, builds wheel - thrown figures 28 MIN
Combining oxides to make glazes 28 MIN

Compotes and attached bases 28 MIN
Construction of Large Pots 28 MIN
Cut and put together pots from thrown shapes 28 MIN
Design and decor principles 28 MIN
Design for mass production 28 MIN
Dora De Larios, guest - builds a slab sculpture 28 MIN
Earthenware 28 MIN
Engobe Decorating on Bowl Forms 28 MIN
Glassblowing - hand and mass production techniques 28 MIN
Glaze application on bisque ware 28 MIN
Hanging Planters, Candlesticks, Lanterns and Other Accessory Forms 28 MIN
Heat Treatments 28 MIN
History of Ceramics 28 MIN
How to Mix an Engobe 28 MIN
How to Roll Coils - Preparing to Hand Build 28 MIN
How to Teach Ceramics - How to Set Up a Studio 28 MIN
Introduction - Overview of Ceramics 27 MIN
Kiln Atmospheres and Temperatures for Glaze Firing 28 MIN
Lidded Pots 28 MIN
Loading and Firing a Bisque Kiln 28 MIN
Low Fire - Enamel on Copper 28 MIN
Mathematical Calculations of Glaze Formulas 28 MIN
Molds and Models - How they are used 28 MIN
Molds and Models - Start to Finish 28 MIN
Other Uses for Ceramics 28 MIN
Porcelain 28 MIN
The Potter's wheel 28 MIN
Raku Glaze Firing 28 MIN
Stoneware 28 MIN
Susan Peterson, Artist - Potter 28 MIN
Teapots 28 MIN
Texturing Clay 28 MIN
Throwing Pitchers, Pulling Handles 28 MIN
Trim Foot of Thrown Bowl 28 MIN
Underglaze and Overglaze Decor 28 MIN
Variety of Glaze Effects - Introduction to Glaze Melts 28 MIN
Wedging the Clay and Making a Pitch Pot 28 MIN
What is Clay 28 MIN
Dist - PBS

Wheels of Business 1 MIN
16mm
Color (H)
LC 80-701273
Describes the Distributive Education Clubs Of America, showing how the free enterprise system spurs competition and how competition spurs incentive to better serve the consumer.
Business and Economics
Dist - PCSI **Prod** - DECA 1980

The Wheels of Toys 29 MIN
VHS / 16mm
Villa Alegre Series
Color (P T)
$46.00 rental _ #VILA - 113
Presents educational material in both Spanish and English.
Education
Dist - PBS

Wheels, Wheels, Wheels 11 MIN
U-matic / VHS / 16mm
Color (P I J)
LC 76-712546
Explores the various forms of wheels that have contributed to our civilization, including the gears, sprockets and winches that drive everything from water wheels to computers. Teaches perceptual values in language arts as well as the value of technical accomplishment.
Science - Physical
Dist - PHENIX **Prod** - KINGSP 1969

Wheels, Wings and Other Things 30 MIN
U-matic
Magic Ring II Series
(K P)
Continues the aim of the first series to bring added freshness to the commonplace and assist children to discover more about the many things in their world. Each program starts with the familiar, goes to the less familiar, then the new, and ends by blending new and old information.
Education; Literature and Drama
Dist - ACCESS **Prod** - ACCESS 1986

Wheels within Wheels 14 MIN
16mm
Color (H C A)
LC FIA65-431
Explains the career opportunities in the trucking industry. Gives an inside view of the business.
Business and Economics; Guidance and Counseling; Psychology; Social Science
Dist - WSUM **Prod** - MTRUCK 1964

The Wheelwright 21 MIN
U-matic / VHS / 16mm
Color (J)
LC 80-701511
Shows two methods of constructing a wheel, either by hand or mass - produced. Points out that both methods require craftsmanship and precision.
Fine Arts; Industrial and Technical Education
Dist - IFB **Prod** - IFB 1975

When a Child Dies 22 MIN
16mm
Color
LC 79-701453
Examines the experiences, feelings and needs of parents and siblings of children who have died. Uses such examples as a child killed in an auto accident, a child who died after suffering from leukemia for 18 months and a child who died as an infant in his crib.
Sociology
Dist - GITTFI **Prod** - GITTFI 1979

When a Child Enters the Hospital 16 MIN
16mm
Color (H C A)
LC 76-703919
Describes what happens when a young child goes into the hospital for a minor operation. Covers hospital procedures, the child's emotions and fears and ways in which parents and hospital personnel help the child before, during and after hospitalization.
Guidance and Counseling; Health and Safety; Psychology
Dist - POLYMR **Prod** - POLYMR 1975

When a group is a team 4 MIN
U-matic / VHS
Meeting breaks series
Color (C A PRO)
$295.00 purchase
Presents a gospel music extravaganza to liven up dull meetings. Uses music, dance and thought provoking lyrics about teamwork. Produced by Media Mix.
Business and Economics; Fine Arts; Psychology
Dist - VIDART

When a Man's a Prince 17 MIN
16mm
B&W (H C)
Features a slapstick comedy with added humorous commentary and a musical score.
Fine Arts
Dist - CFS **Prod** - MSENP

When a trick is not a trick - Part 1 30 MIN
VHS
Kid tricks series
Color (K P I R)
$19.99 purchase, $10.00 rental _ #35 - 891128 - 533
Features famed Christian magician Danny Korem, who uses simple tricks to illustrate Biblical and moral concepts. Demonstrates the difference between good tricks and bad ones, such as lies.
Religion and Philosophy
Dist - APH **Prod** - WORD

When a woman ascends the stairs 110 MIN
VHS
B&W (G) (JAPANESE WITH ENGLISH SUBTITLES)
$79.95 purchase _ #VWA1081
Tells the story of a Ginza bar hostess who struggles to keep her dignity and her appearance as she faces her responsibilities and her age. Directed by Mikio Naruse.
Fine Arts; Sociology
Dist - CHTSUI

When a Woman Fights Back 59 MIN
U-matic / VHS
Color
Discusses the Yvonne Wanrow murder trial which set a legal precedent when her conviction was reversed by the Washington State Supreme Court.
Civics and Political Systems; Sociology
Dist - PBS **Prod** - KCPQTV 1980

When a Word is Worth a Thousand Pictures 29 MIN
U-matic / VHS
Coping with Kids Series
Color (T)
Education
Dist - FI **Prod** - MFFD

When a Word is Worth a Thousand Pictures 30 MIN
VHS / U-matic
Coping with Kids Series
Color
Explains the very significant concept of encouragement. Discusses the importance of both verbal and non - verbal methods in the encouragement process.
Guidance and Counseling; Sociology
Dist - OHUTC **Prod** - OHUTC

When abortion was illegal - Untold stories 28 MIN
VHS
Color (H C G)
$495.00, $95.00 purchase, $45.00 rental
Opens a sealed chapter in women's history by exposing the era of illegal abortions between the turn of the century and the Roe v Wade decision in 1973. Weaves together the stories of women who speak frankly about their experiences for the first time. Reveals that the aura of shame and fear kept most women silent during this time because abortion was deemed a criminal act and women who admitted having abortions risked arrest. Looks at the complications brought about from back alley or self - induced abortions. Produced by Dorothey Fadiman.
Fine Arts; Sociology
Dist - CANCIN **Prod** - KTEHTV 1993

When an individual or small business goes broke - Bankruptcy law for general practitioners 60 MIN
VHS
Color (C PRO A)
$95.00 purchase _ #P266
Provides a succinct explanation of how the various chapters of the Federal Bankruptcy Code are structured and operate. Offers instruction on who can go into bankruptcy and the chapters available. Experienced faculty panelists examine a case chronologically and cover a wide range of pertinent topics. For general practitioners and others dealing with bankruptcy debtors.
Business and Economics; Civics and Political Systems
Dist - ALIABA

When and how to hire temps and freelancers
VHS
Color (G PRO)
$49.95 purchase _ #584 - 67
Shows how to assess when to hire temporary, contract and freelance personnel. Discusses true cost per employee, analyzing the break even point when hiring temps, reviewing terms and definitions in the temporary industry, selecting the right temp service, supervision of temporary workers.
Business and Economics
Dist - MEMIND

When and how to hire temps and freelancers 22 MIN
VHS
Administrative series
Color (PRO A G)
$149.95 purchase _ #SIM4550V-B
Focuses on issues related to office administration. Examines the costs and benefits of hiring temporary or freelance employees. Includes investigations into costs per employee, selecting a temp service, and supervising temps and freelancers. Reveals when temp and freelance workers are most appropriate for a project. Includes written support materials and bonus video Everyone In Your Company Is a Salesperson
Business and Economics
Dist - CAMV

When are they Ready - Reading Readiness 30 MIN
VHS / U-matic
Teaching Early Reading Series
Color (T)
Education; English Language
Dist - CTI **Prod** - CTI

When, Around, Sound 10 MIN
U-matic
Readalong One Series
Color (K P)
Introduces reading and spelling for preschoolers and children in grades 1 to 3 with animation, puppets, humor and music. Comes with teacher's guide and kit.
Education; English Language; Literature and Drama
Dist - TVOTAR **Prod** - TVOTAR 1975

When Baby Comes Home 55 MIN
VHS
(H C A)
$29.95 purchase _ #MH2000V
Presents a series of questions and answers about issues concerning new parents, including handling, bottle and breast feeding, bathing and diapering, special problems, positive reinforcement and more.
Health and Safety; Sociology
Dist - CAMV **Prod** - CAMV

When Billy broke his head ... and other tales of wonder 57 MIN
VHS
Color (G)
$245.00 purchase, $100 rental _ #CE - 136
Focuses on Billy Golfus, an award - winning journalist, who suffered a severe head injury in a motor scooter accident ten years ago. Follows him around the country as he meets disabled people and witnesses first hand the strength and anger that is forging a new civil rights movement for disabled Americans. Produced by David E Simpson and Golfus.
Civics and Political Systems; Health and Safety
Dist - FANPRO

When can we walk home - the Cypriot issue as it affects the Greek American and the Cypriot American community 28 MIN
VHS
Illuminations series
Color (G R)
#V - 1050
Addresses the continuing situation of Cyprus, where the island nation is partitioned into areas of Greek and Turkish influence. Approaches the matter from a pro - Greek perspective. Suggests possible solutions.
Sociology
Dist - GOTEL **Prod** - GOTEL 1990

When Can You Start - Selection Techniques 27 MIN
VHS / 16mm
Color (A PRO)
$790.00 purchase, $220.00 rental
Shows how to hire suitable employees. Considers how to match up job needs with the correct personality type for handling the job. Management training.
Business and Economics; Guidance and Counseling; Psychology
Dist - VIDART **Prod** - VIDART 1990

When children are witnesses 48 MIN
VHS
Color (PRO)
$195.00 purchase _ #2935
Features a training program by Joseph and Laurie Braga that shows how the courtroom and trial proceedings can be made less threatening to children. Describes what instructions and cautions a judge may give attorneys regarding children in the courtroom and more. Produced by Drs Joseph and Lauris Braga and Children's Institute International. Introduction by Richard Dysart.
Civics and Political Systems; Psychology
Dist - GFORD

When children grieve 20 MIN
VHS
Color (H C G)
$295.00 purchase, $60.00 rental
Explores the effects of the death of a parent on a child. Interviews children both before and after their parent's death and observes children's group therapy sessions to provide an understanding of the fears, anger, guilt and aloneness children feel at the death of their mother or father. Health professionals explain the importance of sharing with children the reality of a parent's condition and of preparing them, in some cases, for the inevitability of death. Stresses the need for children to work through their grief, to allay any feelings of responsibility and to assure them that all of their feelings are normal and necessary to the grieving process. Hosted by Art Ulene.
Health and Safety; Psychology; Sociology
Dist - CF **Prod** - FEEFIN 1987

When Children have Cancer 25 MIN
VHS / U-matic
Color
Examines the battle against childhood cancer through profiles of past and current patients.
Health and Safety
Dist - MEDCOM **Prod** - MEDCOM

When Comedy was King 81 MIN
16mm / U-matic / VHS
B&W (P)
Presents a collection of sequences from silent comedies dating from the early Sennett films of 1914 to Roach comedies of 1928. Features such stars as Charlie chaplin, Buster Keaton, Laurel and Hardy, Harry Langdon, Ben Turpin, Fatty Arbuckle, Wallace Berry, Mable Normand, Gloria Swanson and the Keystone Cops.
Fine Arts
Dist - CAROUF **Prod** - YNGSNR

When Commitments Aren't Met 10 MIN
U-matic / VHS
Color
Investigates the problems of meeting deadlines. Shows how to manage time and resources effectively.
Business and Economics; Psychology
Dist - CREMED **Prod** - CREMED

When Crime Pays 48 MIN
U-matic / VHS
Color
$455.00 purchase
Sociology
Dist - ABCLR **Prod** - ABCLR 1981

When Did You Last See Yourself on TV 32 MIN
16mm / U-matic / VHS
Women Series
Color (H C A)
Surveys media stereotypes of women. Presents schoolgirls, a housewife and women in television assessing what television offers and who makes the television image of women. Asks whether television reflects the changes affecting women in recent years or whether women have left television far behind.
Sociology
Dist - LUF **Prod** - LUF 1979

When differences put a strain on relationships - Module V 6 MIN
8mm cartridge / VHS / BETA / U-matic
Brainwaves - case studies in diversity series
Color; PAL (PRO G)
$495.00 purchase
Presents two vignettes 'The Case of Mike and Dolores;' 'The Case of Barbara and Amelia.' Discusses realistic, complex diversity issues, concepts and conflicts. Combines case studies with an interactive learning design to allow trainers to lead participants in a structured, non - threatening exploration of diversity. Part five of six parts. Includes trainer's manual and 20 participant manuals.
Business and Economics; Psychology
Dist - BNA **Prod** - BNA

When Dinosaurs Ruled the Earth 100 MIN
16mm
Color
Describes the adventures of a group of Stone Age people.
Fine Arts
Dist - TWYMAN **Prod** - WB 1970

When Disaster Strikes 17 MIN
16mm
Color
LC 74-706325
Depicts the natural disaster operations of the Army Corps Of Engineers. Shows how they respond to disasters with personnel, equipment, technical assistance and supervision.
Civics and Political Systems; Health and Safety; History - World
Dist - USNAC **Prod** - USAE 1970

When Disaster Strikes - Coping with Loss, Grief and Rejection 33 MIN
VHS
Color (J H)
Probes the human response to personal crisis, focusing on despair, anger, and guilt. Your students learn techniques for coping with crisis, the emotional process of healing, the potential for growth through recovery.
Guidance and Counseling; Health and Safety; Psychology
Dist - HRMC **Prod** - HRMC 1982

When do I respond 10 MIN
VHS
Christian steward's response series
Color (A R)
$19.95 purchase _ #87EE0116
Stresses the importance of good time management as a part of Christian stewardship.
Guidance and Counseling; Literature and Drama; Religion and Philosophy
Dist - CPH **Prod** - CPH

When do I respond - Part 2
VHS
Christian steward's response series
Color (J H C G A R)
$19.95 purchase, $10.00 rental _ #35 - 8116 - 19
Profiles Joan, a woman who must face her mortality after receiving the news of a biopsy. Shows how her pastor helps her reflect on the best ways in which to use whatever time she may have left. Includes planning guide with Bible studies, sermon notes, worship suggestions and other information.
Religion and Philosophy
Dist - APH **Prod** - CPH

When Families Divorce - Part I 30 MIN
VHS
Soapbox With Tom Cottle Series
Color (G)
$59.95 purchase _ #SBOX - 407
Explores the effects divorce can have on teenagers. Features teenagers from divorced families discussing divorce, remarriage and step - families. Hosted by psychologist Tom Cottle.
Psychology; Sociology
Dist - PBS **Prod** - WGBYTV 1985

When Families Divorce - Part II 30 MIN
VHS
Soapbox With Tom Cottle Series
Color (G)
$59.95 purchase _ #SBOX - 408
Features a discussion by teenagers of how their parents' divorces have shaped their own views of relationships and marriages. Continues discussion from 'When Families Divorce - Part I.' Hosted by psychologist Tom Cottle.
Psychology; Sociology
Dist - PBS **Prod** - WGBYTV 1985

When fire breaks out 10 MIN
VHS / U-matic / BETA
Color (IND G A)
$670.00 purchase, $125.00 renta _ #WHE014
States that the possibility of fire exists wherever people work and that employees need to know what to do when fire breaks out. Includes the topics of knowing when to fight or flee, the urgency of reporting a fire, incipient fires, following emergency plans, evacuating and accounting for people, roles and limitations of fire extinguishers.
Health and Safety; Psychology
Dist - ITF **Prod** - ERF 1991

When Fire Starts 18 MIN
16mm / U-matic / VHS
Color
LC 83-700618
Shows how employees have a vital role in preventing small fires from becoming large ones. Shows how such factors as inadequate training in immediate - response action, rapid spread, ignorance of which materials are highly flammable, inadequate equipment and training, late discovery and improper access can lead to fire disaster.
Health and Safety
Dist - IFB **Prod** - MILLBK 1979

When food is an obsession - overcoming eating disorders 28 MIN
VHS
Color (I J H)
$189.00 purchase _ #GW - 121 - VS
Tells why teens - expecially girls - starve and abuse their bodies to achieve a 'perfect body.' Features a 17 - year - old recovering anorexic who discusses the barrage of conflicting messages received from society - food equals pleasure, but beauty, especially feminine beauty, equals thinness. Discusses the symptoms of bulimia and anorexia - puffy eyes, thinning hair and deep - rooted rituals such as those that forbid eating anything except foods of a single color or a certain consistency. Dr Diane Mickley, president of the American Anorexia and Bulimia Assn, stresses the dangers of keeping one's body in a constant state of weakness and explains the social and biological origins of the disease. Produced by Hourglass Productions.
Health and Safety; Sociology
Dist - HRMC

When Friends Die 30 MIN
VHS
Soapbox With Tom Cottle Series
Color (G)
$59.95 purchase _ #SBOX - 502
Inquires how teenagers deal with the death of close friends. Covers the role of family and friends. Hosted by psychologist Tom Cottle.
Psychology; Sociology
Dist - PBS **Prod** - WGBYTV 1985

When Generations Meet 30 MIN
U-matic / VHS / 16mm
Color (PRO)
Documents role - playing sessions with teenage volunteers who express their feelings about working with the elderly.
Health and Safety; Psychology; Sociology
Dist - FEIL **Prod** - FEIL

When governments kill 24 MIN
VHS
Color (C A G)
$20.00 purchase
Teaches college students about the death penalty both internationally and in the United States.
Civics and Political Systems; Sociology
Dist - AMNSTY **Prod** - KAMBER 1989

When Hair Came to Memphis 54 MIN
16mm
Color
LC 70-715451
Portrays the various reactions of the community when the interracial rock musical Hair came to Memphis, Tennessee.
Fine Arts; Geography - United States; Psychology; Sociology
Dist - SHBC **Prod** - SHBC 1971

When Hell was in Session 98 MIN
VHS / U-matic
Color (H C A)
Tells the story of Commander Jeremiah A Denton Jr, a Navy pilot downed near Haiphong and captured by North Vietnamese regulars on July 18, 1965. Reveals that for the next seven - and - a - half years, Denton and his fellow prisoners endured torture, starvation and psychological warfare. Stars Hal Holbrook and Eva Marie Saint.
Fine Arts; History - United States
Dist - TIMLIF **Prod** - TIMLIF 1983

When Heroes Fall 27 MIN
U-matic / VHS / 16mm
Insight Series
Color (H C A) (SPANISH)
Depicts what happens when a boy discovers that the father he idolizes is having an affair. Reveals the boys anger at his father until he realizes that his mother has already forgiven her husband. Stars Panchito Gomez and Jose Perez.
Guidance and Counseling; Religion and Philosophy; Sociology
Dist - PAULST **Prod** - PAULST

When I dream 13 MIN
VHS
Color (J H G)
$15.95 purchase
Examines the problems of teenage pregnancy. Looks at the dreams of teens and children, and the issues which stand in the way of their aspirations.
Health and Safety; Psychology; Sociology
Dist - CDEFF **Prod** - CDEFF

When I Grow Up 30 MIN
VHS
Soapbox With Tom Cottle Series
Color (G)
$59.95 purchase _ #SBOX - 413
Discloses the hopes and aspirations of teenagers. Provides a view of the values that shape society. Hosted by psychologist Tom Cottle.
Education; Guidance and Counseling; Psychology
Dist - PBS **Prod** - WGBYTV 1985

When I Grow Up - Career Aspirations 6 MIN
U-matic / VHS / 16mm
Like You, Like Me Series
Color (K P)
Tells the story of a group of handicapped and nonhandicapped children who dress up as the grownups they would most like to be.
Education; Guidance and Counseling; Psychology
Dist - EBEC **Prod** - EBEC 1977

When I Grow Up I Can be Series
I Can be a Builder 10 MIN
I Can be a Community Service Worker 10 MIN
I Can be a Food Production Worker 10 MIN
I Can be a Hospital Worker 10 MIN
I Can be a Mechanic 10 MIN
Dist - AIMS

When I Need more Money 9 MIN
16mm
Color (I J)
Discusses living within a fixed income, the payment of bills, credit, getting a loan and installment buying.
Business and Economics; Education; Home Economics; Social Science
Dist - SF **Prod** - SF

When I say no, I feel guilty 30 MIN
VHS
Color (A PRO IND)
$525.00 purchase, $130.00 rental
Teaches basic principles of assertive behavior. Based on the book 'When I Say No, I Feel Guilty.'
Business and Economics; Guidance and Counseling; Psychology; Sociology
Dist - VLEARN
CCCD

When I was Young in the Mountains
VHS / 35mm strip
Caldecotts on Filmstrip Series
Color (K)
$35.00 purchase
Presents a children's story. Part of the Caldecott series.
English Language; Literature and Drama
Dist - PELLER

When I was Your Age 28 MIN
U-matic / VHS
Color (G K)
$249.00, $149.00 purchase _ #AD - 1155
Presents today's teenagers and former teenagers Fran Lebowitz, Bob Greene, Maya Angelou and George Plimpton who discuss generational differences.
Education; Psychology; Sociology
Dist - FOTH **Prod** - FOTH

When I was your age - discipline in the family
VHS
Family formula - video basics of parenting series
Color (G)
$79.00 purchase _ #CDFAM110V
Discusses discipline within the family. Integrates cross - cultural and cross - generational wisdom with the street culture of today. Part of a seven - part series.
Education; Guidance and Counseling; Psychology; Sociology
Dist - CAMV

When I'm Calling You 15 MIN
VHS / U-matic
Color (A)
Shows employees how to create a favorable company image over the phone. Illustates both classic errors and exemplary techniques using light humor.
Business and Economics; Psychology
Dist - XICOM **Prod** - XICOM

When I'm Calling You 16 MIN
VHS / U-matic
Color
Shows ways a person can offend or enrage a telephone caller before they get through to the person who can help.
Business and Economics
Dist - VISUCP **Prod** - VISUCP

When I'm Old Enough - Goodby 27 MIN
16mm
B&W
Discusses the problems faced by a young boy who drops out of high school. Emphasizes the value of proper guidance and the importance of the student's seeking this guidance.
Education; Guidance and Counseling; Psychology
Dist - SF **Prod** - STES 1962

When in Doubt, Play Safe 10 MIN
16mm
Dr Bob Jones Says Series
Color (R)
Dr. Bob Jones, Sr. speaks about basic life truths.
Religion and Philosophy
Dist - UF **Prod** - UF

When in Pain 15 MIN
16mm
Color (J)
LC 76-703641
Analyzes aspects of physical and emotional pain and examines the brain's never - ending battle with the pain of anxiety, frustration, fear, distrust and uncertainty. Gives examples of methods of alleviating pain and removing the source of pain.
Guidance and Counseling; Health and Safety; Psychology
Dist - MALIBU **Prod** - KARASC 1975

When in Rome 29 MIN
Videoreel / VT2
Maggie and the Beautiful Machine - Maggie and Her Willing 'Accomplices Series
Color
Physical Education and Recreation
Dist - PBS **Prod** - WGBHTV

When is a Function Integrable
16mm
B&W
Points out the difficulties involved in using the four - stage Lebesgue definition to decide whether a function is a Lebesgue integrable.
Mathematics
Dist - OPENU **Prod** - OPENU

When is help 15 MIN
U-matic / VHS / 16mm
Inside-out series
Color
Presents Karen, Roger and their friends who have decidedly different notions about giving and receiving help. Shows the advantages and disadvantages of their varied attitudes.
Guidance and Counseling; Psychology; Sociology
Dist - AITECH

When Jehovah's Witnesses refuse blood transfusions - medical, ethical and legal issues 16 MIN
VHS / U-matic
Contemporary problems in transfusion medicine series
Color (PRO C)
$395.00 purchase, $80.00 rental _ #C881 - VI - 047
Presents to medical students and physicians the various dimensions of the medical, legal and ethical issues surrounding transfusion and the beliefs of Jehavah's Witnesses. Interviews the parents of a child who was transfused against their wishes. Outlines prominent rules of the sect and sources of physician conflict with Jehovah's Witnesses. Notes conclusions of major court cases and the principal determination that minors should be transfused when necessary, despite parental protests. Part of a three - part series on transfusion medicine presented by Dr James P Crowley.
Civics and Political Systems; Health and Safety; Religion and Philosophy; Science - Natural
Dist - HSCIC

When, Jenny, When 25 MIN
16mm / U-matic / VHS
Reflections Series
Color (J)
LC 79-700813
Presents a dramatization about teenage sexual behavior.
Health and Safety; Psychology; Sociology
Dist - PAULST **Prod** - PAULST 1978

When Jenny When 25 MIN
U-matic / VHS
Color (J A)
Dramatizes the story of two young people who learn to accept themselves and their own sexuality. Stars Maureen McCormick.
Fine Arts; Sociology
Dist - SUTHRB **Prod** - SUTHRB

When Joseph Returns 92 MIN
16mm
Color (HUNGARIAN (ENGLISH SUBTITLES))
Follows the uneasy progress of two women awkwardly thrown together when the newlywed wife of a sailor comes to live with his mother. Directed by Zsolt Kezdi - Kovacs. With English subtitles.
Fine Arts; Foreign Language
Dist - NYFLMS **Prod** - UNKNWN 1976

When Kidneys Fail 25 MIN
U-matic / VHS
Color
Notes that 50,000 people in the US are suffering from chronic renal failure and, in most areas, there are not enough facilities to take care of them. Shows what new hope is offered these people including, among other things, a mobile Belser Unit that can preserve a kidney up to three days after the death of a donor and before the transplant.
Health and Safety; Science - Natural
Dist - MEDCOM **Prod** - MEDCOM

When Kings were Champagne 30 MIN
Videoreel / VT2
Koltanowski on Chess Series
Color
Physical Education and Recreation
Dist - PBS **Prod** - KQEDTV

When Knights were Bold 17 MIN
16mm
Magnificent 6 and 1/2 Series
Color (K P I)
Tells how a member of the magnificent Six - and - A - Half gang encounters many mishaps when he is tempted to try on a suit of armor found outside a vacant house. Depicts how the gang rescues him from an aroused band of his unwitting victims.
Fine Arts; Literature and Drama
Dist - LUF **Prod** - CHILDF 1970

When leaves change colors 20 MIN
VHS
Color (I J H)
$19.95 purchase _ #IV157
Looks at the chemical and physical processes going on inside a leaf which allows changes to take place each autumn.
Science - Natural
Dist - INSTRU **Prod** - INSTRU

When Life Begins 12 MIN
16mm / U-matic / VHS
Color (H)
LC 71-711920
Shows the developing fetus from the earliest moment of fertilization of the egg to the time of birth. Includes the various stages of development of the main external organs of the fetus. Concludes with a live birth sequence.
Science - Natural
Dist - MGHT **Prod** - LFDL 1971

When Life Begins 14 MIN
16mm / U-matic / VHS
Color (H C A)
Looks at the development of the fetus from the earliest moments of fertilization to the time of birth.
Science - Natural
Dist - CRMP **Prod** - GUIGOZ 1972

When Love Needs Care 13 MIN
16mm / U-matic / VHS
Color (J)
LC 72-700677
Focuses on the medical interviews and examination of a boy and girl being examined and treated for venereal diseases. Emphasizes symptoms, treatment and prevention of venereal diseases.
Health and Safety
Dist - PEREN **Prod** - SCHL 1972

When Magoo Flew 7 MIN
U-matic / VHS / 16mm
Mister Magoo Series
Color
LC 79-700045
A reissue of the 1954 motion picture When Magoo Flew. Uses animation to tell a story in which Mr Magoo erroneously boards an airplane instead of entering a movie theater and enjoys the flight as if it were a movie.
Fine Arts
Dist - CF **Prod** - BOSUST 1978

When managers don't respect differences - Module VI 6 MIN
8mm cartridge / VHS / BETA / U-matic
Brainwaves - case studies in diversity series
Color; PAL (PRO G)
$495.00 purchase
Presents two vignettes 'Gavin's Presentation;' 'Gavin's Promotion.' Discusses realistic, complex diveristy issues, concepts and conflicts. Combines case studies with an interactive learning design to allow trainers to lead participants in a structured, non - threatening exploration of diversity. Part six of six parts. Includes trainer's manual and 20 participant manuals.
Business and Economics; Psychology
Dist - BNA **Prod** - BNA

When may Comes, We'll Move to the First Floor 22 MIN
16mm
B&W
LC 78-705715
A narration based on the diary of a severely involved cerebral palsied young woman is used to present the frustrations, hopes and fears that she experiences, as well as her growing anxiety regarding the health of her aging mother who cares for her.
Guidance and Counseling; Health and Safety; Psychology; Sociology
Dist - UCPA **Prod** - UCPA 1969

When Mom and Dad Break Up 32 MIN
VHS
Strong Families, Safe Families Series
Color (K)
$24.95 purchase _ #12562
Tackles the questions frequently asked by children of divorced parents. Features Alan Thicke as host.
Guidance and Counseling; Sociology
Dist - PAR **Prod** - FOXS

When Mom and Dad Break Up 32 MIN
VHS
Color (G)
$24.95 purchase _ #6342
Features Alan Thicke as host. Tackles the questions children of divorced parents frequently ask with kid - to - kid straight talk, music and animation.
Health and Safety; Sociology
Dist - SYBVIS **Prod** - SYBVIS

When Mom and Dad divorce 15 MIN
VHS
Color (I)
$79.95 purchase _ #10241VG
Helps children explore and accept the feelings typically experienced when a divorce occurs. Encourages young people to express their feelings of anger, depression, guilt, and sadness. Shows children who have gone through a divorce and coped successfully. Includes a teacher's guide.
Sociology
Dist - UNL

When Mom has to Work 22 MIN
VHS / U-matic
Color (G)
Examines the work, family, and social lives of three career women with small children, and promotes an understanding of the difficulties facing working mothers today.
Guidance and Counseling; Sociology
Dist - PRI **Prod** - PRI 1986

When Mom Leaves 28 MIN
U-matic / VHS
Color (G)
$249.00, $149.00 purchase _ #AD - 2143
Examines the familial situation when the mother, rather than the father, leaves. Adapts a Phil Donahue program.
Health and Safety; Sociology
Dist - FOTH **Prod** - FOTH

When Mrs Hegarty comes to Japan 58 MIN
VHS / 16mm
Color (G)
$390.00 purchase, $75.00, $125.00 rental
Documents a visit to Japan by the filmmaker's 'adopted' mother in Australia. Examines cross cultural existence and exchange and filled with quirky juxtapositions, generational gaps and diverse outlooks on life. Filmmaker Noriko Sekiguchi searches for her identity, shaped by two worlds of Japan and Australia. In appreciation for Mrs Hegarty's hospitality in Australia, Sekiguchi's parents agreed to host Mrs Hegarty in their Yokohama home for three weeks.
Fine Arts; Geography - World; Sociology
Dist - FIRS

When night is falling 82 MIN
35mm / 16mm
Color (G)
$200.00 rental
Tells the story of a young Christian academic forced to choose between the woman she wants and the man who loves her, and in doing so discovers that the true duty of her soul is desire. Explores how to find courage to make changes. Produced by Barbara Tranter; written and directed by Patricia Rozema.
Fine Arts; Psychology; Religion and Philosophy; Sociology
Dist - OCTOBF

When parents are away 60 MIN
VHS
Mister Rogers' home videos series
Color; CC (K P)
$14.95 purchase _ #HV104
Stars Mister Rogers who helps children and adults deal with times of separation. Part of a series featuring favorite Mister Rogers Neighborhood programs.
Health and Safety; Psychology; Sociology
Dist - FAMCOM **Prod** - FAMCOM 1990

When Parents Divorce
VHS
Daddy Doesn't Live Here Anymore - the Single - Parent Family Series
Color
Shows children's reactions to divorce and examines the response of parents.
Guidance and Counseling; Sociology
Dist - IBIS **Prod** - IBIS

When Parents Grow Old 15 MIN
16mm / U-matic / VHS
Searching for Values - a Film Anthology Series
Color (J)
LC 72-703093
Tells how a young man on the verge of marriage must decide where his responsibilites lie when he is faced with the problem of a suddenly widowed father whose health is failing.
Guidance and Counseling; Psychology; Sociology
Dist - LCOA **Prod** - LCOA 1972

When People Care 33 MIN
16mm
Color (NAVAJO)
LC 77-700065
Explains the role of the Parent Advisory Council of Dilcon Community School in Winslow, Arizona. Shows how the Council plans and operates programs funded by the federal government under Title I.
Education; Foreign Language; Social Science
Dist - BAILYL **Prod** - USBIA 1976

When products harm 33 MIN
VHS
Color (A)
$525.00 purchase
Promotes product liability awareness for manufacturers through a dramatization showing results of a lawsuit aimed at a manufacturer. Covers how such suits can be averted through careful designing, developing, testing and marketing, including the duty to warn and to provide safe operation information. Emphasizes company responsibility.
Business and Economics; Civics and Political Systems; Education
Dist - COMFLM **Prod** - COMFLM

When Sammy Died 20 MIN
U-matic / VHS
Color
$335.00 purchase
From the ABC TV program, 20 20. Presents a program on baby AIDS.
Health and Safety
Dist - ABCLR **Prod** - ABCLR 1984

When Seconds Count 10 MIN
VHS / U-matic
Color (IND)
Discusses Ansul brand vehicle fire suppression systems to be used in mining, forestry, agriculture, construction and sanitation industries. Identifies fire hazard areas and demonstrates Ansul Checkfire electric and pneumatic detection and actuation systems.
Health and Safety
Dist - ANSUL **Prod** - ANSUL 1981

When Sex Means Trouble
U-matic / VHS
Color (J H C)
Introduces the sensitive subject of sexual exploitation. Helps teens understand their own rights, learn to recognize abuse, and develop strategies for protecting themselves. Includes teacher's guide.
Guidance and Counseling; Health and Safety; Psychology; Sociology
Dist - SUNCOM **Prod** - SUNCOM

When Sex was Good, it was Very, Very Good, When it was Bad 29 MIN
U-matic / VHS
Here's to Your Health Series
Color
Examines the psychological and physical causes of sexual problems in adults, assesses the current state of sex therapy and offers common - sense hints for regaining sexual health.
Health and Safety; Sociology
Dist - PBS **Prod** - KERA

When she gets old 28 MIN
VHS
Color (G C PRO)
$225.00 purchase, $50.00 rental
Calls attention to the struggles of older women to survive financially after divorce or widowhood. Highlights social assistance needed by them for shelter, income and nutrition.
Health and Safety
Dist - TNF **Prod** - WTTWTV

When Should Grownups Help 14 MIN
16mm
Studies of Normal Personality Development Series
B&W (C T)
Shows pre - school children in various situations where they may or may not need help. Points out that adult help is necessary in order that the child succeed in projects, but that goals of speed and efficiency should not be forced.
Education; Home Economics; Psychology; Sociology
Dist - NYU **Prod** - NYU 1950

When Should Grownups Stop Fights 15 MIN
16mm
Studies of Normal Personality Development Series
B&W (C T)
Shows four conflicts among two - to five - year - olds. Points out that the teacher must decide whether to intervene, thus must know her children well and must quickly size up the meaning of the conflict.
Education; Home Economics; Psychology; Sociology
Dist - NYU **Prod** - NYU 1950

When Songs and Legends are Silent 30 MIN
U-matic / VHS
Color
Presents ancient Russian architecture, showing masterpieces of the 11th through 13th Centuries in ancient towns such as Novgorod, Chernigov and Kiev and segments of fortress walls in Pskov and and Izborsk.
Fine Arts; Geography - World; History - World
Dist - IHF **Prod** - IHF

When Steve was dancing 120 MIN
VHS
Color (G)
$50.00 purchase
Presents Steve dancing amongst friends in a Michael Mullen production.
Fine Arts
Dist - CANCIN

When Teens Get Pregnant 18 MIN
U-matic / VHS
Color
Presents girls telling about their lives before pregnancy, about their families, school, peer pressure to have sex, the reality of sex as opposed to the fantasy, the differences between their own and their partner's needs and expectations, and the fears and responsibilities introduced by a pregnancy.
Health and Safety; Sociology
Dist - POLYMR **Prod** - POLYMR

When the Animals Talked 28 MIN
16mm / U-matic / VHS
Were You There Series

Color (J)
LC 83-700396
Presents 84 - year - old Rev. Faulkner at his fishing hole as he discusses the sources of his tales and the historically expressive and spiritually sustaining role of Afro - American folklore.
History - United States; Literature and Drama
Dist - BCNFL **Prod** - NGUZO 1982

When the Bay Area quakes 20 MIN
VHS
Color (J H C G A)
$175.00 purchase, $40.00 rental _ #38100
Demonstratres what happens when an earthquake strikes the San Francisco Bay Area. Illustrates the four main geologic effects of such tremblors - ground shaking, liquefaction, landslides, and ground ruptures. Shows how local geology determines how different areas are affected by earthquakes, how buildings are damaged, and how scienctists are monitoring fault zones in order to prepare for and attempt to predict the nex large earthquake in the region. Produced by Dough Prose.
History - United States; Science - Physical
Dist - UCEMC

When the Blues are Running 22 MIN
16mm
Color
LC 78-701334
Shows how the medical community provides a support system for a patient and his family during the critical periods of cancer detection and treatment.
Health and Safety; Psychology
Dist - AMCS **Prod** - AMCS 1977

When the Bough Breaks 11 MIN
16mm
Color
Presents the story of a mother involved in child abuse as she struggles to overcome her guilt.
Sociology
Dist - LUTTEL **Prod** - LUTTEL 1979

When the bough breaks 71 MIN
VHS
Color (C PRO)
$295.00 purchase, $100.00 rental _ #CN - 108
Asks about the right way to give a patient bad news and how to help a patient make appropriate decisions in the face of a poor prognosis. Focuses on the real story of a patient who experienced a stillbirth and dramatically recreates her interactions with several health care providers during the final weeks of pregnancy. Offers a series of ten vignettes to help medical students, residents, nurses, technicians, genetic counselors and others to understand what their patient is going through, and the ways in which their behavior and communication techniques can make a difference. Features Dr Marvin L Hage.
Health and Safety; Social Science
Dist - FANPRO **Prod** - DUKESM

When the bough breaks - Our children, our environment 52 MIN
VHS
Color (H C G)
$275.00 purchase, $75.00 rental
Looks at the major causes of suffering to the children of the world, including pollution, the spread of deserts worldwide and the international debt crisis. Covers five major problems confronted by children worldwide including poison and birth defects; water and children who die from unclean sources; flight from war forcing refugees into camps; debt and the consequences of parents losing their jobs in countries that owe vast sums to international banks; and the vicious cycle of poverty that causes parents to have more children so that they can work to feed the family resulting in over - population. Produced by Lawrence Moore and Robbie Stamp.
Fine Arts; Science - Natural; Sociology
Dist - BULFRG

When the brain goes wrong 45 MIN
VHS / Videodisc
Color (G)
$245.00 purchase, $100.00 rental _ #CE - 131
Offers seven brief segments portraying individuals with a range of brain dysfunctions. Includes schizophrenia, manic depression, epilsepsy, head injury, headaches and addiction and personal stories about what it is like to live with these conditions. Interviews physicians who discuss briefly what is known about the disorders and what can be done to help those who have a brain disorder.
Psychology; Science - Natural
Dist - FANPRO **Prod** - DAVCOO 1994

When the children come home 48 MIN
VHS
Color (A PRO)
$59.95 purchase _ #S01563
Examines the growing phenomenon of post - divorce abduction of a child by the non - custodial parent. Stresses the importance of counseling for children affected by such actions. Deals with related psychological, legal and judicial issues through case histories.
Civics and Political Systems; Sociology
Dist - UILL

When the Circuit Breaks - America's Energy Crisis 28 MIN
16mm
Color (H C A) (SPANISH)
LC 75-704426; 76-703441
Shows the origins and future of America's energy crisis. Examines how some solutions may be reached through the development of coal, oil and natural gas resources. Looks at nuclear, geothermal and solar energy and stresses the importance of conservation.
Geography - United States; Science - Natural
Dist - USNAC **Prod** - USFEAP 1975

When the dance is over 10 MIN
16mm
Cuba - a view from inside series
Color (G)
$150.00 purchase, $25.00 rental
Profiles dancers at the famous Tropicana outdoor nightclub in Havana who discuss the difficulties of their work and dealing with stereotyped public attitudes toward them. Features part of a 17 - part series of shorts by and about Cuban women. Directed by Gerardo Chijona. Illustrated catalog available. Contact distributor for programming advice and discount package rental fees.
Fine Arts; Sociology
Dist - CNEMAG

When the day comes - women as caregivers 28 MIN
VHS / 16mm
Color (H C G)
$595.00 $295.00 purchase, $55.00 rental
Acknowledges the role of women as caregivers of the vast majority of ailing elderly people who are taken care of at home by a family member. Reveals that women have traditionally been expected to cope with family responsibilities and to provide care without financial rewards. While their efforts reduce the cost to society of longterm care costs, these women go largely unnoticed and get little help from others. Features four women who have have provided continuous care for a loved one. Observes their painstaking and exhausting routines as they massage, groom, dress, clean, cook for and respond to demands. The women speak candidly of the physical and emotional stress of this responsibility. Produced by Sharon Ann McGowan.
Health and Safety; History - World; Sociology
Dist - FLMLIB **Prod** - NFBC 1991

When the Day's Work is Done 27 MIN
16mm
Color (A)
Depicts the variety of programs to which union members give their time after working hours.
Social Science; Sociology
Dist - AFLCIO **Prod** - AFLCIO 1964

When the Earth Explodes 22 MIN
U-matic / VHS
Phenomenal World Series
Color (J C)
$129.00 purchase _ #3969
Documents the eruptions of the volcanoes of Mount St Helens and Kilauea through close - up footage to show the creation and concurrent destroyal of land masses.
Science - Physical
Dist - EBEC

When the Earth moves 28 MIN
VHS
Color (J H C)
$24.95 purchase _ #V105
Describes how and where earthquakes, subsidence, landslides, swelling soil, floods, glaciers and volcanoes occur. Explains how the effects of these hazards can be mitigated through intelligent planning and action, using available Earth science information.
Geography - World; Science - Physical
Dist - INSTRU

When the Earth moves - how earthquakes happen 20 MIN
VHS
Color (I J H)
$165.00 purchase _ #A5VH 1312
Presents two parts on earthquakes. Uses computer animation to show the process by which the Earth's lithosphere breaks up into plates which carry continents as they move. The second part focuses on earthquake safety. Shows how principles of earth science can be applied in the erection of safer buildings. Takes students into the field to witness seismic technology at work.
Science - Physical
Dist - CLRVUE **Prod** - CLRVUE 1992

When the fat lady sings 40 MIN
VHS
Adventurers series
Color (A)
PdS65 purchase
Focuses on two young investment executives who fight for their first deals in venture capital. Part of a six-part series on a year in the life of a venture capital house, Grosvenor Venture Managers Ltd, which is approached with up to 600 ideas annually - of which around 20 will receive backing. Explains how the successful ventures are selected, and the drama and conflicts that lie behind the deals.
Business and Economics
Dist - BBCENE

When the harvest comes 30 MIN
VHS / 16mm
Color (G R)
Portrays the efforts of Lutheran World Relief in building wells for drought - stricken Africa. Available on a free - loan basis.
Guidance and Counseling; Literature and Drama; Religion and Philosophy
Dist - CPH **Prod** - LUMIS

When the Honeymoon is Over 32 MIN
16mm / U-matic / VHS
Women Series
Color (H C A)
Presents the personal experiences of mental and physical cruelty experienced by women of different backgrounds. Describes the treatment meted out by their husbands, the fears for their children, the efforts to stop the violence and the attempts to gain help from friends, lawyers, police and social service agencies.
Sociology
Dist - LUF **Prod** - LUF 1979

When the lion roars series
Presents a three - part series on Metro Goldwyn Mayer - MGM which recalls the stars and the wealth of stories behind the movies they made. Includes The Lion's Roar - 1924 - 1936; The Lion Reigns Supreme - 1936 - 1945; and The Lion in Winter - 1946 and Beyond.

The Lion in winter - 1946 and beyond - Part three 121 MIN
The Lion reigns supreme - 1936 - 1945 - Part two 121 MIN
The Lion's roar - 1924 - 1936 - Part one 121 MIN

Dist - INSTRU **Prod** - MGMHU 1979

When the Littlest Camel Knelt 11 MIN
16mm
Color (P I J H)
Tells the story of the little camel who is especially curious about kings and his journey with the wise men which leads him to a most unusual king, a baby sleeping in a stable. Describes how he kneels in adoration, as little camels do to this day.
Literature and Drama; Religion and Philosophy
Dist - CAFM **Prod** - CAFM

When the North Wind Blows 113 MIN
U-matic / VHS / 16mm
Color
Depicts the experiences of an old trapper who decides to parent a Siberian tiger's cubs when it is shot by hunters. Stars Henry Brandon and Dan Haggerty.
Fine Arts; Geography - United States; Physical Education and Recreation
Dist - LUF **Prod** - LUF 1979

When the People Awake 60 MIN
16mm / U-matic / VHS
Captioned; Color (A) (SPANISH (ENGLISH SUBTITLES))
Examines the attempted transition of Chile under Allende from capitalism to socialism, the development of Chile's social classes, and the tragic end of that experiment. Spanish dialog with English subtitles.
Civics and Political Systems; Fine Arts; History - World
Dist - CNEMAG **Prod** - TRIFCW 1972

When the people lead 30 MIN
VHS
Color (J H C G T A)
$29.95 purchase
Portrays a trip by U S "citizen - diplomats" to the U S S R, where they meet and talk with Soviet citizens. Produced by Sharon Tennison.
Civics and Political Systems; Geography - World; Sociology
Dist - EFVP

When the People Lead - a Journey to the Soviet Union 30 MIN
U-matic / VT3
(G)

$95.00 purchase, $45.00 rental
Features 23 Americans who travelled to the Soviet Union to meet the 'enemy.' Challenges many assumptions about the Soviet people and reminds us that individuals can play a leading role in improving international relations.
Civics and Political Systems; Geography - World; Sociology
Dist - EFVP **Prod** - EFVP 1986

When the Pot Boiled Over 14 MIN
16mm
Color; B&W (I J H C G T A)
Seeding and terracing hillsides for flood control at Boise, Idaho in 1960. The summer of 1959 had produced a great mud flood where mud from the hills east of town had flowed down into the residental district, and even threatened the downtown city ares. This was top soil mud caused by a heavy rain on denuded slopes. To prevent future threats of this nature all the concerned worked together to improve the condition of the hillsides.
Geography - United States; Science - Natural; Science - Physical; Social Science
Dist - FO **Prod** - FO 1963

When the pressure's on - groups and you 20 MIN
VHS
Color (I J)
$149.00 purchase _ #2333 - SK
Examines interpersonal group dynamics to show how groups work. Shows that groups can be both positive and negative. Recognizes that an important issue is how to maintain individuality when the group demands conformity. Includes teacher's guide.
Education; Psychology; Sociology
Dist - SUNCOM **Prod** - SUNCOM

When the Rivers Run Dry 29 MIN
U-matic / VHS / 16mm
Color
Presents a cultural history of water use in the semiarid Southwest, a region marked by alternating problems of drought and flood. Demonstrates how, since 300 BC, succeeding cultures have coped with water problems in unique and characteristic ways.
Geography - United States
Dist - UCEMC **Prod** - AROKNG 1979

When the ship comes in 10 MIN
16mm
Color (G)
$15.00 rental
Abounds with magical images, visual metaphors and color from a homemade optical printer in a David McLaughlin production.
Fine Arts
Dist - CANCIN

When the Snake Bites the Sun 57 MIN
VHS
Color (S)
$149.00 purchase _ #188 - 9029
Tells about the genesis of Australian aborigines' nearly obliterated traditions and the odyssey of a young man's commitment to an old man and his world. Features filmmaker Michael Edols who in 1970 first met aborigine Sam Woolgoodja, the undisputed 'bun - man' or spiritual custodian of his people's ancient past. The two men kindled a deep and unusual friendship before Woolagoodja died, and this is Woolagoodja's story.
Geography - World; History - World; Religion and Philosophy; Social Science; Sociology
Dist - FI **Prod** - FLMAUS 1987

When the Snow is Too Deep to Walk 20 MIN
U-matic / VHS
Color (J)
LC 82-706794
Discusses skiing excursions as a practical alternative to motor - powered holidays. Shows how to decide on touring skies vs snowshoes, clothing, camping gear and food. Includes information on skiing techniques, avalanches, hypothermia and telemarking.
Physical Education and Recreation
Dist - AWSS **Prod** - AWSS 1981

When the tide goes out 26 MIN
VHS / U-matic
Survival in nature series
Color (J H)
$275.00, $325.00 purchase, $50.00 rental
Looks at the seashore and rock pools left behind when the tide ebbs, which are occupied by an astounding variety of life. Covers both the familiar animals such as barnacles, limpets, starfish and crabs as well as some of the lesser known ones. Uses time - lapse photography.
Fine Arts; Science - Natural; Science - Physical
Dist - NDIM **Prod** - SURVAN 1990

When the Union has Targeted Your Company 240 MIN
U-matic
How to Keep Your Company Union Free Series
Color (A)
Gives managers the early warning signs of union organizing, the legal rights of parties, how an organizing drive gets started and how to protect a union free status.
Business and Economics
Dist - VENCMP **Prod** - VENCMP 1986

When the White Man Came 13 MIN
U-matic / VHS
America's Indians Series
Color (G)
$199.00, $99.00 purchase _ #AD - 972
Recalls that there were more than a million Indians living in North America when the Europeans arrived. Describes life among the major tribes across what is now the United States. Part of a six - part series on America's Indians.
History - World; Social Science; Sociology
Dist - FOTH **Prod** - FOTH

When the Wind Blows 20 MIN
16mm
B&W
Tells how the Gang's Jackie Cooper captures a burglar. A Little Rascals film.
Fine Arts
Dist - RMIBHF **Prod** - ROACH 1930

When the Wind Stops 11 MIN
16mm / U-matic / VHS
Color (K P I)
$50 rental _ #9840
Shows a young boy asking questions of his mother, revealing the continuity of life. Based on the book by Charlotte Zolotow.
English Language; Guidance and Counseling; Literature and Drama
Dist - AIMS **Prod** - WILETS 1986

When they all still lived 48 MIN
VHS
Color (H C G)
$195.00 purchase, $50.00 rental _ #38185
Relates a poignant chapter in the history of the Chinese in California - the decline and disappearance of the small rural Chinatown in Riverside. Provides extensive historical context for the story, including the history of the Chinese and their bachelor societies throughout California. Dramatizes the narrative through voice - over reflections of the last resident of the doomed Chinatown. Produced by James T Brown and Peter Lang for the Media Resources Center, University of California, Riverside.
Geography - United States; History - United States; Sociology
Dist - UCEMC

When they Interfere 30 MIN
U-matic / VHS
Play Bridge Series
Color (A)
Physical Education and Recreation
Dist - KYTV **Prod** - KYTV 1983

When things get tough - teens cope with crisis 38 MIN
VHS
Color (J H)
$199.00 purchase _ #2272 - SK
Presents three dramatic vignettes in which teenagers must cope with personal crises. Emphasizes the fact that a crisis will pass, and that feeling bad in such times is normal. Provides a four - step plan for coping with crises. Includes teacher's guide.
Psychology; Sociology
Dist - SUNCOM

When to call the doctor if your child is ill 45 MIN
VHS
Color (G)
$79.95 purchase _ #CCP0048V
Describes what to look for when deciding the seriousness of medical conditions for both infants and children of all ages. Teaches what information to gather prior to calling the doctor. Simulates life - like situations where parents must decide whether they should use self - help methods or call the doctor immediately. Explores common illnesses of infants and children and describes warning signs and possible treatment.
Health and Safety; Social Science; Sociology
Dist - CAMV

When tomorrow comes 50 MIN
VHS
Everyman series
Color; PAL (G)
PdS99 purchase
Charts the crises of friendship and loyalty among four 'buddy' relationships centered on one person who has AIDS. Shows what it takes for a person with AIDS to live the sort of life they want to lead. Explores the challenges and rewards of these unusual relationships in which one member is going to die.
Guidance and Counseling; Health and Safety; Psychology
Dist - BBCENE

When 2 become 3 45 MIN
VHS
Color (H C G)
$39.95 purchase _ #UC100V
Discusses the tools to strengthen the bonds between spouses when they become parents for the first time. Offers guidance in preparing and planning for the tremendous changes incurred in parenthood. Discusses managing family happiness through the fundamentals of effective communication, goal setting, targeting objectives and planning.
Health and Safety; Sociology
Dist - CAMV

When We Farmed with Horses 25 MIN
16mm
Color
LC 79-701454
Focuses on the draft horse, around which agricultural practices of the Midwest developed in the late 19th and early 20th centuries. Comments on the evolution of equipment, seasonal activities and the combination of frustrations and pride in workmanship which characterized farming during that period.
Agriculture
Dist - IOWA **Prod** - IOWA 1979

When We First Met 30 MIN
16mm / VHS / U-matic
Color (J H A)
Presents a story which shows how grief can destroy a family. Based on the novel WHEN WE FIRST MET by Norma Fox Mazer.
Guidance and Counseling; Literature and Drama; Psychology; Sociology
Dist - LCOA **Prod** - LCOA 1984

When will the Birds Return 52 MIN
16mm
Color (J)
LC 76-700575
Considers conditions in Darwin, Australia, following the devastating cyclone of Christmas Day, 1974. Shows the extent of the damage, the evacuation arrangements, and the preliminary cleanup and restoration efforts.
Geography - World; History - World
Dist - AUIS **Prod** - FLMAUS 1975

When will they Realize We're Living in the Twentieth Century 24 MIN
U-matic / VHS
Color (A)
Illustrates how avoidable mistakes can lead to labor management strife. Reveals the false assumptions, hardened attitudes and provocative actions that fuel a conflict.
Business and Economics; Sociology
Dist - XICOM **Prod** - XICOM

When will they Realize We're Living in the Twentieth Century 23 MIN
VHS / U-matic
Color
Illustrates how assumptions, actions and attitudes help to precipitate a crisis between management and labor.
Business and Economics
Dist - VISUCP **Prod** - VIDART

When will We Ever Learn 60 MIN
U-matic
Liberation Series
Color
Examines the educational system in the United States as a 'partner of liberation.'.
Education; Sociology
Dist - HRC **Prod** - OHC

When Winning Means no One Loses 29 MIN
VHS / U-matic
Coping with Kids Series
Color (T)
Education
Dist - FI **Prod** - MFFD

When Winning Means no One Loses 30 MIN
VHS / U-matic
Coping with Kids Series
Color
Presents methods of conflict resolution. Shows a family discussing typical problems and gives recommendations for their solution.
Guidance and Counseling; Sociology
Dist - OHUTC **Prod** - OHUTC

When You and I were Young Maggie 29 MIN
Videoreel / VT2
Maggie and the Beautiful Machine - Shape - Up Now for Kids Series

Color
Physical Education and Recreation
Dist - PBS **Prod** - WGBHTV

When You Can't Strike Back - Techniques for Non - Abusive Restraint 59 MIN
VHS / 16mm
Color (C)
$400.00 purchase _ #292201
Introduces techniques to restrain an attacker without physical abuse for health care professionals, paramedics, social workers, teachers, police and private security personnel. Features Neil Dunnigan, a 4th degree black belt in Uechi - Ryu Karate - Do, as instructor.
Computer Science; Guidance and Counseling; Health and Safety; Physical Education and Recreation; Sociology
Dist - ACCESS **Prod** - ACCESS 1989

When You Get Hurt 4 MIN
U-matic / VHS / 16mm
Most Important Person - Health and Your Body Series
Color (K P I)
Explains that the body will heal itself if it has the proper nutrition and rest.
Guidance and Counseling; Health and Safety; Science - Natural
Dist - EBEC **Prod** - EBEC 1972

When You Grow Up 12 MIN
16mm / U-matic / VHS
Color (P I)
LC 74-700033
Points out that though there are many differences in careers, they are in some ways the same. Explains that people feel pride in doing useful work, in doing a good job and in earning money for the things they need. Shows how it takes many different careers to meet our needs in a single main area.
Guidance and Counseling; Psychology; Social Science
Dist - ALTSUL **Prod** - FILMSW 1973

When You Know It's Home 30 MIN
U-matic / VHS
(G)
Reviews the life of former First Lady of Nebraska Ruth Thone. Highlights the people and places of Nebraska.
History - United States; Literature and Drama
Dist - GPN **Prod** - NETV

When You Need Help - Understanding Your Own Mental Health 63 MIN
VHS
Color (H)
Provides guidelines for helping an individual decide whether therapy is needed. Includes descriptions of the major types of therapy and advice in choosing a therapist. Gives a close up look at the process of therapy.
Health and Safety; Psychology
Dist - IBIS **Prod** - IBIS 1982

When You Need Help - Understanding Your Own Mental Health 63 MIN
VHS
Color (J H)
Provides guidelines for helping an individual decide whether therapy is needed. Includes descriptions of the major types of therapy and advice in choosing a therapist. Gives your students a close up look at the process of therapy.
Health and Safety; Psychology
Dist - HRMC **Prod** - HRMC 1982

When You See Arcturus 27 MIN
U-matic / VHS / 16mm
Insight Series
Color; B&W (J)
LC 75-700944
Presents a story about an affluent architect who is so bored with life that he decides to kill himself. Shows how his son and daughter react to his idea and how he is convinced of life's seriousness only after hearing of the senseless murder of his son.
Guidance and Counseling; Psychology; Sociology
Dist - PAULST **Prod** - PAULST 1974

When You Think about it 8 MIN
16mm
Color
LC 75-703443
Shows the functions of the lab of International Business Machines Canada.
Business and Economics; Science
Dist - IBM **Prod** - IBM 1974

When You Walk in that Door - Activities for Senior Citizens 30 MIN
U-matic
(A)
Views the lives of elderly people in the Shangri - La Lodge where they play a major role in determining the direction of their lifestyle.
Health and Safety
Dist - ACCESS **Prod** - ACCESS 1984

When Your Baby is Sick 15 MIN
VHS
Baby Care Workshop Series
Color (I J H A) (SPANISH)
$175.00 purchase
Demonstrates clearly the procedures for taking axillary and rectal temperatures, reading a thermometer, use of bulb syringe and measuring and administering prescription medication. Spanish version available.
Guidance and Counseling; Health and Safety; Home Economics; Sociology
Dist - PROPAR **Prod** - PROPAR 1988

When your baby is sick 11 MIN
VHS
Parents - to - be series
Color (J H C)
$119.00 purchase _ #CG - 925 - VS
Educates new parents about the care of sick infants. Part of a six - part series answering many of the questions and concerns of parents - to - be and new parents regarding the safety and care of their children - before and after birth.
Health and Safety; Sociology
Dist - HRMC **Prod** - HRMC

When your baby is sick 11 MIN
VHS
Color (G C PRO) (SPANISH)
$150.00 purchase _ #CC - 08
Examines the role parents play in attending to their sick child and communicating health problems to their physician. Encourages parents to observe their child carefully, noting physical symptoms as well as changes in appearance and behavior. Underscores the fact that guilt and anxiety are understandable but generally misplaced. Reviews the specific information parents should have ready when calling the doctor.
Health and Safety; Sociology
Dist - MIFE **Prod** - MIFE

When Your Baby Needs a Doctor 14 MIN
Videoreel / VT2
Living Better II Series
Color
Identifies common illnesses of newborn babies and discusses how to treat them. Demonstrates how to use, read and care for a thermometer and the proper ways to burp a baby.
Fine Arts; Home Economics; Sociology
Dist - PBS **Prod** - MAETEL

When Your Car Doesn't Work 20 MIN
U-matic / VHS
Color
$335.00 purchase
From the ABC TV program, 20 20. Discusses the GM diesels.
Health and Safety; Industrial and Technical Education
Dist - ABCLR **Prod** - ABCLR 1984

When your client goes broke - Current issues in individual bankruptcy 50 MIN
VHS
Color (C PRO A)
$95.00 purchase _ #Y122
Provides a general orientation to bankruptcy law with a focus on the statutory provisions that govern cases involving individual debtors. Covers a wide range of topics.
Business and Economics; Civics and Political Systems
Dist - ALIABA **Prod** - CLETV 1990

When Your Friend Moves Away - End - of - the - Year Blues - Clyde's Favorite Toy 15 MIN
U-matic / VHS
Clyde Frog Show Series
Color (P)
Presents stories presented by Muppet - like Clyde Frog presenting stories emphasizing positive self - images, feelings of optimism and self - confidence.
Psychology
Dist - GPN **Prod** - MAETEL 1977

When your head's not a head, it's a nut 57 MIN
VHS
Color (G PRO)
$350.00 purchase, $95.00 rental
Presents filmmaker Garth Stein documenting his 28 - year - old sister's decision to undergo brain surgery to control her epilepsy. Chronicles the events, from her and her family's discussions prior to surgery, through the surgical procedure itself - a cranial resection - to her post - op recovery. Directed by Garth Stein.
Health and Safety; Science - Natural
Dist - CNEMAG

When your parent drinks too much 27 MIN
U-matic / BETA / 16mm / VHS
Color (I J H)
$550.00, $495.00 purchase _ #JR - 5093M
Adapts the book 'When Your Parent Drinks Too Much' by Eric Ryerson. Reveals that most children of alcoholics feel isolated and alone, despite the fact that there are 10 million alcoholics in the United States. Features Alan Thicke as host and emphasizes the three Cs for children of alcoholics - they didn't 'Cause' the drinking, they can't 'Control' the drinking and they can't 'Cure' the drinking.
Guidance and Counseling; Health and Safety; Psychology; Sociology
Dist - CORF **Prod** - CORF 1987

When your unborn child is on drugs, alcohol or tobacco 15 MIN
16mm / VHS
Color (I J H G)
$260.00, $350.00 purchase
Motivates prospective parents to consider healthy alternatives to their own potentially dangerous behaviors. Uses animation to illustrate the adverse impact of drugs, alcohol, and tobacco on the fetus. Interviews parents who miscuss long term psychological and behavioral problems in their children.
Psychology; Sociology
Dist - CF **Prod** - WFP 1991

When You're Alone 15 MIN
16mm / U-matic / VHS
Color
Provides tips for home and personal safety such as securing doors and windows, carrying proper ID, self - defense, nuisance calls and rape prevention.
Health and Safety; Physical Education and Recreation; Sociology
Dist - CORF **Prod** - CORF 1984

When You're Smilin' 6 MIN
U-matic / VHS / 16mm
Color (A)
LC 83-700033
Offers a montage set in motion by Louis Armstrong's song When You're Smilin' which shows that smiling is not only good for one's health but for business as well.
Business and Economics; Fine Arts
Dist - LCOA **Prod** - GLDBGG 1982

When you're turned down - turn on 30 MIN
VHS
Color (G)
$565.00 purchase, $150.00 rental _ #91F6002
Features sales trainer Joe Batten who distinguishes between a true sales rejection and a disguised objection.
Business and Economics; Psychology
Dist - DARTNL **Prod** - DARTNL 1991

When You're Waking Up 4 MIN
U-matic / VHS / 16mm
Most Important Person - Creative Expression Series
Color (K P I)
Describes different waking scenes.
English Language; Fine Arts; Guidance and Counseling; Psychology
Dist - EBEC **Prod** - EBEC 1972

When You're Young 18 MIN
16mm / U-matic / VHS
Color
Highlights the youth activities program of the American Quarter Horse Association, featuring interviews and events at the 1980 American Junior Quarter Horse Association Convention and World Championship Show.
Physical Education and Recreation
Dist - AQHORS **Prod** - AQHORS

Where Action Happens 16 MIN
16mm
PANCOM Beginning Total Communication Program for Hearing Parents of 'Series Level 1
Color (K)
LC 77-700504
Education; Guidance and Counseling; Psychology; Social Science; Sociology
Dist - JOYCE **Prod** - CSDE 1977

Where Airports Begin 20 MIN
16mm
Color
LC 76-702721
Discusses how an airport can be environmentally sound, a good neighbor and an economic stimulus. Stresses the importance of planning and community interaction when building or upgrading an airport.
Industrial and Technical Education; Sociology
Dist - USNAC **Prod** - USFAA 1976

Where Airports Begin 20 MIN
16mm
Color (H)
Portrays how two communities successfully planned and developed their respective airports.

Social Science; Sociology
Dist - MTP **Prod** - FAAFL

Where Am I 5 MIN
16mm
B&W
Shows one of the original Mutt and Jeff cartoons with added musical score.
Fine Arts; Literature and Drama
Dist - CFS **Prod** - CFS

Where America began - Jamestown, colonial Williamsburg and Yorktown 60 MIN
VHS
Color (G)
$29.95 purchase _ #S01629
Visits the historical sites of Jamestown, Yorktown and colonial Williamsburg. Reviews the important events that occurred at these places.
History - United States
Dist - UILL

Where American began - Colonial Virginia 60 MIN
VHS
Color (I J)
$29.95 purchase _ #ST - FF0061
Visits three historic sites - Jamestown, Colonial Williamsburg and Yorktown - in the state of Virginia. Examines their roles during the colonial era of the United States and in the Revolutionary War.
History - United States
Dist - INSTRU

Where and how to look for job leads - looking for jobs in all the right places 30 MIN
VHS
Color (J H C G)
$195.00 purchase _ #JWLJLV
Offers the basics for understanding how the job search works. Provides a mindset for understanding the job search process and reviews the major job search techniques in traditional and non - traditional occupational clusters. Covers the four stages of a job opening and traditional and non - traditional methods of finding a job.
Business and Economics; Guidance and Counseling
Dist - CAMV **Prod** - JISTW

Where Angels Go - Trouble Follows 95 MIN
16mm / U-matic / VHS
Color (J)
Stars Rosalind Russell as the strict Mother Superior who accompanies a group of girls and a progressive young nun on a cross - country trip to attend a youth rally in California.
Fine Arts
Dist - FI **Prod** - CPC 1968

Where angles fear to tread 50 MIN
VHS
Disabled lives series
Color; PAL (G)
PdS99 purchase
Investigates the use of Western methods of prosthesis and care for the 200 people a month who lose limbs due to land mines in Cambodia. Examines the feasibility of modern solutions in an underdeveloped country. Part two of a four part series.
Health and Safety; History - World
Dist - BBCENE

Where Animals Live 15 MIN
U-matic / VHS
Zoo Zoo Zoo Series
Color (P I)
Reveals that where animals live is sometimes determined by their physical characteristics.
Science - Natural
Dist - AITECH **Prod** - WCETTV 1981
NGS

Where are My People 28 MIN
16mm
Color (H C A)
Traces highlights in the history of Armenia from its origins to the massacre of one and one - half million people and the subsequent resurrection of the nation by the starved orphans gathered from desert wastes.
History - World
Dist - ATLAP **Prod** - ATLAP 1965

Where are the jobs - advice for June grads 30 MIN
U-matic
Adam Smith's money world 1985 - 1986 season series; 240
Color (A)
Attempts to demystify the world of money and break it down so that small as well as large businesses and it's people understand and adjust to new social and economic trends. Reports on the major economic stories and discoveries of 1985 and 1986.
Business and Economics
Dist - PBS **Prod** - WNETTV 1986

Where are they coming from - Part 1 30 MIN
VHS
Teaching early reading series
Color (K P I)
#E376; LC 90-712988
Provides a broad spectrum of teaching methods and materials for teaching beginning reading skills. Demonstrates that language development comes from an individual's experience and interaction with other people. Part 1 of a six - part series on teaching early reading.
Education; English Language; Social Science
Dist - GPN **Prod** - CTI 1978

Where are We 14 MIN
VHS / U-matic
Under the Yellow Balloon Series
Color (P)
Shows how a dream, in which Donna's fairy godmother shows her how to find her way with globes, directions and maps, helps her finish her homework.
Geography - United States; Geography - World; Social Science
Dist - AITECH **Prod** - SCETV 1980

Where are Women Going 29 MIN
U-matic
Issue at Hand Series
Color
Discusses the impact of the women's movement on employment, men, family structure and divorce rates.
Sociology
Dist - UMITV **Prod** - UMITV 1976

Where are You in Your Family 4 MIN
16mm / U-matic / VHS
Most Important Person - Identity Series
Color (K P I) (SPANISH)
Explains that whether a person in the family is the oldest or youngest, their place is very special.
Guidance and Counseling
Dist - EBEC **Prod** - EBEC 1972

Where are You - Where are You Going 24 MIN
16mm / U-matic / 8mm cartridge / VHS
Color (DUTCH NORWEGIAN SPANISH SWEDISH)
Shows a model performance appraisal from the preparatory stage to the conclusion of the interview through the story of a young manager who faces her first appraisal interview.
Guidance and Counseling; Psychology; Sociology
Dist - RTBL **Prod** - RTBL

Where babies come from 15 MIN
VHS
Living with your body series
Color (P I)
$69.00 purchase _ #MC312
Gives a simple explanation of the process of birth.
Health and Safety; Psychology; Sociology
Dist - AAVIM **Prod** - AAVIM 1992

Where but the Supermarket 29 MIN
U-matic / VHS / 16mm
Be a Better Shopper Series
Color (H C A)
LC 81-701469
Deals with alternatives to buying in the supermarket. Visits farmers' markets, a roadside stand, a neighborhood store, and a food cooperative.
Home Economics
Dist - CORNRS **Prod** - CUETV 1978

Where Buzzards Fly 60 MIN
U-matic / VHS
L'Amour Series
Stereo (K P I J G C G T A S R PRO IND)
Presents a western short story of the early west.
Literature and Drama
Dist - BANTAP **Prod** - BANTAP 1986

Where Can I Live - a Story of Gentrification 32 MIN
16mm / U-matic / VHS
Color
Describes gentrification as a process by which an underdeveloped urban neighborhood is 'upgraded' by real estate speculation, with higher income individuals moving in and upgrading existing properties. Proceeds to document such a process in Park Slope, Brooklyn. Shows what often happens to existing residents and how they joined together to establish block associations, rent strikes and take legal action. results were a new sense of community and purpose.
Social Science; Sociology
Dist - CNEMAG **Prod** - CNEMAG 1984

Where can we find comfort 80 MIN
VHS
Color (G R)
$59.95 purchase _ #V694
Explores Biblical ways for dealing with feelings of emptiness and desires for personal peace. Includes a study guide and four interactive teaching sessions. Covers topics including God's nature, conscience, sorrow, faith and comfort.
Guidance and Counseling; Literature and Drama; Psychology; Religion and Philosophy
Dist - GF

Where Dead Men Lie 15 MIN
16mm
Color (H C A)
LC 73-702493
Presents a story based on a script written in 1896 by Australian literary figure, Henry Lawson. Tells of a cattle drover who dies of thirst in the desert and is later found by a search party. Follows one of the members of the party who is chosen to take the news to the drover's wife.
Geography - World; Literature and Drama; Sociology
Dist - AUIS **Prod** - FLMAUS 1972

Where Death Wears a Smile 47 MIN
16mm
Color (J H C) (GERMAN)
Relates the story of Australian prisoners of war who were interned in German concentration camps during World War II.
History - World
Dist - CINETF **Prod** - CINETF 1985

Where did I come from 27 MIN
VHS
Color (K P I T)
$24.95 purchase _ #S01559
Uses an animated format to explain conception and birth to children. Based on the book by the same name.
Health and Safety
Dist - UILL

Where did it all come from - where is it all going 7 MIN
16mm
Color (A)
$18.00 rental
Presents an erotic psycho - drama with cut - out animation by Victor Faccinto.
Fine Arts
Dist - CANCIN

Where Did Leonard Harry Go 7 MIN
U-matic
Color (I J H)
Tells how Leonard Harry becomes so bored with his humdrum life that he becomes a master of disguises. Shows what happens when the disguises take over and Leonard disappears.
Fine Arts
Dist - GA **Prod** - DAVFMS

Where did our love go 15 MIN
16mm
Color (G)
$30.00 rental
Presents the filmmaker's second production full of Warhol Factory days; serendipity visits, Janis and Castelli and Bellvue glances; Malanga at work; girl rock group and a disco opening; a romp through the Modern.
Fine Arts
Dist - CANCIN **Prod** - SONBER 1966

Where Did the Colorado Go 59 MIN
U-matic / VHS / 16mm
Nova Series
Color (H C A)
LC 78-700566
Examines suggestions by conservationists as to what should be done to save the Colorado River.
Geography - United States; Science - Natural; Social Science; Sociology
Dist - TIMLIF **Prod** - WGBHTV 1976

Where did they go 5 MIN
VHS
Seahouse series
Color (K P)
$29.95 purchase _ #RB8155
Studies camouflage and other adaptations used for hiding. Focuses on the camouflage techniques of flounder, and shows how a peacock flounder almost disappears against the bottom of the sea. Part of a series of ten parts on marine animals.
Science - Natural
Dist - REVID **Prod** - REVID 1990

Where did they go - a dinosaur update 19 MIN
VHS
Color (P I)

$89.00 purchase _ #RB809
Visits a dinosaur exhibit to discover what dinosaurs were, the different types of dinosaurs and how they lived. Examines a dinosaur dig and the site of a historical dinosaur discovery where it was discovered that dinosaurs stood erect.
Science - Natural; Science - Physical
Dist - REVID **Prod** - REVID

Where Did they Go - a Dinosaur Update 19 MIN
VHS
Color (I)
$80.00 purchase _ #5264V
Explains what dinosaurs are, the different types of dinosaurs, and how they did everything from raising their young to defending themselves from attackers.
Science - Natural; Science - Physical
Dist - SCTRES **Prod** - SCTRES

Where do babies come from 10 MIN
VHS
Learning about sex series
Color (P R)
$12.95 purchase _ #35 - 81023 - 19
Describes the processes of human reproduction in a manner targeted to children ages six to eight.
Health and Safety; Religion and Philosophy
Dist - APH **Prod** - CPH

Where do Babies Come from 29 MIN
U-matic / VHS
Coping with Kids Series
Color (T)
Education
Dist - FI **Prod** - MFFD

Where do I begin - approaching families about organ and tissue donation 27 MIN
VHS
Color (C PRO)
$300.00 purchase, $70.00 rental _ #5274S, #5274V
Discusses organ donation. Presents six dramatic scenes which cover: who should approach the family and which organs and tissues will be discussed; how to provide the correct information and assess the family's understanding; how to begin the process of informed consent; effective questions and good listening skills; how to help the family discuss their fears and how to extend sympathy; how to respond to the family's decision. Features Dr Marget Verbe and Judy Worth.
Health and Safety; Sociology
Dist - AJN **Prod** - STHREE

Where do I Begin - Approaching Families about Organ and Tissue Donation 27 MIN
VHS / 16mm
Color (C PRO)
$300.00 purchase, $60.00 rental _ #5274S, #5274V
Illustrates health care professionals coping with sensitive ethical issues involving organ donation. Demonstrates value of strong, positive attitude in approaching the family, providing correct information, discussing informed consent, and responding to the family's decision.Includes study guide.
Health and Safety
Dist - AJN **Prod** - STHREE 1990

Where do I Belong - Cuban Dropout 29 MIN
U-matic
As We See it Series
Color
Depicts a Chicago high school student traveling to Mexico to examine his feelings of alienation from both his parents and his past culture. Demonstrates problems that Cuban immigrants to Miami face in schools trying to balance the ideas, values and languages of two different cultures.
Sociology
Dist - PBS **Prod** - WTTWTV

Where do I fit in 25 MIN
VHS
Careers 2000 series
Color (J H)
$95.00 purchase _ #FYI1A
Emphasizes personal information gathering, career exploration, and preparing for a future career. Reviews the significance of interests, goal setting, personality style, preference for specific work activities, and skills as they relate to occupational selection. Includes workbook. Part 1 of a 3 - part series.
Business and Economics; Guidance and Counseling
Dist - CFKRCM **Prod** - CFKRCM

Where do I Go from Here 23 MIN
16mm / U-matic / VHS
Color
Helps convince employes that they are responsible for the direction their careers take, show how the employer can supply guidance and resources to support employee goals and provides employees with the strategies for a rigorous self - development program that will help them reach their career objectives.
Business and Economics; Psychology
Dist - EFM **Prod** - EFM

Where do I Go from Here 20 MIN
U-matic / VHS
Color
Provides a concrete, three - step process for setting objectives and creating a plan for successful career development. Includes a leader's guide.
Psychology
Dist - DELTAK **Prod** - DELTAK

Where do I Go from Here 21 MIN
U-matic / VHS / 16mm
Working Series
Color (H C A)
LC 81-700248
Discusses employee review and realistic self - appraisal. Explains how workers can follow their interests and abilities, develop their skills, and choose a career direction.
Guidance and Counseling; Psychology
Dist - JOU **Prod** - JOU 1980

Where do I Go from Here 4 MIN
16mm
Color
LC 76-701578
Conveys the mariner's respect for the rigorous challenge of the sea and depicts a Navy career as one which offers adventure, education and travel.
Civics and Political Systems; Guidance and Counseling
Dist - USNAC **Prod** - USN 1974

Where do I Live 20 MIN
U-matic / VHS
Once upon a Town Series
Color (P I)
Explores literary selections that deal with the effect of geographical, cultural and environmental settings on the way people live.
English Language; Literature and Drama
Dist - AITECH **Prod** - MDDE 1977

Where do I start 72 MIN
VHS
Technical theatre series
Color (J H C G)
$95.00 purchase _ #DSV001V
Discusses economical and effective set construction techniques. Looks at building supplies and tools, flats and platforms, stiffeners and jacks, window frames and door jambs, dutchmaning and more. Includes teacher's guide. Part of a five - part series on theater techniques.
Fine Arts
Dist - CAMV

Where do lost balloons go 11 MIN
VHS
Wonder world of science series
Color; PAL (P)
Follows Wondercat, an animated, curious kitten, who wonders what it means to be 'lighter than air.' Reveals that Wondercat loses a balloon and learns about the atmosphere. Part of a series which encourages youngsters to explore the limitless wonders of the world of science through careful observation, thoughtful comparisons and well - supported conclusions.
Science - Physical
Dist - VIEWTH **Prod** - VIEWTH
CORF

Where do Teenagers Come from 47 MIN
16mm / U-matic / VHS
Teenage Years Series
Color (I)
Presents pediatrician Lendon Smith who discusses the physical and psychological aspects of adolescence. Discusses reproduction, menstruation, nocturnal emissions, mood swings, acne, the need for privacy, and other biological and emotional aspects of becoming a teenager.
Guidance and Counseling; Health and Safety; Psychology
Dist - TIMLIF **Prod** - DEPFRE 1981

Where do they Come from - Language Development 30 MIN
U-matic / VHS
Teaching Early Reading Series
Color (T)
Education; English Language
Dist - CTI **Prod** - CTI

Where do they Go from Here - Motivating the Use of Reading 30 MIN
VHS / U-matic
Teaching Early Reading Series
Color (T)
Education; English Language
Dist - CTI **Prod** - CTI

Where do they go from there - Part 6 30 MIN
VHS
Teaching early reading series
Color (K P I)
#E376; LC 90-712995
Provides a broad spectrum of teaching methods and materials for teaching beginning reading skills. Shows how children can be motivated to experiment with creative, critical and recreational thinking. Part 6 of a six - part series on teaching early reading.
Education; English Language; Social Science
Dist - GPN **Prod** - CTI 1978

Where do We Go from Here 33 MIN
16mm
To Get from Here to There Series
Color (H)
Stresses that driving is the student's responsibility and offers a positive plan for improving highway safety.
Health and Safety; Psychology; Social Science
Dist - PROART **Prod** - PROART

Where do We Go from Here 9 MIN
Videoreel / VHS
Color
Focuses on the elderly and the families who care for them. Presents the story of a family making living arrangements for an elderly parent about to be released from the hospital. Discusses available choices for care of the elderly.
Fine Arts; Health and Safety; Sociology
Dist - EDC **Prod** - EDC

Where do we go from here 30 MIN
VHS
Effective teacher telecourse series
Color (T)
$69.95 purchase, $50.00 rental
Applies the concepts and strategies taught in the series to the future of teaching. Hosted by Dr Loren Anderson.
Education; Psychology
Dist - SCETV **Prod** - SCETV 1987

Where do You Fit into the Organization 20 MIN
VHS / U-matic
Man Management and Rig Management Series
Color (IND)
Shows how first - line supervisors function inside and outside the company. Emphasizes the importance of good communication and cooperation between oil field and office.
Business and Economics; Psychology
Dist - UTEXPE **Prod** - UTEXPE 1983

Where do you go from here - installation and follow up of improvements 16 MIN
16mm
Color
LC 74-706326
Shows how to conduct work simplification programs in the Army.
Business and Economics; Education; Guidance and Counseling; Psychology
Dist - USNAC **Prod** - USA 1973

Where Does all the Money Go 29 MIN
U-matic / VHS / 16mm
Be a Better Shopper Series
Color (H C A)
LC 81-701459
Explores how and where Americans spend their food dollar. Looks at USDA food spending plans, methods for keeping track of spending and information on how the food stamp program works.
Home Economics
Dist - CORNRS **Prod** - CUETV 1978

Where Does Food Come from 15 MIN
VHS / U-matic
Great American Eating Machine - You Series
Color (P)
LC 83-706106
Shows how food is grown, processed and shipped to market. Provides examples of many of the people and places that maintain America's food supply.
Health and Safety; Social Science
Dist - GPN **Prod** - NJPTV 1982

Where Does Food Come from
U-matic / VHS / 16mm
Color
Shows the origins of the foods we take for granted in a supermarket.
Health and Safety; Social Science
Dist - HIGGIN **Prod** - HIGGIN

Where Does Food Go 4 MIN
16mm / U-matic / VHS
Most Important Person - Health and Your Body Series
Color (K P I)
Demonstrates the path that food takes after being eaten, featuring a rabbit chewing, a giraffe swallowing and a hippopotamus shaking his belly.

Guidance and Counseling; Health and Safety; Science - Natural
Dist - EBEC Prod - EBEC 1972

Where Does it Grow 29 MIN
VHS / 16mm
Villa Alegre Series
Color (P T)
$46.00 rental _ #VILA - 144
Presents educational material in both Spanish and English.
Education
Dist - PBS

Where Does it Hurt 90 MIN
16mm
Color (H A)
Tells the story of a profiteering hospital administrator. Black comedy starring Peter Sellers.
Fine Arts
Dist - TIMLIF Prod - TIMLIF 1971

Where Does Life Come from 5 MIN
U-matic / VHS / 16mm
Wonder Walks Series
Color (P)
LC 79-713438
Shows the growth of plants from seeds and animals from eggs.
Science - Natural
Dist - EBEC Prod - EBEC 1971

Where Does My Refrigerator Go from Here 10 MIN
16mm
B&W
Presents a look at the world of garbage, and the people who live with it all day long. Explores not only the kinds of materials that make up garbage and the route across the city it follows from pick - up to final dispositions, but also the relationships of a variety of adults and children to garbage.
Health and Safety; Science - Natural; Social Science; Sociology
Dist - UPENN Prod - UPENN 1969

Where does rain go after it falls 11 MIN
VHS
Wonder world of science series
Color; PAL (P)
Follows Wondercat, an animated, curious kitten, who wonders what happens to the rain after it falls while watching a rainstorm. Teaches about the water cycle. Part of a series which encourages youngsters to explore the limitless wonders of the world of science through careful observation, thoughtful comparisons and well - supported conclusions.
Science - Natural; Science - Physical; Social Science
Dist - VIEWTH Prod - VIEWTH

Where does sand come from 11 MIN
VHS / U-matic / 16mm
Wonder world of science series
Color (P)
$320.00, $250.00 purchase _ #HP - 5708C
Stars Wondercat who discovers that sand consists of tiny bits of rock. Uses animation and live action to portray the creation of sand from rocks by water and air movement - and the creation of some rocks from sand. Part of the Wonder World of Science series. Produced by Bill Walker Productions.
Science - Physical
Dist - CORF

Where Does the Harvest Begin 20 MIN
16mm
Color
Covers in detail the four requirements that must be followed when planting to assure a profitable harvest.
Agriculture
Dist - IDEALF Prod - ALLISC

Where does time fly 17 MIN
VHS / U-matic / 16mm
Language arts through imagination series
Color (P I)
$400.00, $280.00 purchase _ #JC - 67697
Uses live action, animation and clips from classic Disney movies to explore the power and fun of words and literature. Stars the whimsical dragon Figment who flies through time to find the inspiration to write a wonderful story. He visits dinosaurs, the wild west and outer space, but can't come up with an idea he likes. Jessie and Nick are invited to help Figment, and they illustrate past, present and future using apt and specific vocabulary and characterizations. Together they create a pirate story using their collective experiences, imaginations and storytelling techniques.
English Language; Literature and Drama
Dist - CORF Prod - DISNEY 1989

Where eagles fly - an environmental issues program 24 MIN
VHS
Color (J H)
$89.95 purchase _ #10203VG
Shows the debate over development versus preservation of species through the issues of copper mines and bald eagles. Outlines the town of Haines, Alaska's efforts to balance development and conservation. Comes with a teacher's guide, discussion questions and four blackline masters.
Science - Natural
Dist - UNL

Where eagles swim 26 MIN
16mm
Audubon wildlife theatre series
Color (P)
LC 72-709411
Features a search for the bald eagle, taking place in the waters and on the islands off the British Columbia coast about 350 miles north of Vancouver. Shows how the great bird flourishes in this primitive area, relatively undisturbed by man.
Geography - World; Science - Natural
Dist - AVEXP Prod - KEGPL 1969

Where Feeding Problems Begin 7 MIN
U-matic
Take Time Series
(A)
Demonstrates the influence of parents and others caring for pre - schoolers on the physical and emotional development of the child.
Health and Safety; Psychology; Sociology
Dist - ACCESS Prod - ACCESS 1976

Where have all the animals gone - endangered species 25 MIN
VHS
Color (I J)
$89.95 purchase _ #10371VG
Looks at endangered species and wildlife conservation around the world. Explores some of the threats to animals by humans such as pollution; loss of habitat; over hunting; and poaching and exotic pet trade. Comes with a teacher's guide, discussion questions and six blackline masters.
Science - Natural
Dist - UNL

Where have all the Cowboys Gone 29 MIN
U-matic
Like no Other Place Series
Color (J H)
Examines Alberta's two main industries, oil and agriculture.
Geography - World; History - World
Dist - TVOTAR Prod - TVOTAR 1985

Where have all the dolphins gone 58 MIN
VHS
Color (J H C G A)
$59.95 purchase, $30.00 rental
Documents the slaughter of dolphins that often occurs in tuna fishing, with over six million killed in 30 years of fishing. Reveals that while steps have been taken to change this, more than 50 percent of tuna sold worldwide is not dolphin safe. Features accounts of the dolphins' natural charm and intelligence, as well as secret footage shot on tuna boats. Narrated by George C Scott. Produced by the Marine Mammal Fund.
Geography - World; Science - Natural
Dist - EFVP

Where have all the Farmers Gone 20 MIN
16mm
Inherit the Earth Series
Color (I)
Defines the role of agriculture and shows some of its problems. Points out that, industrialized and urbanized, Americans often forget that man biologically is an animal. Explains that through agriculture, man has modified the nature of his food web but remains dependent on the soil and the green plants growing in it for his energy.
Agriculture; Science - Natural
Dist - GPN Prod - KQEDTV

Where have all the Germans Gone 52 MIN
U-matic / VHS / 16mm
Destination America Series
Color (J)
Tells that one - sixth of today's Americans are descended from the German immigrants who came as political and religious refugees. In 1854, half of America's immigrants were German, including teachers, writers and lawyers. The dream of a German society in America was shattered by two world wars.
History - United States; History - World; Sociology
Dist - MEDIAG Prod - THAMES 1976

Where historians disagree series
Facts vs interpretations 35 MIN
Dist - SRA

Where horses fly like the wind 55 MIN
VHS
Silk road II series
Color (J H C A)
$29.95 purchase _ #CPM1058V-S
Presents a video produced by China Central Television to provide sights, sounds, and historic dramas of historic and inaccessible locations on the fabled Silk Road. Features the art, culture, and history that live on in artifacts and the daily lives of the residents. Part of a series.
Geography - World
Dist - CAMV

Where horses fly like the wind - Volume 11 60 MIN
VHS
Silk road series
Color (G)
$29.95 purchase _ #CMP1013
Visits a point along the fabled Silk Road linking Europe and China and traveled by Marco Polo. Features a soundtrack by Kitaro. Part of a series.
Geography - World; History - World
Dist - CHTSUI

Where Hunger Stalks 25 MIN
16mm
Color (H C A)
Tells the true story of P Y Singh, a young Indian boy who found a God who cares and meets human needs.
Guidance and Counseling; Religion and Philosophy
Dist - CBFMS Prod - CBFMS

Where I Want to be 21 MIN
16mm
Color
LC 74-700500
Shows the lives, goals and satisfactions of several women dentists in order to encourage more women of high school and college age to decide on a career in dentistry.
Guidance and Counseling; Health and Safety; Psychology; Sociology
Dist - MTP Prod - ASTF 1973

Where I Want to be - the Story of a Woman Dentist 28 MIN
16mm
Color
LC 74-700500
Describes the career advantages of dentistry to women. Emphasizes the growing need for women in the dental field.
Education; Guidance and Counseling; Psychology; Science; Sociology
Dist - USNAC Prod - USDH 1973

Where I Want to be - the Story of a Woman Dentist 29 MIN
U-matic
Color
LC 77-706194
Describes career advantages for women in the field of dentistry. Emphasizes the growing need for women in the profession. Issued in 1973 as a motion picture.
Health and Safety; Science; Sociology
Dist - USNAC Prod - NIH

Where is Dead 19 MIN
U-matic / VHS / 16mm
Color; Captioned (P)
LC 75-704020
Tells a story about a six - year - old girl's struggle to understand her brother's sudden death, showing her relationship with the adult members of her family as they share their grief and compassion.
Guidance and Counseling; Sociology
Dist - EBEC Prod - EBEC 1975

Where is Home for Me 12 MIN
16mm
Color
LC 76-700442
Pictures Vietnamese refugees awaiting sponsorship and a chance to live in America.
Geography - World; Sociology
Dist - MRS Prod - MRS 1975

Where is Jim Crow - a Conversation with Stokely Carmichael 30 MIN
16mm / U-matic / VHS
Where is Jim Crow Series
B&W (H C T)
Presents Stokely Carmichael, controversial national chairman of the Student Non - violent Coordinating Committee and spokesman for the concept of 'BLACK POWER,' describing the police attack upon civil rights

demonstrators in Montgomery, Alabama in 1965, and discussing the direction of the 'FREEDOM MOVEMENT.' Asserts that racial strife is an accepted part of the United States society.
Civics and Political Systems; History - United States; Sociology
Dist - UCEMC **Prod** - KQEDTV 1964

Where is Jim Crow Series
Where is Jim Crow - a Conversation with Stokely Carmichael 30 MIN
Dist - UCEMC

Where is Larry 14 MIN
VHS / U-matic
Conrad Series
Color (I)
Discusses artificial respiration and the control of bleeding.
Health and Safety
Dist - AITECH **Prod** - SCETV 1977

Where is my child - Vu is mayn kind 90 MIN
16mm
B&W (G) (YIDDISH WITH ENGLISH SUBTITLES)
Features a story of loss, obsession and reconciliation set between 1911, the height of the exodus that brought two million East European Jews to the United States, and 1937, when immigration was still fresh in the audience's memory. Exemplifies the ruptures and betrayals many immigrants experienced. Delia Adler, doyenne of the Yiddish stage, evokes sympathy for the immigrants' suffering. The Vilna Troupe provides comic relief and musical interludes. Produced by Abraham Leff. Contact distributor for rental fee.
Religion and Philosophy; Sociology
Dist - NCJEWF

Where is the Weather Born 8 MIN
16mm / U-matic / VHS
Color (I)
LC 79-701527
Focuses on a team of scientists as they conduct experiments in the North Pacific in an effort to predict weather and climate.
Science; Science - Physical
Dist - AMEDFL **Prod** - NSF 1975

Where it Hurts 29 MIN
16mm
Color
LC 75-700707
Examines a variety of health care delivery issues, including home care, assistant doctors, health planning and health maintenance organizations.
Health and Safety; Sociology
Dist - USNAC **Prod** - USHHS

Where Jesus Lived 15 MIN
16mm
Land of the Bible Series
Color; B&W (P)
Explores the typical environment of the homeland of Jesus. Includes scenes related to the life of Jesus such as a carpenter at work, a synagogue school and a typical family of Galilee.
Geography - World; Religion and Philosophy
Dist - FAMF **Prod** - FAMF

Where Jesus Walked 27 MIN
16mm
Color (J)
LC 79-700515
Describes the land of Palestine by using quotations from the New Testament, paintings of Jesus and scenes of the countryside where Jesus taught.
Geography - World; Religion and Philosophy
Dist - BYU **Prod** - BYU 1978

Where Jesus Walked 40 MIN
VHS / BETA
Color
Tours many of the places mentioned in the Bible, such as Bethlehem and Jericho.
Geography - World; Religion and Philosophy
Dist - DSP **Prod** - DSP

Where Jesus Walked 12 MIN
16mm
Color (J A)
Shows scenes from the Holy Lands and relates them to the Gospel accounts of Jesus' life.
Geography - World; Literature and Drama; Religion and Philosophy
Dist - CBFMS **Prod** - CBFMS

Where land is life 28 MIN
VHS
Color (G)
$14.95 purchase
Highlights traditional agricultural methods practiced by the Quechua and Aymara people of Peru.
Agriculture
Dist - MARYFA

Where land meets sea 19 MIN
VHS
Color (J H)
$45.00 purchase _ #A1VH 9425
Teaches about the constant modification of world shorelines by the actions of waves and currents. Uses footage from around the world to introduce coastal landforms, explain tides and wave action and provide definitions of important terms.
Geography - World; Science - Physical
Dist - CLRVUE **Prod** - CLRVUE

Where Life Still Means Living 24 MIN
16mm / U-matic / VHS
Color
LC FIA65-513
Describes the inner emotional world of an aged couple who are frightened by chronic illness and mental disease and suffer from feelings of rejection and helplessness. Tells about their ultimate admission to a home for the aged where rehabiliattion therapies help to lead them into a life that is meaningful.
Health and Safety; Psychology; Sociology
Dist - FEIL **Prod** - MONTFH 1964

Where Luther walked 35 MIN
VHS
Color (J H C G A R)
$29.95 purchase, $10.00 rental _ #35 - 835 - 8516
Features Luther scholar Dr Roland Bainton in a review of Martin Luther's key moments and turning points. Takes viewers to actual sites in East Germany where many of these events took place.
Literature and Drama; Religion and Philosophy
Dist - APH **Prod** - VISVID

Where Man Lies Buried - Field and Laboratory Treatment of the Ancient Dead 38 MIN
16mm
B&W (H C A)
LC 77-703196
Describes the different kinds of geological and archeological deposits where the bones of ancient man and woman are found. Shows field excavating mortuary sites and examines methods of laboratory analysis of human skeletal remains.
Science; Science - Physical; Sociology
Dist - ITHCOL **Prod** - CORNRS 1974

Where None has Gone Before 60 MIN
U-matic / VHS
Smithsonian World Series
Color (J)
Introduces modern day pioneers. Shows pilots planning a non - stop, non - refueled flight around the world in a specially designed airplane. Interviews astronomers explaining the Hubble Space Telescope. Looks at the discovery of a new class of crustacean by a high school biology teacher.
Industrial and Technical Education; Science - Natural; Science - Physical
Dist - WETATV **Prod** - WETATV
CAMV

Where, oh where and hot dog - Volume 14 45 MIN
VHS
Superbook series
Color (K P I R)
$11.99 purchase _ #35 - 86775 - 979
Uses an animated format to tell the story of Chris and Joy and their time travels through Biblical places and events. 'Where, Oh Where' tells the story of Lot and Abraham, while 'Hot Dog' is an account of Sodom and Gomorrah.
Literature and Drama; Religion and Philosophy
Dist - APH **Prod** - TYHP

Where on earth are we going? series
Explores green alternatives concerning energy, pollution, food, agriculture and industry in the world today. Examines society's acceptance of green politics and its influence on the world.

Energy and pollution 25 MIN
Food and agriculture 25 MIN
Getting there - body politic, immortal soul 25 MIN
Green society 25 MIN
Industry and work 25 MIN
International perspective - one world or no world 25 MIN
Dist - BBCENE

Where Plants and Animals Live 15 MIN
U-matic / VHS
Bioscope Series
Color (I J)
LC 81-707583
Shows how life forms hibernate, migrate, or adapt in response to changing conditions within their own biomes.
Science - Natural
Dist - AITECH **Prod** - MAETEL 1981

Where plants come from 13 MIN
VHS
Debbie Greenthumb series
CC; Color (P I)
$59.95 purchase _ #1123VG
Explains plant distribution and reproduction. Presents seeds, spores, cuttings, runners, roots, and bulbs as ways plants can produce new plants. Comes with a teacher's guide and four blackline masters. Part two of a four - part series.
Science - Natural
Dist - UNL

Where Rainbows Wait for Rain - the Chihuahuan Desert, Pt 2 27 MIN
16mm
Color
LC 82-700535
Focuses on the Chihuahuan Desert with emphasis on moisture in the desert. Reveals little - known facts and strange animals and plants adapted to a special kind of life.
Geography - United States; Geography - World; Science - Natural
Dist - ADAMSF **Prod** - GRDNH 1982

Where Seconds Count 12 MIN
16mm
Color (A)
Describes the public service activities of local REACT teams, such as providing emergency communications for traffic safety and performing vital communications tasks during time of disaster.
Health and Safety; History - World; Psychology
Dist - GM **Prod** - GM

Where shall our child die 25 MIN
VHS
Color (A PRO)
$275.00 purchase, $50.00 rental
Considers the decision whether to allow a terminally ill pediatric patient to die at home or in the hospital. Interviews the parents of four children who died of cancer on the decisions they made and why they made them. Stresses the importance of health care workers' involvement in such decisions. Includes instructional guide.
Health and Safety; Sociology
Dist - UARIZ **Prod** - UARIZ

Where Shipwrecks Abound 50 MIN
U-matic / 16mm / VHS
Color; Mono (G)
MV $250.00 _ MP $975.00 purchase, $50.00 rental
Examines many of the 19th century shipwrecks which are to be found in Lake Huron. It is estimated that 10,000 ships are on the bottom of the Great Lakes and that most of these wrecks occurred in the 19th century and this film discusses reasons for the large numbers of shipwrecks.
Social Science
Dist - CTV **Prod** - MAKOF 1980

Where Should a Squirrel Live 11 MIN
16mm / U-matic / VHS
Color (P I)
Shows the experiences of a squirrel raised in a human's home and then released to its natural world.
Science - Natural
Dist - BARR **Prod** - ADAMSF 1971

Where Should I Sell My Hogs 25 MIN
U-matic / VHS
Color
Discusses the various types of markets and the criteria that should be used to compare markets to increase profits when selling hogs.
Agriculture
Dist - HOBAR **Prod** - HOBAR

Where Should the Money Go 16 MIN
16mm
Color
LC 80-700936
Explores allocation of funds to socially disadvantaged children and schools.
Education; Home Economics; Sociology
Dist - TASCOR **Prod** - TASCOR 1976

Where teachers are targets 29 MIN
VHS
Color (J H C G T A)
$75.00 purchase, $40.00 rental
Follows a group of Canadian teachers as they travel through El Salvador to learn about their Salvadoran teaching peers. Reveals that more than 350 Salvadoran teachers have been killed or "disappeared" since 1979, often because of their desire to teach poor children. Portrays the "disappearance" of a Salvadoran, "death squad" vehicles, and the Canadian teachers working to free a captured Salvadoran teacher. Produced by Lorne Wallace.
Geography - World; History - World
Dist - EFVP

Where the Action is 27 MIN
16mm
Color
LC 74-706327
Depicts work in today's complex technological world and shows how vocational and technical education can prepare young people through proper training, particularly at the post - secondary level, for their place in the world of work. Focuses on the problems of approximately 80 percent of the young people who do not complete college in terms of jobs, training for these jobs and their future.
Guidance and Counseling; Sociology
Dist - USNAC **Prod** - USOE 1967

Where the Action is 39 MIN
16mm
Color
LC 80-700866
Discusses technical details of the coal mining industry.
Industrial and Technical Education; Social Science
Dist - TASCOR **Prod** - IMPACT 1978

Where the Bay Becomes the Sea 30 MIN
U-matic / VHS / 16mm
Color (J H A)
Examines the fertile marine ecosystem where the Bay of Fundy meets the Atlantic Ocean. This area supports an abundance of life from microscopic plants to the 60 ton Right Whale. Explains virtually all marine life depends on small food rich oases like the mouth of the Bay of Fundy. Details past abuses of these oases and makes a powerful case for their preservation.
Guidance and Counseling; Science - Natural; Science - Physical
Dist - BULFRG **Prod** - NFBC 1987

Where the biggest bluefins swim
VHS
Color (G)
$29.90 purchase _ #0380
Travels to the Strait of Canso in the province of Nova Scotia, Canada, where a world record tuna was caught.
Geography - World; Physical Education and Recreation; Science - Natural
Dist - SEVVID

Where the Buffaloes Begin
VHS / 35mm strip
Caldecotts on Filmstrip Series
Color (K)
$35.00 purchase
Presents a children's story. Part of the Caldecott series.
English Language; Literature and Drama
Dist - PELLER

Where the City and Water Meet 18 MIN
VHS / U-matic
Color (J H C)
Presents an historical survey of the constantly changing development of a typical urban waterfront, through industrialization and the current period of transition to recreation.
Sociology
Dist - QUEENU **Prod** - QUAF 1984

Where the Cranberries Grow - an American Story 13 MIN
16mm
Color
LC 82-700283
Uses historical and modern photographs to take a look at both America's and the cranberry's history. Shows how cranberries are harvested by hand and demonstrates their many uses.
Agriculture; Home Economics
Dist - MTP **Prod** - OSC 1981

Where the Fish will be 20 MIN
U-matic / VHS / 16mm
Color
Describes how the U S Fish and Wildlife Service manages fishery programs, including hatcheries, research and cooperative efforts with the states to maintain healthy fish populations.
Civics and Political Systems; Science - Natural
Dist - USNAC **Prod** - USBSFW

Where the Forest Meets the Sea 7 MIN
VHS
Color (K)
$49.00 purchase _ #188 - 9050
Takes a wondrous visual journey through the exotic primeval wilderness of Daintree Tropical Rainforest in Australia. Uses an unusual collage technique. Makes viewers aware that they can play a vital role in preserving nature. Features the animation of Jeannie Baker.
Fine Arts; Geography - World; Literature and Drama; Science - Natural
Dist - FI **Prod** - FLMAUS 1988

Where the Future Begins - Girl Scouts 18 MIN
16mm
Color
Presents scenes of Girl Scouting filmed on location at Girl Scout Councils across the nation.
Fine Arts; Physical Education and Recreation; Psychology; Sociology
Dist - GSUSA **Prod** - GSUSA 1979

Where the Library Dollars are 40 MIN
U-matic
Access Series
Color (T)
LC 76-706265
Discusses ways a small library can supplement its regular operating budget.
Education; Social Science
Dist - USNAC **Prod** - UDEN 1976

Where the Loon Screams 27 MIN
16mm
Color (J H C)
LC 76-709719
Tells of one of the most unusual expeditions ever assembled and its departure for the Canadian Arctic to do extensive Arctic survival studies and to search for the prehistoric musk ox.
Geography - World; Science - Natural
Dist - LSTI **Prod** - LSTI

Where the Memories Live, Pt 1 30 MIN
VHS / U-matic
Franco File Series
Color (I)
Dramatizes contemporary Franco - American life. Emphasizes the theme of faith in self.
Sociology
Dist - GPN **Prod** - WENHTV

Where the Memories Live, Pt 2 30 MIN
U-matic / VHS
Franco File Series
Color (I)
Dramatizes contemporary Franco - American life. Examines the historical perspective.
History - United States; Sociology
Dist - GPN **Prod** - WENHTV

Where the red fern grows 97 MIN
VHS
Color (J H C)
$39.00 purchase _ #05729 - 126
Presents an adaptation of the Wilson Rawls story of a young boy's coming of age during the Depression.
Fine Arts; History - United States; Literature and Drama; Sociology
Dist - GA **Prod** - GA

Where the River Enters the Sea 28 MIN
16mm
Color
Shows how the Eskimo is emerging into modern society and looks at his culture.
Social Science; Sociology
Dist - MTP **Prod** - STOO

Where the river flows clean 17 MIN
U-matic / VHS / BETA
Color (G)
$29.95, $130.00 purchase _ #LSTF74
Explains how rivers have had an influence on human development and that human development now has an enormous impact on rivers. Explains how rivers contribute to the hydrologic cycle, forming watersheds, and how various pollutants degrade water quality. Coproduced by Wyckoff Productions and the Institute of Water Research at Michigan State University.
Science - Natural; Sociology
Dist - FEDU

Where the Sewage Goes 22 MIN
16mm
Color (I)
Presents documentation of the operation of the Washington, D C Blue Plains wastewater treatment plant which is one of America's largest municipal wastewater treatment operations. Emphasizes tertiary treatment.
Industrial and Technical Education; Science - Natural
Dist - FINLYS **Prod** - FINLYS 1977

Where the soul lives 60 MIN
VHS
Moyers - The Power of the word series
Color; Captioned (G)
$59.95 purchase _ #MOPW - 106
Features poets Robert Bly, Lucille Clifton and W S Merwin reading their poetry at the 1988 Geraldine R Dodge Poetry Festival. Interviews the three on their poetic approaches. Includes music by the Paul Winter Consort. Hosted by Bill Moyers.
English Language; Literature and Drama
Dist - PBS

Where the water meets the land 15 MIN
VHS
Junior oceanographer series
CC; Color (P I)
$69.95 purchase_#10366VG
Illustrates how forces, such as water and waves, act up on oceans and land. Explains the formation of waves; how oceans shape the land; and tidepools and their formation. Includes an interactive video quiz, a teacher's guide and six blackline masters. Part two of a four - part series.
Geography - World; Science - Physical
Dist - UNL

Where the waters run 28 MIN
VHS
Moody science classics series
Color (R I J)
$19.95 purchase _ #6119 - 0
Offers a metaphorical comparison between the physical use of water as a vital compound of life and the 'Living Water' of the Christian deity. Features part of a series on creationism.
Literature and Drama; Religion and Philosophy
Dist - MOODY **Prod** - MOODY

Where the wild things are 40 MIN
VHS
Color (K P I J)
Presents Maurice Sendak's story 'Where The Wild Things Are,' in which a young boy named Max discovers the land of wild things. Stars Karen Beardsley, Andrew Gallacher and Hugh Hetherington. Performed by the Glyndebourne Festival Opera. Accompanied by the London Sinfonietta.
Literature and Drama
Dist - UILL **Prod** - BBCTV
FI

Where the Wild Things are 8 MIN
U-matic / VHS / 16mm
Color (K P)
LC 75-701094
Presents an animated adaptation of the story of the same title by Maurice Sendak in which a small boy makes a visit to the land of the wild things. Tells how he tames the creatures and returns home.
Literature and Drama
Dist - WWS **Prod** - WWS 1974

Where there is hatred 57 MIN
VHS
Color (J H C G T A)
$39.95 purchase, $20.00 rental
Presents case studies which support the idea that nonviolent political action is effective for change. Features Harvard professor Dr Gene Sharp, who analyzes recent examples of the success of nonviolent action, and outlines the four steps in the process. Co - produced by Jonathan Miller.
Civics and Political Systems; Sociology
Dist - EFVP **Prod** - ZIVILN 1990

Where There is Hope 20 MIN
16mm
Color
LC 74-706329
Explains that help is available for retarded children from both private and government agencies. Takes a look at some of this help, including the facilities of the John F Kennedy Institute which is associated with the Johns Hopkins Hospital in Baltimore.
Psychology; Sociology
Dist - USNAC **Prod** - USSSA 1968

Where There is Life There is Motion - Function of Microtubules 25 MIN
U-matic
Color (C A)
LC 80-707633
Documents ciliary and flagellar movement, a mechanism mediated by the microtubules in a variety of organisms.
Science - Natural
Dist - PSU **Prod** - TOKYO 1980

Where there is life there is motion - Role of microfilaments in cell motility 25 MIN
VHS / U-matic
Color (H C)
Continues the study of movement in organisms with a detailed examination of the role of actin and myosin microfilaments. Uses sophisticated micrographic techniques to document in a variety of organisms the role of actin and myosin microfilaments in cell motion and in determining cell shape.
Science; Science - Natural
Dist - PSU **Prod** - PSU 1984

Where There's a Wheel There's a Way 19 MIN
Videoreel / VHS
Color
Addresses the physical and psychological benefits obtained by the handicapped through participation in team sports.

Health and Safety; Psychology
Dist - UNDMC Prod - UNDMC

Where There's a will - Leadership and Motivation 29 MIN
VHS / 16mm
Color (A PRO)
Shows that leadership skills can be taught. Demonstrates how to create a staff environment for self - motivation of individual staff members. Management training.
Business and Economics; Guidance and Counseling; Psychology
Dist - VIDART Prod - VIDART 1990
VLEARN

Where there's a will there's an...A - college
VHS
Color (C)
$89.95 purchase _ #DM004
Presents two videocassettes which offer tips on study techniques, note - taking, test - taking. Offers tips and techniques for competing in college. Includes a workbook.
Education
Dist - SIV

Where there's a will there's an...A - grade school
VHS
Color (P I J)
$89.95 purchase _ #DM002
Presents two videocassettes which offer tips on study techniques, note - taking, test - taking. Teaches basic learning skills. Includes a workbook.
Education
Dist - SIV

Where there's a will there's an...A - high school
VHS
Color (H)
$89.95 purchase _ #DM003
Presents two videocassettes which offer tips on study techniques, note - taking, test - taking. Boosts high school grades and helps high school students prepare for college. Includes a workbook.
Education
Dist - SIV

Where there's life series
Alcoholism 25 MIN
Birmingham accident hospital 25 MIN
Facing up to death 25 MIN
Homosexuality 25 MIN
Huntington's chorea 25 MIN
Natural childbirth 25 MIN
Surrogate mothers 25 MIN
What's wrong with ME 25 MIN
Who's your mother 25 MIN
Dist - ACADEM

Where There's Smoke 11 MIN
16mm
Color
Describes basic steps of testing, donning, wearing and using standard breathing apparatus at live fires.
Health and Safety; Social Science
Dist - FILCOM Prod - AREASX

Where There's Smoke 12 MIN
16mm
Color (I)
LC 76-715016
Presents a series of brief television clips, using both live - action and animation, ridiculing the smoking habit.
Health and Safety
Dist - NFBC Prod - CDHW 1970

Where There's Smoke 56 MIN
VHS / 16mm
Color (H C A)
$180.00 purchase, $35.00 rental _ #HC1336
Documents experiences of eight heavy smokers, all nicotine addicts.
Guidance and Counseling; Health and Safety; Psychology
Dist - IU Prod - WCCOTV 1988

Where There's Smoke Firesafety Quiz
U-matic / VHS
Color
Health and Safety
Dist - NFPA Prod - NFPA

Where Timber Wolves Call 25 MIN
16mm / U-matic / VHS
Color (J)
LC 77-701609
Shows Canadian naturalist Tommy Tompkins as he follows a pack of wolves in the Canadian Rockies for three weeks, documenting their habits and behavior and examining their contribution to the balance of nature.
Science - Natural
Dist - WOMBAT Prod - TOMWLF 1977

Where Time Began 91 MIN
16mm
Color
Shows how a British scientist discovers the key to unlock the weird world that exists at the center of the earth.
Fine Arts
Dist - TWYMAN Prod - UNKNWN 1978

Where to begin 30 MIN
Videoreel / VT2
Designing home interiors series; Unit 1
Color (C A)
Introduces field of interior design and the impact it can have on the entire family. Explains psychological effects of interior design. Offers definition of interior design by professional designers and lay people.
Home Economics
Dist - CDTEL Prod - COAST

Where to Begin with Nonverbal Children 17 MIN
16mm
Color (C T)
LC 78-701614
Follows five children through an informal screening - assessment procedure which highlights the capabilities and deficiencies of each subject in the various communication skills.
Education; Psychology
Dist - UKANS Prod - UKANAV 1973

Where to go from here 30 MIN
Videoreel / VT2
Designing home interiors series; Unit 30
Color (C A)
Discusses experience and education required for would - be interior designers, how to work with an interior designer, and the future of careers in the design field.
Home Economics
Dist - CDTEL Prod - COAST

Where to Look - the Territory 15 MIN
U-matic
Job Seeking Series
Color (H C A)
Describes how to seek job openings.
Guidance and Counseling; Psychology
Dist - GPN Prod - WCETTV 1979

Where to put your money if the new tax bill passes 30 MIN
U-matic
Adam Smith's money world 1985 - 1986 season series; 238
Color (A)
Attempts to demystify the world of money and break it down so that small as well as large businesses and it's people understand and adjust to new social and economic trends. Reports on the major economic stories and discoveries of 1985 and 1986.
Business and Economics
Dist - PBS Prod - WNETTV 1986

Where, Turn 10 MIN
U-matic
Readalong One Series
Color (K P)
Introduces reading and spelling for preschoolers and children in grades 1 to 3 with animation, puppets, humor and music. Comes with teacher's guide and kit.
Education; English Language; Literature and Drama
Dist - TVOTAR Prod - TVOTAR 1975

Where Villains Roam 15 MIN
U-matic
Color (I)
Teaches writing skills while telling the story of Chris and his friends who search for the Book Destroyer as they are magically transported through fairy tale worlds.
Education; English Language; Literature and Drama
Dist - TVOTAR Prod - TVOTAR 1982

Where We Live 49 MIN
VHS / U-matic / 16mm
Human Journey Series
Color; Mono (J H C A)
MV $350.00 _ MP $450.00 purchase, $50.00 rental
Presents facts that indicate that the average Canadian's largest expenditure is the purchase of a home and for apartment dwellers the largest expenditure is for rent, therefore it is not surprising to find people are more interested in their homes than anywhere else. Includes conversations with real estate developers, home owners and public officials.
Sociology
Dist - CTV Prod - CTV
FI

Where were You during the Battle of the Bulge, Kid 26 MIN
U-matic / VHS / 16mm
Insight Series
Color; B&W (J) (SPANISH)
Shows the parallels between a father and a son who both must decide whether to conform to society and compromise with evil or follow one's conscience and pay the price.
Fine Arts; Foreign Language; Sociology
Dist - PAULST Prod - PAULST

Where why and how series
A Child's guide to everyday stuff - House - Volume I 9 MIN
Dist - PFP

Where will You Work Tomorrow 60 MIN
Software / VHS
World of Work
(G)
Explores a wide range of high technology job options. Highlights training opportunities and techniques for learning high technology to prepare for future changes in the job market.
Social Science; Sociology
Dist - GPN Prod - TECNVI 1984

Where You are, Where You're Going 15 MIN
U-matic / VHS / 16mm
Color
Stresses the importance of the small businessman keeping up - to - date records. Discusses how to begin record - keeping and to reestablish records that have been destroyed.
Business and Economics
Dist - USNAC Prod - USSBA 1982

Where Your Money Goes 28 MIN
U-matic / VHS / 16mm
Learning to Live on Your Own Series
Color (S) (SPANISH)
LC 80-700258;
Looks at the ways money may be saved or spent. Includes an explanation of payroll deductions, taxes, and the role of banks, savings and loan associations and credit unions with emphasis placed on budgeting.
Business and Economics; Home Economics
Dist - JOU Prod - LINCS 1979

Whereby we thrive - Part VI
VHS
America the bountiful series
Color (G)
$89.95 purchase _ #6 - 402 - 006A
Shows that after World War II, American agriculture became a significant tool in winning the Cold War. Looks at crop improvements yielded by American agricultural research and the export of many United States farm products to Third World nations. The 'Green Revolution' is driven by Nobel laureates such as Norman Borlaug and biotechnology and genetic engineering allow fewer farmers to grow more food. Part of a six - part series on the history of American agriculture hosted by Ed Begley, Jr.
Agriculture; Civics and Political Systems; History - United States; Social Science; Sociology
Dist - VEP Prod - VEP 1993

Where's Charlie 12 MIN
16mm
Color
LC 77-701461
Introduces a new kind of resilient flooring designed to solve the problem of a skilled labor shortage.
Business and Economics; Social Science
Dist - ACOC Prod - ACOC 1976

Where's Danny 16 MIN
16mm / U-matic / VHS
Color
Recommends safe work procedures for interior painting contractors and their employees.
Health and Safety
Dist - IFB Prod - NFBTE

Where's Momma 15 MIN
U-matic / VHS
Color (C G)
$250.00 purchase _ #HH - 6355M
Examines the plight of grandmothers burdened with the responsibility of caring for children whose parents are crack addicts. Interviews grandmothers, family members and medical experts to reveal the stress and physical hardship grandmothers face and emphasize the dangers and devastation of crack addiction.
Guidance and Counseling; Health and Safety; Psychology; Sociology
Dist - CORF Prod - CORF 1990

Where's Pete 26 MIN
16mm / VHS
Family Issues - Learning about Life Series
Color (P I J A)
$395.00, $495.00 purchase, $50.00 rental _ #8047
Portrays normal grieving responses to the death of a loved one; in this case a seven - year - old grieves for his older brother. Also presents attentive, caring adult role modeling.
Guidance and Counseling; Psychology; Sociology
Dist - AIMS **Prod** - NFBC 1988

Where's Picone 112 MIN
VHS / 35mm
Color (G) (ITALIAN WITH ENGLISH SUBTITLES)
$250.00 rental
Stars Giancarlo Gianini as a morgue employee who stumbles into the criminal underworld of Naples. Directed by Nanni Loy.
Fine Arts; Sociology
Dist - KINOIC

Where's poppa 83 MIN
16mm
Color (G)
$125.00 rental
Features a wild imaginative black comedy about a bachelor, played by George Segal, who schemes to eliminate his aging mother. Entertains with sight gags and septuagenarian scene stealer, Ruth Gordon. Also stars Ron Leibman, Vincent Gardenia and Trish Van Devere. Directed by Carl Reiner.
Fine Arts; Health and Safety; Literature and Drama; Religion and Philosophy; Sociology
Dist - NCJEWF

Where's Shelley 13 MIN
U-matic / 16mm / VHS
Color (P I J)
$295.00, $285.00 _ #A554
Tells a realistic story about children who find an opportunity to use alcohol and other drugs. Explores some of the factors which affect such decisions and focuses on the decision not to use alcohol or drugs.
Guidance and Counseling; Health and Safety; Psychology; Sociology
Dist - BARR **Prod** - JOHNIN 1984

Where's the any key - how to use computers to automate your office
VHS
Color (H C A)
$98.00 purchase _ #CD9400V
Presents a comprehensive introduction to the use of computers in the office. Covers the major business uses of computers, and applies them to the different business departments. Defines computer terms.
Business and Economics; Computer Science
Dist - CAMV

Where's the Trouble 9 MIN
16mm
Color (K P)
LC 73-701038
Teaches the concepts of front, back, top and bottom.
Guidance and Counseling; Psychology
Dist - FILMSM **Prod** - FILMSM 1972

Where's the Water 14 MIN
16mm
Color (IND)
LC 70-713370
Examines factors which influence the delivery of water from a water tower to the scene of a fire, relating illustrations of specific principles of hydraulics to actual effects on the fire ground.
Health and Safety; Industrial and Technical Education
Dist - FILCOM **Prod** - IOWAFS 1971
JEWELR

Where's Tommy 11 MIN
16mm / U-matic / VHS
Color (J A)
LC 75-702769
Shows potential dangers surrounding an unattended child while he naps and as his mother visits a neighbor. Explains how children find things fascinating, but lack experience in juding what is harmful and what is safe.
Guidance and Counseling; Health and Safety; Sociology
Dist - HIGGIN **Prod** - HIGGIN 1974

Where's utopia 58 MIN
VHS
Color (G)
$25.00 purchase
Documents Soviet social scientist Dr Peter Gladkov's 1988 whirlwind tour of usccessful cooperative communities in the United States. Looks at a rich diversity of cooperative systems, from housing to farming, food purchasing to insurance plans, neighborhoods and villages, all pointing the way toward a future of people living in reverance for the earth and each other. Produced by Art Rosenblum for the Aquarian Research Foundation.
Civics and Political Systems; Fine Arts; Social Science; Sociology
Dist - CANCIN

Where's Your Loyalty 11 MIN
U-matic / VHS / 16mm
Color (I J) (SPANISH)
LC 72-700976;
Presents vignettes involving dilemmas of loyalty to aid children in formulating and examining their codes of living.
Guidance and Counseling
Dist - EBEC **Prod** - EBEC 1971

Wherever We Find Them 29 MIN
16mm
Color
LC 79-701820
Shows the numerous athletic opportunities available to handicapped individuals, including racketball, skiing, track, swimming, bowling and weightlifting. Describes how exercise and participation in organized competition builds strength and confidence.
Physical Education and Recreation; Psychology
Dist - USNAC **Prod** - USVA 1979

Wherever We Lodge 60 MIN
16mm
Color
Looks at the creative efforts to meet worldwide housing concerns ranging from the visionary to the common - place. Examines the concept of new towns as one possible answer to creative communities.
Sociology
Dist - CCNCC **Prod** - NBCTV

Wherever You are 28 MIN
16mm
Color
LC 77-702172
Tells the story of an arthritis victim who cannot bring herself to seek proper medical treatment. Narrated by Henry Fonda.
Health and Safety
Dist - MTP **Prod** - ARTHF 1977

Whether to Tell the Truth 18 MIN
16mm / U-matic / VHS
Searching for Values - a Film Anthology Series
B&W (J)
LC 72-703148
Tells how a young man painfully gains a sense of himself and his duty to society at the cost of losing his friends and a familiar way of life when he exposes illegal activities taking place on the docks.
Guidance and Counseling; Psychology; Sociology
Dist - LCOA **Prod** - LCOA 1972

Which computer is for me
VHS
Computer series
Color (G)
$29.95 purchase _ #IV - 023
Explains the world of the computer and its usefulness in everyday life.
Computer Science; Home Economics
Dist - INCRSE **Prod** - INCRSE

Which End do I Look in 15 MIN
VHS / U-matic
Movies, Movies Series
Color (J H)
Describes the filmmaking process. Covers planning, filming and editing.
Fine Arts; Industrial and Technical Education
Dist - CTI **Prod** - CTI

Which Energy 23 MIN
16mm
Science of Energy Series
Color
LC 77-700440
Compares different energy sources by visiting field installations and research laboratories. Considers fossil fuels, nuclear fusion, fission, the breeder reactor, solar energy, wind and conservation concepts.
Science - Natural; Science - Physical; Social Science
Dist - FINLYS **Prod** - FINLYS 1976

Which Go Together - Set Building 10 MIN
16mm / U-matic / VHS
Math Readiness Series
Color (P)
$255, $180 purchase _ #3641
Shows how things are grouped into sets. Uses blocks to illustrate the concept of set building.
Mathematics
Dist - CORF

Which governs best 89 MIN
VHS
Color (G)
$79.95 purchase _ #S01083
Examines the concept of democratic government in the US, using the example of New Orleans and Louisiana. Considers the functions, mechanisms, and role of democratic government in the lives of citizens. Stresses the importance of being informed and voting. Hosted and narrated by Steve Allen.
Civics and Political Systems; Geography - United States
Dist - UILL

Which is My World 9 MIN
U-matic / VHS / 16mm
Color (I A)
LC 70-711108
Shows how greed is a major cause of environmental pollution. Tells how our demand for new things leads us to discard still usable items which lie in mounds that scar our environment. Explores the decisions and changes that may be necessary for our safe and pleasant survival.
Science - Natural
Dist - PHENIX **Prod** - PHENIX 1971

Which Mother is Mine 47 MIN
U-matic / VHS / 16mm
Teenage Years Series
Color
LC 79-700936
Relates the story of a girl who has spent most of her life in foster home who must cope with the shock of having her natural mother return to claim her.
Sociology
Dist - TIMLIF **Prod** - TAHSEM 1979

Which Rule Wins 28 MIN
16mm
University of Illinois Arithemtic Project Series
B&W (T)
LC 75-702652
Presents an unrehearsed film in which Miss Phyllis Klein teaches one of the University of Illinois Arithmetic Project topics to a class of third graders.
Education; Mathematics
Dist - AGAPR **Prod** - EDS 1968

Which Side are You on
16mm
B&W
Presents the history of the rank and file, black and white and men and women, as the hands that built America.
History - United States
Dist - CANWRL **Prod** - CANWRL 1970

Which way did the melody go 15 MIN
VHS / U-matic
Music machine series
Color (P)
Discusses musical notation.
Fine Arts
Dist - GPN **Prod** - INDIPS 1981

Which way is east 33 MIN
16mm / VHS
Color (G)
$60.00, $75.00 rental, $195.00 purchase
Travels north from Saigon to Hanoi with the filmmaker and her sister Dana Sachs, a journalist living in Vietnam. Studies Vietnamese culture and the distintive experiences of two women travelers by creating a photographed and narrated travel diary full of personal reflections and childhood remembrances of the war on television.
Geography - World; Psychology; Sociology
Dist - WMEN **Prod** - SACHS 1994

Which Way is Up 94 MIN
16mm
Color
Stars Richard Pryor in a triple role as a farm worker, his old father, and a hypocritical preacher.
Fine Arts
Dist - TWYMAN **Prod** - UPCI 1977

Which Way - Mapping - Geography 14 MIN
U-matic / VHS
Two Cents' Worth Series
Color (P)
Depicts a neighborhood treasure hunt in which two groups of children must interpret and follow simple maps to get free movie passes.
Geography - United States
Dist - AITECH **Prod** - WHATV 1976

Which way now 28 MIN
16mm
Eleventh round series; No 2
Color (C A)
Deals with the problems facing farmers and small towns in the 70's. Discusses main choices in federal farm programs and their effects on farm incomes, taxpayers' cost and food prices.

Agriculture; Business and Economics; Civics and Political Systems
Dist - UNEBR Prod - UNL 1969

Which way to CA 4 MIN
16mm
B&W (G)
$10.00 rental
Fine Arts
Dist - CANCIN Prod - KRENKU 1981

Which Way to the Front 96 MIN
16mm
Color
Stars Jerry Lewis as a patriotic multi - billionaire who tries a variety of schemes to win World War II.
Fine Arts
Dist - TWYMAN Prod - WB 1970

Which Way to Turn 24 MIN
VHS / U-matic
Discovering Physics Series
Color (H C)
Introduces the concept of angular momentum, which helps describe the motion of rotating physical systems in terms more complex than the theory of linear motion will allow. Uses simple examples to show the meaning of basic physics ideas.
Science; Science - Physical
Dist - MEDIAG Prod - BBCTV 1983

Which Witch is which 24 MIN
U-matic / VHS / 16mm
Color
MP=$450.00
Follows cartoon characters Buttons and Rusty as they celebrate Halloween and accidentally assist in catching robbers.
Social Science
Dist - LANDMK Prod - LANDMK 1985

Whiffle Squeek
VHS
Children's Literature on Video Series
Color (K)
$33.00 purchase
Literature and Drama
Dist - PELLER

While at work
VHS
Job strategies set
Color (G A)
$69.50 purchase _ #ES150V
Looks at the traits and skills necessary to succeed in a job. Considers subjects including promotions, personality types, peer and supervisor expectations, and how to make good impressions.
Business and Economics; Psychology
Dist - CAMV

While at Work
VHS / 35mm strip
Pre - Employment Planning Series
$43.50 film purchase, $69.50 VHS purchase _ #XY145 film, #XY155 VHS
Guidance and Counseling
Dist - CAREER Prod - CAREER

While soldiers fought series
Presents a seven - part series which examines the impact of war on American society from historical, literary, artistic and philosophical perspectives. Includes the titles The Artist at War; Coming Home; For God and Country; A Hometown at War; Private Yankee Doodle Dandy; Soldiers' Stories; and Winning the War on Film. Produced by the International University Consortium.

The Artist at war	28 MIN
Coming home	28 MIN
For God and country	28 MIN
A Hometown at war	28 MIN
Private Yankee Doodle	28 MIN
Soldier's stories	28 MIN
Winning the war on film	28 MIN

Dist - PSU

While the Cat's Away 30 MIN
VHS / U-matic
Burglar - Proofing Series
Color
Health and Safety; Sociology
Dist - MDCPB Prod - MDCPB

While the storm clouds gather 30 MIN
VHS
America in World War II - The home front series
Color (G)
$49.95 purchase _ #AWWH - 101
Scans the international political scene in the years before America's involvement in World War II. Focuses on German and Japanese military gains. Illustrates the shift from American neutrality to support of allies. Narrated by Eric Sevareid.

History - United States
Dist - PBS

While You Ride the Bus 12 MIN
16mm
Bellevue Volunteers Series
B&W
Discusses the nonmedical New York City social improvement programs seeking volunteers. Describes their functions, locations and the ways in which prospective volunteers may offer their services.
Social Science; Sociology
Dist - NYU Prod - NYU

While You were Out 9 MIN
Videoreel / VT2
SUCCESS, the AMA Course for Office Employees Series
Color
LC 75-704215
Presents an instructional course for office employees. Presents a case study which shows how communication barriers can cause misunderstanding and confusion even with a simple business message.
Business and Economics; Psychology
Dist - AMA Prod - AMA 1972

Whiplash 16 MIN
U-matic / VHS / 16mm
Color (H A) (SPANISH)
LC 79-700186
Illustrates what happens during a rear - end collision at speeds from 10 to 55 mph. Shows how to minimize whiplash injury and safe driving practices by which rear - end collisions may be avoided.
Health and Safety; Industrial and Technical Education
Dist - AIMS Prod - CAHILL 1968

The Whiplash and trupmet curves 180 MIN
VHS / U-matic
Arctic engineering series
Color (PRO)
Discusses one dimensional heat flow, seasonal changes, geomorphic aspects of cold regions, ice wedges and tabor ice.
Health and Safety; Industrial and Technical Education
Dist - AMCEE Prod - UAKEN

The Whipping boy 15 MIN
VHS
More books from cover to cover series
Color (I G)
$25.00 purchase _ #MBCC - 115
Tells the story of a bratty prince and his whipping boy. Follows them through a series of adventures when they inadvertently trade places. Based on the book 'The Whipping Boy' by Sid Fleischman. Hosted by John Robbins.
Education; English Language; Literature and Drama
Dist - PBS Prod - WETATV 1987

The Whipping Boy 37.56 MIN
First Choice Authors and Books, Unit 33 Series
Color (I J)
LC 88-713637
Tells the story of a spoiled prince and his friendship with a streetwise urchin.
Literature and Drama
Dist - PPIPER Prod - PPIPER 1988

Whirlwind - Bombing Germany, September, 1939 to may, 1944 60 MIN
16mm
World at War Series
Color (H C A) (GERMAN)
LC 76-701778
History - World; Sociology
Dist - USCAN MEDIAG Prod - THAMES 1975

Whirlwind on Mount Egmont 25 MIN
16mm
Color
Presents Japanese professional skier, Yoshiharu Fukuhara, skiing on Mount Egmont which resembles Mt Fuji. Portrays his character through his skiing and interviews.
Geography - World; Physical Education and Recreation
Dist - UNIJAP Prod - UNIJAP 1969

Whiskers and Rhymes
VHS / 35mm strip
ALA Notable Children's Filmstrips Series
Color (K)
$33.00 purchase
Presents a children's story. Part of the American Library Association series.
English Language; Literature and Drama
Dist - PELLER

A Whisper from Space 58 MIN
U-matic / VHS / 16mm
Nova Series
Color (H C A)
LC 79-701905
Explores the history of the universe. Considers whether or not the universe is expanding, the origin of the universe and the creation of various types of matter from the single element, hydrogen.
Science - Physical
Dist - TIMLIF Prod - WGBHTV 1978

Whisper - the waves, the wind 28 MIN
VHS
Color (G C)
$335.00 purchase, $55.00 rental
Documents an art performance involving 154 elderly women dressed in white who express their views of life, love and the future as they grow older.
Health and Safety
Dist - TNF

Whisper - the women 10 MIN
VHS
Color (G C)
$165.00 purchase, $45.00 rental
Allows seven women of different cultures and backgrounds to relate their stories and views of aging. Provides a comprehensive profile of growing older.
Health and Safety
Dist - TNF

The Whisperers 105 MIN
16mm
B&W (J)
Features a perforance by British actress, Dame Edith Evans in a story of a lonely old crone who lives in a cocoon of fantasy in order to establish some meaning in her life. Directed by Bryan Forbes.
Fine Arts
Dist - CANTOR Prod - CANTOR

Whispering mountain 30 MIN
VHS
Color (P I R)
$19.95 purchase, $10.00 rental _ #35 - 822 - 2020
Tells the story of a boy visiting his uncle in the Swiss Alps. Reveals how an act of dishonesty makes an old legend spring to life.
Literature and Drama; Religion and Philosophy
Dist - APH Prod - ANDERK

Whispers of creation 50 MINS
VHS
Horizon series
Color; PAL (H C A)
PdS99 purchase; Not available in the United States or Canada
Reveals the discoveries that were made in 1992 regarding evidence of events leading to the formation of atoms, galaxies and man. Describes how these discoveries have led to the possibility of practical experimentation. Part of the Horizon series.
Science - Physical
Dist - BBCENE

Whispers on the wind - masters of regional writing 45 MIN
VHS
Heritage poetry collection series
Color (J H)
$49.00 purchase _ #60301 - 126
Presents works by D H Lawrence, Alexander Pope, Dubois Heywood, James Dickey and Tennessee Williams.
Literature and Drama
Dist - GA Prod - GA 1992

Whisper's Pacific voyage 95 MIN
VHS
Color (G A)
$39.90 purchase _ #0495
Joins a voyage around the Pacific with writer Hal Roth, his wife Margaret and their cat. Includes some rare footage of remote islands.
Geography - World; Physical Education and Recreation
Dist - SEVVID

Whispers series

The Chumash	30 MIN
The Gabrielino - Tongva	30 MIN

Dist - NAMPBC

Whistle Down the Wind 98 MIN
U-matic / VHS / 16mm
B&W
Presents an allegorical tale about a man who is mistaken for Jesus Christ. Stars Hayley Mills and Alan Bates.
Fine Arts
Dist - FI Prod - JANUS 1960

Whistle for Willie 6 MIN
16mm / U-matic / VHS
Color
Tells the story of a boy who badly wants to learn to whistle so that he can call his dog. Based on the book Whistle For Willie by Ezra Jack Keats.

Literature and Drama
Dist - WWS **Prod** - WWS

Whistle in the Wind 16 MIN
VHS / 16mm
Color (P) (ENGLISH AND SPANISH)
$149.00, $49.00 purchase _ #960 - 9001
Emphasizes the importance of passing along cultural values and understanding of one's heritage. Focuses on a small tract house in California where Rene Aquiree tells his son the Bolivian folktale of a young flute player who lives in the mountains with his beautiful llama.
Fine Arts; Geography - World; Literature and Drama; Social Science
Dist - FI **Prod** - MAKPEC 1984

Whistle of the Wind 15 MIN
16mm
Color
LC 75-704358
Takes a look at gliding.
Industrial and Technical Education; Physical Education and Recreation; Social Science
Dist - YORKU **Prod** - YORKU 1974

Whistle Signals for Approaching Steam Vessels 17 MIN
16mm
B&W
LC FIE52-940
Shows the rules for using one, two and three blast signals, the danger signal and the bend signal in various approaching situations.
Civics and Political Systems; Health and Safety; Social Science
Dist - USNAC **Prod** - USN 1943

Whistleblowers 24 MIN
U-matic / VHS
Color (G)
$249.00, $149.00 purchase _ #AD - 2017
Tells the story of four American whistleblowers who found that the price of integrity was very high. Addresses the question of how whistleblowers can be protected and how distinctions must be drawn in the workplace between honesty and disloyalty.
Business and Economics; Guidance and Counseling; Religion and Philosophy
Dist - FOTH **Prod** - FOTH

Whistling Smith 27 MIN
16mm / U-matic / VHS
Pacificanada Series
Color (H C A)
LC 76-703186
Portrays Bernie Smith, a tough Vancouver policeman as he makes his rounds on foot patrol in a decrepit part of the city.
Civics and Political Systems; Social Science
Dist - WOMBAT **Prod** - NFBC 1976

The Whistling Teakettle and the Witch of Fourth Street 14 MIN
VHS / U-matic
Readit Series
Color (P I)
Presents two stories, one in which Hannah's gift frightens robbers from her mother's candy store while in the other Cathy must choose between giving a daily penny to the monkey she loves or giving it to the woman she believes is a witch. Based on the books The Whistling Teakettle by Mindy Skolsky and The Witch Of Fourth Street by Myron Levoy.
English Language; Literature and Drama
Dist - AITECH **Prod** - POSIMP 1982

The Whitbread Round the World Race 1989 - 1990 111 MIN
VHS
Color (G)
$39.95 purchase _ #0918
Tells the full story of the 1989 - 1990 Whitbread Round the World Race. Includes broken masts, loss of life and the dramatic mid - ocean rescue of a crew when their boat's keel fell off.
Physical Education and Recreation
Dist - SEVVID

White Archer at the Mouth of the Luckiest River 15 MIN
U-matic / VHS
Best of Cover to Cover 1 Series
Color (P)
Literature and Drama
Dist - WETATV **Prod** - WETATV

White as Snow 30 MIN
16mm
Color; B&W (J H T R)
LC FIA65-1581
Tells of a young man going off to college who questions the relevance of his Christian beliefs in his new world of personal freedom, new ideas and new friends. Shows how he answers his own questions regarding the Christian faith.
Guidance and Counseling; Psychology; Religion and Philosophy
Dist - FAMF **Prod** - FAMF 1965

The White balloon 85 MIN
35mm / 16mm
Color (G)
$200.00 rental
Plays out the situation of an endearing little girl who loses a large - denomination banknote on her way to buying a traditional holiday purchase for New Year's Day in Iran. Takes a fascinating look at Iranian culture with a suspenseful production. Produced by Iranian TV - Channel Two; directed by Jafar Panahi; written by Abbas Kiarostami.
Fine Arts; Religion and Philosophy; Sociology
Dist - OCTOBF

White Beach 14 MIN
VHS / U-matic
Color
Documents the engineering of two collaborative performances, the Whisper Project and Freeze Frame - Room For Living Room. Directed by Suzanne Lacy with Doug Smith and Eric La Brecque.
Fine Arts
Dist - ARTINC **Prod** - ARTINC

White birds of winter 30 MIN
VHS
Wildlife on one series
Color; PAL (H C A)
PdS65 purchase
Traces the yearly migration patterns of the snow goose. Describes the beliefs of various indian cultures regarding the 'white bird of winter.'
Science - Natural
Dist - BBCENE

White calligraphy 15 MIN
16mm
B&W (G)
$30.00 rental
Invents a filmic concrete poem by drawing the Japanese characters for the Kojiki, 'the oldest story in Japan,' directly onto the dark leader. Creates a continully changing collage. A Takahiko Iimura film.
Fine Arts; Foreign Language
Dist - CANCIN

The White camel 50 MIN
VHS
Color (P I J)
$195.00 purchase
Tells a Christmas story about young Prince Melchior, heir to a small kingdom in Persia, who desires a white camel. Reveals that when Melchior inherits the kingdom, he decides to obey an ancient prophecy and follow a star on the back of his white camel, traveling with his friends and teachers Caspar and Balthazar.
Literature and Drama; Religion and Philosophy
Dist - LANDMK **Prod** - LANDMK 1993

White Cloud Peaks 22 MIN
16mm
Color; B&W (I J H C G T A)
Presents a mountain ecosystem. Lakes, streams, rivers, forests, details of flora and fauna, strange and unusual rock formations, plant and animal life - all are interrelated and examined in detail.
Agriculture; Science - Natural; Science - Physical; Social Science
Dist - FO **Prod** - FO 1971

White collar grievance 41 MIN
16mm
Color (G A)
$5.00 rental
Portrays the grievance of a woman with seniority who is passed over for a promotion in favor of another woman with comparable experience. Follows the grievance through the steps provided in the contract for arbitration.
Business and Economics; Psychology
Dist - AFLCIO **Prod** - UWISCA 1967

The White Collar Rip - Off 52 MIN
U-matic / VHS / 16mm
Color (J)
LC 76-701275
Presents a television news expose hosted by Edwin Newman which summarizes the hugely profitable white collar crimes that cost American citizens some 40 billion dollars each year. Describes the major types of crime, including employee theft, shoplifting, bribes and kickbacks, fraud and computer crimes.
Sociology
Dist - FI **Prod** - FI 1975

White Crane Spreads Wings 9 MIN
16mm
Color
LC 77-700038
Demonstrates the ancient Chinese art of T'ai Chi Chuan, which aims at complete coordination of mind and body through a system of precise physical movements.
Physical Education and Recreation; Psychology
Dist - CFS **Prod** - CFS 1976

White Dominoes 29 MIN
VHS / 16mm
Sonrisas Series
Color (T P) (SPANISH)
$46.00 rental _ #SRSS - 132
Shows Con Pablo becoming a U S citizen. In Spanish and English.
Sociology
Dist - PBS

White Dwarfs and Red Giants 29 MIN
U-matic
Project Universe - Astronomy Series
Color (C A)
Reviews properties of normal stars on the main sequence. Explains process whereby a star becomes a red giant and progresses to a white dwarf state.
Science - Physical
Dist - CDTEL **Prod** - COAST

White Elephants 30 MIN
U-matic
Inside Japan Series
(H C A)
Explores the breakdown of the traditional pattern of families caring for their old people in Japan and examines the resulting societal problems.
Geography - World; History - World
Dist - ACCESS **Prod** - ACCESS 1980

White Fang 90 MIN
16mm
Color (P I)
Fine Arts
Dist - FI **Prod** - FI

White Fang
Cassette / 16mm
Now Age Reading Programs, Set 3 Series
Color (I J)
$9.95 purchase _ #8F - PN682952
Brings literature to young readers. Filmstrip set includes filmstrip, cassette, corresponding book, classroom exercise materials and a poster. The read - along set includes student activity book, cassette and paperback.
English Language; Literature and Drama
Dist - MAFEX

White Fang 109 MIN
VHS
Color; CC (I J H)
$21.95 purchase _ #516793
Adapts the Jack London story about a ferocious wolf who is transformed into a faithful companion.
Literature and Drama
Dist - KNOWUN

White Fin Dolphin 23 MIN
VHS / 16mm
Let Them Live Series
Color (I)
$465.00, $205.00 purchase
Studies a single specimen of White Fin Dolphin which has survived in captivitity. Reveals that the dolphins of the Yangtzee River in China are threatened with extinction because of pollution.
Geography - World; Science - Natural
Dist - LUF **Prod** - LUF

White Flower Farm 30 MIN
VHS / 16mm
Growing a Business Series
(H C)
$99.95 each, $1,295.00 series
Details the rise to success of a catalog nursery business, White Flower Farm, to epitomize the gains that resourcefulness can bring about.
Business and Economics
Dist - AMBROS **Prod** - AMBROS 1988

White gold 26 MIN
VHS
Commodities series
Color (G)
$220.00 purchase, $50.00 rental
Tells of the initial rise of sugar and slavery, first in Brazil and later in the Caribbean. Traces the history of sugar cane plantations in Brazil. Part of a seven - part series which looks at the way banks, corporations, governments, workers and consumers are affected by such ordinary

items as coffee, tea and sugar. Examines the nature of exchange between Third World commodities producers and the people who control their processing, financing and marketing. Shows how producers try to increase profits. Considers the roles of cartels, financiers and multi - nationals. Produced by Sue Clayton and Jonathan Curling.
Business and Economics; Fine Arts; History - World; Social Science; Sociology
Dist - FIRS **Prod** - CFTV 1986

White heart 53 MIN
16mm
Color (G)
$150.00 rental
Explains filmmaker Barnett, 'A rare reversal print which should only be rented for projection under the best circumstances.'
Fine Arts
Dist - CANCIN **Prod** - BARND 1975

White heat series
Questions the beliefs; hopes and fears of the technology surrounding all of humankind. Uses a unique visual style and music to link elements as diverse as the Ford motor car and hamburgers. Some of the elements explored are basic human skills; technology and culture ; language and technology; standardization; systems; perceptions of technology; war machines; and the future of technology. Eight programs comprise this series.
Beat of the system 50 MIN
The Butcher's blade 50 MIN
Dirt and disorder 50 MIN
Gee whiz - the future 50 MIN
Mothers of invention 50 MIN
Repeat after me 50 MIN
Step right up 50 MIN
War machine 50 MIN
Dist - BBCENE

The White Heron 26 MIN
16mm / U-matic / VHS
Color (I J H)
LC 78-701002
Tells the story of a young girl who helps a hunter find a great white heron but must choose between her friendship with the hunter and her desire to save the bird.
Fine Arts; Guidance and Counseling; Literature and Drama
Dist - LCOA **Prod** - MORRJ 1978

The White hole 10 MIN
VHS
Color (I J H C G)
$250.00, $175.00 purchase, $25.00 rental
Comments on a throw - away society with humor. Shows kids playing in the park when a black hole suddenly appears and gobbles up everything that comes its way. It becomes a way to get rid of waste until one day a white hole appears and starts regurgitating the waste. The message tells us about the misguided way we think about waste. A film by Jurgen Haacks.
Fine Arts; Science - Natural; Sociology
Dist - BULFRG

The White hole in time 27 MIN
VHS
Color (G)
$29.95 purchase _ #P7
Explores the accelerating rate of development in the modern world and how we have arrived at a global crisis. Recommends that we awaken to our spiritual inheritance, inner space, which is the next great frontier. Features Peter Russell and music by Vangelis. Sequel to The Global Brain.
Civics and Political Systems; Fine Arts; Psychology; Sociology
Dist - HP

White House Conference on Mental Retardation 12 MIN
16mm
Color
Depicts the highlights of the White House Conference on Mental Retardation held in 1963.
Psychology
Dist - NMAC **Prod** - NMAC

White Inferno Series
Antarctica - the sixth continent 14 MIN
Beyond the South Pole 49 MIN
Mirny 14 MIN
Trek 14 MIN
Vostok 14 MIN
Dist - TVOTAR

White ivory 15 MIN
VHS
Color (P I J)
Explains why teeth are necessary and how tooth decay can be prevented.
Health and Safety; Science - Natural
Dist - VIEWTH **Prod** - VIEWTH

White Justice 57 MIN
U-matic / VHS
Color (H C A)
$395 purchase, $95 rental
Examines the impact of the Canadian criminal justice system on the Inuit Indians in northern Quebec. Directed by Morgane Laliberte and Francoise Wera.
Civics and Political Systems; History - World
Dist - CNEMAG

The White Lady 26 MIN
U-matic / VHS / 16mm
Color
Dramatizes a Polish story that tells how salt mines came to be.
Geography - World; Literature and Drama
Dist - FOTH **Prod** - FOTH

White Lies 25 MIN
16mm / U-matic / VHS
Color (I J) (FRENCH)
The French version of the videorecording and film White Lies.
Guidance and Counseling; Physical Education and Recreation; Psychology; Sociology
Dist - BCNFL **Prod** - ATLAF 1984

The White Man Moves West 30 MIN
16mm
Great Plains Trilogy, 3 Series Explorer and Settler - the White Man 'Arrives; Explorer and settler - the white man arrives
B&W (H C A)
Sketches America's westward expansion and the problems of living in a new environment. Discusses early explorations for gold, silver and furs. Traces Spanish, French and British penetration of the Great Plains, the discovery of the Missouri River and the early trade with the Indians.
History - United States
Dist - UNEBR **Prod** - KUONTV 1954

White Mane 38 MIN
16mm / VHS
Color (I)
$575.00, $88.00 purchase _ #552 - 0039
Tells the heartrending story of a fierce, wild, white stallion, the ranchers who are determined to break his spirt, and the boy who ultimately tames him with love. Expresses the essence of freedom and friendship.
Fine Arts; Literature and Drama; Science - Natural
Dist - FI **Prod** - JANUS 1983

White Man's Country 51 MIN
U-matic / VHS / 16mm
Color (H C)
Presents the history of Kenya from the viewpoint of the African, through an account of the influence of the white man on Kenya. Covers the period of colonialism up through independence.
History - United States; History - World
Dist - FI **Prod** - FI 1973

White Man's Country 28 MIN
U-matic / VHS / 16mm
Black Man's Land Series
Color
A shortened version of White Man's Country. Shows how a railroad was built through Kenya at the end of the 19th century and how the colonial ideal took root. Explains why colonists thought that Kenya should become a 'white man's country.'.
History - World; Sociology
Dist - FI **Prod** - ADP

White Man's God 30 MIN
16mm
B&W (J H C)
Presents the efforts of missionaries in African jungles to convert natives to Christianity.
Geography - World; Religion and Philosophy
Dist - CPH **Prod** - CPH

White Man's Way 30 MIN
VHS / U-matic
Color (G)
Presents beginning in the late 1800's, an experiment that endeavored to transform the American Indian 'from savagery into civilization' took place across the United States. Shows the heart of what was once Pawnee Indian country, Genoa Nebraska, was built to the U S Indian School, a government supported military style school for Indian children from more than 20 tribes. Here they were taught the White Man's language, traditions and lifestyles and were forbidden to practice their own.
Social Science; Sociology
Dist - NAMPBC **Prod** - NAMPBC 1986

White Man's Way 30 MIN
U-matic / VHS
(G)
Shows the history of the imposition of white values upon Native American lives and cultures. Focuses on government boarding schools, particularly the Genoa Indian School in Genoa, Nebraska. Invites viewers to appraise the merits and consequences of the military's fifty year boarding school program.
History - United States; Social Science; Sociology
Dist - GPN **Prod** - NETV 1986

The White Mountains - a Cultural View 14 MIN
16mm
Color (H C A)
Examines the cultural history of New Hampshire's White Mountain region as it changed from an untrampled wilderness to a well - cultivated playground for thousands of tourists.
Geography - United States; History - United States
Dist - UNH **Prod** - UNH 1980

White Mountains and the City of Gold and Lead 20 MIN
VHS / U-matic
Matter of Fiction Series
B&W (J H)
Presents WHITE MOUNTAINS and THE CITY OF GOLD AND LEAD by John Christopher. Tells about extraterrestrial beings who have taken over most of the earth and how their plan to replace the earth's atmosphere with their own world would end the existence of the human race. Features Well Parker, an English boy, who studies to thwart the plans of the extraterrestial beings. (Broadcast quality).
Literature and Drama
Dist - AITECH **Prod** - WETATV

White night of dance in Leningrad 83 MIN
VHS
Color; Hi-fi; Dolby stereo (G)
$29.95 purchase _ #1305
Records the historic meeting of the Kirov Ballet and the Belgian Ballet in Legningrad's czarist palaces, in parks and on the banks of the Volga River. Includes excerpts from Rite of Spring, Le Corsaire, Swan Lake, Chopiniana, La Bayarde. Stars Farouk Ruzimatov, Olga Chenchikova, Michel Gascard.
Fine Arts
Dist - KULTUR **Prod** - KULTUR 1991

White nights 30 MIN
VHS
Classic short stories
Color (H)
#E362; LC 90-708396
Presents 'White Nights' by Russian writer Fyodor Dostoevsky. Part of a series which combines Hollywood stars with short story masterpieces of the world to encourage appreciation of the short story.
Literature and Drama
Dist - GPN **Prod** - CTI 1988

White Nile Blue Nile 60 MIN
VHS
Giant Nile series
Color (H C)
$250.00 purchase
Travels beyond the Sudan where Nuba villages recently converted to Islam still hold their traditions evidenced by secret wrestling tournaments and stick fights. Observes the Coptic Christian monasteries of Ethiopia and whirling dervishes. Part of a three - part series on the 4200 mile long Nile River.
Geography - World; Religion and Philosophy
Dist - LANDMK **Prod** - LANDMK 1992

White - outpost legionnaire 30 MIN
VHS
Vietnam home movies series
Color (J H C G)
$29.95 purchase _ #BV152V
Features actual footage shot by soldiers during their tour of duty in Vietnam. Tells the story of one soldier in his own words, the combat missions, his friends, his joy after a successful rescue, the devastation after an enemy raid, the sounds of war. Offers footage aboard a UH1 Huey helicopter gunship, a pass dodging sniper fire from the Viet Cong, looking down the rocket sight on a search and destroy mission. Part of a four - part series.
History - United States; Sociology
Dist - CAMV

White rock blues and the cave 20 MIN
VHS
Color (H R)
$19.95 purchase _ #87EE0196
Consists of two short films, 'White Rock Blues' and 'The Cave.' 'White Rock Blues uses an animated format to present a message on who teenagers are and their purpose in life. 'The Cave,' adapted from Plato's 'Republic,' emphasizes the message of the Good News.
Guidance and Counseling; Literature and Drama; Religion and Philosophy
Dist - CPH **Prod** - CPH

The White rose 123 MIN
16mm
Color (G) (GERMAN WITH ENGLISH SUBTITLES)
$175.00 rental
Tells the story about a group of German college students who protested Nazi policies by printing and distributing forbidden leaflets which detailed the Nazis' true intentions during World War II. Focuses on White Rose member Sophie Scholl to add intimacy and humanity to a tragedy about a failed rebellion. Directed by Michael Verhoeven.
Civics and Political Systems; Fine Arts; History - World; Religion and Philosophy
Dist - NCJEWF

The White rose 7 MIN
16mm
B&W (G)
$15.00 rental
Documents a huge painting, weighing over 2300 pounds, being removed from the studio of artist Jay De Feo, eight years after he began the piece in 1957.
Fine Arts
Dist - CANCIN **Prod** - CONNER 1967

The White Seal 26 MIN
U-matic / VHS / 16mm
Color (P I)
LC 76-702624
Tells the story of Kotick, a white seal born on an island in the Bering Sea, who learns during his first migration how to get along in the sea and how to distinguish his friends, various marine mammals, from his enemies, sharks and man. Shows his search for a haven from man.
Literature and Drama
Dist - GA **Prod** - CJE 1976

The White sheik 86 MIN
VHS
B&W (G)
$29.95 purchase _ #WHI090
Features a gentle satire on small - town mentality. Follows a newlywed couple on their honeymoon in Rome where she disappears on the arm of the white sheik, a dashing pulp - fiction hero.
Fine Arts; Literature and Drama; Psychology; Sociology
Dist - HOMVIS **Prod** - JANUS 1952

The White Star Garage 27 MIN
U-matic / VHS / 16mm
Insight Series
Color (J) (SPANISH)
Shows a young couple who are worried because they have no money to pay for the hospital so that the wife can give birth. Explains how the woman winds up giving birth in an auto repair shop. Stars Fausto Bara and Christine Avila.
Psychology; Religion and Philosophy; Sociology
Dist - PAULST **Prod** - PAULST

White tailed deer - flag 16 MIN
U-matic / VHS / BETA
Color (I J H)
$29.95, $130.00 purchase _ #LSTF116
Shows a research area in New York containing a white herd of white tailed deer. Explains the genetics of mutation in a species and plant succession from farmland to forest. Includes teacher's guide. Produced by Nature Episodes assisted by the New York State Dept of Environmental Conservation.
Science - Natural
Dist - FEDU

White - Throat 10 MIN
16mm
Birds of America, 1, their Songs and Sounds Series
Color
Follows a white - throated sparrow through the forest. Pictures a bullfrog, suckers, catfish, grouse, timber wolves, blue jays, sapsuckers, loons, mallards, a fox and a beaver. Uses natural sounds without narration.
Science - Natural
Dist - GIB **Prod** - GIB 1966

White Water and Broke
VHS / U-matic
Pulp and Paper Training, Module 3 - Papermaking Series
Color (IND)
Includes the basic system of white water and broke, savealls, and broke.
Business and Economics; Industrial and Technical Education; Social Science
Dist - LEIKID **Prod** - LEIKID

White Water, Blue Water 14 MIN
16mm
Color
LC 75-704359
Concerns Canada's first school for white water kayaking and canoeing, located on the Madawaska River in northern Ontario.
Geography - World; Physical Education and Recreation
Dist - CANFDC **Prod** - CANFDC 1974

White Water, Grey Hair 20 MIN
16mm / U-matic / VHS
Color (I P I J H C G T A S R PRO IND)
Shows a group of adventuresome senior citizens filmed on a riotous 300 mile raft trip down the incredible Colorado River.
Health and Safety; Physical Education and Recreation
Dist - SF **Prod** - SF 1985

White Water Voyage 8 MIN
16mm
Color
LC 78-700232
Shows the art of guiding a raft through challenging rapids.
Physical Education and Recreation
Dist - SUTHRB **Prod** - SUTHRB 1978

White wilderness - Dutch series
The Arctic Region and its polar bears 28 MIN
Dist - CORF

White wilderness - German series
The Arctic Region and its polar bears 28 MIN
Dist - CORF

White wilderness - Norwegian series
The Arctic Region and its polar bears 28 MIN
Dist - CORF

White wilderness - Portuguese series
The Arctic Region and its polar bears 28 MIN
Dist - CORF

White wilderness series
The Arctic Region and its polar bears 28 MIN
The Lemmings and Arctic Bird Life 21 MIN
Dist - CORF

White wilderness - Swedish series
The Arctic Region and its polar bears 28 MIN
Dist - CORF

White Wildernes
Large Animals of the Arctic 22 MIN
Dist - CORF

White wolf 60 MIN
VHS
National Geographic video series
Color (G)
$29.95 purchase
Portrays a pack of wild arctic wolves as they make their way through their wilderness home.
Science - Natural
Dist - PBS **Prod** - WNETTV

White wolf 59 MIN
VHS / Videodisc / BETA
Color; CLV; Captioned (G)
$35.20, $24.20 purchase _ #C53328, #C50328
Science - Natural
Dist - NGS **Prod** - NGS

The Whitecomers, Episode 4 - the Promised Land 57 MIN
16mm / U-matic / VHS
Images of Canada
(G)
$99.00 1/2 inch, $150.00 3/4 inch, $750.00 16mm, _ #107 73 01
Shows the events and personalities that shaped the prairie provinces. Fur traders come west, Louis Riel leads an uprising of Indians and Metis, thousands of immigrants struggle for existence in a harsh environment.
History - World
Dist - CANBC

The Whitecomers, Episode 1 - the Magic Circle, 1600 - 1867 58 MIN
U-matic / VHS / 16mm
Images of Canada
(G)
$99.00 1/2 inch, $150.00 3/4 inch, $750.00 16mm, _ #107 72 02
Focuses on Canada's European settlers. Looks at those who helped shape the cultural and political traditions of Quebec.
History - World
Dist - CANBC

The Whitecomers, Episode 3 - Peace, Order, and Prosperity Upper Canada 57 MIN
16mm / U-matic / VHS
Images of Canada
(G)
$99.00 1/2 inch, $150.00 3/4 inch, $750.00 16mm, #107 72 04
Shows residents in Upper Canada seeking British order, peace, and good government. After the War of 1812, Ontario places faith in the industrial future of Canada in a strong Confederation.
History - World
Dist - CANBC

Whitecomers, Episode 2 - Ties that Bind, 1600 - 1867 57 MIN
U-matic / VHS / 16mm
Images of Canada
(G)
$99.00 1/2 inch, $150.00 3/4 inch, $750.00 16mm, _ #107 72 03
Shows early settlers in the Atlantic area. Traces the roots of the Maritimes' attitude towards Confederation.
History - World
Dist - CANBC

Whitetail 53 MIN
VHS
Color (H A G)
$69.95 purchase _ #CV902
Teaches about the whitetail deer. Includes the art of hunting with a camera, scent usage, rattling techniques, scoring a typical whitetail rack, trophy deer taxidermy, how to evaluate a taxidermist's work, tips for determining the age of whitetail deer accurately, and yarding tendencies during hard winters. Features Dan Small as host.
Physical Education and Recreation; Science - Natural
Dist - AAVIM **Prod** - AAVIM

Whitetail - Still and Stand Hunting 38 MIN
BETA / VHS
Color
Includes deer signs such as scrapes, rubs, droppings and tracks. Shows many bucks, including one successful rattle and stalk.
Physical Education and Recreation; Science - Natural
Dist - HOMEAF **Prod** - HOMEAF

Whitewater 30 MIN
BETA / VHS
Great Outdoors Series
Color
Talks about getting outfitted for whitewater canoeing. Features a hike and nature study a short ferry ride from San Francisco's Fisherman's Wharf.
Physical Education and Recreation
Dist - CORF **Prod** - WGBHTV

Whitewater Canoeing 11 MIN
16mm
Color (J H C)
Presents the techniques for breaking into and out of a swift current while canoeing, ferry gliding across a swift current and the recovery of a second overturned canoe. Shows how to read the characteristics of rapidly moving water by its surface appearance including rapids, V's, standing waves and back eddies.
Physical Education and Recreation
Dist - SF **Prod** - SF 1974

Whitewater Voyage 8 MIN
VHS / U-matic
Color (P A)
Focuses on whitewater rafting on the Salt River. Narrated by Jay Michael.
Physical Education and Recreation
Dist - SUTHRB **Prod** - SUTHRB

Whitewater...and the winning combination 9 MIN
VHS / U-matic
Color (G)
$350.00 purchase, $95.00 rental
Features Fletcher Anderson, champion kayaker, who rides the Lava Rapids of the Colorado River. Shows the winning combination of traits which makes success possible for everyone - courage, preparedness, determination, a desire to keep on learning and a zeal for the new and unexpected.
Business and Economics; Fine Arts; Psychology; Sociology
Dist - VLEARN **Prod** - VANTCO

Whither Democracy - Pt 10 58 MIN
VHS
Struggle for Democracy Series
Color (S)
$49.00 purchase _ #039 - 9010
Explores the concept of democracy and how it works. Features Patrick Watson, author with Benjamin Barber of 'The Struggle For Democracy,' as host who travels to more than 30 countries around the world, examining issues such as rule of law, freedom of information, the tyranny of the majority and the relationship of economic prosperity to democracy. Part 10 considers whether democracy can survive in our world of nuclear arsenals and widening chasms between rich and poor nations. Watson examines recent experiments in democracy and concludes that democracy's future depens upon the determination of its people to keep the struggle alive.
Business and Economics; Civics and Political Systems; Geography - World; History - World; Science - Physical
Dist - FI **Prod** - DFL 1989

Whither the Mainstream 29 MIN
U-matic / VHS
Mainstreaming the Exceptional Child Series
Color (T)
Education; Psychology
Dist - FI **Prod** - MFFD

Whither Weather 12 MIN
U-matic / 8mm cartridge
Color (H C A)
LC 77-701122
Presents an animated portrayal of the effects of climate upon the world. Emphasizes the need for climate control and international cooperation to ensure the future well - being of the world.
Civics and Political Systems; Geography - World; Science - Natural; Science - Physical; Sociology
Dist - PFP **Prod** - HUBLEY 1977

Whitley, Joyce 29 MIN
U-matic
Like it is Series
Color
Discusses the role and function of the urban planner in modern society.
Sociology
Dist - HRC **Prod** - OHC

Whitney commercial 3 MIN
16mm
Color (G)
$5.00 rental
Features a production commissioned by the Whitney Museum in New York to gain support for their film program. Renders very colorful, naive - looking drawings with heavy outlines. A Suzan Pitt production.
Fine Arts
Dist - CANCIN

Whitney Museum of American Art series
American art today - 1985 biennial exhibition - Pt 2 29 MIN
American art today - 1987 biennial exhibition - Pt 1 24 MIN
Twentieth century American art - highlights of the permanent collection - Pt 3 27 MIN
Dist - FI

Whitney Young 20 MIN
U-matic
Truly American Series
Color (I)
Biography; History - United States
Dist - GPN **Prod** - WVIZTV 1979

Whittaker 50 - Man Escape Capsule
U-matic / VHS
Offshore Operations Series
Color (IND)
Looks at an industry standard all rig hands most know. Covers boarding the capsule, starting the engine, how to safely launch, fire protection systems, how to operate the capsule on water and proper retrieval techniques.
Business and Economics; Industrial and Technical Education; Social Science
Dist - GPCV **Prod** - GPCV

Whittington Designs 12 MIN
16mm
Color (R)
Describes professional stage productions and explores the work of Harrell Whittington of Bob Jones University.
Fine Arts; Religion and Philosophy
Dist - UF **Prod** - UF

Whittlin' 14 MIN
16mm
Color
Shows the new lightweight train which the Santa Fe Railway has designed for piggyback service. Explains the concept and design of this energy - saving idea.
Social Science
Dist - MTP **Prod** - STAFER

Whittling 28 MIN
U-matic
Woodcarver's Workshop Series
Color
Industrial and Technical Education
Dist - PBS **Prod** - WOSUTV

WHMIS - what's it all about - SIMDUT - de quoi s'agit - il 14 MIN
BETA / VHS / U-matic
Canadian specific programs series
Color (IND G) (FRENCH)
$495.00 purchase _ #820 - 52, #820 - 53
Introduces Canadian workers to legislation dealing with hazardous materials in the workplace - WHMIS, SIMDUT. Examines labeling, MSDSs - Material Safety Data Sheets, the requirements for worker education and the duties and responsibilities of the individual employee. Produced by Innovative Video Training, Inc, of Candada.
Health and Safety; Industrial and Technical Education; Psychology
Dist - ITSC

WHMIS - working to protect your health 16 MIN
VHS
Color (IND)
$495.00 purchase _ #820 - 55
Explains all aspects of Canada's Workplace Hazardous Materials Information System regulations. Audit book available separately, #820 - 55.
Health and Safety; Psychology
Dist - ITSC **Prod** - ITSC

Who Am I 29 MIN
Videoreel / VT2
That's Life Series
Color
Guidance and Counseling; Psychology
Dist - PBS **Prod** - KOAPTV

Who Am I 15 MIN
U-matic
Career Planning Series
Color (H)
Dramatizes the senior year of three students and shows how their career plans are confused.
Guidance and Counseling
Dist - TVOTAR **Prod** - TVOTAR 1984

Who Am I 20 MIN
16mm
All that I Am Series
B&W (C A)
Fine Arts; Guidance and Counseling
Dist - NWUFLM **Prod** - MPATI

Who am I 15 MIN
VHS
Understanding who you are - the personality video series
Color (J H)
$79.00 purchase _ #PVS500
Explores the themes of different personalities. Discusses popular myths about personality. Overviews a ten - part series on personality.
Guidance and Counseling; Psychology; Sociology
Dist - CADESF **Prod** - CADESF 1990

Who Am I - Looking at Self - Concept
U-matic / VHS
Color (I J)
Introduces self - concept and the many factors that shape it. Illustrates how self - concept affects everything the individual does or thinks. Helps adolescents analyze what they would like to change about themselves and how to make those changes. Includes teacher's guide.
Guidance and Counseling; Psychology; Sociology
Dist - SUNCOM **Prod** - SUNCOM

Who Am I this Time
BETA / VHS
Color
Presents the American Playhouse production of Kurt Vonnegut's touching story about a shy young man, starring Christopher Walken and Susan Sarandon.
Fine Arts; Literature and Drama
Dist - GA **Prod** - GA
CORF

Who Am I - who I Am 20 MIN
VHS / U-matic
Color
$335.00 purchase
Sociology
Dist - ABCLR **Prod** - ABCLR 1984

Who are My Own - the Life of Saint John Baptist De La Salle 90 MIN
BETA / VHS
Color
Covers the life of Saint John Baptist De La Salle who founded the congregation of Christian Brothers.
Biography; Geography - World; Religion and Philosophy
Dist - DSP **Prod** - DSP

Who are Our Leaders 30 MIN
U-matic
Decision Makers Series
Color
Discusses characteristics of leadership. Introduces The Decision Makers Series.
Biography; Civics and Political Systems
Dist - HRC **Prod** - OHC

Who are the De Bolts, and Where Did they Get 19 Kids, Pt 2 36 MIN
U-matic / VHS / 16mm
Color (J)
LC 78-700876
Focuses on the daily life of the De Bolt family and their adopted, handicapped and multiracial children.
Biography; Guidance and Counseling; Sociology
Dist - PFP **Prod** - KORTY 1978

Who are the Debolts, and Where Did they Get 19 Kids 72 MIN
U-matic / VHS / 16mm
Color (I)
LC 79-707026
Focuses on the daily life of the De Bolt family and their adopted, handicapped and multiracial children.
Psychology; Sociology
Dist - PFP **Prod** - KORTY 1978

Who are the DeBolts - T V Version 54 MIN
U-matic / VHS / 16mm
Color (I) (SPANISH)
Presents a specially edited version, hosted by Henry Winkler, of the story of the DeBolts and their 19 very special children.
Foreign Language; Sociology
Dist - PFP **Prod** - KORTY

Who are the Lutherans 20 MIN
VHS
Lutherans and their beliefs series
Color (J H C G A R)
$39.95 purchase, $10.00 rental _ #35 - 8103 - 2076
Discusses the marks which differentiate Lutherans from their fellow Christians. Features Dr Jerry L Schmalenberger. Produced by Seraphim.
Religion and Philosophy
Dist - APH

Who are these People 22 MIN
16mm
Color
LC 77-702173
Focuses on the special educational needs of gifted children. Shows how these needs often are not met because of misidentification, inadequate programs and general apathy.
Education; Psychology
Dist - SCOTAP **Prod** - GIFTAL 1977

Who are You 9 MIN
16mm / U-matic / VHS
Color (P I)
LC 77-701507
Explores the concept of self - identity through a humorous animated story of a puppy who investigates his new environment in an attempt to discover his mission and identity.
Guidance and Counseling
Dist - FI **Prod** - WHTF 1976

Who are You Calling a Taxpayer 10 MIN
U-matic
Calling Captain Consumer Series
Color (P I J)
Follows two boys who decide that as taxpayers they have a right to complain about the need for repairs in the local playground.
Business and Economics; Civics and Political Systems; Home Economics
Dist - TVOTAR **Prod** - TVOTAR 1985

Who are Your Students 28 MIN
U-matic / VHS
Helping Adults Learn
Color (C G T A)
Explores the characteristics of adult students, their strengths and weaknesses, their motivations, the barriers they face in receiving an education, and the challenges and opportunities these characteristics present to teachers.
Education
Dist - PSU **Prod** - PSU 1986

Who benefits when employees own the company 30 MIN
U-matic
Adam Smith's money world 1985 - 1986 season series; 201
Color (A)
Attempts to demystify the world of money and break it down so that small as well as large businesses and it's people understand and adjust to new social and economic trends. Reports on the major economic stories and discoveries of 1985 and 1986.
Business and Economics
Dist - PBS **Prod** - WNETTV 1986

Who broke it 13 MIN
VHS / U-matic
En Francais series
Color (H C A)
Features a glassmaker's studio in which a country priest's broken stained glass window is fixed.
Foreign Language; Geography - World
Dist - AITECH **Prod** - MOFAFR 1970

Who Built this Place 30 MIN
VHS / 16mm
Color (G)
$55.00 rental _ #WBTP - 000
Uses a combination of animation, historical photographs and news film to present a comedy on the politics of landmark architecture. Focuses on the design process and urban planning.
Civics and Political Systems; Fine Arts; Geography - United States
Dist - PBS **Prod** - KERA

Who Can Catch the Wind 30 MIN
16mm
Color
LC 74-706607
Shows that a young man's dreams come true when he joins the Navy. Describes how he goes through boot camp training, his first sea duty and shore leave.
Civics and Political Systems; Guidance and Counseling; Social Science
Dist - USNAC **Prod** - USN 1973

Who Can Help Harry 20 MIN
16mm
Color
LC 74-706331
Discusses the problem of a manager faced with unplanned organizational growth. Points out the need to apply the Army's position management program to assure sound management of civilian positions.
Business and Economics; Civics and Political Systems; Psychology
Dist - USNAC **Prod** - USA 1968

Who Can I Count on - Lifelong 30 MIN
16mm / U-matic / VHS
Color (C A)
Discusses the ability and right of the mentally retarded to have the freedom, independence and control over their own lives accorded other members of society.
Psychology
Dist - STNFLD **Prod** - NIMR

Who can you trust 9 MIN
16mm / VHS / BETA / U-matic
Color; PAL (P I)
PdS80, PdS88 purchase
Alerts children to the dangers of speaking with suspicious strangers in a police - sponsored production.
Health and Safety; Sociology
Dist - EDPAT
TASCOR

'Who Cares' 20 MIN
16mm / VHS
Color (PRO)
$495.00 purchase, $140.00 rental, $45.00 preview
Discusses patient relation problems in a hospital. Explains the fears and apprehensions of patients when they are admitted into a hospital. Dramatizes the impact of insensitive hospital staff.
Health and Safety; Home Economics; Psychology
Dist - UTM **Prod** - UTM

Who Cares 13 MIN
16mm
Family Life Education and Human Growth Series
Color (J)
LC 73-702564
Shows the conflict of an aging grandfather in the home of a family. Questions where the old man should look for comfort in his old age when his own flesh and blood don't care.
Guidance and Counseling; Psychology; Sociology
Dist - SF **Prod** - SF 1970

Who Cares 21 MIN
16mm
Color (C A)
Describes methods and techniques for driving school buses for maximum fuel economy. Shows that proper driving can increase fuel economy by seven to eight per cent. Claims that if this goal were achieved nationwide, 50 million gallons of fuel could be saved each year.
Health and Safety
Dist - VISUCP **Prod** - VISUCP 1979

Who Cares 15 MIN
VHS / U-matic
It's all Up to You Series
Color (I J)
Examines the rights and responsibilities, personal involvement, and needs of citizens and how these may cause institutions to change.
Sociology
Dist - AITECH **Prod** - COOPED 1978

Who cares 15 MIN
VHS
Color (P I J)
Informs children about some of the personal health services available under the national health program in Great Britain. Emphasizes special services for mothers and young children.
Business and Economics; Geography - World; Health and Safety; Sociology
Dist - VIEWTH **Prod** - VIEWTH

Who cares 20 MIN
VHS
Color (C PRO)
$275.00 purchase _ #6893
Looks at five young people who were clients of the social service system. Details their accounts of being separated from their natural families, shuffled from home to home and having no continuity in caseworkers. Shows how lack of stability in placement erodes a child's ability and willingness to relate to and interact with people.
Psychology; Sociology
Dist - UCALG **Prod** - UCALG 1984

Who Cares about Child Care 33 MIN
16mm / U-matic / VHS
Women Series
Color (H C A)
Views the importance of child care centers to a variety of parents and children and the remarkable qualities of a middle - aged child - care worker.
Home Economics; Sociology
Dist - LUF **Prod** - LUF 1979

Who Cares - about Me 15 MIN
U-matic / VHS
Who Cares Series
Color (I)
Presents ten children selected by their peers who discuss the issues of their lives, including loneliness, boredom, failure, habits and feelings.
Guidance and Counseling
Dist - AITECH **Prod** - GBCTP 1982

Who Cares - about My Habits 15 MIN
U-matic / VHS
Who Cares Series
Color (I)
Presents ten children discussing habits, why people take drugs, why children begin alcohol or drug use, and how friendship can make a difference. Shows three girls role - playing an attempt to persuade a friend to stop drinking.
Guidance and Counseling; Psychology; Sociology
Dist - AITECH **Prod** - GBCTP 1982

Who cares for the caregivers - an Alzheimer's respite weekend 23 MIN
VHS
Color (H C G)
$195.00 purchase, $50.00 rental
Shows that contrary to popular belief, 70 to 80 percent of all sufferers from Alzheimer's are cared for outside of an institution by family members or close friends. Considers the tremendous commitment necessary to be on duty 24 hours a day, without a break from the constant demands and frustrations. In Sonoma County, California, a special two - day respite program was designed to provide free time for caregivers. Witnesses the volunteer care of 12 Alzheimer's sufferers over a weekend. By the end of the weekend, the original family caretakers are refreshed and ready to resume care. Produced by Lifestram Pictures.
Health and Safety; Sociology
Dist - FLMLIB

Who cares for the children - child care in America 55 MIN
VHS
Color (H C G)
$445.00 purchase, $75.00 rental
Reveals that although 80 percent of mothers with pre - school children are now in the workforce, quality child care during these critical developmental years is either unavailable or too expensive. Examines the current child care crisis through the eyes of parents, providers, children and experts. Shows that child care costs generally rank as the second highest expense of the American family, just below housing, yet the wages of child - care providers is barely above minimum wage, resulting in turnover rates of 40 percent a year. Shows that innovative solutions to the child care dilemma are available. Hosted by Rhea Perlman. Produced by Dave Davis.
Sociology
Dist - FLMLIB **Prod** - KCTSTV 1989

Who Cares - How We Get High Together 15 MIN
U-matic / VHS
Who Cares Series
Color (I)
Discusses alternatives to drugs as campers build a community by working and playing together.
Guidance and Counseling; Sociology
Dist - AITECH **Prod** - GBCTP 1982

Who Cares - How We Survive Together 15 MIN
VHS / U-matic
Who Cares Series
Color (I)
Shows children beginning a four - day campout by building shelters and learning about edible wild plants. Shows them gradually learning to cooperate in working together.
Guidance and Counseling; Health and Safety
Dist - AITECH **Prod** - GBCTP 1982

Who Cares - if I Drink 15 MIN
VHS / U-matic
Who Cares Series
Color (I)
Presents ten children discussing their own decisions about alcohol. Deals with how people act when they drink too much, why people drink, how they feel and the effects alcohol has.
Psychology; Sociology
Dist - AITECH **Prod** - GBCTP 1982

Who Cares - if I have an Accident 14 MIN
VHS / U-matic
Who Cares Series
Color (I)
LC 82-706767
Presents students in a sixth - grade classroom finding out what they could do for an injured classmate, what the Emergency Medical Services Center would do and where they can learn more about first aid.
Health and Safety
Dist - AITECH **Prod** - GBCTP 1982

Who Cares Series
Who Cares - about Me 15 MIN
Who Cares - about My Habits 15 MIN
Who Cares - How We Get High Together 15 MIN
Who Cares - How We Survive Together 15 MIN
Who Cares - if I Drink 15 MIN
Who Cares - if I have an Accident 14 MIN
Who Cares - what I Choose to Eat 14 MIN
Who Cares - what I Need 15 MIN
Dist - AITECH

Who Cares - the Counselor's Role in the American School 28 MIN
16mm
Color (T)
LC 77-702330
Presents a series of vignettes portraying a wide variety of actual counselor situations. Depicts the counselor's role in the education process and in the personal process of individual maturation.
Education; Guidance and Counseling; Psychology
Dist - AACD **Prod** - ASCA 1973

Who Cares - what I Choose to Eat 14 MIN
VHS / U-matic
Who Cares Series
Color (I)
Presents fifth - grade students shopping for a family of four at the supermarket and then discussing the reasons for their decisions.
Health and Safety
Dist - AITECH **Prod** - GBCTP 1982

Who Cares - what I Need 15 MIN
VHS / U-matic
Who Cares Series
Color (I)
Offers a fantasy journey in which four 11 - year - olds ask a wizard for feelings they need such as friendship, confidence and love from parents. Seeks to encourage openness and trust in the classroom.
Guidance and Counseling
Dist - AITECH **Prod** - GBCTP 1982

Who Cops Out 11 MIN
16mm / U-matic / VHS
Color (J H)
LC 70-707293
A discussion of the question of the choices today's adolescents make when faced with the confusion and uncertainty of the teen - age years. Focusses on five adolescents who have made five different choices - - a girl who may be asked to leave school, a school drop - out working at a gas station, a high school football star, a scholastic achiever and a drug user.
Guidance and Counseling; Psychology; Sociology
Dist - IFB **Prod** - SMHACM 1969

Who Did what to Whom 17 MIN
16mm
Color (H C A)
LC 74-714963
A training film for educational, religious or industrial leaders which shows how to recognize the four principles of behavior - positive reinforcement, negative reinforcement, extinction and punishment.

Business and Economics; Education; Psychology; Religion and Philosophy; Sociology
Dist - RESPRC **Prod** - MAGER 1972

Who Did what to Whom II - Recognizing Four Behavioral Principles in Action 20 MIN
16mm
Color
Presents four of the basic principles of human behavior and shows how these principles can be applied in the work area. Consists of 33 short scenes followed by discussion time to help understand what occurred, the probability of its happening again and how it could be changed to achieve a more positive result.
Business and Economics; Psychology; Sociology
Dist - RESPRC **Prod** - RESPRC

Who Discovered America 14 MIN
16mm / U-matic / VHS
Color (J)
LC 73-701836
Presents an edited version of 'IN SEARCH OF THE LOST WORLD.' Discusses the origin of the Indians and the influence of voyagers from Africa, Asia and Europe on American culture.
History - United States; Social Science
Dist - FI **Prod** - FI 1972

Who do you listen to - choosing sexual abstinence 34 MIN
VHS
Color (J H)
$295.00 purchase
Uses dramatizations, music and interviews with health professionals and other people to point out facts that must be considered before one chooses whether to be sexually active. Talks about feelings, values and consequences of choices, with emphasis on abstinence as the best choice. Discusses AIDS. For sex education classes. Created by Weiss - Carpenter Productions. Includes discussion guide with videocassette.
Health and Safety
Dist - PFP

Who do you listen to - sex in the age of AIDS 37 MIN
VHS
Color (J H R)
$49.95 purchase, $10.00 rental _ #35 - 8648 - 1518
Uses dramatic vignettes to illustrate the choices teenagers face about engaging in sexual relations. Hosted by Christian author Josh McDowell.
Health and Safety; Religion and Philosophy
Dist - APH **Prod** - GF

Who do You Tell 13 MIN
16mm / U-matic / VHS
Color (P I)
LC 79-700191
Uses animation and documentary footage in discussing various serious family problems, including sexual abuse. Describes community support systems available to help when the child's primary support system, the family, breaks down.
Guidance and Counseling; Psychology; Sociology
Dist - CORF **Prod** - MITCHG 1979

Who do you think you are 11 MIN
16mm / VHS
B&W (G)
$30.00 rental
Investigates heroes presented in commercials advertising cigarettes. Suggests a link between self - destructive behavior and filmmaker's inability to be a hero. Produced by Mary Filippo.
Fine Arts; Health and Safety
Dist - CANCIN

Who Does She Think She is 60 MIN
16mm
Color (C A)
LC 74-703677
Presents a candid look at novelist, singer, painter and ex - wrestler Rosalyn Drexler.
Biography; Sociology
Dist - NYFLMS **Prod** - NYFLMS 1974

Who Does what to what - the Work Distribution Chart 11 MIN
16mm
Color
LC 74-705952
Demonstrates the work distribution chart as a method of observing at a glance what work is actually going on in an organization.
Business and Economics; Psychology
Dist - USNAC **Prod** - USA 1973

Who dunnit 30 MIN
VHS
Join in series
Color (K P)
#362309
Shows that Jacob intends to do some work on a Saturday, but ends up searching for clues when things in the workshop keep disappearing. Features a story about a little girl who uses her detective skills to find some new friends. Part of a series about three artist - performers who share studio space in a converted warehouse.
Fine Arts; Literature and Drama
Dist - TVOTAR **Prod** - TVOTAR 1989

Who Gets Breast Cancer 12 MIN
VHS / 16mm
Understanding Breast Cancer Series
Color (H C A PRO)
$195.00 purchase, $75.00 rental _ #8066
Focuses on the victims of breast cancer.
Guidance and Counseling; Health and Safety
Dist - AIMS **Prod** - HOSSN 1988

Who gets in 52 MIN
VHS / U-matic / 16mm
Color (H C G)
$775.00, $250.00 purchase, $50.00 rental _ #CC426616, #CC4266VU, #CC4266VH
Examines Canadian immigrant and refugee selection processes. Reveals the administrative procedures and policies which determine which applicants will be accepted for citizenship. Reveals that an individual's need to immigrate, no matter how desperate, is far outweighed by the potential contribution of that individual to Canadian society and economy. The selection favors educated, wealthy and politically compatible First World applicants at the expense of those from developing nations.
Geography - World; Sociology
Dist - IU **Prod** - NFBC 1989

Who Happen to be Gay 23 MIN
16mm
Color (A)
LC 80-700853
Features six homosexuals who talk about their lifestyle and its impact upon them.
Sociology
Dist - DIRECT **Prod** - DIRECT 1979

Who has Touched the Sky 8 MIN
16mm
Color
LC 75-702490
Presents scenes of Air Force activity against a background of music by the Anita Kerr Singers.
Civics and Political Systems; Industrial and Technical Education; Social Science
Dist - USNAC **Prod** - USAF 1972

Who Helps who 27 MIN
U-matic / VHS / 16mm
Five Billion People Series
Color
Reveals the benefits that developed countries get from providing international aid to underdeveloped nations. Shows that international aid does little more than maintain and reinforce the present domination of the underdeveloped countries by the developed ones.
Business and Economics; Civics and Political Systems
Dist - CNEMAG **Prod** - LEFSP

Who - Ho - Ray, no 1 and 2 20 MIN
16mm
Color
Deals with two studies using the analog computer as a graphic source for visual astronics and image manipulation.
Industrial and Technical Education; Mathematics; Sociology
Dist - VANBKS **Prod** - VANBKS

Who I Am and Where I Want to Go
VHS / U-matic
Employability Skills Series
Color
Identifies those abilities, interests, values, personal characteristics and experiences that have important implications for choosing a job and?\or career.
Guidance and Counseling
Dist - CAMB **Prod** - ILCS

Who in the world is here - course overview 60 MIN
VHS
Dealing with diversity series
Color (H C G)
$99.00 purchase _ #GSU - 101
Introduces concepts in diverse populations. Presents definitions and discusses the ethnic - racial, religious and cultural origins of members of the class. Features Constance Potter of the National Archives. Part of a 23 - part series hosted by Dr J Q Adams, Western Illinois University, which helps students to develop the awareness that society is strengthened by a free and unfettered expression of individuality in all its diverse manifestations.
Religion and Philosophy; Sociology
Dist - INSTRU

Who Invited Us 60 MIN
16mm / U-matic / VHS
B&W (H C A)
LC 72-708903
Reviews the history of United States military intervention beginning with the takeover of the Philippines and continuing through the Viet nam War. Examines motives for intervention, such as the capitalist - socialist conflict and economic reasons.
Civics and Political Systems; History - United States
Dist - IU **Prod** - NET 1970

Who is Elmer Dunaway and what Does He Want 30 MIN
U-matic
Decision Makers Series
Color
Features an interview with Elmer Dunaway, statewide president, Ohio Fraternal Order of Police.
Biography; Civics and Political Systems
Dist - HRC **Prod** - OHC

Who is God, where is God
VHS
Bippity boppity bunch series
Color (K P I R)
$14.95 purchase _ #35 - 821 - 8579
Deals with questions young people may have about God. Portrays the Bippity Boppity Bunch as they consider questions such as 'Where is God?' and 'What does God look like?'
Literature and Drama; Religion and Philosophy
Dist - APH **Prod** - FAMF

Who is Jesus series
The Death of Jesus 60 MIN
Discipleship - Following Jesus 60 MIN
Easter and Pentecost 60 MIN
Jesus - prophetic teacher 60 MIN
Jesus - teacher of wisdom 60 MIN
Jesus and the Gospel of John 60 MIN
The Resurrection of Jesus 60 MIN
Son of God - Son of Mary 60 MIN
Dist - CTNA

Who is making money in health care 30 MIN
U-matic
Adam Smith's money world series; 123
Color (A)
Attempts to demystify the world of money and break it down so that small as well as large businesses and it's people understand and adjust to new social and economic trends. Reports on the major economic stories and discoveries of the day.
Business and Economics
Dist - PBS **Prod** - WNETTV 1985

Who is Man - an Overview 29 MIN
Videoreel / VT2
Who is Man Series
Color
Explains the concept of the Who Is Man series and surveys the material which will be handled in subsequent programs.
Psychology
Dist - PBS **Prod** - WHROTV

Who is Man Series
Atlantis 29 MIN
Clairvoyant frauds 29 MIN
Clairvoyants 29 MIN
Dreams 29 MIN
Edgar Cayce 29 MIN
ESP and the Artist 29 MIN
ESP Behind the Iron Curtain 29 MIN
ESP I 29 MIN
ESP II 29 MIN
Finger Reading 29 MIN
Gladys Davis Turner 29 MIN
Hypnosis 29 MIN
Primitive Beliefs 29 MIN
Psychokinesis (Russia and Here) 29 MIN
Questions and Answers I 29 MIN
Questions and Answers II 29 MIN
Reincarnation 29 MIN
Research Methods and Probability 29 MIN
The Sensitive 29 MIN
Superstitions 29 MIN
Testing Equipment and Approaches 29 MIN
Who is Man - an Overview 29 MIN
Who is Man - Summary 29 MIN
Dist - PBS

Who is Man - Summary 29 MIN
Videoreel / VT2
Who is Man Series
Color
Features Dr Puryear summing up the material presented in the Who Is Man series.

Psychology
Dist - PBS **Prod** - WHROTV

Who is My Master - Espionage Today 30 MIN
U-matic
Best Kept Secrets Series
Color (H C A)
Profiles the contemporary spy who plays an elaborate and deadly game with complex technologies. He often operates, grows old and dies in isolation. Includes interviews with real spies discussing their friends and enemies.
Civics and Political Systems
Dist - TVOTAR **Prod** - TVOTAR 1985

Who is My Neighbor 30 MIN
16mm
B&W (J H C)
Presents the parable of the Good Samaritan - - a Samaritan finds an injured man lying by the road, a victim of thieves, and takes him to an inn and arranges for his care at his own expense.
Religion and Philosophy
Dist - CAFM **Prod** - CAFM

Who is My Sister 88 MIN
VHS / 16mm
Color (G)
$95.00 rental _ #WIMS - 000
Presents a panel of women from various backgrounds disussing the women's movement. Covers the special problems of minority women and the status of women in the business world as well as at home.
Sociology
Dist - PBS **Prod** - WKARTV

Who is - Oscar Niemeyer 30 MIN
16mm
Who is Series
Color (H C A)
LC 73-708713
Shows how Oscar Niemeyer, a Brazilian architect who contributed to the design of the un building, designed the new city of Brasilia. Illustrates the high aesthetic impact of the new capital's buildings that avoids American and European functional emphasis. Mentions Niemeyer's disappointment in the failure of the project to produce a new, informal and unstratified society.
Fine Arts; Geography - World
Dist - IU **Prod** - NET 1970

Who is Pete 27 MIN
U-matic / VHS / 16mm
Color; B&W (C A)
Introduces the school - wide testing program which reaches each student at regular intervals throughout his school career. A variety of tests are shown in use with students at different grade levels.
Education; Psychology
Dist - IFB **Prod** - NEAPRO 1961

Who is Pulling Your Strings 12 MIN
16mm
Color
Presents Ann Marie Fairchild, a ventriloquist, and her dummy Jackie, making a parallel between Ann Marie pulling Jackie's strings to control him and Jesus controlling our lives if we are willing to let him.
Religion and Philosophy
Dist - BROADM **Prod** - BROADM 1975

Who is responsible 10 MIN
U-matic / VHS / BETA
Color; PAL (C P G)
PdS30, PdS38 purchase
Examines a breakdown of the chain of responsibility in routine work by studying the supervisor and the team.
Psychology
Dist - EDPAT

Who is - Sean Kenny 30 MIN
16mm
Who is Series
Color (H C A)
LC 70-708715
Sean Kenny, designer of the gyrotron at Montreal's Expo 67, explains the philosophies lying behind his design and architectural work. Shows how Kenny has reflected the ideas of his teacher, Frank Lloyd Wright, in his design of stage sets, especially his London Blitz, which is a new form of entertainment - architectural theater. Presents his belief that the different forms and shapes which we contact shape our work, learning and character.
Fine Arts
Dist - IU **Prod** - NET 1970

Who is Series
Who is - Oscar Niemeyer 30 MIN
Who is - Sean Kenny 30 MIN
Dist - IU

Who is Sylvia 30 MIN
16mm
Footsteps Series
Color
LC 79-701561
Explores both the harmful and helpful aspects of television, showing how it shapes children's ideas of what the world is like, as well as their attitudes towards themselves and others. Illustrates how parents can use television to their children's benefit.
Fine Arts; Home Economics; Sociology
Dist - USNAC **Prod** - USOE 1978

Who is Sylvia 27 MIN
16mm / U-matic / VHS
Adolescence Series
B&W (H C)
Studies the dreams, fears and hopes of a 14 - year - old girl. Points out the characteristic lack of communication and understanding between parents and their adolescent children.
Psychology; Sociology
Dist - IFB **Prod** - NFBC 1957

Who is the Real Cinderella 19 MIN
U-matic / VHS
Folk Book Series
Color (P)
Uses puppets to illustrate variations on the Cinderella story.
Literature and Drama
Dist - AITECH **Prod** - UWISC 1980

Who is this Man - John Paul II in America 28 MIN
16mm
Color
LC 80-700649
Reviews the verbal and nonverbal messages of Pope John Paul II during his 1979 visit to the United States.
Biography; Religion and Philosophy
Dist - USCC **Prod** - KNICOL 1979

Who is Tracy Williams 28 MIN
16mm
B&W (C A)
LC 74-702726
Focuses on the problems, frailties and strengths of Tracy Williams, an inmate of the State Correctional Institution at Muncy, Pennsylvania. Depicts prison routine. Interviews William about Muncy and her bitterness about the circumstances surrounding her confinement.
Psychology; Sociology
Dist - PSUPCR **Prod** - PSU 1973
PBS

Who is - Victor Vasarely 30 MIN
16mm
Color (H C)
LC 77-708714
Shows the work of the Hungarian - born artist, Victor Vasarely who is considered to be the founder of op - art and discusses his philosophy.
Fine Arts
Dist - IU **Prod** - NET 1970

Who Killed Determinants 57 MIN
16mm
Maa Calculus Series
B&W
Lectures on the historical patterns of research and growth in the field of determinants, prompted by the apparent demise of determinants as an active field of research.
Mathematics
Dist - MLA **Prod** - MAA

Who Killed Jesus Christ - the New Testament and the Facts
Videoreel / VT2
Jesus Trial Series
Color
LC 79-706738
Religion and Philosophy
Dist - TVBUS **Prod** - TVOTAR 1979

Who Killed Lake Erie, Pt 1 26 MIN
16mm
Color (J)
LC 70-706150
Presents Lake Erie as an example of man's indifferent destruction of his environment. Shows the pollution of the lake, the results of that pollution and what is being done about it.
Science - Natural
Dist - NBCTV **Prod** - NBCTV 1969

Who Killed Lake Erie, Pt 2 26 MIN
16mm
Color (J)
LC 70-706150
Presents Lake Erie as an example of man's indifferent destruction of his environment. Shows the pollution of the lake, the results of that pollution and what is being done about it.
Science - Natural
Dist - NBCTV **Prod** - NBCTV 1969

Who killed Martin Luther King 52 MIN
VHS
Color; B&W (G)
$19.95 purchase _ #1657
Asks - why did James Earl Ray plead guilty to the shooting of Martin Luther King and then, the day after his conviction, claim to have been manipulated and to be innocent. Contains unprecedented interviews with James Earl Ray and other key participants in the case.
Biography; Civics and Political Systems; History - United States
Dist - KULTUR **Prod** - KULTUR 1993

Who killed service
BETA / U-matic / VHS
Color (G)
$325.00 rental
Uses humor to teach about the value of customer service to organizations. Can be purchased in workshop format with supporting materials.
Business and Economics
Dist - AMEDIA **Prod** - AMEDIA

Who killed Vincent Chin 82 MIN
16mm / VHS
Color (H C G)
$550.00, $295.00 purchase, $55.00 rental
Recalls the murder of Vincent Chin, a young Chinese American celebrating his last days of bachelorhood in a Detroit bar. Reveals that an argument between Chin and Ron Ebens, a Chrysler Motors foreman who shouted ethnic insults, culminated in Ebens bludgeoning Chin to death with a baseball bat before onlookers. Ebens was let off with a suspended sentence and a small fine. Outrage moved the Asian - American community to organize an unprecedented civil rights protest. Discusses the failure of the judicial system to value every citizen's right equally, the collapse of the American automobile industry under pressure from Japanese imports and the end of the American dream for blue collar workers. Produced by Christine Choy and Renee Tajima.
History - United States; Sociology
Dist - FLMLIB

Who Kills the Tiger 15 MIN
16mm
Color (H C A)
Employs the graphic arts to illustrate that man's survival is dependent upon his co - operation with his fellow men. Portrays the role of community services.
History - United States; Psychology; Sociology
Dist - WSUM **Prod** - WSUM 1959

Who Listens 30 MIN
U-matic / VHS
Principles of Human Communication Series
Color (H C A)
Focuses on the constituents of good listening and ways to develop good listening habits.
English Language; Psychology
Dist - GPN **Prod** - UMINN 1983

Who lives, who dies - rationing health care 58 MIN
VHS
Color (H C G)
$445.00 purchase, $75.00 rental
Shows that despite the extraordinary medical resources of the United States, its health system fails a large part of its people. Reveals that 1 in 6 Americans has no medical insurance, cannot afford basic care, that low - paid Americans have to rely on public clinics with shrinking funding. Tells of a woman with a malignancy that spread because she couldn't get treatment, a man with hypertension who suffered a cerebral hemorrhage because he couldn't afford medication, a woman in labor turned away from two hospitals because of no insurance. Discloses that poor children are at greatest risk, the US ranks 20th in infant mortality, that two - thirds of infant mortality occur among mothers with little or no prenatal care. James Earl Jones hosts.
Civics and Political Systems; Health and Safety; Sociology
Dist - FLMLIB **Prod** - RWEIS 1988

Who Lives, who Dies, who Decides 14 MIN
U-matic
Bioethics in Nursing Practice Series
Color (PRO)
LC 81-707063
Health and Safety
Dist - BRA **Prod** - BRA 1981

Who Lost a Giraffe 10 MIN
16mm / U-matic / VHS
Color (K P I)
LC 75-702973
Uses animation to tell the story of a small boy who discovers a rubber eraser with the imprint of a giraffe on it.
Fine Arts; Literature and Drama
Dist - PHENIX **Prod** - JURIST 1975

Who Loves Amy Tonight 25 MIN
U-matic / VHS / 16mm
Insight Series
Color (J)
Demonstrates how a spoiled girl has always managed to manipulate her father. Shows how he decides to become firmer with her after she becomes involved in shoplifting and drug dealing. Stars Laura Dern and Tim Van Patten.
Guidance and Counseling; Psychology; Religion and Philosophy; Sociology
Dist - PAULST **Prod** - PAULST

Who, me and Kum Ba Yah 30 MIN
VHS
Davey and Goliath series
Color (P I R)
$19.95 purchase, $10.00 rental _ #4 - 8836
Presents two 15 - minute 'Davey and Goliath' episodes. 'Who, Me?' covers how Davey learns that chores are as much an expression of love as they are a duty. 'Kum Ba Yah' utilizes the words to the hymn of that name to teach Davey to be responsible to the other members of his bell choir. Produced by the Evangelical Lutheran Church in America.
Literature and Drama; Religion and Philosophy
Dist - APH

Who Me - make a Presentation 15 MIN
16mm / U-matic / VHS
Color
Convinces managers that they can overcome the number one fear of most managers, public speaking. Shows managers and salespeople how to sell their ideas to peers, higher management and customers.
Business and Economics; Psychology
Dist - EFM **Prod** - EFM

Who needs a chimney in a head 15 MIN
VHS
Color (P I J)
Portrays an old 'Smoke Maker' who tries to show a boy how smoking would 'help' him by making him unfit for football, swimming and other athletic activities.
Health and Safety; Psychology; Science - Natural
Dist - VIEWTH **Prod** - VIEWTH

Who Needs it 15 MIN
U-matic / VHS
It's all Up to You Series
Color (I J)
Analyzes the conditions necessary for government to function, different types of past and present governments, and the relationship between the ruler and the ruled.
Guidance and Counseling
Dist - AITECH **Prod** - COOPED 1978

Who Needs it
VHS / 16mm
Color (A PRO IND)
Provides information on personnel management. Part of the Employee Assistance Program (EAP) available on videotape.
Guidance and Counseling; Psychology
Dist - HAZELB

Who Needs Math 15 MIN
Videoreel / VT2
Work is for Real Series
Color (J H)
Explains that the ability to handle fundamental math is a real help in any job. Discusses jobs that require varying degrees of math proficiency.
Education; Guidance and Counseling; Mathematics; Psychology
Dist - GPN **Prod** - STETVC

Who Needs Meat 26 MIN
U-matic / VHS / 16mm
Color (H C A)
LC 80-700008
Explains that the key to good health is balanced nutrition and tells how a vegetarian diet can be a healthful one, providing it is nutritionally balanced.
Health and Safety; Social Science
Dist - FI **Prod** - WNETTV 1979

Who Needs Statistics
U-matic / VHS
Statistics for Managers Series
Color (IND)
Discusses some of the applications of statistics and how they can be used at all management levels.
Business and Economics; Mathematics; Psychology
Dist - COLOSU **Prod** - COLOSU

Who Needs to Know - Pt 1 26 MIN
VHS / U-matic
Toxic Chemicals - Information is the Best Defense
Color (J H A)
Explains how concerned groups can work together to develop a community right to know or hazardous materials disclosure ordinance which can prevent accidents and protect public health. Handbook provided.
Civics and Political Systems; Health and Safety; Social Science; Sociology
Dist - BULFRG **Prod** - LWVCA 1986

Who Owns Schools - and what are they Doing about it 34 MIN
16mm
Color
LC 80-700883
Discusses power and responsibility in education. Contrasts mass media portrayals of critical issues in education with the work of teachers who take their jobs seriously.
Education
Dist - TASCOR **Prod** - CANCAE 1979

Who owns the forests 30 MIN
VHS / U-matic
Forests of the world series
Color (J H G)
$270.00, $320.00 purchase, $60.00 rental
Documents different proposals regarding the fate of the forests ranging from unbridled use to total preservation. Lists examples from Japan, Norway, Sweden, England, New Zealand and the United States. Reviews many of the variables that have entered the equation.
Agriculture; Science - Natural; Social Science
Dist - NDIM **Prod** - NRKTV 1993

Who owns the sun 18 MIN
U-matic / 16mm / VHS
Color (P)
$425.00, $280.00 purchase _ #JC - 67286
Adapts the story 'Who Owns the Sun' by 14 - year - old author and illustrator Stacy Chbosky. Joins Joshua, the bright and curious six - year - old son of a plantation slave in the American South, as he explores the concepts of prejudice, freedom and self - respect, and searches for answers to some of life's more difficult questions. Provides important information about a destructive and hate - filled period of American history.
History - United States; Literature and Drama
Dist - CORF **Prod** - DISNEY 1990

Who Pays for AIDS 60 MIN
VHS
Frontline Series
Color; Captioned (G)
$59.95 purchase _ #FRON - 616K
Focuses on the growing costs of treating people with AIDS, showing that taxpeyers will cover at least half of the costs. Reveals that many people with AIDS are forced to rely on government assistance when they lose their jobs and health insurance. Considers how hospitals and AIDS service organizations are attempting to treat a growing number of AIDS cases without assurances of increased funding.
Health and Safety
Dist - PBS **Prod** - DOCCON 1988

Who Profits from Drugs 60 MIN
VHS
Frontline Series
Color; Captioned (G)
$300.00 purchase, $95.00 rental _ #FRON - 706K
Examines how lawyers, bankers, businessmen and other officials have often been involved in laundering of drug money. Features a federal government raid in which $100 million in drug money was traced to offshore banks or dummy corporations. Shows how drug money is invested.
Business and Economics; Civics and Political Systems; Sociology
Dist - PBS **Prod** - DOCCON 1989

Who Protects the Consumer 85 MIN
U-matic / VHS
Milton Friedman Speaking Series
Color (C)
LC 79-708072
Features economist Milton Friedman discussing the consumer advocacy movement. Points out that international competition of free trade is perhaps the best source of protection for the consumer.
Home Economics
Dist - HBJ **Prod** - HBJ 1980

Who Protects the Consumer, Pt 1 42 MIN
U-matic / VHS
Milton Friedman Speaking Series
Color (C)
LC 79-708072
Features economist Milton Friedman discussing the consumer advocacy movement. Points out that international competition of free trade is perhaps the best source of protection for the consumer.
Business and Economics; Home Economics
Dist - HBJ **Prod** - HBJ 1980

Who Protects the Consumer, Pt 2 43 MIN
U-matic / VHS
Milton Friedman Speaking Series
Color (C)
LC 79-708072
Features economist Milton Friedman discussing the consumer advocacy movement. Points out that international competition of free trade is perhaps the best source of protection for the consumer.
Business and Economics; Home Economics
Dist - HBJ **Prod** - HBJ 1980

Who Protects the Worker 82 MIN
U-matic / VHS
Milton Friedman Speaking Series
Color (C)
LC 79-708073
Records economist Milton Friedman discussing the protection of American workers. Looks at labor laws, unions, and government efforts. Concludes that the real way to protect workers is to preserve a free, competitive labor market.
Business and Economics; Sociology
Dist - HBJ **Prod** - HBJ 1980

Who Protects the Worker, Pt 1 41 MIN
U-matic / VHS
Milton Friedman Speaking Series
Color (C)
LC 79-708073
Records economist Milton Friedman discussing the protection of American workers. Looks at labor laws, unions, and government efforts. Concludes that the real way to protect workers is to preserve a free, competitive labor market.
Business and Economics; Sociology
Dist - HBJ **Prod** - HBJ 1980

Who Protects the Worker, Pt 2 41 MIN
U-matic / VHS
Milton Friedman Speaking Series
Color (C)
LC 79-708073
Records economist Milton Friedman discussing the protection of American workers. Looks at labor laws, unions, and government efforts. Concludes that the real way to protect workers is to preserve a free, competitive labor market.
Business and Economics; Sociology
Dist - HBJ **Prod** - HBJ 1980

Who Really Killed Cock Robin 25 MIN
VHS
Color (S)
$79.00 purchase _ #825 - 9572
Reveals that the daily life of a robin is like a soap opera, filled with violence and sex. Follows the fortunes of nearly 40 robins in the magnificent gardens of a British country manor. These hardy birds face many dangers from predators, cold, starvation, disease - even other robins - in their struggle for survival. Narrated by David Attenborough.
Geography - World; Science - Natural
Dist - FI **Prod** - BBCTV 1988

Who Roared 10 MIN
16mm
Color
LC 79-701649
Points out that everyone needs at least one thing in which they are both competent and recognized as being competent. Features a giant bird who tells the story of a boy who had been without confidence in himself but discovered that a goal and a determined effort will produce the desired results.
Guidance and Counseling
Dist - ECI **Prod** - ECI

Who Runs Congress - who Runs Congress / Varieties of Leadership, Pt 1 30 MIN
U-matic / VHS
Congress - We the People Series
Color
Examines several alternative sources of leadership within Congress.
Civics and Political Systems
Dist - FI **Prod** - WETATV 1984

Who Runs Washington 30 MIN
U-matic
Realities
Color (A)
Delves into the political, social, economic and cultural trends of the 1980s. Probes a wide range of contemporary concerns. Each segment includes a guest speaker who is an expert in the field under discussion.
Business and Economics; Civics and Political Systems; Social Science; Sociology
Dist - TVOTAR **Prod** - TVOTAR 1985

Who Said it was Safe? 20 MIN
VHS
Color
From the ABC TV program, 20 20. Discusses the Hoffman La Roche drug, Nisentil.

Health and Safety
Dist - ABCLR **Prod** - ABCLR 1983

Who Says It's Great 29 MIN
U-matic
Visions - the Critical Eye Series
Color (H C)
Explores modernist art and related subjects such as methods of marketing, drawbacks involved in adopting theories of mainstream art, the role of the critic and the ways in which art can express religious experience.
Fine Arts
Dist - TVOTAR **Prod** - TVOTAR 1985

Who Serves in Congress - a Variety of Voices / who Serves in Congress, Pt 1 30 MIN
VHS / U-matic
Congress - We the People Series
Color
Explores characteristics of the members of Congress - how representative or unrepresentative they are of the American people and why they seek office.
Civics and Political Systems
Dist - FI **Prod** - WETATV 1984

Who Sets Your Standards 30 MIN
16mm
Color; B&W (J H T R)
LC FIA67-5757
The Harrison family spends a week together in an isolated mountain cabin. This becomes a time of selfexamination as they discover and evalute the pressures that influence their standards.
Guidance and Counseling; Psychology; Religion and Philosophy
Dist - FAMF **Prod** - FAMF 1967

Who Shall Live and who Shall Die 90 MIN
16mm
B&W
LC 82-700289
Tells the story of the American response to the Holocaust. Includes interviews with government officials, Jewish leaders and concentration camp survivors combined with newsreel footage.
History - United States; History - World
Dist - BLULIT **Prod** - BLULIT 1982

Who Shot Alexander Hamilton 60 MIN
U-matic / VHS / 16mm
B&W
Provides an in - depth look at the Congress of the United States during a time when Congress was dealing with funding for the Vietnam War, Watergate and impeachment proceedings against President Nixon.
Civics and Political Systems; History - United States
Dist - NEWTIM **Prod** - NEWTIM

Who shot President Kennedy 58 MIN
BETA / VHS / U-matic
Nova series
Color (J H C)
$99.00 purchase _ #JY - 5912C
Examines the controversy surrounding the assassination of President Kennedy. Looks at sophisticated techniques of photo enhancement and three-dimensional computer modeling which establish accurate bullet trajectories. Considers recent findings linking accused assasin Lee Harvey Oswald to another gunman.
Biography; History - United States; Sociology
Dist - CORF **Prod** - LCOA 1988

Who should decide 13 MIN
VHS
Discussions in bioethics series
Color (H C A)
$95.00 purchase
Portrays Joanne, a victim of spina bifida, who discovers that her unborn child has the same disease and would, at the very least, be confined to a wheelchair for life if carried to term. Reveals that Joanne and her husband must decide quickly whether to terminate her pregnancy during the second trimester. Comes with discussion guide.
Health and Safety; Psychology; Sociology
Dist - PFP **Prod** - NFBC

Who should pay for college and how 30 MIN
VHS
Adam Smith's money world series
Color (H C A)
$79.95 purchase
Examines the phenomenon of ever - rising college costs. Questions whether the federal government should pick up more of the expense. Features host Jerry Goodman, also known as 'Adam Smith,' and his guests Michael O'Keefe, David Breneman, Steven Trachtenberg, and others.
Business and Economics
Dist - PBS **Prod** - WNETTV

Who Should Survive 10 MIN
16mm
Color
LC 72-700488
Focuses on ethical questions which arise from the increasing effectiveness of modern medicine. Describes the case of a mongoloid child, who was born with an intestinal abnormality. Explains that modern medicine could correct the fatal condition, but that the parents refused permission for surgery because they did not want the mentally retarded child to live.
Health and Safety; Psychology; Religion and Philosophy; Sociology
Dist - KENJPF **Prod** - KENJPF 1972

Who should we defend 28 MIN
VHS
Color (J H C G)
$34.95 purchase _ #ADM526V
Examines the role of the United States military after the end of the Cold War. Asks - what is the purpose of the United States military force; and who should the United States defend.
Civics and Political Systems; History - World; Sociology
Dist - CAMV

Who sold you this, then? 23 MIN
VHS
Color (PRO IND COR A)
$870.00 purchase, $250.00 rental, $50.00 preview
Teaches service, technical and installation staff how to support the salesperson, the product, the organization and the customer. Dramatizes these classic errors that evoke in service, technical and installation staff an understanding of how to become troubleshooters instead of troublemakers. Management and sales staff are also taught to appreciate the problems faced by their after-sales teams.
Sociology
Dist - VIDART

Who Sold You this, Then 22 MIN
U-matic / VHS
Color
Shows how to be the company's best ambassador when dealing with a customer who is unhappy.
Business and Economics
Dist - VISUCP **Prod** - VIDART

Who Sold You this, Theo 23 MIN
U-matic / VHS
Color (A)
Highlights the role of the service representative in ensuring continued good relations between customers and businesses. Shows how service representatives can make or wreck business relationships.
Business and Economics; Psychology
Dist - XICOM **Prod** - XICOM

Who speaks for Earth 60 MIN
U-matic / VHS / 16mm
Cosmos series; Program 13
Color (J)
LC 81-701151
Reviews highlights from the first 12 episodes of the Cosmos series. Weaves together the ideas of cosmic evolution, the scientific approach, history as an exemplary teacher, and the limitedness of human perception. Presents cautionary warnings about the future mankind faces as a species and as a planet. Based on the book Cosmos by Carl Sagan. Narrated by Carl Sagan.
Science - Natural; Science - Physical; Sociology
Dist - FI **Prod** - KCET 1980

Who spooked Rodney? 24 MIN
U-matic / VHS
Young people's specials series
Color
Tells the comic story of Halloween and a young boy who allows himself to be overrun by superstition.
Fine Arts; Social Science; Sociology
Dist - MULTPP **Prod** - MULTPP

Who starts - and why 15 MIN
VHS
Dealing with drugs - teaching kids to say 'no' series
Color; CC (I J H)
$89.95 purchase _ #UW3531
Explores who takes drugs, some of the reasons why people turn to drugs and characteristics of drug dependency. Part of a six - part series using wit and humor to teach students how to say 'no' to drugs.
Guidance and Counseling; Psychology
Dist - FOTH

Who stole the cookies 28 MIN
VHS
Elephant show series
Color (P I)
$95.00 purchase, $45.00 rental
Presents program 33 in the Sharon, Lois and Bram's Elephant Show series. Teaches reading readiness and social skills while engaging children in making music. Each program explores a new theme through adventure, fantasy, mystery and song with recording artists Sharon, Lois and Bram. Uses traditional materials which stress participation - action songs, sing - along songs, story songs, clapping songs, singing games, playground chants and folk songs from many different traditions. Includes teacher's guide co - authored by a music education specialist.
Fine Arts; Sociology
Dist - BULFRG **Prod** - CAMBFP 1991

Who Stole the Quiet Day 18 MIN
16mm / U-matic / VHS
Color (I)
LC 83-700959
Presents an evaluation of the noise pollution problem and how people are affected by it both physically and psychologically. Demonstrates, with the help of leading medical authorities, how loud sound destroys the nerve cells within ears and how young people can begin the deterioration process through thoughtless exposure to loud noises.
Science - Natural
Dist - HIGGIN **Prod** - HIGGIN 1984

Who switched the price tags 200 MIN
VHS
Color (H C G A R)
$199.00 rental _ #36 - 87 - 533
Features sociologist Anthony Campolo in a discussion of how people's values can become mixed - up. Consists of four episodes. 'If I Had It to Live Over Again' discusses how the presence of Jesus in a person's life can awake passion for life. 'The Value of Family Rituals and Traditions' explains how such activities benefit children, while 'Are You Having Fun Yet?' suggests that a lack of job fulfillment will mean family troubles. 'The Church - God's Instrument for Changing the World' envisions how Christians can reach out to others.
Religion and Philosophy
Dist - APH **Prod** - WORD

Who they are - Pt I 30 MIN
VHS
Arab world series
Color (J H C G)
$50.00 purchase _ #MFV210V
Features Bill Moyers and noted scholars and writers who explore the world of Arabia from Morocco to Oman to discover who the Arabs are. Reveals that Arabs may be Christian or Muslim, have black skin or red hair, be as rich as a Saudi prince or as poor as a Palestinian, their only common bond is geography and the Arabic tongue. Part of a five - part series on Arabia.
Geography - World; Religion and Philosophy; Sociology
Dist - CAMV

Who Took the Farmer's Hat 15 MIN
U-matic / VHS
Words and Pictures Series
Color (K P)
Recounts what happens when a farmer asks the animals to help him find his old brown hat. Emphasizes the letter blend br.
English Language; Literature and Drama
Dist - FI **Prod** - FI

Who Wants America Ugly 8 MIN
U-matic / VHS / 16mm
Caring about Our Community Series
Color (P I)
Follows a group of school children as they examine their community and see visual pollution in ugly signs, litter, sidewalk graffiti, bad planning and poor use of open space. Shows that in their classroom, they construct a model community planned to eliminate these abuses and to bring trees and grass into the community center.
Science - Natural; Social Science
Dist - AIMS **Prod** - GORKER 1973

Who Wants to be a Hero 28 MIN
U-matic / VHS / 16mm
Color (I J H)
LC 81-700954
Examines involvement vs non - involvement through the story of Jason, who becomes a hero when he apprehends the thugs who mugged the school janitor. Shows that conflict and trouble set in as he and his mother are threatened when he must testify against the thugs. Based on the book Who Wants To Be A Hero by Robert E Rubinstein.
Guidance and Counseling; Sociology
Dist - LCOA **Prod** - LCOA 1981

Who Wants to Play God 21 MIN
U-matic / VHS
Color (A)
Teaches methods for performance review. Emphasizes positive reinforcement. Shows through a fictionalized situation the five essential elements of an effective performance interview.
Business and Economics; Psychology
Dist - AMEDIA **Prod** - AMEDIA

Who wants unions 27 MIN
VHS / 16mm
Color (G IND)
$5.00 rental
Explores decling union membership in North America. Includes many scenes of management seminars in which personnel are trained by Charles Hughes and other consultants in how to keep unions from organizing a plant or how to bring about decertification. Contrasts these scenes with an organizing drive in a low - wage rural area.
Business and Economics; Social Science
Dist - AFLCIO **Prod** - NFBC 1983

Who was Jack Carrington - Smith 22 MIN
16mm
Color
LC 80-700938
Presents the life and work of noted artist, teacher and Archibald Prize winner Jack Carrington - Smith. Features reminiscences by his friends and family.
Fine Arts
Dist - TASCOR **Prod** - TASCOR 1976

Who We are Series
Are people all the same 9 MIN
Is it OK to be Me 6 MIN
What Color is Skin 9 MIN
What is an American, Pt 1 10 MIN
What is an American, Pt 2 12 MIN
What Makes Me Different 9 MIN
Dist - PFP

Who were the Ones 7 MIN
U-matic / VHS / 16mm
Color (H C A)
LC 73-702462
Presents an Indian's song of protest, expressive of the bitter memories of the past, still alive today. Views North American history as seen from the view of the Indians.
Fine Arts; Social Science
Dist - FI **Prod** - NFBC 1973

The Who, what and Why of Authority 29 MIN
U-matic / VHS / 16mm
Human Relations and School Discipline Series
Color
Presents a compilation of views by leading authorities on discipline regarding power, responsibility, control and rules specifically as they relate to authority, what it is, who has it and why. Explains the concept of natural authority and the conclusion that potentially, in one way or another, teachers will gain authority.
Education; Sociology
Dist - FI **Prod** - MFFD

Who, what, When, Where and Why 15 MIN
VHS / U-matic
Magic Shop Series
Color (P)
LC 83-706159
Employs a magician named Amazing Alexander and his assistants to explore the use of the five W's in writing.
English Language
Dist - GPN **Prod** - CVETVC 1982

Who, what, where, why and when series
The American soldier in combat 29 MIN
Battle for the United States 29 MIN
Greyhounds of the sea 29 MIN
The Presidency - Volume I 28 MIN
The Story of the Stars and Stripes 28 MIN
Dist - INCRSE

Who will be the Teacher 16 MIN
16mm / U-matic / VHS
Learning Laws - Respect for Yourself, Others and the Law Series
Color (I)
Confronts the increasing problem of violence directed against teachers. Tells that in order to join a gang, Terry assaults his teacher. Shows him gradually realizing that this was really an act of cowardice and developing a new respect for his teacher.
Guidance and Counseling; Psychology; Sociology
Dist - CORF **Prod** - DISNEY 1982

Who will care for an aging America - a guide for nurses 25 MIN
VHS
Color (C PRO)
$275.00 purchase, $75.00 rental _ #42 - 2456, #42 - 2456R
Explores how the future of nursing is linked to the 'graying of America.' Showcases the most innovative nursing models in a variety of settings, ranging from a hospital - based geriatric nursing case management center to retirement communities specializing in the needs of the elderly.
Health and Safety
Dist - NLFN **Prod** - NLFN

Who will Cast the First Stone 52 MIN
VHS / 16mm
Color (G)
$350.00 purchase, $85.00 rental; LC 89715588
Examines the impact of Islamization on women in Pakistan. Reveals that in 1979, General Zia al Haq introduced into law the Hudood Ordinances under which Zina - adultery, rape or extramarital sex - became a crime against the state punishable by stoning to death. These laws were aimed at women to promote the middle class image of the ideal Muslim woman, chaste, submissive and confined. Focuses on the case histories of three women.
Geography - World; History - World; Religion and Philosophy; Sociology
Dist - CNEMAG **Prod** - CNEMAG 1989

Who will Comfort Toffel 24 MIN
16mm / VHS
Color (G)
$395.00, $495.00 purchase, $50.00 rental _ #8011
Tells an animated musical story with verse by Tove Jansson who created the Moominfamily. Features Toffel, a lonely little boy who is tormented by nights of bad dreams. Searching for happiness, he meets lots of strange and interesting people but maintains his Swedish reserve. When he decides to get next to and help Miffel he finds happiness in friendship and love. From the Swedish Film Institute.
English Language; Foreign Language; Literature and Drama
Dist - AIMS **Prod** - EDMI 1986

Who will Cry for Me - Avoiding Suicide 50 MIN
VHS
Color (J H)
$209.00 purchase _ #60129
Uses a dramatic original screenplay as the basis for an expert analysis of teenage suicide. Brings a new perspective to a sensitive topic.
Guidance and Counseling; Psychology; Sociology
Dist - GA **Prod** - GA 1989

Who will Help You Start Your Venture 20 MIN
U-matic / VHS / 16mm
Starting a Business Series
Color (H C A)
Explores assistance needed by and avilable to starting business entrepreneurs. Lists help sources and presents creative methods of getting information and evaluating assistance.
Business and Economics
Dist - BCNFL **Prod** - SOMFIL 1983

Who will roll away the stone 60 MIN
VHS
Gospel of Mark series
Color (R G)
$49.95 purchase _ #GMAR10
Examines the structures and the key messages of the Gospel of Mark, as well as examining the life and times of Mark, according to the teachings of the Roman Catholic Church. Features Biblical scholar Father Eugene LaVerdiere, SSS. Part ten of ten parts.
Literature and Drama; Religion and Philosophy
Dist - CTNA **Prod** - CTNA

Who will Your Customers be 18 MIN
U-matic / VHS / 16mm
Starting a Business Series
Color (H C A)
Shows that market research clarifies the goals of a business, forming the basis for almost all other planning.
Business and Economics
Dist - BCNFL **Prod** - SOMFIL 1982

Who Won World War II 26 MIN
VHS / U-matic
World at War Specials Series
Color (H C A)
Presents distinguished American historian Stephen Ambrose, analyzing the consequences of World War II from the perspective of history, arriving at provocative conclusions regarding the effects of world leader's personalities, politics, economics and national characters.
History - World
Dist - MEDIAG **Prod** - THAMES 1974

Who Works at the Zoo 15 MIN
U-matic / VHS
Zoo Zoo Zoo Series
Color (P I)
Outlines the varied duties of zoo workers, including the doctor and the keepers.
Science - Natural
Dist - AITECH **Prod** - WCETTV 1981

Who you are and what you are - understanding sex roles 40 MIN
VHS
Color (J H)
$209.00 purchase _ #06788 - 126
Engages young people in a dialogue concerning the meaning of sexuality and personality. Considers sex - related issues involving career development, marriage, sex, romance and relationships between women and men.
Guidance and Counseling; Health and Safety; Psychology; Sociology
Dist - GA **Prod** - GA

Whodunit - the art of the detective story 36 MIN
35mm strip / VHS
Color (J H C A)
$93.00, $93.00 purchase _ #MB - 513004 - 1, #MB - 512708 - 3
Scrutinizes the art of detective story writing. Outlines the popular techniques used to build suspense, develop characters and clues, present evidence, and more. Traces the evolution of detective stories.
Literature and Drama
Dist - SRA

Whoever says the truth shall die 60 MIN
16mm / VHS
Color (G) (ITALIAN WITH ENGLISH SUBTITLES)
$150.00 rental
Examines the controversial murder of film director Pier Paolo Pasolini in 1975. Reveals that Pasolini was officially pronounced the victim of a homosexual encounter gone sour. Probes the possibility that Pasolini - whose work made him an enemy of the right wing and a frequent target of the Italian government - was in fact assassinated by neo - fascists. Directed by Philo Bregstein.
Civics and Political Systems; Fine Arts; History - World; Sociology
Dist - KINOIC

The Whole approach - a comprehensive and holistic guide to learning the game of golf and lowering scores 35 MIN
VHS
Color (G)
$39.95 purchase
Provides information on the game of golf and how to play it.
Physical Education and Recreation
Dist - DANEHA **Prod** - DANEHA 1993

The Whole Bag 20 MIN
16mm
B&W (H C A)
LC 78-700715
Contrasts life patterns, attitudes and goals of America's Black and white youth.
Guidance and Counseling; Psychology; Sociology
Dist - PSU **Prod** - PSU 1969

Whole Body Manual 17 MIN
16mm / U-matic / VHS
Color (J H C)
LC 77-703412
Uses a magazine format in presenting messages on the human body's many abilities, the four food groups and the importance of a balanced diet and physical exercise.
Health and Safety; Physical Education and Recreation; Science - Natural; Social Science
Dist - PEREN **Prod** - INST 1977

The Whole Damn Human Race and One more 28 MIN
U-matic / VHS / 16mm
Insight Series
B&W (J H A)
LC 73-705458
A dramatization about a humanitarian who attempts to help millions of people but is oblivious of his own daughter's need for love.
Psychology; Sociology
Dist - PAULST **Prod** - PAULST 1967

Whole Earth catalog
CD-ROM
(G A)
$149.00 purchase _ #1961
Reflects a broad range of human interests - education, house design, sea kayaking, digital electronics and more. Updated with new material on music, communications, information technologies, electronics and computer tools. For Macintosh Plus, SE and II computers. Requires at least one M of RAM, one floppy disk drive, and an Apple compatible CD - ROM drive.
Literature and Drama; Sociology
Dist - BEP

Whole Grains 3 MIN
Videoreel / VT2
Beatrice Trum Hunter's Natural Foods Series
Color
Suggests a variety of grains to use as a potato substitute, including brown rice, unpearled barley, millet, bulgar and buckwheat. Shows how they may be cooked in a variety of fluids and served as side dishes, salads and breakfast foods.

Home Economics; Social Science
Dist - PBS **Prod** - WGBH

Whole language - a philosophy that works - Session One 25 MIN
U-matic / VHS / BETA
Whole language - philosophy in practice series
Color (T A G)
$195.00 purchase _ #3116 - CPA
Features teachers, principals, parents and professors who explain whole language while classroom footage shows how to implement the curriculum. Defines the role of the teacher, as well as how to meet district objectives and assess students. Part of a 5 - part teacher inservice training series on whole language.
Education; English Language
Dist - UNIDIM **Prod** - UNIDIM

Whole language - philosophy in practice series 130 MIN
U-matic / VHS / BETA
Whole language - philosophy in practice series
Color (T A G)
$975.00 purchase _ #3116 - CP
Presents a 5 - part teacher inservice training series on whole language. Includes the titles Whole Language - a Philosophy that Works; Developing Literacy Through Meaning I and II; Getting Started - Some Practical Issues; Whole Language the Bilingual Way.
Education; English Language
Dist - UNIDIM **Prod** - UNIDIM

Whole language the bilingual way - Session Five 26 MIN
U-matic / VHS / BETA
Whole language - philosophy in practice series
Color (T A G)
$195.00 purchase _ #3116 - CPE
Shows the whole language philosophy at work in a bilingual or ESL - English as a Second Language - setting. Discusses basic whole language principles and language acquisition theory as applied to a bilingual classroom, as well as how to instruct a second language. Includes when and how to help students make a transition from their native language and novel approaches to grouping. Part of a 5 - part teacher inservice training series on whole language.
Education; English Language
Dist - UNIDIM **Prod** - UNIDIM

A Whole Lot Proud 25 MIN
16mm
Color
Looks at the duties of park rangers who work in the rugged hills of South Dakota and the sprawling beauty of Tennessee.
Geography - United States; Guidance and Counseling
Dist - MTP **Prod** - USAE

Whole Meal Salads 30 MIN
VHS / BETA
Frugal Gourmet Series
Color
Demonstrates how to prepare whole meal salads. Includes broccoli and chicken salad, spaghetti salad with shrimp and pea salad with bacon.
Health and Safety; Home Economics; Psychology
Dist - CORF **Prod** - WTTWTV

Whole meal soups
VHS
Frugal gourmet - entertaining series
Color (G)
$19.95 purchase _ #CCP839
Shows how to prepare soups which comprise a whole meal. Features Jeff Smith, the Frugal Gourmet. Part of a ten - part series on preparing food for entertaining.
History - United States; Home Economics
Dist - CADESF **Prod** - CADESF

A Whole New Ball Game 9 MIN
U-matic / VHS / 16mm
Color (I J)
Shows five youngsters playing tackle together to point out changes in boy - girl relationships that inevitably come with adolescence. Re - examines male - female roles in our rapidly changing society.
Guidance and Counseling; Psychology; Sociology
Dist - PHENIX **Prod** - KINGSP

A Whole new ball game 27 MIN
U-matic / VHS / BETA
Color; PAL (J H C G)
PdS50, PdS58 purchase
Celebrates 'wheelchair basketball' and the courage of disabled people. Features the Harlem Globetrotters.
Health and Safety; Physical Education and Recreation
Dist - EDPAT

A Whole New Image 15 MIN
16mm
Color (H C A)
Presents information about the uniform industry, covering the relative merits of buying or renting, which uniform fabrics are best for comfort, laundering, color and shrinkage suitability, damage resistance and strength.
Home Economics
Dist - KLEINW **Prod** - KLEINW

A Whole New World 17 MIN
16mm / U-matic / VHS
Color (H C A)
LC 75-705717
Uses the experiences of a man whose early contacts turned him away from libraries to show the nonuser the benefits of using a library.
Education; English Language; Sociology
Dist - FEIL **Prod** - CLEVPL 1970

A Whole new world
VHS
Baby's world series
Color (G)
$29.95 purchase _ #DIS24159V-K
Relives birth from the infant's point of view. Explains how newborns get their needs met and shows them battling to gain control of their bodies and conquer movement. Part of a three-part series that demonstrates the process of maturing from infancy into walking, talking, thinking human beings.
Health and Safety; Psychology
Dist - CAMV

Whole Numbers 10 MIN
U-matic / VHS
Basic Shop Math Series
Color (IND)
Explains addition, subtraction, multiplication and divisions. Includes fractions.
Industrial and Technical Education; Mathematics
Dist - LEIKID **Prod** - LEIKID

Whole Numbers 30 MIN
16mm
Mathematics for Elementary School Teachers Series
Color (T)
Studies whole numbers, and examines various other numeration systems. To be used following 'PRE - NUMBER IDEAS.'.
Mathematics
Dist - MLA **Prod** - SMSG 1963

Whole Numbers and Fractions
VHS / U-matic
Basic Shop Math Series
Color
Mathematics
Dist - VTRI **Prod** - VTRI

Whole Numbers and Fractions
U-matic / VHS
Basic Shop Math - Spanish Series
Color (SPANISH)
Foreign Language; Mathematics
Dist - VTRI **Prod** - VTRI

Whole Numbers - Division 30 MIN
VHS
Mathematics Series
Color (J)
LC 90713155
Explains division of whole numbers. Third of 157 installments in the Mathematics Series.
Mathematics
Dist - GPN

Whole numbers - division
VHS
Basic mathematical skills series
Color (I J H)
$125.00 purchase _ #1003
Teaches the concepts of whole numbers and division. Presents part of a series that provides 27 videos, each between 25 and 30 minutes long, that explain and reinforce basic mathematical concepts. Tutors the student through definitions, theorems, step - by - step solutions and examples. Videos are also available in a set.
Mathematics
Dist - LANDMK

Whole numbers - multiplication, order of operations
VHS
Basic mathematical skills series
Color (I J H)
$125.00 purchase _ #1002
Teaches the concepts of whole numbers, multiplication and order of operations. Presents part of a series that provides 27 videos, each between 25 and 30 minutes long, that explain and reinforce basic mathematical concepts. Tutors the student through definitions, theorems, step - by - step solutions and examples. Videos are also available in a set.
Mathematics
Dist - LANDMK

Whole Numbers - Multiplictions, Order of Operations 30 MIN
VHS
Mathematics Series
Color (J)
LC 90713155
Explains multiplication and order of operations with whole numbers. The second of 157 installments in the Mathematics Series.
Mathematics
Dist - GPN

Whole numbers - place value, addition and subtraction, rounding
VHS
Basic mathematical skills series
Color (I J H)
Teaches the concepts of whole numbers, addition and subtraction. Presents part of a series that provides 27 videos, each between 25 and 30 minutes long, that explain and reinforce basic mathematical concepts. Tutors the student through definitions, theorems, step - by - step solutions and examples. Videos are also available in a set.
Mathematics
Dist - LANDMK
GPN

The Whole Picture 10 MIN
U-matic
Color (J H C)
LC 81-706502
Tells how a local council commissions an artist to create murals in an inner city park and beside an inner city road. Shows how the artist works with unemployed and inexperienced people as assistants.
Civics and Political Systems; Fine Arts; Sociology
Dist - TASCOR **Prod** - SYDUN 1980

The Whole Shootin' Match 108 MIN
16mm
B&W
Depicts the rags - to - riches - to - rags story of two 'good ole boys' from America's heartland. Tells how Lloyd and Frank are constantly on the lookout for the gig that will supply them with endless amounts of money.
Sociology
Dist - FIRS **Prod** - FIRS

The Whole Town's Talking 86 MIN
16mm
B&W
Relates the story of a timid little clerk who is mistaken for Public Enemy Number One. Stars Edward G Robinson, Jean Arthur and Wallace Ford. Directed by John Ford.
Fine Arts
Dist - TWYMAN **Prod** - CPC 1935

The Whole Truth 25 MIN
U-matic / VHS / 16mm
Color
LC 78-701107
Looks at the process of producing a television quiz show by offering a backstage glimpse at the TV program To Tell The Truth.
Fine Arts
Dist - TEXFLM **Prod** - WASPEW 1978

The Whole World is Watching 55 MIN
16mm
Public Broadcast Laboratory Series
B&W (H C A)
LC 77-703087
Discusses the question of bias in television new - cast - ing with the help of David Brinkley, Walter Cronkite and critics such as Senator John O Pastore and John Fischer. Shows that a person who is completely objec - tive would be a vegetable and that what is strived for is fairness, not simply objectivity. Discusses tele - vision coverage of the 1968 Democratic National Con - vention and the restraints upon television such as how advertising may influence what news is broadcast.
Psychology; Social Science; Sociology
Dist - IU **Prod** - NET 1969

The Whole World is Watching 18 MIN
16mm
Color (H C A)
LC 72-700399
Combines sounds of rock music, excerpts from various speeches and scenes of the violence and disorder that occurred during the 1968 Democratic National Convention in Chicago to outline the major events and to characterize some of the major attitudes and forces at work there.
Civics and Political Systems; Psychology; Sociology
Dist - MMA **Prod** - MMA 1969

Wholesalers and Distributors
VHS
Retail Video Series
$89.95 purchase _ #RPMP10V
Points out the importance of merchandise selection and lists the marketing activities of a wholesaler. Identifies the role of the industrial distributor.
Business and Economics
Dist - CAREER **Prod** - CAREER

Wholesalers and Distributors 30 MIN
U-matic / VHS
Marketing Perspectives Series
Color
Covers marketing activities performed by wholesalers, the importance of merchandise selection by the wholesaler and the role of the industrial distributor.
Business and Economics; Education
Dist - WFVTAE **Prod** - MATC

Wholesaling 30 MIN
VHS
Color (J H C G)
$69.95 purchase _ #CCP0138V
Shows how related industries contribute to the production of styles that become inventories in retail stores. Reveals that fashion merchandising begins long before styles hit stores. Discloses how it begins with a designer who conceives of garment styles and fabrication and progresses through wholesaling where merchandise is manufactured and sold to retail stores. Discusses how professionals in design and wholesale warehouses buy fabrics, design, sell and produce clothing lines.
Business and Economics; Home Economics
Dist - CAMV **Prod** - CAMV 1994

Who'll Save Our Children 96 MIN
VHS / U-matic
Color (H C A)
Describes what happens when Marjory and Tommy Garver are abandoned by their parents and are literally dumped on the doorstep of the Lavers, a middle - aged, childless couple. Shows what happens when the Lavers must fight for the children when the natural parents attempt to reclaim them. Stars Shirley Jones and Len Cariou. Based on the book WHO'LL SAVE OUR CHILDREN by Rachel Maddux.
Fine Arts; Sociology
Dist - TIMLIF **Prod** - TIMLIF 1982

Wholly Cow 11 MIN
16mm
Color
LC 75-700165
Uses animation and live action to illustrate how food is processed in a cow's four stomachs, how nutrients absorbed from the digestive tract are converted to milk and the role of the udder.
Agriculture; Home Economics; Science - Natural; Social Science
Dist - NDC **Prod** - NDC 1975

Whom shall I send 21 MIN
VHS
Mission videos series
Color (G R)
$12.50 purchase _ #S12370
Profiles Missouri Synod Lutheran missionaries. Stresses the importance of missions. Targets high school and college students, but encourages all to consider how they might serve in missions.
Guidance and Counseling; Literature and Drama; Religion and Philosophy
Dist - CPH **Prod** - LUMIS

A Whopping small dinosaur 27 MIN
VHS
Color; PAL (H)
Follows a team of paleontologists into the Painted Desert to extract the remains of the oldest dinosaur yet discovered. Chronicles how the bones are removed from the ground, shipped to a museum and assembled. Discusses the ancient world of the dinosaur when they were masters of the Earth.
Science - Physical
Dist - VIEWTH **Prod** - VIEWTH

Whore in the gulf 30 MIN
VHS
Color (G)
$30.00 purchase
Features a weekly alternative to mainstream Gulf Crisis coverage, after January 1991, with an irreverent slant. Responds to censorship and the nationalistic zeal produced by the networks by documenting the Bay Area anti - war movement. Children, the elderly, people of color, women, lesbians, gays and white men discuss their views on world peace, Saddam Hussein, the growth of fascism in America, sexual abuse of women by men in the military, and activism in the 1990s. Includes music videos, CNN, peace - positive propaganda and street theater.
Civics and Political Systems; Fine Arts; Sociology
Dist - CANCIN **Prod** - LEIGHC 1991

Whores and healers 28 MIN
VHS
Color (G)
$30.00 purchase
Addresses the role of prostitutes and women as healers and teachers. Includes CAL - PEP - California Prostitutes' Education Project. Takes an insider's look at a model HIV - prevention - education program designed and implemented by prostitutes and ex - prostitutes for prostitutes, IV - drug users, and their partners; POCAAN - People of Color Against AIDS Network; the Yeastie Girlz' safe sex rap, Put a Lid on It; Scarlot Harlot's Safe Sex Slut; prostitutes at the 6th International AIDS Conference; and interviews with women from Thailand and Brazil. Recommended as an educational tool for health, sex, and service classes and programs.
Civics and Political Systems; Fine Arts; Health and Safety; Sociology
Dist - CANCIN **Prod** - LEIGHC 1990

Who's afraid of birthdays 30 MIN
VHS
Color (G A R)
$39.95 purchase, $10.00 rental _ #35 - 85 - 2076
Profiles Ruth Youngdahl Nelson. Reveals aspects of her life, including how Nelson learned to waterski at age 70 and has ministered on three continents.
Religion and Philosophy; Sociology
Dist - APH

Who's afraid of opera series
Features soprano Joan Sutherland and her animal puppets presenting opera highlights - in a series of four programs - designed to make anyone unfamiliar with opera comfortable with this form of musical drama. Uses humor to balance tragedy in some operas and add more fun and suspense to the lighter ones. Each 60-minute video spotlights two operas. Operas include Faust, La Traviata, the Barber of Seville, Mignon and four others. Stories are told in English, with arias sung in original languages.

Barber of Seville, the, and, Lucia Di Lammermoor - Vol 3	60 MIN
Faust, and, Rigoletto - Vol 1	60 MIN
La Traviata, and, Daughter of the Regiment - Vol 2	60 MIN
Mignon, and, La Perichole - Vol 4	60 MIN

Dist - KULTUR

Who's Afraid of Opera Series

The Barber of Seville	30 MIN
Daughter of the regiment	30 MIN
Faust	30 MIN
La Perichole	30 MIN
La Traviata	30 MIN
Lucia Di Lammermoor	30 MIN
Mignon	30 MIN
Rigoletto	30 MIN

Dist - PHENIX

Who's Afraid of the Dark 30 MIN
VHS / BETA
Color
Explores the fear of the dark and gives detailed methods for conquering that fear.
Fine Arts; Literature and Drama
Dist - HOMEAF **Prod** - HOMEAF

Who's Afraid of Virginia Woolf
VHS / U-matic
American Literature Series
B&W (G C J)
$89 purchase _ # 05700 - 85
Screens the film version of Edward Albee's play about a troubled marriage. Stars Richard Burton and Elizabeth Taylor.
Fine Arts
Dist - CHUMAN

Who's afraid of Virginia Woolf 127 MIN
VHS
Color (H C)
$79.00 purchase _ #05700 - 126
Stars Richard Burton and Elizabeth Taylor in an Edward Albee play about a troubled marriage.
Literature and Drama; Sociology
Dist - GA **Prod** - GA

Who's batting for Britain 30 MIN
VHS
Birthrights series
Color; PAL (H C A)
PdS65 purchase
Investigates the meaning of contemporary British identity from the perspective of black Britons who argue that racism and bigotry continue to be pervasive elements in British society. Suggests that many black Britons wish to help in the creation of a new British identity, but cannot do so unless negative attitudes disappear. Part of the Birthrights series.
Social Science; Sociology
Dist - BBCENE

Who's Building Character 15 MIN
16mm
B&W
Presents new understanding for parents and teachers about how the home and the school can best cooperate to instill a sense of responsibility in children.
Religion and Philosophy
Dist - CPH **Prod** - CPH

Who's Caring 22 MIN
VHS / U-matic
Color
Studies the critical shortage of day - care facilities in the Twin Cities.
Geography - United States; Sociology
Dist - WCCOTV **Prod** - WCCOTV 1981

Who's cheating
VHS
Bippity boppity bunch series
Color (K P I R)
$14.95 purchase _ #35 - 820 - 8579
Portrays two friends who discover the negative consequences of cheating.
Literature and Drama; Religion and Philosophy
Dist - APH **Prod** - FAMF

Who's Doing it - Sexual Attitudes in America 13 MIN
U-matic / VHS
Color (C A)
Explores current sexual attitudes in America. Combines animation and live interviews with people of all ages.
Health and Safety; Psychology; Sociology
Dist - MMRC **Prod** - MMRC

Who's for Tennis 7 MIN
16mm
Color (J)
LC 77-709230
Evaluates the condition of tennis in Australia, and discusses the wide popularity of the game and its future prospects.
Geography - World; Physical Education and Recreation
Dist - AUIS **Prod** - ANAIB 1969

Who's for training 25 MIN
VHS
Supervisors series
Color (A)
PdS50 purchase
Features a number of supervisors demonstrating their approach to training in the workplace. Part of an eight-part series designed to help supervisors - particularly newly-appointed ones - to understand the demands of their individual roles through the experience of established supervisors who offer personal insights and strategies from within a framework of good practice.
Business and Economics; Psychology
Dist - BBCENE

Who's going to care for these children - babies with AIDS 14 MIN
VHS
Color (H C G)
$195.00 purchase, $50.00 rental
Introduces individuals who are providing loving homes to desperately needy infants. Meets Darolyn and Bill Sybesma who have five children and have taken in their second foster child with AIDS and others who are caring for such children. Produced by Carolyn Grifel, Cathryn Garland, Chris Riback and others from the Columbia School of Journalism.
Health and Safety; Sociology
Dist - FLMLIB

Who's going to pay for these donuts, anyway 58 MIN
VHS
Color (G)
$75.00 rental, $275.00 purchase
Documents Japanese - American video artist Janice Tanaka's search for her father after a 40 year separation. Tells the story of their reunion when she found him living in a halfway house for the mentally ill on Los Angeles' skid row through the use of a brilliant collage of interviews, family photographs, archival footage and personal narration. A rare look at the connections between racism and mental illness.
Fine Arts; Psychology; Sociology
Dist - WMEN **Prod** - TANAKA 1992

Who's Got the Right to Rhodesia 53 MIN
U-matic / VHS / 16mm
Color (H C A)
LC 77-703311
Documents the racial conflict in Rhodesia. Includes interviews with leaders of both sides and raises the question of U S involvement.
Civics and Political Systems; Geography - World; Sociology
Dist - CAROUF **Prod** - CBSTV 1977

Who's Got the Right to Rhodesia, Pt 1 26 MIN
U-matic / VHS / 16mm
Color (H C A)
LC 77-703311
Documents the racial conflict in Rhodesia. Includes interviews with leaders of both sides and raises the question of U S involvement.
History - World
Dist - CAROUF **Prod** - CBSTV 1977

Who's Got the Right to Rhodesia, Pt 2 27 MIN
16mm / U-matic / VHS
Color (H C A)
LC 77-703311
Documents the racial conflict in Rhodesia. Includes interviews with leaders of both sides and raises the question of U S involvement.
Dist - CAROUF **Prod** - CBSTV 1977

Who's in Charge 15 MIN
U-matic / VHS
It's all Up to You Series
Color (I J)
Discusses government as an institution established by groups of people for themselves.
Civics and Political Systems
Dist - AITECH **Prod** - COOPED 1978

Who's in Charge 24 MIN
U-matic / VHS
Color
Focuses on the problems of a newly promoted foreman under the pressure of three challenges, communicating an unwelcome management decision, handling a breach of discipline and facing an attack on his authority.
Business and Economics
Dist - VISUCP **Prod** - VISUCP

Who's in Charge 56 MIN
U-matic / VHS
We the People Series
Color (G)
$279.00, $179.00 purchase _ #AD - 1424
Explores the distribution of powers in a system that divides authority to govern between the states and the central government, among Congress, the president and the courts, and between the people and the government. Shows citizens fighting to prevent the federal government's locating a nuclear waste dump in their neighborhood. Part of a four - part series on the American Constitution.
Civics and Political Systems
Dist - FOTH **Prod** - FOTH

Who's in Charge - Confrontation Handling for Supervisors and Managers 23 MIN
U-matic / VHS
Color (A)
Shows the right way and the wrong way for a manager to handle challenges to his authority. Treats direct attacks on managerial authority, getting a group to do what it is opposed to doing and breaches of discipline.
Business and Economics; Psychology
Dist - XICOM **Prod** - XICOM

Who's in Charge Here 15 MIN
16mm
Color (H C A)
LC 81-700218
Proposes that U S security depends not only on a well - equipped military but also on an improved and healthy economy. Contends that the United States should turn some of its technology over from arms stockpiling to producing goods for consumers. Narrated by Eli Wallach.
Business and Economics; Civics and Political Systems
Dist - IWO **Prod** - IAM 1980

Who's in Charge of Lincoln and the Lucky Stone 14 MIN
U-matic / VHS
Readit Series
Color (P I)
LC 83-706833
Introduces two stories, the first about a man's adventures involving a sack of stolen money and the second about a lucky stone which provides good fortune for its various owners. Based on the books Who's In Charge Of Lincoln by Dale Fife and The Lucky Stone by Lucille Clifton.
English Language; Literature and Drama
Dist - AITECH **Prod** - POSIMP 1982

Who's in Charge Series
Building self - esteem 30 MIN
Coping with grief and loss 30 MIN
Managing Stress 30 MIN
Surviving Illness with Spirit 30 MIN
Dist - WGTETV

Who's in Our Family 30 MIN
U-matic
Magic Ring II Series
(K P)
Continues the aim of the first series to bring added freshness to the commonplace and assist children to discover more about the many things in their world. Each program starts with the familiar, goes to the less familiar, then the new, and ends by blending new and old information.
Education; Literature and Drama
Dist - ACCESS **Prod** - ACCESS 1986

Who's in the control room 50 MIN
VHS
More than a game series
Color (A)
PdS99 purchase _ Not available in the United States or Canada
Looks at the influence of television on the world of sports. Part of an eight-part series that looks at sports as an integral part of every civilization, offering participation, the opportunity to excel and to belong. Asks if this is a romantic view of sport.
Physical Education and Recreation
Dist - BBCENE

Who's Keeping Score - Documentary 59 MIN
U-matic / VHS
Who's Keeping Score Series
Color
Discusses the minimum competency testing for reading, writing and math, and the questions and objections that have been raised. Hosted by Mike Farrell.
Education; Psychology
Dist - USNAC **Prod** - USHHS 1981

Who's Keeping Score - Hearing Day 1 59 MIN
VHS / U-matic
Who's Keeping Score Series
Color
LC 82-706626
Presents a summary of the first day of hearings held to discuss minimum competency testing and its benefits or harmful effects on students, curricula, teaching and public perception of educational quality. Commentary by Mike Farrell.
Education; Psychology
Dist - USNAC **Prod** - USHHS

Who's Keeping Score - Hearing Day 2 59 MIN
VHS / U-matic
Who's Keeping Score Series WASHINGTON, DC 20409
Color
Presents a summary of the second day of hearings held to discuss minimum competency testing and its benefits or harmful effects on students, curricula, teaching and public perception of educational quality. Commentary by Mike Farrell.
Education; Psychology
Dist - USNAC **Prod** - USHHS

Who's Keeping Score - Hearing Day 3 59 MIN
VHS / U-matic
Who's Keeping Score Series WASHINGTON, DC 20409
Color
Presents a summary of the third day of hearings held to discuss minimum competency testing and its benefits or harmful effects on students, curricula, teaching and public perception of educational quality. Commentary by Mike Farrell.
Education; Psychology
Dist - USNAC **Prod** - USHHS

Who's Keeping Score Series
Who's Keeping Score - Hearing Day 2 59 MIN
Who's Keeping Score - Hearing Day 3 59 MIN
Dist - USNAC

Who's Keeping Score Series
Who's Keeping Score - Documentary 59 MIN
Who's Keeping Score - Hearing Day 1 59 MIN
Dist - USNAC

Who's killing Calvert City 60 MIN
VHS
Frontline series
Color; Captioned (G)
$150.00 purchase _ #FRON - 717K
Focuses on Calvert City, Kentucky, a town which has enjoyed the economic benefit of three chemical plants but now must deal with the resulting toxic waste. Examines the conflict between environmentalists and chemical manufacturers through interviews with experts and local citizens.
Business and Economics; Sociology
Dist - PBS **Prod** - DOCCON 1990

Who's Minding the Farm 60 MIN
VHS / U-matic
(G)
Features field interviews with both management and labor representatives in agricultural industry. Explores structural changes in the farming system, focusing on family, tenant and collective farming. Dicsusses pros and cons of the systems highlighted.
Agriculture; Sociology
Dist - GPN **Prod** - NETV

Who's Ok, Who's not Ok - an Introduction to Abnormal Psychology 43 MIN
VHS
Color (J H)
Teaches your students to identify normal, neurotic, and psychotic behavior. Elucidates such concepts as phobia, depression, obsessive compulsive personality, schizophrenia, paranoia, manic depression, hypochondria, and melancholia.
Psychology
Dist - HRMC **Prod** - HRMC 1976

Who's on First 14 MIN
16mm
Color (J)
Questions the stereotype of girls as non - athletic as seen through the eyes of members of a women's softball team on a nine - game winning streak.
Physical Education and Recreation; Sociology
Dist - JBFL **Prod** - JBFL 1975

Who's on First 8 MIN
16mm / U-matic / VHS
Color (I)
Features Bud Abbott and Lou Costello's routine of mistaken identities on a baseball team.
Fine Arts; Literature and Drama
Dist - SALENG **Prod** - SALENG

Who's Out There 28 MIN
16mm
Color
LC 75-702491
Explores the new view of extraterrestrial life now emerging from the results of probes to the planets. Discusses the conclusion of a number of distinguished scientists that other intelligent civilizations exist in the universe.
History - World; Science - Natural; Science - Physical
Dist - USNAC **Prod** - NASA 1975

Who's Out There
16mm
Color
Presents Nobel Prize winning scientists who conduct an exploration of life in outer space. Narrated by Orson Welles.
Science - Natural; Science - Physical
Dist - DIRECT **Prod** - DREWAS 1973

Who's Out There Listening 15 MIN
VHS / U-matic
Broadcasting Series SPRINGFIELD, VA 22151
Color (J H)
Explains how the effectiveness of radio and television programming is determined.
Fine Arts; Industrial and Technical Education; Social Science; Sociology
Dist - CTI **Prod** - CTI

Who's Responsible 12 MIN
16mm / U-matic / VHS
Color (T)
Attempts to show how to recognize and eliminate negative attitudes about responsibility by telling the story of a worker who becomes a scapegoat when things go wrong at the office.
Psychology
Dist - EBEC **Prod** - VISF 1983

Who's Responsible 15 MIN
U-matic
Workers at Risk Series
(A)
Substitutes foresight for an it can't happen to me attitude and shows job safety as a joint responsibility of workers and employers.
Health and Safety
Dist - ACCESS **Prod** - ACCESS 1982

Who's Supporting the Kids 60 MIN
VHS / U-matic
Color (C A)
Examines the problem of unpaid child support. Shows a tough family court judge at work with this problem. Looks at the personal stories of former families in litigation, of absent fathers, and of mothers in need of money awarded by the court that they have never received.
Civics and Political Systems; Guidance and Counseling; Sociology
Dist - UEUWIS **Prod** - UEUWIS 1984

Who's the Cleanest 7 MIN
U-matic / VHS / 16mm
Little Dog Series
Color (I)

LC 84-707089
Tells the story of Little Dog and his friend Kitten as they become involved with a duck playing in a mudhole and a cow with brown spots on her side.
Fine Arts
Dist - PHENIX **Prod** - KRATKY 1983

Who's There for the Victim 22 MIN
U-matic / VHS / 16mm
Color (A)
LC 81-701512
Demonstrates how the Rape Victim Advocates serve the special needs of the rape victim. Shows the advocates offering immediate emotional and informational support as well as interacting with medical personnel, police and family members.
Social Science; Sociology
Dist - CORF **Prod** - WTTWTV 1981

Who's to Blame 10 MIN
16mm
Techniques of Defensive Driving Film Series
Color (I)
Explains the concepts of defensive driving.
Health and Safety
Dist - NSC **Prod** - NSC

Who's to Blame 59 MIN
VHS / U-matic
Child Welfare Training Tapes Series
Color
Deals with the issue of sexual abuse of children. Shows three interview sessions with a client who is seeking help with family problems. Shows the client's fears about therapy and her self - doubts in the face of problems.
Psychology; Sociology
Dist - UWISC **Prod** - OHIOSU 1980

Who's watching you
VHS
Color (G)
$21.95 purchase _ #SPE000
Examines methods of protection of privacy.
Civics and Political Systems
Dist - SIV

Who's who in the kook capital 30 MIN
16mm
B&W (G)
$50.00 rental
Documents Bay Area people and events such as the Bums and Winos Ball, a Beatitude Poets Reading, a nude beach, the Hooker's Ball. By Richard Beveridge.
Fine Arts; History - United States
Dist - CANCIN

Who's who in the Zoo 12 MIN
U-matic / VHS / 16mm
Color (P I)
$305, $215 purchase _ #74514
Talks about the differnt people who work in the zoo and the animals they take care of.
Science - Natural
Dist - CORF

A Who's who of the Prehistoric World 26 MIN
VHS / 16mm
Color (J)
$149.00 purchase, $75.00 rental _ #0D - 2212
Examines a now extinct line of evolution in the Australian outback, in an effort to better understand the development of Australia's unique animal life.
Geography - World; Science - Natural
Dist - FOTH

Who's your friend
VHS
Jake's world series
Color (K P)
$89.95 purchase
Introduces five short animated stories which illustrate friendships. Features Jake, the gnome, and animals.
Literature and Drama; Psychology
Dist - COLLIE **Prod** - COLLIE

Who's your mother 25 MIN
VHS
Where there's life series
Color; PAL (G)
PdS25 purchase
Discloses that, although making babies used to be an act reserved exclusively for two, in the test - tube age three or even four people can be involved and recently a woman gave birth to her own grandchildren. Ponders the morality surrounding human egg donations. Talks to donors and recipients and asks whether genetic engineering is getting out of hand. Features Dr Miriam Stoppard as host in a series of shows making sense of science and treating controversial subjects in an informed way. Contact distributor about availability outside the United Kingdom.
Health and Safety; Sociology
Dist - ACADEM

Whose Air is it Anyway 23 MIN
VHS / 16mm
Color (PRO)
$495.00 purchase, $125.00 rental, $35.00 preview
Discusses aspects of the controvery around smoking policies in the business place. Addresses the feelings of smokers and non - smokers. Presents medical information about the dangers of smoking and passive inhalation of smoke. Offers ways to smoothly implement a smoking policy. Includes leader's guide.
Business and Economics; Guidance and Counseling; Psychology
Dist - UTM **Prod** - UTM

Whose air is it anyway 23 MIN
8mm cartridge / VHS / BETA / U-matic
Color; CC; PAL (IND G)
$395.00 purchase, $175.00 rental _ #MVP - 001
Introduces employees to the benefits of a smoke - free workplace. Focuses on a definition of passive smoking and its effects on nonsmokers. Discusses the physical effects of exposure to carbon monoxide, why smokers can't simply quit, four simple tactics smokers can employ to resist the urge to smoke, how nonsmokers can help their smoking co - workers, and more. Includes a leader's guide.
Guidance and Counseling; Health and Safety; Psychology
Dist - BNA

Whose America is it 46 MIN
VHS / 16mm
Color (H C A)
$445.00, $330.00
Illustrates that many Americans accuse immigrants of depriving Americans of jobs and threatening America's sense of nationhood by refusing to learn English. Correspondent Bill Moyers examines the problems created by immigrants, legal and illegal, and the question of what to do about the new strangers in our midst.
History - United States; Sociology
Dist - CAROUF **Prod** - CBSTV 1985

Whose bread you eat, their song you'll sing 12 MIN
VHS
Color (J H C G T A)
$65.00 purchase, $35.00 rental
Encourages high school and college students to consider the social implications of their career choices. Suggests, for example, that the winding down of the Cold War will mean fewer job opportunities in the defense industry for science and engineering students. Includes workbook. Narrated by actor Esai Morales. Produced by the Interfaith Center to Reverse the Arms Race.
Guidance and Counseling; Sociology
Dist - EFVP

Whose Child is this 28 MIN
16mm / U-matic / VHS
Color (H C A)
LC 79-701414
Presents a dramatization about a teacher who discovers one of her students is being physically abused by his father. Shows the legal steps which result when the teacher reports her discovery.
Education; Sociology
Dist - LCOA **Prod** - JRLLK 1979

Whose fault is it, anyway 30 MIN
VHS
Color; PAL (H G)
Shows how a typical minor accident involving three cars and a motorcycle resulted from small degrees of negligence and lack of observation by all the drivers concerned, none of whom accepts any responsibility for the accident. Takes on the form of a fantasy as the passing CID Inspector and Sergeant are transformed into Sherlock Holmes and Dr Watson, who arrive on the scene in a vintage car and proceed to unravel 'The Mysterious Case of the Four Cs - Care, Courtesy, Consideration and Concentration' in the traditional Holmes style. Produced for the Company of Veteran Motorists with the Natl Road Safety Officers' Natl Films Committee.
Health and Safety
Dist - BHA

Whose game is it anyway 50 MIN
VHS
More than a game series
Color (A)
PdS99 purchase _ Not available in the United States or Canada
Asks if sports for all can be more than a dream. Part of an eight-part series that looks at sports as an integral part of every civilization, offering participation, the opportunity to excel and to belong. Asks if this is a romantic view of sport.
Physical Education and Recreation
Dist - BBCENE

Whose is it - Possessive Adjectives - 12 30 MIN
VHS
English 101 - Ingles 101 Series
Color (H)
$125.00 purchase
Presents a series of thirty 30 - minute programs in basic English for native speakers of Spanish. Focuses on a specific topic in order to emphasize a particular grammatical point or set of idioms. English is used from the beginning as the primary language of instruction but Spanish translations are included to ensure understanding. Part 12 looks at forms of possessive adjectives, using possessive adjectives correctly, possessive adjectives and possessive nouns.
English Language; Foreign Language
Dist - AITECH **Prod** - UPRICO 1988

Whose liability is it - the practice of nursing and the law 62 MIN
VHS
Color (PRO C G)
$250.00 purchase, $50.00 rental _ #972, #973
Addresses legal aspects of the nursing profession, focusing on the liability issues facing nurses in their day - to - day professional duties. Covers nurses' liability, the legal impact of nursing decisions on the hospital, patient consent, confidentiality with respect to AIDS patients, the right to refuse treatment and no feed - no hydration orders. Includes workbook and discussion guide, testing information and American Journal of Nursing Company CNE credit application.
Civics and Political Systems; Health and Safety; Psychology
Dist - CATHHA

Whose life is it, anyway 118 MIN
VHS
Color (H)
$97.00 purchase _ #04628 - 126
Portrays the fight of a quadriplegic's fight for his right to die with dignity. Stars Richard Dreyfuss.
Health and Safety; Sociology
Dist - GA **Prod** - GA

Whose Neighborhood is this 20 MIN
U-matic / VHS / 16mm
Color
Looks at neighborhood crimes from the perspectives of the victim, the criminal and the police. Shows a variety of neighborhoods reacting to the problem.
Civics and Political Systems; Health and Safety; Social Science; Sociology
Dist - CORF **Prod** - MITCHG

Whose news is it 30 MIN
VHS
Inside story series
Color (G)
$50.00 purchase _ #INST - 401
Reviews how press coverage of the Grenada invasion was restricted by the U S government. Considers whether the restriction was good or bad. Interviews Jimmy Carter, Caspar Weinberger, Walter Cronkite, Patrick Buchanan and others. Hosted by Hodding Carter.
Business and Economics; Literature and Drama; Social Science
Dist - PBS

Whose Problem is it 25 MIN
16mm / U-matic / VHS
Color (A)
Looks at the high cost which substance abuse extracts from American productivity. Deals with individual recognition of the problem, the effects of substance abuse on the individual and his job, role of the supervisor in problem identification and how friends can help bring abuse to the surface.
Business and Economics; Health and Safety
Dist - CORF **Prod** - OLINC 1982

Whose Right to Bear Arms 59 MIN
16mm
Color
LC 77-713329
Discusses gun control legislation and the success of lobbying efforts in the United States. Includes interviews with senators Edward Kennedy, Thomas Dodd and Roman Hruska, and with Franklin Orth, executive director of the National Rifle Association.
Civics and Political Systems
Dist - NBCTV **Prod** - NBCTV 1967

Whose risk is it anyway 17 MIN
VHS
Color; PAL; NTSC (IND G)
PdS40, PdS57 purchase
Presents a common - sense approach to health and safety hazards in the workplace to help save lives as well as to help small firms comply with new legislation in the United Kingdom. Explains risk assessments, which have been compulsory from 1993. Includes booklets.
Business and Economics; Health and Safety
Dist - CFLVIS

Whose Sea this is 26 MIN
VHS / 16mm
Blue Revolution Series
Color (J)
$149.00 purchase, $75.00 rental _ #QD - 2292
Examines law and the sea and the effects of politics, nationalism and economics. The 12th of 16 installments of the Blue Revolution Series.
Civics and Political Systems; Social Science
Dist - FOTH

Whose Shoes 3 MIN
U-matic / VHS / 16mm
Magic Moments, Unit 1 - Let's Talk Series
Color (K P I)
LC 70-705922
Presents situations involving children making decisions. Discusses alternatives and what might have happened in each instance.
English Language
Dist - EBEC **Prod** - EBEC 1969

Whose Standard English 24 MIN
U-matic / VHS / 16mm
Color (T)
LC 77-700501
Focuses on the sensitivity and special skills required in teaching textbook English to dialect - speaking children.
Education; English Language
Dist - GREAVW **Prod** - GREAVW 1975

Whose world view 20 MIN
VHS
Color (G)
$35.00 purchase
Records a Consultation on Global Communication and Justice held in St Lucia, West Indies. Comments on the influence of North American media upon the lives of people in the Caribbean region and upon how the church should respond to the situation.
Civics and Political Systems; History - World; Sociology
Dist - INMED **Prod** - INMED 1992

Why 30 MIN
U-matic / VHS
This is My will Series
Color
Examines the need for a will, the realities, estate administration and mysteries of probate.
Business and Economics; Sociology
Dist - PBS **Prod** - WMHTTV 1983

Why 22 MIN
16mm
Color (J H C A)
Documents the development of the UN from its charter in 1945 to current activity. Tours the UN in New York and the International Court Of Justice in the Hague.
Civics and Political Systems
Dist - UILL **Prod** - UILL 1985

Why 55 15 MIN
16mm
Color
Dramatizes the margin of safety provided by driving at 55 miles per hour and points out that driving at 65 miles per hour does not necessarily get people to their destinations quicker. Examines the economic advantages of driving at the slower speed.
Health and Safety; Psychology
Dist - MATRIX **Prod** - MATRIX

Why a Newspaper 15 MIN
U-matic / VHS
Newspaper - Behind the Lines Series
Color (J H)
Shows how newspapers meet the needs of the public.
Literature and Drama; Social Science; Sociology
Dist - CTI **Prod** - CTI

Why African Heritage 30 MIN
VHS / U-matic
Afro - American Perspectives Series
Color (C)
Discusses the importance of the African heritage to black Americans.
History - United States
Dist - MDCPB **Prod** - MDDE

Why Algorithms
16mm
B&W
Examines the necessity for algorithms and discusses their salient characteristics.
Mathematics
Dist - OPENU **Prod** - OPENU

Why all landfills leak 35 MIN
VHS
Color (G)
$10.00 purchase
Presents a lecture by Dr Peter Montague, Director of the Environmental Research Foundation, who explains about landfills - how they are supposed to work, why they don't work and how toxic wastes can leak into the soil and groundwater of communities.
Science - Natural; Sociology
Dist - GRNPCE **Prod** - GRNPCE 1991

Why Am I Doing this 15 MIN
VHS / 16mm
Color (H C A PRO)
$285.00 purchase, $75.00 rental _ #8040
Examines the lives of several victims of obsessive compulsive disorders, OCDs. Estimates that five million people are plagued by strange and disruptive thoughts that cause them to perform irrational and excessive acts. Includes such behaviors as obsessive cleaning from morning to night, the inability to throw anything out, having to check doors and appliances over and over and over, and ritualized handwashing, the most common OCD.
Psychology; Science - Natural
Dist - AIMS **Prod** - ABCVID 1988

Why Am I Here 9 MIN
16mm
Color
LC 74-705956
Shows Mr Roberts, who has been hospitalized for stomach problems and cannot understand why he has been referred to the dental service for oral examination. Tells of the importance of early detection of cancer in this area.
Health and Safety
Dist - USNAC **Prod** - USVA 1968

Why America Burns 57 MIN
U-matic / VHS / 16mm
Nova Series
Color (H C A)
Looks at why America has more fire - caused deaths than any other industrialized country. Documents how fast certain plastics catch fire, why modern high - rise buildings become towering infernos and how fire caused by cigarettes claims more than 2,000 lives annually.
Health and Safety; Social Science
Dist - TIMLIF **Prod** - WGBHTV 1982

Why Animals Live Where they do 11 MIN
16mm / U-matic / VHS
Color (P)
LC 78-701172
Explains how animals are suited to a particular environment by studying different animals in four envionments, woodpeckers, opossums and carpenter ants in a forest, prairie dogs, grasshoppers and meadowlarks in a grassland, lizards and snakes in a desert, and spoonbills, frogs and fish in a pond.
Science - Natural
Dist - CORF **Prod** - CORF 1969

Why Appeasement 20 MIN
U-matic / VHS / 16mm
Twentieth Century History Series
Color (H C A)
Describes the period in 1938 when Hitler demanded a portion of Czechoslovakia and Great Britain's Prime Minister Neville Chamberlain, eager to avoid war, gave him what he wanted. Tells how Germany absorbed all of Czechoslovakia and invaded Poland, leading to war with Britain.
History - World
Dist - FI **Prod** - BBCTV 1981

Why Appeasement - Pt 5 20 MIN
16mm
Twentieth Century History Series - Vol II
Color (S)
$380.00 purchase _ #548 - 9235
Illuminates the events and issues which shaped our modern world. Uses archival footage, maps, drawings, feature film segments, paintings and posters to illustrate historic events. The first thirteen programs are available separately on 16mm. Part 5 of Volume II of thirteen programs, 'Why Appeasement,' travels the road to World War II, from Hitler's demand for the Sudetenland and Chamberlain's acquiescence to the Nazi invasion of Poland and Britain's declaration of war.
Geography - World; History - World; Sociology
Dist - FI **Prod** - BBCTV 1981

Why Appraise? 8 MIN
U-matic / 35mm strip
Performance Appraisal Series Module 1
Color
Discusses the reasons why performance appraisal is so critical and shows that performance appraisal, when properly used, is an important and effective management tool.
Business and Economics; Psychology
Dist - RESEM **Prod** - RESEM

Why are Team - Teaching and Non - Grading Important 49 MIN
16mm
How to Provide Personalized Education in a Public School Series no 3; No 3
B&W (C T)
LC 79-700100
Presents Dr Goodlad as he explains how team - teaching and non - grading help to bridge the gap between the problems of school organization and individual learning differences.
Education; Psychology
Dist - SPF **Prod** - SPF 1966

Why are we here 3 MIN
16mm
Color (G)
$10.00 rental
Gives an account of a garage band working hard through dream sequences. Stars MX - 80 Sound whose savage musical pleading 'why are we here' collides with poetic impressionistic imagery. Directed by Graeme Whifler.
Fine Arts
Dist - CANCIN

Why are women so weird and men so strange - Part 3 50 MIN
VHS
Maximum marriage series
Color (H C G A R)
$10.00 rental _ #36 - 894003 - 533
Features Tim Timmons in a presentation of his concepts for 'Maximum Marriage.' Discusses differences between men and women.
Guidance and Counseling; Psychology; Sociology
Dist - APH **Prod** - WORD

Why are you so angry 33 MIN
VHS
Color (H G)
$395.00 purchase
Explores both the causes and effect of anger, from its roots to the final stage - dealing with the aftermath. Presents four dramatic vignettes illustrating the various stages of coping with anger - internalizing and hiding the feelings; resentment which is expressed as bitter sarcasm; aggressive behavior; unpredictable rage and impatience. Provides a positive approach to identifying problems and developing action plans to resolve anger. Teaches affected family members, and the perpetrator, the appropriate behavior and strategies for resolving anger in a healthy way. Incorporates realistic situations, ethnic diversity and sound counseling techniques.
Guidance and Counseling; Health and Safety; Sociology
Dist - FMSP

Why Art 29 MIN
16mm
Color
LC 76-703098
Studies the relationship between man and art.
Fine Arts
Dist - SBOE **Prod** - SBOE 1975

Why Battery Should Always be Clean 6 MIN
16mm
B&W
LC 76-703893
Demonstrates how to clean batteries to prevent engine failure. Shows how to wash with solution, wipe dry, check electrolyte level and grease terminals.
Health and Safety; Industrial and Technical Education
Dist - USNAC **Prod** - USA 1955

Why be a Roman Catholic - the Importance of Magisterium for Catholic Living 30 MIN
VHS / U-matic
Up to Date with the Catholic Church Series
Color
Religion and Philosophy
Dist - DSP **Prod** - DSP

Why be Down When You Can be Up 16 MIN
U-matic / VHS / 16mm
Color (J H)
Uses a blend of music and video techniques to present ideas on the use of marijuana by teenagers. Makes the point that there are a number of natural ways to feel good and it's up to each individual to discover what makes him happy or sad.
Health and Safety; Sociology
Dist - CORF **Prod** - DANLSD 1976

Why be Physically Fit 12 MIN
U-matic / VHS / 16mm
Fun to be Fit Series
Color (I)
Shows how being physically fit can help a person have more energy, look better, feel better and cope with stress. Illustrates the effect physical fitness has on the heart,

lungs, joints, tendons, muscular and cardio - respiratory systems.
Physical Education and Recreation
Dist - CORF **Prod** - DISNEY 1983

Why Bees have Stingers 15 MIN
VHS / U-matic
Tales of Wesakechak Series
Color (G)
Emphasizes that long ago bees could not protect themselves or their precious honey. The bees ask Wesakechak for help. After four days of thinking, Wesakechak gives them a gift. He tells them that by working together, using his gift, even Muskwa the bear will not be able to steal their honey.
Social Science
Dist - NAMPBC **Prod** - NAMPBC 1984

Why Believe in God - Why Accept Jesus as Your Lord 60 MIN
BETA / VHS
Up to Date with the Catholic Church Series
Color
Religion and Philosophy
Dist - DSP **Prod** - DSP

Why Bother 10 MIN
VHS
Color (PRO)
$395.00 purchase _ #N900VI051
Explores the needs and feelings of patients in order to sensitize hospital staff.
Health and Safety; Science
Dist - HSCIC

Why bother - Volume 5 40 MIN
VHS
Circle square series
Color (J H R)
$11.99 purchase _ #35 - 86756 - 979
Questions how a person can remain positive in a negative world. Considers this question from a Biblical perspective.
Religion and Philosophy
Dist - APH **Prod** - TYHP

Why boys and girls are different 6 MIN
VHS
Learning about sex series
Color (K)
$12.95 purchase _ #87EE1022
Describes the similarities and differences between boys and girls. Introduces the message that sexuality is a natural gift from God.
Guidance and Counseling; Literature and Drama; Religion and Philosophy; Sociology
Dist - CPH **Prod** - CPH

Why buildings make you sick 50 MIN
VHS
Horizon series
Color; PAL (C H A)
PdS99 purchase
Describes symptoms characteristic of sick building syndrome, an increasingly common problem caused by environmentally incompatible or problematic ventilation systems and construction techniques.
Industrial and Technical Education
Dist - BBCENE

Why Calibrate 16 MIN
16mm
Color
LC FIE67-86
Demonstrates the need for calibrating tests and monitoring equipment and shows how the U S Navy's calibration program is organized.
Civics and Political Systems; Industrial and Technical Education; Mathematics
Dist - USNAC **Prod** - USN 1966

Why Can't I Come to School on Saturday
VHS / 16mm
(T)
$55.00 purchase _ #TV101
Features two of the Christa McAuliffe educators in their science classrooms. Features project - oriented cooperative learning with the aid of technology.
Education
Dist - MECC **Prod** - MECC

Why can't I fly like a bird 13 MIN
U-matic / 16mm / VHS
Wonder world of science series
Color (P)
$320.00, $250.00 purchase _ #HP - 5761C
Stars Wondercat who tries to fly with artificial wings. Looks at different types of flying animals and how they obtain air, water and food. Uses animation and live action to reveal how differences and similarities are used to put animals into groups. Part of the Wonder World of Science series. Produced by Bill Walker Productions.
Science - Natural
Dist - CORF

Why Can't I - Laws 15 MIN
U-matic / VHS
Two Cents' Worth Series
Color (P)
Explains how laws protect the well - being of a community.
Civics and Political Systems; Guidance and Counseling; Social Science
Dist - AITECH **Prod** - WIEC 1976

Why Can't I Learn 51 MIN
U-matic / VHS / 16mm
Color
Defines the classic learning disability symptoms. Examines several approaches to treating these disabilities.
Psychology
Dist - FI **Prod** - MFFD

Why Can't I Learn, Pt 1 25 MIN
16mm / U-matic / VHS
Color
Defines the classic learning disability symptoms. Examines several approaches to treating these disabilities.
Psychology
Dist - FI **Prod** - MFFD

Why Can't I Learn, Pt 2 26 MIN
16mm / U-matic / VHS
Color
Defines the classic learning disability symptoms. Examines several approaches to treating these disabilities.
Psychology
Dist - FI **Prod** - MFFD

Why Can't Jimmy Read 15 MIN
U-matic / VHS / 16mm
B&W (C T S)
LC FIA55-993
The story of a fourth grader and his reading problems is told as a typical case history from the files of the Syracuse University Reading Clinic. Shows diagnostic procedures used and emphasizes the valuable service that can be performed by a reading clinic.
Education; English Language
Dist - IFB **Prod** - SYRCU 1950

Why children can't be creative
VHS
Giftedness - research and practice series
Color (T)
$49.95 purchase
Challenges the cherished belief that all children are creative. Lifts the obligation to be creative from children and offers an alternative premise for developing talent. Presented by Dr David Feldman of Tufts University. Part of a six - part series on gifted children.
Education; Fine Arts; Psychology
Dist - UCALG **Prod** - UCALG 1991

Why Children Play 7 MIN
U-matic
Take Time Series
(A)
Demonstrates the influence of parents and others caring for pre - schoolers on the physical and emotional development of the child.
Health and Safety; Psychology; Sociology
Dist - ACCESS **Prod** - ACCESS 1976

Why Christmas trees aren't perfect 25 MIN
VHS
Color (K P I R)
$14.95 purchase _ #35 - 861476 - 1
Uses an animated format to tell the story of Small Pine, a tree which demonstrates love and charity for its friends. Based on the children's book by Richard H Schneider.
Literature and Drama; Religion and Philosophy
Dist - APH **Prod** - ABINGP

Why Communication Goes Wrong 9 MIN
Videoreel / VT2
SUCCESS, the AMA Course for Office Employees Series
Color
LC 75-704214
Presents an instructional course for office employees. Helps identify and overcome six major barriers to successful communication. Includes a discussion of personal experiences confronting these barriers.
Business and Economics; Psychology
Dist - AMA **Prod** - AMA 1972

Why Decontaminate 20 MIN
VHS
Hazardous Materials Decontamination Series
Color (G PRO)
$125.00 purchase _ #35384
Shows why decontamination is necessary at hazardous materials incidents. Describes 'no exception' policy and other aspects of decontamination. Part of a three - part series that covers all aspects of the decontamination process. Offers information and procedures as required by 29 CFR 1920.120.
Health and Safety; Psychology; Social Science; Sociology
Dist - OKSU **Prod** - OKSU 1989

Why deserts bloom 13 MIN
U-matic / VHS / BETA
Color (G)
$29.95, $130.00 purchase _ #LSTF107
Shows the springtime explosion of flowers in the Saguaro Forest, Organ Pipe Cactus and Joshua Tree Parks. Includes teachers' guide. Produced by Nature Episodes.
Science - Natural
Dist - FEDU

Why Did Gloria Die 27 MIN
16mm / U-matic / VHS
Color (H C A)
LC 73-703206
Points out that the half - million Indians who are leaving reservations seeking a better life in the city are finding the white man's urban world alien and unfriendly. Traces the life of Gloria Curtis, a Chippewa who died of hepatitis at the age of 27, through several crises including unemployment, welfare, inadequate housing and poor medical care, in white - controlled Minneapolis, Minnesota. Features Don and Lucille Goodwin, also members of Minneapolis' Indian ghetto, who discuss how they were able to weather the painful period of adjustment from reservation to urban life.
Social Science
Dist - IU **Prod** - NET 1973

Why Did it Happen 15 MIN
U-matic / VHS
Out and about Series
Color (P)
Depicts the fight which ensues after school when Jason competes with Molly for Sara's friendship and attention. Shows that after knocking over a rack of books in the Library, Sam helps Molly figure out why she and Jason aren't getting along well.
Guidance and Counseling
Dist - AITECH **Prod** - STSU 1984

Why Did You Kiss Me Awake 3 MIN
16mm
Color (C A)
Portrays only the initial movements of an imagined film drama, as the camera which is photographing the mirror image of a totally nude young woman is placed in a drawer, leaving us in total darkness through the rest of the film.
Literature and Drama
Dist - UWFKD **Prod** - UWFKD

Why didn't I think of that 22 MIN
VHS
Color (IND PRO G)
$595.00 purchase _ #AMI138
Instructs on creative problem solving. Offers training on how to change viewpoints, break mental habits, generate alternatives and avoid paradigms. Includes a training leader's guide.
Business and Economics; Fine Arts; Psychology
Dist - EXTR **Prod** - AMEDIA
GA

Why didn't I think of that 28 MIN
VHS
Color (A PRO IND)
$395.00 purchase, $110.00 rental
Encourages viewers to learn to change their viewpoints, break mental habits, generate alternatives, search for similarities, and share ideas.
Business and Economics; Guidance and Counseling; Psychology
Dist - VLEARN

Why Didn't You Tell Me 11 MIN
VHS / U-matic
Color (C A)
Shows a young women who finally gathers the courage to tell her lover that in six months together she has not had an orgasm.
Health and Safety; Psychology; Sociology
Dist - MMRC **Prod** - MMRC

Why Discipline? 10 MIN
U-matic / 35mm strip
Productive Discipline Series Module 1
Color
Offers some of the reasons why discipline is necessary and what happens when it is absent from an organization. Points out some of the reasons why people don't like to discipline others and how to overcome these fears.
Business and Economics; Psychology
Dist - RESEM **Prod** - RESEM

Why do Animals Look Like they do 11 MIN
16mm / U-matic / VHS
Captioned; Color (P I)
LC 79-700319
Discusses the processes of adaptation to environment and evolution of a species.
Science - Natural
Dist - JOU **Prod** - ALTSUL 1978

Why do Birds Sing 27 MIN
16mm / U-matic / VHS
Nova Series
Color (H C A)
LC 78-700572
Discusses the research that has been conducted to decipher the meaning of various types of birdsongs and to discover how fledglings learn adult birdsongs.
Psychology; Science; Science - Natural
Dist - TIMLIF **Prod** - WGBHTV 1976

Why do Birds Sing 30 MIN
U-matic / VHS / 16mm
KnowZone Series
Color (I J H)
$550 purchase - 16 mm, $250 purchase - video _ #5063C
Shows that the songs of birds can be used to assert territory or give warnings. Adapted from the Nova series. Hosted by David Morse.
Science - Natural
Dist - CORF

Why do Cats have Whiskers 11 MIN
U-matic / VHS / 16mm
Wonder World of Science Series
Color (P)
$320 purchase - 16 mm, $250 purchase - video _ #4911C
Explains why certain animals have whiskers. Talks about predators, prey, and survival. Produced by Bill Walker Productions.
Science - Natural
Dist - CORF
VIEWTH

Why do I Feel this Way - Profiles of Depression 48 MIN
U-matic / VHS / 16mm
Color (H C A)
LC 80-701787
Presents profiles of three individuals who are suffering from depression. Includes a commentary by Dr Timothy Johnson of Harvard Medical School who describes various treatments to alleviate the disorder.
Guidance and Counseling; Psychology
Dist - CORF **Prod** - BBINC 1979

Why do I have to cry - Assessment of pain in children 25 MIN
U-matic / VHS
Color (PRO)
$285.00 purchase, $70.00 rental _ #4304S, 4304V
Provides three strategies for determining the level of pain in children of different age groups. Uses real patients in demonstrating pain measurement with the poker chip tool, where one to five chips represent "no hurt" to "the most hurt," the "oucher" tool, which uses pictures of painful facial expressions, and the adolescent pediatric pain tool, using body outlines to determine location, type, and intensity of pain.
Health and Safety
Dist - AJN **Prod** - BELHAN 1989

Why do I respond 10 MIN
VHS
Christian steward's response series
Color (A R)
$19.95 purchase _ #87EE0001
Outlines Christian motivations for giving. Suggests that true Christian stewardship should not be seen as contributions to a cause or activity, but rather as a response from a grateful heart.
Guidance and Counseling; Literature and Drama; Religion and Philosophy
Dist - CPH **Prod** - CPH

Why do People Work 3 MIN
VHS / 16mm
Color (A PRO)
$200.00 purchase
Features John Cleese who discusses why people work. Coffee break material.
Business and Economics; Guidance and Counseling; Psychology
Dist - VIDART **Prod** - VIDART 1991

Why do Spiders Spin Webs 11 MIN
U-matic / VHS / 16mm
Wonder World of Science Series
Color (P)
$320 purchase - 16 mm, $250 purchase - video _ #4981C
Talks about the things that spiders use webs for and the parts of a spider's body that the threads for the web come from.
Science - Natural
Dist - CORF
VIEWTH

Why do We Eat 15 MIN
U-matic / VHS
Great American Eating Machine - You Series Pt 1; Pt 1
Color (P)
LC 83-706105
Establishes the relationship of food to energy, growth and well - being. Shows the need for food and how eating can be fun.
Health and Safety; Social Science
Dist - GPN **Prod** - NJPTV 1982

Why do We Get Sick 30 MIN
U-matic / VHS
Here's to Your Health Series
Color (C T)
Shows how people react to stress. Explores the question, 'Is stress seen as a danger or a challenge for growth?' Addresses the belief that 'people seem to get sick during periods of significant multiple life changes.'.
Health and Safety; Psychology
Dist - DALCCD **Prod** - DALCCD

Why do We Still have Mountains 21 MIN
16mm / U-matic / VHS
Color (I J H) (SPANISH)
Discusses the nature of mountains, using natural photography and laboratory experiments.
Foreign Language; Science - Physical
Dist - EBEC **Prod** - EBEC

Why do We Still have Mountains 20 MIN
U-matic / VHS / 16mm
Earth Science Program Series
Color; B&W (I J H)
Discusses the nature of mountains and the geological concepts dealing with weathering and erosion and with the formation of the earth's crust. Shows that uplift is occurring today at rates which could produce mountains in a geologically short time.
Science - Physical
Dist - EBEC **Prod** - EBEC 1964

Why do You Buy 10 MIN
16mm / U-matic / VHS
Color (J H) (SPANISH)
LC 70-715435;
Uses a comical approach to focus on the emotional elements which enter into the buying decision, and shows how advertising utilizes the emotional appeals to sway purchase decisions.
Business and Economics; Guidance and Counseling; Home Economics; Psychology
Dist - JOU **Prod** - ALTSUL 1971

Why do You Smile, Mona Lisa 14 MIN
16mm / U-matic / VHS
Color
Shows Leonardo da Vinci in his studio in Florence and explains how he got that enigmatic smile on the face of the Mona Lisa.
Fine Arts
Dist - FI **Prod** - FLEET

Why Does Herr R Run Amok 87 MIN
16mm
Color (GERMAN (ENGLISH SUBTITLES))
Presents a statement on the modern - day, bland, ordinary mass murderer. Directed by Werner Herzog. With English subtitles.
Fine Arts; Foreign Language
Dist - NYFLMS **Prod** - UNKNWN 1969

Why Does Mom Drink So Much 30 MIN
VHS
Color (I)
LC 89700229
Uses real stories to help reduce the isolation and stigma experienced by children of alcoholics. Shows that there are things that the children can do to make life better.
Guidance and Counseling; Health and Safety; Psychology; Sociology
Dist - AIMS **Prod** - HRMC 1989
GA

Why Does the Wind Blow 25 MIN
VHS
Active Atmosphere Series
Color (J)
$79.00 purchase _ #2242V
Covers atmospheric dynamics, air parcels, the effects of the real pressure gradient, gravitational and frictional forces and the Coriolis and centrifugal forces. Part of an eight - part series on the atmosphere and the weather it creates. Includes a comprehensive study guide.
Science - Physical
Dist - SCTRES **Prod** - SCTRES

Why doesn't grass grow on the moon 11 MIN
VHS
Wonder world of science series
Color; PAL (P)
Follows Wondercat, an animated, curious kitten, who knows that grass doesn't grow on the moon. Looks at what plants need in order to grow - water, minerals, air and sunlight - and Wondercat imagines how he could get grass to grow on the moon. Part of a series which encourages youngsters to explore the limitless wonders of the world of science through careful observation, thoughtful comparisons and well - supported conclusions.
Science - Natural; Science - Physical
Dist - VIEWTH **Prod** - VIEWTH
CORF

Why Doesn't Grass Grow on the Moon 11 MIN
U-matic / VHS / 16mm
Wonder World of Science Series
Color (P)
$320 purchase - 16 mm, $250 purchase - video
Shows the different things that plants need to grow, such as water, minerals, air, and sunlight, and tells why grass doesn't grow on the moon. Produced by Bill Walker Productions.
Science - Natural
Dist - CORF

Why Doesn't Somebody Ask Me
16mm / U-matic
Color (A)
Uses satire to illustrate how to improve supervisory decision - making skills.
Business and Economics; Psychology
Dist - BNA **Prod** - BNA 1983

Why Doesn't Somebody Trust Me
U-matic / 16mm
Color (A)
Uses satire to illustrate how to improve supervisory decision - making skills.
Business and Economics; Psychology
Dist - BNA **Prod** - BNA 1983

Why don't I fall up 10 MIN
U-matic / 16mm / VHS
Wonder world of science series
Color (P)
$320.00, $250.00 purchase _ #HP - 5762C
Stars Wondercat who falls from a tree and wonders why things fall down instead of up. Discovers through a tug - of - war what holds objects in place, what makes them move and what determines the direction of their motion. The flight of a spaceship helps Wondercat to explore the action of gravity in space and the tug - of - war between the moon's gravity and that of the earth. Part of the Wonder World of Science series. Produced by Bill Walker Productions.
Science - Physical
Dist - CORF

Why Don't You Call Me Skipper Anymore 27 MIN
U-matic / VHS / 16mm
Insight Series
Color; B&W (J)
LC 72-702002
Tells about a girl, who has just graduated from college and cannot find direction for her life, in order to show that work is an important part of one's identity.
Guidance and Counseling; Psychology
Dist - PAULST **Prod** - PAULST 1972

Why Drown 29 MIN
U-matic / VHS
Color
Features an Olympic swimming champion demonstrating a life - saving technique to keep a person afloat for hours even if clothed or injured. Shows how to make water - wings out of trousers.
Health and Safety; Physical Education and Recreation
Dist - IHF **Prod** - IHF

Why E 25 MIN
U-matic / VHS / 16mm
Color
Explains the importance of the number 'e' in the family of functions.
Mathematics
Dist - MEDIAG **Prod** - OPENU 1979

Why employees don't do what they are supposed to do 25 MIN
VHS / 16mm
Color (PRO G A)
$570.00, $595.00 purchase, $130.00 rental
Explores reasons for employee non - performance and suggests ways to overcome problems.Includes a meeting guide.
Business and Economics; Guidance and Counseling; Psychology
Dist - EXTR **Prod** - CCCD

Why employees don't do what they're supposed to do 25 MIN
VHS
Color (A PRO IND)
$570.00 purchase, $130.00 rental
Takes a prevention - oriented approach to the problem of why employees don't always do what they're supposed to do.

Business and Economics; Guidance and Counseling; Psychology
Dist - VLEARN

Why Employees don't do what they're supposed to do 25 MIN
VHS / 16mm
Preventative management series
Color (G)
$595.00, $570.00 purchase, $130.00 rental
Presents a program based on the book 'Why Employees Don't Do What They're Supposed to Do' by Ferdinand Fournies. Stars Fournies and Sam Melville. Shows how to prevent the ten most common reasons for nonperformance. Includes meeting guide. Part of the Preventative Management series.
Business and Economics; Guidance and Counseling; Psychology
Dist - CCCD **Prod** - CCCD

Why Employees Don't Perform 12 MIN
U-matic / Slide
Productive Discipline Series Module 2
Color
Shows supervisors that sometimes employees don't perform properly for reasons which may not suggest discipline and explores the matter of attitudes. Demonstrates that it is difficult to define 'bad' and 'good' attitudes.
Business and Economics; Psychology
Dist - RESEM **Prod** - RESEM

Why Engines are Governed 5 MIN
16mm
B&W
LC FIE55-354
Explains that the governor in military engines limits the speed of the engine at the point where it develops maximum horsepower.
Industrial and Technical Education
Dist - USNAC **Prod** - USA 1955

Why Every Action has a Reaction 5 MIN
U-matic / VHS
Way Things Work Series
Color (K)
$149.95, $49.95 purchase _ #AD - 1647
Demonstrates how the release of pressure in one direction will cause a balloon to move in the opposite direction. Part of a thirty - part series on the way things work hosted by Bob Symes.
Science; Science - Physical
Dist - FOTH **Prod** - FOTH

Why Exercise 11 MIN
U-matic / VHS / 16mm
Fitness and Me Series
Color (P)
Tells the story of Knight Light who is on his way to being in top shape, but his paunchy friend needs some help. Shows how the two knights call upon all their strength and energy when they are sent to recover the king's stolen crown. Points out that exercise strengthens the heart, muscles, and other body systems, giving more energy for work and play.
Physical Education and Recreation
Dist - CORF **Prod** - DISNEY
AIMS

Why Fathers Work 14 MIN
U-matic / VHS / 16mm
Social Studies Series
Color; B&W (P)
LC 78-704166
Shows where a father goes, what he does and how his work helps his family, his community and the city. Illustrates the economic functions of the family as a community unit.
Guidance and Counseling; Psychology; Social Science
Dist - EBEC **Prod** - EBEC 1969

Why Fly 29 MIN
Videoreel / VT2
Discover Flying - Just Like a Bird Series
Color
Social Science
Dist - PBS **Prod** - WKYCTV

Why follow the rules
VHS
Video keys to school success series
Color (H C A)
$98.00 purchase _ #CD8002V
Examines the role of rules in society. Presents a humorous vision of what life would be like without rules.
Education; Sociology
Dist - CAMV

Why Follow the Rules
VHS
(H)
$998.00 purchase _ #KSV 200
Shows students that rules are found in every area of life. Explores the role of rules in these areas with an emphasis on school. Deals with the consequences of following rules and advises students about how to use negotiation. Comes with worksheets and is available as part of a set. Also available in Beta or 3/4".
Education; Sociology
Dist - CADESF **Prod** - CADESF 1989

Why God, why me 27 MIN
VHS
Color (H C G)
$195.00 purchase, $55.00 rental
Dramatizes the life story of childhood sex abuse victims who grew up never feeling safe in their own homes. Presents several women recalling their childhood sexual encounters with adults. Focuses on one survivor who suffered abuse from several relatives, beginning in early childhood, and discovered that the man she married turned out to be a child abuser as well.
Sociology
Dist - FLMLIB **Prod** - VARDIR 1988
VARDIR

Why good marriages often fail 28 MIN
16mm
Color
Explains why good marriages have their own unique problems.
Guidance and Counseling; Sociology
Dist - ECUFLM **Prod** - UMCOM 1982

Why Human Relations 29 MIN
U-matic / VHS / 16mm
Human Relations and School Discipline Series
Color (C)
Identifies the basic need for good human relationships in schools, re - examines goals of public education and shows how discipline and human relations are closely interwoven. Presents documentary scenes of several schools where human relationships have been consciously improved.
Education; Sociology
Dist - FI **Prod** - MFFD 1974

Why is it Always Me 14 MIN
U-matic / VHS / 16mm
Color (I J)
Illustrates better and more effective methods for adolescents to resolve day - to - day personal problems such as conflict situations with their family or peers.
Psychology; Sociology
Dist - CORF
CMPCAR

Why is the ocean salty 30 MIN
VHS
Color (J H)
$29.95 purchase _ #IV161
Looks at the origin of the sea, the sources of the salts, why the sea is not fresh, salinity and how sea life affects seawater composition.
Geography - World; Science - Physical
Dist - INSTRU **Prod** - INSTRU

Why is the Sky Blue 9 MIN
VHS / U-matic
Color
Presented by Ilene Segalove.
Fine Arts
Dist - KITCHN **Prod** - KITCHN

Why it Rains 6 MIN
U-matic / VHS
Way Things Work Series
Color (K)
$149.95, $49.95 purchase _ #AD - 1643
Features Bob Symes, British science broadcaster, who makes rain in his kitchen. Shows that real rain occurs for the same reason - steam when cooled turns into water droplets. Part of a thirty - part series on the way things work hosted by Bob Symes.
Science; Science - Physical
Dist - FOTH **Prod** - FOTH

Why Lightbulbs Glow 6 MIN
U-matic / VHS
Way Things Work Series
Color (K)
$149.95, $49.95 purchase _ #AD - 1667
Shows that when electricity passes through wires inside a bulb, the wires get hot and glow, but do not burn. Demonstrates that the lack of air in the bulb is why. Part of a thirty - part series on the way things work hosted by Bob Symes.
Science; Science - Physical
Dist - FOTH **Prod** - FOTH

Why Lightning is Dangerous 7 MIN
U-matic / VHS
Way Things Work Series
Color (K)
$159.95, $59.95 purchase _ #AD - 1642
Creates lightning in Bob Symes' laboratory. Reveals the secret of the lightning rod - it doesn't conduct the electrical charge, it disperses it. Part of a thirty - part series on the way things work hosted by Bob Symes.
Science; Science - Physical
Dist - FOTH **Prod** - FOTH

Why Lignite 20 MIN
16mm
Color
LC 75-702670
Examines the process of mining and processing lignite and explores its use as a fuel in generating electric power.
Industrial and Technical Education; Social Science
Dist - STOKB **Prod** - STOKB 1975

Why LOTUS 15 MIN
U-matic / VHS
Color
Explains why the Light Of Truth Universal Shrine (LOTUS) is being built.
Religion and Philosophy
Dist - IYOGA **Prod** - IYOGA

Why Man Creates 25 MIN
16mm / U-matic / VHS
Color (I) (SPANISH GERMAN ITALIAN)
Presents a series of explorations, episodes and comments on creativity by a master of conceptual design. Uses humor and satire to explore ideas and important truths.
Fine Arts; Foreign Language; Psychology
Dist - PFP **Prod** - BASSS

Why Man Creates - Man, the Measure of all Things
U-matic / VHS
Color (H C)
Uses great works of art and selected passages to help explain why the history of art is the history of civilization. Based on the Metropolitan Museum of Art's Centennial Exhibition, Masterpieces of Fifty Centuries.
Fine Arts
Dist - GA **Prod** - GA

Why marriage when you can live together - Part 1 50 MIN
VHS
Maximum marriage series
Color (H C G A R)
$10.00 rental _ #36 - 894001 - 533
Features Tim Timmons in a presentation of his concepts for 'Maximum Marriage.' Covers the advantages and disadvantages of both marriage and living together, as well as issues of responsibility and intimacy.
Guidance and Counseling; Psychology; Sociology
Dist - APH **Prod** - WORD

Why Me 10 MIN
16mm / U-matic / VHS
Color (H C A)
LC 79-701216
Presents an animated story about a man who learns that he only has a short time to live. Depicts the emotional stages he experiences, culminating with his resolution to live each remaining moment to its fullest.
Fine Arts; Sociology
Dist - PFP **Prod** - NFBC 1979

Why me 14 MIN
VHS
Color; PAL (IND G PRO)
PdS95 purchase
Trains employers and employees about the problems of sexual harassment in the workplace. Uses short scenarios to illustrate the correct steps to prevent sexual harassment. Offers advice on creating a policy statement on the behavior expected from all members of staff and what procedures to follow if a complaint is made.
Home Economics; Psychology; Social Science
Dist - CFLVIS **Prod** - SCHWOP 1994

Why Me 57 MIN
16mm / U-matic / VHS
Color (A)
LC 75-700654
Presents the case histories of several women who have had cancer of the breast and have experienced a radical mastectomy. Discusses methods of detection, variations of surgical treatment, emotional consequences following a mastectomy and the importance of self - examination. Includes surgical opinions of unidentified physicians.
Guidance and Counseling; Health and Safety
Dist - CAROUF **Prod** - CBSTV 1975

Why Me 16 MIN
16mm
Color
LC 77-702174
Tells the story of an exasperated executive who blames his mistakes on his subordinates, but learns a lesson in accountability when he is visited by an angel.
Business and Economics; Psychology
Dist - ITTSHE **Prod** - ITTSHE 1977

Why Me 24 MIN
16mm
Color (J)
LC 73-702084
Presents an exploratory documentary of a modern police force in action. Exposes the familiar Why Me syndrome experienced by police officers when confronting average citizens in the line of duty.
Psychology; Sociology
Dist - STSF PHENIX **Prod** - NOMIL 1973

Why Me - an Orthopedically Handicapped Child 7 MIN
U-matic / VHS / 16mm
Like You, Like Me Series
Color (K P)
Describes how a little boy with an orthopedic handicap teaches his nonhandicapped friend how to swim.
Education; Guidance and Counseling
Dist - EBEC **Prod** - EBEC 1977

Why me - dealing with an occupational exposure to a blood borne virus 16 MIN
VHS
Color (PRO C)
Informs healthcare workers who have been or are exposed to hepatitis or AIDS - HIV. Shows a cross section of healthcare workers to explain thoroughly the significane of the exposure and possible prevention and treatment methods. Evaluates the likelihood of developing the disease, along with benefits and risks inherent in the treatment. Presents facts on the probability of an exposed healthcare worker developing AIDS from a work - related incident.
Health and Safety
Dist - AJN BAXMED **Prod** - ENVINC

Why Meanings Change 30 MIN
U-matic / VHS
Language and Meaning Series
Color (C)
English Language; Psychology
Dist - GPN **Prod** - WUSFTV 1983

Why Measure 6 MIN
16mm
Measurement Series
Color (J H C A)
LC 78-700704
Deals with the importance of measurement, moving from the ordinary experiences of life to work in the laboratory. Shows the need for and development of standards of measurement and depicts the critical relationship of measurement to science and technology.
Mathematics
Dist - PSU **Prod** - PSU 1972

Why Men Don't Talk to their Wives 28 MIN
U-matic / VHS
Color (G)
$249.00, $149.00 purchase _ #AD - 1686
Shows that men and women communicate differently - they talk about different things in different ways. Features several couples on a Phil Donahue program talking about their problems in communicating. A marriage therapist presents exercises to improve communication.
Psychology; Sociology
Dist - FOTH **Prod** - FOTH

Why Men Rape 40 MIN
U-matic / VHS / 16mm
Color (H C A)
LC 80-701165
Presents ten rapists discussing why they committed their crimes. Offers interviews with authorities who try to present a clearer profile of the rapist. Shows interviews with mixed groups of students who discuss their sexual attitudes.
Psychology; Sociology
Dist - LCOA **Prod** - NFBC 1980

Why Microelectronics Fail 29 MIN
Videoreel / VT2
Interface Series
Color
Business and Economics; Science - Physical
Dist - PBS **Prod** - KCET

Why Moncada 20 MIN
16mm
B&W (H C A)
$50 rental
Deals with Fidel Castro's 1953 attack on the Moncada garrison and the history of the Cuban Revolution. Includes clips from old Cuban TV commercials, newsreels, Hollywood movies, and cartoons. Directed by Sergio Nunez Martinez.
History - World
Dist - CNEMAG

Why Mosquitoes Buzz in People's Ears 10 MIN
16mm / U-matic / VHS
Color (K P)
Reveals that when Mosquito tells Iguana a tall tale and Iquana plugs his ears in disgust, thus sending Python down Rabbit's hole for fear of foul play, the chain reaction leads to jungle disaster. Tells how King Lion calls a meeting where all is set aright.
Literature and Drama
Dist - WWS **Prod** - SCHNDL 1984

Why Mothers Work 19 MIN
U-matic / VHS / 16mm
Color (P I J)
$59.00 purchase _ #3485; LC 76-701793
Follows two working mothers through typical days, observing them at home and at work. Shows how families of both of the women have had to make some adjustments.
Sociology
Dist - EBEC **Prod** - EBEC 1976

Why Muslim women cover
VHS
Color (G)
$15.00 purchase _ #138 - 001
Presents a video lecture by Imam Siraj Wahhaj about the Islamic practice of hijab.
Religion and Philosophy; Sociology
Dist - SOUVIS **Prod** - SOUVIS

Why NATO 26 MIN
16mm
B&W
LC FIE58-372
Tells the story of the North Atlantic Treaty Organization from its inception to its 1957 summit meeting in Paris, France.
Civics and Political Systems; History - World
Dist - USNAC **Prod** - USDD 1958

Why not a woman 26 MIN
VHS / U-matic / 16mm
Color (PRO IND)
$275.00, $110.00 purchase _ #TC010571, #TCA02194, #TCA03725
Discusses the subject of women in non - traditional careers. Portrays women working in such traditionally male - dominated fields as welder, carpenter, and mechanic. Interviews their male peers and supervisors. Dispels myths about women in the workplace.
Business and Economics; Social Science; Sociology
Dist - USNAC **Prod** - USDL 1977

Why not a woman 26 MIN
16mm
Color (G A)
$5.00 rental
Interviews personnel directors and supervisors who were hesitant about hiring women because they expected higher absentee rates and more accidents. Reveals that they found no significant difference in the performance of women and men. Women talk about the challenges of going to work in non - traditional occupations such as carpentry, bus driving, welding, toolmaking, electrical contracting and auto mechanics.
Social Science; Sociology
Dist - AFLCIO **Prod** - PACOWO 1976

Why not be Beautiful 20 MIN
U-matic / VHS / 16mm
Color (J)
LC 73-704600
Explains the importance of cleanliness, good diet and exercise as prerequisites for a healthy body and a beautiful face. Shows basic facial makeup, such as the application of foundation, blush power and eye makeup. Stresses the fact that beauty is more than a pretty face, it's a way of life.
Health and Safety; Home Economics
Dist - HANDEL **Prod** - HANDEL 1969

Why not Live 15 MIN
U-matic
Workers at Risk Series
(A)
Shows that health and safety hazards exist everywhere and exposure to them is often a matter of choice.
Health and Safety
Dist - ACCESS **Prod** - ACCESS 1982

Why not Sign a Union Card 35 MIN
VHS / U-matic
Color
Shows simulation of union authorization card signing campaign demonstrating organizing tactics. Attempts to prepare managers and supervisors to effectively respond and appropriately communicate to employees.
Business and Economics
Dist - SERA **Prod** - SERA

Why not Technology 15 MIN
16mm
Color
LC 76-701495
Documents opportunities for women in scientific and technological fields.
Guidance and Counseling; Science; Sociology
Dist - CNIAG **Prod** - CNIAG 1975

Why not Try 4 MIN
VHS / 16mm / U-matic
Most Important Person - Attitudes Series
Color (K P I) (SPANISH)
Explores a variety of things that many children may never have tried before, including sliding down a slide, finger painting and meeting someone new.
Guidance and Counseling; Psychology
Dist - EBEC **Prod** - EBEC 1972

The Why of Automation Lubrication 24 MIN
16mm
Color (J)
Explains through animation the need for lubrication of automobiles and the uses of oils and greases.
Industrial and Technical Education
Dist - AMROIL **Prod** - AMROIL 1952

Why Patients Get Angry - a Risk Management Program
16mm / U-matic / VHS
Color (PRO)
Discusses experiences in health care facilities which provoke anger on the part of patients. Offers suggestions to health care providers on how to handle situations which may provoke anger.
Health and Safety; Psychology
Dist - FAIRGH **Prod** - FAIRGH

Why Pay 12 MIN
VHS / 16mm
What Now - Deciding What's Right Series
Color (K)
$39.95 purchase
Encourages children to look at their alternatives and to weigh the possible consequences of their actions before reaching a decision or taking an action, by focusing on realistic situations involving shoplifting. The complete series is also available in one video, What Now - Deciding What's Right.
Education; Religion and Philosophy
Dist - JANUP **Prod** - JANUP

Why People are Scared of Hares 6 MIN
U-matic / VHS / 16mm
Color (P I A)
Presents a modern fable about an unusual rabbit that is not well liked by his friends because he does not conform. Describes how he finds a book and teaches himself to read, and when faced with death by a group of hunters, it is his literary skill that saves all of them.
Literature and Drama
Dist - MOKIN **Prod** - SFSP 1983

Why People Buy 20 MIN
U-matic / VHS / 16mm
Color (H C A) (SPANISH)
LC 81-700331
Analyzes the various reasons why people purchase a product.
Business and Economics; Foreign Language; Home Economics; Psychology
Dist - MGHT **Prod** - CRMP 1981

Why People Drink 28 MIN
VHS / U-matic
Color (J A)
Explains rationale behind different drinking styles.
Health and Safety; Psychology; Sociology
Dist - SUTHRB **Prod** - SUTHRB

Why People have Special Jobs - the Man who made Spinning Tops 7 MIN
16mm / U-matic / VHS
Basic Concepts in Social Studies Series
Color (K P)
LC 72-705960
Introduces the basic economic concept of specialization of labor. Shows how one man who made tops became a toymaker and how other fathers began to do one special job.
Business and Economics; Guidance and Counseling; Social Science
Dist - LCOA **Prod** - LCOA 1970

Why People Smoke 10 MIN
U-matic / VHS / 16mm
Color (P I)
LC 78-700370
Uses animation to classify personality traits of people who smoke.
Health and Safety; Psychology
Dist - PFP **Prod** - HARBER 1978

Why people take drugs 15 MIN
VHS
Dealing with drugs - teaching kids to say 'no' series
Color; CC (I J H)
$89.95 purchase _ #UW3530
Covers the definition of drugs, factors that influence opinions about drugs and the problem of drug abuse. Parodies popular TV formats to deliver the message. Part of a six - part series using wit and humor to teach students how to say 'no' to drugs.
Guidance and Counseling; Psychology
Dist - FOTH

Why people work
VHS
Personality games for Macintosh series
Color (H C)
$79 purchase - #CDPVS104M-D
Discusses how each of the six personality orientations is motivated by different monetary or emotional rewards. Looks at different reward systems and how understanding and acceptance is a key to self-fulfilment and getting along with others.
Business and Economics; Guidance and Counseling; Psychology
Dist - CAMV

Why Planes Burn 58 MIN
VHS / U-matic
Nova Series
Color (H C A)
$250 purchase _ #5274C
Shows the dangers of fire resulting from a plane crash. Discusses the airlines' refusal to construct safer planes. Produced by WGBH Boston.
Health and Safety
Dist - CORF

Why Plant a Tree 9 MIN
16mm
Color (P I)
Presents the story of a little boy who uses a stick as a sword and goes about knocking shoots and branches from trees.
Guidance and Counseling; Literature and Drama; Science - Natural; Social Science
Dist - MLA **Prod** - MLA

Why Politics 20 MIN
16mm
Government and Public Affairs Films Series
B&W (H A)
Raymond Moley, journalist, author and political scientist, discusses our need for political information and knowledge of government.
Civics and Political Systems
Dist - MLA **Prod** - RSC 1960

Why Politics - Interview 15 MIN
16mm
Building Political Leadership Series
B&W (H C)
LC FIA68-1335
Civics and Political Systems
Dist - MLA **Prod** - RSC 1966

Why Productivity Increases as Quality Improves 50 MIN
U-matic / VHS
Deming Video Tapes - Quality, Productivity and the Competitive 'Series
Color
Business and Economics
Dist - SME **Prod** - MIOT
MIOT

Why Protect Animals 15 MIN
16mm
Color (J)
Shows how humane societies work effectively to protect animals through education, public action and law. Presents several case histories in their actual settings throughout America.
Science - Natural; Sociology
Dist - KLEINW **Prod** - KLEINW

Why Q A 60 MIN
VHS / U-matic
Quality Assurance Series
Color (IND)
Introduces student to quality assurance. Includes general terminology, standards and specifications. Defines differences between quality assurance and quality control.
Business and Economics; Industrial and Technical Education
Dist - LEIKID **Prod** - LEIKID

Why quality 27 MIN
VHS
Color (A PRO IND)
$625.00 purchase, $150.00 rental
Emphasizes the idea that the ultimate judge of quality is the customer. Features John Guaspari, author of the books 'I Know It When I See It' and 'Why Quality?'
Business and Economics; Guidance and Counseling
Dist - VLEARN **Prod** - EFM
UTM

Why Quality
VHS
Guaspari Series
Color (G)
$625.00 purchase, $150.00 rental
Shows employees the importance of quality from a customer's point of view. Encourages employees to exceed customer expectations. Part of three videos on books written by John Guaspari.
Business and Economics
Dist - VLEARN

Why Quit Quiz 15 MIN
16mm
Color
LC 79-701125
Uses a quiz format to present questions which dramatize the positive health benefits of quitting cigarettes.
Health and Safety; Psychology
Dist - AMCS **Prod** - AMCS 1979

Why Rabbits have Long Ears 15 MIN
U-matic
Magic Carpet Series
Color (P)
Features a Guatemalan folk tale.
Literature and Drama
Dist - GPN **Prod** - SDCSS 1977

Why Read 15 MIN
16mm
Pathways to Reading Series
B&W (I J H)
Examines some of the reasons for reading - - to gain information, to prove or disprove a point, to learn how to do or make something, to satisfy curiosity, to be entertained, to recognize beauty and to gain wisdom and inspiration.
English Language
Dist - AVED **Prod** - CBF 1958

Why reading is important 23 MIN
VHS
Color (J H C A)
$98.00 purchase _ #WRI100
Shows that poor reading ability prevents growth and success. Illustrates the consequences of not developing good reading skills and how the obstacle of poor reading can be overcome.
Education; English Language; Psychology
Dist - CADESF **Prod** - CADESF 1990

Why reading is important
VHS
Why study video series
Color (J H)
$98.00 purchase _ #CD9200V
Demonstrates that self - esteem, work success and life satisfaction depend on reading skills. Answers a question most often asked by poor readers, 'Why do I have to read.' Looks at a variety of educational, social and occupational settings to show that poor reading ability prevents growth and success. Part of a series.
Education; English Language; Psychology
Dist - CAMV

Why Risk a Heart Attack 14 MIN
16mm / U-matic / VHS
Color (J)
Points out the risk factors contributing to a heart attack and what to do about them.
Health and Safety; Physical Education and Recreation; Science - Natural
Dist - TIMLIF **Prod** - AMEDA

Why Roof Control Plans 16 MIN
16mm / U-matic / VHS
Color
Shows that the collapse of roofs and ribs in coal mines can be prevented by following an approved roof - control plan. Explains basic plans, provides examples and describes the implementation of a plan. Describes types of roof support, areas covered, types of rock strata, mining equipment and materials, roof - bolting machines and support timbers.
Health and Safety; Industrial and Technical Education; Social Science
Dist - USNAC **Prod** - USDL 1981

Why Rules 15 MIN
U-matic / VHS
It's Your Move Series
Color (J)
Describes how Jeff ignores basic safety rules while bike riding and goes head over handlebars.
Health and Safety
Dist - AITECH **Prod** - WETN 1977

Why Save Florence 59 MIN
U-matic / VHS / 16mm
Color (H A)
LC 75-711459
Shows the state of affairs in Florence, Italy, following the flood of 1966 which endangered many lives and ruined thousands of priceless art treasures.
Fine Arts; Geography - World; Psychology; Sociology
Dist - IU **Prod** - NET 1971

Why School Fire Safety 15 MIN
U-matic / VHS
Color
Shows the need for school fire safety programs.
Health and Safety; Home Economics
Dist - FPF **Prod** - FPF

Why school is important
VHS
Color (I J H)
$98.00 purchase _ #WSI100
Interviews people from all walks of life to discover why education is important.
Education; Guidance and Counseling; Mathematics; Psychology
Dist - CADESF **Prod** - CADESF 1990

Why schools have rules - the school - work connection
VHS
School solutions video series
Color (I J H)
$98.00 purchase _ #CDSCH102V
Emphasizes how rules help rather than limit. Looks at how learning to follow rules in school prepares students for the future in the very practical, production - oriented world of work. Discusses the positive aspects of rules as well as the consequences of a life without rules. Includes reproducible worksheets. Part of a ten - part series to build student success.
Education; Sociology
Dist - CAMV

Why series

Air pressure on things	15 MIN
Animals from different environments	15 MIN
Different kinds of plants	15 MIN
Electricity into Heat	15 MIN
Electricity into Light	15 MIN
Electricity into Motion	15 MIN
Flowering plants	15 MIN
Fossils tell the story	15 MIN
How do scientists learn about space	15 MIN
How do we know	15 MIN
How does an electric current flow	15 MIN
Inclined plane - a simple machine	15 MIN
A Lake Community	15 MIN
The Lawn and Vacant Lot Community	15 MIN
Lever - a Simple Machine	15 MIN
Light and Color	15 MIN
Light and Heat	15 MIN
Living things and their environment	15 MIN
Making work easier	15 MIN
Measuring Distance	15 MIN
Measuring Temperature	15 MIN
Measuring Time	15 MIN
Measuring Weight	15 MIN
Moving Air Affects the Weather	15 MIN
Pulley - a Simple Machine	15 MIN
Reflected Light	15 MIN
A Seashore Community	15 MIN
Sound and Hearing	15 MIN
Space Neighbors	15 MIN
Static Electricity	15 MIN
A Stream Community	15 MIN
The Sun and the Earth	15 MIN
Water Affects the Weather	15 MIN
Wedge - a Simple Machine	15 MIN
What Happens When Air is Heated and Cooled	15 MIN
What is a Machine	15 MIN
What is Air	15 MIN
What is Sound	15 MIN
What is Weather	15 MIN
What the Earth was Like	15 MIN
The Wheel and Axle - a Simple Machine	15 MIN
A Woodland Community	15 MIN

Dist - AITECH

Why Shoot the Teacher 101 MIN
16mm
Color
Depicts a young teacher's struggle to gain respect when he arrives at a Canadian prairie town during the Great Depression.
Fine Arts
Dist - TLECUL **Prod** - TLECUL

Why should I care 10 MIN
VHS / U-matic
Color (C PRO)
$395.00 purchase, $80.00 rental _ #C920 - VI - 053
Demonstrates some of the worst scenarios a patient or visitor could experience while at a hospital. Shows how poor professional conduct can add undue frustration to an already stressful situation for patients, their family and friends. Presented by Denise Lusk and Tracy Williamson.
Health and Safety
Dist - HSCIC

Why should I stay - crisis intervention with a resistant teenager 26 MIN
VHS
Wediko series
Color (C G PRO)
$175.00 purchase, $28.00 rental _ #35644
Uses an interview to document an episode in the therapeutic work with Priscilla, a 16 - year - old referred to Wediko Children Services because of her repeated running away and abuse of alcohol in the time preceding the video At the Edge of a Desert - Renegotiating a Contract. Part of a series recording spontaneous behavior at Camp Wediko, a pioneer facility for therapeutic camping in Hillsboro, New Hampshire.
Guidance and Counseling; Health and Safety; Physical Education and Recreation; Psychology
Dist - PSU **Prod** - MASON 1987

Why Should I Worry about it 12 MIN
VHS / 16mm
Sexual Harassment - Shades of Gray Series
Color (PRO)
$500.00 purchase, $50.00 rental
Explains the personal costs of sexual harassment for the employer, the victim, co - workers and the harasser. Part of a training program aimed to stop sexual harassment in the workplace.
Business and Economics; Civics and Political Systems; Guidance and Counseling; Psychology; Sociology
Dist - UTM **Prod** - UTM

The Why Show 28 MIN
16mm
Special Delivery Series
Color (P I)
LC 79-701080
Identifies the cause of various handicaps and describes how handicapped individuals adjust to their disabilities.
Education; Psychology
Dist - LAWREN **Prod** - WNVT 1979

Why So many Lab Tests 24 MIN
VHS / U-matic
Color (PRO)
Explains reasons for six commonly used lab tests - hemoglobin level and blood cell count, urinalysis, blood chemistry, serology, blood typing, and microbiological tests.
Health and Safety; Science
Dist - HSCIC **Prod** - HSCIC 1981

Why some people fail to mourn 60 MIN
VHS
Pastoral bereavement counseling series
Color (R G)
$49.95 purchase _ #PSBC7
Helps participants to understand the dynamics of grief and 'tasks' necessary to journey from grief to healing. Develops the personal, technical and pastoral skills necessary to assist the griever. Shows how to design and lead an effective bereavement ministry team. Features Dr Patrick Del Zoppo. Part of eight parts of a complete training program in ministry to the bereaved. Workbook available separately.
Guidance and Counseling; Health and Safety; Religion and Philosophy; Sociology
Dist - CTNA **Prod** - CTNA

Why Space 7 MIN
16mm
Color
LC 74-706332
Shows various scientific milestones which have permitted mankind to approach the age of space. Explains why we are interested in the development of military capabilities in space.
Business and Economics; Industrial and Technical Education; Science - Physical; Social Science
Dist - USNAC **Prod** - USAF 1957

Why Spiders Hide in Dark Corners 15 MIN
U-matic
Magic Carpet Series
Color (P)
Presents an African folk tale.
Literature and Drama
Dist - GPN **Prod** - SDCSS 1977

Why Stay in School 14 MIN
VHS / U-matic
(J H)
$98 _ #CD7V
Points out reasons for students to avoid dropping out of school. Features a scenario in which a teacher attempts a dissatisfied student to stay in school by using examples related to his career future. Reflects key skills that can be exercised in communication and peer relations to improve student enthusiasm.
Education
Dist - JISTW **Prod** - JISTW

Why stay in school 15 MIN
U-matic / VHS / Videodisc / BETA
Color (I J H)
$399.00, $130.00, $98.00 purchase _ #IVV275, #WSV103, #WSV102, WSV101
Examines the close link between work and school. Uses concrete examples to show why it is important to stay in school and how staying in school leads to future success. Reveals that skills learned in school such as setting time priorities, balancing social and study time and meeting deadlines are valuable in the work world.
Education; Guidance and Counseling; Mathematics; Psychology
Dist - CADESF **Prod** - CADESF 1987

Why Stay in School
VHS / U-matic
Study Skills and Job Success Video Series
(H C T)
$98.00 _ #CD810V
Emphasizes the importance of staying in school in relation to job plans. Discusses personal habits, social habits, and leadership habits.
Education; Guidance and Counseling; Sociology
Dist - CAMV **Prod** - CAMV

Why Stay in School
U-matic / VHS
Study Skills Video Series
$98.00 purchase _ #VP003V
Shows the close link between school performance and job performance.
Education
Dist - CAREER **Prod** - CAREER

Why stay in school - building self - esteem for at - risk students
VHS
School solutions video series
Color (I J H)
$98.00 purchase _ #CDSCH100V
Makes a strong case that staying in school develops the skills and responsibilities required for future success by the at - risk student. States that staying in school builds confidence and self - esteem patterns that stay lifelong with an individual, that attendance, homework, following rules, getting along with others all have a purpose. Offers step - by - step reasons as to why school is relevant. Shows how students can seek support from teachers, counselors and other school personnel. Includes reproducible worksheets. Part of a ten - part series to build student success.
Education; Psychology
Dist - CAMV

Why Stories 15 MIN
VHS
Juba Series
Color (G)
Features the folklore stories 'Why Turtle's Shell Is Cracked' and 'Why The Snake Has Rattles.' Illustrates the role of folklore in black culture.
History - United States; Literature and Drama
Dist - PBS **Prod** - WETATV 1978
WETATV

Why study business - skills for the 21st century 30 MIN
VHS
Color (J H)
$98.00 purchase _ #WSB100
Examines various aspects of the business world and the skills that are necessary for each. Emphasizes common skill clusters such as working as part of a team, using computers, and human relations skills. Includes reproducible worksheets.
Business and Economics; Guidance and Counseling; Psychology
Dist - CADESF **Prod** - CADESF 1990

Why Study English
VHS / 16mm
(H C G)
$98.00 purchase _ #EAV 100
Shows the importance of basic communication skills in the workplace. Comes with worksheets.
Business and Economics; English Language
Dist - CADESF **Prod** - CADESF 1989

Why Study English 20 MIN
VHS / 16mm
(J H C)
$98.00 _ #FM217V
Emphasizes the essential need to accurately give and take basic verbal and written instructions in work and life situations.
Guidance and Counseling
Dist - JISTW

Why study English
VHS
Why study video series
Color (J H)
$98.00 purchase _ #CD0005V
Shows many examples of how important basic communiations skills are for the work world. Views scenes from an auto shop, warehouse and a sales office to demonstrate why good English is important on the job. Addresses three key issues - students and workers have to express themselves well in order to do the job right; communications skills help workers to get along with bosses and coworkers; English skills open up new job opportunities. Part of a series.
Education; English Language; Psychology
Dist - CAMV

Why study home economics 30 MIN
VHS
Color (J H C A)
$89.95 purchase _ #CCV700
Illustrates the usefulness of skills taught in home economics. Shows the use of decision making skills in managing money, relationships, parenting children and employment.
Business and Economics; Home Economics
Dist - CADESF **Prod** - CADESF 1990

Why Study Literature 30 MIN
VHS / U-matic
Communicating through Literature Series
Color (C)
Literature and Drama
Dist - DALCCD **Prod** - DALCCD

Why Study Math 20 MIN
VHS / 16mm
(J H C)
$98.00 _ #FM216V
Demonstrates the need for basic math skills in a variety of life and job situations, and the negative consequences for those without these skills.
Guidance and Counseling
Dist - JISTW

Why Study Math
VHS / 16mm
(H C G)
$98.00 purchase _ #MAV 100
Shows that one key to a student's future is in the mastery of basic math skills. Uses on the job work scenes to demonstrate how math is necessary even with the simplest job. Comes with worksheets.
Education; Mathematics
Dist - CADESF **Prod** - CADESF 1989

Why study math
VHS
Why study video series
Color (J H)
$98.00 purchase _ #CD0006V
Illustrates why basic math skills are important to success and advancement on the job. Explains the MPG formula - Mastery, Power and Growth. Shows why professional advancement requires the mastery of numerous math skills, the power to meet expectations from supervisors and coworkers in order to achieve growth and success. Part of a series.
Education; Mathematics; Psychology
Dist - CAMV

Why study series
Presents a six - part series on the importance of school and study. Includes the titles Why Follow the Rules; Why Stay in School; Why Writing Is Important; Why Study Math; Why Study English and Why English is Important.
Why study social studies 30 MIN
Dist - CAMV

Why study social studies 30 MIN
VHS
Why study series
Color (J H G)
$98.00 purchase _ #CDSS100V
Relates the study of social studies to the lives of students. Introduces economics, geography, history, anthropology, sociology and psychology. Illustrates graphically the importance and relevance of each subject upon students by showing that how, where and who they are today is the result of the forces which acted on their ancestors' lives. Offers ethnic balance and a global perspective.
Business and Economics; Geography - World; Psychology; Social Science; Sociology
Dist - CAMV

Why study video series
Why reading is important
Why study English
Why study math
Dist - CAMV

Why Suicide 30 MIN
VHS
Soapbox With Tom Cottle Series
Color (G)
$59.95 purchase _ #SBOX - 411
Covers teenage suicide. Considers the insights of teens who have attempted suicide. Suggests that although there are no certain signs, loneliness, depression and a desire for attention may be common reasons. Hosted by psychologist Tom Cottle.
Psychology; Sociology
Dist - PBS Prod - WGBYTV 1985

Why suicide 30 MIN
VHS
Color (J H C G T A PRO)
$59.95 purchase _ #AH45161
Interviews four teenagers who have attempted suicide at some time in the past. Provides insights on why many teenagers find life unbearable and seek to end it.
Guidance and Counseling; Health and Safety; Sociology
Dist - HTHED Prod - PBS

Why take the risk - sharps safety 18 MIN
VHS / U-matic
Color (PRO)
$250.00 purchase, $60.00 rental _ #4277S, #4277V
Demonstrates preventive procedures and treatment when a needle puncture occurs. Incorporates guidelines of the Centers for Disease Control for the safe handling and disposal of contaminated sharps. Presents practical applications of the guidelines in a hospital setting.
Health and Safety
Dist - AJN Prod - LUGEN 1987

Why the British Lost the War in the South - Pt 20 30 MIN
VHS
And Then There were Thirteen Series
Color (H)
$69.95 purchase
Considers why the British lost the war in the American South. Uses footage shot on battleground locations. Describes command personalities, weapons and uniforms. Part 20 of a twenty - part series on Southern theaters of war during the American Revolution.
Civics and Political Systems; Geography - United States; Guidance and Counseling; History - United States
Dist - SCETV Prod - SCETV 1982

Why the colonies rebelled - causes of the Revolutionary War 18 MIN
VHS
Color (I J)
$58.00 purchase _ #TK103
Reveals that many issues divided England and the American colonies. Discusses the divisive issues of land, trade, taxes and freedom. Covers influences such as the French and Indian War, British troops in the colonies and more. Video transfer from filmstrip.
History - United States
Dist - KNOWUN Prod - KNOWUN 1993

Why the Crow is Black 15 MIN
VHS / U-matic
Tales of Wesakechak Series
Color (G)
Presents long ago, Ah Haw Shiw had beautiful white feathers of which he was very proud. One day the Crow offers to help Wesakechak. He promises to keep the camp fire burning while Wesakechak is away. But because he is careless the fire goes out, and as a result, all of the Crow's feathers are turned black.
Social Science; Sociology
Dist - NAMPBC Prod - NAMPBC 1984

Why the Moose's Skin is Loose 16 MIN
VHS / 16mm
Ukrainian Shadow Puppets Series
Color (I) (ENGLISH AND UKRAINIAN)
$175.00 purchase _ #277102
Introduces some of the cultural heritage of the Cree and Blackfoot people of Alberta, Canada, through a Ukrainian bilingual program to reach the Ukrainian commmunity. Contains a unique blend of myths and legends and original music and artwork commissioned from Cree and Blackfoot artists with Ukrainian silhouette puppets. 'Why The Moose's Skin Is Loose' describes how the woodland animals got their coats. The animals ask Wesakecha to seek the Kechi Manitoo's permission for warmer coats. Each animal orders a coat except for the Moose, who ends up with a coat made from all the leftovers. He is teased so much he goes away to the isolated places where he can still be found. Includes a booklet with Ukrainian language transcripts.
Geography - World; History - World; Literature and Drama; Religion and Philosophy; Social Science; Sociology
Dist - ACCESS Prod - ACCESS 1987

Why the New World was Explored 11 MIN
16mm / U-matic / VHS
Color (I)
LC FIA68-2845
Discusses why so many Europeans risked their wealth and lives to explore the new world. Traces their search for a shorter, safer trade route to the East. Shows how their motives for searching changed from a search for trade routes to a search for gold, furs, forests and farm land.
History - United States; History - World
Dist - PHENIX Prod - FA 1968

Why the Rabbit Turns White 15 MIN
VHS / U-matic
Tales of Wesakechak Series
Color (G)
Shows Wesakechak reminded that as a teacher of the first Indian People, he should have taught them to respect and give thanks for the gifts of the Creator. He is forced to rescue them from a great drought and starvation. He is able to do this with the help of a little brown rabbit.
Social Science; Sociology
Dist - NAMPBC Prod - NAMPBC 1984

Why the Sun and Moon Live in the Sky 11 MIN
U-matic / VHS / 16mm
Children's Storybook Theater Series
Color (P I)
LC 75-711589
A legend of Eastern Nigeria about the sun and moon who lived on land until the sea came to visit them and the inundation forced them up into the sky.
Geography - World; Literature and Drama
Dist - AIMS Prod - ACI 1970

Why the Traditional Approach Fails 30 MIN
U-matic / VHS
Performance Reviews that Build Commitment Series
Color
Looks at why many traditional procedures put the manager on the defensive in performance reviews. Covers the first steps for attaining sound performance standards.
Business and Economics; Psychology
Dist - DELTAK Prod - PRODEV

Why - The United Nations at 40 22 MIN
VHS / U-matic / 16mm
Color (J H G)
$280.00, $330.00, $530.00 purchase, $60.00 rental
Recalls the role of the UN in the momentous events that have shaped history since WWII. Describes how it has dealt with such persistent problems such as human rights, economic development, decolonization, apartheid and world peace.
Civics and Political Systems; History - World; Social Science
Dist - NDIM Prod - UN 1986

Why Us, the Lakens 28 MIN
U-matic / VHS / 16mm
Color
Tells the story of a couple whose tax return is being audited. Gives an overview of IRS functions in general and shows the steps taxpayers may take when they disagree with an IRS examination decision. Narrated by Lyle Waggoner.
Business and Economics; Civics and Political Systems; Social Science
Dist - USNAC Prod - USIRS

Why use computers
VHS
School solutions video series
Color (I J H)
$98.00 purchase _ #CDSCH104V
Explores how computers have become an important part of the world from school to work to the home. Introduces specific computer skills and shows how important they have become for school and work success - word processing, spreadsheets, interactive tutorials, record keeping, subject mastery. Includes reproducible worksheets. Part of a ten - part series to build student success.
Computer Science; Education
Dist - CAMV

Why Use Positive 33 MIN
U-matic / VHS
Learning and Liking it Series
Color (T)
Presents major objections to the use of reinforcement. Demonstrates the objections.
Education; Psychology
Dist - MSU Prod - MSU

Why Vietnam 32 MIN
16mm
B&W
LC 74-705957
Outlines U S policy as stated by President Johnson. Includes Secretary of State, Dean Rusk, and Secretary of Defense, Robert McNamara.
Civics and Political Systems; Geography - World; History - World
Dist - USNAC Prod - USN 1965

Why Vietnam 55 MIN
U-matic / VHS
Color (H C A)
$295.00 purchase (each part separately), $495.00 purchase (both parts)
Discusses the reasons for the Vietnam War.
History - United States; Sociology
Dist - CF

Why Vietnam - Part 1 - the Roots of U S Involvement; the Role of the Press 55 MIN
VHS / U-matic
Color (H C A)
$295.00 purchase
Discusses the events leading up to the Vietnam War. Includes archival footage and interviews with conference participants.
History - United States; Sociology
Dist - CF

Why Vietnam - Part 2 - the Vets; the Vietnamese; Lessons from the War 46 MIN
U-matic / VHS
Color (H C A)
$295.00 purchase
Features veterans discussing the war. Examines the effects of the war on Vietnam and Vietnamese refugees.
History - United States; Sociology
Dist - CF

Why War 26 MIN
16mm / U-matic / VHS
Today's History Series
Color (H C)
Presents rare 1925 footage from New Guinea showing tribal war. Discusses reasons for war and the role of allies. Examines the issues of Cuba, Vietnam and South America.
History - United States; History - World; Sociology
Dist - JOU Prod - JOU 1984

Why was I Born 102 MIN
VHS
Color (G) (MANDARIN CHINESE)
$45.00 purchase _ #6021A
Presents a movie produced in the People's Republic Of China.
Fine Arts; Geography - World; Literature and Drama
Dist - CHTSUI Prod - CHTSUI

Why waste a second chance
VHS
Color (G A)
$80.00 purchase, $45.00 rental
Presents a training module for recycling in small towns with limited resources. Shows how a New Hampshire town with a population of 5,000 consistently recycles 40 percent of its trash and markets these materials to area manufacturers. Includes a book, video and facilitator's guide.
Civics and Political Systems; Geography - United States; Sociology
Dist - NATT Prod - NATT

Why We are the Way We are (Part a)
U-matic / VHS
Behavior Dynamics Series
Color
Reveals the complexity of the human brain, common human factors, how personality and behavior are developed, the formation of individual learned needs and how to protect oneself by the development of coping and defense mechanisms.
Psychology; Science - Natural
Dist - BUSTEL Prod - BUSTEL

Why We Celebrate 55 MIN
VHS / 16mm
Color (P)
$149.95 purchase
Explores the origins and significance of some of the holidays we celebrate. Combines five units previously available separately as filmstrips or enhanced videos - Columbus Day, Halloween, Thanksgiving, Memorial Day, and Independence Day.
Education; Literature and Drama
Dist - JANUP Prod - JANUP

Why we celebrate - video series
Columbus Day
Halloween
Independence Day
Memorial Day
Thanksgiving
Dist - PELLER

Why We Conserve Energy - the Witch of the Great Black Pool 12 MIN
U-matic / VHS / 16mm
Basic Concepts in Social Studies Series
Color (P I)
LC 78-701648
Tells a story about the Land of the Scatterpods, where people use machines which run on Black Soup. Describes what happens when the Scatterpods must start conserving the fuel.
Guidance and Counseling; Literature and Drama; Science - Natural; Social Science
Dist - LCOA **Prod** - LCOA 1978

Why We do what We do 30 MIN
VHS / U-matic
Psychology of Human Relations Series
Color
Examines the elements of motivation, expectancy - value theory of motivation, Maslow's hierarchy of needs, self - actualization, interaction of approach and avoidance motives in conflict situations.
Psychology
Dist - WFVTAE **Prod** - MATC

Why We do what We do 30 MIN
U-matic
Action Options - Alcohol, Drugs and You Series
(H C A)
Explains and contrasts the concept of routine, daily activities as opposed to creating new challenges.
Psychology; Sociology
Dist - ACCESS **Prod** - ACCESS 1986

Why we fight series
The Battle of Russia 80 MIN
Dist - KITPAR
UILL

Why We Fight Series
The Battle of Britain 55 MIN
The Battle of China 67 MIN
The Battle of China, Pt 1 33 MIN
The Battle of China, Pt 2 34 MIN
Divide and conquer 60 MIN
The Nazi Strike 41 MIN
Normandy Invasion 19 MIN
Prelude to war 54 MIN
War Comes to America 67 MIN
War Comes to America, Pt 1 33 MIN
War Comes to America, Pt 2 34 MIN
Dist - USNAC

Why We have Elections - the Kings of Snark 9 MIN
16mm / U-matic / VHS
Basic Concepts in Social Studies Series
Color (K P)
LC 73-700228
Presents a tale set in a mythical kingdom which demonstrates the concept of holding elections to select government officials. Explains that in the land of Snark when bad King Boris dies, the citizens search for a replacement who will rule the country wisely. Explains that after several elections they choose the candidate that will serve them best.
Civics and Political Systems; Guidance and Counseling; Social Science
Dist - LCOA **Prod** - LCOA 1973

Why We have Laws - Shiver, Goble and Snore 7 MIN
16mm / U-matic / VHS
Color; Captioned (P I) (SWEDISH SPANISH)
Notes the various laws in effect in society today.
Civics and Political Systems; Fine Arts; Foreign Language
Dist - LCOA **Prod** - LCOA 1970

Why We have Taxes - the Town that Had no Policeman 7 MIN
U-matic / VHS / 16mm
Basic Concepts in Social Studies Series
Color (K P)
LC 70-705962
Explains how, due to the need of a policeman, everyone gives some money and the idea of taxation is born.
Business and Economics; Civics and Political Systems; Guidance and Counseling; Social Science
Dist - LCOA **Prod** - LCOA 1970

Why We have Taxes - the Town that Had no Policeman 7 MIN
U-matic / VHS / 16mm
Color (P I) (SWEDISH SPANISH)
Introduces the concept of taxation and services provided by public employees for a community.
Business and Economics; Fine Arts; Foreign Language
Dist - LCOA **Prod** - LCOA 1970

Why We Need Doctors - no Measles, no Mumps for Me 11 MIN
16mm / U-matic / VHS
Basic Concepts in Social Studies Series
Color (P)
LC 81-700948
Presents an animated film in which a little boy learns about the value and importance of doctors from his grandmother, who tells him about her childhood when there were no vaccines against such illnesses as whooping cough.
Guidance and Counseling; Health and Safety; Social Science
Dist - LCOA **Prod** - SPORAN 1981

Why We Need each Other - the Animal's Picnic Day 9 MIN
U-matic / VHS / 16mm
Basic Concepts in Social Studies Series
Color (P) (SPANISH SWEDISH)
LC 73-700229
Suggests that individual differences are beneficial to all. Shows forest animals getting together for a picnic on a sunny day. Indicates that certain other animals couldn't join in because they were rejected by the picnickers for looking different. Relates how the ridiculed animals save the others. when danger is imminent.
Guidance and Counseling; Social Science; Sociology
Dist - LCOA **Prod** - LCOA 1973

Why We Need Reading - the Piemaker of Ignoramia 12 MIN
U-matic / VHS / 16mm
Color (P I) (SPANISH)
Shows a child why he or she needs to read and also gives some motivation to do it.
English Language; Fine Arts; Foreign Language
Dist - LCOA **Prod** - LCOA 1976

Why We Take Care of Property - Planet of the Tickle Bops 12 MIN
U-matic / VHS / 16mm
Basic Concepts in Social Studies Series
Color (P I) (SPANISH)
LC 75-704021
Presents an animated story about two children who start damaging property for fun, until they have their own property damaged and learn that everyone is affected sooner or later when people stop caring about their surroundings.
Guidance and Counseling; Science - Natural; Social Science; Sociology
Dist - LCOA **Prod** - LCOA 1975

Why We Take Care of Property - Planet of the Ticklebops 12 MIN
16mm / U-matic / VHS
Color (P I) (SPANISH)
Makes the point that if you don't care about the property of otherthey will not care about yours.
Business and Economics; Foreign Language; Social Science
Dist - LCOA **Prod** - LCOA 1976

Why We Tell the Truth - no more Squareburgers in Straighttalk 12 MIN
U-matic / VHS / 16mm
Basic Concepts in Social Studies Series
Color (A)
LC 78-701710
Tells a story about the inhabitants of Straighttalk, who tell the truth, until one day a spaceship lands and the Master of Lies teaches the people to lie for their own gain. Shows how they are almost doomed by their mistrust of each other until they swear to tell the truth again.
Guidance and Counseling
Dist - LCOA **Prod** - IMAG 1978

Why We Use Money - the Fisherman who Needed a Knife 8 MIN
U-matic / VHS / 16mm
Basic Concepts in Social Studies Series
Color (K P) (SPANISH SWEDISH)
LC 73-705963
Discusses the trading a fisherman must go through in order to get a new knife. Explains how, due to the inconvenience of trading, the idea of money is born.
Business and Economics; Guidance and Counseling; Social Science
Dist - LCOA **Prod** - LCOA 1970

Why we're killing ourselves 29 MIN
VHS
Color (PRO A)
$100.00 purchase _ #HH - 301
Features Host Dr Norman Kaplan who talks with Dr Henry W Blackburn about the risk factors in lifestyles that make individuals targets for cancer and heart disease and what can be done to reduce them.
Health and Safety
Dist - MIFE **Prod** - MIFE

Why We're Killing Ourselves 29 MIN
VHS
Here's To Your Health Series
Color (G)
$59.95 purchase _ #HEAW - 501
Reports that cancer and heart disease are the most common causes of death among adult Americans. Shows that lifestyle choices such as smoking, stress, nutrition and exercise are important in determining whether people develop these conditions.
Health and Safety
Dist - PBS **Prod** - KERA

Why we're killing ourselves 29 MIN
VHS
Color (J H C G A)
$59.95 purchase _ #AH45155
Suggests that modern lifestyles are largely to blame for heart disease and cancer. Blames tobacco, stress, pollution, poor nutrition and lack of exercise as contributors to these problems. Discusses risk reduction strategies.
Health and Safety
Dist - HTHED **Prod** - PBS

Why Women are Dissatisfied with their Gynecologists 29 MIN
U-matic
Woman Series
Color
Discusses health care from the consumer's point of view. Maintains that women should work toward demystifying the profession of medicine and its practitioners.
Health and Safety
Dist - PBS **Prod** - WNEDTV

Why women kill 50 MIN
VHS
Inside story series
Color; PAL (H C A)
PdS99 purchase; Not available in the United States or Canada
Investigates battered women who kill their husbands and uncovers a loophole in the American justice system that prohibits the disclosure of the abuse women suffered to juries. Notes that these women face harsh penalties, often life imprisonment or death. Features women from the Alabama and Texas prison systems who discuss their lives as battered women.
Sociology
Dist - BBCENE

Why Women Stay 30 MIN
U-matic
B&W
Examines the complex reasons why women remain in violent homes. Challenges the prevailing attitudes that accept physical and mental violence toward women. Exposes the social structures that victimize women and contribute to their abuse.
Civics and Political Systems; Sociology
Dist - WMEN **Prod** - WMEN

Why Work 26 MIN
16mm / U-matic / VHS
Today's History Series
Color (H C)
Discusses the future of work, and of the work ethic, especially in light of the considerable unemployment of the late 1970's and early 1980's.
Business and Economics; History - United States; History - World; Sociology
Dist - JOU **Prod** - JOU 1984

Why Work?
VHS / 35mm strip
$119.00 film purchase, $139.00 VHS purchase _ #012 - 584 film, #012 -
Explores work expectations and goals as a basis for making career choices. Features interviews with students and working adults, shows different attitudes toward work, various dreams and goals, and how some people have found job satisfaction and some are still looking.
Guidance and Counseling
Dist - CAREER **Prod** - CAREER

Why work - a professional's guide to motivating unemployed people 48 MIN
VHS
Color (PRO)
$195.00 purchase _ #4000
Captures Dean Curtis live as he trains a group of social service staff. Offers tips for staff personnel who work with unemployed - disadvantaged populations.
Business and Economics; Guidance and Counseling; Psychology
Dist - NEWCAR

Why Work, Pt 1 60 MIN
U-matic / VHS
Bill Moyers' Journal Series
Color
Explores what Bill Moyers calls 'a supreme moment of creation - labor.'.
Psychology; Sociology
Dist - PBS **Prod** - WNETTV 1980

Why Work, Pt 2 60 MIN
U-matic / VHS
Bill Moyers' Journal Series
Color
Explores what Bill Moyers calls 'a supreme moment of creation - labor.'.
Psychology; Sociology
Dist - PBS **Prod** - WNETTV 1980

Why work - six reasons why you're better off employed 15 MIN
VHS
Color (J H C G)
$95.00 purchase _ #2164
Gives positive, practical answers to one of the toughest questions asked by unemployed people, especially chronically unemployed individuals. Affirms six reasons - the employed lifestyle is better; unemployment provides no opportunity for advancement; individuals are more employable when employed; employed individuals are positive role models for their children; employed individuals have higher self - esteem; and there are programs for transition from being unemployed to working.
Business and Economics; Guidance and Counseling
Dist - NEWCAR

Why worship
VHS
Questions of faith III series
Color (J H C G A R)
$10.00 rental _ #36 - 81 - 217
Explores the concept of worship of God. Questions where, when and how it can happen. Features perspectives from a wide variety of contemporary Christian and Jewish thinkers.
Religion and Philosophy
Dist - APH **Prod** - ECUFLM

Why Write 30 MIN
U-matic / VHS
Write Course - an Introduction to College Composition Series
Color (C A)
Discusses the questions of why we write and study, and contemporary theories of the writing process.
English Language
Dist - FI **Prod** - FI 1984

Why Write?
VHS / U-matic
Write Course - an Introduction to College Composition Series
Color (C)
Addresses the questions of why we write and why we study writing, as well as the contemporary theories of the writing process as a whole.
Education; English Language
Dist - DALCCD **Prod** - DALCCD

Why writing is important 20 MIN
VHS
Color (J H C A)
$98.00 purchase _ #WWI100
Demonstrates why writing skills are crucial to work and school success. Illustrates the need for clear and grammatically correct writing in a variety of concrete situations.
Education; English Language; Psychology
Dist - CADESF **Prod** - CADESF 1990
CAMV

Why you - why me 12 MIN
VHS / 16mm
Color (G IND)
$5.00 rental
Shows how to get people to work on political campaigns and set up COPE committees. Produced by the Labor Institute of Public Affairs for COPE.
Business and Economics; Civics and Political Systems
Dist - AFLCIO **Prod** - LIPA 1986

Why You're Feeling Different 26 MIN
16mm / VHS
Facts, Feelings and Wonder of Life - the Early Stages Series
Color (I J PRO)
$295.00, $450.00 purchase, $50.00 rental _ #9980
Looks at the feelings and emotions as well as coping mechanisms for youngsters during puberty. Discusses AIDS and other sexually transmitted diseases.
Guidance and Counseling; Health and Safety; Psychology
Dist - AIMS **Prod** - PVGP 1988

Why You're You 10 MIN
16mm
Family Life and Sex Education Series
Color (I J)
Develops the concept of individual personalities. Examines the nucleus of sperm and egg cells to show that chromosomes contain characteristics. Introduces the influence of environment and discusses the effects of physical growth on personality.
Science - Natural
Dist - SF **Prod** - SF 1968

Why'd the Beetle Cross the Road 8 MIN
U-matic / VHS / 16mm
Color (I)
Presents a bug's - eye view of the meaning of life.
Fine Arts; Psychology; Religion and Philosophy; Science - Natural
Dist - PFP **Prod** - PFP

Why's and How's of Food Preserving 29 MIN
VHS / 16mm
Food Preserving Series
Color (G)
$55.00 rental _ #FODP - 001
Home Economics
Dist - PBS **Prod** - WSWPTV

Wichita Now 26 MIN
16mm
Color (I)
LC 77-705720
Uses visual, sound and editing techniques with a minimum of narration to portray the city of Wichita, describing cultural activities, recreation, education industry, shopping and residential areas.
Geography - United States; Social Science
Dist - SWBELL **Prod** - SWBELL 1969

Wicked queen and a matter of time - Volume 25 45 MIN
VHS
Superbook series
Color (K P I R)
$11.99 purchase _ #35 - 86806 - 979
Uses an animated format to tell the story of Chris and Joy and their time travels through Biblical places and events. Tells the story of Queen Athaliah and presents an account of Hezekiah.
Literature and Drama; Religion and Philosophy
Dist - APH **Prod** - TYHP

Wickersham 28 MIN
VHS
Color (G)
$395.00 purchase, $150.00 rental _ #91F6047
Offers six tried - and - true selling tips.
Business and Economics; Psychology
Dist - DARTNL **Prod** - DARTNL 1991

Wide Angle Saxon 22 MIN
16mm
Color (C)
$582.00
Experimental film by George Owen (aka Owen Land).
Fine Arts
Dist - AFA **Prod** - AFA 1975

Wide Bandpass Filter Photometer 12 MIN
U-matic / VHS
Color
LC 80-706816
Discusses, in detail, the characteristics of the wide bandpass filter photometer and mentions the characteristics of absorption photometers. Outlines contents of the operator's manual and demonstrates instrument calibration.
Science
Dist - USNAC **Prod** - CFDISC 1979

Wide Feelings 20 MIN
16mm
All that I Am Series
B&W (C A)
Fine Arts; Guidance and Counseling
Dist - NWUFLM **Prod** - MPATI

Wide Pastures 21 MIN
16mm
Color (H C A)
LC FIA68-1755
Illustrates the introduction of modern methods to Australian wool growing.
Geography - World; Psychology; Social Science
Dist - AUIS **Prod** - ANAIB 1967

Wide receiver skills and drills 20 MIN
VHS
Quarterback and receiver camp series
Color (H C A)
$39.95 purchase _ #QRC200V
Teaches skills and drills for wide receivers. Covers subjects including alignments, stances, catching the football, basic patterns, releasing from the line, faking, and steps used in the various pass patterns.
Physical Education and Recreation
Dist - CAMV

Wide world of adventure series

The Aggressive impulse	18 MIN
Antarctica - exploring the frozen continent	23 MIN
Bears - kings of the wild	23 MIN
The Big cats - endangered predators	23 MIN
Can Primitive People Survive	24 MIN
Canines - Pets and Predators	23 MIN
Caves - the dark wilderness	24 MIN
Dinosaurs - the terrible lizards	24 MIN
Endangered animals - will they survive	24 MIN
Fire - Friend and Foe	23 MIN
The Great apes - fact vs fantasy	23 MIN
Insects - the Lovely and the Lethal	23 MIN
Is the Ice Age Coming	24 MIN
Jungles - the green oceans	23 MIN
Native American Myths	24 MIN
The Occult - Mysteries of the Supernatural	24 MIN
Physical Fitness - it Can Save Your Life	24 MIN
Quest for Flight	23 MIN
The Snake - Villain or Victim	24 MIN
The Sun - its Power and Promise	24 MIN
Television - Behind the Scenes	23 MIN
Warning - Earthquake	24 MIN

Dist - EBEC

Wide World of Records 17 MIN
VHS / U-matic
Safety for Oilfield Contractors Series
Color
$165.00 purchase _ #40.0151
Focuses on various aspect of servicing and supplying a drilling operation. Provides an overview of the oilfield service and supply industry with emphasis on safe operations.
Health and Safety
Dist - FLMWST **Prod** - FLMWST
UTEXPE

The Widening World of Books 30 MIN
16mm
Starting Tomorrow Series Unit 3 - Individualizing Your Reading 'Program
B&W (T)
LC 70-714210
Illustrates how reading expands knowledge.
Education; English Language
Dist - WALKED **Prod** - EALING 1967

The Widow 102 MIN
U-matic / VHS / 16mm
Color (H C A)
Tells of a widow's experiences with her young children after her husband dies. Reveals that as her loss and financial instability bear down on her, she loses her former values and eventually her sense of identity. Stars Michael Learned. Based on the book The Widow by Lynn Caine.
Sociology
Dist - LUF **Prod** - LUF 1976

Widow 90 MIN
U-matic / VHS
Color (H C A)
Tells of a woman slowly learning to deal with her own grief, her children's traumas and monetary worries after the death of her husband. Stars Michael Learned and Bradford Dillman. Based on the book Widow by Lynn Caine.
Fine Arts; Literature and Drama; Sociology
Dist - TIMLIF **Prod** - TIMLIF 1982

The Widow - factors affecting widowhood - Part 1 32 MIN
BETA / VHS / U-matic
Human development - successful aging series
Color (C PRO)
$150.00 purchase _ #128.3
Presents a video transfer from slide program which considers a variety of factors which determine the social and psychological effects of widowhood. Examines the lives of two very different older women to see how the experience of widowhood has affected them. Interweaves their true stories with conceptual material and reports of gerontological studies. Part one of two parts on widowhood and part of a series on successful aging.
Health and Safety
Dist - CONMED **Prod** - CONMED

The Widow - problems and compensations - Part 2 30 MIN
BETA / VHS / U-matic
Human development - successful aging series

Color (C PRO)
$150.00 purchase _ #128.4
Presents a video transfer from slide program which delineates some of the significant problems occurring when a woman becomes a widow. Explores a number of benefits arising from widowhood. Correlates factors with stories of the women presented in Part 1. Part two of two parts on widowhood and part of a series on successful aging.
Health and Safety
Dist - CONMED **Prod** - CONMED

The Widower 38 MIN
VHS / U-matic / BETA
Human development - successful aging series
Color (C PRO)
$150.00 purchase _ #128.5
Presents a video transfer from slide program which describes the specific problems widowhood creates for older men. Explores methods of coping with the problems. Presents the experiences of two widowers, age 67 and 92, and relates their reactions to widowhood. Part of a series on successful aging.
Health and Safety
Dist - CONMED **Prod** - CONMED

Widowhood 30 MIN
U-matic
Transitions - Caught at Midlife Series
Color
Examines the problems and fears of women alone in their mid - life.
Psychology; Sociology
Dist - UMITV **Prod** - UMITV 1980

Widowhood - Three Personal Perspectives 29 MIN
U-matic
Color (J C)
Interviews three elderly persons coping with widowhood. Explores the ways the widows faced the death of their loved one and coped with grief, loneliness and subsequent changes in their lives. Co - produced by Cedar Community Center, a multiservice center for older persons in San Diego.
Psychology; Sociology
Dist - SDSC **Prod** - SDSC 1978

Widows 28 MIN
U-matic
Are you listening series
Color (J)
LC 80-701127; 80-706742
Presents a group of women discussing their emotional trauma after the deaths of their husbands.
Guidance and Counseling; Psychology; Sociology
Dist - STURTM **Prod** - STURTM 1979

The Widow's Lazy Daughter 27 MIN
U-matic / VHS / 16mm
Storybook International Series
Color
Tells the Irish story of Bridget, who falls in love with a prince but is made to do various tasks of spinning, weaving and knitting by the queen before she can marry him. Relates how she is helped in her tasks by a deformed woman who asks only that she be invited to the wedding feast. Reveals that at the wedding feast, the old woman tells Bridget that she became deformed from too much weaving, spinning and knitting and that the prince forbids Bridget to ever do these tasks again.
Guidance and Counseling; Literature and Drama
Dist - JOU **Prod** - JOU 1982

Wie Kann Man Berliner Luft Sichtbar Machen 15 MIN
16mm / U-matic / VHS
Guten Tag Wie Geht's Series
Color (H C) (GERMAN)
A German language film. Explains that while Herr Hollmann and his students are on a field trip, the students busy themselves with an unusual method of collecting air in Berlin to sell as souvenirs.
Foreign Language
Dist - IFB **Prod** - BAYER 1973

Wield your shield - Volume 7 25 MIN
VHS
Filling station series
Color (K P I R)
$11.99 purchase _ #35 - 811378 - 979
Combines live action and animated sequences to teach the message that faith in God is essential to life.
Literature and Drama; Religion and Philosophy
Dist - APH **Prod** - TYHP

Wieners and buns musical 16 MIN
16mm
B&W (G)
$35.00 rental
Focuses on a housewife heroine named Trixie, who dresses like Dorothy Lamour in the South Sea Islands, and yearns to have her lover rather than her husband.
Fine Arts
Dist - CANCIN **Prod** - MCDOWE 1971

Wife among Wives, a 72 MIN
U-matic / VHS / 16mm
Turkana Conversations Trilogy Series
Color (TURKANA (ENGLISH SUBTITLES))
Investigates how the Turkana of northwestern Kenya view marriage. Shows preparation for marriage and interviews three sisters who discuss why a woman would want her husband to take a second wife and how polygamy can be a source of solidarity among women. Presented in Turkana with English subtitles.
Foreign Language; History - World
Dist - UCEMC **Prod** - MCDGAL 1980

Wife and Auto Trouble 11 MIN
16mm
B&W (J)
Willie Collier, Mae Busch and the Keystone Cops star in a typical slapstick comedy in which a man is caught dining with his secretary and takes off in a model T. A silent film.
Fine Arts
Dist - RMIBHF **Prod** - TRIS 1916

Wife Beating 27 MIN
U-matic / VHS / 16mm
Color (C A)
LC 76-703987
Examines the psychological causes of wife beating and the emotional, as well as physical, repercussions on women and their children. Discusses the emergence of wife beating as a serious social problem and offers possible solutions.
Psychology; Sociology
Dist - FI **Prod** - NBCTV 1976

Wife, Writer, Warrior 1776 30 MIN
U-matic
American Women - Echoes and Dreams Series
Color
Dramatizes three women's contributions to the Revolutionary War effort. Depicts Catherine Schuyler protecting her family. Pictures Mercy Otis Warren, a founder of the Committees of Correspondence. Tells how Deborah Sampson disguised herself in order to fight in the war.
Biography; History - United States; History - World; Literature and Drama
Dist - HRC **Prod** - OHC

Wilber 8 MIN
U-matic / VHS / 16mm
Color (IND)
Demonstrates the many careless mistakes which can lead to accident and loss. Follows Wilber's departure for work through the morning traffic to his attempts to help others. Shows the areas in which safety precautions should be exercised.
Health and Safety
Dist - IFB **Prod** - IAPA 1973

The Wilberforce Pendulum M - 6 3 MIN
16mm
Single - Concept Films in Physics Series
Color (H C)
Indicates resonance between torsional vibration and translational vibration of a rigid body suspended from a helical spring. Shows energy transformations - rotational and translational, kinetic and potential.
Science - Physical
Dist - OSUMPD **Prod** - OSUMPD 1963

Wilbur and Orville - the Air Devils 52 MIN
16mm / U-matic / VHS
Great Americans Series
Color (I)
Presents the story of the Wright Brothers' efforts to build the first working airplane.
History - United States; Industrial and Technical Education
Dist - LUF **Prod** - LUF 1979

Wilbur Shaw - Speed Way Star 15 MIN
BETA / VHS
B&W
Presents one of America's greatest race car drivers, Wilbur Shaw.
Biography; Physical Education and Recreation
Dist - STAR **Prod** - STAR

Wilbur's Story 15 MIN
16mm
Peppermint Stick Selection Series
Color (P I)
LC 77-701722
An excerpt from the motion picture Charlotte's Web. Tells how a pig named Wilbur is saved from the sausage grinder by his literate friend Charlotte the spider, who schemes to save him by weaving into her web words which sing Wilbur's praises. Based on the book Charlotte's Web by E B White.
English Language; Fine Arts; Literature and Drama
Dist - FI **Prod** - FI 1976

Wild America, who Needs it 20 MIN
16mm / U-matic / VHS
Color (J H A)
LC 81-700802
Creates an awareness that although we live with the conveniences and sophisticated alterations to our natural environment brought about by technology, we are still living off the land for our most basic necessities. Points out that everyone is affected by ecologically unsound practices.
Science - Natural
Dist - PHENIX **Prod** - NAS 1979

A Wild and impractical scheme - 1800 - 1845 14 MIN
VHS / 16mm
Railroad series
Color (I J H G)
$280.00, $39.95 purchase
Tells the story of American railroads from its beginning, when the idea of building a railroad was dismissed as 'a wild and impractical scheme,' to a generation or so later when Daniel Webster declared that 'the railroad towered above all other inventions in this or the preceding age.' Part of a series on American railroads.
History - United States; Social Science
Dist - KAWVAL **Prod** - KAWVAL

Wild and Tasty 29 MIN
U-matic
House Botanist Series
Color
Discusses how to identify edible wild plants and how to cook them.
Agriculture; Science - Natural
Dist - UMITV **Prod** - UMITV 1978

The Wild and Wonderful Thirties 28 MIN
16mm
Hollywood and the Stars Series
B&W
LC 73-702038
Examines the film industry in the 1930's, the beginning of sound, describing publicity gimmicks of the stars, films produced through the depression years, and a glimpse of the stars' lives showing their homes, cars and yachts.
Fine Arts
Dist - WOLPER **Prod** - WOLPER 1964

The Wild and Wonderful World of Auto Racing 27 MIN
16mm
Color (J)
LC 70-705721
Examines and compares the four major kinds of auto racing - stocks, sports, drag and Indianapolis championship cars.
Physical Education and Recreation
Dist - SF **Prod** - RAYBEM 1969

The Wild Angels 82 MIN
16mm
Color (H A)
Describes a California motorcycle gang which is run on semireligious, ritualistic, Nazi lines. Stars Peter Fonda, Nancy Sinatra and Bruce Dern in this frequently banned, social drama.
Fine Arts
Dist - TIMLIF **Prod** - AIP 1966

Wild Animal Families 11 MIN
U-matic / VHS / 16mm
Color (K P I) (FRENCH)
Presents common North American animals in family situations, showing the care of the young by both mother and father. Animals shown in natural habitat include bison, antelope, prairie dog, bear, porcupine, elk and Canada goose.
Foreign Language; Science - Natural
Dist - PHENIX **Prod** - FA 1957

Wild Animal Park 15 MIN
VHS / U-matic
Explorers Unlimited Series
Color (P I)
Visits the San Diego Wild Animal Park to learn about an alternative type of animal keeping.
Geography - United States; Science - Natural
Dist - AITECH **Prod** - WVIZTV 1971

Wild Animals Adapt 9 MIN
U-matic / VHS / 16mm
Life Science for Elementary Series
Color (P I)
LC 76-700813
Shows how the physical characteristics of the bighorn sheep, the water ouzel and the squirrel provide effective adaptations in their different environments.
Science - Natural
Dist - AIMS **Prod** - PEDF 1976

Wild Animals Catch Fish 9 MIN
U-matic / VHS / 16mm
Life Science for Elementary Series
Color (P I) (SPANISH)
LC 76-700814
Shows how several different kinds of animals and birds use diverse fishing techniques. Identifies the specialized and adaptive characteristics of each technique.
Foreign Language; Science - Natural
Dist - AIMS **Prod** - PEDF 1976

Wild animals in the zoo 3 MIN
16mm
B&W (G)
$15.00 rental
Mixes charcoal, ink wash and zerographic animation with a muscial score by Basil Bova and George Cordiero. Watches animals that were once wild disintegrate after entering the zoo.
Fine Arts; Science - Natural
Dist - CANCIN **Prod** - JOHNF 1978

Wild Animals of Virginia 26 MIN
16mm
Color (P I J H)
LC FIA67-2017
Presents a survey of the mammals native to Virginia, picturing their habits and natural habitats - - the chipmunk, squirrel, groundhog, beaver, muskrat, otter, mink, elk, deer, bear, grey and red fox, rabbit, opossum, bobcat, raccoon and skunk.
Geography - United States; Science - Natural
Dist - VADE **Prod** - VADE 1967

Wild Animals, Pt 1 15 MIN
Videoreel / VT2
Charlie's Pad Series
Color
Fine Arts
Dist - PBS **Prod** - WSIU

Wild Animals, Pt 2 15 MIN
Videoreel / VT2
Charlie's Pad Series
Color
Fine Arts
Dist - PBS **Prod** - WSIU

Wild at the Wheel 10 MIN
U-matic / VHS / 16mm
Color (H C A)
Examines why people speed, showing the serious accident of a teenager who is a compulsive speeder.
Health and Safety
Dist - AIMS **Prod** - AIMS 1978

Wild Babies 26 MIN
16mm
Color
LC 79-700888
Studies the behavior of the young in a variety of North American animals and notes the similarities between animals and humans.
Psychology; Science - Natural
Dist - STOUFP **Prod** - STOUFP 1979

Wild boar 25 MIN
VHS
Nature watch series
Color (P I J H C)
$49.00 purchase _ #320208; LC 89-715852
Presents a rare and intimate study of wild boars, focusing on the behavior of female boars and their young. Part of a series that explores the curious and uncommon characteristics of a variety of mammals, insects, birds and sea creatures.
Science - Natural
Dist - TVOTAR **Prod** - TVOTAR 1988

The Wild boar - France - Part 4 8 MIN
VHS
Natures kingdom series
Color (P I J)
$125.00 purchase
Reveals that wild boars are hated by French farmers because they destroy planted fields in their search for food. Shows that boars are notorious for their ferocious savagery when cornered. Part of a 26 - part series on animals showing the habitats and traits of various species.
Geography - World; Science - Natural
Dist - LANDMK **Prod** - LANDMK 1992

Wild boy 40 MIN
VHS / U-matic
Color (I J)
$425.00, $395.00 purchase _ #V461
Tells about a boy who is aboard an airplane that disappears near a remote Scottish island. Reveals that two years later, three young men discover the boy who has been living in the wild and learn to respect his survival skills.
Literature and Drama
Dist - BARR **Prod** - CEPRO 1988

The Wild Bunch 143 MIN
16mm
Color
Describes the adventures of a 1913 outlaw gang who plan one last bank robbery.
Fine Arts
Dist - TWYMAN **Prod** - WB 1969

Wild but Friendly 14 MIN
16mm
B&W (H C A)
Presents India's rich wild life as found in the sanctuaries and shows the rich variety of flora and fauna.
Science - Natural
Dist - NEDINF **Prod** - INDIA

Wild California 36 MIN
VHS
Color (J H C G)
$195.00 purchase, $40.00 rental _ #37898
Introduces a dozen natural habitats found in California and the western United States. Provides a captivating and informative profile of the ecology and natural history of the region. Features Peter Coyote as narrator. Produced by Sea Studios, Monterey, California.
Geography - United States; History - United States; Science - Natural
Dist - UCEMC

Wild California - the land 19 MIN
VHS
Color (I J H C G)
$125.00 purchase, $35.00 rental _ #37896
Consists of seven of the natural habitats featured in the complete video program, Wild California. Explores through four seasons the wildlife and ecology of terrestial habitats found in California and the West. Habitats include a Tule marsh, oak woodlands, montane slope, early Sierra winter, the Great Basin and the desert. Includes a vignette on bird migration. Features Peter Coyote as narrator. Produced by Sea Studios, Monterey, California.
Geography - United States; History - United States; Science - Natural
Dist - UCEMC

Wild California - the sea 18 MIN
VHS
Color (I J H C G)
$125.00 purchase, $35.00 rental _ #37897
Introduces wildlife and natural habitats found on and off the Pacific coast, also featured in the complete video program, Wild California. Includes elephant seals on the Farallon Islands, the ecology of beach wrack. Offers sections on the Farallon Islands, sea meadows, between the tides, beach wrack and a salt marsh. Features Peter Coyote as narrator. Produced by Sea Studios, Monterey, California.
Geography - United States; History - United States; Science - Natural
Dist - UCEMC

Wild Cats 26 MIN
16mm
Color
Looks at the seldom - seen but intriguing lives of wild cats including the jaguar, the mountain lion, lynx, bobcat, margay, ocelot and jaguarundi.
Science - Natural
Dist - STOUFP **Prod** - STOUFP 1983

Wild Characters, Patterns, Pipes and Tees 30 MIN
U-matic / VHS
UNIX Series
Color (IND)
Shows that command is - tr (- d, - c, - cs).
Industrial and Technical Education; Mathematics; Sociology
Dist - COLOSU **Prod** - COLOSU

Wild Corners of the Great Lakes 55 MIN
16mm
To the Wild Country Series
Color
LC 76-701078
Views wildlife and Indian relics along Lake Superior's north shore.
Geography - United States; Geography - World
Dist - KEGPL **Prod** - CANBC 1974

Wild Corners of the Great Lakes, Pt 1 27 MIN
16mm
To the Wild Country Series
Color
LC 76-701078
Views wildlife and Indian relics along Lake Superior's north shore.
Geography - United States
Dist - KEGPL **Prod** - CANBC 1974

Wild Corners of the Great Lakes, Pt 2 28 MIN
16mm
To the Wild Country Series
Color
LC 76-701078
Views wildlife and Indian relics along Lake Superior's north shore.
Geography - United States
Dist - KEGPL **Prod** - CANBC 1974

Wild Dogs 26 MIN
16mm
Color
LC 83-700331
Looks at the social behavior of wild dogs and their role in a balanced ecosystem.
Science - Natural
Dist - STOUFP **Prod** - STOUFP 1982

The Wild Duck 60 MIN
VHS / U-matic
Drama - play, performance, perception series; Playrights and plotting
Color (H C A)
Develops an appreciation of the playwright's craft in shaping the elements of plot, theme and character. Uses the play The Wild Duck as an example.
Literature and Drama
Dist - FI **Prod** - BBCTV 1978

The Wild duck 96 MIN
VHS
Color (H C)
$97.00 purchase _ #04636 - 126
Stars Liv Ullmann and Jeremy Irons in a film adaptation of the drama by Henrik Ibsen.
Fine Arts; Literature and Drama
Dist - GA **Prod** - GA

The Wild Duck 106 MIN
16mm
Color (GERMAN (ENGLISH SUBTITLES))
Describes how the family of a photographer leads a life of comfortable delusion until an old friend exposes their lies and hypocrisy. Directed by Hans W Geissendorfer. With English subtitles.
Fine Arts; Foreign Language; Literature and Drama
Dist - NYFLMS **Prod** - UNKNWN 1976

The Wild Duck 108 MIN
VHS / U-matic
Classic Theatre Series
Color
LC 79-706933
Presents Henrik Ibsen's play The Wild Duck, which asks whether humanity can bear 'too much reality.'.
Literature and Drama
Dist - FI **Prod** - BBCTV 1976

Wild Edible Plants 17 MIN
16mm
Color
LC 77-700057
Shows edible wild plants of the United States and notes ways to prepare various plants. Warns against poisonous plants.
Home Economics; Science - Natural
Dist - WESTWN **Prod** - WESTWN 1976

Wild Fire 50 MIN
16mm / U-matic / VHS
Color (J H A)
Documents the tragic saga of the Wenatchee forest fire, one of the worst in history.
History - World
Dist - FI **Prod** - MGM 1972

Wild Foods Form Wild Places 12 MIN
16mm
Color (J)
LC 79-701093
Identifies various types of edible roots, berries, seeds, nuts and greens growing in the wild.
Science - Natural
Dist - COLIM **Prod** - COLIM 1979

Wild geese calling 33 MIN
U-matic / VHS / 16mm
Animal featurettes series; Set 3
Color (I J H)
LC 78-701719
Tells how a nine - year - old boy finds a wild Canadian gander wounded by hunters and unable to fly. Shows how he nurses the gander back to health and then must decide whether to keep it as a pet or set it free to return to its flock.
Literature and Drama; Science - Natural
Dist - CORF **Prod** - DISNEY 1969

The Wild Goose 19 MIN
U-matic / VHS / 16mm
B&W (H C A)
LC 79-700169
Looks at one elderly man's rebellion against life in a convalescent home as he antagonizes other residents and chases nurses in his wheelchair. Depicts the man's struggle against conformity.

Health and Safety; Psychology; Sociology
Dist - FI **Prod** - CRONIN 1975

A Wild goose chase 5 MIN
VHS / 16mm
B&W (G)
$250.00, $225.00 purchase, $75.00 rental
Combines classic film footage featuring W C Fields with Fields - like narration to take an entertaining look at miscommunicating. Teaches the importance of making sure ideas are clearly communicated and clearly understood.
Business and Economics; English Language; Psychology
Dist - CCCD **Prod** - CCCD
VLEARN

Wild - Goose Jack 57 MIN
U-matic / VHS
Color (J)
LC 84-706505
Introduces Canadian Jack Miner who was once a skilled hunter but turned to conservation after the deaths of two of his children and his brother. Discusses Miner's contributions in the field of water fowl migration.
Science - Natural
Dist - DIRECT **Prod** - MURPH 1983

Wild Goose Jack 57 MIN
16mm
(G)
Shows the life of Jack Miner who was an illiterate brickmaker and guide, regarded as the deadliest hunter in Canada, and becomes the world's best known conservationist.
Biography; Science - Natural
Dist - CFLMDC **Prod** - NFBC

Wild gunman 20 MIN
VHS / 16mm
Color (G)
$40.00 rental
Features a manic montage of pop - cultural amusements, cowboy iconography and advertising imagery. Places these found footage fragments with the contemporary geopolitical crisis in a scathing critique of United States' cultural and political imperialism. A Craig Baldwin production. Available for purchase in video format with a group package entitled Three Films.
Business and Economics; Civics and Political Systems; Fine Arts; Psychology; Sociology
Dist - CANCIN

Wild Highlands 21 MIN
U-matic / VHS / 16mm
Color (J H C)
LC FIA65-278
Depicts the variety of wildlife - - flowers, insects and animals - - which is found in the mountains and forests of Western Scotland.
Geography - World; Science - Natural
Dist - IFB **Prod** - BTF 1964

Wild Horses, Broken Wings 30 MIN
16mm / VHS / U-matic
Color (H C A)
LC 79-700952; 79-700951
Explores the life of Davene Bennett, a woman who has been a foster mother for thirty years, taking children of all ages and races into her home.
Guidance and Counseling; Physical Education and Recreation; Sociology
Dist - LCOA **Prod** - VERITN 1979

Wild horses of the Nevada desert 29 MIN
16mm / VHS
Color (J H C G)
$545.00, $200.00 purchase, $40.00 rental
Looks at the conflict between livestock operators and preservationists over the wild horse population on public lands in the Nevada desert.
Agriculture; Geography - United States; Science - Natural
Dist - DIRECT **Prod** - DIRECT 1988

Wild in the City
U-matic / VHS
Color
Looks at the intrusion of the wild raccoon into an urban environment. Follows the nightly lives of a typical urban raccoon family as they get in and out of trouble.
Science - Natural
Dist - NWLDPR **Prod** - NWLDPR

Wild in the Streets 92 MIN
16mm
Color (H A)
Tells the story of a pop singer who becomes president and launches a campaign for teenage emancipation. Social melodrama starring Shelley Winters and Chris Jones.
Fine Arts
Dist - TIMLIF **Prod** - AIP 1968

Wild Indians 29 MIN
Videoreel / VT2
Children's Fair Series
B&W (K P)
Science; Social Science
Dist - PBS **Prod** - WMVSTV

Wild Ireland 50 MIN
U-matic / VHS
Color (H C A)
Portrays the wildlife of Ireland showing a history of human invasion and settlement that cleared the forests, farmed the land and brought new plants and animals. Explains how the landscape is a legacy of the last Ice Age that has undergone dramatic changes. Features arctic plants beside orchids, peat - land with its own animals, birds and plants and mild marshes and estuaries feeding wintering wildfowl of Europe and North America.
Geography - World
Dist - FI **Prod** - BBCTV

A Wild Lens in Algonquin 55 MIN
16mm
To the Wild Country Series
Color
LC 75-704360
Takes a look at the wildlife and vegetation of Algonquin Park in Ontario, Canada.
Geography - World; Science - Natural
Dist - KEGPL **Prod** - CANBC 1974

Wild Life of India 26 MIN
16mm
Color (H C A)
Presents eight wild life sanctuaries in Kashmir, Uttar Pradesh, Assam, Gujaat, Mysore and Kerala in India, with their lush jungles and large varieties of flora and fauna. Includes the bird sanctuary which is frequented by birds of other countries, the Corbett National Park and the Kaziringa Sanctuary and indicates the facilities available for tourists.
Physical Education and Recreation; Science - Natural
Dist - NEDINF **Prod** - INDIA

The Wild Man of the Forest - the Orangutan 23 MIN
VHS / U-matic
Color (K)
Tells of an experiment which may give the orangutan a future. Shows people teaching orangutans, which have been captured, how to live in the wild.
Science - Natural
Dist - NWLDPR **Prod** - NWLDPR 1982

Wild Mountain Sheep 24 MIN
VHS / U-matic
Aerie Nature Series
Color (I J H)
Examines the Rocky Mountain Big Horn Sheep and the Dall Sheep of Alaska from an ecological approach which includes wildlife studies, the mountain sheep's predators such as coyotes, golden eagles and the grizzly bear, survival techniques and mating rituals.
Science - Natural
Dist - CEPRO **Prod** - CEPRO 1982

Wild night in El Reno 6 MIN
VHS
Color (G)
$8.00 rental, $20.00 purchase
Documents a thunderstorm as it rages above a motel in May on the southern plains.
Fine Arts
Dist - CANCIN **Prod** - KUCHAR 1977

The Wild One 79 MIN
16mm
B&W
Demonstrates how the lynch mob response of the townspeople is no less destructive than the wild anarchy of the cycle gangs. Stars Marlon Brando.
Fine Arts
Dist - UAE **Prod** - CPC 1954

Wild Pets 29 MIN
Videoreel / VT2
Observing Eye Series
Color
Science - Natural; Sociology
Dist - PBS **Prod** - WGBHTV

Wild places series

Alligator swamp	10 MIN
Cactus desert	10 MIN
Lily pad pond	10 MIN
Monkey rain forest	10 MIN
Rocky Mountain meadow	10 MIN
Squirrel woodlands	10 MIN

Dist - CORF

Wild Poses 19 MIN
16mm
B&W
Tells what happens when Spanky's parents take him to Otto Phocus' photography studio to have his picture taken. A Little Rascals film.
Fine Arts
Dist - RMIBHF **Prod** - ROACH 1933

Wild refuge series
Draws viewers into the North American wilderness with true life adventures. Shows how animal species cope with their surroundings to survive. Titles include Rocky Mountain Adventures; In Search of the Rare Everglades Kite; Natural Enemies - the Deer and the Wolf; The Oceans - Going Under in the Bahamas; Exploring the Kingdom of the Reptile; The Rain Forest's Green Hell; The Eternal Mysteries of Migration; Long Distance Commuting with the Grey Whale; Come Fly with the Hawk; The Great Bison Herds and the Old West; Saving the Largest Bird in the World; Prowling with the Mighty Polar Bear; and On the Trail of the Bighorn. 13 episodes, each 24 minutes in length, document different areas. Offers a selection of six for $34.95 or purchase individually.

Come fly with the hawk	24 MIN
The Eternal mysteries of migration	24 MIN
Exploring the kingdom of the reptile	24 MIN
The Great bison herds and the old west	24 MIN
In search of the rare Everglades kite	24 MIN
Long distance commuting with the grey whale	24 MIN
Natural enemies - the deer and the wolf	24 MIN
The Oceans - going under in the Bahamas	24 MIN
On the trail of the bighorn	24 MIN
Prowling with the mighty polar bear	24 MIN
The Rain forest's green hell	24 MIN
Rocky Mountain adventures	24 MIN
Saving the largest bird in the world	24 MIN

Dist - CNEMAG **Prod** - HOBELP 1933

Wild rice - The Taming of a grain 18 MIN
VHS / U-matic / 16mm
Color (J H G)
$250.00, $300.00 purchase, $50.00 rental
Traces the history of wild rice, a native North American food rapidly growing in popularity and the first wild grain to be brought into cultivation in modern history. Covers the importance of genetic diversity and the cultural traditions that surround harvesting of the grain. Produced by Waterstone Films.
Home Economics; Science - Natural
Dist - NDIM

A Wild Ride 10 MIN
16mm
B&W
Shows a very young Victoy Moore getting a new automobile.
Fine Arts
Dist - FCE **Prod** - FCE

The Wild Riders 52 MIN
U-matic / VHS
West of the Imagination Series
Color (G)
$279.00, $179.00 purchase _ #AD - 1105
Presents the West of Frederic Remington and Charley Russell, who transformed the cowboy into the most enduring hero - figure in American folklore. Reveals that both created a gallery of heroes who live on in American imagination. Part of a six - part series on the West of imagination, as reported by artists, writers and photographers who went to the frontiers and reported what they saw - or wished they had seen.
Fine Arts; Geography - United States; Industrial and Technical Education; Literature and Drama
Dist - FOTH **Prod** - FOTH

Wild River 52 MIN
U-matic / VHS / 16mm
B&W (I J H C)
LC 79-706853
Shows a family exploring Idaho's Middle Fork Salmon and Salmon Rivers in rafts and kayaks and traveling the Florida everglades.
Geography - United States; Physical Education and Recreation; Science - Natural
Dist - NGS **Prod** - PMI 1970

The Wild river 60 MIN
VHS
Giant Nile series
Color (H C)
$250.00 purchase
Visits Ethiopia, Rwanda, Kenya and the Sudan to travel on the River Omo on a voyage through time to see tribes of huntsmen, labret - wearing women, parades of warriors and Dinkas along the turbulent Nile at its source. Part of a three - part series on the 4200 mile long Nile River.
Geography - World
Dist - LANDMK **Prod** - LANDMK 1992

Wild Russian boars 60 MIN
VHS
Color (H A G)
$49.95 purchase _ #CE104
Films wild boar hunting in Georgia swamps and Texas hills. Demonstrates dog work.
Geography - United States; Physical Education and Recreation
Dist - AAVIM **Prod** - AAVIM

Wild Science 51 MIN
U-matic / VHS
Color (H C)
$79.00 purchase _ #3481
Explores one of science's controversial frontier, phenomena that seem to exist, yet cannot be tested or explained by the scientific method. Presented by actor Peter Falk.
Science; Science - Physical
Dist - EBEC

Wild Science - Communicating with Animals 11 MIN
U-matic / VHS / 16mm
Color (J H)
$59.00 purchase _ #3516; LC 78-700783
Reports on two successful experiments that show that animals can learn language and that interspecies communication is possible. Features Morgan, a whale who helps the Navy locate submarines and guides underwater search - and - retrieve teams, and Lana, a chimpanzee who constructs sentences on a computer. Narrated by Peter Falk.
English Language; Psychology; Science - Natural
Dist - EBEC **Prod** - NBCTV 1976

Wild Science - Mind and Body 10 MIN
16mm / U-matic / VHS
Color (J H)
$59.00 purchase _ #3517; LC 78-700839
Looks at the practices of mind and body regulation of the Tarahumara Indians of Central Mexico, who run distances of 200 miles nonstop, and of yoga practitioners, who control heart rate, blood flow and respiration. Demonstrates that mental and physical health are interrelated. Shows modern science's duplication of these self - regulatory processes by biofeedback training. Narrated by Peter Falk.
Psychology; Science - Natural; Social Science; Sociology
Dist - EBEC **Prod** - NBCTV

Wild south series
Living together 30 MIN
The Robins return 30 MIN
Dist - ALTSUL

Wild strawberries 91 MIN
VHS
B&W (G)
$29.95 purchase _ #WIL140
Follows an aged doctor's journey through a compelling landscape of dream and memory as he travels to receive an honorary degree. Uses haunting flashbacks and incidents along the way, including dramatic effects of light and dark, forcing him to confront his life and its failings. Looks at the eternal questions of loneliness, aging and mortality with a warmth and humanity not often found in director Ingmar Bergman's austere world.
Fine Arts; Health and Safety; Psychology; Sociology
Dist - HOMVIS **Prod** - JANUS 1959

The Wild Swans 9 MIN
16mm / U-matic / VHS
Classic Tales Retold Series
Color (P I)
LC 77-700092
Presents the Hans Christian Andersen story, The Wild Swans, about a young girl's devotion to her 11 brothers who have been placed under an evil spell and turned into wild swans.
Fine Arts; Literature and Drama
Dist - PHENIX **Prod** - PHENIX 1976

The Wild Swans - a Danish Fairy Tale 11 MIN
16mm / U-matic / VHS
Favorite Fairy Tales and Fables Series
Color (K P)
$280.00, $195.00 purchase _ #4149
Presents the Danish fairy tale The Wild Swans. Tells the story of eleven wild swans who are really princes, bewitched by an evil queen. Shows how only their sister's hard work and devotion can return them to human form.
Literature and Drama
Dist - CORF **Prod** - CORF 1980

Wild Synch 10 MIN
16mm
Color
LC 74-702777
Presents an experimental film which shows how to get lip synchronization with a wind up camera and a wild tape recorder as a mother plays piano and her daughter dances.
Education; Fine Arts; Industrial and Technical Education
Dist - CANFDC **Prod** - HANCXR 1973

Wild West 30 MIN
U-matic
Today's Special Series
Color (K P)
Develops language arts skills in children. Programs are thematically designed around subjects of interest to youngsters. Action takes place in a department store where people, mannequins, puppets, comic characters and special guests present a light hearted approach to language arts.
Fine Arts; Literature and Drama; Psychology
Dist - TVOTAR **Prod** - TVOTAR 1985

Wild west woman 7 MIN
16mm / U-matic
Color; B&W (G H C I)
$50.00, $99.00, $125.00 purchase
Pays tribute to the women of all races who lived and emigrated West of the Mississippi between 1850 - 1890. Presents the real women who made history with over 150 black and white 'herstorical' photographs. Produced by Kay Weaver and Martha Wheelock.
History - United States; History - World; Industrial and Technical Education
Dist - ISHTAR

Wild westerns - back to the Saturday matinee 82 MIN
VHS
Color (G)
$29.95 purchase _ #IV - 516
Looks at the Saturday matinee of yesteryear and its dominant item, the B western. Looks at stars such as Ken Maynard, Buck Jones and Randolph Scott. Presents the complete Ken Maynard western, 1934 in Old Sante Fe. Features Tony Thomas as writer and narrator.
Fine Arts; Geography - United States; History - United States; Literature and Drama
Dist - INCRSE **Prod** - INCRSE

Wild westerns - winning the West week by week 58 MIN
VHS
Color (G)
$29.95 purchase _ #IV - 511
Returns to American films made in the 1930s and 1940s for examples of the western serial. Includes excerpts from The Miracle Rider, the last film made by Tom Mix, Harry Carey excaping from The Devil Horse, Johnnie Mack Brown saviing the wagon train from the Indians in Flaming Frontiers, Roy Corrigan discovering the rider of The Painted Stallion, Robert Livingstone saving California from a Russian invasion in The Vigilantes Are Coming, Buck Jones fighting bad guys in Riders of Death Valley, and Dick Foran getting the railroad through in The Winners of the West. Tony Thomas hosts.
Fine Arts; History - United States; Literature and Drama
Dist - INCRSE **Prod** - INCRSE

Wild, Wild World of Animals Series
Cry Wolf 15 MIN
Deadly African Snakes 15 MIN
Kodiak Island 16 MIN
The Octopus 12 MIN
Sea Turtles 13 MIN
The Spider 18 MIN
Dist - TIMLIF

Wild Wings 26 MIN
16mm
Color
Portrays the diversity of bird life on earth including the arctic tern, a roadrunner and a sidewinder.
Science - Natural
Dist - STOUFP **Prod** - STOUFP 1983

Wild Wings 35 MIN
U-matic / VHS / 16mm
Color (J H C)
Explores the wildfowl trust, Slimbridge, England, showing the activities involved in the study and conservation of over 120 species of wildfowl, which migrate to the sanctuary or make it their permanent home.
Science - Natural
Dist - IFB **Prod** - IFB 1967

Wild Women don't have the blues 58 MIN
VHS / 16mm
Color (G)
$850.00, $250.00 purchase, $125.00, $75.00 rental
Recaptures the lives and times of Ma Rainey, Bessie Smith, Ida Cox, Alberta Hunter, Ethel Waters and other women who sang the blues. Reveals that Ma Rainey, Mother of the Blues, first put this folk idiom on the stage in 1902. Celebrity status did not protect these women from segregation and economic exploitation and few of them received much financial reward from their popularity. Produced by Carole van Valkenburgh and Christine Dall.
Fine Arts; History - United States; History - World
Dist - CANWRL

Wild world series
A Colt called lucky 14 MIN
Daisy Discovers the World 14 MIN
A Good thing about spots 14 MIN
A Jungle for Joey 14 MIN
Nina's Strange Adventure 14 MIN
Dist - AIMS

Wildcatter 30 MIN
16mm / U-matic / VHS
Enterprise Series
Color (C A)
Explains how small oil and gas prospectors are playing an increasingly vital role in America's search for energy. Tells the story of one such wildcatter, Bill Brodnax of Taurus Petroleum in Louisiana, as he drills a well in hopes of the big payoff.
Business and Economics; Social Science
Dist - LCOA **Prod** - WGBHTV 1981

Wildebeest 20 MIN
U-matic / VHS / 16mm
Silent Safari Series
Color (P A)
Shows the white - bearded gnu, or wildebeest, in its habitat on the East African plain. Tracks the odyssey of the migrating herds and presents footage of the birth of a wildebeest.
Geography - World; Science - Natural
Dist - EBEC **Prod** - CHE 1984

Wilder Reiter GmbH 106 MIN
16mm
B&W (GERMAN (ENGLISH SUBTITLES))
A German language motion picture with English subtitles. Makes fun of publicity hunters and those making a living from the craze.
Business and Economics; Foreign Language; Literature and Drama
Dist - WSTGLC **Prod** - WSTGLC 1966

The Wilder Summer 54 MIN
16mm / VHS / U-matic
Color (I J H)
An edited version of the motion picture The Wilder Summer. Presents a story set in a summer camp which attempts to show that class differences are not important. Based on the novel The Wilder Summer by Stephen Krensky.
Guidance and Counseling; Literature and Drama; Psychology
Dist - LCOA **Prod** - LCOA 1984

Wilderness 14 MIN
16mm
Color
LC 79-701400
Celebrates the American outdoors. Shares various wilderness experiences, including river running, cross - country skiing, sailing and mountaineering.
Physical Education and Recreation
Dist - FLEX **Prod** - FLEX 1979

Wilderness 30 MIN
VHS / 16mm
Interactions Series
Color (H T PRO)
$180.00 purchase, $35.00 rental
Evaluates land management since 1890 when the last frontiers were tamed. Explains how the fate of the wilderness depends on society's attitudes and why we need to manage our wild lands wisely.
Science - Natural
Dist - AITECH **Prod** - WHATV 1989

Wilderness 30 MIN
16mm
Color
LC 80-700860
Shows the work of the National Parks and Wildlife Service in Kosciusk National Park in Australia. Defines wilderness as a place, a park management technique and a state of mind.
Geography - World; Science - Natural
Dist - TASCOR **Prod** - NSWF 1978

Wilderness - 12 29 MIN
VHS
Interactions in Science and Society - Student Programs series
Color (H T)
$125.00 purchase
Reveals that the United States tamed and exploited its wilderness to the extent that the frontier no longer existed after 1890. Discloses that biologists, medical scientists, psychologists, ecologists and climatologists value untouched nature as a safety factor for continued human existence and that a technological society needs to manage wild land wisely. Part 12 of a 12-part series on interacting technological and societal issues. Includes

teacher in-service. Computer component available which enhances decision - making skills.
Science - Natural; Sociology
Dist - AITECH **Prod** - WHATV 1990

Wilderness - a country in the mind 20 MIN
VHS
Color (G)
$15.00 rental, $20.00 purchase
Induces a mood of informative ecstasy by picturing nature as all of humanity's common ancestor. Encourages a restorative immersion in nature. Aerial sequences are used to produce a feeling of life in the flow of water and clouds. Produced by the Wilderness Society with music by Timothy Marquand.
Fine Arts; Industrial and Technical Education
Dist - CANCIN **Prod** - FULTON 1984

Wilderness - a Country in the Mind 20 MIN
U-matic / VHS
Color (J H C A)
Presents the American wilderness in aerial and time - lapsed photography.
Geography - United States; Science - Natural
Dist - CEPRO **Prod** - CEPRO

Wilderness - an American Ideal 15 MIN
16mm
Color
LC 77-700058
Presents a history of American attitudes on the wilderness, showing the changing attitudes about it.
Science - Natural; Social Science
Dist - WESTWN **Prod** - WESTWN 1975

The Wilderness Below 12 MIN
16mm
Color (I)
LC 77-700948
Presents an impressionistic view of caving. Follows one spelunker as he explores a cavern and shows the beauty, mystery and solitude to be enjoyed in caving.
Physical Education and Recreation; Science - Natural; Science - Physical
Dist - IU **Prod** - INERTH 1977

Wilderness Dawning 14 MIN
16mm
Journal Series
Color
LC 75-704361
Presents glimpses of animal life in Canada's northland.
Geography - World; Science - Natural
Dist - FIARTS **Prod** - FIARTS 1973

Wilderness ecology - coniferous forest 20 MIN
VHS
Wilderness ecology series
Color; PAL (H)
Looks at coniferous forests, those consisting mainly of spruce, pine and other evergreens, which directly and indirectly provide nourishment and shelter to the plants, animals and organisms in their environment. Shows how, in return, conifers receive sustenance from surrounding flora and fauna which allows them to thrive. Examines the breakdown of organic matter which allows for new life, why forest inhabitants have specialized survival mechanisms. Recognizes the importance of forest layering, water cycles and photosynthesis.
Science - Natural
Dist - VIEWTH **Prod** - VIEWTH

Wilderness ecology - deciduous forest 21 MIN
VHS
Wilderness ecology series
Color; PAL (H)
Looks at deciduous forests, those consisting mainly of trees with leaves which die, fall off and regrow during seasonal growing periods, providing nourishment and shelter to the plants, animals and organisms in their environment. Shows the effects of lush, sparse and no leaf foliage upon forest life, the crucial role of fungi and parasites, and considers how the interaction of heat, light and water are necessary for a successful forest.
Science - Natural
Dist - VIEWTH **Prod** - VIEWTH

Wilderness ecology - lakes and streams 21 MIN
VHS
Wilderness ecology series
Color; PAL (H)
Demonstrates the difference between freshwater lakes and running water environments. Looks at the adaptive features of individual plants and animals. Shows what makes one zone rich and another poor and how different seasons present unique survival problems and opportunities.
Geography - World; Science - Natural
Dist - VIEWTH **Prod** - VIEWTH

Wilderness Ecology Series
Coniferous Forest 20 MIN
Deciduous forest 21 MIN
Lakes and Streams 23 MIN
Dist - CORF

Wilderness ecology series
Wilderness ecology - coniferous forest 20 MIN
Wilderness ecology - deciduous forest 21 MIN
Wilderness ecology - lakes and streams 21 MIN
Dist - VIEWTH

Wilderness, Education and Skills 145 MIN
U-matic
University of the Air Series
Color (J H C A)
$750.00 purchase, $250.00 rental
Explores the dangers of unprepared wilderness travel and then demonstrates wilderness skills, equipment and safety procedures. Program contains a series of five cassettes 29 minutes each.
Physical Education and Recreation
Dist - CTV **Prod** - CTV 1978

Wilderness Nomads 18 MIN
16mm / U-matic / VHS
Color (J)
LC 76-700278
Follows the exploits of a group of teenagers calling themselves the wilderness nomads as they make a four - week canoe trip through the northern Canadian woods.
Geography - World; Guidance and Counseling; Physical Education and Recreation
Dist - LCOA **Prod** - LCOA 1976

Wilderness Quest 28 MIN
16mm
Color (G)
Presents Minnesota, Montana and desert wilderness as stars in a conservation effort.
Physical Education and Recreation; Science - Natural
Dist - BOYD **Prod** - RWSHOE

The Wilderness Road 23 MIN
16mm
Color; B&W (I)
Follows Daniel Boone, George Rogers Clark and other pioneers who carved out and traveled the wilderness road through Virginia and Kentucky. Describes their explorations, fight for independence and settlement of the frontier country.
History - United States
Dist - VADE **Prod** - VADE 1953

Wilderness Series
Waters of Yosemite 9 MIN
Winter Geyser 7 MIN
Dist - PHENIX

The Wilderness Trail 15 MIN
U-matic
Color
Takes the viewers on a pack trip into the Bridger wilderness area, Bridger National Forest, Wyoming, which is protected and kept in its natural state. Includes narration by a professional local packer.
Geography - United States; Science - Natural
Dist - USDA **Prod** - USDA 1972

Wildest Dreams 29 MIN
16mm / VHS
Color (J H C A)
$395.00, $495.00 purchase, $75.00 rental _ #9940
Tells a compelling story about self - esteem and believing in yourself. Features orginal rock lyrics. Out of Brigham Young University.
Literature and Drama; Psychology; Religion and Philosophy
Dist - AIMS **Prod** - KKEMP 1987

The Wildest Show on Earth 26 MIN
16mm
Color
LC 74-702528
Shows some of the action at the Texas Prison Rodeo, a contest in which the contestants are prison inmates.
Sociology
Dist - TEXDE **Prod** - TEXDE 1974

Wildfire 60 MIN
VHS
National Audubon video series
Color (J H C G)
$29.98 purchase _ #FFO9056V
Features actor James Woods as host. Takes a look at the 1988 Yellowstone fire that caused over $100 million in damage. Uses dramatic footage to show the power and purpose of fire in the wild and reveals that fire is a powerful evolutionary tool that creates diversity. Discloses that controversy still rages over how humans should, or should not, participate in this process of nature. Part of a five - part series of nature documentaries.
Agriculture; Science - Natural
Dist - CAMV **Prod** - NAS 1991

Wildfire Assessment - Behavior and Initial Attack Strategy
Videodisc
Color (C)
$6550.00 purchase _ #2878
Teaches procedures for the initial assessment and attack of wildfires. Simulates a fire from the first call through extinguishment and comparison with an expert's solution. Suggests changes, if necessary. Can be played on most videodisc players and requires an IBM compatible computer with overlay capability or SONY VIEW 5000 and a second computer, preferably a 386 IBM compatible with VGA monitor, to run the computer graphic fire growth model.
Agriculture; Education; Health and Safety; Psychology; Science - Natural; Science - Physical; Social Science
Dist - ACCESS **Prod** - ACCESS 1990

Wildflower Seed Bank
U-matic / VHS / 16mm
One Second Before Sunrise - Search for Solutions, Program 1 Series
Color (J)
$110.00, $85.00 purchase, $25.00 rental
Describes how Dr Harold Koopowitz started the first cryogenic seed bank in North America and saved 150 species of endangered wildflowers. The seed bank has become a model for many other arboreta and botanical gardens.
Agriculture; Geography - World; Science - Natural; Sociology
Dist - BULFRG **Prod** - HCOM 1990

Wildflowers 30 MIN
U-matic / VHS
Roughing it Series
Color
Physical Education and Recreation
Dist - KYTV **Prod** - KYTV 1984

Wildflowers 11 MIN
U-matic / VHS / 16mm
Color (I J)
LC 72-700114
Shows several kinds of wildflowers blooming in various locations and seasons and explains that each wildflower is suited in some way to life in a particular place.
Science - Natural
Dist - PHENIX **Prod** - PHENIX 1972

Wildfowl sanctuary 26 MIN
16mm
Audubon wildlife theatre series
Color (I)
Features naturalist - photographer Bill Carrcik who is curator of the Kortwright Waterfowl Park in Guelph, Ontario, which harbors a thousand birds of more than 50 species. Observes and studies the Canada goose, black duck, pintail canvasback, redhead, the spectacular looking hooded mergaser and the rare trumpeter swan, among many others.
Geography - World; Industrial and Technical Education; Science - Natural
Dist - AVEXP **Prod** - AVEXP

Wilding 28 MIN
U-matic / VHS
Color (G)
$249.00, $149.00 purchase _ #AD - 2166
Discusses the 'wilding' spree - a group of more than a dozen young males viciously attacked and gang - raped a female jogger in New York's Central Park and left her for dead. Reveals that none of the teenaged suspects had a record and all were considered 'nice kids.' Features Phil Donahue, columnist Peter Hamill, attorneys for two of the accused, and anthropologist Philippe Bourgeois.
Psychology; Sociology
Dist - FOTH **Prod** - FOTH

Wildlands, Our Heritage 26 MIN
16mm
Color (P A)
LC 79-708744
Explores the moods of the wilderness and familiarizes viewers with the wild creatures of Georgian Bay. Includes scenes of white tailed deer, early summer morning mists, the gray jay and the black bear. Features close - ups of various birds.
Science - Natural
Dist - AVEXP **Prod** - KEGPL 1970

Wildlife 24 MIN
16mm
Heading Out Series
Color
LC 76-703337
Shows the flora and fauna of Alberta, Canada.
Geography - World; Science - Natural
Dist - CENTWO **Prod** - CENTWO 1975

Wildlife 29 MIN
Videoreel / VT2
Commonwealth Series
Color
History - United States; Science - Natural
Dist - PBS **Prod** - WITFTV

Wildlife Adventures of Alaska in the Denali Wilderness 28 MIN
VHS / BETA
Color
Invites viewers to join moose, wolves, grizzly bears and caribou in their dramatic struggle for survival in the great Alaskan wilderness.
Geography - United States; Science - Natural
Dist - CBSC **Prod** - CBSC

Wildlife - an American Heritage 14 MIN
U-matic / VHS
Color
Introduces and considers the value of America's vast and diverse wildlife resources.
Science - Natural
Dist - WESTWN **Prod** - WESTWN

Wildlife by air 26 MIN
16mm
Audubon wildlife theatre series
Color (I)
Shows sequences off the shores of Maine with close - ups of plants found in New England, including the cardinal flower, Canada bead Ruby and reindeer moss. Features underwater shots, studying creatures that nature devised to balance the environment. Portrays the shallow spawning beds of many varieties of sharks and rays and examines several bizarre fish amid sea ferns and colorful stony corals off the dry Tortugas Islands.
Geography - United States; Science - Natural
Dist - AVEXP **Prod** - AVEXP

Wildlife Decoy Carvers of the Illinois Flyway 46 MIN
VHS
Color (S)
$19.95 purchase _ #827 - 9002
Celebrates the history of a vanishing American art form, decoy carving, and pays tribute to its remaining practitioners.
Fine Arts; Industrial and Technical Education; Physical Education and Recreation; Science - Natural
Dist - FI **Prod** - PGZ 1986

Wildlife environment series
Presents a three - part series on wildlife in South America. Includes the titles Amazonia - a Celebration of Life, Cry of the Muriqui, and Monkey of the Clouds.

Amazonia - a celebration of life	23 MIN
Cry of the Muriqui	26 MIN
Monkey of the clouds	18 MIN
Wildlife environment series	67 MIN

Dist - LANDMK **Prod** - LANDMK 1986

Wildlife Families 9 MIN
U-matic / VHS / 16mm
Life Science for Elementary Series
Color (P I)
LC 76-700816
Takes a look at several kinds of wildlife families.
Science - Natural
Dist - AIMS **Prod** - PEDF 1976

Wildlife for Sale 30 MIN
U-matic / VHS / 16mm
KnowZone Series
Color (I J H)
$550.00 purchase - 16 mm, $250.00 purchase - video _ #5065C
Shows how the market for rare animals fluorishes. Adapted from the Nova series. Hosted by David Morse.
Science - Natural
Dist - CORF

Wildlife in a Southern Slough 11 MIN
U-matic / VHS / 16mm
Color (I J H)
LC FIA65-279
Presents animal life found in the waterways of several Southern states in the U S. Includes such animals as herons, gallinules, egrets, frogs, turtles, otter, ibis, snakes and alligators.
Geography - United States; Science - Natural
Dist - IFB **Prod** - IFB 1963

Wildlife in the Jungles of Latin America 17 MIN
U-matic / VHS / 16mm
Color (J H C)
LC FIA65-394
Shows how plants and animals native to the rain forests of Latin America adapt to their environment. Uses charts to identify levels of the forest - - ground floor, small tree, lower canopy and upper canopy.
Geography - World; Science - Natural
Dist - IFB **Prod** - IFB 1963

Wildlife in the Managed Forest 10 MIN
16mm
Color
LC 77-702720
Shows the animal and plant life in forest areas.
Science - Natural
Dist - MEPHTS **Prod** - MEPHTS 1976

Wildlife in the Rockies - Animal Census in Alberta 7 MIN
16mm
News Magazine of the Screen Series Vol 3, Issue 2
Color
Depicts the annual spring census of animals in Bann National Park in the Rocky Mountains. Shows how the game wardens cover trail to count the animals, such as moose, bighorn sheep, elk and mountain goats.
Geography - United States; Science - Natural
Dist - HEARST **Prod** - HEARST 1960

Wildlife Island 26 MIN
16mm
Color (P A)
LC 76-710210
Follows a class of intermediate students as they investigate a wildlife island just across the bay from the city of Toronto, Ontario.
Science - Natural
Dist - AVEXP **Prod** - KEGPL 1969

Wildlife Management 30 MIN
VHS / U-matic
Living Environment Series
Color (C)
Considers attempts to manage wildlife in the environment, potential extinction of animal species, destruction of habitats and functions of state parks and wildlife protected areas.
Science - Natural
Dist - DALCCD **Prod** - DALCCD

Wildlife Mothers 9 MIN
16mm / U-matic / VHS
Life Science for Elementary Series
Color (P I)
LC 76-700802
Shows the mothering behavior of animals in their natural habitats, concentrating on the examples of the mallard duck and the burrowing owl.
Science - Natural
Dist - AIMS **Prod** - PEDF 1976

Wildlife on one series

Barrels of crude and wallaroos	30 MIN
The haunted huntress	30 MIN
Malice in wonderland	30 MIN
Orang-utan - out on a limb	30 MIN
Tiger of the highlands	30 MIN
White birds of winter	30 MIN

Dist - BBCENE

Wildlife on Reprieve 12 MIN
U-matic / VHS / 16mm
Color (I)
Shows the need to protect rare, endangered species and their natural habitat.
Science - Natural
Dist - MCFI **Prod** - READER

Wildlife on the Main Stem 27 MIN
U-matic
B&W
Shows how an abundance of wildlife is able to live in harmony with a complex of six multi - purpose dams and resevoirs constructed by the corps of engineers on the upper Mississippi. Features the sharp tailed grouse, beaver, waterfowl, upland game and fish.
Science - Natural
Dist - USNAC **Prod** - USNAC 1972

A Wildlife Photographer at Work 13 MIN
U-matic / VHS / 16mm
Color (I)
Features Kent Durden, naturalist - photographer, showing us the tricks of his trade. Describes how to film the tiny, distant and fast - moving animals.
Industrial and Technical Education
Dist - AIMS **Prod** - PFP 1975

Wildlife sanctuaries of India 26 MIN
16mm
Audubon wildlife theatre series
Color (I)
Portrays wildlife in four wildlife sanctuaries of India, including Kazirange, Periyar Lake, Keoladeo and the Gir forest. Shows some of the crafts and folkways of the villagers who share the vast stretches of rural India with some of the world's rarest wildlife creatures.
Geography - World; Science - Natural; Sociology
Dist - AVEXP **Prod** - AVEXP

The Wilds of Madagascar 59 MIN
VHS / Videodisc / BETA
Color; CLV; Captioned (G)
$35.20, $24.20 purchase _ #C53378, #C50378
Geography - World; Science - Natural
Dist - NGS **Prod** - NGS

The Wildwest show 12 MIN
16mm
Color (G)
$25.00 rental
Retells a 'day in the life' of Television City with an urban landscape that features the most exaggerated moments of Western history iconically portrayed in large billboards. Uses a game show format as the vehicle for the narrative. Portrays American society and culture as totally dominated by audio and visual messages to the extent where truths are indistinguishable from lies and real meaning is lost.
Fine Arts; History - United States; Sociology
Dist - CANCIN **Prod** - RAZUTI 1980

Wildwest suite series

Amarillo - Westcliffe stampede	14 MIN
Blue movie	16 MIN
Ghost dance	25 MIN

Dist - CANCIN

Wildwood nights 29 MIN
U-matic / 16mm / VHS
Color (J H)
$595.00, $425.00, $395.00 _ #C619
Tells the tale of teen Stephanie Miller who is a little bored with the totally wholesome beach vacation with her family. Reveals that she decides to go out with a handsome, older guy - despite her parents' warnings. The date turns out to be a disaster, but Stephanie learns a few things about herself and her peers. Comments on peer pressure and substance abuse. Produced by Karin Kelly.
Guidance and Counseling; Psychology; Sociology
Dist - BARR

Wiley's World - Christopher Columbus 22 MIN
VHS / 16mm
Color (I)
LC 90713247
Uses characters Wiley Beaton - Smith, an investigative reporter, and Professor Pablo Pierpoint to present historical facts about Christopher Columbus.
Computer Science; History - United States; History - World
Dist - ALTSUL

Wiley's World - Why Geography? 20 MIN
VHS / 16mm
Color (I)
Uses characters Wiley Beaton - Smith, an investigative reporter, and Professor Pablo Pierpoint to explain the importance of geography and how humanity has always sought to know its place in the world.
Geography - World
Dist - ALTSUL

Wilf 21 MIN
16mm
Color (J H C)
LC 72-706566
Presents the story of a lonely small farmer who desires to be alone and an old man who does not want to change in a changing world.
Education; Guidance and Counseling; Psychology; Science - Natural; Sociology
Dist - NFBC **Prod** - NFBC 1970

Wilfred Owen - the Pity of War 58 MIN
U-matic / VHS
Color (C)
$279.00, $179.00 purchase _ #AD - 1360
Testifies to the cruelty, horror and insanity of war through excerpts from the poetry, diaries and letters of Wilfred Owen. Reveals that Owen fought, was wounded, and fought again during the front - line conflicts of World War I, 1916 - 1917. He was killed a few days before the Armistice was signed in 1918. Features Peter Florence who edited and presented Owen's material for the program.
Civics and Political Systems; History - United States; Literature and Drama; Sociology
Dist - FOTH **Prod** - FOTH

Wilfredo Castano - 12 - 4 - 74 37 MIN
VHS / Cassette
Poetry Center reading series
B&W (G)
#255 - 206
Features Chicano writer Wilfredo Castano reading his works at the Poetry Center, San Francisco State University. Available only for listening at the Poetry Center; not for sale or rent.
Literature and Drama
Dist - POETRY **Prod** - POETRY 1974

Wilfredo Castano - 9 - 29 - 83 28 MIN
VHS / Cassette
Poetry Center reading series
Color (G)
$15.00 purchase, rental _ #552 - 468
Features Chicano writer Wilfredo Castano reading his works, including selections from Father's Web, at the Poetry Center, San Francisco State University.
Literature and Drama
Dist - POETRY **Prod** - POETRY 1983

Wilfredo Castano - 10 - 24 - 80 8 MIN
VHS / Cassette
Poetry Center reading series
Color (G)
#907 - 344
Features the Chicano writer, Wilfredo Castano, reading his works during the Rebound Project at the Poetry Center, San Francisco State University. Available only for listening purposes at the Center; not for sale or rent.
Literature and Drama
Dist - POETRY **Prod** - POETRY 1980

Wilfredo Castano - 10 - 25 - 78 20 MIN
VHS / Cassette
Poetry Center reading series
Color (G)
$15.00 purchase, rental _ #305 - 255
Features Chicano writer Wilfredo Castano reading his works during the Tin - Tan Magazine reading at the Poetry Center, San Francisco State University.
Literature and Drama
Dist - POETRY **Prod** - POETRY 1978

Wilfrid Gordon Mc Donald Partridge 7 MIN
U-matic / VHS
Color; Mono (K P I)
Tells the story of a little boy and his special friendship with the old folks who live next door, especially Miss Nancy Alison Delacourt Cooper. When Miss Cooper loses her memory, Wilfrid asks his other friends at the old people's home to tell him what a memory is. 'Something that makes you cry,' says Miss Tippett. 'Something that makes you laugh,' says Miss Mitchell. With these and other clues in mind, Wilfrid collects memories of his own and presents them to his friend.
English Language; Guidance and Counseling; Literature and Drama; Sociology
Dist - WWS **Prod** - WWS 1986

Wilkens Coffee with Puppets 1 MIN
VHS / U-matic
Color
Shows a classic television commercial.
Business and Economics; Psychology; Sociology
Dist - BROOKC **Prod** - BROOKC

Wilkinson Fundamentals
16mm
B&W
Presents tips on football, baseball, swimming, diving, basketball, hockey, gymnastics, track and field and other events on 25 different reels.
Physical Education and Recreation
Dist - SFI **Prod** - SFI

Will 5 MIN
16mm
Color
Deals with a color collage of graphics which portrays a dance.
Fine Arts; Industrial and Technical Education
Dist - VANBKS **Prod** - VANBKS

Will defense torpedo the budget 30 MIN
U-matic
Adam Smith's money world series; 119
Color (A)
Attempts to demystify the world of money and break it down so that small as well as large businesses and its people understand and adjust to new social and economic trends. Reports on the major economic stories and discoveries of the day.
Business and Economics
Dist - PBS **Prod** - WNETTV 1985

Will drafting techniques 210 MIN
VHS
Color (A PRO C)
$67.20, $200.00 purchase _ #M744, #P248
Covers selected problems for lawyers. Includes drafting and document planning, how to draft in plain English, bequests and devises, selection of fiduciaries, paying tax liabilities, sheltering the estate tax credit, marital deduction interests and more. A featured highlight is a discussion on drafting the lawyer's own will.
Business and Economics; Civics and Political Systems
Dist - ALIABA **Prod** - ALIABA 1989

Will for Peace 33 MIN
16mm
B&W
LC FIE52-2116
Contrasts the post - war activities of the United States with Russia. Shows how the United States has worked toward peace while Russia has concentrated upon preparations for war.
Civics and Political Systems; History - United States; History - World
Dist - USNAC **Prod** - USA 1951

Will of God 145 MIN
U-matic / VHS
Color
Presents Sri Gurudev answering questions on control of the mind, bowing to the Guru, job - related problems, spontaneous acts and the Will of God.
Religion and Philosophy
Dist - IYOGA **Prod** - IYOGA

Will of iron 30 MIN
VHS
Business matters series
Color (A)
PdS65 purchase
Takes a look at Stanton Ironworks near Notthingham, which has been taken over by its French rival. Reveals that this is the price it paid for the lack of capital investment during the years of nationalization under British Steel. Now the British workforce must learn the difference between British and French management styles and asks, has Britain been looking to Japan and the United States for management techniques when it should have been looking closer to home.
Business and Economics
Dist - BBCENE

The Will of the People 55 MIN
VHS / U-matic
B&W
Recounts the story of the Spanish revolution and the rise of Franco.
History - World
Dist - IHF **Prod** - IHF

Will our children thank us 58 MIN
VHS
Color (G)
$49.95 purchase
Features Dr Benjamin Spock who narrates a documentary about social change.
History - United States; Sociology
Dist - WMMI **Prod** - WMMI 1984

Will protectionism cause the next depression 30 MIN
U-matic
Adam Smith's money world 1985 - 1986 season series; 205
Color (A)
Attempts to demystify the world of money and break it down so that small as well as large businesses and its people understand and adjust to new social and economic trends. Reports on the major economic stories and discoveries of 1985 and 1986.
Business and Economics
Dist - PBS **Prod** - WNETTV 1986

Will Rogers 26 MIN
16mm
History Makers of the 20th Century Series
B&W (I J H)
Uses rare actuality footage to portray the personal life and history - making deeds of Will Rogers.
Biography; Fine Arts; History - United States
Dist - SF **Prod** - WOLPER 1965

Will Rogers 20 MIN
U-matic / VHS
Truly American Series
Color (I)
Biography
Dist - GPN **Prod** - WVIZTV 1979

Will Rogers' 1920's 41 MIN
U-matic / VHS / 16mm
Color (H C A)
$69.95 purchase _ #P10746; LC 76-702942
Depicts Will Rogers as a man who, more than being just a humorist, helped shape the attitudes of America. Features archvive footage accompanied by Will Rogers' comments to provide a visual record of some of the major events and figures of the 1920's.
Biography; History - United States; Literature and Drama
Dist - CF **Prod** - OKSU 1976

Will Rogers' California Ranch 23 MIN
U-matic / VHS / 16mm
American lifestyle series; Cultural leaders
Color (I)
Explores the California ranch built by cowboy comedian Will Rogers and presented to the state as a historic park.
Biography; Industrial and Technical Education; Sociology
Dist - AIMS **Prod** - COMCO 1977
UILL

Will Rogers - Champion of the People 52 MIN
16mm / U-matic / VHS
Great Americans Series
Color (J)
Describes the early years of Will Rogers during which he fights for law and order in his Oklahoma hometown.
Biography; History - United States
Dist - LUF **Prod** - LUF 1979

Will tax reform fly or flop in the Senate 30 MIN
U-matic
Adam Smith's money world 1985 - 1986 season series; 220
Color (A)
Attempts to demystify the world of money and break it down so that small as well as large businesses and its people understand and adjust to new social and economic trends. Reports on the major economic stories and discoveries of 1985 and 1986.
Business and Economics
Dist - PBS **Prod** - WNETTV 1986

Will tax reform sink your state - or save it 30 MIN
U-matic
Adam Smith's money world series; 146
Color (A)
Attempts to demystify the world of money and break it down so that small as well as large businesses and its people understand and adjust to new social and economic trends. Reports on the major economic stories and discoveries of the day.
Business and Economics
Dist - PBS **Prod** - WNETTV 1985

Will the dragon rise again 58 MIN
VHS / U-matic / BETA
Nova - the genius that was China series
Color (H C A)
$250.00 purchase _ #JY - 6184C
Reveals that since the Communist Revolution, China has tried to create a society that is modern, Communist and Chinese. Emphasizes that the current thrust is for modernity. Part of a four - part series which details the rise, fall and re - emergence of science in China.
Civics and Political Systems; Geography - World; History - World
Dist - CORF **Prod** - WGBHTV 1990

Will the farm credit crisis put us all in hock 30 MIN
U-matic
Adam Smith's money world 1985 - 1986 season series; 206
Color (A)
Attempts to demystify the world of money and break it down so that small as well as large businesses and its people understand and adjust to new social and economic trends. Reports on the major economic stories and discoveries of 1985 and 1986.
Business and Economics
Dist - PBS **Prod** - WNETTV 1986

Will the Fishing have to Stop 31 MIN
U-matic / VHS / 16mm
Nova Series
Color (H C A)
LC 78-700565
Discusses the threat of disastrous fish shortages due to indiscriminate and unlimited ocean fishing. Proposes greater international cooperation to deal with the problem.
Science - Natural; Social Science
Dist - TIMLIF **Prod** - WGBHTV 1976

Will the Gator Glades Survive 30 MIN
U-matic / VHS / 16mm
Our Vanishing Wilderness, no 5 Series
Color
LC 70-710659
Explores the dangers to wildlife inhabiting the Florida everglades because of man's interference with the natural water supply and his killing of alligators.
Science - Natural; Social Science
Dist - IU **Prod** - NET 1970

Will the World Starve? 58 MIN
VHS / U-matic
Nova Series
Color (H C A)
$250 purchase _ #5136C
Talks about increasing agricultural production to feed the world's hungry, and discusses the toll high - yield crops take on the soil. Produced by WGBH Boston.
Social Science
Dist - CORF

Will There Always be an England 24 MIN
U-matic / VHS / 16mm
Color (H C A)
LC 77-701262
Outlines the social and economic decline of Great Britain during the 1970's and suggests that this fact may threaten her existence as a democratic nation.
Business and Economics; Geography - World; History - World
Dist - CAROUF **Prod** - CBSTV 1977

Will they Survive 24 MIN
VHS / U-matic
Aerie Nature Series
Color (I J H)
Shows the threat of extinction due to encroachment of human beings on North America's endangered species, such as the alligator, bald eagle, California condor, whooping crane, grizzly bear, the black - footed ferret and the peregrine falcon.
Science - Natural
Dist - CEPRO **Prod** - CEPRO 1982

Will they survive... 27 MIN
35mm strip / VHS
Color (I J H)
$50.00 purchase _ #ACP125 - CV, #ACP125 - C
Shows how the encroachment of human beings upon the environment has placed many animal species in danger. Examines in detail the status of the American alligator, the bald eagle, the grizzly bear, the black - footed ferret and the peregrine falcon.
Science - Natural
Dist - CLRVUE **Prod** - CLRVUE

The Will to be Free 56 MIN
16mm / U-matic / VHS
Color
LC 76-702916
Explores the origins of the ideals which inspired America's founding fathers to sign the revolutionary document they called the Declaration of Independence.
History - United States; Religion and Philosophy
Dist - FI **Prod** - ABCNEW 1976

Will to be Free, the, Pt 1 28 MIN
U-matic / VHS / 16mm
Color
LC 76-702916
Explores the origins of the ideals which inspired America's founding fathers to sign the revolutionary document they called the Declaration of Independence.
History - United States
Dist - FI **Prod** - ABCNEW 1976

Will to be Free, the, Pt 2 28 MIN
U-matic / VHS / 16mm
Color
LC 76-702916
Explores the origins of the ideals which inspired America's founding fathers to sign the revolutionary document they called the Declaration of Independence.
History - United States
Dist - FI **Prod** - ABCNEW 1976

The Will to Win 14 MIN
VHS / U-matic / BETA
Barassi Tapes Series
Color; Stereo (H C G T A S R PRO IND)
Shows Ron Barassi's belief that the will to win is one of the most important elements of success. By wining, he means giving a super best effort all the time. Against a background of winners and losers, he outlines a five point strategy for winning.
Education; Guidance and Counseling; Psychology
Dist - SEVDIM **Prod** - SEVDIM 1983

Will to Win 25 MIN
U-matic
Color
Represents a condensed version of the film Thirteen Minutes To Wait. Shows Toronto's Steve Podborski waiting 13 minutes to find out his World Cup downhill ski racing rival beat him by 28/100ths of a second. Explains how he went on to become ranked best in the world.
Physical Education and Recreation
Dist - LAURON **Prod** - LAURON

Will to win 30 MIN
VHS
Business matters series
Color (A)
PdS65 purchase
Interviews John Scully, recruited for his marketing and management expertise by Apple founder Steve Jobs. Reveals that it was not long before there were substantive disagreements about the way the company should be run - causing Scully to fire Jobs. Scully talks about his desire to create a company that can sustain growth into the next century.
Business and Economics
Dist - BBCENE

The Will to win 28 MIN
VHS
Color (PRO IND A)
$495.00 purchase, $150.00 rental _ #FFH11
Shows that attitude is the key to success. Uses four separate vignettes to help managers and others understand how to learn a positive attitude which they may instill in those with whom they relate.
Business and Economics; Psychology
Dist - EXTR **Prod** - FOTH

The Will to Win 15 MIN
U-matic / VHS / 16mm
Color (J A)
LC 75-712464
Presents a study of men in motion, showing auto and motorcycle racing, tobogganing, skiing, surfing and skydiving.
Physical Education and Recreation
Dist - PFP **Prod** - PFP 1972

Will Venice survive its rescue 60 MIN
Videodisc / VHS
Color (G)
$39.95, $29.98 purchase _ #VA5424
Looks at the controversial efforts to save the romantic 'City of Canals.'
Geography - World
Dist - INSTRU **Prod** - NOVA

Will You Answer True? 16 MIN
U-matic / VHS
Color
Stresses the importance of having relevant information at hand, making notes and checking back on important details in handling telephone sales inquiries.
Business and Economics
Dist - VISUCP **Prod** - VIDART

Will You Answer True? 15 MIN
VHS / U-matic
Color (A)
Employs humor to show how to handle a customer inquiry over the telephone and turn it into a sale.
Business and Economics; Psychology
Dist - XICOM **Prod** - XICOM

Will You Become a Victim, Vol 1 22 MIN
VHS / 16mm
Friend Like Patty Series
Color (G)
$95.00 purchase
Focuses upon positive messages to teenage girls. States that teenage girls are the most vulnerable and victimized segment of our youth. Part of an eight - part series, 'A Friend Like Patty,' featuring Patty Ellis.
Health and Safety; Psychology; Sociology
Dist - PROSOR

Will You Miss Me while I'M in the Pay Toilet 8 MIN
16mm
B&W
Presents a film pantomine shown through abstract images.
Fine Arts; Industrial and Technical Education; Literature and Drama
Dist - VANBKS **Prod** - VANBKS

Will You Take this Woman 17 MIN
16mm
Doctors at Work Series
B&W (H C A)
LC FIA65-1372
A pre - marital examination reveals the presence of an ovarian cyst. Shows the surgical operation in which the benign growth is removed from the ovary.
Health and Safety; Sociology
Dist - LAWREN **Prod** - CMA 1963

Willa Cather 22 MIN
35mm strip / VHS
Color (J H C A)
$93.00, $93.00 purchase _ #MB - 909730 - 8, #MB - 909708 - 1
Portrays the life and work of author Willa Cather. Covers her childhood in Nebraska, her careers as a teacher, editor, and author, and her observations of prairie life that influenced her literature.
Biography; Literature and Drama
Dist - SRA **Prod** - SRA 1990

Willa Cather - a Pictorial Memoir 30 MIN
VHS / U-matic
(G)
Discusses the University of Nebraska Press' book, Willa Cather - A Pictorial Memoir, commemmorating the Willa Cather Centennial Festival. Features editor Virginia Faulkner.
History - United States; Literature and Drama
Dist - GPN **Prod** - NETV 1974

Willa Cather Remembered 60 MIN
U-matic / VHS
(G)
Evokes the life and Nebraska homeland of Willa Cather. Uses reminiscences by the author's friends and family taken from interviews recorded in 1962 and 1966.
History - United States; Literature and Drama
Dist - GPN **Prod** - NETV 1975

Willa Cather's America 60 MIN
16mm / U-matic / VHS
Color (J)
LC 78-701145
Portrays the life, work and times of writer Willa Cather.
Biography; Literature and Drama
Dist - FOTH **Prod** - WNETTV 1978

Willa Cather's America, Pt 1 30 MIN
16mm / U-matic / VHS
Color (J)
LC 78-701145
Portrays the life, work and times of writer Willa Cather.
Literature and Drama
Dist - FOTH **Prod** - WNETTV 1978

Willa Cather's America, Pt 2 30 MIN
U-matic / VHS / 16mm
Color (J)
LC 78-701145
Portrays the life, work and times of writer Willa Cather.
Literature and Drama
Dist - FOTH **Prod** - WNETTV 1978

Willard Gaylin 30 MIN
VHS
World Of Ideas With Bill Moyers - Season I - series
Color (G)
$39.95 purchase _ #BMWI - 107
Interviews author and psychiatrist Willard Gaylin. Discusses interrelationship between biology, medicine and ethics. Explores conflict between the individual and the collective good.
Business and Economics; Guidance and Counseling; Psychology; Religion and Philosophy; Sociology
Dist - PBS

Willem De Kooning 14 MIN
16mm
Color
LC FIA66-1366
A film essay on the artist Willem De Kooning, showing him as he paints and as he comments on the challenges that confront a painter with each new work. Mr De Kooning correlates his observations and solutions with the use of brush work and paint.
Fine Arts
Dist - RADIM **Prod** - FALKNA 1966

Willem De Kooning - the Painter 13 MIN
16mm
Color (C A)
LC 73-703075
Views the painter Willem De Kooning at work on his paintings.
Fine Arts
Dist - MUSLAR **Prod** - MUSLAR 1964

Willi - Busch Report 119 MIN
16mm
Color (GERMAN (ENGLISH SUBTITLES))
A German language film with English subtitles. Tells the story of a small town newspaper publisher who realizes that he can sell more papers and enlarge his newspaper business by using sensationalism, corruption and the power of fiction, but whose initial success eventually turns to his downfall.
Fine Arts; Foreign Language
Dist - WSTGLC **Prod** - WSTGLC 1979

William 13 MIN
16mm
Color (K P I)
LC 73-701880
Tells the story of a small boy who seeks a sense of belonging among the things of nature after facing constant, if unwitting, rejection from peers and family.
Guidance and Counseling; Literature and Drama; Psychology; Sociology
Dist - FRACOC **Prod** - FRACOC 1972

William Bathurst - 2 - 18 - 76 61 MIN
VHS / Cassette
Poetry Center reading series
Color (G)
#168 - 131B
Features poet William Bathurst reading his works at the Poetry Center, San Francisco State University, with an introduction by Lewis MacAdams. Available only for listening purposes at the Center; not for sale or rent.
Literature and Drama
Dist - POETRY **Prod** - POETRY 1976

William Beaumont 23 MIN
16mm / U-matic / VHS
Great Scientists Speak Again Series
Color (H A)
LC 76-702129
Presents Professor Richard M Eakin of the Department of Zoology, University of California giving a lecture in which he impersonates William Beaumont in the words, dress and manner of his time. Recounts Beaumont's classic observations and experiments on gastric digestion, conducted through a hole in a patient's stomach.
Biography; Health and Safety; History - World; Science; Science - Natural
Dist - UCEMC **Prod** - QUICK 1976

William Benton - 11 - 20 - 74 40 MIN
VHS / Cassette
Poetry Center reading series
Color (G)
#89 - 62
Features writer William Benton reading excerpts from his works at the Poetry Center, San Francisco State University, with an introduction by Kathleen Fraser. Available only for listening purposes at the Center; not for sale or rent.
Literature and Drama
Dist - POETRY **Prod** - POETRY 1974

William Benton - 3 - 26 - 74 25 MIN
VHS / Cassette
Poetry Center reading series
B&W (G)
#39 - 29
Features writer William Benton reading excerpts from twelve chapters of Suvon and EJ - A Novel at the Poetry Center, San Francisco State University. Available only for listening purposes at the Center; not for sale or rent.
Literature and Drama
Dist - POETRY **Prod** - POETRY 1974

William Blake 30 MIN
VHS
Famous authors series
Color (J H G)
$225.00 purchase
Looks at the life and career of British poet William Blake through selections from his works. Uses the music and events of his time, up to his death from poverty in 1826. Part of a series of videos about 24 major American and British authors. Videos are also available in a set.
History - World; Literature and Drama
Dist - LANDMK

William Blake 26 MIN
U-matic / VHS / 16mm
Romantic Vs Classic Art - Spanish Series
Color (H C A) (SPANISH)
Fine Arts; Foreign Language
Dist - PFP **Prod** - VPSL

William Blake 57 MIN
U-matic / VHS / 16mm
Third Testament Series
Color
LC 75-703368
Presents the life and thought of William Blake. Tells how the English poet lived a visionary life, describing and painting heaven. Explains how his bizarre lifestyle kept him poor, obscure and solitary, but filled his days with delight.
Biography; Literature and Drama
Dist - TIMLIF **Prod** - NIELSE 1974

William Boddy Reminds the FCC of the 1934 Communications Act 28 MIN
U-matic / VHS
Color
Attacks the ideology and economics of mass media. Presented by Paper Tiger Television.
Fine Arts; Social Science
Dist - ARTINC **Prod** - ARTINC

William Booth - God's Soldier 35 MIN
16mm
B&W (J H C G)
Tells the story of the founding of the Salvation Army and its early development. Reflects life in England before the first World War.
Biography; History - World; Sociology
Dist - VIEWTH **Prod** - GATEEF

William Boyd 35 MIN
VHS
Color (H C G)
$79.00 purchase
Features the British writer with Susan Richards discussing writing about contemporary themes and using comic situations. Talks about his works including A Good Man in Africa; An Ice - Cream War; and the short story collection On the Yankee Station.
Literature and Drama
Dist - ROLAND **Prod** - INCART

William Burroughs 45 MIN
VHS
Color (H C G)
$79.00 purchase
Features the American writer with Kathy Acker discussing the cut up style of writing, using dark humor and his early connections with the beat movement writers. Talks about his works including Junkie; The Naked Lunch; The Soft Machine; The Ticket That Exploded; and others.
Literature and Drama
Dist - ROLAND **Prod** - INCART

William C Palmer 58 MIN
U-matic / VHS
Color (H C A)
$39.95, $59.95 purchase
Presents artist William C Palmer discussing his life, work and personal history. Shows his studio and garden as well as other places that influenced his art. Explores his friendships and calls attention to his murals painted during the Depression.
Fine Arts
Dist - ARTSAM

William Carlos Williams 60 MIN
VHS / 16mm
Voices and Visions Series
Color (H)
$8.00 rental _ #60739
Traces the life and work of poet - physician William Carlos Williams (1883 - 1963), the development of his poetic dictum, 'No ideas but in things', and gives examples of the way he made poetry out of the ordinary objects of everyday life - a kitchen spigot, a car, a red wheelbarrow. Includes documentary footage, surreal dramatization and animation, and interviews.
Literature and Drama
Dist - PSU

William Carlos Williams - Part 13 60 MIN
VHS / U-matic
Voices and visions series
Color (G)
$45.00, $29.95 purchase
Captures the intense life and often visual work of poet William Carlos Williams. Uses a collage of documentary footage, interviews, animation and dramatization to portray Williams. Part of a thirteen - part series on the lives and works of modern American poets.
Biography; History - United States; Literature and Drama
Dist - ANNCPB **Prod** - NYCVH 1988

William Chen's Tai chi Chuan - Volume 1 20 MIN
VHS
Color (G)
$34.99 purchase _ #1102
Features Chen demonstrating his 60 - movement form with front and back views.
Physical Education and Recreation
Dist - WAYF

William Chen's Tai chi Chuan - Volume 2 10 MIN
VHS
Color (G)
$29.99 purchase _ #1103
Demonstrates his Yang style sword form with front and back views.
Physical Education and Recreation
Dist - WAYF

William Christensen 28 MIN
Videoreel / VT2
Art Profile Series
Color
Fine Arts
Dist - PBS **Prod** - KUEDTV

William Cochran - Tenor 29 MIN
Videoreel / VT2
Young Musical Artists Series
Color
Presents the music of tenor William Cochran.
Fine Arts
Dist - PBS **Prod** - WKARTV

William Conway, President, Relates the Nashu Corporation's Experience to Richard Noyes 50 MIN
VHS / U-matic
Deming Video Tapes - Quality, Productivity and the Competitive 'Series
Color
Business and Economics
Dist - SME **Prod** - MIOT

William Dickey - 11 - 14 - 85 18 MIN
VHS / Cassette
Poetry Center reading series
Color (G)
$15.00, $45.00 purchase, $15.00 rental _ #678 - 556
Features poet William Dickey performing in a reading to benefit the San Francisco AIDS Foundation at the Poetry Center, San Francisco State University.
Health and Safety; Literature and Drama
Dist - POETRY **Prod** - POETRY 1985

William Dickey - 4 - 17 - 75 33 MIN
VHS / Cassette
Poetry Center reading series
Color (G)
$15.00, $45.00 purchase, $15.00 rental _ #117 - 90
Features writer William Dickey reading from his works at the Poetry Center, San Francisco State University.
Literature and Drama
Dist - POETRY **Prod** - POETRY 1975

William Dickey - 9 - 19 - 87 40 MIN
VHS / Cassette
Poetry Center reading series
Color (G)
$15.00, $45.00 purchase, $15.00 rental _ #767 - 610
Features writer William Dickey reading from his works at the Poetry Center, San Francisco State University, with an introduction by Frances Phillips.
Literature and Drama
Dist - POETRY **Prod** - POETRY 1987

William Dickey - 10 - 18 - 78 39 MIN
VHS / Cassette
Poetry Center reading series
Color (G)
$15.00, $45.00 purchase, $15.00 rental _ #303 - 254
Features writer William Dickey reading from his works at the Poetry Center, San Francisco State University.
Literature and Drama
Dist - POETRY **Prod** - POETRY 1978

William Dickey - 3 - 2 - 82 60 MIN
VHS / Cassette
Poetry Center reading series
Color (G)
$15.00, $45.00 purchase, $15.00 rental _ #475 - 403
Features writer William Dickey reading from his works at the Poetry Center, San Francisco State University.
Literature and Drama
Dist - POETRY **Prod** - POETRY 1982

William Dickey - 2 - 7 - 89 12 MIN
VHS / Cassette
Poetry Center reading series
Color (G)
$15.00, $45.00 purchase, $15.00 rental _ #839 - 655
Features writer William Dickey reading from his book The Argument For Design, at a reading in honor of new San Francisco State University president Robert Corrigan, at the Poetry Center, San Francisco State University, with an introduction by Robert Gluck.
Literature and Drama
Dist - POETRY **Prod** - POETRY 1989

William E Dillard - a Great Georgian 30 MIN
16mm
Great Georgians Series
Color
Features an account of the career of a man known affectionately to hundreds of railroad employees as 'Bill.' Explains that Mr Dillard began his career as a 17 - year - old night ticket agent in Ellaville, Georgia, and rose to the presidency of the Central of Georgia, now owned by the Southern Railway system. Narrated by Dan Dailey.
Biography; Geography - United States
Dist - WGTV **Prod** - WGTV 1973

The William E Warne Power Plant 6 MIN
U-matic
Color (A)
Discusses the newest addition to the State Water Project in California, the William E Warne power plant. Covers general plant information as well as its energy efficient design.
Geography - United States; Industrial and Technical Education; Social Science
Dist - CALDWR **Prod** - CSDWR

William Everson - Brother Antoninus - 12 - 15 - 76 45 MIN
VHS / Cassette
Poetry Center reading series
Color (G)
$15.00, $45.00 purchase, $15.00 rental _ #235 - 89
Features the writer reading River - Root, including the long preface, at the Poetry Center, San Francisco State University.
Literature and Drama
Dist - POETRY **Prod** - POETRY 1976

William Everson - Brother Antoninus - 5 - 15 - 74 120 MIN
VHS / Cassette
Poetry Center reading series
Color (G)

$15.00, $45.00 purchase, $15.00 rental _ #58 - 36B
Features the writer at the Poetry Center, San Francisco State University, reading The Blowing of the Seed. Presents Poets of the Forties, nine writers in one event, distributed as one tape. Includes James Broughton, Robert Duncan, Madeline Gleason, Robert Horan, Janet Lewis, Richard Moore, Rosalie Moore, and Tom Parkinson.
Literature and Drama
Dist - POETRY **Prod** - POETRY 1974

William Everson - Brother Antoninus - 1 - 25 - 61 55 MIN
VHS / Cassette
NET Outtake series
B&W (G)
$15.00, $125.00 purchase, $15.00 rental _ #189 - 146
Features the writer reading before an audience in the auditorium of the Dominican Monastery at St Albert's College, Oakland, California, during his residency there. Recites Canticle to Waterbirds; What Birds Were There; The Way of Life and the Way of Death, part 1; and In All These Acts. Includes discussion between the poems. Part of a series of films composed of outtakes from the series USA - Poetry, which was produced in 1965 - 66 for National Educational Television, using all retrievable footage to provide rare glimpses of the poets in their own settings.
Literature and Drama
Dist - POETRY **Prod** - KQEDTV 1961

William Faulkner 30 MIN
VHS
Famous authors series
Color (J H G)
$225.00 purchase
Looks at the life and career of American writer William Faulkner through selections from his works. Uses the music and events of his time, including his alcoholism and his struggle with the South's Civil War heritage. Part of a series of videos about 24 major American and British authors. Videos are also available in a set.
History - United States; Literature and Drama
Dist - LANDMK

William Faulkner - a Life on Paper 116 MIN
U-matic / VHS / 16mm
Color (H C A)
LC 82-700304
Offers a portrait of William Faulkner.
Literature and Drama
Dist - FI **Prod** - MAETEL 1981

William Faulkner - a Life on Paper, Pt 1 58 MIN
16mm / U-matic / VHS
Color (H C A)
LC 82-700304
Offers a portrait of William Faulkner.
Literature and Drama
Dist - FI **Prod** - MAETEL 1981

William Faulkner - a Life on Paper, Pt 2 58 MIN
16mm / U-matic / VHS
Color (H C A)
LC 82-700304
Offers a portrait of William Faulkner.
Literature and Drama
Dist - FI **Prod** - MAETEL 1981

William Faulkner's Mississippi 49 MIN
16mm
B&W (J)
LC FIA68-1337
Examines the Southern heritage of William Faulkner, and explores the underlying reasons and the results of the resistance to desegregation by the people of Mississippi and of the South, as interpreted in Faulkner's writings.
Biography; Fine Arts; Literature and Drama
Dist - BNCHMK **Prod** - METROM 1967

William - from Georgia to Harlem 15 MIN
16mm / VHS / U-matic
Color; Captioned (P I J A)
LC 78-709722
Tells the story of a black farmboy who moves to New York City with his family to stay with relatives. Shows how he learns the ways of the city from his swaggering cousin Calvin but he also teaches Calvin something about real courage.
Guidance and Counseling; History - United States; Psychology; Social Science; Sociology
Dist - LCOA **Prod** - LCOA 1971

William Gaddis 32 MIN
VHS
Color (H C G)
$79.00 purchase
Features writer William Gaddis with Malcolm Bradbury, discussing the politics and culture of the US and their effect on writers' works. Talks about his works that include The Recognitions; JR; and Carpenter's Gothic.
Literature and Drama
Dist - ROLAND **Prod** - INCART

William Gibson - 11 - 9 - 89 40 MIN
VHS / Cassette
Poetry Center reading series
Color (G)
$15.00, $45.00 purchase, $15.00 rental _ #863 - 672
Features writer William Gibson reading Skinner's Room, also known as Darwin, and an excerpt from The Difference Engine, co - written with Bruce Sterling, at the Poetry Center, San Francisco State University, with an introduction by Robert Gluck.
Literature and Drama
Dist - POETRY **Prod** - POETRY 1989

William Golding 55 MIN
U-matic / VHS
Color (A)
LC 83-707160
Presents Nobel Prize - winning British author William Golding talking about his career and how it was influenced. Considers themes central to his novels and looks at landmarks in and around the author's native village.
Biography; Literature and Drama
Dist - FOTH **Prod** - LONWTV 1983

William Golding - the man and his myths 17 MIN
VHS
Nobel prize series - literature
Color (J H C)
$49.00 purchase _ #2323 - SK
Features William Golding, Nobel Prize winner, who discusses his writing and the events in his life which have influenced his creativity. Focuses on two of his books - 'Lord of the Flies' and 'The Inheritors.' Includes student notebook and teacher's guide, with additional student workbooks and copies of 'Lord of the Flies' available at an extra charge.
Education; Literature and Drama
Dist - SUNCOM

William H Johnson - art and life of an African American artist 25 MIN
VHS
Color (I J H)
$75.00, $49.99 purchase _ #V90, #V91
Shows what it was like to be a black artist in the United States in the 1920s through the 1940s. Weaves together the social history of the time and the evolution of William H Johnson as an artist. Includes a teacher's guide. Eight 13x15 color reproductions optional.
Fine Arts; History - United States
Dist - KNOWUN

William Hammond and Robert Yesselman 30 MIN
U-matic / VHS
Eye on Dance - Update, Topics of Current Concern Series
Color
Discusses running a dance company. Looks at a performance of 'Esoterica' with Frederick Franklin. Hosted by Ted Striggles.
Fine Arts
Dist - ARCVID **Prod** - ARCVID

William Harvey 19 MIN
16mm / U-matic / VHS
Great Scientists Speak Again Series
Color (H A)
LC 74-702909
Presents Professor Richard Eakin of the Department of Zoology, University of California giving a lecture in which he impersonates William Harvey in the words, dress and manner of his time. Recounts Harvey's ideas regarding the heart and blood vessels and presents his concepts of pulmonary and systematic circuits, using experiments and vividly illustrated descriptions.
Biography; Health and Safety; History - World; Science; Science - Natural
Dist - UCEMC **Prod** - QUICK 1974

William Jennings Bryan's Fairview 24 MIN
VHS
Color (G)
$69.95 purchase _ #S01339
Tours Fairview, the Lincoln, Nebraska home of William Jennings Bryan. Profiles Bryan's life, focusing on his three unsuccessful campaigns for President and his participation in the Scopes evolution trial.
Biography; History - United States; Religion and Philosophy; Science - Natural
Dist - UILL

William Julius Wilson 30 MIN
VHS
World of ideas with Bill Moyers - Season I - series
Color (G)
$39.95 purchase _ #BMWI - 133
Inteviews author and sociologist William Julius Wilson. Suggests that inner city blacks stay poor because of their negative environment. Offers Wilson's views on origins of poverty. Hosted by Bill Moyers.
History - United States; Sociology
Dist - PBS

William Kennedy 50 MIN
VHS
Color (H C G)
$79.00 purchase
Features the writer discussing with Noah Richler how having been a reporter affects his research and his novel writing. Talks about his works including Ironweed; The Ink Truck and the non - fiction O Albany.
Literature and Drama
Dist - ROLAND **Prod** - INCART

William Kolberg 28 MIN
VHS
Touching the future - dialogues on education series
Color (G)
$50.00 purchase, $11.50 rental _ #36377
Features William Kolber, president and CEO of the National Alliance of Business and coauthor of Rebuilding America's Work Force - Busines Strategies to Close the Competitive Gap.' Expresses business' need for high school graduates who can be involved in their jobs, are adept at math and critical thinking, and can perform consistently at the high levels required for the United States to compete in a world market. Emphasizes the increasing desire of business to bear its share of the burden. Part of a series which interviews educational leaders on ways to improve American public school education. Features Dr Rodney Reed, dean of the College of Education at Penn State as host.
Education
Dist - PSU **Prod** - WPSXTV 1991

William Lyon Mackenzie - a Friend to His Country 28 MIN
16mm
B&W (G)
_ #106B 0161 050
Portrays William Mackenzie's election to Parliament of Upper Canada, his later defeat, his exile and his fight for responsible government.
Biography; History - World
Dist - CFLMDC **Prod** - NFBC 1961

William Mayne 16 MIN
16mm
Color (I J T)
LC 77-715122
William Mayne, English author of stories for children, talks about his books, his childhood and the small English village where he lives.
Literature and Drama
Dist - CONNF **Prod** - CONNF 1972

William Mc Kinley and American Imperialism 20 MIN
U-matic / VHS / 16mm
Great Decisions Series
Color (I J H C)
LC 74-709705
Views the decisions President Mc Kinley had to make regarding war with Spain and the course of American imperialism. Discusses manifest destiny and colonization vs freedom.
Biography; Civics and Political Systems; History - United States
Dist - AMEDFL **Prod** - PSP 1970

William Penn and the Quakers 15 MIN
VHS
Color (I J H)
$59.00 purchase _ #MF - 4123
Recreates the settlement of Pennsylvania by Quakers seeking the religious freedom that had been denied them in England. Reveals that they settled on lands granted to William Penn under a proprietary charter.
History - United States
Dist - INSTRU **Prod** - CORF
CORF

William Penn and the Quakers - Pennsylvania Colony 15 MIN
U-matic / VHS / 16mm
Color (I J H)
Uses costumed reenactments and period music to recreate the settlement and development of Pennsylvania. Discusses how Penn's liberal land policies and the freedoms guaranteed by his Frame of Government produced Pennsylvania's diverse ethnic population and aided its rapid growth as a center of trade, industry and culture, and gave it a prominent role in the creation of the United States.
History - United States
Dist - CORF **Prod** - CORF 1982

William Penn - the Passionate Quaker 29 MIN
VHS / 16mm
Color (G)
$55.00 rental _ #WPPQ - 000
Presents a historical account of William Penn, Pennsylvania's founding father. Illustrates how Penn lived and worked. Tours through Pennsbury Manor, illuminating the man whose vision of democracy inspired a revolutionary war.

Biography; History - United States
Dist - PBS **Prod** - WHYY

William Price Fox 15 MIN
VHS
Writer's workshop series
Color (C A T)
$69.95 purchase, $45.00 rental
Features William Price Fox in a lecture and discussion of his work, held as part of a writing workshop series at the University of South Carolina. Introduced by George Plimpton. Concludes a 15 - part telecourse.
English Language; Literature and Drama
Dist - SCETV **Prod** - SCETV 1982

William Price Fox 30 MIN
VHS
Writer's workshop series
Color (G)
$59.95 purchase _ #WRWO - 115
Features author William Price Fox in a lecture and discussion at the University of South Carolina. Discusses storytelling, dialects, Southern writing and ideas for what makes a good story.
Literature and Drama
Dist - PBS **Prod** - SCETVM 1987

William Randolph Hearst's San Simeon 24 MIN
U-matic / VHS / 16mm
American lifestyle series; Industrialists and inventors
Color (I)
LC 79-700026
Features E G Marshall conducting a tour of San Simeon, the residence of tycoon William Randolph Hearst. Describes the family whose tastes are reflected in the mansion.
Biography; Business and Economics; Industrial and Technical Education; Sociology
Dist - AIMS **Prod** - COMCO 1978
UILL

William S Burroughs - 11 - 4 - 74 39 MIN
VHS / Cassette
Poetry Center reading series
Color (G)
$15.00, $45.00 purchase, $15.00 rental _ #84 - 57
Features experimental prose writer William S Burroughs reading Sexual Conditioning; excerpts from Exterminator; and from a novel in progress, Virus B - 23, in an event co - sponsored by the newspaper Gay Sunshine at the Poetry Center, San Francisco State University. Includes an introduction by Winston Leland.
Literature and Drama
Dist - POETRY **Prod** - POETRY 1974

William S Burroughs - 2 - 24 - 83
VHS / Cassette
Poetry Center reading series
Color (G)
$15.00, $45.00 purchase, $15.00 rental _ #521 - 441
Features experimental prose writer William S Burroughs reading from his novel, Place of Dead Roads, at the Poetry Center, San Francisco State University.
Literature and Drama
Dist - POETRY **Prod** - POETRY 1983

William S Hart 27 MIN
16mm
History of the Motion Picture Series
B&W (H C)
Presents highlights from William S Hart's finest films, including the rush sequence from Tumbleweeds.
Fine Arts
Dist - KILLIS **Prod** - SF 1960

William Shakespeare 35 MIN
VHS
Famous Authors Series
Color (J)
$11.50 rental _ #40515
Examines Shakespeare's early years in Stratford, his marriage to Anne Hathaway and the London in which he worked. An installment in the Famous Authors Series, which examines important English writers in the context of their times.
English Language; Fine Arts; Literature and Drama
Dist - PSU **Prod** - EBEC
GA
EBEC

William Shakespeare - Antony and Cleopatra 29 MIN
Videoreel / VT2
One to One Series
Color
Presents readings from Antony And Cleopatra by William Shakespeare.
Literature and Drama
Dist - PBS **Prod** - WETATV

William Shakespeare - Background for His Works 18 MIN
U-matic / VHS / 16mm
Shakespeare Series
Color (J H C)
$425, $250 purchase _ #4989C
Shows how the Renaissance influenced Shakespeare and examines his life and times.
Literature and Drama
Dist - CORF
VIEWTH

William Shakespeare - Background for His Works 14 MIN
U-matic / VHS / 16mm
Shakespeare Series
Color (J H C)
Shows the places of Shakespeare's times and the elements of English life that gave the great poet playwright his language and shaped his character. Brief episodes are given from some of his best known plays.
Literature and Drama
Dist - CORF **Prod** - CORF 1951

William Shatner's mysteries of the way we feel 27 MIN
VHS
Color (K P I T)
$19.95 purchase _ #S01560
Features William Shatner and Wisdom the magic owl in an exploration of feelings. Covers topics including anger, rules, and decision making.
Guidance and Counseling; Psychology
Dist - UILL

William Shatner's mysteries of the way we think and act 25 MIN
VHS
Color (K P I T)
$19.95 purchase _ #S01561
Features William Shatner and Wisdom the magic owl in an exploration of thinking and acting. Covers topics including caring about others, the importance of manners, and caring for pets. Stresses the idea that people's actions affect other people as well.
Guidance and Counseling; Home Economics; Psychology; Social Science; Sociology
Dist - UILL

William Sloan Coffin, Jr, Religion 29 MIN
U-matic / VHS
Quest for Peace Series
Color (A)
Religion and Philosophy
Dist - AACD **Prod** - AACD 1984

William Styron 30 MIN
VHS
Writer's workshop series
Color (G)
$59.95 purchase _ #WRWO - 113
Features author William Styron in a lecture and discussion at the University of South Carolina. Explains his practice of balancing researched information and imagined situations in his writing. Discusses his view that the short story is dying out as a literary form.
Literature and Drama
Dist - PBS **Prod** - SCETVM 1987

William Styron 15 MIN
VHS
Writer's workshop series
Color (C A T)
$69.95 purchase, $45.00 rental
Features William Styron in a lecture and discussion of his work, held as part of a writing workshop series at the University of South Carolina. Hosted by author William Price Fox and introduced by George Plimpton. Part 13 of a 15 - part telecourse.
English Language; Literature and Drama
Dist - SCETV **Prod** - SCETV 1982

William Styron - a Portrait 59 MIN
U-matic / VHS
Color (C)
$279.00, $179.00 purchase _ #AD - 2145
Explores how and why William Styron writes. Reveals his commitment to the belief that the writer is a citizen, his moral view of the human situation, observations on race relations.
Biography; Fine Arts; Literature and Drama
Dist - FOTH **Prod** - FOTH

William Tell 26 MIN
16mm / U-matic / VHS
Mr Magoo in Great World Classics Series
Color
Features Mr Magoo as the brave Swiss peasant who saves his country by the amazing feat of shooting an apple off his son's head with an arrow.
Literature and Drama
Dist - FI **Prod** - FLEET 1965

William Tell 11 MIN
16mm / U-matic / VHS
Color (P I)
The legend of William Tell who must shoot an apple from his son's head to save the boy and himself is told in an animated 12th century Swiss setting.
Literature and Drama
Dist - CORF **Prod** - CORF 1960

William Tell 24 MIN
U-matic / VHS / 16mm
Famous Adventures of Mr Magoo Series
Color (P I J)
LC 79-701874
Presents Mr Magoo in the animated story of William Tell, who refuses to bow before a tyrant's hat and is forced to shoot an apple from his son's head in order to save his son and himself.
Fine Arts
Dist - MCFI **Prod** - UPAPOA 1976

William Tell 25 MIN
16mm
B&W (J) ((ENGLISH NARRATION))
Presents the Metropolitan Opera Company's condensed version of Rossini's William Tell, with English narration.
Fine Arts
Dist - SELECT **Prod** - OFF

William Tell - 1965 27 MIN
16mm
Color
LC 74-706333
Highlights the William Tell interceptor competition. Focuses on preparatory training, aerial intercepts and judging and scoring details. Reviews participating teams, aircraft weapons and targets.
Physical Education and Recreation
Dist - USNAC **Prod** - USAF 1966

William Thomas 28 MIN
16mm
Atrical Film Symposium Series
B&W
LC FIA54-139
In a film talk before students in the Department of Cinema, USC, William Thomas lectures on the distribution and exploitation of the theatrical motion picture.
Fine Arts
Dist - USC **Prod** - USC

William Wegman - Selected Body Works 20 MIN
U-matic / VHS
B&W
Features a variety of works.
Fine Arts
Dist - ARTINC **Prod** - ARTINC

William Wegman - Selected Works, Reel 1 30 MIN
U-matic / VHS
B&W
Features a variety of works.
Fine Arts
Dist - ARTINC **Prod** - ARTINC

William Wegman - Selected Works, Reel 2 30 MIN
U-matic / VHS
B&W
Features a variety of works.
Fine Arts
Dist - ARTINC **Prod** - ARTINC

William Wegman - Selected Works, Reel 3 20 MIN
VHS / U-matic
B&W
Features a variety of works.
Fine Arts
Dist - ARTINC **Prod** - ARTINC

William Wegman - Selected Works, Reel 4 20 MIN
VHS / U-matic
B&W
Features a variety of works.
Fine Arts
Dist - ARTINC **Prod** - ARTINC

William Wegman - Selected Works, Reel 5 30 MIN
U-matic / VHS
B&W
Features a variety of works.
Fine Arts
Dist - ARTINC **Prod** - ARTINC

William Whitaker 30 MIN
U-matic / VHS / 16mm
Profiles in American Art Series
Color
Fine Arts
Dist - KAWVAL **Prod** - KAWVAL

William Wordsworth 28 MIN
U-matic / VHS
Survey of English Verse Series
Color (C)
$249.00, $149.00 purchase _ #AD - 1302
Surveys the works of William Wordsworth within the context of Lake District locations.
Fine Arts; Geography - World; Literature and Drama
Dist - FOTH **Prod** - FOTH

William Wordsworth 29 MIN
VHS
Famous Authors Series
Color (H)
$11.50 rental _ #35513
Depicts the life of William Wordsworth and the era in which he lived. Examines his relationships with his sister Dorothy and with Samuel Taylor Coleridge. Looks at his love of nature. An installment in the Famous Authors Series, which examines important English writers in the context of their times.
English Language; Literature and Drama
Dist - PSU **Prod** - EBEC
EBEC

William Wordsworth and the English Lakes 15 MIN
U-matic / VHS
Color (C)
$249.00, $149.00 purchase _ #AD - 1706
Focuses on the English Lake Country, where William Wordsworth was born and lived most of his life.
Fine Arts; Literature and Drama
Dist - FOTH **Prod** - FOTH

William Wordsworth - William and Dorothy 52 MIN
U-matic / VHS
Color (C)
$299.00, $199.00 purchase _ #AD - 929
Dramatizes some of the major poems of William Wordsworth. Examines his intense and troubled relationship with his sister Dorothy. Features David Warner as Wordsworth. Produced by Ken Russel.
Fine Arts; Literature and Drama
Dist - FOTH **Prod** - FOTH

Williams
VHS
Campus clips series
Color (H C A)
$29.95 purchase _ #CC0060V
Takes a video visit to the campus of Williams College in Massachusetts. Shows many of the distinctive features of the campus, and interviews students about their experiences. Provides information on the composition of the student body, professors, academics, social life, housing, and other subjects.
Education
Dist - CAMV

William's Doll 18 MIN
16mm / U-matic / VHS
Color
LC 81-707553
Tells how a young boy finally gets the doll that he has been longing for when his grandfather comes for a visit. Shows the value of allowing children to grow up without false ideas about masculinity and femininity.
Guidance and Counseling; Literature and Drama; Sociology
Dist - PHENIX **Prod** - CHIESR

William's Doll / Dad and Me 29 MIN
VHS / BETA
Color
$89.00 purchase _ #S01099
Presents a story of a boy who wants a doll, based on the book by Charlotte Zolotow. Tells the story of a seven - year - old and his father in Dad And Me.
Literature and Drama
Dist - PHENIX **Prod** - PHENIX
UILL

Williams, Robert 29 MIN
U-matic
Like it is Series
Color
Discusses how standardized tests discriminate against minorities and the poor.
Education; Sociology
Dist - HRC **Prod** - OHC

Williamsburg 56 MIN
VHS / 16mm
Flower Arranging Series
Color (G)
$69.95 purchase _ #AD100
Demonstrates flower arranging using dried and permanent materials in combination with fresh cut flowers.
Agriculture; Home Economics
Dist - AAVIM **Prod** - AAVIM 1990

The Williamsburg File 45 MIN
U-matic / VHS / 16mm
Nova Series
Color (H C A)
Explains the importance of archaeology to the 50 year restoration and subsequent discovery of Williamsburg as Virginia's colonial capital. Presents descriptions of restoration projects, including Weatherburn's tavern, the cabinetmaker's shop and America's first mental hospital.
Geography - United States; History - United States; Sociology
Dist - CWMS **Prod** - BBCTV 1976

A Williamsburg Sampler 29 MIN
16mm / U-matic / VHS
Color
LC 75-700320
Presents a cross section of Williamsburg's history, architecture, crafts, gardens, people and philosophy.
History - United States
Dist - CWMS **Prod** - CWMS 1975

Williamsburg - the story of a patriot 36 MIN
VHS
Color (I J)
$24.95 purchase _ #ST - KA0208
Uses authentic costumes, furnishings, gardens and architecture to dramatize the story of John Fry, a Virginia plantation owner newly elected to Virginia Colony's governing House of Burgesses.
Biography; History - United States
Dist - INSTRU

Willie 82 MIN
VHS
B&W; Color (G)
$165.00 rental, $59.00 purchase
Focuses on the life of Willie Jaramillo, who, at age 27, is a product of New Mexico's prisons, the most violent prison system in the country. Exemplifies producer Danny Lyon's photographic essays in which life is a collage of abrupt juxtapositions and incongruities. Jaramillo appeared in two previous Lyon films, at age 11 in LLanito and at age 16 in Little Boy.
Geography - United States; Psychology; Sociology
Dist - CANCIN

Willie 49 MIN
16mm
B&W (G)
Follows the adventures of a black youth as he struggles to survive alone in New York City.
Sociology
Dist - EBRAF **Prod** - EBRAG 1980

Willing to learn 27 MIN
VHS
Color (G)
Portrays a young single mother who takes the first step toward self empowerment through literacy. Look at an innovative adult education program - New Horizons Adult Education Progam - in St Vincent, an eastern Caribbean country.
Education; English Language; Geography - World
Dist - ASTRSK **Prod** - ASTRSK 1993

Willis Reed Basketball Series

Dick Van Arsdale - defensive play - Pt 1	12 MIN
Dick Van Arsdale - Defensive Play, Pt 2	11 MIN
Jack Marin - forward play - Pt 1	12 MIN
Jack Marin - forward play - Pt 2	11 MIN
Jo Jo White - Offensive Guard, Pt 1	10 MIN
Jo Jo White - Offensive Guard, Pt 2	12 MIN
Willis Reed - Center Play, Pt 1	11 MIN
Willis Reed - Center Play, Pt 2	12 MIN

Dist - LUF

Willis Reed - Center Play, Pt 1 11 MIN
16mm / U-matic / VHS
Willis Reed Basketball Series
Color (J H C)
LC 73-701358
Features Willis Reed of the New York Knicks illustrating various techniques in center play. Covers shooting, the push shot, the jump shot, the hook shot, the layup and the free throw.
Physical Education and Recreation
Dist - LUF **Prod** - SCHLAT 1972

Willis Reed - Center Play, Pt 2 12 MIN
16mm / U-matic / VHS
Willis Reed Basketball Series
Color (J H C)
LC 73-701368
Features Willis Reed of the New York Knicks illustrating various techniques in center play. Covers defensive rebounding, offensive rebounding, switching on the 'PICK' and proper training techniques.
Physical Education and Recreation
Dist - LUF **Prod** - SCHLAT 1972

The Willmar 8 55 MIN
VHS / 16mm / U-matic
Color (A)
LC 80-701948
Tells how eight women bank employees went out on strike after being passed over for promotion because they were women. Points out that they risked jobs, friends and families and that they challenged the values with which they were raised. Narrated and directed by Lee Grant.
Sociology
Dist - CANWRL **Prod** - CANWRL 1980

The Willmar 8 50 MIN
16mm
Color (G)
Presents an independent production by L Grant. Looks at the struggle against sex descrimination in the workplace.
Fine Arts; Sociology
Dist - FIRS

Willow Point 15 MIN
U-matic / VHS / 16mm
Color (H C A)
LC 74-703668
Stimulates inquiry into the nature of reality and promotes a questioning of the reasons for living. Shows a man on his way to work and explains that when he reaches his destination, the world he is in suddenly takes on aspects of unreality.
Guidance and Counseling; Psychology; Sociology
Dist - PHENIX **Prod** - PHENIX 1974

The Willow Tree 15 MIN
U-matic / VHS
Teletales Series
Color (P)
$125.00 purchase
Features a children's tale indiginous to England and China.
Education; Literature and Drama
Dist - AITECH **Prod** - POSIMP 1984

Wills 15 MIN
VHS / 16mm
You and the Law Series
Color (S)
$150.00 purchase _ #275910
Employs a mixture of drama and narrative to introduce particular aspects of Canadian law. Presents some of the basic concepts and addresses some of the more commonly asked questions. Emphasis is on those elements of the law which are frequently misunderstood. Deals with surrogate court, the role of executors and guardians, and organ donation.
Business and Economics; Civics and Political Systems; Geography - World; Social Science; Sociology
Dist - ACCESS **Prod** - ACCESS 1987

Wills and Estates 19 MIN
VHS / U-matic
Ways of the Law Series
Color (H)
Depicts how in Purgatory, deceased individuals see the consequences of leaving or not leaving a will.
Civics and Political Systems; Sociology
Dist - GPN **Prod** - SCITV 1980

Wills and estates 30 MIN
U-matic / VHS
Consumer survival series; Personal planning
Color
Presents tips on writing wills and planning estates.
Home Economics; Sociology
Dist - MDCPB **Prod** - MDCPB

Wills, Insurance, Witness 44 MIN
16mm
Nursing and the Law Series
B&W
LC 74-703377
Discusses the nurse who acts as a courtroom witness, the nurse who is asked to draft or to witness a will and the insurance needs of nurses.
Civics and Political Systems; Health and Safety
Dist - AJN **Prod** - VDONUR 1968

Will's Mammoth
VHS / 35mm strip
Children's Sound Filmstrips Series
Color (K)
$33.00 purchase
Adapts a children's story by R Martin. Part of a series.
English Language; Literature and Drama
Dist - PELLER

Willy and Miriam 26 MIN
16mm / VHS
Color (G)
$470.00, $260.00 purchase, $55.00 rental
Features an intimate portrait of an impoverished young couple with two children who live in Santiago, Chile. Presents a David Benavente production.
Fine Arts; Sociology
Dist - FIRS

Willy Lindwer collection series
Presents a series of eight documentaries on the Holocaust. Includes the titles The Road to Wannsee - Eleven Million Sentenced to Death; Simon Wiesenthal - Freedom Is Not a Gift From Heaven; Child in Two Worlds; The Lonely Struggle - Marek Edelman, Last Hero of the Warsaw Ghetto Uprising; The Last Seven Months of Anne Frank; Camp of Hope and Despair - Westerbork Concentration Camp, 1939 - 45; Married With a Star; Return to My Shtetl Delatyn.
Camp of hope and dispair - Westerbork Concentration Camp, 1939 - 45 70 MIN
Child in two worlds 60 MIN
The Last seven months of Anne Frank 75 MIN
The Lonely struggle - Marek Edelman , last hero of the Warsaw Ghetto Uprising 60 MIN
Married with a star 33 MIN
Return to my shtetl Delatyn 60 MIN
The Road to Wannsee - eleven million sentenced to death 50 MIN
Simon Wiesenthal - freedom is not a gift from heaven 60 MIN
Dist - ERGOM **Prod** - LINDWE 1984

Willy Mc Bean and His Flying Machine 94 MIN
16mm
Color
Presents the story about Willy Mc Bean, a boy of the jet and space age, and his pal Pablo, a talking monkey. Shows their adventures through time as they encounter General Custer and Sitting Bull, King Arthur and even some cavemen. Incorporates the technique of three - dimensional figures moving against backdrops in a stop - motion photography called animagic.
Literature and Drama
Dist - TWYMAN **Prod** - RANKA

Wilma P Mankiller - Woman of power 29 MIN
VHS
Color (G)
$60.00 rental, $250.00 purchase
Profiles the first female Chief of the Cherokee Nation. Documents Mankiller through one day in her life and shows how she had done groundbreaking work in governance, community development and furthering the cause of her people. Reveals modern tribal life as well as raising questions about women and leadership. Wilma Mankiller provides a strong role model for women and Native Americans as she attempts to find the delicate balance of participating in existing white power structures while maintaining her own cultural identity. By Mary Scott.
Fine Arts; Social Science; Sociology
Dist - WMEN

Wilmar 8 55 MIN
16mm
Color (A)
Documents the two - year strike by eight women against a bank which hired a young man at almost twice the women's salaries, whom they were to train to be their supervisor. Produced by Lee Grant.
Business and Economics; Psychology; Sociology
Dist - AFLCIO

Wilmington 15 MIN
16mm
B&W
Explains how the city of Wilmington, occupied for 11 months by the National Guard after Martin Luther King's assassination, is exposed as the private domain of the Dupont family. Explains how the Dupont Corporation controls the economic and political life of Delaware.
Business and Economics; Civics and Political Systems; History - United States; Sociology
Dist - CANWRL **Prod** - CANWRL

The Wilson Crisis - Stroke 58 MIN
VHS / U-matic
Color
Documents the physical and psychological rehabilitation after a stroke. Presents narratives from the stroke victim and his son.
Health and Safety
Dist - UMDSM **Prod** - UMDSM

Wilson Douglas, Fiddler 8 MIN
U-matic / VHS / 16mm
Color (J)
LC 77-701044
An excerpt from the 1975 motion picture Relations. Presents Kentucky mountain fiddler Wilson Douglas, who performs bluegrass music and discusses the excitement and emotion of this American music form.
Fine Arts
Dist - PHENIX **Prod** - FERTIK 1975

Wilson Hurley 30 MIN
U-matic / VHS / 16mm
Profiles in American Art Series
Color
Fine Arts
Dist - KAWVAL **Prod** - KAWVAL

Wilson - the Road to War 24 MIN
16mm
American Challenge Series
B&W (J H)
Shows how President Woodrow Wilson is drawn inexorably into World War I by such incidents as the sinking of the Lusitania, the resignation of the American secretary of state, the dismissal of the German ambassador and personal criticisms by both political parties. Uses excerpts from the motion picture Wilson starring Alexander Knox and Charles Coburn.
Biography; History - United States
Dist - FI **Prod** - TWCF 1975

Wilson's Creek - a Mean Fowt Fight 14 MIN
16mm
Color (I)
LC 83-700566
Uses the paintings and words of artist George Caleb Bingham to examine the battle at Wilson's Creek, a little - discussed but influential Civil War battle.
History - United States
Dist - USNAC **Prod** - USNPS 1983

Wiltshire 27 MIN
VHS
Color (G)
Tours Wiltshire, with visits to Stonehenge, Salisbury Cathedral Choir and other attractions. Available for free loan from the distributor.
Fine Arts; Geography - World; History - World
Dist - AUDPLN

Wimpy Wendy 18 MIN
VHS / 16mm
Managing Problem People Series
Color (A PRO)
$415.00 purchase, $195.00 rental
Portrays a staff person who knows what to do but won't take the initiative. Part of a series on managing 'problem' employees.
Business and Economics; Guidance and Counseling
Dist - VIDART **Prod** - VIDART 1990

Win at baccarat
VHS
So you wanna be a gambler series
Color (G)
$39.95 purchase _ #JJ011
Part of a series by professional gambler John Patrick, explaining casino games, card games, football, and horse racing.
Physical Education and Recreation; Sociology
Dist - SIV

Win at blackjack - basic course
VHS
So you wanna be a gambler series
Color (G)
$39.95 purchase _ #JJ000
Part of a series by professional gambler John Patrick, explaining casino games, card games, football, and horse racing.
Physical Education and Recreation; Sociology
Dist - SIV

Win at blackjack - card counting
VHS
So you wanna be a gambler series
Color (G)
$39.95 purchase _ #JJ001
Part of a series by professional gambler John Patrick, explaining casino games, card games, football, and horse racing.
Physical Education and Recreation; Sociology
Dist - SIV

Win at craps - advanced I
VHS
So you wanna be a gambler series
Color (G)
$39.95 purchase _ #JJ012
Part of a series by professional gambler John Patrick, explaining casino games, card games, football, and horse racing.
Physical Education and Recreation; Sociology
Dist - SIV

Win at craps - advanced II
VHS
So you wanna be a gambler series
Color (G)
$39.95 purchase _ #JJ005
Part of a series by professional gambler John Patrick, explaining casino games, card games, football, and horse racing.
Physical Education and Recreation; Sociology
Dist - SIV

Win at craps - beginners
VHS
So you wanna be a gambler series
Color (G)
$39.95 purchase _ #JJ030
Part of a series by professional gambler John Patrick, explaining casino games, card games, football, and horse racing.
Physical Education and Recreation; Sociology
Dist - SIV

Win at draw poker
VHS
So you wanna be a gambler series
Color (G)
$39.95 purchase _ #JJ008
Part of a series by professional gambler John Patrick, explaining casino games, card games, football, and horse racing.
Physical Education and Recreation; Sociology
Dist - SIV

Win at Pai Gow - Chinese poker
VHS
So you wanna be a gambler series
Color (G)
$39.95 purchase _ #JJ026
Part of a series by professional gambler John Patrick, explaining casino games, card games, football, and horse racing.
Physical Education and Recreation; Sociology
Dist - SIV

Win at roulette - advanced
VHS
So you wanna be a gambler series
Color (G)
$39.95 purchase _ #JJ003
Part of a series by professional gambler John Patrick, explaining casino games, card games, football, and horse racing.
Physical Education and Recreation; Sociology
Dist - SIV

Win at roulette - basic
VHS
So you wanna be a gambler series
Color (G)
$39.95 purchase _ #JJ002
Part of a series by professional gambler John Patrick, explaining casino games, card games, football, and horse racing.
Physical Education and Recreation; Sociology
Dist - SIV

Win at 7 - card stud poker
VHS
So you wanna be a gambler series
Color (G)
$39.95 purchase _ #JJ007
Part of a series by professional gambler John Patrick, explaining casino games, card games, football, and horse racing.
Physical Education and Recreation; Sociology
Dist - SIV

Win at slots
VHS
So you wanna be a gambler series
Color (G)
$39.95 purchase _ #JJ009
Part of a series by professional gambler John Patrick, explaining casino games, card games, football, and horse racing.
Physical Education and Recreation; Sociology
Dist - SIV

Win at video poker
VHS
So you wanna be a gambler series
Color (G)
$39.95 purchase _ #JJ010
Part of a series by professional gambler John Patrick, explaining casino games, card games, football, and horse racing.
Physical Education and Recreation; Sociology
Dist - SIV

Win some, Lose some 50 MIN
U-matic / 16mm / VHS
Window on the World Series
Color; Mono (J H C A)
MV $350.00 _ MP $600.00 purchase, $50.00 rental
Probes modern man's competitive instincts. Looks at the results of our fear of losing and our burning desire to win.
Business and Economics; Sociology
Dist - CTV **Prod** - CTV 1973

Win teams 23 MIN
VHS
Color (G C PRO)

$595.00 purchase, $140.00 rental
Features workers of the Ericsson GE Mobile Communications plant who show how their employee involvement program radically transformed corporate culture. Reassures viewers that change can be for the better and that employee fears are a natual part of the change process. Includes leader's guide.
Business and Economics; Psychology
Dist - FI **Prod** - VIDVIS 1995

Win teams - how one company made empowerment work 23 MIN
VHS
Color (COR)
$595.00 purchase, $140.00 five - day preview, $35.00 three - day preview _ #VWT/VV
Demonstrates how an employee involvement program transformed a group of workers into committed teams who saved their company. Models one type of employee involvement program and shows how the company changed its corporate culture. Prepares employees for a major cultural change while accepting personal responsibility for improving their workplace. Includes a Leader's Guide. Available for three - day or five - day preview, as well as for purchase.
Business and Economics; Guidance and Counseling
Dist - ADVANM

Win through relationships 43 MIN
VHS
Color (A PRO)
$75.00 purchase _ #588VU
Features Jim Cathcart and Tony Alessandra in an examination of human relationships. Shows how understanding the true nature of people will improve relationships and lead to greater accomplishments. Multimedia package consists of the video, two audiocassettes and two printed guides.
Psychology; Social Science
Dist - NIGCON **Prod** - NIGCON

Win, Win 9 MIN
U-matic / VHS
Color (C A)
Illustrates the need to develop a balance between task and people orientation.
Business and Economics; Psychology
Dist - CORF **Prod** - CORF

Win - win negotiating works 55 MIN
VHS
Color (A PRO)
$169.00 purchase _ #S01132
Suggests that there are four stages to the negotiations process - planning, relationships, agreements and maintenance. Gives examples of ways people try to get what they want, showing what ways are counterproductive. Stresses the idea that good negotiations take time and are worth any short - terms costs. Hosted by Dr Ross Reck and Dr Brian Long.
Business and Economics; Psychology; Social Science
Dist - UILL

Win! with Iron Mike 23 MIN
VHS
Color (COR)
$395.00 purchase, $175.00 rental _ #DWW/DPI
Presents Mike Ditka, former coach of the Chicago Bears, offering motivational advice for approaching successs. Encourages the viewer to know who he or she is and believe in personal accomplishments, commit to peak performance, be patient through the long haul and don't become frustrated by lack of immediate success. Includes a Leader's Guide. Also available in a nine - minute version ($295 purchase, $145 rental).
Business and Economics; Guidance and Counseling; Psychology
Dist - ADVANM

Win with Motivation 15 MIN
VHS / 35mm strip
$43.50 purchase _ #XY856 for filmstrip, $84.95 purchase _ #XY806 for
Emphasizes the importance of motivation in acquiring a job, performing well on the job, and getting promoted to a better position.
Business and Economics; Guidance and Counseling
Dist - CAREER **Prod** - CAREER

Win with motivation
VHS
Career process series
Color (H A)
$84.95 purchase _ #ES1160V
Stresses the importance of motivation on the job. Suggests that motivation is reflected through job security, money, promotion, recognition, and taking pride in one's work.
Psychology
Dist - CAMV

Win with Motivation 15 MIN
VHS
(H C)
$84.95 _ CA130
Gives the importance of motivation for personal job success.
Guidance and Counseling; Psychology
Dist - AAVIM **Prod** - AAVIM 1989

The Winans in concert 108 MIN
VHS
Color (G R)
$39.95 purchase _ #35 - 80 - 94
Features Marvin, Carvin, Ronald and Michael Winans in a performance of their Gospel songs. Includes 'Perfect Love,' 'Question Is,' 'Love Is A Spirit,' and others. Special guest performance by Vanessa Bell Armstrong. Produced by Mercury Films.
Fine Arts; Religion and Philosophy
Dist - APH

Winch Characteristics - Electric, Hydraulic and Steam 25 MIN
16mm
B&W
LC 74-705960
Explains characteristics, preoperation checks and preparations and operation of the two - speed steam winch, unit - type electric winch and hydraulic winch used in military stevedoring. Presents advantages and limitations of each.
Industrial and Technical Education
Dist - USNAC **Prod** - USA 1969

Wind 10 MIN
U-matic
Take a Look Series
Color (P I)
Explains how to make a weather vane and how the wind creates weather.
Science; Science - Physical
Dist - TVOTAR **Prod** - TVOTAR 1986

Wind 4 MIN
16mm
Color
LC 76-703100
Shows how the Ontario countryside is transformed by the wind.
Fine Arts; Geography - World
Dist - CANFDC **Prod** - CANFDC 1975

Wind 8 MIN
16mm / U-matic / VHS
Starting to Read Series
Color (K P)
LC 70-710029
Shows sailboats gliding by, kites soaring above, and branches swaying as photography and a ballad describe the various effects of the wind. Uses simple captions in bold lettering to familiarize the beginning reader with the sound, sight and concept of short words.
English Language
Dist - AIMS **Prod** - ACI 1970

Wind 9 MIN
U-matic / VHS / 16mm
Color (K P)
LC 73-701183
Shows how a gust of wind, swirling clouds and leaves around a small boy enchant his senses and awaken kaleidoscopic visions of magical wind - borne kite and boat trips.
English Language; Literature and Drama; Science - Physical
Dist - LCOA **Prod** - NFBC 1973

Wind 12 MIN
VHS / 16mm
Color (P)
$275.00, $160.00 purchase
Shows a boy chasing his kite out of the city and into the hilly country beyond. Reveals that there he meets the 'wind lady' who shows him how the wind carries the clouds and changes the shape of the land. He sees how wind can do work by turning windmills, rides in a land - sailor, a sailboat and a hot air balloon.
Industrial and Technical Education; Literature and Drama; Science - Physical
Dist - LUF **Prod** - LUF

Wind Across the Everglades 93 MIN
16mm
Color
Tells how a young game warden pursues a gang of plumage hunters deep into Florida's Everglades.
Fine Arts
Dist - TWYMAN **Prod** - WB 1958

Wind - an Energy Alternative 12 MIN
U-matic / VHS / 16mm
Color
Describes wind as an energy alternative and offers a history of its use in the United States. Focuses on developmental efforts by the U S Department of Energy. Defines various terms and concepts, including kilowatt, megawatt and utility interconnect.
Social Science
Dist - USNAC **Prod** - SERI 1980

Wind and the navigator - in - flight analysis 8 MIN
16mm
Beginning Algebra 1 Series
Color
LC FIE58-310
Illustrates the navigator's duties while in flight, including determination of wind changes, drift causes and flight path corrections.
Industrial and Technical Education; Social Science
Dist - USNAC **Prod** - USAF 1957

Wind and the Navigator - Jet Streams 15 MIN
16mm
Color
LC FIE60-342
Explains the high velocity wind currents called jet streams and shows how aircraft navigators save fuel and flight time through use of these forces. Discusses altitude velocity, seasonal changes, direction and turbulence.
Industrial and Technical Education; Science - Physical; Social Science
Dist - USNAC **Prod** - USAF 1957

Wind and the Navigator - Pre - Flight Planning 15 MIN
16mm
Color
LC FIE58-309
Demonstrates how a wind flow chart, using weather data values and scales, is prepared and shows how a flight path is determined.
Industrial and Technical Education; Science - Physical; Social Science
Dist - USNAC **Prod** - USAF 1957

Wind and the Navigator - Wind Theory 15 MIN
16mm
Color
LC FIE58-308
Discusses the theory of wind forces and patterns, pressure gradient force, pressure surfaces, coriolis force, geostrophic winds, friction and centrifugal force.
Industrial and Technical Education; Social Science
Dist - USNAC **Prod** - USAF 1957

The Wind and the River 10 MIN
16mm
B&W (I A)
LC FIA64-1377
Captures the spirit of calm and timeless beauty of the small Himalayan country of Kashmir produces in 1950.
Geography - World
Dist - VIEWFI **Prod** - PFP 1970

Wind and the weather 11 MIN
VHS
Color; PAL (P I)
PdS29.50 purchase
Explains the nature of air and its movement, major wind systems, air pressures, and heating and cooling air.
Science; Science - Physical
Dist - EMFVL **Prod** - STANF

Wind and water energy
Videodisc
Energy series
Color; CAV (P I J)
$189.00 purchase _ #8L202
Examines how wind and water have been used as sources of power and how they are still used today. Looks at how humans have used knowledge of the wind's currents to power windmills and ships and how the energy of water is harnessed to produce electricity. Barcoded for instant random access.
Social Science
Dist - BARR **Prod** - BARR 1991

Wind and what it Does 11 MIN
U-matic / VHS / 16mm
Color (P) (SPANISH)
Discusses the nature of wind and shows how it affects man and his surroundings.
Foreign Language; Science - Physical
Dist - EBEC **Prod** - EBEC

The Wind at One's Fingertips 60 MIN
U-matic / VHS
(G)
Documents the creation of a huge tracker pipe organ, one which works mechanically rather than electrically. Examines the technical workings of the instrument and its year long construction by Nebraska organ builder Gene R. Bedient and his ten person crew. Concludes with installation of the organ and performances by American and French organists.

Fine Arts
Dist - GPN **Prod** - NETV 1986

Wind Chill
16mm
Meteorology Series
Color
Forms the preliminary basis of interdisciplinary investigation of environmental thermal stresses on man. Features concern with atmospheric heat transfer processes and physiological impact on the human body.
Science - Natural; Science - Physical; Sociology
Dist - MLA **Prod** - MLA 1973

Wind energy 30 MIN
VHS
Perspective - energy resources - series
Color; PAL; NTSC (G)
PdS90, PdS105 purchase
Examines the possibility of forests of power feeding high - tech windmills.
Social Science
Dist - CFLVIS **Prod** - LONTVS

Wind Gauge 15 MIN
U-matic
Know Your World Series
(I J)
Investigates several ways to use the wind. In order to understand wind currents better students build a gauge to measure speed and direction.
Science
Dist - ACCESS **Prod** - ACCESS 1981

Wind grass song - the voice of our grandmothers 20 MIN
VHS / 16mm
Color (G)
$225.00 purchase, $60.00 rental
Interviews Oklahoma women aged 85 to 101 years. Looks at United States regional culture through oral history. Includes black, native American and white women. Produced by Jana Birchum and Tori Breitling.
History - United States; Sociology
Dist - WMEN

The Wind in the willows
VHS
Disney classics on video series
Color (K P I)
$29.95 purchase _ #DIS427
Presents the Disney version of The Wind in the Willows on video.
Fine Arts; Literature and Drama
Dist - KNOWUN **Prod** - DISNEY

The Wind in the willows 86 MIN
VHS
Color (K P I J)
$29.95 purchase _ #S02106
Tells the story of Toad, Rat and Mole in a version of the book 'The Wind In The Willows.'
Literature and Drama
Dist - UILL

Wind in the Willows 57 MIN
U-matic / VHS
Wind in the Willows Series
Color (P I)
Contains 1 videocassette.
English Language; Literature and Drama
Dist - TROLA **Prod** - TROLA 1987

Wind in the Willows Series
Wind in the Willows 57 MIN
Dist - TROLA

Wind Instruments - Sound Emission 30 MIN
VHS / U-matic
Musical Sound Series
Color
Demonstrates how the air column in a wind instrument responds to a set of frequencies with a specific relationship. Dr. Arthur Benade has charted frequency sets for several instruments, with important implictions for the ways in which sound is produced and how it is heard in a room.
Fine Arts; Science - Physical
Dist - NETCHE **Prod** - NETCHE 1976

The Wind of Change 30 MIN
16mm
Color (C A)
LC FIA65-519
Pictures the delivery of the first Douglas DC - 8 to Air Afrique. Points out the changes and rapid advancement taking place in the nations of West Africa.
Geography - World; History - United States; Industrial and Technical Education; Psychology; Sociology
Dist - MCDO **Prod** - DAC 1964

Wind power 12 MIN
VHS
Energy and the environment series
Color; PAL (J H)
PdS29.50 purchase
Explores wind power and the problems associated with its use. Includes an examination of wind mills, pumps and turbines. Visits operational windfarms in the mid - Wales area. Part of a three - part series looking into renewable energy sources at the Centre for Alternative Technology in Powys, North Wales. Produced by CV, United Kingdom.
Geography - World; Science; Social Science
Dist - EMFVL

Wind Power - the Great Revival 29 MIN
16mm
Energy Sources - a New Beginning Series
Color
Discusses wind energy and its storability, as well as the aesthetic considerations of windmills in large numbers. Examines the combined use of solar and wind power.
Science - Natural; Social Science
Dist - UCOLO **Prod** - UCOLO

Wind Rose 21 MIN
U-matic / VHS / 16mm
Color (I)
LC 84-707090
Presents Elizabeth and Dan, walking in the woods with their five - year - old daughter, Wind Rose. Tells how the rising of the wind evokes memories in Elizabeth of the stages of her pregnancy. Emphasizes the beauty of family life.
Literature and Drama; Sociology
Dist - PHENIX **Prod** - PHENIX 1983

Wind, Waves, and Water Dynamics 28 MIN
VHS / U-matic
Oceanus - the Marine Environment Series
Color (C A)
Science - Natural; Science - Physical
Dist - SCCON **Prod** - SCCON 1980
CDTEL

Windfalls 21 MIN
U-matic
Color (C)
$310.00
Experimental film by Matthew Geller.
Fine Arts
Dist - AFA **Prod** - AFA 1982

Windfalls 22 MIN
VHS / U-matic
Color
Features two men each telling a long story cutting into one another's. Includes fragments of a scientist's lecture on intelligence and memory.
Fine Arts
Dist - KITCHN **Prod** - KITCHN

Windfalls - Matthew Geller 21 MIN
U-matic
Color
Fine Arts
Dist - AFA **Prod** - AFA 1982

Windflight 13 MIN
U-matic / VHS / 16mm
Color (I)
Deals with windsurfing, the new water sport. Presents a display of physical agility and athletic artistry featuring the first 360 degree flips ever filmed, the largest windsurfing waves ever ridden, and aerial loops, jibes and freestyle performances by some of the top names in sailboarding.
Physical Education and Recreation
Dist - PFP **Prod** - PFP

Windflower 20 MIN
VHS / 16mm
Color (J)
LC 78-701335
Shows a child constructing a model hot air balloon which is magically transformed into full size and which carries him over the autumn countryside.
Fine Arts
Dist - LRF **Prod** - POBAPS

Windflower Song 30 MIN
U-matic / VHS
(G)
Features the work of two Nebraska poets, Ted Kooser and William Kloefkorn. Includes poems and the places where they were written and which inspired them, a bookshop, a barn, a silo, and the Platte River.
Fine Arts; Literature and Drama
Dist - GPN **Prod** - NETV

Windham Hill - Autumn Portrait - Pt 2 55 MIN
VHS
Windham Hill Series
Color (S)
$29.95 purchase _ #384 - 9353
Presents the beautiful and intricately contemporary music produced by the Windham Hill recording company. Combines scenic views and scenic music. Part 2 of an eight - part series.
Fine Arts; Industrial and Technical Education; Religion and Philosophy
Dist - FI **Prod** - PAR 1988

Windham Hill - China - Pt 3 55 MIN
VHS
Windham Hill Series
Color (S)
$29.95 purchase _ #384 - 9558
Presents the beautiful and intricately contemporary music produced by the Windham Hill recording company. Combines scenic views and scenic music. Part 3 of an eight - part series.
Fine Arts; Industrial and Technical Education; Religion and Philosophy
Dist - FI **Prod** - PAR 1988

Windham hill gift set 220 MIN
VHS
Color (H C A)
$99.95 purchase
Presents a four - cassette gift set of New Age music by Windham Hill. Combines natural scenes and the music of artists including Ackerman, Shadowfax, Isham, and more.
Fine Arts
Dist - PBS **Prod** - WNETTV

Windham hill in concert 68 MIN
VHS
Color (H C A)
$29.95 purchase
Presents a collection of live performances of New Age music by Windham Hill musicians. Includes performances from Will Ackerman, Michael Hedges, Scott Cossu, and Shadowfax.
Fine Arts
Dist - PBS **Prod** - WNETTV

Windham Hill - in Concert - Pt 1 68 MIN
VHS
Windham Hill Series
Color (S)
$29.95 purchase _ #384 - 9537
Presents the beautiful and intricately contemporary music produced by the Windham Hill recording company. Combines scenic views and scenic music. Part 1 of an eight - part series.
Fine Arts; Industrial and Technical Education; Religion and Philosophy
Dist - FI **Prod** - PAR 1988

Windham hill - seasons 45 MIN
VHS
Color (H C A)
$19.95 purchase
Presents a collection of New Age music videos from Windham Hill. Includes selections from 'Winter's Path,' 'Winter,' 'Autumn Light,' and 'Western Light.'
Fine Arts
Dist - PBS **Prod** - WNETTV

Windham Hill - Seasons - Pt 4 46 MIN
VHS
Windham Hill Series
Color (S)
$29.95 purchase _ #384 - 9535
Presents the beautiful and intricately contemporary music produced by the Windham Hill recording company. Combines scenic views and scenic music. Part 4 of an eight - part series.
Fine Arts; Industrial and Technical Education; Religion and Philosophy
Dist - FI **Prod** - PAR 1988

Windham Hill Series
Windham Hill - Autumn Portrait - Pt 2 55 MIN
Windham Hill - China - Pt 3 55 MIN
Windham Hill - in Concert - Pt 1 68 MIN
Windham Hill - Seasons - Pt 4 46 MIN
Windham Hill - Tibet - Pt 8 54 MIN
Windham Hill - Water's Path - Pt 5 55 MIN
Windham Hill - Western Light - Pt 6 55 MIN
Windham Hill - Winter - Pt 7 53 MIN
Dist - FI

Windham Hill - Tibet - Pt 8 54 MIN
VHS
Windham Hill Series
Color (S)
$29.95 purchase _ #384 - 9557
Presents the beautiful and intricately contemporary music produced by the Windham Hill recording company. Combines scenic views and scenic music. Part 8 of an eight - part series.
Fine Arts; Industrial and Technical Education; Religion and Philosophy
Dist - FI **Prod** - PAR 1988

Windham Hill - Water's Path - Pt 5 55 MIN
VHS
Windham Hill Series
Color (S)
$29.95 purchase _ #384 - 9355
Presents the beautiful and intricately contemporary music produced by the Windham Hill recording company. Combines scenic views and scenic music. Part 5 of an eight - part series.
Fine Arts; Industrial and Technical Education; Religion and Philosophy
Dist - FI **Prod** - PAR 1988

Windham Hill - Western Light - Pt 6 55 MIN
VHS
Windham Hill Series
Color (S)
$29.95 purchase _ #384 - 9354
Presents the beautiful and intricately contemporary music produced by the Windham Hill recording company. Combines scenic views and scenic music. Part 6 of an eight - part series.
Fine Arts; Industrial and Technical Education; Religion and Philosophy
Dist - FI **Prod** - PAR 1988

Windham Hill - Winter - Pt 7 53 MIN
VHS
Windham Hill Series
Color (S)
$29.95 purchase _ #384 - 9356
Presents the beautiful and intricately contemporary music produced by the Windham Hill recording company. Combines scenic views and scenic music. Part 7 of an eight - part series.
Fine Arts; Industrial and Technical Education; Religion and Philosophy
Dist - FI **Prod** - PAR 1988

Windjammer Fantome
VHS
Color (G A)
$100.00 rental _ #0725
Sails the Bahamas on a four - master, the 282 foot Fantome with 126 shipmates.
Geography - World; Physical Education and Recreation
Dist - SEVVID

Windmill 11 MIN
16mm / U-matic / VHS
Color (I J)
Looks at a well preserved tower mill and shows the details of the mill's operation. Portrays grain being milled into whole meal flour.
Industrial and Technical Education
Dist - VIEWTH **Prod** - VIEWTH

Windmill Summer 15 MIN
VHS / U-matic
Best of Cover to Cover 2 Series
Color (I)
Literature and Drama
Dist - WETATV **Prod** - WETATV

Windmills and Wooden Shoes 15 MIN
VHS / U-matic
Other families, other friends series; Red module; Holland
Color (P)
Presents a tour of Madurodam, a windmill and a wooden shoe factory in Holland.
Geography - World; Social Science
Dist - AITECH **Prod** - WVIZTV 1971

Window 12 MIN
16mm
Color; Silent (C)
$448.00
Experimental film by Ken Jacobs.
Fine Arts
Dist - AFA **Prod** - AFA 1964

Window 30 MIN
U-matic / VHS
Doris Chase concepts series
Color
Reveals memory, not as an act, but as form. Moves script's language through memory - scapes and non - linear thinking, and selected elements are visually abstracted.
Psychology
Dist - WMEN **Prod** - CHASED

A Window 2 MIN
16mm
B&W (G)
$8.00 rental
Delivers an animated haiku about feeling the rain splashing onto one's face.Produced by Philip Perkins. Also distributed by the Northwest Film Study Center in Portland, Oregon.
Fine Arts; Literature and Drama
Dist - CANCIN

Window 20 MIN
16mm
Color
Uses both live action and animation to describe the contribution of education to business, to industry, and to the community as a whole. Stresses that taxes for education provide tangible returns for the entire society.
Business and Economics; Education; Social Science
Dist - WSUM **Prod** - WSUM 1954

Window book library
CD-ROM
(G A)
$99.00 purchase _ #2671
Includes a variety of computer references - the Domestic Mail Manual, WinDos - the comprehensive encyclopedic on - line DOS reference, ADA Language Reference Manual, ADA Source Code supplied by the US government, Federal Information Resources Managemement regulations, Heavens in Hypertext - CALS specificatins, Microsoft's Rich Text Format Specifican, All PC Interrupts and Operating Platform Functions - IntrList. For IBM PCs and compatibles. Requires at least 640K RAM, DOS Version 3.1 or greater, one floppy disk drive - hard disk drive recommended, one empty expansion slot, IBM compatible CD - ROM drive.
Computer Science
Dist - BEP

Window Boxes 29 MIN
Videoreel / VT2
Making Things Grow III Series
Color
LC 80-706151
Features Thalassa Cruso discussing different aspects of gardening. Shows how to make flower and plant arrangements in window boxes.
Agriculture; Science - Natural
Dist - PBS **Prod** - WGBHTV

A Window Full of Cakes 20 MIN
16mm
B&W
Tells the story of Massachusetts nursery shcools for retarded children. Depicts activities in relation to their objectives for the child.
Education; Geography - United States; Psychology
Dist - CMHRF **Prod** - CMHRF

Window of the Living Sea 22 MIN
16mm
Color
LC 74-702529
Explores the educational and research activities at Miami Seaquarium. Examines the care, psychology and training of marine mammals, the collection of specimens and research carried on and the Seaquarium's philosophy of management.
Geography - United States; Science; Science - Natural
Dist - MIAMIS **Prod** - MIAMIS 1974

Window on the Body 26 MIN
VHS / U-matic
Breakthroughs Series
Color
Portrays the excitement of doctors and medical scientists at the staggering implications of a new medical instrument which actually sees the body's chemistry at work.
Science; Science - Natural
Dist - LANDMK **Prod** - NOMDFI

Window on the World Series

Britain, who Shot the Woodcock, Pt 1	25 MIN
Britain, who Shot the Woodcock, Pt 2	25 MIN
Fertility rites for the twenty - first century	50 MIN
The Grains of conflict	50 MIN
Nationalism	50 MIN
The New Europeans	50 MIN
The Oil Weapon	50 MIN
The Pacific Rim	50 MIN
Thine is the Power	50 MIN
Time of the Jackal	50 MIN
Time of the Jackal, Pt 1	25 MIN
Time of the Jackal, Pt 2	25 MIN
Win some, Lose some	50 MIN

Dist - CTV

Window on the World
Britain - who Shot the Woodcock 50 MIN
Dist - CTV

Window Problems 15 MIN
Videoreel / VT2
Making Things Work Series
Color
Home Economics
Dist - PBS **Prod** - WGBHTV

Window Repair 30 MIN
VHS / U-matic
You Can Fixit Series
Color
Presents the basics of window repair.
Industrial and Technical Education
Dist - MDCPB **Prod** - WRJATV

Window to the Universe 15 MIN
VHS / 16mm
Color (I J H C)
LC 77-701519
Traces the origins and development of radio astronomy. Explains the basic parts of a radio telescope and its functions. Examines the ways in which radio astronomy has expanded the knowledge of the universe.
Industrial and Technical Education; Science - Physical; Social Science
Dist - MIS **Prod** - MIS 1977

Window treatments
VHS
Color (G A)
$24.95 purchase _ #NN530V
Teaches the techniques of how to sew window treatments.
Home Economics
Dist - CAMV

Window Water Baby Moving 13 MIN
16mm
Color; Silent (C)
$490.50
Experimental film by Stan Brakhage.
Fine Arts
Dist - AFA **Prod** - AFA 1959

Window wind chimes - Part One 27 MIN
16mm
Color (G)
$50.00 rental
Combines a documentary of the filmmaker and his wife with a personal and poetic vision. Explores their relationship in their apartment by presenting fragments of arguments, apologies and affections.
Fine Arts
Dist - CANCIN **Prod** - GRENIV 1974

Windowmobile 8 MIN
16mm
Color (G)
$16.00 rental
Looks through and at a window, superimposing and conjoining events on both sides of the glass. Presents images by Joel Singer and sounds by James Broughton.
Fine Arts
Dist - CANCIN

Windows 30 MIN
U-matic / VHS / 16mm
Do it Yourself Home Repairs Series
Color
Provides basic information on repairing windows.
Home Economics
Dist - BULFRG **Prod** - ODECA

Windows 3.0
VHS
Color (G)
$149.95 purchase
Provides video PC software training in IBM Windows 3.0. Includes training guide.
Computer Science
Dist - HALASI **Prod** - HALASI

Windows 3.0 58 MIN
VHS
Windows applications series
Color (J H C G)
$29.95 purchase _ #VP141V
Offers concepts in Windows 3.0. Allows viewer to see keyboard and monitor simultaneously so that students can see the result of every keystroke. Part of an eight - part series on Windows.
Computer Science
Dist - CAMV

Windows 3.0 for 286 users
VHS
IBM series
Color (G)
$29.95 purchase _ #60085
Looks at Windows within the scope of IBM and IBM compatible 286 use. Examines requirements and set - up procedures. Teaches about the desktop environment, using the mouse, manipulating the windows.
Computer Science; Mathematics
Dist - CARTRP **Prod** - CARTRP

Windows 3.0 for 386 users 50 MIN
VHS
IBM series
Color (G)
$29.95 purchase _ #60084
Looks at Windows within the scope of IBM and IBM compatible 386 use. Examines requirements and set - up procedures. Teaches about the desktop environment, using the mouse, manipulating the windows.

Computer Science; Mathematics
Dist - CARTRP **Prod** - CARTRP

Windows 3.1 58 MIN
VHS
Windows applications series
Color (J H C G)
$29.95 purchase _ #VP158V
Offers concepts in Windows 3.1. Allows viewer to see keyboard and monitor simultaneously so that students can see the result of every keystroke. Part of an eight - part series on Windows.
Computer Science
Dist - CAMV

Windows 3.1 177 MIN
U-matic / VHS / BETA
Color; NTSC; PAL; SECAM (J H C G)
PdS99.95
Teaches new users and those who want to know more about Windows 3.1.
Computer Science
Dist - VIEWTH

Windows - advanced
VHS
Color (G)
$59.95 purchase _ #VIA018
Teaches the advanced use of computer Windows.
Computer Science
Dist - SIV

Windows - an Introduction to Anesthesia 16 MIN
16mm
Color
LC 79-700348
Shows what happens inside the body when anesthesia is administered during surgical complications. Illustrates reactions caused by inhaled anesthesia and by inhaled plus injected anesthesia.
Health and Safety
Dist - OHMED **Prod** - OHMED 1979

Windows applications series
Introduction to Excel - Windows 58 MIN
Introduction to Lotus 1 - 2 - 3 - Windows 60 MIN
Introduction to WordPerfect 5.1 - Windows 60 MIN
Lotus 1 - 2 - 3 - Windows level II 60 MIN
Microsoft word for Windows introduction 51 MIN
Microsoft word for Windows level II 43 MIN
Windows 3.0 58 MIN
Windows 3.1 58 MIN
Dist - CAMV

Windows easy to use databases
VHS
Computer software training series
Color (J H C G)
$49.95 purchase _ #AAT17V
Teaches Windows database concepts in a comprehensive and easy - to - follow format. Illustrates actual commands and time saving techniques. Part of a 21 - part series on computer software.
Computer Science
Dist - CAMV

Windows for Workgroups 3.1 174 MIN
U-matic / VHS / BETA
Color; NTSC; PAL; SECAM (J H C G)
PdS99.95
Shows how Windows for Workgroups allows users to link a number of computers in a network. Presents Windows and demonstrates how to link PCs and peripherals in a local area network. Features David Bridger.
Computer Science
Dist - VIEWTH

Windows - getting started
VHS
Color (G)
$49.95 purchase _ #VIA035
Teaches about computer Windows.
Computer Science
Dist - SIV

Windows - getting started and advanced
VHS
Color (G)
$109.90 purchase _ #VIA800
Presents two videocassettes teaching beginning and advanced use of computer Windows.
Computer Science
Dist - SIV

Windows - healing and helping through loss 64 MIN
VHS
Color (I J H G)
$199.00 purchase _ #ACG4000V
Presents a video - discussion package which addresses the issue of loss, examines the emotions of a student's experience of divorcing parents and shows effective helping skills as a counselor reaches out to family who has lost a teenage daughter. Includes leader's guide, Windows book, two posters and 24 brochures to promote the program.
Guidance and Counseling; Sociology
Dist - CAMV

Windows in Armour 9 MIN
16mm
Color
LC 77-702723
Deals with urban emotional and societal complexities. Focuses on different personal impressions of metropolitan life and the quest for feelings in the city.
Psychology; Sociology
Dist - CANFDC **Prod** - CANFDC 1974

Windows in the Kitchen 12 MIN
VHS
Color
Features Matt Rurney dancing in the windows of the Kitchen Center for video and Music, New York City.
Fine Arts
Dist - EIF **Prod** - EIF

Windows in the sea 26 MIN
VHS
Challenge of the seas series
Color (I J H)
$225.00 purchase
Takes a look at a new age aquarium, one that the brings people to the natural world of marine ecology. Part of a 26 - part series on the oceans.
Science - Natural; Science - Physical
Dist - LANDMK **Prod** - LANDMK 1991

Windows in Time - Research Today for Energy Tomorrow 29 MIN
16mm
Color
Introduces the contemporary world of research and development. Features five scientists who are seen at work in their labs and in the field where they explain their projects and speak of their lives as researchers.
Science - Physical; Social Science
Dist - MTP **Prod** - ELPORI

Windows into the Mind 15 MIN
U-matic
Process of Reading Series
Color
Explores ways that individuals understand and use what they read. Stresses that children should be encouraged to read often and to read anything that interests them.
English Language; Literature and Drama
Dist - TVOTAR **Prod** - TVOTAR 1976

Windows literacy
VHS
Computer software training series
Color (J H C G)
$49.95 purchase _ #AAT14V
Teaches Windows literacy in a comprehensive and easy - to - follow format. Illustrates actual commands and time saving techniques. Part of a 21 - part series on computer software.
Computer Science
Dist - CAMV

Windows of Change - Survival skills for the future 44 MIN
VHS
Color (PRO IND A)
$1,190.00 purchase, $400.00 rental _ #ENT19 and #ENT20
Describes through the teachings, humor and common sense of Jennifer James, PhD, how to be aware of and utilize change. Teaches individuals in the workplace specific mind - sets and methods for dealing with change. Includes 2 videos.
Business and Economics
Dist - EXTR **Prod** - ENMED

Windows on the Body 26 MIN
U-matic / VHS
Color (C)
$249.00, $149.00 purchase _ #AD - 1887
Examines the revolution in diagnostic technology. Considers Computer X - ray Tomography - CT, nuclear scans, ultrasound, Positron Emission Tomography - PET, Magnetic Resonance Imaging - MRI. Looks at the future of diagnostic technology.
Health and Safety; Science
Dist - FOTH **Prod** - FOTH

Windows on Women 58 MIN
U-matic
Color (J H C A)
Presents a documentary look at the conditions of women over the past ten years. Narrated by Ruby Dee. Spotlights prominent women and discusses what was accomplished by the UN Decade Of Women.
Sociology
Dist - CCMPR **Prod** - CCMPR 1985

Windows personal information managers
VHS
Computer software training series
Color (J H C G)
$49.95 purchase _ #AAT19V
Teaches Windows personal information managing concepts in a comprehensive and easy - to - follow format. Illustrates actual commands and time saving techniques. Part of a 21 - part series on computer software.
Computer Science
Dist - CAMV

Windows presentations
VHS
Computer software training series
Color (J H C G)
$49.95 purchase _ #AAT18V
Teaches Windows presentations concepts in a comprehensive and easy - to - follow format. Illustrates actual commands and time saving techniques. Part of a 21 - part series on computer software.
Computer Science
Dist - CAMV

Windows, Spread Sheets, and Word Processing 60 MIN
VHS / Software / 16mm
Symphony Series
Color (PRO)
$325.00 purchase, $40.00 preview
Trains employees on the use of computer systems. Discusses windows, creating spread sheets, creating and editing a document, combining documents with spread sheets and printing. Includes practice disk and personal training guide.
Business and Economics; Computer Science; Mathematics; Psychology
Dist - UTM **Prod** - UTM

Windows to the sky series
Connecting with invisible worlds - Tape 2 80 MIN
Light Institute exercises with Chris Griscom - Tape 1 80 MIN
Dist - LIGHTI

Windows to understanding 38 MIN
VHS
Color (R) (SPANISH)
$19.95 purchase _ #494 - 5, #498 - 8
Looks at the situations of women who are balancing the work of managing a home and working for pay outside of the home. Includes discussion guide.
Religion and Philosophy; Sociology
Dist - USCC **Prod** - USCC 1992

Windows training videos series
Microsoft Excel 4.0
Microsoft Windows 3.0 or 3.1
Microsoft Word for Windows
WordPerfect for Windows
Dist - AMEDIA

Windows utilities
VHS
Computer software training series
Color (J H C G)
$49.95 purchase _ #AAT20V
Teaches Windows utilities concepts in a comprehensive and easy - to - follow format. Illustrates actual commands and time saving techniques. Part of a 21 - part series on computer software.
Computer Science
Dist - CAMV

Windows word processor and spreadsheets
VHS
Computer software training series
Color (J H C G)
$49.95 purchase _ #AAT16V
Teaches Windows word processor and spreadsheet concepts in a comprehensive and easy - to - follow format. Illustrates actual commands and time saving techniques. Part of a 21 - part series on computer software.
Computer Science
Dist - CAMV

Windowsill Gardening 13 MIN
16mm / U-matic / VHS
Green Thumb Series
Color (P)
Shows an assortment of windowsill plants. Includes various ways of planting, development of seedlings and requirements of light and moisture. Emphasizes plants and procedures which can be used in apartments or school rooms without special equipment or facilities.
Agriculture; Science - Natural
Dist - LUF **Prod** - ACORN

Windrifters - the Bald Eagle Story 20 MIN
U-matic / VHS
Nature Episodes Series
Color
Tells how scientists work to reintroduce the bald eagle, an endangered species, into its former habitat.
Science - Natural
Dist - EDIMGE **Prod** - EDIMGE

Winds and Air Currents 12 MIN
U-matic / VHS / 16mm
Atmospheric Science Series
Color (I J H C)
$400, $250 purchase _ #4621C
Shows how air is set in motion and changes direction and speed.
Science - Physical
Dist - CORF

Winds and air currents 12 MIN
VHS
Atmospheric science series
Color; PAL (H)
Illustrates how different sized convection cells of air produce land - sea breezes, monsoons and, on a giant scale, the trade winds. Shows how winds are lifted by mountains and how unusual warm and cold winds descend from the mountains. Part of a series of eight parts which teaches about the Earth's atmosphere.
Geography - World; Science - Physical
Dist - VIEWTH **Prod** - VIEWTH

Winds and their Causes 11 MIN
16mm / U-matic / VHS
Color (I J)
LC FIA67-122
Pictures a glider soaring over the countryside to provide vivid evidence of moving air currents. Demonstrates that winds are created by unequal heating of air. Shows how local winds are caused by lakes and other features, and how global winds are generated by the sun's heating effects, modified by the earth's rotation and by interaction with other winds.
Science - Physical; Social Science
Dist - CORF **Prod** - CORF 1967

Winds of Change 46 MIN
U-matic / VHS / 16mm
Color
$325 rental - 16 mm, $55 rental - video
Discusses the problems of South Africa. Includes interviews with Bishop Desmond Tutu and World Alliance of Reformed Churches President Dr. Allen Boesak, who discuss apartheid, the relationship between Christianity and politics, and the role of the U. S. Includes a Reflection/Action Guide for study purposes.
History - World; Religion and Philosophy; Sociology
Dist - CCNCC **Prod** - CCNCC 1986
CWS

The Winds of change 9 MIN
U-matic / 16mm / VHS
Color (C A G)
$240.00, $200.00, $170.00 purchase _ #B622
Uses animation to explain that 'Change can be a force to be feared or an opportunity to be seized.' Features Patrick Stewart as narrator.
Business and Economics; Psychology
Dist - BARR **Prod** - WEISSM 1992

The Winds of Change 22 MIN
U-matic / VHS
Phenomenal World Series
Color (J C)
$129.00 purchase _ #3964
Shows the effects of collisions of warm and cold air masses such as the production of violently windy weather in the form of severe thunderstorms, tornadoes, or hurricanes and how weathermen predict their patterns and potential.
Science - Physical
Dist - EBEC

Winds of Change 15 MIN
16mm
B&W (J)
LC FIA64-1081
A documentation of the transformations that have been taking place in all aspects of modern life, with particular emphasis on the implications of these changes on competitive business.
Business and Economics; Psychology; Social Science; Sociology
Dist - GE **Prod** - GE 1963

Winds of change - a matter of choice 60 MIN
VHS
Color (G)
$19.95 purchase _ #PBS 319
Discusses the choices available to young Native Americans - to remain on the reservation or to move out into mainstream American society, and the trade - offs for each choice.
Social Science; Sociology
Dist - INSTRU **Prod** - PBS
CARECS

Winds of change - a matter of promises
VHS
American Indian collection series
Color (J H C G)
$29.95 purchase _ #PAV262V
Explores the plight of Native Americans in modern society. Visits the Onondaga people of New York state, the Navajo nation in Arizona and Lummi nation in Washington state. Witnesses the efforts of many to preserve the traditions and heritage of centuries - old cultures. Part of a five - part series on American Indians.
Social Science
Dist - CAMV

Winds of change series
A Matter of choice 60 MIN
A Matter of promises 60 MIN
Dist - NAMPBC

Winds of memory 52 MIN
VHS
Color (G)
$390.00 purchase, $75.00 rental
Reveals Mayan life and culture in Guatemala today. Tracks the struggle for the Mayan people to regain their lost world - overrun by tourists by day, haunted by death squads at night - by defying their repressors in order to practice ceremonial rites. Filmed over a period of three years and focuses on the Tzutuhil Indians of Santiago Atitlan, a lakeshore village among volcanos. Produced by Felix Zurita.
Civics and Political Systems; Fine Arts; Social Science; Sociology
Dist - FIRS

Windscale AGR 28 MIN
16mm
Color (J)
Illustrates the construction of the advanced gascooled reactor at Windscale, including fuel manufacture and assembly.
Industrial and Technical Education; Science - Physical
Dist - UKAEA **Prod** - UKAEA 1963

Windshield and Sideglass Types - Characteristics and Applications 17 MIN
VHS / 16mm
(A PRO)
$78.50 purchase _ #KTI24
Covers development, braking characteristics, and workability and applications of shatterproof and tempered glass.
Industrial and Technical Education
Dist - RMIBHF **Prod** - RMIBHF

Windshield Water Leak Repair 17 MIN
VHS / BETA
Color (A PRO)
$79.00 purchase _ #AB130
Deals with auto body repair.
Industrial and Technical Education
Dist - RMIBHF **Prod** - RMIBHF

Windsong 19 MIN
U-matic / VHS
Color (J H C A)
Takes a historic look at the use of windmills in the settlement of the west.
Industrial and Technical Education; Social Science
Dist - CEPRO **Prod** - CEPRO

The Windsors 26 MIN
16mm
History Makers of the 20th Century Series
B&W (I)
LC FIA67-1432
Uses footage to portray the personal life and history - making deeds of the Windsors.
Biography; History - World
Dist - SF **Prod** - WOLPER 1966

Windsurfing 30 MIN
VHS
Color (G)
$19.90 purchase _ #0966
Features Robbie Doyle who explores setting sail and anchoring a 29 foot racer - cruiser. Gives an in - depth lesson in boardsailing with Kay Robberson. Looks at navigation.
Physical Education and Recreation
Dist - SEVVID

Windsurfing made easy 54 MIN
VHS
Color (G)
$39.90 purchase _ #0736
Features world champion windsurfer Tom Leudecke. Teaches beginning through advanced techniques in windsurfing from uphauling to duck jibes, wave jumping and small board water starts. Shows how to choose equipment.
Physical Education and Recreation
Dist - SEVVID

Windy Days 15 MIN
U-matic / VHS
Mrs Cabobble's Caboose
(P)
Designed to teach primarty grade students basic music concepts. Highlights melody, rhythm, harmony and the different families of musical instruments. Features Mrs.
Fine Arts
Dist - GPN **Prod** - WDCNTV 1986

Wine - its Selection and Enjoyment 15 MIN
16mm
Color (H C A)
LC 80-701058
Features television host Dan Resin who provides basic information about wines and gives advice on which brands to select, how much each wine should cost, how to taste wine and how to order wine at a restaurant.
Home Economics
Dist - KLEINW **Prod** - KLEINW 1978

Wine - Pure and Simple 50 MIN
VHS
Color (G)
$19.95 purchase
Joins Bob Bellus and Master Sommelier Fred Dame in a tour of some of the world's finest winemaking regions.
Health and Safety; Home Economics; Psychology
Dist - MIRMP **Prod** - MIRMP 1991

Wine - selling it and serving it 12 MIN
35mm strip / VHS
Color (A) (SPANISH)
#FC38
Trains servers new to wine service and provides valuable tips to experienced waiters and waitresses. Demonstrates how to suggest wines, proper presentation to the host, opening techniques and serving.
Industrial and Technical Education
Dist - CONPRO **Prod** - CONPRO

Wine - Where the Extra Profits are 22 MIN
16mm
Color
LC 75-702762
Deals with the major aspects of building a successful wine business, concentrating specifically on the details of merchandising, stocking, selling and serving.
Business and Economics; Home Economics
Dist - SCHABC **Prod** - SCHABC

Wine, Women and Wellness 30 MIN
VHS / U-matic
Color
Explains the symptomatic differences between male and female alcoholism and chemical dependency, their impact on detection and treatment.
Health and Safety; Psychology; Sociology
Dist - WHITEG **Prod** - WHITEG

Winemakers in France 15 MIN
16mm / U-matic / VHS
Man and His World Series
Color (P I J H C)
LC 70-705473
Describes the winemaking process from pruning the vines to the actual bottling of the wine. Tells that the traditional methods have been replaced by modern mass production methods.
Agriculture; Business and Economics; Geography - World
Dist - FI **Prod** - FI 1969

The Winery 21 MIN
VHS
Video Field Trips
Color (J H)
$89.95 purchase _ #6 - 040 - 135P
Visits Llano Estacado, a modern Texas winery. Looks at vineyard grape production, grape crushing and pressing, fermentation, cellar practices, bottling. Part of a series on video field trips which follow raw materials from their natural environment through the processes which transform them into marketable products.
Agriculture; Business and Economics; Health and Safety
Dist - VEP

Winfrith Pipeline 42 MIN
16mm
Color (J)
Shows the disposal of radioactive effluent from the atomic energy establishment at Winfrith by means of a pipeline running two miles out to sea.
Science - Physical
Dist - UKAEA **Prod** - UKAEA 1960

Winfrith Sghwr 100mwe 12 MIN
16mm
Color
Tells the story of the steam generating heavy water reactor. Explains the design of the reactor and illustrates site construction and the manufacture and installation of the principal reactor components. Shows the loading of the fuel elements and the start - up of the completed reactor.
Industrial and Technical Education; Science - Physical
Dist - UKAEA **Prod** - UKAEA 1968

The Wing 27 MIN
16mm
Color
LC 82-700184
Interviews men and women who work at Bitburg Air Force Base in West Germany and give their views of life in the U S Air Force and why they made the choice of military life over civilian life.
Civics and Political Systems
Dist - VARDIR **Prod** - VARDIR 1981

Wing Assembly - the Bow Tip 24 MIN
16mm
B&W
LC FIE52-286
Demonstrates how to fit the bow tip strip to the leading edge strip, make the spar tip joint, install ribs, shape the bow tip, apply and glue the bow tip skins and varnish the surface.
Industrial and Technical Education
Dist - USNAC **Prod** - USOE 1944

Wing Assembly - the Inboard Panel 19 MIN
16mm
B&W
Demonstrates how to install subassemblies in a jig, apply and glue the skins, apply and remove pressure strips, finish the outside surface and inspect the completed assembly.
Industrial and Technical Education
Dist - USNAC **Prod** - USOE 1944

Wing Assembly - the Nose Section 20 MIN
16mm
B&W
LC FIE52-284
Explains how to position the main spar in the jig, install the webbed ribs, junction ribs, regular ribs and leading edge strip, to apply and glue the skins and to finish the surface of the nose section.
Industrial and Technical Education
Dist - USNAC **Prod** - USOE 1944

Wing to Wing 50 MIN
U-matic / VHS
B&W
Tells of the French squadron of 'Normandy - Nieman' which fought together with Soviet Pilots against the Nazis in World War II.
Civics and Political Systems; History - World; Industrial and Technical Education
Dist - IHF **Prod** - IHF

Wingate, I Love You 9 MIN
16mm / U-matic / VHS
Color (J)
LC 76-700737
Uses the experience of a young man running away from family discord in order to emphasize the need of people to express their love for one another.
Guidance and Counseling; Psychology
Dist - AIMS **Prod** - COUNTR 1976

Winged bean - a plant against malnutrition 15 MIN
VHS
Fruits of the earth series
Color (G)
$175.00 purchase
Looks at winged bean (Psophocarpus tetragonolobus) cultivation efforts in Africa aimed at improving the people's nutrition. Focuses on the plant's high - quality proteins and its complete edibility. Considers what is necessary to increase production of this agriculturally important plant. Part of a series of 15 videos that describe everyday conditions in regions throughout the earth and look at plants available for environmentally sound, economically productive development.
Home Economics; Science - Natural
Dist - LANDMK

The Winged Bequest 20 MIN
U-matic / VHS / 16mm
Color (H C A)
Looks at library services to shut - ins and hospital patients.
Health and Safety; Sociology
Dist - FEIL **Prod** - FEIL 1955

The Winged Colt 66 MIN
U-matic / VHS / 16mm
Color (I J)
LC 78-701064
Tells how a colt born with wings bridges the personal differences between a former movie stuntman and his bookish nephew. Based on the book The Winged Colt of Casa Mia by Betsy Byars.
Literature and Drama
Dist - CORF **Prod** - ABCTV 1978

Winged Scourge 10 MIN
U-matic / VHS
Health for the Americas Series
Color
LC 80-707379
Uses animation to show various methods of combatting and eliminating the anopheles mosquito. Issued in 1943 as a motion picture.
Agriculture; Health and Safety
Dist - USNAC **Prod** - USCIAA 1943

Winged Victory on Foot - 43rd Infantry Division 14 MIN
16mm / U-matic / VHS
B&W (H A)
Presents the activities of the 43rd Infantry Division in the Pacific during World War II and as occupation troops in Japan after the war.
Civics and Political Systems; History - United States
Dist - USNAC **Prod** - USA 1950

Wings Across the Sand 5 MIN
U-matic / 16mm / VHS
Color; Mono (G)
MV $85.00 _ MP $170.00 purchase, $50.00 rental
Depicts birds in flight, rest and drifting on the warm air currents of the soutern United States. Film set to a beautiful score.
Science - Natural
Dist - CTV **Prod** - MAKOF 1982

Wings and Things 20 MIN
U-matic / VHS / 16mm
Color
LC 77-700198
Presents model airplanes and their technical creation. Analyzes the characteristics of model airplane enthusiasts.
Physical Education and Recreation; Sociology
Dist - PHENIX **Prod** - OPUS 1976

Wings and Wheels 15 MIN
16mm
Color (H C A)
LC 80-701059
Presents an around - the - world look at the car rental industry, emphasizing the advantages to individuals and business customers.
Business and Economics; Home Economics
Dist - KLEINW **Prod** - KLEINW 1978

Wings for the Doctor - a Story of the Naval Flight Surgeon 28 MIN
16mm
Color
LC 74-706609
Describes training and duties of the naval flight surgeon.
Civics and Political Systems; Health and Safety; Science
Dist - USNAC **Prod** - USN 1971

Wings for the Fleet 29 MIN
U-matic / VHS / 16mm
Color
Shows United States naval aviation flight training from Aviation Officer Candidate School, to winning Navy wings and assignment to fleet operations.
Civics and Political Systems; Industrial and Technical Education
Dist - USNAC **Prod** - USN 1982

Wings in the Grand Canyon 14 MIN
16mm
Color (I)
LC 73-701129
Shows the Grand Canyon as seen from an airplane. Includes views of Angel's Window, the Painted Desert, Hance Rapids, Holy Grail Temple, Thunder Falls, Mt Sinyala, Mooney Falls and Havasupi Falls.
Education; Geography - United States
Dist - MMP **Prod** - MMP 1970

Wings of Eagles, Wings of Gold 28 MIN
16mm
Color
LC 75-704052
Traces the history of naval aviation and emphasizes the importance of preserving this heritage for future generations.
Civics and Political Systems; Industrial and Technical Education
Dist - USNAC **Prod** - USN 1974

The Wings of Mercury 60 MIN
U-matic / VHS
Spaceflight Series
Color
Follows the space program from President John F Kennedy's challenge to N A S A to put a man on the moon before the end of the 1960s through successful space missions, including the Gemini program and the first space docking. Discusses the selection of America's first man in space, Mercury astronaut Alan Shephard, and the first man in space, Russian cosmonaut Yuri Gagarin.
Science - Physical
Dist - PBS **Prod** - PBS

Wings of the Army 45 MIN
U-matic / VHS
B&W
Shows highlights of military and civilian aviation history between the wars. Includes the first flights at Kitty Hawk, first flight across the English Channel, stunt Flyers, air - mail service and others.
History - United States; Industrial and Technical Education
Dist - IHF **Prod** - IHF

Wings of the tropics - Senegal - Part 11 8 MIN
VHS
Natures kingdom series
Color (P I J)
$125.00 purchase
Looks at exotic birds in Senegal - the sacred ibis of ancient Egypt, the hammerhead and snake bird, 'whistling' ducks and male jacana which incubate their young. Part of a 26 - part series on animals showing the habitats and traits of various species.
Geography - World; Science - Natural
Dist - LANDMK **Prod** - LANDMK 1992

The Wings of Youth 15 MIN
16mm
Color (C A)
LC FIA66-691
Shows the activities carried on by the Civil Air Patrol Cadet Program and the initiation of trainees into the world of gliders, sailplanes and powered aircraft.
Guidance and Counseling; Industrial and Technical Education; Physical Education and Recreation
Dist - MCDO **Prod** - DAC 1965

Wings on the water 30 MIN
VHS
Perspectives - transport and communication - series
Color; PAL; NTSC (G)
PdS90, PdS105 purchase
Examines the designing of the optimum sailing craft.
Physical Education and Recreation
Dist - CFLVIS **Prod** - LONTVS

Wings over the pond 14 MIN
VHS
Pond life - a place to live series
Color (I J H)
$119.00 purchase _ #CG - 852 - VS
Examines the hunting and mating of dragon flies. Discusses the different parts of insect's body, how insects mate, lay eggs and eat. Part of a three - part series which looks at life in and around a typical pond in intimate detail.
Science - Natural
Dist - HRMC **Prod** - HRMC

Wings over water 59 MIN
VHS / BETA
Color (G)
$59.95 purchase
Chronicles the 75 year history of United States naval aviation. Combines original footage from the main battles fought by the US with interviews of the personnel involved. Produced by Gordon Bowman.
Civics and Political Systems; History - United States; Industrial and Technical Education
Dist - VARDIR

Wings to Alaska 27 MIN
16mm
Color
LC FIA66-690
Pictures the landscape of Alaska, its mountain ranges, forests and glaciers, and the people who live there - the Eskimo, the Indian and the pioneer. Emphasizes the fact that Alaska is a state with room for individual expression.
Geography - United States
Dist - PANWA **Prod** - PANWA 1965

Wings to Germany 29 MIN
16mm
Color
LC FIA66-688
A tour of West Germany and Berlin showing the beauty of the Rhine and the Black Forest, the old world charm of cities such as Heidelberg and Rothenburg, the winter resorts, the fine restaurants and hotels and the Oktoberfest.
Geography - World
Dist - PANWA **Prod** - PANWA 1965

Wings to Great Britain 28 MIN
16mm
Color
LC FIA67-697
Presents various views of the people and interesting places in Great Britain such as the seacoast, the highlands, the lake country and London.
Geography - World
Dist - PANWA **Prod** - PANWA 1966

Wings to Hawaii 30 MIN
16mm
Color (FRENCH)
LC FIA67-700
Pictures various aspects of life in Hawaii with emphasis on tourist resorts and attractions of the Hawaiian neighbor islands.
Foreign Language; Geography - United States
Dist - PANWA **Prod** - PANWA 1966

Wings to Italy 28 MIN
16mm
Color
LC FIA67-698
Presents views of popular tourist attractions throughout Italy.
Geography - World
Dist - PANWA **Prod** - PANWA 1966

Wings to Scandinavia 28 MIN
16mm
Color
Presents pictures of Norway, Sweden, Finland and Denmark during the summer and winter seasons.
Geography - World; Physical Education and Recreation
Dist - PANWA **Prod** - PANWA

Wings to Spain 29 MIN
16mm
Color
Presents a tour of Spain and its main attractions for the tourist.
Geography - World
Dist - PANWA **Prod** - PANWA

Wings to the Land of the Maya 20 MIN
16mm
Color (J A)
LC FIA64-813
Presents the countries of Mexico, Yucatan, Guatemala and the island of Cozumel, explaining that these countries are growing in popularity yet are among the least exploited areas of Latin America. Shows scenes of typical tourist attractions, including the Mayan ruins of Chichen Itza and Uxmal and an Indian dance ceremony at Uxmal.
Geography - World; History - World; Psychology; Social Science; Sociology
Dist - PANWA **Prod** - VISION 1963

Wings to Venezuela 15 MIN
16mm
Color
LC FIA68-874
Pictures small fishing villages, wind - swept mountain tops, cascading waterfalls and the thriving metropolis of Caracas to provide a view of the people and pleasures of Venezuela. Presents Venezuelan music.
Geography - World
Dist - PANWA **Prod** - PANWA 1967

Wingtip to Canopy 15 MIN
16mm
Color
LC 75-703127
Presents the Blue Angels flight team flying their A - 4 Skyhawks to display the skill of the U S Navy aviator.
Civics and Political Systems; Industrial and Technical Education
Dist - MCDO **Prod** - MCDO 1975

Wingy Manone 30 MIN
U-matic
After Hours with Art Hodes Series
Color
Features the jazz stylings of trumpet player and singer Wingy Manone.
Fine Arts
Dist - FAJAZZ **Prod** - FAJAZZ

Winifred Wise - Anderson on Jane Addams and Hull House 42 MIN
VHS / U-matic
Color
Presents a definitive biography of Jane Addams of Hull House by Winifred Wise - Anderson who worked at Hull House in Chicago while researching her book, JANE ADDAMS OF HULL HOUSE, published in 1935. Shares her personal memories of Jane Addams and the operation of Hull House.
Biography; History - World; Sociology
Dist - UWISC **Prod** - VRL 1982

A Winnable war 60 MIN
VHS
Color (G A R)
$24.99 purchase, $10.00 rental _ #35 - 89608 - 533
Features Christian psychologist Dr James Dobson. Presents Dr Dobson's views that pornography is addictive and negatively affects the home. Offers suggestions for fighting the spread of pornography. Produced by Focus on the Family.
Psychology; Sociology
Dist - APH

Winnebago women - songs and stories 15 MIN
BETA / Cassette / U-matic / VHS
Women's history and literature media series
Color (P I J H G)
$95.00 purchase, $40.00 rental
Presents four Winnebago women who tell their life stories and sing traditional songs. Part of a series about women's history and literature created by Jocelyn Rile. Resource guide available separately.
Biography; History - United States; History - World; Social Science
Dist - HEROWN **Prod** - HEROWN 1992

The Winner and the time machine 30 MIN
VHS
Davey and Goliath series
Color (P I R)
$19.95 purchase, $10.00 rental _ #4 - 8837
Presents two 15 - minute 'Davey and Goliath' episodes. 'The Winner' emphasizes the concept that God gave people individual talents and abilities, while 'The Time Machine' is a story of Davey, Goliath and Sally's trip into the past and future. Produced by the Evangelical Lutheran Church in America.
Literature and Drama; Religion and Philosophy
Dist - APH

Winner by decision - The Tyrell Biggs story 18 MIN
VHS
Color (J H G)
$195.00 purchase
Tells the true story of Olympic Gold Medalist and heavyweight contender Tyrell Biggs who rose from the mean streets of Philadelphia to international fame in the ring, then his addiction to drugs and alcohol put him down for the count. Reveals that Biggs turned his life around and is winning again, both in the ring and in life. Examines peer pressure, denial, disease progression and living clean and sober.
Guidance and Counseling; Health and Safety; Physical Education and Recreation; Psychology
Dist - FMSP **Prod** - FMSP

A Winner Never Quits 18 MIN
U-matic / VHS / 16mm
Color (J)
LC 73-700939
Documents a high school football team, describing the peer group pressure and the role - playing experienced by the athletes, cheerleaders and coaches.
Physical Education and Recreation; Psychology; Sociology
Dist - PHENIX **Prod** - TARORE 1977

The Winner - Problem Solving - Measurement 16 MIN
VHS / U-matic
Expanding Math Skills with the Minicalculator Series
Color (I)
$59.00 purchase _ #3514
Presents the concept of measurement and rates, shows the usefulness of constructing scale models to estimate a solution, and shows how to use a calculator to compare data and solve problems. Animated story.
Mathematics
Dist - EBEC

Winners 24 MIN
VHS / U-matic
Young people's specials series
Color
Focuses on participants in the Special Olympics. Narrated by Tom Seaver.
Physical Education and Recreation; Sociology
Dist - MULTPP **Prod** - MULTPP

The Winners 29 MIN
VHS / 16mm
Sonrisas Series
Color (T P) (SPANISH)
$46.00 rental _ #SRSS - 121
Shows how athletic competition brings out the best and worst in the children. In Spanish and English.
Physical Education and Recreation; Sociology
Dist - PBS

Winners 20 MIN
16mm
Color
LC 80-700861
Shows the commercial and industrial potential of New South Wales. Features ten case histories of companies which have set up successful operations there.
Business and Economics; Geography - World; Social Science
Dist - TASCOR **Prod** - NSWF 1978

Winners all Our Lives 20 MIN
16mm / VHS
Color (PRO)
$475.00, $250.00 purchase, $100.00 rental, $50.00 preview
Depicts middle aged participants of the World Masters Track and Field competitions. Breaks through stereotypes about middle age lethargy. Demonstrates principles of goal - setting and perseverance. Discusses guided imagery and how to change negative attitudes.
Business and Economics; Guidance and Counseling; Health and Safety; Physical Education and Recreation; Psychology; Sociology
Dist - UTM **Prod** - UTM

Winners and losers 54 MIN
VHS
Red empire series
Color (J H C G)
$19.98 purchase _ #FFO9613V
Reveals that war with Germany leads to civil war in Russia. Discloses that Lenin is nearly assassinated while two central groups, the Reds and the Whites, fight for control of the Empire. The Communist Party, under Lenin and Trotsky, gains control. When Lenin dies in 1924, the future of the Communist Party is in doubt, except for a revolutionary on the rise - Joseph Stalin. Part of a seven - part series tracing Russian history from the fall of the Tsar and rise of Lenin, through World War I, the internal war for communism, the emergence of the brutal and ruthless Stalin, World War II, Krushchev, Brezhnev and Gorbachev.
Civics and Political Systems; History - World; Social Science
Dist - CAMV

Winners and losers 40 MIN
VHS
Town hall
Color; PAL (C H)
PdS65 purchase
Follows the Lewisham borough council as decisions are made about which programs will be cut. Captures the uproar following the announcement of program cuts and the establishment of a poll tax. Eighth in the eight - part series Town Hall, which documents the operation of local government in Great Britain.
Civics and Political Systems
Dist - BBCENE

Winners and Losers - a Worldwide Survey 30 MIN
U-matic / VHS
Successful Strategies for Manufacturing Management Series
Color
Examines the nature of manufacturing competition in terms of strategies adopted, maturity of strategies, effectiveness achieved and financial results delivered. Studies the differences between the winners and losers in the new, high - stakes competition of the 80s.
Business and Economics; Industrial and Technical Education
Dist - DELTAK **Prod** - DELTAK

Winners and losers - dealing with substance abuse 30 MIN
VHS
Color (J H C A)
LC 90-700015
Uses interviews and documentary segments to show that some students lose control of their lives to substance addiction. Shows how they work through the slow, painful process of recovery.
Education; Guidance and Counseling; Sociology
Dist - HRMC **Prod** - NBCNEW 1989

Winners and Losers - Poverty in California 59 MIN
VHS / 16mm
Color (G)
$70.00 rental _ #DOCS - 109
Examines the causes and effects of poverty. Focuses on California and some of its black and Chicano ghettos as well as an itinerant worker. Looks at the role of the state in combating poverty.
Business and Economics; Geography - United States; History - United States; Sociology
Dist - PBS **Prod** - KOCETV

The Winner's circle 20 MIN
VHS
Color (A PRO IND)
$195.00 purchase _ #WIN - 721
Presents a motivational tape covering the subject of quick changeover techniques. Compares the quick changeover techniques used by race car crews with what can be done on the assembly line.
Business and Economics; Guidance and Counseling; Psychology
Dist - PRODUC **Prod** - PRODUC

Winner's Circle Series
Going the Distance 8 MIN
The Perfect Balance 8 MIN
Winning Goals 8 MIN
Dist - SFTI

The Winner's Edge 45 MIN
Cassette / VHS
Color (G)
$149.95 purchase _ #6364
Presents an audio seminar for success in the 1990s designed by Dr Denis Waitley as well as 45 - minute video visit with Waitley. Includes 6 audiocassettes which teach self - management skills, two 60 - minute audiocassettes with self - talk affirmations and subliminal suggestions, three new books by Waitley with accompanying audiocassettes and Lifeguide Workbook and the videotape.
Business and Economics; Civics and Political Systems; Psychology; Social Science
Dist - SYBVIS **Prod** - SYBVIS

Winners from Down Under Series
Just Friends 52 MIN
On Loan 52 MIN
The Other Facts of Life 52 MIN
The Paper Boy 52 MIN
Quest Beyond Time 52 MIN
Room to Move 52 MIN
Tarflowers 52 MIN
Top Kid 52 MIN
Dist - FOTH

Winners - Student Athletes with Disabilities 81 MIN
VHS / 16mm
Color (A)
$39.95 purchase, $10.00 rental _ #05421
Describes the sports and recreation programs available to college students with disabilities on the Urbana Campus of the University of Illinois. Features interviews with coaches, competition and practice sessions in men's and women's basketball, track and road racing. Highlights the summer sports camp for the younger disabled which also takes advantage of this setting.
Education; Fine Arts; Health and Safety; Physical Education and Recreation; Psychology
Dist - UILL **Prod** - UILL 1989

Winnie Mandela 15 MIN
VHS / 16mm
Color (H C A)
$225.00, $175.00
Describes how Winnie Mandela has become the leading figure in South Africa's anti - apartheid movement. Profile includes a special interview with Winnie obtained shortly before the South African government crackdown on press coverage. Also depicted are scenes of extreme violence in the strife - torn country.
Biography; Civics and Political Systems; Geography - World; History - United States; Sociology
Dist - CAROUF **Prod** - NBCNEW 1986

Winnie the Pooh and a Day for Eeyore 26 MIN
U-matic / VHS / 16mm
Color (K P I)
Shows how Winnie the Pooh and his friends help celebrate Eeyore the donkey's birthday. Demonstrates that even though things don't go exactly as planned, Eeyore realizes it's the thought that counts.
Fine Arts; Literature and Drama
Dist - CORF **Prod** - DISNEY 1983

Winnie the Pooh and the Blustery Day 25 MIN
16mm / U-matic / VHS
Many Adventures of Winnie the Pooh Series
Color (K P I)
LC 82-700432
Shows what happens when Pooh visits his Thoughtful Spot and then, because of the wind, joins in some antics with Piglet.
Literature and Drama
Dist - CORF **Prod** - DISNEY 1981

Winnie the Pooh and the Honey Tree 26 MIN
16mm / U-matic / VHS
Many Adventures of Winnie the Pooh Series
Color (K P I)
LC 82-700433
Tells about Pooh's attempt to deceive the bees and about his disastrous visit to Rabbit.
Literature and Drama
Dist - CORF **Prod** - DISNEY 1981

Winnie the Pooh and Tigger Too 26 MIN
U-matic / VHS / 16mm
Many Adventures of Winnie the Pooh Series
Color (K P I)
LC 82-700434
Shows that when Rabbit, Pooh and Piglet plan to unbounce Tigger, they discover they like a bouncy Tigger best.
Literature and Drama
Dist - CORF **Prod** - DISNEY 1981

Winnie the Pooh Discovers the Seasons 8 MIN
U-matic / VHS / 16mm
Color (K P)
LC 82-700737
Shows Winnie The Pooh learning to use the calendar to keep track of the passage of days, weeks, months and seasons.
Science - Natural
Dist - CORF **Prod** - DISNEY 1982

Winnie the Pooh's ABC of me 12 MIN
U-matic / 16mm / VHS
Color (P)
$350.00, $250.00 purchase _ #JC - 67274
Uses clips and original songs from Winnie the Pooh adventures to teach the alphabet.
English Language
Dist - CORF **Prod** - DISNEY 1990

Winning 21 MIN
16mm
Color
LC 81-700714
Tells how two mentally handicapped people get married and try to make a life outside the institution.
Health and Safety; Psychology
Dist - TASCOR **Prod** - VICCOR 1980

Winning 50 MIN
VHS
More than a game series
Color (A)
PdS99 purchase _ Not available in the United States or Canada
Takes a look at modern sport in three contrasting worlds. Part of an eight-part series that looks at sports as an integral part of every civilization, offering participation, the opportunity to excel and a chance to belong. Asks if this is a romantic view of sport.
Physical Education and Recreation
Dist - BBCENE

Winning 21 MIN
16mm / VHS / BETA / U-matic
Parenting the child who is handicapped series
Color; PAL (G PRO T)
PdS150, PdS158 purchase
Looks at mentally handicapped people who decide to get married. Reveals that each small step we would take in solving our problems and coping with life is a major step for them. An inspirational film about human beings trying to make a life for themselves outside the world of the institution. Presents part of a six - part series.
Health and Safety; Sociology
Dist - EDPAT

Winning 30 MIN
U-matic / VHS
Commodities - - the Professional Trader Series
Color (C A)
Features Conrad Leslie, Dr. Richard Sander, Francis Wolfe and others explaining the elements for successful speculation.
Business and Economics
Dist - VIPUB **Prod** - VIPUB

Winning all the Time 30 MIN
U-matic / VHS
Sky's the Limit Series
Color
Business and Economics; Psychology
Dist - DELTAK **Prod** - LCOA

Winning - an acquirable habit 38 MIN
VHS / 16mm
Color (PRO)
$475.00 purchase, $110.00 rental, $45.00 preview
Motivates salespeople to become successful through change of attitude. Demonstrates what 'winning' means, healthy self - image, realistic images of others, setting goals and unlocking confidence through enthusiasm. Includes support materials.
Psychology
Dist - UTM **Prod** - UTM

Winning and Losing 15 MIN
VHS / 16mm
Junior High Ethics Resource Package Series
Color (J)
$200.00, $250.00 purchase _ #278404
Presents a comprehensive series on ethics for educators, junior high students and concerned adults. Describes an ethics course introduced in Alberta, Canada, schools and suggests teaching strategies for educators. The last five programs are dramas for students to teach key ethical concepts. 'Winning And Losing' offers opportunities to discuss the concepts of winning and losing and how they effect everyday life.
Business and Economics; Guidance and Counseling; Psychology; Religion and Philosophy; Sociology
Dist - AITECH **Prod** - ACCESS 1989

Winning and Losing 59 MIN
U-matic / VHS
Color (C A)
Focuses on what motivates young people to play high school football. Follows the DuBois Area, Pennsylvania, coach and players through their 1981 season.
Physical Education and Recreation; Sociology
Dist - PSU **Prod** - PSU 1984

Winning and Losing 24 MIN
16mm
Good Time Growing Show Series Show 6; Show 6
Color (K P I)
Reveals that Mickey and Josh are depressed because their team has lost all of its soccer games. Relates that winning a prize is very important to Boaz until he wins a prize he isn't proud of. Stresses that people are never losers in God's eyes.
Psychology; Religion and Philosophy
Dist - WHLION **Prod** - WHLION

Winning and losing - the electoral process and electoral systems 30 MIN
VHS
Remaking of Canada - Canadian government and politics in the 1990s 'series
Color (H C G)
$89.95 purchase _ #WLU - 510
Discusses electoral systems and the electoral process in Canada. Focuses on mechanisms for ensuring fairness in the Canadian electoral process and the effect of differing electoral systems on election results. Part of a 12 - part series incorporating interviews with Canadian politicians and hosted by Dr John Redekop.
Civics and Political Systems; History - World
Dist - INSTRU **Prod** - TELCOL 1992

Winning at Hang Gliding 27 MIN
16mm
Color
Presents hang gliding as a spectator sport as gliders meet to compete in such tasks as the minimum time test, duration flight time and altitude gain flight tests.
Physical Education and Recreation
Dist - MTP **Prod** - WRNGJ

Winning at job hunting in the 90s 60 MIN
VHS
Color (H C G)
$179.00 purchase _ #CCPTU100SV
Features Dr Mel Schnapper, career counselor, who makes his total job hunting system available to the public in this program. Shows how to translate life accomplishments into a powerful resume, how to receive help by networking, how to generate referrals and how to use the telephone most effectively. Discusses the right answers to give and the right questions to ask during interviews, how to negotiate for a higher salary with more benefits. Includes workbook.
Business and Economics; Guidance and Counseling
Dist - CAMV

Winning at soccer with Bobby Charlton series
Mastering the midfield advantage - Part 1
Mastering the midfield advantage - Part 2
Striker tactics - skills to help you score - Part 1
Striker tactics - skills to help you score - Part 2
The Winning formula for fullbacks
Winning strategies for centers
Dist - CAMV

Winning at trial
VHS
Color (PRO C)
$875.00 purchase _ #FVWATOS
Goes step - by - step through the trial of a civil case. Features prominent litigators. Includes six Potter v Shackle case files, one Potter Problems Packet, one program planner's guide, one 'Winning at Trial Teacher's Manual' and nine videocassettes.

Civics and Political Systems
Dist - NITA **Prod** - NITA 1986

Winning at trial series
Uses a wrongful death case to teach the skills of trial advocacy. Includes excerpts from the trial, comments from the lawyers involved, and critiques. Covers topics including jury selection, opening statements, witness examinations, and opening and closing arguments. Nine - part series includes case files, teacher's manual and guide.
Convincing the jury 56 MIN
Examining the defendant 60 MIN
Examining the economic expert 54 MIN
Examining the medical expert 51 MIN
Examining the occurrence witness 59 MIN
Examining the plaintiff 59 MIN
Making the closing argument 59 MIN
Opening statements 58 MIN
Selecting a jury 57 MIN
Dist - NITA **Prod** - NITA 1986

Winning at Work 60 MIN
VHS / U-matic
Road to Achievement Series
Captioned (J H C)
$34.95 _ #KA1210V
Covers preliminary career topics, such as getting hired, using proper company etiquette, managing time and stress and others.
Business and Economics; Guidance and Counseling; Psychology
Dist - CAMV **Prod** - CAMV

A Winning balance 33 MIN
VHS / U-matic / BETA
Color; CC (G IND PRO C)
Helps employees to explore their personal attitudes towards differences and how these attitudes affect their interactions with others. Gives employees the skills they need to become diversity change agents in creating a work environment and organization culture that furthers the development of each and every employee. Includes a trainer's manual and 20 participant manuals.
Business and Economics; Psychology
Dist - BNA **Prod** - BNA 1993

Winning Battles 8 MIN
16mm
Color
Describes a pilot program at Stanford University Children's Hospital where parents of children with cancer are actively involved in the treatment of the child and even discuss the possibility of death, while keeping up hope for the future.
Health and Safety; Sociology
Dist - FLMLIB **Prod** - FRUCTN 1980

Winning by losing - the decision 21 MIN
U-matic / VHS
Caring community - alcoholism and drug abuse series
Color
Defines the role of 'surrender' in the recovery process of the chemically dependent and illustrates the methods that facilitate 'surrender.'.
Psychology; Sociology
Dist - VTRI **Prod** - VTRI

The Winning choice 33 MIN
VHS
Color (P I J H)
$195.00 purchase
Presents the Los Angeles Lakers basketball team with an antidrug rap routine. Features the team and Earvin 'Magic' Johnson, Kareem Abdul - Jabbar, and coach Pat Riley discussing choices, peer pressure and how to live drug - free with young people.
Guidance and Counseling; Health and Safety; Psychology
Dist - PFP

The Winning Combination
16mm
Color
Describes learning center management techniques, hardware, and business courses.
Business and Economics; Education
Dist - HBJ **Prod** - HBJ

A Winning Combination 15 MIN
16mm
Color
LC 75-703551
Discusses the New England Whalers hockey team of the World Hockey Association. Emphasizes the need for physical fitness, skating ability, proper equipment and teamwork.
Physical Education and Recreation
Dist - AETNA **Prod** - AETNA 1975

The Winning combination
VHS
Nanny and Isaiah adventure series
Color (K P I R)
$14.95 purchase _ #87EE0786
Tells how Nanny and Isaiah struggle to form a church softball team, learning along the way how to show love and concern for others. Features a guest appearance by St Louis Cardinals shortstop Ozzie Smith.
Fine Arts; Guidance and Counseling; Literature and Drama; Religion and Philosophy
Dist - CPH **Prod** - CPH

Winning cooperation - communication 30 MIN
VHS
Active parenting series
Color (J H G)
$99.00 purchase _ #05535 - 126
Discusses the role of effective communication in getting children to cooperate. Visits a variety of homes and families to observe parent and child dynamics. Includes excerpts from group discussions to critique parent and child interactions and to help spot common mistakes in parenting. Part of a six - part series on parenting.
Health and Safety; Social Science; Sociology
Dist - GA **Prod** - GA

Winning Customers through Service 15 MIN
16mm / U-matic / VHS
Courtesy Under Pressure Series
(PRO A)
$495, $150 Rental 5 Days, $35 Preview 3 Days
Deals with the issue of service to the client as an asset to the business.
Business and Economics
Dist - ADVANM **Prod** - ADVANM

Winning Customers through Service
VHS
Telephone Courtesy Under Pressure Series
$199.00 purchase _ #012 - 763
Portrays the part customer service people play in informing customers of a company's products and services.
Business and Economics; Social Science
Dist - CAREER **Prod** - CAREER

Winning Defense 60 MIN
VHS
Basketball Series
(H C T J)
#MXS220V
Presents Coach Marv Harshman who demonstrates drills used for training teams on good defensive principles.
Physical Education and Recreation
Dist - CAMV

The Winning Edge 10 MIN
VHS / U-matic
Color (A)
Presents Olympic hockey Coach Herb Brooks explaining his techniques for motivating his team. Discusses leadership, preparation, teamwork and taking risks.
Physical Education and Recreation; Psychology
Dist - SFTI **Prod** - SFTI

The Winning Edge 17 MIN
VHS / U-matic
Color
LC 81-707636
Provides an explanation of wrestling rules, covering such areas as starting position, stalling, control situations, technical violations, illegal holds and pinning situations.
Physical Education and Recreation
Dist - NFSHSA **Prod** - NFSHSA 1981

The Winning edge 14 MIN
VHS
Color (A PRO)
$350.00 purchase, $125.00 rental
Features former U S Olympic gymnast Peter Vidmar in a discussion of success. Stresses that the difference between success and failure in business, just as in sports, can be quite small.
Business and Economics; Physical Education and Recreation; Psychology
Dist - VLEARN

The Winning edge - John McEnroe and Ivan Lendl 45 MIN
VHS
Color (J H A)
$39.95 purchase _ #VV1022V
Features John McEnroe and Ivan Lendl teaching five lessons to improve tennis skills. Covers groundstrokes, volleys, serves, and advanced lessons that put it all together.
Physical Education and Recreation
Dist - CAMV

Winning edge on pocket billiards
VHS
Color (G)
$24.95 purchase _ #KA002
Presents champion Mike Sigel demonstrating pocket billiards.
Physical Education and Recreation
Dist - SIV

Winning edge series
Features Christian celebrities who introduce and profile young people with a passion for excellence. Consists of two tapes and a leader's guide.
Winning edge - Tape 1 48 MIN
Winning edge - Tape 2 48 MIN
Dist - APH **Prod** - CHLGRF

Winning edge - Tape 1 48 MIN
VHS
Winning edge series
Color (J H R)
$10.00 rental _ #36 - 885001 - 533
Features young people with a passion for excellence, introduced by well - known Christian celebrities. Includes introductions by Billy 'White Shoes' Johnson of the Atlanta Falcons, Robert Reid of the Houston Rockets, Storm Davis of the Baltimore Orioles, and others.
Religion and Philosophy
Dist - APH **Prod** - CHLGRF

Winning edge - Tape 2 48 MIN
VHS
Winning edge series
Color (J H R)
$10.00 rental _ #36 - 885002 - 533
Features young people with a passion for excellence, introduced by well - known Christian celebrities. Includes introductions by former Miss America Vonda Kay Van Dyke, recording artist Larnelle Harris, tennis champion Stan Smith, and others.
Religion and Philosophy
Dist - APH **Prod** - CHLGRF

Winning Entrepreneurial Style 60 MIN
U-matic / VHS
Road to Achievement Series
Captioned (J H C)
$34.95 _ #KA1230V
Focuses on techniques useful in business advancement, such as establishing a business plan, marketing and others.
Business and Economics
Dist - CAMV **Prod** - CAMV

The Winning formula 25 MIN
VHS
Color (A PRO IND)
$475.00 purchase, $150.00 rental
Suggests that management success in business depends upon these factors - product quality, customer service, and employee partnership. Interviews Victor Kiam of Remington Razors, Margaret Rudkin of Pepperidge Farm and Mo Siegel of Celestial Seasonings Tea on how their companies have succeeded through this approach.
Business and Economics
Dist - VLEARN

The Winning formula for fullbacks
VHS
Winning at soccer with Bobby Charlton series
Color (J H A)
$29.95 purchase _ #SLS015V
Features English soccer coach Bobby Charlton in an introduction to the fullback position in soccer. Shows that the fullback is responsible for filling in for other defenders as necessary, making defensive plays, and blocking and calling the ball.
Physical Education and Recreation
Dist - CAMV

Winning Goals 8 MIN
VHS / U-matic
Winner's Circle Series
Color (A)
Features Mike Eruzione, captain of America's champion 1980 Olympic hockey team. Shows footage from its final victory. Emphasizes the importance of common goals and team motivation.
Physical Education and Recreation; Psychology
Dist - SFTI **Prod** - SFTI

Winning Golf
16mm
Color
Presents Sam Snead and Billy Casper demonstrating different techniques and styles.
Physical Education and Recreation
Dist - SFI **Prod** - SFI

Winning Grants Series
Choosing the correct funding market - public and private 60 MIN
Developing proposal ideas to find more funding sources 60 MIN
Increasing your success with public funders - pre - proposal contacts 55 MIN
Matching your needs with funding source interests - organizing staff and developing materials 55 MIN

Planning a Persuasive, Realistic Proposal - Budget 60 MIN
Planning a Persuasive, Realistic Proposal Budget 55 MIN
Tailoring Your Proposal to the Funding Source 60 MIN
Dist - GPN

Winning grants
Drafting, Polishing, Submitting, and Following Up Your Proposal 55 MIN
Plotting your strategy - effective management of time and money 55 MIN
Researching public funding sources 55 MIN
Tailoring Your Proposal to the Funding Source 55 MIN
Targeting Private Funding Sources - Foundations and Corporations 55 MIN
Dist - GPN

Winning is Everything 23 MIN
U-matic / VHS / 16mm
Color (J)
Compares organized sports for children which emphasizes competition and winning at any cost with programs that provide all interested children a chance to participate.
Guidance and Counseling; Physical Education and Recreation
Dist - LUF **Prod** - LUF 1978

Winning Isn't Everything - Improving Client Relations 35 MIN
VHS / U-matic
Managing Your Law Firm Series
Color (PRO)
Explores what clients want from their attorney. Relates the preferences of clients, as established by research studies, to practical measures which can be instituted immediately to improve client relations.
Business and Economics; Civics and Political Systems
Dist - ABACPE **Prod** - ABACPE

The Winning Job Interview
BETA / VHS
Color (H)
Gives tips on job interviews for teenagers and leads them through each step of the interview process.
Guidance and Counseling
Dist - GA **Prod** - GA

Winning job interview 60 MIN
VHS
Color (H C A)
$39.95 purchase
Features career counselor John C Crystal in a comprehensive look at the phenomenon of career changing. Explores 10 steps for creating the right image for personal aspirations. Suitable for career changers at all levels and ages.
Guidance and Counseling
Dist - PBS **Prod** - WNETTV

The Winning kick 90 MIN
VHS
Practice makes perfect soccer series
Color (J H A)
$39.95 purchase _ #KWIKS2V
Features soccer stars Shep Messing, Roy Klivecka and Tom Mulroy in a program to teach young players how to improve their skills and techniques. Uses step - by - step instructions and demonstrates skills.
Physical Education and Recreation
Dist - CAMV

The Winning Linebacker 60 MIN
BETA / VHS
Football Fundamentals Series
Color
Covers linebacking play. Demonstrates the methods and techniques of playing the defensive backfield positions.
Physical Education and Recreation
Dist - MOHOMV **Prod** - MOHOMV

The Winning Linebacker 60 MIN
VHS
Tom Landry Football Series
(J H C)
$39.95 _ #MXS150V
Presents Dallas Cowboy star Bob Breunig and Raiders star Mike Haynes who demonstrate methods for reading the play and reacting in defensive backfield positions.
Physical Education and Recreation
Dist - CAMV **Prod** - CAMV

Winning more often 48 MIN
VHS
Speaking of success series
Color (H C G)
$39.95 purchase _ #PD08
Features popular speaker - trainer Mona Moon, discussing how to create win - win situations. Part of a series.
Business and Economics
Dist - SVIP **Prod** - AUVICA 1993

Winning Offense 60 MIN
VHS
Basketball Series
(H C T)
$39.95 _ #MXS240V
Explains how to create a basketball offensive for high school and college players. Analyzes man on man and zone defenses, post play, double stack, and more.
Physical Education and Recreation
Dist - CAMV

A Winning Offense 57 MIN
VHS / BETA
Men's Basketball Basics Series
Color
Shows how to create an offense for a men's basketball team. Demonstrates offensive strategy for man - to - man and zone defenses. Covers topics such as creating a lead, post play and the double stack.
Physical Education and Recreation
Dist - MOHOMV **Prod** - MOHOMV

Winning Soccer 45 MIN
VHS
(J H C)
$29.95 _ #CH2000V
Presents the basics of soccer. Explains dribbling, passing, receiving, ball coordination, goalkeeping, and scoring. Provides drills as demonstrated by famous soccer stars.
Physical Education and Recreation
Dist - CAMV

Winning Softball 45 MIN
VHS
(J H C)
$39.95 _ #MXS800V
Provides examples of improved base running, base hitting, and power hitting in softball. Discusses defensive strategies and player positions. Offers pitching tips from professionals.
Physical Education and Recreation
Dist - CAMV

Winning Softball with Howard's Western Steer
U-matic / VHS
$24.95 purchase
Physical Education and Recreation
Dist - BEEKMN **Prod** - BEEKMN 1988

The Winning Spirit 15 MIN
16mm
Color
Presents Hershey's National Track and Field Youth Program which emphasizes participation and sportsmanship.
Physical Education and Recreation
Dist - MTP **Prod** - HERSHY

Winning sports nutrition - the competition diet 24 MIN
VHS
Color (H)
$209.00 purchase _ #60233 - 025
Teaches students how to eat like winners before, during and after sports competition. Shows how meal schedules affect athletic performance, how to replace fluids, what kind of food to avoid before competing. Includes teacher's guide and a library kit.
Health and Safety; Home Economics; Physical Education and Recreation; Psychology; Social Science
Dist - GA **Prod** - GA 1992

Winning Strategies - 4 50 MIN
VHS
Challege to America series
Color (PRO IND A)
$295.00 purchase, $125.00 rental _ #FFH24D
Presents Hedrick Smith who discloses business strategies used by German and Japanese industries to gain competitive advantage. Challenges American industry through views of foreign technical and automotive companies.
Business and Economics; Psychology
Dist - EXTR **Prod** - FOTH

Winning strategies for centers
VHS
Winning at soccer with Bobby Charlton series
Color (J H A)
$29.95 purchase _ #SLS016V
Features English soccer coach Bobby Charlton in an introduction to the centerback position in soccer. Shows that the centerback must have speed, be aggressive, and must protect the goal while also handling attacks from the side and cross field.
Physical Education and Recreation
Dist - CAMV

A Winning team 8 MIN
VHS
Color (A PRO)
$295.00 purchase, $75.00 rental
Portrays the teamwork of a world - class sailing crew, comparing it to the team process that is necessary to any work group.
Business and Economics; Physical Education and Recreation; Psychology
Dist - VLEARN

Winning telephone tips by Dr Paul R Timm 30 MIN
VHS
Color (A G)
$99.95 purchase _ #JWA 1020AV
Tells how to solve telephone problems. Provides tips such as why it's important to place your own telephone calls; how to avoid unnecessary call screening; how to make your voice mail more efficient; how to deal with the irate caller; innovative ways to prevent callers from wandering off the topic; who calls back if you're disconnected; and more. Includes an audiocassette and book.
Psychology; Social Science
Dist - JWAVID **Prod** - JWAVID 1994

Winning the business jury trial series
Presents a series of nine titles designed to provide sophisticated trial skills training for the business litigator from developing trial strategy to closing arguments. Demonstrates business cases including lender liability, securities fraud and antitrust. Gives the viewer an analytical framework in which to view subsequent demonstrations and discussions, as well as an insider's look at nationally recognized business litigators as they plan their strategies. Includes a psychologist who specializes in persuasive communication strategies and decision - making processes providing analysis based on empirical research and juror interviews. Includes study guides.
Closing arguments 58 MIN
Conducting the cross examination 54 MIN
Conducting the direct examination 58 MIN
Developing trial strategy 56 MIN
Examining the expert witness 58 MIN
Opening statements 56 MIN
Presenting and cross examining the damages claim 56 MIN
Selecting the jury 59 MIN
Using demonstrative evidence and visual aids 55 MIN
Dist - AMBAR **Prod** - AMBAR 1994

Winning the employment game 52 MIN
VHS
Color (H)
$219.00 purchase _ #05511 - 126
Shows students how to identify sources for employment information and how to develop a job search strategy. Stresses the importance of good grooming and the need to create a favorable impression. Uses dramatized job interviews to illustrate typical questions asked by employers.
Business and Economics; Guidance and Counseling; Psychology
Dist - GA

Winning the employment game
VHS
Color (G A)
$219.00 purchase _ #GA600V
Presents tips on identifying sources for employment information and developing a job search strategy. Dramatizes several job interview situations, which offer typical questions and suggest appropriate answers. Considers how a new employee can keep his or her job. Includes a manual.
Business and Economics; Psychology
Dist - CAMV

Winning the Employment Game
VHS
#013 - 210
Uses live action video to dramatize job interviews which illustrate questions asked by employers, and show how one should respond. Teaches how to identify employment information sources and how to develop a job search strategy.
Guidance and Counseling
Dist - CAREER **Prod** - CAREER

Winning the Grocery Game - Revised Edition
VHS / 35mm strip
$69.00 purchase _ #LS60 filmstrip, $79.00 purchase _ #LS60V VHS
Discusses how to survive in the supermarket. Teaches about store layout, impulse buying, food labels, food budgets and finding the best buys.
Home Economics
Dist - CAREER **Prod** - CAREER

Winning the Job Game
U-matic / VHS
Color
Designed to generate behavior that will directly lead to getting a job. Stresses the need for active participation in job hunting.Shows how to organize a job search and write resumes and cover letters. Details job applications and handling references.
Guidance and Counseling
Dist - EDUACT **Prod** - EDUACT

Winning the job you really want 58 MIN
VHS
Color (H C G)
$59.95 purchase _ #JAP100V
Shows how to - identify the perfect job, change careers to make more money, create the perfect resume, turn an interview into a job offer, resign and protect your references, and more. Illustrates how to dress powerfully to make a first impression that lasts and where to find the hot jobs.
Business and Economics; Guidance and Counseling
Dist - CAMV

Winning the Safari Rally 28 MIN
16mm
Color
LC 77-700441
Documents the 24th running of the East African Safari Rally in Kenya in 1976 in which more than 60 cars were raced by world famous professionals, unknown bankers, farmers and businessmen during four days and three nights.
Physical Education and Recreation
Dist - KLEINW **Prod** - KLEINW 1976

Winning the Selective College Admissions Game 75 MIN
VHS / 16mm
(H)
$165.00 _ #CPA213V
Gives advice to young people on selecting and getting into the right college for them. Demonstrates what to expect in admissions interviews, campus visits and many other topics.
Guidance and Counseling
Dist - JISTW

Winning the War on Arson 16 MIN
16mm
Color
LC 79-701171
Explores the problem of arson, the fastest - growing crime in the United States. Shows how the communities of Seattle, Washington, and New Haven, Connecticut, are combatting arson.
Sociology
Dist - AETNA **Prod** - AETNA 1979

Winning the war on film 28 MIN
VHS
While soldiers fought series
Color (H C G)
$180.00 purchase, $19.00 rental _ #35752
Analyzes wartime propaganda. Features Prelude to War by Frank Capra and The Battle of San Pietro by John Huston. Part of a seven - part series which examines the impact of war on American society from historical, literary, artistic and philosophical perspectives. Produced by the International University Consortium.
Fine Arts; Sociology
Dist - PSU

Winning them over 60 MIN
VHS
Color (IND PRO G)
$855.00 purchase, $350.00 rental _ #TWA01
Teaches the art of persuasion in speech making with Paul LeRoux. Includes five videos - delivery skills, visuals, staging, large group presentations, and questions and answers. A hardback copy of Selling to a Group - Presentation Strategies by Paul LeRoux is also provided.
English Language; Psychology; Social Science
Dist - EXTR

Winning through Baldridge 45 MIN
VHS / U-matic / BETA
Color (C A G)
$870.00 purchase, $240.00 rental
Shows case studies of successful quality systems in service organizations. Features Dr Christopher Hart as host. Shows how to use the Baldridge Criteria in organizations.
Business and Economics
Dist - VIDART **Prod** - VIDART

Winning through change series
Includes the two videos Taking the Challenge and Leading the Way in a set with leader's guides. Each is available separately.
Winning through change series
Dist - EXTR **Prod** - AMA

Winning trap 37 MIN
VHS
Color (G)
$59.95 purchase
Features former Olympic figure skater Peggy Fleming and former NFL star Bob Chandler in an examination of the growing 'winning is everything' attitude in children's sports programs. Suggests alternatives to this attitude.
Physical Education and Recreation
Dist - PBS **Prod** - WNETTV

Winning Way to Go 26 MIN
16mm
Color
Highlights sports car racing at America's road racing and oval race courses. Illustrates the intense competition between race teams in their quest to win motor racing's top awards in the International Motor Sports Association series.
Physical Education and Recreation
Dist - MTP **Prod** - MZDAMA

Winning Ways 28 MIN
VHS / U-matic
Please Stand by - a History of Radio Series
(C A)
Fine Arts; History - United States; Psychology; Sociology
Dist - SCCON **Prod** - SCCON 1986

Winning ways 23 MIN
VHS
Color (G)
$525.00 purchase, $150.00 rental _ #91F6094
Features baseball manager Tommy Lasorda. Emphasizes teamwork.
Psychology
Dist - DARTNL **Prod** - DARTNL

Winning Ways - the Rules of Basketball 28 MIN
16mm
National Federation Sports Films Series
Color (I)
LC 77-700468
Describes rules and guidelines used in judging interscholastic and intercollegiate basketball games. Features boys' teams and girls' teams in a demonstration of rules that apply to traveling, dribble restrictions, jump ball, free throw, dunking, division lines, contact situations and officiating mechanics.
Physical Education and Recreation
Dist - NFSHSA **Prod** - NFSHSA 1976

Winning ways to feed a crowd 40 MIN
VHS
Everyday gourmet series
Color (A)
$19.95 purchase _ #KVC0070V-H
Demonstrates fast, easy, and delicious recipes and shows how to entertain with style without spending a lot of time, energy, or money. Offers practical suggestions on everything from shopping and hospitality to decorating and cleaning up.
Home Economics
Dist - CAMV

Winning Ways to Feed a Crowd - a Complete Video Party Package 40 MIN
VHS
Color (C G A)
$14.95_KC200
Suggestions for a crowd pleasing buffet that is easy to prepare. Offers tips on decorating, party themes, and crowd control.
Home Economics; Sociology
Dist - AAVIM **Prod** - AAVIM 1989

Winning with recruiters - a professional's advice on finding employment 60 MIN
VHS
Color (G A)
$99.00 purchase _ #MSR100V
Provides inside information on the techniques job recruiters use to locate, screen, and attract candidates. Covers subjects including screening methods, interview techniques, review of resumes, and more. Focuses on how to gain an advantage with a recruiter. Includes a user's manual to review and apply the principles taught.
Business and Economics; Psychology
Dist - CAMV

Winning your kids back from the media 100 MIN
VHS
Color (G R)
$49.95 purchase
Helps families shut out the media and communicate with each other and God. Features Dr. Quentin Schultze using a straightforward approach including humor and real - life examples to assist family members in becoming more discerning in the areas of media and non - media activities. Contains a five - part video and leader's guide suitable for church, home or school.
Sociology
Dist - GF

Winning Your Wings / Wings Up 36 MIN
U-matic / VHS
B&W
Presents a Hollywood - Government co - production made to attract recruits into the USAF. Features Lieutenant James Stewart. Shows the intense discipline and conditioning techniques at the officer - training school in Miami to recruit officer - candidates for the Air Force. Features footage of men at the school including Mayor Glen Cove, Elmer Meadows, Robert Preston, Gilbert Roland and Clark Gable. Narrated by Clark Gable.
Civics and Political Systems; History - United States; Industrial and Technical Education
Dist - IHF **Prod** - IHF

Winslow Eaves, Sculptor 30 MIN
Videoreel / VT2
World of the American Craftsman Series
Color
Fine Arts
Dist - PBS **Prod** - WENHTV

Winslow Homer 29 MIN
VHS
Color (J)
$29.95 purchase _ #HV - 934; $29.95 purchase _ #667 - 9002
Presents a guide to the artistic progress of Winslow Homer from his civil war drawings to his powerful nature images. Shows how he transformed watercolor from a descriptive medium into a highly expressive vehicle.
Fine Arts; History - United States
Dist - CRYSP **Prod** - CRYSP
KNOWUN

Winsome witnesses
VHS
Evangelism dimensions for discipleship series
Color (G A R)
$39.95 purchase, $10.00 rental _ #35 - 828 - 2076
Features pastor Jack Aamot in presentations on effective evangelism. Produced by Seraphim.
Religion and Philosophy
Dist - APH

Winston Churchill 30 MIN
VHS
Late great britons
Color; PAL (C H)
PdS65 purchase
Covers the life of Winston Churchill. Reassesses the traditional historical view of Churchill. Based on historical research by Martin Gilbert. Third in the six - part series Late Great Britons, which covers the lives of six important figures in British history.
History - World
Dist - BBCENE

Winston Churchill 40 MIN
VHS
Heroes and tyrants of the twentieth century series
Color (J H C G)
$29.95 purchase _ #MH6027V
Chronicles the life Winston Churchill from his days as a World War I POW to his role as Prime Minister of Great Britain, bolstering British forces, addressing the United States Congress and conferring with Roosevelt and Stalin at Yalta. Portrays the destruction of London, the battle of Britain, excerpts from Churchill's most memorable speeches and his funeral procession. Part of a six - part series on 20th - century leaders.
Guidance and Counseling; History - World
Dist - CAMV

Winston Churchill
VHS
Speeches collection series
Color (J H C G)
$29.95 purchase _ #MH1412V
Offers a collection of speeches by Winston Churchill. Part of a ten - part series on the addresses of the 20th - century's most powerful speakers. Witnesses the signing of peace treaties, the inciting of world wars, the making of history with words.
English Language; History - World
Dist - CAMV

Winston Churchill 17 MIN
U-matic / VHS
Color (G)
$229.00, $129.00 purchase _ #AD - 1865
Examines the legacy of Winston Churchill, Prime Minister of England during World War II. Looks at his accomplishments as a strategist, diplomat, historian, Sunday painter and author.
Biography; Civics and Political Systems; History - World
Dist - FOTH **Prod** - FOTH

Winston Churchill 52 MIN
16mm
History Makers of the 20th Century Series

B&W (I)
Uses rare actuality footage to portray the personal life and history - making deeds of Winston Churchill.
Biography; History - World
Dist - SF **Prod** - WOLPER 1965

Winston Churchill - Parts I and II 53 MIN
U-matic / VHS
Biography series
Color (H C)
$79.00 purchase _ #HH - 6223C
Details the remarkable achievements of Winston Churchill in two parts. Reveals that Churchill became Prime Minister of Great Britain during World War II and sustained that country during its greatest wartime crisis with his leadership, rhetoric, courage and optimism. Part of a series portraying a diverse group of personalities who shaped some aspect of world and cultural history.
Guidance and Counseling; History - World
Dist - CORF **Prod** - WOLPER 1963

Winston Churchill - the Valiant Years Series no 1
The Gathering Storm 26 MIN
Dist - SG

Winston Churchill - the Valiant Years Series no 3
Dunkirk 26 MIN
Dist - SG

Winston Churchill - the Valiant Years Series no 4
The French Agony 26 MIN
Dist - SG

Winston Churchill - the valiant years series - No 9
Alone no more 26 MIN
Dist - SG

Winston Churchill - the Valiant Years Series no 10
Out of the East 26 MIN
Dist - SG

Winston Churchill - the Valiant Years Series no 11
The Torch is Lit 26 MIN
Dist - SG

Winston Churchill - the Valiant Years Series no 12
Sand and snow 26 MIN
Dist - SG

Winston Churchill - the Valiant Years Series no 16
Turning of the Tide 26 MIN
Dist - SG

Winston Churchill - the Valiant Years Series no 18
D - Day 26 MIN
Dist - SG

Winston Churchill - the Valiant Years Series no 20
Triumph in France 26 MIN
Dist - SG

Winston Churchill - the Valiant Years Series no 21
Beginning of the End 26 MIN
Dist - SG

Winston Churchill - the Valiant Years Series no 22
Final Christmas 26 MIN
Dist - SG

Winston Churchill - the valiant years series -no 23
Goodbye, Mr Churchill 26 MIN
Dist - SG

Winston Churchill - the valiant years series
Be sure you win 26 MIN
The Combat deepens 26 MIN
The Die is cast 26 MIN
Gotterdammerung 26 MIN
The Ravens remain 26 MIN
Set Europe ablaze 26 MIN
Strike Hard, Strike Home 26 MIN
Struggle at sea 26 MIN
Take One with You 26 MIN
Tying the knot 26 MIN
Yalta 26 MIN
Dist - SG

Winston Cigarettes 1 MIN
U-matic / VHS
Color
Shows a classic television commercial with animated musical notes.
Business and Economics; Psychology; Sociology
Dist - BROOKC **Prod** - BROOKC

Winston's potty chair
VHS
Color (J H C G)
$19.98 purchase _ #PD061
Uses animation to teach parents how to handle toilet training with their toddlers.
Sociology
Dist - SIV

Winter 1000 SEC
16mm
Color (G)
$20.00 rental
Offers a film by David Brooks.
Fine Arts
Dist - CANCIN

Winter 15 MIN
U-matic
Celebrate Series
Color (P)
Social Science
Dist - GPN **Prod** - KUONTV 1978

Winter 30 MIN
U-matic
Polka Dot Door Series
Color (K)
Presents a variety show for pre - school children. Includes songs, mime, stories, film sequences, talk, dance and fantasy figures. Each show emphasizes a particular theme such as numbers, feelings, exploring, music or time. Comes with parent teacher guide.
Fine Arts; Literature and Drama
Dist - TVOTAR **Prod** - TVOTAR 1985

Winter 11 MIN
U-matic / VHS / 16mm
Seasons Series
Color (P I)
$280, $195 purchase _ #79532
Shows the season of winter and its activities from a child's point of view.
Science - Natural
Dist - CORF

Winter 8 MIN
U-matic / VHS / 16mm
Color (J)
LC 81-701241
Presents the story of a bully who is done in by his own envy and love of violence.
Fine Arts
Dist - PHENIX **Prod** - FILBUL 1981

Winter 14 MIN
16mm
Color (P I)
Shows how animals face this winter. Describes what the struggle to survive winter is like during a hard winter with heavy snowfall.
Science - Natural
Dist - VIEWTH **Prod** - GATEEF

Winter 13 MIN
U-matic / VHS / 16mm
Four Seasons Series
Color (P I)
Looks at the activities and changes common to the winter season such as the hibernation of animals and the difficult search for food by creatures which don't hibernate.
Science - Natural
Dist - NGS **Prod** - NGS 1983

Winter - a Museum Experience 15 MIN
U-matic / VHS
Pass it on Series
Color (K P)
Features winter pictures and scenes, months of winter, and a museum visit.
Education; Science - Natural
Dist - GPN **Prod** - WKNOTV 1983

Winter at Squam Lake 15 MIN
VHS / U-matic
Up Close and Natural Series
Color (P I)
$125.00 purchase
Demonstrates the adaptation processes that animals utilize in cold environments.
Agriculture; Science - Natural; Social Science
Dist - AITECH **Prod** - NHPTV 1986

Winter Birds 5 MIN
16mm
Color
LC 77-702724
Shows a variety of eastern North American birds and their behavior during and just after a heavy snowfall.
Science - Natural
Dist - MEPHTS **Prod** - MEPHTS 1977

Winter Carnival Theme 24 MIN
VHS / U-matic
Color
Features a 17 - year - old athlete for all seasons, who competes in the biathlon, an event that combines cross - country skiing and sharp shooting.
Physical Education and Recreation; Sociology
Dist - WCCOTV **Prod** - WCCOTV 1982

Winter City 29 MIN
VHS / 16mm
Discovery Digest Series
Color (S)
$300.00 purchase _ #707617
Explores a vast array of science - related discoveries, challenges and technological breakthroughs. Profiles and 'demystifies' research and development currently underway in many fields. 'Winter City' looks at a city under glass, connective tunnels which 'knit' downtown cores, how winter weather affects our moods and Dr Sandy Murphree with the latest on Northern Lights.
Geography - World; Psychology; Science; Science - Physical; Sociology
Dist - ACCESS **Prod** - ACCESS 1989

Winter Comes to the City 10 MIN
16mm / U-matic / VHS
Seasons in the City Series
Color (P I)
LC 79-704775
Presents the sights, sounds and activities of winter through the eyes of a boy and his family who have moved to Chicago from the South.
Science - Natural; Science - Physical
Dist - CORF **Prod** - CORF 1969

Winter Comes to the Forest 11 MIN
16mm / U-matic / VHS
Seasons Series
Color (P I)
$270, $190 purchase _ #1395
Shows how different animals are able to adapt to living in the winter.
Science - Natural
Dist - CORF

Winter Dangers 16 MIN
VHS / 16mm
Color (J H A)
$295.00 purchase, $75.00 rental _ #8198
Explains the dangers of frostbite and hypothermia and shows how to treat a variety of cold - related injuries. Helps people identify threatening winter situations, how to take action to prevent injury or loss of life and how to advise others in an emergency situation.
Health and Safety
Dist - AIMS **Prod** - AIMS 1990

Winter Days 50 MIN
U-matic / VHS
Color (H C A)
Portrays birds and animals in their winter struggle for survival. Shows swans from Siberia and Scandinavia, ducks from all over Europe and geese from Iceland heading south to the British Isles where the Gulf Stream provides warmth and food.
Science - Natural
Dist - FI **Prod** - WNETTV

Winter Distress Signals 13 MIN
16mm
Color (I J H)
Discusses why many of the distress methods available to the lost camper in summer time are not applicable in winter. Dramatizes the ways in which winter distress signals are employed to summon assistance.
Health and Safety; Physical Education and Recreation; Science - Natural
Dist - SF **Prod** - SF 1968

Winter Driving 11 MIN
16mm / U-matic / VHS
Color (H C A)
LC 80-700257
Discusses winter driving hazards and explores winter safety and maintenance measures.
Health and Safety; Social Science
Dist - JOU **Prod** - NSC 1979

Winter Driving - Keep Your Cool 26 MIN
16mm
Color
Presents expert advice on driving on icy and snowy roads from people with lots of experience.
Health and Safety; Psychology
Dist - NFBC **Prod** - NFBC 1981

Winter Driving Safety - 818 - Clear and En Route 17 MIN
16mm / U-matic / VHS
Color
Follows a Michigan State Trooper as he answers accident and distress calls, illustrating common problems encountered in driving under extreme winter weather conditions.
Health and Safety; Industrial and Technical Education; Psychology; Social Science
Dist - USNAC **Prod** - USAF 1972

Winter driving tactics 14 MIN
16mm / VHS
Color (H A)
$250.00, $300.00 purchase, $50.00 rental _ #9828
Gives detailed instruction on how to prevent winter accidents, how to handle typical winter hazards, and how to ensure that cars are safe for winter. Shows how to winterize cars from adding antifreeze to stocking the trunk with appropriate safety equipment.
Health and Safety; Psychology
Dist - AIMS **Prod** - AIMS 1985

Winter driving tactics update 16 MIN
VHS
Color (H G)
$295.00 purchase, $75.00 rental _ #8403
Replaces the second edition of Winter Driving Tactics. Shows how to winterize vehicles, maintain batteries, check antifreeze, belts and hoses, what to carry in the car during winter, such as tire chains, tools, jumper cables, blankets and non - perishable foods. Recommends using low beams during the winter day.
Health and Safety; Industrial and Technical Education
Dist - AIMS **Prod** - INMARS 1992

Winter driving TV public service announcement 1 MIN
U-matic / VT1
Color (H G)
$14.50, $20.00 purchase _ #626, #625
Presents a set of two 30 second PSAs dealing with two common winter problems in driving. Includes getting out of a skid and stopping on ice and snow.
Fine Arts; Health and Safety; Industrial and Technical Education
Dist - AAAFTS **Prod** - AAAFTS 1982

Winter Encampment, 1779 - 1780 - Jockey Hollow 12 MIN
16mm / VHS / U-matic
B&W
LC 79-706174
Offers a glimpse of the 1779 winter encampment at Jockey Hollow, Morristown, New Jersey. Issued in 1972 as a motion picture.
History - United States
Dist - USNAC **Prod** - USNPS 1972

Winter Fitness 10 MIN
U-matic
Body Works Series
Color (P I J H)
Shows the importance of reading food ingredients labels and how to do some winter sports.
Physical Education and Recreation; Social Science
Dist - TVOTAR **Prod** - TVOTAR 1979

Winter Fun 8 MIN
VHS / U-matic
Happy Time Adventure Series
Color (K P)
$29.95 purchase _ #VW008
Presents an adaptation of the book Winter Fun. Contains a 32 page hardcover book and a video.
English Language; Literature and Drama
Dist - TROLA

Winter Fun 3 MIN
16mm
Of all Things Series
Color (P I)
Gives examples of winter fun.
Physical Education and Recreation
Dist - AVED **Prod** - BAILYL

Winter Garden 11 MIN
16mm / U-matic / VHS
Inventive Child Series
Color (P I)
Reveals that as winter approaches, Boy and his friends search for a way to keep the trees and plants from freezing. Shows that Boy plans a hot water system based on the principle of solar energy. Provides insight into the means by which solar energy can be used for heating and for the generation of power.
History - World; Science - Physical; Social Science
Dist - EBEC **Prod** - POLSKI 1983

Winter Geyser 7 MIN
U-matic / VHS / 16mm
Wilderness Series
Color (P I J)
LC FIA68-173
Shows the end of summer and fall merging into winter. Includes scenes of streams, mud pots and geysers of Yellowstone National Park against the backdrop of snow and ice.
Geography - United States; Science - Natural
Dist - PHENIX **Prod** - PFP 1968

Winter Harvest 15 MIN
16mm / U-matic / VHS
Color (P I J)
Focuses on the life of a farm family in a northern climate and their winter months' activities. Shows how this family's life differs from most in that it has a 300 acre timber area that provides a winter crop. Illustrates other winter activities from ice fishing and ice harvesting to skating and tobogganing.
Agriculture; Science - Natural; Social Science; Sociology
Dist - BCNFL **Prod** - NELVNA 1982

The Winter harvest 20 MIN
VHS
Color (G C)
$125.00 purchase, $15.50 rental _ #24443
Documents the activities of the Bear Creek Ice Company in northeastern Pennsylvania. Interviews former employees who describe working conditions and the process of 'harvesting' the ice from a string of five lakes. Uses archival footage to demonstrate the gathering, cutting and transporting of ice. Although the company folded in the 1950s, reminders of its operations still exist in the area. Produced by Gregory Hansen.
History - United States
Dist - PSU

Winter Heat 28 MIN
16mm
Color
Presents scenes of hot dog skiing on some of the toughest slopes in America. Uses super - slow - motion photography to show every movement as the competitors somersault into space.
Industrial and Technical Education; Physical Education and Recreation
Dist - FFORIN **Prod** - BARP

Winter Ice - a First Film 11 MIN
16mm / U-matic / VHS
Color (P I) (FRENCH)
LC 74-711109
Studies the environment during the winter months when ice covers the landscape. Shows its effects on the community and its benefits on the environment. Discusses frost, snowflakes, frozen streams and lakes, icicles and the rivers and streams resulting from melted ice in the spring.
Science - Natural; Science - Physical
Dist - PHENIX **Prod** - PHENIX 1970

Winter Impressions 12 MIN
16mm
Color (P I)
Follows a little boy as he sets off to discover the joys of winter and finds bare trees in the woods covered with ice, a flock of sheep who stare at him curiously and other children skating on a frozen pond.
Science - Natural
Dist - SF **Prod** - MORLAT 1968

Winter in Nature 12 MIN
16mm / U-matic / VHS
Seasons in Nature Series
Color (P I)
LC 79-701833
Illustrates the changes which occur in plants and animals during winter.
Science - Natural
Dist - ALTSUL **Prod** - CASDEN 1979

Winter is 15 MIN
U-matic / VHS
Stepping into Rhythm Series
Color (P)
Relates rhythm to winter experiences like shoveling snow.
Fine Arts
Dist - AITECH **Prod** - WVIZTV

Winter is Here
16mm / U-matic / VHS
Seasons - an Introductory Series
Color; Captioned (K P)
Explains why seasons occur. Details changes in the activities of people and animals with the turning of the seasons. One of a series of four.
Science - Natural
Dist - IFB **Prod** - BERLET 1971

Winter is Here 11 MIN
16mm / U-matic / VHS
Seasons (2nd Ed Series
Color (P)
LC 80-700464
Focuses on the activities of people and animals and the alterations in nature during winter.
Science - Natural
Dist - IFB **Prod** - IFB 1979

Winter Landscape 8 MIN
16mm
Color
LC 77-702725
Features observation of the winter scene during an ordinary day's activities.
Physical Education and Recreation; Science - Natural; Science - Physical
Dist - MEPHTS **Prod** - MEPHTS 1977

Winter light 81 MIN
VHS
B&W (G)
$29.95 purchase _ #WIN140
Extracts the joylessness of life for a Protestant minister who has lost his faith. Follows the pastor in his darkest hour as he tries to console a suicidal parishioner and struggles to summon a long - dead passion for his desperate mistress. The second film of Ingmar Bergman's religious trilogy, which also includes Through A Glass Darkly and Tho Silence. Digitally remastered with new subtitles.
Fine Arts; Psychology; Religion and Philosophy
Dist - HOMVIS **Prod** - JANUS 1962

Winter light - part 3 9 MIN
16mm
Magenta Geryon series
Color (G)
$20.00 rental
Features a series of three picture - movements where myths of the past meet visions of the present. Contains live - image scenes. Dante and Virgil descended on the back of the monster Geryon into hell. Winter Light explores the endless permutations of light and illumination as representatives of the Demeter - Persephone myth of withdrawal of life through the winter months. Filmed in the dawn hours of a California winter with Vivaldi's winter concerto.
Fine Arts; Religion and Philosophy
Dist - CANCIN **Prod** - JORDAL 1983

Winter Lillies 59 MIN
U-matic / VHS
Color
Examines the life of Wilfred Robertson, fiddle - maker and primitive painter, who carries on the tradition of his aunt, Grandma Moses.
Fine Arts
Dist - KITCHN **Prod** - KITCHN
PBS

Winter Melon 29 MIN
Videoreel / VT2
Joyce Chen Cooks Series
Color
Features Joyce Chen showing how to adapt Chinese recipes so they can be prepared in the American kitchen and still retain the authentic flavor. Demonstrates how to prepare melon.
Geography - World; Home Economics
Dist - PBS **Prod** - WGBHTV

Winter Melts to Spring 29 MIN
U-matic
Edible Wild Plants Series
Color
Explores a swamp and roadside for wild plants that can be used throughout the winter for survival food.
Health and Safety; Science - Natural
Dist - UMITV **Prod** - UMITV 1978

Winter - Nature's Sights and Sounds 14 MIN
U-matic / VHS / 16mm
Nature's Sights and Sounds Series
Color (P I)
Shows how winter may threaten the survival of animals and how each species has a special way to face winter.
Science - Natural
Dist - BCNFL **Prod** - MASLKS 1984

The Winter of despair
Videodisc
Laser learning set 3 series; Set 3
Color; CAV (P I)
$375.00 purchase _ #8L5413
Chronicles the winter of 1777, which the Continental Army spent under terrible conditions of cold and privation. Shows how the courage of the soldiers and their loyalty to General Washington carried them through this difficult time. Part of a series of six theme - based interactive videodisc lessons. Requires a Pioneer LD - V2000 or 2200, with barcode reader and adapter, or a Pioneer LD - V4200 or higher. Includes user's guide, two readers.
History - United States; Sociology
Dist - BARR **Prod** - BARR 1992

Winter of the Witch 25 MIN
U-matic / VHS / 16mm
Color (P A) (SPANISH)
LC 75-705019;
Tells the story of Nicky and his mother who find themselves in a spooky house with a 300 - year - old witch, who eventually turns very loving and creative.
Literature and Drama
Dist - LCOA **Prod** - PARENT 1970

Winter on an Indian Reservation 11 MIN
16mm
Color (P I)
LC 73-702068
Depicts Indian children living on a forest reservation. Portrays the Indian's way of life, communicating its dependence on and harmony with the environment.
Social Science
Dist - ATLAP **Prod** - ATLAP 1973

Winter Park Art Festival 12 MIN
16mm
Color (I J H C)
LC FIA66-681
The story of Winter Park's sidewalk art show and how it won national attention.
Fine Arts; Geography - United States
Dist - FDC **Prod** - FDC 1964

Winter Ride 23 MIN
16mm
Color (FRENCH)
LC 78-701136
Dicusses snowmobiles.
Foreign Language; Physical Education and Recreation
Dist - MILP **Prod** - ISIA 1978

Winter Safety 14 MIN
U-matic / VHS / 16mm
Color (P I J)
LC 80-701815
Discusses the hazards which can occur during winter. Demonstrates safe practices around cars and tells what to do if someone falls through a frozen pond.
Health and Safety
Dist - ALTSUL **Prod** - ALTSUL 1980

Winter Signs 13 MIN
16mm / U-matic / VHS
Discovering Insects Series
Color (I J)
Identifies various structures, marks and other signs made by insects during winter.
Science - Natural
Dist - CORF **Prod** - MORALL 1982

Winter soldier 20 MIN
16mm
B&W (G)
$20.00 rental
Features Vietnam vets giving testimony at the Winter Soldier tribunals. Records military veteranss talking about their personal experiences in Vietnam; what they were made to do as a soldier in an imperialist army; and the atrocities committed against the Vietnamese people. Represents revolutionarky filmmakers in the 1960s whose work provides a window to that period.
Fine Arts; History - United States; Sociology
Dist - CANCIN **Prod** - SINGLE 1971

Winter Storm 14 MIN
U-matic / VHS / 16mm
Your Chance to Live Series
Color (J H T)
Illustrates the many dangers of winter storms using the short story by Jack London, 'TO BUILD A FIRE.' Shows the depths of tragic circumstances possible during winter storms.
Health and Safety; Science - Physical
Dist - CORF **Prod** - USDCPA 1972

Winter storms 29 MIN
VHS
Color (J H C)
$14.95 purchase _ #NA707
Examimines the role of meteorological satellites in tracking winter storms.
History - World; Science - Physical
Dist - INSTRU **Prod** - NASA

Winter Storms 27 MIN
U-matic / VHS / 16mm
Color
LC 80-707113
Recounts the disastrous winter of 1978. Recalls the blizzards in New England and the Midwest, the floods and mudslides in California and the unexpected snowfalls and floods that paralyzed much of the South.
History - United States; Science - Physical
Dist - USNAC **Prod** - USDCPA 1979

Winter - Story of Survival 14 MIN
U-matic / VHS / 16mm
Color (P I J)
Studies winter and its effect on plant and animal life. Shows that some creature migrate during the Winter, some hibernate and others struggle to survive the severe times.
Science - Natural
Dist - AIMS **Prod** - GATEEF 1968

Winter Survival 15 MIN
16mm
Color (J)
Demonstrates how to survive outdoors in winter using the examples of a cross - country skier and a snowmobiler who find themselves stranded. Shows how knowledge means survival.
Health and Safety; Physical Education and Recreation
Dist - NFBC **Prod** - NFBC 1979

Winter Survival in the Bush 20 MIN
U-matic / VHS / 16mm
Color (J)
LC 82-700862
Discusses the dangers of outdoor winter recreation and presents strategies for dealing with a broken automobile, an injured skier and a disabled snowmobile in isolated, snowy locations. Offers advice for treating wounds and shock and preventing hypothermia and frostbite.
Health and Safety; Physical Education and Recreation
Dist - BCNFL **Prod** - GOLDIJ 1982

The Winter there was very little snow 75 MIN
16mm
Color (G)
$100.00 rental
Uses the barest narrative form to convey the feeling and time of crisis for a man in middle age, facing a collapsed marriage, unemployment and the recent death of his father. Mixes images and moments drawn from some space in time that could be his past, present or future. Documents a man's struggle to understand the meaning of his existence as he faces his own mortality.
Psychology; Religion and Philosophy; Sociology
Dist - CANCIN **Prod** - UNGRW 1982

Winter Training - a New Beginning 46 MIN
U-matic
Color (A)
An edited version of Threshold - The Blue Angels Experience.
Industrial and Technical Education; Social Science
Dist - ASVS **Prod** - ASVS 1986

Winter Truck Driving 19 MIN
16mm
Color
Illustrates safe driving techniques for drivers of commercial vehicles such as trucks and semi - trailers. Stresses preparing for winter driving runs.
Health and Safety; Psychology; Social Science
Dist - NSC **Prod** - NSC

Winter Walking 11 MIN
16mm
Color
LC 74-705961
Shows recommended procedures for walking in the ice and snow. Contains spectacular scenery of Vermont combined with scenes of actual tumbles.
Geography - United States; Health and Safety; Physical Education and Recreation; Science - Natural; Science - Physical
Dist - USNAC **Prod** - USPOST 1971

The Winter war and its European context
16mm / VHS
British Universities historical studies in film series
B&W; PAL (G)
PdS495, PdS80 purchase
Studies the relationship of the Soviet Union with its non - Russian neighbors during the inter - war years. Focuses particularly upon the Soviet relationship with Finland and the origins and consequences of its breakdown in the Winter War of 1939 - 1940 and the considerable international significance of the latter. Uses material selected, edited and scripted by D W Spring and George Brandt.
History - World
Dist - BUFVC **Prod** - BUFVC

The Winter Wife 26 MIN
16mm / U-matic / VHS
Color
Dramatizes a legend about a young Chippewa Indian who wanted above all else to be rich. Tells of his betraying his wife and being turned into an elk.
Literature and Drama; Social Science
Dist - FOTH **Prod** - FOTH

Winter Wilderness 30 MIN
BETA / VHS
Great Outdoors Series
Color
Explores Vermont's winter wilderness. Describes riding an elephant and searching for a tiger in Nepal.
Physical Education and Recreation
Dist - CORF **Prod** - WGBHTV

Winter Wipers 30 MIN
BETA / VHS
Last Chance Garage Series
Color
Explains how a four - stroke engine operates. Explores winter wipers. Presents a VW Jetta.
Industrial and Technical Education
Dist - CORF **Prod** - WGBHTV

Winter World 18 MIN
16mm
Color; B&W (I J H C G T A)
Presents basic information for anyone venturing out in a winter climate. Fundamental techniques of protection from freezing are demonstrated. The danger of dampness combined with low temperatures is strongly emphasized at all points, but particularly in the sequence which shows a step by step technique for sleeping beneath the snow in a snow cave. Using the sleeping bag, warming food, running in the sleeping bag, and other techniques for creating a condition for rest and comfort are shown.
Geography - World; Health and Safety; Physical Education and Recreation; Science - Physical
Dist - FO **Prod** - FO 1960

Winter World, Pt 1 14 MIN
Videoreel / VT2
Muffinland Series
Color
Literature and Drama
Dist - PBS **Prod** - WGTV

Winter World, Pt 2 14 MIN
Videoreel / VT2
Muffinland Series
Color
Literature and Drama
Dist - PBS **Prod** - WGTV

Wintercourse 12 MIN
16mm
Color; B&W (G)
$25.00 rental
Concerns the filmmaker's first year of marriage. Contains apprehensions, in a montage style which counterposes 'opposites' such as sexuality and religion.
Fine Arts; Literature and Drama; Sociology
Dist - CANCIN **Prod** - SHARIT 1962

Winterdeath 18 MIN
16mm
Color
LC 77-700443
Tells a story of an old man's imaginary search for a polar bear in the North woods.
Literature and Drama
Dist - WECHO **Prod** - WECHO 1976

Wintering, Diseases, Pests 30 MIN
VHS / U-matic
Bees and Honey Series
Color
Discusses disease symptoms, diagnosis, treatment and wintering problems. Presents methods of moving bee colonies and special practices in beekeeping.
Agriculture; Science - Natural
Dist - MDCPB **Prod** - WGTV

Winterizing your boat 40 MIN
VHS
Color (G A)
$24.95 purchase _ #0925
Teaches professional methods for preparing a boat for winter storage. Introduces the tools, materials and procedures. Covers engines, woodwork, interiors and exteriors, fuel systems, electrical systems.
Physical Education and Recreation
Dist - SEVVID

Winter's End 10 MIN
U-matic / VHS / 16mm
Color (I J H)
LC 74-701764
Shows how animals and ecosystems in the far north of Canada are being endangered by new stresses caused by man's development of the area.
Science - Natural
Dist - JOU **Prod** - MEPHTS 1973

Winter's Soft Mantle 115 MIN
VHS
Tony Couch Watercolor Series
Color (I)
$49.95 purchase _ #VC - - 729
Demonstrates step - by - step how to complete a watercolor of farm buildings in the snow with special instructions on how to paint rough wood, soft snow and cast shadows. Part of a four - part series on watercolor techniques by Tony Couch.
Fine Arts
Dist - CRYSP **Prod** - CRYSP

The Winter's Tale 173 MIN
VHS / 16mm
BBC's Shakespeare Series
(H A)
$249.95; $109.00 purchase _ #DL473
Retells The Winter's Tale, Shakespeare's play about a wife unfairly accused of adultery.
Literature and Drama
Dist - AMBROS **Prod** - AMBROS 1982
BBC

The Winter's Tale 173 MIN
U-matic / VHS
Shakespeare Plays Series
Color (H C A)
LC 82-707356
Presents William Shakespeare's play The Winter's Tale about a king who unjustly accuses his wife of adultery. Reveals that 16 years later, their daughter, missing since infancy, is miraculously restored and reconciled with her dead mother, who is brought back to life again.
Literature and Drama
Dist - TIMLIF **Prod** - BBCTV 1981

The Winter's Tale 29 MIN
Videoreel / VT2
Feast of Language Series
Color
Features Alan Levitan, associate professor of English at Brandeis University discussing The Winter's Tale by Shakespeare.
Literature and Drama
Dist - PBS **Prod** - WGBHTV

Winter's Wildlife 21 MIN
16mm
Color
LC 77-702727
Takes the viewer on a winter hike along a scenic river and through the woods to discover the wildlife that lives there during the season. Shows beaver, deer, foxes, raccoons and a territorial duel between porcupines.
Science - Natural
Dist - GIB **Prod** - GIB 1976

Winterset 30 MIN
VHS / 16mm
Play Series
Color (H)
Presents Maxwell Anderson's play about the son of an executed man punished for a crime he didn't commit. The eighth of eight installments of CTI's The Play Series, which attempts to give students an appreciation of the unique elements of the play through detailed examination of classic and trendsetting productions.
Fine Arts; Literature and Drama
Dist - GPN **Prod** - CTI 1990

Winterspelt 114 MIN
16mm
Color (GERMAN (ENGLISH SUBTITLES))
Discloses the circumstances behind the Ardennen Offensive of World War II, which resulted in 75,000 deaths.
Foreign Language; History - World
Dist - WSTGLC **Prod** - WSTGLC 1978

Wintersports in Sweden 15 MIN
16mm
Color
Points out that Ostersund, in the center of Sweden has much to offer the tourist in the winter, including skating, sleigh riding and skiing practically on your doorstep.
Geography - World; Physical Education and Recreation
Dist - SWNTO **Prod** - SWNTO 1962

Winterwheat 8 MIN
VHS / 16mm
Color (G)
$20.00 rental, $15.00 purchase
Uses an educational film about the farming cycle. Manipulates found footage, by bleaching, scratching and painting directly on the emulsion, to create hypnotic visuals while also suggesting an apocalyptic narrative.
Fine Arts
Dist - CANCIN **Prod** - STREEM 1989

Wipe Out Jargon 24 MIN
U-matic / VHS
Transition Package Series
Color (H C A)
Examines letter and report writing. Demonstrates efficient writing and principles for clear, well structured letters and reports. Includes booklets.
English Language
Dist - SEVDIM **Prod** - SEVDIM

Wipeout 2 MIN
16mm
B&W
LC FIA67-703
A quick succession of images synchronized with music provides impressions of life, death, war, love and hate.
Fine Arts; Religion and Philosophy
Dist - USC **Prod** - USC 1966

Wiping the tears of seven generations 57 MIN
VHS
Color (G I J H)
$24.95 purchase _ #MW14
Documents the journey by 300 Lakota Sioux in December 1990, as they rode 250 miles on horseback through sub zero weather to commemorate the Wounded Knee Massacre of 1890. Inspired by dreams, a group of Lakota decided to bring their people out of mourning through the traditional ceremony of 'Washigila,' or 'Wiping the Tears.'
History - United States; Social Science
Dist - SVIP

The WIPP trail 54 MIN
VHS
Color (H C G A)
$85.00 purchase, $35.00 rental
Scrutinizes the Waste Isolation Pilot Plant, a nuclear waste storage site near Carlsbad, New Mexico. Reveals that nuclear waste bound for WIPP will have to pass through 28 states. Suggests that the safety issues are being ignored or played down by politicians. Interviews scientists, health officials, citizens, and politicians. Narrated by Robert Redford.
Civics and Political Systems; Geography - United States; Health and Safety; Sociology
Dist - EFVP

Wire Joints and Terminals
VHS / 35mm strip
Electronic Soldering Series
$42.00 purchase _ #LXES4 filmstrip, $62.00 purchase _ #LXES4V VHS
Portrays soldering techniques for joining and mounting wire and axial lead components to common terminal types.
Education; Industrial and Technical Education
Dist - CAREER **Prod** - CAREER

Wire Rope 19 MIN
U-matic / VHS
Safety in Rigging Series
Color (A IND)
Discusses wire rope construction and characteristics. Highlights safe loads, inspection, replacement, use, handling and maintenance. Defines terms and abbreviations and demonstrates inspection and testing procedures.
Health and Safety
Dist - IFB **Prod** - CSAO 1984

Wire Rope Terminal Connections 31 MIN
16mm
B&W
LC FIE52-1205
Demonstrates how to make and test the following terminal connections - clips, eye splices and metallic splices.
Civics and Political Systems; Industrial and Technical Education
Dist - USNAC **Prod** - USN 1948

Wire Sculpture 20 MIN
16mm
Color (J)
Depicts the techniques and philosophy of free - lance artist Joe Police as he constructs kinetic wire sculptures with an acetylene torch and steel wire.
Fine Arts; Industrial and Technical Education
Dist - UHAWAI **Prod** - UHAWAI 1973

Wire sizes and voltage drop 13 MIN
16mm
Electrical work - wiring series
B&W
LC FIE52-104
Discusses factors influencing the ability of conductors to carry electron flow, measurement of wire size, voltage drop and ohm's law.
Industrial and Technical Education
Dist - USNAC **Prod** - USOE 1945

The Wired - in World of Zen 25 MIN
U-matic / 16mm
Maclear Series
Color; Mono (J H C A)
$300.00 film, $250.00 video, $50.00 rental
Introduces the philosophy of Zen and how its meditation may be applied to help deal with everyday tension and stress.
Religion and Philosophy
Dist - CTV **Prod** - CTV 1974

Wireladder splint - the injured ankle 7 MIN
U-matic / VHS
EMT video - group two series
Color (PRO)
LC 84-706501
Shows the application of the wireladder splint to an injured foot and ankle, including padding, bending and securing the splint.
Health and Safety
Dist - USNAC **Prod** - USA 1983

Wireless Lizzie 30 MIN
16mm
Classic Christie Comedies Series
B&W
Literature and Drama
Dist - SFI **Prod** - SFI

Wireline Operations with Gas - Lift Valves 17 MIN
Slide / VHS / 16mm
(A IND)
$170.00, $160.00 purchase _ #55.2903, #15.2903
Presents the tools and techniques needed for pulling and running gas - lift valves by means of a wireline unit.
Industrial and Technical Education; Social Science
Dist - UTEXPE

Wires to Our House 14 MIN
16mm / U-matic / VHS
Color (I J H)
LC 77-700227
Explains that the various wires leading into the house are channels for the transmission of power and communication. Shows how the power is distributed safely throughout the house.
Guidance and Counseling; Psychology; Social Science
Dist - IFB **Prod** - VEF 1961

Wiring a House
VHS / 35mm strip
Wiring a House Series
$295.00 purchase _ #DXWAH000 filmstrips, $295.00 purchase _
Presents a series of filmstrips or VHS tapes which provide training on how to wire a house.
Industrial and Technical Education
Dist - CAREER **Prod** - CAREER

Wiring a House Series
Outlet Boxes
Service
Tools and Supplies
Wiring a House
Wiring Fittings
Dist - CAREER

Wiring and Insulation 30 MIN
VHS / BETA
This Old House, Pt 2 - Suburban '50s Series
Color
Discusses wiring a breezeway. Shows how to insulate the garage - turned - family - room.
Industrial and Technical Education; Sociology
Dist - CORF **Prod** - WGBHTV

Wiring and one - line diagrams 60 MIN
U-matic / VHS
Electrical maintenance training series; Module C - Electrical print reading
Color (IND)
Industrial and Technical Education
Dist - LEIKID **Prod** - LEIKID

Wiring, Batteries, Coolant and Upholstery 30 MIN
BETA / VHS
Last Chance Garage Series
Color
Talks about electrical wiring and upholstery. Shows how to check the engine coolant and to recharge a dead battery. Reminisces about a 1964 Triumph Roadster.
Industrial and Technical Education
Dist - CORF **Prod** - WGBHTV

Wiring Fittings
VHS / 35mm strip
Wiring a House Series
$85.00 purchase _ #DXWAH040 filmstrips, $85.00 purchase _ #DXWAH040V
Teaches about wiring switches and receptacles, lighting fixtures, and panels.
Industrial and Technical Education
Dist - CAREER **Prod** - CAREER

Wiring old buildings with armored cable 22 MIN
16mm
Electrical work - wiring series
B&W
LC FIE52-98
Shows how to install outlet boxes, cut and strip armor from cables, attach cable to outlet boxes, run armored cable, repair openings in walls and join conductors at ceiling outlet.
Industrial and Technical Education
Dist - USNAC **Prod** - USOE 1945

Wiring Telltale Panel 17 MIN
16mm
B&W

LC FIE52-207
Explains the purpose of telltale units. Shows how to strip cable, form and lace conductors on a jig, strip the ends of conductors and put on logs.
Industrial and Technical Education
Dist - USNAC **Prod** - USOE 1945

Wiring Up the Organization 25 MIN
VHS / U-matic
Electronic Office Series
Color (H C A)
LC 85-700735
Host Ian McNaught Davis examines how an organization's office work is affected when it provides a network that allows computers to be interconnected with a centralized data base.
Business and Economics; Industrial and Technical Education; Mathematics
Dist - FI **Prod** - BBCTV 1984

Wiring Up the World 25 MIN
VHS / U-matic
Electronic Office Series
Color (H C A)
Examines the implications of increasing use of electronic systems to get information between companies and between companies and their clients. Discusses the factors which have prohibited a revolutionary use of computers in offices, including human scepticism, the lack of standardization and cost.
Business and Economics; Industrial and Technical Education
Dist - FI **Prod** - BBCTV 1984

Wisconsin 60 MIN
VHS
Portrait of America series
Color (J H C G)
$99.95 purchase _ #AMB49V
Visits Wisconsin. Offers extensive research into the state's history. Films key locations and presents segments on its history, government, education, folklore, science, journalism, sociology, industry, agriculture and business. Shows what is unique about Wisconsin and what is distinctive about its regional culture and how it got to be that way. Includes teacher study guides. Part of a 50 - part series.
Geography - United States; History - United States
Dist - CAMV

Wisconsin, a Proud Heritage - the Menomonie People 20 MIN
U-matic / VHS
Color
Presents a summary of the history of the Menomonie people, from their origins to the recent past, and then shows life of the Menomonie as it exists today.
History - United States; Social Science; Sociology
Dist - UWISC **Prod** - NEWIST 1982

Wisconsin Cheese for all Seasons 25 MIN
16mm
Color (H C A)
LC 81-700439
Shows how cheddar and other types of cheese are made and promotes the consumption of cheese by presenting it as a convenient, waste - free and nutritious food available in many flavors, shapes, and sizes and useful in a wide variety of ways. Links cheese with the ethnic groups which brought the old world formulas to America and points out that several kinds originated in Wisconsin.
Agriculture; History - United States; Home Economics
Dist - UWISCA **Prod** - UWISCA 1980

Wisconsin Farming 48 MIN
16mm
Color (I)
LC 79-700106
Presents a survey of Wisconsin's agriculture by showing three farms situated in different parts of the State.
Agriculture; Geography - United States
Dist - UWISC **Prod** - UWISCA 1978

Wisconsin Rural Government - the Town 16 MIN
16mm
Color
Provides an insight into the principle duties and problems of the town officers and the informality of procedures in a form of local government, the town, as it exists in Wisconsin.
Civics and Political Systems; Geography - United States; Social Science
Dist - UWISC **Prod** - UWISC 1964

Wisconsin Town Government 15 MIN
U-matic
Color; Mono (H C)
Presents the history of Wisconsin's town government; how it is structured and its mandated and non - mandated functions. Looks in on a board meeting and annual town meeting in Waupaca County.
Civics and Political Systems; History - United States
Dist - UWISCA **Prod** - UWISCA 1985

Wisconsin's Tort Liability - Road and Street Maintenance 22 MIN
U-matic
Color; Mono (H C)
Can a Wisconsin municipality be sued for alleged negligence in the repair and maintenance of streets? Covers, potholes, construction site safety, obstructions, snow and ice control and more.
Civics and Political Systems; Social Science
Dist - UWISCA **Prod** - UWISCA 1980

Wisdom, freedom and compassion 120 MIN
Cassette
Practicing the heart of healing series
Color; PAL (G)
PdS35, PdS10
Offers the basic precepts for skillful living, non - injury, simplicity, humility, devotion and gratitude. Includes a guided meditation on cultivating compassion and loving kindness. Part of a two - part series.
Fine Arts; Guidance and Counseling; Health and Safety; Religion and Philosophy
Dist - MERIDT

Wisdom from the bench 29 MIN
VHS
America's drug forum second season series
Color (G)
$19.95 purchase _ #210
Reveals that normally reticent United States judges have spoken out against tough mandatory drug sentencing laws which curb judicial decision making power, resulted in unjust jail terms for people caught in the wrong place at the wrong time, and contribute to prison population explosion. Features tough law and order Judge Stanley Sporkin and liberal advocate of legalization Judge Robert Sweet in discussion.
Civics and Political Systems; Psychology
Dist - DRUGPF **Prod** - DRUGPF 1992

Wisdom has no fear of death 39 MIN
U-matic / VHS
Conscious living - conscious dying - the work of a lifetime series
Color
Presents Ram Dass lecturing on the relationship between bodily death and consciousness. Observes that if one is to work effectively with dying persons, one must first work with yourself.
Sociology
Dist - PELICN **Prod** - ORGNLF

The Wisdom of the dream - World of C G Jung series
Inheritance of Dreams - Pt 2 60 MIN
A World of Dreams - Pt 3 60 MIN
Dist - FI

The Wisdom of the dream - World of C G Jung series
A Life of Dreams - Pt 1 60 MIN
Dist - FI

Wise blood 108 MIN
35mm / 16mm
Color (G)
$300.00, $400.00 rental
Presents a John Huston film. Adapts the novel by Flannery O'Connor. Portrays white trash Hazel Motes who returns South after army service to preach for The Church of Jesus Without Christ - 'Where the blind don't see and the lame don't walk and what's dead stays that way.' Reveals that Motes becomes obsessed with a 'blind' preacher and his lustful daughter.
Fine Arts; History - United States
Dist - KINOIC

Wise buying habits series
Presents a three - part series on consumer education. Includes the titles Surviving the Checkout - Wise Food Buying; Clothing Dollars and Sense; and Making the Right Connection - Buying Home Entertainment Components.
Wise buying habits series
Dist - CAMV **Prod** - CAMV 1979

The Wise Use of Credit 11 MIN
16mm
Color; B&W (J H)
LC FIA62-1676
Discusses consumer credit, how it is established, the types and cost, the amount a family can afford and the circumstances under which credit should be used.
Business and Economics; Guidance and Counseling; Home Economics
Dist - SUTHLA **Prod** - SUTHLA 1960

Wise Use of Drugs - a Program for Older Americans 31 MIN
U-matic / VHS / 16mm
Color
LC 80-707247
Provides background information on the use of legal drugs in America and offers advice to the elderly on the use of prescription drugs. Issued in 1979 as a motion picture.
Health and Safety
Dist - USNAC **Prod** - NIDA 1979

Wise use of medications video
VHS
Health care consumerism system series
Color (G)
$179.00 purchase _ #WMV02
Highlights six key principles to taking medications properly, along with answers to the six most commonly asked quesitons about medications. Accelerates the healing process by preparing the viewer to be a partner in treatment. Part of a ten - part series.
Health and Safety; Home Economics
Dist - GPERFO **Prod** - GPERFO

Wise use of the emergency room video
VHS
Health care consumerism system series
Color (G)
$179.00 purchase _ #WMV03
Reveals that emergency rooms are the most expensive service area in any hospital and misuse costs millions of dollars each year. Teaches employees to make the best use of this sometimes necessary, but always expensive service. Part of a ten - part series.
Health and Safety; Home Economics
Dist - GPERFO **Prod** - GPERFO

The Wisest Man in the World 10 MIN
U-matic / VHS / 16mm
Children's Storybook Theater Series
Color (P I)
Retells old legends of the wisdom of Solomon, including visit of the Queen of Sheba and her attempts to outwit him.
Literature and Drama
Dist - AIMS **Prod** - TSE 1970

The Wish 30 MIN
VHS
Join in series
Color (K P)
#362310
Pictures Zack, Jacob, and their new friend Julia trying on Jacob's latest costume designs and acting out the story of Aladdin. Uses songs and dances to show that wishes can come true. Part of a series about three artist - performers who share studio space in a converted warehouse.
Fine Arts; Literature and Drama
Dist - TVOTAR **Prod** - TVOTAR 1989

The Wish Giver
35mm strip / VHS / Cassette
Newbery Award - Winners Series
Color (I)
$66.00, $14.00 purchase
English Language; Literature and Drama
Dist - PELLER

The Wish giver 15 MIN
VHS
More books from cover to cover series
Color (I G)
$25.00 purchase _ #MBCC - 101
Based on the book 'The Wish Giver' by Bill Brittain. Tells the story of a strange little man who grants wishes to three young people. Reveals that the wishes are granted in unusual ways. Hosted by John Robbins.
English Language; Literature and Drama
Dist - PBS **Prod** - WETATV 1987

The Wish - Phone 9 MIN
16mm / U-matic / VHS
Color (K P)
LC 79-700605
Depicts the animated adventures of two children and their dog who receive a magic telephone which carries out their wishes.
Fine Arts; Literature and Drama
Dist - PHENIX **Prod** - KRATKY 1978

Wish you weren't here 30 MIN
VHS
Nature series
Color; PAL (G)
PdS65 purchase; Not available in the United States or Canada
Looks at the environmental costs of tourism. Poses the question of whether the increase of the tourist trade could put a large strain on the ecological balance of the natural world. Addresses means of protecting the planet from the surge in tourists who wish to enjoy it.
Geography - World; Science - Natural
Dist - BBCENE

Wishing won't make it so 28 MIN
16mm / VHS
Color (A G)
$570.00 purchase, $130.00 rental ; $595.00, $570.00 purchase, $130.00 rental
Features management consultant Michael LeBoeuf on customer service. Presents a system for motivating employees to treat customers courteously and a list of suitable stipends for employee courtesy, the Triple Win Reward System.
Business and Economics; Guidance and Counseling; Home Economics; Psychology
Dist - CCCD **Prod** - CCCD 1990
VLEARN

Wit and wisdom 35 MIN
VHS
Color (G C)
$195.00 purchase, $50.00 rental
Presents discussions among a dancer, a rights activist, a nuclear physicist and a gerontologist about their experience of aging. Shows each explaining what life means in the context of his or her personal culture and life principles.
Health and Safety; Literature and Drama
Dist - TNF

The Wit and Wisdom of Aging 26 MIN
U-matic / VHS
Color (C)
$249.00, $149.00 purchase _ #AD - 1591
Features Norman Cousins, writer, editor and survivor of death sentences passed by his doctors. Shows him working with 'terminal' cancer patients who refuse to die as scheduled.
Health and Safety; Sociology
Dist - FOTH **Prod** - FOTH

The Witch of Blackbird Pond 15 MIN
VHS / U-matic
Storybound Series
Color (I)
Tells the story of a girl from the Caribbean in 17th century New England. From the book by Elizabeth George Speare.
Literature and Drama
Dist - CTI **Prod** - CTI
GPN

The Witch who was Afraid of Witches 12 MIN
16mm / U-matic / VHS
Color (P I)
LC 79-700948
Tells the story of Wendy, a young witch who is petrified of witches, especially her two mean witch - sisters. Shows how, on Halloween, Wendy gains confidence in herself and succeeds in outwitching her two mean sisters. Adapted from the book The Witch Who Was Afraid Of Witches by Alice Low.
Guidance and Counseling; Literature and Drama; Social Science
Dist - LCOA **Prod** - NOYES 1979

Witchcraft among the Azande 52 MIN
U-matic / VHS
Disappearing World Series
Color (A)
LC 82-707326
Focuses on the human side of the Azande tribe of the African Sudan and the deep conviction that misfortunes result from witchcraft. Follows a farmer as he seeks magical relief for an ill wife consulting oracles and by the ritual poisoning os a chicken.
Geography - World; Sociology
Dist - FLMLIB **Prod** - GRATV 1982

Witches and mice 15 MIN
VHS
Magic library series
Color (P)
LC 90-707937
Tells a story about witches. Raises children's awareness of a sense of story in order to enrich and motivate language, reading and writing skills. Includes teacher's guide. Part of a series.
Education; English Language
Dist - TVOTAR **Prod** - TVOTAR 1990

Witches, dykes, faggots and poofters 45 MIN
16mm
Color (G)
$800.00 purchase, $75.00 rental
Compares the social and political oppression of lesbians and gay men throughout history with the harassment, victimization and discrimination practiced today. Produced by Digby Duncan of Australia.
Sociology
Dist - WMEN

Witches, New Fashion - Old Religion 52 MIN
U-matic / VHS / 16mm
Color (C A)
Interviews a businessman who studies witchcraft as a hobby and a businesswoman who heads a coven about their beliefs and practices.
Sociology
Dist - MEDIAG **Prod** - THAMES 1972

The Witches of Salem - the Horror and the Hope 34 MIN
16mm / U-matic / VHS
Captioned; Color (J) (SPANISH)
Shows how the hysterical behavior of a few young girls set off the Salem witchcraft trials of 1692.
Fine Arts; History - United States; Sociology
Dist - LCOA **Prod** - AZRELA 1972
UILL

Witchy Weed, the 21 MIN
U-matic / VHS / 16mm
Captioned; Color (A) (PORTUGUESE (ENGLISH SUBTITLES))
Portrays the development of the tobacco industry in Brazil. Discusses the techniques, economics and problems of tobacco production.
Agriculture; Fine Arts
Dist - CNEMAG **Prod** - CNEMAG

With a feminine touch - great women writers 45 MIN
VHS
Heritage poetry collection series
Color (J H)
$49.00 purchase _ #60302 - 126
Presents works by Emily Dickinson, Sylvia Plath, Edna St Vincent Millay, and the Brontes.
Literature and Drama
Dist - GA **Prod** - GA 1992

With a Little Help from My Friends, Pt 1 30 MIN
16mm / U-matic / VHS
Powerhouse Series
Color (I J)
Relates how a new youth center's members are caught up in an adventure with local racketeers.
Guidance and Counseling; Psychology
Dist - GA **Prod** - EFCVA 1982

With a Little Help from My Friends, Pt 2 30 MIN
16mm / U-matic / VHS
Powerhouse Series
Color (I J)
Relates how a new youth center's members are caught up in an adventure with local racketeers.
Guidance and Counseling; Psychology
Dist - GA **Prod** - EFCVA 1982

With a little luck - surviving a hostage situation 36 MIN
VHS
Color (C A)
$295.00 purchase
Dramatizes for police, bank employees, hospital staff, airport workers and similar professionals how to correctly handle a hostage situation and decrease the chance of harm for individuals. Produced by Frank Swaringen.
Health and Safety; Social Science; Sociology
Dist - PFP

With a Long Gray Beard 27 MIN
U-matic / VHS / 16mm
Insight Series
B&W (H C A)
Presents the story of a high - strung super salesman who works too hard, drinks too much and whose wife is leaving him. Shows how the salesman ignores honest concern from those around him except from a dying roomate who offers love and demands acceptance. Concludes with the fact that this man is Christ, the drama of redemption.
Business and Economics; Guidance and Counseling; Psychology; Religion and Philosophy
Dist - PAULST **Prod** - PAULST 1965

With a Vengeance 40 MIN
16mm / VHS
B&W (G)
$600.00, $225.00 purchase, $75.00 rental
Looks at the struggle of women for reproductive freedom since the 1960s. Asks why the battles of the 1980s resemble those of the 1960s. Interviews early abortion rights activists, including members of Redstockings and the JANE Collective, as well as present day young women. Flo Kennedy and Byllye Avery consider the connections between racism, reproductive freedom and healthcare for the poor. Produced by Lori Hiris.
Fine Arts; Health and Safety; Science - Natural; Sociology
Dist - WMEN **Prod** - LOHI 1989

With all Deliberate Speed 59 MIN
Videoreel / VT2
Syngerism - Troubled Humanity Series
Color
Examines the issue of school bussing in Pontiac, Michigan on all levels.
Education; Sociology
Dist - PBS **Prod** - WTVSTV

With America's Enemy, 1954 - 1967 60 MIN
U-matic / VHS / 16mm
Vietnam - a television history series; Episode 6
Color (H C A)
Contrasts the Vietnamese war by offering the views of the followers of Ho Chi Minh and their opponents, U S soldiers and POWs. Depicts the effects of growing socialization in the North and the results of U S bombing, guerilla and conventional warfare.
History - United States; History - World
Dist - FI **Prod** - WGBHTV 1983

With Babies and Banners 45 MIN
16mm
Color (A)
Portrays the everyday life of working women during the 1930's. Tells the story of nine women who were leaders of the Women's Emergency Brigade during the 1937 sitdown strike at General Motors.
Business and Economics; History - World; Psychology; Sociology
Dist - AFLCIO **Prod** - WLHFP 1978
NEWDAY

With Babies and Banners - Story of the Women's Emergency Brigade, Pt 1 23 MIN
16mm
Color (H C A)
LC 78-701221
Uses archival footage and interviews with participants to trace the role of women in the formation of the United Auto Workers. Focuses on the contributions of the Women's Emergency Brigade to the labor movement of the 1930's.
Dist - NEWDAY **Prod** - WLHFP 1978

With Babies and Banners - Story of the Women's Emergency Brigade, Pt 2 22 MIN
16mm
Color (H C A)
LC 78-701221
Uses archival footage and interviews with participants to trace the role of women in the formation of the United Auto Workers. Focuses on the contributions of the Women's Emergency Brigade to the labor movement of the 1930's.
Dist - NEWDAY **Prod** - WLHFP 1978

With Babies and Banners - the Story of the Women's Emergency Brigade 45 MIN
U-matic / VHS / 16mm
Color
Celebrates women's participation in the historic General Motors Sit - Down Strike of 1937. Portrays the transformation of wives and mothers into defiant supporters, looks at their passionate struggle and their ultimate victory.
Business and Economics; Sociology
Dist - CNEMAG **Prod** - GLGLBA

With Bekus in Nepal 14 MIN
U-matic / VHS / 16mm
World's Children Series
Color (P I)
LC 81-700255
Looks at the life of a 13 - year - old boy in Nepal.
Geography - World; Social Science
Dist - JOU **Prod** - ITF 1980

With Bernadette in New Guinea 13 MIN
16mm / U-matic / VHS
World's Children Series
Color (P I)
LC 82-700398
Shows a young girl from Papua, New Guinea as she collects firewood and water, weeds, gardens and feeds her pigs. Shows how the men and boys of the village clear a garden, fly homemade kites, and fish and swim in the warm Pacific waters.
Geography - World; Social Science
Dist - JOU **Prod** - ASTRSK 1981

With Care and Caring - Pediatric Medication 30 MIN
VHS / 16mm
(C)
$385.00 purchase _ #850VI122
Teaches how to administer medication to children of various ages.
Health and Safety
Dist - HSCIC **Prod** - HSCIC 1986

With care and caring ... pediatric medication administration 30 MIN
VHS
Color (PRO C G)
$395.00 purchase _ #R850 - VI - 122
Teaches viewers how to administer medication to children of various ages. Uses real - life situations to demonstrate specific physical techniques, practical considerations and how to approach the child based on developmental stages. Produced with the Univ of Texas at Arlington.
Health and Safety
Dist - HSCIC **Prod** - TEXCU 1986

With Claudia in Australia 13 MIN
16mm / U-matic / VHS
World's Children Series
Color (P I)
LC 82-700399
Introduces an 11 - year - old who lives in North Queensland, a largely rural farming area of Australia. Tells how she learns more about her ancestors, who were rain forest aborigines, as she visits the museum and crafts co - op.
Geography - World; Social Science
Dist - JOU **Prod** - ASTRSK 1981

With Epelli in Fiji 13 MIN
U-matic / VHS / 16mm
World's Children Series
Color (P I)
Shows a young boy who lives in a small village in the South Pacific country of Fiji as he helps with the sugarcane harvest, fishes, attends school, plays soccer, and is introduced to the Kava ceremony, the ancient Fijian ritual of welcome.
Geography - World; Social Science
Dist - JOU **Prod** - ASTRSK 1981

With Every Breath 25 MIN
VHS / U-matic
Color
Covers asthma, emphysema and the effect of smoking in discussing breathing and the lungs. Uses thermography, a photographic process based on heat, to show the actual effect of smoking on the circulation of blood through the body.
Health and Safety; Science - Natural
Dist - MEDCOM **Prod** - MEDCOM

With Eyes Wide Open 58 MIN
U-matic / 16mm
Color (A)
Explores the life and work of handicapped artist Richard Wawro. Reveals the environments that have enabled Richard to grow and express creativity. Narrated by Richard Cactus Pryor.
Fine Arts; Psychology
Dist - CLNGEN **Prod** - CLNGEN 1983

With Fabric and Thread 15 MIN
16mm / U-matic / VHS
Textile Design Series
Color (I)
Explains that creative stitchery is like painting in thread but with greater variety in texture. Explains how to select a background fabric, choose colors and types of yarn and develop a design. Demonstrates such simple stitches as the stem or outline, chain, satin, French knot and couching. Describes such techniques as punch hooking and applique. Shows the creation of a picture in applique from the first sketched design through all stages.
Fine Arts
Dist - AIMS **Prod** - TETKOW 1974

With Gladis in Bolivia 11 MIN
U-matic / VHS / 16mm
World's Children Series
Color (P I)
LC 81-700256
Focuses on a day in the life of a girl in Santa Cruz, Bolivia.
Geography - World; Social Science
Dist - JOU **Prod** - ITF 1980

With God on Our Side 58 MIN
16mm / U-matic / VHS
Color (H C A)
LC 83-706749
Explores the proliferation of the electronic church characterized by television evangelists, radio programs and drive - in churches.
Religion and Philosophy
Dist - PHENIX **Prod** - VONWET 1982

With hand and heart 28 MIN
VHS / U-matic / 16mm
Color (J H G)
$240.00, $290.00, $495.00 purchase, $50.00 rental
Bridges the gap between nomadic Indians who peopled North America nearly two thousand years ago and those who today continue an art cultivated by the land and its forces. Documents the history of Southwestern Native American art as seen through a selected group of contemporary practitioners and storytellers.
Fine Arts; Geography - United States; Social Science
Dist - NDIM **Prod** - OAKCRK 1986

With her own light 20 MIN
16mm
Cuba - a view from inside series
Color (G)
$300.00 purchase, $40.00 rental
Portrays South African Winnie Mandela, her life and struggle, including early footage with Nelson Mandela. Features part of a 17 - part series of shorts by and about Cuban women. Directed by Mayra Vilasis. Illustrated catalog available. Contact distributor for programming advice and discount package rental fees.
Civics and Political Systems; Fine Arts
Dist - CNEMAG

With Just a Little Trust 15 MIN
16mm
Contemporary Family Series
Color
LC 75-703552
Shows how a young, widowed Black woman is brought out of a self - pity by her mother, who urges her to trust in God and have courage in times of adversity.
Guidance and Counseling; Sociology
Dist - FRACOC **Prod** - FRACOC 1975

With kids in mind series

Body talking	6 MIN
A Sense of touch	6 MIN
Sequence and story	6 MIN

Dist - VIEWTH

With liberty and health care for all 21 MIN
VHS
Color (C PRO)
$75.00 purchase _ #42 - 2454
Takes a close look at the Nursing's Agenda for Health Care Reform, which was one of the approaches considered by Clinton administration in the proposed program for health care reform. Interviews families imperiled by spiraling medical costs and examines the painful personal choices and financial nightmares that prompted the reform effort. Illustrates nursing's vital role in the evolving health care delivery system.
Health and Safety; Sociology
Dist - NLFN **Prod** - NLFN

With Love and Hisses 20 MIN
U-matic / VHS / 16mm
B&W (J)
Stars Laurel and Hardy as army rookies, causing a commotion on a troop train, devastating an inspection and burning up all their platoon's clothing.
Fine Arts
Dist - FI **Prod** - ROACH 1927

With Loving Arms 18 MIN
VHS
Color (G PRO)
$34.95 purchase _ #3925
Portrays three foster families caring for HIV - infected children. Looks at the everyday care of these children. Educates about the epidemiology of the disease and the need for loving, stable home environments for infected children. Includes discussion guide.
Health and Safety; Sociology
Dist - CWLOA **Prod** - CWLOA 1989

With Michael in Kyuso, Kenya 13 MIN
U-matic / VHS / 16mm
World's Children Series
Color (P I)
LC 82-700401
Introduces a boy who lives in rural Kyuso, Kenya. Shows how he must walk for an hour to get water for his thirteen brothers and sisters and how his family depends on their farmland for their livelihood.
Geography - World; Social Science
Dist - JOU **Prod** - ASTRSK 1981

With My Red Fires 31 MIN
16mm
Color
LC 78-701639
Presents an adaptation of Doris Humphrey's dance - drama With My Red Fires, performed by the professional Repertory Company of the 1972 American Dance Festival at Connecticut College.
Fine Arts
Dist - DANCE **Prod** - ADFEST 1978

With Nang and Nakorn in Thailand 14 MIN
16mm / U-matic / VHS
World's Children Series
Color (P I)
LC 81-700257
Introduces two children in Thailand and shows the activities of a typical day.
Geography - World; Social Science
Dist - JOU **Prod** - ITF 1980

With needle and yarn 15 MIN
Videoreel / VT2
Art corner series
B&W (P)
Demonstrates how to thread a needle and make running stitches.
Fine Arts
Dist - GPN **Prod** - CVETVC

With no One to Help Us 19 MIN
16mm
Head Start Starts at Home Series
B&W
LC FIE67-140
Demonstrates how the formation of a food - buying club by a group of Newark mothers brought about a necessary change in the community.
Psychology; Sociology
Dist - USNAC **Prod** - USOEO 1967

With one voice 10 MIN
16mm
Cuba - a view from inside series
Color (G)
$150.00 purchase, $25.00 rental
Profiles three musicians on tour in Cuba - Sonia Silvestre from the Dominican Republic, Lucecita Benitez from Puerto Rico, and Sara Gonzalez from Cuba. Features part of a 17 - part series of shorts by and about Cuban women. Directed by Miriam Tlavera. Illustrated catalog available. Contact distributor for programming advice and discount package rental fees.
Fine Arts
Dist - CNEMAG

With Oscar in Peru 11 MIN
16mm / U-matic / VHS
World's Children Series
Color (P I)
LC 81-700258
Visits 13 - year - old Oscar, who lives on the Peruvian altiplano.
Geography - World; Social Science
Dist - JOU **Prod** - ITF 1980

With Our Own Eyes - Pt 1 60 MIN
VHS
Local Heroes - Global Change Series
Color (H)
$75.00 purchase, $40.00 rental
Reveals that culture molds the ways in which people emerge from poverty. Observes that the efforts of industrialized nations to reduce poverty in Third World nations have often been inappropriate to those nations' needs. Part 1 of a four - part series on reducing world hunger.
Business and Economics; Civics and Political Systems; Health and Safety; History - World; Social Science; Sociology
Dist - SCETV **Prod** - SCETV 1990

With Paint on Canvas - Kes Zapkus 42 MIN
16mm
Color (H A)
$650.00 purchase, $65.00 rental
Interviews the artist Kes Zapkus in his downtown New York studio. Produced by Jerry Gambone.
Fine Arts; Industrial and Technical Education
Dist - AFA

With Pastore in Togo 13 MIN
16mm / U-matic / VHS
World's Children Series
Color (P I) (FRENCH)
LC 82-700402
Shows a 13 - year - old boy who lives on the west coast of Africa as he attends his school where the classes are conducted in French and goes home to his house made of mud walls and thatched roof. Observes how his village people work together raising chickens and picking cotton.
Geography - World; Social Science
Dist - JOU **Prod** - ASTRSK 1981

With Patsy in St Vincent 13 MIN
U-matic / VHS / 16mm
World's Children Series
Color (P I)
LC 82-700403
Introduces 13 - year - old Patsy Boyes who lives on the tiny Caribbean Island of St Vincent. Shows her going to school to learn agricultural skills, shopping with her mother, cooking dinner and reading to her young friends.
Geography - World; Social Science
Dist - JOU **Prod** - ASTRSK 1981

With safety, everybody wins 18 MIN
BETA / VHS / U-matic
Australian video programs series
Color; PAL (IND G)

$520.00 purchase _ #325 - 02
Trains employees in Australia. Introduces new employees to company safety policies. Covers common rules and regulations, control measures, emergency procedures and stresses the importance of team work in maintaining a safe and efficient workplace.
Health and Safety; Industrial and Technical Education; Psychology
Dist - ITSC **Prod** - ITSC

With safety, everybody wins 18 MIN
BETA / VHS / U-matic
British video programs series
Color; PAL (IND G)
$520.00 purchase _ #525 - 02
Trains employees in the United Kingdom. Introduces new employees to company safety policies. Covers common rules and regulations, control measures, emergency procedures and stresses the importance of team work in maintaining a safe and efficient workplace.
Health and Safety; Industrial and Technical Education; Psychology
Dist - ITSC **Prod** - ITSC

With safety everybody wins - Con la seguridad todos ganamos 18 MIN
U-matic / BETA / VHS
Safety - live action video series
Color (IND G) (SPANISH)
$495.00 purchase _ #825 - 02, #825 - 03
Gives a basic overview of the safety process to all employees. Describes common rules and procedures, health and safety control measures, protective devices, inspections and emergency procedures. Part of a series on safety.
Health and Safety; Industrial and Technical Education; Psychology
Dist - ITSC **Prod** - ITSC

With scissors and paste 15 MIN
Videoreel / VT2
Art corner series
B&W (P)
Deals with recognizing and cutting shapes.
Fine Arts
Dist - GPN **Prod** - CVETVC

With silk wings - Asian American women at work series 120 MIN
U-matic / VHS
With silk wings - Asian American women at work series
Color (G)
$349.00 purchase
Offers four videos which share vignettes of women in the workplace dealing with professional jobs, non - traditional occupations, assertiveness and the history of Asian immigrant women to the United States. Includes the titles Four Women, Talking History, On New Ground and Frankly Speaking.
Sociology
Dist - CROCUR

With Six You Get Eggroll 95 MIN
16mm
Color
Deals with a widow and widower who fall in love, bringing their teenagers together.
Fine Arts
Dist - SWANK **Prod** - SWAMD

With Spencer in Nairobi, Kenya 13 MIN
16mm / U-matic / VHS
World's Children Series
Color (P I)
LC 82-700404
Introduces a 13 - year - old boy who lives in Nairobi, Kenya and observes his life there.
Geography - World; Social Science
Dist - JOU **Prod** - ASTRSK 1981

With Sylvia in the Philippines 12 MIN
U-matic / VHS / 16mm
World's Children Series
Color (P I)
LC 81-700259
Focuses on a girl living on the island of Luzon in the Philippines.
Geography - World; Social Science
Dist - JOU **Prod** - ITF 1980

With the Dawn 5 MIN
16mm
Song of the Ages Series
B&W (H C A)
LC 73-702125
Presents a modern interpretation of Psalm 29 using a dramatization about a woman and her hospitalized husband.
Religion and Philosophy
Dist - FAMLYT **Prod** - FAMLYT 1964

With the Grain 29 MIN
16mm
Color (T)
Discusses the role of a supervising teacher who works with student teachers. Shows how to improve lesson plans in order to improve pupil rapport and classroom discipline and to avoid lecturing too much. Features supervising teachers having a planning conference and an evaluation session with student teachers.
Education
Dist - WVIZTV **Prod** - WVIZTV

With the Marines - Chosin to Hungnam 58 MIN
U-matic / VHS
B&W
Relates the surprise onslaught by Chinese Communists around Chosin reservoir in Korea and the U S Marines fight back to Hungnam beachhead, where they embarked upon history's most successful evacuation.
History - United States
Dist - IHF **Prod** - IHF

With the Marines - Chosin to Hungnam 24 MIN
16mm
B&W
LC FIE67-140
Presents one of the most famous marches in history, the fight out of Chosin Reserve.
Civics and Political Systems
Dist - USNAC **Prod** - USMC 1951

With their Eyes on the Stars 24 MIN
16mm
Color
Uses folk music to underscore the historic importance of the lunar mission.
History - United States; History - World; Industrial and Technical Education; Social Science
Dist - RCKWL **Prod** - NAA

With their Eyes upon the Stars 20 MIN
16mm
Color
Shows the pioneer spirit applied to the 1960's space age.
History - World; Science; Science - Physical
Dist - THIOKL **Prod** - WB 1964

With these Hands 33 MIN
U-matic / VHS / 16mm
Color (J H C A)
Talks about the struggles of African women to feed their families and reveals that 75% of Africa's food is grown by women. A New Internationalist Publications Limited Film.
Sociology
Dist - CWS
FLMLIB

With these Hands 10 MIN
16mm
Color
LC 78-700387
Presents a series of scenes of people fixing things, such as automobiles, telephones, appliances, clocks and shoes, with musical accompaniment and little narration.
Guidance and Counseling; Industrial and Technical Education
Dist - SANDYC **Prod** - GM 1977

With these Hands 22 MIN
16mm
Color
Examines ways to reduce hand injuries sustained in outside industrial use.
Health and Safety
Dist - USSC **Prod** - USSC

With these Hands 53 MIN
16mm / U-matic / VHS
Color
LC 77-711592
Spotlights the ideals, viewpoints and creative insights of eight American craftsmen.
Fine Arts
Dist - TIMLIF **Prod** - WILSND 1970

With Yau Kai in Hong Kong 13 MIN
16mm / U-matic / VHS
World's Children Series
Color (P I)
LC 81-700260
Visits a boy living in Hong Kong.
Geography - World; Social Science
Dist - JOU **Prod** - ITF 1980

Withdrawal and treatment - Tape 1 66 MIN
VHS
Cocaine, treatment and recovery - Haight - Ashbury training series
Color (C G PRO)
$250.00 purchase
Examines the physiology of withdrawal, medications, environmentally cued craving and relapse. Uses a crack recovery group, animation and professionals to examine treatment strategies. Part of a three - part series on the treatment of cocaine addiction.
Guidance and Counseling; Psychology
Dist - FMSP

Withdrawal Symptoms 30 MIN
U-matic / VHS
Money Puzzle - the World of Macroeconomics Series Module 7
Color
Explains the concept of aggregate demand and aggregate supply. Shows what happens when demand is not the same as supply.
Business and Economics; Sociology
Dist - MDCC **Prod** - MDCC

Withdrawing Medication from a Vial 17 MIN
U-matic / VHS
Basic Nursing Skills Series Tape 15; Tape 15
Color (PRO)
Discusses locating sites for imtramuscular medications. Shows how to administer intramuscular medications.
Health and Safety
Dist - MDCC **Prod** - MDCC

Withdrawing Medication from a Vial, Locating Sites for Intra - Muscular Medications 17 MIN
U-matic / VHS
Basic Nursing Skills Series
Color (PRO)
Health and Safety
Dist - BRA **Prod** - BRA

The Withdrawn Client 30 MIN
16mm
Psychiatric - Mental Health Nursing Series
Color (PRO)
LC 77-700133
Presents course instructors Grayce Sills and Doreen James Wise discussing assessment of the withdrawn clients behavior and intervention and evaluation as aspects of nursing care. Uses dramatic skits to depict clients exhibiting mild to severe withdrawal.
Health and Safety
Dist - AJN **Prod** - AJN 1977

The Withdrawn Patient 20 MIN
U-matic / VHS
Basic Therapeutic Approaches to Abnormal Behaviors Series
B&W
Discusses how to help patients overcome the withdrawn state. Deals with how the feelings of mental health specialists may add to the patients' problems, such as withdrawing from the patient when the patient rejects the counselor.
Psychology; Sociology
Dist - UWISC **Prod** - SCDMH 1979

Within a Lifetime 30 MIN
16mm
Color (GERMAN)
LC 82-700319
Informs about Safeway Stores worldwide operations, presenting some of the company's history as well as its current trends. Emphasizes the diversity and spirit of Safeway employees.
Business and Economics; Foreign Language
Dist - SAFEWS **Prod** - SAFEWS 1981

Within America Series
Crow Dog's paradise 28 MIN
The Land of Heart's Desire 29 MIN
What Can I Tell You - a Portrait of Three Generations of Women 55 MIN
What Can I Tell You - a Portrait of Three Generations of Women, Pt 1 27 MIN
Dist - CEPRO

Within and Without 9 MIN
16mm
Color
LC 76-703169
Presents sculptress Marilynn Stewart discussing her technique and outlook. Shows some of her work.
Fine Arts
Dist - GOLNDA **Prod** - GOLNDA 1974

Within Dialogue - Silence 6 MIN
U-matic
Color (G)
$200.00 purchase, $50.00, $40.00 rental
Considers the lack of communication between the sexes and the isolation of women. Created by Susan Rynard.
Psychology; Sociology
Dist - WMENIF **Prod** - WMENIF 1987

Within Normal Limits 23 MIN
U-matic / VHS / 16mm
Color
Examines the strengths and weakness of diagnostic tests and encourages realistic expectations from the results. Analyzes the referral process, where initiators often do not know whether the specific test they are requesting will provide the needed answers. Shows how parents and teachers may have different views of the testing process than doctors.
Health and Safety
Dist - CORF **Prod** - CORF

Within Our Power 60 MIN
U-matic / VHS
Bill Moyers' Journal Series
Color
Reports on alternative energy sources, featuring a citizen's energy program in Franklin County, Massachusetts, a conversation with Hazel Henderson, author and economist, and an interview with Congressman Richard Ottinger on federal funding for energy projects.
Social Science
Dist - PBS **Prod** - WNETTV 1980

Within Our Reach 17 MIN
16mm
Color
LC 76-702722
Shows what steps are necessary to receive grant funds and describes what individuals can do to ensure cleaner water. Documents the actions of the city officials and citizens of Parsippany - Troy Hills, New Jersey, to clean up its wastewater.
Science - Natural; Sociology
Dist - USNAC **Prod** - USEPA 1976

Within the Circle 12 MIN
16mm
Color
Deals with the production of Israeli coins. Shows how excavations of ancient coins inspire the use of ancient art motifs on the current coins of Israel.
Business and Economics; Fine Arts; Geography - World
Dist - ALDEN **Prod** - ALDEN

Within the Coral Wall - Australia's Great Barrier Reef
U-matic / VHS
Science and Nature Series
Color (G C J)
$197 purchase _ #06868 - 851
Explores the events that are invisible to the naked eye in the everyday world of the Great Barrier Reef.
Science - Natural
Dist - CHUMAN **Prod** - OSF 1988

Within the human brain - a dissection by Dr Marian C Diamond 49 MIN
VHS
Color (I J H C G)
$150.00 purchase, $40.00 rental _ #38115
Features internationally - known brain researcher Marian C Diamond of the University of California, Berkeley, speaking with two elementary school students and two university students. Examines the brain's structure and functions and answers questions from both sets of students as Dr Diamond dissects a human brain. Provides vital knowledge on the brain and illustrates important new research findings in clear and understandable language. Produced by Lawrence Hall of Science, UC Berkeley.
Science - Natural
Dist - UCEMC

Within the Town 25 MIN
16mm
B&W
Shows the planning and development of the Veterans Administration Volunteer Service Program in VA hospitals throughout the country. Discusses the indoctrination and utilization of volunteers at the hospital level explains the urgent need of the volunteer service to supplement the VA hospital program.
Sociology
Dist - USVA **Prod** - USVA 1952

Within this Decade - America in Space 29 MIN
16mm
Color
LC 74-705963
Traces the principal accomplishments of NASA in aeronautics and space research from 1959 until the eve of the first lunar landing. Places emphasis on the progressives experience gained on each manned Apollo mission.
Industrial and Technical Education; Social Science; Sociology
Dist - NASLBJ **Prod** - NASAMS 1969

Within this Earth 12 MIN
16mm
Color (I J H)
Presents ways of using modern equipment and technology to obtain the resources within the earth.
Social Science
Dist - MTP **Prod** - VA 1978

Without a home - On a heym 88 MIN
16mm
B&W (G) (YIDDISH WITH ENGLISH SUBTITLES)
Portrays the hardships facing a people cast adrift in urban America with little hope of preserving their traditional family patterns and values. Juxtaposes the antics of comedy team Dzigan and Shumacher with the story's otherwise unrelieved difficulties. Based on the play by Jacob Gordin, whose bleak outlook permeates the film. First separated and then reunited by immigration, the Rivkin family finds no respite either way. Produced by Adolph Mann. Contact distributor for rental fee.
Religion and Philosophy; Sociology
Dist - NCJEWF

Without an Industry, Without a Highway 29 MIN
U-matic
Like no Other Place Series
Color (J H)
Looks at the effect of the physical environment on British Columbia settlement patterns.
Geography - World; History - World
Dist - TVOTAR **Prod** - TVOTAR 1985

Without consent 25 MIN
VHS
Color (H C G)
$295.00 purchase
Explores the issue of date rape. Centers on two young college students whose developing relationship ends in violation. Does not teach rape - prevention techniques to potential victims. Challenges viewers to consider what rape is, why it occurs, how it might be prevented - who is ultimately responsible. Produced by Chapman College.
Guidance and Counseling; Health and Safety; Sociology
Dist - PFP

Without consent series
Combines three videos showing discussion by rape victims, rapists and abused spouses about the sexual violence involved. Looks at the causes and results of warped male - female relationships. Deals with the sometimes harsh realities of society's handling of sexual crime cases through the police and courts. Videos are also available separately.

The Dark side	36 MIN
Every woman's fear - Pts 1 and 2	86 MIN

Dist - LANDMK

Without due process - Japanese Americans and World War II 52 MIN
VHS / U-matic / 16mm
Color (H G)
$280.00, $330.00 purchase, $50.00 rental
Traces and analyzes the historical events leading up to the incarceration order of over 120,000 Japanese Americans. Covers the internment period, the protests and court challenges to the incarceration and concludes with the formal apology and compensation on behalf of the United States government to those incarcerated and their families. Produced by Northern California Educational TV. Available in two parts.
History - United States
Dist - NDIM

Without Permission 10 MIN
16mm
Color
Presents a documentation of a dance performed in the Ford Foundation Garden.
Fine Arts
Dist - EIF **Prod** - EIF 1971

Without Saying a Word 4 MIN
U-matic / VHS / 16mm
Most Important Person - Creative Expression Series
Color (K P I)
Describes nodding, shrugging and staring as ways of saying a lot without saying a word.
English Language; Fine Arts; Guidance and Counseling; Psychology
Dist - EBEC **Prod** - EBEC 1972

Without Warning 27 MIN
16mm
Color
Describes the dangers of high blood pressure and illustrates what happens, using an example of a busy man who is struck down without warning while preparing a display for a flower show.
Health and Safety; Science - Natural
Dist - MTP **Prod** - CIBA

Without Wheels 12 MIN
VHS
(J H C A)
$160.00 purchase _ #82503
Focuses on the results of a DWI conviction. Discusses how difficult life can be with a revoked driver's license. Emphasizes social and economic problems that result from losing the privelege of driving.
Guidance and Counseling; Health and Safety; Sociology
Dist - CMPCAR **Prod** - CMPCAR

Without witness 97 MIN
35mm / 16mm
Color (G) (RUSSIAN WITH ENGLISH SUBTITLES)
$250.00, $300.00 rental
Uses the ongoing arguments between a divorced couple to reveal details of their past. Directed by Nikita Mikhalkov.
Fine Arts; Sociology
Dist - KINOIC **Prod** - IFEX 1984

Withstanding ovation 24 MIN
VHS
Color (G)
$195.00 purchase, $100.00 rental _ #CA - 107
Profiles two capable young people who have mastered active and creative lives despite severe congenital limb deformities. Shows how they rely minimally on mechanical prostheses and how their physicians and therapists have learned from them how important it is to understand the perspectives of young patients and to treat them as normal children, respecting their abilities but avoiding excessive praise for their accomplishments. Produced by the Texas Scottish Rite Hospital for Children.
Health and Safety
Dist - FANPRO

Witkin on significant developments in California substantive law 480 MIN
VHS
Color (PRO)
$245.00, $395.00 purchase, $295.00 rental _ #CP-55290, #CP-65290
Summarizes ten years of changes in California contract, property, and tort law. Presents B E Witkin discussing new developments and trends of significance to legal practice in the state. Includes a hardcover handbook with either the audio or the video program.
Civics and Political Systems
Dist - CCEB

Witness 6 MIN
16mm
Christian Encounter Series
Color (J)
LC 72-700559
Presents practical implications of Christian love.
Guidance and Counseling; Religion and Philosophy
Dist - FRACOC **Prod** - FRACOC 1969

The Witness 24 MIN
16mm
Color
LC 77-702176
Presents a drama in which a detective story writer finds himself confronted with real criminals in the dark streets of the city.
Literature and Drama; Sociology
Dist - MARTG **Prod** - MARTG 1977

Witness 6 MIN
16mm
Christian Encounter Series,
Color (J)
LC 72-700559
Presents practical implications of Christian love.
Guidance and Counseling; Religion and Philosophy
Dist - FRACOC **Prod** - FRACOC 1969

The Witness 14 MIN
U-matic / VHS / 16mm
Color (J)
LC 76-703965
Presents an open - ended film about a boy who witnesses a classmate assaulting an elderly lady. Shows how out of fear of the larger boy he does not report the incident to the police, but ponders the situation and outcome.
Guidance and Counseling; Sociology
Dist - ALTSUL **Prod** - VITASC 1976

Witness Before a King 17 MIN
16mm
Book of Acts Series
Color; B&W (J H T R)
Presents the adventures of Paul to encourage Christians to keep fresh in their hearts the meaning of their conversion.
Religion and Philosophy
Dist - FAMF **Prod** - BROADM 1957

Witness Examination 97 MIN
U-matic / VHS
James Jean Trial Advocacy Series

Color (PRO)
Civics and Political Systems
Dist - ABACPE **Prod** - ABACPE

Witness Preparation for the Grand Jury 175 MIN
VHS / U-matic
Representing a Client Before a Grand Jury Series
Color (PRO)
Critiques the methodology used in preparing witnesses for testimony before a grand jury. Examines government policy regarding the granting of immunity.
Civics and Political Systems
Dist - ABACPE **Prod** - ABACPE

Witness to Apartheid 56 MIN
U-matic / VHS / 16mm
Color (J H C A)
Details human rights abuses by South African security forces against black school children involved in anti apartheid protests and organizing.
Civics and Political Systems; Geography - World; History - World; Psychology; Sociology
Dist - CANWRL **Prod** - CANWRL 1986
CWS

Witness to Apartheid 34 MIN
U-matic / VHS / 16mm
Color (J H)
Details human rights abuses by South African security forces against black school children involved in anti apartheid protests and organizing.
Geography - World; History - United States; History - World; Social Science; Sociology
Dist - CANWRL **Prod** - CANWRL 1987

Witness to genocide
VHS
Nazis series
Color (J H C G)
$29.95 purchase _ #MH1877V
Exposes the plan of Hitler to eliminate the entire race of Jews through torture and executions. Part of a five - part series on the Nazis.
Civics and Political Systems; History - World; Sociology
Dist - CAMV

Witness to history I series

The Great Depression	9 MIN
Turn - of - the - century America	16 MIN
The United States in World War I	15 MIN
World War II - the Pacific	15 MIN

Dist - GA

Witness to history II series

The New Deal	15 MIN
The Russian Revolution	15 MIN

Dist - GA

Witness to history II series

The Civil rights movement	15 MIN
Europe after World War II	15 MIN

Dist - GA
INSTRU

Witness to History Series

The Cold War	15 MIN
The Roaring '20s	15 MIN
U S Intervention in Latin America	15 MIN
World War II - the Dark Years in Europe	15 MIN

Dist - GA

Witness to History - the Depression
U-matic / VHS
Witness to History Unit
(J H C)
$39.00 purchase _ #06823 94
Documents the devastation countless Americans faced during the Great Depression. Features historic film footage of bank runs, unemployment and food lines, shanty towns. Examines the conflict between the Bonus Army and federal troops and how Americans blamed Hoover for the economic crisis.
Business and Economics; History - United States; Sociology
Dist - ASPRSS **Prod** - ASPRSS

Witness to History - Turn of the Century America
VHS / U-matic
(J H C)
$39.00 purchase _ #06820 94
Documents the changes that took place in the first twenty years of the twentieth century in America. Depicts immigrants entering America at Ellis island. Presents scenes of Henry Ford building the first automobile and the development of the assembly line which revolutionized American industry.
History - United States
Dist - ASPRSS **Prod** - ASPRSS

Witness to History Unit
Witness to History - the Depression
Dist - ASPRSS

A Witness to history with William Shirer - Parts 1 and 2 60 MIN
U-matic / VHS
World of ideas with Bill Moyers - Season 2 series
Color; Captioned (A G)
$59.95, $79.95 purchase _ #WIWM - 220D
Features William Shirer, a journalist in Europe at the beginning of World War II, who broadcast the first on - the - scene radio reports of the war. Expresses Shirer's concerns about German reunification and his reaction to President Reagan's visit to a German cemetary in 1985 in Part 1. Discusses his impressions of Adolf Hitler and the impact of two years Shirer spent in India with Ghandi in Part 2. Part of a series of interviews with Bill Moyers featuring scientists, writers, artists, philosophers and historians. Produced by Public Affairs Television, New York.
Civics and Political Systems; History - World; Religion and Philosophy
Dist - PBS

Witness to History - World War I
VHS / U-matic
(J H C)
$39.00 purchase _ #06821 94
Documents America's involvement in World War I. Depicts 'war fever' on the American homefront, life in the trenches in Europe and the Allies triumph in December, 1918. Follows Wilson's attempts to find lasting peace through the League of Nations.
History - United States; Sociology
Dist - ASPRSS **Prod** - ASPRSS

Witness to History - World War II
U-matic / VHS
(J H C)
$39.00 purchase _ #06822 94
Documents the attack on Pearl Harbour and Roosevelt delivering his war message to Congress. Features historic film footage of troops landing on the beaches of Iwo Jima, Americans coping with rationing and an industrial switch to defense production, the relocation of Japanese Americans, and the nuclear bombing of Hiroshima and Nagasaki. Concludes with footage of the victory celebration on VJ day.
History - United States
Dist - ASPRSS **Prod** - ASPRSS

Witness to the American Experience 30 MIN
U-matic / VHS
Developing Image Series
Color (J H)
Focuses on the use of the photograph as historical data.
History - United States; Industrial and Technical Education
Dist - CTI **Prod** - CTI

Witness to the Holocaust Series

Deportations	19 MIN
The Final Solution	19 MIN
Freedom	
Ghetto Life	19 MIN
Reflections	17 MIN
Resistance	17 MIN
Rise of the Nazis	20 MIN

Dist - CNEMAG

Witness to war 30 MIN
16mm / VHS
Color (G)
$530.00, $290.00 purchase, $60.00 rental
Tells the story of Dr Charlie Clements who, as a pilot in Vietnam, seemed headed for a distinguished Air Force career until he refused further combat missions and was stripped of his military identity. Relates his dedication of his life to non - violence and healing, ultimately to find himself tending wounded behind rebel lines in El Salvador. Produced by Deborah Shaffer and David Goodman.
Fine Arts; Health and Safety
Dist - FIRS

Witness to War - an American Doctor in El Salvador 30 MIN
VHS / 35mm strip
Color
Talks about an American doctor working behind rebel lines in El Salvador. Discusses the causes of the conflict in Central America. Produced by Skylight Pictures and AFSC.
Health and Safety; Sociology
Dist - CWS **Prod** - SKYLIT 1984

Witnesses 58 MIN
VHS
Color (G R)
$29.95 purchase _ #V682
Features actor and author Curt Cloninger in dramatic portrayals of people who knew Jesus. Portrays these characters in contemporary language and dress. Performed before a live audience. Includes discussion guide.
Guidance and Counseling; Literature and Drama; Religion and Philosophy
Dist - GF

Witnesses - Anti - Semitism in Poland, 1946 26 MIN
VHS
Color (H C G)
$295.00 purchase, $55.00 rental
Returns to Kielce Poland, on July 4, 1946. Reveals that a few Jewish survivors of Nazi camps returned to rebuild their lives. Suddenly the rumor ran through the city that Jews were killing Christian children for their blood. A furious crowd gathered to vent their hatred and massacred 42 Jews and gravely wounded many more. Interviews Polish people who were there, a sociologist, a housewife, a baker, a graphic artist, a journalist. They recall the event in grim detail, some expressing horror, others unmoved. Directed by Marcel Lozinsky.
Religion and Philosophy; Sociology
Dist - FLMLIB

Witnesses of Jehovah 58 MIN
VHS
Color (J H C G A R)
$49.95 purchase, $10.00 rental _ #35 - 84 - 2504
Scrutinizes the beliefs of Jehovah's Witnesses, with the implication that the group is a cult. Suggests ways of responding to Witnesses. Produced by Jeremiah Films.
Religion and Philosophy
Dist - APH

Witnesses to Jesus - Tape 3 30 MIN
VHS
Acts of the Apostles series
Color (I J H C G A R)
$29.95 purchase, $10.00 rental _ #35 - 8364 - 1502
Presents stories of the early Christian church as described in the New Testament book of Acts. Covers the events of the trial before the Sanhedrin, teaching in the Temple, the election of the first deacons, and others.
Literature and Drama; Religion and Philosophy
Dist - APH **Prod** - BOSCO

Wittgenstein 45 MIN
VHS
Great philosophers series
Color; PAL (H C A)
PdS99 purchase
Introduces the concepts of Western philosophy and one of its greatest thinkers. Features a contemporary philosopher who, in conversation with Bryan Magee, discusses Wittgenstein and his ideas. Part fifteen of a fifteen part series.
Education; Religion and Philosophy
Dist - BBCENE

The Witwatersrand Basin 30 MIN
VHS / U-matic
Color
Shows detailed geological history of development of the lower Proterozoic basin and deposition of the famous gold - and uranium - bearing quartz - pebble conglomerates.
Geography - World; History - World; Science - Physical
Dist - EDMI **Prod** - EDMI 1982

Wives and Mothers 29 MIN
U-matic
Her Social Security Series
Color
Looks at the benefits available to women who are eligible under their husband's account. Discusses benefits to widows, dependent children and divorced spouses.
Sociology
Dist - UMITV **Prod** - UMITV 1977

Wives of Alcoholics 29 MIN
U-matic
Woman Series
Color
Interviews two women married to alcoholics. Tells how alcoholism nearly destroyed their marriage and how they and their husbands successfully sought help.
Health and Safety; Sociology
Dist - PBS **Prod** - WNEDTV

A Wives' Tale 73 MIN
U-matic / VHS / 16mm
Color (H C A) (FRENCH (ENGLISH SUBTITLES))
$950 purchase - 16 mm, $695 purchase - video, $125 rental
Portray wives of striking miners and how participating in a strike changed their lives. A film by Sophie Bissonnette, Martin Duckworth, and Joyce Rock.
Business and Economics; Social Science; Sociology
Dist - CNEMAG

The Wiz 134 MIN
VHS
Color (H C G)
$49.00 purchase _ #DL242
Presents the 1978 film production of The Wiz, starring Diana Ross and Michael Jackson.

Fine Arts
Dist - INSIM

A Wizard of Earthsea 15 MIN
VHS / U-matic
Best of Cover to Cover 2 Series
Color (I)
Literature and Drama
Dist - WETATV **Prod** - WETATV

The Wizard of no 19 MIN
16mm / U-matic / VHS
Color (P I)
Shows how young Billy learns after smoking a cigarette that his inability to say no to his friends stems from his self - esteem.
Psychology
Dist - CORF **Prod** - CORF

Wizard of Oz 102 MIN
VHS
Color; B&W (G)
$29.95 purchase _ #S01755
Presents the classic Frank L Baum story 'The Wizard of Oz' about Dorothy, the girl from Kansas who encounters high adventure in the land of Oz. Stars Judy Garland, Ray Bolger, Jack Haley, and Bert Lahr.
Fine Arts; Literature and Drama
Dist - UILL

Wizard of Oz 57 MIN
U-matic / VHS
Wizard of Oz Series
Color (P I)
Contains 1 videocassette.
English Language; Literature and Drama
Dist - TROLA **Prod** - TROLA 1987

Wizard of Oz Series
Wizard of Oz 57 MIN
Dist - TROLA

Wizard of the strings 27 MIN
16mm / VHS
Color (H G)
$250.00, $425.00 purchase, $55.00 rental
Profiles Roy Smeck, a former vaudeville star known as The Wizard of the Strings because of his virtuoso talents on the guitar, banjo, ukulele and Hawaiian guitar. Includes film exerpts from 1920s Warner Brothers Vitaphone shorts featuring Smeck; contemporary concert performances; interviews with fellow musicians and composers; and colorful reminiscences by Smeck of the golden age of vaudeville. Directed by Peter Friedman.
Fine Arts
Dist - CNEMAG

The Wizard of Waukesha 58 MIN
16mm
Color
LC 80-700348
Deals with jazz guitarist Les Paul's career as a musician, performer and inventor in the field of music recording.
Biography; Fine Arts
Dist - DIRECT **Prod** - STRAY 1979

The Wizard of Waukesha 59 MIN
U-matic
Color
Pays tribute to Les Paul whose development of the electric guitar and multi - track recording revolutionized popular music.
Fine Arts
Dist - FIRS **Prod** - FIRS

Wizard of Waukesha, the, Pt 1 29 MIN
16mm
Color
LC 80-700348
Deals with jazz guitarist Les Paul's career as a musician, performer and inventor in the field of music recording.
Fine Arts
Dist - DIRECT **Prod** - STRAY 1979

Wizard of Waukesha, the, Pt 2 29 MIN
16mm
Color
LC 80-700348
Deals with jazz guitarist Les Paul's career as a musician, performer and inventor in the field of music recording.
Fine Arts
Dist - DIRECT **Prod** - STRAY 1979

Wizard of Words Series
Nouns and Adjectives 9 MIN
Prepositions 10 MIN
Verbs and Adverbs 9 MIN
Dist - MGHT

The Wizard who Spat on the Floor - Thomas Alva Edison 41 MIN
U-matic / VHS / 16mm
Nova Series
Color (J)
LC 75-702225
Examines the life and work of the American inventor Thomas Alva Edison. Shows some of Edison's many technical inventions, such as the light bulb, fluoroscope and the phonograph, and traces Edison's work in his last years in which his experimentation proved to be less successful.
Biography; Science
Dist - TIMLIF **Prod** - BBCTV 1974

Wizardry with Wood 25 MIN
16mm
Color
Shows that wood is a material of great possibilities and indispensable to our existence.
Geography - World; Industrial and Technical Education
Dist - SIS **Prod** - SIS 1963

The Wizard's Son 10 MIN
U-matic / VHS / 16mm
Color
LC 81-701034
Presents an animated story about a proud and talented wizard who insists that his young son follow in his magical footsteps. Reveals that after a near disaster in which the boy turns the family pig into a rampaging colossus, the father decides to to allow his son to follow his own desires.
Fine Arts; Literature and Drama; Sociology
Dist - PHENIX **Prod** - CANEJ 1981

Wizdom Beats the Blahs 20 MIN
VHS / U-matic
Color (P)
Emphasizes the necessity of choosing a nutritious, well - balanced diet that includes a variety of foods and the importance of reading container labels to determine the nutritive value of the food.
Health and Safety; Social Science
Dist - GPN **Prod** - BCSBIT 1982

Wo Ist Meine Breiftasche 15 MIN
U-matic / VHS / 16mm
Guten Tag Series Part 9; Part 9
Color
Foreign Language
Dist - IFB **Prod** - BAYER 1968

Wo Ist Meine Brieftasche 15 MIN
U-matic / VHS / 16mm
Guten Tag Series no 9; No 9
B&W (H) (GERMAN)
LC 73-707322
A German language film. Presents an episode in which the characters employ frequently used expressions and idioms in order to teach conversational German to beginners. Stresses the correct use of the participle and infinitive at the end of a sentence, participle endings, the pronouns wer, wen and was, and the prepositions auf, mit, ohne, vor and zu.
Foreign Language
Dist - IFB **Prod** - FRGMFA 1970

Wo Spricht Man Deutsch 17 MIN
VHS / 16mm
Color (J) (GERMAN)
LC 89715797
Presents information about the geography, culture and family life in German - speaking countries.
Fine Arts; Geography - World; Guidance and Counseling; History - World
Dist - BARR

The Wobblies 89 MIN
16mm
Color (H C A)
LC 81-700107
Looks at the work of the Industrial Workers of the World, also known as the Wobblies. Interviews former members and traces the causes and effects of the union that welcomed unskilled, black, and female workers into its ranks during the early part of the century.
Business and Economics; History - United States; Sociology
Dist - FIRS **Prod** - FIRS 1981

Woburn Abbey 30 MIN
VHS
Heirs and graces series
Color (A)
PdS65 purchase
Features Lord and Lady Tavistock talking about their home and its contents and their constant program of renovation and maintenance. Examines the way the aristocracy lived in the past and live now. Features anecdotes, beautiful architecture, and objects. Lady Victoria Leatham leads the tour. Part one of a five-part series.
Fine Arts; Home Economics; Industrial and Technical Education
Dist - BBCENE

The Wodaabe 52 MIN
VHS
Disappearing world series
Color (G C)
$99.00 purchase, $19.00 rental _ #51226
Reveals that the Wodaabe are among the last nomadic tribes on Earth and follow their herds hundreds of miles across the harsh landscape of the dought - ravaged Sahel, south of the Sahara. Discloses that the Wodaabe say that their lives are shaped by joy and hardship, and though survival is difficult, they are determined to preserve their way of life. Features anthropologist Mette Bovin. Part of a series working closely with anthropologists who lived for a year or more in societies whose social structures, beliefs and practices are threatened by the expansion of technocratic civilization.
Sociology
Dist - PSU **Prod** - GRANDA 1988

Wodehouse Playhouse Series
Anselm gets his chance 30 MIN
Big business 30 MIN
The Code of the Mulliners 30 MIN
The Editor regrets 30 MIN
Feet of clay 30 MIN
The Luck of the Stiffhams 30 MIN
Mr Potter Takes a Rest Cure 30 MIN
Mulliner's Buck - U - Uppo 30 MIN
The Nodder 30 MIN
Portrait of a Disciplinarian 30 MIN
The Rise of Minna Nordstrom 30 MIN
Rodney Fails to Qualify 30 MIN
Romance at Droitwich Spa 30 MIN
The Smile that Wins 30 MIN
Strychnine in the Soup 30 MIN
Tangled Hearts 30 MIN
Trouble down at Studleigh 30 MIN
The Truth about George 30 MIN
Unpleasantness at Bludleigh Court 30 MIN
A Voice from the Past 30 MIN
Dist - TIMLIF

Woe that is in Marriage - the Wife of Bath and the Nun's Priest's Tale 45 MIN
U-matic / VHS
Survey of English Literature I Series
Color
Analyzes the marriages depicted in The Wife of Bath and The Nun's Priest's Tales.
Literature and Drama
Dist - MDCPB **Prod** - MDCPB

Woebeguf 33 MIN
16mm / VHS
Color (G)
$100.00 rental, $69.95, $199.00 purchase
Narrates a fictional comic adventure of an army colonel, Woebeguf, who is on a secret mission to lead a platoon of war resisters through Vietnam to give peace a chance as a military weapon. Comments on government duplicity. Cast features Moab, Utah community theatre. Original motion picture music score of dulcimer and guitar available on cassette for $3.00.
Fine Arts
Dist - CANCIN

Wok Before You Run 60 MIN
VHS
(H A)
$24.95 purchase _ #WW400V; $19.95 purchase _ #S00893
Illustrates the use of a wok for the preparation of many dishes.
Home Economics
Dist - CAMV **Prod** - CAMV
UILL

Wok on the Wild Side 60 MIN
VHS
(H A)
$24.95 purchase _ #WW100V; $19.95 purchase _ #S00894
Illustrates the use of the wok for the preparation of many dishes.
Home Economics
Dist - CAMV **Prod** - CAMV
UILL

The Wold shadow
16mm
Color (G)
$10.00 rental, $132.00 purchase
Says Brakhage, '...my laboriously painted vision of the god of the forest.'
Fine Arts
Dist - CANCIN **Prod** - BRAKS 1972

Wole Soyinka 50 MIN
VHS
Color (H C G)
$79.00 purchase
Features the Nobel Prize - winning writer, filmmaker, playwright, poet, teacher, novelist and political activist talking about the effect of African culture on American

society and culture, and America's response to African political and social problems. Discusses his works including his novels The Interpreters and A Season of Anomy, along with his plays and poetry.
Civics and Political Systems; History - United States; History - World; Literature and Drama
Dist - ROLAND **Prod** - INCART

Wole Soyinka - a voice of Africa 16 MIN
VHS
Nobel prize series - literature
Color (J H C)
$49.00 purchase _ #2330 - SK
Features Wole Soyinka, Nobel Prize winner, who is the first African to win a literature Laureate. Reveals that his work draws heavily from his background as a Yoruba in Nigeria. Presents excerpts from his novels and poems. Includes student notebook and teacher resource book, with additional student workbooks available at an extra charge.
Education; History - World; Literature and Drama
Dist - SUNCOM

Wolf 22 MIN
16mm / U-matic / VHS
Animals, Animals, Animals Series
Color (P I)
Explores the world of the much - maligned and unjustifiably - feared wolf and tells a new version of the story of Little Red Riding Hood. Visits a resettled pack of wolves in northern Michigan and discusses this animals' highly sophisticated communication network. Hosted by Hal Linden.
Science - Natural
Dist - MEDIAG **Prod** - ABCNEW 1977

The Wolf and the Seven Kids 10 MIN
16mm / U-matic / VHS
Color (P I)
LC 78-701194
Presents an animated folktale of a wolf who tricks seven young goats into opening their door and eats all but one. Shows how Mother Goat finds the wolf, cuts open his stomach to free the kids and fills his stomach with stones.
Literature and Drama
Dist - EBEC **Prod** - GREATT 1978

The Wolf and the Seven Little Goats 10 MIN
U-matic / VHS
Fairy Tale Series
Color (K P I)
Tells the tale of the seven little goats who are eaten by a wolf but rescued by their mother. Comes with teacher materials.
Literature and Drama
Dist - BNCHMK **Prod** - BNCHMK 1985

The Wolf and the Whitetail 26 MIN
16mm
Color
LC 79-700889
Traces the growth and development of the timber wolf and white - tailed deer. Examines their interrelationship as predator and prey.
Science - Natural
Dist - STOUFP **Prod** - STOUFP 1979

Wolf at the door 95 MIN
35mm / 16mm / VHS
Color (G) (DANISH WITH ENGLISH SUBTITLES)
$250.00, $300.00 rental
Stars Donald Sutherland as the painter Paul Gaugin in a film about the troubled life of the painter. Directed by Henning Carlsen.
Fine Arts
Dist - KINOIC

Wolf Mankowitz on Merchant of Venice 25 MIN
VHS
Shakespeare in perspective series
Color (A)
PdS45 purchase _ Unavailable in USA
Films Wolf Mankowitz and his commentary on location and includes extracts of the Shakespeare play The Merchant of Venice. Challenges many of the more traditional interpretations of Shakespeare's works. Part of a series produced between 1978 and 1985.
Literature and Drama
Dist - BBCENE

Wolf Pack 20 MIN
16mm
Color (I)
LC 76-701080
Focuses on the life cycle and social structure of a wolf pack during one year in northern Canada.
Science - Natural
Dist - NFBC **Prod** - CWSO 1976

Wolf Pack - U - Boats in the Atlantic, 1939 to 1944 60 MIN
16mm
World at War Series
Color (H C A)
LC 76-701778
History - World; Sociology
Dist - USCAN **Prod** - THAMES 1975
MEDIAG

The Wolf saga 29 MIN
U-matic / VHS
Survivors series
Color (H C)
$250.00 purchase _ #HP - 6110C
Documents the slaughter of wolves in Sweden and other places. Gives an understanding of wolves and shows why irrational fear and hatred has caused them to be hunted to near extinction. Part of a series on the issue of wildlife conservation discussing the enormity of the task of protecting wildlife and wilderness.
Science - Natural
Dist - CORF **Prod** - BBCTV 1990

Wolf Trap 28 MIN
16mm
Color (A)
LC 77-703135
Documents Wolf Trap Farm Park for the Performing Arts. Highlights performances and other recreational uses of the park.
Fine Arts; Physical Education and Recreation
Dist - USNAC **Prod** - USNPS 1975

Wolfe and Montcalm 30 MIN
16mm 29 MIN
B&W (G)
_ #106B 0157 079 ; _ #106B 0157 070
Recreates the hours before the battle of the Plains of Abraham, in 1759, and then the battle itself in which generals Wolfe and Montcalm were both fatally wounded.
Geography - World
Dist - CFLMDC **Prod** - NFBC 1957

Wolfgang Joop - Joop, Hamburg, Germany 47 MIN
VHS
Tycoons series
Color (J H G)
$225.00 purchase
Tells how east German Wolfgang Joop developed his design and perfume business to a world - wide company, selling in major world markets.
Business and Economics; Home Economics
Dist - LANDMK

Wolves 8 MIN
16mm
Color (G)
$15.00 rental
Offers a portrait of wolves which is 'a labor of respect for creatures far more noble and loving than we.' Produced by Lee Bridgers - Musiek.
Fine Arts; Science - Natural
Dist - CANCIN

Wolves 60 MIN
VHS
National Audubon Society specials series
Color; Captioned (G)
$49.95 purchase _ #NTAS - 504
Focuses on efforts to restore endangered wolf species in the lower 48 states. Features footage shot throughout the U S. Also produced by Turner Broadcasting and WETA - TV. Narrated by Robert Redford.
Science - Natural
Dist - PBS **Prod** - NAS 1988

Wolves 10 MIN
VHS
Animal profile series
Color (P I)
$59.95 purchase _ #RB8108
Studies gray wolves, largest members of the dog family, and one of the most misunderstood animals. Discusses and dispells the myths and legends surrounding wolves. Part of a series on animals which looks at examples from the mammal, snake and bird classes, filmed in their natural habitat.
Science - Natural
Dist - REVID **Prod** - REVID 1990

The Wolves 131 MIN
VHS
Color (G) (JAPANESE WITH ENGLISH SUBTITLES)
$79.95 purchase _ #VWA1070
Presents a film by the 'Sergio Leone of Japan,' Hideo Gosha, set in the late 1920s.
Fine Arts
Dist - CHTSUI

Wolves and Coyotes of the Rockies 15 MIN
16mm / U-matic / VHS
North American Species Series
Color (K P I J)
Illustrates in documentary style the story of the remaining wolves and coyotes, the wild dogs, that inhabit the last great wilderness areas in the Rockies. Cites how numerous moose and elk provide abundant food supplies for predators such as wolves. Shows a pack of wolves bringing down a moose, and how a new wolf pack is formed.
Psychology; Science - Natural
Dist - BCNFL **Prod** - KARVF 1983

Wolves and the Wolfmen 52 MIN
U-matic / VHS / 16mm
Color (K P I J)
LC 70-712023
A documentary about naturalists fighting to save the rapidly vanishing species - wolves.
Science - Natural
Dist - FI **Prod** - MGM 1971

The Wolves of Willoughby Chase 15 MIN
U-matic / VHS
Best of Cover to Cover 2 Series
Color (I)
Literature and Drama
Dist - WETATV **Prod** - WETATV

Wolves on the horizon - reengineering for survival
VHS
Color (PRO IND)
$395.00 purchase, $150.00 rental; $495.00 purchase, $95.00 rental
Reveals how PHH Fleet America and John Crane Belfab used reengineering successfully by viewing their senior management teams and employee teams in action. Shows how both companies have changed the way they work. Includes leader's discussion guide, participants' workbooks and program summary cards.
Business and Economics
Dist - BBP **Prod** - BBP 1995
FI

The Woman 20 MIN
VHS / U-matic
French Revolution - revolutionary witness series
Color (H C)
$250.00 purchase _ #HP - 5959C
Dramatizes the reminiscences of Madame Theroigne de Mericourt from her bleak madhouse cell. Tells how Theroigne, portrayed by Janet Suzman, believed in the Revolution wholeheartedly when it promised political rights to women and led crowds and organized political activist clubs. When women's hopes were abandoned by the Revolution, Theroigne savaged Robespierre for his betrayal and her brother committed her to the asylum for her own protection, where she died. Part of a four - part series on the French Revolution written by playwright Peter Barnes.
History - World; Sociology
Dist - CORF **Prod** - BBCTV 1989

A Woman 25 MIN
16mm / U-matic / VHS
Charlie Chaplin Comedy Theater Series
B&W (I)
Features Charlie Chaplin as a prospective son - in - law. Relates Charlie's desperate but unsuccessful attempt to win the favor of his girlfriend's father.
Fine Arts
Dist - FI **Prod** - MUFLM

A Woman, a Family 108 MIN
16mm
How Yukong Moved the Mountains Series
Color (J A)
LC 80-700575
Offers a personal study of life in the People's Republic of China using direct cinema techniques and dubbed conversations. Shows scenes of the daily routines of a young factory worker living in the suburbs as contrasted with scenes of bustling Peking streets. Emphasizes how the cultural revolution has positively affected living conditions, men's and women's roles and work relationships.
Geography - World; History - World; Sociology
Dist - CINPER **Prod** - CAPI 1978

Woman, a Family, a, Pt 1 27 MIN
16mm
How Yukong Moved the Mountains Series
Color (J A)
LC 80-700575
Offers a personal study of life in the People's Republic of China using direct cinema techniques and dubbed conversations. Shows scenes of the daily routines of a young factory worker living in the suburbs as contrasted with scenes of bustling Peking streets. Emphasizes how the cultural revolution has positively affected living conditions, men's and women's roles and work relationships.

History - World
Dist - CINPER Prod - CAPI 1978

Woman, a Family, a, Pt 2 27 MIN
16mm
How Yukong Moved the Mountains Series
Color (J A)
LC 80-700575
Offers a personal study of life in the People's Republic of China using direct cinema techniques and dubbed conversations. Shows scenes of the daily routines of a young factory worker living in the suburbs as contrasted with scenes of bustling Peking streets. Emphasizes how the cultural revolution has positively affected living conditions, men's and women's roles and work relationships.
History - World
Dist - CINPER **Prod** - CAPI 1978

Woman, a Family, a, Pt 3 27 MIN
16mm
How Yukong Moved the Mountains Series
Color (J A)
LC 80-700575
Offers a personal study of life in the People's Republic of China using direct cinema techniques and dubbed conversations. Shows scenes of the daily routines of a young factory worker living in the suburbs as contrasted with scenes of bustling Peking streets. Emphasizes how the cultural revolution has positively affected living conditions, men's and women's roles and work relationships.
History - World
Dist - CINPER **Prod** - CAPI 1978

Woman, a Family, a, Pt 4 27 MIN
16mm
How Yukong Moved the Mountains Series
Color (J A)
LC 80-700575
Offers a personal study of life in the People's Republic of China using direct cinema techniques and dubbed conversations. Shows scenes of the daily routines of a young factory worker living in the suburbs as contrasted with scenes of bustling Peking streets. Emphasizes how the cultural revolution has positively affected living conditions, men's and women's roles and work relationships.
History - World
Dist - CINPER **Prod** - CAPI 1978

A Woman and a woman - Kobieta i kobieta 99 MIN
VHS
Color (G A) (POLISH WITH ENGLISH SUBTITLES)
$39.95 purchase _ #V031
Examines a ten - year period in the lives of Barbara and Irena, two very dear friends. Asks if their friendship will survive the numerous professional and personal conflicts they encounter. Directed by Ryszard Bugajski.
Fine Arts; Psychology; Sociology
Dist - POLART

Woman and her symbols series
From Earth mother to love goddess 47 MIN
The Great mother Earth 49 MIN
Women Revisioning Ourselves 48 MIN
Dist - QVID

Woman and Man 52 MIN
U-matic / VHS
Human Animal Series
Color (G)
$279.00, $179.00 purchase _ #AD - 1135
Looks at the differences between women and men. Reveals that women generally have a greater response on the logical and analytical side and men on the spatial side. Considers that men are groomed to be astronauts though women have more of the traits desirable in astronauts, and that huge sports arenas are built to cheer the performance of men. Part of a series by Phil Donahue on the Human Animal.
Business and Economics; Civics and Political Systems; Physical Education and Recreation; Psychology; Science; Science - Natural; Sociology
Dist - FOTH **Prod** - FOTH

The Woman and the dress 14 MIN
VHS
B&W (G)
$40.00 purchase
Uses a script from a 1940s drama about teenage rebellion in the world of fashion and parental intervention. Mirrors the conflict in the plot with the clash of colors chosen to decorate this tale.
Fine Arts; Home Economics; Sociology
Dist - CANCIN **Prod** - KUCHAR 1980

Woman as Painter 29 MIN
Videoreel / VT2
Synergism - Profiles, People Series
Color
Examines the often overlooked feminine artist and presents a look at woman as the subject - ornament at the central field of the painter's vision. Studies in detail the American impressionists Mary Cassatt and Berthe Morisot and briefly covers a number of other artists.
Biography; Fine Arts; Sociology
Dist - PBS **Prod** - MAETEL

Woman at the Well 15 MIN
16mm
Living Bible Series
Color; B&W (I)
Jesus and the disciples go through Samaria. Jesus talks with the woman of Sychar at Jacob's well and tells her of the spiritual living water. She goes back to her village and tells the people she has found the Christ.
Religion and Philosophy
Dist - FAMF **Prod** - FAMF

A Woman called Golda 195 MIN
VHS
Color (J H C)
$89.00 purchase _ #05815 - 126
Stars Ingrid Bergman in a portrayal of Golda Meir, prime minister of Israel and major figure in the political history of Israel.
History - World
Dist - GA **Prod** - GA

A Woman called Moses 200 MIN
VHS
Color (J H C G)
$89.95 purchase _ #XE1026V
Tells the story of Harriet Ross Tubman, founder of the Underground Railroad, who led hundreds of slaves to freedom in the North before the Civil War. Reveals that during the Civil War Tubman aided the Union Army as a reconnaissance agent, mobilizing black troops against the Confederates, freeing slaves and staging raids on plantations. Later she became a leader in the women's suffrage movement with connections to many of United States' political figures.
History - United States
Dist - CAMV

Woman Candidate, Running for Office is a Victory 13 MIN
16mm
Color
LC 75-700341
Features Flora Crater being interviewed at her home where she discusses how she decided to run for the office of Lieutenant Governor of Virginia and how she set up her campaign. Follows her as she travels through the state meeting people and discussing the issues. Explains why women should become involved in politics and how to produce social change.
Biography; Civics and Political Systems; Sociology
Dist - BLURIG **Prod** - BLURIG 1974

Woman - Child 15 MIN
16mm / U-matic / VHS
Color
Looks at some of the consequences of adolescent pregnancy through the eyes of six teenagers.
Health and Safety
Dist - NFMD **Prod** - NFMD 1982

Woman demon human 108 MIN
VHS
Color (G) (CHINESE WITH ENGLISH SUBTITLES)
$45.00 purchase _ #6056C
Presents a film from the People's Republic of China.
Geography - World; Literature and Drama
Dist - CHTSUI

The Woman entrepreneur - do you have what it takes 55 MIN
VHS
Color (J H C G)
$29.95 purchase _ #UH400V
Discloses that women - owned businesses are the fastest - growing part of the small business community. Tests women on their abilities to start a business. Evaluates their feelings of independence and control and their willingness to take risks. Emphasizes the critical importance of a sound business plan. Features several successful entrepreneurs who discuss their experiences in starting their own businesses. Based on the book by Dr Robert Hisrich and Candida Brush.
Business and Economics
Dist - CAMV

Woman Facing the Mirror 17 MIN
U-matic / VHS
Color (H C A) (SPANISH (ENGLISH SUBTITLES))
$150 purchase, $30 rental
Examines Cuban National Ballet dancer Rosario Suarez's decision to have a child after considering the effect it will have on her career. Directed by Marisol Trujillo.
Sociology
Dist - CNEMAG

Woman in Green 70 MIN
16mm
B&W
Describes how Sherlock Holmes matches wits against the evil Professor Moriarity in a case that involves the deaths of several attractive girls. Stars Nigel Bruce and Basil Rathbone.
Fine Arts; Literature and Drama
Dist - NAFVC **Prod** - UNKNWN 1945

The Woman in Question 16 MIN
16mm
Color (H C A)
Describes the efforts of three communities to conduct intensive uterine cancer education and case - finding programs.
Health and Safety
Dist - AMCS **Prod** - AMCS

The Woman in Sports, Get Up, Get Out, Get Going 30 MIN
16mm / U-matic / VHS
Color (P)
Motivates women to exercise. Looks at meditation, competition, concentration, coordination and cooperation.
Physical Education and Recreation
Dist - KLEINW **Prod** - KLEINW

The Woman in Sports, Records, Rewards , Heroines 30 MIN
16mm / U-matic / VHS
Color (P)
Documents the evolution of women in sports. Shows women excelling in swimming, basketball, golf, gymnastics, skating, skiing, auto racing, tennis and softball.
Physical Education and Recreation
Dist - KLEINW **Prod** - KLEINW

The Woman in Sports, Reflections of the Champions 30 MIN
U-matic / VHS / 16mm
Color (P)
Observes special moments in the lives of great women athletes including Janet Guthrie at the racetracks and Diane Kallian at softball practice.
Physical Education and Recreation
Dist - KLEINW **Prod** - KLEINW

Woman in Sports, the, Pt 1 30 MIN
16mm
Color (I J)
LC 80-700123
Depicts a young woman who learns to improve her appearance and attitude through physical exercise.
Home Economics; Physical Education and Recreation
Dist - KLEINW **Prod** - KLEINW 1980

Woman in Sports, the, Pt 2 30 MIN
16mm
Color (I J)
LC 80-700123
Documents the activities of women participating in sports, including swimming, basketball, golf, gymnastics, skiing, skating, auto racing, tennis, softball and running. Discusses the benefits of planned physical activity.
Physical Education and Recreation
Dist - KLEINW **Prod** - KLEINW 1980

Woman in Sports, the, Pt 3 30 MIN
16mm
Color (I J)
LC 80-700123
Witnesses special moments in the lives of great women athletes, including Janet Guthrie, Micki King Hogue, Wyomia Tyus, Diane Kallian and Cathy Rigby. Emphasizes that it's never too late to begin participating in sports.
Physical Education and Recreation
Dist - KLEINW **Prod** - KLEINW 1980

Woman in the Boardroom 28 MIN
U-matic / VHS
Color (G)
$249.00, $149.00 purchase _ #AD - 1595
Establishes that sexism in the executive suite is not just an attitude but a weapon. Features Mary Walsh Cunningham, once assistant to the president of the Bendix Corporation, who exploded the myth that a smart, dedicated woman could go as far up the corporate ladder as an equally qualified man. Adapts a Phil Donahue program.
Business and Economics; Civics and Political Systems; Sociology
Dist - FOTH **Prod** - FOTH

Woman in the dunes 123 MIN
VHS
B&W (G) (JAPANESE WITH ENGLISH SUBTITLES)

$35.95 purchase _ #CVC1057
Presents The Woman in the Dunes directed by Hiroshi Teshigahara.
Fine Arts
Dist - CHTSUI

Woman in the mirror 17 MIN
16mm
Cuba - a view from inside series
Color (G)
$200.00 purchase, $40.00 rental
Profiles Cuban ballerina Rosaria Suarez through her first pregnancy - following an earlier abortion - and her return to dancing. Features part of a 17 - part series of shorts by and about Cuban women. Directed by Marisol Trujillo. Illustrated catalog available. Contact distributor for programming advice and discount package rental fees.
Fine Arts; Sociology
Dist - CNEMAG

Woman is 12 MIN
16mm / U-matic / VHS
Color
LC 74-700390
Uses a series of photographic stills in order to illustrate the history and character of the roles that women occupy in society.
Guidance and Counseling; Industrial and Technical Education; Sociology
Dist - PHENIX **Prod** - SILLU 1973

A woman named Mary 19 MIN
VHS
Color (H C G A R)
$24.95 purchase, $10.00 rental _ #4 - 85013
Focuses on the case of Mary as an example of how poverty - stricken women worldwide must cope. Shows that Mary struggles with the church and her faith in God, and is concerned for the future of all poor women.
Religion and Philosophy; Sociology
Dist - APH **Prod** - APH

The Woman next door - La Femme d'a cote 106 MIN
VHS
Color (G)
$39.95 _ #WOM040
Studies obsessive love and human frailty. Stars Fanny Ardant and Gerard Depardieu as former passionate lovers who suddenly find themselves living next door to each other. When they renew their tumultuous affair it brings tragedy for themselves and others. Produced by Les Films du Carrosse.
Fine Arts; Psychology; Religion and Philosophy
Dist - HOMVIS

A Woman of My Platoon 20 MIN
U-matic
Color (G)
$250.00, $200.00 purchase, $50.00 rental
Looks at women's military experience in Canada during World War II. Uses voice over to tell the story of a woman's dishonorable discharge in the 1950s in the first part. The second part counters the invisibility of lesbians in culture and history by looking at classic wartime footage of women. The third part focuses on a debate in Canada's Parliament over a bill that would prevent discrimination against gays in the armed forces - the bill was ultimately voted down. Produced by Marilyn Burgess.
History - United States; History - World; Sociology
Dist - WMEN **Prod** - MBUR 1989

A Woman of Principle 28 MIN
16mm / U-matic / VHS
Insight Series
B&W (H C A)
Presents the elderly widow of a once acclaimed opera star who isolates herself from other people, feeling superior and thinking she does not need them. Shows how her thinking is greatly a mistake, and how she must swallow her pride and principles, and attempt to relate once again to people.
Guidance and Counseling; Psychology
Dist - PAULST **Prod** - PAULST 1970

Woman on the Moon 115 MIN
U-matic / VHS
B&W (GERMAN)
Shows a group of people embark on a journey to the moon. Directed by Fritz Lang.
Fine Arts; Foreign Language
Dist - IHF **Prod** - IHF

Woman series 20024
Sexism in religion, another view 29 MIN
Dist - PBS

Woman series
ACT - action for children's television 29 MIN
Age is money blues 29 MIN
Alternatives to estrogen 29 MIN
Anti - women's liberation 29 MIN
The Battle for the vote, Pt 1 29 MIN
The Battle for the vote, Pt 2 29 MIN
Beyond the Beauty Myth 29 MIN
Birth Experiences 29 MIN
Breast cancer update 29 MIN
Changing Motherhood 29 MIN
Child Custody 29 MIN
Childbirth, Pt 1 29 MIN
Childbirth, Pt 2 29 MIN
Congresswoman Bella Abzug 29 MIN
Controversies within the women's movement, Pt 1 29 MIN
Controversies within the women's movement, Pt 2 29 MIN
A Conversation with Betty Friedan 29 MIN
A Conversation with Elizabeth Janeway, Pt 1 29 MIN
A Conversation with Elizabeth Janeway, Pt 2 29 MIN
A Conversation with Florynce Kennedy 29 MIN
A Conversation with Jeanne Moreau, Pt 1 29 MIN
A Conversation with Jeanne Moreau, Pt 2 29 MIN
A Conversation with Lotte Jacobi 29 MIN
A Conversation with Robin Morgan 29 MIN
Conversation with Simone De Beauvoir 60 MIN
A Conversation with Viveca Lindors 29 MIN
Cosmetic Surgery 29 MIN
The Credit - ability gap 29 MIN
Cris Williamson on women's music 29 MIN
Economics and the American woman 29 MIN
Estrogen Question, the, Pt 1 29 MIN
Estrogen Question, the, Pt 2 29 MIN
Female homosexuality 29 MIN
Feminist press 29 MIN
Florence Luscomb - suffragist 29 MIN
Food for thought 29 MIN
Household workers 29 MIN
Househusbands 29 MIN
Humor by Women 29 MIN
International Tribunals on Crimes Against Women 29 MIN
The Lady Vanishes - Where are the Women in Film 29 MIN
Legislative Report 29 MIN
Legislative Report Update 29 MIN
Lesbian Mothers and Child Custody, Pt 1 29 MIN
Lesbian Mothers and Child Custody, Pt 2 29 MIN
Margaret Sloan on Black Sisterhood 29 MIN
The Marriage Savers 29 MIN
Menopause - How to Cope 29 MIN
Men's Liberation 29 MIN
Menstruation and Premenstrual Tension 29 MIN
Mental Health Care for Women, Pt 2 29 MIN
Mister Midwife 29 MIN
Money 29 MIN
Mothers and Daughters 29 MIN
Mothers who Leave Home 29 MIN
N O W Now 29 MIN
Nora Ephron on Everything 29 MIN
Northern Irish People's Peace Movement, Pt 1 29 MIN
Northern Irish People's Peace Movement, Pt 2 29 MIN
The Northern Irish Question - Another View 29 MIN
Occupation - Mother 29 MIN
Our Bodies, Ourselves 29 MIN
The Perfect Mother - Paradox or Possibility 29 MIN
Political Parties - Women's Clout 29 MIN
Pornography 29 MIN
Pregnancy After 35 29 MIN
The Proper Place for Women in the Church 29 MIN
Puerto Rican Women's Federation 29 MIN
Sexual Suicide 29 MIN
The Single Parent Experience 29 MIN
Sisters in Crime 29 MIN
Sports - What's the Score 29 MIN
Sterilization and Consent 29 MIN
Teenage Pregnancy 29 MIN
Title IX - Fair Play in the Schools 29 MIN
Unlikely Addicts - Middle Class Women 29 MIN
Unnecessary surgery - physicians react 29 MIN
Why Women are Dissatisfied with their Gynecologists 29 MIN
Wives of Alcoholics 29 MIN
Women and Children in China 29 MIN
Women and Insurance 29 MIN
Women and Insurance - the Industry Responds 29 MIN
Women and Taxes 29 MIN
Women in Policing 29 MIN
Women, Money and Power 29 MIN
Women's Astrology 29 MIN
Women's Banks and Credit Unions 29 MIN
Women's Coalition for the Third Century 29 MIN
Women's Studies 29 MIN
Working Class Women 29 MIN
Dist - PBS

Woman Talk Series
Abortion 14 MIN
Birth control 20 MIN
Breast - feeding 17 MIN
Childbirth 17 MIN
Feminine hygiene 17 MIN
Fertility investigation 17 MIN
Menopause 19 MIN
Operative Procedures 17 MIN
Post - natal care 14 MIN
Pre - Natal Care 15 MIN
Preventive Health Care 20 MIN
Sex education 18 MIN
Your first gynecological examination 17 MIN
Dist - CORF

Woman - the Question of Self - Concept 28 MIN
16mm / U-matic / VHS
Inner Woman Series
Color (H C A)
LC 77-702982
Examines the stress imposed on women as a result of freedom of choice brought about by new social values, styles of living and sex roles. Stresses the importance of women's self - concept.
Guidance and Counseling; Psychology; Sociology
Dist - MGHT **Prod** - WXYZTV 1975

A Woman to Remember 30 MIN
16mm
B&W (J)
Depicts the story of Miriam, a vain and selfish woman who loses her wealth and social position by a trick of fate. Shows how she is forced to live in the poorest section of town and how she comes face to face with Jesus.
Religion and Philosophy
Dist - CAFM **Prod** - CAFM

Woman to Woman 48 MIN
16mm
Color
Interviews women in a variety of occupations and explores the nature of women's work. Includes an historical perspective of women's work roles through the decades.
Guidance and Counseling; Sociology
Dist - DETD **Prod** - DETD 1975

Woman to Woman 52 MIN
U-matic / VHS
Color (G)
$249.00, $149.00 purchase _ #AD - 1117
Presents a Phil Donahue program which links 200 women in Boston by satellite with 200 women in Leningrad. Tries to see if women's issues transcend political boundaries. The discussion ranges from the danger of nuclear radiation to rearing children, abortion, divorce, men's role in the home, battered women and freedom of information.
Geography - World; History - United States; History - World; Sociology
Dist - FOTH **Prod** - FOTH

A Woman waiting for her period 23 MIN
VHS
B&W/Color (G)
$50.00 rental, $225.00 purchase
Portrays the videomaker, Wei - Ssu and her close friend, and their lives as Chinese graduate students in the midwestern United States. Weaves fresh observations of US culture and values with poetic meditations, visual and verbal, on silence and displacement and the intimacy between close friends. Waiting for a menstrual period that never comes becomes a metaphor of the suspension and freedom of living in another country.
Education; Geography - United States; Guidance and Counseling; Literature and Drama; Psychology; Sociology
Dist - WMEN **Prod** - CHIEN 1993

The Woman when sacred 6 MIN
16mm
Color (G)
$15.00 rental
Pictures actress Jessie Holladay Loft nine months pregnant in naked respose.Reveals the glowing light of new life in her belly throughout the film which is Walter Gutman's ultimate statement about womanhood.
Fine Arts
Dist - CANCIN

Woman - who is Me 10 MIN
16mm
Color (H C A)
LC 78-700647
Uses animation to explore how men and women see each other and themselves.

Psychology; Sociology
Dist - SERIUS **Prod** - TRICPS 1977

Woman - who is Me? 11 MIN
U-matic / VHS
Color (C A)
Explores the persistence of myths about women and men by comparing classical mythology, biblical themes, Renaissance and 19th century art with pop art and other contemporary images.
Health and Safety; Psychology; Sociology
Dist - MMRC **Prod** - MMRC

The Woman who kept a secret 27 MIN
U-matic / VHS
Color (H C A)
$365.00, $340.00 purchase _ #V384
Documents a firsthand history of how the Atomic Age began during World War II. Interviews Dorothy McKibbin who was assistant - secretary to Robert Oppenheimer and his crew of scientists who worked on the creation of the atomic bomb.
Civics and Political Systems; History - United States; Science - Physical
Dist - BARR **Prod** - CEPRO 1987

Woman with a brush
Videodisc
Laser learning set 1 series; Set 1
Color; CAV (P I)
$375.00 purchase _ #8L5406
Chronicles the experience of Mary Cassatt, a 19th century American woman who challenged tradition and social expectations and became an artist. Illustrates her life as an artist in Europe and her work. Considers character traits. Part of a series of six theme - based interactive videodisc lessons. Requires a Pioneer LD - V2000 or 2200, with barcode reader and adapter, or a Pioneer LD - V4200 or higher. Includes user's guide, two readers.
Biography; Fine Arts; History - World
Dist - BARR **Prod** - BARR 1992

Womancock 15 MIN
16mm
B&W (A)
$20.00 rental
Superimposes images within the frame, juxtaposes pieces of the film with snips of music and talk and uses montage - collage techniques. Constructs a surreality to make a statement about women, who appear erotic and bizarre here. A Carl Linder production.
Fine Arts; Sociology
Dist - CANCIN

Womanpower - a Woman's Place is 28 MIN
16mm
Womanpower Series
Color (J)
LC 77-701391
Addresses the problem of revising rigid social patterns of sexism and promotes women's rights. Shows a Swedish family in which the wife works in heavy industry and the children attend schools teaching new ideas about roles. Encourages men to participate in child rearing with an example of the work of a male nurse.
Sociology
Dist - SF **Prod** - UN 1976

Womanpower - Equality and Development 28 MIN
16mm
Womanpower Series
Color (J)
LC 77-701387
Shows delegates to a preconference for International Women's Year, 1975, convening at the United Nations. Reports on the status of women in their respective countries, revealing remarkably similar conditions. Illustrates issues discussed by a visit to Tunisia.
Sociology
Dist - SF **Prod** - UN 1976

Womanpower Series
Womanpower - a Woman's Place is 28 MIN
Womanpower - Equality and Development 28 MIN
Womanpower - the Hidden Asset 17 MIN
Womanpower - the People's Choice 28 MIN
Dist - SF

Womanpower - the Hidden Asset 17 MIN
16mm
Womanpower Series
Color (J)
LC 77-701388
Shows why the integration of women in the national economy affects a nation's overall development. Focuses on the way in which women of Sri Lanka have attempted to change the traditional system which discounts their contribution to the national economy.
Business and Economics; Sociology
Dist - SF **Prod** - UN 1976

Womanpower - the People's Choice 28 MIN
16mm
Womanpower Series
Color (J)
LC 77-701390
Promotes equality between the sexes with an example of the struggle of three women running for election to political office in Colombia, a country where women were given the right to vote in 1957.
Civics and Political Systems; Sociology
Dist - SF **Prod** - UN 1976

Woman's fitting techniques
VHS
Color (G A)
$24.95 purchase _ #NN820V
Teaches fitting techniques for women's clothing.
Home Economics
Dist - CAMV

A Woman's guide to breast self - examination 18 MIN
VHS
Color (J H C A)
$195.00 purchase
Details how to perform a breast self examination, with emphasis on its importance to an individual's health. Discusses breast normal and abnormal anatomy and physiology. Talks about mammograms and regular checkups as part of one's regular health routine. Created by Nurse Practitioner Creations.
Health and Safety
Dist - PFP

A Woman's guide to firearms
VHS
Color (G)
$39.95 purchase _ #CMP000
Covers recreational and defensive use, safety, types of guns and ammo, shooting, noise, recoil, accuracy and the care and security of guns in the home. Features Gerald McRaney and Lee Purcell.
Physical Education and Recreation; Psychology
Dist - SIV

A Woman's heart 57 MIN
VHS
Color (G)
$149.00 purchase, $75.00 _ #UW5174
Uses animation, special photography and MRI imaging of a woman's heart. Illustrates how heart disease develops in women and discusses myths about women's immunity to heart disease. Examines sexual discrimination in the medical establishment, the physical and psychological causes of heart disease in women, new research on medication, surgery and non - invasive procedures and prevention. Joanne Woodward narrates.
Health and Safety; Sociology
Dist - FOTH

Woman's Hospital 20 MIN
VHS / U-matic
Color (J A)
Orients expectant mothers toward what they can expect from hospital staff before and during childbirth.
Health and Safety
Dist - SUTHRB **Prod** - SUTHRB

The Woman's 'how to' of self - defense 50 MIN
VHS
Color (G)
$39.95 purchase _ #SX100V
Teaches many self defense techniques to women for defending themselves from rapists, muggers, drunks and others. Shows step - by - step techniques for defending against attacks from the front, side and behind. Demonstrates how to avoid attacks in the office, at school, in the park and while jogging in simulated events. Emphasizes being assertive, aggressive and mentally prepared when resisting an attack and avoiding dangerous situations.
Physical Education and Recreation
Dist - CAMV

A Woman's Place 30 MIN
VHS / U-matic
Journey into Japan Series
Color (J S C G)
MV=$195.00
Pictures the Geishas who still reign supreme as Japan's most prestigious entertainers.
Geography - World; History - World
Dist - LANDMK **Prod** - LANDMK 1986

A Woman's Place 25 MIN
U-matic / VHS / 16mm
Color
Pays tribute to noted women of the past and points out that a woman's place is everyplace. Narrated by Julie Harris.
History - World; Sociology
Dist - CCCD **Prod** - CCCD

A Woman's place 25 MIN
VHS
Color (G)
$39.95 purchase _ #S01570
Portrays various women who have 'dared to be first' in their chosen careers. Narrated by Julie Harris. Based on a 'Life' magazine special report.
History - World; Sociology
Dist - UILL

Woman's Place 23 MIN
U-matic / VHS / 16mm
Ancient Lives Series
Color
Deals with the role of women in ancient Egypt.
Geography - World; History - World; Sociology
Dist - FOTH **Prod** - FOTH

Woman's place 8 MIN
16mm
Color (G)
$300.00 purchase, $30.00 rental _ #EPF - 757, #ERF - 757
Discusses the problems of parental sex - typing, mother - daughter generational conflict, the self - image of housewives, the role of the executive wife, and the home responsibilities of the woman who works outside of the home.
Sociology
Dist - ADL **Prod** - ADL

A Woman's place 24 MIN
VHS
Color (A PRO IND)
$795.00 purchase, $185.00 rental
Presents career and personal advice for professional women. Covers subjects including coping with conflicting feelings and demands, identifying skills to be developed, making career and personal decisions, and more.
Business and Economics; Guidance and Counseling; Sociology
Dist - VLEARN **Prod** - MELROS

Woman's Place 52 MIN
U-matic
Color (H C)
Examines the traditional role of women in American society and shows how that role is changing. Narrated by Bess Myerson.
Sociology
Dist - GA **Prod** - ABCTV

A Woman's Place is in the House 30 MIN
U-matic / VHS / 16mm
Color
LC 77-702178
Profiles Massachusetts State Representative Elaine Noble at work, in a discussion with her constituents and at home.
Biography; Civics and Political Systems; Sociology
Dist - TEXFLM **Prod** - WGBHTV 1977

A Woman's Risk 19 MIN
U-matic / VHS
Color (C)
$249.00, $149.00 purchase _ #AD - 1404
Focuses on the cancers which affect women - breast, cervical, ovarian and uterine. Presents candid interviews with three cancer survivors. Compares lumpectomy to mastectomy for treatment of breast cancer. Emphasizes the importance of early detection.
Health and Safety; Psychology; Sociology
Dist - FOTH **Prod** - FOTH

A Woman's secret 85 MIN
VHS
B&W; CC (G)
$19.95 purchase _ #6187
Stars Gloria Grahame as a singer shot by her benefactress Mareen O'Hara who was grooming the vulgar singer as her protege after O'Hara's voice gave out. Reveals that Grahame's character rebelled against attempts to turn her into a lady and singer. Features Melvyn Douglas, Bill Williams and Victor Jory. Directed by Nicholas Ray.
Fine Arts; Literature and Drama
Dist - APRESS

A Woman's Touch 20 MIN
16mm
Patterns Series
Color (J H C)
LC 77-701384
Edited from the motion picture The Battle Of The Sexes. Tells a story about the difficulties which arise when a woman with progressive business ideas tries to work with a man whose manufacturing firm is operated according to his less modern views. Focuses on the conflict between individual efficiency and the systemization of machines.
Fine Arts; Sociology
Dist - SF **Prod** - SF 1977

A Woman's Touch 23 MIN
16mm
Color
Presents Warren Sonbert's film entry selected from the 1985 Whitney Biennial Film and Video Exhibition.
Fine Arts
Dist - AFA **Prod** - AFA 1986

A Woman's Work 20 MIN
16mm
Color
LC 77-702728
Investigates the wage gap between men and women. Interviews working women, lawyers and union leaders in order to provide insight into this subject, emphasizing the problem in Canada.
Business and Economics; Sociology
Dist - CANFDC **Prod** - CANFDC 1976

Womb with a View 40 MIN
VHS / U-matic
Sherry Millner Series
Color (G)
$250.00, $200.00 purchase, $50.00 rental
Explores the social and personal contradictions of pregnancy. Confronts the idealistic societal view of the bliss of pregnancy with the discomfort, confusion and delight of actual pregnancy.
Fine Arts; Health and Safety; Religion and Philosophy; Sociology
Dist - WMEN **Prod** - SHEMIL 1986

Wombats 25 MIN
U-matic
Animal Wonder Down Under Series
Color (I J H)
Shows the wombat, one of Australia's most popular animals.
Geography - World; Science - Natural
Dist - CEPRO **Prod** - CEPRO

Women 13 MIN
VHS / 16mm
Color (G)
$20.00 rental, $25.00 purchase
Comments on the cliches imposed upon women. Produced by Coni Beeson.
Fine Arts; Sociology
Dist - CANCIN

Women 28 MIN
U-matic
Are you listening series
Color (I)
LC 80-707155
Presents a group of women describing their common concerns and the changes that will advance the cause of women's equality. Stresses the need to avoid stereotypical roles for women or men.
Sociology
Dist - STURTM **Prod** - STURTM 1971

Women 13 MIN
U-matic / VHS
Color (C A)
Shows women naked, dressed, laughing, crying, contemporary, ancient, passive. Deals with women's feelings about other women.
Sociology
Dist - MMRC **Prod** - NATSF

Women Abuse - Alcohol and Other Drug Abuse Connections 30 MIN
U-matic / VHS
Color
Explores the relationship between chemical abuse and the continuing cycles of abuse by a review of the research and a discussion of the dynamics that work to maintain the destructive patterns.
Health and Safety; Sociology
Dist - UWISC **Prod** - DACABW 1982

Women Against Women 28 MIN
U-matic / VHS
Color (G)
$249.00, $149.00 purchase _ #AD - 2119
Discusses how women interact with women in the workplace. Asks if they nurture one another or if they compete in the same manner as men do. Considers the portrayal of women as sneaky back - biters to other women and whether the actual trouble comes from men who have problems with women in power. Adapts a Phil Donahue program.
Business and Economics; Civics and Political Systems; Sociology
Dist - FOTH **Prod** - FOTH

Women and AIDS 28 MIN
VHS
Color (H C PRO T A)
$20.00 purchase _ #440 - V8
Targets AIDS health service providers, presenting compelling reasons for developing and expanding AIDS programs directed at women. Discusses how sexism, racism, poverty, and the lack of women's health care aggravate the epidemic for women.
Guidance and Counseling; Health and Safety; Sociology
Dist - ETRASS **Prod** - ETRASS

Women and AIDS - a survival kit 22 MIN
VHS
Color (J H C G) (SPANISH)
$195.00 purchase, $35.00 rental _ #37794
Raises awareness and provides information about the risk of the AIDS epidemic to heterosexual women. Furnishes essential information about at - risk behavior, modes of virus transmission - including perinatal transmission, and prevention guidelines while exploring the psycho - social and emotional aspects of the disease. Combines vignettes illustrating effective communications regarding safer sex and the use of condoms, and commentary by female health professionals and women with AIDS. Covers all issues in a multiethnic, multiracial context. Produced by Terry Looper, University of California, San Francisco.
Health and Safety; Social Science; Sociology
Dist - UCEMC

Women and Alcohol - through the Drinking Glass 28 MIN
16mm
Color (H C A)
LC 80-700043
Focuses on the lives of four recovering alcoholic women, contrasting their drinking habits with those of a group of teenagers who still find drinking fun. Probes the social and psychological factors which affect women's use of and dependence on alcohol. Narrated by Carol Burnett.
Health and Safety; Psychology; Sociology
Dist - FMSP **Prod** - FMSP 1979

Women and Art 25 MIN
16mm / U-matic / VHS
Ways of Seeing Series
Color (H C A)
LC 77-701960
Presents art critic John Berger, who discusses whether paintings and media celebrate or exploit women.
Fine Arts
Dist - FI **Prod** - BBCTV 1974

Women and children at large 7 MIN
16mm
Color (G)
$15.00 rental
Celebrates women, life and film by presenting rapid images from a mythic kingdom where the message of liberation is implicit. Features a musical soundtrack but no dialog. Produced by Freude.
Fine Arts; Sociology
Dist - CANCIN

Women and Children in China 29 MIN
U-matic
Woman Series
Color
Describes the Chinese law, passed after the 1949 revolution, which made husbands and wives equal, abolished arranged marriages, and permitted women to divorce.
Geography - World; Sociology
Dist - PBS **Prod** - WNEDTV

Women and Children - Pt 3 20 MIN
VHS
Greeks Series
Color (I)
$79.00 purchase _ #825 - 9384
Retells some of the great stories of the world and explores one of civilization's richest heritages at an elementary school level. Covers a variety of subjects, including language arts, math, crafts, history, drama and science. Part 3 of four parts takes a fascinating look at domestic life, living standards, and the role of women in ancient Greece. Also begins the story of the Golden Fleece.
Guidance and Counseling; History - World; Sociology
Dist - FI **Prod** - BBCTV 1987

Women and Corporations - Breaking in 30 MIN
VHS / 16mm
(PRO G)
$89.95 purchase _ #DGP10
Examines whether getting into corporate America is any different for a woman than a man. Features Professor Alma Barron, an expert on women in management. Hosted by Dick Goldberg.
Business and Economics; Sociology
Dist - RMIBHF **Prod** - RMIBHF

Women and Corporations - Moving Up 30 MIN
VHS / 16mm
(PRO G)
$89.95 purchase _ #DGP11
Discusses what a woman should and must do after she lands her job in order to reach the boardroom. Features Professor Alma Barron, and expert on women in management. Hosted by Dick Goldberg.
Business and Economics; Sociology
Dist - RMIBHF **Prod** - RMIBHF

Women and Creativity 29 MIN
U-matic / VHS
Creativity with Bill Moyers Series
Color (H C A)
Presents Bill Moyers interviewing three women about the choices between a life of creativity and raising a family. Features artist Judy Chicago, Bernie Lasseau, a rural artist, and best - selling novelist Mary Gordon.
Fine Arts; Literature and Drama; Psychology; Sociology
Dist - PBS **Prod** - CORPEL 1982

Women and Creativity 30 MIN
U-matic / VHS
Creativity with Bill Moyers Series
Color
Fine Arts; Literature and Drama; Psychology
Dist - DELTAK **Prod** - PBS

Women and disease 30 MIN
VHS
Color (G)
$149.00 purchase, $75.00 rental _ #UW3042
Asks if women experience heart disease differently from men. Questions why women have a higher rate of reported depression, if treatments developed exclusively from research on men work for women. Examines the lack of medical research conducted on women and the resulting diminished effectiveness of treatments in the areas of heart disease, depression and alcoholism.
Health and Safety; Sociology
Dist - FOTH

Women and Insurance 29 MIN
U-matic
Woman Series
Color
Discusses sex discrimination in insurance.
Business and Economics; Sociology
Dist - PBS **Prod** - WNEDTV

Women and Insurance - the Industry Responds 29 MIN
U-matic
Woman Series
Color
Features representatives of the insurance industry answering charges of discrimination against women.
Business and Economics; Sociology
Dist - PBS **Prod** - WNEDTV

Women and leadership series
Focuses on issues of interest to working women. Offers practical strategies and skills to help women reach their personal and professional goals. Shows how sucessful women leaders handle difficult people and presents ways to stand one's ground in a conflict - without guilt. Offers the principles of win - win negotiating and strategies for using women's natural negotiating skills and looks at the 'laws of motivation' and examines the reasons why women are excellent natural motivators. Each program 40 minutes in length.
Give and take - the fine art of negotiating 40 MIN
It takes all kinds 40 MIN
The Leadership challenge - motivating a winning team 40 MIN
Shooting straight - guilt - free assertiveness 40 MIN
Dist - CAMV

Women and Minorities 30 MIN
VHS / 16mm
Government by Consent - a National Perspective Series
Color (I J H C A)
Describes how women and minorities historically have been denied their civil rights and traces the constitutional, legislative and judicial remedies for these denials. Describes how the issues of equality have changed to reflect present day problems.
Civics and Political Systems; Sociology
Dist - DALCCD **Prod** - DALCCD 1990

Women and Money 28 MIN
U-matic / VHS
Color (G)
$249.00, $149.00 purchase _ #AD - 1582
Shows that women's money - managing skills have not kept pace with their incomes. Offers advice from an investment counselor, an attorney and a psychologist. Adapts a Phil Donahue program.
Business and Economics; Sociology
Dist - FOTH **Prod** - FOTH

Women and money - things your mother never told you about finances 60 MIN
VHS
Color (G)
$29.95 purchase _ #BC06
Helps women plan a financial future. Discusses organizing important papers, budgeting by categories, retirement income, investments, insurance and choosing a financial counselor. Produced by the National Center for Women and Retirement Research.
Business and Economics
Dist - SVIP

Women and Negotiation - four strategies for success 25 MIN
VHS
Color (IND PRO)
$595.00 purchase, $195.00 rental _ #HAW01
Demystifies the process of negotiating in the workplace through interviews with a television executive, an attorney, a partner in a venture capital firm and a former labor negotiator. Presents Dr Deborah Kolb as the interviewer.
Business and Economics; Social Science; Sociology
Dist - EXTR **Prod** - EXTR

Women and Power in the Nuclear Age 30 MIN
U-matic / VHS
Color
Features Dr Helen Caldicott, a leading figure in the anti - nuclear movement, discussing grassroots tactics for anti - nuclear activity. Recalls her early reactions to the potential horrors of nuclear warfare and her long - term committment to fighting nuclear war technology.
Sociology
Dist - WMENIF **Prod** - HIHOPE

Women and self - care video
VHS
Health care consumerism system series
Color (G)
$179.00 purchase _ #WMV09
Explodes common - and costly - myths regarding women's health issues. Offers step - by - step guidance for breast self - exam and much more. Part of a ten - part series.
Home Economics; Sociology
Dist - GPERFO **Prod** - GPERFO

Women and Sexuality - a Century of Change 36 MIN
16mm
Color (A)
LC 83-700505
Uses selected art reproductions and four unusually articulate and astute modern professional women to express the current state of feminine sexuality.
Sociology
Dist - ALTANA **Prod** - KLUGDP 1983

Women and Society 26 MIN
16mm / U-matic / VHS
Today's History Series
Color (H C)
Explores the true picture of women in history, and looks at social history, including women in everyday life. Shows film clips of unconscious female stereotyping.
History - United States; History - World; Sociology
Dist - JOU **Prod** - JOU 1984

Women and Sports - Basketball 11 MIN
16mm
Color
LC 78-701411
Features highlights from a women's basketball tournament and interviews with players and coaches.
Physical Education and Recreation
Dist - COCA **Prod** - COCA 1977

Women and Sports - Gymnastics 15 MIN
16mm
Color
LC 77-702179
Shows performances in a national women's gymnastics competition. Presents training sessions, comments from coaches and slow - motion scenes of performances.
Physical Education and Recreation
Dist - COCA **Prod** - COCA 1977

Women and Sports - Volleyball 13 MIN
16mm
Color
LC 78-701412
Combines highlights from the National Invitational Volleyball Tournament, practice sessions with the University of Southern California volleyball team, and tips from top players to give a comprehensive view of collegiate women's volleyball.
Physical Education and Recreation
Dist - COCA **Prod** - COCA 1978

Women and Stress 28 MIN
U-matic / VHS
Color (G)
$249.00, $149.00 purchase _ #AD - 1248
Reveals that women experience stress just as men do, but are conditioned by society to conceal their stress reactions. Features Phil Donahue, Dr Georgia Witkin - Laniol, author of 'The Female Stress Syndrome,' and women of various age groups.
Psychology; Sociology
Dist - FOTH **Prod** - FOTH

Women and Taxes 29 MIN
U-matic
Woman Series
Color
Explains changes in federal tax laws that have made tax credits available for child care expenses. Discusses the differences that filing status can make in the amount of due tax and looks at changes in estate laws.
Business and Economics; Sociology
Dist - PBS **Prod** - WNEDTV

Women and the American family 25 MIN
VHS
American foundations - wilderness to world power series
Color (J H C G)
$59.95 purchase _ #BU907V
Recounts the struggle of American women for more control over their lives and destinies and the welfare of their families. Part of a seven - part series on American history.
History - United States; Sociology
Dist - CAMV

Women and the Corporate Game 21 MIN
U-matic / VHS
Color (G)
$249.00, $149.00 purchase _ #AD - 1531
Reveals that women are not only denied equal pay for equal work but are denied the opportunity to show what they can do and blocked by the clubhouse mentality of their male colleagues. Shows that the solution chosen by a growing number of woman executives is to start their own business.
Business and Economics; Civics and Political Systems; Sociology
Dist - FOTH **Prod** - FOTH

Women and the dilemma of difference 60 MIN
VHS
Europe and America in the modern age - 1776 to the present series
Color (H C PRO)
$95.00 purchase
Presents a lecture by David M Kennedy. Focuses on a critical period in European and American history and on leaders of the time. Part of a 20 - part series that looks at the last two centuries in Europe and America. Series presents lectures by David M Kennedy and James Sheehan of Stanford University on such figures as Adam Smith, Marx, Lincoln, Washington, Jefferson, Freud, Margaret Sanger, Susan B Anthony and Jane Adams and their impact on the events of their day. For history resource material and continuing education courses.
Civics and Political Systems; History - United States; History - World; Sociology
Dist - LANDMK

Women and Unions 25 MIN
VHS
Keeping the Home Fires Burning - Women, War, Work and Unions in 'British Columbia Series
Color (G)
$350.00 purchase, $75.00, $60.00 rental
Depicts the role of women in the rapidly growing trade unions of British Columbia during the 1940s. Presented by Sara Diamond.
Business and Economics; Geography - World; Sociology
Dist - WMENIF **Prod** - WMENIF 1988

Women and Weight Loss 28 MIN
U-matic / VHS
Color (C)
$249.00, $149.00 purchase _ #AD - 1254
Examines the differences between the psychological and the physiological problems of being overweight - from a woman's viewpoint. Features Phil Donahue who is joined by Eda Le Shan, author of 'Winning The Losing Battle.'.
Health and Safety; Physical Education and Recreation; Psychology; Social Science; Sociology
Dist - FOTH **Prod** - FOTH

Women and Work 29 MIN
VHS
Keeping the Home Fires Burning - Women, War, Work and Unions in 'British Columbia Series
Color (G)
$350.00 purchase, $75.00, $60.00 rental
Highlights women in nontraditional trades such as aircraft, shipbuilding and wood industries in British Columbia. Presented by Sara Diamond.
Business and Economics; Geography - World; Sociology
Dist - WMENIF **Prod** - WMENIF 1988

Women and Work - Paid and Unpaid 60 MIN
U-matic
Perspectives on Women
Color (A)
Focuses on women in the economy, women and physical well being and how men and women are working to improve women's status in society.
Sociology
Dist - ACCESS **Prod** - ACCESS 1986

Women at arms series
As deadly as the male 50 MIN
Catch 36 - 24 - 36 50 MIN
The Irresistable Force 50 MIN
Dist - FI

Women at risk 56 MIN
VHS
Color (H C G)
$445.00 purchase, $75.00 rental
Reveals that of the 15 million refugees scattered around the world, the majority are women and young girls. Portrays three such refugees - Mai - Lien, a 13 - year - old Vietnamese, who traveled with her 10 - year - old brother to a camp in Malaysia where she is tragically vulnerable; 40 - year - old Pheria, mother of four, living in a camp in Zambia; Juana in Costa Rica, 28, mother of three and pregnant, denied entrance to a more welcoming country. Produced by the Societe de Radio - Television du Quebec.
History - World; Sociology
Dist - FLMLIB

Women at war 45 MIN
VHS
V for victory series
B&W (J H G)
$14.95 purchase _ #ATL331
Examines the role of women during World War II. Presents part of a six - part series featuring select newsreels that depict the leaders, soldiers and battles of World War II. Narrated by Eric Severeid and Edwin Newman.
History - United States; Sociology
Dist - KNOWUN

Women at war - Vietnam - exposure to Agent Orange 30 MIN
U-matic / VHS
Color (G PRO)
#LSTF73
Documents the devastating health effects suffered by women who served in Vietnam and were exposed to Agent Orange. Addresses the scientific, psychological, social and political aspects of the Agent Orange issue. Contact distributor for information about broadcast and distribution rights. Produced by Nancy August Strakosch.
Health and Safety; History - United States
Dist - FEDU

Women at Work 35 MIN
U-matic
Color (A)
LC 80-706692
Discusses the role conflicts of women in business. Emphasizes voluntarism and involvement rather than challenging men employees.
Sociology
Dist - CSULA **Prod** - CSULA 1980

Women at Work - Employment Discrimination 30 MIN
U-matic
B&W
Examines employment discrimination against women in both traditional and non - traditional jobs. Focuses on legal remedies for such discrimination, the comparable value of jobs, employment opportunities for women in skilled trades and affirmative action groups.
Business and Economics; Sociology
Dist - WMENIF **Prod** - SEAFEM

Women Behind Bars 50 MIN
VHS
Color (S)
$79.00 purchase _ #322 - 9302
Examines the attitudes and life - styles of women in America's maximum security prisons. Reveals that although only five percent of the total prison population is female, the number of female inmates has tripled in the last ten years. Features correspondent Maria Shriver who talks to several inmates about their unique problems, rarely perceived by society at large.
Civics and Political Systems; Sociology
Dist - FI **Prod** - NBCNEW 1988

Women, Birth Control and Nutrition 15 MIN
U-matic / VHS / 16mm
Color (H C A)
Discusses the fact that certain birth control methods deplete the female body of vitamins it needs and what women can do about it.
Health and Safety; Social Science; Sociology
Dist - PEREN **Prod** - CINIMA

Women business owners 28 MIN
U-matic
Are you listening series
Color (J)
LC 80-707156
Features a group of women entrepreneurs talking about the rewards of a business career, as well as the motivations, doubts, guilts and surprises they found along the way.
Business and Economics; Sociology
Dist - STURTM **Prod** - STURTM 1977

Women by women 60 MIN
VHS
Color (G)
$35.00 purchase
Features an exhibit of Hispanic artists portraying woman as healer, mother, sister, abuelita, indigena and worker curated by Amalia Mesa Bains and Maria Pineda at San Francisco's Galeria de la Raza. Interviews Judith Baca, Carmen Lomas Garza, Lorraine Garcia, Rita Chavez and others, who explain how each has evolved an individual voice while paying homage to a common cultural heritage.
Fine Arts; Sociology
Dist - CANCIN **Prod** - SHEREL

Women Candidates 35 MIN
U-matic / VHS
Interview - EEO Compliance Series Pt 1; Pt 1
Color (A)
Focuses on avoiding illegal questions while interviewing women candidates for a job.
Business and Economics; Civics and Political Systems; Psychology; Sociology
Dist - XICOM **Prod** - XICOM

Women, Children and War 12 MIN
16mm
Color
Examines the impact of the Yom Kippur War on the women and children of Israel.
History - World; Sociology
Dist - ALDEN **Prod** - UJA

Women - coming out of the shadows 27 MIN
VHS
Color (G)
$195.00 purchase, $100.00 rental _ #CE - 084
Estimates that 6 million American women are alcoholics. Reveals that these women are grandmothers, teenagers, housewives, professional women, poor women, rich women, women from every religion and race. Features Mariette Hartley, a recovering alcoholic, as narrator, with ten women who share their personal stories of addiction and recovery. Produced by Elyse A Williams.
Guidance and Counseling; Health and Safety; Psychology
Dist - FANPRO

Women Composers 30 MIN
U-matic
Color
Presents classical women composers from the middle ages to modern times, and the social barriers which have prevented women from devoting their time to musical pursuits. Includes examples of modern women composers.
Fine Arts; Sociology
Dist - WMENIF **Prod** - WMENIF

Women do know about mechanics 14 MIN
VHS / U-matic
En Francais series
Color (H C A)
Involves a housewife whose car and vacuum cleaner break down and a woman engineer at the Center of Nuclear Studies at Saday.
Foreign Language; Geography - World
Dist - AITECH **Prod** - MOFAFR 1970

Women, Drugs and Alcohol 21 MIN
16mm / U-matic / VHS
Color (A)
LC 80-701277
Looks at the use of alcohol and prescription drugs among women. Narrated by Jessica Walter.
Health and Safety; Psychology; Sociology
Dist - CORF **Prod** - MITCHG 1980

Women, drugs and the unborn child 54 MIN
VHS
Women, drugs and the unborn child series
Color (C A)
$425.00 purchase
Presents a two - part series focusing on the dangers of a pregnant woman's drinking and drug use to the unborn fetus. Combines two videos on one videocassette.
Guidance and Counseling; Health and Safety; Psychology
Dist - PFP **Prod** - FOCPOI

Women, drugs and the unborn child series
Innocent addicts 27 MIN
Treating the chemically dependent woman and her child 27 MIN
Women, drugs and the unborn child 54 MIN
Dist - PFP

Women for America, for the World 29 MIN
U-matic / VHS
Color (J H C A)
Examines women's opinions on national security. Discusses the view that children are an important resource to be protected and nurtured. A Viviene Werdon - Roe film.
Civics and Political Systems; Sociology
Dist - CWS
EFVP

Women generals of the Yang family 135 MIN
VHS
Color (G) (CHINESE)
$45.00 purchase _ #2001C
Presents a film from the People's Republic of China.
Fine Arts; Geography - World; Literature and Drama
Dist - CHTSUI

The Women Get the Vote 27 MIN
U-matic / VHS / 16mm
Twentieth Century Series
B&W (J H C)
Traces the campaign of the suffragettes from the meeting in Seneca Falls to discuss the rights of women to the passage of the Susan B Anthony amendment to the Constitution in 1919.
Civics and Political Systems; History - United States; Social Science; Sociology
Dist - MGHT **Prod** - CBSTV 1962

Women Gold Medalists 50 MIN
16mm / U-matic
Olympiad Series
Color; Mono (J H C A)
$650.00 film, $350.00 video, $50.00 rental
Profiles the women gold medalists in Olympic history highlighting the most dramatic victories.
Physical Education and Recreation
Dist - CTV **Prod** - CTV 1976

Women Gold Medalists, Pt 1 25 MIN
16mm / VHS / BETA
Color
LC 77-702545
Presents a television special from the CTV program Olympiad which gives tribute to women athletes who gained fame in various Olympic competitions for their winning performances.
Physical Education and Recreation
Dist - CTV **Prod** - CTV 1976

Women Gold Medalists, Pt 2 25 MIN
BETA / 16mm / VHS
Color
LC 77-702545
Presents a television special from the CTV program Olympiad which gives tribute to women athletes who gained fame in various Olympic competitions for their winning performances.
Physical Education and Recreation
Dist - CTV **Prod** - CTV 1976

Women, HIV and AIDS 52 MIN
VHS
Color (H C G)
$445.00 purchase, $75.00 rental
Grapples with the special problems of women in the AIDS epidemic - lack of medical care, improper diagnosis, lack of power and control in sexual relationships with men. Discusses safe sex for straight and lesbian women, health care for HIV positive women and advocacy efforts. Produced by Hummingbird Films.
Health and Safety; Sociology
Dist - FLMLIB **Prod** - CFTV 1992

Women I Love
VHS / 16mm
Films of Barbara Hammer Series
Color (G)
$500.00 purchase, $65.00 rental
Features a collective portrayal of four of the lesbian lovers of Barbara Hammer. Produced by Barbara Hammer.
Fine Arts; Health and Safety; Psychology; Sociology
Dist - WMEN

Women in a Changing World 48 MIN
16mm
Color
Presents women from Bolivia, Afghanistan, northern Kenya and the China Coast who express their concern over fundamental rights and human dignity.
Geography - World; Sociology
Dist - WHEELK **Prod** - AUFS

Women in America 30 MIN
U-matic / VHS
America - the second century series
LC 79-700852
Introduces several aspects of the change in status of women since the founding of the People's Republic Of China. Focuses on changing work roles of both men and women, child care as it supports these roles and the use of education to transform ideas.
Geography - World; Sociology
Dist - EDC **Prod** - OPEN 1978

Women in Communications 15 MIN
16mm / U-matic / VHS
Color (J H C)
LC 75-702541
Features three women discussing how they entered their professions, what special problems a woman has in each field and how each job relates to the other.
Guidance and Counseling; Sociology
Dist - PHENIX **Prod** - PHENIX 1975

Women in construction 15 MIN
VHS
Color (J H C G)
$95.00 purchase _ #4206
Features five women - a carpenter, architect, sheetmetal worker and plumbing and electrical apprentices - telling about their work. Presents both the challenges and rewards of working in construction.
Business and Economics; Guidance and Counseling; Sociology
Dist - NEWCAR

Women in construction 15 MIN
Cassette / VHS
Color (P I J H G)
$95.00, $12.00 purchase, $40.00 rental _ #HOW - 13
Interviews five women - a carpenter, sheetmetal worker, architect and plumbing and electrical apprentices - who tell of the challenges and satisfactions of their work in their own words. Features carpenter Carol Arness and architect Pamela K LaRlue who encourage women and girls to study as much mathematics as they can and not to be intimidated by feelings of inadequacy.
Guidance and Counseling; Mathematics; Sociology
Dist - HEROWN **Prod** - HEROWN

Women in engineering 25 MIN
VHS
Career encounters series
Color (J H C A)
$95.00 purchase _ #MG3413V-J; $89.00 purchase _ #4260
Presents a documentary-style program that explores a career in engineering for women. Features professionals at work, explaining what they do and how they got where they are. Emphasizes diversity of occupational opportunities and of women in the field. Offers information about new developments and technologies and about educational and certification requirements for entering the profession. One of a series of videos about professions available individually or as a set.
Business and Economics; Guidance and Counseling; Industrial and Technical Education
Dist - CAMV
NEWCAR

Women in History 145 MIN
U-matic
University of the Air Series
Color (J H C A)
$750.00 purchase, $250.00 rental
Surveys the role of women from Greek and Roman times to the 20th century. Program contains five cassettes 29 minutes each.
History - World; Sociology
Dist - CTV **Prod** - CTV 1976

Women in Management 30 MIN
16mm / VHS
#107585 - 2 3/4
Examines how the increasing number of women in management positions in affecting several different organizations, and explores how the leaders of those organizations are dealing with the situation.
Business and Economics
Dist - MGHT

Women in management 28 MIN
16mm
Are you listening series
Color (J)
LC 80-701129
Features women in high level management positions and asks how it feels to be both a woman and a manager.
Business and Economics; Sociology
Dist - STURTM **Prod** - STURTM 1974

Women in Management - Threat or Opportunity 30 MIN
U-matic / VHS / 16mm
Color (H C A)
Examines the effects of the women's liberation movement on several different organizations and shows the many ways leaders are dealing with these effects.

Business and Economics; Sociology
Dist - CRMP **Prod** - CRMP 1975

Women in Management - Threat or Opportunity 30 MIN
U-matic / VHS / 16mm
Behavior in Business Film Series
Color (H C A) (SPANISH)
Examines the stereotypes commonly associated with women in business. Shows how a program at Weyerhaeuser Lumber Company has helped men and women deal with the new relationships caused by Affirmative Action programs and the new role for women.
Sociology
Dist - CRMP **Prod** - CRMP 1975

Women in Management - Threat or Opportunity 29 MIN
U-matic / VHS / 16mm
Beahvior in Business Film Series
Color (H C A)
LC 75-700173
Examines the stereotypes commonly associated with women in business. Shows how a program at Weyerhaeuser Lumber Company has helped men and women deal with the new relationships caused by Affirmative Action programs and the new role for women.
Sociology
Dist - CRMP **Prod** - CRMP 1975

Women in medicine 28 MIN
VHS
Color (G)
$149.00 purchase, $75.00 rental _ #UW4230
Looks at the lives of women in today's medicine. Talks to both male and female physicians and educators about the impact of women doctors on the world of medical care and research.
Guidance and Counseling; Health and Safety
Dist - FOTH

Women in Medicine, Goals for Today and Tomorrow 50 MIN
U-matic
B&W
Highlights a regional conference on women in medicine sponsored by the Women's Medical Association of New York City. Addresses the problems encountered by women both in the health professions and as consumers of health services.
Health and Safety; Sociology
Dist - WMEN **Prod** - WMANY

Women in Men's Sports 28 MIN
U-matic / VHS
Color (C)
$249.00, $149.00 purchase _ #AD - 1167
Features Beth Balsley who won access to playing on her high school's football team in court only to be cut from the team because she wasn't good enough. Includes Dorothy Harris from the Women's Sports Foundation and Dr Vern Seefeldt from Youth Sport at Michigan State University. Discusses the psychological and physiological needs and abilities of women in the sports arena. A Phil Donahue show.
Business and Economics; Physical Education and Recreation; Sociology
Dist - FOTH **Prod** - FOTH

Women in middle management 28 MIN
16mm
Are you listening series
Color (J)
LC 80-701128
Examines how women rise to middle management positions from often menial positions. Discusses some women's fear of 'coming up from the ranks.'.
Business and Economics; Sociology
Dist - STURTM **Prod** - STURTM 1974

Women in Policing 29 MIN
U-matic
Woman Series
Color
Focuses on the dramatic increase in policewomen and discusses the problems women still face in entering police careers.
Civics and Political Systems; Sociology
Dist - PBS **Prod** - WNEDTV

Women in politics series
Presents a six - part series of documentaries about women politicians. Profiles six women who run the gamut of political involvement. Raises important questions about women and power and what it means to enter the world of male - dominated political institutions. Each part focuses on one politician and includes Benazir Bhutto, Prime Minister of Pakistan; Corazon Aquino of the Philippines; Tatyana Zaslavskaya, an advisor to Gorbachov; Dame Mary Eugenia Charles, Prime Minister of the Commonwealth of Dominica; Simone Veil, a plitician in France and advocate of abortion; and Dr Gudrun Agnarsdottir, a member of the Icelandic parliament. Series by Lowri Gwilym.

Benazir Bhutto 40 MIN
Corazon Aquino 40 MIN
Dame Mary Eugenia Charles 40 MIN
Gudrun Agnarsdottir 40 MIN
Simone Veil 40 MIN
Tatyana Zaslavskaya 40 MIN
Dist - WMEN

Women in Prison 54 MIN
16mm / U-matic / VHS
Color (H C A)
LC 74-703513
Examines the condition of women in prisons. Shows how women are often treated brutally in prison and explores plans which put women offenders under community surveillance rather than behind bars.
Sociology
Dist - CAROUF **Prod** - ABCNEW 1974

Women in Science 35 MIN
U-matic / Kit / 35mm strip / VHS
Time, Space and Spirit
Color (J H)
$82 two color sound filmstrips _ #C537 - 81124 - 9N, $129 one
Presents an account of women in science. The first part covers the history of women in the sciences. The second part assesses the problems and prospects women interested in careers in science can expect today.
Guidance and Counseling; Science; Sociology
Dist - RH

Women in science 33 MIN
VHS
Color; CC (I J H C)
$129.00 purchase _ #605
Shows why women did not play major roles in science in the past because of sexism and how the feminist struggle for women's equality has brought the great increase in women's numbers in the scientific professions. Traces the history of women in science in Part 1, including sections on Marie Anne Lavoisier, Maria Mitchell, Caroline Herschel, Rosalind Franklin and Marie Curie. The segments featuring Curie were shot in her office and laboratory in Paris with the cooperation of the Curie Institute. Part 2 interviews women on the frontiers of science today - chemical engineer Regina Murphy; biochemist Carol Baker; nurse - midwife Kate Dykema; physicist and astronaut Sally Ride; computer technician Emma Earl; microbiologist Brenda Faison. Includes guide.
Science; Sociology
Dist - HAWHIL **Prod** - HAWHIL 1994

Women in science 26 MIN
VHS
Color (J H)
$130.00 purchase _ #A5VH 1016
Traces the history of women in science. Focuses on the increasing number of women entering the traditionally male fields of science and technology. Interviews women on the frontiers of science, including chemical engineer Regina Murphy, ecologist Frances Sharples and physicist and astronaut Sally Ride.
Guidance and Counseling; Science; Sociology
Dist - CLRVUE **Prod** - CLRVUE 1992

Women in science series
Biomedical fields - careers for women 30 MIN
Chemistry - careers for women 30 MIN
Computer Science - Careers for Women 30 MIN
Dentistry - careers for women 30 MIN
Engineering - careers for women 30 MIN
Geosciences - Careers for Women 30 MIN
Physics and Astronomy - Careers for Women 30 MIN
Scientific careers for women - doors to the future 30 MIN
Dist - AITECH

Women in Sports 27 MIN
16mm
Color
LC 81-700564
Tells about women competing in a wide variety of sports where they had never been welcome before. Captures their joy, not necessarily in winning, but in competing, and dispels the myths about what women could not and should not do in athletics.
Physical Education and Recreation; Sociology
Dist - MTP **Prod** - SEARS 1980

Women in Sports 26 MIN
16mm / VHS / U-matic
Sports in America Series
Color (J)
LC 81-700305
Reviews the history of women in sports and examines the status of women athletes and women's athletics. Narrated by James Michener.
Physical Education and Recreation
Dist - PFP **Prod** - EMLEN 1980

Women in Sports - an Informal History 28 MIN
16mm
Color
LC 77-700445
Surveys the participation of women in sports from classical time to the 1970's. Discusses the prejudice against physically active women, the growing awareness of women's rights as sports particpants and the new enthusiasm of women for sports.
Physical Education and Recreation; Sociology
Dist - ALTANA **Prod** - KLUGDP 1976

Women in sports and adventure 60 MIN
VHS
Women of the world series
Color (G)
$59.95 purchase _ #WWRL - 105
Profiles women who have succeeded in sports or careers that have traditionally been considered too dangerous for women. Interviews English equestrian Lucinda Green, French fencing champion Murielle Desmaret and Canadian high jumper Debbie Brill. Features Australian shark photographer Valerie Taylor, U S Air Force pilot Sheila O'Grady and zoologist Joyce Pool. Hosted by Chris Evert.
Physical Education and Recreation; Sociology
Dist - PBS

Women in the City (New York 1880 - 1920, Indianapolis 1880 - 1920) 30 MIN
U-matic / VHS
American City Series
Color (J)
Presents the story of two non - urban women who confront the process of urbanization when they move to the city. Portrays one woman from a small midwestern family farm who moves to Indianapolis, and one woman from a small Eastern European Jewish settlement who moves to New York City.
Geography - United States; History - United States; Sociology
Dist - FI **Prod** - WNETTV 1982

Women in the Corporation - on a Par, not a Pedestal 26 MIN
U-matic / VHS / 16mm
Human Resources and Organizational Behavior Series
Color
Studies women's roles in a large industrial corporation.
Business and Economics
Dist - CNEMAG **Prod** - HOBLEI

Women in the Middle East Series
The Price of Change 26 MIN
A Veiled Revolution 26 MIN
Women Under Siege 26 MIN
Dist - ICARUS

Women in the Military 14 MIN
U-matic / VHS
Color (G)
$249.00, $149.00 purchase _ #AD - 1999
Looks at women succeeding in all those tasks which traditionally have been considered the macho part of the Armed Services. Shows women responding professionally to being put into the equivalent of the front line. Part of a '60 Minutes' program.
Civics and Political Systems; Sociology
Dist - FOTH **Prod** - FOTH

Women in the NDP 28 MIN
U-matic
Color
Presents two long - time associates of the New Democratic Party (Canada) Eileen Sufrin and Olga Nunn, discussing the contributions of women to the party's history.
Civics and Political Systems; History - World; Sociology
Dist - WMENIF **Prod** - WMENIF

Women in the Third World 30 MIN
VHS
Global links series
Color (G)
$39.95 purchase _ #GLLI - 103
Shows how women live in developing nations. Suggests that women are central to most nations' economies and that they are able to bring about societal change.
Social Science; Sociology
Dist - PBS **Prod** - WETATV 1987

Women in the Trades 25 MIN
U-matic

B&W
Looks at the Pre - Trades Program for Women in Winnipeg, which is designed to introduce women to different trades and give them basic skills and experience in entering and working within male - dominated jobs.
Business and Economics; History - World; Sociology
Dist - WMENIF **Prod -** WMENIF

Women in the Work Place 20 MIN
U-matic / VHS
Color
Explains the twelve basic behaviors of the troubled female employee.
Sociology
Dist - WHITEG **Prod -** WHITEG

Women in Trades 57 MIN
U-matic
Color
Shows women from eight different skilled trades demonstrating their jobs, talking about different aspects of their work and commenting on some of the advantages and disadvantages of employment in their trades.
Business and Economics; Sociology
Dist - WMENIF **Prod -** SASWT

Women in war - voices from the front lines - Part I 48 MIN
VHS
Color (H C G)
$295.00 purchase, $55.00 rental
Visits Israel where the Intifada, the Palestinian uprising, has escalated the conflict between Arabs and Jews. Shows women on both sides willing to bear arms for their cause, but also involved in the peacemaking process. Arab and Israeli women, including Yael Dayan, daughter of Moshe, hold a historic conference resulting in a joint statement of strategies for peace. Travels to Northern Ireland to meet Mairead Corrigan and Betty Williams who formed Peace People. Part one of a two - part series produced by Diana Meehan, Pat Mitchell and Mary Muldoon.
Geography - World; History - World; Sociology
Dist - FLMLIB

Women in war - voices from the front lines - Part II 48 MIN
VHS
Color (H C G)
$295.00 purchase, $55.00 rental
Portrays women of the Americas. Visits El Salvador where torture and terrorism are part of every family's history. Shows that Salvadorean women are assuming leadership positions in popular front movements for social justice. Travels to Boston, New York, Washington and Los Angeles where women are working to reclaim their neighborhoods from crime. Interviews welfare mother Kimi Gray who organized tenants to rid her housing development of drug dealers. Part two of a two - part series produced by Diana Meehan, Pat Mitchell and Mary Muldoon.
Geography - United States; Geography - World; History - World; Sociology
Dist - FLMLIB

Women in war - voices from the front lines - Parts I and II 96 MIN
VHS
Color (H C G)
$445.00 purchase, $90.00 rental
Presents a two - part series produced by Diana Meehan, Pat Mitchell and Mary Muldoon. Visits Israel and Ireland in Part I to observe women's efforts to obtain peace in those areas. Travels to El Salvador and Boston, New York, Washington and Los Angeles to meet women leaders who are working for an end to violence and for social justice.
Geography - United States; Geography - World; History - World; Sociology
Dist - FLMLIB

The Women in Your Life is You - Women's Sexuality 33 MIN
U-matic / VHS / 16mm
Women Series
Color (H C A)
Explores the sexual experiences of four women, including a lesbian couple, to answer questions about what goes wrong with sexual relationships and what can be done to develop satisfying contact with partners.
Health and Safety; Sociology
Dist - LUF **Prod -** LUF 1979

Women Inside 60 MIN
16mm / U-matic / VHS
Color (C A)
LC 80-700137
Examines life within a women's prison. Includes the comments of the inmates and wardens.
Sociology
Dist - IU **Prod -** WNETTV 1980

Women Inside, Pt 1 30 MIN
U-matic / VHS / 16mm
Bill Moyers' Journal Series
Color (C A)
LC 80-700137
Examines life within a women's prison. Includes the comments of the inmates and wardens.
Sociology
Dist - IU **Prod -** WNETTV 1980

Women Inside, Pt 2 30 MIN
U-matic / VHS / 16mm
Bill Moyers' Journal Series
Color (C A)
LC 80-700137
Examines life within a women's prison. Includes the comments of the inmates and wardens.
Sociology
Dist - IU **Prod -** WNETTV 1980

Women like that 25 MIN
VHS
Color (G)
$250.00 purchase, $60.00 rental
Presents a sequel to Women Like Us by Suzanne Neild and Rosalind Pearson. Features the eight lesbian participants from the original video who discuss their changed lives since the video. Offers insights into aging, loving and intimacy, and the pain of ending relationships. Discusses homophobia, family support, the lack of housing for elderly lesbians.
Geography - World; Guidance and Counseling; Health and Safety; Sociology
Dist - WMEN

Women like us 49 MIN
VHS / U-matic
Color (G)
$275.00 purchase, $80.00 rental
Tells about the lives of sixteen lesbians of diverse backgrounds, ranging in age from fifty to more than eighty. Explores the experience of women during World War II, butch - femme roles, the emergence of modern feminism and coming out later in life to husbands and children. Produced by Suzanne Neild and Rosalind Pearson and directed by Neild.
Sociology
Dist - WMEN

Women Like Us 43 MIN
U-matic / VHS / 16mm
Color (H C A)
LC 80-701963
Introduces a working wife and mother, a single career woman, and a housewife - mother. Explains why their lifestyles make them happy. Narrated by Betty Rollin.
Sociology
Dist - FI **Prod -** NBCTV 1980

Women make Movies 58 MIN
U-matic / VHS
Color
LC 84-707095
Illustrates life from various perspectives of the physically disabled using dramatizations performed by five variously handicapped women. Portrays day - to - day problems faced by the blind, the hearing impaired, the arthritic and those confined to wheelchairs, including attitudes of the nonhandicapped in their dealings with handicapped.
Education; Guidance and Counseling; Health and Safety
Dist - WMEN **Prod -** WMEN 1982

Women make the Difference 28 MIN
16mm
Color
Looks at 25 years of Community Improvement Projects including crime reduction efforts, protecting the elderly and welcoming soldiers.
Social Science; Sociology
Dist - MTP **Prod -** SEARS

Women Making a Difference 30 MIN
VHS
Color (J)
LC 89716219
Features six successful women who tell their stories of success.
Business and Economics; Sociology
Dist - AIMS **Prod -** HP 1988

Women, Money and Power 29 MIN
U-matic
Woman Series
Color
Discusses the need for women to educate themselves about the nature of the American economic system before they can attain real power.
Sociology
Dist - PBS **Prod -** WNEDTV

Women, myth and reality 30 MIN
VHS / U-matic
Color (C)
$375.00, $345.00 purchase _ #V515
Deals with how many professional women feel about themselves and the world at large. Shares the personal feelings, goals, problems and successes of women from a variety of professions against the background of a song written and performed by Judy Collins.
Sociology
Dist - BARR **Prod -** CEPRO 1990

The Women next door 80 MIN
VHS / 16mm
Color (G) (ARABIC WITH ENGLISH SUBTITLES)
$90.00, $150.00 rental, $295.00 purchase
Looks at how the Intifada Occupation affected women on both sides of the conflict. Features Israeli director, Michal Aviad, traveling through Israel and the Occupied Territories with two other women - a Palestinian assistant director and an Israeli cinematographer - to explore the roles that the Occupation designated for women on both sides and the questions it raises. Provides a unique perspective on women's lives in the Middle East and the critical part they play in rebuilding societies ravaged by war. Includes English narration.
Fine Arts; History - World; Sociology
Dist - WMEN

Women of El Planeta 30 MIN
16mm / VHS
As Women See it - Global Feminism Series
Color (G)
$500.00, $250.00 purchase, $60.00 rental
Reveals that throughout Latin America there are hundreds of thousands of families living on garbage dumps outside of major urban areas. Looks at one such slum, 'El Planeta,' on the outskirts of Lima, Peru. Shows two women, a community leader and a literacy teacher, inspiring the women of 'El Planeta' to take action on the community's many problems, including hunger, illiteracy and contaminated water. Part of a series of films by and about women in Third World countries which include English voice over.
Civics and Political Systems; Geography - World; History - World; Science - Natural; Sociology
Dist - WMEN **Prod -** FAUST

Women of Giriloyu 20 MIN
16mm
Color (J H C A)
Depicts the opportunities for women in Giriloyu, an Islamic village in Indonesia. Focuses on a woman who developed her own batik business and her granddaughter who plans to be a doctor.
Religion and Philosophy; Sociology
Dist - UILL **Prod -** UILL 1985

Women of gold 30 MIN
VHS
Color (A)
$250.00 purchase, $60.00 rental
Features eight Asian Pacific lesbians who participated in the 1990 Gay Games and their passion for sports and women. Discusses growing up female and gay in Asian American families, and attitudes about body image and athletics. Produced by Eileen Lee and Marilyn Abbink.
Fine Arts; Physical Education and Recreation; Sociology
Dist - WMEN

The Women of Hodson 30 MIN
16mm
Color (H C A)
LC 80-701278
Introduces elderly women of the Hodson Senior Citizen Center in the Bronx, NY, who use improvisational theater to portray their life stories and establish a rapport with one another and their audience.
Fine Arts; Health and Safety; Sociology
Dist - FLMLIB **Prod -** DEANJ 1980

Women of intrigue 60 MIN
VHS
Women of the world series
Color (G)
$59.95 purchase _ #WWRL - 106
Profiles the lives of internationally renowned women, including a Brazilian actress, scientists and anthropologists, as well as Yoko Ono. Hosted by Jacqueline Bisset.
Sociology
Dist - PBS

Women of Kerala 27 MIN
VHS
Color (S)
$99.00 purchase _ #386 - 9039
Shows the progress made in the densely populated state of Kerala in India since the women instituted a program of education on sexuality and birth control nearly a decade ago. Reveals that the birthrate has been reduced by 40

percent, and, more importantly, that every child is able to go to school. Many women now have careers and every village has daycare, serving as a model for underdeveloped areas throughout the world.
Geography - World; Health and Safety; Sociology
Dist - FI **Prod** - CANBC 1988

Women of Niger 26 MIN
VHS
Color (G)
$60.00 rental, $250.00 purchase
Documents the fight for women's rights in Niger, a traditionally Islamic country where authorized polygamy and Muslim fundamentalism clash with the country's struggle for democracy. Looks at how women who speak out for their rights have been physically attacked and ex - communicated by the ayatollahs, yet they remain the most ardent defenders of democracy, which offers the best hope of winning the equal rights which are still denied them.
Civics and Political Systems; Fine Arts; History - World; Religion and Philosophy; Sociology
Dist - WMEN **Prod** - FOLLY 1993

Women of Purpose Series
Freedom to Define Myself 14 MIN
Dist - ARNPRO

Women of Russia 12 MIN
16mm
Russia Today Series
Color (J H)
LC 78-701846
Examines the life of Russian women who work hard for their families and country. No narration.
Geography - World; History - World; Sociology
Dist - IFF **Prod** - IFF 1968

Women of Steel 30 MIN
U-matic
Color (A)
Tells the story of four women who escape low paying, dead end jobs through an affirmative action program in the steel mills in the 70's. Shows how they lose their jobs during the 1980 recession and return to the pink collar jobs they had left.
Business and Economics; Sociology
Dist - AFLCIO **Prod** - MONVAL 1985
WMEN

Women of substance 55 MIN
VHS
Color (H G)
$60.00 rental, $195.00 purchase
Opens the door on the struggles and triumphs of women overcoming addiction during pregnancy and motherhood. Points out that over five million women in the United States are affected by drug and alcohol addiction, and that 1,000 babies are born each day with substance abuse in their system. Follows the stories of three women and exposes the legal, moral and health battles being waged to improve treatment opportunities for pregnant addicts and women with children. Narrated by Joanne Woodward. 30 minute version also available.
Fine Arts; Psychology; Sociology
Dist - WMEN **Prod** - KENSMI 1994

Women of summer 55 MIN
16mm / VHS
Color (G IND)
$10.00 rental
Captures an early chapter in the history of workers' education in the United States in a documentary on the Bryn Mawr School for Women Workers which existed 1921 - 1938. Combines photographs and early film footage with interviews of some of the women who participated in the project. Produced by S Bauman and R Heller.
Education; History - United States; Social Science; Sociology
Dist - AFLCIO

The Women of summer - an unknown chapter of American social history 55 MIN
16mm / VHS
Color (H C G)
$850.00, $495.00 purchase, $85.00 rental
Reveals that from 1921 to 1938, 1700 blue collar women participated in a controversial and inspired educational experiment known as the Bryn Mawr Summer School for Women Workers. Shows that the program changed their lives forever and has left a legacy meriting public awareness. The School was funded by prominent capitalists such as the Rockefellers, DuPonts and Carnegies, and introduced women workers of every race and nationality to the realm of humanistic and political thought, including Marxism and trade unionism. In the end it was considered too radical and was discontinued, but not before it had exerted a profound influence on its faculty and students, producing union, community and government leaders. Coproduced with Rita Heller.
Education; History - United States; Sociology
Dist - FLMLIB **Prod** - BAUNSZ 1986

Women of the Bible 60 MIN
VHS
Color (I J H R G A)
$19.95 purchase _ #87EE1015
Profiles four Biblical women who were influential in the shaping of what would become Christianity - Deborah, Ruth, Queen Esther and Mary of Magdala.
Guidance and Counseling; Literature and Drama; Religion and Philosophy
Dist - CPH **Prod** - CPH

Women of the Georgian Hotel 20 MIN
VHS
Color (G C)
$185.00 purchase, $55.00 rental
Highlights the strength and resilience through their life experiences as told by older women who live at the Georgian Hotel.
Health and Safety
Dist - TNF

Women of the Toubou 25 MIN
U-matic / VHS / 16mm
Color (H C A)
LC 74-700405
Presents a documentary on the African tribe known as the Toubou. Explains that the tribe revolves around a strong matriarchy but is extremely protective of their fragilely beautiful, but strong, enduring, graceful women.
History - United States; Sociology
Dist - PHENIX **Prod** - PHENIX 1973

Women of the Western Reserve - Women's Suffrage in Northeastern Ohio in the Late 43 MIN
16mm
Color
Complete title reads The Women Of The Western Reserve - Women's Suffrage In Northeastern Ohio In The Late 1800's. Dramatizes the women's suffrage movement in northeastern Ohio. Discusses whether law changes public opinion or if public opinion is stronger than law.
Civics and Political Systems; History - United States
Dist - HRC **Prod** - OHC

Women of the world series
Features women around the world who have made a name for themselves in whatever field of endeavor. Suggests that all women share a common spirit and values. Seven - part series considers topics such as beauty, families, the battle of the sexes and careers. Produced by Sandra Carter Productions, Inc.
Health, fashion and beauty 60 MIN
Love, marriage and family 60 MIN
Men on women, women on men 60 MIN
Women in change 60 MIN
Women in sports and adventure 60 MIN
Women of intrigue 60 MIN
Women who have it all 60 MIN
Dist - PBS

Women of the yellow earth 50 MIN
VHS
Under the sun series
Color (A)
PdS99 purchase
Describes the situation in rural China where women are restricted to having two children. Reveals that, when Bai conceives for the third time, she refuses to have an abortion. Her punishment is enforced sterilization. Follows her attempts to resist such a drastic measure and her ultimate failure to do so.
Sociology
Dist - BBCENE

Women on Orgasm 15 MIN
16mm
Color (A)
LC 76-701198
Offers information on sex and orgasm. Includes a simulation of a pre - orgasmic women's group, scenes of intercourse and comments by older women on orgasm.
Health and Safety; Psychology
Dist - MMRC **Prod** - DUIPA 1974

Women on the March 60 MIN
16mm
Color (J)
Shows the struggle of women for equal rights from the beginning of the suffragette movement in England to the present. Includes footage dating back to the Victorian Era. Shows how women of the United States, Canada and Europe have achieved status in world councils, politics and many professions.
History - World
Dist - NFBC **Prod** - NFBC 1958

Women on the March, Pt 1 29 MIN
16mm
Color (J)
Shows the struggle of women for equal rights from the beginning of the suffragette movement in England to World War I. Includes footage dating back to the Victorian Era.
Civics and Political Systems; History - World; Psychology; Sociology
Dist - NFBC **Prod** - NFBC 1958

Women on the March, Pt 2 29 MIN
16mm
Color (J)
Depicts the struggle of women for equal rights from World War I to the present. Shows how women of the United States, Canada and Europe have achieved status in world councils, politics and many professions.
Civics and Political Systems; History - United States; History - World; Psychology; Sociology
Dist - NFBC **Prod** - NFBC 1958

Women on Top 26 MIN
U-matic / VHS
Color (G)
$249.00, $149.00 purchase _ #AD - 1927
Examines whether traditional positive female characteristics are undermined by the supposedly male characteristics of aggression, domination and control. Considers whether there is room for 'feminine' behavior in the business world.
Business and Economics; Civics and Political Systems; Sociology
Dist - FOTH **Prod** - FOTH

Women on Top - 202 30 MIN
U-matic
Currents - 1985 - 86 Season Series
Color (A)
Looks at the social and economic state of women today.
Social Science; Sociology
Dist - PBS **Prod** - WNETTV 1985

Women Revisioning Ourselves 48 MIN
VHS
Woman and Her Symbols Series
Color (C)
LC 90708305
Discusses patriarchal oppression of women. Explores female imagery, female creative processes, and social change, as expressed in women's art. Produced by Claire Simon.
Fine Arts; Literature and Drama; Religion and Philosophy; Social Science; Sociology
Dist - QVID **Prod** - SICT 1990

Women seen on television 11 MIN
VHS / U-matic
Color (H G)
$195.00, $245.00 purchase, $45.00 rental
Condenses and edits broadcast footage from two consecutive days of viewing from the three major networks to provide a critical look at how the feminine gender is portrayed. Generates discussion on the role of the media and stereotypes, gender and ethnicity, and the ways in which mass communication is a mirror and - or a molder of opinions. Produced by Letting Go Foundation.
Sociology
Dist - NDIM

Women Series
Marriage - is it a Health Hazard 30 MIN
When Did You Last See Yourself on TV 32 MIN
When the Honeymoon is Over 32 MIN
Who Cares about Child Care 33 MIN
The Women in Your Life is You - Women's Sexuality 33 MIN
Dist - LUF

Women Studies 30 MIN
U-matic
Color
Discusses women's studies courses and the problems of teaching and studying such a topic.
Sociology
Dist - WMENIF **Prod** - WMENIF

Women Take Back the Night 17 MIN
U-matic / VHS
B&W (A)
LC 81-706192
Tells how, united by their common fears and anger, 5,000 women gathered in Minneapolis on August 14, 1979, to protest female victimization. Shows how the women pool their skills and presence in a significant social and political event, which includes an integrated program of music, poetry, speeches, demonstrations in the martial arts, and testimony of those who have suffered and survived criminal assault.
Civics and Political Systems; Sociology
Dist - UCV **Prod** - IBIS 1980

Women Talking 80 MIN
16mm
B&W
Features conversations with leading personalities in the forefront of the Women's Liberation Movement. Seeks to bring an understanding of the vital problem confronting society by relating experiences that contribute to a greater awareness of the social oppression of women.
Sociology
Dist - IMPACT **Prod** - WLIBCC 1971

Women - the Hand that Cradles the Rock 22 MIN
16mm / U-matic / VHS
Color
LC 74-701318
Examines the reconstitution of women's role in society as it relates to men.
Sociology
Dist - CNEMAG **Prod** - HOBLEI 1972

Women - the Hand that Cradles the Rock 20 MIN
16mm / U-matic / VHS
Color
Presents advocates of women's liberation, as well as women satisfied with their traditional roles.
Sociology
Dist - CNEMAG **Prod** - DOCUA

Women - the new poor 28 MIN
VHS
Color (G)
$250.00 purchase, $60.00 rental
Looks at divorced women and single mothers who lack skills and opportunities for economic self - sufficiency. Observes the recent alarming rise in numbers of women in povery in the United States as a result of job discrimination and personal misfortunes. Focuses on four women - Bernice, an unemployed single black mother, Dody, a displaced homemaker with a Connecticut home beyond her means, Paula, a young divorced woman with three part - time jobs, and Alexis, a Latina who moved into a shelter with her teenage daughter after a fire destroyed their home. Stresses the need for education, job training and support for women.
Sociology
Dist - WMEN **Prod** - BEMIL 1990

Women Under Fire 30 MIN
U-matic / VHS
Color (J H C A)
Focuses on four women serving the Madison, Wisconsin Fire Department as firefighters, the first women so employed in the Department's 145 year history. Examines some of the special problems faced by women firefighters and some of the issues their presence has raised, standards for testing and training, physical and emotional stamina, and attitudes about men and women working together.
Guidance and Counseling; Social Science; Sociology
Dist - UEUWIS **Prod** - UEUWIS 1982

Women Under Fire 20 MIN
VHS / U-matic
Color (H C A)
Tells how the Madison, Wisconsin Fire Department hired women as firefighters. Describes the physical strength, technical expertise and tricks - of - the - trade needed to become a firefighter.
Social Science; Sociology
Dist - FILCOM **Prod** - FILCOM

Women Under Siege 26 MIN
16mm / U-matic / VHS
Women in the Middle East Series
Color
Documents the crucial role women play in Rashadiyah, Southern Lebanon, a town which is home to 14,000 Palestinian refugees. Shows the women playing the roles of mothers, teachers, political organizers, farm laborers and fighters.
History - World; Sociology
Dist - ICARUS **Prod** - ICARUS 1982

Women Up in Arms 29 MIN
16mm / U-matic / VHS
B&W
Views the women's place in the Moslem society in a study of a seventeen - year - old Tunisian girl who dances to Beatles' records, her mother who removed her veil seven years before, and her grandmother who maintains the old, traditional ways.
Psychology; Religion and Philosophy; Sociology
Dist - MGHT **Prod** - UN 1966

Women - Up the Career Ladder 30 MIN
16mm
B&W (A)
LC 73-701884
Presents a tool for administrators, personnel managers and consultants for use in implementing affirmative action programs for women. Provides an honest and revealing portrayal of women's experiences in preparation for career mobility.
Guidance and Counseling; Psychology; Sociology
Dist - UCLA **Prod** - UCLA 1972

Women Warriors - 224 30 MIN
U-matic
Currents - 1985 - 86 Season Series
Color (A)
Explores the life of females in the military.
Civics and Political Systems; Social Science
Dist - PBS **Prod** - WNETTV 1985

Women who didn't have an abortion 28 MIN
16mm
Are you listening series
Color (H C A)
LC 80-701130
Presents several women of different backgrounds discussing their reasons for deciding against abortion, touching on the emotional, moral, religious, social, political and practical aspects of this difficult personal question.
Health and Safety; Sociology
Dist - STURTM **Prod** - STURTM 1977

Women who have it all 60 MIN
VHS
Women of the world series
Color (G)
$59.95 purchase _ #WWRL - 107
Profiles women who seem to 'have it all' - beauty, money, fame and love. Includes interviews with rock musician Chrissie Hynde, Catherine Deneuve and others. Hosted by Jane Seymour.
Sociology
Dist - PBS

Women who made the movies 55 MIN
VHS
Color; B&W (G)
$75.00 rental, $250.00 purchase
Traces the careers and films of such pioneer women filmmakers as Alice Guy Blanche, the first person to make a film with a plot - in 1896 - , as well as Ruth Ann Baldwin, Ida Lupino, Leni Riefenstahl, Dorothy Davenport Reid, Lois Webster, Kathlyn Williams, Cleo Madison and many others. Features clips from the films, rare archival footage and stills. Brings to life the works of these remarkable women, some well - known, but many neglected by history.
Fine Arts
Dist - WMEN **Prod** - WWDIXO 1992

Women who smile 50 MIN
VHS
Under the sun series - Hamar trilogy
Color (A)
PdS99 purchase _ Unavailable in USA or Canada
Examines the Hamar, an isolated people living in the dry scrubland of south-western Ethiopia. Concentrates on the proud and outspoken Hamar women. Three women, each at a different stage of her life, talk frankly about their concerns, ambitions and problems.
Psychology
Dist - BBCENE

Women, wine and wellness - a woman's guide to alcohol series 19 MIN
VHS
Women, wine and wellness - a woman's guide to alcohol series
Color (I J H G)
$350.00 purchase
Presents two parts on women and alcohol. Reveals that women are more susceptible than men to the effects of alcohol in Part I, Alcohol and Your Body. Examines the Fetal Alcohol Syndrome - FAS - in Part II.
Guidance and Counseling; Health and Safety; Psychology; Sociology
Dist - FMSP

Women, wine and wellness - a woman's guide to alcohol series

Alcohol and your body - Pt I	10 MIN
Fetal alcohol syndrome - Part II	9 MIN
Women, wine and wellness - a woman's guide to alcohol series	19 MIN

Dist - FMSP

Women with a Message 20 MIN
16mm
Color
LC 74-706610
Depicts training and career opportunities in the field of telecommunications for officers and enlisted women in the U S Navy.
Guidance and Counseling; Psychology; Social Science; Sociology
Dist - USNAC **Prod** - USN 1973

Women with AIDS 28 MIN
VHS / 16mm
Color (PRO G)
$149.00, $249.00, purchase _ #AD - 1471
Reveals that more and more women with AIDS are not users of shared needles but the ultimate victim's victim, infected by their mates who are bi - sexual or drug users. Features Dr Debra Spicehandler who discusses women at risk.
Health and Safety; Psychology; Sociology
Dist - FOTH **Prod** - FOTH 1990

Women within Two Cultures 30 MIN
U-matic
Color
Looks at the situation of the British Columbia West Coast Indian woman and the early white pioneer woman from a white but feminist perspective.
Social Science; Sociology
Dist - WMENIF **Prod** - WMENIF

Women, Work and Babies - Can America Cope 49 MIN
U-matic / VHS
Color (H C A)
Presents interviews with working parents, researchers, authors, business people, professors and politicians on the subject of working mothers. Shows scenes from family homes, day - care centers, classrooms and the work place. Examines re - definition of mother - father roles and the absence of support for single parents. Considers the effect of working parents on children.
Sociology
Dist - FI **Prod** - NBCTV

Women's Astrology 29 MIN
U-matic
Woman Series
Color
Looks at the negativism found in the traditional interpretation of astrology for women. Comments on the appeal of astrology and how it influences its adherents.
Religion and Philosophy; Sociology
Dist - PBS **Prod** - WNEDTV

Women's Banks and Credit Unions 29 MIN
U-matic
Woman Series
Color
Describes the foundation of women's banks and credit unions.
Business and Economics; Sociology
Dist - PBS **Prod** - WNEDTV

Women's Basketball - Defense 6 MIN
16mm / U-matic / VHS
Women's Championship Basketball Series
Color (J H C)
Presents basketball coach Pat Head exploring every phase of defense skills which must be mastered to become an effective defensive team player.
Physical Education and Recreation
Dist - ATHI **Prod** - ATHI 1981

Women's Basketball - Jump Ball 15 MIN
U-matic / VHS / 16mm
Color (J H C)
LC 76-701302
Provides incentive and motivation for women who play and enjoy basketball. Stresses the importance of practice and determination in developing the basic skills of the game and shows how togetherness between teammates and coach can make the difference in winning or losing.
Physical Education and Recreation
Dist - PHENIX **Prod** - PHENIX 1976

Women's Basketball, Pt 1 15 MIN
16mm / U-matic / VHS
Color (J H C)
LC 79-701772
Demonstrates drills for improving techniques in ball handling, dribbling, passing and shooting different types of basket shots.
Physical Education and Recreation
Dist - MCFI **Prod** - LRDKNG 1977

Women's Basketball, Pt 2 15 MIN
U-matic / VHS / 16mm
Color (J H C)
LC 79-701772
Demonstrates competitive basketball shots, including lay - up, underhanded lay - up, reverse lay - up, one hander and jump shot.
Physical Education and Recreation
Dist - MCFI **Prod** - LRDKNG 1977

Women's basketball series
VHS
N C A A instructional video series
Color (H C A)

$64.95 purchase _ #KAR1254V
Presents a three - part series on women's basketball. Focuses on shooting techniques, individual offensive moves, and post moves.
Physical Education and Recreation
Dist - CAMV **Prod** - NCAAF

Women's Championship Basketball Series
Women's Basketball - Defense 6 MIN
Dist - ATHI

Women's Coalition for the Third Century 29 MIN
U-matic
Woman Series
Color
Explains the objectives of the Women's Coalition for the Third Century, which intends to bring together national organizations to identify practical movements for change.
Sociology
Dist - PBS **Prod** - WNEDTV

Women's Discus 4 MIN
16mm
Track & Field Technique Study Films Series
Color; Silent (H C A)
#85 18
Presents a succession of performances by the leading athletes in the women's discus event. Features live film footage.
Physical Education and Recreation
Dist - TRACKN **Prod** - TRACKN 1985

The Women's Films 45 MIN
16mm
B&W
Presents the story of the poor and working women who talk about the oppression they have felt in their homes, on the job and in society. Explains how women are struggling for their liberation on all fronts.
Home Economics; Social Science; Sociology
Dist - CANWRL **Prod** - CANWRL 1970

Women's Golf 60 MIN
VHS / BETA
Color
Features golf champion Patty Sheehan teaching golf techniques.
Physical Education and Recreation
Dist - HOMEAF **Prod** - HOMEAF

Women's golf guide 60 MIN
VHS
Color (A)
$19.95 purchase _ #SLP001V-P
Presents golf tips from LPGA professional Helene Landers. Offers beginners the opportunity to watch four women of different levels of ability play so they can overcome intimidation and learn the basics of the game. Offers advanced players inside information on which balls and clubs are right for different players, proper etiquette on the course, handicap and slope systems, how to warm up, how to make reservations, and how to drive a cart and dress properly.
History - World; Physical Education and Recreation
Dist - CAMV

Women's Golf has Come a Long Way 15 MIN
16mm
Color
Shows women learning to play golf.
Physical Education and Recreation
Dist - NGF **Prod** - NGF

Women's Golf with Patty Sheehan 60 MIN
BETA / VHS
Color
Presents neuromuscular training using Patty Sheehan as the model for an improved golf game. Includes four audiocassettes and personal training guide.
Physical Education and Recreation; Psychology
Dist - SYBVIS **Prod** - SYBVIS

Women's Health - a Question of Survival 49 MIN
U-matic / VHS / 16mm
Color (H C A)
Investigates the questionable health care women may receive, including the administering of potentially dangerous drugs to pregnant women, questionable mastectomies and hysterectomies, and unproven birth control methods. Discusses the disinterest of doctors, drug manufacturers and government regulators.
Health and Safety
Dist - CRMP **Prod** - ABCTV 1977

Women's Health - a Question of Survival, Pt 1 24 MIN
U-matic / VHS / 16mm
Color (H C A)
Investigates the questionable health care women may receive, including the administering of potentially dangerous drugs to pregnant women, questionable mastectomies and hysterectomies, and unproven birth control methods. Discusses the disinterest of doctors, drug manufacturers and government regulators.
Sociology
Dist - CRMP **Prod** - ABCTV 1977
MGHT

Women's Health - a Question of Survival, Pt 2 25 MIN
16mm / U-matic / VHS
Color (H C A)
Investigates the questionable health care women may receive, including the administering of potentially dangerous drugs to pregnant women, questionable mastectomies and hysterectomies, and unproven birth control methods. Discusses the disinterest of doctors, drug manufacturers and government regulators.
Sociology
Dist - CRMP **Prod** - ABCTV 1977
MGHT

Women's health series
Presents an eight - part series offering the most - up - to - date medical information on women's health issues, reviewed and approved by a national panel of health care professionals. Features medical correspondent Dr Holly Atkinson of NBC News Today. Discusses menstruation, contraception, sexually transmitted diseases, infertility, pregnancy, after pregnancy, menopause and breast cancer.
After pregnancy - a new start 35 MIN
Breast cancer - replacing fear with facts 35 MIN
Contraception - know your options 35 MIN
Infertility - the new solutions 35 MIN
Menopause - guidelines to a healthy life 35 MIN
Menstruation - understanding your body 35 MIN
Pregnancy - nine special months 35 MIN
Sexually transmitted diseases - STDs - the keys to prevention 35 MIN
Dist - GPERFO **Prod** - AMEDCO 1977

Women's High Jump 4 MIN
16mm
Track & Field Technique Study Films Series
Color; Silent (H C A)
#85 15
Presents a succession of performances by the leading athletes in the women's high jump event. Features live film footage.
Physical Education and Recreation
Dist - TRACKN **Prod** - TRACKN 1985

Women's history and literature media series
Belle - the life and writings of Belle Case La Follette 15 MIN
Ethel Kvalheim - rosemaler 18 MIN
Her mother before her - Winnebago women's stories 22 MIN
Her own words - pioneer women's diaries 15 MIN
Mountain Wolf Woman - 1884 - 1960 17 MIN
Patchwork - a kaleidoscope of quilts 15 MIN
Prairie cabin - a Norwegian pioneer woman's story 17 MIN
Prairie quilts 15 MIN
Votes for women - the 1913 US Senate testimony 17 MIN
Winnebago women - songs and stories 15 MIN
Zona Gale - 1874 - 1938 15 MIN
Dist - HEROWN

Women's history month 15 MIN
VHS
America's special days series
Color (K P) (SPANISH)
$23.95 purchase
Shows women working in non-traditional roles, including Florence Nightingale and Amelia Earhart. Visits the narrator's mother who is a radio announcer. Challenges students to discuss jobs done by women they know.
Civics and Political Systems; Social Science
Dist - GPN **Prod** - GPN 1993

The Women's How to of Self - Defense 50 MIN
U-matic / VHS
(C A PRO)
$39.95 _ #SX100V
Offers women advice and techniques for defending themselves in various situations, such as traveling to and from work, home, and school, while jogging and others.
Physical Education and Recreation; Sociology
Dist - CAMV **Prod** - CAMV

Women's Hurdle Races 4 MIN
16mm
Track & Field Technique Study Films Series
Color; Silent (H C A)
#85 23
Presents a succession of performances by the leading athletes in women's hurdle racing. Features live film footage.
Physical Education and Recreation
Dist - TRACKN **Prod** - TRACKN 1985

Women's Hurdling 4 MIN
16mm
Track & Field Technique Study Films Series
Color; Silent (H C A)
#85 22
Presents a succession of performances by leading athletes illustrating women's hurdling techniques. Features live film footage.
Physical Education and Recreation
Dist - TRACKN **Prod** - TRACKN 1985

Women's Issues 22 MIN
U-matic / VHS / 16mm
Color (A)
Presents 14 vignettes demonstrating how various women's issues could be handled including sexual harassment, unequal treatment on the job, receiving the dummy treatment from mechanics, being excluded from the husband's business travel and experiencing the to - work - or - not - to - work dilemma.
Psychology; Sociology
Dist - CORF **Prod** - CORF

Women's issues - sexuality series
Five women, five births 29 MIN
Dist - DAVFMS

Women's Javelin 4 MIN
16mm
Track & Field Technique Study Films Series
Color; Silent (H C A)
#85 19
Presents a succession of performances by the leading athletes in the women's javelin event. Features live film footage.
Physical Education and Recreation
Dist - TRACKN **Prod** - TRACKN 1985

Women's Jumps - High Jump, Long Jump, Triple Jump 30 MIN
VHS / U-matic
Track & Field Event Videos Series
Color; B&W; Stereo; Mono; Silent (H C A)
#V86 5
Presents an extensive succession of performances by top athletes of the present and past, illustrating the technique of the women's high jump, arious angles, at various speeds in the vent of. Most show long jump and triple jump. Features many clips photographed from various angles and at speeds.
Physical Education and Recreation
Dist - TRACKN **Prod** - TRACKN 1985

Women's Liberation, Sexuality, and the Family 30 MIN
VHS / U-matic
Ethics in America Series
Color (H C A)
Shows Sol Gordon, director of the Institute for Family Research and Education at Syracuse University, and Jim and Andrea Fordham, authors of The Assault On The Sexes, debating the benefits of women's liberation and changes in sexual attitudes and practices.
Religion and Philosophy; Sociology
Dist - AMHUMA **Prod** - AMHUMA

Women's lives and choices series
A Question of numbers 28 MIN
Rishte - relationships 28 MIN
Dist - MACART
WMEN

Women's lives and choices series
Presents a three - part series dealing with women's health and the social, cultural and economic factors underlying reproductive choices. Includes Ventre Livre - Freeing the Womb - which questions the reproductive rights and social inequality of women in Brazil; Rishte - Relationships - tells the story of a mother who poisoned herself and two of her daughters over the practice of male sex preference in India; and A Question of Numbers which uses the Ibu Eze ceremony in Nigeria honoring women who have borne many children to highlight how family planning issues often conflict with traditional values.
Women's lives and choices series 84 MIN
Dist - WMEN **Prod** - RIESEN

Women's Long Jump 4 MIN
16mm
Track & Field Technique Study Films Series
Color; Silent (H C A)
#85 16
Presents a succession of performances by the leading athletes in the women's long jump event. Features live film footage.
Physical Education and Recreation
Dist - TRACKN **Prod** - TRACKN 1985

Women's Middle and Long Distance Races 4 MIN
16mm
Track & Field Technique Study Films Series
Color; Silent (H C A)
#85 24
Presents a succession of performances by the leading athletes in women's middle and long distance racing. Features live film footage.
Physical Education and Recreation
Dist - TRACKN **Prod** - TRACKN 1985

The Women's Olamal - the Organization of a Masai Fertility Ceremony 110 MIN
VHS / U-matic
Color (G)
Pd99, $800.00 purchase, $90.00 rental
Follows the events that led up to a controversial ceremony in Loita, Kenya to bless the women in order to increase their ability to have children. Examines some of the tensions between men and women in Masai society. Focuses on four women - Nolpiyaya and Kisaju who have four and nine children respectively, Nolmeeya - a barren woman near menopause, and Kisaro who is without a child after ten years of marriage. When the husband of a barren woman dies, the woman is chased away by the sons of her husband's other wives.
History - World; Religion and Philosophy; Sociology
Dist - BBCENE **Prod** - BBCENE 1984
DOCEDR

Women's Power Volleyball Series
Power Volleyball - Individual Defensive Skills 11 MIN
Power Volleyball - Individual Offensive Skills 11 MIN
Dist - ATHI

The Women's Prejudice Film 19 MIN
16mm / VHS / U-matic
Color (I)
LC 74-703293
Examines questionable concepts along with alternative viewpoints that stimulate men and women to re - appraise current attitudes concerning equality. Explores many myths and cliches.
Guidance and Counseling; Sociology
Dist - BARR **Prod** - SAIF 1974

Women's prejudice film - myth vs. realities 18 MIN
16mm
Color (G A)
$10.00 rental
Discusses myths about women. Looks at the beliefs that women are emotional, incapable of planning or accepting responsibility, which beliefs make it acceptable to bar women from jobs traditionally held by men.
Social Science; Sociology
Dist - AFLCIO **Prod** - SAIF 1975

Women's Rally for Action - March 22, 1976 29 MIN
U-matic
Color (G)
Documents the massive mobilization effort of British Columbia feminists to pressure the newly elected Social Credit government to change its policies affecting women.
Civics and Political Systems; History - World; Sociology
Dist - WMENIF **Prod** - WMENIF

Women's Rights 30 MIN
VHS / U-matic
American Government 2 Series
Color (C)
Follows women's struggle for equality from its beginnings in America to the 1977 IWY conference in Houston. Reviews some of the early women's meetings, the public's reaction to the 'suffragettes' and the pros and cons of ERA.
Civics and Political Systems
Dist - DALCCD **Prod** - DALCCD

Women's rights and roles in Islam
VHS
Color (G)
$20.00 purchase _ #110 - 064
Presents a debate between Aminah Assilmi and Deborah Scroggins, Atlanta Journal Constitution. Reveals that the debate is Assilmi's response to a series of articles by Scroggins, Women of the Veil.
English Language; Religion and Philosophy; Sociology
Dist - SOUVIS **Prod** - SOUVIS

Women's Rights in the U S - an Informal History 27 MIN
16mm
Color (H C A)
LC 73-702668
Surveys the conditions and movements which brought about changes in the status of women, such as the frontier, abolition, the Civil War, industrialization and suffragettism. Explores attitudes toward marriage, employment, fashion, education and women's 'proper place' in society.
Civics and Political Systems; History - United States; Psychology; Sociology
Dist - ALTANA **Prod** - KLUGDP 1973

Women's rites or truth is the daughter of time 8 MIN
16mm
Color (G)
$15.00 rental
Celebrates autumn with its colorful fall leaves. Features the poetry of Elsa Gidlow. Shot on witch's land in northern California and pictures chanting circles and tree goddess rites.
Fine Arts; Religion and Philosophy; Sociology
Dist - CANCIN **Prod** - BARHAM 1974

Women's self - defense 60 MIN
VHS
Color (G)
$29.95 purchase _ #CR1210V
Teaches women basic exercises to strengthen their bodies. Shows the basics needed to fight off an attacker. Includes examples of attacks and counter attacks. Finishes with a workout to keep in shape while learning self - defense. Includes instructional booklet.
Physical Education and Recreation
Dist - CAMV

Women's Service to the Nation 10 MIN
16mm
B&W (G)
LC 75-703078
Discusses the contributions of American women to the national welfare from colonial times to the 20th century.
History - United States; History - World; Sociology
Dist - USNAC **Prod** - USA 1964

Women's Service to the Nation - Summary and Conclusion 8 MIN
16mm
Color (G)
LC 75-703077
Describes contributions of America's women to the nation from pioneer days to the 20th century. Recalls their courage and self - sacrifice during times of war and their progressive efforts in times of peace. Emphasizes the expanded role of women in the Armed Forces and in industrial, professional and governmental areas.
History - United States; History - World; Sociology
Dist - USNAC **Prod** - USA 1968

Women's Shot Put 4 MIN
16mm
Track & Field Technique Study Films Series
Color; Silent (H C A)
#85 17
Presents a succession of performances by the leading athletes in the women's shot put event. Features live film footage.
Physical Education and Recreation
Dist - TRACKN **Prod** - TRACKN 1985

Women's Sprint Races 4 MIN
16mm
Track & Field Technique Study Films Series
Color; Silent (H C A)
#85 21
Presents a succession of performances by leading athletes in women's sprint racing. Features live film footage.
Physical Education and Recreation
Dist - TRACKN **Prod** - TRACKN 1985

Women's Sprinting Techniques 4 MIN
16mm
Track & Field Technique Study Films Series
Color; Silent (H C A)
#85 20
Presents a succession of performances by leading athletes illustrating women's sprinting techniques. Features live film footage.
Physical Education and Recreation
Dist - TRACKN **Prod** - TRACKN 1985

Women's Sprints and Hurdles 30 MIN
VHS / U-matic
Track & Field Event Videos Series
Color; B&W; Stereo; Mono; Silent (H C A)
#V86 10
Presents an extensive succession of performances by top athletes of the present and past, illustrating the technique of the women's sprint and from various angles, at various speeds in the vent of. Most show hurdle events. Features many clips photographed from various angles and at various speeds.
Physical Education and Recreation
Dist - TRACKN **Prod** - TRACKN 1985

Women's Studies 29 MIN
U-matic
Woman Series
Color (G)
Discusses the increase in women's studies courses offered at American colleges and universities.
Education; Sociology
Dist - PBS **Prod** - WNEDTV

The Women's Suffrage Movement in Canada 23 MIN
U-matic
Color (G)
Examines the Women's Suffrage Movement, the women who were active at the time and some of the most controversial issues. Draws parallels between the feminist movement today and the roots in the early feminist and suffrage movements.
History - World; Sociology
Dist - WMENIF **Prod** - WMENIF

Women's Throwing Events 30 MIN
U-matic / VHS
Track & Field Event Videos Series
Color; B&W; Stereo; Mono; Silent (H C A)
#V86 8
Presents an extensive succession of performances by top athletes of the present and past, illustrating the technique of the women's shot put, d from various angles, at various speeds in the vent of. Most show discus, and javelin events. Features many clips photographed from various angles and at various speeds.
Physical Education and Recreation
Dist - TRACKN **Prod** - TRACKN 1985

Women's Track and Field Series no 1
Starting, Running and Finishing 17 MIN
Dist - ATHI

Women's Track and Field Series no 3
Long and High Jump 15 MIN
Dist - ATHI

Women's Track and Field Series no 4
Discus, Shot and Javelin 20 MIN
Dist - ATHI

Women's track and field series
Basic strategies 20 MIN
Dist - ATHI

Women's Track and Field Series
Conditioning 33 MIN
Discus / Shot Put 39 MIN
High Jump 23 MIN
Javelin 53 MIN
Long Jump 46 MIN
Middle Distance Running 42 MIN
Sprints, Hurdles and Relays 48 MIN
Talent Search 60 MIN
Dist - MOHOMV

Women's Track & Field Videos Series
Conditioning 33 MIN
Discus and Shot Put 33 MIN
High Jump 33 MIN
Javelin 33 MIN
Long Jump 33 MIN
Middle distance running 33 MIN
Sprints, Hurdles, Relays 33 MIN
Dist - TRACKN

The Women's wear industry 21 MIN
VHS
Business of fashion series
Color (A H)
$120.00 purchase _ #DEP01V-H
Interviews two major designers of women's wear about how they design their collections. Visits on-site production facilities. Explores fashion forecasting. Visits a major trade expostion, The International Boutique Show in New York City, to show buyers making their purchases.
Business and Economics; Home Economics
Dist - CAMV

Women's Workable Wardrobe
VHS / 35mm strip
$69.00 purchase _ #LS75 filmstrip, $79.00 purchase _ #LS75V VHS
Teaches female students how to construct 30 outfits from two suits, two bottoms and five tops, how to choose shoes and accessories.
Home Economics
Dist - CAREER **Prod** - CAREER

Women's World of Golf - Betsy Rawls 20 MIN
16mm
Women's World of Golf Series
B&W (G)
Physical Education and Recreation
Dist - SFI **Prod** - SFI

Women's World of Golf - Mickey Wright 20 MIN
16mm
Women's World of Golf Series
B&W
Physical Education and Recreation
Dist - SFI **Prod** - SFI

Women's World of Golf - Patty Berg 20 MIN
16mm
Women's World of Golf Series
B&W
Physical Education and Recreation
Dist - SFI **Prod** - SFI

Women's World of Golf Series
Women's World of Golf - Betsy Rawls 20 MIN
Women's World of Golf - Mickey Wright 20 MIN
Women's World of Golf - Patty Berg 20 MIN
Dist - SFI

Won Ton 29 MIN
Videoreel / VT2
Joyce Chen Cooks Series
Color
Features Joyce Chen showing how to adapt Chinese recipes so that they can be prepared in the American kitchen and still retain the authentic flavor. Demonstrates how to prepare won ton.
Geography - World; Home Economics
Dist - PBS **Prod** - WGBHTV

Wonder 2 MIN
16mm
Meditation Series
Color (I)
LC 80-700753
Creates a mood for discussion, thought, prayer or meditation on the gifts people take for granted.
Religion and Philosophy
Dist - IKONOG **Prod** - IKONOG 1974

Wonder 5 MIN
16mm
Song of the Ages Series
B&W (P)
LC 75-702120
Inspired by Psalm 8 of the Bible. Pictures the beauty of nature as seen through the eyes of a two - year - old girl, and studies the child as the greatest of all wonders.
Religion and Philosophy
Dist - FAMLYT **Prod** - FAMLYT 1965

Wonder Baby 3 MIN
VHS / U-matic
Metric Marvels Series
Color (P I)
Features the animated superhero Wonder Gram in a discussion of metric measurement.
Fine Arts; Mathematics
Dist - GA **Prod** - NBCTV 1978

Wonder Bar 84 MIN
16mm
B&W (J)
Stars Dick Powell, Al Jolson and Kay Francis. Presents the dance numbers created and staged by Busby Berkeley, including the musical numbers Going To Heaven On A Mule, Why Do I Dream Those Dreams, Don't Say Goodnight, Wonder Bar and Vive La France.
Fine Arts
Dist - UAE **Prod** - WB 1934

Wonder Dog 8 MIN
U-matic / VHS / 16mm
Tales of Pluto Series
Color
Shows Pluto trying to impress his girlfriend by impersonating a circus dog. Demonstrates that the feats he must perform prove trickier than he expected.
Fine Arts; Literature and Drama
Dist - CORF **Prod** - DISNEY

Wonder down under - Part 3 22 MIN
VHS
Complete protozoans series
Color (J H)
$110.00 purchase _ #A2VH 4713
Witnesses the protozoan attack on swarms of bacteria, peranema scavenging for food in a dead rotifer, the huge amoeba pelomyxa enveloping one ciliate after another, and other instances of savage protozoan warfare. Teaches the concepts of conjugation, fission and galvanotaxis in some very interesting experiments. Part three of a three - part series on protozoans.
Science - Natural
Dist - CLRVUE **Prod** - CLRVUE

Wonder Factory 10 MIN
16mm
Color (FRENCH)
Discusses how the leadership of the French Communist Party is aligned with the power structure and does not serve the needs of the people.
Civics and Political Systems
Dist - CANWRL **Prod** - CANWRL

Wonder Gram 3 MIN
U-matic / VHS
Metric Marvels Series
Color (P I)
Tells how Wonder Gram foils a gang of snack thieves and demonstrates the multiples of metric weight.
Fine Arts; Mathematics
Dist - GA **Prod** - NBCTV 1978

The Wonder of Dolphins 11 MIN
16mm / U-matic / VHS
Color (P I J H A)
$280, $195 purchase - #80513
Talks about the behavior, habitat, and sonar communication system of dolphins. A Centron film.
Science - Natural
Dist - CORF

The Wonder of Drag Racing 13 MIN
16mm
Color
LC 73-702400
Depicts the excitement, complexity and intense competition of drag racing as experienced by one participant.
Physical Education and Recreation
Dist - PTRSEN **Prod** - PTRSEN 1973

The Wonder of form 30 MIN
U-matic / VHS
Art of being human series; Module 15
Color (C)
History - World; Literature and Drama; Religion and Philosophy
Dist - MDCC **Prod** - MDCC

Wonder of Insects' Colors and Figures 19 MIN
16mm
Color
Explains that insects possess various devices for protecting themselves from the outside world and describes how they adapt themselves to different circumstances.
Science - Natural
Dist - UNIJAP **Prod** - TOEI 1970

Wonder of living things in the land of Jesus 30 MIN
VHS
Wonder series
Color (K P I R)
$19.95 purchase, $10.00 rental _ #35 - 81 - 2503
Focuses on plants and animals found in the Holy Land, many of which are also described in the Bible.
Religion and Philosophy
Dist - APH

The Wonder of Norway 55 MIN
VHS
Travelouger series
Color (G H)
$24.95 purchase _ #TC15
Travels to Norway, showing maps, geography, museums, sports, landmarks, historical figures, cuisine, etc. Comes with reference booklet.
Geography - World
Dist - SVIP

Wonder of Our Body 13 MIN
VHS / 16mm
Color (I J)
LC 76-702111
Introduces the human body. Reveals the skeleton, the body's lubricating system, the hand, the brain, the eye, the ear and the heart as part of the intricate design that has gone into making the human body.
Science - Natural
Dist - MIS **Prod** - MIS 1976

Wonder of the boy Jesus 30 MIN
VHS
Wonder series
Color (K P I R)
$19.95 purchase, $10.00 rental _ #35 - 80 - 2503
Features a grandfather and his grandchild discussing Jesus' birth and early life. Includes relevant Bible passages and film footage of the Holy Land.
Religion and Philosophy
Dist - APH

Wonder of the days of Jesus 30 MIN
VHS
Wonder series
Color (K P I R)
$19.95 purchase, $10.00 rental _ #35 - 82 - 2503
Features a grandfather and his grandchild discussing the events in the life of Jesus. Covers such events as the entry into Jerusalem and the resurrection. Includes relevant Bible passages and film footage of the Holy Land.
Literature and Drama; Religion and Philosophy
Dist - APH

The Wonder of Words - a Classroom Experience with Bill Martin 21 MIN
VHS / 16mm
Color (C)
$8.50 rental _ #24163
Presents educator Bill Martin showing students how to use his Little Seashore books to improve their skills in listening, reading, writing, spelling, and speaking.
Education; English Language
Dist - EBEC

Wonder of Work 10 MIN
16mm
Color
Deals with the subject of occupational therapy and important developments in treating disabilities which result from disease and accidents.
Health and Safety; Sociology
Dist - IREFL **Prod** - IREFL

The Wonder of you - A Mystery story - A Matter of taste 30 MIN
VHS
Moody science adventures series
Color (R P I)
$14.95 purchase _ #6121 - 2
Examines the complex human machine. Follows the metamorphosis of a caterpillar. Observes the eating habits of five special animals. Credits all of these activities to the creative aspects of the Christian deity. Part of a series.
Literature and Drama; Religion and Philosophy; Science - Natural
Dist - MOODY **Prod** - MOODY

The Wonder Ring 6 MIN
16mm
Color; Silent (C)
$263.00
Experimental film by Stan Brakhage.
Fine Arts
Dist - AFA **Prod** - AFA 1955

Wonder series
Wonder of living things in the land of Jesus 30 MIN
Wonder of the boy Jesus 30 MIN
Wonder of the days of Jesus 30 MIN
Dist - APH

Wonder Walks Series
Bending and reflecting sunlight 7 MIN
How do they move 6 MIN
Let's Find Life 8 MIN
Some Friendly Insects 5 MIN
A Time for Rain 8 MIN
A Time for Sun 6 MIN
What do they Eat 5 MIN
Where Does Life Come from 5 MIN
The World of Up Close 9 MIN
Dist - EBEC

Wonder witness and mighty mouth
VHS
Nanny and Isaiah adventure series
Color (K P I R)
$14.95 purchase _ #87EE0781
Tells how Nanny and Isaiah learn, through a series of adventures, that evangelism should involve everyday lives and relationships.
Fine Arts; Guidance and Counseling; Literature and Drama; Religion and Philosophy
Dist - CPH **Prod** - CPH

Wonder World 25 MIN
16mm
Color
Searches for the secret of the life of antibiotic bacteria and how staphylococci acquire antibiotic - resistance. Shows how bacterial - genes act and how to deal with antibiotic - resistive bacteria.
Science - Natural
Dist - UNIJAP **Prod** - UNIJAP 1972

Wonder world of science series
What good are rocks 12 MIN
What is the Brightest Star? 11 MIN
What's inside a seed 12 MIN
Where does sand come from 11 MIN
Why can't I fly like a bird 13 MIN
Why Doesn't Grass Grow on the Moon 11 MIN
Why don't I fall up 10 MIN
Dist - CORF

Wonder World of Science Series
Can I sit on a cloud 11 MIN
Does it ever rain in the desert 11 MIN

How big were the dinosaurs 11 MIN
Where do lost balloons go 11 MIN
Why do Cats have Whiskers 11 MIN
Why do Spiders Spin Webs 11 MIN
Why doesn't grass grow on the moon 11 MIN
Dist - CORF
VIEWTH

Wonder world of science series
What is the brightest star 11 MIN
What's the biggest living thing 11 MIN
Where does rain go after it falls 11 MIN
Dist - VIEWTH

Wonderful baby 30 MIN
VHS / U-matic
Say it with sign series; Pt 9
Color (H C A) (AMERICAN SIGN)
Presents Lawrence Solow and Sharon Neumann Solow introducing American Sign Language used by the hearing - impaired. Emphasizes signs that have to do with a new baby in the family.
Education
Dist - FI **Prod** - KNBCTV 1982

A Wonderful Bird was the Pelican 26 MIN
16mm / U-matic / VHS
Color
LC 79-701783
Shows the effects of DDT in the diet of the brown pelican, once common along the coast of California.
Science - Natural
Dist - MCFI **Prod** - UPA 1975

A Wonderful Construction 15 MIN
16mm
Color
LC 72-702454
Celebrates as creative artists the men who build buildings, comparing them to the men in Leger's painting 'LES CONSTRUCTEURS.'.
Fine Arts; Industrial and Technical Education
Dist - RADIM **Prod** - RADIM

The Wonderful Crook 112 MIN
16mm
Color (FRENCH (ENGLISH SUBTITLES))
Describes a modern Robin Hood's double life and loves. Directed by Claude Goretta.
Fine Arts; Foreign Language
Dist - NYFLMS **Prod** - UNKNWN 1975

The Wonderful flight to the Mushroom Planet 15 MIN
U-matic / VHS
Book bird series
Color (I)
Tells a story of two boys who discover the secret of a doomed planet. From the book by Elinor Cameron.
English Language; Literature and Drama
Dist - CTI **Prod** - CTI

The Wonderful kangaroo 60 MIN
VHS
Color (G)
$24.95 purchase _ #S02002
Portrays the Australian giant red kangaroo in its outback habitats.
Geography - World; Science - Natural
Dist - UILL **Prod** - SIERRA

The Wonderful Lollypop Rooster 8 MIN
16mm
Color (P)
Presents the nonnarrated story of a mysterious organ grinder who gives the children of a colorless village lollypops. Reveals that one of the lollypops is shaped like a rooster and has magic powers.
Literature and Drama
Dist - SF **Prod** - SF 1972

Wonderful things 50 MIN
VHS
Face of Tutankhamun series
Color; PAL (G)
PdS99 purchase
Examines the treasures which brought fame and fortune to the discoverers of the boy king Tutankhamun's tomb. Explores the death of expedition member Carnarvon and the ensuing rumor of a curse on the antiquities. Part two of a five - part series.
History - World
Dist - BBCENE

The Wonderful Walking Stick - a Bulgarian Folk Tale 10 MIN
16mm
Folk Tales from Around the World Series
Color (P I)
LC 80-700352
Tells the tale of a magic stick that by a mere touch changes anger into laughter.
Literature and Drama
Dist - SF **Prod** - FILBUL 1980

The Wonderful Weather Machine 13 MIN
U-matic / VHS / 16mm
Color (P I J)
LC 83-700636
Describes how gravity, water, land, air and the sun all act together to create different weather conditions. Explains how the tilt of the earth determines whether it's summer or winter. Reveals how clouds, rain, wind and snow are generated and the causes of thunderstorms, tornadoes and hurricanes.
Science - Physical
Dist - BARR **Prod** - LEARN 1983

Wonderful Winter Haven 15 MIN
16mm
Color
Explores Lakeland, the citrus center of Florida.
Agriculture; Geography - United States; Sociology
Dist - FLADC **Prod** - FLADC

Wonderful Womenfolk 19 MIN
U-matic / VHS
Folk Book Series
Color (P)
Literature and Drama
Dist - AITECH **Prod** - UWISC 1980

The Wonderful Word and Wordless Story Wagon 10 MIN
U-matic / VHS
Book, Look and Listen Series
Color (K P)
Focuses on the ability to respond to language games with one word, a phrase or complete sentence stories.
English Language; Literature and Drama
Dist - AITECH **Prod** - MDDE 1977

The Wonderful World God Gave Us - Grandpa O'Shea Tells a Story 19 MIN
BETA / VHS
Color (K P)
Shows a group of children discovering the wonders of creation in their own neighborhood, and teaches children from a religious perspective about judging a person's true worth.
Literature and Drama; Religion and Philosophy
Dist - DSP **Prod** - DSP

Wonderful World of Adventure 32 MIN
16mm
Color
LC FIA68-627
Views the floats, bands and horses of the floral festival and parade held in Pasadena, California, on New year's Day, 1968.
Civics and Political Systems; Geography - United States
Dist - TRA **Prod** - TRA 1968

Wonderful world of exhibitions 25 MIN
VHS
Color (A PRO)
$595.00 purchase, $155.00 rental
Discusses exhibitions and what can make them a success. Uses humor and real - life vignettes to illustrate what works and what doesn't. Stresses the importance of advance preparation and thorough follow - up after the exhibition.
Business and Economics; Psychology
Dist - VLEARN **Prod** - RTBL

Wonderful world of liquid air 45 MIN
VHS
Chemistry 101 series
Color (C A)
$50.00 purchase _ #S01896
Presents a basic introduction to the chemistry concepts of 'liquid air,' as taught in the introductory freshman - level class at the University of Illinois. Utilizes both lectures and demonstrations to illustrate the various concepts.
Science; Science - Physical
Dist - UILL **Prod** - UILL

The Wonderful world of the butterfly 30 MIN
U-matic / VHS / BETA
Color; NTSC; PAL; SECAM (J H C)
PdS58
Explores the colorful world of the butterfly. Illustrates in close - up the detailed life cycle of the insect. Captures the birth of the caterpillar from a pin - head sized egg, the transformation of the caterpillar to a pupa, the emergence of the fully - grown butterfly from its dormant stage as a pupa and many other aspects.
Science - Natural
Dist - VIEWTH

Wonderful World of Water Sports 15 MIN
16mm
Color
Features the wide variety of water sports available to the enthusiast in Florida.
Geography - United States; Physical Education and Recreation
Dist - FLADC **Prod** - FLADC

The Wonderful World of Wet 30 MIN
U-matic
Magic Ring II Series
(K P)
Continues the aim of the first series to bring added freshness to the commonplace and assist children to discover more about the many things in their world. Each program starts with the familiar, goes to the less familiar, then the new, and ends by blending new and old information.
Education; Literature and Drama
Dist - ACCESS **Prod** - ACCESS 1986

Wondering about Air 13 MIN
16mm
Color (P)
LC 85-703265
Presents a lesson about air. Uses the setting of three clowns on a beach. Shows motion of a hat, balloon and kite moving in the air.
Science - Physical
Dist - EBEC **Prod** - EBEC 1986

Wondering about Light 10 MIN
16mm
Color (P)
LC 85-703266
Learn about light from the four children playing hide and seek and from the girl who enters the garage.
Science - Physical
Dist - EBEC **Prod** - EBEC 1986

Wondering about Things 22 MIN
VHS / 16mm
Color (H)
$418.00, $293.00 purchase, $40.00 rental _ #192 E 0110, 193 E 2016, 140 E 6400
Asks a number of creative persons in many walks of life the questions, 'Are you concerned about the possible misuses of science,' and 'Are you satisfied with life as it is today.' Stimulates creative thinking in all age groups.
Psychology; Science - Physical
Dist - WARDS

Wonders and wildlife of Yellowstone and the Grand Teton 42 MIN
VHS
Color (G)
$29.95 purchase _ #S01013
Portrays the geological wonders and wildlife of Yellowstone and the Grand Tetons.
Geography - United States; Science - Natural
Dist - UILL

Wonders are many - science in antiquity 20 MIN
VHS
Soul of science series
Color; CC (H C)
$79.00 purchase _ #183
Takes a trip through the history of science in ancient times. Stresses the importance of artisans on all continents as well as the philosopher - scientists of ancient Ionian Greece. Part one of a four - part series on the history of science. Includes a book of the same title from the Learning Power series.
History - World; Religion and Philosophy; Science
Dist - HAWHIL **Prod** - HAWHIL 1994

Wonders in a country stream; 3rd ed. 10 MIN
U-matic / VHS / 16mm
Color (K P I)
$79.95 purchase _ #Q10428; LC 77-703304
Provides basic scientific facts about amphibians, reptiles and other water creatures. Features children at a country stream where they comment on turtles, water bugs, salamanders, newts, and crawfish. Utilizes song and pictures. No adult narration.
Science - Natural
Dist - CF **Prod** - CF

Wonders in your own backyard 11 MIN
VHS
Color (P I)
$210.00, $145.00 purchase, $60.00 rental
Observes a number of children having an adventure in the backyard. Show thatthey discover a snail, sowbug, millipede, earthworm and house spider.
Science; Science - Natural
Dist - CF

Wonders in Your Own Backyard; 3rd ed. 11 MIN
U-matic / Videodisc / VHS / 16mm

Color (K P I)
$99.95, $79.95 purchase _ #Q10427; LC 77-700126
Provides scientific information about animals and insects that can be found in an ordinary backyard. Utilizes songs and the conversation of children to discuss how snails, butterflies, worms, sow bugs and spiders look and feel. No adult narration.
Science - Natural
Dist - CF **Prod** - CF

Wonders of Florida 3 MIN
16mm
Of all Things Series
Color (P I)
Shows some of the wonders of the state of Florida.
Geography - United States
Dist - AVED **Prod** - BAILYL

The Wonders of God's creation 195 MIN
VHS
Color (R)
$59.95 purchase _ #9292 - 2
Offers a creationist view of the planet, attributing all to the Christian deity.
Literature and Drama; Religion and Philosophy
Dist - MOODY **Prod** - MOODY

Wonders of Growing Plants ; 3rd ed. 14 MIN
16mm / U-matic / VHS
Color (P I)
$79.95 purchase _ #Q10429; LC 75-704269
Utilizes time - lapse photography to illustrate the ways in which plants grow from stems, leaves, seeds or roots. Provides basic scientific information about plant growth.
Science - Natural
Dist - CF **Prod** - CF 1995

The Wonders of Islamic science
VHS
Color (J H G)
$27.00 purchase _ #510 - 003
Discloses how the Quran inspired Muslims to lead the world in science and civilization. Describes the achievements of Muslims in astronomy, medicine, mathematics, geography, botany, zoology and many other fields. Shows how these accomplishments were a direct result of Quranic teachings. Includes the book The Miracle of Islamic Sciences by Dr K Ajram.
Religion and Philosophy; Science
Dist - SOUVIS **Prod** - SOUVIS

Wonders of learning CD-ROM library series
Presents a series of CD-ROMs, including such titles as A World of Animals, Our Earth, The Human Body, A World of Plants, Animals and How They Grow, and People Behind the Holidays. Includes activity guide, user's guide, poster and color booklet and library cards for each unit. Designed for use with Macintosh computer.
Animals and how they grow
The Human body
Our Earth
A World of animals
A World of plants
Dist - NGS

Wonders of life series
The Bones and the muscles get rhythm 11 MIN
The Brain and the nervous system think science 11 MIN
The Heart and lungs play ball 11 MIN
Dist - CORF

Wonders of man's creation 60 MIN
VHS
Great wonders of the world series
Color (J H C G)
$24.95 purchase _ #IVN943V
Visits the Kremlin's Red Square, Versailles, the Eiffel Tower, Mt Rushmore, the Great Wall of China, Manchu Picchu and the Statue of Liberty. Part of a three - part series traveling to 21 of the Earth's most inspiring natural wonders, engineering marvels and shrines of sacred beauty.
Business and Economics; Fine Arts
Dist - CAMV **Prod** - READER 1993

Wonders of nature 60 MIN
VHS
Great wonders of the world series
Color (J H C G)
$24.95 purchase _ #IVN946V
Journeys to the Sahara Desert, the Grand Canyon. Witnesses the migration of thousands of animals in the Serengeti. Travels to the Himalayas, the Amazon, Iguazo Falls and Ayres Rock in Australia. Part of a three - part series traveling to 21 of the Earth's most inspiring natural wonders, engineering marvels and shrines of sacred beauty.
Geography - World
Dist - CAMV **Prod** - READER 1993

The Wonders of Norway 60 MIN
VHS
Color (G)
$29.95 purchase _ #QU018
Presents a video vacation combining history, geography, scenery and people.
Geography - World
Dist - SIV

Wonders of plastic surgery 60 MIN
VHS
Nova video library
Color (G)
$29.95 purchase
Focuses on the techniques of plastic surgery. From the PBS series 'NOVA.'
Health and Safety
Dist - PBS **Prod** - WNETTV

Wonders of the unseen world 40 MIN
VHS
B&W (G)
$60.00 purchase
Combines sounds and images gathered from ten years of journeys around the world with pre - existing stock material from various sources. Experiments with using the compilation documentary form. The soundtrack reflects the current interest in world music and includes sounds of nature, industry and liturgy from a wide cross - section of traditions. Produced by Richard Beveridge.
Fine Arts; Geography - World
Dist - CANCIN

The Wonders of Wheat 14 MIN
16mm
Color
Looks at the development of wheat and explores its importance in early cultures. Explores present day uses and kinds of wheat, how bread is made and its importance in the daily diet.
Agriculture
Dist - MTP **Prod** - OIWWC

Wonders of Wilderness 21 MIN
U-matic
Color
Portrays the frustration and tension of living and working in crowded urban areas. Suggests a trail riding vacation into one of the forest service wilderness areas.
Physical Education and Recreation; Science - Natural; Sociology
Dist - USDA **Prod** - USDA 1972

Wonders sacred and mysterious 60 MIN
VHS
Great wonders of the world series
Color (J H C G)
$24.95 purchase _ #IVN944V
Visits the Taj Mahal, Stonehenge, the Great Pyramids of Giza, St Peter's Basilica, Istanbul's Hagia Sofia and Borobudur, Buddha's cosmic mountain. Part of a three - part series traveling to 21 of the Earth's most inspiring natural wonders, engineering marvels and shrines of sacred beauty.
Fine Arts
Dist - CAMV **Prod** - READER 1993

Wonderstruck presents series
Animals 26 MIN
Cold show 26 MIN
Digging into the past 26 MIN
Environmental alert 26 MIN
Hawaii 26 MIN
Living Ocean 26 MIN
Making music 26 MIN
Mummies and Mayas 26 MIN
Space trek 26 MIN
Understanding animals 26 MIN
Dist - CF

Wonderstruck presents series
Watching birds 26 MIN
Dist - CF
FI

Wonderstruck Presents Series
Digging into the past - Pt 6 30 MIN
Environmental alert - Part 2 30 MIN
The Living Ocean - Pt 8 30 MIN
Making Music - Pt 1 30 MIN
Mummies and Maya - Pt 5 30 MIN
Space Trek - Pt 7 30 MIN
Understanding Animals - Pt 3 30 MIN
Dist - FI

Wonderworks collection series
African journey 174 MIN
Bridge to Terabithia 58 MIN
Brother future 116 MIN
Daniel and the towers 60 MIN
The Fig tree 58 MIN
Gryphon 55 MIN
Home at last 58 MIN
The House of Dies Drear 116 MIN
Maricela 62 MIN
The Mighty pawns 60 MIN
Runaway 59 MIN
Taking care of terrific 61 MIN
Words by heart 116 MIN
You must remember this 106 MIN
Dist - KNOWUN

WonderWorks Series
And the children shall lead 55 MIN
A Girl of the limberlost 110 MIN
Hiroshima Maiden 55 MIN
The Hoboken Chicken Emergency 55 MIN
Jacob have I loved 55 MIN
A Little Princess 160 MIN
Miracle at Moreaux 55 MIN
Necessary Parties 110MIN
Sweet 15 110 MIN
Walking on Air 55 MIN
A Waltz through the Hills 110 MIN
Dist - FI

A Wondrous Complexity 29 MIN
U-matic
Future Without Shock Series
Color
Discusses the numerous analytical tools used by the operations engineer to aid handling of complex systems.
Industrial and Technical Education; Sociology
Dist - UMITV **Prod** - UMITV 1976

Wondrous works of nature - Volume 4 70 MIN
VHS
Animals of Africa series
Color (G)
$29.95 purchase
Tours several of the major natural sites of Africa, including the Kalahari Desert, the Botswana swamplands, and the Fever Tree Forest.
Science - Natural
Dist - PBS **Prod** - WNETTV

Won't know till I get there 15 MIN
VHS
More books from cover to cover series
Color (I G)
$25.00 purchase _ #MBCC - 103
Focuses on how fourteen - year - old Stephen, his foster brother and friends are all required to help out at an old age home after being caught in vandalism. Based on the book 'Won't Know Till I Get There' by Walter Dean Myers. Hosted by John Robbins.
Education; English Language; Literature and Drama
Dist - PBS **Prod** - WETATV 1987

The Wood 10 MIN
VHS
Stop, look, listen series
Color; PAL (P I J)
Visits the woods in the spring to observe the variety of life. Returns in the fall to see the changes that have taken place. Part of a series of films which start from some everyday observation and show more of what is happening, how and why. Builds vocabulary and encourages children to be more observant.
English Language; Science - Natural; Social Science
Dist - VIEWTH

Wood 17 MIN
16mm / VHS
Color (P I J)
$260.00, $29.95 purchase
Explores the origin and uses of wood. Looks at forest preservation and reforestation.
Agriculture; Industrial and Technical Education; Science - Natural
Dist - KAWVAL **Prod** - KAWVAL

Wood 30 MIN
U-matic
Today's Special Series
Color (K P)
Develops language arts skills in children. Programs are thematically designed around subjects of interest to youngsters. Action takes place in a department store where people, mannequins, puppets, comic characters and special guests present a light hearted approach to language arts.
Fine Arts; Literature and Drama; Psychology
Dist - TVOTAR **Prod** - TVOTAR 1985

Wood and Glass 29 MIN
Videoreel / VT2
Directions in Design Series
Color
Provides a glimpse of Hawaiian craftsmen working with wood and glass.
Fine Arts; Geography - United States; Industrial and Technical Education
Dist - PBS **Prod** - HETV

Wood and metal stud rough - in techniques 20 MIN
VHS
Color (H A T)
$95.00 purchase _ #VC300
Uses step - by - step demonstrations to teach new construction rough - in techniques. Includes a detailed section on box - fill calculations using the 1990 National Electrical Code. Gives many code references in the discussion of proper nonmetallic cable routing and protection, EMT conduit connection, box selection and sizing, layout, mounting, grounding, tools and laborsaving tips.
Industrial and Technical Education
Dist - AAVIM **Prod** - AAVIM 1992

Wood and Paper Characteristics 60 MIN
VHS
Basic Theory and Systems Series
Color (PRO)
$600.00 - $1500.00 purchase _ #POWPC
Focuses on how the processes in a pulp mill and a paper mill influence the characteristics of wood, pulp and paper. Examines the basic components of wood. Differentiates between the two major groups of trees. Considers a Kraft pulp, a semichemical pulp and a mechanical pulp mill. Describes common pulp and paper tests. Includes ten textbooks and an instructor guide to support four hours of instruction.
Education; Industrial and Technical Education; Psychology
Dist - NUSTC **Prod** - NUSTC

Wood and Tee Shots 55 MIN
VHS
Name of the Gme is Golf Series
(H C A)
$49.95 purchase _ #SWC450V
Discusses wood and tee shots in golf. Explains playing the wind, the rough and the fairway, and improving eye and hand coordination and more. Features slow motion photography.
Physical Education and Recreation
Dist - CAMV

Wood and wooden objects 29 MIN
U-matic
Sketching techniques series; Lesson 20
Color (C A)
Focuses on wood grain as a natural art element. Teaches how to draw some wooden objects such as a table, box, or stool, and how to draw grain on the wood to add to its appearance.
Fine Arts
Dist - CDTEL **Prod** - COAST

Wood Bending - a New Twist 13 MIN
16mm / U-matic / VHS
Color (H C)
LC 74-707262
Shows the new process of bending wood by using anhydrous ammonia.
Industrial and Technical Education
Dist - IFB **Prod** - SUNY 1969

Wood Chip Mulch for Erosion Control 13 MIN
16mm
Color
LC 74-705965
Demonstrates how wood chip mulch provides a solution to erosion during and after highway construction. Shows that air and water pollution can be controlled and a natural resource put to use instead of being wasted or burned.
Industrial and Technical Education; Science - Natural; Social Science
Dist - USNAC **Prod** - USDTFH 1972

Wood Finishes 14 MIN
16mm
Hand Tools for Wood Working Series, no 10; No 10
Color (H C A)
LC FIA67-968
Stains, shellac, varnish, lacquer, wax and oil for use on wood.
Industrial and Technical Education
Dist - SF **Prod** - MORLAT 1967

Wood Finishing
VHS
Video Workshops Series
$39.95 purchase _ #FW500
Shows a master craftsman demonstrating his technique for finishing wood.
Education; Industrial and Technical Education
Dist - CAREER **Prod** - CAREER

Wood Finishing with Frank Klausz 110 MIN
VHS / BETA
Color (H C A)
Shows how to create a number of professional quality finishes for wood projects. Comes with booklet.
Industrial and Technical Education
Dist - TANTON **Prod** - TANTON

Wood frame building collapse 21 MIN
VHS
Collapse of burning buildings video series
Color (IND)
$140.00 purchase _ #35607
Presents one part of a five - part series that is a teaching companion for the Collapse of Burning Buildings book, as well as to the IFSTA Building Construction manual. Explains the most common US building construction. Illustrates types and features of construction and how buildings collapse. Demonstrates safety procedures and special dangers. Produced by Fire Engineering Books & Videos.
Health and Safety; Science - Physical; Social Science
Dist - OKSU

Wood Heat 28 MIN
U-matic / VHS / 16mm
Home Energy Conservation Series
Color (A)
LC 81-700073
Offers tips on firewood and wood stoves.
Home Economics
Dist - BULFRG **Prod** - RPFD 1980

Wood is Too Good to Burn 29 MIN
U-matic / VHS
Color
LC 82-706621
Explains how, in the face of rising materials' costs and resource depletion, timber offers a renewable and versatile alternative to plastics and fibers in the making of many products.
Agriculture; Science - Natural; Social Science
Dist - PBS **Prod** - WETN 1980

Wood Joints 13 MIN
16mm
Hand Tools for Wood Working Series
Color (J)
Joining wood - - butt, rabbet, dado and groove, dowel and half lap joints.
Industrial and Technical Education
Dist - SF **Prod** - MORLAT 1967

The Wood Lathe 17 MIN
VHS / BETA
Woodworking Power Tools Series
Color (IND)
Industrial and Technical Education
Dist - RMIBHF **Prod** - RMIBHF

The Wood Lathe
VHS
Woodworking Power Tools Series
(C G)
$59.00 _ CA180
Demonstrates the handing and operation of the wood lathe.
Industrial and Technical Education
Dist - AAVIM **Prod** - AAVIM 1989

Wood Lathe and Accessories - Operation and Safety
VHS
Woodworking Power Tools Videos Series
$89.00 purchase _ #LX6105
Provides instruction on basic and advanced operational techniques for the wood lathe and accessories. Uses close up photograpy to show how each machine performs cutting, forming, or shaping operations. Stresses safety procedures and considerations including use of each machine's safety guards.
Industrial and Technical Education
Dist - CAREER **Prod** - CAREER

Wood Lathe Safety
VHS / Slide
Wood Safety Series
Color
$28.00 purchase _ #TX1B10 filmstrip, $58.00 purchase _ #TX1B10V VHS
Industrial and Technical Education
Dist - CAREER **Prod** - CAREER

Wood - Masterpiece of Creation 28 MIN
U-matic / VHS / 16mm
Color (H C A)
Examines the various properties of wood including its complex components, different cuts, the distinction between hard and soft types and its diversity of uses in the home.
Industrial and Technical Education; Psychology; Social Science
Dist - IFB **Prod** - SUCF 1966

Wood Plastic - a New Dimension 12 MIN
U-matic / VHS / 16mm
Color (H C)
LC 78-707263
Demonstrates the use of the catalyst heat system in making wood plastic. Shows how the usual disadvantages of wood are minimized by this process and presents a commercial use for the new material.
Business and Economics; Science - Physical
Dist - IFB **Prod** - HOLTMB 1969

Wood Preservation - Control of Marine Organisms 21 MIN
16mm
Color
LC FIE61-135
Describes corrective measures for effective control of damage by marine organisms to wood.
Industrial and Technical Education; Science - Natural
Dist - USNAC **Prod** - USN 1959

Wood Preservation - Control of Wood Destroying Organisms 24 MIN
16mm
Color
LC FIE57-33
Outlines methods which can be employed to control wood destroying organisms.
Agriculture; Industrial and Technical Education; Science - Natural
Dist - USNAC **Prod** - USN 1959

Wood Preservation - Effects of Marine Organisms 20 MIN
16mm
Color
LC FIE61-134
Shows the habits, characteristics and economic significance of marine organisms in waterfront structures.
Industrial and Technical Education; Science - Natural
Dist - USNAC **Prod** - USN 1959

Wood Preservation - Inspection for Wood Destroying Organisms 18 MIN
16mm
Color
LC FIE57-34
Describes problems faced by the navy in maintaining its wooden structures.
Agriculture; Industrial and Technical Education; Science - Natural
Dist - USNAC **Prod** - USN 1959

Wood, Pt 1
VHS / U-matic
Pulp and Paper Training, Module 1 - Kraft Pulping Series
Color (IND)
Covers types of wood, wood structure and wood characteristics.
Business and Economics; Industrial and Technical Education; Social Science
Dist - LEIKID **Prod** - LEIKID

Wood Safety Series
Circular table saw safety
Hand - Held Power Tool Safety
Hand Tool Safety
Introduction to Woodshop - Carpentry Safety
Jointer Safety
Planer, Disc Sander, Drill Press, Grinder Safety
Power Equipment Safety
Radial Arm and Band Saw Safety
Shaper - Scroll Saw Safety
Wood Lathe Safety
Dist - CAREER

Wood Sculptor 6 MIN
U-matic / VHS / 16mm
Color (I)
LC 76-701937
Follows sculptor Nick Edmunds through the creation of a massive wood sculpture.
Fine Arts
Dist - PHENIX

Wood series
Choosing and cutting firewood 25 MIN
Fireplaces and woodstoves 24 MIN
Dist - MOKIN

The Wood Shell 31 MIN
16mm
House Construction Series
Color
LC 81-700821
Depicts the carpentry construction of a home. Illustrates architectural plans, the installation of wood sills, girders, floor joists, stud walls, framing of ceiling joists and roof rafters, and plywood sheathing of walls and roof. Shows the daily progress on a residential building site and the basic steps and procedures in wood frame construction.
Industrial and Technical Education
Dist - COPRO **Prod** - COPRO 1980

Wood shop - safety and operations series
Center Guiding of Drawers 9 MIN
Safety and operation of faceplate turning - Pt 1 8 MIN

Safety and operation of faceplate turning - Pt 2 12 MIN
Safety demonstration on the band saw 14 MIN
Safety demonstration on the jointer 12 MIN
Safety demonstration on the radial saw 12 MIN
Safety demonstration on the single surface planer 15 MIN
Safety demonstration on the table saw 20 MIN
Safety demonstration on the table saw - Pt 1 11 MIN
Safety demonstration on the wood lathe 11 MIN
Safety demonstration on the wood shaper - Pt 1 11 MIN
Safety demonstration on the wood shaper - Pt 2 10 MIN
Using the Shaper to make Drawers 14 MIN
Using the shaper to make panel doors 16 MIN
Using the shaper to make raised panels for doors 9 MIN
Dist - AIMS

Wood stork - Barometer of the Everglades 60 MIN
VHS
National Audubon Society specials series
Color; Captioned (G)
$49.95 purchase _ #NTAS - 302
Shows how environmental damage to the Florida Everglades has made the indigenous wood stork an endangered species. Describes biological, conservationist and political efforts to address the damage. Also produced by Turner Broadcasting and WETA - TV. Narrated by Richard Crenna.
Science - Natural
Dist - PBS **Prod** - NAS 1988

Wood Stove Wisdom 15 MIN
16mm
Color (A)
Introduces Ezra Winter, a Maine backwoodsman and volunteer firefighter who presents safety rules pertaining to wood stove wisdom. Discusses buying, installing and maintaining wood stoves.
Health and Safety
Dist - NFPA **Prod** - NFPA 1981

Wood Turning 10 MIN
16mm
Color; B&W (J)
Hugh Baird, industrial arts instructor for the Los Angeles school system, demonstrates the technique of wood turning, using one of the new multiple unit power tools.
Industrial and Technical Education
Dist - AVED **Prod** - ALLMOR 1957

Wood, Woodyard and Pulping
U-matic / VHS
Pulp and Paper Training, Module 1 - Kraft Pulping Series
Color (IND)
Covers wood, wood preparation, chipping and pulping methods.
Business and Economics; Industrial and Technical Education; Social Science
Dist - LEIKID **Prod** - LEIKID

Wood work - machine tools series
Band saw 13 MIN
Dist - SF

Woodblock Mandala - the World of Shiko Munkata 30 MIN
16mm
Japanese Woodblock Series
Color (H C A)
Explains the process of Japanese woodblock prints.
Fine Arts; Industrial and Technical Education
Dist - FI **Prod** - NHK 1973

Woodcarver's Workshop Series
Decoy carving 28 MIN
Finishing Techniques 28 MIN
Review 29 MIN
Sculpture in the round 28 MIN
Tools of the Trade 30 MIN
Whittling 28 MIN
Dist - PBS

The Woodcock 6 MIN
16mm / U-matic / VHS
Color (J H C)
Observes the plumage pattern, natural camouflage, nesting and feeding habits of the woodcock.
Science - Natural
Dist - IFB **Prod** - CRAF 1956

The Woodcuts of Antonio Frasconi 25 MIN
16mm
Color (H A)
$600.00 purchase, $65.00 rental
Captures a wide range of the works of Antonio Frasconi, who creates woodblock prints of impressionistic landscapes and compelling images of the victims of war and terrorism. Produced by his son, Pablo Frasconi.
Fine Arts
Dist - AFA

The Woodcutter and the Magic Tree - a North African Folk Tale 7 MIN
16mm
Folk Tales from Around the World Series
Color (K P I)
LC 80-700848
Presents an animated story about a poor woodcutter who spares an ancient tree and is rewarded with a magic platter that constantly replenishes itself with food.
Literature and Drama
Dist - SF **Prod** - ADPF 1980

Woodcutters of the Deep South 90 MIN
16mm
Color
Shows how poor black and white working people of the deep South are trying to overcome the forces of racism among themselves to organize into a cooperative association to dispel the bonds ot their economic captors - the paper and the pulpwood companies. Features interviews with the men directly involved in the formation of this group, the Gulf - Coast Pulpwood Association.
Social Science; Sociology
Dist - IMPACT **Prod** - ROGOSN 1973

The Wooden gun 91 MIN
VHS
Color (G) (HEBREW WITH ENGLISH SUBTITLES)
$79.95 purchase _ #529
Recreates the tense atmosphere of Tel Aviv of the late 1950s. Focuses on two rival groups of teens whose behavior, motivated by the concepts of heroism, nationalism and friendship, raises hard questions. Portrays first generation sabras - native born Israelis - and Jews who came to Israel from Europe, many of them Holocaust survivors. Features Eric Rosen, Judith Solng, Leo Yung and Ophelia Strahl. Directed by Ilan Moshenson.
Fine Arts; History - World; Literature and Drama; Sociology
Dist - ERGOM **Prod** - ERGOM 1979

Wooden House 10 MIN
U-matic
Get it together series
Color (P I)
Teaches children how to make a house with rooms and a roof from sticks and glue.
Fine Arts
Dist - TVOTAR **Prod** - TVOTAR 1978

Wooden Lullaby 7 MIN
16mm
B&W (H C A)
Presents a short vignette about a whorish mother, her lonely son and his wooden rocking horse.
Sociology
Dist - CFS **Prod** - CFS 1964

The Wooden Overcoat 14 MIN
16mm
Color
LC 74-705967
Shows that a container having six - inch - thick shells of fir plywood will adequately protect the inner metal container of radioactive material. Shows the development and testing of the wooden containers as well as how they are made.
Industrial and Technical Education; Science; Science - Physical
Dist - USNAC **Prod** - USNRC 1965

Wooden Ships and Men of Iron 14 MIN
16mm / U-matic / VHS
Color (J A)
Portrays the Cape Cod whaling industry through archival footage of ships under sail, harpooners on the attack and shipwrecks. Presents the US Livesaving Service in action rescuing victims of these shipwrecks.
Business and Economics; Geography - United States; Social Science
Dist - USNAC **Prod** - USNPS 1984

Wooden Shoe (Clog) Study 24 MIN
VHS / U-matic
Color (PRO)
LC 80-707598
Demonstrates the improvement in walking ability exhibited by multiple sclerosis patients wearing wooden clogs with a special ankle strap.
Health and Safety
Dist - USNAC **Prod** - USVA 1980

A Woodland Community 15 MIN
VHS / U-matic
Why Series
Color (P I)
Discusses the living things found in a forest.
Science - Natural
Dist - AITECH **Prod** - WDCNTV 1976

Woodland Ecology - Fauna 19 MIN
16mm
Color (P I J)
Shows the kinds of animals found in a typical oak wood. Describes methods of locating the animals.
Science - Natural
Dist - VIEWTH **Prod** - GATEEF

Woodland Ecology - Flora 19 MIN
16mm
Color (P I J)
Describes the seasonal variations and life cycles of the plants found in a typical wood.
Science - Natural
Dist - VIEWTH **Prod** - GATEEF

Woodland Indians of Early America 10 MIN
U-matic / VHS / 16mm
Color (P I)
$265, $185 purchase _ #4055
Shows how the Chippewa Indians lived and their agricultural way of life.
Social Science
Dist - CORF

The Woodlands 28 MIN
16mm
Spadework for History Series
Color (C A)
Emphasizes planning and initial reconnaissance that form the early part of work in any reservoir project. All the stages of the project, through final publications are included. Covers the stories of two reservoir projects - - the Allegheny Reservoir, a public flood control project in northwestern Pennsylvania, and the Gaston Reservoir, a private power project in North Carolina.
Health and Safety; Industrial and Technical Education; Sociology
Dist - UTEX **Prod** - UTEX 1964

Woodlawn sisterhood 28 MIN
16mm
Are you listening series
Color (J)
LC 80-701132
Presents a primer on do - it - yourself community organization as delivered by the women who created their own organization on the south side of Chicago. Discusses summer programs for girls, a lunch program for children, a drop - in center, male and female relations in the community effort, the problems of jealousy and gossip among women, child care and the importance of cohesiveness.
Sociology
Dist - STURTM **Prod** - STURTM 1972

Woodlot harvesting kit series
Felling and limbing - Pt 2 27 MIN
Management, Gear and Maintenance, Pt 1 44 MIN
Dist - VEP

Woodpecker 25 MIN
VHS
Nature watch series
Color (P I J H C)
$49.00 purchase _ #320211; LC 89-715855
Demonstrates the unique characteristics of the well - known woodpecker, and shows how useful its special traits are. Part of a series that explores the curious and uncommon characteristics of a variety of mammals, insects, birds and sea creatures.
Science - Natural
Dist - TVOTAR **Prod** - TVOTAR 1988

The Woodpecker Gets Ready for Winter 9 MIN
VHS / 16mm
Color (P I)
Reveals the unique manner in which the el carpentero woodpecker stores acorns for winter. Shows the interrelationship between animals and plants of the forest.
Science - Natural
Dist - MIS **Prod** - MIS 1958

Woodpeckers 3 MIN
16mm
Of all Things Series
Color (P I)
Discusses the birds known as woodpeckers.
Science - Natural
Dist - AVED **Prod** - BAILYL

Woodpeckers and Spiders 10 MIN
VHS
Tiny tales series
Color (K P I)
$195.00 purchase
Presents two short animated stories narrated in rhyme by Ivor the spider. Tells a story about woodpeckers in A Woodpecker's Worry and about spiders in Ivor Goes to School.
Literature and Drama
Dist - LANDMK **Prod** - LANDMK

The Woodpile 29 MIN
16mm / U-matic / VHS
Insight Series
B&W (J H A)
LC FIA66-684
Dramatizes the problem faced by the board of directors of a large electronic firm which must decide whether or not to hire its first Negro executive.
Business and Economics; History - United States; Psychology; Sociology
Dist - PAULST **Prod** - PAULST 1965

Woodrow Cornett - Letcher County Butcher 10 MIN
16mm
B&W (H C A)
LC 79-700978
Presents a documentary about a butcher's art in the Appalachian mountains. Features Woodrow Cornett who makes a living by butchering hogs and steers. Includes Appalachian songs played on the harmonica by Ashland Fouts.
Agriculture; Fine Arts; Geography - United States; Sociology
Dist - APPAL **Prod** - APPAL 1971

Woodrow Wilson 26 MIN
VHS / U-matic
Biography series
Color (H C)
$79.00 purchase _ #HH - 6226C
Explores the life of Woodrow Wilson. Reveals that during his presidency, Wilson curbed giant holding companies and inaugurated the first income tax. Part of a series portraying a diverse group of personalities who shaped some aspect of world and cultural history.
Biography; Business and Economics; History - United States
Dist - CORF **Prod** - WOLPER 1963
MGHT

Woodrow Wilson 50 MIN
VHS / U-matic
Profiles in Courage Series
Color; B&W (I J H)
LC 83-706548
Dramatizes the controversy surrounding President Woodrow Wilson's nomination of Louis Brandeis, a Jew, to the Supreme Court. Shows how Wilson braved religious prejudice and political opposition to defend Brandeis. Based on book Profiles In Courage by John F Kennedy.
Biography; Civics and Political Systems; History - United States
Dist - SSSSV **Prod** - SAUDEK 1965

Woodrow Wilson and the Treaties 29 MIN
Videoreel / VT2
Course of Our Times I Series
Color
History - World
Dist - PBS **Prod** - WGBHTV

Woodrow Wilson - idealism and American democracy 38 MIN
VHS
Color (J H)
$89.00 purchase _ #06009 - 026
Includes teacher's guide and library kit.
Biography; Education; History - United States
Dist - GA

Woodrow Wilson - Peace and War and the Professor President 23 MIN
16mm / U-matic / VHS
American lifestyle series; U S Presidents
Color (J)
Present mementoes of Woodrow Wilson's distinguished and inspiring career.
Biography
Dist - AIMS **Prod** - COMCO 1984
UILL

Woodrow Wilson, Pt 1 25 MIN
16mm
Profiles in Courage Series
Color (I)
Portrays Woodrow Wilson standing by his nomination of Louis D Brandeis to the U S Supreme Court despite widespread religious prejudice against Brandeis.
Biography; Civics and Political Systems; History - United States
Dist - SSSSV **Prod** - SAUDEK 1965

Woodrow Wilson, Pt 2 25 MIN
16mm
Profiles in Courage Series
Color (I)
Portrays Woodrow Wilson standing by his nomination of Louis D Brandeis to the U S Supreme Court despite widespread religious prejudice against Brandeis.
Biography; Civics and Political Systems; History - United States
Dist - SSSSV **Prod** - SAUDEK 1965

Woodrow Wilson - the Fight for a League of Nations 20 MIN
U-matic / VHS / 16mm
Great Decisions Series
Color (I J H C)
LC 71-709707
Focuses on the problem Woodrow Wilson had in making his dream of a new League of Nations into a reality. Presents facts and asks the viewer to decide whether or not he would have voted for the League.
Biography; Civics and Political Systems; History - United States; History - World
Dist - AMEDFL **Prod** - PSP 1970

The Woods 15 MIN
VHS / U-matic / VT1
Walking with Grandfather series
Color (G)
$39.95 purchase, $35.00 rental
Emphasizes the importance of forgiveness in the story of the Corn Maidens. Reveals that in the beginning people had only grass and seeds to eat. They made offerings and prayer for better food. Six beautiful Corn Maidens came to Earth to show how to grow corn. The people were grateful and worked hard to take care of the corn, but they become lazy and scornful and the Corn Maidens left because they can't stay where they are not respected. The people realize they have sinned but only the flute player, always loyal to the Corn Maidens, can call them back. They come back and graciously forgive the people, who celebrate each year the generosity of the Corn Maidens. Part of a series on storytelling by elders produced by Phil Lucas Productions, Inc.
Guidance and Counseling; Literature and Drama; Social Science
Dist - NAMPBC

Woods Guiding - Fishing 19 MIN
U-matic
Occupations Series
Color (J H)
Interviews an occupational course student, his employer and two guests at a fishing resort on the duties of woods guiding.
Guidance and Counseling
Dist - TVOTAR **Prod** - TVOTAR 1985

Woods Guiding - Hunting 19 MIN
U-matic
Occupations Series
B&W (J H)
Interviews an occupational course student at a flying camp about a moose hunt and his work as a guide.
Guidance and Counseling
Dist - TVOTAR **Prod** - TVOTAR 1985

Woods - Review 13 MIN
16mm
B&W
Highlights of Byron Nelson's professional career with Jimmy Demaret giving a lesson on the use of irons and woods.
Physical Education and Recreation
Dist - SFI **Prod** - SFI

Woodsmen and river drivers - another day, another era 30 MIN
VHS
Color; B&W (G)
$19.95 purchase
Brings out the dangers and discomforts of lumber camp life during the 1920s through interviews with men of the Machias Lumber Company in Maine.
Fine Arts; History - United States
Dist - NEFILM

The Woodwind family 15 MIN
VHS / U-matic
Music machine series
Color (P)
Teaches recognition of woodwind musical instruments.
Fine Arts
Dist - GPN **Prod** - GPN

The Woodwind Family - 16 15 MIN
VHS
Music and Me Series
Color (P)
$125.00 purchase
Looks at musical instruments in the woodwind family. Encourages student participation to develop skills in singing, listening, rhythmic expression and playing simple instruments. Part of the Music And Me Series.
Fine Arts
Dist - AITECH **Prod** - WDCNTV 1979

Woodwinds and dance 10 MIN
U-matic / 16mm / VHS / BETA
Indians of the Orinoco - the Makiritare tribe series
Color (G H C)
Records two Makiritare Indians making bassoon - like reed instruments, which are made from green wood. Shows that they last only a short time and are used right after their manufacture in a village dance. Without narration. Part of an eight - part series on the Makiritare Indians of Venezuela.
Fine Arts; Social Science; Sociology
Dist - IFF **Prod** - IFF 1972
EDPAT

Woodwinds in Multiples 29 MIN
Videoreel / VT2
American Band Goes Symphonic Series
B&W
Fine Arts
Dist - PBS **Prod** - WGTV

Woodwork - machine tools series
Portable electric sander 13 MIN
Power Drills for Woodwork 13 MIN
The Scroll saw 13 MIN
Woodworking Lathe - Face Plate Turning 13 MIN
Woodworking Lathe - Spindle Turning 13 MIN
Dist - SF

Woodworking
VHS
Around the home series
Color (G)
$29.95 purchase _ #IV - 012
Introduces the materials and basic construction of woodworking. Demonstrates power tools and emphasizes safety in their use.
Home Economics; Industrial and Technical Education
Dist - INCRSE **Prod** - INCRSE

Woodworking Explained - Building a Better Bookshelf 99 MIN
VHS / 35mm strip
(H A IND)
#701XV7
Shows how to draw a working plan (pt 1 and 2), basic layout techniques, how to cut stock, planing, drilling and boring, sanding, basic assembly techniques, and finishing (9 tapes). Includes a Study Guide.
Education; Industrial and Technical Education
Dist - BERGL

Woodworking Hand Tools Explained 72 MIN
VHS / 35mm strip
Color (J H A IND)
#703XV7
Introduces the types and proper uses of various woodworking hand tools. Includes measuring tools, marking tools, cutting tools, wood planes, forming and shaping tools, and files and finishing tools (6 tapes). Includes a Study Guide.
Education; Industrial and Technical Education
Dist - BERGL

Woodworking Lathe - Face Plate Turning 13 MIN
16mm
Woodwork - Machine Tools Series
Color (J)
Presents five concepts dealing with the woodworking lathe - face plate turning - - mounting the face plate, mounting work on the face plate, setting up, turning to diameter and finishing edge to shape. The projector may be stopped after each concept.
Industrial and Technical Education
Dist - SF **Prod** - SF 1967

Woodworking Lathe - Spindle Turning 13 MIN
16mm
Woodwork - Machine Tools Series
Color (J)
LC 73-712982
Presents six concepts dealing with the woodworking lathe - spindle turning - - parts, cutting tools, centering stock, mounting the work, rough turning, and cutting curves, grooves and shoulders. The projector may be stopped after each concept.
Industrial and Technical Education
Dist - SF **Prod** - MORLAT 1967

Woodworking Machine Operations 87 MIN
VHS / 35mm strip
Color (J H A IND)
#702XV7
Introduces and explains the safe operating procedures of many commonly used woodworking machines. Includes operating the circular saw, the scroll saw, the band saw, the jointer, the drill press, the woodworking lathe, and faceplate turning on the woodworking lathe (7 tapes). Includes a Study Guide.
Education; Industrial and Technical Education
Dist - BERGL

Woodworking Power Tools Series
Circular saws
Drilling machines
Planing Machines
Router and Shaper

Sanding Machines
The Wood Lathe
Dist - AAVIM

Woodworking Power Tools Series
Band, jig and saber saws 18 MIN
Circular saws 19 MIN
Drilling Machines 15 MIN
Planing Machines 15 MIN
Router and Shaper 14 MIN
Sanding Machines 13 MIN
The Wood Lathe 17 MIN
Dist - RMIBHF

Woodworking Power Tools Videos
VHS
Woodworking Power Tools Videos Series
$395.00 purchase _ #LX6100
Provides instruction on basic and advanced operational techniques for the woodworking power tools. Uses close up photograpy to show how each machine performs cutting, forming, or shaping operations. Stresses safety procedures and considerations including use of each machine's safety guards.
Industrial and Technical Education
Dist - CAREER **Prod** - CAREER

Woodworking Power Tools Videos Series
Band saw - operation and safety
Jointer - Surfacer and Accessories - Operation and Safety
Radial Arm Saw - Operation and Safety
Table Saw and Accessories
Wood Lathe and Accessories - Operation and Safety
Woodworking Power Tools Videos
Dist - CAREER

Woodworking powers tools series
Band, jig, and saber saws
Dist - AAVIM

Woodworking Projects 30 MIN
VHS
$39.95 purchase _ #DI - 406
Discusses how to build various woodworking projects. Includes bandsaw boxes, towel racks, cassette racks and turning bowls.
Industrial and Technical Education
Dist - CAREER **Prod** - CAREER

Woodworking Series
Attic conversion 36 MIN
Basic carpentry 44 MIN
Basic home repair 30 MIN
Building bookcases
Building cabinets
Building tables
Ceramic Tile - Floors and Countertops 27 MIN
Ceramic Tile - Walls 27 MIN
Decorating - selecting the right carpet 25 MIN
Easy to build woodworking projects
Energy conservation 30 MIN
Exterior projects 45 MIN
Furniture refinishing 22 MIN
Garages - Wall Framing, Roof Framing and Sheathing, Roofing, Siding and Finishing 60 MIN
Interior Paint and Wallpaper 30 MIN
Interior Projects 45 MIN
Kitchens 52 MIN
Molding and Picture Frame - Molding
Outdoor Furniture - Hexagonal Picnic Table
Paneling 30 MIN
Dist - AAVIM

Woodworking series
Basic tools 88 MIN
Dovetails 80 MIN
Finishing and Polishing 80 MIN
Hinging, Clamping and Screwing 74 MIN
Mortice and Tenon - Dados 56 MIN
Preparation of surfaces - planing 63 MIN
Sharpening - Inlaying and Detailing 86 MIN
Dist - ANVICO

Woodworking series
Gives students the knowledge necessary to increase and refine their woodworking skills.
Woodworking series
Dist - CAREER **Prod** - CAREER

Woodworking series
Creative sculpturing for everyone, Pt 1 13 MIN
Creative sculpturing for everyone, Pt 2 13 MIN
How to hang a door 13 MIN
How to Use Chisels and Gouges 13 MIN
How to Use Hand Boring Tools 13 MIN
How to Use Planes 13 MIN
Dist - VISIN

Woodworking Tools 30 MIN
U-matic / VHS
Antique Shop Series
Color
Presents guests who are experts in their respective fields who share tips on collecting and caring for antique woodworking tools.
Fine Arts
Dist - MDCPB **Prod** - WVPTTV

Woodworking - Trees to Lumber 10 MIN
BETA / VHS
Color (IND)
Shows the processes involved in woodworking, from logging to lumber.
Agriculture; Business and Economics
Dist - RMIBHF **Prod** - RMIBHF

Woodworking video series
Building bookcases 40 MIN
Building cabinets 35 MIN
Building tables 40 MIN
Easy to build woodworking projects 30 MIN
Molding and picture frame 30 MIN
Outdoor projects 40 MIN
Dist - DIYVC

Woody Allen - an American Comedy 33 MIN
U-matic
Color (J)
LC 77-701974
Presents Woody Allen talking about his life and work as a writer, dramatist and filmmaker and discusses his creative sources, theoretical approaches and working methods. Shows scenes from some of his major films, including Take The Money And Run, Sleeper, Love And Death and Annie Hall.
Biography; English Language; Fine Arts; Literature and Drama
Dist - FOTH **Prod** - FOTH 1977

Woody el pajaro loco y sus amigos 30 MIN
VHS
Color (G) (SPANISH)
$9.95 purchase _ #W1461
Features the adventures of cartoon character Woody Woodpecker.
Fine Arts; Foreign Language; Literature and Drama
Dist - GPC

Woody Guthrie 52 MIN
U-matic / VHS
Rainbow quest series
Color
Features a solo performance by Pete Seeger in which he sings some of the hundreds of songs composed by Woody Guthrie. Includes film and photos of Woody.
Fine Arts
Dist - NORROS **Prod** - SEEGER

Woody Guthrie 13 MIN
U-matic / VHS
Color (G)
$229.00, $129.00 purchase _ #AD - 1754
Profiles Woody Guthrie, musician and singer who wrote anthems for the poor and oppressed of America.
Biography; Fine Arts; History - United States
Dist - FOTH **Prod** - FOTH

Woody plant production series
Presents two parts on woody plant production. Includes the titles Container Grown Plants and Field Grown Plants.
Container grown plants
Field grown plants
Dist - VEP **Prod** - VEP

Woody Vasulka - Artifacts 23 MIN
U-matic / VHS
Color
Presented by Woody Vasulka.
Fine Arts
Dist - ARTINC **Prod** - ARTINC

Woody Vasulka - the Commission 45 MIN
U-matic / VHS
Color
Employs an operatic form to tell the story of a 19th century commission offered to the violinist Niccolo Paganini.
Fine Arts
Dist - ARTINC **Prod** - ARTINC

Wool 10 MIN
VHS
Stop, look, listen series
Color; PAL (P I J)
Follows the processing of wool from the sheep's back to a human's back. Shows hand processes as the sheep is sheared, the wool washed, carded, combed and spun on a spinning wheel. Shows the variety of things made from wool. Part of a series of films which start from some everyday observation and show more of what is happening, how and why. Builds vocabulary and encourages children to be more observant.
Agriculture; English Language; Industrial and Technical Education; Social Science
Dist - VIEWTH

Wool and mutton 16 MIN
VHS
Color; PAL (P I J H)
Examines the use of sheep as sources of meat and wool.
Agriculture; Industrial and Technical Education; Social Science
Dist - VIEWTH **Prod** - VIEWTH

Wool in Australia 19 MIN
U-matic / VHS / 16mm
Man and His World Series
Color (P I J H C)
LC 72-705463
Describes life in an isolated area of Australia and the living conditions of a family who raise sheep. Tells how the sheep are sheared, the wool is sorted, graded, baled and shipped to a market in Melbourne or Sydney to be auctioned to buyers from all over the world.
Agriculture; Geography - World
Dist - FI **Prod** - FI 1969

A Wooley tale - Volume 1 25 MIN
VHS
Filling station series
Color (K P I R)
$11.99 purchase _ #35 - 811300 - 979
Combines live action and animated sequences to teach the message that people are the symbolic sheep of God's pasture.
Literature and Drama; Religion and Philosophy
Dist - APH **Prod** - TYHP

Woolf 23 MIN
VHS / 16mm
Color; B&W (G)
$45.00 purchase, $46.00 rental
Entertains with a comedy about a larger - than - life character reminiscent of Buchner's Woyzeck. Presents Woolf as a blue collar heroine who doesn't fit in and doesn't want to. Highlights include rubber chickens, a skyscraper - high pan of Coke cans, newspapers, food and other items of concern to Woolf. The entire cast and crew are women in this production by Virginia Sandman.
Fine Arts; Social Science; Sociology
Dist - CANCIN

Worcester State College
VHS
Campus clips series
Color (H C A)
$29.95 purchase _ #CC0110V
Takes a video visit to the campus of Worcester State College in Massachusetts. Shows many of the distinctive features of the campus, and interviews students about their experiences. Provides information on the composition of the student body, professors, academics, social life, housing, and other subjects.
Education
Dist - CAMV

Word Analysis Skills 20 MIN
U-matic / VHS / 16mm
Literacy Instructor Training Series
Color (T)
LC 78-700888
Introduces formal diagnostic procedures, such as listening to the students read to determine specific instructional needs. Uses word analysis skills to aid reading fluency and comprehension.
Education; English Language
Dist - IU **Prod** - NEWPAR 1978

Word Elements 11 MIN
U-matic / VHS
Better Spelling Series Lesson 3A; Lesson 3A
Color
English Language
Dist - DELTAK **Prod** - TELSTR

Word Families / Compound Words 19 MIN
BETA / VHS
Color
Teaches basic vocabulary skills. Uses stories and visuals to show how words are formed.
English Language
Dist - PHENIX **Prod** - PHENIX

Word from Our Sponsor 4 MIN
16mm
Color (H C A)
Presents the role of the television commercial in modern love life.
Fine Arts; Literature and Drama
Dist - UWFKD **Prod** - UWFKD

A Word from the Sponsor 28 MIN
U-matic / VHS
Please Stand by - a History of Radio Series

(C A)
Fine Arts; History - United States; Psychology; Sociology
Dist - SCCON **Prod** - SCCON 1986

Word grouping road 20 MIN
U-matic / VHS
Efficient reading - instructional tapes series; Tape 9
Color
Demonstrates how to read groups of words to help structure the author's main idea.
English Language
Dist - TELSTR **Prod** - TELSTR

The Word Hunt (Similar Meanings) 13 MIN
16mm / U-matic / VHS
Fun with Words Series
Color (P)
$315, $220 purchase _ #3490
Describes synonyms, regional variations, and how words add richness to the language.
English Language
Dist - CORF

A Word in Edgewise 26 MIN
VHS / 16mm
Color (G)
$250.00 purchase, $60.00 rental
Documents sex - biased language as well as alternatives to bias. Offers the example of over 200 terms vilifying women compared to only twenty terms vilifying men. Interviews university professors and people on the street, looks at everyday language and the historical development of English to convey how the unconscious use of biased language affects our perceptions of the world and promotes inequality between the sexes. Produced by Heather MacLeod.
English Language; History - World; Psychology; Sociology
Dist - WMEN **Prod** - HML 1986

A Word in Time 24 MIN
VHS / 16mm
Color (A PRO)
$435.00 purchase, $160.00 rental
Shows how to organize and manage projects. Illustrates time management, delegation, communication, management and supervision for working efficiently and effectively. Management training.
Guidance and Counseling; Psychology
Dist - VIDART **Prod** - VIDART 1990

Word is Out 45 MIN
16mm 130 MIN
Color
Chronicles what it's like to be a homosexual. Presents interviews with gay men and lesbians of various life - styles, races, ages, and socio - economic backgrounds.
Psychology; Sociology
Dist - NYFLMS **Prod** - UNKNWN 1978

Word Magic (2nd Ed Series
Your Face Speaks 15 MIN
Dist - GPN

Word Meaning 30 MIN
U-matic / VHS
Teaching Reading Comprehension Series
Color (T PRO)
$180.00 purchase,$50.00 rental
Demonstrates techniques for development of word meaning in students and its effects on reading skills and comprehension.
English Language
Dist - AITECH **Prod** - WETN 1986

Word movie - Fluxfilm 29 4 MIN
16mm
Color (G)
$9.00 rental
Features fifty words visually repeated in varying sequential and positioned relationships. Looks at each frame as a different word.
Fine Arts
Dist - CANCIN **Prod** - SHARIT 1966

Word of honor - Volume 11 40 MIN
VHS
Circle square series
Color (J H R)
$11.99 purchase _ #35 - 867640 - 979
Reveals the importance of trustworthiness in dealings with friends. Contains Biblical principles as the underlying theme.
Religion and Philosophy
Dist - APH **Prod** - TYHP

Word of Life - People of Rivers 28 MIN
VHS / U-matic
Real People Series
Color (G)
Serves as an introduction to the history of the seven tribes and a map for future growth. It is a good foundation for in depth studies of each tribe. It offers a new perspective on Indian history, past and future, rather than the conventional historical survey of battles and defeats.
Social Science
Dist - NAMPBC **Prod** - NAMPBC 1976

Word on the street... - HIV - AIDS prevention for very high - risk youth 18 MIN
VHS
Color (I J H)
$189.00 purchase
Aims at high - risk teens in non - school settings - medical and social work situations, foster care, the juvenile justice system, emergency shelters. Portrays a dangerous day in the life of a group of kids on the street. Looks at their encounters with drugs, sex, AIDS, HIV, pregnancy and death, drawn from the real stories of young people across the country.
Health and Safety; Psychology; Sociology
Dist - SELMED **Prod** - ODNP 1992

Word Order, the Pause and the Importance of Meaning 15 MIN
U-matic / VHS
Treatment of the Borderline Patient Series
Color
Discusses the use and implications of altered or unusual work sequences, double entendres, timing of words, pauses and accentuations.
Health and Safety; Psychology
Dist - HEMUL **Prod** - HEMUL

Word Play 15 MIN
VHS / U-matic
Strawberry Square II - Take Time Series
Color (P)
Fine Arts
Dist - AITECH **Prod** - NEITV 1984

Word Power - Vocabulary Building Series
Be Brief 30 MIN
Be Concrete 30 MIN
Be lively 30 MIN
Be orderly 30 MIN
Be personal 30 MIN
Be poetic 30 MIN
Be simple 30 MIN
Be tactful 30 MIN
Dist - DELTAK

Word Power - Vocabulary Building Series
Be Exact 30 MIN
Dist - TELSTR

Word Power Workouts, Tape 1 30 MIN
U-matic / VHS
Efficient Reading - Expediter Tapes Series
Color
Focuses on increasing fluency through working with antonyms. Shows tachistoscopic flashes of 20 digits with the shutter speed set at one tenths of a second.
English Language
Dist - TELSTR **Prod** - TELSTR

Word Power Workouts, Tape 2 30 MIN
VHS / U-matic
Efficient Reading - Expediter Tapes Series
Color
Discusses how to increase fluency through working with synonyms. Shows how to look at words in phrase groups to increase speed.
English Language
Dist - TELSTR **Prod** - TELSTR

Word Power Workouts, Tape 3 30 MIN
U-matic / VHS
Efficient Reading - Expediter Tapes Series
Color
Shows how to increase word power by use of contextual clues. Discusses geometric forms.
English Language
Dist - TELSTR **Prod** - TELSTR

Word Power Workouts, Tape 4 30 MIN
U-matic / VHS
Efficient Reading - Expediter Tapes Series
Color
Focuses on understanding the word - meaning in a sentence. Looks at digits as perception promoters.
English Language
Dist - TELSTR **Prod** - TELSTR

Word Power Workouts, Tape 5 30 MIN
VHS / U-matic
Efficient Reading - Expediter Tapes Series
Color
Covers finding the right meaning when reading. Looks at span developers, or spreading out what the eye takes in, as perception promoters.
English Language
Dist - TELSTR **Prod** - TELSTR

Word Power Workouts, Tape 6 30 MIN
VHS / U-matic
Efficient Reading - Expediter Tapes Series
Color
Discusses how to use the context of a passage for comprehension. Presents sentences as perception promoters.
English Language
Dist - TELSTR **Prod** - TELSTR

Word Power Workouts, Tape 7 30 MIN
U-matic / VHS
Efficient Reading - Expediter Tapes Series
Color
Focuses on word parts, how to look for meaning and the prefix 'ex.' Covers digits as perception promoters.
English Language
Dist - TELSTR **Prod** - TELSTR

Word Power Workouts, Tape 8 30 MIN
U-matic / VHS
Efficient Reading - Expediter Tapes Series
Color
Focuses on the prefix 'pre - .' Looks at span developers as perception promoters.
English Language
Dist - TELSTR **Prod** - TELSTR

Word Power Workouts, Tape 9 30 MIN
U-matic / VHS
Efficient Reading - Expediter Tapes Series
Color
Uses the prefix 'de' to improve word power. Studies how to read complete sentences for speed.
English Language
Dist - TELSTR **Prod** - TELSTR

Word Power Workouts, Tape 10 30 MIN
U-matic / VHS
Efficient Reading - Expediter Tapes Series
Color
Focuses on the LDE Formula for word power workouts. Uses geometric forms as perception promoters.
English Language
Dist - TELSTR **Prod** - TELSTR

Word Power Workouts, Tape 11 30 MIN
U-matic / VHS
Efficient Reading - Expediter Tapes Series
Color
Studies roots of words in order to increase word power. Looks at span developers as perception promoters.
English Language
Dist - TELSTR **Prod** - TELSTR

Word Power Workouts, Tape 12 30 MIN
U-matic / VHS
Efficient Reading - Expediter Tapes Series
Color
Focuses on word suffixes in order to increase word power and speed. Uses digits at 1/100 a second for perception promoters.
English Language
Dist - TELSTR **Prod** - TELSTR

Word problems 30 MIN
VHS
College algebra series
Color (C)
$125.00 purchase _ #4007
Explains word problems. Part of a 31 - part series on college algebra.
Mathematics
Dist - LANDMK **Prod** - LANDMK

Word problems
VHS
Beginning algebra series
Color (J H)
$125.00 purchase _ #2015
Teaches fundamental principles used to set up and solve word problems. Part of a series of 31 videos, each between 25 and 30 minutes long, that explain and reinforce basic concepts of algebra. Tutors the student through definitions, theorems, step - by - step solutions and examples. Videos are also available in a set.
Mathematics
Dist - LANDMK

Word Problems 30 MIN
VHS
Mathematics Series
Color (J)
LC 90713155
Explains word problems. The 69th of 157 installments in the Mathematics Series.
Mathematics
Dist - GPN

Word Processing
U-matic / VHS

Work - a - Day America
$59.95 purchase _ #VV121V
Helps students achieve career vocational preparation. Stresses the four main points of career awareness and exploration, specific skills intended, employability skills needed, and real people sharing on the job experiences.
Guidance and Counseling
Dist - CAREER **Prod** - CAREER

Word Processing
16mm
Color
Introduces vital concepts and skills required in word processing, describes on - the - job settings, and contains personal statements, which convey the excitement and challenge of the word processing environment. Takes a close look at the equipment of a word processing center, and shows how a central dictating system works.
Business and Economics
Dist - HBJ **Prod** - HBJ

Word - processing 30 MIN
VHS
Computing for the less terrified series
Color (A)
PdS65 purchase
Asks if using WP can make the viewer a better writer, and if it makes writers more critical of their work. Part of a seven-part series which aims to allay everyone's fear of the computer, whether an individual is an experienced user or relative novice. Explores the numerous applications of the computer and illustrates some of the pitfalls.
Computer Science; English Language; Guidance and Counseling
Dist - BBCENE

Word Processing 30 MIN
U-matic / VHS
On and on about Instruction - Microcomputers Series
Color (C)
Demonstrates word processing and discusses its successful application to educational problems.
Industrial and Technical Education; Mathematics; Psychology
Dist - GPN **Prod** - VADE

Word processing - communication and technology
VHS / U-matic
Computer literacy - computer language series
Color
Discusses word processing and computer use.
Industrial and Technical Education; Mathematics
Dist - LIBFSC **Prod** - LIBFSC

Word Processing in Office Systems 30 MIN
U-matic / VHS
Making it Count Series
Color (H C A)
LC 80-707582
Discusses the application of computer technology to the production of written communications needed by business and industry. Compares the different types of word processing equipment in terms of display and output methods, storage and access methods, and text editing and formatting capabilities. Discusses the factors affecting successful implementation of a system and looks at some future applications of computer technology to office systems.
Business and Economics; Mathematics
Dist - BCSC **Prod** - BCSC 1980

Word Processing on Your Microcomputer - from Keyboard to Printout
VHS / U-matic
Color
Familiarizes with the general applications and techniques of word processing programs. Explores several common editing commands and the interrelationship between word processors and dictionary, mail - merge and communications software.
Mathematics
Dist - GA **Prod** - GA 1984

Word processing series
MicroSoft Word 4.0 introduction 53 MIN
MicroSoft Word 4.0 level II 58 MIN
MicroSoft Word 5.0 introduction 60 MIN
Microsoft Works word processing 1.05 50 MIN
PFS - first choice - word processor introduction 54 MIN
WordPerfect 4.2 introduction 39 MIN
WordPerfect 4.2 level II 56 MIN
WordPerfect 4.2 level III 57 MIN
WordPerfect 5.0 introduction 80 MIN
WordPerfect 5.0 level II 80 MIN
WordPerfect 5.0 level III 60 MIN
WordPerfect 5.1 introduction 57 MIN
WordPerfect 5.1 level II 58 MIN
WordPerfect 5.1 level III 58 MIN
WordStar Pro 4.0 introduction 58 MIN
Dist - CAMV

Word processing series
WordStar Pro 4.0 level II 58 MIN
Dist - CAMV
INSTRU

Word Processing Series
Dictation - Napoleon to now - WP - 8 12 MIN
'In' Side Word Processing - WP - 9 9 MIN
It's Really People - WP - 7 12 MIN
Kissing 'the Girls' Goodbye - WP - 3 13 MIN
'Out' Side Word Processing 13 MIN
The Pivot Point - WP - 5 12 MIN
The Rules of the Game - WP - 6 11 MIN
Take it from the Top - WP - 2 15 MIN
What's it all about - WP - 1 11 MIN
Dist - MONAD

Word Processing - with Microcomputers
U-matic / VHS
Color
Presents the possibilities for doing word processing with microcomputers.
Industrial and Technical Education; Mathematics
Dist - LIBFSC **Prod** - LIBFSC

Word Processing with Microcomputers
VHS / 35mm strip
$40.00 purchase _ #XX6390 filmstrip, $59.00 purchase _ #RM6390V VHS
Shows how word processing can be done on most microcomputers with the proper software and printer.
Computer Science
Dist - CAREER **Prod** - CAREER

The Word processor
VHS
Computer series
Color (G)
$29.95 purchase _ #IV - 001
Overviews the separate components of the computer, their functions and how they interrelate. Illustrates and demonstrates the keyboard, video screen, programs and computer memory systems.
Computer Science
Dist - INCRSE **Prod** - INCRSE

Word Recognition 11 MIN
16mm / U-matic / VHS
Reading Self - Improvement Series
Color (I J H)
$315, $220 purchase _ #3537
Discusses context, phonetic analysis, and the use of the dictionary.
English Language
Dist - CORF

The Word shop series
Uses puppet characters to teach primary school children language skills. Presents information about stories, poems, plays, folktales and books. Thirty - part series is hosted by John Robbins.
The Word shop series 450 MIN
Dist - PBS **Prod** - WETATV 1979

Word Shop Series
Action in stories 15 MIN
Books about animals 15 MIN
Books about fantasy 15 MIN
Books about people 15 MIN
Books about places 15 MIN
Books that answer questions 15 MIN
Character Playing 15 MIN
Characters in Stories 15 MIN
Comic strips 15 MIN
Fantasy stories 15 MIN
Folk tales 15 MIN
Making a Book 15 MIN
Mystery Books 15 MIN
Mystery Stories 15 MIN
News Stories 15 MIN
Nonsense and made - Up Words in Poetry 15 MIN
Playwrights 15 MIN
Poems as Descriptions 15 MIN
Poems as Rhythm 15 MIN
Poems as Sounds 15 MIN
Poems as Stories 15 MIN
Poets 15 MIN
Scene Playing 15 MIN
Setting in Stories 15 MIN
Signs 15 MIN
Story Maker 15 MIN
Story Playing 15 MIN
Story Telling 15 MIN
Structure in Stories 15 MIN
Tall Tales 15 MIN
Dist - WETATV

Word Strategy
U-matic / VHS
Write Course - an Introduction to College Composition Series
Color (C)
Shows common abuses of words with a continuation of a previous lesson.
Education; English Language
Dist - DALCCD **Prod** - DALCCD

Word Strategy 30 MIN
VHS / U-matic
Write Course - an Introduction to College Composition Series
Color (C A)
Emphasizes common abuses of words.
English Language
Dist - FI **Prod** - FI 1984

The Word - Tape 1 20 MIN
VHS
Journeys in faith - Volume II
Color (J H C G A R)
$29.95 purchase, $10.00 rental _ #35 - 8118 - 2076
Examines the Christian concept of Jesus as the Word of God. Produced by Seraphim.
Religion and Philosophy
Dist - APH

Word that Describe Sounds 12 MIN
16mm / U-matic / VHS
Fun with Words Series
Color (P I)
$295, $210 purchase _ #3270
Describes onomatopoeia with demonstrations of the various sounds.
English Language
Dist - CORF

A Word to the Wise 14 MIN
16mm
Color
Shows how to choose a dentist, how to reduce dental bills, what to do if one has a disagreement with his or her dentist and how to know which oral health products to buy.
Health and Safety
Dist - MTP **Prod** - AMDA

Word Twins 10 MIN
U-matic / VHS / 16mm
Fun with Words Series
Color (P)
$265, $185 purchase _ #1941
Discusses antonyms, synonyms, and homonyms.
English Language
Dist - CORF

Word Understanding 14 MIN
16mm / U-matic / VHS
Reading Self - Improvement Series
Color (I J H)
$315, $220 purchase _ #3538
Discusses the meaning of words and how to increase vocabulary.
English Language
Dist - CORF

Word weaving - the art of storytelling 25 MIN
VHS
Color (C G)
$125.00 purchase, $35.00 rental _ #37071
Teaches step - by - step the essential techniques of storytelling. Includes a booklet supplement. Features Catherine Farrell, storyteller and trainer, who also produced the program.
Fine Arts; Literature and Drama
Dist - UCEMC

Word Wise - Antonyms 12 MIN
16mm / U-matic / VHS
Vocabulary Skills Series
Color (P I)
LC 78-700925
Tells the story of the search for the missing Professor Updown in the Antonyms, where all the animals talk in antonyms.
English Language
Dist - PHENIX **Prod** - PHENIX 1977

Word Wise - Compound Words 10 MIN
U-matic / VHS / 16mm
Vocabulary Skills Series
Color (P I)
LC 76-702143
Uses the story of a canoe trip to teach the concept of compound words.
English Language
Dist - PHENIX **Prod** - PHENIX 1976

Word Wise - Homographs 12 MIN
U-matic / VHS / 16mm

Vocabulary Skills Series
Color (P I)
LC 78-700926
Tells the story of Joey Patterson, by who seeks a solution to an attack on Australia by words that are spelled alike but have different meanings, called homographs.
English Language
Dist - PHENIX **Prod** - PHENIX 1977

Word Wise - Homonyms 11 MIN
U-matic / VHS / 16mm
Vocabulary Skills Series
Color (P I)
LC 77-700853
Tells the story of Daisy Daring, who finds a book of secret homonym passwords that if used correctly will lead her to the sunken city of Homonym Bay. Includes Caribbean scenery and underwater photography.
English Language
Dist - PHENIX **Prod** - PHENIX 1977

Word Wise - Prefixes 11 MIN
U-matic / VHS / 16mm
Vocabulary Skills Series
Color (P I)
LC 76-703176
Presents 15 prefixes in a story of a forgetful secret service agent who forgets the secret code, a prefix he must use to identify himself to his fellow agent.
English Language
Dist - PHENIX **Prod** - PHENIX 1976

Word Wise - Root Words 12 MIN
16mm / U-matic / VHS
Vocabulary Skills Series
Color (P I)
LC 77-700094
Follows the adventures of a spaceman disguised as an Earthling as he attempts to learn about root or base words. Presents 20 root or base words, forming more than 44 different words.
English Language
Dist - PHENIX **Prod** - PHENIX 1976

Word Wise - Suffixes 12 MIN
16mm / U-matic / VHS
Vocabulary Skills Series
Color (P I)
LC 76-703175
Tells the Great Suffix Mystery about what happens when all the suffixes disappear from our language. Presents 13 suffixes and basic rules for affixing them to words.
English Language
Dist - PHENIX **Prod** - PHENIX 1976

Word Wise - Synonyms 13 MIN
U-matic / VHS / 16mm
Vocabulary Skills Series
Color (P I)
LC 78-700927
Tells the story of Colonel Daring and his search for Lord and Lady Synonym to find out how the Synonym diamond is like a synonym.
English Language
Dist - PHENIX **Prod** - PHENIX 1977

Word Wise - Word Families 9 MIN
U-matic / VHS / 16mm
Vocabulary Skills Series
Color (P I)
LC 76-701291
Introduces the concept of families of words which have the same ending letters. Provides an understanding of how words are put together and offers aids in rapid word recognition.
English Language
Dist - PHENIX **Prod** - PHENIX 1976

Wordcruncher disc
CD-ROM
(G C)
$239.00 purchase _ #2861
Contains literary, biblical and political texts. Includes the definitive editions of works by Shakespeare, Benjamin Franklin, Willa Cather, Melville, Twain and others, the King James and New International versions of the Bible, and historical documents such as the Federalist Papers and Common Sense. For IBM PCs and compatibles, requires 604K RAM, DOS 3.1 or later, one floppy disk drive - hard disk recommended, one empty expansion slot, and an IBM compatible CD - ROM drive.
History - United States; Literature and Drama
Dist - BEP

Wordly Wise 14 MIN
16mm / VHS / U-matic
Serendipity Series
Color (P)
LC 76-701768
Focuses on the many ways in which life is made up of words.
English Language
Dist - MGHT **Prod** - MGHT 1976

The Wordmaker 90 MIN
VHS
Color (G) (ENGLISH AND HEBREW)
$200.00 purchase
Delves into the language war that raged in Palestine at the beginning of the 20th century. Portrays the champion fighter for modern Hebrew, Eliezer Ben - Yehuda, stubborn, zealous and courageous and who wished, above all else, to breathe life into the ancient Biblical tongue. Denounced as a heretic, Ben - Yehuda pressed on tirelessly, often at great personal expense of health and family. Set in 1917, New York, where Ben - Yehuda is ill and convinced that his life's work has been a failure. He recalls the joys, conflicts and tragedies from his extraordinary past in Russia, Paris, Vienna and Jerusalem. Directed by Eli Cohen.
Fine Arts; Foreign Language; Religion and Philosophy; Sociology
Dist - NCJEWF

WordPerfect
BETA / U-matic / VHS
MS - DOS training video series
Color (G)
$1195.00 purchase, $275.00 rental
Offers introductory and advanced training in WordPerfect MS - DOS. Teaches WordPerfect's extensive document features and how to format text. Shows keyboard shortcuts, how to import spreadsheet files from other programs.
Computer Science; Psychology
Dist - AMEDIA **Prod** - AMEDIA

WordPerfect 4
Videodisc
(H A)
$2195.00
Demonstrates using search and replace procedures in addition to basic word processing functions. Also covers more advanced techniques for editing and formatting documents, merging files, and using the verification features. Six to eight hour course for those with basic knowledge of personal computers and the disk operating system.
Computer Science; Education
Dist - CMSL **Prod** - CMSL

WordPerfect 4.2 introduction 39 MIN
VHS
Word processing series
Color (J H C G)
$29.95 purchase _ #VP104V
Introduces concepts in WordPerfect 4.2. Allows viewer to see keyboard and monitor simultaneously so that students can see the result of every keystroke. Part of a series on word processing.
Business and Economics; Computer Science
Dist - CAMV

WordPerfect 4.2 level II 56 MIN
VHS
Word processing series
Color (J H C G)
$29.95 purchase _ #VP105V
Discusses intermediate concepts in WordPerfect 4.2. Allows viewer to see keyboard and monitor simultaneously so that students can see the result of every keystroke. Part of a series on word processing.
Business and Economics; Computer Science
Dist - CAMV

WordPerfect 4.2 level III 57 MIN
VHS
Word processing series
Color (J H C G)
$29.95 purchase _ #VP114V
Discusses advanced concepts in WordPerfect 4.2. Allows viewer to see keyboard and monitor simultaneously so that students can see the result of every keystroke. Part of series on word processing.
Business and Economics; Computer Science
Dist - CAMV

WordPerfect 5
Videodisc
(H A)
$2395.00
Explains basic and advanced features of WordPerfect versions 5.0 and 5.1, including desktop publishing features. More useful for those with basic knowledge of personal computers and the disk operating system. Ten to twelve hour course.
Computer Science; Education
Dist - CMSL **Prod** - CMSL

WordPerfect 5.0 introduction 80 MIN
VHS
Word processing series
Color (J H C G)
$29.95 purchase _ #VP121V
Introduces concepts in WordPerfect 5.0. Allows viewer to see keyboard and monitor simultaneously so that students can see the result of every keystroke. Part of a series on word processing.
Business and Economics; Computer Science
Dist - CAMV

WordPerfect 5.0 level II 80 MIN
VHS
Word processing series
Color (J H C G)
$29.95 purchase _ #VP126V
Offers intermediate concepts in WordPerfect 5.0. Allows viewer to see keyboard and monitor simultaneously so that students can see the result of every keystroke. Part of a series on word processing.
Business and Economics; Computer Science
Dist - CAMV

Wordperfect 5.0, Level II 60 MIN
VHS
Master Computer Software Easily Series
Color (G)
$29.95 purchase _ #60007
Shows how to use Wordperfect 5.0 software's color font attributes, fast save, initial setting and codes, auxiliary files. Demonstrates margins, tabs, page numbering, working on two documents at once and search - replace. Part of a nine - part series which breaks down into three sets of three units which discuss Lotus, DOS and Wordperfect. Any three units of the series can be purchased for $79.95.
Business and Economics; Computer Science; Education
Dist - CARTRP **Prod** - CARTRP

WordPerfect 5.0 level III 60 MIN
VHS
Word processing series
Color (J H C G)
$29.95 purchase _ #VP131V
Offers advanced concepts in WordPerfect 5.0. Allows viewer to see keyboard and monitor simultaneously so that students can see the result of every keystroke. Part of a series on word processing.
Business and Economics; Computer Science
Dist - CAMV

Wordperfect 5.0, Level III 60 MIN
VHS
Master Computer Software Easily Series
Color (G)
$29.95 purchase _ #60008
Shows how to use Wordperfect 5.0 software for creating merge files. Demonstrates setting print for labels, forms design, special tab techniques, spreadsheets, automatic outlining and paragraph numbers and using styles. Part of a nine - part series which breaks down into three sets of three units which discuss Lotus, DOS and Wordperfect. Any three units of the series can be purchased for $79.95.
Business and Economics; Computer Science; Education
Dist - CARTRP **Prod** - CARTRP

WordPerfect 5.1
VHS
Color (G)
$149.95 purchase _ #WP51
Provides video PC software training in WordPerfect 5.1 word processing. Includes training guide.
Computer Science
Dist - HALASI **Prod** - HALASI

WordPerfect 5.1 introduction 57 MIN
VHS
Word processing series
Color (J H C G)
$29.95 purchase _ #VP140V
Introduces concepts in WordPerfect 5.1. Allows viewer to see keyboard and monitor simultaneously so that students can see the result of every keystroke. Part of a series on word processing.
Business and Economics; Computer Science
Dist - CAMV

WordPerfect 5.1 level II 58 MIN
VHS
Word processing series
Color (J H C G)
$29.95 purchase _ #VP142V
Offers intermediate concepts in WordPerfect 5.1. Allows viewer to see keyboard and monitor simultaneously so that students can see the result of every keystroke. Part of a series on word processing.
Business and Economics; Computer Science
Dist - CAMV

WordPerfect 5.1 level III 58 MIN
VHS
Word processing series
Color (J H C G)

$29.95 purchase _ #VP143V
Offers advanced concepts in WordPerfect 5.1. Allows viewer to see keyboard and monitor simultaneously so that students can see the result of every keystroke. Part of a series on word processing.
Business and Economics; Computer Science
Dist - CAMV

WordPerfect 5.1 series
Journey through 5.1 - Volume 1
Journey through 5.1 - Volume 2
Journey through 5.1 - Volumes 1 and 2
Learning 5.1
Learning WordPerfect for Windows
Quick start to WordPerfect for Windows
Secrets and timesavers
Dist - SIV

WordPerfect 5.1 training series
Offers a series of training videos for users of WordPerfect. Shows how to create professional reports, letters, memos and deskstop - published documents such as newsletters. Includes 6 videocassettes, a diskette and 6 guides. Published by Learn - PC.
WordPerfect 5.1 training series
Dist - VIDEOT

WordPerfect 5.1 transition
VHS / U-matic
Color (H C G)
$445.00, $395.00 purchase _ #08 - WPT
Teaches users of WordPerfect who are upgrading from previous versions. Includes a videocassette, a diskette and a guide. Published by Learn - PC.
Business and Economics; Computer Science
Dist - VIDEOT

WordPerfect 6.0 for DOS 177 MIN
U-matic / VHS / BETA
Color; NTSC; PAL; SECAM (J H G C)
PdS99.95
Presents the most - used and the new features of the latest DOS version. Features Daniel Sumner of WordPerfect - UK.
Computer Science
Dist - VIEWTH

Wordperfect 6.0 for DOS learning system 115 MIN
VHS
Color (G H C IND PRO)
$595.00 purchase _ #MIC19
Teaches first time users and those upgrading the software in this two video set.
Computer Science
Dist - EXTR **Prod** - MICROV

WordPerfect 6.0 for Windows 177 MIN
U-matic / VHS / BETA
Color; NTSC; PAL; SECAM (J H G C)
PdS99.95
Presents the most - used and the new features of the latest version. Features Greg Johns of WordPerfect - UK.
Computer Science
Dist - VIEWTH

WordPerfect 5 0 - Beginning through Advanced Skills 180 MIN
VHS / U-matic
(A PRO)
$895.00, $1,045.00
Shows work enhancing innovations of the software. Teaches skills necessary for professional reports,letters and desktop publishing.
Computer Science
Dist - VIDEOT **Prod** - VIDEOT 1988

WordPerfect 5 Advanced Features 100 MIN
U-matic / VHS
(A PRO)
$495.00, $595.00
Assumes basic knowledge of software. Includes desktop features.
Computer Science
Dist - VIDEOT **Prod** - VIDEOT 1988

WordPerfect 5 - Complete Anderson Set
U-matic / VHS
(A PRO)
$495.00
Complete instructions for use of WordPerfect software.
Computer Science
Dist - VIDEOT **Prod** - VIDEOT 1988

WordPerfect 5 - complete set
VHS
Color (H C G)
$595.00 purchase _ #08 - WP5 - WAP
Offers two training videos for users of WordPerfect 5. Includes the titles Mastering Word Processing and Advanced Features on 2 videocassettes, 2 diskettes and 2 guides.
Business and Economics; Computer Science
Dist - VIDEOT **Prod** - ANDRST

WordPerfect 5 Learning Systems 60 MIN
VHS / U-matic
(A PRO)
$495, $595
Teaches user the writing, editing, spell checking and other features of the software.
Computer Science
Dist - VIDEOT **Prod** - VIDEOT 1988

WordPerfect 5 - Mastering the Basics 60 MIN
U-matic / VHS
(A PRO)
$275.00
Aids trainee master all skills for creating, revising and formats of documents. Includes use of thesaurus speller and customizing page layouts and printing.
Computer Science
Dist - VIDEOT **Prod** - VIDEOT 1988

WordPerfect for Windows
BETA / U-matic / VHS
Windows training videos series
Color (G)
$995.00 purchase, $250.00 rental
Offers introductory and advanced training in WordPerfect Windows. Explores word wrapping, changing fonts and manipulating text, wrapping text around graphics, using tables and moving columns.
Computer Science; Psychology
Dist - AMEDIA **Prod** - AMEDIA

WordPerfect - intermediate macros, merging and menus
VHS
Color (H A T G)
$30.00 purchase _ #PM510
Teaches intermediate WordPerfect users about menus in 5.1, four kinds of merges - boilerplate, keyboard, mail merge and label merge, and how to write five macros. Produced by Diskmasters.
Computer Science
Dist - AAVIM

WordPerfect - Level II 56 MIN
VHS
Video professor's WordPerfect series
Color (G)
$29.95 purchase _ #6600
Uses slow, clear narration and graphics to go step - by - step through each operation in an introduction to WordPerfect, part two in a three - part series.
Computer Science
Dist - ESPNTV **Prod** - ESPNTV

WordPerfect - Level III 57 MIN
VHS
Video professor's WordPerfect series
Color (G)
$29.95 purchase _ #6601
Uses slow, clear narration and graphics to go step - by - step through each operation in an introduction to WordPerfect, part three in a three - part series.
Computer Science
Dist - ESPNTV **Prod** - ESPNTV

WordPerfect literacy
VHS
Computer software training series
Color (J H C G)
$49.95 purchase _ #AAT02V
Teaches WordPerfect literacy in a comprehensive and easy - to - follow format. Illustrates actual commands and time saving techniques. Part of a 21 - part series on computer software.
Business and Economics; Computer Science
Dist - CAMV

WordPerfect - version 4 thru 5.1
VHS
Excellence in computer literacy series
Color (G)
$49.95 purchase
Covers WordPerfect, version 4 through 5.1. Shows how to write a simple letter and enhanced editing - Italicizing, underlining, moving, deleting. Examines desktop publishing - changing fonts and the use of graphics. Discusses special commands and shortcuts.
Computer Science
Dist - SMPUB **Prod** - SMPUB

WordPerfer 5 - Basic and Advanced 120 MIN
U-matic / VHS
(A PRO)
$495.00, $595.00
Covers basic and advanced wordprocessing features of the software.
Computer Science
Dist - VIDEOT **Prod** - VIDEOT 1988

Wordplay A
VHS
Wordplay - teaching children to read series
Color (P I)
$19.95 purchase _ #JWATVPAV-K
Consists of five lively stories with illustrations designed to increase a child's listening, speaking, and reading vocabularies. Uses stories to introduce 50 study words that are selected for their benefits to intellectual growth. Based on a book series of the same name. Part one of a two-part series.
English Language
Dist - CAMV

Wordplay B
VHS
Wordplay - teaching children to read series
Color (P I)
$19.95 purchase _ #JWATVPBV-K
Offers assistance with increasing children's listening, speaking, and reading vocabularies. Uses illustrated stories to present 50 study words. Imparts definition of words through combination of illustration and sentence and story context. Based on the book series of the same name. Approximately 15-20 minutes in length. Part two of a two-part series.
Education; English Language; Health and Safety
Dist - CAMV

Wordplay - teaching children to read series
VHS
Wordplay - teaching children to read series
Color (P I)
$29.95 purchase _ #JWATVPSV-K
Offers assistance with increasing children's listening, speaking, and reading vocabularies. Uses illustrated stories to present selected study words and imparts definition of words through combination of illustrations and sentence and story context. Consists of two videos based on the book series of the same name. Each program 15-20 minutes in length.
English Language; Health and Safety
Dist - CAMV

Wordplay - teaching children to read series
Wordplay - teaching children to read series
Wordplay A
Wordplay B
Dist - CAMV

Words 14 MIN
16mm / U-matic / VHS
Joy of Writing Series
Color (K P I)
LC 77-703303
Shows children working with a teacher and making letters and words with their bodies, brainstorming words for alliterative sentences, pantomiming words, using words as inspirations for stories, composing cinquains and visiting a printer to have their cinquain realized in type.
English Language
Dist - CF **Prod** - CF 1977

Words 10 MIN
16mm
Cues to Reading Series
B&W (I J H)
Stresses the importance of understanding words and gives ways to develop a wider vocabulary.
English Language
Dist - AVED **Prod** - CBF 1958

Words 1 30 MIN
VHS / U-matic
Writing for a Reason Series
Color (C)
English Language
Dist - DALCCD **Prod** - DALCCD

Words 2 30 MIN
VHS / U-matic
Writing for a Reason Series
Color (C)
English Language
Dist - DALCCD **Prod** - DALCCD

Words about Herbs 29 MIN
U-matic
House Botanist Series
Color
Shows how to plant, maintain and use an herb garden.
Agriculture; Science - Natural
Dist - UMITV **Prod** - UMITV 1978

Words and Ideas 6 MIN
16mm
Color (K P I)
Outlines several familiar objects, producing circles, to encourage the learning of the relationship between geometric shapes and concrete objects.
Education; Psychology
Dist - SF **Prod** - SF 1968

Words and letters 30 MIN
VHS
Bill Cosby picture pages series
Color (K P)
$9.95 purchase _ #FRV16001V - K
Helps prepare children for the skills required to recognize words and letters. Features Bill Cosby and builds on the fact that children enjoy learning. Includes two activity books. Part of a six - part series of building skills in reading and counting and in color, animal, word and letter recognition.
English Language; Psychology
Dist - CAMV

Words and Letters - their Origin 23 MIN
VHS / 16mm
Color (I)
LC 90713814
Describes the origins of language. Surveys various writing systems throughout history. Documents the development of Champollion's methods for deciphering hieroglyphics.
Computer Science; English Language; Psychology; Sociology
Dist - BARR

Words and Meaning
VHS / U-matic
Write Course - an Introduction to College Composition Series
Color (C)
Supplies a heightened awareness of words as a stylistic device and an increased sense of the finer points of style.
Education; English Language
Dist - DALCCD **Prod** - DALCCD

Words and Meanings 30 MIN
U-matic / VHS
Write Course - an Introduction to College Composition Series
Color (C A)
Emphasizes a heightened awareness of style.
English Language
Dist - FI **Prod** - FI 1984

Words and meanings - word strategy - Parts 19 and 20 60 MIN
VHS / U-matic
Write course - an introduction to college composition
Color (C)
$45.00, $29.95 purchase
Covers word choices as a stylistic device and the finer points of style in Part 19. Reveals that jargon, euphemism, wordiness and triteness are foes of good communication in Part 20. Parts of a 30 - part series on college composition.
Education; English Language
Dist - ANNCPB **Prod** - DALCCD 1984

Words and more Words 15 MIN
U-matic / VHS
Hidden Treasures Series no 15; No 15
Color (T)
LC 82-706555
Uses the adventures of a pirate and his three friends to explore the many facets of language arts. Focuses on verbs and adverbs, and shows what they are and how they are used in oral and written expression.
English Language
Dist - GPN **Prod** - WCVETV 1980

Words and Music 29 MIN
U-matic
Song Writer Series
Color
Discusses the importance of the right word fitting the write sounds.
Fine Arts
Dist - UMITV **Prod** - UMITV 1977

Words and music with Jeannette Haien 30 MIN
U-matic / VHS
World of ideas with Bill Moyers - Season 2 series
Color; Captioned (A G)
$39.95, $59.95 purchase _ #WIWM - 223
Features Jeannette Haien, a teacher and musician, and now a writer with her novel, The All of It. Discusses how the structure of music helped Haien write her novel. Shares her views on the form, composition and performance of music. Part of a series of interviews with Bill Moyers featuring scientists, writers, artists, philosophers and historians. Produced by Public Affairs Television, New York.
English Language; Fine Arts
Dist - PBS
FOTH

Words and Pictures Series
I Am Better than You 15 MIN
The Letter 15 MIN
The Little Girl and the Tiny Doll 15 MIN
Master Salt and the Sailor's Son - Pt 7 16 MIN
Mog - the Forgetful Cat - Pt 6 17 MIN
The Monkey and the Crocodile - Pt 1 15 MIN
The Three Little Pigs - Pt 5 15 MIN
Too much noise 15 MIN
Who Took the Farmer's Hat 15 MIN
Dist - FI

Words and place series
By this song I walk - Navajo song 25 MIN
A Conversation with Vine Deloria Jr 29 MIN
Iisaw - Hopi coyote stories 18 MIN
Natwaniwa - a Hopi philosophical statement 27 MIN
Origin of the crown dance - an Apache narrative and Ba'ts'oosee - an Apache trickster 40 MIN
Running on the edge of the rainbow - Laguna stories and poems 28 MIN
Seyewailo - the flower world 51 MIN
Songs of my hunter heart - Laguna songs and poems 34 MIN
Dist - NORROS

Words and Symbols 19 MIN
U-matic / VHS
Reading Approach to Math Series
Color (J H)
Shows students in everyday situations where their problems can be solved by using mathematics. Key words are identified which will enable students to decide which operation to use in order to solve a given problem.
Mathematics
Dist - GPN **Prod** - WNVT 1979

Words and their Meaning 32 MIN
16mm
Principles and Methods of Teaching a Second Language Series
B&W (H T)
Shows the deficiencies of word - for - word translation. Discusses how the meanings of words change with usage. Demonstrates in a French class for English speakers how words are taught in meaningful contexts and how ranges of meanings are developed appropriately.
Education; English Language; Foreign Language
Dist - IU **Prod** - MLAA 1962

Words as Force Option 25 MIN
VHS / 16mm
Verbal Judo Series
Color (C PRO)
$375.00 purchase _ #9863
Leads police officers through a variety of situations in which verbal skills are used in lieu of phsysical force. Part 3 of three parts.
Civics and Political Systems; Computer Science; Guidance and Counseling; Psychology
Dist - AIMS **Prod** - AIMS 1985

Words by heart 116 MIN
VHS
Wonderworks collection series
Color (I J H)
$29.95 purchase _ #WOR300
Portrays youth as the hope for a better future in a story about an early 19th - century black family living in an all - white Missouri town.
Guidance and Counseling; Literature and Drama; Sociology
Dist - KNOWUN **Prod** - PBS 1991

Words - four stories about becoming literate 30 MIN
VHS
Color (H C G)
$150.00 purchase, $55.00 rental
Gives voice to four people who are struggling with illiteracy. Shows what it is like to lack reading and writing skills that are often taken for granted. Janet came from a close - nit family that helped her 'cover up' her disability. Jerry suffered from headaches all during school and didn't discover until much later that he was nearsighted and couldn't see the blackboard. Deanna moved off the reservation, lost a year in school and never caught up with her class. Cyntra's family believed that girls didn't need education because they only minded the house - her mother is also illiterate. Shows how all these persons reaped the benefits of community - based literacy programs.
English Language; Psychology; Sociology
Dist - FLMLIB **Prod** - ASTRSK 1992

Words into Symbols 15 MIN
VHS
Power of Algebra Series
Color (J)
LC 90712872
Uses computer animation and interviews with professionals who use algebra to explain words into symbols. The tenth and final installment of The Power Of Algebra Series.
Mathematics
Dist - GPN

Words must be clear 18 MIN
VHS
Color (H C A)
$39.95 purchase - #KAR599V-J
Demonstrates the importance of good written and oral communication skills in everyday situations and in careers. Presents vignettes and interviews with professionals that challenge students to think about communication issues. Includes vignettes with student actors, workplace interviews, and a music video. Comes with teacher's guide.
Business and Economics; Social Science
Dist - CAMV

Words of a True Friend 20 MIN
16mm
Color (A)
Presents one of the last speeches given by the late Senator Hubert Humphrey at the state convention of the Minnesota AFL - CIO.
Biography; Business and Economics; Sociology
Dist - AFLCIO **Prod** - AFLCIO 1978

Words of Fire 20 MIN
VHS / U-matic
American Literature Series
Color (H C A)
LC 83-706250
Offers dramatizations of the words of Samuel Adams, Thomas Paine, Patrick Henry, James Rivington and Benjamin Franklin, as well as from the Declaration of Independence and the Constitution.
Literature and Drama
Dist - AITECH **Prod** - AUBU 1983

Words of Leadership - 10 15 MIN
VHS
Wordscape Series
Color; Captioned (I)
$125.00 purchase
Uses the word 'cell' approach to teach vocabulary, opening each program - sixteen 15 - minute programs - with several word cells familiar to fourth graders and using these 'cells' to form compound words, birdhouse, girlfriend. Employs animated graphics to dramatize how compounds are 'built' of cells that form a seemingly endless series of new words and to teach that understanding cell words can help to understand the new words composed of them. Program 10 'leads' through word cells having to do with leadership, using familiar and humorous scenarios to define and model pronunciation of words.
English Language; Psychology
Dist - AITECH **Prod** - OETVA 1990

Words of Life, People of Rivers 30 MIN
U-matic
Real People Series
Color
Discusses the value of land and water to the Indian.
Social Science; Sociology
Dist - GPN **Prod** - KSPSTV 1976

Words of Music - 14 15 MIN
VHS
Wordscape Series
Color; Captioned (I)
$125.00 purchase
Uses the word 'cell' approach to teach vocabulary, opening each program - sixteen 15 - minute programs - with several word cells familiar to fourth graders and using these 'cells' to form compound words, birdhouse, girlfriend. Employs animated graphics to dramatize how compounds are 'built' of cells that form a seemingly endless series of new words and to teach that understanding cell words can help to understand the new words composed of them. Program 14 considers music and word cells associated with music.
English Language; Psychology
Dist - AITECH **Prod** - OETVA 1990

Words of Space - 11 15 MIN
VHS
Wordscape Series
Color; Captioned (I)
$125.00 purchase
Uses the word 'cell' approach to teach vocabulary, opening each program - sixteen 15 - minute programs - with several word cells familiar to fourth graders and using these 'cells' to form compound words, birdhouse, girlfriend. Employs animated graphics to dramatize how compounds are 'built' of cells that form a seemingly endless series of new words and to teach that understanding cell words can help to understand the new words composed of them. Program 11 highlights word cells having to do with heavenly bodies and discusses the Latin, Greek and Old English roots of the cells.
English Language; Psychology
Dist - AITECH **Prod** - OETVA 1990

Words of the Language
U-matic / VHS
'C' Language Programming Series
Color
Defines identifier and data type, identifying the two categories of data types in 'C' language. Describes the difference between literal and symbolic constants and the categories of key words in a 'C' language program.
Industrial and Technical Education; Mathematics; Sociology
Dist - COMTEG **Prod** - COMTEG

Words of Time - 3 15 MIN
VHS
Wordscape Series
Color; Captioned (I)
$125.00 purchase
Uses the word 'cell' approach to teach vocabulary, opening each program - sixteen 15 - minute programs - with several word cells familiar to fourth graders and using these 'cells' to form compound words, birdhouse, girlfriend. Employs animated graphics to dramatize how compounds are 'built' of cells that form a seemingly endless series of new words and to teach that understanding cell words can help to understand the new words composed of them. Program 3 emphasizes words related to time in humorous scenarios involving weekends, music, sports and other activities.
English Language; Psychology
Dist - AITECH **Prod** - OETVA 1990

Words that Add Meaning 11 MIN
U-matic / VHS / 16mm
Fun with Words Series
Color (P)
$270, $190 purchase _ #1994
Discusses adjectives and adverbs, how they add meaning to sentences, and how they help with sentence building.
English Language
Dist - CORF

Words that Name and do 11 MIN
16mm / U-matic / VHS
Fun with Words Series
Color (P)
$270, $190 purchase _ #1884
Expounds on the differences between nouns and verbs.
English Language
Dist - CORF

Words that Rhyme 10 MIN
U-matic / VHS / 16mm
Fun with Words Series
Color (P)
$265, $185 purchase _ #3309
Discusses rhyme, pronunciation, and word endings.
English Language
Dist - CORF

Words that Work 180 MIN
VHS / U-matic
Your Speaking Image - When Women Talk Business Series
Color (H C A)
Business and Economics; Education; Psychology; Sociology
Dist - UEUWIS **Prod** - UEUWIS 1984

Words that Work 30 MIN
VHS / U-matic
Your Speaking Image Series
(C A PRO)
$180.00 purchase
Focuses on language that is considered to be sheepish and ineffective and then demonstrates speech that is effective and direct.
English Language
Dist - AITECH **Prod** - WHATV 1986
DELTAK

Words - they Come and Go 30 MIN
VHS / U-matic
Language and Meaning Series
Color (C)
English Language; Psychology
Dist - GPN **Prod** - WUSFTV 1983

Words, Words, Words 30 MIN
U-matic / VHS
Reading is Power Series no 4
Color (T)
LC 81-707519
Uses interviews and candid classroom scenes to show how innovative teachers are employing word recognition and vocabulary - building exercises to help children learn to read.
English Language
Dist - GPN **Prod** - NYCBED 1981

Words words words 10 MIN
16mm
Amazing life game theater series
Color (K)
LC 72-701741
Illustrates language, communication and association of letter sounds with words as seen through the eyes of an animated boy.
English Language; Guidance and Counseling; Psychology
Dist - HMC **Prod** - HMC 1971

Wordscape series

Animal words - 15	15 MIN
Building words - 1	15 MIN
Clothing Words - 9	15 MIN
A Family of words - 16	15 MIN
Food words - 6	15 MIN
Friendship words - 13	15 MIN
Loud Talk - 8	15 MIN
Movie Words - 2	15 MIN
Mystery Words - 7	15 MIN
Sports Words - 4	15 MIN
Talk Words - 5	15 MIN
Words of Leadership - 10	15 MIN
Words of Music - 14	15 MIN
Words of Space - 11	15 MIN
Words of Time - 3	15 MIN
Writing words - 12	15 MIN

Dist - AITECH

Wordsmith Series

Module Blue - Body I	15 MIN
Module Blue - Body II	15 MIN
Module Blue - Fire	15 MIN
Module Blue - Looking	15 MIN
Module Blue - Sound	15 MIN
Module Brown - Leading	15 MIN
Module Brown - Nature	15 MIN
Module Brown - Position	15 MIN
Module Brown - Transportation I	15 MIN
Module Brown - Transportation II	15 MIN
Module Green - Numbers I	15 MIN
Module Green - Numbers II	15 MIN
Module Green - Numbers III	15 MIN
Module Green - Walk and Run	15 MIN
Module Green - Water	15 MIN
Module Orange - Communication	15 MIN
Module Orange - Connection	15 MIN
Module Orange - Measure and Metrics	15 MIN
Module Orange - Relatives	15 MIN
Module Orange - Twist and Turn	15 MIN
Module Red - Animals I	15 MIN
Module Red - Animals II	15 MIN
Module Red - Cutting	15 MIN
Module Red - Serendipity	15 MIN
Module Red - Time	15 MIN
Module Yellow - Food	15 MIN
Module Yellow - Form	15 MIN
Module Yellow - Potpourri	15 MIN
Module Yellow - Size	15 MIN
Module Yellow - Talking	15 MIN

Dist - AITECH

Wordstar
U-matic / VHS
Color
Illustrates the overall concept of word processing and the basic text editing function of WordStar. Shows how to open a document file, set margins and tabs, find and replace and do general text editing. Shows how to mark, copy, move and delete blocks of text, or paragraphs.
Industrial and Technical Education; Mathematics
Dist - ANDRST **Prod** - LANSFD

WordStar
Videodisc
(H A)
$1995.00
Teaches word processing using WordStar version 3xx. Includes topics such as entering, editing and printing text as well as formatting documents and using dot commands. Five to six hour course.
Computer Science; Education
Dist - CMSL **Prod** - CMSL

WordStar Pro 4.0 introduction 58 MIN
VHS
Word processing series
Color (J H C G)
$29.95 purchase _ #VP108V
Introduces concepts in WordStar Pro 4.0. Allows viewer to see keyboard and monitor simultaneously so that students can see the result of every keystroke. Part of a series on word processing.
Business and Economics; Computer Science
Dist - CAMV

WordStar Pro 4.0 level II 58 MIN
VHS
Word processing series
Color (J H C G)
$29.95 purchase _ #VP111V
Offers intermediate and advanced concepts in WordStar Pro 4.0. Allows viewer to see keyboard and monitor simultaneously so that students can see the result of every keystroke. Part of a series on word processing.
Business and Economics; Computer Science
Dist - CAMV
INSTRU

Wordstar Professional - Level II 75 MIN
VHS
Wordstar Professional series
Color (G)
$29.95 purchase _ #6765
Uses slow, clear narration and graphics to go step - by - step through each operation in a Level II explanation of Wordstar Professional.
Computer Science
Dist - ESPNTV **Prod** - ESPNTV

Wordstar Professional series
Presents a two - part series which uses slow, clear narration and graphics to go step - by - step through each operation in an introduction to Wordstar Professional. Includes an introduction in part one, a Level II explanation in part two.

Introduction to Wordstar Professional	58 MIN
Wordstar Professional - Level II	75 MIN

Dist - ESPNTV **Prod** - ESPNTV

Wordsworth's Lake Country - Image of Man and Nature 20 MIN
16mm
Color (J H C)
LC 75-713540
Presents scenes of Dove Cottage, Duddon Valley, Cokermouth, Grasmere and Lakeland scenery in the England lake country and portrays the influence of these settings on Wordsworth as a romantic poet.
Literature and Drama
Dist - PERFET **Prod** - PERFET 1971

Wordworks, the, Pt 01 11 MIN
16mm
Color (P)
LC 74-703086
Uses animation and live action to present lessons for the beginning reader. Focuses on beginning letter - sound associations for F, M, B, T, N and D, as well as the high - frequency words 'a' and 'to.'.
English Language
Dist - HMC **Prod** - ALGC 1974

Wordworks, the, Pt 02 10 MIN
16mm
Color (P)
LC 74-703087
Uses animation and live action to present lessons for the beginning reader. Focuses on beginning letter - sound associations for P, W, C and S, and high - frequency words, such as 'is,' 'go,' 'I' and 'in.'.
English Language
Dist - HMC **Prod** - ALGC 1974

Wordworks, the, Pt 03 11 MIN
16mm
Color (P)
LC 74-703088
Uses animation and live action to present lessons for the beginning reader. Focuses on beginning letter - sound associations for L, R, Y, Wh, H and K, and the high - frequency words 'he,' 'we,' 'on,' 'will' and 'not.'.
English Language
Dist - HMC **Prod** - ALGC 1974

Wordworks, the, Pt 04 10 MIN
16mm
Color (P)
LC 74-703090
Uses animation and live action to present lessons for the beginning reader. Focuses on beginning letter - sound associations for V and the clusters Ch, Th and Sh, as well as the high - frequency words 'the,' 'and' and 'you.'.
English Language
Dist - HMC **Prod** - ALGC 1974

Wordworks, the, Pt 05 10 MIN
16mm
Color (P)
LC 74-703091
Uses animation and live action to present lessons for the beginning reader. Focuses on letter - sound associations for words ending in Z, S and ing, the clusters st and tr, the phonograms at and an, and examples of the comma to show address.
English Language
Dist - HMC **Prod** - ALGC 1974

Wordworks, the, Pt 06 9 MIN
16mm
Color (P)
LC 74-703092
Uses animation and live action to present lessons for the beginning reader. Focuses on sound association for 'ay,' 'ee,' 'oa,' and for the use of C to attain an S sound. Explains using Y as a vowel and discusses words with more than one meaning.

English Language
Dist - HMC **Prod** - ALGC 1974

Wordworks, the, Pt 07 9 MIN
16mm
Color (P)
LC 74-703093
Uses animation and live action to present lessons for the beginning reader. Focuses on compound words, 'all' and 'ake' sounds, words ending in 'er' and verbs ending in 'ed.'.
English Language
Dist - HMC **Prod** - ALGC 1974

Wordworks, the, Pt 08 10 MIN
16mm
Color (P)
LC 74-703094
Uses animation and live action to present lessons for the beginning reader. Focuses on sound association for 'oo,' the word endings 'en' and 'ly,' the clusters Bl and Br and the phonograms 'et' and 'old.'.
English Language
Dist - HMC **Prod** - ALGC 1974

Wordworks, the, Pt 09 10 MIN
16mm
Color (P)
LC 74-703095
Uses animation and live action to present lessons for the beginning reader. Focuses on sound association for A, 'ee' and G, the prefixes 'be' and A, and the common syllables 'un' and 'ful.'.
English Language
Dist - HMC **Prod** - ALGC 1974

Wordworks, the, Pt 10 10 MIN
16mm
Color (P)
LC 74-703096
Uses animation and live action to present lessons for the beginning reader. Focuses on sound association for I, O, U, Kn and mb, the clusters Qu and Squ, words with more than one meaning, and following directions.
English Language
Dist - HMC **Prod** - ALGC 1974

Work 15 MIN
U-matic
Chemistry 102 - Chemistry for Engineers - Series
Color (C)
Discusses the efficiency of machines including the human body. Defines work, discussing its relationship to path taken. Describes the reversibility of thermodynanmic processes. Introduces fule cells as an efficient source of energy.
Industrial and Technical Education; Science - Physical
Dist - UILL **Prod** - UILL 1984

Work 30 MIN
U-matic
Today's Special Series
Color (K P)
Develops language arts skills in children. Programs are thematically designed around subjects of interest to youngsters. Action takes place in a department store where people, mannequins, puppets, comic characters and special guests present a light hearted approach to language arts.
Fine Arts; Literature and Drama; Psychology
Dist - TVOTAR **Prod** - TVOTAR 1985

Work 20 MIN
16mm
Color (H C A)
$400 purchase, $50 rental
Examines the unsatisfying aspects of factory work, and tells about one successful attempt to make work more meaningful and satisfying.
Social Science; Sociology
Dist - CNEMAG **Prod** - DOCUA 1988

Work 5 MIN
U-matic
Eureka Series
Color (J)
Presents the physics definition of work, work equals force times distance.
Science; Science - Physical
Dist - TVOTAR **Prod** - TVOTAR 1980

Work 60 MIN
U-matic
Challenge Series
Color (PRO)
Shows a discussion by six men on work related issues.
Psychology
Dist - TVOTAR **Prod** - TVOTAR 1985

Work 30 MIN
16mm / U-matic / VHS
Charlie Chaplin Comedy Theatre Series
B&W (I)
LC 76-711888
Presents Charlie Chaplin, the paper - hanger's helper as he tries to do his job amidst havoc in the streets, flying paste, an exploding stove and domestic chaos.
Fine Arts
Dist - FI **Prod** - ENY

Work 25 MIN
VHS
Dragon's tongue series
Color (J H G)
$195.00 purchase
Teaches basics of Putonghua, China's official language. Presents one video in a series of nineteen helping students develop comprehension skills by using only Chinese - no subtitles. Shows authentic scenes of Chinese homes, cities and the countryside. Features Colin Mackerras of Griffith University.
Foreign Language
Dist - LANDMK

Work 15 MIN
U-matic / VHS
Watch Your Language Series
Color (J H)
$125.00 purchase
Introduces the use of proper language on a professional level encouraging the viewer to make use of it on job applications and in interview situations.
English Language; Social Science
Dist - AITECH **Prod** - KYTV 1984

Work - a - Day America
Auto body repair
Auto mechanics
Banking and bookkeeping
Carpentry
Computer Maintenance
Cosmetology
Diesel mechanics
Food services
Home Appliance Repair
Hospital Information Services
Law Enforcement
Lawn and Gardening
Machinist
Medical Assistant
Medical Records
Nurse's Assistant
Printing
Production Art
Retail Sales
Secretarial
Word Processing
Dist - CAREER

Work and energy 7 MIN
VHS
Discovering simple machines series
CC; Color (P)
$55.00 purchase _ #1283VG
Shows the scientific views of work and energy. Teaches that work is accomplished when an object with resistance is moved a distance. Covers potential and kinetic energy, and forces such as friction that slow objects down. Comes with a teacher's guide and four blackline masters. Part one of a four - part series.
Science - Physical
Dist - UNL

Work and energy 10 MIN
VHS
Work, energy, and the simple machine series
Color (I J)
$55.00 purchase _ #1153VG
Discusses the scientific definition of work and the related formulas. Defines energy in both potential and kinetic forms. Presents efficiency and the power of machines. Comes with a teacher's guide and six blackline masters. Part one of a four - part series.
Science - Physical
Dist - UNL

Work & family 21 MIN
VHS
Color (COR)
%i $295.00 purchase, $95.00 five - day rental, $35.00 three - day preview _ #GWF
Assists companies in recognizing the need to help employees successfully balance work and family. Demonstrates how businesses can benefit by arranging temporary flexible work - at - home time for eligible support staff and managers. Discusses telecommuting via phone and computer, which enables working parents to remain on the job as highly productive personnel. Helps supervisors to help employees cope with temporary family situations and avoid choosing between job and family. Includes a Leader's Guide.
Business and Economics; Guidance and Counseling
Dist - ADVANM

Work and family - walking the tightrope 30 MIN
VHS / 16mm
Color (G IND)
$10.00 rental
Outlines the problems facing working parents and suggests solutions which have been implemented through collective bargaining, legislation and corporate policies. Available to unions only.
Business and Economics; Social Science; Sociology
Dist - AFLCIO **Prod** - BNA 1986

Work and Fulfillment 59 MIN
U-matic / VHS
Young and Old - Reaching Out Series
Color (H C A)
LC 80-707181
Discusses what the American Dream means to the old and the young. Examines changing values about work, money, education, business and success.
Psychology
Dist - PBS **Prod** - CRFI 1979

Work and Motherhood - the Dilemma of the New Professional Woman 28 MIN
U-matic
Color (J C)
Discuss how many high achieving women desire children yet know that being a good mother will make tremendous demands on their professional lives. They are faced with a dilemma - How do they manage both? Three top professional mothers in their 30's and their husbands talk about how they are dealing with this balancing act. Two experts, Natasha Josefowitz and Majorie Hansen Shaevitz offer coping strategies.
Sociology
Dist - SDSC **Prod** - SDSC 1986

Work and pay 34 MIN
VHS
Color; PAL (J H)
PdS29.50 purchase
Outlines economic principles and theories relating to pay determination. Discusses the factors that in practice influence the level of earnings of professionals in the private and public sectors. Includes notes. Intended as a teaching and learning aid for students of economics and business at the GCSE and advanced level, and for those on the first year of a degree course. Also suitable for use on the BTEC courses.
Business and Economics; Guidance and Counseling
Dist - EMFVL **Prod** - GLAMOR

Work and Power 14 MIN
U-matic / VHS / 16mm
Color (I J H)
Shows practical examples of scientific formulas in action - - inertia on the inclined planes, pulleys used to transfer power and cables used as levers.
Science - Physical
Dist - IFB **Prod** - VEF 1960

Work and Retirement
16mm
Aging in the Future Series
Color
Raises questions about the quality of life in retirement and the effects of inflation on this work - retirement decision.
Health and Safety; Sociology
Dist - UMICH **Prod** - UMICH

Work and Retirement 21 MIN
U-matic
Aging in the Future Series
Color
Looks at historical achievement of a society that can afford retirement for its workers. Discusses the importance for some older citizens to continue working.
Health and Safety; Sociology
Dist - UMITV **Prod** - UMITV 1981

Work, Bike and Eat 45 MIN
16mm
B&W
LC 77-702730
Presents the adventures of a man as he copes with shoplifters, family dinners, beer fights, hush puppy stories, infantile bikers, brief encounters and calisthenics.
Fine Arts
Dist - CANFDC **Prod** - CANFDC 1972

Work, Bike and Eat, Pt 1 23 MIN
16mm
B&W
LC 77-702730
Presents the adventures of a man as he copes with shoplifters, family dinners, beer fights, hush puppy stories, infantile bikers, brief encounters and calisthenics.
Fine Arts
Dist - CANFDC **Prod** - CANFDC 1972

Work, Bike and Eat, Pt 2 22 MIN
16mm
B&W
LC 77-702730
Presents the adventures of a man as he copes with shoplifters, family dinners, beer fights, hush puppy stories, infantile bikers, brief encounters and calisthenics.
Fine Arts
Dist - CANFDC **Prod** - CANFDC 1972

Work Center Supervisor's Job 60 MIN
BETA / VHS
Manufacturing Series
(IND)
Describes the work center supervisor's responsibilities for producing a quality product on time at the most economical cost.
Business and Economics
Dist - COMSRV **Prod** - COMSRV 1986

Work Climate Improvement Process Video Tape Previews
U-matic / VHS
$75.00 purchase
Previews of the WCIP video tape programs are availale for a one week period.
Business and Economics
Dist - BAUERA **Prod** - BAUERA 1985

Work Climate Improvement Process Video Tape Set
U-matic / VHS
$2,000.00 purchase
Helps work group leaders and participants to visualize their roles in the Work Climate Improvement Process.
Business and Economics
Dist - BAUERA **Prod** - BAUERA 1985

Work Communications 19 MIN
VHS / U-matic
Jobs - Seeking, Finding, Keeping Series
Color (H)
Tells how Roland can't get along with his foreman and then becomes a foreman himself. Shows that he is a terrible boss until he begins working on his communication skills.
Guidance and Counseling; Psychology
Dist - AITECH **Prod** - MDDE 1980

Work - Coping with the Twenty - Hour Week
U-matic / VHS / 16mm
Color
Examines the tremendous reorganization of priorities required by the 20 - hour work week. Shows that the four - day week will result in an increase in the participation in government, an increase in choice and a chance for people to develop themselves to their greatest potential.
Business and Economics; Social Science; Sociology
Dist - CNEMAG **Prod** - DOCUA

The Work Crisis 30 MIN
16mm
Color (J H T R)
LC FIA67-5756
Documentary study of the effects of technological development on work and leisure. Explores the biblical meaning of work and the necessity of dignity of the individual in an increasingly automated work world.
Business and Economics; Guidance and Counseling; Psychology; Religion and Philosophy; Sociology
Dist - FAMF **Prod** - FAMF 1967

Work - Don't Let Your Attitude Intrude (Documentary) 18 MIN
U-matic / VHS
Work - Don't Let Your Attitude Intrude Series
Color
Presents a documentary explaining what is involved in putting together a program telling how to seek employment and right and wrong job - seeking techniques.
Guidance and Counseling; Psychology
Dist - USNAC **Prod** - USDL 1979

Work - Don't Let Your Attitude Intrude (Musical) 40 MIN
VHS / U-matic
Work - Don't Let Your Attitude Intrude Series
Color (H T)
Presents a musical that shows how to seek employment.
Guidance and Counseling; Psychology
Dist - USNAC **Prod** - USDL 1979

Work - Don't Let Your Attitude Intrude Series
Work - Don't Let Your Attitude Intrude (Documentary) 18 MIN
Work - Don't Let Your Attitude Intrude (Musical) 40 MIN
Work - Don't Let Your Attitude Intrude (Skits) 21 MIN
Dist - USNAC

Work - Don't Let Your Attitude Intrude (Skits) 21 MIN
VHS / U-matic
Work - Don't Let Your Attitude Intrude Series
Color (H T)
Shows skits that tell how to seek employment and use group discussions to determine the right and wrong job - seeking techniques.
Guidance and Counseling; Psychology
Dist - USNAC **Prod** - USDL

Work, energy, and the simple machine series
Introduces the concepts of work and energy in the scientific definition. Presents and demonstrates the six simple machines and compound machines. Comes with four videos, a teacher's guide, and 25 blackline masters.
Compound machines 12 MIN
Inclined plane, wedge, screw 7 MIN
Lever, wheel and axle, pulley 11 MIN
Work and energy 10 MIN
Work, energy and the simple machine series 40 MIN
Dist - UNL

Work Environment 19 MIN
U-matic / VHS
Jobs - Seeking, Finding, Keeping Series
Color (H)
Presents people from many kinds of work talking about their jobs, the importance of on - the - job surroundings, and the need for new workers to be realistic about what they expect in their jobs.
Guidance and Counseling
Dist - AITECH **Prod** - MDDE 1980

The Work Ethic 30 MIN
U-matic / VHS
Focus on Society Series
Color (C)
Discusses the Protestant Ethic. Examines affluence, alienation, individualism, hedonism and other variables.
Sociology
Dist - DALCCD **Prod** - DALCCD

Work Execution 30 MIN
U-matic / VHS
Maintenance Management Series
Color
Considers work execution. Focuses on job assignment, communication, supervision and overtime.
Business and Economics; Psychology
Dist - ITCORP **Prod** - ITCORP

Work Experience 11 MIN
VHS / 16mm
Color (G)
Follows an unemployed man from a job interview to his stroll among city shops. Explores the problem of gaining work experience when lack of such experience limits employment opportunities.
Business and Economics; Guidance and Counseling; Sociology
Dist - FLMWST

Work hard, play hard - 30 10 MIN
VHS / U-matic
Life's little lessons - self - esteem K - 3 - series
Color (K P)
$129.00, $99.00 _ #V629
Tells about sergeants and brothers Fred and Ned Matheson, Fred the merciless tyrant, Ned the lazy good for nothing. Shows how they learned the necessity of both working and playing hard. Part of a 30 - part series on self - esteem.
Guidance and Counseling; Psychology
Dist - BARR **Prod** - CEPRO 1992

Work Hardening 10 MIN
BETA / VHS
Color (A PRO)
$61.00 purchase _ #KTI65
Deals with auto body repair. Defines and demonstrates work hardening.
Industrial and Technical Education
Dist - RMIBHF **Prod** - RMIBHF

Work in progress 15 MIN
VHS
Color; B&W (G) (ENGLISH & SPANISH W/ENG SUBTITLES)
Employs the legislative events of 1986, in which the first major revision of the Immigration Law in 20 years was enacted, as a springboard for reflection on the resonances of the word 'alien' in American cultural and political life. Uses a collage of melodramatic grade - B science fiction movies, government propaganda films, INS surveillance footage and the testimony of illegal immigrants to underline the xenophobia that denies humanity to those risking their lives for a better future. Produced and directed by Luis Valdovino.
Fine Arts; History - United States; Sociology
Dist - THWONE

Work, Income, and Your Career 28 MIN
U-matic / VHS
Personal Finance and Money Management Series
Color (C A)
Business and Economics; Civics and Political Systems
Dist - SCCON CDTEL **Prod** - SCCON 1987

Work is for real series
Computing the future 15 MIN
D E develops 'know - how' 15 MIN
Who Needs Math 15 MIN
Dist - GPN

The Work I've Done 58 MIN
16mm
Color (G)
Presents an independent production by K Fink. Examines the complex issues of retirement.
Fine Arts; Guidance and Counseling; Sociology
Dist - FIRS

Work Measurement Works 23 MIN
16mm
B&W
LC 74-706335
Illustrates work measurement in four areas, improving work methods, scheduling and controlling work, determining productivity and forecasting resource requirements.
Business and Economics; Guidance and Counseling; Psychology
Dist - USNAC **Prod** - USA 1969

Work of Gomis 47 MIN
U-matic
Color (C A)
Documents a healing ceremony in Sri Lanka utilizing dance, theater and decorations made of clay, flowers and leaves.
Geography - World; Sociology
Dist - HANMNY **Prod** - HANMNY 1972

The Work of ice 11 MIN
VHS
Color; PAL (P I J)
PdS29
Compares an area of active glaciation in the French Alps - Mer de Glace - with the result of ice action that can be seen around Snowdon and Nant Ffrancon in North Wales. Shows glacial deposition in a lowland region - Flamborough Head.
Geography - World
Dist - BHA

The Work of Love - a M Sullivan, Poet 26 MIN
16mm
Color
LC 80-700182
Presents the poetry of A M Sullivan.
Literature and Drama
Dist - GUINEA **Prod** - GUINEA 1979

The Work of rivers 15 MIN
VHS
Color; PAL (P I J)
PdS29
Films along the Rivers Severn and Brett to contrast the western giant with its smaller Suffolk cousin. Opens with scenes of rainclouds over the mountains of North Wales washing rocks, stones and soil into the infant Severn. Reveals that many of these solids - the river's load - will be deposited lower down the river to build new land near the sea. Shows that the Severn and Brett display the same characteristics - broadening as they merge with tributaries, following the wide valleys cut by past floods, and being subjected to manmade controls to minimize the dangers of future flooding. Examines both rivers from both ground level and from the air, the latter including shots of the Shrewbury, Worcester and Bristol regions.
Geography - World; Science - Physical
Dist - BHA

The Work of Rivers 3 MIN
16mm
Of all Things Series
Color (P I)
Shows the work of rivers.
Geography - United States; Geography - World
Dist - AVED **Prod** - BAILYL

The Work of running water 27 MIN
VHS
Scenes of the plateaulands and how they came to be series
Color (J H)
$19.95 purchase _ #IVSPL - 2
Looks at the various landforms created by running water. Includes cliffs, mesas and buttes, canyons and badlands. Part of a five - part series which overview the geological forces that formed and are still working on the Colorado Plateau. Includes footage of Colorado, Utah and Arizona, Grand Canyon, Bryce Canyon, Zion National Park, Arches, Bridges, Dinosaur, Petrified Forest and Canyonlands National Parks.

Geography - United States
Dist - INSTRU

The Work of the Goethe Institute in Germany 5 MIN
16mm / U-matic / VHS
European Studies - Germany Series
Color (H C A) (GERMAN)
LC 76-700770
Describes the functioning of the Goethe Institute and its efforts to foster appreciation of the German language and culture.
Geography - World
Dist - IFB **Prod** - MFAFRG 1973

Work of the heart 21 MIN
VHS
Color (J H) (SPANISH)
$99.00 purchase _ #4264 - 026
Uses animation to illustrate the processes and parts of the heart and how they relate to the lungs, arteries and veins. Includes teacher's guide.
Education; Fine Arts; Science - Natural
Dist - GA **Prod** - EBEC
EBEC

The Work of the kidneys 20 MIN
16mm / U-matic / VHS
Biology Series Unit 8 - Human Physiology; Unit 8 - Human physiology
Color (H C) (SPANISH)
LC 73-701184
Demonstrates the essential work of the kidneys in maintaining the fluid environment body cells must have. Examines the kidneys' major structures and the function of each.
Science - Natural
Dist - EBEC **Prod** - EBEC 1972

The Work of the sea 11 MIN
VHS
Color; PAL (P I J)
PdS29
Examines the effects of marine destruction and construction on the coasts of East Anglia - a soft rock area - and Cornwall - a hard rock area - and at Chesil Bank in Dorset. Considers human effort to halt destruction by the sea.
Geography - World; Science - Natural; Science - Physical
Dist - BHA

Work of the wind 20 MIN
VHS
Color (J H)
$29.95 purchase _ #IV116
Visits the site of the Great Sand Dunes in Colorado. Reveals that many of the dunes are almost 700 feet high. Shows how a dune is formed, the various kinds of dunes - barchan, transverse and longitudinal - as well as the origin of these dunes near the Sangre de Christo range.
Geography - United States; Science - Physical
Dist - INSTRU

The Work of the Wind - a Visit to the Great Sand Dunes 15 MIN
VHS
Color (C PRO)
$154.00 purchase _ #193 E 2111
Takes the viewer to the Great Sand Dunes in central Colorado to investigate sand dune formation and how the wind plays an important role in shaping the earth's surface.
Science - Physical
Dist - WARDS

Work of the Wind and Running Water 19 MIN
16mm / U-matic / VHS
Color (J H)
LC 74-706762
Explains and illustrates the processes involved in the geologic work of wind and running water and their effects on landforms.
Science - Physical
Dist - MEDIAG **Prod** - WILEYJ 1970

Work or Play 5 MIN
16mm
Color
LC 74-706884
Discusses hobbies and their relaxing effects. Stimulates oral language skills.
English Language; Psychology; Sociology
Dist - MLA **Prod** - DBA 1969

The Work pace 14 MIN
VHS
Color (H A)
$80.00 purchase _ #WRK100V
Interviews seven employers who hire young people for entry - level positions. Discusses what employers expect of young workers. Companies represented include United Parcel Service, McDonald's, Centennial Bank, and others.
Psychology
Dist - CAMV

Work Performance Rating 27 MIN
16mm
Color; B&W (IND)
LC 72-701863
Shows time - study personnel in action under simulated shop conditions measuring 40 operations from ten basic categories common in many industrial organizations.
Business and Economics; Guidance and Counseling; Psychology
Dist - VOAERO **Prod** - VOAERO 1968

The Work Place 14 MIN
VHS / 16mm
Skills for First Time Job Seekers Series
(H A)
$89.00 _ #WRK2V
Provides students with tips from employers for success on their first job. Features real - life managers from UPS, McDonalds and other entry level employers telling what they look for and expect from workers.
Guidance and Counseling
Dist - JISTW **Prod** - LGFAMS 1984

Work Planning and Scheduling 30 MIN
U-matic / VHS
You - the Supervisor Series
Color (PRO)
Suggests some approaches for work planning and scheduling that are practiced during the discussion period following the session.
Business and Economics; Psychology
Dist - DELTAK **Prod** - PRODEV

Work practice guidelines for handling antineoplastic agents 11 MIN
VHS / U-matic / BETA
Nursing education series
Color (C PRO)
$280.00 purchase _ #601.4
Discusses reasons antineoplastic agents can be considered harmful and gives examples of ways hospital personnel are exposed. Describes newest guidelines for handling these agents based on OSHA recommendations. Presents procedures for handling spills and for washing the drug from skin and eyes if they become contaminated. Produced by Ohio State University Hospitals.
Health and Safety
Dist - CONMED

The Work Prejudice Film 13 MIN
U-matic / VHS / 16mm
Color (I)
LC 74-703294
Investigates the work world as it relates to sterotypes, attitudes and opportunities. Explores preconceived misconceptions. Presents statistics to indicate that women are succeeding in business and that a variety of ethnic groups are achieving in a broad assortment of jobs, crafts and professions.
Business and Economics; Education; Guidance and Counseling; Sociology
Dist - BARR **Prod** - SAIF 1974

Work Procedures for a Derrickman
U-matic / VHS
Working Offshore Series
Color (IND)
Discusses derrickman's duties in the derrick and in the pump room. Looks at safe work procedures for handling drill pipe during tripping operations. Details pump room equipment and maintenance procedures.
Business and Economics; Industrial and Technical Education; Social Science
Dist - GPCV **Prod** - GPCV

Work Procedures for a Roustabout
VHS / U-matic
Working Offshore Series
Color (IND)
Looks at a roustabout's life in terms of personal safety equipment and responsibilities, housekeeping procedures, painting procedures and safety, assisting the crane operator, working with slings and hitches, crane communica - tion and safety, and unloading crews and workboats.
Business and Economics; Industrial and Technical Education; Social Science
Dist - GPCV **Prod** - GPCV

Work, Pt 1
U-matic
Calculus Series
Color
Mathematics
Dist - MDCPB **Prod** - MDDE

Work, Pt 2
U-matic
Calculus Series
Color
Mathematics
Dist - MDCPB **Prod** - MDDE

Work Songs 29 MIN
U-matic
Folklore - U S a Series
B&W
Surveys the old work songs, chanties and chain gang songs by using guitar and field recordings from the Library of Congress.
Literature and Drama
Dist - UMITV **Prod** - UMITV 1967

The Work Supervisor 8 MIN
16mm / U-matic / VHS
Career Job Opportunity Film Series
Color
LC 79-707889
Depicts a variety of actual work and training situations where Neighborhood Youth Corps supervisors teach trainees. Issued in 1970 as a motion picture.
Business and Economics
Dist - USNAC **Prod** - USDLMA 1970

Work - the inside story series
Fitting in 15 MIN
Getting the facts 15 MIN
Leaving school 15 MIN
Moving on 15 MIN
Dist - TVOTAR

Work, Work, Work 59 MIN
U-matic / VHS
Color
Examines the concept of work from ancient times to the 20th century. Discusses the work ethic and introduces individual workers who explore their feelings about their jobs.
Sociology
Dist - PBS **Prod** - NJPBA

Work, Work, Work - Income 15 MIN
VHS / U-matic
Two Cents' Worth Series
Color (P)
Explores the gap between income and the expenses of life.
Social Science
Dist - AITECH **Prod** - WIEC 1976

Work World - Vocational Reading Resource Kit, Pt 1
U-matic / VHS
Color (J H)
Gives information about job hunting and keeping a job. Reinforces vocabulary. Includes getting a job, how to fill out forms, and on - the - job behavior.
English Language; Guidance and Counseling; Psychology
Dist - EDUACT **Prod** - EDUACT

Work World - Vocational Reading Resource Kit, Pt 2
U-matic / VHS
Color (J H)
Gives information about job hunting and keeping a job. Reinforces vocabulary skills. Includes strategies for developing appropriate on - the - job behavior.
English Language; Guidance and Counseling; Psychology
Dist - EDUACT **Prod** - EDUACT

Work worth doing 30 MIN
VHS / 16mm
Color (G IND)
$5.00 rental
Examines labor - management cooperation at several different American companies. Uses a before and after approach to demonstrate that union - management cooperation can enhance productivity, improve competitiveness and upgrade the quality of worklife for employees.
Business and Economics; Social Science
Dist - AFLCIO **Prod** - USDL 1987

Work worth doing 60 MIN
VHS
Color (A PRO IND)
$495.00 purchase, $150.00 rental
Presents a two - part documentary on six companies and their unions. Reveals that the companies have cooperated with the unions in developing cooperative labor practices and quality - of - work - life programs.
Business and Economics; Psychology
Dist - VLEARN **Prod** - FI

Work worth doing - Part one 28 MIN
VHS / U-matic
Color (PRO IND)
$110.00 purchase _ #TCA16639, #TCA16638
Documents the advantages of several different types of joint labor - management programs. Shows how such programs can increase both productivity and quality of life at work. Includes discussion guide.
Business and Economics; Social Science
Dist - USNAC **Prod** - USDL 1987

Work worth doing - Part two 27 MIN
VHS / U-matic
Color (PRO IND)
$110.00 purchase _ #TCA16642, #TCA16641
Focuses on the underlying principles of labor - management programs. Covers subjects including organizational readiness, management philosophy, employee attitudes, and more. Includes discussion guide.
Business and Economics; Social Science
Dist - USNAC **Prod** - USDL 1987

Work zone safety
BETA / VHS / U-matic
Safety meetings series
Color (G IND)
$495.00 purchase, $95.00 rental _ #WHP4
Emphasizes the importance of keeping a workspace clean, neat and free from safety hazards.
Business and Economics; Health and Safety; Psychology
Dist - BBP **Prod** - BBP 1990

The Workable Way 19 MIN
16mm
Color
LC 74-711594
Demonstrates the action taken by a group of Virginia and North Carolina farmers in solving local labor problems. Told in first person and by narration. Describes the background planning of a youth work center, putting the plan into effect and some of the final results.
Agriculture; Business and Economics; Social Science; Sociology
Dist - VAEC **Prod** - VAEC 1971

Worker to worker 25 MIN
16mm
Color (G IND)
$5.00 rental
Looks at the many kinds of safety and health problems encountered by workers on the job. Shows how these problems sometimes travel home with the worker and affect the health of spouses and children. Chemicals causing cancer and birth defects are frequently used by workers unaware of their deadly properties. Discusses OSHA and NIOSH.
Health and Safety; Social Science; Sociology
Dist - AFLCIO **Prod** - USDL 1981

Worker to Worker 29 MIN
16mm
Color
Tells the stories of Americans who know their rights are more that words on paper, they are rights to be used for protection on the job. Gives case histories and is narrated by Studs Terkel.
Guidance and Counseling; Health and Safety
Dist - DURRIN **Prod** - DURRIN

Workers '80 - Robotnicy '80 94 MIN
VHS
(G A) (POLISH)
$24.95 purchase _ #V130
Takes a look back at the beginnings of the Solidarity Movement through the lenses of cameramen who were at the shipyard during the 1980 strikes in Gdansk led by Lech Walesa.
Civics and Political Systems; Fine Arts; History - World; Social Science; Sociology
Dist - POLART

Workers at Risk Series
It's all in Your Head 15 MIN
That's a Killer 15 MIN
Those Other Guys 15 MIN
Who's Responsible 15 MIN
Why not Live 15 MIN
You Bet Your Life 15 MIN
Dist - ACCESS

The Workers Comp Connection 30 MIN
16mm
Color
Focuses on the physician's key role in the worker's compensation system and attempts to promote closer teamwork among physicians, insurers, employers and others working within the system.
Business and Economics
Dist - EMW **Prod** - EMW

Workers' Compensation - it Should be Your Right 12 MIN
16mm
Color
Explains the process of claiming for workers' compensation in Australia. Follows the case of Spiros Tripos, a Greek migrant who speaks little English. Shows how he has an accident at work and has difficulty in following the correct procedure for lodging his claim. Re - enacts the procedure Spiros should have taken to lodge his claim and gain benefit.
Business and Economics; Geography - World; Sociology
Dist - TASCOR **Prod** - NSWF 1978

Workers Depend on each Other 10 MIN
16mm / U-matic / VHS
Color (P)
LC 73-701637
Presents the workers necessary to make a doll house to show their dependence on one another.
Education; Psychology
Dist - CORF **Prod** - CORF 1973

Workers in Tropical Medicine - Calista E Causey, D Sc 60 MIN
VHS / U-matic
Color
LC 81-707187
Presents a biographical interview with Dr Calista E Causey, who recalls her years of research working with a field team in Brazil and later in Ibadam, Nigeria, which led to the discovery of many virus/vector/host relationships of significance to man.
Health and Safety
Dist - USNAC **Prod** - NMAC 1979

Workers of Our Community 12 MIN
16mm / U-matic / VHS
Color (P)
$305, $215 purchase _ #3593
Shows the many different people and services that are necessary for the welfare of the community.
Civics and Political Systems; Social Science
Dist - CORF

The Workers' State - 1970 - 1987 60 MIN
VHS
Struggles For Poland Series
Color (G)
$59.95 purchase _ #STFP - 109
Focuses on Poland's shift from a rural to an industrial society. Shows that Western economic difficulties, most notably the Arab oil embargo, strongly affected the Polish economy as well. Describes the beginnings of the Solidarity trade union, as well as its impact on Polish society.
Business and Economics; History - World
Dist - PBS **Prod** - WNETTV 1988

Workfare, Welfare - What's Fair 26 MIN
U-matic / VHS
Color (G)
$249.00, $149.00 purchase _ #AD - 1941
Focuses on a workfare program to get people off welfare and into jobs. Examines the costs, the prospects, the problems.
Guidance and Counseling; Sociology
Dist - FOTH **Prod** - FOTH

Workforce diversity - the corporate response 24 MIN
VHS
Color (COR)
$595.00 purchase, $165 rental _ #GWD
Presents a case-study showing how GTE has integrated the workplace, including diversity in selected workplaces. Provides information for managers and supervisors which focuses on collective thinking; flexible job arrangements; mentoring; accomodating employees' disabilities; multiculturalism; and financial benefits of diversity. Includes a Leader's Guide. Available for three - day preview, as well as rental, purchase, or lease.
Business and Economics; Psychology
Dist - ADVANM

Workforce diversity - the corporate response 24 MIN
VHS
Color (COR)
$595.00 purchase, $165.00 five - day rental, $35.00 three - day preview _ #GWD
Shows how GTE has achieved full integration of the workplace by embracing change. Focuses on two workplaces, Corning and Pitney Bowes. Demonstrates that different ideas are needed to collectively produce the best ideas; diversity is an outcome of embracing change and yields positive economic results; and that supporting flexibility in the workplace makes good business sense. Describes examples of flexibility, including job - sharing, telecommuting, mentoring, accomodating employees with disabilities, and highlighting ethnicity. Includes a Leader's Guide. Available for three - day preview and five - day rental, as well as purchase or lease.
Business and Economics; Guidance and Counseling; Psychology
Dist - ADVANM

Working 57 MIN
16mm / VHS
Heart of the Dragon Series
(J H C)
$99.95 each, $595.00 series
Looks at the working life of some Chinese people in a Mongolian factory.
Geography - World; History - World
Dist - AMBROS **Prod** - AMBROS 198-

Working 57 MIN
U-matic / VHS / 16mm
Heart of the Dragon Series Pt 6; Pt 6
Color (H C A)
Looks at China's industrial workers, focusing on those in the cities of Datong. Views Datong's two main industries, coal mining and railways. Introduces a young woman who wanted to be writer, but stoically accepts the State's decision that she should train to become a welder.
Civics and Political Systems; Geography - World; History - World
Dist - TIMLIF **Prod** - ASH 1984

Working 90 MIN
VHS / U-matic
Color (H C A)
LC 83-706567
Offers a musical which explores the world of work using actual interview responses which reveal the attitudes, aspirations and aggravations of people on the job. Based on the book Working by Studs Terkel.
Fine Arts; Sociology
Dist - FI **Prod** - WNETTV 1982

Working a Program - How to Get Well and Stay Well 30 MIN
VHS
(A)
$395.00 _ #83238
Presents a seminar on alcohol addiction recovery by Earnie Larsen. Discusses what a recovery program really means and how to make it work.
Guidance and Counseling; Health and Safety; Psychology
Dist - CMPCAR **Prod** - CMPCAR

Working a Program - How to Get Well and Stay Well
VHS / 16mm
Color (G)
$395.00 purchase, $70.00 rental _ #4973, 4977, 0439J, 0443J
Outlines a pattern of consistent daily and weekly practice in overcoming chemical dependency. Produced by Earnie Larsen.
Guidance and Counseling; Health and Safety; Psychology; Sociology
Dist - HAZELB

The Working actor - actors on acting 27 MIN
VHS
Color (PRO G)
$149.00 purchase, $49.00 rental _ #735
Presents four Australian actors in separate intercut interviews talking about their craft. Emphasizes specific techniques for bring a character to life and evoking authentic and believable emotional responses on stage. Discusses approaches to bodily movement and physiognomic control, research, work with the script, rehearsal techniques and modes of actor - director communication. Produced by the Australian Film, Television and Radio School.
Fine Arts
Dist - FIRLIT

The Working actor - teachers on acting 21 MIN
VHS
Color (PRO G)
$149.00 purchase, $49.00 rental _ #736
Presents scenes from acting workshops led by Dean Carey of Actors Centre, Sydney, Australia; Murray Hutchison, director of special training, ABC - TV; and Hayes Gordon, Ensemble Studios, Sydney. Emphasizes specific improvisational techniques and the building of a character step - by - step. Includes a thumbnail sketch of a 19th century portrayal of emotions and the evolution of modern acting styles resulting from the pioneering work of Stanislavsky. Produced by the Australian Film, Television and Radio School.
Fine Arts
Dist - FIRLIT

Working and breast - feeding - what you need to know 18 MIN
VHS
Color (G)
$120.00 purchase, $15.00 rental _ #24493
Looks briefly at the nutritional advantages of human milk, breast pumps and their costs, and important issues in milk storage. Interviews nursing mothers and their spouses, points out fears and concerns, difficulties in scheduling time, how they make it work and the special joys they experience.
Health and Safety
Dist - PSU **Prod** - UMINN 1986

Working and Playing to Health 35 MIN
16mm / U-matic / VHS

B&W (C A)
Illustrates the ways recreational, occupational and industrial therapy are used to help mental hospital patients back to health.
Health and Safety; Psychology
Dist - IFB **Prod** - MHFB 1954

Working artist series
Carole Morisseau and the Detroit City Dance Company 14 MIN
Dist - LRF
MARXS

Working Artist Series
Gerhardt Knodel - an Artist and His Work 13 MIN
Jim Pallas - Electronic Sculptor 12 MIN
John Glick - an Artist and His Work 9 MIN
John Voelker (Alias Robert Traver) - Anatomy of an Author 20 MIN
Lavinia Moyer and the Attic Theater 22 MIN
Dist - MARXS

Working as a Beautician
VHS / U-matic
Careers Without College
$30.00 purchase _ #CX503
Discusses a vocational field which does not require a college degree. Includes - on the job - interviews with workers who describe their jobs and the training they receive.
Guidance and Counseling
Dist - CAREER **Prod** - CAREER

Working as a Broadcast Technician
U-matic / VHS
Careers Without College
$30.00 purchase _ #CX501
Discusses a vocational field which does not require a college degree. Includes - on the job - interviews with workers who describe their jobs and the training they receive.
Guidance and Counseling
Dist - CAREER **Prod** - CAREER

Working as a Computer Programmer
U-matic / VHS
Careers Without College
$30.00 purchase _ #CX504
Discusses a vocational field which does not require a college degree. Includes - on the job - interviews with workers who describe their jobs and the training they receive.
Guidance and Counseling
Dist - CAREER **Prod** - CAREER

Working as a Dental Hygienist
U-matic / VHS
Careers Without College
$30.00 purchase _ #CX505
Discusses a vocational field which does not require a college degree. Includes - on the job - interviews with workers who describe their jobs and the training they receive.
Guidance and Counseling
Dist - CAREER **Prod** - CAREER

Working as a Paramedic
VHS / U-matic
Careers Without College
$30.00 purchase _ #CX500
Discusses a vocational field which does not require a college degree. Includes - on the job - interviews with workers who describe their jobs and the training they receive.
Guidance and Counseling
Dist - CAREER **Prod** - CAREER

Working as a Paraprofessional Teacher
VHS / U-matic
Careers Without College
$30.00 purchase _ #CX507
Discusses a vocational field which does not require a college degree. Includes - on the job - interviews with workers who describe their jobs and the training they receive.
Guidance and Counseling
Dist - CAREER **Prod** - CAREER

Working as a Secretary
U-matic / VHS
Careers Without College
$30.00 purchase _ #CX502
Discusses a vocational field which does not require a college degree. Includes - on the job - interviews with workers who describe their jobs and the training they receive.
Guidance and Counseling
Dist - CAREER **Prod** - CAREER

Working as an Auto Mechanic
U-matic / VHS
Careers Without College
$30.00 purchase _ #CX506
Discusses a vocational field which does not require a college degree. Includes - on the job - interviews with workers who describe their jobs and the training they receive.
Guidance and Counseling
Dist - CAREER **Prod** - CAREER

Working at the Car Wash Blues 15 MIN
U-matic
Success in the Job Market Series
Color (H)
LC 80-706454
Looks at various jobs and features counselers and educators commenting about the relationship between work and self - fulfillment.
Guidance and Counseling
Dist - GPN **Prod** - KUONTV 1980

Working class chronicle 43 MIN
16mm
Color & B&W (G)
$75.00 rental
Reconstructs the past of the filmmaker through the organizing concept of selective memory. Uses found footage; rephotographed home movies; optically printed materials; static copy - stand icon photography; live action camera work; voiceover narration; and reprocessed music from the time period. Combines personal history with historical events. Produced by Jack Walsh.
Fine Arts; Literature and Drama; Sociology
Dist - CANCIN

Working Class Women 29 MIN
U-matic
Woman Series
Color
Looks at the role of the working woman. Cites conditioning, culture mores and the lack of communication among women as factors contributing to the voicelessness of working class women.
Sociology
Dist - PBS **Prod** - WNEDTV

Working Couples - Urban and Family Life 28 MIN
16mm
Human Face of Japan Series
Color (H C A)
LC 82-700641
Deals with the pressures of urban life in Japan. Focuses on a typical middle - income couple and what their life is like on a day - to - day basis.
Geography - World; History - World; Social Science; Sociology
Dist - LCOA **Prod** - FLMAUS 1982

Working Cow Horse 25 MIN
U-matic / VHS / 16mm
Color
Discusses the origination of the working cow horse and its training.
Physical Education and Recreation
Dist - AQHORS **Prod** - AQHORS

Working Effectively with Different Managerial Styles
U-matic / VHS
Team Building for Administrative Support Staff Series
Color
Helps employees to work more productively with their own supervision and with other managers. Shows how three different types deal with a variety of work situations.
Business and Economics; Psychology
Dist - AMA **Prod** - AMA

Working effectively with others - Part 8 14 MIN
VHS
Employment development series
Color (PRO IND A)
$495.00 purchase, $150.00 rental _ #ITC34
Presents part eight of a ten - part series designed to prepare employees to cope with workplace demands in a skillful and confident manner. Enables supervisors and managers to improve their skills and abilities as they work with their peers. Includes a leader's guide, instructions for self - study and participant's booklet.
Business and Economics; Guidance and Counseling; Psychology
Dist - EXTR **Prod** - ITRC

Working for a better community 8 MIN
VHS / 16mm
Color (G IND)
$5.00 rental
Shows how thousands of unemployed workers who have exhausted their savings receive food from union food centers set up by labor and United Way. Looks at union representatives taking courses in counseling to help union members with problems.
Business and Economics; Guidance and Counseling; Social Science; Sociology
Dist - AFLCIO **Prod** - UWAMER 1986

Working for a Living - Job Skills for the Real World 48 MIN
VHS / U-matic
Color (J H)
LC 81-706153
Provides an inside look at a variety of entry - level jobs, and shows how to transfer the skills learned in school to new environments. Discusses job dissatisfaction and how to leave a job gracefully.
Guidance and Counseling
Dist - GA **Prod** - GA 1981

Working for America 17 MIN
VHS / U-matic
Color (G A)
$45.00, $95.00 purchase _ #TCA18219, #TCA18218
Interviews Federal government employees on why they work for the government. Includes interviews with a clerk - typist, a lab technician, a computer programmer, a warehouse foreman, and others. Co - produced by the Department of the Army.
Civics and Political Systems; Education; Guidance and Counseling
Dist - USNAC **Prod** - USDD 1989

Working for life - biology - No 1 20 MIN
BETA / VHS / U-matic
Career encounters series
Color (H C)
$110.00, $95.00 purchase
Interviews working biologists. Overviews the many job opportunities which exist in the field of biology. Tells how to prepare for a career in biology, what kind of background prospective employers look for and the salaries which accompany a career in biology.
Business and Economics; Guidance and Counseling; Psychology; Science
Dist - PLEXPU **Prod** - PLEXPU 1988

Working for the Lord 52 MIN
U-matic / VHS / 16mm
American Documents Series
Color (J H A)
Analyzes religious societies which originated because of dissatisfaction with greater society and survived by vigorous enterprise and commerce.
Guidance and Counseling; Religion and Philosophy
Dist - LUF **Prod** - LUF 1976

Working for the U S a 14 MIN
16mm
B&W
LC FIE57-151
Tells of Federal Civil Service employment. Includes how positions are obtained, wage scales, opportunities for advancement and fringe benefits.
Civics and Political Systems; Guidance and Counseling; Psychology
Dist - USNAC **Prod** - USA 1957

Working for the United States 25 MIN
16mm
Working for the United States Series
Color (H A)
LC 77-700711
Presents the new or prospective civil service employee with information on the executive branch and its relation to the other branches of the U S government. Discusses the role of the Federal employee in the political system and the work of the Federal workforce.
Civics and Political Systems; Guidance and Counseling
Dist - USNAC **Prod** - USCSC 1976

Working for the United States Series
Benefits you earn 16 MIN
The Road Ahead 17 MIN
Working for the United States 25 MIN
You and the Merit System 15 MIN
Your Rights and Responsibilities 17 MIN
Dist - USNAC

Working I and II
VHS / Kit
Color (S T PRO)
$599.00 purchase
Presents a two - part series on employment for the developmentally disabled, learning disabled and educationally handicapped. Looks at attitudes and habits for getting and holding a job and interpersonal skills assessment and training for job tenure. Part I is available in either a kit with six filmstrips and two videos or in eight videocassettes. Part II includes the TICE - Test of Interpersonal Competence for Employment - assessment for identifying the skills of individuals and a teacher's guide.
Education; Guidance and Counseling; Psychology
Dist - STANFI **Prod** - STANFI

Working I - attitudes and habits for getting and holding a job
VHS / Kit
Working series
Color (S T PRO)
$399.00 purchase _ #1012
Presents eight programs on getting employment for the developmentally disabled, learning disabled and educationally handicapped. Discusses grooming, punctuality, positive attitudes, working with other people, on the job behavior, understanding directions and producing quality work. Available in a kit with six filmstrip programs and two video programs or all eight programs on video. Includes teacher's guide.
Education; Guidance and Counseling; Psychology
Dist - STANFI **Prod** - STANFI

Working II - interpersonal skills assessment and training for job tenure 60 MIN
VHS
Working series
Color (S T PRO)
$399.00 purchase _ #1013
Focuses on 24 separate interpersonal skills identified as important for job tenure. Trains the developmentally disabled, learning disabled and educationally handicapped. Includes the TICE - Test of Interpersonal Competence for Employment - assessment for identifying the skills of individuals and a teacher's guide.
Education; Guidance and Counseling; Psychology
Dist - STANFI **Prod** - STANFI

Working in 3D sculpture - 6 30 MIN
U-matic / VHS
Think new series
Color (C G)
$129.00, $99.00 purchase _ #V581
Gives theoretical motivation and practical ideas about working in three - dimensional sculpture. Draws content from mathematics, science, history, human feelings, every human endeavor. Part of an 11 - part series that treats art as an essential mode of learning.
Fine Arts
Dist - BARR **Prod** - CEPRO 1991

Working in Communications and Media 20 MIN
16mm / U-matic / VHS
Working Series
Color (I)
Takes a look at the duties of a photojournalist, a film editor, a television engineer and a telephone installer.
Guidance and Counseling; Industrial and Technical Education; Social Science; Sociology
Dist - LCOA **Prod** - NICKWA 1982

Working in Food Services 21 MIN
U-matic / VHS / 16mm
Working Series
Color (I)
Looks at the duties of a restaurant manager, a baker and a meat wrapper.
Guidance and Counseling; Industrial and Technical Education
Dist - LCOA **Prod** - NICKWA 1982

Working in Groups 9 MIN
VHS / 16mm
English as a Second Language Series
Color (A PRO)
$165.00 purchase _ #290317
Demonstrates key teaching methods for English as a Second Language - ESL teachers. Features a teacher - presenter who introduces and provides a brief commentary on the techniques, then demonstrates the application of the technique to the students. 'Working In Groups' identifies some key principles to facilitate more effective small group discussions and then demonstrates the principles in a classroom setting.
Education; English Language; Mathematics
Dist - ACCESS **Prod** - ACCESS 1989

Working in Marketing and Distribution 22 MIN
U-matic / VHS / 16mm
Working Series
Color (I)
Looks at the duties of a clothing buyer, a window display designer, a graphic artist and a toy designer.
Business and Economics; Guidance and Counseling; Industrial and Technical Education
Dist - LCOA **Prod** - NICKWA 1982

Working in Science 20 MIN
U-matic / VHS / 16mm
Working Series
Color (I)
LC 83-700574
Introduces the duties of a mechanical engineer, a computer scientist, an industrial engineer and a physicist.
Guidance and Counseling; Psychology; Science
Dist - LCOA **Prod** - NICKWA 1982

Working in the hazard zone series
Presents an eight - part series on working with and around hazardous materials. Includes the titles - Beyond the Training Room - Introduction; Breathing Easy - Respirators; Fashions for Living - Personal Protective Equipment; Drum Beat - Container Handling; Tightrope - Physical Hazards; Nurse Vera Explains It All - Chemical Hazards; Incident at Building 13 - Emergency Response; Decon - Decontamination. Each program includes a leader's guide and ten participant manuals.

Beyond the training room	18 MIN
Decon - decontamination	15 MIN
Drum beat - container handling	17 MIN
Fashions for living - personal protective equipment	14 MIN
Incident at building 13 - emergency response	13 MIN
Nurse Vera explains it all - chemical hazards	15 MIN

Dist - BNA **Prod** - BNA 1982

Working in the hazard zone series

Tightrope	12 MIN

Dist - BNA
ITF

Working in the hazard zone series

Breathing easy	19 MIN
Drum beat	17 MIN
Fashions for living	14 MIN
Working safely within a hazardous environment	18 MIN

Dist - ITF

Working in the Integrated Classroom 29 MIN
U-matic / VHS / 16mm
Survival Skills for the Classroom Teacher Series
Color (T)
Examines the dynamics of the integrated classroom environment. Shows practical options for promoting positive intergroup relations in a climate which encourages academic achievement and individual self - esteem. Covers dealing with both student and teacher expectations, grouping strategies which avoid resegregation, parent and peer influence, and the place of extracurricular activities in a successful integration program.
Education
Dist - FI **Prod** - MFFD

Working in the USA 30 MIN
U-matic / BETA / 16mm / VHS
Color (G)
$600.00, $500.00 purchase, $100.00 rental
Introduces non - United States citizens to the values and dynamics of the US workplace. Shares the experiences and advice of foreign nationals through documentary footage filmed in diverse work environments. Also available in STSC, PAL and SECAM formats.
Business and Economics; Guidance and Counseling; History - United States; Social Science; Sociology
Dist - COPGRG **Prod** - COPGRG

Working in Transportation 21 MIN
16mm / U-matic / VHS
Working Series
Color (I)
Looks at the duties of a fishing boat captain, an auto repair shop owner, a construction equipment operator, an air traffic controller and a truck driver.
Guidance and Counseling; Industrial and Technical Education; Social Science
Dist - LCOA **Prod** - NICKWA 1982

Working in Washington 13 MIN
VHS / U-matic
Under the Yellow Balloon Series
Color (P)
Shows Joanne visiting Washington where Dad has just begun to work and learning about the presidency, seeing laws being made and explained, and visiting famous monuments and the Smithsonian Institution.
Civics and Political Systems; Fine Arts; Geography - United States
Dist - AITECH **Prod** - SCETV 1980

Working in Watercolor 18 MIN
U-matic / VHS / 16mm
Color (J H C)
Presents basic tools and materials and demonstrates novel and new manipulations of water color. Stimulates students to use water color in an individual and personal style.
Fine Arts
Dist - IFB **Prod** - IFB 1959

Working in Wax 13 MIN
U-matic / VHS
Color
Offers a behind - the - scenes look at London's Wax Museum, where the famous and the infamous stand side by side.
Fine Arts; Geography - World
Dist - JOU **Prod** - UPI

Working it Out 15 MIN
U-matic
Job Skills Series
(H C A)
Examines the reasons for working and discusses how work fulfills physical and emotional needs.
Business and Economics; Guidance and Counseling; Science - Physical
Dist - ACCESS **Prod** - ACCESS 1982

Working it Out 18 MIN
16mm
Color
LC 78-700400
Provides information on the Comprehensive Employment and Training Act (CETA), which provides federal money to fund jobs in private industry. Shows what happens when three people try the CETA program.
Business and Economics; Civics and Political Systems; Sociology
Dist - MGMO **Prod** - MGMO 1977

Working it out - support groups for nursing aides 30 MIN
VHS
Color (G C PRO)
$89.00 purchase, $35.00 rental
Demonstrates the benefits to nursing aides of support groups in which they can discuss problems and issues related to their work. Encourages use of such groups to reduce job stress and turnover among staffmembers.
Health and Safety
Dist - TNF

Working Late 24 MIN
VHS / 16mm / U-matic
Color (H C G)
$520, $365, $395 _ #A534
Explores the issue of age discrimination in the workplace both toward the over 45 age group and also toward those approaching senior citizen status. Points out that many in the over 45 age group are passed over, despite their knowledge and experience, in favor of their younger counterparts.
Business and Economics; Guidance and Counseling; Psychology; Social Science; Sociology
Dist - BARR **Prod** - BARR 1988

Working model of the thorax 3 MIN
16mm
Dukes physiology film series
Color (C)
LC 77-710185
Uses a bell, jar and balloon model to illustrate the role of the chest cavity and diaphragm in normal respiration, pneumothorax, the return of blood to the heart, and regurgitation in ruminants.
Science - Natural
Dist - IOWA **Prod** - IOWA 1971

Working Mom's Survival Guide 45 MIN
VHS
Color (G)
$24.95 purchase _ #6320
Shows how to find 'guilt - free' time, how to get organized. Shares secrets for success with mates, what experts are saying about quality time with children, stress prevention, fitness and more.
Sociology
Dist - SYBVIS **Prod** - SYBVIS

Working more Effectively with People 46 FRS
VHS / U-matic
Human Side of Management Series
Color
Discusses why and how an effective supervisor can change unacceptable employee attitudes and behavior to acceptable ones. Emphasizes that it is important for the employee to see problems as their own as well as the organization's.
Business and Economics; Psychology
Dist - RESEM **Prod** - RESEM

The Working Mother 28 MIN
16mm
Look at Me Series no 2
Color (A)
LC 77-700464
Describes how mothers can have fun with their children. Shows different game experiences possible at various locations.
Guidance and Counseling; Physical Education and Recreation; Psychology; Sociology
Dist - USNAC **Prod** - PARLTF 1975

Working Mother Series

The Spring and Fall of Nina Polanski	6 MIN

Dist - MEDIAG

Working Mother Series
And they lived happily ever after 13 MIN
It's not Enough 16 MIN
Mothers are People 7 MIN
They Appreciate You more 16 MIN
Dist - NFBC

The Working of Magnesium 27 MIN
16mm
B&W
LC FIA55-1029
Portrays the correct technique for matching, forming, arc and spot welding, riveting, chemical treating and painting of magnesium alloys.
Industrial and Technical Education; Science - Physical
Dist - DCC **Prod** - DCC 1953

Working offshore series
Making a Connection
Safe Use of Drill Pipe Tongs
Trip into the hole
Trip out of the hole
Work Procedures for a Derrickman
Work Procedures for a Roustabout
Dist - GPCV

Working on Aerial Lifts, Cranes and Swing Stages 15 MIN
16mm / VHS
Safety on the Job Series
Color (H C A PRO)
$295.00, $350.00 purchase, $75.00 rental _ #8035
Teaches workers safety rules to follow when operating aerial lifts, cranes and swing stages.
Health and Safety; Psychology
Dist - AIMS **Prod** - AIMS 1989

Working on Ladders, Poles and Scaffolds 15 MIN
16mm / VHS
Safety on the Job Series
Color (H C A PRO)
$295.00, $350.00 purchase, $75.00 rental _ #8034
Provides important safety guidelines for working on ladders, poles and scaffolding.
Health and Safety; Psychology
Dist - AIMS **Prod** - AIMS 1989

Working on oneself quartet 120 MIN
BETA / VHS
Color (G)
$69.95 purchase _ #Q324
Presents a four - part discussion about working on the self. Includes 'The Gurdjieff Work' with Dr Kathleen Speeth, 'The Transmission of Knowledge' with Dr Claudio Naranjo, 'Overcoming Compulsive Behavior' with Shinzen Young, and 'Intuitive Risk Taking' with Patricia Sun.
Psychology; Religion and Philosophy
Dist - THINKA **Prod** - THINKA

Working on oneself series
The Gurdjieff work 30 MIN
Intuitive risk taking 30 MIN
Overcoming compulsive behavior 30 MIN
The Transmission of knowledge 30 MIN
Dist - THINKA

Working on Working 29 MIN
16mm
Color (T)
LC 80-701397
Focuses on the mainstreaming of handicapped students in vocational education programs.
Education; Psychology
Dist - USNAC **Prod** - USHHS 1979

Working on your career series
Presents a three - part series on careers. Includes the titles 'Take This Job and Keep It,' 'Go For It' and 'Choices in Health.'
Choices in health - 3 10 MIN
Go for it - 2 9 MIN
Take this job and keep it - 1 20 MIN
Dist - BARR **Prod** - NYSED 1979

Working out an epistemology 45 MIN
VHS / U-matic
Artificial intelligence series; Fundamental concepts, Pt 1
Color (PRO)
Discusses role of natural constraints in solving perception problems, coping with thousands of possibilities, increased constraint, and illustration.
Mathematics; Psychology
Dist - MIOT **Prod** - MIOT

Working Outdoors 20 MIN
16mm / U-matic / VHS
Working Series
Color (I)
LC 83-700572
Introduces the duties of a tree surgeon, a zoo tour guide and a trash collector.
Guidance and Counseling; Psychology
Dist - LCOA **Prod** - NICKWA 1982

Working Partners - the Secretary - Manager Team 1986
16mm / VHS
#109089 - 4 3/4
Shows how productivity and personal job satisfaction can be markedly increased when manager and secretary work together as a team. Follows two secretary - manager pairs as they develop into teams, demonstrating the methods they use to make work easier and more effective.
Business and Economics
Dist - MGHT

The Working Process 28 MIN
U-matic / VHS
Beethoven by Barenboim Series
Color (C)
$249.00, $149.00 purchase _ #AD - 1224
Shows Beethoven's working methods through the Second and Third Leonore Overtures. Part of a thirteen - part series placing Beethoven, his music and his life within the context of his time and the history of music, Beethoven by Barenboim.
Fine Arts; History - World
Dist - FOTH **Prod** - FOTH

Working River 59 MIN
16mm
Color
Provides a modern history of the Ohio River as told by the people who live and work on it including a towboat crew, a retired river captain and a homesteading author/artist.
Geography - United States
Dist - UPITTS **Prod** - LNGRDL 1982

Working safely with electricity - II 10 MIN
8mm cartridge / VHS / BETA / U-matic
Rules of danger series
Color; CC; PAL (IND G PRO)
$395.00 purchase, $175.00 rental _ #MEL - 104
Reinforces respect and awareness for electricity. Illustrates safe work procedures such as bonding flammable liquid containers, wearing proper personal protection equipment, keeping work areas clean and dry, using lockout - tagout procedures and more. Part two of two parts. Includes a leader's guide and ten participant workbooks.
Health and Safety; Science - Physical
Dist - BNA

Working safely with hand and power tools 15 MIN
8mm cartridge / VHS / BETA / U-matic
Color; PAL (IND G)
$295.00 purchase, $175.00 rental _ #MAR - 102
Demonstrates the proper use and maintenance of hand and power tools. Gives new insights into the ergnomics of proper tool use to reduce the potential for repetitive stress. Includes a leader's guide and ten workbooks.
Health and Safety; Psychology
Dist - BNA

Working safely with HIV in the research laboratory 20 MIN
U-matic / VHS
Color (IND PRO C)
$395.00 purchase, $80.00 rental _ #C900 - VI - 004
Discusses routes of contamination and demonstrates proper procedures for avoiding contamination with HIV - Human Immunodeficiency Virus - and other microbiological agents in the microbiological research laboratory. Trains researchers and lab technicians. Features Biosafety Level 2 and 3 laboratories.
Health and Safety; Science
Dist - HSCIC **Prod** - NIH 1990

Working Safely with Pesticides 18 MIN
VHS
Color (G) (SPANISH)
$89.95 purchase _ #6 - 300 - 306P, #6 - 300 - 307P - Spanish Version
Presents a training film on pesticide safety for agricultural workers. Includes record - keeping on material safety data sheets, pesticide labels and containers, employee safety training and pesticide storage and disposal. Meets the OSHA Hazard Communication Standard.
Agriculture; Health and Safety; Psychology
Dist - VEP **Prod** - VEP

Working Safely with Scaffolds 19 MIN
U-matic / VHS
Safety Action for Employees Series
Color (IND)
Describes and demonstrates correct safety procedures for working with scaffolds, how to build a scaffold according to safety regulations, and how to safely work the scaffold.
Health and Safety
Dist - GPCV **Prod** - GPCV

Working Safely with Unibolt Couplings 15 MIN
U-matic / VHS
Color (IND)
Explains safe and proper procedures to use when changing out a choke housed in a unibolt coupling.
Health and Safety; Industrial and Technical Education; Social Science
Dist - UTEXPE **Prod** - UTEXPE 1983

Working safely within a hazardous environment 18 MIN
BETA / VHS / U-matic
Working in the hazard zone series
Color (IND G A)
$775.00 purchase, $175.00 rental _ #WOR064
Introduces the health and safety aspects of hazardous waste operations and emergency response. Part of a fivo - part series on working with hazardous substances.
Health and Safety; Psychology
Dist - ITF **Prod** - BNA 1991

Working series
Decision making 20 MIN
Doing your eight 20 MIN
Rules of the Game 19 MIN
Where do I Go from Here 21 MIN
Dist - JOU

Working series
Communications and media 20 MIN
Working in Communications and Media 20 MIN
Working in Food Services 21 MIN
Working in Marketing and Distribution 22 MIN
Working in Science 20 MIN
Working in Transportation 21 MIN
Working Outdoors 20 MIN
Working with Animals 20 MIN
Dist - LCOA

Working series
Working I - attitudes and habits for getting and holding a job
Working II - interpersonal skills assessment and training for job tenure 60 MIN
Dist - STANFI

A Working Solution 15 MIN
16mm
Color (H C A)
Provides information on temporary help companies, showing how they organize part - time work for people. Discusses how to get temporary or part - time employment.
Guidance and Counseling; Sociology
Dist - KLEINW **Prod** - KLEINW

The Working Solution 27 MIN
VHS / U-matic
Color (IND)
Studies the effects of on - the - job injuries. Explores the cost to the company, the emotional and physical cost to the worker, and the role of supervisor in the return to work program.
Business and Economics; Health and Safety; Psychology
Dist - CHARTH **Prod** - CHARTH

Working - Soviet Style 27 MIN
U-matic / VHS / 16mm
Soviet Style Series
Color (J)
Examines the role of workers and natural resources in the development of the Soviet economy. Studies the interrelationships of government, management and trade unions and examines a coal mine, a refrigerator factory, a timber processing plant and dock workers on the Odessa waterfront.
Business and Economics; Civics and Political Systems; Geography - World; History - World; Sociology
Dist - JOU **Prod** - JOU 1982

Working stiffs 62 MIN
VHS
Color (G)
$25.00 purchase
Uses a B - movie horror facade to portray an unscrupulous temporary employment agency that discovers the secret to cheap labor by using voodoo spells to turn dead employees into living workaholics. Entertains with an offbeat satire of the American work ethic gone wild. Produced by Sideshow Cinema.
Fine Arts; Literature and Drama
Dist - CANCIN

Working Teens 30 MIN
VHS
Soapbox With Tom Cottle Series
Color (G)
$59.95 purchase _ #SBOX - 210
Analyzes the importance of jobs to many high school students. Reports that teenagers who work must balance their job responsibilities with their schoolwork and family obligations. Hosted by psychologist Tom Cottle.
Business and Economics; Education; Guidance and Counseling; Psychology
Dist - PBS **Prod** - WGBYTV 1985

Working the booth 16 MIN
BETA / U-matic / VHS
Color (G)
$375.00 purchase, $130.00 rental
Shows how trade show exhibitors can obtain solid sales leads. Trains in trade show etiquette, maintaining a professional presence, attract positive attention, qualify prospects as sales leads, involve prospects in a dialogue, sell solutions to customer problems.
Business and Economics; Psychology
Dist - AMEDIA **Prod** - AMEDIA 1992

Working the Double Shift 20 MIN
U-matic / VHS
Color
Projects images from the home which conflict with mass media 'home life.' Presented by Lisa Steele and Kim Tomczak.
Fine Arts
Dist - ARTINC **Prod** - ARTINC

Working the fast food counter 12 MIN
35mm strip / VHS
Color (A)
#FC40
Demonstrates that employees working the fast food counter must be able to serve their customers quickly but with courtesy and good service. Teaches the proper steps of counter service - greeting the customer, asking for the order, suggesting additional items, getting the order together, bagging, taking payment and thanking the customer. Includes cleaning and stocking.
Industrial and Technical Education
Dist - CONPRO **Prod** - CONPRO

Working through change 32 MIN
VHS
Working through change series
Color (PRO IND A)
$795.00 purchase, $175.00 rental _ #GP101A & B
Features Dr Harry Woodward who reveals how change affects people and organizations. Helps employees and managers - supervisors identify the phases of change and how to handle transitions.
Business and Economics
Dist - EXTR **Prod** - GPERFO

Working through change - employee video 16 MIN
VHS
Color (G)
$495.00 purchase, $150.00 rental _ #WTEV, #WTEVR
Addresses the needs of survivors of mergers, acquisitions, down - sizing, out - sourcing and other sources of change in the corporate world. Prepares these employees to survive and even thrive on change. Created by Dr Harry Woodward.
Business and Economics; Guidance and Counseling; Psychology
Dist - GPERFO

Working through change - manager's video 16 MIN
VHS
Color (G)
$495.00 purchase, $150.00 rental _ #WTMV, #WTMVR
Addresses the needs of survivors of mergers, acquisitions, down - sizing, out - sourcing and other sources of change in the corporate world. Prepares these employees to survive and even thrive on change. Created by Dr Harry Woodward.
Business and Economics; Guidance and Counseling; Psychology
Dist - GPERFO

Working through change series
How to help your people get back on track - Part 2 - manager - supervisor version 16 MIN
How to move from endings to new beginnings - Part 1 - employee version 16 MIN
Working through change 32 MIN
Dist - EXTR

Working through College 20 MIN
16mm
B&W
LC FIE52-2117
Tells the story of a college student and the assistance provided him by a student employment adviser in finding a job which helps meet his expenses and enables him to acquire practical experience in the field he has chosen as a career.
Guidance and Counseling
Dist - USNAC **Prod** - USA 1954

Working to Save Your Back 10 MIN
VHS
Color (PRO)
$395.00 purchase _ #N900VI047
Introduces nurses and hospital staff to techniques for the safe and efficient moving of patients. Demonstrates bed positioning and various states of mobility. Shows procedures for one and two person patient transfers. Emphasizes the maintenance of postural curves and protecting the backs of staff.
Health and Safety; Science
Dist - HSCIC

Working Together 16 MIN
VHS / U-matic
Funny Business Series
Color
Business and Economics; Psychology
Dist - DELTAK **Prod** - LCOA

Working together 29 MIN
16mm / VHS
Color (G IND)
$5.00 rental
Examines labor - management cooperation on the state and local government level. Looks at four examples of teamwork - the city government of Madison, Wisconsin, county government in Jackson County, Oregon, New York state government and a school district in Dade County, Miami, Florida. Reveals that each situation is different but all of their cooperative efforts result in workers doing a better job, managers making better decisions and taxpayers getting the best service possible for their tax dollar. Produced by the State and Local Government Labor - Management Committee.
Business and Economics; Civics and Political Systems; Social Science
Dist - AFLCIO

Working Together 30 MIN
16mm
We Can Help Series
Color (PRO)
LC 77-703249
Features multiagency and multidiscipline approaches to child abuse and neglect. Discusses consultation teams, community coordinating and professional and public education.
Home Economics; Sociology
Dist - USNAC **Prod** - NCCAN 1977

Working Together 18 MIN
VHS / 16mm
Color (PRO)
$459.00 purchase, $125.00 rental, $45.00 preview
Offers ways to improve relationships between employees and supervisors. Shows how to coach employees going through difficult times, how to improve communications in the office, offer criticism and correct mistakes.
Business and Economics; Guidance and Counseling; Psychology
Dist - UTM **Prod** - UTM

Working Together 24 MIN
VHS / 16mm / U-matic / BETA
Working Together Series
Color; Stereo
Shows the problems of small group decision making, individual receiving information from a group, generating group discussion, eliciting opinions from within a group, effectively ending a communication session, and the necessity for preparation in a group information session.
English Language; Psychology; Sociology
Dist - SEVDIM **Prod** - SEVDIM 1983

Working Together 20 MIN
16mm
Color
LC FIE63-108
Shows how the cooperative effort of the hospital and nursing home is beneficial to the hospital, the nursing home and the patient.
Health and Safety; Sociology
Dist - USNAC **Prod** - USPHS 1962

Working Together 12 MIN
16mm / U-matic / VHS
Simple Machines Series
Color (I J)
$315, $215 purchase _ #4485
Shows how simple machines form complex mechanical devices.
History - World
Dist - CORF

Working together - 65 9 MIN
U-matic / VHS
Life's little lessons - self - esteem 4 - 6 series
Color (I)
$129.00, $99.00 purchase _ #V694
Reveals that unity is when a group of people works together toward a common goal. Looks at a TV crew working to produce the best show that they can, but the star keeps changing the script and adding material so she can look good and become a singing star. Part of a 65 - part series on self - esteem.
Guidance and Counseling; Psychology
Dist - BARR **Prod** - CEPRO 1992

Working together for action series
Deciding what to do 25 MIN
Starting to Work Together 20 MIN
Taking Action 15 MIN
Dist - UWISC

Working together - managing cultural diversity 23 MIN
VHS
Color (PRO IND A)
Emphasizes the need to work together productively 'because of' rather than 'in spite of' ethnic diversity.
Business and Economics
Dist - ACTIVM **Prod** - ACTIVM 1990
EXTR
INCUL

Working together - Saturn and the UAW 31 MIN
U-matic / VHS
Color (IND G)
$225.00 purchase, $120.00 rental
Interviews assembly - line workers, union officers and line managers to show how labor problems are handled at Saturn. Observes the give - and - take at a weekly team meeting to illustrate how workers make decisions on work issues - even on the rearrangement of the plant for the model change. Two of the chief negotiators, Reid Rundell of General Motors and Donald Ephlin of the United Auto Workers, tell how management and the union put the innovative jointness agreement together. Some principal critics of jointness explain why they oppose it. Written and directed by Henry Bass.
Business and Economics; Social Science
Dist - ROLAND **Prod** - MRMKF

Working together series
Presents six comic aspects of the difficulties encountered by group leaders and participants in meetings.
Any Questions 4 MIN
Be prepared 4 MIN
The Briefing 4 MIN
The Decision makers 4 MIN
Just One more Thing 4 MIN
Well, if You Ask Me 4 MIN
Working Together 24 MIN
The Working together series 19 MIN
Dist - SEVDIM **Prod** - SEVDIM

Working together - video and book
VHS
Color (PRO G)
$495.00 purchase _ #W09
Shows how to become more effective in a multicultural organization. Teaches that acknowledging, understanding and appreciating diversity is fundamental to working well together. Section one looks into differences, two examines how people talk to and about each other, and section three helps workers identify and deal with major differences in unspoken language - gestures, touches, looks and tone of voice.
Psychology; Social Science
Dist - NEWRP **Prod** - NEWRP

Working together works 24 MIN
VHS
Color (PRO A G)
$520.00 purchase, $140.00 rental
Presents the benefits of working together through dramas, animated sequences, personal interviews and documentaries. Encourages development of good working relationships. Includes a leader's guide and workshop materials.
Business and Economics; Psychology
Dist - EXTR **Prod** - DARTNL
VLEARN

Working Together - Works 28 MIN
VHS / 16mm
Color (PRO)
$520.00 purchase, $85.00 rental, $50.00 preview
Teaches employees to work with each other as a team. Shows how to develop a positive work attitude.
Business and Economics; Psychology
Dist - UTM **Prod** - UTM

Working toward a Career
VHS / 16mm
Color (H C A PRO)
$89.00 purchase _ #MC600
Demonstrates the value of co - op, work study, work experience and related programs in providing skills to students as they move toward independent living.
Business and Economics; Guidance and Counseling
Dist - AAVIM **Prod** - AAVIM 1990

The Working Unit 30 MIN
U-matic / VHS
Business Management Series Lesson 9; Lesson 9
Color (C A)
Looks at the practical steps involved in creating a working organizational structure and examines certain key organizational concepts such as unity of command and span of control. Explores various types of organizational structures.

Business and Economics; Psychology
Dist - SCCON **Prod** - SCCON

Working with Animals 20 MIN
16mm / U-matic / VHS
Working Series
Color (I)
LC 83-700573
Introduces the duties of a dairy farmer, a horse trainer, a zoo keeper, a dog groomer and a vet.
Guidance and Counseling; Physical Education and Recreation; Psychology; Science; Science - Natural
Dist - LCOA **Prod** - NICKWA 1982

Working with Animals 11 MIN
U-matic / VHS / 16mm
Zoom Series
Color
LC 78-700147
Presents three young people who talk about their experiences working with animals.
Physical Education and Recreation; Sociology
Dist - FI **Prod** - WGBHTV 1977

Working with assertiveness 19 MIN
VHS
Color (A PRO IND)
$495.00 purchase, $175.00 rental
Features assertiveness training for managers. Hosted by Rennie Fritchie.
Business and Economics; Guidance and Counseling; Psychology
Dist - VLEARN

Working with Chains 5 MIN
U-matic / VHS
Steel Making Series
Color (IND)
Looks at chain inspection and discusses possible causes for damages. Identifies and stresses safe working procedures.
Business and Economics; Health and Safety; Industrial and Technical Education
Dist - LEIKID **Prod** - LEIKID

Working with creative imagery 30 MIN
BETA / VHS
Working with the unconscious series
Color (G)
$29.95 purchase _ #S338
Considers that the images one visualizes serve as blueprints for events which manifest in one's life. Features Shakti Gawain who says that one can consciously influence the process of imagery by visualizing the positive situations desired. Provides instruction for a basic visualization technique. Part of a four - part series about working with the unconscious.
Psychology; Religion and Philosophy
Dist - THINKA **Prod** - THINKA

Working with difficult people 20 MIN
VHS
Color (A PRO IND)
$495.00 purchase, $95.00 rental
Explains why 'difficult' people behave as they do, and gives suggestions for dealing with their behavior. Reveals the five most common reasons people put up defense mechanisms.
Business and Economics; Guidance and Counseling; Psychology
Dist - VLEARN **Prod** - BBP

Working with Difficult People 1984
16mm / VHS
#109037 - 1 3/4
Explains four simple steps that minimize the negative effects of working with people with difficult personalities.
Business and Economics
Dist - MGHT

Working with dreams 30 MIN
BETA / VHS
Working with the unconscious series
Color (G)
$29.95 purchase _ #S333
Points out that dreams are held in disrepute by mainstream institutions because they challenge closed systems of thought. Features Jeremy Taylor who suggests that techniques such as lucid dreaming can be used for healing and overcoming addictions. Taylor believes that dreams connect the dreamer with the world of nature and with God. Part of a four - part series about working with the unconscious.
Health and Safety; Psychology; Religion and Philosophy
Dist - THINKA **Prod** - THINKA

Working with Einstein 60 MIN
U-matic
Color
Presents men who worked with Albert Einstein. Illustrates his philosophies and methods of working.
Biography; Science
Dist - HRC **Prod** - OHC

Working with electricity 16 MIN
VHS
Safety on the job series
Color (G IND)
$99.95 purchase _ #6 - 203 - 019A
Details the hazards associated with using electricity on the job. Illustrates problem - solving procedures and how most electrical disasters are preventable. Discusses insufficient wire insulation, faulty breakers, overloaded outlets and water. Reviews OSHA regulations. Part of a series on job safety.
Health and Safety; Industrial and Technical Education
Dist - VEP **Prod** - VEP 1993

Working with Electricity 16 MIN
VHS / 16mm
Safety on the Job Series
Color (H C A PRO)
$295.00 purchase, $75.00 rental _ #8132
Details the hazards associated with using electricity on the job.
Health and Safety; Psychology
Dist - AIMS **Prod** - AIMS 1989

Working with Groups 30 MIN
Videoreel / VHS
One Strong Link Series
B&W
Guidance and Counseling; Social Science
Dist - CORNRS **Prod** - CUETV 1971

Working with Groups - a Behavioral Approach 60 MIN
U-matic / VHS
Color
Gives an overview of the various types of group work. Outlines operant role modeling, communication and problem solving groups. Covers model target, interest groups, cross age tutoring and group desensitization.
Sociology
Dist - UWISC **Prod** - UWISC 1979

Working with hostile and resistant teens 30 MIN
VHS
Working with hostile and resistant teens series
Color (T PRO G)
$99.00 purchase _ #ATC01EV - K
Features Stephen Campbell, a therapist who has worked with hostile, resistant and explosive children for 25 years and developed an effective anger management strategy. Consists of role plays with teens who are, in most cases, acting out their own personal histories. Campbell leads the role plays, provides an analysis, and shows how to effectively work with hostile and resistant individuals. Part of two parts.
Guidance and Counseling; Health and Safety; Psychology
Dist - CAMV

Working with hostile and resistant teens series
Presents two parts featuring Stephen Campbell, a therapist who has worked with hostile, resistant and explosive children for 25 years and developed an effective anger management strategy. Consists of role plays with teens who are, in most cases, acting out their own personal histories. Campbell leads the role plays, provides an analysis, and shows how to effectively work with hostile and resistant individuals.
Working with hostile and resistant teens 30 MIN
Dist - CAMV

Working with hostile and resistant teens series
Working with resistant teens 30 MIN
Dist - CAMV
FANPRO

Working with hostile teens 45 MIN
VHS
Color (G)
$89.00 purchase _ #CA - 104
Features dramatized counseling sessions between Steven Campbell and teenagers acting out incidents from their own personal histories. Trains counselors, therapists, teachers, administrators, psychology and social work students, parents and anyone who works with teenagers. Includes a study guide. Produced by Tom Kinney.
Health and Safety
Dist - FANPRO

Working with Intrinsic Forecasting Techniques 60 MIN
BETA / VHS
Manufacturing Series
(IND)
Teaches the principles and methods used in intrinsic forecasting, including computer based techniques and their applications in planning, production and management of inventory.
Business and Economics
Dist - COMSRV **Prod** - COMSRV 1986

Working with Japan series
Presents a six - part series on business relations with Japan produced by Intercultural Training Resources, Inc. Includes the titles Preparation, First Meeting, Negotiating, Business Entertaining, Women in Business, Managing the Relationship.
Business entertaining - 4 33 MIN
First meeting - 2 35 MIN
Managing the relationship - 6 45 MIN
Negotiating - Parts I and II - 3 68 MIN
Preparation - 1 47 MIN
Women in business - 5 35 MIN
Dist - INCUL

Working with Lead 14 MIN
U-matic / VHS
Steel Making Series
Color (IND)
Discusses special safety precautions when working with lead. Examines the use of respirators in detail.
Business and Economics; Health and Safety; Industrial and Technical Education
Dist - LEIKID **Prod** - LEIKID

Working with machinery 17 MIN
VHS
Safety on the job series
Color (G IND) (SPANISH)
$79.95 purchase _ #6 - 203 - 400A, #6 - 203 - 401A
Identifies dangers to ears, eyes, hands and lungs when working with machinery. Demonstrates precautions. Shows safeguards against injury on forklifts and machinery which shears, rotates, presses and grabs. Part of a series on job safety.
Health and Safety
Dist - VEP **Prod** - VEP

Working with Modern School Mathematics 20 MIN
16mm
Duncan - Modern School Math Films Series
Color; B&W
LC 72-701740
Lelon Capps gives an overview of the content and objectives of the text entitled 'MODERN SCHOOL MATHEMATICS, STRUCTURE AND USE' and explains how to use the teacher's annotated edition of the text.
Mathematics
Dist - HMC **Prod** - HMC 1971

Working with Nebraska's Water 29 MIN
16mm
Nebraska Water Resources Series
Color (H C A)
LC 74-700163
Describes current water - management practices in Nebraska and the problems encountered. Discusses three manageable reservoirs of water - the soil moisture reservoirs, stream reservoirs and groundwater reservoirs. Shows these reservoirs in relation to water use.
Geography - United States; Science - Natural
Dist - UNEBR **Prod** - UNL 1971

Working with Nonverbal Behavior 60 MIN
VHS
Color (PRO)
$150.00 purchase
Introduces specific methods for working with nonverbal behavior within the normal processes of individual, group, or family psycotherapy. Features Dr. Steere, author of Bodily Expressions in Psycotherapy, who discusses the nature of movement behavior. Provides instruction for the psycotherapist on working effectively with nonverbal behavior.
Psychology
Dist - BRUMAZ **Prod** - STEERE

Working with Offshore Cranes
U-matic / VHS
Offshore Operations Series
Color (IND)
Familiarizes new operator with work procedures and specific job responsibilities associated with electric and hydraulic cranes. Discusses crane components, how load requirements are determined, wire ropes and slings and how to properly secure a load. Looks at lift planning, the personnel basket, hand signals, maintenance and safety.
Business and Economics; Industrial and Technical Education; Social Science
Dist - GPCV **Prod** - GPCV

Working with Others
U-matic / VHS
Team Building for Administrative Support Staff Series
Color
Shows how to improve teamwork throughout an organization by sensitizing participants to the problems and pressures faced by both managers and co - workers. Dramatizes the operating realities of the modern manager.
Business and Economics; Psychology
Dist - AMA **Prod** - AMA

Working with Others 10 MIN
U-matic / VHS / 16mm
Guidance for Primary Grades Series no 3; No 3
Color (P)
An open - end approach to four situation - type episodes involving respect for other races, the opposite sex, the handicapped and 'becoming involved.'.
Guidance and Counseling; Sociology
Dist - AIMS **Prod** - CAHILL 1969

Working with Others 30 MIN
VHS / U-matic
Professional Skills for Secretaries Series Pt 3
Color (A)
LC 81-707648
Explains that interpersonal skills make a secretary's workday easier and more pleasant and contribute to the good will and good public relations of the organization itself. Urges the proofreading of typewritten correspondence and the use of a dictionary to check spelling and usage.
Business and Economics; Guidance and Counseling
Dist - TIMLIF **Prod** - TIMLIF 1981

Working with People 30 MIN
16mm
Success in Supervision Series
B&W
LC 74-706339
Discusses the way people become supervisors and relates some of the common mistakes made by supervisors who are inexperienced or untrained.
Business and Economics; Guidance and Counseling
Dist - USNAC **Prod** - WETATV 1965

Working with People 15 MIN
U-matic
Job Skills Series
(H C A)
Deals with on the job communications. Examines some of the fears and concerns that block effective comunication.
Business and Economics; Guidance and Counseling; Science - Physical
Dist - ACCESS **Prod** - ACCESS 1982

Working with Positive and Negative Exponents 30 MIN
16mm
B&W (H)
Discusses rules for manipulating numbers with positive exponents. Shows that negative exponents equal reciprocals with a corresponding positive power. Gives examples to illustrate the rules.
Mathematics
Dist - MLA **Prod** - CALVIN 1959

Working with Radiation - and Protecting the Unborn 24 MIN
16mm
Color
LC 79-701199
Deals with the effects of ionizing radiation on workers in medical, university, governmental and industrial facilities. Includes discussion of mutagenetic effects and the necessity of avoiding excessive exposure, especially for pregnant women.
Health and Safety
Dist - RADIAM **Prod** - RADIAM 1979

Working with resistant teens 30 MIN
VHS
Working with hostile and resistant teens series
Color (T PRO G)
$99.00 purchase _ #ATC02EV - K; $89.00 purchase _ #CA - 103
Features Stephen Campbell, a therapist who has worked with hostile, resistant and explosive children for 25 years and developed an effective anger management strategy. Consists of role plays with teens who are, in most cases, acting out their own personal histories. Campbell leads the role plays, provides an analysis, and shows how to effectively work with resistant individuals. Part of two parts.
Guidance and Counseling; Health and Safety; Psychology
Dist - CAMV
FANPRO

Working with Scale 11 MIN
16mm / U-matic / VHS
Color (I J)
LC 70-700651
Introduces the concepts and practical uses of scale. Compares a scale model car to the fullsize car and explains methods of writing scale. Shows other examples of the use of the scale - - the laying out of a floor plan from a scale drawing, and finding locations on a map after measuring the distances by interpretation of the map scale.
Mathematics; Social Science
Dist - PHENIX **Prod** - BOUNDY 1969

Working with shapes 15 MIN
VHS / 16mm
Art - i - facts series
Color (I)
$125.00 purchase, $25.00 rental
Introduces organic and geometric shapes, encouraging students to look for them in nature and man - made environments.
Fine Arts
Dist - AITECH **Prod** - HDE 1986

Working with shapes 17 MIN
VHS
Art - i - facts series; Pt 2
Color (I)
$125.00 purchase
Introduces organic and geometric shapes to encourage students to look for them in nature and artificial environments. Uses works by Picasso to illustrate the unique expressive potential of shapes. Part of the Art - I - Facts Series to give third and fourth graders a foundation in the visual arts.
Fine Arts; Geography - United States; History - United States
Dist - AITECH **Prod** - HDE 1986

Working with the beginning teacher series
Working with the beginning teacher - teaching story analysis - a series
Dist - SPF

Working with the beginning teacher - teaching story analysis - a series
Working with the beginning teacher series
Color
Demonstrates an effective framework for the productive supervision of the beginning teacher. Instructional Conference; Lesson And Analysis.
Education
Dist - SPF **Prod** - SPF

Working with the Beginning Teacher - Teaching Story Analysis Series
Instructional Conference 29 MIN
Lesson and Analysis 29 MIN
Dist - SPF

Working with the Computer Series
The Computer and Your Job 30 MIN
Using a Computer 30 MIN
What is a Computer? 30 MIN
Dist - DELTAK

Working with the Public 25 MIN
VHS / 16mm
Verbal Judo Series
Color (C PRO)
$375.00 purchase _ #9861
Leads police officers through a variety of situations in which verball skills are needed for dealing with the public. Part 1 of three parts.
Civics and Political Systems; Computer Science; Guidance and Counseling; Psychology
Dist - AIMS **Prod** - AIMS 1985

Working with the System 93 MIN
U-matic
Skills of Helping Series Program 3
Color (C A)
LC 80-707460
Describes how social workers can better work with the professionals both within and outside their own agencies.
Sociology
Dist - SYRCU **Prod** - MCGILU 1980

Working with the System, Pt 1 46 MIN
U-matic
Skills of Helping Series Program 3
Color (C A)
LC 80-707460
Describes how social workers can better work with the professionals both within and outside their own agencies.
Guidance and Counseling
Dist - SYRCU **Prod** - MCGILU 1980

Working with the System, Pt 2 47 MIN
U-matic
Skills of Helping Series Program 3
Color (C A)
LC 80-707460
Describes how social workers can better work with the professionals both within and outside their own agencies.
Guidance and Counseling
Dist - SYRCU **Prod** - MCGILU 1980

Working with the troubled family 20 MIN
VHS / U-matic / BETA
Pediatrics - psychosocial implications series
Color (C PRO)
$150.00 purchase _ #136.6
Presents a video transfer from slide program which describes guidelines for identifying families unable to meet children's needs for stability and emotional support. Suggests techniques for avoiding negative attitudes towards these families and stresses the importance of the interdisciplinary approach. Focuses on the nurse's role in teaching parenting skills, providing emotional suppport and acting as an advocate for parents and children. Part of a series on the psychosocial implications of pediatric nursing.
Guidance and Counseling; Health and Safety
Dist - CONMED **Prod** - CONMED

Working with the unconscious quartet 120 MIN
BETA / VHS
Color (G)
$69.95 purchase _ #Q234
Presents a four - part discussion on working with the unconscious. Includes 'Working with Creative Imagery' with Shakti Gawain, 'On Dreams and Dreaming' with Dr Patricia Garfield, 'The Power of Ritual' with Anna Halprin, and 'Working with Dreams' with Jeremy Taylor.
Fine Arts; Health and Safety; Psychology; Religion and Philosophy
Dist - THINKA **Prod** - THINKA

Working with the unconscious series
On Dreams and dreaming 30 MIN
The Power of ritual 30 MIN
Working with creative imagery 30 MIN
Working with dreams 30 MIN
Dist - THINKA

Working with Trigonometric Identities 29 MIN
16mm
Trigonometry Series
B&W (H)
Reviews the fundamental trigonometric identities and shows techniques of manipulating them, such as working on only one side of the identity, watching the form of the terms and checking results. Develops geometric illustrations of the identities on the unit circle and shows alternate proofs of the identities.
Mathematics
Dist - MLA **Prod** - CALVIN 1959

Working with Your Supervisor 13 MIN
VHS
$89.95 purchase _ #005 - 710
Portrays how to get along with one's supervisors. Points out that understanding what the boss wants, expects, and needs from employees helps them get along with the supervisor. Uses hidden - camera and reenactment episodes.
Business and Economics; Guidance and Counseling
Dist - CAREER **Prod** - CAREER

Working with Your Supervisor - Part II 12 MIN
16mm / VHS
You and Your Job Series
Color (PRO)
$325.00 purchase, $95.00 rental, $35.00 preview
Gives newly hired employees understanding of relationship with the supervisor. Explains that the employee's behavior reflects on the supervisor. Communicates importance of following instructions, asking questions and being enthusiastic while developing positive relationships with supervisor.
Business and Economics; Psychology
Dist - UTM **Prod** - UTM

The Working Woman 29 MIN
U-matic
Her Social Security Series
Color
Discusses importance of Social Security benefits for the working woman.
Sociology
Dist - UMITV **Prod** - UMITV 1977

Working Women 25 MIN
U-matic / VHS
Color
Looks at some of the underlying causes of why most women are still employed in what is called 'women's work,' work with less pay, less chance for advancement and subtle and not so subtle discrimination.
Sociology
Dist - WCCOTV **Prod** - WCCOTV 1979

Working words 300 MIN
VHS
Color; PAL (H C G)
PdS55 purchase
Presents ten 30 - minute programs providing basic training in oral and written and oral communication skills, introduced by Richard Briers. Concentrates on working environment communication. Covers a range of skills in the first seven programs - from words used by secretaries to the language of reporters and public speaking techniques. The three final programs are comedy dramas

set in the factor of Wainwright and Laidlaw. Meeting Points shows that communication can be frustrating or productive, depending on a shared agreement in the rules. We'll Let You Know tackles the problem of being interviewed. How Do You Mean look at the chaos that can result from misunderstanding. Contact distributor about availability outside the United Kingdom.
English Language; Guidance and Counseling; Social Science
Dist - ACADEM

Working Worlds Series

Helping hands - careers in health	13 MIN
Welcome to the Working Worlds	17 MIN

Dist - COUNFI

Working Worlds Series

At your service - careers in business and personal services	13 MIN
Culture and Conscience - Careers in Education, Fine Arts and Social Scienies	13 MIN
Earth people - careers in natural resources and the environment	13 MIN
The First step - careers in construction	13 MIN
The Foodmakers - careers in agribusiness and food production	13 MIN
Good time people - careers in hospitality and recreation	13 MIN
The Marketeers - Careers in Marketing	13 MIN
On the Move - Careers in Transportation	13 MIN
The Organizers - Careers in Business Office	13 MIN
People and Things - Careers in Manufacturing	13 MIN
People to People - Careers in Communications and Media	13 MIN
We, the People - Careers in Public Service	13 MIN

Dist - FFORIN

The Workmanship Myth 18 MIN
16mm
Color
LC 76-702920
Documents the quality of American workmanship in the making of automotive and other products. Use photography taken on location in Japan, South America, West Germany and elsewhere.
Industrial and Technical Education
Dist - MTP **Prod** - CMD 1976

Workout Challenge 90 MIN
BETA / VHS
Color
Presents a program for advanced exercisers. Includes 20 minutes of advanced aerobics.
Physical Education and Recreation
Dist - GA **Prod** - GA

Workout with light weights 30 MIN
VHS
Esquire great body series
Color (H C A)
$19.99 purchase _ #EQGB09V
Presents the ninth of a nine - part exercise series oriented to women. Combines stretches and a workout program utilizing light weights. Developed by Deborah Crocker.
Physical Education and Recreation; Science - Natural
Dist - CAMV

Workover Fluids 19 MIN
U-matic / VHS
Color (IND)
Defines workover fluids and points out the many factors that must be considered in the selection of a good workover fluid.
Industrial and Technical Education; Social Science
Dist - UTEXPE **Prod** - UTEXPE 1975

Workpace fundamentals 20 MIN
BETA / 16mm / VHS / U-matic
Color; Silent (A PRO)
$200.00, $275.00 purchase, $10.00 rental
Presents an orientation film for understanding performance rating in plants manufacturing metal products or involved in small machine work and assemblies. Uses silent feature to permit seminar leaders to inject appropriate comments.
Business and Economics; Psychology
Dist - TAMMFG **Prod** - TAMMFG

Workpace rating exercises A - H, J and K 20 MIN
BETA / 16mm / VHS / U-matic
Color; Silent (A PRO)
$200.00, $275.00 purchase, $10.00 rental
Offers 20 separate performance rating practice films to be used in conjunction with Workplace Fundamentals or Fair Day's Work Concept films. Films A - F are for use with Workplace Fundamentals in plants manufacturing metal products. Films D, G and H are for use with Workplace Fundamentals in operations involving small machine work and assemblies. Films J and K are for use with Fair Day's Work Concepts in electronics operations. Silent feature permits seminar leaders to inject appropriate comments.
Business and Economics; Psychology
Dist - TAMMFG **Prod** - TAMMFG

The Workplace 60 MIN
VHS
America by Design Series
Color (H)
$11.50 rental _ #60953, VH
Examines the American work place and the changes undergone in 300 years. Depicts the effects of technological developments. Looks at the balance between productivity and work environment design. Final part of the America By Design Series.
Agriculture; Computer Science; Fine Arts; History - United States; Industrial and Technical Education
Dist - PSU **Prod** - PBS

Workplace 30 MIN
VHS
How do you do - learning English series
Color (H A)
#317722
Observes CHIPS as he learns about working conditions, employee benefits and how to read a paycheck. Discusses working conditions and safety equipment in a factory. Part of a series that helps newcomers learn English or improve their ability. Includes viewer's guide with grammar explanations and vocabulary drills, worksheets, and two audio cassettes.
English Language; Guidance and Counseling
Dist - TVOTAR **Prod** - TVOTAR 1990

Workplace diversity - Price Cobbs 50 MIN
U-matic / VHS / Cassette
Color; PAL (C G PRO)
$89.95, $69.95, $16.00 purchase _ #92AST-V-T0, #92AST-T0
Reminds that 'the creative genius in our American experience has always been in our diversity.' Looks at three major trends to emerge from the 1980s - the increasingly competitive global marketplace, a dramatically changing workforce and the celebration rather than the mere acknowledgement of differences and their effects on the workplace of the 90s. Discusses the role that HRD - human relations development - can play in fostering the varied talents of the diverse workforce and in breaking down the barriers that inhibit the transfer of important skills among employees. Features the President of Pacific Management Systems, San Francisco.
Business and Economics; Psychology
Dist - MOBILE **Prod** - ASTD 1992

The Workplace environment - 2
U-matic / VHS / BETA
Synergy - EEO, diversity and management series
Color; CC; PAL (IND PRO G)
$895.00 purchase
Reveals that to manage effectively, supervisors need to manage differences in the workplace so that mutual respect and understanding replace resentment, mistrust and fear, or any negative stereotypes that interfere with work. Uses case studies to help managers develop the skills, sensitivity and understanding they need to address common EEO - diversity issues such as - segregated departments; affirmative action - gender issues; hostile environments; the glass ceiling and subtle discrimination. Includes 20 participant manuals. Part of a series showing managers how to apply EEO guidelines in managing a diverse workforce.
Business and Economics; Guidance and Counseling
Dist - BNA **Prod** - BNA

Workplace hustle 30 MIN
16mm
Color (G IND)
$5.00 rental
Explores the many varieties of sexual harassment which women encounter on the job and its emotional and economic impact on their lives. Gives examples which can provide a background for discussion of the issue and how women can handle the problem individually and through the union. Features Ed Asner as narrator.
Business and Economics; Sociology
Dist - AFLCIO **Prod** - CLRKCO 1981
CORF
AIMS

Workplace precautions against bloodborne pathogens 24 MIN
U-matic / VHS
Color (C PRO)
$395.00 purchase, $80.00 rental _ #C921 - VI - 033
Provides an overview of how the Occupational Safety and Health Administration's Standards on Bloodborne Pathogens applies in different occupations - law enforcement, fire fighting, emergency medical care, hospital laboratory, housekeeping, dentistry and medical waste disposal. Demonstrates the importance of taking universal precautions in the workplace. Instructs users to contact their nearest OSHA office for more information on how the Standard applies to their specific environment. Presented by Steve Thurston.
Health and Safety; Science - Natural
Dist - HSCIC

Workplace ready - job skills for the 21st century series

Foundation skills - Part Two	50 MIN
Up and running - Part One	45 MIN

Dist - HRMC

Workplace teams - building successful teams - Part 1 29 MIN
VHS
Workplace teams - Partnership series
Color (PRO IND A)
$645.00 purchase, $190.00 rental _ #AMA54
Presents part one of a two - part series which uses team members and managers to actualize the challenges and achievements of workplace teams. Informs and guides all those involved in the workplace team process. Includes Discussion Guide.
Business and Economics; Psychology
Dist - EXTR **Prod** - AMA

Workplace teams - helping your team succeed - Part 2 26 MIN
VHS
Workplace teams - Partnership series
Color (PRO IND A)
$645.00 purchase, $190.00 rental _ #AMA55
Presents part two of a two - part series which uses team members and managers to actualize the challenges and achievements of workplace teams. Informs and guides all those involved in the workplace team process. Includes Discussion Guide.
Business and Economics; Psychology
Dist - EXTR **Prod** - AMA

Workplace teams - Partnership series 55 MIN
VHS
Workplace teams - Partnership series
Color (PRO IND A)
$975.00 purchase, $380.00 rental _ #AMA54 - 55
Details in a two - part series the challenges and achievements of actual team members and managers. Informs and guides all those involved in the workplace team process. Includes Discussion Guide. Part of the Partnership Series.
Business and Economics; Psychology
Dist - EXTR **Prod** - AMA

Workplace teams - Partnership series

Workplace teams - building successful teams - Part 1	29 MIN
Workplace teams - helping your team succeed - Part 2	26 MIN
Workplace teams - Partnership series	55 MIN

Dist - EXTR

Workplace violence 20 MIN
CD-ROM
Color (PRO IND A)
$695.00 purchase, $195.00 rental _ #KEN01, #KEN02
Gives legal and incident management advice on recognizing and preventing violence in the workplace. Utilizes the legal expertise of Garry Mathiason and counseling insights of Chris Hatcher - along with an interview of a convicted offender and a dramatization - to address the problem. Includes Leader' Guide.
Business and Economics
Dist - EXTR **Prod** - EXTR

Workplace Violence - customer service & field personnel 25 MIN
VHS
Color; CC (IND)
$495.00 purchase, $125.00 rental _ #AIM11
Teaches employees of service - oriented businesses how to recognize potential violence and how to protect themselves accordingly.
Business and Economics; Guidance and Counseling; Health and Safety; Social Science; Sociology
Dist - EXTR **Prod** - AIMS

Workplace violence - developing a trauma response plan 29 MIN
VHS
Color (IND)
$695.00 purchase, $195.00 rental _ #LMC01
Teaches how to develop an organized response to workplace violence and a Critical Incident Stress Debriefing - CISD - following a crisis, with Dr. Thomas Harpley. Includes leader and management resource guides.
Business and Economics; Guidance and Counseling; Health and Safety; Social Science; Sociology
Dist - EXTR **Prod** - LUMBMC

Workplace violence - employee awareness 25 MIN
VHS
Color; CC (IND)
$495.00 purchase, $125.00 rental _ #AIM10
Outlines techniques to help employees avoid becoming victims of violent abuse. Includes a training manual and tests.
Business and Economics; Guidance and Counseling; Health and Safety; Social Science; Sociology
Dist - EXTR **Prod** - AIMS

Workplace violence - first line of defense 30 MIN
VHS
Color (COR)
$695.00 purchase, $195.00 rental _ #EWV/ETC
Presents information to enhance the organization's awareness of the potential for violence. Assists employees in recognizing early warning signs of possibly violent persons or situations. Discusses reporting and recording of incidents. Provides information on enhancing security at the workplace. Offers advice from legal and psychiatric viewpoints. Includes a Leader's Guide and Participant Workbook. Available for three - day preview, as well as rental, purchase, or lease. Also available on interactive compact disc and with closed captioning.
Guidance and Counseling; Psychology; Sociology
Dist - ADVANM

Workplace violence - recognizing and diffusing aggressive behavior 26 MIN
VHS
Color; CC (IND)
$495.00 purchase, $125.00 rental _ AIM13
Teaches supervisors and managers to recognize the warning signs of potential violent behavior. Includes a training manual and tests.
Business and Economics; Guidance and Counseling; Health and Safety; Social Science; Sociology
Dist - EXTR **Prod** - AIMS

Workplace violence - the calm before the storm 25 MIN
VHS
Color (COR)
$495.00 purchase, $95 rental _ #CWV/COA
Presents a re - enactment of an episode of workplace violence, the true story of Angela Bowman, who was held at gunpoint at her work. Graphically recreates the terror of the situation. Encourages all employers to establish a Violence Prevention Program. Includes a Leader's Guide.
Business and Economics; Guidance and Counseling; Sociology
Dist - ADVANM

Workplace violence - the risk from within 26 MIN
VHS
Color (A)
$525.00 purchase
Increases managers' awareness of situations that can lead to violence in the workplace, helps managers identify at - risk employees, and shows how many of the problems can be dealt with to resolve the issues. Suggests guidelines for obtaining help as soon as possible. Includes one user's reinforcement guide. Additional copies available separately.
Business and Economics; Education
Dist - COMFLM **Prod** - COMFLM

Workplace violence - understanding, preventing, surviving 47 MIN
VHS
Color (COR)
$495.00 purchase, $150.00 rental _ #SWV
Describes three categories of workplace violence, and provides guidelines to reduce risks and create a safe environment for employees. Deals with robbery, disgruntled workers and ex - employees, and domestic violence spilling over into the workplace. Includes a Leader's Guide.
Business and Economics; Guidance and Counseling; Sociology
Dist - ADVANM

Works for Windows
VHS
Color (G)
$39.95 purchase _ #VIA040
Explains the use of Works for Windows.
Computer Science
Dist - SIV

Works of Calder 20 MIN
16mm
Color
Interprets Calder's mobiles. Rhythmical sequences suggest parallels between familiar forms and movements in nature and the movements of the artist's works.
Fine Arts
Dist - MOMA **Prod** - MERB 1950

The Works of La Fontaine 26 MIN
U-matic / VHS
Color (C)
$279.00, $179.00 purchase _ #AD - 2123
Profiles the life and work of La Fontaine, fabulist, who rendered Aesop in verse and created other stories. Views splendidly illustrated 18th - century books.
Biography; Foreign Language; History - World; Industrial and Technical Education; Literature and Drama
Dist - FOTH **Prod** - FOTH

Works of Sadie Benning series
Jollies 11 MIN
Me and Rubyfruit program 18 MIN
A Place called lovely 20 MIN
Welcome to normal 19 MIN
Dist - WMEN

Works on paper 4 MIN
16mm
B&W (G)
$10.00 rental
Consists of animation of an abstract brush drawing in motion. Presents a series of subtle changes and variations on the theme of black ink on white paper. Produced by Philip Perkins. Also distributed by the Northwest Film Study Center in Portland, Oregon.
Fine Arts
Dist - CANCIN

The Works series
Shows engineers in a creative light as they apply their knowledge, skills and experience to help solve society's varied technological problems. Explores the areas of liquid engineering; random movement; fixing agents; engineering accidents; and perspective. Six programs constitute the series.
Accidents will happen 20 MIN
Beating the bounce 20 MIN
The Fix 20 MIN
Inside the box 20 MIN
Slippery when wet 20 MIN
Waiting to work 20 MIN
Dist - BBCENE

Workshop for Peace 23 MIN
16mm / U-matic / VHS
Color (I J H)
LC 75-702176
Presents a pictorial study of the United Nations describing its varied activities in the maintenance of peace. Introduces the variety of organizations and activities that make up the structure and function of the United Nations.
Civics and Political Systems
Dist - JOU **Prod** - UN 1975

Workshop in oils with William Palluth - autumn landscape 60 MIN
VHS
Color (G)
$29.95 purchase _ #S01767
Features landscape artist William Palluth, who paints an autumn landscape scene with oil paints. Provides a step - by - step guide to making realistic forms, mixing colors, and selecting the best colors.
Fine Arts
Dist - UILL

Workshop in oils with William Palluth - oil painting techniques 60 MIN
VHS
Color (G)
$29.95 purchase _ #S01765
Features landscape artist William Palluth, who teaches oil painting techniques. Focuses on techniques which can help the developing painter obtain a higher form of realism.
Fine Arts
Dist - UILL

Workshop in oils with William Palluth series
Presents a six - part series on oil painting by landscape artist William Palluth. Includes the titles Starting to Paint, Oil Painting Techniques, Autumn Landscape, Winter Landscape, Sunset, Mountains.
Mountains 60 MIN
Sunset 60 MIN
Dist - CAMV

Workshop in oils with William Palluth - starting to paint 60 MIN
VHS
Color (G)
$29.95 purchase _ #S01764
Features landscape artist William Palluth, who teaches basic oil painting skills. Depicts the basic equipment and brushstrokes. Tells how to apply colors to canvas while keeping them clean and rich.
Fine Arts
Dist - UILL

Workshop in oils with William Palluth - winter landscape 60 MIN
VHS
Color (G)
$29.95 purchase _ #S01766
Features landscape artist William Palluth, who paints a winter landscape scene with oil paints. Provides a step - by - step guide to making realistic forms, mixing colors, and selecting the best colors.
Fine Arts
Dist - UILL

A Workshop with Martin Booth 30 MIN
U-matic / VHS
Booth and Bly - Poets Series
Color
Uses an ancient Spanish coin forged from Aztec gold as the focus for a discussion of the poet as myth - maker. Reveals bits and pieces of the coin's history as the students compose, contemplating the personal history of the coin and its various owners. Focuses on the history of the object and the description of images from the past.
Education; Literature and Drama
Dist - NETCHE **Prod** - NETCHE 1978

A Workshop with Robert Bly 30 MIN
U-matic / VHS
Booth and Bly - Poets Series
Color
Uses an old, gnarled tree stump as a prop and the five senses to discover a new writing experience. Focuses on strong, sensory descriptions of the stump, including word selection, points of view and images.
Education; Literature and Drama
Dist - NETCHE **Prod** - NETCHE 1978

The Workup and NANDA nomenclature 14 MIN
BETA / VHS / U-matic
Nursing diagnosis and care planning series
Color (C PRO)
$150.00 purchase _ #144.2
Presents a video transfer from slide program which presents the process in selecting a diagnosis from the NANDA list - the most confusing and revolutionary aspect of the system. Gives guidelines for gathering data, eliciting and clustering cues prior to the selection and delineates pitfalls. Part of a series on nursing diagnosis and care planning.
Health and Safety
Dist - CONMED **Prod** - CONMED

The World - a television history series 780 MIN
16mm / VHS
The World - a television history series
Color (J H C)
$3395.00, $10250.00 purchase
Provides 26 programs covering world history from the earliest evidence of humans to the most recent times. Includes Human Origins; The Agricultural Revolution; The Birth of Civilization; The Age of Iron; Greece and Rome; The World Religions; Islam; The End of the Ancient World; Europe Recovers; The Mongol Onslaught; Expansion of Europe; China in Transition; China and Japan; The Ottoman Empire; Africa Before the Europeans; The Americas Before the Europeans; Europe - State and Power; The West and Wider World; Asia; The Age of Revolutions; The Making of Russia; The Making of the United States of America; Industry and Empire; The End of the Old Order; The World in Conflict; and The Modern World.
History - World
Dist - LANDMK

World - A Television history series 780 MIN
VHS
World - A Television history series
Color (C A)
$750.00 rental
Presents a 26 - part telecourse on the geography and history of the earth. Based on "The Times Atlas of World History." Also available for lease on a five - year and semester basis. Available only to institutions of higher education.
History - World; Sociology
Dist - SCETV **Prod** - SCETV 1986

World - A Television history series
Asia, 1600 - 1800 26 MIN
The End of the ancient world - AD 100 - AD 600 30 MIN
Islam, 600 - 1200 26 MIN
Dist - LANDMK
SCETV

The World according to Bob Dole 30 MIN
U-matic
Adam Smith's money world series; 139
Color (A)
Attempts to demystify the world of money and break it down so that small as well as large businesses and it's people

understand and adjust to new social and economic trends. Reports on the major economic stories and discoveries of the day.
Business and Economics
Dist - PBS **Prod** - WNETTV 1985

The World according to David Stockman 30 MIN
U-matic
Adam Smith's money world 1985 - 1986 season series; 235
Color (A)
Attempts to demystify the world of money and break it down so that small as well as large businesses and it's people understand and adjust to new social and economic trends. Reports on the major economic stories and discoveries of 1985 and 1986.
Business and Economics
Dist - PBS **Prod** - WNETTV 1986

World according to Nicholas series
Comes in all colors, shapes and sizes 25 MIN
Fraidy Cats 24 MIN
Just Like Me 26 MIN
Magic Man 24 MIN
Dist - LUF

The World After Nuclear War - the Nuclear Winter 28 MIN
U-matic / VHS
Color
Reveals that the use of a small fraction of the world's nuclear arsenal would have such devastating climatic consequences that civilization as we know it would be destroyed and the human species would probably become extinct. From the conference on the Long Term World Wide Biological Consequences of nuclear war.
Civics and Political Systems; Sociology
Dist - EFVP **Prod** - EFVP 1984

The World almanac and book of facts
CD-ROM
(G A)
$69.00 purchase _ #2222
Contains the 1990 edition with more than one million up - to - date facts. For IBM PCs and compatibles. Requires at least 640K RAM, DOS Version 3.1 or greater, one floppy disk drive - hard disk drive recommended, one empty expansion slot, and an IBM compatible CD - ROM drive.
History - World; Literature and Drama
Dist - BEP

The World and Basic Facts 12 MIN
16mm
Color (P I J)
Depicts education as a building process starting with a child's blank mind which, as it acquires a few basic facts, triggers a quest for more information. Explains basic facts about the origin of the earth and its geography.
Education; Psychology
Dist - AVED **Prod** - AVED 1963

A World Apart - a World of Caves 21 MIN
16mm
Color (J H C G)
Follows the progress of a party of cavers through the underground limestone caves of the Mendip Hills in Somerset.
Geography - World; Physical Education and Recreation; Science - Physical
Dist - VIEWTH **Prod** - GATEEF

The World Arena 60 MIN
VHS
Global Rivals Series
Color; Captioned (G)
$59.95 purchase _ #GLBR - 103
Reveals that while the Cold War remains a top priority for the two superpowers, the same cannot be said of other industrial nations. Shows that these nations are more concerned about domestic and regional issues. Examines the unsuccessful attempts by the U S and Soviet Union to control events in the Third World.
Civics and Political Systems; Sociology
Dist - PBS **Prod** - WNETTV 1988

The World Around Us 25 MIN
U-matic / VHS / 16mm
Smithsonian Series
Color (I J H)
Identifies the subject of ecology, or environmental biology, and defines its limits and relationships with other life sciences. Discusses the interdependence of living things.
Science; Science - Natural
Dist - MGHT **Prod** - NBCTV 1967

World Around Us Series
Tuareg 46 MIN
Tuareg - Pt 1 23 MIN
Tuareg - Pt 2 23 MIN
Dist - ICARUS

World around us series
Alternative energy sources - geothermal, water and wind
Bicycle repair made easy
Sharks
Slight of hand - the magic of cards
Solar energy - hope for the future
The Stock market
Dist - INCRSE

The World at his fingertips 28 MIN
VHS / 16mm
Color; Captioned (H C G)
$500.00, $295.00 purchase, $55.00 rental
Reveals that Mike Van Orman, married and the father of two sons, lost both his sight and hearing when he was in his thirties. Shows that with the help of the Helen Keller National Center Mike found a new sense of purpose through relearning the skills needed for daily life and discovered that he could still enjoy close human relationships, achieve a measure of independence and participate in recreational and social activities.
Guidance and Counseling; Health and Safety
Dist - FLMLIB **Prod** - HKELNT 1987

The World at war 44 MIN
VHS
B&W (G)
$19.95 purchase _ #S00405
Uses archival footage to document the events leading up to World War II. Narrated by Paul Stewart.
Civics and Political Systems; History - World
Dist - UILL

The World at war 45 MIN
U-matic / VHS / 16mm
B&W
LC FIE52-755
Shows the events in Europe and Asia from 1931 to 1941 which preceded the second World War. Includes a discussion of the Japanese invasion of Manchuria and the bombing of Pearl Harbor.
History - World
Dist - USNAC IHF **Prod** - USOWI IHF 1943

A World at war - 1942 - 1945 16 MIN
U-matic / VHS / 16mm
World War II series
Color (J H C A)
$350.00, $245.00 purchase _ #4475
Shows how Americans prepared for war, and how the war ended when two atomic bombs were dropped on Japan.
History - United States; History - World
Dist - CORF

World at War Series
Alone - May 1940 - 1941 52 MIN
Banzai - Japan, 1931 - 1942 52 MIN
Barbarossa - June - December 1941 52 MIN
The Bomb - February - September 1945 52 MIN
The Desert - North Africa, 1940 - 1943 52 MIN
Distant war - september 1939 - may 1940 52 MIN
Home fires - Britain, 1940 - 1941 52 MIN
Inside the Reich - Germany, 1940 - 1944 52 MIN
It's a Lovely Day Tomorrow - Burma, 1942 - 1944 52 MIN
Japan, 1941 - 1945 52 MIN
Morning - June - August 1944 52 MIN
Nemesis - Germany, February - May 1945 52 MIN
On Our Way - U S A, 1939 - 1942 52 MIN
Pacific, February 1942 - 1945 52 MIN
Red Star - the Soviet Union, 1941 - 1943 52 MIN
Remember 52 MIN
Stalingrad - June 9 1942 - 1943 52 MIN
Tough Old Gut - Italy, November 1942 - June 1944 52 MIN
Dist - MEDIAG

World at War Series
France Falls - may - June 1940 52 MIN
Genocide - 1941 - 1945 52 MIN
A New Germany - 1933 - 1939 52 MIN
Occupation - Holland, 1940 - 1944 52 MIN
Pincers - August 1944 - March 1945 52 MIN
Reckoning - 1945 and After 52 MIN
Whirlwind - Bombing Germany, September, 1939 to may, 1944 60 MIN
Wolf Pack - U - Boats in the Atlantic , 1939 to 1944 60 MIN
Dist - MEDIAG USCAN

World at War Series
Alone 60 MIN
Banzai 60 MIN
Barbarossa 60 MIN
Desert - North Africa, 1940 to 1943 60 MIN
Distant war - September, 1939 to May, 1940 60 MIN
Home fires - Britain, 1940 to 1942 60 MIN
Inside the Reich 60 MIN
Japan 60 MIN
Morning - June to August, 1944 60 MIN
Nemesis - Germany, February to May, 1945 60 MIN
On Our Way 60 MIN
Pacific 60 MIN
Red Star 60 MIN
Remember 60 MIN
Stalingrad 60 MIN
Tough Old Gut 60 MIN
Dist - USCAN

World at War Specials Series
The Final Solution - Auschwitz 208 MIN
Hitler's Germany 156 MIN
Secretary to Hitler 26 MIN
Two Deaths of Adolph Hitler 52 MIN
Warrior 52 MIN
Who Won World War II 26 MIN
Dist - MEDIAG

World at Your Feet 23 MIN
U-matic / VHS / 16mm
Color (I)
Shows how plants, insects, animals and man depend on the soil and contribute to its productivity. Describes different types of soil, the effects of wind and water on soil and the importance of bacteria and insects to the soil.
Agriculture; Science - Natural; Science - Physical
Dist - IFB **Prod** - NFBC 1953

A World at Your Fingertips 15 MIN
U-matic / VHS / 16mm
Color (J)
Features the workings of the book club relationship.
Literature and Drama
Dist - KLEINW **Prod** - KLEINW

World atlas
CD-ROM
Color (G)
$109.00 purchase _ #2231
Contains over 240 full - color maps and hundreds of pages of information. Uses a graphic interface. Sources include world organizations and US government agencies. Includes map data in five subject areas - geography, people, government, economics, and transportation. IBM PC and compatibles require at least 640K of RAM, DOS 3.1 or greater, one floppy disk drive - hard disk recommended, one empty expansion slot, an IBM compatible CD - ROM drive, and an EGA or VGA monitor.
Geography - World; Literature and Drama
Dist - BEP **Prod** - BEP

World atlas 3.0 multimedia
CD-ROM
Color (J H C G)
$149.95 purchase _ #BO34R5CD
Zooms from the ocean depths to world's largest peaks in a flash. Charts, analyzes and compares thousands of facts and statistics in over 200 countries. Combines graphs, reports and maps quickly and easily. Includes a multimedia feature for Windows that allows the auditory pronunciation of countries and cities, the listening to national anthems as well as animated maps. Offers 240 VGA color reference maps, over 4,400 statistical maps, easy - to - read comparison graphs, audio help and comprehensive city data.
Geography - World; Social Science
Dist - CAMV

World beat - great decisions in foreign policy series 240 MIN
VHS
World beat - great decisions in foreign policy series
Color (G)
$240.00 purchase _ #WDBT - 000
Examines some of the most important international issues facing the United States. Considers matters of the environment, world trade, and U S foreign policy, both in general and toward individual nations or regions. Eight - part series uses interviews, regional maps and state - of - the - art graphics. Hosted by Georgetown University School of Foreign Service Dean Peter Krogh.
Business and Economics; Civics and Political Systems; Science - Natural
Dist - PBS **Prod** - WETATV 1988

World Beat - Great Decisions In Foreign Policy
The Soviet Union - Gorbachev's Reforms and the Eastern Bloc 30 MIN
Western Europe - between the 30 MIN

Superpowers
Dist - PBS

World Beneath the Sea 23 MIN
VHS
Ocean Studies Series
Color
$69.95 purchase _ #4031
Shows camouflage, predation, aggression, and mimicry, protection and survival mechanisms for all life forms, including the life beneath the sea.
Science - Physical
Dist - AIMS **Prod** - AIMS

World Beneath the Sea 29 MIN
16mm
Color
Tells the story of man's search for oil off the coasts of the United States. Illustrates the history of offshore drilling and explains how industry has learned to produce oil efficiently and safely in deep water.
Business and Economics; Geography - United States; Science - Physical; Social Science
Dist - EXXON **Prod** - EXXON 1973

World Beneath the Sea 23 MIN
U-matic / VHS / 16mm
Color (I) (SPANISH)
LC 77-700990
Explores the world of life beneath the sea and among reefs. Features the camouflage, predation, aggression and minicry used as protection and survival mechanisms within this ecological system.
Science - Natural; Science - Physical
Dist - AIMS **Prod** - DUTCHE 1976

The World between 26 MIN
16mm / U-matic / VHS
Color
Dramatizes an Ojibway Indian legend that begins in The Path Of Souls. Tells, in this second part, of a man journeying between the land of the living and the dead to search for his wife. Continues in The Path Of Life.
Literature and Drama; Social Science
Dist - FOTH **Prod** - FOTH

World Beyond Death 52 MIN
16mm
Fourth Dimension Series
Color
LC 79-700408
Explores life - after - death experiences, including mediumship, ectoplasm, spirit entities, hypnotic regression and mind over matter. Features Will Geer and Dr Elizabeth Kubler - Ross.
Sociology
Dist - INTTFP **Prod** - INTTFP 1978

World Beyond Death, Pt 1 26 MIN
16mm
Fourth Dimension Series
Color
LC 79-700408
Explores life - after - death experiences, including mediumship, ectoplasm, spirit entities, hypnotic regression and mind over matter. Features Will Geer and Dr Elizabeth Kubler - Ross.
Sociology
Dist - INTTFP **Prod** - INTTFP 1978

World Beyond Death, Pt 2 26 MIN
16mm
Fourth Dimension Series
Color
LC 79-700408
Explores life - after - death experiences, including mediumship, ectoplasm, spirit entities, hypnotic regression and mind over matter. Features Will Geer and Dr Elizabeth Kubler - Ross.
Sociology
Dist - INTTFP **Prod** - INTTFP 1978

The World Car is Born 26 MIN
16mm / U-matic / VHS
Color
Presents the story of a new automobile, built because American industry has responded to the ever - changing energy environment, rising costs, consumer needs and preferences. Covers four years of planning, development engineering, testing and manufacturing of engines, transmissions, suspension and interior and other parts of a motor car.
Industrial and Technical Education; Social Science
Dist - FORDFL **Prod** - FORDFL

World Changes Series Japan - Nation in Transition
Japan's Food from Land and Sea 12 MIN
Dist - SF

World city, 1970's 20 MIN
16mm / U-matic / VHS
Artist as a reporter series
Color (J)
LC 73-713474
Artist - reporter Franklin Mc Mahon views and comments on 'world city', drawings and paintings made in the United States, England, Europe and South America.
Fine Arts; Geography - World; Sociology
Dist - PHENIX ROCSS **Prod** - ROCSS 1971

World City - an Artist's Report 17 MIN
16mm / U-matic / VHS
Color (H C A)
Shows how artist - reporter Franklin McMahon captures the sights and sounds of cities in the United States, Europe, South America and the Far East.
Fine Arts; Literature and Drama; Sociology
Dist - PHENIX **Prod** - PHENIX 1978

World class excellence - The Florida Power and Light Model 60 MIN
VHS
Color (PRO G A)
$1495.00 purchase, $150.00 rental
Looks at Florida Power and Light, which made quality its goal in every facet of its operation. Includes three 20 - minute videos and a copy of the case study by the American Productivity and Quality Center.
Business and Economics; Guidance and Counseling; Psychology
Dist - EXTR **Prod** - EBEC

World conquerors 45 MIN
VHS
Storm from the east
Color; PAL (C H)
PdS99 purchase; Not available in the United States or Pacific Rim countries
Describes the Mongol empire's plans for world domination. Includes the story of Ghengis Khan's son Ogedei, who constructed the city of Quarakorum as his capitol for world rule. Second in the four - part series Storm from the East, which presents the history of the Mongol empire.
Civics and Political Systems; History - World
Dist - BBCENE

World Cultures and Youth Series

Amy the photographer	25 MIN
Amy the photographer (USA)	25 MIN
Anessi's Barkcloth Art	25 MIN
Anessi's barkcloth art - Tonga	25 MIN
Francesco the Potter	25 MIN
Gilberto's Mayan dream	25 MIN
Gopal's golden pendant	25 MIN
Hasan the carpetweaver	25 MIN
Igor and the Dancing Stallions	25 MIN
Jafar's blue tiles	25 MIN
Joshua's Soapstone Carving	23 MIN
Julia the gourdcarver	25 MIN
Kathy's Pacing Horse	25 MIN
Kathy's Pacing Horse (Australia)	25 MIN
Kurtis, Hollywood Stuntboy (U S a)	25 MIN
Laroussie the Saddlemaker	25 MIN
Lee's Parasol	25 MIN
Lena the Glassblower	25 MIN
Lena the Glassblower - Sweden	25 MIN
Ming - Oi the Magician	25 MIN
Richard's Totem Pole	25 MIN
Richard's Totem Pole - Canada	25 MIN
Serama's mask - Bali	25 MIN
Shao Ping the Acrobat	25 MIN
Slima the Dhowmaker	25 MIN
Steffan the Violinmaker	25 MIN
Tanya the Puppeteer	25 MIN
Valerie's Stained Glass Window	25 MIN
Yang - Xun the Peasant Painter	25 MIN
Yohannes the Silversmith	25 MIN
Yoshiko the Papermaker	25 MIN

Dist - CORF

World cultures - similarities and differences 50 MIN
VHS
People and cultures series
Color (I J)
$105.00 purchase _ #UL80903
Presents two videos which provide a thorough explanation of culture - what culture is, why cultures are alike and different and what roles religion, environment, historical events and other factors play in shaping culture. Includes a teacher's guide and 15 duplicating masters. Part of three parts on people and culture.
Geography - World; Sociology
Dist - KNOWUN

World debt 30 MIN
U-matic
Adam Smith's money world series; 104
Color (A)
Attempts to demystify the world of money and break it down so that employees of small businesses can understand and adjust to new social and economic trends. Reports on the major economic stories and discoveries of the day.
Business and Economics
Dist - PBS **Prod** - WNETTV 1985

World debt time bomb 30 MIN
U-matic
Adam Smith's money world series; 128
Color (A)
Attempts to demystify the world of money and break it down so that employees of small businesses can understand and adjust to new social and economic trends. Reports on the major economic stories and discoveries of the day.
Business and Economics
Dist - PBS **Prod** - WNETTV 1985

World discovery - the last African flying boat 50 MIN
VHS
Color (J H C G)
$29.95 purchase _ #ABC123V - S
Traces the history of the Empire flying boats of Imperial Airways in the late 1930s. Reveals that the airline linked the British colonies of East Africa from Eqypt to South Africa and that it carried passengers in country - club comfort on a five - day journey featuring luxurious accommodations, five - star service, landings on the Nile - and a privileged rite of passage along the journey. Follows, 50 years later, the attempt of journalist Alexander Frater, producer - director David Wallace and a camera crew to recreate the trek, in a harrowing journey over five independent states and two war zones. Includes vintage footage of the original airline.
History - World; Industrial and Technical Education; Social Science
Dist - CAMV

World Drums 57 MIN
16mm / U-matic / VHS
Color; Stereo (J)
$850.00, $310.00 purchase, $85.00 rental
Documents an Expo '86 performance by 250 drummers from around the world. Features composer John Wyre as coordinator.
Fine Arts
Dist - BULFRG **Prod** - RHOMBS 1989

World exchange series
The Third coast - Pt 1 28 MIN
The Third coast - Pt 2 27 MIN
Dist - DIRECT

World feminists 29 MIN
U-matic
Are you listening series
Color (J H C)
LC 80-707409
Presents an international group of feminists exploring some of the primary issues facing women. Discusses the need for collaboration among all women, the role of male feminists, and the ways in which the women's movement is transforming societies.
Sociology
Dist - STURTM **Prod** - STURTM 1980

World food - Part 1 44 MIN
VHS
Introductory principles of nutrition series
Color (C PRO G)
$70.00 purchase, $16.00 rental _ #50708
Discusses malnutrition, its various symptoms, and the nutritional states of deficiency diseases. Part of a 20 - part series on basic principles of nutrition, evaluation of dietary intake, nutritional status, nutrition through the life cycle and world food supplies.
Health and Safety; Social Science
Dist - PSU **Prod** - WPSXTV 1978

World food - Part 2 60 MIN
VHS
Introductory principles of nutrition series
Color (C PRO G)
$70.00 purchase, $16.00 rental _ #60370
Overviews the world food supply in relation to population. Part of a 20 - part series on basic principles of nutrition, evaluation of dietary intake, nutritional status, nutrition through the life cycle and world food supplies.
Health and Safety; Social Science; Sociology
Dist - PSU **Prod** - WPSXTV 1978

The World from One Point of View
U-matic
Growth and Development - a Chronicle of Four Children Series Series '8
Color
Describes growth and development of a child from 34 to 35 months.
Psychology
Dist - LIP **Prod** - JUETHO

The World from One Point of View - Gregory, 34 Months 6 MIN
16mm
Growth and Development - a Chronicle of Four Children Series Series '8
Color
LC 78-700689
Psychology
Dist - LIP **Prod** - JUETHO 1976

The World from One Point of View - Joseph, 35 Months 7 MIN
16mm
Growth and Development - a Chronicle of Four Children Series Series '8
Color
LC 78-700689
Psychology
Dist - LIP **Prod** - JUETHO 1976

The World from One Point of View - Melissa, 34 Months 6 MIN
16mm
Growth and Development - a Chronicle of Four Children Series Series '8
Color
LC 78-700689
Psychology
Dist - LIP **Prod** - JUETHO 1976

The World from One Point of View - Terra, 35 Months 6 MIN
16mm
Growth and Development - a Chronicle of Four Children Series Series '8
Color
LC 78-700689
Psychology
Dist - LIP **Prod** - JUETHO 1976

The World goes to war - 1900 - 14 52 MIN
VHS
Century of warfare series
Color (G)
$19.99 purchase _ #0 - 7835 - 8429 - 6NK
Examines the worldwide buildup to World War I from 1900 to 1914. Covers strategy, tactics, weapons, personalities, battles and campaigns, victories and defeats. Part of a 20 - part series on 20th - century warfare.
Civics and Political Systems; History - World; Sociology
Dist - TILIED

World Health 10 MIN
16mm
Problems of World Order Series
Color (J H)
LC 73-703430
Introduces the concept of environmental health to stimulate discussions about the implications of world health problems in the modern context. Details the nature and achievements of the World Health Organization (WHO.) Discusses structure and staff training, population and birth control, international drug standards, food, pesticides, pollution and sewage. Illustrates the need for a new approach to international cooperation.
Civics and Political Systems; Science - Natural; Social Science; Sociology
Dist - AGAPR **Prod** - VISNEW 1972

World Health Organization 28 MIN
Videoreel / VHS
International Byline Series
Color
Interviews a senior information officer at the World Health Organization of the United Nations and a diabetes specialist from a Boston clinic. Presents a film clip on the last known case of smallpox.
Civics and Political Systems; Geography - World
Dist - PERRYM **Prod** - PERRYM

World hot spots - update 20 MIN
35mm strip / VHS
Color (J H C T A)
$57.00, $48.00 purchase _ #MB - 909457 - 0, #MB - 909454 - 6
Examines the world's 'hot spots' - nations where change is occurring and hard to predict. Considers relevant history for each nation and offers prospects for resolving each situation successfully.
Civics and Political Systems; History - World
Dist - SRA **Prod** - NYT 1989

World Hunger 30 MIN
U-matic
Realities
Color (A)
Delves into the political, social, economic and cultural trends of the 1980s. Probes a wide range of contemporary concerns. Each segment includes a guest speaker who is an expert in the field under discussion.
Business and Economics; Civics and Political Systems; Social Science; Sociology
Dist - TVOTAR **Prod** - TVOTAR 1985

World Hunger - who will Survive 90 MIN
U-matic
Color (G)
$95.00 rental _#WHWS - 000
Focuses on the world food crisis, questioning whether nations are equipped to deal with the problem of rocketing population combined with static and even faltering food production. Uses the nations of Niger, Columbia and India as case studies. Narrated by Bill Moyers.
Agriculture; Sociology
Dist - PBS **Prod** - CPT

World in a Marsh 22 MIN
16mm / U-matic / VHS
Color (J H C)
Shows a variety of life forms which inhabit a marsh, such as insects, amphibious creatures and birds, and records their activities.
Science - Natural
Dist - MGHT **Prod** - NFBC 1968

World in a Schoolroom 17 MIN
16mm
B&W
LC FIE52-2118
Portrays citizens demonstrating their skills in the classroom so that students may see the application of the principles and techniques taught in school.
Education
Dist - USNAC **Prod** - USA 1951

The World in a water drop 30 MIN
U-matic / VHS / BETA
Color; PAL (G H C)
PdS50, PdS58 purchase
Explores the secret universe of the underwater world of ponds and lakes. Features three leading actors - Daphnia, Utricularin vulgaris and Chlorohydria. Produced in Switzerland.
Science - Natural
Dist - EDPAT

The World in Conflict - 1929 - 1945 26 MIN
VHS / 16mm / U-matic
World - a Television History Series
Color (J H C)
MP=$475.00
Portrays a three - cornered contest of Liberal, Nazi and Communist for control of the world, ending with Communist control of China.
History - World
Dist - LANDMK **Prod** - NETGOL 1985

The World in Conflict, 1929 - 1945 26 MIN
U-matic / VHS / 16mm
World - a Television History Series
Color (J H C)
MP=$475
Portrays a three - cornered contest of Liberal, Nazi and Communist for control of the world, ending with Communist control of China.
History - World
Dist - LANDMK **Prod** - NETGOL 1985

The World in conflict - 1929 - 1945 30 MIN
VHS
World - A Television history series
Color (C A T)
$55.00 rental
Covers the period from 1929 to 1945, emphasizing World War II. Based on "The Times Atlas of World History." Serves as part 25 of a 26 - part telecourse. Available only to institutions of higher education.
History - World; Sociology
Dist - SCETV **Prod** - SCETV 1986

A World in One Country 27 MIN
VHS
Color (G)
Features aerial photography of South African scenery. Available for free loan from the distributor.
Geography - World
Dist - AUDPLN

A World in our backyard - a wetlands educational and stewardship program 24 MIN
VHS
Color (I J H T)
$29.95 purchase _ #WB101
Shows middle - school students and their teachers how to use local wetlands as outdoor classrooms. Includes a 16 - minute program for teachers and a 7 - minute program, Fabulous Wetlands, for students. Features Bill Nye, the Famous and Wacky Science Guy as host.
Science; Science - Natural
Dist - ENVIMC **Prod** - USEPA 1992

World in your kitchen series

Austrian cooking	28 MIN
Chinese cooking	28 MIN
Danish cooking	28 MIN
French Canadian cooking	28 MIN
Greek cooking	28 MIN
Hungarian cooking	28 MIN
Indian cooking	28 MIN
Indonesian cooking	28 MIN
Jamaican cooking	28 MIN
Jewish cooking	28.5 MIN
Portuguese cooking	28.5 MIN

Dist - RMIBHF

World in your kitchen series

Italian cooking	28 MIN
Ukrainian cooking	28 MIN

Dist - RMIBHF
TVOTAR

World in your kitchen series

Austrian cooking	30 MIN
Chinese cooking	30 MIN
Danish cooking	30 MIN
French Canadian cooking	30 MIN
Greek cooking	30 MIN
Hungarian cooking	30 MIN
Indian cooking	30 MIN
Indonesian cooking	30 MIN
Jamaican cooking	30 MIN
Jewish cooking	30 MIN
Portuguese cooking	30 MIN

Dist - TVOTAR

The World is a Bank 9 MIN
U-matic / VHS / 16mm
Color (P I)
LC 72-700113
Explores some of the ways we can safeguard our wealth of natural resources so that we can enjoy them for many more years.
Science - Natural; Science - Physical; Social Science
Dist - PHENIX **Prod** - PHENIX 1972

The World is a Stage 13 MIN
U-matic / VHS / 16mm
Zoom Series
Color
Interviews two creative teenagers, one a member of a children's dance theater and the other a member of a clown club.
Fine Arts; Sociology
Dist - FI **Prod** - WGBHTV 1978

A World is born 20 MIN
U-matic / VHS / 16mm
Color (I)
Pictures the 'Rites Of Spring' sequence from the 1940 feature film Fantasia which depicts the birth of the earth and the first living creatures to inhabit it.
Fine Arts; Science - Natural; Science - Physical
Dist - CORF **Prod** - DISNEY 1955

A World is Built 30 MIN
16mm
Great Plains Trilogy, 1 Series in the Beginning - the Primitive Man; In the beginning - the primitive man
B&W (H C A)
Tells how the seas have advanced and withdrawn through the ages. Illustrates how the world scene changed as mountains were built and how life began in the plains of Central North Ameria.
Science - Physical
Dist - UNEBR **Prod** - KUONTV 1954

The World is full of oil 58 MIN
U-matic / VHS
Nova series
Color (H C A)
$250.00 purchase _ #HP - 5915C
Investigates new theories on how oil is formed and found, including a theory that oil can be found anywhere if you dig deep enough.
Industrial and Technical Education; Science - Physical; Social Science
Dist - CORF **Prod** - WGBHTV 1989

The World is Watching 30 MIN
VHS / 16mm
Color (G)
$50.00 rental
Examines how the news business works and reveals the inevitable distortions that become part of the process. Shows journalists questioning the enormous pressures they face.
Literature and Drama; Sociology
Dist - ICARUS

The World is Watching 59 MIN
16mm / VHS
Color (G)

$390.00 purchase, $125.00, $75.00 rental
Focuses on journalists covering Nicaragua during the Arias Peace Plan negotiations in November, 1987. Follows John Quinones of ABC in Managua, records the editorial decisions made by Peter Jennings and other senior editors in New York. Includes journalists Randolph Ryan, Edith Coron, and photographer Bill Gentile. Reveals how the news business works and exposes the distortions that are inevitable.
Civics and Political Systems; Geography - World; Literature and Drama; Sociology
Dist - FIRS **Prod** - FIRS 1988

World Leaders Series
Churchill and British history - 1874 - 1918 29 MIN
Churchill and British history - 1919 - 1965 32 MIN
Queen Victoria and British History - 1837 - 1901 28 MIN
Roosevelt and U S History - 1882 - 1929 28 MIN
Roosevelt and U S History - 1930 - 1945 32 MIN
Stalin and Russian History - 1879 - 1927 29 MIN
Stalin and Russian History - 1928 - 1953 31 MIN
Dist - CORF

World medicine - disease recognition 17 MIN
16mm
Color
LC 74-706611
Describes signs, symptoms and laboratory findings on the virus borne Japanese B encephalitis.
Health and Safety; Sociology
Dist - USNAC **Prod** - USN 1965

The World Moses built 58 MIN
VHS
American experience series
Color (H)
$9.50 rental _ #60948, #60947
Examines the career of New York builder Robert Moses and his use of the law of eminent domain to push through many of his projects despite community resistance. The fifth installment of The American Experience Series.
Sociology
Dist - PSU **Prod** - PBS
PBS

The World Needs Help 20 MIN
16mm
Cellar Door Cine Mites Series
Color (I)
LC 74-701552
Fine Arts
Dist - CELLAR **Prod** - CELLAR 1972

World of a primitive painter 20 MIN
16mm / VHS / U-matic
Color (I) (ENGLISH, SPANISH)
LC 72-702169
Examines the work of Jose Antonio Velasquez, a primitive Honduran painter, placing his art against the background of the mining town in which he lives and works. Narrated by Shirley Temple Black.
Fine Arts; History - World
Dist - MOMALA **Prod** - OOAS 1972

The World of Absolute Zero 26 MIN
U-matic / VHS
Color (C)
$249.00, $149.00 purchase _ #AD - 1980
Examines the latest developments in cryogenics and their applications in the areas of superconductivity, developing rocket fuels, steel manufacturing and other industrial processes.
Business and Economics; Psychology; Science - Physical
Dist - FOTH **Prod** - FOTH

World of Andrew Wyeth 26 MIN
U-matic / VHS / 16mm
Color (I J H C)
LC 74-706206
Covers the significant facts in Andrew Wyeth's life, especially the influence of his father, N C Wyeth, the well - known illustrator. Explores more than 35 paintings, giving both an overall impression of each canvas and a close look at specific details of Wyeth's technique.
Biography
Dist - IFB **Prod** - ABCTV 1968

A World of animals
CD-ROM
Wonders of learning CD-ROM library series
Color (K P) (ENGLISH, SPANISH)
$89.95 purchase _ #T05736
Tells real stories about spiders, butterflies, farm animals, whales and dinosaurs. Includes activity guide, user's guide, poster and booklets. Designed for use with Macintosh computer.
Science - Natural
Dist - NGS

The World of Anne Frank 28 MIN
VHS / U-matic
Color (G)
$60.00, $40.00 purchase _ #HVC - 755, #HHC - 755
Remembers Anne Frank and the millions who died during World War II. Dramatizes segments of her diary, documents World War II through photos of Frank, her family and Nazi Germany, historical film footage of Hitler and the rise of Nazism. Interview Anne's father, Otto Frank, and Miep Gies and Victor Kraler who hid the Frank family from the Nazis.
Civics and Political Systems; History - World; Religion and Philosophy; Sociology
Dist - ADL **Prod** - ADL

The World of Anne Frank 28 MIN
VHS
Color (I J H)
$39.95 purchase _ #611
Interweaves dramatic recreations from Anne Frank's diary, documentary information including rare film footage, photographs and interviews with Frank's father and those who risked their lives to hide the Frank family in World War II Amsterdam.
History - World; Literature and Drama; Sociology
Dist - ERGOM **Prod** - ERGOM

The World of Apu (the honeymoon) 14 MIN
16mm
Film study extracts series
B&W (J)
Presents an excerpt from the 1959 motion picture The World Of Apu. Tells how Apu and his wife set up a household in Apu's tiny tenement apartment. Directed by Satyajit Ray.
Fine Arts
Dist - FI **Prod** - UNKNWN

The World of Archery 30 MIN
16mm
Color
LC FIA68-2708
Introduces archery and distinguistes between the different types - - tournament, hunting and fishing archery.
Physical Education and Recreation
Dist - AMARCH **Prod** - AMARCH 1968

The World of Birds 25 MIN
16mm / U-matic / VHS
Untamed World Series
Color; Mono (J H C A)
$400.00 film, $250.00 video, $50.00 rental
Illustrates the bird kingdom by focusing on a variety of species and their behaviours.
Science - Natural
Dist - CTV **Prod** - CTV 1969

The World of Buckminster Fuller 85 MIN
BETA / VHS
Color (G)
$39.95 purchase _ #211
Presents a lecture by Buckminster Fuller. Includes footage of the Dymaxion car, house, the Expo dome and Fuller at his summer home in Maine.
Religion and Philosophy; Science
Dist - BFINST **Prod** - BFINST

World of C++ 120 MIN
VHS
Vision video series
Color (A PRO)
$99.95 purchase
Outlines the process of updating C programming skills to C++ programs, as well as the power of object-oriented programming. Presents 21 video lessons, which detail how C++ works, and how to streamline programs and speed through development cycles. Provides easy-to-understand examples presented in clear, everyday language with high-tech production techniques and animation graphics. Includes workbook written by Bruce Eckel. Hosted by David Intersimone. Part of a six-part series of training videos.
Computer Science
Dist - BORLND **Prod** - BORLND 1992

A World of Care in Brewing 20 MIN
16mm
Color
LC 77-700446
Presents the history of beermaking, with emphasis on the complex and quality - conscious process of brewing.
Home Economics
Dist - SCHLTZ **Prod** - SCHLTZ 1976

World of Carl Sandburg, the 59 MIN
U-matic / VHS / 16mm
Color (J)
LC 76-702516
Presents a portrait of the American writer, Carl Sandburg and a look, through his eyes, at America and its people.
Biography; Fine Arts; History - United States; Literature and Drama
Dist - PHENIX **Prod** - KROLL 1976

World of Change, World of Promise 22 MIN
16mm
Color
LC 79-701694
Shows the different goals and activities of members of the World Association of Girl Guides and Girl Scouts. Visits troops of Girl Guides and Girl Scouts in various parts of the world and shows them teaching reading and hygiene, practicing first aid, preserving traditional customs and acquiring income - producing skills.
Guidance and Counseling; Sociology
Dist - GSUSA

The World of Charles Dickens 14 MIN
U-matic
Great English Writers Series
Color (J H C)
Tells how Dickens recorded the two great transformations of 19th century England, the Industrial Revolution and the Victorian Age. His writings helped shape needed social reforms while chronicling the times.
Biography; History - World; Literature and Drama
Dist - CEPRO **Prod** - CEPRO

The World of Charles Dickens - 1 14 MIN
U-matic / VHS
Great English writers series
Color (H C G)
$225.00, $200.00 purchase _ #V321
Examines the life of Charles Dickens who lived through, and provided a vivid record of, two great periods of transformation in England's history - the Industrial Revolution and the Victorian Age. Reveals that he devoted his literary career to exposing the injustices and extremities of the class structure, helping to shape needed social reforms. Part one of a three - part series looking at Chaucer, Shakespeare and Dickens.
Literature and Drama
Dist - BARR **Prod** - CEPRO 1986

The World of chemistry - color - Parts 1 and 2 60 MIN
U-matic / VHS
World of chemistry series
Color (C)
$45.00, $29.95 purchase
Presents parts 1 and 2 of the 26 - part World of Chemistry series. Presents highlights of key sequences and themes from programs in the series. Shows the relationship of chemistry to the other sciences. Looks at the mid - 1800s search for new colors which indirectly led to the development of modern chemistry. Two thirty - minute programs hosted by Nobel laureate Roald Hoffmann.
History - World; Science - Physical
Dist - ANNCPB **Prod** - UMD 1990

World of chemistry series
Presents a 26 - part series on the world of chemistry. Features Nobel laureate Roald Hoffmann as host. Explores the foundations of chemical structure.
The Busy electron - the proton in chemistry - Parts 15 and 16 60 MIN
Carbon - the age of polymers - Pts 21 and 22 60 MIN
Chemistry and the environment - futures - Parts 25 and 26 60 MIN
The Driving forces - molecules in action - Parts 13 and 14 60 MIN
A Matter of state - the atom - Parts 5 and 6 60 MIN
Measurement - the foundation of chemistry - modeling the unseen - Parts 3 and 4 60 MIN
Metals - on the surface - Parts 19 and 20 60 MIN
The Mole - water - Parts 11 and 12 60 MIN
Molecular architecture - signals from within - Parts 9 and 10 60 MIN
The Periodic table - chemical bonds - Parts 7 and 8 60 MIN
The Precious envelope - the chemistry of the Earth - Pts 17 and 18 60 MIN
Proteins - structure and function - the genetic code - Parts 23 and 24 60 MIN
The World of chemistry - color - Parts 1 and 2 60 MIN
Dist - ANNCPB **Prod** - UMD 1990

World of Children 29 MIN
U-matic
Folklore - U S a Series
B&W
Discusses the games, rhymes and chants of children. Features a group of nine - year - olds demonstrating some favorites.

Literature and Drama
Dist - UMITV Prod - UMITV 1967

The World of Comic Books 16 MIN
16mm / U-matic / VHS
Color (J)
LC 80-701171
Examines the highly competitive world of comic book publishing and briefly chronicles the development of comic book art and writing. Shows the devotion of comic book fans and collectors at a comics convention.
Fine Arts; Literature and Drama
Dist - LUF Prod - MEDLIM 1980

World of Cooking Series
Brazil - a Bahian Menu 28 MIN
Finland - a Karelian Menu 28 MIN
France - an Alpine Menu 28 MIN
Germany - a Southern Menu 28 MIN
Hong Kong - a Cantonese Menu 28 MIN
India - a Northern Menu 28 MIN
Italy - a Venetian Menu 28 MIN
Japan - a Banquet Menu 28 MIN
Mexico - a Family - Style Menu 28 MIN
The Netherlands - a Traditional Menu 28 MIN
Spain - a Catalonian Menu 28 MIN
Dist - CORF

The World of Cousteau 28 MIN
16mm
Color (J)
Shows that the sea is a source of natural resources as the earth's resources are being depleted and the population continues to grow.
Psychology; Science - Natural; Sociology
Dist - AETNA Prod - AETNA 1967

A World of Credit 12 MIN
16mm
Color
LC 81-701404
Looks at Dun and Bradstreet's information gathering and disseminating operations. Includes actual reporter interviews, filmed throughout the United States. Points out the importance of credit to the American economy.
Business and Economics; Social Science
Dist - MTP Prod - DBI 1981

The World of CRS - People First 24 MIN
16mm
Color
Looks at the humanitarian efforts of Catholic Relief Services in Thailand, Egypt, Kenya, Colombia and Costa Rica.
Sociology
Dist - MTP Prod - CATHRS

The World of Darkness 25 MIN
U-matic / VHS / 16mm
Color
LC 72-702937
A shortened version of the 1973 motion picture Strange Creature Of The Night. Uses night - vision camera devices in presenting studies of bats, owls, hyenas and sightless cave - dwelling fish during their nighttime activities.
Science - Natural
Dist - NGS Prod - NGS 1973

World of database management 29 MIN
VHS
Visions video series
Color (A PRO)
$19.95 purchase
Outlines the concepts of database management, including object-oriented technology and Windows database technology. Details how databases can be used to manage corporate information efficiently and profitably. Provides easy-to-understand examples presented in clear, everyday language with high-tech production techniques and animation graphics. Hosted by Philippe Kahn. Part of a six-part series of training videos.
Computer Science
Dist - BORLND Prod - BORLND 1992

World of David Milne 13 MIN
16mm
Color
_ #106C 0163 008N
Geography - World
Dist - CFLMDC Prod - NFBC 1963

The World of David Rockefeller - Pt 1 60 MIN
VHS / U-matic
Bill Moyers' Journal Series
Color
Looks at the power and influence of David Rockefeller. Shows Bill Moyers as he accompanies Rockefeller on a whirlwind trip through five European countries.
Biography; Business and Economics
Dist - PBS Prod - WNETTV

The World of David Rockefeller - Pt 2 60 MIN
VHS / U-matic
Bill Moyers' Journal Series
Color
Looks at the power and influence of David Rockefeller. Shows Bill Moyers as he accompanies Rockefeller on a whirlwind trip through five European countries.
Biography; Business and Economics
Dist - PBS Prod - WNETTV

The World of Deaf - Blind Children - Growing Up 29 MIN
16mm
Color
LC 76-702950
Shows programs for deaf - blind children at the Perkins School for the Blind. Covers career education, skills for home life and mobility skills.
Education; Guidance and Counseling; Psychology
Dist - CMPBL Prod - PERKNS 1975

The World of Deaf - Blind Children - How they Communicate 29 MIN
16mm
Color
LC 74-702530
Shows how the educational programs at the Perkins School for the Blind can help deaf - blind children learn to deal with the world around them.
Education; Guidance and Counseling; Home Economics; Psychology
Dist - CMPBL Prod - PERKNS 1974

A World of Difference 9 MIN
16mm
Child Abuse and Neglect Series
Color (C A)
LC 78-701591
Explains the signs of child abuse, including descriptions of the typical abused child, the typical abusive parent and the external circumstances that may provoke the parent to violence or willful neglect. Provides a legal definition of child abuse and neglect and explains what may happen to an abusive family if a report is made against them.
Guidance and Counseling; Sociology
Dist - UKANS Prod - UKANS 1977

A World of Difference 27 MIN
16mm
Color
LC 74-700496
Helps motivate distributor prospects for amway corporation, a maker of household products and cosmetics.
Business and Economics; Home Economics
Dist - AMWAY Prod - AMWAY 1973

A World of Difference - B F Skinner and the Good Life 58 MIN
16mm / U-matic / VHS
Nova Series
Color (C A)
LC 79-701898
Traces the life of behavioral psychologist B F Skinner, who believes that environment alone molds behavior. Visits Twin Oaks, a rural cooperative where Skinner's theories were put into practice.
Psychology; Social Science
Dist - TIMLIF Prod - WGBHTV 1979

The World of Dreams
VHS
Ater of the Night - the Science of Sleep and Dreams Series
Color
Deals with research on dreams. Compares Freud's theories to those of modern physiological psychologists.
Health and Safety; Psychology
Dist - IBIS Prod - IBIS

A World of Dreams - Pt 3 60 MIN
VHS
Wisdom of the Dream, the - World of C G Jung Series
Color (S)
$29.95 purchase _ #833 - 9550
Captures the essential spirit of C G Jung, a psychiatrist, a scholar, a painter and a traveler, but above all a healer and a dreamer. Part 3 of three parts reveals Jung's enduring influence on modern life. Analyst John Beebe considers a key scene in 'Notorious' by Alfred Hitchcock in Jungian terms. Dr Harry Wilmer explains his remarkable research into the 'healing nightmares' of Vietnam veterans.
Fine Arts; History - United States; History - World; Literature and Drama; Psychology; Religion and Philosophy
Dist - FI Prod - RMART 1989

World of Dredging 18 MIN
U-matic / VHS / 16mm
Color
Shows how the Corps of Engineers on its own and in cooperation with the private dredging industry maintains our waterways and harbors.
Civics and Political Systems; Social Science
Dist - USNAC Prod - USAE

A World of Energy 28 MIN
16mm
Energy - an Overview Series
Color (J H)
Portrays major developments and turning points in the history of energy production. Talks about protection of the environment, resource recovery, the role of transportation and efficient use of energy.
Home Economics; Science - Physical; Social Science
Dist - CONPOW Prod - CENTRO

A World of Energy - the Breeder Reactor 13 MIN
16mm
Color
Uses a tour of the 1982 World's Fair to show international advancements in breeder reactor technology. Presents Dr Alvin Weinberg explaining what the breeder means to Americans. Closes with President Reagan calling for the development of safe nuclear energy.
Industrial and Technical Education; Social Science
Dist - MTP Prod - MTP

World of Extremes Series
Ultra - Low Temperatures 12 MIN
Ultra - Strong Magnetic Fields 12 MIN
Very High Pressures 12 MIN
Dist - FOTH

World of F Scott Fitzgerald Series
The Death of heroism 60 MIN
The End of an Era 60 MIN
The Golden boom 60 MIN
He Called it the Jazz Age 60 MIN
The Last Novelist 60 MIN
Lost and Lucky 60 MIN
The Most Famous Forgotten Writer in America 60 MIN
The Spoiled Priest 60 MIN
Dist - DALCCD

World of festivals series
Presents a 12 - part series on European festivals. Visits Germany, Switzerland, Spain, Scotland, Italy, Yugoslavia, Wales, Belgium, Netherlands, Ireland, Austria and France.
Belgium salutes an emperor 30 MIN
Carnival in France 30 MIN
A Day for being Irish 30 MIN
Demon Christmas in Austria 30 MIN
Dutch pirates are heroes 30 MIN
Ghost of the Spanish warrior 30 MIN
Masked madness in Switzerland 30 MIN
Oktoberfest in Munich 30 MIN
Sing out for Wales 30 MIN
The Venice gondola pageant 30 MIN
Viking sacrifice in Shetland 30 MIN
Yugoslavia's mountain homecoming 30 MIN
Dist - LANDMK Prod - LANDMK

The World of Ford 30 MIN
16mm / U-matic / VHS
Color
Relates the story of the Ford Motor Company, within the context of an American dream come true.
Business and Economics; Industrial and Technical Education
Dist - FORDFL Prod - FORDFL

The World of Franklin and Jefferson 28 MIN
U-matic / VHS / 16mm
Color (J)
LC 76-703170
Traces the interlocking careers of Benjamin Franklin and Thomas Jefferson. Presents the background and accomplishments of these two men.
Biography; History - United States
Dist - PFP Prod - EAMES 1976
MTP IBMCOP

The World of Geoffrey Chaucer 13 MIN
U-matic
Great English Writers Series
Color (H C A)
Tells how Chaucer detailed the people and events of 14th Century England into his Canterbury Tales.
Biography; History - World; Literature and Drama
Dist - CEPRO Prod - CEPRO

The World of Geoffrey Chaucer - 2 13 MIN
U-matic / VHS
Great English writers series
Color (H C G)
$215.00, $195.00 purchase _ #V322
Examines the life of Geoffrey Chaucer who was born in London in 1340, during a century of transition between the medieval period and the threshold of the modern world. Reveals that he wrote the first great epic of English

poetry, 'The Canterbury Tales,' which has become an important reference for its detailed descriptions of the people and events of his time. Part one of a three - part series looking at Chaucer, Shakespeare and Dickens.
Literature and Drama
Dist - BARR **Prod** - CEPRO 1986

A World of gestures 28 MIN
VHS
Color (H C G)
$295.00 purchase, $50.00 rental _ #38112
Explores gestures from cultures around the world. Shows people from dozens of countries performing gestures that are by turns powerful, provocative, poignant - and sometimes outrageous. Illustrates many types of gestures, including those for beauty, sexual behavior, suicide, aggression and love. Examines the meaning and function of gestures as a form of nonverbal communication and studies their origins and emotional significance. Produced by Dane Archer, Prof of Sociology, University of California, Santa Cruz.
Social Science; Sociology
Dist - UCEMC

The World of green 28 MIN
U-matic / VHS
Life of plants series
Color (C)
$249.00, $149.00 purchase _ #AD - 1683
Shows that the plant world has its own rules. Reveals that trees can live as long as 2000 years. Even when a tree's branches appear to be dead and only part of the trunk is alive, it continues to grow and produce viable seeds. Part of a series on plants.
Science - Natural
Dist - FOTH **Prod** - FOTH

The World of Hare Krishna 34 MIN
16mm
Color
Studies the International Society for Krishna Consciousness.
Religion and Philosophy
Dist - BHAKTI **Prod** - ISKCON 1982

World of Health Series
Birth Control - Five Effective Methods 10 MIN
Dist - PRORE
SF

World of Health Series
Cholesterol - eat your heart out 14 MIN
The Common cold 9 MIN
Run for Your Life 15 MIN
Dist - SF

World of 'Hip Hop,' the - Rapping, Break Dancing and Electric Boogie 30 MIN
U-matic / VHS
Popular Culture in Dance Series
Color
Fine Arts
Dist - ARCVID **Prod** - ARCVID

The World of I T W 2 MIN
16mm
Color
LC 72-700330
An industry management - oriented film which shows how the world has changed in the past thirty - five years and indicates the changes that will occur in the next thirty - five years.
Business and Economics; Psychology; Sociology
Dist - ITW **Prod** - ITW 1971

World Of Ideas With Bill Moyers - Seaon I - series
Noam Chomsky - Parts I and II 30 MIN
Dist - PBS

World of ideas With Bill Moyers - Season I - series
Anne Wortham - Parts I and II 60 MIN
Arturo Madrid 30 MIN
August Wilson 30 MIN
Barbara Tuchman 30 MIN
Carlos Fuentes 30 MIN
Chen Ning Yang 30 MIN
Derek Walcott 30 MIN
E L Doctorow 30 MIN
Elaine Pagels - Parts I and II 60 MIN
Forrest McDonald 30 MIN
Forrester Church 30 MIN
Isaac Asimov - Parts I and II 60 MIN
James MacGregor Burns 30 MIN
Jessica Tuchman Mathews 30 MIN
John Lukacs 30 MIN
John Searle 30 MIN
Joseph Heller 30 MIN
Leon Kass - Parts I and II 30 MIN
Louise Erdrich and Michael Dorris 30 MIN
Martha C Nussbaum 30 MIN
Mary Catherine Bateson 30 MIN
Maxine Singer 30 MIN
Michael Josephson 30 MIN
Northrop Frye 30 MIN
Peter Berger 30 MIN
Peter Drucker 30 MIN
Robert Bellah 30 MIN
Sara Lightfoot 30 MIN
Sheldon Wolin 30 MIN
Sissela Bok 30 MIN
Steven Weinberg 30 MIN
Summing Up 30 MIN
T Berry Brazelton - Parts I and II 60 MIN
Vartan Gregorian 30 MIN
Willard Gaylin 30 MIN
William Julius Wilson 30 MIN
Dist - PBS

World of ideas with Bill Moyers - Season II - series
Hope for the Long Run with Cornel West 30 MIN
Inventing the future with Robert Lucky - Parts I and II 60 MIN
Invitation to education with Mike Rose 30 MIN
Justice with Michael Sandel 30 MIN
A Mind for music with Peter Sellars - Parts I and II 60 MIN
The Mind of Patricia Churchland 30 MIN
The Peace Dividend with Seymour Melman 30 MIN
The Science of hope with Jonas Salk 30 MIN
Spiritual democracy with Steven Rockefeller 30 MIN
The Stories of Maxine Hong Kingston - Pts I and II 60 MIN
World of ideas with Bill Moyers series - Season II 1560 MIN
A Writer's work with Toni Morrison 30 MIN
Dist - PBS

World of ideas with Bill Moyers - season 1 series
David Puttnam - Parts 1 & 2 240 MIN
Mary Ann Glendon 30 MIN
Dist - PBS

World of ideas with Bill Moyers - Season 2 series
Words and music with Jeannette Haien 30 MIN
Dist - FOTH
PBS

World of ideas with Bill Moyers, season 2 series
An American story with Richard Rodriguez - Parts 1 and 2 60 MIN
The Broken cord with Louise Erdrich and Michael Dorris 30 MIN
Changing agendas with Gro Harlem Brundtland 30 MIN
A Concern for community with Ernie Cortes - Parts 1 & 2 60 MIN
A Confucian life in America with Tu Wei - ming 30 MIN
Conquering America with Bharati Mukherjee 30 MIN
Ethics and work with Joanne Ciulla 30 MIN
Fame with Leo Braudy 30 MIN
Food for thought with M F K Fisher 30 MIN
The Islamic mind with Seyyed Hossein Nasr 30 MIN
Money with Jacob Needleman 30 MIN
Mortal choices with Ruth Macklin - Part 1 and Public policy, private choices with Ruth Macklin - Part 2 60 MIN
On being a white African with Nadine Gordimer 30 MIN
Quarks and the universe with Murray Gell - Mann 30 MIN
Science and gender with Evelyn Fox Keller 30 MIN
The State of the world with Lester Brown 30 MIN
A Witness to history with William Shirer - Parts 1 and 2 60 MIN
Words and music with Jeannette Haien 30 MIN
Dist - PBS

World of ideas with Bill Moyers series - Season II 1560 MIN
VHS
World of ideas with Bill Moyers - Season II - series
Color; Captioned (G)
$1,500.00 purchase _ #WIWM - 200
Interviews scientists, writers, artists, philosophers and others who discuss ideas and values that could shape the future. Consists of 52 half - hour interviews. Hosted by Bill Moyers.
Computer Science; English Language; Fine Arts; Guidance and Counseling; Religion and Philosophy; Science
Dist - PBS

World of ideas with Bill Moyers series
Chinua Achebe 30 MIN
Henry Steele Commager 30 MIN
Tom Wolfe 60 MIN
Dist - PBS

World of ideas with Bill Moyers, session 2 series
Labor's future with Gus Tyler 30 MIN
Thoughts on capitalism with Louis Kelso 30 MIN
Dist - PBS

World of Illusion 28 MIN
16mm
Color (J)
LC 73-701568
Portrays the difference between the world of illusion and the world of reality. Features Mr Kole, one of the foremost inventors of magical effects, who displays his talent in mystifying his audience with a series of illusions.
Psychology; Sociology
Dist - CCFC **Prod** - CCFC 1970

The World of Impressionism 18 MIN
VHS
Color (I J H)
$22.95 purchase _ #IMP01
Examines the Impressionistic movement and the works of five of its greatest artists - Monet, Renoir, Degas, Manet and Cassatt. Contains nude subjects.
Fine Arts
Dist - KNOWUN

The World of insectivorous plants 20 MIN
U-matic / VHS
Color (C)
$249.00, $149.00 purchase _ #AD - 1614
Presents photographic images of the battle for survival between plants and insects.
Science - Natural
Dist - FOTH **Prod** - FOTH

The World of Insects 25 MIN
16mm / U-matic / VHS
Untamed World Series
Color; Mono (J H C A)
$400.00 film, $250.00 video, $50.00 rental
Focuses on four varieties of insects, caterpillars, beetles, wasps, and termites.
Science - Natural
Dist - CTV **Prod** - CTV 1969

The World of Insects 20 MIN
U-matic / VHS / 16mm
Color (J)
LC 79-701615
Examines the anatomy and life cycles of the insect. Explains how insect numbers are kept in check and evaluates the advantages and disadvantages of biological pest control and chemical spraying.
Science - Natural
Dist - NGS **Prod** - NGS 1979

World of Insects Series
Provides detailed investigation of insect anatomy, activity, and defense through close up views and time lapse techniques.
Insects - Body Structure and Function 15.5 MIN
Insects - Cycles of Life 19.5 MIN
Insects - Defenses Against Enemies 12.5 MIN
Dist - BARR **Prod** - BARR 1979

World of Islam Series
The Five pillars of Islam 30 MIN
Islam Today 30 MIN
Islamic Art 30 MIN
The Islamic City 30 MIN
Islamic Science and Technology 30 MIN
Orient - Occident 30 MIN
Dist - FOTH

World of Jacques - Yves Cousteau 53 MIN
U-matic / VHS / 16mm
Color (J A)
LC FIA67-5240
Records the day - by - day events in the lives of six aquanauts who pioneered an inner space expedition 328 feet below the surface of the Mediterranean for 27 days.
Geography - World; Science; Science - Natural; Science - Physical
Dist - NGS **Prod** - NGS 1966

World of Jai - Alai 14 MIN
16mm
Color
LC 80-700312
Gives a brief history of the sport of jai - alai from its origins in the Basque region to the game played in the United States in the 1970s. Culminates with the first American amateur to become a professional world champion.
Physical Education and Recreation
Dist - FLADC **Prod** - WJAIAL 1979

The World of James Joyce 120 MIN
U-matic
Color (H C A)
Blends narrative, readings, interviews, and archival recordings to show the life and works of James Joyce.

Biography; Literature and Drama
Dist - CEPRO Prod - CEPRO 1985

The world of Jesus and John 59 MIN
VHS
Time travel through the Bible series; 02
Color (G)
$19.95 purchase
Profiles John the Baptist and his ministry prior to Christ's birth. Considers the significance of the discoveries of the Dead Sea scrolls and the home of Peter.
Guidance and Counseling; Literature and Drama; Religion and Philosophy
Dist - CPH Prod - LUMIS

The World of Jesus Christ 42 MIN
U-matic / VHS / 16mm
Color (J)
Offers a fresh view of the nativity, events leading to it and the early years of Christ's ministry. Shows how biblical events have inspired paintings by Giotto, Michelangelo, Grunewald and El Greco. Presents music that springs from the Christian tradition.
Religion and Philosophy
Dist - CORF Prod - ABCNEW 1978

World of Joseph Campbell Series
Introduction - the Hero's Journey 57 MIN
The Soul of the Acients - Vol I - Pt I 109 MIN
The Soul of the Acients - Vol I - Pt II 109 MIN
The Soul of the Acients - Vol I - Pt III 58 MIN
Dist - FI

World of Joseph Campbell - Volume III series
The World of Joseph Campbell - Volume III - the western way - Part I 118 MIN
The World of Joseph Campbell - Volume III - the western way - Part II 58 MIN
Dist - HOMVIS

The World of Joseph Campbell - Volume III - the western way - Part I 118 MIN
VHS
World of Joseph Campbell - Volume III series
Color (G)
$29.95 purchase _ #CAM07
Presents part I of the third volume of the World of Joseph Campbell. Focuses on the roots of modern western society through a probe of the Arthurian legends, Parsifal, Tristan and Isolde.
History - World; Literature and Drama; Religion and Philosophy
Dist - HOMVIS Prod - MYTHL 1990

The World of Joseph Campbell - Volume III - the western way - Part II 58 MIN
VHS
World of Joseph Campbell - Volume III series
Color (G)
$19.95 purchase _ #CAM08
Presents part II of the third volume of the World of Joseph Campbell. Focuses on the roots of modern western society through a probe of the Arthurian legends, Parsifal, Tristan and Isolde.
History - World; Literature and Drama; Religion and Philosophy
Dist - HOMVIS Prod - MYTHL 1990

World of Light - a Portrait of may Sarton 30 MIN
16mm
Color (H C A)
Follows the activities of writer May Sarton at her home in Maine as she explores her life and works. Features Sarton discussing her creative process, presenting her views and experiences on solitude, aging, the woman writer, discipline, integrity and relationships, and reading from her poetry and novels.
Biography; Literature and Drama
Dist - ISHTAR Prod - ISHTAR

World of Little Things 16 MIN
VHS / 16mm
Color (I J H)
Introduces the microscopic world. Shows examples of the amoeba, volvox, paramecium and didinium. Studies the structure and nature of marine life, such as flatworms, medusa and protozoans. Shows algae and diatoms in relation to their variety and usefulness to man.
Science - Natural
Dist - MIS Prod - MIS 1976

The World of Living Things 15 MIN
U-matic / VHS
Bioscope Series
Color (I J)
LC 81-707651
Describes some of the remarkable features of living organisms. Focuses on seed dispersal mechanisms, plants that defend themselves, and plants that attack and kill animals for food. Offers information on jellyfish, army ants, dolphins and anacondas.
Science - Natural
Dist - AITECH Prod - MAETEL 1981

The World of magazines 30 MIN
VHS
Exploring mass communication series
Color (H C)
$39.95 purchase _ #IVMC24
Introduces the magazine publishing industry. Explores the history and structure of the business. Examines trends in the magazine field and how the magazine has changed over the years.
Guidance and Counseling; Sociology
Dist - INSTRU

The World of Mark Twain
VHS / U-matic
Color (H C)
Shows how Mark Twain's boyhood, journalistic and riverboat experiences formed his writings, and presents excerpts from his fiction, essays and letters.
Literature and Drama
Dist - GA Prod - GA

The World of Mark Twain
U-matic / VHS / 35mm strip
American Literature Series
(G C J)
$109, $139 purchase _ #06205 - 85
Examines the themes and best - known works of Mark Twain through readings of his essays, books, and letters.
Literature and Drama
Dist - CHUMAN Prod - GA

The World of Martin Luther 30 MIN
16mm
B&W (I)
LC 72-701664
Re - creates in Luther's own words his work, life and era. Retraces Luther's footsteps from St Peter's Church in Eisleben, where he was baptized, to the room where he died.
Biography; History - World
Dist - CPH Prod - LUTHER 1966

World of Medicine Series
Walk Your Way to Weight Control
Dist - INFORP

The World of molecules 12 MIN
VHS
Color (I)
$230.00, $160.00 purchase, $60.00 rental
Explores molecules through the experience of children, experiments and the observation of common phenomena. Considers the size of molecules, their attraction for each other, behavior in solids, liquids and gases and changes of states.
Science - Physical
Dist - CF

World of Molecules 12 MIN
U-matic / VHS / 16mm
Color (I)
LC 77-703305
Explores molecules, using children's experiments to illustrate their size, their behavior in solid, liquid and gaseous forms and their changes of state.
Science; Science - Physical
Dist - CF Prod - CF 1977

The World of molecules ; Rev. 2nd ed. 12 MIN
U-matic / VHS / 16mm
Color (I)
$79.95 purchase _ #Q10292
Utilizes experiments and observation of common phenomena to explain what molecules are. Illustrates their size; attraction for each other; behavior in solids, liquids and gases; and changes of states. Features live action footage to demonstrate principles.
Science - Physical
Dist - CF

The World of Mother Teresa 59 MIN
U-matic / VHS / 16mm
Color (J)
LC 81-700554
Shows scenes of Mother Teresa being awarded the Nobel Peace Prize in 1979. Follows the missionary as she tours facilities she founded for the poor, sick and dying in India.
History - World; Religion and Philosophy; Sociology
Dist - FI Prod - PTRIA MGM 1981

World of Motion 27 MIN
16mm
Color
LC 73-701878
Presents a kaleidoscopic chronicle of the past history and present world - wide operations of the General Motors Corporation.
Business and Economics; Industrial and Technical Education; Social Science
Dist - GM Prod - GM 1973

World of Muffins 14 MIN
Videoreel / VT2
Muffinland Series
Color
English Language; Literature and Drama
Dist - PBS Prod - WGTV

World of Music 15 MIN
U-matic
Music Box Series
Color (K P)
Introduces a magic Music Box which produces a variety of music and musical instruments.
Fine Arts
Dist - TVOTAR Prod - TVOTAR 1971

World of Music Series
The Music Lesson 30 MIN
Music of Shakespeare's Time 30 MIN
The Philadelphia Woodwind Quintet 30 MIN
The Renaissance Band 30 MIN
Secular Music of the Renaissance - Josquin Des Pres 30 MIN
Dist - IU

The World of Norman Lear - Part I - the creative process 29 MIN
VHS
Creativity with Bill Moyers series
Color (G)
$49.95 purchase _ #CWBM - 111C
Goes behind the scenes with television writer and producer Norman Lear to show how he and his associates produce a television program. Includes excerpts from the story conference, casting call and director's rehearsals. Hosted by Bill Moyers.
Fine Arts; Literature and Drama
Dist - PBS Prod - CORPEL 1981

The World of Norman Lear - Part II - the creative person 29 MIN
VHS
Creativity with Bill Moyers series
Color (G)
$49.95 purchase _ #CWBM - 112C
Profiles television writer and producer Norman Lear. Focuses on the various creative influences contained in his life, including his early life as a small businessman and unsuccessful salesman. Considers his philosophy of writing and creativity.
Fine Arts; Literature and Drama
Dist - PBS Prod - CORPEL 1981

The World of Numbers 28 MIN
16mm
Color (R)
Compares such developments as the laser beam, computers that draw and talk, and the scientific machinery that controls navigation with the claims of Jesus Christ.
Guidance and Counseling; Religion and Philosophy
Dist - OUTRCH Prod - OUTRCH

World of objects 20 MIN
VHS
Visions video series
(A PRO)
$19.95 purchase
Describes the uses and concepts behind object-oriented programming. Features Philippe Kahn and his special guests who take the viewer on a guided tour. Provides easy-to-understand examples presented in clear, everyday languagae with high-tech production techniques and animation graphics. Part of a six-part series of training videos.
Computer Science
Dist - BORLND Prod - BORLND 1992

World of ObjectVision 85 MIN
VHS
Visions video series
Color (A PRO)
$39.95 purchase
Teaches viewers how to create their own Windows applications without programming with quick, easy lessons. Provides easy-to-understand examples presented in clear, everyday language with high-tech production techniques and animation graphics. Hosted by John Mandell. Includes sample ObjectVision applications. Part of a six-part series of training videos.
Computer Science
Dist - BORLND Prod - BORLND 1992

World of ObjectWindows for C++ 120 MIN
VHS
Visions video series
Color (A PRO)
$99.95 purchase
Provides Windows users an interface with C++ . Provides examples presented in clear, everyday language with high-tech production techniques and animation graphics. Includes two videotapes, workbook written by Tom Swan, and sample source codes. Hosted by David Intersimone. Part of a six-part series of training videos.

Computer Science
Dist - BORLND **Prod** - BORLND 1992

World of ObjectWindows for Turbo Pascal 120 MIN
VHS
Vision videos series
Color (A PRO)
$99.95 purchase
Offers easy installation interfaces with Turbo Pascal for Windows users. Describes how to use software to improve your computer's abilities. Provides examples presented in clear, everyday language with high-tech production techniques and animation graphics. Includes workbook written by Tom Swan, as well as a sample source code. Hosted by David Intersimone. Part of a six-part series.
Computer Science
Dist - BORLND **Prod** - BORLND 1992

The World of Paul Delvaux 12 MIN
16mm
Color (FRENCH)
Pictures the dream world through poetry and music.
Fine Arts; Literature and Drama
Dist - GROVE **Prod** - GROVE

World of Pets Series
Cats 15 MIN
Dogs 16 MIN
Fish 16 MIN
Dist - NGS

The World of Piri Thomas 60 MIN
U-matic / VHS / 16mm
Color; B&W (H C A)
LC 71-701051
Piri Thomas, a painter, poet, author, ex - con and ex - junkie, describes the life of a puerto Rican in the Spanish Harlem ghetto in New York City.
Psychology; Sociology
Dist - IU **Prod** - NET 1968

The World of plant and animal communities 13 MIN
U-matic / VHS / 16mm
Color (P I)
Shows how living things depend on one another for food and shelter in forests, deserts, oceans and grasslands. Stresses the importance of food chains in a community and the interrelationship among people, plants and animals in the food chains of the human community.
Science - Natural
Dist - EBEC **Prod** - EBEC 1981

A World of plants
CD-ROM
Wonders of learning CD-ROM library series
Color (K P) (ENGLISH, SPANISH)
$89.95 purchase _ #T05751
Teaches about plants. Examines growth from seed to maturity, how trees change with the seasons. Includes activity guide, user's guide, poster and booklets. Designed for use with Macintosh computer.
Science - Natural
Dist - NGS

A World of Polo 56 MIN
BETA / VHS
Color
Covers the history of polo and modern polo events.
Physical Education and Recreation
Dist - EQVDL **Prod** - ROLEX

The World of Print 18 MIN
U-matic / VHS / 16mm
Color (H C A)
LC 80-700599
Presents a short history of printing from early Chinese woodblocks, through the Gutenberg press, to linotype machines. Illustrates printing methods and discusses the wide variety of knowledge and skills needed in printing and allied industries.
History - World; Industrial and Technical Education
Dist - IFB **Prod** - MOOREN 1979

The World of protozoa 18 MIN
VHS
Color (I J)
$295.00 purchase, $50.00 rental _ #8380
Reveals that a drop of pond water contains thousands of minute, single - celled creatures called protozoa. Defines protozoa, how they move, ingest food, grow and reproduce.
Science - Natural
Dist - AIMS **Prod** - GREATT 1991

The World of Real - Time 15 MIN
16mm
Color
Describes SITA, an organization dealing with interline communications for major airlines, Kesko, a shopping chain in Finland and Lockheed, and a manufacturer in Georgia, showing how they use the various capabilities of UNIVAC real - time systems.
Business and Economics; Mathematics; Social Science
Dist - UNIVAC **Prod** - SPGYRO 1969

The World of Rembrandt 30 MIN
16mm
Eternal Light Series
B&W (H C A)
LC 77-700976
A documentary filmed in Amsterdam. Presents some of the masterpieces of the Dutch artist, Rembrandt Van Rijn, including many of his portraits. Also shows Amsterdam's historic Spanish Portugese Synagogue and deals with the history of the Jews in Holland. (Kinescope).
Fine Arts; Religion and Philosophy
Dist - NAAJS **Prod** - JTS 1968

The World of remote control 22 MIN
VHS
Color (G)
$39.95 purchase _ #S01853
Covers the spectrum of remote control modeling, including boats, cars and airplanes. Describes how to get started in the hobby successfully.
Fine Arts; Sociology
Dist - UILL

The World of Semiconductors 38 MIN
U-matic / VHS / 16mm
Color (J H)
Describes the electrical properties of semiconductor materials, the effect of adding various controlled impurities, and the ways in which semiconductors can be used for rectification or as amplifiers.
Industrial and Technical Education; Science - Physical
Dist - IFB **Prod** - AEIND 1964

World of semiconductors 38 MIN
16mm / U-matic / VHS
Color (H C A)
Presnts an illustrated lecture and demonstration on semiconductors, transistors and their uses. Electrical properties, effects of adding controlled impurities, rectification and amplification are discussed.
Industrial and Technical Education
Dist - IFB **Prod** - IEEE 1962

World of Sholom Aleichem 30 MIN
16mm
B&W
Brings to life some of the folk characters in the East - European town of Kasrilevka, created by Sholom Aleichem. A companion film to 'Visit To The World Of Sholom Aleichem.' Based on the book of the same title. (Kinescope).
Literature and Drama; Religion and Philosophy
Dist - NAAJS **Prod** - JTS 1952

A World of Silence 30 MIN
VHS / 16mm
First International Mime Clinic and Festival Series
Color (G)
$55.00 rental _ #FMFI - 001
Fine Arts
Dist - PBS **Prod** - KTCATV

World of stories 78 MIN
VHS
Color (K P I)
$19.95 purchase _ #1665
Features Katharine Hepburn as narrator of six children's stories illustrated by different artists. Includes Beauty and the Beast, Jack and the Beanstalk, The Musicians of Bremen, The Emperor's New Clothes, The Nightingale and Tattercoats.
Literature and Drama
Dist - KULTUR **Prod** - KULTUR 1993

The World of Strawberry Shortcake 24 MIN
16mm
Color (K P I)
Uses animation to present a story about Strawberry Shortcake. Shows how her surprise birthday party is spoiled and the valley where she lives is flooded because of the Peculiar Purple Pieman's evil doings with a fantastic watering can. Tells how a special birthday wish that the Sun grants to Strawberry Shortcake turns everything right and converts the Purple Pieman into a friend.
Literature and Drama
Dist - CORF **Prod** - CORF 1982

World of the 30s Series
Airplanes and the rising sun 30 MIN
America in the Thirties - depression and optimism 30 MIN
China - the agony of a giant 30 MIN
The Dawn of tomorrow 30 MIN
Disaster in a Pleasant Climate - Trouble in Italy and Spain 30 MIN
Dreams and Nightmares 30 MIN
The End of a Revolution 30 MIN
The End of the World 30 MIN
The Fuehrer's Germany 30 MIN
Losing the peace 30 MIN
Master in the Colonies 30 MIN
Old Peoples, New Consciousness 30 MIN
Years of Gloom and Hope 30 MIN
Dist - FOTH

World of the American Craftsman Series
Barbara Scarponi, jewelry and metal worker 30 MIN
Dorothy Young, Weaver 30 MIN
Vivika Heino, Potter 30 MIN
Walker Weed, Wood Worker 30 MIN
Winslow Eaves, Sculptor 30 MIN
Dist - PBS

The World of the Beaver 32 MIN
U-matic / VHS / 16mm
Color (P I J H C)
LC 73-709816
A shortened version of the film The World Of The Beaver. Shows the world of the small furry conservationist, the beaver, who engineered many of the waterways of our continent and who is an industrious, intelligent, social creature who benefits most of the animals around him, including man. Presents the life cycle of the beaver with emphasis on the beaver's ecological role and the excellent example which he presents to mankind. Narrated by Henry Fonda.
Industrial and Technical Education; Science - Natural
Dist - PHENIX **Prod** - CBSTV 1969

The World of the Dark Crystal 55 MIN
16mm
Color
Shows the evolution of the story, sets and characters of the motion picture The Dark Crystal, from conception to the work of the same puppeteers who work with the Muppets.
Fine Arts
Dist - FLMLIB **Prod** - HENASS 1982

The World of the Diving Spider 12 MIN
U-matic / VHS / 16mm
Color (J H)
LC 78-700645
Studies the 'diving spider' (argyoneta aquatica), an air - breathing member of the animal kingdom that lives its entire life under water. Reveals the spider's habits and life - cycle, from the creation of its mobile air supply and its bubble - chamber submarine house to its food hunting techniques, mating, birth of its young and its death.
Science - Natural
Dist - AIMS **Prod** - AIMS 1977

World of the forest - Pt 1 14 MIN
Videoreel / VT2
Muffinland series
Color
English Language; Literature and Drama
Dist - PBS **Prod** - WGTV

World of the forest - Pt 2 14 MIN
Videoreel / VT2
Muffinland series
Color
English Language; Literature and Drama
Dist - PBS **Prod** - WGTV

The World of the Future 19 MIN
16mm / U-matic / VHS
Color
Interviews author Alvin Toffler, who explains that in a society exploding with change it becomes difficult for people to maintain their equilibrium. Suggests that society, rather than the individual, will be the effective cushion against the phenomenon of future shock.
Sociology
Dist - CNEMAG **Prod** - DOCUA

The World of the Future - Crisis in the 800th Lifetime 22 MIN
16mm / U-matic / VHS
Color
Examines the type of problems the individual and society will face as a result of never - ending change. Presents interviews with Dr Arnold Friedman of the Montefiore Hospital in New York, Frank Ogden, an art teacher, and Dr Irving Buchan of Fairley Dickinson College in Madison, New Jersey, as well as Alvin Toffler, author of the book Future Shock.
Biography; Sociology
Dist - CNEMAG **Prod** - DOCUA

The World of the Koala 25 MIN
U-matic
Animal Wonder Down Under Series
Color (I J H)
Observes the behavior of a mother Koala and her young.
Geography - World; Science - Natural
Dist - CEPRO **Prod** - CEPRO

The World of the microscope 12 MIN
16mm
Color (P I J)
LC FIA67-706
Explains the principles and use of the microscope by relating the instrument to things familiar to the student - light from the sun and a magnifying glass. Uses line drawings and live action.
Science
Dist - BAL VIEWTH **Prod** - STNFRD 1966

The World of the protozoa 30 MIN
VHS
Color (J H)
$125.00 purchase _ #10212VG
Shows the world of the protozoa and pond water ecosystems. Uses microphotography to reveal a variety of freshwater invertebrates. Discusses the need to research microorganisms. Comes with an interactive video quiz, teacher's guide and ten blackline masters.
Science - Natural
Dist - UNL

World of the Sea 27 MIN
16mm
Color
LC 74-706612
Shows the development of new diving techniques and systems which will enable divers to live and work in the sea for extended periods of time.
Business and Economics; Physical Education and Recreation; Science
Dist - USNAC **Prod** - USN 1973

World of the Seance 30 MIN
16mm
Color (R)
Reveals how people are tricked into believing they are communicating with the dead during a seance.
Guidance and Counseling; Religion and Philosophy
Dist - GF **Prod** - GF

World of the unborn 52 MIN
VHS
Color; PAL (G H)
PdS30 purchase
Follows the story of the creation of a new human life. Starts with the birth of a baby to show how each child can inherit a unique genetic constitution from its parents. Contact distributor about availability outside the United Kingdom.
Science - Natural; Sociology
Dist - ACADEM

World of the yeshiva 12 MIN
16mm
Color (G)
$25.00 rental
Depicts the life in an institution with a 2,000 - year - old tradition, the old world of the yeshivot or rabbinical academies. Introduces students in a Jerusalem yeshiva, looks at their daily life, how they pray and study, their revered teachers and the unceasing study of Torah for its own sake. Made for Beth Hatefutsth, the Museum of the Jewish Diaspora in Tel Aviv.
Fine Arts; Religion and Philosophy; Sociology
Dist - NCJEWF

The World of Theodore Wores 26 MIN
16mm
Color (H A)
$475.00 purchase, $50.00 rental
Features San Francisco artist Theodore Wores, 1859 - 1939. Produced by Ben Shenson and A. Jess Shenson.
Fine Arts; Industrial and Technical Education
Dist - AFA

The World of Tomorrow 84 MIN
Color; B&W (J A G)
Documents the great New York World's Fair of 1939 and the more than 40 million people who glimpsed the future there. Incorporates home movies, newsreels, cartoons, photographs, and vintage graphics to evoke that fragile moment when the world stood poised between black and white and color, between the Great Depression and the Second World War.
History - United States
Dist - DIRECT **Prod** - NIERNG 1985

World of two kings - Tape 2 30 MIN
VHS
Jesus Christ series
Color (J H C G A)
$39.95 purchase, $10.00 rental _ #35 - 860542 - 1
Attempts to give a profile of the people who heard Jesus. Suggests that such a profile can provide a valuable perspective on who he was.
Literature and Drama; Religion and Philosophy
Dist - APH **Prod** - ABINGP

The World of U S holsteins 19 MIN
16mm
Color (PORTUGUESE SPANISH)
Shows details concerning the export of U S Holsteins to other countries.
Agriculture
Dist - HFAA **Prod** - HFAA

The World of Up Close 9 MIN
U-matic / VHS / 16mm
Wonder Walks Series
Color (P I)
LC 75-713437
Views commonly seen objects in extra close - up range.
Industrial and Technical Education; Science - Natural; Social Science
Dist - EBEC **Prod** - EBEC 1971

The World of Vatican II - an artist's report 30 MIN
U-matic / VHS / 16mm
Artist as a reporter series
Color (J)
LC FIA67-1107
Presents artist - reporter Franklin Mc Mahon discussing the Vatican Councils and its world - wide implications. Includes paintings and drawings made by the artists in Rome, Japan, India and the United States.
Fine Arts; Religion and Philosophy
Dist - PHENIX **Prod** - ROCSS 1967

The World of William Shakespeare 15 MIN
U-matic
Great English Writers Series
Color (H C A)
Tells how Shakespeare's writings brought the occurrences of the Elizabethan Age into personal terms.
Biography; History - World; Literature and Drama
Dist - CEPRO **Prod** - CEPRO

The World of William Shakespeare - 3 15 MIN
VHS / U-matic
Great English writers series
Color (H C G)
$240.00, $215.00 purchase _ #V323
Examines the life of William Shakespeare, born in Stratford - on - Avon around 1574. Tells how he went to London and became the city's leading playwright. Shows how he touched on the universal themes of tragedy, humor, compassion and understanding and how his writings continue to live on over the centuries. Part three of a three - part series looking at Chaucer, Shakespeare and Dickens.
Literature and Drama
Dist - BARR **Prod** - CEPRO 1986

World of William Shakespeare Series
Fair is Foul, and Foul is Fair 20 MIN
Hamlet 35 MIN
Macbeth 36 MIN
Romeo and Juliet 36 MIN
Shakespeare of Stratford and London 32 MIN
Star - Crossed Love 20 MIN
The Time is Out of Joint 20 MIN
Dist - NGS

The World of work 14 MIN
16mm
Library of career counseling films series
Color (J H)
LC 74-702068
Divides the world of work into major categories and shows selected occupations in each. Examines many possibilities and suggests how to go about each. Considers both the satisfaction people derive from work and the relationship between their own talent, interests and values and the requirements of major career fields.
Guidance and Counseling; Psychology
Dist - COUNFI **Prod** - COUNFI 1974

World of work 30 MIN
U-matic / VHS
Making a living work series; Program 105
Color (C A)
Focuses on working women and transferable skills. Shows several women talking about their experiences as working mothers. Examines the need for changes in the world of work as the needs of the work force change. Includes such ideas as flextime.
Guidance and Counseling; Sociology
Dist - OHUTC **Prod** - OHUTC

The World of Work 12 MIN
VHS
$89.95 purchase _ #005 - 715
Uses a cartoon format to explain how to find and keep a job. Points out why it is sometimes necessary to start at the bottom and work toward advancement.
Guidance and Counseling
Dist - CAREER **Prod** - CAREER

World of work 30 MIN
VHS
Making a living work series
Color (G A C)
$150.00 purchase _ #JW850V; $225.00 purchase _ #013 - 536; $225.00 purchase _ JWOT5V; $150.00 purchase _ #PAOT5V
Suggests that the rapid changes in the work world make transferrable skills - especially people - oriented ones - essential. Considers how learning and leisure relate to these matters.
Business and Economics; Psychology
Dist - CAMV CAREER JISTW **Prod** - CAREER OHUTC

World of Work 19 MIN
U-matic / VHS
Jobs - Seeking, Finding, Keeping Series
Color (H)
Profiles three young people who aren't sure what they want to do with their lives but who agree that they should seek careers by choice, not chance.
Guidance and Counseling
Dist - AITECH **Prod** - MDDE 1980

The World of work - feelings and problems involved in getting a job 12 MIN
VHS
Color (H C A)
$89.95 purchase _ #333VEG
Presents an animated cartoon to explain finding and keeping a job. Covers issues of personal hygiene, dress and attitude. Looks at tips for successful job hunting.
Psychology; Sociology
Dist - UNL

The World of work - intercultural aspects 15 MIN
16mm
Job hunt game series; Show 5
Color
Discusses how employees affect others, how to bridge cultural gaps and the importance of punctuality and reliability.
Guidance and Counseling; Psychology
Dist - ICVT **Prod** - ICVT 1982

World of Work Series
Country Vet 12 MIN
Intern - a Long Year 20 MIN
Rescue Squad 14 MIN
Tugboat Captain 14 MIN
Dist - EBEC

World of Work Series
Guide to tomorrow's jobs - the hidden job - how to find it 60 MIN
Dist - GPN

World of Work
Is technology stealing your job? 60 MIN
Where will You Work Tomorrow 60 MIN
Dist - GPN

World Orthodoxy 28 MIN
VHS
Illuminations series
Color (G R)
#V - 1029
Provides insights into Eastern Orthodox Christianity. Notes that all Orthodox churches, though somewhat loosely organized, accept the Patriarch of Constantinople as their spiritual leader. Focuses on the unique Orthodox outlook on Christian faith.
Religion and Philosophy
Dist - GOTEL **Prod** - GOTEL 1989

The World Outside 31 MIN
16mm
B&W (C A)
LC FIA65-1588
Illustrates some central concepts of therapy with severely emotionally disturbed children. Filmed at the Marianne Frostig School of Educational Therapy in Los Angeles.
Education; Psychology
Dist - SLFP **Prod** - SLFP 1963

The World Outside 34 MIN
16mm
To Get from Here to There Series
Color (H)
Discusses street and highway design with stress on necessary improvements.
Health and Safety; Psychology
Dist - PROART **Prod** - PROART

World peace 60 MIN
VHS / BETA
Color; PAL (G)
PdS2 purchase
Follows the Dalai Lama's tour of Britain in 1984. Records his final public talk in Westminster Abbey, London. Sums up the difficulties facing the world today. He points out that whether conflicts are personal or national, political or

religious, between East and West or North and South, they are all created by ourselves and therefore always open to change. For positive change, He stresses the need for hope, courage and determination together with good human qualities such as kindness and a warm heart. At the end, questions stimulate some thought - provoking views on global politics, economics and education. His replies and most of the talk are in English. Translated by Prof Jeffrey Hopkins.
Civics and Political Systems; Fine Arts; Religion and Philosophy; Social Science
Dist - MERIDT

World peace is a local issue 20 MIN
U-matic / VHS / 16mm
Color
Documents a textbook example of democracy at its best, the grassroots impact of the citizenry upon units of government. Shows how an aroused citizenry in California espoused their views in a prolonged presentation to a city council and got support for a resolution endorsing a Soviet/American Bilateral Nuclear Weapons freeze.
Civics and Political Systems
Dist - CNEMAG **Prod** - FADMND 1984

The World peace march 6 MIN
VHS
Color (G)
$14.95 purchase
Looks at the World Peace March as it arrived in the Hudson Valley en route to the United Nations Special Session on Disarmament in 1982.
History - United States; Religion and Philosophy; Sociology
Dist - WMMI **Prod** - WMMI 1982

World population 4 MIN
16mm / U-matic / VHS
Color (J)
LC 73-702083
Condenses 200 years of world population growth with statistical accuracy and stresses the importance of population control as fundamental to the solution of environmental crisis.
Science - Natural; Sociology
Dist - CORF **Prod** - PERSPF 1973

World population 7 MIN
VHS
Color (P I J H C G A)
$29.95 purchase
Uses strong graphic images to show how the world's population is growing at an alarming rate. Reveals that the population has increased fourfold since 1900, and is expected to double again by the year 2030. Includes activity and discussion guide. Produced by Zero Population Growth, Inc and Southern Illinois University.
History - World; Social Science
Dist - EFVP

World population 7 MIN
16mm / VHS
Color (G)
Updates the 1972 version. Provides graphic simulation of the history of human population growth, from 1 AD to the year 2020. Includes activity and discussion guide.
Sociology
Dist - ZPG **Prod** - ZPG

World Population, 1000 B C - 1965 a D 4 MIN
16mm
Color
LC FIA67-707
Uses an animated population record on a dymaxion air ocean world map to trace the growth of the world's population from the year 1,000 B C to 1965 A D.
History - World; Psychology; Science - Natural; Social Science; Sociology
Dist - SIUFP **Prod** - SILLU 1965

The World religions - 600 BC - AD 500 30 MIN
VHS
World - A Television history series
Color (C A)
$55.00 rental
Covers the historical development of the world religions in the period from 600 B C to A D 500. Based on The Times Atlas Of World History. Serves as part six of a 26 - part telecourse. Available only to institutions of higher education.
History - World; Sociology
Dist - SCETV **Prod** - SCETV 1986

The World religions - 600 BC - AD 500 26 MIN
U-matic / VHS / 16mm
World - a television history series
Color (J H C)
$475.00, $400.00 purchase
Describes the great world religions of Hinduism, Buddhism, Judaism, Christianity, Islam, Zoroastrianism and Taoism which were all developed in Asia within a thousand years.
History - World; Religion and Philosophy
Dist - LANDMK **Prod** - NETGOL 1985

The World religions - 600 BC to AD 500 26 MIN
VHS
Color (J H C G A R)
$10.00 rental _ #36 - 80 - 216
Reveals that seven of the world's great religions - Hinduism, Buddhism, Judaism, Christianity, Islam, Zoroastrianism and Taoism - all developed in Asia during a thousand year period.
Religion and Philosophy
Dist - APH **Prod** - LANDMK

World Series
Three Days in Szczecin
Dist - GRATV

World Series
The Search for Sandra Laing
Dist - INTENC

World series
The Chinese way 58 MIN
Dist - PBS

The World shadow 3 MIN
16mm
Color; Silent (C)
$112.00
Presents an experimental film by Stan Brakhage.
Fine Arts
Dist - AFA **Prod** - AFA

A World Society 29 MIN
U-matic
On to Tomorrow Series
Color
Looks at political, cultural and value dimensions of technology. Discusses the importing of technology by developing nations.
Business and Economics; Sociology
Dist - UMITV **Prod** - UMITV 1976

World song 15 MIN
VHS
Color (G)
$295.00 purchase
Shows people of many lands and cultures celebrating the life experiences common to all peoples - growing up, falling in love, giving birth, sorrowing at death. Reminds the viewer that all peoples have more commonalities than differences. Produced by BRC Imagination Arts.
Sociology
Dist - PFP

World Streets and Avenues 20 MIN
U-matic
Understanding Our World, Unit I - Tools We Use Series
Color (I)
Discusses latitude and longitude with host John Rugg.
Social Science
Dist - GPN **Prod** - KRMATV

World Sugar 11 MIN
16mm
Color (J H)
Discusses the sugar industry. Covers both sugar cane and sugar beets.
Agriculture; Home Economics
Dist - VIEWTH **Prod** - GATEEF

The World that Moses Built 60 MIN
VHS
American Experience Series
Color; Captioned (G)
$59.95 purchase _ #AMEX - 115
Focuses on the career of urban planner Robert Moses, who designed and constructed many public projects in New York City. Discusses how his projects often displaced people, particularly in ghettos. Probes the potential conflict between individual liberty and public order.
Geography - United States; Industrial and Technical Education; Sociology
Dist - PBS **Prod** - WGBHTV 1988

The World, the flesh and Jimmy Jones 13 MIN
16mm
B&W
Reviews the life of one of America's 600,000 victims of cerebral palsy from the day the diagnosis was made through the therapies, special education and vocational training through the frustrating period of job - seeking.
Education; Health and Safety; Psychology
Dist - UCPA **Prod** - UCPA

A World to Perceive - Perception 29 MIN
U-matic / VHS / 16mm
Focus on Behavior Series
B&W (H C A)
Discusses basic theories and methods for investigating perception. Explains the role of perception in handling and processing information from the environment and the way in which our personalities affect our perception.
Psychology
Dist - IU **Prod** - NET 1963

World Tour 90 MIN
VHS / U-matic
Color
Documents Swami Satchidananda's 1970 World Service Tour. Portrays Sri Gurudev's life of dedication to humanity.
Religion and Philosophy
Dist - IYOGA **Prod** - IYOGA

World Track and Field Cups, 1977, 1979, 1981 165 MIN
U-matic / VHS
IAAF Videocassettes Series
Color (H C A)
Features highlights of world track and field cups.
Physical Education and Recreation
Dist - TRACKN **Prod** - TRACKN 1984

The World Tree - a Scandinavian Creation Myth 10 MIN
U-matic / VHS
Color
Depicts the beginning of the world according to a Scandinavian creation myth. Using animation, it shows opposing forces of fire and ice, frost giant and ice cow, trolls and the most important Scandinavian Gods. Covers how the Gods created the earth, mountains, rivers, the sky, grass, animals and plants, and dividing time into night and day. Concludes with gods transforming two trees into man and woman and, finally, bringing a world tree into being to form a bridge between the gods and the universe they had created.
Geography - World; History - World; Literature and Drama; Religion and Philosophy
Dist - IFF **Prod** - IFF

The World Tree - the Scandinavian Creation Myth 10 MIN
16mm
Color (J)
LC 78-700234
Uses Scandinavian rock and cave drawings to illustrate the Scandinavian creation myth.
History - World; Literature and Drama; Religion and Philosophy; Sociology
Dist - IFF **Prod** - NOITA 1977

A World Turned Upside Down 35 MIN
VHS / U-matic
Color (G PRO)
$795.00, $695.00 purchase, $200.00 rental
Features Tom Peters in a speech to the Royal Society for the Encouragement of Arts, Manufacture and Commerce, England. States that only those organizations which create an environment that welcomes change will thrive.
Business and Economics; Guidance and Counseling; Sociology
Dist - VPHI **Prod** - VPHI 1989

The World turned upside down 52 MIN
16mm
American heritage series
Color (H C)
Continuation of the film Washington - Time Of Triumph. Follows George Washington to provide a view of General Cornwallis' surrender. Portrays how Washington, after the surrender, refused absolute power in order that democracy might work.
Civics and Political Systems; History - United States
Dist - FI **Prod** - WOLPER 1974

The World Turned Upside Down 15 MIN
U-matic / VHS / 16mm
American Scrapbook Series
Color (I)
Follows British and American soldiers during the Revolutionary War. Re - creates battle scenes in New York and Virginia.
History - United States
Dist - GPN **Prod** - WVIZTV 1977

A World turned upside down 35 MIN
VHS / 16mm
Color (PRO)
$695.00 purchase, $185.00 rental, $50.00 preview
Discusses how the slow response of American companies to economic change damages the US economy. Explains how organizations must welcome change. Includes a viewer's guide.
Business and Economics; Education; Guidance and Counseling; Psychology
Dist - UTM **Prod** - UTM

The World upside down 30 MIN
U-matic / VHS
Color (A)
Tells what is happening to disciples' ministries overseas. Looks at the church in Zaire. Stresses the values of church and scriptures.

Religion and Philosophy
Dist - ECUFLM **Prod** - DCCMS 1982

World vista
CD-ROM
Color (J H C G)
$79.95 purchase _ #BO12R5, #BO13R5
Uses maps and data from Rand McNally, Inc. Includes more than 1000 full - color images of landmarks, scenery, people, examples of music and 12 standard phrases spoken in the native languages of all the countries in the world. Allows easy access through visual interface. Designed for latest multimedia platforms in PCs and the MAC. Requires 2MN.
Foreign Language; Geography - World; History - World; Social Science
Dist - CAMV

A World war 60 MIN
VHS
Eagle's nest series
Color (G)
$29.95 purchase _ #1629
Portrays events during the 1940s and World War II. Part of a four - part series on Hitler, the German Reich and World War II considered from the perspective of the Nazi inner - circle.
Biography; Foreign Language; History - World
Dist - KULTUR **Prod** - KULTUR 1991

World War 2 30 MIN
VHS / U-matic
America - the second century series
Color (C H)
$34.95 purchase
Shows how the U S, the super nation with the super weapon, emerged from World War II with a responsibility to help reshape the postwar world.
History - United States
Dist - DALCCD **Prod** - DALCCD
GPN

World War I 25 MIN
16mm / U-matic / VHS
American History Series
Color (J H)
LC 75-702076
Discusses the domestic situation in the United States in 1914, the efforts of President Wilson to enact progressive reforms and to stay out of the European war, and the effects of the war on the domestic program.
Civics and Political Systems; History - United States; History - World
Dist - MGHT **Prod** - PSP 1969

World War I 25 MIN
VHS
Coburn collection series
Color (G)
Contact distributor about rental cost _ #N92 - 001
Highlights Indiana's contribution to World War I, including training scenes at Fort Benjamin Harrison, patriotic activities, Armistice Day, and construction of the Indiana War Memorial.
History - United States; Sociology
Dist - INDI

World War I 45 MIN
U-matic / Kit / VHS
Western Man and the Modern World in Video
Color (J H)
$1378.12 the 25 part series _ #C676 - 27347 - 5, $89.95 the individual
Uses battlefield photos, the poetry of Sassoon and Owen and contemporary sketches to depict the human toll taken by World War I.
History - World
Dist - RH

World War I 45 MIN
35mm strip / VHS
Western man and the modern world series - Unit V
Color (J H C T A)
$102.00, $102.00 purchase _ #MB - 510390 - 7, #MB - 510267 - 6
Presents an 'at - the - front' account of the human costs of World War I. Features battlefield photographs, sketches, and written accounts. Shows that new war technologies such as aircraft, tanks, and poison gas changed war forever.
History - World; Sociology
Dist - SRA

World War I - a documentary on the role of the U S A 28 MIN
16mm / U-matic / VHS
B&W (J H C) (ENGLISH, SPANISH)
Describes the events which led the United States into war, the course of the war and Wilson's role at the peace conference.
Civics and Political Systems; History - United States; History - World
Dist - EBEC **Prod** - EBEC 1957

World War I - Armistice 30 MIN
U-matic / VHS
How Wars End Series
Color (G)
$249.00, $149.00 purchase _ #AD - 912
Reveals that the war that began without any war aims other than winning ended in a rush to armistice, with different warring nations simply signing with the nearest available member of the Allies. Reports that the armistice neither defined nor resolved the war aims, but left everything to the peace treaty. Part of a six - part series on how wars end, hosted by historian A J P Taylor.
History - United States; History - World; Sociology
Dist - FOTH **Prod** - FOTH

World War I - background tensions 13 MIN
VHS
World War I series
Color; PAL (H)
Examines the assassination of Archduke Ferdinand at Sarajevo which drew the nations of Europe into World War I. Uses archival footage and dramatic narrative to portray the leaders who talked of peace but gave way to war after the assassination.
Civics and Political Systems; History - World; Sociology
Dist - VIEWTH

World War I - fighting on two fronts 18 MIN
VHS
World War I series
Color; PAL (H)
Chronicles the world's first mechanized war with battles on land, sea and in the air, which began in the summer of 1914. Reveals that both Allied and Central powers believed it would be a short war.
Civics and Political Systems; History - World; Sociology
Dist - VIEWTH

World War I - Here and 'Over There' 28 MIN
16mm
B&W (H A)
Presents 'Oregon's finest' in training and on the parade ground, combined with U S Army Signal Corps footage which was unreleased at the time of WW I.
History - United States
Dist - OREGHS **Prod** - OREGHS

World War I - historically speaking 30 MIN
U-matic / VHS
Historically speaking series; Pt 19
Color (H)
Looks at the general causes of World War I and the assassination of Archduke Ferdinand. Reveals the permanent changes the war caused in European life.
History - World
Dist - AITECH **Prod** - KRMATV 1983

World War I Overseas Fliers Reunion 12 MIN
16mm
Color
LC 74-705970
Reviews exploits of America's first fighter pilots as World War I airmen hold their first reunion at USAF Museum at Wright - Patterson AFB. Features presentation of awards and excerpts of speeches.
Civics and Political Systems; History - United States; Industrial and Technical Education
Dist - USNAC **Prod** - USAF 1962

World War I series
The Politics of peace making 14 MIN
Dist - CORF

World War I Series
Assassination at Sarajevo - pretext for war 16 MIN
The Day the Guns Stopped Firing - 1918 18 MIN
Doomed dynasties of Europe 16 MIN
Home front, 1917 - 1919 - war transforms American life 17 MIN
Revolution in Russia, 1917 19 MIN
The Sinking of the Lusitania 17 MIN
The Sinking of the Lusitania - Unrestricted Submarine Warfare 17 MIN
Soviet Union - Civil War and Allied Intervention 17 MIN
Soviet Union, 1918 - 1920 - Civil War and Allied Intervention 17 MIN
U S Neutrality, 1914 - 1917 17 MIN
Dist - FI

World War I series
World War I - background tensions 13 MIN
World War I - fighting on two fronts 18 MIN
World War I - the politics of peacemaking 14 MIN
Dist - VIEWTH

World War I - the politics of peacemaking 14 MIN
VHS
World War I series
Color; PAL (H)
Recalls the arrival in 1917 of American troops, with representatives of every ethnic group, into the European theater of World War I. Looks at the signing of the armistice in November, 1918, and the highly politicized negotiations at Versailles of a flawed treaty which led to World War II.
Civics and Political Systems; History - World; Sociology
Dist - VIEWTH

World War II 30 MIN
U-matic / VHS
Historically speaking series; Pt 22
Color (H)
Shows how the Western policy of appeasement failed to prevent aggression by Axis nations. Views the persecution of the Jews, the war itself and its results.
History - World
Dist - AITECH **Prod** - KRMATV 1983

World War II 52 MIN
VHS
History machine series
B&W (H C G)
Documents the American home front during the war in 1941 - 1945, the Casablanca Summit meeting in January of 1943, the East - West summit in Cairo and Teheran in November, 1943, D - Day on June 6, 1944, the atomic bomb project in 1939 - 1945, the Crimean conference in Yalta in February, 1945, and the situation of Japanese - Americans, 1941 - 1945. Part of a seven - part historical series on American history produced by Arthur M Schlesinger, Jr, and a team of historians and film editors.
History - United States; Sociology
Dist - VIEWTH **Prod** - VIEWTH

World War II 30 MIN
VHS
Color (J H G)
$98.00 purchase _ #TK105
Surveys World War II. Discusses the rise of Hitler and the Nazi party, the Holocaust, blitzkrieg warfare, the first use of the atomic bomb, rationing, mass production and patriotism in the United States. Video transfer from filmstrip.
Civics and Political Systems; History - United States; History - World; Sociology
Dist - KNOWUN

World War II - 1922 - 1945
VHS
Hearst News library series
Color (G)
$29.95 purchase _ #TK039
Presents dramatic war footage and rare news clips tracing the history of World War II from the rise of Hitler to V - J Day. Part of a series excerpted from 350 newsreels from the Hearst News Library.
Civics and Political Systems; History - United States; History - World
Dist - SIV

World War II - a fragile peace - 1918 - 1929 11 MIN
VHS
World War II series
Color; PAL (H)
Focuses on the growing world unrest which eroded the spirit of optimism following the signing of the Treaty of Versailles. Examines the problems of homelessness, unemployment and war debts in Europe and the debacle of the 'Roaring '20s' in the United States with the stock market crash.
Business and Economics; Civics and Political Systems; History - World; Sociology
Dist - VIEWTH

World War II - a personal journey 184 MIN
VHS
Color (J H C G)
$98.95 purchase _ #IVN065SV
Presents four volumes on World War II. Includes 1941 - 42; 1943; 1944; and 1945 recalled through interviews with participants in the war - Gerald Ford, Senator Robert Dole, Mike Wallace and others.
History - United States; History - World; Sociology
Dist - CAMV

World War II - a world at war - 1942 - 1945 16 MIN
VHS
World War II series
Color; PAL (H)
Watches as the United States prepares for war. Reveals that as men are inducted into the military and trained, women are accepted as military volunteers and workers in the war industries. By May, 1945, Italy and Germany have surrendered, and in August, 1945, the atomic age begins with the dropping of two bombs on Nagasaki and Hiroshima, Japan. Six months later World War II ends, after 50 million casualties and massive destruction.

Civics and Political Systems; History - United States; History - World; Sociology
Dist - VIEWTH

World War II - G I Diary Series

The Bulge	30 MIN
D - Day - One Bad Day in June	30 MIN
The Flying fortress	30 MIN
Hell in the Arctic	30 MIN
Iwo jima - eight square miles of hell	30 MIN
The Last Barrier - Crossing the Rhine	30 MIN
Medal of Honor	30 MIN
Nightmare at San Pedro	30 MIN
Peleliu - the Killing Ground	30 MIN
Road to Berlin	30 MIN
Savage Road to China	30 MIN
The Toughest Target	30 MIN

Dist - AMBROS

World war II - G I diary series

The Battle for Saipan	30 MIN
Big ben	30 MIN
Sicily - the Yanks are coming	30 MIN

Dist - AMBROS
TIMLIF

World War II - G I diary series

The Flying fortress	30 MIN
Iwo Jima - eight square miles of hell	30 MIN

Dist - TIMLIF

World War II - GI Diary Series

Americans in Paris	30 MIN
Anzio to Rome	30 MIN
The Bulge	30 MIN
D - Day - One Bad Day in June	30 MIN
Desert war	30 MIN
The Double strike - air force raids on Schweinfurt - Regensburg	30 MIN
GI Christmas	30 MIN
Hell in the Arctic	30 MIN
Kamikaze - Flower of Death	30 MIN
The Last Barrier - Crossing the Rhine	30 MIN
Medal of Honor	30 MIN
Midway	30 MIN
Nightmare at San Pietro	30 MIN
Okinawa - at the Emperor's Doorstep	30 MIN
Peleliu - the Killing Ground	30 MIN
Return to the Philippines	30 MIN
Road to Berlin	30 MIN
Savage Road to China	30 MIN
Target - Tokyo	30 MIN
The Toughest Target	30 MIN

Dist - TIMLIF

World War II in the Pacific 15 MIN
U-matic / VHS
Color (PRO)
Portrays Japan's rise as an industrial power from the opening of foreign trade to expansionism and defeat in WWII. Uses seldom seen WWII photographs. Looks at modern Japan.
Civics and Political Systems; History - United States; History - World; Sociology
Dist - USNAC **Prod** - USNPS 1983

World War II planes series
Presents three videos on World War II aircraft. Includes the Curtiss P - 40 Warhawk, the Mitchell B - 25 Bomber and the B - 17 Flying Fortress.
B-17 Flying Fortress
Curtiss P - 40 Warhawk
Mitchell B - 25 Bomber
World War II planes series
Dist - SIV

World War II - prologue, U S A 29 MIN
16mm / U-matic / VHS
B&W (J H C) (ENGLISH, SPANISH)
Reviews the events that led the U S into the war, showing the different stages of public opinion as events in Europe took place. Follows the conflict of World War II from Japan's invasion of Manchuria to the bombing of Pearl Harbor and the entry of the U S.
History - United States; History - World
Dist - EBEC **Prod** - EBEC 1956

World War II Series

The Expanding Conflict - 1940 - 1941	12 MIN
A Fragile Peace - 1918 - 1929	11 MIN
The Inevitable War - 1939 - 1940	13 MIN
The Roots of Aggression - 1929 - 1939	14 MIN
A World at war - 1942 - 1945	16 MIN

Dist - CORF

World War II series

World War II - a fragile peace - 1918 - 1929	11 MIN
World War II - a world at war - 1942 - 1945	16 MIN
World War II - the expanding conflict - 1940 - 1941	12 MIN
World War II - the inevitable war - 1939 - 1940	13 MIN
World War II - the roots of aggression - 1929 - 1939	14 MIN

Dist - VIEWTH

World War II - The Allies 21 MIN
VHS
Color (I J H G)
$49.95 purchase _ #3035D
Offers biographies of the leaders of the World War II Allies - Winston Churchill, Josef Stalin, Franklin D Roosevelt, Chiang Kai - shek, Charles de Gaulle and Harry S Truman. Features Bob Considine as host.
Biography; Civics and Political Systems; History - World
Dist - INSTRU

World War II - The Axis 14 MIN
VHS
Color (I J H G)
$49.95 purchase _ #3036D
Offers biographies of the leaders of the World War II Axis powers - Adolph Hitler, Hermann Goering, Hideki Tojo and Benito Mussolini. Features Bob Considine as host.
Civics and Political Systems; History - World
Dist - INSTRU

World War II - the Dark Years in Europe 15 MIN
VHS
Witness to History Series
Color (J H)
$49.00 purchase _ #60155
Presents scenes of the Blitzkrieg, Dunkirk, The Battle of Britain, and the German invasion of Russia.
History - United States; History - World; Sociology
Dist - GA **Prod** - GA 1989

World War II - the Eastern Front 30 MIN
16mm / VHS
Color (H A)
$395.00, $495.00 purchase, $50.00 rental _ #8045
Uses historic footage to trace World War II on the eastern front. Shows through animated maps the sieges of Leningrad and Moscow and the attacks on the Caucasian oilfields. Evokes the incredible losses suffered by the Soviet Union during the war.
Geography - World; History - United States; History - World
Dist - AIMS **Prod** - AIMS 1983

World War II - the expanding conflict - 1940 - 1941 12 MIN
VHS
World War II series
Color; PAL (H)
Reveals that in October, 1940, Hitler and Germany dominated Europe to the Russian border, Italian troops invaded Egypt and Greece, and Japan had taken the French colonies south of China. Looks at spring, 1941, when Hitler, believing Britain to be nearly defeated, mobilized German forces to attack Russia. The United States placed an embargo on the sale of oil to Japan, and Japan planned to retaliate in an attack upon the Americans and British in the Pacific on December 7 and 8 of 1941.
Civics and Political Systems; History - United States; History - World; Sociology
Dist - VIEWTH

World War II - the inevitable war - 1939 - 1940 13 MIN
VHS
World War II series
Color; PAL (H)
Examines the fall of Western Europe and Poland under German domination in the early years of World War II. Recalls the dramatic rescue of French and British troups at Dunkirk and the intense bombing of Britain. Then, a pact among Japan, Germany and Italy creates a formidable and, perhaps, undefeatable alliance.
Civics and Political Systems; History - World; Sociology
Dist - VIEWTH

World War II - the Pacific 15 MIN
VHS
Witness to history I series
Color (J H)
$49.00 purchase _ #06822 - 026
Views the attack at Pearl Harbor from an attacking aircraft. Shows Roosevelt delivering his war message to Congress, troops landing at Iwo Jima and the bombing of Nagasaki and Hiroshima, along with the joyous celebrations on V - J Day. Part of a four - part series. Includes teacher's guide and library kit.
Education; Fine Arts; History - United States
Dist - GA

World War II - the Pacific 15 MIN
VHS
Color (J H)
$49.00 purchase _ #06822 - 026
Presents an eyewitness view from an enemy aircraft attacking Pearl Harbor. Includes footage of Franklin Delano Roosevelt delivering his war message to Congress, troops landing at Iwo Jima and the atomic bombs dropped on Nagasaki and Hiroshima, the celebrations on V - J Day. Includes teachers' guide and library kit.
Civics and Political Systems; History - United States; Sociology
Dist - INSTRU

World War II - the Propaganda Battle 58 MIN
VHS / U-matic
Walk through the 20th Century with Bill Moyers Series
Color
Describes how World War II saw two motion picture experts from Germany and the United States battle to make films that would inspire and instill the desire to win the war. Features filmmakers Frank Capra of the United States and Fritz Hippler of Germany.
Fine Arts; History - United States; History - World; Sociology
Dist - PBS **Prod** - CORPEL 1982

World War II - the roots of aggression - 1929 - 1939 14 MIN
VHS
World War II series
Color; PAL (H)
Looks at the end of the 1920s and world prosperity. Follows the occupation of Manchuria by Japan and its war with China, and the rise in power of Hitler in economically depressed Germany. After the formation of the 'Axis' between Italy and Germany, Italy invades Ethiopia and Germany invades Austria and, after signing a pact with Russia, Poland. World War II has begun.
Business and Economics; Civics and Political Systems; History - World; Sociology
Dist - VIEWTH

World War II with Walter Cronkite Series

Europe - the Allies Close in	90 MIN
Walter Cronkite Remembers and the Battle of the Bulge	60 MIN

Dist - CBSVL

World War One 28 MIN
16mm
Glory and the Dream - Ohio's Response to War Series
Color
Describes Ohio's response to World War I. Covers events leading to the war, the war itself, and the period immediately following the war.
History - United States; History - World
Dist - HRC **Prod** - OHC

World War Two 25 MIN
16mm
Glory and the Dream - Ohio's Response to War Series
Color
Describes Ohio's reaction to World War II. Discusses conscientious objectors, war protests and prisioners of war.
History - United States; History - World
Dist - HRC **Prod** - OHC

The World was all before them 30 MIN
U-matic / VHS
Art of being human series; Module 15
Color (C)
History - World; Literature and Drama; Religion and Philosophy
Dist - MDCC **Prod** - MDCC

World was there 28 MIN
U-matic / VHS
Color
LC 80-707384
Shows how the news media of the world covered the manned space launches of NASA's Project Mercury. Covers the flights of astronauts Shepard, Grissom, Glenn, Carpenter, Schirra and Cooper. Narrated by Alexander Scourby. Issued in 1975 as a motion picture.
Industrial and Technical Education; Science - Physical
Dist - USNAC **Prod** - NASA 1980

The World We Live in 15 MIN
U-matic / VHS
Arts Express Series
Color (K P I J)
Fine Arts
Dist - KYTV **Prod** - KYTV 1983

World We Live in Series

Animal war, animal peace	30 MIN
Antarctica - because it's there	29 MIN
The Child watchers	30 MIN
The Dam Builders	30 MIN
Life in Parched Lands	30 MIN
Questions of time	30 MIN
Riddle of Heredity	29 MIN
The Sun Watchers	30 MIN

Survival in the Sea	30 MIN
Water - Old Problems, New Approaches	30 MIN
The Weather Watchers	30 MIN

Dist - MGHT

The World We Live in - Venture Read - Alongs 110 MIN
U-matic / VHS
Venture Read - Alongs Series
(P I)
Contains a read along cassette and 8 paperbacks.
Social Science
Dist - TROLA **Prod** - TROLA 1986

World weather disc
CD-ROM
(PRO A)
$289.00 purchase _ #1373
Describes the climate of the Earth today and during the past few hundred years. Teaches HVAC engineers, climatologists and TV weatherpeople. For IBM PCs and compatibles. Requires at least 640K RAM, DOS Version 3.1 or greater, one floppy disk drive - a hard drive is recommended, one empty expansion slot, and an IBM compatible CD - ROM drive.
Geography - World; Science - Physical
Dist - BEP

World - Wide Fallout from Nuclear Weapons 41 MIN
16mm / U-matic / VHS
Color
Explains what is and is not known about the long - term consequences of world - wide fallout. Discusses only the fallout on which a substantial amount of information is available, to correct any factually unsupported statements which may have been issued.
Civics and Political Systems; Industrial and Technical Education; Science - Physical; Sociology
Dist - USNAC **Prod** - USDD

World - Wide Naval Operations in Peace and War - 1815 - 1860 23 MIN
16mm
History of the United States Navy
Color
Describes contributions to naval science, such as the development of steam power, and the navy's role in protecting American citizens and promoting trade.
Civics and Political Systems; History - United States
Dist - USNAC **Prod** - USN 1956

A World within a World 10 MIN
16mm
Color
LC 79-701314
Depicts the function of duty - free shops and seastores around the world.
Geography - World; Home Economics
Dist - PHILMO **Prod** - PHILMO 1979

World within a World - the Maximum Containment Laboratory 24 MIN
16mm
Color
LC 78-701150
Describes principles and procedures used to safely operate a class IV laboratory which handles virulent viruses and hazardous DNA.
Science
Dist - USNAC **Prod** - CFDISC 1978

World within a World - the Maximum Containment Laboratory 5 MIN
VHS / U-matic
Color
LC 80-706767
Describes the need for and construction of a modular laboratory. Longer version issued in 1978.
Science
Dist - USNAC **Prod** - CFDISC 1979

The World within - C G Jung in his own words and Remembering Jung - Laurens van der Post discusses Jung 80 MIN
16mm / VHS
Color; B&W (G)
$300.00 rental
Portrays Carl Gustav Jung. Directed by Suzanne Wagner.
Fine Arts; Psychology
Dist - KINOIC

World within World - Pt 1 26 MIN
16mm / U-matic
Ascent of Man Series
Color (H C A)
LC 74-702263
Explores the world within the atom and traces the history of humanity and ideas that have made 20th-century physics. Narrated by Dr Jacob Bronowski of the Salk Institute.
Science; Science - Physical
Dist - TIMLIF **Prod** - BBCTV 1973

World within World - Pt 2 26 MIN
16mm / U-matic
Ascent of Man Series
Color (H C A)
LC 74-702263
Explores the world within the atom and traces the history of humanity and ideas that have made 20th-century physics. Narrated by Dr Jacob Bronowski of the Salk Institute.
Science; Science - Physical
Dist - TIMLIF **Prod** - BBCTV 1973

World within Worlds 23 MIN
U-matic / VHS / 16mm
Color (H C A)
LC 81-700382
Shows how different photographic techniques, such as microphotography, time - lapse photography, Kirlian photography, and ultraviolet photography, can overcome obstacles of size and time and depict things that were previously invisible.
Industrial and Technical Education
Dist - NGS **Prod** - NGS 1981

World Without Sun 93 MIN
16mm
Color
Illustrates Cousteau and his divers testing themselves and a new underwater vehicle by remaining submerged for a month.
Physical Education and Recreation; Science - Natural; Science - Physical
Dist - TWYMAN **Prod** - CPC 1964

World Without Sun 8 MIN
16mm
Color
Presents an abridged version of a segment from The Undersea World Of Jacques Cousteau. Analyzes life beneath the Red Sea.
Geography - World; Science - Physical
Dist - TIMLIF **Prod** - TIMLIF 1982

World without walls - Beryl Markham's African memoir 60 MIN
VHS
Color (G)
$29.95 purchase _ #S01768
Profiles the life of Beryl Markham. Notes her accomplishments of being the only female to hunt with the men of Kenya's Nandi Morani tribe, the first female horse trainer in Kenya, and the first person to complete a solo trans - Atlantic flight from England to the US.
History - World; Industrial and Technical Education
Dist - UILL

Worlds apart 50 MIN
VHS
Redemption song series
Color; PAL (H C A)
PdS99 purchase
Examines the history of dissonance between Black and Asian populations in Trinidad and Guyana. Features interviews with residents who discuss their histories and the modern - day tensions between the two groups. Fifth in a series of seven programs documenting the history of the Caribbean.
History - World; Sociology
Dist - BBCENE

Worlds Apart 55 MIN
16mm / VHS
Living Planet Series
(J H C)
$99.95 each, $595.00 series
Explains the existence and survival of life forms on islands. Hosted by David Attenborough.
Science; Science - Natural; Science - Physical
Dist - AMBROS **Prod** - AMBROS 1984

Worlds apart 96 MIN
16mm
Color
LC FIA68-880
Tells the story of Captain Paul Matthews, an army doctor, whose battlefield surgery won decorations for bravery including a Purple Heart. Wounded in action, he was forced to return to the United States, where he renewed an acquaintance with Denise Henley, a college classmate whose rise to stardom in show business came while Paul was in combat. Paul's dedication to Christ soon brings them into conflict.
Religion and Philosophy
Dist - GF **Prod** - YOUTH 1967

Worlds apart 55 MIN
U-matic / VHS / 16mm
Living planet series; Pt 10
Color (H C A)
Visits Aldabra Island in the Indian Ocean to find giant tortoises that have reached their zenith in a hostile landscape of jagged coral rock where survival may mean eating your neighbor.
Science - Natural
Dist - TIMLIF **Prod** - BBCTV 1984

Worlds Apart Series

A Connemara Family	55 MIN
The Muria	55 MIN
The Panare - Scenes from the Frontier	60 MIN
Raj Gonds	55 MIN
The South - East Nuba	60 MIN

Dist - FI

Worlds below 50 MIN
VHS
Color (G)
$29.95 purchase
Takes a tour of the underwater worlds off California's central coast, focusing on the Monterey Bay area.
Geography - World
Dist - PBS **Prod** - WNETTV

The Worlds Beyond the Sea 26 MIN
VHS / 16mm
Blue Revolution Series
Color (J)
$149.00 purchase, $75.00 rental _ #QD - 2282
Documents the changing attitudes about the sea that accompanied developments in technology. The second of 16 installments of the Blue Revolution Series.
Geography - World; Science - Physical; Social Science
Dist - FOTH

World's children series
Presents a 13 - part series about children around the world. Offers a 'day in the life' look at children in various nations.
World's children series 169 MIN
Dist - ASTRSK **Prod** - ASTRSK 1990

World's Children Series

With Bekus in Nepal	14 MIN
With Bernadette in New Guinea	13 MIN
With Claudia in Australia	13 MIN
With Epelli in Fiji	13 MIN
With Gladis in Bolivia	11 MIN
With Michael in Kyuso, Kenya	13 MIN
With Nang and Nakorn in Thailand	14 MIN
With Oscar in Peru	11 MIN
With Pastore in Togo	13 MIN
With Patsy in St Vincent	13 MIN
With Spencer in Nairobi, Kenya	13 MIN
With Sylvia in the Philippines	12 MIN
With Yau Kai in Hong Kong	13 MIN

Dist - JOU

The World's Columbia exposition 30 MIN
U-matic / VHS
Art America series
Color (H C A)
Deals with the Columbia Exposition and with architecture in the early 1900s.
Fine Arts
Dist - CTI **Prod** - CTI

The World's Columbian Exposition 30 MIN
VHS
Art America series
Color (H C)
$43.00 purchase
Focuses on 19th century painting, sculpture and architecture as seen during the 1893 Chicago World's Fair. Provides background information on US social and cultural history of the period. Part of a 20-part series on art in America.
Fine Arts; History - United States
Dist - GPN

The World's Favorite Prune 22 MIN
16mm
Color
LC 82-700113
Presents the story of prunes from their development in 1860 to the present and traces the development of the prune industry. Looks at the cultivation, harvest and processing of prunes.
Agriculture; Home Economics
Dist - MTP **Prod** - MTP 1982

The World's favorite walnut 23 MIN
16mm
Color
Focuses on the commitment of the members of the Diamond Walnut Growers in all phases of cultivation, harvesting and processing one third of the world's walnuts.
Agriculture
Dist - MTP **Prod** - SDG

World's funniest TV commercials
VHS
Color (G)
$19.95 purchase _ #EK101
Collects 41 spots from ad man Joe Sedelmier.
Business and Economics; Fine Arts; Literature and Drama
Dist - SIV

The World's Greatest Freak Show 11 MIN
U-matic
Desire to Read Series
Color (P)
Tells how a magician presents a freak show and learns that the wildly applauding audience is as deformed as his three 'freaks.' Examines the nature of beauty and selfish vanity.
Literature and Drama
Dist - GA **Prod** - BOSUST

World's greatest photography course 90 MIN
VHS
Color (H C A)
$14.95 purchase; $29.95 purchase _ #SOO119
Presents a comprehensive look at amateur photography. Covers subjects including composition, lighting, exposure, lenses, filters, and more. Hosted by Lief Ericksen.
Industrial and Technical Education
Dist - PBS **Prod** - WNETTV
UILL

The World's Greatest Photography Course
VHS / BETA
Color (H)
Gives a hands - on introduction to photography. Offers demonstrations and professional tips on all the basics by photographer Lief Ericksenn.
Fine Arts; Industrial and Technical Education
Dist - GA **Prod** - GA

The World's Greatest Photography Course
VHS
(H C A)
$29.98 purchase _ #VID701V
Examines the art of photography in three categories including Seeing the Picture, Knowing Your Equipment, and Shooting the Photo. Discusses various subjects and techniques.
Fine Arts
Dist - CAMV

World's Greatest Supercross Races 60 MIN
VHS
Motocross Series
Color (G)
$19.98 purchase _ #TT8113
Presents the world's greatest supercross races.
Industrial and Technical Education; Literature and Drama; Physical Education and Recreation
Dist - TWINTO **Prod** - TWINTO 1990

The World's Largest Nest - the Sociable Weaverbird 9 MIN
U-matic / VHS / 16mm
Aspects of Animal Behavior Series
Color (I)
Examines the colonial nest of the sociable weaverbird of southern Africa, including the details of nest structure, the variety of nest configurations, the process of nest building and the ecological contributions of the nest to the success of the bird in the Kalahari Desert.
Geography - World; Science - Natural
Dist - UCEMC **Prod** - UCLA 1976

The World's most mysterious places 180 MIN
VHS
Color (G)
$59.95 purchase _ #P51
Features a boxed set of three videos that trace the facts and legends of Europe's fascinating locations. Includes Sacred Sites of Europe which explores Aachen, Germany, Charlemagne's City, France's Chartres Cathedral, Santiago and the Shrine of St James in Spain; Mysterious Places of England, which delves into Stonehenge, Glastonbury, the Isle of Avalon, the mysteries of the Land's End Peninsula and many stone circles; and Mysterious Places of the Mediterranean, which explores Pompeii, Menorca the island of stones, Apollo and the Oracle of Delphi. 60 minutes each.
Fine Arts; Geography - World
Dist - HP

The World's most Versatile Horse 13 MIN
16mm / U-matic / VHS
Color
Features some of the quarter horse breed's finest individuals cutting, roping, reining and barrel racing.
Physical Education and Recreation; Science - Natural
Dist - AQHORS **Prod** - AQHORS

The Worlds of Martha Schlamme 30 MIN
16mm
Eternal Light Series
B&W (H C A) (YIDDISH)
LC 70-700958
Shows Martha Schlamme, folk singer, who presents selections in Yiddish, Hebrew, English and German. (Kinescope).
Fine Arts; Religion and Philosophy
Dist - NAAJS **Prod** - JTS 1966

The Worlds of Rudyard Kipling 30 MIN
U-matic / VHS / BETA
B&W (G H C)
PdS50, PdS58 purchase
Delves into the world of Kipling. Looks at his India; the America that he married into; his world of steam, sail and hardbitten Scottish engineers; and at the Boers in South Africa.
Literature and Drama
Dist - EDPAT

The World's still young 5 MIN
16mm
B&W
LC 73-702401
Presents a montage of international scenes leading to a review of world - wide production facilities of the Levi Strauss Organization, followed by marketing differences among various countries. Includes views of children around the world wearing Levis.
Business and Economics; Home Economics; Social Science
Dist - LEVI **Prod** - LEVI 1972

World's Winter Strawberry Capital 14 MIN
16mm
Color
Highlights the Hillsborough County Fair and Florida Strawberry Festival.
Geography - United States; Physical Education and Recreation
Dist - FLADC **Prod** - FLADC

The Worlds within 29 MIN
16mm
Color
LC FIE64-185
A nontechnical description of the design, construction and use of the Stanford linear accelerator. Presents a background account on its development and a discussion on the theory of its operation and the problems encountered in its construction and use. Examines the fabrication and testing of a two - mile long copper tube through which atomic particles will be fired, and of high - power radio tubes, called klystrons, which are used to project electrons down the tube. Compares various methods of projecting particles of minute dimensions.
Industrial and Technical Education; Science - Physical
Dist - EDUC **Prod** - STNFRD 1963

World's Young Ballet
VHS
Color (G)
$29.95 purchase _ #1275
Looks at the world of international ballet competitions. Features footage of young Mikhail Baryshnikov, pre - defection, competing in Moscow in 1969. Ballet legends Maya Plisetskaya and Alicia Alonso are among the judges.
Fine Arts; Geography - World; Physical Education and Recreation
Dist - KULTUR

Worldview
VHS
Inside Genesis series
Color (G R)
$14.95 purchase
Presents basic ideas underlying Christian belief. Helps in individual study, small groups and teaching Bible concepts. 10 - 13 minutes in length. Part of a four - part series.
Religion and Philosophy
Dist - GF

Worldwide Competition 30 MIN
VHS / U-matic
Information Industry - Strategic Planning Considerations Series
Color
Describes the six major groups in the information industry. Identifies the challenges faced by each industry group and explains how these challenges, if not met, provide competitive opportunities for other firms.
Business and Economics; Industrial and Technical Education
Dist - DELTAK **Prod** - DELTAK

Worm fishing techniques 30 MIN
BETA / VHS
Color
Features the U.S. Bass World Champion demonstrating his techniques. Shows proper selection of plastic worms, casting and retrieving and the hook set.
Physical Education and Recreation; Science - Natural
Dist - HOMEAF **Prod** - HOMEAF

Worm fishing - techniques and patterns
VHS
Color (G)
$29.80 purchase _ #0135
Shows how to fish, using worms as bait. Describes equipment and techniques.
Physical Education and Recreation; Science - Natural
Dist - SEVVID

Worms and how they live 18 MIN
Videodisc / 16mm / VHS
Animals and how they live series
Color (I J)
$395.00, $295.00 purchase, $50.00 rental _ #8223
Observes the building of a worm farm to study the way worms eat, move and reproduce. Examines the head, segments and bristles of earthworms under the microscope. Explains the functions which make earthworms highly valued by farmers and gardeners. Studies brandling worms and tubifex. Part of a series on invertebrates produced by Cicada Productions and VATV.
Science - Natural
Dist - AIMS

Worms - flat, round and segmented 16 MIN
U-matic / VHS / 16mm
Major phyla series
Color (J H C)
$365.00, $250.00 purchase _ #1597; LC 78-706712
Emphasizes regeneration and tropism in flatworms, parasitism in roundworms and evolutionary advances of segmented worms.
Science - Natural
Dist - CORF **Prod** - CORF 1970

Worms - the Annelida 13 MIN
U-matic / VHS / 16mm
Color; B&W (J H C)
A study of the four classes of annelid worms showing their structure, distinguishing characteristics, behavior and habitats. Shows the various ways in which annelids move, breathe, gather food and reproduce. Explains how the earthworm contributes to the conservation of the soil.
Science - Natural
Dist - EBEC **Prod** - EBEC 1955

Worms to Wings 13 MIN
VHS / 16mm
Color (P I J H)
Shows the metamorphic process of the anise swallowtail butterfly in its entirety.
Science - Natural
Dist - MIS **Prod** - MIS 1955

The Worrell 1000
VHS
Color (G)
$39.80 purchase _ #0235
Presents the Sun Media coverage of the Worrell 1000. Reveals that the race originated as an informal Hobie 16 race and evolved into a 1,000 mile classic for 20 foot catamarans.
Physical Education and Recreation
Dist - SEVVID

Worried Man 30 MIN
U-matic / VHS
Bluegrass banjo - level one series
Color (H C A)
Shows how to master various banjo fingering exercises and presents the song Worried Man.
Fine Arts
Dist - GPN **Prod** - OWL 1980

Worries and Wonders - WP - 4 12 MIN
U-matic
(PRO)
$235.00 purchase
Portrays the experience of working in word processing. Discusses fears, doubts and satisfactions.
Business and Economics
Dist - MONAD **Prod** - MONAD

Worry - I'm in Big Trouble Now 12 MIN
U-matic
Color (I J)
Tells what happens when Billy is entrusted with the care of his little brother and his brother disappears into the woods.
Fine Arts; Guidance and Counseling
Dist - GA **Prod** - GA

Worship and the arts - liturgical dance 11 MIN
VHS
Color (H C G A R)
$10.00 rental _ #36 - 816 - 1521
Demonstrates the various ways in which dance and interpretive movement may be used in church worship. Filmed during actual worship services.
Religion and Philosophy
Dist - APH **Prod** - MMM

Worship - giving our hearts and minds to God 30 MIN
VHS
Color (G R)
$24.95 purchase
Presents a collection of five hymns - O the Deep, Deep Love of Jesus; Let the Flame Burn Brighter; O For a Thousand Tongues; Levantare Mi Voz; and O Sacred Head. Uses recordings of singing at Urbana and images from around the world. Interspersed with suggestions for worship leaders from InterVarsity staff Alison Siewart and Phil Dyer. A useful tool for personal or corporate worship.
Fine Arts; Religion and Philosophy
Dist - GF

Worship II - a resource for worship through image and song 30 MIN
VHS
Color (G R)
$24.95 purchase
Combines diverse styles of expression and compelling images for a fresh approach to prayer and praise. Includes Holy, Holy, Holy; Jesus Shall Reign; Betapa Hatiku; a dramatic Psalm 104 reading; and Mourning to Dancing - from groups including Indonesian Christian Fellowship and Integrity Music.
Fine Arts
Dist - GF

The Worship of nature 52 MIN
16mm / U-matic / VHS
Civilisation series; No 11
Color (J A)
LC 79-708448
Surveys the development of Western civilization during the late 1700s and the 1800s as characterized by a romantic belief in the divinity of nature and evidenced in the work of Rousseau, Goethe and Wordsworth, and in the paintings of Constable, Casper David Friederich and William Turner.
Fine Arts; History - World; Literature and Drama; Religion and Philosophy
Dist - FI **Prod** - BBCTV 1970

The Worship of nature - Pt 1 24 MIN
U-matic / VHS / 16mm
Civilisation series; No 11
Color (J A)
LC 79-708448
Surveys the development of Western civilization during the late 1700s and the 1800s as characterized by a romantic belief in the divinity of nature and evidenced in the work of Rousseau, Goethe and Wordsworth, and in the paintings of Constable, Casper David Friederich and William Turner.
Fine Arts; History - World; Literature and Drama
Dist - FI **Prod** - BBCTV 1970

The Worship of nature - Pt 2 28 MIN
U-matic / VHS / 16mm
Civilisation series; No 11
Color (J A)
LC 79-708448
Surveys the development of Western civilization during the late 1700s and the 1800s as characterized by a romantic belief in the divinity of nature and evidenced in the work of Rousseau, Goethe and Wordsworth, and in the paintings of Constable, Casper David Friederich and William Turner.
Fine Arts; History - World; Literature and Drama
Dist - FI **Prod** - BBCTV 1970

Worship the king 55 MIN
VHS
Color (R)
$19.95 purchase _ #5018 - 9
Features instrumental and vocal selections of Christian music.
Fine Arts; Religion and Philosophy
Dist - MOODY **Prod** - MOODY

The Worst Child Killer 9 MIN
16mm
Doctors at Work Series
B&W (PRO)
Presents a visit to a hospital, a doctor's office and a poison information center to warn of common accidents and hazards that affect children, such as bicycle - auto collisions, knocking pots off stoves and investigating medicine chests.
Health and Safety
Dist - LAWREN **Prod** - CMA

The Worst loan I ever made 33 MIN
VHS
Color (IND PRO)
$445.00 sale, $245.00 rental _ #BTC02
Gives an overview of the lending process. Examines three case studies of loans that went sour. Produced by Banctraining.
Business and Economics
Dist - EXTR

The Worst of Crimes 30 MIN
U-matic
Explorations in Shaw Series
Color (H)
Dramatizes George Bernard Shaw's encounters with poverty in London, his early attacks on capitalism, and his first successes as a young socialist playwright.
Literature and Drama
Dist - TVOTAR **Prod** - TVOTAR 1974

The Worst of Hollywood - Volume one
VHS
B&W (G)
$29.95 purchase _ #SM - 508
Offers two Hollywood bombs, Maniac and Protect Your Daughter.
Fine Arts
Dist - INCRSE **Prod** - INCRSE

The Worst of Hollywood - Volume three
VHS
B&W (G)
$29.95 purchase _ #SM - 510
Offers two Hollywood bombs, Probation, featuring the first screen appearance of Betty Grable, and Nation Aflame, depicting incompetent fascists against the social norm.
Fine Arts
Dist - INCRSE **Prod** - INCRSE

The Worst of Hollywood - Volume two
VHS
B&W (G)
$29.95 purchase _ #SM - 509
Offers two Hollywood bombs, Fugitive Road and The Crime of Dr Crespi.
Fine Arts
Dist - INCRSE **Prod** - INCRSE

Worst Winter of the Century 5 MIN
16mm
Screen news digest series; Vol 5; Issue 8
B&W
Tells the story of the coldest winter of the twentieth century which assaulted most of the world with unprecedented cold weather. Shows that man may be able to forecast and prepare for all kinds of weather but he cannot yet control it.
Science - Physical
Dist - HEARST **Prod** - HEARST 1963

Worth a Thousand Words 18 MIN
16mm
Color
Explains the uses of automated computer graphical output and describes a system developed at the Culham Laboratory for achieving it. Includes a number of examples of computer - produced cine output, drawn from the fields of astronomy, geometry and plasma physics.
Industrial and Technical Education
Dist - UKAEA **Prod** - UKAEA 1968

Worth it 30 MIN
VHS
Color (J H R)
$24.95 purchase _ #87EE0501; $24.95 purchase _ #35 - 8501 - 19
Portrays Danny and Karen, two teenagers who are struggling with their self - esteem. Shows that one of them attempts suicide at a youth retreat. Divided into several viewing segments to allow discussion of self - worth, possible warning signs of suicide, and where to turn for help. Includes leader's guide.
Guidance and Counseling; Literature and Drama; Psychology; Religion and Philosophy
Dist - CPH **Prod** - CPH
APH FAMF

Worth of a Child 22 MIN
16mm
Color
LC 77-702180
Features a young woman who has made a friend of a mentally handicapped person. Shows how she goes on to become a teacher of the mentally and physically handicapped.
Education; Psychology
Dist - BYU **Prod** - BYU 1977

The Worth of Waste 18 MIN
16mm
Color
Examines the efforts of industry and government to reclaim and re - use much of the material previously considered junk.
Science - Natural
Dist - GM **Prod** - GM

Worth quoting series 243 MIN
VHS
Programs with Hazel Henderson series
Color (H C G)
$195.00 purchase
Features Hazel Henderson, economic analyst, futurist and author of 'Paradigms in Progress,' In four videocassettes hosted by Carol Miner, provost of the Open University. Discusses global democracy, planet ecology, creative management, trends shaping the 21st century and green economics. Produced by Florida Community College at Jacksonville.
Civics and Political Systems; Fine Arts; Science - Natural
Dist - BULFRG

Worth quoting - Videocassette 1 90 MIN
VHS
Programs with Hazel Henderson series
Color (H C G)
$89.00 purchase, $45.00 rental
Presents Hazel Henderson, economic analyst, futurist and author of 'Paradigms in Progress,' in the first of four in a series hosted by Carol Miner, provost of the Open University. Features Henderson with biologist Elisabet Sahtouris, author of 'Gaia - The Human Journey from Chaos to Cosmos.' Covers Planet Earth as Our Teacher, Planetary Ecology vs. World Trade, Citizen's Groups and the Growth of Democracy. Produced by Florida Community College at Jacksonville.
Business and Economics; Civics and Political Systems; Fine Arts; Science - Natural
Dist - BULFRG

Worth quoting - Videocassette 2 60 MIN
VHS
Programs with Hazel Henderson series
Color (H C G)
$59.00 purchase, $35.00 rental
Presents Hazel Henderson, economic analyst, futurist and author of 'Paradigms in Progress,' in the second of four in a series hosted by Carol Miner, provost of the Open University. Features Henderson with management consultant Peter Russell, author of 'The Global Brain' and 'The White Hole in Time.' Covers Inner Roots of our Global Crises and Creative Management. Produced by Florida Community College at Jacksonville.
Civics and Political Systems; Fine Arts; Home Economics; Science - Natural
Dist - BULFRG

Worth quoting - Videocassette 3 60 MIN
VHS
Programs with Hazel Henderson series
Color (H C G)
$59.00 purchase, $35.00 rental
Presents Hazel Henderson, economic analyst, futurist and author of 'Paradigms in Progress,' in the third of four in a series hosted by Carol Miner, provost of the Open University. Features Henderson with Dutch businessman Eckhart Wintzen, President of Origin International. Covers Globalization and Restructuring - Trends Shaping the 21st Century and Business and the Environment - Green Economics. Produced by Florida Community College at Jacksonville.
Civics and Political Systems; Fine Arts; Science - Natural
Dist - BULFRG

Worth quoting - Videocassette 4 60 MIN
VHS
Programs with Hazel Henderson series
Color (H C G)
$59.00 purchase, $35.00 rental
Presents Hazel Henderson, economic analyst, futurist and author of 'Paradigms in Progress,' in the fourth of four in a series hosted by Carol Miner, provost of the Open University. Features Henderson with Ashok Khosla, President of Development Alternatives in New Delhi, India. Covers The Road from Rio - To a Sustainable Future and Agenda 21 - North and South Views of the 21st Century. Produced by Florida Community College at Jacksonville.
Civics and Political Systems; Fine Arts; Science - Natural
Dist - BULFRG

Worth the Effort 16 MIN
16mm
Color
Presents the story of one major corporation's efforts to develop vitally needed energy sources and resources, while at the same time, protecting and preserving the environment through reforestation, land renewal and enhancement of the areas it owns and leases.
Science - Natural; Social Science
Dist - MTP **Prod** - GRACE

Worth the Effort 16 MIN
16mm
Color
LC 81-701213
Presents three examples of how the Grace Corporation, a large chemical corporation, has spent over $350 million insuring minimal impact of their activity on the environment.
Business and Economics; Science - Natural; Social Science
Dist - GRACE **Prod** - GRACE 1981

Worth Waiting for 28 MIN
16mm
B&W (J H A)
Describes the problems that arose for a high school couple when they decided to become engaged .
Guidance and Counseling; Psychology
Dist - CMPBL **Prod** - BYU 1962

Worthington - the New Eden 29 MIN
U-matic
Color
Describes the settling of Worthington, Ohio, in 1803.
History - United States
Dist - HRC **Prod** - OHC

Worthington - the Virtuous Society in Transition 29 MIN
U-matic
Color
Discusses the economic, cultural, religious, social, educational and political life of the town of Worthington, Ohio, from 1803 to the mid - century.
History - United States
Dist - HRC **Prod** - OHC

A Worthy Destination
VHS / BETA
Color
Deals with setting and achieving goals, Focuses on developing positive attitudes, creating opportunities and planning.
Psychology
Dist - NIGCON **Prod** - NIGCON

Wot - no Art 55 MIN
16mm / VHS
Color (H A)
$1020.00 purchase, $70.00 rental
Shows the struggle of the British government to bring art to the people in the aftermath of World War II. Illustrates the large gap between the public and the artist as perceived at the time.
Fine Arts; History - World
Dist - AFA **Prod** - ACGB 1979

Wot u lookin at 55 MIN
VHS
Horizon series
Color; PAL (H C A)
PdS99 purchase
Addresses the issue of youth violence and focuses on perpetrators who are young, poor, and male. Presents experts who assert that factors other than poverty, such as gene make - up, can account for violent behavior. Investigates gene research aimed at discovering the 'violent' gene which some claim targets racial minorities.
Sociology
Dist - BBCENE

Woton's wake 32 MIN
16mm
B&W (H C)
Features a new experimental film which combines the sardonic humor of James Broughton's 'The Pleasure Garden' with the mysterioso of 'The Stranger Left No Card.'
Fine Arts
Dist - CFS **Prod** - DEPALB

Would I Work with Me
VHS / 16mm
(H)
$99.00 _ #CA101V
Teaches job survival skills and shows both teenagers' and employers' points of view. Designed for teenagers who have never worked and for employers who have never employed teenagers.
Guidance and Counseling; Psychology
Dist - JISTW

Would I work with me - teens in the work world 22 MIN
VHS
Color (H C A)
$99.00 purchase _ #AM463VG
Features working teens telling about what to expect in the adult working world and what it takes to be a good employee. Covers responsibility, dependability, initiative, communication, and customer service. Includes a leader's guide and 25 booklets.
Psychology; Sociology
Dist - UNL

Would I work with me - the teens' point of view 19 MIN
VHS
Color (COR H)
$395.00 purchase, $100.00 rental - #WWW
Presents information to young people entering the workforce on expectations of coworkers and desirable employee traits. Demonstrates to managers the importance of communication with young employees. Stresses employee dependability, initiative, self - discipline, and responsibility. Includes a Leader's Guide. Available for three - day preview, as well as for rental, purchase, or lease.
Guidance and Counseling; Psychology
Dist - ADVANM

Would you bet your life 17 MIN
16mm / U-matic / VHS
Color (IND)
Compares bets to the chances taken when an electrical lineman does not heed the safety rules. Presents linemen who have had accidents who tell how the accident occurred.
Health and Safety
Dist - IFB **Prod** - EUSA
EDPAT

Would you like to make a book 15 MIN
Videoreel / VT2
Art corner series
B&W (P)
Demonstrates manipulating paper to achieve a simple four - page book to decorate with drawings or prints.
Fine Arts
Dist - GPN **Prod** - CVETVC

Wouldn't it be Nice 15 MIN
U-matic / VHS / 16mm
Color (P)
Informs about the methodology and mechanism of catalog purchasing that make it a successful process.
Business and Economics
Dist - KLEINW **Prod** - KLEINW

Wouldn't you like to meet your neighbor - a New York subway tape 15 MIN
U-matic
Color (G)
$35.00 purchase
Features a series of interviews with New York City subway riders asking them if they talk to other passengers, what they are reading, and attempting to get strangers to talk to one another.
Fine Arts; Psychology
Dist - CANCIN **Prod** - BARHAM 1985

Wound Care for Nurses 29 MIN
VHS / 16mm
(C)
$385.00 purchase _ #870VI055
Offers nurses a complete guide to wound care. Covers aseptic technique, wound healing, dressing functions, dressing applications, irrigation techniques, packing procedures, and procedures for documenting wound condition.
Health and Safety
Dist - HSCIC **Prod** - HSCIC 1987

Wound care series
Presents three parts on wound care. Includes the titles Assessment of Complex Wounds; Management of Complex Wounds; and Prevention and Treatment of Pressure Ulcers.

Assessment and management of complex wounds	56 MIN
Assessment of complex wounds	28 MIN
Management of complex wounds	28 MIN
Prevention and treatment of pressure ulcers	28 MIN

Dist - AJN **Prod** - AJN 1987

Wound Healing by Primary Intention 27 MIN
16mm
Color
LC 75-703130
Shows the critical differences between healing by secondary and primary intention.
Health and Safety
Dist - MMAMC **Prod** - BAYUCM 1975

Wound healing I - by secondary intention 27 MIN
U-matic
Color (PRO)
Visualizes by animation the six processes involved in wound healing when tissue heals without approximation.
Health and Safety
Dist - MMAMC **Prod** - MMAMC

Wound healing II - by primary intention 23 MIN
U-matic
Color (PRO)
Combines animation and live action to discuss the six phases of healing when sutures or wound closure strips are used to approximate tissue.
Health and Safety
Dist - MMAMC **Prod** - MMAMC

Wound packing and irrigation 20 MIN
VHS
Color (C PRO)
$250.00 purchase, $70.00 rental _ #4339S, #4339V
Shows a variety of open wounds and how to irrigate, pack and secure them properly. Covers essential steps in wound care, including collection, containment and assessment of drainage; protecting the wound from further trauma, maintaining patient comfort and promoting a healing environment. Shows and describes various types of debridement such as surgical, chemical and enzymatic, autolytic digestion and mechanical, as well as different irrigation methods. Discusses topical agents and packing the wound, key observations to make and record and the general need for documentation. Produced by St Francis Regional Medical Center.
Health and Safety
Dist - AJN

Wound rotor controllers 17 MIN
16mm
Electrical work - motor control series; No 4
B&W
LC FIE52-179
Discusses wound rotor motor principles, operation of a faceplate controller, drum - type nonreversing controller, drum - type reversing controller and automatic magnetic starter for a wound rotor motor.
Industrial and Technical Education
Dist - USNAC **Prod** - USOE 1945

The Wounded healer 30 MIN
VHS
Conversations with Rollo May series
Color (A PRO)
$95.00 purchase _ #77654
Discusses well known helping professionals and how their background and childhood experiences enabled them to become 'healers.' Rollo May also discusses the relationship between creativity and pain.
Psychology
Dist - AACD **Prod** - AACD 1984

The Wounded Knee Affair 17 MIN
U-matic / VHS
Color (H C A)
Describes the 1973 protest at Wounded Knee, South Dakota, during which American Indians tried to draw international attention to the problems facing their culture.
History - United States; Social Science
Dist - JOU **Prod** - UPI

Wounds and Bleeding 30 MIN
VHS / U-matic
First Aid in the Classroom Series
Color
Shows how to recognize 'life threatening situations' and how to treat punctures, abrasions, incisions and lacerations.
Health and Safety
Dist - NETCHE **Prod** - NETCHE 1973

Wounds from within 48 MIN
U-matic / VHS
Color
$455.00 purchase
Sociology
Dist - ABCLR **Prod** - ABCLR 1981

Woven Gardens 55 MIN
16mm / VHS / U-matic
Tribal Eye Series
Color
LC 77-701591; 79-707120
Examines the woven rugs of the Qashqa tribe of Iran and explains how the rugs are made, what functions they serve and the significance of the traditional symbols used in their design.
Fine Arts; History - World; Sociology
Dist - TIMLIF **Prod** - BBCTV 1976

Woven Hangings 25 MIN
VHS / U-matic
Craft of the Weaver Series
Color (J)
Portrays innovation in weaving today. Demonstrates the shaft - switching technique which makes possible the complex design on the rugs of series consultant Peter Collingwood. Includes Ann Sutton talking about her own work, and looks at the range and variety of woven hangings.
Fine Arts
Dist - FI **Prod** - BBCTV 1983

Woyzeck 82 MIN
16mm
Color (GERMAN (ENGLISH SUBTITLES))
Depicts the tragedy of an ordinary man's headlong plunge into madness and murder. Directed by Werner Herzog.
Fine Arts
Dist - NYFLMS **Prod** - UNKNWN 1978

Woyzeck 60 MIN
VHS / U-matic
Drama - play, performance, perception series; Dramatis personae
Color (H C A)
Explores methods of character development. Uses the play Woyzeck as an example.
Literature and Drama
Dist - FI **Prod** - BBCTV 1978

Woyzeck 97 MIN
16mm
B&W
Based on the case of Johann Christian Woyzeck, a soldier who murdered his mistress in a jealous rage, and the ensuing medical controversy as to whether or not he was insane. Depicts the pervasive influence of a hostile environment. A television production of Georg Buechner's drama Woyzeck, which inspired Alban Berg's famous opera version of the story, Wozzeck.
Fine Arts
Dist - WSTGLC **Prod** - WSTGLC 1967

Woza Albert 50 MIN
16mm / U-matic / VHS
Color (H C A)
Discusses what would happen if Christ were to visit South Africa, and examines the problems of blacks living under apartheid. Based on a play by two black South Africans. Produced by David M. Thompson, BBC.
Religion and Philosophy; Sociology
Dist - CWS

Woza Albert 52 MIN
U-matic / VHS
Everyman series
Color (J H C A)
Presents a documentary about an award winning play by two black South Africans. Includes scenes from the play and video footage from South Africa showing the play's origins in actual situations and events.
Fine Arts; Geography - World
Dist - CANWRL **Prod** - CANWRL 1982

Wozzeck - Vienna State Opera 98 MIN
VHS
Color (G)
$39.95 purchase _ #WOZ01
Presents the modern opera 'Wozzeck' by Alban Berg which displays the gruesome detail, horror and passion of German Expressionism. Tells the story of Wozzeck, a soldier driven insane by manipulative superiors and an unfaithful mistress. He stabs the mistress, then drowns while trying to wash away the blood of his slaughter. Stars Franz Grundheber, Heldegard Behrens, Philip Langridge. Claudio Abaddo conducts.
Fine Arts; History - World
Dist - HOMVIS **Prod** - RMART 1990

Wrap it Up 15 MIN
Videoreel / VT2
Umbrella Series
Color
Fine Arts
Dist - PBS **Prod** - KETCTV

Wrapped in steel 115 MIN
VHS
Color (G)
$89.00 purchase _ #S00166
Portrays four Chicago steelworker neighborhoods and the residents' struggle to retain their livelihoods and standard of living in the face of a highly competitive world steel market.
Business and Economics; Geography - United States; Social Science
Dist - UILL

Wrapping a permanent wave - on a mannequin
U-matic / VHS
Lessons on a mannequin series; Lesson IV
Color
Explains the relationship of rod size to block size. Shows how hair is held while wrapping, the application of end papers, proper wrapping technique and the fastening of bands to avoid breakage and indentations. Illustrates wrong procedures. Demonstrates how the comb is used to protect the scalp during styling with a hot brush.
Education; Home Economics
Dist - MPCEDP **Prod** - MPCEDP 1984

Wrapping it up 29 MIN
U-matic
Beginning piano - an adult approach series; Lesson 30
Color (H A)
Reviews Beethoven and Kabalevsky pieces. Gives suggestions regarding newly acquired piano playing skills.
Fine Arts
Dist - CDTEL **Prod** - COAST

Wrappings 15 MIN
Videoreel / VT2
Making Things Work Series
Color
Fine Arts
Dist - PBS **Prod** - WGBHTV

Wraps 11 MIN
16mm
Color
LC 79-700349
Discusses the versatility of aluminum wrap and describes its artistic and scientific uses.
Business and Economics
Dist - MTP **Prod** - REYMC 1978

Wrath of grapes 15 MIN
16mm / VHS
Color (G IND)
$5.00 rental
Documents the toxic spraying of fruits and vegetables in fields where farm laborers are working. Shows how such pesticide usage has spread beyond the fields to menace nearby communities. Urges the ban of five cancer causing chemicals and the boycotting of table grapes.
Agriculture; Health and Safety; Social Science; Sociology
Dist - AFLCIO **Prod** - UFWA 1987

Wrath of Hunger 6 MIN
16mm
Color
LC 74-700333
Tells of the poverty, disease and hunger of the third world countries.
Social Science; Sociology
Dist - MARYFA **Prod** - MARYFA 1973

Wreck 5 MIN
16mm / BETA / U-matic / VHS
Color; Mono (G)
MV $85.00 _ MP $170.00 purchase, $50.00 rental
Follows a lone driver as he probes the depths of a shipwreck. Filmed in Lake Huron. The camera explores the spartan remains of a 19th century sailing barque.
Geography - United States; Social Science
Dist - CTV **Prod** - MAKOF 1982

The Wreck and rescue of the schooner J H Hartzell 58 MIN
VHS
Color (G)
$39.95 purchase _ #0776
Recreates the true story of a 19th century shipwreck on the Great Lakes, the wreck and rescue of the schooner J H Hartzell.
Geography - United States; Physical Education and Recreation
Dist - SEVVID

Wreck of a Marriage
The Divorce 12 MIN
Rudolf 13 MIN
Sofie 12 MIN
Dist - CEPRO

The Wreck of the New York Subway 17 MIN
16mm
B&W
Explains how fares increase, conditions become more perilous and how subway workers and riders organize to educate the public about municipal corruption and cynicism.
Sociology
Dist - CANWRL **Prod** - CANWRL

Wreck Raisers 45 MIN
16mm
Color (P I)
Presents Tom and his pals attempting to raise a wrecked boat in order to prove they aren't to blame for its destruction.
Literature and Drama
Dist - LUF **Prod** - LUF

Wreckers 30 MIN
VHS
Skirt through history
Color; PAL (H C A)
PdS65 purchase
Utilizes personal writings to document the lives of two women active in the suffrage movement. Features Ethel Smith, an acclaimed composer outside her native Britain, and Sarah Bennett, a social worker seeking to improve working conditions for the poor in the Staffordshire potteries. Fourth in a series of six programs covering four centuries of women's history.
Civics and Political Systems; History - World
Dist - BBCENE

Wrecks of the Caribbean 30 MIN
VHS
Scuba world series
Color (G)
$24.90 purchase _ #0437
Visits some of the better known wrecks of the Caribbean. Presents underwater archaeology.
History - World; Physical Education and Recreation
Dist - SEVVID

Wrenches 14 MIN
16mm
Hand operations - woodworking series
Color
LC 75-704363
Illustrates the versatility and practicality of a variety of wrenches.
Industrial and Technical Education
Dist - SF **Prod** - MORLAT 1974

Wrenches 19 MIN
16mm
B&W
Explains the uses and advantages of various wrenches and shows the damage which may result from incorrect and dangerous practices in using them.
Industrial and Technical Education
Dist - USNAC **Prod** - USA 1943

Wrens, thrushes, warblers, finches - Volume 5 60 MIN
VHS
Audubon society videoguides to the birds of North America series
Color (G)
$29.95 purchase
Combines live footage and color photography in an Audubon Society bird watching program. Focuses on wrens, thrushes, warblers, finches, and several other bird types. Uses bird sights and sounds, visual graphics, and maps to aid in the identification of bird types. Narrated by Michael Godfrey.
Science - Natural
Dist - PBS **Prod** - WNETTV

Wrestling 13 MIN
16mm
B&W
National AAU champion Danny Hodge wrestles according to amateur rules.
Physical Education and Recreation
Dist - SFI **Prod** - SFI

The Wrestling Abeline Paradox 21 MIN
Software
Sports 1 2 3 Individual Sports Series
(T G)
#109039 - 8 3/4
Organizes team activities. Requires Lotus 1 - 2 - 3 software and MS - DOS. Comes on a 5.25" disk. Explains how the reluctance of group members to express their reservations and objections leads to dangerous decision making. Shows how to spot false consensus and teaches strategies for avoiding the problem.
Computer Science; Education; Physical Education and Recreation; Psychology
Dist - MECC **Prod** - MECC 1984

Wrestling Fundamentals 11 MIN
U-matic / VHS / 16mm
Color (J H) (SPANISH)
LC 76-704310
Explains that good wrestling requires a series of moves and counter - moves and the basic ones are, the take downs, double leg, single leg, arm drag and whip over, the escapes, sit out and roll out, the reverses, switch short switch and side roll, and the pin holds, bar arm and half nelson, and the cradle.
Physical Education and Recreation
Dist - PHENIX **Prod** - RICH 1969

Wrestling series
VHS
N C A A instructional video series
Color (H C A)
$64.95 purchase _ #KAR2504V
Presents a three - part series on wrestling. Focuses on takedowns, escapes and reverses, and riding and pinning techniques.
Physical Education and Recreation
Dist - CAMV **Prod** - NCAAF

Wrestling Series no 3
Rides and Escapes 22 MIN
Dist - ATHI

Wrestling Series no 4
Pinning Combinations 20 MIN
Dist - ATHI

Wrestling series
Fundamentals of wrestling 19 MIN
Takedown techniques 22 MIN
Dist - ATHI

Wrestling Today 17 MIN
16mm
Color (J H C)
LC 74-703506
Discusses the rules of interscholastic wrestling. Illustrates the decisions of officials and shows the bases for these decisions.
Physical Education and Recreation
Dist - NFSHSA **Prod** - NFSHSA 1973

Wrestling videos series
Features former collegiate and Olympic wrestlers in a series covering basic wrestling skills. Includes live - action demonstration of skills including setups, takedowns, reversals, pins, and more. Consists of 11 videocassettes.
Attack from square stance - Tim Vanni 60 MIN
Basics with the Keller twins 60 MIN
Defensive offense - John Smith 60 MIN
Hands on with Joe Gonzales 60 MIN
A I A - Gene Davis and Don Shuler 60 MIN
Take downs with Joe Seay 60 MIN
Tilt and turn with Gene Mills 60 MIN
Two on one with Gene Mills 60 MIN
Two supermen with Jim and Bill Scherr 60 MIN
Wrestling videos series 660 MIN
Wrestling with Adam Cuestas 60 MIN
Wrestling with Mark Shultz 60 MIN
Dist - CAMV

Wrestling with Adam Cuestas 60 MIN
VHS
Wrestling videos series
Color (H C A)
$39.95 purchase _ #DP006V
Features Adam Cuestas covering basic wrestling skills. Includes live - action demonstration of these skills.
Physical Education and Recreation
Dist - CAMV

Wrestling with Mark Shultz 60 MIN
VHS
Wrestling videos series
Color (H C A)
$39.95 purchase _ #DP004V
Features Mark Shultz covering basic wrestling skills. Includes live - action demonstration of these skills.
Physical Education and Recreation
Dist - CAMV

The Wretched Refuse 15 MIN
VHS / U-matic
Los Peregrinos Modernos - the Modern Pioneers Series
Color (I)
Shows the character Roberto announcing that his own family has made it safely to America while a church group discusses plans for resettling a family. Emphasizes the strength and support among the Martinez family members as they endure the difficult journey to America.
Geography - World; Sociology
Dist - GPN **Prod** - NETV

The Wright Brothers Airplane 10 MIN
16mm
B&W
Gives a complete reel showing the first successful flight with the government award for reaching a speed of 42 miles per hour.
Fine Arts
Dist - FCE **Prod** - FCE 1909

The Wright brothers - the birth of aviation 24 MIN
U-matic / VHS
Color (I J)
$325.00, $295.00 purchase _ #V183; LC 90-706273
Dramatizes the story of the development of the airplane by the Wright brothers. Explains basic concepts of aerodynamics.
Biography; Fine Arts; History - United States; Industrial and Technical Education
Dist - BARR **Prod** - GLOBET 1989

A Wrinkle in Time 15 MIN
U-matic / VHS
Storybound Series
Color (I)
Presents a science fiction story about the adventures of a girl and her family. From the book by Madeline L'Engle.
Literature and Drama
Dist - CTI **Prod** - CTI

A Wrinkle in time 15 MIN
VHS
Storybound series
Color (I)
#E375; LC 90-713289
Presents a science fiction thriller, 'A Wrinkle in Time' by Madeleine L'Engle, which follows the imaginative adventures of Meg Murray and her family. Part of a 16 - part series designed to lead viewers to the library to find and finish the stories they encounter in the series.
English Language; Literature and Drama; Social Science
Dist - GPN **Prod** - CTI 1980
CTI

The Wrinkle squad 28 MIN
U-matic / VHS / 16mm
Insight series
B&W (J)
LC 74-713915
A dramatization about three old men who run afoul of state bureaucracy when they open a child - care center as a way of halting the feeling of uselessness that can accompany old age.
Civics and Political Systems; Sociology
Dist - PAULST **Prod** - PAULST 1971

Wrinkles 29 MIN
U-matic
Sketching techniques series; Lesson 28
Color (C A)
Demonstrates two different kinds of wrinkles used in drawing, those in fabric and skin.
Fine Arts
Dist - CDTEL **Prod** - COAST

The Wrist Driven Flexor Hinge Splint 10 MIN
U-matic
Color (C)
Demonstrates criteria for determining appropriate, candidates for the use of the wrist driven flexor hinge splint.
Health and Safety; Science - Natural
Dist - UOKLAH **Prod** - UOKLAH 1984

Write a Letter 20.25 MIN
VHS / 16mm / U-matic
Elementary Language Skills Series
Color (K P I)
$475, $335, $365 _ #A405
Teaches all about writing both business and personal letters. Shows the fun of letter writing.
Business and Economics; English Language; Literature and Drama
Dist - BARR **Prod** - BARR 1986

Write a Story 22.5 MIN
VHS / 16mm / U-matic
Elementary Language Skills Series
Color (K P I)
$505, $355, $385 _ #A511
Explains the basic elements of story writing. Describes the differences between prose and poetry, fiction and nonfiction.
English Language; Fine Arts; Literature and Drama
Dist - BARR **Prod** - BARR 1987

Write an essay 22 MIN
16mm / VHS
Color (I)
LC 89715692
Teaches fundamentals of essay writing. Encourages students to write and to raise questions about values.
Computer Science; English Language; Guidance and Counseling
Dist - BARR

Write Arabic 90 MIN
VHS
Color (G) (ARABIC)
$160.00 purchase _ #SAR203
Teaches beginning students of Arabic using authentic situations and information on local customs. Developed and produced by Tim Francis. Includes videocassette, two audiocassettes and text.
Foreign Language
Dist - NORTNJ

The Write channel - Pt 01 15 MIN
U-matic / VHS
Color (P I)
Discusses the use of 'and' for compound subjects, objects and verbs. Points out the need to start a sentence with a capital letter and end a statement with a period.
English Language
Dist - AITECH **Prod** - MAETEL 1979

The Write channel - Pt 02 14 MIN
U-matic / VHS
Color (P I)
Explains adjective modification and looks at the correct use of the period and capital letter.
English Language
Dist - AITECH **Prod** - MAETEL 1979

The Write channel - Pt 03 14 MIN
U-matic / VHS
Color (P I)
Describes the use of conjunctions 'and' and 'but' in a compound sentence and focuses on the comma.
English Language
Dist - AITECH **Prod** - MAETEL 1979

The Write channel - Pt 04 15 MIN
U-matic / VHS
Color (P I)
Tells how to add when, where and how information to a base sentence. Describes the capitalization of the days and months and the use of a comma between the day and the year.
English Language
Dist - AITECH **Prod** - MAETEL 1979

The Write channel - Pt 05 15 MIN
VHS / U-matic
Color (P I)
Discusses the addition of adjective clauses introduced by 'who' or 'that' to a base sentence. Considers the use of the question mark and the exclamation point.
English Language
Dist - AITECH **Prod** - MAETEL 1979

The Write channel - Pt 06 14 MIN
U-matic / VHS
Color (P I)
Focuses on the use of the prepositional phrase introduced by 'with.' Describes the use of a comma after an introductory 'yes' or 'no.'.
English Language
Dist - AITECH **Prod** - MAETEL 1979

The Write channel - Pt 07 15 MIN
U-matic / VHS
Color (P I)
Examines the addition of prepositional phrases to a base sentence. Tells how to capitalize the name of a city or a state and discusses the use of a comma between a city and a state.
English Language
Dist - AITECH **Prod** - MAETEL 1979

The Write channel - Pt 08 15 MIN
U-matic / VHS
Color (P I)
Exemplifies the variety of sentence types and emphasizes the need to choose the one that best expresses an idea. Discusses the use of a capital letter to begin a person's name and the use of a comma to separate a series of adjectives.
English Language
Dist - AITECH **Prod** - MAETEL 1979

The Write channel - Pt 09 15 MIN
VHS / U-matic
Color (P I)
Focuses on the use of the subordinating conjunctions 'when,' 'after' and 'before.' Explains the capitalization of 'I.'.
English Language
Dist - AITECH **Prod** - MAETEL 1979

The Write channel - Pt 10 14 MIN
VHS / U-matic
Color (P I)
Describes the use of the subordinating conjunctions 'because,' 'although' and 'if.' Explores the use of the apostrophe in a contraction.
English Language
Dist - AITECH **Prod** - MAETEL 1979

The Write channel - Pt 11 15 MIN
U-matic / VHS
Color (P I)
Looks at the use of infinitives and participial phrases, as well as the use of the apostrophe in possessives.
English Language
Dist - AITECH **Prod** - MAETEL 1979

The Write channel - Pt 12 15 MIN
U-matic / VHS
Color (P I)
Discusses the use of appositives and the use of commas to set off an appositive.
English Language
Dist - AITECH **Prod** - MAETEL 1979

The Write channel - Pt 14 15 MIN
VHS / U-matic
Color (P I)
Describes the use of 'that' in a noun clause. Offers information on the capitalization and underlining of a book title.
English Language
Dist - AITECH **Prod** - MAETEL 1979

The Write channel - Pt 15 15 MIN
U-matic / VHS
Color (P I)
Reviews sentence combining techniques, capitalization, and punctuation rules.

English Language
Dist - AITECH **Prod** - MAETEL 1979

The Write course - an introduction to college composition series 900 MIN
VHS / U-matic
The Write course - an introduction to college composition series
Color (C)
$575.00, $375.00 purchase
Presents a 30 - part series on college composition. Uses a comedy series format interspersed with interviews to emphasize the process method. Offers practical advice from contemporary writers such as Irving Wallace, Larry Gelbart and Irving Stone, while mini - documentaries filmed on location tackle real - life writing problems.
Education; English Language
Dist - ANNCPB **Prod** - DALCCD 1984

Write Course - an Introduction to College Composition Series
Discovering the Library
Dist - ANNCPB
DALCCD

Write Course - an Introduction to College Composition Series
The Audience
Audience and style
Beginning and Ending
Definition
Developing form
The Drama of Thinking
The Essay Test
Narration and Description
New Directions
Paragraph Patterns
Report and Proposal Writing
Revision Strategies 30 MIN
Structuring the Topic
Using the Writer's Tools
Why Write?
Word Strategy
Words and Meaning
Dist - DALCCD

Write course - an introduction to college composition series
Argumentation 30 MIN
Discovering Ideas 30 MIN
Process and analysis 30 MIN
Sentence patterns 30 MIN
Sentence strategy 30 MIN
Sharpening the focus
Writing a research paper 30 MIN
Writing about books 30 MIN
Writing at work
The Writing process 30 MIN
Dist - DALCCD
FI

Write Course - an Introduction to College Composition Series
Audience and style 30 MIN
The Beginning 30 MIN
Beginning and Ending 30 MIN
Definition 30 MIN
Developing form 30 MIN
The Drama of Thinking 30 MIN
The Essay Test 30 MIN
Narration and Description 30 MIN
New Directions 30 MIN
Paragraph Patterns 30 MIN
Report and Proposal Writing 30 MIN
Structuring the Topic 30 MIN
Style 30 MIN
Using the Writer's Tools 30 MIN
Why Write 30 MIN
Word Strategy 30 MIN
Words and Meanings 30 MIN
Dist - FI

Write course - an introduction to college composition
Argumentation - paragraph patterns - Parts 15 and 16 60 MIN
Audience and style - discovering ideas - Parts 5 and 6 60 MIN
Developing form - narration and description - Pts 11 and 12 60 MIN
The Drama of thinking - sharpening the focus - Parts 7 and 8 60 MIN
Process and analysis - definition - Parts 13 and 14 60 MIN
Revision strategies - using the writer's tools - Parts 21 and 22 60 MIN
Sentence patterns - sentence strategy - Parts 17 and 18 60 MIN
Structuring the topic - beginning and ending 60 MIN
Style - new directions 60 MIN
Words and meanings - word strategy - Parts 19 and 20 60 MIN
Dist - ANNCPB

The Write course - Pt 1 - the beginning 30 MIN
VHS / 16mm
Write Course Series
Color (C)
$8.00 rental _ #34345
Provides an overview of the series and explains how to use the information presented. Views teaching of composition as a process. Each videotape contains real - life adaptations of the writing process at work.
Education; English Language
Dist - FI **Prod** - ANNCPB 1984

The Write course - Pt 2 - why write 30 MIN
VHS / 16mm
Write Course Series
Color (C)
$8.00 rental _ #34346
Addresses the question of why we write and why we study, and examines theories of the writing process as a whole.
Education; English Language
Dist - FI **Prod** - ANNCPB 1984

The Write course - Pt 3 - the writing process 30 MIN
VHS / 16mm
Write Course Series
Color (C)
$8.00 rental _ #34347
Provides current research information on how to be a successful writer. Clarifies concepts about the writing process.
Education; English Language
Dist - FI **Prod** - ANNCPB 1984

The Write course - Pt 4 - the audience 30 MIN
VHS / 16mm
Write Course Series
Color (C)
$8.00 rental _ #34348
Examines the relationship of the writer to his or her audience and the relationship of the audience to the written message. The different kinds of audience - writer relationships are described.
Education; English Language
Dist - FI **Prod** - ANNCPB 1984

The Write course - Pt 5 - audience and style 30 MIN
VHS / 16mm
Write Course Series
Color (C)
$8.00 rental _ #34349
Studies how the audience affects the style of writing (specifically the diction and the use of language), with emphasis placed on the fact that the "correct" use of language is the use that is appropriate to the audience.
Education; English Language; Literature and Drama
Dist - FI **Prod** - ANNCPB 1984

The Write course - Pt 6 - discovering ideas 30 MIN
VHS / 16mm
Write Course Series
Color (C)
$8.00 rental _ #34350
Focuses on the prewriting stage of composition, showing free and unfocused techniques to use for generating ideas on composition topics. First of three lessons on the prewriting phase.
Education; English Language
Dist - FI **Prod** - ANNCPB 1984

The Write course - Pt 7 - the drama of thinking 30 MIN
VHS / 16mm
Write Course Series
Color (C)
$8.00 rental _ #34351
Focuses on the prewriting stage of composition, showing more structured ways to generate ideas on a given subject. Presents idea - generating devices based on sound knowledge. Second of three lessons on the prewriting phase.
Education; English Language; Fine Arts
Dist - FI **Prod** - ANNCPB 1984

The Write course - Pt 8 - sharpening the focus 30 MIN
VHS / 16mm
Write Course Series
Color (C)
$8.00 rental _ #34352
Shows how to develop a specific topic from a wide range of ideas during the prewriting phases. The relationship of the composition to the audience is also reinforced. Third of three lessons on the prewriting stage.
Education; English Language
Dist - FI **Prod** - ANNCPB 1984

The Write course - Pt 9 - structuring the topic 30 MIN
VHS / 16mm
Write Course Series
Color (C)
$8.00 rental _ #34353
Explains why the audience needs clearly structured writing by showing 'how - to' strategies to plan and organize the writing.
Education; English Language
Dist - FI **Prod** - ANNCPB 1984

The Write course - Pt 10 - beginning and ending 30 MIN
VHS / 16mm
Write Course Series
Color (C)
$8.00 rental _ #34354
Emphasizes the usefulness of introductory and concluding paragraphs to the writer and the reader and their place in the writing process.
Education; English Language
Dist - FI **Prod** - ANNCPB 1984

The Write course - Pt 11 - developing form 30 MIN
VHS / 16mm
Write Course Series
Color (C)
$8.00 rental _ #34355
Introduces four traditional patterns of development, encouraging the view of the writer as the one who chooses and controls the composition, not the one who imitates predefined modes of discourse.
Education; English Language
Dist - FI **Prod** - ANNCPB 1984

The Write course - Pt 12 - narration and description 30 MIN
VHS / 16mm
Write Course Series
Color (C)
$8.00 rental _ #34356
Introduces the study of traditional rhetorical patterns, using a pragmatic approach. The lesson emphasizes the use of traditional patterns to develop individual writing styles. First of four lessons on this subject.
Education; English Language
Dist - FI **Prod** - ANNCPB 1984

The Write course - Pt 13 - process and analysis 30 MIN
VHS / 16mm
Write Course Series
Color (C)
$8.00 rental _ #34357
Explores uses of the process and analysis pattern to write a practical paper outside the classroom. Second of four lessons on this subject.
Education; English Language
Dist - FI **Prod** - ANNCPB 1984

The Write course - Pt 14 - definition 30 MIN
VHS / 16mm
Write Course Series
Color (C)
$8.00 rental _ #34358
Presents several methods of writing extended definitions, showing uses for academic and nonacademic settings. Definition is used in the broad sense.
Education; English Language
Dist - FI **Prod** - ANNCPB 1984

The Write course - Pt 15 - argumentation 30 MIN
VHS / 16mm
Write Course Series
Color (C)
$8.00 rental _ #34359
Studies the relationship of formal logic to clear writing, showing how common logical fallacies make expository writing less powerful. Includes treatment of the components of persuasive writing and audience appeal.
Education; English Language; Religion and Philosophy
Dist - FI **Prod** - ANNCPB 1984

The Write course - Pt 16 - paragraph patterns 30 MIN
VHS / 16mm
Write Course Series
Color (C)
$8.00 rental _ #34360
Examines the paragraph's flexibility and realistic use in writing, and traditional misconceptions about its role as a unit.
Education; English Language
Dist - FI **Prod** - ANNCPB 1984

The Write course - Pt 17 - sentence patterns 30 MIN
VHS / 16mm
Write Course Series
Color (C)
$8.00 rental _ #34361
Explores the sentence and its rhetorical aspects to help gain an understanding about the importance of sentence style and its relationship to grammar.
Education; English Language
Dist - FI **Prod** - ANNCPB 1984

The Write course - Pt 18 - sentence strategy 30 MIN
VHS / 16mm
Write Course Series
Color (C)
$8.00 rental _ #34362
Continues the previous lesson, emphasizing sentence revision to fit rhetorical context.
Education; English Language
Dist - FI **Prod** - ANNCPB 1984

The Write course - Pt 19 - words and meanings 30 MIN
VHS / 16mm
Write Course Series
Color (C)
$8.00 rental _ #34363
Teaches a heightened awareness of words as a stylistic device and an increased sense of the finer points of style.
Education; English Language; Literature and Drama
Dist - FI **Prod** - ANNCPB 1984

The Write course - Pt 20 - word Strategy 30 MIN
VHS / 16mm
Write Course Series
Color (C)
$8.00 rental _ #34364
Continues the previous lesson, showing common abuses of words.
Education; English Language; Literature and Drama
Dist - FI **Prod** - ANNCPB 1984

The Write course - Pt 21 - revision strategies 30 MIN
VHS / 16mm
Write Course Series
Color (C)
$8.00 rental _ #34365
Focuses on the revision stage of the writing process. Treats revision as more than just proofreading and editing.
Education; English Language; Industrial and Technical Education
Dist - FI **Prod** - ANNCPB 1984

The Write course - Pt 22 - using the writer's tools 30 MIN
VHS / 16mm
Write Course Series
Color (C)
$8.00 rental _ #34366
Focuses on editing, proofreading, and the books that can help with these tasks, giving specific practical instructions in using common reference books. Complements the previous lesson.
Education; English Language; Industrial and Technical Education
Dist - FI **Prod** - ANNCPB 1984

The Write course - Pt 23 - discovering the library 30 MIN
VHS / 16mm
Write Course Series
Color (C)
$8.00 rental _ #34367
Studies the 'why' and 'how' of preparing a research paper, presenting the steps for acquiring the information from researching a topic in the library to preparing the information.
Education; English Language
Dist - FI **Prod** - ANNCPB 1984

The Write course - Pt 24 - writing a research paper 30 MIN
VHS / 16mm
Write Course Series
Color (C)
$8.00 rental _ #34368
Explains the nature of the research paper and the steps necessary to produce it.
Education; English Language
Dist - FI **Prod** - ANNCPB 1984

The Write course - Pt 25 - writing about books 30 MIN
VHS / 16mm
Write Course Series
Color (C)
$8.00 rental _ #34369
Provides practical advice on writing book reports, challenging commonly held misconceptions about the task and encouraging students to go beyond summarization.
Education; English Language
Dist - FI **Prod** - ANNCPB 1984

The Write course - Pt 26 - the essay test 30 MIN
VHS / 16mm
Write Course Series
Color (C)
$8.00 rental _ #34370
Shows the particular requirements of the essay test in relation to the basic organizational and writing techniques learned throughout the course.
Education; English Language; Literature and Drama
Dist - FI **Prod** - ANNCPB 1984

The Write course - Pt 27 - writing at work 30 MIN
VHS / 16mm
Write Course Series
Color (C)
$8.00 rental _ #34371
Provides a practical approach to writing common forms of business communications, integrating this with information from research on successful business writers.
Business and Economics; Education; English Language
Dist - FI **Prod** - ANNCPB 1984

The Write course - Pt 28 - report and proposal writing 30 MIN
VHS / 16mm
Write Course Series
Color (C)
$8.00 rental _ #34372
Shows how to write proposals and reports in academia, business, and science, using proper format, audience appeal, and occasion.
Business and Economics; Education; English Language; Science
Dist - FI **Prod** - ANNCPB 1984

The Write course - Pt 29 - style 30 MIN
VHS / 16mm
Write Course Series
Color (C)
$8.00 rental _ #34373
Examines how to achieve an individual style appropriate to the writing situation, using voice, tone, and point of view.
Education; English Language; Literature and Drama
Dist - FI **Prod** - ANNCPB 1984

The Write course - Pt 30 - new directions 30 MIN
VHS / 16mm
Write Course Series
Color (C)
$8.00 rental _ #34374
Stresses the future uses of newly acquired writing skills and shows how these skills can be transferred to other writing situations.
Education; English Language
Dist - FI **Prod** - ANNCPB 1984

Write Course Series
The Write course - Pt 11 - developing form 30 MIN
The Write course - Pt 12 - narration and description 30 MIN
The Write course - Pt 13 - process and analysis 30 MIN
The Write course - Pt 14 - definition 30 MIN
The Write course - Pt 15 - argumentation 30 MIN
The Write course - Pt 16 - paragraph patterns 30 MIN
The Write course - Pt 17 - sentence patterns 30 MIN
The Write course - Pt 18 - sentence strategy 30 MIN
The Write course - Pt 19 - words and meanings 30 MIN
The Write course - Pt 21 - revision strategies 30 MIN
The Write course - Pt 22 - using the writer's tools 30 MIN
The Write course - Pt 23 - discovering the library 30 MIN
The Write course - Pt 24 - writing a research paper 30 MIN
The Write course - Pt 25 - writing about books 30 MIN
The Write course - Pt 26 - the essay test 30 MIN
The Write course - Pt 27 - writing at work 30 MIN
The Write course - Pt 28 - report and proposal writing 30 MIN
The Write course - Pt 29 - style 30 MIN
The Write course - Pt 30 - new directions 30 MIN
The Write course - Pt 8 - sharpening the focus 30 MIN
The Write course - Pt 5 - audience and style 30 MIN
The Write course - Pt 4 - the audience 30 MIN
The Write course - Pt 9 - structuring the topic 30 MIN
The Write course - Pt 1 - the beginning 30 MIN
The Write course - Pt 7 - the drama of thinking 30 MIN
The Write course - Pt 6 - discovering ideas 30 MIN
The Write course - Pt 10 - beginning and ending 30 MIN
The Write course - Pt 3 - the writing process 30 MIN
The Write course - Pt 20 - word Strategy 30 MIN
The Write course - Pt 2 - why write 30 MIN
Dist - FI

Write in Water 10 MIN
16mm
Color
Presents nature's forms as they are reflected by the flux of the landscape over the changing seasonal periods.
Fine Arts; Science - Natural
Dist - RADIM **Prod** - DAVISJ

Write it right 15 MIN
U-matic / VHS
Hidden treasures series; No 7
Color (T)
LC 82-706547
Uses the adventures of a pirate and his three friends to explore the many facets of language arts. Focuses on observation and organization in writing a story, including the determination of who, what, when, which and why.
English Language
Dist - GPN **Prod** - WCVETV 1980

Write it Right - it all Starts with Paragraphs 55 MIN
U-matic / VHS
Color (J H)
LC 83-707019
Uses a step - by - step approach to describe the essentials of paragraph writing. Stresses the importance of considering audience and purpose, and of narrowing one's subject. Demonstrates proper paragraph construction.
English Language
Dist - GA **Prod** - CHUMAN 1983

Write it Right - it all Starts with Paragraphs
VHS / Slide / 35mm strip / U-matic
Writing Skills Series
(G C J)
$229 purchase _ #00315 - 85
Revised edition of Communication Skills - Write it Right. Describes the essentials of paragraph writing in a step by step approach. Compares and contrasts subjective and objective writing approaches.
English Language
Dist - CHUMAN

The Write Move 24 MIN
16mm
Color
LC 78-700235
Presents several situations which demonstrate the need for basic writing skills. Explains that four facets of good writing are mechanics, organization, vocabulary and expression.
English Language
Dist - BYU **Prod** - BYU 1977

Write now - pay later 27 MIN
VHS
Color (A)
$525.00 purchase
Brings out the importance and liability surrounding document writing in business situations, illustrating how carelessly written items can be misinterpreted. Draws on real - life situations to show how such items as memos, telephone logs and vouchers can create legal trouble.
Business and Economics; Civics and Political Systems; Education
Dist - COMFLM **Prod** - COMFLM

Write on 14 MIN
U-matic / 16mm / VHS
Serendipity Series
Color (P)
LC 76-701769
Considers the activity of writing as a part of communication.
English Language
Dist - MGHT **Prod** - MGHT 1976

Write on 260 MIN
VHS
Color; PAL (J H)
PdS55 purchase
Presents ten programs of 26 minutes each to help take the pain out of writing, whether a business report, letters to a friend, a complaint, or something creative. Encourages style and clarity and helps to boost viewer confidence in writing ability while stimulating an interest in writing. Includes a set of teacher's background notes and a summary of each program and ideas for discussion and follow - up work. Contact distributor about availability outside the United Kingdom.
English Language; Fine Arts
Dist - ACADEM

Write on series - Set 1
Goodbye, cruel world 5 MIN
Dist - CTI

Write on series - Set 2
The Almost dangerous game 5 MIN
Dist - CTI

Write on series
Calling Dr Kent 5 MIN
Cinderella Newton 5 MIN
Gone with the paragraph 5 MIN
The Pharaoh's daughter 5 MIN
Show business 5 MIN
Dist - CTI

Write on, set 1 series
The Bard 5 MIN
Captain Kent 5 MIN
The Comma kid 5 MIN
Comrades X and B 5 MIN
Dracula's Defeat 5 MIN
The Escaped Convict 5 MIN
The Foolish suitor 5 MIN
Fragment Fred 5 MIN
Henry Chan 5 MIN
Irma Faust 5 MIN
King Kane 5 MIN
La Bellicosa 5 MIN
Lucretia 5 MIN
The Mad Bomber 5 MIN
The Making of Flaws 5 MIN
Miss Grouse 5 MIN
Miss Newton's Trial 5 MIN
Paolo Carbonara 5 MIN
Peter Berton 5 MIN
Reginald Parse 5 MIN
Rhubarb Power 5 MIN
The Robber's Guide 5 MIN
Slick Stagger 5 MIN
The Spice of Life 5 MIN
Stocky Mariano 5 MIN
The UFO 5 MIN
You Bet Your Life 5 MIN
Dist - CTI

Write on - Set 2 series
Beau Jest 5 MIN
The Case of the missing editor 5 MIN
A Critical lapse 5 MIN
Curses, foiled again 5 MIN
The Devil and Henry Kent 5 MIN
Dream on 5 MIN
Dream Weaving 5 MIN
The Dreamer 5 MIN
Happy Daze 5 MIN
Henry Kent, tycoon 5 MIN
Henry's angels 5 MIN
I, Henry 5 MIN
Jungle madness 5 MIN
Leo Claws 5 MIN
MacHenry 5 MIN
The Night Before 5 MIN
The Old Man and the Paragraph 5 MIN
Perchance to Dream 5 MIN
The Revengers 5 MIN
The Rocking Horse Writer 5 MIN
The Scarlet Pen Pal 5 MIN
Scribbling Beauty - Pt 1 5 MIN
Scribbling Beauty - Pt 2 5 MIN
An SOS 5 MIN
Their Finest Paragraph 5 MIN
Transition Trek 5 MIN
Dist - CTI

Write poems, sing songs 22 MIN
VHS
Color (P I C G)
$195.00 purchase, $40.00 rental _ #38093
Motivates children to enjoy reading and writing. Shows how David Williams, acclaimed poet, songwriter, performer, and English teacher, works as a visiting artist - in - residence with fifth graders. Motivates students labeled as underachievers to write and read poetry. Prepared for two audiences - for elementary level language arts teachers, the film shows how poetry and songwriting can be imaginatively incorporated into the classroom; for students, it shows a new way of looking at language arts. Produced by Janyce Hamilton.
Education; English Language; Fine Arts; Literature and Drama
Dist - UCEMC

The Write stuff 39 MIN
VHS
Color (G)
$195.00 purchase _ #91F61107
Shows how to improve business writing. Includes a video, audiocassette, 5 copies of The Write Stuff, 5 copies of How to Take the Frog Out of Writing.
Business and Economics; English Language
Dist - DARTNL **Prod** - DARTNL

Write your own ticket 14 MIN
VHS / U-matic / BETA
Barassi tapes series
Color; Stereo (H)
Shows a passenger from Rutville agonize over buying his ticket to nowhere. His goals are restricted by an unwillingness to see possibilities. He and a woman traveler use Ron Barassi's strategy for setting and achieving goals. Highly appropriate for anyone who wants to achieve success.
Guidance and Counseling; Psychology
Dist - SEVDIM **Prod** - SEVDIM 1983

Writer in America Series
Eudora Welty 29 MIN
Ross MacDonald 29 MIN
Dist - CORF

Writers 0 MIN
U-matic
Teachers Teaching Writing Series
Color (T)
Demonstrates classroom techniques of several teachers who have been judged superior in their methods of teaching writing. Each of the six programs, which were taped in regular classes, features a single teacher conducting an actual writing process.
Education; English Language
Dist - AFSCD **Prod** - AFSCD 1986

Writer's Block 7 MIN
U-matic / VHS / 16mm
Color (J H C A)
$190, $135 purchase _ #4044
Tells about the frustrations of writer's block. A Perspective film.
English Language
Dist - CORF

Writers - John Updike 30 MIN
16mm / U-matic / VHS
USA Series
B&W (H C A)
Presents interviews with John Updike during which he discusses some of the beliefs, concepts and attitudes which have influenced his novels. Shows him in and about his home at Ipswich, Mass. He reads selections from several of his short stories, accompanied by scenes which depict the things described.
Literature and Drama
Dist - IU **Prod** - NET 1966

Writers of today series
Offers a five - part series, produced in the 1950s, in which dialogues take place between drama and literary critic Walter Kerr and a well - known male writer. Provides insights into these men as they speak about contemporary literature and society at the time of their own writing peaks. Writers featured are W H Auden, Archibald MacLeish, Arthur Miller, Frank O'Connor and Robert Penn Warren.
Archibald MacLeish 30 MIN
Arthur Miller 30 MIN
Frank O'Connor 30 MIN
Robert Penn Warren 30 MIN
W H Auden 30 MIN
The Writers of today series 150 MIN
Dist - FIRS

Writers on Writing 20 MIN
VHS / U-matic
Color (H C A)
Presents seven of American's finest contemporary authors discussing their lives, sources of inspiration and writing methods. Includes Catherine Drinker Bowen and James Houston.
Literature and Drama
Dist - DAVFMS **Prod** - DAVFMS

Writers on writing series
Features leading Australian and American writers in a three - part series on writing for film, television and radio. Produced by the Australian Film, Television and Radio School.
Writing for film 52 MIN
Writing for radio 44 MIN
Writing for television 48 MIN
Dist - FIRLIT

Writers - Philip Roth 30 MIN
16mm
USA Series
B&W (H C A)
A conversation between writer Philip Roth and Jerre Mangione, novelist and professor of English at the University of Pennsylvania, during which Roth discusses his stories and plays and explains the covert and ostensible meanings of his works. Discusses the relationship of his work to that of Saul Bellow and Roth's reactions to critics' reviews.
Literature and Drama
Dist - IU **Prod** - NET 1966

Writer's plan road 20 MIN
U-matic / VHS
Efficient reading - instructional tapes series; Tape 11
Color
Shows how to understand the writer's style and key word signs in order to get the whole picture.
English Language
Dist - TELSTR **Prod** - TELSTR

Writer's realm series
Asking the right question 15 MIN
Checking it out 15 MIN
Details, details 15 MIN
Everything in its Place 15 MIN
It's Like this 15 MIN
Just the Right Tone 15 MIN
Let's Get Organized 15 MIN
A Little Help from Your Friends 15 MIN
Picture this 14 MIN
Put it in Writing 15 MIN
The Search Begins 15 MIN
See what I'm Saying 15 MIN
Show me what you mean 15 MIN
That's Worth Noting 15 MIN
What's the Idea? 15 MIN
Dist - AITECH

Writers - Science Fiction 30 MIN
16mm
USA Series
B&W (H C A)
Presents a discussion of science fiction by a panel of writers, a scientist and an English professor which includes both historical and future perspectives and definitions of science fiction.
Literature and Drama
Dist - IU **Prod** - NET 1966

Writer's Tools 15 MIN
VHS / U-matic
Zebra Wings Series
Color (I)
Illustrates the steps in writing a report or article. Emphasizes the importance of research and creative organization and presentation of non - fiction material.
English Language; Literature and Drama
Dist - AITECH **Prod** - NITC 1975

The Writer's view 15 MIN
VHS / U-matic
America past series
(J H)
$125.00 purchase
Explains the development of the American literary tradition.
History - United States; Literature and Drama
Dist - AITECH **Prod** - KRMATV 1987

A Writer's work with Toni Morrison 30 MIN
VHS
World of ideas with Bill Moyers - Season II - series
Color; Captioned (G)
$39.95 purchase _ #WIWM - 207
Interviews author Toni Morrison. Presents her observations on her books' characters, her personal life and her philosophy of love as a metaphor. Hosted by Bill Moyers.
Literature and Drama
Dist - PBS

Writer's workshop - how to write a short story 36 MIN
VHS
Color (J H C A)
$93.00 purchase _ #MB - 540797 - 5
Teaches basic techniques in short story writing. Uses two short stories by Hawthorne and Poe to exemplify techniques and devices - Hawthorne's 'Young Goodman Brown' and Poe's 'Masque of the Red Death.'
Literature and Drama
Dist - SRA **Prod** - SRA 1988

Writer's workshop series
Presents 15 contemporary writers in lectures and discussion at the University of South Carolina. Features the writers' observations on writing, literary trends, the ins and outs of getting published, and other subjects. Fifteen - part series is hosted by USC writer - in - residence William Price Fox and introduced by George Plimpton.
George Plimpton 30 MIN
James Alan McPherson 30 MIN
James Dickey 30 MIN
John Gardner 30 MIN
John Hawkes 30 MIN
Nora Ephron 30 MIN
Pauline Kael 30 MIN
Reynolds Price 30 MIN
Stephen Spender 30 MIN
Susan Sontag 30 MIN
Tom Wolfe 30 MIN
William Price Fox 30 MIN
William Styron 30 MIN
Dist - PBS **Prod** - SCETVM 1988

Writer's workshop series
Kurt Vonnegut 30 MIN
Dist - PBS
SCETV

Writer's workshop series
Features 15 major fiction and nonfiction writers in lectures and discussions of their work, in a writing workshop series held at the University of South Carolina. Hosted by author William Price Fox and introduced by George Plimpton, with special appearances by James Dickey. Presents a 15 - part telecourse.
George Plimpton 15 MIN
James Dickey 15 MIN
James McPherson 15 MIN
John Gardner 15 MIN
John Hawkes 15 MIN
John Irving 15 MIN
Nora Ephron 15 MIN
Pauline Kael 15 MIN
Reynolds Price 15 MIN
Stephen Spender 15 MIN
Susan Sontag 15 MIN
Tom Wolfe 15 MIN
William Price Fox 15 MIN
William Styron 15 MIN
Dist - SCETV **Prod** - SCETV 1988

Writing 29 MIN
VHS / U-matic
Teaching Writing - a Process Approach Series
Color
Focuses on the role the teacher assumes when guiding students to write. Explains how the teacher can create an environment conducive to writing by removing obstacles to writing and by providing reinforcing stimuli.
Education; English Language
Dist - PBS **Prod** - MSITV 1982

Writing a bibliograpy 20 MIN
VHS / 16mm
Study research library skills series
Color (J)
Teaches how to write a bibliography using different formats.
Education; English Language
Dist - COMEX **Prod** - COMEX 1987

Writing a Play 15 MIN
U-matic
You Can Write Anything Series
Color (P I)
Teaches writing techniques through Keith and Amanda who learn how to write dialogue, set precise stage directions and the correct play form.
Education; English Language
Dist - TVOTAR **Prod** - TVOTAR 1984

Writing a Research Paper 7 MIN
U-matic / VHS
Library Skills Tapes Series
Color
Teaches the basic steps of writing a research paper. Includes choosing a topic, outlining, footnotes, typing, and proofreading.
Education; English Language
Dist - MDCC **Prod** - MDCC

Writing a research paper 30 MIN
U-matic / VHS
Write course - an introduction to college composition series
Color (C A)
LC 85-700909
Explains the nature of the research paper and the steps required to produce it.
English Language
Dist - FI **Prod** - FI 1984
DALCCD DALCCD

Writing a timed essay 23 MIN
VHS
Color (H C G)
$435.00, $295.00 purchase, $60.00 rental
Looks at effective techniques for writing a timed essay. Demonstrates how to assess a topic, plan and organize ideas, use standard paragraph format, and proofread. Appropriate preparation for the essay sections of the CAP, GED, SPE and TASP exams. Written and produced by Bobrow Test Preparation Services.
Education; English Language; Literature and Drama
Dist - CF

Writing about books 30 MIN
U-matic / VHS
Write course - an introduction to college composition series
Color (C A)
Discusses commonly held misconceptions about book reviews and encourages students to go beyond summary in their writing.
English Language
Dist - FI **Prod** - FI 1984
DALCCD DALCCD

Writing about books - the essay test 60 MIN
U-matic / VHS
Write course - an introduction to college composition - series; Pt 25 and 26
Color (C)
$45.00, $29.95 purchase
Reveals that writing an effective book review requires the ability to differentiate between summary and evaluation in Part 25. Looks at preparation, organization and writing techniques which make a powerful essay in Part 26. Parts of a 30 - part series on college composition.
Education; English Language
Dist - ANNCPB **Prod** - DALCCD 1984

Writing about Drama 30 MIN
U-matic / VHS
Communicating through Literature Series
Color (C)
Literature and Drama
Dist - DALCCD **Prod** - DALCCD

Writing about Fiction 30 MIN
U-matic / VHS
Communicating through Literature Series
Color (C)
English Language; Literature and Drama
Dist - DALCCD **Prod** - DALCCD

Writing about Film 30 MIN
VHS / U-matic
Communicating through Literature Series
Color (C)
English Language; Fine Arts
Dist - DALCCD **Prod** - DALCCD

Writing about Literature 30 MIN
U-matic / VHS
Communicating through Literature Series
Color (C)
English Language; Literature and Drama
Dist - DALCCD **Prod** - DALCCD

Writing about literature - interpreting and explaining 30 MIN
VHS
Color (H C G)
$69.95 purchase _ #RWR - 23
Shows how to interpret and explain poems, short stories and books. Discusses reader participation - take notes, paraphrasing and recording initial reactions, the importance of rereading, writing about character and point of view.
English Language; Literature and Drama
Dist - INSTRU **Prod** - FLCCJA 1991

Writing about Poetry 30 MIN
U-matic / VHS
Communicating through Literature Series
Color (C)
English Language; Literature and Drama
Dist - DALCCD **Prod** - DALCCD

Writing - an interview with Irving Stone 19 MIN
16mm / U-matic / VHS
Color (H C A)
$435.00, $250.00 purchase _ #3895; LC 77-703418
Interviews novelist Irving Stone and his wife, Jean, who discuss Stone's writings and speak on the functions of a writer, the hard work and perseverance which professional writing entails and the problems involved in transforming books into screenplays.
Biography; Guidance and Counseling; Literature and Drama
Dist - CORF **Prod** - CORF 1978

Writing and Executing Programs 180 MIN
U-matic
Microprocessors - a Comprehensive Introduction Series
Color (A)
Introduces a timing control exercise. Discusses implementing a delay routine and accomplishing control changes by simple software modifications. A motor speed control program illustrates performing speed/power conversion and controlling the motor power.
Computer Science
Dist - INTECS **Prod** - INTECS

Writing and Sharing 0 MIN
U-matic
Teachers Teaching Writing Series
Color (T)
Demonstrates classroom techniques of several teachers who have been judged superior in their methods of teaching writing. Each of the six programs, which were taped in regular classes, features a single teacher conducting an actual writing process.
Education; English Language
Dist - AFSCD **Prod** - AFSCD 1986

Writing and speaking 14 MIN
U-matic / VHS
En Francais series
Color (H C A)
Shows two feuding neighbors and a sequence at the French Space Telecommunications Center at Pleumeur - Bodou in Brittany.
Foreign Language; Geography - World
Dist - AITECH **Prod** - MOFAFR 1970

Writing and stems 30 MIN
VHS / 16mm
Art of decorating cakes series
(G)
$49.00 purchase _ #BCD8
Instructs in the art of cake decorating. Shows how to pattern construction for assembly of stems and writing on cake. Shows how to write and print 'Happy Birthday' on cakes. Taught by Leon Simmons, master cake decorator.
Home Economics; Industrial and Technical Education
Dist - RMIBHF **Prod** - RMIBHF

Writing as a process - a step - by - step guide 45 MIN
VHS
Color (G A)
$219.00 purchase _ #GA332V
Takes a comprehensive look at writing. Reveals the various steps of the process, including planning, getting information, writing a first draft, revisions, and copy editing.
Education; English Language
Dist - CAMV

Writing as process - a step - by - step guide 41 MIN
VHS
Color (J H)
$129.00 purchase _ #00332 - 026
Gives practical tips on how to master the three major stages of the writing process - prewriting, writing and revising. Shows how to generate ideas, gather and organize information, prepare a plan, write a first draft, make revisions and prepare a final draft. Includes teacher's guide and library kit.
Education; English Language
Dist - GA

Writing at work
VHS / U-matic
Write course - an introduction to college composition series
Color (C A)
Integrates a practical approach to the writing of common forms of business communications with information from current research on successful business writers.
Education; English Language
Dist - DALCCD **Prod** - DALCCD 1984
FI FI

Writing at work - report and proposal writing - Parts 27 and 28 60 MIN
VHS / U-matic
Write course - an introduction to college composition - series
Color (C)
$45.00, $29.95 purchase
Covers the common ingredients of good business writing with current research in the field and tips on writing a simple, accurate and professional business letter in Part 27. Identifies the skills necessary for effective report and proposal writing in Part 28. Parts of a 30 - part series on college composition.
Education; English Language
Dist - ANNCPB **Prod** - DALCCD 1984

Writing behavioral objectives 25 MIN
U-matic / VHS
How to of patient education series
Color
Centers around the formulation of objectives in patient education. Describes points to remember when writing objectives and explains and examines three domains of behavioral objectives, including cognitive, affective and psychomotor.
Health and Safety
Dist - FAIRGH **Prod** - FAIRGH

Writing Challenging Specific Objectives 30 MIN
VHS / U-matic
Performance Reviews that Build Commitment Series
Color
Defines and examines specific objectives. Shows the relationship of job descriptions, performance standards, specific objectives and corporate goals.
Business and Economics; Guidance and Counseling; Psychology
Dist - DELTAK **Prod** - PRODEV

Writing checks right 30 MIN
VHS
Color (I J H)
$89.95 purchase _ #CDS300
Teaches basic banking skills. Shows how to open checking and savings accounts, make deposits and withdrawals, write checks, keep a check register and reconcile a bank statement. Includes blank checks and workbook. Additional checks and workbooks available separately.
Business and Economics; Education
Dist - CADESF **Prod** - CADESF 1990

Writing Clearly 30 MIN
VHS / U-matic
Business of Better Writing Series
Color
Deals with writing clearly as part of improving business writing skills.
Business and Economics
Dist - KYTV **Prod** - KYTV 1983

Writing commentary 30 MIN
U-matic / VHS
BBC TV production training course series
Color (C)
$279.00, $179.00 purchase _ #AD - 2073
Demonstrates how to prepare a shot list and write commentary to fill the shot - listed program. Examines the use of wild tracks, sound effects, graphics and music. Includes sequences from distinguished commentary writers. Part of a twelve - part series on TV production by the BBC.
Fine Arts; Geography - World; Industrial and Technical Education
Dist - FOTH **Prod** - FOTH

Writing Compilers 30 MIN
U-matic / VHS
Pascal, Pt 3 - Advanced Pascal Series
Color (H C A)
LC 81-706049
Tells more about parsing activities within compilers. Shows Pascal code representation for common syntax diagram constructs. Illustrates an example code generation for a simple Pascal program.
Industrial and Technical Education; Mathematics; Sociology
Dist - COLOSU **Prod** - COLOSU 1980

Writing Concisely 30 MIN
U-matic / VHS
Business of Better Writing Series
Color
Deals with writing concisely as part of improving business writing skills.
Business and Economics
Dist - KYTV **Prod** - KYTV 1983

Writing Correctly 30 MIN
U-matic / VHS
Business of Better Writing Series
Color
Deals with writing correctly as part of improving business writing skills.
Business and Economics
Dist - KYTV **Prod** - KYTV 1983

Writing - Cursive Capital Letters a - M 30 MIN
VHS / U-matic
Printing and Writing Series
Color
English Language
Dist - KITTLC **Prod** - KITTLC

Writing - Cursive Capital Letters N - Z 30 MIN
VHS / U-matic
Printing and Writing Series
Color
English Language
Dist - KITTLC **Prod** - KITTLC

Writing - cursive small letters a - m 30 MIN
U-matic / VHS
Printing and writing series
Color
English Language
Dist - KITTLC **Prod** - KITTLC

Writing - cursive small letters n - z 30 MIN
U-matic / VHS
Printing and writing series
Color
English Language
Dist - KITTLC **Prod** - KITTLC

Writing - Everyman's Art 28 MIN
16mm
Alphabet - the Story of Writing Series
Color
Discusses the mechanical age and electronic pen making, inks and inkwells, the problems of portability, the arrival of the fountain pen, modern pen making, modern calligraphy and the alphabet of the future.
English Language; History - World
Dist - FILAUD **Prod** - CFDLD 1982

Writing for a Reason Series

The Beginning	30 MIN
Coherence	30 MIN
The Dictionary	30 MIN
The English Language - a Brief History	30 MIN
Epistomology and logic	30 MIN
The Essay	30 MIN
The Evaluative Essay	30 MIN
Fallacies	30 MIN
Language Options	30 MIN
The Letter of Application	30 MIN
The Nature of Communication	30 MIN
Order	30 MIN
The Paper of Analysis	30 MIN
The Paper of Classification	30 MIN
The Paper of Comparison	30 MIN
The Paper of Definition	30 MIN
The Paragraph	30 MIN
The Persuasive Paper	30 MIN
Readiness - Audience and Persona	30 MIN
The Report	30 MIN
The Sentence 1	30 MIN
The Sentence 2	30 MIN
Special Paragraphs - Conclusions and Transitions	30 MIN
Special Paragraphs - Introductions	30 MIN
Unity	30 MIN
Words 1	30 MIN
Words 2	30 MIN

Dist - DALCCD

Writing for business 18 MIN
VHS
Color (PRO IND A)
$595.00 purchase, $150.00 rental _ #VCO07
Addresses the difficulty people have with written communication. Shows through humorous examples what would happen if verbal communication were the same as written communication, and teaches business people a conversational style of writing. Includes Leader's Guide. By Video Communicators.
Business and Economics; Literature and Drama; Social Science
Dist - EXTR

Writing for children - Robert Leeson, Maurice Sendak, Gillian Avery, Penelope Farmer and Jill Paton Walsh 45 MIN
VHS
Color (H C G)
$79.00 purchase
Features the writers talking about writing for children, with observations on fantasy and realism, writing within a moral framework and children's preferences. Includes a group of seven - year - old children talking about how they choose a book to read.
Literature and Drama
Dist - ROLAND **Prod** - INCART

Writing for film 52 MIN
VHS
Writers on writing series
Color (PRO G C)
$149.00 purchase, $49.00 rental _ #715
Interviews four top screen writers including Frank Pierson and David Williamson. Discusses the nuts and bolts of their craft. Covers finding a story, research techniques, character development, dialog, the three - act script structure, plot and subplot, formula scripts. Part of a three - part series on writing for film, television and radio. Produced by the Australian Film, Television and Radio School.
English Language; Fine Arts; Literature and Drama
Dist - FIRLIT

Writing for Hollywood 83 MIN
VHS
Color (G PRO)
$79.95 purchase
Provides an insider's look at writing and selling scripts for motion pictures and television. Discusses the process of scriptwriting, collaboration and TV sitcoms.
Business and Economics; English Language; Fine Arts
Dist - WRITEC

Writing for Others 30 MIN
U-matic / VHS
Introduction to Technical and Business Communication Series
Color (H C A)
Business and Economics; English Language
Dist - GPN **Prod** - UMINN 1983

Writing for radio 44 MIN
VHS
Writers on writing series
Color (PRO G C)
$149.00 purchase, $49.00 rental _ #731
Interviews four expert radio writers who discuss their craft. Focuses on writing radio drama. Emphasizes the unlimited potential of radio as a medium of the imagination. Discusses how to work within the limitations of time slots and tight budgets, plot development, proper use of stage directions in a radio script, the use of music and sound effects. Part of a three - part series on writing for film, television and radio. Produced by the Australian Film, Television and Radio School.
English Language; Fine Arts; Literature and Drama
Dist - FIRLIT

Writing for Results 30 MIN
U-matic / VHS
Effective Writing for Executives Series
Color (C A)
LC 80-707288
Discusses effective and ineffective writing and analyzes the cost of writing in business, emphasizing that effective writing saves time and money and usually gets results. Focuses on organization of ideas and use of effective language. Hosted by Ed Asner.
Business and Economics; English Language
Dist - TIMLIF **Prod** - TIMLIF 1980

Writing for results - the winning written report 30 MIN
VHS
90s communications series
Color (J H C G)
$79.00 purchase _ #CPP0059V
Stresses that good writing skills are critical to job success and that employers seek job applicants who have such skills. Shows how to produce quality written reports by analyzing the reader, determining the purpose, selecting and narrowing topics, gathering, recording and filing information; and organizing the paper. Part of a three - part series on communication.
English Language; Social Science
Dist - CAMV **Prod** - CAMV 1991

Writing for television 48 MIN
VHS
Writers on writing series
Color (PRO G C)
$149.00 purchase, $49.00 rental _ #701
Interviews four veteran television writers who discuss the components of a successful TV script and reveal their own working methods. Covers telling a story with pictures, creating a character, generating dialog, collaboration and role playing, the rewrite process, adapting a novel, researching and developing a major miniseries. Part of a three - part series on writing for film, television and radio. Produced by the Australian Film, Television and Radio School.
English Language; Fine Arts; Literature and Drama
Dist - FIRLIT

Writing for the humanities - the explication 30 MIN
VHS
Color (H C G)
$69.95 purchase _ #RWR - 16
Discusses the explication as an interpretative paper in literature, fine arts or philosophy. Shows how to critique a manuscript for style, use of symbolism and analysis of meaning. Examines the explication as commentary and its differences from a research paper, using examples from novels and poems. Features a panel of professionals who discuss concerns unique to writing for the humanities.

English Language; Literature and Drama
Dist - INSTRU **Prod** - FLCCJA 1991

Writing for the information age 210 MIN
VHS
Color (A PRO IND)
$1,990.00 purchase, $350.00 rental
Presents a multi - media writing program for professionals and managers. Covers the four phases of the writing process, and presents basic writing tools. Consists of seven half - hour videotapes. Participant handbooks available at an extra charge.
Business and Economics; English Language; Guidance and Counseling; Industrial and Technical Education
Dist - VLEARN

Writing for the Modern Harp 30 MIN
VHS / U-matic
Sounds they make Series
Color (C T)
Demonstrates fingering, visual location of strings and tactile relationships, advance finger placement, pedal slides, the glissando and the arpeggiated chord. Explores the harp's capability for special effects. Offers some general advice for the harp composer.
Fine Arts
Dist - OHUTC **Prod** - OHUTC

Writing for the pedal harp 45 MIN
VHS / U-matic
Color
Presents step - by - step demonstration of harp notation and technique. Shows 135 examples of harp notation that the American Harp Society would like to standardize. Gives notation and demonstration on the screen simultaneously.
Fine Arts
Dist - OHUTC **Prod** - OHUTC

Writing for the sciences 30 MIN
VHS
Color (H C G)
$69.95 purchase _ #RWR - 20
Shows how to treat the laboratory report as a scientific paper. Discusses writing with the idea of being published. Features a panel of experts who discuss the special concerns of writing for the sciences.
English Language; Literature and Drama; Science
Dist - INSTRU **Prod** - FLCCJA 1991

Writing for the social sciences - the abstract 30 MIN
VHS
Color (H C G)
$69.95 purchase _ #RWR - 18
Discusses restating or paraphrasing a written work from history, sociology, political science or psychology and condensing it into a summary. Illustrates steps in writing, using lively examples. Features a panel of professional writers and professors who discuss concerns unique to writing for the social sciences.
English Language; Literature and Drama; Social Science
Dist - INSTRU **Prod** - FLCCJA 1991

Writing for Work Series Pt 5
Organizing Ideas 30 MIN
Dist - TIMLIF

Writing for Work Series Pt 7
Revising and Editing 30 MIN
Dist - TIMLIF

Writing for work series
Complete sentences 30 MIN
First drafts 30 MIN
Tools of writing 30 MIN
Writing for your reader 30 MIN
Writing paragraphs 30 MIN
Dist - TIMLIF

Writing for your reader 30 MIN
U-matic / VHS
Writing for work series; Pt 4
Color (A)
LC 81-706737
Presents basic writing skills for office workers, emphasizing the importance of clearly stating the purpose of the communication and knowing as much as possible about the who will be reading the letter, memo or report. Points out that tone and style can play a significant part in the success or failure of any communication. Hosted by Cicely Tyson.
Business and Economics; English Language
Dist - TIMLIF **Prod** - TIMLIF 1981

Writing for Yourself 30 MIN
U-matic / VHS
Introduction to Technical and Business Communication Series
Color (H C A)
Business and Economics; English Language
Dist - GPN **Prod** - UMINN 1983

Writing - from assignment to composition 21 MIN
VHS
Color (J H)
$99.00 purchase _ #06240 - 026
Presents a practical guide to choosing a subject, collecting supportive details and selecting an appropriate outlining style. Shows how to compose a logical and concise presentation. Includes teacher's guide and library kit.
Education; English Language
Dist - GA

Writing in the upward years series
May Sarton - writing in the upward years 30 MIN
Molly Harrower - writing in the upward years 23 MIN
Richard Eberhart - writing in the upward years 27 MIN
Dist - TNF

Writing Interestingly 30 MIN
U-matic / VHS
Business of Better Writing Series
Color
Deals with writing interestingly as part of improving business writing skills.
Business and Economics
Dist - KYTV **Prod** - KYTV 1983

Writing it Down 29 MIN
U-matic
Music Shop Series
Color
Shows composer Jerry Bilik as he sets a poem to music.
Fine Arts
Dist - UMITV **Prod** - UMITV 1974

Writing it right 28 MIN
U-matic / BETA / VHS
Communication skills 2 - advanced series
Color (H C G)
$101.95, $89.95 purchase _ #CA - 15
Defines narrative, descriptive and expository writing, as well as denotation and connotation, and distinguishes each form of writing from the other. Demonstrates the writing of narrative, descriptive and expository paragraphs. Part of a 26 - part series.
English Language; Social Science
Dist - INSTRU

Writing - journalism 15 MIN
VHS / U-matic / BETA
Career success series
(H C A)
$29.95 _ #MX314; $29.95 _ #CS314
Portrays occupations in writing and journalism by reviewing their required abilities and interviewing people employed in these fields. Tells of the anxieties and rewards involved in pursuing a career as a writer or journalist.
Education; English Language; Guidance and Counseling; Literature and Drama
Dist - CAMV RMIBHF **Prod** - CAMV RMIBHF

Writing Letters that Get Results 28 MIN
U-matic / 16mm / 8mm cartridge
Color; B&W (H A S C) (DUTCH)
LC fia67-5712; FIA67-5712
Features Waldo J Marra, nationally known communications consultant, discussing and illustrating the principles and techniques of writing effective business letters. Points out that the objectives of writing a letter are to create interest, to present facts and figures and to stimulate action.
Business and Economics; English Language; Foreign Language
Dist - RTBL **Prod** - RTBL 1967

Writing magic with Figment and Alice in Wonderland 16 MIN
U-matic / 16mm / VHS
Color (P)
$400.00, $280.00 purchase _ #JC - 67254
Uses animation and live action to solve the dilemma of Alice in Wonderland. Reveals that she has ended up in Figonia and the whimsical dragon Figment uses magic to disclose that in order to return to Wonderland, Alice must write a new story, using brainstorming, writing and rewriting.
English Language; Literature and Drama
Dist - CORF **Prod** - DISNEY 1989

Writing Number Sentences 15 MIN
U-matic
Math Factory, Module IV - Problem Solving Series
Color (P)
Presents the language and symbolism of addition and subtraction.
Mathematics
Dist - GPN **Prod** - MAETEL 1973

Writing papers without them riding you
VHS
School solutions video series
Color (I J H)
$98.00 purchase _ #CDSCH116V
Teaches the importance of good writing skills. Shows how, by following some simple steps, students can increase their ability to communicate with teachers, as well as with future bosses. Presents the different stages of writing a paper - picking a topic, preliminary research, outlining, major research, rough drafts, further research and final copy. Includes reproducible worksheets. Part of a ten - part series to build student success.
Education; English Language
Dist - CAMV

Writing paragraphs 30 MIN
VHS / U-matic
Writing for work series; Pt 3
Color (A)
LC 81-706736
Presents basic writing skills for office workers, emphasizing how paragraphs are structured, their aim and ways to create smooth transitions between sentences. Hosted by Cicely Tyson.
Business and Economics; English Language
Dist - TIMLIF **Prod** - TIMLIF 1981

Writing Persuasively 30 MIN
U-matic / VHS
Business of Better Writing Series
Color
Deals with writing persuasively as part of improving business writing skills.
Business and Economics
Dist - KYTV **Prod** - KYTV 1983

Writing - Plain and Fancy 9 MIN
16mm / U-matic / VHS
Color (I)
LC 82-700165
Looks at the development of writing including the introduction of capital letters by the ancient Romans, the standardization of the print manuscript alphabet by Charlemagne and the refinement of writing into a distinctive cursive flow by Renaissance Italians.
English Language
Dist - CORF **Prod** - PEREZ 1981

Writing Plain Letters 5 MIN
16mm
B&W
Shows the administrator of veterans affairs who explains the purpose and advantages of the information gained in the plain letters (4 - S) course and gives his personal views on the value of short, simple, strong and sincere letter writing.
Education
Dist - USVA **Prod** - USVA 1958

Writing Poetry 30 MIN
VHS / U-matic
Engle and Poetry Series
Color
Describes the process of writing poetry as making ordinary words do things they were never intended to do.
Literature and Drama
Dist - NETCHE **Prod** - NETCHE 1971

Writing position descriptions - a helping hand 22 MIN
U-matic / VHS
Position management series
Color (A)
Discusses the skills required for writing good position descriptions. Emphasizes interaction between supervisor, employee and personnel specialist. Describes how good position descriptions facilitate the personnel and management process.
Business and Economics; English Language; Guidance and Counseling; Psychology
Dist - USNAC **Prod** - USOPMA 1984

Writing positions in a newspaper 28 MIN
VHS
Color (J H C)
$39.95 purchase _ #IVMC19
Looks at professions in the newspaper industry. Features journalists who explain their jobs, including that of reporter, city editor and features reporter. Looks at other jobs in a contemporary newspaper, including advertising copywriters, advertising layout and design, plate making, printing. Examines the education necessary to be successful in the newspaper job market and offers suggestions to students who want to enter the profession. Visits the locations of several newspapers, including the Wall Street Journal.
Business and Economics; English Language; Guidance and Counseling; Industrial and Technical Education; Literature and Drama; Social Science
Dist - INSTRU

Writing Principles 30 MIN
U-matic / VHS
Business of Better Writing Series
Color
Deals with bettering writing principles as part of improving business writing skills.
Business and Economics
Dist - KYTV **Prod** - KYTV 1983

The Writing Process 28 MIN
VHS / U-matic
Next Steps with Computers in the Classroom Series
Color (T)
Industrial and Technical Education; Mathematics; Sociology
Dist - PBS **Prod** - PBS

The Writing Process 360 MIN
VHS / U-matic
Next Steps with Computers in the Classroom Series
Color (C T)
Computer Science; Education; Mathematics
Dist - UEUWIS **Prod** - UEUWIS 1985

The Writing Process 47 MIN
U-matic
Color (T)
Demonstrates how to teach the writing process to students. Illustrates the four steps in writing, pre - writing, draft, revision and publication.
Education; English Language
Dist - AFSCD **Prod** - AFSCD 1986

The Writing process 30 MIN
VHS / U-matic
Write course - an introduction to college composition series
Color (C A)
Discusses how to be a successful writer. Clarifies concepts about the writing process.
English Language
Dist - FI **Prod** - FI 1984
DALCCD DALCCD

The Writing process - a conversation with Mavis Jukes 20 MIN
U-matic / 16mm / VHS
Color (P I)
$450.00, $325.00 purchase _ #JC - 67264
Interviews children's writer Mavis Jukes. Shares her perspectives on creative writing and how she empathizes with young writers and their feelings. According to Jukes, the basic elements of good writing include being able to pretend, a love of words, and the ability to draw from personal experiences.
English Language; Literature and Drama
Dist - CORF **Prod** - DISNEY 1989

The Writing Process - an Overview 29 MIN
U-matic / VHS
Teaching Writing - a Process Approach Series
Color
Introduces writing as an extension of speaking, emphasizing the five interdependent stages of writing - diagnosis, prewriting, writing, rewriting and evaluation.
Education; English Language
Dist - PBS **Prod** - MSITV 1982

The Writing process - the audience - Pts 3 and 4 60 MIN
VHS / U-matic
Write course - an introduction to college composition series
Color (C)
$45.00, $29.95 purchase
Dispels commonly held misconceptions about the writing process as successful writers reveal what stages they go through to craft a finished work in Part 3. Focuses on the triangular relationship among writer, writing, and audience in Part 4. Parts of a 30 - part series on college composition.
English Language
Dist - ANNCPB **Prod** - DALCCD 1984

The Writing Program 20 MIN
U-matic / VHS
Color
Illustrates rules which are keys to good writing. Focuses on longer written communications, especially report writing, proposal writing and long letters.
English Language
Dist - VISUCP **Prod** - MELROS

Writing - resumes and cover letters 12 MIN
VHS
From pink slip to paycheck series
Color (A G)
$69.00 purchase _ #4184
Shows how to create resumes and write cover letters for older workers experiencing unemployment. Features Richard Bolles, author of What Color Is Your Parachute; William Morin - Drake Beam Morin; and others who offer practical, upbeat advice on developing a job search strategy, feeling positive about oneself, communicating clearly and learning to present oneself as an asset and a resource to potential employees. Part of a five - part series.
Business and Economics; Guidance and Counseling
Dist - NEWCAR

Writing reviews 15 MIN
U-matic / VHS
Tuned - in series; Lesson 9
Color (J H)
Presents a student - produced television program which includes a sitcom with an original theme song, a commercial for a student body office candidate, a news report, a commercial, a documentary about students with unusual jobs and a slightly censored sports report.
Fine Arts; Sociology
Dist - FI **Prod** - WNETTV 1982

Writing says it all 24 MIN
U-matic / 16mm / VHS
Color (I)
$540.00, $410.00, $380.00 purchase _ #A323
Helps youngsters to understand the importance of writing in communicating with others and in gaining better self - awareness. Teaches why spelling, punctuation, and good sentence and paragraph structure are crucial to good writing skills. Produced by Mark Chodzko.
English Language; Social Science
Dist - BARR **Prod** - DONMAC 1982

Writing Skills - Kindergarten Starting Points 15 MIN
U-matic / VHS
Young Writer's Workshop Series
Color (T)
Shows kindergarten authors engaged in a variety of language experiences including beginning reading and writing. Stresses writing stages.
English Language
Dist - BCNFL **Prod** - BCNFL 1986

Writing Skills - Reluctant Writers 15 MIN
U-matic / VHS
Young Writer's Workshop Series
Color (T)
Demonstrates that student understanding of punctuation is enhanced when learned in context.
English Language
Dist - BCNFL **Prod** - BCNFL 1986

Writing Skills Series
Write it Right - it all Starts with Paragraphs
Dist - CHUMAN

Writing Skills Series
Capitalization with Ralph and Stanley 12 MIN
Paragraphs with Ralph and Stanley 14 MIN
Punctuation with Ralph and Stanley 14 MIN
Sentences with Ralph and Stanley 15 MIN
Dist - PHENIX

Writing Skills - the Final Touch - Editing, Rewriting and Polishing
VHS / U-matic
Color (H C)
Stresses the need for clear, direct and concise communication and gives pointers on achieving it through consideration of the structure of the composition as a whole, then each paragraph, and finally the polishing of sentences and words.
Education; English Language
Dist - GA **Prod** - GA

Writing Skills - the Stages of Writing 15 MIN
VHS / U-matic
Young Writer's Workshop Series
Color (T)
Deals with six key stages of the writing process - prewriting, drafting, editing, proofreading, publishing and presenting.
English Language
Dist - BCNFL **Prod** - BCNFL 1986

Writing Skills - the Writing Process 15 MIN
VHS / U-matic
Young Writer's Workshop Series
Color
Shows three teachers working together to help students develop a sense of belonging to a school language family. Includes working on writing projects and grammar.
English Language
Dist - BCNFL **Prod** - BCNFL 1986

Writing Skills - Young Authors 15 MIN
U-matic / VHS
Young Writer's Workshop Series
Color (T)
Follows students through the writing process. Gives audience feedback. Deals with students on first and sixth grade level.
English Language
Dist - BCNFL **Prod** - BCNFL 1986

Writing skills - young editors 15 MIN
U-matic / VHS
Young writer's workshop series
Color (T)
Shows students in a workshop, editing their work and the work of fellow students.
English Language
Dist - BCNFL **Prod** - BCNFL 1986

Writing skills - young poets 15 MIN
U-matic / VHS
Young writer's workshop series
Color (T)
Observes a fourth grade class involved in a writer's workshop. Includes narrowing a poem topic, brainstorming, prewriting, editing, and final draft.
English Language
Dist - BCNFL **Prod** - BCNFL 1986

Writing the argumentative essay 30 MIN
VHS
Color (H C G)
$69.95 purchase _ #RWR - 7
Shows how to recognize the difference between arguable and non - arguable statements, how to understand the audience in order to be persuasive. Discusses methods for establishing credibility, proving a thesis through inductive or deductive reasoning and avoiding the dangers of jumping to conclusions. Examines logical fallacies and personal attacks and how to strengthen an essay by acknowledging opposing views.
English Language; Literature and Drama
Dist - INSTRU **Prod** - FLCCJA 1991

Writing the essay exam 30 MIN
VHS
Color (H C G)
$69.95 purchase _ #RWR - 22
Examines the differences and similarities between writing an essay for class and writing an essay exam. Suggests note - taking, making an outline, using a timeline and other techniques. Identifies key and strategic terms - define, discuss, analyze and compare and contrast.
Education; English Language; Literature and Drama
Dist - INSTRU **Prod** - FLCCJA 1991

Writing the first draft 30 MIN
VHS
Color (H C G)
$69.95 purchase _ #RWR - 10
Shows how to write the first draft, working from the outline. Discusses separating note cards by topic headings, matching detailed notes to outline, interpreting information, using transitions, crediting sources, avoiding plagiarisms. Presents guidelines for selecting and incorporating quotations in a paper with suggestions for paragraph development and unity.
English Language
Dist - INSTRU **Prod** - FLCCJA 1991

Writing the Letter 30 MIN
U-matic / VHS
Business of Better Writing Series
Color
Deals with writing letters as part of improving business writing skills.
Business and Economics
Dist - KYTV **Prod** - KYTV 1983

Writing the paper
VHS
Using your library to write a research paper series
Color (J H C G)
$49.95 purchase _ #VA774V
Shows how to write a research paper, using the library. Walks viewers through the process, offering tips, tricks and insights that make the researach and writing process fast and more productive. Part of a four - part series.
Education; English Language
Dist - CAMV

Writing the Report 30 MIN
U-matic / VHS
Business of Better Writing Series
Color
Deals with writing business reports as part of improving business writing skills.
Business and Economics
Dist - KYTV **Prod** - KYTV 1983

Writing the research paper - preparing a working bibliography - stating the thesis 30 MIN
VHS
Color (H C G)
$69.95 purchase _ #RWR - 4
Shows how to classify and categorize material into overview, as well as how to focus on a topic and use supporting material. Discusses preparing a preliminary bibliography, formatting index cards for books, periodicals, nonprint materials and personal interviews. Illustrates how to format the thesis and use precise language, support the thesis with facts and limit its consideration.
English Language; Social Science
Dist - INSTRU **Prod** - FLCCJA 1991

Writing the research paper - selecting and narrowing a topic 30 MIN
VHS
Color (H C G)
$69.95 purchase _ #RWR - 3
Shows how to gather information, sift through the data and arrive at a conclusion. Discusses common misconceptions about writing and the importance of selecting a subject of interest to the student, asking focusing questions and resource availability.
English Language; Social Science
Dist - INSTRU **Prod** - FLCCJA 1991

Writing the research paper - taking notes 30 MIN
VHS
Color (H C G)
$69.95 purchase _ #RWR - 5
Shows how to judge the quality of source material for relevance and timeliness, as well as how to rank the sources. Discusses the use of index cards for note taking, direct quotations, paraphrasing, summarizing and key terms. Emphasizes the importance of avoiding plagiarism and distinguishing between fact and opinion.
English Language
Dist - INSTRU **Prod** - FLCCJA 1991

Writing Time Series
Introduction of Cursive Writing - Paper, Pencil and Writing Positions, Stick Stroke 15 MIN
Review of Writing Position and the Last 13 Lower Case Letters Learned 15 MIN
Dist - GPN

Writing to Different Executive Levels 30 MIN
VHS / U-matic
Business of Direct Mail Series
Color
Shows how to write to different executive levels when using direct mail.
Business and Economics
Dist - KYTV **Prod** - KYTV 1983

Writing - uses and importance 17 MIN
VHS
CC; Color (P)
$89.95 purchase _ #10112VL
Presents the purpose, importance and methods of writing. Uses video experiences to illustrate the need for writing as a tool; a means of communication; and a way to store information. Comes with a teacher's guide; student activities; discussion questions; and a set of blackline masters.
English Language; Social Science
Dist - UNL

Writing Well
U-matic / VHS / 16mm
Color (I)
$645 purchase - video (entire series), $920 purchase - 16 mm (entire
Discusses writing techniques.
English Language
Dist - CF

Writing well - paragraphs 15.5 MIN
16mm / U-matic / VHS
Color (I)
$325.00 purchase - 16 mm, $240.00 purchase - video
Discusses organizing sentences in logical order, omitting extraneous ideas, and constructing a paragraph. Directed by William Haugse.
English Language
Dist - CF

Writing Well - Paragraphs 16 MIN
U-matic / VHS / 16mm
Writing Well Series
Color (I)
Explains topic sentences and paragraph organization and unity. Illustrates various sentence constructions.
English Language
Dist - CF **Prod** - CF

Writing Well - Planning 8 MIN
U-matic / VHS / 16mm
Writing Well Series
Color (I)
Spells out how to gather and develop ideas before starting to write. Tells how a girl first clusters her possible general choices and then makes another cluster to develop the details in her chosen subject.
English Language
Dist - CF **Prod** - CF 1985

Writing Well - Sentences 14 MIN
U-matic / VHS / 16mm
Writing Well Series
Color (I)
Demonstrates run - on and choppy sentences. Involves sentence combining. Stresses using descriptive words.
English Language
Dist - CF **Prod** - CF

Writing Well - Sentences 14 MIN
U-matic / VHS / 16mm
Color (I)
$290 purchase - 16 mm, $210 purchase - video
Tells how to use descriptive words, avoid run - on and choppy sentences, and how to achieve a distinctive writing style. By William Haugse.
English Language; Literature and Drama
Dist - CF

Writing Well Series
Writing Well - Paragraphs 16 MIN
Writing Well - Planning 8 MIN
Writing Well - Sentences 14 MIN
Writing Well - Sharing 11 MIN
Dist - CF

Writing Well - Sharing 11 MIN
16mm / U-matic / VHS
Writing Well Series
Color (I)
Shows the post - writing process of sharing writing in a small group. Tells how positive comments and constructive criticism help each writer to rewrite.
English Language
Dist - CF **Prod** - CF 1985

Writing with both sides of your brain 30 MIN
VHS
Color (J H C A)
$93.00 purchase _ #MB - 512994 - 9
Encourages students to use both sides of their brains in writing. Shows that one hemisphere of the brain controls analytical thinking, and is important for technique, while the other hemisphere controls creativity. Focuses on developing one's innate creativity.
Fine Arts; Literature and Drama
Dist - SRA **Prod** - SRA 1988

Writing words - 12 15 MIN
VHS
Wordscape series
Color; Captioned (I)
$125.00 purchase
Uses the word 'cell' approach to teach vocabulary, opening each program - sixteen 15 - minute programs - with several word cells familiar to fourth graders and using these 'cells' to form compound words, such as 'birdhouse' and 'girlfriend.' Employs animated graphics to dramatize how compounds are 'built' of cells that form a seemingly endless series of new words and to teach that understanding cell words can help to understand the new words composed of them. Program 12 presents the language of writing, some history of writing and a mini - documentary featuring S E Hinton, writer of books popular with adolescents.
English Language; Psychology
Dist - AITECH **Prod** - OETVA 1990

Writing your letter 15 MIN
U-matic / VHS
Fins, feathers and fur series
(P)
$125.00 purchase
Explains the writing and reading of letters to children focusing on a thank you letter.
English Language
Dist - AITECH **Prod** - WXXITV 1986

Writing your letter 30 MIN
VHS / U-matic
Fins, feathers and fur series
Color (P)
Features a pet shop for teaching writing to second and third graders. Shows children writing letters.
English Language; Psychology
Dist - AITECH **Prod** - WXXITV 1986

Writing your poem 15 MIN
VHS / U-matic
Fins, feathers and fur series
(P)
$125.00 purchase
Features a discussion of rhyme and rhythm and how to construct a poem on paper. Designed for children.
English Language
Dist - AITECH **Prod** - WXXITV 1986

Writing Your Poem 30 MIN
VHS / U-matic
Fins, Feathers and Fur
Color (P)
Features a pet shop for teaching writing to second and third graders. Shows children discussing rhyme and rhythm and writing poetry.
English Language; Psychology
Dist - AITECH **Prod** - WXXITV 1986

Writing your sentences 15 MIN
VHS / U-matic
Fins, feathers and fur series
(P)
$125.00 purchase
Demonstrates the structure of a paragraph for children learning to write. Shows the use of an idea web to compose a newspaper column.
English Language
Dist - AITECH **Prod** - WXXITV 1986

Writing your story 15 MIN
U-matic / VHS
Fins, feathers and fur
Color (P)
$125.00 purchase
Features a pet shop for teaching writing to second and third graders. Shows children reviewing principles taught in earlier programs.
English Language; Psychology
Dist - AITECH **Prod** - WXXITV 1986

Writing your way up the job ladder
VHS
(G A)
$84.95 purchase _ #XY808; $84.95 purchase _ #ES1180V
Discusses written communications in the job search and on the job. Considers subjects such as resumes, cover letters, interview follow - up letters, forms, letters, memoranda, and more. Stresses clarity and neatness.
English Language; Psychology
Dist - CAREER CAMV **Prod** - CAREER 1987

Written Communication 28 MIN
16mm
You in Public Service Series
Color (A)
LC 77-700970
Presents basic techniques for communication using letters, forms, memos and reports.
Business and Economics
Dist - USNAC **Prod** - USOE 1977

Written Language 30 MIN
VHS / U-matic
Rainbow Road Series Pt 3
Color (A)
LC 82-707395
Demonstrates how young children can be introduced to written language and books through simple family activities and specially planned trips.
Home Economics; Sociology
Dist - GPN **Prod** - KAIDTV 1982

Written Language Disabilities 30 MIN
VHS / U-matic
Characteristics of Learning Disabilities Series
Color (C A)
Discusses specific written language disorders in children.
Education; Psychology
Dist - FI **Prod** - WCVETV 1976

The Written law - for out of Zion 15 MIN
VHS
Color (G)
$29.95 purchase _ #853
Introduces the Torah and its centrality in Jewish life. Examines the Torah as the idea, aesthetic and liturgical object, and wellspring of Jewish religious ritual and tradition.
Religion and Philosophy; Sociology
Dist - ERGOM **Prod** - ERGOM

The Written Word 30 MIN
VHS / U-matic
Language - Thinking, Writing, Communicating Series
Color
English Language
Dist - MDCPB **Prod** - MDCPB

The Written Word 20 MIN
U-matic / VHS
Art of Learning Series
Color (H A)
Deals with the preparation of written assignments. Defines different types of short papers and demonstrates a step - by - step method of preparing a term paper.
Education; English Language
Dist - GPN **Prod** - WCVETV 1984

Wrong adventures 21 MIN
U-matic / VHS
Contemporary arts series
Color (G)
$200.00, $140.00 purchase, $75.00, $50.00 rental
Explores themes in the work of Bruce Charlesworth, identity shifts, surveillance and psychiatry. Gives the question of artistic identity an ironic twist by making Charlesworth the protagonist of elliptical dramas staged for the camera. Portrays a central character caught up in a spiraling depression that leads him through a landscape of sparse urban interiors and chaotic rain forests in search of his father.
Fine Arts; Health and Safety; Psychology
Dist - IAFC

Wrong again 24 MIN
16mm
B&W
LC 73-713143
Presents a comedy in which two boys confuse the painting 'Blue Boy' with a horse of the same name.
Fine Arts; Literature and Drama
Dist - RMIBHF **Prod** - ROACH 1960

Wrong again 20 MIN
U-matic / VHS / 16mm
B&W (J)
Stars Laurel and Hardy who confuse the famous painting 'Blue Boy' with a horse of the same name.
Fine Arts
Dist - FI **Prod** - ROACH 1929

The Wrong Box 105 MIN
16mm
Color (J)
Stars John Mills and Ralph Richardson as elderly heirs, involved in a winner - take - all kind of insurance whereby the sole survivor inherits the total fortune.
Fine Arts
Dist - TIMLIF **Prod** - CPC

The Wrong idea 20 MIN
VHS
Color (C G)
$130.00 purchase, $15.50 rental _ #24405
Uses a culturally diverse cast to portray campus sexual harassment in nine vignettes to stimulate discussions of differing perceptions. Strives to sensitize American and international students, faculty and staff to cultural and gender rights and responsibilities. Includes training manual.
Sociology
Dist - PSU **Prod** - UMINN 1988

The Wrong Man 105 MIN
16mm
B&W
Stars Henry Fonda as a man who is arrested and convicted for a crime he did not commit.
Fine Arts
Dist - TWYMAN **Prod** - WB 1956

Wrong Route 30 MIN
U-matic
Color (I J)
Shows children the importance of finishing what they have started without enlisting help from their friends.
Psychology; Sociology
Dist - TVOTAR **Prod** - TVOTAR 1986

Wrong stuff 50 MIN
VHS
Horizon series
Color (A PRO IND)
PdS99 purchase
Shows that people working in small teams with sophisticated technology in crisis situations may experience accidents. Examines work being done by psychologists to analyze and prevent such catastrophes. Of interest to persons involved with automated equipment, crises handling, communication skills and teamwork.
Health and Safety
Dist - BBCENE

The Wrong Stuff - American Architecture 13 MIN
U-matic / VHS / 16mm
Color (H C A)
LC 83-700322
Introduces social critic Tom Wolfe who examines current styles of American architecture and finds it bland.
Fine Arts; Industrial and Technical Education
Dist - CAROUF **Prod** - CBSTV

The Wrong Way Kid 42 MIN
U-matic / VHS / 16mm
Color (J H)
LC 83-700943
Uses children's stories to point out that growing up, at any age, is a process of change and learning. Shows that the turmoil young people may feel is normal and that there are ways to deal with these feelings.
Guidance and Counseling; Literature and Drama
Dist - CF **Prod** - BOSUST 1983

Wrong Way Kid Series
Hardlucky 11 MIN
I'm not Oscar's Friend Anymore 7 MIN
Martha Ann and the Mother Store 7 MIN
Someone New 4 MIN
Dist - CF

Wrongful dismissal 15 MIN
VHS / 16mm
You and the law series
Color (S)
$150.00 purchase _ #275906
Employs a mixture of drama and narrative to introduce particular aspects of Canadian law. Presents some of the basic concepts and addresses some of the more commonly asked questions. Emphasis is on those elements of the law which are frequently misunderstood. Reviews the recommended options open to those who feel they may have been dismissed from a job unfairly. Topics include - the Employment Standards Act, grievance procedures, the concepts of constructive dismissal, adequate notice and unions.
Business and Economics; Civics and Political Systems; Geography - World; Guidance and Counseling; Sociology
Dist - ACCESS **Prod** - ACCESS 1987

Wrongful termination series
Details company and individual policies and actions that could lead to wrongful termination litigation under the law. Outlines seven principles for hiring, reviewing and firing. Shows a panel discussion of particular problem areas in hiring and firing. Set of two videos - Termination on Trial (Part I) and Termination - Six Expert Views (Part II).
Termination - six expert views 30 MIN
Termination on trial 25 MIN
Dist - COMFLM **Prod** - COMFLM 1987

Wu Shu 10 MIN
16mm
Color
LC 80-700314
Shows the ancient Chinese discipline of physical training as studied by a group of American students under the direction of a dedicated Chinese teacher of martial arts.
Physical Education and Recreation
Dist - WHITNM **Prod** - WHITNM 1980

Wu Song 115 MIN
VHS
Color (G) (MANDARIN CHINESE)
$45.00 purchase _ #2015B
Presents an opera movie produced in the People's Republic of China.
Fine Arts; Geography - World; Literature and Drama
Dist - CHTSUI **Prod** - CHTSUI

Wunder Des Fliegens 80 MIN
U-matic / VHS
B&W (GERMAN)
Presents flight routine footage of world - famous stunt pilot Ernst Udet.
Fine Arts
Dist - IHF **Prod** - IHF

Wuthering Heights
Cassette / 16mm
Now Age Reading Programs, Set 3 Series
Color (I J)
$9.95 purchase _ #8F - PN682960
Brings a classic tale to young readers. Filmstrip set includes filmstrip, cassette, corresponding book, classroom exercise materials and a poster. The read - along set includes student activity book, cassette and paperback.
English Language; Literature and Drama
Dist - MAFEX

Wuthering heights 104 MIN
16mm
B&W (J H)
$24.95 purchase _ #500290
Stars Merle Oberon as the headstrong Cathy, who traps the brooding Heathcliffe (Laurence Olivier) with her love and then cruelly rejects him. Directed by William Wyler.
Fine Arts
Dist - TWYMAN
UILL

Wuxing people's commune 57 MIN
16mm
Color (H C A)
$775.00, $400.00 purchase, $60.00 rental
Deals with daily life in a rural Chinese commune, touching on the political and social organization of this unique institution.
Geography - World; Sociology
Dist - NFBC **Prod** - NFBC 1980
DOCEDR

WWII after Pearl Harbor - 1941 - 1945
VHS
Color; B&W (G)
$19.95 purchase _ #NA003
Chronicles events in World War II after the bombing of Pearl Harbor. Plunges directly into front lines from the carriers at Midway to the beachhead at Anzio to the cockpit of the Enola Gay. Includes enemy footage and the audiocassette Radio Goes to War, Volume 2.
Civics and Political Systems; History - United States; History - World
Dist - SIV

WWII before - 1939 - 1941 - and after - 1941 - 1945 - Pearl Harbor
VHS
Color; B&W (G)
$39.90 purchase _ #NA200
Presents two videos on World War II. Chronicles events before and after the bombing of Pearl Harbor. Tape one covers the Japanese invasion of China, the Nazi blitzkrieg across Europe and the attack on Pearl Harbor that pulled the United States into the war. Tape two goes into the front lines from the carriers at Midway to the beachhead at Anzio to the cockpit of the Enola Gay. Includes enemy footage and the audiocassettes Radio Goes to War, Volume 1 and 2.
Civics and Political Systems; History - United States; History - World
Dist - SIV

WWII before Pearl Harbor - 1931 - 1941
VHS
Color; B&W (G)
$19.95 purchase _ #NA002
Chronicles events in World War II before the bombing of Pearl Harbor. Witnesses Japan's invasion of China, the Nazi blitzkrieg across Europe and the attack on Pearl Harbor that plunged the United States into the war. Includes enemy footage and the audiocassette Radio Goes to War, Volume 1.
Civics and Political Systems; History - United States; History - World
Dist - SIV

WWII - The Music video - Volume 2
VHS
Color (G)
$19.95 purchase _ #NA000
Features Danny Kaye, Harry James, Abbott and Costello, Betty Grable, Count Basie, and more.
Fine Arts
Dist - SIV

WWII - The Music video - Volume I
VHS
Color (G)
$19.95 purchase _ #NA004
Features Bing Crosby, the Andrews Sisters, Peggy Lee, and more.
Fine Arts
Dist - SIV

WWII - The Music video - Volumes 1 & 2
VHS
Color (G)
$39.00 _ #NA100
Offers both volumes of WWII music.
Fine Arts
Dist - SIV

The Wyeth phenomenon 26 MIN
U-matic / VHS / 16mm
Color (H C A)
LC FIA68-881
Displays more than forty of N C Wyeth's paintings which provide an in - depth study of the famous artist. His paintings have a large amount of detail and his subjects are the people and places he knows best.
Biography; Fine Arts
Dist - PHENIX **Prod** - CBSTV 1967

The Wyeths - a father and his family 60 MIN
VHS
Smithsonian world series
Color (G)
$49.95 purchase _ #SMIW - 301
Tells the story of the Wyeth family. Focuses on N C Wyeth, the father, but also notes the accomplishments of his

children, who are composers, painters, engineers and contemporary artists.
Fine Arts
Dist - PBS **Prod** - WETATV

Wyland, the artist and 'Save the Whales' 20 MIN
VHS
Color (K P I J)
$24.95 purchase
Discusses whales and their marine environment. Interviews Wyland, the muralist, who is completing the world's largest mural in Long Beach, California. Discusses Wyland's motivation for painting the whaling walls and his deep love of the oceans and their inhabitants. Interviews Maris Sidenstecker II, a marine biologist and co - founder of the Save the Whales group. Workbook available separately.
Science - Natural
Dist - SUGAWE **Prod** - SUGAWE 1992

Wyld Ryce Series
Celebration 13 MIN
Circle of the winds 16 MIN
Heart of the Earth Survival School 16 MIN
The Pipe is the Alter 13 MIN
Dist - UCV

Wyman - Gordon - the Problem Solvers 24 MIN
16mm
Color
LC 75-701597
Promotes the capabilities of the Wyman - Gordon Co in producing high quality forgings for the gas turbine, nuclear power and airframe industries.
Business and Economics
Dist - WYMGOR **Prod** - WYMGOR 1975

Wynken, Blynken and Nod 4 MIN
16mm / U-matic / VHS
B&W (K P)
LC 70-715123
Uses the pictures and text of the poem by Eugene Field to tell the story about Wynken, Blynken and Nod.
Literature and Drama
Dist - WWS **Prod** - WWS 1971

Wynn Bullock - Photographer 24 MIN
U-matic / VHS / 16mm
Color (H C A)
LC 79-700657
Presents photographer Wynn Bullock commenting on his work and demonstrating unusual photographic techniques. Includes views of some of his photographs and scenes of the artist with his family.
Fine Arts; Industrial and Technical Education
Dist - PHENIX **Prod** - TYSONT 1978

Wyoming 60 MIN
VHS
Portrait of America series
Color (J H C G)
$99.95 purchase _ #AMB50V
Visits Wyoming. Offers extensive research into the state's history. Films key locations and presents segments on its history, government, education, folklore, science, journalism, sociology, industry, agriculture and business. Shows what is unique about Wyoming and what is distinctive about its regional culture and how it got to be that way. Includes teacher study guides. Part of a 50 - part series.
Geography - United States; History - United States
Dist - CAMV

Wyoming's geography 30 MIN
VHS
Color (J H C)
$29.95 purchase _ #IVWYG
Focuses on Wyoming as one of the most geographically diverse states in the country. Explores Wyoming's rivers, plains and mountains, including the Black Hills; the Laramie, Medicine Bow, Sierra Madre and Bighorn Mountains; the Wind River, Teton ranges, the Beartooth Mountains and mountains on the Idaho - Wyoming border and the Absaroka Range. Investigates the many basins of Wyoming - Wind River, Powder River and Bighorn Basin.
Geography - United States; History - United States; Science - Physical
Dist - INSTRU

X

X 8 MIN
16mm
Color (G)
$20.00 rental
Experiments with a woman's despair, rage and exhibitionism and transforms her pain into a self - healing ritual.
Fine Arts; Health and Safety; Religion and Philosophy; Sociology
Dist - CANCIN **Prod** - BARHAM 1974

X 9 MIN
16mm
B&W (G)
$20.00 rental
Perceives a black line as delineation or as a shape in itself, among other things. Considers the rectangle of the film screen itself transforming into a trapezoid.
Fine Arts
Dist - CANCIN **Prod** - GRENIV 1976

X-15 - Man into Space 8 MIN
16mm
Color (J)
Shows an X - 15 rocket plane being carried aloft by a B - 52 bomber and its actual 'drop.' Uses graphic animation to take the viewer along as the X - 15 climbs to a height of more than 100 miles above the earth.
Civics and Political Systems
Dist - IBM **Prod** - IBM

The X-15 Story 27 MIN
16mm
Color (I)
Documents the development and flight testing of the X - 15.
Industrial and Technical Education
Dist - RCKWL **Prod** - NAA

The X-17 Story 14 MIN
16mm
Color
LC FIE59-235
Traces the development of the X - 17, a three - stage test missile designed to solve the re - entry problem.
Science - Physical
Dist - USNAC **Prod** - USDD 1958

X - Et 17 MIN
16mm
Color
Points out that Sven Erixon is one of Sweden's best known artists. Features the artist in his studio and conducts a tour through his paintings into his special world.
Fine Arts; Geography - World
Dist - AUDPLN **Prod** - ASI 1963

X - people 25 MIN
VHS
UFO series
Color (G)
$35.00 rental, $40.00 purchase
Deals with mystery people that haunt the characters, who wander around reading books which have to do with mystery people. Part of the UFO series.
Fine Arts; Literature and Drama
Dist - CANCIN **Prod** - KUCHAR 1985

X - Ray Examinations - a Guide to Good Practice 15 MIN
16mm
Color (PRO)
Examines the proper procedures and safe practices which help reduce the potential hazards of radiation in x - ray examinations.
Health and Safety; Industrial and Technical Education; Science
Dist - SQUIBB **Prod** - SQUIBB

X - Ray Inspection 21 MIN
16mm
Engineering Series
B&W
LC FIE52-170
Discusses the use of radiographs in industry, the generation of X - rays in the X - ray tube and the wave nature of X - rays. Explains how radiographs are made and how they are interpreted for defects in metal.
Industrial and Technical Education
Dist - USNAC **Prod** - USOE 1944

X - Ray Procedures in Layman's Terms Series
Abdomimal ultrasound
Barium enema
Bone scan
Brain Scan
Cardiac stress test and imaging
Cholecystogram
CT Scan
Diagnostic Radiology 22 MIN
IVP
Liver Scan
Lung Ventilation Scan
Mammography
Nuclear Medicine 26 MIN
Pelvic Ultrasound
Thyroid Uptake and Scan
Ultrasound and the CT Scanner 15 MIN
Upper GI
Dist - FAIRGH

X - Ray Spectroscopy - the Inside Story 26 MIN
16mm
Adventure in Research Series
Color (J H C)
LC 74-705971
Explains how and why the spectroscope is used to study X - ray beams. Describes how specially grown crystals are used to diffuse the beam in the spectrometer, isolate a single wavelength, scan the spectrum and record its characteristics.
Science; Science - Physical
Dist - NASA **Prod** - NASA 1968

X - Ray Technician 15 MIN
U-matic / 16mm / VHS
Career Awareness
(I)
$130 VC purchase, $240 film purchase, $25 VC rental, $30 film rental
Presents an empathetic approach to career planning, showing the personal as well as professional qualities of x - ray technicians. Highlights the importance of career education.
Guidance and Counseling
Dist - GPN

X - ray technologist 5 MIN
U-matic
Good work series
Color (H)
Provides useful, up to date information on various occupations to aid high school students in career selection. Available in five series of ten jobs each.
Education; Guidance and Counseling; Industrial and Technical Education
Dist - TVOTAR **Prod** - TVOTAR 1981

X - ray technologist 14 MIN
VHS
Get a life - a day in the career guidance series
Color (H C A)
$89.00 purchase _ #886696-07-1
Profiles the field of radiology from the perspective of three x - ray technologists. Features a department manager who reveals the qualities necessary to be sucessful in this allied health profession. Describes the educational and other professional requirements for the job. Uses candid, casual interviews. Part of a ten-part series.
Business and Economics; Guidance and Counseling; Health and Safety
Dist - VOCAVD **Prod** - VOCAVD 1995

X - ray technologist 5 MIN
VHS / 16mm
Good works series; No 3
Color (H VOC)
$40.00 purchase _ #BPN213908
Presents the occupation of an X - ray technologist. Gives a profile of a young person who is either undergoing an apprenticeship or has recently completed training in this field. Takes the viewer on a tour of this person's workplace and explains the practical skills and training offered by employers and schools. Gives a better understanding of the demand for skilled workers today and the potential for personal growth.
Guidance and Counseling
Dist - RMIBHF **Prod** - RMIBHF

X - ray technologist
VHS
Day in a career series
Color (H VOC)
$89.00 purchase _ #VOC03V-G
Presents information about the occupation of x-ray technologist, one of the careers that the United States Department of Labor projects as potentially successful by the year 2000. Profiles in detail the work day of a real person, with candid interviews and work situations and information about the educational requirements, credentials, job outlook, salaries, important associations, and contacts in the field. One of a series of ten videos, lasting 15 to 22 minutes, available individually or as a set.
Business and Economics; Guidance and Counseling; Science
Dist - CAMV

X - Ray, Ultrasound and Thermography in Diagnosis 22 MIN
16mm
Upjohn Vanguard of Medicine Series
Color (PRO)
LC 76-705728
Demonstrates for physicians the potential of three electronic diagnostic techniques. Reveals the movement of a twelve - week - old human fetus as it was recorded with ultrasound. Explains the significant advantages of thermography in mass screening for early breast cancer and shows examples of color thermography.
Health and Safety; Science; Science - Natural
Dist - UPJOHN **Prod** - UPJOHN 1969

X - Rays and Energy Levels 24 MIN
U-matic / VHS
Discovering Physics Series
Color (H C)
Documents the discovery of X - rays and its implications for the newly emerging quantum theory.
Industrial and Technical Education; Science - Physical
Dist - MEDIAG **Prod** - BBCTV 1983

X - rays - do I have to 17 MIN
VHS / U-matic
Color (PRO C G)
Provides beginning students in dentistry and related dental professionals as well as patients with an appreciation for the purpose and value of dental X - rays. Addresses concerns many patients have - why and how are X - rays necessary, how much radiation is absorbed during X - rays, what effects do X - rays have on the body and what can be done to reduce these effects. Presented by Dr William K Bottomly.
Health and Safety
Dist - HSCIC **Prod** - DPVA 1987
USNAC

X - Rays - How Safe 28 MIN
16mm
Consultation Series
Color
LC 75-702444
Discusses reduction of unnecessary radiation exposure to the public from diagnostic radiology. Describes the federal standard for the manufacture of x - ray systems as a major contribution in reducing unnecessary radiation exposure to patients and operators.
Business and Economics; Health and Safety; Science
Dist - USNAC **Prod** - USBRH 1974

X - the Man with the X - Ray Eyes 80 MIN
16mm
Color
Features Ray Milland as a crusading opthamologist who tests a special sight - improvement serum on himself and acquires x - ray vision.
Fine Arts
Dist - TWYMAN **Prod** - AIP 1963

X, Y, Z 15 MIN
VHS / U-matic
Cursive writing series
Color (P)
Presents techniques of handwriting, focusing on the lower case letters x, y and z.
English Language
Dist - GPN **Prod** - WHROTV 1984

Xala 123 MIN
16mm
Color (FRENCH (ENGLISH SUBTITLES) WOLOF)
Discusses the supposed myth of African independence as black African leaders adopt white colonial policies. Shows the sometimes unfortunate blending of the French and Senegalese cultures in the central character.
Fine Arts; Foreign Language; History - World; Sociology
Dist - NYFLMS **Prod** - NYFLMS 1974

Xam Cartier - 11 - 17 - 88 30 MIN
VHS / Cassette
Poetry Center reading series
Color (G)
$15.00, $45.00 purchase, $15.00 rental _ #833 - 652
Features the writer at the Poetry Center, San Francisco State University, reading from her works, including selections from A Void Dance - a novel in progress later retitled Muse - Echo Blues - and Be - Bop Re - Bop, with an introduction by Robert Gluck.
Literature and Drama
Dist - POETRY **Prod** - POETRY 1988

Xam Cartier - 2 - 7 - 89 16 MIN
VHS / Cassette
Poetry Center reading series
(G)
#838 - 655
Features the writer at the Poetry Center at San Francisco State University, reading selections from Be - Bop Re - Bop in honor of the new president Robert Corrigan, with an introduction by Robert Gluck. Available only for listening purposes at the Center; not for sale or rent.
Literature and Drama
Dist - POETRY **Prod** - POETRY 1989

Xaviera on Campus 12 MIN
16mm
B&W (H C A)
LC 76-701498
Documents a visit by Xaviera Hollander to the campus of Niagara College.
Education; Psychology; Sociology
Dist - CNIAG **Prod** - CNIAG 1975

XB - 70 Phase One 13 MIN
16mm
Color (I)
Tells the story of the engineering development of the XB - 70.
Industrial and Technical Education
Dist - RCKWL **Prod** - NAA

XB - 70A roll - out 10 MIN
16mm
Color (G)
Presents the unveiling of the USAF XB - 70A at the NAA - Palmdale facility in May, 1964.
Social Science
Dist - RCKWL **Prod** - NAA

Xenon tetrafluoride 6 MIN
16mm
Color (J H)
Explains that XEF is an 'impossible' compound involving a supposedly inert element - xenon - with fluorine. Tells how their recently discovered reaction has led to experiments yielding other compounds such as XEF2 (produced under ultraviolet light) and experiments with radon and fluorine. Provides science with new insight into the nature of chemical bonding.
Science; Science - Physical
Dist - USNAC **Prod** - USNRC 1962
USERD ANL

Xeriscape - appropriate landscaping to conserve water 26 MIN
VHS
Color (G)
$89.95 purchase _ #6 - 070 - 102P
Examines xeriscaping, a method of landscaping which conserves water, lowers maintenance, reduces labor and saves money. Emphasizes the appropriateness of xeriscaping because of periodic drought and water shortages. Discusses plant selection, drought tolerant plants and their cultural requirements, climatic factors, soil testing, hydrozoning for water savings, irrigation, soil management and mulches, ground covers, 'hardscaping.'
Agriculture; Geography - United States; Science - Natural
Dist - VEP **Prod** - VEP

A Xerox Report 45 MIN
16mm
Color
LC 80-701308
Provides insight and understanding into the complex strategy that is guiding the Xerox Corporation toward the close of the century as told through the unscripted reflections of the key people who created and experienced it.
Business and Economics
Dist - GITTFI **Prod** - XEROX 1980

Xfilm 14 MIN
16mm
Color (G)
$18.00 rental
Features a personal exploration of film as an abstract, kinetic medium. Manipulates individual frames and groups of frames to create a sense of momentum. Produced by John Luther Schofill.
Fine Arts
Dist - CANCIN

Xi Xiang Ji 190 MIN
VHS
Color (G) (MANDARIN CHINESE)
$80.00 purchase _ #6034S
Presents a movie produced in the People's Republic of China.
Fine Arts; Geography - World; Literature and Drama
Dist - CHTSUI **Prod** - CHTSUI

Xian 58 MIN
U-matic / VHS / 16mm
Cities in China Series
Color (J)
LC 82-700346
Explores the Chinese urban experience, past and present. Focuses on the historical sites, scenery and culture in Xian, China, and observes the activities of its modern residents.
Geography - World; History - World; Sociology
Dist - UCEMC **Prod** - YUNGLI 1981

The Xi'an incident 190 MIN
VHS
Color (G) (MANDARIN CHINESE (ENGLISH SUBTITLES))
$80.00 purchase _ #1024S
Presents a movie produced in the People's Republic of China.
Fine Arts; Geography - World; Literature and Drama
Dist - CHTSUI **Prod** - CHTSUI

The Xinguana - Aborigines of South America 29 MIN
16mm / U-matic / VHS
Color (J)
LC 70-712933
Presents an ethnographic study of the Xinguana, farmer - Fishermen of the Xingu River in Brazil whose culture remained unchanged until recently. Explores their horticulture, bodily ornamentation, puberty rites and the Kwarup ceremony.
Geography - World; Sociology
Dist - MGHT **Prod** - VISION 1971

Xochicalco 56 MIN
U-matic / VHS
Color (C) (SPANISH)
$279.00, $179.00 purchase _ #AD - 2192
Looks at the astronomical observatories of the Aztecs at Xochicalco. Reveals that they reached a high degree of sophistication in their computations. Looks at the murals and architecture which still remain.
Geography - World; History - World; Psychology; Science; Science - Physical; Social Science; Sociology
Dist - FOTH **Prod** - FOTH

XTX - Expect the Unexpected
U-matic / 16mm
Color (A)
Alerts workers to prepare for the unexpected by illustrating the potential for accidents in everyday activities at work and at home.
Health and Safety
Dist - BNA **Prod** - BNA 1983

Xu Mao and his daughters 95 MIN
VHS
Color (G) (CHINESE)
$45.00 purchase _ #1010C
Presents a film from the People's Republic of China.
Geography - World; Literature and Drama
Dist - CHTSUI

Xue cheng 960 MIN
VHS
Color (G) (CHINESE)
$240.00 purchase _ #5112
Presents a film from the People's Republic of China. Includes 8 videocassettes.
Geography - World; Literature and Drama
Dist - CHTSUI

The XVII Karmapa's return to Tsurphu 110 MIN
VHS / BETA
Color; PAL (G)
PdS25 purchase
Looks at the first reincarnation inside Tibet since 1959. Records the arrival and enthronement of the young reincarnation at the partially restored Tsurphu monastery, traditional home of the Karmapas in Tibet.
Fine Arts; Religion and Philosophy
Dist - MERIDT

XVII - 3 - get the facts 20 MIN
16mm
Color (H C A)
LC 74-702681
Presents two grievances in which Postal Union representatives solve a problem according to the Postal Manual and union contract, pointing out that one grievance is resolved at the local level while the second requires arbitration.
Business and Economics; Social Science
Dist - NALC **Prod** - NALC 1974

Y

Y E S Inc Series
All the difference 30 MIN
Nature's Rhythms 30 MIN
Neighborhood Drums 30 MIN
Time for Myself 30 MIN
Top of the Line 30 MIN
Dist - GPN

The Y - Riders 14 MIN
16mm
Color
LC 76-713472
Traces the history of the Y - Rider Program designed to fight drug abuse among teenagers. Features interviews with the young program directors.
Guidance and Counseling; Health and Safety; Sociology
Dist - AHONDA **Prod** - AHONDA 1970

Ya like totally hafta talk about it - sex 20 MIN
VHS
Color (J H C)

$195.00 purchase
Visits small town America where high school and college students talk about sex. Uses interviews, testimonials and group discussions to examine fears and attitudes about sexual responsibility and AIDS.
Guidance and Counseling; Health and Safety; Sociology
Dist - SELMED

Yacht building 15 MIN
VHS
Field trips series
Color (I J)
$34.95 purchase _ #E337; LC 90-708557
Visits a modern boat yard where the building of a fiberglass yacht is followed through its various stages from the molding of a fiberglass hull through the addition and construction of the various elements to the final launching and testing. Part of a series which provides visual opportunities for children to 'visit' a variety of locations and activities as if they were on a field trip.
Education; Geography - United States; Industrial and Technical Education; Physical Education and Recreation; Social Science
Dist - GPN **Prod** - MPBN 1983

Yacht chartering - Turqoise Coast - Turkey - Istanbul and the British Virgin Islands
VHS
Color (G)
$19.80 purchase _ #0873
Focuses on the Turqoise Coast of Turkey and the British Virgin Islands. Shows how to charter a yacht complete with crew and other amenities and bareboat yachts.
Geography - World; Physical Education and Recreation
Dist - SEVVID

Yachting in the 30s 45 MIN
VHS
Color; B&W (G)
$19.95 purchase
Presents several short films including Weetamoe, a 1930 film about the J - boat built by Herreshoff.
Fine Arts; Physical Education and Recreation
Dist - NEFILM

Yachting in the Thirties
VHS / BETA
B&W
Presents four short sailing programs, including Dorade - A Most Significant Yacht, Yankee Cruise To England, Brilliant In The Thirties, and The Last J - Boat Race.
Geography - World; Physical Education and Recreation; Social Science
Dist - MYSTIC **Prod** - MYSTIC 1983

Yachting in the thirties
VHS
Color (G)
$21.90 purchase _ #0072
Examines the boat classics of the thirties. Includes J boats, the yawl Dorace, the three masted schooner Atlantic, the 65 foot schooner Brilliant. Visits Transatlantic and Fastnet races.
Physical Education and Recreation
Dist - SEVVID

YAG laser capsulotomy 5 MIN
VHS
3 - part cataract series
Color (G)
$100.00 purchase, $40.00 rental _ #5311S, #5311V
Discusses how, if the posterior capsule becomes opacified after successful surgery, the laser is used to painlessly restore clear vision. Part of a three - part series.
Health and Safety; Science - Natural
Dist - AJN **Prod** - VMED

Yahoo 28 MIN
16mm
Color
Follows two ski instructors, Dave Wheeler and Ted Mc Coy, on the freewheeling hot dog circuit. Shows how they use their winnings to finance a trip to the spectacular Caribou Mountains in Canada for helicopter skiing in untracked powder. Features Jeff Jobe flying his hand kite at Snowbird, Utah, and depicts a hot dog contest at Aspen, Colorado.
Physical Education and Recreation
Dist - FFORIN **Prod** - BARP

Yakkety - yak 20 MIN
VHS / U-matic
Catalyst series
Color (I J H)
$260.00, $310.00 purchase, $50.00 rental
Covers the subject of communication. Includes computers, computers and jobs, telephone communication and the disabled, communication in outer space and future technology for sending messages.
Computer Science; History - World; Industrial and Technical Education; Social Science
Dist - NDIM **Prod** - ABCTV 1991

The Yakuza 112 MIN
16mm
Color
Tells how Robert Mitchum takes a martial arts expert to Tokyo to save Brian Keith from Japanese gangs.
Fine Arts
Dist - TWYMAN **Prod** - WB 1975

Yale
VHS
Campus clips series
Color (H C A)
$29.95 purchase _ #CC0016V
Takes a video visit to the campus of Yale University in Connecticut. Shows distinctive features of the campus and interviews students about their experiences. Provides information on the composition of the student body, professors, academics, social life, housing, and other subjects.
Education
Dist - CAMV

Yalom - an interview 40 MIN
VHS
Understanding group psychotherapy series
Color (C PRO)
$150.00 purchase, $60.00 rental _ #38162
Interviews Dr Irvin D Yalom who discusses his existential perspective on group psychotherapy. Shares the early influences that helped shape his professional life as well as his insights into the training of group therapists, the healing factors in group work, death anxiety and his work in bereavement. Part of a three - part series on group psychotherapy produced by the Brooks Cole Publishing Co.
Psychology
Dist - UCEMC

Yalta 26 MIN
16mm
Winston Churchill - the valiant years series; No 23
B&W (J H G)
LC FI67-2121
Uses documentary footage to describe the Yalta Conference of February 1945, where Churchill, Roosevelt and Stalin discussed final military moves against Germany and the structure of the proposed United Nations. Based on the book The Second World War by Winston S Churchill.
History - World
Dist - SG **Prod** - ABCTV 1961

Yamaguchis' story 50 MIN
VHS
Everyman series
Color (A)
PdS99 purchase
Traces what happens to the marriage of workaholic, conformist Japanese businessman, Mr. Yamaguchi, when his wife becomes a 'born-again Buddhist.' Asks how the new sects are answering the spiritual needs of the Japanese people who have suffered the flip-side of the economic miracle.
Psychology; Religion and Philosophy; Sociology
Dist - BBCENE

Yang short form with self defense 120 MIN
VHS
Color (G)
$39.95 purchase _ #1122
Features a Yang style short form host Robert Klein learned from William Chen and Herb Ray. Demonstrates several fighting applications and theory. Shows push hands with beginning exercises and applications. Solo form is shown twice from different angles, then verbal instructions follow.
Physical Education and Recreation
Dist - WAYF

Yang style long form by Terry Dunn 120 MIN
VHS
Color (G)
$39.95 purchase _ #1108
Teaches the Yang style long form. Explains breathing, posture, warmup, advanced training techniques, and circling exercises. Includes step by step instruction with video windows showing different angles.
Physical Education and Recreation
Dist - WAYF

Yang style sword and broadsword 20 MIN
VHS
Color (G)
$39.95 purchase _ #1110
Demonstrates but does not teach traditional Yang style T'ai chi ch'uan sword and broadsword forms. Repeats the two weapons forms several times and some techniques for the sword are isolated. With York Why Loo.
Physical Education and Recreation
Dist - WAYF

Yang style T'ai chi ch'uan 60 MIN
VHS
Color (G)
$39.95 purchase _ #1160
Teaches the 37 - movement Yang style short form. Shows key self defense applications, including kicking and punching. By Yu Cheng Hsiang, a student of Cheng Man - ch'ing.
Physical Education and Recreation
Dist - WAYF

Yang style with applications 60 MIN
VHS
Color (G)
$50.00 purchase _ #1159
Demonstrates but does not teach basic stances, breathing drills, and stationary and moving drills of T'ai chi. Shows several fighting applications with windows in slow motion and at combat speed. By Dr Yang Jwing - ming. Book also available.
Physical Education and Recreation
Dist - WAYF

Yang - Xun the Peasant Painter 25 MIN
16mm / U-matic / VHS
World Cultures and Youth Series
Color (J)
Introduces Yang - Xun, a Chinese boy who wants to be skilled in the style of art known as peasant painting. Shows how he gets advice from his aunt, an accomplished peasant painter, on how to put feeling in his painting. Depicts Yang - Xun putting the advice to use when he is taken on a field trip to sketch a bridge.
Geography - World; Sociology
Dist - CORF **Prod** - SUNRIS 1981

Yangju Sandae Nori - Masked Drama of Korea 33 MIN
16mm
Ethnic Music and Dance Series
Color (J)
LC 72-700264
Describes the masked drama of Korea, which probably derived from old Buddhist morality plays, and explains how it has evolved into a folk drama consisting of a number of short acts using stock characters.
Geography - World; Literature and Drama
Dist - UWASHP **Prod** - UWASH 1971

Yangtze River - a documentary 540 MIN
VHS
Color (G) (MANDARIN)
$165.00 purchase _ #5007
Presents a documentary on the Yangtze River produced for television in the People's Republic of China. Includes four videocassettes.
Geography - World
Dist - CHTSUI

Yankee Calling 29 MIN
16mm
Color
Recalls the history of Yankee craftsmen, inventors and peddlers who made Connecticut into a manufacturing state during the period from the end of the revolution to the start of the Civil War.
Business and Economics; Fine Arts; Geography - United States
Dist - FENWCK **Prod** - FENWCK

Yankee Clipper 27 MIN
16mm
History of the Motion Picture Series
B&W
Presents William Boyd in a film about early clipperships. Features a typhoon, a mutiny and a race between British and American ships for China tea trade.
Fine Arts; Social Science
Dist - KILLIS **Prod** - SF 1960

Yankee Craftsman 18 MIN
U-matic / VHS / 16mm
Color
LC 72-701778
A documentary film about a man who has spent his life making furniture in the old way with old tools in his own shop. Contrasts the furniture maker's life - style and his product with that of a modern factory worker on the production line.
Business and Economics; Social Science; Sociology
Dist - JOU **Prod** - CHAPWW 1972

Yankee do 28 MIN
16mm
Color

LC FIE62-49
Illustrates the importance of the attack carrier as the backbone of the fast carrier task force as seen through the eyes of a Canadian naval aviator. Shows how the men of the navy maintain and operate these carriers.
Civics and Political Systems; Social Science
Dist - USNAC **Prod** - USN 1962

Yankee Doodle 10 MIN
16mm / U-matic / VHS
Color
LC 76-703542
Travels with Yankee Doodle as he goes to town riding on a pony. Presents a pictorial representation of the Revolutionary era in American history.
History - United States; Literature and Drama
Dist - WWS **Prod** - WWS 1976

Yankee Doodle 26 MIN
VHS / 16mm
Children's Classics Series
Color (P)
$195.00 purchase
Creates twelve year old Danny and his Midnight Militia friends and their version of the American Revolutionary War. Features Fred Halliday as creator. Animated.
Fine Arts; Literature and Drama
Dist - LUF **Prod** - BROVID

Yankee Doodle Cricket 26 MIN
U-matic / VHS / 16mm
Color (P I)
LC 76-703280
Uses animation in presenting a story about the experiences of a mouse, a cat and a cricket during the American Revolution.
Civics and Political Systems; Fine Arts; Literature and Drama
Dist - GA **Prod** - CJE 1976

Yankee Doodle Dandy 126 MIN
16mm
B&W (I J H C)
Stars James Cagney as America's great patriot and composer, George M Cohan.
Biography; Fine Arts
Dist - UAE **Prod** - WB 1942

Yankee Go Home - Communist Propaganda 45 MIN
VHS / U-matic
B&W
Features George V Allen, the first director of the United States Information Agency, explaining the purpose of his organization and the ways he hopes to counter anti - American propaganda in the popular media, especially motion pictures. Examines various Soviet documentary and feature films, including segments from an International Youth Festival in Moscow Stadium, Meeting On The Elbe, The Partisan and The Forty First.
Civics and Political Systems; History - World
Dist - IHF **Prod** - IHF

Yankee Ingenuity 52 MIN
U-matic / VHS
Color (G)
$249.00, $149.00 purchase _ #AD - 1265
Features Arlo Guthrie as host of this chronicle of Yankee - New England - ingenuity. Includes the invention of the telephone, sewing machine, steamboat, the game of basketball, the pacemaker, electric motor. Introduces some modern inventor - scientists.
Business and Economics; History - United States; History - World
Dist - FOTH **Prod** - FOTH

Yankee Painter - the Work of Winslow Homer 27 MIN
16mm / U-matic / VHS
Color (H C A)
LC 81-700672
Presents drawings, watercolors and oils of Winslow Homer to show the progress of his career, his artistic development and the breadth of his interests.
Fine Arts
Dist - IFB **Prod** - UARIZ 1976

Yankee thunder - rebel lightning
VHS
Color (G)
$59.95 purchase _ #CI010
Reenacts key battles of the Civil War in the United States.
History - United States; Sociology
Dist - SIV

The Yankee Years 58 MIN
U-matic / VHS
Crisis in Central America Series
Color (A)
Looks at the turbulent years from the Spanish - American War in 1898 to the 1950s when U S preeminence in Central America was never successfully challenged. Covers the building of the Panama Canal, the early Marine occupation of Nicaragua and the Cold War crisis in Guatemala in 1954 which resulted in the CIA's first 'covert' war in the region.
Civics and Political Systems; History - United States; History - World
Dist - FI **Prod** - WGBHTV

The Yankees at Bat 15 MIN
16mm
Color (J H C)
Yankee players, such as Mickey Mantle, Elston Howard and Roger Maris, talk about their approach to various facets of baseball.
Physical Education and Recreation
Dist - MOKIN **Prod** - MOKIN 1965

Yanki no
16mm
Color (J H G) (SPANISH)
Looks at people who are in political and social turmoil in Latin America.
Civics and Political Systems; History - World; Sociology
Dist - DIRECT **Prod** - DREWAS 1960

The Yanks are Coming 52 MIN
16mm
Color (H C)
Tells of a world plunging from peace into a catastrophic war, World War I.
History - United States
Dist - FI **Prod** - WOLPER 1974

The Yankton Sioux 30 MIN
VHS
Indians of North America video series
Color; B&W; CC (G)
$39.95 purchase _ #D6660; $49.95 purchase _ #LVCD6659V-S
Overviews the history of the Yankton Sioux. Combines interviews with leading authorities on Native American history with live footage and historic stills. Part of a ten - part series.
Social Science
Dist - KNOWUN
CAMV

The Yankwon Sioux - Ihanktonwon Dakota 30 MIN
VHS
Indians of North America series
Color (J H C G)
$49.95 purchase _ #LVCD6659V - S
Interviews Yankwon Sioux leaders who discuss their nation's history. Includes location footage at reservations where children and elders discuss what it means to be Native American today. Part of a 10 - part series on Indian culture.
History - United States; Social Science
Dist - CAMV

Yanomama - a Multidisciplinary Study 45 MIN
U-matic / VHS / 16mm
Color
Describes the field techniques and findings of teams from such disciplines as human genetics, anthropology, epidemiology, dentistry, linguistics and medicine as they conduct a biological - anthropological study of the jungles.
Science; Science - Natural; Social Science; Sociology
Dist - USNAC **Prod** - USNRC

Yanomama I 25 MIN
U-matic / VHS / 16mm
Untamed World Series Series
Color; Mono (J H C A)
$400.00 film, $250.00 video, $50.00 rental
Examines the Yanomama Indians of South America. Looks at their religion, arts, and social traditions.
Geography - World; Sociology
Dist - CTV **Prod** - CTV 1973

Yanomama II 25 MIN
16mm / U-matic / VHS
Untamed World Series
Color; Mono (J H C A)
$400.00 film, $250.00 video, $50.00 rental
Focuses on the societal changes that the Yanomama tribe of South America has undergone during the modern age.
Geography - World; Sociology
Dist - CTV **Prod** - CTV 1973

Yanomama series
A Father washes his children 13 MIN
Dist - PSUPCR

Yanomamo - a multidisciplinary study 45 MIN
16mm / VHS
Yanomamo series
Color (G)
$650.00, $350.00 purchase, $60.00, $40.00 rental
Illustrates the field techniques used by a multidisciplinary team of researchers from the University of Michigan in collaboration with Venezuelan colleagues. Includes specialists in human genetics, serology, epidemiology, demography, dentistry, physical and cultural anthropology and linguistics. Describes the team's objectives and the methods used to obtain data. Includes a brief sketch of Yanomamo culture and society. Part of a series on the Yanomamo Indians of Venezuela by Timothy Asch and Napoleon Chagnon.
Geography - World; Psychology; Social Science; Sociology
Dist - DOCEDR **Prod** - DOCEDR 1968

Yanomamo - a Multidisciplinary Study 43 MIN
16mm
Color (J)
LC 70-713631
Describes the field techniques and findings of teams from such disciplines as human genetics, anthropology, epidemiology, dentistry, linguistics and medicine as they conduct a biological - anthropological study of the jungles of Venezuela and Brazil.
English Language; Geography - World; Health and Safety; Science; Science - Natural; Sociology
Dist - USERD **Prod** - BRNDSU 1971

Yanomamo Indians - Moonblood 14 MIN
16mm
Yanomamo Series
Color
LC 76-702852
Features a Yanomamo headman explaining creation and accounting for the human capacity for violence.
Social Science; Sociology
Dist - DOCEDR **Prod** - DOCEDR 1975

Yanomamo of the Orinoco 29 MIN
VHS
Yanomamo series
Color (J H C)
$150.00 purchase, $20.00 rental
Utilizes film footage from the series on the Yanomamo Indians of Venezuela by Timothy Asch and Napoleon Chagnon for use by seventh grade teachers to show land use in a South American rain forest. Depicts many of the daily activities of the Yanomamo - slash - burn - gardening, body decorating, gathering firewood, bathing in the river and preparing for a feast.
Geography - World; Science - Natural; Social Science; Sociology
Dist - DOCEDR **Prod** - DOCEDR 1987

Yanomamo series
The Ax fight 30 MIN
Bride service 10 MIN
Climbing the peach palm 9 MIN
A Father washes his children 15 MIN
Firewood 10 MIN
Jaguar - a Yanomamo twin cycle myth as told by Daramasiwa 22 MIN
Magical Death 28 MIN
A Man Called Bee - Studying the Yanomamo 40 MIN
Myth of Naro as told by Dedeheiwa 22 MIN
Myth of Naro as Told by Kaobawa 22 MIN
New tribes mission 12 MIN
Tapir distribution 15 MIN
Tug of War 9 MIN
Weeding the garden 14 MIN
Yanomamo - a multidisciplinary study 45 MIN
Yanomamo Indians - Moonblood 14 MIN
Yanomamo of the Orinoco 29 MIN
Dist - DOCEDR

Yanomamo series
Arrows 10 MIN
Children's magical death 8 MIN
A Man and his wife weave a hammock 12 MIN
Ocamo is my town 23 MIN
Dist - DOCEDR
PSUPCR

Yanomamo series
The Feast 29 MIN
Dist - USNAC

Yantra 8 MIN
16mm
Color (C)
$202.00
Presents an experimental film by James Whitney.
Fine Arts
Dist - AFA **Prod** - WHITNY 1957
CFS

Yantra Tibetan yoga - system of Namkhai Norbu
VHS
Color (G)
$35.00 purchase _ #NNYY
Presents five senior Yantra Yoga practitioners who demonstrate the movements of Yantra Tibetan yoga. Differs from hatha yoga in its emphasis on more continuous movement.

Physical Education and Recreation; Religion and Philosophy
Dist - SNOWLI **Prod** - SNOWLI

Yanzhi 105 MIN
VHS
Color (G) (MANDARIN CHINESE (ENGLISH SUBTITLES))
$45.00 purchase _ #1038B
Presents a movie produced in the People's Republic of China.
Fine Arts; Geography - World; Literature and Drama
Dist - CHTSUI **Prod** - CHTSUI

Yardening with Jeff Ball series
How to design and build a vegetable garden 53 MIN
Dist - AAVIM

Yardening with Jeff Ball Series
How to Care for Your Lawn 53 MIN
Dist - AAVIM
BAKERT
VEP

Yarn Preparation for Weaving and Warp Knitting
U-matic / VHS
ITMA 1983 Review Series
Color
Fine Arts; Industrial and Technical Education
Dist - NCSU **Prod** - NCSU

Yasir Arafat - Friday, January 8, 1988 80 MIN
VHS
Nightline series
Color (H C G)
$14.98 purchase _ #MP6161
Focuses on Palestine Liberation Organization leader Yasir Arafat, considered persona non grata in the United States.
Fine Arts; History - World
Dist - INSTRU **Prod** - ABCNEW 1988

The Yavapai story 58 MIN
VHS
Color (J H G)
$250.00 purchase
Relates the history of the Yavapai Indians who fought the encroachment of the pioneers. Looks at events up to 1992, including the Yavapai defense of their territory against the Fifth Cavalry in Arizona in 1872. Traces more modern economic developments led by women of the tribe.
Social Science
Dist - LANDMK

Yawn Wave Theory 20 MIN
16mm
Color
LC 76-703102
Presents a humorous insight into the various levels of consciousness in a young man who tries to stay awake for 48 hours.
Fine Arts; Literature and Drama; Psychology
Dist - CFDEVC **Prod** - SHERCL 1976

Yea, Verily 13 MIN
16mm
B&W
Presents an irreverent parody of Catholicism.
Fine Arts; Literature and Drama; Religion and Philosophy
Dist - NYU **Prod** - NYU

Yeager - an autobiography by General Chuck Yeager and Leo Janos 60 MIN
U-matic / VHS
Stereo (A COR G)
Presents interview materials and narrative from the book featuring Chuck Yeager, Glennis Yeager and Bud Anderson.
Biography; History - United States; Literature and Drama
Dist - BANTAP **Prod** - BANTAP

Yeah you rite 29 MIN
VHS / U-matic
Color (H C A)
$295.00 purchase, $55.00 rental
Explores the various dialects spoken in New Orleans, and shows how the English language has been influenced by the city's history. Shows how some dialects are considered more prestigious than others. Directed by Louis Alvarez and Andrew Kolker.
English Language; Geography - United States; Sociology
Dist - CNEMAG **Prod** - CNAM 1988

The Year 2000 and beyond 71 MIN
VHS
Color (H C G A R)
$24.95 purchase, $10.00 rental _ #4 - 9934
Takes a look at how daily life might be in the 21st century. Covers five subjects - the earth, peacemaking, culture and technology, persons and institutions, and how to make a difference in the church. Includes study book.
Business and Economics; Sociology
Dist - APH **Prod** - APH

The Year Ahead - the Competitive Edge 45 MIN
VHS / U-matic
(PRO G)
$395.00 purchase, $165.00 rental
Examines possible future trends with a focus on critical decision making and strategic planning. Features John Naisbitt.
Business and Economics
Dist - CREMED **Prod** - CREMED 1987

Year book 1990 edition
CD-ROM
(PRO)
$395.00 purchase _ #1953cpm
Contains 18 complete year books from Mosby Year Book - Year Book of Dermatology, Diagnostic Radiology, Drug Therapy, Emergency Medicine, Family Practice, Medicine, Neurology and Neurosurgery, Obstetrics and Gynecology, Pediatrics, Psychiatry and Applied Mental Health, Oncology, Cardiology, Critical Care, Infectious Diseases, Infertility, Orthopedics, Sports Medicine, and Surgery. Produced by CMC. For Macintosh Plus, SE, and II computers. Requires 1MB RAM, floppy disk drive, Apple compatible CD - ROM drive. IBM PCs and compatibles require 640K RAM, DOS 3.1 or later, floppy disk drive - hard disk recommended, one empty expansion slot, and an IBM compatible CD - ROM drive.
Health and Safety
Dist - BEP

Year in review - 1974 28 MIN
U-matic / VHS
Color (H C A)
Presents highlights of the final Nixon White House days and a review of the events just prior to President Richard Nixon's resignation. Includes an overview of accelerated Middle East tensions, the OPEC - influenced international economic crisis and the violent changes in many governments.
Civics and Political Systems; History - United States; History - World
Dist - JOU **Prod** - JOU

Year in Review - 1975 50 MIN
U-matic / VHS
Color (H C A)
Presents the major news event of 1975, the final withdrawal of all United States personnel from Vietnam. Shows footage of those final days and the fall of Hanoi. Captures a year of international terrorism and continued armed hostilities in the Middle East.
History - United States; History - World; Sociology
Dist - JOU **Prod** - JOU

Year in Review - 1976 28 MIN
VHS / U-matic
Color (H C A)
States that the United States elected a president while she celebrated 200 years of independence. Describes how Africa struggled in many civil wars and political upheavals while Lebanon became embroiled in her own war and Middle East tensions focused on it. Tells how many changes in European governments occurred as China lost her leaders, Mao and Chairman Chou En Lai. Features the many technological advances of the year.
History - United States; History - World
Dist - JOU **Prod** - JOU

Year in Review - 1977 28 MIN
U-matic / VHS
Color (H C A)
Tells that this was the year Jimmy Carter was sworn in as the 39th President of the United States. Shows that tensions continued in the Middle East though signs of hope emerged when Anwar El Sadat visited Israel and addressed the Knesset, the first Egyptian president ever to do so. Recounts the strife and political upheavals that plagued Africa.
History - United States; History - World
Dist - JOU **Prod** - JOU

Year in review - 1978 28 MIN
U-matic / VHS
Color (H C A)
Portrays 1978 as a year best remembered as one of hope for peace in the Middle East as Carter, Begin and Sadat participated in the historic summit meeting at Camp David. Tells how instability continued in Central America and Africa as terrorism swept the international scene. The year ended on a happy note as Louise Joy Brown, the first test - tube baby, was born in London.
History - United States; History - World
Dist - JOU **Prod** - JOU

Year in Review - 1980 28 MIN
U-matic / VHS
Color
Presents a capsulized summary of the key events of the year. Focuses on those stories that have the greatest impact on the world. Covers those changes and milestones that have occurred in religion, politics, science and sports. Reports the events and charts the trends of a year that is a most significant one in the world's history.
History - United States; History - World
Dist - JOU **Prod** - JOU

Year in Review - 1982 50 MIN
VHS / U-matic
Color (H C A)
Reports that late in the year Leonid Brezhnev died after 18 years as leader of the Soviet Union. Describes how conflict in the Middle East escalated as Israel invaded Lebanon and international support for the Israelis began to waiver. Presents the Falklands crisis, the anti - nuclear weapons movement and Central American instability. Shows also the headline news in science, sports, politics and religion.
History - United States; History - World
Dist - JOU **Prod** - JOU

Year in Review - 1983 50 MIN
VHS / U-matic
Color (H C A)
Shows the year beginning with continued protests over armaments, instability in Central America, United States presidential candidates from the Democratic Party making themselves known and Republicans awaiting a decision from Ronald Reagan. Presents international headlines, background for the upcoming Olympic Games, as well as news in science.
Civics and Political Systems; History - United States; History - World
Dist - JOU **Prod** - JOU

Year in science 1990 - space exploration 30 MIN
VHS
Color (G A)
$19.95 purchase _ #TCC124CE
Uses live and animated footage of planetary observations to examine the future of space exploration. Suggests that interplanetary travel is already a reality. Hosted by CNN correspondents Charles Crawford and Mark Levenson.
History - World; Science; Science - Physical
Dist - TMM **Prod** - TMM

Year in science 1990 - the changing earth 30 MIN
VHS
Color (G A)
$19.95 purchase _ #TCC123CE
Explores the causes and effects of both natural and manmade disasters. Focuses on the effects these disasters have on the earth's plants and animals. Hosted by CNN correspondent Charles Crawford.
History - World; Science - Physical; Social Science
Dist - TMM **Prod** - TMM

The Year of 53 Weeks - USAF Supersonic Pilot Training 37 MIN
16mm
Color
LC 74-706340
Describes day - to - day experiences of an Air Force ROTC graduate enrolled in the Air Training Command's 53 week supersonic pilot training program. Focuses on the program's academic, flying, military and physical training courses.
Civics and Political Systems; Guidance and Counseling; Industrial and Technical Education
Dist - USNAC **Prod** - USAF 1966

Year of Birth 28 MIN
16mm
B&W
LC FIE63-109
Depicts facts of pregnancy, delivery and the first year of life. Shows research being done at the National Institute of Neurological Diseases and Blindness for prevention and control of cerebral palsy and other neurological diseases in infants.
Psychology; Sociology
Dist - USNAC **Prod** - USPHS 1958

Year of Change - 1932 17 MIN
U-matic / VHS
B&W
Reviews prohibition, Adolf Hitler's rise and world threat, the ominous signs inherent in the Olympics, the optimism associated with the remarkable flight of Amelia Earhart and the election of Franklin D. Roosevelt.
History - United States; History - World
Dist - KINGFT **Prod** - KINGFT

Year of fulfillment 23 MIN
16mm
Color (J H G)
Summarizes events and progress in the Manned Space Flight Program between the late 1950s and early 1969.
History - United States; Industrial and Technical Education; Science - Physical
Dist - NASA **Prod** - NASA

The Year of the Big Surprise 27 MIN
16mm
Color (J)
LC FIA68-1411
Highlights the 1965 professional baseball season featuring team and individual performances of the New York Giants.
Physical Education and Recreation
Dist - NFL **Prod** - NFL 1966

Year of the Buffalo 25 MIN
16mm
Color (H C A)
Follows Fred Bear to Portuguese East Africa where he stalks the wily cape buffalo, rated by experienced hunters as one of the most dangerous beasts of the African bush. Includes scenes of Fred as he battles spectacular tiger fish in the hippo - infested Save River.
Geography - World; Physical Education and Recreation
Dist - GFS **Prod** - GFS

The Year of the dragon 24 MIN
U-matic / VHS
Young people's specials series
Color
Tells of an orphaned Chinese boy's involvement in the building of the Transcontinental Railroad in nineteenth century America.
Fine Arts; History - United States; Sociology
Dist - MULTPP **Prod** - MULTPP

Year of the Eagle 27 MIN
U-matic
Color (J H C A)
Follows the life of the bald eagle from birth through maturity. Focuses on environmental issues.
Science - Natural
Dist - CEPRO **Prod** - CEPRO 1982

The Year of the Hyena 25 MIN
U-matic / VHS / 16mm
Ancient Lives Series
Color
Documents a time of decay and change in ancient Egypt.
Geography - World; History - World; Sociology
Dist - FOTH **Prod** - FOTH

The Year of the jeep 20 MIN
U-matic / VHS
Matter of fiction series; No 11
B&W (J H)
Presents Year Of The Jeep, a film by Keith Robertson. Concerns two boys who find a jeep and restore it to running order. Tells that when the owner wants the jeep back to sell at a public auction, the boys try to earn money to buy it. Relates their money - earning adventures, which include capturing and selling bats to a biologist and assisting in the arrest of a gang of thieves.
Literature and Drama; Social Science
Dist - AITECH **Prod** - WETATV

Year of the quiet sun - Rok spokojnego slonca 106 MIN
VHS
Color (G A) (POLISH WITH ENGLISH SUBTITLES)
$34.95 purchase _ #V275
Tells the story of a Polish widow after WW II who meets an American soldier involved in war crimes investigation. Shows that although they can communicate only through gesture, they find much to share. Directed by Krzysztof Zanussi.
Fine Arts; History - World; Psychology; Religion and Philosophy
Dist - POLART
KINOIC

The Year of the wildebeest 30 MIN
VHS
Color (I J H)
Shows a large herd of wildebeest as they migrate 2000 miles through East Africa.
Geography - World; Science - Natural
Dist - BNCHMK **Prod** - BNCHMK 1984

The Year of the wildebeest 55 MIN
16mm
Color (I)
LC 76-701908
Examines the migration of millions of wildebeest in Kenya on their search for grass and water during the dry summer months.
Geography - World; Science - Natural
Dist - BNCHMK **Prod** - ROOTA 1976

Year one 25 MIN
U-matic / VHS
Color
Shows Dr Richard Koch of Children's Hospital demonstrating physical and mental development in the first year of life, with nine guests ranging in age from two weeks to twelve months. Includes pediatrician Carter Wright explaining common health problems in infancy.
Home Economics; Psychology
Dist - MEDCOM **Prod** - MEDCOM

Year one, boys and girls inversion with body shape - Unit D 57 MIN
VHS
Secondary gymnastics series
Color; PAL (I J H T)
PdS35.00 purchase
Features observation material allowing an opportunity to consider technical aspects of gymnastics and to provide a basis for discussion on the place and nature of gymnastics in education. Consists of a series of four units.
Physical Education and Recreation
Dist - EMFVL

Year one, traveling with changes of body shape - Unit A 40 MIN
VHS
Secondary gymnastics series
Color; PAL (J H T)
PdS35.00 purchase
Features observation material allowing an opportunity to consider technical aspects of gymnastics and to provide a basis for discussion on the place and nature of gymnastics in education. Consists of a series of four units.
Physical Education and Recreation
Dist - EMFVL

The Year they discovered people 14 MIN
16mm
Color
LC 75-700338
Presents a documentary on employee attitudes within the Western Electric Company over the past 50 years, indicating advances and opportunities which have resulted. Features recollections of participants in the Hawthorne Studies of the 1920s, film footage, photographs and re - creations of factory conditions.
Guidance and Counseling; Psychology; Social Science
Dist - MTP **Prod** - WESTEC 1974

Year three, partner work with twisting and turning - Unit C 50 MIN
VHS
Secondary gymnastics series
Color; PAL (J H T)
PdS35.00 purchase
Features observation material allowing an opportunity to consider technical aspects of gymnastics and to provide a basis for discussion on the place and nature of gymnastics in education. Consists of a series of four units.
Physical Education and Recreation
Dist - EMFVL

The Year Times Changed 27 MIN
16mm
Color
LC 79-700351
Uses still photographs, archival footage, and animation to document the nature of America during the years 1900 to 1910. Highlights events and inventions which made this period a turning point in the history and development of the United States.
History - United States
Dist - MTP **Prod** - PENN 1978

A Year Towards Tomorrow 29 MIN
16mm
Color
Describes difficulties and satisfactions experienced by three VISTA volunteers. Shows two girls on a Navajo reservation in Arizona and an ex - navy volunteer in the slums of Atlanta.
History - United States; Psychology; Sociology
Dist - USNAC **Prod** - USVIST 1966

Year two, twisting and turning - Unit B 41 MIN
VHS
Secondary gymnastics series
Color; PAL (J H T)
PdS35.00 purchase
Features observation material allowing an opportunity to consider technical aspects of gymnastics and to provide a basis for discussion on the place and nature of gymnastics in education. Consists of a series of four units.
Physical Education and Recreation
Dist - EMFVL

The Yearling
U-matic / VHS
Adolescent literature series
Color (J H G)
Follows the lives of a young boy and his adopted fawn. Stars Gregory Peck and Jane Wyman. Based on the story by Marjorie Kinnan Rawlings.
Fine Arts; Literature and Drama
Dist - CHUMAN **Prod** - GA
GA
UILL

Yearning to breathe free 15 MIN
U-matic / VHS
Los peregrinos modernos - the modern pioneers series
Color (I)
Outlines new immigrant Mr. Martinez's problems with the new culture, including expecting that his wife should also work to support the family. Focuses on difficulties such as prejudice and a new language.
Geography - World; Sociology
Dist - GPN **Prod** - NETV

The Years 1904 - 1914 - the Drums Begin to Roll 52 MIN
VHS / 16mm
Europe, the Mighty Continent Series no 4; No 4
Color (GERMAN)
LC 77-701559
Analyzes the European events and conditions that set the stage for World War I. Discusses the Russian defeat in the Russo - Japanese War, which convinced Asians, Africans and Indians that Europe was not invincible and which inspired confidence in Germany.
History - World
Dist - TIMLIF **Prod** - BBCTV 1976

The Years 1904 - 1914 - the drums begin to roll - Pt 1 26 MIN
U-matic / VHS
Europe - the mighty continent series
Color (H C A)
Special two - part version of the film and videorecording The Years 1904 - 1914 - The Drums Begin To Roll.
History - World
Dist - TIMLIF **Prod** - BBCTV 1976

The Years 1904 - 1914 - the drums begin to roll - Pt 2 26 MIN
U-matic / VHS
Europe - the mighty continent series
Color (H C A)
Special two - part version of the film and videorecording The Years 1904 - 1914 - The Drums Begin To Roll.
History - World
Dist - TIMLIF **Prod** - BBCTV 1976

The Years Ahead 30 MIN
16mm
Color
LC 80-701492
Provides biographical sketches of six senior citizens who have confronted various problems in the later years and have found constructive and satisfying solutions.
Health and Safety; Sociology
Dist - CPTEL **Prod** - CPTEL 1980

Years in Review - the Thirties, 1934 8 MIN
8mm cartridge / 16mm
Years in Review - the Thirties Series
B&W (C)
LC 75-703316
History - United States; History - World
Dist - KRAUS **Prod** - KRAUS 1975

Years in Review - the Thirties, 1935 9 MIN
16mm
Years in Review - the Thirties Series
B&W (C)
LC 75-703317
History - United States; History - World
Dist - KRAUS **Prod** - KRAUS 1975

Years in Review - the Thirties Series
Years in Review - the Thirties, 1934 8 MIN
Years in Review - the Thirties, 1935 9 MIN
Dist - KRAUS

Years of change series
America in 1968 - Pt 1 - World Affairs 20 MIN
America in 1968 - Pt 3 - People and Culture 20 MIN
America in 1968 - Pt 2 - Government and Politics 22 MIN
Dist - PHENIX

Years of destiny 21 MIN
16mm

B&W
Tells why and how an independent Jewish state rose again, in modern times. Presents the record of the struggle for that independence and its results.
Geography - World; History - World
Dist - ALDEN **Prod** - ALDEN

Years of Gloom and Hope 30 MIN
VHS / 16mm
World of the 30s Series
Color (J)
$149.00 purchase, $75.00 rental _ #OD - 2261
Describes how British workers maintained hope despite the serious economic problems caused by aging plants of the Industrial Revolution. Reveals that workers in Holland and Belgium did not feel the same. The fourth of 13 installments of The World Of The 30s Series.
History - United States; History - World
Dist - FOTH

The Years of Reconstruction - 1865 - 1877 25 MIN
U-matic / VHS / 16mm
American history series
Color (J H)
LC FIA68-2289
Shows the economic, social and political problems facing the freed slaves after the Civil War, and illustrates how resentment and bitterness on both sides frustrated attempts to reach a reasonable peace. Features the presidential election of 1875 as the official end of Reconstruction.
History - United States
Dist - MGHT **Prod** - MGHT 1969

Years of revolt and revolution 30 MIN
35mm strip / VHS
Western man and the modern world series; Unit V
Color (J H C T A)
Documents the unrest in Europe between 1830 and 1872. Focuses on three critical figures of the era - Metternich, Garibaldi, and Bismarck.
History - World; Sociology
Dist - SRA
RH

Yeast Dough Shaping made Easy 15 MIN
16mm
Color (J H A)
Shows techniques for making dinner rolls, cinnamon buns, sticky buns, coffee cakes and foreign specialties from two basic, simple doughs.
Home Economics
Dist - MTP **Prod** - FLSMNY

Yeats Country 18 MIN
16mm / U-matic / VHS
Color (H C A)
The scenes and impressions which inspired Yeats' writing are related to the history and social environment of his time.
History - World; Literature and Drama
Dist - IFB **Prod** - AENGUS 1965

Yehuda Amichai - 11 - 22 - 77 45 MIN
VHS / Cassette
Poetry Center reading series
Color (G)
$15.00, $45.00 purchase _ #272 - 226
Features the poet reading his works at the Poetry Center, San Francisco State University.
Literature and Drama
Dist - POETRY **Prod** - POETRY 1977

Yehuda Amichai - 3 - 15 - 89 58 MIN
VHS / Cassette
Lannan Literary series
Color (G)
$15.00, $19.95 purchase, $15.00 rental _ #898
Features the poet addressing a small group at the Folger Shakespeare Library in Washington, DC and reading from his Selected Poetry of Yehuda Amichai at Georgetown University. Includes an interview by Esther Robbins, Adjunct Professor in the Arabic and Hebrew Department at Georgetown University. Part of a series of literary videotapes presenting major poets and writers from around the globe reading and talking about their work; readings were sponsored by The Lannan Foundation of Los Angeles, a private contemporary arts organization.
Guidance and Counseling; Literature and Drama
Dist - POETRY **Prod** - METEZT 1989

Yehudi Menuhin - Brahms Violin Concerto in D, Op 77 60 MIN
VHS
Color (G)
$29.95 purchase _ #1127
Presents Yehudi Menuhin performing the 'Violin Concerto In D, Op 77' by Brahms at the Gewandhaus in Leipzig, East Germany. Reveals that the concerto was given its first performance at the old Gewandhaus in Leipzig conducted by Brahms himself. The concerto is preceded by a personal introduction by Menuhin, and two unaccompanied Bach pieces make up the encores.
Fine Arts; Geography - World
Dist - KULTUR

Yelling fire 5 MIN
16mm
Color (G)
$12.00 rental
Plays with the rhyming of simple existence.
Fine Arts
Dist - CANCIN **Prod** - RAYHER 1980

Yellow aria
16mm
Color (G A) (ITALIAN SUBTITLES)
$30.00 rental
Presents the work of filmmaker Tina Bastajian. Presents an oratory of female lament over the loss of love.
Fine Arts; History - United States; Industrial and Technical Education; Psychology; Religion and Philosophy; Sociology
Dist - PARART **Prod** - CANCIN 1986

The Yellow Ball Cache 18 MIN
16mm
Color (P I J H)
LC FIA67-5040
Presents a demonstration of the creativity and skill of children, ages 5 to 15, as observed in their work in the planning and production of 13 short animated films which they created using cut - out techniques. Features instructor Yvonne Andersen.
Fine Arts
Dist - YELLOW **Prod** - YELLOW 1965

Yellow Creek, Kentucky 29 MIN
VHS / 16mm
Color (G)
$100.00 purchase _ #YELLOWV
Documents the efforts of the citizens of Yellow Creek, Kentucky, to stop toxic waste dumping in their creek. Shows a takeover of the Middlesboro city government by a bipartisan citizens' coalition.
Business and Economics; Geography - United States; Sociology
Dist - APPAL

Yellow earth 90 MIN
VHS
Color (G) (MANDARIN CHINESE)
$45.00 purchase _ #1079A; $45.00 purchase _ #6074C
Presents a movie produced in the People's Republic of China.
Fine Arts; Geography - World; Literature and Drama
Dist - CHTSUI **Prod** - CHTSUI

Yellow - Headed Blackbird 3 MIN
16mm
Of all Things Series
Color (P I)
Discusses the bird known as the yellow - headed blackbird.
Science - Natural
Dist - AVED **Prod** - BAILYL

Yellow horse 9 MIN
16mm
Color (G)
$15.00 rental
Depicts a cycle scrambling poem with bass solo by Pat Smith, Los Angeles.
Fine Arts
Dist - CANCIN **Prod** - BAILB 1965

Yellow Pages Commercial 1 MIN
U-matic / VHS
Color
Shows a classic animated television commercial.
Business and Economics; Psychology; Sociology
Dist - BROOKC **Prod** - BROOKC

Yellow rain 29 MIN
VHS / U-matic
Inside story series
Color
Considers the fact that the alleged use of 'yellow rain,' a poisonous substance used in chemical - biological warfare is a major story of critical international importance that has received spotty media coverage.
Fine Arts; Literature and Drama; Social Science; Sociology
Dist - PBS **Prod** - PBS 1981

Yellow river 15 HRS
VHS
Color (G) (MANDARIN CHINESE)
$550.00 purchase _ #6037X
Presents a geo-cultural documentary television program produced in the People's Republic of China.
Fine Arts; Geography - World; History - World; Industrial and Technical Education; Literature and Drama
Dist - CHTSUI **Prod** - CHTSUI

The Yellow School Bus 10 MIN
16mm / U-matic / VHS
Color (K P I)
LC 75-702499
Shows safety practices and considerate behavior while riding a school bus.
Guidance and Counseling; Health and Safety
Dist - ALTSUL **Prod** - RUGLSG 1975

Yellow Slippers 45 MIN
U-matic / VHS / 16mm
CBS Children's Film Festival Series
Color (P I J)
LC 73-702062
Dramatizes the story of an orphan boy, apprenticed to a sculptor, who witnesses a church robbery by a mysterious pilgrim, is kidnapped and trained by the robber after his release from jail, and is finally rescued.
Fine Arts
Dist - MGHT **Prod** - WRLDP 1969

The Yellow star 16 MIN
16mm
Color (G)
$25.00 rental
Presents a documentary made in Israel.
Dist - NCJEWF

The Yellow Submarine 85 MIN
16mm
Color
Presents the animated story of how Pepperland is saved from the evil Blue Meanies when the Beatles arrive in a yellow submarine.
Fine Arts
Dist - TWYMAN **Prod** - KINGFT 1968

Yellow tale blues - two American families 30 MIN
VHS
Color (H C G)
$295.00 purchase, $55.00 rental
Presents ethnically stereotyped clips from Hollywood movies which reveal nearly a century of disparaging images of Asians which are juxtaposed with portraits of the Choys, an immigrant, working class family, and the Tajimas, a fourth - generation middle class California family. Driected by Christine Choy and Renee Tajima and produced by Quynh Thai.
History - United States; Sociology
Dist - FLMLIB

The Yellow Wallpaper 15 MIN
16mm / VHS
Color (G)
$350.00, $195.00 purchase, $45.00 rental; #E373
Portrays 'The Yellow Wallpaper' created by Charlotte Perkins Gilman. Tells the story of Elizabeth, an aspiring writer who becomes ill and is forced by her doctor and her husband to take a 'rest cure.' Rigorously isolated, Elizabeth creates a world inside the wallpaper of her room - in which a woman is trapped and unable to escape.
History - United States; Literature and Drama; Sociology
Dist - WMEN **Prod** - MARSH 1978
GPM CTI

The Yellow Wallpaper by Charlotte Perkins Gilman 15 MIN
U-matic / VHS / 16mm
Short Story Series
Color (J)
LC 83-700041
Presents a tale of a woman's gradual mental breakdown as a result of confinement and denial of her creative energies by her husband and doctors. Based on the short story The Yellow Wallpaper by Charlotte Perkins Gilman.
Literature and Drama
Dist - IU **Prod** - IITC 1982

Yellowstone 55 MIN
VHS
Reader's digest great national parks series
Color (G)
$24.95 purchase
Tours the Yellowstone National Park in Wyoming. Presents extensive footage of the natural wonders located there, and gives an explanation of how natural forces created the park. Offers advice on where to stay, hours of operation, permits, trails, campsites, and more.
Geography - United States
Dist - PBS **Prod** - WNETTV

Yellowstone 11 MIN
U-matic / VHS / 16mm
Color (J)
Provides an introduction to a study of America's park policy. Shows Norris Geyser Basin, Yellowstone Falls, Old Faithful and the Grand Canyon.
Geography - United States; Science - Natural
Dist - IFB **Prod** - MOYER 1950

Yellowstone 3 MIN
16mm
Of all Things Series
Color (P I)
Shows Yellowstone National Park in the state of Wyoming.
Geography - United States
Dist - AVED **Prod** - BAILYL

Yellowstone Adventure 15 MIN
16mm
Color
Shows rare shooper swans, bears, osprey with fish in its tallons in Yellow stone Park.
Geography - United States; Science - Natural
Dist - SFI **Prod** - SFI

Yellowstone aflame 30 MIN
VHS
Color (G)
$29.95 purchase
Tells the story behind the Great Yellowstone Fires. Reveals the causes and extreme conditions that set the stage for the fires. Discusses the positive ecological role of fire and its effect on wildlife. Portrays Yellowstone before, during, and after the fires.
History - United States
Dist - PBS **Prod** - WNETTV

Yellowstone and Grand Teton National Parks 60 MIN
VHS
Beautiful America series
Color (G)
$29.95 purchase
Offers scenic views of Yellowstone and Great Teton National Parks from the air, at water's edge and at the top of famous peaks and waterfalls. Mixes musical scores with scenes of nature to enhance the park's beauties. Part of a series.
Geography - United States
Dist - WIVI **Prod** - WIVI 1993

The Yellowstone Concerto 32 MIN
16mm
Color
LC 77-702181
Follows the course of the Yellowstone River from its many mountain tributaries. Shows the diversity of life which depends on the river and makes a plea for future preservation.
Geography - United States; Science - Natural
Dist - MDFG **Prod** - MDFG 1977

Yellowstone cubs 47 MIN
U-matic / VHS / 16mm
Animal featurettes series; Set 2
Color
LC 76-701287
Presents the adventures of two mischievous bear cubs as they blaze a hilarious trail through Yellowstone National Park after they become separated from their mother.
Literature and Drama
Dist - CORF **Prod** - DISNEY 1967

Yellowstone cubs - Pt 1 23 MIN
16mm / U-matic / VHS
Animal featurettes series; Set 2
Color
LC 76-701287
Presents the adventures of two mischievous bear cubs as they blaze a comical trail through Yellowstone National Park after they become separated from their mother.
Geography - United States; Psychology; Science - Natural
Dist - CORF **Prod** - DISNEY 1967

Yellowstone cubs - Pt 2 23 MIN
16mm / U-matic / VHS
Animal featurettes series; Set 2
Color
LC 76-701287
Presents the adventures of two mischievous bear cubs as they blaze a comical trail through Yellowstone National Park after they become separated from their mother.
Geography - United States; Science - Natural
Dist - CORF **Prod** - DISNEY 1967

Yellowstone in Winter 27 MIN
16mm / U-matic / VHS
Color (I)
LC 83-700269
Offers views of Yellowstone National Park during the winter season. Shows the fall courting prances of male elk and bighorn sheep and the desperate food foraging of buffalo, deer and elk during the winter.
Geography - United States
Dist - EBEC **Prod** - BAYERW 1983

Yellowstone National Park 28 MIN
BETA / VHS
Color
Captures the best of this geological showcase and teaches the fascinating story behind Yellowstone's wonderland of beauty and nature. Tours the park in its entirety.
Geography - United States
Dist - CBSC **Prod** - CBSC

Yellowstone National Park 19 MIN
U-matic / VHS / 16mm
Color
Describes Yellowstone National park, where animals roam with freedom and dignity.
Geography - United States
Dist - KAWVAL **Prod** - KAWVAL

Yellowstone National Park
VHS
America's great national parks series
Color (J H C G)
$39.95 purchase _ #QV2233V
Visits Yellowstone National Park. Part of a three - part series on national parks in the United States.
Geography - United States
Dist - CAMV

Yellowstone National Park 19 MIN
VHS
Color (P I J)
$89.00 purchase _ #RB826
Studies Yellowstone National Park which has the largest collection of hydrothermal features in the world, the Grand Canyon of the Yellowstone, dozens of spectacular waterfalls and the largest lake in North America at such a high elevation.
Geography - United States
Dist - REVID **Prod** - REVID

Yellowstone - the first national park 60 MIN
VHS
Great national parks - Set I series
Color; CC (G)
$24.95 purchase _ #906
Visits Yellowstone National Park. Views Mammoth Hot Springs, Old Faithful, Norris Geyser Basin, the 'Grand Canyon' of Yellowstone from Inspiration Point and Artist Point. Part of a series on national parks.
Geography - United States
Dist - APRESS **Prod** - READ 1988

Yellowstone - the Living Sculpture 9 MIN
U-matic
Color
LC 79-706176
Highlights Yellowstone National Park as a living sculpture, showing how ground water seeps through subsurface ducts to trigger natural phenomena such as bubbling mud pots, hot springs and geysers. Uses animation to demonstrate how these phenomena operate. Issued in 1972 as a motion picture.
Geography - United States; Science - Physical
Dist - USNAC **Prod** - USNPS 1979

Yellowstone under fire 60 MIN
VHS
Frontline series
Color; Captioned (G)
$150.00 purchase _ #FRON - 712K
Examines the conflict between preservation and development around the Yellowstone Park area. Shows that the Reagan Administration aggressively sought development of surrounding areas, selling or trading more than 68 million acres. Considers the arguments of ecologists and environmentalists that the wildlife and ecosystem of Yellowstone extends beyond the park's original borders.
Geography - United States; Science - Natural
Dist - PBS **Prod** - DOCCON

Yellowstone's burning question 60 MIN
Videodisc / VHS
Color (G)
$39.95, $29.98 purchase _ #VA5423
Explores the consequences of the most extensive wilderness fire in human history.
Geography - United States; History - United States
Dist - INSTRU **Prod** - NOVA

Yeman - happy Arabia 30 MIN
U-matic
Countries and peoples series
Color (H C)
$90.00 purchase _ #BPN128110
Shows that Yeman has managed to keep its doors closed to foreigners for centuries.
Geography - World; History - World
Dist - TVOTAR RMIBHF **Prod** - TVOTAR RMIBHF 1982

Yemen Arab Republic 28 MIN
Videoreel / VHS
International Byline Series
Color
Interviews Ambassador Ahmed Al - Haddad, permanent representative to the United Nations. Includes a film clip on the architecture of Yemen. Hosted by Marilyn Perry.
Business and Economics; Civics and Political Systems; Geography - World
Dist - PERRYM **Prod** - PERRYM

A Yen for harmony 26 MIN
U-matic / VHS / 16mm
Human resources and organization behavior series
Color
LC 77-702826
Shows how Japanese management techniques were implemented in a factory In the United States.
Business and Economics; Psychology
Dist - CNEMAG **Prod** - HOBLEI DOCUA 1976

YES 26 MIN
U-matic / VHS
Color
Celebrates the inherent unity of mankind and documents All Faith's Day at Satchidananda Ashram - Yogaville.
Religion and Philosophy
Dist - IYOGA **Prod** - IYOGA

Yes 54 MIN
16mm
Color; B&W
Presents a surrealistic tale of a teenage girl nearing break - down in a room containing by a TV set. Shows other teens who wander in and hallucinatory images.
Fine Arts
Dist - NWUFLM **Prod** - NWRTVF

Yes and no 7 MIN
U-matic
Color (I J H)
Stresses the importance of self - discipline by describing the kingdom of Yesland, where people can do anything they want.
Fine Arts
Dist - GA **Prod** - DAVFMS

Yes, but 30 MIN
16mm
B&W (A)
LC FIA65-1617
Shows how a white chief engineer and his newly - appointed negro research assistant learn to recognize the proper approach to the problems of race relations.
Business and Economics; History - United States; Psychology; Sociology
Dist - CPH **Prod** - CPH 1964

Yes, I Can 13 MIN
VHS / U-matic
Under the Blue Umbrella Series
Color (P)
Tells how six - year - old Tommy gains self confidence when he finds that he has his own abilities to contribute to the family.
Guidance and Counseling; Sociology
Dist - AITECH **Prod** - SCETV 1977

Yes, I can 15 MIN
VHS / 16mm / U-matic
Inside-out series
Color
Presents David who insists that he is ready to go out on his own for an overnight stay at summer camp at the age of nine. Shows what happens when he gets his chance, but comes up against problems he hadn't counted on. Considers the limits of independent actions and recognizes the prudence of thorough preparation.
Guidance and Counseling; Psychology
Dist - AITECH

Yes Ma'am 48 MIN
16mm
Color (H C A)
LC 81-700402
Presents a study of black domestics employed in the stately, old houses of New Orleans. Shows how old - timers resent those newcomers who work only for money and not for pride in their work and the care of the family, while younger household workers feel exploited and are offended by the 'mammy' role they are expected to play as part of their job.
Sociology
Dist - FLMLIB **Prod** - FLMLIB 1982

Yes means yes, no means no 8 MIN
VHS
Color (G)
$30.00 purchase
Features a powerful interracial date - rape drama written and directed by the filmmaker and San Francisco performance artist Dee Russell. Provides a portrayal of sexual assault and a sharp satire on interracial sexual perceptions.

Fine Arts; Literature and Drama; Sociology
Dist - CANCIN **Prod** - LEIGHC 1990

Yes, no, maybe - decision - making skills 18 MIN
VHS
Color (I J)
$149.00 purchase _ #2311 - SK
Covers decision - making skills. Presents a five - step decision - making process. Stresses the importance of self - awareness, values, and goal - setting in making sound decisions. Includes teacher's guide.
Education; Guidance and Counseling; Psychology
Dist - SUNCOM **Prod** - SUNCOM

Yes, no - Stop, Go 13 MIN
U-matic / VHS / 16mm
Color (K P)
LC 73-700510
Offers a visual interpretation of the words yes, no, stop and go. Helps the child relate the sights and sounds of the words to reading the words.
English Language
Dist - AIMS **Prod** - EVANSA 1971

Yes or no - choosing success sooner 26 MIN
VHS
Color (COR)
$695.00 purchase, $195.00 five - day rental, $40.00 fifteen - day preview
Presents a system to facilitate decision - making for people at every organizational level. Features John Debello explaining Dr Spencer Johnson's five - step method for making successful choices sooner, enabling everyone to handle more responsibility with less dependence on management. Provides examples of successful and unsuccessful decision - making in various corporations. Helps viewers make better decisions to save time, money, and error.
Business and Economics; Psychology
Dist - ADVANM

Yes or no, Jean Guy Moreau 58 MIN
16mm
Color
_ #106C 0179 254N
Geography - World
Dist - CFLMDC **Prod** - NFBC 1979

Yes to life - Montreal stadium youth rally 92 MIN
VHS / BETA
Pope John Paul II - a pilgrimage of faith, hope, and love
(R G) (FRENCH)
$29.95 purchase, _ #VHS 5PV 123 _ #Beta 5PV 223
Shows the visit of Pope John Paul II to the Montreal Stadium Youth Rally in Canada in 1984.
History - World; Religion and Philosophy
Dist - CANBC

Yes, Virginia, There is a Santa Claus 25 MIN
16mm
Color (P I)
LC 76-701135
Presents the story of eight - year - old Virginia O'Hanlan and her attempt to find out if there really is a Santa Claus. Shows how she tried several sources before finally getting an answer from the editor of the New York Sun.
Literature and Drama; Social Science
Dist - FI **Prod** - WOLPER 1975

Yes We Can 31 MIN
U-matic
B&W
Shows six women speaking of the difficulties they encounter, the changes they hope for and the growth and self - worth brought about by their pursuit of traditionally 'masculine' trades.
Business and Economics; Sociology
Dist - WMENIF **Prod** - VIDFEM

Yes - we're walking 24 MIN
VHS
Color (H C A)
$29.95 purchase _ #FV200V
Presents a comprehensive program for walking as exercise. Covers how to develop proper walking stride, technique, and a walking program that meets individual fitness needs. Includes a copy of the Rockport Fitness Walking Test booklet.
Physical Education and Recreation; Science - Natural
Dist - CAMV

Yes, you are 30 MIN
VHS
Celebrating with children series
Color (G A R)
$39.95 purchase, $10.00 rental _ #35 - 898 - 2076
Features teacher Kathy Wise in lessons on how to maintain order in a classroom and how to encourage children's development of positive self - images. Produced by Seraphim.
Education; Sociology
Dist - APH

Yes You Can 28 MIN
16mm
You Can do it - if Series
Color (J)
LC 81-700095
Explains how people can pinpoint areas in their lives they would like to change, and suggests how to carry out these changes.
Psychology
Dist - VANDER **Prod** - VANDER 1980

Yes, you can afford college - a complete guide to student financial aid 33 MIN
VHS
Color (H C A)
$69.95 purchase _ #CCP0168V-D
Tells parents and prospective college students of the avenues available to them to finance a college education. Interviews financial aid experts. Details resources available to college students, costs of college, how much aid students and families can expect to receive, and more. Includes a workbook that lists financial aid resources and a glossary of financial aid terminology.
Education
Dist - CAMV

Yes, You Can Change a Flat 29 MIN
VHS / 16mm
What to do 'Till the Wrecker Comes Series
Color (G)
$55.00 rental _ #WTDT - 004
Industrial and Technical Education
Dist - PBS **Prod** - GAEDTN

Yes, You Can make a Difference 15 MIN
16mm
Color
Demonstrates that performance coaching is, or should be, a part of every manager's day - to - day responsibilities. Emphasizes skills development.
Business and Economics; Psychology
Dist - EFM **Prod** - EFM

Yes you can microwave 60 MIN
VHS
Color (A)
$29.95 purchase _ #S00307
Teaches basic cooking skills for the microwave oven. Demonstrates the preparation of several recipes. Includes a cookbook.
Home Economics; Industrial and Technical Education; Social Science
Dist - UILL

Yes you can say no 19 MIN
VHS
Color (P I)
$195.00 purchase, $50.00 rental _ #204; $75.00 rental _ #9873
Teaches assertiveness and communication and reporting skills to prevent the sexual abuse of children.
Guidance and Counseling; Psychology; Sociology
Dist - SICACC **Prod** - SICACC 1990
AIMS

Yes you can video series
Presents a five - part series on custom slipcovering and drapery, cushion and pillow making. Covers basic slipcovers, zippers, cushions and pillows, fitting slipcovers for complex chairs and draperies.

Basic slipcovers - yes you can	94 MIN
Creative solutions to difficult areas	60 MIN
Cushions and pillows	60 MIN
Pinch pleated draperies	60 MIN
Zippers like a pro	60 MIN

Dist - CAMV

Yeshua - Part 5
VHS
Color; Captioned (S R)
Presents a captioned account of part 5 of 'Yeshua.' Available on a free - loan basis from the Lutheran Church - Missouri Synod's Deaf Ministry.
Guidance and Counseling; Literature and Drama; Religion and Philosophy
Dist - CPH **Prod** - LUMIS

Yeshua - Parts 1 and 2
VHS
Color; Captioned (S R)
Presents a captioned account of parts 1 and 2 of 'Yeshua.' Available on a free - loan basis from the Lutheran Church - Missouri Synod's Deaf Ministry.
Guidance and Counseling; Literature and Drama; Religion and Philosophy
Dist - CPH **Prod** - LUMIS

Yeshua - Parts 3 and 4
VHS
Color; Captioned (S R)
Presents a captioned account of parts 3 and 4 of 'Yeshua.' Available on a free - loan basis from the Lutheran Church - Missouri Synod's Deaf Ministry.
Guidance and Counseling; Literature and Drama; Religion and Philosophy
Dist - CPH **Prod** - LUMIS

Yeshua series
Presents a miniseries of Biblical history, spanning from the time of Abraham to the resurrection of Jesus. Also available in individual hour segments.

Yeshua series	300 MIN

Dist - CPH **Prod** - LUMIS

Yesterday and today
U-matic / VHS
Pre - war German featurettes series
B&W
Presents an argument for National Socialism using film clips contrasting the new prosperity under Nazi rule compared with an earlier Weimar Republican Germany inflicted with economic depression and unemployment.
History - World
Dist - IHF **Prod** - IHF

Yesterday and Today Series

The Birch canoe builder	22 MIN
Cider maker	18 MIN
Grist Miller	18 MIN
The Maple Sugar Farmer	29 MIN

Dist - AIMS

Yesterday Lives Again 14 MIN
16mm
Color
Recaptures the day - to - day world of our ancestors at the Oldest Store Museum in St Augustine, Florida.
Geography - United States; History - United States
Dist - FLADC **Prod** - FLADC

Yesterday the coyote sang - Pt 1 30 MIN
16mm
Glory trail series
B&W (I)
LC FIA66-975
Describes the 'great American cowboy,' focusing on cattle drives and their leaders.
History - United States
Dist - IU **Prod** - NET 1965

Yesterday the coyote sang - Pt 2 30 MIN
16mm
Glory trail series
B&W (I)
LC FIA66-974
Discusses the cattleman's economic troubles and his chief enigma -- the incoming farmer with his plows, wire fences and sod homes.
History - United States
Dist - IU **Prod** - NET 1965

Yesterday, Today 58 MIN
16mm
Color (J)
LC 72-703039
Studies a day in the life of a Netsilik Eskimo family.
Geography - United States; Social Science; Sociology
Dist - EDC **Prod** - NFBC 1971

Yesterday, today and tomorrow - the women of Papua, New Guinea 27 MIN
VHS / U-matic
Color (H C A)
$420.00, $390.00 purchase _ #V445
Examines some of the ancient customs and rituals of tribal women in Papua, New Guinea. Contrasts the traditional women with a few women who have entered the modern world and are faced with the conflict of balancing ancient customs with new ideals.
Geography - World; History - World; Sociology
Dist - BARR **Prod** - CEPRO 1988

Yesterday, Today - the Netsilik Eskimo 57 MIN
U-matic
Color
Examines one day in the life of a Netsilik family in a government village ten years after settlement in Pelly Bay, Canada. Shows that the inter - dependency and specialization of modern living have replaced the self - sufficiency of traditional Eskimo family life.
Social Science; Sociology
Dist - EDC **Prod** - EDC

Yesterday, tomorrow, and you 52 MIN
16mm / U-matic / VHS
Connections series; No 10
Color (H C A)

$99.95, $595.00 purchase _ #9; LC 79-700865
Illustrates common factors that create change at different times and in different places. Explains why people are becoming increasingly incapable of understanding complex changes in the modern world. Points out the need for a radical change in the availability and use of information in the future. Hosted by James Burke.
Sociology
Dist - TIMLIF **Prod** - BBCTV 1979
AMBROS

Yesterday's dream, today's reality 20 MIN
VHS / U-matic
Space stations series
Color (I J H G)
$245.00, $295.00 purchase, $50.00 rental
Traces the historical origins of space exploration, with emphasis on the United States Space Station. Includes the Skylab, Apollo and Space Shuttle Programs. Looks at the factors that determine space station design. Part of a three - part series. Produced by Media Craft Communications.
Industrial and Technical Education; Science
Dist - NDIM

Yesterday's Farm 17 MIN
U-matic / VHS / 16mm
Color (P I J)
LC 73-701289
Points out that the old farms that spread across North America are rich sources of information about our past, showing the ruggedness of life, the trials of the movement westward, the values that were held by early settlers and the hopes and ambitions of generations.
Agriculture; History - United States; Social Science; Sociology
Dist - PHENIX **Prod** - PHENIX 1972

Yesterday's Farm 20 MIN
16mm
Color
LC 76-702579
Discusses the need to preserve the farm heritage.
Agriculture; Social Science; Sociology
Dist - HRAWC **Prod** - ATKINS 1974

Yesterday's Heroes 23 MIN
U-matic / VHS
Color
Focuses on the wild descendants of the animals that helped build the continent of Australia, such as horses, donkeys and camels.
Geography - World; Science - Natural
Dist - NWLDPR **Prod** - NWLDPR

Yesterday's Wings 20 MIN
VHS / U-matic
Color (J)
LC 82-706795
Discusses vintage aircraft, including Curtiss, Waco, Ryan and Beechcraft, among others.
Industrial and Technical Education; Social Science
Dist - AWSS **Prod** - AWSS 1981

Yesterday's witness - a tribute to the American newsreel 52 MIN
16mm
B&W; Color
LC 76-700447
Uses newsreel footage and interviews with newsreel personages in presenting the history of the American newsreel from the silent days to mid-century.
Fine Arts; History - United States
Dist - BLACKW **Prod** - BLACKW 1976

Yesterday's Witness in America Series
Gold rush at Cripple Creek 50 MIN
The Long March of the Suffragists 50 MIN
A Question of Loyalty 50 MIN
A Very Public Private Affair 50 MIN
Dist - TIMLIF

Yet 2 MIN
16mm
Color
Presents a short film.
Fine Arts; Industrial and Technical Education
Dist - VANBKS **Prod** - VANBKS

Yetta Bernhard, MA - Conflict Resolution with a Couple 60 MIN
U-matic / VHS
Perceptions, Pt a - Interventions in Family Therapy Series Vol VI, 'Pt A12
Color (PRO)
Illustrates the concepts outlined in Yetta Bernhard's book, Self Care. Includes an interview with a reconstituted family. Discusses communication and contracts with family members.
Guidance and Counseling; Psychology; Sociology
Dist - BOSFAM **Prod** - BOSFAM

Yetta Bernhard, MA, Private Practice, Los Angeles, California 60 MIN
U-matic / VHS
Perceptions, Pt B - Dialogues with Family Therapists Series Vol VI, 'Pt B12
Color (PRO)
Traces the evolution of a school teacher to a family therapist who combines the experiences of her family of origin and her marriage.
Guidance and Counseling; Psychology; Sociology
Dist - BOSFAM **Prod** - BOSFAM

Yevgeny Yevtushenko 29 MIN
16mm / U-matic / VHS
B&W (C)
$485.00, $289.00, $189.00 purchase _ #AD - 117
Presents a close - up view of popular poet Yevgeny Yevtushenko. Examines his roots in Siberia, Babi Yar, Moscow and his relationship to other Russian poets from Pushkin to Pasternak.
Biography; Foreign Language; History - World; Literature and Drama
Dist - FOTH **Prod** - FOTH

Yevtushenko - a Poet's Journey 29 MIN
16mm / U-matic / VHS
Color (J) (RUSSIAN)
LC 74-708460
An account of Yevtushenko's travels around the world, his working methods in his moscow apartment, the Siberia of his youth and his conversations with friends and admirers. Includes sequences of the poet reading his works in Russian, over which English interpretations are imposed.
Literature and Drama
Dist - FOTH **Prod** - MANTLH 1970

The Yew tree 27 MIN
VHS / U-matic
Color (J H G)
$275.00, $325.00 purchase, $50.00 rental
Covers all aspects of the Yew tree, found only in the ancient forests of the Pacific Northwest and nearly extinct from overcutting and overuse. Discloses that taxol, a substance found in the bark and needles of the tree, may be one of the major new treatments for ovarian and other cancers. Produced by Aspect Productions.
Fine Arts; Health and Safety; Science - Natural
Dist - NDIM

The Yiddish cinema 60 MIN
VHS
Color; B&W (G)
$25.00 purchase
Documents the history of Yiddish film production in Eastern Europe and the United States, nourished by Yiddish literature and theater, and flourishing between the two world wars. Uses interviews, archival photographs and film clips to include all aspects of the history, such as music and tradition, comedy and tragedy, actors and directors. Traces the decline of the cinema and language, along with other cultural decimations. Narrated by David Mamet.
Fine Arts; Foreign Language; Religion and Philosophy; Sociology
Dist - NCJEWF

Yiddish - the Mame - Loshn 58 MIN
VHS
Color (G)
$49.95 purchase _ #434
Uses interviews, excerpts from Yiddish films, poetry and music to portray Yiddish as a language and as a culture. Features author Leo Rosten, actor Herschel Bernardi and comedian David Steinberg.
Sociology
Dist - ERGOM **Prod** - ERGOM

Yiddish theater series
Presents five videos recording Yiddish theater from the 1930s. Includes the titles His Wife's Lover, Le Golem, Tevye, Green Fields and Mirele Efros.
Yiddish theater series 444 MIN
Dist - ERGOM **Prod** - ERGOM

The Yiddisher boy 3 MIN
16mm
B&W (G)
$7.00 rental
Features Moses, growing up on the Lower East Side, who helps support his family by selling papers. Presents a sympathetic portrayal of urbane, American Jewish life. Produced by the Lubin Company.
Fine Arts; Sociology
Dist - NCJEWF

Yiddle with his fiddle, Mamele, A Letter to mother, The Purimspieler 388 MIN
VHS
B&W (G)
$250.00 purchase
Presents a special package offer of four Yiddish film classics by Joseph Green, made between 1936 - 1938 in his native Poland, restored with complete English subtitles. See individual titles for descriptions. 16mm and 35mm prints also available; contact distributor for more information.
Fine Arts; Religion and Philosophy; Sociology
Dist - NCJEWF

Yiddle with his fiddle - Yidl mitn fidl 92 MIN
35mm
B&W (G) (YIDDISH WITH ENGLISH SUBTITLES)
Portrays Molly who, seeking to help her aging father and finding few options for young women in the shtetl, disguises herself as a boy, Yiddle, to join a band of klezmorim. Travels from shtetl to shtetl until their musical lands on Warsaw's Yiddish stage. Producer Joseph Green returned to his native Poland to film on location in Warsaw and Kazimierz, where he employed shtetl inhabitants as extras. This classic folk comedy and romance is the most commercially successful musical in the history of Yiddish cinema. Contact distributor for rental fee.
Fine Arts; Religion and Philosophy; Sociology
Dist - NCJEWF

The Yidishe Gauchos 28 MIN
VHS
Color (H)
$195.00 purchase, $55.00 rental
Narrates the story of Jews who fled Russia to become ranchers and farmers on the pampas in Argentina. Features Eli Wallach as narrator. Produced by Mark Freeman.
Geography - World; Sociology
Dist - FLMLIB

Yidl mitn fidl - Yidl with a fiddle 92 MIN
VHS
Joseph Green Yiddish film classics series
B&W (G) (YIDDISH WITH ENGLISH SUBTITLES)
$89.95 purchase _ #710
Stars Molly Picon who portrays a young woman who poses as a man in order to join a band of musicians travelling the Polish countryside. Reveals that she fall in love with one of colleagues with humorous results. With Simche Fostel, Max Bozyk and Leon Liebgold. Directed by Joseph Green.
Fine Arts; Sociology
Dist - ERGOM **Prod** - ERGOM 1936

Yield - Research to Reality 17 MIN
16mm
Color
Shows how hybrid corn is developed at Dekalb AgResearch and the factors involved in developing these plants.
Agriculture
Dist - MTP **Prod** - MTP

Yin Hsien 9 MIN
U-matic / VHS / 16mm
Color
LC 75-700499
Uses an image synthesizer to create abstract moving forms from live action. Presents a Chinese master of the martial art of T'ai chi chu'uan and transforms him into kinetic figures, mists and hieroglyphs.
Fine Arts; Industrial and Technical Education
Dist - PFP **Prod** - WHIT 1975

Yin - Yang 5 MIN
16mm
Color (H C A)
Presents a psychedelic time - painting, using positive, negative and black light illuminated alternating frames.
Fine Arts
Dist - CFS **Prod** - CFS 1969

Yippie Film 15 MIN
16mm
Color
Views what took place in the streets of Chicago during the 1968 Democratic Convention. Records original songs by the Fugs, Phil Ochs, Lawrence Welk, Wolf Lowenthal and Rennie Davis.
Geography - United States; Sociology
Dist - CANWRL **Prod** - CANWRL 1968

Yirrkala Adventure 30 MIN
VHS
Color (J)
$79.00 purchase _ #188 - 9030
Follows the adventures of a group of Australian teenagers from the city as they live in the bush with aborigines. Shares the youngsters' new experiences as they learn the aborigine ways of eating, dancing, playing and working.
Geography - World; History - World; Social Science; Sociology
Dist - FI **Prod** - FLMAUS 1987

Yizkor - Jiskor 100 MIN
16mm
Silent; B&W (G) (ENGLISH INTERTITLES)
Recounts the Volhynian legend that inspired the yearly memorial prayer of the same name and which teaches fidelity to one's self, religion and community. Looks at a young Jewish guardsman, Leybke, favored by employment with a Count who ignores the obsessive attentions of the Count's daughter and remains true to Kreyndl, his first love. His loyalty costs him dearly as he is imprisoned, then rescued and hidden. He finally surrenders to prevent others from suffering but his love for Kreyndl never wavers and the Count's daughter resorts to suicide to ensure vengeance from the grave. Produced by Joseph Green and Jacob Kalish. Contact distributor for rental fee.
Religion and Philosophy; Sociology
Dist - NCJEWF

Yo Contemplare Su Gloria 55 MIN
16mm
Color (J) (SPANISH)
Presents a Spanish version of 'I Beheld His Glory.' A Roman centurion describes events which led up to the death of Jesus and tells about His crucifixion, resurrection and appearance to Thomas.
Foreign Language
Dist - CAFM **Prod** - CAFM 1965

Yo Me Recuerdo 13 MIN
16mm
B&W
LC 78-701581
Presents a day in the life of a Tucson, Arizona, shoeshine boy.
Sociology
Dist - RUBIOA **Prod** - RUBIOA 1978

Yo Soy 60 MIN
U-matic / VHS
Color (H C A)
$395 purchase, $90 rental
Explores the key issues, problems, and concerns of the Mexican American community in the United States. Reviews the progress Chicanos have made during the past two decades in politics, education, labor and economic development. Summarizes the responses of Chicanos to the challenges of the 1980s. Directed by Jesus Salvador Trevino and Jose Luis Ruiz.
Sociology
Dist - CNEMAG

Yo Soy Chicano 60 MIN
16mm
Color (H C A) (SPANISH)
LC 73-700537
Portrays the Chicano experience, from its roots in pre - Columbian history to the present, by actors who recreate key events in Mexican history and through interviews with Chicano leaders.
Geography - World; History - World; Sociology
Dist - IU **Prod** - KCET 1972
CNEMAG

Yo Soy Pablo Neruda 29 MIN
16mm / U-matic / VHS
Color
Shows Chilean author Pablo Neruda in his native habitat on the fierce rocky shores of Isla Negra, in the flea market of Santiago surrounded by a world of entrancing everyday objects and in the streets of Chile's capital.
Biography; Literature and Drama
Dist - FOTH **Prod** - FOTH 1984

Yo trabajo la tierra - I work the land 13 MIN
VHS
Color (R) (SPANISH WITH ENGLISH SUBTITLES)
$14.95 purchase _ #472 - 4
Portrays a farm - working family in a meditation on the dignity of work and faith. Includes a bilingual study guide.
Agriculture; Religion and Philosophy; Social Science
Dist - USCC **Prod** - USCC 1991

A Yo - Yo and a Physical Fitness Program 8 MIN
16mm
Crystal Tipps and Alistair Series
Color (K P)
LC 73-700454
Follows Crystal as she tries to break the yo - yo record only to realize she is out of shape and needs to start on a physical fitness program.
Guidance and Counseling; Literature and Drama
Dist - VEDO **Prod** - BBCTV 1972

Yo yo paradise 17 MIN
16mm
Color (G)
$40.00 rental
Captures a pet rat, Homer, on film despite all the AM radio noise and TV commercials flooding the filmmaker's mind.
Fine Arts
Dist - CANCIN **Prod** - WONGAL 1972

Yoga companion 70 MIN
VHS
Color (H C A)
$29.95 purchase
Features Gloria Goldberg and Bonnie Anthony in nine practice sessions of Iyengar yoga exercises. Each session lasts between five and ten minutes, and is designed for a particular lifestyle demand.
Health and Safety; Physical Education and Recreation
Dist - YOGAJ **Prod** - YOGAJ

Yoga for Beginners 75 MIN
VHS
Color (G)
$29.95 purchase _ #6029
Demonstrates yoga for developing strength, flexibility, to reduce stress, increase energy and concentration. Includes 52 - page Handbook. Suitable for all ages and levels of fitness.
Physical Education and Recreation
Dist - SYBVIS **Prod** - SYBVIS

Yoga for health 11 MIN
16mm
B&W (H C A)
Introduces the time - honored science of yoga and shows how certain 'asanas,' if practiced correctly, can help to build up physical health, mental alertness and stamina.
Physical Education and Recreation
Dist - NEDINF **Prod** - INDIA

Yoga for Riders 40 MIN
VHS / BETA
Color
Deals with yoga for horse riders. Teaches hip and lower back stretching to loosen and strengthen the pelvic area.
Physical Education and Recreation
Dist - EQVDL **Prod** - MHRSMP

Yoga in Daily Life 30 MIN
U-matic / VHS
Color
Presents Sri Gurudev speaking on Yoga in daily life.
Religion and Philosophy
Dist - IYOGA **Prod** - IYOGA

Yoga journal's yoga for beginners 75 MIN
VHS
Color (G)
$29.95 purchase; $24.95 purchase
Presents an introductory course in Hatha yoga. Covers breathing techniques and yoga postures, intended for both beginning and more advanced students. Includes a 52 - page companion booklet. Hosted by Patricia Walden.
Physical Education and Recreation
Dist - PBS **Prod** - WNETTV
YOGAJ

Yoga with Richard Freeman 85 MIN
VHS
Color (G)
$39.95 purchase _ #X002
Offers nearly 50 postures from ashtanga yoga, which incorporate continuous, dynamic, precise flow and special breathing techniques. Features Richard Freeman. Includes booklet.
Physical Education and Recreation
Dist - STRUE **Prod** - DELPHI 1993

The Yogic Approach to Happiness and Healing 120 MIN
U-matic / VHS
Color
Shows Sri Gurudev speaking to the Johns Hopkins University faculty and student body emphasizing that he is a skilled Naturopath. Depicts him speaking on laughter, health, breathing, selflessness and Yoga in action.
Religion and Philosophy
Dist - IYOGA **Prod** - IYOGA

Yogurt 4 MIN
Videoreel / VT2
Beatrice Trum Hunter's Natural Foods Series
Color
Demonstrates a simple method for making yogurt at home. Shows the three steps involved, heating the milk, culturing it with a bit of completed yogurt and incubating it long enough for the process of fermentation to happen and the liquid to thicken. Suggests saving a bit of yogurt to use as a culture in the next batch.
Home Economics; Social Science
Dist - PBS **Prod** - WGBH 1974
PBS

Yogurt and Cheese, make Your Own 30 MIN
VHS / BETA
Frugal Gourmet Series
Color
Shows how to make yogurt without special equipment. Demonstrates making a cheese spread, yogurt sauce and yogurt balls in garlic oil.
Health and Safety; Home Economics; Psychology
Dist - CORF **Prod** - WTTWTV

Yohannes the Silversmith 25 MIN
U-matic / VHS / 16mm
World Cultures and Youth Series
Color (J)
Introduces an Ethiopian who is working to become a master silversmith.
Geography - World; Sociology
Dist - CORF **Prod** - SUNRIS 1981

Yojimbo 111 MIN
VHS / Videodisc
B&W; CLV (G) (JAPANESE WITH ENGLISH SUBTITLES)
$55.95, $22.95 purchase _ #CC1211L, #NEL6143
Tells of a mercenary samurai who turns a town feud to his own advantage. Directed by Akira Kurosawa.
Guidance and Counseling; Literature and Drama; Religion and Philosophy
Dist - CHTSUI

Yokneam 50 MIN
16mm
Color (H C A)
Takes a look at the election process as lived out in a small town called Yokneam near Haifa, Israel. Present local party members who explain how they recruit new voters and describe the process by which people get involved with a particular party.
Civics and Political Systems; History - World
Dist - NJWB **Prod** - NJWB 1981

Yolanda 22 MIN
16mm / VHS
Color (G)
$25.00 rental, $40.00 purchase
Portrays a housewife obsessed with the idea of a large hairy creature that stands twelve feet tall. Chronicles her eventual breakdown.
Fine Arts; Psychology
Dist - CANCIN **Prod** - KUCHAR 1981

The Yom Kippur war 28 MIN
VHS
Color (G)
$29.95 purchase _ #218
Reveals that at 2 pm on Yom Kippur day in October, 1973, when the people of Israel stood in solemn prayer, the armies of Egypt and Syria invaded the borders of Israel. Documents the battle on the homefront and on the field of battle - in Sinai, the Golan Heights, in the air and at sea.
History - World; Sociology
Dist - ERGOM **Prod** - ERGOM 1993

Yonder
VHS
Children's Literature on Video Series
Color (K)
$33.00 purchase
Literature and Drama
Dist - PELLER

Yonder Come Day 26 MIN
U-matic / VHS / 16mm
Color (H C A)
LC 75-704367
Documents the efforts of 72 - year - old Bessie Jones to pass along to new generations the rich heritage of black slave songs and culture. Shows how the music, games, songs and traditions of an earlier time reveal the roots of black music, the role played in the time of slavery and its significance today.
Fine Arts; History - United States; Sociology
Dist - MGHT **Prod** - CAPCC 1975

Yonge Street 7 MIN
16mm
B&W
LC 77-702732
Presents scenes of Toronto's Yonge Street, from Bloor Street south to the lake.
Geography - World
Dist - CANFDC **Prod** - CANFDC 1972

Yoo Hoo, I'm a Bird 28 MIN
Videoreel / VT1
Color
Shows winter in Colorado, including skiing.
Physical Education and Recreation
Dist - MTP **Prod** - UAL

orick's Skull - Gallows Humor in Hamlet 45 MIN
U-matic / VHS
Survey of English Literature I Series
Color
Looks at gallows humour in Shakespeare's work Hamlet.
Literature and Drama
Dist - MDCPB **Prod** - MDCPB

'ork 30 MIN
U-matic
South by northwest series
Color
Focuses on the life of York, the Black servant of Lieutenant William Clark, who accompanied the Lewis and Clark expedition which reached the Pacific Ocean in November, 1805. Tells how due to his active role in the success of the expedition, York was given his freedom upon the party's return to Missouri in 1806.
Biography; History - United States
Dist - GPN **Prod** - KWSU

'orkshire 20 MIN
VHS
Regional geography of England series
Color; PAL (P I J)
PdS29
Focuses on the regional geography of Yorkshire in England. Offers teacher's notes upon request. Part of a series.
Geography - World
Dist - BHA

'orkshire glory 52 MIN
VHS
Color; PAL (H)
PdS9.99 purchase
Examines the many moods of Yorkshire - from the rugged east coast to the stark skyline of the coal and steel town - in a musical journey through Britain's largest county. Captures a variety of life and landscapes in the county backed by a symphonic picture painted by composer Christopher Gunning in a specially commissioned classical score in six movments. Matches the music with footage of some of Yorkshire's best - known landmarks, including York Minster, the Bronte house at Howarth and the Dales, as well as a huge variety of industries and culture in the county. Contact distributor about availability outside the United Kingdom.
Geography - World
Dist - ACADEM

The Yorkshire of the Bronte Sisters 15 MIN
U-matic / VHS
Color (C)
$249.00, $149.00 purchase _ #AD - 1705
Looks at the landscape of Yorkshire, home to Charlotte, Emily and Anne Bronte.
Fine Arts; Literature and Drama
Dist - FOTH **Prod** - FOTH

Yorktown - the World Turned Upside Down 13 MIN
U-matic / VHS / 16mm
Color (J)
LC 72-701250
Re - creates the events and atmosphere of the victory of the French and American forces over the British army on October 19, 1781. Shows the battleground and surrounding landscape at Yorktown.
History - United States
Dist - CORF **Prod** - TERF 1971

Yosemite 3 MIN
16mm
Of all Things Series
Color (P I)
Shows Yosemite National Park in the state of California.
Geography - United States
Dist - AVED **Prod** - BAILYL

Yosemite 48 MIN
16mm
Color
LC FIE54-257
Depicts scenes from Yosemite National Park, including Sentinel Peak, Half Dome, Cathedral Spires, El Capitan and Mirror Lake, and explains the three major geologic changes in the Yosemite Valley.
Geography - United States
Dist - USNPS **Prod** - USNPS 1954

Yosemite 55 MIN
VHS
Reader's digest great national parks series
Color (G)
$24.95 purchase
Tours the Yosemite National Park in California. Presents extensive footage of the natural wonders located there, and gives an explanation of how natural forces created the park. Offers advice on where to stay, hours of operation, permits, trails, campsites, and more.
Geography - United States
Dist - PBS **Prod** - WNETTV

Yosemite 24 MIN
VHS
Color (P I J)
$89.00 purchase _ #RB822
Studies Yosemite in terms of science, history, geology and geography.
Geography - United States; History - United States
Dist - REVID **Prod** - REVID

Yosemite 24 MIN
VHS / 16mm
Color (I J H G)
$450.00, $29.95 purchase
Visits Yosemite, one of America's most popular national parks, equal in size to Rhode Island, containing Yosemite Valley.
Geography - United States
Dist - KAWVAL **Prod** - KAWVAL

Yosemite 10 MIN
16mm
B&W
Presents a scenic tour of Yosemite National Park in California and explains, using maps, models and animated drawings, the three major geologic changes in the Yosemite Valley.
Geography - United States; Science - Natural; Science - Physical
Dist - USNPS **Prod** - USNPS

Yosemite - a gift of creation 60 MIN
VHS
Great national parks - Set I series
Color; CC (G)
$24.95 purchase _ #905
Views Yosemite Fall, tallest falls in North America, and Bridalveil Falls. Visits Mariposa Grove, home of the Grizzly Giant Sequoia. Traces the history of Yosemite's discovery. Discusses how the canyon was formed. Part of a series on national parks.
Geography - United States
Dist - APRESS **Prod** - READ 1988

Yosemite and the fate of the Earth 14 MIN
VHS
Color (J H C G)
$95.00 purchase, $25.00 rental
Delves into Yosemite Park's threatened ecosystem. Looks at auto and evening campfire pollution, the decline of migratory songbirds and all species of frogs and pine trees with ozone damage. The fate of Yosemite is tied to the fate of the Earth. Produced by the Yosemite Guardian Project of Earth Island Institute.
Fine Arts; Science - Natural; Sociology
Dist - BULFRG

Yosemite National Park
VHS
America's great national parks series
Color (J H C G)
$39.95 purchase _ #QV2235V
Visits Yosemite National Park. Part of a three - part series on national parks in the United States.
Geography - United States
Dist - CAMV

Yosemite National Park 17 MIN
U-matic / VHS / 16mm
Color (I)
LC 79-701767
Pictures the scenic beauty and wildlife of Yosemite National Park through the changing seasons. Explains the geological development of Yosemite Valley and surrounding terrain and shows views of the Sierra Nevada Mountains, Half Dome, El Capitan, Merced River, Yosemite Falls and the sequoias.
Geography - United States
Dist - MCFI **Prod** - HOE 1973

Yosemite National Park 60 MIN
VHS
Beautiful America series
Color (G)
$29.95 purchase
Offers scenic views of Yosemite National Park from the air, at water's edge and at the top of famous peaks and waterfalls. Mixes musical scores with scenes of nature to enhance the park's beauties. Part of a series.
Geography - United States
Dist - WIVI **Prod** - WIVI 1993

Yosemite National Park 14 MIN
VHS / U-matic
Science in Our National Parks
Color (I J H C A)
Studies the movement of the Merced River and the formation of V shaped valleys and polished granite walls in Yosemite Valley. Discusses the peeling process that forms domes, wild animals found in the park, and the diversity of forests and wildflowers.
Science - Natural
Dist - IFB **Prod** - CSPC 1986

Yosemite - seasons and splendor 40 MIN
VHS
Color (G)
$29.95 purchase _ #S01566
Explores Yosemite and its scenic beauty. Notes the geologic and natural history of the region.
Geography - United States
Dist - UILL

Yoshiko Chuma, Yves Musard and Jack Waters 30 MIN
VHS / U-matic
Eye on Dance - Dance and the Plastic Arts Series
Color
Discusses counter - culture dance at the clubs and alternate locations of New York. Hosted by Celia Ipiotis.
Fine Arts
Dist - ARCVID **Prod** - ARCVID

Yoshiko the Papermaker 25 MIN
U-matic / VHS / 16mm
World Cultures and Youth Series
Color (I J A) (JAPANESE)
LC 80-700085
Introduces a young Japanese girl named Yoshiko who is learning the ancient art of papermaking from a local master. Shows her making a paper panel from a kozo tree and designing a bamboo forest to adorn it.
Geography - World; Sociology
Dist - CORF **Prod** - SUNRIS 1980

Yoshiko the Papermaker 25 MIN
16mm
Color (H A)
$500.00 purchase, $65.00 rental
Narrates the apprenticeship of thirteen - year - old Yoshiko Fujimoto with master papermaker Ando.
Fine Arts
Dist - AFA **Prod** - SUNRIS 1979

Yosl Cutler and his puppets 18 MIN
16mm
(G) (YIDDISH WITH ENGLISH SUBTITLES)
Documents a solo puppet show by poet and Yiddish Art Theater designer Yosl Cutler. Illustrates his work with the marionettes he designed, built and brought to life in plays ranging from 'Purimshpiln' to political satire. Contact distributor for rental fee.
Fine Arts; Literature and Drama; Religion and Philosophy
Dist - NCJEWF

You 4 MIN
U-matic / VHS / 16mm
Color
$225.00 purchase; $75.00 rental; LC 80-700076
Suggests that adults would be happier and would have richer lives if they recaptured the imagination and curiosity characteristic of children.
Psychology
Dist - CCCD **Prod** - CCCD 1979
VLEARN

You 17 MIN
U-matic / VHS / 16mm
Color (P I) (SPANISH)
Examines the concepts of empathy in human relations through observation of young brothers engaged in a typical sibling argument. Shows that when their anger cools, they begin to explore each other's feelings and viewpoints.
Foreign Language; Guidance and Counseling
Dist - CORF **Prod** - PHENIX 1973

You and Addiction 29 MIN
Videoreel / VT2
You Series
Color
Presents a study of the various services of the Department of Health, Education and Welfare. Includes a discussion on addicts.
Civics and Political Systems; Health and Safety; Psychology; Sociology
Dist - PBS **Prod** - WRCTV

You and Alcohol 29 MIN
Videoreel / VT2
You Series
Color
Presents a study of the various services of the Department of Health, Education and Welfare. Includes a discussion of alcohol.
Civics and Political Systems; Health and Safety; Psychology; Sociology
Dist - PBS **Prod** - WRCTV

You and Disaster 29 MIN
Videoreel / VT2
You Series
Color
Presents a study of the various services of the Department of Health, Education and Welfare.
Civics and Political Systems; Sociology
Dist - PBS **Prod** - WRCTV

You and Drugs 29 MIN
Videoreel / VT2
You Series
Color
Presents a study of the various services of the Department of Health, Education and Welfare. Includes a discussion on drugs.
Civics and Political Systems; Health and Safety; Psychology; Sociology
Dist - PBS **Prod** - WRCTV

You and Family Health 29 MIN
Videoreel / VT2
You Series
Color
Presents a study of the various services of the Department of Health, Education and Welfare. Emphasizes the family health services which are available.
Civics and Political Systems; Health and Safety; Sociology
Dist - PBS **Prod** - WRCTV

You and Kentucky Justice 60 MIN
VHS / U-matic
Color
Contains a question - answer self - test on jury duty, the Kentucky court system, and humorous stories on historic area justice, lawyers, and magistrates.
Civics and Political Systems; History - United States
Dist - EASTKU **Prod** - EASTKU

You and M - Das 15 MIN
16mm
Color
LC 76-700448
Demonstrates the use of data from Earth scanners on the LANDSAT satellite. Shows how computer analysis and categorization can be used with color video displays in order to depict Earth resources and features in detail. Emphasizes the system's great versatility in the fields of agriculture, land - use planning, oil exploration and pollution control.
Foreign Language; Industrial and Technical Education; Mathematics
Dist - CYBRN **Prod** - CYBRN 1975

You and Manana 29 MIN
Videoreel / VT2
You Series
Color
Presents a study of the various services of the Department of Health, Education and Welfare.
Civics and Political Systems; Sociology
Dist - PBS **Prod** - WRCTV

You and Me 30 MIN
16mm
Color (J H C)
Discusses careers in engineering, showing some of America's largest engineering projects and some of the nation's foremost mechanical engineers. Presents noted engineers who reveal how they prepared themselves for their careers while still in school and how that training paid off.
Guidance and Counseling; Industrial and Technical Education; Psychology
Dist - KLEINW **Prod** - KLEINW

You and Mental Retardation 29 MIN
Videoreel / VT2
You Series
Color
Shows how the Department of Health, Education and Welfare is becoming increasingly concerned with mental retardation.
Civics and Political Systems; Health and Safety; Psychology; Sociology
Dist - PBS **Prod** - WRCTV

You and Mobility 29 MIN
Videoreel / VT2
You Series
Color
Presents a study of the various services of the Department of Health, Education and Welfare.
Civics and Political Systems; Sociology
Dist - PBS **Prod** - WRCTV

You and Mr Rat 29 MIN
Videoreel / VT2
You Series
Color
Presents a study of the various services of the Department of Health, Education and Welfare. Shows various techniques of rat extermination.
Civics and Political Systems; Health and Safety; Sociology
Dist - PBS **Prod** - WRCTV

You and Office Safety 9 MIN
U-matic / VHS / 16mm
Color (H C A)
LC FIA67-1281
Illustrates common hazards in offices and demonstrates constructive corrective measures.
Business and Economics; Health and Safety
Dist - GA **Prod** - ACAMC 1966

You and Only You 14 MIN
16mm
Color (I)
LC 72-701109
Demonstrates the social and economic value of forest land by showing the dependency of the American way of life upon the forest. Emphasizes methods and needs of reforestation.
Agriculture; Science - Natural; Social Science
Dist - VADE **Prod** - VADE 1972

You and Quackery 29 MIN
Videoreel / VT2
You Series
Color
Presents a study of the various services of the Department of Health, Education and Welfare.
Civics and Political Systems; Home Economics; Sociology
Dist - PBS **Prod** - WRCTV

You and Returning Veterans 29 MIN
Videoreel / VT2
You Series
Color
Presents a study of the various services of the Department of Health, Education and Welfare. Includes a discussion on veterans who are returning home.
Civics and Political Systems; Guidance and Counseling; Sociology
Dist - PBS **Prod** - WRCTV

You and Rx Learning 29 MIN
Videoreel / VT2
You Series
Color
Presents a study of the various services of the Department of Health, Education and Welfare.
Civics and Political Systems; Health and Safety; Sociology
Dist - PBS **Prod** - WRCTV

You and Services 29 MIN
Videoreel / VT2
You Series
Color
Presents a study of the services of the Department of Health, Education and Welfare.
Civics and Political Systems; Sociology
Dist - PBS **Prod** - WRCTV

You and Surplus Property 29 MIN
Videoreel / VT2
You Series
Color
Presents a study of the various services of the Department of Health, Education and Welfare. Includes a discussion of property.
Business and Economics; Civics and Political Systems; Sociology
Dist - PBS **Prod** - WRCTV

You and the Computer 9 MIN
16mm
Color (I J H C)
LC 79-704300
Uses live action and animated art to show the issuance of a paycheck, a basic function of a computer.
Mathematics
Dist - GE **Prod** - GE 1969

You and the Courts 30 MIN
VHS / U-matic
Making Government Work
(H)
Uses dramatizations and interviews to familiarize high school students with the functions of government. Focuses on trials and the role of juries.
Civics and Political Systems
Dist - GPN

You and the Delinquents 29 MIN
Videoreel / VT2
You Series
Color
Presents a study of the various services of the Department of Health, Education and Welfare. Includes a discussion of delinquents.
Civics and Political Systems; Sociology
Dist - PBS **Prod** - WRCTV

You and the Drivotrainer System 20 MIN
16mm
New Aetna Drivotrainer Film Series no 1
Color
LC FI67-867
Introduces the Drivotrainer System. Includes elementary procedures such as readying cars for either manual or automatic shift. Shows the correct use of several control devices. Designed for use with the Aetna Drivotrainer System.
Health and Safety
Dist - AETNA **Prod** - AETNA 1964

You and the Future
U-matic / VHS
Computers at Work Series
Color
Explains the traditional types of jobs in business data processing and discusses the job responsibilities of the systems analyst. Outlines the duties of a typical computer center operations manager.
Business and Economics; Industrial and Technical Education; Mathematics; Sociology
Dist - COMTEG **Prod** - COMTEG

You and the Handicapped 29 MIN
Videoreel / VT2
You Series
Color
Presents a study of the various services of the Department of Health, Education and Welfare. Includes a discussion of the handicapped.
Civics and Political Systems; Psychology; Sociology
Dist - PBS **Prod** - WRCTV

You and the Job Market
VHS
Choosing Careers Series
(J C)
AAVIM
Teaches students decision making skills and outlines procedures to getting a job.
Education
Dist - AAVIM

You and the Law 29 MIN
U-matic / VHS / 16mm
Color; Captioned (H C A)
LC 79-700320
Dramatizes various types of practical legal problems which deaf persons may encounter, including job discrimination, consumer rights violations and civil actions. Explains how and where a deaf person can find help to protect his rights under the law.
Civics and Political Systems; Guidance and Counseling
Dist - JOU **Prod** - LINCS 1978

You and the Law 16 MIN
16mm
Captioned; Color (A)
Uses four different stories that bring up a different legal issue - job discrimination, consumer rights, landlord - tenant disagreements, and criminal law. Discusses importance of reading and understanding legal papers before signing them.
Civics and Political Systems; Guidance and Counseling; Psychology
Dist - GALCO **Prod** - GALCO 1976

You and the Law 17 MIN
16mm
Color (H C A)
LC 75-701990
Creates an understanding of the rights and duties of citizens and police officers. Discusses probable cause, search and seizure, warrants, arrest procedures and juvenile and adult court procedures.
Civics and Political Systems; Social Science
Dist - MCCRNE **Prod** - MCCRNE 1974

You and the law - lesson 5 series
Administrative law 29 MIN
Dist - CDTEL

You and the Law Series Lesson 11
Minors' Rights 29 MIN
Dist - CDTEL

You and the Law Series Lesson 3
The Lawyer 29 MIN
Dist - CDTEL

You and the law series lesson 4
Dealing with lawyers 29 MIN
Dist - CDTEL

You and the Law Series Lesson 8
Torts - You as a Victim 29 MIN
Dist - CDTEL

You and the Law Series Lesson 9
Torts - You as Accused 29 MIN
Dist - CDTEL

You and the law series lesson 12
Contracts and the consumer 29 MIN
Dist - CDTEL

You and the Law Series Lesson 14
Life Insurance 29 MIN
Dist - CDTEL

You and the Law Series Lesson 16
Landlords and Tenants 29 MIN
Dist - CDTEL

You and the Law Series Lesson 17
Housing 29 MIN
Dist - CDTEL

You and the Law Series Lesson 18
Mortgages 29 MIN
Dist - CDTEL

You and the Law Series Lesson 19
Investments 29 MIN
Dist - CDTEL

You and the Law Series Lesson 21
Owning a Car 29 MIN
Dist - CDTEL

You and the Law Series Lesson 22
Car Accidents 29 MIN
Dist - CDTEL

You and the Law Series Lesson 23
The Employee 29 MIN
Dist - CDTEL

You and the Law Series Lesson 24
The Employer 29 MIN
Dist - CDTEL

You and the Law Series Lesson 25
Retirement 29 MIN
Dist - CDTEL

You and the law series
Contract and consumer law 15 MIN
Divorce 15 MIN
Domestic violence 15 MIN
Insurance 15 MIN
Labour Law 15 MIN
Landlord and Tenant Law 15 MIN
Marriage and Common - Law 15 MIN
Small claims court 15 MIN
Wills 15 MIN
Wrongful dismissal 15 MIN
Dist - ACCESS

You and the Law Series
Presents a series designed for the layperson who desires knowledge of the legal principles on which law is based and some understanding of the system that administers the law.
Checks and notes 29 MIN
Credit laws 29 MIN
Criminal law 29 MIN
Criminal proceedings 29 MIN
Estate Planning 30 MIN
Family law 29 MIN
Health and Property Insurance 29 MIN
The Judicial System 30 MIN
What is the Law 30 MIN
Dist - CDTEL **Prod** - COAST 1974

You and the Merit System 15 MIN
16mm
Working for the United States Series
Color (H A)
LC 77-700712
Presents the new or prospective civil service employee with information on the Federal merit principles, probationary period, career status, pay systems, classification systems and equal employment opportunities.
Civics and Political Systems; Guidance and Counseling
Dist - USNAC **Prod** - USCSC 1976

You and the Pap Test 29 MIN
Videoreel / VT2
You Series
Color
Presents a study of the various services of the Department of Health, Education and Welfare. Explains how the pap test is used as a safeguard against cancer and other abnormalities.
Civics and Political Systems; Health and Safety
Dist - PBS **Prod** - WRCTV

You and the Police - Victim or Witness of a Crime 37 MIN
U-matic / VHS
Captioned; Color (S)
Shows deaf persons what they are to do if they are victims or witnesses of crime. Urges deaf person to give the police as much help as possible. Signed.
Guidance and Counseling; Psychology; Social Science; Sociology
Dist - GALCO **Prod** - NCLD 1978

You and the Question Mark Kids 29 MIN
Videoreel / VT2
You Series
Color
Presents a study of the various services of the Department of Health, Education and Welfare.
Civics and Political Systems; Education; Sociology
Dist - PBS **Prod** - WRCTV

You and the Red Schoolhouse 29 MIN
Videoreel / VT2
You Series
Color
Presents a study of the various services of the Department of Health, Education and Welfare. Discusses educational opportunities which are available.
Civics and Political Systems; Education; Sociology
Dist - PBS **Prod** - WRCTV

You and the Road Children 29 MIN
Videoreel / VT2
You Series
Color
Presents a study of the various services of the Department of Health, Education and Welfare.
Civics and Political Systems; Sociology
Dist - PBS **Prod** - WRCTV

You and the telephone 21 MIN
16mm
Golden triangle teller training series
Color (IND)
LC 76-700453
Points out the six basic guidelines that can produce top telephone performance. Suggests that every phone call is another chance to build the respect and trust which can attract and hold customers.
Business and Economics; Guidance and Counseling
Dist - PART **Prod** - PART

You and Traffic Safety 60 MIN
VHS / U-matic
Color
Presents a question - answer traffic safety self - test with film illustrations on Kentucky driving law.
Health and Safety; History - United States
Dist - EASTKU **Prod** - EASTKU

You and what You do it with
16mm / U-matic
Color (A)
Presents five accident victims who are given a second chance after learning how to treat their machinery or equipment with respect. Shows how to care for equipment and heed any warning signals it gives.
Health and Safety
Dist - BNA **Prod** - BNA 1983

You and When it Matters 29 MIN
Videoreel / VT2
You Series
Color
Presents a study of the various services of the Department of Health, Education and Welfare.
Civics and Political Systems; Sociology
Dist - PBS **Prod** - WRCTV

You and Women's Lib 29 MIN
Videoreel / VT2
You Series
Color
Presents a study of the Department of Health, Education and Welfare. Includes a discussion on the Women's Liberation Movement.
Civics and Political Systems; Sociology
Dist - PBS **Prod** - WRCTV

You and Your Aging Parents 59 MIN
U-matic / VHS
Color (A)
Discusses some of the myths and describes stresses associated with growing old. Addresses the challenges of those who must raise their own children while caring for their aging parents.
Health and Safety; Sociology
Dist - USNAC **Prod** - USPHS 1985

You and Your Baby Come Home 18 MIN
16mm
Color (H C A)
LC FIA66-1185
Emphasizes the new mother's needs for sleep, rest, proper exercise and correct diet. Uses a baby boy and a baby girl in demonstrations of handling, bathing, bottle and breast feeding, and preparation for sleep.
Psychology; Sociology
Dist - SF **Prod** - MORLAT 1960

You and Your Breath 29 MIN
Videoreel / VT2
You Series
Color
Presents a study of the various services of the Department of Health, Education and Welfare.
Civics and Political Systems; Sociology
Dist - PBS **Prod** - WRCTV

You and Your Car Series
What'll You do if 12 MIN
Dist - PART

You and Your Cat 51 MIN
VHS / 16mm
(G)
$29.95 purchase _ #HT29
Takes pet owners through every aspect of cat care, from adoption and selection to grooming and illness. Taught by Dr Michael Fox, veterinarian.
Physical Education and Recreation; Science - Natural
Dist - RMIBHF **Prod** - RMIBHF

You and Your Co - Workers - Part III 11 MIN
16mm / VHS
You and Your Job Series
Color (PRO)
$325.00 purchase, $95.00 rental, $35.00 preview
Gives newly hired employees understanding of how their actions in the workplace affect their co - workers. Explains that an employee works as part of a team, that tardiness, absenteeism, carelessness, gossiping and wasting time disrupt work flow of a company.
Business and Economics; Psychology
Dist - UTM **Prod** - UTM

You and Your Dog 51 MIN
VHS / 16mm
(G)
$29.95 purchase _ #HT28
Takes pet owners through every aspect of dog care, from adoption and selection to grooming and illness. Taught by Dr Michael Fox, veterinarian.
Physical Education and Recreation; Science - Natural
Dist - RMIBHF **Prod** - RMIBHF

You and your ears 14 MIN
U-matic / 16mm / VHS
This is you series
Color (P)
$400.00, $280.00 purchase _ #JC - 67262
Visits a magical place where anything can happen - the World of Books. Uses computer animation, live action and Jiminy Cricket animation to help Molly and Zach explore the different parts of the ear, how it works, why the sense of hearing is valuable, how it helps in safety and how ears can be protected. Part of the This Is You series.
Fine Arts; Health and Safety; Science - Natural
Dist - CORF **Prod** - DISNEY 1990

You - and your ears 8 MIN
16mm / U-matic / VHS
This is you - health series
Color (P I J) (DUTCH SPANISH FRENCH ARABIC THAI)
Jiminy Cricket explains the structure of the ear and shows how sound waves affect the ear.
Health and Safety; Science - Natural
Dist - CORF **Prod** - DISNEY 1957

You - and your eyes 8 MIN
U-matic / VHS / 16mm
This is you - health series
Color (P I J) (ARABIC DUTCH SPANISH FRENCH)
Jiminy Cricket explains the structure and anatomy of the eye by comparing it with a camera. Stresses the safety features designed by nature to protect the eyes and the rules for care of the eyes.
Health and Safety; Science - Natural
Dist - CORF **Prod** - DISNEY 1958

You and your eyes 13 MIN
U-matic / 16mm / VHS
This is you series
Color (P)
$400.00, $280.00 purchase _ #JC - 67261
Visits a magical place where anything can happen - the World of Books. Uses computer animation, live action and Jiminy Cricket animation to explore the eye, how it works, why eyes are so important, how to keep eyes safe and how eyes protect people. Part of the This Is You series.
Fine Arts; Health and Safety; Science - Natural
Dist - CORF **Prod** - DISNEY 1990

You and Your Family 15 MIN
U-matic / Kit / VHS
Growing Up
(J)
Discusses the structure of the family and highlights ways to resolve conflict. Stresses individual responsibility. First in a six part series.
Sociology
Dist - GPN

You and Your Feelings 15 MIN
U-matic / VHS
All about You Series
Color (P)
Explains emotions and discusses consideration of the feelings of other people. Indicates that as children grow up their feelings grow up too. Introduces a character puppet named Muggsy. (Broadcast quality).
Guidance and Counseling; Psychology
Dist - AITECH **Prod** - NITC 1975

You - and your five senses 8 MIN
U-matic / VHS / 16mm
This is you - health series
Color (P I J) (ARABIC FRENCH SPANISH)
Discusses man's five senses. Explains that some are more highly developed than others and that man compensates accordingly.
Health and Safety; Science - Natural
Dist - CORF **Prod** - DISNEY 1956

You and your five senses 13 MIN
VHS / U-matic / 16mm
This is you series
Color (P)
$400.00, $280.00 purchase _ #JC - 67280
Visits a magical place where anything can happen - the World of Books. Stars Pinocchio, now a real boy, and Jiminy Cricket and Captain Nonsense who learn about the five senses, how the senses work and how to protect sensory organs. Part of the This Is You series.
Fine Arts; Health and Safety; Science - Natural
Dist - CORF **Prod** - DISNEY 1990

You - and Your Food 8 MIN
U-matic / VHS / 16mm
This is You - Health Series
Color (P I J) (THAI HUNGARIAN SPANISH ARABIC DUTCH FRENCH)
Jiminy Cricket stresses the value of foods which are necessary to good health. Uses the analogy of the construction of an automobile to point out that proper foods must be eaten to build the body, to supply energy and to maintain the body in good condition.
Health and Safety
Dist - CORF **Prod** - DISNEY 1959

You and your food 12 MIN
VHS / U-matic / 16mm
This is you series
Color (P)
$400.00, $280.00 purchase _ #JC - 67279
Visits a magical place where anything can happen - the World of Books. Stars Pinocchio, Jiminy Cricket and 'food expert' Samantha as they explore nutrition. Shows the four main food groups, how to select a well - balanced diet and how food provides fuel for the body. Part of the This Is You series.
Fine Arts; Health and Safety; Home Economics; Science - Natural; Social Science
Dist - CORF **Prod** - DISNEY 1990

You and Your Friends 15 MIN
U-matic / Kit / VHS
Growing Up
(J)
Discusses peer pressure and friendship. Stresses individual responsibility. Second in a six part series.
Sociology
Dist - GPN

You and Your Heritage 29 MIN
Videoreel / VT2
You Series
Color
Presents a study of the various services of the Department of Health, Education and Welfare.
Civics and Political Systems
Dist - PBS **Prod** - WRCTV

You and your horse series
Presents a six - part series on training the western horse featuring B F Yeates, Extension Horse Specialist Emeritus of Texas A&M University. Includes the titles Owning Your First Horse, Bits and Bitting, Collection and Flying Lead Change, Rider Skills, Basic Maneuvers and More Basic Maneuvers.
Basic maneuvers
Bits and bitting
Collection and flying lead change
More basic maneuvers
Owning your first horse
Rider skills
Dist - VEP **Prod** - VEP

You and Your Job Series
Getting a Good Start - Part I 13 MIN
Working with Your Supervisor - Part II 12 MIN
You and Your Co - Workers - Part III 11 MIN
Dist - UTM

The You and your new job series
Prepares young job seekers for the realities of the job market. Covers issues of job hunting, worker relations, and communication with supervisors. Consists of three videos, leader's guides, and blackline masters.
The You and your new job series 37 MIN
Dist - UNL

You and your new job series
Getting a good start, working with your supervisor and you and your co - workers
Dist - VLEARN

You and Your Parents - Making it through the Tough Years
VHS / 35mm strip
$119.00 purchase _ #014 - 903 filmstrip, $139.00 purchase _ #014 -
Instructs how to understand and deal with the problems of parent - child relationships that occur during adolescence. Provides examples of how sending more adult messages to parents can reduce friction.
Sociology
Dist - CAREER **Prod** - CAREER

You and Your Parents - Making it through the Tough Years
U-matic / VHS
Color (I J)
Helps aid in understanding and coping with tensions in parent - child relationships that accompany the years from ages eleven to fourteen.
Guidance and Counseling; Psychology; Sociology
Dist - SUNCOM **Prod** - SUNCOM

You and Your Personal Computer Series Part I
The Machine 12 MIN
Dist - VISUCP

You and Your Personal Computer Series Pt II
The Machine at Work 14 MIN
Dist - VISUCP

You - and Your Sense of Smell and Taste 8 MIN
16mm / U-matic / VHS
This is You - Health Series
Color (P I J) (ARABIC)
Jiminy Cricket explains the senses of smell and taste in humans as compared to other animals. He shows how these two senses act together.
Health and Safety; Science - Natural
Dist - CORF **Prod** - DISNEY 1963

You - and your sense of touch 8 MIN
16mm / U-matic / VHS
This is you - health series
Color (P I J) (ARABIC FRENCH)
Jiminy Cricket explains the importance of the sense of touch, the four sensations involved and their effects.
Health and Safety; Science - Natural
Dist - CORF **Prod** - DISNEY 1962

You and your sense of touch 13 MIN
U-matic / 16mm / VHS
This is you series
Color (P)
$400.00, $280.00 purchase _ #JC - 67263
Visits a magical place where anything can happen - the World of Books. Stars Jiminy Cricket and two children who discover through computer animation and live action how the skin and sense of touch work, their importance and how to protect them. Part of the This Is You series.
Fine Arts; Health and Safety; Science - Natural
Dist - CORF **Prod** - DISNEY 1990

You and your senses of smell and taste 14 MIN
U-matic / 16mm / VHS
This is you series
Color (P)
$400.00, $280.00 purchase _ #JC - 67278
Visits a magical place where anything can happen - the World of Books. Stars Jiminy Cricket and two children who discover through computer animation and live action how the nose and tongue work, their importance and how to protect them. Part of the This Is You series.
Fine Arts; Health and Safety; Science - Natural
Dist - CORF **Prod** - DISNEY 1990

You and your values
VHS
Big changes, big choices series
Color (I J)
$69.95 purchase _ #LVB - 2A
Looks at the elements of an identity - clothes, values, beliefs, group or gang membership. Part of a 12 - part video series designed to help young adolescents work their way though the many anxieties and issues they face. Encourages them to make positive and healthful life choices. Features humorist and youth counselor Michael Pritchard.
Guidance and Counseling; Psychology
Dist - CFKRCM **Prod** - CFKRCM

You and Yours 20 MIN
VHS / U-matic
Color
Tells about preventing fires, burns and clothing fires, baby sitters, home fire detection systems, escape planning and what to do if fire strikes.
Health and Safety; Home Economics
Dist - FPF **Prod** - FPF

You are a Band Member 15 MIN
U-matic / VHS
Imagine that Series Program 12; Program 12
Color (P)
Uses a multisensory approach to help children develop mind - body coordination. Integrates an imaginary theme with indoor classroom activities and calisthenics.
Education; Psychology
Dist - GPN **Prod** - WBRATV 1981

You are a Dancer 15 MIN
VHS / U-matic
Imagine that Series Program 14; Program 14
Color (P)
Uses a multisensory approach to help children develop mind - body coordination. Integrates an imaginary theme with indoor classroom activities and calisthenics.
Education; Psychology
Dist - GPN **Prod** - WBRATV 1981

You are a - do Your Own Thing - using Imagine that 22 MIN
U-matic / VHS
Imagine that Series Program 15; Program 15
Color (T)
Introduces the Imagine That Series and explains how teachers can use its multisensory approach to help children develop mind - body coordination.
Education; Psychology
Dist - GPN **Prod** - WBRATV 1981

You are a Happy Farmer 15 MIN
VHS / U-matic
Imagine that Series Program 13; Program 13
Color (P)
Uses a multisensory approach to help children develop mind - body coordination. Integrates an imaginary theme with indoor classroom activities and calisthenics.
Education; Psychology
Dist - GPN **Prod** - WBRATV 1981

You are a Skeleton 15 MIN
U-matic / VHS
Imagine that Series Program 11; Program 11
Color (P)
LC 82-706437
Uses a multisensory approach to help children develop mind - body coordination, focusing on the body and the identification of its parts. Integrates an imaginary theme with indoor classroom activities and calisthenics.
Education; Psychology
Dist - GPN **Prod** - WBRATV 1981

You are a Zoo Animal 15 MIN
U-matic / VHS
Imagine that Series Program 7; Program 7
Color (P)
LC 82-706473
Uses a multisensory approach to help children develop mind - body coordination, focusing on gross motor movements and spatial awareness. Integrates an imaginary zoo theme with the use of rhythmic music, pantomime, and indoor classroom activities and calisthenics.
Education; Psychology
Dist - GPN **Prod** - WBRATV 1981

You are Changing 15 MIN
16mm
Color
LC 74-700487
Portrays the attitudes and concerns of a group of students as they research and film a class assignment on how they feel about the physical and emotional changes that take place as they enter puberty.
Education; Guidance and Counseling
Dist - WSTGLC **Prod** - WSTGLF 1972

You are Free 29 MIN
U-matic / VHS / 16mm
Color (P A G)
Shows how the sorrow of the Nazi concentration camps becomes a human reality. Features interviews with four Allied soldiers and one camp prisoner and powerful archival footage of holocaust realities. Award nominated.
History - United States; Psychology
Dist - DIRECT **Prod** - NIERNG 1984

You are here - X marks the spot 10 MIN
16mm
B&W (G)
$35.00 rental
Presents a psycho - drama concerned with focalization; dream representation; the positioning of the camera in the view of the spectator; concealment and revelation; the targeting of the gaze; and the manipulation of refracted light. Features the 'X' and the bull's eye as the thematic basis.
Fine Arts; Psychology
Dist - CANCIN **Prod** - NIGRIN 1986

You are in Outer Space 15 MIN
U-matic / VHS
Imagine that Series Program 10; Program 10
Color (P)
LC 82-706438
Uses a multisensory approach to help children develop mind - body coordination, focusing on gross motor activities such as skipping, walking, hopping and running, along with rhythmical movements and pantomimes. Integrates an outer space theme with indoor classroom activities and calisthenics.
Education; Psychology
Dist - GPN **Prod** - WBRATV 1981

You are in the Computer 60 MIN
U-matic / VHS
Frontline Series
Color
Examines computerized information systems and the issue of privacy.
Business and Economics; Industrial and Technical Education; Sociology
Dist - PBS **Prod** - DOCCON

You are not alone 10 MIN
VHS
Color (H C PRO)
$195.00 purchase
Brings out thoughts of women who have been raped along with information about the steps involved in healing from an assault. Shows steps followed by a professional in a post - rape examination and in collecting evidence. Useful for rape crisis counseling and for training those who deal with victims.
Sociology
Dist - LANDMK

You are not Alone 27 MIN
16mm
Sudden Infant Death Syndrome Series
Color
LC 79-700567
Explores the physical and emotional aspects of grief experienced by parents who have had an infant die because of sudden infant death syndrome. Assures parents that the death was not their fault and discusses problems which may arise with a spouse, siblings, in - laws and friends.
Sociology
Dist - USNAC **Prod** - USBCHS 1976

You are not Alone 29 MIN
Videoreel / VT2
That's Life Series
Color
Guidance and Counseling; Psychology
Dist - PBS **Prod** - KOAPTV

You are not alone 92 MIN
16mm
Color (DANISH (ENGLISH SUBTITLES))
Explores the boundaries of friendship and love within a private boys school in Copenhagen where a headmaster's inability to cope with his students leads to their rebellion.
Fine Arts; Foreign Language
Dist - IFEX **Prod** - AWARD 1980

You are Old, Father William 50 MIN
U-matic / VHS / 16mm
Color (A)
LC 82-700534
Investigates the complex physical and mental changes of growing old. Interweaves various gerontological studies and individual experiences to explain such visible signs of aging as a shambling gait to less apparent internal processes, concluding that there is no one biological mechanism that is the key to longevity.
Health and Safety; Sociology
Dist - FI **Prod** - BBCTV 1981

You are Someone Else 15 MIN
U-matic / VHS
Imagine that Series Program 1; Program 1
Color (P)
LC 82-706467
Uses a multisensory approach to help children develop mind - body coordination, focusing on the identification and movement of specific body parts, the development of spatial awareness and experience of movement through mirror imaging with a partner. Integrates an imaginary theme with the use of rhythmic music, pantomime and indoor classroom activities and calisthenics.
Education; Psychology
Dist - GPN **Prod** - WBRATV 1981

You are Something Else 15 MIN
U-matic / VHS
Imagine that Series Program 3; Program 3
Color (P)
LC 82-706469
Uses a multisensory approach to help children develop mind - body coordination, focusing on axial movements, basic locomotor experiences and the movement of the body to form floor designs. Integrates an imaginary theme with the use of rhythmic music, pantomime, and indoor classroom activities and calisthenics.
Education; Psychology
Dist - GPN **Prod** - WBRATV 1981

You are Somewhere Else 15 MIN
VHS / U-matic
Imagine that Series Program 4; Program 4
Color (P)
LC 82-706470
Uses a multisensory approach to help children develop mind - body coordination, focusing on hand - eye coordination, rhythmical movements, and the demonstration of creative shapes with the body. Integrates an imaginary theme with the use of rhythmic music, pantomime, and indoor classroom activities and calisthenics.
Education; Psychology
Dist - GPN **Prod** - WBRATV 1981

You are Special 13 MIN
16mm
I Am, I Can, I will, Level I Series
Color (K P S)
LC 80-700562
Presents Mr Rogers discussing with children the qualities which make them unique and different, including differences relating to handicaps.
Guidance and Counseling; Psychology
Dist - HUBDSC **Prod** - FAMCOM 1979

You are the difference - leadership 10 MIN
U-matic / VHS
Color (G)
$275.00 purchase, $150.00 rental
Presents two motivation meeting openers with Buck Rogers. Urges taking control rather than letting situations and other people control in 'Difference.' Shows how to select the right people, why responsibility and authority must be tied together, and how to give - and get - the ultimate compliment in 'Leadership.'
Business and Economics; Guidance and Counseling; Psychology
Dist - VLEARN **Prod** - AMA

You are the Game - Sexual Harassment on Campus 59 MIN
U-matic / VHS
Color (C A)
Dramatizes the situation of two college women students who have experienced different forms of sexual harassment from male professors.
Education; Psychology; Sociology
Dist - IU **Prod** - IU 1985

You are the key - lockout - tagout safety 15 MIN
U-matic / BETA / VHS
Color (IND G)
$395.00 purchase _ #600 - 25
Informs employees on essential lockout - tagout procedures for shutting off energy sources required to ensure safety while repairing or maintaining equipment.
Health and Safety; Industrial and Technical Education; Psychology
Dist - ITSC **Prod** - ITSC

You are the Teacher 13 MIN
16mm
Color (PRO)
Demonstrates the practical application of audio - visual devices and tools in a teaching situation. Shows several methods of incorporating teaching tools into programs which supplement in - service training.
Education; Health and Safety; Science
Dist - ACY **Prod** - ACYDGD 1969

You are there series
Assassination of Julius Caesar 27 MIN
Death of Socrates 27 MIN
The Rise of Adolph Hitler 27 MIN
Salem Witch Trials 28 MIN
Dist - MGHT

You are there series
Columbus and Isabella 22 MIN
The Fall of Troy 22 MIN
Galileo and his universe 22 MIN
Harriet Tubman and the Underground Railroad 21 MIN
Lewis and Clark at the Great Divide 22 MIN
The Mystery of Amelia Earhart 22 MIN
The Nomination of Abraham Lincoln 22 MIN
Ordeal of a President 22 MIN
Paul Revere's Ride 22 MIN
The Record Ride for the Pony Express 22 MIN
The Siege of the Alamo 21 MIN
The Torment of Joan of Arc 22 MIN
The Trial of Susan B Anthony 22 MIN
The Vision of Dr Koch 22 MIN
Dist - PHENIX

You are There - with Your Fair Share 15 MIN
16mm
Color
LC FIA66-702
Demonstrates the many ways in which money donated to the Heart of America United Fund campaign is used to help people.
Psychology; Social Science; Sociology
Dist - HAUFC **Prod** - HAUFC

You are what You Eat 29 MIN
VHS / 16mm
Villa Alegre Series
Color (P T)
$46.00 rental _ #VILA - 109
Presents educational material in both Spanish and English.
Education; Home Economics
Dist - PBS

You are what You Eat 25 MIN
U-matic
Not Another Science Show Series
Color (H C)
Explains the basic food groups, ways to get in shape without starving and that a balanced diet is as important as exercise.
Home Economics; Science
Dist - TVOTAR **Prod** - TVOTAR 1986

You as a Manager 30 MIN
U-matic / VHS
Business Management Series Lesson 3; Lesson 3
Color (C A)
Discusses skills that are important to success. Suggests ways in which prospective and working managers can improve their performance.
Business and Economics; Education; Psychology
Dist - SCCON **Prod** - SCCON

You be the Judge 15 MIN
VHS / U-matic
It's Your Move Series
Color (I)
Tells how Tom is found guilty of endangering himself on the street and is sentenced by the judge of a very strange court.
Health and Safety
Dist - AITECH **Prod** - WETN 1977

You be the Judge 13 MIN
U-matic / VHS / 16mm
Color (I J)
LC 72-701047
Uses a stop - projector technique to present three cases involving juveniles in order to give the viewer an opportunity to witness the events and discuss possible decisions by the judge.
Civics and Political Systems; Guidance and Counseling; Psychology; Sociology
Dist - AIMS **Prod** - CAHILL 1972

You be the judge - the legal side of interviewing 27 MIN
BETA / U-matic / VHS
Color; CC (G PRO) (ENGLISH WITH JAPANESE SUBTITLES)
$595.00 purchase, $130.00 rental; $550.00 purchase, $110.00 rental
Shows job interviewers how to base their decisions solely on job - related issues. Trains in taking objective notes that are only job related, asking legally correct questions, recognizing what is illegal to ask. Demonstrates how to avoid both intentional and unintentional discrimination,

handle questions of age, sex, race, religion and national origin and use a structured interview plan. Includes desk reminder cards, training guide on computer disk and slide charts of legal and illegal questions.
Business and Economics; Guidance and Counseling; Psychology
Dist - AMEDIA EXTR UTM **Prod** - AMEDIA UTM

You belong 15 MIN
VHS / 16mm / U-matic
Inside-out series
Color
Explores the vital connections between human beings and their surroundings. Stresses the increase of a sense of responsibility which all people must feel for the environment.
Guidance and Counseling; Psychology; Sociology
Dist - AITECH

You Bet My Life 15 MIN
16mm
Color (IND)
LC 72-701860
Demonstrates the importance of production cleanliness. Shows that because one assemblyman failed to retrieve a dropped rivet, a pilot was killed and a multi - million dollar airplane was destroyed. Emphasizes that only the worker's constant attention can ensure a quality product free of potentially dangerous manufacturing scraps.
Business and Economics; Industrial and Technical Education; Psychology
Dist - VOAERO **Prod** - VOAERO

You Bet - they Wynn Dollars 26 MIN
16mm
Color
LC 80-701448
Takes a look at the gambling industry, focusing on a rural bingo parlor in Maryland and a large Las Vegas casino, both owned and operated by the Wynn brothers.
Sociology
Dist - WJLATV **Prod** - WJLATV 1979

You bet your baby 35 MIN
VHS / U-matic
Color (H G)
$280.00, $330.00 purchase, $50.00 rental
Uses a television quiz show format as a vehicle for a dramatic production on prenatal, maternal and early childhood health.
Health and Safety
Dist - NDIM **Prod** - PARGRO 1990

You Bet Your Burger 28 MIN
VHS / 16mm
Sonrisas Series
Color (T P) (SPANISH)
$46.00 rental _ #SRSS - 134
Shows how factions can cooperate. In Spanish and English.
Sociology
Dist - PBS

You Bet Your Life 60 MIN
U-matic / VHS
Color
Features two great episodes of the comedy TV series starring Groucho Marx.
Fine Arts
Dist - IHF **Prod** - IHF

You Bet Your Life 13 MIN
16mm / U-matic / VHS
Color (H C A)
LC 81-701507
Looks at the prospects for kicking the gambling habit. Shows that gamblers will steal, lie and cheat to get money to support their habit. Demonstrates how gamblers are taught to abstain from gambling and substitute new activities for it.
Psychology; Sociology
Dist - CAROUF **Prod** - CAPLNJ 1981

You Bet Your Life 5 MIN
U-matic / VHS
Write on, Set 1 Series
Color (J H)
Teaches correct word usage. Explains 'Already' and 'All ready' and 'Further' and 'Farther'.
English Language
Dist - CTI **Prod** - CTI

You Bet Your Life 15 MIN
U-matic
Workers at Risk Series
(A)
Introduces three main characters in a portrayal of the values and lifestyles of the 17 to 25 year old age group.
Health and Safety
Dist - ACCESS **Prod** - ACCESS 1982

You Bring Your Lunch, I'll Bring Mine 13 MIN
16mm / U-matic / VHS
Growing Up with Sandy Offenheim Series
Color (K P)
LC 82-707059
Explores the ideas about differences in people and points out that individual characteristics are to be appreciated. Visits a playground where everyone is having fun, demonstrating self - expression of emotions, and physical activity.
Education; Fine Arts; Psychology; Sociology
Dist - BCNFL **Prod** - PLAYTM 1982

You Call that Art 29 MIN
U-matic / VHS / 16mm
Color (H C A G)
$55.00 rental _ #YCLA - 000; LC 80-707183
Surveys different approaches to contemporary art, with examples drawn from exhibits at Chicago's Museum of Contemporary Art.
Fine Arts
Dist - PBS **Prod** - WTTWTV

You Can 28 MIN
U-matic / VHS / 16mm
Color
Features a summer marine biology program for disabled youths. High school students are shown discovering marine biology, ways of communicating and good times at the beach. These students have disabilities such as blindness, hearing impairments and paralysis.
Guidance and Counseling; Health and Safety; Psychology; Science - Natural; Sociology
Dist - USNAC **Prod** - USNOAA 1980

You can be a better parent in 30 minutes 30 MIN
VHS
Color (G)
$29.95 purchase _ #FAS100V
Identifies problems parents face in getting the behavior and discipline they want from their children. Offers viable solutions, drawn from a panel of experts, that can be used right away. Covers ten of the common problems faced by parents of 6 - 12 - year - old children - following directions; parents yelling at children; behaving in public; school performance; taking 'no' for an answer; doing chores; using discipline that causes more problems; not recognizing and praising good behavior; expecting too much from children and comparing children. Includes a free subscription to Family America Newsletter, a bumper sticker and a refrigerator magnet with ten parenting tips.
Health and Safety; Sociology
Dist - CAMV

You can be too thin - understanding anorexia and bulimia 57 MIN
VHS
Color (H)
$219.00 purchase _ #60117 - 126
Teaches the causes and consequences of serious eating disorders and the coping skills necessary for avoiding such disorders. Dramatizes two days in the life of Maggie, a high school senior who is obsessive about her weight, her looks, dieting, boys and achieving perfect grades.
Health and Safety; Sociology
Dist - GA **Prod** - GA

You can choose - being responsible 28 MIN
VHS
You can choose - series
Color (P I J)
$59.95 purchase _ #476 - V8
Shows Rhonda and her friends trying to complete a science project over the weekend - then another friend invites Rhonda to go to Disneyland. Centers around responsible decision making. Part of a series which builds self - esteem and life skills. Allows children to share in a problem - solving session with comedian and youth counselor Michael Pritchard.
Guidance and Counseling; Psychology
Dist - ETRASS **Prod** - ETRASS

You can choose - Cooperation 28 MIN
VHS
You can choose - series
Color (P I J)
$59.95 purchase _ #477 - V8
Shows Moose planning to quit the school quartet when he's asked to sing backup instead of leading a song. Centers around the benefits of cooperation. Part of a series which builds self - esteem and life skills. Allows children to share in a problem - solving session with comedian and youth counselor Michael Pritchard.
Guidance and Counseling; Psychology
Dist - ETRASS **Prod** - ETRASS

You can choose - Dealing with feelings 25 MIN
VHS
You can choose - series
Color (P I J)
$59.95 purchase _ #478 - V8
Shows Moose and Tuggie preparing for a camping trip, but Tuggie panics about spending the weekend away from home. Encourages viewers to honestly communicate about their feelings. Part of a series which builds self - esteem and life skills. Allows children to share in a problem - solving session with comedian and youth counselor Michael Pritchard.
Guidance and Counseling; Psychology
Dist - ETRASS **Prod** - ETRASS

You can choose - Saying no to smoking 28 MIN
VHS
You can choose - series
Color (P I J)
$59.95 purchase _ #479 - V8
Shows Missy's best friend trying to get her to try smoking. Gives viewers specific ways to say 'no' to smoking or other risky behavior. Part of a series which builds self - esteem and life skills. Allows children to share in a problem - solving session with comedian and youth counselor Michael Pritchard.
Guidance and Counseling; Health and Safety; Psychology
Dist - ETRASS **Prod** - ETRASS

You can choose series
Cooperation 25 MIN
Dist - CORF

You can choose series
Being responsible 28 MIN
Dist - CORF REVID

You can choose - series
Presents a series which helps to teach self discipline, decision making, responsibility, cooperation, self esteem, life skills, and critical thinking for grades K - 5. Entertains and challenges students with comedy, drama, peer education, and role modeling. Each program features a skit in which a character faces a tough decision. Between acts, real children solve problems with comedian and youth counselor Michael Pritchard. Titles include Being Responsible; Cooperation; Dealing with Feelings; Saying No to Smoking; Doing the Right Thing; Dealing with Disappointment; Appreciating Yourself; Asking for Help; Being Friends; and Resolving Conflicts. Titles also available individually.
You can choose - being responsible 28 MIN
You can choose - Cooperation 28 MIN
You can choose - Dealing with feelings 25 MIN
You can choose - Saying no to smoking 28 MIN
Dist - ETRASS **Prod** - ETRASS

You can choose series
Appreciating yourself 28 MIN
Asking for help 28 MIN
Being friends 28 MIN
Cooperation 28 MIN
Dealing with disappointment 28 MIN
Dealing with feelings 28 MIN
Doing the right thing 28 MIN
Resolving conflicts 28 MIN
Saying no 28 MIN
Dist - REVID

You can compose a dance - Pt 1 10 MIN
16mm
B&W (P I)
Illustrates how young children can create their own dances. Shows how to start with an idea.
Education; Physical Education and Recreation
Dist - SLFP **Prod** - WINTER 1970

You can compose a dance - Pt 2 10 MIN
16mm
B&W (P I)
Illustrates how young children can create their own dances. Shows dance structure.
Education; Physical Education and Recreation
Dist - SLFP **Prod** - WINTER 1970

You Can Count on Computers 30 MIN
16mm / U-matic / VHS
Mr Microchip Series
Color (I J H)
Presents various types and uses of computer software, especially educational programs, such as games which teach math or science skills, and speed reading programs. Demonstrates simple computer programming.
Mathematics
Dist - JOU **Prod** - JOU

You can dance - cha cha
VHS
Color (G A)
$29.95 purchase
Presents step - by - step instruction in the Cha Cha. Taught by Vicki Regan and Ron De Vito.

Fine Arts
Dist - PBS **Prod** - WNETTV

You can dance - foxtrot
VHS
Color (G A)
$29.95 purchase
Presents step - by - step instruction in the Foxtrot. Taught by Vicki Regan and Ron De Vito.
Fine Arts
Dist - PBS **Prod** - WNETTV

You can dance - jitterbug
VHS
Color (G A)
$29.95 purchase
Presents step - by - step instruction in the Jitterbug. Taught by Vicki Regan and Ron De Vito.
Fine Arts
Dist - PBS **Prod** - WNETTV

You can dance - mambo and dirty dancing
VHS
Color (G A)
$29.95 purchase
Presents step - by - step instruction in the Mambo and in 'dirty dancing.' Taught by Vicki Regan and Ron De Vito.
Fine Arts
Dist - PBS **Prod** - WNETTV

You can dance - nightclub - disco and slow
VHS
Color (G A)
$29.95 purchase
Presents step - by - step instruction in nightclub dancing, both disco and slow styles. Taught by Vicki Regan and Ron De Vito.
Fine Arts
Dist - PBS **Prod** - WNETTV

You can dance - rumba
VHS
Color (G A)
$29.95 purchase
Presents step - by - step instruction in the Rumba. Taught by Vicki Regan and Ron De Vito.
Fine Arts
Dist - PBS **Prod** - WNETTV

You can dance series
Features Vicki Regan and Ron de Vito in an eight - part series on ballroom dancing. Includes Cha Cha, Foxtrot, Jitterbug - Swing, Nightclub, Rhumba, Tango, Waltz and Mambo and Dirty Dancing.
You can dance series
Dist - SIV

You can dance - tango
VHS
Color (G A)
$29.95 purchase
Presents step - by - step instruction in the Tango. Taught by Vicki Regan and Ron De Vito.
Fine Arts
Dist - PBS **Prod** - WNETTV

You can dance - waltz
VHS
Color (G A)
$29.95 purchase
Presents step - by - step instruction in the Waltz. Taught by Vicki Regan and Ron De Vito.
Fine Arts
Dist - PBS **Prod** - WNETTV

You Can do Anything 15 MIN
U-matic / VHS
Imagine that Series Program 6; Program 6
Color (P)
LC 82-706472
Uses a multisensory approach to help children develop mind - body coordination, focusing on simple stunts, spatial awareness and creative stunt combinations. Integrates an imaginary theme with the use of rhythmic music, pantomime, and indoor classroom activities and calisthenics.
Education; Psychology
Dist - GPN **Prod** - WBRATV 1981

You Can do it
VHS
Color (H)
$250.00 purchase _ #V019
Uses Rational - Emotive Therapy - RET concepts to motivate success in high school students. Produced in Australia.
Guidance and Counseling; Psychology
Dist - IRL **Prod** - IRL 1990

You Can do it - if Series
Accept and excel 28 MIN
Acquiring greatness 28 MIN
All successful people have it 28 MIN
Detour - a challenge 28 MIN
If You Don't, who will 28 MIN
The Surprises of Failure Can Lead to the Secrets of Success 28 MIN
Try it, They'll Like it 28 MIN
What is the most Important Priority of a Teacher 28 MIN
Yes You Can 28 MIN
You Decide 28 MIN
Dist - VANDER

You Can do Something about Acne 16 MIN
16mm / U-matic / VHS
Color (J H)
LC 73-701708
Outlines the physiological reasons for acne and offers health care suggestions.
Health and Safety
Dist - AIMS **Prod** - WHITEP 1973

You can drive the big rigs 15 MIN
16mm
Color (G)
$45.00 rental
Looks at the small town cafes in the rural Midwest which function as a focal point for many aspects of the rural subculture and which also reveal the limits and somewhat closed nature of that culture.
Fine Arts; Geography - United States; History - United States; Sociology
Dist - CANCIN **Prod** - PIERCE 1989

You can even run for President - Greek Americans in politics 28 MIN
VHS
Illuminations series
Color (G R)
#V - 1046
Describes the participation of Greek Americans in U S politics. Shows that Greek Americans have run for office at every level of government, and often been elected. Traces this political participation to the ancient Greeks' focus on politics. Interviews Greek American politicians including Michael Dukakis, Senator Paul Sarbanes, and Helen Boosalis, former mayor of Lincoln, NE.
Civics and Political Systems
Dist - GOTEL **Prod** - GOTEL 1990

You Can Fight City Hall 30 MIN
VHS / 16mm
Color (G)
$195.00 purchase, $60.00 rental
Documents the gay community's struggle to add the words 'sexual orientation' to job protection legislation at a Columbus, Ohio, City Council Meeting. Contrasts the homophobic rhetoric of the political right with the conviction of the activists.
Civics and Political Systems; Fine Arts; Sociology
Dist - WMEN **Prod** - VIVS 1986

You Can Fixit Series
Chairs and Other Furniture 30 MIN
Counter Tops 30 MIN
Dead bolts 30 MIN
Doors and windows 30 MIN
Electrical Outlets 30 MIN
Faucets 30 MIN
Floor cover 30 MIN
Hot water time switch 30 MIN
Lighting 30 MIN
Sheet rock 30 MIN
The Tool Box I 30 MIN
The Tool Box II 30 MIN
Window Repair 30 MIN
Dist - MDCPB

You Can Fly 4 MIN
16mm / U-matic / VHS
Color
Uses a comic character to dispel the notion that only a special breed of person can fly a plane. Shows some of the basic maneuvers of flying through aerial photography.
Industrial and Technical Education; Physical Education and Recreation; Social Science
Dist - USNAC **Prod** - NASM 1981

You Can Handle it 10 MIN
16mm
B&W
Combines cartoons and real - life action to demonstrate safe material handling methods.
Business and Economics; Health and Safety
Dist - NSC **Prod** - NSC

You can have all of the numbers all of the time
16mm
B&W
Demonstrates how set theory can be used to set up natural numbers and arithmetic. Pays special attention to the recursion theorem and to comparing recursion with induction.
Mathematics
Dist - OPENU **Prod** - OPENU

You can heal your life - study course 120 MIN
VHS
Color (G)
$24.95 purchase _ #400
Presents an 'at home' workshop by Louise L Hay. Includes exercises to help persons with emotional and physical problems dissolve the fears and causes at the root of the dis-ease.
Health and Safety; Psychology
Dist - HAYHSE **Prod** - HAYHSE

You Can Hear Again 30 MIN
16mm
B&W
Presents the story of Harry Walker and his recognition and conquest of defective hearing with the aid of the VA Aural Rehabilitation Program. Shows how he was finally forced to admit his defective hearing to himself and how the VA program restored him to normal living.
Health and Safety; Science - Natural
Dist - USVA **Prod** - USVA 1949

You Can Help 15 MIN
16mm
Color (J H C)
Describes careers in property and liability insurance.
Business and Economics; Guidance and Counseling; Psychology
Dist - III **Prod** - III 1973

You can last longer - Solutions for ejaculatory control 38 MIN
VHS
Color (C A)
$29.95 purchase
Illustrates clearly the treatment program for premature ejaculation. Features Drs Derek C Polansky, Harvard Medical School, and Marian E Dunn, sex therapist, who lead the viewer through a step - by - step program for achieving better ejaculatory control. Produced by Dr Mark Schoen.
Health and Safety; Sociology
Dist - FCSINT

You Can Lead a Horse to Water 28 MIN
U-matic / 8mm cartridge
Color (A)
Demonstrates performance modification in six basic steps. Discusses productivity, behavior modification, performance feedback and positive reinforcement.
Business and Economics; Psychology
Dist - AMEDIA **Prod** - AMEDIA

You Can Learn a Lot from a Lobster - the Family Puppet Interview 28 MIN
U-matic / VHS
Color
Shows how the Family Puppet Interview technique is useful in facilitating communication and interaction among family members in therapy. Shows a typical interview session with a family of four. Demonstrates the four parts of the Family Puppet Interview, including selection, planning, presentation and discussion.
Psychology; Sociology
Dist - PSU **Prod** - PSU

You Can make Music
U-matic / VHS
You Can make Music Series
Color (K P I)
$1,995, $2,175 purchase _ #S837
Demonstrates how to make music. Encourage viewers to participate in the lessons being offered. Provides directions so viewers can learn while they make music.
Fine Arts
Dist - BARR **Prod** - BARR 1987

You Can make Music Series
Harmony 24 MIN
Melody and Pitch 21.5 MIN
Melody and Scale 25 MIN
Rhythm - the Beat 21 MIN
Rhythm Pattern 22 MIN
Rythm - strong and weak beats 22 MIN
You Can make Music
Dist - BARR

You can marry for keeps 28 MIN
VHS
Color (J H C)

$189.00 purchase _ #2299 - SK
Interviews three young couples and a marriage counselor to explore potential problems and conflicts in marriage. Raises issues of sexual equality, changing marital patterns, and commitment. Stresses the concept that marriage is a serious step, not one to be taken lightly. Includes teacher's guide.
Guidance and Counseling; Sociology
Dist - SUNCOM **Prod** - SUNCOM

You can play bluegrass mandolin series
Presents a two - part series featuring mandolinist Butch Baldassari. Shows how to hold and tune a mandolin and basic chords, scales, melodies and techniques in Video One. Demonstrates 'chopping' rhythm chords, chord positions up and down the neck, soloing, slides, hammer - ons, open chords, open - string harmonies, tremolo, licks and more in Video Two. Includes music and tablature.
You can play bluegrass mandolin - Video One 60 MIN
You can play bluegrass mandolin - Video Two 55 MIN
Dist - HOMETA **Prod** - HOMETA

You can play bluegrass mandolin - Video One 60 MIN
VHS
You can play bluegrass mandolin series
Color (G)
$39.95 purchase _ #VD - BAL - MN01
Features mandolinist Butch Baldassari. Shows how to hold and tune the mandolin, basic chords, scales, melodies, open - strings and double - stop techniques. Includes the songs John Henry, Nine - Pound Hammer, Old Joe Clark and Sally Goodin and music and tablature. Part one of a two - part series.
Fine Arts
Dist - HOMETA **Prod** - HOMETA

You can play bluegrass mandolin - Video Two 55 MIN
VHS
You can play bluegrass mandolin series
Color (G)
$39.95 purchase _ #VD - BAL - MN02
Features mandolinist Butch Baldassari. Shows 'chopping' rhythm chords, chord positions up and down the neck, soloing, slides, hammer - ons, open chords, open - string harmonies, tremolo, licks and more. Includes the songs Bury Me Beneath the Willow, Soldier's Joy and Whiskey before Breakfast. Music and tablature. Part two of a two - part series.
Fine Arts
Dist - HOMETA **Prod** - HOMETA

You can play guitar - Part 1 60 MIN
VHS
You can play guitar series
Color (J H C G)
$49.95 purchase _ #HSPHO1V
Shows the beginning guitar student how to play chords on the guitar and how they fit together in creating music. Includes songs, exercises, playing ideas and advice. Part one of a three - part series taught by Happy Traum.
Fine Arts
Dist - CAMV

You can play guitar - Part 2 60 MIN
VHS
You can play guitar series
Color (J H C G)
$39.95 purchase _ #HSPTO1V
Demonstrates strumming and picking techniques and how they can be used to enhance songs and make them more exciting. Includes rhythmic variations, left and right - hand damping, alternating bass notes, hammering - on and more. Part two of a three - part series taught by Happy Traum.
Fine Arts
Dist - CAMV

You can play guitar - Part 3 60 MIN
VHS
You can play guitar series
Color (J H C G)
$39.95 purchase _ #HSPNO1V
Explores the fingerboard to provide a solid understanding of the relationships of notes, frets and strings. Part three of a three - part series taught by Happy Traum.
Fine Arts
Dist - CAMV

You can play guitar series
Presents a three - part series on guitar taught by Happy Traum. Shows the beginner how to play chords in Part 1. Part 2 demonstrates strumming and picking techniques. Explores the fingerboard to provide a solid understanding of the relationships of notes, frets and strings in Part 3.
You can play guitar - Part 1 60 MIN
You can play guitar - Part 2 60 MIN
You can play guitar - Part 3 60 MIN
Dist - CAMV

You can play jazz guitar series
Presents a three - part series featuring jazz guitarist Mike DeMicco. Covers scales, modes and voicings in Video One. Teaches jazz guitar in styles ranging from bebop to jazz blues in Video Two. Shows how to build creative solos while challenging the viewer to find an individual voice in Video Three. Includes music and diagrams.
Improvisation - developing your style - Video Two 80 MIN
Putting it all together - Video Three 60 MIN
Scales, modes and other essentials - Video One 82 MIN
Dist - HOMETA **Prod** - HOMETA

You can play jazz piano 90 MIN
VHS
Color (J H C G)
$49.95 purchase _ #HSP01V
Teaches the basics of pop and jazz piano. Covers basic hand positions, ascending and descending diatonic 3rds, triads and inversion, chord voicings, melodic improvisation, the II - V - I chord progression, playing the blues, using tri - tones and blues scales, melodic ornamentation and more. Features Warren Bernhardt.
Fine Arts
Dist - CAMV

You can play jazz piano series
Presents a three - part series featuring jazz pianist Warren Bernhardt. Covers basic hand positions and scales in Video One. Looks at chord voicings, progressions, substitutions and inversions in Video Two. Examines scales for soloing and improvisation; 'setting up' a solo; preparing a song for performance; playing with other musicians and more in Video Three. Includes music.
Basic keyboard harmony - video two 90 MIN
Getting started - video one 90 MIN
Soloing and performing - Video Three 90 MIN
You can play jazz piano series 270 MIN
Dist - HOMETA **Prod** - HOMETA

You can say no - here's how 25 MIN
VHS
Color (I J)
$169.00 purchase _ #2310 - SK
Dramatizes three situations in which adolescents are forced to 'stand up' for what they believe in. Teaches assertiveness techniques that can be effective in such situations. Stresses that people have the right to act in their own best interests, but must also accept responsibility for their own decisions. Includes teacher's guide.
Education; Guidance and Counseling; Psychology; Sociology
Dist - SUNCOM **Prod** - SUNCOM

You can say no to a drink or a drug 30 MIN
U-matic / Videodisc / 16mm / VHS
Color (I J H)
$550.00, $425.00 purchase _ #JR - 4996M
Adapts the book 'You Can Say No to a Drink or a Drug,' by Susan Newman. Dramatizes situations where teenagers must make difficult decisions on whether or not to go along with the crowd, to accept the actions of friends and family, or to stand up for themselves and what they know is right. Features professional baseball player Keith Hernandez as host.
Guidance and Counseling; Psychology; Sociology
Dist - CORF **Prod** - CORF 1987

You Can See Tomorrow 24 MIN
16mm
Color
Demonstrates how parents, teachers and health professionals can work together to observe, detect and prevent health problems in children in the early elementary school years.
Health and Safety; Home Economics
Dist - MTP **Prod** - MLIC

You can sell them - why and how US firms export 18 MIN
U-matic / VHS
Export now series
Color (PRO)
$65.00, $95.00 purchase _ #TCA17675, #TCA17674
Portrays four American companies which became successful exporters with the help of US Department of Commerce programs.
Business and Economics
Dist - USNAC

You can sing 60 MIN
VHS
Color (G)
$29.95 purchase _ #VD - PEN - TI01
Features Penny Nichols. Shows the viewer how to break down inhibitions and teaches pitch perception and basic music theory.
Fine Arts
Dist - HOMETA **Prod** - HOMETA

You Can Speak Well 13 MIN
U-matic / 35mm strip
Effective Speaking Series
Color
Stresses the importance of being able to speak well and offers four practical rules to improve speaking ability.
English Language; Psychology
Dist - RESEM **Prod** - RESEM

You Can Stop Rubella 29 MIN
Videoreel / VT2
You Series
Color
Presents a study of the various services of the Department of Health, Education and Welfare. Shows how it is attempting to put a stop to rubella epidemics.
Civics and Political Systems; Health and Safety; Sociology
Dist - PBS **Prod** - WRCTV

You Can Surpass Yourself 28 MIN
8mm cartridge / 16mm
From the Eden Ryl Behavioral Series
Color (I J H C A) (SPANISH)
LC 77-703333
Presents Dr Eden Ryl, who examines the learning process and the forces and strategies that render people more teachable.
Foreign Language; Guidance and Counseling
Dist - RAMIC **Prod** - RAMIC 1975

You Can Take it with You 15 MIN
16mm
B&W
Tells a humorous story of the worker who won't leave the plant after a series of nerve - shattering accidents at home.
Business and Economics; Health and Safety; Psychology
Dist - NSC **Prod** - NSC

You can teach hitting series
Presents a three - part series on baseball and batting. Includes A Systematic Approach to Hitting; Ten Common Mistakes and How to Correct Them; Twenty Hitting Drills; and the book You Can Teach Hitting.
A Systematic approach to hitting
Ten common mistakes and how to correct them
Twenty hitting drills
Dist - CAMV

You Can Use it Now 20 MIN
U-matic
Metric System Series
Color (J)
Points out that the metric system can be used in daily life. Reviews the content of the Metric System series.
Mathematics
Dist - GPN **Prod** - MAETEL 1975

You Can Win Elections 22 MIN
U-matic / VHS / 16mm
Color; B&W (J)
Demonstrates how a single citizen can influence elections when he uses professional political techniques. Shows how the electoral process works. Suggests that precinct workers should get people registered and to the polls. Sponsored by Roosevelt University, independent voters of Illinois and labor division, AFLCIO.
Civics and Political Systems
Dist - IFB **Prod** - EMERFC 1954

You Can Write Anything Series
Beginnings 15 MIN
Getting Ideas 15 MIN
The Power of Words 15 MIN
Reports 15 MIN
Stories 1 - Planning 15 MIN
Stories 3 - Endings 15 MIN
Stories 2 - Characters 15 MIN
Unlock Your Imagination 15 MIN
Using Words 15 MIN
Writing a Play 15 MIN
Dist - TVOTAR

You Can't Always Get what You Want 30 MIN
VHS / U-matic
Money Puzzle - the World of Macroeconomics Series Module 2
Color
Explains the law of demand and the law of supply.
Business and Economics; Sociology
Dist - MDCC **Prod** - MDCC

You Can't be Too Careful 20 MIN
U-matic / VHS / 16mm
Color
Uses flashback sequences to show the dangers in rehabilitating older buildings. Uses the example of a worker who was working on an older building where the electricity had been supposedly out off.
Health and Safety
Dist - IFB **Prod** - NFBTE

You Can't Bite Back 10 MIN
16mm
Color
LC 74-705980
Shows the employee the most effective way to handle neighborhood dogs. Points out that dogs have various personalities and the tactics that are useful when each type of dog is encountered.
Science - Natural; Social Science
Dist - USNAC **Prod** - USPOST 1969

You Can't Buy Friendship 15 MIN
16mm
Our Children Series
Color; B&W (P I R)
Tells of a boy visiting his cousins in another city who learns that winning friends involves Christian attitudes of respect.
Guidance and Counseling; Psychology; Religion and Philosophy
Dist - FAMF **Prod** - FAMF

You can't buy health 27 MIN
16mm
Color
Tells how corporations, government, other organizations and other individuals can help contain health costs. Interviews physicians and directors of fitness programs that give practical ideas for health promotion and cost containment.
Health and Safety
Dist - NABSP BCBSA **Prod** - NABSP BCBSA

You Can't Catch it 40 MIN
16mm
Color
LC 73-702069
Portrays the experience of two sickle cell anemia victims in an attempt to clarify many misconceptions about the incurable disease which afflicts blacks. Presents a modern dance sequence to dramatize how sickle cell anemia is inherited.
Health and Safety; History - United States; Science - Natural; Sociology
Dist - EDC **Prod** - EDC 1973

You Can't Get There from Here 30 MIN
16mm
Glory Trail Series no 2; No 2
B&W (I)
LC FIA66-1238
Traces the growth of transportation and communication methods and their influence upon the West.
History - United States; Psychology; Social Science
Dist - IU **Prod** - NET 1965

You can't get there from here 60 MIN
VHS
Color; B&W (G)
$39.95 purchase _ #S02288
Presents selected clips from American movies made between 1946 and 1960. Shows how these movies reflected the culture Americans aspired to, as well as how they influenced consumer preferences. Clips selected by Richard Prelinger.
Fine Arts; History - United States
Dist - UILL

You can't grow home again 58 MIN
VHS
Color (P I J H C G A)
$19.95 purchase
Teaches children about the rain forests and related scientific matters. Features insect collection "safaris" to Costa Rica, visits to an iguana farm, and demonstrations of basic scientific principles. From the PBS "3 - 2 - 1 Contact" series.
Agriculture; Science - Natural; Social Science
Dist - EFVP **Prod** - CTELWO 1990

You can't shift the blame 16 MIN
16mm
Color; PAL (IND)
LC 81-700715
Explores some of the dangers faced by crane drivers.
Health and Safety
Dist - TASCOR EDPAT **Prod** - TASCOR 1981

You Can't Take it with You 127 MIN
16mm
B&W (I)
Stars James Stewart as the young man who wants to marry the daughter of a family of eccentrics.
Fine Arts
Dist - TIMLIF **Prod** - CPC 1938

You can't win 40 MIN
16mm
B&W (R)
Presents a dramatized film sermon by Dr. Bob Jones Sr., about the 'game of sin.'
Literature and Drama; Religion and Philosophy
Dist - UF **Prod** - UF

You Catch a Thief - Unit 5 13 MIN
VHS / 16mm
Robbery and Fraud Preparedness Series
Color (PRO)
$695.00 purchase, $325.00 rental $35.00 preview
Presents former con man Frank Abagnale who shows bank employees how to avoid fraud. Covers six subtopics on various types of fraud. Topics include forgeries, government checks, photocopies, traveler's checks, counterfeit money, short change, paper crime update, and electronic crime update. Includes support material.
Business and Economics; Computer Science; Psychology; Sociology
Dist - UTM **Prod** - UTM

You choose 20 MIN
VHS
Color (G)
$360.00 purchase, $45.00 rental
Discourages young people from using chewing tobacco. Uses the theme of respect and love for oneself, for the earth and for other people in the use of tobacco. Follows a grandfather and his Yurok grandson on a visit to a Rosebud Sioux friend and the corner market where a rap music debate ensues between Indian teens, with images of Trickster Coyote and Wise Eagle entering into the debate.
Health and Safety; Literature and Drama; Psychology; Social Science; Sociology
Dist - SHENFP **Prod** - SHENFP

You could be arrested 22 MIN
VHS
Color (H A)
$20.00 purchase
Teaches high school students about Amnesty International. Interviews former prisoners of conscience, high school group members and rock musicians involved in the human rights movement. Produced and directed by Paul Stern.
Civics and Political Systems; Fine Arts; Sociology
Dist - AMNSTY

You Decide 28 MIN
16mm
You Can do it - if Series
Color (J)
LC 81-700096
Explains that accomplishment comes from persistence.
Psychology
Dist - VANDER **Prod** - VANDER 1980

You Decide - Open Ended Tales 73 MIN
VHS / U-matic
You Decided - Open Ended Tales Series
Color (P I)
English Language
Dist - TROLA **Prod** - TROLA 1987

You Decided - Open Ended Tales Series
You Decide - Open Ended Tales 73 MIN
Dist - TROLA

You deserve 48 MIN
VHS
Les Brown series
Color (G)
$69.95 purchase _ #TVL 1011
Brings home the message that just about anything anyone desires can be theirs if they put forth the energy, time, effort and tenacity to go after it.
Guidance and Counseling; Psychology
Dist - JWAVID **Prod** - JWAVID

You determine your success - John Wooden 18 MIN
16mm / VHS
Color (PRO)
$500.00, $550.00 purchase, $150.00 rental, $75.00 preview
Presents coach John Wooden. Discusses the importance of realistic goal setting, hard work, discipline, team spirit, self - confidence, initiative and perseverence.
Psychology
Dist - UTM **Prod** - UTM

You dirty rat 52 MIN
VHS
Color (G)
$55.00 purchase
Features a hilarious parody of 1930s gangster movies. Enlivens the rags - to - riches story of the rise and fall of Frankie the Feet with puppet animation by animator Tom Triman. Music by Craig Inglis, Ron Mandlecorn, Jim Valley. Produced by Tom Triman.
Fine Arts; Literature and Drama
Dist - CANCIN

You Discovered Something New 15 MIN
U-matic / VHS
Imagine that Series Program 2; Program 2
Color (P)
LC 82-706468
Uses a multisensory approach to help children develop mind - body coordination, focusing on movement experiences using newspaper and the development of small muscle skills and hand - eye coordination. Integrates an imaginary theme with the use of rhythmic music, pantomime, and indoor classroom activities and calisthenics.
Education; Psychology
Dist - GPN **Prod** - WBRATV 1981

You do believe the press, don't you - newsroom notes on sensationalism, cynicism, subjectivity and survival 60 MIN
VHS
Color (G)
$15.00 purchase _ #V94 - 21
Presents the 17th annual Frank E Gannett Lecture, by Shelbey Coffy III, Los Angeles Times. Part of a series on freedom of the press, free speech and free spirit.
Literature and Drama; Social Science; Sociology
Dist - FREEDM **Prod** - FREEDM 1994

You don't have to feel fright, dear - an interview with Dr Albert Ellis 28 MIN
VHS
Color (H C G)
$150.00 purchase, $55.00 rental
Portrays Dr Albert Ellis, founder of Rational Emotive Therapy, as author, psychotherapist and human being. Produced by Gudrun Sprank.
Psychology
Dist - FLMLIB

You don't have to smoke to be cool - peer pressure and smoking 30 MIN
VHS
Color (I J H)
$209.00 purchase _ #06128 - 126
Uses interviews with teens and experts, vignettes, charts and graphs to discuss the use of tobacco and its effects upon health. Describes how students started smoking and techniques for quitting. Illustrates role modeling for alternative behavior.
Guidance and Counseling; Health and Safety; Psychology; Sociology
Dist - GA **Prod** - GA

You Got the same Thing, Aincha 17 MIN
U-matic / VHS
Social Seminar Series
Color
LC 80-707340
Focuses on an urban school in which students and teachers alike experience the frustrations of teaching and learning in an environment marked by change. Issued in 1974 as a motion picture.
Education
Dist - USNAC **Prod** - NIMH 1980

You got to move 87 MIN
16mm / VHS
Color (G IND)
$5.00 rental
Documents and affirms the fact that one person can make a difference. Tells the story of ordinary people - housewives, blue collar workers - who got involved in solving social problems. Looks at Highlander Folk School which teaches grassroots intervention methods and includes sections on organizing, toxic waste and civil rights.
Civics and Political Systems; Social Science; Sociology
Dist - AFLCIO **Prod** - FIRS 1987

You Got to Move 87 MIN
16mm
Color (G)
Presents an independent production by Lucy Phenix and Veronica Selver. Retells the story of the struggle for civil rights in the American South. Features black and white Southerners, recast to deal with contemporary social problems.
Civics and Political Systems; Fine Arts; History - United States; Sociology
Dist - FIRS

You Got what 23 MIN
16mm
Color (J)
LC 75-711597
Presents graphic sequences on the development of venereal diseases, describes the confidential treatment that is provided by clinics and stresses the importance of naming one's sexual contacts.
Health and Safety; Sociology
Dist - FRAF **Prod** - CINIKA 1970

You Gotta Think about it 21 MIN
16mm
Color
LC 74-706613
Discusses the need for serious thought in making necessary decisions in life.
Guidance and Counseling; Sociology
Dist - USNAC **Prod** - USN 1973

You have a chance 22 MIN
U-matic / VHS
Color (H G R PRO)
$195.00 purchase _ #C850 - VI - 125
Discusses drug and alcohol abuse and rehabilitation. Presented by Drs Susan J Stockman and Ronald Forbes.
Guidance and Counseling; Psychology
Dist - HSCIC

You have a choice 16 MIN
VHS / U-matic
Color (J H)
$235.00, $285.00 purchase, $50.00 rental
Presents a multi - ethnic exploration of the experiences and options open to teenagers should they become pregnant. Includes interviews with teen parents and compelling facts to discourage pregnancy at an early age. Produced by Children Having Children.
Health and Safety
Dist - NDIM

You have a choice - Pt 1 25 MIN
U-matic / VHS
Color (J A)
Shows right and left brain research used in the prevention of teenage alcohol and drug abuse. Discusses peer pressure.
Psychology; Science - Natural; Sociology
Dist - SUTHRB **Prod** - GOLDTO

You have a choice - Pt 2 25 MIN
U-matic / VHS
Color (J A)
Shows right and left brain research used in the prevention of teenage alcohol and drug abuse. Discusses peer pressure.
Psychology; Science - Natural; Sociology
Dist - SUTHRB **Prod** - GOLDTO

You have a Favorite Partner 15 MIN
VHS / U-matic
Imagine that Series Program 8; Program 8
Color (P)
LC 82-706474
Uses a multisensory approach to help children develop mind - body coordination, focusing on partner activities and basic locomotor activities. Integrates an imaginary theme with the use of rhythmic music, pantomime, and indoor classroom activities and calisthenics.
Education; Psychology
Dist - GPN **Prod** - WBRATV 1981

You have a Job Offer - Now what 13 MIN
VHS / U-matic
Making it Work Series
Color (H A)
Shows Marcie and Diane considering the pros and cons of a sales job each has been offered. Explains gross and net pay and common deductions. Presents Joe and his wife Gail reviewing their deductions to understand his paycheck.
Guidance and Counseling; Psychology
Dist - AITECH **Prod** - ERF 1983

You have a Little Friend 15 MIN
U-matic / VHS
Imagine that Series Program 9; Program 9
Color (P)
LC 82-706475
Uses a multisensory approach to help children develop mind - body coordination, focusing on simple exercise patterns, gross motor movements and the development of listening skills. Integrates an imaginary theme of friendship with the use of rhythmic music, pantomime, and indoor classroom activities and calisthenics.
Education; Psychology
Dist - GPN **Prod** - WBRATV 1981

You have gingivitis - 4 8 MIN
16mm / VHS / BETA / U-matic
UK dental care series
Color; PAL (G)
PdS60, PdS68 purchase
Discusses the nature of chronic gingivitis and why plaque control is vital for treatment and prevention in part of a four - part series.
Health and Safety
Dist - EDPAT

You have Got the Power 27 MIN
U-matic / VHS / 16mm
Color
Demonstrates the nature of the rehabilitation process, both physical and psychological, for the bone cancer amputee. Shows the experiences of five individuals and the impact of amputation upon their lives.
Health and Safety; Psychology
Dist - STNFLD **Prod** - STNFLD

You have more Power than You Think 25 MIN
16mm / U-matic / VHS
Negotiating Successfully Series Part 3
Color (A)
LC 76-702387
Presents a lecture by Chester L Karrass explaining the use of power in negotiating, showing the sources of power, the illusions of power and the techniques of power.
Business and Economics; Guidance and Counseling
Dist - TIMLIF **Prod** - TIMLIF 1975

You have something to offer 14 MIN
16mm / U-matic / VHS
Learning Values with Fat Albert and the Cosby Kids, Set II Series
Color (P I)
Suggests that excellence comes from identifying one's real talents and stresses that accepting oneself is important.
Guidance and Counseling
Dist - MGHT **Prod** - FLMTON 1977

You have Struck a Rock 28 MIN
VHS / 16mm / U-matic
Color
Recounts the experiences of women who took the lead in mobilizing mass opposition to apartheid during the 1950s when the South African regime attempted to extend the hated pass system to them.
History - United States; History - World
Dist - CANWRL **Prod** - MAYDEB 1981

You have to start so small to even make an inch 30 MIN
VHS / U-matic
Color (G)
$195.00 purchase _ #C850 - VI - 126
Features Dr Eric Schopler who briefly discusses autism, discusses its traditional diagnosis and treament and explains the conclusions of recent research and clinical observations. Explains fully each step of North Carolina's comprehensive program for autistic children, TEACCH.
Psychology
Dist - HSCIC

You Haven't Changed a Bit 15 MIN
16mm
Marriage Series
Color (H C)
LC 72-700515
Presents a dramatization about a young couple who after a quarrel take separate vacations at their parents' homes, showing how they learn that their real identity lies in their relationship with each other.
Guidance and Counseling; Psychology; Sociology
Dist - FRACOC **Prod** - FRACOC 1970

You Hide Me 20 MIN
U-matic / VHS / 16mm
B&W (C A)
LC 74-702318
Analyzes the policy of European colonial regimes which, in establishing their rule, wiped out all traces of African civilization, religion, language and art.
Civics and Political Systems; Geography - World; Sociology
Dist - CNEMAG **Prod** - TRIFCW 1973

You in Japan 19 MIN
16mm
B&W
LC FIE56-323
Tours major Japanese cities and scenic rural areas. Describes the cultural, social and religious background of Japan. Explains her political, military and economic structure.
Geography - World
Dist - USNAC **Prod** - USDD 1956

You in mind 70 MIN
VHS
Color (H C A)
PdS99 purchase
Discusses common mental health problems and how people deal with them, including anxiety, fear, insomnia, and depression.
Health and Safety; Psychology
Dist - BBCENE

You in OPD 22 MIN
16mm
Color
LC 74-706342
Shows how to develop techniques for an effective relationship between staff and patients in the outpatient department.
Guidance and Counseling; Health and Safety; Psychology; Sociology
Dist - USNAC **Prod** - USN 1969

You in Public Service Series

Applying for a public service job	28 MIN
Basic record keeping	28 MIN
Basic report writing	28 MIN
Good grooming	28 MIN
Interviewing Skills	28 MIN
Introduction - You in Public Service	28 MIN
Oral Communication	28 MIN
Person - to - Person Relationships	28 MIN
Techniques of Decision Making	28 MIN
Written Communication	28 MIN

Dist - USNAC

You irresistible you 11 MIN
16mm
Color (J)
LC 75-702797
Features comedian Marshall Efron as he points out that an increasing number of men are willing to pay high prices for furnishings and cosmetics which promise to make them irresistible to the opposite sex. Spotlights suntan lotions, stereos, waterbeds and various grooming aids.
Home Economics; Sociology
Dist - BNCHMK **Prod** - WNETTV 1972

You Just Love Your Children 12 MIN
16mm
Color
LC 79-701126
Presents two short studies of homosexuals as parents.
Psychology; Sociology
Dist - TEMPLU **Prod** - TEMPLU 1979

You know what I mean 20 MIN
VHS
Color (A PRO IND)
$660.00 purchase, $155.00 rental
Uses a racecar motif to present the message that good communication is important to the success of a work team. Stresses the concept that each employee must ensure that he or she is heard and understood by others.
Business and Economics; English Language; Psychology; Social Science
Dist - VLEARN **Prod** - RTBL

You Light Up My Life 90 MIN
16mm
Color
Tells how a young singer - songwriter beats all the odds to make it to the top of the charts.
Fine Arts
Dist - TWYMAN **Prod** - CPC 1977

You Look Ridiculous Said the Rhinocerus to the Hippopotamus 15 MIN
U-matic / VHS
Magic Pages Series
Color (P)
Literature and Drama
Dist - AITECH **Prod** - KLVXTV 1976

You made some Other Noise 15 MIN
U-matic / VHS
Imagine that Series Program 5; Program 5
Color (P)
LC 82-706471
Uses a multisensory approach to help children develop mind - body coordination, focusing on gross and small motor movements and the development of listening skills. Integrates an imaginary theme with the use of rhythmic music, pantomime, and indoor classroom activities and calisthenics.
Education; Psychology
Dist - GPN **Prod** - WBRATV 1981

You make Me Sick 30 MIN
U-matic / VHS / 16mm
Powerhouse Series
Color (I J)
Shows how the Powerhouse Kids race the clock to find the source of a deadly illness.
Health and Safety
Dist - GA **Prod** - EFCVA 1982

You make the Difference 9 MIN
VHS / U-matic
Color
Introduces library circulation assistants and their job. Emphasizes a good public service attitude.
Education; Social Science
Dist - LVN **Prod** - BCPL

You make the difference - food handling and you - safety in housekeeping - pt 1
U-matic / VHS
We care series
Color
Portrays the role of the health care employee as it relates to the care and well - being of a patient. Emphasizes the importance of cleanliness, shows the importance of being safety conscious.
Health and Safety
Dist - VTRI **Prod** - VTRI

You make the difference - valuing diversity - Part IV 30 MIN
VHS
Valuing diversity series
Color (A PRO IND)
$695.00 purchase, $100.00 rental
Presents the fourth of a seven - part series on diversity in the workplace. Argues that diversity can be a strength if properly handled. Dramatizes situations leading to conflict and poor performance, showing how they can be better handled. Focuses on entry level employees.
Business and Economics; Guidance and Counseling; Sociology
Dist - VLEARN

You may call her Madam Secretary 57 MIN
VHS / 16mm
Color (G IND)
$10.00 rental
Tells the story of the first woman to serve in a President's cabinet, Secretary of Labor Frances Perkins, 1933 - 1945. Reveals that she devoted her life championing legislation to improve the lives of workers, and that her tenure as secretary saw the passage of retirement pensions, wage and hour legislation, unemployment compensatin and workers' compensation. Produced by R and M Potts.
Business and Economics; History - United States; History - World; Social Science
Dist - AFLCIO

You, me, and technology series

China, Japan and the West	20 MIN
Communications - the expanding world	20 MIN
Decisions, decisions, decisions	20 MIN
Energy for societies	19.50 MIN
Exploring Space	20 MIN
Feeding the world	20 MIN
Health and Technologies	19.44 MIN
Living with technology	20 MIN
Population, Patterns and Technology	20 MIN
Risk, safety and technology	20 MIN
The Technology spiral	20 MIN

Dist - AITECH

You Meant what 15 MIN
U-matic / VHS
Communication at Work Series
Color (H)
Discusses the difference between clarity and ambiguity and considers the problems of misconstrued meaning.
Guidance and Counseling; Psychology
Dist - AITECH **Prod** - OHSDE 1979

You, mother 10 MIN
16mm
B&W (G)
$18.00 rental
Offers a look at parents and children in a variety of daily activities with voices offscreen of women explaining why they have children. Aims to raise questions about why people have children.
Fine Arts; Religion and Philosophy; Sociology
Dist - CANCIN **Prod** - HOLMEK 1970

You must have been a bilingual baby 46 MIN
VHS
Color (H C G)
$395.00 purchase, $65.00 rental
Investigates how babies become bilingual, how school children fare in immersion classes and how adults cope with learning foreign languages. Features Dr Michel Paradis, specialist in the brain and bilingualism at McGill University, who believes that 'The younger you are the easier it is to acquire not just language but any kind of skill.'
Foreign Language; Psychology
Dist - FLMLIB **Prod** - CANBC 1992

You must remember this 106 MIN
VHS
Wonderworks collection series
Color (I J H)
$29.95 purchase _ #YOU040
Portrays a young girl who discovers that her great - uncle was a great black film director 50 years earlier. Reveals that she helps him to accept his past and, in the process, unearths a rich cultural legacy.
Guidance and Counseling; History - United States; Literature and Drama
Dist - KNOWUN **Prod** - PBS 1992

You must remember this - inside Alzheimer's Disease 57 MIN
VHS
Color (H C G)
$445.00 purchase, $75.00 rental
Visits people in Australia who are suffering at various stages of Alzheimer's Disease. Meets John Hooper who is in the early stages and can still read and drive, but 'doesn't do things as well as he used to.' Iris Sweetman, in a later stage, can still play tennis but may come to the court inappropriately equipped. Arch Palmer no long recognizes his wife of 35 years, Steve Stephenson is becoming disoriented. Produced and directed by Helen Bowden and Susan MacKinnon.
Health and Safety
Dist - FLMLIB

You must Take it with You 14 MIN
16mm
Color
Traces the need for creating artificial environment not only in aircraft but also in space vehicles. Describes the environment on earth and explains how it is reproduced in pressurized aircraft and space vehicles.
Science - Physical
Dist - GARET **Prod** - GARET 1964

You Need Me - Selling Your Talents to an Employer 30 MIN
VHS
Color
Problem solving approach to finding, securing, and keeping a good job. Offers strategies in areas of effective resume writing, creating a network of personal contacts, defining and following a career path, and improving communications skills.
Education; Guidance and Counseling
Dist - HRMC **Prod** - HRMC 1986

You Need to Know Series

Drawworks	24 MIN
F - FA mud pumps	55 MIN
FB mud pumps	47 MIN
Mechanical Compounds	8 MIN
Swivels, Blocks, Rotaries	25 MIN

Dist - UTEXPE

You Never Miss the Water 15 MIN
16mm
Color (J)
LC 80-701061
Tells how to reduce water usage in the home and thus save on water bills while at the same time helping to preserve the environment.
Home Economics; Science - Natural; Social Science
Dist - KLEINW **Prod** - KLEINW 1978

You Only Live Once 11 MIN
16mm
Color
LC 70-714166
Shows the difference between a professional driver and the complacent driver, and demonstrates driving errors and correct procedures.
Health and Safety; Psychology; Social Science
Dist - USPOST **Prod** - USPOST 1971

You Owe it to Yourself 23 MIN
16mm
Color (PRO)
LC FIE68-70
Explains benefits made available to servicemen by the US government whether they remain in the service or are discharged.
Civics and Political Systems; Guidance and Counseling; Psychology
Dist - USVA **Prod** - VA 1968

You owe it to yourself series

Banking and savings institutions	29 MIN
Budgeting	29 MIN
Credit	28 MIN
Estate Planning	29 MIN
Health Insurance	29 MIN
Housing for Family Needs	29 MIN
Investments and Risk Capital	24 MIN
Life Insurance	29 MIN
Property and Liability Insurance	29 MIN
Social Security	29 MIN

Dist - PBS

You Pack Your Own Chute 30 MIN
U-matic
Eden Ryl Behavioral Series
Color (SPANISH PORTUGUESE)
Shows cinema verite coverage of the first parachute jump into the ocean by Eden Ryl. Uses this jump as a symbol, with discussion and illustrative vignettes, to show how to recognize and overcome unrealistic fears.
Guidance and Counseling; Psychology
Dist - RAMIC **Prod** - RAMIC 1972

You - parents are special series
VHS / U-matic / BETA
You - parents are special series
Color (K P G)
$525.00 purchase _ #V409; $125.00 _ #YPAS - 000
Presents a series of brief conversations with children and parents about topics of concern to families. Features Fred Rogers. Includes Imaginary Friends, Divorce, Moving, School Experiences, Discipline, Friends Who Fight, Nurturing Creatively, Siblings.
Psychology; Sociology
Dist - FAMCOM **Prod** - FAMCOM 1982
PBS

You - parents are special series

Discipline	10 MIN
Divorce	10 MIN
Friends who fight	10 MIN
Imaginary Friends	10 MIN
Moving	10 MIN
Nurturing Creativity	10 MIN
School Experiences	10 MIN
Siblings	10 MIN

Dist - FAMCOM

You - parents are special series
You - parents are special series
Dist - FAMCOM
PBS

You - Poor Kids Can Learn 29 MIN
Videoreel / VT2
You Series
Color
Presents a study of the various services of the Department of Health, Education and Welfare. Discusses educational opportunities which are available for needy children.
Civics and Political Systems; Education; Sociology
Dist - PBS **Prod** - WRCTV

You Really Shouldn't do that 15 MIN
VHS / U-matic
Hidden Treasures Series no 14; No 14
Color (T)
LC 82-706554
Uses the adventures of a pirate and his three friends to explore the many facets of language arts. Shows what can happen in 'shouldn't do' situations, focusing on their use in oral and written expression.
English Language
Dist - GPN **Prod** - WCVETV 1980

You Run for Your Life 14 MIN
16mm
Color
Shows the components necessary to create good running shoes for running as well as other sports.
Physical Education and Recreation
Dist - MTP **Prod** - MTP

You See I've Had a Life 32 MIN
16mm
Color (J H C)
LC 73-700635
Presents Paul Hendricks, a teenager who has leukemia.
Health and Safety; Science - Natural; Sociology
Dist - TEMPLU **Prod** - TEMPLU 1972

You See what You Say - an Introduction to Latin Prepositions 13 MIN
16mm / U-matic / VHS
Color (J H)
LC 80-700691
Presents an animated introduction or review of the Latin prepositions ab, ad, de, in and ex and illustrates the correct usage of these prepositions.
Foreign Language
Dist - IFB **Prod** - VPI 1979

You Sell Shoes 15 MIN
16mm
Color
LC 78-700322
Demonstrates techniques for selling shoes to customers of various ages, sizes and lifestyles.
Business and Economics; Home Economics; Psychology
Dist - USSHOE **Prod** - USSHOE 1978

You Series
You - Poor Kids Can Learn 29 MIN
You and Addiction 29 MIN
You and Alcohol 29 MIN
You and Disaster 29 MIN
You and Drugs 29 MIN
You and Family Health 29 MIN
You and Manana 29 MIN
You and Mental Retardation 29 MIN
You and Mobility 29 MIN
You and Mr Rat 29 MIN
You and Quackery 29 MIN
You and Returning Veterans 29 MIN
You and Rx Learning 29 MIN
You and Services 29 MIN
You and Surplus Property 29 MIN
You and the Delinquents 29 MIN
You and the Handicapped 29 MIN
You and the Pap Test 29 MIN
You and the Question Mark Kids 29 MIN
You and the Red Schoolhouse 29 MIN
You and the Road Children 29 MIN
You and When it Matters 29 MIN
You and Women's Lib 29 MIN
You and Your Breath 29 MIN
You and Your Heritage 29 MIN
You Can Stop Rubella 29 MIN
Dist - PBS

You the Better 33 MIN
16mm
Color
Presents Ericka Beckman's film entry selected from the 1985 Whitney Biennial Film and Video Exhibition.
Fine Arts
Dist - AFA **Prod** - AFA 1986

You - the discussion group 28 MIN
U-matic / BETA / VHS
Communication skills 2 - advanced series
Color (H C G)
$101.95, $89.95 purchase _ #CA - 08
Overviews proper attitude in approaching a discussion situation. Identifies the four basic rights of group discussion. Presents the four knowledge requirements for a group member. Shows how to apply the basic communication skills to discussions. Demontrates effective participation in group discussion. Part of a 26 - part series.
Guidance and Counseling; Social Science
Dist - INSTRU

You - the discussion leader 28 MIN
U-matic / BETA / VHS
Communication skills 2 - advanced series
Color (H C G)
$101.95, $89.95 purchase _ #CA - 07
Distinguishes a group leader from a chairperson or moderator. Identifies several different styles of leadership. Presents the characteristic qualities of a leader and identifies the duties of a leader in a group discussion. Applies the theories of leadership to discussions. Part of a 26 - part series.
Guidance and Counseling; Social Science
Dist - INSTRU

You - the human animal 8 MIN
U-matic / VHS / 16mm
This is you - health series
Color (P I J) (FRENCH ARABIC SPANISH)
LC 74-714360
Discusses the differences between the human animal and other animals, emphasizing ability to think.
Health and Safety; Science - Natural
Dist - CORF **Prod** - DISNEY 1957

You, the Law, and Criminals 60 MIN
U-matic / VHS
Color
Explores ways citizens can aid themselves and the police in dealing with crime. Deals with burglary precautions and the Kentucky Uniform And Crime Reporting System.
Civics and Political Systems; History - United States; Sociology
Dist - EASTKU **Prod** - EASTKU

You - the living machine 8 MIN
U-matic / VHS / 16mm
This is you - health series
Color (P I J) (FRENCH ARABIC)
Jiminy Cricket shows the difference between a living machine and a manufactured machine. He explains how to take care of the body and shows the functions of the digestive and circulatory systems.
Health and Safety; Science - Natural
Dist - CORF **Prod** - DISNEY 1959

You - the Supervisor - Introduction 30 MIN
VHS / U-matic
You - the Supervisor Series
Color
Shows a newly promoted supervisor trying to handle his job. Discusses the common concerns of supervisors and the anxieties they experience on the job. Introduces the concept of promotion depression.
Business and Economics; Guidance and Counseling; Psychology
Dist - DELTAK **Prod** - PRODEV

You - the supervisor series
Building a productive climate 30 MIN
Counseling and Coaching 30 MIN
Interviewing and Selecting 30 MIN
Leadership and Growth 30 MIN
Orientation and Training 30 MIN
Performance Reviews that Get Results 30 MIN
Work Planning and Scheduling 30 MIN
You - the Supervisor - Introduction 30 MIN
Dist - DELTAK

You - the Supervisor Series
Personal Growth for the Supervisor 30 MIN
Dist - PRODEV

You too can make a map 16 MIN
16mm / U-matic / VHS
Color (I J)
$59.95 purchase _ #P10930
Demonstrate how to make a topographical map from available resources and provides instruction on how to interpret legends and symbols on maps. Discusses street maps, topographical maps and other types of maps. Emphasizes the importance of maps in meteorology, outdoor recreation, and flying.
Geography - United States; Geography - World
Dist - CF **Prod** - CYPRES

You Touched Me 24 MIN
16mm
Color (A)
Explores a volunteer program providing recreation for the mentally retarded.
Health and Safety; Physical Education and Recreation; Psychology
Dist - OMNIFS **Prod** - OMNIFS

You want ME to help with housework - no way 15 MIN
VHS
Boy's town parenting series
Color (G)
$29.95 purchase _ #FFB205V
Presents a systematic way to teach children to help out more around the house. Shows how having children share in household responsibilities builds thei self - esteem and gives today's busy parents more time to enjoy their families. Part of an 11 - part series.
Guidance and Counseling; Health and Safety; Home Economics; Psychology; Sociology
Dist - CAMV **Prod** - FFBH

You Want to be a Volunteer 8 MIN
16mm
Bellevue Volunteers Series
B&W
Instructs new volunteers in the correct grooming, behavior and attitude necessary for effective service.
Guidance and Counseling; Social Science
Dist - NYU **Prod** - NYU

You were Never Lovelier 97 MIN
16mm
B&W
Features a music comedy starring Fred Astaire and Rita Hayworth.
Fine Arts
Dist - TWYMAN **Prod** - CPC 1942

You were Never Lovelier 18 MIN
16mm
B&W
An abridged version of the motion picture You Were Never Lovelier. Relates how a hotel tycoon tries to keep his daughter happy with fake romance but that the plan backfires when real love blossoms.
Fine Arts
Dist - TIMLIF **Prod** - TIMLIF 1982

You Won't Feel a Thing 26 MIN
VHS / 16mm
Color (A)
$149.00 purchase, $75.00 rental _ #OD - 2235
Documents the efforts of a team of anesthesiologists preparing for surgery. Examines how new anesthetic agents have led to new monitoring devices.
Health and Safety
Dist - FOTH

You would if you loved me - making decisions about sex 60 MIN
VHS
Color (I J H)
$209.00 purchase _ #496 - V8
Helps teens examine sexual messages, myths, and misconceptions. Encourages teens to get the facts from dependable sources and to trust their own good judgment. As they are asked to consider the meaning and consequences of sexual activity, teens gain insight in to how to counter pressures with their own values and common sense. Includes Teacher's Guide.
Guidance and Counseling; Health and Safety; Psychology; Social Science
Dist - ETRASS **Prod** - ETRASS

You would if You Loved Me - Making Decisions about Sex 31 MIN
U-matic / VHS
Color (I J H)
LC 81-706154
Deals with the sexual pressures of modern society, discussing the consequences of early pregnancy and venereal disease, and the effect of peer pressure. Stresses the importance of getting accurate information about sexual behavior and emphasizes the need for strong personal values.
Guidance and Counseling; Health and Safety; Sociology
Dist - GA **Prod** - GA 1981

You'll Find it in the Library 13 MIN
U-matic / VHS / 16mm
Color (I)
Demonstrates how to find books in a library by title, author and subject matter.
Education; English Language; Guidance and Counseling; Psychology; Social Science
Dist - CORF **Prod** - CORF 1966

You'll Get Yours When You're 65 40 MIN
U-matic / VHS / 16mm
Color (P I J H C)
LC 73-703132
Depicts America's treatment of its senior citizens. Contrasts this treatment with that of other countries, such as West Germany. Dispels some of the misconceptions about the American health and retirement systems.
Sociology
Dist - CAROUF **Prod** - CBSTV 1973

You'll Soon Get the Hang of it 29 MIN
16mm
Color (A)
Presents John Cleese who uses a variety of situations to show how to organize training to fit in with the three ways people learn and how to employ different sorts of motivation at the three different stages of training.
Business and Economics; Psychology
Dist - VISUCP **Prod** - VIDART 1982

You'll Soon Get the Hang of it 24 MIN
VHS / U-matic
Color (A)
Humorously presents the major mistakes most people make in training new recruits. Discusses both how to organize training to fit the basic ways people learn and when to use different motivational techniques at different stages of training.
Business and Economics; Education; Psychology
Dist - XICOM **Prod** - XICOM

Young adult cliffhangers series
The Cat ate my gymsuit
Dist - PELLER

Young adult issues series
Presents five videos for young adults dealing with challenges they face in today's society. Includes the following titles and topics - Too Much - alcohol abuse; Echo in the Night - teen suicide; Innocent Again - sexual abuse; Jason's Choice - family values; Sink or Swim - ethics. Each video ends with an epilogue by a Christian recording artist, designed to promote discussion.
Echo in the night 30 MIN
Innocent again 30 MIN
Jason's choice 28 MIN
Sink or swim 28 MIN
Too much 30 MIN
Dist - GF

Young adults 30 MIN
VHS / U-matic
Issues of cystic fibrosis series
Color (PRO C)
$395.00 purchase, $80.00 rental _ #C891 - VI - 043
Discusses young adult cystic fibrosis patients. Offers insights into how young adults cope with cystic fibrosis. Looks at the doctor - patient relationship, the disease's variability from patient to patient and patient autonomy. Part of a 13 - part series on cystic fibrosis presented by Drs Ivan Harwood and Cyril Worby.
Health and Safety; Science - Natural
Dist - HSCIC

The Young Akbar 30 MIN
VHS
Great Moghuls series
Color (H C G)
$195.00 purchase
Recalls that when the second Emperor Humayun died suddenly, his 13 - year - old son Akbar was crowned Emperor. Reveals that Akbar - meaning great - came to be the greatest of the Great Moghuls. Part of a six - part series on the Moghul Empire.
History - World
Dist - LANDMK **Prod** - LANDMK 1990

The Young Alcoholic - a Family Dilemma 30 MIN
U-matic / VHS / 16mm
Color
Focuses on the intervention process as the major step toward treating minors addicted to alcohol and helping their families. Examines the physical and emotional effects of chemical dependency, explores the dynamics occuring in families beset by this problem and shows why typical reactions often backfire.
Health and Safety; Psychology; Sociology
Dist - CORF **Prod** - CBSTV

The Young Alcoholics
16mm / U-matic / VHS
(J H)
$295.00 purchase _ #80929 3/4 inch and #80911 VHS and #80523 film,
Introduces the issue of teenage alcoholism.
Guidance and Counseling; Health and Safety; Psychology
Dist - CMPCAR

Young and angry 29 MIN
VHS / 16mm
A Different understanding series
Color (G)
$90.00 purchase _ #BPN178014
Examines antisocial behavior as an extension of adolescence. Presents a case study of one teenager's journey through the juvenile justice system and his struggle to come to terms with adult society and its demands. Taken from the program `Sharp And Terrible Eyes.'
Sociology
Dist - RMIBHF **Prod** - RMIBHF
TVOTAR TVOTAR

Young and Just Beginning 29 MIN
16mm
Color
LC 76-701499
Features the work of a ten - year - old gymnast, examining her summer training and her prospects for the 1980 Olympics.
Physical Education and Recreation
Dist - OVTNF **Prod** - OVTNF 1975

Young and Old - Reaching Out Series
Love and Loneliness 29 MIN
Raising Children 59 MIN
Work and Fulfillment 59 MIN
Dist - PBS

Young and Old - Reaching Out - Work and Fulfillment 60 MIN
U-matic / VHS
Color
Deals with the American Dream and what it means to the old and the young. Discusses changing values about work, money, education, business and success. Features Senator Sam Ervin and George Willing, the man who scaled New York's World Trade Center. Brings together young adults and the elderly from diverse backgrounds to share life experiences.
Guidance and Counseling; Health and Safety; Sociology
Dist - DELTAK **Prod** - PBS

The Young Art - Children make their Own Films 16 MIN
16mm
Color
LC 73-714116
Demonstrates how to set up and run a filmmaking class for young students. Shows students developing their ideas, such as shooting, splicing and editing film, and discussing their results. Includes scenes from student films.
Education; Fine Arts
Dist - VANREN **Prod** - VANNOS 1971

Young aspirations - young artists 40 MIN
VHS
Color (J H C G)
$49.95 purchase _ #YA100V; $99.95 purchase _ #YA001V
Portrays a group of talented inner - city kids from New Orleans who design, draw and dream together under the watchful eye of an inspirational teacher. Reveals that what starts as a small after - school class carries the kids to the castles and canals of Amersterdam on a mission of art, racial understanding and self - discovery.
Education
Dist - CAMV

Young at Art 29 MIN
VHS / U-matic
Creativity with Bill Moyers Series
Color (H C A)
Explores the creativity of self - discovery exhibited by students at New York City's High School of Performing Arts in the classroom, rehearsals and in performance.
Fine Arts; Psychology; Sociology
Dist - PBS **Prod** - CORPEL 1982

Young at Art - Introduction 14 MIN
U-matic / VHS
Young at Art Series
Color (P I)
Introduces the Young At Art Series.
Fine Arts
Dist - AITECH **Prod** - WSKJTV 1980

Young at Art - New York High School for the Performing Arts 59 MIN
VHS
Creativity With Bill Moyers Series
Color (G)
$49.95 purchase _ #CWBM - 117C
Depicts the students of the New York High School for the Performing Arts as they balance rehearsals, performances and their academic classwork.
Education; Fine Arts; Geography - United States; Psychology
Dist - PBS **Prod** - CORPEL 1981

Young at Art Series
Aquarium classroom 15 MIN
Clay figures 15 MIN
Combed patterns 14 MIN
Crayon and tempera resist 15 MIN
Cubist Flips 15 MIN
Discovering Design 14 MIN
Environmental art 14 MIN
Foil and string relief 15 MIN
Found object masks 14 MIN
Innertube Prints 15 MIN
Line Prints 15 MIN
Look at Lines 15 MIN
Magic of Color 15 MIN
Moon Creatures 14 MIN
Name Designs 15 MIN
Near and Far 14 MIN
Op Art 15 MIN
Paint Engravings 15 MIN
Paper Sculpture Animals 14 MIN
Papier - Mache Birds 14 MIN
Pop Art 14 MIN
Prehistoric Magic 14 MIN
Snap Art 14 MIN
Super Bugs 14 MIN
Super realists 15 MIN
Tempera as Watercolor 15 MIN
Textile Art 15 MIN
Young at Art - Introduction 14 MIN
Dist - AITECH

Young at heart 28 MIN
VHS / U-matic / 16mm
Color (H G)
$295.00, $345.00, $545.00 purchase, $65.00 rental; $245.00 purchase, $55.00 rental
Tells the story of a widow and widower, both artists, who meet in their 80s, court and marry. Reaffirms that love and romance can happen at any age for the clear - eyed and open - hearted.
Health and Safety; Literature and Drama; Religion and Philosophy; Sociology
Dist - NDIM **Prod** - MARXS 1987
TNF

The Young at heart comedians 77 MIN
VHS
Color (G)
$29.95 purchase _ #S02107
Features George Gobel, Jackie Vernon, Norm Crosby, Henny Youngman, Jackie Gayle, Carl Ballantine, and Shelley Berman in a tribute to America's stand - up comics. Hosted by David Brenner.
Fine Arts; Literature and Drama
Dist - UILL

Young audiences - muralist 30 MIN
U-matic / VHS
Kaleidoscope series
Color
Fine Arts
Dist - SCCOE **Prod** - KTEHTV

The Young Bullfighters 45 MIN
16mm
Color
Presents the story of two young men, one Mexican and one American, who train to become toreadors. Shows how the bulls are raised and selected and also other people involved in the bullfights.
Physical Education and Recreation; Social Science; Sociology
Dist - FILCOM **Prod** - SCORPO 1970

Young Caesar 11 MIN
16mm
B&W (J H)
A Latin classic for classroom use.
Foreign Language; History - World; Literature and Drama
Dist - FCE **Prod** - FCE

The Young Champions 30 MIN
16mm / U-matic / VHS
Color (FRENCH JAPANESE SPANISH)
LC 80-701534
Depicts the World Youth Soccer Championships held in Tokyo, Japan.
Physical Education and Recreation
Dist - AMEDFL **Prod** - COCA 1980

Young Chemists - in Transition 28 MIN
16mm
Color (C)
LC 79-701627
Presents young industrial chemists offering their views on the transition from the academic to the industrial community, while company recruiters describe what they look for in young chemists. Offers suggestions about job hunting in industrial fields.
Science
Dist - AMCHEM **Prod** - AMCHEM 1979

A Young Child is 30 MIN
16mm
Color (A)
LC 83-700678
Shows infant and pre - school children in the process of learning.
Education; Psychology
Dist - LAWREN **Prod** - EDIMP 1983

The Young child - vol 1 52 MIN
VHS / 16mm
Art of parenting video series
Color (G)
$69.95 purchase
Offers tips, suggestions and solutions to parenting problems. Focuses on infants to five - year - olds. Considers bedtime conflicts, controlling adult anger, the whining child, TV, sibling rivalry, toilet training, and more. Part of a three - part series on the art of parenting which features Evelyn Peterson, family life education expert.
Social Science; Sociology
Dist - PROSOR

Young Children in Brief Separation Series
John, 17 Months - 9 Days in a Residential Nursery 45 MIN
Kate, a Two Year Old in Foster Care 33 MIN
Dist - NYU

Young Children in Brief Separation Series
Jane - Aged 17 Months in Fostercare for 10 Days 37 MIN
Thomas - aged two years, four months, in foster care for 10 days 38 MIN
Dist - NYU
PSU

Young children in brief separation series
John - aged 17 months, in a residental nursery for 9 days 45 MIN
Kate - aged 2 years, 5 months, in foster care for 27 days 33 MIN
Lucy - aged 21 months, in foster care for 19 days 31 MIN
Dist - PSU

Young Children on the Kibbutz 26 MIN
16mm
Exploring Childhood Series
B&W
LC 73-702071
Describes the life of four - year - old children on an Israeli kibbutz. Shows how they are trained in groups and live in quarters separated from their parents.
Agriculture; Geography - World; Sociology
Dist - EDC **Prod** - EDC 1973

Young Children with Special Needs 14 MIN
16mm
Exceptional Learners Series
Color (T S)

LC 79-700718
Presents a look at the importance of early intervention, showing preschoolers in home - and center - based programs for handicapped children.
Education; Psychology
Dist - MERILC **Prod** - MERILC 1978

Young Children with Special Needs - Conceptual Development 30 MIN
U-matic
Color
LC 79-706215
Deals with the importance of sequential instruction and methods used to facilitate concept development in the developmentally disabled child.
Education; Psychology
Dist - MERILC **Prod** - VACOMU 1978

Young children with special needs - No 01 - introduction 30 MIN
U-matic
Color
LC 79-706207
Deals with the identification of young children with developmental disabilities.
Education; Psychology
Dist - MERILC **Prod** - VACOMU 1978

Young children with special needs - No 02 - children at high risk 30 MIN
U-matic
Color
LC 79-706208
Deals with the child with developmental disabilities, including the rationale for early identification and intervention, procedures for securing services and the child's right to an education.
Education; Psychology
Dist - MERILC **Prod** - VACOMU 1978

Young children with special needs - No 03 - who can help 30 MIN
U-matic
Color
Introduces the types of professionals who deal with children with developmental disabilities, including pediatricians, nurses, physical and occupational therapists, language pathologists, psychologists, psychiatrists, social workers and child development specialists.
Education; Psychology
Dist - MERILC **Prod** - VACOMU 1978

Young children with special needs - No 04 - assessment, diagnosis, remediation 30 MIN
U-matic
Color
LC 79-706210
Discusses the use of developmental scales and the information provided by ancillary professionals to determine the educational requirements of the child with developmental disabilities.
Education; Psychology
Dist - MERILC **Prod** - VACOMU 1978

Young children with special needs - No 05 - community resources 30 MIN
U-matic
Color
LC 79-706211
Describes the home as the first school for children with developmental disabilities and surveys possible and existing facilities, telling how facilities can be improved to provide quality services for these children.
Psychology
Dist - MERILC **Prod** - VACOMU 1978

Young children with special needs - No 06 - how do children learn 30 MIN
U-matic
Color
LC 79-706212
Deals with the ways in which all children acquire knowledge, skills and attitudes and examines barriers to learning, effects of early learning and readiness for learning.
Psychology
Dist - MERILC **Prod** - VACOMU 1978

Young children with special needs - No 07 - motor skills 30 MIN
U-matic
Color
LC 79-706213
Focuses on both gross and fine motor skills and ways of working with the developmentally disabled child to facilitate development in these areas.
Education; Psychology
Dist - MERILC **Prod** - VACOMU 1978

Young children with special needs - No 08 - language and verbal skills 30 MIN
U-matic
Color
LC 79-706214
Distinguishes between receptive and expressive language in the developmentally disabled child. Focuses on inner language and aspects of nonverbal language.
Psychology
Dist - MERILC **Prod** - VACOMU 1978

Young children with special needs - No 10 - self - help skills 30 MIN
U-matic
Color
LC 79-706216
Deals with self - help skills for the developmentally disabled child, including self - feedings, dressing and toilet training. Demonstrates homemade aids for facilitating self - feeding.
Education; Home Economics; Psychology
Dist - MERILC **Prod** - VACOMU 1978

Young children with special needs - social and emotional development - No 11 30 MIN
U-matic
Color (PRO)
LC 79-706217
Deals with the development of the mental health of the developmentally disabled child. Covers differences in techniques needed to encourage growth in various settings such as home, foster home, institution.
Education; Guidance and Counseling; Psychology; Sociology
Dist - MERILC **Prod** - MERILC 1978

Young children with special needs - No 12 - child's play 30 MIN
U-matic
Color
LC 79-706219
Deals with the relationship between play and development for the developmentally disabled child and focuses on various attitudinal issues.
Education; Psychology
Dist - MERILC **Prod** - VACOMU 1978

Young children with special needs - No 13 30 MIN
U-matic / VHS
Color (PRO)
LC 79-706220
Deals with a variety of considerations with a developmentally disabled child, including nutrition and hygiene, the child's role in the family and concern for the siblings and other family members. Points out differences in the family life of the institutionalized child.
Education; Guidance and Counseling; Psychology; Sociology
Dist - MERILC **Prod** - VACOMU 1978

Young children with special needs - No 14 - health, safety, nutrition 30 MIN
U-matic
Color
LC 79-706221
Deals with practices that are appropriate in the health care and safety of all young children but especially important for handicapped children because of their special needs.
Home Economics
Dist - MERILC **Prod** - VACOMU 1978

Young children with special needs - No 15 - review 30 MIN
U-matic
Color
LC 79-706222
Reviews and summarizes the Young Children With Special Needs programs dealing with the developmentally disabled child.
Education; Psychology
Dist - MERILC **Prod** - VACOMU 1978

Young children's reactions to hospitalization 14 MIN
VHS / U-matic
Color (PRO)
$200.00 purchase, $60.00 rental _ #4257S, #4257V
Interviews parents and children to portray how a hospitalized child can change behaviorally because of hospitalization - decline in toilet skills, demanding behavior, withdrawal. Urges parents to be candid with their children about when they must leave and when they will return, as separation is the most difficult aspect of hospitalization for children.
Health and Safety; Psychology; Sociology
Dist - AJN **Prod** - PACKRH 1985

The Young Conqueror 60 MIN
VHS / U-matic
Search for Alexander the Great Series Pt 2
Color (C A)
LC 82-707381
Follows Alexander's ascendancy to the throne after his father's assassination. Shows that against formidable obstacles, the young conqueror emerges victorious in his military campaign and begins his lifelong quest to conquer the world.
Biography; History - World
Dist - TIMLIF **Prod** - TIMLIF 1981

Young Dillinger 102 MIN
16mm
B&W (H C A)
Focuses on John Dillinger's younger years and on the influences at work which led him into a life of crime.
Fine Arts; Sociology
Dist - CINEWO **Prod** - CINEWO 1965

Young Dr Freud 98 MIN
U-matic / VHS / 16mm
Color (H C A)
LC 77-701972
Re - creates Sigmund Freud's childhood, youth, school years and medical school years. Dramatizes his associations with Breuer, Bruke, Meynert and Charcot, as well as his seminal findings which led to the development of psychoanalysis. First released under the title Der Junge Freud.
Biography; Health and Safety; History - World; Psychology
Dist - FOTH **Prod** - ATASGN 1977

Young entrepreneurs 15 MIN
VHS
Skills - work - related themes series
Color (H C)
$49.00 purchase, $15.00 rental _ #316635; LC 91-712583
Features a variety of young entrepreneurs who discuss the advantages and disadvantages of running your own business and the personality traits, skills and experience that can increase chances for success. Part of a series created to complement the Skills - Occupational Programs series, focusing on ways to develop these skills and demonstrate their effectiveness in the workplace. Includes teacher's guide with reproducible worksheets.
Business and Economics; Guidance and Counseling; Psychology
Dist - TVOTAR **Prod** - TVOTAR 1990

Young explorers' journey to Bible times music video 30 MIN
VHS
Color (K P R)
$14.99 purchase _ #SPCN 85116.00434
Presents seven Bible Times songs perfomed by host Barry McGuire on a visit to a Bible Times village. Includes demonstrations of musical steps and hand motions by merchants, children and puppets.
Fine Arts; Religion and Philosophy
Dist - GOSPEL **Prod** - GOSPEL

Young Fathers - Teenage Love 15 MIN
VHS
Color (C A)
$75.00 purchase, $35.00 rental
Addresses teen fatherhood. Focuses on the feelings and changed conditions experienced by young men.
Health and Safety; Sociology
Dist - CORNRS **Prod** - EDCC 1985

Young Fingers on a Typewriter - a New Concept in Learning 36 MIN
U-matic / VHS / 16mm
B&W
LC 76-702985
Demonstrates a typewriter's ability to develop general learning processes. Shows how beginning typewriter activities are turned into exercises for developing language skills of spelling, reading and writing as well as powers of concentration, memory and visual imagery.
Education; Psychology
Dist - UCEMC **Prod** - PETITG 1975

Young Goodman Brown 30 MIN
16mm / U-matic / VHS
Color (H C A)
LC 73-701123
Probes the heart and captures the complexities and ambiguities in Hawthorne's story of man's involvement with hidden evil.
Literature and Drama
Dist - PFP **Prod** - PFP 1973

Young hearts - what you must know about cholesterol 30 MIN
VHS
Color (J H C)

$189.00 purchase _ #673 - SK
Presents the facts about cholesterol, revealing that many children and adolescents are at risk for high cholesterol levels. Suggests that cholesterol levels are based not only upon diet, but other lifestyle factors as well. Demonstrates how to determine one's cholesterol levels, and how to make changes in one's lifestyle. Includes teacher's guide.
Health and Safety; Psychology; Science - Natural; Social Science
Dist - SUNCOM **Prod** - HRMC
AIMS

Young Japanese women 29 MIN
VHS / U-matic
Are you listening series
Color (H C A) (JAPANESE)
LC 84-706131
Shows Japanese women in their 20s and 30s discussing issues of concern to them, such as marriage, careers, children and the uniquely Japanese concept of daughter - in - law.
Geography - World; History - World
Dist - STURTM **Prod** - STURTM 1983

The Young Job Seekers 60 MIN
VHS / U-matic / BETA
Young Job Seekers Series
Color; Stereo (H)
Deals with steps to follow to a successful job interview. Book available to work with the video.
Guidance and Counseling; Psychology
Dist - SEVDIM **Prod** - SEVDIM 1984

Young job seekers series
Answering questions 10 MIN
Improving Performance 10 MIN
Preparation 10 MIN
Presentation 10 MIN
Showing initiative 10 MIN
The Young Job Seekers 60 MIN
Your first job interview 10 MIN
Dist - SEVDIM

The Young Lady and the Cellist - La Demoiselle Et La Violoncelliste 10 MIN
16mm / U-matic / VHS
Color (J H C)
LC 77-701540
Presents an animated tale about a musician who, inspired by the sight of the sea, improvises a concerto on his cello, only to provoke a wild storm which sweeps away a lovely girl.
Fine Arts; Literature and Drama
Dist - TEXFLM **Prod** - LESFG 1977

Young Life - a Commitment 28 MIN
16mm
Color
LC 73-702406
Shows how a nonsectarian Christian organization, Young Life, communicates and carries on its work with youth.
Guidance and Counseling; Religion and Philosophy; Social Science; Sociology
Dist - YLC **Prod** - YLC 1973

The Young Lion 60 MIN
U-matic / VHS
Search for Alexander the Great Series Pt 1
Color (C A)
LC 82-707380
Introduces Alexander the Great as a young boy when he begins his Spartan training. Shows him learning the power of knowledge from Aristotle and the power of the lance from his father, King Philip.
Biography; History - World
Dist - TIMLIF **Prod** - TIMLIF 1981

The Young lions 167 MIN
16mm
Color (G)
$150.00 rental
Adapts Irwin Shaw's big novel of World War II. Stars Marlon Brando, Montgomery Clift, Dean Martin, Maximilian Schell, Hope Lange, Mai Britt. Directed by Edward Dmytryk.
Fine Arts; History - United States
Dist - NCJEWF

Young Man and Death 16 MIN
16mm
Color (H C A)
LC 76-701273
Dramatizes in dance the story of a young man's encounter with death.
Fine Arts; Sociology
Dist - FI **Prod** - MACM 1976

Young Man with a Future 8 MIN
U-matic / VHS / 16mm
Color (J)
LC 72-703180
Explains that the young man with a future seems invincible. Shows how he moves through life with the force of a great engine, devouring his mother, throttling his enemies, conquering his artistic and philosophical weaknesses and crushing his debilitating attraction toward women. Points out that finally a giant foot comes down out of the sky and crushes him.
Fine Arts; Guidance and Counseling; Psychology; Sociology
Dist - TEXFLM **Prod** - FI 1972

Young Marriage - When's the Big Day 14 MIN
U-matic / VHS / 16mm
Conflict and Awareness Series
Color (I J H)
Portrays a young couple who, just prior to their marriage, visit old friends whose marriage is not going well. Probes why so many marriages fail, what the chances for success are and men's and women's different expectations from marriage.
Guidance and Counseling; Sociology
Dist - CRMP **Prod** - CRMP 1974

Young Musical Artists Series
Anne elgar - soprano 29 MIN
Arthur Thompson - Baritone 29 MIN
Blanca Uribe - Pianist 29 MIN
Jeffry and Ronald Marlowe - Duo - Pianists 29 MIN
Jessy Norman - Soprano 29 MIN
Joseph Kalichstein - Pianist 29 MIN
Nerine Barrett - Pianist 29 MIN
New York Trio Da Camera 29 MIN
Nicolai Neilsen - Guitarist 29 MIN
Ralph Votapek - Pianist 29 MIN
Trio - Easley Blackwood 29 MIN
Walter Verkehr - Violinist and David Renner - Pianist 29 MIN
William Cochran - Tenor 29 MIN
Dist - PBS

The Young one 96 MIN
16mm
Films of Luis Bunuel series
B&W (G)
$200.00 rental
Portrays a black musician fleeing from the law who is drawn into a dangerous web of intrigue on an island preserve. Directed by Luis Bunuel.
Fine Arts; Literature and Drama
Dist - KINOIC **Prod** - IFEX 1961

Young People Can do Anything 16 MIN
U-matic / VHS / 16mm
Color
LC 74-700486
Shows how two young people helped raise money for the establishment of a performing arts center for talented Black students as well as talented White students. Stimulates discussion about images of minority groups, career guidance, problems of the disadvantaged and schools.
Sociology
Dist - AMEDFL **Prod** - AMEDFL 1973

Young people in A A 27 MIN
VHS
Color (G)
$15.00 purchase _ #2900
Shows A A members telling their stories and what life was like when they were drinking. Reveals how A A works and how it changes the lives of the chemically dependent. Demonstrates that addiction cuts across racial, cultural, regional and socio - economic barriers and shows how to find a local A A group.
Guidance and Counseling; Health and Safety; Psychology; Sociology
Dist - HAZELB **Prod** - HAZELB

Young People's Concert Series
Concerto for Orchestra, Pt 1 - the Music of Bela Bartok 25 MIN
Concerto for Orchestra, Pt 2 - the Music of Bela Bartok 25 MIN
A Copland celebration - Pt 1 29 MIN
A Copland celebration - Pt 2 29 MIN
Dist - PHENIX

Young People's Concerts Series
What is American Music 54 MIN
What is American Music, Pt 1 27 MIN
What is American Music, Pt 2 27 MIN
Dist - MGHT

Young people's special series
Goodbye carnival girl 24 MIN
Dist - MULTPP

Young people's specials series
My mother, the witch 24 MIN
Nightmare - the immigration of Joachim and Rachael 24 MIN
Zerk the jerk 24 MIN
Dist - FOTH

Young people's specials series
I'm sooo ugly 24 MIN
Dist - FOTH
MULTPP

Young people's specials series
The Achievers 50 MIN
All about dogs 24 MIN
The Americanization of elias 24 MIN
Andrew 24 MIN
Atomic legs 24 MIN
The Boy who couldn't lose 24 MIN
Cajun cousins 24 MIN
The Championship 24 MIN
The Crime 24 MIN
The Edison adventures 24 MIN
The Fisherman's son 24 MIN
Four children 50 MIN
Goin' along 24 MIN
Jenny and me 24 MIN
Joshua's confusion 24 MIN
Just another stupid kid 24 MIN
The Land, the sea, the children there 24 MIN
The Little match girl 24 MIN
Melinda's blind 24 MIN
My father, my brother, and me 24 MIN
My special world 24 MIN
Navajo moon 24 MIN
Nightmare - the immigration of Joachim and Rachael 24 MIN
Palm trees and icebergs 24 MIN
Pilgrim journey 24 MIN
PR 24 MIN
The Rebel slave 24 MIN
Rodeo girl 24 MIN
Sacajawea 24 MIN
The Sellin' of Jamie Thomas, Pt 1 24 MIN
The Sellin' of Jamie Thomas, Pt 2 24 MIN
The Skater 24 MIN
Suzy's war 24 MIN
Tinseltown and the Big Apple 24 MIN
The Trouble with Mother 24 MIN
The Undersea adventures of Pickle and Bill 24 MIN
Valley Forge - the young spy 24 MIN
Westward wagons 24 MIN
Who spooked Rodney? 24 MIN
Winners 24 MIN
The Year of the dragon 24 MIN
Dist - MULTPP

The Young Philadelphians 136 MIN
U-matic / VHS / 16mm
B&W (H C A)
Stars Paul Newman in the story of a man's career as a Philadelphia main line lawyer.
Literature and Drama; Sociology
Dist - FI **Prod** - WB 1959

Young Puppeteers of South Vietnam 20 MIN
16mm
B&W
Explains how teenagers in the NLF liberated areas of Vietnam, armed with puppets made from scraps of war material, perform puppet plays for the local children while U S planes 'search and destroy.' Shows a view of the war even more powerful than images of atrocities.
Civics and Political Systems; Fine Arts; Sociology
Dist - CANWRL **Prod** - CANWRL

Young red beasts - France - Part 22 8 MIN
VHS
Natures kingdom series
Color (P I J)
$125.00 purchase
Shows that wild boar go from life in the litter to solitary adulthood. Reveals that cute little piglets grow into foul - tempered and ugly adults who live for about 15 years and show their rivals no mercy. Part of a 26 - part series on animals showing the habitats and traits of various species.
Geography - World; Science - Natural
Dist - LANDMK **Prod** - LANDMK 1992

Young Sam Gompers 30 MIN
16mm
B&W
Presents the early life of Samuel Gompers. Tells of his job as a cigar maker, his role in the cigar makers union and his participation in the American Federation of Labor. (Kinescope).
Biography; Religion and Philosophy
Dist - NAAJS **Prod** - JTS 1961

The Young Self - made Millionaire 30 MIN
VHS / 16mm
(PRO G)
$89.95 purchase _ #DGP47
Features Lenny Mattioli discussing the hows, whys, and costs of building his American TV empire.
Business and Economics
Dist - RMIBHF **Prod** - RMIBHF

Young, Single and Pregnant 18 MIN
U-matic / VHS / 16mm
Color (J H C)
LC 73-703141
Focuses on the lives of four girls who became pregnant when they were teenagers. Discusses each girl's reasons for choosing the life she had, whether abortion, marriage or single parenthood. Describes each girl's relationship with her boyfriend in the context of her decision.
Guidance and Counseling; Science - Natural; Sociology
Dist - PEREN **Prod** - SCHL 1973

Young, Single and Pregnant - a New Perspective
VHS / 35mm strip
$209.00 purchase _ #IE5784, $209.00 purchase _ #IE6784V
Uses case studies to illustrate the multitude of problems and questions encountered with any teenage sexual activity or pregnancy. Discusses and describes birth control methods. Points out that two to three million teenagers become pregnant mothers or unwed fathers every year.
Health and Safety; Psychology; Sociology
Dist - CAREER **Prod** - CAREER

Young, Single and Pregnant - a New Perspective 48 MIN
U-matic / VHS
Color (J H C)
LC 81-706756
Presents several case histories which illustrate common problems and questions that attend any teenage pregnancy. Describes reliable birth control methods, examines the complex decisions that must be made by the mother and father - to - be, and offers reliable sources of assistance and guidance for pregnant teenagers.
Health and Safety; Sociology
Dist - GA **Prod** - GA 1982

Young Torless 85 MIN
16mm
B&W
Displays the violence and confused sensuality of adolescence under a repressive educational system. Explores the question of individual guilt and the possible roots of totalitarianism.
Fine Arts
Dist - NYFLMS **Prod** - UNKNWN 1966

Young Uruguay 17 MIN
16mm
B&W
LC FIE52-716
Portrays the young people of Uruguay at home, play and school. Emphasizes progressive steps being made in education. Includes scenes of primary schools, special classes for children from families whose histories show tuberculosis, rural schools, athletics in secondary schools and music education.
Fine Arts; Geography - World; Health and Safety; History - World; Physical Education and Recreation; Social Science
Dist - USOIAA **Prod** - UWF 1943

The Young Veterans Program 24 MIN
U-matic / VHS
Color (PRO)
LC 82-706315
Describes a specialized in - patient psychiatric unit for Vietnam veterans, established at the VAMC, Northport, NY, in 1975.
Guidance and Counseling; Psychology
Dist - USNAC **Prod** - VAMCNY 1982

Young Vietnam 28 MIN
VHS
Color (G)
$250.00 purchase, $50.00 rental
Takes an inside look at the last generation of Vietnamese to remember the horrors of the Vietnam War and the first to hope for an end to the country's isolation by increasing trade and communication with the West. Features interviews with students.
Fine Arts; History - World; Sociology
Dist - CNEMAG

Young viewer series 65 MIN
BETA / VHS / U-matic / 16mm
Young viewers series
Color (K P)
$1102.50, $306.00 purchase _ #C50765, #C51501
Presents a five - part series which introduces concepts essential to academic and social life. Includes the titles Directions - Up, Down, All Around, I Can Make Friends, I Can Take Care of Myself, Shapes, Senses - How We Know.
Mathematics; Psychology; Science - Natural
Dist - NGS **Prod** - NGS 1992

Young viewers series

Directions - up, down, all around	15 MIN
I can make friends	15 MIN
I can take care of myself	15 MIN
Senses - how we know	15 MIN
Shapes	15 MIN
Young viewer series	65 MIN

Dist - NGS

The Young Vote - Power, Politics and Participation 15 MIN
U-matic / VHS / 16mm
Color (J H C)
LC 72-701151
Raises questions about attitudes and values relating to voting, politics and the democratic process itself. Examines disillusionment, apathy, commitment, involvement and idealism.
Civics and Political Systems; Social Science
Dist - PHENIX **Prod** - PHENIX 1972

Young Women in Sports 16 MIN
16mm / U-matic / VHS
Color (I)
LC 74-703829
Examines the attitudes of four young women athletes about strength, competition and themselves as women and as athletes.
Physical Education and Recreation; Sociology
Dist - PHENIX **Prod** - SILSHA 1974

Young Wonders, Inc 29 MIN
VHS / U-matic
Color
Shows 35 students from a Manhattan public school who formed an opera company, the Young Wonders Inc, and then wrote, produced and performed their own opera with the help of the Metropolitan Opera Guild. Shows the opera performance.
Fine Arts
Dist - MOG **Prod** - MOG 1983

Young writer's workshop series

Writing Skills - Kindergarten Starting Points	15 MIN
Writing Skills - Reluctant Writers	15 MIN
Writing Skills - the Stages of Writing	15 MIN
Writing Skills - the Writing Process	15 MIN
Writing Skills - Young Authors	15 MIN
Writing skills - young editors	15 MIN
Writing skills - young poets	15 MIN

Dist - BCNFL

Younger Brother 19 MIN
16mm
Color (J H A)
Presents the story of Jiro, one of the many lost and puzzled second sons in modern Japan, and the struggle he has to make a place for himself and to find a faith to replace the old order.
Geography - World; Sociology
Dist - YALEDV **Prod** - YALEDV

The Younger Romantics 28 MIN
U-matic / VHS
Survey of English Verse Series
Color (C)
$249.00, $149.00 purchase _ #AD - 1303
Focuses on Shelley, Keats, and peripherally on Byron and Wordsworth. Considers the poetic conceit of rebel, martyr and impractical dreamer.
Fine Arts; Geography - World; Literature and Drama
Dist - FOTH **Prod** - FOTH

Your aching back 30 MIN
VHS
Color (G A)
$29.95 purchase _ #MAP100V
Defines the most common causes of muscular lower back pain. Explains why back pain occurs and why most treatment programs for it fail. Teaches exercises to prevent back pain from happening in the first place.
Health and Safety; Physical Education and Recreation
Dist - CAMV

Your active body - bones and movement 10 MIN
VHS
Your active body series
Color; PAL (H)
Examines human bones within the context of other vertebrates. Shows how the human skeleton allows upright posture and a wide range of movement. Uses live - action, animation and X - rays to illustrate how bones are held together by ligaments, how different kinds of joints function and how bones are cushioned from shock. Demonstrates how bones heal and the positive effect of gravity upon bone strength. Part of a series on the human body encouraging a self - awareness of the sensitivities of the body and its reactions to physical demands.
Science - Natural
Dist - VIEWTH

Your active body - breathing and respiration 10 MIN
VHS
Your active body series
Color; PAL (H)
Uses animation and X - ray motion pictures to illustrate the process that enables the body to release energy from nutrients through breathing and respiration. Follows the breathing process, when oxygen is brought into the lungs, and shows the respiration phase where oxygen is transferred into the blood and made available to living cells. Part of a series on the human body encouraging a self - awareness of the sensitivities of the body and its reactions to physical demands.
Science - Natural
Dist - VIEWTH

Your active body - digestion and absorption 10 MIN
VHS
Your active body series
Color; PAL (H)
Shows how the body responds to the sight and smell of food by stimulating appetite. Follows the digestive process from the initial point of ingestion to the entry of nutrients into the cells. Examines the role of digestive juices, the small intestine, capillaries and blood, and the importance of supplying cells with the proper nutrients. Part of a series on the human body encouraging a self - awareness of the sensitivities of the body and its reactions to physical demands.
Science - Natural
Dist - VIEWTH

Your active body - heart and circulation 10 MIN
VHS
Your active body series
Color; PAL (H)
Shows that for the human body to remain alive and active, its cells have to be supplied with nutrients and oxygen, and waste products must be carried away. Demonstrates how the process is accomplished by the blood and the heart which keeps blood traveling through two complete circuits. Uses animation and observations of a stress test to illustrate pulse and blood pressure. Visits a hematology lab to relate blood tests to blood composition and show the relationship between gravity and blood flow through astronauts in orbit. Part of a series on the human body encouraging a self - awareness of the sensitivities of the body and its reactions to physical demands.
Science - Natural
Dist - VIEWTH

Your active body - muscles and energy 10 MIN
VHS
Your active body series
Color; PAL (H)
Demonstrates the ability of muscles to move large and small body parts. Introduces the role and function of muscles, the relationship between muscles and energy and the dynamics of exercises that improve muscle strength, flexibility, coordination and endurance. Observes a sleep lab to demonstrate how voluntary muscles relax and how involuntary muscles maintain breathing and heartbeat. Part of a series on the human body encouraging a self - awareness of the sensitivities of the body and its reactions to physical demands.
Physical Education and Recreation; Science - Natural
Dist - VIEWTH

Your active body series

Your active body - bones and movement	10 MIN
Your active body - breathing and respiration	10 MIN
Your active body - digestion and absorption	10 MIN
Your active body - heart and circulation	10 MIN
Your active body - muscles and energy	10 MIN

Dist - VIEWTH

Your Air Force 18 MIN
16mm
Color
LC 74-706345
Presents a panorama of the major Air Force commands and their contributions to the USAF team.
Civics and Political Systems; Social Science
Dist - USNAC **Prod** - USAF 1966

Your Air Weather Service 30 MIN
16mm
Color
LC 74-706346
Pictures the operation of Air Weather Service (AWS). Portrays the AWS control center at SAC command post where worldwide weather conditions are gathered, computer - processed and transmitted to subordinate weather units.
Science - Physical; Sociology
Dist - USNAC **Prod** - USDD 1962

Your and Your Co - Workers 11 MIN
VHS
$89.95 purchase _ #005 - 753
Emphasizes the importance of getting and keeping the support and good will of fellow employees.
Business and Economics; Guidance and Counseling
Dist - CAREER **Prod** - CAREER

Your appearance after a mastectomy 10 MIN
U-matic / VHS
Color
Explains and provides information on how a mastectomy patient looks as attractive after her surgery as she did before. Shows clothing that is suitable in the hospital and during early recovery, and describes various breast prostheses. Emphasizes that after recovery the woman can still dress appropriately for any activity.
Health and Safety; Physical Education and Recreation; Science; Science - Natural
Dist - MEDCOM **Prod** - MEDCOM

Your appearance I - the interview
VHS
Career process series
Color (H A)
$84.95 purchase _ #ES1130V
Focuses on the importance of personal appearance in a job interview - proper attire, personal cleanliness, and good grooming.
Psychology
Dist - CAMV

Your Appearance I - the Inverview 15 MIN
VHS
(H C)
$84.95 _ CA125
Discusses the importance of one's appearance when being interviewed for a job.
Education; Guidance and Counseling
Dist - AAVIM **Prod** - AAVIM 1989

Your appearance II - on the job
VHS
Career process series
Color (H A)
$84.95 purchase _ #ES1140V
Stresses the importance of maintaining personal appearance on the job. Suggests that neat appearance and a clean work area are just as important as ability in determining retention and promotion.
Home Economics; Psychology
Dist - CAMV

Your Appearance II - on the Job 15 MIN
VHS
(H C)
$84.95 _ CA126
Shows how appearance influences retention and promotion.
Education
Dist - AAVIM **Prod** - AAVIM 1989

Your Appearance on the Interview 11 MIN
U-matic / VHS
(H C)
$98 _ #EA5V
Presents basic tips that are useful in presenting oneself during an interview.
Business and Economics
Dist - JISTW **Prod** - JISTW

Your Appearance on the Job 12 MIN
U-matic / VHS
(H C A)
$98 _ #EA3V
Uses dramatized job situations and narration to stress the relevance of appearance to job success.
Business and Economics; Education
Dist - JISTW **Prod** - JISTW

Your appearance on the job 15 MIN
VHS / 35mm strip
$43.50 purchase _ #XY854 for filmstrip, $84.95 purchase _ #XY804 for
Emphasizes that many times supervisors and fellow workers base their impressions strictly on appearance. Gives many on the job situations in which appearance has an important effect on job retention and promotion.
Business and Economics; Guidance and Counseling
Dist - CAREER **Prod** - CAREER

Your Appearance - the Interview 15 MIN
VHS / 35mm strip
$43.50 purchase _ #XY853 for film, $84.95 for VHS
Points out how an applicant's appearance determines their chances for employment. Discusses the importance of good grooming, proper dress and cleanliness.
Business and Economics; Guidance and Counseling
Dist - CAREER **Prod** - CAREER

Your Apple Computer - a User's Guide
VHS / U-matic
Color
Clarifies important Apple functions and hardware including keyboards, CRTs, disk drives, printers and modems. Shows how the disk operating system works.
Mathematics
Dist - GA **Prod** - GA

Your Aptitudes - Related to Learning Job Skills
VHS
Color
$89.00 purchase _ #012 - 621; $89.00 purchase _ #3254
Uses self - assessment booklets and videos to teach students the value of early career planning. Helps evaluate interests, temperament, and abilities, and apply them to course selection and career decisions. Individualized Career Exploration Booklets - package of 10 - can be ordered for $13.95 using order #012 - 664.
Guidance and Counseling
Dist - CAREER MERIDN **Prod** - CAREER MERIDN 1988

Your Aptitudes - Related to Learning Job Skills
U-matic / VHS
CEPP Video Series
(J H C A)
$89.00 _ #MG3254V
Uses live action to introduce the viewer to the major issues regarding job skills in relation to his aptitudes.
Business and Economics; Guidance and Counseling
Dist - CAMV **Prod** - CAMV

Your are There Series
Treason of Benedict Arnold 22 MIN
Dist - PHENIX

Your army reports - No 12 29 MIN
16mm
Big picture series
Color
LC 74-706347
Shows General Harold K Johnson, Army Chief of Staff, speaking at the annual convention of the Association of the United States Army. Shows Vietnamese civilians working with the United States Army and describes the work of the Army combat photographer.
Civics and Political Systems; History - United States; History - World; Industrial and Technical Education; Sociology
Dist - USNAC **Prod** - USA 1967

Your army reports - No 13 29 MIN
16mm
Big picture series
Color
LC 74-706348
Shows General Harold K Johnson, Army Chief of Staff, decorating Warrant Officer Jerome R Daley for gallantry in action. Pictures Army combat photographers moving forward with the first Cavalry Division and Vietnamese troops during an amphibious landing and search for Viet Cong. Depicts the mission of harbor pilots in the port of Qui Nhon.
Civics and Political Systems; History - United States; History - World; Sociology
Dist - USNAC **Prod** - USA 1967

Your army reports - No 14 29 MIN
16mm
Big picture series
Color
LC 74-706349
Features training activities of the 205th Infantry Brigade of the U S Army Reserve as it prepares to meet its mission in defense of America.
Civics and Political Systems; History - United States; History - World; Sociology
Dist - USNAC **Prod** - USA 1967

Your Attitude - Your Job
VHS
Job Skills Series
(H C)
$59.00 _ CA119
Shows how job attitude and the willingness to help are important in job progress and development.
Business and Economics
Dist - AAVIM **Prod** - AAVIM 1989

Your Baby 30 MIN
VHS
(H C A)
$29.95 purchase _ #FV100V
Presents a series of exercises that can be used to promote natural parent child bonding and infant development.
Health and Safety; Home Economics; Psychology; Sociology
Dist - CAMV **Prod** - CAMV

Your baby - a video guide to care and understanding 77 MIN
VHS
Color (G)
$24.95 purchase _ #PA03
Demonstrates techniques of everyday care, including - meeting your baby; feeding; comforting; cleanliness; bringing your baby home to the family; sleep; diapers; health; and development. With Dr Penelope Leach.
Home Economics; Sociology
Dist - SVIP

Your baby - an infant wellness program 30 MIN
VHS
Color (G)
$19.95 purchase _ #KAR508
Informs on positive reinforcement of a child's motor capability and psychological well - being. Features Dr Marvin I Clein.
Health and Safety; Physical Education and Recreation; Psychology; Sociology
Dist - CADESF **Prod** - CADESF

Your baby - video guide to care and understanding 75 MIN
VHS
Color (G)
$39.95 purchase _ #SPC100V
Features child development expert Penelop Leach who demonstrates every day baby care techniques. Discusses Meeting Your Baby; Sleep - Yours and Your Baby's; Crying and Comforting; Diapering; Keeping Your Baby Healthy; Your Baby's Development.
Health and Safety; Sociology
Dist - CAMV

Your baby well born - steps to a healthy pregnancy 10 MIN
U-matic / VHS
Color (H C A)
Identifies maternal behaviors and characteristics known to increase the risk of low birth rate, neurological abnormality and/or perinatal death. Gives recommendations for reducing risks.
Health and Safety; Home Economics
Dist - UARIZ **Prod** - UARIZ

Your Baby with a Congenital Heart Defect 29 MIN
U-matic / VHS
Color (A)
Designed for parents of infants with congenital heart defects. Shows families relating their feelings and experiences resulting from caring for their infants with a heart defect.
Health and Safety; Science - Natural
Dist - UMICHM **Prod** - UMICHM 1981

Your baby's first days 21 MIN
U-matic / VHS
Color
Uses close - ups of various newborn infants to explain normal appearance, behavior and development. Presents information on caring for both the physical and emotional needs of new infants.
Health and Safety; Home Economics
Dist - MIFE POLYMR **Prod** - MIFE POLYMR 1980

Your baby's first six months 50 MIN
VHS
Growth and development of your new baby series
Color (G)
$29.95 purchase _ #COV011V-K
Presents information for new parents about approaches to the daily situations they will encounter. Includes how to get to know the baby's body; breastfeeding; engorgement of the breasts; expressing milk; bottle feeding; the transition of weaning; how and when to start feeding solid food; changing diapers; keeping the baby clean; family outings; discovering the baby's temperament; crying; and games to play with a new baby. Part of a three-part series.
Health and Safety; Social Science; Sociology
Dist - CAMV

Your baby's first six months 59 MIN
VHS
Color (H C A PRO)

$29.95 purchase
Presents three - parts on a baby's first six months and ensuring normal development. Considers the baby's development at two, four, and six - month stages. Covers topics including baby formulas. sleep patterns, feeding, safety, and medical care.
Health and Safety; Psychology
Dist - UARIZ **Prod** - UARIZ

Your baby's first steps 50 MIN
VHS
Growth and development of your new baby series
Color (A G)
$29.95 purchase _ #COV022V-K
Presents information about child development from six months to two years. Teaches parents and caregivers about physical development and growth, including teeth; how to ensure the child hears and sees properly; personality and discipline; games and sociability; daycare; babysitters; disease prevention; diet; and communication and language. Part of a three-part series.
Psychology; Social Science; Sociology
Dist - CAMV

Your Back at Work 18 MIN
VHS / 16mm
Color (PRO)
$450.00 purchase, $110.00 rental, $35.00 preview
Trains workers how to protect their backs from injury both at work and at home. Illustrates how the back works and how it can be damaged. Demonstrates safe lifting techniques, exercises for prevention of injury, how to increase overall flexibility and strength through lifestyle changes, and medical resources.
Business and Economics; Guidance and Counseling; Health and Safety; Psychology; Science - Natural
Dist - UTM **Prod** - UTM

Your Beautiful Lawn 48 MIN
BETA / VHS
Lawn and Garden Series
Color
Shows how to seed and maintain a lawn. Includes topics such as liming and moss control, raking and thatching.
Agriculture
Dist - MOHOMV **Prod** - MOHOMV

Your beautiful roses 56 MIN
VHS / BETA
Lawn and garden series
Color
Explains the differences among different kinds of roses. Tells how to grow climbing and tree roses. Includes fertilization and insect control.
Agriculture
Dist - MOHOMV **Prod** - MOHOMV

Your Best Shot 30 MIN
VHS
(J H C T)
$39.95 _ #NS100V
Demonstrates the proper execution of six basic basketball shots. Features basketball stars.
Physical Education and Recreation
Dist - CAMV

Your bicycle and you 13 MIN
16mm
Color (P I J)
Gives rules of the road for cyclists and compares these rules with automobile rules. Points out dangerous bike riding practices that lead to accidents and injuries.
Health and Safety
Dist - MLA **Prod** - CARSON 1962

Your Biological Guide to AIDS 25 MIN
VHS
Color (S)
$129.00 purchase _ #825 - 9639
Uses three - dimensional models of the AIDS virus, the skin and the white blood cells to illustrate what causes AIDS, how it gets into the body and what happens inside an infected body. Treats the subject frankly and dispels the myths as well as providing sufficient information to allow individuals to judge the risks for themselves.
Health and Safety; Sociology
Dist - FI **Prod** - BBCTV 1987

Your Birthday Suit 15 MIN
U-matic / VHS
All about You Series
Color
Introduces the concept that skin is a living organ which protects one's body from germs and puts one in touch with the world. Explains the scientific basis for differences in skin color.
Science - Natural
Dist - AITECH **Prod** - WGBHTV

Your Body - an Introduction
VHS / 35mm strip
Your Body - an Owner's Manual Series
$29.00 purchase _ #010 - 580 filmstrip, $49.00 purchase _ #010 - 585
Shows how body parts contribute to a person's well - being and how the systems are interdependent.
Health and Safety
Dist - CAREER **Prod** - CAREER

Your Body - an Owner's Manual Series
Your Body - an Introduction
Dist - CAREER

Your Body and its Parts 12 MIN
U-matic / VHS / 16mm
Color (P) (SPANISH)
Introduces the five systems of the human body, describing the muscles, the respiratory system, circulation, the skeleton and the nervous system. Demonstrates the interdependence between these systems.
Foreign Language; Science - Natural
Dist - EBEC **Prod** - EBEC

Your Body Belongs to You 30 MIN
VHS 24 MIN
Safe Child Program - Preschool - Series
Color (K A)
$395.00 purchase
Shows parents, teachers and professionals how to teach preschool youngsters to avoid sexual, emotional and physical abuse, and safety for children in self care. Uses videotapes to guarantee the accurate introduction of the concepts to children and classroom role - playing to develop individual mastery of safety skills. Part of a complete package of four videotapes in the Safe Child - Preschool - Program.
Education; Health and Safety; Psychology; Sociology
Dist - LUF **Prod** - LUF 1989

Your body - Series 1 54 MIN
VHS
Your body series
Color (I J H)
$120.00 purchase _ #A5VH 1053
Presents three parts which overview the human body and focuses on the muscular and skeletal systems. Includes The Human Organism; Your Skeletal System - Support and Protection; Your Muscular System - A Body in Action. Part of a three - part series on the body.
Science - Natural
Dist - CLRVUE **Prod** - CLRVUE

Your body - Series 2 54 MIN
VHS
Your body series
Color (I J H)
$160.00 purchase _ #A5VH 1054
Presents four parts which explores the operations of the digestive and circulatory systems of the human body. Includes Your Digestive System - A Food Factory; Your Blood - Liquid Tissue; Your Circulatory System - The Body's Highways. Part of a three - part series on the body.
Science - Natural
Dist - CLRVUE **Prod** - CLRVUE

Your body - Series 3 54 MIN
VHS
Your body series
Color (I J H)
$160.00 purchase _ #A5VH 1055
Presents four parts which examine the complex workings of the communications system of the human body. Includes Your Nervous System; Your Brain - A Personal Computer; Your Endorine System - The Control System. Part of a three - part series on the body.
Science - Natural
Dist - CLRVUE **Prod** - CLRVUE

Your body series
Presents a three - part series on the human body. Includes a total of 11 parts which examine the various systems of the body.
Your body - Series 1 54 MIN
Your body - Series 2 54 MIN
Your body - Series 3 54 MIN
Dist - CLRVUE **Prod** - CLRVUE

Your body series
Circulatory and respiratory systems 20 MIN
Digestive system 20 MIN
Muscular and skeletal systems 20 MIN
Nervous system 20 MIN
Reproductive systems 20 MIN
Dist - NGS

Your Body Systems at Work
U-matic / VHS / 35mm strip
3 - 2 - 1 Contact Series
(G J)
$197 purchase _ #27025 - 851, #27023 - 851
Introduces students to the basic systems of the human body. Includes the skeletal, circulatory, nervous, digestive, respiratory, muscular and reproductive systems. Highlights the interdependence of the various parts on one another.
Science - Natural
Dist - CHUMAN **Prod** - CTELWO 1988

Your Breast Biopsy 9 MIN
U-matic / VHS
Color
LC 79-730753
Suggests program should be viewed by women who must have a breast biopsy, and provides details of what the woman can expect when admitted to the hospital.
Health and Safety; Science; Science - Natural
Dist - MEDCOM **Prod** - MEDCOM

Your Busy Brain 15 MIN
VHS / U-matic
All about You Series
Color (P)
Presents a diagram of the brain and nerve network which shows that the brain is like a control center, receiving and sending messages all the time. Explains that the brain is able to store information. Describes the functions of specialized cells.
Science - Natural
Dist - AITECH **Prod** - WGBHTV 1975

Your Cancer Diet 13 MIN
U-matic / 35mm strip
Patient Education Programs - Clinical Diet Series
Color
Helps the cancer patient understand the importance of minimizing weight loss during therapy, and recommends ways of increasing calories and protein in the diet. Suggests ways to overcome eating problems that may occur during cancer treatments.
Health and Safety
Dist - POAPLE **Prod** - POAPLE

Your Car and Clean Air 13 MIN
16mm
Color
Presents the report of the automobile manufacturers association and the American petroleum Institute's work aimed at removing automobiles from the list of air polluters.
Home Economics; Science - Natural
Dist - GM **Prod** - GM 1970

Your Car in Motion 10 MIN
16mm / U-matic / VHS
Driving Tips Series
Color
Health and Safety; Industrial and Technical Education; Psychology
Dist - FORDFL **Prod** - FORDFL

Your care during pregnancy 18 MIN
U-matic / VHS / BETA
Color; NTSC; PAL; SECAM (H C G)
PdS83
Highlights the importance of antenatal care to prospective mothers. Covers home pregnancy testing, the initial visit to the general practitioner and subsequent stages of antenatal care. Shows the various screening tests and preparation for childbirth.
Health and Safety
Dist - VIEWTH

Your Career as a Secretary 27 MIN
16mm
Color (J H)
Shows classwork in typing, shorthand, bookkeeping, business law and arithmetic, and points out that the modern high school offers more complete training for a job in the secretarial field than in any other.
Business and Economics; Guidance and Counseling; Psychology
Dist - MLA **Prod** - WFPC 1954

Your Career as an Electronics Technician 27 MIN
16mm
Color (J H)
Shows how interest in physics, electricity and shop, an ability to make precise measurements and a facility with tools are advantageous for an electronics career. Gives suggestions for training after high school.
Guidance and Counseling; Industrial and Technical Education; Psychology
Dist - MLA **Prod** - WFPC 1954

Your Career in Aeronautical Engineering 27 MIN
16mm
Your Career Series
Color (J H)
LC 73-701179
Explorers careers in aeronautical engineering, including the importance of mathematics, highlights of college course material and scenes from industry showing graduate application of technical training.

Industrial and Technical Education; Science; Science - Physical
Dist - MLA Prod - RARIG 1962

Your Career in Architecture 27 MIN
16mm
Your Career Series
Color (H)
LC 78-701180
Reviews the education needed for a career as an architect. Includes a view of the five - year college course and the three - year apprentice period.
Fine Arts; Guidance and Counseling; Psychology
Dist - MLA Prod - RARIG 1962

Your Career in Elementary Teaching 27 MIN
16mm
Color (J H)
Describes the personal attributes and preparation necessary for elementary school teachers - - ability to understand people, broad academic background and good teaching skills. Illustrates practice teaching, and tells what a graduate may expect in job - seeking.
Education; Guidance and Counseling; Psychology
Dist - MLA Prod - WFPC 1954

Your Career in Forestry 27 MIN
16mm
Color (J H)
Tells why college schools of forestry require good preparation in English, math, botany and physics. Illustrates the application of forestry skills in both private and public employment.
Guidance and Counseling; Psychology; Science - Natural
Dist - MLA Prod - WFPC 1954

Your Career in Hotel Management 27 MIN
16mm
Your Career Series
Color (H)
LC 79-701183
Reviews the education recommended for a career in hotel management. Surveys preparatory courses and shows many of the career opportunities available to a person trained in this field.
Guidance and Counseling; Psychology
Dist - MLA Prod - RARIG 1962

Your Career in Instrumentation and Control
VHS
Color (J)
$39.95 purchase _ #YOUR - VA
Examines the various careers in instrumentation and control.
Guidance and Counseling; Industrial and Technical Education; Mathematics; Psychology
Dist - ISA Prod - ISA

Your Career in Journalism 27 MIN
16mm
Your Career Series
Color (H)
LC 71-701181
Reviews the liberal arts education recommended for a career in journalism. Presents a view of beginning jobs in reporting and describes some specialized jobs.
Guidance and Counseling; Psychology; Social Science
Dist - MLA Prod - RARIG 1962

Your Career in Law 27 MIN
16mm
Your Career Series
Color (H)
Stresses reading comprehension and capacity, love for words and respect for truth as the mark of the future lawyer. A mock trial in a law school illustrates professional study of torts, contracts, property rights and other aspects of the law.
Civics and Political Systems; Guidance and Counseling; Psychology
Dist - MLA Prod - RARIG 1962

Your Career in Meteorology 27 MIN
16mm
Your Career Series
Color (H)
LC 72-701184
Reviews the education necessary for a career in the field of meteorology. Describes preparatory courses and shows various areas of specialization within each field.
Guidance and Counseling; Psychology; Science; Science - Physical
Dist - MLA Prod - RARIG 1962

Your Career in Nursing 27 MIN
16mm
Color (J H)
Examines both avenues to a nursing degree - - college training and hospital apprenticeship. Explores specialization in specific fields and explains the importance of a background of science in high school.
Guidance and Counseling; Health and Safety; Psychology
Dist - MLA Prod - WFPC 1954

Your career in printing 27 MIN
16mm
Color (J H)
Shows how a high school student becomes interested in the industry while working with a printer to publish his school paper. He sees the importance of high school courses in art and photography in relation to printing. Names six separate, but related, skilled trades in the industry.
Guidance and Counseling; Industrial and Technical Education; Psychology
Dist - MLA Prod - WFPC 1954

Your Career, J Kenneth Lund
U-matic / VHS
Management Skills Series
Color (PRO)
Business and Economics; Psychology
Dist - AMCEE Prod - AMCEE

Your Career Series
Your Career in Aeronautical Engineering 27 MIN
Your Career in Architecture 27 MIN
Your Career in Hotel Management 27 MIN
Your Career in Journalism 27 MIN
Your Career in Law 27 MIN
Your Career in Meteorology 27 MIN
Dist - MLA

Your Chance to Live Series
Earthquake 14 MIN
Flood 14 MIN
Forest fire 14 MIN
Heat Wave 14 MIN
Hurricane 14 MIN
Pollution 14 MIN
Tornado 14 MIN
Winter Storm 14 MIN
Dist - CORF

Your child - 12 - 18 months 11 MIN
VHS
Color (G C PRO) (SPANISH)
$150.00 purchase _ #CC - 05
Covers the increased independence of the child and its tendency to test limits. Shows how the development in language, coordination and socialization is rapidly increasing. Emphasizes the importance of effective parent - child interaction including reading, talking and bedtime preparation. Reviews sibling rivalry, self - image, individualism, eating patterns and further safety precautions. Concludes with toilet training and bedtime problems.
Health and Safety; Sociology
Dist - MIFE Prod - MIFE

Your child - 18 - 24 months 11 MIN
VHS
Color (G C PRO) (SPANISH)
$150.00 purchase _ #CC - 06
Focuses on the transformation of baby into child. Reveals that language skills and mobility are accelerating dramatically, necessitating a greater need for parental awareness and interaction. This is often the time of nighttime fears, pretend friends and active rebellion. Examines the increased assertiveness of the child and offers suggestions for discipline. Recommends more challenging toys and increased play space. Stresses importance of child - proofing and close supervision.
Health and Safety; Sociology
Dist - MIFE Prod - MIFE

Your Child and Diabetes 23 MIN
U-matic / 35mm strip
Color (SPANISH)
LC 83-730081;
Provides an understanding of diabetes, its cases and how it will affect the family's lifestyle. Prepares parents to provide the guidance, encouragement, and direction that the child requires.
Foreign Language; Health and Safety; Sociology
Dist - MEDCOM Prod - MEDCOM

Your Child has a Fever 15 MIN
U-matic / VHS / 16mm
Color (A)
Demonstrates how to recognize a fever, use a thermometer and reduce a fever. Indicates when to call a doctor.
Health and Safety; Home Economics
Dist - CF Prod - CF

Your Child has a Fever 20 MIN
U-matic / VHS
Color (A)
$235 purchase
Describes the differences between dangerous and non - threatening fevers, how to reduce a fever, and when to call a doctor. A film by Richard Usatine, M.D. and Martin Smietenka, M.D.
Health and Safety
Dist - CF

Your child - 6 - 12 months 11 MIN
VHS
Color (G C PRO) (SPANISH)
$150.00 purchase _ #CC - 04
Examines how the child is becoming more expressive, assertive and curious and is not necessarily the 'team player' Mom and Dad expected. Prepares parents for the slowdown in both appetite and growth which often accompanies this period, along with an interest of the child in feeding itself. Cautions on proper safeguards to match the child's emerging mobility.
Health and Safety; Sociology
Dist - MIFE Prod - MIFE

Your child - 2 - 6 months 12 MIN
VHS
Color (G C PRO) (SPANISH)
$150.00 purchase _ #CC - 03
Covers basic motor and muscular developmental milestones such as head control, grasping, sitting with support. Reviews travel, toys, teething, safety measures, immunizations and baby receptivity to language - spoken or otherwise. Stresses need for parents to find time away from caretaking.
Health and Safety; Sociology
Dist - MIFE Prod - MIFE

Your child - 2 weeks - 2 months 14 MIN
VHS
Color (G C PRO) (SPANISH)
$150.00 purchase _ #CC - 02
Shows parents that a child's needs are mostly simple things such as nutrition, sleep and warm comfort in the first two months of life. Stresses the importance of a consistent pattern of growth rather than gains in weight or height. Includes safety tips.
Health and Safety; Sociology
Dist - MIFE Prod - MIFE

Your Children Come Back to You 27 MIN
16mm
B&W
Tells the story of Tovi, a little black girl caught between European and African values within her own family.
History - United States; Sociology
Dist - BLKFMF Prod - BLKFMF

Your children come back to you 27 MIN
VHS / 16mm
B&W (G)
$75.00 rental, $250.00 purchase
Literalizes the meaning of a 'mother country' by telling the story of a young girl who is torn between two surrogate mothers - one comfortably bourgeois, the other nationalist. Considers the psychological and emotional bonds between mothers and daughters while probing contemporary African American culture. An allegory about values and assimilation. By Alile Sharon Larkin.
Guidance and Counseling; Literature and Drama; Sociology
Dist - WMEN

Your Child's First Few Steps 15 MIN
U-matic / VHS / 16mm
Color (J)
Explores infant footwear. Discusses the walking process.
Home Economics; Psychology
Dist - KLEINW Prod - KLEINW

Your Child's Growth and Development 10 MIN
U-matic / VHS / 16mm
Color (PRO)
A revised edition of Growth And Development/Toilet Training. Describes the basic elements vital to a child's growth and social progress and provides guidelines for toilet training using positive reinforcement.
Health and Safety; Home Economics; Psychology; Science - Natural
Dist - PRORE Prod - PRORE

Your child's ostomy 12 MIN
VHS
Color (G C PRO)
$200.00 purchase, $70.00 rental _ #4338S, #4338V
Explains and shows what an ostomy is and how to care for it. Demonstrates step - by - step the care of a child's ostomy on both a model and a child. Continues with the care and maintenance of the ostomy pouch, materials needed for stoma care and care and evaluation of the site. Discusses practical tips, such as type of clothing best suited for a child with an ostomy. Produced by the Children's Hospital of Alabama.
Health and Safety
Dist - AJN

Your Child's Safety 10 MIN
16mm
Color
LC 79-711598
Provides education and motivation for parents, especially new mothers, regarding child care and accident prevention, as part of an audiovisual system of learning.
Education; Guidance and Counseling; Health and Safety; Psychology; Sociology
Dist - SUTHLA **Prod** - ROCOM 1971

Your child's school experiences 30 MIN
VHS
Parents' point of view series
Color (T A PRO)
$69.95 purchase
Presents advice on caring for children under five years old. Targeted to both parents and care givers. Covers children's school experiences. Hosted by Nancy Thurmond, ex - wife of Senator Strom Thurmond.
Education; Guidance and Counseling; Health and Safety
Dist - SCETV **Prod** - SCETV 1988

Your choice - decision - making - anthropology - sociology 15 MIN
U-matic / VHS
Two cents' worth series
Color (P)
Reveals that Pat decides to go hiking alone rather than help his family set up camp. Shows that when he does not return, a search party is organized.
Psychology; Sociology
Dist - AITECH **Prod** - WHATV 1976

Your choice - our chance series
The Big break - media 15 MIN
The Big break - media - 4 15 MIN
Decisions - decisions and actions - 8 15 MIN
Fitting in - stress 15 MIN
A Friend indeed - response - ability - 9 15 MIN
A Friend indeed - responsibility 15 MIN
Good Practice Today - Refusal Skills - 6 15 MIN
I Think, I Am - Self - Concept - 2 15 MIN
I Think I Am - Self Concept 15 MIN
Like You, Dad - Wellness - 10 15 MIN
Parents and School - Community Program 30 MIN
Partners - Community Program 30 MIN
Penalty Kick - Risk Factors 15 MIN
Sister, Sister - Enhancing Alternatives - 7 15 MIN
Sister, Sister - Health - Enhancing Alternatives 15 MIN
Sunrise House - Community Program 30 MIN
Sunrise House - Salinas, California 30 MIN
Thanks - but no Thanks - Peer Pressure 15 MIN
Thanks, but no Thanks - Peer Pressure - 5 15 MIN
Dist - AITECH

Your Church and the Mentally Retarded 20 MIN
16mm
Color
Literature and Drama; Religion and Philosophy
Dist - BROADM **Prod** - BROADM 1977

Your Clothing Can Burn 16 MIN
16mm / U-matic / VHS
Color (I A)
LC 81-700333
Presents laboratory demonstrations showing burning characteristics of various fabrics. Describes what to do if clothes catch on fire.
Health and Safety; Home Economics
Dist - HIGGIN **Prod** - HIGGIN 1981

Your Communication Skills - Listening 11 MIN
16mm / U-matic / VHS
Color (I J)
LC 77-703332
Points out that listening is as important for communication as speaking, and shows some of the listening skills that can help improve communication.
English Language
Dist - CORF **Prod** - CORF 1969

Your Complete Denture 10 MIN
16mm
Dental Health Series
Color (P I J H)
LC 75-700037
Provides the patient having a new complete denture, with methods for adjusting to appearance, speech, eating and other activities. Uses animation to portray the problems of a denture in the mouth and shows the proper care and cleaning of the denture.
Health and Safety; Home Economics
Dist - MIFE **Prod** - MIFE 1973

Your complete guide to CPR
VHS
Color (J H C G)
$49.00 purchase _ #CCP0123V
Shows how to identify the early signs of a heart attack and how to administer CPR to infants, children and adults. Features certified instructors who demonstrate proper CPR procedures as outlined by the Journal of the American Medical Association. Includes manual.
Health and Safety
Dist - CAMV **Prod** - CAMV 1993

Your Congressman at Work 20 MIN
16mm
Color
LC FIE59-1
Presents a typical day in the life of a member of Congress. Stresses the importance of voting in elections and of being informed about candidates and issues.
Civics and Political Systems
Dist - USNAC **Prod** - USDD 1956

Your Congressman at Work 22 MIN
U-matic
B&W
Presents a typical day in the life of a member of Congress. Urges all members of the armed forces to become familiar with the issues and candidates in forthcoming elections and to vote.
Civics and Political Systems; History - United States
Dist - USNAC **Prod** - USNAC 1972

Your Contact Lens Procedures - Hard Lens 7 MIN
U-matic / VHS
Color
Instructs patient on proper technique of application and removal of contact lenses. Discusses proper hygiene and care.
Health and Safety; Science - Natural
Dist - MEDCOM **Prod** - MEDCOM

Your Coronary Care Diet 11 MIN
U-matic / 35mm strip
Patient Education Programs - Clinical Diet Series
Color
Discusses the restrictions on sodium, saturated fats and cholesterol in the coronary care diet. Talks about the significance of dietary fiber and the importance of achieving and maintaining one's ideal body weight.
Health and Safety
Dist - POAPLE **Prod** - POAPLE

Your Credit is Good - a Film about Paying Later 15 MIN
U-matic / VHS / 16mm
Color; Captioned (J H C)
LC 73-700990
Demonstrates in a series of dramatic vignettes, that the lure of extended credit can hold many hazards for the unwary consumer.
Business and Economics; Home Economics; Social Science
Dist - JOU **Prod** - ALTSUL 1972

Your Credit is Good, Unfortunately 10 MIN
U-matic / VHS / 16mm
Consumer Fraud Series
Color (I)
LC 76-700809
Warns against fraudulent credit practices which can leave credit buyers with enormous monthly payments.
Business and Economics; Home Economics; Social Science
Dist - PFP **Prod** - PART 1976

Your credit record 20 MIN
VHS
Credit series
Color (A H C)
$79.95 purchase _ #CCP0161V-D
Reveals that whenever an individual establishes credit by opening a charge account or borrowing through a bank or finance company, each transaction is reported to the credit bureau. Explains that as payments are made, debts are paid off and applications are made for further credit, the bureau will continue to keep a complete record of an individual's financial history. Discusses the credit report and stresses the importance of keeping a credit record clean. Part of a three-part series on credit.
Business and Economics
Dist - CAMV

Your credit record - keeping it clean 30 MIN
VHS
Credit series
Color (H A C)
$79.95 purchasse _ #CCPO161V
Addresses issues related to credit. Explains to viewers that as they make payments, pay off debts and apply for further credit, the bureau will continue to keep a complete record of their financial history. Advises how to obtain credit reports and the importance of establishing credit and keeping their record clean. Part of a three-part series.
Business and Economics; Home Economics; Social Science
Dist - CAMV

Your Dental X - Ray Exam 8 MIN
U-matic / VHS / 16mm
Color
Helps answer patients' questions and concerns about the necessity and safety of dental radiographic procedures. Emphasizes the important information that can be gained from X - rays, as well as the ways modern safety standards have minimized patient exposure and risk.
Health and Safety
Dist - PRORE **Prod** - PRORE

Your Diet - Carbohydrates 12 MIN
U-matic / VHS / 16mm
Your Diet Series
Color (J)
LC 82-700393
Explains the various forms of carbohydrates and the roles they play in one's diet. Tells of some good sources of carbohydrates.
Health and Safety
Dist - JOU **Prod** - ALTSUL 1982

Your Diet - Exercise 12 MIN
16mm / U-matic / VHS
Color (J)
Looks at various forms of exercise and recreation and their effects on health. Emphasizes that people of all ages need daily exercise for healthy bodies and minds.
Health and Safety; Physical Education and Recreation
Dist - JOU **Prod** - ALTSUL 1982

Your Diet - Fats 12 MIN
16mm / U-matic / VHS
Your Diet Series
Color (J)
LC 82-700395
Looks at the effects of the overconsumption of fats and offers alternative foods to help reduce intake of fats while still maintaining the proper amount of proteins in the daily diet.
Health and Safety
Dist - JOU **Prod** - ALTSUL 1982

Your diet - fiber 12 MIN
U-matic / VHS / 16mm
Your diet series
Color (J)
LC 82-700396
Examines what fiber is and the role it plays in one's diet. Tells how fast foods have caused the fiber content in diets to decrease and what diseases and conditions are attributed to lack of fiber. Names some good sources of fiber.
Health and Safety
Dist - JOU **Prod** - ALTSUL 1982

Your Diet Series
Calories - enough is enough 10 MIN
Food labeling - understanding what you eat 13 MIN
Snacks Count Too 12 MIN
Your Diet - Carbohydrates 12 MIN
Your Diet - Fats 12 MIN
Your diet - fiber 12 MIN
Your Diet - Water 10 MIN
Dist - JOU

Your Diet - Water 10 MIN
16mm / U-matic / VHS
Your Diet Series
Color (J H A)
Discusses the importance of water in people's diets.
Health and Safety
Dist - JOU **Prod** - ALTSUL 1981

Your Driving Habits 15 MIN
16mm
B&W
LC FIE52-315
Shows the elements of good driving. Demonstrates how to start the engine, use the clutch, shift gears and use the brakes. Explains how to drive under hazardous conditions.
Health and Safety
Dist - USNAC **Prod** - USOE 1945

Your Ear and Noise 50 MIN
U-matic / VHS
Color (PRO)
Discusses the concepts of industrial noise and its effect on hearing. Presents controls and methods of determining harmful industrial noise levels.
Health and Safety; Science - Natural
Dist - HOUSEI **Prod** - HOUSEI

Your Ear - what Can Go Wrong 55 MIN
U-matic / VHS
Color (PRO)
Discusses the mechanism of hearing, the causes of hearing impairment and the medical and surgical treatment of otologic problems.
Guidance and Counseling; Health and Safety; Science - Natural
Dist - HOUSEI **Prod** - HOUSEI

Your ears 6 MIN
U-matic / VHS / 16mm
Color; B&W (P) (SPANISH)
Children discover their dependence on ears for hearing. Animation is used to show the function of the ear, explaining what happens when sound enters it. Good health habits are stressed.
Health and Safety; Science - Natural
Dist - EBEC **Prod** - EBEC 1964

Your educational skills - don't leave home without them 20 MIN
VHS
Color (I J)
$99.95 purchase _ #TMESA
Helps bridge the gap between what students have learned in high school and occupational success. Illustrates how specific levels of math, language and reasoning competencies are related to the fifty fastest growing jobs in the US. Real - life scenarios are used to reinforce the need for sound high school course selection.
Business and Economics; Guidance and Counseling
Dist - CFKRCM **Prod** - CFKRCM

Your Environment is the Earth 12 MIN
16mm / U-matic / VHS
Color (I J)
LC 74-710755
Takes the viewer on a journey from the polar ice caps to the Northern Tundra, from the forests of the temperate zone to tropical jungles and from outer space to the ocean depths in order to demonstrate that our environment is our surroundings.
Science - Natural
Dist - JOU **Prod** - WER 1969

Your Erroneous Zones 97 MIN
BETA / 16mm
Color (A)
Presents Wayne Dyer, psychologist and author, discussing how to avoid such unhealthy behavioral patterns as guilt, anger, anxiety and insecurity. Based upon his book Your Erroneous Zones.
Psychology
Dist - CBSFOX **Prod** - CBSFOX

Your ever well wisher 57 MIN
16mm
Color
Presents a biography of A C Bhaktivedanta Swami from his childhood days in Calcutta through his achievements as the founder and leader of the Hare Krishna movement.
Religion and Philosophy
Dist - BHAKTI **Prod** - ISKCON 1983

Your exercises after a mastectomy 10 MIN
VHS / U-matic
Color
Recommends a program to be viewed on the second or third postoperative day by the woman who has had a mastectomy. Reviews the physical therapy that will help the woman return to her normal activities as soon as possible after her operation. Describes passive exercises and nature of normal recovery, and concludes with demonstrations of the five different exercises frequently prescribed.
Health and Safety; Physical Education and Recreation; Science; Science - Natural
Dist - MEDCOM **Prod** - MEDCOM

Your Eyes 7 MIN
U-matic / VHS / 16mm
Color (P) (SPANISH)
Demonstrates ways in which man depends on his eyes. Shows how the eye works and illustrates good eye care.
Foreign Language; Health and Safety; Science - Natural
Dist - EBEC **Prod** - EBEC

Your Face Speaks 15 MIN
Videoreel / VT2
Word Magic (2nd Ed Series
Color (P)
Provides an enrichment program in the communitive arts area by using facial expressions.
English Language; Social Science
Dist - GPN **Prod** - CVETVC

Your Feet's Too Big 3 MIN
16mm / U-matic / VHS
Color (I A)
Features story of a monkey who rejects an amorous elephant because of his large feet.
Fine Arts
Dist - MTOLP **Prod** - MTOLP 1984

Your Fire Service 20 MIN
U-matic / VHS
Color
Shows people in their communities what it costs to run a fire department, risks firefighters take and other fire department public information.
Health and Safety
Dist - FPF **Prod** - FPF

Your Fireman 12 MIN
16mm
B&W (I)
Depicts the jobs of a fire department other than putting out fires. Includes rescue work, fire inspection and prevention programs, maintaining equipment and continuous education of firemen.
Social Science
Dist - RVIERA **Prod** - RVIERA 1953

Your first baby
VHS
To your health series
Color (G)
$29.95 purchase _ #IV - 036
Shows how to prepare the home and parents for their first baby.
Health and Safety; Home Economics; Sociology
Dist - INCRSE **Prod** - INCRSE

Your first baby 40 MIN
VHS
Color (J H G)
$49.00 purchase _ #04650 - 126
Shows what to expect from a newborn baby and how to deal with problems.
Health and Safety; Psychology; Sociology
Dist - GA **Prod** - GA

Your First Baby 40 MIN
VHS
(H C A)
$39.95 purchase _ #IV100V
Discusses many aspects of infant care including breast feeding or bottle feeding, newborn diets, diapering, common illnesses and treatments, and more.
Health and Safety; Home Economics; Sociology
Dist - CAMV **Prod** - CAMV

Your first cruise - a beginner's guide to the Internet 30 MIN
VHS
Information Superhighway series
Color (G A)
$79.95 purchase _ #CCP0119V; # CCP0229V-D
Guides beginners through learning about how the Internet was developed, why people use it, how to access it, popular features, and how to navigate. Explains what services are offered and how to obtain the right connection for viewer's needs. Available individually or as a set with Connect on the Net - On-line Employment.
Computer Science
Dist - CAMV

Your first gynecological examination 17 MIN
16mm / U-matic / VHS
Woman talk series
Color (H C A)
Gives a brief animated explanation of the female internal and external genitalia, and follows Jenny through her first gynecological visit. Details the initial consultation, breast examination and pap smear and states the importance of each procedure. statedGives special attention to the necessity for frank, honest communication between doctor and patient.
Health and Safety; Sociology
Dist - CORF **Prod** - CORF 1983

Your first interview 15 MIN
VHS
Becoming independent series
Color (H G)
$79.00 purchase _ #CDHEC506V
Presents practical and reassuring interview tips at a basic level for entry into the working world. Discusses how to dress, questions to prepare for and ask, how to create a good impression and what to do after the interview. Part of a 13 - part series featuring practical life and consumer skills for teens venturing out into independence.
Guidance and Counseling; Home Economics
Dist - CAMV

Your First Job
VHS
Job Skills Series
(H C)
$59.00 _ CA118
Shows the importance of one's attitude while on the job as well as the importance of relationships between the employee, customers, fellow workers, and the boss.
Business and Economics; Guidance and Counseling
Dist - AAVIM **Prod** - AAVIM 1989

Your first job 15 MIN
VHS
Becoming independent series
Color (H G)
$79.00 purchase _ #CDHEC508V
Emphasizes the role of the boss in establishing a good working relationship leading to career opportunities. Stresses work attitude, behaviors and first job mechanics. Covers punctuality, dependability, W - 4 forms, wage computation, overtime, pay stubs, and more. Part of a 13 - part series featuring practical life and consumer skills for teens venturing out into independence.
Business and Economics; Guidance and Counseling
Dist - CAMV

Your first job interview 10 MIN
VHS / U-matic / BETA
Young job seekers series
Color; Stereo (H C A)
Shows three school leavers attend interviews for the same job. The interviewer gives his opinion of each applicant.
Guidance and Counseling; Psychology
Dist - SEVDIM **Prod** - SEVDIM 1984

Your first pelvic exam 6 MIN
VHS
Color (C PRO G)
$250.00 purchase
Presents a reassuring introduction to the pelvic exam for younger patients. Uses animated 3 - D graphics and tasteful visuals to help the patient understand pelvic anatomy, bi - manual examination, Pap smears and culture samples.
Health and Safety
Dist - LPRO **Prod** - LPRO

Your First Pony
VHS / BETA
Captain Mark Phillips Horsemanship Training Series
Color
Physical Education and Recreation
Dist - EQVDL **Prod** - EQVDL

Your First Six Years 10 MIN
16mm
Family Life and Sex Education Series
Color (K P I J)
Considers the development of abilities, emotions and self - expression during the first six years of life. Shows changing attitudes and expanding roles of children of different ages at play, in school and in their relationship to their parents. Emphasizes the role of the parents in the development of young children.
Psychology; Science - Natural
Dist - SF **Prod** - SF 1968

Your first steps to watercolors 112 MIN
VHS
Color (H C G T A)
$79.95 purchase _ #S00897
Presents basic techniques for watercolor painting. Includes close - up demonstrations of specific strokes and techniques. Hosted by artist and teacher Gene Pollock.
Fine Arts
Dist - UILL **Prod** - UILL

Your Fluoride Carriers - Purpose, Use and Care 6 MIN
U-matic
Color (C)
Provides an understanding of the purpose, use and care of fluoride carriers. The steps involved in construction of a custom fluoride carrier as well as tips for greater patient comfort during irradiation therapy are discussed.
Health and Safety; Science - Natural
Dist - UOKLAH **Prod** - UOKLAH 1984

Your Food 7 MIN
U-matic / VHS / 16mm
Basic Life Science Series
Color; B&W (P)
LC FIA65-337
Shows what happens to food when it enters the digestive system, and relates this system to other body systems. Presents examples of a balanced diet.
Health and Safety; Home Economics; Science - Natural
Dist - EBEC **Prod** - EBEC 1964

Your Food Allergies 7 MIN
VHS / U-matic
Color
Explains what food allergy is and how it acts. Presents a method for finding causes of food allergy through a food diary.

Health and Safety
Dist - MEDFAC **Prod** - MEDFAC 1978

Your friend the forest - save it or destroy it 6 MIN
U-matic / VHS / 16mm
Color (P I) (SPANISH)
Presents an animated cartoon story to demonstrate the importance of preventing forest fires.
Health and Safety; Science - Natural
Dist - EBEC **Prod** - EBEC 1954

Your Friend the Water - Clean or Dirty 6 MIN
16mm / U-matic / VHS
Color (P I)
An animated cartoon of a little boy who learns the factors behind a good supply of pure water, as well as the conditions which produce dirty, polluted water.
Health and Safety; Science - Natural
Dist - EBEC **Prod** - EBEC 1954

Your furniture, their lives 40 MIN
VHS
Open space series
Color; PAL (G)
PdS50 purchase
Investigates the decline of mahogany reserves in Brazil due to its popularity as a material for furniture. Delves into the controversy surrounding the illegal cutting of mahogany by sawmill owners operating on Amazonian tribal lands. Focuses on tribes such as the Arara that face economic loss and ecological disaster from the threatening encroachment of timber bandits.
Agriculture; Geography - World; Industrial and Technical Education
Dist - BBCENE

Your Future in Art - a Career for the 80's 22 MIN
16mm
Color
Focuses on a group of commercial artists, photographers and interior designers working at their jobs in various cities and describing opportunities, responsibilities and achievements in their respective fields. Shows the skills and training essential for a career in commercial art.
Fine Arts; Guidance and Counseling; Home Economics
Dist - MTP **Prod** - MTP

Your Future - Planning through Career Exploration
VHS / U-matic
CEPP Video Series
(J H C A)
$89.00 _ #MG3251V
Uses live action to introduce the viewer to the major issues relating to career exploration.
Business and Economics; Guidance and Counseling
Dist - CAMV **Prod** - CAMV

Your future - planning through career exploration
VHS / 16mm
Color (H C A)
$89.00 purchase _ #3251; $89.00 purchase _ #012 - 645
Presents the concepts key to planning for the future through career exploration.
Guidance and Counseling
Dist - MERIDN **Prod** - MERIDN 1988
CAREER

Your guardian angel 15 MIN
16mm / U-matic / VHS
Harry Sparks series
Color (IND) (SPANISH)
LC 82-700854
Reviews the characteristics of 600 - volt lines and illustrates basic safety techniques in handling them.
Health and Safety; Industrial and Technical Education
Dist - IFB **Prod** - IAPA 1974

Your guide to antique shopping in Britain 60 MIN
VHS
Color (G)
$29.95 purchase _ #407
Focuses on the leading antique centers in Great Britain. Shows how to locate the places and organizations which deal with antiques and reviews publications. Presents examples of antiques and interviews experts.
Geography - World; History - World; Home Economics; Industrial and Technical Education
Dist - IHF

Your guide to parallel skiing 60 MIN
VHS
Color (H C A)
$34.95 purchase _ #GINAP01V
Presents a comprehensive introduction to parallel skiing. Covers clothing, equipment, and basic techniques as well as skills to practice. Tells what to do if the skiing doesn't feel right. Video is accompanied by a 60 - minute audiocassette, and a 17 - page booklet.

Physical Education and Recreation
Dist - CAMV

Your health care after a mastectomy 11 MIN
U-matic / VHS
Color
LC 79-730753
Describes some precautions which can contribute to a woman's health care after a mastectomy. Discusses precautions to help the patient avoid injury and infection of the affected hand and arm, followed by a demonstration of breast self - examination. Stresses follow - up therapy and follow - up physician visits.
Health and Safety
Dist - MEDCOM **Prod** - MEDCOM

Your health matters - Attention a votre sante 14 MIN
U-matic / BETA / VHS
Canadian specific programs series
Color (IND G) (FRENCH)
$C635.00 purchase _ #601 - 09
Discusses the safe handling of chemicals in the workplace. Provides information on basic industrial hygiene concepts and the importance of using personal protective equipment to minimize exposure to potentially hazardous chemicals.
Health and Safety; Industrial and Technical Education; Psychology
Dist - ITSC **Prod** - ITSC

Your health matters - Su salud importa - manejo seguro de substancias quimicas 14 MIN
BETA / VHS / U-matic
Hazard communication - live - action video series
Color (IND G) (SPANISH)
$495.00 purchase _ #820 - 22, #820 - 42
Discusses safe handling of chemicals in the workplace. Informs on basic industrial hygiene concepts, the importance of using personal protective equipment to minimize exposure. Part of a series on hazard communication.
Health and Safety; Industrial and Technical Education; Psychology
Dist - ITSC **Prod** - ITSC

Your health series
A Doctor - patient partnership 15 MIN
Lifestyle Choices - Your Health, Baby's Health 29 MIN
Managing stress 15 MIN
Dist - ACCESS

Your Healthy Best 27 MIN
16mm
Color
Features people who tell how practical rules regarding diet, exercise and stress reduction helped them reach new levels of wellness.
Health and Safety
Dist - BCBSA **Prod** - BCBSA

Your Heart - the Mighty Muscle 15 MIN
U-matic / VHS
All about You Series
Color (P)
Utilizes an X - ray, siphon pump and heart model to describe the functions of the heart and blood and to show how blood is circulated through the body.
Science - Natural
Dist - AITECH **Prod** - WGBHTV 1975

Your heart - your health 59 MIN
VHS
Color (A)
$29.95 purchase _ #S01366
Describes the causes and dangers of heart disease. Features the perspectives of a wide variety of heart experts, including heart surgeon Michael DeBakey. Hosted by Frank Gifford. Includes a booklet designed to help people assess their risk of heart attacks.
Health and Safety
Dist - UILL

Your hemodiolysis therapy 9 MIN
VHS / U-matic
Color
LC 80-730458
Introduces hemodialysis therapy with an overview of normal kidney function, followed by an explanation of the purpose and function of the artificial kidney. Emphasizes the patient's participatory role in his health care and gives guidelines to apply to one's own treatment. Focuses attention on scheduling of treatment sessions, care of the circulatory access site and diet modification.
Health and Safety; Science - Natural
Dist - MEDCOM **Prod** - MEDCOM

Your Hero Heart 15 MIN
U-matic / VHS
Cardio Series
Color (K P)
Health and Safety; Science - Natural
Dist - PCATEL **Prod** - NCSDPI

Your Home Beautiful 15 MIN
16mm
Color (J)
LC 80-701062
Presents a talking house which personifies the modern, American, single - family home and how it is decorated. Provides information on home buying and decorating.
Home Economics
Dist - KLEINW **Prod** - KLEINW 1975

Your House in Order 18 MIN
U-matic / VHS / 16mm
Color
Shows how industrial accidents can be the result of poor housekeeping and sloppiness. Uses the examples of a reckless forklift operator, a careless maintenance man, two workers unloading pipe without looking, a lathe operator who doesn't clean up the scrap and other workers leaving tools and trucks in dangerous places.
Health and Safety
Dist - IFB **Prod** - MILLBK

Your house, your health
VHS
Color (G)
$19.95 purchase
Features healthy house expert John Bower who guides the viewer on a tour of a recently completed Model Healthy House. Offers information about roofing, siding, filters, doors, ventilation, cabinets and more to prevent suffering from allergies, respiratory symptoms or chemical sensitivities because of poor indoor air quality.
Sociology
Dist - HHOUSE **Prod** - HHOUSE 1994

Your image at work 23 MIN
U-matic / 16mm / VHS
Color (H C A G)
$595.00, $405.00, $375.00 purchase _ #A611
Provides practical guidelines for a professional image - a good physical impression, effective communication and appropriate job behavior. Includes the topics of wardrobe, cleanliness, hairstyle - makeup, verbal skills, body language and developing a positive work attitude. Shows how to fit into a work environment while maintaining individuality. Produced by Timothy Armstrong.
Business and Economics; Guidance and Counseling; Home Economics; Psychology; Social Science
Dist - BARR **Prod** - ARMPIC 1992

Your Image - make it Work for You 17 MIN
16mm / U-matic / VHS
Color (H C A)
LC 83-700166
Explores how grooming, dress, verbal communication and body language come together to create an image of a person in the minds of others.
Guidance and Counseling; Psychology
Dist - BARR **Prod** - BARR 1983

Your Interests - Related to Work Activities
VHS / 16mm
Color (H C A PRO)
$89.00 purchase _ #MC117; $89.00 purchase _ # 012 - 640; $89.00 purchase _ 3252
Ties the concept of basic interests to work interests. Illustrates how past experiences - mostly nonwork - can be a starting point for examining viewers' interests in work and potential career fields.
Business and Economics; Guidance and Counseling
Dist - AAVIM **Prod** - AAVIM 1990
CAREER CAREER
MERIDN MERIDN

Your Interests - Related to Work Activities
U-matic / VHS
CEPP Video Series
(J H C A)
$89.00 _ #MG3252V
Uses live action to introduct the viewer to the major issues concerning work activities.
Business and Economics; Guidance and Counseling
Dist - CAMV **Prod** - CAMV

Your IPPB Therapy 12 MIN
U-matic / VHS
Color
LC 73-732792
Illustrates the techniques of Intermittent Positive Pressure Breathing. Presents an IPPB therapy machine and shows its use. Notes that patient must be instructed in his role during treatment and need of cooperation.

Health and Safety; Science - Natural
Dist - MEDCOM Prod - MEDCOM

Your Job 20 MIN
U-matic / VHS
Color
Shows what to do in case of fire at the job site. Illustrates the value of fire protection equipment.
Health and Safety
Dist - FPF Prod - FPF

Your Job - Applying for it 14 MIN
U-matic / VHS / 16mm
Your Job Series
Color (H C A)
LC FIA68-3037
Uses interviews with workers of varying ages and education to show that the way to apply for a job and get it is by following a planned procedure which includes getting enough good leads, sticking with it, selling oneself and making the most of what one has.
Guidance and Counseling; Psychology
Dist - CORF Prod - CORF 1968

Your job - finding the right one 14 MIN
16mm / U-matic / VHS
Your job series
Color (H C A)
LC FIA68-3036
Shows how young people can locate jobs suited to their needs and abilities. Shows how to organize a plan of action that will get the 'right' job.
Guidance and Counseling; Psychology
Dist - CORF Prod - CORF 1968

Your job - fitting in 16 MIN
16mm / U-matic / VHS
Your job series
Color (H C A)
LC FIA68-3038
Examines two situations wherein an employee is fired for doing 'too little' and another is fired for trying to do 'too much.' Challenges the viewer to decide how he would respond to each situation.
Guidance and Counseling; Psychology
Dist - CORF Prod - CORF 1968

Your Job - Getting Ahead 16 MIN
U-matic / VHS / 16mm
Your Job Series
Color (H C A)
LC FIA68-3041
Interviews experienced workers at their jobs, and gives tips on getting ahead. Discusses questions about changing jobs, recognizing dead - end jobs, picking areas for advancement and planning for additional education.
Guidance and Counseling; Psychology
Dist - CORF Prod - CORF 1968

Your Job - Good Work Habits 14 MIN
U-matic / VHS / 16mm
Your Job Series
Color (H C A)
LC FIA68-3040
Interviews two high school graduates on their first full - time jobs regarding their opinions about good work habits. Shows that working steadily, concentration, and planning ahead can lead to promotions, raises and/or other benefits.
Guidance and Counseling; Psychology
Dist - CORF Prod - CORF 1968

Your Job in Germany 15 MIN
16mm / U-matic / VHS
B&W
Presents a film made for American occupation troops to discourage fraternization with our former enemies. Unlike earlier Frank Capra films that blamed the war on German leaders, this film condemned the German people as a whole. Considered one of the most bitter and angry films to be made during the war.
Civics and Political Systems; Geography - World; History - World
Dist - USNAC Prod - USAPS 1982

Your job in Germany - Our job in Japan 32 MIN
U-matic / VHS
B&W
Promotes anti - German sentiments intended to discourage American occupation troops from fraternizing with their former enemies, made shortly before Germany's surrender. Blames World War II on the 'inherent belligerism' of Germans. Portrays Japanese as victims of cynical leaders who filled their minds with thoughts of world conquest. Suggests that these ideas must be changed so Japan can join the community of peaceful nations.
Civics and Political Systems; History - United States; History - World; Sociology
Dist - IHF Prod - IHF

Your Job Interview
VHS
Job Skills Series
(H C)
$59.00 _ CA117
Shows students how to mentally prepare for a job interview.
Business and Economics; Guidance and Counseling
Dist - AAVIM Prod - AAVIM 1989

Your Job - Keys to Advancement 30 MIN
VHS
Color
Details step by step strategies which include identifying and clarifying goals, creating a career path, outlining a plan, and performing for promotion.
Education; Guidance and Counseling
Dist - HRMC Prod - HRMC 1986

Your job - keys to advancement
VHS
(G)
$139.00 purchase _ #HR801V
Discusses the critical skills needed to advance and succeed on the job. Provides step by step strategies such as identifying and clarifying goals, creating a career path, outlining a plan, and performing for promotion. Discusses promotion, motivation, how to identify the interests of your company and how to be a problem solver and develop leadership skills.
Guidance and Counseling
Dist - CAREER Prod - CAREER

Your job - now it's up to you
VHS
Career process series
Color (H A)
$84.95 purchase _ #ES1230V
Examines the qualities that help employees keep their jobs and receive promotions.
Psychology
Dist - CAMV Prod - CAMV 1987

Your job - now it's up to you 15 MIN
VHS
(H C)
$84.95 _ CA129; $84.95, $43.50 purchase _ #XY863
Helps show students how to develop good working relationships by stressing the importance of appearance, positive attitude, accepting criticism positively, etc.
Education
Dist - AAVIM Prod - AAVIM 1989
CAREER CAREER

Your Job Series
Your Job - Applying for it 14 MIN
Your job - finding the right one 14 MIN
Your job - fitting in 16 MIN
Your Job - Getting Ahead 16 MIN
Your Job - Good Work Habits 14 MIN
Your Job - You and Your Boss 16 MIN
Dist - CORF

Your Job - You and Your Boss 16 MIN
16mm / U-matic / VHS
Your Job Series
Color (H C A)
LC FIA68-3039
Discusses the qualifications of leadership and many of the employee qualities that the leader seeks in those who work under his supervision. Stresses the need for mutual understanding.
Guidance and Counseling; Psychology
Dist - CORF Prod - CORF 1968

Your Knees, Injury and Treatment 17 MIN
VHS
Color (G PRO)
$195.00 purchase _ #N900VI046
Explains common knee injuries, forms of treatment and indicates what degree of recovery can be expected. Describes first aid for minor injuries, such as the RICE treatment - Rest, Ice - packs, Compression, Elevation. Illustrates the anatomy of the knee and shows endoscopic images of injured knees for a better understanding of the injuries, as well as surgical, investigative and repair procedures.
Health and Safety; Physical Education and Recreation; Science - Natural
Dist - HSCIC

Your last breath - forever 12 MIN
BETA / VHS / U-matic
Color (IND G A)
$510.00 purchase, $125.00 rental _ #YOU038
Explains the dangers of entering confined spaces previously filled with inert gases. Demonstrates the nature of oxygen - deficient atmospheres, the effects of inert gases on humans and proper procedures to follow to prevent accidents involving confined spaces.
Health and Safety; Psychology; Science - Natural
Dist - ITF Prod - ERF 1991

Your Last Chance 30 MIN
16mm
Color; B&W (J H T R)
LC FIA67-5754
Motivates church members to be alert to the needs of others.
Guidance and Counseling; Psychology; Religion and Philosophy
Dist - FAMF Prod - FAMF 1967

Your Library and Media Center - How to Get the most from Them
U-matic / VHS / 35mm strip
Library Skills Series
(G J)
$229 purchase _ #04008 - 85
Introduces students to the basic library skills by involving them in specific research. Covers the use of the Dewey Decimal System, the card catalog, and reference texts in relation to English and social studies projects.
Education
Dist - CHUMAN

Your library and media center - how to get the most from them 54 MIN
VHS
Color (H)
$249.00 purchase _ #04008 - 126
Involves students in specific research to introduce basic library skills. Explains the Dewey Decimal system and how to use it in research. Explores the resources available in the reference collection. Provides exercises to give students opportunities to practice what they have learned.
Education; Social Science
Dist - GA Prod - GA

Your lifestyle 26 MIN
VHS
Surviving in the real world - basic skills series
Color (J H)
$169.00 purchase _ #CG - 885 - VS
Looks at various lifestyle choices, emphasizing those realistic for young people just starting out on their own. Focuses on decisions involving major purchases, such as appliances, clothing and insurance. Discusses consumer scams to avoid, and contracts and warranties. Concludes with choices available for various types of insurance, including medical, tenant and life insurance. Part of a three - part series on consumer and life skills.
Business and Economics; Guidance and Counseling; Home Economics
Dist - HRMC Prod - HRMC

Your Living - Room 17 MIN
VHS / 16mm
Color (J)
$395.00 purchase, $75.00 rental
Suggests almost all rear - end collisions could be avoided if drivers maintained a certain distance between themselves and other automobiles to give time and space for necessary responses. Lists three - step sequence of events necessary to make a safe stop. Suggests related activities.
Health and Safety; Industrial and Technical Education; Social Science
Dist - IFB Prod - IFB 1989

Your Main Idea 15 MIN
VHS / U-matic
Fins, Feathers and Fur Series
(P)
$125.00 purchase
Discusses the formation of the main idea for a composition and the organization of basic opening paragraphs. Designed for children learning basic writing skills.
Education; English Language
Dist - AITECH Prod - WXXITV 1986

Your marriage - no 6 series
Accommodate or assimilate 29 MIN
Dist - UNL

Your money matters
VHS
Career process series
Color (H A)
$84.95 purchase _ #ES1240V
Helps viewers understand the deductions and differing wages of paychecks, as well as begin to develop a family budget.
Psychology
Dist - CAMV

Your Money Matters 11 MIN
U-matic / VHS
(H C A)

$98 _ #EA1V
Illustrates methods for keeping books, time schedules, budgets, and other financial records.
Business and Economics
Dist - JISTW **Prod** - JISTW

Your money matters 15 MIN
VHS
$43.50 purchase _ #XY864 for filmstrip, $84.95 _ #XY814 purchase for video
Stresses proper management of money in order to achieve a desired lifestyle. Shows students how a paycheck is calculated and guides them through the development of a personal or family budget of anticipated income and expenditures.
Business and Economics
Dist - CAREER **Prod** - CAREER

Your Money Matters Series
ABC'S of life insurance 25 MIN
Best investments for the small saver 25 MIN
Creative financing 25 MIN
Especially for Women 25 MIN
Evaluating Employee Benefits 25 MIN
Investments for Seniors 25 MIN
Money Management in Troubled Times 25 MIN
Old and New Investments 25 MIN
Planning Your Estate 25 MIN
Practical tax shelters - Pt I 25 MIN
Practical tax shelters - Pt II 25 MIN
Pre - Retirement Planning 25 MIN
Real Estate Investments 25 MIN
Stock Strategies for Individuals 25 MIN
Things You Should Know about Your Financial Institution 25 MIN
Dist - FILMID

Your Money or Your Life 14 MIN
16mm / U-matic / VHS
Color
Reports on the types of investments corporations are making to protect themselves. Discusses ways to minimize the risk of being kidnapped.
Business and Economics
Dist - CORF **Prod** - CBSTV

Your Money or Your Life 45 MIN
16mm / U-matic / VHS
Color
Presents an illuminating and provocative story about urban crime in America and how the resulting atmosphere of fear that pervades cities encourages racial antagonism. Shows two examples supporting such views. Counters with an alternative viewpoint of a black Mugger/Philosopher/Economist who compares mugging to the American economic system and justifies his actions as a means of redistributing wealth.
Sociology
Dist - CNEMAG **Prod** - CNEMAG 1984

Your Money Series
Bonds 59 MIN
Marketplace, the 55 MIN
Mutual Funds 51 MIN
Understanding the Business World and Stocks 58 MIN
Dist - CAMV

Your Mouth 16 MIN
16mm / U-matic / VHS
Color (I J H C)
LC 72-703068
Examines many aspects of the development of the human mouth from babyhood to maturity. Describes the growth of temporary and permanent teeth, the function of gums, tongue, lips, muscles, nerves and peridontal membrance, the attack of tooth enamel by bacteria and acids and the importance of saliva as a protector. Discusses the part played by the mouth in more complex activities, such as taste, smell and speech.
English Language; Health and Safety; Science - Natural
Dist - PHENIX **Prod** - LEVER 1972

Your Move
VHS / 16mm
Color (A PRO IND)
Provides information on personnel management. Part of the Employee Assistance Program (EAP) available on videotape.
Guidance and Counseling; Psychology
Dist - HAZELB

Your Move 25 MIN
16mm / U-matic / VHS
New Partnerships Series
Color (J)
LC 83-700511
Presents a fictional story of a young couple struggling with sex roles in contemporary family life. Focuses on the professional as well as personal issues confronting dual - career couples. Points out the pitfalls that can ensnare marriages when one partner sacrifices a successful career for the sake of the other.
Sociology
Dist - UCEMC **Prod** - BERKS 1982

Your Move 22 MIN
16mm / U-matic / VHS
Color
LC 76-703190
Presents myths and taboos which have prevented women from enjoying competitive and recreational sports. Shows a variety of sports activities and encourages girls and women to move and enjoy physical activity.
Physical Education and Recreation; Sociology
Dist - FI **Prod** - NFBC 1976

Your New Baby 19 MIN
VHS / U-matic
Color
Presents details of caring for a new baby during the first few weeks after birth. Describes basic materials which will be needed. Discusses common problems such as diaper rash, fever and feeding problems.
Home Economics; Sociology
Dist - MEDFAC **Prod** - MEDFAC 1981

Your new baby, your new life - 3 58 MIN
VHS
Project future series
Color (J H G)
$400.00 purchase
Presents two parts on teen parenting. Provides a practical overview of essential parenting skills, teaching the characteristics and basic care of the newborn in Your New Baby. Concentrates on the changes and challenges following birth, covering postpartum care for mothers and fathers, social and emotional responses to parenting, strategies for continuing education, day care options, contraception, AIDS prevention. Part of a series on teen pregnancy, childbirth and parenting coproduced by the National Organization of Gynecologic, Obstetric and Neonatal Nurses.
Health and Safety; Sociology
Dist - VHC **Prod** - VHC

Your new job 17 MIN
VHS / U-matic / 16mm
Color; Captioned (J H C)
$385.00, $300.00, $270.00 purchase _ #A982
Follows Michelle to her first day on the job. Reveals that she is excited and nervous and feels a little overwhelmed. Shows that meeting standards of punctuality, personal cleanliness and dress are basic considerations, as are being open - minded, attentive and polite. Michelle learns to ask questions and to not be afraid of making mistakes.
Business and Economics; Guidance and Counseling; Psychology
Dist - BARR **Prod** - SAIF 1985

Your newborn baby 60 MIN
VHS
Color (G)
$29.95 purchase _ #KAR504; $19.95 purchase _ #6331
Discusses the care of a newborn baby. Shows how to choose a doctor, feed, bathe, deal with crying and sleeping. Features Joan Lunden.
Health and Safety; Sociology
Dist - CADESF SYBVIS **Prod** - CADESF SYBVIS

Your newborn baby 45 MIN
VHS
(H C A)
$29.95 purchase _ #JJ200V
Explains how to chose a new born baby's doctor and prepare the home. Discusses the moment of childbirth, how to bathe an infant and how to deal with crying and sleeping patterns.
Health and Safety; Home Economics; Psychology; Sociology
Dist - CAMV **Prod** - CAMV

Your Newborn Baby 60 MIN
VHS
Color (G)
$19.95 purchase _ #6331
Stars Joan Lunden of Good Morning America. Covers diapering, feeding, bathing and safely baby - proofing the home.
Health and Safety; Psychology; Sociology
Dist - SYBVIS **Prod** - SYBVIS

Your Next Two Years 14 MIN
16mm
Color
LC 78-701455
Introduces Queensborough Community College by describing the college's academic, athletic and cultural programs. Presents faculty and students who explain what attracted them to the college.
Education
Dist - QUEECC **Prod** - QUEECC 1977

Your Operational Action Plan - Module 4 70 MIN
U-matic
Planning the Future and the Opportunities for Your Enterprise Series
Color (A)
Consists of four lessons - The Need For Planning, Operational Action Planning Steps, The Market Concept Of Managing and An Operational Action Plan Model.
Business and Economics
Dist - VENCMP **Prod** - VENCMP 1986

Your own business - getting started 45 MIN
VHS
Color (PRO)
$69.95 purchase _ #AISB100V-B
Teaches viewers how to establish their own business. Provides information from successful small business entrepreneurs, bankers, lawyers, accountants, and business consultants. Includes information not only on establishing a business but in making it successful and profitable.
Business and Economics
Dist - CAMV

Your Own Worst Enemy 26 MIN
VHS / U-matic
Color (J A)
Gives an overview of stress and how it manifests itself in people's lives. Demonstrates ways of dealing with stress.
Psychology
Dist - SUTHRB **Prod** - SUTHRB

Your Own Worst Enemy - Stress 24 MIN
16mm / U-matic / VHS
Color (H C A)
LC 77-702308
Documents the stories of individuals who have suffered the debilitating effects of stress and have taken steps against it, including counseling, recreation, religion, acupuncture, biofeedback, meditation and other Eastern spiritual and physical exercises.
Health and Safety; Physical Education and Recreation; Psychology
Dist - CF **Prod** - FIVSON 1976

Your participation in recovery from surgery 18 MIN
U-matic / VHS
Color (PRO)
$250.00 purchase, $60.00 rental _ #4297S, #4297V
Reveals that patients who take an active part in their own care recover more quickly. Prepares patients for surgery and encourages them to take an active part in their recovery. Depicts a 40 year old woman who is having gall bladder surgery. Follows her through the process step by step - her anxiety the night before, her concerns about pain and the exercises she learns, and her reactions two weeks after the operation.
Health and Safety
Dist - AJN **Prod** - COCO 1983

Your PC - inside out 120 MIN
BETA / VHS
Color (G)
$295.00 purchase
Provides personal computer - PC - independence in three steps. Shows how to diassemble the PC, troubleshooting and maintenance techniques and installing add - ons. Includes troubleshooting handbook, PC tool kit, and diagnostic, preventive maintenance and help programs on a diskette. Presented by Mark Minasi.
Computer Science; Mathematics; Psychology
Dist - DATEIN **Prod** - DATEIN 1990

Your PC - inside out 120 MIN
VHS
Self - teaching video learning package series
Color (G PRO)
$295.00 purchase _ #1YP54
Features PC expert Mark Minasi who takes the viewer inside a PC and presents a step - by - step demonstration of all of its inner workings. Uncovers and explains everything you need to know about PC maintenance and repair, including a discussion on components, power supply, drives, memory, boards, and chips. Includes a comprehensive course workbook, a precision tool kit, a diagnostic utilities disk and video. Part of a series.
Computer Science
Dist - TECHIN

Your PC - inside out - troubleshooting and maintaining your IBM PC compatibles
VHS / U-matic
Color (H C G)
$445.00, $295.00 purchase _ #06 - TMC
Shows how to perform most PC repairs, maintenance and troubleshooting procedures immediately. Trains non - technical users of IBM PCs and compatibles including the PS - 2. Features Mike Minasi. Includes a diskette with over 600K of diagnostic, preventive maintenance and help programs, a workbook and tool kit. Published by Data - Tech Institute.

Computer Science; Industrial and Technical Education
Dist - VIDEOT

Your Pelvic and Breast Examination 12 MIN
U-matic / VHS / 16mm
Color (J)
LC 75-704180
Provides a step - by - step description and explanation of the routine pelvic and breast examination. Emphasizes the importance of breast self - examination and of a regular check - up, including a pap smear.
Guidance and Counseling; Health and Safety
Dist - PEREN Prod - CROMIE 1975

Your Pelvic Examination 7 MIN
VHS / U-matic
Color
Describes reason for doing a pelvic examination. Explains the PAP test.
Health and Safety; Science - Natural; Sociology
Dist - MEDFAC Prod - MEDFAC 1977

Your Peritoneal Dialysis Therapy 9 MIN
U-matic / 35mm strip
Color
LC 80-730459
Introduces peritoneal dialysis with overview of normal kidney function and explanation of peritoneal dialysis. Emphasizes patient's participatory role in his health care and demonstrates guidelines he can apply to his own treatment. Focuses attention to scheduling of treatment sessions, care of the peritoneal catheter and diet modifications.
Health and Safety; Science - Natural
Dist - MEDCOM Prod - MEDCOM

Your Permit to Drive 14 MIN
16mm
Color (H)
Emphasizes the privileges and responsibilities of a driver's license.
Health and Safety; Social Science
Dist - GM Prod - GM 1969

Your Personal Affairs Officer 22 MIN
16mm
B&W
LC FIE63-279
Depicts how the personal affairs officer assists servicemen and their families during illness, accident or death, acts as counselor in insurance and retirement planning, assists in oversea transfer preparations, coordinates saving bonds campaigns and briefs new personnel.
Civics and Political Systems
Dist - USNAC Prod - USDD 1962

Your personal appearance 10 MIN
U-matic / VHS / 16mm
Communications and selling program series
Color (SPANISH)
LC 77-700447
Illustrates principles for dressing appropriately for different business situations, for different kinds of jobs and for different cultures. Emphasizes the importance of first impressions and discusses proper fit and dressing economically as well as tastefully.
Guidance and Counseling; Home Economics
Dist - NEM Prod - NEM 1977

Your personal health history 6 MIN
VHS / U-matic
Color
Emphasizes the patient's responsibility to provide complete and accurate information and cites the importance for accurate health history.
Health and Safety
Dist - MEDCOM Prod - MEDCOM

Your Pet - Forty Million BC 30 MIN
16mm
Great Plains Trilogy, 1 Series in the Beginning - the Primitive Man; In the beginning - the primitive man
B&W (H C A)
Traces the evolution of dogs and cats from primitive stages to domestication by man. Views the flesh - eating relatives of household pets.
Science - Natural
Dist - UNEBR Prod - KUONTV 1954

Your pet, your pal 30 MIN
VHS
Color (K P I J)
$29.95 purchase _ #S00601
Teaches children about different kinds of pets and to realize their responsibilities as pet owners.
Health and Safety; Science - Natural
Dist - UILL

Your pet, your pal
VHS
Children's discovery series
Color (P I J)
$29.95 purchase _ #IV - 037
Discusses the questions that should be asked when buying a pet. Looks at types of pets, sizes and shapes, potential owner allergies, and owner lifestyle.
Home Economics; Science - Natural
Dist - INCRSE Prod - INCRSE

Your place in the family 23 MIN
VHS
Color (J H)
$89.00 purchase _ #60410 - 026
Addresses brothers and sisters, birth order and family dynamics. Teaches how birth order and early family experiences shape attitudes and actions well into adulthood.
Sociology
Dist - GA

Your Place in the Nuclear Age 26 MIN
16mm
Careers in Nuclear Science and Nuclear Engineering Series
Color (J)
LC 74-706770
Pictures the professional environment of a career employee in nuclear science or engineering. Covers the three major employment areas - - contractors' laboratories of the United States Atomic Energy Commission, commerical nuclear industries and colleges and universities.
Guidance and Counseling; Psychology; Science; Science - Physical
Dist - USERD Prod - USNRC 1970

Your Planning Control - Module 5 70 MIN
U-matic
Planning the Future and the Opportunities for Your Enterprise Series
Color (A)
Consists of one lesson - Feedback And Measurement Of Your Goals.
Business and Economics
Dist - VENCMP Prod - VENCMP 1986

Your Police 11 MIN
16mm
B&W (I)
Presents information about the police department and its services to citizens.
Psychology; Social Science; Sociology
Dist - RVIERA Prod - RVIERA 1957

Your pregnancy, your plan - 1 43 MIN
VHS
Project future series
Color (J H G)
$400.00 purchase
Presents two parts on teen pregnancy. Focuses on prenatal care and health during pregnancy and the effects of substance abuse in Your Pregnancy. Considers the emotional, social and practical life - issues surrounding pregnancy, stressing the role of the young father throughout in Your Plan. Addresses concerns about continuing education, family relationships and finances. Reviews basic clothing and equipment needs of the newborn. Part of a series on teen pregnancy, childbirth and parenting coproduced by the National Organization of Gynecologic, Obstetric and Neonatal Nurses.
Health and Safety; Psychology; Sociology
Dist - VHC Prod - VHC

Your prescription and generic drugs 4 MIN
VHS / U-matic
Color
Explains the pharmacist's role in selecting drug products, including the use of generics and economic considerations.
Health and Safety
Dist - MEDCOM Prod - MEDCOM

Your Present Thinking Creates Future Events 55 MIN
VHS
Self - Esteem Video Series
Color (G)
$69.95 purchase _ #6 - 080 - 104P
Considers that most people look at the future as though it is largely determined by what others do and by circumstances beyond control. Reveals that most people are where they are because of their past choices, and where they will be in the future is controlled by present choices. Features Marilyn Grosboll.
Health and Safety; Psychology
Dist - VEP

Your price is right - sell it 30 MIN
U-matic / VHS / 16mm
Tough - minded salesmanship series
Color
Features Joe Batten who uses his tough - minded approach to convince salesmen that their price is right. Demonstrates a classic technique salesmen can use to overcome even the most stubborn price resistance.
Business and Economics
Dist - DARTNL Prod - DARTNL

Your product or service 73 MIN
VHS
How to start your own business series
Color (H A T)
$69.95 purchase _ #NC117
Considers products and services. Part of a ten - part series on starting a business.
Business and Economics
Dist - AAVIM Prod - AAVIM 1992

Your Protection Against Disease 8 MIN
16mm / U-matic / VHS
Color (P) (SPANISH)
Shows some of the ways in which germs spread disease, as well as examples of health habits to prevent disease. Describes how the body controls the microorganisms entering it.
Foreign Language; Health and Safety; Science - Natural
Dist - EBEC Prod - EBEC

Your recovery and growth 60 MIN
VHS
Passages - A National course of healing and hope for teens, their 'parents, friends and caregivers series
Color (R G)
$49.95 purchase _ #PASS3
Addresses how teens understand and experience loss through death. Features Dr Patrick Del Zoppo. Part of three parts.
Guidance and Counseling; Religion and Philosophy; Sociology
Dist - CTNA Prod - CTNA

Your Renal Diet 9 MIN
U-matic / 35mm strip
Patient Education Programs - Clinical Diet Series
Color
Presents the dietary restrictions imposed by kidney failure and considers the complications of not following the special renal diet. Discusses the key nutrients, including protein, sodium, and potassium and emphasizes calorie fluid intakes.
Health and Safety
Dist - POAPLE Prod - POAPLE

Your resume - a self portrait 30 MIN
U-matic / VHS / BETA
Color (G)
#CCP2000V; $98.00 purchase _ #XP300V; $98.00 purchase _ #CC4V
Presents information the job seeker needs to compose an ideal resume, stressing resume appearance. Features exercises and tips on skill identification, organization and presentation. Contrasts the functional resume with the chronological resume and presents information on the cover letter. Comes with manual.
Guidance and Counseling
Dist - CADESF Prod - CADESF 1987
CAREER CAREER
JISTW JISTW

Your right to a hearing 10 MIN
U-matic / VHS / 16mm
Consumer education series
Captioned; Color (J) (SPANISH)
LC 72-703422
Stresses the debtor's right to a hearing before creditor actions such as repossession and garnishment of wages are taken. Illustrates the hearing of an 18 - year - old unable to pay off a purchase. Points out the pressures and confusion of sales techniques, the responsibilities inherent in the new legal status of the 18 - year - old and the help he is given at the hearing by a young attorney from the neighborhood legal services.
Civics and Political Systems; Home Economics
Dist - ALTSUL Prod - ALTSUL 1972

Your Right to Know 17 MIN
VHS / 16mm
Haz - Comp Solution Series
Color (PRO)
$350.00 purchase, $125.00 rental, $40.00 preview
Presents information and materials needed for a company to comply with OSHA's Hazard Communication Standard. Shows the need for employees and the public to know about the presence of hazardous wastes. Includes support items.
Business and Economics; Computer Science; Guidance and Counseling; Health and Safety; Psychology; Sociology
Dist - UTM Prod - UTM

Your right - to - know
VHS
Right - to - know series
Color (H A G T)
$225.00 purchase _ #BM503
Trains educational market personnel about the potential chemical hazards they might encounter on the job.
Business and Economics; Education; Health and Safety; Psychology
Dist - AAVIM **Prod** - AAVIM 1992

Your Rights and Responsibilities 17 MIN
16mm
Working for the United States Series
Color (H A)
LC 77-700713
Presents the new or prospective civil service employee with information on employee conduct, grievance procedures, Equal Employment Opportunity complaints, adverse actions, reduction in force (RIF), privacy, political activity, unions and safety.
Civics and Political Systems; Guidance and Counseling
Dist - USNAC **Prod** - USCSC 1976

Your Safety Systems 10 MIN
U-matic / VHS / 16mm
Color (P I J)
LC 76-702164
Presents rules of the road for pedestrians and bicyclists. Shows how youngsters in the course of a typical day use a number of their safety systems to handle correctly the traffic situations they meet.
Health and Safety
Dist - AIMS **Prod** - DAVP 1973

Your School Safety Patrol 17 MIN
16mm
Color (P I)
Presents guidelines for the organization and safe operation of school safety patrol programs designed to protect children as they travel to and from school.
Guidance and Counseling; Health and Safety
Dist - AAAFTS **Prod** - AAAFTS 1975

Your Self Image 8 MIN
16mm
Color
Deals with the individual's confidence in himself. Tells the story of James, a small boy with self - image problems, who is continually rejected by others with whom he seeks to play. Shows how James opens a closet door while alone in his room and finds mirror man, a superman - type hero in charge of telling people about self - image.
Guidance and Counseling; Sociology
Dist - ECI **Prod** - ECI

Your Self - Images 30 MIN
VHS / U-matic
Personal Development and Professional Growth - Mike McCaffrey's 'Focus Seminar Series
Color
Psychology
Dist - DELTAK **Prod** - DELTAK

Your Share in Space 30 MIN
U-matic / VHS
History of Space Travel Series
Color
Science - Physical
Dist - MDCPB **Prod** - NASAC

Your Silent Partner 52 MIN
16mm
Color (I)
LC 73-702809
Creates public awareness of organized crime and its impact on society. Features the chief of the Organized Crime Division of the Michigan Attorney - General's Office answering questions regarding mutual numbers rackets, the effect of the two dollar bet, illicit narcotics, sports and off - track betting, police corruption, loan sharking, infiltration into legitimate businesses and other related topics.
Civics and Political Systems; Sociology
Dist - MOCJP **Prod** - MOCJP 1972

Your Skin and the Sun 13 MIN
16mm / VHS
Color (J A)
$295.00, $265.00 purchase, $50.00 rental
Warns young people that excessive exposure to sunlight is very damaging to the skin and can cause skin cancer. Shows how sunlight affects the skin, how skin cancer develops, and how to prevent it. Explains the use of sunscreen and protective clothing.
Health and Safety; Home Economics; Science - Physical; Social Science
Dist - HIGGIN **Prod** - HIGGIN 1988

Your Softlens Contact Lens Procedures 9 MIN
U-matic / VHS
Color
Provides instructions for application and removal of B and L Softlens with emphasis placed on proper hygiene and care.
Health and Safety; Science - Natural
Dist - MEDCOM **Prod** - MEDCOM

Your Speaking Image Series
Vocal Quality Counts 30 MIN
Dist - AITECH

Your Speaking Image Series
Finding Your Public Voice 30 MIN
Words that Work 30 MIN
Dist - AITECH
DELTAK

Your Speaking Image Series
Interactions that Count 30 MIN
Dist - AITECH
DELTAK
UEUWIS

Your Speaking Image - When Women Talk Business 180 MIN
U-matic / VHS
Color (H C A)
Covers the total range of speech competence, helping employees to build important communication skills. Increases employees' effectiveness by adding confidence, control and power to their speech. It is a practical and informative communication training series for both men and women.
Business and Economics; Education; English Language; Psychology; Sociology
Dist - UEUWIS **Prod** - UEUWIS 1984

Your Speaking Image - When Women Talk Business Series
The Sounds of Success 30 MIN
Dist - AITECH
DELTAK

Your Speaking Image - When Women Talk Business Series
Sounds of Success 30 MIN
Vocal Quality Counts 30 MIN
Your Vocal Assets 30 MIN
Dist - DELTAK

Your Speaking Image - When Women Talk Business Series
Finding Your Public Voice 180 MIN
Sounds of Success 180 MIN
Words that Work 180 MIN
Your Vocal Assets 180 MIN
Dist - UEUWIS

Your Spelling Profile 7 MIN
U-matic / VHS
Better Spelling Series
Color
English Language
Dist - DELTAK **Prod** - TELSTR

Your Stake in the Political Process 15 MIN
U-matic / VHS
By the People Series
Color (H)
Deals with the ways political events and conditions affect the life of the individual.
Civics and Political Systems; Social Science
Dist - CTI **Prod** - CTI

Your Stay in the Hospital 10 MIN
U-matic / VHS / 16mm
Color (SPANISH)
Clarifies the role of the hospital in modern medical care. Discusses reasons for hospital charges, emphasizes the importance of following hospital routine and procedures, and answers many questions asked by patients.
Foreign Language; Health and Safety
Dist - PRORE **Prod** - PRORE

Your Sterling Heritage 27 MIN
16mm
Color
Tells the story of how Sterling designs are developed, including many of the manufacturing steps. Presents a historical background of many famous Sterling patterns.
Business and Economics; Guidance and Counseling; Home Economics
Dist - MTP **Prod** - REEBAR

Your study skills - taking tests 11 MIN
U-matic / VHS / 16mm
Color (I J)
$280, $195 purchase _ #3575
Shows the different types of tests that students take, and suggestions for studying for them.
Education
Dist - CORF **Prod** - CORF 1977

Your surgical experience 12 MIN
VHS
Color (PRO A)
$200.00 purchase _ #GS - 07
Follows a patient through the three stages of surgery. Shows patients what to expect during the pre - operative period, in the operating suite itself and in the post - operative recuperation period. Familiarizes the viewers with the customary routines of each phase and describes the sensory input the patient will experience. Produced by the New England Baptist Hospital, Boston, MA.
Health and Safety
Dist - MIFE

Your Teeth 6 MIN
U-matic / VHS / 16mm
Color (P) (SPANISH)
Points out how first teeth are formed, how teeth serve different purposes, how decay starts and how to protect teeth.
Foreign Language; Health and Safety; Science - Natural
Dist - EBEC **Prod** - EBEC

Your temperaments - related to work situations
VHS
$89.00 purchase _ #012 - 626; $89.00 purchase _ #3253
Uses self - assessment booklets and videos to teach students the value of early career planning. Helps evaluate interests, temperament, and abilities, and apply them to course selection and career decisions.
Guidance and Counseling
Dist - CAREER MERIDN **Prod** - CAREER MERIDN 1988

Your Temperaments - Related to Work Situations
U-matic / VHS
CEPP Video Series
(J H C A)
$89.00 _ #MG3253V
Uses live action to introduce the viewer to the major ideas regarding work situations in relation to his temperament.
Business and Economics; Guidance and Counseling; Psychology
Dist - CAMV **Prod** - CAMV

Your Thoughts Create Your Life 51 MIN
Cassette / VHS
Conversations On Living Lecture Series
Color (G)
$19.95, $10.00 purchase _ #404, #210
Considers the physiology and organ systems of the human body and describes the emotional causes underlying the problems experienced in specific areas. Features Louise L Hay. Part of a four - part series.
Health and Safety; Psychology
Dist - HAYHSE **Prod** - HAYHSE

Your touch 10 MIN
U-matic
Readalong One Series
Color (K P)
Introduces reading and spelling for preschoolers and children in grades 1 to 3 with animation, puppets, humor and music. Comes with teacher's guide and kit.
Education; English Language; Literature and Drama
Dist - TVOTAR **Prod** - TVOTAR 1975

Your Town 25 MIN
16mm / U-matic / VHS
Color (I)
LC 84-706562
Describes how a small town in New Hampshire is divided in the townspeoples' opinions as to whether to allow an electronics plant to locate in their town or to preserve the rural quality of their lives.
Sociology
Dist - PHENIX **Prod** - CINEWO 1984

Your town I series
Presents a five - part series on community services. Includes the titles The Fire Station, The Police Station, The Hospital, The Library, The Post Office.
The Fire station 13 MIN
The Hospital 15 MIN
The Library 14 MIN
The Police station 15 MIN
The Post office 15 MIN
Dist - NGS **Prod** - NGS 1984

Your town II series
Presents a five - part series on community services. Includes the titles Recreation, Communiations, Schools, Transportation, Public Works.
Communications 15 MIN
Public works 15 MIN
Recreation 15 MIN
Schools 15 MIN
Transportation 15 MIN
Dist - NGS **Prod** - NGS 1984

Your Turn in the Box 17 MIN
U-matic / VHS / 16mm
Color (J)
LC 75-702528
Features baseball player Hank Aaron demonstrating the proper methods for hitting a baseball. Suggests the need for discipline and the desire to succeed.
Physical Education and Recreation
Dist - MCFI **Prod** - LRDKNG 1971

Your Turn, My Turn 101 MIN
16mm
Color (FRENCH (ENGLISH SUBTITLES))
Focuses on two veterans of unhappy marriages who pursue an affair in the face of hostile children, unpleasant spouses, and troublesome new moralities. Directed by Francois Leterrier. With English subtitles.
Fine Arts; Foreign Language
Dist - NYFLMS **Prod** - UNKNWN 1978

Your turn on the court - Film 1 - the serve and volley 16 MIN
U-matic / VHS / 16mm
Color (J)
Presents Ken Stuart demonstrating the fundamentals of the serve and volley in tennis.
Physical Education and Recreation
Dist - MCFI **Prod** - LRDKNG 1978

Your turn on the court - Film 2 - the ground strokes 22 MIN
16mm / U-matic / VHS
Color (J)
Demonstrates the fundamentals of the tennis forehand and backhand ground strokes, including proper grips, footwork, racquet position, swing, ball contact and follow through.
Physical Education and Recreation
Dist - MCFI **Prod** - LRDKNG 1978

Your Two Cents Worth 11 MIN
16mm
Color (J)
Shows highlights of the first decade of man in space, which was financed by just two cents out of every tax dollar. Enumerates some of the resulting benefits to mankind and describes our future goals in space.
History - World; Industrial and Technical Education; Science; Science - Physical
Dist - RCKWL **Prod** - NAA

Your ulcer diet 63 FRS
U-matic / VHS
Patient education programs - clinical diet series
Color
Discusses an ulcer diet intended for the patient who needs to be treated for peptic ulcer disease.
Health and Safety
Dist - POAPLE **Prod** - POAPLE

Your Upper Body 10 MIN
Videoreel / VT2
Janaki Series
Color
Physical Education and Recreation
Dist - PBS **Prod** - WGBHTV

Your Vision, Your Life 25 MIN
16mm
Color
Presents the full scope of optometric care with dramatic vignettes ranging from how the profession serves the child with a vision problem that interferes with learning to the older person with a potentially blinding disease.
Health and Safety; Science
Dist - MTP **Prod** - AOA 1982

Your Vocal Assets 30 MIN
U-matic / VHS
Your Speaking Image - When Women Talk Business Series
Color
English Language; Psychology
Dist - DELTAK **Prod** - WHATV

Your Vocal Assets 180 MIN
U-matic / VHS
Your Speaking Image - When Women Talk Business Series
Color (H C A)
Business and Economics; Education; Psychology; Sociology
Dist - UEUWIS **Prod** - UEUWIS 1984

Your vocational job search campaign - successful guerilla tactics 30 MIN
VHS
Color (H C G)
$79.95 purchase _ #CCP0057V
States that conducting a successful job search requires the same steps as running an effective military campaign. Shows vocational students how to locate and investigate potential employers; how to contact them by phone and in person; the importance of strategy, goals and self assessment; how to write a resume and cover letter; how to prepare for and what to wear to an interview; the do's and don'ts of interview techniques; how to best present themselves and their skills. Interviews employers who discuss the qualities they look for when selecting applicants.
Business and Economics; Education; Guidance and Counseling; Industrial and Technical Education
Dist - CAMV **Prod** - CAMV 1991

Your Vote Counts - State and Local Government
VHS / U-matic
Color (H)
Outlines the structures and functions of state, county and city government. Discusses urban and suburban problems, and the facts and values of real local political disputes.
Civics and Political Systems
Dist - GA **Prod** - GA

Your Way or Mine 17 MIN
16mm / U-matic / VHS
Color
Dramatizes a grievance incident, from the employee's point of view as well as from the supervisor's point of view.
Business and Economics; Psychology
Dist - USNAC **Prod** - USDL 1981

Your weekly weaver series
Ancient art of tablet weaving - also called card weaving 29 MIN
Frame Looms and How to Build, Buy or Find One 29 MIN
An Introduction to a Small Lap Loom Called the Inkle Loom 29 MIN
An Introduction to the four - harness loom - both floor and table models 29 MIN
Rigid Heddle Looms and How to Warp Them for Fabric Weaving 29 MIN
Versatility and the Variety of Weaves Possible with the Four - Harness Loom are 29 MIN
Dist - PBS

Your Weight Reduction Diet 74 FRS
VHS / U-matic
Patient Education Programs - Clinical Diet Series
Color
Discusses how a weight reduction diet reduces the health risks of obesity by urging the overweight patient to become involved in a comprehensive program, including calorie counting, behavior modification, and increased physical activity.
Health and Safety; Physical Education and Recreation
Dist - POAPLE **Prod** - POAPLE

Your will and Estate 25 MIN
U-matic / VHS
Money Smart - a Guide to Personal Finance Series
Color (H C A)
Focuses on estate planning. Covers what should be included in a will and who should be chosen as executors and guardians. Includes trust funds and revisions.
Business and Economics; Civics and Political Systems; Education; Home Economics
Dist - BCNFL **Prod** - SOMFIL 1985

Your work and your health - the role of the industrial hygienist 16 MIN
U-matic / BETA / VHS
Color (IND G)
$495.00 purchase _ #859 - 37
Discusses the role of the industrial hygienist in protecting workplace health. Explains the concepts of hazard and risk in regard to handling materials and workplace exposure.
Health and Safety; Industrial and Technical Education; Psychology
Dist - ITSC **Prod** - ITSC 1990

You're a Big Boy Now 96 MIN
16mm
Color
Tells how an innocent library worker falls in love with a man - hating go - go dancer and then hits the road to find maturity.
Fine Arts
Dist - TWYMAN **Prod** - WB 1967

You're Accountable 51 MIN
VHS
Color (H C A) (SPANISH)
$60.00 purchase, $20.00 rental ; $12.00 rental ; $60.00 purchase, $20.00 rental
Teaches how to select and use financial accounts.
Business and Economics; Home Economics
Dist - CORNRS **Prod** - CORNRS 1986

You're Being Asked 25 MIN
U-matic / VHS
Color
Shows blood donors and recipients telling why giving blood is important, because ten pints of blood are used every minute in the US, 16,000 pints per day, to save lives of people threatened by illness or injury.
Health and Safety; Science - Natural
Dist - MEDCOM **Prod** - MEDCOM

You're Coming Along Fine 23 MIN
VHS / 16mm / U-matic
Color; B&W (H C A) (NORWEGIAN PORTUGUESE SWEDISH GERMAN DUTCH FRENCH)
LC FIA68-2709; fia68-2709
Examines a manager's problem in appraising employee work, discussing employee achievement with higher management and explaining unsatisfactory work to the employees themselves.
Business and Economics; Psychology
Dist - RTBL **Prod** - RTBL 1968

You're Costing Me Money 15 MIN
U-matic / VHS
Communication at Work Series
Color (H)
Explores the principles of on - the - job persuasion, including saving face, considering the other person, establishing a common ground, and avoiding name - calling.
Guidance and Counseling; Psychology
Dist - AITECH **Prod** - OHSDE 1979

You're Eating for Two 20 MIN
U-matic / VHS / 16mm
Color (H C A)
Discusses the importance of nourishment during pregnancy for both the mother and the baby. Shows the consequences of poor nutrition on the unborn baby.
Health and Safety; Home Economics; Social Science
Dist - PEREN **Prod** - NFBC

You're Growing Up with Dr Joyce Brothers 12 MIN
VHS / BETA
Color
Presents six articulate adolescent girls, who discuss growing up with psychologist Dr Joyce Brothers, including topics such as menstruation, other physical changes, and relationships with boys, friends and family.
Health and Safety; Psychology; Science - Natural; Sociology
Dist - WSTGLC **Prod** - WSTGLC

You're Hired 30 MIN
VHS
Speaking American English at Work Series
Color (G)
$79.50 purchase _ #SV7210
Focuses on communication skills required to get a job and the importance of appearing confident at an interview. Tells the story of a Vietnamese refugee's experiences in the US job market. Provides practice using students from different language backgrounds as well as written and oral exercises. Includes teacher's manual. Part of a two - part series.
Business and Economics; English Language; Guidance and Counseling; Psychology
Dist - NORTNJ

You're hired - customer service for youth 51 MIN
VHS / U-matic / BETA
Color (H C G)
Shows young, potential jobholders the practical skills they'll need to know once hired. Looks at a variety of service sectors.
Guidance and Counseling; Social Science
Dist - TRIUNE **Prod** - TRIUNE

You're hired - customer service for youth series 50 MIN
VHS
You're hired - customer service for youth series
Color (H C A)
$399.00 purchase _ #10353VG
Helps youth entering the job market and trains teenagers in maintaining a customer service perspective. Uses scenarios from a variety of stores and offices to show how to treat customers in person and on the phone. Includes four videos, leader's guides and blackline masters. Tape One can not be purchased separately.
Business and Economics; Psychology
Dist - UNL

You're hired series
Help wanted - offre d'emploi 15 MIN
Dist - CDIAND

You're in Charge 12 MIN
16mm
Secondary School Safety Series

B&W
Rules for safe, successful baby sitting. Shows both a girl and a boy in situations with children.
Health and Safety; Home Economics
Dist - NSC **Prod** - NSC 1955

You're in Charge of Your Life, Believe it or not 55 MIN
VHS
Self - Esteem Video Series
Color (G)
$69.95 purchase _ #6 - 080 - 102P
Reveals that people have choices about the things happening in their lives but frequently fail to recognize those choices. Realizing that there is choice, even if it's an unpleasant choice, puts one back in control of one's life. Features Marilyn Grosboll.
Health and Safety; Psychology
Dist - VEP

You're Never Too Young 10.5 MIN
VHS / 16mm
Taking Care FOCUS Series
(PRO G)
$270.00 purchase
Encourages employees to adopt healthier lifestyles. Gives suggestions and strategies to help employees reach their health goals. Focuses on the adult years.
Business and Economics; Health and Safety
Dist - CNTRHP **Prod** - CNTRHP

You're Nobody Till Somebody Loves You 12 MIN
16mm
B&W
Documents the marriage of Timothy Leary to a model. By D A Pennebaker.
Fine Arts; History - United States
Dist - PENNAS **Prod** - PENNAS

You're not alone 26 MIN
VHS / U-matic
Color (PRO C G)
$195.00 purchase _ #C890 - VI - 002
Introduces patients awaiting spine surgery to the situations and emotions they can expect to experience as they prepare for surgery. Follows two women who face similar surgery through the time leading up to and following their operations. They candidly discuss the fears, frustrations and depression experienced as a result of their debilitating conditions. Presented by Sheila Bjoklund, RN, Carolyn Dietz, RN, William Johnson, RN, Darlene Swanson, RN, Laury Christensen and Lisa M Brown.
Health and Safety
Dist - HSCIC

You're not alone with herpes
VHS / 16mm / U-matic
Color (H C A)
Discusses various aspects of herpes, including the definition of the Herpes virus, related diseases, transmission of the disease, initial attack and ways of keeping the virus under control.
Health and Safety
Dist - PEREN **Prod** - SKYLTE 1983

You're not communicating 23 MIN
16mm / VHS
Color (H)
$545.00, $410.00, $380.00 purchase _ #A559; LC 89715694
Teaches five different skills used in the communication process.
Computer Science; Psychology
Dist - BARR

You're not communicating - second edition 23 MIN
VHS
Color (A PRO IND)
$595.00 purchase, $140.00 rental
Presents five humorous vignettes illustrating communication problems. Covers five keys to effective communication, including specificity, presenting one idea at a time, and keeping words and body language in sync.
Business and Economics; Guidance and Counseling; Literature and Drama; Psychology; Social Science
Dist - VLEARN **Prod** - BARR

You're not Listening 30 MIN
VHS
Soapbox With Tom Cottle Series
Color (G)
$59.95 purchase _ #SBOX - 412
Examines family communication. Tells how many teenagers feel their parents are overprotective. Hosted by psychologist Tom Cottle.
Psychology; Sociology
Dist - PBS **Prod** - WGBYTV 1985

You're not Listening 32 MIN
16mm
Color
LC 76-702309
Shows how a young second - grade teacher with a problem child in her class comes to learn and recognize aspects of brain dysfunction which are afflicting the boy.
Education; Psychology
Dist - MTP **Prod** - CIBA 1976

You're not There Yet 32 MIN
16mm
Color (C A)
LC 79-701855
Follows one man with a drinking problem through his day as he gradually becomes aware of, and at the same time denies, his drinking problem.
Health and Safety; Psychology; Sociology
Dist - FILCOM **Prod** - LENWAY 1978

You're Only Old Once 60 MIN
VHS / U-matic
Color
Attempts to dispel some of the myths about aging through an examination of the issues and concerns of Minnesota's large and active population of senior citizens. Gives insight into the loneliness and hardship that often dominate old age.
Health and Safety; Sociology
Dist - WCCOTV **Prod** - WCCOTV 1979

You're right and so am I 15 MIN
VHS
Respect series
CC; Color (I)
$89.95 purchase _ #10417VG
Gives strategies for showing respect for others' ideas and learning to deal with differences in taste and opinion. Uses live - action, narration, music and graphics to teach sensitivity. Comes with a teacher's guide and a set of blackline masters. Part three of a four - part series.
Guidance and Counseling; Home Economics; Psychology
Dist - UNL

You're the Doctor - Prevention 30 MIN
VHS / U-matic
Color
Tells how the 'lifestyle' disease brought on by abuse of the body can be avoided through preventive maintenance by the individual. Discusses the dangers of smoking, the importance of moderation in drinking alcohol and the need for adequate sleep. Explains the merits of a well balanced diet and discusses how people are led astray by television commercials and the importance of the right kind of exercise.
Health and Safety; Physical Education and Recreation
Dist - FAIRGH **Prod** - FAIRGH

You're the Key Man 10 MIN
16mm
Key Man Series
B&W
Shows how a foreman's decision to become active in the safety program paid off.
Business and Economics; Health and Safety
Dist - NSC **Prod** - NSC

You're Under Arrest 15 MIN
U-matic / VHS / 16mm
Color
Provides a close - up look at America's drunk driving problem, with a special focus on efforts aimed at toughening and enforcing drunk driving laws. Shows how alcohol seriously impairs the reflexes, judgment and control of drivers behind the wheel. Witnesses the procedure law enforcement officers follow after pulling over individuals suspected of being under the influence. Originally shown on the CBS program 60 Minutes.
Civics and Political Systems; Health and Safety; Social Science
Dist - CORF **Prod** - CBSTV

You're Why We're Here 25 MIN
16mm
Color
Introduces the physical structure and academic attractions of Cuyahoga Community College, Metro campus. Describes the academic programs, student services and registration processes at Cuyahoga Community College.
Education; Guidance and Counseling
Dist - CUYAHO **Prod** - CUYAHO 1971

Yours for a Song 22 MIN
16mm
Color (P I J H)
Shows a backyard bird sanctuary established to attract migrating and resident birds throughout the year. Explains that birds are attracted to yards and gardens if they are provided with food, water and shelter. Includes views of 24 different species of birds.
Science - Natural
Dist - FENWCK **Prod** - WILCOX 1954

Yours Truly 15 MIN
VHS / U-matic
Magic Shop Series no 12
Color (P)
LC 83-706157
Employs a magician named Amazing Alexander and his assistants to explore letter writing.
English Language
Dist - GPN **Prod** - CVETVC 1982

Yours Truly, Andrea G Stern 38 MIN
U-matic / VHS / 16mm
Color (J)
LC 80-700045
Dramatizes some common problems of single - parent families in a story about the conflicts that arise between a young girl, her mother and her mother's live - in lover.
Fine Arts; Sociology
Dist - PHENIX **Prod** - SEIDS 1979

Youth and grief 32 MIN
VHS / U-matic / 16mm
Color (J H)
$280.00, $330.00 purchase, $50.00 rental
Records teenagers sharing with the viewer their experiences with the dying and death of a family member. Discusses the grieving and coping processes. A social worker, who himself lost a parent at an early age, covers some of the special concerns that teachers, family and friends need to consider. Produced by Top Shelf Productions.
Guidance and Counseling; Sociology
Dist - NDIM

Youth and music in Detroit 24 MIN
16mm
Color (H C A)
Depicts the music department activities of a Detroit high school. Shows various choral, instrumental and dance groups.
Fine Arts
Dist - WSUM **Prod** - WSUM 1956

Youth and the future 26 MIN
VHS
Turning 16 series
Color; CC (G T)
$175.00 purchase, $50.00 rental
Asks how teens feel about their future. Unites all six teenagers featured in the series to discuss their global concerns and examine the impact American culture has on their lives. Part eight of an eight - part series that questions whether there is a global teenager. Examines the lives of teens from Jamaica, Niger, Egypt, Brazil, Thailand and India, and explores the major issues facing young people everywhere - including education, culture, sex and marriage, sports, religion, work and the future.
Civics and Political Systems; Fine Arts; Geography - World; Sociology
Dist - BULFRG **Prod** - HARCOT 1994

Youth and the global village 26 MIN
VHS
Turning 16 series
Color; CC (G T)
$175.00 purchase, $50.00 rental
Looks at how teens around the world listen to the same music, watch similar videos, and make idols of the same pop stars. Asks if they hold similar views on marriage, culture and religion. Features part one of an eight - part series that questions whether there is a global teenager. Examines the lives of six teens from different countries and explores major issues facing young people everywhere - including education, culture, sex and marriage, sports, religion, work and the future.
Fine Arts; Geography - World; Sociology
Dist - BULFRG **Prod** - HARCOT 1994

Youth and the Law 36 MIN
16mm / U-matic / VHS
B&W (C A)
Dramatizes the role of the police as they work with community organizations to guide youthful energies into constructive channels and to prevent delinquency.
Civics and Political Systems; Psychology; Sociology
Dist - IFB **Prod** - MHFB 1962

Youth Communications 36 MIN
16mm
Color
LC 74-705984
Uses illustrations from the pre - 1970 era to emphasize the more important general youth communications patterns that continue to this day. Developed to assist in understanding the drug problem and to close the understanding gap that exists between adults and today's youthful media audience.
Health and Safety; Psychology; Sociology
Dist - USNAC **Prod** - USDD 1969

The Youth Drug Scene 30 MIN
16mm
Color (J H)
Shows that Mark has overcome his three year addiction to drugs because he has found a personal relationship with Jesus Christ. Discusses the risks and dangers of drug experimentation.
Guidance and Counseling; Health and Safety; Psychology; Religion and Philosophy; Sociology
Dist - FAMF **Prod** - FAMF

Youth gives a damn 25 MIN
VHS / U-matic
Color
Tells about VD, pollution, sex education, drugs, filmed at YGAD camp, which was simultaneously a mountain retreat, health learn - in, weekend rap session, and if not quite a bridge, at least a rope ladder across that so - called chasm, the 'generation gap.'
Health and Safety
Dist - MEDCOM **Prod** - MEDCOM

Youth leadership - Part I 23 MIN
VHS / U-matic
Teen - family life series
Color (J H G)
$179.00, $229.00 purchase, $60.00 rental
Explores the development of leadership skills for youth. Interviews leaders in youth leadership programs and explores skills essential for leadership. Part of a two part series.
Guidance and Counseling; Sociology
Dist - NDIM **Prod** - FAMLIF 1993

Youth leadership - Part II 25 MIN
VHS / U-matic
Teen - family life series
Color (J H G)
$179.00, $229.00 purchase, $60.00 rental
Focuses on skills essential to leadership such as self - esteem, communication, conflict resolution and the significance of assuming responsibility. Features teenagers talking about the importance of respect in developing leadership roles. Part of a two part series.
Guidance and Counseling; Psychology; Sociology
Dist - NDIM **Prod** - FAMLIF 1993

Youth Lifeskills Series
Streetproofing 28 MIN
Dist - HMDI

Youth, maturity, old age, death 8 MIN
U-matic / VHS / 16mm
Art of silence, pantomimes with Marcel Marceau series
Color (J H C)
LC 75-703448
Features Marcel Marceau presenting symbolically the cycle of life.
Fine Arts
Dist - EBEC **Prod** - EBEC 1975

Youth, Sex and Chastity 40 MIN
BETA / VHS
Color (G)
Introduces the religious and psychological counseling of Father Groeschel, PhD in Psychology, as he talks with three young adults on sexual morality.
Psychology; Religion and Philosophy; Sociology
Dist - DSP **Prod** - DSP

Youth sports - is winning everything 30 MIN
VHS
Color (H C G)
$69.95 purchase _ #DH100V
Asks if young athletes have been pressured into becoming miniature professionals who compete, not for themselves, but for Mom and Dad and the hometown. Reveals that too many youth coaches are caught in the 'win at all cost' syndrome, sacrificing the emotional and physical development of children for league titles. Discusses the values adults place on winning and what effect those values can have on children involved in sports.
Guidance and Counseling; Physical Education and Recreation
Dist - CAMV

Youth Sports - is Winning Everything 28 MIN
16mm
Color (A)
LC 80-701873
Explains that many sports coaches ignore a child's emotional needs and physical limitations, often disregarding the recreational value of sports.
Physical Education and Recreation
Dist - COXBAR **Prod** - COXBAR 1980

Youth Stress 24 MIN
16mm / U-matic
Color (J H A)
Illustrates causes and results of adolescent stress and offers suggestions to counteract the stress teenagers are likely to experience.
Psychology; Sociology
Dist - PEREN **Prod** - SCCL

Youth Terror - the View from Behind the Gun 48 MIN
U-matic / VHS / 16mm
Color (J)
LC 78-701183
Views teenage crime.
Sociology
Dist - MGHT **Prod** - ABCTV 1978

Youth terror - the view from behind the gun - Pt 1 29 MIN
U-matic / VHS / 16mm
Color (J)
LC 78-701183
Offers a view of teenage crime.
Sociology
Dist - MGHT **Prod** - ABCTV 1978

Youth terror - the view from behind the gun - Pt 2 19 MIN
16mm / U-matic / VHS
Color (J)
LC 78-701183
Offers a view of teenage crime.
Sociology
Dist - MGHT **Prod** - ABCTV 1978

Youth - the Future 28 MIN
VHS
Illuminations series
Color (G R)
#V - 1040
Interviews three young Greek Americans on the importance of the Greek Orthodox Church to their lives. Shares their visions of the future of the church.
Religion and Philosophy; Sociology
Dist - GOTEL **Prod** - GOTEL 1989

Youth to Maturity 29 MIN
U-matic / VHS / 16mm
History of U S Foreign Relations Series
Color (J)
LC 73-702970
Portrays the evolution of the United States from a small, weak nation into a world power. Covers Admiral Perry's trip to Japan, Civil War diplomacy, the Spanish - American War, the Philippines expedition, the construction of the Panama Canal and the U S role as international peacemaker in the Portsmouth negotiations, the Algeciras Conference and the two Hague Conferences.
History - United States
Dist - CORF **Prod** - USDS 1972

Youth Under the Influence Series
Hard Drugs - It's not the Going Up that Hurts, It's the Coming Down 16 MIN
Dist - CNEMAG

The Youth who wanted to shiver 9 MIN
16mm / U-matic / VHS
Grimm's fairy tales series
Color (K P I) (SPANISH)
LC 79-700384
Presents an animated adaptation of the classic fairy tale by the Brothers Grimm, about a young boy who sets out into the world to learn how to fear and shiver.
Literature and Drama
Dist - CF **Prod** - BOSUST 1978

Youth's finest hour 20 MIN
16mm
Color
Shows the opportunities of a young athlete to learn and then apply the 'language of victory.'
Physical Education and Recreation
Dist - FELLCA **Prod** - FELLCA

You've come a long way, maybe 55 MIN
U-matic / VHS
Moore report series
Color (J)
LC 82-707399
Explores the issue of comparable worth, focusing on women and their role in the U S work force. Includes comments of women, their supporters and detractors, attorneys, and policy - making executives, who voice their opinions about the validity of comparable worth claims as opposed to need to let supply and demand or the market determine salaries.
Sociology
Dist - IU **Prod** - WCCOTV 1981

You've come a long way, Rene 22 MIN
U-matic / 16mm / VHS
Color (P I J)
$495.00, $375.00, $345.00 _ #A344
Tells the story of Rene and her best friend Carol. Reveals that Rene's goal is to become a championship runner, while Carol wants to be accepted by the kids at school and has begun to smoke. When Rene won't smoke, Carol shuns her. Rene decides not to smoke, and when she sets a track record, Carol and the gang want to be her friend.
Guidance and Counseling; Health and Safety; Psychology; Sociology
Dist - BARR **Prod** - HAMRL 1983

You've got a nerve 30 MIN
VHS
Bodymatters series
Color (H C A)
PdS65 purchase
Discusses nervo cells and the nervous system. Part of a series of 26 30-minute videos on various systems of the human body.
Science - Natural
Dist - BBCENE

You've got to be taught to hate 12 MIN
16mm
Color & B&W (J H G)
$150.00 purchase, $30.00 rental _ #PPF - 762, #PRF - 762
Presents an edited version of The Victims. Demonstrates that prejudice is like a disease which is subtly transmitted.
Sociology
Dist - ADL **Prod** - ADL

You've Got to be Up 15 MIN
16mm
Color
LC 80-700939
Takes a look at the game of bowls.
Physical Education and Recreation
Dist - TASCOR **Prod** - TASCOR 1976

You've got to live somewhere forever 10 MIN
16mm
Dr Bob Jones says series
Color (R)
Presents Dr. Bob Jones, Sr. speaking about basic life truths.
Religion and Philosophy
Dist - UF **Prod** - UF

You've Sold Me, Mrs Marlowe 9 MIN
16mm
People Sell People Series
Color (H A)
Emphasizes the importance of making the most of each contact with each customer and describes the necessary requirements for making a sale completely successful.
Business and Economics
Dist - MLA **Prod** - SAUM 1965

Yrs Truly 26 MIN
16mm
Color (G)
LC 73-702403
Presents the value of keeping schools open all year. Features Senator Charles Percy who describes the need and outlines the values inherent in this way of looking to the future educational system. Interviews administrators and teachers in three areas of the United States where schools have been operating on a year - round basis - Prince William County Schools in Virginia, the San Diego School District and the Valley View School District in Romeoville, Illinois.
Education; Sociology
Dist - GOLDES **Prod** - GOLDES 1973

Yucatan Ruins 15 MIN
16mm
Color (J)
Pictures Merida, Capital of Yucatan, and Chichen - Itza, America's Egypt. Shows fields where the game Pelota was played, the observatory, pyramids and the Temple.
Geography - World; Science - Physical; Sociology
Dist - AVED **Prod** - BARONA 1957

The Yucatec Maya - a Case Study in Marriage 30 MIN
U-matic
Faces of Culture - Studies in Cultural Anthropology Series Lesson 10; Lesson 10
Color (C A)
Explores characteristics of an extended family in an agricultural society. Describes pressures on the traditional extended family to change.
Sociology
Dist - CDTEL **Prod** - COAST

Yue Fei 203 MIN
VHS
Color (G) (CHINESE)
$60.00 purchase _ #5186
Presents a film from the People's Republic of China. Includes two videocassettes.
Geography - World; Literature and Drama
Dist - CHTSUI

Yugoslav Farm Family 12 MIN
16mm
How We Live Series
Color (P I J H)
LC FIA66-1855
Pictures farmers of the Dalmation Coast, who must struggle with a harsh land and an oppressive government. No narration is used, but a musical score based on Yugoslav folk melodies is provided.
Geography - World; Psychology; Social Science; Sociology
Dist - IFF **Prod** - IFF 1964

Yugoslav - Pt 1 29 MIN
Videoreel / VT2
Grand master chess series
Color
Physical Education and Recreation
Dist - PBS **Prod** - KQEDTV

Yugoslav - Pt 2 29 MIN
Videoreel / VT2
Grand master chess series
Color
Physical Education and Recreation
Dist - PBS **Prod** - KQEDTV

Yugoslavia ; 1988 19 MIN
16mm
Modern Europe series
Color (I J H)
LC 88-712607; 88-712609
Illustrates the economic system, natural resources, government and customs of Yugoslavia.
History - World
Dist - JOU **Prod** - SOLFIM 1987

Yugoslavia 28 MIN
16mm
Color (C A)
LC 72-702166
Tours Yugoslavia's historic and scenic areas, including views of the Adriatic coast, the Roman Coliseum at Pula, the inland parks and the Dubrovnik Music FestiVal.
Geography - World; Social Science
Dist - MCDO **Prod** - MCDO 1972

Yugoslavia 27 MIN
U-matic / VHS
Nations of the World Series
Color (I J H A)
Introduces the viewers to today's Yugoslavs in their cities, farms, and factories and shows the remarkable phusical bearty of this striving socialist state.
Geography - World
Dist - NGS **Prod** - NGS

Yugoslavia 18 MIN
U-matic / VHS / 16mm
Families of the World Series
Color (I)
Presents a girl in the city of Bor in southern Yugoslavia, where the parents work in a huge copper manufacturing plant. Features a class trip and a visit to her grandparents' farm revealing a lot about her life and her country.
Geography - World
Dist - NGS **Prod** - NGS

Yugoslavia 20 MIN
16mm
Color (I)
Highlights the various groups of people who live in Yugoslavia. Depicts how shy, isolated cultures have survived invasion in fortified mountain cities.
Geography - World; Sociology
Dist - AVED **Prod** - WIANCK 1963

Yugoslavia 18 MIN
U-matic / VHS
Families of the World Series, Pt 1; Pt 1
Color (I)
$172.00 purchase _ #51069
Follows the daily life of a Yugoslavian family.
Geography - World; Sociology
Dist - NGS

Yugoslavia 25 MIN
16mm / U-matic
Untamed World Series
Color; Mono (J H C A)
$400.00 film, $250.00 video, $50.00 rental
Features the Plitzwitze national park in the mountains of Yugoslavia and the wildlife of southeastern Europe that reside there.
Geography - World
Dist - CTV **Prod** - CTV 1973

Yugoslavia - crossroads of civilizations 30 MIN
U-matic
Countries and peoples series
Color (H C)
$90.00 purchase _ # BPN213304
Studies how Yugoslavia developed into a country with no official language and a mixture of cultures from Europe and the Mediterranean.
Geography - World; History - World
Dist - TVOTAR RMIBHF **Prod** - TVOTAR RMIBHF 1982

Yugoslavia - Land of Contrasts 27 MIN
16mm
Color (J)
LC FIA66-1683
Depicts 26 cities and towns in Yugoslavia and points out the contrasts in people, traditions, customs, history, art and architecture of each.
Geography - World; Social Science
Dist - AVED **Prod** - BAILYL 1965

Yugoslavia - Life After Tito 15 MIN
VHS / U-matic
Color (H C A)
Discusses the post - Tito era in Yugoslavia, focusing on politics, people, economy and life style.
Geography - World
Dist - JOU **Prod** - UPI

Yugoslavia - the road to nowhere 50 MIN
VHS
Blood and belonging series
Color (A)
PdS99 purchase _ Available in UK only
Features host Michael Ignatieff taking a dangerous and dramatic journey of discovery to examine nationalism in Yugoslavia. Travels through a war zone, meeting with the warlords who rule on either side of the Serbian and Croatian front line.
Civics and Political Systems; History - World
Dist - BBCENE

Yugoslavian Coastline 14 MIN
16mm / U-matic / VHS
Man and His World Series
Color (P I J H C)
LC 73-705474
Describes life in the towns along the Adriatic Sea. Contrasts the old face of the city with narrow streets, stone houses and market places with produce and fish displayed with a modernized area which has a fish - canning factory and bauxite mine.
Business and Economics; Geography - World
Dist - FI **Prod** - PMI 1969

Yugoslavia's mountain homecoming 30 MIN
VHS
World of festivals series
Color (J H C G)
$195.00 purchase
Observes the Festival of Bohinj in Yugoslavia which celebrates the return of the herdsmen from the mountains. As they return, villagers in costume dance to meet them. Part of a 12 - part series on European festivals.
Geography - World; Social Science
Dist - LANDMK **Prod** - LANDMK 1988

Yuki Shimoda - Asian American actor 30 MIN
VHS / U-matic
Color (G)
$125.00 purchase, $75.00 rental
Explores the life and 30-year acting career of Yuki Shimoda. Reveals that he was offered limited roles by the Hollywood establishment during certain times of his career, but he persevered to take on challenging roles. Follows his journey from Sacramento's J - Town, his imprisonment in an American concentration camp and his experiences on Broadway and in Hollywood. Interviews Mako, Beulah Quo, Nobu McCarthy and Soon Teck Oh.
Biography; Fine Arts; Sociology
Dist - CROCUR **Prod** - VISCOM 1985

Yukon Jake 21 MIN
16mm
B&W
LC 70-713142
Presents a comedy about the complications that arise when Sheriff Cylone Bill tries to capture Yukon jake.
Literature and Drama
Dist - RMIBHF **Prod** - SENN 1960

Yukon Passage 59 MIN
U-matic / VHS / 16mm
Color
LC 78-700776
Presents a documentary about four young men who retrace the passage of oldtime prospectors to the gold - rich Klondike during the period 1897 - 1898.
Geography - World; History - World
Dist - NGS **Prod** - NGS 1977

Yukon passage 60 MIN
VHS
National Geographic video series
Color (G)
$29.95 purchase
Features the efforts by four adventurers to travel across the Alaskan Yukon, going more than 1,800 miles on foot, skis, raft, and dogsled. Narrated by Jimmy Stewart.
History - World
Dist - PBS **Prod** - WNETTV

Yukon passage 60 MIN
VHS
Color (G)
$29.90 purchase _ #0310
Explores the frozen reaches of Canada and Alaska, inspired by the hardship and romance experienced by the women and men lured by the 1898 gold rush. Braves the roaring rapids of the Yukon River, travels 1,800 miles on foot, skis, long raft and dogsled.
Geography - United States; Geography - World; History - World; Physical Education and Recreation
Dist - SEVVID **Prod** - NGS

Yukon passage 60 MIN
VHS
Color; Captioned (G)
$29.95 purchase _ #S01162
Tells the story of four young men who decided to make their way through the Yukon region of Canada. Narrated by Jimmy Stewart.
Geography - World; History - World; Physical Education and Recreation
Dist - UILL **Prod** - NGS

Yukon Passage - Pt 1 30 MIN
16mm / U-matic / VHS
Color
LC 78-700776
Presents a documentary about four young men who retrace the passage of oldtime prospectors to the gold - rich Klondike during the period 1897 - 1898.
History - United States
Dist - NGS **Prod** - NGS 1977

Yukon Passage - Pt 2 29 MIN
16mm / U-matic / VHS
Color
LC 78-700776
Presents a documentary about four young men who retrace the passage of oldtime prospectors to the gold - rich Klondike during the period 1897 - 1898.
History - United States
Dist - NGS **Prod** - NGS 1977

The Yukon territory 15 MIN
VHS
Color (G)
$29.95 purchase _ #S01847
Explores the flora and fauna of Canada's Yukon wilderness.
Geography - World; Science - Natural
Dist - UILL

The Yukon Territory 15 MIN
U-matic / VHS / 16mm
Natural Environment Series
Color (I)
LC 77-703490
Presents different ecological regions of the Yukon Territory, from the ice fields to the vast, treeless plains, and describes the animals native to each area.
Geography - World; Science - Natural
Dist - JOU **Prod** - WILFGP 1977

Yukon - the invisible history 30 MIN
U-matic
North of sixty degrees - destiny uncertain series
Color (H C)
Examines the influences of the gold rush, the building of the Alaska highway and the fight for responsible government by the Yukon's native people.
Geography - United States; Geography - World; History - World
Dist - TVOTAR **Prod** - TVOTAR 1985

Yule Rules 15 MIN
16mm
Color (C)
LC 81-700484
Parodies safety films by looking at a typical suburban family and the many risks involved in trying to enjoy a typical suburban Christmas. Explores the hazards of sending Christmas cards, cuddling under the mistletoe, giving gifts and eating Christmas dinner.
Fine Arts
Dist - RWLNSJ **Prod** - NYU 1981

Yuletide Reflections - Vietnam 16 MIN
16mm
Color
LC 74-706350
Describes impressions of the chief of Navy chaplains concerning the war in Vietnam.

History - World
Dist - USNAC Prod - USN 1968

Yum, yum, yum 31 MIN
16mm / U-matic / VHS
Louisiana films series
Color (G)
$500.00, $250.00, $150.00 purchase
Marries the passion of Les Blank for spicy, down - home food with his admiration for the Cajuns and Creoles to create a mouth - watering, visceral exploration of the cooking and culture of southern Louisiana. Focuses on the multi - faceted Marc Savoy as he prepares his deceptively simple one - pot Cajun gumbos and sauce piquantes while serving up his own zesty commentary on Cajun cooking. Also features Chef Paul Prudhomme, Queen Ida and local Louisiana cooks.
Geography - United States; Home Economics
Dist - FLOWER **Prod** - BLNKL 1991

Yuma crossing 28 MIN
U-matic / VHS
Color (J H C G)
$355.00, $325.00 purchase _ #V486
Looks at the cultural and historical significance of the crossing between the Colorado and Gila Rivers in Southwestern Arizona. Presents dramatizations, first person accounts and archival material.
Geography - United States; History - United States; Literature and Drama
Dist - BARR **Prod** - CEPRO 1989

Yuri Grigorovich - Master of the Bolshoi 67 MIN
VHS
Color (G)
$29.95 purchase _ #1261
Profiles the ballet master and choreographer of the Bolshoi, Yuri Grigorovich. Features excerpts from Bolshoi productions.
Fine Arts; Foreign Language; Geography - World; Physical Education and Recreation
Dist - KULTUR

Yuri Kochiyama - passion for justice 57 MIN
VHS
Color (G)
$75.00 rental, $250.00 purchase
Portrays Yuri Kockiyama, a Japanese American woman who has lived in Harlem for more than forty years with a long history of activism on a wide range of issues. Chronicles her contribution to social change through some of the most significant events of the 20th century - including the Black Liberation movement, the struggle for Puerto Rican independence, and the Japanese American Redress movement - through extensive interviews with friends and family, archival footage, music and photographs.
Civics and Political Systems; Fine Arts; History - United States; Sociology
Dist - WMEN **Prod** - SAUTAJ 1994

Yuri Schmidt Show 30 MIN
VHS / U-matic
Cookin' Cheap Series
Color
Presents cooks Larry Bly and Laban Johnson who offer recipes, cooking and shopping tips.
Home Economics
Dist - MDCPB **Prod** - WBRATV

Yusuf Islam on the Seerah of Prophet Muhammad
VHS
Video lectures of Yusuf Islam series
Color (G)
$15.00 purchase _ #110 - 084
Features Islamic lecturer Yusuf Islam presenting a keynote speech in the Seerah Conference organized by the Muslim community of Orange County, California.
Religion and Philosophy
Dist - SOUVIS **Prod** - SOUVIS 1995

Yves Saint Laurent 50 MIN
VHS
Look series
Color (A)
PdS99 purchase _ Unavailable in the USA
Profiles the undisputed king of couture, Yves Saint Laurent. Strips away the glitz and glamor of the fashion business to look behind the scenes. Explores the mystique of the designer label and debates the meaning of style. Reveals the mysteries of material and unveils the interdependence between the fashion industry, the media, financiers, and the consumer. Part of a six-part series.
Home Economics
Dist - BBCENE

Yvonne Jacquette - Autumn Expansion 14 MIN
VHS
Color (H C A)
$39.95
Shows Yvonne Jacquette discussing her work 'Autumn Expansion' during its 1981 exhibition at the Brooke Alexander Gallery.
Fine Arts
Dist - ARTSAM

Yvonne Jacquette - Autumn Expansion 10 MIN
16mm
Color (H A)
$55.00 rental
Narrates the history of the large triptych Autumn Expansion by Yvonne Jacquette, which was commissioned for the Bangor, Maine Post Office. Produced and directed by Rudy Burckhardt.
Fine Arts; Industrial and Technical Education
Dist - AFA

Yvonne Jacquette - Autumn Expansion - at the Brooke Alexander, Inc Gallery 13 MIN
U-matic
Color (H A)
$200.00 purchase, $45.00 rental
Features artist Yvonne Jacquette discussing her work, Autumn Expansion, during its 1981 exhibition at the Brooke Alexander Gallery.
Fine Arts; Industrial and Technical Education
Dist - AFA

Z

Z is for Zoo 8 MIN
16mm / U-matic / VHS
Starting to Read Series
Color (K P)
LC 79-706155
Describes various activities performed by animals in a zoo and spells out the action words.
English Language; Science - Natural
Dist - AIMS **Prod** - ACI 1970

Z - tansform properties 56 MIN
U-matic / VHS
Digital signal processing series
Color (PRO)
Industrial and Technical Education; Mathematics
Dist - GPCV MIOT **Prod** - GPCV MIOT

The Z was Zapped
VHS
Color (P)
$45.00 purchase
Depicts a mysterious transformation of each letter of the alphabet. By Chris Van Allsburg.
English Language; Literature and Drama
Dist - PELLER

Zaa, the little white camel 25 MIN
16mm
Color
Presents the escape of Zaa, a baby camel, from a camel merchant. Shows the terrain of an arid land and the daily living habits of the Islamic people.
Religion and Philosophy; Science - Natural
Dist - RADIM **Prod** - BELLNY

Zack and the Magic Factory 50 MIN
U-matic / VHS / 16mm
Color (I)
Reveals that when Zack visits his eccentric aunt one summer, he discovers her magic factory is deeply in debt and in danger of take - over by her arch - enemy. Shows Zack becoming a hero when he stages a magic show to raise money to save the factory.
Literature and Drama
Dist - CORF **Prod** - ABCLR 1983

Zadie and the Bar Mitzvah 25 MIN
VHS
B&W (G)
$34.95 purchase
Portrays the videomaker's grandfather, Zadie, and the nephew of the videomaker and his non - traditional Bar Mitzvah.
Religion and Philosophy; Sociology
Dist - WMMI **Prod** - WMMI 1975

Zagreb Collection Series
Pickles 11 MIN
Dist - PHENIX

Zaire 60 MIN
VHS
Under African skies series
Color (A)
PdS99 purchase
Reviews the music of Zaire. Explores how African music reflects its culture, religion, and politics. Seeks out the diverse music of Africa to find out where it comes from, what it means, and where it's going. Part of a five-part series.
Fine Arts; Geography - World
Dist - BBCENE

Zajota and the boogie spirit 20 MIN
VHS / 16mm
Color (H C G)
$550.00, $295.00 purchase, $50.00 rental
Incorporates African rhythms and dance and animation to portray the history of Afro - Americans from their African origins to present day life, watched over by the goddess Zajota who keeps alive the boogie spirit.
Fine Arts; History - United States
Dist - FLMLIB **Prod** - AYCH 1990

Zakopane 45 MIN
VHS
Color (G A)
$24.95 purchase _ #V261
Features film impressions from Zakopane and the neighborhood. Shows Giewont, Morskie Oko and the unique architecture of Zakopane and the folklore of the mountaineers.
Geography - World
Dist - POLART

Zakopane - Part 2 30 MIN
VHS
Color (G A)
$24.95 purchase _ #V262
Features film impressions from Zakopane and the neighborhood. Flies in a helicopter over selected parts of the Tatra mountains to see the Chocholowska Valley, Giewont, Kasprowy Wierch and Morskie Oko.
Geography - World
Dist - POLART

Zalman P Usiskin
U-matic / VHS
Third R - Teaching Basic Mathematics Skills Series
Color
Focuses on the way mathematics can be used in real situations. Illustrates ways in which computational skills and other basic skills can be used in a wide range of everyday situations.
Education; Mathematics
Dist - EDCPUB **Prod** - EDCPUB

The Zambezi Express 60 MIN
16mm / U-matic / VHS
Color (J H A)
Travels with historian Michael Woods aboard the Blue Train, the most luxurious train in the world, from Cape Town, South Africa to Victoria Falls. Traverses the wilderness area of the Karoo, the diamond fields of Kimberly and the gold city of Johannesberg.
Geography - World; Social Science
Dist - FI **Prod** - BBCTV 1981

Zambia 28 MIN
Videoreel / VHS
International Byline Series
Color
Interviews Mr. Muuka L M Muchimba, tourist officer of Zambia for North America. Presents film clips on the Zambia National Parks, Victoria Falls and safaris.
Business and Economics; Civics and Political Systems; Geography - World
Dist - PERRYM **Prod** - PERRYM

Zambia 28 MIN
Videoreel / VHS
Marilyn's Manhattan Series
Color
Interviews Ambassador Gwendoline Chomba Konie. Includes a film clip on Zambia. Hosted by Marilyn Perry.
Business and Economics; Civics and Political Systems; Geography - World
Dist - PERRYM **Prod** - PERRYM

Zambia - Namibia 28 MIN
Videoreel / VHS
International Byline Series
Color
Interviews Ambassador Paul Lusaka, permanent representative of Zambia to the United Nations and president of the United Nations Council for Namibia. Includes a film clip. Hosted by Marilyn Perry.
Business and Economics; Civics and Political Systems; Geography - World
Dist - PERRYM **Prod** - PERRYM

Zane forbidden 10 MIN
16mm
Color & B&W (G)

$15.00 rental
Presents a production in which the filmmaker states, 'I love home movies.'
Fine Arts; Sociology
Dist - CANCIN **Prod** - WILEYJ 1972

Zantray '88 - a portrait of modern Haiti 52 MIN
VHS / U-matic
Color (C G)
$425.00, $395.00 purchase _ #V454
Portrays Haiti, the poorest country in the Western Hemisphere. Shows how the country continues to suffer under a repressive military dictatorship. Looks at the Macoutes - brutal political terrorists, disease, poverty and voodoo beliefs which continue to hold Haitians in their thrall.
Civics and Political Systems; Geography - World; Religion and Philosophy; Sociology
Dist - BARR **Prod** - CEPRO 1988

The Zany Fiancee 11 MIN
U-matic / VHS / 16mm
Color (I J H C)
LC 83-700382
Chronicles the ceaseless misfortunes of a would - be bridegroom who experiences a change of heart concerning his bad luck when he observes that his misadventures may have prevented him from getting in even deeper trouble.
Fine Arts
Dist - PHENIX **Prod** - PHENIX 1981

Zap 10 MIN
16mm
Color
LC 77-702309
Tells the story of how a young hero in a park loses his girl, but wins her back when he finds a shrinking machine that falls out of a flying saucer.
Literature and Drama
Dist - LBRD **Prod** - LBRD 1975

Zap - Static Awareness 20 MIN
16mm
Color
LC 79-701821
Discusses the nature and generation of static electricity and the hazard which it presents to electronic equipment. Shows how an electrostatic charge accumulates on people and nonconducting materials. Demonstrates precautions for minimizing this hazard.
Industrial and Technical Education; Science - Physical
Dist - USNAC **Prod** - USN 1978

Zapp - the human lightning of empowerment - and how it works for you - William C Byham 90 MIN
VHS
Color; PAL (C G PRO)
$89.95, $69.95, $16.00 purchase _ #91AST - V - M25, #91AST - M25
Takes empowerment beyond a theoretical concept into practical action. Discusses the importance of empowerment to a self - motivated workforce working toward constant improvement, the linkage of empowerment with self - directed work teams and the role people - rather than technology - play in keeping companies competitive. Features William C Byham, President, Development Dimensins International, Pittsburgh.
Business and Economics; Guidance and Counseling; Psychology
Dist - MOBILE **Prod** - ASTD 1991

Zara dhyan dein series
Presents seven 5 - minute programs about health and social issues affecting Asian families in Britain. Includes Paan Chewing - an addictive substance associated with oral cancer and gum disease; Screening for Handicap - screening to facilitate early intervention; Immunisation - the importance of immunizing children; Post - Natal Depression - addresses the problem of post - natal depression and offers advice to parents on how to cope; Child Safety at Home - highlights the importance of safety measures in the home; Fostering - explains the 'need' and 'how' of providing foster care for children; Domestic Violence - recognizing domestic violence and getting help. Contact distributor about availability outside the United Kingdom.
Zara dhyan dein series 35 MIN
Dist - ACADEM

Zara Nelsova 54 MIN
VHS / 16mm
Visiting Artists Series
Color (G)
$70.00 rental _ #VSTA - 002
Profiles concert cellist Zara Nelsova discussing her philosophy of music and teaching. Shows Nelsova working with master classes and performing.
Fine Arts
Dist - PBS **Prod** - NETCHE

Zarabanda 660 MIN
VHS
Color (S) (SPANISH)
$990.00 purchase _ #548 - 9093
Teaches basic Spanish conversation and comprehension by engaging students in the continuing mystery story of Ramiro, a teenage mechanic. Shows Ramiro's adventures and difficulties with love, jobs, strange places and people. Each program devotes more than half its time to teaching and practicing grammatical structures and developing listening comprehension. Twenty - five 25 minute programs, four programs per tape.
Foreign Language; Geography - World; History - World
Dist - FI **Prod** - BBCTV 1981

Zarabanda - the Adventures of Ramiro - the Story 360 MIN
VHS
Color (S) (SPANISH)
$499.00 purchase _ #825 - 9634
Tells the story of Ramiro, a young Spaniard who leaves his small village for the big city of Seville. Reveals that there he finds a job as a mechanic, falls in love and becomes entangled in a dangerous extortion scheme. Edited from the complete 'Zarabanda' series. Combines an exciting story in Spanish without subtitles and beautiful location footage of Spain. Five volumes containing 25 episodes.
Foreign Language; Geography - World; History - World
Dist - FI **Prod** - BBCTV 1989

Zarda - a nomadic tribes feast days 50 MIN
VHS
Color (H C G)
$445.00 purchase, $75.00 rental
Captures the sights and sounds of a spectacular event in southern Tunisia. Reveals that every fall the nomads of this area celebrate their ancestral ties, caravans roll through the desert loaded with food, tents and high - spirited families for matchmakng, religious devotion and competitive horsemanship. Produced by Sophie Ferchiou.
Geography - World; Physical Education and Recreation; Sociology
Dist - FLMLIB

Zardips quest 15 MIN
VHS
Zardips search for healthy wellness series
Color (P I)
LC 90-707981
Presents an episode in a series. Helps young children understand basic health issues and the value of taking good care of their bodies. Includes teacher's guide.
Education; Health and Safety
Dist - TVOTAR **Prod** - TVOTAR 1989

Zardips search for healthy wellness series

The dentist	15 MIN
The Doctor	15 MIN
Ears	15 MIN
Environmental health	15 MIN
Exercise	15 MIN
Eyes	15 MIN
Feelings	15 MIN
Food	15 MIN
Germs	15 MIN
Growth	15 MIN
Hospital visit	15 MIN
The Human body	15 MIN
Laurie's operation	15 MIN
More food	15 MIN
More germs	15 MIN
Safety	15 MIN
The Secret discovered	15 MIN
Sleep	15 MIN
Teeth	15 MIN
Zardips quest	15 MIN

Dist - TVOTAR

The Zax 5 MIN
U-matic / VHS / 16mm
Dr Seuss on the Loose Series
Color
LC 74-700290
Deals with stubbornness and the inability to change. Presents an animated cartoon about the North - going zax and the South - going zax, who meet and quarrel with one another on their journeys, each stubbornly refusing to let the other pass. Edited from the 1974 motion picture Dr Seuss On The Loose.
Guidance and Counseling; Literature and Drama
Dist - PHENIX **Prod** - CBSTV 1974

The Zayre Credit Story 12 MIN
16mm
Color
LC 74-702668
Discusses the success of private enterprise in terms of the availability of consumer goods and services on credit. Encourages Zayre employees to promote the use of Zayre credit cards.
Business and Economics
Dist - ZAYRE **Prod** - ZAYRE 1969

Zazie 85 MIN
16mm
Color (FRENCH)
Tells of Zazie, a foul - mouthed cynic, age 11, who comes to Paris for a weekend with her uncle, a female impersonator. Points out that nobody is quite like what they seem to be.
Fine Arts; Foreign Language; Literature and Drama
Dist - NYFLMS **Prod** - NYFLMS 1960

Zbigniew in Love 4 MIN
16mm
Color (H C A)
LC 80-700720
Uses animation and experimental techniques to tell the story of Zbigniew, who enjoys creating shadow figures. Shows how he becomes absorbed in the fantasy of a shapely female who assumes a reality for him, only to turn him into a shadowy substance that disappears.
Fine Arts
Dist - CFS **Prod** - LIBBYE 1979

Zea 6 MIN
16mm
Color
LC 82-700597
Zeros in on a blimp - shaped object whose orange - rust skin becomes coated with a clear fluid. Scans around the increasingly changing pellet until the kernel bursts open in a cloud of white.
Fine Arts
Dist - NFBC **Prod** - NFBC 1981

Zea - a study in perception 5 MIN
U-matic / VHS / 16mm
(G)
Illustrates that each of us sees reality from a slightly different perspective. Helps relate perceptual insights to managerial problem solving in work situations.
Business and Economics; Fine Arts; Social Science
Dist - SALENG **Prod** - NFBC 1981

Zebra 18 MIN
16mm
B&W (G)
$40.00 rental
Pictures a visual keening for the exterminated quagga, an extinct striped wild ass from South Africa in a silent dirge by Louis Hock.
Fine Arts
Dist - CANCIN

Zebra in your stable 30 MIN
VHS
Amazing animal shows series
Color; PAL (H C A)
PdS65 purchase
Travels to Africa, France and North America to compare domestic and wild horse breeds. Demonstrates that parallel behavior among the different breeds helps to trace back to a single common ancestor.
Science - Natural
Dist - BBCENE

Zebra - Part 8 8 MIN
VHS
Safari TV series
Color (P I)
$125.00 purchase
Studies the daily life of the zebra. Part of a 13 - part series on African animals.
Geography - World; Science - Natural
Dist - LANDMK **Prod** - LANDMK 1993

Zebra Wings Series

Humor I	15 MIN
Humor II	15 MIN
Journal	15 MIN
Myths and Fables	15 MIN
Newspaper Writing	15 MIN
Persuasive Writing	15 MIN
Plays	15 MIN
Poetry I	15 MIN
Poetry II	15 MIN
Script Writing	15 MIN
Short Story I	15 MIN
Short Story II	15 MIN
Writer's Tools	15 MIN

Dist - AITECH

Zebras 10 MIN
U-matic / VHS
Eye on Nature Series
Color (I J)
$250 purchase
Discusses the family behavior, eating habits, care for young, and dangers from predators among zebras. Produced by the BBC.
Science - Natural
Dist - CORF

Zebras 10 MIN
VHS
Animal profile series
Color (P I)
$59.95 purchase _ #RB8128
Studies zebras. Explores why zebras have never been successfully domesticated. Looks at three different types of zebras. Part of a series on animals which looks at examples from the mammal, snake and bird classes, filmed in their natural habitat.
Science - Natural
Dist - REVID **Prod** - REVID 1990

Zeca 19 MIN
16mm / U-matic / VHS
Color (H C A)
LC 74-701566
Traces the professional, social and family life of Zeca, a cowherder from the northeast of Brazil.
Social Science; Sociology
Dist - PHENIX **Prod** - SLUIZR 1974

ZEGOTA - a time to remember 52 MIN
VHS
Color (G)
$49.00 purchase
Chronicles ZEGOTA, the only government - sponsored agency created to aid Jewish refugees in German - occupied Europe. Reveals that it was formed by the Polish government - in - exile in London and first tried to make the Allied powers aware of Hitler's intention to annihilate European Jews. Then, during 1943 and 1944, ZEGOTA operatives worked at great personal risk to provide safety, sustenance and medical attention to Jewish escapees from Nazi ghettos and concentration camps. Features interviews with former ZEGOTA operatives. Includes discussion guide.
History - World; Sociology
Dist - DOCINT **Prod** - DOCINT

Zeit Der Schuldlosen 95 MIN
16mm
B&W (GERMAN)
Scrutinizes the situation of nine hostages from all walks of life who are imprisoned with the would - be assassin of the governor of a country. Traces the story of their murder of the man and their subsequent lives and deaths.
Foreign Language; Literature and Drama
Dist - WSTGLC **Prod** - WSTGLC 1964

Zeitaufnahme - Time exposure 3 MIN
16mm
Color (G)
$10.00 rental
Constructs a 21 - day film in which the camera, mounted in front of a window, records the view outside. Uses the same three rolls of film one after the other each day while a mask in front of the camera is also changed daily.
Fine Arts; Industrial and Technical Education
Dist - CANCIN **Prod** - KRENKU 1973

Zelig 79 MIN
16mm
Color; B&W (G)
$75.00 rental
Present's Woody Allen's satire of the media with a send - up of the newsreel format. Tells the story of Leonard Zelig, played by Allen, a neurotic conformist who becomes famous for his chameleon - like ability to physically and mentally adapt to any crowd by changing his appearance at will. Provides humor with faked newreel footage of Zelig with Chaplin, Babe Ruth and even Hitler. Stars Mia Farrow.
Fine Arts; Literature and Drama; Sociology
Dist - NCJEWF

Zen 45 MIN
VHS / BETA
Color; PAL (G)
PdS30 purchase
Features Alan Watts in a 3 - part program. Includes Mood of Zen, which explains the basic teachings of Zen; Zen and Now, a meditation of being here now; and The Flow of Zen, in which Watts begins his talk on the philosophy of Zen Buddhism with a poem comparing the qualities of water with the qualities evolved through practising Zen.
Fine Arts; Literature and Drama; Religion and Philosophy
Dist - MERIDT **Prod** - HP

Zen and Now 14 MIN
16mm
Color (H C)
LC 76-703348
Discusses the Zen philosophy of living for the present, developing sensory awareness, and appreciating the beauty of nature.
Religion and Philosophy
Dist - HP **Prod** - HP 1969

The Zen Archer 11 MIN
U-matic
Color (H A)
Captures a Japanese woman's exercise in the art of Zen archery. Shows her executing the ordered, ancient procedures utilized by Samurai warriors. Contrasts the silence surrounding the ceremonial practice with the woman's journey home, which takes her through the clamor of traffic and hurrying commuters, past video arcades and the sounds of rock music. Without narration.
Physical Education and Recreation; Religion and Philosophy; Sociology
Dist - MOBIUS **Prod** - MOBIUS 1982

Zen center 53 MIN
VHS
Color (G)
$39.95 purchase
Takes an in - depth, honest and sympathetic look at Zen as it is practiced in America. Explores Zen principles of awareness, attention to detail, and the interconnectedness of all life.
Fine Arts; Religion and Philosophy
Dist - HP

Zen guts 3 MIN
16mm
Color (G)
$3.00 rental
Entertains with a film - painting by Henry Yeaton. Consists of color, shapes and textures moving with the rhythm of Yugoslav folk - music. A David Ringo production.
Fine Arts
Dist - CANCIN

Zen journey 99 MIN
VHS / BETA
Color; PAL (G)
PdS20 purchase
Features Susan Postal, a Buddhist practitioner for over 20 years, beginning with Tibetan vajrayana and ending up as a Zen priest in Rye, New York. Alternates between her personal story and scenes of chanting, a tea ceremony and formal dharma talk.
Fine Arts; Religion and Philosophy; Sociology
Dist - MERIDT

Zen Master 3 MIN
16mm
Color (J)
LC 79-700701
Shows Zen Buddhist master Roshi Joshu Sasaki doing everyday chores and conducting Zen meditation.
Religion and Philosophy
Dist - IA **Prod** - IA 1966

Zen Mountain Center 45 MIN
Videoreel / VT2
Color
Explores Zen life and teaching at the Tassajara Zen monastery, the only Zen monastery in America.
Religion and Philosophy
Dist - PBS **Prod** - KQEDTV

Zen shiatsu acupressure
VHS
Acupressure Institute series
Color (G)
$39.95 purchase _ #ACU000
Presents the first of a series of four tapes explaining the ancient Oriental art of therapeutic acupressure and how it stimulates the body's natural healing abilities. Explains how to release tension in shoulders, neck, back and legs with simple pressure techniques.
Health and Safety; Psychology
Dist - SIV

Zen - the best of Alan Watts 60 MIN
VHS
Color (G)
$24.95 purchase
Creates a single program of Watts' finest work. Distills his insights from the Mood of Zen; Zen and Now; Buddhism, Man and Nature; and The Art of Meditation.
Literature and Drama; Religion and Philosophy
Dist - HP

Zen - three films with Alan Watts 45 MIN
VHS
Color (G)
$59.95 purchase
Features Alan Watts, leading authority on Zen Buddhism and counterculture hero. Includes Mood of Zen, which explains the basic teachings of Zen; Zen and Now, a meditation on being here now; and The Flow of Zen, the qualities of flowing water versus human qualities that come from Zen.
Fine Arts; Literature and Drama; Religion and Philosophy
Dist - HP

A Zenana - scenes and recollections 36 MIN
16mm / VHS
Color (G)
$550.00, $300.00 purchase, $55.00, $35.00 rental
Chronicles the lives of women in the zenana - women's quarters - of Dhrangadra, northern India. Uses songs, dances and the stories of several palace women, including the Maharini - also the mother of one of the filmmakers. Reflects upon traditional women's roles, the strictness of their former seclusion and the ideals of purity of women and inner strength. Produced by Roger Sandall and Jayasinhji Jhala.
History - World; Sociology
Dist - DOCEDR **Prod** - DOCEDR

Zengbu after Mao 27 MIN
VHS / U-matic
Color (H G)
$275.00, $325.00 purchase, $50.00 rental
Portrays a rural village in the Republic of China and the socio - economic changes that have occurred since the death of Mao Tse Tung ten years earlier. Generates discussion on the changes in the largely rural population of China as it has moved from a Maoist socialism into contact with a world economy. Produced by the Center for Visual Anthropology.
Business and Economics; Civics and Political Systems; History - World
Dist - NDIM

Zerda's Children 53 MIN
U-matic / VHS / 16mm
Color (H C A)
LC 81-700928
Focuses on the life of Sixto Ramon Zerda, a modern - day peasant in Argentina. Shows how his serfdom to his employer, his lack of protected rights, his poverty and his hope for his children are common to the majority of rural families living in South America, Asia and Africa.
Geography - World; Social Science; Sociology
Dist - PHENIX **Prod** - PRELJ 1978

Zerk the jerk 24 MIN
U-matic / 16mm / VHS
Young people's specials series
Color (K)
$495.00, $349.00, $249.00 purchase _ #AD - 1789
Takes place during World War II. Tells of a young refugee from Austria who is mistaken for a spy and becomes the object of a clandestine and comic conspiracy. Part of the Young People's Specials series.
History - United States; Literature and Drama
Dist - FOTH **Prod** - FOTH

Zero Defects for the Air Force 28 MIN
16mm
B&W
LC 75-703737
Presents a panel discussion explaining the value of the zero defects program to the Air Force and contractor personnel. Stresses perfection in the production of complex weapon systems.
Civics and Political Systems
Dist - USNAC **Prod** - USAF 1965

Zero Defects - Right the First Time 22 MIN
16mm
Color
LC 74-705985
Explains the purpose of the zero defects program. Emphasizes the responsibility of each individual to do his job right the first time.
Business and Economics; Education; Psychology; Social Science
Dist - USNAC **Prod** - USAF 1966

Zero Defects - Right Time the First Time 22 MIN
U-matic
Color
Describes the purpose of the zero defects program emphasizing responsibility of each individual to do his job right the first time. Depicts how errors result from inadequare equipment and wrong attitudes.
Business and Economics; Guidance and Counseling; Psychology
Dist - USNAC **Prod** - USNAC 1972

Zero Defects - the Personal Commitment to Economy, Readiness and Effectiveness 32 MIN
16mm
B&W
LC 74-706351
Explains the zero defects program and relates its benefits to national defense, industrial cooperation, improved production and worker motivation.
Civics and Political Systems
Dist - USNAC **Prod** - USAF 1965

Zero Draft 14 MIN
16mm
Screen news digest series; Vol 15; Issue 8
B&W (I)
LC 73-701275
Examines military conscription in the United States from the Civil War to the modern volunteer army.
Civics and Political Systems; History - United States
Dist - HEARST **Prod** - HEARST 1973

The Zero factor 60 MIN
VHS
Time of AIDS - the medical and political aspects of AIDS series
Color (G C PRO)
$149.00 purchase, $75.00 rental _ #UW4563
Travels from the bathhouses of San Francisco and New York to Fire Island. Meets the physicians who first saw the symptoms of Karposi's sarcoma and pneumonia in their gay patients, as well as men whose friends have died of AIDS. Interviews the woman from the CDC who did her own checking on patient histories and found that they all had one thing in common - Gaeton Dugas, or Patient Zero. Part of four parts on the history of AIDS.
Health and Safety; Sociology
Dist - FOTH

Zero for conduct 44 MIN
U-matic / VHS / 16mm
B&W (J) (FRENCH (ENGLISH SUBTITLES))
LC 75-703866
Satirizes the oppressive life in a French boarding school from the viewpoint of the school boys. Shows the boys' revolt against the school administration.
Education; Foreign Language; Sociology
Dist - FI **Prod** - MACM 1973

Zero for conduct - the dormitory revolt 10 MIN
16mm
Film study extracts series
B&W (J)
Presents an excerpt from the 1959 motion picture Zero For Conduct. Depicts the revolt in the dormitory, including the famed pillow fight. Directed by Jean Vigo.
Fine Arts
Dist - FI **Prod** - UNKNWN

Zero G 50 MIN
16mm / U-matic / VHS
Color (C A)
Presents a humorous explanation of how astronauts can do such things as salt their food when the salt refuses to fall downwards in weightless space. Examines the mystery of disappearing body fluids, hormonal imbalances and other problems which must be studied. Filmed aboard Skylab.
Science - Physical
Dist - FI **Prod** - BBCTV 1981

Zero - g 15 MIN
U-matic / VHS
Skylab Science Demonstrations Series
Color
LC 80-706411
Presents a tour of the Skylab spacecraft and an introduction to its laboratory which is effectively free from the Earth's gravitational field. Explains the dynamics of the Earth's orbit and the meaning of the term zero - g. Issued in 1975 as a motion picture.
Science - Physical
Dist - USNAC **Prod** - NASA 1980

Zero gravity - The Space station's environment 20 MIN
VHS / U-matic
Space stations series
Color (I J H G)
$245.00, $295.00 purchase, $50.00 rental
Looks at how zero gravity affects all aspects of life - support systems in space. Explores the challenges of living in space for long periods. Part of a three - part series. Produced by Media Craft Communications.
Industrial and Technical Education; Science
Dist - NDIM

Zero Hour 20 MIN
U-matic / VHS / 16mm
Color (I J H C)
LC 78-700929
Presents a story about a girl and her friends who play a game called 'Invasion.' Shows how the girl's mother becomes alarmed when she discovers that the invasion is to come from outer space, and she begins to wonder what will happen at zero hour.
Literature and Drama
Dist - BARR **Prod** - WILETS 1978

Zero hour 30 MIN
VHS / 16mm
B&W (G)
$45.00 rental
Examines the changing face of war documentation by deconstructing a United States Navy - sponsored film promoting Victory Bonds, which depicts World War II orphans wandering through rubble searching for food, migrating and caring for their siblings. Constructs an apocalyptic reality in which the 1945 footage becomes timeless by optically printing and intercutting other footage. Produced by Dana Plays.
Fine Arts; History - United States; Sociology
Dist - CANCIN

Zero hour - Part 10 60 MIN
VHS / U-matic
War and peace in the nuclear age series
Color (G)
$45.00, $29.95 purchase
Focuses on Europe in the 1970s and 1980s. Chronicles the controversy surrounding the North Atlantic Treaty Organization - NATO - decision to deploy additional weapons to defend the continent and subsequent negotiations to withdraw USSR - US intermediate - range missiles. Part ten of a thirteen - part series on war and peace in the nuclear age.
Civics and Political Systems; History - World
Dist - ANNCPB **Prod** - WGBHTV 1989

Zero in 10 MIN
16mm
Color
LC 72-701068
Strives to motivate workers toward plant and factory safety by showing a series of fabricated hazards. Gives a review of normal plant safety methods. Shows how the individual workers can prevent accidents by paying attention to everyday hazards.
Business and Economics; Guidance and Counseling; Health and Safety
Dist - NSC **Prod** - NSC 1971

Zero in on Safety 10 MIN
16mm
Color
LC 72-711599
Dramatizes major causes of industrial accidents and gives an organized plan to be followed by companies or departments in order to improve safety records. Features Howard W Pyle, President of the National Safety Council.
Business and Economics; Education; Health and Safety; Industrial and Technical Education
Dist - NSC **Prod** - NSC 1970

Zero Power Reactor 3 - ZPR - 3 10 MIN
16mm
Color
LC FIE63-194
Illustrates the ZPR - 3 operating method to study fuel configurations and their effect upon critical assembly, particularly operation and current applications in the Argonne National Laboratory's fast reactor program.
Industrial and Technical Education; Science; Science - Physical
Dist - USNAC **Prod** - USNRC 1958

Zero - Something for Nothing 8 MIN
U-matic
Color (P)
Shows how a 'mathemagician' demonstrates the property of zero in the operations of addition and multiplication.
Mathematics
Dist - GA **Prod** - DAVFMS

Zero, the Troublemaker 11 MIN
U-matic / VHS / 16mm
Color (P)
$280, $195 purchase _ #3157
Shows the usefulness of zero and how it is used as a place holder.
Mathematics
Dist - CORF

Zero Waste in Railroad Fueling 27 MIN
8mm cartridge / 16mm
Color (IND)
LC 76-703961
Presents an industrial training film that explores basic causes of diesel fuel waste. Shows ways of preventing and reducing oil leaks and spills, covers all types of high - speed automatic railroad fueling equipment and several types of manual fueling operations.
Business and Economics; Home Economics; Industrial and Technical Education; Social Science
Dist - VCI **Prod** - SUNOIL 1976

Zeros and roots - 1
VHS
Quadratics series
Color; PAL (J H G)
Introduces quadratic equations and their corresponding functions on the Cartesian plane. Uses computer animation. Part one of a six - part series.
Industrial and Technical Education; Mathematics
Dist - EMFVL **Prod** - TVOTAR

A Zest for Living 29 MIN
Videoreel / VT2
That's Life Series
Color
Psychology
Dist - PBS **Prod** - KOAPTV

Zeus, by Jove 60 MIN
U-matic / VHS / 16mm
I, Claudius Series Number 9; No 9
Color (C A)
Tells how Claudius is drawn perilously closer to power as his mad nephew Caligula proclaims himself a deity equal to Zeus.
Literature and Drama
Dist - FI **Prod** - BBCTV 1977

Zhao Si xiaojie yu Zhang Xue Liang jiangjun 686 MIN
VHS
Color (G) (CHINESE)
$240.00 purchase _ #5183
Presents a film from the People's Republic of China. Includes eight videocassettes.
Geography - World; Literature and Drama
Dist - CHTSUI

Zhenzhen's beauty parlor 107 MIN
VHS
Color (G) (MANDARIN CHINESE (ENGLISH SUBTITLES))
$45.00 purchase _ #6028A
Presents a movie produced in the People's Republic of China.
Fine Arts; Geography - World; Literature and Drama
Dist - CHTSUI **Prod** - CHTSUI

Zhou Enlai 172 MIN
VHS
Color (G) (MANDARIN)
$85.00 purchase _ #0294S
Presents a documentary about Zhou Enlai produced in the People's Republic of China.
Fine Arts
Dist - CHTSUI

Zhu ge liang 526 MIN
VHS
Color (G) (CHINESE WITH ENGLISH SUBTITLES)
$120.00 purchase _ #5092
Presents a film from the People's Republic of China. Includes four videocassettes.
Geography - World; Literature and Drama
Dist - CHTSUI

Zhu geliang 526 MIN
VHS
Color (G) (MANDARIN)
$150.00 purchase _ #5092
Presents a program produced for television in the People's Republic of China. Includes four videocassettes.
Geography - World
Dist - CHTSUI

Zhu yuan Zhang 240 MIN
VHS
Color (G) (CHINESE)
$60.00 purchase _ #5117
Presents a film from the People's Republic of China. Includes two videocassettes.
Geography - World; Literature and Drama
Dist - CHTSUI

Ziehl - Neelsen Staining Procedure 6 MIN
VHS / U-matic
Color
LC 80-706598
Demonstrates the various steps in the Ziehl - Neelsen staining procedure.
Science
Dist - USNAC **Prod** - CFDISC 1979

Ziel in Den Wolken 101 MIN
VHS / U-matic
B&W (GERMAN)
Presents a drama about a young cavalry officer trying to convince his superiors of the role of aircraft in army reconnaissance, in the pioneer age of aviation in Germany. Shows how he leaves the military to pursue aviation development independently, forsaking the

conservative old order to realize a progressive ideal without support from his contemporaries. No subtitles.
Civics and Political Systems; Fine Arts; History - World; Industrial and Technical Education
Dist - IHF **Prod** - IHF

Ziggy Stardust and the Spiders from Mars 91 MIN
35mm / 16mm
Color (G)
$250.00, $300.00 rental
Captures the 1973 tour of rocker David Bowie. Includes 17 songs. Directed by D A Pennbaker.
Fine Arts; History - United States
Dist - KINOIC **Prod** - CORINT 1983

Zigzag 7 MIN
16mm
Color
Creates an abstract experiment on film using the colors and movement of neon advertising signs at night. Expresses the frenzied pace of our modern cities.
Fine Arts; Sociology
Dist - RADIM **Prod** - STAHER

Zikkaron 6 MIN
U-matic / VHS / 16mm
Color
LC 73-700997
Prsents an allegorical film in which ephemeral images depict the cycle of life. Without narration.
Fine Arts; Literature and Drama; Religion and Philosophy; Science - Natural
Dist - IFB **Prod** - NFBC 1971

Zimbabwe 60 MIN
VHS / 16mm
No Easy Walk Series
Color (G)
$395.00 purchase, $90.00 rental
Reveals that in March of 1896 the Ndebele of the country known then as Rhodesia rose in armed rebellion against European settlers such as Cecil Rhodes. Discloses that the First Chimurenga ended in defeat and it took another 84 years and a guerilla war in the 1970s before independence was gained for the country now known as Zimbabwe. Part of a three - part series which chronicles the history of colonialism and struggle for independence in three African countries.
Geography - World; History - United States; History - World; Social Science; Sociology
Dist - CNEMAG **Prod** - CNEMAG 1988

Zimbabwe 60 MIN
VHS
Under African skies series
Color (A)
PdS99 purchase
Reviews the music of Zimbabwe. Explores how African music reflects Africa's culture, religion, and politics. Seeks out the diverse music of Africa to find out where it comes from, what it means, and where it's going. Part of a five-part series.
Fine Arts; Geography - World
Dist - BBCENE

Zimbabwe - Africa's wildlife sanctuary 54 MIN
VHS
Color (G)
$29.95 purchase _ #ST - IV1302
Visits Hwange and Mana Pools. Views herds of elephants and fish in Lake Kariba. Tours the capital of Zimbabwe, Harare, a city of flowering trees, skyscrapers and international commerce.
Geography - World
Dist - INSTRU

Zimbabwe - the New Struggle 58 MIN
VHS / BETA
Color
Deals with the most compelling aspects of Zimbabwe's current political, social, and economic development, which include social and economic development in Matabeleland, the 'dissident' problem in Matabeleland, and the debate over Zimbabwe's possible future as a Marxist one - party state. Includes interviews with Prime Minister Mugabe, opposition leader Joseph Nkomo, Mozambican President Samora Machel and many people at the grass roots level.
Civics and Political Systems; Geography - World
Dist - ICARUS **Prod** - ICARUS

Zion - Nature's Garden - Utah 29 MIN
U-matic / VHS / BETA
National park series
Color (G)
$29.95, $130.00 purchase _ #LSTF102
Tours Zion National Park, an area filled with huge sandstone structures sculpted by nature. Produced by KHR, Enterprises.
Geography - United States
Dist - FEDU

Zip Code - the Swing Six 13 MIN
16mm
Color
LC 74-705986
Shows the need for ZIP code and how ZIP code works.
Social Science
Dist - USNAC **Prod** - USPOST

Zip plus plus
CD-ROM
(G A)
$195.00 purchase - #2071
Offers a cleaned and compressed version of the complete, official USPS national files, with every viable address range in the US. Enables user to correct addresses, insert or correct Zip+4 zip codes for postal discounts and greater accuracy, insert carrier route codes for faster delivery of mail, and clean lists for easy detection of near - duplicates. For IBM PC and compatibles. Requires 640K RAM, DOS Version 3.1 or greater, floppy disk drive - hard disk drive recommended, an empty expansion slot, IBM compatible CD - ROM drive.
Computer Science; Literature and Drama
Dist - BEP

Zip your lip to gossip - Volume 20 30 MIN
VHS
Our friends on Wooster Square series
Color (K P I R)
$34.95 purchase, $10.00 rental _ #35 - 87269 - 460
Presents religious concepts through storylines, songs and Scripture. Features puppet characters including Smedly, Troll and Sizzle.
Fine Arts; Literature and Drama; Religion and Philosophy
Dist - APH **Prod** - FRACOC

Zipper 25 MIN
16mm
Color (G)
$50.00 rental
Ranges from snow in the Catskills, with stop - overs in Boulder, Colorado and San Francisco, to Easter in New York, flowers and cows in Maine, a Caribbean carnival in Brooklyn, country fairs with men splitting wood and women weight - lifting. Portrays the classic Renaissance Venus and the Nordic, Gothic Venus of the Broken Trees. Employs a diary or collage style and the music ranges from Spike Jones to Hector Berlioz' Nuits d'Ete.
Fine Arts
Dist - CANCIN **Prod** - BURCKR 1987

Zipper Applications 28 MIN
U-matic / VHS
Clothing Construction Techniques Series
Color (C A)
Covers applying a lapped zipper (open and closed seam methods), hand stitching a lapped zipper, applying an exposed zipper, and applying a fly front zipper.
Home Economics
Dist - IOWASP **Prod** - IOWASP

Zipper Installation 29 MIN
Videoreel / VT2
Sewing Skills - Tailoring Series
Color
Features Mrs Ruth Hickman demonstrating how to install a zipper.
Home Economics
Dist - PBS **Prod** - KRMATV

The Zipper Special 29 MIN
Videoreel / VT2
Designing Women Series
Color
Home Economics
Dist - PBS **Prod** - WKYCTV

Zippers 5 MIN
U-matic / VHS / 16mm
How It's made Series
Color (K)
Business and Economics
Dist - LUF **Prod** - HOLIA

Zippers like a pro 60 MIN
VHS
Yes you can video series
Color (H C G)
$39.00 purchase _ #TMCV102V
Shows how to install zippers in cushions, slipcovers and pillows. Part of a five - part series on custom slipcovering and drapery, cushion and pillow making.
Home Economics
Dist - CAMV

Zipview
CD-ROM
(G A)
$899.00 purchase _ #2821
Lets users display the geographic distribution of existing data in seconds and turns complex data base information into easy - to - understand color maps. Accepts almost any ASCII file that contains ZIP Code information. For IBM PCs and compatibles. Requires 640K RAM, DOS Version 3.1 or greater, one floppy disk drive - a hard drive is recommended, one empty expansion slot, and an IBM compatible CD - ROM drive.
Mathematics; Social Science
Dist - BEP

Zit life 14 MIN
16mm
B&W (G)
$20.00 rental
Presents a story about the ugly side of life, including stupid ruthless men and nagging women. Uses clay animation. Producod by Michael Connor.
Fine Arts
Dist - CANCIN

Ziveli - medicine for the heart 51 MIN
16mm / VHS
Color (G)
$99.95 purchase, $100.00 rental
Features the culture and music of Serbian - American communities in Chicago and California. Focuses on the vital cultural strengths of these Yugoslavian immigrants who helped form the backbone of industrial America. Made in association with anthropologist Andrej Simic and the University of Southern California.
Fine Arts; Sociology
Dist - CANCIN **Prod** - BLNKL 1987

Zlateh the Goat 20 MIN
U-matic / VHS / 16mm
Color (I J)
Presents a jewish folk tale by the Yiddish author, Isaac Bashevis Singer, about village life in pre - war Poland. Tells a deceptively simple story about a goat taken by its owner's son to be sold to the town butcher. Reveals the ecological balance that exists throughout nature and which links man to all living things.
Literature and Drama; Religion and Philosophy
Dist - WWS **Prod** - WWS

Zocalo 15 MIN
16mm
Color (G)
$15.00 rental
Presents a color, optically - printed experiment that uses as its base the Zocalo Square in Mexico City.
Fine Arts; Geography - World
Dist - CANCIN **Prod** - MYERSR 1972

Zodiak 9 MIN
16mm
Color
LC 74-701328
Presents a rhythmic fantasy created by the metamorphosis of images with drumbeats.
Fine Arts; Industrial and Technical Education
Dist - CANFDC **Prod** - DORAYA 1972

Zoll surfaces by Victor Guellemin 60 MIN
VHS
AMS - MAA joint lecture series
Color (PRO G)
$59.00 purchase _ #VIDGUELLEMIN - VB2
Presents a historical perspective on Zoll surfaces. Discloses that a two - dimensional surface is a Zoll surface if all its geodesics are closed geodesics. Traces the origin of this idea to Darboux in the 19th century and describes Zoll's generalization of Darboux's work, Funck's systematic treatment of the subject and the modern characterization using Riemann manifolds. Discusses recent developments in the spectral theory of Zoll manifolds. Recorded in New Orleans.
Mathematics
Dist - AMSOC **Prod** - AMSOC 1986

Zoll zeyn - Let it be 135 MIN
VHS
Color (G) (YIDDISH WITH ENGLISH SUBTITLES)
$72.00 purchase
Traces the 'kulturkampf' between 'Hebraists' and 'Yiddishists.' Documents the present state of Yiddish culture in Israel - from the Bundists in Tel Aviv, still fighting for a socialist utopia, to the Orthodox fundamentalists living in the Mea Shearim neighborhood of Jerusalem. In between these two extremes are the Yiddish poets, singers, revolutionaries, journalists and actors for whom Yiddish is still a living language. A film by Henryk M Broder and Frans van der Meulen.
Fine Arts; History - World; Religion and Philosophy; Sociology
Dist - NCJEWF

Zollinger - Ellison Syndrome 23 MIN
U-matic / VHS
Color (PRO)
Discusses Zollinger - Ellison Syndrome.
Health and Safety
Dist - WFP **Prod** - WFP

Zona Gale - 1874 - 1938 15 MIN
Cassette / U-matic / BETA / VHS
Women's history and literature media series
Color (P I J H G)
$95.00 purchase, $40.00 rental
Examines the life, work and philosophy of novelist, journalist, poet and playwright Zona Gale, who was the first woman to win a Pulitzer prize in drama. Part of a series about women's history and literature created by Jocelyn Rile. Resource guide available separately.
Biography; History - United States; History - World; Literature and Drama
Dist - HEROWN **Prod** - HEROWN 1992

The Zonal centrifuge 6 MIN
16mm
Color (H C A)
Explains that one of the most powerful tools of the molecular biologist is the zonal ultracentrifuge, and that its improved separation capabilities are playing an ever - increasing vital role in the fractionation of cell constituents and the purification of vaccines.
Science; Science - Physical
Dist - USERD **Prod** - USNRC 1971
USNAC ANL

Zone gap offense - how to beat any zone defense - Scott
VHS
Basketball small college winners series
Color (H C G)
$29.95 purchase _ #SAM080V - P
Features Coach Scott who discusses zone gap offense and how to beat zone defense in basketball. Part of an 11 - part series featuring innovative basketball coaches at the small college level.
Physical Education and Recreation
Dist - CAMV

Zoo 14 MIN
VHS / U-matic
Color (J)
$250.00 purchase _ #HH - 6264L
Adapts a story by Edward D Hoch. Takes a zany trip into the future to look at what zoos might be like, with the question being just who is on display - the animals or the humans. Seeks to change the way individuals think about how they might be perceived by others and to look beyond preconceived notions and prejudices. Adapted by Mel Gilden.
Literature and Drama; Psychology; Science - Natural; Sociology
Dist - LCA **Prod** - LCA 1990

Zoo 130 MIN
VHS / 16mm
Color (G H)
$350.00 purchase, $150.00 rental
Documents the routine of the Miami, Florida zoo as keepers and veterinarians go about the business of caring for over 780 animals. Directed by Frederick Wiseman.
Fine Arts; Science - Natural
Dist - ZIPRAH **Prod** - WISEF

The Zoo 6 MIN
U-matic / VHS / 16mm
Public Places Series
Color (P I)
LC 70-712843
Portrays the varied personalities of animals at the zoo.
Science - Natural; Social Science
Dist - PHENIX **Prod** - KINGSP 1971

The Zoo 11 MIN
U-matic / VHS / 16mm
Color (K P I)
LC 79-701861
Features the Brookfield Zoo near Chicago, pointing out the pleasures, pastimes and purposes of a zoo. Looks at the animals' habitats, the necessary jobs humans perform, and special sights, such as the Children's Zoo and animal shows. Emphasizes the importance of zoos in conserving and protecting endangered species.
Science - Natural
Dist - EBEC **Prod** - EBEC 1979

Zoo 15 MIN
U-matic / VHS
Picture Book Park Series Brown Module; Brown module
Color (P)
Presents the children's stories May I Bring A Friend by Beatrice De Regniers and Zoo, Where Are You by Ann Mc Govern.
Literature and Drama
Dist - AITECH **Prod** - WVIZTV 1974

Zoo 28 MIN
VHS
Elephant show series
Color (P I)
$95.00 purchase, $45.00 rental
Presents program 9 in the Sharon, Lois and Bram's Elephant Show series. Teaches reading readiness and social skills while engaging children in making music. Each program explores a new theme through adventure, fantasy, mystery and song with recording artists Sharon, Lois and Bram. Uses traditional materials which stress participation - action songs, sing - along songs, story songs, clapping songs, singing games, playground chants and folk songs from many different traditions. Includes teacher's guide co - authored by a music education specialist.
Fine Arts; Sociology
Dist - BULFRG **Prod** - CAMBFP 1988

Zoo 12 MIN
U-matic / VHS / 16mm
B&W (I)
LC 75-704033
Presents a visual essay on the comic characters at the zoo, including those on both sides of the bars. Filmed in Holland.
Guidance and Counseling; Sociology
Dist - PFP **Prod** - HA 1975

Zoo 22 MIN
16mm / U-matic / VHS
Color
LC 75-701598
Takes a look at the behind - the - scenes activity at the National Zoological Park in Washington, D C. Shows how the animals are fed and doctored and how the Zoo conducts research in the areas of animal behavior and reproduction.
Geography - United States; Science - Natural
Dist - AIMS **Prod** - FNZOO 1974

Zoo 60 MIN
VHS
Smithsonian world series
Color; Captioned (G)
$49.95 purchase _ #SMIW - 501
Commemorates the 100th anniversary of Washington, D C's National Zoological Park. Features zoo director Michael Robinson, who shares his vision of zoos as bioparks where humans can gain a better understanding of their relationship with nature.
Science - Natural
Dist - PBS **Prod** - WETATV

Zoo animals behind the scenes 14 MIN
U-matic / VHS / 16mm
Color (P I)
$340.00, $240.00 purchase _ #3256; LC 76-711494
Shows the needs of zoo animals, telling how zoo workers prepare various foods for different animals, provide proper surroundings and necessary medical care. Relates this care to facts about the animals.
Science - Natural
Dist - CORF **Prod** - CORF 1971

Zoo animals in rhyme 11 MIN
U-matic / VHS / 16mm
Color (P)
$270.00, $290.00 purchase _ #1588
Presents rhymes telling about zoo animals such as the lion, monkey, elephant, kangaroo, giraffe and bear.
English Language; Science - Natural
Dist - CORF **Prod** - CORF 1965

Zoo animals in the wild 10 MIN
U-matic / VHS / 16mm
Color (P I)
LC 80-700114
Discusses the natural habitats of North American mammals intercutting scenes of the animals in the zoo with scenes of the same types of animals in their natural environments.
Science - Natural
Dist - IFB **Prod** - BERLET 1979

Zoo Animals in the Wild Series
Apes 5 MIN
Baboons 7 MIN
Bears 6 MIN
Beavers 6 MIN
Crocodiles 6 MIN
Elephants 5 MIN
Giant turtles 5 MIN
Lions and Tigers 6 MIN
Monkeys 5 MIN
Ostriches 5 MIN
Pelicans 6 MIN
Rhinos and Hippos 6 MIN
Zoo Babies 8 MIN
Dist - CORF

Zoo animals in the wild series
Baboons - apes - monkeys - Cassette 1
Bears - lions and tigers - elephants - Cassette 2
Giant turtles - Beavers - Crocodiles - Cassette 4
Pelicans - Ostriches - Rhinos and hippos - Cassette 3
Dist - VIEWTH

Zoo animals series
Presents a six - part series on zoo animals. Includes the titles 'Chimpanzee,' 'Elephant,' 'Hippopotamus,' 'Lion,' 'Tiger' and 'Herbivores.'
Chimpanzee - 1 10 MIN
Elephant - 2 10 MIN
Herbivores 10 MIN
Hippopotamus - 3 10 MIN
Lion - 4 10 MIN
Tiger - 5 10 MIN
Dist - BARR **Prod** - GREATT 1979

Zoo Babies 8 MIN
U-matic / VHS / 16mm
Color (K P)
Describes zoo babies and their relationships to their parents. Observes monkeys, gnus, kudus, peacocks, alligators and bears.
Science - Natural
Dist - CORF **Prod** - CORF 1978

Zoo Babies 8 MIN
U-matic / VHS / 16mm
Zoo Animals in the Wild Series
Color (P)
$215, $155 purchase _ #3993
Talks about the offspring of different animals and how they are protected.
Science - Natural
Dist - CORF

Zoo Babies 15 MIN
VHS / U-matic
Zoo Zoo Zoo Series
Color (P I)
Views the various amounts of care which the babies of different species receive. Reveals that snakes, ducklings and goslings need little mothering while robins, alpacas, lions, gorillas and humans need lots of care.
Science - Natural
Dist - AITECH **Prod** - WCETTV 1981

Zoo Babies - Large and Small 11 MIN
U-matic / VHS / 16mm
Color (P I)
Views some of the baby animals which can be found in zoos including bears, antelopes, zebras, giraffes, elephants and monkeys. Shows animals being fed at the children's zoo.
Science - Natural
Dist - MCFI **Prod** - DEU

Zoo day 14 MIN
VHS / 16mm / U-matic
Color (K P)
$230, $260 purchase _ #V133
Uses narration to introduce viewers to many exotic animals and animal groups. Describes which areas of the world each animal comes from, as well as distinguishing features. Teaches viewers about the people necessary to keep a zoo properly running - the zookeeper, the veterinarian, the office staff, and those who run concession and souvenir stands. Introduces the zoo's important role in protecting endangered species.
Science - Natural
Dist - BARR **Prod** - BARR 1988

Zoo Families 9 MIN
U-matic / VHS / 16mm
Color (P)
LC 78-700930
Shows a group of children visiting a zoo, where they learn to recognize some of the animals and understand their ways of behaving.
Science - Natural
Dist - PHENIX **Prod** - PHENIX 1977

Zoo medicine 27 MIN
U-matic / VHS / BETA
Stationary ark series
Color; PAL (G H C)
PdS50, PdS58 purchase
Discusses the recreation of humankind, nature and wildlife in part of a 12 - part series. Features Gerald Durrell. Filmed on location in Jersey, England.
Science - Natural
Dist - EDPAT

Zoo Time 17 MIN
16mm
Color (P I)
Describes how Mr and Mrs Graham convince the children that Alice the chimp should be returned to the zoo. Explains how Alice escapes, taking four other chimps with her.
Fine Arts
Dist - LUF **Prod** - LUF 1977

Zoo Zoo Zoo Series
All about ears 15 MIN
All about eyes 15 MIN
All about feet 15 MIN
All about tails 15 MIN
Animal costumes 15 MIN
Animal defenses 15 MIN
Animal groups 15 MIN
Animal homes 15 MIN
Do animals talk 15 MIN
How and what Animals Eat 15 MIN
How Animals Move 15 MIN
How Animals Need each Other 15 MIN
The Importance of Predators 15 MIN
Who Works at the Zoo 15 MIN
Zoo Babies 15 MIN
Dist - AITECH

Zoo Zoo Zoo Series
Where Animals Live 15 MIN
Dist - AITECH
NGS

The Zookeeper 15 MIN
U-matic
Harriet's Magic Hats III Series
(P I J)
Details how zoos care for animals including those that are endangered.
Guidance and Counseling
Dist - ACCESS **Prod** - ACCESS 1985

Zookeepers 29 MIN
16mm / U-matic / VHS
Color
LC 81-701573
Offers a visit to Chicago's Lincoln Park Zoo. Highlights the relationships between the animals and the men and women who care for them. Includes brief chats with the zoo's administrators and veterinarian in order to provide insight into the goals and management of the park.
Science - Natural
Dist - FI **Prod** - ROSAD 1981
LINCPK

Zoolab Series
And then there were none 30 MIN
Animal engineering 30 MIN
Can you teach an old dog new tricks 30 MIN
Community - how do you live with your neighbors 30 MIN
Environment - there's no place like home 30 MIN
How do you get a white tiger 30 MIN
How to Trace a Family Tree 30 MIN
Life among the Test Tubes 30 MIN
Nutrition, Fitness and Stress 30 MIN
What Can You Learn from an Aardvark? 30 MIN
Dist - AITECH

Zoological abstracts 6 MIN
16mm
Color (G)
$9.00 rental
Deals with images photographed at a zoo for their visual content. Depicts editing decisions based on color, motion, texture and temporal rhythms. Produced by David Gerstein.
Fine Arts
Dist - CANCIN

Zoom in on Video 15 MIN
U-matic / VHS
Color (H C A)
Demonstrates techniques of video production.
Fine Arts; Industrial and Technical Education
Dist - SEVDIM **Prod** - SEVDIM

Zoom series
Alone in the family 13 MIN
Animal partners 13 MIN
The Best I can 12 MIN
Country Families 13 MIN
Everybody Likes Jazz 10 MIN
Experiments in Design 9 MIN
Fast - talking jobs 11 MIN
Finding My Way 8 MIN
First it seemed kinda strange 6 MIN
For love or money 12 MIN
From generation to generation 11 MIN
Helping my parents 7 MIN
I'm on the Waltons 7 MIN
It's Harder for Patrick 7 MIN
Martha 9 MIN
Messages by Hand 8 MIN
More than a Snapshot 10 MIN
Nobody Treats Me Different 8 MIN
On Stage and Screen 10 MIN
People are People 8 MIN
Rooted in the Past 13 MIN
Working with Animals 11 MIN
The World is a Stage 13 MIN
Dist - FI

Zooms on Self - Similar Figures 8 MIN
16mm / U-matic / VHS
Topology Short Films Series
Color (C A)
LC 81-700618
Gives insight into philosophical levels of the infinite in space.
Mathematics
Dist - IFB **Prod** - IFB 1979

A Zoo's - Eye View - Dawn to Dark 11 MIN
U-matic / VHS / 16mm
Color (P)
Depicts the drama of a typical day at the zoo.
Physical Education and Recreation; Science - Natural
Dist - EBEC **Prod** - EBEC 1973

Zoos of the World 52 MIN
U-matic / VHS / 16mm
Color (I)
LC 78-710389
Travels around the globe to some of the best zoos, which are striving to fill a new role that relates directly to environmental education.
Science - Natural
Dist - NGS **Prod** - NGS 1970

Zoot Sims Quartet 29 MIN
VHS / 16mm
Jazz on Stage Series
Color
Fine Arts
Dist - RHPSDY **Prod** - RHPSDY

Zora is my name 90 MIN
VHS
Color (J H)
$19.95 purchase _ #PLAH - 901
Shows how Zora Neale Hurston, a turn - of - the century black woman, captured the folklore of the rural United States South in unforgettable stories. Uses anecdotes and musical performances to portray the life and times of Hurston.
History - United States; Literature and Drama
Dist - KNOWUN **Prod** - PBS 1989

Zorro rides again 28 MIN
VHS
Cliffhangers I series
B&W (G)
Features six episodes from the Republic Golden Age serial 'Zorro.'
Fine Arts
Dist - SCETV **Prod** - SCETV 1983

Zorro's black whip 216 MIN
35mm
Republic cliffhanger serials series
B&W (G)
Features a woman disguised as the Black Whip fighting a reign of terror. Offers 12 episodes, 18 minutes each. Contact distributor for rental price.
Fine Arts
Dist - KITPAR **Prod** - REP 1944

Zorro's legion
VHS
Cliffhangers II series
B&W (G)
Features Zorro and his men in a battle against Don Del Oro, who has persuaded the Indians that he is a god. Follows Zorro in his adventures of saving the gold train from attack, defending the mission against an explosion, and his escape from a torture chamber. Concludes with Zorro exposing Del Oro's fraud. Includes seven episodes.
Fine Arts
Dist - SCETV **Prod** - SCETV 1987

Zou Zou 92 MIN
35mm / 16mm / VHS
B&W (G)
$250.00, $300.00 rental
Co - stars Josephine Baker with Jean Gabin in a play about a talented Cinderella who takes the place of the lead on the opening night of a musical revue. Includes the musical number 'Haiti.' Directed by Marc Allegret.
Fine Arts
Dist - KINOIC

Zounds 120 MIN
VHS / U-matic
(I J H)
Shows students hear, create, and produce sounds they never imagined. Musical adventures include playing classroom instruments in unusual ways, creating home made instruments from junk, composing simulated electronic music using tape recorders plus much more. Teacher guide supplies directions, cassette transcript, list of materials and follow up ideas.
Fine Arts
Dist - WALCHJ **Prod** - WALCHJ 1976

Zu Spat, Zu Spat 15 MIN
U-matic / VHS / 16mm
Guten Tag Series no 5; No 5
B&W (H) (GERMAN)
LC 78-707318
Presents an episode in which the characters employ frequently used expressions and idioms in order to teach conversational German to beginners. Stresses the correct use of strong present verb forms, the prepositions in, von, zum, nach, vor and um, the numbers 1 to 12 and 2, 20, 200, 220, and introduces variations on questions about time.
Foreign Language
Dist - IFB **Prod** - FRGMFA 1970

Zubin and the IPO 59 MIN
16mm / U-matic
Color
LC 83-707098
Discusses the history of the Israel Philharmonic Orchestra. Focuses on its place in the musical world and on its relationship with conductor Zubin Mehta. Presents interviews with Mehta, other well - known musicians, and members of the orchestra.
Fine Arts; Geography - World
Dist - ADL **Prod** - ADL

Zubin Mehta and His Masters - Piatigorsky and Rubinstein 29 MIN
16mm
Search of Zubin Mehta Series
Color (J)
LC 78-700994
Interviews musician and conductor Zubin Mehta, who reveals how Gregor Piatigorsky, Arthur Rubinstein and others have influenced his life. Includes footage showing the interaction between Mehta, Piatigorsky and Rubenstein, as well as portions of a concert conducted by Mehta.
Biography; Fine Arts
Dist - ESMRDA **Prod** - ESMRDA 1978

Zubin Mehta - Commitment and Fulfillment as a Way of Life 22 MIN
16mm
Search of Zubin Mehta Series
Color (J)
LC 78-700996
Shows musician and conductor Zubin Mehta conducting the Los Angeles Philharmonic Orchestra and presents a discussion by Mehta on the need for fulfillment and commitment to a goal.
Biography; Fine Arts; Guidance and Counseling
Dist - ESMRDA **Prod** - ESMRDA 1978

Zubin Mehta - if You are Going to Lead, Lead 36 MIN
16mm
Search of Zubin Mehta Series
Color (J)
LC 78-700997
Presents musician and conductor Zubin Mehta, who talks about the need for an orchestra conductor to be a strong, resourceful leader and about the demands that conducting make upon his life. Shows Mehta leading the Los Angeles Philharmonic Orchestra in excerpts from music by Beethoven, Mahler and others.
Biography; Fine Arts
Dist - ESMRDA **Prod** - ESMRDA 1978

Zubin Mehta Rocks the Gospel 21 MIN
16mm
Search of Zubin Mehta Series
Color (J)
LC 78-700998
Shows musician and conductor Zubin Mehta as he conducts the rock gospel music of the Inter - Denominational Gospel Choir.
Biography; Fine Arts
Dist - ESMRDA **Prod** - ESMRDA 1978

Zucker Aus Ruben 5 MIN
16mm / U-matic / VHS
European Studies - Germany (German Series
Color (H C A) (GERMAN)
Presents a German - language version of the motion picture Sugar From Beets. Describes the processes involved in obtaining sugar from beets.
Foreign Language; Geography - World; Home Economics
Dist - IFB **Prod** - MFAFRG 1973

Zuckerkandl 15 MIN
U-matic / VHS / 16mm
Color (H C)
LC 77-701738
Presents a spoof on academic pomposity with Professor Zuckerkandl's life's work as the example. Based on a satirical essay by educator Dr Robert M Hutchins.
Education; Fine Arts
Dist - TEXFLM **Prod** - HUBLEY 1976

Zulu 138 MIN
16mm
Color
Tells the stirring story of the battle of Rorke's Drift and the handful of men who defended the mission station against 4,000 Zulu warriors during the British conquest of Zululand in 1879. Stars Stanley Baker, Jack Hawkins and Ulla Jacobsson.
Fine Arts
Dist - TWYMAN **Prod** - AVCEP

Zur Sache Schaetzchen 80 MIN
16mm
B&W (GERMAN (ENGLISH SUBTITLES))
Shows Martin, a typical beatnik, fleeing to the public swimming pool to escape his girlfriend and her reminders of his promise to marry her. Continues with him meeting the pretty and adroit Barbara, with whom he spends the rest of the day.
Foreign Language; Literature and Drama
Dist - WSTGLC **Prod** - WSTGLC 1967

Zurich 3 MIN
16mm
Of all Things Series
Color (P I)
Discusses the city of Zurich in Switzerland.
Geography - World
Dist - AVED **Prod** - BAILYL

Zwischengleis 109 MIN
16mm
Color (GERMAN (ENGLISH SUBTITLES))
Examines the life of a 31 - year - old woman who commits suicide for no apparent reason. Stars Pola Kinski and Mel Ferrer.
Foreign Language; Sociology
Dist - WSTGLC **Prod** - WSTGLC 1978

Zydeco 57 MIN
U-matic / VHS / BETA
Color (G)
$400.00, $250.00 purchase
Explores Louisiana Creole culture and fast - paced Zydeco music. Combines cinema verite style footage, interviews and musical performances shot on location in rural southwestern Louisiana. Looks at zydeco gigs in local clubs and a Mardi Gras celebration in rural Louisiana. Features BeBe Carriere, Amedee Ardoin and Alphonse 'Bois Sec' Ardoin. Produced by Nicholas R Spitzer and Steven Duplantier. Narrated in English; interviews in Cajun - Creole French with English subtitles.
Fine Arts
Dist - FLOWER

Zydeco gumbo 28 MIN
VHS
Color (G)
$24.95 purchase
Features Clifton Chenier and his zydeco combo.
Fine Arts
Dist - KINOIC **Prod** - RHPSDY

Zydrasis Horizontas 70 MIN
VHS / U-matic
B&W (LITHUANIAN)
Relates a popular children's adventure story. Presents the Lithuanian film studio's first independently - produced feature film.
Fine Arts; Foreign Language
Dist - IHF **Prod** - IHF

Zygosis 26 MIN
VHS / 16mm
Color (G)
$280.00 purchase, $50.00 rental
Pays tribute to John Heartfield, the anti - Nazi German satirist who pioneered the photomontage. Uses radical and humorous electronic methods via animation of archival material, contemporary interviews and footage shot in Berlin during the opening of the Wall and the upheavals in East Germany. Fuses modern video techniques such as scratch editing, chroma - key, paintbox and three dimensional computer animation. Produced by Gavin Hodge and Tim Morrison.
Fine Arts; Industrial and Technical Education; Literature and Drama
Dist - FIRS

Zyzomys electronic French dictionary
CD-ROM
(G) (FRENCH)
$495.00 purchase _ #2271
Gathers data from the Dictionnaire de Notre Temps, Dictionnaire des Synonymes, and the Atlas Pratique onto one disc. Includes CD - Navigator software that allows users to browse, search for synonyms, conjugate verbs, display maps, consult practical rules and letter writing conventions. For IBM PCs and compatibles, requires 640K RAM, DOS 3.1 or later, one floppy disk drive - hard disk recommended, one empty expansion slot, and an IBM compatible CD - ROM drive. Mouse recommended.
Foreign Language
Dist - BEP

NOTES

Notes

NOTES

NOTES

NOTES

Notes

NOTES

Notes

Notes

Notes

NOTES

NOTES